The Almanac of American Politics
★ 2012 ★

THE **Senators,** THE **Representatives**

AND THE **Governors:**

THEIR **Records** AND **Election Results,**

THEIR **States** AND **Districts**

Michael Barone
Chuck McCutcheon

The University of Chicago Press

Chicago and London

National Journal Group, Inc.

The University of Chicago Press, Chicago 60637
The University of Chicago Press, Ltd., London
©2011 by National Journal Group, Inc.
All rights reserved. Published 2011.

Printed in the United States of America

20 19 18 17 16 15 14 13 12 11   1 2 3 4 5

ISBN-13: 978-0-226-03807-0   (cloth)

ISBN-13: 978-0-226-03808-7   (paper)

ISBN-10: 0-226-03807-6   (cloth)

ISBN-10: 0-226-03808-4   (paper)

Library of Congress Control Number: 2011929193

♾ This paper meets the requirements of ANSI/NISO Z39.48-1992 (Permanence of Paper).

THE ALMANAC OF AMERICAN POLITICS 2012

Author	Michael Barone
Coauthor	Chuck McCutcheon
Editor	Jackie Koszczuk
Managing Editor	Gregg Sangillo
Researchers	Brendan Sasso, John Ryan
Contributing Writers	Olga Belogolova, Scott Bland, Lindsey Boerma, Althea Fung, Christopher Snow Hopkins, Cameron Joseph, Rebecca Kaplan, Naureen Khan, Andy Leonatti, Clifford Marks, Katy O'Donnell, John Ryan, Brendan Sasso, Sara Sorcher, Ben Terris
Contributing Editors	Jim Humes, Deron Lee, Andy Leonatti, Tom Madigan, Mike Magner, Tonia E. Moore, S. Scott Rohrer, Monica Sullivan
Photo Editor	Liz Lynch
Information Technology Editor	Thomas Allen
Data Assistants	Christopher Peleo-Lazar, Dan Roem
Election Results, Demographics, Maps	Polidata
Interns	Leslie Tamura, Katherine Morison, Sonia Mugabo, Joshua Nosie
Founding Editor	Grant Ujifusa

Atlantic Media Company
Chairman: David G. Bradley
President: Justin B. Smith

National Journal Group, Inc.
Editor-in-Chief: Ron Fournier

TABLE OF CONTENTS

x   **Contents**

xii **Contents**

GUIDE TO USAGE

The following guide explains the information sources used by *The Almanac of American Politics*. Much of the tabular information was provided by Polidata, a Virginia-based political statistics and demographics firm. Other major sources of information include the U.S. Census Bureau, and the staffs of *National Journal* and *The Cook Political Report*. The 2012 *Almanac* uses the latest available data and offers significant updates from the last edition of the book, published in 2009. Figures released by the Census Bureau may vary slightly from those used by *The Almanac* due to different methods of data aggregation or tabulation.

Biography

This section lists the date each governor, senator and representative was elected or appointed, the date and place of birth, current hometown, college degrees earned, religion, marital status and, if applicable, spouse's name and number of children. Also provided is a brief outline of the subject's past elected offices, professional career and military service, as well as office addresses, telephone numbers and Web sites. Committee and subcommittee assignments are current as of June 2011. (Note: On many committees, the chairman and ranking minority member are ex officio members of subcommittees. Committee listings do not appear for the congressional leaders who are not assigned to committees.)

Vote Ratings

Group Ratings: The congressional ratings by 10 interest groups provide insight into a legislator's general ideology and the degree to which he or she reflects the individual group's point of view. Some organizations provided just one rating for 2009 and 2010, the two sessions of the 111th Congress.

ADA: Americans for Democratic Action
Liberal: Since its founding in 1947, ADA has pushed for less defense spending, protection of civil liberties and human rights. The ADA used 20 votes during the 111th Congress for its analysis.

ACLU: American Civil Liberties Union
Pro-individual liberties: ACLU seeks to protect individuals from what it views as legal, executive and congressional infringements on civil liberties. The ACLU ratings are published once every Congress.

AFS: American Federation of State, County and Municipal Employees (AFSCME)
Liberal labor: The nation's largest public service employees union, AFSCME is committed to improving working conditions through collective bargaining. Its analysis is based on a sample of roll call votes.

LCV: League of Conservation Voters
Environmental: Formed in 1970, LCV is the national, non-partisan arm of the environmental movement that works to elect pro-environmental protection candidates to Congress. LCV ratings are based on key votes on energy, environment and natural resources legislation.

ITIC: Information Technology Industry Council
High-tech industry: ITIC represents the leading U.S. providers of information technology products and services. Its mission is to help shape policies that advance electronic commerce and foster innovation.

NTU: National Taxpayers Union
Pro-taxpayer rights: The NTU is the nation's oldest taxpayers' rights group, with members in all 50 states. It analyzes roll call votes that significantly affect federal taxes, regulations, and spending and debt.

COC: U.S. Chamber of Commerce
Pro-business: Founded in 1912, COC represents local, regional and state chambers of commerce in addition to trade and professional organizations.

ACU: American Conservative Union
Conservative: Since 1971, ACU ratings have provided a means of gauging the conservatism of members of Congress. Foreign policy, social and budget issues are analyzed.

CFG: Club for Growth
   Pro-tax limitation: CFG supports limited government, lower taxes and policies it deems
favorable to economic growth. CFG ratings are based on key votes on bills dealing with taxes,
trade and the economy.
FRC: Family Research Council
   Conservative: Founded in 1983, the FRC promotes marriage and family and advocates
for policies that uphold Judeo-Christian values. It bases its ratings on votes on abortion and
family issues.

National Journal Vote Ratings

National Journal's rating system is an objective method of analyzing congressional voting.
A panel of the magazine's editors and writers compiled a list of congressional roll call votes
and classified them as economic, social or foreign policy-related. The votes in each issue
area were subjected to a principal-components analysis, a statistical procedure designed to
determine the degree to which each vote resembled other votes in the same category (the same
members tending to vote together). The analysis also revealed which yea votes correlated with
which nay votes within each issue area (members voting yea on certain issues tended to vote
nay on others). The yea and nay positions on each roll call were then identified as conservative
or liberal. Each roll call vote was assigned a weight from 1 (lowest) to 3 (highest), based on
the degree to which it correlated with other votes in the same issue area. A higher weight
meant that vote was more strongly correlated with other votes and was therefore a better
test of economic, social or foreign-policy ideology. Members of Congress who participated in
at least half of the votes in each area received ratings. Members who missed more than half
the votes were not scored (shown as *). Absences and abstentions were not counted.
   Members of Congress were then ranked according to relative liberalism and conservatism. Finally, they were assigned percentiles showing their rank relative to others in the
chamber. The liberal percentage score means that the member's votes were more liberal than
that percentage of his or her colleagues' votes in that issue area in 2010. The conservative
score means that the member's votes were more conservative than that percentage of his or
her colleagues' votes. The composite score is an average of a member's six issue-based scores.

Key Votes

The key votes section illustrates a legislator's stances on important issues and provides clues
to his or her general ideology. The following list of key votes is from the 111th Congress
(2009–10) and was selected by *The Almanac* staff. A member who was absent, voted present,
or was not in office at the time of a vote receives an *. Roll call data were obtained from the
House clerk and Senate secretary. NV means "did not vote," and P means voted "present."

House Votes

2009:

1. **Overturn *Ledbetter* decision:** (House Vote 9/HR 11) Reverse the U.S. Supreme
   Court's decision in *Ledbetter v. Goodyear Tire & Rubber* by extending the statute of
   limitations in pay discrimination cases beyond 180 days. Jan. 9, 2009. (247-171) (D: 244-
   5; R: 3-166)
2. **Pass $820 billion stimulus:** (House Vote 46/HR 1) Approve an $820 billion bill to
   revive the U.S. economy. Jan. 28, 2009. (244-188) (D: 244-11; R: 0-177, NV-1)
3. **Allow guns in national parks:** (House Vote 277/HR 627) Permit people to carry guns
   in national parks and wildlife refuges. May 20, 2009. (279-147) (D: 105-145, NV-5; R:
   174-2, NV-2)
4. **Establish cap-and-trade system:** (House Vote 477/HR 2454) Allow industries to "buy
   and sell" pollution allowance credits as a way of reducing greenhouse gases. June 26,
   2009. (219-212) (D: 211-44, NV-1; R: 8-168, NV-2)
5. **Bar federal funds for abortion:** (House Vote 884/HR 3962) Prohibit the use of federal
   funds for health insurance plans that cover abortion. Nov. 7, 2009. (240-194) (D: 64-194;
   R: 176-0, P-1)
6. **Pass health care bill**: (House Vote 887/HR 3962) Approve a health care overhaul,
   including a government-run option for people without private insurance. Nov. 7, 2009.
   (220-215) (D: 219-39; R: 1-176)

2010:

1. **Regulate financial services industry:** (House Vote 413/HR 4173) Approve new federal regulations on financial services firms. June 30, 2010. (237-192) (D: 234-19, NV-2; R: 3-173, NV-2)
2. **Extend Bush-era tax cuts for middle class:** (House Vote 604/HR 4853) Continue the Bush-era income tax cuts for individuals earning less than $200,000 and households earning less than $250,000. Dec. 2, 2010. (234-188) (D: 231-20, NV-4; R: 3-168, NV-8)
3. **Stop Guantanamo transfers:** (House Vote 335/HR 5136) Prohibit the use of defense funds to transfer or release detainees at the U.S. facility at Guantanamo Bay, Cuba. May 28, 2010. (282-131) (D: 114-130, NV-10; R: 168-1, NV-8)
4. **Legalize kids of illegal immigrants:** (House Vote 625/HR 5281) Approve a bill to give children of illegal immigrants a path to legal status. Dec. 8, 2010. (216-198) (D: 208-38, NV-9; R: 8-160, NV-11)
5. **Repeal "Don't ask, don't tell":** (House Vote 638/HR 2965) Lift the ban on openly gay people serving in the military. Dec. 15, 2010. (250-175) (D: 235-15, NV-5; R: 15-160, NV-4)
6. **Limit campaign funds:** (House Vote 391/HR 5175) Pass the DISCLOSE Act requiring sponsors of campaign ads to identify themselves. June 24, 2010. (219-206) (D: 217-36, NV-2, R: 2-170, NV-6)

Senate Votes

2009:

1. **Overturn *Ledbetter* decision:** (Senate Vote 14/S 181) Reverse the U.S. Supreme Court's decision in *Ledbetter v. Goodyear Tire & Rubber* by extending the statute of limitations in pay discrimination cases beyond 180 days. Jan. 22, 2009. (61-36) (D: 54-0, NV-1; R: 5-36; I: 2-0)
2. **Pass $787 billion stimulus:** (Senate Vote 64/HR 1) Approve a $787 billion plan to revive the U.S. economy. Feb. 13, 2009. (60-38) (D: 55-0, NV-1; R: 3-38; I: 2-0)
3. **Repeal DC gun laws:** (Senate Vote 72/S 160) Repeal the District of Columbia's limits on firearms and its ban on semiautomatic weapons. Feb. 26, 2009. (62-36) (D: 22-33, NV-1; R: 40-1; I: 0-2)
4. **Confirm Sonia Sotomayor:** (Senate Vote 262/PN 506) Confirm Sonia Sotomayor to the U.S. Supreme Court. Aug. 6, 2009. (68-31) (D: 57-0, NV-1; R: 9-31; I: 2-0)
5. **Pass health care bill:** (Senate Vote 396/HR 3590) Approve a health care overhaul, including a provision letting private firms offer insurance policies regulated by the government. Dec. 24, 2009. (60-39) (D: 58-0; R: 0-39, NV-1; I: 2-0)

2010:

1. **Regulate financial services industry:** (Senate Vote 162/HR 4173) Approve new federal regulations on financial services firms. May 20, 2010. (59-39) (D: 53-2, NV-2; R: 4-37; I: 2-0)
2. **Extend Bush-era tax cuts except top 2%:** (Senate Vote 275/HR 4853) Continue the Bush-era tax cuts for everyone except the top 2% of income-earners. Dec. 15, 2010. (43-57) (D: 42-14; R: 0-42; I: 1-1)
3. **Legalize kids of illegal immigrants:** (Senate Vote 278/HR 5281) End debate on a bill to give children of illegal immigrants a path to legal status. Dec. 18, 2010. (55-41) (D: 50-5, NV-1; R: 3-36, NV-3; I: 2-0)
4. **Ratify New START:** (Senate Vote 298/Treaty Doc. 111-5) Ratify the New START treaty with Russia. Dec. 22, 2010. (71-26) (D: 56-0; R: 13-26, NV-3; I: 2-0)
5. **Confirm Elena Kagan:** (Senate Vote 229/PN 1768) Confirm Elena Kagan to the U.S. Supreme Court. Aug. 5, 2010. (63-37) (D: 56-1; R: 5-36; I: 2-0)
6. **Oppose EPA regulating greenhouse gases:** (Senate Vote 184/SJR 26) Pass a resolution opposing the EPA's decision to regulate greenhouse gases under the Clean Air Act. June 10, 2010. (47-53) (D: 6-51; R: 41-0; I: 0-2)
7. **Repeal "Don't ask, don't tell":** (Senate Vote 281/HR 2965) Lift the ban on openly gay people serving in the military. Dec. 18, 2010. (65-31) (D: 55-0, NV-1; R: 8-31, NV-3; I: 2-0)

NOTE: Freshman members of the House and Senate, because they were newly arrived in 2011, do not have key votes or vote scores from the interest groups and *National Journal* for the 111th Congress (2009–10).

Election Results

Listed for House members are results of the 2010 general, runoff and primary elections, as well as any special elections held since November 2008. The most recent election results are listed for senators and governors. Due to rounding decisions, some totals may equal more or less than 100%. Candidates in primaries receiving less than 5% of the total vote and candidates in general elections receiving less than 2% of the total were excluded. Election results were supplied by Polidata.

Prior winning percentage: This is winning percentage for the incumbent in past elections.

Presidential vote: Results were compiled from state and local election authorities; caucus results are not provided. Polidata estimates the presidential vote by congressional district from information collected from state and local election offices. A handful of states provide district-level presidential vote data. By necessity, other results are aggregated from precinct-level returns. Voting data from districts with split precincts and centrally counted absentee votes should be considered estimates; the allocation of these unassigned votes is determined by Polidata.

Campaign Finance: All data were derived from the candidates' and parties' filings with the Federal Election Commission. The dollar figure, in parentheses to the right of the election results, represents the candidates' total receipts for the period Jan. 1, 2009 to Dec. 31, 2010. The figures do not include all corrections or amendments filed with the FEC after May 2010. The total receipts figures for senators are from the Center for Responsive Politics, which tabulates receipts over the six years prior to a Senate election.

Demographics and Politics (Boxed)

Population: Figures are from the 2010 census and the U.S. Census Bureau's 2007–09 American Community Survey (ACS).

Urban/rural population: The percentage of total population living in areas defined by the bureau as urban or as rural. Figures for congressional districts are from the 2010 census. Some urban/rural figures had not been updated for 2010 at press time for *The Almanac* and are labeled as (2000).

Native of state: People born in a state of residence as a percentage of total population.

Not a citizen: People who are foreign born and not a citizen as a percentage of total population.

Area size: Area size is in square miles, including water.

Most populous cities: City population figures are from the 2010 census.

Household income: Household income as a percentage of all households.

Home value: Refers to self-estimated market value of owner-occupied units.

Work sector: A classification of employed persons 16 years and older. *Private* refers to people employed by private for-profit or not-for-profit organizations on a wage or salary basis. *Government* refers to federal, state and local government employees.

Unemployment: Unemployed, non-military people 16 years and older as a percentage of the labor force.

Poverty status: The percentage of people 16 years and older for whom poverty status has been determined and who fall below the poverty line, defined by the federal government in 2009 as a family of four living on $22,050 or less a year.

Occupation ("collar"): The percentage of employed persons 16 years and older. *White collar* refers to managerial, professional, sales and administrative occupations. *Blue collar* refers to construction, production and transportation occupations. *Khaki collar* refers to active-duty military personnel. *Other* refers to the balance of employed people, such as those in the farming or in health care, protective service or food preparation occupations.

Race/ethnicity: As defined by the Census Bureau, race reflects individual respondents' perceptions of their racial identity. Hispanic origin is defined as an ethnicity, and includes those who classified themselves in one of three specific Hispanic categories—Cuban, Mexican, or Puerto Rican—or as of "other Spanish/Hispanic origin." Persons of Latino or Hispanic origin may be of any race for census purposes, but *The Almanac* includes only non-Hispanic blacks in the black population category and only non-Hispanic whites in the white population category. The numbers provided for each racial or ethnic group represent a percentage of all people in a state or a congressional district.

Ancestry: Ethnic origin or descent. This category provides data for groups that were not included in the Census Bureau's Hispanic origin and race questions. Thus, it does not reflect diversity within Hispanic and Asian subgroups. The *USA* designation refers to "American" as a unique ethnicity if it was cited alone as a response, in the absence of other ethnicity. *Sub-Saharan* refers to the census category of "Sub-Saharan African." *West Indian* excludes Hispanic groups.

Language: The percentage of households speaking a certain language. The abbreviation *Other Eur.* refers to other Indo-European languages.

Education: *H.S. grad* refers to people with a high school diploma or higher and *college grad* refers to people with a bachelor's degree or higher, both as a percentage of people 25 years and older.

Military veterans: People who were in the Armed Forces as a percentage of voting-age population.

Registered Voters: The number of registered voters by party. The individual states' election bureaus or political parties provide figures. Some states have no voter registration. *D* refers to Democrat; *R* refers to Republican; and *other* refers to independent voters or those from minor parties.

Turnout: The share of the total voting age population that voted in the 2008 and 2010 elections. Basing calculations on voting age population permits comparisons across states and across districts, but it does not account for voting age persons who are not eligible to vote due to the status of their residency and citizenship, for example.

State information: Each legislature is referred to according to its proper name, with a breakdown of membership by party affiliation. Partisan composition figures are current as of June 2011. *D* refers to Democrat; *R* refers to Republican; *I* or *Indep.* refers to independents. *V* is used to indicate a vacancy in a seat as of June 2011.

Cook Partisan Voting Index: Developed in 1997 by political analyst Charlie Cook, the partisan voting index (PVI) is designed to provide a quick, overall assessment of a state or district's generic partisan strength. The PVI measures a state or district's recent partisan performance at the presidential level (district value) against that of the nation as a whole (national value). For this volume, the calculations are based on an average of 2004 and 2008 presidential election data for each district. Both years carry equal weight. Only votes for major party nominees are considered. The national Democratic value is 51.2 (an average of John Kerry's 48.8% share and Barack Obama's 53.7% share) and the national Republican value is 48.8. Thus, if Kerry and Obama won an average of 56.2% of the two-party vote in a given district, the district's PVI would be D +5, because it voted five percentage points more Democratic than the national average. A PVI value of "even" indicates an evenly balanced district.

Abbreviations

ACLU	American Civil Liberties Union	IC	Independent Conservative
ACU	American Conservative Union	ID	Independent Democrat
ADA	Americans for Democratic Action	IG	Independent Green
AFDC	Aid to Families with Dependent Children	IMC	Independent Maine Course
		Ind	Independence Party
AFL-CIO	American Federation of Labor and Congress of Industrial Organizations	IAP	Independent American Party (NV)
		IVP	Independent Voters Party
AFS	American Federation of State, County & Municipal Employees (AFSCME)	L	Liberal Party
		LCV	League of Conservation Voters
AID	Agency for International Development	LHOB	Longworth House Office Building
		Lib	Libertarian Party
AMI	American Independent (CA)	Mod	Moderate Party
ANWR	Arctic National Wildlife Refuge	NAFTA	North American Free Trade Agreement
BL	Better Life Party		
C	Conservative Party (NY)	NARAL	NARAL Pro-Choice America
CAFE	Corporate Average Fuel Economy	NFIB	National Federation of Independent Business
CAFTA	Central America Free Trade Agreement	NL	Natural Law Party
CFL	Connecticut for Lieberman	NP	Non-Partisan
CHOB	Cannon House Office Building	NPA	No Party Affiliation
CIA	Central Intelligence Agency	NRCC	National Republican Congressional Committee
CNP	Constitution Party		
CPF	Constitution Party of Florida	NRSC	National Republican Senatorial Committee
COC	Chamber of Commerce of the United States	NSA	National Security Agency
		NTU	National Taxpayers Union
COLA	Cost of Living Adjustment	PDP	Popular Democratic Party (PR)
DCCC	Democratic Congressional Campaign Committee	PF	Peace and Freedom Party
		PJ	Peace and Justice Party (NY)
DFL	Democratic-Farmer-Labor Party (MN)	POP	Populist Party
DLC	Democratic Leadership Council	PRG	Progressive Party
DNC	Democratic National Committee	Ref	Reform Party
DSCC	Democratic Senatorial Campaign Committee	RHOB	Rayburn House Office Building
		RMM	Ranking Minority Member
DSOB	Dirksen Senate Office Building	RNC	Republican National Committee
EMILY	EMILY's List (Early Money is Like Yeast)	RSOB	Russell Senate Office Building
		RTL	Right-to-Life Party
ERISA	Employee Retirement Income Security Act	S	Capitol Building Room, Senate side
		SOC	Socialist Party
FEC	Federal Election Commission	SW	Socialist Workers Party
FERC	Federal Energy Regulatory Commission	TEA	Tea Party
		UAW	United Auto Workers
Green	Green Party	WF	Working Families
H	Capitol Building Room-House side	WI	Write In
HSOB	Hart Senate Office Building		
I	Independent		

Open Field Politics...Continued

By Michael Barone

Americans voted in record numbers for Democrats in 2008. They voted in record numbers for Republicans in 2010. Not so long ago, in the years from 1995 to 2005, it seemed inconceivable that there could be such extreme oscillation in American voting behavior. That decade was described in *The Almanac of American Politics* as a period of trench warfare politics, in which the political parties resembled two equally sized armies in a culture war, with very little variation in partisan preference from one election to the next and with the capture of very small pieces of political ground—a few hundred votes in Florida—spelling the difference between victory and defeat.

Since 2005, we have experienced what *The Almanac* in 2007 described as open field politics, in which issue focus has changed constantly and voting behavior has varied widely from one election to the next. In 2006 and 2008, Americans veered sharply toward the Democrats. In 2010, they veered sharply to the Republicans.

In 2008, Democrat Barack Obama won 53% of the popular vote, more than any other presidential nominee of the world's oldest political party except Andrew Jackson, Franklin Roosevelt and Lyndon Johnson. He outpolled Grover Cleveland, Woodrow Wilson, Harry Truman, John Kennedy, Jimmy Carter and Bill Clinton. The popular vote for the House of Representatives has been a key political metric since the middle 1990s, when the parties' percentages for president and for the House converged. In 2008, Democratic candidates won 54% of the popular vote for the House and Republicans won only 43%. This was the Democrats' best showing since 1986, when they carried the House popular vote in the South (defined here as the 11 Confederate states plus West Virginia, Kentucky and Oklahoma). In the 36 non-Southern states, Democrats in 2008 carried the popular vote for the House by 57%-40%, their biggest margin in those states since the beginning of the 20th century. Just two years later, Republicans posted a record performance. They won the popular vote for the House in 2010 by 52%-45%, the same percentage split as in 1994 and their best showing since the election of 1946.

There was speculation after the 2008 election, not without some basis, that a new Democratic era had begun, just as there was speculation after George W. Bush's re-election and the Republican victories of 2004 that a new Republican era was at hand. In both instances, the speculation was squelched, first by the Democratic victories in 2006 and most recently by the Republican triumphs in 2010.

Obama carried 28 states with 361 electoral votes, plus three from the District of Columbia and one from Nebraska's proportional voting system, for a total of 365 electoral votes. John McCain carried 22 states with 173 electoral votes. Democrats did even better in House elections in 2008. They carried the popular vote for the House in 35 states with 401 electoral votes; add the District of Columbia and the total is 404. Republicans carried the popular vote for the House in only 15 states with 134 electoral votes. Democrats won the House popular vote in the North 57%-40%, their best showing since the beginning of the 20th century, and they only narrowly lost the House popular vote in the South by 50%-47%, their best showing in the region since 1992. Republicans carried the House popular vote in only two Obama states (Delaware and Florida), while Democrats carried the House popular vote in eight McCain states—four in the South (Georgia, Mississippi, Tennessee and West Virginia) and four outside the South (Arizona, Missouri, North Dakota and South Dakota).

The House popular vote expressed in electoral vote terms looked very different in 2010. Democrats carried the popular vote for the House in only 15 states and the District of Columbia, for a total of 187 electoral votes. Republicans carried the popular vote for the House in 35 states with 351 electoral votes. Of the 15 Democratic states, eight were in the Northeast, three were on the Pacific coast, one was Hawaii, and only three—Illinois, Minnesota and New Mexico—were in the vast interior or on the southern rim of the country. It is an exaggeration, but perhaps a revealing one, to say that the Republicans swept everything from the George Washington Bridge to the Donner Pass.

Between the 2008 and 2010 elections, the Democratic percentage of the House popular vote fell by 9% and the Republican percentage rose by 9%. This may not seem like a lot, but it is the largest shift in partisan preference since the elections of 1946 and 1948. By way of comparison, in the five House elections during the trench warfare period between 1995 and 2005, the Democratic percentage of the popular vote oscillated between 46% and 49%, and the Republican percentage varied between 48% and 51%, with the Republicans coming out ahead narrowly all five times. Similarly, in the four elections between 1984 and 1990, the Democratic percentage fluctuated between 52% and 55%, and the Republican percentage between 45% and 47%, with the Democrats ahead all four times.

Government Expansion: Then and Now

There is an interesting similarity between the 2008-10 and 1946-48 periods. In both, to a greater extent than at any time in between, voters were faced with a choice between a Democratic Party that mostly wanted to greatly increase the size and scope of government and a Republican Party that almost unanimously opposed government expansion. In his 1944 State of the Union address, Franklin Roosevelt set forth a program for postwar America that included graduated income taxes, government controls on crop prices and food prices and continued controls on wages. He asserted that every citizen had a right to health care, decent housing and an education. It was the American equivalent of the British Labour Party's contemporaneous program, based on the wartime Beveridge Report, for a cradle-to-grave welfare state, though without Labour's proposals to nationalize the commanding heights of the economy. Roosevelt's program was embraced by his successor, Truman, and it was arguably rejected by American voters in November 1946.

The 80th Congress that was installed after that election was labeled by Truman as the "Do Nothing Congress" for refusing to enact the Democrats' program, but it in fact did a lot. The Republican majorities, with support from at least half of the Southern Democrats (the 14 Southern states elected 10 Republicans and 113 Democrats to the House), cut taxes more than any other Congress in history, abolished wage and price controls, passed the Taft-Hartley Act (over Truman's veto) limiting the power of labor unions, and rejected public housing, federal aid to education, and national health insurance. Democrats won a major victory in the 1948 elections, sweeping back to majorities in Congress. But they were split between Northern and Southern Democrats, and they were unable to repeal Taft-Hartley or to pass the housing, education and health insurance bills that liberals supported. Congress didn't raise tax rates until after the outbreak of the Korean War.

Republicans were able to win congressional majorities only once more, in 1952, until they captured a majority in the Senate in 1980 and majorities in both houses in 1994. During that long period, there was a substantial expansion in government after the election of 1964, and a limited contraction after the election of 1980. But the share of gross domestic product represented by federal revenues and federal government spending oscillated within a relatively narrow band.

The election of Obama and of what amounted to Democratic supermajorities in Congress (although they held a 60-vote Senate supermajority sufficient to overcome a Republican filibuster only from July 2009, when Minnesota Democrat Al Franken was sworn in, until February 2010, when Massachusetts Republican Scott Brown took office) presented Americans once again with the question of whether the size and scope of government should be vastly expanded. The Obama Democrats were faced as well with the very difficult question of how to respond to a financial crisis that had plunged the country into a deep recession in the short period between the national conventions in late summer 2008 and the inauguration of the 44th president in January 2009. They responded with the $787 billion economic stimulus bill in February 2009 and a budget that greatly increased government's share of GDP. This reflected in part a sharp, recessionary reduction in GDP, but it also reflected a steep increase in government spending. In addition, the Democrats continued to superintend the major banks, the failed insurance company AIG, the government-sponsored enterprises Fannie Mae and Freddie Mac, and the bankruptcy proceedings of General Motors and Chrysler—all of them initiated during the final months of the Bush administration. And the Democrats embarked on ambitious plans for national health care legislation, for reducing carbon dioxide emissions, for adjusting financial regulation and for increasing tax rates on high-income earners. This agenda was not exactly Roosevelt's 1944 platform, but it did represent a major escalation in the size and scope of government.

Rise of the Tea Party

There was every indication that Obama and the Democratic leaders in Congress expected these efforts to stimulate economic recovery and to be popular with voters. They had talked about many of these initiatives during the congressional campaigns of 2006 and the presidential campaign of 2008. They viewed the Republican defeats in those years as not just a verdict on perceived GOP incompetence on matters ranging from the Iraq war and Hurricane Katrina to the surge in spending earmarks, but as a verdict on ideology, a rejection of Bush's 2001 and 2003 tax cuts, of various forms of economic deregulation, and of intervention in Iraq. And they seemed to have absorbed the lesson taught by the historians of the New Deal: Economic distress would make American voters more supportive of, or at least amenable to, big-government policies.

This proposition turned out to be mistaken. On Feb. 19, 2009, soon after passage of the stimulus legislation, CNBC reporter Rick Santelli, speaking from the floor of the Chicago Mercantile Exchange, delivered his famous rant calling for a "tea party." Interestingly, he was complaining not about high government spending but about mortgage modification and bailouts of improvident homeowners, and by implication, bailouts of large financial firms and auto companies, which of course were initiated before Obama became president. Thousands of people took part in tea party protests on tax day, April 15, taking aim at the stimulus bill, federal budget deficits and the Democrats' health care proposals. And they turned out in droves at town hall meetings held by Democratic members of Congress during the July and August recesses.

Public opinion polls showed the policies to be increasingly unpopular until in August 2009, Obama's job approval, well over 60% in his first months in office, fell to just over 50%. Even more surprising was the inrush into political activity of a multitude of previously uninvolved citizens symbolized by, but not limited to, the tea party movement. This was a mass phenomenon that in some ways resembled the peace movement that emerged in the late 1960s and early 1970s, although admirers of each movement tend to resent the comparison. In both cases, large numbers of people were motivated to enter into political activity because of their strong beliefs, not on peripheral issues, but on the most serious public policy questions of the day—war or peace, the size and scope of government. In both movements, the participants by and large were ordinary citizens, some of whom turned out to have fine political instincts: Democratic Rep. Patricia Schroeder of Colorado was elected to the House as a peace candidate in 1972, and Republican Ron Johnson, an Oshkosh plastics manufacturer, ran for the Senate in 2010 and beat three-term Democratic incumbent Russ Feingold.

Both movements also included, as self-directed mass movements often do, a certain number of fringe characters. Christine O'Donnell, who won the September 2010 Republican Senate primary in Delaware, proceeded to lose the general election by a wide margin after a campaign highlighted by revelations that she dabbled in witchcraft as a young woman. Initially, the peace and tea party movements were avowedly nonpartisan. Republican Rep. Pete McCloskey of California ran against Richard Nixon for the 1972 Republican nomination as a peace candidate. But soon, the bulk of their energies were concentrated within one of the two major parties. Both movements produced insurgent candidates who beat moderates in party primaries and then lost in the general election. The peace movement had a profound and lasting effect on the Democratic Party, which had been the more interventionist party on foreign policy in the 50 years from 1917 to 1967 and has been the more anti-interventionist party in the 44 years since. Whether the tea party movement will have such a powerful and lasting effect on the Republican Party remains to be seen, but it certainly had a strong impact on Republicans in 2010.

The Democratic Slide of 2010

As Democrats struggled and missed deadlines in passing complex health care and carbon emissions legislation, their standing in public opinion polls declined. When Obama took office, psephologists extrapolating from the 2006 and 2008 election results speculated that Democrats might gain Senate seats in the 2010 cycle. And indeed, they did gain two seats and attained the 60 they needed to overcome a filibuster when Pennsylvania Republican Arlen Specter switched parties in April 2009 and Franken was finally judged the winner in the close Minnesota contest. By August 2009, the Democrats' prospects for gains in the Senate and House had dimmed, although few predicted that Republicans would gain the 11 Senate seats and 40 House seats they needed to claim majorities. By a narrow margin, the House in June 2009 passed a bill establishing a carbon emissions trading system, a clear priority of Speaker Nancy Pelosi. By a similarly narrow margin, and after concessions by Pelosi on a contentious abortion funding issue, the House in November passed major health care legislation. The Senate, after concessions to individual senators to secure the last handful of votes, passed its version of health care legislation just before Christmas. Democrats reckoned they could reconcile the two versions and produce a final health care bill early in the new year.

Then came a thunderbolt. Liberal stalwart Edward Kennedy of Massachusetts died in office in August 2009, and in the January 2010 special election for the Senate seat Kennedy held for 47 years, Brown beat Democrat Martha Coakley 52%-47%. The upset resulted from a convergence of factors: an attractive Republican candidate, a mistake-prone and overly confident Democrat and the involvement of tea party activists. A Rasmussen poll released on Jan. 5, 2010, two weeks before the election, showed Brown trailing by just 50%-41% and a flood of contributions—over $1 million a day—flowed into his campaign over the Internet. The fact that this upset occurred in Massachusetts, which Obama carried 62%-36% and which had not elected a Republican senator in 38 years, made it all the more striking. Brown had campaigned explicitly as the 41st vote to block the Democratic health care initiative. Obama and Pelosi continued to press for the legislation, and finally settled on a strategy of having the House pass the Senate bill and then having both houses pass a reconciliation measure altering it somewhat, which under Senate rules would require only 50 votes. With perseverance, Pelosi squeezed out the necessary votes—an impressive feat of legislative leadership.

After this achievement, the Democratic leadership in Congress was in some disarray, as Republican leaders had been in 2006, their last year in the majority. Neither the House nor the Senate passed a budget resolution, which was not only contrary to the dictates of the 1974 budget law, but also meant that the Senate could pass no more legislation with a simple majority under the budget reconciliation process. The appropriations bills were not brought forward. The Senate also could not pass promised bills on cap-and-trade and immigration, much less a bill sought by labor unions to make it easier to organize workers. Plans to raise tax rates on high-income earners, long a staple of Democratic platforms, by extending the 2001 and 2003 tax cuts except for those earning more than $250,000 annually were left until after the election. By September 2010, it was clear that Democrats were at serious risk of losing their majority in the House and at some risk of losing their majority in the Senate. The Democrats' campaign committee in the House, under the able leadership of Maryland Rep. Chris Van Hollen, even cut off funding to several incumbents—triage suggesting there might be many casualties in store.

The November elections produced massive Republican gains. The Republicans gained six seats in the Senate, enough to reduce the Democrats' majority to 53-47. Republicans prevailed in Arkansas, where incumbent Blanche Lincoln was defeated 58%-37%; in Illinois, where Mark Kirk claimed Obama's former seat, 48%-46%; in Indiana, where Dan Coats took the seat vacated by Evan Bayh, 55%-40%; in North Dakota, where Gov. John Hoeven ended Republicans' 30-year losing streak in Senate contests with a 76%-22% victory; in Pennsylvania, where Specter lost the Democratic primary and Pat Toomey captured his seat, 51%-49%; and in Wisconsin, where Johnson beat Feingold, 52%-47%. In Delaware, O'Donnell predictably lost, where the moderate Rep. Mike Castle, whom she beat in the September primary, would probably have won. In Nevada, Sharron Angle lost by a wide margin to Senate Majority Leader Harry Reid, who was aided by an all-out effort by casino owners and unions to retain a powerful incumbent, especially as the state's other senator, Republican John Ensign, was increasingly enmeshed in a scandal that ultimately led to his resignation in May 2011. In Colorado, Republican nominee Ken Buck lost 48%-46% to appointed incumbent Michael Bennet.

Republicans won 63 seats in the House, by a considerable margin the largest gain for either party since 1948. The national map of congressional districts, which was about half red and half blue after the 2008 election, was closer to 80% red after the election. Democrats held geographically compact central-city and inner-suburban districts and black-majority districts in the South, but only a few clusters of rural and small-town seats.

Republican gains were even more impressive at the state level. They went into the 2010 elections with 24 governorships and emerged with 29; Democrats went in with 26 governorships and emerged with 20. One of them, Rhode Island's, was won by former Republican Sen. Lincoln Chafee running as an independent. Democrats won governorships in California, Connecticut, Hawaii, Minnesota and Vermont, states in which Republicans were not running for re-election, while Republicans picked up governorships in Iowa, Kansas, Maine, Michigan, New Mexico, Ohio, Oklahoma, Pennsylvania, Tennessee, Wisconsin and Wyoming.

Implications for Redistricting

Lower down the ballot, Republicans captured more than 675 seats in state legislatures, attaining a level of dominance they have not enjoyed since the 1920s. Republicans had majorities in both houses of the legislature and control of the governorship in 20 states, Democrats in only 11. This obviously had serious implications for congressional redistricting. In the reapportionment following the 2010 census, the states won by Obama in 2008 lost a net six House seats, while the states won by McCain gained six House seats. And control of redistricting heavily favored Republicans. Two of the three largest states where Democrats hold the legislature and governorship, California and Washington, have redistricting commissions that are at least theoretically nonpartisan. Of the other 10 states with Democrats in power, Delaware and Vermont have just one congressional district each, Hawaii and Rhode Island have just two a piece, West Virginia has three and Arkansas four. There is not much room for gaining partisan advantage there. The four other states where Democrats have control are: Illinois (18 seats after reapportionment), Massachusetts (nine), Maryland (eight), and Connecticut (five). And even in these states, there is little opportunity for partisan gains. The existing plans in Illinois and Maryland were drawn by Democrats, and Massachusetts and Connecticut already have achieved all-Democratic House delegations. Plus, Massachusetts lost one of those seats in reapportionment.

Although the prospects for Republican gains in redistricting are considerably greater than for the Democrats, they may not be as great as they first appear. The 20 states where Republicans have control of both the legislature and governorship will have 196 representatives in the 113th Congress (2013-14). But chances for GOP pickups are minimal to nonexistent in Idaho (two seats after reapportionment), Kansas (four), Maine (two), North Dakota (one), South Dakota (one), Utah (four) and Wyoming (one). Existing plans were drawn by Republicans in Florida (27), Georgia (14), Michigan (14), Ohio (16), Pennsylvania (18), and Texas (36).

The Voting Rights Act, which under prevailing interpretations requires maximizing the number of majority-black and majority-Hispanic districts, will affect redistricting in several states. This works to the Republicans' advantage in some cases: Cordoning off heavily Democratic black voters or somewhat less heavily Democratic Hispanic voters into one or two districts tends to make adjacent districts more Republican. But rising numbers of Hispanics in Arizona, Florida and Texas may mean that the seven seats those three states gained from reapportionment will not all go to Republicans. And the new seat in South Carolina may end up as a second black-majority district. Plans passed in spring 2011 in Indiana and Missouri seem likely to cost Democrats one seat in each state, and it was possible to imagine similar small gains for Republicans in Ohio and Wisconsin. Republicans' best prospect for additional seats may be in North Carolina, where the Democratic governor under the state constitution does not have the power to veto redistricting legislation passed by the Republican-controlled legislature. And the existing plan was artfully drawn by Democrats.

Lessons for 2012

What explains the wildly different responses of voters in 2008 and 2010? And what comes next?

One explanation is voters repudiated Republicans in 2008 more on grounds of competence than of ideology, and they rejected Democrats in 2010 more on ideology than on competence. The Obama Democrats, in this view, misinterpreted the results of the 2008 election and, tempted by their large majorities, advanced policies that voters never actually endorsed. Voters certainly may have heard Democrats promoting such policies, but for the preceding 14 years, when Republicans either controlled the House or held the White House, there was no real chance they would be enacted, and so voters paid them little heed until the first months of 2009. Polling in the late summer also revealed voters' anxiety about the economy, which was only sluggishly emerging from the deep recession of 2007-09. Sixty percent of Americans reported having little faith that Obama's economic stimulus legislation would work, and most opposed any additional stimulus spending by the federal government.

Another explanation is that American voters tend to express considerable unhappiness with the status quo and favor change in the abstract, but when they are presented with the prospect of substantial change in either political direction, they tend to balk. In this view, they administered significant setbacks to Ronald Reagan's Republicans in 1982 and to Clinton's Democrats in 1994. They did not punish Republicans in 1990, after George H.W. Bush had compromised with Democrats on raising tax rates. They may have been inclined to go against George W. Bush and his party in 2002, but the September 11 attacks had the effect of rallying Americans behind the president. Voters did in fact repudiate Bush and his party in 2006. Americans tend to favor divided government, in this view, not just as an abstract proposition but also in practice. When one party or the other moves away from the status quo, in spite of all their grumbling about the way things are, voters seem to find it preferable to substantial change. After all, most Americans neither live in a state of material misery nor suffer political oppression as, arguably, most human beings in history have.

A third way to explain these results is to say that the electorate that turned out to vote in the midterm election of 2010 was not representative of the larger electorate that turned out in the presidential year of 2008 (and will likely turn out in the presidential year of 2012). There is something to this: Turnout among black Americans was unusually high in 2008, both because of the organizational efforts of the Obama campaign and because of spontaneous enthusiasm for the first black major-party presidential candidate in American history. Turnout among young voters in 2008 also increased from 2004. The age group 18 to 24 was the only one to post a statistically significant uptick, perhaps as a result of the Obama campaign targeting residents of college towns and singles' apartment zones in big metro areas.

But in the past two decades, increases in the number of votes cast have not necessarily correlated with Democratic victories. Voter participation was high both in the Democratic year of 1992 and the Republican year of 1994. It declined 8% between 1992 and 1996, when Clinton won a second term, and 7% between 1994 and 1998, when Republicans held on to their popular vote plurality and majority in the House. The number of ballots cast rose 9% between the presidential years of 1996 and 2000, and it went up somewhat more, 11%, between the midterm elections of 1998 and 2002. The biggest increase was the 16% from 2000 to 2004, when George W. Bush won a second term and Republicans won a majority of the House popular vote. The number of voters was up only 7% between 2004 and 2008, when Obama and the Democrats won big. And it rose 9% between the midterm elections of 2002 and 2006, culminating in a Democratic victory, and 8% between 2006 and 2010, culminating in a Republican victory. Overall, the electorate increased at a slower rate than population growth between 1994 and 2000 and at a faster rate than population growth since 2000.

From all of this, it is possible to imagine two different scenarios for 2012. In one, the Democrats continue to be rejected on ideological grounds, as they arguably were in 2010. Obama is denied a second term in favor of the Republican nominee, and Republicans hold onto their House majority and win a majority in the Senate. In the second scenario, voters reject as overreach the policies advanced by Republicans in 2011 and 2012 just as they rejected as overreach the policies advanced by Democrats in 2009 and 2010. Obama wins a second term, the Republicans' House majority is reduced or eliminated, and the Senate remains divided approximately as it is now. Other scenarios may take shape. A public disenchanted with both political parties may rally toward an independent candidate, as it did toward Ross Perot in the spring of 1992. International events or another outbreak of terrorism may vastly strengthen or weaken the incumbent president. An egregious mistake may disqualify the Republican challenger or even the Democratic president. In a period of open field politics, surprises have become the norm.

President

Barack Obama (D)

Elected 2008, term expires Jan. 2013, 1st term; b. Aug. 4, 1961, Honolulu, HI; home, Chicago, IL; Attended Occidental College, 1979-81, Columbia U., B.A. 1983, Harvard U., J.D. 1991; United Church of Christ; married (Michelle); 2 children.

Elected Office: IL Senate, 1996-2004; U.S. Senate, 2005-08.

Professional Career: Dir., Illinois Project Vote!, 1992; Practicing atty., 1993-2004; Lecturer, U. of Chicago, 1992-2004.

Vice President

Joe Biden (D)

Elected 2008, term expires Jan. 2013, 1st term; b. Nov. 20, 1942, Scranton, PA; home, Wilmington, DE; U. of DE, B.A. 1965, Syracuse U., J.D. 1968; Catholic; married (Jill); 3 children.

Elected Office: New Castle Cnty. Cncl., 1970-72; U.S. Senate, 1973-2009.

Professional Career: Practicing atty., 1968-72.

Population		Household Income		Work	
Pop. 2010:	308,745,538	Under $15k:	13%	Private:	78.3%
Change since 2000:	Up 9.5%	$15k to $50k:	35.8%	Government:	15%
Urban (2000):	79%	$50k to $100k:	31%	Self-employed:	6.4%
Rural (2000):	21%	$100k to $200k:	16.3%	Unemployment (2010):	9.6%
Native of U.S.:	59%	Over $200k:	4%		
Foreign born::	12.5%	Median income:	$51,369	Blue collar:	21.5%
Not a citizen:	7%	**Home Value**		White collar:	60.3%
Most populous cities		Under $100k:	22.6%	Khaki collar:	0.4%
New York	8,175,133	$100k to $300k:	47.5%		
Los Angeles	3,792,621	$300k to $500k:	17.2%		
Chicago	2,695,598	$500k to $1 mil:	10.3%		
Houston	2,099,451	Over $1 million:	2.5%		
		Median:	$191,900		

Race/Ethnicity				Military Veterans		Voters in 2010 and 2008	
White:	63.7%	**Language**		% of Pop:	9.7%	Number of voters	
Black:	12.2%	English:	80.2%	*Veterans by Period*		in 2010:	90,321,305
Hispanic:	16.3%	Spanish:	12.3%	WWII and before:	10.8%	Turnout as % of	
Asian:	4.7%	Asian:	3%	Korea:	11.4%	voting age:	38.5%
Native Am.:	0.7%	Other European:	3.7%	Vietnam:	32.8%	Number of voters	
Hawaiian:	0.2%	**Education**		Gulf (pre-2001):	11.7%	in 2008:	131,312,554
Two+ races:	1.9%	H.S. grad:	85%	Gulf (post-2001):	8.2%	Turnout as % of	
Age		College grad:	27.8%	Peace time:	25.2%	voting age:	57.1%
Median age:	36.7 yrs.	Grad degree:	10.2%				
More than 65 yrs:	12.7%						
Less than 18 yrs:	24.4%						

2008 Presidential Vote

Obama (D)............................69,498,215 (53%)
McCain (R).........................59,948,240 (46%)

2004 Presidential Vote

Bush (R) 62,040,606 (51%)
Kerry (D) 59,028,109 (48%)

★ ALABAMA ★

In 1813, Andrew Jackson and his army defeated the Red Stick band of the Creek Indians at Horseshoe Bend, in what is now Tallapoosa County—and set the course for the future of Alabama. The Indians were removed, as Jackson insisted, and white settlers poured in. The first wave was from the north as farmers from Tennessee swept into the red clay hills. You can see their early Greek Revival buildings in historic Huntsville, surrounded by the boomtown that has grown up around the Marshall Space Flight Center. But Jacksonian Alabama was anything but civil and classical. The settlers brought the fighting faith of the Scots-Irish, a hot-spirited willingness to fight to the death against any perceived insult or threat. The other surge of settlement into Alabama came a decade later, when entrepreneurial Southern planters brought slaves in to pick cotton in the fertile Black Belt (so named for its soil) east and west of Montgomery in the middle of the state. The interplay between the offspring of these two streams of settlers has been the stuff of Alabama politics ever since. The Jacksonians' fighting spirit led them to join the planters to support secession. The first Confederate Congress convened, and Jefferson Davis took the oath of office as president of the Confederacy, in the Alabama Capitol in February 1861.

After the Civil War, Alabama, like other Southern states, became solidly Democratic, with an angry populist accent. Birmingham, with its solid-iron Red Mountain, became the South's first steel producer in the 1880s. Alabama politics in the first half of the 20th century was a struggle between plantation owners of the Black Belt and populists who favored New Deal government spending to help the little guy. Among the latter group was the senator and later Supreme Court Justice Hugo Black, Sens. Lister Hill and John Sparkman, Gov. "Kissin' Jim" Folsom, and the local economic potentates they called the "Big Mules."

Alabama went on to become, kicking and screaming, one of the birthplaces of the civil rights movement. Down the hill from the capitol is the Dexter Avenue King Memorial Baptist Church, where in December 1956 the 27-year-old Martin Luther King Jr. led the boycott following Montgomery seamstress Rosa Parks' refusal to move to the back of the bus. A hundred miles north in Birmingham, while King was held in jail in May 1963, Birmingham Police Commissioner Bull Connor, then Alabama's Democratic national committeeman, ordered police dogs and fire hoses to be turned on peaceful demonstrators. Four months later, four girls were killed when a bomb exploded in Birmingham's 16th Street Baptist Church. (The bombers were convicted in 1977, 2001 and 2002.) In March 1965, a civil rights marcher was murdered in Montgomery two weeks after police beat dozens of people at Selma's Edmund Pettus Bridge. Another activist was shot and killed in Lowndes County that August. These events had reverberations far beyond Alabama. In June 1963, President Kennedy endorsed what would become the Civil Rights Act of 1964, and in March 1965, Congress passed the Voting Rights Act.

While Alabamians like Parks were leading the nation toward civil rights, Alabama's most prominent politician of the time, George Wallace, was pulling the other way. Elected governor in 1962, he made national news in June 1963 by standing in a schoolhouse door to defy a federal court desegregation order. In 1964, Wallace ran in the Democratic presidential primaries against Lyndon Johnson. In 1968, he ran for president as a third-party candidate and won 13.5% of the vote. He ran in the Democratic primaries again in 1972, and was partially paralyzed by a gunshot wound while campaigning in May. He took delegates to the national convention, and did not lose his potency as a national politician until Jimmy Carter beat him in the March 1976 Florida primary. But he remained the key figure in Alabama for three decades, running his wife to succeed him in 1966 (she died midterm), regaining the governorship in 1970 and again in 1974, and then running and winning one last time in 1982. He spent his last, sad years apologizing for his acts, meeting with the student he tried to block in the schoolhouse door, and proclaiming, "The South has changed, and for the better." He died in September 1998.

It was during Wallace's last term as governor, in 1983, that the state government started publishing a black heritage guide. Today, heritage tourism commemorating the civil rights movement is one of the fastest-growing segments of the tourism industry, and Alabama is leading the way. Montgomery boasts artist Maya Lin's circular Civil Rights Memorial, Troy University's Rosa Parks Museum, the Dexter Parsonage, and the end point of the Selma-to-Montgomery trail. The Edmund Pettus Bridge in Selma, the Selma-to-Montgomery interpretive center in Lowndes County, and the Tuskegee Airmen National Historic Site are all on the Alabama Civil Rights Museum Trail. In 2007, the Alabama Legislature passed a resolution apologizing for slavery.

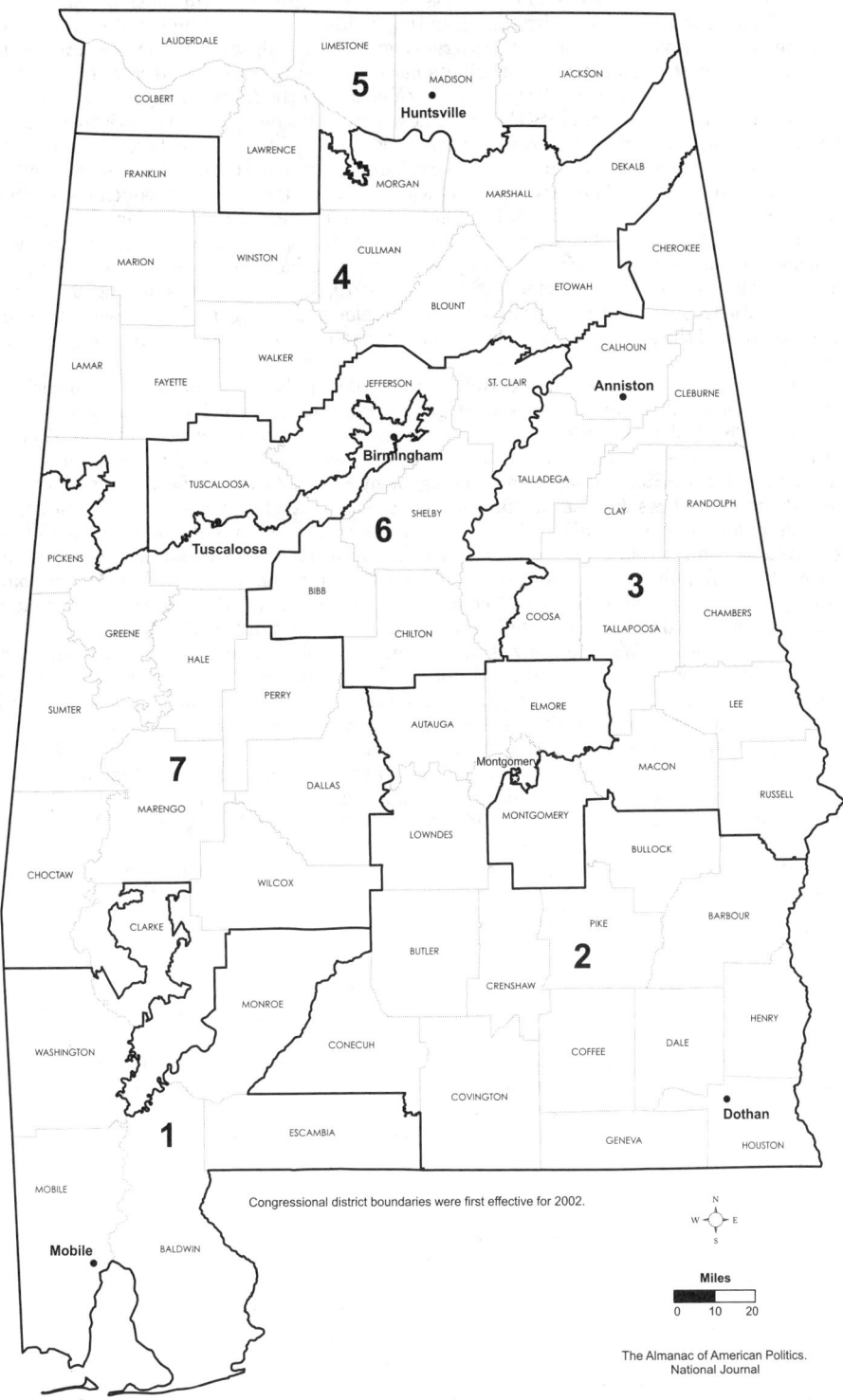

Congressional district boundaries were first effective for 2002.

Miles
0   10   20

Economically, Alabama in recent years has been gaining ground lost during the Wallace years. While Atlanta was peacefully desegregating and beginning decades of vibrant white-collar growth, Birmingham was violently resisting the civil rights movement, only to see its once substantial blue-collar base in the steel industry shrink and its most talented residents of all races flee to calmer climes. But Alabama's economy has been moving ahead recently. Autos have played a major part, and not just at the Talladega NASCAR racetrack or the Porsche Sport Driving School in Leeds. Big, new automobile manufacturing plants have opened with Mercedes in Tuscaloosa, Honda in Talladega County, and Hyundai in Montgomery. Unions have tried to organize them without success. A state that produced no cars in 1994 now is the second largest auto-producing state in the nation, with 140,000 auto-related jobs. In addition, ThyssenKrupp is building a large steel processing plant near Mobile and General Electric is building a plant near Auburn to make coatings for components in military jet engines. During the recent recession, unemployment zoomed upward from an historic low of 3.1% in October 2007, but in 2010, the economy was moving ahead faster than the national average. Domestic in-migration accelerated during the decade, with an increasing percentage of the population born out-of-state, though Alabama still has relatively few immigrants.

Alabama's economic progress was rudely interrupted in the spring of 2011 by a major storm system that hatched deadly tornadoes throughout the state. After the tornadoes struck on April 27, at least 250 Alabama residents were dead and property damage was estimated at $5 billion, with the greatest destruction in the metro areas of Tuscaloosa and Birmingham. Rural areas were hardly spared. The Alabama Emergency Management Agency declared disaster areas in 38 of the state's 67 counties. President Barack Obama went to Tuscaloosa two days later and declared, "I've never seen destruction like this." Whole neighborhoods were obliterated, and 5,000 homes were destroyed. The storm system hit several states in the South, but Alabama took the brunt of the fury. Newly elected Republican Gov. Robert Bentley, confronting a massive rebuilding effort, toured Tuscaloosa neighborhoods with the Democratic president and said, "When you see areas of the city where you have lived for 35 years totally demolished, it makes it difficult."

Politically, George Wallace delayed for a generation Alabama's move toward the Republican Party. But in the two decades after he last appeared on the ballot, Alabama developed two-party politics and then, starting with presidential elections and going down the ballot to state legislative elections, became a solidly Republican state by 2010. Democrats remained competitive in governor races from 1990 through 2002, with virtually unanimous support from black voters and backing from the well-organized teachers' unions and trial lawyers. Republicans for a time were rent by divisions between affluent suburbanites and white evangelical Protestants. But they made breakthroughs in state Supreme Court races and down-ballot statewide offices in the 2000s. Democrats removed Republican Gov. Guy Hunt from office in 1993 and elected Don Siegelman governor in 1998. But Siegelman lost narrowly to Republican Bob Riley in 2002, despite carrying the central cities, the Black Belt, and many of the poor, white rural counties in the north—the coalition of blacks and poor whites that political scientist V.O. Key, Jr. longed for in his mid-century classic *Southern Politics*.

In 2010, the spotlight was on two very different candidates for governor: Artur Davis, the black U.S. House member running as a moderate, and former Chief Justice Roy Moore, a Republican whose placing of a huge model of the Ten Commandments in the Supreme Court building in 2001 triggered a controversy that resulted in his removal from the bench. But in the GOP primary in June, Moore finished fourth, with only 19% of the vote. The more consequential result was the 166-vote margin by which state Rep. Robert Bentley beat Tim James, the son of former Republican Gov. Fob James, in the first round of primary voting. The results moved Bentley ahead to a runoff, and in that contest, he prevailed 56%-44% over Bradley Byrne, a former state senator and college system chancellor who had Riley's backing. In the Democratic primary, Davis was beaten 62%-38% by Agriculture Commissioner Ron Sparks, a white candidate who was supported by prominent black organizations. Some 493,000 votes were cast in the Republican primary, more than the 318,000 cast in the Democratic primary—a vivid contrast with 1986, the year that Wallace retired, when 830,000 Alabamians voted in the Democratic primary and only 25,000 participated in the GOP primary.

In the general election, Bentley beat Sparks 58% to 42%. Voters rejected by a similar margin a ballot proposition, supported by Sparks, to divert $100 million of Gulf natural gas royalties to highway construction. They evidently preferred Bentley's no-new-taxes pledge and his proposal for business tax deductions for firms hiring unemployed workers.

There were Republican victories up and down the line. Democratic Lt. Gov. Jim Folsom Jr., who served as governor when the Mercedes plant deal was made, was defeated for re-election 51%-

48%. And GOP Sen. Richard Shelby was re-elected with 65%. In 2008, Democrats secured three of the state's seven seats in the U.S. House. But in 2010, 5th District Rep. Parker Griffith switched parties and then lost the Republican primary to Mo Brooks, and 2nd District Democratic Rep. Bobby Bright lost to Republican Martha Roby, a Montgomery City Council member. That left only the black-majority 7th District in Democratic hands, with the election there of Terri Sewell to Davis' former seat.

In the state legislature, the Democrats' 20-15 majority in the Senate and 60-45 edge in the House were reversed and more, as Republicans ended up ahead 22-12-1 in the Senate and 66-39 in the lower chamber—the first Republican majorities since 1874. In northern Alabama, the old TVA country, white voters stuck with Democrats for years, but abandoned them in 2010. Even the Democratic House majority leader, Ken Guin, lost 69%-31% to a UPS truck driver, and Senate Majority Leader Zeb Little also lost handily. To be sure, the statehouse Democrats had more working against them than Republican ascendancy in the South. Several incumbents were undone by a double-dipping scandal that revealed legislators were paid lucrative sums for part-time jobs in the state's two-year college system. In 2007, the state school board passed a policy banning incoming legislators from employment at state two-year colleges but several lawmakers had continued to draw paychecks for suspect jobs.

Population		Household Income		Work	
Pop. 2010:	4,779,736	Under $15k:	17.7%	Private:	77.1%
State rank:	23rd	$15k to $50k:	40.2%	Government:	16.9%
Change since 2000:	Up 7.5%	$50k to $100k:	28.3%	Self-employed:	5.9%
Urban:	54.8%	$100k to $200k:	11.7%	Unemployment (3-yr. average):	5.1%
Rural:	45.2%	Over $200k:	2.2%	Poverty:	16.7%
Native of state:	70.7%	Median income:	$41,458	Blue collar:	26.7%
Not a citizen:	2.1%			White collar:	56.7%
Area size:	52,420 sq. mi.	**Home Value**		Khaki collar:	0.5%
		Under $100k:	42.2%	Other:	16.2%
Most populous cities		$100k to $300k:	47.0%		
Birmingham	212,237	$300k to $500k:	7.4%	**Age**	
Montgomery	205,764	$500k to $1 mil:	2.6%	Median age:	37.3 yrs.
Mobile	195,111	Over $1 million:	0.7%	More than 65 yrs:	13.6%
Huntsville	180,105	Median:	$118,700	Less than 18 yrs:	24.1%

Race/Ethnicity				Military Veterans		Registered Voters in 2010	
White:	67.0%	*Language*		% of Pop:	11.3%	No Party registration	
Black:	26.0%	English:	95.6%			Voter turnout:	1,494,273
Hispanic:	3.9%	Spanish:	2.7%	*Veterans by Period*		Turnout as % of	
Asian:	1.1%	Asian:	0.7%	WWII and before:	8.5%	voting age:	41.0%
Native Am.:	0.5%	Other European:	0.8%	Korea:	10.5%		
Hawaiian:	0.0%			Vietnam:	32.2%	**Legislature**	
Two+ races:	1.3%	**Education**		Gulf (pre-2001):	14.0%	Senate:	12 D 22 R 1 I
		H.S. grad:	81.5%	Gulf (post-2001):	9.9%	House:	39 D 66 R
Ancestry		College grad:	21.8%	Peace time:	25.1%		
USA	11.1%	Grad degree:	7.8%				
Irish	9.3%						
English	8.5%						

Presidential politics   Alabama has become a solidly Republican state in presidential politics. George W. Bush carried it twice by wide margins. John McCain carried it 60%-39%, his best show-ing in all but four other states—Oklahoma, Wyoming, Utah, and Idaho. There was clear polarization by race, with McCain carrying whites 88%-10% and Barack Obama carrying blacks 98%-2%. Obama carried the Black Belt, Montgomery County, and Birmingham's Jefferson County. It was the first time it had gone Democratic since 1952, as whites had moved out to suburbs. McCain carried everything else. But this was not just a vote on race. Here as elsewhere Obama ran poorly among voters with Jacksonian roots.

Alabama's presidential primary for years was held in June, too late to count for much. It might have counted for something in 2008 if the Legislature had left it there. But in 2006, it moved the contest to February 5, Super Tues-

2008 Presidential Vote		
John McCain (R) 1,266,546	(60%)
Barack Obama (D) 813,479	(39%)

2008 Presidential Primary		
Barack Obama (D) 300,319	(56%)
Hillary Clinton (D)................223,089	(42%)

2008 Presidential Primary		
Mike Huckabee (R)................227,766	(41%)
John McCain (R) 204,867	(37%)
Mitt Romney (R)......................98,019	(18%)

2004 Presidential Vote		
George W. Bush (R)............1,176,394	(62%)
John Kerry (D) 693,933	(37%)

day, in the hope of getting some national attention. It didn't work. Alabama was overshadowed by big states such as New York and California that had also joined Super Tuesday. For the first time, more Alabamians voted in the Republican presidential primary, 552,000, than in the Democratic presidential primary, 537,000. Polls showed four different Republicans leading at some point in the cycle, but Mike Huckabee ended up edging McCain 41%-38%, with Mitt Romney at 18%. McCain carried the Black Belt, and the race was very close in the counties including Birmingham and Montgomery. Huckabee ran up big margins in northern, Jacksonian counties. On the Democratic side, blacks mostly voted for Barack Obama and whites mostly for Hillary Rodham Clinton, and Obama won, 56%-42%. A June primary might have turned out differently. The Republican contest would have been over by then, and with no party registration, more whites might have opted for the Democratic primary and boosted Clinton's total.

Congressional districting   Democrats drew the boundaries of the state's seven congressional districts after the 2000 Census with a shrewd eye to partisan advantage—but not shrewd enough to overcome Alabama's Jacksonian trend toward the Republican Party. They held on to the 5th District until the incumbent changed parties in 2010 and gained the Montgomery-based 2nd District for a term when it came open in 2008. Now Republicans will be in charge of drawing the lines, and Democrats seem unlikely to gain a second seat unless the Obama administration's Justice Department or a court can argue plausibly that a second black-majority district can be created—a tall order given the state's demography.

112th Congress Lineup	
6 R	1 D
111th Congress Lineup	
4 R	3 D

Governor

Robert Bentley (R)

Elected 2010, term expires Jan. 2015, 1st term; b. Feb. 3, 1943, Columbiana; home, Tuscaloosa; U. of AL, B.S. 1964; U. of AL (Birmingham), M.D. 1968; Southern Baptist; Married (Dianne); 4 children.

Military Career: U.S. Air Force, 1969-71.

Elected Office: AL House, 2002-10.

Professional Career: Intern, Carraway Methodist Hospital, 1968-69; Resident, dermatology, U. of AL Hospital, 1971-74; Founding partner/pres., AL Dermatology Assoc., 1974-2009.

Office: 600 Dexter Ave., 36130, 334-242-7100; Fax: 334-353-0004.

Election Results

2010 general	Robert Bentley (R)	860,472	(58%)
	Ron Sparks (D)	625,710	(42%)
2010 primary	Robert Bentley (R)	261,233	(56%)
	Bradley Byrne (R)	204,503	(44%)
2010 primary	Bradley Byrne (R)	137,451	(28%)
	Robert Bentley (R)	123,958	(25%)
	Tim James (R)	123,792	(25%)
	Roy Moore (R)	95,163	(19%)

Republican Robert Bentley came out of nowhere to be elected governor of Alabama in 2010, succeeding term-limited GOP Gov. Bob Riley. Bentley joked that not even his wife gave him a chance when he launched his campaign. He grew up in rural Columbiana, southeast of Birmingham, where his father worked at a sawmill. He put himself through college at the University of Alabama, majoring in chemistry and biology and earning a bachelor's degree in three years. Fulfilling a childhood dream to become a doctor, he went on to Alabama's medical school and received his M.D. in 1968. It was the height of the Vietnam era, and Bentley joined the Air Force. He was commissioned as a captain and served as a general medical officer at Pope Air Force Base at Fort Bragg in North Carolina. After completing his three-year residency, he moved to Tuscaloosa to start what became a successful dermatology practice.

Bentley entered politics in 2002 by winning a seat in the state House of Representatives with nearly 65% of the vote. He was an advocate of conservative causes, such as lowering taxes, and the main force behind revising the state's organ-donor laws. But he was never known as a rhetorical firebrand, displaying a low-key and mild-mannered style. He was re-elected without opposition in 2006, and in 2010 introduced a constitutional amendment to freeze property taxes for homeowners. He sponsored another constitutional amendment banning requirements that people or businesses participate in health-care plans, a slap at President Obama's health plan then being debated in Congress. Another of his proposals offered an income tax credit to businesses that hire unemployed workers and keep them on the payroll for one year.

As Bentley neared retirement from his dermatology practice in late 2008, he began thinking seriously about running for governor. He cited his experience in working with Democrats in the legislature and his desire to provide more Alabamians with access to health care. He announced his candidacy in May 2009, promising to develop better relations with lawmakers than Riley had. He played up his medical credentials, using the slogan "Alabama is sick, and we need a doctor." But he struggled to raise money, with most of it coming from individuals and companies around Tuscaloosa. By May 2010, he had loaned his campaign nearly $800,000 out of his personal fortune. Also by that time, he had two better-known and better-funded GOP primary opponents—businessman Tim James, the son of former Gov. Fob James, and Bradley Byrne, a former state senator and college system chancellor who had Riley's backing. Three other Republicans also vied for the seat, including former state Supreme Court Justice Roy Moore, who drew national attention for his refusal to remove a monument of the Ten Commandments from the state courthouse in defiance of a federal judge's order.

In the June primary, Byrne captured 28% of the vote while Bentley and James were tied with 25% each. Bentley had a slim advantage over James of fewer than 200 votes out of almost half a million cast. Moore finished a distant fourth with 19%. The results set up a runoff between Byrne and Bentley. At a time when political outsiders were gaining visibility in other political races nationwide, Bentley was perceived as being less tied to the state's GOP establishment. He also portrayed Byrne as less of a Republican than himself, citing Byrne's votes for Democrats Bill Clinton and Michael Dukakis in previous presidential elections. And he had two outside groups help do the dirty work of negative campaigning. One of them, the True Republican PAC, ran advertisements questioning whether Byrne believed the Bible is fact as well as whether he opposed teaching creationism in public schools. Meanwhile, the Alabama Education Association carried on a verbal war with Byrne over an overhaul of two-year colleges that diminished the teachers group's clout while he was chancellor. Bentley won the runoff, 56% to Byrne's 44%.

Bentley's opponent in the general election was Democrat Ron Sparks, the state agriculture commissioner. Sparks was a fellow underdog who had managed in his party's primary to topple U.S. Rep. Artur Davis, who abandoned a promising House career in the hope of becoming governor. Sparks relentlessly advocated for a vote to legalize and tax gambling to fund education and state services, prompting *The Anniston Star* to label him "a one-trick pony who is riding into what he promises will be a gambling wonderland." Bentley accused Sparks of taking money from gambling interests who faced indictment in a federal public corruption investigation. He also supported a public vote on gambling, but said he felt there were better ways to improve Alabama's economy. He promised not to take a salary as governor until the state's unemployment returned to normal levels. Given the state's overwhelmingly Republican makeup, Sparks faced long odds in winning, which were only exacerbated by the Democratic Party's national unpopularity in 2010. Bentley won with ease, 58%-42%.

Early in his term, Bentley tried to keep his focus on his promises to make government more efficient and to create jobs. He faced some daunting obstacles, topped by a projected shortfall in state revenue of some $450 million. In March 2011 he announced cuts of as much as 15% to many state departments. The next month, more than a dozen Alabama counties were devastated by tornadoes, killing more than 130 people and causing billions of dollars in damage. Bentley pushed back against the suggestion that the state was unprepared, citing its long history of being victim to such natural disasters. "We were very prepared . . . but it was just the force of the storms," he told reporters. Bentley also stumbled in public remarks he made to a church group on inauguration day on January 17, 2011. Speaking to a crowd at Dexter Avenue King Memorial Baptist Church, where late civil rights leader Rev. Martin Luther King Jr. once was pastor, Bentley said, "So anybody here today who has not accepted Jesus Christ as their savior, I'm telling you, you're not my brother and you're not my sister, and I want to be your brother." He later explained that he was using the terminology of his religious faith and meant no offense to non-Christians. Bentley held a meeting with Jewish leaders later the same week and apologized. "If you're not a person who can say you are sorry, you're not a very good leader," the new governor told news reporters.

Senior Senator

Richard Shelby (R)

Elected 1986, term expires 2016, 5th term; b. May 6, 1934, Birmingham; home, Tuscaloosa; U. of AL, B.A. 1957, LL.B. 1963; Presbyterian; married (Annette Nevin); 2 children.

Elected Office: AL Senate, 1970–78; U.S. House of Reps., 1979–87.

Professional Career: Practicing atty., 1963–78; City prosecutor, Tuscaloosa, 1963-71; U.S. magistrate 1966-70; Spec. asst. to Alabama atty. gen., 1969-71.

DC Office: 304 RSOB, 20510, 202-224-5744; Fax: 202-224-3416; Web site: shelby.senate.gov.

State Offices: Birmingham, 205-731-1384; Huntsville, 256-772-0460; Mobile, 251-694-4164; Montgomery, 334-223-7303; Tuscaloosa, 205-759-5047.

Committees: *Aging (Special). Appropriations:* Commerce, Justice, Science & Related Agencies; Defense; Energy & Water Development; Homeland Security; Labor, Health & Human Services, Education & Related Agencies (RMM); Transportation, HUD & Related Agencies. *Banking, Housing & Urban Affairs* (RMM). *Rules & Administration.*

Group Ratings

	ACLU	ACU	ADA	CFG	AFS	FRC	LCV	ITIC	NTU	COC
2010	7	96	0	90	23	95	14	33	96	100
2009	–	88	10	83	9	–	18	–	74	86

National Journal Ratings

	2010 LIB	—	2010 CONS	2009 LIB	—	2009 CONS
Economic	20%	—	79%	21%	—	78%
Social	26%	—	73%	6%	—	92%
Foreign	0%	—	72%	0%	—	84%
Composite	20%	—	80%	12%	—	88%

Key Votes of the 111th Congress

1. Overturn Ledbetter	N	5. Pass health care bill	N
2. Pass $787 billion stimulus	N	6. Regulate financial firms	N
3. Repeal DC gun laws	Y	7. Pass tax cuts for some	N
4. Confirm Sonia Sotomayor	N	8. Legalize immigrants' kids	N

9. Ratify New START	N
10. Confirm Elena Kagan	N
11. Stop EPA climate regs	Y
12. Repeal don't ask, tell	N

Election Results

2010 general	Richard Shelby (R)	968,181	(65%)	($8,557,473)
	William Barnes (D)	515,619	(35%)	($5,870)
2010 primary	Richard Shelby (R)	405,398	(84%)	
	N. C. 'Clint' Moser (R)	75,190	(16%)	

Prior Winning Percentages: 2004 (68%); 1998 (63%); 1992 (65%); 1986 (50%); House: 1984 (97%); 1982 (97%); 1980 (73%); 1978 (94%)

Alabama senior Sen. Richard Shelby's political career spans nearly 40 years. He grew up in Birmingham, the son of a steelworker. After earning two degrees from the University of Alabama, he stayed in Tuscaloosa and practiced law with Walter Flowers, who was later a conservative Democratic congressman. Shelby, a Democrat at that time, was elected to the state Senate in 1970 at age 36. When Flowers ran, unsuccessfully, for the U.S. Senate in 1978, Shelby ran for his House seat. The critical contest was the Democratic runoff against Chris McNair, an African American state legislator whose daughter, Denise, was one of the four young girls killed in the 1963 Birmingham church bombing. Although the district had the highest black percentage in Alabama at the time, Shelby won 59%-41%. In the House, Shelby had a conservative voting record, opposing the Voting Rights Act extension and the Martin Luther King Jr. holiday. He ran for the Senate in 1986 and won the Democratic primary with 51% of the vote after then-Secretary of State (and later governor) Don Siegelman withdrew. In the general election, he ran ads against incumbent Republican Jeremiah Denton, a retired admiral who had been a prisoner of war in Vietnam, for voting to cut Social Security and for owning two Mercedes-Benz cars. Shelby won by 7,000 votes.

As one of a half a dozen or so conservative Southern Democrats in the Senate in the mid-1980s, Shelby at first attracted little notice. He voted for the confirmation of Clarence Thomas to the Supreme Court in the wake of sexual harassment claims against Thomas by a former colleague. And Shelby voted for the 1991 resolution to go to war in the Persian Gulf after Iraq invaded Kuwait. In 1992, he was re-elected 65%-33%, breaking a jinx on a seat that before Shelby's election in 1986 had had four different occupants in 10 years.

Soon after President Bill Clinton took office in 1993, Shelby broke ranks with the Democratic Party. At a meeting with Vice President Al Gore, he turned to the assembled Alabama television cameras and opposed the Clinton program as "high on taxes, low on spending cuts." In response, the administration announced that a multimillion-dollar space facility would be built not in Alabama but in Texas (although it eventually was built in Alabama). The more he defied Clinton, the better Shelby's favorable ratings were at home. He lined up with the Republicans and against the administration on vote after vote. The day after Republicans regained control of the Senate in 1994, Shelby announced he was switching parties, increasing the GOP majority to 53-47. Republicans happily allowed him to keep his seniority on the Banking Committee and gave him seats on Appropriations and its Defense Subcommittee. He got a seat on the Senate Intelligence Committee as well, putting him on a course to assume the chairmanship of Intelligence in 1997.

By the time of the September 11 attacks, the Senate was back in Democratic hands, but Shelby, as the ranking Republican on the Intelligence panel, was an important player in the ensuing weeks and months. He had adopted an adversarial posture toward the intelligence agencies during the Clinton and Bush presidencies, and soon after September 11, Shelby stopped just short of calling for the resignation of Central Intelligence Agency Director George Tenet, who was appointed by Clinton and retained by Bush. He was negatively impressed when, after India conducted three underground nuclear tests, U.S. officials "didn't have a clue," as Tenet put it. Shelby also was critical of the lack of information about the February 1993 World Trade Center bombing and the 2000 attack on the *U.S.S. Cole*. In June 2004, when Tenet announced his resignation, Shelby said, "What was a surprise was that he held onto the job as long as he did."

Aside from his positions on the intelligence agencies, Shelby was mostly supportive of the Bush administration's conduct of the war on terrorism. In December 2001, he was one of 10 senators to sign a letter calling for a plan "to eliminate the threat from Iraq." But he clashed with the two Intelligence Committee chairmen, Democratic Sen. Bob Graham and Republican Rep. Porter Goss, both of Florida. He helped push aside their choice of staff director for the joint probe of intelligence agencies, and he installed his own candidate. At first, he opposed the appointment of an independent September 11 Commission as unnecessary, but relented in 2002. He was out front in calling for the creation of a director of national intelligence after the intelligence agencies, in his view, were unable to work together and to share information. That position was later upheld by the 9/11 Commission and adopted in the intelligence bill approved by Congress in 2004. That bill included a Shelby proposal to give the DNI ombudsman access to all intelligence for analytical reviews, but he was displeased that the new director would not be a Cabinet member.

On domestic issues, Shelby has compiled a conservative record. But he is not a free market purist. Despite his party switch, he has remained friendly with trial lawyers, who usually support Democrats in Alabama. He opposed Alabama colleague Jeff Sessions' amendment to cap lawyers' fees in tobacco cases, and insisted tort reform was a state issue. He voted against a 2004 bill to protect gun manufacturers from liability for actions of users of their products. He was the only Senate Republican to vote against financial services deregulation in 1999, and he opposed allowing federally insured banks to sell real estate or insurance.

Since January 2003, Shelby has been either the chairman or the ranking minority member of the Banking, Housing and Urban Affairs Committee, and from that perch, has been at the center of congressional attempts to stem problems in the mortgage and insurance industries. On a hotly lobbied issue in 2003, he supported defining stock options as expenses, a measure opposed by the high-technology industry. The same year, he presciently quizzed Federal Reserve Chairman Alan Greenspan about the increasing number of home loans to borrowers with weak credit histories, a trend that sent the home mortgage market into a tailspin by 2008. In July 2005, the committee voted along party lines for Shelby's legislation to impose tighter limits on Fannie Mae's and Freddie Mac's portfolios, but it foundered on the side issue of creating an affordable housing fund. In 2008, Democratic Chairman Christopher Dodd of Connecticut pushed a compromise housing bill that would allow bankruptcy judges to restructure mortgages and another proposal to refinance mortgages for millions of homeowners at risk of defaulting. Consumer groups pushed for both, but could not get by Shelby. The government, he said, should not engage in a "taxpayer funded bailout of investors or homeowners." He later reached agreement with Dodd on a bill to allow Fannie Mae and Freddie Mac to fund the refinancing of home mortgages, but he also got a provision increasing capital requirements for the two quasi-public mortgage giants.

Shelby opposed the $700 billion rescue of the financial markets in September 2008, though President Bush was pushing the legislation. Two months later, he opposed a massive government loan for the Big Three domestic automakers, which he called "dinosaurs." After the automakers presented their plan for recovery in December 2008, he said, "I wouldn't loan them any money. They're either failed or failing." He threatened to filibuster and the bill did not pass the Senate. When he was criticized on the grounds that he was defending foreign automakers with plants in Alabama, he pointed out that he had voted against an earlier bailout of Chrysler long before the plants were built. In 2010, Shelby again came under fire for blocking the nomination of esteemed economist Peter Diamond to the board of the Federal Reserve. He insisted Diamond was not ready to serve and lacked experience and knowledge in monetary economics, comments that were derided by national media outlets after Diamond won the Nobel Prize in economics in October 2010.

As the ranking Republican on the committee during the Obama administration, Shelby became a key player in efforts to reform the nation's financial regulatory system in 2009-2010. The bill reined in the over-the-counter derivatives market as well as granted regulators the power to take over firms and liquidate them as a way to prevent future government rescues. Shelby and Dodd appeared ready to work together during the early stages of negotiations on the bill. When the Obama administration wanted to designate the Federal Reserve as the top regulator of systemic risk in the financial system, both Shelby and Dodd opposed the idea. The two supported a move toward ending future government bailouts, and they reached an agreement in May 2010 on a provision that would remove a $50 billion fund designed to pay for orderly liquidations carried out by the Federal Deposit Insurance Corporation. Instead, they offered a substitute amendment that would give the FDIC a line of credit from the Treasury Department, which would then recoup costs by the sales of assets. Shelby and Dodd also agreed, in theory, with the creation of a consumer financial protection division or agency. However, a persistent sticking point surfaced over the details of creating the new entity. While Dodd and the Obama White House wanted the new consumer protection agency to be housed within the Federal Reserve and given more independence, Shelby wanted to create a consumer protection division within the FDIC. The amendment failed 61-38.

Shelby expressed other reservations about the bill, including its failure to address Fannie Mae and Freddie Mac, which received substantial rescue funds. When the initial financial services reform bill was passed by the Senate in late May, Shelby voted against it. Meanwhile, Dodd was criticized by House Financial Services Chair Barney Frank, D-Mass., for dealing with Shelby and other Republicans who voted against the original bill. Still, Shelby was one of five Senate Republican conferees involved in hashing out the differences between Senate and House bills. In the final version, Shelby fought for and won an amendment giving the Securities and Exchange Commission greater powers and independence in monitoring the financial markets. His provision allowed the SEC to circumvent the White House and submit its budget request directly to Congress, and it gave the commission authority to use up to $100 million a year in reserve funds to respond quickly to unforeseen problems in the markets.

A few years earlier, Shelby was deeply involved in another major change in SEC operations. In 2006, he pushed to enact a bill to direct the commission to designate ratings agencies as Nationally Recognized Statistical Ratings Organizations if they meet certain standards over three years. The SEC had been enforcing a 1975 rule that prevented many ratings agencies from qualifying, and that left 80% of the business in the hands of Moody's and Standard & Poor's. "The dominant rating agencies failed millions of investors by neglecting to lower their ratings on Enron, WorldCom and other companies headed for bankruptcy. The absence of timely downgrades in these cases was the product of an industry that was beset by conflicts of interest and a lack of competition," Shelby said.

In his role on the Appropriations Committee, Shelby looks out for Alabama's interests. When the sock industry in DeKalb County—which calls itself the "Sock Capital of the World"—stood to be hurt by a 2002 free trade bill, he held up the bill to get protection from socks produced in the Caribbean, and in 2004, he got country-of-origin labeling for imported and domestic socks. He has obtained some $70 million for University of Alabama at Birmingham medical campus buildings, one of which is named for him, and funds for refurbishing the Vulcan statue on Birmingham's Red Mountain—a favorite target of Sen. John McCain, R-Ariz., the 2008 presidential candidate who has crusaded against earmarks, the special provisions tucked into spending bills by individual lawmakers. In 2007, Shelby voted for a measure to force senators to disclose their earmarks, but he was the only Republican senator to oppose a bill to allow the president to send back individual spending items for up-or-down votes in Congress. He registers near the top of the annual list of wasteful spending earmarks compiled by the watchdog group Citizens Against Government Waste.

Shelby's party switch caused him no trouble in increasingly Republican Alabama. In 1998, he was reelected 63%-37% over a retired ironworker who mortgaged his pickup truck to pay the $2,672 filing fee. For the 2004 election, his Democratic opponent was Wayne Sowell, Alabama's first black Senate nominee and a telephone claims representative for the Social Security Administration in Birmingham. Shelby spent only $2.3 million of the $11 million he had stockpiled for the contest, and won 68%-32%, running behind in only nine black-majority counties in the Black Belt. He easily won re-election in 2010 against Democrat William Barnes, a Birmingham lawyer.

Junior Senator

Jeff Sessions (R)

Elected 1996, term expires 2014, 3rd term; b. Dec. 24, 1946, Hybart; home, Mobile; Huntingdon Col., B.A. 1969, U. of AL, J.D. 1973; Methodist; married (Mary); 3 children.

Military Career: Army Reserves, 1973–86.

Elected Office: AL atty. gen., 1994–96.

Professional Career: Practicing atty., 1973–75, 1977–81, 1993–94; Asst. U.S. atty., 1975–77; U.S. atty., 1981–93.

DC Office: 326 RSOB, 20510, 202-224-4124; Fax: 202-224-3149; Web site: sessions.senate.gov.

State Offices: Birmingham, 205-731-1500; Huntsville, 256-533-0979; Mobile, 251-414-3083; Montgomery, 334-244-7017.

Committees: *Armed Services:* Airland; Seapower; Strategic Forces (RMM). *Budget* (RMM). *Environment & Public Works:* Clean Air & Nuclear Safety; Green Jobs & the New Economy; Transportation & Infrastructure; Water & Wildlife (RMM). *Judiciary:* Administrative Oversight & the Courts (RMM); Crime & Terrorism; Immigration, Refugees & Border Security.

Group Ratings

	ACLU	ACU	ADA	CFG	AFS	FRC	LCV	ITIC	NTU	COC
2010	7	100	5	94	3	91	14	67	96	82
2009	–	96	5	100	0	–	9	–	91	60

National Journal Ratings

	2010 LIB	—	2010 CONS	2009 LIB	—	2009 CONS
Economic	0%	—	87%	5%	—	94%
Social	21%	—	74%	20%	—	79%
Foreign	0%	—	72%	0%	—	84%
Composite	15%	—	85%	11%	—	89%

Key Votes of the 111th Congress

1. Overturn Ledbetter	N	5. Pass health care bill	N	9. Ratify New START	N
2. Pass $787 billion stimulus	N	6. Regulate financial firms	N	10. Confirm Elena Kagan	N
3. Repeal DC gun laws	Y	7. Pass tax cuts for some	N	11. Stop EPA climate regs	Y
4. Confirm Sonia Sotomayor	N	8. Legalize immigrants' kids	N	12. Repeal don't ask, tell	N

Election Results

2008 general	Jeff Sessions (R)	1,305,383	(63%)	($6,370,595)
	Vivian Figures (D)	752,391	(37%)	($332,750)
2008 primary	Jeff Sessions (R)	199,690	(92%)	
	Earl Gavin (R)	16,718	(8%)	

Prior Winning Percentages: 2002 (59%), 1996 (52%)

Republican Jeff Sessions, Alabama's junior senator, is the ranking Republican on the Judiciary Committee. He grew up in the state's Black Belt, the son of a country-store owner, and recalls walking to school barefoot. He graduated from Huntingdon College and the University of Alabama Law School, and then practiced law in a small town near the Tennessee Valley and later in Mobile. He was appointed U.S. attorney in Mobile in 1981, at age 35, and became known as a tough, aggressive prosecutor over the next dozen years. In 1985, he was nominated for a federal judgeship but was attacked by liberals for "gross insensitivity" in racial matters when he prosecuted vote fraud cases. With Alabama's Democratic Sen. Howell Heflin voting against him in the Judiciary Committee, his nomination never went to the Senate floor. In 1994, Sessions challenged state Attorney General Jimmy Evans, a Democrat who had successfully prosecuted Republican Gov. Guy Hunt the year before, and won 57%-43%. In March 1995, when Heflin announced his retirement, Sessions ran for his seat.

In the contested GOP primary, Sessions relied on his base in southern Alabama, territory that not so long ago cast almost no Republican primary votes. Long-distance carrier executive Sid McDonald spent more than $1 million on his campaign. From Birmingham north, the primary was a close race: McDonald led 30%-29%. But in the rest of the state, Sessions led 48%-12%, for a 38%-22% statewide victory. In the runoff, McDonald extended his lead north from Birmingham, 54%-

46%. But almost half the total votes were cast farther south, and there Sessions led 73%-27%, for a 59%-41% win.

The Democratic nominee, trial lawyer and state Sen. Roger Bedford, was financed by trial lawyers and endorsed by key public employee unions and African-American organizations—the heart of today's Alabama Democratic Party. In the general election, Bedford was competitive in fundraising and was the better campaigner. He opposed abortion rights, gun control, and gays in the military. Sessions avoided debates and attacked the Democrat as a "Ted Kennedy" supporter, a reference to the Massachusetts liberal senator that suggested Bedford was too far to the left for Alabama. Sessions won 52%-45%, running best in the suburban counties around Alabama's cities. Bedford carried the Black Belt and other rural counties.

Sessions has a very conservative voting record in the Senate, and must derive a certain satisfaction from holding the top minority party slot on the committee that once rejected his nomination for a judgeship. Just as Heflin earlier judged him to be too conservative, Sessions has loudly complained on Judiciary about President Obama's "far-left nominees" to the bench.

In 2006, Sessions emerged as one of the most vocal opponents of the bipartisan immigration bill sponsored by Kennedy and Sen. John McCain, R-Ariz. He staunchly opposed a provision granting immigrants who had entered the country illegally a process to achieve citizenship. Over the next two years, as Congress debated changes in immigration policy, Sessions was a major roadblock to proposals easing immigration restrictions. In January 2007, he got the Senate to pass a bill banning federal contracts for 10 years to contractors who do not use the E-Verify system and hire illegal immigrants. Later in the year, he fought a bill that came to the floor that created a guest-worker program for illegal immigrants. He objected to a provision that 30% of immigrants be admitted on the basis of marketable skills, saying the percentage should be much higher, and he also said that immigrants with temporary legal status should be ineligible for the Earned Income Tax Credit. "The American people have been clear that they want us to restore the rule of law to our immigration system before legalization programs are considered," Sessions said. In March 2008, he succeeded in getting passed an amendment to the budget to fund completion of a fence along the border with Mexico, to impose mandatory prison terms for illegal border crossers, and to deport illegal immigrants convicted of a felony.

Although Sessions has sponsored few major bills, he has had considerable success at inserting into other legislation provisions he favors that set new federal policy. He typically targets bills that are likely to pass, an effective strategy. When the Medicare prescription drug bill came to the floor in 2003, Sessions inserted a provision for higher Medicare reimbursement for rural hospitals and threatened to vote against the final version of the bill unless it stayed in. It did, sending $738 million to Alabama, more than any other states except Texas and Florida. He had less success in teaming with Missouri Democrat Claire McCaskill in 2010 in adding to a measure to raise the federal debt limit an amendment to impose multi-year caps on discretionary spending. The pair offered the measure several times until it fell just one vote short of the 60 required to pass.

As a member of the Energy and Natural Resources Committee, Sessions has been a staunch defender of the oil, gas and nuclear power industries, but has occasionally shown willingness to compromise. He was one of four Republicans on the panel who supported the committee's massive energy bill in 2009. After the BP Deepwater Horizon oil spill in 2010, he joined Louisiana Republican David Vitter in introducing a bill to raise the amount in damages for spill-related losses apart from cleanup costs. He rejected the idea that BP should lead the cleanup effort, saying the government should take on that role. Sessions is one of the Senate's leading backers of more nuclear generated power. "Nuclear does all four: It's all-American, it creates high-paying American jobs, it emits no CO2, and it's cost-effective," he once told the *Birmingham News*.

On the Armed Services Committee, Sessions has been a big advocate for missile defense, and has also focused on building up defense installations in Alabama. He supported the Bush administration on the Iraq war, and was one of nine senators voting against an amendment banning "cruel, inhuman, or degrading treatment" of prisoners. Along with Republicans Tom Coburn of Oklahoma and Jim DeMint of South Carolina, he is one of the Senate's biggest critics of earmarks, the special provisions inserted into spending bills by lawmakers for their districts or states. Nevertheless, on Armed Services Sessions supports major projects with an impact on Alabama.

During the fight in Congress in late 2008 over the government rescue of private industries, Sessions opposed the $700 billion bill for the ailing financial markets. He opposed as well a multibillion-dollar government loan for General Motors, Chrysler, and Ford, citing the fact that foreign manufacturers with plants in Alabama weren't seeking similar treatment. "It strikes me as unfair to our auto industry," Sessions said. "They propose taxing Alabama's healthy auto industry to subsidize a sick one in Detroit." However, during the first year and a half of Obama's presidency, Sessions was generally supportive of the administration's policies in Iraq and Afghanistan.

In 2002, Sessions was opposed by Democrat Susan Parker, the state auditor and a fundraiser for colleges. She had the support of teachers' unions, but Sessions outspent her 4-to-1 and won 59%-40%. Parker carried two Tennessee River counties in the north and 12 Black Belt counties in the center of the state, but Sessions won everything else. He raised early money in advance of the 2008 election, warding off possible challenges by prominent Democrats Artur Davis, then a House member, and Ron Sparks, the state agriculture commissioner. His opponent was state Sen. Vivian Davis Figures of Mobile. Sessions raised $6.4 million and spent $3.8 million, while Figures spent $331,000. Sessions won 63%-37%.

FIRST DISTRICT

Jo Bonner (R)

Elected 2002, 5th term; b. Nov. 19, 1959, Selma; home, Mobile; U. of AL, B.A. 1982; Episcopalian; married (Janee); 2 children.

Professional Career: Sr. aide, U.S. Rep. Sonny Callahan, 1984-2002.

DC Office: 2236 RHOB, 20515, 202-225-4931; Fax: 202-225-0562; Web site: bonner.house.gov.

State Offices: Foley, 251-943-2073; Mobile, 251-690-2811.

Committees: *Appropriations:* Commerce, Justice, Science & Related Agencies (VChmn); Defense; Financial Services & General Government. *Ethics* (Chmn).

Group Ratings

	ACLU	ACU	ADA	CFG	AFS	FRC	LCV	ITIC	NTU	COC
2010	6	95	0	83	0	100	20	33	85	88
2009	–	92	0	90	22	–	0	–	85	87

National Journal Ratings

	2010 LIB	—	2010 CONS	2009 LIB	—	2009 CONS
Economic	19%	—	80%	15%	—	84%
Social	18%	—	77%	20%	—	78%
Foreign	12%	—	79%	0%	—	75%
Composite	19%	—	81%	16%	—	84%

Key Votes of the 111th Congress

1. Overturn Ledbetter	N	5. Bar federal abortion funds	Y	9. Stop detainee transfers	Y
2. Pass $820 billion stimulus	N	6. Pass health care bill	N	10. Legalize immigrants' kids	N
3. Let guns in national parks	Y	7. Regulate financial firms	N	11. Repeal don't ask, tell	N
4. Pass cap-and-trade	N	8. Pass tax cuts for some	N	12. Limit campaign funds	N

Election Results

2010 general	Jo Bonner (R)	129,063	(83%)	($913,053)
	David Walter (CNP)	26,357	(17%)	($21,321)
2010 primary	Jo Bonner (R)	56,937	(75%)	
	Peter Gounares (R)	18,725	(25%)	

Prior Winning Percentages: 2008 (98%), 2006 (68%), 2004 (63%), 2002 (60%)

Population		Race/Ethnicity		Work	
Pop. 2010:	687,841	White:	65.8%	Private:	79.5%
Change since 2000:	Up 8.3%	Black:	27.6%	Government:	14.7%
Urban:	64.4%	Hispanic:	2.8%	Self-employed:	5.6%
Rural:	35.6%	Asian:	1.3%	Blue collar:	26.1%
Area size:	7,183 sq. mi.	Native Am.:	1.1%	White collar:	56.2%
		Hawaiian:	0.0%	Khaki collar:	0.1%
Age		Two+ races:	1.3%	Other:	17.6%
Median age:	37.5 yrs.				
More than 65 yrs:	14.0%	*Ancestry*		Median income:	$41,307
Less than 18 yrs:	25.1%	USA	10.2%	Median Home Value:	$130,200
		Irish	9.6%		
Education		German	7.7%	**Military Veterans**	
H.S. grad:	83.1%			% of Pop:	12.3%
College grad:	20.6%				
Grad degree:	6.7%				

Election Results

2010 general	Martha Roby (R)	111,645	(51%)	($1,253,557)
	Bobby Bright (D)	106,865	(49%)	($1,413,032)
2010 primary	Martha Roby (R)	39,169	(60%)	
	Rick Barber (R)	26,091	(40%)	
2010 primary	Martha Roby (R)	36,295	(49%)	
	Rick Barber (R)	21,313	(29%)	
	Stephanie Bell (R)	13,797	(18%)	

Population		Race/Ethnicity		Work	
Pop. 2010:	673,877	White:	63.1%	Private:	72.0%
Change since 2000:	Up 6.1%	Black:	30.8%	Government:	21.4%
Urban:	50.1%	Hispanic:	3.4%	Self-employed:	6.4%
Rural:	49.9%	Asian:	0.9%	Blue collar:	26.9%
Area size:	10,608 sq. mi.	Native Am.:	0.4%	White collar:	54.8%
		Hawaiian:	0.0%	Khaki collar:	1.3%
Age		Two+ races:	1.4%	Other:	17.1%
Median age:	36.9 yrs.				
More than 65 yrs:	13.9%	*Ancestry*		Median income:	$39,381
Less than 18 yrs:	24.5%	USA	13.8%	Median Home Value:	$107,900
		Irish	7.9%		
Education		English	7.3%	**Military Veterans**	
H.S. grad:	80.8%			% of Pop:	13.1%
College grad:	19.7%				
Grad degree:	7.0%				

Southeast Alabama; Montgomery

Thick green countryside blankets southern Alabama. Even in Montgomery, the stone and brick buildings of the downtown district do not mask the contours of the hills or hide the lush foliage. One can look downhill from the restored Greek Revival capitol toward Dexter Avenue Baptist Church, where the young Martin Luther King Jr. was pastor in the 1950s, or out past the impressive Carolyn Blount Theater, host of the Alabama Shakespeare Festival, toward new sub-

2008 Presidential Vote		
John McCain (R)	182,618	(63%)
Barack Obama (D)	107,669	(37%)
2004 Presidential Vote		
George Bush (R)	170,427	(67%)
John Kerry (D)	84,043	(33%)
Cook Partisan Voting Index: R+16		

divisions and shopping malls, and easily imagine when this land was covered with cotton fields and pine trees. The atmosphere is even more rural in southeast Alabama's Wiregrass region, named for the stiff native grass. There is the fishing town of Eufaula, along the Chattahoochee River; the Army's Fort Rucker, the home of Army aviation flight training; and Enterprise, site of the Boll Weevil Monument that commemorates the insect that destroyed two-thirds of the cotton crop in 1915 and then spread throughout the South. Timber is an important resource here, and peanuts are now the main crop in the area surrounding Dothan. The region ranks second in the nation in acres harvested for peanuts. But the area is diversifying: Hyundai built its first U.S. assembly plant in southwest Montgomery County, with about 3,000 local jobs. Then in 2010, Hyundai Heavy Industries, announced plans for a $90 million plant to manufacture large power transformers. The company, which will employ about 500 people when the plant opens in 2012, was lured to the area by over $9 million in tax incentives from local governments and by Montgomery's familiarity with Korean business culture, gleaned from its experience with Hyundai's auto plant. The unemployment rate in greater Montgomery fell a whole percentage point to 9% in late 2010, due in part to the rebound in auto manufacturing.

The 2nd Congressional District covers the southeast corner of the state. It includes most of the city of Montgomery but only a small part of Montgomery County. Democratic redistricters put the rest, including the capitol and many black precincts, into the 3rd District in an attempt to make that seat more Democratic. The result was to make the 2nd District strongly Republican. The Montgomery County precincts, plus suburban Elmore and Autauga counties, vote heavily Republican, as does the area around Dothan and Houston County in the Wiregrass region. The area out-votes by a large number the district's "black belt" counties—Lowndes, Bullock, with a large black majority, and Barbour on the Georgia border, which was George Wallace's home base. It would be a mistake to see these preferences as purely racial, however. African-Americans here tend to support a larger and more generous government, and hence vote Democratic. Alabama whites tend to take a hard line on defense and crime and want government to promote traditional cultural values, and hence vote Republican.

Martha Roby (R)

The new congresswoman from Alabama's 2nd District is Martha Roby, a Republican who beat one-term Democratic Rep. Bobby Bright in this conservative bastion in the 2010 election. Bright managed to win two years earlier by attracting strong crossover support from Republicans in what then was a favorable climate for Democrats.

Roby is the daughter of Joel Dubina, a judge on the U.S Court of Appeals for the 11th Circuit. She grew up in Montgomery, and received a bachelor's degree in music from New York University in 1998. After earning a law degree from Samford University in Birmingham, she returned to her hometown to practice law. In 2003, she was elected to the Montgomery City Council. In that role, she led efforts to adopt an ordinance barring city businesses from hiring undocumented workers. In 2007, she won a second term in a landslide election, garnering 82% of the vote.

Immigration emerged as a major issue in the House race. Bright, a former mayor of Montgomery, criticized Roby for moving too slowly on her undocumented-workers initiative. The National Republican Congressional Committee, which helped Roby, branded the incumbent a "flip-flopper" because he expressed misgivings in a *Washington Post* story about Arizona's law giving law enforcement significant new powers to crack down on illegal immigrants.

Roby and the Republicans kept Bright on the defensive. He felt it necessary to become the first Democrat to announce he would not vote for a second time to elect California liberal Nancy Pelosi as speaker of the House. The election of speaker is typically a unanimous vote of the party in power. Bright voted to elevate Pelosi to speaker in January 2009, and Roby charged that the vote was proof of Bright's flawed judgment. In one campaign ad, Bright boasted of having voted with House Republican Leader John Boehner of Ohio 80% of the time. He also played up his endorsements from the National Rifle Association and the National Right to Life PAC. He sometimes campaigned in a "Fire Congress" T-shirt.

Bright has deep political roots in the district, but some political observers attribute his 2008 win to a bitter feud between state lawmakers Jay Love and Harri Anne Smith, who savaged each other in the Republican primary. This time around, the GOP closed ranks around Roby.

The race attracted the attention of some Republican heavyweights, including former Alaska Gov. Sarah Palin and former House Speaker Newt Gingrich of Georgia, both of whom endorsed Roby. The Democratic Congressional Campaign Committee spent about $1 million for Bright. But Roby won in a close race, 51%-49%.

THIRD DISTRICT

Mike Rogers (R)

Elected 2002, 5th term; b. July 16, 1958, Hammond, IN; home, Anniston; Jacksonville St. U., B.A. 1981, M.P.A. 1984, Birmingham Schl. of Law, J.D. 1991; Baptist; married (Beth); 3 children.

Elected Office: Calhoun Cnty. Commission, 1986-90; AL House of Reps., 1994-2002, Min. ldr., 1998-2000.

Professional Career: Practicing atty., 1991-2002.

DC Office: 324 CHOB, 20515, 202-225-3261; Fax: 202-226-8485; Web site: mike-rogers.house.gov.

State Offices: Anniston, 256-236-5655; Montgomery, 334-277-4210; Opelika, 334-745-6221.

Committees: *Armed Services:* Readiness; Strategic Forces. *Homeland Security:* Border & Maritime Security; Transportation Security (Chmn).

Group Ratings

	ACLU	ACU	ADA	CFG	AFS	FRC	LCV	ITIC	NTU	COC
2010	6	96	5	81	0	100	20	0	85	75
2009	–	80	15	62	44	–	7	–	68	93

National Journal Ratings

	2010 LIB	—	2010 CONS		2009 LIB	—	2009 CONS
Economic	22%	—	77%		34%	—	66%
Social	23%	—	77%		24%	—	73%
Foreign	12%	—	79%		33%	—	63%
Composite	21%	—	79%		32%	—	69%

Key Votes of the 111th Congress

1. Overturn Ledbetter	N	5. Bar federal abortion funds	Y	9. Stop detainee transfers	Y
2. Pass $820 billion stimulus	N	6. Pass health care bill	N	10. Legalize immigrants' kids	N
3. Let guns in national parks	Y	7. Regulate financial firms	N	11. Repeal don't ask, tell	N
4. Pass cap-and-trade	N	8. Pass tax cuts for some	N	12. Limit campaign funds	N

Election Results

2010 general	Mike Rogers (R) 117,736	(59%)	($1,141,732)
	Steve Segrest (D) 80,204	(41%)	($8,750)
2010 primary	Mike Rogers (R) .... unopposed		

Prior Winning Percentages: 2008 (53%), 2006 (59%), 2004 (61%), 2002 (50%)

Population		Race/Ethnicity		Work	
Pop. 2010:	681,298	White:	62.6%	Private:	74.6%
Change since 2000:	Up 7.2%	Black:	31.7%	Government:	20.1%
Urban:	53.3%	Hispanic:	2.8%	Self-employed:	5.1%
Rural:	46.7%	Asian:	1.3%	Blue collar:	29.0%
Area size:	7,988 sq. mi.	Native Am.:	0.3%	White collar:	53.3%
		Hawaiian:	0.0%	Khaki collar:	0.5%
Age		Two+ races:	1.2%	Other:	17.2%
Median age:	36.4 yrs.				
More than 65 yrs:	13.4%	*Ancestry*		Median income:	$37,816
Less than 18 yrs:	23.0%	USA	11.5%	Median Home Value:	$102,500
		Irish	8.6%		
Education		English	8.6%	**Military Veterans**	
H.S. grad:	78.3%			% of Pop:	11.3%
College grad:	19.4%				
Grad degree:	7.8%				

East Alabama; Auburn

Forty years ago, Lineville, Alabama, in the red hills of Clay County, was Ku Klux Klan country, with whites determined to resist race-mixing and blacks under constant threat of violence. More recently in Lineville, integrated crowds regularly cheer mixed black and white high school teams, and people of all races work together, though they tend to pray separately on Sundays. Lineville's progress perhaps echoes that of America's most integrated institution,

2008 Presidential Vote

John McCain (R) 161,154	(56%)
Barack Obama (D) 124,973	(43%)

2004 Presidential Vote

George Bush (R) 146,380	(58%)
John Kerry (D) 103,456	(41%)

Cook Partisan Voting Index: R+9

the military. The small town produced more men and women per capita for Operation Desert Storm than any other community in the nation. When the United States invaded Iraq in 2003, Alabama was the nation's top contributor of National Guard personnel. Clay County has one of the highest concentrations of Guard enlistments and reservists in the state.

The 3rd Congressional District of Alabama is centered geographically and philosophically in Lineville. The military presence is unmistakable: Calhoun County is home to the Anniston Army Depot and formerly home to Fort McClellan, which closed in 1999. Horseshoe Bend is where Andrew Jackson won a climactic battle against the Upper Creek Indians. Fort Mitchell, a 19th-century frontier military outpost, is the site of a national military cemetery sometimes referred to as the "Arlington of the South." Phenix City, across the Chattahoochie River from Georgia's Fort Benning, served as a "sin city" in the 1940s and 1950s, with virtually every imaginable vice for pleasure-seeking soldiers, a place so sleazy that Gen. George Patton threatened to level it with his tanks. Today, the huge military installation plays a more constructive role in the local economy.

There are other places of distinction in the district: Tuskegee is the home of Booker T. Washington's Tuskegee Institute (now Tuskegee University), the training ground for the Tuskegee Airmen, the first black pilots trained to fly for the U.S. military. Auburn is the home of Auburn University and its renowned sports teams and veterinary school. Talladega is the site of the Alabama Institute for the Deaf and Blind, and is perhaps America's most user-friendly city for the disabled. NASCAR fans know it as the home of a famed speedway and for the International Motorsports Hall of Fame—the Cooperstown of auto racing.

This looks and feels like rural country, though few people here make a living off their farms. Rather, they work at Tyson Foods or Wal-Mart or in dozens of small and medium-sized factories. An economy once dependent on cotton mills is today more diverse, and interstates have brought in new businesses, including a huge Honda assembly plant in Talladega County, where good wages boosted local personal income by 22% in the three years after it opened. In Montgomery, state government is the largest employer, while Calhoun County's Anniston Army Depot and its partner companies are responsible for about 7,000 jobs. The small town of Ohatchee in Calhoun County was hit especially hard by a deadly tornado on April 27, 2011, when a severe storm system spawned twisters throughout Alabama. Entire neighborhoods in Ohatchee were destroyed, and nine people died in Calhoun County.

Politically, this was long one of the heartlands of the Democratic Party, the home of conservative white Democrats who are patriotic supporters of the military and cautious supporters of some domestic programs. There is also a large population of African-American descendants of slaves from plantations. But the area has become Republican, except for Tuskegee's Macon County and portions of Montgomery County added by the 2002 redistricting in an attempt by Democrats to make the district competitive. Democrats have remained competitive in some state elections. George W. Bush won 52% here in 2000, and 58% in 2004. Barack Obama increased the black turnout in 2008, but John McCain still won with 56% of the vote.

Mike Rogers (R)

The congressman from the 3rd District is Mike Rogers, a Republican elected in 2002. He is a fifth-generation resident of Calhoun County who, at the age of 28 in 1986, was the first Republican elected to the county commission. In 1994, he won a seat in the Alabama House, and in his second term, he became minority leader. In 2002, after Republican Bob Riley gave up the 3rd District seat to run for governor, Rogers easily won the GOP nomination to succeed him. But in the general election, he had stiff competition from Democrat Joe Turnham Jr., who served three years as state party chairman and challenged Riley unsuccessfully in 1998. Turnham and Rogers tried to "out-bubba" each other, with Turnham calling for a congressional auto racing caucus and demanding that Rogers prove he had hunting and fishing licenses. Rogers touted his working-class values and support from the National Rifle Association. He also emphasized his opposition to abortion rights and support for a constitutional amendment permitting prayer in the public schools.

Though both national parties targeted the district, Turnham did not risk bringing in national Democrats to campaign for him in this socially conservative district, while Rogers got frequent visits from national Republican leaders. The contrast in national party support was evident in Rogers's big fundraising advantage. Still, Rogers won, but only 50%-48%. He did well in his base, Calhoun County, where he got 60% of the vote. In contrast, Turnham lost Lee County, his home, 52%-46%, but carried the district's portion of Montgomery County 57%-42%.

Rogers is one of two Republicans of the same name in the House; the other is from the 8th District of Michigan. Alabama's Mike Rogers has a conservative voting record, and his views occasionally light up the liberal blogosphere. He told a local audience in 2009 that Speaker Nancy Pelosi is "crazy" and "mean as a snake," and in 2010 was an early supporter of Republican Rep. Michele Bachmann's bill to repeal the health care overhaul law. Rogers is more centrist on economic issues. He bucked the Bush administration and won local praise by opposing the free-trade agreement with Morocco on the grounds that it would reduce local textile and apparel jobs. In 2009, he proposed allowing new car buyers a tax deduction of up to $7,500. On the Armed Services Committee, he won House passage of a bill to ensure that universities provide access to their facilities for military recruiters and ROTC personnel. He took over in 2009 as ranking Republican on the Subcommittee on Emergency Communications, Preparedness and Response. The following year, he attacked as "indefensible" the Obama administration's proposal to reduce Federal Emergency Management Agency grants for firefighter personnel and equipment by 25%.

In this ancestrally Democratic district, Rogers has worked hard to entrench himself and raise money to discourage strong Democratic opposition. In his first two re-election campaigns, his Democratic challengers were inadequately funded and never posed serious threats. But in 2008, Rogers faced a serious contest with Josh Segall, a 29-year-old Montgomery bankruptcy lawyer who stuck with Democratic doctrine on most issues except gay rights and gun control, spent over $1 million, and had the support of the Democratic Congressional Campaign Committee. He attacked Rogers for backing the $700 billion government rescue of the financial markets, and also accused him of harming the local textile industry with his support of the Central America Free Trade Agreement. Rogers attacked Segall for his "Hollywood and New York" campaign contributions and his liberal views that "don't reflect east Alabama's conservative values." Segall took Montgomery County 62%-38% and three nearby counties, but Rogers won 53%-47% overall.

FOURTH DISTRICT

Robert Aderholt (R)

Elected 1996, 8th term; b. July 22, 1965, Haleyville; home, Haleyville; Birmingham-Southern Col., B.A. 1987, Samford U., J.D. 1990; Congregationalist; married (Caroline); 2 children.

Professional Career: Haleyville Municipal Judge, 1992–96; Asst. legal advisor, Gov. Fob James, 1995–96.

DC Office: 2264 RHOB, 20515, 202-225-4876; Fax: 202-225-5587; Web site: aderholt.house.gov.

State Offices: Cullman, 256-734-6043; Decatur, 256-350-4093; Gadsden, 256-546-0201; Jasper, 205-221-2310.

Committees: *Appropriations:* Agriculture, Rural Development, FDA & Related Agencies; Commerce, Justice, Science & Related Agencies; Homeland Security (Chmn).

Group Ratings

	ACLU	ACU	ADA	CFG	AFS	FRC	LCV	ITIC	NTU	COC
2010	6	92	0	86	0	100	0	33	85	88
2009	–	92	5	79	22	–	0	–	82	92

National Journal Ratings

	2010 LIB	—	2010 CONS		2009 LIB	—	2009 CONS
Economic	18%	—	81%		26%	—	74%
Social	18%	—	77%		20%	—	78%
Foreign	29%	—	68%		0%	—	75%
Composite	23%	—	77%		20%	—	80%

Key Votes of the 111th Congress

1. Overturn Ledbetter	N	5. Bar federal abortion funds	Y	9. Stop detainee transfers	Y
2. Pass $820 billion stimulus	N	6. Pass health care bill	N	10. Legalize immigrants' kids	N
3. Let guns in national parks	Y	7. Regulate financial firms	N	11. Repeal don't ask, tell	N
4. Pass cap-and-trade	N	8. Pass tax cuts for some	N	12. Limit campaign funds	N

Election Results

2010 general	Robert Aderholt (R)..167,714	(99%)	($828,588)
2010 primary	Robert Aderholt (R).....................................unopposed		

Prior Winning Percentages: 2008 (75%), 2006 (70%), 2004 (75%), 2002 (87%), 2000 (61%), 1998 (56%), 1996 (50%)

Population		Race/Ethnicity		Work	
Pop. 2010:	660,162	White:	86.4%	Private:	78.5%
Change since 2000:	Up 3.9%	Black:	5.0%	Government:	13.2%
Urban:	26.5%	Hispanic:	6.4%	Self-employed:	8.1%
Rural:	73.5%	Asian:	0.4%	Blue collar:	35.6%
Area size:	8,523 sq. mi.	Native Am.:	0.6%	White collar:	48.0%
		Hawaiian:	0.0%	Khaki collar:	0.1%
Age		Two+ races:	1.2%	Other:	16.3%
Median age:	39.3 yrs.				
More than 65 yrs:	15.4%	*Ancestry*		Median income:	$37,433
Less than 18 yrs:	24.0%	USA	12.3%	Median Home Value:	$93,500
		Irish	12.1%		
Education		English	9.8%	**Military Veterans**	
H.S. grad:	74.9%			% of Pop:	10.6%
College grad:	13.2%				
Grad degree:	4.9%				

North Central Alabama; Gadsden

The Appalachian Mountains' corduroy ridges, dividing the Atlantic coast from the interior, make up America's coal-and-steel industrial spine, from the black coal country of western Pennsylvania to the red hill country of northern Alabama. Here rose America's two premier steel cities, Pittsburgh and Birmingham. Around both, and for many miles in between them, is countryside settled by feisty Scots-Irish farmers in the years between the Revolution and the

2008 Presidential Vote		
John McCain (R) 205,362	(76%)
Barack Obama (D) 60,207	(22%)
2004 Presidential Vote		
George Bush (R) 186,509	(71%)
John Kerry (D) 73,504	(28%)
Cook Partisan Voting Index: R+26		

Civil War. In valley land accessible to railroads, great steel factories were built in the 80 years after the Civil War, along with smaller factories that produced socks, tires, glass, chemicals and butchered chickens. Northern Alabama was solidly Democratic through the 1950s. It was populist on economics, conservative on cultural issues. Since then, the region has moved toward the Republicans, even though it has benefited from massive federal public works programs. The movement is most pronounced in counties close to Birmingham and along the interstates.

Alabama's 4th Congressional District is a collection of small towns—Cullman, Jasper, Russellville, Fort Payne, and Albertville. The last is the home of a military helicopter plant and other aerospace facilities. Gritty Gadsden (pop. 37,000) is the biggest city, with a large Goodyear tire plant built in 1929. The investor service Moody's in 2010 identified Gadsden as one of 22 metro areas at risk of slipping back into recession. Sandwiched between Huntsville to the north and Birmingham to the south, the 4th District crosses the state and the Appalachian ridges, from the Georgia state line to the Mississippi state line. Decades of coal mining scarred 150 square miles of landscape, about one-fourth of which has been reclaimed.

The district was hard hit by a spate of deadly tornadoes that struck Alabama on April 27, 2011. Of the estimated 250 people who died statewide, 135 of them lived in northwest Alabama, and property damage there was extensive. The outbreak's strongest tornado, with peak wind speeds exceeding 250 mph, touched down in Marion County. The EF-5 twister, the strongest there is, cleared a three-quarter-mile wide path, 25 miles long across the county, killing 23 people. In nearby Franklin County, 28 people died. In the small town of Hackleburg in Marion County, there weren't enough body bags for the dead, and officials were forced to store some of them in a refrigerated truck. Hackleburg was already struggling with nearly 13% unemployment when the storm destroyed a Wrangler jeans distribution center that employed 150 people. On the eastern edge of the district, 33 people were killed in DeKalb County.

This is Alabama's premier Scots-Irish district, with the lowest African-American population percentage of the state's seven congressional districts. Though family income is low and poverty above national averages, high marriage rates give some social stability. There are few vestiges of its Democratic heritage. George Bush won here with 71% in 2004. John McCain won many of these counties with over 70% of the vote in 2008.

Robert Aderholt (R)

The congressman from the 4th District is Robert Aderholt, a Republican first elected in 1996 to replace 30-year Democratic Rep. Tom Bevill, a longtime senior appropriator and federal benefactor for the region. Aderholt is from Winston County, the one ancestrally Republican county in north Alabama; it opposed secession in the Civil War and declared itself the Free State of Winston. His father was a circuit judge for more than 30 years; his wife's father was a state senator and state commissioner of Agriculture and Industry. In 1992, Aderholt was appointed Haleyville municipal judge. Three years later, he became a top aide to Republican Gov. Fob James. With that pedigree, he decided to run for Congress when Bevill retired. As the Republican nominee, he faced state Sen. Bob Wilson Jr., who called himself a Democrat "in the Tom Bevill tradition." In this culturally conservative district, Aderholt didn't hedge on cultural issues, opposing abortion rights, gun control, same-sex marriage, and prohibitions against school prayer. "We want to go to Washington to deliver a message, and that is, don't mess with our traditional family values," he said. He also attacked Wilson for his support from labor unions and trial lawyers. This was a nationally targeted race, seriously contested, and Aderholt won 50%-48%.

Aderholt's voting record is generally conservative, and he was among the first House Republicans to join the Tea Party Caucus in July 2010. But he often votes with labor on trade issues, mainly because of local imperatives. He has supported quotas on steel imports and sponsored a bill assessing additional antidumping duties on foreign steel. He voted against normalizing trade relations with China, and opposed free-trade agreements with Chile, Morocco, and Singapore. In 2005, however, he was a crucial vote for the Central America Free Trade Agreement after he got a last-minute letter from President George W. Bush delaying the phase-out of tariffs on socks. Still, the agreement ultimately proved devastating for Fort Payne, which once had 150 plants and proclaimed itself the "Sock Capital of the World." By 2007, sock imports from Central America and China closed more than 100 of those mills. Aderholt said that he was "disappointed" that the administration failed to give the mills more time to adjust. He also went to bat for the region's aerospace industry in 2010, criticizing the Obama administration's decision to cancel the Constellation space program without congressional approval.

Recognizing Aderholt's electoral vulnerability, Republican leaders put him on the Appropriations Committee, where he has been able to secure more highway and sewer money than most of his GOP colleagues. In 2009, Aderholt became ranking Republican on the Legislative Branch Subcommittee at Appropriations. In his first year, he praised his Democratic counterpart, Debbie Wasserman Schultz of Florida, for her fairness. But he voted against the conference report on the fiscal 2010 version of the Legislative Branch appropriations bill because it included a continuing resolution to fund other government agencies. In January 2011, after Republicans took majority control of the House from the Democrats, Aderholt became chairman of the Appropriations Subcommittee on Homeland Security.

And he hasn't forgotten the social issues. When Alabama's chief justice Judge Roy Moore called for a new law to prevent federal judges from interfering with public displays of the Ten Commandments, Aderholt sponsored legislation toward that goal. "The acknowledgment of God is not a legitimate subject of review by the federal courts," Aderholt said. He was the only House member from Alabama in 2008 to vote against the $700 billion rescue of the financial markets. He cited public "discontent" with the plan, and the need for a more market-based approach.

Aderholt faced serious challenges in his first two re-elections, but has won easily since.

FIFTH DISTRICT

Mo Brooks (R)

Elected 2010, 1st term; b. April 29, 1954, Charleston, SC; home, Huntsville; Duke U., B.A. 1975; U. of AL, J.D. 1978.; Christian; Married (Martha); 4 children.

Elected Office: AL House, 1983-90; Madison Cnty. Commissioner, 1997-2010.

Professional Career: Tuscaloosa Cnty. asst. district atty., 1978-80; Madison Cnty. district atty., 1991-93; AL special asst. atty. gen., 1995-2002; practicing atty., 1993-2010.

DC Office: 1641 LHOB, 20515, 202-225-4801; Fax: 202-225-4392; Web site: brooks.house.gov.

State Offices: Decatur, 256-355-9400; Huntsville, 256-551-0190; Shoals Office, 256-381-3450.

Committees: *Armed Services:* Oversight & Investigations; Strategic Forces. *Homeland Security:* Transportation Security. *Science & Technology:* Research & Science Education (Chmn); Space & Aeronautics.

Election Results

2010 general	Mo Brooks (R)	131,109	(58%)	($961,211)
	Steve Raby (D)	95,192	(42%)	($929,084)
2010 primary	Mo Brooks (R)	35,746	(51%)	
	Parker Griffith (R)	23,525	(33%)	
	Les Phillip (R)	11,085	(16%)	

Population		Race/Ethnicity		Work	
Pop. 2010:	718,724	White:	73.4%	Private:	75.7%
Change since 2000:	Up 13.1%	Black:	17.6%	Government:	18.4%
Urban:	59.4%	Hispanic:	4.6%	Self-employed:	5.7%
Rural:	40.6%	Asian:	1.5%	Blue collar:	25.1%
Area size:	4,689 sq. mi.	Native Am.:	0.9%	White collar:	59.4%
		Hawaiian:	0.1%	Khaki collar:	0.8%
Age		Two+ races:	2.0%	Other:	14.7%
Median age:	38.2 yrs.				
More than 65 yrs:	13.6%	*Ancestry*		Median income:	$46,401
Less than 18 yrs:	23.6%	USA	12.0%	Median Home Value:	$127,800
		Irish	10.4%		
Education		English	8.9%	**Military Veterans**	
H.S. grad:	83.6%			% of Pop:	12.2%
College grad:	26.8%				
Grad degree:	9.3%				

North Alabama; Huntsville

The federal government long has had a hand in shaping the destiny of northern Alabama. In 1933, it created the Tennessee Valley Authority, which took the World War I federal munitions plant at Muscle Shoals, on the Tennessee River, and built a series of dams to control flooding and to produce cheap hydroelectric power. This was backward country then. Poor white farmers scratched an existence out of hardscrabble land, were housed in shacks without electricity or running water, and lived off a diet that produced pellagra and rickets. The TVA was intended to showcase what an enlightened, generous federal government could do. Today, the TVA is still government owned, and provides electricity to seven Southern states through a combination of sources, including coal, gas, nuclear and hydroelectric. In 2010, it began engineering work on the Bellefonte Nuclear Plant in Jackson County, one of just a few new nuclear plants approved for construction around the country.

2008 Presidential Vote		
John McCain (R)	190,225	(61%)
Barack Obama (D)	117,838	(38%)

2004 Presidential Vote		
George Bush (R)	167,552	(60%)
John Kerry (D)	110,633	(40%)

Cook Partisan Voting Index: R+12

After the Soviets put up Sputnik in 1957, the Redstone Arsenal in Huntsville became the nation's foremost missile development center. Huntsville, then a sleepy town huddled around a well-preserved, early-19th-century settlement, grew to become Alabama's fourth-largest city. Residents are fond of referring to their hometown as "Rocket City." The first of the large U.S. ballistic missiles were developed here. On the grounds of Redstone, NASA built its Marshall Space Flight Center in the 1960s, and the Huntsville-Decatur area soon achieved high-tech critical mass. With leadership from Wernher von Braun and other German engineers, Redstone and Marshall built Explorer 1, the first American orbiting satellite; the Mercury-Redstone vehicle that boosted astronaut Alan Shepard into suborbital flight; and the Saturn V rocket that sent man to the moon. In the 1970s, Marshall produced Skylab and developed the space shuttle's main engines and solid-rocket boosters. The Boeing research center here has been a prime contractor for the space station. In 1990, it helped launch the Hubble Space Telescope. Boeing produces the Delta IV booster at its factory in Decatur.

With the retirement of the space shuttle, NASA expected that Marshall would have a major role in preparing the next generation of space vehicles, including the Ares I rocket and the Constellation project aimed at returning man to the moon. But Marshall and Huntsville have been on edge since the Obama administration, wary of large-scale space exploration programs funded entirely by the government, announced it wants to scuttle Constellation. Congress disagrees, and has blocked NASA from curtailing the program through its power of the purse. Still, the uncertainty has created angst for Huntsville officials, who estimate the program employs over 2,000 people locally. All told, Marshall and its related contractors employ 7,500 in the area. Yet Huntsville has done a smart job of diversifying its high-tech economy in recent years, and so can weather setbacks like Constellation better than most cities its size. Space-related jobs have evolved with a broader defense focus. In 2005, the Pentagon base-closing commission moved 1,800 jobs in the Missile Defense Agency from northern Virginia to Redstone. In 2009 and 2010, about two dozen companies either located or expanded in Hunstville, adding 2,000 jobs. Over several decades, city leaders carefully cultivated the Cummings Research Park, now home to 285 companies specializing in technology-based manufacturing, biotechnology and pharmaceuticals. In addition to the usual tax incentives and grants, the city took the novel approach of offering to train or retrain high-tech manufacturing employees at city facilities for free. The city and surrounding area were dealt a serious economic setback on April 27, 2011 when a spate of deadly tornadoes struck Alabama. At least six tornadoes ripped through Madison County, which includes Huntsville, killing seven people and injuring 82.

The 5th Congressional District of Alabama takes in most of the state's TVA and space counties. TVA and the space program were primarily Democratic projects, and for years most voters here were staunch New Deal Democrats, liberal on economics and not much interested in race issues, like longtime Sen. John Sparkman, the party's vice presidential nominee in 1952. But professional and technical people in the space business tended to be conservative, and this made much of northern Alabama marginal-to-Republican country in the 1990s. The district has voted Republican for president since 1980, but hadn't elected a Republican to Congress until recently. In 2008, John McCain won this district, 61%-38%.

Mo Brooks (R)

The new congressman from 5th District is Mo Brooks, the first Republican to be elected to the seat since 1868. He dispatched Rep. Parker Griffith in the May 2010 primary after Griffith changed his party affiliation from Democrat to Republican. Brooks then bested his Democratic opponent in the general election, political consultant Steve Raby.

Brooks was born in Charleston, S.C. His father, Jack Brooks, was raised "dirt poor" in Chattanooga, Tenn., and his mother, Betty Brooks, grew up without electricity or indoor plumbing. "Out of that poverty, my parents learned that you'd better work, and work hard," Brooks said. "That's the beauty of America. Anybody can succeed if they work hard and take advantage of their free education." In 1963, when Mo was 9, the family moved to Huntsville, Ala., where Jack worked as an electrical engineer and Betty taught high school economics and government. Brooks was a student at Grissom High School during the Vietnam War, and he says the experience influenced his decision to make a career in government. He quit the basketball team to join the debate team, and wound up participating in two state-championship debates. Brooks went on to study economics and political science at Duke University, graduating in three years. While he was a senior, he met Martha Jenkins of Ohio at a fraternity event, and a few years later, the two married.

In 1980, they moved to Brooks's hometown of Huntsville, where he landed a Circuit Court clerkship. Two years later, he ran for the Alabama House, becoming one of only 11 Republicans elected that year out of 147 legislators. Brooks was re-elected three times, and says he was most proud of his No. 1 ranking from the Alabama Taxpayers' Defense Fund for his efforts to fight tax increases. He left the Legislature when Republican Gov. Guy Hunt appointed him Madison County district attorney in 1991. He succeeded Democrat Bud Cramer, who had been elected to the U.S. House. Brooks lost a bid to keep the D.A.'s job two years later, hampered by Cramer's endorsement of his Democratic opponent. He returned to public office in 1996, when he was elected to the Madison County Commission. In spite of Alabama's history of electing conservative Democrats until relatively recently, Brooks says he has always felt more at home in the Republican Party. "It's the difference between Jimmy Carter and policies that fail, and Ronald Reagan and policies that work," he says.

Brooks got into the contest for Cramer's former seat after Griffith announced in December 2009 that he was switching to the Republican Party in an ill-disguised attempt to improve his re-election prospects in 2010. *The Cook Political Report* noted that Republican presidential nominee John McCain carried the district with 61% in 2008 and that "Democrats are holding this district on borrowed time." During the GOP primary campaign, Brooks criticized Griffith's party switch and campaigned on the theme that the district "deserves a congressman who acts honorably." He won with 51% of the vote to Griffith's 33% and was able to avoid a runoff.

His opponent in the general election, Raby, was raised on farm and was the longtime chief of staff to Sen. Howell Heflin of Alabama. The Democrat shunned his party label in most of his ads, focusing almost exclusively on local issues. Brooks, for his part, took on hot-button issues, declaring that he is in favor of repealing President Obama's health care overhaul and deporting all immigrants who are in the country illegally. He says that the country is veering dangerously toward socialism and that the trend must be reversed. Brooks won with 58% of the vote to Raby's 42%.

SIXTH DISTRICT

Spencer Bachus (R)

Elected 1992, 10th term; b. Dec. 28, 1947, Birmingham; home, Columbus; Auburn U., B.A. 1969, U. of AL, J.D. 1972; Baptist; married (Linda); 3 children.

Military Career: Natl. Guard, 1969–71.

Elected Office: AL Senate, 1983–84; AL House of Reps., 1984–87.

Professional Career: Owner, Lumber Co.; Practicing atty., 1972–92; AL Repub. Party chmn., 1991–92.

DC Office: 2246 RHOB, 20515, 202-225-4921; Fax: 202-225-2082; Web site: bachus.house.gov.

State Offices: Birmingham, 205-969-2296; Clanton, 205-280-0704.

Committees: *Financial Services* (Chmn).

Group Ratings

	ACLU	ACU	ADA	CFG	AFS	FRC	LCV	ITIC	NTU	COC
2010	13	96	0	85	13	93	20	33	85	88
2009	–	92	5	84	0	–	0	–	84	80

National Journal Ratings

	2010 LIB — 2010 CONS	2009 LIB — 2009 CONS
Economic	28% — 71%	16% — 84%
Social	18% — 77%	27% — 73%
Foreign	21% — 77%	32% — 68%
Composite	24% — 76%	25% — 75%

Key Votes of the 111th Congress

1. Overturn Ledbetter	*	5. Bar federal abortion funds	Y	9. Stop detainee transfers	Y
2. Pass $820 billion stimulus	N	6. Pass health care bill	N	10. Legalize immigrants' kids	N
3. Let guns in national parks	Y	7. Regulate financial firms	N	11. Repeal don't ask, tell	N
4. Pass cap-and-trade	N	8. Pass tax cuts for some	N	12. Limit campaign funds	N

Election Results

2010 general	Spencer Bachus (R)	205,288	(98%)	($1,415,672)
2010 primary	Spencer Bachus (R)	80,725	(76%)	
	Stan Cooke (R)	25,997	(24%)	

Prior Winning Percentages: 2008 (98%), 2006 (100%), 2004 (100%), 2002 (90%), 2000 (88%), 1998 (72%), 1996 (71%), 1994 (79%), 1992 (52%)

Population		Race/Ethnicity		Work	
Pop. 2010:	754,482	White:	80.2%	Private:	80.6%
Change since 2000:	Up 18.8%	Black:	12.6%	Government:	13.5%
Urban:	62.1%	Hispanic:	4.2%	Self-employed:	5.7%
Rural:	37.9%	Asian:	1.6%	Blue collar:	19.9%
Area size:	4,649 sq. mi.	Native Am.:	0.3%	White collar:	67.9%
		Hawaiian:	0.0%	Khaki collar:	0.2%
Age		Two+ races:	1.0%	Other:	12.0%
Median age:	37.6 yrs.				
More than 65 yrs:	12.7%	*Ancestry*		Median income:	$57,167
Less than 18 yrs:	24.2%	USA	11.6%	Median Home Value:	$174,000
		English	11.5%		
Education		Irish	10.6%	**Military Veterans**	
H.S. grad:	88.2%			% of Pop:	10.6%
College grad:	33.6%				
Grad degree:	12.2%				

Central; Birmingham suburbs

Birmingham, once one of America's booming industrial cities, was better known in the latter half of the last century as a bastion of white resistance to the civil-rights movement. It has more hopeful prospects in the 21st century. This is a new city by Southern standards. Before the Civil War, there was nothing here but a few creeks running below Red Mountain. But Red Mountain is almost pure iron ore, and by 1890, Birmingham had the South's largest steel mills. In

2008 Presidential Vote		
John McCain (R) 268,791	(77%)	
Barack Obama (D) 78,150	(22%)	
2004 Presidential Vote		
George Bush (R) 248,095	(78%)	
John Kerry (D) 69,449	(22%)	
Cook Partisan Voting Index: R+29		

the early 20th century, as the statue of Vulcan, the Roman god of fire and metalworking, looked out over the smokestack-filled valley, Birmingham seemed the most progressive city in the South. But the worldwide overcapacity of steel and technological obsolescence at home sent the American steel industry into long-term decline starting in the 1950s. Meanwhile, Birmingham's political leaders plotted to avoid desegregation, and the city's violent reaction to the civil rights movement made a vivid impression on the rest of the country, watching it unfold on the relatively new medium of television. Police Commissioner (and Democratic National Committeeman at the time) Bull Connor set dogs and fire hoses against peaceful demonstrators, and Ku Klux Klansmen bombed the 16th Street Baptist Church, killing four young girls in 1963. Those images haunted Birmingham for a generation.

In recent years, Birmingham has worked to improve race relations and has developed a new economic base. Health care is a major industry. The city has some of the largest and most advanced medical care centers in the South, and is especially renowned for its sports medicine facilities and specialists who tend to the ailments of famous athletes. Banking is also important. While Atlanta's banks foundered and were acquired by outsiders, Birmingham became the largest Southern banking center outside Charlotte, N.C. But city leaders worry that the viability of the downtown area and white movement to newer suburbs have caused an uptick in racial polarization. The city's population has declined by 100,000 since 1960 and was 74% African-American in 2000. Whites have been moving out of Birmingham's Jefferson County southeast to Shelby County, which grew 44% in the 1990s and 34% from 2000 to 2009—the fastest growth in the state. (However, the migration to Shelby has not been entirely white flight. Its African-American population increased significantly as well.) Jefferson County, once more Republican than most of Alabama, votes Democratic in close statewide elections, while Shelby County is one of the most Republican counties in the state. Metropolitan planners project an 85% population increase for Shelby County from 2005 to 2035, but only a 2% increase for Jefferson, whose development growth is limited by its hills. The area was hard hit by a batch of deadly tornadoes that touched down in Alabama on April 27, 2011, destroying entire neighborhoods in the Birmingham and Tuscaloosa metro areas. The greatest loss of life was in Tuscaloosa County, where 39 people died, but Jefferson County lost 20 residents and also had considerable damage. Statewide, more than 250 people were killed and property damage surpassed $5 billion.

The 6th Congressional District of Alabama, which once included all of Birmingham and most of Jefferson County, is now the suburban Birmingham-area district and strongly Republican. It includes parts of Jefferson County, such as prosperous Mountain Brook, and stretches southwest to Tuscaloosa and south along Interstate 65 halfway to Montgomery. Its largest city, Hoover, houses the corporate offices of Blue Cross and Blue Shield of Alabama. In 2002, the Democratic line-drawers made it even more Republican by removing the last part of Birmingham and some black precincts in Tuscaloosa, and adding most of fast-growing St. Clair County north of Shelby County. Today, this is one of the most Republican districts in the nation. It voted 74% for George W. Bush in 2000—his second-best district outside of Texas—and four years later, gave Bush 78%. In 2008, John McCain won this district, 77%-22%.

Spencer Bachus (R)

The congressman from the 6th District is Republican Spencer Bachus, the chairman of the House Financial Services Committee.

A Birmingham native, he owned a sawmill company and for two decades was a trial lawyer. An early beneficiary of the region's transition away from its southern Democratic roots, Bachus (*BACK-us*) was the first Republican elected to the state school board in more than 100 years. He won a seat in the state Legislature in 1982, and was also the campaign manager to Guy Hunt when

Hunt was elected governor in 1986. After running unsuccessfully for attorney general in 1990, Bachus became Republican state chairman. When the 6th District was radically redrawn in 1992, he won a Republican runoff and defeated incumbent Ben Erdreich, a moderate Democrat.

Bachus has a conservative voting record and has been an aggressive lawmaker whose habit of negotiating across party lines to pass bills has sometimes gotten him into hot water with fellow conservatives. As the top Republican on the Financial Services Committee, he angered Republicans in 2007 during debate on a bill to ban predatory mortgage lending practices when he cut a deal with then committee Chairman Barney Frank, D-Mass. Bachus was also deeply involved in the government's response to the housing foreclosure crisis and collapse of the financial markets. On what became a $700 billion rescue of the financial industry, he was the only House Republican to participate in the initial September 2008 discussions, and he entered into a tentative agreement with Democrats. The move angered House GOP leaders, who opposed the deal as it stood and wanted modifications to satisfy the party's conservative wing. As a result, Bachus was replaced by then-Minority Whip Roy Blunt during the final negotiations on the legislation, an outcome Bachus called "very frustrating."

Having lost the confidence of Minority Leader John Boehner, who felt Bachus was too quick to compromise with the Democrats, he was at risk of being ousted from his leadership role on the committee, and speculation swirled about who would succeed him. But he showed skill as a survivor, which included a promise to toe the party line. He also rallied other influential Republicans to his side, including Virginia Republican Eric Cantor, who replaced Blunt as whip. Bachus made further amends in the 111th Congress (2009-10) by naming conservative firebrands Jeb Hensarling of Texas and Scott Garrett of New Jersey to chair two key subcommittees. Then in 2009, his rehabilitation reached new heights when he declared that he knew of 17 "socialists" in Congress. Pressed to produce proof, he identified only one by name–Vermont Sen. Bernie Sanders, a political independent. Frank complained that Bachus had become "a wholly owned subsidiary" of the conservative House Republican Study Committee.

In 2010, Bachus criticized the Obama administration for failing to move faster to develop legislation to control mortgage giants Fannie Mae and Freddie Mac, which he said had been "hooked on easy money and cheap credit." As an alternative to the 2009 Democratic financial overhaul bill crafted by Frank, Bachus unsuccessfully proposed a streamlined bankruptcy process as well as ending federal conservatorship for Fannie and Freddie. The Dodd-Frank bill ultimately passed. Shortly after taking over as chairman from Frank in 2010, Bachus vowed to conduct a "title by title" review of the legislation "to correct, replace, or repeal the job killing provisions that unnecessarily punish small businesses and community banks that did nothing to cause the financial crisis."

Bachus finds it difficult to stifle his impulse to legislate for long, and that invariably involves compromise. He cooperated with Democrats on a bill to deter abuses by credit card companies and in 2009 backed an effort to tighten credit rating agency regulations. At a July 2009 hearing, he rattled fellow Republicans when he recounted at length a private conversation he had had with Frank in which Bachus candidly told the chairman that action probably was needed to rein in bank executives' large bonuses, but such a move placed Republicans in a politically difficult situation. Earlier, Bachus helped to enact changes in the Fair Credit Reporting Act, which provided consumers additional access to their credit reports. In 2006, he pushed enactment of the controversial ban on Internet gambling.

In the 1990s, Bachus showed another side as an able investigator on the committee. He discovered that the Community Development Financial Institute, which President Clinton established in 1994, directed $11 million in loans to four banks with ties to then-first lady Hillary Rodham Clinton without proper documentation. The two top CDFI officials resigned as a consequence. He is also something of a maverick on foreign policy. He has been an unlikely crusader for international debt relief for poor Third World nations, and he criticized the Bush administration's dealings with the genocidal regime in Sudan. In 2007, he joined a bipartisan one-day fast to promote international debt relief.

Bachus beat out fellow Republican Richard Baker of Louisiana for the top spot on Financial Services after the 2006 election. He benefited from his early support of Boehner in Boehner's contest with Blunt for majority leader in 2006; Baker had backed Blunt. He also was helped by his more generous campaign contributions to other Republicans, more than $800,000.

SEVENTH DISTRICT

Terri Sewell (D)

Elected 2010, 1st term; b. Jan. 1, 1965; Princeton U., B.A. 1986; Oxford U., M.A. 1988; Harvard U., J.D. 1992.; African Methodist Episcopal Church; Single.

Professional Career: Clerk, U.S. District Court judge, 1993-94; practicing atty., 1994-2010.

DC Office: 1133 LHOB, 20515, 202-225-2665; Fax: 202-226-9567; Web site: sewell.house.gov.

State Offices: Birmingham, 205-254-1960; Demopolis, 334-287-0860; Livingston, 205-652-5834; Marion, 334-683-2157; Selma, 334-877-4414; Tuscaloosa, 205-752-5380.

Committees: *Agriculture:* General Farm Commodities & Risk Management; Rural Development, Research, Biotechnology & Foreign Agriculture. *Science & Technology:* Research & Science Education; Space & Aeronautics.

Election Results

2010 general	Terri Sewell (D)	136,696	(72%)	($1,802,819)
	Don Chamberlain (R)	51,890	(28%)	($45,555)
2010 primary	Terri Sewell (D)	32,366	(55%)	
	Shelia Smoot (D)	26,481	(45%)	
2010 primary	Terri Sewell (D)	31,531	(37%)	
	Shelia Smoot (D)	24,490	(29%)	
	Earl Hilliard (D)	22,981	(27%)	
	Martha Bozeman (D)	6,672	(8%)	

Population		Race/Ethnicity		Work	
Pop. 2010:	603,352	White:	32.7%	Private:	77.7%
Change since 2000:	Down 5.0%	Black:	62.6%	Government:	17.8%
Urban:	72.2%	Hispanic:	3.0%	Self-employed:	4.3%
Rural:	27.8%	Asian:	0.7%	Blue collar:	26.5%
Area size:	8,780 sq. mi.	Native Am.:	0.2%	White collar:	53.3%
		Hawaiian:	0.0%	Khaki collar:	0.1%
Age		Two+ races:	0.8%	Other:	20.1%
Median age:	34.5 yrs.				
More than 65 yrs:	12.5%	*Ancestry*		Median income:	$31,674
Less than 18 yrs:	24.4%	USA	5.8%	Median Home Value:	$88,900
		Irish	4.7%		
Education		English	4.5%	**Military Veterans**	
H.S. grad:	80.2%			% of Pop:	9.2%
College grad:	17.1%				
Grad degree:	6.0%				

West Alabama; Birmingham

Alabama has learned to celebrate its black heritage, building striking memorials to the civil-rights movement in Montgomery and Birmingham, acknowledging its history as ground zero of white resistance to the empowerment of blacks in the 1950s and 1960s. Blacks first came here as slaves. The last slave ship to the United States, the *Clotilde*, docked in Mobile in 1859, where its cargo was then set free. Blacks were part of the great migration into the cotton lands

2008 Presidential Vote
Barack Obama (D)	207,732	(74%)
John McCain (R)	72,801	(26%)

2004 Presidential Vote
John Kerry (D)	160,875	(65%)
George Bush (R)	88,433	(35%)

Cook Partisan Voting Index: D+18

after the Jacksonians swept the Indians out of the Southeast and sent them on their Trail of Tears to what is now Oklahoma. Today, Alabama's rural African-Americans are still clustered in the Black Belt of fertile dark soil across the center of the state. In Selma, founded by Alabama's one vice president, William Rufus King, Sheriff Jim Clark's troops beat up peaceful marchers on the Edmund Pettus Bridge in demonstrations that led to the march on Montgomery and the 1965 Voting Rights Act. All 10 of Alabama's majority-black counties are in the rich farm country of the Black Belt, but most Alabama blacks now live in urban areas—one-quarter of them in metropolitan Birmingham.

After decades of urban decline, Birmingham has undergone a renaissance in recent years. The city pulled itself out of the spiral of abandoned neighborhoods, soaring joblessness and crime through the savvy use of public-private partnerships and other incentives. Numerous vacant and boarded up buildings were supplanted by lofts and cafes for young professionals and empty-nesters, slowing the trend of migration to the suburbs. Some 4,000 people live in downtown Birmingham now. Crime zones like the Metropolitan Gardens public housing project were leveled and replaced by mixed-income apartments. On the drawing board are a baseball park and a new Westin Hotel. But in late 2009, the city took it hard on the chin when its controversial mayor, Larry Langford, was convicted of accepting $230,000 in bribes for steering millions of dollars of Jefferson County sewer bond business to an investment banker buddy when Langford headed the county commission. That and other shady deals with large investment houses on Wall Street forced the county to the brink of bankruptcy, dealing Birmingham both a tough financial and public relations blow to the civic optimism that had fueled its revival. Compounding the city's financial woes were recovery efforts after a deadly series of tornadoes touched down in Alabama on April 27, 2011, destroying entire neighborhoods in the Birmingham and Tuscaloosa metro areas. The greatest loss of life was in Tuscaloosa County, where 39 people died, but Jefferson County also lost 20 people and sustained considerable damage. Statewide, more than 250 people were killed and property damage surpassed $5 billion.

The 7th Congressional District of Alabama was created in 1992 as a majority-African-American district. It includes Black Belt counties where the Alabama and Tombigbee rivers flow past old plantations and the catfish industry has thrived, plus part of Tuscaloosa, home of the University of Alabama, and nearby Vance, site of a Mercedes factory. Most of its people are in Birmingham and surrounding Jefferson County. It is 63% African-American, and solidly Democratic. John Kerry won 65%-35% here in 2004, one of his best showings in the Deep South. In 2008, Barack Obama swept each of the Black Belt counties by large margins, including 87%-13% in Macon County, which is in the 3rd District. Overall, he won this district, 74%-26%.

Terri Sewell (D)

The congresswoman from the 7th District is Terri Sewell, one of the first women sent to Congress from Alabama. She vaulted over several better-known Democrats to win the 2010 primary, which was tantamount to securing the seat of Rep. Artur Davis, a Democrat who ran unsuccessfully for governor.

Sewell was born in Huntsville, Ala., and raised in Selma, a hotbed of activity for the civil-rights movement. She grew up near the famed Edmund Pettus Bridge, the site of the "Bloody Sunday" clash between protest marchers and state troopers. Sewell's family on her maternal side offered shelter for wayward travelers making the famed march from Selma to Montgomery in 1965. Hailing from such a place, "you appreciate the significance of your elders' fight for voting rights and civil rights," Sewell said. Her mother, Nancy Sewell, was the first African-American woman elected to the Selma City Council. Her father was the high school basketball coach at Selma High School, where Sewell was the first black valedictorian. "Well, when you can get no dates because your daddy is a coach, all you can really do is study, right?" she joked.

Sewell earned her undergraduate degree from Princeton University. During that time, she took part in a Big Sister program and drew inspiration from the mentor assigned to her, Michelle Robinson, now first lady Michelle Obama. While Sewell was writing her senior thesis at Princeton, she also met former Rep. Shirley Chisholm, D-N.Y., the first African-American woman elected to Congress, who was retired by then and teaching at Mount Holyoke College. "I don't know if anybody could ever follow in Shirley Chisholm's footsteps, but I can tell you that I was inspired by her whole life story," Sewell said. "It really made a lasting impression on me."

Sewell later studied politics at the University of Oxford on a scholarship, earning a master's degree. A theater buff, she dabbled in drama while at Oxford, directing and starring in the play *For Colored Girls Who Have Considered Suicide When the Rainbow is Enuf* by Ntozake Shange. Later, while earning her law degree from Harvard, Sewell was a classmate of future President Obama. At Harvard, she took a year off to turn her master's thesis into a book called *Black Tribunes: Race and Representation in British Politics.*

After graduating, Sewell clerked for a U.S. District Court judge in Birmingham, and then in 1994 moved to New York City to work as a lawyer on Wall Street. But she returned home to Alabama to help take care of her ailing father, who has survived several strokes. Most recently, Sewell was a bond lawyer and a partner in the Birmingham law firm Maynard, Cooper, and Gale.

When Davis decided to leave the House after four terms to run for governor, Sewell jumped into the Democratic primary contest against eight other candidates. They included prominent local figures Earl Hilliard Jr., son of former Rep. Earl Hilliard, D-Ala., and Jefferson County Commissioner Sheila Smoot. Sewell had lower name recognition than Hilliard or Smoot, but she made up for it through an effective fund-raising campaign. She outraised the other candidates with both a local and national fund-raising network, which included big name donors such as Starbucks CEO Howard Schultz, Washington, D.C., lawyer Vernon Jordan, and former Gov. Roy Barnes, D-Ga. On June 1, 2010, Sewell finished first in the Democratic primary with 37% of the vote. Smoot snagged second place with 29%, setting up a July 13 runoff. Smoot got the endorsement of House Majority Whip Jim Clyburn, D-S.C., but Sewell outspent Smoot by nearly $1 million. In a relatively congenial runoff race, Sewell bested Smoot, 55% to 45%. She went on to easily defeat Republican opponent Don Chamberlain, a Selma businessman, with 72% of the vote.

★ ALASKA ★

Sarah Palin's Alaska is the title of the television series, but Alaska had been a distinctive state for nearly half a century before Palin was elected governor in 2006 and nominated for vice president in 2008. Alaska in 2009 celebrated the 50th anniversary of its admission as the 49th state in the Union. With 16% of the nation's land area and just .23% of its population, Alaska is a state created by the federal government that it often resents, and it is an individualistic society that has responded to its unique situation in creative ways. Alaska would not be American at all but for the expansive dream of Secretary of State William Seward, who took advantage of a fleeting opportunity to create an American Pacific empire by purchasing the region from Russia in 1867 for $7.2 million. (The Russian Orthodox Church still claims 30,000 members in Alaska, many of them Alaska Natives.) The Alaska Territory owed most of its early growth to decisions made by the federal government. It started growing feverishly with the Klondike gold rush in 1897, just as President McKinley reaffirmed the gold standard. Anchorage, the largest city, had its beginnings in 1913 as the chief worksite of the federal government's Alaska Railroad, completed in 1923. The Army built the Alcan Highway, connecting Alaska to the lower 48 states, in the grim war days of 1942, when the Aleutian Islands of Attu and Kiska were invaded by the Japanese, the only part of the United States occupied by a foreign enemy since the War of 1812. By 1943, 152,000 U.S. troops were stationed in a territory whose prewar population was only 72,000. Alaska is the only state abutting Russia, across the Bering Strait and over the North Pole—there actually is a part of Alaska where you can see Russian land—and Alaska continues to occupy a strategic geographic position. The military is a major presence at Fort Richardson and Elmendorf Air Force Base near Anchorage and at Fort Wainwright and Eielson Air Force Base near Fairbanks, with interceptors for the national missile defense system not far to the south at Fort Greely.

Alaska's size is hard for most Americans to comprehend. If superimposed on the lower 48, the state would stretch from Florida to California. The westernmost Aleutians are closer to Tokyo than to Juneau and farther west than Wellington, New Zealand. One-third of Alaskans have no access to state roads and are reachable only by boat or airplane. Alaska has, per capita, six times the number of pilots and 16 times the number of aircraft as the rest of the nation. Moose walk around residential neighborhoods in Anchorage, and a much higher rate of people go missing here than in the lower 48, or simply "Outside" as Alaskans say. Only 710,000 people live in Alaska, with more than 60% of the population in Anchorage and the nearby (by Alaska standards) Kenai Peninsula and Matanuska-Susitna Valley. This plus Fairbanks, with 13% of the population, is the fastest-growing part of Alaska, with a dynamic private-sector economy. The Panhandle, with 11% of the people, is the old Alaska, with towns settled by Russians and the old state capital of Juneau built up against steep mountains on inlets from the Pacific. The other 15% live in the bush, scattered in small towns and the oil port of Valdez, in Native settlements and on hundreds of lakes. About half the people here are Alaska Natives. They are greatly outnumbered and outvoted on many issues, and yet are the object of respect for their achievements in building viable civilizations with impressive art traditions in such a forbidding environment. Considering its remoteness, Alaska has impressive racial diversity. Its population is 3% black, 14% Native, 5% Asian, and 5.5% Hispanic.

Alaska won statehood in January 1959, after a valiant campaign. But statehood did not end federal decision-making power over Alaska—or the widespread resentment of it. Alaska's economy depended on fishing, oil production in Cook Inlet around Anchorage, and the military—all federally regulated or controlled. Less than a decade later, however, Alaska's economy and public life were reshaped by the discovery of North Slope oil. It began suddenly, accidentally. On the day after Christmas 1967, at Prudhoe Bay on the Arctic coast, a tremendous roar as loud as four jumbo jets drew a crowd of 40 men, heavily clothed against the 30-below weather, to an oil rig. A natural gas flare shot 30 feet straight up. This was the great 12 billion-barrel North Slope oil field. Earlier, oil companies had drilled seven dry wells on Prudhoe Bay, and Arco chief executive Robert Anderson wouldn't have ordered this last try, except that he had a drilling rig nearby. This was the greatest oil strike in U.S. history and the beginning of much of today's Alaska.

Finding oil in Prudhoe Bay was somewhat akin to finding it on the moon. It was not clear in 1967 who owned the oil or how it could be taken out. The Statehood Act of 1959 gave the state the right to choose its own public lands, but only after settling Native land claims. The only feasible way to get the oil out—the Arctic Ocean ice breaks up in late July for only six weeks—was a pipeline. But environmentalists opposed that option for fear it would destroy the delicate permafrost and interfere with caribou migrations. Development-minded Alaskans got a pipeline bill through Con-

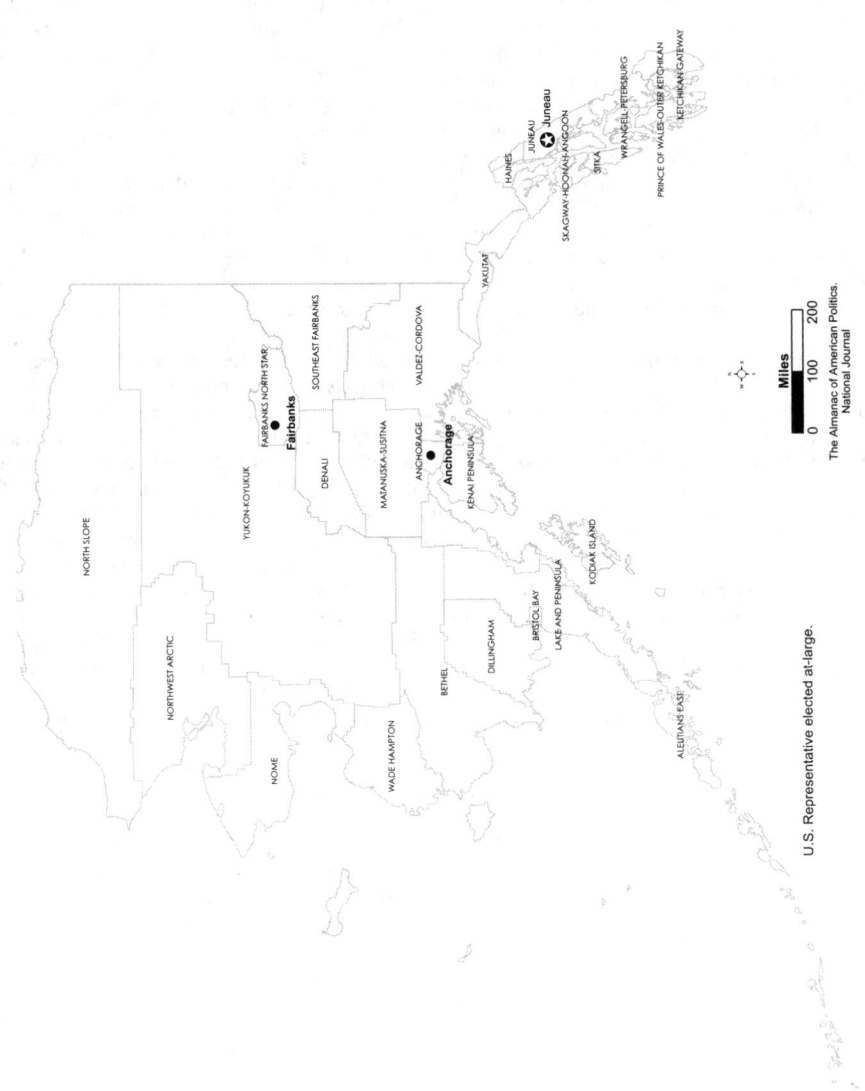

U.S. Representative elected at-large.

The Almanac of American Politics.
National Journal

Miles

0   100   200

gress in 1973, by just a one-vote margin in the Senate, but the pipeline had to be built on stilts and wasn't opened until 1977. Then in 1980, after astute lobbying by environmentalists, Congress passed—over the objections of Alaska's two senators and Rep. Don Young—the Alaska Lands Act, which set aside 159 million acres as national parks, national monuments, or wilderness: One-third of the state was protected (or barred) from development. Much, if not all of this, turned out to be for the best. The pipeline came on line just as oil prices were approaching a peak, thus generating maximum revenues to the state, which gets 100% of the royalties. The environment was protected far better than it would have been without the safeguards. The Western Arctic herd of caribou grew to 401,000 animals in 2009, and Native Alaskans got more autonomy than the non-Native majority of Alaskans would have given them. With oil providing some 85% of its revenue, the state government abolished its income tax in 1980 and created a low-tax regime that has helped Alaska to grow even as oil revenues and military spending have declined.

Wisely, Alaska did not squander its windfall. In 1976, Republican Gov. Jay Hammond persuaded the legislature to establish a Permanent Fund for most of the oil revenues. Each year, it presents every resident with a dividend of 20% of the average of profits for the preceding five years—$1,281 in 2010. Even though $18.8 billion has been paid in dividends, most of the money was put into investments worth $35.7 billion in 2010. North Slope oil production has been declining since it peaked in 1988, so most of its income now comes from investments rather than oil. Some speculated that Alaska voters would pressure legislators for bigger payouts. But Alaskans have acted like investors. They want their dividend checks not just now but in the future. Voters have rejected proposals to spend Permanent Fund earnings, and no one has dared to suggest tapping the capital.

Similarly, 12 regional Native corporations created by the Alaska Native Claims Act have proved to be successful not just in providing income for Natives but in helping them preserve Native traditions and adapt to Alaska's market economy at their own pace. On Indian reservations in the lower 48, all land is held by the tribe and supervised by the government; elections held on the political model have produced a winner-take-all politics that is often corrupt and incapable of pursuing long-range strategies. The corporate model, on the other hand, allows more continuity in office for the Alaska Native corporations' managers—although some have made bad decisions and been thrown out. But the cumulative voting method, by which a minority can get a seat on the board, has produced management that is sensitive to all opinions. Huge windfalls are avoided because 70% of profits from mineral sales are shared by all corporations. The corporation itself, not a distant federal bureaucracy, is left with the choice of how much ancestral land to retain and how much to exploit economically. Individual Natives can make the transition from their traditional communal economy, living on subsistence fishing and hunting, or make their way in the market economy: 43% of Natives now live in Anchorage, Fairbanks, Juneau, Matanuska-Susitna, or the Kenai Peninsula. In 2004, the 42 regional and village Native corporations had revenues of $4.5 billion and employed 13,000 Alaskans. But not all is rosy. Native villages in the bush have little in the way of a private-sector economy, and alcoholism and suicide rates remain high.

The federal government continues to make decisions that shape Alaska's economy—and not always in Alaska's favor, despite the efforts of such formidable senior elected officials as Sens. Ted Stevens (1968-2009) and Frank Murkowski (1981-2002) and Rep. Don Young, first elected in 1973. These three Republicans failed to get approval of oil drilling in a sliver of the Arctic National Wildlife Refuge—an area the size of Washington's Dulles International Airport in an area the size of Delaware—although it was on the verge of being approved in 1989, when the *Exxon Valdez* ran aground in Prince William Sound. Environmental groups made ANWR oil drilling one of their main issues in their direct-mail fundraising. ANWR is estimated to have 9 billion to16 billion barrels of oil, the most by far in any untapped U.S. oil field. In 2005 and 2006, the Senate approved ANWR drilling as part of its budget resolution, but it was stricken by the House when liberal Republicans threatened to withhold their votes. The Democratic takeover of both chambers in the 2006 elections killed the issue for four years. Now, while it might pass the House, it is unlikely to pass the Senate, where Alaska has less seniority than at any time since the 1970s. Republican Sen. Lisa Murkowski was appointed by her father in 2002 and elected in 2004 and 2010. Democratic Sen. Mark Begich was elected in 2008. The Obama administration is firmly opposed to ANWR drilling, and its 2010 ban on offshore drilling is blocking development in the Chukchi Sea between Nome and Barrow.

Although the North Slope's oil has been pumped out through the pipeline since 1977, there has been no way to get its vast quantities of natural gas out. So it's been burned off at the wellhead or pumped back into the ground. An estimated 30 trillion cubic feet is in Prudhoe Bay and another 70 trillion cubic feet is elsewhere on the Slope. In 2004, after years of effort, Stevens and Lisa

Murkowski got an 80% federal loan guarantee for a gas pipeline through Congress. That left the ball in the state government's court. Gov. Frank Murkowski accepted two proposals—one from the three North Slope oil companies and another from a pipeline company with Native corporations involved—to build the pipeline, and he urged that the state take an equity interest in the project. But Palin, then mayor of Wasilla, and others argued that this was a giveaway to the oil companies. It became the issue that enabled Palin to defeat Murkowski 51%-19% in the August 2006 Republican primary, with 30% going to a third candidate. She went on to defeat former Democratic Gov. Tony Knowles in November, and, working with the legislature, enacted the Alaska Gasline Inducement Act, which offers up to $500 million in seed money to help build the natural-gas pipeline as well as freeze production taxes for 10 years. The state received five applications to build the pipeline, none of them from the North Slope oil producers. In 2008, Alaska approved a bid from Calgary-based TransCanada, a major victory for Palin.

Alaska's economy is also dependent on fishing, long its largest private employer. Alaska produces half of America's seafood, and the salmon fisheries here, unlike so many elsewhere, have not been dangerously depleted. Tourism, the No. 2 private employer, has been on the rise, with over 1.5 million tourists a year, many arriving on cruise ships from which they view glaciers in the southeast, troop into Russian-settled Sitka, and make side trips to Denali National Park and Mount McKinley. In 2006, voters by just 52%-48% approved a $50 per passenger cruise ship tax. Ted Stevens International Airport in Anchorage, near the top of the world, is seven hours from New York City, Tokyo, and London, and it is a major cargo transfer point for UPS, FedEx, Northwest Airlines, and the U.S. Postal Service. More wide-bodied, all-cargo aircraft move through it than any other U.S. airport.

Sarah Palin's election in 2006 was one of several earthquakes that reshaped Alaska's political landscape. That year, three state legislators were convicted of bribery. Bill Allen, head of the oil field services company VECO, was handing out $100 bills to legislators to get them to vote against higher taxes on oil companies. In June 2007, *The New York Times* reported that a Young aide altered the 2005 transportation bill with a $10 million addition for roadwork on Interstate 75 near Naples, Fla., that would help real estate developer Daniel Aronoff, who had raised $40,000 for Young. But no charges were brought against him. Stevens was convicted of concealing $250,000 in gifts from VECO and Allen, including extensive renovations on his home—which undoubtedly accounted for his 48%-47% defeat in November. But his conviction was thrown out in 2009 because prosecutors had withheld key evidence from Stevens's defense attorneys. Stevens, who flew transport planes in World War II and survived a 1978 crash that killed his first wife, died in a plane crash in Alaska in August 2010.

The last half of the 2000s saw something of a political revolution in Alaska, starting with Palin's defeat of the two previous governors in 2006 and continuing with Stevens' narrow loss to Begich in 2008. Holding on, narrowly, in 2008, was Young, who from his positions as chairman of the Resources Committee (1995-2001) and Transportation Committee (2001-07), fought for oil and gas exploration and sponsored countless infrastructure projects. He narrowly won the August primary over then-Lt. Gov. Sean Parnell, 45.5%-45.2%, and defeated Democratic legislator Democrat Ethan Berkowitz 50%-45% in November. He returned to Congress without a ranking member post or chairmanship, having exhausted Republicans' term limits. And of course Stevens's defeat marked the end of a highly productive, 44-year career in which he played major roles in the Alaska Native Claims Act, approval of the oil pipeline and dozens of other Alaska issues. Most famous, not just in Alaska but nationally, was the "bridge to nowhere," as critics called it, between Ketchikan and Gravina Island (pop. 50, plus the local airport), to the tune of some $250 million in the

Population		Household Income		Work	
Pop. 2010:	710,231	Under $15k:	7.40%	Private:	64.70%
State rank:	47th	$15k to $50k:	29.30%	Government:	28.19%
Change since 2000:	Up 13.3%	$50k to $100k:	35.10%	Self-employed:	6.70%
Urban:	65.20%	$100k to $200k:	23.89%	Unemployment (3-yr. average):	6.20%
Rural:	34.79%	Over $200k:	4.40%	Poverty:	8.69%
Native of state:	39.5%	Median income:	$66,565	Blue collar:	22.89%
Not a citizen:	3.29%			White collar:	57.10%
Area size:	665,384 sq. mi.	**Home Value**		Khaki collar:	2.39%
		Under $100k:	12.6%	Other:	17.60%
Most populous cities		$100k to $300k:	57.60%		
Anchorage	291,826	$300k to $500k:	23.10%	**Age**	
Fairbanks	31,535	$500k to $1 mil:	6.0%	Median age:	32.70 yrs.
Juneau city and boro	31,275	Over $1 million:	0.5%	More than 65 yrs:	7.20%
		Median:	$232,600	Less than 18 yrs:	26.39%

Race/Ethnicity				Military Veterans		Registered Voters in 2010	
White:	64.09%	*Language*		% of Pop:	14.0%	Democrats:	74,802 (15%)
Black:	3.10%	English:	84.09%			Republicans:	126,486 (26%)
Hispanic:	5.5%	Spanish:	3.79%	*Veterans by Period*		Ind./other:	286,287 (59%)
Asian:	5.3%	Asian:	4.70%	WWII and before:	3.29%	Voter turnout:	258,746
Native Am.:	14.4%	Other European:	2.20%	Korea:	4.70%	Turnout as % of	
Hawaiian:	1.0%			Vietnam:	34.10%	voting age:	49.5%
Two+ races:	6.40%	**Education**		Gulf (pre-2001):	17.89%		
		H.S. grad:	91.09%	Gulf (post-2001):	19.19%	**Legislature**	
Ancestry		College grad:	26.5%	Peace time:	20.80%	Senate:	10 D 10 R
German	15.19%	Grad degree:	9.5%			House:	16 D 24 R
Irish	9.80%						
English	7.90%						

2005 transportation bill—a project that gave the Republican Congress a reputation for out-of-control pork-barrel spending and contributed to the Democratic takeover in 2006. Palin's resignation as governor in July 2009 caught Alaskans as well as those Outside by surprise. She turned the governor's office over to Lt. Gov. Sean Parnell, a political ally, who was elected to a full term 59%-38% over Democrat Ethan Berkowitz.

In partisan terms, Alaska is pretty solidly Republican. It hasn't voted Democratic for president since 1964, or come close since 1968. Begich is the first Alaska Democrat elected to the Senate since 1974. His father, Nick Begich, who died in a plane crash with House Majority Leader Hale Boggs in 1972, was the last Alaska Democrat elected to the House. Yet in the legislature, divisions are not always along party lines. Palin worked more with Democrats, including Berkowitz, than with Republican leaders on the natural-gas pipeline and tougher ethics laws. And, anyway, Alaska is quirky, with its own special issues that are not always congruent with issues Outside. Alaska has a libertarian streak—people don't move all the way there to let other people tell them how to live their lives. Palin, sometimes painted as an extremist in what she calls the "lamestream media," never pressed for restrictions on abortion rights or for banning same-sex marriage. Oil company workers in their two-week stints on the North Slope are not allowed to have alcohol, illegal drugs, or guns. But don't try to take those things away from Alaskans when they're back home. Arguments that seem so consuming in the lower 48 seem beside the point in Alaska, where the wilderness is always nearby and the possibilities for the future seem limitless.

Presidential politics   When Alaska and Hawaii were admitted to the union in 1959, it was expected that Alaska would vote Democratic and Hawaii Republican. It has turned out to be pretty much the other way around. Alaska voted near the national average in the close elections of 1960 and 1968. Since then, it has voted primarily on Alaska issues, which means against the national Democrats. In 1980, the year of the Alaska Lands Act, it gave only 26% of its votes to Democratic incumbent Jimmy Carter. In 1992, third-party candidate Ross Perot won 28% here, his second-best showing in the country. In 2000,

2008 Presidential Vote		
John McCain (R) 193,841	(59%)
Barack Obama (D) 123,594	(38%)

2004 Presidential Vote		
George W. Bush (R)...............190,889	(61%)
John Kerry (D) 111,025	(36%)

George W. Bush won 59%-28%, but Ralph Nader got 10% of the vote, Nader's best showing. In 2004, Bush got 61% and John Kerry improved on Al Gore's showing with 36%.

So critics scoffed in 2008 when Democratic National Chairman Howard Dean included Alaska in his 50-state strategy and, on a visit to Anchorage, encouraged the state Democratic Party to hire more than one staffer. But Dean turned out to have a point, even if no presidential candidates showed up in the state before the February 5 caucuses on Super Tuesday. Some 8,900 voters turned out for the Democratic caucuses—not many fewer than the 11,600 who turned out for Republican caucuses, and a whole lot more than the 700 who showed up in 2004. Barack Obama, whose campaign opened an Anchorage office in December 2007, beat Hillary Rodham Clinton by 75%-25%. On the Republican side, Mitt Romney, whose son, Josh, did visit Alaska, won with 44% of the vote to 22% for Mike Huckabee, 17% for Ron Paul (that libertarian streak again), and 16% for John McCain—not coincidentally, the only Republican opposed to oil drilling in ANWR.

In the general election campaign, the Obama campaign shrewdly targeted Alaska, and he ran about even with McCain in spring and early-summer polls. It was the first race since 1968 in which the oil-drilling issue did not work heavily in favor of the Republican nominee. By August, Obama had 60 paid staffers in Alaska and his volunteers were busy canvassing voters in the long hours of summer daylight. But McCain's selection of Palin as his vice presidential nominee switched Alaska safely to the Republican side. Even as Stevens and Young were battling for re-election after 40 and 35 years in Congress, respectively, McCain, their adversary on ANWR, was running well ahead in September and October. Despite Palin's presence on the ticket and despite the close Senate and House races, turnout was up only 4% over 2004 in Alaska. McCain won 59%-38%, his sixth-biggest-percentage margin in the nation. He carried 32 of Alaska's 40 legislative districts, losing only blue-collar areas in Anchorage and Fairbanks, the trendy quarter (such as it is) of Anchorage, state-employee-heavy Juneau, and two heavily Native areas in the Bush.

Governor

Sean Parnell (R)

Assumed office July 2009, term expires Dec. 2014, 1st full term; b. Nov. 19, 1962, Hanford, CA; home, Juneau; Pacific Lutheran U., B.B.A. 1984; U. of Puget Sound, J.D. 1987; married (Sandy); 2 children.

Elected Office: AK House of Reps., 1992-96; AK Senate, 1996-2000; Lt. gov, 2006-09

Professional Career: Practicing atty., 1987-present; ConocoPhillips, atty. & lobbyist; Deputy dir., AK Div. of Oil & Gas.

Office: Alaska State Capitol Building, Third Floor, 99811-0001, 907-465-3500; Fax: 907-465-3532; Web site: www.gov.state.ak.us.

State Offices: Anchorage, 907-269-7450; Fairbanks, 907-451-2920.

Election Results
2010 general	Sean Parnell (R)	151,318	(59%)
	Ethan Berkowitz (D)	96,519	(38%)
2010 primary	Sean Parnell (R)	54,125	(50%)
	Bill Walker (R)	35,734	(33%)
	Ralph Samuels (R)	15,376	(14%)

Republican Sean Parnell took over as governor of Alaska on July 26, 2009, from Sarah Palin, who unexpectedly resigned with 18 months left in her term. Parnell had been elected lieutenant governor in 2006 on a Republican ticket with Palin, who later was swept into the swirl of the 2008 presidential campaign as GOP nominee John McCain's running mate. Although she connected well with party conservatives, Palin's stumbling performance on the national stage raised doubts about her suitability for vice president. She cited residual negative attention from the presidential campaign in announcing her resignation as governor in early July.

Parnell was born in Hanford, Calif., just south of Fresno. His father, Pat, was stationed at the Army's Fort Richardson in Anchorage and fell in love with Alaska. He moved his family there in 1973, when Sean was 10 years old. The elder Parnell opened a law practice in Anchorage and got involved in politics. He served in the Anchorage Assembly and in Alaska's House of Representatives as a Democrat. In 1980, Pat Parnell unsuccessfully challenged Republican Don Young for the state's lone congressional seat. Even then, Alaska tilted heavily Republican, and Young won with 74% of the vote. Meanwhile, Sean Parnell attended college and law school in Washington state. Following his father's career path, he returned to Anchorage, opened a legal practice, and ran for office. But, unlike his father, he ran as a Republican. In 1992, at age 29, he was elected to the state House, where he served two terms. In 1996, he was elected to the state Senate. Parnell championed legislation to toughen domestic violence penalties, citing the effect his grandfather's alcoholism and physical abuse had on his own family. In the state Senate, he rose to become co-chairman of the powerful Finance Committee, where he worked to increase state oil revenues and to balance the state budget.

In 2000, citing a desire to spend more time with his family, Parnell announced that he would not seek a second Senate term. He returned to work as a commercial contract lawyer in Anchorage, and later took a job with ConocoPhillips as an attorney and lobbyist. In 2003, then-Gov. Frank Murkowski, a Republican, appointed him as deputy director of Alaska's Division of Oil and Gas, a post that got him deeply involved in negotiations over the state's proposed natural-gas pipeline. Two years later, Parnell parlayed his knowledge of energy issues into a job at the Anchorage branch of the Washington, D.C.-based law firm Patton Boggs, which handled such high-profile cases as the defense of what is now ExxonMobil in the 1989 *Exxon Valdez* oil spill in Alaska's Prince William Sound.

Parnell returned to politics in 2006 with his successful campaign for lieutenant governor. His primary opponent was state Sen. Jerry Ward, who accused Parnell of being too cozy with oil companies. But Ward had his own record to defend—he had been arrested on a burglary charge, which was later dropped, and he had served probation for a gun conviction. Still, polls showed the two in a tight race, although Parnell ultimately won 57%-43%. After his victory, Parnell joined with Palin, who had won the Republican gubernatorial nomination by defeating the scandal-scarred incumbent, Murkowski. Palin and Parnell faced a Democratic ticket led by former Gov. Tony Knowles, with state Rep. Ethan Berkowitz as his running mate. Knowles entered the race late but argued that he was the best candidate to negotiate a pipeline deal that could deliver Alaska's great natural-gas reserves to market. Palin started off trailing in the polls and with plenty of political enemies in her own party. But in an election year in which the national mood seemed to be running against incumbent Republicans, Palin's outsider status was an asset to the party. On Election Day, Palin and Parnell defeated Knowles and Berkowitz, 48%-41%, with 9% going to Andrew Halcro, a former Republican legislator running as an independent.

Throughout the first two years of their administration, Parnell was a loyal Palin ally. He supported her tax increase on oil companies and her plan to give Alaskans $100-a-month debit cards to use for gasoline as part of an energy relief plan. But in March 2008, he shocked much of Alaska's political establishment when he announced a primary challenge to Young, hoping to oust the 17-term congressman who had defeated his father 28 years earlier. Young had been tainted by scandals involving appropriations earmarks favoring a Florida company that had been a substantial donor to his campaigns. Parnell ran as a fiscal conservative and pointed to his budgetary experience in the state legislature as a contrast to Young's decades-long history of effusive earmarking. Palin endorsed her lieutenant over Young, and early polls showed Parnell leading the incumbent. Young forcefully attacked Parnell as inexperienced. On Alaska Public Radio, he called Parnell "Captain Zero," and Young told his challenger during the GOP state convention, "I beat your dad, and I'm going to beat you." Parnell had strong support from the national anti-tax group Club for Growth and was also endorsed by the conservative *National Review*. On the night of the August 26 primary, Young had a narrow lead of 152 votes; after absentee ballots were counted, he prevailed by 304 votes. Parnell decided against requesting a recount, saying that the cost to the state could not be justified. Young went on to defeat Democrat Berkowitz in November.

For his part, Parnell was still the lieutenant governor, and, as it turned out, his responsibilities multiplied rapidly. After McCain chose Palin as his running mate in August 2008, Parnell took over many of the day-to-day duties of governor while Palin was on the road campaigning. He was thrust into the top job by Palin's sudden decision to step down midterm. Parnell said he learned he would be taking over as governor only two days before Palin's hastily arranged press conference on July 3 at her Wasilla home on Alaska's Lake Lucille. Palin cited numerous reasons for her premature departure, including not wanting to be a lame-duck governor, frustration with media scrutiny of her family, and state and personal resources that had been spent battling ethics claims against her. Palin also praised Parnell's capability as her successor, saying he would carry out their "good, positive agenda for Alaska."

Parnell signaled that he planned to continue many of Palin's policies, including pursuing a natural-gas pipeline for the state. In recent years, Parnell had come under fire from some fellow Republicans for being too close to Palin and her positions. But all sides agreed that his bland, non-confrontational style was distinctly different from his predecessor. "I've never been about standing up and just yelling for the sake of yelling," Parnell told *The New York Times* in April 2010. "That's not who I am. I'm about getting the job done."

Parnell's dealings with the legislature were aided by rising oil prices that put Alaska in much better shape than the cash-strapped states in the lower 48. He still faced some rocky moments, however. When lawmakers sent him a bill to alter the state's system of taxing oil and gas production together, he issued a veto, agreeing with critics that it would send the industry the wrong signal. Lawmakers also thumbed their noses at his pleas for fiscal restraint by passing more than $3 billion in capital spending projects. But the 2010 legislative session ended with Parnell obtaining a number of his priorities, including a reduction in the state's head tax on cruise ship passengers and anti-domestic violence and sexual assault bills. Lawmakers also agreed in principle to his proposal for an ambitious new education program that would award scholarships to high school students with good grades, but they did not provide the funding for it.

Parnell then turned to the task of seeking a full term as governor. After a primary campaign in which he faced criticism for not being bold enough, he fended off five other Republicans with

50% of the vote. His closest challenger was former Valdez Mayor Bill Walker, who poured $300,000 of his own money into the race and finished with 33%. Parnell's opponent in the general election again was Berkowitz, who had earlier vied with him for lieutenant governor and Don Young's House seat. Berkowitz sought to persuade voters that Parnell lacked leadership qualities, and offered plans to expand wind power statewide as well as to expand preschool opportunities for Alaska children. Parnell maintained that his opponent's ideas typified Democratic big government. In addition to all the traditional disadvantages facing Democrats in Alaska, Berkowitz had another handicap. The governor's race was thoroughly overshadowed by the Senate battle between Republican Joe Miller and GOP Sen. Lisa Murkowski, who lost to Miller in the primary but waged an ultimately successful write-in campaign. Parnell won easily with 59%. Thanks to high oil prices, he entered the 2011 legislative session with the luxury of a $10 billion state budget reserve.

Senior Senator

Lisa Murkowski (R)

Appointed Dec. 2002, term expires 2016, 2nd full term; b. May 22, 1957, Ketchikan; home, Anchorage; Willamette U., 1975-77, Georgetown U., B.A. 1980, Willamette U., J.D. 1985; Catholic; married (Verne Martell); 2 children.

Elected Office: AK House of Reps., 1998-02.

Professional Career: Anchorage Dist. Court Clerk's Office, atty., 1987-89; Practicing atty., 1989-98.

DC Office: 709 HSOB, 20510, 202-224-6665; Fax: 202-224-5301; Web site: murkowski.senate.gov.

State Offices: Anchorage, 907-271-3735; Fairbanks, 907-456-0233; Ketchikan, 907-225-6880; Wasilla, 907-376-7665.

Committees: *Appropriations:* Commerce, Justice, Science & Related Agencies; Defense; Energy & Water Development; Homeland Security; Interior, Environment & Related Agencies (RMM); Military Construction, Veterans Affairs & Related Agencies. *Energy & Natural Resources* (RMM). *Health, Education, Labor & Pensions:* Primary Health & Aging. *Indian Affairs.*

Group Ratings

	ACLU	ACU	ADA	CFG	AFS	FRC	LCV	ITIC	NTU	COC
2010	43	73	20	72	20	83	0	33	89	100
2009	–	68	35	82	36	–	36	–	71	71

National Journal Ratings

	2010 LIB	—	2010 CONS		2009 LIB	—	2009 CONS
Economic	35%	—	64%		35%	—	64%
Social	37%	—	62%		37%	—	62%
Foreign	35%	—	64%		32%	—	66%
Composite	36%	—	64%		35%	—	65%

Key Votes of the 111th Congress

1. Overturn Ledbetter	Y	5. Pass health care bill	N	9. Ratify New START	Y
2. Pass $787 billion stimulus	N	6. Regulate financial firms	N	10. Confirm Elena Kagan	N
3. Repeal DC gun laws	Y	7. Pass tax cuts for some	N	11. Stop EPA climate regs	Y
4. Confirm Sonia Sotomayor	N	8. Legalize immigrants' kids	Y	12. Repeal don't ask, tell	Y

Election Results

2010 general	Lisa Murkowski (WI)	101,091	(39%)	($4,072,428)
	Joe Miller (R)	90,839	(35%)	($3,367,483)
	Scott McAdams (D)	60,045	(23%)	($1,331,272)
2010 primary	Joe Miller (R)	55,878	(51%)	
	Lisa Murkowski (R)	53,872	(49%)	

Prior Winning Percentages: 2004 (49%)

Lisa Murkowski is a Republican who was appointed to the Senate in December 2002 by her father, then-Alaska Gov. Frank Murkowski, to fill the vacancy caused by his own resignation from the Senate to become governor. She won a full term in her own right in 2004 to become the first woman elected to Congress from Alaska. In her 2010 bid for re-election, she lost the GOP primary to a tea party-backed challenger, only to come back to win the general election as a write-in candidate.

The second of six children, Murkowski grew up in Ketchikan in Alaska's Panhandle and in Fairbanks. In her senior year of high school, she worked for five weeks as an intern in the late Republican Sen. Ted Stevens' Washington office. She attended Willamette University in Salem, Oregon, and graduated from Georgetown in 1980, the year her father was first elected to the Senate. Murkowski went on to get a degree from Willamette law school in 1985. She served as an Anchorage District Court attorney, worked for an Anchorage law firm for eight years, and then established her own law practice. In 1998, she was elected to the state House from a north Anchorage district that included her neighborhood of Government Hill.

Alaska's state government depends heavily on revenues from North Slope oil and in early 2002 was facing a budget shortfall of $1.1 billion. Murkowski was one of the leaders of the bipartisan Fiscal Policy Caucus, which sought tax increases—a position opposite to that of her father, who was running for governor on a platform of no new taxes. Murkowski pushed hard for increasing the alcohol tax from 3 cents a drink to 10 cents, and her bill was enacted, giving Alaska the nation's highest alcohol tax. She also angered conservatives when she voted against a bill restricting publicly funded abortions. She said, "I may have a very short-lived political future here. But you know, I've got great kids and a great husband, and I'm going to have a good heart, and I'm going to stand up for the women of the state of Alaska, and I'm going to vote no." But she has also said that abortion should be legal only when a mother's life is in danger or in cases of rape or incest. Still, Alaska Right to Life opposed her. She had a tough fight for re-election in 2002 against conservative Nancy Dahlstrom, who attacked her for favoring tax increases and tapping the state's Permanent Fund to pay its bills. Murkowski won by only 57 votes. After the election, she was chosen state House majority leader.

That same year, her father, with two years left in his U.S. Senate term, was elected governor. (Republican state legislators saw to it that he, and not outgoing Democratic Gov. Tony Knowles, appointed a successor. Earlier in the year, they passed, over Knowles' veto, a law barring a governor from appointing a successor until five days after the vacancy occurred.) Murkowski said he was looking for someone with legislative experience who was young enough to serve many years and who shared his views on Alaska issues. He unveiled a short list of 26 potential nominees that included Gen. Joseph Ralston, NATO's Supreme Allied Commander in Europe; retired Gen. Mark Hamilton, president of the University of Alaska; and also, his daughter. On Dec. 20, 2002, he announced that he had decided to appoint Lisa Murkowski. It was the first time a governor had appointed his or her child to the Senate. Most Republicans and many Democrats praised Murkowski's abilities, but others called it a case of nepotism that would undermine public trust in the office. For her part, Murkowski stressed that she and her father kept their political lives separate. "We have always maintained very separate identities, at least for the time I have been in the legislature," she said. "I haven't called him for counseling, and typically he doesn't offer."

As she served the remaining two years of her father's term, Murkowski was acutely aware that she would be closely watched by her critics for signs that she was not up to the job. She proved not only competent, but with help from powerful fellow Senate Republicans, she exceeded expectations. She got seats on the Energy, Environment, Veterans and Indian Affairs committees, putting her at the center of most issues important to Alaska. Longtime family friend Stevens took her under his wing. As a senior member of the Appropriations Committee, Stevens was then one of the most influential members of Congress. Her biggest success came in October 2004, when she sponsored a bill creating federal loan guarantees for a 3,500-mile pipeline to bring natural gas from the North Slope to the lower 48, a major economic venture for the state. Her pipeline bill, with the guiding hand of Stevens, passed as part of the appropriations for military construction projects that year. Murkowski also got out front on efforts to pass legislation opening the Arctic National Wildlife Refuge to oil and gas exploration, an idea popular in Alaska but long opposed by environmental and wilderness groups, which have blocked its passage. Stevens praised the work of his former intern, saying that Murkowski "is a hell of a lot better senator than her dad ever was." (She returned his loyalty in 2009, when she asked President Bush to pardon Stevens after his conviction for concealing $250,000 in gifts from an oil executive. Bush declined, but the conviction was later thrown out because of prosecutors' errors.)

No Alaska Republican senator had ever been defeated for re-election, but Murkowski entered the 2004 campaign in weak condition. She had primary opposition from conservative former legislator Mike Miller, who attacked her stands on abortion, gun rights and taxes. Miller was even supported by her father's lieutenant governor, Loren Leman. But Murkowski was better financed and had the support of Stevens and Rep.-at-Large Don Young. She won the primary 58%-37%.

Her opponent in the general election was former Gov. Tony Knowles, the most successful Alaska Democrat in recent times. A Vietnam veteran and Yale classmate and friend of George W.

Bush, Knowles ran a restaurant in Anchorage and had been twice elected the city's mayor in the 1980s and twice elected governor in the 1990s. Knowles criticized Murkowski for not supporting more spending for veterans' health care. In her defense, Stevens said that Murkowski had supported over $1 billion for veterans' health. Knowles said that, knowing what he did in 2004, he would not have voted for the Iraq war resolution two years earlier; Murkowski said she would have.

Looming over the campaign was the nepotism issue. Knowles' pollster said that 54% of people found it a convincing reason to vote against Murkowski, and she trailed, usually by narrow margins, in most polls during the campaign. Organizers obtained 50,000 signatures for a ballot measure to ban governors from appointing new senators, which later passed with 56% of the vote. Against this, Republicans raised the issue of party and seniority. Stevens said Alaska would be hurt if Democrats gained a majority that year in the Senate and made the point that Murkowski, at age 47, would have a chance of amassing more seniority than would 61-year-old Knowles.

This was one of the national Democrats' best chances to pick up a Republican seat in 2004, but this red state ended up giving its GOP junior senator a full term, by 49%-46%. Like her father in the 2002 governor's race, Murkowski ran behind by a wide margin in the Bush and by a lesser margin in the Panhandle. In historically Republican Anchorage and Fairbanks, she ran only narrowly ahead. Her winning margins came in south-central Alaska, in the fast-growing arc around Anchorage.

Murkowski has established a moderate voting record, considerably closer to the middle of the road than her father's. She assumed a much larger role in the Senate on Alaska-centric issues after Stevens lost his bid for re-election in 2008 amid the corruption scandal. By 2009, she had won the respect of many of her colleagues and was moving up the ladder. She secured a seat on the Appropriations Committee, and she rose to become the ranking member of the Senate Energy and Natural Resources Committee after three Republicans with more seniority were suddenly off the committee. (Craig Thomas of Wyoming died of leukemia, Larry Craig of Idaho left the Senate after being arrested in a homosexual-sex sting, and Pete Domenici of New Mexico retired.) The move gave Murkowski the top job for the minority party on a committee vital to Alaska's energy interests.

Republican leaders sought to help her in other ways. She was invited into the Senate GOP leadership by becoming a counsel to Minority Leader Mitch McConnell. When Arizona Republican John Ensign stepped down as Republican Policy Committee chairman in 2009 after acknowledging an extramarital affair, Murkowski replaced South Dakota's John Thune as the conference vice chair while Thune moved into Ensign's old slot.

She pursued the Alaska delegation's long-standing goal of opening up ANWR to drilling, an issue widely thought to be off-limits with Democrats controlling Congress. She tried a new tack in 2008, promoting a bill that would automatically open the area to drilling if world oil prices topped $125 a barrel for five days, a strategy designed to take advantage of pressure Congress was feeling from soaring consumer prices at the pump. On the Energy Committee, Murkowski developed a cordial relationship with New Mexico's Jeff Bingaman, the panel's similarly pragmatic chairman. The two share an interest in pressing for a wide range of energy solutions, including renewable sources and nuclear power, in addition to oil and gas drilling. They successfully reported a bipartisan energy bill out of the committee in 2009. But she split with him on the issue of letting the Environmental Protection Agency regulate greenhouse-gas emissions without congressional approval. She led Republican opposition to the proposal.

But her first full term was also marred by an ethics controversy. In late 2006, Murkowski and her husband purchased an acre of waterfront land on Alaska's Kenai River from developer Bob Penney, a friend of Stevens. An ethics watchdog group charged that the $179,500 the couple paid for the lot was well below the market value of approximately $350,000. Penney told local newspaper reporters that he had sold Murkowski the land, next to property he owned on the river, for the assessed value. However, in early 2007, just weeks after the sale, the assessed value on the lot went up to $215,000. In July 2007, Murkowski called the deal "nothing nefarious or underhanded" but said she had decided to sell the land back to Penney for the purchase price of $179,500.

Murkowski's independence and centrist positions put her in the center of high-profile national debates. Suspicious of her abortion stance, the conservative Christian group Focus on the Family called her a "squishy Republican" and ran ads in the state that said she was likely to support Democratic obstruction of nominees. When Bush asked Congress to reauthorize the USA PATRIOT Act, Murkowski was one of four Republican senators to insist the anti-terrorism bill include more civil liberties protections. She teamed with Iowa Democratic Sen. Tom Harkin in 2007 on an amendment to the farm bill to raise nutritional standards for food and beverages sold in school vending machines and cafeterias.

Murkowski has been aggressive on Alaska issues. In June 2008, she sponsored an amendment to a Senate tax bill that would have eased the tax burden on plaintiffs sharing $2.5 billion in punitive damages in the *Exxon Valdez* oil-spill case. However, the Senate tax bill did not pass. She is also the leading advocate in the Senate for joining the Convention on the Law of the Sea, an international treaty that sets policy for ocean resources, including vast untapped supplies of oil in the Arctic. Some 155 countries, including Russia, have ratified the treaty, but American conservatives have long argued that the United States needs no such document to assert its claims over the Arctic and its natural resources. She used her position on Appropriations in 2010 to try to restore funding to Alaska's Denali Commission, a program that funds primary care clinics in the state. But she was unsuccessful. In 2006, not to be out-Alaska'ed by anyone, Murkowski bested eight other senators during a Kenai River conservation fundraiser by catching a 63-pound king salmon.

She hoped that her work on such issues, together with frequent trips home to make the case for her growing influence, would insulate her against a strenuous re-election challenge in 2010. She caught a break in 2009 when then-Alaska Gov. Sarah Palin, who had defeated her father, chose not to run against Murkowski. However, Palin, by then a national figure as a former vice presidential nominee for the GOP in 2008, backed Murkowski's Republican primary opponent, Fairbanks attorney Joe Miller, a self-described "constitutional conservative." Palin did relatively little campaigning for Miller, but her followers in the tea party movement flocked to his camp, pouring in donations and funding television and radio advertisements in the weeks leading to the August 24, 2010 primary.

Miller's challenge by itself would probably not have proven fatal for Murkowski. In the closing weeks of the campaign, Miller failed to come within striking distance of Murkowski. But the presence on the ballot of an anti-abortion referendum likely tipped the balance in Miller's favor in the final days. The measure, which called for parental notification for minors seeking abortions, brought thousands of voters to the polls, most of them in favor of Measure 2. Murkowski's ads touting her record of accomplishment were insufficient to overcome her record on abortion rights, and Miller managed to pull ahead of her by less than 1,668 votes out of 90,000 cast. A count of absentee and provisional ballots cut the margin to about 1,200. Nevertheless, she conceded on August 30.

In the weeks that followed, however, Murkowski publicly floated potential ways to run in the general election. One option for her was to run as a Libertarian, though officials from that party rejected the idea because they disagreed with her on taxes and the Iraq war. The other choice was a write-in bid, a strategy that had not been successful since Republican Strom Thurmond won in South Carolina in 1954. After saying she agonized over the decision, she announced on September 17 that she would run, contending that voters had encouraged her to do it because they couldn't support Miller or the Democratic nominee, Sitka Mayor Scott McAdams. Murkowski resigned her Senate Republican Conference vice chairmanship position, but her GOP colleagues let her remain as the Energy Committee's ranking Republican. With the slogan "Let's Make History," she embarked on a spirited effort to educate voters on how to properly spell her name and cited the considerable seniority that federally dependent Alaska would lack if she lost.

Miller, meanwhile, became enmeshed in several embarrassing controversies. Confronted with news reports that he had been disciplined in a previous job for using government computers for political purposes, he initially lied about it. He subsequently declared he would no longer discuss his background with the media, only to have his security guards handcuff a reporter who questioned him. On Election Day, state officials reported that 41% of the votes went to a write-in candidate, though the ballots had to be read manually to determine the name. Miller filed a federal lawsuit asking for any votes that didn't clearly spell her name to be discounted. The counting began. By November 17, Murkowski had established a lead of more than 10,000 votes, including 8,153 that were awarded to her after Miller's challenge was overruled. The Associated Press declared that her lead was insurmountable and she claimed victory.

Junior Senator

Mark Begich (D)

Elected 2008, term expires 2014, 1st full term; b. March 30, 1962, Anchorage; home, Anchorage; Steller H.S. (Anchorage), 1980.; Catholic; married (Deborah Bonito); 1 child.

Elected Office: Anchorage Assembly, 1988-98; Anchorage mayor, 2003-08.

DC Office: 114 RSOB, 20510, 202-224-3004; Fax: 202-224-2354; Web site: begich.senate.gov.

State Offices: Anchorage, 907-271-5915; Fairbanks, 907-456-0261.

Committees: *Armed Services:* Personnel; Readiness & Management Support; Strategic Forces. *Budget. Commerce, Science & Transportation:* Aviation Operations, Safety & Security; Communications, Technology & the Internet; Competitiveness, Innovation & Export Promotion; Oceans, Atmosphere, Fisheries & Coast Guard (Chmn); Surface Transportation & Merchant Marine Infrastructure, Safety & Security. *Homeland Security & Governmental Affairs:* Contracting Oversight (Ad Hoc); Federal Financial Management, Government Information, Federal Services & International Security; Investigations (Permanent); Oversight of Government Management, the Federal Workforce & the District of Columbia. *Veterans' Affairs.*

Group Ratings

	ACLU	ACU	ADA	CFG	AFS	FRC	LCV	ITIC	NTU	COC
2010	93	4	85	3	100	0	71	67	13	27
2009	–	12	100	6	100	–	82	–	7	57

National Journal Ratings

	2010 LIB	—	2010 CONS		2009 LIB	—	2009 CONS
Economic	56%	—	43%		61%	—	37%
Social	63%	—	35%		57%	—	41%
Foreign	47%	—	0%		55%	—	0%
Composite	65%	—	35%		66%	—	34%

Key Votes of the 111th Congress

1. Overturn Ledbetter	Y	5. Pass health care bill	Y	9. Ratify New START	Y
2. Pass $787 billion stimulus	Y	6. Regulate financial firms	Y	10. Confirm Elena Kagan	Y
3. Repeal DC gun laws	Y	7. Pass tax cuts for some	Y	11. Stop EPA climate regs	N
4. Confirm Sonia Sotomayor	Y	8. Legalize immigrants' kids	Y	12. Repeal don't ask, tell	Y

Election Results

2008 general	Mark Begich (D)	151,767	(48%)	($4,576,970)
	Ted Stevens (R)	147,814	(47%)	($3,858,991)
	Bob Bird (Ind)	13,197	(4%)	
2008 primary	Mark Begich (D)	63,747	(84%)	
	Ray Metcalfe (D)	5,480	(7%)	
	Bob Bird (D)	4,216	(6%)	

Mark Begich, a Democrat elected in 2008, is Alaska's junior senator. He was born five years after his parents moved to the Alaska Territory in 1957 to teach school. His father, Nick Begich, was a major figure in the state's political history. He was elected to the Alaska Senate and, in 1970, was elected Alaska's at-large representative to Congress. In October 1972, Nick Begich was killed along with U.S. House Majority Leader Hale Boggs of Louisiana as they were flying to a campaign fundraiser. Their plane disappeared over the Gulf of Alaska. The terrible loss initially turned a young Mark Begich away from politics as a potential career. "I was 10 years old, my mother was thirty-four, and she had six kids, and the job that took my dad away from me was politics. So probably subconsciously I had no interest, zero, because of that," Begich said.

As a young man, Begich was more interested in business. Showing his entrepreneurial side at age 16, he opened a teen nightclub called the Motherlode. When the property he leased was sold to someone who wanted to shut the nightclub down and replace it with a strip club, Begich gathered signatures on a petition protesting the award of a liquor license for the bar, testified in front of the city Assembly, and ultimately succeeded in having conditions attached to the granting of the license. When he graduated from high school in 1980, the Alaskan economy had hit a low point and his mother's real estate business was in serious trouble. Begich recalled, "She was a single parent, and in order to help, I had a choice." Rather than go to college like many of his classmates, Begich went to work in every aspect of his mother's business, from maintenance to management of the properties. He helped several of his brothers and sisters with their college expenses, although it meant giving up his own chance to earn a degree. That experience, he said, led him to place a high value on educational opportunity and is one of the main reasons he says he's a Democrat in a conservative state like Alaska. But he's quick to note that he's an Alaska-*style* Democrat, which is to say, "pro-gun rights, pro-oil and gas, pro-business, small business."

Despite his prior disinterest in politics, it turned out that Begich inherited his father's knack for it. He was appointed by the Anchorage mayor to the youth commission at age 17, and then landed a spot in the city health department. When he was 20, Begich was hired as the personal assistant to Mayor Tony Knowles, who would later become governor. A few years later, Begich, frustrated that the roads in his neighborhood were not being paved, ran for the Anchorage Assembly and won, becoming the body's youngest member ever. He served for 10 years and was chosen chairman.

In the 1990s, Gov. Knowles appointed Begich to the Student Loan Corporation and tasked him with dealing with its serious financial problems. Begich identified a debilitating lack of coordination between the corporation and the Post-Secondary Education Commission, and dealt with the problem by appointing himself chairman of the commission. He held meetings of the two organizations at the same time, compelling them to get along. When he left the Student Loan Corporation, he had significantly lowered interest rates for borrowers and raised its bond rating. In 1994, Begich ran for Anchorage mayor and lost with 42% of the vote. He ran again in 2000 and lost with 48%. In his third attempt in 2003, Begich beat incumbent George Wuerch. As mayor, Begich claimed credit for getting voters to twice pass bond issues, for holding down property taxes, for hiring 65 additional police officers, and for setting up a multi-agency anti-gang initiative. He was easily re-elected to a second term in 2006.

In late 2007, national Democratic leaders began courting Begich for a possible challenge to U.S. Sen. Ted Stevens, a six-term Republican who was vulnerable as a result of a federal corruption investigation into his relationship with Bill Allen, the head of VECO, an oil services company. Stevens was later indicted for failing to report on his Senate financial disclosure forms thousands of dollars in renovation work that VECO employees did on his home. Despite this baggage, Stevens was still a formidable figure to cross in Alaskan politics. He had represented the state for four decades and had won re-election by wide margins; in one race he carried every precinct in the state. He could claim credit for the legislation that allowed the building of the Alaska oil pipeline and that established Alaska Native corporations. As a senior member of the Appropriations Committee, he funneled vast sums of money into the state. Begich was encouraged to take him on by Democratic Senatorial Campaign Committee Chairman Charles Schumer of New York. Begich also traveled the state, testing the waters for a possible candidacy in areas where he had little or no name recognition.

In early 2008, Begich made the decision to challenge Stevens on an anti-corruption platform. "We've seen here in Alaska the ultimate result of unfettered greed—grainy videotapes of state legislators in hotel rooms laughing at the citizens of our great state," he said. "And we've seen in Washington the ultimate result of special influence and legislative indifference." He issued an "Alaska Ethics Pledge" in which he vowed to make public both his and his wife's finances "to the dollar" and to disclose the beneficiary of his congressional earmarks, the special spending provisions tucked into appropriations bills by lawmakers. But he was careful not to attack the revered Stevens personally, and he paid tribute to Stevens' long service to the state.

Begich also zeroed in on Alaska issues. He called for increased spending for rural health care, an important matter for many Alaskan natives, and for loans for energy-efficient community buildings. He spoke out strongly against the No Child Left Behind Act, which he argued had hurt rural schools. He said that the national Democratic Party was "wrong" on gun rights, and wrong in opposing drilling in the Arctic National Wildlife Refuge. With help from the DSSC, he proved to be a solid fundraiser, spending $4.4 million to Stevens' $5.7 million. National Democrats ran ads showing federal agents raiding the incumbent's house. National Republicans ran ads accusing Begich of rezoning downtown Anchorage land to aid two developers, and highlighting $16,000 in tax liens on his businesses in the 1990s.

Stevens was indicted on July 29, 2008. He proclaimed his innocence, but polls showed him running slightly behind or even with Begich. In the August Democratic primary, Begich got 84% of the vote against four opponents. In the GOP primary, Stevens beat David Cuddy, a businessman who had run against him 12 years before, 64%-27%. Some national Republicans expressed hope that Stevens would resign and let Alaska Republicans pick a new, untarnished candidate. But Stevens refused to quit even though he spent much of the fall campaign season on trial in a Washington, D.C., courtroom. On October 27, 2008, Stevens was convicted on all seven counts. He accused Justice Department lawyers of "unconscionable" conduct, and aired a two-minute television ad recounting what he had done for Alaska for 40 years. Last-minute polls showed a dead heat.

For much of Election Night on November 3, returns put Stevens ahead of Begich 48%-46%, but the race was too close to call even into the next morning. Presidential candidate Barack Obama's superb organization in Alaska had ensured that many Democrats cast early votes or absentee votes, and as they were counted, Begich gained ground. By November 12, Begich was ahead, and on November 18, he led by more than the number of votes left to count. He became the first Democratic senator elected in Alaska since Mike Gravel was re-elected in 1974.

In April 2009, the Justice Department dismissed Stevens' conviction after it was revealed that prosecutors had failed to turn over key documents to his defense lawyers. The Alaska GOP and then-Gov. Sarah Palin called for a special election in light of the new information. Begich responded with a statement saying, "I got into the Senate race long before Sen. Stevens' legal troubles began because Alaskans were looking for a change and a senator as independent as Alaska." No special election was held.

In the Senate, Begich moved briskly to put his stamp on energy legislation and other issues vital to the Alaskan economy. "I'm not bashful about telling people what I think," Begich says. "I'm very blunt about who and what I believe in. I don't believe in all the protocols and that stuff around here." He succeeded in getting Senate Democratic leaders interested in a bill he co-sponsored with Democratic Sen. Mary Landrieu of Louisiana that spelled out the liability of oil companies in the wake of a spill like the one caused by BP in the Gulf of Mexico in 2010. Their plan, adapted from the nuclear industry, ensured that sky-high insurance costs would not shut out small and mid-sized oil companies from drilling opportunities. The BP escrow account President Obama announced with BP on June 16, 2010, was an idea that Begich discussed in the Democratic Caucus right after the blowout. He introduced a bill that forces companies responsible for spills to put money in an escrow account in order to obtain future leases.

In 2009, Begich introduced several bills aimed at improving life in the Arctic. They would coordinate the plethora of scientific research projects currently being conducted in the Arctic, create a U.S. ambassador to the Arctic, provide for new icebreakers and Coast Guard facilities, and promote research into oil spill response in Arctic waters. He also pushed to ensure that the Senate's energy bill would include revenue-sharing, a top priority for him. With fellow Alaska Sen. Lisa Murkowski, a Republican, he voted against a ban on earmark spending, saying it would have a negative effect on Alaska's economy.

Democratic leaders took note of the energetic newcomer and in 2010 named Begich chairman of the Democratic Steering and Outreach Committee, a 15-member panel made up of the chairs of major Senate committees. The slot puts him in the Senate Democratic leadership.

REPRESENTATIVE-AT-LARGE

Don Young (R)

Elected Mar. 1973, 19th full term; b. June 9, 1933, Meridian, CA; home, Fort Yukon; Yuba Jr. Col., A.A. 1952, Chico St. Col., B.A. 1958; Episcopalian; widowed; 2 children.

Military Career: Army, 1955–57.

Elected Office: Fort Yukon City Cncl., 1960–64; Fort Yukon mayor, 1964–68; AK House of Reps., 1966–70; AK Senate, 1970–73.

Professional Career: School teacher, Fort Yukon, 1960-68; Riverboat captain, 1960-68.

DC Office: 2314 RHOB, 20515, 202-225-5765; Fax: 202-225-0425; Web site: donyoung.house.gov.

State Offices: Anchorage, 907-271-5978; Fairbanks, 907-456-0210; Juneau, 907-586-7400; Kenai, 907-283-7701.

Committees: *Natural Resources:* Fisheries, Wildlife, Oceans & Insular Affairs; Indian & Alaska Native Affairs (Chmn); National Parks, Forests & Public Lands. *Transportation & Infrastructure:* Coast Guard & Maritime Transportation; Highways & Transit; Water Resources & Environment.

Group Ratings

	ACLU	ACU	ADA	CFG	AFS	FRC	LCV	ITIC	NTU	COC
2010	20	75	10	65	25	93	0	33	74	100
2009	–	75	10	64	38	–	29	–	60	90

National Journal Ratings

	2010 LIB	—	2010 CONS		2009 LIB	—	2009 CONS
Economic	37%	—	63%		31%	—	69%
Social	39%	—	61%		35%	—	65%
Foreign	38%	—	61%		0%	—	75%
Composite	38%	—	62%		26%	—	74%

Key Votes of the 111th Congress

1. Overturn Ledbetter	Y	5. Bar federal abortion funds	Y	9. Stop detainee transfers	Y
2. Pass $820 billion stimulus	N	6. Pass health care bill	N	10. Legalize immigrants' kids	N
3. Let guns in national parks	Y	7. Regulate financial firms	*	11. Repeal don't ask, tell	N
4. Pass cap-and-trade	N	8. Pass tax cuts for some	N	12. Limit campaign funds	N

Election Results

2010 general	Don Young (R)	175,384	(69%)	($1,001,015)
	Harry Crawford (D)	77,606	(31%)	($240,439)
2010 primary	Don Young (R)	74,310	(70%)	
	Sheldon Fisher (R)	24,709	(23%)	
	John Cox (R)	6,605	(6%)	

Prior Winning Percentages: 2008 (50%), 2006 (57%), 2004 (71%), 2002 (75%), 2000 (70%), 1998 (63%), 1996 (59%), 1994 (57%), 1992 (47%), 1990 (52%), 1988 (63%), 1986 (57%), 1984 (55%), 1982 (71%), 1980 (74%), 1978 (55%), 1976 (71%), 1974 (54%), 1973 (51%)

Cook Partisan Voting Index: R+13

Don Young has been Alaska's congressman-at-large since 1973 and is now the second-most-senior Republican in the House, after Bill Young of Florida. His long political career was nearly destroyed by an influence-peddling scandal in 2008, when he only narrowly survived re-election. But Young came roaring back politically in 2010 and, with the GOP ascendant in the House, is again poised to be a forceful figure in Washington.

Young grew up on his family's farm in the Sacramento Valley of California, served in the Army, and graduated from college. He had a thirst for adventure and the rugged outdoors—he remembers that *The Call of the Wild* by Jack London was a favorite book growing up. He moved to Alaska in 1959, the year that the vast, untamed U.S. territory became a state. Young worked in construction, fishing, trapping, and gold prospecting. He taught elementary school to indigenous Alaskan children in Fort Yukon, pop. 700. After spring thaws, he worked as a tugboat captain on the Yukon. He is the only licensed mariner in Congress and, in his words, is definitely "not one of these smooth, namby-pamby politicians." He is temperamental and salty-tongued, given to tough talk. To critics who once proposed shifting money for Alaska bridges to Hurricane Katrina recovery efforts, he said, "They can kiss my ear." Young was elected mayor of Fort Yukon in 1964, to the state House in 1966, and to the state Senate in 1970. He ran for Congress in 1972. His opponent, incumbent Democrat Nick Begich, was killed in a plane crash in October and was re-elected posthumously. Young won the March 1973 special election to succeed him. Young is not a free-market conservative and has recently voted with liberals on some cultural issues. But he is a consistent, fierce advocate for Alaska's interests.

Soon after taking his seat in the House, Young voted for building the Alaska pipeline. But he often found that his aggressive pursuit of economic development for his state conflicted with the environmental lobby and its interest in preserving wildlife. On what was then the Interior Committee, he called his critics a "self-centered bunch, the waffle-stomping, Harvard-graduating, intellectual idiots." During 12 years of Republican control of Congress, Young occupied power positions that allowed him to work around his adversaries. He led the Resources Committee from 1995 to 2001 and the Transportation and Infrastructure Committee from 2001 to 2007. He steered to passage in the House bills allowing oil drilling in the Arctic National Wildlife Refuge in 1995, 2001, and 2006, only to see them defeated or bottled up in the Senate. His attempts to roll back some environmental rulings, such as allowing logging in the Tongass National Forest, were frustrated in the 1990s by Democratic President Clinton, or by adverse votes cast by Republicans from the Northeast, Arizona, and Florida. But on both committees, Young also proved capable of forging bipartisan consensus. In 2000, he got Congress to pass the Conservation and Reinvestment Act to dedicate royalties from offshore oil and gas wells to state purchases of land.

After the 2000 election, Young took over the Transportation and Infrastructure Committee, arguably the most bipartisan panel in the House because its chairmen traditionally larded their bills to make sure every cooperating committee member received plenty of highway or mass transit projects for his or her district. In 2003, Young proposed a surface transportation bill with $375 billion in spending, financed with a gas-tax increase. But the Bush administration and the House Republican leadership were stoutly opposed to any such hike. (A memo that surfaced in 2010 written by a former Young aide at the time said the GOP leadership considered Young a "rogue member.") In March 2004, the committee approved Young's bill by voice vote. But the House approved a $275 billion bill, without Young's gas-tax increase. A House-Senate conference committee agreed to $284 billion, a number the administration threatened to veto. The bill languished as members of the House and Senate bickered over funding formulas that granted states a certain share of gas-tax revenues. The conference deadlocked, and no bill passed when Congress adjourned in 2004. Young's proposal for a gas-tax increase was dead.

In 2005, he tried again and got the House to pass a $284 billion bill in March. But there was mounting criticism of the bill's earmarks—special projects for certain lawmakers—particularly of two bridges in Alaska. One was from Anchorage to the largely uninhabited land across the Knik Arm; the other was from the town of Ketchikan (pop. 14,000) to the island of Gravina (pop. 50) with its airport, which could already be reached by local ferry. They were derisively dubbed the "bridges to nowhere." Negotiations with the Senate and the Bush administration continued, and in July, both chambers passed by near-unanimous votes a $286 billion bill with more than 6,300 earmarks. They included $230 million for the Knik Arm bridge and $220 million for the Ketchikan-Gravina bridge. All told, the bill contained about $941 million for Young's Alaska, more than any other state except California, Illinois, and New York.

That likely would have been the end of the earmark controversy, except that Hurricane Katrina struck the Gulf Coast in August. Suddenly, there were demands that money be shifted from Alaska's "bridges to nowhere" to New Orleans and other parts of the devastated region. "That is the dumbest thing I ever heard," Young said. But for the next year, criticism of earmarks and the bridges continued. Conservative Republicans as well as Democrats chimed in, and profligate spending, symbolized by the two spans, emerged as an issue in the 2006 election. It was among the factors that helped wipe out the Republican majorities that year.

For an incumbent who has been around as long as he has, Young has had a bumpy history with Alaska voters and drew serious challengers in 1978, 1984, 1986, 1990, and 1992. He looked safe for a period in the early 2000s, but in 2006, he again ran into trouble. His Democratic opponent, Diane Benson, a Green Party candidate for governor in 2002, attracted attention as the mother of a soldier who lost both legs in an explosion in Iraq, and she called for a graceful exit strategy from that conflict. Then, the *Anchorage Daily News* (the "Daily Screw," as Young calls it) ran a story detailing Young's receipt of $20,000 in campaign contributions from Indian tribes that were clients of disgraced lobbyist Jack Abramoff; his use of Abramoff's skybox at MCI Center (now Verizon Center) to hold two fundraisers; and his behind-the-scenes work pressuring a government agency to give preferential treatment to tribes on proposals to redevelop Washington's Old Post Office. Young spent nearly $2 million on heavy advertising while avoiding joint appearances with Benson. She spent only $197,000 and did not tape her first television ad until late October. Young appeared upbeat and predicted in October that Republicans would lose no seats in the House. Ultimately, Young won but by the considerably reduced ratio of 57%-40%.

His problems had just begun. In April 2007, a former Young aide pleaded guilty to accepting cash from Abramoff in exchange for inside government information. Records released in April 2008 showed 120 contacts between Young and his staff with Abramoff and his clients. In May 2007, Rick Smith, an associate of Young's and a former lobbyist with the oil-services firm VECO, a major Young contributor since 1989, pleaded guilty to bribing Alaska state legislators. In July, *The Wall Street Journal* reported that the investigation had expanded to include Young. *The New York Times* published a story about a Young staffer altering the 2005 transportation bill to add $10 million for an interstate interchange in Florida that would help real estate developer Daniel Aronoff, who had raised $40,000 for the lawmaker. Young dismissed the allegations, telling the *Anchorage Daily News* that it was just "a recycled story." Plus, he said, Florida Gulf Coast University supported the Coconut Road interchange. In April 2008, Democratic Speaker Nancy Pelosi ordered an investigation, and the Senate voted 64-28 and the House 358-51 for a U.S. Justice Department inquiry.

Former Alaska House Minority Leader Ethan Berkowitz, a Democrat, lined up to run against him in the general election in 2008, and Republican Lt. Gov. Sean Parnell announced he would challenge Young in the primary. Parnell was endorsed by GOP Gov. Sarah Palin. Polls in the summer of 2008 showed Young trailing both Parnell and Berkowitz, but he professed to be unfazed, saying he was used to tough re-elections. During a debate with Parnell, he said: "I've been accused of being arrogant, being a bully, and sometimes I'll plead to being both of those. Most of the time and every time I've done that is because I'm fighting for this state." An Alaska TV station reported that Young told Parnell during the GOP state convention: "I beat your dad, and I'm going to beat you." Pat Parnell was the Democratic nominee against Young in 1980. Sean Parnell spent $572,000, with strong support from the anti-tax Club for Growth. "We're tired of being the nation's symbol of excess and greed," Parnell said in an August debate, after the indictment of Republican Sen. Ted Stevens in an influence-peddling case. Young beat Parnell by just 304 votes, 45.47% to 45.19%. Only when the last 350 votes were counted on September 17 was it clear that Young had won.

His battle was far from over, however. Gearing up for the general election, Berkowitz was well funded, with $1.6 million, while Young's resources were being steadily depleted by legal fees and by the primary contest. The Democratic Congressional Campaign Committee spent $1.4 million on ads charging that Young was the subject of four investigations, basing its claim on allegations by Citizens for Responsibility and Ethics in Washington. Berkowitz and Young were not far apart on the issues. Berkowitz framed the choice as one of style, contrasting his consensus-building approach to Young's tendency to "bully and intimidate." He said he would seek earmarks if communities and citizens asked for them, but not for lobbyists. Young responded during a debate, tongue in cheek, that he is "one of the nicest, kindest persons in the world." He added, "But when you mess with the state, you're messing with me."

In October, polls showed Young trailing Berkowitz. But either most polls were wrong or public opinion changed in the final days. Perhaps Alaskans feared losing the clout of both Young and Stevens, who that month had been convicted on corruption charges. Young defeated Berkowitz 50%-45%. Young ran only even in usually Republican Anchorage and carried the Fairbanks area 50%-44%, thanks largely to support from his hometown of Fort Yukon. But he held Berkowitz's margins down in the Panhandle, carrying Ketchikan, and he won the Matanuska-Susitna area 62%-33%. Most important, he carried the Bush 49%-45%, even as Stevens was losing it to Democratic challenger Mark Begich 54%-41%.

Young returned to Washington, but he was under a cloud. In November, he lost his seat on the Republican Steering Committee to Mike Simpson of Idaho; in December, he lost the ranking minority member position on Resources, the committee on which he had served for 36 years, to Rep. Doc Hastings of Washington state. Young issued a press release saying he would regain the post when "my name is cleared." He remained as feisty as ever. When the GOP caucus voted to hold a moratorium on special-interest earmark requests, Young scoffed at the idea. "To do that would be turning my back on the state that I love while handing over control to President Obama and his appointed government officials," he wrote in a *Daily News* column. He also drew bipartisan criticism when he argued the massive BP oil spill in the Gulf of Mexico was "not an environmental disaster" but "a natural phenomenon."

It turned out Young's prediction about his name being cleared wasn't idle talk. In August 2010, he issued a statement saying the Justice Department had concluded its investigation and would not prosecute him. He was already a strong favorite in the Republican primary against Sheldon Fisher, a former telecommunications executive and political newcomer, and the news only bolstered his prospects despite Fisher's attempts to characterize Young as practicing "special interest politics." Young ended up with more than 70% of the primary vote and went on to easily defeat Democratic state Rep. Harry Crawford.

★ ARIZONA ★

Arizona, home to one of America's most ancient civilizations, is also arguably on the cutting edge of change in 21st century America. The Hopi Indians, America's oldest continuous community, thrived as shepherds on the plateaus east of the Grand Canyon and have been rooted in northeastern Arizona for more than 900 years. They have spurned Christianity since 1680, when they killed the local Franciscan priests and burned their churches. More recently, they have been involved in land disputes with the more numerous Navajo tribe. The Hopi are the oldest Arizonans, and the newest are moving in every day, into subdivisions rising from the empty desert east, north, and west of Phoenix, hemmed in only by dry riverbeds, upcroppings of mountains, and Indian reservation boundaries.

For most of the 1990s and 2000s Arizona was one of the nation's boom states, nearly doubling in population from 3.7 million in 1990 to 6.4 million in 2010. It grew at a faster percentage rate than any other state except Nevada from 1990 to 2004, and faster than Nevada from 2004 to 2008. But then disaster in the form of the collapse of the housing market struck. Policies encouraging low-down-payment mortgages to dicey borrowers left many homeowners underwater. House prices fell to 50% of 2005 levels, and together with Nevada, Arizona led the nation in foreclosures. It was only the seventh fastest growing state in 2008-09 and seemed poised to slip further down the list. In the boom years, construction and real estate accounted for a third of the state's economy. When they slowed down toward zero, unemployment rose and state government revenues plummeted. At the same time, Arizona faced what many considered a crisis in illegal immigration, as effective border control measures in California and Texas funneled the illegal trade across the Arizona desert. Arizona's response was controversial, but Census Bureau estimates suggest it has reduced the state's population of illegal immigrants significantly.

Just about no one would have envisioned either Arizona's boom times or the problems it faces now in 1912 when it was admitted to the Union. For decades, its growth was attributable to the five Cs, memorialized in the state seal. The first C was copper: The dome of the state Capitol is encased in copper, and one of Arizona's leading public figures was Lewis Douglas—copper heir, congressman, Franklin D. Roosevelt's first budget director, and Harry Truman's ambassador to Britain. The second C was cattle: As late as the mid-1960s, a dozen or so cattlemen ran the state legislature. The third C was cotton: Carl Hayden, a Democratic senator from 1927 to 1969, concentrated on bringing public works to Arizona; his signal achievement was the Central Arizona Project, a massive irrigation program that brought cotton farms to the flatlands around Phoenix. The water also helped with the fourth C: citrus. The fifth C was climate, which kept people out of Arizona for many years.

Then came air conditioning. In the years after World War II, Arizona became less dependent on federal largesse, except for its military bases and defense contracts. Businessmen, lawyers, developers, and water companies, notably the Salt River Project, built Arizona based on the opposite of New Deal principles: with minimal government and precious little regulation of business, a welcoming of new technological ideas, and a shunning of cultural liberalism. Their political champion was Barry Goldwater, Phoenix City Council member and senator and the nation's most recognizable conservative for much of the 1950s and 1960s. He helped to make Arizona solidly Republican, the only state to vote Republican for president in every election from 1952 to 1992.

Modern Arizona grew phenomenally, from 700,000 people immediately after the war to 3.7 million in 1990 and 6.4 million in 2010. For years, its growth was based on high technology and low taxes. Contrary to popular perception, this was not growth based on an influx of elderly retirees. Arizona may have Sun City, but just 13% of its residents are over 65, compared to 12% nationally. Neither was it based on subsidized farming, since cotton farms have been bought out by subdivision developers; the Valley of the Sun around Phoenix lost nearly half its farmland between 1975 and 2000. It still produces two-thirds of the nation's copper, but this is not a labor-intensive enterprise. Arizona's growth is explained partly, but only partly, by immigration. Arizona has attracted immigrants from Mexico and Latin America eager for entry-level jobs, so eager that many cross the lightly guarded border in the desert at the risk of death. For many years, the engine of Arizona's growth has been technology. Phoenix started attracting high-tech industries when Motorola built a research center for military electronics there in 1948. Big employers included Honeywell, Raytheon, Motorola, Intel, Avnet, and Northrop Grumman. Defense industries are important here, especially the manufacture of unmanned aircraft. The state counts two Air Force bases and a Marine air station plus the huge Barry M. Goldwater Range, where many of America's pilots have

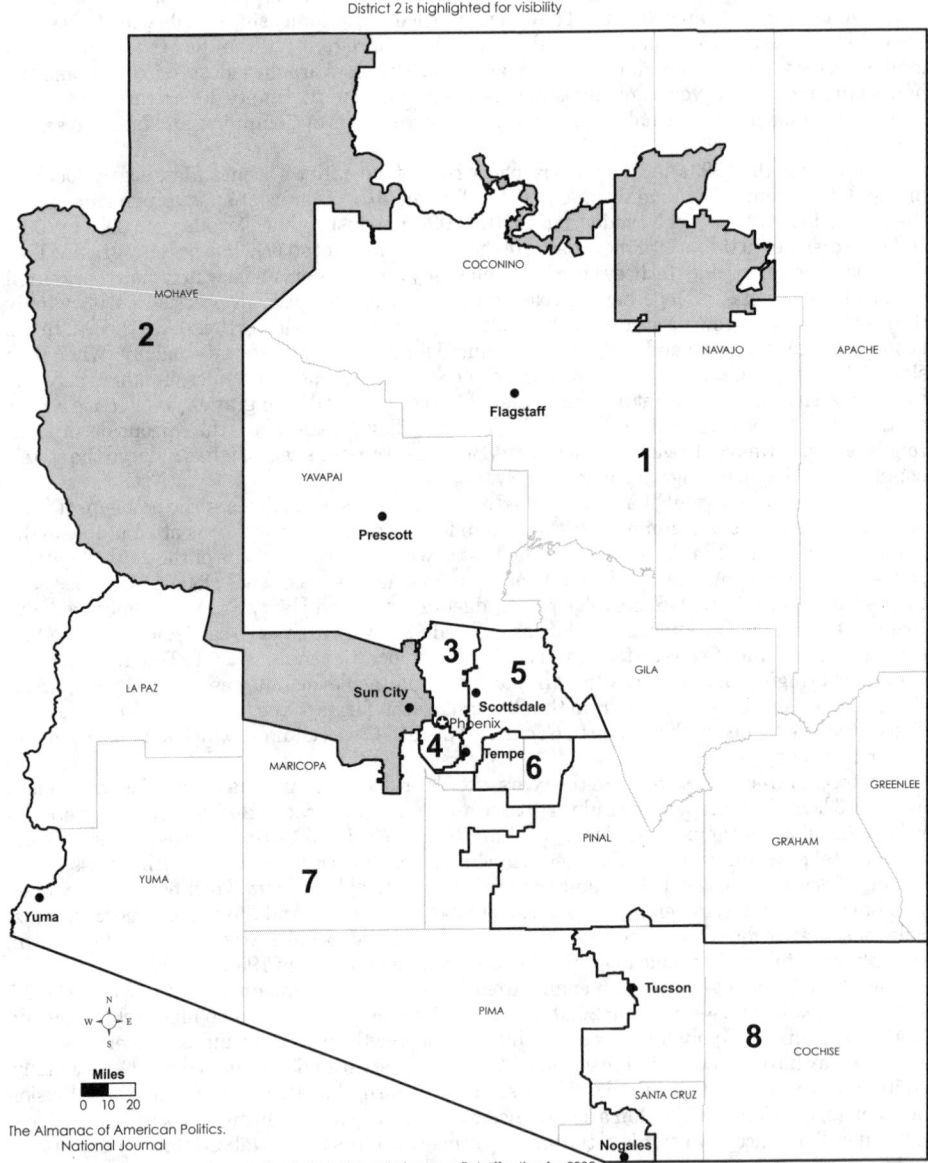

District 2 is highlighted for visibility

COCONINO

MOHAVE

2

NAVAJO   APACHE

• Flagstaff

YAVAPAI

1

• Prescott

3   **5**

GILA

LA PAZ

Sun City •   Scottsdale •
              Phoenix
4   Tempe • **6**

MARICOPA

GREENLEE

PINAL   GRAHAM

7

YUMA

Yuma •

Tucson •

8   COCHISE

PIMA

SANTA CRUZ

Miles
0 10 20

The Almanac of American Politics.
National Journal

Nogales •

Congressional district boundaries were first effective for 2002.

been trained. By the 1990s, real estate and construction were overshadowing technology, with bounteous results until the 2007-08 crash.

In the past decade, Arizona has become a focal point of illegal immigration. With stronger border enforcement in Texas and a fence going up near San Diego, the hilly Arizona desert in Cochise and Santa Cruz counties became a major entry point for illegal immigrants. Thousands streamed in over ranchlands, heading north to Phoenix or west to California. Local residents formed a Minuteman organization, reporting illegal border crossings to authorities and demanding stronger enforcement by the federal government. Anger at the flood of illegal immigrants contributed to the passage of ballot propositions denying welfare benefits, requiring government employees to report illegal residents, and denying punitive damages to illegal immigrants. Other ballot measures declared English Arizona's official language and denied illegal residents in-state tuition at state colleges. These were characterized by some as signs of bigotry, but they were supported by at least 40% of Hispanics as well as majorities of Anglo whites. The legislature in 2007 required employers to use the increasingly accurate E-Verify system to validate the immigration status of new employees, and in 2008, a ballot proposition to repeal the law was soundly defeated.

The state's two Republican senators, John McCain and Jon Kyl, laid the problem at the doorstep of Congress, but were stymied again and again in legislating a solution in the absence of a political consensus on the right approach. Meanwhile, the crisis deepened. Illegal immigrants tramped through ranches near the border and murdered a local rancher. Kidnappings involving illegal aliens became common, and "coyotes" harbored immigrants in boarded-up houses in the desert. In 2010, the legislature took matters into its own hands and passed Senate Bill 1070 authorizing law enforcement officials to check the immigration status of people stopped for other reasons. After some hesitation, Republican Gov. Jan Brewer signed the bill. Up for re-election that year, she had been running poorly in Republican primary polls and was trailing Democratic Attorney General Terry Goddard. After signing the crackdown bill, she zoomed into big leads. President Barack Obama and his Justice Department denounced Arizona's law as encouraging racial profiling and brought a lawsuit to stop its enforcement. A federal judge overturned the law for infringing on the federal prerogatives.

Arizona has been competitive in recent elections. Democrat Bill Clinton carried it narrowly in 1996 and Democrats have looked to the increasing Hispanic population and the influx of newcomers from California as a sign it might tip their way permanently. But they weren't able to prevent George W. Bush from carrying Arizona twice. (They didn't bother to target it in 2008 with favorite son McCain in the race.) But the state has sported a persistent progressive side in one respect:

Population		Household Income		Work	
Pop. 2010:	6,392,017	Under $15k:	12.1%	Private:	78.5%
State rank:	16th	$15k to $50k:	37.5%	Government:	15.2%
Change since 2000:	Up 24.6%	$50k to $100k:	31.8%	Self-employed:	6.2%
Urban:	82.1%	$100k to $200k:	15.2%	Unemployment (3-yr. average):	4.7%
Rural:	17.9%	Over $200k:	3.4%	Poverty:	15.2%
Native of state:	36.6%	Median income:	$50,356	Blue collar:	20.4%
Not a citizen:	10.2%			White collar:	59.9%
Area size:	113,990 sq. mi.	**Home Value**		Khaki collar:	0.3%
		Under $100k:	15.1%	Other:	19.3%
Most populous cities		$100k to $300k:	54.3%		
Phoenix	1,445,632	$300k to $500k:	19.4%	**Age**	
Tucson	520,116	$500k to $1 mil:	9.1%	Median age:	34.8 yrs.
Mesa	439,041	Over $1 million:	2.2%	More than 65 yrs:	12.9%
Chandler	236,123	Median:	$221,100	Less than 18 yrs:	26.4%

Race/Ethnicity				Military Veterans		Registered Voters in 2010	
White:	57.8%	*Language*		% of Pop:	11.4%	Democrats:	1,002,937
Black:	3.7%	English:	71.9%			Republicans:	1,131,802
Hispanic:	29.6%	Spanish:	21.8%	*Veterans by Period*		Ind./other:	1,011,679
Asian:	2.7%	Asian:	1.6%	WWII and before:	10.9%	Voter turnout:	1,750,840
Native Am.:	4.0%	Other European:	2.1%	Korea:	12.4%	Turnout as % of	
Hawaiian:	0.2%			Vietnam:	32.3%	voting age:	36.8%
Two+ races:	1.8%	**Education**		Gulf (pre-2001):	12.1%		
		H.S. grad:	83.9%	Gulf (post-2001):	8.3%	**Legislature**	
Ancestry		College grad:	25.6%	Peace time:	23.9%	Senate:	9 D 21 R
German	12.9%	Grad degree:	9.3%			House:	20 D 40 R
Irish	8.7%						
English	8.1%						

Arizona has had only women governors since 1997, when Republican Secretary of State Jane Hull succeeded Fife Symington. In 1998, Arizona became the first state to elect women to all of its top five statewide down-ballot offices. Democrat Janet Napolitano, after serving as attorney general, was elected governor in 2002 and re-elected by a solid margin in 2006. When Napolitano resigned to become Obama's Homeland Security secretary in 2009, she was succeeded by Brewer, the Republican secretary of state.

Brewer's vigorous support of the immigration crackdown carried her to a re-election victory of 54%-42% over Attorney General Goddard, a former Phoenix mayor, in 2010. McCain was re-elected the same year, 59%-35%. McCain performed better than Brewer mainly because Latinos voted 40% for McCain but only 28% for her. Whites voted 65% for McCain and 61% for Brewer. Republicans won all of the statewide offices, most by wide margins, and widened their majorities in the state legislature to 21-9 in the Senate and 40-20 in the House.

Presidential politics   Arizona has tried every so often to make itself another Iowa or New Hampshire in presidential politics, with little success. In 1972, it had an early Democratic primary, and the improbable winner was Republican-turned-Democrat New York Mayor John Lindsay. His campaign went nowhere from there. In 1996, Arizona tried to set its primary on the same date as New Hampshire's; when that failed, the state set it one week later. The intended beneficiary was Texas Republican Sen. Phil Gramm, a conservative running with McCain's support. But Gramm pulled out of the race a week before New Hampshire, and Arizona became a battleground between Kansas Sen. Bob Dole, who now had McCain's support; conservative pundit Pat Buchanan; and magazine publisher Steve Forbes, who peppered the state with ads boosting his flat tax and attacking Washington politicians. Buchanan finished third, with 28%, and it was clear he had no

2008 Presidential Vote		
John McCain (R) 1,230,111	(54%)
Barack Obama (D) 1,034,707	(45%)

2008 Presidential Primary		
Hillary Clinton (D)...............229,501	(50%)
Barack Obama (D) 193,126	(42%)

2008 Presidential Primary		
John McCain (R) 255,197	(47%)
Mitt Romney (R)...................186,838	(34%)
Mike Huckabee (R).................48,849	(9%)

2004 Presidential Vote		
George W. Bush (R)...........1,104,294	(55%)
John Kerry (D) 893,524	(44%)

chance to win the nomination. Dole finished second with 30%. Forbes won 33% and all the delegates, after which his campaign, like that of his fellow Easterner Lindsay a quarter-century before, went nowhere.

In 2000, Arizona tried again. McCain had irritated local Republicans enough that Gov. Jane Hull and other party leaders endorsed George W. Bush. McCain, however, won a solid victory in his home state in the February primary, but it was overshadowed by his victory the same day in Michigan. Arizona Democrats ran and paid for their own primary in March, because the state's February date was outside the "window" permitted by national Democratic Party rules. They allowed voting via the Internet, and about 35,000 Arizonans mouse-clicked their choices, another 20,000 voted by mail, and still others voted by computer or paper ballot at the polls. But the Internet voting was not flawless, and the primary didn't matter because Al Gore had already clinched the nomination. In 2004, a regular primary was held one week after New Hampshire, on Feb. 3, the same day as contests in Delaware, Missouri, New Mexico, North Dakota, Oklahoma, and South Carolina. Democrats John Kerry and Wesley Clark were the only candidates who targeted the state, and Kerry got 43% of the vote to Clark's 26%. Only 603,000 voted in a state of 5.6 million people. In 2006, Arizona Democrats made a bid to have their state designated as the site for a caucus election soon after Iowa. But in August of that year, the Democratic National Committee picked Nevada instead.

So in 2008, Arizona settled for being another Super Tuesday state. The Republican primary was conceded to McCain, but having aroused the lasting hostility of some conservatives, he beat Mitt Romney by only 47% to 34%. Romney carried the 6th Congressional District (Mesa, Chandler) and rural Graham County, both with large Mormon populations. On the Democratic side, Hillary Rodham Clinton, with heavy support from Latinos, beat Obama 50%-42%. Obama carried the upscale 5th Congressional District (Scottsdale, Tempe) and Coconino and Yavapai counties.

Native-son Barry Goldwater, born when Arizona was still a territory, carried the state in 1964, and it voted Republican in every presidential election from 1952 to 1992. But it has become more seriously contested since. Clinton was competitive in 1992 and, with increased support in Phoenix and other metro areas, carried it 47%-44% in 1996. Bush won here by only 51%-45% in 2000. He increased that victory to 55%-44% in 2004, as John Kerry's campaign thought about targeting Arizona and then thought better of it. In 2008, Obama's campaign conceded the state to McCain, but he won by just 54%-45%, leaving Democrats hopeful that Arizona, with its increasing number of Latino voters and without McCain on the ticket, could be within reach in 2012. But the Republican trend in 2010 and the Obama administration's lawsuit against the broadly popular immigration bill made that seem less likely.

Congressional districting

112th Congress Lineup	
5 R	3 D
111th Congress Lineup	
5 D	3 R

Arizona has gained House seats in reapportionment after every census since 1960. It gained two after the 2000 census and seemed likely to gain another two in the next decade—only to fall short because of the housing bust and gain only one. So in the course of five decades, it has gone from two House members to nine. Since passage of a 2000 ballot proposition, redistricting is the responsibility of a five-member Independent Redistricting Commission. Two Republican and two Democratic legislators appoint four members, and the fifth, to be neither a Democrat nor a Republican, is picked by the other four. In 2001, Democrats were disappointed because the commission's plan didn't create a competitive seat in the Phoenix area, but commissioners said such a district was possible only by drawing grotesque lines that, in their view, would be gerrymandering. Democrats challenged the plan for not creating sufficient competitive seats, and the case bounced around the courts for years. As it turned out, they were more competitive congressional districts than the Democrats, or the Republicans, had thought. Democrats captured the 5th and 8th Districts in 2006 and the 1st District in 2008, and for two years had a majority of the Arizona delegation for the first time since 1966. Then in 2010, Republicans recaptured the 1st and 5th Districts, and came close in the 7th District, where incumbent Democrat Raul Grijalva got in trouble for supporting a tourist boycott of Arizona in protest of the immigration bill.

The commission is scheduled to redraw the House districts again for the 2012 election. Maricopa County is entitled to about 5.5 districts and Pima to 1.5. Arizona's redistricting issues often also involve its two major Indian tribes. The Hopi have had disputes for many years with the far more numerous Navajo, whose reservation surrounds theirs. The 2000 redistricting commission decided that the Hopi should have a U.S. representative who doesn't also represent the Navajo. (Confusingly, most of the Hopi Reservation is in Navajo County and most of the Navajo Reservation is in Apache County.)

Governor

Jan Brewer (R)

Assumed office Jan. 2009, term expires Jan. 2015, 1st full term; b. Sept. 26, 1944, Hollywood, CA; home, Glendale; Lutheran; married (John); 3 children (1 deceased).

Elected Office: AZ House, 1983-86; AZ Senate, 1987-96; Maricopa Co. Bd. of Supervisors, 1996-2002; AZ sec. of st., 2002-09.

Office: State Capitol, 1700 W. Washington, Phoenix, 85007, 602-542-4331; Fax: 602-542-1381; Web site: governor.state.az.us.

Election Results

2010 general	Jan Brewer (R)	938,934	(54%)
	Terry Goddard (D)	733,935	(42%)
	Barry Hess (Lib)	38,722	(2%)
2010 primary	Jan Brewer (R)	479,202	(82%)
	Buz Mills (R)	51,010	(9%)
	Dean Martin (R)	36,028	(6%)

Jan Brewer is the Republican governor of Arizona. She ascended to governor on Jan. 21, 2009, from the post of secretary of state after Democratic Gov. Janet Napolitano resigned to head the Homeland Security Department in the Obama administration. Brewer is the fifth secretary of state to succeed a governor—Arizona has no lieutenant governor—in state history. She was elected to a full term in her own right on Nov. 2, 2010.

Brewer grew up in Los Angeles. Her father, a civilian supervisor at a Navy munitions depot, died of lung cancer when she was 11, and her mother started a small dress shop, where Brewer cleaned dressing rooms and worked the cash register. Her father's premature death from lung disease influenced her to go into the medical field, and she got a degree in radiology from a California community college. In 1970, she married John Brewer and took a job as an office manager to put him through school to become a chiropractor. The couple moved to his hometown of Glendale in the West Valley near Phoenix. As a stay-at-home mother of three, she started attending school board meetings in 1981 and thought about running for the school board herself. Instead, a seat in the state legislature opened, and she successfully ran for a House seat in 1982. She was re-elected in 1984 and then in 1986, she won a seat in the state Senate, to which she was re-elected four times. In 1993, she became majority whip. She is a conservative who advocated tax cuts and voted against a Martin Luther King state holiday. She also opposed the 1988 impeachment of Republican Gov. Evan Mecham, who was charged with obstruction of justice and misuse of government funds. She backed charter schools and Arizona's open-enrollment law, which allows students to attend any public school of their choice. She sponsored the first living-will statute in the nation.

In 1996, residents of Sun City were incensed when the Maricopa County Board of Supervisors approved a .25% sales tax to build the Bank One Ballpark. Brewer decided to run for the West Valley seat on the board, was elected, and went on to become chairman. She helped persuade voters to support a .2% sales tax increase to build and upgrade county jails. Maricopa County is the fourth-largest county in the United States, and in 1996, it had serious financial problems, issuing $165 million in bonds to maintain cash flow. Brewer was regarded as a fiscal hawk, and by 2002 *Governing* magazine called Maricopa "one of the two best-managed large counties in the United States." Brewer also took the lead in planning a homeless shelter campus in downtown Phoenix and preserving open space in the West Valley. In February 2002, she resigned to run for secretary of state.

Brewer had two opponents in a spirited Republican primary: Sal DiCiccio, a former Phoenix councilman, and Sharon Collins, an aide to Republican Gov. Jane Hull. She won with 45% of the vote, to 34% for DiCiccio and 21% for Collins. The Democratic nominee was state Sen. Chris Cummiskey, who promised a summer academy for high school students and cooperation with colleges and universities to encourage young people to vote. Brewer won, 49%-46%.

As secretary of state, Brewer continued to have a listed telephone number and drove to work in a convertible with the top down playing her favorite music, songs by ABBA in the musical *Mamma Mia*. Relations between Napolitano and Brewer were sometimes testy; Brewer battled to keep her Tucson office open in 2003 after Napolitano took over the space and gave her a conference room. In 2004, Democrats criticized Brewer for serving as state co-chairman of the Bush-Cheney campaign and for implementing Proposition 200, passed by voters in 2004, which required voters to show identification and proof of citizenship to vote. In 2005, she and Democratic Attorney General Terry Goddard agreed that showing one piece of photo identification or two pieces of non-photo identification was sufficient. She was re-elected in 2006 by a comfortable 57%-39%, while Napolitano was re-elected, 63%-35%. The following year, Brewer and her family suffered a terrible personal tragedy when they lost their three sons, John, to cancer.

She rose to the top job after Obama chose Napolitano as his secretary of Homeland Security. Democratic fears about Brewer at the helm were soon realized. She moved quickly to approve restrictions on abortion that Napolitano had blocked. She signed into law bills imposing a 24-hour waiting period on women seeking an abortion and requiring parental consent for minors. She also liberalized Arizona's already liberal gun law by signing legislation eliminating the need for a permit to carry a concealed weapon. Also this year, Brewer withdrew the state from the regional Western Climate Initiative's effort to impose a cap-and-trade system on carbon emissions. Brewer said that regulating carbon emissions would hurt an already ailing state economy.

Throughout 2009, Brewer mostly focused on the state's grave budget problems. The real estate bubble in fast-growing Arizona had burst as the recession set in. The considerable share of its economy in construction stagnated. Napolitano's final budget before leaving for Washington had a $4.6 billion shortfall, a huge amount considering that the annual general fund is $9.9 billion. Shortly after taking office, Brewer told the *Arizona Daily Star*: "First I was worried, then I was concerned, and now I'm just angry to see what has happened and the irresponsible management that has led us to the brink of bankruptcy." In her first address to the legislature, Brewer said raising taxes would have to be an option and two GOP lawmakers huffed out in protest, touching off a feud between the new governor and fellow conservatives that would rage for several weeks. Republican lawmakers wanted deeper spending cuts, while Brewer maintained that the state could not simply cut its way out of the crisis. She was particularly reluctant to make further cuts in education, which had already been trimmed by $300 million. "We're not going to let our education system fail if I have any say on it," Brewer told *The Arizona Republic*. "In order to get businesses here, we have to have an educated workforce." Brewer was criticized for her rough-and-tumble dealings with fellow GOP lawmakers and conceded she had not spent enough time at the Capitol courting support for her ideas.

In her second year as governor, Brewer mended fences with lawmakers, and in March 2010, they approved a nearly $9 billion spending plan with relatively little fuss. Facing a $2.6 billion shortfall, Brewer and lawmakers ended Arizona's children's health insurance program for 47,000 low-income children and also removed 310,000 low-income adults from state medical coverage.

Some state parks were closed and motor-vehicles branches laid off hundreds of workers. The legislature balked at her plan to temporarily increase the sales tax by a penny to 6.6 cents on the dollar for three years. But voters in May approved the increase in a victory for Brewer. Her crusade for the tax increase invited challenges from the right as Brewer geared up to run for election to the post in November. Yet she burnished her conservative credentials in other ways that would prove crucial to her prospects.

After Congress passed Democratic President Obama's overhaul of the health insurance system, Brewer joined a multi-state lawsuit aimed at stopping implementation of the changes. Goddard, her likely Democratic rival in the fall, adamantly opposed the move. Next, she signed into law one of the most restrictive immigration laws in the country, touching off an explosion of national news coverage and debate. Ignoring the outcry from immigration groups and raucous protests at the state capital, she signed in April 2010 a bill requiring local police to enforce federal immigration laws, including giving them power to check the immigration status of anyone stopped for other reasons. Pro-immigration groups charged that the law would result in racial profiling and other civil rights abuses. The Mexican American Legal Defense and Educational Fund accused Brewer of caving "to the radical fringe," and the Obama Justice Department filed a lawsuit to block it on grounds that the federal government had sole authority on immigration. Liberal groups led by U.S. Rep. Raul Grijalva, who represents a border district in Arizona, announced a boycott of business in the state.

Defenders of the new law countered that it expressly prohibited racial profiling, and Brewer herself dismissed the fallout as "hysteria and misinformation." Politically, the news was all good for the governor. Her job approval rating shot from 40% to 56% in a state where most residents consider illegal immigration a major problem. The boycott was less disruptive economically than expected, although it cost the state some $140 million in lost meeting and convention business. By late summer, Brewer had not only shored up her standing with voters, local commentators were describing her as Arizona's "popular" governor. She beat her closest GOP rival, businessman Owen Mills, in the Republican primary, 82% to 9%.

However, she still faced a tough competitor in the November 2010 election—Goddard, the attorney general, who accused Brewer of taking the state backward to a less enlightened time when Arizona was ridiculed nationally for refusing to accept Martin Luther King Day as a holiday. Brewer also stumbled on a few occasions. During a debate with Goddard, she fell silent for 10 seconds, seemingly uncertain about what to say next, an episode that got wide distribution on YouTube and on the political satire program, *The Daily Show*. And Brewer had to backtrack from an assertion that law enforcement agencies investigating illegal border traffic had found beheaded bodies in the Arizona desert. She called the statement an "error." But Brewer's steady handling of the fiscal crisis and her association with the illegal-immigration law carried her to an unexpectedly easy victory over Goddard. She won 54% to 42%. Libertarian candidate Barry Hess got 2.2%. Exit polls by the Associated Press showed that 75% of people who strongly supported the new law voted for Brewer. Goddard won nine out of 10 voters who strongly opposed the law, plus nearly three-fourths of Latinos. Brewer's win was a historic breakthrough: Of the five Arizona secretaries of state who have ascended to the governorship, only one, Hull in 1998, was elected governor in her own right.

Her victory celebration was short-lived. Just days into the new year, Arizona was the scene of a shocking outbreak of violence when a gunman opened fire at a public forum hosted by U.S. Rep. Gabrielle Giffords, killing six people and seriously wounding Giffords, who was shot through the head. She was treated at a Tucson hospital and faced months of rehabilitation. Brewer devoted her State of the State address to the Jan. 8, 2011, shooting, describing Arizona as "a place with a bruised, battered heart that I know will get past this hideous moment."

When she returned to work, things hadn't gotten any easier on the fiscal front. A projected $1.1 billion budget deficit loomed, and Brewer predicted there would be steep cuts in even last-resort programs like education and health care for the mentally ill. In early 2011, she formally sought a waiver from the new federal health care law to make some $540 million in reductions in the Arizona Medicaid program, which would remove 280,000 people from the rolls, including 5,200 of the mentally ill. She called for shifting $10 million to psychiatric medication for that population, although they would lose their coverage for physical ailments and for transportation and housing. Brewer's adult son, Ronald, has lived at the Arizona State Hospital for two decades and she has described the help he got from a drug developed to treat schizophrenia. What little new spending there was in her budget proposal was devoted to helping stem the loss of jobs in the state. She called for a reduction in the corporate income tax and $25 million in grants to businesses expanding or relocating to Arizona.

Senior Senator

John McCain (R)

Elected 1986, term expires 2016, 5th term; b. Aug. 29, 1936, Panama Canal Zone; home, Phoenix; U.S. Naval Academy, B.S. 1958, Natl. War Col., 1973-74; Episcopalian; married (Cindy); 7 children.

Military Career: Navy, 1958–80 (Vietnam).

Elected Office: U.S. House of Reps., 1982–86.

Professional Career: Dir., Navy Senate Liaison Ofc., 1977–81.

DC Office: 241 RSOB, 20510, 202-224-2235; Fax: 202-228-2862; Web site: mccain.senate.gov.

State Offices: Phoenix, 602-952-2410; Tempe, 480-897-6289; Tucson, 520-670-6334.

Committees: *Armed Services* (RMM). *Health, Education, Labor & Pensions:* Children & Families. *Homeland Security & Governmental Affairs:* Contracting Oversight (Ad Hoc); Federal Financial Management, Government Information, Federal Services & International Security; Investigations (Permanent). *Indian Affairs.*

Group Ratings

	ACLU	ACU	ADA	CFG	AFS	FRC	LCV	ITIC	NTU	COC
2010	7	100	0	97	15	95	14	67	100	100
2009	–	96	15	100	9	–	9	–	93	71

National Journal Ratings

	2010 LIB	—	2010 CONS		2009 LIB	—	2009 CONS
Economic	0%	—	87%		10%	—	89%
Social	0%	—	79%		28%	—	71%
Foreign	0%	—	72%		0%	—	84%
Composite	10%	—	90%		16%	—	84%

Key Votes of the 111th Congress

1. Overturn Ledbetter	N	5. Pass health care bill	N	9. Ratify New START	N
2. Pass $787 billion stimulus	N	6. Regulate financial firms	N	10. Confirm Elena Kagan	N
3. Repeal DC gun laws	Y	7. Pass tax cuts for some	N	11. Stop EPA climate regs	Y
4. Confirm Sonia Sotomayor	N	8. Legalize immigrants' kids	N	12. Repeal don't ask, tell	N

Election Results

2010 general	John McCain (R)	1,005,615	(59%)	($21,878,921)
	Rodney Glassman (D)	592,011	(35%)	($1,334,034)
	David Nolan (Lib)	80,097	(5%)	
2010 primary	John McCain (R)	333,744	(56%)	
	J. D. Hayworth (R)	190,229	(32%)	
	Jim Deakin (R)	69,328	(12%)	

Prior Winning Percentages: 2004 (77%); 1998 (69%); 1992 (56%); 1986 (60%); House: 1984 (78%); 1982 (66%)

John McCain is Arizona's senior senator and in 2008 was the 26th person to be nominated for the presidency by the Republican Party. McCain was born in the Canal Zone, the son and grandson of Navy admirals. (His married-to-the-military mother, Roberta McCain, at age 96, was one of his hardest-working campaign supporters; she danced at the podium at the Republican National Convention celebrating his nomination.) McCain graduated from the Naval Academy, fifth from the bottom of his class academically but high in demerits, and trained to be a fighter pilot. He volunteered for service in Vietnam, and flew ground-attack aircraft from carriers at sea. In July 1967, he was severely injured in a flight-deck explosion on the carrier USS *Forrestal*. McCain could have returned home, but refused. He continued to fly bombing runs over North Vietnam. That October, on his 23rd bombing mission, his A-4E Skyhawk was shot down by a missile, and McCain ejected from the plane, breaking both of his arms and a leg in a fall into Truc Bach Lake near Hanoi. After pulling him from the water, his North Vietnamese "rescuers" crushed one of his shoulders with a rifle butt, bayoneted him, and then refused McCain medical treatment during his stay at a prison dubbed by U.S. soldiers the Hanoi Hilton. He spent the next five and a half years in prisoner-of-war camps, most of it in suffering as a result of repeated torture by his Communist captors. He spent two of those years in solitary confinement. That chapter of McCain's life is recounted in Robert Timberg's *The Nightingale's Song,* and in McCain's 1999 best-seller *Faith of My Fathers*. When he was offered release because of his father's rank, he refused to be let out ahead of those who had been imprisoned longer, and he returned to the United States in March 1973 with other POWs.

McCain recovered in military hospitals, and despite intensive physical therapy, suffered permanent injuries, including restricted movement of his arms. On top of the many medals and commendations he received, his heroism was rewarded with a final assignment in a high-profile, non-combat role as the Navy's liaison to the Senate in 1977. McCain says the job launched his career in politics. He became close to several senators, including Republicans John Tower of Texas and William Cohen of Maine and Democrat Gary Hart of Colorado. On the personal front, McCain's first marriage failed. In 1980, he was remarried, to Cindy Lou Hensley, the wealthy daughter of a beer distributor from Phoenix. Two years later, he ran for an open House seat in Arizona. Attacked as an outsider, he responded, "The longest place I ever lived in was Hanoi." He won a four-way primary 32%-26%, and then the general election in November. In 1986, he easily defeated former Arizona state legislator Democrat Richard Kimball to win the Senate seat of conservative icon Barry Goldwater, who was retiring.

In Congress, McCain established a conservative voting record and, at first, a low profile. He was a strong supporter of the Reagan administration, and surprised some by opposing the president's dispatch of troops to Lebanon in 1982, arguing there were too few to be effective and too vulnerable to attack. Later, he backed President George H.W. Bush's war in the Persian Gulf in 1991, and his decision not to oust Iraqi leader Saddam Hussein. In the 1990s, he worked with Massachusetts Sen. John Kerry, a Democrat and also a decorated Vietnam veteran, to end the trade embargo on Vietnam, and pressed for establishing diplomatic relations. He supported air strikes against Serbia in 1999, but criticized the Clinton administration for ruling out ground troops in Bosnia and for not using "all necessary force" against the Serbs.

McCain strongly supported President George W. Bush in the war on terrorism after September 11, and in his later decision to go to war with Iraq. McCain repeatedly pushed for more ground troops in Afghanistan and signed a letter urging that Iraq be the next target. He called for a special commission to investigate intelligence failures before the terrorist attacks. The final version of the law provided, at the insistence of relatives of 9/11 casualties, that McCain and Richard Shelby of Alabama get a veto over appointees to the commission. When Bush decided to invade Iraq in 2003, McCain continually pushed for a larger army and more troops to get the job done. He clashed frequently with Defense Secretary Donald Rumsfeld.

McCain finally concluded that the administration's handling of the war "will go down as one of the worst" mistakes in U.S. military history. He dismissed the recommendations of the Iraq Study Group in December 2006 and called for the surge of troops that Bush ordered in January 2007. To those who said the troops were already overextended, he replied, "There's only one thing worse than an overstressed Army and Marine Corps, and that's a defeated Army and Marine Corps." He strongly opposed Democratic calls for a troop withdrawal. When critics speculated that his support for the war would hurt his chances to become president, McCain said, "I would much rather lose an election than lose a war."

In the last two decades, McCain built a reputation in Congress as someone who refused to engage in business as usual, making him a popular figure outside of Washington. But at one time, engaging in business as usual nearly ended his career. In the mid-1980s, McCain was one of the Keating Five senators investigated for allegedly pressuring regulators on behalf of Charles Keating's Arizona savings and loan. Ultimately, he was cited for exercising bad judgment for attempting to influence regulators overseeing Keating's thrift. Vindicated by his re-election in 1992, McCain reinvented himself as a reformer.

When Republicans won control of Congress two years later, McCain sought out Democrat Russ Feingold of Wisconsin, who had a bill to clamp down on campaign finance abuses. For the next several years, the McCain-Feingold bills went through several transformations. Key features included prohibitions on soft money—the large, unregulated contributions to political parties that were ripe for abuse—and limits on advertising by independent organizations within 60 days of an election. The changes were fiercely opposed as an infringement on free speech and as a threat to the Republican Party by the powerful Mitch McConnell of Kentucky, who used threats of filibusters to prevent the bill from coming to a vote.

In early 2001, McCain threatened to tie up the Senate unless Majority Leader Trent Lott, R-Miss., set aside time for debate on the issue. In March 2001, after two weeks of civilized but spirited debate, during which McCain and Feingold fended off several poison-pill amendments, the legislation passed April 2 by a 59-41 vote. An amendment by Fred Thompson, R-Tenn., and Dianne Feinstein, D-Calif., was passed to raise limits on individual contributions from $1,000 to $2,000, but the bill passed mostly intact. The House passed its version in February 2002, and the bill became law. For years, it withstood multiple court challenges. But then in January 2010, the Supreme Court, reversing earlier precedents, struck down a key reform when it ruled that curbs on political spending by corporations are an unconstitutional infringement on free speech. The 2002 law banned the broadcast, cable or satellite transmission of election messages paid for by corporations or labor unions from their general funds in the 30 days before a presidential primary and in the 60 days before the general elections.

Another of his legislative crusades was a war on earmarks, the practice among lawmakers of slipping high-dollar projects into bills to benefit a particular congressional district or state. Each year, McCain highlighted the pork-barrel spending he found in the appropriations bills, to the growing irritation of his colleagues in both parties, who were accustomed to using earmarks to curry favor with voters back home. But eventually McCain's lonely campaign was joined by conservatives in the House, and the issue was a factor in 2006 and in every election since.

McCain's generally conservative voting record has as many quirks as the man himself. He supported funding of embryonic stem cell research, in opposition to most other Republicans. With liberal Democrat Kerry, he proposed fuel efficiency standards of 36 miles per gallon for cars and light trucks by 2015. And with independent Sen. Joe Lieberman of Connecticut, he co-authored a bill to reduce carbon dioxide emissions. McCain opposed the constitutional amendment to ban same-sex marriage as "antithetical in every way to the core philosophy of Republicans" to respect states' rights to govern themselves.

His biggest act of ideological heresy in recent years came on the issue of immigration. "The truth is, border enforcement alone does not work," McCain said, as most conservatives were pursuing tougher enforcement strategies. He opposed Arizona's Proposition 200, which would cut off public benefits to illegal immigrants, arguing that it would "delay, possibly derail, the search for a solution." In 2005, McCain and liberal Sen. Edward Kennedy of Massachusetts sponsored an immigration bill that gave illegal immigrants a path to legalization, allowing them to obtain two three-year visas and then "get in the back of the line" of legal immigrants. "Some Americans believe we must find all these millions, round them up, and send them back to the countries they came from. I don't know how you do that. And I don't know why you would want to," McCain said. But a comprehensive bill failed in 2006 and again in 2007.

McCain's quest for the presidency began with the 2000 election. In 1999, he decided to skip the caucuses in dovish and ethanol-loving Iowa (McCain had long denounced ethanol subsidies as pork barrel spending) to concentrate on New Hampshire, where he traveled around in his "Straight Talk Express" bus. At first, only a few reporters traveled with him and crowds were sparse. But McCain struck a chord. To increasingly larger and more enthusiastic crowds, he told his personal story in self-deprecating terms, and pledged, "I will never tell you a lie." He talked about defense and foreign-policy issues—the only candidate to spend much time doing so—and invariably called for campaign finance regulation. McCain did not have much support from his colleagues. Only four fellow senators endorsed him. Back home, Republican Gov. Jane Hull, who had had her fill of McCain's sometimes abrasive treatment, endorsed Texas Gov. George W. Bush, and *The Arizona Republic* wrote editorials warning of McCain's "volcanic" temper. But the strength of feeling among his ever-larger crowds was real, and on Feb. 1, McCain beat Bush by an impressive 49%-31%. Suddenly he became, if not the front-runner, at least the front-runner's most serious opponent.

From there, the "Straight Talk Express" had mixed success. It went to South Carolina, where both the Republican establishment and Christian conservatives lined up with Bush. The campaigning got negative, but what hurt even more was McCain's failure to win over self-identified Republicans. His emphasis on campaign finance regulation and his criticisms of Bush's tax cuts for giving too much to the rich helped with independents, but sounded like enemy talk to Republicans. On Feb. 18, Bush won 53%-42% in South Carolina, in what turned out to be a decisive victory.

The race continued, with McCain running about even with Bush among Republicans, way ahead among independents, but way behind among Republicans in Southern states. McCain's most striking win was in Michigan that February, where he prevailed 50%-43%, among an atypical electorate: 17% of Republican primary voters were self-identified Democrats, 35% were independents, and only a minority were Republicans.

McCain might have done better had he emphasized other issues on which he had consistently taken stands in line with most Republicans' thinking, such as national defense, tax cuts (he had a tax-cut plan himself, but he spent less time on it than on attacking Bush's), abortion rights, and Social Security individual investment accounts. Instead, after South Carolina, he gave a speech in Virginia Beach attacking the religious right, and in an offhand comment to reporters on the bus, called Pat Robertson and Jerry Falwell "forces of evil." McCain lost in Virginia and Washington on February 29. On Super Tuesday, March 7, McCain won in Massachusetts, Connecticut, Rhode Island, and Vermont. But he lost decisively in New York, Ohio, and California. He suspended his campaign in March, and two months later, grudgingly endorsed Bush.

Four years later, as Bush headed into his 2004 re-election campaign, McCain was a major national figure, with high positives among Republicans and very low negatives among Democrats. Always enchanted with him, the press gave McCain plenteous coverage. As Kerry, his fellow Vietnam veteran, clinched the Democratic nomination in March 2004, there was speculation that he would ask McCain to be his vice presidential nominee. After some days of speculation, McCain firmly rejected the idea. "I am a pro-life, deficit-hawk, free-trade Republican," he said. Subsequently, the Bush and McCain camps made peace. But he also maintained his relationship with fellow vet Kerry. When the Swift Boat Veterans for Truth ads appeared against Kerry, McCain called them "dishonorable" and said they should be dropped from the air.

As the 2008 presidential contest neared, McCain voiced more frequently and fervently his long-standing opposition to abortion rights. Even so, many conservatives were not enthusiastic about McCain, given his stands on campaign finance, immigration, and carbon dioxide emissions. Their skepticism doomed McCain's early strategy in 2007, which was to campaign as the next-in-line Republican for the presidential nomination. He fell behind New York's Rudolph Giuliani in the polls, and he fell far short of his fundraising goals, raising just $13.6 million in the first quarter of 2007, behind Giuliani and Massachusetts' Mitt Romney. By late June, the McCain campaign was broke. Its opulent headquarters was closed, and the campaign's top managers were fired, replaced with McCain stalwart Rick Davis and Bush-Cheney veteran Steve Schmidt. Backed into a corner, McCain adopted the campaign strategy that some of the best consultants rely on—campaign on what you believe in. And, he had a backup strategy that even the worst consultants are ashamed to advance—wait for all the other candidates' strategies to fail.

They both worked. After a spring trip to Iraq, McCain commented in July 2007 that he was convinced the troop surge strategy was working and praised the outcome despite near-universal skepticism in the press. In September, he launched his "No Surrender" tour. In the GOP primary debates, McCain was treated respectfully and uncritically by his opponents, while he was quick to jab at any who expressed skepticism about the surge. Meanwhile, his opponents' strategies started to fail. Romney's poll numbers were stalled at about 30%. Tennessee's Fred Thompson took months to announce he was running, then seemed strangely unenergetic. Judging that the field was stacked against him in early contests, New York's Giuliani decided to wait until the Florida primary. Only Mike Huckabee, the former minister and Arkansas governor, exceeded expectations, running second in the Iowa straw poll in August 2007 and first, ahead of the free-spending Romney, in the Iowa caucuses on Jan. 3, 2008. As in 2000, McCain had written off dovish Iowa. He focused on the New Hampshire primary, and campaigned hard in that state. On January 8, he beat Romney, who owned a vacation home in New Hampshire, 37%-32%. "Mac is back," chanted the crowd on Election Night.

Next up was Michigan, where Romney had grown up and where his father was governor 40 years before. Romney promised to bring back jobs in the state's important automobile industry, while McCain stated bluntly that many jobs would never return. With fewer crossovers than in 2000, Michigan gave Romney 39% and McCain 30%. From Michigan, it was on to South Carolina, where McCain had lost decisively in 2000. This was the one real four-way Republican contest in 2008. McCain, with 33%, came out ahead of Huckabee, with 30%. Thompson undoubtedly took votes away from fellow Southerner Huckabee and got 16%. Romney was fourth with 15%.

In critical and always baffling Florida on January 29, GOP Gov. Charlie Crist delivered a surprise endorsement of McCain. Meanwhile, support was draining from Giuliani, who was depending heavily on the state. That was especially true among Miami's Cuban-Americans, who were going to McCain. The result was a 36%-31% victory for McCain over Romney. A few days later on Super Tuesday, February 5, McCain effectively sewed up the nomination, winning absolute majorities (his first) in New York, New Jersey, and Connecticut and winning a 1% victory over Huckabee in Missouri. He racked up victories in states as diverse as California, Illinois, Oklahoma, and Delaware. Two days later, Romney withdrew. Huckabee stayed in the race for another month.

The Republican Party's winner-take-all delegate allocation rules allowed McCain to clinch the nomination with narrow pluralities—5% in New Hampshire, 3% in South Carolina, 5% in Florida, 1% in Missouri, and 7% in California. This gave Republicans a nominee out of sync with the party's base supporters on some important issues. Yet he was admired by some hard-core conservatives for his support of the troop surge and for enduring his increasingly negative treatment by the national press. By late spring, McCain had consolidated the Republican base, but it was smaller than in 2004, and not sufficiently motivated to come anywhere close to matching the fundraising feats of Democrat Barack Obama. Working against McCain were Bush's low job rating, an increasing Democratic advantage in party identification, doubts about the course of the economy, the continuing unpopularity of the war in Iraq, and the enthusiasm among young and black voters for Obama. Another factor was McCain's own campaign finance law. Obama eschewed federal funding and was able to massively outspend McCain, who had little choice but to take public financing.

In these circumstances, what is perhaps surprising is that McCain made a contest of it and that he was actually leading during part of the fall campaign. He sought to portray himself, more than Obama, as an agent of change. After Obama chose 36-year Senate veteran Joe Biden of Delaware as his running mate, McCain chose the two-year governor of Alaska, Sarah Palin. Her initial appearance in Ohio and her speech before the Republican National Convention sparked huge enthusiasm among the Republican base and, for the first time, enabled the McCain campaign to muster volunteer and fundraising efforts competitive with Obama's. Palin's record of defeating powerful Republicans in Alaska underlined McCain's message of change and reform, and polls after the convention showed a sharp narrowing of the race in states like Washington, Oregon, North Dakota, Minnesota, Wisconsin, and Michigan. For about two weeks, the McCain-Palin ticket actually led Obama-Biden by narrow margins.

Then, on September 15, Lehman Brothers went into bankruptcy, and a financial crisis ensued. The same day, McCain said, "The fundamentals of our economy are strong." Four days later, Treasury Secretary Henry Paulson and Federal Reserve Chairman Ben Bernanke called for a $700 billion rescue of the financial markets. Obama's campaign scoffed at McCain's "strong" comment, surged in the polls and never relinquished the lead after that. On September 24, McCain announced he was suspending his campaign, pulling his television ads, and returning to the Capitol to work on the financial industry bill. He said he might not appear at the first presidential debate scheduled two days later. Obama coolly said that the president had to tend to more than one thing at a time, and the debate went off. When the House rejected the financial rescue on September 29, McCain was blamed for not bringing along a sufficient number of House Republicans. He received precious little credit when revised legislation passed the Senate on October 1 and the House on October 3.

In the rhetoric war, McCain attacked Obama sharply on taxes, energy, and other issues in October. But he also subtly raised questions about Obama's character, asking voters whether they knew the "real Barack Obama" and could trust him. When fringe activists started loudly protesting that Obama might be a socialist or a terrorist and perhaps was not even an American citizen, McCain modulated his comments, saying on October 10, "I want to be president of the United States and obviously I do not want Senator Obama to be, but I have to tell you, I have to tell you he is a decent person, and a person that you do not have to be scared of as president of the United States." He criticized Obama for saying he wanted to "spread the wealth around," but when asked in a debate about the economy, McCain fell back on his determination to stop spending on earmarks, which could hardly be viewed as a comprehensive economic agenda.

In the final days of the campaign, Obama avoided mistakes. He won 53%-46%, the best Democratic percentage since 1964. Obama got 95% support from African-American voters, and he won 66%-32% among voters under age 30. Among those older than 30, McCain lost by only 50%-49%. On Election Night, McCain made a gracious concession speech, saying, "Senator Obama has achieved a great thing for himself and for his country."

After the election, McCain continued to weigh in on major issues, but he took a more conservative line than he had in earlier years. He called for a payroll tax cut in January 2009 and opposed the Democrats' $787 billion economic stimulus bill. In April 2009, despite his support of past legislation to reduce carbon emissions, he called Democrats' cap-and-trade bill irresponsible, and said the plan to auction all emissions credits was "bad economic policy that would cost businesses billions of dollars and allow for little to no transition into a low carbon system."

As the ranking Republican on the Armed Services Committee, McCain remained heavily involved in defense issues. He worked with Chairman Carl Levin, D-Mich., to support Defense Secretary Robert Gates' decision in 2009 to end production of the F-22 fighter. And, after his many criticisms of Bush's handling of the Iraq war, he gave the former president credit for ending it well. "Though most Democrats still cannot bear to admit it, the war in Iraq is ending successfully because the surge worked," he told *The Wall Street Journal*. In another interview, McCain added, "If we had done what President Obama wanted, we would have failed in Iraq." McCain supported Obama's decisions to send more troops to Afghanistan in March and December 2009, but criticized the president's call for troop reductions starting by July 2011. "Dates for withdrawal are dictated by conditions," McCain said. He also spoke out strongly against repeal of the ban on openly gay military personnel.

McCain's positive image with the public had been built on his tendency toward political independence, and that image acquired chinks in 2010. He disappointed many of his longtime supporters when, faced with a primary challenge in his re-election, McCain backed away from some of his earlier stances and told *Newsweek* in April 2010, "I never considered myself a maverick." One of his most telling changes of heart was on immigration. McCain retreated from his earlier out-front support for a path to citizenship and other elements of a bipartisan approach to illegal immigration, saying bluntly that voters had spoken and that the border must be protected first, before any comprehensive bill would be passed. Most Republican primary voters in Arizona and practically all talk radio hosts there strongly opposed legalization as a form of amnesty, and McCain no doubt was angling to eliminate an easy line of attack for his primary opponent, conservative talk radio host J.D. Hayworth, a former House member. In March 2009, McCain snipped to a Hispanic group, "You people made your choice during the election," a reference to exit polls that showed he lost Latinos to Obama 67%-31%.

In April 2009, McCain and fellow Republican Jon Kyl called for sending 3,000 National Guard troops to the Arizona border. He also supported Arizona's controversial new law allowing police to look into the immigration status of people stopped for other reasons, and he opposed the Obama administration's lawsuit to block it from going into effect. "The Obama administration has not done everything it can do to protect the people of Arizona from the violence and crime illegal immigration brings to our state," McCain said. "Until it does, the federal government should not be suing Arizona on the grounds that immigration enforcement is solely a federal responsibility."

If McCain was hoping to mitigate Hayworth's attacks, it didn't work. Known for a bombastic streak during his House years, Hayworth chortled over McCain's "double talk express" and dubbed him "weenie of the week." He assailed him on immigration, campaign finance and his earlier opposition to the Bush tax cuts. Polling in early 2009 showed McCain just clearing 50% among GOP primary voters.

But Hayworth had his own problems. Before losing his seat—including usually Republican Scottsdale—to Democrat Harry Mitchell in 2006, he had received contributions from disgraced lobbyist Jack Abramoff. As a House member, Hayworth had requested and received many spending earmarks for his district—a no-no for tea party conservatives in 2010. Most damaging for Hayworth was an ad for a business he had made in which he promised "free government money." McCain, once so critical of big spending campaigns, raised plenty of money. He brought Palin, his former running mate, into the state to campaign for him and Kyl traveled constantly for him. With his long Senate career on the line, McCain campaigned nonstop. McCain beat Hayworth in the August primary 57%-32%, a solid victory but not an overwhelming one. A third candidate who claimed tea party affiliation got 12%.

In the general election campaign, Democratic nominee Rodney Glassman, the former vice mayor of Tucson, could attract little funding in a year many other Democratic Senate candidates were struggling, and he never became well-known in the Phoenix market. McCain won by 59%-35%. He has made it plain that his days of presidential campaigning are over, but as the ranking Republican on the Armed Services Committee in the 112th Congress (2011-12), he may have many years of active lawmaking ahead.

Junior Senator

Jon Kyl (R)

Elected 1994, term expires 2012, 3rd term; b. April 25, 1942, Oakland, NE; home, Phoenix; U. of AZ, B.A. 1964, L.L.B. 1966; Presbyterian; married (Caryll); 2 children.

Elected Office: U.S. House of Reps., 1986–94.

Professional Career: Practicing atty., 1966–86; Chmn., Phoenix Chamber of Commerce, 1984–85.

DC Office: 730 HSOB, 20510, 202-224-4521; Fax: 202-224-2207; Web site: kyl.senate.gov.

State Offices: Phoenix, 602-840-1891; Tucson, 520-575-8633.

Committees: *Finance:* Health Care; Social Security, Pensions & Family Policy; Taxation & IRS Oversight (RMM). *Judiciary:* Constitution, Civil Rights & Human Rights; Crime & Terrorism (RMM); Immigration, Refugees & Border Security.

Group Ratings

	ACLU	ACU	ADA	CFG	AFS	FRC	LCV	ITIC	NTU	COC
2010	7	96	0	97	0	91	14	67	97	100
2009	–	92	5	94	0	–	0	–	91	71

National Journal Ratings

	2010 LIB	—	2010 CONS	2009 LIB	—	2009 CONS
Economic	14%	—	84%	11%	—	87%
Social	21%	—	74%	24%	—	73%
Foreign	0%	—	72%	0%	—	84%
Composite	18%	—	83%	15%	—	85%

Key Votes of the 111th Congress

1. Overturn Ledbetter	N	5. Pass health care bill	N	9. Ratify New START	N
2. Pass $787 billion stimulus	N	6. Regulate financial firms	N	10. Confirm Elena Kagan	N
3. Repeal DC gun laws	Y	7. Pass tax cuts for some	N	11. Stop EPA climate regs	Y
4. Confirm Sonia Sotomayor	N	8. Legalize immigrants' kids	N	12. Repeal don't ask, tell	N

Election Results

2006 general	Jon Kyl (R)	814,398	(53%)	($15,524,019)
	Jim Pederson (D)	664,141	(44%)	($14,709,628)
2006 primary	Jon Kyl (R)	unopposed		

Prior Winning Percentages: 2000 (79%); 1994 (54%); House: 1992 (59%); 1990 (61%); 1988 (87%); 1986 (65%)

Jon Kyl is Arizona's junior senator, and although he's often overshadowed by his home-state colleague John McCain, Kyl is a political force in his own right. He was the unanimous choice of his colleagues in late 2007 for minority whip, the No. 2 ranking post in the Senate Republican leadership. Unlike McCain, Kyl prefers to operate behind the scenes and relies on intellect rather than emotion to get his points across. Minority Leader Mitch McConnell of Kentucky, lauding Kyl in *Time* magazine in 2010, said, "Jon demonstrates continually that the essence of Senate power is the power to persuade." Kyl has served two terms in the Senate, and announced in February 2010 that he would not seek a third when his seat is up in the 2012 election.

Kyl (*KILE*) was born in Nebraska, but his family moved to Iowa when he was young. His father was a school principal who went on to become active in politics and was elected to the U.S. House in 1958 and again in 1966. He encouraged his son's interest in politics and brought him to Washington with him during the summers. Kyl fell in love with Arizona when he did his undergraduate work at the University of Arizona, and then stayed to get his law degree there. He settled in Phoenix and practiced law while also working on Republican campaigns and heading that city's Chamber of Commerce. Kyl won the heavily Republican 4th District seat in the U.S. House in 1986. In the decisive GOP primary, he defeated former Rep. John Conlan (1973-77), who had support from Christian conservatives, 60%-28%. While in the House, Kyl had a solidly conservative voting record and developed expertise in missile defense systems. He was a vocal critic of fellow members who had overdrafts at the House bank, which grew into a major scandal in 1992 and helped him establish credibility as a reformer. He was well positioned two years later to run for the Senate seat of Dennis DeConcini, a three-term Democrat who was retiring after being named one of the "Keating

Five" senators accused of pressuring regulators on behalf of a shady savings and loan owner. Kyl had no primary opposition. His Democratic opponent was one-term Rep. Sam Coppersmith. With far more money, Kyl ran ads with a home-movie flavor showing him traveling through the Arizona desert, dressed in jeans and working on ranches, and talking about how he and his wife fell in love with the state. Kyl won easily, 54%-40%.

In the Senate, the unassuming Kyl quietly built a reputation for hard work, for his knowledge of the nuances of policy, and for his ability to play the inside game. After surveying congressional aides in 2008, *Washingtonian* magazine said that he was considered one of the smartest, most hardworking members of Congress. In 2007, GOP senators unanimously chose Kyl to be minority whip, making him the chamber's highest-ranking Republican after McConnell. Kyl also sits on the influential Finance Committee, where he is the senior Republican on the Subcommittee on Taxation and Internal Revenue Service Oversight. He started his rise in the leadership as chairman of the Republican Steering Committee in 2001. He became Republican Policy Committee chairman in 2003, and chairman of the Republican Conference, the third-ranking post, in 2007. (For a fairly reserved conservative, Kyl has an adventurous side: He is a big fan of fast cars and has been spotted driving the lead car around the track in warm-up laps at Phoenix International Raceway.)

In the leadership, Kyl did his share to promote President George W. Bush's agenda in Congress, but he sometimes took principled stands in opposition to the Republican president. In 2007, he was harshly critical of the administration's ouster of eight U.S. attorneys around the country, which many viewed as retribution for their failure to aggressively prosecute Democratic officeholders. Two years earlier, he led the move to derail Bush's choice of White House counsel Harriet Miers to serve on the Supreme Court, helping orchestrate efforts to paint her as insufficiently conservative. She eventually withdrew her nomination.

Kyl is a major player on defense policy. He was one of the staunchest congressional champions of a missile defense system to protect the United States from nuclear attack. In 1997, he and Republican Sen. Jesse Helms of North Carolina led the losing fight against the Chemical Weapons Convention. Learning from that experience, Kyl organized the winning battle to reject the Comprehensive Test Ban Treaty, an international agreement to halt all underground nuclear tests with a maximum force equal to 150,000 tons of TNT. President Bill Clinton sent the treaty to the Senate for ratification in 1997. Kyl studied the details and convinced Republican colleagues that compliance by other nuclear-armed countries would not be verifiable and the terms of the treaty not enforceable. Senate Democrats and the Clinton White House eventually discovered that Kyl had done his work well: The CTBT did not even get a majority of votes, much less the two-thirds required for ratification. It was defeated 48-51. In 2010, Kyl took a dim view of President Barack Obama's efforts to get the Senate to ratify the New START nuclear-arms reduction treaty with Russia, declaring that Obama should commit to more funding to modernize the U.S. nuclear weapons complex to make his case for the pact.

Kyl strongly supported the Bush administration on the wars in Afghanistan and Iraq, and defended Bush when no weapons of mass destruction were found in Iraq. "The reality is, no one was duped," he said. "We were all working off the same data. Reasonable people reached different conclusions about what to do based on a commonly understood set of facts." He is the ranking Republican on the Judiciary Committee's Crime and Terrorism Subcommittee. After the September 11 attacks, he and Democratic Sen. Dianne Feinstein introduced a bill to establish a comprehensive lookout database that would combine information from the Central Intelligence Agency, the Federal Bureau of Investigation, and the State Department. In that period, Kyl continually pointed out problems with lax State Department visa policies—notably the Visa Express program in Saudi Arabia, which delegated visa issuance to travel agents and enabled most of the September 11 hijackers to enter the United States.

Immigration is Kyl's other big focus on Judiciary, and it has brought him both success and great political pain. He generally took a dim view of bipartisan bills in recent years that attempted to address illegal immigrants already in the country by allowing them into guest worker programs and giving them a path to citizenship. He was often at odds with his powerful home-state colleague, McCain, who sponsored a bipartisan bill with liberal Democratic Sen. Edward Kennedy of Massachusetts. Kyl favored a guest worker program only if it required immigrants to first return home and apply for work permits before seeking jobs in the United States. That proposal failed, but Kyl did succeed in attaching an amendment to a defense spending bill that provided $1.8 billion for 370 miles of fencing along the U.S.-Mexico border.

Once he reached the upper echelon of leadership, Kyl came under increased pressure to find a compromise on immigration. In 2007, he surprised his supporters by backing a compromise immigration bill that established a temporary guest worker program and a path to legalization for millions of undocumented workers. The bill ultimately died in Congress, but not before Kyl took a thumping. Fellow Republicans accused him of supporting "amnesty" for illegal immigrants, and one state senator said that the legislation would foster an "invasion by illegal aliens." Describing the reaction back home, Kyl said, "Yes, I have learned some new words from some of my constituents." In 2010, Kyl and McCain sought instead to emphasize enforcement, unsuccessfully offering amendments to a supplemental spending bill that called for more than $3 billion in border security funds, including money to deploy 6,000 National Guard troops and to buy more unmanned drones.

Water is one of the most sensitive issues in Arizona. For years Kyl had worked mostly behind the scenes on settling American Indian claims to Colorado and Gila river water and an ongoing intergovernmental dispute about how much money Arizona should pay the federal government for the Central Arizona Project, completed in 1993 at a cost of $3.6 billion. With McCain as co-sponsor and with the support of the Arizona House delegation, Kyl succeeded in passing the Arizona Water Settlement Act in 2004, which resolved Indian lawsuits against Arizona and New Mexico and set Arizona's reimbursement to the federal government at $1.65 billion. It was the most far-reaching Indian water settlement in history.

Kyl was the lead Senate sponsor of an Internet gambling ban and a bill prohibiting credit card companies from processing online wagers. The House in 2006 overwhelmingly passed a similar bill, and later that year Bush signed legislation that included a ban on interstate and international online gambling transactions. In 2010, Kyl drew Democrats' anger over several public comments. He said that paying people unemployment insurance is "a disincentive for them to seek new work." Later, he said extending Bush's 2001 tax cuts was important even if the result added to the budget deficit: "You should never have to offset the cost of a deliberate decision to reduce tax rates on Americans."

Kyl had no difficulty winning re-election in 2000: No Democrat filed to run against him, and he won 79% of the vote. His opponent in 2006 was former state Democratic Chairman Jim Pederson, a wealthy real estate developer who had revitalized the state party by pouring millions of dollars of his personal wealth into it. Kyl portrayed Pederson as inexperienced and ran ads accusing him of attempting to buy the Senate seat and of supporting amnesty for illegal immigrants because he favored a guest worker program. Pederson painted Kyl as a Washington insider and part of its "special-interest" culture, while also tying him to the unpopular president. Surveys showed Kyl leading Pederson throughout the campaign but polling less than 50%. Pederson spent nearly $15 million on the race, $11 million of it his own money; Kyl spent slightly more. Five days before the election, the Democratic Senatorial Campaign Committee poured $1 million into the state to boost Pederson. Kyl won 53%-43%, carrying all but four counties and the Phoenix metro area. He lost Flagstaff's Coconino County and Tucson's Pima County.

FIRST DISTRICT

Paul Gosar (R)

Elected 2010, 1st term; b. Nov. 27, 1958, Rock Springs, WY; home, Flagstaff; Creighton U., B.S. 1981, D.D.S. 1985.; Catholic; Married (Maude); 3 children.

Professional Career: Owner, dental practice.

DC Office: 504 CHOB, 20515, 202-225-2315; Fax: 202-226-9739; Web site: gosar.house.gov.

State Offices: Casa Grande, 520-836-5289; Flagstaff, 928-214-6055; Prescott, 928-445-1683.

Committees: *Natural Resources:* Energy & Mineral Resources; Indian & Alaska Native Affairs; Water & Power. *Oversight & Government Reform:* Government Organization, Efficiency & Financial Management; Health Care, District of Columbia, Census & the National Archives (VChmn); National Security, Homeland Defense & Foreign Operations.

Election Results

2010 general	Paul Gosar (R)...112,816	(50%)	($1,173,026)
	Ann Kirkpatrick (D)..99,233	(44%)	($1,992,860)
	Nicole Patti (Lib)..14,869	(7%)	
2010 primary	Paul Gosar (R)...21,941	(31%)	
	Sydney Hay (R)..16,328	(23%)	
	Bradley Beauchamp (R)....................................11,356	(16%)	
	Russell Bowers (R)...10,552	(15%)	
	Steve Mehta (R)..5,846	(8%)	

Population		Race/Ethnicity		Work	
Pop. 2010:	774,310	White:	57.1%	Private:	70.0%
Change since 2000:	Up 20.7%	Black:	1.5%	Government:	23.1%
Urban:	55.5%	Hispanic:	19.5%	Self-employed:	6.7%
Rural:	44.5%	Asian:	0.9%	Blue collar:	23.6%
Area size:	58,711 sq. mi.	Native Am.:	19.1%	White collar:	53.8%
		Hawaiian:	0.2%	Khaki collar:	0.1%
Age		Two+ races:	1.6%	Other:	22.4%
Median age:	38.1 yrs.				
More than 65 yrs:	15.2%	*Ancestry*		Median income:	$41,739
Less than 18 yrs:	24.9%	German	12.6%	Median Home Value:	$178,700
		English	9.7%		
Education		Irish	8.7%	**Military Veterans**	
H.S. grad:	82.7%			% of Pop:	12.7%
College grad:	18.8%				
Grad degree:	7.4%				

Northeast Arizona; Flagstaff, Prescott

Beyond Phoenix, Arizona is a vast state of stunning beauty: the awe-inspiring Grand Canyon, the subtle pastel hues of the Painted Desert, the sheer cliff walls of Canyon de Chelly, the still waters of Lake Powell, the mountainous pine forests around Flagstaff, and the rust-and-rosy red rocks of Sedona. It also has man-made landmarks: The celebrated U.S. 66, now mostly superseded by Interstate 40, and the old gold mining camp of Prescott, home since 1888 of America's oldest annual rodeo. Jerome, a mining town built improbably on hillside stilts, has been reborn as an artist colony. There are old copper mining towns like Globe.

2008 Presidential Vote		
John McCain (R) 157,160	(54%)	
Barack Obama (D) 127,790	(44%)	
2004 Presidential Vote		
George Bush (R) 139,221	(54%)	
John Kerry (D) 117,673	(46%)	
Cook Partisan Voting Index: R+6		

All of these places are in the 1st Congressional District of Arizona, which includes over half the state, an area larger than Pennsylvania. It covers most of northern Arizona, except for Mohave County and the Hopi Indian Reservation and a narrow band of land connecting them. It reaches south to the northern edges of the Phoenix and Tucson metro areas. It encompasses Flagstaff, a college town and growing retirement mecca that has lured snowbirds with its climate and well-priced housing. The median home price in Flagstaff was $259,000 in 2010. But it was particularly vulnerable to the housing bust of the late 2000s; from 2009 to 2010, Flagstaff lost the highest percentage of construction jobs of any metropolitan area.

The 1st is the home of the nation's largest Indian population, and a full 20% of its residents identify themselves as American Indians. There are several reservations here—Fort Apache, San Carlos, Zuni—but by far the largest is the Navajo Nation. (The Hopi are excluded because they have a long and angry boundary dispute with the Navajo and agreed to be part of the 2nd District.) Most of the Navajo are in Apache County, with the rest in Navajo and Coconino counties. They have a history of fiercely contested tribal elections and considerable social problems. Unemployment on the Navajo Reservation in 2010 topped 57%; a large number of dwellings were without telephone service, and 21% of homes lacked complete plumbing systems. Alcoholism and drug abuse remain rampant, and there is little economic development.

The 1st District was designed to be closely divided between the two parties, but today is solidly Republican in presidential elections. The copper mining counties of Greenlee, Graham, and Gila are historically Democratic and still register that way, but they tend to vote Republican. Apache County, with its Navajo majority, is heavily Democratic. Coconino County includes Flagstaff, part of the Navajo Reservation, and Sedona, where the Army drove the Apaches off the land in the 1870s after gold was discovered; it is increasingly Democratic. Yavapai County is heavily Republican. It includes Prescott, where conservative icon Barry Goldwater always began his Arizona campaigns. President Bush won the district easily in 2004 with 54% of the vote, and Arizona native son John McCain won it similarly with 54% in 2008.

Paul Gosar (R)

The new congressman from the 1st District is Republican Paul Gosar, who unseated one-term Democratic Rep. Ann Kirkpatrick in 2010 with the backing of the national GOP glitterati, including former Alaska Gov. Sarah Palin.

Gosar (*GO sar*) grew up in Pinedale, Wyo., a town of fewer than 2,000 residents near the headwaters of the Green River. He was the first of 10 children in the "Fighting Gosars," a family he describes as close and also "rough and rowdy." He and his brothers were altar boys in their Roman Catholic parish in nearby Rock Springs, but they weren't beyond a little mischief, such as sneaking swigs of wine in the sacristy. Gosar's father, a geologist with Belco Petroleum and Union Pacific, was often away working on rigs, and an uncle, who was a dentist, stepped in as a role model during those absences. Gosar went on to study dentistry at Creighton University with the expectation that he would return to Wyoming to go into practice with his uncle. His father, however, advised him to seek a more vibrant economy. "My dad took me aside and said, 'I don't think the right time is here. I think the minerals, the oil, and gas are going to crash," Gosar recalled.

After receiving his D.D.S. in 1985, Gosar landed in Flagstaff, Ariz. Appealing to a local banker for financing to launch his practice in 1985, Gosar says he emphasized his frugality, vowing to eat nothing but peanut-butter-and-jelly sandwiches until his business was established. He married an antiques dealer and the couple now has three children, the oldest of whom is a senior at Creighton.

Gosar didn't like the health care overhaul that the Democratic Congress passed in December 2009, and he cites it as one of the big reasons he decided to challenge Kirkpatrick. In his campaign, he sharply criticized her votes for President Obama's agenda in Congress, including the health care bill. He also took a hard line on immigration, in contrast to Kirkpatrick, touting his endorsement from Maricopa County Sheriff Joe Arpaio, who has become well-known nationally for his aggressive pursuit of illegal immigrants in Arizona.

Kirkpatrick refused to follow many other Democrats in tight re-election contests who distanced themselves from the administration. Her ads highlighted her support for Obama's $787 billion economic stimulus bill "that prevented our economy from falling off a cliff." But she also talked about her independence, such as her vote against the Democratic cap-and-trade bill to curb industrial carbon emissions. She cast Gosar as an irresponsible millionaire who was late paying business and property taxes 12 times.

Kirkpatrick, who won the seat in 2008 after scandal-plagued Republican Rep. Rick Renzi resigned, maintained a significant cash advantage over Gosar. Going into the fall contest, she had $870,000 to spend, compared with his $49,000. But Gosar received help from the American Dental Association and other medical groups that oppose the health care law. He also was boosted by a prevailing trend of Republican expansion in suburban, high-growth areas in the district, and he got help from tea party activists. "Give me 10 tea party folks who really care and you can conquer mountains," he told a dental newsletter after the election. Gosar is one of two dentists in Congress; the other is Idaho Rep. Mike Simpson, also a Republican.

Before Kirkpatrick, the last Democrat to be elected from northern Arizona was Karan English, a moderate, in 1992. Two years later, after voting for President Clinton's budget and a ban on assault weapons, she lost to conservative Republican J.D. Hayworth.

SECOND DISTRICT

Trent Franks (R)

Elected 2002, 5th term; b. June 19, 1957, Uravan, CO; home, Pioria; Ottawa University, 1989-90; Baptist; married (Josie); 2 children.

Elected Office: AZ House of Reps., 1984-86.

Professional Career: Director, AZ Governor's Office for Children, 1987-88; Exec. director, AZ Family Research Institute, 1989-93; Writer-commentator, AZ radio station KTKP; Co-owner, Franks Brothers Independent Drilling; Pres.-CEO, Liberty Petroleum Corp.

DC Office: 2435 RHOB, 20515, 202-225-4576; Fax: 202-225-6328; Web site: franks.house.gov.

State Offices: Glendale, 623-776-7911.

Committees: *Armed Services:* Emerging Threats & Capabilities; Strategic Forces. *Judiciary:* Constitution (Chmn); Courts, Commercial & Administrative Law.

Group Ratings

	ACLU	ACU	ADA	CFG	AFS	FRC	LCV	ITIC	NTU	COC
2010	6	100	5	97	0	100	0	–	90	75
2009	–	100	0	97	0	–	0	–	94	73

National Journal Ratings

	2010 LIB	—	2010 CONS	2009 LIB	—	2009 CONS
Economic	0%	—	97%	0%	—	96%
Social	0%	—	85%	0%	—	93%
Foreign	0%	—	88%	0%	—	75%
Composite	5%	—	95%	6%	—	94%

Key Votes of the 111th Congress

1. Overturn Ledbetter	N	5. Bar federal abortion funds	Y
2. Pass $820 billion stimulus	N	6. Pass health care bill	N
3. Let guns in national parks	Y	7. Regulate financial firms	N
4. Pass cap-and-trade	N	8. Pass tax cuts for some	N

9. Stop detainee transfers	Y
10. Legalize immigrants' kids	N
11. Repeal don't ask, tell	N
12. Limit campaign funds	N

Election Results

2010 general	Trent Franks (R)	173,173	(65%)	($964,398)
	John Thrasher (D)	82,891	(31%)	($22,021)
	Powell Gammill (Lib)	10,820	(4%)	
2010 primary	Trent Franks (R)	81,252	(81%)	
	Charles Black (R)	19,220	(19%)	

Prior Winning Percentages: 2008 (59%), 2006 (59%), 2004 (59%), 2002 (60%)

Population		Race/Ethnicity		Work	
Pop. 2010:	972,839	White:	69.3%	Private:	77.7%
Change since 2000:	Up 51.7%	Black:	3.5%	Government:	15.5%
Urban:	89.0%	Hispanic:	20.8%	Self-employed:	6.7%
Rural:	11.0%	Asian:	2.5%	Blue collar:	20.6%
Area size:	20,387 sq. mi.	Native Am.:	1.7%	White collar:	60.4%
		Hawaiian:	0.2%	Khaki collar:	0.4%
Age		Two+ races:	1.9%	Other:	18.6%
Median age:	38.1 yrs.				
More than 65 yrs:	17.1%	*Ancestry*		Median income:	$53,298
Less than 18 yrs:	25.5%	German	15.1%	Median Home Value:	$217,700
		Irish	9.9%		
Education		English	8.8%	**Military Veterans**	
H.S. grad:	87.2%			% of Pop:	14.5%
College grad:	21.4%				
Grad degree:	7.0%				

Northwest Arizona; Phoenix suburbs

Beyond the cities of Phoenix and Tucson, much of Arizona looks as it did a century ago. Some is intentionally preserved in its natural state, such as the sere uplands of the Hopi Indian Reservation. Other places maintain a timeless Western look, like Wickenburg, the oldest Arizona town north of Tucson. Still others preserve antiquated ways of life, such as the polygamist community of Colorado City, just south of Utah. In some cases, nature and settlement juxtapose

2008 Presidential Vote		
John McCain (R) 220,667	(61%)
Barack Obama (D) 138,275	(38%)
2004 Presidential Vote		
George Bush (R) 182,326	(62%)
John Kerry (D) 112,620	(38%)
Cook Partisan Voting Index: R+13		

jarringly: The real London Bridge has been transplanted to Lake Havasu City, a retirement community on the Colorado River.

All of these areas are part of the 2nd Congressional District of Arizona, which stretches from the Hoover Dam and Lake Mead in the northwest corner of the state to the western suburbs of Phoenix, where 80% of its voters live. Astride Grand Avenue, the only diagonal street in the rigorous grid of metro Phoenix, is the mushrooming suburb of Glendale, not so long ago just a crossroads but now home to 253,000 people. The Phoenix Coyotes hockey stadium went up in Glendale in 2003, followed in 2006 by the University of Phoenix Stadium, where Super Bowl XLII was played in February 2008, and a new baseball facility where the Los Angeles Dodgers and Chicago White Sox set up spring training in 2009. The nearby Westgate City Center is now one of several edge cities in Phoenix's Valley of the Sun. Just west in the former desert are Peoria, as middle American as its namesake in Illinois, and the huge retirement community of Sun City, started in the 1950s. This had been a growth area, but the mid-2000s housing boom was followed by a bust. The resulting economic downturn seriously affected the area. The negative fallout for its tourism industry was made worse by angry boycotts in reaction to Arizona's controversial 2010 immigration law, the nation's strictest, which gave law enforcement added powers to detain suspected illegal immigrants.

The 2nd District also includes the corridor along the Interstate 10 Papago Freeway, taking in Luke Air Force Base, which has the largest fighter training wing in the Air Force and the only active duty F-16 training base in the United States. It extends to the once open spaces of Goodyear and Buckeye and Mohave County, with its growing Las Vegas suburbs, and the Hopi Indian Reservation, connected to the rest of the district by a narrow, oddly shaped corridor that runs along the bottom of the Grand Canyon.

This is Republican territory. The retirees here remember the culturally conservative, Ozzie-and-Harriet lifestyle of the 1950s, and the upwardly striving, family-oriented young migrants who have populated new towns in the desert are trying to replicate it. Culture, more than affluence, which by national standards is not all that striking here, accounts for their political conservatism. Republicans also dominate the new cities along the Colorado River.

Trent Franks (R)

The congressman from the 2nd District is Trent Franks, a Republican first elected in 2002. He grew up in Colorado, attended college briefly, and started his own oil-and-gas exploration business. His political career began when he won a single term in the Arizona House in 1984. There, he was known for wearing a tie tack in the shape of the feet of a fetus, as a constant reminder of his anti-abortion-rights views. In 1987, he was the director of the Governor's Office for Children under Evan Mecham, a conservative Republican who was later impeached. In 1989, he became executive director of the Arizona Family Research Institute, an organization associated with James Dobson's Focus on the Family, and he was a consultant to conservative Pat Buchanan's presidential campaign. Franks fought unsuccessfully for a 1992 ballot initiative to limit abortion rights. He designed the state's 1997 scholarship tax credit legislation, a much litigated measure that ultimately was upheld by the U.S. Supreme Court. The plan provides tax credits for donations to nonprofit organizations to help families pay for private education. In 1994, he ran for an open U.S. House seat but lost to John Shadegg in the Republican primary, 43%-30%.

In 2002, Republican Rep. Bob Stump announced he was retiring and endorsed Lisa Atkins, his chief of staff throughout his 26-year congressional career. When the campaign started, Franks was not in the top tier of candidates. But his base of Christian conservatives and abortion opponents, plus an infusion into his campaign of $300,000 of his own money, made him a contender. Franks spent heavily on radio ads, and he benefited from the distribution of a voter guide by the

Center for Arizona Policy, which described itself as "the only organization in Arizona actively fighting in the Legislature and media for conservative, traditional views on gambling, homosexuality, and pornography." Franks called for overturning the Supreme Court's *Roe v. Wade* decision legalizing abortion and for constitutional protection for fetuses. He endorsed a flat tax as a step toward eliminating the federal income tax, supported individual investment accounts in Social Security, and called for tougher enforcement of immigration laws. His base of activists made the difference. He finished first with 28% of the vote, only 797 votes ahead of Atkins, who got 26%. In November, he won 60%-37%.

In the House, Franks has accumulated one of the GOP's most conservative voting records while emerging as one of its fiercest rhetorical firebrands. He was among the first House Republicans to join the Tea Party Caucus in 2010. He introduced a bill in 2009 making it a crime for practitioners to perform abortions based on the sex or race of a child. And he wrote an anti-child pornography bill. In the 111th Congress (2009-10), he disappointed members of the Surprise City Council when he withdrew several submitted earmark requests in response to the House GOP's self-imposed earmark ban, including a $10 million project to build an interchange at a busy intersection. He proved his outsider stripes by announcing he had no interest in serving on the Appropriations Committee, which controls the government purse strings and is ground zero for earmarked spending. But he succumbed to pressure from Republican leaders and earned their gratitude in December 2003 by switching his vote to support the Medicare prescription drug bill during a tension-filled, three-hour roll-call vote. Many conservatives opposed the massive expansion of the program to pay for prescription drugs for senior citizens.

On the Armed Services Committee, Franks has strongly supported missile defense and he unsuccessfully sought in 2009 to amend the defense authorization bill to restore a proposed $1.2 billion cut in the program. After his appointment to a House GOP group on national security in April 2010, he said President Barack Obama "has enacted policies that embolden our enemies and alienate and endanger many of America's most cherished allies." From 2007 to 2009, he was the ranking Republican on the Constitution Subcommittee of Judiciary, where he worked to promote building a fence along the country's borders to stem illegal immigration. In 2009, Franks became the ranking Republican on the Commercial and Administrative Law Subcommittee of Judiciary. On a personal note, he has encouraged public awareness of facial deformity similar to the one he has battled. Franks has had multiple surgeries to correct a cleft palate.

In his first bid for re-election in 2004, Franks faced a competitive primary against Rick Murphy, a free-spending radio station owner, who hammered Franks for supporting the prescription drug bill. Murphy was endorsed by several local Republican officials who complained about their lack of contact with Franks. Murphy also attacked Franks for abandoning his promise not to take money from political action committees. Franks won 64%-36%. He narrowly lost Mohave County, but he took 68% in Maricopa, which cast 76% of the total vote. In November, Franks won 59%-39%.

Franks has won re-election easily in recent years. In the early maneuvering for the 2008 Republican presidential nomination, Franks backed Duncan Hunter of California, the top Republican on the Armed Services Committee, as "an unequivocal social conservative and fiscal conservative" over home-state favorite Sen. John McCain. In November 2008, he called newly elected Obama "the most dangerous president the country has ever had," and in September 2009, he castigated Obama as "an enemy of humanity" because of his support for abortion rights. Franks also angered African-Americans when he declared in 2010 that their population has been decimated more by abortions than by slavery.

THIRD DISTRICT

Ben Quayle (R)

Elected 2010, 1st term; b. Nov. 5, 1976, Fort Wayne, IN; home, Phoenix; Duke U., B.A. 1998; Vanderbilt U., J.D. 2002.; Protestant; Married (Tiffany).

Professional Career: Practicing atty., 2003-07; founder, Tynwald Capital.

DC Office: 1419 LHOB, 20515, 202-225-3361; Fax: 202-225-3462; Web site: quayle.house.gov.

State Offices: Phoenix, 602-263-5300.

Committees: *Homeland Security:* Border & Maritime Security (VChmn); Counterterrorism & Intelligence. *Judiciary:* Crime, Terrorism & Homeland Security; Intellectual Property, Competition & the Internet. *Science & Technology:* Research & Science Education; Technology & Innovation (Chmn).

Election Results

2010 general	Ben Quayle (R)	108,689	(52%)	($2,653,070)
	Jon Hulburd (D)	85,610	(41%)	($1,670,024)
	Michael Schoen (Lib)	10,478	(5%)	
2010 primary	Ben Quayle (R)	17,400	(22%)	
	Steve Moak (R)	14,211	(18%)	
	Jim Waring (R)	13,850	(18%)	
	Vernon Parker (R)	13,411	(17%)	
	Pamela Gorman (R)	6,473	(8%)	
	Paulina Morris (R)	6,138	(8%)	

Population		Race/Ethnicity		Work	
Pop. 2010:	707,919	White:	70.7%	Private:	83.3%
Change since 2000:	Up 10.4%	Black:	3.1%	Government:	10.3%
Urban:	96.5%	Hispanic:	19.3%	Self-employed:	6.4%
Rural:	3.5%	Asian:	3.4%	Blue collar:	16.3%
Area size:	599 sq. mi.	Native Am.:	1.3%	White collar:	66.5%
		Hawaiian:	0.1%	Khaki collar:	0.0%
Age		Two+ races:	1.9%	Other:	17.1%
Median age:	35.9 yrs.				
More than 65 yrs:	10.7%	*Ancestry*		Median income:	$57,261
Less than 18 yrs:	24.8%	German	14.9%	Median Home Value:	$279,500
		Irish	10.5%		
Education		English	8.3%	**Military Veterans**	
H.S. grad:	87.6%			% of Pop:	9.7%
College grad:	32.4%				
Grad degree:	11.7%				

North Phoenix; Paradise Valley

In May 1998, conservative trailblazer Barry Goldwater died at his home in the Phoenix suburb of Paradise Valley. His life had spanned almost the whole history of Arizona. He was born on New Year's Day 1909, when Arizona was still a territory, and he could remember when it was the "baby state," with fewer people than any state except Delaware, Wyoming, and Nevada. When he returned from service in World War II, Paradise Valley was still undeveloped, and

Phoenix—founded after the Civil War as a hay market for cavalry horses at Fort McDowell—was not much more than a tiny outpost of American civilization, a metropolitan area of fewer than 300,000 in a sizzling desert. By 2010, Arizona had 6.4 million people, with more than 4 million in metropolitan Phoenix. The city had been transformed from a frontier outpost to a diversified high-tech center, an example of how creativity and ingenuity can build a sophisticated city even in the most unwelcoming desert environs. In recent years, the city has tried with some success to market its most abundant natural resource, the sun. A $6 million plant making rooftop solar-power systems was expected to begin production in 2011, bringing with it 350 new jobs.

Like Los Angeles and San Francisco, Phoenix is dotted with mountains that rise grandly from the plains and are preserved as undeveloped parkland. Some, such as Shaw Butte, contain archaeological evidence that Indians used them as a base for sophisticated astronomical observations. From Camelback Mountain, 1,800 feet above Phoenix and Paradise Valley, one can get with equal awe a sense of what the land was originally like and an understanding of how impressively Phoenix has grown. East of Camelback, subdivisions were often built with grass and greenery. In the affluent areas north of Camelback and spreading out along Scottsdale Road and the Black Canyon Freeway, the natural desert look is more common. The planned community of Anthem, 35 miles north of downtown and established in 1998, already has about 40,000 residents. Grass is discouraged and often banned by subdivision covenant; planting anything but desert flora is frowned upon. The architecture of the houses tends toward unadorned stucco with picture windows facing away from the sun. The idea is to suggest that there is a horse corral over in the next lot, and sometimes, especially in the northern edges of Phoenix, there is.

The 3rd Congressional District of Arizona includes the northern part of Phoenix plus Paradise Valley, bounded on the south by a zigzag line that approximates the Arizona Canal. The 3rd also includes the communities of New River, Cave Creek, and Carefree, so named in 1955 by developers who hoped to lure snowbird retirees. Here the stores are more likely to feature horse feed than designer clothes, but that is changing fast as metro Phoenix moves inexorably north, bringing with it more-upscale malls. This is an affluent, and largely Republican, district.

Ben Quayle (R)

The new congressman from the 3rd District is Republican Ben Quayle, the son of former Vice President Dan Quayle, who prevailed in a tough 2010 contest for the seat of retiring GOP Rep. John Shadegg. Quayle was born days after his father was first elected to the House in 1976. He grew up in Washington with Secret Service protection and attended Gonzaga College High School, a Catholic boys school. He has said that his politics are similar to his father's, but he told *The New York Times* in March that he was "even more free-market" than the elder Quayle. He graduated from Duke University in 1998 with a bachelor's degree in history and a minor in political science and went on to earn a law degree from Vanderbilt in 2002. Quayle moved to California, where he joined a law firm, focusing primarily on commercial litigation. He then went back east to New York City to pursue his interest in corporate law, where he focused on securities, and mergers and acquisitions. In 2006, he took a job at a law firm in Arizona, and in 2007, he and his brother, Tucker Quayle, started an investment company, where he is now a managing partner.

Having lived in the state full time for just the past four years, Quayle sought to avoid the "carpetbagger" label in his bid for the House seat. Dan Quayle used his political connections to help his son raise substantial amounts of money. Nearly $900,000, or almost half, of Quayle's campaign donations came from outside Arizona. Former President George H.W. Bush hosted a fundraiser at his Houston home, and donors included former Defense Secretaries William Cohen and Donald Rumsfeld. Former President George W. Bush and Laura Bush also donated $1,000.

Like his father, the younger Quayle weathered his share of controversy. He was attacked during the Republican primary for distributing campaign literature with a picture of him with two young girls, depicting him as a family man; many believed that the girls were his daughters. In fact, Quayle and his wife are childless, and after his campaign initially said that the girls were the children of a campaign staffer, it came to light they are Quayle's nieces. Opponents also accused him of making offensive comments on a racy nightlife website, *DirtyScottsdale.com*. The site's owner said that Quayle posted lewd comments under the pseudonym "Brock Landers," a reference to a fictional porn star in the 1997 film *Boogie Nights*. Quayle denied using the pseudonym and at first also denied any connection with the site; later he acknowledged that he had done some writing for it. He sought to divert attention from the negative publicity with an ad in which he called President Obama "the worst president in history." He managed to emerge from a 10-person August GOP primary with nearly 22% of the vote. He got 17,400 votes, more than his two closest challengers, businessman Steve Moak, who got 14,211 (18%), and former state Sen. Jim Waring, who got 13,850 (17%).

In the general election, Quayle's Democratic opponent was businessman and lawyer Jon Hulburd, who liked to remind voters about the *DirtyScottsdale.com* charges. He asserted that Quayle lacked the maturity and experience for the job, and also questioned Quayle's contention that it will be possible to repeal the Democrats' health care law. Quayle, in spite of his family connections and formative years in Washington, cast himself as a political outsider who would fight Obama and the Democrats in control of Congress.

The makeup of the wealthy, conservative district gave Quayle an edge. He won with 52% of the vote to Hulburd's 41%; a Libertarian candidate received 5%.

FOURTH DISTRICT

Ed Pastor (D)

Elected Sept. 1991, 10th full term; b. June 28, 1943, Claypool; home, Phoenix; AZ St. U., B.A. 1966, J.D. 1974; Catholic; married (Verma); 2 children.

Elected Office: Maricopa Cnty. Bd. of Supervisors, 1976–91.

Professional Career: High schl. teacher, 1966–69; Asst., AZ Gov. Castro, 1975.

DC Office: 2465 RHOB, 20515, 202-225-4065; Fax: 202-225-1655; Web site: www.pastor.house.gov.

State Offices: Phoenix, 602-256-0551.

Committees: *Appropriations:* Energy & Water Development; Financial Services & General Government; Transportation, HUD & Related Agencies.

Group Ratings

	ACLU	ACU	ADA	CFG	AFS	FRC	LCV	ITIC	NTU	COC
2010	94	0	85	5	100	0	100	100	10	14
2009	–	0	100	0	100	–	100	–	2	33

National Journal Ratings

	2010 LIB	—	2010 CONS	2009 LIB	—	2009 CONS
Economic	63%	—	37%	71%	—	28%
Social	67%	—	31%	75%	—	20%
Foreign	78%	—	17%	87%	—	9%
Composite	71%	—	30%	79%	—	21%

Key Votes of the 111th Congress

1. Overturn Ledbetter	Y	5. Bar federal abortion funds	N	9. Stop detainee transfers	N
2. Pass $820 billion stimulus	Y	6. Pass health care bill	Y	10. Legalize immigrants' kids	Y
3. Let guns in national parks	N	7. Regulate financial firms	Y	11. Repeal don't ask, tell	Y
4. Pass cap-and-trade	Y	8. Pass tax cuts for some	Y	12. Limit campaign funds	Y

Election Results

2010 general	Ed Pastor (D)	61,524	(67%)	($1,014,291)
	Janet Contreras (R)	25,300	(28%)	($82,896)
	Joe Cobb (Lib)	2,718	(3%)	
	Rebecca DeWitt (Green)	2,365	(3%)	
2010 primary	Ed Pastor (D)	unopposed		

Prior Winning Percentages: 2008 (72%), 2006 (73%), 2004 (70%), 2002 (67%), 2000 (69%), 1998 (68%), 1996 (65%), 1994 (62%), 1992 (66%), 1991 (56%)

Population		Race/Ethnicity		Work	
Pop. 2010:	698,314	White:	21.5%	Private:	82.7%
Change since 2000:	Up 8.9%	Black:	8.6%	Government:	10.6%
Urban:	99.5%	Hispanic:	63.9%	Self-employed:	6.5%
Rural:	0.5%	Asian:	2.2%	Blue collar:	34.9%
Area size:	199 sq. mi.	Native Am.:	2.1%	White collar:	42.3%
		Hawaiian:	0.1%	Khaki collar:	0.1%
Age		Two+ races:	1.4%	Other:	22.7%
Median age:	28.0 yrs.				
More than 65 yrs:	5.4%	*Ancestry*		Median income:	$37,257
Less than 18 yrs:	33.6%	German	4.9%	Median Home Value:	$173,900
		Irish	3.9%		
Education		English	2.8%	**Military Veterans**	
H.S. grad:	63.6%			% of Pop:	5.9%
College grad:	12.0%				
Grad degree:	4.2%				

Downtown Phoenix

Phoenix is a relatively new American metropolis; it's grown to big-city size just in the past generation. Yet it is also an ancient city, or built on top of one. The Arizona Canal, several miles north of downtown Phoenix, runs along the route of a canal built about 600 years ago by the Hohokam aboriginal people. They distributed irrigated water diverted from the Salt River in its wet moments to farmers in what today is called the Valley of the Sun, and they made sophisti-

2008 Presidential Vote		
Barack Obama (D) 86,815	(65%)
John McCain (R) 43,610	(33%)
2004 Presidential Vote		
John Kerry (D) 71,805	(62%)
George Bush (R) 43,967	(38%)
Cook Partisan Voting Index: D+13		

cated astronomical observations from the mountains that jut up from the plains. This society disappeared for reasons unknown less than half a century before the Spaniards arrived in North America. So today's Phoenix is the second civilization to prosper in this desert region. Maricopa County had 331,000 people in 1950 and nearly 4 million by 2010. Half a century ago, Phoenix spread six miles north, west, and east of the downtown and only a few miles south. Downtown was its only office district and its main shopping area, and people blew fans over boxes of ice to cool off. Today, the view from downtown Phoenix's office towers stretches as far as the eye can see, toward groupings of other office towers to the north, northeast, and northwest.

The 4th Congressional District of Arizona is centered in downtown Phoenix and is based entirely in Maricopa County. It covers the Capitol, in a rundown neighborhood a couple of miles to the west, and busy Sky Harbor International Airport, situated in an industrial corridor several miles east. It includes most of southern Phoenix, and its boundaries follow approximately the southern and western city limits. It extends as far north as Bethany Home Road and Northern Avenue. It stretches south into Guadalupe and northwest into Glendale. Geographically, it covers most of the land between South Mountain and Camelback Mountain. The area was hit extremely hard by the economic downturn in recent years. A 2009 Brookings Institution study rated its economy among the weakest of any of the nation's large metropolitan areas, thanks in part to a plunge in housing prices of more than 40% in three years. The district is one of Arizona's two Hispanic districts; its population by 2010 was 64% Hispanic. Most are Mexican, but there has been an influx of Guatemalans. Politically, this is a solidly Democratic district, the most Democratic in Arizona.

Ed Pastor (D)

The congressman from the 4th District is Ed Pastor, a Democrat who won a 1991 special election to succeed Morris (Mo) Udall, the revered, 14-term liberal who championed environmental causes. (At the time, the district's boundaries were different.) Pastor grew up in Claypool, a mining town in Gila County. The oldest of Enrique and Margarita Pastor's three children, he was the first in his family to graduate from college. He got a bachelor's degree in chemistry from Arizona State University in 1966, and later earned a law degree at ASU. Pastor taught chemistry at North High School and then was the deputy director of a non-profit community organization called the Guadalupe Organization. He was an assistant to Democratic Gov. Raul Castro, the first Hispanic governor of Arizona, in 1975. He was elected in 1976 to the Maricopa County Board of Supervisors, where he served until his election to Congress. In 1991, he defeated Republican Pat Connor, 56%-44%. He has not faced serious competition since.

Pastor has been a faithful follower of the Democratic leadership and has a mostly liberal voting record. He supported the North American Free Trade Agreement of 1993 despite strong labor opposition, but he opposed normal trade relations with China and the free-trade agreement with Central America. He vigorously opposed Arizona's English Only law and in 2010 joined fellow Arizona Democrat Raul Grijalva in imploring President Barack Obama to stop Arizona's stringent immigration law from taking effect. Pastor called the law, which expanded law enforcement powers to detain suspect illegal immigrants, "a severe setback to civil rights in America." He has sponsored legislation to provide amnesty to immigrants who were in the United States prior to January 2000. After a 2002 trip to Cuba, where he met with President Fidel Castro for three hours, Pastor urged the immediate end of the U.S. trade embargo with that country. Pastor serves in the Democratic leadership as a chief deputy whip, and is also active in the Hispanic Caucus.

Much of Pastor's work has been on the Appropriations Committee, where he has often earmarked funds for local projects. He has evolved into the "go-to guy" for federal funds for Arizona because he is the only House or Senate appropriator from the state, and because most influential fellow Arizonans, like GOP Sen. John McCain and Republican Rep. Jeff Flake, ideologically oppose earmarks. When money is needed, said a Maricopa County supervisor, "you go to Ed." In early 2009, Pastor took temporary control of the chairmanship of the Subcommittee on Energy and Water after Chairman Peter Visclosky of Indiana stepped aside for the duration of a grand jury probe into possible corruption in the appropriations process. The arrangement put Pastor at the helm of a $30 billion energy and water projects bill that year. Pastor supports alternative energy but also has noted that because coal and nuclear power will fulfill most of the nation's energy needs for at least the near future, those two sources must be made more efficient.

FIFTH DISTRICT

David Schweikert (R)

Elected 2010, 1st term; b. March 3, 1962, Los Angeles, CA; home, Fountain Hills; AZ St. U., B.A. 1986, M.B.A. 2005.; Catholic; Married (Joyce).

Elected Office: AZ House, 1989-94; treasurer, Maricopa Cnty., 2004-07.

Professional Career: Owner, Sheridan Equities and Sheridan Equities Holdings.

DC Office: 1205 LHOB, 20515, 202-225-2190; Fax: 202-225-0096; Web site: schweikert.house.gov.

State Offices: Scottsdale, 480-946-2411.

Committees: *Financial Services:* Capital Markets and Government Sponsored Enterprises (VChmn); Domestic Monetary Policy & Technology.

Election Results

2010 general	David Schweikert (R)	110,374	(52%)	($1,732,731)
	Harry Mitchell (D)	91,749	(43%)	($2,174,509)
	Nick Coons (Lib)	10,127	(5%)	
2010 primary	David Schweikert (R)	26,678	(37%)	
	Jim Ward (R)	18,480	(26%)	
	Susan Bitter Smith (R)	17,297	(24%)	
	Chris Salvino (R)	7,156	(10%)	

Population		Race/Ethnicity		Work	
Pop. 2010:	656,833	White:	70.3%	Private:	82.6%
Change since 2000:	Up 2.4%	Black:	3.8%	Government:	11.6%
Urban:	97.2%	Hispanic:	16.5%	Self-employed:	5.7%
Rural:	2.8%	Asian:	4.4%	Blue collar:	13.0%
Area size:	1,421 sq. mi.	Native Am.:	2.5%	White collar:	70.4%
		Hawaiian:	0.2%	Khaki collar:	0.1%
Age		Two+ races:	2.1%	Other:	16.5%
Median age:	35.9 yrs.				
More than 65 yrs:	11.8%	*Ancestry*		Median income:	$62,067
Less than 18 yrs:	21.3%	German	14.2%	Median Home Value:	$327,400
		Irish	10.0%		
Education		English	9.1%	**Military Veterans**	
H.S. grad:	91.7%			% of Pop:	9.1%
College grad:	42.5%				
Grad degree:	15.8%				

Phoenix suburbs; Scottsdale, Tempe

As metropolitan Phoenix has expanded in the Valley of the Sun, it has absorbed the crossroads towns that were separate and distinct 50 years ago. Two such towns are Tempe and Scottsdale. Tempe is east of downtown Phoenix, south of the Arizona Canal. It was founded in 1871 as Hayden's Ferry, by the father of the future Democratic Sen. Carl Hayden (1927-1969), and was renamed in 1879 for an ancient Greek vale. The old town centered on Arizona State University, and both the town and the university have ex-

2008 Presidential Vote

John McCain (R)	153,736	(51%)
Barack Obama (D)	140,287	(47%)

2004 Presidential Vote

George Bush (R)	152,576	(54%)
John Kerry (D)	127,811	(45%)

Cook Partisan Voting Index: R+5

panded greatly. The university sits astride a rise with a fine view of much of metropolitan Phoenix. Tempe is relatively affluent and still growing, with 178,500 people in 2009, up from 142,000 in 1990. It has eight stations along Phoenix's 20-mile light-rail system and new high-rises in its downtown.

Scottsdale is east of the affluent part of Phoenix and north of Tempe and the Salt River Indian Reservation; it encompasses Frank Lloyd Wright's Taliesin West, which was beyond the reach of electricity and telephone lines when it was built in the 1940s. Scottsdale, which grew in population from 130,000 in 1990 to 238,000 in 2009, features luxury shopping malls and resorts, lots of nightlife, the Buffalo Bill Historical Center, and the WestWorld equestrian center. Local politicians argue over whether Scottsdale should keep marketing itself as a Western town or emphasize its new live-work downtown. It also likes to tout its importance in the Cactus League of warm-weather cities that host spring training camps for Major League Baseball. Scottsdale is the winter home of the San Francisco Giants; the Chicago Cubs work out in nearby Mesa; and the Texas Rangers train in Surprise.

The 5th Congressional District of Arizona includes Tempe, Scottsdale, and the northeast corner of Maricopa County—Fountain Hills, the Salt River and Fort McDowell Indian Reservations, and part of the Tonto National Forest. Politically, this has been a Republican district, though less so than a dozen years ago. The 5th has the highest percentage of college graduates and high-income households of any district in Arizona, and some affluent people here, like those on both coasts, have been attracted to the Democrats by their stands on cultural issues. This was the only Arizona district to vote for Barack Obama over Hillary Rodham Clinton in the Democratic presidential primary.

David Schweikert (R)

The new congressman from the 5th District is Republican David Schweikert, who defeated two-term Democratic Rep. Harry Mitchell in 2010.

Schweikert was born in a Catholic home for unwed mothers in downtown Los Angeles; he was adopted and raised by a family in Arizona. As a young man in Scottsdale, he was involved in sports and joined a club for Republican teens. He credits his early affinity for politics to former President Ronald Reagan. "We had a president [Jimmy Carter], who would go on television wearing a sweater and demanding that we adjust our thermostats because we were living in a world of shortages," Schweikert recalled. Along came Reagan, who galvanized a "wave of young people," he said. As an undergraduate at Arizona State University, Schweikert focused on finance and real estate. "I have spent almost all my life within a 20-mile radius," he said. But he was "fiercely independent," refusing to accept his parents' help to finance his education. He acquired a real estate license at the age of 18 and worked full-time while taking classes at night. He graduated in six years. "There was never a time I wasn't working six days a week," Schweikert said.

He ventured into the political arena at age 26, when he lost a bid to represent the Scottsdale area in the Arizona House. Two years later, he was elected to an open seat, and at the end of his freshman term, he became majority whip. He was 30 and one of the youngest whips in state history, yet his greatest legislative allies were party elders. "Oddly enough, the oldest members were often the greatest to work with because they were less concerned about their personal ambitions. ...If you were the hyperenergetic young guy, you were their best friend," Schweikert said. He worked to pass legislation that laid the foundation for tax cuts, tort reform, and charter schools, as well as a bill shortening the legislative session from 170 to 98 days. In the course of his public service, Schweikert returned to ASU to get a master's degree in business administration. He was persuaded by Doug Todd, the outgoing treasurer of Maricopa County, to run as his successor; Schweikert did and won. In that role from 2004 to 2007, he managed a $4 billion budget, created a program to help low-income seniors pay their property taxes, and corrected thousands of deed errors.

In 2008, Schweikert was the Republican nominee to challenge Mitchell, who had dethroned six-term GOP Rep. J.D. Hayworth two years earlier. Schweikert lost by 9 points in an inhospitable year for Republicans. Two years later, Democrats could not catch a break from a disillusioned, recession-weary electorate, and Schweikert's rematch with Mitchell told the larger tale of Election 2010: It featured an incumbent under fire for supporting the Obama administration agenda and a conservative challenger touting his outsider credentials.

The economy was the main issue in the Tempe-based district, and Schweikert made Mitchell's vote for President Obama's $787 billion economic-stimulus bill a central point in his campaign. His campaign signs called Mitchell a "lap dog" for liberal House Speaker Nancy Pelosi, and among what Schweikert calls Mitchell's "list of sins" were his votes in favor of the financial-industry rescue in 2008 and Obama's health care overhaul. Mitchell countered that he had been among the Democrats most likely to buck his party, emphasizing his support for extending the Bush-era tax cuts and his opposition to the Democrats' bill to impose limits on carbon emissions. The incumbent had the money edge. Mitchell raised $1.4 million, and Schweikert raised just under half that amount, according to the campaign finance reports in late fall. Schweikert won over Mitchell, 52% to 43%. A Libertarian candidate got 5%.

SIXTH DISTRICT

Jeff Flake (R)

Elected 2000, 6th term; b. Dec. 31, 1962, Snowflake; home, Mesa; Brigham Young U., B.A. 1986, M.A. 1987; Mormon; married (Cheryl); 5 children.

Professional Career: Pub. plcy. exec., Shipley, Smoak & Henry, 1987-89; Exec. dir., Fndt. for Democracy (Namibia), 1989-90; Owner, Interface Pub. Affairs, 1990-92; Exec. dir., The Goldwater Inst., 1992-99.

DC Office: 240 CHOB, 20515, 202-225-2635; Fax: 202-226-4386; Web site: flake.house.gov.

State Offices: Mesa, 480-833-0092.

Committees: *Appropriations:* Interior, Environment & Related Agencies; Labor, HHS, Education & Related Agencies; Military Construction, Veterans Affairs & Related Agencies.

Group Ratings

	ACLU	ACU	ADA	CFG	AFS	FRC	LCV	ITIC	NTU	COC
2010	20	96	10	100	0	100	0	0	97	75
2009	–	100	0	100	0	–	0	–	99	71

National Journal Ratings

	2010 LIB	—	2010 CONS	2009 LIB	—	2009 CONS
Economic	3%	—	97%	0%	—	96%
Social	18%	—	77%	13%	—	84%
Foreign	26%	—	72%	40%	—	60%
Composite	17%	—	83%	19%	—	81%

Key Votes of the 111th Congress

1. Overturn Ledbetter	N	5. Bar federal abortion funds	Y	9. Stop detainee transfers	Y
2. Pass $820 billion stimulus	N	6. Pass health care bill	N	10. Legalize immigrants' kids	N
3. Let guns in national parks	Y	7. Regulate financial firms	N	11. Repeal don't ask, tell	Y
4. Pass cap-and-trade	*	8. Pass tax cuts for some	N	12. Limit campaign funds	N

Election Results

2010 general	Jeff Flake (R)	165,649	(66%)	($538,758)
	Rebecca Schneider (D)	72,615	(29%)	
	Darell Tapp (Lib)	7,712	(3%)	
2010 primary	Jeff Flake (R)	62,285	(65%)	
	Jeff Smith (R)	34,137	(35%)	

Prior Winning Percentages: 2008 (62%), 2006 (75%), 2004 (79%), 2002 (66%), 2000 (54%)

Population		Race/Ethnicity		Work	
Pop. 2010:	971,733	White:	69.3%	Private:	82.7%
Change since 2000:	Up 51.5%	Black:	3.1%	Government:	11.7%
Urban:	96.8%	Hispanic:	20.7%	Self-employed:	5.5%
Rural:	3.2%	Asian:	3.6%	Blue collar:	18.5%
Area size:	724 sq. mi.	Native Am.:	1.0%	White collar:	64.5%
		Hawaiian:	0.2%	Khaki collar:	0.1%
Age		Two+ races:	2.0%	Other:	16.9%
Median age:	34.4 yrs.				
More than 65 yrs:	13.1%	*Ancestry*		Median income:	$60,000
Less than 18 yrs:	28.3%	German	15.6%	Median Home Value:	$236,200
		English	10.4%		
Education		Irish	9.6%	**Military Veterans**	
H.S. grad:	88.9%			% of Pop:	11.7%
College grad:	27.6%				
Grad degree:	9.2%				

Southeast Phoenix suburbs; Mesa

The city of Phoenix is exceedingly young. Conservative trailblazer Barry Goldwater, born in 1909, grew up knowing people who remembered when the Valley of the Sun—or the Valley, as most people say—was virtually empty, with a few parched settlements set above the dry riverbed. As late as 1950, only 106,000 people lived in Phoenix and 331,000 in all of Maricopa County. But the air conditioner and military technology transformed Phoenix from a sleepy

2008 Presidential Vote		
John McCain (R)	220,718	(61%)
Barack Obama (D)	135,178	(37%)
2004 Presidential Vote		
George Bush (R)	188,372	(64%)
John Kerry (D)	102,902	(35%)
Cook Partisan Voting Index:	R+15	

whistle-stop to today's high-rise-studded metropolis, with 1.5 million city dwellers and nearly 4 million people in Maricopa County. From 2000 to 2009, Maricopa's population grew by 31%. This is not, as some people think, a giant retirement village, nor is it overrun by crooked land salesmen and fast-buck artists, though Phoenix has attracted its share of each.

The second-largest city in Maricopa County is Mesa, south of the Salt River and east of Phoenix. It was founded by Mormons in 1878 on a square mile, and was laid out Salt Lake City-style on broad streets with large lots. A gleaming white Mormon temple was built in 1927, one of the few in the United States then. In 1950, Mesa had 17,000 people, enough to make it Arizona's third-largest city. In 2008, it had 463,000 people, more than Minneapolis and Pittsburgh. Mesa has been making plans to grow even more. A former Air Force base is now Phoenix-Mesa Gateway Airport, with plans for it to become a major multimodal center for passengers and freight. In 2005, developers won approval to build the giant Mesa Riverview shopping center after voters agreed to offer them rebates. By mid-2010, the center had contributed around $6.8 million to the city, less than projected because of the economic downturn. In November of that year, Mesa voters passed a ballot measure agreeing to spend up to $84 million to help build a new stadium for the Chicago Cubs, which do their spring training in Mesa.

The 6th Congressional District of Arizona is made up of the southeast suburbs of Phoenix, with distinct incorporated towns like Mesa, Chandler, Gilbert, and Queen Creek. It crosses the Pinal County line and includes fast-growing Apache Junction, Gold Camp, and Sun Lakes. For years, growth has been constant here: In 2007, Chandler and Gilbert had populations of 246,000 and 208,000, respectively. But with the collapse of the local housing market and the departure of many Latinos after Arizona adopted tough enforcement policies on illegal immigrants, growth is slowing considerably. The 6th includes some high-income precincts, and Asians lead whites in income in Chandler and Gilbert. But the district's cultural tone is resolutely middle class. By most measures, it is the most Republican district in Arizona.

Jeff Flake (R)

The congressman from the 6th District is Jeff Flake, a Republican first elected in 2000 and known in his party as a maverick. A fifth-generation Arizonan, he is a Mormon who was born and raised on a ranch in Snowflake, a town named after his great-great-grandfather. The fifth of 11 children, Flake graduated with a degree in international studies from Brigham Young University and did missionary work in South Africa and Zimbabwe. In 1989, he moved to Namibia to become executive director of the Foundation for Democracy, which monitored democratic progress in that country. After Namibia gained independence in 1990, Flake returned to Arizona and became executive director of the Goldwater Institute, where he led the fight for Arizona's charter school law. In 2000, when conservative Republican Matt Salmon kept his pledge to serve only three terms in Congress, he handpicked Flake to succeed him. Flake faced four opponents in a hard-fought September primary, in which he ran as the most conservative candidate. He had the support of several prominent Republican state leaders and was bolstered by more than $200,000 from the anti-tax organization Club for Growth. Flake won with 32% to 24% for Phoenix Councilman Sal DiCiccio. In the general election, Flake won 54%-42% over Democrat David Mendoza, a longtime lobbyist for public employees.

Flake promised to serve no more than three terms and to "continue to rock the boat" as Salmon had as a principled conservative who bucked the Republican leadership. In his first year in the House, as Congress debated the first round of President George W. Bush's tax cuts, Flake said that it would be a mistake for the Republican president to limit his proposed tax cut to the "easy things," such as repeal of the marriage penalty, and estate and gift taxes. He called for replacing the income tax with a national sales tax, a proposal that never got off the ground. In 2009, as the House debated a bill to limit greenhouse gases by forcing polluting companies to trade emissions allowances among themselves, Flake went even further, introducing a bill to tax carbon while reducing payroll taxes by a corresponding amount.

Flake has a habit of taking lonely stands. He was one of two members who voted against a bill to punish Sudan for its human rights abuses. Flake said he had seen in Africa the adverse impact of economic sanctions on poor nations. He was one of 33 Republicans who voted against final passage of Bush's No Child Left Behind education bill in 2001, and one of 25 Republicans who opposed the GOP's Medicare prescription drug bill in 2003. In 2010, he was one of only three Republicans to oppose a bill overhauling the Pentagon's method of buying goods and services by expanding authority for its acquisition workforce. And he has not confined his iconoclasm to voting: In 2009 he spent a week alone on a tiny deserted island in the Pacific with just a few supplies. "I've always wondered if I could do that, if I could really survive for a while on my own with the bare essentials," he told NBC News afterward.

For many years, Flake's loneliest stand was his battle against congressional earmarks, the special spending provisions slipped into bills by lawmakers to benefit their individual districts or states. Earmarking is extremely popular among lawmakers as a way of scoring points with voters. From the beginning of his service in the House, Flake vowed never to ask members of the Appropriations Committee for earmarks. He has sponsored numerous amendments to delete them from bills, and in 2004, he began naming an "Egregious Earmark of the Week." Almost all of his amendments have been overwhelmingly defeated. But with public distrust of Congress reaching new heights in 2010, Flake's colleagues started to heed his concerns. In March 2010, Democratic leaders announced a one-year moratorium on earmarking, followed by the House Republicans' adoption of Flake's proposal to disallow all earmark requests for the coming fiscal year.

Immigration is a big issue in Arizona, which shares a border with Mexico, and Flake has joined with Republican Sen. John McCain of Arizona in backing comprehensive bills with legalization and guest worker programs as well as enforcement provisions. He warned that Republicans faced negative political consequences from Latino voters if they failed to go beyond simply punishing illegal immigrants. In 2007, he and Illinois Rep. Luis Gutierrez, a liberal Democrat, introduced a bill requiring illegal immigrants to pay fines and back taxes and return to their countries before being granted legal status. With Democrats in the majority, Flake said "the planets were aligned" for the legislation, but it failed to pass the Senate, and the House leadership never brought it to the floor for a vote. After Arizona state lawmakers enacted the nation's toughest immigration law in 2010, Flake criticized the Obama administration for filing suit to block it. Another important issue for Flake is his effort to get Congress to lift restrictions on travel by U.S. citizens to Cuba.

Flake has paid a price for his independence. In January 2007, the Republican leadership took away his seat on the Judiciary Committee, though six other members had less seniority than he did. In January 2008, after Republican Rep. Roger Wicker of Mississippi was appointed to the Senate and resigned from the House, Flake sought his seat on Appropriations—ground zero for earmarks. The seat went instead to Alabama Republican Jo Bonner, an energetic practitioner of earmarking. In November 2008, Flake once again sought a seat on Appropriations but seemed to realize that his chances were nil. So that month, he called for the replacement of the Republican leadership.

Flake gave some thought to challenging McCain in the 2004 Senate primary but decided against it. Instead he faced a serious primary challenge himself. Former state Sen. Stan Barnes called Flake "fringe, libertarian, and just a bit kooky," and attacked him for his stance on immigration. Flake won 59%-41%. But he had no Democratic opponent in November. Just days after the election, he announced that he would abandon his term limit pledge. "As much as I hate to admit making a mistake, I made a big one here," he said, repeating a theme often invoked by lawmakers who find they like being in Washington more than they thought they would.

In 2006, Flake had no opposition in the primary and no Democratic opponent in the general election. Unlike some Arizona Republicans, he supported McCain for president early on, and campaigned for him in New Hampshire, an early primary state, when McCain's chances appeared slight. In 2008, Flake had a Democratic opponent, but won 62%-35%. He now appears comfortably ensconced in his district.

SEVENTH DISTRICT

Raúl Grijalva (D)

Elected 2002, 5th term; b. Feb. 19, 1948, Tucson; home, Tucson; U. of AZ, B.A. 1985; Catholic; married (Ramona); 3 children.

Elected Office: Tucson Unified Schl. Dist. Governing Bd., 1974-86; Pima Cnty. Bd. of Supervisors, 1988-2002.

Professional Career: Asst. dean of Hisp. Affairs, U. of AZ., 1987.

DC Office: 1511 LHOB, 20515, 202-225-2435; Fax: 202-225-1541; Web site: grijalva.house.gov.

State Offices: Tucson, 520-622-6788; Yuma, 928-343-7933.

Committees: *Education & the Workforce:* Early Childhood, Elementary & Secondary Education; Higher Education & Workforce Training. *Natural Resources:* National Parks, Forests & Public Lands (RMM); Water & Power.

Group Ratings

	ACLU	ACU	ADA	CFG	AFS	FRC	LCV	ITIC	NTU	COC
2010	94	0	90	0	100	0	80	67	7	13
2009	–	0	100	0	100	–	100	–	3	33

National Journal Ratings

	2010 LIB — 2010 CONS		2009 LIB — 2009 CONS	
Economic	77%	— 23%	73%	— 27%
Social	89%	— 7%	89%	— 0%
Foreign	66%	— 29%	78%	— 17%
Composite	79%	— 21%	83%	— 17%

Key Votes of the 111th Congress

1. Overturn Ledbetter	Y	5. Bar federal abortion funds	N	9. Stop detainee transfers	N
2. Pass $820 billion stimulus	Y	6. Pass health care bill	Y	10. Legalize immigrants' kids	Y
3. Let guns in national parks	N	7. Regulate financial firms	Y	11. Repeal don't ask, tell	Y
4. Pass cap-and-trade	Y	8. Pass tax cuts for some	Y	12. Limit campaign funds	Y

Election Results

2010 general	Raúl Grijalva (D)	79,935	(50%)	($1,470,861)
	Ruth McClung (R)	70,385	(44%)	($744,066)
	Harley Meyer (I)	4,506	(3%)	
	George Keane (Lib)	4,318	(3%)	
2010 primary	Raúl Grijalva (D)	unopposed		

Prior Winning Percentages: 2008 (63%), 2006 (61%), 2004 (62%), 2002 (59%)

Population		Race/Ethnicity		Work	
Pop. 2010:	855,769	White:	32.6%	Private:	74.1%
Change since 2000:	Up 33.4%	Black:	3.7%	Government:	19.7%
Urban:	83.6%	Hispanic:	56.0%	Self-employed:	6.1%
Rural:	16.4%	Asian:	1.8%	Blue collar:	25.2%
Area size:	22,890 sq. mi.	Native Am.:	4.3%	White collar:	50.7%
		Hawaiian:	0.1%	Khaki collar:	0.5%
Age		Two+ races:	1.5%	Other:	23.6%
Median age:	31.3 yrs.				
More than 65 yrs:	11.4%	*Ancestry*		Median income:	$39,534
Less than 18 yrs:	29.7%	German	8.4%	Median Home Value:	$156,300
		Irish	5.8%		
Education		English	5.0%	**Military Veterans**	
H.S. grad:	73.6%			% of Pop:	10.0%
College grad:	15.3%				
Grad degree:	5.2%				

Southwest; Yuma, Part Tucson

Southern Arizona, though technically part of Mexico for hundreds of years, was never a home to Latin American civilization as northern New Mexico was. Here the hot desert land was inhabited mainly by Native American tribes such as the Apache and Cocopah. They kept their culture and language alive in the region until they were uprooted by English-speaking whites who came in on cavalry horses and in miners' wagons

2008 Presidential Vote		
Barack Obama (D)	123,202	(57%)
John McCain (R)	89,725	(42%)
2004 Presidential Vote		
John Kerry (D)	105,532	(57%)
George Bush (R)	79,674	(43%)
Cook Partisan Voting Index: D+6		

and railroad cars in the late 19th century. In 1854, the Gadsden Purchase—$10 million to Mexico for 30,000 square miles of desert—cleared the way for a southern transcontinental railroad. Today's Hispanic Arizonans are mostly descendants of later emigrants from Mexico, some of whom came over the border in the sleepier days before World War II, when *la frontera* was scarcely patrolled. Many more have come since the 1980s to partake in the dazzling economic growth in the region over a quarter-century. That immigration pattern has slowed considerably in recent years, with the collapse of the real estate market in Arizona and stronger law enforcement against illegal aliens.

The 7th Congressional District of Arizona was created in 2002 and is the state's second Hispanic-majority district. Its population in 2010 was 56% Hispanic. It is geographically a giant of a district—larger than Rhode Island, Delaware, Hawaii, Connecticut, and New Jersey put together—and shares 300 miles of border with Mexico. The district is a collection of four distant communities connected by many square miles of uninhabited Sonoran desert. One is the suburb of Tolleson just west of downtown Phoenix. The second is the heavily Latino west and south sides of Tucson. The largest employer in southern Arizona is the University of Arizona in Tucson. The third community is Yuma, located at a Colorado River crossing in an irrigated agricultural valley, often the hottest place in the country. The lower Colorado produces much of the nation's lettuce and in the winter is one of the nation's biggest RV centers. The fourth is the Mexican border town of Nogales, which is 94% Hispanic and located near many maquiladora plants, long an entry point for the drug trade and the scene of many illegal border crossings in recent years. The twin smuggling tides—drugs and people—have inflicted damage on the fragile desert ecosystem. Its port of entry, built in 1973 and one of the busiest cargo ports along the Mexican border, received $200 million in federal stimulus money in 2009 for upgrades.

Out in the desert there is the Organ Pipe Cactus National Monument, the Tohono O'odham Indian Reservation, and the Barry M. Goldwater Air Force Range, the largest aerial gunnery range after Nevada's Nellis Air Force Range. It is twice the size of Delaware. However, 95% of it is not used for target practice in order to protect the habitat of the endangered Sonoran pronghorn antelope. Near Nogales, other unique forms of wildlife are found in the Tumacacori Highlands, including endangered species such as the jaguar, peregrine falcon, Chiricahua leopard frog, and Mexican spotted owl. With its brutal desert heat, the Baboquivari trail that runs north to the Tohono O'odham nation has been the deadliest immigrant crossing in the nation. Trash left behind by illegal crossers has caused growing environmental problems. The 7th District, home to seven Indian tribes, is one of two overwhelmingly Democratic districts in Arizona.

Raúl Grijalva (D)

The congressman from the 7th District is Raúl Grijalva, a Democrat first elected in 2002. He grew up in Tucson, the son of a *bracero*, or guest worker, who emigrated from Mexico in 1945. He graduated from the University of Arizona and has lived in the city all of his life; he has deep roots in the immigrant community on the city's southwest side. He was director of El Pueblo Neighborhood Center and assistant dean for Hispanic student affairs at the university. In 1974, he was elected to the Tucson school board and served 12 years. In 1988, he was elected a Pima County supervisor and served 14 years. As supervisor, he backed an effort to extend medical and dental benefits to same-sex domestic partners of county employees and focused on affordable health care, family and children services, and economic growth. Developers and builders helped elect him to office, but his support for planned growth and impact fees later alienated them.

When the district was created in 2002, the Democratic primary (in effect) determined who would get the seat. Grijalva entered with a home-court advantage: 64% of the primary votes were cast in Pima County. His chief opponent was state Sen. Elaine Richardson, who was endorsed by the women's fundraising group EMILY's List. Although outspent nearly 3-to-1, Grijalva had a well-organized grassroots effort and endorsements from labor unions, teachers' unions, and the Sierra Club. Mocking his opponent's national funding, Grijalva created "Adelita's List," invoking a name alluding to the independent women who fought in the Mexican Revolution. He opposed the partial privatization of Social Security and a proposed increase in the retirement age, and he supported amnesty for illegal immigrants. He won the primary with 41% to Richardson's 21%. He won easily in November and his daughter, Adelita, won a seat on the school board.

In the House, Grijalva's voting record is strongly liberal. On the Education and Labor Committee, he and other liberals complained loudly that the Bush administration's 2001 No Child Left Behind law, which tied federal funding to student performance on standardized tests, was too underfunded to be effective. Grijalva dubbed it the "No Child Left Untested" law. Much of his effort has been focused on immigration policy. He has co-sponsored bills to raise the number of low-skill visas from 5,000 to 400,000 and to allow legalization for some illegal immigrants, provided they pay a $500 civil fine. After Arizona state lawmakers passed a controversial immigration bill in 2010 expanding law enforcement's powers to detain suspected immigrants, he joined his Democratic colleague Ed Pastor in urging the Obama administration to prevent its implementation. Then, Grijalva took the unusual step of urging a boycott of his state, calling on "civic, religious, labor, Latino, organizations of color to refrain from using Arizona as a convention site, to refrain from spending their dollars in the state of Arizona until Arizona turns the clock forward instead of backwards and joins the rest of the union." He abandoned the boycott idea after a federal judge in July halted the implementation of most of the immigration law.

Another strong area of interest for Grijalva is his work as chairman of the Subcommittee on National Parks, Forests and Public Lands, which is a part of the Natural Resources Committee. He has worked to stop uranium mining in the Kaibab National Forest and on federal lands near the Grand Canyon. He also has sought wilderness designation for the Tumacacori Highlands, to prevent mining claims in the Coronado National Forest, and, more generally, to prevent oil and gas drilling without environmental review on public lands. He and his Tucson-area colleague, Democratic Rep. Gabrielle Giffords, got the House to vote in favor of creation of a Santa Cruz Valley National Heritage Area in 2007. He has opposed the 4,000-acre Rosemont copper mine on U.S. Forest Service land southeast of Tucson, and has sought to protect Tumamoc Hill from development by trading federal lands with the developer. He has worked to create a Sonoran Desert conservation system, which would protect 3.3 million acres and 56 miles of trails in Arizona.

In 2008, Grijalva was widely mentioned as a possible nominee for Interior secretary, and was supported by several national Hispanic organizations and by Natural Resources Committee Chairman Nick Rahall, D-W.Va. But in December, Obama announced then-Sen. Ken Salazar, D-Colo., as his choice. The same month, he turned down an offer of a seat on the Ways and Means Committee, saying he preferred to stay on Natural Resources. "You come to Congress for the things that you care about—resources, education, and labor," he said. "Ways and Means is prestigious and powerful. It ain't my cup of tea."

Grijalva is on the far left in the Democratic Caucus. In 2007, he joined 22 other Democrats in the move to impeach Vice President Dick Cheney. In 2008, he was elected co-chair with Rep. Lynn Woolsey, D-Calif., of the 75-member Progressive Caucus. In that position, he initially insisted in 2009 that any health care overhaul legislation include a government-run public insurance option to compete with private insurers, but he later backed away from that demand. He also espoused a "war tax" that year to finance military operations in Afghanistan, an effort he considered immoral.

He had been re-elected by wide margins until 2010, when he drew an aggressive challenge from Republican Ruth McClung, a 28-year-old physicist. Using the slogan "Boycott Grijalva, not Arizona," she got help from tea party groups, along with a televised endorsement from GOP Sen. John McCain, to pull nearly even with him in polls. At the same time, Grijalva's abandonment of the boycott also did not help him with his Hispanic base of supporters. But national Democrats raced to his assistance with ads, and he eked out a 49%-46% victory, with two other candidates splitting the remainder.

EIGHTH DISTRICT

Gabrielle Giffords (D)

Elected 2006, 3rd term; b. June 8, 1970, Tucson; home, Tucson; Scripps Col., B.A. 1993, Cornell U., M.S. 1996; Jewish; married (Mark Kelly); 2 children.

Elected Office: AZ House of Reps., 2000-02; AZ Senate, 2002-05.

Professional Career: Price Waterhouse Coopers, 1996-97; CEO and pres., El Campo Tire, 1997-2000.

DC Office: 1030 LHOB, 20515, 202-225-2542; Fax: 202-225-0378; Web site: giffords.house.gov.

State Offices: Sierra Vista, 520-459-3115; Tucson, 520-881-3588.

Committees: *Armed Services:* Air & Land Forces; Readiness. *Science & Technology:* Space & Aeronautics (RMM); Technology & Innovation.

Group Ratings

	ACLU	ACU	ADA	CFG	AFS	FRC	LCV	ITIC	NTU	COC
2010	88	13	75	16	100	0	80	100	24	38
2009	–	20	95	12	100	–	100	–	14	40

National Journal Ratings

	2010 LIB	—	2010 CONS	2009 LIB	—	2009 CONS
Economic	46%	—	54%	50%	—	50%
Social	49%	—	49%	54%	—	43%
Foreign	44%	—	55%	50%	—	48%
Composite	47%	—	53%	52%	—	48%

Key Votes of the 111th Congress

1. Overturn Ledbetter	Y	5. Bar federal abortion funds	N	9. Stop detainee transfers	Y
2. Pass $820 billion stimulus	Y	6. Pass health care bill	Y	10. Legalize immigrants' kids	Y
3. Let guns in national parks	Y	7. Regulate financial firms	Y	11. Repeal don't ask, tell	Y
4. Pass cap-and-trade	Y	8. Pass tax cuts for some	Y	12. Limit campaign funds	Y

Election Results

2010 general	Gabrielle Giffords (D)	138,280	(49%)	($3,504,410)
	Jesse Kelly (R)	134,124	(47%)	($1,692,504)
	Steven Stoltz (Lib)	11,174	(4%)	
2010 primary	Gabrielle Giffords (D)	unopposed		

Prior Winning Percentages: 2008 (55%), 2006 (54%)

Population		Race/Ethnicity		Work	
Pop. 2010:	754,300	White:	68.2%	Private:	72.2%
Change since 2000:	Up 17.6%	Black:	3.3%	Government:	21.5%
Urban:	87.3%	Hispanic:	22.7%	Self-employed:	6.2%
Rural:	12.7%	Asian:	2.7%	Blue collar:	15.0%
Area size:	9,057 sq. mi.	Native Am.:	0.8%	White collar:	65.0%
		Hawaiian:	0.2%	Khaki collar:	1.2%
Age		Two+ races:	2.1%	Other:	18.8%
Median age:	41.1 yrs.				
More than 65 yrs:	17.9%	*Ancestry*		Median income:	$51,126
Less than 18 yrs:	21.7%	German	15.5%	Median Home Value:	$226,600
		Irish	10.5%		
Education		English	9.5%	**Military Veterans**	
H.S. grad:	91.2%			% of Pop:	15.9%
College grad:	33.3%				
Grad degree:	13.5%				

Southeast Arizona; Tucson

Arizona's first frontier was just south of today's Tucson, where Franciscan friars built Mission San Xavier del Bac in the 18th century. To the east, the late-19th-century mining towns of Tombstone and Bisbee sprang up on mountainsides, where miners dug up gold and silver and much of America's copper. Cochise County, where Tombstone and Bisbee are located, was the most populous county when Arizona became the 48th state in 1912. Here the white man

2008 Presidential Vote		
John McCain (R)	181,771	(52%)
Barack Obama (D)	161,164	(46%)
2004 Presidential Vote		
George Bush (R)	167,647	(53%)
John Kerry (D)	147,300	(47%)
Cook Partisan Voting Index: R+4		

finally quashed the rebellion of the land-starved American Indian, when the Apache leader Geronimo faced the U.S. Army in 1900. In the last decade, Cochise County has been an active frontier again. After the Border Patrol reduced illegal crossings in California and Texas, Mexicans trying to enter the United States illegally came to Agua Prieta, just across the border from the town of Douglas. There they fan out, cross the border, and use the area's numerous roads, mountain trails, and ranch lands to get to Tucson and Phoenix. The Border Patrol's Tucson sector has become the most active on the border in both apprehensions and illegal drug seizures. Stepped-up border enforcement has resulted in decreases in these metrics since 2004, but many bodies are still found in the mountains and in the desert. The Homeland Security Department's controversial border technology surveillance network, SBInet, is based in the area, though repeated delays and cost overruns have left its future in doubt.

One immigrant destination is Tucson itself, Arizona's second metropolis. It is much smaller, more rough-hewn, and politically less conservative than Phoenix. Tucson is a high-tech city and home to the University of Arizona. Defense giant Raytheon Co. has a huge missile plant at Tucson International Airport. A smaller company, Paragon Space Development Corp., designs systems to keep astronauts breathing in space. Other companies have flocked to the city in recent years to work on solar energy projects. It is also a tourist destination, with famed resorts. For nearly 40 years, Tucson was the political base of the brothers Udall: Stewart, a representative in the 1950s and the Interior secretary in the 1960s; and Morris, a representative for 30 years and pioneering environmentalist who retired in 1991 because of Parkinson's disease and died in 1998. Now their sons, Tom and Mark Udall, represent New Mexico and Colorado in the Senate; a cousin, Stephen Udall, finished second in the 2002 Democratic primary in Arizona's 1st District.

The 8th Congressional District of Arizona includes all of Tucson, except the Latino-dominated west and south sides, which are in the 7th District. The 8th also includes the eastern half of surrounding Pima County and much southeastern Arizona desert real estate: all of Cochise County, Douglas, and Sierra Vista near Fort Huachuca, which is the site of the Army Military Intelligence Center, where military interrogators are trained. It also takes in small portions of Santa Cruz and Pinal counties. Politically it is closely divided, voting narrowly for George W. Bush in 2000 and 2004 and for Arizona favorite son John McCain in 2008.

Gabrielle Giffords (D)

The congresswoman from the 8th District is Gabrielle Giffords, a Democrat elected in 2006. Her name is indelibly tied to the shocking events of January 8, 2011, when Giffords was shot through the head by a deranged constituent at a public forum at a Tucson grocery store. Giffords survived the attack, but faced months, if not years, of recovery. The events renewed interest in tougher gun laws and more treatment options for the mentally ill, and also sparked a debate about the lack of civility in American political discourse.

Giffords grew up in Tucson, a third-generation southern Arizonan. Her life was shaped by the culture of the West. She rode horses competitively from age 8, mucking stalls to pay for her lessons. Wide open spaces also influenced her fondness for motorcycles and old cars; she's partial to Corvairs. Giffords' father ran a Tucson tire business and her mother was a conservator of Latin American art. The couple split up when Giffords was 15. Her father moved to Mexico, remarried and had a son, and Giffords learned to speak Spanish fluently in part through her relationship with her brother. Today, she also owns a home in Mexico.

Giffords graduated from Scripps College in California, and then won a Fulbright scholarship to study demographics in Chihuahua, Mexico. She spent another year studying the impact of Operation Gatekeeper on the border at San Ysidro, an experience that led her to return to school to get a master's degree in regional planning from Cornell University. After working briefly in New York,

Giffords returned home to Tucson to take over the family tire business. Her entry into state politics was inspired by her observation of problems in Arizona schools, which awarded diplomas to students barely able to read. Then a Republican, Giffords changed her party affiliation in 1999 because she said the state GOP was too conservative for her moderate views. (She voted for Bill Clinton twice.) Giffords was elected as a Democrat to the state House in 2000, and two years later, at age 32, became the youngest woman ever elected to the state Senate.

When 11-term moderate Republican Rep. Jim Kolbe announced his retirement in November 2005, Giffords was a serious contender for the swing district. In the Democratic primary, she faced local television news anchor Patty Weiss. Giffords was supported by labor unions, the women's fundraising group EMILY's List, and the Sierra Club. She had a nearly 3-to-1 fundraising advantage, and won the six-candidate primary in September by 54%-31%. The Republican primary was a battle between state Rep. Randy Graf, supported by the Minuteman Project border patrol group, and two moderate Republicans who wound up splitting the moderate vote and allowing Graf to win.

In the general election campaign, national Republicans initially ran ads against Giffords, but by October gave up the contest and canceled reserved airtime. Kolbe pointedly refused to endorse Graf. Giffords portrayed herself as a pro-business moderate who could work across party lines and publicized her experience running the family tire store. Her campaign featured photos of her with her motorcycle and with her fiancé, Discovery astronaut Mark Kelly (they were married in November 2007). She won 54%-42%, even carrying Cochise County, where the Minuteman Project was active.

In the House, Giffords got a seat on the Armed Services Committee, where she could keep watch on the two large military bases in the district. She was the first freshman to travel to the Iraq war zone in February 2007, and she spent four days in Afghanistan and Pakistan in April 2008. She joined the Blue Dog Coalition of fiscally conservative Democrats but backed her party on most social legislation. However, she has joined with gun-rights advocates, noting that her district has "a very strong gun culture." A pet project of hers is funding for solar energy, which is a potential economic boon for sunny Arizona. Giffords also supported the 2009 energy bill containing a "cap and trade" program aimed at limiting greenhouse gas emissions, a move that drew sharp criticism from businesses.

She gets involved in immigration issues, perhaps the biggest concern in her district. In 2007, she negotiated a settlement between border-area communities in her district and the Border Patrol, which wanted to open a permanent checkpoint in the area but agreed to move it six miles south. The Tucson sector of the border was the only one without a permanent interior checkpoint. Residents in towns along Interstate 19 south of Tucson feared that one would cause illegal immigrants to cross their property, and Kolbe long had used his seat on the powerful Appropriations Committee to prevent the Border Patrol from building one.

Giffords favors a change in immigration law to create a guest-worker program and a path to legalization as well as enforcement provisions. She has also called for a doubling of the number of H-1B visas for high-tech workers, and extension of the E-Verify system, which allows employers to check the immigration status of new hires. When Arizona lawmakers passed the nation's most restrictive immigration law in 2010, Giffords came out against it, a position that cost her the potential support of some independents and conservative Democrats. But she also said a national boycott of the state—a position backed by 7th District Democratic colleague Raul Grijalva—was misguided, which left Hispanics disappointed. Giffords supported the Obama administration's decision to deploy National Guard troops on the border.

Her active first term in Congress made Giffords one of the newcomers to watch in Washington. "I wouldn't be surprised if she's the first or second female president of the United States," said former Labor Secretary Robert Reich, a Giffords mentor, in 2007.

Both political parties made the 8th District a priority in 2008. The Service Employees International Union began running ads for Giffords as early as July 2007, and she raised $1.2 million by October 2007. Her Republican opponent was state Senate President Tim Bee, a popular moderate. After Giffords voted against the massive rescue of the financial markets, then voted in favor of an amended bill, Bee criticized her switch in positions. Giffords said she did so because the October bill included an extension of the solar energy tax credit. She won 55%-43%, narrowly carrying Cochise County and winning solidly in Pima County.

Two years later, Republicans came after Giffords again, hoping the sluggish economy could be a political weapon in their favor. Her Republican opponent was Jesse Kelly, a former Marine sergeant who upset the GOP's establishment candidate, state Sen. Jonathan Paton, in the primary. Kelly's aggressive, anti-politician stance drew support from tea party activists, who poured money into his campaign. He also caught the eye of former Alaska Gov. Sarah Palin, who put Giffords on her "Take Back the 20" list with ads that targeted incumbent lawmakers she found lacking. On a map, the districts of the Democratic lawmakers were pinpointed with rifle sights. Later, in a television interview, Giffords criticized Palin's use of gun imagery in the ad. "When people do that, they have to realize there are consequences to that action," she said.

In his campaign, Kelly blasted Giffords for opposing Arizona's immigration law and backing the health care overhaul. He tied her to President Obama with some especially fierce rhetoric. He told *National Journal* in an interview, "We've elected a radical to the White House and better do everything we can [to] stop his agenda. Everything's possible if we remove liberals....Giffords lied through her teeth. She's no moderate!" But Giffords showed her toughness. Within hours of Kelly's upset win in the August primary, she went on the air to warn voters that he would raid the Social Security trust fund, and seized on a videotape of Kelly telling voters he supports a national sales tax.

Democrats also accused Kelly of "Nazi ties" after he accepted an endorsement from an anti-immigration group, Americans for Legal Immigration PAC (ALIPAC). Kelly angrily refuted the allegations, but could not surmount Giffords' huge cash advantage. Three days after the polls closed, she declared victory with 48.7% to Kelly's 47.2%.

Days after being sworn in to a third term in January 2011, Giffords was shot while hosting her first "Congress on Your Corner" event outside a Tucson Safeway store. Witnesses said a man walked up to Giffords, shot her in the face and then kept firing into the small crowd that had turned out to meet her. Six people were killed, including federal Judge John Roll, 9-year-old Christina Taylor Green, and Gabe Zimmerman, Giffords' community outreach director. Two other Giffords staffers were wounded. Jared Lee Loughner, 22, of Tucson, was charged with attempted assassination of Giffords and murder in the deaths of the others.

Quick action by Giffords intern Daniel Hernandez has been credited with helping save her life. The University of Arizona junior stemmed some of the bleeding from her head and held her upright so she could breathe while they waited for help. Giffords underwent emergency surgery at the University Medical Center in Tucson, where doctors said a single bullet had traveled completely through her brain on one side. Giffords responded well to treatment, regained consciousness and on January 26, was transferred to Houston's TIRR Memorial Hermann, which is nationally recognized for its rehabilitation program for brain trauma victims. Husband Kelly became Giffords' liaison to a national audience eager for frequent news about her progress.

The fallout from the shooting was immediate and intense, with versions of a single question being examined everywhere: Was the polarization of the country in recent elections and the stridency of the political debate leading to violence? President Obama went to Arizona and delivered a stirring speech calling on Americans to talk with each other "in a way that heals, not in a way that wounds." Prominent members of both parties pledged to tone it down rhetorically, and Palin felt compelled to release a video in which she accused her political enemies of unfairly portraying her as responsible for the charged political environment. Republicans and Democrats sat together for the first time at Obama's State of the Union address in late January, although most political experts predicted the civility truce would be fleeting.

Several bills were introduced to step up background checks for gun purchases, to create no-gun zones around lawmakers and to ban high-volume magazines like the one that allowed Loughner to shoot several people within seconds. The shooting also kicked off a national debate about access to guns by people with mental health issues and whether the government is doing enough to protect society from people with a history of mental illness.

★ ARKANSAS ★

Jutting out over the banks of the Arkansas River, in Little Rock's Market District, is the William J. Clinton Presidential Center, home of the nation's largest presidential library. It is a monument to the 42nd president, the most talented and accomplished politician produced by a small state that has produced more than its share of them. Bill Clinton's presidential library is the first with electronic records as well as paper documents. In its alcoves are exhibits and electronic connections to what Clinton considers his greatest achievements, along with a treatment of "the politics of persecution," his take on his 1998 impeachment. Clinton, a notoriously hearty eater, decreed that planners set aside space on the grounds for picnics and cookouts. He may not have returned to live in Arkansas after his presidency ended (eight other presidents also chose not return to their home states), but he is clearly regarded here and elsewhere as an Arkansan, a man whose eloquence and earthiness, outsized ambitions and overly visible faults, are redolent of the state from which he began his unlikely ascent to prominence. That rise has been on the whole a source of pride to Arkansans. For many of them, Clinton's success wiped away the stain of Gov. Orval Faubus, whose defiance of an order desegregating Little Rock's Central High School prompted President Eisenhower to dispatch federal troops to enforce it in 1957.

Arkansas, like Clinton, began life without many advantages. In area, it's the smallest state between the Mississippi River and the Pacific Ocean. In population, it's the smallest state in the South. It has not been blessed with great natural resources, unless you count flame-retarding bromine, of which the state produces half the world supply. Historically, it has been home to no major industry. Arkansas is the land left over when Louisiana and Missouri were carved out of the Louisiana Purchase and what is now Oklahoma was fenced off as Indian Territory. Its first two senators could not agree on how to pronounce the state's name, but since 1881 it's been illegal to call it *ar-KAN-sas*. Settled by poor farmers with large families, few slaves, and little cash, Arkansas has had no Atlanta or Dallas or even Memphis as a focal point of growth. Arkansas consistently has the second- or third-lowest income levels and percentage of college graduates of any state. However, its economy is far more vibrant and productive than it was in the Faubus years half a century ago. Northwest Arkansas, around Bentonville and Fayetteville, is a boom area, housing the headquarters of Wal-Mart Stores, Tyson Foods, and J.B. Hunt trucking. Population growth has been rapid, with Wal-Mart leading the way. Food processing is a big business; so is the manufacturing of auto parts and medical and construction equipment, and the growing of federally subsidized rice and cotton. In southern Arkansas, Murphy Oil promises to pay for college for graduates of El Dorado public schools.

Culturally, Arkansas is Jacksonian and religious, settled more by dirt farmers than plantation owners, people who are proud of their independence and willing to fight to maintain it. It is the birthplace of Pentecostal denominations. The Church of God in Christ was started in Little Rock in 1907, and the Assembly of God (now headquartered in Springfield, Mo.) in Hot Springs in 1914. The state has the highest married rate after heavily Mormon Utah and Idaho, but also a high divorce rate, as highlighted in 2005 when Gov. Mike Huckabee, a former Baptist minister who, like Clinton, was born in the town of Hope, declared "a state of marital emergency" in Arkansas. Huckabee also is an advocate of weight loss, as a 2008 presidential candidate and later as a host on a Fox News program.

As the late political scientist Diane Blair noted, Arkansas never had a power elite of great plantation owners or economic robber barons. That has left it a heritage without honored traditions or tight standards, but it has also made Arkansas a place of great opportunities, where talented people can move up fast and amass huge fortunes with breakthrough ideas. Sam Walton believed that rural and small-town America would support a chain of giant discount stores that, through tough bargaining with vendors and ultra-quick distribution, could undersell competitors. Walton was the richest American when he died in April 1992, and Wal-Mart Stores today is the largest private employer in the world, with a payroll of 2 million people. The brothers Jack and Witt Stephens started an investment banking house in Little Rock specializing in underwriting municipal bonds and investing in businesses that are a mix of private enterprise, government subsidies, and public regulation. They amassed a billion-dollar fortune. Don Tyson took over his father's chicken business and made it one of the biggest food producers in America. J.B. Hunt established his trucking empire in Arkansas. These business giants have cultivated a down-home, laid-back style, but they have also skillfully united their interests with those of the state's politicians.

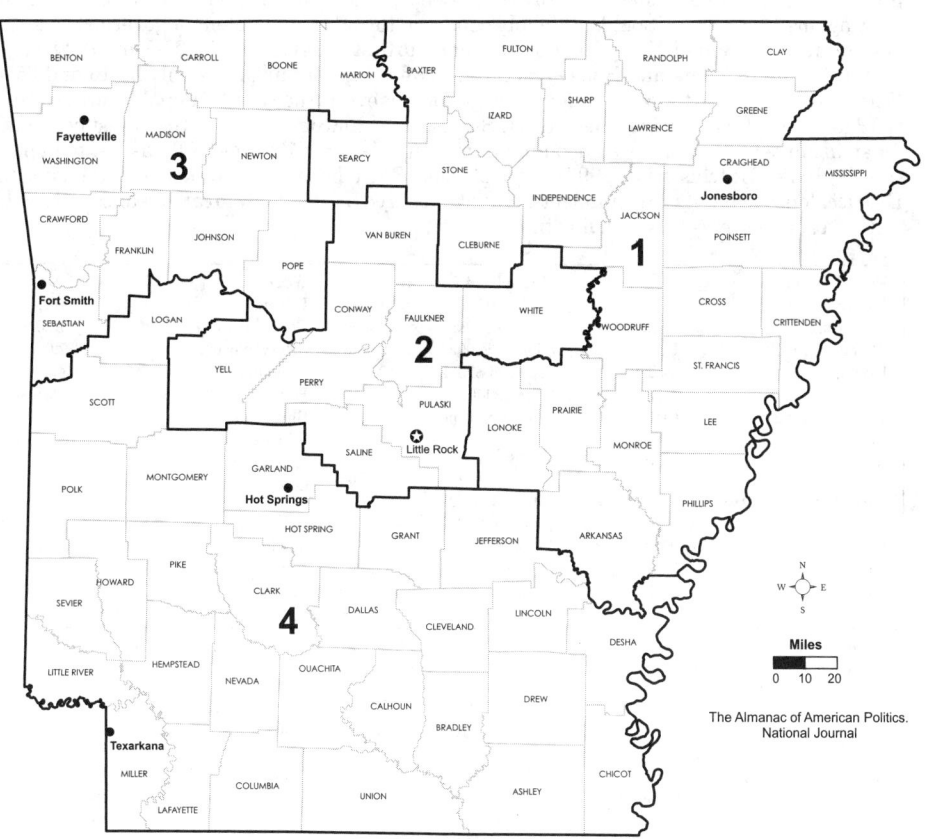

Congressional district boundaries were first effective for 2002.

Politically, Arkansas was long solidly Democratic, with Republican pockets in the mountains of the northwest. For years, it produced Democratic politicians who accumulated great seniority and power in Washington—longtime House Ways and Means Chairman Wilbur Mills; Sens. John McClellan and William Fulbright, who represented the state for a total of 65 years from the 1940s to the 1970s; and Sens. Dale Bumpers and David Pryor, who served a total of 42 years from the 1970s to the 1990s. Republicans won some governor races—Winthrop Rockefeller in the 1960s, Frank White in 1980, and Mike Huckabee in 1998 and 2002. But presidentially, Arkansas remained one of the most Democratic states in the South, with solidly Democratic congressional delegations. But President Barack Obama has not been popular here, perhaps partly because he ran against Hillary Rodham Clinton in the primaries. Arkansas had the biggest drop in Democratic percentage between the presidential years 1996 and 2008. Like other parts of Jacksonian America, Arkansas in 2010 was less impressed with Obama as president than it had been with him as a presidential candidate. Democratic Gov. Mike Beebe, widely popular, was re-elected overwhelmingly against weak opposition. But Republicans won the offices of lieutenant governor, secretary of state and lands commissioner. Democrats went into the 2010 election with 27-8 and 72-28 majorities in the state Senate and House respectively, and came out ahead by only 20-15 and 55-44. Democrats' 5-1 edge in the congressional delegation was overturned to a 4-2 Republican advantage. GOP Rep. John Boozman beat Democratic Sen. Blanche Lincoln 58%-37%, the lowest percentage for an incumbent senator since appointed Democratic Sen. Bob Krueger of Texas lost to Republican Kay Bailey Hutchison in a 1993 special election. Republicans easily picked up the 1st and 2nd District House seats where incumbent Democrats retired. It's too early to call Arkansas a Republican state, but it seems to be heading that way.

Population		Household Income		Work	
Pop. 2010:	2,915,918	Under $15k:	18.39%	Private:	76.70%
State rank:	32nd	$15k to $50k:	43.29%	Government:	16.0%
Change since 2000:	Up 9.1%	$50k to $100k:	27.0%	Self-employed:	7.0%
Urban:	52.29%	$100k to $200k:	9.5%	Unemployment (3-yr. average):	4.70%
Rural:	47.70%	Over $200k:	1.8%	Poverty:	18.10%
Native of state:	61.10%	Median income:	$38,577	Blue collar:	27.89%
Not a citizen:	2.89%			White collar:	54.60%
Area size:	53,179 sq. mi.	**Home Value**		Khaki collar:	0.20%
		Under $100k:	48.70%	Other:	17.30%
Most populous cities		$100k to $300k:	44.0%		
Little Rock	193,524	$300k to $500k:	4.90%	**Age**	
Fort Smith	86,209	$500k to $1 mil:	1.8%	Median age:	37.10 yrs.
Fayetteville	73,580	Over $1 million:	0.5%	More than 65 yrs:	14.1%
Springdale	69,797	Median:	$102,900	Less than 18 yrs:	24.69%

Race/Ethnicity				Military Veterans		Registered Voters in 2010	
White:	74.5%	*Language*		% of Pop:	11.4%	No Party registration	
Black:	15.30%	English:	93.40%			Voter turnout:	784,333
Hispanic:	6.40%	Spanish:	4.79%	*Veterans by Period*		Turnout as % of	
Asian:	1.2%	Asian:	0.90%	WWII and before:	9.90%	voting age:	35.60%
Native Am.:	0.69%	Other European:	0.69%	Korea:	11.30%		
Hawaiian:	0.20%			Vietnam:	33.5%	**Legislature**	
Two+ races:	1.60%	**Education**		Gulf (pre-2001):	11.9%	Senate:	20 D 15 R
		H.S. grad:	81.79%	Gulf (post-2001):	8.5%	House:	54 D 45 R 1 V
Ancestry		College grad:	19.0%	Peace time:	24.80%		
Irish	11.30%	Grad degree:	6.29%				
German	10.19%						
English	8.69%						

Presidential politics From Reconstruction up through 1960, Arkansas like most Southern states voted more Democratic than the nation as a whole in presidential elections. Since then, it has done so four times, when Southerner Jimmy Carter and Arkansas' own Bill Clinton were the Democratic nominees. However, except for 1968, when Orval Faubus was governor and George Wallace carried the state, its Democratic percentage for president trailed the national average only by single digits—until 2008, when Obama lost Arkansas 59%-39%. It is an understatement to say that Arkansas, like other states with Jacksonian roots, was unenchanted with Obama. This was the best state for former Arkansas First Lady Hillary Rodham Clinton, notwithstanding her relocation to New York, in the 2008 primary on Super Tuesday, which she won 70%-26%. Polls looking ahead to the general election suggested that Clinton might well have won Arkansas against John McCain or any other

2008 Presidential Vote		
John McCain (R)	638,017	(59%)
Barack Obama (D)	422,310	(39%)

2008 Presidential Primary		
Hillary Clinton (D)	220,136	(70%)
Barack Obama (D)	82,476	(26%)

2008 Presidential Primary		
Mike Huckabee (R)	138,557	(60%)
John McCain (R)	46,343	(20%)
Mitt Romney (R)	30,997	(14%)

2004 Presidential Vote		
George W. Bush (R)	572,898	(54%)
John Kerry (D)	469,953	(45%)

Republican candidate, except perhaps former Arkansas Gov. Huckabee, who captured the state's 2008 Republican presidential primary easily.

Arkansas' presidential primary used to be in May, and it attracted little attention. The legislature in 2005 voted to hold it on Feb. 5, which in 2008 came on Super Tuesday. Arkansas Democrats tried to get the Democratic National Committee to make it one of the first four states to vote, but the national Democrats instead chose South Carolina because of its higher African-American percentage and its tradition of early Republican primaries.

Congressional districting In April 2001, the Democratic legislature slightly adjusted the boundaries of Arkansas' four congressional districts to meet the equal population standard. Because it didn't split counties, the legislature's plan had the highest population difference in the nation between the districts—6,698 people—but it also contained a backup provision: If a court found the plan invalid, it would be repealed and 4,400 voters would be shifted between districts. A court challenge never materialized, however. Republican Gov. Huckabee, lacking the votes to prevent an override of his veto, let the plan become law without his signature. Arkansas grew at a faster rate than the national average from 2000 to 2010 and retains its four districts. The Democratic legislature could try to change the boundaries to weaken one of the three Republican congressmen, two of them first elected in 2010, but it is not clear how without weakening Democrat Mike Ross in the 4th District.

112th Congress Lineup	
3 R	1 D
111th Congress Lineup	
1 R	3 D

Governor

Mike Beebe (D)

Elected 2006, term expires Jan. 2015, 2nd full term; b. Dec. 28, 1946, Amagon; home, Searcy; AR St. U., B.A. 1968, U. of AR, J.D. 1972; Episcopalian; married (Ginger); 3 children.

Military Career: Army Reserve, 1968-74.

Elected Office: AR Senate, 1982-2002; AR atty. gen., 2002-06.

Professional Career: Practicing atty., 1972-2002.

Office: State Capitol, Rm. 250, Little Rock, 72201, 501-682-2345; Fax: 501-682-1382; Web site: www.governor.arkansas.gov.

Election Results

2010 general	Mike Beebe (D)	506,336	(65%)
	Jim Keet (R)	262,784	(34%)
2010 primary	Mike Beebe (D)	.... unopposed	

Prior Winning Percentages: 2006 (56%)

Democrat Mike Beebe (*BEE-bee*) was elected governor of Arkansas in 2006 and reelected in 2010. He was born to a single mother in his great-grandmother's country shack outside of tiny Amagon in Jackson County. He never met his father and moved frequently as a child—to St. Louis, Detroit, Houston, and Alamogordo, N.M., where his mother worked through a succession of waitressing jobs and marriages; he recalls going to five different schools in the fifth grade alone. "It taught me to adapt, to be resilient, and it taught me to make friends fast," he told the *Arkansas Democrat-Gazette*. His mother returned to Arkansas in time for him to enroll in high school. He put his life on a track to success: Beebe graduated from Arkansas State University, and then the University of Arkansas Law School, and joined the U.S. Army Reserves. He launched a career as a trial lawyer, and won a record-breaking $4.1 million verdict in 1981. He then beat that record in 1986.

Beebe was elected to the state Senate in 1982, where he served for two decades and developed a reputation as an expert on state government and as a consensus builder; he never had Republican opposition for the seat. He helped write laws setting a uniform property tax rate for school funding and creating a $300 homestead property tax exemption. Beebe considered running against Republican Gov. Mike Huckabee in 2002, but with low statewide name recognition decided to run for attorney general and was elected without opposition in either the primary or general election.

In 2006, Huckabee was barred from running again by term limits. This was the first election in which the incumbent governor wasn't running since Bill Clinton won in 1978 at age 32. Beebe was an obvious candidate and was unopposed in the Democratic primary. Republican Lt. Gov. Win Rockefeller dropped out of the race because of illness in July 2005 and the Republican nominee was former 3rd District Rep. Asa Hutchinson, who also had been the under secretary for border and transportation security in the George W. Bush administration. Beebe reminded voters of his humble upbringing and called for pre-kindergarten programs, a new state health care plan, a $50 million discretionary fund to attract business and a phase-out of the state's grocery tax. Hutchinson questioned Beebe's commitment to tax relief, and Beebe suggested Hutchinson chose to run for governor because Bush had not made him a Cabinet secretary. The two candidates argued over how best to combat illegal immigration, debated Hutchinson's record at Homeland Security, and sparred over past gun control votes. Beebe spent $6.3 million to Hutchinson's $3.3 million. Former President Clinton campaigned for Beebe, while Bush stumped for Hutchinson. Beebe won 56%-41%.

Beebe inherited a $919 million budget surplus and capitalized on his 20 years of experience in the Legislature—he was the first governor with legislative experience since Clinton's predecessor David Pryor. He won a grocery tax cut from 6% to 3% and the homestead property tax was reduced. The income tax was eliminated for people below the poverty level. Legislators also approved $456 million to build and improve public school buildings and gave the governor discretion to spend nearly $188 million on other projects. Beebe kept a low profile on a Republican proposal banning gays from serving as foster parents, which died in committee. Lawmakers wrapped up work in 86 days, making for the Legislature's shortest session since Clinton was governor.

In the next legislative session, with the national recession producing a bleaker revenue picture, Beebe obtained an $86 million increase in the cigarette and tobacco tax to pay for improvements in emergency care. He also won an expansion of Medicaid health insurance for children and community health centers. He worked with the Legislature to establish a state lottery, which was approved by voters and was used to fund college scholarships. Beebe also hoped to reduce the grocery sales tax by another 1%, bringing it to 2%. The reduction would cut state revenues by $35 million, but Beebe had long argued that the tax was regressive and unfair to lower income workers. The Legislature also imposed a 5 percent royalty on the surging production of natural gas. When the Legislature also pushed for a 3-cent tax on milk and dairy products, Beebe found funds already appropriated to help dairy farmers and the tax was sidelined.

Beebe entered election year 2010 with a job approval rating of 74% and easily raised $2.4 million for his campaign by summer. Republicans had trouble finding an opponent. Their nominee, restaurant owner and former legislator Jim Keet, raised almost no money. When Republicans charged that Beebe allowed officials to use state cars for private purposes, the governor signed an executive order limiting such use. He won re-election 65%-34%, carrying every county. But Republicans won the offices of lieutenant governor, secretary of state and commissioner of state lands and gained seven seats in the state Senate and 16 in the state House, leaving Democrats with their smallest majorities since Reconstruction.

Senior Senator

Mark Pryor (D)

Elected 2002, term expires 2014, 2nd full term; b. Jan. 10, 1963, Fayetteville; home, Little Rock; U. of AR, B.A. 1985, J.D. 1988; Christian; married (Jill); 2 children.

Elected Office: AR House of Reps., 1990-94; AR atty. gen., 1998-02.

Professional Career: Practicing atty., 1988-96.

DC Office: 255 DSOB, 20510, 202-224-2353; Fax: 202-228-0908; Web site: pryor.senate.gov.

State Offices: Little Rock, 501-324-6336.

Committees: *Appropriations:* Agriculture, Rural Development, Food and Drug Administration & Related Agencies; Commerce, Justice, Science & Related Agencies; Labor, Health & Human Services, Education & Related Agencies; Military Construction, Veterans Affairs & Related Agencies; Transportation, HUD & Related Agencies. *Commerce, Science & Transportation:* Communications, Technology & the Internet; Competitiveness, Innovation & Export Promotion; Consumer Protection, Product Safety & Insurance (Chmn); Science & Space; Surface Transportation & Merchant Marine Infrastructure, Safety & Security. *Ethics (Select). Homeland Security & Governmental Affairs:* Contracting Oversight (Ad Hoc); Disaster Recovery & Intergovernmental Affairs (Ad Hoc) (Chmn); Federal Financial Management, Government Information, Federal Services & International Security. *Rules & Administration. Small Business & Entrepreneurship.*

Group Ratings

	ACLU	ACU	ADA	CFG	AFS	FRC	LCV	ITIC	NTU	COC
2010	60	29	65	29	91	4	14	67	22	60
2009	–	8	90	14	91	–	100	–	9	57

National Journal Ratings

	2010 LIB	—	2010 CONS		2009 LIB	—	2009 CONS
Economic	45%	—	54%		52%	—	47%
Social	42%	—	57%		55%	—	44%
Foreign	47%	—	0%		48%	—	51%
Composite	54%	—	46%		52%	—	48%

Key Votes of the 111th Congress

1. Overturn Ledbetter	Y	5. Pass health care bill	Y	9. Ratify New START	Y
2. Pass $787 billion stimulus	Y	6. Regulate financial firms	Y	10. Confirm Elena Kagan	Y
3. Repeal DC gun laws	Y	7. Pass tax cuts for some	Y	11. Stop EPA climate regs	Y
4. Confirm Sonia Sotomayor	Y	8. Legalize immigrants' kids	N	12. Repeal don't ask, tell	Y

Election Results

2008 general	Mark Pryor (D)...804,678	(80%)	($4,998,992)
	Rebekah Kennedy (Green)................................207,076	(20%)	($13,745)
2008 primary	Mark Pryor (D)... unopposed		

Prior Winning Percentages: 2002 (54%)

Mark Pryor is the Democratic senior senator from Arkansas, elected in 2002. He is the son of former Democratic Sen. David Pryor, and grew up in southern Arkansas, Little Rock and the Washington area, the latest in several generations of politically active Pryors in Arkansas. His grandmother, Susie Newton Pryor, was the first woman in Arkansas to run for office after women won the right to vote. David Pryor was elected to the U.S. House in 1966, as governor in 1974 and to the Senate in 1978. Mark Pryor graduated from the University of Arkansas and its law school in the 1980s. He practiced law in Little Rock and was elected to the Arkansas House in 1990 and 1992. He became the state attorney general at age 35, the youngest attorney general in the nation (but not in Arkansas history: Bill Clinton won the office at 30). In 1995, he was diagnosed with clear-cell sarcoma, a rare form of cancer. He underwent tendon transplant surgery in his left heel in 1996; the cancer has not returned.

As attorney general, Pryor implemented the state's "Do Not Call Registry." He also pushed for legislation to increase penalties for nursing home accidents and to strengthen background checks for long-term care employees. He worked to reduce utility rates and to remove unsafe products from day care centers. In July 2001, Pryor announced that he would run against Sen. Tim Hutchinson, the first Republican to win an Arkansas Senate seat since 1879. A Baptist minister, radio station owner and founder of a Christian school in Rogers, Hutchinson represented that conservative area in the Legislature and then for two terms as the 3rd District representative in Congress. Hutchinson's conservative voting record would ordinarily have made him a favorite for reelection. But in June 1999, Hutchinson filed for divorce from his wife of 29 years, and in August 2000, he married a former member of his staff. Pryor never mentioned Hutchinson's divorce and remarriage, but a recurrent theme in his campaign was "Tim Hutchinson has changed"—even though the incumbent's positions on issues had not changed much at all.

However, one of Pryor's earlier positions had changed, rather dramatically. Running for attorney general in 1998, Pryor had called himself a "pro-choice" candidate. But in the Senate contest, he emphasized his belief that abortion was wrong except in cases of rape, incest, or to save the life of the mother. He avoided saying whether or not the *Roe v. Wade* Supreme Court ruling legalizing abortion should be overturned. Pryor also campaigned on his support for gun rights, increased military spending, and for the Iraq war resolution. He accused Hutchinson of working for special interests, especially the pharmaceutical companies, and for supporting plans that would risk Social Security benefits. Pryor called Hutchinson "way too conservative" for Arkansas.

But he also appealed to cultural conservatives unhappy with Hutchinson's personal life by emphasizing his marriage and his Christian religion. One of Pryor's ads showed him, his wife and their two children saying grace before a meal. Pryor, holding a Bible, says, "The most important lessons in life are in this book right here." The Pryors belonged to an evangelical church in Little Rock and sent their children to a private Christian school. He turned down an invitation to appear with Hutchinson on *Meet the Press*, explaining that voters wouldn't be able to watch "because they're in church Sunday morning." He pulled ahead in polls in mid-year and never really fell behind. He won 54%-46%, a solid victory in a year when Democrats lost their majority in the Senate. A survey by pollster John Zogby showed that 12% said Hutchinson's divorce affected their vote—enough by itself to explain his drop from 53% in 1996 to 46% in 2002. Hutchinson's losses were particularly great in his home area. In 1996, he had won 65%-35% in the 3rd Congressional District; in 2002, he carried the district 56%-44%.

In the Senate, Pryor established a conservative voting record for a Democrat. He backed efforts to weaken Clinton-era environmental controls (although he later voted against oil drilling in the Arctic National Wildlife Refuge). He voted against a resolution supporting *Roe v. Wade,* and in 2006, Pryor voted with Republicans for a bill that would make it a crime to help a minor avoid parental notification laws by traveling to another state for an abortion. He voted against a constitutional amendment barring same-sex marriages, saying the issue should be left to the states, and then supported a state ballot measure in 2004 banning same-sex marriage in Arkansas. In 2003, Pryor voted against the omnibus appropriations bill that contained $300 million for Arkansas projects and against the $350 billion Bush tax cut. "I just can't support these budgets that send our deficits and national debt soaring out of control," he said.

The crowning achievement of Pryor's first term was a bill imposing sweeping changes on the Consumer Product Safety Commission. Passed in 2008, the legislation mandated that products be tested by independent laboratories, restricted levels of lead allowed in children's toys, and increased the budget for consumer safety to $105 million from $80 million. He has also advocated stronger parental controls for the Internet, and has encouraged movie rental chains and retailers to put up signs warning parents about the content of video games. Pryor has led efforts on legislation to prevent price gouging in the oil supply chain, to make the national "Do Not Call" list permanent, and to require employers to use the federal E-Verify system to curb hiring of illegal immigrants.

Pryor has been deeply involved in energy policy, meeting with a group of seven other senators from both parties to come up with proposals for moving the United States away from its reliance on oil-based energy. The group in 2009 proposed a bill to cut industrial carbon emissions and promote energy conservations and efficiency. But as a centrist, he drew the line when the Environmental Protection Agency moved that year to begin regulating greenhouse gases after Congress failed to enact a Democratic bill imposing caps on carbon emissions. Pryor said that Congress, not the EPA, should be in charge of setting broad policy on the issue. The issue of gun control also has Pryor sometimes straddling the political divide. In August 2009, he switched his vote to support Republican Sen. John Thune's bill to allow gun owners with concealed-carry permits to bring firearms into states with similar laws after it was apparent that it lacked the 60 votes needed to pass.

His centrist voting record has put him in the center of the several other high-profile debates. In 2007, Pryor joined all the other Senate Democrats in co-sponsoring a bill backed by labor unions to effectively abolish the secret ballot in union elections by eliminating a company's ability to demand a secret ballot before employees can join a union. But as the issue heated up, and major companies including Arkansas-based Wal-Mart Stores came out strongly against the unions' so-called card check bill, Pryor indicated he would not co-sponsor it again. In March 2010, he said, "There are more pressing issues relating to the economy that the Senate should be addressing." In 2009, Pryor waded into the health care battle by saying he would support a government-financed health insurance option backed by many Democrats only if the states could opt out. Although the public option had been dropped by the time the Senate voted on a final bill, Pryor joined two other Senate Democrats in voting no. He said he objected to the bill's increased Medicaid costs to the states, new taxes, and fees on employers who do not offer health insurance. Pryor also took conservative stances on other key issues, voting in September 2010 to block debate on the repeal of the ban on openly gay military personnel and advocating extension of all the Bush-era tax cuts, even those for wealthy Americans that the Obama administration had said should be allowed to expire.

Republicans hoped to target Pryor in 2008, but failed to field a candidate. He raised $5.5 million and, opposed by only a Green Party candidate, was re-elected with 80% of the vote. He was the only senator who did not draw a major-party challenge to his re-election that year. It was quite a contrast with the fate in 2010 of his Democratic colleague, Blanche Lincoln, who lost to GOP Rep. John Boozman by 58%-37%. Pryor comes up for re-election in 2014.

Junior Senator

John Boozman (R)

Elected 2010, term expires 2016, 1st full term; b. Dec. 10, 1950, Shreveport, LA; home, Rogers; U. of AR, 1969-72; Southern Col. of Optometry, O.D. 1977; Baptist; married (Cathy); 3 children.

Elected Office: Rogers School Bd., 1994-2001; U.S. House, 2001-11

Professional Career: Optometrist, Boozman-Hof Regional Eye Clinic, 1977-2001.

DC Office: 320 HSOB, 20510, 202-224-4843; Fax: 202-228-1371; Web site: boozman.senate.gov.

State Offices: El Dorado, 870-863-4641; Ft. Smith, 479-573-0189; Lowell, 479-725-0400; Mountain Home, 870-424-0129; Jonesboro, 870-268-6925; Stuttgart, 870-672-6941.

Committees: *Agriculture, Nutrition & Forestry:* Commodities, Markets, Trade & Risk Management; Conservation, Forestry & Natural Resources (RMM); Livestock, Dairy, Poultry, Marketing. *Commerce, Science & Transportation:* Aviation Operations, Safety & Security; Communications, Technology & the Internet; Competitiveness, Innovation & Export Promotion; Consumer Protection, Product Safety & Insurance; Oceans, Atmosphere, Fisheries & Coast Guard; Science & Space (RMM); Surface Transportation & Merchant Marine Infrastructure, Safety & Security. *Environment & Public Works:* Green Jobs & the New Economy (RMM); Oversight; Superfund, Toxics & Environmental Health; Transportation & Infrastructure. *Veterans' Affairs.*

Group Ratings (House)

	ACLU	ACU	ADA	CFG	AFS	FRC	LCV	ITIC	NTU	COC
2010	13	100	0	82	0	100	10	33	86	88
2009	–	96	0	91	11	–	7	–	86	80

National Journal Ratings (House)

	2010 LIB	—	2010 CONS	2009 LIB	—	2009 CONS
Economic	23%	—	77%	15%	—	84%
Social	0%	—	85%	20%	—	78%
Foreign	12%	—	79%	0%	—	75%
Composite	16%	—	84%	16%	—	84%

Key Votes of the 111th Congress (House)

1. Overturn Ledbetter	N	5. Bar federal abortion funds	Y	9. Stop detainee transfers	Y
2. Pass $820 billion stimulus	N	6. Pass health care bill	N	10. Legalize immigrants' kids	N
3. Let guns in national parks	Y	7. Regulate financial firms	N	11. Repeal don't ask, tell	N
4. Pass cap-and-trade	N	8. Pass tax cuts for some	N	12. Limit campaign funds	N

Election Results

2010 general	John Boozman (R)	451,618	(58%)	($3,057,796)
	Blanche Lincoln (D)	288,156	(37%)	($10,752,803)
	Trevor Drown (I)	25,234	(3%)	
2010 primary	John Boozman (R)	75,010	(53%)	
	Jim Holt (R)	24,826	(17%)	
	Gilbert Baker (R)	16,540	(12%)	
	Conrad Reynolds (R)	7,128	(5%)	

Prior Winning Percentages: House: 2008 (79%); 2006 (62%); 2004 (59%); 2002 (99%); 2001 (56%)

Republican John Boozman is Arkansas' new junior senator, having ousted two-term Democrat Blanche Lincoln in 2010 by the largest majority of any Senate challenger over a defeated incumbent.

Boozman (*BOZ-man*) was born in Shreveport, La., but grew up in Fort Smith, Ark., the state's second-largest city. He credits his upbringing—his father was Air Force Master Sgt. Fay Boozman Jr.—for his appreciation of the issues that military families face. Boozman graduated from Northside High School in Fort Smith and attended the University of Arkansas, where he played football. He left college after completing his pre-optometry requirements and went on to graduate from the Southern College of Optometry in 1977.

He opened the Boozman Eye Clinic in Rogers, Ark., with his brother, Fay Boozman, an ophthalmologist. The brothers merged with another eye clinic in 1981 to form the Boozman-Hof Regional Eye Clinic. Boozman also established a low-vision program for the Arkansas School for the Blind. His first public office was a seat on the Rogers Board of Education in 1994. He served until 2001, when he won a November special election to succeed Republican Rep. Asa Hutchinson, who vacated the seat to head the Drug Enforcement Administration.

Boozman was easily re-elected every two years in the reliably conservative 3rd District, which contains Bentonville, the home of Wal-Mart Stores' corporate headquarters. He compiled a conservative voting record, opposing a bill to impose caps on carbon emissions, the Obama administration's $787 billion economic stimulus bill, and the health care overhaul. He broke with his party by favoring the end of the U.S. trade embargo with Cuba. During the Bush administration, Boozman voted in favor of the 2008 bill rescuing the U.S. financial system, a vote that tea party supporters used in other Republican primaries to blast incumbents. Previously, he opposed President Bush's attempt at comprehensive immigration legislation, which included a pathway to legal residency for illegal immigrants.

Boozman entered the 2010 Senate race in February, ending months of speculation and forcing Lincoln to run against a Boozman for the second time. Fay Boozman, then a state senator, was her opponent when she first ran for the Senate in 1998. Lincoln won that contest, 55% to 42%. Fay, a close friend of then-Gov. Mike Huckabee, went on to become director of the Arkansas Health Department. He was killed in a barn collapse in 2005.

In the primary season, Lincoln got bogged down in a bruising fight with Lt. Gov. Bill Halter, which she barely won. She pressed the importance of her role as chairman of the Senate Agriculture Committee for a state reliant on farming. She also tried to distance herself from Obama and the Democratic Party, noting her opposition to the carbon emissions bill and her support for cutting estate tax rates. Halter spent nearly $3 million on his campaign, forcing Lincoln to drain $7 million from her re-election fund. He managed to hold her to 45% of the vote to his 42%, which, because neither one hit 50%, forced the two into a runoff the following month. She won the runoff 52%-48%.

Meanwhile, Boozman topped an eight-candidate GOP primary in June with 53%, avoiding a runoff of his own. Not only was he the best known of the candidates running, he benefited from the fact that his congressional district was home to the largest share of Republican voters in the state. Tea party supporters were unhappy with his vote for the financial sector rescue, but his credibility with that group was bolstered by an endorsement from former Alaska Gov. Sarah Palin, a tea party favorite.

In the fall campaign against Boozman, Lincoln again stressed her role as chairwoman of the Agriculture Committee and she criticized Boozman for agreeing to a House GOP moratorium on earmarked spending. Boozman painted Lincoln as insufficiently conservative for Arkansas, and frequently mentioned his endorsements from the National Rifle Association and Arkansas Right to Life. He hammered Lincoln for her vote for the health care overhaul, which he said he would work to repeal. "I listened to your concerns on 'Obamacare,' fought for you in Washington, and voted against this bill," Boozman said. "But the Senate has let you down. Arkansas did not have a voice in that chamber willing to stand up to" Obama and congressional Democratic leaders. Boozman also slammed Lincoln for voting for Obama's economic stimulus bill. And he said he would not only vote to extend the expiring tax cuts enacted under Bush, he would consider additional tax cuts as well.

Arkansas' political trends were in Boozman's favor. The state had voted Republican in the two previous presidential elections, and two open House seats held by retiring Democrats also went Republican in 2010. Boozman maintained a double-digit lead in polls from the outset. To offset Lincoln's emphasis on her chairmanship, Minority Leader Mitch McConnell promised Boozman a seat on the panel. On Election Day, he prevailed with 58%, winning over independents by nearly 2-to-1, as well as older voters. Lincoln carried only 14 counties to Boozman's 61, and she won only nine of the 26 counties in the 1st District, which she once represented, according to the *Arkansas Democrat-Gazette*. Boozman's strongest showing was in his home of Benton County and his boyhood home of Sebastian County, where his share of the vote topped 70%.

FIRST DISTRICT

Rick Crawford (R)

Elected 2010, 1st full term; b. Jan. 22, 1966, Homestead Base, FL; home, Jonesboro; AR St. U., B.A. 1996.; Southern Baptist; Married (Stacy); 2 children.

Military Career: Army, 1985-89.

Professional Career: Owner, AgWatch Network.

DC Office: 1408 LHOB, 20515, 202-225-4076; Fax: 202-225-5602; Web site: crawford.house.gov.

State Offices: Cabot, 501-843-3043; Jonesboro, 870-203-0540.

Committees: *Agriculture:* Department Operations, Oversight & Credit; General Farm Commodities & Risk Management; Nutrition & Horticulture. *Transportation & Infrastructure:* Economic Development, Public Buildings & Emergency Management (VChmn); Highways & Transit; Water Resources & Environment.

Election Results

2010 general	Rick Crawford (R)	93,224	(52%)	($1,330,038)
	Chad Causey (D)	78,267	(43%)	($1,631,222)
	Ken Adler (Green)	8,320	(5%)	
2010 primary	Rick Crawford (R)	14,461	(72%)	
	Princella Smith (R)	5,682	(28%)	

Population		Race/Ethnicity		Work	
Pop. 2010:	687,694	White:	78.59%	Private:	75.09%
Change since 2000:	Up 2.9%	Black:	16.5%	Government:	16.30%
Urban:	44.5%	Hispanic:	2.70%	Self-employed:	8.30%
Rural:	55.5%	Asian:	0.5%	Blue collar:	29.60%
Area size:	17,521 sq. mi.	Native Am.:	0.40%	White collar:	51.89%
		Hawaiian:	0.0%	Khaki collar:	0.20%
Age		Two+ races:	1.2%	Other:	18.30%
Median age:	38.60 yrs.				
More than 65 yrs:	15.6%	*Ancestry*		Median income:	$34,495
Less than 18 yrs:	24.39%	Irish	11.5%	Median Home Value:	$85,200
		USA	10.4%		
Education		German	10.19%	**Military Veterans**	
H.S. grad:	79.0%			% of Pop:	11.69%
College grad:	13.69%				
Grad degree:	4.29%				

Northeast Arkansas; Jonesboro

The Mississippi Delta, the flat, mucky, river-crossed lowland on both sides of the great river, was some of the country's first industrial farmland. This land was uncultivated in most of the 19th century, when plows were still pulled by mules and muddy flatlands were impassable. Then, big landowners used machines to drain the marshlands and persuaded poor blacks to move here to tend fields of cotton, rice, and later, soybeans. The results were bountiful agricul-

2008 Presidential Vote
John McCain (R) 145,340   (59%)
Barack Obama (D) 95,102   (38%)

2004 Presidential Vote
George Bush (R) 127,179   (52%)
John Kerry (D) 115,994   (47%)

Cook Partisan Voting Index: R+8

ture and impoverished people. Around 1940, the Delta began to slowly change: the first minimum-wage and war-industry jobs up North drew young people out of the Delta, and the introduction of the mechanical cotton picker idled many farm workers.

But this land—stretching flat as far as the eye can see, along ribbons of asphalt that shimmer in the heat—remains poor by national standards. The people are undereducated, and the area has substantial pockets of unemployment. Local rice farmers are among the largest recipients of federal farm subsidies: The congressional district ranked fifth in the nation, pulling in $5.2 billion from 1995 to 2006. Riceland Foods, in the town of Stuttgart, is the world's largest rice miller and marketer and the largest recipient of subsidies in the United States, having received $554 million from 1995 to 2006. The rice producer has attracted an unusual partner in recent years, Colusa Biomass, which hopes to make ethanol out of rice hulls and plans to move its corporate headquarters to Stuttgart. The local rice fields also attract ducks, helping put Arkansas on the map as the most productive state for mallard hunters. Several big auto-parts plants have been built in Marion, across the Mississippi River from Memphis. And the area recently seemed to be discovering a manufacturing niche as a supplier of wind turbine components. Nordex USA, a German subsidiary, opened a turbine manufacturing plant in Jonesboro in 2010, with plans to eventually employ 700 people, and Mitsubishi was building a $100 million wind turbine assembly plant in Fort Smith. The companies will supply neighboring states like Texas and Oklahoma, where wind farms are being developed.

The 1st Congressional District of Arkansas includes most of the state's Delta lands and stretches west to the cool, green Ozarks. The largest city in the district is Jonesboro, whose cheap labor and flat land have made it a hub for food-processing companies like Nestle and Frito-Lay. In 2008, the StarTek call center brought a few hundred more jobs to the area. The district's natural beauty draws outdoorsmen to the sleepy Ozark town of Mountain Home, named *Outdoor Life* magazine's best place to live in 2008. The Delta, with its large black population, is the most Democratic part of Arkansas. Some of the hill counties are ancestrally Republican, and there is a Republican trend in Jonesboro and in Lonoke County, which is part of the Little Rock metro area. The result is that the district is closely divided in national politics. It voted 50%-48% for Democrat Al Gore in 2000 but 52%-47% for Republican George W. Bush in 2004. In 2008, the district voted 59% for Republican John McCain.

Rick Crawford (R)

The new congressman from the 1st District is Rick Crawford, the first Republican to win this northeastern Arkansas district since Reconstruction. In 2010, he soundly defeated Democrat Chad Causey, the former chief of staff for Rep. Marion Berry, whose retirement after seven terms sparked the battle for a successor.

Crawford was born in Florida on the former Homestead Air Force Base, where his father, a munitions expert, was stationed. Growing up in a military family meant a lot of "bouncing around," says Crawford, who attended a dozen schools as a child. The frequent uprooting provided a crash course in making friends quickly and adapting to new environments, skills that he says have become second nature. After graduating from high school in Hudson, N.H., enlisting in the military seemed a natural next step. Crawford's older siblings had already signed up, one joining the Air Force and one the Navy. So he chose the Army. "I guess if there had been a fourth brother, he'd have gone into the Marine Corps," he quipped.

In the service, Crawford was trained as a bomb-disposal technician, disabling suspected live explosive devices, a line of work that was introduced to a mass audience in the acclaimed 2008 film *The Hurt Locker*. Crawford achieved the rank of sergeant, did a tour of duty in Pakistan, and later served on U.S. Secret Service details for Presidents Reagan and George H.W. Bush. When his military service ended, he moved to southern Missouri and enrolled at Arkansas State University, in Jonesboro, to study agribusiness and economics. He competed on the college rodeo circuit until injuries forced him to quit. At the time, he says, he was "grossly under-employed," and his medical bills and other obligations piled up. In 1994, he declared personal bankruptcy, but he eventually found full-time employment—and discovered he had some skills—in rodeo announcing. He worked some 100 shows a year before returning to school to finish his degree. In 1995, he met his wife, Stacy, on a date orchestrated by their mothers, who were co-workers at the time. Stacy was then a fellow student at Arkansas State, and today is a licensed social worker and school-based therapist. The couple has two children, ages 4 and 2.

Working the rodeo-broadcasting gigs helped Crawford land a news-anchor job in Jonesboro after graduation. That eventually led him to agricultural broadcasting and to starting his own business called the AgWatch Network, a farm-news outlet that broadcasts on 39 radio stations in Arkansas, Kentucky, Mississippi, Missouri, and Tennessee, as well as on television stations in Little Rock and Jonesboro.

When Crawford decided to challenge Berry for the 1st District seat, national Republicans were at first cool to the idea, hoping to recruit a more seasoned candidate. But Crawford gained traction after Berry announced he wouldn't run, which made the district ripe for a GOP takeover. Crawford coasted to an easy primary victory over 26-year-old congressional aide Princella Smith, and he launched a general election campaign with the theme that Democrats had lost touch with the region's rural and small-town conservative voters.

In the general election campaign, Causey made an issue of Crawford's personal bankruptcy, attacking the Republican for failing to release his financial records. Democratic ads also suggested that Crawford would privatize Social Security and Medicare. Crawford, meanwhile, sought to portray Causey as a Washington insider beholden to national Democrats. The national parties jumped in with independent expenditures for ads, and former President Clinton returned to his home state to help raise money for Causey to no avail. Crawford beat Causey, 52% to 44%.

SECOND DISTRICT

Tim Griffin (R)

Elected 2010, 1st full term; b. Aug. 21, 1968, Charlotte, NC; home, Little Rock; Hendrix Col., B.A. 1990; Oxford U., attended 1991; Tulane U., J.D. 1994.; Baptist; Married (Elizabeth); 2 children.

Military Career: Army Reserve, 1996-present.

Professional Career: Cnsl., Office of Independent Cnsl., 1995-97; cnsl., House Oversight and Gov. Reform Cmte., 1997-99; dep. research dir., RNC, 2000; asst. U.S. atty., 2001-02; dep. communications dir., RNC, 2004; special asst. political affairs, White House, 2005; U.S. atty., AR Eastern District, 2006-07; gen. cnsl., Mercury Public Affairs, 2007-08; owner, law firm.

DC Office: 1232 LHOB, 20515, 202-225-2506; Fax: 202-225-5903; Web site: griffin.house.gov.

State Offices: Little Rock, 501-324-5941.

Committees: *Armed Services:* Readiness; Seapower & Projection Forces. *Foreign Affairs:* Africa, Global Health & Human Rights; Europe and Eurasia (VChmn); Terrorism, Nonproliferation & Trade. *Judiciary:* Crime, Terrorism & Homeland Security; Intellectual Property, Competition & the Internet.

Election Results

2010 general	Tim Griffin (R)	122,091	(58%)	($1,855,578)
	Joyce Elliott (D)	80,687	(38%)	($1,019,594)
	Lance Levi (I)	4,421	(2%)	
2010 primary	Tim Griffin (R)	24,610	(62%)	
	Scott Wallace (R)	15,285	(38%)	

Population		Race/Ethnicity		Work	
Pop. 2010:	751,377	White:	70.5%	Private:	76.09%
Change since 2000:	Up 12.8%	Black:	20.69%	Government:	18.0%
Urban:	66.20%	Hispanic:	5.20%	Self-employed:	5.70%
Rural:	33.79%	Asian:	1.4%	Blue collar:	23.0%
Area size:	6,045 sq. mi.	Native Am.:	0.40%	White collar:	60.20%
		Hawaiian:	0.0%	Khaki collar:	0.40%
Age		Two+ races:	1.60%	Other:	16.39%
Median age:	35.70 yrs.				
More than 65 yrs:	12.69%	*Ancestry*		Median income:	$43,161
Less than 18 yrs:	24.60%	German	10.4%	Median Home Value:	$122,300
		Irish	10.19%		
Education		English	8.69%	**Military Veterans**	
H.S. grad:	86.59%			% of Pop:	11.6%
College grad:	25.5%				
Grad degree:	9.0%				

Central Arkansas; Little Rock

Little Rock has been the capital of Arkansas and also its largest city for more than a century. It is at the geographic center of an otherwise rural state, and it is home to the presidential library of Bill Clinton, the former Arkansas governor. The city is best known for its role at the dawn of the civil rights movement. In September 1957, Democratic Gov. Orval Faubus sent in the National Guard to block a desegregation order at Central High School. President Eisenhower sent in U.S.

2008 Presidential Vote
John McCain (R)	161,540	(54%)
Barack Obama (D)	131,891	(44%)

2004 Presidential Vote
George Bush (R)	145,392	(51%)
John Kerry (D)	134,478	(48%)

Cook Partisan Voting Index: R+5

troops and federalized the National Guard to enforce the order, and Little Rock became a synonym for bigotry around the world. Forty years later, the Little Rock Nine who had integrated the high school returned for an anniversary commemoration with President Clinton. "It was Little Rock that made racial equality a driving obsession in my life," he said. Today, Little Rock is still the political center of Arkansas, setting the tone of the public life of its state as do only a few other state capitals—Boston, Providence, Atlanta, Denver, and Honolulu. It is home to the *Arkansas Democrat-Gazette*, the feisty, conservative paper whose editor Paul Greenberg christened Clinton

"Slick Willie." On the banks of the Arkansas River is the Clinton Presidential Center and Park, opened in 2004 and designed to promote local economic revitalization and with architecture evocative of a "bridge to the 21st century."

The 2nd Congressional District of Arkansas includes Little Rock and North Little Rock, a kind of industrial suburb across the Arkansas River and known informally for years as Dog Town. The metropolitan area suffered a nearly 6% decline in jobs since employment peaked in 2008. But as local leaders work to diversify the economy, the metro area is on track to recover those losses by early 2015. The district also takes in Saline (named for its early salt works) and Faulkner (named for fiddle player Sanford C. Faulkner, the original Arkansas Traveler) counties, which have grown rapidly as people move farther out on the freeways. This is the seat once held by legendary Ways and Means Chairman Wilbur Mills, who retired in 1976. In 2004, the district favored President Bush 51%-48%—the same as in the national popular vote. In 2008, John McCain defeated Barack Obama, 54%-44%.

Tim Griffin (R)

The new congressman from the 2nd District is Tim Griffin, a Republican who won the 2010 election to succeed retiring Democratic Rep. Vic Snyder.

Griffin, the son of a Baptist minister and a teacher, was born in Charlotte, N.C., and grew up in Magnolia, Ark., near the Louisiana border. He graduated cum laude from Hendrix College, north of Little Rock, and Tulane University Law School, and later studied at Oxford University. Griffin spent the past 14 years as a judge advocate in the Army and served in Mosul, Iraq. In 2003, Shannon Boozman, the daughter of Rep. John Boozman, R-Ark., set Griffin up on a blind date with Elizabeth, a sorority sister from the University of Arkansas. Two years later, they married.

In the late 1990s Griffin worked for Independent Counsel David Barrett in his investigation of Housing and Urban Development Secretary Henry Cisneros, a Democrat. Griffin then became an investigator for the House Oversight and Government Reform Committee under then-Chairman Dan Burton, R-Ind. He later worked for the Republican National Committee, helping with George W. Bush's recount effort in Florida during the 2000 election and doing opposition research for Bush's 2004 campaign. When Bush won a second term, Griffin became a deputy to Karl Rove, the president's top political operative.

Griffin gained national attention in early 2007, shortly after Bush fired nine U.S. attorneys, including Bud Cummins of the Eastern District of Arkansas, an action that Democrats charged was politically motivated. Paul McNulty, a Bush deputy attorney general, later acknowledged that Cummins had not been fired over performance. Griffin was picked as Cummins' successor, but the state's senators, Blanche Lincoln and Mark Pryor, both Democrats, refused to support his nomination. Bush appointed him anyway. Griffin resigned after six months, saying that the Bush administration had "mishandled" his appointment and that partisan senators were uninterested in giving him a fair hearing. A special prosecutor said in July that no criminal charges would be filed over the firings.

After leaving government, Griffin ran his law firm and a public affairs business. He considered challenging Lincoln in 2010 but eventually decided to run against Snyder, who, he contended, had not properly represented the Republican-leaning district's views because Snyder supported President Obama's agenda. His road to Congress was a sign of just how deep the dissatisfaction with Democrats was in red states in 2010. Despite his notoriety from the 2006 firings, Griffin had an easy path to victory. Well-connected in Republican circles, Griffin had no trouble raising money, and he mostly avoided being tagged as a Washington insider.

In the May Republican primary, Griffin outraised opponent Scott Wallace, a restaurant owner, nearly 7-to-1 and won with 62% of the vote. That set up a general-election matchup with state Sen. Joyce Elliott, a former public-school teacher who was forced to spend most of her money on a Democratic primary battle against state House Speaker Robbie Wills. Griffin defeated Elliott, 58% to 38%.

THIRD DISTRICT

Steve Womack (R)

Elected 2010, 1st full term; b. Feb. 18, 1957, Russellville; home, Rogers; AR Tech U., B.A. 1979.; Southern Baptist; Married (Terri); 3 children.

Military Career: AR Army Natl. Guard, 1979-2009.

Elected Office: Rogers Mayor, 1998-2010.

Professional Career: Reporter, mgr., KURM Radio, 1979-90; exec. officer, Army ROTC, U. of AR, 1990-96; financial consultant, Merrill Lynch, 1997.

DC Office: 1508 LHOB, 20515, 202-225-4301; Fax: 202-225-5713; Web site: womack.house.gov.

State Offices: Fort Smith, 479-424-1146; Harrison, 870-741-6900; Rogers, 479-464-0446.

Committees: *Appropriations:* Energy & Water Development (VChmn); Financial Services & General Government; Transportation, HUD & Related Agencies.

Election Results

2010 general	Steve Womack (R)	148,581	(72%)	($717,894)
	David Whitaker (D)	56,542	(28%)	($81,705)
2010 primary	Steve Womack (R)	18,334	(52%)	
	Cecile Bledsoe (R)	17,080	(48%)	
2010 primary	Steve Womack (R)	19,414	(31%)	
	Cecile Bledsoe (R)	8,253	(13%)	
	Gunner Delay (R)	8,088	(13%)	
	Bernie Skoch (R)	7,092	(11%)	
	Doug Matayo (R)	6,088	(10%)	
	Kurt Maddox (R)	6,037	(10%)	
	Mike Moore (R)	4,801	(8%)	

Population		Race/Ethnicity		Work	
Pop. 2010:	822,564	White:	79.5%	Private:	80.90%
Change since 2000:	Up 22.3%	Black:	2.39%	Government:	11.6%
Urban:	54.39%	Hispanic:	11.9%	Self-employed:	7.20%
Rural:	45.60%	Asian:	2.20%	Blue collar:	28.19%
Area size:	8,661 sq. mi.	Native Am.:	1.3%	White collar:	55.60%
		Hawaiian:	0.59%	Khaki collar:	0.10%
Age		Two+ races:	2.10%	Other:	16.10%
Median age:	35.10 yrs.				
More than 65 yrs:	12.69%	*Ancestry*		Median income:	$41,171
Less than 18 yrs:	25.69%	Irish	12.0%	Median Home Value:	$131,000
		German	11.9%		
Education		English	10.0%	**Military Veterans**	
H.S. grad:	81.70%			% of Pop:	10.80%
College grad:	21.30%				
Grad degree:	7.20%				

Northwest Arkansas; Fort Smith

In the mid-2000s, the northwest corner of Arkansas became one of America's boom areas, with major corporate headquarters and dozens of small factories, tourist attractions and retirement developments in the Ozarks. The Fayetteville-Springdale-Rogers metropolitan region grew by nearly 7% in 2005, outpacing the rest of the state. The region also had a rapidly growing population of Hispanics, who made up more than 20% of the population of Springdale and

2008 Presidential Vote
John McCain (R)	185,055	(64%)
Barack Obama (D)	96,485	(34%)

2004 Presidential Vote
George Bush (R)	171,853	(62%)
John Kerry (D)	100,656	(37%)

Cook Partisan Voting Index: R+16

Rogers. Driving the local economy are three major employer anchors: Wal-Mart Stores, J.B. Hunt Transport Services and Tysons Foods. This is also home to the mountain-bound resort town of

Eureka Springs and the handsome University of Arkansas in Fayetteville, where young lawyers Bill Clinton and Hillary Rodham married in the living room of a brick bungalow.

For most of the 20th century, the rounded green mountains and pleasant wide valleys, farmhouses and small towns of northwest Arkansas seemed left behind. But the friendly atmosphere and strong religious faith of these communities have proved to be assets, not liabilities, conducive to economic creativity and personal serenity. There have also been touches of genius. Sam Walton, who opened his first Wal-Mart on the town square of Bentonville (it's now a small museum), had the inspiration to build a retail chain in tradition-minded small towns and rural areas using sophisticated computerized management. It made him the richest man in America, though he still drove a pickup truck and kept the corporate headquarters in a deliberately unglitzy building in Bentonville. His company employs some 48,000 Arkansans, many in the northwest corner of the state. Don Tyson built Tyson Foods, with headquarters outside Springdale, into the world's leading chicken producer and processor. In 2007, Tyson Foods announced it would invest $150 million to build the first plant to refine animal and vegetable fats into fuel. Other firms have flocked in, especially to do business with Wal-Mart, now the world's largest food retailer. Lately though, local leaders have worried about the area's reliance on the three mainstay companies, whose job growth in the future is limited. In 2011, they launched an effort to diversify the northwest Arkansas economy into new realms like professional services and tourism.

The 3rd Congressional District covers northwest Arkansas, including Bentonville, Fayetteville and Springdale, plus Fort Smith on the Oklahoma line. It extends as far east as Marion County, home to Ranger Boats, the renowned manufacturer of tournament-quality fishing boats. Politically, this area has been the most Republican part of Arkansas since the Civil War. John Paul Hammerschmidt was elected to the U.S. House in 1966 as one of the first Republican congressmen from the South. He was strong enough even in Democratic 1974 to beat Bill Clinton, then 28, in Clinton's first election, though Clinton did get an impressive 48% of the vote. Lately, this area has become even more Republican, as Christian conservatives have entered politics and new migrants and millionaires have voted heavily Republican. After voting narrowly for Clinton in 1992 and narrowly against him in 1996, the 3rd twice voted strongly for George W. Bush and gave John McCain 64% in 2008.

Steve Womack (R)

The new congressman from the 3rd District is Republican Steve Womack, the winner of the 2010 contest to fill the seat left vacant by GOP Rep. John Boozman, who ran successfully for the Senate.

Womack was born in Russellville, Ark., and spent a good portion of his childhood in Moberly, Mo., before returning with his family to Russellville in his junior year of high school. His father, a local radio broadcaster, introduced him to popular political figures in the region, including former Sens. Tom Eagleton and Stuart Symington and Gov. Warren Hearnes, all Missouri Democrats. "If I 'Dr. Phil' myself about what got me involved in public service, it's that I always admired political leaders," Womack said, recalling those visits with his father. After high school, Womack stayed in Russellville to earn his bachelor's degree at Arkansas Tech University. He and his father subsequently established KURM Radio, which focused on community news, the weather, the county fair, and high school football and Little League baseball games. Womack covered local politics for the station. "I always would second-guess things, and say, 'Could I do that better?' " he recalled.

In 1990, Womack, by then a member of the Army National Guard, did a stint as executive officer of the Army ROTC program at the University of Arkansas. Later, in 2002, he led a peacekeeping task force of 500 troops in the Sinai Desert in Egypt—a mission established by the peace accords negotiated between Israel and Egypt in 1979. In the late 1990s, he worked briefly as a financial consultant for Merrill Lynch, but quit the job when he got the chance to test whether he could "do better" than the local politicians he had covered as a reporter. In 1998, Womack was elected mayor of Rogers, a city in the high-growth Fayetteville metropolitan area. He was re-elected twice. As Rogers and Benton County were experiencing significant population growth, Womack accurately anticipated a spike in demand for retail outlets in the area and worked to turn the city into a shopping destination. The city issued bonds to develop infrastructure to attract retail business.

He also had a reputation for tough enforcement of immigration laws. Local Hispanic leaders were incensed when Womack maintained that a majority of crimes in the city were committed by illegal immigrants, which they said was untrue. In 2007, Womack directed city officials to cooperate with raids by federal immigration agents on a Northwest Arkansas Mexican restaurant chain. Four years earlier, Hispanic motorists filed a lawsuit against Rogers and its police department, charging racial profiling. A settlement was reached without an award of damages or an admission of guilt, though Womack formed a committee to build better relations with the immigrant community.

When Boozman gave up his House seat after four terms to challenge Democratic Sen. Blanche Lincoln, Womack stepped into a crowded field of Republicans interested in the seat. His opponents included former state Sen. Gunner DeLay, a distant cousin of former House Majority Leader Tom DeLay, R-Texas; Steve Lowry, an ex-Drug Enforcement Administration agent; and Cecile Bledsoe, a state senator endorsed by former Alaska Gov. Sarah Palin and former Rep. Asa Hutchinson, R-Ark.

Womack and Bledsoe finished first and second, respectively, setting up a June runoff. The two candidates, who live less than a mile from each other, took to the airwaves in an unneighborly way. Bledsoe tried to portray herself as the true conservative in the race, promising to repeal "Obamacare," the derisive term national Republicans gave to President Obama's health care overhaul. Womack touted his record of job creation and attacked Bledsoe for her votes on tax issues, saying that she supported a $100 million tax increase and also a tax on milk when she was in the state Legislature. Womack eked out a victory, 52% to 48%.

Once he had prevailed in the primary, the hard work was behind him. Voters in the northwest corner of Arkansas had not elected a Democrat to the House since 1967. Womack easily prevailed in the general election over Democrat David Whitaker, a former assistant city attorney in Fayetteville, 72% to 28%.

FOURTH DISTRICT

Mike Ross (D)

Elected 2000, 6th full term; b. Aug. 2, 1961, Texarkana; home, Prescott; U. of AR, B.A. 1987; Methodist; married (Holly); 2 children.

Elected Office: Nevada County Quorum Court, 1983-85; AR Senate, 1990-2000.

Professional Career: Chief of staff, AR Lt. Gov. Winston Bryant, 1984-89; Owner, Holly's Health Mart, 1993-2007.

DC Office: 2436 RHOB, 20515, 202-225-3772; Fax: 202-225-1314; Web site: mikeross.house.gov.

State Offices: El Dorado, 870-881-0681; Hot Springs, 501-520-5892; Pine Bluff, 870-536-3376; Prescott, 870-887-6787.

Committees: *Energy & Commerce:* Commerce, Manufacturing & Trade; Health; Oversight & Investigations.

Group Ratings

	ACLU	ACU	ADA	CFG	AFS	FRC	LCV	ITIC	NTU	COC
2010	38	25	45	37	75	62	70	100	39	88
2009	–	20	60	26	78	–	71	–	14	80

National Journal Ratings

	2010 LIB	—	2010 CONS	2009 LIB	—	2009 CONS
Economic	47%	—	52%	48%	—	51%
Social	43%	—	57%	44%	—	56%
Foreign	48%	—	51%	48%	—	52%
Composite	46%	—	54%	47%	—	53%

Key Votes of the 111th Congress

1. Overturn Ledbetter	Y	5. Bar federal abortion funds	Y	9. Stop detainee transfers	Y
2. Pass $820 billion stimulus	Y	6. Pass health care bill	N	10. Legalize immigrants' kids	N
3. Let guns in national parks	Y	7. Regulate financial firms	N	11. Repeal don't ask, tell	N
4. Pass cap-and-trade	N	8. Pass tax cuts for some	Y	12. Limit campaign funds	Y

Election Results

2010 general	Mike Ross (D)	102,479	(58%)	($2,426,280)
	Beth Anne Rankin (R)	71,526	(40%)	($603,000)
	Joshua Drake (Green)	4,129	(2%)	
2010 primary	Mike Ross (D)	unopposed		

Prior Winning Percentages: 2008 (86%), 2006 (75%), 2004 (100%), 2002 (61%), 2000 (51%)

Population		Race/Ethnicity		Work	
Pop. 2010:	654,283	White:	68.70%	Private:	73.40%
Change since 2000:	Down 1.8%	Black:	24.19%	Government:	19.30%
Urban:	44.70%	Hispanic:	4.59%	Self-employed:	7.09%
Rural:	55.29%	Asian:	0.59%	Blue collar:	32.0%
Area size:	20,951 sq. mi.	Native Am.:	0.5%	White collar:	48.70%
		Hawaiian:	0.0%	Khaki collar:	0.10%
Age		Two+ races:	1.3%	Other:	19.19%
Median age:	39.60 yrs.				
More than 65 yrs:	16.10%	*Ancestry*		Median income:	$34,861
Less than 18 yrs:	23.69%	Irish	11.30%	Median Home Value:	$77,700
		English	8.5%		
Education		German	7.79%	**Military Veterans**	
H.S. grad:	79.90%			% of Pop:	11.5%
College grad:	14.9%				
Grad degree:	4.5%				

South Arkansas; Pine Bluff

West from the Delta flatlands along the Missis-sippi River, where the water-soaked fields pro-duce America's largest rice crop, are small cities like Pine Bluff and El Dorado and the Ouachita Mountains. Southern Arkansas might well be called the northwest corner of the Deep South. It includes the state's largest African-American population, a reminder that parts of southern Arkansas were once plantation country. There is also oil production, and the broiler-chicken in-

> **2008 Presidential Vote**
> John McCain (R) 146,082 (58%)
> Barack Obama (D) 98,832 (39%)
>
> **2004 Presidential Vote**
> George Bush (R) 128,474 (51%)
> John Kerry (D) 118,825 (48%)
>
> **Cook Partisan Voting Index:** R+7

dustry looms large in these parts. The accent is clearly Arkansan: El Dorado, Nevada and Lafayette are all pronounced with long a's and accents on the penultimate syllable, and Ouachita, with a bow to the original French rendition of the Indian name, is *wa-SHEE-ta*.

The district includes the little railroad-crossing county-seat town of Hope, where former Presi-dent Clinton and his first White House Chief of Staff Mack McLarty were classmates in Miss Mary's kindergarten and where former Gov. Mike Huckabee grew up a decade later. Hot Springs is the spa resort and gambling haven where Clinton's stepfather sold Buicks, his mother bet on the horses, and he excelled in high school. To the east is Pine Bluff, where unemployment has been higher than in the rest of the state despite the presence of poultry giant Tyson Foods. It has taken several unwelcome hits to its economy, including the November 2010 decision to lay off 1,100 work-ers at the Pine Bluff Chemical Agent Disposal Facility, which began operations in 2005 as part of an international effort to eradicate chemical weapons. The city hopes to capitalize on tourism, particularly the coming 150th anniversary of the Battle of Pine Bluff, when Union soldiers with-stood a Confederate attack on the fortified courthouse square.

The 4th Congressional District occupies almost all of the southern half of Arkansas, from the Mississippi River to Texarkana. It is historically a Democratic district, and one that for most of the 20th century elected young men to the House and kept them there for years, to cut deals with the Democratic leadership and bring home the bacon. But like much of the rest of the state, it has turned more Republican. President Obama failed to break 40% here in 2008, eight years after Al Gore carried the district.

Mike Ross (D)

The congressman from the 4th District is Mike Ross, a Democrat who in 2000 defeated Republican Jay Dickey, the only House Republican outside California to be defeated that year. A fifth-genera-tion Arkansan, Ross was born in Texarkana. He graduated from Hope High School and the Univer-sity of Arkansas at Little Rock. He got his start in local politics in 1982 as a travel aide to Bill Clinton during his successful bid for governor. While in college, Ross was on the staff of Lt. Gov. Winston Bryant and was executive director of the Arkansas Youth Suicide Prevention Commission. Later, Ross sold insurance and worked as a sales manager for a pharmaceutical company. He and his wife, who is a pharmacist, ran Holly's Health Mart in rural Prescott until they sold the business in 2007. Ross was elected to the state Senate in 1990. When term limits forced him out a decade later, he ran for Congress.

This was perhaps the only district in the nation where impeachment played a pivotal role in 2000. Dickey, representing Clinton's boyhood homes, had voted for impeachment, angering the White House. Although Dickey often was a thorn to Republican leaders, Ross tied him to them and argued that "the real Jay Dickey" voted to cut Medicare and Social Security benefits to fund tax cuts for the rich. Dickey responded that Ross was getting his script from "his liberal masters in Washington." Clinton had an impact. He helped bring in $300,000 for Ross at fundraisers, orchestrated endorsements from administration officials with Arkansas roots, and campaigned for Ross in Pine Bluff on the Sunday before the election. There were plenty of independent expenditures as well. Ross won, 51%-49%.

In the House, Ross joined the conservative Blue Dog Democrats and became a vocal proponent of prescription drug legislation, often citing his experiences as a small-town pharmacist. He also is influenced by his country roots. Ross regularly shoots skeet from the back of his pickup truck, and in 2009, his aversion to gun laws inspired him to join 65 House Democrats in warning Attorney General Eric Holder to refrain from reinstituting the expired ban on assault weapons. On the Energy and Commerce Committee, he introduced legislation in 2008 to open the Arctic National Wildlife Refuge in Alaska and the outer continental shelf to oil drilling. On the home front, Ross in 2002 won approval of his proposal to remove Arkansas' constitutional limit on interest rates, which local bankers and consumer groups agreed had made financing difficult. His action won wide support from political leaders in Arkansas, the only remaining state to mandate such terms.

In recent years, Ross became active in the Democratic leadership, putting him out front on national issues and campaigns. In 2006, Ross was a top lieutenant to Illinois Democrat Rahm Emanuel, who as chairman of the Democratic Congressional Campaign Committee helped orchestrate the party's successful takeover of the House majority that year. He consistently has tried to move the leadership to the center on issues. In 2007 and 2008, he was one of three co-chairs of the Blue Dogs, the group of roughly 50 conservative Democrats in the House. "We're in the middle, where the American people are," said Ross, who handled communications and message for the faction.

As Blue Dogs sought to expand their influence beyond budgetary matters in 2009, Ross headed the group's task force on health care. That assignment gave him a pivotal role in the health care debate. He denounced the House Democrats' plan in July 2009, declaring it did not curtail the escalating costs of Medicare and other spending. But Emanuel and Energy and Commerce Chairman Henry Waxman of California got Ross to the negotiating table and, after two weeks, hammered out a deal. The Blue Dogs won several concessions, including easing mandates on employers and cutting $100 billion in costs. The bill made it out of committee on a 31-28 vote.

Republicans blasted Ross for being a "lapdog" that allowed the proposal to move forward, while liberal Democrats angrily accused him of doing the health insurance industry's bidding. Amid the controversy, the investigative reporting group ProPublica raised questions about the sale of Ross' family pharmacy to a drug chain with a stake in the debate's outcome. Ross was one of 24 Blue Dogs who opposed the final House bill in November 2009, and held firm in refusing to back the ultimate version in March 2010.

Ross was elected the Blue Dog group's co-chair for communications in the 112th Congress (2011-12). He also began expanding his portfolio into international issues, picking up a seat on the Foreign Affairs Committee in 2009. The following year, he was elected vice president of the NATO Parliamentary Assembly.

After Ross' first term in office, he faced a repeat challenge from Dickey in 2002. Both candidates again raised substantial sums. Dickey constantly reminded voters that he had delivered federal money to the district from his Appropriations Committee seat and had secured a pledge from then-GOP House Speaker Dennis Hastert to get back his seat on the committee. Ross won by a convincing 61%-39%. Ross had no Republican opposition in 2004, and Dickey became a Washington lobbyist. Ross has been re-elected easily since, even as the rest of the state's Democratic House delegation has vanished. He has made little secret of his ambition to someday run for governor, possibly in 2014.

★ CALIFORNIA ★

California, America's largest state, is a great success story and, at least in some eyes, a story of unanticipated failure. It is the birthplace of much of the world's most advanced technology, yet it is a place with plenty of Third World neighborhoods. It is home to some of the most creative people and industries ever imagined, but also posted the nation's second highest unemployment rate, behind only Nevada, in 2010. Among the states, it has attracted the largest number of immigrants from Mexico, Latin America and Asia, but it also has seen the second largest exodus, after New York, of citizens to other states. At mid-century, California was the promised land for an American middle class that supported the New Deal and liked Ike, that embraced and personified all-American values in 1940s movies and 1950s television. By the early 21st century, California has become a two-tiered society, with an affluent elite that embraces culturally liberal values—gentry liberals in Californian Joel Kotkin's inspired term—and immigrant masses living in Spanish-language neighborhoods and striving to hold onto low-paying jobs in a stagnant economy. California, we have been told for decades, is the America of the future—and for many years it was. But not necessarily anymore. The decade of the 2000s was the first since California was admitted to the Union in 1850 that it did not grow faster than the national average.

With one out of eight people in America, California is a demographic giant, which means that its achievements—and problems—are the nation's. The U.S. Census Bureau estimated California's population in 2010 at 37 million, far ahead of second-place Texas, with 25 million. Metro Los Angeles had 18 million people, second only to metro New York City's 19 million. The San Francisco Bay Area had 7.4 million, not so far behind Chicagoland's 9.6 million. San Diego and Orange counties, with 3 million people each, are the nation's sixth and seventh largest counties. California owes its preeminence not only to its natural advantages, including its vast geographic area and pleasant climate, but also to its human ingenuity. Despite having little in the way of natural resources and no natural harbor, Los Angeles is both a busy port and the nation's biggest manufacturer. The city is also known as the world's entertainment center. The Bay Area, which once made its living by exporting food, is now the global leader in computers and high technology. In the half-century after World War II, California was a magnet for migrants, a promised land where dreams could be realized. But from 2000 to 2009, some 1.5 million Americans left California for places east and north, even as 1.8 million foreign immigrants moved in. As a result the state's population is currently 38% Hispanic and 13% Asian.

Change has been a constant in California's history. Its economy has been transformed several times over, its population has been transformed by one group of newcomers after another, and its politics are periodically transformed with the suddenness of an earthquake. In 1848, when California passed from Mexico to the United States by the Treaty of Guadalupe Hidalgo, it was sparsely populated, inhabited by a few thousand Indians and Mexicans and by a few hundred U.S. soldiers and men on the make. Then in 1849, gold was found in Sutter's Mill and thousands of people arrived in the Gold Rush. Within months, San Francisco became one of America's 25 largest cities. The big money was made not by the miners but by the grocers and dry-goods merchants and transportation entrepreneurs who provisioned them, such as the Big Four—Crocker, Hopkins, Huntington, Stanford—who built the Central and Southern Pacific Railroads. Many of the laborers were Chinese, and California whites, angry at low-wage competition and fearful of an Asian tidal wave, were the impetus behind the aptly-named Chinese Exclusion Act of 1882, which suspended legal Chinese immigration and was not fully repealed until 1965.

The railroads sold off vast chunks of the Central Valley to large farming operations and enticed settlers with low fares to newly platted suburbs in the Los Angeles Basin. Engineers built great aqueducts that stretched hundreds of miles, from Yosemite to San Francisco and from the Owens River to Los Angeles. Without a water supply, the cities would not exist. Early-20th-century California was affluent and cultured, containing great universities such as the University of California (Berkeley) and Stanford and fine museums and libraries. It was America's window on the Pacific, alert to developments in China and Japan, Hawaii and the Philippines, and it was eager to extend America's economic reach and military strength. Nevertheless, as author Carey McWilliams wrote, California was an "island" separated from the rest of the country. Then in World War II, California became one of the great defense industry states, building ships and airplanes by the thousands. Millions of Americans came and millions stayed. The population rose from 7 million in 1940 to 17 million in 1963, when California passed New York as the nation's most populous state.

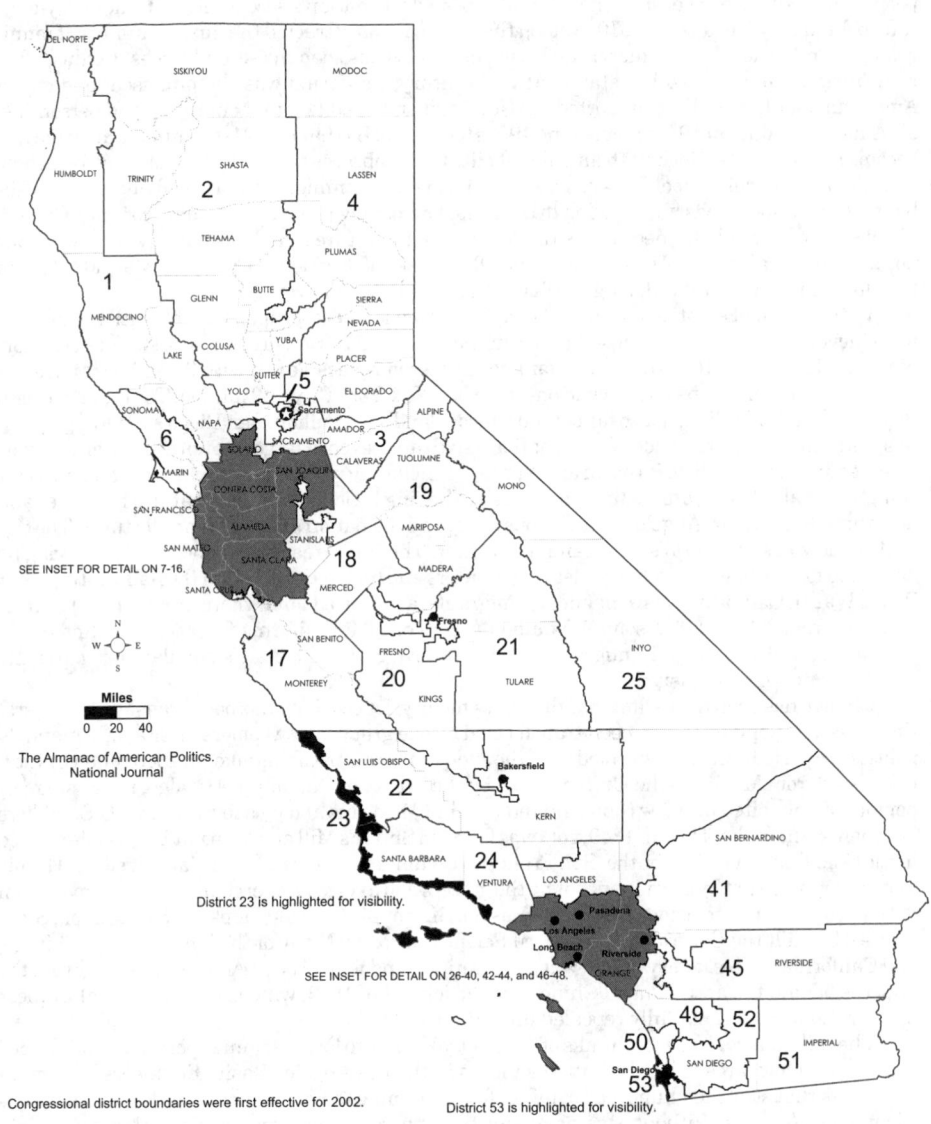

SEE INSET FOR DETAIL ON 7-16.

Miles
0   20   40

The Almanac of American Politics.
National Journal

District 23 is highlighted for visibility.

SEE INSET FOR DETAIL ON 26-40, 42-44, and 46-48.

District 53 is highlighted for visibility.

Congressional district boundaries were first effective for 2002.

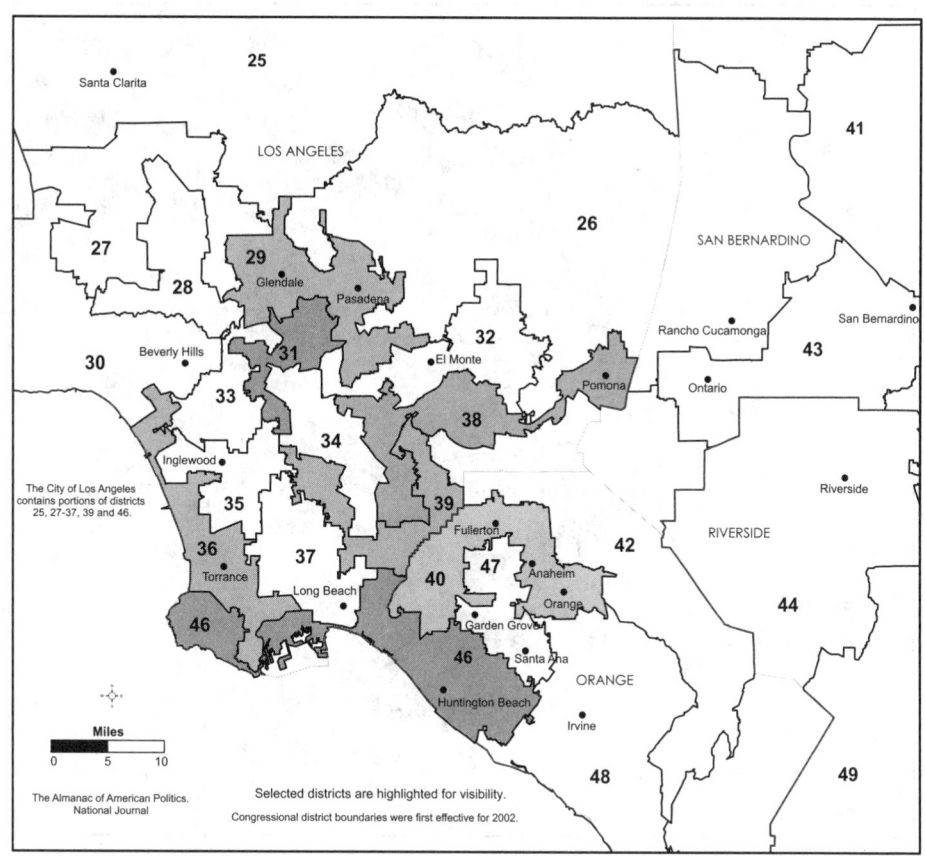

The heads of the big units of government and business planned California's future—leaders such as President Franklin D. Roosevelt and industrial mogul Henry J. Kaiser, who constructed vast shipyards and steel and aluminum factories. Republican Gov. Earl Warren husbanded tax monies to build schools and freeways in the years after the war. Educators Robert Sproul and Clark Kerr transformed the University of California into what Kerr called "the multiversity," and Democratic Gov. Pat Brown completed the vast system of canals and aqueducts that brought water from the wet north to the dry south. But the real engine of growth was the little people who took advantage of this infrastructure and built a humming economy. When California's defense plants closed down after World War II, government and civic leaders imagined that hundreds of thousands of jobs would head back east. Instead, as urbanologist Jane Jacobs pointed out, one-eighth of all the new jobs in the nation in the late 1940s were created in metro Los Angeles. This small-scale growth, multiplied thousands of times over, helped make California the nation's largest state.

The infusion of migrants transformed California politically. Before the war, it was a Republican state, with progressive leanings. Political struggles took place inside the Republican Party. The in-rush of the GI generation, with its allegiance to the New Deal, and the building of auto and steel factories, which unionized their workforces, transformed California into a two-party state. These new migrants were middle- and working-class, family men and women enjoying a life in suburbs in the lovely California climate. Warren's progressive Republicans remained dominant through the mid-1950s, but with Brown's election as governor in 1958, a group of talented, liberal Democrats took over. Things turned sour in the mid-1960s, when student rebellions starting at Berkeley and the Watts riot upset the New Deal order. Californians responded by calling in a disillusioned New Dealer espousing the conformist cultural conservatism of the GI generation, Ronald Reagan. California was a harbinger: It showed the nation where it would go next in the 1980s.

In 1974, California elected Democrat Jerry Brown as governor, entranced for a time by his fresh vision of Baby Boomer liberalism. California's laid-back lifestyles became a magnet for highly educated Boomers, lawyers, scientists, techies, and show-biz types. But they were not the domi-

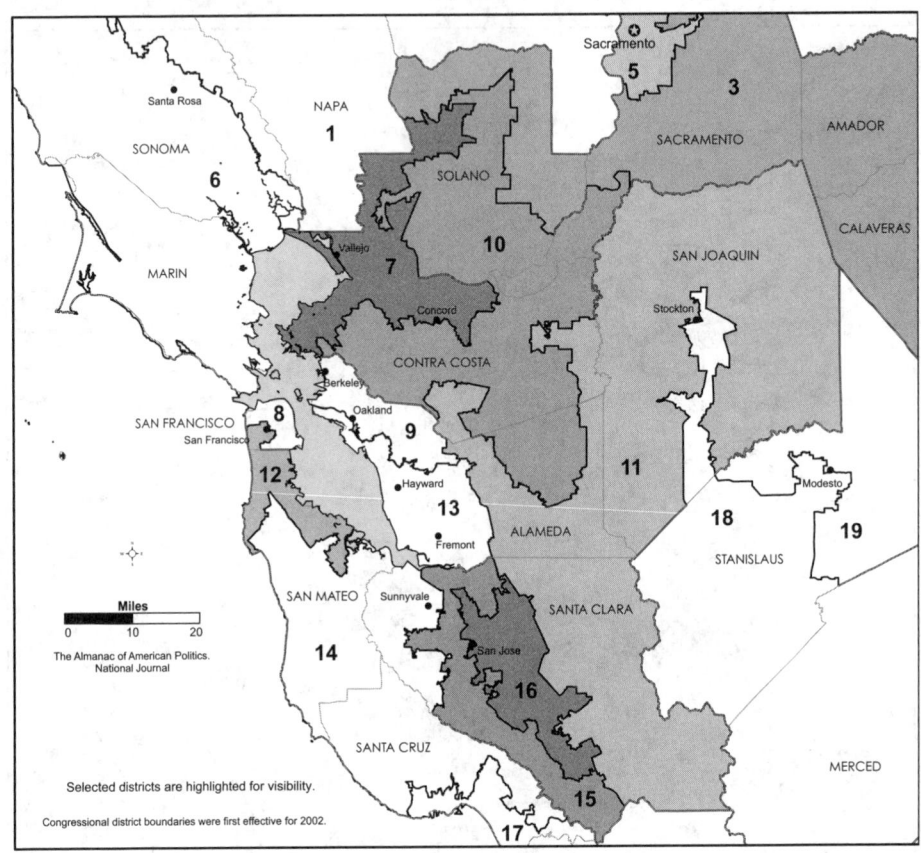

nant force in the state's politics for some time. California voted Republican in every presidential election from 1968 to 1988. Brown's administration was not wholly successful on policy. Voters froze property taxes by passing Proposition 13 in 1978, and ousted three of his state Supreme Court justices in 1986. Republicans followed Brown in the governorship: George Deukmejian, elected in 1982 and 1986, and Pete Wilson, elected in 1990 and 1994.

In the 1980s, California's defense industry boomed and Silicon Valley flowered south of San Francisco. Immigration continued, in vast numbers, with newcomers living in the dirty stucco bungalows and garden apartments that white, blue-collar workers left behind in neighborhoods south and east of downtown Los Angeles. Large swaths of the San Fernando Valley and Santa Ana in Orange County became mostly Latino. Public policy increasingly was set by Willie Brown, speaker of the California Assembly from 1980 to 1995, and later by the Democratic legislature. In the 1990s, disaster struck in several forms. Defense industry cutbacks hit the Los Angeles area hard, costing hundreds of thousands of jobs and sending housing values plummeting. Television screens were filled with news of floods and earthquakes, of riots and trials. California government responded competently to the natural disasters, less well to those that were man-made. Lou Cannon's *Official Negligence*, the definitive story of the Rodney King case, is a story of public-sector incompetence as dismaying as that spotlighted for the nation in the O.J. Simpson murder trial. In the 1990s, California also lost many of its trademark big businesses to mergers and relocations.

In the past two decades, California's current demographic and political trends were set. Since 1990, California has had an outflow of people to other states offset by an even larger inflow of people from other countries. The lingering recession of the early 1990s started the outflow, with about 2 million Californians, mostly white and affluent, leaving for other Western states or moving farther east, while immigrants kept arriving. California's Hispanic population rose from 16% in 1980 to 32% in 2000 and to 37% in 2009, the Asian percentage rose from 5% in 1980 to 11% in 2000 and 13% in 2009. The pace accelerated from 2000 to 2009, when domestic out-migration was 1.5 million and foreign in-migration was 1.8 million. Los Angeles County is what New York City was 100 years ago: the great entry point in the United States. The county has the world's largest numbers of Mexicans, Iranians, Samoans, Filipinos, Salvadorans, Armenians, Guatemalans, Koreans, and Thais outside their native lands. Even far Northern California is 15% Hispanic. The farmlands of Imperial County are three-quarters Hispanic. Asians make up half the population of the west side of San Francisco and Los Angeles County's San Gabriel Valley, and more than one-third in the south end of San Francisco Bay, from Palo Alto and Fremont south to San Jose.

If California seemed to lean Republican in the two decades after Ronald Reagan's election as governor in 1966, in the past two decades California has become increasingly Democratic, with gentry liberals of the Baby Boom generation and their younger counterparts joining an increasing number of Latino and Hispanic voters. Bill Clinton accelerated the process. After carrying California 46%-33% in the 1992 general election, at a time when the state was presumed to be part of a Republican "lock" on the presidency, he assiduously returned again and again, courting Silicon Valley entrepreneurs, Hollywood celebrities, feminist icons, Asian contributors, and Latino politicians. The Democratic trend was helped along by the response to Proposition 187, which barred non-emergency government spending on illegal immigrants and their children and became a central issue in state politics in 1994. Republican Gov. Wilson, trailing state Treasurer Kathleen Brown (Jerry Brown's sister) in polls and concerned about fast-rising state spending on illegal immigrants, supported Prop 187; although he was careful to differentiate between illegal and legal immigrants, he also ran ads showing Mexicans sprinting across the border, as the voice-over says, in ominous tones, "They keep coming." Voters made that distinction, too: Nearly 60% of all voters and about one-third of Hispanics voted for the proposition. Wilson won a decisive victory, 55%-41%, but one that came with considerable collateral damage to his party. In 1996, Clinton carried California, and Republicans lost their brief majority in the state Assembly. Republican George W. Bush's courtship of Hispanics enabled him to run with 29% and 34% of the Latino vote in 2000 and 2004, respectively, but GOP nominee John McCain's share fell to 23% in 2008. Asians, who seemed to rally to Republicans when predominately black rioters looted Los Angeles' "Koreatown" in 1992, went with Democrat Al Gore in 2000, and cast nearly two-thirds of their votes for the Democratic presidential tickets in 2000, 2004, and 2008.

Gentry liberals provided the other building block for California's Democratic majorities. They were repelled by the Republican Party of U.S. House Speaker Newt Gingrich and President George W. Bush, of Christian conservatives and gun-rights activists. They were similarly repelled by the conservative brand of California Republican, who habitually denounced immigration and championed opposition to abortion rights. Democrat Gray Davis was elected governor by a margin of 58%-38% in 1998, and Gore carried the state by 53%-42% in 2000, even though Bush spent $20 million on California media and Gore not a penny. In 2002, Davis, with low job ratings after the 2001 electricity crisis, was re-elected by only 47%-42%. But Democrats won every statewide office for the first time since 1882.

Those results seemed to establish California as a solidly Democratic state. The cataclysmic event of 2003—the recall of Gov. Davis and the election of Republican Arnold Schwarzenegger to replace him—was a major exception. The recall was sparked in early 2003 by isolated protests and gained strength when U.S. Rep. Darrell Issa, a Republican, donated his own money to finance a recall petition drive. Davis unwittingly stimulated it by signing a bill authorizing driver's licenses for illegal aliens and by unilaterally raising the license-plate fee. In August, Schwarzenegger went on the *Tonight Show* to say he would run. Two months later, Davis was recalled by a 55%-45% margin, and on the replacement ballot, Schwarzenegger won 49% of the vote to 32% for Democratic Lt. Gov. Cruz Bustamante and 14% for conservative Republican Tom McClintock. Cowed by Schwarzenegger's popularity, the legislature repealed driver's licenses for illegal immigrants and voted for changes in workmen's compensation laws. But in 2005 Schwarzenegger's frontal attack on the power structure in Sacramento—ballot measures giving the governor new powers to cut spending, to increase the time it took teachers to get tenure, and to create a redistricting commission—were defeated after public employees unions spent more than $100 million on anti-Schwarzenegger ads. His job rating sunk under 50% and he hired one of Davis' top aides as his chief of staff. Thenceforward, Schwarzenegger governed much as Davis had, backing liberal measures like carbon emissions reduction legislation and bonds for high-speed rail lines and trying, without great success, to hold down spending by the Democratic legislature. He won re-election in 2006, 56%-39%, over state Treasurer Phil Angelides.

When the housing bubble burst in 2007, unemployment in the state shot above the national average and eventually hit some of the highest levels in the nation. California's high taxes and stringent regulations helped drive businesses out of the state. In 2010, former eBay CEO Meg Whitman spent $141.5 million of her own money running for governor, and promised to take on the power brokers in Sacramento and reduce the costs of doing business. But a revived Jerry Brown, unopposed for the Democratic nomination, ran devastating ads showing Whitman mouthing the same phrases Schwarzenegger had in 2003, while hinting that with his experience he might be able to tame the legislature. It worked; Brown won 54%-41%. There were limits, however, to California's liberalism. Proposition 19, which would have legalized marijuana, was rejected 53%-47%. It carried in coastal counties from Sonoma to Santa Barbara, but it was rejected by narrow majorities of whites, blacks, and Latinos, and by 61% of Asians.

Once upon a time, people used to analyze California politics by distinguishing between Northern California and Southern California. Northern California—the Central Valley and the North Coast as well as the San Francisco Bay Area—tended to vote for John F. Kennedy, Hubert Humphrey, Jimmy Carter, and other Democrats. Southern California—Los Angeles County as well as the smaller suburban and desert counties—tended to vote for Richard Nixon, Gerald Ford, and other Republicans. Today, the geographic divisions run the other way. The two sides are coastal California and interior California. Coastal California is defined as all of the counties that touch the coast or San Francisco Bay. From 2000 to 2007, coastal California had an immigrant inflow of 6% and a domestic outflow of 9%. That's a lot of people: 1.4 million immigrants moving in, 1.8 million Americans moving out. The latter moved to places with lower housing prices and more middle-class accommodations: to the Central Valley, to Arizona, Nevada, Texas, and the Rocky Mountain states. Interior California from 2000 to 2007 saw quite different movements—an immigrant inflow of 3% overshadowed by a domestic inflow of 9%. The result was that coastal California grew 4% in those years, less than the national average of 6%, while interior California grew by 17%, more than any state except Nevada and Arizona.

The huge immigrant inflow and domestic outflow from coastal California has contributed to making the region an increasingly two-tiered society economically. Nonetheless, affluent elites and low-income immigrants remain united in voting Democratic. Coastal California voted 65%-33% for Barack Obama over John McCain for president in 2008, a higher percentage than in any other state except Obama's native Hawaii and tiny Vermont. The transformation of coastal California over the past generation can be measured another way: Reagan in 1984 lost the Bay Area 51%-48%; McCain in 2008 lost it 74%-24%. The Democratic trend is even apparent in the far south coast. Orange County and San Diego County voted 75%-24% and 65%-33%, respectively, for Reagan. McCain carried Orange County by only 50%-48% and lost San Diego County by 54%-44%. Coastal California did move toward Republicans in 2010, but still voted 57%-38% for both Brown and Sen. Barbara Boxer, enough to give them solid margins statewide.

Interior California is a very different kind of place, with twice as many native-born Americans moving in as immigrants. The income gap is not nearly as wide as in coastal California, and low-income immigrants enjoy at least a somewhat lower cost of living—no Neiman Marcuses here and not so many swap-meets. Until the recession of the late 2000s, population growth was vibrant, even frenetic. Interior California grew 18% between 2000 and 2008, accounting for two-thirds of the statewide population growth. But the explosion turned out to have negative consequences. The Inland Empire and large parts of the Central Valley from Bakersfield to Sacramento were subprime mortgage territory. The collapse of the housing market hit hard here, and the Inland Empire and the Central Valley had some of the highest foreclosure rates in the country. The result has been some violent political swings. In 2008, interior California trended Democratic, voting for Obama 50%-48%. In 2010, it swung the other way. Whitman carried interior California 49%-45% and Fiorina beat Boxer there 53%-40%.

Coastal California, more than twice as populous as interior California, is dominant politically. Even with a significant swing toward Republicans in 2010, the coalition of gentry liberals and low-income Hispanics put the state as far out of reach of the Republicans as it was for George W. Bush in 2004. Only one statewide race was close, in which San Francisco District Attorney Kamala Harris beat Los Angeles District Attorney Steve Cooley 46%-45%, for state attorney general. Otherwise no Republican candidate for the down ballot offices got even 40% of the vote. But there were troubling signs for the dominant coalition. Some municipalities are sinking toward bankruptcy and the state government has a credit rating lower than any other state's. The cost of local governments was spotlighted in summer 2010 when it was revealed that the tiny Los Angeles County city of Bell was paying its city manager $787,000 a year. California's determination to reduce carbon dioxide emissions, which in the short run are relatively benign, threaten to impose huge costs on the state. The slow-growth policies of coastal California, together with the subprime mortgage abuses prevalent in interior California, have left residents with housing prices in urban areas well above the average person's reach. California's expensive public schools yield some of the lowest test scores in the nation, and its state universities have been raising tuition sharply. High-tech employment has remained about static for a decade, as Silicon Valley firms outsource research and work to more economically affordable sites. State government's "descent into insolvency," as Kotkin puts it, seems unstoppable, as thousands of youngish state and local employees qualify for six-figure pensions every year. California, which has always prided itself on setting trends for the rest of the country, is in danger of getting left behind. It may not be coincidental that its leading officeholders—Brown, Dianne Feinstein, Boxer, House Minority Leader Nancy Pelosi, and Reps. Pete Stark, Henry Waxman, Howard Berman—are all in their 70s and got started in politics in the 1960s and 1970s. California, which likes to think of itself as the future, is in danger of becoming the past.

Population		Household Income		Work	
Pop. 2010:	37,253,956	Under $15k:	10.5%	Private:	76.3%
State rank:	1st	$15k to $50k:	31.5%	Government:	14.9%
Change since 2000:	Up 10.0%	$50k to $100k:	30.4%	Self-employed:	8.6%
Urban:	92.7%	$100k to $200k:	21.2%	Unemployment (3-yr. average):	5.6%
Rural:	7.3%	Over $200k:	6.4%	Poverty:	13.3%
Native of state:	53.2%	Median income:	$60,422	Blue collar:	19.7%
Not a citizen:	15.0%			White collar:	61.0%
Area size:	163,695 sq. mi.	**Home Value**		Khaki collar:	0.4%
		Under $100k:	5.9%	Other:	18.9%
Most populous cities		$100k to $300k:	20.6%		
Los Angeles	3,792,621	$300k to $500k:	28.8%	**Age**	
San Diego	1,307,402	$500k to $1 mil:	35.1%	Median age:	34.7 yrs.
San Jose	945,942	Over $1 million:	9.6%	More than 65 yrs:	11.1%
San Francisco	805,235	Median:	$461,400	Less than 18 yrs:	25.8%

Race/Ethnicity				Military Veterans		Registered Voters in 2010	
White:	40.1%	*Language*		% of Pop:	7.4%	Democrats:	7,620,240
Black:	5.8%	English:	57.4%			Republicans:	5,361,875
Hispanic:	37.6%	Spanish:	28.4%	*Veterans by Period*		Ind./other:	4,303,768
Asian:	12.8%	Asian:	9.0%	WWII and before:	11.5%	Voter turnout:	10,302,324
Native Am.:	0.4%	Other European:	4.3%	Korea:	11.7%	Turnout as % of	
Hawaiian:	0.3%			Vietnam:	33.2%	voting age:	36.8%
Two+ races:	2.6%	**Education**		Gulf (pre-2001):	10.6%		
		H.S. grad:	80.5%	Gulf (post-2001):	7.8%	**Legislature**	
Ancestry		College grad:	29.9%	Peace time:	25.1%	Senate:	25 D 15 R
German	8.2%	Grad degree:	10.7%			Assembly:	52 D 28 R
Irish	6.6%						
English	5.8%						

Presidential politics   California has 55 electoral votes, substantially more than any other state. And that fact supposedly gave Republicans a lock on the presidency from 1968 to 1988. Then, from 1992 to 2008, California gave the Democrats, if not a lock on the presidency, then at least a way to be competitive at the presidential level. The state's percentages for Democratic presidential candidates have been on an upward trajectory—46% in 1992, 51% in 1996, 53% in 2000, 54% in 2004, and 61% in 2008. In 2000, George W. Bush's chief strategist, Karl Rove, spent $20 million on ads in California media. Democrat Al Gore's campaign, coolly assessing the polls, put in nothing at all, and he won the state 53%-42%. Eight years later, Republican John McCain's strategists didn't give California a second thought.

Even so, the size of Obama's victory merits examination. Obama won California 61%-37%. He did better than favorite-son Reagan in 1984 and Democrat Lyndon Johnson in 1964, and he received a higher percentage of votes than any presidential candidate since Franklin Roosevelt won 67% in California in 1936. The exit polls provided insight. Some 10% of California voters were black—lower than in any of the other 10 largest

2008 Presidential Vote
Barack Obama (D) 8,274,473   (61%)
John McCain (R) 5,011,781   (37%)

2008 Presidential Primary
Hillary Clinton (D).............2,608,184   (51%)
Barack Obama (D) 2,186,662   (43%)

2008 Presidential Primary
John McCain (R) 1,238,988   (42%)
Mitt Romney (R).................1,013,471   (35%)
Mike Huckabee (R)...............340,669   (12%)

2004 Presidential Vote
John Kerry (D) 6,745,485   (54%)
George W. Bush (R)...........5,509,826   (44%)

states but significantly higher than blacks' 7% share of the California population. They voted 94% for Obama. Another 18% of the voters were self-identified Latinos, and they voted for Obama 74%-25%. About 6% of the voters were Asian, and they went 64%-35% for Obama. These three groups, amounting to 34% of the electorate, accounted for about 13% of Obama's 24-percentage-point margin of victory.

Another large quantum of the Obama vote came from the gentry liberals. That's not an exit poll category, of course, but some exit poll categories do provide useful proxies. White college graduates voted 57% for Obama, more than white non-graduates. And voters with annual incomes over $200,000 voted 58% for Obama. Perhaps the most illuminating group was the 50- to 64-year-old age group, which is roughly congruent with the Baby Boom Generation. It includes relatively few Hispanics and Asians (immigrants tend to be younger than average). This cohort voted conspicuously out of line with adjacent age groups: 62% of them voted for Obama, compared with 55% of voters in their 40s (roughly congruent with Generation X) and 48% of Obama voters age 65 and over. When the Baby Boom voters are added to the ethnic minorities and the sum is adjusted for overlap, the resulting group accounts for almost the entire Obama margin. Pretty much all the rest can be attributed to vote-switchers in the mortgage crisis epicenters in interior California. Is it an enduring majority? Quite possibly, although the shakeout from the mortgage crisis might impel marginalized immigrants, more than cranky conservatives, to move out of the state. And in time, the Baby Boom generation will diminish in numbers and may fade into political irrelevance.

A few old-timers can still recall when California's June primary was the national tiebreaker. In 1964, the state was the center of national attention when Nelson Rockefeller lost here to Barry Goldwater in the Republican primary. California returned to the limelight in 1968, when Robert Kennedy prevailed over Eugene McCarthy in the Democratic primary, then was assassinated by Palestinian terrorist Sirhan Sirhan on primary night. Four years later, George McGovern edged Hubert Humphrey in the Democratic primary. But the state waned in importance following two developments—Democrats got rid of winner-take-all primaries after the 1972 election, and in the next five election cycles, both parties' nominations were clinched long before California voted. For the 1996 campaign, California moved its presidential primary from the first week in June to March 26, which was still too late to make a difference. So in 2000 and 2004, California held its primary in the first week of March, and it became one of several states that clinched nominations for Bush in 2000 and Democrat Kerry in 2004. In 2008, California joined other major states, including New York and New Jersey, in holding its primary on February 5, Super Tuesday.

As it turned out that year, both parties' races were still competitive when Californians voted. But the state's leverage in the Democratic race was limited because all but 11 of its delegates were allotted by proportional representation within each of the 53 congressional districts. The enthusiasm for Obama in Silicon Valley and Hollywood, and his endorsement by Schwarzenegger's wife, Maria Shriver, a Kennedy clan member, were not reflected in the results. Turnout was enormous—5 million, compared with 3 million in 2004. Hillary Rodham Clinton won 51%-43%. Obama narrowly lost the San Francisco Bay Area 46% to 48%, while Clinton won 55% in Los Angeles County and Southern California generally. She took the Central Valley as well. Obama carried six congressional districts in Northern California, the coastal Santa Barbara district, one San Diego beachfront district and the three Los Angeles County districts that have African-American House members.

In enormous California, the organizational edge that Obama enjoyed in caucus states made little difference. Voting ran more along ethnic lines. Obama won among African-Americans, but Clinton carried Latinos, who outnumber blacks in the electorate by about 4-to-1. She carried Asians 71%-25%. Obama's advantage among upscale liberals was minimal because Jewish voters, as in New York and Florida, preferred Clinton. Clinton carried 42 congressional districts to Obama's 11, but proportional representation limited her delegate advantage to 204-166. If the Republican winner-take-all rules had been in force, she would have led 279-91, perhaps enough to have given her the delegate lead and put her in the favor of super delegates in the months to come.

The Republican primary attracted far fewer voters—2.9 million, only slightly more than the 2.8 million who voted in 2000. Far fewer dollars were spent by Republican candidates than by Democratic candidates, and there was far less in the way of GOP organizing efforts. Polling showed a close race between McCain and Mitt Romney, with Mike Huckabee not a serious factor. McCain won 42%-35%. McCain's margin was widest, 53%-28%, among the relatively few Republican voters in the San Francisco Bay Area. (Three times as many Democrats as Republicans voted in the Bay Area.) McCain led 44%-35% in Los Angeles County and by a narrow 40%-37% in the rest of Southern California. The race was closest in the Central Valley and mountains, where McCain led 39%-35%.

But McCain's 7% margin enabled him to carry 48 of the 53 congressional districts. He lost in only one Central Valley district and in four in Orange and San Diego counties. Republican winner-take-all rules gave McCain a 155-15 delegate lead in the 53 congressional districts, an outcome that left Romney so far behind in delegates that he had little choice but to fold his campaign.

Congressional districting

112th Congress Lineup		
33 D	19 R	1 V
111th Congress Lineup		
34 D	19 R	

In 2010, for the first time since it was admitted to the Union in 1850, California did not gain House seats following the decennial census. Granted one seat when it became a state, it went to three after the 1850 Census and to 53 after the 2000 Census, gaining as many as eight at a time, after the 1960 Census. In 2011, also for the first time, California will not have a partisan redistricting fight. Voters in 2010 approved, 61%-39%, a ballot proposition that leaves congressional redistricting to a nonpartisan commission.

It's not clear that the commission will make as much of a difference as is commonly supposed. The House redistricting plan approved after the 2000 census was an incumbent-protection plan; it sacrificed a Republican district in Los Angeles County that could not be protected, but created a new one in the Central Valley. And, the one additional seat the state gained from the 2000 reapportionment was allotted to a heavily Hispanic and Democratic area in Los Angeles County. The boundaries of most districts are relatively regular, in some cases even elegant, with the major exceptions being districts affected by the prevailing interpretations of the Voting Rights Act and the coastal 23rd District, which united demographically and politically similar areas along the Pacific coast and separates them from the demographically and politically quite different areas on the other side of the mountains.

There will be some significant changes, because interior California has grown more rapidly than coastal California. This may lead to the elimination of one heavily Hispanic or black district in Los Angeles County, and the creation of a new district in the Central Valley or the Inland Empire. The San Francisco Bay area will probably shed a district, which could imperil Democrat Jerry McNerney, who barely held on in 2010 in a district partly in the Bay area and partly in the Central Valley. The redistricting commission process might benefit Republicans, because redistricters will be under pressure from the Voting Rights Act and the Obama Justice Department to create as many heavily Hispanic districts as possible in interior California. In contrast, even the most nonpartisan redistricter is unlikely to create more Republican districts in coastal California than currently exist; that would require some pretty grotesque boundary lines. Critics of California's 2000 redistricting have bemoaned the fact that there has been a shift in party control in only one of California's 53 congressional districts in the last five elections, leaving Democrats with a solid 33-19 advantage. But that is unlikely to change much after the commission does its work.

Governor

Jerry Brown (D)

Elected 2010, term expires Jan. 2015, 3rd term; b. April 7, 1938, San Francisco; home, Oakland; U. of CA, Berkeley, B.A. 1961; Yale U., J.D. 1964; Catholic; Married (Anne Gust).

Elected Office: Los Angeles Comm. Col. Bd. of Trustees, 1969-71; Secy. of st., CA, 1970-74; CA gov., 1974-82; Chmn., CA Dem. Party, 1989-1991; Oakland mayor, 1998-2006; Atty. gen., CA, 2006-2010.

Professional Career: Law clerk, CA Supreme Court; Practicing atty., Tuttle & Taylor; practicing atty., Fulbright & Jaworski; Radio host, KPFA, Berkeley, 1995-1998.

Office: State Capitol, Suite 1173, 95814, 916-445-2841; Fax: 916-558-3160; Web site: gov.ca.gov/.

Election Results

2010 general	Jerry Brown (D)	5,428,458	(54%)
	Meg Whitman (R)	4,127,371	(41%)
2010 primary	Jerry Brown (D)	2,021,189	(84%)

Prior Winning Percentages: 1978 (56%); 1974 (50%)

Jerry Brown, a Democrat, was elected governor of California in 2010. He had previously been elected governor in 1974 and 1978. He first won statewide office, as secretary of state, in 1970, went on to serve two terms as governor, and then was defeated in a bid for U.S. senator in 1982. He's also been the mayor of Oakland and a three-time presidential candidate. Only a few of today's top political figures have elective careers that go back further than Brown's (Sens. Daniel Inouye of Hawaii and Jay Rockefeller of West Virginia; U.S. Reps. John Dingell and John Conyers, both of Michigan, and Rep. Bill Young of Florida) or go back as far (Sen. Harry Reid of Nevada and Rep. Charles Rangel of New York).

Edmund G. Brown Jr. grew up in San Francisco, in the upper-middle-class and heavily Catholic neighborhood of St. Francis Wood, the grandson of a cigar store owner and a policeman, and the son of lawyer Edmund G. Brown, universally known as Pat. In 1943, when Edmund G. Jr. was 5, Pat Brown ran for district attorney of the city and county of San Francisco and won. This was a prominent position: Nearly 10% of Californians then lived in San Francisco and another 15% in the rest of the San Francisco Bay area. And in a state where Democrats had been the minority party, Pat Brown was a natural contender for statewide office. He went on to serve two terms as state attorney general, and beginning in 1959, two terms as governor of California. With a liberal Democratic legislature, he embarked on a vast program of public spending—a water system transferring northern California water to the Central Valley and Los Angeles, a public university and state college system promising higher education for all who qualified, and a freeway program to connect the sprawling metropolitan areas that were growing up rapidly in the interstices between mountain ranges and the Pacific Ocean. Voters heartily endorsed this record when they re-elected Brown 52%-47% in 1962 over Richard Nixon, the future U.S. president.

At first, Pat Brown's son was uninterested in following his political heritage. A year after graduating from St. Ignatius High School in 1955, Jerry Brown entered the Sacred Heart Novitiate, a Jesuit seminary, where he set out to become a priest. But after several years, he changed course and entered the University of California at Berkeley, where he earned a degree in classics in 1961. This was before the tumultuous Berkeley rebellion of 1964, but Brown was something of a rebel against his father's policies. He championed the cause of Caryl Chessman, who was sentenced to death for rape. His father delayed the execution for a time, but finally ordered it to go forward in 1960. After college, Brown went to Yale Law School, where he graduated in 1964 in the same class with Gary Hart. In only a decade, one would be elected governor and the other a U.S. senator from Colorado.

After law school, Brown clerked for a state Supreme Court justice and then traveled in Latin America. When he returned to California, he settled not in his native San Francisco, but in Los Angeles. He worked for a large law firm, and in 1969, three years after his father was defeated by Republican Ronald Reagan 58%-42%, Brown ran for the board of trustees of Los Angeles Community College and finished first among 124 candidates. In 1970, he ran statewide for secretary of state, and won easily even as Reagan was winning a second term. The victory put Brown in position to run for governor in 1974, when it was presumed Reagan would retire, many presumed from political life forever, at the age of 63. In the Democratic primary, Brown had serious competition from San Francisco Mayor Joseph Alioto, state Assembly Speaker Bob Moretti and U.S. Rep. Jerome Waldie. He won with 38% of the vote, to 19% for Alioto, 17% for Moretti, and 8% for Waldie. It was a very favorable year for Democrats, but California then was not nearly as Democratic as it is now, and in the general election, Brown faced Controller Houston Flournoy, a moderate Republican. He won by only 50%-47%.

At 36, Brown was governor of California. He turned out to be not at all the same kind of Democrat as his father. Brown refused to stay in the governor's mansion and instead hung out in a sparely furnished apartment. He refused to use the governor's limousine, and drove around in a Plymouth. He largely stopped highway construction and tried to encourage mass transportation. He created a Wellness Commission and an Office of Appropriate Technology. Brown also legalized the practice of acupuncture. He opposed the death penalty, but his veto of a capital punishment bill was overridden by the legislature. If he was liberal on cultural issues, Brown was relatively conservative on economic issues. He was surprisingly tight-fisted on spending, but he also gave bargaining rights to public employee unions.

Brown's eccentricity and his unusual policy positions made him a regular subject of late night comics' monologues. Still, in 1976, at age 38, he ran for president. In the primaries, he won his first victory in May in Maryland, 48%-37%, over front-runner Jimmy Carter of Georgia with the help of San Francisco housewife Nancy Pelosi, who later became speaker of the House. Two weeks later, he won in Nevada and ran a fairly close third to Frank Church of Idaho and Carter in dovish Oregon. Brown won 59% of the vote in the California primary, making him second in the national popular vote to Carter. But he was unable to stay ahead of Carter in subsequent contests, and he finished third at the 1976 Democratic convention with about 300 delegates.

His political career was not exactly washed up. In 1978, Brown won a second term as governor, defeating GOP state Attorney General Evelle Younger 56%-37%. That year, a taxpayers' revolt led to passage of Proposition 13 to freeze property taxes in a period of rapidly rising housing prices. Brown, like most Democrats, opposed it, but when it passed, he sounded like its biggest booster and set about cutting state spending in order to funnel revenue to localities. His second term is considered less successful than his first. For example, Brown in 1981 came under harsh attack by the state's important farm sector for refusing to order use of the pesticide malathion when California crops were hit by an infestation of medflies. But Brown was also ahead of his time in some ways. He appointed openly gay judges to the state courts and he embraced satellite technology for emergency communications systems before it was in common use around the world. His novel and sometimes far-fetched ideas inspired Chicago columnist Mike Royko to dub him "Governor Moonbeam," a nickname that, unfortunately for Brown, stuck. He ran for president again in 1980 and finished far behind Carter and Massachusetts Sen. Edward Kennedy everywhere, even in California. He won just 3% of the popular vote. In 1982, Brown ran for the Senate seat being vacated by Republican S. I. Hayakawa. He was far better known than his Republican opponent, San Diego Mayor Pete Wilson. But Wilson out-debated him and won 52%-45%. Brown carried Los Angeles County and the San Francisco Bay area narrowly, but lost in all but one county in the rest of the state.

In the middle 1980s, when Reagan was basking in public approval in the White House, Brown traveled to China, Japan, Russia, and India, where he worked with Mother Teresa's humanitarian projects. He practiced law in Los Angeles, and in 1989, embarked on a two-year stint as California Democratic chairman. In 1992, he ran for president a third time, refusing contributions over $100 and inviting listeners to call his 800 number to send him money. He finished a poor fifth in New Hampshire, but beat Arkansas' Bill Clinton and Massachusetts' Paul Tsongas in the Colorado and Connecticut primaries and in the caucuses in Maine, Vermont, and Nevada. He also aroused Clinton's ire by suggesting that there might be something improper about Hillary Rodham Clinton's work at the Rose Law Firm in Little Rock. By the time California voted in June, Clinton was the sure nominee, but he beat Brown there by only 47%-40%.

During most of the Clinton administration, Brown was a political outsider, utterly out of favor at the White House. In time, he moved to Oakland, and in 1998, ran for mayor of that troubled city. In an 11-candidate primary, he was elected with 59% of the vote. He won passage of a proposal creating a strong mayor form of government, ordered innovative policing that sharply reduced crime, stimulated significant development in the bedraggled downtown and established both the Oakland School for the Arts and the Oakland Military Institute as an alternative high school option. He won a second term as mayor in 2002 with 64% of the vote.

All the while, Brown remained an interested and informed spectator of California state government. His successor as governor, Republican George Deukmejian, presided over a relatively quiet and successful administration during the 1980s, as California boomed with the defense spending of the Reagan military buildup and started attracting hundreds of thousands of immigrants, particularly Asians and Mexicans and other Latin Americans. Republican Pete Wilson, who beat former San Francisco Mayor Dianne Feinstein 49%-46% for governor in 1990, had a rockier time. California was hit by defense cutbacks, the Northridge earthquake, the Rodney King race riots in Los Angeles, and huge revenue shortfalls. Wilson was re-elected 55%-41% over Brown's sister, state Treasurer Kathleen Brown, after he backed Proposition 187, which barred public spending on illegal immigrants and their children. The campaign for the proposition tainted the Republican label for many of the slowly rising number of Latino voters in California. Perhaps more important, in the middle 1990s, reaction against the Southern and religious conservative Republicans who dominated the party's new congressional majorities pushed affluent, educated voters in metro Los Angeles and San Francisco toward the Democratic Party. And as the years wore on, conservative white voters, repelled by California's high taxes, started leaving the state in large numbers for more congenial territory in the mountain West or Texas. California, a target state in elections from the 1940s through the 1990s, became a safe Democratic state except under the most unusual circumstances by 2000.

Term limits, imposed by voters in 1990, made a difference as well. They rotated Wilson out of the governorship and installed Brown's chief of staff as governor, Democrat Gray Davis, who was elected to the Assembly in 1982 and as lieutenant governor in 1994. Davis' strategy was to try to hold down spending by the heavily Democratic legislature. He won a second term in 2002 by the uninspiring margin of 47%-42% by stressing his opponent's opposition to abortion rights. But early in 2003, as the state budget deficit ballooned and he increased the vehicle tax and came out for driver's licenses for illegal immigrants, conservatives launched a successful drive for a recall election. Voters were given the opportunity to choose a replacement for Davis. One of their choices was Republican Arnold Schwarzenegger, a former movie star, a successful investor, and the husband of Maria Shriver, a member of the Kennedy clan. He called for cutting taxes to create a more favorable business climate. In October, Davis was recalled 55%-45%; and Schwarzenegger was elected with 49% of the vote on the replacement ballot, to 32% for Democratic Lt. Gov. Cruz Bustamante and 13% for conservative state Sen. Tom McClintock.

In his two terms, Schwarzenegger reversed Davis' unpopular policies, including repeal of driver's licenses for illegal immigrants. But he and the Democratic legislature struggled over his two terms to balance the books. He was determined not to raise taxes, and so forced changes in worker's compensation laws and cut state employees' pay. He tried to drastically reduce the power of the public employee unions but failed. He later imposed a temporary sales tax increase and launched an aggressive multi-billion-dollar bond program to build a high-speed rail system and other infrastructure. Schwarzenegger also presided over the fiscal debacle caused by the collapse of the housing market in California. The state was one of the epicenters of subprime mortgage lending, with reduced standards or outright fraud in providing financing for marginal buyers, a large percentage of them Latino. Housing prices peaked in 2006, and soon many borrowers found themselves under water, with more debt than their houses were worth. Foreclosures skyrocketed, construction plummeted, and tax revenues fell far below projections. The robust spending increases that Schwarzenegger, like Davis, had allowed became unsustainable. As the recession deepened, and foreclosures proliferated, his job ratings sagged.

In 2006, Brown, finishing his second term as Oakland mayor, ran for attorney general and won over state Sen. Chuck Poochigian 56%-38%. As attorney general, Brown in 2009 asked the Supreme Court to stay a three-judge federal court decision requiring the state to release 40,000 inmates from California prisons. He sued the city of San Bernardino for its zoning plan for encouraging sprawl. After voters in 2008 passed Proposition 8 overturning the state Supreme Court decision authorizing same-sex marriage, Brown initially promised to defend it in court, but reversed himself in December, making the novel argument that the people could not revoke rights discovered by the courts to be "inalienable." With Schwarzenegger term-limited, it was clear that Brown was once again running for governor, as he had done 36 years before. "Why do it?" said the 72-year-old Brown. "I've been doing this most of my life. I think some of these people who have not been governor, who've not really been at the heart of California politics, have no idea what's in store for them. Our state is in serious trouble and the next governor must have the preparation and the knowledge and the know-how to get California working again."

Two Democratic mayors, Antonio Villaraigosa of Los Angeles and Gavin Newsom of San Francisco, considered running for governor. Villaraigosa opted out and Newsom ran briefly before dropping out. Meanwhile, the Republicans had a fierce primary fight between two Silicon Valley magnates, former eBay chief Meg Whitman and state Insurance Commissioner Steve Poizner. Both spent their own money, but Whitman spent much more and pointed out that Poizner had supported Democrats in the past while she backed Mitt Romney in the 2008 presidential election. Spending some $60 million, Whitman won the June primary 64%-27%, while Brown won with 84% against seven relatively unknown candidates.

In the 2010 general election, Whitman ultimately spent $160 million, $141.5 million of it her own money. She ran saturation advertising, including one showing Bill Clinton attacking Brown for raising taxes as governor. Brown's attacks were equally hard-hitting. Talking with a KCBS reporter, he said, "She'll have people believing whatever she wants about me. It's like Goebbels. Goebbels invented this kind of propaganda."

Whitman faced problems on immigration, as California Republicans have since 1996. In the primary, she ran an ad showing former Gov. Wilson saying she would be "tough as nails" on illegal immigration. But after the primary, worried about Latino voters, she made a point of opposing Arizona's controversial new law authorizing police to inquire about the immigration status of people stopped for other reasons. Her support from Latinos plummeted in September, when lawyer Gloria Allred brought forward Whitman's former nanny, an illegal immigrant who claimed she had been fired after Whitman entered politics.

Brown led in most polls, but by uninspiring margins. Then, late in the campaign, he ran an ad that struck at the central premise of Whitman's campaign. She said that California's economy needed to be liberated from the burden of high taxes and lavish public employee pensions, and that she would usher in fundamental change. The promises were quite similar to those Schwarzenegger made in the 2003 recall campaign, but by 2010, had failed to deliver on. Brown's ad showed first Schwarzenegger and then Whitman saying almost precisely the same things.

Most of America voted Republican in 2010, but California remained staunchly Democratic. Brown beat Whitman 54%-41%, while Democratic Sen. Barbara Boxer beat former Hewlett-Packard CEO Carly Fiorina by an almost identical 52%-42%. The comparison with his 1974 run is interesting: Brown ran far better in coastal California in 2010 than he did years earlier, and far worse in interior California. In 2010, Brown won 63% of the vote in Los Angeles County and 67% in the San Francisco Bay area, way up from 53% in both places in 1974. In 2010, he won only 42% in the rest of Southern California, down from 44% in 1974. In the rest of the state, he lost with 47% compared with 1974, when he carried the area with 50%.

So once again, as he had 36 years before, Brown replaced a movie actor as governor of California. "I still carry with me that missionary zeal to kind of transform the world," he said during the campaign. But he also said, "You've got to find ways of doing more with less. I was the original guy on that." In his first weeks in office, Brown called for $12.5 billion in spending cuts, including reductions in welfare programs, health care for the poor, community colleges and a $1 billion cut from the budgets for the University of California and California State University systems. He also planned to seek voter approval to extend temporary increases in taxes on income, retail sales, and vehicles, which would raise another $12 billion. He followed this up with a state hiring freeze in February 2011.

Senior Senator

Dianne Feinstein (D)

Elected Nov. 1992, term expires 2012, 3rd full term; b. June 22, 1933, San Francisco; home, San Francisco; Stanford U., B.A. 1955; Jewish; married (Richard C. Blum); 4 children.

Elected Office: San Francisco Bd. of Supervisors, 1970–78, Pres., 1970–71, 1974–75, 1978; San Francisco mayor, 1978–88.

Professional Career: CA Women's Parole Bd., 1960–66.

DC Office: 331 HSOB, 20510, 202-224-3841; Fax: 202-228-3954; Web site: feinstein.senate.gov.

State Offices: Fresno, 559-485-7430; Los Angeles, 310-914-7300; San Diego, 619-231-9712; San Francisco, 415-393-0707.

Committees: *Appropriations:* Agriculture, Rural Development, Food and Drug Administration & Related Agencies; Commerce, Justice, Science & Related Agencies; Defense; Energy & Water Development (Chmn); Interior, Environment & Related Agencies; Transportation, HUD & Related Agencies. *Intelligence (Select)* (Chmn). *Judiciary:* Crime & Terrorism; Immigration, Refugees & Border Security. *Rules & Administration.*

Group Ratings

	ACLU	ACU	ADA	CFG	AFS	FRC	LCV	ITIC	NTU	COC
2010	87	8	90	5	89	0	100	67	7	27
2009	–	0	100	3	100	–	100	–	6	43

National Journal Ratings

	2010 LIB	—	2010 CONS	2009 LIB	—	2009 CONS
Economic	70%	—	27%	70%	—	29%
Social	47%	—	52%	79%	—	19%
Foreign	47%	—	0%	55%	—	0%
Composite	64%	—	36%	76%	—	24%

Key Votes of the 111th Congress

1. Overturn Ledbetter	Y	5. Pass health care bill	Y	9. Ratify New START	Y
2. Pass $787 billion stimulus	Y	6. Regulate financial firms	Y	10. Confirm Elena Kagan	Y
3. Repeal DC gun laws	N	7. Pass tax cuts for some	Y	11. Stop EPA climate regs	N
4. Confirm Sonia Sotomayor	Y	8. Legalize immigrants' kids	Y	12. Repeal don't ask, tell	Y

Election Results

2006 general	Dianne Feinstein (D)	5,076,289	(59%)	($12,200,678)
	Dick Mountjoy (R)	2,990,822	(35%)	($198,630)
2006 primary	Dianne Feinstein (D)	2,176,829	(87%)	
	Colleen Fernald (R)	191,170	(8%)	
	Martin Luther Church (D)	127,291	(5%)	

Prior Winning Percentages: 2000 (56%); 1994 (47%); 1992 (54%)

Dianne Feinstein, California's senior senator, is a Democrat first elected in 1992. Feinstein grew up in San Francisco in lush Presidio Heights, the daughter of a doctor who hoped she would follow him into the profession. In her first semester at Stanford University, Feinstein got a D in genetics and decided she did not have the aptitude for medicine. But she did love a class she took on American political thought. She graduated with a degree in criminology and then, while doing an internship, wrote a paper about post-conviction phases of the justice system that she thought contained valuable ideas for the state of California. Feinstein sent her paper to Gov. Pat Brown. Despite her youth—she was just 27—the governor appointed her to the California Women's Board of Terms and Parole. In 1969 she won her first election, to the San Francisco County Board of Supervisors. Feinstein went on to become president of the board and in 1978, was suddenly catapulted to mayor when Mayor George Moscone and Supervisor Harvey Milk were shot to death by former Supervisor Dan White. Feinstein discovered Moscone's body and in the subsequent weeks, displayed a steadiness and a sense of command that calmed the city. She was elected to full terms in 1979 and 1983. In 1984, Democratic presidential candidate Walter Mondale seriously considered her for vice president, but passed over her for Geraldine Ferraro because of qualms about the business dealings of Feinstein's husband, Richard Blum. She presided gracefully that year over the Democratic National Convention in San Francisco, while ironically, Ferraro juggled questions about *her* family's business dealings.

Ineligible for a third term, Feinstein left the mayor's office in 1987 and ran for governor in 1990. She won the Democratic primary impressively, then lost 49%-46% to Republican Pete Wilson. When Wilson appointed Orange County state Sen. John Seymour—an unknown and bland choice—to replace him in the Senate, Feinstein quickly announced for the seat. She had primary competition from Gray Davis, then state controller, who ran an ad against her campaign-finance practices and compared her to haughty New York billionaire Leona Helmsley, who went to jail for tax evasion. Feinstein won 58%-33%, and after that, her relations with Davis, elected governor in 1998 and 2002, were never warm. Davis was forced out of office in a 2003 recall election. In the 1992 general election, nothing worked for the hapless Seymour, the appointed GOP incumbent—not his switch from having opposed abortion rights to favoring them, not his attempt to play on fears of illegal immigration and not his attacks on Feinstein's arguably tricky financing of her 1990 gubernatorial campaign, which resulted in a $190,000 fine. Feinstein won 54%-38%, coming close even in Seymour's Southern California base.

In the Senate, Feinstein kept a distance from the Clinton administration, negotiating for changes before voting for its 1993 budget, voting against the North American Free Trade Agreement, and withdrawing her support of the Clinton health care plan. Feinstein had two significant legislative achievements in her first two years. One was a ban on assault weapons in 1994. When Idaho Republican Larry Craig argued that her definition of assault weapons was not rigorous enough and challenged her knowledge of firearms, she stopped the argument in its tracks by reminding the Senate of the horrific tragedy earlier in her political career. "I know something about what firearms can do," Feinstein said. "I came to be mayor of San Francisco as a product of assassination." (In 2000, she sponsored an unsuccessful bill to require licensing of all guns and in 2004 pressed fervently for reauthorization of the 1994 assault-weapons ban. The act expired in September 2004.) Her other achievement in her early Senate years was the California Desert Protection Act, which had long been held up by the state's Republican senators as too restrictive.

Feinstein has had a moderate to liberal voting record and has differed on some issues from her colleague and Bay Area neighbor, Democratic Sen. Barbara Boxer. She supported the Bush tax cuts in 2001 and the Iraq war resolution in 2002, although two years later she said she had been misled into voting for the war by an exaggeration of the threat and regretted her vote. Feinstein supported the GOP's Medicare prescription drug bill in 2003 as well. With Republican Sen. Jon Kyl of Arizona, she co-sponsored a bill to bar entry to the United States for people from nations that sponsor terrorism, which became law in 2002.

On the Judiciary Committee, Feinstein took an active role in the immigration debate in recent years. She favors a guest worker program for agricultural workers and would allow illegal aliens with U.S. work history to obtain "blue cards" to allow them to work for two years. In the debate on immigration in 2006, she and Boxer proposed a 20-year sentence for people caught building or financing underground cross-border tunnels, which became part of the border fence bill that passed both houses. On other issues, Feinstein disagreed with other Democrats who claimed the USA PATRIOT Act, the Bush administration's centerpiece anti-terrorism law, had led to violations of civil liberties, a statement cited by President Bush in pressing for renewal of the act. She also was the only Democrat on the committee to vote in 2006 for the amendment authorizing prosecutions for flag desecration.

In 2005, Feinstein was less bipartisan in the war over some of President Bush's judicial nominees, but she also was frequently willing to compromise in the end. With other Judiciary Democrats, she opposed several nominees to the federal appeals court. But then, with Boxer, she made an arrangement with the Bush administration to set up six-member panels to decide on the potential merits of federal trial judges in California. Three members were appointed by each side, and four votes were required to approve a nominee. In May 2005, Feinstein voted against the nomination of conservative nominee Priscilla Owen, but declined to take the harsher step of a filibuster. After an interview with Supreme Court nominee John Roberts in July 2005, she called him "very impressive" but opposed his confirmation nonetheless, out of concern that he might overturn the *Roe v. Wade* decision legalizing abortion. After Harriet Miers' nomination for the high court was withdrawn in October 2005, Feinstein said, "I don't believe they would have attacked a man the way she was attacked."

In January 2009, Feinstein became chair of the Senate Intelligence Committee and indicated she wanted to clean house at the intelligence agencies. "My view is that it's time for a new start," she said. "I want to see the Senate Intelligence Committee with much closer oversight and a much closer relationship with the intelligence community." When former Clinton White House chief of staff Leon Panetta was announced as Obama's choice for director of the Central Intelligence Agency, she said that she thought Obama should have appointed "an intelligence professional." But after Vice President Joseph Biden said it was a mistake not to have informed her in advance of the appointment, she was conciliatory, saying, "I'm very respectful of the president's authority, and if this is the man he wants, then that means a lot to me."

Feinstein doesn't hesitate to go her own way on the committee. In 2007, she supported immunity for telecommunications companies that had allowed the government to listen in on telephone calls from suspected terrorists abroad to persons in the United States, though many Democrats opposed immunity. Feinstein attached amendments to the 2007 and 2008 intelligence authorization bills to require that all government interrogations be conducted under the rules of the Army Field Manual, and she attempted to apply that standard to government contractors as well. In January 2009, she called for closing the detention camp at Guantanamo Bay, Cuba, which she called a "failed experiment," and for banning the CIA from using private contractors as interrogators. In February 2009, she was criticized for disclosing that Predator drones directed at extremists near the Pakistan-Afghanistan border were launched from bases in Pakistan; a Feinstein aide said that the fact had been revealed in *The Washington Post* months earlier. In December 2009, she supported President Obama's decision to prosecute the war in Afghanistan. "It's very important that women's rights be considered and be part of this," she said.

Feinstein frequently joins with Republicans in the time-honored method of getting legislation passed through compromise. In January 2009, she and conservative Sen. John Cornyn of Texas co-sponsored a bill to create a permanent commission to guarantee the financial viability of Social Security and Medicare. In March 2009, she and Judiciary Committee Chairman Patrick Leahy of Vermont hammered out a compromise creating clearer requirements in patent infringement cases. With Republican Sen. Judd Gregg of New Hampshire, she introduced a bill in 2009 to reduce gradually the tariff on Brazilian sugar ethanol, and with Republican Sen. Kit Bond of Missouri, she called for duty-free imports of apparel from Afghanistan and Sri Lanka. In 2010, she co-sponsored a ban on BPA plastic widely used in food containers, though it was not included in the food safety bill passed in 2010. Also that year, she won wide agreement on a national registry for convicted arsonists and bombers.

On the Senate Rules Committee, Feinstein has worked on institutional reforms. She co-sponsored a requirement that earmarks added to spending bills be posted on the Internet for at least 24 hours. She was in the spotlight in January 2009, when former Illinois Attorney General Roland Burris, a Democrat, was appointed by Gov. Rod Blagojevich to fill Obama's Senate seat. Democratic leaders initially said they would refuse to seat him because his appointment was tainted by allegations that Blagojevich had demanded political favors in exchange. Feinstein argued that Burris should be seated, and prevailed. She said: "The question, really, is one, in my view, of law. And that is, does the governor have the power to make the appointment? And the answer is yes. Is the governor discredited? And the answer is yes. Does that affect his appointment power? And the answer is no, until certain things happen." Burris, after being turned back at the door of the Capitol, was seated. As Rules chairman, Feinstein also presided over Obama's inauguration ceremonies on Jan. 20, 2009.

With a seat on the powerful Appropriations Committee, Feinstein has sought public and private funding to protect old-growth redwoods in the Headwaters Forest and salt ponds in the San Francisco Bay area and to prohibit development, including solar plants and wind farms, on an additional 1 million acres in the Mojave Desert. In September 2009, she urged the Interior Department to reconsider decisions cutting off water to the Central Valley to protect the allegedly endangered delta smelt and in February 2010, she backed an amendment to increase water delivery to the Valley.

She is more accommodating of trade ties with China than San Francisco neighbor Nancy Pelosi, the House minority leader. Feinstein has supported trade with China since she established a sister-city relationship in 1990 between San Francisco and Shanghai. She opposed Pelosi's efforts to impose penalties on China because of its human rights violations. In 2005, Feinstein called on China to crack down on piracy of intellectual property and to revalue its currency, but she opposed a bipartisan bill to impose 27.5% tariffs on Chinese goods if it did not revalue.

Feinstein has had only one serious challenge since she was elected to the Senate, in the Republican year of 1994. U.S. Rep. Michael Huffington spent $30 million of his own money running against her and pulled even in the polls in September. Feinstein was frustrated that she could not count on outspending him. Huffington slipped when it was revealed that he and his wife, Arianna Huffington, employed an illegal alien as a nanny. (Arianna Huffington now runs the liberal *Huffington Post* blog.) On the Thursday before the election, it was revealed that Feinstein, despite her earlier denials, had employed a woman whose work permit had expired. The media ran stories casting doubt on assertions that the woman was an illegal alien. That probably made the difference. Feinstein won 47%–45%. She carried Los Angeles County 52%-40% and the San Francisco Bay Area 63%-30%, offsetting Huffington's margins in Southern California and the rest of the state.

Since then, Feinstein has enjoyed positive poll ratings. In 2000, Republican U.S. Rep. Tom Campbell, a libertarian Stanford Law professor, challenged her. Feinstein far outspent him, $10.3 million to $4.4 million, and won 56%-37%, carrying all of the major regions of the state. In her 2006 re-election contest, Republicans nominated conservative former state Sen. Richard Mountjoy. Feinstein spent $8 million on her campaign, while Mountjoy spent just $195,000. She won 59%-35%. In 2009, Feinstein was being mentioned as a possible candidate for governor in 2010. Polls showed her ahead but in February 2010 she declined to run. Her Senate seat comes up in 2012.

Junior Senator

Barbara Boxer (D)

Elected 1992, term expires 2016, 4th term; b. Nov. 11, 1940, Brooklyn, NY; home, Rancho Mirage; Brooklyn Col., B.A. 1962; Jewish; married (Stewart); 2 children.

Elected Office: Marin Cnty. Bd. of Supervisors, 1976–82; U.S. House of Reps., 1982–92.

Professional Career: Stockbroker & researcher, 1962–65; Journalist, *Pacific Sun,* 1972–74; Dist. aide, U.S. Rep. John Burton, 1974–76.

DC Office: 112 HSOB, 20510, 202-224-3553; Fax: 202-224-0454; Web site: boxer.senate.gov.

State Offices: Fresno, 559-497-5109; Los Angeles, 213-894-5000; Sacramento, 916-448-2787; San Bernardino , 909-888-8525; San Diego, 619-239-3884; San Francisco, 415-403-0100.

Committees: *Commerce, Science & Transportation:* Aviation Operations, Safety & Security; Communications, Technology & the Internet; Consumer Protection, Product Safety & Insurance; Surface Transportation & Merchant Marine Infrastructure, Safety & Security. *Environment & Public Works* (Chmn). *Ethics (Select)* (Chmn). *Foreign Relations:* East Asian & Pacific Affairs; International Operations & Organizations, Democracy & Global Women's Issues (Chmn); Near Eastern & South & Central Asian Affairs; Western Hemisphere, Peace Corps & Global Narcotics Affairs.

Group Ratings

	ACLU	ACU	ADA	CFG	AFS	FRC	LCV	ITIC	NTU	COC
2010	93	0	95	0	99	0	100	67	6	18
2009	–	0	100	3	100	–	100	–	5	43

National Journal Ratings

	2010 LIB	—	2010 CONS	2009 LIB	—	2009 CONS
Economic	78%	—	21%	76%	—	23%
Social	48%	—	49%	78%	—	21%
Foreign	47%	—	0%	55%	—	0%
Composite	67%	—	33%	78%	—	23%

Key Votes of the 111th Congress

1. Overturn Ledbetter	Y	5. Pass health care bill	Y	9. Ratify New START	Y
2. Pass $787 billion stimulus	Y	6. Regulate financial firms	Y	10. Confirm Elena Kagan	Y
3. Repeal DC gun laws	N	7. Pass tax cuts for some	Y	11. Stop EPA climate regs	N
4. Confirm Sonia Sotomayor	Y	8. Legalize immigrants' kids	Y	12. Repeal don't ask, tell	Y

Election Results

2010 general	Barbara Boxer (D)...	5,218,441	(52%)	($29,331,343)
	Carly Fiorina (R)...	4,217,366	(42%)	($21,521,397)
2010 primary	Barbara Boxer (D)...	1,957,920	(81%)	
	Brian Quintana (D)..	338,442	(14%)	
	Robert Kaus (D)	123,573	(5%)	

Prior Winning Percentages: 2004 (58%); 1998 (53%); 1992 (48%); House: 1990 (68%); 1988 (73%); 1986 (74%); 1984 (68%); 1982 (52%)

Barbara Boxer, California's junior senator, is a Democrat first elected to the House in 1982 and a decade later to the Senate. She is the chairman of the Environment and Public Works Committee. Boxer grew up in Brooklyn, N.Y. In 1962, she graduated from Brooklyn College, where she met her husband, Stewart. The couple moved to Marin County, Calif. in 1968. Boxer, a stockbroker, volunteered for Eugene McCarthy's presidential campaign that year. In 1970, she and some neighbors formed the Marin Alternative to oppose the Vietnam War. Marin County was only on its way to being trendy then; the overall political tone was liberal Republican, but heading left. In 1972, Boxer ran for the Board of Supervisors and lost to an incumbent Republican. She then went to work as an aide to Democratic U.S. Rep. John Burton. In 1976, she ran again for the county board and won. When Burton retired unexpectedly in 1982, Boxer ran for the House seat and was easily elected. In the House, she was known for her aggressive investigation into wasteful spending, unearthing the Air Force's $7,622 coffee pot in 1984, and for her vocal opposition to the Gulf War in the early 1990s. She also led a group of women House members in a march to the steps of the Senate to demand hearings into law professor Anita Hill's sexual-harassment allegations against Clarence Thomas, who was in the process of being confirmed to the Supreme Court.

In 1992, Boxer ran for the Senate. She started off as neither the best-known nor the best-financed candidate, but 1992 turned out to be the "Year of the Woman," in which the enthusiasm of the feminist left helped produce important victories for Democratic candidates. Boxer won the June primary with 44% of the vote, to 31% for Lt. Gov. Leo McCarthy and 22% for U.S. Rep. Mel Levine. In the general election, her opponent was Bruce Herschensohn, a Los Angeles television and radio commentator. The Boxer-Herschensohn race was a battle of opposites, the far left versus the far right of the ideological spectrum. Herschensohn opposed abortion rights and advocated a flat tax and offshore oil drilling. Boxer's positions were precisely the opposite. Her bid was helped by the poor showing of President George H.W. Bush's campaign in California and by the revelation late in the campaign that Herschensohn had frequented nightclubs that featured nude dancers. She won with 48% of the vote.

Boxer's voting record is among the most liberal in the Senate, and she has long been one of the chamber's most outspoken members. She objected to Army Brigadier Gen. Michael Walsh calling her "ma'am" at a June 2009 hearing. "Could you say 'senator' instead of 'ma'am?'" she asked Walsh. "It's just a thing. I worked so hard to get that title." Conservative bloggers called the remark arrogant, but she saw no need to apologize. Boxer is one of the strongest proponents of abortion rights in Congress and a prime sponsor of the Freedom of Choice Act, which would nullify all state restrictions on abortion.

She was a staunch defender of President Bill Clinton during the impeachment proceedings in 1998, when the president was accused of lying about an extramarital affair with a White House intern. In 2001, Boxer supported the use of force in Afghanistan. But in October 2002, she voted against the use of force in Iraq, and she later cast votes against funding for the war. In January 2005, as the electoral vote count was read out to a joint session of Congress, she was the one senator to protest the awarding of Ohio's electoral votes to Republican President George W. Bush. She recalled that four years earlier, no senator had protested the Florida vote in the bitterly contested presidential contest of 2000, and Boxer said she regretted not having protested then. Her protest triggered the dissolution of the joint session and a debate in each of the two chambers. The Senate voted 74-1 to accept the Ohio count, with Boxer as the lone dissenter, and the House voted 267-31 on the same question. "I hate inconveniencing my friends, but I think it's worth a couple of hours to shine some light on these issues," Boxer said.

Boxer has supported gun control and has sponsored amendments to require childproof safety locks on all handguns and to ban sales of guns to people who are intoxicated. But in summer 2002, she and Kentucky Republican Sen. Jim Bunning emerged as the Senate's leading advocates of allowing airline pilots to carry guns. Boxer argued that pilots could be trusted with that responsibility and that they could protect passengers against terrorists. The measure passed in both the House and Senate.

During the Clinton years, Boxer was frustrated when Republicans held up nominations to the Ninth Circuit Court of Appeals, long the most liberal in the country. During the Bush years, she held up nominations of judges she considered too conservative. In 2001, she opposed the nomination of Rep. Christopher Cox of California to the Ninth Circuit. When Democratic Sen. Dianne Feinstein said she might oppose him too, Cox withdrew. In 2005, Boxer said she would "use all the parliamentary tools I've been given as a U.S. senator" to delay a vote on the confirmation of John Roberts to the Supreme Court, and she voted against both Roberts and Samuel Alito. In 2005, Boxer published a novel called *A Time to Run* about a liberal, woman senator from California opposing a conservative Supreme Court nominee. Four years later, she came out with another *roman a clef* political thriller, "Blind Trust," about the same senator battling a Republican White House on homeland security and civil liberties.

In recent years, Boxer has concentrated on environmental issues. As the ranking member on the Environment and Public Works Committee during the years of Republican control of Congress, she sparred continually with conservative Chairman James Inhofe of Oklahoma over the issue of reducing carbon emissions to combat global warming. Inhofe famously said that the theory of human-caused global warming was a "hoax." The committee's emphasis changed abruptly when Democrats won the Senate majority in 2006. Boxer made addressing the causes of global warming her top legislative priority. "I really have two major goals," she said. "They are to protect the health of the American people. And the second is to make the environment a bipartisan issue again on Capitol Hill."

But her aggressive style did not always foster bipartisanship. In December 2007, she harshly criticized then-Environmental Protection Agency chief Stephen Johnson for refusing to grant a waiver allowing California's tough carbon emissions law to go into effect. She sought access to an EPA staff document recommending a waiver and accused Johnson of lying. She fumed during the summer and fall of 2008 when he refused to appear before the committee and testify. Inhofe boycotted the hearings as well. Boxer's primary goal was to enact a cap-and-trade system to reduce carbon emissions, which she has called "the greatest challenge of our generation." Such a system would allow companies to trade emissions "credits," depending on the amount of pollution they generate. Boxer called former Vice President Al Gore to testify in a highly publicized hearing in March 2007, showering him with praise for his campaign to spur action on global warming. In 2007, Boxer's committee took up a cap-and-trade bill sponsored by Connecticut Independent Sen. Joe Lieberman and Virginia Republican John Warner, and in nearly 10 hours of hearings, she fended off more-restrictive amendments from independent Vermont Sen. Bernie Sanders and less-restrictive amendments from others. In May 2008, she advanced a version with changes she hoped would increase support. In early June, her bill attracted only 48 votes in the Senate, well short of the 60 needed to proceed.

In the next Congress (2009-2010), senators from states that are heavily dependent on coal-generated electricity wanted to stop any cap-and-trade bill that would put their states at a competitive disadvantage, but during the early months of the Obama administration in 2009, Boxer continued to push the legislation. As the year progressed, however, she ceded control of the issue to Lieberman and Massachusetts Democratic Sen. John Kerry, a more accomplished negotiator who did not have a re-election to worry about, unlike Boxer. Kerry and Lieberman enlisted South Carolina Republican Sen. Lindsey Graham in the hope that his support could bring aboard more Republicans. The three worked to develop a method of pricing carbon while increasing production of nuclear power, a compromise Boxer said she could accept. However, when Majority Leader Harry Reid proposed bringing up a comprehensive immigration bill for debate in April 2010, Graham said the climate bill was far closer to being ready and angrily accused Reid of catering to Hispanics in order to win his own re-election, essentially killing any deal.

Boxer pursued other bipartisan initiatives, working in 2007 with the Bush White House to increase the energy efficiency of federal buildings. Boxer co-sponsored, with Republican John Ensign of Nevada, a bill to reduce the tax on corporate profits earned abroad if they were invested in creating American jobs. She and Ensign estimated the 10-year revenue loss as $18 billion. But after Congress' Joint Committee on Taxation pegged the revenue loss at $28 billion, the measure was not included in the president's February 2009 economic stimulus bill. Boxer has long been interested in enacting a "bill of rights" for stranded airline passengers, and in 2009 joined Republican Sen. Olympia Snowe of Maine in seeking support for a measure allowing passengers to deplane after every three hours on the ground and to be given food, water and other amenities while they wait. It was incorporated as part of a reauthorization bill for the Federal Aviation Administration that passed the Senate in 2010 but stalled in negotiations with the House. The Obama administration issued a rule modeled after their legislation that took effect in April of that year.

In 2007 and 2008, Boxer was entrusted with considerable institutional responsibilities when Reid appointed her to temporarily replace the disabled Tim Johnson of South Dakota as chairman of the Senate Ethics Committee. (Johnson suffered a brain hemorrhage in late 2006 but recovered.) In February 2008, she led the committee in admonishing Republican Larry Craig of Idaho for attempting to withdraw his guilty plea following his arrest in a homosexual sex sting in a Minneapolis airport men's room. He had pleaded guilty to a disorderly conduct charge, a misdemeanor, and later, after the incident was publicized, tried to change the plea. Under Boxer, the panel also admonished New Mexico Republican Pete Domenici for contacting a federal prosecutor who was investigating state Democrats in a corruption case. In June 2008, after public revelations that Democrats Christopher Dodd of Connecticut and Kent Conrad of North Dakota had received favorable terms on home mortgages, committee members voted unanimously to require more disclosure of members' mortgage terms.

During her first three years in the Senate, Boxer's job ratings were among the Senate's lowest. But California, with its large metropolitan areas, trended sharply toward the Democrats in the mid-1990s. From about 1997 on, Boxer generally has had positive job ratings, though they are somewhat lower than those of her more centrist colleague Feinstein. In 1998, Boxer was challenged by Republican state Treasurer Matt Fong. She raised $15 million and ran ads attacking Fong for what she called his ambiguous stances on issues like abortion rights. Fong attacked her for what he called the hypocrisy of her support for Clinton. (The president's brother-in-law, Tony Rodham, married Boxer's daughter.) But Fong failed to raise much money. Boxer won 53%-43%. She won 61% of the vote in Los Angeles County and 63% in the San Francisco Bay Area, and was not far behind in Southern California and the rest of the state—an impressive performance for a Democrat dismissed a few years before as too left-wing for much of the state.

When she was up for re-election in 2004, Boxer raised impressive amounts of money early, and well-known Republicans declined to make the race against her. Her opponent was Bill Jones, who had been elected secretary of state by narrow margins in 1994 and 1998 and was not well known outside his home base in Fresno County. Boxer spent $16 million to Jones' $7 million. She won 58%-38%.

In early November 2009, Carly Fiorina, the former chief executive officer of Hewlett-Packard, decided to seek the GOP nomination to challenge Boxer in 2010. The well-connected former CEO had the potential to be a well-financed and formidable opponent, and after investing $5.5 million of her own savings, breezed past her Republican rivals in the June primary with 54% to former Rep. Tom Campbell's 26% and Assemblyman Chuck DeVore's 17%.

The political climate appeared ripe for Fiorina, with public distrust of Washington and its longtime inhabitants reaching a crescendo in the summer. Fiorina ran as an outsider with business experience, calling Boxer "one of the most bitterly partisan" senators and attacking her record of getting only a handful of original bills passed into law. She even was caught on an open microphone criticizing Boxer's hairstyle as "so yesterday." Fiorina blasted the senator as being partly to blame for the recession through her party's enactment of policies such as the $787 billion economic stimulus. But Fiorina also embraced such conservative causes as opposing abortion rights and backing offshore drilling that risked alienating moderates and independents. Boxer attacked her opponent on those issues, but focused on Fiorina's tenure at Hewlett-Packard, citing the company's decision to lay off 28,000 workers and moving jobs overseas. Boxer refuted criticism of her thin legislative record, citing "1,000 Boxer provisions" enacted as amendments or other additions to legislation. She got a boost from President Obama, whose popularity in the Golden State was above his national ratings and who campaigned for her in the state. Polls through the summer and fall showed Fiorina within a few points of Boxer. In the end, she could not overcome the state's Democratic tilt and Boxer handily won a fourth term, finishing with 52% to Fiorina's 43%. Boxer noted that voters also returned former Democratic Gov. Jerry Brown to office and said, "I think as (voters) looked at Jerry and they looked at me, they said, 'you know, these are two imperfect people ⋯ but we trust them.'"

FIRST DISTRICT

Mike Thompson (D)

Elected 1998, 7th term; b. Jan. 24, 1951, St. Helena; home, St. Helena; CA St. U., B. A. 1982, M. A. 1996.; Catholic; married (Janet); 2 children.

Military Career: Army, 1969-73 (Vietnam).

Elected Office: CA Senate, 1990-98.

Professional Career: Supervisor, Beringer Winery; CA Assembly fellow, 1982-83; Chief of staff, CA Assemblyman Lou Papan, 1984-87; Chief of staff, CA Assemblywoman Jackie Speier, 1987-90.

DC Office: 231 CHOB, 20515, 202-225-3311; Fax: 202-225-4335; Web site: mikethompson.house.gov.

State Offices: Eureka, 707-269-9595; Fort Bragg, 707-962-0933; Napa, 707-226-9898; Woodland, 530-662-5272.

Committees: *Permanent Select Committee on Intelligence:* Oversight; Terrorism, HUMINT, Analysis & Counterintelligence (RMM). *Ways & Means:* Health; Select Revenue Measures.

Group Ratings

	ACLU	ACU	ADA	CFG	AFS	FRC	LCV	ITIC	NTU	COC
2010	88	0	100	10	88	0	90	67	9	13
2009	–	0	100	4	100	–	100	–	4	40

National Journal Ratings

	2010 LIB	—	2010 CONS	2009 LIB	—	2009 CONS
Economic	64%	—	36%	75%	—	21%
Social	77%	—	21%	75%	—	20%
Foreign	78%	—	17%	91%	—	0%
Composite	74%	—	26%	83%	—	17%

Key Votes of the 111th Congress

1. Overturn Ledbetter	Y	5. Bar federal abortion funds	N	9. Stop detainee transfers	N
2. Pass $820 billion stimulus	Y	6. Pass health care bill	Y	10. Legalize immigrants' kids	Y
3. Let guns in national parks	N	7. Regulate financial firms	Y	11. Repeal don't ask, tell	Y
4. Pass cap-and-trade	Y	8. Pass tax cuts for some	N	12. Limit campaign funds	Y

Election Results

2010 general	Mike Thompson (D)	147,307	(63%)	($1,912,475)
	Loren Hanks (R)	72,803	(31%)	($114,869)
	Carol Wolman (Green)	8,486	(4%)	
	Mike Rodrigues (Lib)	5,996	(3%)	
2010 primary	Mike Thompson (D)	unopposed		

Prior Winning Percentages: 2008 (68%), 2006 (66%), 2004 (67%), 2002 (64%), 2000 (65%), 1998 (62%)

Population		Race/Ethnicity		Work	
Pop. 2010:	704,012	White:	63.1%	Private:	67.6%
Change since 2000:	Up 10.2%	Black:	1.6%	Government:	21.1%
Urban:	76.0%	Hispanic:	23.6%	Self-employed:	11.0%
Rural:	24.0%	Asian:	5.9%	Blue collar:	19.3%
Area size:	12,194 sq. mi.	Native Am.:	2.3%	White collar:	58.1%
		Hawaiian:	0.2%	Khaki collar:	0.1%
Age		Two+ races:	3.1%	Other:	22.5%
Median age:	37.0 yrs.				
More than 65 yrs:	13.3%	*Ancestry*		Median income:	$50,419
Less than 18 yrs:	22.6%	German	11.8%	Median Home Value:	$400,100
		Irish	10.0%		
Education		English	9.0%	**Military Veterans**	
H.S. grad:	84.9%			% of Pop:	9.8%
College grad:	28.2%				
Grad degree:	10.9%				

North Coast; Napa, Davis

The North Coast of California is unlike any other place in America. It is the only part of the lower 48 states first settled by Russians, who built Fort Ross in 1812. They sold it in 1841 to a Swiss pioneer named John Augustus Sutter, whose discovery of gold near Sacramento eight years later started the Gold Rush. It is the only part of the world with large numbers of redwood trees, shooting up hundreds of feet in the drizzly air. It

2008 Presidential Vote		
Barack Obama (D) 199,835	(66%)
John McCain (R) 96,530	(32%)
2004 Presidential Vote		
John Kerry (D) 173,926	(60%)
George Bush (R) 111,754	(38%)
Cook Partisan Voting Index: D+13		

is wet country, and for years it was one of America's prime lumbering areas. Eureka and smaller lumber towns are filled with filigreed Victorian houses and old mills, but also art galleries, hiking trails, pubs, and waterfront hotels. Humboldt County is known for its quality marijuana fields, and the local economy relies heavily on the product, as depicted in the 2008 movie *Humboldt County*. Local voters that year in next-door Mendocino County pulled back from the nation's most liberal marijuana law by falling in line with the state limit of six plants per resident—instead of 24, which had been the county law since 2000—because of concern about nonmedical abuses of the crop.

The region has moved on to other crops. In sunny valleys sealed off from the Coast Range, some of the nation's premium wine grapes are grown on ridges. Thirty years ago, there were only 20 wineries in Napa Valley. Today, there are several hundred, with more just west of the ridges in Sonoma County. Wineries were a favorite investment for Silicon Valley millionaires until the recession caused production cutbacks and thousands of job layoffs in 2008. Olive trees are also grown here. Some of California's earliest literary haunts were in the valleys. Robert Louis Stevenson took his honeymoon near Calistoga in Napa, and Jack London owned a giant house in Sonoma that mysteriously burned down in 1913. Along the coast, a 2006 law designated 273,000 acres of wilderness and restored the rights of commercial fishermen to drive trucks on the beaches of the Redwood National Park.

The 1st Congressional District of California consists of the North Coast from Mendocino County to the Oregon border. To the south, it includes Napa County and the eastern edge of Sonoma County—Healdsburg, the Alexander Valley, and part of Sonoma Valley—plus part of the Yolo County flatlands, including the University of California at Davis and industrial West Sacramento. Just above Napa is Lake County, which, in contrast to numerous other California counties, has clean air—the nation's 10th cleanest in 2010, according to the American Lung Association. But the county also has fewer jobs than most; its unemployment rate soared above 16% in late 2009. The North Coast lumbering area, from Mendocino on north, was once filled with rough-hewn working men, and was historically Democratic. But the timber business was hurt in the 1980s by environmental protections for the northern spotted owl, and the local backlash prompted more interest in Republican politics. Now, the focus is on sustainable forestry. And the area remains largely Democratic. The Pacific Lumber Company, the longtime landlord of the town of Scotia, one of the last company-owned towns in the United States, sold all of its 275 houses in 2008 and planned to continue limited timber production. Inland, the wine-growing country around Healdsburg and in Napa County, was Republican in the 1970s, but now partakes of the San Francisco Bay Area's liberal consensus. This district changed partisan hands four times during the 1990s, thanks largely to splits among Democrats, but redistricting in 2001 made it solidly Democratic.

Mike Thompson (D)

The congressman from the 1st District is Mike Thompson, a Democrat first elected in 1998. Thompson grew up in the Napa Valley town of St. Helena, dropped out of high school, served in the Army in Vietnam, and earned a Purple Heart. Later, he got a bachelor's and master's degree from what is now California State University at Chico. He owned a vineyard and worked as a maintenance supervisor for Beringer, a big winery in the valley. From 1984 to 1990, he was the chief of staff to two Bay Area state Assembly members. In 1990, he was elected to the state Senate, where he chaired the Budget Committee. In 1998, he ran for the U.S. House seat of Republican Frank Riggs, who planned to challenge Democratic Sen. Barbara Boxer that year. Thompson faced only weak opposition and had support from almost every interest group that matters in the district: unions, medical providers, vintners, oil and timber interests, environmental advocates, law enforcement groups, and fishermen. His issue stands—opposition to oil drilling off the California coast, support of abortion rights and the death penalty—were broadly popular. He won the primary 78%-22% and the general election 62%-33%. He has not been seriously challenged since then.

In the House, Thompson is a moderate Democrat whose voting record is among the least liberal of coastal Californians. He joined both the New Democrats and the Blue Dog Coalition of conservative Democrats. He is among the members of his party who agree with Republicans on the need to abolish the estate tax, which he said unfairly burdens family farms. With Republican Rep. George Radanovich of California, he started the Congressional Wine Caucus, and wineries such as Gallo and Sutter Home have been among his largest campaign contributors. For the past several years, Thompson and the caucus have battled lawmakers allied with beer and alcohol wholesalers over a bill giving states new power to restrict sales over the Internet. He said the bill "allows states to discriminate against (wine) producers in ways that promote economic protectionism." In 2009, Thompson added provisions to a solar technology bill aimed at preventing thefts of solar panels at wineries, a growing problem in the Napa Valley. He also joined California GOP Rep. Jerry Lewis on a proposal to create a $1 billion fund for making buildings more resistant to earthquakes.

Thompson has been a close ally of former House Speaker Nancy Pelosi, D-Calif., which gives him influence among House Democrats. She tapped him in 2009 to coordinate redistricting efforts for Democrats following the 2010 census. But his ambition to head the Democratic Congressional Campaign Committee after the 2002 election was dashed by an ill-timed visit to Iraq. Thompson traveled to Baghdad in 2002, before the United States went to war with Iraq, with a group that included Reps. David Bonior, D-Mich., and Jim McDermott, D-Wash., who criticized President Bush's Iraq policy—statements that were deemed impolitic with tensions running high between the two countries. Although Thompson did not make the controversial comments and later conceded it was a bad idea to criticize the president from Iraq, the trip dashed his chances of assuming a high-profile party role.

As consolation, Thompson was asked to lead the DCCC's incumbent protection program, and got a seat on the House Ways and Means Committee. On the powerful panel, he was able to enact a tax break for landowners who place their land under conservation easements, a way to preserve farmland. In 2007, Thompson sponsored the Airline Passenger Bill of Rights, which requires airlines to provide basic necessities, like food, water, and well-ventilated facilities, when flights are delayed for long periods. Although it stalled in Congress, the Obama administration issued a rule modeled after the legislation in 2010. After Republicans talked up increased domestic oil drilling, Thompson in early 2009 proposed to ban all drilling along the North Coast, saying it made little sense economically or environmentally.

On the Intelligence Committee, Thompson sponsored a successful addition to the 2008 defense bill that cracked down on abuses by private contractors in Iraq and expanded the authority of a special inspector general. Later, he joined several other Democrats in 2010 to amend the House's fiscal 2011 defense bill to permit the Government Accountability Office to investigate the operations of spy agencies.

Following the 2008 election, Thompson was mentioned as a contender for Interior secretary in the Obama administration, a position that ultimately went to then-Sen. Ken Salazar, D-Colo.

SECOND DISTRICT

Wally Herger (R)

Elected 1986, 13th term; b. May 20, 1945, Yuba City; home, Chico; American River Comm. Col., A.A. 1967, CA St. U., 1968-69; Mormon; married (Pamela); 9 children.

Elected Office: CA Assembly, 1980–86.

Professional Career: Rancher; Owner, Herger Gas Inc., 1969–present.

DC Office: 242 CHOB, 20515, 202-225-3076; Fax: 202-226-0852; Web site: herger.house.gov.

State Offices: Chico, 530-893-8363; Redding, 530-223-5898.

Committees: *Joint Committee on Taxation. Ways & Means:* Health (Chmn); Trade.

Group Ratings

	ACLU	ACU	ADA	CFG	AFS	FRC	LCV	ITIC	NTU	COC
2010	6	100	0	100	0	100	0	33	94	88
2009	–	100	0	97	11	–	0	–	90	73

National Journal Ratings

	2010 LIB	—	2010 CONS	2009 LIB	—	2009 CONS
Economic	6%	—	94%	9%	—	89%
Social	0%	—	85%	10%	—	90%
Foreign	0%	—	88%	0%	—	75%
Composite	7%	—	94%	11%	—	89%

Key Votes of the 111th Congress

1. Overturn Ledbetter	N	5. Bar federal abortion funds	Y	9. Stop detainee transfers	Y
2. Pass $820 billion stimulus	N	6. Pass health care bill	N	10. Legalize immigrants' kids	N
3. Let guns in national parks	Y	7. Regulate financial firms	N	11. Repeal don't ask, tell	N
4. Pass cap-and-trade	N	8. Pass tax cuts for some	N	12. Limit campaign funds	N

Election Results

2010 general	Wally Herger (R)	130,837	(57%)	($1,010,414)
	Jim Reed (D)	98,092	(43%)	($155,554)
2010 primary	Wally Herger (R)	57,272	(65%)	
	Pete Stiglich (R)	30,487	(35%)	

Prior Winning Percentages: 2008 (58%), 2006 (64%), 2004 (67%), 2002 (66%), 2000 (66%), 1998 (63%), 1996 (61%), 1994 (64%), 1992 (65%), 1990 (64%), 1988 (59%), 1986 (58%)

Population		Race/Ethnicity		Work	
Pop. 2010:	708,596	White:	70.2%	Private:	69.7%
Change since 2000:	Up 10.9%	Black:	1.3%	Government:	19.7%
Urban:	67.7%	Hispanic:	19.0%	Self-employed:	10.4%
Rural:	32.3%	Asian:	4.3%	Blue collar:	21.1%
Area size:	21,979 sq. mi.	Native Am.:	1.7%	White collar:	55.5%
		Hawaiian:	0.2%	Khaki collar:	0.4%
Age		Two+ races:	3.2%	Other:	23.0%
Median age:	37.7 yrs.				
More than 65 yrs:	14.3%	*Ancestry*		Median income:	$43,470
Less than 18 yrs:	24.2%	German	14.1%	Median Home Value:	$265,000
		Irish	10.7%		
Education		English	9.2%	**Military Veterans**	
H.S. grad:	83.7%			% of Pop:	11.8%
College grad:	20.2%				
Grad degree:	6.4%				

Central Calif.; Redding, Chico

Rising 14,000 feet over low foothills and the Central Valley, visible for 100 miles, is the snow-capped volcanic cone of Mount Shasta, one of a string of (supposedly) burnt-out volcanoes up and down the Pacific Coast states. This is the far northern end of California, where truck traffic on Interstate 5 is the only reminder of the choked metropolitan areas where most of the state's people live. This is lumber country mostly, where the mountains that rise on all sides—the

2008 Presidential Vote		
John McCain (R) 161,636	(55%)
Barack Obama (D) 125,291	(43%)
2004 Presidential Vote		
George Bush (R) 173,528	(62%)
John Kerry (D) 102,254	(37%)
Cook Partisan Voting Index: R+11		

Coast Range to the west, the Sierra Nevada to the east, the scattered mountains sealing off the Central Valley north of Redding—are carpeted with trees. It's rugged, flannel-shirt, two-lane-road country that was left behind economically when Los Angeles and San Francisco boomed after World War II. North of Shasta, the tiny town of Weed became a logging center and a noted locale for racial integration a half-century ago, but the loss of jobs has led younger blacks and whites to move out. Farther south are the flat farm fields of the Sacramento Valley, spread across the 50 miles between the Sierra Nevada and the Coast Range. Since the 1980s, this northern end of California has been attracting people, mostly young families who come here to raise their children in a small-town environment, but also retirees looking for a calm atmosphere and low cost of living.

The 2nd Congressional District of California covers most of this area. The district has three major population areas. One is Redding, south of Mount Shasta, where increased high-altitude snowfall has allowed the Whitney Glacier to defy global warming trends by growing in the past century, the only glacier to do so. The second is farther south, at the edge of the Sierra foothills, around the Butte County communities of Paradise and Chico, home to a state university campus and Sierra Nevada Pale Ale. In 2008, surrounding areas suffered devastating forest fires. Between Redding and Chico is Red Bluff, which has been the recent beneficiary of state and federal largesse. It received almost $110 million in federal stimulus money in 2009 to build a pumping plant to improve fish passage conditions. Still farther south are the farm counties of Colusa, Yuba, and Sutter, not far north of Sacramento. The locally cultivated rice hybrids from Colusa County, the leading rice-producing county in the nation, are a lucrative export. The region has a Democratic heritage but is culturally conservative, angry at intrusions by urban environmentalists. Until 1980, it elected rough-and-ready Democrats who pulled strings in Sacramento and Washington to build roads and dams. Since then, it has elected abstemious Republicans who have solidly conservative voting records and tend to local needs. George W. Bush won 62% of the vote here in 2004, and John McCain won 55% in 2008, their best showings in a northern California district.

Wally Herger (R)

The congressman from the 2nd District is Wally Herger, a Republican first elected in 1986. He grew up in the farm country north of Sacramento, where he was a local farmer and rancher. He also owned a propane gas company. Herger married young, and his first marriage did not last. Then he met his present wife, Pamela, a nurse, who like him was a Mormon who wanted a large family. The couple had three children from their first marriages and together had six more, although they mourned the loss of one child who died as a toddler. In 1980, he was elected to the California Assembly. Six years later, Herger was elected to the U.S. House after winning solid margins over the mayor of Redding in the primary and beating a Shasta County supervisor in the general.

Herger has a solidly conservative voting record and was among the first House Republicans to join the Tea Party Caucus in 2010. He drew liberal Democrats' scorn for complimenting a constituent as a "great American" at an August town hall meeting after the man described himself as a "proud right-wing terrorist." The constituent later said that he was using satire to describe liberal portrayals of his views as extreme. The burst of attention was unusual for Herger, who has served quietly on the Ways and Means Committee, voting for balanced budgets and lower taxes. When federal budget deficits were wiped out in the late 1990s, Herger was a leader of the battle to stop the government from spending surpluses in the Social Security and Medicare trust funds. That debate became moot with the return of big deficits. As chairman of the Human Resources Subcommittee, he helped write the Republican welfare reform law in 1996, which increased work requirements for recipients and incentives for states to reduce caseloads.

His advancement on the committee, however, has been slowed by more aggressive and charismatic Republicans. Junior lawmakers have twice leapfrogged him to take the top Republican post on the committee. In 2007, Rep. Jim McCrery of Louisiana jumped over him, with the leadership's blessing, to become the ranking Republican. When McCrery retired two years later, Dave Camp of Michigan, a more aggressive party spokesman and campaign contributor, ascended to the top minority slot. In 2009, Herger did become the ranking Republican on one of the most important subcommittees, responsible for health care policy. Two years later, after Republicans gained majority control of the House in the 2010 election, Herger became chairman of the Health Subcommittee. He was a regular critic of President Obama's health care overhaul, including its emphasis on "comparative effectiveness research," a study tool to determine strategies for treating patients that he and other Republicans said would eventually leave decision-making to bureaucrats who could ration health care. He sought in 2009 to amend the legislation to bar such research, but his proposal failed on a party-line vote on the committee.

On local issues, Herger has tended to water projects and called for exemption of flood control programs from the Endangered Species Act. He also helped to enact a program to aid about 750 counties that have suffered loss of revenue from timber sales. In 2009, Herger introduced a bill to expedite hazardous-fuels reduction and forest-thinning projects during wildfire emergencies. He has been easily re-elected every two years, usually with more than 60% of the vote.

THIRD DISTRICT

Dan Lungren (R)

Elected 2004, 9th term; b. Sept. 22, 1946, Long Beach; home, Gold River ; Notre Dame U., A.B. 1968, Georgetown U., J.D. 1971; Catholic; married (Bobbi); 3 children.

Elected Office: U.S. House of Reps.1978-88; CA Atty. Gen. 1990-98.

Professional Career: Staff, U.S. Sen. George Murphy, 1969-70; Staff, U.S. Sen. Bill Brock, 1971; Spec. asst. RNC, 1971-72; Practicing atty., 1973-78.

DC Office: 2313 RHOB, 20515, 202-225-5716; Fax: 202-226-1298; Web site: lungren.house.gov.

State Offices: Gold River, 916-859-9906.

Committees: *Homeland Security:* Cybersecurity, Infrastructure Protection & Security Technologies (Chmn); Transportation Security. *House Administration* (Chmn). *Judiciary:* Crime, Terrorism & Homeland Security; Immigration Policy & Enforcement.

Group Ratings

	ACLU	ACU	ADA	CFG	AFS	FRC	LCV	ITIC	NTU	COC
2010	6	96	0	83	14	93	0	33	84	88
2009	–	100	5	91	11	–	0	–	85	80

National Journal Ratings

	2010 LIB — 2010 CONS		2009 LIB — 2009 CONS	
Economic	28%	— 71%	19%	— 80%
Social	16%	— 82%	7%	— 90%
Foreign	29%	— 68%	33%	— 63%
Composite	25%	— 75%	21%	— 79%

Key Votes of the 111th Congress

1. Overturn Ledbetter	N	5. Bar federal abortion funds	Y	9. Stop detainee transfers	Y
2. Pass $820 billion stimulus	N	6. Pass health care bill	N	10. Legalize immigrants' kids	N
3. Let guns in national parks	Y	7. Regulate financial firms	N	11. Repeal don't ask, tell	N
4. Pass cap-and-trade	N	8. Pass tax cuts for some	N	12. Limit campaign funds	N

Election Results

2010 general	Dan Lungren (R)	131,169	(50%)	($2,025,541)
	Ami Bera (D)	113,128	(43%)	($2,942,764)
	Jerry Leidecker (AMI)	6,577	(3%)	
	Douglas Tuma (Lib)	6,275	(2%)	
2010 primary	Dan Lungren (R)	unopposed		

Prior Winning Percentages: 2008 (49%), 2006 (59%), 2004 (62%), 1986 (73%), 1984 (73%), 1982 (69%), 1980 (72%), 1978 (54%)

Population		Race/Ethnicity		Work	
Pop. 2010:	783,317	White:	62.4%	Private:	69.7%
Change since 2000:	Up 22.6%	Black:	5.8%	Government:	21.3%
Urban:	86.4%	Hispanic:	15.6%	Self-employed:	8.8%
Rural:	13.6%	Asian:	10.8%	Blue collar:	16.8%
Area size:	3,422 sq. mi.	Native Am.:	0.6%	White collar:	66.5%
		Hawaiian:	0.5%	Khaki collar:	0.0%
Age		Two+ races:	4.0%	Other:	16.6%
Median age:	37.8 yrs.				
More than 65 yrs:	12.5%	*Ancestry*		Median income:	$66,025
Less than 18 yrs:	25.4%	German	12.8%	Median Home Value:	$352,600
		Irish	10.2%		
Education		English	8.9%	**Military Veterans**	
H.S. grad:	89.3%			% of Pop:	11.8%
College grad:	28.6%				
Grad degree:	8.9%				

Sacramento Suburbs

Until recently, Sacramento was chiefly the metropolis of a fertile valley that produced a marvelous variety of crops: rice, plums, almonds, olives, asparagus, pears, hops, beans, celery, onions, and potatoes, plus caviar-yielding sturgeon in pools of filtered water. The farmlands remain, and the capital city flourishes as a center of government. Until recessionary forces struck in 2007, greater Sacramento was one of the fastest-growing metro areas in the country.

2008 Presidential Vote
Barack Obama (D) 165,617   (49%)
John McCain (R) 164,025   (49%)

2004 Presidential Vote
George Bush (R) 176,512   (58%)
John Kerry (D) 123,671   (41%)

Cook Partisan Voting Index: R+6

Almost all of the growth has been away from the floodplain of the Sacramento River, in the higher land east of the city that eventually turns into hills rising toward the Sierra Nevadas. But home sales plunged and foreclosures soared in 2007, which led to service cutbacks in Sacramento County. After the county opened a $22 million animal shelter in 2009, so many animals came in from people who couldn't afford their upkeep—an estimated 30 per day—that the shelter had to double up animals in kennels. Amador and Calaveras counties are in Mother Lode Country, which filled up with people in the gold rush days, when Mark Twain was inspired to write his story about the famous jumping frog of Calaveras County. In rapidly growing Rancho Cordova, local leaders created a "new urbanist" development plan to replace aging strip malls with a traditional downtown. It won an All-America City award in 2010.

The 3rd Congressional District of California includes much of suburban Sacramento, some territory in Solano County and some of the Mother Lode Country to the east. The district reaches over the Sierras to Alpine County, the smallest county in California (1,061 people in 2008), with the state's highest mountain ridgeline. The district stops at the Nevada line. Population in the district grew 23% from 2000 to 2010. More than 80% of the people in the district live in Sacramento County, in suburbs like Carmichael, Citrus Heights, Arden-Arcade, and the old town of Folsom, where Intel established a campus of about 6,000 employees and created a prosperous company town. Historically, Sacramento was Democratic. But Sacramento County, with its rapid growth, continues to shift politically. The district voted 58% for George W. Bush in 2004, but Barack Obama prevailed over John McCain, 49.3%-48.8%, in 2008.

Dan Lungren (R)

The congressman from the 3rd District is Dan Lungren, a Republican elected in 2004 who previously was the representative from the 42nd District for 10 years. Lungren grew up in Long Beach, and his father was President Nixon's personal physician. Young Dan worked on the staffs of Sens. George Murphy of California and Bill Brock of Tennessee, both Republicans. After a few years of law practice in Long Beach, he unsuccessfully challenged Democrat Mark Hannaford in the U.S. House in 1976, then came back and won rather easily in 1978 with a boost from the anti-tax Proposition 13. He entered a freshman class that included Reps. Dick Cheney of Wyoming and Newt Gingrich of Georgia, as well as Jerry Lewis and Bill Thomas of California. During his initial years in Congress, Lungren focused on criminal-code reform on the Judiciary Committee.

Lungren was also a member of the Conservative Opportunity Society, the influential group of young House conservatives organized by Gingrich, who went on to lead Republicans to capture majority control of the House in 1994. He played a key role on major immigration legislation in 1986, which made it illegal to knowingly hire illegal immigrants. He left the House in 1989 after he was nominated to be California state treasurer, but he was deemed too partisan and was not confirmed by the state Senate. In 1990, he was elected to the first of two terms as California attorney general. After losing 58%-38% to Democrat Gray Davis in the 1998 race for governor, Lungren worked in the Sacramento area as a visiting professor and radio talk show host. He joined a Washington, D.C.-based law firm.

In 2004, 3rd District incumbent Republican Doug Ose honored his pledge to retire after serving three terms, and Lungren ran for the seat. His toughest competition was in the Republican primary, in which he faced Mary Ose, the incumbent's sister, and state Sen. Rico Oller. Ose, a real estate developer, raised more than $2 million, much of it from her own pocket. Despite an almost 2-to-1 fundraising advantage over the others, she won only 23% of the votes. Oller, with a geographic base in Amador and Calaveras counties, attacked Lungren as soft on immigration. Lungren ran an ad with praise from Gingrich for his work on the 1986 immigration bill, and beat Oller 39%-36%, winning 42%-32% in Sacramento County, which cast 82% of the total vote. In the GOP-leaning district, Lungren easily won the general election over Democrat Bill Lockyer, 62%-35%. He returned to Congress representing a district nearly 400 miles north of his old one.

Lungren quickly resumed his status as an influential Republican player and usually voted with conservatives. He got credit for his previous service and gained senior positions on the Judiciary and the Homeland Security committees, though he lost a bid in 2005 to chair Homeland Security. Subsequently, he worked with Rep. Jane Harman, D-Calif., to enact a bill enhancing port security, including requirements to scan cargo containers for radioactive materials. He also talked up the growing threat of cyber attacks on telecommunications systems and other infrastructure.

On Judiciary, he opposed restrictions on the USA PATRIOT Act as "compromising our ability to investigate terrorist cases," and helped to write the House-passed bill for warrantless surveillance, which has been controversial with civil liberties groups. Lungren sided with most House Republicans in 2006 in opposing the Senate-passed immigration bill that included a guest worker program. He emphasized the need to "get control of our border." He also was a sponsor of a proposed constitutional amendment to ban gay marriage. After the 2010 health care overhaul became law, he introduced a bill to repeal a controversial provision requiring businesses to file a 1099 IRS form for anyone paid more than $600 a year, a burden he said was onerous.

Sometimes a maverick, Lungren criticized his party for the huge growth of earmark spending during the years Republicans controlled the majority. That may be one of the reasons his leadership ambitions have been stymied. In November 2006, he ran fourth of four candidates for chairman of the Republican Conference, the third-ranking leadership post. And he ran a seemingly futile last-minute challenge to Minority Leader John Boehner of Ohio in November 2008. Lungren cited the need for the party to adopt more fiscally conservative policies. In 2009, Boehner tapped him as the ranking Republican on the House Administration Committee, the housekeeping panel that controls perks for fellow members. Campaign finance issues are part of the committee's jurisdiction, and Lungren said in October 2010 that he backed a free-market, deregulated approach that would eliminate all spending caps, an action that he said would ensure that independent groups would not play an outsized role. Campaign finance activists decried the effect of such a scenario.

In 2006, Lungren was re-elected 59%-38% against Bill Durston, an emergency-room physician who served with the Marines in Vietnam and was endorsed by a national group calling for the impeachment of President Bush. He had an unexpectedly close rematch with Durston in 2008. Durston tried to connect Lungren to special interests in Washington, and Lungren accused him of "McCarthyism on the left." Lungren this time won by only 49%-44%.

Two years later, he found himself in yet another tight race, even in the highly favorable climate for Republicans in 2010. His Democratic challenger, physician and political neophyte Ami Bera, showed surprising strength as a fundraiser, drawing on donations from Indian-Americans across the country to become the only Democratic challenger in mid-2010 to out raise a sitting House Republican. He accused Lungren of being out of touch with district voters and duplicated Durston's ad showing Lungren poolside on a lobbyist-financed vacation in Hawaii. Though Lungren's trip was cleared in advance by the House Ethics Committee, Bera accused Lungren of violating the spirit of the law. The incumbent didn't help his case when he was stopped by police for speeding while conducting a live radio interview. He responded to Bera's attacks by portraying his opponent as a vote for Speaker Nancy Pelosi's agenda. Lungren also got financial help from Karl Rove's American Crossroads organization, which spent nearly $700,000 for him—more than it devoted to any other candidate. That helped Lungren eke out a win with 51% of the vote to Bera's 43%.

FOURTH DISTRICT

Tom McClintock (R)

Elected 2008, 2nd term; b. July 10, 1956, Bronxville, NY; home, Granite Bay; U.C.L.A., B.A. 1978.; Baptist; married (Lori); 2 children.

Elected Office: CA Assembly, 1982-92, 1996-2000; CA Senate 2000-08.

Professional Career: Newspaper columnist, journalist.

DC Office: 428 CHOB, 20515, 202-225-2511; Fax: 202-225-5444; Web site: mcclintock.house.gov.

State Offices: Granite Bay, 916-786-5560.

Committees: *Budget. Natural Resources:* Indian & Alaska Native Affairs; National Parks, Forests & Public Lands; Water & Power (Chmn).

Group Ratings

	ACLU	ACU	ADA	CFG	AFS	FRC	LCV	ITIC	NTU	COC
2010	13	100	0	100	0	100	0	33	94	88
2009	–	100	0	100	0	–	0	–	95	73

National Journal Ratings

	2010 LIB	—	2010 CONS	2009 LIB	—	2009 CONS
Economic	7%	—	92%	5%	—	94%
Social	18%	—	77%	0%	—	93%
Foreign	26%	—	72%	0%	—	75%
Composite	18%	—	82%	7%	—	93%

Key Votes of the 111th Congress

1. Overturn Ledbetter	N	5. Bar federal abortion funds	Y	9. Stop detainee transfers	Y
2. Pass $820 billion stimulus	N	6. Pass health care bill	N	10. Legalize immigrants' kids	N
3. Let guns in national parks	Y	7. Regulate financial firms	N	11. Repeal don't ask, tell	N
4. Pass cap-and-trade	N	8. Pass tax cuts for some	N	12. Limit campaign funds	N

Election Results

2010 general	Tom McClintock (R)	186,397	(61%)	($1,871,623)
	Clint Curtis (D)	95,653	(31%)	($32,176)
	Benjamin Emery (Green)	22,179	(7%)	
2010 primary	Tom McClintock (R)	89,443	(78%)	
	Michael Babich (R)	24,528	(22%)	

Prior Winning Percentages: 2008 (50%)

Population		Race/Ethnicity		Work	
Pop. 2010:	774,261	White:	78.0%	Private:	71.3%
Change since 2000:	Up 21.2%	Black:	1.4%	Government:	18.1%
Urban:	67.4%	Hispanic:	12.1%	Self-employed:	10.3%
Rural:	32.6%	Asian:	4.2%	Blue collar:	17.0%
Area size:	17,156 sq. mi.	Native Am.:	1.0%	White collar:	64.6%
		Hawaiian:	0.2%	Khaki collar:	0.1%
Age		Two+ races:	2.9%	Other:	18.4%
Median age:	41.5 yrs.				
More than 65 yrs:	14.8%	*Ancestry*		Median income:	$64,094
Less than 18 yrs:	23.0%	German	15.0%	Median Home Value:	$410,600
		Irish	11.7%		
Education		English	11.4%	**Military Veterans**	
H.S. grad:	91.4%			% of Pop:	12.8%
College grad:	29.5%				
Grad degree:	9.4%				

Northeast California; Roseville

California sprang into existence with the Gold Rush of 1849. Statehood and the creation of the first 27 counties followed in 1850. The new state's first boom area was the Mother Lode Country in the foothills of the Sierra Mountains above Sacramento. Mining camps the size of Eastern cities grew up almost overnight in vacant valleys locked amid steep hills, with thousands of would-be millionaires gathered to find gold, though most of those who actually got rich

2008 Presidential Vote		
John McCain (R) 206,385	(54%)
Barack Obama (D) 167,604	(44%)
2004 Presidential Vote		
George Bush (R) 216,838	(61%)
John Kerry (D) 132,267	(37%)
Cook Partisan Voting Index: R+10		

did so by providing goods and services that catered to miners' needs. In Placerville, John Studebaker had a buggy shop, Philip Armour ran a butcher shop, and Mark Hopkins had a dry goods store. The biggest mine in California was in Grass Valley in 1857 and was worked for half a century. But long before that, most of the Mother Lode Country emptied out, leaving ghost towns and villages with hundreds of deserted houses, an antique vacation country left behind in time.

When local residents celebrated the sesquicentennial, the area had been resurrected as a booming exurban and tourist mecca. "The American River near Coloma becomes a virtual freeway of whooping rafters on summer weekends," wrote *USA Today*. "The Mother Lode also offers modern-day prospectors an intriguing pastiche of bed-and-breakfast inns, musty antique stores and such blink-and-you'll-miss-'em outposts as Volcano, Fiddletown, Rough and Ready." Thousands of Californians—many of them families from smog-filled, middle-class suburbs of the Los Angeles Basin and the San Francisco Bay Area—went looking for a more pleasant, small-town, orderly environment and found it along fast-flowing creeks where the '49ers camped. Placer County, which includes Sacramento suburbs and part of the Mother Lode Country, grew 40% from 2000 to 2009, and was among the fastest-growing counties in California. It also has the highest percentage of registered Republicans in the state and ranks among its wealthiest counties. On Lake Tahoe, Truckee has grown with the development of ski resorts. Politically, this growth has changed the Mother Lode Country from Democratic to Republican. In 1976, nine Mother Lode counties from Sierra to Mariposa cast 118,000 ballots and voted 50%-47% for Jimmy Carter over Gerald Ford. In 2008, they cast 445,000 votes and backed John McCain over Barack Obama, 54%-44%. California as a whole favored Obama over McCain 61%-37%. The culture here could not be more different from that of the Bay Area, less than 50 miles away.

The 4th Congressional District of California consists of the northern half of the Mother Lode Country and the Placer County suburbs of Sacramento, plus a small slice of Sacramento County. It extends north through thinly populated mountain counties like Modoc, site of a World War II detention facility for Japanese-Americans. Modoc County shares a border with Oregon and Nevada. Most residents live within the Interstate 80 corridor, clustered near Sacramento in suburbs like Roseville, the district's most populous city, which grew 34% from 2000 to 2006 and completed a $240 million addition to its upscale mall that features Tiffany and Co. Some 33% of district residents live in areas classified as rural, the largest percentage of the state's 53 districts.

Tom McClintock (R)

The congressman from the 4th District is Republican Tom McClintock, who was first elected in 2008. He spent his early childhood in White Plains, N.Y., where he lived until he was 9. His earliest exposure to politics came at a young age, when his mother took him to a campaign rally for Republican presidential candidate Richard Nixon at a local airport in 1960. After graduating from the University of California at Los Angeles, he worked briefly as a political columnist and a state Senate aide before leaping into elected office at age 26 with a successful run for the California Assembly in 1982. From his earliest days in the legislature, McClintock established himself as perhaps its most vocal, if not the most effective, budget hawk, railing against tax increases and high spending under Democratic and Republican administrations alike. Supporters saw an eloquent champion of conservative ideas, a policy wonk with a penchant for quoting Abraham Lincoln. Detractors viewed him as an ideological obstructionist with few legislative accomplishments.

McClintock tested the limits of his appeal in a liberal state through a relentless effort to win higher office. His name has appeared on a ballot in California in every state election since 1982. He ran twice for a U.S. House seat in Southern California, dropping out of the 1986 race during the Republican primary and losing the 1992 race to Democratic Rep. Anthony C. Beilenson. He ran for state controller in 1994 and again in 2002, narrowly losing both times. In 2006, he was unsuccessful as his party's nominee for lieutenant governor, even as Republican Gov. Arnold Schwarzenegger sailed to re-election. But no race elevated McClintock's profile in the state as much as his quixotic campaign for governor in the 2003 recall election. As star-struck Republicans lined up behind former actor Schwarzenegger, McClintock forged ahead unbowed, presenting himself as the true Republican in a field of hopefuls that at one point included political commentator Arianna Huffington and actor Gary Coleman. He finished with 13.5%.

Opportunity struck yet again for McClintock in 2008. In February, after nine-term Republican Rep. John Doolittle announced he would step down amid a federal probe of disgraced Republican lobbyist Jack Abramoff, several Republicans in the district urged McClintock to get into the race. Barred by term limits from seeking re-election to the state Senate, McClintock got in and faced an intense, three-month primary campaign against former Rep. Doug Ose, a Republican moderate who held the neighboring 3rd District seat from 1999 to 2005. Ose attacked McClintock as a career politician and carpetbagger, although Ose also lived outside the district. McClintock, who noted that he had lived in the district's Sacramento suburbs while serving in the legislature, ran ads branding Ose as a liberal who had voted to raise taxes and had earmarked millions of dollars for federal projects in his district. McClintock won the primary 54%-39% over Ose.

In the general election, McClintock faced Democrat Charlie Brown, a retired Air Force officer who came within 10,000 votes of beating Doolittle in 2006. Brown, who raised his family in the Sacramento suburb of Roseville, renewed criticism of McClintock as an opportunist who didn't live in the district. McClintock ran ads calling attention to Brown's attendance at a 2005 protest by Code Pink, the fiercely anti-war group, and asserted that Brown supported gay marriage but not the troops in Iraq. McClintock's expected easy victory actually took weeks to unfold. He won by precisely 1,800 votes, 50.2%-49.8%, and took six of the nine counties.

In the House, McClintock has proven to be a faithful Republican vote, and with other conservatives joined the Tea Party Caucus in July 2010. "The bigger government gets, the more it takes from working folks," he told Fox News that year. "And the more it takes from working folks, the worse the economy does." He promised to eschew earmarks, the funding requests that members often tack on to major spending bills for special projects in their districts, and called for the earmarking process to be abolished instead of simply reformed. As a member of the Education and Labor Committee, he introduced a bill in 2009 with Sen. David Vitter, R-La., that would allow employers to give merit-based bonuses or other compensation increases above any collective bargaining agreement. He was a vociferous critic of the Democrats' health care overhaul, and sought without success in 2009 to suspend the original House bill's employer mandate and health exchange provisions if they were found to add to the deficit over the next decade.

In 2011, McClintock became the chairman of the Water and Power Subcommittee of the Natural Resources Committee. On the panel, he has complained that about half of the state's water supply is consumed to meet various environmental regulations, a particular problem during the state's frequent droughts. In 2010, he called for local water district officials and farmers to lobby Congress to amend the Endangered Species Act to permit water deliveries from the Sacramento-San Joaquin delta to farmers.

And even from Washington, McClintock could not resist jumping into California's political fray. He supported state Insurance Commissioner Steve Poizner for the GOP gubernatorial nomination over the more moderate former eBay executive Meg Whitman, saying in April 2010: "We can't afford another Republican governor who actively undermines the ticket." Despite his efforts, Whitman beat Poizner in the primary.

FIFTH DISTRICT

Doris Matsui (D)

Elected March 2005, 3rd full term; b. Sept. 25, 1944, Poston, AZ; home, Sacramento; U. of CA, B.A. 1966; United Methodist; widowed; 1 child.

Professional Career: Transition team, President-elect Bill Clinton, 1992-93; Dep. asst. to the pres., dep. dir. of public liaison, White House, 1993-98; Lobbyist, 1998-2005.

DC Office: 222 CHOB, 20515, 202-225-7163; Fax: 202-225-0566; Web site: matsui.house.gov.

State Offices: Sacramento, 916-498-5600.

Committees: *Energy & Commerce:* Communications & Technology; Environment & the Economy.

Group Ratings

	ACLU	ACU	ADA	CFG	AFS	FRC	LCV	ITIC	NTU	COC
2010	88	0	100	0	100	0	100	67	6	13
2009	–	0	100	4	100	–	100	–	2	40

National Journal Ratings

	2010 LIB	—	2010 CONS	2009 LIB	—	2009 CONS
Economic	90%	—	0%	88%	—	9%
Social	89%	—	7%	84%	—	11%
Foreign	84%	—	11%	91%	—	0%
Composite	91%	—	9%	91%	—	10%

Key Votes of the 111th Congress

1. Overturn Ledbetter	Y	5. Bar federal abortion funds	N	9. Stop detainee transfers	N
2. Pass $820 billion stimulus	Y	6. Pass health care bill	Y	10. Legalize immigrants' kids	Y
3. Let guns in national parks	N	7. Regulate financial firms	Y	11. Repeal don't ask, tell	Y
4. Pass cap-and-trade	Y	8. Pass tax cuts for some	Y	12. Limit campaign funds	Y

Election Results

2010 general	Doris Matsui (D)	124,220	(72%)	($835,400)
	Paul Smith (R)	43,577	(25%)	($23,941)
	Gerald Frink (PF)	4,594	(3%)	
2010 primary	Doris Matsui (D)	unopposed		

Prior Winning Percentages: 2008 (74%), 2006 (71%), 2005 special (68%)

Population		Race/Ethnicity		Work	
Pop. 2010:	700,443	White:	35.8%	Private:	70.4%
Change since 2000:	Up 9.6%	Black:	13.7%	Government:	23.2%
Urban:	99.7%	Hispanic:	27.4%	Self-employed:	6.2%
Rural:	0.3%	Asian:	16.4%	Blue collar:	18.3%
Area size:	150 sq. mi.	Native Am.:	0.6%	White collar:	60.9%
		Hawaiian:	1.3%	Khaki collar:	0.1%
Age		Two+ races:	4.6%	Other:	20.7%
Median age:	32.7 yrs.				
More than 65 yrs:	10.7%	*Ancestry*		Median income:	$47,286
Less than 18 yrs:	25.8%	German	8.1%	Median Home Value:	$277,700
		Irish	6.5%		
Education		English	5.1%	**Military Veterans**	
H.S. grad:	80.5%			% of Pop:	8.8%
College grad:	25.2%				
Grad degree:	8.1%				

Sacramento

Sacramento, capital of the nation's most populous state, is the focus of California's third-largest media market. It has a national sports franchise (the NBA's Sacramento Kings) and an 18-mile light-rail system. It is no longer just a small city with a lot of civil servants and a vegetable-packing economy — it is a historically vibrant metropolis that has struggled recently along with the rest of the Golden State. Sacramento started as a river port on the sluggish waters of the Sacramento and American rivers. It was the destination of many overland migrants, the site of Sutter's Fort, where John Augustus Sutter found the gold that set off the Gold Rush of 1848, and the western terminus of the Pony Express in 1860. This was the natural choice at the time to be California's capital, halfway between the San Francisco Bay and the Mother Lode Country in the foothills of the Sierras, and in the middle of California's vast valley. It has the world's largest almond processing plant, and agriculture continues to be important in Sacratomato, as some locals call it.

2008 Presidential Vote		
Barack Obama (D)	165,776	(70%)
John McCain (R)	67,625	(28%)
2004 Presidential Vote		
John Kerry (D)	125,378	(61%)
George Bush (R)	77,788	(38%)
Cook Partisan Voting Index:	D+15	

In the old days, government was not a big business. Just a few lobbyists hung out in saloons on K or J streets, the governor's mansion was a musty antique, and the summers of 100-plus degrees emptied out what there was of the city. But air conditioning has replaced awnings, and freeways and shopping malls have followed the city's growth east and north toward the Sierra foothills. In the 1980s, metropolitan Sacramento grew by 35% and in the 1990s by 22%, so that it now has 2 million people, about the same as metro Cincinnati or Orlando. Today, Sacramento is one of America's higher-income metropolitan areas. High-tech firms have moved east from Silicon Valley, with Intel and Hewlett-Packard maintaining large campuses. Bay Area refugees have welcomed less expensive and more comfortable living standards. The increase has continued in recent years, but at a slower pace due to housing shortages and the nationwide recession. In June 2010, the region's six county governments said they would be forced to cut spending by a total of $900 billion in the coming fiscal year.

But Sacramento has been protected to some degree by state government's expansion. Platoons of lobbyists, lawyers, and consultants have set up permanent shop, and new hotels have been built to serve them. Today, 1,000 registered lobbyists prowl the halls of the capitol, transforming this once working-class bastion. In 1966, Sacramento was just about the only part of California beyond the Bay Area that stuck with Pat Brown over challenger Ronald Reagan. But when John Kerry carried California 54%-44% in 2004, he carried Sacramento County by only 49.6%-49.3%. In the 2003 recall election, 60% of county voters voted to remove Gray Davis, and Arnold Schwarzenegger won 52% of the vote on the replacement ballot. In 2008, Barack Obama won the county 58%-39%.

The 5th Congressional District of California consists of all of the city of Sacramento and some of its close-in suburbs. It contains affluent neighborhoods and scattered low-income black and Latino neighborhoods, plus new condominiums north of the American River and middle-class subdivisions south of downtown. This is a true majority-minority district. In 2010, 64% of the population was Hispanic, Asian, African-American, or "some other race." According to the Public Policy Institute of California, Sacramento's neighborhoods are more ethnically diverse than those of any other big city in the state. They are home to, among others, recent Hmong refugees from Laos, Vietnamese, and since the late 1980s, Russians and Ukrainians. This is the solidly Democratic part of metro Sacramento, and the 5th is the most Democratic district in the great valley from Bakersfield north to Oregon.

Doris Matsui (D)

The congresswoman from the 5th District is Doris Matsui, who won a special election in March 2005 to replace her late husband, Democrat Robert Matsui. She was born in a Japanese internment camp in Arizona and was a well-known political figure during her husband's career in Congress. She grew up in Dinuba in Fresno County and graduated from the University of California at Berkeley. In Sacramento, she chaired the board of the local public television station and participated in many civic organizations. After working on Bill Clinton's presidential campaign, she joined his transition team and then served as deputy director of public liaison, where she worked on economic and budget issues. When she left the White House in 1998, she became a senior adviser at a Washington law firm. Robert Matsui died of complications from a rare blood disorder in January 2005, after serving 13 terms. He was a senior member of the House Ways and Means Committee and a confidant to then-Minority Leader Nancy Pelosi.

A few days after the Washington and Sacramento memorial services for her husband, Doris Matsui announced that she would run in the special election. With her strong support from Pelosi, other prominent Sacramento Democrats decided not to run. None of Matsui's 10 opponents in the nonpartisan contest had significant political experience or name recognition. Matsui emphasized her support for local water projects and her opposition to President George W. Bush's proposal for personal retirement accounts in Social Security. She also opposed the war in Iraq. Her investment in a partnership with a longtime friend who was a Sacramento land developer sparked a brief flurry of criticism, but she emphasized that her husband had nothing to do with the deal while he was in office, and that there was no conflict of interest. Some called the contest a "coronation," but the lack of competition surely reflected the respect the Matsuis had won over the years. She won the all-party primary with 68% of the vote to 9% for the runner-up.

In the House, she has a reliably liberal voting record. From her seat on the Transportation and Infrastructure Committee, she tended to the many highway and water-resource needs of her district. In 2009, she moved to the Energy and Commerce Committee, where she became involved in telecommunications and technology issues. She introduced legislation in 2010 to create a $15 million fund to bolster the U.S. clean-tech manufacturing industry, which lags behind countries such as China and Germany. The bill was included as part of House Democrats' "Make It in America" campaign to showcase the party's concern for lost manufacturing jobs. And she sponsored another bill to extend two Federal Communications Commission programs that subsidize telephone service to include broadband.

Matsui also previously served on the Rules Committee, where she helped carry out the leadership's wishes in shaping legislation for floor debate when her party was in the majority. The leadership granted her a rare waiver to its policy of limiting members to service on only one major committee. She earned that goodwill by taking on leadership assignments and fighting for party priorities such as federal funding for embryonic stem cell research and reduced prescription drug prices. She cited her family's experience in internment camps to warn of potential civil liberties abuses in the USA PATRIOT Act and with detainees at Guantanamo. Matsui has been re-elected easily. In 2008, she chaired the Asian-American voter outreach campaign for Democratic candidate Hillary Rodham Clinton.

SIXTH DISTRICT

Lynn Woolsey (D)

Elected 1992, 10th term; b. Nov. 3, 1937, Seattle, WA; home, Petaluma; U. of San Francisco, B.S. 1981; Presbyterian; divorced; 4 children.

Elected Office: Petaluma City Cncl., 1985–92, Vice Mayor, 1986, 1991.

Professional Career: Human Resources Mgr., Harris Digital Telephone, 1969–80; Owner, Woolsey Personnel Svc., 1980–92.

DC Office: 2263 RHOB, 20515, 202-225-5161; Fax: 202-225-5163; Web site: woolsey.house.gov.

State Offices: San Rafael, 415-507-9554; Santa Rosa, 707-542-7182.

Committees: *Education & the Workforce:* Early Childhood, Elementary & Secondary Education; Workforce Protections (RMM). *Science & Technology:* Energy & Environment.

Group Ratings

	ACLU	ACU	ADA	CFG	AFS	FRC	LCV	ITIC	NTU	COC
2010	93	0	100	0	100	6	100	67	6	14
2009	–	0	100	0	100	–	100	–	4	33

National Journal Ratings

	2010 LIB	—	2010 CONS	2009 LIB	—	2009 CONS
Economic	90%	—	0%	82%	—	14%
Social	93%	—	0%	89%	—	0%
Foreign	77%	—	22%	61%	—	39%
Composite	90%	—	10%	80%	—	20%

Key Votes of the 111th Congress

1. Overturn Ledbetter	Y	5. Bar federal abortion funds	N	9. Stop detainee transfers	N
2. Pass $820 billion stimulus	Y	6. Pass health care bill	Y	10. Legalize immigrants' kids	Y
3. Let guns in national parks	N	7. Regulate financial firms	*	11. Repeal don't ask, tell	*
4. Pass cap-and-trade	Y	8. Pass tax cuts for some	Y	12. Limit campaign funds	Y

Election Results

2010 general	Lynn Woolsey (D)	172,216	(66%)	($846,466)
	Jim Judd (R)	77,361	(30%)	($151,843)
	Eugene Ruyle (PF)	5,915	(2%)	
	Joel Smolen (Lib)	5,660	(2%)	
2010 primary	Lynn Woolsey (D)	unopposed		

Prior Winning Percentages: 2008 (72%), 2006 (70%), 2004 (73%), 2002 (67%), 2000 (64%), 1998 (68%), 1996 (62%), 1994 (58%), 1992 (65%)

Population		Race/Ethnicity		Work	
Pop. 2010:	664,468	White:	68.5%	Private:	74.1%
Change since 2000:	Up 4.0%	Black:	2.0%	Government:	11.9%
Urban:	89.8%	Hispanic:	21.1%	Self-employed:	13.8%
Rural:	10.2%	Asian:	4.5%	Blue collar:	16.2%
Area size:	2,119 sq. mi.	Native Am.:	0.5%	White collar:	65.1%
		Hawaiian:	0.3%	Khaki collar:	0.1%
Age		Two+ races:	2.8%	Other:	18.6%
Median age:	41.1 yrs.				
More than 65 yrs:	14.0%	*Ancestry*		Median income:	$70,878
Less than 18 yrs:	21.5%	German	11.8%	Median Home Value:	$647,100
		Irish	11.4%		
Education		English	9.5%	**Military Veterans**	
H.S. grad:	88.8%			% of Pop:	8.6%
College grad:	40.5%				
Grad degree:	15.6%				

Marin and Sonoma Counties

When the Golden Gate Bridge was opened in 1937, San Francisco was one of the nation's best-known cities, but few knew much about the land beyond the bridge's north pier head. There were fewer than 50,000 people in Marin County then and another 65,000 just to the north in Sonoma County. For San Franciscans, Marin was known for the ferry terminus in Sausalito, a fishing village and art colony, and as the beginning of the Redwood Empire, with its giant trees in Muir

2008 Presidential Vote		
Barack Obama (D)	253,087	(76%)
John McCain (R)	73,345	(22%)

2004 Presidential Vote		
John Kerry (D)	226,051	(70%)
George Bush (R)	90,432	(28%)

Cook Partisan Voting Index: D+23

Woods that grow taller than any others in the world (the largest is more than 300 feet tall and 30 feet in diameter), and with a dense concentration of spotted owls that demand quiet during the mating season. Near the Bay and adjacent to the Interstate 580 bridge is the state prison at San Quentin, one of the oldest in the nation, with its famous gas chamber and crowded death row. Plans in 2007 for a $337 million overhaul of the facility were sidetracked, and led to local calls to demolish it so that the valuable land could be used for commercial enterprises. Inverness has old wooden storefronts and attracts weekenders escaping city life. Farther north is the Point Reyes peninsula with its organic farming and recreational activities, and the wine country of Sonoma County, sunny valleys protected from the fog by the Coast Range. In one such valley is Santa Rosa, which was destroyed by the 1906 earthquake and later the site of agronomist Luther Burbank's laboratory, a town that looked Middle American enough to be the set for dozens of movies. Politically, the area was then typical of the nation: traditionally Republican, but favoring Franklin D. Roosevelt in the 1930s.

Today, this part of California is far more populous, with 252,409 people in Marin County and 483,878 in Sonoma, and is affluent beyond the dreams of post-World War II Americans. It has joined the rest of the state in experiencing hard times—unemployment in Sonoma County jumped 15% between April 2009 and May 2010. Marin, meanwhile, saw expansion in the biotechnology area in 2010, with BioMarin Pharmaceutical opening a new $100 million manufacturing facility in Bel Marin Keys. The area is also extreme in its cultural attitudes, with relatively few racial minorities compared to other counties in the Bay Area. Until it was surpassed by Silicon Valley in the late 1990s, it was the nation's most expensive housing market.

Santa Rosa is thriving, thanks to the wine and telecommunications industries. Trendy Marin is economically affluent and culturally liberal. When the war in Iraq began, a group of antiwar feminists decided to "bare witness" by using their nude bodies to spell out "PEACE." After a while, such an image feeds on itself. Marin attracts affluent people who share its values, while those who don't go elsewhere—in the Bay Area to the more conservative San Ramon Valley, beyond the mountains east of Oakland. Indeed the Bay Area as a whole seems to attract liberals and repel conservatives, just as the Dallas-Fort Worth Metroplex does the opposite. Marin and Sonoma attract the most liberal of the liberal—anti-military, averse to traditional religious denominations, and indifferent to traditional sexual and marriage mores.

The 6th Congressional District of California includes all of Marin County and all of Sonoma County except for its rural eastern border. These counties have been transformed politically over the past generation. In 1980, they voted for Ronald Reagan over Jimmy Carter 47%-36%. Then they moved left and voted in 1988 for Michael Dukakis over George H. W. Bush by 57%-41%. Now Republicans seem almost an endangered species here. In 2004, the district voted for John Kerry over George W. Bush by 70%-28%. Barack Obama's 2008 victory over John McCain in Marin and Sonoma was a stunning 76%-22%.

Lynn Woolsey (D)

The congresswoman from the 6th District is Lynn Woolsey, a Democrat first elected in 1992. Woolsey grew up in the Pacific Northwest, moved to Marin, and was a stay-at-home mother with three children under age six when her marriage ended in 1968. She went on welfare, got a low-paying job, and was often struggling to find decent child care. Deliverance appeared in the form of a job with a high-tech start-up firm, where she rose to become a top executive. She remarried and moved to a house in Petaluma, where her mother could live in and look after the kids. She put herself through business school at night, earned a degree in human resources, and started her own personnel service. In 1984, Woolsey won a seat on the Petaluma Council. In 1992, she won the U.S. House Democratic nomination in a nine-candidate primary with 26%, well ahead of 19% for the runner-up. In the general election, she faced liberal Republican Assemblyman Bill Filante. He was prevented from campaigning when he fell ill and had to have surgery for a brain tumor. She won 65%-34%.

An apt representative of her district, Woolsey has one of the most liberal voting records in the House. In the 111th Congress (2009-10), she co-chaired the Congressional Progressive Caucus. As the first former welfare recipient in Congress, she opposed the 1996 welfare overhaul and supports easing work requirements and providing more child care. She says she thinks a parent ought to be at home until children reach age 11. She lobbied against banning gays in the military, accompanied by her son, who is gay. Republicans sought to embarrass Democrats by calling for a vote on Woolsey's bill to revoke the federal charter for the Boy Scouts because the group excludes gays, and her bill was defeated 362-12. On the Science, Space and Technology Committee, Woolsey has worked to promote energy efficiency and increase support for alternative-energy sources. She is an unabashed liberal who after the 2008 election said that it would be a mistake for President Barack Obama to take then-Democratic House Speaker Nancy Pelosi's advice that "the country must be governed from the middle." One of the few issues on which she sides with Republicans is repealing the estate tax, which she said would benefit her district's small family farms where "their wealth is only in their land."

With Reps. Barbara Lee and Maxine Waters, fellow California Democrats, she created the Out of Iraq Caucus in 2005, and antiwar groups called it "the conscience" of the Democratic Caucus. For President Bush's State of the Union message in 2006, she gave a ticket to the House spectator gallery to antiwar protestor Cindy Sheehan, who was arrested during the speech. When President Obama announced a buildup of forces in Afghanistan in late 2009, she called for a "smart security" approach that abandoned the military-only strategy and emphasized humanitarian aid, economic development, and reconstruction. During the 2009 health care debate, she led liberal calls for a government-run "public option" to compete with private insurers, but accepted a compromise to get a bill passed in the House. In September 2008, Woolsey was one of 13 Democrats who voted against passage of a bill to lift the moratorium on offshore drilling. She wrote that the plan "continues the myth . . . that we can drill our way out of our nation's energy crisis." With her occasionally fractious relationship with Pelosi, she has failed in her quest to win a seat on the influential Appropriations Committee.

But Woolsey did manage to get the House to authorize $15 million to renovate the immigration complex on Angel Island, where countless Chinese arrivals were detained in deplorable conditions. She has been easily re-elected. In the 2008 Democratic presidential primary contest, she endorsed Sen. Hillary Rodham Clinton, though Woolsey said that her own views were closer to those of Rep. Dennis Kucinich, the liberal Ohio Democrat and long-shot candidate in the race.

SEVENTH DISTRICT

George Miller (D)

Elected 1974, 19th term; b. May 17, 1945, Richmond; home, Martinez; San Francisco St. U., B.A. 1968, U. of CA at Davis, J.D. 1972; Catholic; married (Cynthia); 2 children.

Professional Career: Legis. aide, CA Senate Majority Ldr., 1969–74; Practicing atty., 1972–74.

DC Office: 2205 RHOB, 20515, 202-225-2095; Fax: 202-225-5609; Web site: georgemiller.house.gov.

State Offices: Concord, 925-602-1880; Richmond, 510-262-6500; Vallejo, 707-645-1888.

Committees: *Education & the Workforce* (RMM): Higher Education & Workforce Training; Workforce Protections.

Group Ratings

	ACLU	ACU	ADA	CFG	AFS	FRC	LCV	ITIC	NTU	COC
2010	93	0	100	0	100	6	100	67	6	13
2009	–	0	95	0	100	–	86	–	3	33

National Journal Ratings

	2010 LIB	—	2010 CONS		2009 LIB	—	2009 CONS
Economic	90%	—	0%		87%	—	12%
Social	93%	—	0%		72%	—	28%
Foreign	92%	—	3%		91%	—	0%
Composite	95%	—	5%		85%	—	15%

Key Votes of the 111th Congress

1. Overturn Ledbetter	Y	5. Bar federal abortion funds	N	9. Stop detainee transfers	N
2. Pass $820 billion stimulus	Y	6. Pass health care bill	Y	10. Legalize immigrants' kids	Y
3. Let guns in national parks	N	7. Regulate financial firms	Y	11. Repeal don't ask, tell	Y
4. Pass cap-and-trade	Y	8. Pass tax cuts for some	Y	12. Limit campaign funds	Y

Election Results

2010 general	George Miller (D)	122,435	(68%)	($972,502)
	Rick Tubbs (R)	56,764	(32%)	($130,515)
2010 primary	George Miller (D)	52,210	(85%)	
	John Fitzgerald (D)	9,188	(15%)	

Prior Winning Percentages: 2008 (73%), 2006 (84%), 2004 (76%), 2002 (71%), 2000 (76%), 1998 (77%), 1996 (72%), 1994 (70%), 1992 (70%), 1990 (61%), 1988 (68%), 1986 (67%), 1984 (66%), 1982 (67%), 1980 (63%), 1978 (63%), 1976 (75%), 1974 (56%)

Population		Race/Ethnicity		Work	
Pop. 2010:	655,708	White:	35.3%	Private:	74.8%
Change since 2000:	Up 2.6%	Black:	14.8%	Government:	17.1%
Urban:	98.7%	Hispanic:	29.7%	Self-employed:	8.0%
Rural:	1.3%	Asian:	14.9%	Blue collar:	21.0%
Area size:	443 sq. mi.	Native Am.:	0.4%	White collar:	57.7%
		Hawaiian:	0.6%	Khaki collar:	0.7%
Age		Two+ races:	4.0%	Other:	20.7%
Median age:	37.0 yrs.				
More than 65 yrs:	11.0%	*Ancestry*		Median income:	$63,914
Less than 18 yrs:	24.6%	German	7.6%	Median Home Value:	$412,400
		Irish	6.2%		
Education		English	5.3%	**Military Veterans**	
H.S. grad:	83.3%			% of Pop:	9.0%
College grad:	25.1%				
Grad degree:	7.2%				

East Bay; Vallejo, Richmond

The journey inward from the Pacific Ocean to the vast flatness of California's Central Valley passes through a wondrous variety of terrain. The traveler starts at the Golden Gate Bridge, with the lush green Presidio on one side and the bluffs of mountains in Marin County on the other. The journey continues through the San Francisco Bay, through the narrow Carquinez Strait to Suisun Bay, with its sloughs and marshes and ships ready for scrap, and finally

2008 Presidential Vote		
Barack Obama (D)	179,037	(72%)
John McCain (R)	66,272	(27%)
2004 Presidential Vote		
John Kerry (D)	153,988	(67%)
George Bush (R)	72,994	(32%)
Cook Partisan Voting Index: D+19		

past the mountains, to the flat, fertile expanse of California's great interior. This is not a journey most tourists make, but it was a familiar route to the first Americans in California, and it passes by much of the industrial base of the Bay Area. On the east side of the bay is Richmond, developed almost instantaneously during World War II when Henry J. Kaiser built a shipyard in its deepwater port and 91,000 people from all over the country were put to work building ships for the Pacific theater. What became known as Rosie the Riveter Memorial Park is now a national park. The recession landed a severe blow here—median household earnings plummeted by more than $3,000 over the two years it lasted, according to census figures. But Contra Costa County, at least, fared better than most of the rest of the Bay Area; of its nine counties, it joined Marin and Sonoma as the only three with more people coming in than going out between July 2008 and July 2009.

Across Carquinez Strait is Vallejo, named for a Mexican general and member of the first California Senate, the site from 1853 to 1996 of the giant Mare Island Naval Shipyard, where 41,000 worked during World War II. In 2008, the city filed for bankruptcy, which was caused in part by the closing of the shipyard and in part by huge public employee salaries and pensions—292 of 411 city workers earned more than $100,000 a year. In 2010, unemployment in the city topped 14%. Farther up the bay, to the south, is Concord, the largest city in Contra Costa County, whose city officials were unique in that they lobbied the Pentagon to close the mostly unused Concord Naval Weapons Station. They wanted to use the land for business and residential development, which is banned beyond the urban limit that county voters imposed in 1990. The Defense Department complied and included about half of the site on the 2005 base-closure list. This is the industrial part of the Bay Area, with tank farms and refineries. The towns are among the most ethnically diverse in the country, with large percentages of African-Americans, Hispanics, Asians, and Filipinos.

The 7th Congressional District includes most of this territory, from Richmond to Vallejo, Hercules, Martinez, and Pittsburg. It also proceeds inland through the mountain interstices of Contra Costa County to include part of Concord. Northeast of Vallejo, it includes Vacaville on flatland beneath Vaca Mountain. Politically, this industrial area was blue-collar Democratic back in the days when San Francisco, with its larger white-collar population, often voted Republican. Today, it remains heavily Democratic, but not as leftist on cultural issues as other San Francisco areas. John Kerry won the district 67%-32% over George W. Bush in 2004, and Barack Obama won it 72%-27% over John McCain in 2008.

George Miller (D)

The congressman from the 7th District is George Miller, one of just two remaining Democrats of the Watergate class of 1974 who came to power in the backlash over the Nixon-era scandal. (The other is Henry Waxman of California.) Miller is the top Democrat on the Education and the Workforce Committee, and considered the most trusted confidant of Democratic leader Nancy Pelosi. The late conservative columnist Robert Novak described him as "her *consigliere*, always at her side."

Miller is heir to a tradition of Bay Area working-class politics. His father was chairman of the state Senate Finance Committee. When his father died in 1969, Miller lost the race to succeed him, but became a staffer for Senate Leader George Moscone, who was later the mayor of San Francisco. Miller was a protégé of Rep. Phillip Burton, D-Calif., who helped establish liberal hegemony in the U.S. House in the 1970s. Miller has one of the most liberal voting records in the House, and he brings a zest for political combat reminiscent of Burton. He is a strong backer of protecting the environment against what he sees as greedy private-sector operators, and of furthering the causes of labor unions. Like Burton, Miller has grasped for top party leadership posts but hasn't made it. But he has learned a legislator's virtues of patience, timing, and creativity. He played a central role in getting several of President Obama's most significant initiatives into law, including an overhaul of the health insurance system, an expansion of Pell grants for education in 2010, and the Lilly Ledbetter Fair Pay Act restoring employee rights to challenge pay discrimination in 2009. His strong support influenced the tilt toward huge education spending in the economic stimulus law that year as well.

Pelosi relies on Miller for his advice, judgment, and protection from potential adversaries within the Democratic Caucus. "She is the leader that I've been waiting for for 30 years," Miller once said of Pelosi. "She is the complete package. She understands policy, politics, and has a core of values that is clear and solid." Pelosi named Miller chairman of the Democratic Policy Committee, where he was instrumental in preparing the "New Direction" agenda for the 2006 campaign. During the 2009 health care battle, he was faced with the task of telling abortion-rights advocates that they needed to compromise, reportedly touching off an angry shouting match with liberal Rep. Rosa DeLauro, D-Conn., who opposed the idea. That tactical decision, however, enabled the bill to pass the House and eventually become law. Because Miller rarely does anything that runs contrary to Pelosi's interests, his early support for Waxman's ultimately successful bid to oust John Dingell of Michigan as chairman of the Energy and Commerce Committee in November 2008 was a strong signal of Pelosi's otherwise unstated view: She preferred Waxman for the job. When criticism of Pelosi mounted among Democrats after the party lost its majority in the 2010 elections, Miller was among those who forcefully countered that the blame instead lay with the White House. He complained that the Obama administration neglected to defend the speaker and her accomplishments.

On the education committee a priority for Miller has been an overhaul of the Bush-era No Child Left Behind Act, and he has pushed for increased funding for mandates in the law and incentives for improved teacher quality. Bush's opposition to additional funding led Miller to defer renewal of the act until the inauguration of a new president in 2009. But the legislation took a backseat to other priorities and did not move. Miller doesn't always follow the dictates of the teachers' unions, especially if he thinks they are getting in the way of improving public schools. He has long advocated more spending on education, but he has also wanted more rigorous standards, with measurable results. During the Bush administration, he worked with then-committee Chairman John Boehner, R-Ohio, to write No Child Left Behind, and Bush praised Miller for his contributions at the bill signing in January 2002. Though he thinks the act's mandates were underfunded by the Republicans, Miller also has lauded its impact on test scores for minority and poor students.

In the 110th Congress (2007-08), Miller focused on higher education programs and efforts to help more students pay for college and to foster loan forgiveness programs for graduates who work as teachers. His bill, enacted in May 2008, increased the amounts that students could borrow to pay for college. In response to the recent recession, Miller got through the House a bill with $10 billion to help local governments preserve teachers' jobs and more than $16 billion in health assistance to states. With Republicans back in power in the 112th Congress (2011-12), Miller is the most likely Democrat to lead opposition to any efforts among tea party conservatives to make good on their campaign pledge to abolish the Education Department.

On labor issues, Miller in 2007 won enactment of an increase in the hourly minimum wage from $5.15 to $7.25. He has pressed for enactment of the card check bill, which would require an employer to recognize a union if a majority of workers sign union authorization cards. Secret-ballot elections would be held only if requested by unions, which would have little incentive to do so. His agenda on behalf of organized labor also included a bill mandating new safety features in mines and stepped-up oversight of mine safety, which passed the House in 2008. The legislation was a response to the Crandall Canyon Mine disaster, in which six miners died in Utah in 2007 after a cave-in blocked all exits.

As a longtime member of the Natural Resources Committee, Miller crusaded against water reclamation projects that provided cheap water to farmers. In 1992, during a California drought, he passed a Central Valley Project law that raised farmers' prices closer to those of urban users and imposed environmental restrictions, over the fierce opposition of Central Valley politicians and Republican Gov. Pete Wilson. When Republicans were in the majority, Miller was a major obstacle to attempts to scale back the reach of environmental regulations and the Endangered Species Act, and to GOP efforts to open up the Arctic National Wildlife Refuge to oil drilling and the Tongass National Forest to more logging. After the BP oil spill disaster in the Gulf of Mexico in mid-2010, the House passed Miller's measure to deny new offshore leases or drilling permits to companies with egregious safety records. It also beefed up whistleblower protections to offshore oil and gas workers.

EIGHTH DISTRICT

Nancy Pelosi (D)

Elected June 1987, 12th full term; b. March 26, 1940, Baltimore, MD; home, San Francisco; Trinity Col., B.A. 1962; Catholic; married (Paul); 5 children.

Professional Career: CA Dem. Party, Northern Chmn., 1977–81, St. Chmn., 1981–83; DSCC Finance Chmn., 1985–87; PR exec., Ogilvy & Mather, 1986–87.

DC Office: 235 CHOB, 20515, 202-225-4965; Web site: pelosi.house.gov.

State Offices: San Francisco, 415-556-4862.

Vote Ratings and Key Votes: *As House speaker, she frequently did not vote.*

Election Results

2010 general	Nancy Pelosi (D)	167,957	(80%)	($2,597,319)
	John Dennis (R)	31,711	(15%)	($2,369,385)
	Gloria LaRiva (PF)	5,161	(2%)	
	Philip Berg (Lib)	4,843	(2%)	
2010 primary	Nancy Pelosi (D)	unopposed		

Prior Winning Percentages: 2008 (72%), 2006 (80%), 2004 (83%), 2002 (80%), 2000 (85%), 1998 (86%), 1996 (84%), 1994 (82%), 1992 (82%), 1990 (77%), 1988 (76%), 1987 (63%)

Population		Race/Ethnicity		Work	
Pop. 2010:	666,827	White:	41.7%	Private:	79.5%
Change since 2000:	Up 4.3%	Black:	6.5%	Government:	12.1%
Urban:	100.0%	Hispanic:	16.6%	Self-employed:	8.4%
Rural:	0.0%	Asian:	31.1%	Blue collar:	10.1%
Area size:	114 sq. mi.	Native Am.:	0.2%	White collar:	71.9%
		Hawaiian:	0.4%	Khaki collar:	0.1%
Age		Two+ races:	3.2%	Other:	17.9%
Median age:	37.9 yrs.				
More than 65 yrs:	13.6%	*Ancestry*		Median income:	$68,593
Less than 18 yrs:	13.9%	German	7.3%	Median Home Value:	$775,100
		Irish	7.0%		
Education		English	5.2%	**Military Veterans**	
H.S. grad:	84.6%			% of Pop:	4.8%
College grad:	50.4%				
Grad degree:	19.0%				

San Francisco

On Feb. 20, 1915, a crowd of 150,000 gathered on the grounds of the Panama-Pacific International Exposition to see the Spanish-Italian baroque-style structure built on reclaimed land in what was to become San Francisco's Marina district. The Exposition ostensibly celebrated the completion of the Panama Canal, but it was clearly intended to show off San Francisco's recovery from the 1906 earthquake. It also spotlighted the city as the central focus of America's efforts

2008 Presidential Vote
Barack Obama (D)	266,210	(85%)
John McCain (R)	38,665	(12%)

2004 Presidential Vote
John Kerry (D)	244,009	(85%)
George Bush (R)	40,558	(14%)

Cook Partisan Voting Index: D+35

to open an economic door to the eastern part of the world, especially in light of the acquisition of Hawaii and the Philippines and of its interest in an open-door policy with China and trade with Japan. The Exposition established the physical style of San Francisco, encouraging the use of Mediterranean color, accent, and detail that characterizes many of the post-Victorian houses and commercial structures in The City, as the *San Francisco Examiner* called it for years. It set the tone for the picturesque Marina district, whose old buildings had been among those damaged in the 1989 earthquake, and for Fisherman's Wharf and Ghirardelli Square. On a sunny day, San Francisco can look almost tropical, with brown mountains baking in the sun and light shining off the pastel stucco buildings. When the clouds scud in from the Pacific, it can look sinister, full of dark corners where a private detective's partner might be ambushed by a pretty woman. The buildings can be majestic, like the monumental Beaux Arts City Hall, or tawdry, like the hotels of the Tenderloin district. It is a city that at first looks exotic but, when you look closely, can only be American.

San Francisco grew from nothing to a major city in the single year of 1850, an instant product of the California Gold Rush. Within just a few years, culture was flourishing in the city, and San Francisco developed a parochial pride in the great writers who worked there—Jack London, Ambrose Bierce, Frank Norris—and in giving birth to the Arts and Crafts movement. Later, San Francisco newspaper scribe Herb Caen coined the term "beatnik" to describe the youthful penchant for freedom in the 1950s and wrote definitively about the hippies who thronged Haight-Ashbury in 1967. In the 1970s, the city was among the first to embrace the gay rights movement, in the Castro district (although lately, gays have been moving to the suburbs and straights have been moving in). Over the years, the city's booming economy—based initially on food processing, but now on finance, high-tech, and clothing (Levi Strauss, the Gap)—attracted talented newcomers, though its population is increasingly polarized between high-income and low-income. The dot-com crash in 2000 took a brutal toll, but the city rallied in mid-decade, as new high-rise office buildings and condominiums sprang up on the waterfront and south of Market. The housing bust in 2008 did not hit as hard here as in California's Central Valley subdivisions, where many modest-income Bay Area residents had been fleeing. San Francisco has had the lowest percentage of children (16%) of any major city, but the number of births has been rising in the past decade, with more strollers on the streets of the Noe Valley and the Castro. The population on the west side is nearly half Asian. But overall, proudly tolerant San Francisco is one of California's whitest cities, with only about half as many black residents as it had in 1970.

Politically, San Francisco was a progressive Republican town, like the two men who led the way into the Exposition: Mayor "Sunny Jim" Rolph and California Gov. Hiram Johnson. The sour-tempered Johnson made his name as a reformer, throwing out crooked city politicians. His administration gave California primary elections, referenda and recall, and strong civil-service laws. Rolph, mayor from 1911-30 and then governor, built the civic center, parks, schools, streetcars, and the Hetch Hetchy aqueduct—the antique infrastructure of San Francisco today (though the water quality is terrific). Sympathetic to the conservation movement, willing to deal with organized labor in a union town that had America's only general strike in 1934, and tolerant of California's diversity, these progressive Republicans were the recognizable ancestors of, though certainly not identical to, the generally liberal San Franciscans of today.

The city has elected strong liberal politicians, notably Mayor George Moscone and the first openly gay supervisor, Harvey Milk. Both were shot to death in 1978 by Dan White, a former city supervisor, who was found guilty of the lesser crime of voluntary manslaughter after his lawyers successfully argued that he suffered from depression. (As evidence of his diminished mental capacity, they cited White's addiction to Twinkies and other junk food. It was widely and derisively dubbed "the Twinkie defense," although the lawyers never claimed that Twinkies *caused* White's mental problems.) Over the next decade, the city's cultural liberalism was tempered by Democratic Mayor Dianne Feinstein, who vetoed a domestic partnership ordinance and opposed commercial rent control. In 1995, Willie Brown, ousted after 15 years as speaker of the state Assembly, returned home and was elected mayor. Brown's political flair was always in evidence, but high taxes and an increasing homeless population drove out middle-class families and immigrants. As his successor, San Francisco installed Gavin Newsom, who in February 2004 started issuing marriage licenses to same-sex couples, although California voters had outlawed same-sex marriage. The state Supreme Court ordered him to stop and voided the marriages. In 2008, Newsom was vindicated when the state Supreme Court declared the state's ban on same-sex marriage unconstitutional. But his victory statement—"This door's wide open, it's going to happen, whether you like it or not"—was featured in ads for proponents of Proposition 8, which by a 52%-48% vote reversed the court's decision. In November 2010, Newsom was elected California's lieutenant governor. The Board of Supervisors subsequently appointed City Administrator Ed Lee as interim mayor. Lee is the first Asian-American to serve as San Francisco mayor; his appointment was to last until November 2011, when a mayoral election was scheduled.

The 8th Congressional District of California takes in four-fifths of San Francisco, all but the southwest corner. It includes all of San Francisco's high-rise downtown area, the crowded and bustling Chinatown, Telegraph Hill, Nob Hill and Russian Hill, North Beach, Pacific Heights, and the Marina District (which does not have a very big marina). In the valleys are the mostly black Fillmore and Western Addition areas. The district is 7% African-American, 17% Hispanic and 31%

Asian. The 8th also has Noe Valley; the Castro, still mainly gay; Haight-Ashbury, once the bedraggled center of hippie culture and now another gentrifying San Francisco neighborhood; and Potrero Hill, with its restored houses overlooking downtown. Farther south are the old residential areas overlooking Interstate 280, with pastel houses strewn along grid streets that hug the steep hills. The district is overwhelmingly Democratic and voted 85%-12% for Democratic presidential nominee Barack Obama in 2008.

Nancy Pelosi (D)

The 8th District is represented by Nancy Pelosi, the speaker of the House from 2007 to 2011 and the minority leader since Democrats lost control of the House in January 2011. Pelosi was the first woman in history to achieve the post of House speaker.

First elected to Congress in June 1987, she has the energy and shrewdness of one who has handled the most delicate of political chores, and the charm and unflappability of one who is the mother of five and grandmother of seven. Pelosi grew up on Albemarle Street in Baltimore's Little Italy, just east of downtown. Her father, Thomas D'Alesandro Jr., served in the House from 1939 to 1947 and was mayor of Baltimore for 12 years after that. Her mother, Annunciata D'Alesandro, was an indefatigable political organizer, and her brother, Thomas, was mayor from 1967 to 1971. Pelosi says of her parents, "What I got from them was about economic fairness. That was the difference between Democrats and Republicans all those years ago." She graduated from Trinity College (now Trinity Washington University) in Washington, D.C., where she met her husband. After marrying, they moved to his hometown of San Francisco. There he became a successful real estate investor, and she raised their children and got into local Democratic politics.

At first, Pelosi impressed rough-hewn Rep. John Burton of California as just another stylish hostess in a city that had many of them. But she soon got Burton's attention and that of his older brother, U.S. Rep. Phillip Burton, the de facto liberal leader of the House, who lost his race for majority leader to Texas Democrat Jim Wright by one vote in 1976. That year, Pelosi returned east to run the Maryland campaign of presidential candidate Jerry Brown, then and now once again governor of California. She was able to relate both to "Governor Moonbeam," as Brown was dubbed, and to the practical-minded politicians she had met through her parents. In 1977, she became chairman of the Northern California Democratic Party, and four years later, she became chairman of the California Democratic Party. The positions required a considerable amount of diplomacy. Assembly Majority Leader Howard Berman of Los Angeles was attempting to oust Assembly Speaker Leo McCarthy of San Francisco, a protracted struggle out of which Democrat Willie Brown of San Francisco emerged with the speakership. Pelosi managed to remain on good terms with all of them and to help Democrats hold majorities in the legislature.

Then in 1982, John Burton declined to run for re-election in a new Marin-and-San-Francisco-based district. Some Democrats sounded out Pelosi, whose Presidio Heights home was in the district, but she declined to run, and the seat went instead to Marin-based Democrat Barbara Boxer. In the next few years, Pelosi worked with Mayor Dianne Feinstein to land the 1984 Democratic National Convention for San Francisco. In 1985, she ran for Democratic National Chairman, but lost to Paul Kirk. Technically, Pelosi was still a stay-at-home mother, but she was dealing with politicians of the first order of magnitude or soon to become so: Brown was a presidential candidate in 1976 and 1992, Phil Burton was a major power in the House, and John Burton was later president of the California Senate; Berman was elected in 1982 to the House, where he still serves, McCarthy became lieutenant governor, Willie Brown remained speaker for 15 years, and Feinstein has been in the Senate since 1992. This was a fast political track. In April 1983, Phil Burton, who chain-smoked Pall Malls and drank vodka from tumbler glasses, dropped dead at 57. Elected to succeed him was his widow, Sala Burton, who idolized his record and whose political instincts were as shrewd as his own. But her health failed too. In 1987, as she was dying of cancer, she told her friends whom she wanted to succeed her: Nancy Pelosi.

Only two years before, Pelosi had told the press, "I won't be running for office." Her children were not yet grown, her husband's business interests kept him mostly in California, and their net worth was not yet such that she could afford to self-finance a campaign. (The couple eventually became extremely wealthy, with houses in San Francisco, a vineyard in the Napa Valley, a town-home in the Sierras and a condominium in Washington.) But she ran, moving her residence from Presidio Heights to a Pacific Heights rental apartment (Presidio Heights is back in her district now). Her chief opponent in the Democratic primary was San Francisco Supervisor Harry Britt, who had succeeded Harvey Milk after the assassination. San Francisco's gay community at that time was not as mainstream as it is now, but Britt, who was gay, had a good record in office, and Pelosi had to work hard to beat him 35%-31%.

There seemed to be no clue in Pelosi's early work in the House that she would seek a leadership position as Phil Burton had. Instead she took the lead on important issues of local sensitivity. One was the Presidio. Burton had inserted into legislation a provision that transferred the Presidio from the military to the Interior Department. The problem was that it was so expensive to maintain, it threatened to exceed the National Park Service's budget. Through several Congresses, Pelosi worked to get bipartisan support for a funding source, and in 1997 created the Presidio Trust, with a declining appropriation scheduled to be phased out in 2012.

Another sensitive issue was human rights, especially in China. After the Tiananmen Square massacre, she sponsored an amendment to give Chinese students the right to remain in the United States. President George H. W. Bush vetoed it. In 1991, she became the lead sponsor of the bill to make China's most-favored-nation status conditional on human rights reforms. The House overrode Bush's veto, but it was upheld in the Senate. After that, Pelosi led the annual fight against normalizing trade relations with China. She did all this at some political risk. Pelosi's position was by no means universally popular with Asian-Americans in her district; many thought that the United States should trade and negotiate quietly with China. One of her chief adversaries was her San Francisco neighbor, Sen. Feinstein; for many years, they lived in houses just a few blocks apart in Presidio Heights. Pelosi courted support from people on the opposite end of the ideological spectrum, especially religious conservatives in the Republican caucus who also wanted to remain vigilant on China's human rights record.

At the time of the September 11 attacks, Pelosi was the senior Democrat on the Intelligence Committee. She joined in the committee's conclusion that, while the intelligence community did not have specific evidence in advance, it did have information that was relevant to the attacks. On other issues, Pelosi maintained an almost perfectly liberal voting record and established herself as a leader in encouraging family planning overseas and environmental protection.

Her move into the leadership was persistent, shrewd and well-organized. In 1997, as a member of the Committee on Standards of Official Conduct, she doggedly pursued ethics charges against Republican Speaker Newt Gingrich and worked with Minority Whip David Bonior in using scorched-earth tactics against him. (Gingrich had used a nearly identical strategy to weaken former Democratic Speaker Jim Wright of Texas, who ultimately stepped down amid an ethics investigation.) In 1999, she launched a campaign for majority whip, anticipating that Democrats would win a majority in 2000, which they nearly did. Her opponent was Democrat Steny Hoyer of Maryland. They were old acquaintances, having served as interns for Sen. Daniel Brewster of Maryland in the 1960s, but not confreres: there were considerable stylistic and ideological differences. Many of the Democratic women in the House felt there should be a woman in the leadership. Pelosi, who raised $3 million for Democratic candidates that cycle, said she was not running as a woman, but "the fact that I am a woman is an enhancement, because we absolutely must have diversity in the leadership."

But in 2000, Republicans held on to their majority, and the race for majority whip was moot. Not for long, though. Michigan's Republican Legislature, in drawing new congressional districts, put Bonior in a district it was plain he could not win, and he decided to run for governor. He resigned as minority whip, and Pelosi was off and running against Hoyer. Pelosi said that Democrats needed to refocus on grassroots organization, money, and message. Some supporters played up her potential to become a celebrity—"a glamorous grandmother who knocks people off their feet," as Hawaii Rep. Neil Abercrombie put it. With nearly unanimous support from the 32 California Democrats and from most female members, Pelosi started off with a strong base. Her support also crossed ideological lines. She was nominated by John Murtha, a mostly hawkish and culturally conservative Vietnam veteran from the coal country of western Pennsylvania, with a following among old-line Democrats. Pelosi and Murtha formed an alliance similar to that between Phil Burton and the hard-bitten conservative Wayne Hays from the coal country of eastern Ohio a quarter-century earlier. In October 2001, Pelosi won by a convincing 118-95.

As whip, Pelosi moved quickly to assert herself, sometimes independently from Minority Leader Dick Gephardt of Missouri. She sparked a controversy when she contributed $10,000 to Lynn Rivers in a redistricting-forced Michigan primary against John Dingell, the powerful ranking Democrat on the Energy and Commerce Committee who had been a strong supporter of Hoyer for whip. Normally, party leaders do not take sides in such primaries. Dingell won handily. Pelosi's biggest conflict came in the fall of 2002, when she actively encouraged opponents of the resolution authorizing the use of force in Iraq, which Gephardt had enthusiastically endorsed. Pelosi contended that supporters had not made the case for using force and that she had seen no evidence that Iraq "poses an imminent threat to our nation." To the surprise of many, her efforts helped win 126 Democratic votes against the resolution, while only 81 backed Gephardt's position. In retrospect, the split signaled a transition in the caucus. Once the disappointing 2002 election results were in and Gephardt said that he was stepping down, Pelosi had all but locked up the support of a majority of the caucus. Rep. Martin Frost of Texas announced his candidacy with warnings that the selection of Pelosi might create a "permanent minority party." He withdrew from the contest a day later, conceding that he could not win. Harold Ford of Tennessee made a belated, quixotic bid designed to appeal to a combination of blacks and New Democrats, but Pelosi won 177-29.

As the Democratic leader in the House, she brought a burst of energy—and favorable press coverage—to a party that badly needed it. She showed hands-on management in selecting members for House committee vacancies and in developing a Democratic message criticizing the Bush agenda. There were bruised feelings over some committee assignments, but even allies of Hoyer and Frost credited her with bringing a breath of fresh air and enthusiasm to party deliberations. As Republicans pressed their agenda, Pelosi declared that Democrats would take "a party position" in opposition to the Republican Medicare prescription-drug bill. But 16 Democrats voted for the final deal in November 2003, providing the critical margin for passage. She was largely silent about the renegades, many of whom were responding to local pressures.

In 2004 Pelosi traveled the country raising money and boosting local candidates. If she became speaker, Pelosi pledged, she would reform the House to give a greater voice to all members and to assure fairness. She cited Democratic gains of open seats in Kentucky and South Dakota in special elections in early 2004 as proof that the political tide was turning their way. But the three-seat loss in the November election that year turned out to be yet another disappointment for House Democrats, though Pelosi noted correctly that they won a net gain apart from the effects of the 2003 Texas redistricting.

In early 2005, she firmly insisted that House Democrats would not sit down with Republicans on a plan for overhauling Social Security until they removed President Bush's proposal to introduce private investment accounts into the program. Bush's declining job approval ratings and the rising prospects of Democrats in the 2006 election helped Pelosi maintain party discipline. She saluted her longtime supporter Murtha for a November 2005 speech calling for a redeployment of troops out of Iraq, and she suggested without saying so that it would be the party's position. Hoyer was adamantly opposed to withdrawing from Iraq, which he said would be a "disaster."

In the summer of 2006, Hoyer declared that he had no intention of challenging Pelosi if once again Democrats failed to win a majority that fall. "If we lose, it will not be Nancy Pelosi's fault. She's done everything she possibly can. Win, lose, or draw, she's going to be our leader." Just days later, Murtha announced he would run for majority leader if Democrats won, presumably against Hoyer. For months House Democrats worked to come up with a platform to run on in 2006 and after many postponements, emerged with a "Six for '06" program of increasing the minimum wage and enacting the remaining recommendations of the 9/11 Commission. Pelosi campaigned tirelessly across the country and was rewarded when Democrats gained 31 seats, enough for a Democratic majority, on Election Day.

As she assumed the office that put her third in line for the presidency, Pelosi said, "This is an historic moment, for Congress, and for the women of this country. It is a moment for which we have waited more than 200 years. For our daughters and granddaughters, today we have broken the marble ceiling. To our daughters and granddaughters, the sky is the limit." Minority Leader John Boehner of Ohio echoed the sentiment, saying, "In a few moments, I'll have the high privilege of handing the gavel of the House of Representatives to a woman for the first time in history. Whether you're a Republican, a Democrat, or an independent, this is a cause for celebration."

Much of her leadership team was already in place. Although she had vigorously supported Murtha for majority leader, Hoyer had the support of most of the conservative Blue Dog Democrats, most freshmen, and senior incoming committee chairmen like Dingell and Henry Waxman of California. Hoyer won 149-86, putting him in the No. 2 spot, just after Pelosi. Whether they liked it or not, Pelosi and Hoyer were a team. The third-ranking spot, majority whip, went to the well-liked James Clyburn of South Carolina, an African-American who brought some racial diversity to the new lineup. Influential Illinois Rep. Rahm Emanuel had wanted to be whip, but Pelosi persuaded him to take the fourth-ranking job, that of caucus chairman, with new responsibilities.

There was some awkwardness in Pelosi's first months as speaker. The 100 hours to pass the "Six for '06" program turned out to be 100 legislative hours, stretched over a couple of weeks. A request for a military plane to fly her to her district seemed an extravagant request, although the previous speaker, Republican Dennis Hastert, had had use of military planes to travel to his Illinois district, and Pelosi, not unreasonably, wanted an aircraft that could fly nonstop to San Francisco. Beneath the velvet glove, Pelosi continued to operate with an iron fist. One of her key issues was reducing carbon dioxide emissions to curb global warming. So she announced the creation of a

Select Committee on Energy Independence and Global Warming, to be headed by Energy and Commerce member Edward Markey of Massachusetts. Her old nemesis, Energy and Commerce Chairman Dingell, protested that he was being sidelined.

She had some early impressive legislative successes. But there were also disappointments, especially when Democratic leaders in the closely divided Senate failed to rally the 60 votes needed to pass bills sent over from the House. The minimum wage was finally raised after many years, and an ethics reform bill that banned lobbyists' gifts and required public disclosure of the identity of lawmakers sponsoring spending earmarks was enacted. Her greatest frustration was being unable to end military involvement in Iraq. The House passed measures with timetables for withdrawal, but they failed in the Senate. She disappointed antiwar liberals by bringing to the floor war-funding bills she opposed because, as she said, she had promised to protect the troops. In September, after Gen. David Petraeus testified about the success of Bush's troop surge strategy, public pressure for withdrawal from Iraq diminished. Pelosi conceded that she had underestimated the Republicans' willingness to stick with the president on the war, a position at odds with statements they had made to her privately and also at odds with the public mood in some Republican districts.

On domestic policy, Pelosi and her Democratic leadership ran a tight ship and were largely successful, at least in the House. She held back on the issue of addressing illegal immigration, about which many Democrats were skittish, and watched as the Senate failed to act. The Democrats' bill to expand the State Children's Health Insurance Program was passed by both chambers, but Bush vetoed it. In April 2008, she prevailed when she ignored the law giving the president broad authority over trade and refused to bring the Colombia Free Trade Agreement to the floor. When gasoline hit $4 a gallon in 2008 and public opinion began to favor more offshore oil drilling, Pelosi refused to allow a roll call vote. "I'm trying to save the planet," she said. Republicans screamed foul, and during the August recess, though Congress had technically gone home, they made speeches to curious tourists in the House chamber urging a vote. Pelosi ordered the lights turned out. But Democrats too were coming under pressure to act on gas prices, and on August 16, Pelosi agreed to allow a vote on a bill that gave the individual states a role in offshore drilling decisions.

In September 2008, the House was confronted with a request by Treasury Secretary Henry Paulson and Federal Reserve Chairman Ben Bernanke for $700 billion to bail out financial firms on the brink of collapse in the weakening economy. Pelosi, with Financial Services Committee Chairman Barney Frank of Massachusetts, decided to grant the request. But a few days later, it became clear that many Democrats were unwilling to vote for it. Pelosi announced she would bring Democrats along if 100 Republicans supported it as well. When the bill came to a vote on Sept. 29, it was defeated, and Republicans blamed Pelosi for speaking harshly about Bush administration economic policies. The Senate changed some of the terms of the bill, and it passed on October 1. The House took up the Senate version and, with some vote switches prompted by Pelosi, passed it two days later.

In the November 2008 election, Democrats gained 21 House seats, and Pelosi entered the 111th Congress in 2009 as the leader of 257 Democrats—the biggest majority a speaker has enjoyed since Democrat Thomas Foley of Washington in 1993-94. Pelosi made it plain to the new Obama administration that she expected it to work through her and not make side deals with conservative Democratic factions, much less Republicans. In January, Pelosi pushed through House rules changes repealing the six-year term limit on committee chairmen that Republicans had imposed in 1995 and placing restrictions on motions to recommit, which Republicans had used frequently to delay or stop legislation. As labor unions pressed for a card-check bill effectively abolishing the secret ballot in unionization elections, Pelosi let it be known that the Senate would have to act before she would ask Democrats in the House to cast what for some would be a politically dangerous vote. She said, "A country must be governed from the middle." Pelosi went on to preside over a record of legislative accomplishments that many consider the most impressive since the Great Society Congress of 1965-66.

The first order of business was President Obama's massive economic stimulus bill. Pelosi largely delegated the specifics to Appropriations Chairman David Obey of Wisconsin, but did succeed in reducing the tax cut component from $300 billion to $275 billion. The $819 billion measure was passed without a single Republican vote. The size of the stimulus was reduced in the Senate, and Pelosi negotiated hard to get the price tag to $787 billion. The measure became law at that amount in mid-February, less than a month after Obama's inauguration.

On the issue of Iraq, Pelosi said she was unhappy with Obama's decision to leave 50,000 troops in the country and also with the Justice Department's decision not to prosecute Bush administration officials for approving enhanced interrogation techniques. She was embarrassed in May 2009 when the Central Intelligence Agency released documents indicating that she had been present at a September 2002 briefing where water boarding was discussed. In a tense press conference, she said, "In that or any other briefing, we were not and, I repeat, were not told that water boarding or any of these other enhanced interrogation techniques were used"—only that they were legal. She did admit that other Intelligence Committee members were briefed in February 2003 on techniques that included water boarding, but said she made no protest because it would have been ineffective. Republicans' call for an inquiry was voted down 252-172 on partisan lines. Despite her views on Iraq, Pelosi worked with the administration to convince antiwar Democrats to help pass the $105.9 billion supplemental defense bill for the war in June 2009.

As in the previous Congress, Pelosi pushed hard for legislation restricting carbon emissions, her "signature" issue. She quietly supported California Rep. Henry Waxman's successful campaign to replace Dingell as chairman of the Energy and Commerce, with prime jurisdiction over the issue. And she worked closely with Waxman and Markey of Massachusetts on the contents of the bill. In June 2009, she approved Waxman's concessions to win over conservative Democrats and even met with 11 Republican moderates to get their support. In late June, she brought the bill to the floor where it passed, 219-212, with eight Republicans voting yes. But the Senate failed to act, and the bill died.

The other major initiative for Pelosi in the Congress was President Obama's health care insurance overhaul, which she had hoped to pass before the August 2009 recess. But finding agreement on complex and far-reaching changes to the present medical insurance system, including a controversial proposal to let people opt into a federally sponsored plan, bogged the bill down in committee for many weeks. Waxman finally reported one out of the Energy and Commerce Committee on July 31, too late for a pre-recess floor vote. As Pelosi had feared, opposition to the bill reared its head at town hall meetings across the country during the recess period, including those in Democratic districts. Lawmakers were more skittish about the legislation when they returned. Still, Pelosi worked hard in September and October gathering up votes. She agreed to changes in the controversial public option, but refused to give in to pressure from conservative Democrats to drop it from the bill. And, in the 11th hour and to the dismay of feminists, she agreed to accept Michigan Rep. Bart Stupak's amendment barring coverage for abortions. A 1,990-page draft was unveiled on Oct. 29 and the bill was passed 220-215 on Nov.7, with 39 Democrats voting no.

The public option proved to be an even tougher sell in the Senate, and after 25 consecutive days of debate on the bill, the upper chamber ultimately voted on Christmas Eve for a health care overhaul minus the government insurance provision. Normally, a House and Senate conference committee would have begun immediately to hammer out a final version settling differences between the chambers. But on Jan. 19, 2010, Republican Scott Brown won the special Senate election for the seat vacated by the death of liberal Democrat Edward Kennedy of Massachusetts. In his campaign, Brown had promised to be the 41st vote against the health care bill, denying Democrats the 60 votes they needed to stop a filibuster. The obstacles seemed great. But Pelosi characteristically braced for the fight. "We're in the majority," she told Obama. "We'll never have a better majority in your presidency in numbers than we've got right now. We can make this work."

In early 2010, public opinion polls showed the public to be increasingly wary of the changes to the health care system. Each day of the week leading to a final House vote, Pelosi orchestrated statements of support from previously uncommitted Democrats, most of whom were facing tough opposition in the November 2010 election. Rules Committee Chairman Louise Slaughter of New York prepared a version in which the House would, in one roll call, deem the Senate bill to have been passed and add changes to it. But this procedural sleight of hand was abandoned in favor of two roll calls, one on the Senate version of the bill and one on a set of House changes to the legislation. She agreed to drop a House-passed surtax on high-income earners, which was replaced by an excise tax on high-end insurance plans. Pelosi also got Stupak and other anti-abortion rights lawmakers to agree to changes to their provision that they had previously deemed unacceptable. On the day of the vote, March 21, Pelosi marched with fellow Democrats from their offices to the Capitol, while an angry crowd, held back by Capitol police, chanted "Kill the bill." Pelosi's attitude toward the anti-Obama health care forces was clear in a statement in January of that year: "We will go through the gate. If the gate is closed, we will go over the fence. If the fence is too high, we will pole vault in. If that doesn't work, we will parachute in. But we are going to get health care reform passed for the American people." The final roll call was 219-212, without a single Republican vote. The Senate acquiesced to the House changes and Obama signed the health care bill.

Its passage was the climactic moment of Pelosi's speakership and showcased her skills at putting together complex legislation and rounding up reluctant votes, amid a volatile climate of public opinion. Polls around the country showed a disturbing number of incumbent Democrats trailing their Republican challengers. Pelosi brought the House back into session briefly in August 2010 to pass a $26 billion bill, already approved in the Senate, to help states pay teacher salaries and make Medicare payments. The following month, she hoped to send Democrats home to campaign on a high note by having them vote to extend the Bush-era income tax cuts except for upper income-earners of $200,000 or more. But when it became clear the votes weren't there—a counter proposal to extend the cuts for everyone regardless of income was attracting Republicans and some Democrats— she moved to adjourn a week earlier than scheduled, and then voted for adjournment herself, although traditionally the speaker votes on only major issues. It was acknowledgement that her ability to control a majority, after four years of doing so time and again, was now in the hands of a restless electorate in November.

That fall, Pelosi campaigned for Democrats across the country, but she was more a liability than an asset in conservative-leaning districts where Democratic incumbents were bombarded with GOP-orchestrated ads labeling them as "Pelosi-Reid Democrats." Even as Pelosi was expressing optimism publicly, the political tide was turning dramatically against Democrats who had voted for the health care bill and other elements of the Obama agenda. On election day, the Democrats lost 63 seats, the most the party had lost since 1938. They surrendered majority control to the Republicans the following January.

It was widely expected that Pelosi would not try to hold onto her leadership position. The last speakers to become minority leaders after their parties lost the majorities were Democrat Sam Rayburn in 1947 and 1953 and Republican Joseph Martin in 1949 and 1955. The previous speaker, Republican Dennis Hastert of Illinois, resigned shortly after his party's defeat in 2006. But after two days of prayer and conversations, Pelosi announced she wanted to run for minority leader again. Her ally Clyburn announced he would run for minority whip against Hoyer. Wishing to avoid a bitter leadership fight, Pelosi announced she would create a new leadership post for Clyburn, enabling Hoyer to run for whip unopposed. But she could not stop North Carolina's Heath Shuler, a conservative Democrat, from running against her although it was doubtful he had sufficient support in the caucus to topple her. Pelosi prevailed in the caucus vote 150-43. When asked to explain why she won, she said, "Because I'm an effective leader, because we got the job done on health care and Wall Street reform and consumer protection, the list goes on. Because they know that I'm the person that can attract the resources, both intellectual and otherwise, to take us to victory because I have done it before."

Back home, Pelosi was re-elected with 80% or more of the vote from 1992 to 2006. In 2008, antiwar protester Cindy Sheehan ran against her as an independent. Pelosi refused to debate or acknowledge Sheehan, who wound up getting 16% of the vote, more than the Republican nominee's 10%. Pelosi got 72%. It was her lowest percentage since the 1987 special election when she first won the seat. In 2010, she won 80%-15%.

NINTH DISTRICT

Barbara Lee (D)

Elected April 1998, 7th full term; b. July 16, 1946, El Paso, TX; home, Oakland; Mills Col., B.A. 1973, U. of CA-Berkeley, M.S.W. 1975; Baptist; divorced; 2 children.

Elected Office: CA Assembly, 1990–96; CA Senate, 1996–98.

Professional Career: Chief of staff, U.S. Rep. Ron Dellums, 1975–87.

DC Office: 2267 RHOB, 20515, 202-225-2661; Fax: 202-225-9817; Web site: lee.house.gov.

State Offices: Oakland, 510-763-0370.

Committees: *Appropriations:* Financial Services & General Government; Labor, HHS, Education & Related Agencies.

Group Ratings

	ACLU	ACU	ADA	CFG	AFS	FRC	LCV	ITIC	NTU	COC
2010	94	0	95	0	100	6	90	67	8	0
2009	–	0	100	0	100	–	100	–	4	33

National Journal Ratings

	2010 LIB	—	2010 CONS	2009 LIB	—	2009 CONS
Economic	77%	—	23%	75%	—	21%
Social	93%	—	0%	89%	—	0%
Foreign	63%	—	35%	62%	—	35%
Composite	79%	—	21%	78%	—	22%

Key Votes of the 111th Congress

1. Overturn Ledbetter	Y	5. Bar federal abortion funds	N	9. Stop detainee transfers	N
2. Pass $820 billion stimulus	Y	6. Pass health care bill	Y	10. Legalize immigrants' kids	Y
3. Let guns in national parks	N	7. Regulate financial firms	Y	11. Repeal don't ask, tell	Y
4. Pass cap-and-trade	Y	8. Pass tax cuts for some	Y	12. Limit campaign funds	Y

Election Results

2010 general	Barbara Lee (D)	180,400	(84%)	($1,156,049)
	Gerald Hashimoto (R)	23,054	(11%)	
	Dave Heller (Green)	4,848	(2%)	
2010 primary	Barbara Lee (D)	unopposed		

Prior Winning Percentages: 2008 (86%), 2006 (86%), 2004 (85%), 2002 (81%), 2000 (85%), 1998 (83%), 1998 (67%)

Population		Race/Ethnicity		Work	
Pop. 2010:	648,766	White:	34.6%	Private:	72.5%
Change since 2000:	Up 1.5%	Black:	20.3%	Government:	17.0%
Urban:	99.9%	Hispanic:	22.0%	Self-employed:	10.3%
Rural:	0.1%	Asian:	18.0%	Blue collar:	15.9%
Area size:	152 sq. mi.	Native Am.:	0.3%	White collar:	67.8%
		Hawaiian:	0.5%	Khaki collar:	0.1%
Age		Two+ races:	4.0%	Other:	16.1%
Median age:	35.8 yrs.				
More than 65 yrs:	10.9%	*Ancestry*		Median income:	$55,101
Less than 18 yrs:	21.4%	German	6.2%	Median Home Value:	$588,400
		Irish	5.6%		
Education		English	4.9%	**Military Veterans**	
H.S. grad:	83.1%			% of Pop:	5.7%
College grad:	42.4%				
Grad degree:	19.2%				

East Bay; Oakland, Berkeley

On the East Bay opposite San Francisco, Oakland and Berkeley stand today on one of the lushest sites in America, overlooking the San Francisco-Oakland Bay Bridge and the Golden Gate Bridge and basking in the sunshine that is more common here than across the bay. Both cities host great institutions, but in different ways they are also museum pieces, antiques from a moment in the 1960s when both, especially Berkeley, gained identities that became hard to shake.

2008 Presidential Vote		
Barack Obama (D) 260,662	(88%)
John McCain (R) 29,186	(10%)
2004 Presidential Vote		
John Kerry (D) 228,642	(86%)
George Bush (R) 33,450	(13%)
Cook Partisan Voting Index: D+37		

Berkeley was founded as a university town, named after the 18th-century Irish philosopher Bishop George Berkeley for his proclamation, "Westward the course of empire takes its way." Famous for years as the home of first-rate scholarship at the University of California, Berkeley became famous politically in 1964 as ground zero of student rebellion when an administrator's refusal to let students set up a table to sign up volunteers for Democrat Lyndon Johnson's presidential campaign led to months of riots, student strikes, and classroom confrontation. In 1969, students led protests at "People's Park," a lot owned by the university, and Republican Gov. Ronald Reagan sent in the National Guard to protect state property, an episode in which both sides relished the confrontation. Berkeley gave birth to a street culture that still exists. Its denizens made common cause with the quasi-political Black Panthers from nearby Oakland, and smoked marijuana with the Hell's Angels motorcycle gang. With its view of the bay, the campus is beautiful, and old buildings like the shingled Claremont Hotel are grand, although construction of new offices and apartment buildings created a more modern feel by 2008. All of those yoga classes, bean sprouts, and healthy lifestyles add up to a life expectancy in Berkeley of 83 years, five years longer than the national average.

Oakland has a different history, centered on commerce. (Gertrude Stein was wrong: There is a there there.) It became the western terminus of the transcontinental railroad in 1870 and was connected by ferry to San Francisco. It has always had heavy industry, and its port today is the busiest on the bay. The docks attracted young roustabouts like the writer Jack London, after whom a downtown square is named. Civic affairs were run by the local elite, like the Knowland family who owned the *Oakland Tribune*. With the Bay Area's largest black community, Oakland spawned the Black Panthers. African-American leaders began to dominate city government in the 1970s and the *Tribune* in the 1980s. Then Jerry Brown came on the scene. Governor of California 20 years earlier and an unsuccessful presidential candidate several times over, he ran an unorthodox campaign for mayor, and won. Brown irritated local factions by firing department heads and ignoring long-standing alliances, but he seemed to take seriously his mission of propelling Oakland to prominence. With his tough talk on crime and advocacy of big commercial development projects that drove up rents, he sounded like a conservative. He even set up a military high school. Crime rates dropped, and the local economy thrived, partly with the growth of middle-income refugees from the exorbitant housing costs of San Francisco. But many longtime residents, especially African-Americans, complained about rising costs, and they in turn moved to the outskirts. The black population fell from 47% in 1980 to about 28% in 2010. Brown's successor as mayor was former Democratic U.S. Rep. Ron Dellums. He and other community leaders in 2007 created a public-private initiative called the Oakland Partnership, with the goal of attracting 10,000 jobs to Oakland over five years. In its first two years, it almost reached that figure, but the recession threatened its future prospects.

The 9th Congressional District of California consists of Oakland and Berkeley, plus Castro Valley. It has the largest African-American percentage of any northern California district (22% in 2007), and also has high percentages of Hispanics (21.5%) and Asians (16.2%). Politically, it may be the most left-wing district in the nation. It voted 86%-13% for John Kerry in 2004 and 88%-10% for Barack Obama in 2008.

Barbara Lee (D)

The congresswoman from the 9th District is Barbara Lee, a Democrat who won an April 1998 special election. Lee spent her childhood in Texas and says her political thinking was shaped by her early exposure to race discrimination. While in labor with her, Lee's mother was at first denied treatment at an El Paso hospital. Lee attended a segregated school in that city until her parents sent their children to a Catholic school. In 1960, the family moved to Southern California, where Lee was the first black cheerleader in her high school, a distinction she won after enlisting the help of the local chapter of the NAACP. In 2008, Lee authored a memoir, *Renegade for Peace and Justice,* in which she discussed her experiences as a single welfare mother raising two children while attending college, and her early days of social advocacy. "In order to go the policy front, I had to do the personal," she said. Lee graduated from Mills College in Oakland and got a degree in social work at the University of California at Berkeley. She started a community mental health center in Berkeley and then worked as a staffer for 12 years for Rep. Ron Dellums, who chaired the House Armed Services Committee. She was elected to the California Assembly in 1990 and to the Senate in 1996. After Dellums announced he was resigning, he endorsed Lee as his successor, and she won the special election with 67% of the vote.

In the House, Lee is at the far left of the ideological spectrum. She wants to reduce the nation's weapons stockpiles and cut Pentagon spending sharply. She supports increased funding for international AIDS programs, and after a visit to Cuba, called for steps to end the 40-year trade embargo. She led a delegation of Democrats there in 2009 to discuss trade and other issues with its Communist-run government. As the co-chairman of the Progressive Caucus, she laid out an agenda with three priorities: economic justice and security, protection of civil rights and liberties, and promotion of global peace. She was a founder of the Out of Iraq Caucus, a group of the most vocal antiwar House members.

Lee has consistently opposed military action to the point of being a lonely but principled voice. As most Democrats voted to authorize bombing of Serbia in 1999, Lee was the only House member to oppose a resolution supporting U.S. troops. In September 2001, she was the only member of Congress to vote against the resolution authorizing the use of force in response to the terrorist attacks. "If we rush to launch a counterattack, we run too great a risk that women, children, and other noncombatants will be caught in the crossfire," she said. Her vote brought a torrent of national attention. Lee received threats of violence, and the Capitol police provided her with 24-hour protection. But there were supportive rallies in her district. During the debate in October 2002 to authorize the use of force in Iraq, Lee offered an alternative calling for diplomatic action, which was defeated 355-72.

In 2008, Lee became chairman of the Congressional Black Caucus, which she calls "the conscience of the Congress." In February 2009, she criticized Senate cuts in the House-passed version of President Obama's $787 billion economic stimulus bill. She and other caucus members subsequently lamented Obama's plans to add troops in Afghanistan and they have pressured Obama to pay more attention to minorities.

In 2007, House Speaker Nancy Pelosi gave Lee a seat on the powerful Appropriations Committee. She was one of 14 Democrats to vote against the Iraq war funding bill on the House floor. "My conscience is that we can't put up more money to fund this war," Lee said. In July 2008, the House passed, 399-24, her bill to prevent permanent U.S. military bases in Iraq or U.S. control of Iraqi oil. The House also passed her bill to encourage states to divest from companies that do business in Sudan, in protest of the genocide in the Darfur region. As Republican criticism mounted over earmarked spending, the special-interest provisions added to spending bills, Lee remained a staunch defender of the practice. "I'll tell them to come to my community and see what we can accomplish with whatever federal dollars we can get," she said in 2009.

TENTH DISTRICT

John Garamendi (D)

Elected 2009, 1st full term; b. Jan. 24, 1945, Mokelumne Hill; home, Walnut Grove; U of CA-Berkeley, B.A. 1966; Harvard U., M.B.A. 1974; Christian; married (Patti); 6 children.

Elected Office: CA Assembly, 1974-76; CA Senate, 1976-88; CA insurance commissioner, 1991-95, 2002-06; CA lt. gov, 2006-09

Professional Career: U.S. Peace Corps volunteer, Ethiopia 1966-68; Deputy Secy., U.S. Dept. of Interior, 1995-98

DC Office: 228 CHOB, 20515, 202-225-1880 ; Fax: 202-225-5914; Web site: garamendi.house.gov.

State Offices: Antioch, 925-757-7187 ; Fairfield, 707-438-1822; Walnut Creek, 925-932-8899 .

Committees: *Armed Services:* Air & Land Forces; Strategic Forces. *Natural Resources:* National Parks, Forests & Public Lands; Water & Power.

Group Ratings

	ACLU	ACU	ADA	CFG	AFS	FRC	LCV	ITIC	NTU	COC
2010	71	0	100	0	100	0	90	50	5	0
2009	–	0	–	–	100	–	100	–	0	14

National Journal Ratings

	2010 LIB	—	2010 CONS	2009 LIB	—	2009 CONS
Economic	90%	—	0%	*	—	*
Social	66%	—	33%	*	—	*
Foreign	78%	—	17%	*	—	*
Composite	81%	—	19%	*	—	*

Key Votes of the 111th Congress

1. Overturn Ledbetter	*	5. Bar federal abortion funds	N	9. Stop detainee transfers	Y
2. Pass $820 billion stimulus	*	6. Pass health care bill	Y	10. Legalize immigrants' kids	Y
3. Let guns in national parks	*	7. Regulate financial firms	Y	11. Repeal don't ask, tell	Y
4. Pass cap-and-trade	*	8. Pass tax cuts for some	Y	12. Limit campaign funds	Y

Election Results

2010 general	John Garamendi (D)	137,578	(59%)	($1,764,354)
	Gary Clift (R)	88,512	(38%)	($53,250)
	Jeremy Cloward (Green)	7,716	(3%)	
2010 primary	John Garamendi (D)	unopposed		

Prior Winning Percentages: 2009 (52%)

Population		Race/Ethnicity		Work	
Pop. 2010:	714,750	White:	52.8%	Private:	75.5%
Change since 2000:	Up 11.8%	Black:	7.2%	Government:	16.2%
Urban:	96.5%	Hispanic:	21.3%	Self-employed:	8.1%
Rural:	3.5%	Asian:	13.3%	Blue collar:	15.5%
Area size:	1,085 sq. mi.	Native Am.:	0.3%	White collar:	67.8%
		Hawaiian:	0.5%	Khaki collar:	0.5%
Age		Two+ races:	4.3%	Other:	16.3%
Median age:	37.9 yrs.				
More than 65 yrs:	12.1%	*Ancestry*		Median income:	$81,297
Less than 18 yrs:	25.6%	German	10.6%	Median Home Value:	$552,200
		Irish	9.0%		
Education		English	7.8%	**Military Veterans**	
H.S. grad:	89.9%			% of Pop:	9.3%
College grad:	39.6%				
Grad degree:	14.7%				

East Bay; Fairfield, Antioch

In the 1950s, when San Francisco and Oakland were already thriving cities, the rolling grasslands east of the mountain ridges were still mostly empty. In the years since, they have filled up. Freeways took the first commuters through the Caldecott Tunnel to the woodsy, trail-like roads of Orinda and Lafayette. Interstate 580 brought people east from the southern East Bay towns to the Amador Valley and Livermore, site of the Lawrence Livermore National Labora-

2008 Presidential Vote		
Barack Obama (D) 204,138	(65%)
John McCain (R) 104,628	(33%)

2004 Presidential Vote		
John Kerry (D) 169,373	(59%)
George Bush (R) 117,037	(40%)

Cook Partisan Voting Index: D+11

tory, which conducts nuclear warhead and energy research. Since the 1980s, anti-nuclear protestors have gathered at Livermore on the anniversary of the bombing of Hiroshima, Japan. Interstate 680 running north-south provided a spine for businesses and shopping centers up and down the San Ramon Valley, from burgeoning Concord to Walnut Creek in Contra Costa County to points south. BART stations in Walnut Creek and Orinda took commuters to downtown San Francisco. Not all of the inhabitable areas are filled up yet, and local voters have passed measures to set limits on growth. But what has evolved in this sunny land, shielded by the mountains from the ocean fogs and rains, is a civilization of highly skilled and educated people. They are affluent and generally less culturally liberal than San Francisco, but they are concerned about preserving their pleasant physical environment.

This territory is the heart of the 10th Congressional District of California. Redistricting in 2001 removed the San Ramon Valley south of Walnut Creek and added part of the Sacramento River Delta and parts of booming Solano County to the north. Fairfield is the largest city in the 10th, but suffered a big drop in residential property values when the recession hit in 2008. Travis Air Force Base, with its C-17 cargo haulers and constant traffic to and from Iraq, adds $1.4 billion annually to the local economy. From 2000 to 2010, about three-fourths of the population growth was attributable to Hispanics, who increased from 15% to 21% of the total. The district is largely Democratic. In 2004, Democratic presidential nominee John Kerry carried it 59%-40%, and in 2008, Democrat Barack Obama won it 65%-33%.

John Garamendi (D)

The congressman from the 10th District is John Garamendi, a Democrat and former California lieutenant governor. He won the San Francisco Bay-area seat in a Nov. 3, 2009 special election to replace Democrat Ellen Tauscher, who left Congress in June to join President Obama's State Department. Though he is relatively new to Washington, Garamendi is politically seasoned, with more than 30 years of public service, most of it in California.

Garamendi was raised on his family's cattle ranch in Calaveras County, Calif. At the University of California at Berkeley, he was an All-American offensive guard in football and was also a competitive wrestler. After graduating, he joined the Peace Corps in Ethiopia, where his wife, Patti, also was a volunteer. The experience launched him on a career in public service. After returning to California, he won his first campaign in 1974 to the state Assembly. In 1976, he was elected to the state Senate, where he eventually became majority leader. During his career, he did two stints as the state's insurance commissioner, and also was President Clinton's deputy secretary of the Interior. But he ultimately failed twice in his bid to become governor of California. In the 2006 Democratic primary for lieutenant governor, Garamendi narrowly defeated Jackie Speier, who represents the 12th District in the House. He went on to beat Republican Tom McClintock in the general election. Garamendi was planning another run for governor in 2010 when Tauscher resigned her House seat in June 2009 to become Obama's undersecretary for state for arms control and international security.

In the jockeying before the all-party primary in September, state Sen. Mark DeSaulnier was an early favorite among Democrats and gained endorsements from Tauscher and from neighboring 7th District Rep. George Miller, a close ally of Democratic House Speaker Pelosi. While DeSaulnier was better known locally, Garamendi had higher name identification statewide, and he also had endorsements from Clinton and former Vice President Gore. Garamendi was criticized for living outside the district, although California does not make residency a requirement. He insisted that he did live in the district, at least partially. Garamendi said that his front lawn was in the 10th District although his house was not.

In the Sept. 1 primary, Garamendi prevailed among Democrats, winning 26% to DeSaulnier's 18%. But no candidate received the requisite 50%, and Garamendi moved on to a runoff election against Republican attorney David Harmer, who earned the most votes among the Republican candidates.

Harmer had some name recognition as the son of former GOP Lt. Gov. John Harmer, but otherwise was not well known. He was competitive financially, raising $800,000 to Garamendi's $1 million. Still, he faced an uphill battle in a suburban San Francisco district where Democrats hold an 18-percentage-point advantage over Republicans. During the campaign, Garamendi embraced Obama's agenda, including support for the public option in the health care legislation. Harmer campaigned in opposition to the president, criticizing the government bailouts of the financial and auto industries. Garamendi won with 53% of the vote to Harmer's 43%.

Garamendi has been a more reliable Democratic vote than Tauscher, whom the *San Francisco Chronicle* once described as "the closest thing the Bay Area has to a Republican." Garamendi was among the strongest critics of offshore oil drilling in the wake of the BP oil spill in the Gulf of Mexico, drawing attention for his proposal to bar new federal drilling leases off the coasts of California, Oregon and Washington state. As a member of the Science and Technology Committee, he also called for more research into renewable energy technologies at Lawrence Berkeley and elsewhere. "As long as we depend on oil, our energy future is locked into the fate of Saudi Arabia, Iran, Venezuela and the Gulf Coast," he told MSNBC in June 2010.

In 2010, Garamendi joined the Armed Services Committee, where he added an amendment to the fiscal 2011 defense authorization bill to authorize the Energy Department to create technology transfer centers at Livermore and other labs. He also supported repeal of the "don't ask, don't tell" ban on openly gay soldiers from serving in the military and worked with other area Democrats to obtain money to modernize Travis Air Force Base.

ELEVENTH DISTRICT

Jerry McNerney (D)

Elected 2006, 3rd term; b. June 18, 1951, Albuquerque, NM; home, Pleasanton; Attended U.S. Military Academy, 1969-71, U. of NM, B.S. 1973, M.S. 1975, Ph.D. 1981; Catholic; married (Mary); 3 children.

Professional Career: National security contractor, Sandia National Laboratories, 1979-85; Engineer, U.S. Windpower, Kenetech, 1985-94; Energy consultant, 1994-99; CEO, start-up wind turbine manufacturer, 2000-06.

DC Office: 1210 LHOB, 20515, 202-225-1947; Fax: 202-225-4060; Web site: mcnerney.house.gov.

State Offices: Pleasanton, 925-737-0727; Stockton, 209-476-8552.

Committees: *Science & Technology:* Energy & Environment; Investigations & Oversight. *Veterans' Affairs:* Disability Assistance & Memorial Affairs (RMM); Oversight & Investigations.

Group Ratings

	ACLU	ACU	ADA	CFG	AFS	FRC	LCV	ITIC	NTU	COC
2010	88	8	85	9	88	0	100	100	11	25
2009	–	12	100	8	100	–	93	–	9	40

National Journal Ratings

	2010 LIB	—	2010 CONS		2009 LIB	—	2009 CONS
Economic	50%	—	49%		56%	—	44%
Social	54%	—	42%		54%	—	43%
Foreign	49%	—	49%		48%	—	52%
Composite	52%	—	48%		53%	—	47%

Key Votes of the 111th Congress

1. Overturn Ledbetter	Y	5. Bar federal abortion funds	N	9. Stop detainee transfers	Y
2. Pass $820 billion stimulus	Y	6. Pass health care bill	Y	10. Legalize immigrants' kids	Y
3. Let guns in national parks	Y	7. Regulate financial firms	Y	11. Repeal don't ask, tell	Y
4. Pass cap-and-trade	Y	8. Pass tax cuts for some	Y	12. Limit campaign funds	Y

Election Results

2010 general	Jerry McNerney (D)	115,361	(48%)	($3,209,478)
	David Harmer (R)	112,703	(47%)	($2,931,475)
	David Christensen (AMI)	12,439	(5%)	
2010 primary	Jerry McNerney (D)	unopposed		

Prior Winning Percentages: 2008 (55%), 2006 (53%)

Population		Race/Ethnicity		Work	
Pop. 2010:	796,753	White:	50.3%	Private:	77.8%
Change since 2000:	Up 24.7%	Black:	4.6%	Government:	14.2%
Urban:	90.1%	Hispanic:	26.3%	Self-employed:	7.8%
Rural:	9.9%	Asian:	14.3%	Blue collar:	18.8%
Area size:	2,317 sq. mi.	Native Am.:	0.4%	White collar:	65.5%
		Hawaiian:	0.4%	Khaki collar:	0.1%
Age		Two+ races:	3.5%	Other:	15.6%
Median age:	35.4 yrs.				
More than 65 yrs:	10.5%	*Ancestry*		Median income:	$77,407
Less than 18 yrs:	28.3%	German	11.1%	Median Home Value:	$471,700
		Irish	8.3%		
Education		English	6.8%	**Military Veterans**	
H.S. grad:	86.4%			% of Pop:	8.3%
College grad:	31.3%				
Grad degree:	10.4%				

Central California; Part Stockton

California is often defined by its cosmopolitan cities, its gorgeous Pacific coastline, and its world-class vineyards, but beyond Beverly Hills and Nob Hill, there is another California that likes to get its hands dirty. This is an old part of the state, settled in the 1840s beginning with the Gold Rush. When the fortune seekers departed, the land was left to a determined population of farmers. Crisscrossed with railroads and canals, the Central Valley became one of the world's greatest agricultural regions. The San Joaquin River channel was deepened to 37 feet, and Stockton today is the Central Valley's port. (The city is named after Robert Stockton, the second U.S. military governor of California, who captured Santa Barbara and Los Angeles from Mexico and proclaimed California U.S. territory.) The rich land attracted immigrants from all over: Mexicans came up Route 99 and joined North Dakotans flocking to the town of Lodi. Italian and Yugoslavian immigrants brought their Old World crops. Yankees and Okies brought their distinct churches and beliefs. Later, Southeast Asian refugees crowded into the older streets of Stockton.

2008 Presidential Vote		
Barack Obama (D)	169,183	(54%)
John McCain (R)	139,863	(44%)
2004 Presidential Vote		
George Bush (R)	151,397	(54%)
John Kerry (D)	127,102	(45%)
Cook Partisan Voting Index: R+1		

More recently, Stockton has positioned itself to take advantage of the region's economic strength by turning into a warehouse and distribution center for Northern California. This growth came even though the farm economy was threatened by actions to reduce water subsidies, the growing difficulty of attracting migrant workers for harvests, and a devastating drought that began in 2007 and has reduced the acreage of useable land. Many of the valley's crops, especially fruits and vegetables, are not subject to the vagaries of federal controls, though the area is still a big cotton producer. And the Central Valley has also become a suburban zone. Because of the high cost of living in San Francisco, Bay Area workers with modest incomes bought lower-priced houses around Tracy and Stockton and commute to work on Interstate 580, past the windmills of Altamont. Still, crime and unemployment remain barriers—*Forbes* magazine named Stockton the most miserable city in America in 2011. San Joaquin County's jobless rate topped 16% in 2010. The area also was hard hit by the housing foreclosure crisis, but it has begun to slowly recover. In the second quarter of 2010, San Joaquin led the nation's 100 largest metropolitan areas in a decline in bank-owned foreclosures.

The 11th Congressional District of California includes much of this area plus the Bay Area suburbs of San Ramon Valley in Contra Costa County. The central part of Stockton is in the 18th District, connected by a thin corridor to the valley further south. But the 11th does include northwest Stockton and most of the rest of San Joaquin County—Tracy, Lodi, and the almond center of Manteca. Lodi has a sizeable Muslim community. The district also takes in the adjacent town of Brentwood in Contra Costa County, the fastest-growing city in the Bay Area in the 1990s and early 2000s. Brentwood nearly doubled in population from 2000 to 2006, but growth slowed considerably after the housing bust in 2007.

The farm town of Morgan Hill anchors the far southern edge of the 11th in Santa Clara County. The San Ramon Valley towns—Danville and San Ramon in Contra Costa County, and Dublin and Pleasanton in Alameda County—are much more affluent than the Central Valley parts of the district. The district has moved cautiously toward Republicans on cultural issues and on the strength of farmers' hostility to environmental restrictions that impede their livelihoods. The San Ramon Valley is the most Republican part of the Bay Area, but that is not very Republican by national standards; it is fairly liberal on cultural issues. This district, whose odd lines were drawn by Republicans in 2001 as their only Bay Area district, voted 54% for George W. Bush in 2004. But Democrat Barack Obama carried it with 54% in 2008.

Jerry McNerney (D)

The congressman from the 11th District is Jerry McNerney, a Democrat who won in one of the most hard-fought contests of 2006 and in another protracted battle four years later. McNerney's father was a union organizer in the 1930s and later worked for the U.S. Geological Survey in Albuquerque, where Jerry McNerney was born. Along with his twin brother, McNerney was sent to a military boarding school in Hays, Kan., and later won an appointment to the U.S. Military Academy. He left West Point after two years because he opposed the war in Vietnam. He transferred to the University of New Mexico, where he eventually earned a doctoral degree in differential geometry. He spent several years as a contractor for Sandia National Laboratories, working on national security programs. In 1985, he moved to the private sector with U.S. Windpower. He later became chief executive of a firm that planned to manufacture wind turbines. McNerney, who named his daughter Windy, claimed that his work contributed to saving the equivalent of 8.3 million tons of carbon dioxide. Before running for Congress, he had never held elected office.

McNerney was an unlikely winner against Republican Rep. Richard Pombo, a local rancher in an area where he was so well known, it was dubbed "Pombo Country." As the chairman of the House Resources Committee, Pombo was the leader of the property-rights movement backed by ranchers and farmers. When McNerney first challenged Pombo in 2004, he was crushed, 61%-39%. In the 2006 primary, the Democratic Congressional Campaign Committee endorsed Steve Filson, an airline pilot and political neophyte who turned out to be a disappointment. McNerney, endorsed by the state party and by local organized labor, soundly defeated Filson, 53%-28%.

In the general election, Pombo outspent McNerney by nearly 2-to-1. McNerney managed nevertheless to turn the election into a referendum on the controversial seven-term incumbent. Pombo had been targeted by national environmental groups, which called him an "eco-thug" and "Wildlife Enemy No. 1." The campaign contributions he received from disgraced Republican lobbyist Jack Abramoff also came under close scrutiny. Over the summer, McNerney captured the imagination of liberal Internet activists and got a boost in fundraising. As he inched closer to Pombo in the polls, the DCCC began to air ads against the Republican. McNerney emphasized his background as an energy consultant and focused his attacks on Pombo's environmental voting record. The two candidates disagreed on virtually every issue, including the Iraq war, the partial privatization of Social Security, and oil exploration in Alaska. But Pombo was running against a strong anti-Republican wind. McNerney won 53%-47%. In San Joaquin County, which cast a bit more than half of the vote, Pombo led 51%-49%. But McNerney won comfortably in counties closer to the Bay Area, with 54% in Contra Costa, 63% in Alameda, and 61% in Santa Clara.

In the House, McNerney established the most moderate voting record in California's delegation, especially on cultural issues. Democratic leaders gave him an early opportunity to sponsor a bill that won House passage—a pilot program to help communities with endangered water supplies find alternative sources. In the 2007 energy bill, he added a provision to promote research and development of geothermal energy. And in 2009, with crucial help from Bay Area neighbor Speaker Nancy Pelosi, McNerney got a coveted slot on the influential Energy and Commerce Committee. There, he won a provision in the House-passed bill regulating carbon emissions to encourage electric vehicle usage and fund clean-energy job training programs. But he continued his independent streak. He was one of just 20 House Democrats in December 2010 to oppose a bill that denied tax cuts to the wealthiest Americans. McNerney lost his seat on the committee when Republicans claimed the majority in 2011.

Widely viewed as one of the rare vulnerable Democrats in 2008, McNerney worked the district aggressively with "Congress on Your Corner" events and citizen advisory panels for agriculture, health care, and small-business issues. He was also able to tout the $15 million for asparagus growers that he inserted in the final version of the 2008 farm bill, an earmark of great interest to asparagus farmers in the Central Valley. California Assemblyman Dean Andal, the Republican nominee, called McNerney a "Pelosi clone," and emphasized his reputation as a budget hawk who supporter lower taxes in the Assembly. But Andal's campaign was poorly financed and disorganized. McNerney won handily, 55%-45%.

Republicans came after McNerney with a vengeance in 2010. They fielded a credible challenger in David Harmer, son of John Harmer, who was Ronald Reagan's lieutenant governor. The younger Harmer had been an aide to Sen. Orrin Hatch, R-Utah. He later became a high-profile education activist and author, as well as a financial executive at JPMorgan Chase. Harmer lost to Lt. Gov. John Garamendi in the 2009 general election to replace 10th District Democratic Rep. Ellen Tauscher after her appointment to the State Department, but drew an impressive 43% in the heavily Democratic district.

Harmer campaigned as a conservative who would focus on ending the government's fiscal problems. He promised to shun earmarks, calling them "the gateway drug of federal spending." Democratic interest groups attacked him for his earlier writings on education, including a 2000 op-ed column in which he called for the abolition of public education. Polls showed him deadlocked with McNerney right up to Election Night on Nov. 2. McNerney eked out a 121-vote lead, which grew to 2,269 votes as Alameda, Contra Costa and Santa Clara counties updated their counts. San Joaquin County also revised its totals and Harmer gained about 800 votes, not enough to close the gap. McNerney claimed victory on Nov. 10, but Harmer refused to concede. On Dec. 4, more than a week after the Associated Press called the race for McNerney, his opponent finally threw in the towel.

TWELFTH DISTRICT

Jackie Speier (D)

Elected April 2008, 2nd full term; b. May 14, 1950, San Francisco; home, Hillsborough; U. of CA-Davis, B.A., 1972, U of CA-Hastings Col. of Law, J.D., 1976.; Catholic; married (Barry Dennis); 2 children.

Elected Office: San Mateo Cnty. Bd. of Supervisors, 1980-86, CA Assembly, 1986-96, CA Senate, 1998-2006.

Professional Career: Staff aide, Rep. Leo Ryan, 1973-78, Dir. government affairs, Community Gatepath, 1996-98, Dir. government affairs, Electronic Arts, 1996-98, attorney, 2007-08.

DC Office: 211 CHOB, 20515, 202-225-3531; Fax: 202-226-4183; Web site: speier.house.gov.

State Offices: San Mateo, 650-342-0300.

Committees: *Homeland Security:* Counterterrorism & Intelligence (RMM); Transportation Security. *Oversight & Government Reform:* Regulatory Affairs, Stimulus Oversight & Government Spending; TARP, Financial Services & Bailouts of Public & Private Programs.

Group Ratings

	ACLU	ACU	ADA	CFG	AFS	FRC	LCV	ITIC	NTU	COC
2010	94	0	95	0	100	0	90	67	5	13
2009	–	4	95	7	100	–	93	–	7	33

National Journal Ratings

	2010 LIB	—	2010 CONS	2009 LIB	—	2009 CONS
Economic	84%	—	16%	72%	—	27%
Social	87%	—	12%	71%	—	28%
Foreign	91%	—	8%	78%	—	17%
Composite	88%	—	12%	75%	—	25%

Key Votes of the 111th Congress

1. Overturn Ledbetter	Y	5. Bar federal abortion funds	N	9. Stop detainee transfers	N
2. Pass $820 billion stimulus	Y	6. Pass health care bill	Y	10. Legalize immigrants' kids	Y
3. Let guns in national parks	*	7. Regulate financial firms	Y	11. Repeal don't ask, tell	Y
4. Pass cap-and-trade	Y	8. Pass tax cuts for some	Y	12. Limit campaign funds	Y

Election Results

2010 general	Jackie Speier (D)	152,044	(76%)	($1,060,953)
	Mike Moloney (R)	44,475	(22%)	
	mark Williams (Lib)	4,611	(2%)	
2010 primary	Jackie Speier (D)	unopposed		

Prior Winning Percentages: 2008 (75%)

Population		Race/Ethnicity		Work	
Pop. 2010:	651,322	White:	40.9%	Private:	76.5%
Change since 2000:	Up 1.9%	Black:	2.2%	Government:	14.2%
Urban:	99.9%	Hispanic:	18.5%	Self-employed:	9.2%
Rural:	0.1%	Asian:	33.4%	Blue collar:	13.8%
Area size:	363 sq. mi.	Native Am.:	0.2%	White collar:	71.0%
		Hawaiian:	1.0%	Khaki collar:	0.0%
Age		Two+ races:	3.5%	Other:	15.2%
Median age:	40.0 yrs.				
More than 65 yrs:	14.2%	*Ancestry*		Median income:	$86,625
Less than 18 yrs:	20.2%	Irish	7.5%	Median Home Value:	$783,500
		German	7.2%		
Education		Italian	5.8%	**Military Veterans**	
H.S. grad:	90.0%			% of Pop:	6.3%
College grad:	46.0%				
Grad degree:	17.1%				

Part San Francisco, Suburbs

The city of San Francisco sits at the tip of the San Francisco Peninsula on the California coast. This is geologically interesting country. The San Andreas Fault runs just east of the Coast Range, underneath the reservoirs that store San Francisco's water supply. To the west are green mountains running down to the ocean. To the east is a zone of flat land between mountain and bay, an unbroken chain of suburbs and urban settlement, with light industry and salt flats

along the bay front. Daly City and Pacifica on the ocean are a kind of extension of San Francisco's old working-class districts, with boxy houses on streets looking out on the ocean or the freeway. Today, these neighborhoods are home to many of the Bay Area's Asian immigrants. Pacific Islanders are prominent, too. The nation's biggest concentration of Samoans is in Daly City, and the biggest concentration of Tongans is in San Bruno. A strip of Highway 1 that winds along the coastal cliffs south of Pacifica passes through an area known as "Devil's Slide" for the mudslides that often follow heavy storms. A tunnel bypassing Devil's Slide was scheduled to open in early 2012.

On the Bay side is South San Francisco, where Herb Boyer and Bob Swanson sketched on a napkin their plans for the first biotechnology company, Genentech. They bought space in an old warehouse on the waterfront near a Bethlehem Steel plant. In 2009, Genentech was purchased by the Swiss pharmaceutical firm Roche and had a market capitalization exceeding $100 billion. The area is one large biotech campus overlooking the Bay, with lawns, parkways, and earth-toned office complexes, the center of the industry. *YouTube*, started in 2005, is headquartered in San Bruno. Oracle, a computer software company, is based in a cluster of gleaming glass buildings in Redwood City. *Forbes* ranked Oracle co-founder Larry Ellison the sixth-richest person in the world in 2010, with an estimated net worth of $28 billion. Between the Bayshore Freeway and Interstate 280 are middle-class suburbs that grew up to be cities with office complexes—Millbrae, Burlingame, San Mateo, and San Carlos. On September 9, 2010, a ruptured gas line in San Bruno caused a massive explosion that killed eight people and destroyed 38 homes. Federal investigators found cracks in welds that held sections of the pipe together, and it was revealed that pipeline owner Pacific Gas and Electric Co. had cut corners in its safety inspections.

The 12th Congressional District of California consists of these northern peninsula suburbs plus the southwest quadrant of the city of San Francisco, the middle-income Sunset district. It is ethnically and racially diverse; 33% of its residents are Asian, one of the highest ratios among congressional districts, and another 17% are Hispanic. The economic orientation here was historically toward San Francisco, then later south toward Silicon Valley, but now the district has its own burgeoning biotech industry. Income levels are among the highest in the state. Politically, the peninsula was long a bastion of progressive Republicanism, but the 12th District votes overwhelmingly Democratic now.

Jackie Speier (D)

The congresswoman from the 12th is Jackie Speier *(SPEER)*, a Democrat who won a special election in April 2008 to succeed Tom Lantos, the chairman of the House Foreign Affairs Committee who died during his 14th term in office. Born in San Francisco's Sunset district, she graduated from the University of California at Davis and got her law degree at U.C.'s Hastings College of Law. While an undergraduate, she interned in Sacramento for Democratic Assemblyman Leo Ryan and later joined his staff after he was elected to Congress. In November 1978, Speier accompanied third-term Rep. Ryan on a trip to Jonestown, Guyana, to investigate claims that some of Ryan's constituents, who were members of a church called the Peoples Temple, were being held against their will by the Rev. Jim Jones of San Francisco. Some defectors from the church joined Ryan's entourage for the journey home, but the group made it only as far as the airport. Four assassins sent by Jones opened fire on the defenseless group. Ryan and four others, including two journalists, were killed. Speier was shot five times and left for dead on the airstrip, where she waited 15 hours before the Guyana police rescued her. In the meantime, Jones, back at his jungle camp, set in motion events that shocked the world. He forced his cult followers to commit "revolutionary suicide" by drinking poison-laced punch, which resulted in the deaths of more than 900 followers, some of them babies and children.

Once back in California, Speier underwent 10 surgeries, including skin grafts. Despite her injuries, she ran in the special election to succeed Ryan, but she got only 15% of the total vote and finished third among Democrats in the primary. She returned to the Bay Area and built her political career, starting on the San Mateo County Board of Supervisors and then serving 18 years in the Legislature. Her pinnacle achievement was legislation protecting consumers' privacy from invasive practices by banks and insurance companies. In 2006, she unsuccessfully sought the nomination for lieutenant governor.

When Lantos, the only Holocaust survivor to serve in Congress, announced his retirement in early January 2008, he endorsed Speier as his successor. He died in February of complications from cancer of the esophagus. Speier immediately became the front-runner. Stanford University law professor Larry Lessig, who has crusaded against the influence of money in politics, briefly considered a challenge, but candidly conceded that he would probably have lost to Speier. She won the all-party election with 75% of the vote against four little-known opponents.

In the House, Speier quickly established her mark as an ardent and sometimes outspoken liberal. Immediately after she took her oath of office, she caused a ruckus when she launched a sharp partisan attack on President George W. Bush's handling of the war in Iraq. "History will not judge us kindly if we sacrifice four generations of Americans because of the folly of one," she declared. Her remarks triggered a volley of boos among Republican members on the floor and prompted Republican Rep. Darrell Issa of California to walk out of the chamber, claiming she had violated House rules of decorum. Speier responded that she had been "forthright." Later, in March 2010, Speier joined 59 other Democrats in voting for a resolution requiring the withdrawal of troops from Afghanistan.

In February 2011, during a House floor debate over funding for abortion providers, Speier emotionally discussed her own experience with abortion. She said that she had to terminate a wanted pregnancy in the second trimester due to a serious medical complication, and suggested that ardent anti-abortion rights Rep. Chris Smith, R-N.J., was mischaracterizing the procedure she underwent. "For you to stand on this floor and to suggest, as you have, that somehow this is a procedure that is either welcomed or done cavalierly or done without any thought is preposterous," Speier said. She later told MSNBC, "It's time we stop demonizing women who have to endure this procedure," which she described as a D&C, the common term for "dilation and curettage."

In her first term, Speier called for a national speed limit of 60 miles per hour on freeways in urban areas to reduce gasoline consumption. On the Financial Services Committee, her opposition scuttled a bipartisan 2008 proposal to create an office of insurance information in the Treasury Department. She objected that the measure could pre-empt state laws that limit rate increases. During debate on a major financial services regulatory bill in 2009, Speier passed in the House an amendment requiring big banks to have at least $1 in capital for every $15 in assets. In the final bill, lawmakers watered down the requirement, giving federal regulators the option of enforcing the limit only if a firm posed a "grave threat" to financial stability.

In February 2009, Speier joined 20 mostly moderate House Democrats who voted against the omnibus spending bill because it was chock full of earmarks for individual lawmakers' districts. She created her own citizens' panel to review congressional earmarks and chose Lessig to chair it. But Speier has not completely eschewed directing money to her own district. In April 2010, she sponsored a bill with other Bay Area lawmakers authorizing $100 million to clean up the San Francisco Bay.

Speier considered running for state attorney general in 2010, but opted to stay in the House, easily winning re-election.

THIRTEENTH DISTRICT

Pete Stark (D)

Elected 1972, 20th term; b. Nov. 11, 1931, Milwaukee, WI; home, Fremont; MIT, B.S. 1953, U. of CA, M.B.A. 1960; Atheist; married (Deborah); 7 children.

Military Career: Air Force, 1955–57.

Professional Career: Founder, Beacon Savings & Loan Assn., 1961; Founder & pres., Security Natl. Bank, Walnut Creek, 1963–72.

DC Office: 239 CHOB, 20515, 202-225-5065; Fax: 202-226-3805; Web site: stark.house.gov.

State Offices: Fremont, 510-494-1388.

Committees: *Ways & Means:* Health (RMM); Social Security.

Group Ratings

	ACLU	ACU	ADA	CFG	AFS	FRC	LCV	ITIC	NTU	COC
2010	93	0	90	0	100	12	80	67	9	0
2009	–	10	70	18	100	–	71	–	13	43

National Journal Ratings

	2010 LIB	—	2010 CONS		2009 LIB	—	2009 CONS
Economic	70%	—	30%		64%	—	36%
Social	93%	—	0%		89%	—	0%
Foreign	73%	—	27%		53%	—	47%
Composite	80%	—	20%		71%	—	30%

Key Votes of the 111th Congress

1. Overturn Ledbetter	Y	5. Bar federal abortion funds	N	9. Stop detainee transfers	N
2. Pass $820 billion stimulus	Y	6. Pass health care bill	Y	10. Legalize immigrants' kids	Y
3. Let guns in national parks	*	7. Regulate financial firms	Y	11. Repeal don't ask, tell	Y
4. Pass cap-and-trade	N	8. Pass tax cuts for some	Y	12. Limit campaign funds	Y

Election Results

2010 general	Pete Stark (D)	118,278	(72%)	($487,385)
	Forest Baker (R)	45,575	(28%)	(no FEC report)
2010 primary	Pete Stark (D)	48,603	(84%)	
	Justin Jelincic (D)	9,021	(16%)	

Prior Winning Percentages: 2008 (76%), 2006 (75%), 2004 (72%), 2002 (71%), 2000 (70%), 1998 (71%), 1996 (65%), 1994 (65%), 1992 (60%), 1990 (58%), 1988 (73%), 1986 (70%), 1984 (70%), 1982 (61%), 1980 (55%), 1978 (65%), 1976 (71%), 1974 (71%), 1972 (53%)

Population		Race/Ethnicity		Work	
Pop. 2010:	665,318	White:	26.3%	Private:	81.2%
Change since 2000:	Up 4.1%	Black:	6.9%	Government:	12.6%
Urban:	99.3%	Hispanic:	24.9%	Self-employed:	6.1%
Rural:	0.7%	Asian:	36.0%	Blue collar:	19.9%
Area size:	281 sq. mi.	Native Am.:	0.3%	White collar:	65.6%
		Hawaiian:	1.2%	Khaki collar:	0.1%
Age		Two+ races:	4.2%	Other:	14.4%
Median age:	36.6 yrs.				
More than 65 yrs:	11.2%	*Ancestry*		Median income:	$76,671
Less than 18 yrs:	24.3%	German	6.1%	Median Home Value:	$574,000
		Irish	4.6%		
Education		English	4.1%	**Military Veterans**	
H.S. grad:	86.0%			% of Pop:	6.4%
College grad:	36.6%				
Grad degree:	12.8%				

East Bay; Fremont, Hayward

The East Bay is the workaday, unglamorous side of the San Francisco Bay Area—a narrow strip of land between the Bay and the surprisingly high mountains that rise just to the east. The shoreline is not picturesque, with its closed-down Navy bases and its docks, airports, and salt evaporators. The Bay Bridge cuts an inspiring figure, though it requires constant patching; work is under way to add a new span, with completion scheduled in 2013. The San Mateo

2008 Presidential Vote		
Barack Obama (D) 175,838	(74%)
John McCain (R) 56,299	(24%)
2004 Presidential Vote		
John Kerry (D) 153,598	(71%)
George Bush (R).....................60,559	(28%)
Cook Partisan Voting Index: D+22		

Bridge to the south is at best utilitarian. In World War II, when the shipyards of Richmond were buzzing, the East Bay south of Oakland was still largely uninhabited farm fields. After the war, the area filled up, south along old Route 17: San Leandro, originally settled by Portuguese; Hayward with its California State University campus and seafood industry; Union City with its rail yards; and Newark, with dozens of industrial plants ranging from salt processing to computer network servers. Also in the district is Fremont, where a General Motors/Toyota auto plant closed in April 2010 and a month later was taken over by Tesla Motors, which has plans to build high-end electric cars there. That development, said the newsletter *California Planning & Development Report*, could make the city "the Detroit of the 21st century." Hit hard by the dot-com bust, the East Bay revived with biotech, construction, and health care, only to suffer like the rest of California during the recession. Underneath the East Bay is the Hayward Fault, not as famous as the San Andreas, but just as dangerous. An earthquake there in 1868 registered about 7.0 on the Richter scale.

The 13th Congressional District of California is made up of this string of East Bay towns in Alameda County. The district is racially and ethnically mixed. Fremont is home to the Little Kabul neighborhood of Afghans. Koreans and other Asians have moved in large numbers to Fremont and Hayward. In 2009, the district was 35% Asian, 23% Hispanic, and 7% African-American. This has long been a Democratic area. Democrat John Kerry got 71% of the vote here in 2004, and Democrat Barack Obama won it with 74% in 2008.

Pete Stark (D)

The congressman from the 13th District is Pete Stark, a liberal Democrat first elected in 1972 and now the dean of California's congressional delegation. Stark grew up in Wisconsin, served in the Air Force, and then got an engineering degree at the Massachusetts Institute of Technology and a master's degree in business administration from the University of California at Berkeley. In 1963, he started a bank in Walnut Creek, which he later sold. An early opponent of the Vietnam War, he attracted attention, and accounts, all over the Bay Area when he put a giant peace symbol atop his bank headquarters and peace symbols on all of the checks. In 1972, he ran for Congress, spending his own money freely and beating 81-year-old incumbent George Miller in the primary 56%-22%. Stark held on in the George McGovern undertow that year to win the general election with 53% of the vote. By his third term, he had a safe seat and was on the powerful Ways and Means Committee, eventually becoming the top Democrat on the Health Subcommittee.

In the House, Stark is a vocal advocate for the liberal wing of his party. For many years, his major focus has been using the power of the federal government to make health care more affordable and more broadly available. He has been effective in expanding Medicare benefits and making sure younger workers have continued coverage under COBRA health insurance plans. His major achievement was the Catastrophic Health Care Act of 1988, which created a new benefit for Medicare recipients. But it was overwhelmingly repealed in 1989 after an outpouring of protests from the elderly, who didn't like its tax on high-income seniors and thought that the benefits were insufficiently generous.

After 1995, when Democrats lost the majority, Stark mostly criticized Republican policies, found few areas of agreement with the opposing party, and had testy personal dealings with his GOP counterparts. When President George W. Bush presented his proposal for prescription drug coverage for seniors, Stark countered with a plan that would guarantee affordable and comprehensive coverage for all seniors under Medicare. But other than voicing criticism from the sidelines, he had little role in the debate on the Medicare prescription drug bill in 2003. He continued to push for the importation of U.S. prescription drugs from other countries, where they are sold more cheaply. When AARP, the venerable advocacy group for the elderly, offered its own prescription drug plan, he attacked the group for seeking to "leverage a trusting membership of America's seniors to pass legislation that you know will do little more than line your own pocket."

When Democrats gained the majority in 2007, Stark played a central role in pushing the bill to expand the State Children's Health Insurance Program. After Congress failed to override Bush's veto of the legislation, Barack Obama in early 2009 enacted the SCHIP legislation with one of his first signatures as president. And Stark went to work on a bill to provide universal health insurance in the United States, which he predicted would become law during Obama's first term. He advocated a government-run public option to compete with private insurers, but quickly found himself at odds with conservative Blue Dog Democrats who opposed the idea. That led Stark to tell reporters, "They're just looking to raise money from insurance companies and promote a right-wing agenda that isn't very useful in this process." The bill ultimately passed the House in March 2010.

Stark has a distinct maverick streak. He was one of two House members to vote against repeal of the 3% telephone excise tax, and he opposed the Democrats' cap-and-trade industrial emissions regulation bill in 2009 on the grounds that it didn't go far enough to address global warming. His willingness to go his own way extended to cultural issues. He was one of three House members who opposed the resolution denouncing the 9th Circuit Court of Appeals decision that declared the Pledge of Allegiance unconstitutional. In 2003, he called the bombing of Iraq "an act of extreme terrorism." Stark co-sponsored a plan to reinstate the military draft as a way of criticizing what he viewed as the disproportionate burden the war placed on the poor and minorities. The House defeated the measure 402-2. During the debate on SCHIP, he harshly chided Republicans who opposed the bill, saying they preferred to spend government money "to blow up innocent people if we can get enough kids to grow old enough for you to send to Iraq, to get their heads blown off for the president's amusement." Angry Republicans filed a resolution to censure Stark, which 173 House members, including five freshman Democrats, supported; Stark apologized.

Known for his incendiary debating style, he concedes that his remarks are sometimes "unnecessary." At a town hall event in June 2010, he tauntingly asked a border security activist, "Who are you gonna kill today?" In 1995, he called mild-mannered Republican Rep. Nancy Johnson of Connecticut a "whore for the insurance industry." And after Rep. Scott McInnis, R-Colo., told him to "shut up" in 2003, Stark replied, "You think you are big enough to make me, you little wimp. Come over here and make me, I dare you, you little fruitcake." The *San Francisco Chronicle* then reported "rumblings that it might be time for the veteran congressman to retire." But Stark said he had no intention of leaving Congress. "I've got to keep running," he said. "I've got 2-year-old twins and I've got to get them through college. Our retirement plan is good, but it ain't that good."

In March 2007, he again attracted attention for describing his religious affiliation as "a Unitarian who does not believe in a supreme being." Atheist groups then claimed that Stark was the first member of Congress and the highest-ranking American politician to say he does not believe in God.

When ethics problems forced Ways and Means Chairman Charles Rangel of New York to step aside from the post in March 2010, Stark held the gavel for one day. But the job quickly went to Sander Levin of Michigan, largely because House Democrats openly said they were unwilling to put up with Stark's volatility. Democratic Congressional Campaign Committee Chairman Chris Van Hollen reportedly told Stark it would be in their party's best interests if he went along with the deal. Stark kept his chairmanship of Ways and Means' Health Subcommittee, and he is now the ranking Democrat on the panel.

FOURTEENTH DISTRICT

Anna Eshoo (D)

Elected 1992, 10th term; b. Dec. 13, 1942, New Britain, CT; home, Menlo Park; Canada Col., A.A. 1975; Catholic; divorced; 2 children.

Elected Office: San Mateo Cnty. Bd. of Supervisors, 1982–92, pres., 1986.

Professional Career: Chmn., San Mateo Cnty. Dem. Party, 1980; Chief of staff, CA assembly speaker, 1981.

DC Office: 205 CHOB, 20515, 202-225-8104; Fax: 202-225-8890; Web site: eshoo.house.gov.

State Offices: Palo Alto, 650-323-2984.

Committees: *Energy & Commerce:* Communications & Technology (RMM).

Group Ratings

	ACLU	ACU	ADA	CFG	AFS	FRC	LCV	ITIC	NTU	COC
2010	81	0	95	0	100	0	90	67	6	13
2009	–	0	100	4	100	–	100	–	3	33

National Journal Ratings

	2010 LIB	—	2010 CONS	2009 LIB	—	2009 CONS
Economic	90%	—	0%	75%	—	21%
Social	89%	—	7%	75%	—	20%
Foreign	78%	—	17%	91%	—	0%
Composite	89%	—	11%	83%	—	17%

Key Votes of the 111th Congress

1. Overturn Ledbetter	Y	5. Bar federal abortion funds		
2. Pass $820 billion stimulus	Y	6. Pass health care bill	N	9. Stop detainee transfers	N
3. Let guns in national parks	N	7. Regulate financial firms	Y	10. Legalize immigrants' kids	Y
4. Pass cap-and-trade	Y	8. Pass tax cuts for some	Y	11. Repeal don't ask, tell	Y
			Y	12. Limit campaign funds	Y

Election Results

2010 general	Anna Eshoo (D)	151,217	(69%)	($1,464,393)
	Dave Chapman (R)	60,917	(28%)	
	Paul Lazaga (Lib)	6,735	(3%)	
2010 primary	Anna Eshoo (D)	unopposed		

Prior Winning Percentages: 2008 (70%), 2006 (71%), 2004 (70%), 2002 (68%), 2000 (70%), 1998 (69%), 1996 (65%), 1994 (61%), 1992 (57%)

Population		Race/Ethnicity		Work	
Pop. 2010:	653,935	White:	50.9%	Private:	81.0%
Change since 2000:	Up 2.3%	Black:	2.3%	Government:	8.9%
Urban:	93.6%	Hispanic:	20.8%	Self-employed:	10.0%
Rural:	6.4%	Asian:	21.5%	Blue collar:	10.9%
Area size:	1,031 sq. mi.	Native Am.:	0.2%	White collar:	74.6%
		Hawaiian:	0.8%	Khaki collar:	0.0%
Age		Two+ races:	3.3%	Other:	14.5%
Median age:	37.6 yrs.				
More than 65 yrs:	12.5%	*Ancestry*		Median income:	$94,547
Less than 18 yrs:	23.0%	German	9.3%	Median Home Value:	$908,800
		English	7.9%		
Education		Irish	7.0%	**Military Veterans**	
H.S. grad:	90.4%			% of Pop:	6.6%
College grad:	56.4%				
Grad degree:	28.2%				

Silicon Valley; Sunnyvale

Silicon Valley is a place and a state of mind, an area that had no distinctive identity three decades ago but that people all over the world today recognize and imitate. In the 1980s and 1990s, Silicon Valley emerged as the center of America's computer industry, a place where creative minds developed products that large corporations never thought would sell. Its beginnings can be traced back to 1939, when William Hewlett and David Packard started their electronics

2008 Presidential Vote		
Barack Obama (D) 213,671	(73%)
John McCain (R) 72,707	(25%)

2004 Presidential Vote		
John Kerry (D) 188,864	(68%)
George Bush (R) 83,326	(30%)

Cook Partisan Voting Index: D+21

firm in a Palo Alto garage, or perhaps even to 1891, when Stanford University was founded on the estate of a California governor and senator. Not every aspect of the computer business is centered here. Microsoft, routinely disparaged in every Palo Alto espresso shop and bar, is in Redmond, Wash., and the downsized IBM is in Armonk, N.Y., But Silicon Valley is where most of the giants and much of the creativity of the high-tech business—as well as many dot-coms—have been based.

How did Silicon Valley come to be where it is? One factor is Stanford, the students it attracts and produces, and its tradition of encouraging faculty members to pursue profit-making activity. Another key component is venture capital, widely available from innovation-minded old San Francisco money. A third ingredient is the presence of smart young innovators, attracted to the Valley's lifestyle. Elite law and medical school graduates head to the prestigious, high-salary jobs of central cities. But techies are free to live in this pleasant, healthy environment. Sheltered by hills from coastal fogs and rains, Silicon Valley boasts a sunny climate with perceptible but gentle seasons, perfect for year-round outdoor sports. There may well be more jogging trails and bicycle paths here than anywhere else in the country. A Gallup study in February 2010 ranked the district the highest in the nation for overall health and happiness. These communities were rustic but never poor, rural but not small-minded, country-like but still easily accessible to urban luxuries. People here were ahead of the rest of the nation in fighting for the environment, in favoring natural over processed foods, and in incorporating regular exercise into busy lives.

And the area has been quick to adapt to change. In the 1980s, in the face of threats from Japanese firms, Silicon Valley shifted to microprocessors and personal computers. In the 1990s, when PCs became a low-profit commodity business, Silicon Valley shifted to the Internet. Yahoo and Hotmail reportedly were conceived at Buck's restaurant, the networking nexus in Woodside. When the Internet bubble burst in 2000, however, Silicon Valley fell on hard times. By one estimate, the area lost 220,000 jobs, nearly two-thirds of the 350,000 created during the dot-com boom. Stock prices plummeted and real estate prices did too, though they are still among the highest in the nation. The area actually lost population from 2000 to 2003. Billions of dollars in paper wealth disappeared, and technology exports from California fell. The question became whether Silicon Valley still had the ability to adapt. Before the 2008 recession, the Valley was in an upturn, with rising profits and a net gain of jobs, including increased research and investment in clean energy. But the recession took a toll in home values and start-up businesses. Unemployment in the San Jose-Sunnyvale-Santa Clara region remained above 11% in 2010. But there have been some bright spots. Telecommunications giant Nokia Corp. announced plans in May 2010 to move most of its Bay Area operations to Sunnyvale, the district's largest city.

The 14th Congressional District of California includes much of Silicon Valley, along with Menlo Park, Palo Alto, and most of Redwood City. Further south along El Camino Real are Mountain View and the several thousand employees of Google. Its median income of $98,000 is California's highest. There are some ultra wealthy enclaves here: Woodside, with its mansions dotting the hills, and Portola Valley and Los Altos Hills, with stark contemporary homes overlooking San Francisco Bay. Over the mountains, the district takes in the little town of Half Moon Bay, with its pumpkin farms rising over the ocean. Imposing redwoods grow within five miles of spectacular beaches. The 14th's political heritage is progressive, with a sort of environmentalist, dovish, culturally liberal but entrepreneurial Republicanism, typified by former Reps. Pete McCloskey, Ed Zschau, and Tom Campbell, each of whom quit the House to run unsuccessfully for the Senate between 1982 and 2000. But this kind of Republican is now virtually extinct, and Silicon Valley has become Democratic. In 2008, Barack Obama won this district 73%-25%.

Anna Eshoo (D)

The congresswoman from the 14th District is Anna Eshoo, a Democrat first elected in 1992. Born in Connecticut, Eshoo (*EH-shoo*) is the only member of Congress of Assyrian descent. Her father, a jeweler and an FDR Democrat, sparked her interest in politics at a young age by taking her to political rallies. The family moved to California. Eshoo married and had two children, and for a while was a stay-at-home mother working on a degree in English literature. (She later divorced.) Eshoo was active in civic groups, then chaired the San Mateo County Democratic Party and in 1982 was elected to the San Mateo Board of Supervisors. In 1988, she ran for the U.S. House against incumbent Republican Tom Campbell. The two spent a total of $2.5 million. Campbell won 52%-46%. In 1992, Campbell gave up his seat to run for the Senate, and Eshoo again ran. In the primary, she beat Assemblyman Ted Lempert, who had strong backing from environmentalists but lost ground by making unsubstantiated attacks against Eshoo. She prevailed 40%-36%. In the general election, Eshoo had a tough contest against Republican Tom Huening, the San Mateo supervisor who was backed by David Packard and other Silicon Valley business leaders. But Eshoo won by a convincing 57%-39%. She has not had a serious challenge for re-election.

In the House, Eshoo's voting record has been mostly liberal with more-moderate inclinations on issues such as taxes that affect high-income earners in her district. She joined Republicans and high-tech interests in votes on securities litigation and normalizing trade relations with China. She opposed a proposal to charge stock options against earnings, which would have hit hard in Silicon Valley. Eshoo also fought telecommunications legislation that would have allowed Internet carriers to use a two-tier pricing system, contending that it would disadvantage start-up firms.

As a senior member of the Energy and Commerce Committee, Eshoo has sponsored legislation to increase the number of electric cars as well as to require broadband installation on federal highway projects. She has also been active on health technology issues, and in 2009 prevailed over committee Chairman Henry Waxman in winning passage of a measure allowing makers of "biologic" drugs up to 12 years of protection from competition from the generic drug industry. In 2008, the House passed her bill to increase research and support services for arthritis victims, and she also sponsored a bill to reduce the volume of television commercials. Eshoo's other legislative work includes enactment of bills to increase Internet access for schools and to allow the use of electronic signatures in business transactions. Another bill required insurance companies to pay for reconstructive surgery for cancer patients.

Eshoo is a member of House Speaker Nancy Pelosi's inner circle. The two women have been close friends and confidants since they met at a Democratic event in the Bay Area in the early 1970s, and Eshoo officiated at the marriage ceremony for Pelosi's daughter Christine in 2008. Eshoo is a fierce and loyal advocate for Pelosi, and represented her interests as a member of the House Intelligence Committee until Republicans took majority control of the House in 2011. Eshoo sought greater transparency at spy agencies, leading a drive in 2010 to give the Government Accountability Office the power to investigate intelligence work.

FIFTEENTH DISTRICT

Mike Honda (D)

Elected 2000, 6th term; b. June 27, 1941, Walnut Creek; home, San Jose; San Jose St. U., B.S. 1969, B.A. 1970, M.A. 1973; Protestant; widowed; 2 children.

Elected Office: San Jose Unified Sch. Bd., 1981-90; Santa Clara Cnty. Bd. of Supervisors, 1990-96; CA Assembly, 1996-2000.

Professional Career: Peace Corps, 1965-67; Elem. schl. principal, 1978-90.

DC Office: 1713 LHOB, 20515, 202-225-2631; Fax: 202-225-2699; Web site: honda.house.gov.

State Offices: Campbell, 408-558-8085.

Committees: *Appropriations:* Commerce, Justice, Science & Related Agencies; Legislative Branch (RMM). *Budget.*

Group Ratings

	ACLU	ACU	ADA	CFG	AFS	FRC	LCV	ITIC	NTU	COC
2010	88	0	95	0	100	0	100	67	6	0
2009	–	0	100	6	100	–	100	–	3	33

National Journal Ratings

	2010 LIB	—	2010 CONS	2009 LIB	—	2009 CONS
Economic	90%	—	0%	88%	—	9%
Social	93%	—	0%	89%	—	0%
Foreign	78%	—	17%	78%	—	17%
Composite	91%	—	9%	88%	—	12%

Key Votes of the 111th Congress

1. Overturn Ledbetter	Y	5. Bar federal abortion funds	N	9. Stop detainee transfers	N
2. Pass $820 billion stimulus	Y	6. Pass health care bill	Y	10. Legalize immigrants' kids	Y
3. Let guns in national parks	N	7. Regulate financial firms	Y	11. Repeal don't ask, tell	Y
4. Pass cap-and-trade	Y	8. Pass tax cuts for some	Y	12. Limit campaign funds	Y

Election Results

2010 general	Mike Honda (D)...126,147	(68%)	($773,921)
	Scott Kirkland (R)..60,468	(32%)	($66,867)
2010 primary	Mike Honda (D).. unopposed		

Prior Winning Percentages: 2008 (72%), 2006 (72%), 2004 (72%), 2002 (66%), 2000 (54%)

Population		Race/Ethnicity		Work	
Pop. 2010:	677,605	White:	36.6%	Private:	82.9%
Change since 2000:	Up 6.0%	Black:	2.3%	Government:	10.3%
Urban:	99.3%	Hispanic:	20.7%	Self-employed:	6.6%
Rural:	0.7%	Asian:	36.4%	Blue collar:	13.8%
Area size:	289 sq. mi.	Native Am.:	0.2%	White collar:	72.8%
		Hawaiian:	0.4%	Khaki collar:	0.0%
Age		Two+ races:	3.2%	Other:	13.4%
Median age:	36.4 yrs.				
More than 65 yrs:	10.6%	*Ancestry*		Median income:	$87,558
Less than 18 yrs:	24.4%	German	7.4%	Median Home Value:	$701,800
		Irish	5.8%		
Education		English	5.3%	**Military Veterans**	
H.S. grad:	88.9%			% of Pop:	5.8%
College grad:	45.8%				
Grad degree:	18.8%				

Santa Clara County; Part San Jose

A few decades ago, the broad valley of Santa Clara County around San Jose was mostly orchards and vineyards. Sheltered by mountains from the chilly ocean fogs, with soil incredibly fertile once it was irrigated, this valley produced peaches, plums, prunes, apricots, and grapes and made San Jose the nation's biggest fruit-packing center. Today, subdivisions, shopping centers, and office buildings have replaced the orchards, and Santa Clara County has a population of 1.9 million. San Jose, with a growing downtown, an arena for its National Hockey League team, and 965,000 people, has become a major American city. In 2005, it replaced Detroit on the list of the nation's 10 largest cities. After price declines triggered by the recession, real estate prices in Santa Clara County went up between 2009 and 2010, with the average sales price for single-family homes climbing to more than $695,000—a 12.5% increase in a year's time.

2008 Presidential Vote		
Barack Obama (D)	174,571	(68%)
John McCain (R)	75,753	(30%)
2004 Presidential Vote		
John Kerry (D)	145,007	(63%)
George Bush (R)	82,742	(36%)
Cook Partisan Voting Index:	D+15	

The 15th Congressional District consists of the central slice of still-growing Santa Clara County, which is the sixth biggest in the state and has large numbers of Chinese, Vietnamese, and Mexican immigrants. Nearly half of the district's population is in San Jose, and the majority of those residents live in the city's affluent neighborhoods. West of San Jose, the district includes the cities of Santa Clara and Cupertino, where Steve Jobs started Apple in a garage in the 1970s and where the company is still headquartered. The district also includes the salt flats of San Jose, now the site of a Great America theme park; the heavily Asian city of Milpitas; and, far to the south, connected by a swath of mountains, Gilroy, the garlic capital of the world. Outside of Hawaii, this district has the highest percentage of Asians in the nation, 34%. In Cupertino, where Asians are nearly a majority, their influence has made them a political force. This area was once marginal political territory but is now heavily Democratic. John Kerry got 63% of the vote here in 2004, and Barack Obama got 68% in 2008.

Mike Honda (D)

The congressman from the 15th District is Mike Honda, a Democrat first elected in 2000. Honda's grandparents came to the United States from Japan's Kumamoto Prefecture, which served as the primary battleground for the Seinan Civil War in the 1870s (memorialized in the film *The Last Samurai*). Honda was born in Walnut Creek and spent 14 months during his childhood in a World War II internment camp in Colorado. His wife, Jeanne, who died of cancer in 2004, was born in Hiroshima and survived the atomic attack before immigrating to the United States several years later. Honda received his bachelor's and master's degrees from San Jose State University and served two years in the Peace Corps in El Salvador, where he became fluent in Spanish and gained a passion for teaching.

In 1971, San Jose Mayor Norman Mineta appointed him to the city Planning Commission. Honda worked as a science teacher, and then was a principal at two area elementary schools from 1978 to 1986. During that period, he also served on the San Jose Unified School Board. He was then elected to the Santa Clara County Board of Supervisors. In 1996, he was elected to the California Assembly, where he worked to reduce classroom sizes and increase teacher benefits.

In 2000, Republican Rep. Tom Campbell decided to run against Sen. Dianne Feinstein, D-Calif. At first Honda was reluctant to run for the House, but persuasive telephone calls from several leading House Democrats and, finally, from President Clinton, changed his mind. Honda won the primary over Bill Peacock, a venture capitalist, 67% to 24%. His Republican opponent was Assemblyman Jim Cunneen, a Campbell protégé who was strongly supported by national GOP leaders and many Silicon Valley capitalists. Cunneen had liberal positions on cultural issues, and he tried to depict the contest as a referendum on the old economy versus the new. Honda, despite his close ties to unions, supported normal trade relations with China, a position strongly backed by the high-tech industry. He won 54%-42%.

Honda has been among the most liberal members of the House. He has chaired the Congressional Asian Pacific American Caucus, which advocates for underrepresented groups on issues such as immigration. He denounced Arizona's decision to broaden police powers to detain suspected illegal immigrants in 2010 and said centrist congressional Democrats should not fear the political consequences of tackling comprehensive immigration reform. "Leadership is not only following what constituents want, but also leading them," he said. He helped to enact a cyber-security law that funds training and programs to protect computer data and networks. He was a major architect of the Nanotechnology Research and Development Act of 2003 to encourage the development of networked facilities, which involve the manipulation of matter at the atomic level. This has become a booming technology in the Bay Area.

On foreign policy, Honda opposed the 2009 troop surge in Afghanistan and chaired the Congressional Progressive Caucus' task force on that country. In 2007, with help from House Speaker Nancy Pelosi, he got a seat on the powerful Appropriations Committee. He has focused on trying to win full funding for education programs, many of which are financed at levels well below what is called for in the enabling legislation.

An important cause for Honda is eliciting apologies for past abuses from Japan, and he has publicized the cause of American POWs in World War II who were transported on "hell ships" to work as slave laborers in Japan. In 2007, Honda won House passage of a resolution calling on Tokyo to apologize for forcing as many as 200,000 women into sexual slavery during the war. His efforts have generated controversy in Japan, and *The New York Times* referred to Honda as "one of the most famous American congressmen in his ancestral land." In March 2010, he rebuked Sen. Lindsey Graham, R-S.C., after Graham said Pelosi had members "liquored up on sake" to make a "suicide run" on passing a health care bill.

Another of his passions is addressing low voter turnout in national elections, a situation he calls a "serious illness." As vice chairman of the Democratic National Committee during the 2008 campaign, Honda crisscrossed the nation to try to spark more participation by Asian-Americans in the election. Larry Gerston, a political scientist at San Jose State University, told the *San Jose Mercury News* that rather than take high-profile leadership roles, Honda prefers to put together coalitions for causes that might not otherwise get attention. "He really puts the K in 'Kumbaya,'" Gerston said.

SIXTEENTH DISTRICT

Zoe Lofgren (D)

Elected 1994, 9th term; b. Dec. 21, 1947, San Mateo; home, San Jose; Stanford U., B.A. 1970, U. of Santa Clara Law Schl., J.D. 1975; Protestant; married (John Collins); 2 children.

Elected Office: Santa Clara Bd. of Supervisors, 1980–94.

Professional Career: Staff Asst., U.S. Rep. Don Edwards, 1970–78; Practicing atty., 1978–80; Prof., U. of Santa Clara Law Schl., 1981–94.

DC Office: 1401 LHOB, 20515, 202-225-3072; Fax: 202-225-3336; Web site: lofgren.house.gov.

State Offices: San Jose, 408-271-8700.

Committees: *House Administration:* Oversight (RMM). *Judiciary:* Immigration Policy & Enforcement (RMM); Intellectual Property, Competition & the Internet. *Science & Technology:* Energy & Environment; Investigations & Oversight.

Group Ratings

	ACLU	ACU	ADA	CFG	AFS	FRC	LCV	ITIC	NTU	COC
2010	87	4	95	0	100	6	70	67	7	0
2009	–	0	95	4	100	–	100	–	5	40

National Journal Ratings

	2010 LIB	—	2010 CONS		2009 LIB	—	2009 CONS
Economic	90%	—	0%		79%	—	20%
Social	88%	—	11%		84%	—	11%
Foreign	92%	—	3%		76%	—	24%
Composite	93%	—	7%		81%	—	19%

Key Votes of the 111th Congress

1. Overturn Ledbetter	Y	5. Bar federal abortion funds	N	9. Stop detainee transfers	N
2. Pass $820 billion stimulus	Y	6. Pass health care bill	Y	10. Legalize immigrants' kids	Y
3. Let guns in national parks	N	7. Regulate financial firms	Y	11. Repeal don't ask, tell	Y
4. Pass cap-and-trade	Y	8. Pass tax cuts for some	Y	12. Limit campaign funds	Y

Election Results

2010 general	Zoe Lofgren (D) 105,841	(68%)	($782,100)
	Daniel Sahagun (R) 37,913	(24%)	(no FEC report)
	Edward Gonzalez (Lib) 12,304	(8%)	
2010 primary	Zoe Lofgren (D) .... unopposed		

Prior Winning Percentages: 2008 (71%), 2006 (73%), 2004 (71%), 2002 (67%), 2000 (72%), 1998 (73%), 1996 (66%), 1994 (65%)

Population		Race/Ethnicity		Work	
Pop. 2010:	676,880	White:	25.6%	Private:	82.4%
Change since 2000:	Up 5.9%	Black:	2.9%	Government:	10.8%
Urban:	98.7%	Hispanic:	39.9%	Self-employed:	6.6%
Rural:	1.3%	Asian:	28.3%	Blue collar:	21.7%
Area size:	232 sq. mi.	Native Am.:	0.3%	White collar:	60.5%
		Hawaiian:	0.4%	Khaki collar:	0.0%
Age		Two+ races:	2.5%	Other:	17.8%
Median age:	33.9 yrs.				
More than 65 yrs:	9.5%	*Ancestry*		Median income:	$75,909
Less than 18 yrs:	25.7%	German	5.6%	Median Home Value:	$621,000
		Irish	4.0%		
Education		English	3.8%	**Military Veterans**	
H.S. grad:	78.0%			% of Pop:	5.2%
College grad:	30.8%				
Grad degree:	11.0%				

San Jose

With more people than San Francisco, a tradition of high-tech innovation, and a professional sports team, San Jose finally has claims on national attention and respect. Yet San Jose does not register on the national consciousness as it should. At the southern end of the Bay, it remains in the shadow of the city on the Golden Gate. San Francisco is every tourist's idea of a city: geographically compact, with picturesque housing; old and new immigrant groups; an

2008 Presidential Vote		
Barack Obama (D) 154,324	(70%)
John McCain (R) 63,975	(29%)
2004 Presidential Vote		
John Kerry (D) 125,415	(63%)
George Bush (R) 70,190	(36%)
Cook Partisan Voting Index: D+16		

economy historically based on heavy industry and sea trade; a large city bureaucracy; and a monumental City Hall. San Jose is quite different. It got its start as a farm-market town, with canneries and fruit-packing operations for the produce from the surrounding fertile plains. Farm-labor icon Cesar Chavez settled with his family in the East San Jose barrio of Sal Si Puedes ("Get out if you can"). San Jose sits not on the Bay but on the Southern Pacific rail line above the marshes and salt evaporators. Its major transportation arteries are the freeways—U.S. 101, Interstates 280, 680, and 880, California 17—that encircle its revitalized downtown.

Starting in the 1950s, San Jose grew in every direction, with developers hopscotching across the farmland and at times putting up subdivisions faster than the few city employees could update the street maps. Economically, San Jose has been sustained by everything from its traditional agriculture to manufacturing to the high-tech businesses that are centered in Silicon Valley towns just to the west and are omnipresent here: an American city, 21st-century style. Santa Clara County had the highest median household income in the Bay Area, and it held up comparatively well when the recession hit in 2007. By mid-2010, technology jobs in Silicon Valley appeared to be returning more strongly than in the rest of the nation, as improved global demand for their products led Intel Corp. and Google to beef up recruiting efforts.

For many years, San Jose has been viewed as a focal point for immigration issues. It has Northern California's largest Mexican-American community, many of whose members are farmworkers. Now there is a diverse immigrant presence, with large numbers from Latin America and East and South Asia. Nearly half of all Santa Clara County residents speak a language other than English at home, mostly Spanish, Vietnamese, or Chinese, and one in three are foreign-born.

The 16th Congressional District of California consists of about two-thirds of San Jose, plus a nearby unincorporated area to the south. More than 90% of its residents live inside the jagged city limits of San Jose. It includes the old and new downtowns and the heavily Mexican-American areas to the east. It has the largest Hispanic share (39%) of any district in the Bay Area, and the largest concentration of Vietnamese in the country. Politically, it is solidly Democratic.

Zoe Lofgren (D)

The congresswoman from the 16th District is Zoe Lofgren, a Democrat first elected in 1994. Lofgren grew up in the Bay Area, where her father was a Teamsters truck driver and her mother worked for the Machinists Union. She graduated from Stanford University, and then moved to Washington to work for Democratic Rep. Don Edwards while he was a leader on the Judiciary Committee that voted to impeach President Richard Nixon. She stayed on for eight years as an aide to Edwards. She met her husband, a lawyer, one Election Night. Lofgren returned to California to get a law degree, and then specialized in immigration law. In 1980, she was elected to the Santa Clara County Board of Supervisors. When Edwards retired, Lofgren ran for his House seat. Her chief Democratic opponent, former San Jose Mayor Tom McEnery, was better known. But Lofgren raised twice as much money, with support from national women's organizations and women in the California delegation. She gained considerable recognition after she insisted on listing herself as a county supervisor/mother on the ballot. Election officials refused, and the national press covered the ensuing controversy. Lofgren won the primary 45%-42%, and easily won the general election.

Lofgren's voting record, while mostly liberal, includes bipartisan free-market positions responsive to local businesses. Working with Republican David Dreier, a fellow Californian, she won expanded allotments of visas for high-tech workers. She pushed for looser controls on encryption exports, securities litigation limitations, and relaxation of trade restraints on supercomputers, all big Silicon Valley causes. When the House split 210-210 on a proposal to restrict government access to library records, Lofgren was the only House member to vote "present." She said that the amendment went too far in preventing legitimate law enforcement searches.

When Democrats won the majority in 2006, Lofgren, a trusted lieutenant of House Speaker Nancy Pelosi, became chairwoman of the Judiciary Subcommittee on Immigration, Citizenship, Refugees, Border Security, and International Law. She hoped to see a major overhaul of immigration policy, but the politically charged issue bogged down. Hoping to shed some light on the problems facing immigrant farmworkers, the normally serious-minded Lofgren took a novel tack: She invited Comedy Central's faux-conservative comedian Stephen Colbert to testify at a September 2010 hearing on the topic. His quip-filled appearance attracted the reams of publicity she had hoped for, but it also drew bipartisan criticism from observers and lawmakers who said it made a mockery of Congress. Lofgren usually is a reliable liberal vote in the House Democratic Caucus, although that does not prevent her from pursuing bipartisan compromises. She was part of a group in July 2010 that introduced legislation aimed at curbing restrictive technology standards affecting the Internet.

In January 2009, Pelosi picked Lofgren to chair the House Committee on Standards of Official Conduct, informally known as the Ethics Committee. She took over as a politically sensitive inquiry was under way involving House Ways and Means Chairman Charles Rangel, D-N.Y., and questions were being raised about other senior Democrats' connections to lobbyists. Lofgren's skills as a former staffer and law professor were tested by the politically combustible cases. She revealed in testimony before the House Administration Committee in early 2010 that at least 36 lawmakers—around 8% of the House—had been subjected to scrutiny the previous year. Many were associated with the PMA Group lobbying firm, a group accused of exchanging campaign contributions for earmarks. She announced in February 2009 that she would return $7,000 in contributions from the firm. Her panel subsequently found that no House members colluded with the group.

Of the lawmakers under investigation, none proved more difficult for Lofgren than Rangel. She hoped to avoid a drawn-out and embarrassing ethics trial, but the defiant and crafty political veteran was unwilling to bargain. An ethics subcommittee determined in July 2010 that Rangel violated ethics rules on a variety of allegations related to his personal finances, a judgment that some Democrats worried could cloud their already-shaky chances for holding the majority. The case dragged on for months, with the ethics panel's ranking Republican, Jo Bonner of Alabama, complaining that Lofgren had refused to set the trial before the November election. Finally, just after the election, Rangel was afforded a trial, but walked out in protest after complaining that he hadn't been granted enough time to hire a new attorney. Lofgren and the rest of the panel refused to back down, and a few days later voted 9-1 to censure him—a decision Lofgren called "quite wrenching."

As if that wasn't enough, Lofgren had to wrestle with another touchy ethics case involving Maxine Waters, D-Calif., who was investigated for her efforts to get federal bailout money for a bank. Like Rangel, she vehemently denied any wrongdoing. Lofgren led a subcommittee formed in August 2010 to try Waters.

In 2003, Lofgren tried to get a foothold in leadership by running for vice chairman of the Democratic Caucus. But Pelosi, who is also from the Bay Area, had already been elected minority leader, and the Congressional Black Caucus pressed to have one of its members in the leadership. Lofgren got 53 votes to 95 for James Clyburn, an African-American from South Carolina, who won the post. Lofgren has had no trouble winning re-election every two years.

SEVENTEENTH DISTRICT

Sam Farr (D)

Elected June 1993, 9th full term; b. July 4, 1941, San Francisco; home, Carmel; Willamette U., B.S. 1963; Episcopalian; married (Shary); 1 child.

Elected Office: Monterey Cnty. Bd. of Supervisors, 1975–80, chmn., 1979; CA Assembly, 1980–93.

Professional Career: Peace Corps, Colombia, 1963–65; staff, CA Assembly, 1965–75.

DC Office: 1126 LHOB, 20515, 202-225-2861; Fax: 202-225-6791; Web site: farr.house.gov.

State Offices: Salinas, 831-424-2229; Santa Cruz, 831-429-1976.

Committees: *Appropriations:* Agriculture, Rural Development, FDA & Related Agencies (RMM); Military Construction, Veterans Affairs & Related Agencies.

Group Ratings

	ACLU	ACU	ADA	CFG	AFS	FRC	LCV	ITIC	NTU	COC
2010	94	0	90	9	100	0	100	67	7	13
2009	–	0	100	0	100	–	100	–	3	33

National Journal Ratings

	2010 LIB	—	2010 CONS	2009 LIB	—	2009 CONS
Economic	73%	—	25%	87%	—	12%
Social	93%	—	0%	84%	—	11%
Foreign	97%	—	0%	78%	—	17%
Composite	90%	—	10%	85%	—	15%

Key Votes of the 111th Congress

1. Overturn Ledbetter	Y	5. Bar federal abortion funds	N	9. Stop detainee transfers	N
2. Pass $820 billion stimulus	Y	6. Pass health care bill	Y	10. Legalize immigrants' kids	Y
3. Let guns in national parks	N	7. Regulate financial firms	Y	11. Repeal don't ask, tell	Y
4. Pass cap-and-trade	Y	8. Pass tax cuts for some	Y	12. Limit campaign funds	Y

Election Results

2010 general	Sam Farr (D)	118,734	(67%)	($704,177)
	Jeff Taylor (R)	53,176	(30%)	($183,520)
2010 primary	Sam Farr (D)	52,689	(89%)	
	Arthur Dunn (D)	6,653	(11%)	

Prior Winning Percentages: 2008 (74%), 2006 (76%), 2004 (67%), 2002 (68%), 2000 (69%), 1998 (65%), 1996 (59%), 1994 (52%), 1993 (52%)

Population		Race/Ethnicity		Work	
Pop. 2010:	664,240	White:	39.2%	Private:	72.5%
Change since 2000:	Up 3.9%	Black:	2.0%	Government:	18.0%
Urban:	90.0%	Hispanic:	50.4%	Self-employed:	9.2%
Rural:	10.0%	Asian:	5.1%	Blue collar:	18.7%
Area size:	5,386 sq. mi.	Native Am.:	0.3%	White collar:	52.8%
		Hawaiian:	0.3%	Khaki collar:	1.1%
Age		Two+ races:	2.3%	Other:	27.4%
Median age:	33.0 yrs.				
More than 65 yrs:	10.4%	*Ancestry*		Median income:	$59,031
Less than 18 yrs:	26.1%	German	7.9%	Median Home Value:	$586,800
		Irish	7.2%		
Education		English	6.3%	**Military Veterans**	
H.S. grad:	73.6%			% of Pop:	7.3%
College grad:	26.7%				
Grad degree:	10.2%				

Monterey and Santa Cruz Counties

The California coast around Monterey Bay is for many a working definition of paradise. This kernel of California, site of the first state capital, still makes a fine living off the land and sea, as it has for 150 years. The locale for *The Grapes of Wrath* and many other John Steinbeck novels, the fields around Salinas provide much of the nation's lettuce and cauliflower. The area is often referred to as "the salad bowl of the world."

2008 Presidential Vote
Barack Obama (D) 171,180   (72%)
John McCain (R) 61,163   (26%)

2004 Presidential Vote
John Kerry (D) 149,029   (66%)
George Bush (R) 75,005   (33%)

Cook Partisan Voting Index: D+19

Nearby, the farmlands around Castroville supply the country with its artichokes, and the vast greenhouses around Watsonville produce a goodly portion of its roses. The fishing fleet and the 18 now-closed canneries of Monterey (the last sardines were canned in 1964) have generated a new industry. Once described by Steinbeck as "a poem, a stink, a grating noise, a quality of light, a tone, a habit, nostalgia, a dream," Cannery Row now is refurbished with upscale shops and hotels. The magnificent Monterey Bay Aquarium is one of California's top tourist destinations, and the National Marine Sanctuary holds more than 400 shipwrecks and ditched aircraft.

The Monterey Bay area calls itself the world's language learning capital, with the Defense Language Institute, Language Line Services, and Cal State's Monterey Bay Center for Intensive Language and Culture. Perhaps the main attraction of the Monterey peninsula is the lush 17-Mile Drive along the Pacific Coast Highway, with Pebble Beach's golf courses, the Del Monte Lodge, and Carmel, whose restrictive laws—no house numbers, no door-to-door mail delivery, no live entertainment, no stoplights, no cutting trees without City Council permission—reflect an effort to maintain the atmosphere of nearly a century ago, when it was an artists' colony. Not immune to California's propensity for destructive wildfires, the Big Sur area, heavily dependent on tourism, suffered major fire damage in 2008, including the loss of trees on more than 220,000 acres of national park land. To prevent such damage from recurring, 19 local agencies and groups subsequently drafted a wildfire protection plan.

The 17th Congressional District of California includes the entire coast of Monterey Bay and follows the stunning Big Sur coastline south along the steep slopes almost to William Randolph Hearst's castle, San Simeon, taking in some of the most beautiful scenery in America. To the north along Monterey Bay, it runs past Watsonville to Santa Cruz. The district extends inland, into sunny valleys sheltered from ocean mists, and covers some of the nation's richest farmland. Most of the farmworkers are Latino, mainly Mexican, and in the 1990s, the Hispanic population rose from 31% to 43%, the largest increase in any Northern California district; by 2010, the share had grown to 50%.

The gap between rich and poor in Monterey County is wide. It has thousands of homes valued at more than $1 million but also usually ranks high in the share of households below the poverty line. Forty years ago, this was a solidly Republican area, dominated politically by the landowners in Salinas and the townspeople who sympathize with them, plus retirees in Santa Cruz and on the Monterey peninsula. But an influx of young people, attracted less by the economy than by the atmosphere, moved the coast to the left. Monterey and Santa Cruz counties have become steadily more Democratic than the nation, and each now exceeds the national Democratic presidential vote by more than 10 percentage points. A district that once consistently voted for Ronald Reagan gave Democratic presidential nominees John Kerry 66% of the vote in 2004 and Barack Obama 72% in 2008.

Sam Farr (D)

The congressman from the 17th District is Sam Farr, a Democrat first elected in June 1993. A fifth-generation Californian, he grew up in Monterey County, where his father was a state senator for many years. Farr signed up for the Peace Corps after college, learned Spanish at the Monterey Institute of International Studies, and served two years in Colombia. He was a California Assembly staff member for a decade, became a Monterey County supervisor in 1975, and was elected to the Assembly in 1980. There, he wrote one of the nation's strictest oil-spill liability laws. In 1993, when Democratic Rep. Leon Panetta resigned from the House to become director of the Office of Management and Budget, Farr ran for his seat. He entered the race as the overwhelming favorite, and won 26% of the vote in the all-party primary to defeat two other Democrats. But in the runoff, which came after President Clinton's budget and tax increase had arrived in Congress, he had trouble against Republican Bill McCampbell, whom Panetta had defeated 72%-24% seven months earlier. Farr won, but by just 52%-43%.

In the House, Farr has a solidly liberal voting record. He is a close ally of Democratic Leader Nancy Pelosi and a longtime advocate of normalizing relations with Cuba; he sent President Obama a letter in 2009 signed by 46 House members outlining a 10-step process for doing so. On the Appropriations Committee, Farr is a senior member on subcommittees dealing with two major local concerns: farming and military bases. He helped to negotiate the final agreement that conveyed the former Fort Ord to civilian hands, and he took the lead in transferring the lands to local governments and in refusing to permit the Navy to establish a practice bombing range near Big Sur. In 2006, Farr helped to write the law revising rules for offshore fisheries, and in 2009, the House passed his bill to encourage a research and recovery program for endangered sea otters.

After the local spinach crop was affected by an E. coli outbreak in 2006, Farr pushed for $25 million to aid producers, a provision that generated controversy after it was added to an emergency war spending bill. It was stripped from the measure that passed in April 2007. "It's easy to make fun of spinach," Farr said in defense of the subsidy. "But if we had eaten more of it, we would be a stronger society." He also introduced a bill in 2009 calling for more fruits and vegetables in school breakfasts and lunches.

Nationally, Farr gets attention for some of his relatively extreme liberal positions. In 2007, he co-sponsored a resolution calling for the impeachment of Vice President Dick Cheney, and in 2009 introduced a bill to permit medical marijuana smokers convicted under federal laws to offer evidence that their use of the drug followed state laws. Farr has been re-elected easily.

EIGHTEENTH DISTRICT

Dennis Cardoza (D)

Elected 2002, 5th term; b. March 31, 1959, Merced; home, Atwater; U. of MD, B.A. 1982, CA St. U. Stanislaus; Catholic; married (Kathleen McLoughlin); 3 children.

Elected Office: Atwater City Cncl., 1984-86; Merced City Cncl., 1994-95; CA Assembly, 1996-2002.

Professional Career: Agribusiness owner.

DC Office: 2437 RHOB, 20515, 202-225-6131; Fax: 202-225-0819; Web site: cardoza.house.gov.

State Offices: Merced, 209-383-4455; Modesto, 209-527-1914; Stockton, 209-946-0361.

Committees: *Agriculture:* General Farm Commodities & Risk Management; Livestock, Dairy & Poultry (RMM). *Foreign Affairs:* Asia & the Pacific; Middle East & South Asia.

Group Ratings

	ACLU	ACU	ADA	CFG	AFS	FRC	LCV	ITIC	NTU	COC
2010	67	0	75	19	100	12	100	100	10	25
2009	–	8	90	11	100	–	86	–	7	43

National Journal Ratings

	2010 LIB	—	2010 CONS	2009 LIB	—	2009 CONS
Economic	57%	—	42%	59%	—	40%
Social	59%	—	40%	54%	—	46%
Foreign	66%	—	29%	52%	—	47%
Composite	62%	—	38%	55%	—	45%

Key Votes of the 111th Congress

1. Overturn Ledbetter	Y	5. Bar federal abortion funds	Y	9. Stop detainee transfers	Y
2. Pass $820 billion stimulus	Y	6. Pass health care bill	Y	10. Legalize immigrants' kids	Y
3. Let guns in national parks	Y	7. Regulate financial firms	Y	11. Repeal don't ask, tell	*
4. Pass cap-and-trade	Y	8. Pass tax cuts for some	Y	12. Limit campaign funds	Y

Election Results

2010 general	Dennis Cardoza (D)..72,853	(58%)	($1,180,308)
	Michael Berryhill (R)...51,716	(42%)	($930,355)
2010 primary	Dennis Cardoza (D)..................................... unopposed		

Prior Winning Percentages: 2008 (100%), 2006 (65%), 2004 (68%), 2002 (51%)

Population		Race/Ethnicity		Work	
Pop. 2010:	723,607	White:	29.5%	Private:	80.1%
Change since 2000:	Up 13.2%	Black:	5.5%	Government:	13.6%
Urban:	91.3%	Hispanic:	52.7%	Self-employed:	6.1%
Rural:	8.7%	Asian:	8.8%	Blue collar:	29.6%
Area size:	3,107 sq. mi.	Native Am.:	0.5%	White collar:	44.1%
		Hawaiian:	0.5%	Khaki collar:	0.1%
Age		Two+ races:	2.4%	Other:	26.2%
Median age:	29.8 yrs.				
More than 65 yrs:	9.2%	*Ancestry*		Median income:	$42,444
Less than 18 yrs:	31.9%	German	6.1%	Median Home Value:	$236,300
		Irish	5.4%		
Education		English	3.7%	**Military Veterans**	
H.S. grad:	65.7%			% of Pop:	6.9%
College grad:	10.7%				
Grad degree:	3.1%				

Central Valley; Stockton, Modesto

The Central Valley of California is a miraculous landscape, an outdoor factory stretching as far as the eye can see. Nature created the vast flatlands, rimmed by mountains rising in the distant haze. In the 20th century, people disciplined the land with a remorseless mile-square grid of roads, the California Aqueduct, and dozens of arrow-straight canals. Pipes fitted with valves and gauges pump water, fertilizer, and pesticides to the fields in measured quantities with

2008 Presidential Vote		
Barack Obama (D) 104,299	(59%)
John McCain (R) 68,629	(39%)
2004 Presidential Vote		
George Bush (R) 80,157	(50%)
John Kerry (D) 79,764	(49%)
Cook Partisan Voting Index: D+4		

industrial precision. The crops grow in carefully spaced rows. The rich soil and the irrigated water were too precious to waste on decorative fountains or flower gardens. Throughout history, farming here has been a business, not a way of life. In the 19th century, the U.S. government did not give the land to 160-acre homesteaders but rather sold it to large enterprises in thousands-of-acres parcels. Among the most famous local capitalists were the Gallo brothers, Ernest and Julio, who started a winery in Modesto in 1933 with virtually no money. It now covers more than 10,000 acres of vineyards and produces 80 million cases of wine each year.

In recent years, the Central Valley was one of California's surprise boom areas, not just for crops but also for people. Middle-income employees in the San Francisco Bay area drive east at the end of the day on Interstate 580, past surreal windmills whirling on the bare hills of the Altamont Pass, to modestly priced homes in Modesto, the town immortalized (when it was much smaller) in the 1973 film *American Graffiti*. Warehouses and factories have sprung up on land that for all its farming value is cheaper than industrial land in the Bay Area. With increases in water prices, some croplands have been given over to pasture. But there are costs. Traffic is a problem, air-pollution levels on bad days can be among the worst in the nation, and the pace of life has become more hectic. In 2009 and 2010, the impact of the national recession on the Central Valley in some ways was more severe than elsewhere in the country. Stockton, pop. 243,000, suffered a higher rate of housing foreclosures than any other city in the United States. By early 2011, the city had taken first place on *Forbes* magazine's list of "most miserable cities" to live. Rural areas were not immune to hardship. A severe drought severely reduced agricultural water supplies.

The 18th Congressional District of California includes a large chunk of the Central Valley from Stockton, south to Modesto, through Merced County, to the fringes of Fresno. The political tradition here had been Democratic: In the 1960s, Democrats in Washington and Democratic Gov. Pat Brown built the irrigation canals and authorized the water subsidies; Democrats owned the McClatchy newspapers, the predominant Central Valley chain; and Democrats staffed the Bank of America, long the dominant financial force here. The district produced two U.S. House Democratic whips, John McFall in the late 1970s and Tony Coelho in the late 1980s. But the Central Valley, with the highest proportion of families and children in California, also is more culturally conservative than other parts of the state. In the 1980s and 1990s, it trended Republican, and even the Latinos here were less solidly Democratic than those in Los Angeles. The 18th District is still modestly Democratic, because of very careful redistricting and because of a recent influx of liberals from the Bay Area. In 2004, Republican President George W. Bush carried the district only narrowly, 50%-49%, and in 2008, Democrat Barack Obama won it 59%-39%. One cause of the voter shift was the increase in the Hispanic population from 42% in 2000 to 53% in 2010, while total population grew 13%.

Dennis Cardoza (D)

The congressman from the 18th District is Dennis Cardoza, a Democrat first elected in 2002. Cardoza grew up in Atwater, the son of farmers who raised sweet potatoes and dairy cows. Like many people in the Central Valley, he is descended from Portuguese immigrants from the Azores Islands (as are Democrat Jim Costa of the adjacent 20th District and Republican Devin Nunes of the 21st). Interested in politics as a youth, Cardoza attended the University of Maryland just outside of Washington, D.C., and interned on Capitol Hill. In the mid-1980s, he was an aide to Democrat Gary Condit, who was then a California assemblyman. He worked on Condit's 1989 special-election campaign and served on his Washington staff. In 1996, Cardoza was elected to the Assembly. He very likely would have remained close to Condit had it not been for the case of Chandra Levy. She was a Modesto resident who was working as an intern in the executive branch when she and Condit began an affair. She vanished in Washington in April 2001 and was later found murdered in the city's Rock Creek Park. During the investigation of her disappearance, the affair came to light, and the married Condit was hounded by the media, though it turned out he had nothing to do with Levy's tragic death. A sexual predator was convicted of the crime in 2010. But the revelations about his personal life destroyed Condit's career.

National and local Democrats urged Cardoza to enter the contest because they feared that Condit, who was running for re-election despite his tattered reputation, would lose the seat to the Republicans. When he decided to run, Cardoza received immediate endorsements from many members of the House delegation. He beat Condit in the primary 53%-39%. In the general election, Republicans nominated state Sen. Dick Monteith, whose seat included three-quarters of the congressional district. Monteith claimed that Cardoza was too liberal for an agriculture-oriented constituency, but Cardoza cited his pro-business reputation in the legislature. In October, Condit's children released a letter that harshly criticized Cardoza and urged a vote against him. But Cardoza won 51%-43%. Stockton made the difference. Cardoza led 67%-27% in San Joaquin County, which gave him a 10,000-vote margin that wiped out Monteith's 2,000-vote lead elsewhere.

In the House, Cardoza established his independence from the liberal Democratic leadership and racked up a centrist voting record, though he became a more reliable party vote after Democrats regained control of the House in 2007. He sided with the majority on major initiatives such as the 2009 economic stimulus bill and the cap-and-trade legislation to reduce greenhouse gas emissions. He joined the moderate Democrats' Blue Dog Coalition and emphasized the need for fiscal discipline, opposing a massive $410 billion omnibus spending bill for fiscal 2009. He was among the last holdouts on the health care overhaul, but backed it after President Obama included money for a new medical school at UC Merced.

Cardoza naturally gravitated to the issues of agriculture and resources. He bucked environmentalists and worked with Republicans on farmer-friendly revisions to the Endangered Species Act, including changes in designating critical habitats. He advocated solar power and other sources of renewable energy. The father of two adopted children, Cardoza also worked on legislation encouraging placement of more children in foster care.

When Democrats assumed the majority on Capitol Hill in 2007, Cardoza became chairman of the Agriculture Subcommittee on Horticulture and Organic Agriculture, a title that gave him a seat at the table in drafting the 2007-08 farm bill. He helped secure more than $2 billion in new federal subsidies for "specialty crops," which include the fruits and vegetables grown in his district. With other Blue Dogs, he pushed for some constraints on overall spending and supported a provision that stops federal payments to farmers with annual incomes of $1 million or more. Cardoza also implored the Obama administration in 2010 to resolve the issue of Mexican truckers operating in the United States. After Congress terminated funding in 2009 for a pilot program allowing trucks from that country into the U.S. to deliver loads beyond the commercial trade zone, Mexico imposed steep tariffs on U.S. exports in retaliation.

Cardoza has had occasional differences with Democratic Leader Nancy Pelosi. He publicly supported Maryland Rep. Steny Hoyer in his pitched battle against Pennsylvania Rep. John Murtha for majority leader in 2007 (Pelosi backed Murtha). Still, Pelosi gave Cardoza a seat on the leadership-run Rules Committee, and he later patched things up with her by co-chairing the Democratic Congressional Campaign Committee's program to help endangered incumbents. After House Democrats lost their majority in 2010, though, he voted for Rep. Jim Costa, D-Calif. for Democratic leader as a signal of his concern over the direction of the party. Cardoza has won re-election handily.

NINETEENTH DISTRICT

Jeff Denham (R)

Elected 2010, 1st full term; b. July 29, 1967, Hawthorne; home, Atwater; CA Polytechnic St. U., San Luis Obispo, B.A. 1991.; Presbyterian; Married (Sonia); 2 children.

Military Career: Air Force, 1984-89; Air Force Reserve, 1989-2000 (Persian Gulf).

Elected Office: CA Senate, 2002-10.

Professional Career: Project mgr., Fresh Express, 1992-98; owner, Denham Plastics.

DC Office: 1605 LHOB, 20515, 202-225-4540; Fax: 202-225-3402; Web site: denham.house.gov.

State Offices: Fresno, 559-449-2490; Modesto, 209-579-5458.

Committees: *Natural Resources:* Indian & Alaska Native Affairs; Water & Power. *Transportation & Infrastructure:* Economic Development, Public Buildings & Emergency Management (Chmn); Railroads, Pipelines & Hazardous Materials; Water Resources & Environment. *Veterans' Affairs:* Economic Opportunity; Health.

Election Results

2010 general	Jeff Denham (R)	128,394	(65%)	($1,256,745)
	Loraine Goodwin (D)	69,912	(35%)	($44,492)
2010 primary	Jeff Denham (R)	26,594	(36%)	
	Jim Patterson (R)	22,355	(31%)	
	Richard Pombo (R)	15,196	(21%)	
	Larry Westerlund (R)	9,126	(12%)	

Population		**Race/Ethnicity**		**Work**	
Pop. 2010:	757,337	White:	49.8%	Private:	72.9%
Change since 2000:	Up 18.5%	Black:	3.7%	Government:	17.9%
Urban:	80.6%	Hispanic:	37.3%	Self-employed:	9.0%
Rural:	19.4%	Asian:	5.5%	Blue collar:	21.3%
Area size:	6,780 sq. mi.	Native Am.:	0.8%	White collar:	57.7%
		Hawaiian:	0.2%	Khaki collar:	0.1%
Age		Two+ races:	2.4%	Other:	21.0%
Median age:	34.5 yrs.				
More than 65 yrs:	11.5%	*Ancestry*		Median income:	$52,592
Less than 18 yrs:	27.5%	German	10.1%	Median Home Value:	$299,400
		Irish	7.6%		
Education		English	6.7%	**Military Veterans**	
H.S. grad:	80.0%			% of Pop:	8.3%
College grad:	21.3%				
Grad degree:	7.3%				

Central Valley; Fresno, Modesto

The city of Fresno started as a farm-marketing center—one high-income neighborhood is called Fig Garden because that's what it used to be—and as a tourist rest stop on the way to Yosemite National Park. But it has long since grown out north, east, and west from its old downtown, and its economy has diversified. Like all of the Central Valley, Fresno has always been ethnically diverse, with a telephone book that reads like the United Nations directory. It is home to the second-largest Armenian community in the United States. (Only Los Angeles surpasses it.) Its already large Latino population has more than doubled in the past 20 years, and Fresno County was 50% Hispanic in 2010. Asians, including Chinese, Filipinos, Vietnamese, and Hmong, were 10% of the county's population. The city has grown 12% since 2000, despite some serious problems: high unemployment, violent teenage gangs, and air pollution that made the Sierra Nevada invisible on many days. Fresno has had some success addressing those problems, but the poverty rate remains high. Among the nation's largest cities, it ranked third in the percent-

2008 Presidential Vote		
John McCain (R)	141,013	(52%)
Barack Obama (D)	124,533	(46%)

2004 Presidential Vote		
George Bush (R)	151,603	(61%)
John Kerry (D)	93,918	(38%)

Cook Partisan Voting Index: R+9

age of children in poverty in 2008. Tighter border patrolling has encouraged illegal Mexican immigrants to remain in Fresno County year-round, even during the off-season for farm work. Migrants have been crowding into trailers and makeshift homes on formerly vacant farmland. The growing Hispanic presence has increased the popularity of the Spanish *charreadas,* which are part-rodeo and part-fiesta and are not advertised to the general public. Historically, Fresno was a Democratic town, the prime Democratic bastion in the Central Valley south of Sacramento. Since the 1990s, it has moved toward the Republicans. It voted for George W. Bush twice and for Republican gubernatorial candidates in 1998 and 2002. But in 2008, Barack Obama narrowly won the county, 50%-48%.

The 19th Congressional District of California includes all of Tuolumne and Mariposa counties. In the Central Valley, it takes in parts of Fresno, Stanislaus and Madera counties. It has nearly half of Fresno, the relatively affluent north side of the city, and several farm towns in Madera County. This area is one of the two heavily populated parts of the district. The other, nearly 100 miles away, is the northern and eastern half of Stanislaus County, including the northern edge of Modesto and the towns of Turlock, Riverbank, and Oakdale. These two areas are linked by mountainous areas that include the Sierra foothills, the peaks of the Sierra Nevadas, and Yosemite National Park. It is generally safe Republican territory.

Jeff Denham (R)

The new congressman from the 19th District is Jeff Denham, a Republican elected in 2010 to succeed the retiring George Radanovich, also a Republican. Denham was born near Los Angeles and lived in Indiana for five years, but he spent most of his childhood in the Northern California town of Pescadero. His parents were just 17 and 18 years old when he was born. He is the oldest of three children; his mother worked at car dealerships and his father was at various times a farmer, a construction worker, and a meat-cutter. His parents divorced when he was in high school, and Denham spent much of his time at his grandparents' home. His grandfather served in World War II and the Korean War before joining the Los Angeles Police Department. At age 17, Denham enlisted in the Air Force. "The influence of my grandparents is why I joined up," he says.

Denham was on active duty for three-and-a-half years and was in the Air Force Reserve for more than a dozen. He was a crew chief, preparing and maintaining aircraft such as F-4 fighter jets and C-5 transport planes. After transitioning to the Reserve, Denham attended community college and then transferred to Cal Poly (San Luis Obispo), where he was active in the college Republicans and received a bachelor's degree in political science. During the Persian Gulf War, he was called to active duty and worked on an air base in Saudi Arabia. He also maintained aircrafts involved in the peacekeeping mission in Somalia in 1992. Back home after his service, Denham became the manager of a packaged salad company, and in 1998, he founded his own business, Denham Plastics, an agricultural container supply firm. In 2004, he bought a ranch in Merced County, where he grows almonds.

Denham first ran for public office in 2000, losing a bid for the California Assembly. Two years later, he ran for the state Senate and eked out a victory in a district where Democrats held a 12-point registration advantage. In the Senate, Denham sponsored a bill that would have required convicted pedophiles to wear electronic tracking devices for their entire lives. In 2007, during one of California's numerous budget crises, Democrats needed Republican support to approve a budget. Because of the makeup of Denham's district, Democratic leaders hoped that he would agree to a compromise that included spending cuts and tax increases to balance the state's books. Denham refused, and as a result, Democratic Senate Leader Don Perata organized a recall campaign against him. The petition drive acquired sufficient signatures to qualify for the ballot in June 2008, but a resounding 75% of district voters chose not to recall Denham.

In December 2009, Radanovich announced he would retire at the end of the term to care for his ailing wife. He called Denham shortly before Christmas and asked him to run. Denham did not have a clear path to Congress, however. The rare open congressional seat interested former Rep. Richard Pombo and former Fresno Mayor Jim Patterson. Pombo had been ousted from the neighboring 11th District by Democrat Jerry McNerney in 2006. His primary opponents criticized Denham for flying on a corporate jet with Republican strategist Karl Rove, a possible violation of federal election law, and for his ties to an Indian tribe that sponsored ads attacking his opponents. But with strong fundraising and the support of the popular Radanovich, Denham won the primary with 36%, ahead of Patterson, who finished with 31%. Pombo placed third with 21%. In the general election, Denham easily defeated Democrat Loraine Goodwin, a physician, 65% to 35%.

TWENTIETH DISTRICT

Jim Costa (D)

Elected 2004, 4th term; b. April 13, 1952, Fresno; home, Fresno; CA State U. Fresno, B.A. 1974; Catholic; single.

Elected Office: CA Assembly, 1978-94; CA Senate, 1994-2002.

Professional Career: Consultant, 2002-04.

DC Office: 1314 LHOB, 20515, 202-225-3341; Fax: 202-225-9308; Web site: costa.house.gov.

State Offices: Bakersfield, 661-869-1620; Fresno, 559-495-1620.

Committees: *Agriculture:* Conservation, Energy & Forestry; Rural Development, Research, Biotechnology & Foreign Agriculture (RMM). *Natural Resources:* Energy & Mineral Resources; Water & Power.

Group Ratings

	ACLU	ACU	ADA	CFG	AFS	FRC	LCV	ITIC	NTU	COC
2010	69	8	70	17	100	12	80	100	16	50
2009	–	12	85	19	100	–	71	–	11	67

National Journal Ratings

	2010 LIB	—	2010 CONS	2009 LIB	—	2009 CONS
Economic	50%	—	50%	55%	—	45%
Social	49%	—	49%	52%	—	48%
Foreign	56%	—	38%	53%	—	44%
Composite	53%	—	47%	54%	—	46%

Key Votes of the 111th Congress

1. Overturn Ledbetter	Y	5. Bar federal abortion funds	Y	9. Stop detainee transfers	Y
2. Pass $820 billion stimulus	Y	6. Pass health care bill	Y	10. Legalize immigrants' kids	Y
3. Let guns in national parks	Y	7. Regulate financial firms	Y	11. Repeal don't ask, tell	Y
4. Pass cap-and-trade	N	8. Pass tax cuts for some	Y	12. Limit campaign funds	Y

Election Results

2010 general	Jim Costa (D)	46,247	(52%)	($1,845,156)
	Andy Vidak (R)	43,197	(48%)	($900,648)
2010 primary	Jim Costa (D)	19,599	(79%)	
	Steve Haze (D)	5,122	(21%)	

Prior Winning Percentages: 2008 (74%), 2006 (100%), 2004 (53%)

Population		Race/Ethnicity		Work	
Pop. 2010:	744,350	White:	16.6%	Private:	75.3%
Change since 2000:	Up 16.5%	Black:	6.0%	Government:	18.5%
Urban:	91.2%	Hispanic:	70.4%	Self-employed:	6.1%
Rural:	8.8%	Asian:	5.1%	Blue collar:	26.9%
Area size:	4,982 sq. mi.	Native Am.:	0.6%	White collar:	34.4%
		Hawaiian:	0.1%	Khaki collar:	0.8%
Age		Two+ races:	1.2%	Other:	37.9%
Median age:	27.5 yrs.				
More than 65 yrs:	7.1%	*Ancestry*		Median income:	$34,834
Less than 18 yrs:	33.8%	German	3.6%	Median Home Value:	$197,900
		Irish	3.1%		
Education		English	2.3%	**Military Veterans**	
H.S. grad:	55.6%			% of Pop:	5.7%
College grad:	7.3%				
Grad degree:	2.0%				

Central Valley; Fresno, Bakersfield

By car, California's Central Valley is a monotonous landscape: mile after mile of farmland with mile-square grid roads, intersected by railroads and canals, with an occasional cluster town. The land is hilly and gets more water near the Sierra Nevada Mountains, and this is where the larger cities are. On the other side are the Westlands, where the land is flatter and the water scarcer. Its 600,000 acres are the nation's largest irrigation district. Here the land was always devel-

2008 Presidential Vote		
Barack Obama (D)	77,158	(60%)
John McCain (R)	50,146	(39%)
2004 Presidential Vote		
John Kerry (D)	58,534	(51%)
George Bush (R)	56,045	(49%)
Cook Partisan Voting Index:	D+5	

oped and sold in big plots; today it has some of the world's largest farming operations. The land produces abundantly: alfalfa, cantaloupes, cotton, grapes, lima beans, olives, peaches, plums, raisins, sugar beets, tomatoes, walnuts, wheat. The landowners are a hardy and politically independent lot, but they have been happy to receive government help over the years, with money for crop price supports (in the case of cotton), agricultural research, irrigation systems, and, most important, subsidized and plentiful water. Landowners have fought hard against liberals' efforts at change, from Democratic Gov. Jerry Brown's encouragement of Cesar Chavez's United Farm Workers in the 1970s to former House Natural Resources Committee Chairman George Miller's 1992 law to draw off more water to the Sacramento delta and charge higher prices for it in the valley. They were also stymied when conservatives controlled Congress, and it deadlocked on expansion of guest-worker programs pushed by valley farmers. Landowners also worry that Los Angeles users might outbid them for scarce water. In the Westlands, several hundred thousand acres have gone fallow.

The 20th District of California includes most of the Westlands of the Central Valley, from Bakersfield to a point northwest of Fresno. Its irregular boundaries were drawn to maximize the Hispanic population and Democratic percentage, so the 20th includes the old downtown neighborhoods of Bakersfield and Fresno but not their more affluent neighborhoods. Unemployment here has been among the nation's highest, hitting 18% in Fresno County in early 2009 and still above 15% in late 2010. Many of those lost jobs are not expected to return until mid-2012. The district includes heavily Latino towns such as Delano, Chavez's old headquarters. Just 36% of Fresno's population is included within the 20th, and just 18% of Bakersfield's. The district's Hispanic population is 70%, about double that of other Central Valley districts. In 60% of homes, the main language is not English. This is the most Democratic valley seat between Sacramento and Los Angeles, although in 2004 George W. Bush won 49% here and in 2006 Republican Gov. Arnold Schwarzenegger won 54%. As in most of California, Democratic presidential candidate Barack Obama won easily here in 2008, 60%-39%.

Jim Costa (D)

The congressman from the 20th District is Jim Costa, a Democrat elected in 2004. Born in Fresno, he was raised on his family's dairy farm. He is the grandson of Portuguese immigrants who settled in the San Joaquin Valley near the turn of the 20th century. In 1978, Costa was elected to the state Assembly, where he was known as a moderate Democrat. In 2002, after he was forced to retire that year because of term limits, Costa founded a consulting firm. Two years later, when Democratic Rep. Cal Dooley retired after 14 years, Costa entered the race and started off with solid name recognition—his former state Senate district covered the entire congressional district. But in the March primary, he faced a bruising challenge from Lisa Quigley, Dooley's chief of staff. Quigley grew up in the Central Valley, but she hadn't lived in the district in nearly two decades. Costa, a third-generation farmer and a Fresno native, questioned her residency and her agricultural credentials. Quigley was endorsed by Dooley and national abortion rights groups, and painted Costa as a special-interest lobbyist. In the campaign's final days, Quigley ran ads mentioning Costa's 1986 arrest for soliciting a prostitute and a 1994 incident in which police found drug paraphernalia in his home. Costa shrugged off the attacks and won the primary by an unexpectedly large 73%-27%.

In the general election, Costa began as a clear favorite in this Democratic-leaning district. But the Republican nominee, state Sen. Roy Ashburn, ran a formidable campaign. He criticized Costa for supporting tax policies that he said hurt low-income families. The National Republican Congressional Committee ran $1.5 million in ads saying, "Jim Costa—he's gonna cost ya." But Costa's lengthy legislative record didn't readily lend itself to the "liberal" label. In a relatively low turnout event, Costa won 53%-47%.

In the House, Costa got seats on the Agriculture and the Natural Resources committees, both important to the valley. His voting record is one of the most conservative among California House Democrats and placed him near the political center of the House as a whole, though he was more of a loyalist in the years his party controlled the House. He and his close friend and fellow Blue Dog Democrat Dennis Cardoza were among the last undecided votes on the health care overhaul before agreeing to back it. Republicans charged that Cardoza and Costa were given extra public water allocations for their region, though both denied there was any connection. When another California Democrat, George Miller of the Bay Area, said in April 2010 that tougher restrictions were needed on water diversions, Costa was indignant. "If he wants a fight with the Latino community and Valley farmworkers whose futures depend on water allocations, we'll give him a fight," he said.

As chairman of Natural Resources' Energy and Mineral Resources Subcommittee, Costa supported lifting the ban on oil drilling 50 to 100 miles off the nation's coast, but he sought to maintain the federal ban on drilling within 25 miles of shore. He also pushed to require mining companies to pay royalties on mines near national parks in 2007. On the Agriculture Committee, he worked with Rep. Adam Putnam, R-Fla., and with industry groups in 2009 on a bipartisan approach to toughen food safety regulation, including the creation of a quality assurance program that would hold food imports to the same safety standards as domestic products. The House-passed food safety bill included many of the stricter fruit and vegetable standards that he and Putnam had written.

On other issues, Costa co-sponsored a bill that would require states to establish independent commissions like California's to handle redistricting after the 2010 census. The highly partisan process used by many state legislatures after the 2000 census resulted in heavily gerrymandered districts across the country. On the Foreign Affairs Committee, Costa was part of the chorus of lawmakers condemning Iran for human rights violations and pursuing nuclear weapons.

After his initial tough contests in 2004, Costa did not face a significant re-election challenge until 2010. Republican rancher Andy Vidak did his best to blame Costa for the area's weak economy, running billboards depicting him as the pitchfork-holding "American Gothic" farmer with Speaker Nancy Pelosi at his side. Vidak surged in the polls, and in the closing weeks the race became a toss-up. But Costa put in a month of heavy retail politicking and handshaking, and got last-minute help from the Democratic Congressional Campaign Committee. The Obama administration also chipped in: It announced a few days before the election that California would get an additional $715 million for high-speed rail, contingent on money being spent quickly on a San Joaquin Valley segment.

In a race that dragged on for three weeks past Election Day, Costa won 52%-48%. While Vidak got nearly 70% in strongly Republican Kings County, Costa topped 60% in both Fresno and Kern counties. But Republicans sense Costa is now vulnerable. Republican Kevin McCarthy of Bakersfield, the incoming majority whip, told *The Fresno Bee* that Costa's district "will be our No. 1 target in California."

TWENTY-FIRST DISTRICT

Devin Nunes (R)

Elected 2002, 5th term; b. Oct. 1, 1973, Tulare; home, Tulare; Col. of the Sequoias, A.D. 1993, CA Poly. U., B.S. 1995, M.A. 1996.

Elected Office: Col. of the Sequoias Governing Bd., 1996-2002.

Professional Career: State Dir., USDA Rural Dev., 2001

DC Office: 1013 LHOB, 20515, 202-225-2523; Fax: 202-225-3404; Web site: nunes.house.gov.

State Offices: Clovis, 559-323-5235; Visalia, 559-733-3861.

Committees: *Permanent Select Committee on Intelligence:* Oversight; Technical & Tactical Intelligence. *Ways & Means:* Health; Trade.

Group Ratings

	ACLU	ACU	ADA	CFG	AFS	FRC	LCV	ITIC	NTU	COC
2010	13	100	0	97	0	100	0	33	90	100
2009	–	96	0	87	0	–	7	–	89	73

National Journal Ratings

	2010 LIB	—	2010 CONS	2009 LIB	—	2009 CONS
Economic	0%	—	97%	8%	—	92%
Social	18%	—	82%	16%	—	83%
Foreign	0%	—	88%	0%	—	75%
Composite	9%	—	92%	12%	—	88%

Key Votes of the 111th Congress

1. Overturn Ledbetter	N	5. Bar federal abortion funds	Y	9. Stop detainee transfers	Y
2. Pass $820 billion stimulus	N	6. Pass health care bill	N	10. Legalize immigrants' kids	N
3. Let guns in national parks	Y	7. Regulate financial firms	N	11. Repeal don't ask, tell	N
4. Pass cap-and-trade	N	8. Pass tax cuts for some	N	12. Limit campaign funds	N

Election Results

2010 general	Devin Nunes (R)... unopposed	($1,223,376)
2010 primary	Devin Nunes (R)... unopposed	

Prior Winning Percentages: 2008 (68%), 2006 (67%), 2004 (73%), 2002 (70%)

Population		Race/Ethnicity		Work	
Pop. 2010:	784,176	White:	37.3%	Private:	73.2%
Change since 2000:	Up 22.7%	Black:	2.0%	Government:	19.6%
Urban:	79.9%	Hispanic:	51.2%	Self-employed:	7.1%
Rural:	20.1%	Asian:	6.7%	Blue collar:	21.9%
Area size:	8,090 sq. mi.	Native Am.:	0.8%	White collar:	51.3%
		Hawaiian:	0.1%	Khaki collar:	0.2%
Age		Two+ races:	1.7%	Other:	26.7%
Median age:	30.4 yrs.				
More than 65 yrs:	10.0%	*Ancestry*		Median income:	$47,632
Less than 18 yrs:	31.1%	German	7.8%	Median Home Value:	$244,400
		Irish	5.8%		
Education		English	5.4%	**Military Veterans**	
H.S. grad:	73.3%			% of Pop:	7.3%
College grad:	17.4%				
Grad degree:	5.5%				

Central Valley; Fresno, Visalia

In California's Central Valley, between the flat Westlands and the Sierras, is Fresno, a city that is both agricultural and industrial, middle American and ethnically diverse. Although it began as a farm-marketing center, the city has long since grown out to the north, east, and west from its downtown, and its economy has diversified. It is a creation of the Industrial Age and the Central Pacific Railroad. Historian Kevin Starr described the San Joaquin Valley, at the heart of the Central Valley, as "the most productive unnatural environment on Earth." Fresno's city fathers bred the local wine grape, developed the raisin industry, and introduced the Smyrna fig. These are among the area's 300-plus crops, which include cotton, lima beans, nectarines, almonds, tomatoes, cantaloupes, plums, peaches, and alfalfa. Dairy, however, is now the biggest commodity. Fresno County produces more farm products in dollar value than any other county in the United States; neighboring Tulare County is close behind. Central Valley agriculture is industrial in its thoroughness and in its ownership by large corporations. The vineyards outside Fresno radiate in mechanical precision, with vines just 10 feet apart and exposed to the relentless summer sun: nothing romantic or quaint about it. Until recently, times were good. The weak dollar boosted farm exports, large citrus groves benefited from losses in hurricane-plagued Florida, and nuts found new export markets. The recession, plus a serious continuing drought, hit the area hard. The city of Fresno was forced to cut its workforce by almost 16% in 2010.

2008 Presidential Vote		
John McCain (R)	125,347	(56%)
Barack Obama (D)	93,578	(42%)

2004 Presidential Vote		
George Bush (R)	133,004	(66%)
John Kerry (D)	68,501	(34%)

Cook Partisan Voting Index: R+13

The 21st District, the most productive farm district in the nation, covers most of Fresno County east of Fresno and all of Tulare County to the south; 42% of the population is in Fresno County and 58% is in Tulare. Here and there amid the farm fields are small cities, and connecting many of these places is state Route 99, the old Farm-to-Market Corridor. Past Kings Canyon and Sequoia National Parks loom the giant peaks of the Sierra Nevada Mountains, including Mount Whitney, at 14,494 feet, the highest point in the lower 48 states. This part of the Central Valley grew over 15% in past decade, and is about 51% Hispanic. In 2004, George W. Bush got 66% of the vote, his second-highest percentage in a California district. In 2008, Republican John McCain defeated Democrat Barack Obama here, 56%-42%, McCain's second-highest percentage in the state, after the neighboring 22nd District.

Devin Nunes (R)

The congressman from the 21st District is Devin Nunes, a Republican first elected in 2002. Nunes (*NEW-nez*) is the descendant of Portuguese immigrants from the Azores. His grandfather established the 600-acre-plus dairy farm that his parents ran when he was growing up in Tulare County. He graduated from California Polytechnic State University (San Luis Obispo) with degrees in agriculture, worked on the family farm, and married a local elementary schoolteacher whose family roots are also in Portugal. In 1998, at age 25, Nunes ran for the U.S. House in the 20th District and finished second in the primary, losing 52%-48%. In 2000, he was the Tulare County campaign chairman for former Republican Rep. Bill Thomas, who chaired the powerful Ways and Means Committee before he retired. In 2001, with Thomas' help, Nunes was appointed California director of rural development for the U.S. Agriculture Department. When California's redistricting plan was unveiled in September 2001, the 21st District was left without an incumbent, and Nunes moved quickly. He was supported by Thomas, whose deep-pocketed campaign contributors in the pharmaceutical and insurance industries agreed to help Nunes. At home, Nunes won the endorsement of the California Farm Bureau, the state's largest farm organization and a powerful voice in Central Valley politics.

But Nunes had serious primary competition from Jim Patterson, Fresno's conservative former mayor, who was backed by the anti-tax group Club for Growth, and California Assembly member Mike Briggs. There were few differences among them on policy. All three promised to seek new water sources for farmers about to lose the San Joaquin River as a primary source after environmentalists successfully lobbied to restore the river, which for years had been dammed for irrigation. The candidates also called for tax cuts, fewer federal regulations, and expanded guest-worker programs for immigrants. Nunes won with 37% of the vote to 33% for Patterson and 26% for Briggs. Against a Democratic opponent in November, Nunes won easily, 70%-26%.

Nunes has a mostly conservative voting record, although it tends to be more centrist on social issues. Arriving in the House, he developed a good working relationship with then-House Speaker

Dennis Hastert and through the years continued to keep a hand in leadership. In 2009, he co-led an effort with Mike Rogers, R-Mich., to investigate initiatives by governors and states that could also work on the federal level. Nunes can deliver a cutting sound bite, once comparing government spending with the actions of "a broke gambler who desperately keeps doubling down in a vain effort to break even."

Legislatively, Nunes dove into the district's most pressing issue: the use of water from the San Joaquin. He got a feasibility study for a new water reservoir near Temperance Flat, which would help farmers if the river was restored to its original flow. But he clashed with Rep. George Radanovich, a Republican from the adjacent, downstream district, over Radanovich's push to increase water flow over the Friant Dam so that salmon could be returned to the parched lower reaches of the San Joaquin. Nunes contended that the move would seriously deplete the area's water supply for irrigation. During California's severe drought in 2009, Nunes lashed out at the Obama administration for allying with "radical environmentalists" in preventing farmers from getting sufficient water. At an April 2009 Natural Resources subcommittee hearing, he introduced a fishbowl of smelt for the record as a symbolic protest of how groups have used potential harm to fish to limit water deliveries for farming.

Nunes' major committee assignment is Ways and Means. In 2008, he enacted a bill guaranteeing GI benefits to soldiers who leave the military after a sibling dies in combat, a move inspired by Jason Hubbard, a surviving brother who returned home from Iraq after his two brothers died there and was denied benefits usually given to honorably discharged soldiers. At the outset of the health care debate in 2009, Nunes joined Paul Ryan, R-Wisc., in introducing a bill providing tax credits for people to buy insurance and ending the tax exemption for businesses providing workers with the benefit. Their strategy frustrated Ways and Means' ranking Republican, Michigan's Dave Camp, who preferred to take more time to craft a plan. Nunes has been easily re-elected every two years.

TWENTY-SECOND DISTRICT

Kevin McCarthy (R)

Elected 2006, 3rd term; b. Jan. 26, 1965, Bakersfield; home, Bakersfield; Attended Bakersfield Col., 1984-85, CA St. U., B.S. 1989, M.B.A. 1994; Baptist; married (Judy); 2 children.

Elected Office: Kern Comm. Col. Board, 2000-02, CA Assembly, 2002-06, min.ldr., 2003-06.

Professional Career: Owner, Kevin O's Deli, 1986-87, Mesa Marin Batting Range, 1991-92; Dist. dir., U.S. Rep. Bill Thomas, 1987-2002.

DC Office: 326 CHOB, 20515, 202-225-2915; Fax: 202-225-2908; Web site: kevinmccarthy.house.gov.

State Offices: Atascadero, 805-461-1034; Bakersfield, 661-327-3611.

Committees: *Financial Services:* Capital Markets and Government Sponsored Enterprises; Financial Institutions & Consumer Credit.

Group Ratings

	ACLU	ACU	ADA	CFG	AFS	FRC	LCV	ITIC	NTU	COC
2010	13	95	0	96	0	100	0	33	86	100
2009	–	100	0	90	11	–	0	–	87	80

National Journal Ratings

	2010 LIB	—	2010 CONS		2009 LIB	—	2009 CONS
Economic	14%	—	86%		4%	—	95%
Social	16%	—	82%		13%	—	84%
Foreign	28%	—	72%		0%	—	75%
Composite	20%	—	80%		11%	—	90%

Key Votes of the 111th Congress

1. Overturn Ledbetter	N	5. Bar federal abortion funds	Y	9. Stop detainee transfers	Y
2. Pass $820 billion stimulus	N	6. Pass health care bill	N	10. Legalize immigrants' kids	N
3. Let guns in national parks	Y	7. Regulate financial firms	N	11. Repeal don't ask, tell	N
4. Pass cap-and-trade	N	8. Pass tax cuts for some	N	12. Limit campaign funds	N

Election Results

2010 general	Kevin McCarthy (R)..173,490	(99%)	($2,091,010)
2010 primary	Kevin McCarthy (R).....................................unopposed		

Prior Winning Percentages: 2008 (100%), 2006 (71%)

Population		Race/Ethnicity		Work	
Pop. 2010:	797,084	White:	54.3%	Private:	67.9%
Change since 2000:	Up 24.7%	Black:	6.2%	Government:	23.5%
Urban:	82.5%	Hispanic:	32.0%	Self-employed:	8.5%
Rural:	17.5%	Asian:	3.9%	Blue collar:	22.2%
Area size:	10,454 sq. mi.	Native Am.:	0.7%	White collar:	56.3%
		Hawaiian:	0.2%	Khaki collar:	0.7%
Age		Two+ races:	2.5%	Other:	20.8%
Median age:	34.2 yrs.				
More than 65 yrs:	10.6%	*Ancestry*		Median income:	$55,088
Less than 18 yrs:	27.4%	German	10.7%	Median Home Value:	$272,600
		Irish	8.5%		
Education		English	7.5%	**Military Veterans**	
H.S. grad:	81.2%			% of Pop:	10.7%
College grad:	19.9%				
Grad degree:	6.5%				

Kern and San Luis Obispo Counties

Bakersfield, near the southern end of California's Central Valley, has been the focus of great migrations four times—in the gold rush of 1885, in the boomlet that followed the discovery of oil in 1899, in the 1930s flight of Dust Bowl refugees from Oklahoma, Kansas and Texas and in a flood of newcomers in the last two decades, when Bakersfield and Kern County grew more rapidly than California's biggest metro areas. The migration that made the deepest imprint was in the

2008 Presidential Vote
John McCain (R) 172,792   (60%)
Barack Obama (D) 110,910   (38%)

2004 Presidential Vote
George Bush (R) 180,584   (68%)
John Kerry (D) 82,356   (31%)

Cook Partisan Voting Index: R+16

1930s. The Okies drove over a thousand miles of brown landscape, then through the Tehachapi Pass, and found this vast green valley, with its irrigated fields and its eucalyptus-shaded towns—the richest farming country in the world. The story is told vividly in novelist John Steinbeck's *The Grapes of Wrath* and in Dan Morgan's *Rising in the West*, which explains how the Okies' descendants prospered in California. As a result, the area around Bakersfield is the one (partly) Southern-accented part of California, the home of country singers Buck Owens and Merle Haggard and a thriving country-music scene. People here are culturally conservative with little empathy for Los Angeles-style cultural liberalism. More recently, Latinos have been coming here in large numbers, to work on farms and in off-seasons, to take advantage of California's safety net. The result is that the Central Valley, including Bakersfield, has had both high population growth and high unemployment for a decade—with the latter climbing even higher when the housing market collapsed.

The 22nd Congressional District of California, the southernmost district in the Central Valley, includes most of Bakersfield and Kern County, plus most of the land area of San Luis Obispo County and a slice of northern Los Angeles County, including half the desert town of Lancaster and the tiny desert town of Gorman. At the eastern end, in the Mojave Desert, is Edwards Air Force Base, where Chuck Yeager flew the X-1 and where the Space Shuttle has frequently landed. The 22nd includes oil fields and high-income subdivisions. The rich farmland produces most of the olives grown in the United States and more than 70% of the carrots (this is where the baby carrot was born). Politically, Kern County was Democratic territory, but by the late 1960s, it had become solidly Republican in national politics. The inland portion of San Luis Obispo County has always been Republican. This has been the most heavily Republican California congressional district in the last two presidential races.

Kevin McCarthy (R)

The congressman from the 22nd District is Kevin McCarthy, a Republican who won the seat in 2006. He is an up-and-coming leader in the Republican Party who rocketed to the No. 3 spot in the

House GOP leadership by making himself indispensable to the party's campaign planning operations.

McCarthy grew up in Bakersfield, where his blue-collar family has lived for generations and often voted Democratic. He moved in the other direction. At 19, he won $5,000 in the state lottery and invested it in a deli, which helped pay for business school at Cal State, Bakersfield. In college, he was elected chairman of the California Young Republicans and later headed the national Young Republicans organization. After he sold the deli, he got a job in the local office of U.S. Rep. Bill Thomas, who was then on his way to chairing the powerful House Ways and Means Committee. McCarthy eventually became Thomas' district director and protégé. In 2000, McCarthy was elected to the Kern County Community College Board and in 2002, he, like Thomas before him, was elected to the Assembly. He was immediately chosen Republican leader (which is a little easier than it looks—because of California's term limits, no assemblyman at the beginning of a session has served more than two terms). McCarthy worked with Republican Gov. Arnold Schwarzenegger on the budget, workers' compensation issues and redistricting procedures.

When Thomas announced his retirement in March 2006, just four days before the filing deadline, McCarthy was the obvious candidate to succeed him. He faced only token opposition in the Republican primary. In November, he won 71%-29%. Looking ahead, he raised more than $1 million and traveled the country campaigning for other Republican congressional candidates. That attracted the attention of party leaders. After the election, he was chosen the freshman representative on the Republican Steering Committee, a leadership-run group that makes all-important committee assignments. He also chaired the Platform Committee at the 2008 Republican National Convention, winning praise for soliciting a wide spectrum of views and uniting conservatives and moderates. In 2009, he landed a leadership position when Minority Whip Eric Cantor appointed him chief deputy whip—an unusual amount of responsibility bestowed on a House member serving only his second term.

McCarthy also took on some legislative initiatives. He introduced a bill to streamline the voting process for military personnel stationed overseas, and he tried to amend a Democratic bill with a provision to prohibit unions from political spending of dues money derived from government-administered payroll deductions. On the Financial Services Committee, he sponsored an amendment to deny the Treasury Department the power to block access to U.S. markets for companies whose home countries are deemed to undermine the stability of financial markets.

His main focus has been on his first love, politics. His Republican colleague from the Central Valley, Devin Nunes, has said that McCarthy "lives and breathes politics." McCarthy was the head of recruiting for the National Republican Congressional Committee in what turned out to be a highly successful election for the GOP in 2010. He traveled widely looking for candidates, identifying people capable of taking on Democrats used to winning against weak opposition. Ultimately, Republicans had candidates in 430 of the 435 congressional districts, the highest number ever. With Cantor and Wisconsin Rep. Paul Ryan, he was named head of the party's Young Guns program to spotlight otherwise obscure Republican challengers.

House Minority Leader John Boehner also assigned McCarthy and Rep. Peter Roskam of Illinois to draw up a document similar to the House Republicans' 1994 Contract with America. They solicited ideas from the public on the Internet, and ultimately compiled the "Pledge to America" policy manifesto. Kept deliberately vague to deter Democratic attacks, it did not make as big an impression as the Contract, but it did tend to commit incoming and veteran Republicans to a single set of policies, such as extending the Bush-era tax cuts and repealing President Obama's health care overhaul.

McCarthy was handsomely rewarded for his impressive efforts in improving the party's electoral fortunes. When Cantor ascended to majority leader after Republicans won control of the House, McCarthy was chosen by his peers to replace Cantor as whip, the third-ranking position in the House after speaker and majority leader. Rep. Pete Sessions of Texas, another influential Republican, wanted the post, but was persuaded by Boehner to stay on for a second term as chairman of the NRCC, clearing the way for McCarthy to run unchallenged for whip. In his home district, McCarthy was re-elected without Democratic opposition in 2008 and 2010.

TWENTY-THIRD DISTRICT

Lois Capps (D)

Elected March 1998, 7th full term; b. Jan. 10, 1938, Ladysmith, WI; home, Santa Barbara; Pacific Lutheran U., B.S. 1959, Yale U., M.A. 1964, U. of CA at Santa Barbara, M.A. 1990; Lutheran; widowed; 3 children (1 deceased).

Professional Career: Staff nurse, Visiting Nurses Assn., 1963–64; Head nurse, Yale New Haven Hospital, 1960–63; Instructor, Santa Barbara City Col., 1983–95; Nurse, Santa Barbara Schl. Dist., 1979–96.

DC Office: 2231 RHOB, 20515, 202-225-3601; Fax: 202-225-5632; Web site: capps.house.gov.

State Offices: San Luis Obispo, 805-546-8348; Santa Barbara, 805-730-1710; Ventura County, 805-985-6807.

Committees: *Energy & Commerce:* Energy & Power; Environment & the Economy; Health.

Group Ratings

	ACLU	ACU	ADA	CFG	AFS	FRC	LCV	ITIC	NTU	COC
2010	93	0	95	0	100	0	100	100	5	25
2009	–	0	100	4	100	–	100	–	2	29

National Journal Ratings

	2010 LIB — 2010 CONS		2009 LIB — 2009 CONS	
Economic	84%	— 15%	91%	— 0%
Social	93%	— 0%	84%	— 11%
Foreign	83%	— 16%	91%	— 0%
Composite	88%	— 12%	93%	— 8%

Key Votes of the 111th Congress

1. Overturn Ledbetter	Y	5. Bar federal abortion funds	N	9. Stop detainee transfers	N
2. Pass $820 billion stimulus	Y	6. Pass health care bill	Y	10. Legalize immigrants' kids	Y
3. Let guns in national parks	N	7. Regulate financial firms	Y	11. Repeal don't ask, tell	Y
4. Pass cap-and-trade	Y	8. Pass tax cuts for some	Y	12. Limit campaign funds	Y

Election Results

2010 general	Lois Capps (D)	111,768	(58%)	($955,565)
	Tom Watson (R)	72,744	(38%)	($611,864)
	John Hager (I)	5,625	(3%)	
2010 primary	Lois Capps (D)	unopposed		

Prior Winning Percentages: 2008 (68%), 2006 (65%), 2004 (63%), 2002 (59%), 2000 (53%), 1998 (55%), 1998 (53%)

Population		Race/Ethnicity		Work	
Pop. 2010:	695,404	White:	41.1%	Private:	74.3%
Change since 2000:	Up 8.8%	Black:	1.6%	Government:	17.0%
Urban:	98.0%	Hispanic:	49.5%	Self-employed:	8.4%
Rural:	2.0%	Asian:	5.3%	Blue collar:	18.8%
Area size:	2,479 sq. mi.	Native Am.:	0.3%	White collar:	55.6%
		Hawaiian:	0.2%	Khaki collar:	0.4%
Age		Two+ races:	1.9%	Other:	25.2%
Median age:	32.4 yrs.				
More than 65 yrs:	12.3%	*Ancestry*		Median income:	$55,670
Less than 18 yrs:	23.7%	German	9.0%	Median Home Value:	$558,900
		Irish	6.9%		
Education		English	6.5%	**Military Veterans**	
H.S. grad:	76.8%			% of Pop:	7.9%
College grad:	27.8%				
Grad degree:	11.2%				

South Coast; Santa Barbara

In a state where stunning coastal landscapes and charming small towns are a dime a dozen, Santa Barbara stands out as someplace special. It is a collection of red tile roofs and leafy live oaks, sheltered by towering mountains just above the sea. The impression is a bit misleading, for Santa Barbara has its problems. Most of its quaint white stucco buildings were put up not as part of 18th-century mission settlement, but after a 1925 earthquake leveled much of the

2008 Presidential Vote		
Barack Obama (D) 172,348	(66%)
John McCain (R) 85,261	(32%)
2004 Presidential Vote		
John Kerry (D) 147,361	(58%)
George Bush (R) 101,817	(40%)
Cook Partisan Voting Index: D+12		

town. Like Disneyland, Santa Barbara is not an authentic antique, but rather a bigger, more attractive, cleaner version of a historical artifact, one that is maintained not by a company, but by an architectural review board. This has long been one of the nation's richest retirement communities, one determined to preserve its pristine environment and serenity. Both features came under threat spectacularly in 1969, when an underwater oil well ruptured, coating the beach with oil. Pictures of the oil slick in the channel, and of volunteers trying to wash oil off grounded birds, helped to launch the 1970s environmental movement. Almost all of the wells are closed now (though some old 19th-century wells still send globs of oil to the beach at nearby Summerland). But the oil spill left a long-lasting residue in Santa Barbara's politics. This was once a mostly Republican community, uninterested in redistribution of wealth, but always concerned about the environment (it has the nation's largest desalination plant) and having moderate-to-liberal impulses on cultural issues. Like most of coastal California, it has moved decisively to the left in the past decade.

The 23rd Congressional District of California is a thin strip of Pacific coastline, two to 12 miles wide, that runs from the industrial ports of Oxnard and Port Hueneme southeast of Santa Barbara to the north end of San Luis Obispo County on the Big Sur coast, just north of William Randolph Hearst's San Simeon. Nearly half of the population lives in upscale Santa Barbara County. But the largest city is Oxnard, in Ventura County, which, with a large number of immigrants, is anything but upscale. Overall, the district is 50% Hispanic. Much of the Santa Barbara coastline is occupied by Vandenberg Air Force Base, which launches unmanned government and commercial satellites into polar orbit. The largest towns in northern Santa Barbara County, like San Luis Obispo to the north, are pleasant, comfortable places, as untrendy as you can find in coastal California. In San Luis Obispo County, the challenge will be coping with future state budget cuts. One-fifth of the workforce holds government jobs at Cal Poly and other schools as well as at a state hospital and prison. This was a marginal district, seriously contested several times in the 1990s. But in its current iteration, it is safely Democratic. In 2008, Democrat Barack Obama won the district by a solid 66%-32% over Republican John McCain.

Lois Capps (D)

The congresswoman from the 23rd District is Lois Capps, a Democrat first chosen in a March 1998 special election to replace her late husband, Walter Capps. Lois Capps grew up in Wyoming and Montana, the daughter of a Lutheran minister. She graduated from college with a nursing degree and was the head nurse at Yale New Haven Hospital when she met Walter Capps, a student at Yale Divinity School. In 1964, he became a professor at the University of California at Santa Barbara. Lois Capps became the head elementary school nurse for the Santa Barbara school system, director of the county's teenage pregnancy and parenting project, and a part-time instructor at Santa Barbara City Community College. In 1996, Walter Capps ran for the U.S. House and defeated Andrea Seastrand, a conservative state Assemblywoman. He died of a heart attack in his first year in office, in October 1997.

Lois Capps ran for his seat against Republican Assemblyman Tom Bordonaro, the favorite of Christian conservatives. Bordonaro, a paraplegic since a car accident in college, emphasized his "blue-collar roots and common values." Capps had help from labor unions and environmental groups. In the January 1998 primary, she finished first with 45% to 29%. In the runoff, Bordonaro was hurt by divisions in the local GOP, and Capps won a surprisingly large 53%-45% victory. The same two candidates were on the ballot in November. But national Republicans had little hope of winning by then, and it was not a priority race. Capps won 55%-43%.

She is a solid liberal, but she has worked more successfully with Republicans when Democrats are in the minority than has the typical California Democrat. Perhaps it is her disposition. An annual survey of congressional aides by *Washingtonian* magazine has three times named Capps "the nicest member of Congress."

With her background as a nurse and her seat on the Energy and Commerce Committee, Capps has focused on the national nursing shortage, mental health issues and reforming the Medicare program for the elderly and disabled. She won enactment of a bill to attract more students into the nursing profession. In 2007, she became vice chair of the Health Subcommittee of Energy and Commerce, an important perch for shaping health care policy. During the 2009-2010 health care overhaul debate, she emerged as a leading opponent of efforts by anti-abortion Rep. Bart Stupak, D-Mich., to prevent federal subsidies to insurance carriers providing abortion coverage to women. She developed what she called "an abortion-neutral compromise" that would have barred direct payments of federal funds in most cases. She succeeded in drawing support from several pro-abortion rights moderates. But Stupak and his allies remained unsatisfied, contending that her proposal would have allowed indirect payments. They held up the final bill's fate until President Obama brokered a last-minute deal.

In keeping with her district's interests, another of Capps' major interests is environmental policy. In 2004, the House passed her amendment to stop a comprehensive inventory of oil and gas resources beneath the outer continental shelf. She also opposed the Bush administration plan to drill in the Los Padres National Forest and has been outspoken against offshore drilling along the California coast. After the 2010 BP oil spill disaster, she pushed for an aggressive federal response, calling for an independent commission to make recommendations on how to avoid future mishaps. Along with Washington Democrat Jay Inslee, she also led a Democratic effort to postpone exploratory drilling in the Arctic Ocean. In 2005, she successfully opposed an attempt by California Republicans to convert part of the Channel Islands into a private recreation area for the military.

Capps has had an up-and-down relationship with organized labor. After she voted for normalizing trade relations with China, the Teamsters claimed that she'd betrayed them. She later patched things up, and in recent years she co-sponsored organized labor's "card check" legislation aimed at making it easier for workers to join unions.

In her first re-election bid, in 2000, Capps had serious competition from moderate Republican Mike Stoker, a former Santa Barbara County supervisor. She had a big fundraising edge and won 53%-44%. After promising in 1998 to serve only three terms, she abandoned that pledge. Since 2002, she has not been seriously challenged.

TWENTY-FOURTH DISTRICT

Elton Gallegly (R)

Elected 1986, 13th term; b. March 7, 1944, Huntington Park; home, Simi Valley; Los Angeles St. Col., 1962-63; Protestant; married (Janice); 4 children.

Elected Office: Simi Valley City Cncl., 1979–80; Simi Valley mayor, 1980–86.

Professional Career: Owner, real estate firm.

DC Office: 2309 RHOB, 20515, 202-225-5811; Fax: 202-225-1100; Web site: house.gov/gallegly.

State Offices: Solvang, 805-686-2525; Thousand Oaks, 805-497-2224.

Committees: *Foreign Affairs* (VChmn): Europe and Eurasia; Western Hemisphere. *Judiciary:* Courts, Commercial & Administrative Law; Immigration Policy & Enforcement (Chmn).

Group Ratings

	ACLU	ACU	ADA	CFG	AFS	FRC	LCV	ITIC	NTU	COC
2010	8	95	0	86	0	93	0	33	87	88
2009	–	96	5	88	13	–	7	–	84	79

National Journal Ratings

	2010 LIB	—	2010 CONS		2009 LIB	—	2009 CONS
Economic	13%	—	87%		16%	—	83%
Social	33%	—	66%		27%	—	72%
Foreign	12%	—	79%		0%	—	75%
Composite	21%	—	79%		19%	—	81%

Key Votes of the 111th Congress

1. Overturn Ledbetter	*	5. Bar federal abortion funds	
2. Pass $820 billion stimulus	N	6. Pass health care bill	
3. Let guns in national parks	Y	7. Regulate financial firms	
4. Pass cap-and-trade	N	8. Pass tax cuts for some	

Y 9. Stop detainee transfers	Y
N 10. Legalize immigrants' kids	N
N 11. Repeal don't ask, tell	N
N 12. Limit campaign funds	N

Election Results

2010 general	Elton Gallegly (R)	144,055	(60%)	($783,257)
	Timothy Allison (D)	96,279	(40%)	($178,734)
2010 primary	Elton Gallegly (R)	unopposed		

Prior Winning Percentages: 2008 (58%), 2006 (62%), 2004 (63%), 2002 (65%), 2000 (54%), 1998 (60%), 1996 (60%), 1994 (66%), 1992 (54%), 1990 (58%), 1988 (69%), 1986 (68%)

Population		Race/Ethnicity		Work	
Pop. 2010:	681,622	White:	60.3%	Private:	75.7%
Change since 2000:	Up 6.7%	Black:	1.5%	Government:	14.7%
Urban:	94.2%	Hispanic:	28.8%	Self-employed:	9.5%
Rural:	5.8%	Asian:	6.1%	Blue collar:	15.4%
Area size:	4,157 sq. mi.	Native Am.:	0.4%	White collar:	66.3%
		Hawaiian:	0.1%	Khaki collar:	0.5%
Age		Two+ races:	2.5%	Other:	17.8%
Median age:	38.3 yrs.				
More than 65 yrs:	12.4%	*Ancestry*		Median income:	$78,535
Less than 18 yrs:	25.5%	German	11.9%	Median Home Value:	$576,000
		Irish	8.9%		
Education		English	8.7%	**Military Veterans**	
H.S. grad:	87.8%			% of Pop:	9.5%
College grad:	34.4%				
Grad degree:	12.7%				

Ventura and Santa Barbara Counties

The city of Simi Valley is a product of the 1960s, the expansive postwar years when migrants from points across the United States went west to Los Angeles and then spread beyond city and county limits to fill up barren valleys between the mountains. With their work ethic, varied skills, and appreciation of the local environment, they brought a distaste for the crime and civil strife that seemed all too common in Los Angeles during that turbulent decade in U.S. his-

2008 Presidential Vote

Barack Obama (D)	160,738	(51%)
John McCain (R)	151,678	(48%)

2004 Presidential Vote

George Bush (R)	165,430	(56%)
John Kerry (D)	127,875	(43%)

Cook Partisan Voting Index: R+4

tory. The valleys of Ventura County, west of Los Angeles, filled up with people building new communities in what had been orange and lemon groves. Like California overall, the Ventura County population has trended socially liberal and economically conservative. To the south is upscale Thousand Oaks, one of the safest large cities in the nation and the headquarters of biotechnology giant Amgen Inc. Farther west in Pleasant Valley is Camarillo, which is home to numerous technology firms. In the inland valleys still farther west are Santa Paula and Ojai. Academy Award nominee *Sideways*, which dealt with the abundant consumption of local wines by two friends, was filmed in nearby Buellton. Looking out toward these valleys and to the Pacific beyond is the Ronald Reagan Presidential Foundation and Library in Simi Valley. Housed there are 55 million pages of presidential documents and a large piece of the Berlin Wall, which Reagan famously urged Mikhail Gorbachev to tear down. Despite its affluence, the area did not escape the recession. The number of Ventura County residents on food stamps grew by more than 50% between 2007 and 2009, with some of the biggest increases in Thousand Oaks and Simi Valley.

The 24th Congressional District of California includes the interior of Ventura and Santa Barbara counties (most of their coastlines are in the 23rd District), plus a stretch of the Ventura County coastline and the Point Mugu Naval Weapons Test Center. The Santa Barbara County interior is lightly inhabited. It includes the small towns of Lompoc, Solvang, and Santa Ynez, near Reagan's beloved cabin in the mountains. It shares Vandenberg Air Force Base and the five Channel Islands and their steep cliffs with the 23rd. Most of the population is in eastern Ventura County. Politically, these areas trended Republican, but were more marginal in 2008. The district voted

56% for President George W. Bush in 2004, but gave Democrat Barack Obama a 51%-48% edge four years later.

Elton Gallegly (R)

The congressman from the 24th District is Elton Gallegly, a Republican first elected in 1986. Gallegly *(GAL-eh-glee)* grew up in the working-class suburb of Huntington Park in Los Angeles County, the son of Dust Bowl migrants from Oklahoma who resettled in California. He dropped out of college and became a real estate broker, then started his own successful real estate business. In 1979, he was elected to the Simi Valley City Council and a year later became mayor. He built his campaign for the U.S. House on his record on economic development for Simi Valley. In the Republican primary, he ran against Tony Hope, son of comedian and actor Bob Hope, and won. He went on to win the general election overwhelmingly.

Gallegly has a moderate-to-conservative voting record and has played a mostly backstage role on major issues. As a member of the Judiciary Committee, he has been one of the Republican hardliners on the issue of illegal immigration in recent years. He once proposed that public schools be given the option of turning away the children of illegal immigrants because of the cost of educating them. He also advocated a constitutional amendment to deny citizenship to the children of illegal immigrants, an issue that gained currency with conservatives in 2010. His other cause is preventing animal cruelty. He sponsored a 1999 law banning the practice, which the Supreme Court struck down as overly broad. He came back in 2010 with a bill, which he got signed into law, making it a federal crime to sell videos depicting the torture of small animals.

Gallegly passed up several opportunities to chair a Judiciary subcommittee over the years. He was more interested in becoming chairman of the Natural Resources Committee. But in 2003, Republican leaders passed over Gallegly and other more senior Republicans to give the gavel to Richard Pombo of California, a favorite of then-Majority Leader Tom DeLay. Gallegly was passed over again in 2009 for the top Republican slot on the committee, which went to Rep. Doc Hastings of Washington state. The leadership's treatment of him contributed to Gallegly's decision to retire from the House in 2006. But he was persuaded to stay by contrite leaders, who faced a tough battle for control of the House that year and did not want another seat to defend. After they won control of the House in 2010, Republicans made him vice chairman of the Foreign Affairs Committee and also gave him the gavel of the Subcommittee on Immigration Policy and Enforcement.

In 2003, Gallegly spent a few days campaigning for governor in the recall election, but withdrew because he lacked statewide name recognition. In his re-election campaign in 2008, Democratic challenger Marta Jorgensen accused him of ignoring the district, but she spent less than $12,000 compared with Gallegly's $737,000, and he won 58%-42%. He had little trouble in 2010.

TWENTY-FIFTH DISTRICT

Buck McKeon (R)

Elected 1992, 10th term; b. Sept. 9, 1938, Los Angeles; home, Santa Clarita; Brigham Young U., B.S. 1985; Mormon; married (Patricia); 6 children.

Elected Office: William S. Hart Schl. District Bd., 1979–87; Santa Clarita mayor, 1987–88; Santa Clarita City Cncl., 1988–92.

Professional Career: Small businessman; Owner, Howard & Phil's Western Wear, 1973–00; Chmn., Valencia Natl. Bank, 1987–88.

DC Office: 2184 RHOB, 20515, 202-225-1956; Fax: 202-226-0683; Web site: mckeon.house.gov.

State Offices: Palmdale, 661-274-9688; Santa Clarita, 661-254-2111.

Committees: *Armed Services* (Chmn). *Education & the Workforce:* Higher Education & Workforce Training.

Group Ratings

	ACLU	ACU	ADA	CFG	AFS	FRC	LCV	ITIC	NTU	COC
2010	13	96	0	86	0	93	0	33	85	86
2009	–	96	15	86	11	–	14	–	82	87

National Journal Ratings

	2010 LIB	—	2010 CONS	2009 LIB	—	2009 CONS
Economic	11%	—	88%	22%	—	77%
Social	25%	—	71%	24%	—	73%
Foreign	21%	—	77%	0%	—	75%
Composite	20%	—	80%	20%	—	80%

Key Votes of the 111th Congress

1. Overturn Ledbetter	N	5. Bar federal abortion funds	Y	9. Stop detainee transfers	Y
2. Pass $820 billion stimulus	N	6. Pass health care bill	N	10. Legalize immigrants' kids	N
3. Let guns in national parks	Y	7. Regulate financial firms	N	11. Repeal don't ask, tell	N
4. Pass cap-and-trade	N	8. Pass tax cuts for some	N	12. Limit campaign funds	N

Election Results

2010 general	Buck McKeon (R)	118,308	(62%)	($1,254,681)
	Jackie Conaway (D)	73,028	(38%)	($3,890)
2010 primary	Buck McKeon (R)	unopposed		

Prior Winning Percentages: 2008 (58%), 2006 (60%), 2004 (64%), 2002 (65%), 2000 (62%), 1998 (75%), 1996 (62%), 1994 (65%), 1992 (52%)

Population		Race/Ethnicity		Work	
Pop. 2010:	844,320	White:	41.7%	Private:	73.6%
Change since 2000:	Up 32.1%	Black:	9.7%	Government:	18.7%
Urban:	88.2%	Hispanic:	39.2%	Self-employed:	7.5%
Rural:	11.8%	Asian:	5.6%	Blue collar:	22.9%
Area size:	21,622 sq. mi.	Native Am.:	0.7%	White collar:	57.3%
		Hawaiian:	0.2%	Khaki collar:	0.5%
Age		Two+ races:	2.6%	Other:	19.3%
Median age:	32.2 yrs.				
More than 65 yrs:	8.1%	*Ancestry*		Median income:	$61,347
Less than 18 yrs:	30.9%	German	9.3%	Median Home Value:	$337,600
		Irish	6.7%		
Education		English	5.9%	**Military Veterans**	
H.S. grad:	81.3%			% of Pop:	8.6%
College grad:	21.2%				
Grad degree:	6.5%				

Los Angeles County; Santa Clarita

For decades, as the mild-temperature flatlands of the Los Angeles Basin and San Fernando Valley filled up with people, the rugged mountains and hot desert to the north in Los Angeles County remained mostly empty. But as L.A. and the Valley filled up, people began moving north through the Newhall pass on Interstate 5 and northeast on Route 14 to the high desert country. Immediately north of the pass is Santa Clarita, with 170,000 residents, and the Six Flags Magic Mountain theme park. Northeast on Route 14, past the former gold-mining center of Acton, the mountains stop at the San Andreas Fault and the desert stretches out low and flat. This is Antelope Valley, with huge aerospace plants and military bases around Palmdale and Lancaster, where more than 290,000 people live. Not far from upscale shopping centers, there has been a resurgence of specialty farm crops such as baby carrots, organic onions, and parsnips. The adjacent Air Force Plant 42 is home to many defense contractors, with projects that include the B-2 Stealth Bomber, the F-117 Stealth Fighter, and the F-35 Joint Strike Fighter. This was a fast-growing area for most of the last decade, with housing prices well below those in the San Fernando Valley and mortgages easy to come by. But when housing prices collapsed, it had one of the nation's highest foreclosure rates. It was further set back in 2009 when the Palmdale airport closed, two months after United Airlines ended flights there. North of the Antelope Valley the desert stretches for miles, with clumps of human settlement—Edwards Air Force Base, where Chuck Yeager flew the X-1 and where the Space Shuttle has frequently landed. To the east are the desert towns of Victorville and Apple Valley; to the north, off Interstate 15 heading to Las Vegas, are Barstow, the military training center at Fort Irwin and the Naval Air Warfare Center at China Lake.

2008 Presidential Vote		
Barack Obama (D)	134,222	(49%)
John McCain (R)	131,201	(48%)
2004 Presidential Vote		
George Bush (R)	142,052	(59%)
John Kerry (D)	96,355	(40%)
Cook Partisan Voting Index:	R+6	

The 25th Congressional District of California covers these areas, sharing Edwards AFB with the 22nd District. Geographically, it is vast, the largest in the state. It extends far to the north, across the almost uninhabited Mojave Desert and mountains to include Death Valley (where the International Dark-Sky Association laments the visibility of lights from Las Vegas) and the Owens Valley (the source of Los Angeles's water supply), and the Mammoth ski resort area. Politically, this has been a Republican district, though in the 2008 presidential election, Democrat Barack Obama carried it 49%-48%.

Buck McKeon (R)

The congressman from the 25th District is Howard (Buck) McKeon, a Republican first elected in 1992 and now chairman of the Armed Services Committee. McKeon grew up in Southern California, graduated from Brigham Young University, and then went to work in the family business, Howard and Phil's Western Wear. He later took over the chain, which at its peak had 52 stores in California, Arizona, Nevada, and Utah. (The business closed in 2000.) McKeon was the first mayor of Santa Clarita after it was incorporated in 1987. He ran for a new U.S. House seat in 1992 and won the crucial Republican primary, 40%-38%, over Assemblyman Phil Wyman.

McKeon has had a reliably conservative voting record and long played a lead role on the Education and Labor Committee. In 2001, he handled the renewal of the higher-education bill and advocated steps to penalize hundreds of universities and colleges that have raised tuition much faster than inflation. Many schools and Democrats complained loudly that he was advocating price controls. When the Bush administration also objected, he abandoned the proposal, claiming that many colleges had moved to rein in tuition hikes. In February 2006, when committee Chairman John Boehner was elected majority whip to replace Tom DeLay, McKeon succeeded Boehner as chairman, leapfrogging two more senior Republicans. In the remaining months of the Republican majority, he completed an overhaul of employment training programs and a sweeping rewrite of pension laws, with the support of Boehner, who had initiated the legislation as chairman.

In 2007, after Republicans lost the majority, McKeon became ranking Republican. He cooperated with new Democratic Chairman George Miller on the renewal of the Higher Education Act, which took steps to control college costs and to increase financial aid for students. Despite strong criticism from the Bush administration, the House overwhelmingly approved the legislation, which raised the maximum Pell grant from $4,000 to $8,000 a year and prohibited gifts and profit-sharing arrangements between student loan lenders and colleges. On an issue of great local interest, McKeon joined Democratic Sen. Barbara Boxer to support wilderness protection for 430,000 acres in the Sierra Nevada and San Gabriel mountains. Their measure was enacted in March 2009.

When the ranking Republican on the Armed Services Committee, John McHugh of New York, resigned to become the Army secretary in June 2009, McKeon vied with the more senior Roscoe Bartlett of Maryland and the less senior Mac Thornberry of Texas for the post. McKeon was selected by the Republican Steering Committee.

He was one of 44 Republicans who voted for the Obama administration's defense supplemental spending bill that year. McKeon complained that Democrats were loading unrelated items onto the defense authorization bill, but he nonetheless worked closely with Democratic Chairman Ike Skelton on the legislation. When the administration released the Quadrennial Defense Review, McKeon cautioned, "Choosing to win in Iraq and Afghanistan should not mean our country must also choose to assume greater risk in the conventional national defense challenges of today and tomorrow." He joined Skelton when the committee in May 2010 added billions of dollars to the Pentagon's budget request, increased the military's pay raise and authorized an alternate engine for the F-35. In March 2010, he argued that earmarks for military construction projects should not be covered by the House Republicans' ban on earmarks if they are part of the "future years" defense plan. In another hotly contested area of military policy, McKeon opposed repeal of the ban on openly gay service personnel. When Republicans regained the majority in 2011, he became Armed Services chairman without significant opposition.

At home McKeon has been re-elected without serious opposition. His closest margin, 58%-42%, came in 2008; in 2010 he was re-elected 62%-38%.

TWENTY-SIXTH DISTRICT

David Dreier (R)

Elected 1980, 16th term; b. July 5, 1952, Kansas City, MO; home, San Dimas; Claremont McKenna Col., B.A. 1975, Claremont Grad. Schl., M.A. 1976; Christian Scientist; single.

Professional Career: Corp. relations dir., Claremont McKenna Col., 1976–78; Mktg. dir., Industrial Hydrocarbons, 1978–80; V.P., Dreier Development Co., 1985–present.

DC Office: 233 CHOB, 20515, 202-225-2305; Fax: 202-225-7018; Web site: dreier.house.gov.

State Offices: San Dimas, 909-575-6226.

Committees: *Rules* (Chmn).

Group Ratings

	ACLU	ACU	ADA	CFG	AFS	FRC	LCV	ITIC	NTU	COC
2010	19	96	5	97	0	100	20	33	89	88
2009	–	92	5	81	11	–	0	–	80	86

National Journal Ratings

	2010 LIB	—	2010 CONS	2009 LIB	—	2009 CONS
Economic	27%	—	72%	21%	—	79%
Social	25%	—	71%	13%	—	84%
Foreign	0%	—	88%	0%	—	75%
Composite	20%	—	80%	16%	—	84%

Key Votes of the 111th Congress

1. Overturn Ledbetter	N	5. Bar federal abortion funds	Y	9. Stop detainee transfers	Y
2. Pass $820 billion stimulus	N	6. Pass health care bill	N	10. Legalize immigrants' kids	N
3. Let guns in national parks	Y	7. Regulate financial firms	N	11. Repeal don't ask, tell	Y
4. Pass cap-and-trade	N	8. Pass tax cuts for some	N	12. Limit campaign funds	N

Election Results

2010 general	David Dreier (R)	112,774	(54%)	($1,243,191)
	Russ Warner (D)	76,093	(37%)	($315,157)
	David Miller (AMI)	12,784	(6%)	($42,074)
	Randall Weissbuch (Lib)	6,696	(3%)	
2010 primary	David Dreier (R)	42,400	(72%)	
	Mark Butler (R)	16,220	(28%)	

Prior Winning Percentages: 2008 (53%), 2006 (57%), 2004 (54%), 2002 (64%), 2000 (57%), 1998 (58%), 1996 (61%), 1994 (67%), 1992 (58%), 1990 (64%), 1988 (69%), 1986 (72%), 1984 (71%), 1982 (65%), 1980 (52%)

Population		Race/Ethnicity		Work	
Pop. 2010:	691,452	White:	42.8%	Private:	75.5%
Change since 2000:	Up 8.2%	Black:	4.6%	Government:	16.5%
Urban:	98.8%	Hispanic:	30.7%	Self-employed:	7.8%
Rural:	1.2%	Asian:	19.0%	Blue collar:	15.0%
Area size:	755 sq. mi.	Native Am.:	0.2%	White collar:	71.6%
		Hawaiian:	0.1%	Khaki collar:	0.0%
Age		Two+ races:	2.4%	Other:	13.4%
Median age:	37.2 yrs.				
More than 65 yrs:	11.4%	*Ancestry*		Median income:	$76,247
Less than 18 yrs:	25.2%	German	9.0%	Median Home Value:	$558,200
		English	6.5%		
Education		Irish	6.4%	**Military Veterans**	
H.S. grad:	89.4%			% of Pop:	7.1%
College grad:	36.8%				
Grad degree:	14.6%				

Inland Empire; Rancho Cucamonga

It was the great route west to California in the first half of the 20th century: Passengers on the Santa Fe railroad's *Super Chief* or motorists on U.S. 66, after hours and days in barren desert, descended through the Cajon Pass into the Los Angeles Basin, then moved in a stately procession beneath the 10,000-foot snow-capped San Gabriel Mountains, marveling at orange groves and exotic plants. The railroad and highway ran

2008 Presidential Vote
Barack Obama (D) 149,249   (51%)
John McCain (R) 137,329   (47%)

2004 Presidential Vote
George Bush (R) 148,352   (55%)
John Kerry (D) 117,532   (44%)

Cook Partisan Voting Index: R+3

through a line of towns built by Midwestern Protestants as independent communities that today have been transformed into high-income suburbs with their own civic institutions. There is Claremont, home of the academically renowned Claremont Colleges— "the City of Trees and Ph.D.'s." There are La Verne, Glendora and San Dimas, with its rodeo and horse trails. Arcadia has the Santa Anita racetrack and the Los Angeles County Arboretum and Botanic Gardens. Luxurious San Marino is the home of the Huntington Library, one of the world's great museums and scholarly institutions, with more than 150 acres of botanical gardens. The district also includes the new suburb of Walnut to the south and, far to the west, the mountain-enclosed suburb of La Canada Flintridge, home of NASA's Jet Propulsion Laboratory.

The 26th Congressional District of California covers these Foothill communities in the San Gabriel Valley. It includes, east of Claremont, the newer San Bernardino cities of Upland, Montclair and Rancho Cucamonga, the largest city in the district, where the local baseball team, the Quakes, play at the Epicenter. Much of the last decade was a boom era here, drawing Latinos who found jobs in construction and got mortgages with little or no down payment. But when the housing market collapsed, jobs disappeared and warehouses built in huge numbers to store goods offloaded in the port of Los Angeles-Long Beach stood empty. Foreclosures rose to some of the highest levels in the nation.

Historically, the towns running east from Los Angeles were heavily Republican. But the area now has large and growing Hispanic and Asian populations; a foreign language is spoken in 36% of homes in the district. In 2010, the Census Bureau estimated that 31% of its population was Hispanic and 19% was Asian. San Marino, Arcadia, San Dimas and Walnut have sizable Chinese populations. And its communities are no longer solidly Republican. George W. Bush won 55% of the vote here in 2004, but Barack Obama won 51%-47% in 2008.

David Dreier (R)

The congressman from the 26th District is David Dreier, a Republican first elected in 1980 and the chairman of the House Rules Committee. Dreier grew up in Kansas City, Mo., the son of a former Marine Corps drill instructor who ran a real estate investment firm. Dreier spent a decade mostly on the Claremont McKenna campus, first as a student and then as an administrator, before he was elected to Congress. He first ran in 1978, at age 26, and lost to Democratic incumbent Jim Lloyd 54%-46%. Two years later, in the Reagan landslide, he beat Lloyd 52%-45%. Dreier personifies the intellectually rigorous conservatism and free-market economics that have thrived at Claremont, and he maintains a California-style cheerfulness and good humor. In 1991, he won a seat on the

Rules panel, which sets the terms and conditions under which bills can come to the floor. The committee had been dominated since the 1970s by the leadership of the majority party, which has a 9-4 edge in membership. Dreier was at least two decades younger than the two senior Republicans and so in a position to move up, but the Democrats seemed to have a perpetual majority in the House. That changed in 1994, when Republicans won majority control. In 1999, after Chairman Gerald Solomon of New York retired, Dreier took over the gavel. He became a top lieutenant of Republican Speaker Dennis Hastert from 1999 to 2006. In that time, the committee produced hundreds of rules, and Dreier lost only two rules fights with the Democrats. In 2005, House Republicans suspended the six-year term limit for the Rules chairman, allowing Dreier to continue in the post.

The same year, Rep. Tom DeLay of Texas was forced to step down as majority leader amid an ethics scandal. Hastert wanted to name Dreier as acting majority leader, but conservatives objected to him as insufficiently conservative on cultural issues, and Hastert agreed to give the job to Roy Blunt of Missouri.

When Republicans lost the majority in 2006, Dreier became the ranking Republican on Rules. He frequently clashed with Chair Louise Slaughter, and displayed a zest in challenging the Democrats' procedural moves and occasionally outmaneuvering them with motions to recommit legislation to committee with changes designed to embarrass the opposition. In January 2009, he opposed Democrats' rules changes allowing the pay-as-you-go rule to be waived in case of "emergencies" and restricting motions to recommit, calling them "a host of new procedural gimmicks to stifle debate and perpetuate partisanship." In summer 2009, he decried Democrats' closed rules on appropriations, designed to prevent large numbers of Republican amendments targeting earmarks. In March 2010, he loudly opposed Slaughter's proposal to have the House "deem" the Senate health care bill passed by the House. Now, once again in the majority, Dreier and the Republican leadership will be tested on whether they allow bills to be more open to amendment, as Speaker John Boehner promised before the election.

Dreier's voting record is mostly conservative, though it's more centrist on cultural issues. His policy agenda is focused on free trade, promotion of high technology and issues related to diminishing water supplies in the San Gabriel Valley. On trade, he was actively involved in efforts to normalize trade relations with China in the 1990s and to give the president broader powers to negotiate trade deals in the early 2000s. In 2009 Dreier joined Sen. John Kerry, D-Mass. in urging freer trade with the country of Georgia. On high-tech issues, he was a leading sponsor of legislation increasing the number of visas for high-technology workers from overseas and he helped win enactment in 2005 of the "Real ID" bill to prevent states from issuing drivers' licenses to illegal immigrants. On local issues, Dreier has sought federal disaster funds for victims of the 2010 mudslides and backed federal funds for metro Los Angeles' rail transit system.

Dreier took the lead for California Republicans on redistricting in 2001 and reached an agreement with the Democrats under which 19 of the 20 Republican incumbents got safe districts and Republicans got a newly created seat in the Central Valley. That helped Dreier, whose district was becoming more Hispanic and more Democratic. Nonetheless, Dreier has faced more serious electoral competition in the past decade than in the 1990s. In 2004, two Los Angeles radio talk show hosts attacked his stands on illegal immigration and launched a "Fire Dreier" campaign. Democratic nominee Cynthia Matthews spent only $26,000, while he spent $1.3 million, but he won by only 54%-43%. He did better in a 2006 rematch, winning 57%-38%. In 2008, Democrat Russ Warner spent $1.2 million against him. Republicans sent out flyers citing tax problems in Warner's business dealings. Dreier won 53%-40% as Barack Obama was carrying the district. In the more Republican year of 2010, he beat Warner in a rematch, 54%-37%.

These were solid but not overwhelming margins for a party leader, and Dreier could be weakened by the post-2010 census redistricting. He remains the head of the California Republican delegation, but presumably will take little part in redistricting; voters in 2010 approved a ballot proposition giving that task to an independent commission. Los Angeles County will lose nearly a whole seat in representation, and Dreier probably would benefit if his district is moved farther into San Bernardino County or north into desert country, which is more Republican than the increasingly Latino towns in the Foothills.

TWENTY-SEVENTH DISTRICT

Brad Sherman (D)

Elected 1996, 8th term; b. Oct. 24, 1954, Los Angeles; home, Sherman Oaks; U.C.L.A., B.A. 1974, Harvard U., J.D. 1979; Jewish; married (Lisa); 2 children.

Elected Office: CA St. Board of Equalization, 1990–95, chmn., 1991–95.

Professional Career: Accountant, 1980–90.

DC Office: 2242 RHOB, 20515, 202-225-5911; Fax: 202-225-5879; Web site: sherman.house.gov.

State Offices: Sherman Oaks, 818-501-9200.

Committees: *Financial Services:* Capital Markets and Government Sponsored Enterprises; Insurance, Housing & Community Opportunity. *Foreign Affairs:* Asia & the Pacific; Terrorism, Nonproliferation & Trade (RMM).

Group Ratings

	ACLU	*ACU*	*ADA*	*CFG*	*AFS*	*FRC*	*LCV*	*ITIC*	*NTU*	*COC*
2010	94	0	90	0	100	0	100	100	5	25
2009	–	0	100	0	100	–	100	–	2	33

National Journal Ratings

	2010 LIB	—	2010 CONS		2009 LIB	—	2009 CONS
Economic	86%	—	13%		87%	—	12%
Social	89%	—	7%		80%	—	18%
Foreign	56%	—	38%		53%	—	44%
Composite	79%	—	21%		74%	—	26%

Key Votes of the 111th Congress

1. Overturn Ledbetter	Y	5. Bar federal abortion funds	N	9. Stop detainee transfers	N
2. Pass $820 billion stimulus	Y	6. Pass health care bill	Y	10. Legalize immigrants' kids	Y
3. Let guns in national parks	N	7. Regulate financial firms	Y	11. Repeal don't ask, tell	Y
4. Pass cap-and-trade	Y	8. Pass tax cuts for some	Y	12. Limit campaign funds	Y

Election Results

2010 general	Brad Sherman (D)..	102,927	(65%)	($1,743,592)
	Mark Reed (R)..	55,056	(35%)	($112,837)
2010 primary	Brad Sherman (D)....................................... unopposed			

Prior Winning Percentages: 2008 (69%), 2006 (69%), 2004 (62%), 2002 (62%), 2000 (66%), 1998 (57%), 1996 (49%)

Population		**Race/Ethnicity**		**Work**	
Pop. 2010:	684,496	White:	38.0%	Private:	78.7%
Change since 2000:	Up 7.1%	Black:	4.3%	Government:	10.4%
Urban:	99.7%	Hispanic:	42.3%	Self-employed:	10.8%
Rural:	0.3%	Asian:	12.3%	Blue collar:	19.3%
Area size:	152 sq. mi.	Native Am.:	0.2%	White collar:	63.0%
		Hawaiian:	0.1%	Khaki collar:	0.0%
Age		Two+ races:	2.5%	Other:	17.7%
Median age:	35.7 yrs.				
More than 65 yrs:	11.3%	*Ancestry*		Median income:	$58,604
Less than 18 yrs:	24.5%	German	5.7%	Median Home Value:	$517,700
		Irish	4.5%		
Education		English	4.0%	**Military Veterans**	
H.S. grad:	80.9%			% of Pop:	5.0%
College grad:	29.6%				
Grad degree:	8.6%				

San Fernando Valley; Part L.A.

In the early 20th century, when the movie business was young, the San Fernando Valley was a vast expanse of empty land that had been annexed to Los Angeles in 1915. Moviemakers, looking for filming sites for a western, drove past the vacant lots of Westwood, up narrow roads through the Santa Monica Mountains and over into the vast Valley, sheltered from ocean breezes and rain-bearing clouds by the mountains. Since then, this vast bowl of land has been

2008 Presidential Vote		
Barack Obama (D) 157,100	(66%)
John McCain (R) 75,286	(32%)

2004 Presidential Vote		
John Kerry (D) 130,567	(59%)
George Bush (R) 86,397	(39%)

Cook Partisan Voting Index: D+13

transformed, first into 1950s suburbia, and then into a postmodern city of its own, economically vital and yeastily ethnic. Even in its suburban years, the San Fernando Valley was not entirely residential. Big factories provided jobs—the now shuttered General Motors Van Nuys assembly plant, the Anheuser-Busch brewery, Rockwell (now Boeing) and Litton (now Northrop Grumman) defense plants. In those years, this was fast-growing, family-friendly territory. And politically, it was turf fought over by Republicans and Democrats.

There is plenty of upscale territory left in the uplands of the Valley, in Granada Hills and Tarzana. The office blocks and mini-malls show unmistakable signs of affluence. In what had been the culturally arid Valley, lounges and bars have become prevalent. Urban planners have revived the planned community of Panorama City, which was the busy center of the Valley during the 1950s. In the inner lowlands of the Valley, new immigrants have moved to the growing communities of Reseda and Van Nuys. Some old neighborhoods have become rough enclaves, with youth gangs and boarded-up houses and apartments. Iranians and Chinese, Mexicans and Koreans, Israelis and Filipinos are keeping other neighborhoods diverse and solidly middle class. Even this multiethnic Valley has been unhappy to be linked with the city of Los Angeles, whose City Council imposes high taxes and irksome regulations. A Valley secession movement arose, and the issue was put on the November 2002 ballot. The Valley voted 51%-49% for it, with stronger support in the western part. But it needed a majority in all of Los Angeles to pass, and so it failed, though some embers of secession interest remain. In 2007, the Valley had 1.76 million residents, more than 40% of them foreign-born. After being hit hard by the recession, the Valley's economy began improving in 2010, thanks in part to a massive expansion in California's enterprise zone program. Nevertheless, thousands of middle-class residents have relocated in recent years to less-costly places. That prompted *LA Weekly* to warn in 2009: "At the current rate, within 60 years the Valley will have no discernible middle class."

The 27th Congressional District of California on the map looks like an inverted "U" over the San Fernando Valley, between the Santa Monica and San Gabriel mountains. On the east it includes part of Burbank, the home of NBC studios and Disney headquarters, and also blue-collar and heavily Hispanic neighborhoods filled with renters. To the north are Sunland and Tujunga at the base of the San Gabriel Mountains. The larger and more settled parts of the district are west of the 405 Freeway (roughly the dividing line between the East and West valleys), including most of Granada Hills, Northridge, Van Nuys, and Tarzana. This is a diverse district, indeed: 42% of residents are Hispanic, most of them Mexican, and 12% are Asian, roughly half of them Filipino or Korean. The district is comfortably Democratic, and traces of the Valley as the onetime base for President Ronald Reagan long ago disappeared.

Brad Sherman (D)

The congressman from the 27th District is Brad Sherman, a Democrat first elected in 1996. Sherman grew up in Monterey Park, in the San Gabriel Valley east of Los Angeles. He started working on Democratic campaigns at age 6, licking stamps and stuffing envelopes for U.S. Rep. George Brown. He set up his own stamp-wholesaling firm at age 14. He graduated with high honors from the University of California at Los Angeles, worked as an accountant, then went to Harvard Law School. He came back to the Los Angeles area to practice tax law, and he represented the Philippines in its successful effort to seize the assets of deposed president Ferdinand Marcos.

In 1990, Sherman was elected from Los Angeles County to the state Board of Equalization, which is a sort of tax court. He was known as a stickler for detail, a "tax nerd," as one former staffer said, who used the office with a keen scent for political advantage. He irritated cartoonists with a ruling that exempted artwork from the state tax but not illustrations. They took their revenge by setting up a website, the Sherman Gallery, where they vied in caricaturing the balding and bespectacled Sherman. In 1996, he moved his residence from Santa Monica to Sherman Oaks, where a U.S. House seat had opened. Both he and his Republican opponent, businessman Rich Sybert, were self-financers; Sherman spent $578,000 of his own money. And both stressed their moderation. Sherman ran against then-House Speaker Newt Gingrich and the Republican Congress, but he also supported the death penalty, called for phasing out racial quotas and preferences, and favored tough measures on illegal immigration. Sybert stressed his independence from Gingrich as well as his support of abortion rights and environmental protections. Sherman won 49%-44%.

In the House, his voting record has been more moderate than those of most other Los Angeles County Democrats, and he has shown occasional independence from party leaders. One of the few certified public accountants in Congress, Sherman serves on the Financial Services Committee, where his experience has been useful in congressional attempts to unravel recent corporate accounting scandals. In 2008, he was an outspoken foe of the bill creating the Troubled Assets Relief Program to bail out the financial services industry, dubbing it "cash for trash." He was regularly critical of Treasury Secretary Timothy Geithner's subsequent efforts on behalf of Wall Street, calling Geithner's proposal allowing the government to take over large firms "TARP on steroids." When domestic auto company executives testified in favor of a proposed bailout for that industry in November 2008, Sherman got them to concede that they had all flown separately to Washington in private airplanes, a revelation that sparked a public backlash. In March 2009, he advocated a 70% surtax on all compensation exceeding $1 million for executives of financial institutions receiving large federal bailouts. Sherman also helped form the new Consumer Financial Protection Bureau as part of the 2010 financial overhaul bill.

He has taken an interest in some of the more arcane aspects of government; he sponsored bills for several years to overhaul the presidential succession process and another measure in 2010 to set up a commission to reduce delays in processing Freedom of Information Act requests. On the Foreign Affairs Committee, Sherman is the top Democrat on the Terrorism, Nonproliferation, and Trade Subcommittee, where his priority has been preventing Iran from obtaining nuclear weapons. One of Israel's leading congressional defenders, he also has sought tougher economic sanctions against Iran, and in 2009, he sponsored a bill to punish companies that sell the Iranian government equipment to block Internet or cell phone access for Iranian citizens.

Sherman has won re-election easily, even after redistricting following the 2000 census gave him a district that was two-thirds new to him and 37% Hispanic. He has not had serious opposition. The area's growing Hispanic population and ambitious redistricters in Sacramento could place him at risk in 2012.

TWENTY-EIGHTH DISTRICT

Howard Berman (D)

Elected 1982, 15th term; b. April 15, 1941, Los Angeles; home, Hollywood; U.C.L.A., B.A. 1962, LL.B. 1965; Jewish; married (Janis); 2 children.

Elected Office: CA Assembly, 1973–82, maj. ldr., 1974–79.

Professional Career: Practicing atty., 1967–72.

DC Office: 2221 RHOB, 20515, 202-225-4695; Fax: 202-225-3196; Web site: www.house.gov/berman.

State Offices: Van Nuys, 818-994-7200.

Committees: *Foreign Affairs* (RMM). *Judiciary:* Intellectual Property, Competition & the Internet.

Group Ratings

	ACLU	ACU	ADA	CFG	AFS	FRC	LCV	ITIC	NTU	COC
2010	93	0	90	0	100	0	90	100	6	25
2009	–	0	100	4	100	–	100	–	2	33

National Journal Ratings

	2010 LIB	—	2010 CONS	2009 LIB	—	2009 CONS
Economic	84%	—	15%	88%	—	9%
Social	87%	—	12%	84%	—	11%
Foreign	71%	—	28%	91%	—	0%
Composite	81%	—	19%	91%	—	10%

Key Votes of the 111th Congress

1. Overturn Ledbetter	Y	5. Bar federal abortion funds	N	9. Stop detainee transfers	*
2. Pass $820 billion stimulus	Y	6. Pass health care bill	Y	10. Legalize immigrants' kids	Y
3. Let guns in national parks	N	7. Regulate financial firms	Y	11. Repeal don't ask, tell	Y
4. Pass cap-and-trade	Y	8. Pass tax cuts for some	Y	12. Limit campaign funds	Y

Election Results

2010 general	Howard Berman (D)	88,385	(70%)	($1,914,073)
	Merlin Froyd (R)	28,493	(22%)	($39,636)
	Carlos Rodriguez (Lib)	10,229	(8%)	
2010 primary	Howard Berman (D)	26,092	(83%)	
	Richard Valdez (D)	5,203	(17%)	

Prior Winning Percentages: 2008 (100%), 2006 (74%), 2004 (71%), 2002 (71%), 2000 (84%), 1998 (82%), 1996 (66%), 1994 (63%), 1992 (61%), 1990 (61%), 1988 (70%), 1986 (65%), 1984 (63%), 1982 (60%)

Population		Race/Ethnicity		Work	
Pop. 2010:	660,194	White:	30.5%	Private:	79.6%
Change since 2000:	Up 3.3%	Black:	3.4%	Government:	7.6%
Urban:	99.9%	Hispanic:	57.5%	Self-employed:	12.7%
Rural:	0.1%	Asian:	6.5%	Blue collar:	25.2%
Area size:	78 sq. mi.	Native Am.:	0.2%	White collar:	55.0%
		Hawaiian:	0.1%	Khaki collar:	0.0%
Age		Two+ races:	1.6%	Other:	19.7%
Median age:	32.8 yrs.				
More than 65 yrs:	9.1%	*Ancestry*		Median income:	$52,223
Less than 18 yrs:	26.0%	German	3.9%	Median Home Value:	$532,100
		Irish	3.5%		
Education		English	3.0%	**Military Veterans**	
H.S. grad:	70.3%			% of Pop:	3.6%
College grad:	27.0%				
Grad degree:	8.6%				

San Fernando Valley; Part L.A.

A hiker looking north from the crest of the Santa Monica Mountains in 1912 would have seen a valley almost totally empty and barren, 20 miles long and 12 miles wide. Separated by the Cahuenga Pass from rapidly growing Los Angeles and Hollywood, the San Fernando Valley was bought up in massive tracts by civic leaders as they were urging city engineer William Mulholland to build a huge 250-mile aqueduct from the Owens Valley to bring water to Los Angeles and

2008 Presidential Vote

Barack Obama (D)	147,958	(76%)
John McCain (R)	42,815	(22%)

2004 Presidential Vote

John Kerry (D)	125,351	(71%)
George Bush (R)	49,220	(28%)

Cook Partisan Voting Index: D+23

persuading the city in 1915 to annex 200 square miles of the Valley. In the years after World War II, this was modern suburbia, filled with *Leave It to Beaver* families. Today the San Fernando Valley is postmodern urban, with Disney headquarters in Burbank and Universal Studios' CityWalk shopping and entertainment center. The driver topping the crest today sees office towers looming out over slightly hazy air, shopping centers, occasional palm trees, stucco subdivisions, and the squat factory and warehouse buildings that once made Los Angeles County a top manufacturing locale.

But many of the big plants have closed and the Valley has changed. The 1950s white Anglo families with stay-at-home moms have been replaced by hard-working Latino families with parents juggling two jobs and trying to raise children who will have a better chance than they had. Pacoima, at the northern end of the Valley, is mostly Latino. Farther south, in Canoga Park, Van Nuys, and Burbank, was the industrial base—the GM plants were mostly shut down in the 1980s, and only one of the defense plants remains open, the old Rocketdyne plant, which is now owned by Pratt and Whitney. But now there are hundreds of small factories and multimedia plants where thousands of jobs have been created. The southern rim of the Valley, around Studio City and North Hollywood, is still heavily Jewish and is attracting new families who often send their kids to religious schools. There is a trendy and lively shopping strip along Ventura Boulevard. People with money cluster near the foot of the mountains around the Valley; those less well off settle on the flatlands beyond. This leads to some disputes. Neighborhoods have been petitioning the Los Angeles City Council for name changes, with a particularly bitter dispute about whether a chunk of heavily Latino Van Nuys should be changed to swank Sherman Oaks. The Valley was hit hard when the housing bubble burst in 2007, with prices dropping 50% or more in some areas. This was a big area for subprime mortgages which have left homeowners, many of them Hispanic, underwater.

The 28th Congressional District of California consists of about half of the San Fernando Valley and some of the mountains to the south. It includes parts of Van Nuys and several miles of land on either side of the Hollywood Freeway, from the point where it comes through the Cahuenga Pass from Hollywood to the junction with the Golden State Freeway. Much of the northern end of the Valley, including Pacoima and the small city of San Fernando, is in the district. Mulholland Drive, which runs along the crest of the Santa Monica Mountains and the Ventura Freeway, is the southern border, until the district dips south to Hollywood Boulevard. Within these borders are affluent North Hollywood, Studio City, Sherman Oaks, and Encino, with big houses on twisting streets overlooking the Valley and just above the shops of Ventura Boulevard. The population of the district is about 58% Hispanic, mostly concentrated in the central and northern sections. But Hispanics are still not the majority voting bloc here, because many are not citizens, and many are children or young people not yet in the voting stream. The high Democratic percentages here are due as much to Jewish as to Latino voters. This part of the Valley voted against secession from the city of Los Angeles when it was on the ballot in 2002.

Howard Berman (D)

The congressman from the 28th District is Howard Berman, a Democrat first elected in 1982. He has endured as one of the most creative members of the House and one of the most clear-sighted operators in American politics. Berman grew up in Los Angeles in modest circumstances. His father was a Polish immigrant who worked in the textile industry. Berman got interested in politics in high school and went to the University of California at Los Angeles, where he befriended Henry Waxman, who has been an ally in politics ever since and has represented an adjacent congressional district since 1975. While in law school, Berman got an internship at the California Assembly and was assigned to farm-labor issues with César Chávez's movement. "From then on, I was hooked," Berman said. In 1972, he was elected to the Assembly at age 31, beating the Assembly's Republican leader in a Hollywood Hills district. Waxman was already serving in the Assembly. This was the beginning of the so-called Berman-Waxman political machine—not so much a precinct organization as a group of consultants who raised money, redrew district lines, and endorsed candidates through direct mail. Their core constituency was liberal Westside Jews. A key player was Berman's brother Michael Berman, who became an expert on redistricting and drew the new congressional and legislative district lines for California after the 2000 census. Howard Berman became majority leader in his first term. In 1980, he tried to unseat Speaker Leo McCarthy, but ultimately they both lost to Willie Brown, who remained in the post for 15 years. Berman's consolation prize was a Valley-based congressional seat in 1982. The machine fell on hard times in the early 1990s, when Republican Gov. Pete Wilson prevented Democrats from controlling redistricting. "We don't have a machine anymore, if we ever did," Berman said in 2004. "We just helped some friends."

Berman has been an active legislator on all manner of issues, but not one who gets much publicity. On foreign policy, he started off less as a Vietnam War dove than as a backer of Israel. With Republican Henry Hyde, he wrote the law authorizing embargoes on nations that condone terrorism. In April 1990, he called for sanctions on Iraq, four months before Saddam Hussein invaded Kuwait, and he voted for the Gulf War resolution in January 1991. Later, he played a critical role in winning passage by a wide margin of the Iraq War resolution in October 2002. He had organized a group of Democrats who shared his views, and those discussions led to Minority Leader Richard Gephardt's agreement with the administration on the terms of the resolution—talks that undercut the demands of other senior Democrats, including then-Minority Whip Nancy Pelosi.

Berman has been a major player on immigration as well. In 1988, he sponsored the legislation allowing 20,000 immigrant visas for migrants without close relatives in the United States, to be selected randomly by computer—"Berman visa applications," they are called. In 2003, he and Sen. Edward Kennedy, D-Mass., worked out a bipartisan agreement to temporarily legalize farm workers and give them a way to eventually become legal residents. But it was set aside in favor of President George W. Bush's broader guest-worker program, although that legislation failed to be enacted after many months of debate. More recently, he and Republican Rep. Adam Putnam of Florida co-sponsored a farm workers bill that would give permanent residency status to up to 1.35 million illegal immigrants who could show they have worked on U.S. farms for 150 days a year or for 100 days in the last five years. And with GOP Rep. Lincoln Diaz-Balart of Florida, he co-sponsored the DREAM Act to create a path to citizenship for undocumented immigrant students who have been living in the United States since they were young.

Berman also focuses on intellectual-property issues of vital concern to the entertainment and high-tech industries, both with a strong presence in this district. From his seat on the Judiciary Committee, he won passage of an anti-cyber-squatting law to discourage pouncing on website names, a 2003 law creating new judgeships to determine copyright royalty rates, and a bipartisan bill creating criminal penalties for mass downloaders of music and requiring file-sharing software to contain warnings of security risk. Electronics-industry lobbyist John Palafoutas described what it's like being on the opposing side of Berman on an issue: "There are two problems with Howard Berman," he told the *Los Angeles Times.* "One, he's really smart. And two, he knows how to represent his constituents, which in this case is Hollywood."

In 2007 Berman became chairman of the Subcommittee on Courts, the Internet and Intellectual Property. He won passage in the House of major changes in patent law, creating a new review process and giving legal priority to the "first inventor to file," thereby replacing what some said was the outdated "first to invent" standard. A major beneficiary would have been the technology industry, which had been the target of a slew of nuisance lawsuits for patent-infringement claims. But the Senate did not act. Berman continued to pursue other intellectual property issues, arguing that "intellectual property protection is an economic stimulus." He criticized Canada for transshipping Chinese-made pirated materials and got the House to vote for a resolution opposing provisions of a carbon emissions treaty that would weaken intellectual property protection of American green technology. In May 2009, the Judiciary Committee approved a measure he co-sponsored to eliminate radio stations' exemption from paying royalties to performers and music companies (they do pay them to composers). The action built pressure for negotiations between the content providers and radio broadcasters.

From 1997 to 2003, Berman was the ranking Democrat on the House Ethics Committee. During his tenure, few complaints were filed for partisan reasons. After he left the committee in 2003, that no longer was the case. Then in 2006, when Ethics Committee senior Democrat Alan Mollohan of West Virginia resigned the post because of ethics questions raised about him, Pelosi asked Berman to take the post. "This is an honor I could have done without," Berman said. "The ethics committee should be neither a member protection agency nor a forum for deciding partisan and ideological battles." He worked amicably with Chairman Doc Hastings, a Washington state Republican, and the committee staff.

In March 2008, Berman took over as chairman of the Foreign Affairs Committee following the death of his California colleague Tom Lantos. Berman staked out positions concerning several of the world's trouble spots. Despite his more supportive views of the war in Iraq, he avoided proposals that could create conflict with Pelosi and the Democratic Caucus. His own views had evolved by that time, and he harbored doubts about the prospects for U.S. success. Berman helped craft measurable benchmarks for progress in Iraq.

Berman's most significant legislative achievement during his first year as chairman was approval of the civilian nuclear agreement with India. As part of the deal, he insisted on increased congressional oversight, including a requirement that the president notify Congress of new discussions with India. As a strong supporter of Israel, Berman in January 2009 sponsored a resolution supporting its retaliatory strikes against Palestinians in Gaza, which passed 390-5. Berman has long been concerned about Iran's nuclear program and supports sanctions against the mullah regime. He supported the Obama administration's attempts to negotiate with the Iranians on ending their nuclear weapons programs. But he also prepared a bill authorizing tougher sanctions, including a ban on U.S. contracts with firms exporting gasoline to refinery-poor Iran, which he called "the first key step to ensure that President Obama is empowered with the full range of tools he needs to address the looming nuclear threat from Iran." It passed 412-12 in December 2009.

Berman supported Obama administration proposals to increase foreign aid to Pakistan, and his bill to triple it to $6 billion over four years passed the House in June 2009. He also opposed a Democratic move to require the Obama administration to state an exit strategy in Afghanistan, saying it would "complicate our efforts to help (the Afghans) create a stable and secure nation." After President Obama announced a new Afghanistan strategy in December 2010, Berman held extensive hearings. On other issues, he led the committee in approving full payment of United Nations dues, expanding the Peace Corps, and passing a resolution condemning the Ottoman Turks' genocide against Armenians in 1915.

When Democrats lost majority control of the House in 2011, Berman became ranking member on Foreign Affairs. And he is second in seniority to Democrat John Conyers of Michigan on Judiciary. He remains a go-to guy on many state issues. But in 2009, he was a target of criticism for an earmark he put in the economic stimulus bill: $200,000 for the tattoo removal program at Providence Holy Cross Medical Center in North Hollywood. He argued that it helped curb gang activity in the area.

Redistricting, a Berman specialty, will be different for him this time around. After the 2000 census, his brother, Michael, was hired as redistricting consultant by California's U.S. House and state Senate Democrats, and Berman ended up with a district that enhanced his electability. That scenario won't be repeated. In 2008, California voters passed Proposition 11 creating an independent commission to oversee redistricting. At the insistence of then-House Speaker Pelosi, the commission was limited to drawing state legislative districts, not congressional districts. But in 2010, Proposition 20 was introduced to give the commission jurisdiction over congressional lines. Berman responded by pushing his own Proposition 27 to repeal Proposition 11. He lost resoundingly. Proposition 20 was approved 61%-39%, while Berman's proposition was defeated 60%-41%.

TWENTY-NINTH DISTRICT

Adam Schiff (D)

Elected 2000, 6th term; b. June 22, 1960, Framingham, MA; home, Burbank; Stanford U., B.A. 1982; Harvard U., J.D. 1985; Jewish; married (Eve); 2 children.

Elected Office: CA Senate, 1996-00.

Professional Career: Prosecutor, U.S. Atty. Gen. Ofc., L.A., CA 1987-93; Practicing atty., 1986-87, 1995-96.

DC Office: 2411 RHOB, 20515, 202-225-4176; Fax: 202-225-5828; Web site: schiff.house.gov.

State Offices: Pasadena, 626-304-2727.

Committees: *Appropriations:* Commerce, Justice, Science & Related Agencies; State, Foreign Operations & Related Programs. *Permanent Select Committee on Intelligence:* Technical & Tactical Intelligence (RMM).

Group Ratings

	ACLU	ACU	ADA	CFG	AFS	FRC	LCV	ITIC	NTU	COC
2010	87	0	90	0	100	0	100	100	6	25
2009	–	0	100	4	100	–	100	–	3	33

National Journal Ratings

	2010 LIB	—	2010 CONS	2009 LIB	—	2009 CONS
Economic	80%	—	18%	73%	—	25%
Social	61%	—	39%	75%	—	20%
Foreign	78%	—	17%	78%	—	17%
Composite	74%	—	26%	77%	—	23%

Key Votes of the 111th Congress

1. Overturn Ledbetter	Y	5. Bar federal abortion funds	N	9. Stop detainee transfers	N
2. Pass $820 billion stimulus	Y	6. Pass health care bill	Y	10. Legalize immigrants' kids	*
3. Let guns in national parks	N	7. Regulate financial firms	Y	11. Repeal don't ask, tell	Y
4. Pass cap-and-trade	Y	8. Pass tax cuts for some	Y	12. Limit campaign funds	Y

Election Results

2010 general	Adam Schiff (D)	104,374	(65%)	($1,378,951)
	John Colbert (R)	51,534	(32%)	($675,596)
	William Cushing (Lib)	5,218	(3%)	
2010 primary	Adam Schiff (D)	unopposed		

Prior Winning Percentages: 2008 (69%), 2006 (63%), 2004 (65%), 2002 (63%), 2000 (53%)

Population		Race/Ethnicity		Work	
Pop. 2010:	642,138	White:	39.5%	Private:	76.9%
Change since 2000:	Up 0.5%	Black:	4.6%	Government:	13.2%
Urban:	99.4%	Hispanic:	25.0%	Self-employed:	9.8%
Rural:	0.6%	Asian:	27.7%	Blue collar:	14.4%
Area size:	102 sq. mi.	Native Am.:	0.1%	White collar:	70.0%
		Hawaiian:	0.1%	Khaki collar:	0.0%
Age		Two+ races:	2.7%	Other:	15.6%
Median age:	39.1 yrs.				
More than 65 yrs:	14.5%	*Ancestry*		Median income:	$59,209
Less than 18 yrs:	20.2%	German	4.7%	Median Home Value:	$621,800
		Irish	4.3%		
Education		English	4.1%	**Military Veterans**	
H.S. grad:	83.6%			% of Pop:	4.4%
College grad:	38.4%				
Grad degree:	14.2%				

Glendale, Pasadena, Alhambra

In the early part of the 20th century, when Los Angeles was growing rapidly and on its way to becoming one of America's major cities, its richest citizens settled not on the beach (too clammy and cold) or on the west side (too dusty and remote), but in communities they built at the base of the San Gabriel Mountains. Their snow-capped peaks, rising 10,000 feet above the city, are visible most of the year. The place to be was Pasadena, home of the Rose Bowl, Cal Tech, and

2008 Presidential Vote
Barack Obama (D) 159,947   (68%)
John McCain (R) 71,860   (30%)

2004 Presidential Vote
John Kerry (D) 136,796   (61%)
George Bush (R) 83,448   (37%)

Cook Partisan Voting Index: D+14

a baroque-domed city hall. Pasadena and South Pasadena have carefully preserved their bungalow neighborhoods, and Pasadena preserved and rebuilt the 80-year-old curving Colorado Boulevard Bridge over Arroyo Seco. More middle-class is Glendale, north of downtown Los Angeles, site of Forest Lawn Cemetery and DreamWorks Animation. To the west, beneath the Verdugo Mountains, is Burbank, the "media capital of the world" and the headquarters for NBC Studios, ABC Studios, Warner Brothers, and Disney, plus many small entertainment and multimedia companies. With their lower taxes and business-friendly attitude, Glendale and Burbank were booming before the nationwide recession struck in 2007 and 2008. The downturn also hit local governments hard; Pasadena's sales tax revenue dropped almost 24% in 2009. Still, the city pushed ahead in 2010 with a $170 million renovation of the Rose Bowl stadium, one of the area's economic mainstays.

The 29th Congressional District of California includes Pasadena, South Pasadena, Glendale, and the eastern half of Burbank. Historically, these were solidly Republican cities, but they have become more Democratic in recent years, for various reasons—Pasadena because of the cultural liberalism of affluent voters and the Democratic preference of the growing black community; Glendale because of large communities of Armenians (the nation's largest), Iranians, Koreans, and Filipinos; and Burbank from its reliance on show business. The district also includes, south of South Pasadena, cities with large Asian populations: Vietnamese in San Gabriel and Chinese in Alhambra, Temple City, and the northern edge of Monterey Park (which the locals call Little Taipei). This is a polyglot district—25% Hispanic, 28% Asian, 11% Armenian, and 5% African-American. It has become solidly Democratic, casting only 37% of its votes for President Bush in 2004 and 30% for Republican presidential candidate John McCain in 2008.

Adam Schiff (D)

The congressman from the 29th District is Adam Schiff, a Democrat elected in 2000. Schiff's father was a traveling salesman and later owned a lumberyard. Schiff grew up throughout the country, eventually graduating from high school in Northern California. He went on to Stanford University and Harvard Law School. From 1987 to 1993, he worked in the U.S. attorney's office in Los Angeles. He ran for the California Assembly and lost three times. But in 1996, he was elected to the state Senate. In his first two years, he authored dozens of measures that Republican Gov. Pete Wilson signed into law, including a bill guaranteeing up-to-date textbooks in classrooms and another reforming the child support system. Schiff also taught political science at Glendale Community College.

Schiff ran for the House in the first election following the 1998 impeachment of President Clinton, and the issue became a factor in a number of races in 2000. Schiff challenged incumbent Republican James Rogan, who was a leader in the Judiciary Committee's deliberations and a persuasive voice for the case against Clinton, which centered on the president's affair with a White House intern. Rogan had won re-election in 1998 by just 51%-46%, and Clinton pal and entertainment mogul David Geffen was promising to raise millions of dollars to oppose him. The Schiff-Rogan race became a fundraising marathon, and was then the most expensive House race on record. The candidates raised more than $10 million combined, and much more was spent independently by Clinton's supporters as well as his detractors.

In addition to their opposing positions on Clinton's impeachment, the candidates disagreed on health care, abortion rights, gun control, and taxes. Rogan branded his opponent as a traditional tax-and-spend liberal, who would "run naked through the Treasury, spending everything he can." Schiff attacked Rogan for calling abortion a Holocaust for the African-American community. And he said Rogan's focus on Washington led him to ignore local problems. Schiff won by an unexpectedly large 53%-44% vote, and has been easily re-elected since.

In the House, Schiff's voting record has been moderate, especially on defense and foreign policy. He joined the Blue Dog Coalition of moderate to conservative Democrats, and has sometimes worked across party lines. He was instrumental in bipartisan legislation that made identity theft a crime. And on a bill to implement recommendations of the 9/11 commission, he was the only Democrat voting with Judiciary Committee Republicans on added immigration restrictions. The final bill included his provisions to establish new penalties for developing a "dirty bomb," and to give new tools to law enforcement to crack down on weapons of mass destruction.

Schiff stirred complaints from liberal constituents when he supported the resolution approving the use of force in Iraq in 2002 and for voting for the USA PATRIOT Act, the anti-terrorism law giving law enforcement broad new powers. He also was the only Democrat on the Judiciary Committee in 2009 to join Republicans in opposing legislation giving Americans greater power to challenge charges of alleged spying or illegal detention. But he also has been a solid party activist, contributing to the Democratic Congressional Campaign Committee's re-election efforts by co-chairing a mentoring program for prime candidates. His contribution to congressional ethics reform was a bill, passed by the House in 2007, preventing lawmakers from placing their spouses on campaign payrolls. He has an interest in intellectual property issues and serves as co-chairman of the Congressional International Anti-Piracy Caucus, which in 2010 released a list of foreign websites that provide access to pirated materials.

As the co-founder of a Democratic study group on national security and with seats on both the Intelligence and Appropriations committees, Schiff has focused especially on legislation to secure nuclear materials in the former Soviet Union and elsewhere to keep them out of the hands of terrorists. In 2010, Schiff got a bill into law to have the Homeland Security Department develop better ways to "fingerprint" nuclear material. He has also pressed the cause for recognition of the Armenian genocide as the responsibility of the Ottoman Empire, a move Turkey adamantly opposes. His resolution was approved by the House Foreign Affairs Committee in 2007, but he agreed to postpone further action after a strong reaction from Turkey. He did get a bill signed into law in 2010 that calls for the State Department to expand its monitoring of press freedom and media independence as it tracks human rights violations.

THIRTIETH DISTRICT

Henry Waxman (D)

Elected 1974, 19th term; b. Sept. 12, 1939, Los Angeles; home, Los Angeles; U.C.L.A., B.A. 1961, J.D. 1964; Jewish; married (Janet); 2 children.

Elected Office: CA Assembly, 1968–74.

Professional Career: Practicing atty., 1965–68.

DC Office: 2204 RHOB, 20515, 202-225-3976; Fax: 202-225-4099; Web site: waxman.house.gov.

State Offices: Los Angeles, 310-652-3095; 818-878-7400; 323-651-1040.

Committees: *Energy & Commerce* (RMM): Commerce, Manufacturing & Trade; Communications & Technology; Energy & Power; Environment & the Economy; Health; Oversight & Investigations.

Group Ratings

	ACLU	ACU	ADA	CFG	AFS	FRC	LCV	ITIC	NTU	COC
2010	94	0	90	0	100	6	90	100	9	25
2009	–	0	100	4	100	–	100	–	1	33

National Journal Ratings

	2010 LIB — 2010 CONS	2009 LIB — 2009 CONS
Economic	90% — 0%	91% — 0%
Social	93% — 0%	89% — 0%
Foreign	71% — 28%	91% — 0%
Composite	88% — 12%	95% — 5%

Key Votes of the 111th Congress

1. Overturn Ledbetter	Y	5. Bar federal abortion funds	N	9. Stop detainee transfers	N
2. Pass $820 billion stimulus	Y	6. Pass health care bill	Y	10. Legalize immigrants' kids	Y
3. Let guns in national parks	N	7. Regulate financial firms	Y	11. Repeal don't ask, tell	Y
4. Pass cap-and-trade	Y	8. Pass tax cuts for some	Y	12. Limit campaign funds	Y

Election Results

2010 general	Henry Waxman (D)	153,663	(65%)	($1,538,103)
	C. Wilkerson (R)	75,948	(32%)	($368,248)
	Erich Miller (Lib)	5,021	(2%)	($13,517)
2010 primary	Henry Waxman (D)	unopposed		

Prior Winning Percentages: 2008 (100%), 2006 (71%), 2004 (71%), 2002 (70%), 2000 (76%), 1998 (74%), 1996 (68%), 1994 (68%), 1992 (61%), 1990 (69%), 1988 (72%), 1986 (88%), 1984 (63%), 1982 (65%), 1980 (64%), 1978 (63%), 1976 (68%), 1974 (64%)

Population		Race/Ethnicity		Work	
Pop. 2010:	662,319	White:	72.1%	Private:	77.1%
Change since 2000:	Up 3.6%	Black:	2.9%	Government:	8.6%
Urban:	97.5%	Hispanic:	10.1%	Self-employed:	14.0%
Rural:	2.5%	Asian:	10.8%	Blue collar:	5.1%
Area size:	388 sq. mi.	Native Am.:	0.1%	White collar:	85.1%
		Hawaiian:	0.1%	Khaki collar:	0.0%
Age		Two+ races:	3.5%	Other:	9.7%
Median age:	39.8 yrs.				
More than 65 yrs:	15.3%	*Ancestry*		Median income:	$80,343
Less than 18 yrs:	17.5%	German	9.0%	Median Home Value:	$888,300
		Irish	7.1%		
Education		English	6.9%	**Military Veterans**	
H.S. grad:	94.9%			% of Pop:	6.0%
College grad:	59.2%				
Grad degree:	24.6%				

Part Los Angeles, Santa Monica

The Westside (often written as one word) of Los Angeles is perhaps the most glamorous and flashiest concentration of affluence in the world. It is the heartland of one of America's most productive and creative industries and one of the nation's major exports, show business. The first moviemakers came here looking for a place to shoot silent films where the sunlight was more dependable than in Astoria, Queens, or Englewood, New Jersey. They found it in Hollywood, a

2008 Presidential Vote		
Barack Obama (D) 242,022	(70%)
John McCain (R) 95,869	(28%)
2004 Presidential Vote		
John Kerry (D) 220,181	(66%)
George Bush (R) 109,014	(33%)
Cook Partisan Voting Index: D+18		

suburb just annexed by burgeoning Los Angeles when the first movie studio was built in 1911. In 1923 came the "Hollywood" sign, overlooking the soon-famous intersection of Hollywood and Vine. By the 1930s, big studio lots were scattered around town, over the mountains in Burbank, or out toward the ocean in Westwood and Culver City. Miraculously, the studio bosses of that era—most of them Jewish immigrants with little ancestral experience of America—created a popular culture that was universally accessible and embodied the American spirit in a way that still rings true.

Showbiz still sets the tone for the Westside. It remains tremendously profitable, and not just for the big conglomerate-owned studios. There are thousands of entrepreneurs, actors, writers, and craftsmen who are the best in the world at what they do and who tend to cluster on the Westside because so many of the others they do business with are there. Not everyone is in show business, of course. The Westside is metro Los Angeles's biggest office center, with horrific traffic inbound in the morning and outbound in the evening. Most office workers can't afford to live anywhere nearby. Los Angeles ranks first in the nation in the percentage of people who work at home.

There are large numbers of singles and gays here. It is the center of the nation's second-largest Jewish community, or actually, communities. The old Fairfax district, where corner delis have long been a hub of political discourse, is now home to many Russian Jewish immigrants. Orthodox Jews are building communities, amid protests of overdevelopment, along Pico Boulevard. Iranian Jews have poured in since 1979, and now make up about one-quarter of the population of Beverly Hills, which elected an Iranian-American mayor in 2007. Beverly Hills and the Westside remain the locus of some of America's most expensive residential real estate, where people buy houses for multiples of $1 million, knock them down, and build something new for many more millions. And it has one of the world's premier high-priced shopping areas, Rodeo Drive.

The 30th Congressional District of California contains most of Westside Los Angeles plus territory to the west. It includes the Fairfax neighborhood east to La Brea Avenue, heavily gay West Hollywood, Beverly Hills, Westwood and UCLA, Bel Air, Brentwood, Santa Monica, and the whole 27 miles of Malibu on the ocean. The district also includes the western end of the San Fernando Valley, with the high-income neighborhoods of Woodland Hills and Chatsworth up against the mountains that rim the Valley. And it includes the high-income suburbs of Hidden Hills, Calabasas, Agoura Hills, and Westlake Village, nestled amid mountains along the Ventura Freeway. By today's definitions, it is the least diverse district in metro Los Angeles. Only 3% of its residents are African-American, and only 10% are Hispanic, by a considerable margin the lowest percentages in Southern California. Many Latinos work in the district, but few are interested in paying the prices for housing. Politically, the 30th District is heavily Democratic, but not as heavily as San Francisco. (The Westside was the home of a former president who did not at all exemplify its politics: Ronald Reagan. Until he withdrew from public view, suffering from Alzheimer's disease, he regularly went to his office on the former Fox lot that is now Century City.) The 30th District voted 66%-33% for John Kerry in 2004 and 70%-28% for Barack Obama in 2008.

Henry Waxman (D)

The congressman from the 30th District is Henry Waxman, a Democrat first elected in 1974, long one of the ablest members of the House and a shrewd political operator. He is the ranking Democrat on the powerful House Energy and Commerce Committee, which he chaired before Democrats lost the majority in the 2010 election.

There is no Westside glitz about him. The son of Russian immigrants, Waxman grew up over his family's store in Watts. He graduated from the University of California at Los Angeles and its law school, where he met Howard Berman, his longtime political ally and colleague from the adjacent 28th District. They became immersed in the Federation of Young Democrats, and Waxman chaired the group for a year. He moved up rapidly in politics by spying openings before others did.

He ran against Assemblyman Lester McMillan in the mostly Jewish Fairfax area in 1968, at age 28, and won 64% in the primary. From 1971 to 1972, he chaired the Assembly's redistricting committee, a good place to make friends. In 1974 he was elected to Congress. Waxman's biggest break in Congress came after the 1978 election, when he was elected chairman of the Commerce Committee's Health and Environment Subcommittee. This was one of the first times House Democrats decided to ignore seniority in handing out subcommittee chairs. Waxman argued his case on the issues. And in a move quite unprecedented at the time, though common in Sacramento, he made campaign contributions to other Democrats on the full committee. (The practice is all but expected today of anyone trying to get a committee gavel or role in party leadership in Congress.) Waxman won the post, 15-12, over the widely respected Richardson Preyer of North Carolina.

In the 1970s and 1980s, Waxman and Berman built their own political machine in Los Angeles. Its power came not from patronage but from fundraising and savvy. They raised huge sums on the Westside for favored candidates. They put out carefully targeted direct mail, with customized letters and endorsement slates sent out to different lists of people. In California, where television advertising is exceedingly expensive and political activists are widely dispersed geographically, this made them critical players. But the organization withered in the 1990s. Waxman is less active now in Los Angeles-area politics, though he did endorse former Assembly Speaker Antonio Villaraigosa in his successful 2005 mayoral race.

From 1978 to 1994, Waxman was part of the Democratic majority in the House and the chairman of an important subcommittee, making him a major national policy maker, usually from behind the scenes. In 1981 and 1982, he prevented the Reagan administration and Commerce Committee Chairman John Dingell, D-Mich., from revising the Clean Air Act, because he wanted tougher pollution controls. Biding his time, Waxman worked to strengthen the law in the 1990 revision. He also had a hand in legislation addressing chemicals in drinking water, radon abatement, and lead contamination. Another Waxman project was expanding Medicaid for the poor. Between 1984 and 1990, he got coverage for all poor children up to 18 and pregnant women living in poverty. This helped raise Medicaid from 9% to 14% of state spending in the 1980s, and explains why Waxman was unpopular with many governors.

Waxman has secured funding for AIDS research, important in a district with a large gay population. In early 1994, in widely publicized hearings, he lined up the chief executive officers of leading tobacco companies and accused them of adding nicotine and other substances to cigarettes and of lying in their testimony. All of this had no immediate legislative result, and when Republican Thomas Bliley of Virginia became Commerce Committee chairman, the hearings stopped. But Waxman brought the tobacco issue into public view, and he helped inspire the lawsuits against tobacco companies that resulted in a massive redistribution of corporate assets—from the tobacco companies to state governments and trial lawyers.

When Republicans took over Congress in 1995, there was no slackening of effort on Waxman's part, though he was largely shut out of the legislative process. In 1996, he gave up the ranking position on the health subcommittee to become the ranking Democrat on the Government Reform Committee, where he concentrated on holding hearings and publicizing Government Accountability Office reports. Waxman sharply attacked GOP Chairman Dan Burton's investigation of President Clinton's fundraising operation, arguing that Burton had given himself unprecedented subpoena power and was misusing it. He emerged as Clinton's most articulate House defender during the campaign finance scandal. In 2001, with Republican George W. Bush as the new president, Waxman frequently fired off letters to Burton demanding investigations of alleged White House misdeeds. He and Dingell instigated a GAO investigation of company executives who had been consulted by Vice President Cheney's energy task force. In February 2002, the GAO brought a lawsuit against Cheney, but a federal judge ruled against the agency.

In January 2003, Virginia Republican Tom Davis took over as committee chairman and promised a more constructive relationship with Waxman. Nevertheless, Waxman indefatigably wrote multipage letters with dozens of footnotes and questions, called for GAO investigations, and invoked a 1920s rule that entitles any seven members of the committee to seek information from the executive branch. He assembled a staff of dozens of investigators, squirreled in tiny offices around the Capitol Hill complex. He and Democrat Sherrod Brown of Ohio demanded that 10 pharmaceutical companies reveal how much they paid in consulting fees and stock options to National Institutes of Health scientists, which led to a stricter NIH policy on ethics and disclosure in 2005. Waxman was a leading critic of Halliburton and other government contractors in Iraq, pointing out tirelessly that Cheney was once Halliburton's chief executive officer and alleging that State Department documents revealed Halliburton employees tried to extract bribes for fuel contracts. But Waxman and Davis managed to work together on investigations on mad-cow disease and D.C. drinking water.

Democrats took control of the House in 2007, giving Waxman the gavel at the Oversight and Government Reform Committee. Davis, who became the ranking minority member, said, "There is no question that life is going to be different for the administration. Henry is going to be tough ···and he's been waiting a long time to do this." Waxman reduced the number of subcommittees from seven to five and doubled the staff reporting to him. His first hearings were on whether the administration had interfered with the work of climate scientists and on fraud and waste in reconstruction projects in Iraq.

That was only the beginning. Waxman's bottomless portfolio included hearings into secret agent Valerie Plame's complaints that the revealing of her name had violated national security and testimony by Secretary of State Condoleezza Rice on prewar intelligence in Iraq. Few subjects seemed too far afield for a Waxman investigation: He probed the health effects of uranium mines on Navajo lands, the pricing of government contracts with Sun Microsystems, and steroid use in professional baseball. Probably his most publicized hearing came in February 2008, when baseball pitcher Roger Clemens and his former trainer gave conflicting testimony on drug use. In 2008, Waxman turned his focus to the collapse of major financial institutions as a result of shaky lending practices and sought information on the compensation of executives of Fannie Mae and Freddie Mac, the government-backed mortgage issuers.

With the arrival of a Democratic administration in 2009, Waxman could achieve more of his policy goals on the Energy and Commerce Committee than on the oversight panel. He remained particularly interested in issues related to air pollution and global warming. He had co-sponsored bills limiting carbon emissions and supported the bill passed by the California Legislature and signed by Republican Gov. Arnold Schwarzenegger in 2006. In addition, he had long been eager to advance national health insurance legislation. All of this suggested that Waxman wanted to be chairman of Energy and Commerce. But there was a hitch. An equally savvy and effective Democrat, John Dingell of Michigan, was next in line for the job. But working against Dingell was his rocky relationship with Democratic House Speaker Nancy Pelosi, who, by contrast, was a big fan of Waxman's. And Dingell, who represents a Detroit-area district dependent on auto manufacturing, was less enthusiastic about air-pollution regulation than Pelosi. The long-brewing clash came after the November 2008 elections. House Democratic rules provided for committee chairmen to be chosen by a vote of the Democratic Caucus, and Waxman had quietly sought support and made contributions to Democrats in close elections. Waxman then went public that he was challenging Dingell for the chairmanship.

In the past, some Democratic members had retired before they reached the point where they could be humiliated by being deprived of a gavel because they were seen as less competent than a challenger, but this was not the issue here: Both men were regarded as highly competent. On Nov. 19, 2008, the Democratic Steering and Policy Committee voted 25-22 for Waxman. This was seen as a signal that Pelosi was supporting Waxman, though the margin was pretty small. There were signs that President-elect Obama was leaning Waxman's way. Obama had just reiterated his support for tougher carbon emissions legislation and had hired Waxman's longtime chief of staff, Phil Schiliro, as the White House liaison to Congress. The caucus vote was scheduled for November 20. Dingell had the support of many members of the Congressional Black Caucus, of the conservative "Blue Dogs," and of the moderate New Democrats. He also had the backing of lawmakers from industrial and coal states that would be hit hard by carbon emissions legislation. Waxman had the support of most of the 33 Democrats in the California delegation, and of the bulk of the Democratic freshmen. Waxman won 137-122.

As chairman, Waxman played a key role in much of the major legislation of the 111th Congress (2009-10). In March 2009, he and Democratic Rep. Edward Markey of Massachusetts proposed a cap-and-trade bill that created an emissions trading system among industries with the aim of reducing carbon dioxide emissions 20% by the year 2020, 42% by 2030 and 83% by 2050. Many emission permits would be auctioned off and utilities would be required to produce 6% of their electricity from renewable sources by 2012. Republicans called it a national energy tax, and even some Energy and Commerce Democrats were dubious. To gain votes, Waxman agreed to changes. He lowered the emissions target to 17% by 2020 and agreed that 35% of emissions credits would be granted free to electric utilities and 15% to producers of steel, aluminum, chemicals and glass. To gain support from Texans, he agreed to provide 2% of emission credits to oil refiners; to get Dingell on board, he agreed to free credits for automakers that produce cars in the United States. The committee approved his bill 33-25, with one Republican voting yes and four Democrats voting no.

As the bill headed for a final floor showdown, Waxman made further concessions. To placate lawmakers from industrial districts, he agreed to tariffs against countries that don't reduce carbon emissions. He gave Democrat Alan Grayson a $50 million hurricane research center in his Florida district. Amid intensive administration lobbying, the bill passed on June 26, 2009 by 219-212. "Today we have taken decisive and historic action to promote America's energy security and to create millions of clean energy jobs that will drive our economic recovery and long-term growth," Waxman said. Despite all of his efforts, the Senate, where opposition to the bill ran deep, never took it up.

Waxman also had a hand in the Democrats' sweeping health care overhaul in 2009 and 2010. Speaker Pelosi hoped to pass it in the House before the August 2009 recess, but Waxman encountered problems in committee. Negotiations with conservative Blue Dog Democrats were on and off, and when Waxman agreed that a newly created government-run insurer would negotiate fees with providers rather than base them on Medicare rates, liberals complained loudly. Waxman propitiated them with more amendments. It finally passed in committee 31-28 on July 31, too late to come to the floor before the recess. Then, over the recess, some Democrats encountered strong opposition to the bill in town hall meetings. More changes were necessary to secure a majority, including the addition of an amendment by Michigan Democrat Bart Stupak barring any federal involvement in abortions. The bill finally came to the floor on Nov. 7, 2009, and passed 220 to 215. The Senate passed its own version on Dec. 24, 2009, and Congress ultimately approved a final version that was signed by Obama on March 23, 2010.

In addition to major initiatives on energy and health care, Waxman influenced several smaller legislative efforts. He has long worked on drug patent legislation, and the development of biologics raised the issue of their patent life. Companies and universities developing biologics wanted 14 years. Waxman, opposed to patent protection, initially proposed zero but ultimately agreed to a White House-engineered compromise of 10 years. Energy and Commerce also weighed in on the financial regulatory rewrite in December 2009, and Waxman prevailed over Financial Services Committee Chairman Barney Frank, D-Mass., in having a board rather than a single chairman run a new consumer protection agency. On other issues, the committee passed a bill requiring black boxes to be installed on cars to provide a record in crashes, voted unanimously to give the Federal Energy Regulatory Commission authority to shield the nation's electric grid from terrorist attacks, and approved a rewrite of the Clean Water Act. The House in 2010 passed Waxman's "cash for caulkers" bill granting $6 billion in tax rebates for taxpayers installing energy-efficient home improvements. The Senate did not take it up by the close of the 111th Congress.

Waxman has always won re-election easily, and has continued to contribute generously, and strategically, to other Democrats' campaigns. In July 2009, he published *The Waxman Report: How Congress Really Works*, a memoir written with the assistance of *Atlantic* staff writer Joshua Green.

THIRTY-FIRST DISTRICT

Xavier Becerra (D)

Elected 1992, 10th term; b. Jan. 26, 1958, Sacramento; home, Eagle Rock; Stanford U., B.A. 1980, J.D. 1984; Catholic; married (Carolina Reyes); 3 children.

Elected Office: CA Assembly, 1990–92.

Professional Career: Staff atty., Legal Assistance Corp. of Central MA; Dist. dir., CA Sen. Art Torres, 1986; CA dep. atty. gen., 1987–90.

DC Office: 1226 LHOB, 20515, 202-225-6235; Fax: 202-225-2202; Web site: becerra.house.gov.

State Offices: Los Angeles, 213-483-1425.

Committees: *Ways & Means:* Oversight; Social Security (RMM).

Group Ratings

	ACLU	ACU	ADA	CFG	AFS	FRC	LCV	ITIC	NTU	COC
2010	93	0	95	5	100	0	100	67	6	13
2009	–	4	100	6	100	–	100	–	2	33

National Journal Ratings

	2010 LIB	—	2010 CONS	2009 LIB	—	2009 CONS
Economic	78%	—	20%	91%	—	0%
Social	93%	—	0%	89%	—	0%
Foreign	92%	—	3%	83%	—	16%
Composite	90%	—	10%	91%	—	9%

Key Votes of the 111th Congress

1. Overturn Ledbetter	Y	5. Bar federal abortion funds	N	9. Stop detainee transfers	N
2. Pass $820 billion stimulus	Y	6. Pass health care bill	Y	10. Legalize immigrants' kids	Y
3. Let guns in national parks	N	7. Regulate financial firms	Y	11. Repeal don't ask, tell	Y
4. Pass cap-and-trade	Y	8. Pass tax cuts for some	Y	12. Limit campaign funds	Y

Election Results

2010 general	Xavier Becerra (D)	76,363	(84%)	($1,716,196)
	Stephen Smith (R)	14,740	(16%)	($15,361)
2010 primary	Xavier Becerra (D)	20,550	(88%)	
	Sal Genovese (D)	2,795	(12%)	

Prior Winning Percentages: 2008 (100%), 2006 (100%), 2004 (80%), 2002 (81%), 2000 (83%), 1998 (81%), 1996 (72%), 1994 (66%), 1992 (58%)

Population		Race/Ethnicity		Work	
Pop. 2010:	611,336	White:	11.3%	Private:	80.7%
Change since 2000:	Down 4.3%	Black:	3.8%	Government:	8.2%
Urban:	100.0%	Hispanic:	68.2%	Self-employed:	10.9%
Rural:	0.0%	Asian:	15.0%	Blue collar:	28.8%
Area size:	40 sq. mi.	Native Am.:	0.2%	White collar:	45.2%
		Hawaiian:	0.1%	Khaki collar:	0.1%
Age		Two+ races:	1.1%	Other:	25.9%
Median age:	32.3 yrs.				
More than 65 yrs:	8.3%	*Ancestry*		Median income:	$35,932
Less than 18 yrs:	25.7%	German	1.8%	Median Home Value:	$493,600
		Irish	1.8%		
Education		English	1.3%	**Military Veterans**	
H.S. grad:	59.6%			% of Pop:	2.6%
College grad:	19.6%				
Grad degree:	5.1%				

Northeast and South Los Angeles

Surrounding downtown Los Angeles are neighborhoods built in the mid-20th century that are
just now starting to take on the patina of the historic. Downtown L.A., with its pink cylinders jutting up to 70 stories from what was once a low-
rise business district, has become surprisingly
pedestrian-friendly, with attractive plazas like
the one around the redesigned Los Angeles Library. But downtown remains detached from
the ethnically diverse neighborhoods around it.

2008 Presidential Vote		
Barack Obama (D) 113,941	(80%)
John McCain (R) 25,441	(18%)

2004 Presidential Vote		
John Kerry (D) 92,894	(77%)
George Bush (R) 26,054	(22%)

Cook Partisan Voting Index: D+29

They seem to change character with every new immigration flow. South of downtown is the garment district, with factories in nondescript buildings, an economically vibrant area that has helped
make Los Angeles the largest manufacturing city in America today. To the north is Lincoln
Heights, a heavily Hispanic area centered on the busy shopping street of North Broadway, where
residents have been fighting gangs and graffiti with some success; crime in much of Los Angeles
dropped significantly in 2009. Highland Park and Eagle Rock, which were white middle-class enclaves 30 years ago, are now ethnically mixed middle-class enclaves with large numbers of Latinos
and Asians. Eagle Rock is the home of Occidental College, where President Obama attended his
first two years of college. West of downtown are Pico Union, an entry point for new immigrants
where Greeks, Mexicans and Central Americans co-mingle, united by their passion for soccer; University Park, which surrounds the University of Southern California campus; and Thai Town,
along Hollywood Boulevard between Normandie and Western. Lower Sunset Boulevard and gentrifying Echo Park have become lively shopping strips filled with that rare L.A. commodity: pedes-
trians. Historic Filipinotown, known locally as Hi-Fi, was settled by Filipinos in the early 1900s
and has become more of a polyglot. Hollywood has long had a seedy look—it has not sprouted the
office buildings like Burbank or Glendale—but has recently been spiffed up.

Almost all of these areas, centering geographically on Dodger Stadium, are part of California's
31st Congressional District. In Los Angeles' booming 1980s, these neighborhoods were suddenly
thronged with immigrants, with small houses and garden apartments full of large families and
many children. In the 1990s, the population surge stopped, and this became the slowest-growing
district in California, as the newcomers of the decade before moved out to middle-class neighborhoods and incoming immigrants spread more evenly around the Los Angeles Basin. Nearly one-
quarter of the district's families lived below the poverty level in 2008. And more than half the population was foreign-born.

Xavier Becerra (D)

The congressman from the 31st District is Xavier Becerra, a Democrat first elected in 1992. As the
vice chairman of the House Democratic Caucus, he is a member of the minority leadership team
headed by Nancy Pelosi of California.

Becerra *(beh-SEH-ra)* grew up in Sacramento. His mother was a Mexican immigrant, and his
father, who was born in the United States, supported the family with construction and other jobs.
Becerra worked his way through college and law school at Stanford University, becoming the first
in his family to get a college degree. He married a Harvard Medical School graduate who became
vice president of California's largest health care foundation. Becerra started his career at a legal
services clinic in Massachusetts, doing work for mentally disabled clients. When he returned to
California, Becerra was an aide to state Sen. Art Torres and then to Attorney General John Van
de Kamp. In 1990, he was elected to the California Assembly. In 1992, when U.S. Rep. Edward
Roybal, California's first Latino congressman and a Democrat, announced his retirement, Becerra
jumped into the race. His main competitor, Leticia Quezada, was a member of the Los Angeles
school board. Becerra had the endorsements of Roybal and County Supervisor Gloria Molina. Becerra won the primary with 32% of the vote to 22% for Quezada. He went on to defeat Republican
Morry Waksberg in the general election with 58% of the vote.

In the House, Becerra has been a consistent liberal. He has also been successful in moving
into the House Democratic leadership, winning praise for his hard-working, cerebral style. Some
Congressional Hispanic Caucus members dubbed him "Harvard," though he did not attend that
school. When Democrats won majority control of the House, fellow Californian and House Speaker
Nancy Pelosi gave him the newly created position of assistant to the speaker, where he helped
to set the party's legislative agenda. In a November 2008 leadership shuffle, Becerra ran for vice

chairman of the Democratic Caucus, and with Pelosi's help, defeated Rep. Marcy Kaptur of Ohio, 175-67. Pelosi also put him on the presidential deficit reduction panel formed in 2010. But he has not always seen eye-to-eye with his mentor; she was reportedly angry in 2009 when he intimated to Progressive Caucus members that the leadership abandoned a government-run "public option" for the health care overhaul bill too quickly.

President Obama also recognized Becerra as a standout and offered him the post of U.S. trade representative in 2008. But he declined after deciding that trade policy would not be a major White House priority in Obama's early years. Becerra had been Obama's campaign liaison to the Hispanic community and urged him to get behind a comprehensive immigration bill. He acknowledged in 2010 that Latinos regarded Obama with "a lot of suspicion" because of his failure to make immigration a priority in his first term.

Becerra was the first Hispanic to win a seat on the powerful House Ways and Means Committee. He has advocated tax changes to curtail the overseas exodus of jobs in the entertainment industry, including a tax credit for labor costs of independent film producers. He supported normalizing trade relations with China and won House approval of a resolution supporting reunification efforts between North and South Korea. His support for free trade deals with Chile and Singapore led to local protests by union activists, and he demanded improvements in the labor standards in the Central American Free Trade Agreement in return for his support. "Trade has to be sold as something that's good for us," he told *The Washington Post* in 2007. During the health care debate in 2009, he and Rep. Charles Boustany, R-La., convened a bipartisan group of lawmakers that sought in vain to find common ground on the issue.

In May 2008, Becerra won enactment of a bill establishing a commission to develop a national museum of the American Latino, which would be located on the National Mall and would be part of the Smithsonian Institution. The commission convened in 2009.

The one career setback for Becerra in recent years was his failed run for mayor of Los Angeles in 2001. He did not raise enough money to establish name recognition outside his district, and he was overshadowed by former Assembly Speaker Antonio Villaraigosa. In the primary, Becerra finished fifth, with just 6% of the vote.

THIRTY-SECOND DISTRICT

Judy Chu (D)

Elected July 2009, 1st full term; b. July 7, 1953, Los Angeles, CA; home, Monterey Park, CA; U.C.L.A., B.A. 1974; M.A. 1977; Ph.D. 1979.; No religious affiliation; married (Mike Eng); 0.

Elected Office: Garvey Schl. Bd., 1985-88; Monterey Park City Cncl. 1988-2001; CA Assembly, 2001-06; CA St. Bd. of Equalization, 2006-09.

Professional Career: Faculty member, Los Angeles Community College District, 1981-2001; Los Angeles City College, Psychology Dept., 1981-1988; E. Los Angeles College, Psychology Dept., 1988-2001.

DC Office: 1520 LHOB, 20515, 202-225-5464; Fax: 202-225-5467; Web site: chu.house.gov.

State Offices: El Monte, 626-448-1271.

Committees: *Judiciary:* Crime, Terrorism & Homeland Security; Intellectual Property, Competition & the Internet. *Small Business:* Agriculture, Energy & Trade; Contracting & Workforce (RMM); Economic Growth, Tax and Capital Access.

Group Ratings

	ACLU	ACU	ADA	CFG	AFS	FRC	LCV	ITIC	NTU	COC
2010	89	0	100	0	100	7	100	50	5	0
2009	–	0	–	0	100	–	100	–	2	40

National Journal Ratings

	2010 LIB — 2010 CONS		2009 LIB — 2009 CONS	
Economic	90% —	0%	* —	*
Social	93% —	0%	* —	*
Foreign	97% —	0%	* —	*
Composite	97% —	3%	* —	*

Key Votes of the 111th Congress

1. Overturn Ledbetter	*	5. Bar federal abortion funds	N	9. Stop detainee transfers	N
2. Pass $820 billion stimulus	*	6. Pass health care bill	Y	10. Legalize immigrants' kids	Y
3. Let guns in national parks	*	7. Regulate financial firms	Y	11. Repeal don't ask, tell	Y
4. Pass cap-and-trade	*	8. Pass tax cuts for some	Y	12. Limit campaign funds	Y

Election Results

2010 general	Judy Chu (D)..77,759	(71%)	($2,503,421)
	Edward Schmerling (R) 31,697	(29%)	(no FEC report)
2010 primary	Judy Chu (D)... unopposed		

Prior Winning Percentages: 2009 special (62%)

Population		Race/Ethnicity		Work	
Pop. 2010:	642,236	White:	10.5%	Private:	80.6%
Change since 2000:	Up 0.5%	Black:	1.9%	Government:	12.7%
Urban:	100.0%	Hispanic:	64.2%	Self-employed:	6.6%
Rural:	0.0%	Asian:	22.1%	Blue collar:	29.7%
Area size:	93 sq. mi.	Native Am.:	0.2%	White collar:	50.5%
		Hawaiian:	0.1%	Khaki collar:	0.0%
Age		Two+ races:	1.0%	Other:	19.8%
Median age:	32.8 yrs.				
More than 65 yrs:	10.3%	*Ancestry*		Median income:	$51,858
Less than 18 yrs:	27.3%	German	2.8%	Median Home Value:	$428,500
		Irish	1.9%		
Education		English	1.7%	**Military Veterans**	
H.S. grad:	66.2%			% of Pop:	4.1%
College grad:	16.6%				
Grad degree:	4.3%				

East Los Angeles, El Monte

Straight east from downtown Los Angeles on Interstate 10 is a string of suburbs that grew up in the 1940s and 1950s as white middle-class communities and today are a melting pot of immigrant groups that have achieved the American dream of home ownership and decent schools. The stucco houses were once filled with Midwest and East Coast migrants who discovered California during World War II. Now, they are more likely to be occupied by Mexican-American

2008 Presidential Vote

Barack Obama (D) 119,726	(68%)
John McCain (R) 52,356	(30%)

2004 Presidential Vote

John Kerry (D) 99,286	(62%)
George Bush (R) 58,341	(37%)

Cook Partisan Voting Index: D+15

families who spread out from their original East Los Angeles base to blue-collar suburbs like El Monte, Baldwin Park, Azusa and West Covina. Chinese and other Asians are the majority in Monterey Park and 49% of the population in Rosemead. The late *New York Times* food maven R.W. Apple Jr. described "a memorable week in the gastronomic trenches" of the local Asian restaurant scene, and reported that "it is easier to buy bok choy than iceberg" in Monterey Park. Almost every neighborhood here is mixed, with people whose origins are in different continents and cultures. The relatively recent arrivals have upgraded neighborhoods, bringing in energy and money, the enthusiasm of the young and the community-spiritedness of the homeowner. There are newly painted homes with carefully tended gardens, and neighborhoods filled with children. When blacks and Latinos were rioting in South Central and Hollywood in 1992, East Los Angeles and the San Gabriel Valley were quiet and orderly. But the nation's recent economic downturn hit this area of modest incomes like a sledgehammer, with unemployment climbing above 13% in several cities in 2009. The city of El Monte cut 17 police officers from its ranks that year, while other cities have sought to save money by cutting salaries as much as 10%.

The 32nd Congressional District of California covers much of this territory. It includes part of East Los Angeles and a small part of Los Angeles, most of Monterey Park and all of Rosemead, El Monte, Baldwin Park, Azusa, West Covina and Covina. It is 64% Hispanic and 22% Asian—the second-highest Asian percentage (after the adjacent 29th District) in southern California. Forty-two percent of its residents are foreign born. Politically, the new Latinos and Asians have been up for grabs. In the early 1990s, Asians, dismayed that civic leaders seemed more interested in the complaints of rioters than in compensating the store owners whose property was destroyed, moved toward the Republicans. In the middle 1990s, Latinos, because of Republican-inspired immigration and welfare laws halting aid to legal immigrants, moved heavily toward the Democrats. George W. Bush got 37% here in 2004. Four years later, Republican presidential nominee John McCain got 30%, while Democrat Barack Obama cleaned up with 68%.

Judy Chu (D)

The congresswoman from the 32nd District is Democrat Judy Chu. In this left-leaning district, Chu won a competitive Democratic primary in May 2009, and then cruised to an easy win in the July 2009 special election to succeed Democrat Hilda Solis, who became President Obama's new secretary of Labor. Chu is the second Chinese-American member of the House, after Rep. David Wu, an Oregon Democrat, and the first Chinese-American woman. She graduated from the University of California at Los Angeles, got a Ph.D. in psychology, and then taught for 13 years at East Los Angeles College. She served on the Garvey School District board for three years and was mayor of Monterey Park for 12 years. In 2000, Chu was elected to the California Assembly, where she focused on criminal justice and environmental protection issues. As the chairman of the Appropriations Committee, she sponsored a tax amnesty program that brought in significant sums for the state. In 2006, she was elected to the state Board of Equalization, where she worked on closing tax loopholes.

After Solis' Cabinet appointment, the contest for the Democratic nomination quickly settled into a race between Chu and state Sen. Gil Cedillo. He was the leading Hispanic candidate after state Sen. Gloria Romero decided to focus on her 2010 bid for state schools superintendent. Although many observers viewed the election as an ethnic showdown between an Asian and a Latino, the race actually was more nuanced. Chu gained the endorsement of much of the Democratic establishment and the state party, including some prominent Hispanics, such as Los Angeles Mayor Antonio Villaraigosa and members of Solis' family. The Los Angeles County Labor Federation, which was impressed by Chu's support for farm workers, supported her, as did EMILY's List, the national advocacy group for pro-abortion rights Democratic women. Cedillo's decade in the legislature proved to be less of an asset than expected, given that the Democratic primary was held on the same day that voters overwhelmingly defeated five state referenda on controversial tax and spending policies. A third candidate was also a Hispanic and siphoned support from likely Cedillo voters: political novice Emanuel Pleitez, a 26-year-old financial analyst who had worked on Obama's presidential campaign. Chu had raised nearly $1 million, Cedillo more than $700,000, and Pleitez $200,000. Chu won with 32%, to 23% for Cedillo and 14% for Pleitez.

Because she failed to receive a majority of the total primary vote, she faced a runoff with Republican Betty Chu, a Monterey Park councilwoman who is Chu's distant cousin by marriage. Little known by most district voters, Betty Chu got 10% of the vote in the primary, edging out Republican-endorsed Teresa Hernandez who got 9%. Hispanic groups lamented the likely loss of a seat in the House. Judy Chu easily bested Betty Chu by a nearly 2-to-1 ratio, 62% to 33%.

Chu has continued Solis' strongly liberal voting record. She joined the Out of Afghanistan Caucus and voted against a July 2010 spending bill to fund military operations there. When she served on the Education and Labor Committee, she worked to extend a program using economic stimulus funds to put unemployed workers in new jobs, co-sponsored Democratic Rep. Barney Frank's bill to bar discrimination on the basis of sexual orientation, and introduced legislation to maintain funding levels for school lunch programs. Chu co-sponsored Illinois Rep. Luis Gutierrez's comprehensive immigration reform bill and added an amendment to a 2010 bill requiring the Census Bureau and other federal offices to consider the needs of non-English speakers in writing instructions and rules.

THIRTY-THIRD DISTRICT

Karen Bass (D)

Elected 2010, 1st term; b. Oct. 3, 1953, Los Angeles; home, Los Angeles; U. of Southern CA, physician's asst. certificate; CA St. U., Dominguez Hills, B.A. 1990.; Baptist; Divorced; 5 children.

Elected Office: CA Assembly, 2005-10, speaker 2008-10.

Professional Career: Physician's asst., Los Angeles Cnty. Gen. Hospital; instructor, U. of Southern CA; exec. dir., Comm. Coalition, 1990-2004.

DC Office: 408 CHOB, 20515, 202-225-7084; Fax: 202-225-2422; Web site: karenbass.house.gov.

State Offices: Los Angeles, 323-965-1422.

Committees: *Budget. Foreign Affairs:* Africa, Global Health & Human Rights; Oversight & Investigations.

Election Results

2010 general	Karen Bass (D)..131,990	(86%)	($932,281)
	James Andion (R)..21,342	(14%)	(no FEC report)
2010 primary	Karen Bass (D)..41,250	(85%)	
	Felton Newell (D)..3,096	(6%)	

Population		Race/Ethnicity		Work	
Pop. 2010:	637,122	White:	21.6%	Private:	77.2%
Change since 2000:	Down 0.3%	Black:	24.5%	Government:	11.1%
Urban:	100.0%	Hispanic:	37.4%	Self-employed:	11.6%
Rural:	0.0%	Asian:	13.2%	Blue collar:	16.3%
Area size:	48 sq. mi.	Native Am.:	0.2%	White collar:	60.5%
		Hawaiian:	0.1%	Khaki collar:	0.0%
Age		Two+ races:	2.4%	Other:	23.1%
Median age:	34.2 yrs.				
More than 65 yrs:	10.4%	*Ancestry*		Median income:	$42,959
Less than 18 yrs:	21.4%	Subsaharan	5.0%	Median Home Value:	$601,700
		German	3.6%		
Education		Irish	3.3%	**Military Veterans**	
H.S. grad:	77.6%			% of Pop:	4.0%
College grad:	32.4%				
Grad degree:	10.5%				

West Central L.A., Culver City

Since the Los Angeles riots of 1992 and 1965, the city has had to live down its reputation as being inhospitable to African-Americans, a problem exacerbated by racial tensions in the city's infamous police department. But by other measures—levels of income and degree of residential integration with nonblacks—blacks in Los Angeles are doing better than blacks elsewhere in the United States. The city's black-owned businesses have the highest revenues of any city

2008 Presidential Vote		
Barack Obama (D) 205,470	(87%)
John McCain (R) 27,672	(12%)
2004 Presidential Vote		
John Kerry (D) 172,382	(83%)
George Bush (R) 33,132	(16%)
Cook Partisan Voting Index: D+35		

in the nation. Among states, Californians have historically shown less prejudice toward African-Americans. And job opportunities in Los Angeles—up to and including the office of mayor for 20 years—have been relatively good for blacks. This is apparent in the hills just west of Crenshaw, an Art Deco neighborhood built in the 1920s and 1930s and the birthplace of West Coast hip-hop music. Here, in Baldwin Hills, where on clear days one can see the snow-capped San Gabriel Mountains, is a high-income, African American neighborhood. Near Windsor Hills along Slauson Avenue are other comfortable black-majority neighborhoods. In the more rundown Crenshaw area, former L.A. Lakers basketball player Magic Johnson built his successful multiplex theaters. At Hollywood Boulevard, near the tourist mecca of the famed Grauman's Chinese Theatre, is a huge complex anchored by the Kodak Theatre, which hosts the Academy Awards and many television and award events, including the finals of the Fox network's *American Idol* program.

These parts of central Los Angeles are the heart of the 33rd Congressional District, which is bisected by the Santa Monica Freeway, and runs from the Golden State Freeway southwest to the economically revived Culver City and almost to Venice on the Pacific Ocean. It includes most of Koreatown, centered on Western Avenue and Olympic Boulevard, which has become a hub for the city's cultural and business life and an investment opportunity for many South Koreans. It takes in some of Hollywood and the affluent Los Feliz neighborhoods. Its population in 2010 was 37% Hispanic, 25% black, and 13% Asian. But many of the district's Latinos are not citizens or registered voters, and a majority of Democratic primary voters are African-American. This is one of the most Democratic districts in the nation: John Kerry got 83% of the vote in 2004, and Barack Obama got 87% in 2008.

Karen Bass (D)

The new congresswoman from the 33rd District is Karen Bass, a Democrat elected in 2010 to succeed retiring Rep. Diane Watson, also a Democrat. Bass is a Watson protégé and the former speaker of the California Assembly.

She was born and raised in Los Angeles. Her father was a letter carrier and her mother was a homemaker. Her father had moved to California from Texas after World War II; her mother was a Los Angeles native who learned to speak Spanish as a child. In an interview, Bass said that the most influential part of her childhood was watching television news coverage of the civil rights movement with her father, which "absolutely, positively shaped who I am today and why I'm interested in politics." In middle school, Bass was a student representative on a committee overseeing integration of the school. At age 14, she got involved in Democratic Sen. Robert F. Kennedy's 1968 presidential campaign by signing up her mother as a precinct captain and then doing all the neighborhood canvassing herself. At her high school in West Los Angeles, Bass joined her teachers in protests against the Vietnam War. Bass attended San Diego State University and stayed active in community organizing. "School wound up being rather secondary for me," she said. Bass served on a committee that investigated accusations of police abuses in Los Angeles and participated in groups that advocated for the end of apartheid in South Africa.

Bass ultimately received a nursing certificate from the University of Southern California and her bachelor's degree from California State University. She was married in 1980 and had a daughter; the couple divorced in 1986. She and her ex-husband stayed in contact, cooperating on raising their daughter and four stepchildren. In 2006, Bass's daughter and son-in-law died in a car accident.

In 1990, Bass founded the Community Coalition, a nonprofit that works with African-American and Latino communities in South Los Angeles to combat drug use and gang violence by shutting down liquor stores and motels. The group also campaigned against Proposition 187, which sought to deny public services to illegal immigrants, and Proposition 209, which prohibited affirmative action admissions policies in public universities. Bass served as executive director of the organization for 14 years.

In 2004, she won election to the state Assembly. In the legislature, she sponsored several bills aimed at reforming the state's foster care system and expanding health insurance programs for children. In her first term, she was the majority whip; in her second, she was majority leader; and in her third term, she became the first black female speaker of the Assembly. Trying to balance California's budget in the midst of a fiscal crisis consumed much of her tenure. She negotiated budget compromises that included deep cuts to education and social spending. Bass described her two years as speaker as "painful" and said, "I ran for office because I wanted to create, build, and expand programs, not tear them apart."

In February, Watson announced she would retire from Congress at the end of her term. A few days later, Watson joined Bass at a press conference where Bass declared her candidacy. Other prominent Democrats stayed out of the race, assuming that Bass would easily win on turf she had represented in the legislature. She won the June Democratic primary with 85% of the vote; her nearest challenger was Felton Newell, a prosecutor with the Los Angeles city attorney's office, who finished with about 6%. In the general election, she easily defeated Republican lawyer James Andion.

THIRTY-FOURTH DISTRICT

Lucille Roybal-Allard (D)

Elected 1992, 10th term; b. June 12, 1941, Los Angeles; home, Los Angeles; CA State L.A., B.A. 1965; Catholic; married (Edward Allard); 4 children.

Elected Office: CA Assembly, 1986–92.

DC Office: 2330 RHOB, 20515, 202-225-1766; Fax: 202-226-0350; Web site: roybal-allard.house.gov.

State Offices: Los Angeles, 213-628-9230.

Committees: *Appropriations:* Homeland Security; Labor, HHS, Education & Related Agencies.

Group Ratings

	ACLU	ACU	ADA	CFG	AFS	FRC	LCV	ITIC	NTU	COC
2010	88	0	100	0	100	0	100	67	2	13
2009	–	0	100	0	100	–	93	–	1	33

National Journal Ratings

	2010 LIB	—	2010 CONS	2009 LIB	—	2009 CONS
Economic	88%	—	10%	91%	—	0%
Social	89%	—	7%	89%	—	0%
Foreign	73%	—	24%	78%	—	17%
Composite	85%	—	15%	90%	—	10%

Key Votes of the 111th Congress

1. Overturn Ledbetter	Y	5. Bar federal abortion funds	N
2. Pass $820 billion stimulus	Y	6. Pass health care bill	Y
3. Let guns in national parks	N	7. Regulate financial firms	Y
4. Pass cap-and-trade	Y	8. Pass tax cuts for some	Y

9. Stop detainee transfers	N
10. Legalize immigrants' kids	Y
11. Repeal don't ask, tell	Y
12. Limit campaign funds	Y

Election Results

2010 general	Lucille Roybal-Allard (D)	69,382	(77%)	($577,788)
	Wayne Miller (R)	20,457	(23%)	(no FEC report)
2010 primary	Lucille Roybal-Allard (D)	14,309	(71%)	
	David Sanchez (D)	5,917	(29%)	

Prior Winning Percentages: 2008 (77%), 2006 (77%), 2004 (74%), 2002 (74%), 2000 (85%), 1998 (87%), 1996 (82%), 1994 (81%), 1992 (63%)

Population		Race/Ethnicity		Work	
Pop. 2010:	654,303	White:	8.8%	Private:	83.6%
Change since 2000:	Up 2.4%	Black:	4.7%	Government:	10.0%
Urban:	100.0%	Hispanic:	78.7%	Self-employed:	6.1%
Rural:	0.0%	Asian:	6.5%	Blue collar:	36.6%
Area size:	59 sq. mi.	Native Am.:	0.2%	White collar:	43.5%
		Hawaiian:	0.1%	Khaki collar:	0.1%
Age		Two+ races:	0.8%	Other:	19.8%
Median age:	29.9 yrs.				
More than 65 yrs:	8.1%	*Ancestry*		Median income:	$37,599
Less than 18 yrs:	30.3%	German	1.6%	Median Home Value:	$435,800
		USA	1.3%		
Education		Irish	1.2%	**Military Veterans**	
H.S. grad:	55.0%			% of Pop:	3.4%
College grad:	11.5%				
Grad degree:	3.2%				

East Central L.A., Downey

A block from the 452-foot trademark white tower of the Los Angeles City Hall is the huge retail shopping street of Broadway. The sidewalks are thronged with Latinos, the signs are mostly in Spanish, and the merchandise is displayed on tables. This could be Mexico City or Lima. It is Latin America transplanted just a short walk from City Hall and the 60- and 70-story post-modern pink cylinders that define downtown L.A. these days. Broadway is neither the geo-

2008 Presidential Vote		
Barack Obama (D)	106,695	(75%)
John McCain (R)	33,056	(23%)
2004 Presidential Vote		
John Kerry (D)	82,942	(69%)
George Bush (R)	35,926	(30%)
Cook Partisan Voting Index:	D+22	

graphical nor spiritual center of Los Angeles's Latino communities, and it is just one of many shopping and dining areas. But it is an emblem of the entry-level Latino neighborhoods of the nation's second-largest city, the places where many immigrants, not only from Mexico but also from Central and South America, come to find a cheap place to live—doubling and tripling up with other families, close enough to drive an old car to work in factories and warehouses that fill the acreage south and east of downtown. In recent years, the Gold Line extension of Los Angeles's transit agency brought light rail service to the area.

Broadway and many of these entry-level neighborhoods are part of the 34th Congressional District of California. It includes downtown and Boyle Heights, once an entry neighborhood for Irish and Jewish immigrants and for the past 40 years predominantly Mexican-American. Near the Hollywood Freeway is the Cathedral of Our Lady of the Angels, the $190 million center of the nation's largest and most ethnically diverse Roman Catholic archdiocese, which Cardinal Roger Mahony dedicated as an "anchor for the ages." Another new landmark is the Walt Disney Concert Hall, home of the Los Angeles Philharmonic. The 34th also includes the giant factories south of downtown along the Santa Ana Freeway. And it takes in part of East Los Angeles, which like the rest of the district has been crippled by the faltering economy. In May 2010, Homeboy Industries, a 20-year-old Boyle Heights organization that finds work for former gang members, announced it was laying off most of its employees.

To the south it includes the garment factories of Vernon and the 1940s working-class suburbs of Huntington Park, with its shopping strip on the wide Pacific Boulevard, Bell and Bell Gardens, Commerce, Maywood, and Cudahy, all of which are now heavily Latino. Bell drew national attention in 2010 when its residents were shocked to learn their city manager was paid an annual salary of $787,000, while their police chief received $457,000; both subsequently resigned. City officials have declared Maywood a "sanctuary city" for illegal immigrants. Beyond those areas are the more affluent suburbs of Downey, home of the Boeing (formerly Rockwell) plant that built the space shuttle, and Bellflower, a formerly prime shopping area struggling for a comeback. Bisecting much of the district is the concrete-lined Los Angeles River. City officials plan to clean up the river and return it to a more natural condition, with adjacent parkland, while preserving its flood-control assets.

The 34th District is 79% Hispanic, the highest percentage in any California district, and 80% of the residents speak a language other than English at home. A Gallup-Healthways survey of well-being and livability in 2009 found its residents were sadder and angrier than those in any other Golden State congressional district. Politically, this area is heavily Democratic. It is not clear what the future political preferences of people here will be, for the large majority of adults here do not vote. In 2008, in a constituency of 654,000 people, only 143,000 voted in the general election, far fewer than the 344,000 who voted in the Westside 30th District or even the 237,000 who voted in the downtown 33rd District.

Lucille Roybal-Allard (D)

The congresswoman from the 34th District is Lucille Roybal-Allard, first elected in 1992. She is the first Mexican-American woman to be elected to Congress, and, in 1999, became the first woman to chair the Congressional Hispanic Caucus. Roybal-Allard grew up in the Los Angeles area, the daughter of longtime U.S. Rep. Edward Roybal, who was the first Latino to serve on the Los Angeles City Council. She dreamed of a show business career as a teenager and later worked as a department store clerk and for nonprofit organizations. After raising a family—two of her children are lawyers—she followed her father into politics when she was 45 years old. She was elected to the California Assembly in 1986. Six years later, she ran for a newly created House district that took in much of the Los Angeles area that her father had represented for 30 years. Her father retired in 1992, the year she ran for the House. Roybal-Allard won easily with 75% of the vote in the primary and 63% in the general election.

Roybal-Allard has compiled a solidly liberal voting record. On the Appropriations Committee, she has focused on immigration issues, and she has pushed aggressively for a bill that would include a path to citizenship for illegal immigrants currently in the country. The bill has not passed despite repeated attempts in recent years. When Senate Finance Committee Democrats proposed restrictions on illegal immigrants participating in health care programs as part of the 2009-2010 health care overhaul, she joined a group of Hispanics who succeeded in modifying the provision. With Reps. Howard Berman, D-Calif., and Lincoln Diaz-Balart, R-Fla., she is the sponsor of the Dream Act, which would provide a path to legal immigration for college-bound students. In the past, she also has pushed for in-state college tuition rates for illegal immigrants. In 2009, Roybal-Allard introduced a measure aimed at raising labor standards and protections for children of migrant farm workers to the same level set for children in occupations outside of agriculture. Conservatives attacked the measure as an effort to give labor unions more power.

Roybal-Allard worked with officials in Maywood and Bell in 2010 to explore the idea of combining police departments as a way to cut costs. She also got a bill signed into law to coordinate federal programs and research on underage drinking as well as to fund a media campaign on its dangers. Another of her recent successes was a bill enacted in 2008 that authorizes federal grants for newborn health screening for congenital, genetic, and metabolic disorders. She introduced a separate bill in 2010 aimed at expanding federal research of maternity practices. "The future of our country depends on the health and well-being of our mothers and their children," she said.

Unlike several other Democratic women in the California delegation, Roybal-Allard isn't as close to House Minority Leader Nancy Pelosi and her powerful inner circle, which sometimes limits her leverage in the House. In 2006, Roybal-Allard seconded the nomination of Democrat Steny Hoyer of Maryland for majority leader, indicating her support for Hoyer over Pelosi's preferred candidate, Democrat John Murtha of Pennsylvania. However, Hoyer won the contest, so Roybal-Allard still has a friend or two in high places.

THIRTY-FIFTH DISTRICT

Maxine Waters (D)

Elected 1990, 11th term; b. Aug. 15, 1938, St. Louis, MO; home, Los Angeles; CA State L.A., B.A. 1970; Christian; married (Sidney Williams); 2 children.

Elected Office: CA Assembly, 1976–90.

Professional Career: Head Start teacher, 1966; Dpty., City Councilman David Cunningham, 1973–76.

DC Office: 2344 RHOB, 20515, 202-225-2201; Fax: 202-225-7854; Web site: waters.house.gov.

State Offices: Los Angeles, 323-757-8900.

Committees: *Financial Services:* Capital Markets and Government Sponsored Enterprises (RMM); Insurance, Housing & Community Opportunity; Oversight & Investigations. *Judiciary:* Immigration Policy & Enforcement; Intellectual Property, Competition & the Internet.

Group Ratings

	ACLU	ACU	ADA	CFG	AFS	FRC	LCV	ITIC	NTU	COC
2010	94	4	90	3	100	6	90	67	6	25
2009	–	0	90	0	100	–	93	–	5	36

National Journal Ratings

	2010 LIB	—	2010 CONS	2009 LIB	—	2009 CONS
Economic	76%	—	23%	64%	—	36%
Social	75%	—	25%	84%	—	11%
Foreign	97%	—	0%	59%	—	39%
Composite	83%	—	17%	70%	—	30%

Key Votes of the 111th Congress

1. Overturn Ledbetter	Y	5. Bar federal abortion funds	N	9. Stop detainee transfers	N
2. Pass $820 billion stimulus	Y	6. Pass health care bill	Y	10. Legalize immigrants' kids	Y
3. Let guns in national parks	N	7. Regulate financial firms	Y	11. Repeal don't ask, tell	Y
4. Pass cap-and-trade	Y	8. Pass tax cuts for some	Y	12. Limit campaign funds	N

Election Results

2010 general	Maxine Waters (D)	98,131	(79%)	($698,821)
	K. Bruce Brown (R)	25,561	(21%)	($17,340)
2010 primary	Maxine Waters (D)	unopposed		

Prior Winning Percentages: 2008 (83%), 2006 (84%), 2004 (81%), 2002 (78%), 2000 (87%), 1998 (89%), 1996 (86%), 1994 (78%), 1992 (83%), 1990 (79%)

Population		Race/Ethnicity		Work	
Pop. 2010:	662,413	White:	9.0%	Private:	78.4%
Change since 2000:	Up 3.6%	Black:	28.4%	Government:	13.6%
Urban:	100.0%	Hispanic:	54.5%	Self-employed:	7.9%
Rural:	0.0%	Asian:	5.6%	Blue collar:	27.9%
Area size:	55 sq. mi.	Native Am.:	0.2%	White collar:	48.8%
		Hawaiian:	0.4%	Khaki collar:	0.1%
Age		Two+ races:	1.6%	Other:	23.2%
Median age:	30.6 yrs.				
More than 65 yrs:	8.4%	*Ancestry*		Median income:	$42,091
Less than 18 yrs:	29.7%	USA	3.6%	Median Home Value:	$447,300
		Subsaharan	2.5%		
Education		German	2.1%	**Military Veterans**	
H.S. grad:	68.3%			% of Pop:	4.7%
College grad:	16.8%				
Grad degree:	5.3%				

South Los Angeles, Inglewood

In the years just after World War II, Los Angeles was the fastest-growing metropolitan area in America. LAX, today the nation's third-busiest airport, with eight central terminals, was then a small airfield amid open country. The mile-square grids east, north, and south of the airport were just filling up with rapidly multiplying subdivisions. Also north of the airport were the wetlands along Ballona Creek, where Howard Hughes took his Spruce Goose, the largest airplane ever built, up for its one and only flight. The rapidly growing suburb of Inglewood, just east of the airport around the Hollywood Park racetrack, was filling up with the young families of people who had moved to Los Angeles during the war—workers in the giant aircraft factories or in the small factories that every day were making California less dependent on goods from back East. In Hawthorne, home of a big Northrop Grumman plant, future celebrities were growing up—Sonny Bono and the Beach Boys. Gardena, east of Hawthorne, was known for its legal poker clubs and its Japanese-American residents, back from the wartime internment camps.

East of Gardena is the part of Los Angeles called South Central or, more recently, South Los Angeles, after the City Council in 2003 officially renamed the community to rid it of the stigma of gang wars and race riots. The area continues to have some of the highest crime rates in the L.A. region. In the days of residential segregation, much of this area was the home of Los Angeles's black community, its numbers greatly expanded by migration from the South during and after the war. In the Central Avenue entertainment district were clubs and theaters hosting Ella Fitzgerald, Sarah Vaughan, Duke Ellington and Louis Armstrong. Later, it was the epicenter of L.A.'s two postwar riots, in the Watts district of Los Angeles in 1965 and at the corner of Florence and Normandie in 1992. In the past 20 years, Latinos have been arriving in increasing numbers, buying homes and opening businesses. The Crips and Bloods gangs have been replaced by Hispanic counterparts such as Florencia 13, six of whose members were sentenced to life in prison in February 2010 after a long spate of violence that left dozens of people dead.

The 35th Congressional District of California today is made up of all these areas, with a landscape and population very different from 60 years ago. At its west and east ends are two of the

2008 Presidential Vote

Barack Obama (D)	165,761	(84%)
John McCain (R)	27,789	(14%)

2004 Presidential Vote

John Kerry (D)	130,764	(79%)
George Bush (R)	33,110	(20%)

Cook Partisan Voting Index: D+31

Los Angeles area's great transportation facilities. One is LAX and the cluster of hotels and office buildings all around (LAX's swooping arches, intended in 1961 to symbolize the jet era, are now a historic landmark). The other is the Alameda Corridor, the 20-mile express rail line connecting the ports of Los Angeles and Long Beach with rail distribution points near downtown Los Angeles. Once mostly white working class and middle class, the district's population in 2010 was 28% African-American and 55% Hispanic. Almost 20% of its residents speak a language other than English at home. The recent recession struck the area with brutal force. Subprime lending led to widespread foreclosures, and in 2010 eager investors began "flipping" homes there for quick resale. Politically, this is an overwhelmingly Democratic district.

Maxine Waters (D)

The congresswoman from the 35th District is Maxine Waters, a Democrat first elected in 1990. She grew up in St. Louis, one of 13 children. She has said, "I know all about welfare. I remember the social workers peeking in the refrigerator and under the beds." She moved to California in 1961, worked in a garment factory, and raised two children. Waters got a sociology degree at California State University in Los Angeles and became an assistant Head Start teacher after the Watts riot of 1965. She likes to call herself "The Organizer" and has shown the capacity to draw big supportive crowds to her protests over the years. From 1973 to 1976, she worked on the staff of a Los Angeles city councilman. In 1976, she won a seat in the California Assembly, where she helped pass legislation divesting state pension funds from South Africa, setting up a child-abuse-prevention training program, and prohibiting police strip searches for nonviolent offenses. When Democratic Rep. Augustus Hawkins retired in 1990 after 28 years in the U.S. House, Waters was the obvious choice for the seat and won it easily. Her husband, a former professional football player and Mercedes-Benz salesman, became President Clinton's ambassador to the Bahamas.

Having grown up in poverty and lived under segregation laws, Waters believes with fervor in federal aid for the poor and for racial preferences to help blacks overcome years of slavery, segregation, and discrimination. She has favored drastic reductions in defense spending in favor of domestic spending. She voted against the Gulf War resolution in 1991, asking how urban gang members could be expected to stop fighting when America's own leaders were waging battles. She has been a staunch opponent of the Iraq war as well as a subsequent troop buildup in Afghanistan. She brings an intensity bordering on fury to her work, asserting herself regardless of protocol. Her anger is a political weapon she uses shrewdly to get both publicity and results. "I don't have time to be polite," Waters says.

She came to Washington shortly before the 1992 race riots in L.A., which occasioned her best and worst moments. She flew home immediately and roused the Department of Water and Power to restore water to the riot area, and she was effective in gaining provisions to the post-riot emergency act that were eventually signed into law. But she also suggested rioters were morally justified and claimed ominously, "Los Angeles is under siege....The violence could spill over to many other cities in this country."

Waters isn't afraid to step on toes in pursuit of her legislative or political agenda. When House Appropriations Chairman David Obey of Wisconsin sought to ban earmarks named after members in 2009, she heatedly confronted him over his refusal to fund her request for the Maxine Waters Employment Preparation Center. Obey eventually prevailed. She has pushed for federal loan guarantees to cities for economic and infrastructure development. In a rare legislative success in the Republican-controlled House, Waters sponsored an amendment to triple spending for the erasure of the debts of poor nations, mostly in Africa. She has sponsored bills to repeal mandatory minimum sentences for drug crimes, and charges that the war on drugs has created "apartheid." In 2009, the House passed her bill to require the federal Bureau of Prisons to develop a program for inmate HIV/AIDS testing. She has been an occasional thorn in the side of President Obama. She and other Congressional Black Caucus members held up a vote on the financial services overhaul in November 2009 because they said the administration wasn't addressing the needs of segments of the black community. Waters repeatedly discussed the need to "educate" people advising Obama.

As a senior member of the Financial Services Committee, Waters sponsored measures to overhaul discredited housing finance programs, expand affordable-housing programs, and aid local governments to rehabilitate foreclosed homes. She harshly criticized the Federal Reserve Board and big bankers for their financing practices and the tight credit that resulted. She told a panel of banking executives in February 2009, "To the captains of the universe sitting here before all of us, all of my political life I have been in disagreement with the banking industry." With Rep. Ron Klein, D-Fla., she got a bill through the committee in 2010 to crack down on fraudulent brokers and lenders, and she successfully amended the financial services bill in 2009 to beef up protection for securities investors.

But in recent years, her personal finances have become the target of watchdogs. In 2005, the liberal-leaning Citizens for Responsibility and Ethics criticized the fact that members of her family had made more than $1 million in eight years doing business with companies, candidates, and causes that she had helped. Her reply: "They do their business and I do mine." In March 2009, news stories raised the issue of whether Waters had urged federal regulators to give favorable treatment to a bank in which she and her husband had a financial interest. Federal regulators told *The New York Times* that Waters in 2008 helped set up a meeting with bankers, including one whose chief executive asked them for $50 million in government bailout funds. Waters defended her actions, saying, "I have been an outspoken advocate for minority communities and businesses in California and nationally for decades."

The Ethics Committee launched an investigation in 2009, and subsequently charged her with three counts of breaking House rules barring lawmakers from taking actions in their own financial interest. Hoping to seize political advantage, Republicans clamored to have ethics trials of Waters and Rep. Charles Rangel, D-N.Y., held before the November 2010 elections and accused ethics Chairwoman Zoe Lofgren, D-Calif., of stalling. While Rangel's case went forward, Waters' trial was postponed when Lofgren and Alabama's Jo Bonner, the committee's ranking Republican, cited the discovery of additional evidence. Waters contended that the delay proved the case against her was weak. "I have been denied basic due process," she told reporters. Meanwhile, it came to light that two Ethics Committee lawyers on the case were placed on administrative leave. The highly secretive panel did not disclose the reason.

Waters is a force to be reckoned with in L.A. politics. Other politicians are eager to be included on her Progressive Connections slate of candidates that are mailed out to many thousands of black voters. Politicians pay to be included—a common California practice. She has been re-elected without difficulty. The biggest potential threat to her tenure is the rising Hispanic percentage in the district.

THIRTY-SIXTH DISTRICT
Vacant

Election Results

2010 general	Jane Harman (D)	114,489	(60%)	($1,203,707.21)
	Mattie Fein (R)	66,706	(35%)	($170,618.04)
	Herb Peters (Lib)	10,840	(6%)	
2010 primary	Jane Harman (D)	27,146	(59%)	
	Marcy Winograd (D)	18,792	(41%)	

Prior Winning Percentages: 2008 (69%), 2006 (63%), 2004 (62%), 2002 (61%), 2000 (48%), 1996 (52%), 1994 (48%), 1992 (48%)

Population		Race/Ethnicity		Work	
Pop. 2010:	659,385	White:	43.7%	Private:	77.3%
Change since 2000:	Up 3.2%	Black:	4.0%	Government:	11.5%
Urban:	100.0%	Hispanic:	32.0%	Self-employed:	11.0%
Rural:	0.0%	Asian:	16.2%	Blue collar:	13.9%
Area size:	122 sq. mi.	Native Am.:	0.2%	White collar:	70.5%
		Hawaiian:	0.4%	Khaki collar:	0.1%
Age		Two+ races:	3.2%	Other:	15.5%
Median age:	36.5 yrs.				
More than 65 yrs:	10.9%	*Ancestry*		Median income:	$69,119
Less than 18 yrs:	22.7%	German	8.7%	Median Home Value:	$682,500
		Irish	7.2%		
Education		English	5.9%	**Military Veterans**	
H.S. grad:	86.5%			% of Pop:	6.4%
College grad:	43.0%				
Grad degree:	15.2%				

Torrance, Redondo Beach

For many Southern Californians, there is no better place to be than the beach. It is not a perfect environment: In the morning there may be mists, the winter air is damp and clammy, and even in summer the weather can be chilly. The water is never very warm and it is sometimes polluted. But for many this is echt-California, and in this democratic polity, there is a beach to suit the taste of just about everyone, many of them with their unique piers and athletes, especially volleyball. The funkiest of all is Venice: "Muscle Beach," with its beach houses and expensive new mansions jammed together, sharing the shoreline with homeless people in cars and campers who have staked out spots along the beach in recent years. Venice is known for its chaotic boardwalk, where skateboarding got its start and in-line skating sports are de rigueur.

2008 Presidential Vote		
Barack Obama (D)	176,924	(64%)
John McCain (R)	92,105	(34%)

2004 Presidential Vote		
John Kerry (D)	154,010	(59%)
George Bush (R)	103,425	(40%)

Cook Partisan Voting Index: D+12

To the south is Marina Del Rey, with sleek modern apartment complexes and expensive yacht moorings, and south of LAX Airport, El Segundo, named for Chevron's second oil refinery and now with big office buildings. Next is South Bay, with Manhattan Beach, a favorite of the Beach Boys, who grew up a couple of miles inland in Hawthorne. Tiny Hermosa Beach, with tightly packed frame houses originally the homes of elderly retirees, is now filled with the young and the trying-to-stay-young. Many of the beaches enforce no-smoking rules. Farther south are the flower-planted rises of Redondo Beach and the larger city of Torrance, whose vast inland expanse is the home of large Korean and Japanese communities and of the North American headquarters of both Toyota and Honda. Overlooking L.A.'s modern container port are Wilmington and San Pedro, once working class, but moving up as well.

The 36th Congressional District of California includes most of this beach territory, from Venice south to San Pedro (both of which are within the Los Angeles city limits, though the area in between is not). The district is multiethnic: 32% of residents are Hispanic, 14% Asian, and 28% foreign-born. But the beach communities, as if in the 1950s, are still filled mostly with white Anglos. Culturally, the area is libertarian—against restrictions or even aspersions on its various lifestyles. This has been one of America's leading defense and aerospace areas, where Howard Hughes built planes half a century ago and where much of the 1980s defense buildup took place. With its many military and space facilities for electronics research and development, Boeing is the largest private employer in the area, including its assembly operation in El Segundo. Nearby is Northrop Grumman, which announced plans in 2010 to relocate its headquarters to Washington, D.C., though most of its work will remain in California. Not all of the district's big employers are in the defense business. In El Segundo, Mattel Inc., the nation's largest toymaker, saw an uptick in sales in 2010 thanks to its ever-popular Barbie dolls and Hot Wheels toys.

The 36th District was represented by Democrat Jane Harman until February 2011, when she resigned the seat to head the Woodrow Wilson International Center for Scholars, a Washington, D.C.-based think tank. Her retirement set up a special election for the seat, the results of which were not known at press time for the Almanac. The winner will serve the remainder of Harman's two-year term ending in January 2013 and will be well-positioned to run for a full term in the November 2012 general election.

A primary was held in May 2011. Democrat Janice Hahn, a three-term Los Angeles City Councilwoman, won with 24.6% of the vote; tea party-backed Republican Craig Huey came in second with 22.2%. The two advanced to a special election scheduled for July 12, 2011.

The primary outcome was a major defeat for California Secretary of State Debra Bowen, a Democrat who was expected to finish at least well enough to advance to a runoff. But she trailed Huey by 709 votes, and eventually conceded. The related surprise element of the primary was the strong showing by Huey, a conservative website publisher from Rolling Hills Estates, in the heavily Democratic district. He spent $500,000 from his own pocket on his "cut spending, grow jobs" campaign. His presence in the run-off made it easier for Democrat Hahn to prevail in a two-way matchup. Hahn told The Daily Breeze that she preferred Huey as an opponent: "I think the choice for voters is more clear," she said, although she acknowledged that Huey's personal wealth could make him a tough competitor.

The establishment favorite, Hahn had the support of elected officials such as U.S. Sen. Dianne Feinstein and L.A. Mayor Antonio Villaraigosa, who ran in two mayoral elections against Janice Hahn's brother, former L.A. Mayor James Hahn. She also had support from the locally powerful Los Angeles County Federation of Labor. Although Huey faced tough odds going into the July runoff, he told the Los Angeles Times that the primary proved that the "district does not belong to any one party or political machine."

The contest was the first test of the state's new open primary elections system that allows voters, irrespective of party affiliation, to choose candidates of any political party. The top two finishers then compete for the seat, even if they belong to the same party. Six Republicans, five Democrats and five third-party or independent candidates entered the race for Harman's seat. A moderate Democrat, Harman served eight terms and was a leader on national security issues. In the early 2000s, she was the ranking member of the House Intelligence Committee. Harman was first elected in 1992, and regained the seat in 2000 after running unsuccessfully for governor in 1998. Her husband, Sidney, died in April 2011, not long after she resigned from Congress, and she assumed her late husband's seat on the board of Newsweek Daily Beast Co.

THIRTY-SEVENTH DISTRICT

Laura Richardson (D)

Elected Aug. 2007, 2nd full term; b. April 14, 1962, Los Angeles; home, Long Beach; U.C.L.A., B.A. 1984, U. of S. CA, M.B.A. 1996; Christian; divorced.

Elected Office: Long Beach City Cncl., 2000-06; CA Assembly, 2006-07.

Professional Career: Teacher, 1984-87; Mktg. rep., Xerox Corp., 1987-2001; Field Dpty., Rep. Juanita Millender-McDonald, 1996-98; Southern CA dir., Lt. Gov. Cruz Bustamante, 2001-05.

DC Office: 1330 LHOB, 20515, 202-225-7924; Fax: 202-225-7926; Web site: richardson.house.gov.

State Offices: Long Beach, 562-436-3828.

Committees: *Homeland Security:* Cybersecurity, Infrastructure Protection & Security Technologies; Emergency Preparedness, Response & Communications (RMM). *Transportation & Infrastructure:* Highways & Transit; Railroads, Pipelines & Hazardous Materials; Water Resources & Environment.

Group Ratings

	ACLU	ACU	ADA	CFG	AFS	FRC	LCV	ITIC	NTU	COC
2010	94	0	95	0	100	0	90	100	7	25
2009	–	0	100	2	100	–	100	–	3	31

National Journal Ratings

	2010 LIB	—	2010 CONS	2009 LIB	—	2009 CONS
Economic	66%	—	33%	67%	—	32%
Social	76%	—	24%	64%	—	34%
Foreign	77%	—	22%	65%	—	35%
Composite	73%	—	27%	66%	—	34%

Key Votes of the 111th Congress

1. Overturn Ledbetter	Y	5. Bar federal abortion funds	N	9. Stop detainee transfers	Y
2. Pass $820 billion stimulus	Y	6. Pass health care bill	Y	10. Legalize immigrants' kids	Y
3. Let guns in national parks	N	7. Regulate financial firms	Y	11. Repeal don't ask, tell	Y
4. Pass cap-and-trade	Y	8. Pass tax cuts for some	Y	12. Limit campaign funds	Y

Election Results

2010 general	Laura Richardson (D)	85,799	(68%)	($639,928)
	Star Parker (R)	29,159	(23%)	($1,851,459)
	Nicholas Dibs (I)	10,560	(8%)	($3,549)
2010 primary	Laura Richardson (D)	22,574	(67%)	
	Peter Mathews (D)	6,144	(18%)	
	Lee Davis (D)	2,848	(9%)	
	Terrance Ponchak (D)	1,955	(6%)	

Prior Winning Percentages: 2008 (75%), 2007 (67%)

Population		Race/Ethnicity		Work	
Pop. 2010:	648,847	White:	13.7%	Private:	79.5%
Change since 2000:	Up 1.5%	Black:	21.3%	Government:	14.0%
Urban:	100.0%	Hispanic:	49.4%	Self-employed:	6.3%
Rural:	0.0%	Asian:	11.8%	Blue collar:	25.9%
Area size:	75 sq. mi.	Native Am.:	0.2%	White collar:	52.6%
		Hawaiian:	1.2%	Khaki collar:	0.0%
Age		Two+ races:	2.1%	Other:	21.4%
Median age:	30.2 yrs.				
More than 65 yrs:	8.1%	*Ancestry*		Median income:	$46,937
Less than 18 yrs:	30.2%	Subsaharan	3.8%	Median Home Value:	$411,900
		German	3.2%		
Education		Irish	2.7%	**Military Veterans**	
H.S. grad:	71.1%			% of Pop:	5.6%
College grad:	19.1%				
Grad degree:	5.6%				

L.A. County; Long Beach, Compton

With 463,000 people, Long Beach would be a major metropolis almost anywhere but in Los Angeles County, where it seems just the largest of many suburbs. But it has an identity of its own. Started as a beach resort in 1888, it soon became a port when Los Angeles civic leaders decided that if their town was to be a world-class city, it must have a world-class harbor. Since nature had not provided one, they built it where the

Los Angeles River flows into the ocean at the western edge of Long Beach. By 1909, Los Angeles had annexed the harbor towns of San Pedro and Wilmington on the other side of the river. Over the next decades, the two cities persuaded the federal government to dredge channels and build a breakwater and turning basins. Long Beach was developing other businesses as well. It sprouted oil derricks in the 1920s and briefly became one of the nation's big oil producers. It was the site of major aircraft plants in the 1940s and beyond.

Since then, the Los Angeles-Long Beach port has become the nation's largest, the fastest-growing major cargo center in the world, with huge steel-gray container ships pulling quietly up to enormous automated loading facilities—a 21st-century contrast to the rotting docks of New York and San Francisco. The length of three football fields, these ships unload a daily average of 20,000 containers, which account for about a quarter of West Coast shipping. From there, about half of the cargo leaves by rail in 50 daily trains along the $2.4 billion high-speed 20-mile Alameda Corridor to the large rail yards near downtown Los Angeles. The recession hit these ports hard, and reduced volume by almost a third in early 2009. But the ports have shown signs of rebounding, with the number of empty containers shipped out to other countries up by 20% in 2009 and 16% in 2010. With three major highways threading through the port, cargo security is a major local concern. The *Queen Mary,* converted into a floating hotel, is a big tourist attraction, and there is a glittering array of high-rises and a huge new aquarium along the beach.

The 37th Congressional District of California includes 80% of the city of Long Beach and Signal Hill, surrounded by Long Beach, where the oil rigs are still pumping. It includes the two industrial suburbs of Compton and Carson. Compton became a majority black city in the 1960s, but by the 1980s was heavily Latino. Today, it struggles with a poor economy and unemployment that topped 20% in 2009. Carson, with recent subdivisions amid freeway interchanges, has a multiethnic population. The district includes the south end of South Central Los Angeles, including the Watts tower, where the riot of 1965 broke out. In 2010, the district's population was 21% African-American and 49% Hispanic. But many of the Latinos are not U.S. citizens and were only an estimated 22% of registered voters in 2007. It is a heavily Democratic district.

Laura Richardson (D)

The congresswoman from the 37th District is Laura Richardson, a Democrat who won the seat in an August 2007 special election after the death of Rep. Juanita Millender-McDonald, also a Democrat. A former field deputy for Millender-McDonald, Richardson majored in political science at the University of California at Los Angeles, worked as a marketing representative for Xerox, and got an MBA from the University of Southern California. In 2000, she began her career in elected office by winning a seat on the Long Beach City Council and simultaneously served as Southern California director for Democratic Lt. Gov. Cruz Bustamante. In 2006, Richardson ran for an open Assembly seat and won the primary 54% to 46%; she won the general with 68% of the vote.

In the special election, the June primary was the critical test of African-American and Hispanic voting clout in a district where power is shifting from blacks to Hispanics. Seventeen candidates filed for the election, but the front-runners were Richardson, who is African-American, and state Sen. Jenny Oropeza, who is Latina. Both hailed from Long Beach. Each candidate sought to downplay the racial component of the contest, but Richardson's endorsements came chiefly from African-American leaders while Oropeza got her support mostly from Hispanics.

Oropeza and Richardson both called for an end to the war in Iraq and said that they would focus on the needs of the local port, such as additional security. Organized labor's opposition to a proposed Indian-run casino led national and county labor federations to back Richardson. In the low-turnout voting, Richardson won 37% to secure the Democratic nomination, while Oropeza got 31%. Valerie McDonald, daughter of the late congresswoman, finished third with 9%. John Kanaley, a Long Beach police officer and Iraq war veteran, finished first among Republicans with 8%. Since no candidate received more than 50% of the vote, each party's leading candidate competed in an August 21 runoff. This was a pro forma contest in this solidly Democratic district, with Richardson winning 67% to Kanaley's 25%.

In the House, Richardson has a relatively moderate voting record for a Los Angeles-area Democrat. She joined the locally useful Transportation and Infrastructure Committee, where she pledged to educate House members about the "national significance" of her district's transportation infrastructure. She introduced a bill with California Republican Dana Rohrabacher in May 2009 to raise money for land and sea port cities through maintenance fees, though it did not advance. On the Homeland Security Committee, where she chaired the emergency response subcommittee before Democrats lost the majority in 2011, she questioned the Federal Communications Commission about selling commercial firms access to communications spectrum in July 2010 without resolving key technical and legal issues.

But most of the early attention Richardson drew was unwanted. Her personal finances were a mess, especially her home ownership. Local news reports detailed that she had defaulted on mortgage payments six times in eight years. Her home in Sacramento was foreclosed on by a bank, which sold it but then reversed that action after Richardson objected. The *Los Angeles Times* quoted neighbors as calling it a blight on the neighborhood in 2009. She also abandoned her car after failing to pay a repair bill. The liberal-leaning Citizens for Responsibility and Ethics in Washington called her a "deadbeat," and filed an ethics complaint alleging lenders may have given her preferential treatment. But the House Ethics Committee cleared her of any violation in July 2010. Her constituents did not seem to mind her personal problems. She has been re-elected easily.

THIRTY-EIGHTH DISTRICT

Grace Napolitano (D)

Elected 1998, 7th term; b. Dec. 4, 1936, Brownsville, TX; home, Norwalk; Brownsville H.S.; Catholic; married (Frank); 5 children.

Elected Office: Norwalk City Cncl., 1986-92; Norwalk mayor, 1989-92; CA Assembly, 1992-98.

Professional Career: Employee, Ford Motor Co., 1970-1992.

DC Office: 1610 LHOB, 20515, 202-225-5256; Fax: 202-225-0027; Web site: napolitano.house.gov.

State Offices: Santa Fe Springs, 562-801-2134.

Committees: *Natural Resources:* Water & Power (RMM). *Transportation & Infrastructure:* Highways & Transit; Railroads, Pipelines & Hazardous Materials; Water Resources & Environment.

Group Ratings

	ACLU	ACU	ADA	CFG	AFS	FRC	LCV	ITIC	NTU	COC
2010	88	0	100	0	100	0	90	67	6	13
2009	–	0	100	0	100	–	100	–	2	33

National Journal Ratings

	2010 LIB — 2010 CONS		2009 LIB — 2009 CONS	
Economic	90%	— 0%	91%	— 0%
Social	89%	— 7%	82%	— 17%
Foreign	92%	— 3%	86%	— 13%
Composite	94%	— 7%	88%	— 12%

Key Votes of the 111th Congress

1. Overturn Ledbetter	Y	5. Bar federal abortion funds	N	9. Stop detainee transfers	N
2. Pass $820 billion stimulus	Y	6. Pass health care bill	Y	10. Legalize immigrants' kids	Y
3. Let guns in national parks	N	7. Regulate financial firms	Y	11. Repeal don't ask, tell	Y
4. Pass cap-and-trade	Y	8. Pass tax cuts for some	Y	12. Limit campaign funds	Y

Election Results

2010 general	Grace Napolitano (D)..85,459	(74%)	($391,824)
	Robert Vaughn (R)...30,883	(27%)	(no FEC report)
2010 primary	Grace Napolitano (D)................................. unopposed		

Prior Winning Percentages: 2008 (82%), 2006 (75%), 2004 (100%), 2002 (71%), 2000 (71%), 1998 (68%)

Population		Race/Ethnicity		Work	
Pop. 2010:	641,410	White:	9.5%	Private:	80.7%
Change since 2000:	Up 0.4%	Black:	2.8%	Government:	12.6%
Urban:	100.0%	Hispanic:	75.4%	Self-employed:	6.5%
Rural:	0.0%	Asian:	11.0%	Blue collar:	30.8%
Area size:	105 sq. mi.	Native Am.:	0.2%	White collar:	50.6%
		Hawaiian:	0.1%	Khaki collar:	0.1%
Age		Two+ races:	0.9%	Other:	18.5%
Median age:	31.9 yrs.				
More than 65 yrs:	10.3%	*Ancestry*		Median income:	$53,589
Less than 18 yrs:	28.5%	German	2.1%	Median Home Value:	$413,200
		Irish	1.8%		
Education		USA	1.4%	**Military Veterans**	
H.S. grad:	66.1%			% of Pop:	4.7%
College grad:	14.6%				
Grad degree:	4.1%				

L.A. County; Pomona, Norwalk

One of the great population trends in the United States is the upward social movement of hundreds of thousands of immigrants in the Los Angeles Basin, from crowded entry-level neighborhoods out on freeways to suburban cul-de-sacs. It is visible east and southeast of Los Angeles, in suburbs that over a generation have changed from solidly white Anglo to largely Latino. Many people here have climbed the economic ladder by working in small smokeless factories along railroad tracks and riverbeds and beneath roaring freeways, and in small business offices and stores. These workers have made Los Angeles the nation's top metropolitan area for manufacturing, surpassing Chicago. Their values resemble those of working-class Americans of the 1960s: pro-family and traditional (L.A.-area Latinos have lower-than-average divorce rates), patriotic and hardworking (Latino males have the highest workforce participation of any measured group, and the incomes of U.S.-born Los Angeles County Latinos are at the county average).

2008 Presidential Vote		
Barack Obama (D) 130,092	(71%)
John McCain (R) 48,599	(27%)
2004 Presidential Vote		
John Kerry (D) 106,652	(65%)
George Bush (R) 54,869	(34%)
Cook Partisan Voting Index: D+18		

Many of these relatively new residents live in the 38th Congressional District of California, where the percentage of Hispanics in 2010 was 75%. This is a swath of Los Angeles County anchored by four primarily Hispanic suburbs. To the northwest is Montebello (Italian for "beautiful hill"), a working-class suburb just beyond East Los Angeles and once the site of oil drilling. To the east is La Puente, a center of the light manufacturing economy that created thousands of jobs in the Los Angeles Basin. Increasing numbers of its small businesses are owned by Asians, Latinos, and African-Americans. Farther east is the old town of Pomona, the district's largest city and the site of the Los Angeles County Fair as well as a $30 million conference center that broke ground in February 2010. Pomona has been troubled for decades by gang wars, and because of rising costs the city mulled contracting with the Sheriff's Department instead of having its own police force; the City Council rejected the idea in 2010. Nearby is the aptly named city of Industry, which won a rare waiver from state environmental laws in 2009 for a 75,000-seat football stadium. To the south are Norwalk, a rail crossroad astride the Santa Ana Freeway, and Santa Fe Springs.

Grace Napolitano (D)

The congresswoman from the 38th District is Grace Napolitano, a Democrat first elected in 1998. She grew up in the lower Rio Grande Valley of Texas, married at age 18, and eventually had five children. When she was 23, the family moved to California. She got a job as a secretary at Ford Motor and stayed for 22 years. After her first husband died, she married Frank Napolitano, and in 1980, they started a pizzeria. She served on the Norwalk City Council from 1986 to 1992, and also served one term as mayor, becoming the first Latino to hold the position. In 1992, she was elected to the California Assembly from a district that covered much of her current congressional district.

Term-limited in 1998, she got the opportunity to run for Congress when 16-year Democratic Rep. Esteban Torres announced three days before the filing deadline that he was retiring. Torres's surprise move seemed designed to promote the election of Jamie Casso, his son-in-law and chief of staff, who immediately announced his candidacy. Napolitano was not deterred. She persuaded the state AFL-CIO to vote an "open endorsement," although the executive board had backed Casso and Torres had been a senior United Auto Workers official in the 1960s. Napolitano and Casso waged a fierce campaign. She criticized him for not living in the district, and he criticized her $180,000 loan to her campaign at an unusual 18% interest rate. (Later, a 2009 *Los Angeles Times* article said she took advantage of a Federal Election Commission ruling to charge her campaign 18% for her personal loans, collecting tens of thousands of dollars in interest.) Napolitano had the financial backing of national women's organizations, including EMILY's List, plus the benefit of higher name recognition. The two candidates had few differences on major issues. Napolitano signed a pledge to serve only three terms. She won the primary by 618 votes, and her victory in November was assured in this Democratic district.

Napolitano has a liberal voting record; she was ranked by *National Journal* as the 12th most liberal member of the House in 2010. She is a former chairman of the Congressional Hispanic Caucus, and has been more consensus-oriented on immigration legislation than some caucus members.

On the Natural Resources Committee, Napolitano was active in the 2004 reauthorization of the California Bay-Delta water-allocation program, which featured unusual bipartisanship among

Californians. When Democrats took majority control in 2007, she became the chairman of the Natural Resources panel's Water and Power Subcommittee, with a focus on Southern California's acute need for an adequate water supply of good quality. During California's severe drought in 2009 and 2010, she held hearings to examine possible long-term solutions to address the state's water needs. Also in 2010, she got a bill through the House to set aside 5% of the Hoover Dam's hydroelectric power for Indian tribes and other groups that had lacked access.

Napolitano gets involved in issues related to the mentally ill, an interest that was sparked by a report that one in three Hispanic girls contemplates suicide. "Mental health is treatable. But [the Latino community has] a stigma attached to it," Napolitano said. During the 2010 health care overhaul debate, she said affordable health care was "critical to the future of women who suffer in silence from mental illness."

Napolitano's work has played well at home. In February 2003, she abandoned her earlier pledge to serve only three terms; she ran for a fourth in 2004 and won. She has not been seriously challenged for re-election. In 2007, she was criticized by the watchdog group Citizens for Responsibility and Ethics in Washington for paying her daughter, Yolanda Dyer, and her daughter's consulting firm nearly $53,000 for work on her campaigns between 2002 and 2006. Napolitano said her daughter ran her campaigns.

THIRTY-NINTH DISTRICT

Linda Sánchez (D)

Elected 2002, 5th term; b. Jan. 28, 1969, Orange; home, Lakewood; U. of CA, B.A. 1991, U.C.L.A., J.D. 1995; Catholic; married (Jim Sullivan); 4 children.

Professional Career: Practicing atty., 1995-98; Exec. secy. treas. of Orange Cnty. AFL-CIO, 2000-02.

DC Office: 2423 RHOB, 20515, 202-225-6676; Fax: 202-226-1012; Web site: lindasanchez.house.gov.

State Offices: Cerritos, 562-860-5050.

Committees: *Ethics* (RMM). *Judiciary:* Intellectual Property, Competition & the Internet. *Veterans' Affairs:* Economic Opportunity.

Group Ratings

	ACLU	ACU	ADA	CFG	AFS	FRC	LCV	ITIC	NTU	COC
2010	93	0	100	0	100	0	80	67	5	13
2009	–	5	85	6	100	–	79	–	3	36

National Journal Ratings

	2010 LIB	—	2010 CONS		2009 LIB	—	2009 CONS
Economic	90%	—	0%		91%	—	0%
Social	93%	—	0%		89%	—	0%
Foreign	97%	—	0%		91%	—	0%
Composite	97%	—	3%		95%	—	5%

Key Votes of the 111th Congress

1. Overturn Ledbetter	Y	5. Bar federal abortion funds	N	9. Stop detainee transfers	N
2. Pass $820 billion stimulus	Y	6. Pass health care bill	Y	10. Legalize immigrants' kids	Y
3. Let guns in national parks	*	7. Regulate financial firms	Y	11. Repeal don't ask, tell	Y
4. Pass cap-and-trade	Y	8. Pass tax cuts for some	Y	12. Limit campaign funds	Y

Election Results

2010 general	Linda Sánchez (D)..81,590	(63%)	($723,863)
	Larry Andre (R) 42,037	(33%)	($53,711)
	John Smith (Lib)..5,334	(4%)	
2010 primary	Linda Sánchez (D)......................................unopposed		

Prior Winning Percentages: 2008 (70%), 2006 (66%), 2004 (61%), 2002 (55%)

Population		Race/Ethnicity		Work	
Pop. 2010:	643,115	White:	15.8%	Private:	81.0%
Change since 2000:	Up 0.6%	Black:	5.4%	Government:	12.7%
Urban:	100.0%	Hispanic:	66.5%	Self-employed:	6.1%
Rural:	0.0%	Asian:	10.5%	Blue collar:	29.8%
Area size:	65 sq. mi.	Native Am.:	0.2%	White collar:	53.5%
		Hawaiian:	0.3%	Khaki collar:	0.1%
Age		Two+ races:	1.2%	Other:	16.6%
Median age:	31.6 yrs.				
More than 65 yrs:	9.0%	*Ancestry*		Median income:	$55,311
Less than 18 yrs:	29.3%	German	3.6%	Median Home Value:	$459,100
		Irish	2.6%		
Education		English	2.3%	**Military Veterans**	
H.S. grad:	68.6%			% of Pop:	4.7%
College grad:	17.0%				
Grad degree:	4.7%				

L.A. County; South Gate, Lakewood

In the years just after World War II, much of southeast Los Angeles County was farmland—citrus groves and dairy farms. The Zamboni ice-resurfacing machine for skating rinks was invented not in some frozen Northern clime, but by local businessmen Frank and Lawrence Zamboni, who, in 1949, found an innovative new use for the refrigeration technology they were using to service the local dairy industry. In the next two decades, housing subdivisions were

2008 Presidential Vote		
Barack Obama (D)	128,579	(66%)
John McCain (R)	63,680	(32%)
2004 Presidential Vote		
John Kerry (D)	102,660	(59%)
George Bush (R)	70,635	(40%)
Cook Partisan Voting Index: D+12		

built and new cities incorporated so that what had been a few towns separated by farmland became one continuous swath of suburbia. The towns were different in character. Whittier, founded by Midwestern Quakers, was the hometown of Richard Nixon, a young lawyer thinking about running for Congress in early 1946 who later became president. South Gate and Lynwood, with new auto plants and other factories, filled up with newcomers from the south. Lakewood, just north of Long Beach, used to be an area of lima bean fields. Developers built it up so rapidly in the 1950s that *Life* magazine featured it as one of the first mass-produced suburbs. Other towns were late-bloomers. There were still dairy farms in Cerritos in the 1970s, though few remain now. Car dealerships sprung up around Whittier. When four of them closed on one main street in the economic downturn, city officials began exploring replacing their vacant lots with office buildings, shops and homes.

The 39th Congressional District of California is made up of a heterogeneous and oddly fashioned collection of these suburbs. It is shaped like a U. Two-thirds of Whittier, all of South and West Whittier, and La Mirada are on the east. The bottom part of the U includes Lakewood and, in former dairy country, Cerritos, Artesia, and Hawaiian Gardens. The west end includes South Gate, Lynwood, Paramount, and the eastern fringe of South Central Los Angeles. These were once working-class white communities, then mostly black, then heavily Latino. The district's population is 67% Hispanic and 11% Asian. More evidence of the 39th's diversity can be found at a local motor vehicles office, where the written exam can be taken in 33 languages. As this area grew in the postwar years, it was pretty closely divided between the parties. But in the 1990s, it trended Democratic. On the presidential level, it voted 59%-40% for Democrat John Kerry in 2004 and 66%-32% for Democrat Barack Obama in 2008.

Linda Sánchez (D)

The congresswoman from the 39th District is Linda Sánchez, a Democrat first elected in 2002 and the junior member of the first pair of sisters ever elected to Congress. Her sister is Loretta Sanchez, who is nine years older and was elected to the House from Orange County in 1996. They are two of the seven children of Mexican immigrant parents Ignacio Sánchez, a machinist, and Maria Macias, a bilingual education aide in an elementary school. Their parents met while trying to organize a union at a tire shop where they worked when they were young. Their mother once took little Linda to a rally to hear famed migrant farmworker organizer César Chávez speak. Linda Sánchez earned her undergraduate and law degrees at the University of California (Los Angeles), working her way through school with jobs as a security guard, nanny, and teacher's aide. She became a civil-rights lawyer and was executive secretary-treasurer of the Orange County Federation of Labor. "She's definitely the more liberal one," Loretta has said. She's also considered the funnier one. Sanchez has won kudos from Washington insiders for her routines at the D.C. Improv, a professional comedy club that often hosts charity fundraisers featuring members of Congress.

When the district lines were unveiled for this new seat after the 2000 census, Linda Sánchez was one of six Democrats who ran for it. Her most important asset was her sister's support. She tapped Loretta's extensive fundraising network, walked precincts with her, and appeared in a television commercial with her. In a Spanish ad, their mother urged voters to send both of her daughters to Capitol Hill. All of this work gave Linda Sánchez an advantage over her two chief opponents, who were better known when the race began: two-term Assemblywoman Sally Havice and South Gate Councilman Hector De La Torre, a former legislative aide and Labor Department official. The three candidates differed very little on the issues.

Sánchez's ties to labor helped her build a strong voter-turnout operation, and she also won the endorsement of then-House Minority Whip Nancy Pelosi of California. Her opponents noted that no Latino members of Congress endorsed Sánchez, and they charged that she was a political opportunist who changed her name and residence to run in the newly created district. Sánchez had used her non-Latino married name until she ran for the House. But she won the primary with 33% of the vote; De La Torre received 29% and Havice 19%. This district is not as Democratic as the four other L.A.-based Hispanic-majority districts, and the negative primary campaign may have hurt Sánchez in the general election. Republican Tim Escobar, a financial adviser and former Army helicopter pilot, called her an inexperienced liberal extremist. But Sánchez won 55%-41%, and she has been re-elected easily since then.

Sánchez has a strongly liberal voting record. The first law she sponsored as a member of Congress would have provided federal funds to help stop bullying in schools. She was able to get the proposal into the Justice Department authorization bill, but it died in the Senate. Later, in 2009, Sánchez introduced bills to use existing federal funds for bullying- and gang-prevention programs and to punish severe "cyberbullying" online. Neither bill was successful. With Democrats in the majority in 2007, Sánchez gained more influence as the chairwoman of the Judiciary Committee's Commercial and Administrative Law Subcommittee, where she worked with senior Democrats on hearings to oversee the Bush administration's allegedly politically motivated firings of U.S. attorneys around the country. When senior White House political adviser Karl Rove refused to cooperate, Sánchez initiated a contempt of Congress action. When Rove capitulated in March 2009, the House dropped its lawsuit against him.

In January 2009, Sánchez won a plum assignment to the House Ways and Means Committee. As co-founder of the House Trade Working Group, she pledged tougher review of proposed international trade deals. She also sponsored a bill to permit consumer lawsuits against overseas manufacturers of defective products. And she proposed creation of a New Deal-style Civilian Conservation Corps, which would spend $5 billion on repairs and construction projects in parks and wilderness areas. She lost her spot on the committee when Republicans took majority control of the House in 2011.

In 2010, Sánchez stirred up the conservative blogosphere in 2010 when she said that an Arizona state law expanding law enforcement's power to detain suspected immigrants was drafted "by people who have ties to white supremacy groups." She stood by her remark, explaining she was referring to Arizona state Sen. Russell Pearce, who in 2006 apologized after sending an email containing an article from a supremacist group.

FORTIETH DISTRICT

Ed Royce (R)

Elected 1992, 10th term; b. Oct. 12, 1951, Los Angeles; home, Fullerton; CA State Fullerton, B.A. 1977; Catholic; married (Marie).

Elected Office: CA Senate, 1982–92.

Professional Career: Tax mgr., 1979–82.

DC Office: 2185 RHOB, 20515, 202-225-4111; Fax: 202-226-0335; Web site: royce.house.gov.

State Offices: Orange, 714-744-4130.

Committees: *Financial Services:* Capital Markets and Government Sponsored Enterprises; Financial Institutions & Consumer Credit. *Foreign Affairs:* Asia & the Pacific; Terrorism, Nonproliferation & Trade (Chmn).

Group Ratings

	ACLU	ACU	ADA	CFG	AFS	FRC	LCV	ITIC	NTU	COC
2010	6	100	0	86	0	100	0	33	90	88
2009	–	100	0	96	11	–	7	–	94	80

National Journal Ratings

	2010 LIB — 2010 CONS		2009 LIB — 2009 CONS	
Economic	5%	— 94%	11%	— 89%
Social	0%	— 85%	0%	— 93%
Foreign	12%	— 79%	26%	— 68%
Composite	10%	— 90%	15%	— 86%

Key Votes of the 111th Congress

1. Overturn Ledbetter	N	5. Bar federal abortion funds	Y	9. Stop detainee transfers	Y
2. Pass $820 billion stimulus	N	6. Pass health care bill	N	10. Legalize immigrants' kids	N
3. Let guns in national parks	Y	7. Regulate financial firms	N	11. Repeal don't ask, tell	N
4. Pass cap-and-trade	N	8. Pass tax cuts for some	N	12. Limit campaign funds	N

Election Results

2010 general	Ed Royce (R)	119,455	(67%)	($1,797,849.31)
	Christina Avalos (D)	59,400	(33%)	(no FEC report)
2010 primary	Ed Royce (R)	unopposed		

Prior Winning Percentages: 2008 (63%), 2006 (67%), 2004 (68%), 2002 (68%), 2000 (63%), 1998 (63%), 1996 (63%), 1994 (66%), 1992 (57%)

Population		Race/Ethnicity		Work	
Pop. 2010:	665,653	White:	39.1%	Private:	80.5%
Change since 2000:	Up 4.2%	Black:	2.2%	Government:	11.9%
Urban:	100.0%	Hispanic:	35.2%	Self-employed:	7.4%
Rural:	0.0%	Asian:	20.5%	Blue collar:	19.7%
Area size:	102 sq. mi.	Native Am.:	0.2%	White collar:	64.6%
		Hawaiian:	0.4%	Khaki collar:	0.0%
Age		Two+ races:	2.2%	Other:	15.7%
Median age:	35.6 yrs.				
More than 65 yrs:	11.7%	*Ancestry*		Median income:	$69,639
Less than 18 yrs:	25.4%	German	8.6%	Median Home Value:	$566,000
		Irish	6.6%		
Education		English	5.9%	**Military Veterans**	
H.S. grad:	82.8%			% of Pop:	7.1%
College grad:	30.8%				
Grad degree:	9.7%				

Orange County; Orange

Orange County is the sixth-most-populous county in the United States, having grown steadily from 130,000 people in 1940, to nearly 2 million in 1980, to just over 3 million in 2010. It is now a community with the patina of maturity, and in some places an aging community, fraying around the edges. The county can no longer double its population, as it did for several decades when Disneyland sprung up on empty land and when orange groves and bean fields were trans-

2008 Presidential Vote		
John McCain (R)	125,066	(51%)
Barack Obama (D)	114,025	(47%)
2004 Presidential Vote		
George Bush (R)	138,766	(60%)
John Kerry (D)	88,631	(39%)
Cook Partisan Voting Index: R+8		

formed into subdivisions, shopping centers and office towers. Ranchers and farmers have given way to aerospace engineers. Until relatively recently, the communities of Orange County were mostly white and middle class. The area has been transformed by its openness to economic and ethnic change. Its economy has been constantly reshaped by the inevitable upheavals of capitalism, and that pattern continues. Tourism remains key, but there is no single industry that is responsible for Orange County's prosperity. The region was hit hard by the defense spending cutbacks and recession of the early 1990s but it bounced back, fueled by start-ups and small entrepreneurial successes not anticipated by government or corporate planners. Orange County was again rocked by recession in 2008, when the hyperinflation of the local housing market abruptly burst and home values slid as much as 20% from 2007 levels. Two major hospitals closed in 2009, putting nearly 1,100 people out of work. But because of rapid moves by local governments to cut costs and draw new projects, as well as continuing increases in green jobs such as solar power manufacturing, Orange County is expected to recover more quickly than other California counties.

Always Republican, Orange County became a symbol of conservatism, first in California and then nationally. This was a solid base for Ronald Reagan in his campaigns for governor and president. In 1988, the district's 317,000-vote plurality for George H.W. Bush was his largest in any county in the nation. Orange County's conservatism reflected a belief in technological progress and traditional values as unyielding as the mile-square grid that the county's founders imposed on most of its land, and a belief in market economies that produced wonders such as the area's advanced military technologies. Over the years, Orange County has become racially and ethnically more diverse. The all-white Orange County stereotype is now thoroughly out of date, exemplified by the election in 2007 of the county's first Vietnamese-American supervisor. In 2004, Orange County gave George W. Bush a 222,000-vote margin, well below his father's margin 16 years before. The GOP advantage dwindled significantly in 2008, when John McCain prevailed over Barack Obama by only 29,500 votes.

The 40th Congressional District of California is located entirely in Orange County. At the geographic center is Fullerton, with 36,000 students at its own branch of California State University. The campus's business school is the largest in the state. To the southwest are Buena Park, home of Knott's Berry Farm, the earliest theme park (1940), plus Cypress, Los Alamitos, La Palma, Stanton, and parts of Garden Grove and Westminster. Southeast of Fullerton, the district includes most of Placentia, part of eastern Anaheim, and all of Villa Park and Orange, the district's largest city. Overall, the 40th District is 34% Hispanic, 19% Asian (primarily Korean, Vietnamese and Filipino) and 3% African-American.

Ed Royce (R)

The congressman from the 40th District is Ed Royce, a Republican first elected in 1992. His lifetime almost precisely spans the area's growth. He grew up in Fullerton and belonged to the conservative Young Americans for Freedom at Cal State Fullerton. He was later the head of Youth for Reagan in California during Reagan's 1976 challenge to Gerald Ford. Royce worked several years as a tax and capital projects manager for a cement company. In 1982, a bunch of conservative state legislators known as the "Cave Men" took him to a Black Angus restaurant—no avocado-and-sprout sandwiches for them—and persuaded him to run for the state Senate. He won at age 31. When the legislature refused to pass Royce's bill allowing crime victims to object to trial delays, giving grand juries more power, and ending "jury-shopping," he got the measure on the ballot as an initiative and it passed by a wide margin. He also wrote the first law making it a felony to stalk someone. In 1992, Royce ran for the U.S. House. With the blessing of Orange County Republican leaders, he was unopposed in the primary and easily won the general. He has been re-elected by wide margins ever since.

In the House, Royce has a conservative voting record, and he has been a faithful fundraiser for Republicans. He has been a vocal critic of the Obama administration's approach to immigration, calling for it to tightly enforce current laws rather than propose new ones. On the Financial Services Committee, he has worked with Democrats to expand lending authority for credit unions and to put them on an equivalent status with banks. With Rep. Melissa Bean, D-Ill., in 2009, Royce proposed a federal regulator for insurance companies to replace the patchwork state regulatory system. During conference committee negotiations on the 2010 financial industry overhaul, he tried without success to persuade conferees to make substantive changes to government-backed mortgage giants Fannie Mae and Freddie Mac, arguing that reshaping those oft-criticized institutions was crucial to any reform effort.

The last time Republicans held the majority, Royce was the chairman of the International Relations Subcommittee on Africa. Although he had never set foot in Africa, he was widely praised for getting up to speed on the issues. He was instrumental in getting bipartisan support to enact an Africa free trade bill. He also sponsored bills to encourage oil production, promote human rights, and condemn the genocide in Sudan. He was among the sponsors of a bipartisan bill in 2009 requiring Obama to develop a comprehensive plan to end the brutal two-decade war in Uganda.

Back in the majority after the 2010 election, Royce became chairman of the Foreign Affairs Subcommittee on Terrorism, Nonproliferation, and Trade, where he has focused on the spread of radical Islam. He won enactment of a bill establishing Radio Free Afghanistan and another measure to promote nuclear nonproliferation in North Korea. He has also urged stronger strategic and trade relationships between the United States and India, and condemned the discrimination against Hindus in Pakistan, Bangladesh and Bhutan. He helped win the release of two journalists from a North Korean prison in 2009. The following year, Royce joined in an effort to get money into a defense spending bill for a California State University initiative training students in Arabic, Persian and other languages considered important to national security.

FORTY-FIRST DISTRICT

Jerry Lewis (R)

Elected 1978, 17th term; b. Oct. 21, 1934, Seattle, WA; home, Redlands; U.C.L.A., B.A. 1956; Presbyterian; married (Arlene); 7 children.

Elected Office: San Bernardino Sch. Bd., 1964-68; CA Assembly, 1968–78.

Professional Career: Insurance exec., 1959–78; Field rep., U.S. Rep. Jerry Pettis, 1968.

DC Office: 2112 RHOB, 20515, 202-225-5861; Fax: 202-225-6498; Web site: jerrylewis.house.gov.

State Offices: Redlands, 909-862-6030.

Committees: *Appropriations:* Defense (VChmn); Energy & Water Development; Interior, Environment & Related Agencies; Labor, HHS, Education & Related Agencies; State, Foreign Operations & Related Programs.

Group Ratings
	ACLU	ACU	ADA	CFG	AFS	FRC	LCV	ITIC	NTU	COC
2010	13	96	0	97	0	93	0	33	89	88
2009	–	84	5	81	22	–	7	–	80	80

National Journal Ratings
	2010 LIB	—	2010 CONS	2009 LIB	—	2009 CONS
Economic	11%	—	88%	24%	—	75%
Social	0%	—	85%	22%	—	77%
Foreign	0%	—	88%	0%	—	75%
Composite	8%	—	92%	20%	—	80%

Key Votes of the 111th Congress
1. Overturn Ledbetter	N	5. Bar federal abortion funds	Y	9. Stop detainee transfers	Y
2. Pass $820 billion stimulus	N	6. Pass health care bill	N	10. Legalize immigrants' kids	N
3. Let guns in national parks	Y	7. Regulate financial firms	N	11. Repeal don't ask, tell	N
4. Pass cap-and-trade	N	8. Pass tax cuts for some	N	12. Limit campaign funds	N

Election Results

2010 general	Jerry Lewis (R)..127,857	(63%)	($688,155)
	Pat Meagher (D)..74,394	(37%)	($48,279)
2010 primary	Jerry Lewis (R)..42,462	(66%)	
	Eric Stone (R)..21,607	(34%)	

Prior Winning Percentages: 2008 (62%), 2006 (67%), 2004 (83%), 2002 (67%), 2000 (80%), 1998 (65%), 1996 (65%), 1994 (71%), 1992 (63%), 1990 (61%), 1988 (70%), 1986 (77%), 1984 (85%), 1982 (68%), 1980 (72%), 1978 (61%)

Population		Race/Ethnicity		Work	
Pop. 2010:	797,133	White:	50.7%	Private:	67.4%
Change since 2000:	Up 24.7%	Black:	6.0%	Government:	24.1%
Urban:	89.4%	Hispanic:	34.9%	Self-employed:	8.3%
Rural:	10.6%	Asian:	4.7%	Blue collar:	23.0%
Area size:	13,350 sq. mi.	Native Am.:	0.8%	White collar:	55.6%
		Hawaiian:	0.3%	Khaki collar:	2.0%
Age		Two+ races:	2.5%	Other:	19.4%
Median age:	34.3 yrs.				
More than 65 yrs:	12.8%	*Ancestry*		Median income:	$50,505
Less than 18 yrs:	27.9%	German	11.2%	Median Home Value:	$275,500
		Irish	9.0%		
Education		English	7.9%	**Military Veterans**	
H.S. grad:	82.6%			% of Pop:	11.2%
College grad:	20.1%				
Grad degree:	7.7%				

San Bernardino County; Redlands

In the 1970s, as the coastal portions of the Los Angeles Basin became fully developed and in the 1980s as real estate values skyrocketed, people with modest incomes and young families increasingly moved east, from the high-cost, high-crime coast to the sunnier, smoggier, hotter valleys inland. There was much empty, low-priced land in what people began calling the Inland Empire, defined usually as San Bernardino and Riverside counties, and even more in the desert to the north and east of the passes through the mountains that rim the Basin. This has been a high-growth area, with population growing from 1.6 million in 1980 to 3.2 million in 2000 to 4.2 million in 2010. In the century's first decade, there was a boom in commercial real estate, especially warehouses to store merchandise offloaded at the port of Los Angeles-Long Beach. The uptick in construction attracted many Latinos, both citizens and immigrants; the Inland Empire had the nation's biggest increase in Latino population in 2000-08. New subdivisions sprang up and subprime mortgages were readily available with little or no money down. Then in 2007 the housing bubble burst, and in the ensuing recession commercial real estate went sour. Millions of square feet of warehouses stood empty. The Inland Empire had one of the nation's highest foreclosure rates and housing values fell by half.

2008 Presidential Vote		
John McCain (R) 147,982	(54%)
Barack Obama (D) 119,255	(44%)

2004 Presidential Vote		
George Bush (R) 149,673	(62%)
John Kerry (D) 89,424	(37%)

Cook Partisan Voting Index: R+10

The 41st Congressional District covers some of the Inland Empire and the desert beyond the San Bernardino Mountains. It includes most of the land area of San Bernardino County, which with 20,052 square miles is the largest county in the United States—more than twice the size of New Jersey. Nearly half its population is concentrated in its southwest corner, inside the Los Angeles Basin, including the northern and eastern edges of San Bernardino and all of Loma Linda, Redlands, Highland, and Yucaipa; many of these small towns were founded by Midwesterners at the base of 10,000-foot mountains. The district also includes a number of towns in Riverside County just to the south: Calimesa, Beaumont, Banning, and San Jacinto.

East of the mountains is the vast Mojave Desert, mostly uninhabited but with growing clusters of population. In the Victor Valley are Hesperia and Apple Valley, new towns in the desert with 159,000 people between them, and Victorville, another high-growth, high-desert community that was once home to cowboy stars Roy Rogers and Dale Evans. The district includes the mountain country around Lake Arrowhead and Big Bear Lake; Desert Hot Springs, the rustic town north of posh Palm Springs; and Twentynine Palms with its huge Twentynine Palms Marine Corps Base, the largest Marine base in the world. It also takes in the city of Needles, pop. 4,800, which often has the hottest temperature in the nation. About one-third of the district's residents are Hispanic, a much lower percentage than in the adjacent 43rd District. Historically the Inland Empire has been more Republican than central Los Angeles, and the 41st district was drawn to exclude Democratic areas. It voted 62%-37% for George W. Bush in 2004 and 54%-44% for John McCain in 2008.

Jerry Lewis (R)

The congressman from the 41st District is Jerry Lewis, a Republican first elected in 1978 and a former chairman of the Appropriations Committee. Lewis grew up in San Bernardino, worked as a lifeguard and graduated from the University of California at Los Angeles. (He maintains his swimming skills and once saved former Speaker Jim Wright off the shore of Hawaii.) He was an insurance agent in Redlands, where he joined civic groups and was elected to the school board in the early 1960s. He won a seat in the California Assembly in 1968, at age 34. A decade later, he was elected to the U.S. House after the incumbent congressman retired. In 1980, Lewis got a seat on the Appropriations Committee, where bipartisan cooperation was the norm, enabling even minority members to confer favors on their districts. With a small-city background and an accommodating attitude toward Democrats, he steadily won leadership positions: chairman of the Republican Research Committee in 1984, chairman of the Republican Policy Committee in 1986, and Republican Conference chairman in 1988. Lewis seemed destined to rise to the minority leader post. But a small group of young conservatives, followers of Newt Gingrich, rebelled against the bipartisan cooperation that Lewis and other more senior Republicans practiced, believing that it would prevent the party from ever gaining a House majority. In March 1989, when the minority whip position came open after Dick Cheney of Wyoming was appointed Defense secretary, Lewis considered running, but aware of the growing unrest in the GOP conference, declined. Gingrich won on an 87-85 vote. In December 1992, Rep. Dick Armey of Texas, with support from Gingrich, challenged Lewis for the Conference chairmanship and won 88-84. Those two votes put in place the two top leaders of the House when Republicans won their first majority in 40 years in 1994.

Lewis then became chairman of the Appropriations subcommittee in charge of veterans and housing programs. That made him a member of the so-called "college of cardinals" of appropriations subcommittee chairmen known for their collective power to control government spending. As part of the new majority's call for tighter federal budgets, Lewis made deep cuts in agency spending, including in popular agencies like NASA. In 1999, Lewis became chairman of the Defense Subcommittee. With a nose for a deal, Lewis led the panel through several relatively uneventful years of making defense budgets. Lewis' job got increasingly difficult during the Iraq war years, as the mounting bill for the war aroused opposition among Democrats and some Republicans. In 2004, Lewis warned Defense Secretary Donald Rumsfeld that "people will be targeting our budget in a serious way." But that year he managed to get through the House a $417 billion appropriation that included $25 billion for Iraq. However, Lewis insisted that only $1 billion of the money be available for "flexible" use; the Bush administration wanted discretion over how the entire amount was spent.

As an appropriator, Lewis was long unapologetic about channeling funds into his district in the form of earmarks. One special beneficiary has been Loma Linda University, where he has promoted cancer treatment and NASA research. He played a role in converting the former George and Norton Air Force bases into successful airports. Some of his projects are sentimental. He got $1 million to rebuild the Perris Hill Plunge, a WPA-built pool where he had been a lifeguard and taught dozens of children to swim.

In 2004, when Bill Young of Florida reached the end of his six-year term limit as Appropriations chairman, Lewis was third in seniority among committee Republicans. But he made a play for the gavel, vying with the more senior Ralph Regula of Ohio, who voted less often with the Republican leadership, and the less senior Harold Rogers of Kentucky. The contest turned on who had contributed the most money to fellow Republicans. Regula had contributed little. Lewis had contributed $1.35 million to Republicans that election season. He was chosen chairman.

Lewis had a rocky two years at the helm of the influential committee. He wanted to streamline the appropriations process and end the growing dependence on omnibus spending bills, which were taking the place of individual spending bills as the House grew more politically polarized. He failed to achieve either goal. The combination of Iraq war funding and Hurricane Katrina relief added more than $200 billion to the original budget in 2005. The next year, Lewis' committee finished most of its work, but breakdowns in the Republican-controlled Senate meant that most spending decisions were deferred to the Democrats after they took majority control in the House in 2007. In 2006, the Justice Department reportedly began investigating Lewis and his associates for their work on earmarks benefitting clients of lobbyist Bill Lowery, a former Appropriations Committee colleague of Lewis' from California. Lewis denied wrongdoing and said he had not been contacted by the FBI, but since then, he has paid legal fees of $1.2 million.

Once in the minority, Lewis became the ranking Republican on the committee. In 2007, he criticized Democrats for their defense bill that "ties the hands of our commander-in-chief during a time of war, places military decisions in the hands of politicians and attempts to buy votes for its passage, on the left and on the right, by literally promising something for everyone." In 2008 he called the committee's failure to handle most of its bills in the usual manner "an historic dereliction of duty." Democrats blamed the inaction in part on Lewis for pushing votes on controversial proposals, like one to increase offshore oil drilling.

In May 2009, Lewis supported the Democrats' $96 billion supplemental defense spending bill but objected to some of their policies. On other appropriations bills, Lewis offered amendments that were usually voted down on party lines, although he did get $34 million to hire 200 Border Patrol officers. His amendment to prohibit spending on any new government-run health plan lost. He called for non-defense appropriations in fiscal 2010 to be held to a 2% increase over 2009 levels as a way of freeing up funds for President Obama's troop deployment to Afghanistan. In 2010, Lewis sought unsuccessfully to limit transportation spending to ensure that at least $4 billion remained in the highway trust fund. But with help from fellow California Republican David Dreier, he secured a measure increasing federal compensation to states for the cost of incarcerating illegal immigrants from $300 million to $400 million; California stood to get nearly half the funds.

Lewis secured more than $18 million in earmarks in the economic stimulus bill of 2009. The same year, he requested 70 projects despite growing public anger at earmarking, assuring critics, "Every project on this list has been carefully reviewed to ensure that they fit federal programs created by law to fund these types of projects." Then in 2010, he joined fellow House Republicans in swearing off earmarks. Lewis hoped that he might become chairman again when the GOP won control of the House in the election that year, but the influx that year of young conservative Republicans who had waged campaigns critical of earmarks worked against Lewis. The Republican Steering Committee awarded the chairmanship to Rogers.

Lewis remains popular in his district. In the 1990s, he took note of the rising Hispanic population in his district and took Spanish lessons. House Democrats thought Lewis might be vulnerable in 2008 because of the federal probe of his ties to lobbyists. But Lewis was re-elected 62%-38%. In 2010, he won 63%-37%.

FORTY-SECOND DISTRICT

Gary Miller (R)

Elected 1998, 7th term; b. Oct. 16, 1948, Huntsville, AR; home, Diamond Bar; Mt. San Antonio Col. 1971, 1988-89; Christian; married (Cathy); 4 children.

Military Career: Army, 1967.

Elected Office: Diamond Bar City Cncl., 1989-95; Diamond Bar Mayor, 1992; CA Assembly, 1995-98.

Professional Career: Businessman, real estate developer, G. Miller Development Co., 1971-98.

DC Office: 2349 RHOB, 20515, 202-225-3201; Fax: 202-226-6962; Web site: garymiller.house.gov.

State Offices: Brea, 714-257-1142; Mission Viejo, 949-470-8484.

Committees: *Financial Services:* Insurance, Housing & Community Opportunity; International Monetary Policy & Trade (Chmn). *Transportation & Infrastructure:* Highways & Transit; Railroads, Pipelines & Hazardous Materials; Water Resources & Environment.

Group Ratings

	ACLU	ACU	ADA	CFG	AFS	FRC	LCV	ITIC	NTU	COC
2010	15	96	0	97	0	100	0	33	89	100
2009	–	90	5	84	13	–	0	–	82	77

National Journal Ratings

	2010 LIB	—	2010 CONS		2009 LIB	—	2009 CONS
Economic	24%	—	75%		21%	—	78%
Social	0%	—	85%		18%	—	82%
Foreign	0%	—	88%		0%	—	75%
Composite	13%	—	87%		17%	—	83%

Key Votes of the 111th Congress

1. Overturn Ledbetter	*	5. Bar federal abortion funds	Y	9. Stop detainee transfers	Y
2. Pass $820 billion stimulus	N	6. Pass health care bill	N	10. Legalize immigrants' kids	N
3. Let guns in national parks	Y	7. Regulate financial firms	N	11. Repeal don't ask, tell	N
4. Pass cap-and-trade	N	8. Pass tax cuts for some	N	12. Limit campaign funds	N

Election Results

2010 general	Gary Miller (R)	127,161	(62%)	($767,700)
	Michael Williamson (D)	65,122	(32%)	(no FEC report)
	Mark Lambert (Lib)	12,115	(6%)	
2010 primary	Gary Miller (R)	32,669	(49%)	
	Phil Liberatore (R)	25,181	(38%)	
	Lee McGroarty (R)	7,113	(11%)	

Prior Winning Percentages: 2008 (60%), 2006 (100%), 2004 (68%), 2002 (68%), 2000 (59%), 1998 (53%)

Population		Race/Ethnicity		Work	
Pop. 2010:	667,638	White:	45.1%	Private:	77.2%
Change since 2000:	Up 4.5%	Black:	2.4%	Government:	14.6%
Urban:	98.7%	Hispanic:	29.3%	Self-employed:	8.0%
Rural:	1.3%	Asian:	20.2%	Blue collar:	13.2%
Area size:	317 sq. mi.	Native Am.:	0.2%	White collar:	73.5%
		Hawaiian:	0.1%	Khaki collar:	0.0%
Age		Two+ races:	2.5%	Other:	13.2%
Median age:	37.3 yrs.				
More than 65 yrs:	10.0%	*Ancestry*		Median income:	$87,364
Less than 18 yrs:	25.3%	German	9.8%	Median Home Value:	$593,400
		Irish	7.9%		
Education		English	6.9%	**Military Veterans**	
H.S. grad:	89.4%			% of Pop:	6.7%
College grad:	38.3%				
Grad degree:	12.8%				

Inland Empire; Mission Viejo, Chino

The fastest growth in the Los Angeles metropolitan area over the past 25 years has been in the Inland Empire, at the eastern end of the Los Angeles Basin. Mostly orange groves and dairy farms a few decades ago, this territory is now the site of a robust economy, personal upward mobility, and ethnic and cultural diversity. The main ingredient of the growth has been small entrepreneurial businesses, usually started by people with no particular connections or advantages

2008 Presidential Vote
John McCain (R) ... 152,256 (53%)
Barack Obama (D) ... 128,474 (45%)

2004 Presidential Vote
George Bush (R) ... 164,998 (62%)
John Kerry (D) ... 98,108 (37%)

Cook Partisan Voting Index: R+10

and often of Asian or Latino immigrant background. California has never been a land of leisure, as stereotype would have it, but rather a place for hard work, where the fertility of the soil and the productivity of the people have led to prosperity and, more recently, relative tolerance toward newcomers. (Anti-Asian sentiment expressed itself in the Chinese Exclusion Act of 1882 and the Japanese-American internment camps of 1942-44. Despite occasional tensions since World War II, this has been one of the more welcoming destinations for immigrants.)

The 42nd Congressional District of California is centered in the Inland Empire where Los Angeles, San Bernardino and Orange counties come together. In San Bernardino County, it includes Chino, site of a large youth prison that is expected to undergo a $110 million conversion into an adult facility. It also has large meatpacking plants, whose smell can carry across the valley on a windy day, and Chino Hills, incorporated in 1991 and full of subdivisions for commuters who battle the heavy traffic on Interstate 5 to Orange and L.A. counties. In Los Angeles County, it includes Diamond Bar, La Habra Heights and the eastern part of Whittier. Nearly two-thirds of the district's population is in Orange County. The county includes Yorba Linda, the birthplace of Richard Nixon and the site of his presidential library. Only 40,000 people lived there in 1913 when Nixon was born; just over 3 million live there today. Other Orange County towns in the 42nd are Brea and La Habra; the eastern part of Anaheim; and the newer condominium communities of Mission Viejo and Rancho Santa Margarita. Ethnically diverse, the district is 28% Hispanic and 19% Asian, and relatively stable socially: It has the highest percentage of married people in the state. It leans Republican. In 2004, George W. Bush won the district with 62% here, and in 2008 John McCain won by 53%-45%.

Gary Miller (R)

The congressman from the 42nd District is Gary Miller, a Republican first elected in 1998. He was born in Arkansas but grew up in Whittier. In his early 20s, he became a home builder and later developed planned communities. He is among the wealthiest members of the House. He began his public service in 1988, when he was appointed to the Diamond Bar Municipal Advisory Council. A year later, after Diamond Bar was incorporated, Miller was elected to the City Council and served as mayor. In 1995, he was elected to the California Assembly in a special election. After chairing the Assembly's Budget Committee, he decided in 1997 to run for the U.S. House against scandal-tarred incumbent Republican Jay Kim, who had pleaded guilty to accepting and conceal-ing $230,000 in illegal campaign contributions. Miller emphasized standard Republican themes—lower taxes, tougher penalties for crime, improved local education—and financed his campaign largely with his own money. He won the all-party primary with 48% to 26% for Kim. Democrats did not pose a serious challenge in November.

Since then, Miller has come under scrutiny for questionable ethics himself. Several of his land deals have been investigated by the media and the Justice Department. One involved Miller's sale of 165 acres to the city of Monrovia, Calif. According to several published reports, he made $10 million on the deal, then avoided paying capital gains taxes by claiming the land had been threat-ened by an eminent domain action by Monrovia. In another case, he got a $1.28 million earmark in an appropriations bill to improve streets in front of development property he co-owned in the town of Diamond Bar. Miller has maintained that he did nothing wrong and that he was the victim of a smear campaign by Democrats. He was named in 2009 in a leak of information about members under investigation by the House ethics committee.

Miller has a conservative voting record in the House, and became one of the Tea Party Caucus' early members in July 2010. He drew national attention for his bill calling for an end to birthright citizenship for children of illegal immigrants born on U.S. soil. Miller has advanced some original proposals: He sponsored a bill giving Internet service providers a cause of action against spammers, with $500 per message in penalties. A Civil War buff, Miller sponsored a bill to preserve Civil War battlefields after discovering that nearly 20% of the major battle sites have been lost.

On the Financial Services Committee, he was active on legislation to address the mortgage crisis and sought to increase the maximum mortgage-loan limits for Fannie Mae and Freddie Mac in high-cost areas such as California. In 2009, he got a bill through the House to allow banks and mortgage services to temporarily enter into leases on foreclosed properties, a move intended to give families a chance to stay in their homes.

Democrats talked about trying to unseat Miller in 2008 in light of his ethics troubles. But they failed to put up much of a fight. Miller won easily, 60%-40%, over Montebello lawyer and school-board member Ed Chau in a low-budget contest.

Two years later, however, anti-incumbency sentiment led Miller to draw three GOP primary challengers: Whittier business owner Phil Liberatore, Chino investment services executive Lee McGroarty and Diamond Bar salesman David Su. They criticized him for his support of the massive government rescue of the financial industry. And they seized on an article in *Harper's* that said several biographical entries portrayed him as serving in the Army during Vietnam, though Miller was in the service for just seven weeks before being discharged. But Miller poured money into the race, lending his campaign $475,000, and said he had not inaccurately described his military service, which he said was ended by health problems. He held on to win with 49%, with Liberatore drawing 37%, McGroaty 11%, and Su 3%.

Miller suffered two personal tragedies in 2007. His 33-year-old daughter died for reasons that were not made public, and the children of one of his sons were abducted by their mother after a bitter custody dispute.

FORTY-THIRD DISTRICT

Joe Baca (D)

Elected Nov. 1999, 6th full term; b. Jan. 23, 1947, Belen, NM; home, Rialto; CA State L.A., B.A., 1971; Catholic; married (Barbara); 4 children.

Military Career: Army, 1966-68.

Elected Office: CA Assembly, 1992-98; CA Senate, 1998-99.

Professional Career: Community affairs rep., General Telephone and Electric, 1974-89; Co-owner, Interstate World Travel, 1989-present.

DC Office: 2366 RHOB, 20515, 202-225-6161; Fax: 202-225-8671; Web site: baca.house.gov.

State Offices: San Bernardino, 909-885-2222.

Committees: *Agriculture:* Department Operations, Oversight & Credit; Livestock, Dairy & Poultry; Nutrition & Horticulture (RMM). *Financial Services:* Financial Institutions & Consumer Credit; Oversight & Investigations.

Group Ratings

	ACLU	ACU	ADA	CFG	AFS	FRC	LCV	ITIC	NTU	COC
2010	81	0	90	0	100	6	80	100	5	14
2009	–	4	90	2	100	–	100	–	3	40

National Journal Ratings

	2010 LIB — 2010 CONS		2009 LIB — 2009 CONS	
Economic	75%	— 24%	80%	— 20%
Social	61%	— 35%	59%	— 37%
Foreign	49%	— 49%	85%	— 14%
Composite	63%	— 37%	76%	— 25%

Key Votes of the 111th Congress

1. Overturn Ledbetter	Y	5. Bar federal abortion funds	Y	9. Stop detainee transfers	Y
2. Pass $820 billion stimulus	Y	6. Pass health care bill	Y	10. Legalize immigrants' kids	Y
3. Let guns in national parks	Y	7. Regulate financial firms	Y	11. Repeal don't ask, tell	Y
4. Pass cap-and-trade	Y	8. Pass tax cuts for some	Y	12. Limit campaign funds	Y

Election Results

2010 general	Joe Baca (D) 70,026	(66%)	($758,696)
	Scott Folkens (R) 36,890	(35%)	($23,852)
2010 primary	Joe Baca (D) .... unopposed		

Prior Winning Percentages: 2008 (69%), 2006 (64%), 2004 (66%), 2002 (66%), 2000 (60%), 1999 (51%)

Population		Race/Ethnicity		Work	
Pop. 2010:	735,581	White:	14.6%	Private:	80.2%
Change since 2000:	Up 15.1%	Black:	9.9%	Government:	13.2%
Urban:	99.3%	Hispanic:	69.4%	Self-employed:	6.4%
Rural:	0.7%	Asian:	4.0%	Blue collar:	34.5%
Area size:	193 sq. mi.	Native Am.:	0.3%	White collar:	46.3%
		Hawaiian:	0.3%	Khaki collar:	0.1%
Age		Two+ races:	1.4%	Other:	19.1%
Median age:	28.1 yrs.				
More than 65 yrs:	6.0%	*Ancestry*		Median income:	$49,318
Less than 18 yrs:	33.3%	German	4.2%	Median Home Value:	$307,700
		Irish	3.4%		
Education		English	2.4%	**Military Veterans**	
H.S. grad:	66.8%			% of Pop:	5.5%
College grad:	11.3%				
Grad degree:	3.0%				

Inland Empire; Ontario

The gateway to the Los Angeles Basin for decades was San Bernardino. Passengers on the Santa Fe Railroad and motorists on U.S. 66 traveled from the hot and dusty desert, through the twisting, windy Cajon Pass, and wound up in the green, tree-lined Los Angeles Basin. This was an agricultural zone until World War II, when Henry J. Kaiser built the West Coast's first major steel mill between the Santa Fe and Southern Pacific rail lines in Fontana, just west

2008 Presidential Vote		
Barack Obama (D) 112,020	(68%)
John McCain (R) 49,594	(30%)
2004 Presidential Vote		
John Kerry (D) 79,946	(58%)
George Bush (R) 55,952	(41%)
Cook Partisan Voting Index: D+13		

of San Bernardino. Today, these lands have largely filled up. The Inland Empire, as it is called, may be where the smog piles up against the mountains, but it also has some of the lowest real estate prices in the Los Angeles Basin and an energetic small-business economy. Business growth has been spurred by huge distribution and warehouse centers that service overseas cargo from the Long Beach port. Within 26 miles of San Bernardino, there are more than 15 Walmarts. The area's farmlands and dairy pastures have been reduced substantially. From 1990 to 2005, jobs in the county grew from 408,000 to 643,000. But the recession hit hard and early in the Inland Empire, with home foreclosures among the highest in the nation in 2007. There were signs of hope in 2010: San Bernardino's sales tax revenue appeared to stabilize after plummeting 44% in four years, and two companies signed leases for large distribution facilities in the Ontario area.

The 43rd Congressional District of California includes most of San Bernardino and Colton and the towns running west—Rialto, Ontario, and Fontana, where many new businesses have supplanted the steel mill that was closed in 1994. Northrop Grumman has opened a Missile Engineering Center. The shuttered Norton Air Force Base has been redeveloped as San Bernardino's airport, and the city has built a new baseball stadium. Politically this area trended Republican in the 1980s. But as the Latino population grew—the district was 69% Hispanic in 2010—it became Democratic. Barack Obama's 68% showing in the 43rd District was his second-best Southern California district outside Los Angeles in 2008.

Joe Baca (D)

The congressman from the 43rd District is Joe Baca, a Democrat first elected in 1999. He was born in Belen, N.M., the youngest of 15 children. His family moved to Barstow, Calif., in the desert, when he was 4 years old. His father worked as a laborer for the Santa Fe Railroad. At age 10, Baca went to work, first shining shoes and then selling newspapers and working as a janitor. He served in the Army as a paratrooper during the Vietnam War but did not see combat. After graduating from California State University at Los Angeles, Baca moved to the San Bernardino area, where he spent 15 years as a community affairs representative for General Telephone and Electric. He was elected four times to the San Bernardino Community College board. After two unsuccessful campaigns, the persistent Baca was elected to the state Assembly in 1992. He rose to become speaker pro tempore of the Assembly, the first Latino to hold the position. He earned a reputation as a hard worker, introducing legislation to reduce welfare rolls, lower taxes on middle-income earners and increase penalties for drug dealers.

Facing term limits in 1998, he ran for the state Senate, spending $2 million to win the seat and raise his profile. His opportunity to run for Congress came in July 1999, when Democratic Rep. George Brown died in his 18th term. His widow, Marta Macias Brown, ran for the seat. Widows of members had won in 35 of the previous 36 such races, but Minority Leader Richard Gephardt refused her request to clear the field, and Baca ran. He won the endorsement of organized labor and had a base among Latino voters. Brown attacked him for his endorsement from the National Rifle Association. Baca won the all-party primary with 32% of the vote to Brown's 30%. He then focused on Republican nominee Elia Pirozzi, a real estate developer. Brown did not endorse Baca, who emphasized his centrist voting record and his support for targeted tax cuts, a minimum wage increase and abortion rights. Baca won 51%-45%.

In the House, Baca has one of the more conservative voting records among California Democrats. He voted with Republicans against a 2010 bill ending the ban on travel to Cuba, and he also joined the GOP in backing an amendment to housing legislation in 2009 to allow guns in public housing projects. But he is strongly pro-labor and introduced a bill to create a national holiday honoring United Farm Workers founder Cesar Chavez. He also strongly criticized Arizona's 2010 enactment of the nation's toughest immigration law, saying he would boycott the state and handing out wristbands printed with a message making that point.

Personally, Baca is known for his athleticism. He is an avid golfer and former semipro baseball player who underwent elbow surgery in 2005 partly so he could continue to pitch in the annual congressional charity game. He achieved a high-profile role of another kind in the 110th Congress (2007-08), when he was chosen as chairman of the Congressional Hispanic Caucus. His tenure was marked by internal discord. In 2007, several women members complained about allegedly sexist remarks, and all but one woman member abstained from the vote naming him chairman. A year earlier, when Baca was running the group's political action committee, some members protested when funds were used to support bids for office by two of his sons.

In 2007, Baca became chairman on the Agriculture Subcommittee on Department Operations, Oversight, Nutrition and Forestry and was the most senior Californian working on the farm bill that year. He focused on greater opportunities for socially disadvantaged farmers and won support for a new program to give minority farmers better access to Agriculture Department services. With a seat as well on Financial Services, Baca sought relief for people facing home foreclosures. He voted for a bill bailing out the financial markets in 2008 after securing a commitment for subsequent mortgage relief legislation. But he drew some unwanted publicity in 2009 when the *Wall Street Journal* published a lengthy article suggesting that his push to make it easier for first-time homebuyers to obtain loans contributed to the more than 9,000 foreclosures in his district.

Baca wins re-election easily every two years. In 2006, Baca's two sons lost bids for the state Legislature. But in 2009, Joe Baca Jr. became the mayor of Rialto.

FORTY-FOURTH DISTRICT

Ken Calvert (R)

Elected 1992, 10th term; b. June 8, 1953, Corona; home, Corona; Chaffey Col., 1972-73; San Diego St. U., B.A. 1975; Protestant; divorced.

Professional Career: Restaurant owner, 1975–80; Real estate broker, 1980–92; Chmn., Riverside Cnty. Repub. Party, 1984–88.

DC Office: 2269 RHOB, 20515, 202-225-1986; Fax: 202-225-2004; Web site: calvert.house.gov.

State Offices: Las Flores, 949-888-8498; Riverside, 951-784-4300.

Committees: *Appropriations:* Defense; Interior, Environment & Related Agencies (VChmn); Legislative Branch. *Budget.*

Group Ratings

	ACLU	ACU	ADA	CFG	AFS	FRC	LCV	ITIC	NTU	COC
2010	13	96	0	85	0	93	0	33	86	100
2009	–	92	10	82	22	–	14	–	80	87

National Journal Ratings

	2010 LIB — 2010 CONS		2009 LIB — 2009 CONS	
Economic	13%	— 87%	28%	— 71%
Social	16%	— 82%	20%	— 78%
Foreign	21%	— 77%	0%	— 75%
Composite	17%	— 83%	21%	— 79%

Key Votes of the 111th Congress

1. Overturn Ledbetter	N	5. Bar federal abortion funds	Y	9. Stop detainee transfers	Y
2. Pass $820 billion stimulus	N	6. Pass health care bill	N	10. Legalize immigrants' kids	N
3. Let guns in national parks	Y	7. Regulate financial firms	N	11. Repeal don't ask, tell	N
4. Pass cap-and-trade	N	8. Pass tax cuts for some	N	12. Limit campaign funds	N

Election Results

2010 general	Ken Calvert (R)	107,482	(56%)	($1,663,591)
	Bill Hedrick (D)	85,784	(44%)	($546,701)
2010 primary	Ken Calvert (R)	37,327	(66%)	
	Chris Riggs (R)	18,994	(34%)	

Prior Winning Percentages: 2008 (51%), 2006 (60%), 2004 (62%), 2002 (64%), 2000 (74%), 1998 (56%), 1996 (55%), 1994 (55%), 1992 (47%)

Population		Race/Ethnicity		Work	
Pop. 2010:	844,756	White:	40.5%	Private:	76.1%
Change since 2000:	Up 32.2%	Black:	5.2%	Government:	15.4%
Urban:	97.7%	Hispanic:	43.5%	Self-employed:	8.2%
Rural:	2.3%	Asian:	7.8%	Blue collar:	23.8%
Area size:	549 sq. mi.	Native Am.:	0.3%	White collar:	60.0%
		Hawaiian:	0.3%	Khaki collar:	0.3%
Age		Two+ races:	2.2%	Other:	16.0%
Median age:	32.2 yrs.				
More than 65 yrs:	8.2%	*Ancestry*		Median income:	$71,004
Less than 18 yrs:	29.4%	German	9.6%	Median Home Value:	$431,300
		Irish	7.0%		
Education		English	6.1%	**Military Veterans**	
H.S. grad:	80.1%			% of Pop:	7.4%
College grad:	25.6%				
Grad degree:	9.3%				

Inland Empire; Riverside, Corona

Riverside was a sleepy town of 34,000 people, a couple hours' drive from Los Angeles, when Richard and Pat Nixon were married there in 1940 at the Mission Inn, built in 1876 and adorned with bell towers, fountains, and stained glass windows. Riverside was not much larger, with 46,000 people, when Ronald and Nancy Reagan spent their honeymoon at the Mission Inn a dozen years later, in 1952. Riverside then was a citrus center, a market town amid orange

2008 Presidential Vote		
Barack Obama (D)	133,535	(50%)
John McCain (R)	131,003	(49%)

2004 Presidential Vote		
George Bush (R)	139,476	(59%)
John Kerry (D)	94,374	(40%)

Cook Partisan Voting Index: R+6

groves, where the local agricultural college developed, among other things, the navel orange. Today the Mission Inn is again doing business, after being shuttered from 1985 to 1992, but Riverside has changed completely. The city has grown to 300,000 people, and Riverside County now has over 2 million, more than double its population in 1980. This has been a boom part of California, where modest-income families found new houses in inexpensive developments and small businesses expanded. Near Moreno Valley, the former March Air Force Base became a business park and regional hub for shipping giant DHL. But the recent recession halted that progress. Unemployment in the Riverside area was above 14% in 2010, and it had a high level of home foreclosures. The county cut 1,600 public jobs over two years and concentrated limited resources on public safety. Those moves helped reduce violent crime by 21%. On the upside, the University of California announced plans for a new medical school in Riverside that is expected to enroll its first students in fall 2012.

The 44th Congressional District of California, which covers much of this area, has been one of the fastest-growing congressional districts in the nation in the past two decades; from 2000 to 2008, it grew another 28%. Much of the increase was in the Hispanic population, which went from 35% to 42% of the total. Some 40% of district residents live in the city of Riverside and most others in nearby towns like Corona and Norco, the home of a Naval Surface Warfare Center, which evaluates weapons systems. The district includes the eastern edge of Orange County all the way to the ocean, much of it uninhabited mountainsides. But it also takes in San Clemente, where President Nixon lived after he resigned the presidency, and half of San Juan Capistrano, to which the swallows famously return every March. This has been a solidly Republican district, which President George W. Bush won 59%-40% in 2004. However, Democrat Barack Obama did unexpectedly well in 2008, edging out Republican John McCain, 49.5%-48.6%. Obama won the Riverside portion of the district by more than 13,000 votes, while McCain led in Orange County by nearly 11,000 votes. Local Republicans blamed the shift on the region's high unemployment and foreclosure rates.

Ken Calvert (R)

The congressman from the 44th District is Ken Calvert, a Republican first elected in 1992. Calvert grew up in Corona. While in college, he was a congressional intern at the Senate Watergate hearings of 1973. Later, he ran the family restaurant back home and, in 1980, got into the commercial real estate business. In 1982, at age 29, he ran for Congress in a district that included almost all of Riverside County and lost a nine-candidate primary to Al McCandless by 868 votes. In 1992, he ran in a new district and won the primary with 28% of the vote. His Democratic opponent was Mark Takano, an eighth-grade teacher who had the support of teachers' unions and Japanese-Americans. Calvert beat Takano by 519 votes. Calvert ran into trouble at home soon after he was elected, when the Riverside *Press-Enterprise* reported that he had been stopped by police with a prostitute in his car. Calvert apologized and said that he was upset because his wife had divorced him the month before and his father had recently committed suicide. His opponents in 1994 used the incident against him. Calvert won the primary 51%-49%, with only an 884-vote margin, against business Professor Joseph Khoury. Takano, running again in the general election, ran an ad that accused Calvert of "flagrant womanizing." But with the Republican tide that year, Calvert won 55%-38%.

In the House, Calvert has compiled a moderate-to-conservative voting record. He broke with most GOP colleagues in 2008 by supporting housing finance legislation, citing his district's high foreclosure rate. But he has usually been a Republican team player and is an ally of GOP Speaker John Boehner, who put him on the leadership-run Steering Committee charged with making committee assignments.

In 2001, Calvert took over as chairman of the Water and Power Subcommittee of the Resources Committee, where he focused intensively on building support for reauthorization of the vital water-supply program (CALFED) for California's Central Valley. With the water issues largely resolved, Calvert in 2005 became chairman of the Science and Technology Committee's Space and Aeronautics Subcommittee. That year, he enacted a reauthorization of NASA programs, which included the goal of returning an astronaut to the moon by 2020 and incentives for private entrepreneurs to develop space technologies.

Calvert left the two panels in 2007 after snagging a coveted seat on the Appropriations Committee, where he aggressively sought spending earmarks for his district. In fiscal year 2010, taxpayer groups criticized him for more than $33 million in solo provisions, the third-largest amount in the California delegation behind then Speaker Nancy Pelosi and Appropriations ranking Republican Jerry Lewis. But he found fault with President Obama's spending initiatives and in 2010, he signed on to Lewis' bill to return billions of unspent economic stimulus dollars to the Treasury. Calvert has been a major backer of E-Verify, an online system he helped create that allows employers to confirm the eligibility of new hires. In 2009, he also worked to get a statue of Ronald Reagan placed in the Capitol's Statuary Hall.

In 2003, Calvert abandoned his 1992 pledge to serve only 12 years. But he was re-elected easily anyway. In recent years, his ethics have been called into question, which could hamper his efforts to move up the ladder in the House. In 2006, the *Los Angeles Times* reported that he and his real estate partner had bought a four-acre tract for $550,000, then sold it less than a year later for $985,000, after Calvert secured an $8 million spending earmark for expansion of a nearby freeway interchange. Calvert denied wrongdoing, noting that it was not illegal for a member of Congress to make personal investments. A year later, when Calvert was tapped to replace the ethically tainted Rep. John Doolittle, R-Calif., on Appropriations, the story came back to haunt him. Conservative bloggers reacted angrily to his selection.

In 2008, Calvert had a close contest against Democrat Bill Hedrick, a Corona-Norco school board member who was poorly funded and had no national party help. Hedrick benefited not just from Calvert's ethics problems, but also from Obama's success in the district. Calvert won by only a little more than 6,000 votes, 51.2% to 48.8%. He was rescued by his nearly 15,000 vote-lead in the heavily Republican Orange County portion of the district.

Hedrick returned for a rematch in 2010. This time, he got help from the Democratic Congressional Campaign Committee, which ran ads slamming Calvert for voting against the economic stimulus bill, children's health legislation and other initiatives. But the National Republican Congressional Committee stepped in to help Calvert, and the DCCC eventually turned its focus to more-winnable races. Calvert won 55%-45%, spending more than $1.5 million to Hedrick's $493,000. Shifting demographics could make him a prime target for Democratic redistricters in 2012.

FORTY-FIFTH DISTRICT

Mary Bono Mack (R)

Elected April 1998, 7th full term; b. Oct. 24, 1961, Cleveland, OH; home, Palm Springs; U. of S. CA, B.F.A. 1984; Protestant; married (Connie Mack); 4 children.

Professional Career: Gen. mgr., Bono restaurant, 1986–90.

DC Office: 104 CHOB, 20515, 202-225-5330; Fax: 202-225-2961; Web site: bonomack.house.gov.

State Offices: Hemet, 951-658-2312; Palm Springs, 760-320-1076.

Committees: *Energy & Commerce:* Commerce, Manufacturing & Trade (Chmn); Communications & Technology; Environment & the Economy.

Group Ratings

	ACLU	ACU	ADA	CFG	AFS	FRC	LCV	ITIC	NTU	COC
2010	19	91	20	91	13	81	30	33	82	88
2009	–	79	30	58	33	–	43	–	70	80

National Journal Ratings

	2010 LIB	—	2010 CONS	2009 LIB	—	2009 CONS
Economic	31%	—	69%	34%	—	66%
Social	36%	—	64%	37%	—	62%
Foreign	32%	—	67%	0%	—	75%
Composite	33%	—	67%	28%	—	72%

Key Votes of the 111th Congress

1. Overturn Ledbetter	N	5. Bar federal abortion funds	Y	9. Stop detainee transfers	Y
2. Pass $820 billion stimulus	N	6. Pass health care bill	N	10. Legalize immigrants' kids	N
3. Let guns in national parks	Y	7. Regulate financial firms	N	11. Repeal don't ask, tell	Y
4. Pass cap-and-trade	Y	8. Pass tax cuts for some	N	12. Limit campaign funds	N

Election Results

2010 general	Mary Bono Mack (R)	106,472	(52%)	($2,427,224)
	Steve Pougnet (D)	87,141	(42%)	($1,846,142)
	Bill Lussenheide (AMI)	13,188	(6%)	
2010 primary	Mary Bono Mack (R)	42,981	(71%)	
	Thibodeau (R)	17,940	(29%)	

Prior Winning Percentages: 2008 (58%), 2006 (61%), 2004 (67%), 2002 (65%), 2000 (59%), 1998 (60%), 1998 (64%)

Population		Race/Ethnicity		Work	
Pop. 2010:	914,209	White:	41.1%	Private:	75.6%
Change since 2000:	Up 43.0%	Black:	6.4%	Government:	14.8%
Urban:	89.9%	Hispanic:	45.2%	Self-employed:	9.5%
Rural:	10.1%	Asian:	4.4%	Blue collar:	21.3%
Area size:	6,062 sq. mi.	Native Am.:	0.5%	White collar:	54.3%
		Hawaiian:	0.2%	Khaki collar:	0.3%
Age		Two+ races:	2.1%	Other:	24.2%
Median age:	34.9 yrs.				
More than 65 yrs:	14.3%	*Ancestry*		Median income:	$54,722
Less than 18 yrs:	28.3%	German	8.9%	Median Home Value:	$314,800
		English	6.7%		
Education		Irish	6.5%	**Military Veterans**	
H.S. grad:	79.3%			% of Pop:	10.5%
College grad:	21.1%				
Grad degree:	7.0%				

Inland Empire; Moreno Valley

From the air three decades ago, a night flight east from Los Angeles flew over the lights of homes of 10 million people and then into almost perfect darkness. The city then was a vast metropolis surrounded by almost uninhabited territory. Today the sprinkled pattern of white lights has spread into the Inland Empire around Riverside and San Bernardino and is multiplying outward into the desert. The Inland Empire has filled up with instant towns like family-oriented Moreno Valley, which did not exist in 1980 but had 193,000 people in 2010. Over the 10,000-foot San Jacinto Mountains, desert communities boomed: Palm Springs was once the lone winter resort for the stars but now is popular for its retro architecture and as a destination for gays. It is one of a string of communities along Highway 111 and Frank Sinatra and Bob Hope drives. Among rich retirees, the coast's cachet lessened as beach cities filled up with rollerbladers and rent-control crusaders. The clean, dry, roomy desert, where the days are almost always crystal clear and the sky usually blue and cloudless, became more attractive with the prevalence of air-conditioning. Two presidents retired to the desert here: Dwight Eisenhower, who wintered in Palm Desert, and Gerald Ford, who resided for 30 years after his presidency in nearby Rancho Mirage. The population is nearly 300,000 for the entire desert corridor if the count includes Indio and Coachella, the heavily Latino and fast-growing cities in the agricultural Coachella Valley. The valley has 75% of the country's date palms. The annual music and arts festival in Coachella, which began in 1999, drew a record 75,000 people per day in 2010.

> **2008 Presidential Vote**
> Barack Obama (D) 142,305 (52%)
> John McCain (R) 129,664 (47%)
>
> **2004 Presidential Vote**
> George Bush (R) 132,288 (56%)
> John Kerry (D) 101,679 (43%)
>
> **Cook Partisan Voting Index:** R+3

The 45th Congressional District of California covers almost the entire desert in Riverside County, from Blythe on the Nevada border to Palm Springs. Joshua Tree National Park, with its high-desert sands, is a popular tourist spot (it's shared with the 41st District, though most of it is in the 45th). Like other parts of California, the mortgage crisis hit hard here, and unemployment in 2010 ranged from below 10% in Palm Desert to more than 22% in Coachella. About half the district's population lives west of the 10,000-foot peak that looms above Palm Springs, in fast-growing Moreno Valley, socially conservative Murrieta and the old town of Hemet. This area has grown rapidly since 2000. Hispanics contributed much of that growth and now make up 42% of the district's population. It has tended to vote Republican, but in 2008, Democratic presidential candidate Barack Obama won the district by an unexpectedly comfortable 52%-47%.

Mary Bono Mack (R)

The congresswoman from the 45th District is Mary Bono Mack, who won the seat in an April 1998 special election after the death of her husband, Sonny Bono, the onetime pop music celebrity who became a member of the U.S. House. In 2008, she married U.S. Rep. Connie Mack, a Florida Republican.

Bono Mack grew up as Mary Whitaker in South Pasadena, the daughter of a surgeon and a chemist. She was an accomplished gymnast and remains a fitness buff and a certified personal fitness instructor who has studied karate and Tae Kwan Do. She met Sonny Bono when she was celebrating her college graduation at his Los Angeles restaurant in 1984. They were married two years later. The couple was on a family vacation when he was killed in a skiing accident in South Lake Tahoe, Calif. At the time of his death, she had no political experience and was little known in Washington. House Republican leaders encouraged her to run for her husband's seat, believing she was the only one who could avert a divisive Republican primary. In the special election, Democrats backed actor Ralph Waite, best known as Pa Walton in *The Waltons*. Waite was hurt during the brief campaign because he kept a commitment to play Willy Loman in *Death of a Salesman* six times a week in a New Jersey theater. The campaign's biggest controversy came when Sonny's 83-year-old mother said that her son would have opposed Mary's candidacy, preferring that she care for their children. But it was no contest. Mary Bono won 64%-29%, a bigger margin than Sonny's two victories.

Bono Mack has a moderate voting record, especially on social issues, and is the least conservative of the California Republicans. She helped pass the reauthorization of the Ryan White AIDS research law in 2006, and she supported embryonic stem cell research and increases in the federal minimum wage. Her initial legislative priority was passage of Sonny Bono's bill to restore the Salton Sea, a body of water in the desert that had been shrinking and getting polluted by agricultural runoff. Although some Democrats objected to taking funds from other California projects, Bono Mack secured $13 million for what became the Sonny Bono Salton Sea National Wildlife Refuge.

On the Energy and Commerce Committee, Bono Mack in 2009 caused considerable consternation in Republican circles for supporting the Democrats' cap-and-trade bill to reduce carbon emissions. She said that the bill, while "far from perfect," prevented the Environmental Protection Agency from having sole regulatory authority over greenhouse gas emissions. By April 2010, she was less supportive of the bill, writing in a letter to GOP negotiators that she had "serious reservations" about proceeding with the talks. Though she joined Republicans in opposing the health care overhaul that year, she worked with Democrats on bills aimed at improving children's health and combating eating disorders and obesity.

In 2007, the House passed her legislation to crack down on invasive computer "spyware," which can hijack a computer and tamper with its operations. Bono Mack, who collects about $100,000 annually from her late husband's royalties, has opposed legislation to relax controls on digital piracy. The House passed her bill in December 2009 to educate consumers about privacy and security risks associated with digital file-sharing. During the immigration debate in recent years, she supported tougher enforcement at the border as well as an expanded guest worker program.

Bono Mack usually has been re-elected with ease, though she has faced tougher battles in recent elections. In 2008, she was challenged by former Assemblywoman Julie Bornstein, a Democrat who ran an ad depicting Bono Mack as a bubblehead for Bush's policies. Bornstein spent nearly $400,000, but Bono Mack won 58%-42%.

Two years later, her moderate record led to a primary challenge from Clayton Thibodeau, who moved from San Diego County to Hemet at the urging of tea-party activists. But she trounced Thibodeau in the June 2010 primary, setting up a race against Palm Springs Mayor Steve Pougnet. He raised serious money, bringing in nearly $1.7 million. Openly gay, he was able to neutralize some of the support she had built up in that community. Encouraged by Obama's showing in 2008, national Democrats hoped they could wage a competitive race, and ran ads highlighting her opposition to the 2009 financial reform overhaul. But Bono Mack proved difficult to pigeonhole as a lock-step conservative. She won with 51.5%, having raised more than $2.2 million.

FORTY-SIXTH DISTRICT

Dana Rohrabacher (R)

Elected 1988, 12th term; b. June 21, 1947, Coronado; home, Huntington Beach; Long Beach St. Col. B.A. 1969, U. of S. CA, M.A. 1975; Christian; married (Rhonda); 3 children.

Professional Career: Radio & print journalist, 1970–80; Sr. speechwriter, special asst. to Pres. Reagan, 1981–88.

DC Office: 2300 RHOB, 20515, 202-225-2415; Fax: 202-225-0145; Web site: rohrabacher.house.gov.

State Offices: Huntington Beach, 714-960-6483.

Committees: *Foreign Affairs:* Middle East & South Asia; Oversight & Investigations (Chmn). *Science & Technology:* Energy & Environment; Space & Aeronautics.

Group Ratings

	ACLU	ACU	ADA	CFG	AFS	FRC	LCV	ITIC	NTU	COC
2010	13	96	5	86	0	93	0	33	91	88
2009	–	100	5	88	0	–	7	–	88	73

National Journal Ratings

	2010 LIB — 2010 CONS		2009 LIB — 2009 CONS	
Economic	20%	80%	26%	74%
Social	0%	85%	0%	93%
Foreign	36%	63%	39%	61%
Composite	21%	79%	23%	77%

Key Votes of the 111th Congress

1. Overturn Ledbetter	N	5. Bar federal abortion funds	Y	9. Stop detainee transfers	Y
2. Pass $820 billion stimulus	N	6. Pass health care bill	N	10. Legalize immigrants' kids	N
3. Let guns in national parks	Y	7. Regulate financial firms	N	11. Repeal don't ask, tell	N
4. Pass cap-and-trade	N	8. Pass tax cuts for some	N	12. Limit campaign funds	N

Election Results

2010 general	Dana Rohrabacher (R)	139,822	(62%)	($404,285.00)
	Ken Arnold (D)	84,940	(38%)	($18,405)
2010 primary	Dana Rohrabacher (R)	unopposed		

Prior Winning Percentages: 2008 (53%), 2006 (60%), 2004 (62%), 2002 (62%), 2000 (62%), 1998 (59%), 1996 (61%), 1994 (69%), 1992 (55%), 1990 (59%), 1988 (64%)

Population		Race/Ethnicity		Work	
Pop. 2010:	648,663	White:	55.8%	Private:	78.8%
Change since 2000:	Up 1.5%	Black:	1.5%	Government:	12.1%
Urban:	99.9%	Hispanic:	20.2%	Self-employed:	8.9%
Rural:	0.1%	Asian:	18.8%	Blue collar:	13.9%
Area size:	825 sq. mi.	Native Am.:	0.2%	White collar:	70.9%
		Hawaiian:	0.3%	Khaki collar:	0.2%
Age		Two+ races:	2.9%	Other:	15.0%
Median age:	39.7 yrs.				
More than 65 yrs:	14.9%	*Ancestry*		Median income:	$75,726
Less than 18 yrs:	20.9%	German	11.5%	Median Home Value:	$665,800
		Irish	8.8%		
Education		English	8.0%	**Military Veterans**	
H.S. grad:	89.8%			% of Pop:	8.3%
College grad:	39.8%				
Grad degree:	14.3%				

Huntington Beach, Part Long Beach

In the 1950s, when The Beach Boys were at Hawthorne High School, surfers would drive far down the coast to the vast expanse of Huntington Beach in Orange County to catch a wave. This was empty country then, vegetable fields and orange groves mainly, with nary a freeway or shopping center in sight. Today, the 42-mile shoreline of Orange County is pretty much filled in with pricey coastal resorts and other development. Huntington Beach, a city of 190,000, is a mixture of family subdivisions and garden apartments and home of the International Surfing Museum. Its eight miles of beach and self-depiction as Surf City make it a tourist draw in the summer. To the north is Westminster, the center of the nation's most prominent Vietnamese-American community, with miles of shops with Vietnamese names and its own Vietnamese-language daily newspaper. Southeast along San Diego Freeway is Fountain Valley, the central focus of many Asian-owned high-technology businesses. Near the coast is Costa Mesa, site of South Coast Plaza's luxury stores and a grand performing arts center. Like other California cities, it experienced a huge influx of Hispanic immigrants in the last decade. Adapting has been rocky; the Costa Mesa City Council shut down a day labor center and declared itself a "rule of law city" rather than a sanctuary city.

The 46th Congressional District of California includes all of this beachfront plus the Long Beach Harbor area and the Palos Verdes Peninsula. It also includes inland territory: the eastern end of Long Beach and next-door Seal Beach, areas settled by many retirees; most of Westminster; all of Fountain Valley and Costa Mesa; the southwest corner of Santa Ana; and a tiny slice of Los Angeles. The eastern part of the district is connected to the Palos Verdes Peninsula by a thin strip of beach or the port area. Politically, the two ends of the district are solidly Republican, from high-income Palos Verdes to Westminster. This is no longer the monoracial Orange County of the 1960s. The district's population is 20% Hispanic and 19% Asian (nearly half of whom are Vietnamese). Unlike other coastal California districts, this one has remained Republican. In 2008, GOP presidential candidate John McCain won it, albeit narrowly, 50%-48%.

2008 Presidential Vote

John McCain (R)	150,937	(50%)
Barack Obama (D)	145,393	(48%)

2004 Presidential Vote

George Bush (R)	168,158	(57%)
John Kerry (D)	122,991	(42%)

Cook Partisan Voting Index: R+6

Dana Rohrabacher (R)

The congressman from the 46th District is Dana Rohrabacher, a Republican first elected in 1988. He calls himself a surfer Republican and sports an American-flag surfboard on his lapel. He grew up in Southern California, went to college and experimented with drugs, and once had a folk band called the Goldwaters. By the mid-1970s, he was on a far straighter path as a press aide in Ronald Reagan's 1976 and 1980 presidential campaigns. He wrote editorials for the *Orange County Register* and later was a speechwriter in the Reagan White House. He returned to Southern California in 1988, when GOP Rep. Dan Lungren was appointed acting state treasurer, leaving open a heavily Republican seat. Rohrabacher won the primary with 35% of the vote, and went on to prevail in the general with 64%. During the campaign, one of his volunteers, a surfer, entered him in a surfing contest. They later married and, in 2004, became the parents of triplets.

A self-styled free spirit, Rohrabacher likes to make waves in the House. His website once featured the motto: "Fighting for freedom and having fun." His voting record can be unpredictable, especially on cultural issues. He supports medical marijuana and joined with liberal Rep. Barney Frank of Massachusetts on a bill to decriminalize possession of less than 100 grams. He invited Frank, who is gay, and his partner, a surfer, to visit Huntington Beach. As a maverick, Rohrabacher has never gotten a seat on a top committee. In 2006, he lost the ranking minority position on the full Science and Technology Committee to the more senior Ralph Hall of Texas. When Republicans regained the House majority in 2011, Hall became chairman.

Rohrabacher has been skeptical of theories of anthropogenic global warming, and in 2009 sought unsuccessfully to get the National Academy of Sciences to certify state climate monitoring stations. Rohrabacher has taken on some unusual causes. With Democrat Brian Baird of Washington, he called for measures to assure continuity of Congress in case of a catastrophic attack or disaster. And he sponsored a bill that would give District of Columbia residents full voting rights in Maryland but would maintain a separate District government.

Rohrabacher's other main focus has been the Foreign Affairs Committee, where he has taken a special interest in efforts to fight the Taliban in Afghanistan. After the September 11 attacks, he visited the exiled king of Afghanistan in Rome, encouraged him to return to Kabul and promised that the United States would oust the Taliban and help rebuild the country. He opposed President Obama's troop increase in 2009, saying, "The way to win in Afghanistan is to help rebuild the country from the bottom up." Rohrabacher has been a longtime critic of China's rulers. He strongly opposed normal trade relations with China and has backed strong export controls to bar advanced technology from non-democratic governments.

For years Rohrabacher has called for stronger action against illegal immigration. In 2003, he delayed his support for the Republicans' Medicare prescription drug bill until Republican leaders, in exchange for his vote, gave him a vote on his bill to require hospitals to report potential illegal immigrants to the Homeland Security Department. He also has led voter initiatives to remove illegal aliens from California's welfare and school rolls, and he successfully urged President George W. Bush to commute the sentences of two former Border Patrol agents who shot a Mexican drug dealer.

Rohrabacher has been routinely re-elected by wide margins. But in 2008 he faced Huntington Beach Mayor Debbie Cook, a Democratic lawyer and environmental activist who claimed he had done little during his time in Congress. With no help from the national party, she raised $482,000. Rohrabacher criticized Cook's opposition to more oil drilling and her support for the rescue of the financial markets. He won by a reduced 53%-43%. In 2010, he won by something more like his customary margins, 62%-38%.

FORTY-SEVENTH DISTRICT

Loretta Sanchez (D)

Elected 1996, 8th term; b. Jan. 7, 1960, Lynwood; home, Garden Grove; Chapman U., B.A. 1982, American U., M.B.A. 1984; Catholic; divorced.

Professional Career: Mgr. & financial analyst, Orange Cnty. Transp. Auth., 1984–87; Asst. vice pres., Fieldman, Rolapp & Assoc., 1987–90; Assoc., Booz, Allen & Hamilton, 1990–93; Principal, Amiga Advisors, 1993-96.

DC Office: 1114 LHOB, 20515, 202-225-2965; Fax: 202-225-5859; Web site: www.lorettasanchez.house.gov.

State Offices: Garden Grove, 714-621-0102.

Committees: *Armed Services:* Emerging Threats & Capabilities; Oversight & Investigations; Strategic Forces (RMM). *Homeland Security:* Border & Maritime Security; Counterterrorism & Intelligence. *Joint Economic Committee.*

Group Ratings

	ACLU	ACU	ADA	CFG	AFS	FRC	LCV	ITIC	NTU	COC
2010	93	0	95	0	100	0	100	67	4	0
2009	–	0	90	2	100	–	100	–	4	36

National Journal Ratings

	2010 LIB — 2010 CONS		2009 LIB — 2009 CONS	
Economic	82% —	17%	67% —	33%
Social	75% —	24%	72% —	26%
Foreign	92% —	3%	76% —	23%
Composite	84% —	16%	72% —	28%

Key Votes of the 111th Congress

1. Overturn Ledbetter	Y	5. Bar federal abortion funds	N	9. Stop detainee transfers	N
2. Pass $820 billion stimulus	Y	6. Pass health care bill	Y	10. Legalize immigrants' kids	Y
3. Let guns in national parks	N	7. Regulate financial firms	Y	11. Repeal don't ask, tell	Y
4. Pass cap-and-trade	Y	8. Pass tax cuts for some	Y	12. Limit campaign funds	Y

Election Results

2010 general	Loretta Sanchez (D)	50,832	(53%)	($2,056,345)
	Van Tran (R)	37,679	(39%)	($1,404,741)
	Cecilia Iglesias (I)	7,443	(8%)	($118,889)
2010 primary	Loretta Sanchez (D)	unopposed		

Prior Winning Percentages: 2008 (69%), 2006 (62%), 2004 (60%), 2002 (61%), 2000 (60%), 1998 (56%), 1996 (47%)

Population		Race/Ethnicity		Work	
Pop. 2010:	631,422	White:	12.4%	Private:	87.1%
Change since 2000:	Down 1.2%	Black:	1.3%	Government:	7.2%
Urban:	100.0%	Hispanic:	67.6%	Self-employed:	5.6%
Rural:	0.0%	Asian:	17.0%	Blue collar:	34.0%
Area size:	301 sq. mi.	Native Am.:	0.2%	White collar:	40.1%
		Hawaiian:	0.4%	Khaki collar:	0.0%
Age		Two+ races:	1.0%	Other:	25.8%
Median age:	29.7 yrs.				
More than 65 yrs:	7.2%	*Ancestry*		Median income:	$52,185
Less than 18 yrs:	31.0%	German	2.8%	Median Home Value:	$435,200
		Irish	2.2%		
Education		English	1.9%	**Military Veterans**	
H.S. grad:	56.4%			% of Pop:	3.6%
College grad:	12.6%				
Grad degree:	3.3%				

Orange County; Santa Ana, Anaheim

When Walt Disney began planning Disneyland in the late 1940s, he did not have to drive far from downtown Los Angeles before finding agricultural land. Dairy farms and orange groves covered most of southeast Los Angeles County and adjacent Orange County, which had only 216,000 people in 1950. As Disneyland opened there in 1955 and became a vast success, the area around it—a mass of flatland surrounded by mountains and sea—found itself directly in

2008 Presidential Vote		
Barack Obama (D)	77,144	(60%)
John McCain (R)	48,461	(38%)
2004 Presidential Vote		
George Bush (R)	56,226	(50%)
John Kerry (D)	54,623	(49%)
Cook Partisan Voting Index:	D+4	

the path of the most explosively growing metropolitan area in the United States. Now, with 3 million people, Orange County is the nation's fifth-largest county, just a bit ahead of San Diego County.

Just as Orange County was once transformed by newcomers from Los Angeles County and the Midwest, so it is again being transformed by immigrants, from Mexico and other parts of Latin America, and from Vietnam, Taiwan, Korea, and other parts of East Asia. By 2010, the county was 34% Hispanic and 18% Asian. The county seat of Santa Ana is a major arrival point for immigrants from Mexico, and is 78% Hispanic. Others immigrants have moved farther out, like so many Southern Californians before them, working hard jobs, commuting on freeways, and living in stucco subdivisions. There are concentrations in various places—Latinos in Santa Ana and much of Anaheim; Vietnamese in Westminster and Garden Grove, who constitute the largest Vietnamese community in the nation—but many of these new Californians are scattered throughout the county. These demographic changes have made for some political wobble. Until the mid-1990s, Asians were split between the parties, and few Latinos were registered to vote. After the 1994 approval of Proposition 187, which sought to deny most social services to illegal immigrants, many more Latinos began voting, and voting mostly Democratic. Asian voters were less predictable.

The 47th Congressional District of California is the geographic heart of Orange County. About half its people live in Santa Ana. The district includes most of Garden Grove and Anaheim and many Orange County landmarks—Angel Stadium of Anaheim, Disneyland, and Disney's California Adventure. Unemployment was in double digits in most cities through 2010. Disneyland did report "modestly better" attendance in late summer 2010 compared to the previous year, though the park would not release specific numbers. The district's population in 2008 was 69% Hispanic and 15% Asian, primarily Vietnamese. This core area has always been the most Democratic part of Orange County. But it is not overwhelmingly Democratic like most majority-Hispanic districts in Los Angeles County. Republican President George W. Bush won the district in 2004, but by only 50%-49% over Democrat John Kerry. In 2008, Barack Obama returned the district to the Democrats by winning over Republican John McCain 60%-38%.

Loretta Sanchez (D)

The congresswoman from the 47th District is Loretta Sanchez, a Democrat first elected in 1996. She and her sister, Linda Sánchez, are the first sisters to serve in Congress. (Linda uses the accent mark with her surname; Loretta does not.) Loretta is nine years older than Linda, who represents California's 39th District. They co-authored a 2008 memoir titled *Dream in Color.*

Sanchez was raised in Anaheim. Her parents were Mexican immigrants, her father a machinist and her mother a secretary who worked to organize a union at the plant where she worked. Sanchez graduated from Chapman University in Orange, and got an M.B.A. from American University in Washington, D.C. She worked as a financial analyst, providing advice on municipal finances to public agencies and private businesses, and then started her own firm in the early 1990s. In 1994, she ran for the Anaheim City Council under her married name, Loretta Sanchez-Brixey, and lost. In 1996, she ran for the U.S. House, this time as Loretta Sanchez, against one of the most vocal conservatives, Rep. Robert Dornan. In the primary against three Anglo male Democrats, she won with 35%. That victory attracted little attention, not even from Dornan. But she shrewdly counted on increasing Latino turnout, plus attracting contributions from the many enemies that Dornan had made over a political career that went back to 1976. President Bill Clinton came to Santa Ana late in the campaign to stump for Sanchez, and may have made the difference. She won by 984 votes, 47%-46%. Dornan charged vote fraud, and, using the privileges afforded to former members, he regularly appeared on the House floor trying to persuade his former colleagues to call for a special election. But in February 1998, the House Administration Committee upheld Sanchez's victory.

In the House, Sanchez's voting record has been in the Democratic middle, though she has been slightly more loyal to her party in recent years. She was among the last Democratic holdouts on the health care overhaul in March 2010 after having supported the earlier House version. She backed it at the last minute, though she criticized it for lacking a government-run public option and not adequately reimbursing California hospitals for Medicare. U.S.-Vietnam relations have been a focus for her. She accompanied Clinton on his 2000 visit there, and met with dissidents to discuss human rights. In 2007, after three times having been denied a visa, she returned to Vietnam and again stirred controversy by attempting to meet with the wives of imprisoned dissidents and criticizing the government's lack of openness. The same year, Sanchez was at the center of a controversy at the Congressional Hispanic Caucus. She and other women in the caucus complained that Chairman Joe Baca of California was dismissive of them. Further, she accused Baca of calling her a "whore," which he denied. She resisted entreaties in 2009 to rejoin the caucus.

As the senior woman on the Armed Services Committee, she has tried to update the sexual assault crimes in the Uniform Code of Military Justice to comply with the way civilian sexual assault crimes are handled at the federal level. Sanchez is also the No. 2 Democrat on the Homeland Security Committee, where she has focused on port security, including her proposal for a secure, long-range automated vessel-tracking system. She also was outspokenly critical of Homeland Security's problem-plagued SBInet border technology tracking program. In 2010, she took over the terrorism subcommittee of Armed Services. After Chairman Ike Skelton and the panel's other senior members lost their bids for re-election in 2010, she jockeyed to become the ranking Democrat on the panel. In the Steering and Policy Committee, she narrowly lost to Washington's Adam Smith, 28-23, but took the fight to the full caucus. Smith and Sanchez tied on the first ballot, but Smith prevailed, 97-86, on the second round of votes.

Until 2010, Sanchez had been re-elected comfortably. Voters had grown accustomed to her spirited and unconventional style, including her quirky Christmas cards, which feature her aging white cat Gretzky. Ever ambitious, Sanchez in 2009 briefly considered a run for California governor. A year later, however, she found herself in a tough fight. Republican Assemblyman Van Tran, who fled Saigon with his family in 1975, raised over $1 million. An independent candidate, Cecilia Iglesias, threatened to siphon off Hispanic voters while many Vietnamese were backing Tran. The situation irked Sanchez, who asserted on a Spanish-language Univision show in September that "the Vietnamese and the Republicans are, with an intensity, [trying] to take this seat." Tran responded that the district "belongs to the people and not an individual ethnicity." But she recovered from that stumble, got party help—Bill Clinton headlined a rally for her—and raised more than $1.7 million. She won with 53% to Tran's 39% and Iglesias' 8%.

FORTY-EIGHTH DISTRICT

John Campbell (R)

Elected Dec. 2005, 3rd full term; b. July 19, 1955, Los Angeles; home, Irvine; U.C.L.A., B.A. 1976, U. of S. CA, M.B.T., 1977; Presbyterian; married (Catherine); 2 children.

Elected Office: CA Assembly, 2000-04; CA Senate, 2004-05.

Professional Career: Tax accountant, 1977-78; Auto dealership executive, 1978-2003.

DC Office: 1507 LHOB, 20515, 202-225-5611; Fax: 202-225-9177; Web site: campbell.house.gov.

State Offices: Newport Beach, 949-756-2244.

Committees: *Budget. Financial Services:* Capital Markets and Government Sponsored Enterprises; International Monetary Policy & Trade. *Joint Economic Committee.*

Group Ratings

	ACLU	ACU	ADA	CFG	AFS	FRC	LCV	ITIC	NTU	COC
2010	19	95	10	100	0	93	0	0	93	83
2009	–	92	10	84	11	–	0	–	88	86

National Journal Ratings

	2010 LIB	—	2010 CONS	2009 LIB	—	2009 CONS
Economic	10%	—	90%	26%	—	73%
Social	23%	—	76%	0%	—	93%
Foreign	35%	—	65%	37%	—	63%
Composite	23%	—	77%	22%	—	78%

Key Votes of the 111th Congress

1. Overturn Ledbetter	N	5. Bar federal abortion funds	Y	9. Stop detainee transfers	Y
2. Pass $820 billion stimulus	N	6. Pass health care bill	N	10. Legalize immigrants' kids	N
3. Let guns in national parks	Y	7. Regulate financial firms	N	11. Repeal don't ask, tell	Y
4. Pass cap-and-trade	N	8. Pass tax cuts for some	N	12. Limit campaign funds	N

Election Results

2010 general	John Campbell (R)	145,481	(60%)	($1,547,266)
	Beth Krom (D)	88,465	(36%)	($704,262)
	Mike Binkley (Lib)	8,773	(4%)	
2010 primary	John Campbell (R)	unopposed		

Prior Winning Percentages: 2008 (56%), 2006 (60%); 2005 (44%)

Population		Race/Ethnicity		Work	
Pop. 2010:	727,833	White:	58.0%	Private:	79.5%
Change since 2000:	Up 13.9%	Black:	1.4%	Government:	11.2%
Urban:	99.9%	Hispanic:	17.9%	Self-employed:	9.1%
Rural:	0.1%	Asian:	18.8%	Blue collar:	9.0%
Area size:	301 sq. mi.	Native Am.:	0.2%	White collar:	79.3%
		Hawaiian:	0.2%	Khaki collar:	0.1%
Age		Two+ races:	3.3%	Other:	11.6%
Median age:	38.4 yrs.				
More than 65 yrs:	13.1%	*Ancestry*		Median income:	$86,690
Less than 18 yrs:	21.9%	German	11.3%	Median Home Value:	$682,500
		Irish	8.9%		
Education		English	8.4%	**Military Veterans**	
H.S. grad:	93.6%			% of Pop:	7.5%
College grad:	52.1%				
Grad degree:	20.1%				

Orange County; Irvine

Forty years ago, the area south of Santa Ana and the John Wayne Airport was open land, a vacant landscape of flat plains and low mountains, all beneath the 4,600-foot Trabuco Peak in the distance. This was the Irvine Ranch, purchased by Gold Rush merchant James Irvine from the Sepulveda and Yorba families and maintained as a ranch until the early 1970s, the last large plot of vacant land in metro Los Angeles. Ten miles

2008 Presidential Vote		
Barack Obama (D)	163,063	(49%)
John McCain (R)	160,584	(49%)
2004 Presidential Vote		
George Bush (R)	178,739	(58%)
John Kerry (D)	123,664	(40%)
Cook Partisan Voting Index: R+6		

along the Pacific Coast and 22 miles inland to the mountains, a traveler on the freeway could still get a sense of what the first American settlers to reach California saw. As Orange County grew up to the limits of the Irvine Ranch, the Irvine family was sitting on some immensely valuable land. In 1959, they donated a site for the University of California at Irvine, which today has over 25,000 students. In the 1970s, they sold the rest to developers. The resulting city of Irvine was a planned community, with eight-lane parkways, huge office parks, shopping malls and attractive subdivisions. Irvine has attracted high-tech and high-growth businesses, highly educated and affluent people, and also Asian immigrants. Its population is 37% Asian, with enough Chinese to support a Chinese supermarket and a Chinese-language library.

Irvine is set amid a raft of affluent communities, except for low-income Santa Ana, which is majority Hispanic and was one of California's fastest-growing cities in 2009. To the north is Tustin, an older town built on Irvine land. To the south is Newport Beach, one of California's richest cities, which has resisted the rapid development of Irvine. Newport Harbor is chock-full of expensive boats, and nearby Balboa Island is filled with multimillion-dollar homes. To the east is Lake Forest; the name used to be El Toro, and some residents now complain that it has few lakes or forests. To the southeast on the ocean is Laguna Beach, with its art galleries and cute shops, and more conventionally affluent Dana Point. Inland are Laguna Niguel, Laguna Hills, and the Laguna Woods retirement community. The El Toro Marine Corps Air Station that closed in 1999 is being developed as 1,300 acres of parkland ringed by 2,400 acres of development, 3,600 homes, and 3 million square feet of commercial and industrial space.

The 48th Congressional District of California, entirely contained within Orange County, is centered geographically on the Irvine Ranch lands and includes all of these communities. A 2010 Gallup-Healthways survey ranked its residents as among the most content in the country. Politically, this is a conservative area, and for a long time it was one of the most Republican districts in the United States. Since the 1990s, like most of metro Los Angeles, it has trended to the Democrats. In 2010, it was 18% Hispanic and 19% Asian. It is still Republican, but far from the most Republican district in the state. Republican George W. Bush won with 58% here in 2000 and 2004, but Democrat Barack Obama won the district by 2,500 votes in 2008, 49.3% to 48.6% for Republican John McCain.

John Campbell (R)

The congressman from the 48th District is John Campbell, a Republican who won a special election in December 2005. He has deep roots in Southern California. His great-grandfather was a Republican member of the state Assembly in the mid-1800s, and his grandfather was the managing editor of the now-defunct *Herald-Examiner*, W.R. Hearst's rival to the *Los Angeles Times*. Campbell's father was an oil field geologist and investor who later edited the *Herald-Examiner*'s financial pages. John Campbell graduated from the University of California at Los Angeles and got a master's degree in business taxation from the University of Southern California. A certified public accountant, he did a stint with Ernst & Young, one of the big accounting firms, and then joined an Orange County automobile dealership group as controller in 1978. Reviewing the company's books, Campbell discovered that the company's management had diverted $500,000 toward personal expenses. He alerted shareholders, including his father. The chief executive officer was fired, and Campbell was given the job. In the 1990s, he sold off Campbell Automotive's Mazda, Ford, and Nissan dealerships to focus on its remaining Saab franchises—and on politics. In 2000, Campbell won an Irvine-based seat in the California Assembly, and four years later was elected to the state Senate.

Campbell got his opportunity to run for Congress when President Bush selected Rep. Christopher Cox to chair the Securities and Exchange Commission in June 2005. Campbell was instantly the front-runner. Also in the primary was Marilyn Brewer, a former state Assembly member who supported abortion rights, and drew support from the moderate Republican Main Street Partnership. Campbell was endorsed by Republican Gov. Arnold Schwarzenegger, whom he had worked closely with in Sacramento, and by the state and Orange County Republican parties. With 19 candidates running for the seat in the all-party October 4 special primary, Campbell finished first with 45%, well above Brewer's 17%, to win the Republican nomination. Steve Young was the Democratic nominee after winning 9%. Jim Gilchrist, founder of the anti-illegal-immigrant Minuteman Project, finished third with 15% and was the nominee of the American Independent Party.

In the campaign for the December 4 runoff, Gilchrist criticized Campbell for his votes in the Assembly, prompting Campbell to say that he made a mistake in 2001 when he voted to allow illegal immigrants to receive in-state college tuition. Gilchrist's single-issue campaign caught Campbell off guard and turned the contest into a referendum on immigration. Campbell won, though, with a surprisingly modest 44% to 28% for Democrat Young and 25% for Gilchrist.

In the House, Campbell's voting record is mostly conservative. He drew widespread scorn from liberals when he said on MSNBC at the height of the far-right controversy over President Obama's birthplace that Obama is a U.S. citizen "as far as I know." He moved quickly into a leadership role among conservatives as the chairman of the budget and spending task force of the Republican Study Committee. He led Republicans angry about Congress' lack of spending restraint, offering a series of amendments designed to embarrass sponsors of questionable spending earmarks. Campbell rarely got many more than 100 votes, but made a point about wasteful spending. When he learned that Democrats planned to embarrass him by highlighting his support for a $2.5 million water project for his district, he withdrew his support for it. But he parted company with most fiscal conservatives in September 2008 when he backed the Troubled Assets Relief Program for the financial industry, which he said was vital to stop the rapid slide of the economy. With that shift, he abandoned his bid to chair the conservative Republican Study Committee.

But he remained an outspoken critic of big spending. Campbell came out against the Southern California-manufactured Air Force C-17 transport plane, and he touted "Project YouCut," a 2010 effort by House Republicans to get citizens to vote for proposed spending votes. However, he raised eyebrows in 2009 when he amended a bill to exempt the lending practices of auto dealers from a new consumer protection financial watchdog agency. He justified the move by arguing that auto dealers already were struggling with the economic downturn and did not need additional regulation. He later joined an unsuccessful GOP effort to amend the bill on the floor to replace the new agency with a council of regulators. Meanwhile, he was one of a group of at least eight lawmakers who were informed in 2010 that the Office of Congressional Ethics was investigating them for attending fundraisers just before a vote on the financial overhaul legislation.

At home, Campbell has been re-elected easily.

FORTY-NINTH DISTRICT

Darrell Issa (R)

Elected 2000, 6th term; b. Nov. 1, 1953, Cleveland, OH; home, Vista; Sienna Heights U., B.A. 1976; Antioch Orthodox Christian; married (Kathy); 1 child.

Military Career: Army, 1970-72; 1976-80.

Professional Career: Founder & pres., Directed Electronics, 1982-99.

DC Office: 2347 RHOB, 20515, 202-225-3906; Fax: 202-225-3303; Web site: issa.house.gov.

State Offices: Vista, 760-599-5000.

Committees: *Judiciary:* Intellectual Property, Competition & the Internet. *Oversight & Government Reform* (Chmn).

Group Ratings

	ACLU	ACU	ADA	CFG	AFS	FRC	LCV	ITIC	NTU	COC
2010	19	100	0	100	0	93	0	33	90	88
2009	–	100	5	91	11	–	7	–	89	73

National Journal Ratings

	2010 LIB — 2010 CONS		2009 LIB — 2009 CONS	
Economic	17%	— 83%	16%	— 83%
Social	23%	— 76%	13%	— 84%
Foreign	26%	— 72%	0%	— 75%
Composite	23%	— 78%	15%	— 86%

Key Votes of the 111th Congress

1. Overturn Ledbetter	N	5. Bar federal abortion funds	Y	9. Stop detainee transfers	Y
2. Pass $820 billion stimulus	N	6. Pass health care bill	N	10. Legalize immigrants' kids	N
3. Let guns in national parks	Y	7. Regulate financial firms	N	11. Repeal don't ask, tell	N
4. Pass cap-and-trade	N	8. Pass tax cuts for some	N	12. Limit campaign funds	N

Election Results

2010 general	Darrell Issa (R)	119,088	(63%)	($1,495,193)
	Howard Katz (D)	59,714	(31%)	($15,359)
	Dion Clark (AMI)	6,585	(4%)	
	Mike Paster (Lib)	4,290	(2%)	
2010 primary	Darrell Issa (R)	unopposed		
2010 primary	Darrell Issa (R)	unopposed		

Prior Winning Percentages: 2008 (58%), 2006 (63%), 2004 (63%), 2002 (77%), 2000 (61%)

Population		Race/Ethnicity		Work	
Pop. 2010:	797,428	White:	47.9%	Private:	70.5%
Change since 2000:	Up 24.8%	Black:	4.3%	Government:	21.2%
Urban:	90.3%	Hispanic:	38.5%	Self-employed:	8.1%
Rural:	9.7%	Asian:	5.0%	Blue collar:	22.4%
Area size:	1,778 sq. mi.	Native Am.:	0.8%	White collar:	54.3%
		Hawaiian:	0.5%	Khaki collar:	4.3%
Age		Two+ races:	2.8%	Other:	19.0%
Median age:	32.1 yrs.				
More than 65 yrs:	11.1%	*Ancestry*		Median income:	$60,913
Less than 18 yrs:	28.3%	German	11.1%	Median Home Value:	$386,100
		Irish	8.2%		
Education		English	7.4%	**Military Veterans**	
H.S. grad:	82.4%			% of Pop:	10.8%
College grad:	23.0%				
Grad degree:	7.6%				

San Diego County, Riverside County

The California coast between Los Angeles and
San Diego has never entirely filled up with development—and never will as long as the Marine Corps retains custody of Camp Pendleton,
the giant training base just south of the Orange-
San Diego County line and the Corps's largest
expeditionary training facility on the West
Coast. The land along the coast and inland in
northern San Diego County, usually referred to
as North County, was largely empty territory a

2008 Presidential Vote		
John McCain (R) 137,739	(53%)
Barack Obama (D) 117,283	(45%)
2004 Presidential Vote		
George Bush (R) 149,283	(63%)
John Kerry (D) 86,998	(37%)
Cook Partisan Voting Index: R+10		

half-century ago—never fertile enough to produce a large farm community, never endowed with
much manufacturing, never actively promoted as a retirement community. But North County has
been growing rapidly since then. Today about 1 million people live here, and who can blame them?
This is one of America's most beautiful and comfortable environments, with ocean and mountain
scenery, sunny and warm weather, and low crime. Amid dry but not desert landscape, there are
miles of rolling hills, with occasional sagebrush-like bushes. It has attracted thousands of new
migrants—many, but by no means all, retirees.

The 49th Congressional District of California occupies the northern part of San Diego County
and the southwestern corner of Riverside County. It was the fastest-growing California district in
the 1990s, with a population increase of 35%; its growth slowed in the 2000s. On the coast next to
Camp Pendleton is Oceanside, a lower-middle-income town heavily dependent on the base. Inland
is Vista, a higher-income community that calls itself the "climatic wonderland of the United
States," with day after day of blue skies, sunshine, and average high temperatures that range from
68° in January to 82° in July. About 35% of the district's population is in these two areas. About
25% is in small communities in North County, including a small portion of San Diego.

Another 40% of the population is in southwest Riverside County. Until the housing bubble
burst in 2007, this was one of the hottest growth parts of the country. Tens of thousands of people
came for cheap housing, even at the cost of long commutes, and for construction jobs, of which there
were plenty of those while the boom lasted. For most of the past decade Temecula, Murrieta, Lake
Elsinore and Perris made the list of America's fastest-growing cities, zooming up toward or over
100,000 population from almost nothing. When the housing market collapsed, construction jobs
disappeared and young Latino or Anglo homebuyers with subprime mortgages found they were
under water. At one point, Murrieta ranked first, Temecula third and Perris fifth in foreclosure
rates nationally.

Politically, this has been a heavily Republican area, but in the economic turmoil of 2008, it
voted only 53% for John McCain.

Darrell Issa (R)

The congressman from the 49th District is Darrell Issa *(ICE-sah)*, a Republican first elected in
2000. He grew up in a working-class section of Cleveland, the son of an X-ray technician. Hampered
by dyslexia, Issa found academics difficult, and he dropped out of high school to join the Army.
After his service, the military paid for him to finish school, and he graduated from Siena Heights
University in Michigan. A brother's run-ins with the law for car theft spurred Issa's idea for his first
business venture. He invested all of his savings, some $7,000, in a car-alarm business in Cleveland,
eventually taking it over with his wife, Kathy, and relocating the business to Vista, Calif., north of
San Diego. Their Directed Electronics became the nation's largest manufacturer of vehicle security
systems, including the popular Viper system, and earned them a fortune estimated at $200 million.
Issa became active in the high-technology industry, serving as chairman of the Consumer Electronics Association.

In the early 1990s, he turned to politics, contributing to Republicans and chairing the 1996
campaign to pass Proposition 209, which banned the use of racial quotas and preferences in California. In 1998, he ran for the Republican nomination to challenge Sen. Barbara Boxer and spent $9.8
million of his own money. He lost the primary 45%-40% to Matt Fong. In November 1999, when
Ron Packard of the heavily Republican 48th District announced his retirement, 10 candidates ran
in the Republican primary. This turned into a contest between Issa and state Sen. Bill Morrow.
Morrow questioned Issa's business practices, and Issa raised questions about Morrow's honesty.
On most issues, the candidates took similar positions. Issa spent $1.5 million of his own money
on the primary and beat Morrow 46%-30%. In the fall, the Democratic nominee abandoned his

campaign after getting little national party support, and Issa won 61%-28%. He has been re-elected easily.

In the House, Issa's voting record has been relatively moderate, especially on the foreign affairs issues that capture his attention. Of Lebanese descent, Issa has been vocal in condemning the sponsorship of terrorism by Arab nations while also urging the United States to reach out to build coalitions with friendly Arab nations. That earned him enemies among pro-Israel groups, including extremists on that side of the conflict. Two members of the militant Jewish Defense League were charged with plotting to blow up Issa's office in San Clemente, a Culver City mosque, and a Muslim public affairs building. One of them died in 2002 and the other pleaded guilty to civil rights and weapons violations in 2005.

Issa also has been active on patent reform issues. Drawing on his experience as a patent holder (he holds 37 of them), he sponsored a bipartisan bill that became law in 2011 giving district court judges hearing patent cases access to clerks trained in patent law. With Democrat Howard Berman of California he co-sponsored legislation to create a review process of already-issued patents and to tighten rules for calculating damages in patent lawsuits. The technology industry had led the charge for patent reform, contending it is being held hostage by "patent trolls" who obtain patents solely for the purpose of launching infringement suits to cash in on multibillion-dollar damage awards. Issa also supported requiring radio stations to pay royalties to record companies and performers as well as to composers of music, and he joined in a Democratic amendment to allow low-income stations to pay a small, fixed yearly fee.

After the 2008 election, Republican leaders chose Issa over several more senior Republicans to be the ranking member on the Oversight and Government Reform Committee, with broad jurisdiction over the federal government. The Democratic majority was reluctant to launch investigations of an incoming Democratic administration, so Issa hired staff capable of conducting investigations. Inevitably, Issa sought investigations and subpoenas that Chairman Edolphus Towns of New York declined to grant. The two disagreed sharply on opening an investigation of Countrywide Financial, a bank that had given favorable treatment to Democratic Sens. Christopher Dodd of Connecticut and Kent Conrad of North Dakota. In October 2009, Republicans filmed Democrats leaving the hearing room after they canceled a hearing on Countrywide. In retaliation, Towns ordered the locks changed and barred the Republicans from the room. In March 2010, Issa called, to no avail, for a special prosecutor to investigate whether White House aides violated the law when they tried to induce Rep. Joe Sestak, D-Pa., not to run against Sen. Arlen Specter after Specter changed his party affiliation to Democrat. But Issa and Towns found agreement in some areas, including Issa's 2009 bill requiring agencies to standardize information in their reports to create more transparency and another bill giving the Government Accountability Office authority to probe the inner workings of the Federal Reserve.

Gradually, Issa worked to increase the size of his staff, expanding his power and making it possible for him to leap into investigative mode when Republicans won majority control of the House in 2010 and he moved up to chairman of the committee. He suggested that he would follow the aggressive tactics of Democrat Henry Waxman of California, who chaired the panel in 2007 and 2008 during the Bush administration. He pointed out that he had worked with Towns on some matters that reflected negatively on the Bush White House and that there was sufficient corruption and inefficiency to be ferreted out in government without regard for partisan blame. But in the early days of the Republican Congress, he called the Obama administration "one of the most corrupt administrations ever." He later said that he meant it was guilty of overspending and inefficiency.

Issa has harbored ambitions for statewide office. In early 2003, he spent $1.7 million of his own money to get the signatures needed for a recall election of Democratic Gov. Gray Davis. His hopes of getting unified support as a replacement candidate foundered when others stayed in the race and then were utterly dashed when Arnold Schwarzenegger got in. Issa tearfully announced that he would not run. He has been re-elected easily to his House seat.

FIFTIETH DISTRICT

Brian Bilbray (R)

Elected June 2006, 6th full term; b. Jan. 28, 1951, Coronado; home, Carlsbad; Attended SW Commun. Col., 1970-72, 1974; Catholic; married (Karen); 5 children.

Elected Office: Imperial Beach City Cncl., 1976–78; Imperial Beach Mayor, 1978–84; San Diego Cnty. Bd. of Supervisors, 1984–94; U.S. House of Reps., 1994-2000.

Professional Career: Tax consultant, 1972–present; Lobbyist, 2001-05.

DC Office: 2410 RHOB, 20515, 202-225-0508; Fax: 202-225-2558; Web site: bilbray.house.gov.

State Offices: Solana Beach, 858-350-1150.

Committees: *Energy & Commerce:* Communications & Technology; Energy & Power; Oversight & Investigations.

Group Ratings

	ACLU	ACU	ADA	CFG	AFS	FRC	LCV	ITIC	NTU	COC
2010	7	85	15	77	13	93	30	33	78	100
2009	–	88	10	78	22	–	21	–	75	93

National Journal Ratings

	2010 LIB	—	2010 CONS	2009 LIB	—	2009 CONS
Economic	34%	—	66%	28%	—	71%
Social	31%	—	69%	24%	—	73%
Foreign	33%	—	65%	0%	—	75%
Composite	33%	—	67%	22%	—	78%

Key Votes of the 111th Congress

1. Overturn Ledbetter	N	5. Bar federal abortion funds	Y	9. Stop detainee transfers	Y
2. Pass $820 billion stimulus	N	6. Pass health care bill	N	10. Legalize immigrants' kids	*
3. Let guns in national parks	Y	7. Regulate financial firms	N	11. Repeal don't ask, tell	N
4. Pass cap-and-trade	N	8. Pass tax cuts for some	N	12. Limit campaign funds	N

Election Results

2010 general	Brian Bilbray (R)	142,247	(57%)	($1,207,757)
	Francine Busby (D)	97,818	(39%)	($615,606)
	Lars Grossmith (Lib)	5,546	(2%)	
	Miriam Clark (PF)	5,470	(2%)	
2010 primary	Brian Bilbray (R)	unopposed		

Prior Winning Percentages: 2008 (50%), 2006 (53%), 2006 (50%), 1998 (49%), 1996 (53%), 1994 (49%)

Population		Race/Ethnicity		Work	
Pop. 2010:	753,135	White:	58.5%	Private:	76.2%
Change since 2000:	Up 17.8%	Black:	1.8%	Government:	14.0%
Urban:	97.8%	Hispanic:	22.2%	Self-employed:	9.6%
Rural:	2.2%	Asian:	13.6%	Blue collar:	13.7%
Area size:	365 sq. mi.	Native Am.:	0.3%	White collar:	70.2%
		Hawaiian:	0.2%	Khaki collar:	1.1%
Age		Two+ races:	3.1%	Other:	15.1%
Median age:	37.1 yrs.				
More than 65 yrs:	11.9%	*Ancestry*		Median income:	$78,806
Less than 18 yrs:	25.0%	German	11.2%	Median Home Value:	$590,300
		English	8.9%		
Education		Irish	8.5%	**Military Veterans**	
H.S. grad:	89.8%			% of Pop:	9.7%
College grad:	45.4%				
Grad degree:	17.9%				

North San Diego; Escondido

The affluent San Diego neighborhood of La Jolla is spectacularly situated between Soledad Mountain and the Pacific Ocean. A 15-minute drive from the city's downtown, La Jolla (*la-HOY-uh*) is known for its beaches, upscale shopping, and restaurants, but mostly for its physical beauty and temperate climate. La Jolla is also home to the University of California at San Diego and the Scripps Institution of Oceanography, as well as biotech companies such as Synthetic Genomics Inc., which formed a $600 million partnership with ExxonMobil Corp. in 2009 to study how to derive fuel from algae. West of La Jolla are several inland communities, such as Escondido and San Marcos, that are also pleasant, affluent, and attractively planned with houses of red tile roofs that contrast with the tan hillsides. Also to the west, beyond the mountain, is the Miramar Marine Corps Air Station.

2008 Presidential Vote		
Barack Obama (D)	172,962	(51%)
John McCain (R)	158,845	(47%)
2004 Presidential Vote		
George Bush (R)	169,935	(55%)
John Kerry (D)	135,007	(44%)
Cook Partisan Voting Index: R+3		

The 50th Congressional District of California covers much of this part of San Diego County. About 40% of its population is in the city of San Diego, including most of scenic La Jolla, hillside Clairemont, Carmel Valley, University City, Mira Mesa, Rancho Penasquitos, and part of Rancho Bernardo. About 25% lives on or near the coast, from Del Mar to Encinitas and Carlsbad, home of the La Costa resort and a big tourist destination. Immigrants from Mexico in smuggling boats are periodically apprehended on Carlsbad beaches. Just inland is Rancho Santa Fe, one of the wealthiest communities in the nation, with multimillion-dollar mansions set amid rolling hills and lush greenery. About 30% of the district's people are in Escondido and fast-growing San Marcos. Politically, this has been Republican territory but not overwhelmingly so; it is more liberal on the coast and more conservative inland. Democrat Barack Obama prevailed in 2008 by 51% to 47% over Republican John McCain.

Brian Bilbray (R)

The congressman from the 50th District is Brian Bilbray, a Republican who served in Congress from 1995 to 2001 and then returned to win a June 2006 special election. Bilbray grew up in Imperial Beach, south of San Diego. A former lifeguard and an avid surfer, Bilbray owned his own tax preparation business and then at age 25 was elected to the Imperial Beach Council in 1976. Two years later, he became mayor. In 1984, he was elected to the San Diego County Board of Supervisors, where he worked on environmental protection and economic development issues. In 1994, Bilbray ousted first-term U.S. Rep. Lynn Schenk, a moderate Democrat who had voted for the 1993 Clinton budget and tax increases. Once in office, Bilbray went to the other extreme in his approach to the Clinton administration, voting to impeach the president in 1998. He said at the time that in his politically marginal district (he was then in the 49th District), the vote might be the issue that "drives a nail through my political coffin." That comment proved prescient as Bilbray lost 50%-46% in 2000 to Democrat Susan Davis, who said that Bilbray "talks moderate in San Diego but votes conservative in Washington."

Bilbary stayed on in Washington as a lobbyist and as the co-chairman of the Federation for American Immigration Reform, which lobbies for limiting immigration levels and toughening border controls. The 50th District House seat opened when Republican Rep. Randy (Duke) Cunningham pleaded guilty in November 2005 to taking more than $2 million in bribes to help a defense contractor. Bilbray got into the race and was an early front-runner, but he faced competitive contests in both the primary and the special general election. His chief Republican opponents were more conservative. State Sen. Bill Morrow, former Assemblyman Howard Kaloogian and wealthy businessman Eric Roach all criticized Bilbray for becoming a lobbyist and claimed his voting record had been too liberal. Bilbray highlighted his work with FAIR, and won the nomination with 15% of the total vote, to 14% for Roach, 7% for Kaloogian, and 5% for Morrow.

Spotting an opportunity to take a longtime Republican seat in the wake of the Cunningham scandal, national Democrats invested heavily in Francine Busby, a professor of women's studies and local school board member who had lost two years earlier to Cunningham. The fundraising powerhouse EMILY's List, which had ignored Busby in 2004, became an active supporter. By mid-May, Busby had collected more than $2 million. She embraced the theme that the GOP-controlled Congress was mired in a "culture of corruption." Bilbray said that Busby had no ideas of her own to offer on immigration and pollution at the border with Mexico. Then, five days before the June 6 election, Busby made a critical mistake when she told a crowd that "you don't need papers for voting, you don't need to be a registered voter to help." Bilbray and the Republicans seized on the remark as an invitation for illegal aliens to vote, and blitzed the airwaves with a final round of ads. Bilbray won 50%-45%.

Once he was back in the House, Bilbray's voting record became more conservative on social issues. In 2007, he replaced Republican Rep. Tom Tancredo of Colorado as chairman of the Immigration Reform Caucus. Although less of a rhetorical firebrand than Tancredo, he has advocated tough enforcement on the U.S. border and stronger curbs on illegal immigration. He drew widespread attention for declaring in a 2010 television interview that illegal immigrants could be distinguished by their clothing. (Several months later, he was in the headlines again for his role in forming a Congressional Cigar Association, which became a conduit for industry lobbyists to organize lavish events for staffers and members. He denied any impropriety.)With Democratic Rep. Heath Shuler of North Carolina in 2007, he sponsored the Secure America with Verification and Enforcement (SAVE) Act, which requires employers to use the E-Verify program to verify the immigration status of new hires. Democratic leaders blocked House action on the bill.

Bilbray was re-elected 53%-44% in a rematch with Busby in 2006. Two years later, he had a close race against attorney Nick Leibham, who raised $1.3 million and criticized Bilbray's opposition to the financial industry rescue of 2008. Bilbray won 50%-45%.

FIFTY-FIRST DISTRICT

Bob Filner (D)

Elected 1992, 10th term; b. Sept. 4, 1942, Pittsburgh, PA; home, San Diego; Cornell U., B.A. 1963, Ph.D. 1973, U. of DE, M.A. 1969; Jewish; married (Jane Merrill); 2 children.

Elected Office: San Diego Schl. Bd., 1979–83, Pres., 1982–83; San Diego City Cncl., 1987–92, Dpty. mayor, 1991.

Professional Career: Prof., San Diego St. U., 1970–92; Legis. asst., U.S. Sen. Hubert Humphrey, 1974; Legis. asst., U.S. Rep. Don Fraser, 1975; Spec. asst., U.S. Rep. Jim Bates, 1984.

DC Office: 2428 RHOB, 20515, 202-225-8045; Fax: 202-225-9073; Web site: www.house.gov/filner.

State Offices: Chula Vista, 619-422-5963; Imperial, 760-355-8800.

Committees: *Transportation & Infrastructure:* Aviation; Economic Development, Public Buildings & Emergency Management; Highways & Transit; Water Resources & Environment. *Veterans' Affairs* (RMM): Oversight & Investigations.

Group Ratings

	ACLU	ACU	ADA	CFG	AFS	FRC	LCV	ITIC	NTU	COC
2010	94	0	100	0	100	12	90	67	9	13
2009	–	0	95	0	100	–	100	–	5	33

National Journal Ratings

	2010 LIB	—	2010 CONS		2009 LIB	—	2009 CONS
Economic	71%	—	28%		75%	—	21%
Social	93%	—	0%		84%	—	11%
Foreign	65%	—	34%		78%	—	17%
Composite	78%	—	22%		81%	—	19%

Key Votes of the 111th Congress

1. Overturn Ledbetter	Y	5. Bar federal abortion funds	N	9. Stop detainee transfers	N
2. Pass $820 billion stimulus	Y	6. Pass health care bill	Y	10. Legalize immigrants' kids	Y
3. Let guns in national parks	N	7. Regulate financial firms	Y	11. Repeal don't ask, tell	Y
4. Pass cap-and-trade	Y	8. Pass tax cuts for some	Y	12. Limit campaign funds	Y

Election Results

2010 general	Bob Filner (D)	86,423	(60%)	($943,216)
	Nick Popaditch (R)	57,488	(40%)	($366,749)
2010 primary	Bob Filner (D)	unopposed		

Prior Winning Percentages: 2008 (73%), 2006 (67%), 2004 (62%), 2002 (58%), 2000 (68%), 1998 (99%), 1996 (62%), 1994 (57%), 1992 (57%)

Population		Race/Ethnicity		Work	
Pop. 2010:	757,891	White:	15.2%	Private:	70.0%
Change since 2000:	Up 18.6%	Black:	7.0%	Government:	23.2%
Urban:	95.6%	Hispanic:	62.4%	Self-employed:	6.5%
Rural:	4.4%	Asian:	12.2%	Blue collar:	21.4%
Area size:	4,896 sq. mi.	Native Am.:	0.4%	White collar:	52.9%
		Hawaiian:	0.5%	Khaki collar:	2.1%
Age		Two+ races:	2.1%	Other:	23.6%
Median age:	32.3 yrs.				
More than 65 yrs:	10.6%	*Ancestry*		Median income:	$49,566
Less than 18 yrs:	29.2%	German	4.1%	Median Home Value:	$353,600
		Irish	3.2%		
Education		English	2.3%	**Military Veterans**	
H.S. grad:	71.5%			% of Pop:	8.8%
College grad:	17.8%				
Grad degree:	5.2%				

San Diego and Imperial Counties

Anchoring a corner of the continental United States, San Diego not so long ago was a small Navy town known for its good harbor and splendid weather. It, of course, is now a major metropolis of 1.3 million people and the center of a county of 3 million. To its occasional discomfort, it is also one of the largest cities directly on an international border, situated between countries with strikingly different economic conditions, political systems, and cultural traditions.

2008 Presidential Vote
Barack Obama (D) 135,960 (63%)
John McCain (R) 76,438 (36%)

2004 Presidential Vote
John Kerry (D) 100,062 (53%)
George Bush (R) 85,762 (46%)

Cook Partisan Voting Index: D+8

San Diego sits on the busiest border crossing in the world, and on a daily basis, agents for the Border Patrol play a sometimes violent cat-and-mouse game with people trying to cross illegally. The recent economic downturn has slowed traffic considerably. Apprehensions by the Border Patrol in the San Diego sector, which numbered around 300,000 per year in the 1980s, dropped to 118,721 in 2009. Thousands of legal workers cross the border daily to reach the industrial zone on San Diego's southern edge, on brown hills in Otay Mesa and San Ysidro, and the industrial suburbs of Chula Vista and National City. Despite the recession, Otay Mesa has become a food production center, with more than 1,000 workers employed at seven food factories in 2010. Many children from Mexico cross daily to attend public and private schools. Latinos pour billions of dollars into the San Diego economy and are scattered in various parts of the city, in the southern corridor, and in Encanto and Chollas Park in the eastern section. Oddly, there is not much evidence of Mexican style in San Diego—less than in Los Angeles.

The 51st Congressional District of California covers California's entire border with Mexico, including the southeast corner of San Diego, and also National City and Chula Vista. The district extends east to the Arizona border and includes all of Imperial County, with its string of farms and towns running south from the Salton Sea to Mexicali, Mexico. Water comes from the Colorado River through the All-American Canal. With farmland being turned into moderately priced subdivisions, rapidly growing Imperial County in 2009 had 167,000 people, 76% of them Hispanic. El Centro, the county seat of Imperial, had unemployment above 22% in 2009 and 2010—the highest in the nation—resulting from drought, the decline of the Mexican peso, and the national recession. Hispanics are a majority in the district, which was created to be solidly Democratic. In 2004, Democratic presidential nominee John Kerry won 53% of the district's vote, and in 2008 Democrat Barack Obama won 63%.

Bob Filner (D)

The congressman from the 51st District is Bob Filner, a Democrat first elected in 1992. Filner grew up in New York City, and became politically active early in his adult life by joining the civil rights movement. He was a fundraiser for the Rev. Martin Luther King Jr. and in 1961 joined the Freedom Riders, the groups of whites and blacks that traveled to the South to ride public transportation and use public facilities to challenge the lack of compliance with Supreme Court rulings outlawing segregation. The protests often sparked violent reactions from local citizens. Filner was arrested in Mississippi while trying to integrate a lunch counter, and was imprisoned for two months. He earned a Ph.D. at Cornell University, taught history at San Diego State University, and directed the Lipinsky Institute for Judaic Studies. He worked on Democratic Sen. Hubert Humphrey's staff in the 1970s, and was elected to the San Diego school board in 1979 and to the City Council in 1987. Redistricting in 1992 created a new Democratic seat in San Diego County, and Filner was strongly backed by local activists even though he had better-known rivals in the Democratic primary. Filner won with 26% of the vote, to 23% for Waddie Deddeh, a state senator and assemblyman; 20% for Jim Bates, a four-term congressman defeated in 1990 after being disciplined for sexual harassment; and 19% for Juan Carlos Vargas. Filner went on to win the general election easily.

Filner is politically savvy, with some original ideas about policy. He is also one of the most liberal members of the House, though he has seen his ranking on roll call votes fall as he has stuck with his principles rather than the Democratic leadership on key votes. For example, he was one of 13 Democrats to vote against a 2008 energy bill that allowed for some offshore drilling, which he strongly opposes. Filner has a reputation for being confrontational. He once got into a heated argument with Republican Rep. Joe Wilson of South Carolina on C-SPAN, and once was reported by immigration officials at a detention facility after demanding to see a detainee. In August 2007, he made headlines when he was charged with assault and battery after an altercation with an airline employee at Dulles International Airport. He later paid a $100 fine but did not plead guilty. The Committee on Standards of Official Conduct looked into the matter and determined that Filner had shown "poor judgment."

In 2007, Filner became chairman of the Veterans' Affairs Committee following a contest with Rep. Michael Michaud, D-Maine. Bolstered by support from then-House Speaker Nancy Pelosi, with whom he sometimes had a testy relationship, Filner won the Democratic Caucus vote over Michaud, 112-69.

Filner has long been a vocal advocate of veterans' rights and benefits, a popular cause in a district with many members of the military and military retirees. In 2008, he won enactment of a major overhaul of the GI Bill, which dates to 1944 and has boosted countless veterans to the middle class by paying for college and first homes. Filner's legislation gave veterans the full cost of any public college, up from half the cost previously, plus an average $1,100-a-month living stipend depending on the local housing market. The benefit is expected to cost $62 billion over a decade. Outraged by the treatment of Filipino veterans, who in the past did not get full benefits, Filner in 2009 got included in the economic stimulus bill lump-sum bonus payments for Filipino veterans. Given his district's location, Filner also has been active on border and immigration issues. He introduced bills in 2009 to cut down on border air pollution and reduce visa costs for poor Mexicans seeking medical aid.

Filner has survived several political challenges at home. In the 1996 primary, he was again opposed by Vargas, by then on the San Diego Council. Filner won, but by just 55%-45%. After redistricting placed heavily Latino parts of San Diego in his district in 2002, he faced Danny Ramirez, an Imperial County businessman. Filner won 70%-30%. In 2006, Vargas challenged Filner a third time. The bitter primary contest featured negative campaigning on each side, but Filner benefited from his constituent work in Imperial County, where Vargas was not well known despite his Hispanic ties, and won 51%-43%. He has had easy re-election victories since then.

FIFTY-SECOND DISTRICT

Duncan D. Hunter (R)

Elected 2008, 2nd term; b. Dec. 7, 1976, San Diego; home, Lakeside; San Diego St. U., B.S. 2000.; Protestant; married (Margaret); 3 children.

Military Career: Marine Corps, 2002-05 (Iraq); Marine Reserves, 05-present (Afghanistan).

Professional Career: Business analyst, Cayenta Inc., 2000-02; Residential developer, 2005-07.

DC Office: 223 CHOB, 20515, 202-225-5672; Fax: 202-225-0235; Web site: hunter.house.gov.

State Offices: El Cajon, 619-448-5201.

Committees: *Armed Services:* Emerging Threats & Capabilities; Seapower & Projection Forces. *Education & the Workforce:* Early Childhood, Elementary & Secondary Education (Chmn). *Transportation & Infrastructure:* Water Resources & Environment.

Group Ratings

	ACLU	ACU	ADA	CFG	AFS	FRC	LCV	ITIC	NTU	COC
2010	13	100	0	86	0	93	0	33	89	88
2009	–	100	5	82	11	–	0	–	85	80

National Journal Ratings

	2010 LIB	—	2010 CONS	2009 LIB	—	2009 CONS
Economic	7%	—	92%	15%	—	84%
Social	0%	—	85%	13%	—	84%
Foreign	12%	—	79%	0%	—	75%
Composite	11%	—	90%	14%	—	86%

Key Votes of the 111th Congress

1. Overturn Ledbetter	N	5. Bar federal abortion funds	Y	9. Stop detainee transfers	Y
2. Pass $820 billion stimulus	N	6. Pass health care bill	N	10. Legalize immigrants' kids	N
3. Let guns in national parks	Y	7. Regulate financial firms	N	11. Repeal don't ask, tell	N
4. Pass cap-and-trade	N	8. Pass tax cuts for some	N	12. Limit campaign funds	N

Election Results

2010 general	Duncan D. Hunter (R)................................139,460	(63%)	($766,759)
	Ray Lutz (D)...70,870	(32%)	($42,049)
	Michael Benoit (Lib) 10,732	(5%)	
2010 primary	Duncan D. Hunter (R)................................72,506	(91%)	
	Terri Linnell (R)..7,355	(9%)	

Prior Winning Percentages: 2008 (56%)

Population		Race/Ethnicity		Work	
Pop. 2010:	673,893	White:	64.1%	Private:	73.7%
Change since 2000:	Up 5.4%	Black:	4.3%	Government:	18.0%
Urban:	93.6%	Hispanic:	19.4%	Self-employed:	8.1%
Rural:	6.4%	Asian:	7.3%	Blue collar:	15.9%
Area size:	251 sq. mi.	Native Am.:	0.6%	White collar:	67.0%
		Hawaiian:	0.4%	Khaki collar:	1.1%
Age		Two+ races:	3.7%	Other:	16.0%
Median age:	37.0 yrs.				
More than 65 yrs:	11.5%	*Ancestry*		Median income:	$70,501
Less than 18 yrs:	25.3%	German	13.9%	Median Home Value:	$477,300
		Irish	10.3%		
Education		English	8.4%	**Military Veterans**	
H.S. grad:	90.2%			% of Pop:	12.4%
College grad:	32.5%				
Grad degree:	11.9%				

Eastern San Diego, Suburbs

San Diego began as a port, but today most metropolitan-area residents live out of sight of the sea, in hilltop neighborhoods that look out over distant ridges and freeways or in warm, sunny valleys amid the mountains that become dense and taller as one travels east from the Pacific Ocean. There is a discernible difference in attitudes and values between those who have settled inland and those who live nearer the ocean, part of the split between coastal California and interior

2008 Presidential Vote		
John McCain (R) 161,332	(53%)
Barack Obama (D) 135,848	(45%)
2004 Presidential Vote		
George Bush (R) 177,055	(61%)
John Kerry (D) 108,806	(38%)
Cook Partisan Voting Index: R+9		

California that has been at the heart of the state's political struggles and culture wars. In San Diego, both groups have tended to identify as Republicans. Coastal residents tend to be more affluent, and those who settle inland are more likely to be culturally traditional, supportive of the military, and dubious about the ability of government to help society's have-nots. They are more conservative and therefore more reliably Republican. Part of it can be explained by the large military presence there. Of the county's 140,000 federal employees, 100,000 are in the armed forces.

The 52nd Congressional District of California takes in many of the inland San Diego suburbs and most of the mountain and desert interior of San Diego County. It includes the part of San Diego north of Interstate 8 and east of Interstate 15. It has Santee, an East County city of 53,000; and El Cajon, which has the nation's second-largest (after the Detroit area) community of Chaldeans, Catholic Arabs from Iraq. An estimated 7,000 Iraqis arrived there in 2009. The district also includes high-income Poway, north of San Diego, and more modest La Mesa, east of San Diego. The mountains and the desert to the east are lightly inhabited. In the mountains is tiny Alpine. In the desert is the town of Borrego Springs amid the giant Anza-Borrego Desert State Park. Politically, this is a solidly Republican district. Republican presidential candidate John McCain in 2008 posted a smaller win than either of George W. Bush's here, but he still prevailed easily, 53%-45%, over Democrat Barack Obama.

Duncan D. Hunter (R)

The congressman from the 52nd District is Duncan D. Hunter, a Republican who was elected to the seat that his father held for 28 years. The senior Duncan Hunter, the longtime chairman of the House Armed Services Committee, gave up the seat to compete for the GOP presidential nomination in 2008.

The younger Hunter grew up in El Cajon and got a degree in business administration from San Diego State University, after having started a Web design company with a friend during his sophomore year. He worked in the computer industry for several years during the technology boom of the late 1990s. He says that the September 11 terrorist attacks prompted him to rethink his career plans. The next day, Hunter quit his job and enlisted in the Marine Corps. After completing officer training, Hunter was commissioned as a lieutenant. He was deployed to Iraq in 2003, served in Baghdad after the fall of the city, and in 2004 fought in the battle of Falluja. In 2006, he was promoted to captain and placed on reserve status. Though he earlier had shown little interest in following his father into politics, he said his experiences on the battlefield led him to reconsider public service. But shortly after announcing his candidacy in March 2007 for his father's House seat, Hunter was again called to active duty, this time in Afghanistan. Hunter was prohibited from any campaign activities, including fundraising and planning, and held only one event before leaving. In his absence, the management of his nascent campaign fell to his wife, Margaret Hunter. She took over all appearances and campaign duties in addition to caring for their three young children. When Hunter called home from Afghanistan, it was still illegal for him even to inquire how the campaign was going, and he remained largely in the dark about its status until his duty ended in December 2007. He returned home to resume campaigning full-time.

In the June primary, Hunter faced two competitors, Santee Councilman Brian Jones and San Diego Board of Education President Bob Watkins. Although both were well known locally and campaigned actively, Hunter and his family surrogates effectively ran on the basis of his military credentials. Hunter also benefited from his father's political and congressional connections, raising nearly three times as much as his Republican challengers. Hunter cruised to victory in the June primary with 72% percent of the vote. In the general election, Hunter faced another military veteran, retired Navy SEAL Commander Mike Lumpkin, a former Republican turned Democrat. He agreed with Hunter on many issues, including gun rights and the need for a fence along the U.S.-

Mexico border. But national Democrats paid little attention to the contest, and Hunter prevailed, 56%-39%. He had less trouble in 2010, winning re-election with 64%.

Hunter shares not only his father's name but also many of his political beliefs. Both were 31 years old when they were elected to Congress. He followed in his father's footsteps with a seat on the Armed Services Committee, and cites national security as his top priority. "I can tell you what the guys on the ground, the men and women out there fighting, actually need," Hunter said. "We have a whole lot of brass out there at the Pentagon and in the DOD (Department of Defense) who haven't left their offices in six or seven years." In one of his first legislative efforts, Hunter in 2009 introduced a bill to bar the transfer of terrorism suspects from the military prison camp in Guantanamo Bay, Cuba to San Diego County. He said that the Obama administration's proposal would make the region a bigger target for terrorists crossing the U.S.-Mexico border. He later introduced a bill to ensure military recruiters have proper access to student information and called for an independent review panel to potentially speed up awarding Congressional Medals of Honor to deserving Iraq and Afghanistan combat veterans. He strongly opposed repealing the "don't ask, don't tell" policy prohibiting openly gay military personnel, telling National Public Radio that the bond between soldiers "is broken if you open up the military to transgenders, to hermaphrodites, to gays and lesbians."

Hunter's other interests include tougher immigration laws and finding ways to halt the outflow of jobs overseas. He drew attention in May 2010 when he declared at a tea party rally that he supported deporting the children of illegal immigrants, even if they are citizens by virtue of being born on U.S. soil. His spokesman later modified the remarks, saying Hunter believes that U.S.-born children of illegal immigrants should stay with their parents unless they have a legal guardian.

FIFTY-THIRD DISTRICT

Susan Davis (D)

Elected 2000, 6th term; b. April 13, 1944, Cambridge, MA; home, San Diego; U. of CA, B.A. 1964, U. of NC, M.A. 1968; Jewish; married (Steven); 2 children.

Elected Office: San Diego School Bd., 1983-92; CA Assembly, 1994-2000.

Professional Career: Devel. assoc., KPBS Radio, 1980-82.; Exec. dir., Aaron Price Fellows, 1990-94.

DC Office: 1526 LHOB, 20515, 202-225-2040; Fax: 202-225-2948; Web site: house.gov/susandavis.

State Offices: San Diego, 619-280-5353.

Committees: *Armed Services:* Emerging Threats & Capabilities; Military Personnel (RMM); Seapower & Projection Forces. *Education & the Workforce:* Early Childhood, Elementary & Secondary Education; Higher Education & Workforce Training.

Group Ratings

	ACLU	ACU	ADA	CFG	AFS	FRC	LCV	ITIC	NTU	COC
2010	88	0	90	0	100	0	100	100	5	25
2009	–	0	100	4	100	–	93	–	3	40

National Journal Ratings

	2010 LIB	—	2010 CONS	2009 LIB	—	2009 CONS
Economic	87%	—	12%	82%	—	14%
Social	71%	—	25%	75%	—	20%
Foreign	66%	—	29%	78%	—	17%
Composite	76%	—	24%	81%	—	19%

Key Votes of the 111th Congress

1. Overturn Ledbetter	Y	5. Bar federal abortion funds	N	9. Stop detainee transfers	N
2. Pass $820 billion stimulus	Y	6. Pass health care bill	Y	10. Legalize immigrants' kids	Y
3. Let guns in national parks	N	7. Regulate financial firms	Y	11. Repeal don't ask, tell	Y
4. Pass cap-and-trade	Y	8. Pass tax cuts for some	Y	12. Limit campaign funds	Y

Election Results

2010 general	Susan Davis (D)	104,800	(62%)	($623,886)
	Michael Crimmins (R)	57,230	(34%)	($147,384)
	Paul Dekker (Lib)	6,298	(4%)	
2010 primary	Susan Davis (D)	unopposed		

Prior Winning Percentages: 2008 (68%), 2006 (68%), 2004 (66%), 2002 (62%), 2000 (50%)

Population		Race/Ethnicity		Work	
Pop. 2010:	662,854	White:	47.7%	Private:	72.7%
Change since 2000:	Up 3.7%	Black:	6.4%	Government:	19.5%
Urban:	99.9%	Hispanic:	31.9%	Self-employed:	7.6%
Rural:	0.1%	Asian:	9.9%	Blue collar:	14.2%
Area size:	251 sq. mi.	Native Am.:	0.3%	White collar:	63.3%
		Hawaiian:	0.4%	Khaki collar:	3.6%
Age		Two+ races:	3.0%	Other:	18.9%
Median age:	32.3 yrs.				
More than 65 yrs:	9.9%	*Ancestry*		Median income:	$50,891
Less than 18 yrs:	18.5%	German	10.0%	Median Home Value:	$480,500
		Irish	7.9%		
Education		English	6.6%	**Military Veterans**	
H.S. grad:	85.4%			% of Pop:	9.7%
College grad:	39.4%				
Grad degree:	15.5%				

Downtown San Diego

When the United States was dictating the terms of the Treaty of Guadalupe Hidalgo in 1848, after its successful war with Mexico, it made sure the southern boundary of its new California territory was just south of the port of San Diego. This is one of three splendid natural harbors on the Pacific Coast, and in 1914 the Marine Corps established a base on North Island. This was just the first of many military bases in San Diego, with its mild climate, deep harbor, and plentiful

2008 Presidential Vote		
Barack Obama (D)	177,863	(68%)
John McCain (R)	77,930	(30%)
2004 Presidential Vote		
John Kerry (D)	146,160	(61%)
George Bush (R)	89,890	(38%)
Cook Partisan Voting Index: D+14		

land for aircraft maneuvers. This has been the major West Coast U.S. Navy base for more than 50 years, the second-largest Navy port behind Norfolk, and home to about 30,000 active-duty Navy and Marine Corps personnel on shore. Also based here are the retired aircraft carriers *Midway* and *Constellation*, plus the *Ronald Reagan*, which was commissioned in 2003, with a flight deck that covers 4.5 acres.

The port and Navy base in the sheltered harbor remain the central focus of a rapidly growing metropolis that now stretches far inland and to the north. Downtown features post-modern buildings like the Horton Plaza amid a few well-preserved early-20th-century relics like the Spreckels Theatre. Across the harbor, on the sand spit that guards it against the ocean, is the white frame castle of the Hotel Del Coronado, with its surprisingly dark wooden interior—the U.S.'s largest wooden structure, opened in 1888 and a favored resort of past American presidents.

San Diego is not all harbor and Navy. To the north, the Pacific waves pound against the beach beneath erose cliffs of unique rock formations along the coast. Located here are some of San Diego's great cultural institutions: the Scripps Institute of Oceanography, the University of California San Diego campus, the Salk Institute, and the Torrey Pines reserve, home of the unique, wide-spreading pine tree. To the south are raffish Mission Beach; Ocean Beach, with its strong rip currents; and Point Loma, overlooking the entrance to the harbor. The weather—a sunny 70 degrees most of the time—lures tourists and new residents. But this also is a working town, a sophisticated high-tech center with growing biotechnology, electronics, software, and telecommunications industries. It is a manufacturing center as well, with *maquiladora* factories clustering near the Mexican border.

The 53rd Congressional District of California consists of the center of San Diego, the beaches from Blacks Beach to Ocean Beach, the port, La Jolla beach (but not the neighborhood itself), and Balboa Park. It includes the heavily Latino neighborhoods south and east of downtown; the Gaslamp District, with its glitzy nightlife scene; and the older neighborhoods of University Heights and East San Diego. Altogether, 85% of the district's population is within the city limits. It also includes Coronado and Imperial Beach, just north of the Mexican border, and the inland suburbs of La Presa and Lemon Grove, site of a celebrated school desegregation case in the 1930s. The district is 32% Hispanic. Blacks make up less than 7%, and UCSD experienced an outbreak of racial incidents in 2010 that began with a "Compton Cookout" to mock Black History Month, prompting the school to take steps in response. Historically, this was a Republican district, but with coastal California's trend toward cultural liberalism and with more Democratic areas added in the most recent redistricting, it is now more solidly Democratic than San Diego's other districts. In 2004, Democratic nominee John Kerry won the district 61%-38%, and in 2008, Democrat Barack Obama won it 68%-30%.

Susan Davis (D)

The congresswoman from the 53rd District is Susan Davis, a Democrat first elected in 2000. She grew up in Richmond, Calif., the daughter of a pediatrician. She graduated from the University of California at Berkeley and got a degree in social work at the University of North Carolina. After she married, she and her husband lived for a time in Japan while he served as an Air Force doctor during the Vietnam War. In 1972, they moved to San Diego. She was a producer for a local television station while also volunteering in civic groups, including as president of the local League of Women Voters. In 1983, she was elected to the San Diego school board. In 1994, she won the first of three terms in the California Assembly, where she chaired the Consumer Protection Committee. Facing term limits, Davis in 2000 challenged U.S. Rep. Brian Bilbray, a Republican who had won three close elections. She portrayed him as too conservative for the district, though he took liberal and moderate positions on abortion rights and environmental protection. But Bilbray had voted with conservatives to impeach President Clinton in 1998, and Davis attacked him as well for supporting bills that would deny citizenship to U.S.-born children of illegal immigrants. The AFL-CIO ran so much advertising on her behalf that Davis requested it stop. Davis won 50%-46%, and has been re-elected easily. Bilbray returned to Congress in June 2006 when he won a special election in the neighboring 50th District.

In the House, Davis has a liberal voting record but tends to be more centrist on foreign policy. Assigned to the Armed Services and Education and Labor committees, she set herself priorities that have included higher military pay, increased aid for school districts with a large military presence, increased student loans, and incentives for better teachers. She angered organized labor by voting to give President George W. Bush wide authority to negotiate international trade deals, which unions opposed. She called the vote "agonizing," but one that served the interests of a city that has been built on trade. Organized labor rescinded its endorsement of her. She has taken an interest in COBRA, and introduced a bill in May 2010 allowing people enrolled in it to keep the health benefit until they find another job offering coverage or become eligible for the an insurance exchange created under the new health reform law.

On Armed Services, she voted against the use of force in Iraq in 2002 and against Bush's troop "surge" strategy in 2007, but Davis stopped short of cutting off funding for the war, which some Democrats advocated. She supported President Obama's troop buildup in Afghanistan in 2009, but cautioned that greater civilian support and involvement from U.S. allies was essential. In 2009, as chair of Armed Services' Personnel Subcommittee, she helped secure a higher military pay raise than Obama requested. She also sponsored a bill allowing service members to appeal courts martial convictions directly to the Supreme Court. On the House Administration Committee, she proposed allowing universal voting by mail in federal elections.

★ COLORADO ★

Colorado, with its distinct and variable geography, its sea of Great Plains, and its majestic Rocky Mountains, has long been at the front edge of economic, cultural, and political change in the West. With vistas of vast emptiness, it is mostly an urban state. About half of its 5 million people live in metropolitan Denver, and four-fifths of them are in the urban strip paralleling the Front Range, where the Rockies rise suddenly from the mile-high plateau. The state's ruggedness means there is room for more settlement. While the eastern Plains continue to lose population, the valley crevices between the mountains are filling up with second-home condominiums and ranchettes, and the rolling land on three sides of metro Denver is being platted into subdivisions.

Colorado started off with a boom, and its recent history has been one of booms punctuated by pauses of moderate growth. The first boom came after the discovery of gold and silver in the Rocky Mountains after the Civil War. You can still see evidence of this mining boom in the opera houses and storefronts of Cripple Creek and Central City, Aspen and Telluride, built when Denver was just a village on the South Platte River. After mining towns went bust, Denver grew as a meatpacking, banking, and manufacturing center, and as the state capital and regional headquarters of the federal government. In comparatively recent times, the 1970s' spike in energy prices sparked interest in Colorado's natural gas, oil, and shale. Half a million people moved in and the Denver skyline sprouted buildings overlooking the Capitol's golden dome, while entrepreneurs built premier ski resorts and year-round mountain residences. Colorado's economy sagged during the period of low energy prices in the 1980s, but with an influx of telecommunications and high-tech companies, it rebounded in the 1990s.

The visible signs of this boom are all around—in the skyscrapers of downtown Denver, bearing at various times, the names of Qwest and TCI and other high-tech companies; in the retro Coors Field baseball park set amid Denver's LoDo neighborhood, where warehouses have been renovated into restaurants and clubs; in the startling architecture of the Denver International Airport far out on the plains; in the sprawling Denver Tech Center south of the city; and in the fast-growing tracts of subdivisions and office parks in Douglas County on the city's southern rim. Colorado's economy grew robustly in the 1990s, and the state attracted well-educated newcomers from around the country, including many from California. The bursting of the high-tech bubble hit Colorado hard in 2001 and 2002, but its moderate growth in the ensuing years insulated it from the worst effects of the collapse of the housing market in the late 2000s. If growth in Denver was not as robust as in Phoenix or Las Vegas, Denver has also seen a far lower foreclosure rate than its Western counterparts. With its relatively young and highly educated population and its stunning environment, Colorado is also the leanest state, with the lowest incidence of obesity, and arguably the healthiest, with relatively low rates of cancer and heart disease. Coloradans like to ride, jog, bike, and, of course, ski. There are bike paths not only in Denver, but also in the mountains, and Boulder is a national center for bungee jumping, mountain biking, snowshoe running, and hot-air ballooning.

Colorado has been reshaped, economically and politically, by its successive waves of newcomers. The conservative and boosterish Colorado of the 1960s was transformed in the 1970s by a wave of young liberal migrants who swept the state's politics by calling for environmental protections and slow growth. Its national leaders reflected this trend—slow-growth Gov. Dick Lamm, Sen. Gary Hart, Rep. Patricia Schroeder, Sen. Tim Wirth. Democrats controlled the governorship for 24 years but Republicans held on to control of the legislature. Then, in the 1990s, a new wave of migrants—tech-savvy, family-oriented cultural conservatives looking for an environment to prosper—moved Colorado's politics to the right. In the 1990s, public school enrollment rose 14%, while private school enrollment was up 33% and the number of home-schooled children tripled. If the spirit of the 1970s newcomers was embodied in Boulder, with its pedestrian mall, outdoor sports shops, and vegetarian restaurants, and was dominated politically by environmentalist liberals, the spirit of the 1990s newcomers was embodied in Colorado Springs, the home of the Air Force Academy, Fort Carson, and the Focus on the Family advocacy organization, and was dominated politically by religious conservatives. Both of these politically divergent communities have some reason to believe that they exemplify the state. Colorado elections can be viewed as contests to determine which one does.

The victories of the liberal Democrats in the 1970s, starting with the 1972 referendum blocking the Winter Olympics from Denver, were followed by a long period in which Republicans held control of the legislature and the congressional delegation. The victories of the conservative Repub-

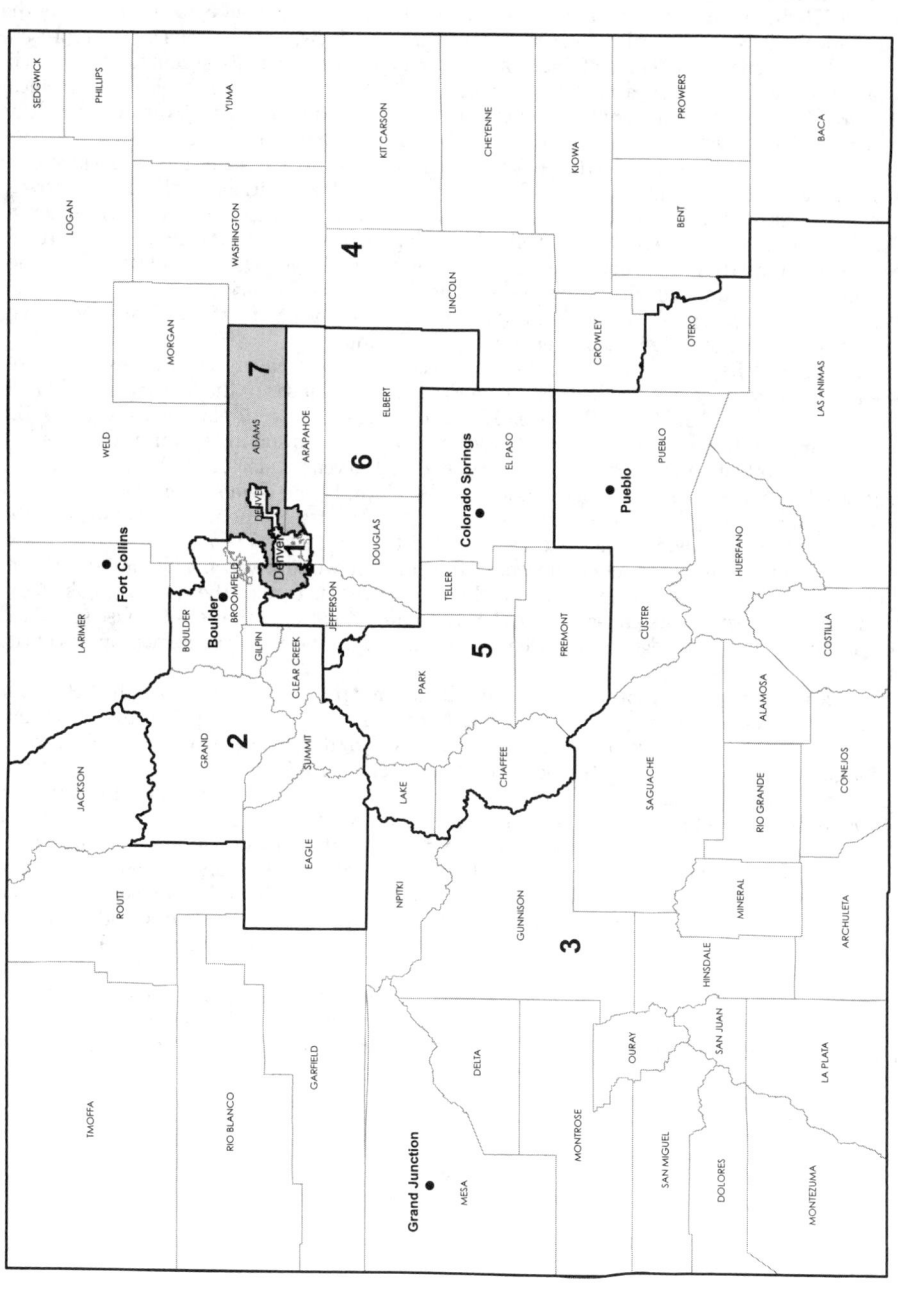

Congressional district boundaries were first effective for 2002.

District 7 is highlighted for visibility.

Miles

0   20   40

The Almanac of American Politics.
National Journal

licans in the 1990s, starting with the 1990 referendum imposing term limits and the 1992 Taxpayers' Bill of Rights requiring referenda to raise taxes, have been followed by a resurgence of the Democratic Party, led by liberal entrepreneurs such as Jared Polis, now the 2nd District representative. Polis was one of the "Gang of Four," a group of high-powered political contributors who financed the resurgence of the party. The other three were QuarkXPress founder Tim Gill, medical technology heiress Patricia Stryker, and geophysicist and MicroMAX software creator Rutt Bridges. The group nurtured a web of liberal activist organizations, framed issues, chose their targets shrewdly, and helped reshape the political landscape. They took advantage of some favorable demographic trends. Colorado has one of the nation's youngest populations, with large university enclaves. The state is 21% Latino, according to 2010 census data. People support environmental causes of all kinds, sometimes to the point of endangering their own species. Boulder used to protect the local bears until they killed not only dogs and cats but also a jogger. Denver and Boulder attract young professionals imbued with liberal values; the ski resorts—Telluride, Aspen, Vail, Crested Butte, Steamboat Springs—are inhabited by the wealthy and the people who wait on them in restaurants, and both groups tend to be Democratic in Colorado.

Looking back, Republicans were dominant as recently as 2002, when Gov. Bill Owens was re-elected overwhelmingly and the GOP had majorities in both houses of the legislature, and held both U.S. Senate seats and five of the seven House seats. After the 2008 elections, it was just the other way around. Democrats voted to hold their national convention in Denver, unbothered by the fact that their last national convention there, exactly 100 years before, in 1908, nominated the losing ticket of William Jennings Bryan and John W. Kern. In the Democratic primary, Barack Obama's campaign targeted Colorado early on. He beat Hillary Rodham Clinton 2-to-1 in the state's Super Tuesday Democratic caucuses, which attracted 120,000 people, more than in any other caucus state except Iowa and Minnesota. His campaign worked with the like-minded liberal groups that had sprung up during the decade. In the fall, Obama carried the state by a solid 54%-45% margin, and Democrats ended up with both Senate seats, five of the seven House seats and solid margins in the state legislature. Obama was helped by the changing demographics of the state.

The 2010 election saw another turnaround. Democrats prevailed at the top of the ticket, but with unimpressive percentages. Appointed Sen. Michael Bennet held on against tea party-supported Weld County District Attorney Ken Buck, 48%-46%, and Denver Mayor John Hickenlooper won the governorship relinquished by Democrat Bill Ritter with 51% of the vote. Hickenlooper was helped by the implosion of the Republican candidates: Just weeks before the primary, front-runner Scott McInnis admitted plagiarizing a piece of writing for which he was paid a $300,000 fee and Dan Maes was revealed to have concealed damaging information about his career. Former Rep. Tom Tancredo, long a loud crusader against illegal immigration, ran as an independent and got 36% of the vote to 11% for Maes—but of course that meant an easy win for Hickenlooper, a former brewpub proprietor in a state that loves beer. (It has the world's largest brewery and the Great American Beer Festival features more varieties of beer than available anywhere else.) The further down the ballot, the greater the evidence of a Republican sweep. Republicans won all four statewide races below the gubernatorial contest. They regained the 3rd and 4th district House seats that they lost in 2006 and 2008, and thus were rewarded with a 4-3 edge in the delegation. They won the popular vote in races for the state Senate 55%-45%, but after the election the party still had five fewer seats. They won the popular vote in races for the state House 57%-42% and gained six seats there, converting a 37-27-1 Democratic majority to a 33-32 Republican majority.

Population		Household Income		Work	
Pop. 2010:	5,029,196	Under $15k:	11.2%	Private:	78.1%
State rank:	22nd	$15k to $50k:	33.3%	Government:	14.7%
Change since 2000:	Up 16.9%	$50k to $100k:	32.3%	Self-employed:	7.0%
Urban:	80.4%	$100k to $200k:	18.8%	Unemployment (3-yr. average):	4.4%
Rural:	19.6%	Over $200k:	4.4%	Poverty:	12.2%
Native of state:	42.3%	Median income:	$56,334	Blue collar:	19.4%
Not a citizen:	6.7%			White collar:	62.7%
Area size:	104,094 sq. mi.	**Home Value**		Khaki collar:	0.7%
		Under $100k:	9.4%	Other:	17.1%
Most populous cities		$100k to $300k:	56.1%		
Denver	600,158	$300k to $500k:	22.2%	**Age**	
Colorado Springs	416,427	$500k to $1 mil:	9.8%	Median age:	35.6 yrs.
Aurora	325,078	Over $1 million:	2.4%	More than 65 yrs:	10.4%
Fort Collins	143,986	Median:	$237,800	Less than 18 yrs:	24.6%

Race/Ethnicity		Language		Military Veterans		Registered Voters in 2010	
White:	70.0%	*Language*		% of Pop:	11.0%	Democrats:	812,389
Black:	3.8%	English:	83.3%			Republicans:	874,962
Hispanic:	20.7%	Spanish:	11.9%	*Veterans by Period*		Ind./other:	789,851
Asian:	2.7%	Asian:	1.8%	WWII and before:	7.8%	Voter turnout:	1,787,730
Native Am.:	0.6%	Other European:	2.4%	Korea:	8.7%	Turnout as % of	
Hawaiian:	0.1%			Vietnam:	34.0%	voting age:	47.0%
Two+ races:	2.0%	**Education**		Gulf (pre-2001):	16.2%		
		H.S. grad:	89.1%	Gulf (post-2001):	9.4%	**Legislature**	
Ancestry		College grad:	35.7%	Peace time:	23.8%	Senate:	20 D 15 R
German	17.7%	Grad degree:	12.7%			House:	32 D 33 R
Irish	9.9%						
English	9.2%						

Presidential politics   When it comes to presidential contests, Colorado tends to swing from one political party to the other more than the nation as a whole: It cast higher percentages for Democrat Barack Obama and Republican George W. Bush than their national averages, as it did for Republicans Ronald Reagan, Richard Nixon and Dwight Eisenhower, and for Democrats Lyndon Johnson and Harry Truman. Perhaps the state's large number of young voters or newcomers accounts for these higher-than-average swings. In 2000, Colorado was not a target state, as Bush carried it 51%-42% (with 5% for Ralph Nader). In 2004, the "Gang of Four" liberal campaigners brought out higher turnouts in heavily Democratic areas, and John Kerry's campaign gave thought to targeting the state late in the campaign; Bush ended up winning by only 52%-47%.

National Democrats had Colorado in their sights long before 2008, as was apparent when they chose to hold their national convention in

2008 Presidential Vote
Barack Obama (D) 1,288,576   (54%)
John McCain (R) 1,073,589   (45%)

2008 Presidential Primary
Barack Obama (D) 80,113   (67%)
Hillary Clinton (D) 38,839   (32%)

2008 Presidential Primary
Mitt Romney (R).....................33,288   (60%)
John McCain (R) 10,621   (18%)
Mike Huckabee (R)..................7,266   (13%)
Ron Paul (R) 4,670   (8%)

2004 Presidential Vote
George W. Bush (R)...........1,101,255   (52%)
John Kerry (D) 1,001,732   (47%)

Denver. After Obama's triumph in Colorado's caucuses, polling showed him ahead or at least competitive in Colorado for months. Polling just after the Republican National Convention suggested that the state might be within reach for John McCain, but he fell behind significantly after the crisis in the financial markets broke in September. Liberals were energized and conservatives were dejected. Turnout was up from 2004 by 14% in Denver County and by 8% in Boulder County, where population growth has been low. It also surged well ahead of population growth in the Denver suburbs. Obama's percentage increase over Kerry's in 2004 was biggest in metro Denver and the Front Range from Fort Collins down to Colorado Springs. Obama carried all of the suburban counties except fast-growing Douglas County, where he got a respectable 41% of the vote.

Colorado had an early March presidential primary from 1992, when long-shot California Democrat Jerry Brown won it, until 2000; it never attracted much national attention. In 2003, to save money, the legislature voted to eliminate the presidential primary the following year. In 2007, the legislature passed a law leaving it to the major parties to decide when to hold 2008 caucuses; both selected February 5. The Democratic caucuses attracted 120,000 voters, the Republican caucuses only 70,000, a sign of the prevailing trend in a state where Republicans four years earlier had 120,000 participants. Enthusiasm for Obama and his campaign's organizational skill gave him a 67%-32% victory over Clinton. Ninety percent of the votes were cast in 13 of the 64 counties, and Obama carried them all except industrial Pueblo. Clinton ran well among Latinos but not among other ethnic groups. The highest turnouts were in Denver and Boulder counties, where Obama won 69% and 74%, respectively. Mitt Romney, the only Republican with much of an organization in Colorado, won the Republican caucuses with 60% of the vote; McCain got only 18%, and Mike Huckabee got 13%.

Congressional districting

Colorado gained a single House seat in the reapportionments that followed the censuses of 1970, 1980 and 2000, but not after the censuses of 1990 and 2010. After the 2000 census, Republicans fell short of controlling the process by a single seat in the state Senate. Curiously, Democrats found themselves in the same predicament after the 2010 Census. The legislature was unable to agree on a plan in 2002, at which point a state court judge selected a Democrat-designed plan. Republicans responded angrily. They wanted the new district drawn in the fast-growing Republican counties on the south side of Denver. Instead, the newly created 7th District was anchored in the inner Denver suburbs to the north of the city. It was very competitive early in the decade, but it trended more Democratic as the years went on. After taking over the legislature, Republicans passed a new plan in May 2003, but in December of that year, the state Supreme Court threw out the new map on the grounds that the state constitution prohibited more than one plan every 10 years. The results of this plan show that in Colorado, with its wide political swings, prediction is difficult. Three of the seven congressional districts—the 3rd, 4th and 7th—elected both Republicans and Democrats during the decade, while the 1st and 2nd remained solidly Democratic and the 5th and 6th solidly Republican.

There have not been wide variations in growth rates in different parts of the state over the past decade, so it would be possible to create a plan closely resembling the current lines by expanding the relatively slow-growth 1st and 7th districts into the faster-growing 6th District. Democrats would not want to add too much Republican territory to the 7th, however, and may try for a more favorable alignment than one that leaves them currently at a 4-3 disadvantage. Their problem is that there is not much heavily Democratic territory outside the three currently Democratic districts—just Pueblo, a few small Hispanic counties and some ski resorts like Aspen and Crested Butte, all of which are in the current 3rd District and were not enough to keep it in Democratic hands in 2010.

Governor

John Hickenlooper (D)

Elected 2010, term expires Jan. 2015, 1st term; b. Feb. 7, 1952, Narberth, PA; home, Denver; Wesleyan U., B.A. 1974, M.A. 1980; Episcopalian; Married (Helen Thorpe); 1 child.

Elected Office: Denver mayor, 2003-2010.

Professional Career: Geologist, restauratuer, 1980-2003.

Office: 136 State Capitol, Denver, 80203, 303-866-2471; Fax: 303-866-2003; Web site: www.colorado.gov/governor.

Election Results

2010 general	John Hickenlooper (D)	912,005	(51%)
	Tom Tancredo (CNP)	651,232	(36%)
	Dan Maes (R)	199,034	(11%)
2010 primary	John Hickenlooper (D)	unopposed	

John Hickenlooper, a Democrat, was elected governor of Colorado in 2010. He grew up in the Philadelphia suburbs, raised by a frugal widowed mother. He is a descendant of the Revolutionary War financier Robert Morris and went to the Haverford School. "My great-grandparents were Quakers. And I tried to take that ethic into business. Quaker honesty, Quaker mindfulness, that effort to build community across differences....I get that from my Philly background," he told *The Philadelphia Inquirer*. He graduated from Wesleyan University, first studying English, and then getting a master's degree in geology. He moved to Colorado in 1981 and took a job in the oil industry. When oil prices fell in the 1980s, he was laid off by Buckhorn Petroleum. On a trip to the San Francisco Bay area, he stopped in at a brewpub, then a rarity. He thought the concept might work in Denver, and in 1988, opened the Wynkoop Brewery in the warehouse district northwest of downtown Denver, the first brewpub in Colorado. He put ads for nearby restaurants in his bar to encourage development of the Lower Downtown as an attractive entertainment district. He ended up starting 14 restaurants himself and today LoDo is buzzing with activity.

Looming over LoDo in the 1990s was Mile High Stadium. At the time, the Denver Broncos owners wanted a new football field, with lots of lucrative skyboxes. They asked corporations to put in bids for naming rights, which got Hickenlooper's attention. He brought a lawsuit to stop the sale of the stadium naming rights to the highest bidder, a move he hoped would preserve the name "Mile High" as a unique identifier for Denver. He argued that the owners' plan to pay off a $15 million, no-interest construction loan with proceeds from the naming rights was "a conflict of interests that verges on corruption." Ultimately, the deal was brokered and the structure, where Democratic presidential candidate Barack Obama gave his acceptance speech in August 2008, was called INVESCO Field at Mile High Stadium.

Hickenlooper's work got his friends talking about him running for mayor of Denver in 2003, when incumbent Wellington Webb was barred by term limits from running for a fourth term. Hickenlooper got into a contest with six other candidates and was among the top two finishers, with city Auditor Don Mares. The two competed in a June 2003 runoff campaign noteworthy for its lack of vitriol. Hickenlooper refused to run negative ads. "In the restaurant business, we spend our whole lives trying never to have an enemy," he later told *The Denver Post*. "It always struck me that that was a more useful paradigm in politics." He campaigned against "the nonsense of government," including parking meter rates. One television ad showed Hickenlooper with a change maker around his waist, thrusting quarters into meters. He also pledged to cut the city payroll by 4%. In the runoff, he beat Mares, 65%-35%.

As mayor, he reached out to suburban officials and to Republican Gov. Bill Owens. In 2004, he got all 32 mayors in metro Denver to support a ballot proposition instituting a 0.4% sales tax to raise $4.7 billion for a light rail system. He also got voters to approve the largest bond issue in the city's history, a permanent property tax increase and a tax increase for early-childhood education. Hickenlooper also took control of the city's troubled public schools and installed his chief of staff, Michael Bennet, now a U.S. senator, as superintendent and charged him with using innovative ways to increase school performance. His 2005 program to increase energy efficiency and decrease carbon emissions reduced energy use per passenger 11% at Denver International Airport and increased recycling in the city by 69%.

In 2007, Hickenlooper won a second term as mayor. When Democrat Bill Ritter was elected governor, the two worked together successfully to bring the 2008 Democratic National Convention to Denver. But they differed on other issues. Ritter favored restrictions on abortion rights, a position that put him at odds with many Democrats, and he favored limits on oil and gas drilling, which the business community opposed. Hickenlooper tended to take the opposite stands. In December 2008, when President Obama appointed Democratic Sen. Ken Salazar as Interior secretary, it was widely expected that Ritter would appoint Hickenlooper to fill Salazar's Senate seat. Instead Ritter, keeping his own counsel, appointed schools chief Bennet.

In January 2010, Ritter surprised political insiders again when he said he would not seek a second term. Obama called Hickenlooper and asked him to run. A week later, he agreed and was quickly endorsed by Ritter. Hickenlooper said that he wanted to make Colorado a center for innovation, entrepreneurship and small-business development. He criticized Ritter's rulemaking process and said he was "coming from a very different place than Governor Ritter" on oil and gas issues, saying he wanted to cut red tape not increase it. Running on his record as mayor, he claimed to have closed budget gaps of more than $350 million.

Despite Hickenlooper's popularity in the Denver media market, which covers most of the state, Republicans seemed to have a serious chance to regain the office they lost in 2006. In 2009, state Senate Minority Leader Josh Penry, only 33, started running aggressively, but in November he bowed out and endorsed former U.S. Rep. Scott McInnis. In the winter and spring of 2010, McInnis was competitive with Hickenlooper in the polls. But in July, it was revealed that a paper on water issues for which McInnis had been paid $300,000 by a think tank was in large part plagiarized. After some hesitation, he admitted it and claimed to have been confused. This provided an opening for his one primary opponent, businessman Daniel Maes, who espoused strong conservative positions and enjoyed support from tea party activists. It also prompted former U.S. Rep. Tom Tancredo, who ran a quixotic presidential campaign in 2008 on the illegal immigration issue, to announce that he would run on a third party line because both McInnis and Maes were unacceptable.

In August, Maes won the Republican primary, 51%-49%, and promptly fell into serious trouble himself. He charged that a city program that encouraged bicycle riding, which was sponsored by a United Nations affiliate and was begun long before Hickenlooper became mayor, was "converting Denver into a United Nations community." His personal finances—incomes of $19,000 in 2005, $20,000 in 2006, $11,000 in 2008—suggested he wasn't the business success he claimed. He failed to file paperwork with the state government on businesses, including one that produced educational videos on how to maintain a good credit rating. Then it was revealed that a lien was placed on his property after he fell seven months behind on dues to a homeowners' association. On top of that, newspaper reports indicated that he misstated seriously his work as a police officer in Liberal, Kansas some years before.

Maes' money dried up. In early September, state Republican Chairman Dick Wadhams publicly urged him to get out of the race. The head of the Republican Governors Association, Mississippi's Haley Barbour, said he was done spending the group's money on the Colorado race. And by mid-September, Maes was trailing even Tancredo in the polls. Former Alaska Gov. Sarah Palin endorsed Tancredo, but over the years Tancredo's spirited denunciations of illegal immigration did not project the calm demeanor or studied judgment that most voters look for in a governor. Still, he was attractive in comparison to Maes, and by mid-October, Tancredo was considered the leading Republican and Maes the fringe candidate.

Meanwhile, Hickenlooper was much better financed than the Republicans and was happily adhering to his policy of "No negative ads!" His first ad showed him dressed in a suit, in the shower, saying how negative ads make him feel dirty. Hickenlooper won by a wide margin, 15% ahead of Tancredo, but with barely an absolute majority, 51%, of the vote. Tancredo got 36% and Maes 11%. Tancredo carried Colorado Springs' El Paso County and exurban Douglas County, but lost the main Denver suburban counties to Hickenlooper.

Hickenlooper was the only statewide Democratic candidate to run above 50% in a very poor political year for his party. Republicans won a 33-32 majority in the state House, upsetting the Democrats' 37-27-1 advantage. Democrats kept control of the state Senate, however, with a margin of five seats. Hickenlooper's transition team included Republicans such as former Gov. Owens and former U.S. Rep. Bob Schaffer as well as Democrats such as his predecessor as mayor, Webb. He set about inviting legislators of both parties to work with him on cutting an estimated $715 million budget deficit for the state in early 2011.

Senior Senator

Mark Udall (D)

Elected 2008, term expires 2014, 1st term; b. July 18, 1950, Tucson, AZ; home, Eldorado Springs; Williams Col., B.A. 1972; no religious affiliation; married (Maggie L. Fox); 2 children.

Elected Office: CO House of Reps., 1996-98; U.S. House of Reps., 1998-2008.

Professional Career: CO Outward Bound course dir., 1975-85, exec. dir., 1985-95.

DC Office: 328 HSOB, 20510, 202-224-5941; Fax: 202-224-6471; Web site: markudall.senate.gov.

State Offices: Denver, 303-650-7820; Grand Junction, 970-245-9553.

Committees: *Aging (Special)*. *Armed Services:* Emerging Threats & Capabilities; Readiness & Management Support; Strategic Forces. *Energy & Natural Resources:* Energy; National Parks (Chmn); Public Lands & Forests. *Intelligence (Select)*.

Group Ratings

	ACLU	ACU	ADA	CFG	AFS	FRC	LCV	ITIC	NTU	COC
2010	93	8	90	10	96	0	57	33	15	18
2009	–	16	95	3	100	–	100	–	8	43

National Journal Ratings

	2010 LIB	—	2010 CONS		2009 LIB	—	2009 CONS
Economic	48%	—	51%		61%	—	37%
Social	59%	—	38%		57%	—	41%
Foreign	47%	—	0%		55%	—	0%
Composite	61%	—	39%		66%	—	34%

Key Votes of the 111th Congress

1. Overturn Ledbetter	Y	5. Pass health care bill	Y	9. Ratify New START	Y
2. Pass $787 billion stimulus	Y	6. Regulate financial firms	Y	10. Confirm Elena Kagan	Y
3. Repeal DC gun laws	Y	7. Pass tax cuts for some	Y	11. Stop EPA climate regs	N
4. Confirm Sonia Sotomayor	Y	8. Legalize immigrants' kids	Y	12. Repeal don't ask, tell	Y

Election Results

2008 general	Mark Udall (D)	1,230,994	(53%)	($11,787,048)
	Bob Schaffer (R)	990,755	(42%)	($7,387,843)
	Douglas Campbell (CNP)	59,733	(3%)	
	Bob Kinsey (Green)	50,004	(2%)	
2008 primary	Mark Udall (D)	unopposed		

Prior Winning Percentages: House: 2006 (68%); 2004 (67%); 2002 (60%); 2000 (55%); 1998 (50%)

Mark Udall, Colorado's senior senator, is a Democrat first elected to the House in 1998 and to the Senate in 2008. Udall grew up in Tucson, Ariz., in a family with deep political roots in the West. His grandfather, Levi Stewart Udall, a Republican, was a justice on Arizona's Supreme Court from 1947 to 1960. An uncle, Democrat Stewart Udall, was the representative from the Tucson district from 1955 to 1961 and then secretary of the Interior for eight years. Stewart was succeeded in the House by Morris Udall, Mark's father, who served from 1961 until 1991. He was the longtime Democratic chairman of the Interior Committee and an unsuccessful presidential candidate in 1976. As a child, Mark listened in on living room conversations between his father and prominent political figures like Robert Kennedy and Supreme Court Justice William Douglas. In Tucson, the two Udall brothers lived a bike-ride apart, and young Mark used to ride over to see Stewart's son, cousin Tom Udall, who was elected to the Senate from New Mexico in 2008. Mark Udall says he and his cousin have been as close as brothers throughout their lives.

Udall graduated from Williams College in 1972. The same year, he was arrested for possession of marijuana, and after pleading guilty to a misdemeanor, moved to Boulder, Colo., where he worked for the Colorado Outward Bound School and became an accomplished mountaineer. He has climbed Mount Aconcagua, the highest peak in the Western Hemisphere, and Kanchenjunga, the third-highest peak in the world, and he has scaled the north face, though he did not reach the top, of Mount Everest. He was executive director of the school from 1985 to 1995. In 1996, Udall ran for the state House and with his family's connections raised 40% of his money out of state and won. When 2nd District Democratic Rep. David Skaggs retired in 1998, Udall ran for his seat against Republican Bob Greenlee, the mayor of Boulder. Udall stressed environmental protection, growth management, and education. Greenlee was popular in usually Democratic Boulder. But Udall won Boulder, and he defeated Greenlee 50%-47%.

In the House, Udall compiled a mostly liberal voting record. On environmental issues, he opposed allowing states to designate roads in wilderness areas, but dismayed some local environmental groups by supporting cutbacks in forests to combat infestation by bark beetles and to reduce the threat of wildfires. In 2004, he championed Colorado's Amendment 37, which imposed a renewable energy standard on the state, and he helped persuade the U.S. House to pass renewable energy standards in 2007. Udall served on the House Armed Services Committee and voted against the Iraq war resolution in October 2002, citing his father's regret over supporting the Tonkin Gulf resolution in 1964. But by May 2007, he had softened his anti-war stance somewhat, voting in favor of funding for the war and against an amendment that called for troops to be withdrawn within 180 days. "We rushed into this war, and we need to withdraw in a phased fashion so we don't leave the Middle East aflame," he told *The Denver Post*. In response, anti-war protesters stormed his Washington office and were arrested.

Udall was often mentioned as a contender for statewide office. In 2003, he declined to challenge Republican Sen. Ben Nighthorse Campbell, but the following year, when Campbell suddenly announced he would retire, Udall entered the race. Within 24 hours, however, under pressure from Democrats who thought they needed a more moderate candidate, Udall dropped out and endorsed state Attorney General Ken Salazar, who went on to win the Senate seat in 2004. But Udall made it clear he would run for the Senate seat up in 2008, when Republican Sen. Wayne Allard would be at the end of the two terms he had said he would serve.

Udall was unopposed in the Democratic primary. Former Rep. Scott McInnis, considered the front-runner for the Republican nomination, dropped out of the race, which cleared the way for former Rep. Bob Schaffer, who retired from the House in 2002 in line with his pledge to serve only three terms. In 2004, Schaffer ran for the Senate and lost the nomination to beer company executive Pete Coors. So, two candidates who were passed over in the 2004 Senate race faced each other in 2008.

There was a fairly sharp contrast between the candidates' views. Republicans constantly referred to Udall as a "Boulder liberal," while Democrats referred to Schaffer as "Big Oil Bob." Udall emphasized his support of renewable energy sources, but said he also supported clean coal development and nuclear power. In July 2008, he came out for allowing additional forms of recreation beyond skiing, such as mountain biking and concerts, in ski-permit areas on U.S. Forest Service land. Schaffer, who had earlier in his career attacked conservation programs as infringement on property rights, cited his work after he left Congress on seismic technology, and said he supported renewable energy. The Democratic Senatorial Campaign Committee ran an ad criticizing Schaffer for supporting tax breaks for energy companies and then subsequently earning $800,000 as an oil-company executive.

Then in May 2008, gas prices hit $4 a gallon, and public opinion shifted in favor of offshore oil drilling. Schaffer attacked Udall for his long opposition to offshore drilling. In August, as Congress was about to adjourn, Udall cast one of the last votes for the Democratic leadership's move to adjourn without, as Republicans demanded, voting on offshore drilling. In mid-August he switched and supported proposals for offshore and more domestic drilling, a move that Schaffer derided as a "fig leaf."

But Udall won 53%-42%, while Democratic presidential nominee Barack Obama was carrying the state 54%-45%. Schaffer ran well ahead in Colorado Springs, in exurban Douglas County and the eastern plains, and also in mining areas on the Western Slope. But Udall carried the other Denver suburbs by impressive margins, and his big margins in ski resort areas and Pueblo enabled him to carry the 3rd Congressional District, something many Democrats feared impossible. It was the widest margin for a Democrat in a Colorado Senate race since Gary Hart's victory in 1974.

When home-state colleague Ken Salazar was confirmed as Interior secretary and resigned from the Senate in early 2009, Udall became a senior senator after just 16 days as a junior senator. His new cohort was Michael Bennet, the Denver schools chief who was appointed to replace Salazar in the Senate. Udall and Bennet voted together on many issues, and Udall endorsed Bennet for a full term when he ran for election to the seat in 2010. Like other Western Democrats, they depart from their party on gun issues. In May 2009, they supported an amendment to allow guns in national parks, and in July 2009, they supported one to allow holders of concealed weapons permits in one state to possess guns in states that have reciprocal laws. But on another divisive social issue, Udall joined most Democrats in 2010 in supporting repeal of the ban on openly gay service personnel in the military.

On other issues, Udall sought additional federal funds to remove dead trees stricken by bark beetles to reduce the risk of wildfires. And his amendment to require numerical credit scores on credit reports passed by a voice vote. In spring 2010, as the Senate debated a major energy bill to cap carbon emissions, Udall expressed support for bipartisan versions of the bill and emphasized the importance of carbon pricing. "If you don't put a price on carbon, you don't unleash this job creation engine that all the economists tell us will unfold if we put a price on carbon," he said. Having supported "responsible and environmentally sensitive offshore oil drilling" in 2008, he called for closer regulation of offshore apparatus after the massive BP oil spill in the Gulf of Mexico in 2010. "This is a case where we ought to trust, but we ought to verify," Udall said. After China cut off sales of rare earth minerals in the fall of 2010, Udall called for the reopening of a shuttered rare earth mineral mine in California owned by the Colorado firm Molycorp.

With a seat on the Armed Services Committee, Udall has supported the Obama administration's policies on Iraq and Afghanistan. He also voted for the New START treaty with Russia. He said, "Failure to ratify the treaty would make the broad 'resetting' of U.S.-Russian relations harder. The distrust it would engender would also reduce or even eliminate the possibility of further bilateral strategic weapons reductions."

Junior Senator

Michael Bennet (D)

Appointed Jan. 2009, term expires 2016, 1st full term; b. Nov. 28, 1964, New Delhi, India; home, Denver; Wesleyan U., B.A. 1987; Yale U., J.D. 1993.; No religious affiliation; married (Susan Daggett); 3 children.

Professional Career: Dep. atty. gen., U.S. Dept. of Justice, 1995-97; Managing dir., Anschutz Investment Co., 1997-2003; Chief of staff, Denver Mayor John Hickenlooper, 2003-05; Superintendent, Denver Public Schl., 2005-09.

DC Office: 702 HSOB, 20510, 202-224-5852; Fax: 202-228-5036; Web site: bennet.senate.gov.

State Offices: Alamosa, 719-587-0096; Colorado Springs, 719-328-1100; Denver, 303-455-7600; Durango, 970-259-1710; Fort Collins, 970-224-2200; Fort Morgan, 970-542-9446; Grand Junction, 970-241-6631; Pueblo, 719-542-7550.

Committees: *Aging (Special). Agriculture, Nutrition & Forestry:* Commodities, Markets, Trade & Risk Management; Conservation, Forestry & Natural Resources (Chmn); Nutrition, Specialty Crops, Food & Ag Research. *Banking, Housing & Urban Affairs:* Housing, Transportation & Community Development; Securities, Insurance & Investment; Security & International Trade & Finance. *Health, Education, Labor & Pensions:* Children & Families; Employment & Workplace Safety.

Group Ratings

	ACLU	ACU	ADA	CFG	AFS	FRC	LCV	ITIC	NTU	COC
2010	93	8	85	8	89	0	43	67	20	36
2009	–	8	95	12	91	–	100	–	10	57

National Journal Ratings

	2010 LIB	—	2010 CONS	2009 LIB	—	2009 CONS
Economic	49%	—	49%	64%	—	35%
Social	54%	—	43%	61%	—	38%
Foreign	47%	—	0%	55%	—	0%
Composite	60%	—	40%	68%	—	32%

Key Votes of the 111th Congress

1. Overturn Ledbetter	Y	5. Pass health care bill	Y
2. Pass $787 billion stimulus	Y	6. Regulate financial firms	Y
3. Repeal DC gun laws	Y	7. Pass tax cuts for some	N
4. Confirm Sonia Sotomayor	Y	8. Legalize immigrants' kids	Y

9. Ratify New START	Y
10. Confirm Elena Kagan	Y
11. Stop EPA climate regs	N
12. Repeal don't ask, tell	Y

Election Results

2010 general	Michael Bennet (D)	851,590	(48%)	($11,536,750)
	Ken Buck (R)	822,731	(46%)	($4,953,818)
	Bob Kinsey (Green)	38,768	(2%)	
2010 primary	Michael Bennet (D)	184,714	(54%)	
	Andrew Romanoff (D)	156,419	(46%)	

Colorado's junior senator is Michael Bennet, a Democrat appointed by Gov. Bill Ritter in January 2009 to succeed Ken Salazar, who'd been named Interior secretary by President Obama. Bennet was born in New Delhi, India, where his father, Douglas Bennet, was an aide to Ambassador Chester Bowles. His mother and her family were Jews who emigrated from Poland after World War II. Michael grew up and attended private schools in Washington, D.C., while his father pursued his career in public service. Douglas Bennet was a staffer for Vice President Hubert Humphrey, assistant secretary of state in the Carter administration and later president of National Public Radio. The younger Bennet graduated from Wesleyan University, and went to work as an aide to Democratic Gov. Richard Celeste of Ohio, a family friend. In 1990, Bennet entered Yale Law School, where he was editor-in-chief of the *Yale Law Journal.* He clerked for a federal judge in Baltimore, where he met his wife, Susan Daggett, and then joined Lloyd Cutler's influential law firm in Washington. In 1995, he was named counsel to Deputy Attorney General Jamie Gorelick in the Clinton administration and wrote speeches for Attorney General Janet Reno. In 1997, he moved to Denver, where his wife, a natural resources lawyer, went to work for the Sierra Club Legal Defense Fund. Bennett took a job with the investment company headed by billionaire Philip Anschutz, a political conservative. Bennet had never read a balance sheet, and Anschutz told him to attend accounting school at night at his own expense. Eventually, Bennet got such assignments as restructuring

$3 billion in debt for several companies, including Forcenergy, Regal Cinemas, United Artists and Edwards Theaters. He also oversaw the consolidation of the three theater chains into Regal Entertainment Group, the world's largest movie theater company.

In 2003, a fellow Wesleyan alumnus, John Hickenlooper, was elected Denver mayor and asked Bennet to be his chief of staff. Bennet says he gave up millions in stock options to accept "an opportunity that wouldn't come around again." He worked on balancing the budget, mediating a dispute between United and Frontier airlines at Denver International Airport and brokering agreements with public-employee unions. "I have referred to him as the second mayor, the hidden mayor," Hickenlooper told *The Denver Post*. In 2005, the position of Denver Public Schools superintendent came open, and among the 14 top candidates was Bennet—even though he had no experience in education, had himself attended private schools, and was sending his daughter to a private kindergarten. In 2005, the board picked him to head a system of 73,000 students, three-quarters of them Latino or African-American and two-thirds of them eligible for the school lunch program. When he closed the predominately minority Manual High School in 2006, black community leaders protested and called Bennet a "dictator." But the school reopened in 2008 with a new emphasis on student achievement, and Bennet mended fences with the community leaders. He instituted a "Denver Plan," which boosted performance standards in the schools and created workshops to teach principals how to lead schools to reform. An early-childhood education program was put in place, and more than 90% of five-year-olds got full-day kindergarten. By 2008, enrollment was at its highest point since 1976, and test scores rose faster than or at the state average in 140 of 164 schools. Still, Denver schools performed below statewide levels: Only 46% of Denver students showed proficiency in reading and 35% in math, compared to the statewide averages of 68% and 53%, respectively.

When Obama was running for president in 2008, Bennet co-hosted a fundraiser for the then-Illinois senator. He was later included in the Democratic candidate's weekly education conference calls with innovative big city school heads. After Obama was elected, Bennet was on the short list for secretary of Education, although Obama ultimately chose Chicago schools chief Arne Duncan. Yet Bennet was not even considered a long shot for U.S. senator after Obama named Salazar his Interior secretary. That left it up to Democratic Gov. Ritter to appoint a replacement to serve until Salazar's Senate seat came up for re-election in 2010. Bennet had limited national experience, consisting mainly of a 2004 speech he gave to a group of business leaders denouncing the Iraq War and President George W. Bush. In Colorado political circles, Bennet was on exactly no one's radar.

The more obvious candidates were outgoing state House Speaker Andrew Romanoff, who had ties to Democratic politicians and activists across the state, and Hickenlooper, Bennet's mentor, who was well-known and popular throughout the state. On Jan. 2, 2009, Ritter astonished just about everyone by naming Bennet, saying he was impressed with his record of bringing diverse interests together to solve problems and by his pragmatic approach to turning around troubled public and private enterprises. Republican leaders relished the prospect of taking on a candidate far less formidable electorally than Hickenlooper or Romanoff in 2010.

On Jan. 22, 2009 he was sworn in as a senator. The other Colorado senator, Democrat Mark Udall, had been elected in November 2008, and so, after just 16 days on the job, Udall became the senior senator from Colorado and Bennet the junior senator. (Vice President Joe Biden, who swore Bennet in, served 28 years before he became the senior senator from Delaware).

In his early days as senator, Bennet began setting up a campaign organization heavy with veterans of the Obama campaign, who had helped the new president carry Colorado by 54%-45%. During his first two years in the Senate, Bennet tackled a number of government reforms. He joined Udall in pushing to change the rules of the filibuster, which had frustrated the Democratic majority by ensuring that almost any piece of legislation needed 60 votes for passage. He also sponsored a bill eliminating annual cost-of-living adjustments for members of Congress until unemployment rates fell significantly. Bennet was a strong supporter of the DISCLOSE Act, which would rewrite campaign finance laws in the aftermath of the Supreme Court's ruling in *Citizens United v. Federal Election Committee*. The high court struck down laws barring corporate and union campaign spending. In late July, the bill garnered 57 votes, a solid majority but not enough to break a threatened filibuster.

As a member of the Health, Education, Labor, and Pensions Committee, he introduced a bill in August 2010 that would strengthen the Food and Drug Administration's ability to identify and prevent tainted drugs from reaching consumers. During the 2009-2010 fight over health insurance reform, he secured Senate passage of an amendment that established a deficit-neutral reserve fund to address inequities in Medicare and Medicaid reimbursements to providers. It also required Medicare savings to be invested back into the program.

In March 2009, Bennet joined a coalition of 15 moderate Senate Democrats that met every other week to focus on fiscal discipline and budget matters. He occasionally broke from liberal orthodoxy. In July 2009, he supported an amendment by Sen. John Thune, R-S.D., to allow concealed gun laws in one state to apply to other states with concealed gun laws. On an important state issue, Bennet said he would follow Ritter's and Udall's go-slow approach on oil-shale leasing in western Colorado.

Still, Bennet's frog leap over more prominent state Democrats to the Senate was not forgotten. As he prepared to seek election to the seat in his own right in 2010, he drew a ferocious challenge from state House Speaker Romanoff, who portrayed himself as the outsider in the race and attacked Bennet, a one-time investment banker, as a tool of Wall Street. He also accused Bennet of failing to support the public health insurance option component of health care reform, which many liberals favored. Bennet proved to be a strong fundraiser and heavily outspent Romanoff. He vehemently defended his health care record and claimed he had indeed supported the public option, which was left out of the final health care law because of opposition from party conservatives. One setback for him was a damaging *New York Times* article that said Bennet's efforts to eliminate a $400 million hole in the pension fund when he was Denver schools chief ended up forcing the school district further into debt. The story ran just four days before the primary, as Romanoff was surging in the polls. The two candidates appeared to be in a dead heat as the Aug. 10 primary neared. However, in a year that was widely viewed as tough for incumbents, Bennet defeated Romanoff 54% to 46%.

In November, he faced another tough contest against Weld County District Attorney Ken Buck, who had won the GOP nomination over the establishment Republican candidate, former Lt. Gov. Jane Norton, with the backing of tea party activists. Buck portrayed Bennet as part of the problem in big-spending Washington, and attacked his votes for Obama's $767 billion economic stimulus bill and the overhaul of the health insurance system. Buck called for dismantling the U.S. Department of Education and replacing the income tax with a national sales tax. But Buck was also gaffe-prone, and his record in office, including his opposition to abortion in all circumstances, was more susceptible than Norton's to being painted as extremist, which Bennet and his Democratic allies did at every turn.

During the primary fight with Norton, Buck first raised eyebrows when he said Republican women should vote for him because he didn't "wear high heels." Democrats later made an issue of his 2005 decision as district attorney not to prosecute an accused rapist because a jury would likely conclude that her complaint was a case of "buyer's remorse." In an appearance on *Meet the Press*, Buck compared homosexuality to alcoholism, saying, "I think that birth has an influence over it, like alcoholism and some other things. But I think that basically, you have a choice."

With $11.5 million in campaign funds, Bennet saturated the airwaves with Buck's missteps and a picture of a candidate who would turn back the clock on abortion rights and who was too extreme for Colorado's independent-minded voters. *Denver Post* columnist Vincent Carroll wrote, tongue-in-cheek: "During the height of the onslaught on TV, it was sometimes hard to tell if Buck was a candidate for office or a fugitive from justice." Buck himself raised $5 million and had help from the GOP-friendly American Crossroads, which invested $5 million in negative ads against Bennet. But the Democrat held the upper hand in the air war in spite of his votes for major elements of the Obama agenda, which were hurting Democratic incumbents elsewhere in the country. Colorado College political scientist Bob Loevy told *The Denver Post*, "To a very large extent, Bennet made the issue not about the national economy, but about the characteristics of Ken Buck."

Bennet won 48% to 46%. Exit polls showed that he was heavily favored by independent voters and benefited from a significant gender gap. Women voted for Bennet over Buck 56% to 40%. He carried unaffiliated voters 52% to 41% in the exit polls.

FIRST DISTRICT

Diana DeGette (D)

Elected 1996, 8th term; b. July 29, 1957, Tachikawa, Japan; home, Denver; CO Col., B.A. 1979, N.Y.U., J.D. 1982; Presbyterian; married (Lino Lipinsky); 2 children.

Elected Office: CO House of Reps., 1992–96, asst. min. ldr., 1994–95.

Professional Career: Practicing atty., 1982–96.

DC Office: 2335 RHOB, 20515, 202-225-4431; Fax: 202-225-5657; Web site: degette.house.gov.

State Offices: Denver, 303-844-4988.

Committees: *Energy & Commerce:* Communications & Technology; Environment & the Economy; Oversight & Investigations (RMM).

Group Ratings

	ACLU	ACU	ADA	CFG	AFS	FRC	LCV	ITIC	NTU	COC
2010	81	0	95	0	100	0	100	67	3	13
2009	–	0	100	4	100	–	100	–	2	33

National Journal Ratings

	2010 LIB	—	2010 CONS	2009 LIB	—	2009 CONS
Economic	83%	—	16%	82%	—	14%
Social	86%	—	13%	75%	—	20%
Foreign	90%	—	10%	87%	—	9%
Composite	87%	—	13%	84%	—	17%

Key Votes of the 111th Congress

1. Overturn Ledbetter	Y	5. Bar federal abortion funds	N	9. Stop detainee transfers	N
2. Pass $820 billion stimulus	Y	6. Pass health care bill	Y	10. Legalize immigrants' kids	Y
3. Let guns in national parks	Y	7. Regulate financial firms	Y	11. Repeal don't ask, tell	Y
4. Pass cap-and-trade	Y	8. Pass tax cuts for some	Y	12. Limit campaign funds	Y

Election Results

2010 general	Diana DeGette (D)	140,073	(67%)	($825,016)
	Mike Fallon (R)	59,747	(29%)	($196,993)
2010 primary	Diana DeGette (D)	unopposed		

Prior Winning Percentages: 2008 (72%), 2006 (80%), 2004 (73%), 2002 (66%), 2000 (69%), 1998 (67%), 1996 (57%)

Population		Race/Ethnicity		Work	
Pop. 2010:	662,039	White:	53.6%	Private:	82.1%
Change since 2000:	Up 7.7%	Black:	9.4%	Government:	11.0%
Urban:	100.0%	Hispanic:	30.7%	Self-employed:	6.7%
Rural:	0.0%	Asian:	3.3%	Blue collar:	18.7%
Area size:	173 sq. mi.	Native Am.:	0.6%	White collar:	62.5%
		Hawaiian:	0.1%	Khaki collar:	0.1%
Age		Two+ races:	2.1%	Other:	18.7%
Median age:	33.3 yrs.				
More than 65 yrs:	10.5%	*Ancestry*		Median income:	$45,093
Less than 18 yrs:	22.7%	German	12.3%	Median Home Value:	$239,200
		Irish	8.3%		
Education		English	6.9%	**Military Veterans**	
H.S. grad:	84.0%			% of Pop:	7.7%
College grad:	39.3%				
Grad degree:	15.4%				

Denver

Denver is serious about being the mile-high city: There are three markers on the granite steps of the gold-domed Capitol that proclaim the elevation of 5,280 feet. Denver is situated a few miles from where the High Plains yield to the sharp peaks of the Front Range of the Rockies, with a freshwater supply adequate for a town one-tenth of its size. With 610,000 people in 2009, the city for a century has been the economic and cultural capital of the Rocky Mountain region. On

2008 Presidential Vote		
Barack Obama (D)	222,009	(74%)
John McCain (R)	72,573	(24%)
2004 Presidential Vote		
John Kerry (D)	180,064	(68%)
George Bush (R)	81,265	(31%)
Cook Partisan Voting Index:	D+21	

top of its Old West heritage and early-20th-century elegance, Denver has developed an exuberant postmodern style. The National Western Stock Show held here every year and the LoDo entertainment district along the South Platte River evoke the Old West. The Capitol, the spacious parks, the aspens that line the streets, give the city a lush, burnished air, in contrast to the dry high plains and the stark Rocky peaks. Amid its downtown grid, slanted on a 45-degree angle to align with the South Platte and the railroads, are the skyscrapers of the 1970s energy boom and the 1990s high-tech boom, plus the new-old Coors Stadium, the Elitch Gardens amusement park and the expanded Museum of Nature and Science. Rather than losing population as many central cities have, Denver has gained people since 1990. Most of its neighborhoods have vitality, including the African-American neighborhoods of northeastern Denver, filled with neat 1950s bungalows, and the Hispanic quarter northwest of downtown. But more than three-quarters of the metro area's people now live in the suburbs, and Denver has disproportionate numbers of singles and cultural liberals who value an urban and physically active lifestyle in the gentrified areas south of the Capitol.

Denver is the liberal heart of Colorado, heavily Democratic. The city remains majority Anglo, but has elected Hispanic and black mayors. In the early 1970s, Denver liberals were hostile to growth and boosterism. Today's Denver, from the wealthy enclave of Cherry Creek to the night life of LoDo, has shown that growth can produce more of the distinctiveness that people here appreciate. Civic pride was rampant during the 2008 Democratic convention in Denver, with an emphasis on its green projects. There was good reason: Denver has been ranked among the nation's top 10 cities in business climate, livability, libraries, and bikeways. In the lower downtown near Coors Field, dilapidated bars have been replaced by art galleries in the past decade.

The 1st Congressional District of Colorado includes all of Denver and extends northeast to take in Denver International Airport. The district extends to affluent suburbs, long-settled Englewood and newly settled Cherry Hills Village in Arapahoe County. It counts most of metro Denver's African-Americans and Hispanics, singles and gays; the Hispanic share of the district has grown to 31%. The percentage of households with married couples and children has been among the lowest in America, and was lower in 2000 than in 1990. In an era when cultural attitudes are a better clue to voting behavior than economic status, this district, which last elected a Republican in 1970, is solidly Democratic.

Diana DeGette (D)

The congresswoman from the 1st District is Diana DeGette, a Democrat first elected in 1996. She is a fourth-generation resident of Denver, though she was born on a military base in Japan. DeGette (*de GET*) says that she was inspired at age 13 by the television show *Storefront Lawyers* to "crusade for justice," and decided she would be a public interest lawyer. She attended New York University's law school on a full scholarship, and then returned to Denver to practice employment law. In 1992, at age 35, DeGette was elected to the Colorado House. Her signature accomplishment was the Bubble Bill, which was aimed at protecting women at abortion clinics by making it illegal for protesters to come within eight feet of a person entering or leaving a health care facility. DeGette worked across the aisle with Republicans in the legislature to overcome the efforts by the GOP majority leadership to kill the bill. The legal battle over its constitutionality eventually reached the U.S. Supreme Court, which upheld the law in a 6-3 decision. In 1995, when U.S. Rep. Patricia Schroeder, a pioneer of the feminist left, announced she was retiring after 24 years in the U.S. House, DeGette decided to run for the seat. Organizationally adept, legislatively creative and politically liberal, she proved a worthy successor to Schroeder, one of the most well-known figures in Colorado politics.

In both the minority and the majority, she has managed to achieve legislative successes in the House. On the Energy and Commerce Committee, she has focused on health care issues. Teaming with Republican Mike Castle of Delaware, DeGette established a bipartisan coalition to expand federal funds for stem cell research, which employs excess embryos from in vitro fertilization. President George W. Bush opposed more money for such research, but in 2005, DeGette and Castle won majority support in the House, and the Senate passed the bill a year later. Bush vetoed the bill, his first veto as president, and the House fell 51 votes short of an override. In 2007, after Democrats won majority control of Congress, her bill passed again, but was still short the two-thirds necessary to override Bush's veto. Ultimately, President Obama removed most federal restrictions on stem cell research in 2009. In August 2010, a federal judge blocked Obama's executive order, but an appeals court later lifted the injunction. DeGette says she was inspired to take on the cause after one of her daughters was diagnosed with diabetes at age 4. She wrote a book on the topic in 2008 called *Sex, Science, and Stem Cells*.

On other health issues, DeGette was a leading advocate for expanding the State Children's Health Insurance Program. In 2009, she co-sponsored, with her congressional mentor John Dingell, D-Mich., the Food Safety Enhancement Act. She secured two key provisions giving the Food and Drug Administration the power to mandate product recalls and authorizing the FDA to establish a food-tracking system. The bill was passed by the House but stalled in the Senate. Mandatory recall authority for the FDA became law in the Food Safety Modernization Act in 2011.

During the health care overhaul debate in 2009 and 2010, DeGette played a major role in shaping the final abortion provisions in the legislation. In November 2009, she led more than 40 pro-abortion rights Democrats in opposing an abortion restriction that was added to the bill by Democratic leaders to appease Rep. Bart Stupak, D-Mich., and other anti-abortion Democrats. It banned coverage of abortions in any new government-subsidized insurance plans. During negotiations to reconcile the House and Senate bills, Stupak pressed to have his abortion restriction preserved. He and DeGette held their respective ground and the president's health care agenda stalled. Finally, a compromise was reached in which Stupak agreed to forgo the provision in the bill in exchange for Obama's promise to sign an executive order reaffirming the law prohibiting the use of federal funds for abortion. DeGette supported the compromise.

DeGette's legislative skills put her on a leadership track in the House, although she also has been on the losing side of some big internal party battles. On the energy panel, she has helped broker the frequent clashes among the panel's Democrats. But she had to rebuild some of those relationships after the bitter fight between Dingell and California Rep. Henry Waxman for the chairmanship in late 2008. DeGette backed Dingell, but Waxman won. In 2001, DeGette supported Maryland's Steny Hoyer in his unsuccessful bid for Democratic whip against California's Nancy Pelosi, who went on to become speaker of the House. When Hoyer eventually got the job as party whip in 2002, Hoyer added DeGette to his whip team, and she moved into the role of party strategist.

When Democrats gained control of the House in 2007, Hoyer decided to run for majority leader, and DeGette seriously considered running to succeed him as whip against South Carolina's James Clyburn. She said she ultimately decided that it would have been disruptive to have another internal struggle at the same time Pennsylvania's John Murtha was challenging Hoyer for the majority leader's post. Clyburn made DeGette his chief deputy whip, putting her in position to take over as whip should Clyburn retire or step down for any reason. "If the opportunity arose I would love to be whip," DeGette told *National Journal*. "I love to whip!"

As a mother of two children, who were just 2 and 6 years old when she was elected, DeGette tries to help newer members of Congress with children find a balance between family and public life. She advises newcomers to "carve out family time" because while service in Congress is finite, family relationships last a lifetime. One of the ways DeGette finds family time is through her love of sports. The family has season tickets to the Denver Broncos and the Colorado Rockies.

In 2002, DeGette fared impressively against credible primary and general election opponents. Ramona Martinez, a 15-year member of the Denver City Council and a Democratic National Committeewoman, criticized her for having lost touch with the district. DeGette returned her family to Denver from the Maryland suburbs in 2001 and won by an unexpectedly large 73%-27% split. That November, she faced Republican Ken Chlouber, a rural state senator known for folksy humor and a flame-painted pickup truck. He also had the Teamsters union endorsement. Still, DeGette won 66%-30% and has not been seriously challenged since.

SECOND DISTRICT

Jared Polis (D)

Elected 2008, 2nd term; b. May 12, 1975, Boulder; home, Boulder; Princeton U., B.A. 1996.; Jewish; partner (Marlon Reis).

Elected Office: CO Bd. of Education, 2001-07; Chmn., 2004; Vice chmn., 2005-06.

Professional Career: Entrepreneur, 1996-2008.

DC Office: 501 CHOB, 20515, 202-225-2161; Fax: 202-225-7840; Web site: polis.house.gov.

State Offices: Boulder, 303-484-9596; Frisco, 970-668-3240; Thonrton, 303-287-4159.

Committees: *Rules.*

Group Ratings

	ACLU	ACU	ADA	CFG	AFS	FRC	LCV	ITIC	NTU	COC
2010	94	4	90	14	88	0	100	100	14	25
2009	–	4	95	9	100	–	100	–	8	47

National Journal Ratings

	2010 LIB — 2010 CONS		2009 LIB — 2009 CONS	
Economic	57% —	43%	54% —	46%
Social	67% —	31%	89% —	0%
Foreign	84% —	11%	78% —	17%
Composite	71% —	30%	76% —	24%

Key Votes of the 111th Congress

1. Overturn Ledbetter	Y	5. Bar federal abortion funds	N	9. Stop detainee transfers	N
2. Pass $820 billion stimulus	Y	6. Pass health care bill	Y	10. Legalize immigrants' kids	Y
3. Let guns in national parks	*	7. Regulate financial firms	Y	11. Repeal don't ask, tell	Y
4. Pass cap-and-trade	Y	8. Pass tax cuts for some	Y	12. Limit campaign funds	Y

Election Results

2010 general	Jared Polis (D)	148,720	(57%)	($1,248,539)
	Stephen Bailey (R)	98,171	(38%)	($130,886)
	Jenna Goss (CNP)	7,080	(3%)	
2010 primary	Jared Polis (D)	unopposed		

Prior Winning Percentages: 2008 (63%)

Population		Race/Ethnicity		Work	
Pop. 2010:	733,805	White:	72.4%	Private:	79.9%
Change since 2000:	Up 19.4%	Black:	1.0%	Government:	13.3%
Urban:	87.3%	Hispanic:	20.3%	Self-employed:	6.6%
Rural:	12.7%	Asian:	3.9%	Blue collar:	19.5%
Area size:	5,664 sq. mi.	Native Am.:	0.4%	White collar:	64.7%
		Hawaiian:	0.1%	Khaki collar:	0.1%
Age		Two+ races:	1.7%	Other:	15.7%
Median age:	34.0 yrs.				
More than 65 yrs:	7.6%	*Ancestry*		Median income:	$65,428
Less than 18 yrs:	23.9%	German	17.7%	Median Home Value:	$268,600
		Irish	9.9%		
Education		English	9.2%	**Military Veterans**	
H.S. grad:	90.6%			% of Pop:	8.4%
College grad:	41.3%				
Grad degree:	15.2%				

Denver Suburbs; Boulder

Nestled against the Front Range of the Rocky Mountains is Boulder, home of the 29,000-student University of Colorado, once billed by the city as "a combination of Lycra-clad athletes, New Age artists, and thoughtful intellectuals sipping cappuccinos." Boulder is one of the nation's leading centers for bungee jumping, mountain biking, snowshoeing, rock and ice climbing, downhill skiing, land surfing, and hot-air ballooning. It has been called the nation's No. 1

2008 Presidential Vote		
Barack Obama (D) 235,165	(64%)
John McCain (R) 125,048	(34%)
2004 Presidential Vote		
John Kerry (D) 188,538	(58%)
George Bush (R) 132,642	(41%)
Cook Partisan Voting Index:	D+11	

town for outdoor sports by *Outdoor* magazine, and in 2010 topped *Portfolio.com*'s list of mid-sized metropolitan areas with the best quality of life. Marathoners from around the world train in several camps here. It is also the home of the Buddhist Naropa Institute and the Boulder School of Massage Therapy. All have come because of the terrain. The streets of Boulder literally look up at craggy peaks rising to 14,000 feet from a mile-high plain stretching farther east than the eye can see. Five of the 10 counties in the nation with the highest life-expectancy rates are in this district. It has become a magnet for technology firms dissatisfied with the more congested Silicon Valley; in the first three months of 2010, 11 startup companies brought in $57 million in venture capital.

The 2nd Congressional District is centered in Boulder. It includes most of Boulder County and extends west along Interstate 70 on its awesome course through the mountains as it takes in picturesque Rocky Mountain acreage, including the old mining town of Central City, the nearby casino mecca of Black Hawk, and the lodges and resorts of Vail. There is talk of widening the often congested I-70. Once dependent on mining and agriculture, Vail evolved into an international resort after the 10th Mountain Division ski troops were introduced to the Eagle River Valley in the 1940s. After World War II, a group of Army buddies returned and developed a ski resort. The district also contains some of Denver's northwest suburbs—Northglenn, Federal Heights, Lafayette, and most of Westminster and Thornton. It includes the old Rocky Flats nuclear weapons plant, so toxic that it required a $7 billion cleanup before being transformed into a national wildlife refuge. Politically, the Metro North area is marginal, while Boulder is heavily Democratic. The mountain counties have been trending Democratic. Overall, this remains one of a half-dozen safe Democratic districts in the Rocky Mountain states.

Jared Polis (D)

The congressman from Colorado's 2nd District is Jared Polis, a Democrat first elected in 2008. Polis was born in Boulder, but grew up in San Diego, returning to Colorado with his family during the summers. His mother, a poet, and his father, an artist, were both politically active during the antiwar movement of the late 1960s and early 1970s. Polis and his younger brother and sister frequently accompanied their parents to demonstrations and rallies. Their activism spurred Polis' interest in politics and liberal ideas. He graduated from high school in three years, and headed off to Princeton University to study political science. Also fascinated by technology and business, Polis and two friends banded together in their sophomore year to launch an Internet start-up called American Information Systems, an Internet access provider. Soon afterward, he founded *bluemountainarts.com*, an electronic greeting card site that at its height was the eighth most popular site on the Internet. His next venture was *Proflowers.com*, a service enabling customers to order fresh flowers directly from growers. All three were successful, and Polis sold them for profits of upwards of $300 million.

Financial security from his business ventures allowed Polis to focus on his other passions. "I was always interested in public service. Education is an issue I feel very passionately about, providing an opportunity to all Americans," he said. In 2000, he was elected to the Colorado state board of education, serving for six years and as chairman for one year. During his tenure, Polis says he was most proud of his advancement of school choice through the establishment of charter schools and his work improving accountability standards for schools. In part with his own money, he founded two innovative charter schools in Colorado, which were geared toward helping new immigrants assimilate. One of the schools, the New America School, targeted 16- to 21-year-old immigrants with flexible day or evening programs, day-care reimbursement and teachers trained to help students learn English. "We really needed a school to cater to their unique needs," Polis said. At the same time, he partnered with three other Colorado multimillionaires—who were dubbed the "Gang of Four" in newspapers—and built a massive political fundraising operation that raised $3.6 million in 2004.

When Democratic Rep. Mark Udall in Colorado's 2nd District decided to run for an open Senate seat in 2008, Polis decided to run for Udall's seat. In the Democratic primary, he faced former state Senate President Joan Fitz-Gerald and conservationist Will Shafroth. Most of the state's Democratic establishment backed Fitz-Gerald, based on her political seasoning. Pouring his own money into the campaign, he outspent his opponents 4-to-1. In the August 2008 primary, he got 42% of the vote, followed by Fitz-Gerald with 38% and Shafroth with 20%. In the general election, Republican nominee Scott Starin, an engineer, raised less than $100,000 and provided little serious opposition. Polis won 63% to 34%. All in all, he spent $7 million, $6 million of it his own. The nonpartisan watchdog, Center for Responsive Politics, ranked Polis in 2009 as the third-wealthiest member of the House, pegging his wealth in the range of $97 million to $254 million, based on his financial disclosure reports. He had little trouble winning re-election in 2010, dispatching tea party-backed Republican Stephen Bailey with 57%.

In Washington, Polis jumped into the health care debate, taking a leading role in fighting a proposal by his own party that would pay for elements of the overhauled health care system with a tax on wealthy Americans. Polis maintained that the tax would hurt small-business owners who aren't large enough to organize as corporations. He was chided by many in the liberal blogosphere, but he succeeded in corralling 21 other freshman Democrats to sign a letter to House Speaker Nancy Pelosi calling on her to purge the surtax from the bill, and it was not included as part of the sweeping overhaul of health care that passed the House on Nov. 7, 2009.

Polis also has been a leader in gay and lesbian rights. He is the first openly gay man elected to Congress (Rep. Barney Frank, D-Mass., is also openly gay but came out after he was elected to the House. Rep. Tammy Baldwin, D-Wis., is the first openly gay woman elected to Congress.) Polis is a co-sponsor of a proposed repeal of the Defense of Marriage Act, the 1996 law that permits states to refuse to recognize gay marriages. President Obama has said he will sign the repeal if it passes, and Polis says the measure has thus far attracted more than 100 co-sponsors. "It becomes more and more of an issue, the more states that allow same-sex couples to marry," he said.

Using new media has also been a central element of Polis' time in office. He has more than 1,900 "friends" on Facebook and more than 6,900 followers on Twitter. "It's a very tech-savvy district, a very wired district," he says. Along with Utah Republican freshman Rep. Jason Chaffetz, Polis was featured on CNN.com as part of a series called *Freshman Year,* which chronicled the behind-the-scenes lives of newly elected lawmakers. Polis also has displayed an impressive fundraising ability, collecting from liberal interest groups, investment companies and others and donating money to politically vulnerable Democrats through his Jared Polis Victory Fund. In 2010, he made it onto *Time* magazine's "40 Under 40" list of young movers and shakers.

Democratic leaders gave Polis a seat on the influential Rules Committee, which controls the rules of debate for major bills that reach the floor of the House. On the Judiciary Committee in 2010, he sought to protect the rights of medical marijuana dispensaries. He also worked on a proposal to designate more than 340,000 acres of Colorado land as wilderness. Polis hopes to broaden his focus into immigration and education. He introduced a bill in 2010 offering non-dairy alternatives to milk as part of school lunches and drew controversy later that year when he blasted Arizona's stringent immigration law as "reminiscent" of Nazi Germany. Following the 2010 election, Polis was an early supporter of letting Rep. Nancy Pelosi continue to lead House Democrats, saying she "has led the Democrats out of the wilderness before, and I am confident she can do it again."

THIRD DISTRICT

Scott Tipton (R)

Elected 2010, 1st term; b. Nov. 9, 1956, Espanola, NM; home, Cortez; Fort Lewis Col., B.A. 1978.; Christian; Married (Jean); 2 children.

Elected Office: CO House, 2009-11.

Professional Career: Owner, CEO, Mesa Verde Pottery.

DC Office: 218 CHOB, 20515, 202-225-4761; Fax: 202-226-9669; Web site: tipton.house.gov.

State Offices: Alamosa, 719-587-5105; Grand Junction, 970-241-2499; Pueblo, 719-542-1073.

Committees: *Agriculture:* Conservation, Energy & Forestry. *Natural Resources:* National Parks, Forests & Public Lands; Water & Power. *Small Business:* Agriculture, Energy & Trade (Chmn); Healthcare & Technology; Investigations, Oversight & Regulations.

Election Results

2010 general	Scott Tipton (R)..129,257	(50%)	($1,232,113)
	John Salazar (D)..118,048	(46%)	($2,067,198)
	Gregory Gilman (Lib) 5,678	(2%)	
2010 primary	Scott Tipton (R)..39,346	(56%)	
	Bob McConnell (R)..31,214	(44%)	

Population		Race/Ethnicity		Work	
Pop. 2010:	706,186	White:	71.6%	Private:	74.6%
Change since 2000:	Up 14.9%	Black:	0.7%	Government:	16.1%
Urban:	61.0%	Hispanic:	24.2%	Self-employed:	9.1%
Rural:	39.0%	Asian:	0.6%	Blue collar:	24.3%
Area size:	54,100 sq. mi.	Native Am.:	1.3%	White collar:	55.4%
		Hawaiian:	0.1%	Khaki collar:	0.1%
Age		Two+ races:	1.4%	Other:	20.1%
Median age:	38.3 yrs.				
More than 65 yrs:	13.8%	*Ancestry*		Median income:	$48,029
Less than 18 yrs:	24.2%	German	16.4%	Median Home Value:	$206,300
		English	10.5%		
Education		Irish	10.1%	**Military Veterans**	
H.S. grad:	87.6%			% of Pop:	12.0%
College grad:	26.4%				
Grad degree:	8.7%				

Western Colorado; Pueblo

On a clear night from the air, they look like tiny mottled veins, thickest near Denver. These are the lights of the civilization Americans have built on the Western Slope of the Rockies in Colorado. The lights follow the trails of valley roads and mountainside switchbacks. The nodes mark the dozens of little towns built during mining boom years: the gold rush of the 1870s, the uranium boom of the 1950s, and the oil-shale boomlet of the 1970s. The Western Slope—everything

2008 Presidential Vote		
John McCain (R) 170,852	(50%)
Barack Obama (D) 162,254	(48%)
2004 Presidential Vote		
George Bush (R) 171,115	(55%)
John Kerry (D) 135,755	(44%)
Cook Partisan Voting Index: R+5		

west of the Front Range, with dozens of peaks over 14,000 feet—has always blocked east-west movement. Except for mining and skiing, few would have followed the Ute Indians and settled here. The miners who tracked gold and silver and lead ores also built Victorian towns with opera houses and gingerbread storefronts in Aspen and Telluride, in valleys and defiles scarcely accessible to the outside world. Now many of these towns have been restored by ski resort operators and joined by dozens of new condominiums and shopping malls. Cries of overdevelopment have followed. Amid the tourism, some resource development continues, of gas deposits trapped beneath the Roan Plateau. More than half of the area's iconic aspen trees have died in recent years due to fire or natural causes.

The political map of the Western Slope is as diverse as its history. Aspen and Telluride are liberal and Democratic. The former coal-mining centers of Crested Butte and Steamboat Springs, today sporting contemporary condominiums and ski lodges, were formerly Republican, but are now Democratic as well. Durango, an old frontier town, has moved in the same direction. Republicans still have a voter registration edge in surrounding La Plata County. Some areas are still heavily Republican and hostile to environmentalists and others of the liberal ilk: the rough-handed mining area around Grand Junction, where piles of tailings still crackle with radioactivity; Glenwood Springs, with its old hot springs hotel once visited by President Taft; and the northwest corner of the state, where people remember the oil shale boom with nostalgia. Generally on the Western Slope, the high-income areas, with lots of liberals opposed to new oil and gas drilling, are the most Democratic, while more modest-income, working-class towns are the most Republican.

The 3rd Congressional District of Colorado is the state's largest—roughly the size of Arkansas—and includes most of the Western Slope. It extends east of the Front Range to include the small industrial city of Pueblo. There, on the banks of the Arkansas River, the Rockefellers built large steel factories before World War I to make barbed wire and rails. Today, this blue-collar town survives on large medical centers and some industrial plants, but still suffers the highest unemployment rates of any metro area in the state—9.5% in 2010. Pueblo is heavily Democratic, and so are the counties on the plains and in the San Luis Valley to the south. These inhabitants are Hispanic but not necessarily Mexican-Americans: Spanish-speaking people have been living here, as in northern New Mexico, for 350 years. The 3rd District voted for Democrat Bill Clinton in 1992, for Republican Bob Dole in 1996 and for Republican George W. Bush in 2000 and 2004. In 2008, John McCain took 15 counties and Barack Obama won 14 counties here. The two largest counties are resource-heavy Mesa, which McCain took 64%-34%, and Pueblo, which Obama won 56%-42%. On balance, it is a Republican district, but it can be unpredictable. McCain won the district, 50%-48%.

Scott Tipton (R)

The congressman from the 3rd District is Scott Tipton, a Republican who ousted three-term Democrat John Salazar in 2010. Tipton was born in Española, N.M. His family moved to Cortez, Colo., three months after he was born. His father was a construction worker for a Denver-based company, but the family's finances were often strained by the medical needs of Tipton's brother, who was diabetic. "Until I was about 7 years old, we ate oatmeal every morning for breakfast," Tipton said. "It wasn't because we needed to lower our cholesterol." Tipton's mother and father were doting and attentive parents, "who never missed a parent-teacher conference," he said. When Tipton enrolled in Fort Lewis College in Durango, he became the first member of his family to go beyond high school, an achievement he attributes to his stable home life.

After getting his degree, Tipton returned to his hometown to establish a production facility for Native American pottery and jewelry, employing childhood friends who belonged to the Ute and Navajo tribes. But his fledgling business was encumbered by onerous and redundant government paperwork, he says. "We spent hours filling out forms (asking) how many thousands of pounds of clays we went through each year," an experience that made Tipton a critic of government intrusion into the affairs of small businesses.

In 2006, he mounted his first political campaign, challenging Salazar, then a freshman. Salazar won handily, receiving 62% of the vote, but Tipton's campaign increased his visibility. Two years later, the local Republican Party in nearby Montrose recruited him to run for the Colorado House, and he was soon on his way to Denver. As a Republican legislator, Tipton says he sometimes felt marginalized by the Democratic Party's hegemony in the state following the 2008 election. He was the ranking Republican on the Agriculture Committee and worked on legislation that streamlined government paperwork through increased reliance on the Internet. He was also a sponsor of the bipartisan "Katie's Law," which requires collection of DNA from anyone arrested on suspicion of a felony.

In the August primary to run against Salazar, retired Army lawyer Bob McConnell was the preferred candidate of tea party activists and Tipton's main opponent. Some tea partiers viewed Tipton suspiciously as a member of the Republican establishment, but he refrained from criticizing McConnell. The race never grew overly negative and *The Pueblo Chieftain* dubbed Tipton's win a "bloodless victory."

In the fall campaign, Tipton portrayed Salazar as too deferential to the Democratic leadership, "voting as (House Speaker Nancy) Pelosi and Obama would have him vote." The Republican slammed the incumbent for his votes in favor of President Obama's $787 billion economic-stimulus bill and his major health care overhaul. Of the 220 House supporters of the health care law, only 11 represented districts that are more Republican than Salazar's, according to *The Cook Political Report*. Salazar also was perceived as having close ties to the Obama administration because his younger brother, Ken Salazar, is Interior secretary. For his part, John Salazar suggested in his ads that Tipton would reduce Social Security retirement benefits, and he deemphasized his party label, calling himself "An Independent Voice for Rural Colorado." The incumbent was also well-funded, with $1.8 million compared with Tipton's $1 million.

Although Salazar enjoyed decisive victories in two previous re-election bids, the district's conservative voters were energized, and Tipton prevailed, with 50% to 46% for Salazar.

FOURTH DISTRICT

Cory Gardner (R)

Elected 2010, 1st term; b. Aug. 22, 1974, Yuma; home, Yuma; CO St. U., B.S. 1997; U. of CO, J.D. 2001.; Lutheran; Married (Jaime); 1 child.

Elected Office: CO House, 2005-10.

Professional Career: Communications dir., Natl. Corn Growers Assn., 2001-02; staffer, Sen. Wayne Allard, R-Colo., 2002-05; owner, Farmers Implement dealership.

DC Office: 213 CHOB, 20515, 202-225-4676; Fax: 202-225-5870; Web site: gardner.house.gov.

State Offices: Ft. Collins, 970-221-7110; Greeley, 970-351-6007; Lamar, 719-931-4003; Sterling, 970-522-0203.

Committees: *Energy & Commerce:* Energy & Power; Environment & the Economy; Oversight & Investigations.

Election Results

2010 general	Cory Gardner (R)	138,634	(52%)	($2,426,591)
	Betsy Markey (D)	109,249	(41%)	($3,601,721)
	Doug Aden (CNP)	12,312	(5%)	
2010 primary	Cory Gardner (R)	unopposed		

Population		Race/Ethnicity		Work	
Pop. 2010:	725,041	White:	75.0%	Private:	75.8%
Change since 2000:	Up 18.0%	Black:	1.1%	Government:	16.0%
Urban:	75.1%	Hispanic:	20.2%	Self-employed:	8.0%
Rural:	24.9%	Asian:	1.5%	Blue collar:	21.8%
Area size:	31,048 sq. mi.	Native Am.:	0.5%	White collar:	59.2%
		Hawaiian:	0.1%	Khaki collar:	0.1%
Age		Two+ races:	1.4%	Other:	19.0%
Median age:	34.8 yrs.				
More than 65 yrs:	10.8%	*Ancestry*		Median income:	$51,275
Less than 18 yrs:	24.4%	German	22.1%	Median Home Value:	$210,300
		Irish	9.8%		
Education		English	8.8%	**Military Veterans**	
H.S. grad:	87.7%			% of Pop:	9.9%
College grad:	31.5%				
Grad degree:	11.4%				

Eastern Colorado; Fort Collins

The High Plains of eastern Colorado are dusty brown, gently rolling grasslands that seem flat but actually slope imperceptibly up toward the Rocky Mountains. The land is fertile, but dry. Rainfall is rare, the rivers are just a trickle most of the year, and in many places, groundwater is scarce. It is fine wheat country when irrigated, and one of the foremost beef cattle regions. But it has been squeezed in recent decades by declining prices for wheat, declining demand for beef and increased prices for water due to the high demand in Denver and along the Front Range. Bitter confrontations have erupted over who gets access to the South Platte River, leading to limitations

2008 Presidential Vote
John McCain (R)	171,981	(50%)
Barack Obama (D)	169,113	(49%)

2004 Presidential Vote
George Bush (R)	180,017	(58%)
John Kerry (D)	128,002	(41%)

Cook Partisan Voting Index: R+6

on pumping from the basin. Local farmers are now finding that the value of their water rights to metro Denver far exceeds what they could hope to gain by farming. Their neighbors condemn them for selling out and betraying a way of life. The prairie lands and small towns of the High Plains have small reminders of their past: the Pawnee National Grasslands, where antelope, coyotes, and prairie dogs still roam, and Burlington's 1905 carousel, one of the few with the original paint. But the free market that once peopled the High Plains with farmers and ranchers and made it the scene of farm protests and revolts is now causing it to empty out and revert to untamed land, ready again for increasingly numerous buffalo, elk, deer and bighorn sheep.

The 4th Congressional District of Colorado contains almost all of the High Plains plus the medium-sized and fast-growing developments around Greeley, Fort Collins and Loveland—the northern end of the densely populated Front Range, off Interstate 25 as it heads toward Cheyenne, Wyo. It includes all of fast-growing Larimer County east of the mountains and reaches into Boulder County to pick up the city of Longmont. Fort Collins became a center for California transplants seeking a different lifestyle at start-up telecommunications firms. It also is home to a Centers for Disease Control and Prevention lab that conducts cutting-edge research to combat bioterrorism. *Fast Company* magazine in 2007 named Fort Collins a research and development "hot spot." To the east is Weld County, still mostly rural and more conservative in its politics. By heritage and usually by inclination, this was once reliably Republican territory, but it is getting friendlier to Democrats as liberal and independent-minded Denver residents migrate to northern Colorado for cheaper real estate. The district was evenly split in 1992, though it later gave solid margins to George W. Bush. In 2008, Barack Obama won Larimer County with 54% of the vote, but McCain won the district, 50%-49%.

Cory Gardner (R)

The new congressman from the 4th District is Republican Cory Gardner, who toppled freshman Democrat Betsy Markey in 2010. Gardner grew up in Yuma, Colo., a tiny farming and ranching town 150 miles east of Denver. His family owns and operates a farm implement dealership founded by his great-grandfather, who settled north of Yuma in 1886. After high school, Gardner enrolled in the University of Colorado at Boulder, but the raucous campus was "a little bit of a big change" from sleepy Yuma, and he eventually transferred to Colorado State University in Fort Collins, where he joined a chapter of the Farm House Fraternity. After graduating summa cum laude in 1997, Gardner returned to Yuma in pursuit of a pastoral lifestyle. But his father urged him to consider a profession less closely tied to the vagaries of Colorado's eastern plains. Several seasons of drought were beginning to take a toll, and his father suggested he indulge his longtime interest in the law.

In 2001, Gardner got a law degree from the University of Colorado and took a job as communications director for the National Corn Growers Association. The following year, he became an aide to then-U.S. Sen. Wayne Allard, a Republican. In the summer of 2005, Gardner was appointed to fill a vacancy in the Colorado House, and a year later he was elected to a full term. As a lawmaker, Gardner helped establish the Colorado Clean Energy Authority, which facilitated the investment of millions of dollars in renewable energy projects. He also championed telemedicine, advancing legislation that allowed Medicaid reimbursements for patients who were examined remotely using a machine that measures and relays blood pressure and other vital signs to a doctor.

Believing Markey to be vulnerable in early 2010's worsening climate for Democrats, state Republicans coalesced around Gardner. They viewed him as a rising star in the state party and emphasized his deep roots in the district's heavily Republican eastern plains. By mid-October, Markey had significantly outraised her challenger, $3.2 million to $2 million. Two years earlier, she had clobbered then Rep. Marilyn Musgrave, beating the Republican by 12 percentage points in an election that was viewed as a repudiation of the ultraconservative Musgrave. But conservative voters in 2010 were energized in opposition to the Obama administration; Gardner pounded Markey for supporting the president's spending policies while skirting the social issues that could potentially alienate suburban voters. Markey struggled to reconcile her credentials as a conservative Blue Dog Democrat with her votes in favor of Obama's $787 billion economic stimulus bill, his health insurance overhaul and a proposal to limit carbon emissions. Gardner won, 52% to 41%.

FIFTH DISTRICT

Doug Lamborn (R)

Elected 2006, 3rd term; b. May 24, 1954, Leavenworth, KS; home, Colorado Springs; U. of KS, B.S. 1978, J.D. 1986; Christian; married (Jeanie); 5 children.

Elected Office: CO House of Reps., 1994-98; CO Senate, 1998-2006.

Professional Career: Practicing atty., 1987-2007.

DC Office: 437 CHOB, 20515, 202-225-4422; Fax: 202-226-2638; Web site: lamborn.house.gov.

State Offices: Colorado Springs, 719-520-0055.

Committees: *Armed Services:* Air & Land Forces; Strategic Forces. *Natural Resources:* Energy & Mineral Resources (Chmn); National Parks, Forests & Public Lands. *Veterans' Affairs:* Disability Assistance & Memorial Affairs; Oversight & Investigations.

Group Ratings

	ACLU	ACU	ADA	CFG	AFS	FRC	LCV	ITIC	NTU	COC
2010	13	100	5	100	0	100	0	0	91	75
2009	–	100	0	100	0	–	0	–	93	73

National Journal Ratings

	2010 LIB — 2010 CONS			2009 LIB — 2009 CONS		
Economic	0%	—	97%	0%	—	96%
Social	0%	—	85%	0%	—	93%
Foreign	0%	—	88%	0%	—	75%
Composite	5%	—	95%	6%	—	94%

Key Votes of the 111th Congress

1. Overturn Ledbetter	N	5. Bar federal abortion funds	Y
2. Pass $820 billion stimulus	N	6. Pass health care bill	N
3. Let guns in national parks	Y	7. Regulate financial firms	N
4. Pass cap-and-trade	N	8. Pass tax cuts for some	N

9. Stop detainee transfers	Y
10. Legalize immigrants' kids	N
11. Repeal don't ask, tell	N
12. Limit campaign funds	N

Election Results

2010 general	Doug Lamborn (R)	152,829	(66%)	($338,476)
	Kevin Bradley (D)	68,039	(29%)	(no report)
	Brian Scott (CNP)	5,886	(3%)	
	Jerell Klaver (Lib)	5,680	(2%)	
2010 primary	Doug Lamborn (R)	unopposed		

Prior Winning Percentages: 2008 (60%), 2006 (60%)

Population		Race/Ethnicity		Work	
Pop. 2010:	725,902	White:	73.6%	Private:	71.4%
Change since 2000:	Up 18.1%	Black:	5.2%	Government:	22.1%
Urban:	85.7%	Hispanic:	14.6%	Self-employed:	6.3%
Rural:	14.3%	Asian:	2.4%	Blue collar:	17.3%
Area size:	7,733 sq. mi.	Native Am.:	0.7%	White collar:	60.9%
		Hawaiian:	0.3%	Khaki collar:	4.5%
Age		Two+ races:	3.2%	Other:	17.3%
Median age:	36.1 yrs.				
More than 65 yrs:	10.4%	*Ancestry*		Median income:	$54,331
Less than 18 yrs:	25.0%	German	17.6%	Median Home Value:	$215,800
		Irish	10.7%		
Education		English	9.5%	**Military Veterans**	
H.S. grad:	91.4%			% of Pop:	17.0%
College grad:	33.2%				
Grad degree:	12.5%				

Central Colo.; Colorado Springs

In 1893, Katherine Lee Bates took the cog railway up from Colorado Springs to the top of
14,110-foot Pikes Peak, and looking out at the
purple mountain's majesty above amber waves
of grain, she wrote the lines of "America the
Beautiful." Pike's Peak, espied by Zebulon Pike
in 1806, and Colorado Springs, with the Garden
of the Gods and the Broadmoor Hotel, have been
tourist attractions for more than 100 years. In
the second half of the 20th century, Colorado

2008 Presidential Vote		
John McCain (R) 189,498	(59%)
Barack Obama (D) 129,095	(40%)
2004 Presidential Vote		
George Bush (R) 190,190	(66%)
John Kerry (D) 93,684	(33%)
Cook Partisan Voting Index: R+14		

Springs, safe in the vastness of North America, also became a great American military fortress.
During the height of the Cold War in the 1960s, the Pentagon constructed the North American
Aerospace Defense Command more than 1,000 feet below Cheyenne Mountain, a fortified bunker
theoretically able to survive a nuclear strike from a Soviet missile. The Pentagon, in part because
of local traffic congestion, moved NORAD's surveillance operations to nearby Peterson Air Force
Base, site of space-based defense research, with the option of a rapid return to secure Cheyenne
Mountain in an emergency. Other military installations dominate the landscape as well: rapidly
growing Fort Carson, site of the Air Force Academy, and Schriever Air Force Base, named in 1998
for Gen. Bernard A. Schriever, a pioneer in the development of ballistic missile programs.

Colorado Springs has built a high-tech, innovative economy. Although it was hit hard by job
losses during the recession, in 2010 the city came in sixth among medium-sized metropolitan areas
in *Portfolio.com*'s best quality-of-life rankings. With the arrival of Dr. James Dobson's Focus on
the Family in 1994 and other Christian organizations, it has been a center of conservative Christianity, the home of Colorado's young conservatism and the counterpoint to Denver's aging liberalism. This was the birthplace of Colorado's anti-tax initiatives and of Amendment 2, which in 1992
repealed the city's gay rights ordinances only to be later overturned by the U.S. Supreme Court. It
is one of America's most Republican metropolitan areas. In 2004, Colorado Springs' El Paso County
cast more votes than Denver County, and its 83,000-vote margin for George W. Bush almost balanced out Denver's 96,000-vote margin for John Kerry. The Democrats regained the advantage in
2008, as Barack Obama made gains among white evangelicals. John McCain won El Paso County
by only 59% with 51,000 votes, while Obama took Denver by 135,000 votes.

The 5th Congressional District consists of Colorado Springs and El Paso County, plus all or
most of four mountain counties to the west. One of them, Lake County, includes the old mining
town of Leadville and usually votes Democratic. But 87% of the district's population is in El Paso
County, and in effect, this is the Colorado Springs congressional district. The 5th District is the
most Republican district in Colorado.

Doug Lamborn (R)

The congressman from the 5th District is Doug Lamborn, a Republican first elected in 2006. The
son of a prison guard, Lamborn was born in Leavenworth, Kansas. He studied journalism at the
University of Kansas and ultimately earned a law degree. He said he voted in 1976 for Jimmy
Carter, but was then drawn to the Republican politics of Ronald Reagan in the 1980s. In 1987,
Lamborn moved his family to Colorado Springs, where he practiced business and real estate law
and became an avid mountain climber. In 1994, he won the first of two terms in the Colorado House
and, in 1998, was appointed to a vacant state Senate seat. Lamborn ran unopposed in the next
election and later served as state Senate president pro tem. During 12 years in the legislature,
Lamborn compiled a reliably conservative record on social and fiscal issues. He opposed abortion
rights, sponsoring bills to limit late-term abortions, and advocated tax cuts, including a reduction
in state income taxes. He backed legislation that would have ended some benefits to illegal immigrants and increased penalties for illegal immigrant smugglers.

When Republican U.S. Rep. Joel Hefley retired, Lamborn ran for his seat. In the primary,
Hefley endorsed Jeff Crank, his former aide. Lamborn had the backing of the anti-tax Club for
Growth and the Colorado Christian Coalition. At the May GOP party convention, Crank won the
delegate vote 46%-40%, but Lamborn had more than the minimum 30% needed to secure a place
on the primary ballot. Lamborn emphasized his conservative voting record and vowed never to
raise taxes. The state Christian Coalition sent a mailer suggesting Crank backed the "radical homosexual lobby." In the August primary, Crank won five of the district's six counties and appeared
headed to victory. But once absentee ballots were counted, the results flipped and Lamborn won
by 892 votes, defeating Crank 27%-25%.

In the general election, Lamborn faced Democrat Jay Fawcett, an Air Force Academy graduate who won a Bronze star during the Persian Gulf War. In most years, the Democratic nominee would not have drawn a second look; no Democrat had won the seat since it was created in 1972. But the bruising Republican primary and a tough national environment for Republicans made for an unusually competitive general election. Hefley accused Lamborn of running a "sleazy" primary campaign and refused to endorse him. Fawcett sought to take advantage of the Republican discord, purchasing a newspaper ad featuring the names and photos of three dozen prominent local Republicans who also declined to endorse Lamborn. He tried to appeal to Republicans and unaffiliated voters by emphasizing his military experience, a strong selling point in the military-oriented district. In October, polls showed a dead heat, an alarming result for a district that national Republicans were unaccustomed to worrying about. But on Election Day, voters overcame lingering animosity toward Lamborn and gave him a 60%-40% victory.

In the House, Lamborn established a record as one of his party's most conservative members. He was an original member of the Tea Party Caucus and endorsed former Rep. Tom Tancredo, known for his incendiary opposition to immigration, for Colorado governor in 2010. He tried, but lost overwhelmingly, to pass amendments to eliminate funding for the National Endowment for the Arts and the Corporation for Public Broadcasting, two government-sponsored entities that conservatives consider too liberal. He also sponsored a bill to bar federal funds to schools that provide access to emergency contraception services. In 2009, he led Colorado's House delegation in adding earmarks to spending bills, particularly military-related projects, according to the watchdog group Citizens Against Government Waste. On defense issues, Lamborn led an effort to gather support for Mosab Hassan Yousef, the son of a founder of the terrorist group Hamas who converted to Christianity and became an anti-Hamas informer. He had been threatened with deportation from the United States but was granted political asylum in 2010.

Back home, lingering resentment over the 2006 primary led to a rematch with Crank in 2008. The challenger attacked Lamborn's job performance. This time, Lamborn won all of the counties except Lake, and won the district overall with 44% to 30% for Crank. He won easily in November against token Democratic opposition. In 2010, he trounced Democrat Kevin Bradley with nearly 66%.

SIXTH DISTRICT

Mike Coffman (R)

Elected 2008, 2nd term; b. March 19, 1955, Fort Leonard Wood, MO; home, Aurora; U. of CO, B.A., 1979.; Methodist; married (Cynthia).

Military Career: Army, 1972-79, Marine Corps, 1979-94, 2005-06 (Iraq).

Elected Office: CO House 1988-94; CO Senate, 1994-98; CO treasurer, 1998-05; CO secy. of st., 2006-08.

Professional Career: Property management firm owner, 1983-2000.

DC Office: 1222 LHOB, 20515, 202-225-7882; Fax: 202-226-4623; Web site: coffman.house.gov.

State Offices: Lone Tree, 720-283.9772.

Committees: *Armed Services:* Military Personnel; Oversight & Investigations; Seapower & Projection Forces. *Natural Resources:* Energy & Mineral Resources; National Parks, Forests & Public Lands. *Small Business:* Contracting & Workforce; Economic Growth, Tax and Capital Access; Investigations, Oversight & Regulations (Chmn).

Group Ratings

	ACLU	ACU	ADA	CFG	AFS	FRC	LCV	ITIC	NTU	COC
2010	13	100	0	87	0	93	0	33	90	88
2009	–	92	5	89	11	–	7	–	88	73

National Journal Ratings

	2010 LIB	—	2010 CONS		2009 LIB	—	2009 CONS
Economic	20%	—	80%		13%	—	87%
Social	25%	—	71%		24%	—	73%
Foreign	29%	—	68%		0%	—	75%
Composite	26%	—	74%		17%	—	83%

Key Votes of the 111th Congress

1. Overturn Ledbetter	N	5. Bar federal abortion funds	Y	9. Stop detainee transfers	Y
2. Pass $820 billion stimulus	N	6. Pass health care bill	N	10. Legalize immigrants' kids	N
3. Let guns in national parks	Y	7. Regulate financial firms	N	11. Repeal don't ask, tell	N
4. Pass cap-and-trade	N	8. Pass tax cuts for some	N	12. Limit campaign funds	N

Election Results

2010 general	Mike Coffman (R)...217,368	(66%)	($904,466)
	John Flerlage (D)..104,104	(31%)	($153,657)
	Rob McNealy (Lib)...9,466	(3%)	
2010 primary	Mike Coffman (R)... unopposed		

Prior Winning Percentages: 2008 (61%)

Population		Race/Ethnicity		Work	
Pop. 2010:	797,813	White:	81.9%	Private:	80.7%
Change since 2000:	Up 29.8%	Black:	2.7%	Government:	12.3%
Urban:	84.7%	Hispanic:	8.7%	Self-employed:	6.9%
Rural:	15.3%	Asian:	4.0%	Blue collar:	12.4%
Area size:	4,111 sq. mi.	Native Am.:	0.3%	White collar:	75.0%
		Hawaiian:	0.1%	Khaki collar:	0.2%
Age		Two+ races:	2.1%	Other:	12.4%
Median age:	37.9 yrs.				
More than 65 yrs:	8.9%	*Ancestry*		Median income:	$85,255
Less than 18 yrs:	27.0%	German	19.8%	Median Home Value:	$303,000
		Irish	11.3%		
Education		English	10.6%	**Military Veterans**	
H.S. grad:	96.3%			% of Pop:	11.2%
College grad:	48.6%				
Grad degree:	16.6%				

South Denver Suburbs; Part Aurora

Two generations ago, most people in metro Denver lived in the city itself. At the city limits, the tree-shaded sidewalks gave way to the empty High Plains. Today, more than three-quarters of metro Denver residents live outside the city, some in long-settled suburbs, some in large new subdivisions raised up in the 1990s and 2000s on rolling land with magnificent views of the Rocky Mountains. Littleton, originally a small, long-settled suburb just south of Denver, now extends

2008 Presidential Vote

John McCain (R) 229,791	(53%)
Barack Obama (D) 202,122	(46%)

2004 Presidential Vote

George Bush (R) 223,156	(60%)
John Kerry (D) 144,683	(39%)

Cook Partisan Voting Index: R+8

to vast new tracts. Just south of Littleton is Douglas County, which until the 1970s was a sparsely populated patch of the High Plains just east of the Front Range. From 2000 to 2008, it grew 51%, making it the fastest growing county in the state, and it also largely avoided the housing slump, as young families moved into 35-acre "ranchettes," or to subdivisions around Castle Rock and Parker. There were high-paying telecommunications jobs at local employers Echo Star and AT&T Broadband, now a part of Comcast. Lockheed has attracted scientists to build the Orion space exploration vehicle in Jefferson County. In 2000, Douglas was the nation's most affluent county in median household income ($84,645) and had the smallest percentage of people living in poverty (1.8%). This is Patio Land, as conservative writer David Brooks has described it: an area with a high-tech economy, a highly educated population with relatively conservative cultural values, and families looking for a safe environment for children, with the serenity, if not the close personal ties, of the traditional small town and the creativity of a metropolis. But the economic downturn was felt here. Unemployment jumped and the Douglas County School District had to cut $36 million for the 2010 school year, trimming 260 jobs.

The 6th Congressional District of Colorado is centered on Littleton and Douglas County. To the west, it includes much of Jefferson County, including part of affluent Evergreen in the mountains. To the east, it includes much of Arapahoe County and, southeast, Elbert County, long empty land but now sprouting new subdivisions. After the Colorado Springs-based 5th District, this is the state's second most Republican district. President George W. Bush got 60% of the vote here in 2004, and Republican candidate John McCain won it, 53% to 46%, in 2008.

Mike Coffman (R)

The congressman from the 6th District is Mike Coffman, a Republican first elected in 2008 to succeed retiring five-term Republican Tom Tancredo, who ran a long-shot race for president that year. The son of an Army doctor, Coffman enlisted in the Army before he finished high school and completed his diploma in the military. He went to the University of Colorado on the G.I. Bill, and then officers' school in the Marine Corps. After his active duty service ended, he started several Denver-area property management firms, which he sold in 2000. In 1988, Coffman was elected to the Colorado House. Two years later, he was called back to active duty with the Marines to serve in the first Gulf War. His colleagues draped his desk with a Marine Corps flag and yellow ribbons, and read his letters from the front lines on the House floor. After his service, Coffman returned to public life, first as a state senator and then as Colorado treasurer. But military duty called again in 2005. Coffman resigned as treasurer to go to Iraq on a six-month deployment, during which he helped facilitate elections in the Al Anbar Province and establish local governments in the Western Euphrates River Valley. When he got home, he was elected secretary of state, touting his experience with the Iraqi elections.

During his two-year tenure, Coffman drew criticism for taking several voting machines out of commission because of possible problems with them and not having replacement machines ready as the election approached. County clerks lobbied for an all-mail ballot voting system, but he strongly opposed it, instead supporting paper ballots at polling places. The August 2008 primary was plagued with errors, and many voters did not receive their absentee ballots.

In 2007, Coffman announced his candidacy for Congress. In the GOP primary, he first had to ward off a challenge from businessman Wil Armstrong, the son of former Republican Sen. Bill Armstrong. Also running were state senators Ted Harvey and Steve Ward. The four were nearly uniformly conservative. All supported the Iraq war and like Tancredo were staunch opponents of giving citizenship to illegal aliens. But Coffman had the highest name recognition, thanks to his statewide offices, and he also outraised his challengers. He won with 40% of the vote, with Armstrong coming in at 33%, a victory that all but assured Coffman the seat in this Republican district.

Amid his campaigning, Coffman had to balance his duty to carry out the election in a crucial swing state in the presidential race. He was criticized for the alleged purging of thousands of names from voter rolls shortly before the November election because they were suspected of being duplicate or erroneous registrations. He disputed the number of names purged and said their removal was valid. Still, the Advancement Project, a national voting-rights group, sued Coffman over the purged registrations, and a judge four days before the election ordered him to reinstate 146 voters. The controversy apparently had no effect on Coffman's own election. In the general election, he cruised to victory against Democrat Hank Eng with 61% of the vote. Unlike in the primary, elections around the state proceeded relatively smoothly.

Once in Congress, Coffman opposed President Obama's initiatives, telling the conservative publication *Human Events* in 2009 that "they are taking us down the road to a European-style social welfare state." Given his military background, Coffman was a natural to be appointed to the House Armed Services Committee. He was named to a bipartisan panel of the committee in 2009 that reviewed Pentagon acquisition practices, and got a bill through the House in March 2010 to extend re-employment protections for National Guard members. He also pushed for action that year on safeguarding "rare earths," mainly Chinese-produced mineral elements used in developing military technologies. He was also named to the House Natural Resources Committee, of special importance to his district. He criticized the Interior Department for what he called its persistent efforts to delay and prevent domestic energy production.

In 2010, he cruised to re-election with 66% of the vote.

SEVENTH DISTRICT

Ed Perlmutter (D)

Elected 2006, 3rd term; b. May 1, 1953, Denver; home, Golden; U. of CO, B.A. 1975, J.D. 1978; Protestant; divorced; 3 children.

Elected Office: CO Senate, 1994-2002.

Professional Career: Practicing atty., 1979-2006.

DC Office: 1221 LHOB, 20515, 202-225-2645; Fax: 202-225-5278; Web site: perlmutter.house.gov.

State Offices: Lakewood, 303-274-7944.

Committees: *Financial Services:* Capital Markets and Government Sponsored Enterprises; International Monetary Policy & Trade.

Group Ratings

	ACLU	ACU	ADA	CFG	AFS	FRC	LCV	ITIC	NTU	COC
2010	88	4	95	0	100	0	60	67	4	29
2009	–	0	95	5	89	–	100	–	3	40

National Journal Ratings

	2010 LIB	—	2010 CONS		2009 LIB	—	2009 CONS
Economic	60%	—	39%		68%	—	30%
Social	52%	—	46%		67%	—	31%
Foreign	77%	—	22%		62%	—	35%
Composite	64%	—	36%		67%	—	33%

Key Votes of the 111th Congress

1. Overturn Ledbetter	Y	5. Bar federal abortion funds	N	9. Stop detainee transfers	N
2. Pass $820 billion stimulus	Y	6. Pass health care bill	Y	10. Legalize immigrants' kids	Y
3. Let guns in national parks	Y	7. Regulate financial firms	Y	11. Repeal don't ask, tell	Y
4. Pass cap-and-trade	Y	8. Pass tax cuts for some	Y	12. Limit campaign funds	Y

Election Results

2010 general	Ed Perlmutter (D)	112,667	(53%)	($2,443,962)
	Ryan Frazier (R)	88,026	(42%)	($1,771,943)
	Buck Bailey (Lib)	10,117	(5%)	
2010 primary	Ed Perlmutter (D)	unopposed		

Prior Winning Percentages: 2008 (63%), 2006 (55%)

Population		Race/Ethnicity		Work	
Pop. 2010:	678,410	White:	58.7%	Private:	81.2%
Change since 2000:	Up 10.4%	Black:	6.8%	Government:	12.8%
Urban:	97.7%	Hispanic:	28.4%	Self-employed:	5.9%
Rural:	2.3%	Asian:	3.1%	Blue collar:	23.7%
Area size:	1,265 sq. mi.	Native Am.:	0.6%	White collar:	58.3%
		Hawaiian:	0.2%	Khaki collar:	0.3%
Age		Two+ races:	2.1%	Other:	17.7%
Median age:	35.5 yrs.				
More than 65 yrs:	11.4%	*Ancestry*		Median income:	$50,457
Less than 18 yrs:	24.8%	German	16.3%	Median Home Value:	$216,200
		Irish	8.9%		
Education		English	8.1%	**Military Veterans**	
H.S. grad:	85.2%			% of Pop:	10.7%
College grad:	27.2%				
Grad degree:	8.4%				

Inner Denver Suburbs; Lakewood

The inner circle of suburbs around Denver was developed between the 1950s and 1970s. West of Denver, on broad avenues running toward the mountains, is Lakewood, where growth was sparked by the Denver Federal Center. The suburbs are affluent in the south, more marginal near the Denver city limits. Out to the west is the town of Golden, with the old Colorado School of Mines and the Coors brewery. To the north are Arvada (which is shared with the 2nd District)

2008 Presidential Vote		
Barack Obama (D) 168,819	(59%)
John McCain (R) 113,848	(40%)
2004 Presidential Vote		
John Kerry (D) 130,984	(51%)
George Bush (R) 122,772	(48%)
Cook Partisan Voting Index: D+4		

and Wheat Ridge, middle-income suburbs with an increasing number of Latinos. On the other side of Denver, to the east of the now-closed Stapleton Airport, is Aurora, as vast as Lakewood and somewhat newer, with its huge regional mall and an increasing number of middle class African-Americans. Construction began in 2009 on a new 1,800-acre renewable energy testing center where public- and private-sector entities will work on commercializing technologies. East of Aurora are rolling, empty plains that stretch to the Kansas state line.

The 7th Congressional District of Colorado, created after the 2000 census, covers parts of three counties and most of the inner Denver suburbs. The bulk of its land area, but only 15% of its voters, are in Adams County, which includes the industrial zone along the South Platte River and the Rocky Mountain Arsenal National Wildlife Refuge. Adams County has long been the most Democratic of the suburban Denver counties, but its politics are in flux. It is beginning to fill up with new subdivisions. Aurora, partly in Adams County with a larger part in Arapahoe County, has long been Republican. But with more black and Latino residents, it has been trending Democratic. Lakewood is the largest city in the district, and with the other towns in Jefferson County (or Jeffco, as people call it), it is perhaps Colorado's premier political battleground. Denver's new light rail line extends to Lakewood, which is sparking more growth in technology. Long solidly Republican, Lakewood is now more marginal. And it is crucial here: Jeffco has 62% of the 7th District's voters. The judge who handed down the redistricting plan deliberately chose to make the 7th evenly divided between the parties, and so it has been.

Ed Perlmutter (D)

The congressman from the 7th District is Ed Perlmutter, a Democrat first elected in 2006. He grew up in Jefferson County, walking precincts with his father on Democratic campaigns. He attended the University of Colorado and earned a law degree in 1978, and then went into private practice. In 1994, Perlmutter won election to the state Senate from a northern Jefferson County district that had not elected a Democrat in nearly 30 years. In the legislature, where he gained a reputation as a mediator, he chaired the renewable energy caucus and worked on legislation protecting consumer rights and promoting responsible growth. He won a second term in 1998 and served two years as Senate president pro tem, then retired in 2002 when term limits forced him from office. Perlmutter was considered the early front-runner for the newly created 7th District, but he opted not to run in 2002, citing the time it would take him away from his three daughters. The new district elected Republican Bob Beauprez by just 121 votes. When Beauprez ran for governor in 2006, Democrats immediately touted it as one of their top pickup opportunities. This time, Perlmutter got into the race.

His most significant primary opposition came from Peggy Lamm, a former state representative who used to be the sister-in-law of former Democratic Gov. Richard Lamm. Perlmutter campaigned in favor of embryonic stem cell research, and in his first commercial, his oldest daughter talked about how stem cell research might find a cure for her epilepsy. EMILY's List endorsed Lamm, but she trailed Perlmutter in fundraising. He won the primary by a solid 53%-38%.

In the general election, he faced Republican Rick O'Donnell, a rising star who left his post as executive director of the Colorado Higher Education Department to run. At a time of multiple ethics scandals in Congress, O'Donnell argued that Perlmutter's marriage to a Denver lobbyist for a D.C.-based lobbying firm would lead to conflicts of interest. The two candidates also debated illegal immigration. Perlmutter supported a guest worker program for immigrants, while O'Donnell opposed it. By October, the two were closely matched in fundraising, each with well over $2 million. However, the strength of Perlmutter's candidacy, Beauprez's poor showing in the governor's race, and President George W. Bush's unpopularity all worked against O'Donnell. Perlmutter won by 55%-42%. He carried Jefferson County by nearly 15,000 votes, 55%-43%.

In the House, Perlmutter has been a fairly consistent but not automatic Democratic vote. Inspired by his daughter's struggles with epilepsy, he won passage of a bill creating epilepsy centers for returning combat veterans. In sync with local interests in energy, he sponsored a bill to offer incentives to lenders who create a market for green buildings. He also got a provision in the Waxman-Markey energy and climate bill in 2009 to benefit green banks, drawing criticism from Republicans when it was revealed that he was an investor in one of them. Democratic leaders put him on the influential Rules Committee in the 111th Congress (2009-10).

On the Financial Services Committee, Perlmutter worked with Republicans to add protections for taxpayers to the $700-billion government rescue of the financial markets. He and Frank Lucas, R-Okla., proposed in 2009 to create a council of regulators to monitor risk in the U.S. financial markets. He also worked with Colorado Republican Mike Coffman on legislation to temporarily allow small banks to amortize commercial real estate losses over seven years instead of writing them down all at once. And in 2010, he worked on a proposal to assist the victims of disgraced financier Bernard Madoff's multibillion-dollar Ponzi investment scheme.

In 2010, Perlmutter mulled a bid for Colorado's governorship but decided against it. His reelection race that year proved considerably tougher than his 2008 contest. His challenger, Aurora GOP Councilman Ryan Frazier, an African-American Navy veteran, attacked him for contributing to excess government overspending. Perlmutter, meanwhile, accused his opponent's company, software developer Takara Systems, of outsourcing its consulting services. Frazier got considerable help from national Republicans and outside groups, with the free-market conservative American Future Fund spending more than $500,000 on the race. Things turned nasty when Perlmutter slapped Frazier's hand away during a debate, something for which the incumbent immediately apologized. But Frazier couldn't keep pace financially with Perlmutter, who raised more than $2 million. He won with 53% of the vote.

★ CONNECTICUT ★

Connecticut is arguably America's highest achieving state, with its highest incomes by many measures and great accumulations of wealth. But it is also the state with the fastest-rising inequality between rich and poor. It is high on lists of states competitive in the global knowledge economy, yet it has grown achingly slowly. Connecticut has drawn freely on its Yankee heritage of inventiveness and openness to technical innovation. But it did not generate an appreciable gain in jobs between the recessions of 1990-91 and 2007-09. Yet at times it seems headed for a comfortable retirement, as hedge-fund managers on their estates in Greenwich savor life untormented by the travails of low-income workers in Stamford and Hartford.

Connecticut was founded by Puritans who considered Massachusetts too lenient and backsliding. Connecticut Yankees for years were flintier and more unyielding, more tightfisted and set in their ways than other New Englanders. Yet they were also open to certain reforms. In 1784, Connecticut voted for gradual emancipation of the state's slaves, becoming one of the first societies anywhere to do so. Life here still bears the imprint of the 17th-century settlers, even though most Connecticut residents today are descendants of Catholic immigrants who arrived between 1840 and 1924. This small chunk of rocky terrain has been an odd duck politically, the last state to back the Federalist Party (in 1816), one of the few to vote to re-elect Herbert Hoover (1932), and one of the last states to impose an income tax (1991).

Connecticut's affluence came not from any windfall but from a knack for tinkering and making good productive use of savings. George Washington called it the "provision state" for the supplies of food and cannon it provided his Revolutionary War forces. Connecticut made clocks, hats, combs, cigars, silk thread, pins, matches, and furniture. It invented and still manufactures Pez candy in the town of Orange, Nivea skin cream in Norwalk, and the Wiffle Ball in Shelton. The quintessential Connecticut Yankee, Eli Whitney, was the inventor not only of the cotton gin but also of rifles with interchangeable parts. The state has been a major arms maker ever since Samuel Colt won a War Department contract to manufacture guns for the Mexican-American War. During the Reagan defense buildup of the 1980s, Connecticut produced Air Force jets and Army helicopters and, in the Electric Boat Shipyard in New London, most of the Navy's nuclear submarines. These industries, like Connecticut's civilian manufacturers, depend heavily on meticulous work. Through decades of immigration, its workers never lost the Yankee knack: Connecticut ranks first in patents per capita. Over the years, the state has accumulated capital and invested shrewdly, with great skill at assessing risk. It is the home of several of the nation's great insurance companies, and its laws are unusually friendly to creditors and harsh on debtors.

But Connecticut has been finding its success at accumulating wealth hard to sustain. Its insurance companies have been hit by huge casualty losses from natural disasters, and cuts in defense spending cost Connecticut nearly 150,000 manufacturing jobs. Its small central cities—New Haven, Hartford, Bridgeport—have been plagued by crime and have been bleeding manufacturing jobs and people. In 1950, the three cities had 500,000 people in a state of 2 million; in 2009, they had 384,000 in a state of 3.5 million. Connecticut's post-1990 economic growth has been concentrated in two corners of the state, on opposite sides of the invisible divide that separates Yankee fans and Red Sox fans. In the southeast is the state's biggest employer and taxpayer, the Foxwoods Resort Casino, which opened in 1992 and is run by the 785-member Mashantucket Pequot tribe. Its big competitor is Mohegan Sun, owned by the 1,600-member Mohegans. In the southwest, Stamford and Greenwich have become major financial services centers and the headquarters of the hedge fund industry. But both were hard hit by the collapse of the financial markets and the recession that began in 2007. Some hedge funds closed their doors and employment fell by 10,000, while gambling revenues have been in decline since 2008. The casinos have laid off employees and fended off debt problems.

It's not clear that Connecticut's top-and-bottom work force, with many highly educated people and many with little education, is poised to spark growth. In recent years, its 18-to-34-year-old population has declined by about 200,000. An influx of immigrants from Mexico, Peru, the Dominican Republic, and other parts of Latin America has filled jobs that would otherwise go begging. Hispanics are now 13% of the state's population, slightly higher than African-Americans, at 10%. Its state and local tax burden per capita is ranked third in the nation by the Tax Foundation, trailing only New York and New Jersey. Small business growth is inhibited by high taxes, heavy regulation, and requirements that health insurance policies cover every imaginable contingency. Corruption has been widespread. Mayors of Waterbury and Bridgeport were sent to prison, and the

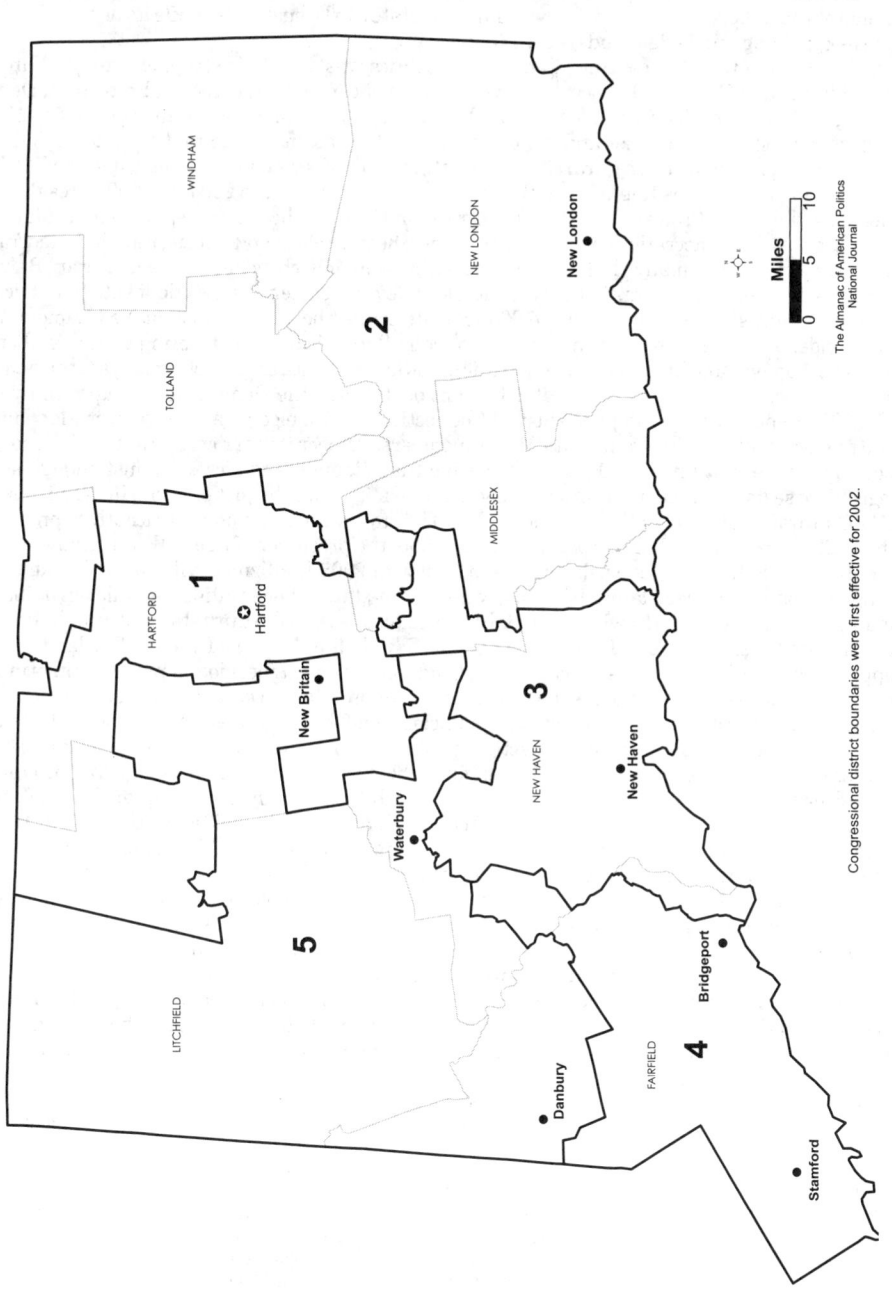

Congressional district boundaries were first effective for 2002.

The Almanac of American Politics
National Journal

Hartford mayor was arrested on bribery charges in January 2009. Republican Gov. John Rowland went to prison in 2005 for corruption. As former Republican state legislator Kevin Rennie wrote, "Affluence, high scholastic scores, and verdant hills have masked an increasingly corrupt political system that thrives on a complacent public and political elite." The question is whether the achievements of the tinkerers and investors who built this state can be sustained while its new lead industries—gambling and hedge funds—are reeling.

For most of the 20th century, Connecticut politics was an ethnic struggle between Yankee Republicans and Catholic Democrats. Slowly, as Catholic birthrates exceeded Protestant, Democrats gained ground. Their great leader was John Bailey, state party chairman from 1946 to 1975, a master legislative strategist and ticket-balancer, who was one of the first to endorse John F. Kennedy for president. The central cities and Catholic suburbs voted Democratic, and the WASPy suburbs and rural towns Republican. But those days are gone. In the 2004 and 2008 presidential elections, the state's Protestants voted Democratic and its Catholics voted Republican; secular voters went heavily Democratic. Now, the central cities, heavily black and Latino, remain Democratic and are joined by many high-income suburbs—Greenwich voted for Democrat Barack Obama—while old mill towns in the Naugatuck Valley and eastern Connecticut vote Republican. Similar patterns were apparent in the 2006 Senate contest between Democrat Ned Lamont and independent Joe Lieberman, with many historically Republican areas favoring the more liberal, anti-war Lamont, and historically Democratic areas favoring moderate Lieberman, a former Democrat who became an independent after Lamont beat him in the Democratic primary that year. The 2010 Republican tide stopped short of Connecticut, which elected a new Democratic senator and re-elected all five of its Democratic House members. Democrats narrowly recaptured the governorship for the first time in 20 years. Offsetting that, Republicans picked up just enough state legislative seats to put Democrats short of veto-proof majorities (by just one vote in each house).

Cultural issues have played a role in this. The state whose ban on contraceptives produced the U.S. Supreme Court's *Griswold* decision in 1965, the precursor of *Roe v. Wade*, is now solidly for abortion rights, and its legislature passed a law in 2005 legalizing civil unions for same-sex couples. Connecticut legislators have also voted for in-state college tuition for children of illegal immigrants and, after the Rowland scandal, Connecticut became the third state with public financing of state legislative races. Former Republican Gov. Jodi Rell, who succeeded Rowland, either approved or acquiesced in these decisions, and had some of the highest job-approval ratings in the nation. Her decision to retire opened the way for Stamford Mayor Dannel Malloy, a Democrat, to take the governorship after he defeated Republican Tom Foley, a former ambassador to Ireland.

The major national news in Connecticut politics has been its Senate races. Democratic Sen. Christopher Dodd, faced with revelations of favorable treatment on his mortgage from Countrywide Financial, decided to retire after 30 years, even while sponsoring a major financial regulation bill that passed in 2010 as the Dodd-Frank Act. Self-financer Linda McMahon, the head of World Wrestling Entertainment, beat former Rep. Rob Simmons for the Republican nomination for the open seat, but was not able to overcome Democrat Richard Blumenthal, who during 20 years as state attorney general had been looking for openings at the top of the ticket. Lieberman, whose ascent from attorney general to the Senate in 1988 opened the way for Blumenthal, held his seat in 2006 by running as an independent after he lost the Democratic primary to antiwar candidate Ned Lamont. Lieberman further antagonized local Democrats by supporting Arizona Republican John McCain for president in 2008 and by ostentatiously blocking the inclusion a publicly funded insurance option as part of the health care bill in December 2010. In early 2011, he announced he would not run for re-election in 2012. Running as a Democrat seemed not to be an option, so he

Population		Household Income		Work	
Pop. 2010:	3,574,097	Under $15k:	9.5%	Private:	80.1%
State rank:	29th	$15k to $50k:	27.5%	Government:	13.3%
Change since 2000:	Up 4.9%	$50k to $100k:	31.3%	Self-employed:	6.5%
Urban:	87.0%	$100k to $200k:	23.5%	Unemployment (3-yr. average):	5.1%
Rural:	13.0%	Over $200k:	8.1%	Poverty:	9.0%
Native of state:	55.7%	Median income:	$67,724	Blue collar:	18.0%
Not a citizen:	7.0%			White collar:	65.0%
Area size:	5,543 sq. mi.	**Home Value**		Khaki collar:	0.2%
		Under $100k:	3.3%	Other:	16.9%
Most populous cities		$100k to $300k:	46.5%		
Bridgeport	144,229	$300k to $500k:	30.2%	**Age**	
New Haven	129,779	$500k to $1 mil:	14.7%	Median age:	39.2 yrs.
Hartford	124,775	Over $1 million:	5.3%	More than 65 yrs:	13.7%
Stamford	122,643	Median:	$301,000	Less than 18 yrs:	23.3%

Race/Ethnicity				Military Veterans		Registered Voters in 2010	
White:	71.2%	*Language*		% of Pop:	8.7%	Democrats:	749,889
Black:	9.4%	English:	80.0%			Republicans:	418,297
Hispanic:	13.4%	Spanish:	9.8%	*Veterans by Period*		Ind./other:	853,895
Asian:	3.8%	Asian:	2.1%	WWII and before:	14.5%	Voter turnout:	1,163,320
Native Am.:	0.2%	Other European:	7.5%	Korea:	13.3%	Turnout as % of	
Hawaiian:	0.0%			Vietnam:	32.8%	voting age:	42.2%
Two+ races:	1.7%	**Education**		Gulf (pre-2001):	7.6%		
		H.S. grad:	88.4%	Gulf (post-2001):	5.1%	**Legislature**	
Ancestry		College grad:	35.5%	Peace time:	26.7%	Senate:	23 D 13 R
Italian	14.5%	Grad degree:	15.5%			House:	100 D 51 R
Irish	13.1%						
English	7.8%						

would have had to either run as a Republican or again as an independent. But this time, he might have faced a serious Republican opponent, possibly McMahon, as well as a strong Democrat, perhaps rising star Rep. Chris Murphy.

Presidential politics Why does the nation's highest income state vote Democratic for president? Because liberal stands on cultural issues have trumped any hunger for tax cuts among most of Connecticut voters and because many of its voters are members of ethnic groups with a historic Democratic heritage. And because of the selective outmigration since the adoption of the state income tax in the early 1990s of economic conservatives: perhaps much of the erstwhile Republican base in the 4th and 5th districts of Connecticut now reside in the sunny 4th and 5th districts of Florida. The Obama-Biden ticket carried Connecticut 61%-38%, better than Kerry-Edwards' 54%-44% in 2004 or Gore-Lieberman's 56%-38% in 2000.

Though it comes fairly early in the calendar, Connecticut's presidential primary has not been quite early enough to make a great difference. Only registered Democrats or Republicans can vote, and here, as in Massachusetts, large plu-

2008 Presidential Vote
Barack Obama (D) 997,772 (61%)
John McCain (R) 629,428 (38%)

2008 Presidential Primary
Barack Obama (D) 179,742 (51%)
Hillary Clinton (D)...............165,426 (47%)

2008 Presidential Primary
John McCain (R) 78,836 (52%)
Mitt Romney (R).....................49,891 (33%)
Mike Huckabee (R)................10,607 (7%)

2004 Presidential Vote
John Kerry (D) 857,488 (54%)
George W. Bush (R)..............693,826 (44%)

ralities do not register to vote in either party. Democrats who have won Connecticut's primary include Edward Kennedy in 1980, Gary Hart in 1984, and Jerry Brown in 1992. Republican John McCain won in 2000. But they all ultimately fared no better than the Federalists whom Connecticut favored in 1816. Two recent presidential candidates from Connecticut, Lieberman in 2004 and Dodd in 2008, failed to keep their candidacies alive long enough to contest their home state.

In 2008, Connecticut played a greater role, with its primary set for Super Tuesday, February 5. Thanks to Greenwich and the hedge funds, it was vital in the money primary. By the end of 2007, Democrats Barack Obama and Hillary Clinton raised $2 million and $1.8 million in the state, respectively; Republicans Mitt Romney and John McCain raised $1.5 million and $1.1 million, respectively. As the numbers indicate, interest was greater on the Democratic side and, with polls showing a close race, Obama held a rally in Hartford on the day before the primary and Clinton had an event at Yale. Democratic turnout was 355,000, far more than the past record of 241,000 in 1988. Obama won 51%-47%. Obama carried central cities and affluent suburbs, African-Americans, and secular voters; Clinton carried ethnic areas and mill towns, Latinos, and Catholics. The Republican primary was less seriously contested and attracted only 151,000 voters, less than the record 178,000 in 2000. McCain won 52% of the vote. Romney, though governor of neighboring Massachusetts for four years, won only 33%.

Congressional districting

Connecticut has devised a bipartisan process for redistricting. Two Republicans and two Democrats from each chamber of the legislature meet to draw the lines. If their map is approved by a two-thirds vote in both chambers, it becomes law. Otherwise, a ninth member is chosen by the other eight, and they try to reach consensus. The process worked in 1991, when the legislature approved a plan that made minimal changes in the congressional district lines. And it worked in 2001, with a nudge from the state Supreme Court, when the task was much harder: Connecticut had lost one of its six seats in the 2000 census, and two incumbents had to be put together in one district. The commission decided to create a new seat out of the 5th District represented by Democrat Jim Maloney and the 6th District represented by Republican Nancy Johnson. It failed to come up with a plan by the September 2001 deadline, and it appointed as its tiebreaker former state House Speaker Nelson Brown, a Republican, who came up with a plan with which both incumbents said they were satisfied.

Connecticut held onto its five House seats in the reapportionment following the 2010 census, and with all five seats now held by Democrats, and with Democratic majorities in both houses of the legislature and a Democratic governor, redistricting is likely to be non-controversial.

Governor

Dannel Malloy (D)

Elected 2010, term expires Jan. 2015, 1st term; b. July 21, 1955, Stamford; home, Hartford; Boston Col., B.A. 1977, J.D. 1980; Catholic; Married (Cathy); 3 children.

Elected Office: Mayor, Stamford, 1995-2009.

Professional Career: Asst. district atty., Brooklyn, NY, 1980-84; Partner, Abate and Fox, 1984-95.

Office: State Capitol, 210 Capitol Avenue , 6106, 860-566-4840; Fax: 860-524-7395; Web site: www.governor.ct.gov/malloy/site/default.asp.

Election Results

2010 general	Dannel Malloy (D)	567,278	(50%)
	Tom Foley (R)	560,874	(49%)
2010 primary	Dannel Malloy (D)	103,154	(57%)
	Ned Lamont (D)	77,772	(43%)

Dannel Malloy, a Democrat, was elected governor of Connecticut in 2010. Malloy, the youngest of eight children, grew up in Stamford with a learning disability; he had difficulties with reading and motor coordination and after several years was diagnosed as dyslexic. He graduated from Boston College and its law school, taking the bar exam orally. He was an assistant district attorney in Brooklyn from 1980 to 1984, and in that role, obtained 22 convictions in 23 felony cases. He moved back to Stamford to practice law. In 1995, he beat Republican incumbent Mayor Stanley Esposito and served in that job until 2009. In those years, Malloy recruited big financial houses to set up shop in Stamford, eventually generating about 5,000 new jobs. He sponsored citywide preschool and a Stamford Urban Transitway. The one blight on his record was an accusation of favoritism to campaign contributors and contractors who did work on his house. After a 17-month investigation, prosecutors said there was no evidence of wrongdoing.

Stamford is not Connecticut's largest city, but it often casts a high number of votes, which was helpful for Malloy when he turned his sights to statewide office. In 2006, he ran for governor, won the endorsement of the Democratic state convention by a single vote and then lost the Democratic primary to New Haven Mayor John DeStefano, 51%-49%. DeStefano went on to be defeated 63%-35% by Republican incumbent Jodi Rell, who was widely popular after replacing disgraced and jailed Republican Gov. John Rowland in July 2004.

Rell announced in November 2009 she would not run again. In March 2010, Malloy got into the contest as an underdog in the Democratic primary against investor Ned Lamont, who had beaten Sen. Joe Lieberman in the 2006 Senate primary, but then lost to him when Lieberman ran as an independent in the general election. On the Republican side, a contest shaped up between Lt. Gov. Mike Fedele and former Ambassador to Ireland Tom Foley. Lamont attacked Malloy for allegedly awarding no-bid contracts in Stamford, and Malloy attacked Lamont's business practices. Lamont spent $8.6 million of his own money, which triggered Connecticut's Citizens' Election Program and the allocation of $2.5 million in public funds to Malloy. He also had the support of public employee unions, which had backed DeStefano in 2006. That helped him beat Lamont by more than a 2-1 margin at the May Democratic state convention. Although Lamont led in initial polls, Malloy won the August 10 primary 57%-43%. At the same time, Foley edged Fedele in the Republican primary, 42%-39%.

There were sharp issue differences between the candidates in the fall 2010 campaign. Malloy opposed the death penalty, while Foley said he would veto any bill repealing the death penalty as Rell had. The issue was especially vivid because of the conviction in October of a career criminal for killing a mother and two daughters in a 2007 home invasion in Cheshire. "There is absolutely no connection between the death penalty and preventing or discouraging homicides from taking place," Malloy said. He also favored legalizing same-sex marriage and a union-backed bill to require companies with more than 50 employees to grant employees paid sick days. He called for requiring 20% of Connecticut's electricity to be produced from renewable sources by 2020 and presented a 12-point economic development plan. Foley promised no tax increases and called for $2 billion in spending cuts in the state budget. He charged that Stamford had lost 13,000 jobs since 2000, its peak employment year. Malloy charged that Foley had driven a Georgia textile company into bankruptcy while earning $20 million himself from the firm. Foley said that Malloy misstated the facts and that he had lost control of the company before the bankruptcy.

By September, Foley had loaned his campaign $5.3 million. The Democratic-controlled legislature approved a bill revising the Citizens Election Program to conform with recent court decisions and freeing up some $6 million in public financing for Malloy. Rell called the bill "a welfare program for politicians and a war chest for the impending, inevitable barrage of nasty negative advertising and robo-calls."

Malloy was well ahead in the polls in early fall, but the race tightened in October and the result turned out to be extremely close. Officials in heavily Democratic Bridgeport failed to print sufficient ballots and, with Secretary of State Susan Bysiewicz, got a judge to hold the polls open until 10 p.m. Bysiewicz, the state's chief election officer, declared on Nov. 3, the day after the election, that Malloy had won. But Foley insisted he had prevailed and questioned the integrity of the ballot-counting. Bysiewicz withdrew her statement, but on Friday, with the count for Bridgeport in, officially declared Malloy the winner. Foley and state Republicans examined the results over the weekend, and on Monday, they announced that they concurred. Malloy had indeed won, albeit narrowly, 50%-49%. In early 2011, his first order of business was figuring out ways to address a projected $3.5 billion budget shortfall.

Senior Senator

Joe Lieberman (I)

Elected 1988, term expires 2012, 4th term; b. Feb. 24, 1942, Stamford; home, Stamford; Yale U., B.A. 1964, LL.B. 1967; Jewish; married (Hadassah); 4 children.

Elected Office: CT Senate, 1970–80, Maj. ldr., 1974–80; CT atty. gen., 1982–88.

Professional Career: Practicing atty., 1967-70, 1980-82.

DC Office: 706 HSOB, 20510, 202-224-4041; Fax: 202-224-9750; Web site: lieberman.senate.gov.

State Offices: Hartford, 860-549-8463.

Committees: *Armed Services:* Airland (Chmn); Personnel; Strategic Forces. *Homeland Security & Governmental Affairs* (Chmn). *Small Business & Entrepreneurship.*

Group Ratings

	ACLU	ACU	ADA	CFG	AFS	FRC	LCV	ITIC	NTU	COC
2010	57	4	75	12	85	8	57	67	19	30
2009	–	20	95	12	100	–	100	–	10	43

National Journal Ratings

	2010 LIB	—	2010 CONS	2009 LIB	—	2009 CONS
Economic	51%	—	48%	49%	—	50%
Social	51%	—	47%	63%	—	36%
Foreign	36%	—	62%	37%	—	61%
Composite	47%	—	53%	50%	—	50%

Key Votes of the 111th Congress

1. Overturn Ledbetter	Y	5. Pass health care bill	Y	9. Ratify New START	Y
2. Pass $787 billion stimulus	Y	6. Regulate financial firms	Y	10. Confirm Elena Kagan	Y
3. Repeal DC gun laws	N	7. Pass tax cuts for some	N	11. Stop EPA climate regs	N
4. Confirm Sonia Sotomayor	Y	8. Legalize immigrants' kids	Y	12. Repeal don't ask, tell	Y

Election Results

2006 general	Joe Lieberman (CFL)	564,095	(50%)	($20,219,460)
	Ned Lamont (D)	450,844	(40%)	($20,580,603)
	Alan Schlesinger (R)	109,198	(10%)	($221,019)
2006 primary	Ned Lamont (D)	146,404	(52%)	
	Joe Lieberman (D)	136,490	(48%)	

Prior Winning Percentages: 2000 (63%); 1994 (67%); 1988 (50%)

Joe Lieberman, Connecticut's senior senator, is an independent. He was a Democrat until 2006, when he lost a primary fight to an anti-war candidate and went on to be re-elected anyway as a political independent. Since then, he has gravitated between the two political parties on an issue-by-issue basis while failing to find a secure home in either one. Lieberman announced on January 19, 2011 that he would not seek re-election to a fifth term in 2012, when he likely would have drawn strong challengers from one or both parties. Speaking to a group of supporters in Stamford, Lieberman said that he believes there is no longer a place for his independent brand of politics in Congress. "The politics of President Kennedy — service to country, support of civil rights and social justice, pro-growth economic and tax policies, and a strong national defense — are still my politics, and they don't fit neatly into today's partisan political boxes any more either," Lieberman said. "... I have not always fit comfortably into conventional political boxes, maybe you've noticed that, Democrat or Republican, liberal or conservative. I have always thought that my first responsibility is not to serve a political party but to serve my constituents, my state, and my country, and then to work across party lines to make sure good things get done for them."

Lieberman grew up in Stamford, the son of a liquor store owner, and was interested in politics early on. He remembers coming home from school at age 9 eager to watch the televised Kefauver hearings looking into organized crime in the United States. He graduated from Yale College and Yale Law School, became chairman of the *Yale Daily News,* and worked summers for Sen. Abraham Ribicoff and the Democratic National Committee. Even then, his political ambitions were no secret—other students called him "the senator." In college, he wrote an admiring yet academically solid biography of that quintessential political boss John Bailey, the Connecticut Democratic chairman from 1946 to 1975. Still, he was unafraid to challenge the political establishment, founding an anti-war Caucus of Connecticut Democrats. In 1970, he ran for the state Senate in New Haven against state Senate Majority Leader Edward Marcus and won, with help from, among others, a Yale law student volunteer named Bill Clinton. In 1980, he ran for an open U.S. House seat and lost 52%-46% in a Republican year. In 1982, he was elected Connecticut attorney general.

In 1988, Lieberman challenged Republican Sen. Lowell Weicker, another maverick but of a different sort. Weicker was well to the left of most Republicans on economic and cultural issues; Lieberman was to the right of most Democrats on cultural issues and foreign policy. He ran witty ads, one showing a bear sleeping through work—a takeoff on the growling and erratic Weicker. Lieberman won 50%-49%.

In his first years in the Senate, Lieberman made a mark in foreign policy. He was one of the leaders in favor of the Gulf War resolution in 1991, and without his earnest and vehement support, it might not have passed. Presciently, he called for "final victory" over Iraqi Leader Saddam Hussein. An Orthodox Jew, he is a strong supporter of Israel. After the September 11 attacks, he avidly supported the war on terrorism in Afghanistan and in December 2001 was one of 10 members who signed a letter urging President George W. Bush to target Iraq next. The following year, he urged the administration to move its putative allies in the Arab world toward political freedom to prevent a "theological iron curtain" behind which terrorism could build.

Lieberman played a key role on homeland security as it developed into a major issue. He initiated the call in Congress for a Department of Homeland Security with a bill in October 2001 that became one of the working documents in the debate over the creation of the department. As the ranking Democrat on Governmental Affairs in 2005 and 2006, Lieberman worked closely with Chairman Susan Collins, a Maine Republican. They investigated the government's response to Hurricane Katrina and recommended the appointment of an inspector general to monitor recovery efforts. In 2006, they called for an independent Office of Public Integrity, in which nonmembers would conduct investigations requiring final approval by the Senate Ethics Committee, but the plan was rejected. Lieberman was also part of the "Gang of 14" that promised to prevent the filibuster of judicial nominees except in extreme cases.

Lieberman has spoken out eloquently on moral issues and has said, "We in government should look to religion as a partner, as I think the founders of our country did." In highly publicized Commerce, Science and Transportation Committee hearings in September 2000, Lieberman denounced the marketing of violent movies, music, and video games to children. He refused to be a lockstep defender of President Clinton when Clinton was accused of lying about extramarital relations with a White House intern. He called Clinton's behavior "wrong and unacceptable" and said the president deserved "some measure of public rebuke and accountability." But he stopped well short of backing impeachment or resignation. Lieberman has long believed, as he said in 2002, that "faith-based groups can help government solve pressing social problems," but he opposed the Bush administration's faith-based charities bill in 2001, calling instead for tax incentives for corporate giving.

Al Gore's decision to make Lieberman his vice presidential nominee in 2000 was history-making. He was the first Jew on a major party ticket. Plus, Lieberman's reputation for probity and his denunciation of Clinton gave the ticket some insulation from the scandals of the Clinton era. Lieberman's moderate record on issues was an asset. He generally supported Democratic policies on economic issues but backed such measures as capital gains tax cuts for small business. "You can't be pro-jobs and anti-business," he said. Another asset proved to be Lieberman's fervent avowals that religious faith had a rightful place in politics. For Democrats, what might have been resented from a Christian conservative seemed attractive coming from an Orthodox Jew.

His poll ratings were high, and if there was general agreement that Dick Cheney excelled at the October 6 vice presidential debate, Lieberman also performed well. Lieberman's Judaism seems not to have hurt the ticket anywhere, and it probably helped in crucial Florida. He made memorable campaign appearances in heavily Jewish Broward and Palm Beach counties, which together voted 65%-32% for Gore-Lieberman. But there was some tension between positions Lieberman had taken before 2000 and his campaign rhetoric. He had questioned racial quotas and preferences, and he supported publicly funded private school vouchers for students in failing District of Columbia schools.

As he contemplated his own bid for the presidency four years later, Lieberman was not a clear choice for the party, especially given widespread doubts about his unswerving support of the Iraq war. He had supported Bush on going into Afghanistan and going into Iraq, not just perfunctorily or after the fact, but fervently, even as many Democrats soured on the war. He stuck to those positions in the summer of 2003, even as Vermont's Howard Dean attracted a mass constituency over the Internet and rose in the polls in part on his stringent criticism of Bush on Iraq. In August 2003, though, Lieberman said, "I share the anger of my fellow Democrats with George Bush and the wrong direction he has taken our nation. But the answer to his outdated, extremist ideology is not to be found in outdated extremes of our own. That path will not solve the challenges of our time and it could well send us Democrats back to the political wilderness for a long time." He told unions that foreign trade is good for the American economy. He cautioned Democrats not to abandon Clinton-era principles that "made our party once again fiscally responsible, pro-growth, strong on values, for middle-class tax cuts," adding that "Howard Dean is against all of these."

Like other hawkish candidates—Gore in 1988, McCain in 2000—Lieberman decided to avoid dovish Iowa. He was stung in December 2003 when Gore, without notice, endorsed Dean. "I don't have anything to say today about Al Gore's sense of loyalty, I really don't, and I have no regrets about the loyalty that I had to him when I waited until he decided whether he would run (in 2004) to make my decision because that was the right thing to do," he said. While Dean, Kerry, John Edwards, and Dick Gephardt were attracting attention in Iowa, Lieberman spent the month before the January 27 primary living in a basement apartment in New Hampshire, chatting with voters over coffee, speaking to groups wherever he could. But Dean was attracting far more volunteers and far larger crowds, and Kerry, after his come-from-behind victory in Iowa, was also better organized. "We have JOE-mentum," Lieberman would proclaim cheerfully, but it wasn't enough. He finished fifth in New Hampshire with 9% of the vote. For another week he persisted in campaigning for the February 3 primaries in six states, but the best he could do was a second-place finish in Delaware, and he ended his campaign.

In 2005, after he delivered his State of the Union address, Bush embraced Lieberman as he was leaving the House floor. Many thought Bush had kissed him—and "the kiss" became one of the war cries of Lieberman's critics in the blogosphere. The Democratic leadership was not pleased when he continued to support the Iraq war, voted to confirm Alberto Gonzales as attorney general, and supported faith-based initiatives. Still, the well-financed Lieberman was initially thought to be a safe bet for re-election in 2006. But money was not a problem for Ned Lamont, the great-grandson of J. P. Morgan partner Thomas Lamont and the owner of a successful cable television installation business. He had been a selectman in Greenwich from 1987 to 1989, and had contributed to many Democratic candidates, including Lieberman in 2000. He recruited Tom Swan, head of the Connecticut Citizen Action Group, to manage his campaign and challenged Lieberman for the Democratic nomination.

At first, Lamont's campaign seemed a long shot. To get on the primary ballot, he had to get 15% of the votes at the state party convention in May (or signatures from 2% of registered Democrats, an avenue he didn't pursue). That was not an overwhelming obstacle, given the anti-war views of most Connecticut Democrats, but Lieberman had been deeply involved in Connecticut Democratic politics for 40 years and had built up many close personal relationships. Given his easy re-elections in 1994 and 2000, he seemed certain to keep the seat out of the hands of the Republicans. Lieberman's work on saving the Groton submarine base from closing in 2005 would pay dividends in eastern Connecticut, and he had support from key Democratic groups, from the state AFL-CIO to the Human Rights Campaign. Also, Lamont was an inexperienced candidate not given to easy repartee, and he made some mistakes along the way—for instance, calling job losses from free trade agreements a necessary "transition cost."

But he had enthusiastic support from Weicker, the man whom Lieberman beat in 1988 and who in 1990 was elected governor as an independent. Video clips championing Lamont's candidacy got wide airing on YouTube, and Lieberman was booed at the state Jefferson-Jackson-Bailey dinner. At the May 19 state convention, Lamont won a third of the delegates. Lieberman emphasized his Democratic credentials and his votes against some of Bush's policies, and said that he hoped troops could be pulled out by the end of the year. He also had some $4 million, which he used on television advertising. At a July debate, while Lamont attacked him on Iraq, Lieberman said, "The people of Connecticut and I have known each other for a long time. We have laughed and cried together. We prayed and dreamed together. And, most of all, we have worked together." But Lamont was also spending liberally, both his own money—he ultimately put in $17 million—and funds raised over the Internet.

It turned out to be a close election. Lamont won 52%-48%. Lieberman declared that he would run in the general on the "Connecticut for Lieberman" party line, and said he offered "a new politics of unity and purpose." In a tough blow for him, his close friend and fellow home-state senator, Democrat Christopher Dodd, endorsed Lamont and most Democrats shunned Lieberman when he returned to Washington in September. Some called for him to drop out of the race.

Most polls from primary day through November showed Lieberman leading Lamont. Liberal bloggers speculated hopefully that the mostly ignored Republican candidate, Derby Mayor Alan

Schlesinger, would surge and take votes from Lieberman, but that never happened. Lamont seemed unprepared for this second struggle, and Swan admitted that 98% of his planning was for the primary. Lieberman researchers revealed that Lamont had missed a vote on increasing property taxes on the Greenwich Board of Selectmen. He also resigned from the Round Hill Club in Greenwich, having discovered after many years that it didn't have many black members. And Swan was quoted as saying that the industrial town of Waterbury was "where the forces of slime meet the forces of evil." This was a reference to crooked local politicians, but it looked like a slur against a working-class, and largely Democratic, city. The polls proved to be on point. Lieberman won 50%-40%, with only 10% for the hapless Schlesinger.

Lieberman was welcomed back to the Democratic Caucus by Majority Leader-elect Harry Reid, who said, "We're all family." Senate Democrats—and Republicans—were very much aware that it was Lieberman's vote alone that gave them a Senate majority. Lieberman continued his independent ways. He co-sponsored, with Republicans John McCain of Arizona and Lindsey Graham of South Carolina, a resolution opposing the Democrats' calls for withdrawal from Iraq, and he strongly supported President Bush's troop "surge" to try to restore order in the country, which was on the brink of civil war. As the chairman of the Homeland Security and Governmental Affairs Committee, Lieberman declined to initiate investigations of Bush administration policies, prompting North Dakota Sen. Byron Dorgan to use the Democratic Policy Committee to launch a probe of private contractors in Iraq.

Then, in December 2007, Lieberman's estrangement from the Democratic Party intensified when he endorsed McCain for president. The two senators had worked together on many issues over the years, and had often traveled together. "When it comes to leading America to victory against the Islamist terrorists who attacked us on 9/11, there's no one better prepared than John McCain," Lieberman said. Moreover, he campaigned for McCain in New Hampshire, Florida, and other states. There was speculation that McCain might give him the vice presidential nomination, which Lieberman tried to parry. "Been there, done that," Lieberman said in August 2008. But inside the McCain camp, Graham pushed hard for Lieberman, who evidently made McCain's short list before being passed over for Alaska Gov. Sarah Palin.

In any case, Lieberman, having attended eight Democratic conventions from 1976 to 2004 and having been nominated for vice president at the 2000 event, attended his first Republican National Convention in 2008 and spoke at the end of Tuesday night's proceedings. He called Obama "a gifted and eloquent young man"—which enraged many Democrats—and said, "When colleagues like Barack Obama were voting to cut off funding for our troops on the battlefield"—the audience started booing—"John McCain had the courage to stand against the tide of public opinion and support the surge. And because of that, today our troops are at last beginning to come home, and they are coming home with honor."

After the speech, Democratic net-roots groups launched a campaign to have his committee chairmanship stripped in 2009, when it was widely expected that he would no longer hold the 51st vote in determining party control of the Senate. A "Lieberman Must Go" online petition accumulated 47,000 signatures by July 2008. Reid said he was "disappointed" in Lieberman. But two days after the election, Reid and Lieberman held a meeting at which Lieberman reportedly said losing the chairmanship was "unacceptable," and that he might consider joining the Republican Party—a decision that, with the Georgia, Alaska, and Minnesota races then still undecided, would have made it impossible for Democrats to reach a 60-seat filibuster-proof majority. Dodd and others began lobbying colleagues to let Lieberman keep his gavel, and word leaked that the Obama transition team did not want him punished. On Nov. 18, 2008, the Senate Democratic Caucus voted 42-13 to let him remain as chairman of the Homeland Security panel. For his part, Lieberman apologized for some of the things he had said about Obama.

On the committee in the 111th Congress (2009-2010), Lieberman was the lead sponsor of the bill giving the District of Columbia congressional representation, which passed 61-37 in February 2009 with an amendment repealing most of the District's gun control laws. Lieberman also worked to gain support for Obama's economic stimulus bill from moderate Republicans. But hard feelings in his former party remained. Democratic Rep. John Larson, who represents Connecticut's 1st District, told the *Hartford Courant*, "I think Joe is on a different roster. He's made a conscious choice to go over to the other side."

He broke with Democrats on issue after issue. He and Graham threatened to block the 2009 military supplemental spending bill unless it prevented the release of photos of detainees in anti-terrorism investigations. Liberals criticized him harshly for opposing the creation of a government-run insurance plan in the Democrats' health care bill in the fall of 2009. An unfazed Lieberman said, "I think it's such a mistake that I would use the power I have as a single senator to stop a final vote." However, he supported the final health care bill in December 2009 after the public option was dropped. On the Homeland Security panel, where he continued to reign as chairman, Lieberman in April 2010 called for building more reinforced physical fencing on the Arizona-Mexico border. Two months later, he criticized the Obama administration's national security strategy as too soft on domestic terror threats and, in the fall, he opposed the call by some Democrats to allow Bush-era tax cuts to expire in 2011.

On other matters, Lieberman's work on the committee was less controversial. In 2009, he and Collins of Maine sought greater security regulations on biological weapons laboratories. Lieberman also worked with Graham of South Carolina and Kerry of Massachusetts in summer 2010 on carbon emissions legislation designed to be a centrist alternative to the bill proposed by liberal Democrat Barbara Boxer of California. Later in the year, he and Collins sponsored a measure to repeal the ban on openly gay people serving in the military.

But Lieberman's standing with Democrats at home remained strained at best. Polls showed him faring poorly in the 2012 primary and in late 2010, some Connecticut political observers said he could win re-election only as a Republican. In January 2011, Lieberman announced that he would not seek re-election in 2012.

Junior Senator

Richard Blumenthal (D)

Elected 2010, term expires 2016, 1st term; b. Feb. 13, 1946, Brooklyn, NY; home, Greenwich; Harvard U., B.A. 1967; Yale U., J.D. 1973.; Jewish; Married (Cynthia); 4 children.

Military Career: Marine Corps Reserve, 1970-76.

Elected Office: CT House, 1984-88; CT Senate, 1988-91; CT atty. gen., 1991-2010.

Professional Career: Teacher, Washington, D.C., public schl., 1968-69; staff asst., White House Office of Econ. Opportunity, 1969-70; law clerk, 1973-75; administrative asst., Sen. Abraham Ribicoff, D-Conn., 1975-76; U.S. atty., CT, 1977-81; practing atty., 1981-1990.

DC Office: 702 HSOB, 20510, 202-224-2823; Fax: 202-224-9673; Web site: http://blumenthal.senate.gov.

State Offices: Hartford, 860-258-6940.

Committees: *Aging (Special). Armed Services:* Airland; Personnel; Seapower. *Health, Education, Labor & Pensions:* Children & Families; Employment & Workplace Safety. *Judiciary:* Antitrust, Competition Policy & Consumer Rights; Constitution, Civil Rights & Human Rights; Immigration, Refugees & Border Security; Privacy, Technology & the Law.

Election Results

2010 general	Richard Blumenthal (D) 636,040	(55%)	($8,733,486)
	Linda McMahon (R)..498,341	(43%)	($50,285,122)
2010 primary	Richard Blumenthal (D) .... unopposed		

The junior senator from Connecticut is Democrat Richard Blumenthal, the former state attorney general who won an open-seat contest against tea party-backed Republican Linda McMahon in 2010. He succeeded retiring Sen. Christopher Dodd, also a Democrat.

Blumenthal was born in Brooklyn, N.Y., to Jane and Martin Blumenthal. His father fled Nazi Germany in 1935 and became wealthy by trading commodities in his adopted country. He sent his son to Harvard, where Blumenthal earned a bachelor's degree in political science, and to Yale Law School, where he edited the *Yale Law Journal.* Blumenthal's post-college list of employers reads like a Who's Who of the Washington elite in the 1970s: He worked at *The Washington Post* for longtime publisher Katharine Graham; he was a staff assistant to Daniel Patrick Moynihan when Moynihan was a top adviser in the Nixon White House; and he clerked for Supreme Court Justice William Brennan. Blumenthal's résumé impressed President Carter, who appointed him U.S. attorney in Connecticut in 1977.

Blumenthal went on to do some legal work for the NAACP Legal Defense Fund while in private practice in the early 1980s, where he gained wider fame by dismantling the case against an innocent prisoner on Connecticut's death row. A stay was granted just 15 hours before Joseph Brown's scheduled execution in 1983, and he was later released. Blumenthal went on to win election to the Connecticut Assembly in 1984 and to the state Senate in 1987 before his successful run for attorney general in 1990. As the state's top lawyer, Blumenthal actively pursued consumer protection lawsuits, including cases against tobacco companies, polluters, health insurers, and banks charging automatic teller fees. The lawsuits won Blumenthal increased popularity with Connecticut Democrats—and earned him the nickname "Sue 'Em All Blumenthal" from his detractors. He had long been considered a candidate for higher office, but other figures, notably independent Sen. Joe Lieberman, who remained on Connecticut's Senate ballot in 2000 while also running for vice president, long stood in his way. He was elected and re-elected state attorney general five times since 1990, never with less than 59% of the vote.

He finally got his shot to run for the Senate in 2010 after Dodd, first elected to the Senate in 1980, announced he was retiring after five terms. But it was also the year when the tea party took flight, and what should have been a stroll in the park for Blumenthal, given his popularity in blue Connecticut, turned into a bruising fight against McMahon, the former head of World Wrestling Entertainment. The Republican nominee harnessed an upswing in GOP voter energy to make it a real contest, one that was monitored nationally as a possible gauge of the strength of the fledgling tea party movement.

The first sign things were not going to be easy for Blumenthal was his apparent exaggeration of his military service. A member of the Marine Corps Reserve from 1970 to 1975, Blumenthal claimed on several occasions to have served in Vietnam, though he never in fact deployed. The McMahon campaign attacked him for distorting his record, putting a chink in his best asset: his long record of public service compared to McMahon's recent embrace of politics as a second career. Blumenthal apologized, but the episode sparked a nasty back-and-forth campaign. Blumenthal's camp went after McMahon for the sexism and use of steroids in professional wrestling, where McMahon earned her wealth as WWE president. He chided her for heavy personal spending on her campaign, saying voters deserved "an election, not an auction."

Though Blumenthal enjoyed a wide lead over McMahon at the beginning of the race, it tightened considerably in the wake of the Marine Reserve flap. In the fall, Blumenthal attacked McMahon for what he called her support of lowering or abolishing the hourly minimum wage. In a bad year for Democrats, Blumenthal stressed his independence from the national party on a handful of issues, including his opposition to the financial industry rescue. He also said that unlike McMahon, he would support letting the Bush-era tax cuts expire for households earning over $250,000 a year; she supported making them permanent for all income levels. Still, by late September, Blumenthal was ahead by just 3 percentage points.

McMahon emphasized her business savvy as a CEO who created jobs, and talked about her middle-class upbringing by two civil service workers in North Carolina. To appeal to Democrats and independents, she billed herself as a centrist Republican who supported abortion rights and the prerogative of states to decide the same-sex marriage issue. Her readiness for the job was called into question with revelations that she had failed to even vote in elections in 2006 and 2008. But McMahon proved to be a tireless campaigner with an easy manner in the endless meet-and-greet aspects of the role.

Still, she could not overcome Connecticut's Democratic tilt even in 2010's poor climate for President Obama and his party. *The Hartford Courant* noted that "she had persistent trouble winning over women voters, despite the fact she would have become the first female senator in the state's history. Some women were turned off by some of the racier images of WWE; others didn't like her aggressive advertising strategy." Blumenthal won with 55% of the vote to 43% for McMahon. When the results were in, the *Courant* summed things up this way: "In the beginning, Richard Blumenthal looked unbeatable. At the end, he was. In between, there was quite a battle."

FIRST DISTRICT

John Larson (D)

Elected 1998, 7th term; b. July 22, 1948, Hartford; home, E. Hartford; Central CT St. U., B.S. 1971; Catholic; married (Leslie); 3 children.

Elected Office: E. Hartford Bd. of Ed., 1977-79; E. Hartford Town Cncl., 1979-83; CT Senate, 1983-95, Pres. pro-tem 1986-95.

Professional Career: H.S. teacher, 1972-77; Insurance broker, 1977-98; Sr. fellow, Yale Bush Ctr., 1995-1998.

DC Office: 1501 LHOB, 20515, 202-225-2265; Fax: 202-225-1031; Web site: larson.house.gov.

State Offices: Hartford, 860-278-8888.

Committees: *Ways & Means:* Select Revenue Measures; Trade.

Group Ratings

	ACLU	ACU	ADA	CFG	AFS	FRC	LCV	ITIC	NTU	COC
2010	94	0	100	0	100	0	100	67	5	13
2009	–	0	100	4	100	–	100	–	2	33

National Journal Ratings

	2010 LIB	—	2010 CONS		2009 LIB	—	2009 CONS
Economic	90%	—	0%		88%	—	9%
Social	89%	—	7%		72%	—	26%
Foreign	92%	—	3%		84%	—	15%
Composite	94%	—	7%		82%	—	18%

Key Votes of the 111th Congress

1. Overturn Ledbetter	Y	5. Bar federal abortion funds	N	9. Stop detainee transfers	N
2. Pass $820 billion stimulus	Y	6. Pass health care bill	Y	10. Legalize immigrants' kids	Y
3. Let guns in national parks	N	7. Regulate financial firms	Y	11. Repeal don't ask, tell	Y
4. Pass cap-and-trade	Y	8. Pass tax cuts for some	Y	12. Limit campaign funds	Y

Election Results

2010 general	John Larson (D)	138,440	(61%)	($2,401,252)
	Ann Brickley (R)	84,076	(37%)	($314,097)
2010 primary	John Larson (D)	unopposed		

Prior Winning Percentages: 2008 (72%), 2006 (74%), 2004 (73%), 2002 (67%), 2000 (72%), 1998 (58%)

Population		Race/Ethnicity		Work	
Pop. 2010:	710,951	White:	64.8%	Private:	80.8%
Change since 2000:	Up 4.4%	Black:	13.9%	Government:	14.1%
Urban:	93.4%	Hispanic:	14.7%	Self-employed:	4.9%
Rural:	6.6%	Asian:	4.4%	Blue collar:	17.2%
Area size:	673 sq. mi.	Native Am.:	0.2%	White collar:	65.5%
		Hawaiian:	0.0%	Khaki collar:	0.1%
Age		Two+ races:	1.7%	Other:	17.2%
Median age:	39.4 yrs.				
More than 65 yrs:	14.3%	*Ancestry*		Median income:	$61,225
Less than 18 yrs:	23.1%	Italian	12.9%	Median Home Value:	$247,900
		Irish	11.8%		
Education		Polish	7.2%	**Military Veterans**	
H.S. grad:	87.1%			% of Pop:	8.5%
College grad:	32.6%				
Grad degree:	13.8%				

Hartford, Bristol

In 1871, Mark Twain moved to Hartford to become director of an insurance company, and in time, became the Connecticut capital's most famous citizen. And Hartford became the nation's best-known insurance center. This was not what the Puritans who founded Hartford had in mind, but Connecticut's Yankees turned out to be shrewd businessmen. Hartford is the boyhood home of financier J.P. Morgan and also home to the nation's longest-circulating newspaper, the

2008 Presidential Vote		
Barack Obama (D) 218,794	(66%)
John McCain (R) 108,572	(33%)
2004 Presidential Vote		
John Kerry (D) 187,089	(60%)
George Bush (R) 121,263	(39%)
Cook Partisan Voting Index: D+13		

Hartford Courant, established in 1764. Thanks to the broad Connecticut River, Hartford also became a seaport. Its merchants wrote fire insurance, using the capital they had accumulated in the Napoleonic Wars to finance their ventures. One was Samuel Colt's gun factory just south of downtown Hartford, which became one of the nation's great arms plants.

Although each sector has downsized, insurance and arms are still economic mainstays of Hartford, Connecticut's biggest metropolitan area. Connecticut has the largest concentration of financial and insurance firms in the nation, mostly in the Hartford area. The Hartford Financial Services Group, Aetna, and St. Paul Travelers are among the top employers in Connecticut, and the insurance industry employed over 64,000 statewide in 2009. Across the river is the Pratt & Whitney jet engine plant in East Hartford, cornerstone of Connecticut-based United Technologies. Though its local workforce is less than one-fourth its size in 1980, it still builds engines for more than 600 customers around the world. The central core of Hartford is suffering, however, with bedraggled, high-crime neighborhoods filled with abandoned buildings, a troubled school system, and downtown landmarks, such as the Civic Center and Broadcast House in Constitution Plaza, that are in jeopardy. Many words have been written about the sad decline of this once rich city. Where 177,000 people lived in 1950, there were 124,000 in 2009. Its population is 37% African-American and 41% Hispanic. Beyond Hartford, the metropolitan area is more affluent but growing slowly.

The 1st Congressional District of Connecticut is centered on Hartford and upscale West Hartford. On the map it looks like a lobster claw. The claw extends west, excluding some affluent suburbs while including small towns and part of Torrington in the north. Southwest of Hartford, the district includes Bristol, site of the sprawling headquarters of ESPN, the multimedia network that revolutionized sports broadcasting and employs about 3,400 locally. East of the Connecticut River are East Hartford and more affluent suburbs. Politically, the Hartford area has long been more Democratic than the rest of Connecticut. It owes some of its Democratic character to John Bailey, an old-fashioned political boss with a scandal-free career who promoted a raft of first-class candidates. Bailey was state Democratic chairman from 1946 to 1975 and national Democratic chairman from 1961 to 1968.

John Larson (D)

The congressman from the 1st District is John Larson, who as the chairman of the Democratic Caucus is the No. 3-ranking leader in the House minority.

One of eight children, Larson grew up in the Mayberry Village public-housing project in East Hartford, and is fond of saying that he is a "product of public housing, public education, and public service." His father was a fireman at Pratt & Whitney and also worked as an auto mechanic and butcher. His mother had a job at the state Capitol and served on the town council. Growing up, Larson recalls, the family shared a bathroom the size of a telephone booth but never wanted for anything. Teachers had a great influence on his life, and after graduating from Central Connecticut State University, Larson taught high school and coached athletics. He also worked in the hometown industry as an insurance agent. In 1982, at age 34, Larson was elected to the state Senate. The Republican landslide in 1984 wiped out half of the Democratic seats in the Senate, and Larson led a successful effort two years later to regain a Democratic majority, which earned him a promotion to Senate president. He sponsored one of the nation's first family medical leave laws, a prototype for the federal bill sponsored by Sen. Christopher Dodd, D-Conn., and signed into law by President Bill Clinton in 1993.

Larson's politics are a product of his upbringing. Family members benefited from President Franklin D. Roosevelt's New Deal programs and were great admirers of their fellow Irish Catholic, President John F. Kennedy. He says that he doesn't believe in big government or small government, but the "effective use of government on behalf of the people you are sworn to serve." Larson seemed headed for the governorship and, in 1994, won the party designation at the state convention. But Comptroller Bill Curry built an organization of unionists and liberal activists and beat him 55%-45% in the primary. When Democratic U.S. Rep. Barbara Kennelly (the daughter of state Democratic boss John Bailey) decided to run for governor in 1998, Larson ran for her seat. In the primary, he faced Secretary of State Miles Rapoport, who led in the polls and fundraising. But Larson raised impressive sums as well, built a local organization, campaigned door-to-door, and got help from Hartford Mayor Mike Peters. He won 46%-43%. In the general election, he competed against Kevin O'Connor, a 31-year-old former law clerk and Securities and Exchange Commission lawyer who was endorsed by *The Hartford Courant.* Larson won 58%-41% and has not been seriously challenged since.

One of his first endeavors was working with members of both parties to establish an official history of the U.S. House of Representatives after Larson realized that the Senate had one and that House did not. His voting record places him near the center of his party. In 2002, he actively opposed authorizing the use of force in Iraq, saying that unilateral action could unite Arab countries against the United States. In 2005, Larson secured a seat on the powerful tax-writing Ways and Means Committee. That year's energy bill included his provisions expanding tax incentives for fuel cell technologies.

Among his legislative interests are issues related to campaign finance and election reform. In 2009, Larson introduced a bill with Rep. Walter Jones, R-N.C. that would allow the federal government to match $400 for every $100 raised by a candidate who agrees to accept contributions of only $100 or less. He also has proposed a constitutional amendment that would give members of the House four-year terms with elections staggered every two years. Longer terms would make legislators more effective by allowing them to spend less time running for re-election every two years, Larson says.

On an important parochial issue in 2008, he won National Historic Landmark status for the original Colt factory and grounds. Larson is also a defender of his district's aerospace industry, which is led by Pratt & Whitney. In 2009, he lost a battle with Defense Secretary Robert Gates to maintain funding for the Air Force's F-22 fighter plane, whose engine is manufactured by the company. Gates argued the military does not need the plane. Larson also supported a Boeing-Pratt & Whitney alliance to build a new Air Force refueling tanker over the European owned company, EADS.

In 2003, Larson became the senior Democrat on the House Administration Committee, the congressional housekeeping panel that handles office space assignments and other perks of interest to colleagues. Leadership on the committee can be a stepping-stone to higher positions in the Democratic hierarchy. Then-Minority Leader Nancy Pelosi brought Larson into her circle of advisers, and his influence grew. In 2006, he won a hotly contested race for Democratic Caucus vice chairman. His competitors were the better-known Jan Schakowsky of Illinois and Joseph Crowley of New York. When Schakowsky finished third on the first ballot and was eliminated, she threw her support to Larson. With Schakowsky's former supporters, Larson prevailed on the second ballot 116-87 over Crowley, who was allied with Maryland's Steny Hoyer, Pelosi's arch rival in leadership. In 2007, Larson planned to run for caucus chairman, but stepped aside when it became clear that Rahm Emanuel of Illinois had locked up support for the job. When Emanuel quit the House in November 2008 to become chief of staff to President-elect Obama, then-Speaker Pelosi persuaded Chris Van Hollen, D-Md., to remain as chairman of the Democratic Congressional Campaign Committee, clearing the field for Larson to finally become caucus chairman.

Larson has taken on a number of assignments for Pelosi, including coordinating the Democrats' 2008 strategy on energy policy and dealing with party dissidents who complained that Pelosi's Iraq strategy was too accommodating to President George W. Bush. In 2010, along with most House Democrats, Larson supported the party's health care overhaul. He said that although imperfect, the legislation was an historic achievement on par with creation of the Medicare and Social Security programs and with passage of the Civil Rights Act. Some Democrats privately deride him as Pelosi's cheerleader, but he shrugs off such comments, saying that his "bottom-up, member's member" approach is very different from the imperious style Emanuel was known for, but no less effective. "If you were using generals as analogy, (Emanuel) would be Patton. I would be Omar Bradley," he says. Larson believes that Pelosi will be judged by history as one of the great speakers, saying "Nobody, I mean nobody, outworks Nancy Pelosi."

When Democrats lost control of the House in 2010, Pelosi became minority leader and Larson remained as caucus chairman, making him one of the top four leaders of the House Democrats.

SECOND DISTRICT

Joe Courtney (D)

Elected 2006, 3rd term; b. April 6, 1953, Hartford; home, Vernon; Tufts U., B.A. 1975, U. of CT, J.D. 1978; Catholic; married (Audrey); 2 children.

Elected Office: CT House of Reps., 1986-94.

Professional Career: Practicing atty., 1978-2006; CT coordinator, John Edwards pres. campaign, 2004.

DC Office: 215 CHOB, 20515, 202-225-2076; Fax: 202-225-4977; Web site: courtney.house.gov.

State Offices: Enfield, 860-741-6011; Norwich, 860-886-0139.

Committees: *Agriculture:* General Farm Commodities & Risk Management; Livestock, Dairy & Poultry. *Armed Services:* Readiness; Seapower & Projection Forces.

Group Ratings

	ACLU	ACU	ADA	CFG	AFS	FRC	LCV	ITIC	NTU	COC
2010	87	0	90	4	100	0	100	100	10	25
2009	–	0	95	5	88	–	100	–	4	33

National Journal Ratings

	2010 LIB	—	2010 CONS	2009 LIB	—	2009 CONS
Economic	62%	—	37%	73%	—	25%
Social	61%	—	35%	66%	—	33%
Foreign	56%	—	38%	70%	—	24%
Composite	62%	—	39%	71%	—	29%

Key Votes of the 111th Congress

1. Overturn Ledbetter	Y	5. Bar federal abortion funds	N	9. Stop detainee transfers	Y
2. Pass $820 billion stimulus	Y	6. Pass health care bill	Y	10. Legalize immigrants' kids	Y
3. Let guns in national parks	Y	7. Regulate financial firms	Y	11. Repeal don't ask, tell	Y
4. Pass cap-and-trade	Y	8. Pass tax cuts for some	Y	12. Limit campaign funds	Y

Election Results

2010 general	Joe Courtney (D)	147,748	(60%)	($1,781,959)
	Janet Peckinpaugh (R)	95,671	(39%)	($247,391)
2010 primary	Joe Courtney (D)	unopposed		

Prior Winning Percentages: 2008 (66%), 2006 (50%)

Population		Race/Ethnicity		Work	
Pop. 2010:	729,771	White:	84.3%	Private:	76.5%
Change since 2000:	Up 7.1%	Black:	3.6%	Government:	17.2%
Urban:	66.7%	Hispanic:	6.7%	Self-employed:	6.3%
Rural:	33.3%	Asian:	2.9%	Blue collar:	19.0%
Area size:	2,143 sq. mi.	Native Am.:	0.4%	White collar:	62.5%
		Hawaiian:	0.0%	Khaki collar:	0.6%
Age		Two+ races:	1.9%	Other:	17.8%
Median age:	40.0 yrs.				
More than 65 yrs:	13.3%	*Ancestry*		Median income:	$70,283
Less than 18 yrs:	21.9%	Irish	14.7%	Median Home Value:	$276,000
		Italian	12.0%		
Education		English	10.5%	**Military Veterans**	
H.S. grad:	90.2%			% of Pop:	11.4%
College grad:	32.9%				
Grad degree:	14.6%				

East Connecticut; Norwich

One of the longest-settled parts of the United States, eastern Connecticut has experienced great, and sometimes painful, change in recent years—change comparable to that of the 1640s or 1810s or 1950s. When the Puritan settlers from Massachusetts and England arrived, these flinty hills were the home of small Indian tribes, whose numbers were decimated by warfare and even more by disease. This was never fertile

2008 Presidential Vote		
Barack Obama (D) 204,221	(59%)
John McCain (R) 139,945	(40%)
2004 Presidential Vote		
John Kerry (D) 180,235	(54%)
George Bush (R) 147,819	(44%)
Cook Partisan Voting Index: D+6		

farming country, but New London and Norwich were among the 13 Colonies' leading workshops and ports. Factories developed around mills in little villages on the fast-flowing Quinebaug and Shetucket rivers. Sandbars kept oceangoing ships out of the rivers, but they docked at New London. In the mid-20th century, new technology shaped the area. Four nuclear power plants were built here, more than in any similarly populated part of the United States. In Groton, the "Submarine Capital of the World" situated across the Thames River from New London, is General Dynamics' Electric Boat company, which built its first submarines in 1915 and later, nuclear submarines.

In the 1990s, the local economy was in trouble. Nuclear plants were wearing out and being shut down across the country. After the end of the Cold War, many in the Electric Boat workforce were laid off, though some remained to work on the next-generation, Virginia-class submarine. About 10,000 are employed at both the Groton and Rhode Island facilities today. Even with the Navy's December 2008 announcement of a $14 billion contract for additional production, the port's long-term survival is in doubt. Meanwhile, drug maker Pfizer Inc. eliminated a longtime manufacturing plant in Groton in 2007 and announced it would close its former worldwide R&D headquarters in New London by the end of 2012. The area's economic base shifted to entertainment, specifically to gambling. The Foxwoods Resort Casino, built by the 650-member Mashantucket Pequot tribe and opened in 1992, is the largest casino in the world, with hotels, golf courses, and a convention center. In 2008, Foxwoods completed a $700 million expansion and is now the largest employer in Connecticut. Eight miles away, near Norwich, is the Mohegan Sun casino, the second largest casino in the world, which opened in 1996. Gambling now provides a significant share of tax dollars to the state. But competition from nearby states is slowing the growth of gaming in the area. New London has taken steps to become a cruise ship destination. A University of Connecticut report in 2010 said the Norwich-New London area is likely to lead the rest of the state in recovering from the recession.

The 2nd Congressional District includes most of the eastern part of the state, centering on the small cities of New London and Norwich and including mill towns and the University of Connecticut in Storrs. The northeastern edge of Windham County, long known as "Quiet Corner" for its small towns and dairy farms, has lured away many Rhode Island and Massachusetts residents looking to escape high taxes and housing prices. The district stretches west to the outskirts of Hartford and to antique-filled small towns like Essex and Old Lyme on Long Island Sound. For many years, this was a politically marginal district, with close battles between Yankee Republicans and Catholic Democrats. More recently, it has trended Democratic and has become volatile.

Joe Courtney (D)

The congressman from the 2nd District is Joe Courtney, a Democrat elected in 2006. Courtney was raised in West Hartford, the youngest of five boys. He studied at Tufts University, graduated from the University of Connecticut law school and went into private practice. In 1986, he won the first of four terms in the state House, where he served as chairman of the public health and human services committees. He ran unsuccessfully for lieutenant governor in 1998, and then unsuccessfully against Republican Rep. Rob Simmons in 2002. Simmons, who earned two Bronze Stars in Vietnam and later served as a CIA operations officer, had defeated 20-year Democratic Rep. Sam Gejdenson two years earlier. Courtney ran on the Democratic themes of Social Security restructuring, better prescription drug coverage for seniors and opposition to President Bush's tax cuts. The environmental group Friends of the Earth gave Simmons a boost, saying that he had the most pro-environment record of the freshmen Republicans. Simmons won 54%-46%. Courtney stepped aside for Democrat Jim Sullivan to take on Simmons in 2004, but Sullivan lost by the same 54%-46% total.

Courtney came back for a rematch with Simmons in 2006, getting his campaign under way early in 2005. Democrats worked diligently to nationalize the race by exploiting voter anger over the Iraq war and GOP ethics scandals in Congress. Simmons was attacked for donating $1,000 to the legal defense fund for Republican House Majority Leader Tom DeLay, who was caught up in dual ethics and fundraising investigations. After DeLay left Congress in disgrace, Democrats sought to tether Simmons to the increasingly unpopular Republican president. Simmons touted his independence by pointing to votes he took on partial-birth abortion and same-sex marriage in opposition to the administration's positions. He also touted his successful lobbying to keep the district's submarine base off the 2005 base-closing list.

On Election Night, Courtney held a slim 167-vote lead, a margin that was small enough to trigger an automatic recount. A week later, Courtney's lead was cut in half, but official results gave him a winning margin of 83 votes out of the more than 242,000 cast. He was the survivor of the closest House race of the 2006 elections.

In the House, Courtney's new colleagues gave him a nickname, "Landslide Joe." But he also got a seat on the prestigious Armed Services Committee, where he could more effectively lobby for more money for the Navy's shipbuilding program at Groton. In 2007, he worked with other Connecticut and Rhode Island lawmakers to successfully secure an extra $588 million in the Defense appropriations bill for submarines, paving the way for the Navy to double its submarine production from one a year to two a year. Democratic leaders were eager to help the rookie representative secure his hold on the district. Courtney was able to get Armed Services Chairman Ike Skelton, D-Mo., and Defense Appropriations Subcommittee Chairman John Murtha, D-Pa., to visit the district, and both of the powerful chairmen backed improvements at Electric Boat.

In 2008, Courtney won enactment of a bill giving environmental protection to 25 miles of the Eightmile River, bringing it under the Wild and Scenic Rivers Act. He was the only member of the Connecticut delegation who voted against the $700 billion Wall Street rescue, which he said focused too much on "a square mile of New York City." He worked with a bipartisan group of House and Senate members on expanding the "Troops to Teachers" program, which gives soldiers bonuses for agreeing to teach in schools with low-income students, and on raising the maximum amounts available in Pell grants for college students. During the 2009 health care debate, Courtney led House Democratic opposition to a proposed "Cadillac tax" on high-cost health insurance plans, which he said would harm millions of middle-class people. He helped change it to a 3.8 percent tax on unearned income.

In 2008, Republicans put up Sean Sullivan, former commander of the Groton submarine base, against Courtney. Sullivan depicted him as a lockstep loyalist for Democratic leaders. Courtney cited his accomplishments and said he had been elected to "stand up to Bush's policies." He won 66%-32%, establishing a firm grip on this formerly competitive seat. Two years later, his GOP opponent was Janet Peckinpaugh, a former television news anchor who was able to raise just over $215,000 for her campaign without getting the national GOP support she had hoped for. Courtney collected $1.7 million and cruised to victory 60%-39%.

THIRD DISTRICT

Rosa DeLauro (D)

Elected 1990, 11th term; b. March 2, 1943, New Haven; home, New Haven; Marymount Col., B.A. 1964, London Sch. of Econ., 1962-63, Columbia U., M.A. 1966; Catholic; married (Stanley Greenberg); 3 children.

Professional Career: Exec. asst., New Haven Mayor Frank Logue, 1976–77; Exec. asst. & develop. admin., City of New Haven, 1977–79; Chief of staff, U.S. Sen. Christopher Dodd, 1980–87; Exec. dir., Countdown '87, 1987–88; Exec. dir., EMILY's List, 1989.

DC Office: 2413 RHOB, 20515, 202-225-3661; Fax: 202-225-4890; Web site: delauro.house.gov.

State Offices: New Haven, 203-562-3718; Stratford, 203-378-9005.

Committees: *Appropriations:* Agriculture, Rural Development, FDA & Related Agencies; Labor, HHS, Education & Related Agencies (RMM).

Group Ratings

	ACLU	ACU	ADA	CFG	AFS	FRC	LCV	ITIC	NTU	COC
2010	81	0	100	0	100	0	100	67	5	13
2009	–	0	100	0	100	–	100	–	2	33

National Journal Ratings

	2010 LIB	—	2010 CONS	2009 LIB	—	2009 CONS
Economic	90%	—	0%	88%	—	9%
Social	89%	—	7%	75%	—	20%
Foreign	73%	—	24%	84%	—	15%
Composite	87%	—	13%	84%	—	16%

Key Votes of the 111th Congress

1. Overturn Ledbetter	Y	5. Bar federal abortion funds	N	9. Stop detainee transfers	N
2. Pass $820 billion stimulus	Y	6. Pass health care bill	Y	10. Legalize immigrants' kids	Y
3. Let guns in national parks	N	7. Regulate financial firms	Y	11. Repeal don't ask, tell	Y
4. Pass cap-and-trade	Y	8. Pass tax cuts for some	Y	12. Limit campaign funds	Y

Election Results

2010 general	Rosa DeLauro (D)	143,565	(65%)	($1,309,373)
	Jerry Labriola (R)	74,107	(34%)	($204,422)
2010 primary	Rosa DeLauro (D)	unopposed		

Prior Winning Percentages: 2008 (77%), 2006 (76%), 2004 (72%), 2002 (66%), 2000 (72%), 1998 (71%), 1996 (71%), 1994 (63%), 1992 (66%), 1990 (52%)

Population		Race/Ethnicity		Work	
Pop. 2010:	712,339	White:	68.8%	Private:	80.9%
Change since 2000:	Up 4.6%	Black:	12.5%	Government:	13.2%
Urban:	96.6%	Hispanic:	12.7%	Self-employed:	5.9%
Rural:	3.4%	Asian:	3.8%	Blue collar:	19.3%
Area size:	485 sq. mi.	Native Am.:	0.2%	White collar:	64.0%
		Hawaiian:	0.0%	Khaki collar:	0.0%
Age		Two+ races:	1.7%	Other:	16.7%
Median age:	38.2 yrs.				
More than 65 yrs:	13.8%	*Ancestry*		Median income:	$62,328
Less than 18 yrs:	21.7%	Italian	19.4%	Median Home Value:	$286,400
		Irish	13.3%		
Education		German	7.0%	**Military Veterans**	
H.S. grad:	88.7%			% of Pop:	8.5%
College grad:	32.5%				
Grad degree:	14.8%				

South Connecticut; New Haven

The beginnings of Connecticut's defense industry date to more than two centuries ago, in 1798,
when Eli Whitney, a young Yale graduate, won
an order from the young United States government to produce 10,000 muskets at $13.40 each.
Six years before, Whitney had invented the cotton gin, which revolutionized the South but for
years embroiled him in a patent suit. On the mu-
sket contract, he was determined to make a
profit right off, so he set up a system of inter-

2008 Presidential Vote		
Barack Obama (D) 201,741	(63%)
John McCain (R) 117,114	(36%)
2004 Presidential Vote		
John Kerry (D) 174,382	(56%)
George Bush (R) 128,960	(42%)
Cook Partisan Voting Index: D+9		

changeable parts and invented a milling machine and gauges: the birth of standardized American
manufacturing. It also launched New Haven, established more than 150 years earlier as a religious
haven for strict Puritans, as a manufacturing center; Whitney set up his factory along a small,
rapidly flowing river just north of town. For the next 150 years or so, New Haven mass-produced
rifles, clocks, locks, hardware and toys—anything its tinkerers and entrepreneurs could fashion.
Few factories remain in New Haven, and the state's defense contracts are modest compared to
those of the city's heyday. The factory that produced Winchester rifles and guns for 140 years closed
in 2006. In recent years, southern Connecticut around New Haven discovered a new source of prosperity in scores of small technology and biomedical firms. The result has spurred growth in outer-
ring suburban towns, with the fastest being East Windsor, whose population jumped more than
4% between 2007 and 2009.

But the city itself, with significant crime rates and many neighborhoods scarred by abandoned
homes, has shrunk in population: It had 164,000 people in 1950 and 123,000 in 2007. Yale, with
its Gothic spires and red-brick halls, has always been the visual focus of New Haven and is now its
largest employer. Some local revival has been sparked by a state development program that has
turned old retail and office buildings into residences and by $1 billion in investments by biotech
firms. After limping through the recent recession, local officials began seeing small signs of hope.
Home prices were down almost 7% from a year earlier, but the number of housing permits nearly
doubled in October 2010 from the previous year. Unemployment remained close to 9%, but total
employment grew by half a percent from 2009, and on the drawing board was a $45 million over-
haul of the old Winchester factory, which will convert it into residential units and the headquarters of the Higher One education financing firm.

The 3rd Congressional District of Connecticut covers the New Haven metropolitan area,
which has long since spread beyond the narrow city limits into what were once Yankee villages
and countryside. New Haven proper cast only 13% of the district's votes in 2008. For many years,
the 3rd was a marginal district, regularly changing partisan hands in the 1980s. But it is now a
strongly Democratic district. Barack Obama got 63% of the vote here in 2008, and John Kerry won
56% in 2004 against fellow Yale graduate George W. Bush.

Rosa DeLauro (D)

The congresswoman from the 3rd District is Rosa DeLauro, first elected in 1990. She is well connected in New Haven and Washington. She grew up in New Haven's Wooster Square. Both her
parents were New Haven aldermen. Her mother, Luisa DeLauro, retired from the Board of Aldermen in 1999 after 35 years, the longest tenure in New Haven history. Rosa DeLauro's husband,
Stanley Greenberg, was Bill Clinton's chief pollster from 1991 to 1994 and worked for Al Gore's
presidential campaign in 2000 and John Kerry's in 2004. Former Obama White House Chief of
Staff Rahm Emanuel, a family friend, officiated at the wedding of Greenburg's daughter Anna, a
political consultant. DeLauro has been in politics nearly all of her life. She was a development
administrator in New Haven in the 1970s, chief of staff to Democratic Sen. Christopher Dodd from
1980 to 1987, and then spent a year working to stop U.S. military aid to Nicaraguan contras before
going on to become director of EMILY's List, the women's campaign fundraising group. When 3rd
District incumbent Bruce Morrison ran for governor in 1990, DeLauro ran for his seat and won,
52%-48%, over anti-tax and anti-abortion rights state Sen. Tom Scott. Her last serious competition
came in 1992, when she won a rematch against Scott, 66%-34%.

DeLauro has a consistently liberal voting record, is a close ally of House Minority Leader
Nancy Pelosi, and is one of the Democratic leadership's most vocal champions in debate. She is an
active and ardent supporter of feminist issues. A cancer survivor, she sponsored the law to require
that patients and doctors, not insurance companies, decide on 48-hour hospital stays for mastecto-

mies. She also lobbied for insurance coverage of early-detection tests for cervical cancer, and helped to enact "Johanna's Law" to increase awareness of gynecological cancers. In 2009, she introduced a bill to require employers to give workers seven paid sick days annually. Also that year, the House passed her Paycheck Fairness Act, which provided remedies to victims of wage discrimination. A similar bill, the Lilly Ledbetter Fair Pay Act, was signed into law, reversing a Supreme Court decision that had made it more difficult to ensure that women and men doing the same job are paid comparable wages.

As chairperson from 2007 to 2010 of the Appropriations Subcommittee on Agriculture, Rural Development, Food and Drug Administration, and Related Agencies, DeLauro took a keen interest in food safety, which she said should have the same priority as prescription drug and medical device safety. Her subcommittee in 2008 increased by $1.8 billion President George W. Bush's funding request for the FDA. But she said a year later that the agency remained "badly broken," and faulted the Obama administration for not doing enough to address food safety in its fiscal 2010 budget, which had 19% more funding for the agency. After the Centers for Disease Control and Prevention released figures in late 2010 showing that food-borne disease remained a public health threat, she introduced a bill to create a single agency to regulate the food supply.

As a political strategist and advocate of Democratic causes, DeLauro is "a live wire whose words rush out like sparks," as a *New York Times* profile described her. In November 2009, as Pelosi reluctantly announced her support for an amendment strictly limiting insurance coverage for abortions as part of the health care overhaul, DeLauro reportedly got into an angry confrontation with California Rep. George Miller, another trusted Pelosi ally who called for more pragmatism. When home-state Senate colleague Joe Lieberman, a political independent, held up the legislation a month later, DeLauro demanded that Lieberman be recalled.

DeLauro has run twice for chair of the Democratic Caucus and suffered two painfully close losses. In 1998, she lost 108-97 to Martin Frost of Texas, but then Minority Leader Dick Gephardt named her an assistant leader in charge of the party's message. In 2002, she lost 104-103 to Robert Menendez of New Jersey after an intense yearlong contest. DeLauro has been an active supporter of Pelosi in her leadership races through the years, which helped cement the bond between the two Italian-American liberal women. Pelosi has leaned on DeLauro for important appointive leadership roles and made her co-chair of the Democratic Steering Committee, a powerful panel that makes committee assignments. In 2007, DeLauro also became a vice chair of the Democratic Congressional Campaign Committee, the House Democrats' fundraising and recruiting arm. Three years earlier, DeLauro led the drafting of the Democratic platform when John Kerry was nominated for president.

She has expressed interest in running for the Senate, an option that could become increasingly attractive to her if Republicans retain majority control in coming elections, crimping her influence in the House. In addition, with Lieberman's announcement that he will not seek re-election in 2012, there will be an open Senate seat.

FOURTH DISTRICT

Jim Himes (D)

Elected 2008, 2nd term; b. July 5, 1966, Lima, Peru; home, Greenwich; Harvard U., B.A. 1988; Oxford U., M.Phil. 1990.; Presbyterian; married (Mary); 2 children.

Elected Office: Greenwich Bd. of Estimates in Taxation, 2005-07.

Professional Career: Financial analyst and V.P., Goldman Sachs, 1990-2002; V.P., Enterprise Community Partners, 2004-08.

DC Office: 119 CHOB, 20515, 202-225-5541; Fax: 202-225-9629; Web site: himes.house.gov.

State Offices: Bridgeport, 866-453-0028; Stamford, 266-453-0028.

Committees: *Financial Services:* Capital Markets and Government Sponsored Enterprises; Oversight & Investigations.

Group Ratings

	ACLU	ACU	ADA	CFG	AFS	FRC	LCV	ITIC	NTU	COC
2010	81	13	90	0	100	0	80	100	13	29
2009	–	4	95	10	89	–	100	–	10	40

National Journal Ratings

	2010 LIB — 2010 CONS		2009 LIB — 2009 CONS	
Economic	54%	— 45%	57%	— 42%
Social	52%	— 46%	64%	— 34%
Foreign	54%	— 46%	77%	— 23%
Composite	54%	— 46%	67%	— 34%

Key Votes of the 111th Congress

1. Overturn Ledbetter	Y	5. Bar federal abortion funds	N
2. Pass $820 billion stimulus	Y	6. Pass health care bill	Y
3. Let guns in national parks	N	7. Regulate financial firms	Y
4. Pass cap-and-trade	Y	8. Pass tax cuts for some	Y

9. Stop detainee transfers	N
10. Legalize immigrants' kids	Y
11. Repeal don't ask, tell	Y
12. Limit campaign funds	Y

Election Results

2010 general	Jim Himes (D)	115,351	(53%)	($3,685,473)
	Dan Debicella (R)	102,030	(47%)	($1,965,915)
2010 primary	Jim Himes (D)	unopposed		

Prior Winning Percentages: 2008 (51%)

Population		Race/Ethnicity		Work	
Pop. 2010:	706,740	White:	64.6%	Private:	81.8%
Change since 2000:	Up 3.8%	Black:	11.2%	Government:	9.2%
Urban:	95.9%	Hispanic:	17.5%	Self-employed:	8.9%
Rural:	4.1%	Asian:	4.6%	Blue collar:	14.4%
Area size:	539 sq. mi.	Native Am.:	0.1%	White collar:	69.7%
		Hawaiian:	0.0%	Khaki collar:	0.0%
Age		Two+ races:	1.4%	Other:	15.9%
Median age:	38.8 yrs.				
More than 65 yrs:	13.1%	*Ancestry*		Median income:	$84,957
Less than 18 yrs:	25.7%	Italian	13.9%	Median Home Value:	$576,200
		Irish	12.0%		
Education		German	7.4%	**Military Veterans**	
H.S. grad:	88.5%			% of Pop:	6.4%
College grad:	46.2%				
Grad degree:	20.6%				

Southwest Connecticut; Bridgeport

No one in colonial America imagined that the rocky shore of southern Connecticut on Long Island Sound would some day lodge one of the largest concentrations of wealth in the world. The soil was stony, the terrain unaccommodating, and the harbors not as convenient as those in New York, Rhode Island, and Massachusetts. For 200 years, this was the home of unnoticed Yankee farmers, sailors, and tinkerers. Then, factories were built on its fast-running stream.

2008 Presidential Vote		
Barack Obama (D)	190,995	(60%)
John McCain (R)	126,849	(40%)
2004 Presidential Vote		
John Kerry (D)	162,166	(52%)
George Bush (R)	143,280	(46%)
Cook Partisan Voting Index: D+5		

In the 19th century, Bridgeport became famous as the home of P.T. Barnum, who was the city's mayor before he started his circus. Around that time, rich New Yorkers began taking the train north to country houses in Connecticut. In the 20th century, Greenwich and other Yankee villages clustered around commuter railroad stations became the home of some of New York's elite.

Greenwich has over a dozen private clubs and nearly a dozen private schools. Houses routinely sell at high prices and are then torn down to make way for grander mansions. Starting in the 1950s, New York City-based executives, eager to minimize their commutes and avoid New York's income taxes, moved their headquarters to Greenwich and beyond, including General Electric in Fairfield and several firms in Stamford. Greenwich, sometimes referred to as "Wall Street by the Sea" for its proliferation of hedge fund offices and financial firms, is closest to New York and commands the highest commercial rents of all these places. Not all of the businesses are financial powerhouses, though. In Shelton, Wiffle Ball Inc. sells millions of wiffle balls and bats each year. The Brookings Institution's Global MetroMonitor in late 2010 ranked the Bridgeport area behind Boston in climbing out of the recession, but ahead of regional neighbors Providence and New York.

The 4th Congressional District covers Connecticut along Long Island Sound, from industrial Bridgeport, the state's largest city, to affluent Greenwich. It goes inland to take in Ridgefield, Redding, Monroe, and Oxford. This is the wealthiest district in the nation's wealthiest state. More than 40% of Connecticut's state taxes are collected in Fairfield County. It includes bustling and pricey Stamford, woodsy Darien, modest Norwalk, artsy-craftsy Westport, Fairfield, and then Bridgeport. An odd duck, Bridgeport is an industrial and low-income town, though spruced up when the state-financed Harbor Yard sports complex opened for minor league baseball and a major downtown rehabilitation resulted. The basic political balance has been the same since the 1940s, when the heavily affluent suburbs outvoted Bridgeport and elected Republican Clare Boothe Luce to Congress. More than the rest of Connecticut, the 4th is oriented to New York City rather than to Hartford or Boston. They are Yankees, not Red Sox, fans. Their political attitudes are shaped by what is happening in New York as much as in Hartford. Opposition to high taxes has helped Republicans to win here. But the influence of Christian conservatives in the GOP has repelled Episcopalians and other mainline Protestants, and they have been increasingly voting Democratic. This is the district where George H. W. Bush grew up and one that he carried in 1988 and 1992. But George W. Bush lost it in 2000 and 2004, and Democrat Barack Obama defeated Republican John McCain 60%-40% in 2008.

Jim Himes (D)

The congressman from the 4th District is Jim Himes, a Democrat elected in 2008. Though he represents one of the wealthiest areas of the country, Himes grew up in different surroundings. Born in Lima, Peru, he spent his early years in Peru and Colombia, where his father worked for the Ford Foundation, the automotive pioneer's international development organization. Around the time of his 10th birthday, after his parents divorced, he came to the United States with his mother and two sisters and settled in Pennington, N.J. His early experience in Latin America had an enduring effect. He speaks fluent Spanish and maintains a deep interest in the region. Himes earned his undergraduate degree from Harvard University and then got a Rhodes scholarship to study at Oxford. When he returned to the United States, he went to work for Goldman Sachs as a financial analyst. He spent 12 years at the powerful investment house, and left the company in 2002 as a vice president. The following year, he joined Enterprise Community Partners, a Columbia, Md.-based nonprofit dedicated to alleviating urban poverty. Beginning in 2004, he managed its offices in the Northeast.

Like many other Wall Street executives, Himes moved in 1998 to the affluent suburb of Greenwich to raise a family with his wife, Mary. He became active in the town Democratic committee after the 2000 presidential election, and served as committee chairman from 2003 to 2007. On Sept. 11, 2001, Himes left his Goldman Sachs office against company orders to provide assistance to victims. In 2006, he worked as a campaign volunteer for Democrat Diane Farrell, who finished roughly 7,000 votes behind Rep. Christopher Shays, a GOP moderate who had withstood repeated Democratic assaults on his seat. The following April, Himes announced his own campaign against Shays, promising the third competitive race in a row in this Democratic district.

Himes set a torrid fundraising pace, aided in large measure by his Wall Street connections. The Democratic Congressional Campaign Committee also made him one of its top prospects in 2008. After easily dispatching a minor challenger in the August primary, Himes focused on Shays and the Bush administration and attempted to link the two over the Iraq war. Himes embraced the national Democratic establishment, frequently reminding voters that he would appear on the same ticket as presidential nominee Obama. The efforts of national Democrats helped Himes slightly out raise Shays, and the DCCC further tipped the scales by investing $1.2 million in the race.

Sensitive to his district's politics, Shays made his own overtures to Democrats, running ads that touted him as the candidate with "the hopefulness of Obama" and "the straight talk of McCain." But he made a questionable move in September 2008, when he echoed McCain's claim that the fundamentals of the United States' economy were strong. Himes and the DCCC criticized that assessment amid widespread economic suffering in the district and nationally, but Shays stuck to it and even reiterated it at a debate in late October. In past years, Shays' moderate record and seniority on Capitol Hill helped him weather severe political storms. But in 2008, the surge of enthusiasm for Obama's candidacy provided a powerful final push. Himes defeated Shays 51%-48%. He won the district's urban regions by substantial margins and also managed to stay competitive in the affluent suburbs that tend to break Republican.

Himes has taken a centrist approach in Congress, supporting Obama's major priorities but also asserting his independence. He riled some Democratic leaders when he joined several other junior lawmakers in July 2010 to form a working group to propose large spending cuts in defense, energy, housing and agriculture. He also explored ways to put his Wall Street background to use. On the Financial Services Committee, he worked with Rep. Alan Grayson, D-Fla., in March 2009 during the furor over bonuses paid to executives at AIG International Inc. and other firms receiving federal rescue money. Their measure required all future compensation to be performance-based; it passed the House but stalled in the Senate. When the committee took up a sweeping financial overhaul bill, he helped craft a provision regulating the complex financial instruments known as derivatives. As the bill entered delicate House-Senate negotiations in 2010, Himes faced criticism from consumer advocates who said he and other centrist Democrats backed weaker derivatives controls passed by the Senate and intended to appease Wall Street. Himes argued that the legislation still took significant steps to crack down on abuses at investment firms.

Republicans hoped that Obama's absence from the ballot in 2010 would give them a shot at unseating Himes. But the GOP nomination went to state Sen. Dan Debicella of Shelton over the more moderate former state Sen. Rob Russo of Bridgeport. Himes wasted little time in portraying Debicella as an inconsistent extremist, saying that Debicella had welcomed federal economic stimulus money in his district while criticizing the Democrats' stimulus bill. Debicella raised questions about Himes' centrism and called him a "rubber stamp" for liberal House Speaker Nancy Pelosi. Debicella was able to raise $800,000 in the campaign's last few months, but he was no match for Himes, who again relied on his Wall Street connections to bring in more than $3.3 million. He won with 53% of the vote.

FIFTH DISTRICT

Chris Murphy (D)

Elected 2006, 3rd term; b. Aug. 3, 1973, White Plains, NY; home, Cheshire; Attended Exeter College (England), 1994-95; Williams Col., B.A. 1996; U. of CT, J.D. 2002; Protestant; married (Cathy Holahan); 1 child.

Elected Office: CT House of Reps., 1998-2002; CT Senate, 2002-06.

Professional Career: Southington zoning commission, 1997-99; Practicing atty., 2002-06.

DC Office: 412 CHOB, 20515, 202-225-4476; Fax: 202-225-5933; Web site: chrismurphy.house.gov.

State Offices: Danbury, 203-798-2072; Meriden, 203-630-0815; New Britain, 860-223-8412; Waterbury, 203-759-7541.

Committees: *Foreign Affairs:* Middle East & South Asia. *Oversight & Government Reform:* Health Care, District of Columbia, Census & the National Archives; Technology, Information Policy, Intergovernmental Relations & Procurement Reform.

Group Ratings

	ACLU	ACU	ADA	CFG	AFS	FRC	LCV	ITIC	NTU	COC
2010	81	4	95	0	100	0	90	67	8	13
2009	–	4	100	7	89	–	100	–	5	40

National Journal Ratings

	2010 LIB	—	2010 CONS		2009 LIB	—	2009 CONS
Economic	60%	—	40%		70%	—	29%
Social	82%	—	14%		75%	—	20%
Foreign	66%	—	29%		59%	—	41%
Composite	71%	—	29%		69%	—	31%

Key Votes of the 111th Congress

1. Overturn Ledbetter	Y	5. Bar federal abortion funds	N	9. Stop detainee transfers	N
2. Pass $820 billion stimulus	Y	6. Pass health care bill	Y	10. Legalize immigrants' kids	Y
3. Let guns in national parks	N	7. Regulate financial firms	Y	11. Repeal don't ask, tell	Y
4. Pass cap-and-trade	Y	8. Pass tax cuts for some	Y	12. Limit campaign funds	Y

Election Results

2010 general	Chris Murphy (D)	122,879	(54%)	($3,034,971)
	Sam Caligiuri (R-I)	104,402	(46%)	($1,320,420)
2010 primary	Chris Murphy (D)	unopposed		

Prior Winning Percentages: 2008 (59%), 2006 (54%)

Population		Race/Ethnicity		Work	
Pop. 2010:	714,296	White:	73.2%	Private:	80.8%
Change since 2000:	Up 4.9%	Black:	5.9%	Government:	12.4%
Urban:	85.9%	Hispanic:	15.6%	Self-employed:	6.6%
Rural:	14.1%	Asian:	3.1%	Blue collar:	19.8%
Area size:	1,282 sq. mi.	Native Am.:	0.1%	White collar:	63.5%
		Hawaiian:	0.0%	Khaki collar:	0.1%
Age		Two+ races:	1.6%	Other:	16.6%
Median age:	39.6 yrs.				
More than 65 yrs:	14.0%	*Ancestry*		Median income:	$65,759
Less than 18 yrs:	24.0%	Italian	14.6%	Median Home Value:	$292,800
		Irish	13.3%		
Education		German	8.4%	**Military Veterans**	
H.S. grad:	87.5%			% of Pop:	8.6%
College grad:	33.5%				
Grad degree:	13.7%				

West Connecticut; Waterbury

Over the years, Connecticut's stony soil has become home to some of the most affluent people in the nation and the world. This is true even in the hills of northwest Connecticut, off the interstates and far from Connecticut's small urban capital of Hartford and its sometime booming edge city of Stamford. In Litchfield County are exquisite Yankee towns like Washington and Kent, which were prosperous in the post-Revolutionary era, when Connecticut's shipowners accumulated capital and invested it in factories and mills. They now are considered the "anti-Hamptons," a country-home mecca for ultrarich New Yorkers seeking to avoid the glitz of Southampton and East Hampton. Avon and Simsbury have become comfortable bedroom communities and home to champion international ice skaters.

2008 Presidential Vote		
Barack Obama (D) 182,022	(56%)
John McCain (R) 136,966	(42%)

2004 Presidential Vote		
John Kerry (D) 153,616	(49%)
George Bush (R) 152,504	(49%)

Cook Partisan Voting Index: D+2

Not too far away are small industrial cities like New Britain, America's ball-bearing capital for years; Meriden, which turned from making ivory combs, clocks and cutlery to producing electrical signaling equipment, biotech filters, and nuclear instruments; and Waterbury, once the nation's largest producer of brass, whose unemployment rate hovered above 11% in 2010, higher than any other Connecticut city. Danbury, once the nation's leading producer of hats, is now attracting an eclectic mix of recent immigrants from South America, the Caribbean and Southeast Asia. The city of 75,000 attracted as many as 10,000 illegal immigrants by 2009, prompting local police to partner with federal immigration officers in a crackdown, which sparked community protests and spurred numerous immigrants to leave.

The 5th Congressional District of Connecticut covers much of the western side of the state, dipping down to include the northern towns of Fairfield County. It has two arms that reach into the hills of central Connecticut—one to Democratic Meriden and the other to the affluent and Republican-leaning Farmington Valley suburbs of Hartford. This district was carefully drawn by a bipartisan redistricting commission to provide a "fair fight" between two incumbents forced into the same district after Connecticut lost a House seat in the 2000 census. Until recently, small towns like Kent and Salisbury in Litchfield County were dominated by Republicans, but the influx of newcomers has altered voting patterns. Barack Obama won this district by 45,056 votes in 2008; George W. Bush lost it in 2004 by only 1,112 votes.

Chris Murphy (D)

The congressman from the 5th District is Chris Murphy, an ambitious young Democrat elected in 2006. Murphy grew up in Wethersfield, and his father is a prominent member of a Hartford law firm. He graduated from Williams College in 1996 and the same year, at age 22, became the campaign manager for Democrat Charlotte Koskoff, who came 1,587 votes short of ousting veteran Republican Rep. Nancy Johnson. (Back then, he lived in a converted funeral home in Southington that later became the basis for a 2009 horror film, *The Haunting of Connecticut*.) The lessons of Koskoff's campaign would serve Murphy well in his political career. He won a seat in the state House in 1998, got a law degree in 2002 and, later that year, won election to the state Senate. He served as co-chairman of the public health committee, where he worked to curb hospital collection practices, ban smoking in workplaces, and increase investment in embryonic stem cell research.

In early 2005, Murphy moved into Johnson's 5th District, announcing in April that he planned to challenge her. He was backed by the Democratic establishment and faced no primary opposition. Unlike Connecticut's other two competitive congressional races in 2006, this one did not revolve around the Iraq war and President Bush. Much of the debate focused instead on the Medicare prescription drug benefit that moderate Republican Johnson had helped design in 2003 as chairman of the House Ways and Means Health Subcommittee. Murphy contended that the Republicans' prescription drug program's enrollment deadlines penalized seniors, and he spotlighted drug industry contributions to Johnson to portray her as a shill for the industry.

But Johnson effectively introduced national security as an issue in the campaign with an ad timed on the fifth anniversary of the September 11 terrorist attacks that criticized Murphy for opposing the Bush administration's warrantless wiretapping program. The spot suggested that the delay in investigations caused by the process of getting court warrants for surveillance would jeopardize national security, and put Murphy on the defensive. He struck back with an ad that implied Johnson was reluctant to help a mother obtain health coverage for surgery to fix her infant's cleft palate. Just before the election, another Johnson ad accused Murphy of voting to raise taxes 27 times. By that time, all the negative campaigning may have undermined Johnson's image as a cool-headed, seasoned legislator. She outspent Murphy $5 million to $2.5 million, but he beat her, 54%-44%.

In the House, Murphy has established a record as a fairly loyal Democrat, particularly as he has allied with home-state colleagues Rosa DeLauro and John Larson, both senior leaders of the Democratic Caucus. But Murphy has at times taken pains to distance himself from the leadership, declaring in 2010 that he would not support a federal budget that did not cut non-entitlement spending by at least 1%. He took the lead in organizing freshman Democrats for ethics reform, especially the creation of an outside commission to review ethics complaints against House members. Although his proposal failed, the House did create an Office of Congressional Ethics, with independent investigators. In April 2008, the House passed his Government Contractor Accountability Act requiring disclosure of the names and salaries of top officers of large companies that made most of their money from contracts with the government.

In 2009, Murphy won a seat on the influential Energy and Commerce Committee, where he worked on health care issues. He supported a government-run public option to compete with private insurers when the House debated the health care overhaul, and he got into the bill his provision requiring lawmakers and their staffs who accept government health insurance benefits to receive them only through the exchanges created by the legislation. He also introduced a bill in 2010 requiring federal contracting officials to solicit information from businesses regarding how many American jobs would be retained or created if their bids were chosen. And he won House passage the same year of "Billy's Law," authorizing $14.4 million over six years to help families find missing relatives. Murphy lost his seat on the panel when Republicans claimed the majority in 2011

National Republicans initially saw an opportunity when state Sen. David Cappiello challenged Murphy in 2008. Cappiello ran as a John McCain-style maverick, and he criticized Murphy's campaign contributions from finance firms as well as his support for the 2008 rescue of the financial and insurance industries. Murphy emphasized the need for sweeping policy change in the tax and trade policies that contributed to the crisis. National party interest waned in the closing weeks as Cappiello failed to gain traction, and Murphy won 59%-39%.

Two years later, Murphy drew another GOP state senator as an opponent—Sam Caligiuri, who prevailed in a competitive three-way primary. He ran on the standard Republican themes of 2010, depicting Murphy as a big-spending liberal close to then-Speaker Nancy Pelosi. He got some outside help; the conservative American Action Network ran an ad falsely claiming that the health care law required jail time for people who did not buy health insurance. Murphy called the ad part of a "smear campaign." Late polls showed Murphy trailing Caligiuri, but he campaigned vigorously on his support of "Buy American" laws and his efforts to save jobs at East Hartford's Pratt & Whitney jet engine factory. Murphy outspent his opponent 2-to-1 and eked out a victory with 54% of the vote.

★ DELAWARE ★

Delaware, the first state to ratify the Constitution, the second-smallest state in area, and the sixth- smallest in population, is a small corner of America but with some considerable claims on U.S. history. The mouth of the Delaware River was explored by Henry Hudson, and the Dutch and Swedes built settlements on the west bank in the 1630s. But the three counties of Delaware owe their separate existence to the politics of the proprietors of William Penn's colony of Pennsylvania, and to Delawareans' own speed in ratifying the Constitution, which made it literally the "First State."

Throughout most of its history, Delaware has been unusually affluent. It had the nation's highest income levels during the early 20th century and still has relatively high income levels. The many members of the du Pont clan occupy beautiful cobblestone mansions in its chateau country. Delaware's racial and ethnic mix is not radically different from the rest of the nation's: its population is 21% African-American and 8% Hispanic. It has a mixture of suburbs, old immigrant neighborhoods, urban neighborhoods, attractive beach towns, and farmlands. Sussex County in southern Delaware is a world of its own. It produces more chickens than any other county in the country—chickens outnumber people 300-to-1 in Delaware—and also thousands of tons of processed chicken dung (or "broiler litter"). Its beach communities are bustling with growth, and there is a move toward historic preservation in the old, inland towns.

For much of the past two centuries, the central focus of Delaware's economy was the business started by Eleuthère Irénée du Pont, the practical-minded son of a dreamy, idealistic French immigrant. He built a gunpowder mill on the banks of Brandywine Creek in 1802, which was the first enterprise of the du Pont family. Over time, it became one of America's great munitions and chemical companies. It switched from gunpowder to dynamite in the 1880s, and the company grew especially rapidly during World War I, generating so much capital that it bought a large share of General Motors stock in the 1920s and controlled GM for 30 years, when GM was the country's largest corporation. DuPont capital also financed what was arguably the world's finest research and development program. In the years on either side of World War II, DuPont prospered by bringing to the consumer and industrial markets new synthetics and plastics such as rayon, nylon, synthetic dyes, cellophane, Lucite, Teflon, and Dacron: "Better Living Through Chemistry."

Business trends in Delaware have had an outsized impact on national policy. In the late 19th century, the state passed pioneering laws of incorporation, giving more flexibility and power to managers and owners. Most companies in the *Fortune* 500 and on the New York Stock Exchange and Nasdaq are incorporated in Delaware. Their legal births take place in a federal-style building near the Capitol in Dover, which means that much of the nation's corporate law, especially on mergers and acquisitions, is made in Delaware's Chancery Court. Delaware takes care in choosing judges and writing corporate law to produce a reliable legal environment. Recently, the Chancery Court's jurisdiction has been extended to intellectual property, and the Wilmington bar has boned up on corporate bankruptcy law.

In the quarter-century boom starting in the early 1980s, Delaware fostered a new industry: credit cards. In 1981, Gov. Pete du Pont pushed through a law abolishing Delaware's usury laws and lowering its bank franchise tax. Inflation was high, and banks were looking for a state with no limit on interest rates to locate their credit card operations. Although South Dakota abolished its usury law in 1980, the state didn't have a labor force large enough to support many banks. Delaware did. MBNA moved there from Maryland in 1982 and invented the affinity card in 1983. It became the nation's largest credit card issuer; its chief executive officer, Charles Cawley, replaced the du Pont family as Delaware's most visible philanthropist and community leader. Cawley retired in 2003, and Bank of America acquired MBNA in 2005. The 2007 financial crisis hit the credit card business hard, helping to send Delaware into recession, and the troubles in the domestic auto industry reverberated in the state as well. More than 1,000 people lost their jobs when Chrysler closed its Dodge manufacturing plant in Newark at the end of 2008, and another 550 were laid off at General Motors' Wilmington plant in 2009. Still, DuPont is keeping the state on the cutting edge by developing alternative fuels, and life sciences businesses are growing. Unemployment in the state rose in 2010 to the highest level since 1976, but it was still below the national average.

One way Delaware thrives is by "exporting taxes." Journalist Jonathan Chait, irritated at the exorbitant tolls and traffic jams at the tollbooths on Interstate 95 through Delaware, wrote in *The New Republic:* "The organizing principle of Delaware government is to subsidize its people at the rest of the country's expense." State government gets 3% of its operating budget from the turnpike

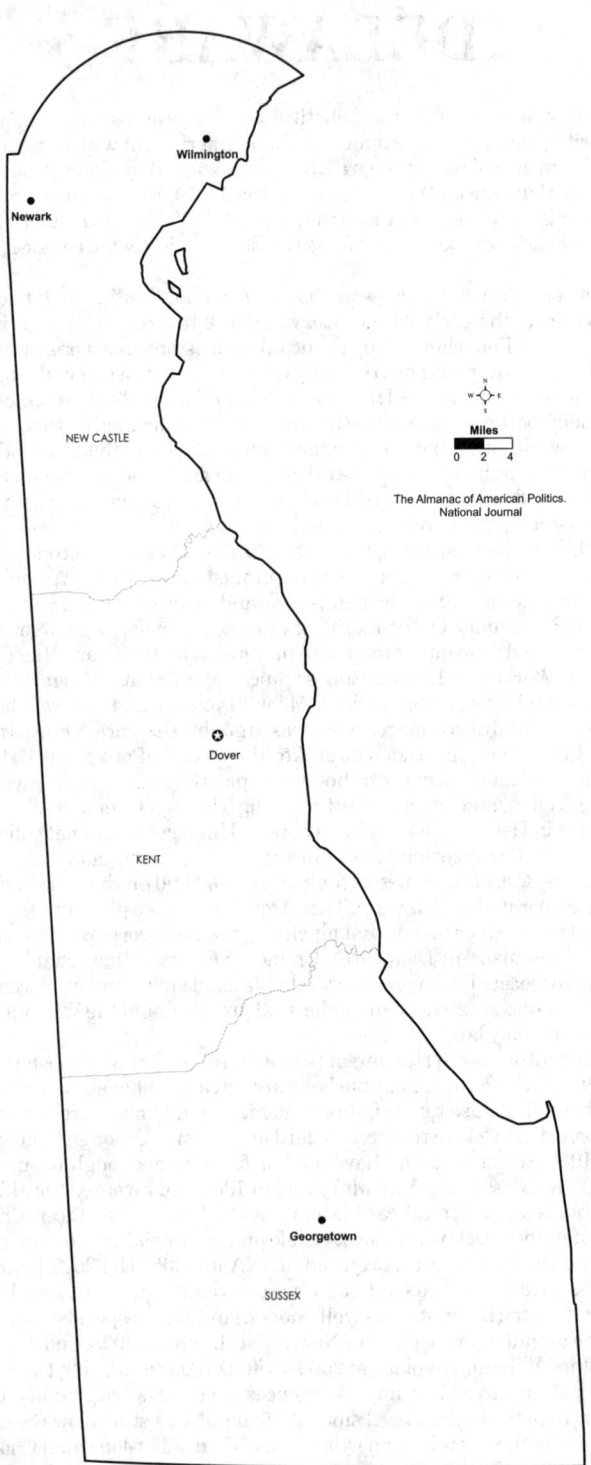

Wilmington

Newark

NEW CASTLE

Miles
0   2   4

The Almanac of American Politics.
National Journal

Dover

KENT

Georgetown

SUSSEX

U.S. Representative elected at-large.

tolls, 22% from corporate and franchise taxes, and 7% from the lottery and slot machines. A 1993 U.S. Supreme Court decision sanctioned Delaware's tax on unclaimed property from other states. Exporting taxes has allowed Delaware to be one of the five states with no sales tax. And it has lowered its income tax several times in recent years, first under du Pont, then under Republican Gov. Michael Castle and Democratic Gov. Thomas Carper. Property taxes are low, with no reassessments since 1974 in Sussex County, since 1983 in New Castle County, and since 1986 in Kent County. The Census Bureau reports that Delaware's state government has the fourth-highest revenue per capita of any state. Delaware boosters can argue that its state policies have provided credit to millions of people and businesses, enabled America's industrial economy to grow robustly, and led the nation in a virtuous cycle of lowering taxes. Certainly Delaware has done well. Its population grew 18% in the 1990s and 13% from 2000 to 2010.

Delaware is on both sides of the Mason-Dixon line. It was a slave state with many emancipation sympathizers. On his Wilmington stop during his train ride to Washington in January 2009, President-elect Barack Obama, joined by Delaware's own Joe Biden, paid tribute to Delaware's Underground Railroad. They did not mention that Abraham Lincoln, during his 1861 train ride to Washington, decided not to risk a stop in slaveholding Delaware. Delaware also has immigrant communities in the Wilmington area, and it has Southern-accented farmers in Kent and Sussex counties, plus Latino migrants working in its chicken plants. Its New Castle County suburbs range from very affluent to not-so-affluent. Well-preserved 18th-century buildings line the streets of New Castle, the capital from 1704 to 1777. Newark has grown from a country crossroads to a small city as the University of Delaware has expanded.

From the 1950s through the 1980s, the state's considerable variety produced robust, two-party politics in which tiny Delaware's vote mirrored that of the nation's. But in the 1990s, Delaware, like many of America's largest metro areas, trended toward the Democrats. Now it is virtually a one-party state. Delaware has not elected a Republican governor since 1988, when GOP moderate Castle won. Jack Markell, who had been the Democratic state treasurer, effectively clinched the office when he defeated Lt. Gov. John Carney in the 2008 primary. Democrats hold both U.S. Senate seats: Carper won it by beating incumbent Republican William Roth in 2000, and Christopher Coons was easily elected to the last four years of Biden's term over eccentric Republican nominee Christine O'Donnell in 2010. Democrats have solid majorities in the tiny state legislature and increased their margin in the state House in 2010. The major exception to Democratic rule for many years was Castle, who was elected to the state's lone House seat in 1992 after two terms as governor. National Republicans were delighted when he was persuaded to seek Biden's seat, held temporar-

Population		Household Income		Work	
Pop. 2010:	897,934	Under $15k:	9.9%	Private:	80.9%
State rank:	45th	$15k to $50k:	33.6%	Government:	14.8%
Change since 2000:	Up 14.6%	$50k to $100k:	33.6%	Self-employed:	4.2%
Urban:	76.4%	$100k to $200k:	19.1%	Unemployment (3-yr. average):	4.6%
Rural:	23.6%	Over $200k:	3.8%	Poverty:	10.7%
Native of state:	46.1%	Median income:	$57,176	Blue collar:	19.7%
Not a citizen:	4.7%			White collar:	62.7%
Area size:	2,489 sq. mi.	**Home Value**		Khaki collar:	0.3%
		Under $100k:	10.5%	Other:	17.3%
Most populous cities		$100k to $300k:	54.6%		
Wilmington	70,851	$300k to $500k:	25.8%	**Age**	
Dover	36,047	$500k to $1 mil:	7.4%	Median age:	38.0 yrs.
Newark	31,454	Over $1 million:	1.7%	More than 65 yrs:	14.0%
		Median:	$246,000	Less than 18 yrs:	23.6%

Race/Ethnicity				Military Veterans		Registered Voters in 2010	
White:	65.3%	*Language*		% of Pop:	11.6%	Democrats:	293,885
Black:	20.8%	English:	88.6%			Republicans:	183,645
Hispanic:	8.2%	Spanish:	5.7%	*Veterans by Period*		Ind./other:	146,945
Asian:	3.2%	Asian:	1.8%	WWII and before:	9.8%	Voter turnout:	310,946
Native Am.:	0.3%	Other European:	3.1%	Korea:	12.6%	Turnout as % of	
Hawaiian:	0.0%			Vietnam:	32.6%	voting age:	44.9%
Two+ races:	2.0%	**Education**		Gulf (pre-2001):	10.6%		
		H.S. grad:	87.3%	Gulf (post-2001):	8.4%	**Legislature**	
Ancestry		College grad:	27.5%	Peace time:	26.0%	Senate:	14 D 7 R
Irish	14.6%	Grad degree:	10.9%			House:	26 D 15 R
German	12.8%						
English	9.8%						

ily by longtime Biden aide Ted Kaufman, in the 2010 election. But they were dismayed when he lost the Republican primary to the tea party-backed O'Donnell, whose performance on the stump was at best uneven. Any chance the party had for the seat was gone. O'Donnell did actually carry Kent and Sussex counties, but she lost New Castle County by more than 2-to-1. Coons won 57%-40%, while Carney won the state's single House seat by an almost identical 57%-41%.

Delaware elections are not usually bitter contests (Castle's primary defeat was an exception). Thanks to the state's small size, politics remain intimate. Personal campaigning is important, and voters are not at all surprised to run into their senators in the supermarket. Successful Delaware politicians are almost always nice people; they couldn't get elected otherwise. Then there is Delaware's unique custom, dating back to 1792, of "Return Day." On the Thursday after an election, winning and losing candidates go to the Sussex County seat of Georgetown and ride together in carriages to receive the bipartisan cheers of the voters and, literally, bury a hatchet in a box of Lewes Beach sand. Not a bad example for the other 49 states.

Presidential politics   Until 2000, Delaware could claim it was a presidential bellwether: It had voted for every winner from 1952 to 1996, the longest winning streak of any state. But starting in 2000, this affluent state has been voting significantly more Democratic than the national average. The New Castle County suburbs, like other affluent parts of major metropolitan areas, starting in the middle 1990s tilted toward the Democrats and away from the Republicans on cultural issues. Most Delaware voters still see plenty of ads, because in the past three elections all candidates have targeted Pennsylvania and most of the state is in the Philadelphia media market. But it seldom sees presidential or vice presidential candidates, except for Biden, whom voters saw often during his 36 years in the Senate.

In 2004, Delaware scheduled its primary one week after New Hampshire's, on Feb. 3, but it was only one of several states voting that day.

2008 Presidential Vote		
Barack Obama (D) 255,459	(62%)
John McCain (R) 152,374	(37%)

2008 Presidential Primary		
Barack Obama (D) 51,124	(53%)
Hillary Clinton (D).................40,751	(42%)

2008 Presidential Primary		
John McCain (R) 22,626	(45%)
Mitt Romney (R).....................16,344	(33%)
Mike Huckabee (R)...................7,706	(15%)

2004 Presidential Vote		
John Kerry (D) 200,152	(53%)
George W. Bush (R)..............171,660	(46%)

Joe Lieberman, endorsed by Carper, Carney, and Markell, paid several trips to Delaware. Other candidates were scarcer. John Kerry won the primary with 50% of the vote; Lieberman ran second with 11%, in what amounted to a tie with John Edwards, Howard Dean, and Wesley Clark.

In 2008, Delaware held its primary on Feb. 5, Super Tuesday. Little campaigning occurred until after the Iowa caucuses, and Biden had already withdrawn from the race. On Jan. 31, Michelle Obama appeared at a theater in Wilmington and drew a crowd of 2,600. Encouraged, the Obama campaign scheduled a February rally in Rodney Square, and 10,000 thronged to see the candidate. Obama was endorsed by gubernatorial primary rivals Markell and Carney. Hillary Rodham Clinton was endorsed by outgoing Gov. Ruth Ann Minner, and her daughter, Chelsea Clinton, put in an appearance on Feb. 4. But it was not enough. Obama carried the state 53%-42%, winning by a big margin in both black neighborhoods and affluent suburbs in New Castle County. Clinton carried Southern-accented Sussex County. Some 96,000 Delawareans voted in the Democratic primary, while only 50,000 turned out for the GOP primary. The Republican candidates did little campaigning here. John McCain, endorsed by Castle, won with 45% of the vote, to 33% for Mitt Romney and 15% for Mike Huckabee.

In recent general elections, Democrats Al Gore and Kerry carried Delaware by decisive margins, 55%-42% and 53%-46%, respectively, in 2000 and 2004. In 2008, with Biden on the ticket—the first Delawarean on a national ticket—Obama carried the state 62%-37%. Regional patterns did emerge in the voting. Obama carried New Castle County—once marginal political ground—by an astonishing 70%-29%, much better than in demographically similar areas in southeast Pennsylvania or southern New Jersey. But Obama carried Kent County by only 54%-45%, and he lost Sussex County by 45%-54%.

Governor

Jack Markell (D)

Elected 2008, term expires Jan. 2013, 1st term; b. Nov. 26, 1960, Newark; home, Wilmington; Brown U., B.A. 1981; U. of Chicago, M.B.A. 1985; Jewish; married (Carla); 2 children.

Elected Office: DE treas., 1999-2008.

Professional Career: Officer, First Natl. Bank Chicago, 1982-86; Assoc., McKinsey & Co., Inc., 1986-1988; Sr. v.p., Nextel, 1989-95; V.P., Comcast, 1996-1998.

Office: Tatnall Bldg., William Penn Street, 2nd Floor, Dover, 19901, 302-744-4101; Fax: 302-739-2775; Web site: www.state.de.us/governor.

State Offices: Wilmington, 302-577-3210.

Election Results

2008 general	Jack Markell (D)	266,861	(68%)
	William Lee (R)	126,662	(32%)
2008 primary	Jack Markell (D)	37,849	(51%)
	John Carney (D)	36,112	(49%)

Jack Markell, a Democrat, was elected governor of Delaware in 2008. Markell (*mar-KEL*) was raised in a split-level house in Newark, the youngest of three children. His father was a professor at the University of Delaware and his mother was a state social worker. Growing up, Markell came to appreciate Delaware's small-town familiarity; he went to kindergarten with his future wife, Carla. His first foray into politics came at age 17, when he was elected president of his high school's student body. The same year, he accompanied his father on an overseas sabbatical, living half the year in Britain and half in New Zealand. After graduating from Brown University and earning an M.B.A. from the University of Chicago, Markell set off on a 16-year career in business. He worked briefly in banking and consulting before joining a telecommunications startup called Fleet Call in 1989. Over the next decade, Fleet Call grew into a major cellular service provider and rebranded itself as Nextel, a name Markell coined. He struck up a lasting friendship there with one of Fleet Call's early investors, Mark Warner, later governor of Virginia and now a senator. Following a brief stint as an executive for cable service provider Comcast, Markell defeated Republican state Treasurer Janet Rzewnicki in 1998 in his first campaign for public office.

Markell brought his business acumen to the treasurer's office and played an influential role in shaping the state's finances. Shortly after taking office, he sought to cut state spending by consolidating purchases across agencies. He helped pioneer a program that provides every state employee a detailed health assessment in an effort to provide better care while reducing the state's costs. Believing that most citizens knew relatively little about monetary issues, he sought to improve financial literacy in the state where most of the nation's credit cards are issued. Together with community and church leaders in Wilmington, he led a campaign to encourage eligible families to apply for the Earned Income Tax Credit. He created the Delaware Money School, which offers free classes on a range of personal financial topics. He was re-elected by wide margins in 2002 and 2006.

When Democratic Gov. Ruth Ann Minner was barred by term limits from running again in 2008, Markell was a natural to get into the contest to succeed her. But there was someone of equal political stature ahead of him in line. John Carney, the lieutenant governor, was the Democratic favorite. In a small state where most elected officials are on personal terms with one another, office seekers defer to the wishes of party elders, who hoped to avoid the first contested Democratic gubernatorial primary since 1992. They urged Markell to run for lieutenant governor instead. But he was steadfast about wanting the top job. Deprived of his anticipated coronation, Carney lined up support from much of the party establishment, including Minner, state legislators, and unions. But Markell campaigned tirelessly across the state and raised more than $4 million, including $725,000 of his own money, a record fundraising haul in a Delaware governor's race. Carney could not keep pace with Markell's fundraising, but enjoyed the backing of the state party's executive committee, which ran ads against Markell. As Minner's popularity flagged after two terms in office, Markell subtly distanced himself from her by campaigning on a theme of change, and in June released a detailed compendium of policy proposals called the "Blueprint for a Better Delaware." Still,

Markell's victory in the September primary was a stunner. He took 51% of the vote to Carney's 49%, a margin of about 1,700 votes.

The party rallied behind Markell for the general election, where he faced Republican Bill Lee, a retired Superior Court judge making his third straight run for the office. On the campaign trail, Markell and Matt Denn, the Democratic candidate for lieutenant governor, touted a plan they claimed would save taxpayers over $100 million while simultaneously balancing a state budget faced with a massive deficit. The 12-page document drew heavily on previous Markell proposals for health care, education, and energy. The Republican Party tried to taint Markell with ads that referenced a 1994 lawsuit alleging that he and other Nextel executives had made false statements to boost the company's stock price. The executives settled the lawsuit for $27 million without admitting wrongdoing.

In the weeks leading up to the general election, few doubted that Markell would keep the governor's mansion in Democratic hands. He entered October with a commanding lead in the polls and 10 times as much money as his opponent. During a debate in late October, Lee pushed Markell to pledge not to levy any new taxes in order to fund his proposed programs. Markell refused, but still defeated Lee, 68%-32%.

Markell took office at a time of deepening economic uncertainty for the state, whose reliance on the financial services industry for its tax revenue left it disproportionately affected by volatility on Wall Street. Facing a budget deficit estimated at $800 million, Markell cut state workers' pay and raised taxes. Taking advantage of a provision in a 1992 federal law, he proposed legalizing sports betting in Delaware, as well as increasing the number of slot machines. The National Collegiate Athletic Association threatened a tournament boycott if betting were allowed on college games; a federal appeals court in August 2009 limited the betting to three-game parlays on National Football League contests. Markell also promoted wind farms off the Delaware coast, in partnership with the governors of Maryland and Virginia, and got local utilities to commit to buying wind energy. In 2010, he signed a law requiring 25% of the state's electricity to come from renewable sources by 2025. He promoted a one-time tax amnesty in 2009 that netted $22 million and signed a bill in 2010 allowing mutual insurance companies headquartered in Delaware to demutualize, in line with Delaware's tradition of encouraging companies to incorporate in the state.

When General Motors announced in June 2009 that it would close the Boxwood Road plant, Markell encouraged Fisker Automotive to buy the facility. He enlisted Vice President Joe Biden's help, and in September got a $529 million loan from the Department of Energy on top of a $12.5 million state loan for infrastructure and other financial incentives. In October, the company announced it was moving in and CEO Henrik Fisker told *The News Journal* of Wilmington, "The governor pulled (things) together faster than I can take my family of four people to dinner."

In December 2009, Markell became head of the Democratic Governors Association. His party lost not quite as many governorships in 2010 as some predicted it would. And in Delaware, Democrats did fine, with New Castle County Executive Christopher Coons beating Christine O'Donnell for Biden's Senate seat and John Carney taking the U.S. House seat vacated by Republican Michael Castle. Democrats even gained seats in the state legislature. Markell comes up for re-election in 2012.

Senior Senator

Thomas Carper (D)

Elected 2000, term expires 2012, 2nd term; b. Jan. 23, 1947, Beckley, WV; home, Wilmington; OH St. U., B.A. 1968, U. of DE, M.B.A. 1975; Presbyterian; married (Martha); 2 children.

Military Career: Navy, 1968–73 (Vietnam); Naval Reserves, 1973–91.

Elected Office: DE treas., 1976–82; U.S. House of Reps., 1982–92; DE gov. 1992-2000.

Professional Career: Industrial devel. specialist, DE Div. of Econ. Devel., 1975–76.

DC Office: 513 HSOB, 20510, 202-224-2441; Fax: 202-228-2190; Web site: carper.senate.gov.

State Offices: Dover, 302-674-3308; Georgetown, 302-856-7690; Wilmington, 302-573-6291.

Committees: *Environment & Public Works:* Clean Air & Nuclear Safety (Chmn); Green Jobs & the New Economy; Superfund, Toxics & Environmental Health; Transportation & Infrastructure. *Finance:* Energy, Natural Resources & Infrastructure; Health Care; Taxation & IRS Oversight. *Homeland Security & Governmental Affairs:* Contracting Oversight (Ad Hoc); Federal Financial Management, Government Information, Federal Services & International Security (Chmn); Investigations (Permanent).

Group Ratings

	ACLU	ACU	ADA	CFG	AFS	FRC	LCV	ITIC	NTU	COC
2010	93	0	90	5	91	0	100	67	12	27
2009	–	4	90	8	91	–	100	–	9	57

National Journal Ratings

	2010 LIB	—	2010 CONS		2009 LIB	—	2009 CONS
Economic	67%	—	31%		50%	—	49%
Social	65%	—	0%		85%	—	0%
Foreign	47%	—	0%		55%	—	0%
Composite	75%	—	25%		74%	—	27%

Key Votes of the 111th Congress

1. Overturn Ledbetter	Y	5. Pass health care bill	Y	9. Ratify New START	Y
2. Pass $787 billion stimulus	Y	6. Regulate financial firms	Y	10. Confirm Elena Kagan	Y
3. Repeal DC gun laws	N	7. Pass tax cuts for some	Y	11. Stop EPA climate regs	N
4. Confirm Sonia Sotomayor	Y	8. Legalize immigrants' kids	Y	12. Repeal don't ask, tell	Y

Election Results

2006 general	Thomas Carper (D)	170,567	(70%)	($4,752,942)
	Jan Ting (R)	69,734	(29%)	($203,289)
2006 primary	Thomas Carper (D) .... unopposed			

Prior Winning Percentages: 2000 (56%); Governor: 1996 (70%); 1992 (65%); House: 1990 (66%); 1988 (68%); 1986 (66%); 1984 (59%); 1982 (52%)

Democrat Thomas Carper is Delaware's senior senator. He grew up in Southside Virginia and Ohio and graduated from Ohio State University. He first came to Delaware as an ensign in the Navy, then returned to get his M.B.A. at the University of Delaware after service in Southeast Asia, where he was a mission commander piloting submarine-hunting planes. In 1976, he was elected state treasurer, at age 29. He ran for the U.S. House in 1982 and beat a scandal-tarred incumbent. In office, Carper established a moderate voting record and worked to let banks into the securities business and to prevent ocean sludge-dumping, both causes supported by Delaware constituencies. In 1992, when Republican Gov. Michael Castle was term-limited and ran for the House, Carper ran for governor and won the general election with 65% of the vote.

As governor, Carper pursued an agenda that was in many ways more conservative than liberal. He continued former Republican Gov. Pete du Pont's policy of cutting taxes, reducing income tax rates by about 10%, and also cutting small-business and utility taxes. Delaware's strong economy helped him keep the budget in the black, and he boosted the state's credit rating to a historic high even as state spending rose 40% in eight years. He also signed a bill authorizing charter schools. He was re-elected 70%-30% over then-Treasurer Janet Rzewnicki. Barred from a third term, he ran in 2000 for the U.S. Senate seat held by Republican William Roth since 1970.

This was a battle of positives. Both candidates had very high approval ratings at home, and both were familiar figures to many voters; they brought a combined total of 58 years in statewide office to the race. Roth had a record of achievements that paid direct benefits to people in this generally affluent state: the Kemp-Roth tax cut of 1981, the Roth IRA enacted in 1997, the reform of the Internal Revenue Service passed in 1998, $2.3 billion for Amtrak capital improvements in 1998. Roth's main problem was that he was 79 years old. The then 53-year-old Carper was careful not to campaign negatively against Roth or to attack him for his age, but his slogan, "A Senator for Our Future," spotlighted the contrast between their ages. Carper's 16-hour campaign days contrasted with Roth's approach. He stayed in Washington and made only a few campaign appearances with his trademark St. Bernard dogs. Roth outspent Carper, $4.3 million to $2.5 million, but the Democratic Party spent some $4 million in Delaware, more than evening the score. In October, Roth fainted twice on the campaign trail, once in full view of cameras. Polls showed the race close to even in September and October, but in November, Carper won by a solid 56%-44%.

In the Senate, Carper has had one of the more moderate voting records among Democrats, and has been actively involved over the years with centrist organizations like the Democratic Leadership Council. He is often at the center of efforts to build bipartisan coalitions when important legislation bogs down, such as efforts to pass a health care overhaul bill in 2009 and 2010. He has expressed frustration with the pace of getting things done in Congress, and has complained to colleagues on occasion, "My worst day as governor was better than my best day as a United States senator."

During work on a major revision of health insurance policy, Carper bucked liberals in his party by opposing creation of a government-run insurance plan for people who could not afford private plans. But rather than attack the public option idea, he tried to broker a compromise that he and other centrist Democrats could support. He advanced an alternative that would allow states to individually decide whether to offer such an option to compete with private insurers. The public option was ultimately dropped from the final legislation because of opposition from Republicans and other centrist Democrats. On the sweeping financial regulation bill in 2010, Carper opposed an amendment restricting banks' charges to merchants and sought to prevent state officials from imposing more stringent regulations than the federal government.

Carper has taken a major role in clean air legislation. In 2006, he co-sponsored with Republican Lamar Alexander of Tennessee a bill to limit emissions of sulfur dioxide, nitrous oxide, mercury and carbon dioxide. The legislation has gone nowhere year after year, but Carper keeps trying. In February 2010, he and Alexander reprised their bill to substantially reduce emissions from power plants, and when it failed to attract sufficient bipartisan support to pass, they put it on hold—again. When the Environmental Protection Agency announced new power plant pollution regulations in July 2010, Carper called it "a step in the right direction," but said he preferred to keep trying to enact a law that would be more resilient to court challenges than the agency's rule.

In recent years, Carper also supported cap and trade, a proposal to cap greenhouse gas emissions but allow companies to get emissions "credits" from companies that pollute less. In 2007, he co-sponsored the bill with Republican John McCain and independent Joe Lieberman, but later declined to back a version of the bill that did not include limits on mercury, sulfur dioxide and nitrous oxide, which he thought necessary. On the issue of car emissions, Carper in May 2007 proposed credits for cars that can run on both gasoline and renewable fuels and $50 million in financing for advanced battery technology research; he supported a compromise bill that passed in December 2007. He also has called for increased use of nuclear energy, and with his Delaware colleagues, he has promoted offshore wind energy.

On the Governmental Affairs Committee, Carper worked with moderate Republican Susan Collins of Maine to pass in December 2006 the first major revision of Postal Service business operations since 1970. (More than half of credit card issuers have operations in Delaware, and that industry provides one-quarter of the Postal Service's mail.) Their bill provided for a streamlined rate increase procedure and for holding increases below inflation for 10 years. It passed after last-minute compromises with postal unions and retiree groups. In March 2010, Carper endorsed Postmaster General John Potter's plan to cut postal delivery from six to five days a week to cover revenue shortfalls, an idea that has been blocked by opposition in Congress. "It is not productive for Congress to act like a 535-member board of directors and constantly second-guess these necessary changes," Carper said. Also that year, Carper sponsored a successful bill, signed into law by President Barack Obama, requiring government agencies to conduct audits to identify some $125 billion that was expected to be lost through waste and fraudulent claims. He also teamed up with Lieberman and Collins on a bill to improve cybersecurity for Internet users, including giving the president authority to shut down Internet services in a national emergency. Critics said the bill went too far in allowing the government to control the Internet.

In earlier battles, Carper, with five Republicans and five other Democrats, managed in the early 2000s to condition the Bush tax cuts on deficit reduction. In 2001, he and Republican Judd Gregg of New Hampshire got $125 million for public school choice programs and $400 million for charter schools. And in 2005, he was more open to Social Security privatization than many Democrats, saying he would not "rule out at some point having private accounts."

Delaware is a small state in which unusually large percentages of voters actually meet with their elected representatives in person. It has a unique tradition of "Return Day," the day after the election, in which losing candidates along with winners take part in a parade in the town of Georgetown. It is a familiar ritual for Carper, who has been elected to statewide office 12 times and has ties to just about every prominent Democrat in the state. He even keeps a database with several hundred birthdays, so he can make congratulatory calls to friends and supporters. And Carper is a fierce defender of Delaware's interests. He was quick to complain in 2007 when the Department of Homeland Security issued a rule that would require buyers of more than 7,500 pounds of propane gas to register with the department. The rule was opposed by chicken growers in Delaware, where there are about 300 chickens to every person. He has worked with others in the Delaware delegation to bring millions on dollars in earmarked projects home to the state. In 2008, after the practice of earmarking became controversial, Carper said he would disclose his earmarks.

In 2006, Carper was re-elected, 70%-29%. He comes up for re-election in 2012.

Junior Senator

Christopher Coons (D)

Elected 2010, term expires 2014, 1st term; b. Sept. 9, 1963, Greenwich, CT; home, Wilmington; Amherst Col., B.A. 1985; Yale U., J.D. 1992; Yale Divinity Schl., M.A. 1992.; Presbyterian; Married (Annie); 3 children.

Elected Office: New Castle Cnty. Cncl., 2001-05; New Castle Cnty. exec., 2005-10.

Professional Career: Practicing atty., 1996-2004.

DC Office: 127A RSOB, 20510, 202-224-5042; Fax: 202-228-3075; Web site: coons.senate.gov.

State Offices: Milford, 302-424-8090; Wilmington, 302-573-6345.

Committees: *Budget. Energy & Natural Resources:* Energy; National Parks; Public Lands & Forests. *Foreign Relations:* African Affairs (Chmn); East Asian & Pacific Affairs; International Development & Foreign Assistance, Economic Affairs & International Environmental Protection; Near Eastern & South & Central Asian Affairs. *Judiciary:* Administrative Oversight & the Courts; Constitution, Civil Rights & Human Rights; Crime & Terrorism.

Election Results

2010 general	Chris Coons (D)	174,012	(57%)	($3,852,049)
	Christine O'Donnell (R)	123,053	(40%)	($7,539,252)
	Glenn Miller (Ind)	8,201	(3%)	
2010 primary	Chris Coons (D)	unopposed		

The junior senator from Delaware is Christopher Coons, a Democrat who won Vice President Joe Biden's former seat in 2010. Coons defeated the tea party-backed Christine O'Donnell.

Coons was born in Greenwich, Conn., the middle son of Ken and Sally Coons. His mother was a schoolteacher; his father held a variety of jobs, including managing a cannery and manufacturing kitchen furniture. After the family moved to Delaware in Coons' early childhood, bankruptcy wiped out much of his father's business success. His parents later divorced. In high school, Coons considered himself a Republican like his parents, and volunteered for Ronald Reagan's 1980 presidential campaign. His conversion to the Democratic Party came while he was a student at Amherst College. Visiting Kenya for a semester in 1984, Coons said that observing his host family changed the way he thought about poverty and free markets, and led him to write a tongue-in-cheek column for the college newspaper, titled "Chris Coons: The Making of a Bearded Marxist."

After graduating in 1985, Coons did relief work with a church group in South Africa, and then returned to the United States to attend Yale Law School. He also enrolled in the Divinity School and graduated from both programs in 1992. He moved to New York City to work with low-income students with the "I Have a Dream" Foundation. Delaware beckoned, though, and Coons moved back in 1996 after getting married; he and his wife had met while serving on a state community service commission the year before. Coons joined his stepfather's Newark-based fabrics company, W.L. Gore and Associates, as a lawyer. His first foray into politics came in 2000, when he ran for the New Castle County Council. After four years, he was elected county executive on an anti-corruption platform. Despite promising in his campaign not to increase taxes, Coons wound up raising taxes to close a budget gap.

When Biden was chosen to join Barack Obama's presidential ticket, the heavy favorite on the Democratic side for the open seat was state Attorney General Beau Biden, the incumbent's son. But the younger Biden declined to run, perhaps influenced by the appraisal by leading Democrats that the race was probably unwinnable against Republican Rep. Michael Castle, who had been elected statewide 12 times in 30 years and was the prohibitive favorite in the general election. But in one of 2010's big upsets, Castle lost the GOP primary to tea party favorite Christine O'Donnell, a local television commentator and perennial Senate candidate who hadn't been taken seriously until her stunning primary win. By that time, Coons was already in the race, having decided to run after Biden's announcement in February, and now, he had a real shot at winning.

Coons got the attention of the national media and an immediate double-digit lead over O'Donnell. Predictions that she would be a weak opponent were fulfilled in spades. O'Donnell was put on the defensive by old footage showing her condemning masturbation and claiming to have dabbled in witchcraft. She was compelled to tape a now famous campaign ad in which she reassured her supporters, "I am not a witch.... I'm nothing you've heard. I am you." A conservative, she also criticized judicial activism but could not answer a question about which Supreme Court cases she disagreed with.

O'Donnell focused on Coons' record raising of taxes as county executive, dubbing him "The Tax Man." Republicans also tried to use his "Bearded Marxist" essay as a line of attack, but he insisted the title was hyperbolic for humor's sake. "I am a clean-shaven capitalist," he retorted. Mostly, Coons kept a low profile while O'Donnell's campaign came apart with one controversy after another. She did make some headway with voters and ardent tea party activists who praised her for a common touch. And, she was no slouch at fundraising. O'Donnell raised over $7 million for her campaign, almost double that of Coons, who raised $3.8 million.

But on Election Day, it wasn't close. Coons won, 57% to 40%. Exit polls showed that he attracted significant crossover votes from Republicans and was heavily favored by women, who split 63%-35% in Coons' favor. O'Donnell fared somewhat better with men, who voted 53%-44% for Coons. However, the two ran about evenly among independents. Unaffiliated voters split 49% for Coons and 46% for O'Donnell.

REPRESENTATIVE-AT-LARGE

John Carney (D)

Elected 2010, 1st full term; b. May 20, 1956, Wilmington; home, Wilmington; Dartmouth Col., B.A. 1978; U. of DE, M.P.A. 1987.; Catholic; Married (Tracey); 2 children.

Elected Office: DE secy. of finance, 1997-2000; DE lt. gov., 2001-09.

Professional Career: Staff asst., Sen. Joe Biden, D-Del., 1986-89; dep. chief admin. officer, New Castle Cnty. Exec., 1989-94; dep. chief of staff, Gov. Thomas Carper, D-Del., 1994-97; pres., COO, Transformative Technologies, 2009-10.

DC Office: 1429 LHOB, 20515, 202-225-4165; Fax: 202-225-2291; Web site: johncarney.house.gov.

State Offices: Wilmington, 302-428-1902.

Committees: *Financial Services:* Financial Institutions & Consumer Credit; Oversight & Investigations.

Election Results

2010 general	John Carney (D)	173,543	(57%)	($2,140,065)
	Glen Urquhart (R)	125,442	(41%)	($1,369,932)
2010 primary	John Carney (D)	unopposed		

The new at large congressman from Delaware is John Carney, a Democrat elected to succeed nine-term Republican Rep. Michael Castle after Castle gave up the seat to run for the Senate in 2010. Carney, the second of nine children born to two teachers, has lived in Wilmington for most of his life. He was careful to stress his humble upbringing and the fact that he, his wife, and their two children live in a modest row house. Still, Carney has spent nearly his entire adult life in public office, except for brief stints as president and chief operating officer of Transformative Technologies, a Delaware green technology firm, and as executive vice president of a wind farm start-up called DelaWind. After getting a degree in English at Dartmouth College and a master's degree at the University of Delaware, Carney went to work as an aide to Joe Biden, then a Democratic senator from Delaware. In the 1990s, Carney became a top aide to then Gov. Thomas Carper, now a U.S. senator. Carney was also the state secretary of finance under Carper, from 1997 to 2000. That year, he won the first of two terms as Delaware's lieutenant governor. In 2008, Carney tried to move up to the top job but lost a high-profile primary against Jack Markell for governor. Markell went on to win.

His track record in office earned him the scorn of tea party activists who labeled him a "career politician" in his campaign against Glen Urquhart for Delaware's at large seat in the House. Carney faced Urquhart in the contest to succeed Castle, a Republican moderate, after Castle gave up the post to run what ultimately was a losing bid for the Senate. Carney ran on his support for the development of renewable energy technology and green jobs and his opposition to oil drilling off the Delaware shoreline.

Urquhart, a Rehoboth Beach developer, lambasted him for collecting government paychecks for years in his various capacities rather than creating jobs in the private sector. He called Carney "part of the problem" with government. Urquhart also called attention to Carney's attempt to lobby the state for money in 2009, when he worked for DelaWind. The deal fell apart after the primary investor dropped out, forcing the company to withdraw its application to the U.S. Energy Department for tax credits and its application for $1.4 million in state funding.

But Carney's government-heavy résumé was not the liability it was for candidates elsewhere in the country in an election year marked by anti-incumbent fervor. Left-leaning Delaware was skittish about some of Urquhart's conservative positions. He said he would vote to repeal the health care law passed by Congress in 2010 and support abolishing the departments of Energy and Education. The Republican's social agenda and lack of polish also probably hurt him: He said he opposed abortion even in cases of rape or incest. And in widely circulated comments, he compared liberals to Nazis while claiming that Hitler, not Thomas Jefferson, first coined the phrase "separation of church and state."

Carney declared Urquhart too "radical" and "extreme" to represent the state. He said he supported the health care law, although he didn't agree with every aspect of it and would work in Congress to make it more effective. Carney also favored the Democrats' financial regulation bill, a controversial stance in a state heavily reliant on finance and corporate headquarters. Most of the companies in the *Fortune* 500 and on the New York Stock Exchange were incorporated in Delaware, and the DuPont business empire has shaped politics there for more than a century. On the issue of extending the Bush-era tax cuts, Urquhart taunted Carney in a debate by asking his foe to refuse to play the "class warfare card" and to commit to extending the cuts permanently. Carney kept to his position of extending them temporarily to give Congress time to come up with a deficit reduction plan.

Carney had the upper hand in the money chase. He raised over $2 million, while Urquhart had $1.3 million, $1 million of that from his own pocket. Urquhart criticized his opponent for taking money from political action committees, saying that Carney couldn't be a voice independent of those "paying his way." On Election Day, Carney prevailed with 57% of the vote to 41% for his opponent, a rare instance of a Democrat seizing Republican territory in 2010.

★ DISTRICT OF COLUMBIA ★

The capital of the most powerful and affluent nation in history, Washington is a physically beautiful city of great achievements and astonishing contrasts. Those achievements and that contrast go back more than 200 years. In 1787, the Constitution's framers, familiar with contemporary London and Paris mobs and remembering how unruly crowds had threatened the Continental Congress in Philadelphia, purposely gave the new federal government control of the 10-mile-square enclave that came to be called the District of Columbia. (The portion across the Potomac River was retroceded to Virginia in 1846 on the grounds that the federal government would never need it.)

Over the years, Congress kept control of the District for its own advantage and, at times, out of distrust of the city's large African-American population. In the 1790s, blacks made up one-quarter of Washington's population, and the city was a center for free blacks before the Civil War and right after emancipation. Radical Republicans gave the District self-government during Reconstruction in 1871, but Gov. Alexander (Boss) Shepherd, in building great public works, spent the District into bankruptcy, and the experiment ended in 1874. Later, Washington's growth spurts, starting with the New Deal and especially after World War II, resulted in the development of large, mostly white suburbs, and blacks became a larger percentage of the city's population, reaching a majority in the 1960 census. Amid the 1960s civil rights revolution, it began to seem absurd to deny the vote to the District of Columbia. So in 1964, after the Constitution was amended, District residents began to cast three electoral votes for president; in 1968, they were allowed to vote for the school board; in 1971 they got to elect a nonvoting delegate to Congress; and in 1974 they got home rule and could vote for a mayor and a city council.

For some time, this self-government worked no better than it did in the 1870s. The Boss Shepherd of modern times was Marion Barry, a talented politician but a disastrous mayor who held office for 16 of 20 years between 1978 and 1998. Under Barry, the District was a dysfunctional polity, a city with above-average incomes and a vibrant commercial property base, but with a local government so bloated with employees (up to 51,000 at its peak) and so indifferent to its responsibilities that it destroyed one marginal neighborhood after another. Violent crime flourished despite a 1978 law that essentially outlawed possession of handguns acquired after that date. Barry raised money from public employee unions and real estate developers and increasingly won votes from poor blacks by attacking any critic as a racist. In January 1990, he was arrested in a D.C. hotel for using crack cocaine, and was prosecuted and sent to prison. A reform-minded mayor, Sharon Pratt Kelly, was elected that fall but flinched when it came time to cut the payroll. Barry, out of prison and elected to the D.C. Council in 1992, won a fourth term as mayor in 1994.

The District's fiscal crisis after Barry's return led Congress in 1995 to take most of the government from his control. This was not a hostile takeover. House Speaker Newt Gingrich appointed Tom Davis as chairman of the D.C. subcommittee. Davis was a Republican member of Congress from Northern Virginia long sympathetic to the District, and he worked closely with D.C.'s elected delegate, Eleanor Holmes Norton. They got Congress to establish a five-member financial control board in April 1995, and the board's chief financial officer, Anthony Williams, hacked away at the payroll, reformed management practices, and cleaned up messes in District government offices. When Barry announced in May 1998 that he wouldn't run again, there was a push, encouraged by *The Washington Post,* to draft Anthony Williams as mayor. An unlikely candidate who was diffident in crowds and partial to wearing a bow tie, Williams had lived in Washington for only a few years, but he won the Democratic primary and the general election. The control board immediately delegated power to the new mayor, and in the fall of 2000, the courts returned control of most District departments to the city.

Over the last dozen years, the District thrived. Its population has been increasing since 2000, and affluent professionals and young people in large numbers flowed in, gentrifying and giving vitality to neighborhoods long given up to decline—Penn Quarter, Columbia Heights, Logan Circle, Shaw and the H Street corridor. New apartment buildings sprang up on land left empty for years. In the process, the black percentage fell from a peak of 71% in 1970 to 55% in 2007 and to 50% in 2010 as whites moved back to the city, low-income black neighborhoods emptied out and middle-income blacks moved to majority-black Prince George's County, Md. and other suburbs. High-rise condominiums and rental apartments targeted at singles (only 23% of District households are married-couple families, while 49% of adults have college degrees) were built in what had once been high-crime areas. The District's population topped the 600,000 mark in the 2010 census, although that was still well short of its peak of 802,000 in 1950. One corollary is that whites now cast approximately half or almost half of the District's votes and blacks will probably cast less than half some time in the next decade. But the electorate remains overwhelmingly Democratic. In 2004, John Kerry carried the District over George W. Bush 89%-9%. In 2008, Barack Obama won it 92%-7%. Whites voted 80% for Kerry and 86% for Obama. The District is the one jurisdiction in the nation where Hispanics vote more Republican than whites.

Williams declined to seek another term in 2006. The front-runner to succeed him was council President Linda Cropp, who had years of experience in city government, going back to the time her husband was a top aide to Barry. But also jumping into the fray was 35-year-old council member Adrian Fenty, the son of a black father and a white mother who grew up over their athletic shoe store in the diverse Mount Pleasant area. He represented the affluent, mostly black Ward 4 east of Rock Creek Park. Fenty started campaigning early and hard. Accompanied often by some of his many volunteers, he knocked on about half the doors in the District of Columbia. He ran less on issues than on energy. Cropp had the support of most of the local business community. But in the September primary, Fenty trounced Cropp 57%-31%. He carried all eight wards and all 142 precincts in the city. Electoral politics in Washington has often divided voters on lines of race. Fenty did not do so. He won the general election with 89% of the vote.

In office, Fenty moved to shake things up. His greatest initiative as mayor was on education. The D.C. public schools for years, despite some of the highest spending levels in the nation, had low achievement levels and plunging enrollments. By 2006, 25% of the students were enrolled in charter schools, one of the highest rates in the country. In 2007, Fenty persuaded the council to give him, rather than the independent board of education, control over the schools, and he carried the issue by a 9-2 council vote. Fenty installed as his schools superintendent Michelle Rhee, an alumna of the Teach for America program and the founder of the New Teacher Project. An outside-the-mainstream choice who didn't come from a government background, she promptly ordered the closing of 23 schools and declared her support for charter schools. She took on the teachers union in another area: Rhee promised teachers higher pay in return for relinquishing their right to tenure. She eventually negotiated a contract with the union giving teachers the option of earning merit pay and giving her power to dismiss under-performing teachers, which she did in significant numbers.

Population		Household Income		Work	
Pop. 2010:	601,723	Under $15k:	15.5%	Private:	68.2%
Change since 2000:	Up 5.2%	$15k to $50k:	28.4%	Government:	26.8%
Urban:	100.0%	$50k to $100k:	26.1%	Self-employed:	4.9%
Rural:	0.0%	$100k to $200k:	20.2%	Unemployment (3-yr. average):	6.3%
Native of state:	40.3%	Over $200k:	9.8%	Poverty:	17.4%
Not a citizen:	8.0%	Median income:	$58,422	Blue collar:	7.6%
Area size:	68 sq. mi.			White collar:	75.5%
		Home Value		Khaki collar:	0.6%
Age		Under $100k:	1.9%	Other:	16.2%
Median age:	35.4 yrs.	$100k to $300k:	20.7%		
More than 65 yrs:	11.8%	$300k to $500k:	33.7%		
Less than 18 yrs:	19.2%	$500k to $1 mil:	33.4%		
		Over $1 million:	10.4%		
		Median:	$457,100		

Race/Ethnicity		Language		Military Veterans		Registered Voters in 2010	
White:	34.8%	*Language*		% of Pop:	6.9%	Democrats:	344,630
Black:	50.0%	English:	86.4%			Republicans:	29,972
Hispanic:	9.1%	Spanish:	6.7%	*Veterans by Period*		Ind./other:	79,270
Asian:	3.5%	Asian:	1.5%	WWII and before:	11.6%	Turnout:	135,846
Native Am.:	0.2%	Other European:	3.9%	Korea:	11.2%	Turnout as % of	
Hawaiian:	0.0%			Vietnam:	28.7%	voting age:	27.1%
Two+ races:	2.1%	**Education**		Gulf (pre-2001):	10.2%		
		H.S. grad:	86.4%	Gulf (post-2001):	10.3%		
Ancestry		College grad:	48.3%	Peace time:	28.0%		
Irish	5.9%	Grad degree:	27.0%				
German	5.8%						
English	4.5%						

Fenty's flaw was his aloofness from other elected officials, which stood in negative contrast to his energetic door-to-door campaigning. *The Washington Post*'s editorial writers, while sympathetic to his policies, criticized his "silly fights" with the council, his penchant for "unnecessary secrecy" and for "shutting out community voices." Rhee's teacher firings seemed insensitive to many African-American Washingtonians raised in an environment where public sector jobs seemed the only means to upward mobility. In addition, the highly visible gentrification that made the city so attractive to young whites made it seem an increasingly alien place to blacks with deep roots in gentrifying neighborhoods. Rhee became a lightning rod for discontent with Fenty, and in the Democratic primary in 2010, he was challenged by council President Vincent Gray.

2008 Presidential Vote		
Barack Obama (D) 245,800	(92%)
John McCain (R) 17,367	(7%)

2008 Presidential Primary		
Barack Obama (D) 93,386	(75%)
Hillary Clinton (D).................29,470	(24%)

2008 Presidential Primary		
John McCain (R) 4,198	(68%)
Mike Huckabee (R)....................1,020	(16%)
Ron Paul (R) 494	(8%)
Mitt Romney (R).........................398	(6%)

2004 Presidential Vote		
John Kerry (D) 202,970	(89%)
George W. Bush (R)................21,256	(9%)

Cook Partisan Voting Index: D+41

Gray's political base was in Anacostia, the far eastern edge of the city, a low-income and high-crime area, and he was supported by public employee unions unhappy with Fenty's policies. But he was not nearly so divisive a figure as Barry had been, and he was also supported by Councilwoman Mary Cheh from Ward 3, the affluent area west of Rock Creek Park. Fenty was urged by advisers to hire pollsters and campaign consultants, but he insisted on concentrating on door-to-door campaigning while not releasing his schedule to the press, as in the past. He hoped that drops in crime rates, rising test scores in the schools and construction of new school buildings, recreation centers, swimming pools and shopping centers would commend him to voters. So it came as a shock when in late August 2010 a *Post* poll showed him trailing Gray. The next month, Gray beat Fenty decisively, 54%-44%, carrying just about every black-majority precinct and losing just about all the others. Fenty won 79%-20% in the predominately white neighborhoods west of Rock Creek Park; Gray won 82%-16% east of the Anacostia River. The gentrified and gentrifying areas of Capitol Hill, Adams Morgan and Columbia Heights voted heavily for Fenty, but Ward 4 on either side of 16th Street, Fenty's home area, voted about as heavily for Gray. After the election, Rhee resigned her post.

Widespread hopes in the District that a sympathetic Democrat in the White House would quickly result in approval of a full-voting member in Congress for D.C. were dashed in 2009. After Democratic President Barack Obama was inaugurated, the Senate cast a filibuster-proof 61 votes for a bill giving full voting rights to D.C.'s representative to Congress. But the conservatives in the House and Senate wanted to amend the bill to include repeal of the District's strict gun laws. D.C. Delegate Eleanor Holmes Norton and other leading city officials objected, and the bill was shelved. Liberals won a victory on the issue of same-sex marriage, however. In May 2009, the Council approved recognition of same-sex marriages from other states, and in December 2009, by a vote of 11-2, with the two members from wards east of the Anacostia River, the poorest in the city, voting no, it passed an act recognizing same-sex marriages.

DELEGATE

Eleanor Holmes Norton (D)

Elected 1990, 11th term; b. June 13, 1937, Washington, D.C.; home, Washington, D.C.; Antioch Col., B.A. 1960, Yale, M.A. 1963, LL.B. 1964; Episcopalian; divorced; 2 children.

Professional Career: Asst. legal dir., ACLU, 1965–70; New York City Human Rights Comm., 1970–77; Equal Empl. Oppor. Comm., 1977–81; Sr. fellow, The Urban Inst., 1981–82; Prof., Georgetown U. Law Ctr., 1982–present.

DC Office: 2136 RHOB, 20515, 202-225-8050; Fax: 202-225-3002; Web site: www.norton.house.gov.

State Offices: NW Washington, D.C., 202-783-5065; SE Washington, D.C., 202-678-8900.

Committees: *Oversight & Government Reform:* Federal Workforce, U.S. Postal Service & Labor Policy; Government Organization, Efficiency & Financial Management; Health Care, District of Columbia, Census & the National Archives. *Transportation & Infrastructure:* Aviation; Economic Development, Public Buildings & Emergency Management (RMM); Water Resources & Environment.

Election Results

2010 general	Eleanor Holmes Norton (D)	117,990	(89%)	($425,600)
	Missy Smith (R)	8,109	(6%)	($74,726)
	Rick Tingling-Clemmons (Green)	4,413	(3%)	
2010 primary	Eleanor Holmes Norton (D)	116,277	(90%)	
	Douglass Sloan (D)	11,857	(9%)	

Prior Winning Percentages: 2008 (92%), 2006 (100%), 2006 (100%), 2004 (91%), 2002 (93%), 2000 (90%), 1998 (90%), 1996 (90%), 1994 (89%), 1992 (85%), 1990 (62%)

Eleanor Holmes Norton, a Democrat who was first elected delegate from the District of Columbia in 1990, grew up in Washington. The daughter of a District government employee and a school teacher, she graduated from Dunbar High School, famed for its distinguished black graduates, and went on to get a law degree at Yale. She worked for the American Civil Liberties Union and the New York City Commission on Human Rights, and was head of the Equal Employment Opportunity Commission in the Carter administration. Afterward, she taught law at Georgetown University. When the delegate seat came open in 1990, she ran for it, and drew criticism because her husband hadn't filed their income taxes for several years. But in the primary, she edged past Council Member Betty Anne Kane, 39%-33%. Norton has been re-elected easily since.

In her early terms in the House, she had the difficult and sometimes vexing task of responding to the fiscal collapse of the District government just as Republicans took over Congress in 1995. But she was seen as hardworking, competent, intellectually honest, able to get along with opponents as well as fellow partisans, and willing to take personal and political risks. She established good relations with Republicans active on District matters. She led the drive to give the D.C. delegate and the four territorial delegates to the House—all of whom were then Democrats—votes on most legislation in the House. In 1995, she worked with Republican Tom Davis of Virginia and Speaker Newt Gingrich to create the fiscal control board to oversee District finances in the aftermath of the disastrous reign of the city's drug-using mayor, Marion Barry. In 1997, she and Davis came up with the legislation that rescued the District's finances and removed control over most of the government from Barry. The measure also included tax breaks for downtown and other neighborhoods. The District recovered financially, and in the next decade under Mayors Anthony Williams and Adrian Fenty, prospered. Norton successfully pushed several local projects, including the Southeast Federal Center Public-Private Development Act that promoted development around the Washington Navy Yard and the decision to place the Coast Guard headquarters on the grounds of the old St. Elizabeth's Hospital. She protested vigorously when the House voted to repeal the District's ban on handguns.

Throughout her decades in the House, Norton has sought to move the District toward statehood, to secure full representation in Congress and to prevent Congress from overriding decisions of the District government. "We must never retreat from our full citizenship rights, and we must always seize any part of our rights that we can get," she told *The Washington Post.* Those goals seemed far out of reach during the District's fiscal crisis and during the 12 years of Republican majorities in the House. Nonetheless she had some successes. She and Davis worked to pass a law providing in-state tuition for District students at colleges and universities in any state. And in 2007 she got the Democratic-controlled House to remove the ban on the District's needle exchange program intended to reduce AIDS transmission.

But Norton has been frustrated in one of her top priorities, securing full voting rights for D.C. in the House of Representatives, even after Democrats won majorities in both houses of Congress in 2006 and won the presidency in 2008. Davis came up with the idea of creating two new House seats, one for the District of Columbia and the other for the state entitled to the 436th district under the statutory reapportionment formula, which after the 2000 census, happened to be heavily Republican Utah. That gave Republicans a strong incentive to vote for the bill. In 2007, the House passed her bill 241-177. But in the Senate that year, it fell three votes short of the 60 necessary to prevent a filibuster. In 2009, with increased Democratic majorities, Norton revived it and it passed the House Judiciary Committee in February 2009. In March, the Senate also approved it, 61-37, but with an amendment sponsored by conservative Sen. John Ensign of Nevada overturning the District's strict gun control laws. Norton looked for a path to compromise, but then, House conservatives added even more constraints on the District's ability to regulate guns in its jurisdiction, and Norton threw up her hands. Democratic Majority Leader Steny Hoyer said he would not bring it to the floor so long as District officials were opposed, and the legislation died.

In April 2011, Norton was furious when President Barack Obama, striking a budget deal with House Republicans to avert a government shutdown, made concessions that allowed the GOP conservatives to revive a school voucher program in the District and to prohibit the city from using its own funds to provide abortions for low-income women. She said both parties were using the District as a bargaining chip. She said, "It's time that the District of Columbia told the Congress to go straight to hell."

Nonetheless, Norton had a number of successes on local issues. In 2009, the House passed her bill freeing District employees from the federal Hatch Act limiting political activity once the District passed its own law on the subject. Her bill to allow the District to take over Kingman and Heritage islands in the Anacostia River passed the House as well, and her bill to restore retirement credits lost by District employees when their agency was transferred to the federal government became law. Democratic appropriators agreed to bar amendments affecting the District referendum authorizing medical marijuana and its ability to continue its needle exchange program. In addition, Norton got senators and the White House to recognize her recommendations for federal trial judges and the U.S. attorney for the District of Columbia.

★ FLORIDA ★

Within the lifespan of an octogenarian, Florida has been transformed, from a swampy, under-settled, mostly rural state of 1.5 million people, the smallest population in the South, to a mostly high-tech, mostly metropolitan giant of 18.8 million people. Today, it's the fourth most populous state in the nation, and close enough to the third largest, New York, that it will have the same number of seats in Congress after redistricting. The result is a kind of nation-state, historically Southern, demographically Northeastern and Midwestern, and culturally, at least partly, Latin American. It has been economically vibrant for most of the past century, but subject to sudden contractions, as in the mid-1920s, the mid-1970s and since the most recent recession hit in 2007. It has the nation's largest percentage of elderly citizens, but its exotic past reaches back to Ponce de León's quest for the Fountain of Youth. It is the only Atlantic Coast state that was not part of the colonial United States. In 1819, it was acquired from Spain, through the exertions of John Quincy Adams and Andrew Jackson. Adams thought that in foreign hands, Florida could block the Gulf of Mexico and the Mississippi Valley, while Jackson saw it as a launching place for runaway slaves and Indians to raid the farmers and planters of what was then the American Southwest.

As history has unfolded, Florida has served different functions. A minor agricultural state until the early 20th century, its frost-free climate made it the center of America's citrus industry and inspired millionaires—Henry Flagler, Henry Plant—to build winter resort hotels. Miami experienced a real estate boom and, after a hurricane hit, a sudden bust in 1926; in the 1930s New Yorkers started retiring to art deco apartments in Miami Beach. But the real breakthrough for Florida was air conditioning. In 1950, only 20% of Florida houses had it; in 2000, 95% did.

At first, a flood of retirees arrived looking forward to sunny, year-round warmth after years of gray skies over factories and office buildings. Then in the 1980s and 1990s, the percentage of children and young couples as a share of Florida's population grew rapidly as people migrated from the South, from various points north and from Latin America. They were lured by jobs and opportunities in communities that hadn't existed a generation earlier. Some 17% of Florida's population today is over age 65, more than the national average of 13%, but not extraordinarily more. The state's percentage of children under age 18 is 22%, not much below the national average of 24%. For refugees from Cuba and Haiti and for immigrants from the Caribbean and Latin America, Florida has been a land of freedom and security from authoritarian regimes. Florida has been continually replenished with people from out of state, one-third from foreign countries. Miami has long been the economic and commercial capital of Latin America, as well as a mecca for its political exiles. You can fly nonstop from Miami to just about anyplace in Latin America, both English and Spanish are commonly understood, and it has been one place where many Latinos could be sure their money and their persons were safe from government takeover. Recent ructions in their countries have brought thousands of Venezuelans, Bolivians, and Ecuadorans, some affluent and some struggling, to South Florida. Large numbers of Puerto Ricans have been moving to central Florida's Interstate 4 corridor, and Mexicans to the Tampa Bay area; as a result, Cubans now account for only about a third of Florida's Hispanics.

For almost two decades, Florida had one of America's most buoyant economies, though its economy often seems a puzzle to outsiders. That economy has been based heavily on small business, with a significant high-tech sector and a substantial amount of international trade. But as in all fast-growing states, Florida's economy has been built on construction and real estate—which makes it subject to sudden busts. Looking back on the past decade, growth slowed down in Florida in 2005, but the real estate and construction industries kept going. One-sixth of all housing units in 2008 were built since 2000. Speculators built and bought houses and condos in Miami and Cape Coral, Orlando and Port St. Lucie on the assumption that growth would accelerate and that they could turn over heavily mortgaged properties for fast profits, even as property taxes and insurance premiums rose. But suddenly, housing values plummeted, with prices falling nearly 50% and condominium prices falling 61% by 2009. A flood of foreclosures followed, and Florida became one of the "sand states"—the others are Nevada, Arizona and California—that have the nation's highest foreclosure rates by far, accounting for more than half of all foreclosures from 2007 to 2010. Local tax receipts, heavily dependent on property values and the construction industry, sagged. Unemployment rose from 5% in January 2008 to 12.1% in August 2010. Florida's population growth slowed down, according to census estimates, from a torrid 2.3% annually in mid-decade to one-third that rate. And starting in 2007, more Americans left Florida than moved there—for the first time, probably, since the 1926 Miami real estate collapse.

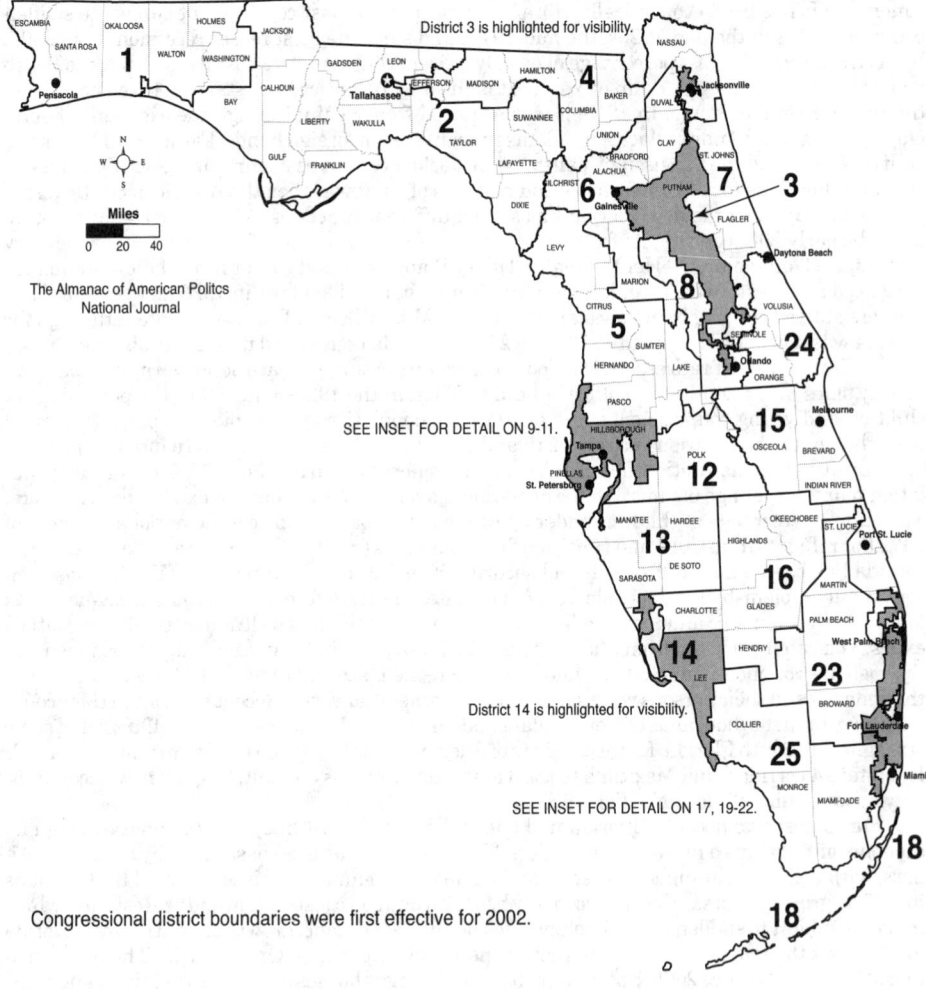

District 3 is highlighted for visibility.

SEE INSET FOR DETAIL ON 9-11.

District 14 is highlighted for visibility.

SEE INSET FOR DETAIL ON 17, 19-22.

Congressional district boundaries were first effective for 2002.

The Almanac of American Politcs
National Journal

Miles
0   20   40

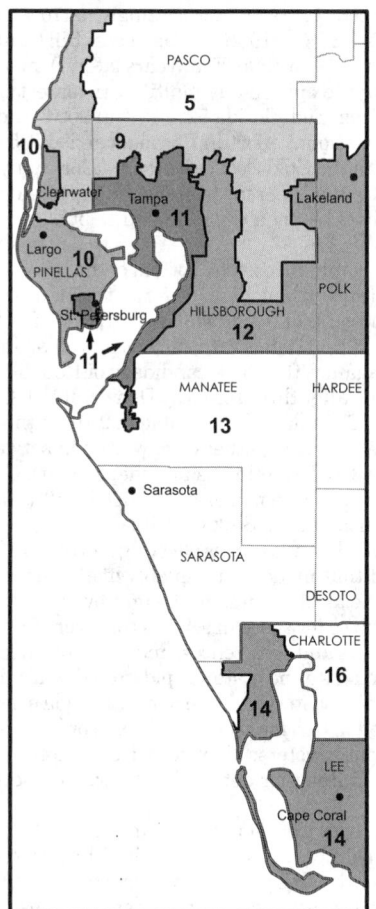 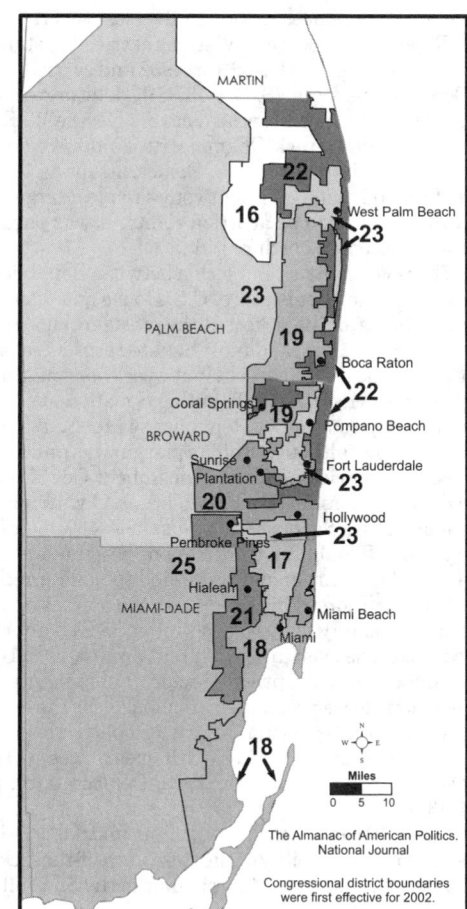

All this was happening in a state with a fragile civil society. Florida can be disorderly and chaotic in the best of times. Most people do not have deep roots in the state—most communities sprang into existence within living memory—and if Florida gives people more freedom and options than elsewhere, it also gives them more disruption and crime than they anticipated. Its largest urban focus, Miami, is geographically off to one corner, and a large part of it is culturally uniquely Cuban. The rest of the Gold Coast, Broward and Palm Beach counties, with one-sixth of Florida's population, is also atypical, with a population drawn heavily from New York and other Northeastern cities, plus non-Latino migrants from Miami-Dade and large numbers of Jews and retirees. Central Florida—the I-4 corridor from Tampa-St. Petersburg through citrus and tourist country and Orlando—is mostly family, not retiree, country. It depends on high-tech industries as well as tourism, and is a year-round rather than seasonal megalopolis of 5 million people. There is also the Gulf Coast, the affluent and burgeoning communities south of Tampa Bay and the more modest retirement counties to the north. The western Panhandle, the so-called Redneck Riviera around Pensacola and Panama City, is culturally very Southern. State government is headquartered in Tallahassee, chosen because it was midway between the two population centers of Jacksonville and Pensacola at a time when almost no one lived in the Florida peninsula; it and the university town of Gainesville are liberal bastions in a sea of conservatism.

Politically, this all adds up to a state that is closely divided between the parties and politically volatile. The trend in Florida politics since the 1990s has been toward the Republicans, who captured the state House in 1994, the state Senate in 1996, and the governorship in 1998 and now hold almost all the statewide offices and have big majorities in the legislature: 28-12 in the Senate, 81-39 in the House. They have been helped by term limits and redistricting, which Republicans influenced after the 1990 census and controlled after the 2000 and 2010 censuses: African-American and Jewish areas are concentrated in a few districts. But Democrats have remained competitive in statewide races, although they lost several in recent years by excruciatingly narrow margins. Republican George H. W. Bush carried the state 61%-39% in 1988, but Democrat Bill Clinton lost the state by only 41%-39% in 1992 and carried it 48%-42% in 1996. Four years later, Democrat Al Gore lost the state 48.85%-48.84%, determined after the epic 36-day multi-court contest that decided the 2000 presidential election. George W. Bush carried Florida 52%-47% in 2004—not a landslide—and Barack Obama, with a massive organizational effort in Florida, carried it 51%-48% in 2008. The move toward Democrats in the 1990s in the Gold Coast and the I-4 Corridor was part of a trend among affluent voters in most large metropolitan areas based on liberal stands on cultural issues such as abortion rights. It was partially offset by a trend toward Republicans in Southern-accented north Florida.

There is a contrast in Florida between Republican dominance at the bottom of the ticket—in races for the state legislature, U.S. House and statewide down ballot offices—and the many close races at the top of the ticket. At the presidential level, no candidate has won more than 52% of the vote here since 1988, and most Senate races have been close. Democrat Bill Nelson won an open seat 51%-46% in 2000 and held it by a wider margin against the weak candidacy of Republican Katherine Harris in 2006. The other Senate seat, vacated after three terms by Democrat Bob Graham in 2004, was won by Republicans Mel Martinez in 2004 and Marco Rubio in 2010 with just 49% of the vote (although Rubio's margin was much greater because other votes were split between Democrat Kendrick Meek and incumbent Gov. Charlie Crist running as an independent). Crist won the governorship as a Republican and with a reputation as a moderate in 2006 by 52%-45%; Republican Rick Scott won it by just 49%-48% over Democrat Alex Sink in 2010.

The one Republican who has done better has been Jeb Bush, who was elected governor in 1998 by a 55%-45% margin and proceeded to build a record that made him arguably one of the most effective governors of his time. Over the opposition of the teachers' unions, he improved the rigor and accountability of the schools and provided alternatives for those in schools that were failing. He cut taxes, he overturned, to great protest, racial quotas and preferences, and he involved local governments and the private sector in helping accommodate the state's rapid growth with new infrastructure. He prepared meticulously for the natural disasters that are part of Florida's natural heritage. And, personally, he was a particularly good match for Florida—the son of one president and brother of another, with special ties to Hispanic voters; his wife is from Mexico and he speaks fluent Spanish. In 2002, Democrats targeted Bush for defeat, but he was re-elected 56%-43.

The 2010 campaign season, in the midst of Florida's worst economic times in nearly 40 years, illustrated the instability of the state's top-of-the-ticket politics. The story begins in February 2009, when Barack Obama, widely popular in the first full month of his presidency, decided to visit Fort Myers, one of the nation's metro areas hardest hit by underwater housing prices and foreclosures. Stumping his economic stimulus bill, he was welcomed and literally embraced by Republican Gov. Charlie Crist. Some of Crist's policies—notably his program making state government the insurer of last resort against hurricane damage—were unpopular with many conservatives, including Jeb Bush, but he enjoyed high job approval among Democrats and independent voters as well as Republicans. In May 2009, Crist announced that, instead of running for what seemed certain re-election as governor, he would run for the Senate seat being vacated by the retiring Martinez. Crist was widely expected to win easily, and other Republicans dropped out of contention. But Marco Rubio, former speaker of the state House, defiantly stayed in the race, encouraged by Bush. He adopted the mantle as the one true conservative in the contest, and circulated video of the Crist-Obama hug. Rubio struggled to raise money, but slowly rose in the polls. By early 2010, Rubio had jumped to a huge lead over Crist in polls of Republican primary voters, and in April 2010, Crist took himself out of the GOP race and announced that he was running as an independent. He enjoyed a burst of favorable publicity with his handling of the Gulf oil spill from April to July, while Rubio husbanded his funds for the fall campaign.

In the contest to succeed Crist as governor, state Attorney General Bill McCollum was the favorite in the Republican primary while state Chief Financial Officer Alex Sink was the only serious candidate for the Democratic nomination. But there were two wild card, self-financing candidates in the August primary: entrepreneur Jeff Greene ran against U.S. Rep. Kendrick Meek for the Democratic nomination for senator, while insurance executive Rick Scott, who had run national ads against the Democrats' health care bill, ran for the Republican nomination for governor. Both had some problems. Greene had entertained dubious characters on a yacht and was not long established in Florida. Scott had been the head of Columbia/HCA in the late 1990s when massive Medicare fraud was uncovered at the firm. Meek beat Greene, 58%-31%, helped by a 70%-21% margin in the Gold Coast. But Scott's attack on the national health care legislation and his charges that

McCollum was insufficiently conservative helped him to a 46%-44% upset victory. McCollum won solidly in the Gold Coast, but it accounted for only 15% of Republican primary votes, while Scott held McCollum even in his home area in the I-4 corridor, which cast one-third of the primary votes. Scott won solidly in the remainder of the state, which cast half the primary vote. Interestingly, Republican primary voters outnumbered Democrats by about 1.3 million to 900,000, although there were more registered Democrats than Republicans.

The Senate race, which in August looked like a close contest between Rubio and Crist, instead turned out to be a rout for Rubio. Crist said he would caucus with Democrats to organize the Senate, but state and national Democrats could hardly abandon Meek, their only African-American Senate nominee. Rubio won with 49% of the vote; Crist got 30% and Meek 20%. Rubio got only 39% in the Gold Coast, his home area, to 33% for Crist and 27% for Meek; but he led Crist 48%-31% in the I-4 corridor, Crist's home area, and led him by 55%-27% in the rest of the state. Whites and Latinos both voted 55% for Rubio; blacks voted 74% for Meek.

The race for governor was much closer. Sink had serious experience in state government and a united Democratic party behind her. She was endorsed by the major newspapers, and the huge fine levied against Columbia/HCA while Scott was in charge was given much coverage. But Scott's barrage of ad buys and the state's underlying Republican leanings enabled him to win by 49%-48%—the closest Florida governor race since Republicans began serious competing for the office. Sink carried the Gold Coast 60%-38%, but ran only even in the I-4 corridor, her home territory. In the rest of the state, Scott prevailed 55%-41%.

Not since 1970 had Florida had two rip-roaring races for governor and senator in the same year. That year, two moderate Democrats from rural central and north Florida prevailed, Gov. Reubin Askew and Sen. Lawton Chiles. In subsequent years, Democrats of similar stripes tended to dominate Florida politics. From 1970 until 1998, Republicans won the governorship only once and won only three in 10 Senate races. Did 2010 usher in a long period of Republican dominance? The fact that neither Rubio nor Scott won 50% of the vote suggests not; the fact that Republicans dominated the races further down the ticket suggests it might. It certainly seems likely that Florida, now with 29 electoral votes, will be the nation's largest target state in the presidential contest of 2012. And Nelson will likely get serious competition in his bid to win a third Senate term.

Population		Household Income		Work	
Pop. 2010:	18,801,310	Under $15k:	13.1%	Private:	80.3%
State rank:	4th	$15k to $50k:	39.7%	Government:	13.6%
Change since 2000:	Up 17.6%	$50k to $100k:	30.2%	Self-employed:	6.0%
Urban:	86.1%	$100k to $200k:	13.5%	Unemployment (3-yr. average):	5.4%
Rural:	13.9%	Over $200k:	3.5%	Poverty:	13.6%
Native of state:	34.7%	Median income:	$47,051	Blue collar:	19.2%
Not a citizen:	10.0%			White collar:	60.6%
Area size:	65,758 sq. mi.	**Home Value**		Khaki collar:	0.4%
		Under $100k:	16.8%	Other:	19.8%
Most populous cities		$100k to $300k:	54.0%		
Jacksonville	821,784	$300k to $500k:	18.7%	**Age**	
Miami	399,457	$500k to $1 mil:	8.0%	Median age:	39.9 yrs.
Tampa	335,709	Over $1 million:	2.5%	More than 65 yrs:	17.0%
St. Petersburg	244,769	Median:	$210,800	Less than 18 yrs:	22.1%

Race/Ethnicity				Military Veterans		Registered Voters in 2010	
White:	57.9%	*Language*		% of Pop:	11.5%	Democrats:	4,631,068
Black:	15.2%	English:	73.8%			Republicans:	4,039,259
Hispanic:	22.5%	Spanish:	19.1%	*Veterans by Period*		Ind./other:	2,547,057
Asian:	2.4%	Asian:	1.4%	WWII and before:	14.1%	Voter turnout:	5,460,573
Native Am.:	0.3%	Other European:	5.1%	Korea:	13.5%	Turnout as % of	
Hawaiian:	0.1%			Vietnam:	29.5%	voting age:	36.9%
Two+ races:	1.5%	**Education**		Gulf (pre-2001):	11.1%		
		H.S. grad:	85.2%	Gulf (post-2001):	6.9%	**Legislature**	
Ancestry		College grad:	25.7%	Peace time:	25.0%	Senate:	12 D 28 R
German	10.0%	Grad degree:	9.0%			House:	39 D 81 R
Irish	9.1%						
English	7.4%						

Presidential politics   Of the 10 largest states, only Florida and Ohio gave their winning presidential candidates margins of less than 5% in the 2000, 2004 and 2008 presidential elections, and Florida is far larger, with 29 electoral votes to Ohio's 18 after the 2010 census. The key in the past two contests was not so much persuading undecided voters, but turning out base supporters at the polls. In the process, turnout rose from 6 million in 2000 to 7.6 million in 2004 to 8.4 million in 2008, a 40% increase during a time when population rose 15%. In 2004, George W. Bush's campaign out-organized the other side and beat Democrat John Kerry. In 2008, Illinois Democrat Barack Obama's campaign exceeded those efforts. Spending some $39 million on television ads and organization, and targeting potential supporters early, Obama raised turnout and the Democratic percentage sharply in Orlando and Osceola County, Tampa, Jacksonville and Miami. Over the period from 2000 to 2008, the Democratic percentage rose most in counties with many African-Americans and His-

2008 Presidential Vote		
Barack Obama (D) 4,282,074	(51%)
John McCain (R) 4,045,624	(48%)
2008 Presidential Primary		
Hillary Clinton (D)................870,986	(50%)
Barack Obama (D) 576,214	(33%)
John Edwards (D) 251,562	(14%)
2008 Presidential Primary		
John McCain (R) 701,761	(36%)
Mitt Romney (R)....................604,932	(31%)
Rudy Giuliani (R).................286,089	(15%)
Mike Huckabee (R)................262,681	(13%)
2004 Presidential Vote		
George W. Bush (R)............3,964,522	(52%)
John Kerry (D) 3,583,544	(47%)

panics and along the southern Gulf Coast, while the Republican percentage went up markedly in most of north Florida and the smaller counties of central Florida.

Florida's presidential primary, held from 1988 to 2004 on Super Tuesdays, also produces very large delegations to the two parties' national conventions. But it has not been crucial in determining a nomination since 1976, when Democrat Jimmy Carter defeated George Wallace and ended Wallace's career in national politics.

Determined to give Florida more clout in the 2008 election, the legislature decided to move the primary to an earlier date, to Jan. 29. Democratic legislators protested, because their party's rules forbade the state from voting before Feb. 5, but to no avail. In August 2007, the Democratic National Committee under Chairman Howard Dean voted to strip Florida of its delegates, and in September, all of the major Democratic candidates agreed not to campaign in the state. In October, Sen. Nelson and Democratic Rep. Alcee Hastings sued the DNC, but lost. Meanwhile, in November, the Republican National Committee took the less onerous step of depriving Florida of half its delegates without demanding that candidates boycott the state. The national parties' decisions had the result of making Florida decisive in the race for the Republican nomination and making it a bone of contention for Democrats until their nominee was decided in June.

For much of 2007, Florida didn't look like much of a contest among Republicans, with New York's Rudolph Giuliani leading in all the polls. But Giuliani's standing began to slip in December, and when he failed to win an appreciable number of votes in any state before Florida, his support in the state collapsed, even as he campaigned heavily there in January 2008. Meanwhile, Massachusetts' Mitt Romney here, as elsewhere, outspent the other candidates and campaigned as a mainstream conservative. Arkansas' Mike Huckabee, with little money but considerable charm, struggled to extend his appeal beyond evangelical Christians in a state with eight media markets and a Republican electorate drawn from many parts of the nation. On Jan. 19, 10 days before the Florida primary, Arizona's John McCain beat Huckabee in South Carolina 33%-30%. Tennessee's Fred Thompson won 16% of the votes there, leading some to conclude that Huckabee would have beaten McCain if Thompson had not been in the race. Thompson promptly dropped out, and for 10 days the spotlight was on Florida. On Saturday, January 26, Crist endorsed McCain.

That may have tipped the balance, and presumably affected at least a few votes in a fluid race with a crowded field. Turnout was large: 1.9 million, nearly triple the 690,000 who had voted in the 2000 Republican presidential primary. McCain won with 36% of the vote to 31% for Romney. Giuliani got 15% and Huckabee 13%. McCain carried metro Tampa, Crist's home area, but his highest percentages were in South Florida. Polls suggest that many original Giuliani supporters there voted for McCain, especially Cuban-Americans. Romney carried metro Jacksonville and southwest Florida. Under the state Republicans' winner-take-all rules, McCain won all of the state's delegates. McCain's Florida victory put him in position to clinch the nomination a week later, on Super Tuesday. Romney ended his campaign. Anticlimactically, the Republicans voted in August 2008 to restore all of Florida's delegates.

Democratic candidates mostly kept their promises to not campaign in Florida. Turnout in the primary was 1.75 million, less than in the Republican contest despite impressive gains in Democratic party registration, though still far ahead of the 754,000 who turned out in 2004. New York Sen. Hillary Rodham Clinton won 50% of the vote, Barack Obama 33%, and former North Carolina Sen. John Edwards 14%. Obama carried counties with large black populations (Jacksonville, Pensacola, rural north Florida counties) and those with universities or state employees (Gainesville, Tallahassee). Edwards won 11 small counties in north Florida. Clinton won every county south of Gainesville. She carried Latino and Jewish voters 2-to-1. Young voters were evenly split. Clinton, barred from the state during the campaign by her September promise, made an election night appearance to celebrate her victory.

The desire of Florida Democrats to be counted in the nomination process guaranteed continued controversy. It was suggested that Florida could stage another primary, or have a mail-in rerun, but the cost—$18 million for a primary, $5 million for a mail-in—was prohibitive for the state Democratic party. Democratic legislators filed a lawsuit in May, but it was quickly dismissed. Florida Democrats appealed to the DNC in May to have half the delegation seated, but the Obama campaign, aware that the proposal would give Clinton a delegate edge, resisted. On May 31, a few days before the last primary, a compromise was reached giving Clinton a 52.5-33.5 delegate edge over Obama (Edwards got 6.5 delegates), not quite what her showing in the Florida and Michigan primaries would have justified and not enough to change the outcome of the nomination fight as superdelegates moved toward Obama. On August 2, when it no longer mattered, Obama asked that all the Florida delegates be seated, and so they were at the party's convention in Denver.

When Obama started the general election campaign in Florida, trends in party registration were going his way. Many more new voters registered as Democrats than as Republicans, and by May 2008, registered Democrats for the first time outnumbered registered Republicans among Hispanics. There also was a disparity in spending in the state between the two candidates. The Obama campaign planned to spend about $39 million in Florida and flooded the airwaves from summer on. The McCain campaign, aware that it was behind in other states that had voted more heavily for Bush in 2004, gambled and spent almost nothing. As McCain anticipated, the swing away from the Republican ticket was far smaller in Florida than it was in states like Virginia, North Carolina and Indiana. But the assumption that the swing would be too small to allow Obama to win turned out to be wrong.

The Obama campaign did an excellent job of increasing African-American turnout in Miami, Tampa, and Jacksonville. But it also concentrated on increasing Hispanic turnout, especially in the Orlando area, where the many new Puerto Rican voters had little in common with Republican-favoring Miami Cubans. Obama's weakness among Jewish voters, evident in the primary results, was transfigured by the nomination of Alaska Gov. Sarah Palin as McCain's running mate. Despite her pro-Israel views, she seemed to tip them heavily against the Republican ticket. Broward and Palm Beach counties delivered huge majorities to Obama, as they had to the Gore-Lieberman ticket in 2000. The Obama campaign neglected no critical angle, running early-voter efforts in black barbershops, getting Creole speakers to call voters in Haitian neighborhoods, and taping comedian Sarah Silverman urging young Jews to tell their grandparents in Florida to vote for Obama. The Republicans held big rallies for their ticket, with 60,000 appearing at the Villages, northwest of Orlando, in sizzling heat to hear Palin speak.

The final results revealed the Florida electorate to be more polarized than ever, with hugely Democratic areas (Broward and Palm Beach counties) balanced against hugely Republican areas (the Panhandle). White evangelical Protestants voted more than 3-to-1 for McCain; Jews about 3-to-1 for Obama. Cuban-Americans voted 65% for McCain—less than in the past—but young Hispanics voted more than 3-to-1 for Obama. Here, perhaps, was the biggest difference from the previous election: In 2004, Hispanics voted 56% for Bush; in 2008, despite McCain's support of immigration legislation offering a path to citizenship for illegal immigrants, they voted 57% for Obama. This was one state without much of a gender gap, perhaps because elderly voters, most of them women, voted 53%-45% for McCain. In Florida, as nationally, voters with incomes over $200,000 voted for Obama. Did organization matter? An amazing 29% of voters said they'd been contacted by the Obama campaign, and 20% by the McCain campaign.

Congressional districting   Florida has gained congressional districts after every census

112th Congress Lineup	
19 R	6 D
111th Congress Lineup	
15 R	10 D

since 1930, when it elected just four House members. In the 2000 census, it gained two seats, for a total of 25. Then, the redistricting process was controlled by Republicans, who passed a plan in March 2002. Disagreement between the state House and Senate was resolved when senators agreed to create a district tailor-made for Republican House Speaker Tom Feeney; the other new district was tailor-made for Republican Mario Diaz-Balart, chairman of the House Congressional Redistricting Committee. Democrats filed lawsuits against the plan in state and federal courts, but lost those challenges. The plan was solidly in place by the July 9 filing deadline for 2002 contests. The plan produced a congressional delegation of 18 Republicans and seven Democrats, a lopsided GOP majority in a state that had been evenly divided in the 2000 presidential election.

But, as often happens with partisan redistricting plans, the effects wore off after a while. In 2006, Republican Clay Shaw was defeated and Democrats picked up the seat of Republican Mark Foley, tarred in a congressional page sex scandal. In 2008, Republicans regained the Foley seat after the Democratic incumbent was caught up in his own scandal, but they lost two seats anchored in Orlando. The 18-7 Republican edge was reduced over the course of two elections to 15-10.

Florida gained two seats in the reapportionment following the 2010 census, leaving the state with a delegation the same size as New York's. Scott's narrow victory and the big Republican margins in the legislature mean that Republicans can once again control the process. But the passage in November 2010 of ballot propositions requiring legislators to draw compact districts conforming to county or geographic boundaries could reduce their options. The most egregiously shaped districts in the current plan—the 3rd, 11th and 23rd—owe their shape to the prevailing judicial interpretations of the Voting Rights Act, which require that the number of black-or Hispanic-majority districts be maximized. That result can be obtained in a state with Florida's demographics only by creating districts that are anything but compact and that cut across many political and geographic boundaries. Presumably, the federal Voting Rights Act trumps the state redistricting law, in which case Republicans would be able to draw a plan resembling the current one.

Governor

Rick Scott (R)

Elected 2010, term expires Jan. 2015, 1st term; b. Dec. 1, 1952, Bloomington, IL; home, Tallahassee; U. of MO, Kansas City, B.A. 1975; Southern Methodist U., J.D. 1978; Christian; Married (Ann); 2 children.

Military Career: U.S. Navy, 1971-74.

Professional Career: Co-founder, chmn. and CEO, Columbia/HCA, 1987-97; Venture capitalist, 1997-2010; Practicing atty., Johnson & Swanson, Dallas.

Office: The Capitol, 400 S. Monroe St., 32399-0001, 850-488-7146; Fax: 850-487-0801; Web site: flgov.com.

Election Results

2010 general	Rick Scott (R)	2,619,335	(49%)
	Alex Sink (D)	2,557,785	(48%)
	Peter Allen (I)	123,831	(2%)
2010 primary	Rick Scott (R)	599,909	(46%)
	Bill McCollum (R)	563,538	(44%)
	Mike McCalister (R)	130,991	(10%)

Rick Scott, a Republican, was elected governor of Florida in 2010. He grew up in Kansas City, Mo., the son of a truck driver and JCPenney clerk. He enlisted in the Navy after one year of community college. After his military service, Scott enrolled at the University of Missouri-Kansas City, and, displaying an early entrepreneurial streak, financed his education by buying two donut shops and hiring his mother to manage them. Undergraduate degree in hand, he went to Southern Methodist University in Texas for a law degree. After college, he went to work for a large firm, where he specialized in health care mergers and acquisitions. In 1987, Scott put together a $6 billion bid to purchase Nashville-based HCA, the hospitals firm founded by Drs. Thomas Frist and Thomas Frist

Jr., father and brother of former Sen. Bill Frist of Tennessee. When that offer was rejected, Scott and Texas billionaire Richard Rainwater started their own hospital company called Columbia with $125,000 in savings.

Columbia started off in 1988 with two hospitals in El Paso, and for the next nine years, bought up dozens of hospitals, many of them nonprofit operations, and offered ownership shares to doctors who made referrals. Columbia became highly profitable, and in 1994, made a successful bid for HCA. The merged Columbia/HCA firm added 80 more hospitals, mainly in rural areas, by the end of the next year. Scott worked to reduce costs and to require more accountability while opening up bypass surgery facilities. By 1997, Columbia/HCA was the nation's largest health care company and its seventh largest employer, with 340 hospitals, $20 billion in revenues and 285,000 employees

But the FBI was investigating charges that Columbia/HCA overbilled the Medicare and Medicaid programs, and in that year, twice raided the firm's hospitals seeking evidence. Nine days after the second raid, Scott was ousted by the board of directors, and Thomas Frist Jr. was made chief executive officer. In settlements in 2000 and 2002, the firm pleaded guilty to federal fraud charges and paid $1.7 billion in fines. The company admitted to systematically overcharging the government by claiming marketing costs as reimbursable, by filing false data about how hospital space was being used, and by exaggerating the seriousness of the illnesses they were treating, among other abuses, according to *Forbes.com*. In a deposition in a civil suit in which he was a witness, Scott invoked his Fifth Amendment right against self-incrimination 75 times rather than answer questions. His business associates told *The New York Times* at the time that Scott was a brilliant and incisive businessman who was undone by his fatal flaws, including an arrogance and aggressiveness that permeated the company. One of his most controversial strategies was giving ownership stakes in hospitals to doctors, which critics said compromised the doctors ethically.

Still, Scott was richly rewarded for his work at Columbia/HCA, leaving with $10 million in cash and $300 million in stock and options. In rehabilitating his image later, Scott maintained that he was never charged with wrongdoing. "I learned very hard lessons from what happened and those lessons have helped me become a better businessman and leader," he said. He went on to new business ventures. Scott bought control of the America's Health Network cable channel and in 2001, co-founded Solantic, which operates walk-in urgent care centers throughout Florida and specializes in patients without insurance. In 2003, Scott moved to Naples, Fla.

In March 2009, Scott pitched in $5 million to found Conservatives for Patients' Rights, which ran TV ads featuring Scott criticizing the Democrats' health care bills, particularly the provision creating a government-financed insurance option, and spotlighting negative results of government health care in Canada and Britain. It spent $1.6 million on ads through May 2009. The Democrats' health care bill passed in March 2010, and the next month, Scott announced that he was running for governor as a Republican to succeed Charlie Crist, a Republican who was running for the Senate. Scott, who announced that his net worth was $218 million, immediately spent $4.7 million on ads. The front-runner in the primary was Attorney General Bill McCollum, a former U.S. House member and the GOP nominee for the Senate in 2000. Scott's ad barrage sent McCollum tumbling 26% in the polls within a month. By June, polls showed Scott ahead. Scott called McCollum a career politician and attacked him for his connections to former state GOP Chairman Jim Greer, who was indicted on fraud charges. McCollum responded with ads recalling the Columbia/HCA fiasco and its record fine for fraud. By June, Scott had spent $16 million. Republican luminaries Jeb Bush, Newt Gingrich and Mitt Romney all endorsed McCollum, and Republican state legislators made scathing attacks on Scott.

In July, Scott sought unsuccessfully to get a federal judge to overturn Florida's campaign finance law, which provides matching funding to the opponent of a self-financing candidate who spends more than $24.9 million. He unveiled a catchy economic plan with seven steps to create 700,000 jobs in seven years, with corporate and property tax cuts, public payroll reductions and the streamlining of government agencies. "Let's get to work" was the tag line on his ads. McCollum complained that Scott was copying his proposals. In all, Scott spent about $50 million before the primary and beat McCollum 46%–44%. McCollum carried Miami-Dade County solidly and the other two Gold Coast counties narrowly, but he won by only a small margin in the I-4 Corridor and, except for the counties containing Tallahassee and the University of Florida, was virtually shut out in the rest of the state. Scott ran especially strong in the Naples and Jacksonville areas. Soon afterward, he picked as his running mate GOP state Sen. Jennifer Carroll, a black immigrant from Trinidad who had served in the Navy and started her own business.

The fact that more votes were cast in the Republican primary than the Democratic primary, although there were more registered Democrats than Republicans in the state, boded well for

Scott's general election campaign, as did the unpopularity of President Obama among Republicans. The Democratic nominee, state Chief Financial Officer Alex Sink, won her primary without serious opposition and with minimal spending, but as a result, voters knew little about her. Her husband, Tampa lawyer Bill McBride, had beaten former Attorney General Janet Reno in the 2002 Democratic primary, and then lost the general election 56%-43% to incumbent Republican Gov. Jeb Bush. Sink had had a successful career in banking, rising to the position of head of Florida operations for the Bank of America. In 2006, she was elected to the new position of chief financial officer, the only Democrat elected to statewide office that year other than Sen. Bill Nelson, D-Fla.

This was one of the most negative campaigns in the country. Democratic ads, some featuring law enforcement officials, attacked Scott for his conduct at Columbia/HCA. In their first debate, Sink said, "Rick, the people of Florida can't trust you." She also called him "a corporate raider" who "bought hospitals all over the country and shut many of them down." Scott tried to sully Sink's reputation in return, alleging she was responsible for questionable sales practices by NationsBank Securities, for which it was fined $6.7 million. Newspaper reports saying that the company in question was separate from the one Sink headed took some punch out of the allegation. Scott also attacked her for losses in the state pension funds; her defenders pointed out that almost all pension funds lost money when the stock market cratered in 2008. Perhaps his most effective negative strategy was painting Sink as a "Tallahassee insider" and a booster of Obama's policies. He said she would increase state spending in the billions of dollars, while he would slash agencies like the state Department of Community Affairs, responsible for approving development projects, because "it's really killing jobs."

In another year, Scott's business record might have made him unelectable. But in 2010, political insiders were unpopular, and Sink had been in office for four years. National Democratic policies were also unpopular, and Scott could deflect criticism by saying, as he did in their second debate, "Obama math doesn't work here." Polls showed the race tight all through September and October. Perhaps the crucial moment came in the third debate on Oct. 25. The campaigns had agreed not to allow the candidates to accept cell phone messages during the debate. But during a commercial break, an aide handed a Droid phone to Sink, who read a message on it. Scott charged her with cheating, and the issue dominated news coverage for much of the last week of the campaign. Meanwhile, Scott ran ads featuring his mother, wife and adult daughters to soften his image from the highly negative portrayals by Democrats. Scott's total spending ultimately reached $73 million.

Scott won another squeaker, 49%-48%. Interestingly, he carried Latinos 50%-48% and won 62% among whites with no college degree. Sink won 60% of the vote in the Gold Coast, but Scott ran just barely ahead of her in the I-4 Corridor, and won 55% of the vote in the rest of the state. "I won't rest until we make Florida a model for the country in job creation and education," he said on Election Night. Republicans also increased their already large margins in both houses of the legislature.

In his first actions, Scott said he would sign two pieces of legislation that had been vetoed by Crist—a merit pay for teachers opposed by the teachers' union and a bill requiring women seeking an abortion to view an ultrasound of the fetus. Scott also said he wanted to make windstorm insurance "actuarially sound," a reversal of Crist's policy, which made the state the largest insurer and liable for enormous claims if a hurricane devastated a major metropolitan area.

Senior Senator

Bill Nelson (D)

Elected 2000, term expires 2012, 2nd term; b. Sept. 29, 1942, Miami; home, Orlando; Yale U., B.A. 1965; U. of VA, J.D. 1968; Protestant; married (Grace Cavert); 2 children.

Military Career: U.S. Army, 1968-70; U.S. Army Reserves, 1965-71.

Elected Office: FL House of Reps., 1972-78; U.S. House of Reps., 1978-90; FL treasurer, insurance comm. & fire marshal, 1994-2000.

Professional Career: Practicing atty., 1970-79, 1991-94; Legis. asst., FL Gov. Reubin Askew, 1971; Crew member, Space Shuttle Columbia, 1986.

DC Office: 716 HSOB, 20510, 202-224-5274; Fax: 202-228-2183; Web site: billnelson.senate.gov.

State Offices: Coral Gables, 305-536-5999; Davie, 954-693-4851; Fort Myers, 239-334-7760; Jacksonville, 904-346-4500; Orlando, 407-872-7161; Tallahassee, 850-942-8415; Tampa, 813-225-7040; West Palm Beach, 561-514-0189.

Committees: *Aging (Special). Budget. Commerce, Science & Transportation:* Aviation Operations, Safety & Security; Communications, Technology & the Internet; Oceans, Atmosphere, Fisheries & Coast Guard; Science & Space (Chmn). *Finance:* Energy, Natural Resources & Infrastructure; Fiscal Responsibility & Economic Growth (Chmn); International Trade, Customs & Global Competitiveness; Taxation & IRS Oversight. *Intelligence (Select).*

Group Ratings

	ACLU	ACU	ADA	CFG	AFS	FRC	LCV	ITIC	NTU	COC
2010	87	8	90	14	92	0	86	67	16	36
2009	–	4	100	10	100	–	100	–	10	43

National Journal Ratings

	2010 LIB — 2010 CONS		2009 LIB — 2009 CONS	
Economic	57%	— 42%	68%	— 30%
Social	54%	— 43%	69%	— 28%
Foreign	47%	— 0%	46%	— 52%
Composite	62%	— 38%	62%	— 38%

Key Votes of the 111th Congress

1. Overturn Ledbetter	Y	5. Pass health care bill	Y	9. Ratify New START	Y
2. Pass $787 billion stimulus	Y	6. Regulate financial firms	Y	10. Confirm Elena Kagan	Y
3. Repeal DC gun laws	N	7. Pass tax cuts for some	N	11. Stop EPA climate regs	N
4. Confirm Sonia Sotomayor	Y	8. Legalize immigrants' kids	Y	12. Repeal don't ask, tell	Y

Election Results

2006 general	Bill Nelson (D)..	2,890,548	(60%)	($18,031,681)
	Katherine Harris (R)	1,826,127	(38%)	($8,666,803)
2006 primary	Bill Nelson (D)..	unopposed		

Prior Winning Percentages: 2000 (51%); House: 1988 (61%); 1986 (73%); 1984 (61%); 1982 (71%); 1980 (70%); 1978 (61%)

Bill Nelson was first elected to the Senate in 2000. He grew up in Melbourne, Fla. His mother was a schoolteacher, and his father was a lawyer and real estate investor who died when Bill was 14. Nelson likes to recall that his great-grandfather arrived in Florida from Denmark as a stowaway on a ship. From his family home in Rock Point, Nelson could see rockets blast off in the 1950s and 1960s from what is now the Kennedy Space Center. He was active in student government and has always been something of a straight arrow; he doesn't drink, smoke or swear. He attended the University of Florida for two years, and then graduated from Yale and the University of Virginia law school. After a two-year hitch in the Army, he returned to Melbourne and briefly practiced law and worked on the staff of Democratic Gov. Reubin Askew. In 1972, at age 30, he was elected to the state House of Representatives.

In 1978, when Republican Rep. Louis Frey retired, Nelson ran for the U.S. House in a district that then included the Space Coast's Brevard County and most of Orlando's Orange County. His religious faith and traditional values, his indefatigable campaigning and folksy manner made him popular in an area that was trending Republican. He won the seat 61%-39%; in five succeeding elections, he captured 61% to 73% of the ballots in a district that voted just 29% for Democrat Michael Dukakis in the 1988 presidential race. In the House, he became chairman of the Science

Committee's Space Subcommittee, obviously of prime importance to the district. Nelson not only boosted the space program in every possible way but also rode the space shuttle *Columbia* himself, spending six days orbiting the Earth in early 1986. Less than two weeks later, space shuttle *Challenger* exploded as it took off. After the *Columbia* was lost in February 2003, he called for continued manned space flight despite the risks.

In 1989, with the support of leading Florida Democrats, Nelson set out to run against Republican Gov. Bob Martinez, who was not faring well in polls. But in early 1990, some Democrats became antsy about Nelson's prospects and persuaded Lawton Chiles, who had retired from the Senate in 1988 after three terms, to run. Chiles was always far ahead in their race and won the September primary 69%-31%. Nelson returned to his 77-acre oceanfront home in Melbourne, his political career seemingly over. But in 1994, he found an opening when state Insurance Commissioner Tom Gallagher, a Republican, ran for governor. Nelson was elected in November to an office whose full title was treasurer, insurance commissioner, and state fire marshal, and proceeded to compile an activist record.

Nelson's chance to run for higher office came in March 1999, when Republican Sen. Connie Mack said he would not run for re-election in 2000. Mack's retirement left a seat up for grabs in a state that, as Election Night 2000 returns would show, was closely divided between the parties. Republicans nominated 20-year, Orlando-based Rep. Bill McCollum, one of the House managers of the impeachment of President Bill Clinton.

Washington observers considered the race a contest about the wisdom of impeachment but mostly it was a battle of competing styles. Running his fourth statewide race in 10 years, Nelson's easygoing manner contrasted favorably with McCollum's stiff, often aggressive demeanor. With a long conservative record on abortion rights and gun control, McCollum attempted to moderate his positions but only succeeded in antagonizing his base supporters. This was the most expensive Florida Senate race to that point, with the two candidates spending more than $15 million between them. Nelson won 51%-46%. He prevailed 60%-37% in the Gold Coast. In the Interstate 4 corridor, which included McCollum's congressional district and most of the district that Nelson had represented in the House, Nelson won 51%-46%. In the rest of the state, Nelson lost by only 52%-46%, compared with the 55%-42% ratio by which Democratic presidential nominee Al Gore lost there that year. Folksiness and Florida roots counted.

In the Senate, Nelson has become known as a careful, deliberative lawmaker who has compiled a moderate-to-liberal voting record. He is not especially well known nationally, but his activity on issues directly relevant to segments of Florida's population—including space, oil drilling, health care and national security—has raised his profile. He sided with President George W. Bush on the Iraq war resolution but later opposed Bush's troop "surge" strategy. But he looked with favor on military involvement elsewhere, calling in May 2007 for United Nations peacekeeping troops on both sides of the Sudan-Chad border and a no-fly zone over the area. In recent years he has raised concerns about warming relations with Cuba. In March 2009, he and Sen. Robert Menendez, D-N.J., held up a $410 billion omnibus spending bill because of provisions that loosened travel and export restrictions with Cuba. The pair relented only after Treasury Secretary Timothy Geithner assured them in writing that the provisions would have little effect on current law.

Since January 2007, Nelson has been chairman of the Commerce subcommittee with jurisdiction over the space program. After the loss of *Columbia,* he called for accelerated development of a reusable space vehicle to ferry astronauts to the International Space Station. In 2004, Nelson won passage of an amendment calling on NASA to report to Congress on the costs of extending the space shuttle program beyond 2010, but he did not get approval of another amendment requiring NASA to find laid-off shuttle workers similar jobs in the agency. When President Obama took office, Nelson sharply criticized his administration's commitment to NASA and got a bill through the Senate in 2010 providing enough money for another space shuttle flight in 2011, jump-starting NASA's new heavy-lift rocket, and developing the commercial rocket industry.

Starting in 2005, Nelson worked with Republican colleague Mel Martinez of Florida to block oil and gas exploration in the eastern part of the Gulf of Mexico. After Republican Gov. Charlie Crist came out in favor of offshore drilling in June 2008, Nelson continued to oppose it. Then, in September 2008, Nelson said he would back a bipartisan deal allowing some offshore drilling in the Gulf of Mexico, provided it was limited to 125 miles, rather than 50 miles, from the Florida coast. Then came the massive BP oil spill disaster in the Gulf of Mexico in 2010. Nelson joined Menendez and Frank Lautenberg, D-N.J., in leading the opposition to expanded drilling along the East Coast and the Gulf. Over objections from Republicans, Nelson also sought to increase the cap on damages from oil spills from $75 million to $10 billion.

As a new member of the powerful Finance Committee, Nelson emerged as a player in the 2009-2010 health care debate. He amended an early version of the bill to lessen the impact of cuts to

Medicare Advantage, a privatized Medicare program that covers more than 900,000 seniors in Florida. But Republicans castigated it as a backroom deal intended to benefit Florida, and his amendment was killed. He did successfully add an amendment to the Finance version of the bill exempting seniors from a hike in the itemized medical deduction limit from 7.5 % to 10%.

Florida seems to have more than its share of disputes over elections. During the 2008 presidential campaign, Nelson objected vigorously when the Democratic National Committee stripped Florida of its national delegates and urged presidential candidates to boycott the state after the legislature set the state's primary for January 29 rather than the earliest date permitted by party rules, February 5. He and Democratic Rep. Alcee Hastings sued the DNC, but a judge ruled against them. Nelson then pressed for a second primary or a mail-in vote, which the committee refused to pay for, and he argued to have half of the delegates seated, which the DNC ultimately agreed to do.

In June 2005, two-term Republican Rep. Katherine Harris announced she would challenge Nelson. Polling data indicated that Harris' prominent role as Florida secretary of state during the disputed 2000 presidential election had left her too unpopular to win, but she enjoyed celebrity status among many rank-and-file Republican voters. Efforts to persuade Gov. Jeb Bush, House Speaker Allen Bense, and former Rep. Joe Scarborough to run failed, and Harris became the nominee. Harris announced she would use $10 million of her own money on her campaign; she ended up spending a third of that amount. Nelson won in a landslide, 60%-38%. He lost in the Panhandle but carried 57 of 67 counties, including Harris' home county of Sarasota. He may have a considerably more difficult challenge in 2012—the Republican National Convention will be held in Tampa that year, energizing the state's GOP, and Nelson is the lone Democrat left in statewide office in Florida.

Junior Senator

Marco Rubio (R)

Elected 2010, term expires 2016, 1st term; b. May 28, 1971, Miami; home, West Miami; U. of FL, B.A. 1993; U. of Miami, J.D. 1996.; Catholic; Married (Jeanette); 4 children.

Elected Office: West Miami city commissioner, 1998-2000; FL House, 2000-08, speaker, 2006-08.

Professional Career: Practicing atty., 1997-2010; prof., FL Intl. U., 2009-10.

DC Office: B40A DSOB, 20510, 202-224-3041; Fax: 202-228-0285; Web site: rubio.senate.gov.

State Offices: Jacksonville, 904-398-8586; Miami, 305-418-8553; Orlando, 407-254-2573; Pensacola, 850-433-2603; Tampa, 813-977-6450.

Committees: *Commerce, Science & Transportation:* Communications, Technology & the Internet; Oceans, Atmosphere, Fisheries & Coast Guard; Science & Space; Surface Transportation & Merchant Marine Infrastructure, Safety & Security. *Foreign Relations:* East Asian & Pacific Affairs; International Development & Foreign Assistance, Economic Affairs & International Environmental Protection; Near Eastern & South & Central Asian Affairs; Western Hemisphere, Peace Corps & Global Narcotics Affairs (RMM). *Intelligence (Select).* *Small Business & Entrepreneurship.*

Election Results

2010 general	Marco Rubio (R)	2,645,743	(49%)	($21,741,330)
	Charlie Crist (I)	1,607,549	(30%)	($13,680,424)
	Kendrick Meek (D)	1,092,936	(20%)	($8,860,405)
2010 primary	Marco Rubio (R)	1,069,936	(85%)	
	William Kogut (R)	112,080	(9%)	
	William Escoffery (R)	82,426	(7%)	

The junior senator from Florida is Marco Rubio, who won a riveting contest in 2010 in an early test of the strength of the fledgling tea party movement. Rubio was mostly brought up in a working-class Cuban-American neighborhood in Miami, the son of immigrants who fled from Fidel Castro. His parents had grown up poor and struggled to make ends meet. His father worked long days as a bartender and his mother was a hotel maid with a second job at Kmart. The family moved to follow work; Rubio spent six years in Las Vegas while his parents worked in the hotel industry before returning to Miami for high school. His upbringing is a cornerstone of his stump speech in public life. "I was raised by exiles, by people who know what it is like to lose their country," Rubio said in February 2010. "By people who have a unique perspective on why elections matter, or lack thereof, by people who clearly understand how different America is from the rest of the world."

Rubio played football in high school, and despite his small stature, earned a football scholarship to Tarkio College in Missouri. He returned home after the school went bankrupt, spent a year at a junior college, and got his undergraduate degree in 1993 at the University of Florida. He then went to the University of Miami for a law degree. He interned for Republican Rep. Ileana Ros-Lehtinen, and in his last year of law school, ran the Dade County operation for Republican Sen. Bob Dole's presidential campaign in 1996. There, he met future Florida Gov. Jeb Bush, who later became his political mentor.

Rubio landed a position at the law firm of Al Cardenas, a prominent Republican he got to know on the campaign. He soon met Jeanette Dousdebes, a former Miami Dolphins cheerleader, and they married in 1998. That year, at age 26, he ran for city commissioner in West Miami, a tiny, heavily Cuban town just south of Miami International Airport, and beat an incumbent. Two years later, he won an open state House seat. Rubio quickly endeared himself to party leaders by working tirelessly on redistricting plans. In 2007, he became speaker of the Florida House, making him the youngest person and the first Hispanic in that position. He toured the state, holding "idea-raisers" with voters to find budget-neutral ideas to improve the state. The 100 ideas he liked best were bundled into a book, which former House Speaker Newt Gingrich called "a work of genius." Many of the smaller proposals passed easily, but his personal favorite, replacing the state property tax with a sales tax, stalled.

Rubio announced his campaign for the Senate in May 2009. He caught the tea party movement's lightning in its nascent days and used it to power his upstart primary campaign against then-popular Republican Gov. Charlie Crist, who had long been planning his bid for the Senate. Crist began the race with a huge cash and name recognition advantage, and the National Republican Senatorial Committee endorsed him early on. But Crist was never a favorite of conservatives, and his embrace of President Obama's $787 billion economic-stimulus bill (and his literal embrace of the president at a public event) infuriated many of them. Rubio received early support from Sen. Jim DeMint, R-S.C., a conservative stalwart who was backing insurgent GOP candidates. By the time Crist realized the conservative base was slipping away, it was too late. Rubio had gone from underdog to front-runner. On the verge of losing the primary, Crist quit the Republican Party in late April to run as an independent.

In the general election campaign, Rubio faced both Crist and Democratic nominee Kendrick Meek, a U.S. House member. Crist started off with an early lead in the polls, but his support plummeted as he got caught in the crossfire from Rubio on the right and from Meek on the left, both of whom painted Crist as a political opportunist. Crist tried to become the de facto Democratic candidate with appeals to independents and moderate Republicans, but Meek refused to get out of the race, regularly polling at around 20% of the likely vote and denying Crist a one-on-one contest with Rubio.

Tea party activists, multiplying by the week, embraced Rubio's campaign and his theme of "Reclaim America." And although he benefited from the association, Rubio at the same time stood apart from the tea party. Polished and measured in his rhetoric, he was careful to avoid some of the plundering aspects of the tea partiers that could repel moderate voters. But he was diplomatic in giving them their due. He said that early in the campaign, "I noticed a real frustration that neither party spoke to the mainstream of America, their aspirations for their country and their families. And the tea party movement became an expression of that." Rubio stressed fiscal responsibility, although he sidestepped specific policy proposals. He indicated support for raising the eligibility age for Social Security beneficiaries and giving the president the line-item veto over spending bills. He opposed abortion rights and took a more conservative position than Crist on immigration, supporting Arizona's crackdown on illegal immigrants. Prominent Republicans got on board with Rubio, including former Vice President Dick Cheney, former Massachusetts Gov. Mitt Romney and former Alaska Gov. Sarah Palin.

After August, Rubio did not trail in a single independent poll and most polls showed him holding a double-digit lead. On Election Night, he won with 49% of the vote. Crist got 30% and Meek, 20%. At his victory celebration, Rubio made clear he would continue to be his own brand of Republican in the Senate, as he was in the campaign. "We make a great mistake if we believe that tonight these results are somehow an embrace of the Republican Party," he said. "What they are is a second chance, a second chance for Republicans to be what they said they were going to be not so long ago."

FIRST DISTRICT

Jeff Miller (R)

Elected Oct. 2001, 5th full term; b. June 27, 1959, St. Petersburg; home, Chumuckla; U. of FL, B.A. 1984; Methodist; married (Vicki); 2 children.

Elected Office: FL House of Reps., 1998-2001.

Professional Career: Real estate broker, Henry Co. homes; Owner, Jeff Miller Real Estate; Deputy sheriff.

DC Office: 2416 RHOB, 20515, 202-225-4136; Fax: 202-225-3414; Web site: jeffmiller.house.gov.

State Offices: Ft. Walton Beach, 850-664-1266; Pensacola, 850-479-1183.

Committees: *Armed Services:* Emerging Threats & Capabilities. *Permanent Select Committee on Intelligence:* Oversight. *Veterans' Affairs* (Chmn).

Group Ratings

	ACLU	ACU	ADA	CFG	AFS	FRC	LCV	ITIC	NTU	COC
2010	6	96	0	84	0	100	10	33	89	88
2009	–	100	0	97	0	–	0	–	91	73

National Journal Ratings

	2010 LIB — 2010 CONS	2009 LIB — 2009 CONS
Economic	12% — 87%	0% — 96%
Social	0% — 85%	7% — 90%
Foreign	12% — 79%	0% — 75%
Composite	12% — 88%	8% — 92%

Key Votes of the 111th Congress

1. Overturn Ledbetter	N	5. Bar federal abortion funds	Y	9. Stop detainee transfers	Y
2. Pass $820 billion stimulus	N	6. Pass health care bill	N	10. Legalize immigrants' kids	N
3. Let guns in national parks	Y	7. Regulate financial firms	N	11. Repeal don't ask, tell	N
4. Pass cap-and-trade	N	8. Pass tax cuts for some	N	12. Limit campaign funds	N

Election Results

2010 general	Jeff Miller (R)	170,821	(80%)	($567,898)
	Joe Cantrell (NPA)	23,250	(11%)	($11,179)
	John Krause (NPA)	18,253	(9%)	($38,631)
2010 primary	Jeff Miller (R)	unopposed		

Prior Winning Percentages: 2008 (70%), 2006 (69%), 2004 (77%), 2002 (75%), 2001 (66%)

Population		Race/Ethnicity		Work	
Pop. 2010:	694,158	White:	74.6%	Private:	70.5%
Change since 2000:	Up 8.6%	Black:	14.3%	Government:	23.7%
Urban:	77.5%	Hispanic:	5.1%	Self-employed:	5.7%
Rural:	22.5%	Asian:	2.3%	Blue collar:	20.9%
Area size:	5,241 sq. mi.	Native Am.:	0.8%	White collar:	55.5%
		Hawaiian:	0.1%	Khaki collar:	3.8%
Age		Two+ races:	2.7%	Other:	19.7%
Median age:	37.5 yrs.				
More than 65 yrs:	13.6%	*Ancestry*		Median income:	$45,617
Less than 18 yrs:	22.8%	Irish	10.5%	Median Home Value:	$164,800
		German	10.5%		
Education		USA	10.2%	**Military Veterans**	
H.S. grad:	86.4%			% of Pop:	17.6%
College grad:	22.1%				
Grad degree:	7.7%				

Panhandle; Pensacola

The "Redneck Riviera" is the affectionate local
name for the Gulf Coast beaches of Florida's
Panhandle, stretching from Pensacola east to
Destin. This has been military country ever
since John Quincy Adams persuaded Spain to
sell Florida to the United States in 1819 with the
goal of getting the port of Pensacola. In October
1861, the Union defeated the Confederates in a
battle to control Santa Rosa Island, the outer-
most spit of land protecting Pensacola Bay.

2008 Presidential Vote		
John McCain (R) 234,257	(67%)
Barack Obama (D) 112,726	(32%)

2004 Presidential Vote		
George Bush (R) 231,199	(72%)
John Kerry (D) 88,686	(28%)

Cook Partisan Voting Index: R+21

(A quarter century later, the site of that clash, Fort Pickens, became Apache warrior Geronimo's
prison.) In the 20th century, the Pensacola Naval Air Station was turned into the nation's first
naval-aviation training base, giving birth to carrier aviation. Today, about 20,000 people are employed at Eglin Air Force Base, which spreads over three counties and, with approximately 100,000
square miles of airspace stretching over the Gulf of Mexico to the Florida Keys, is considered the
largest air base in the free world. Eglin developed the BLU-82 "Daisy Cutter" bomb that was used
in Afghanistan, and it was the test site for the largest conventional bomb in the U.S. arsenal, the
21,000-pound ordnance that is dropped from the rear of a C-130 cargo plane and is referred to as
the "Mother of All Bombs." Base realignment was expected to add more than 4,000 troops and 100
F-35 jet fighters to Eglin by 2011. But unemployment in Pensacola's Escambia County, where
about half the district's people live, soared over 11% in 2010. When oil giant BP sought to hire 90
workers for temporary cleanup jobs from its massive oil spill in July 2010, an estimated 600 people
showed up.

The western panhandle of Florida is closer to Houston than to Miami, and is culturally part
of Dixie. A columnist for the *Pensacola News Journal* once recommended the creation of an independent commonwealth of West Florida. "We don't have much in common with the people inhabit-
ing what I call peninsular Florida," wrote Jerry Maygarden. "I'm convinced that the further south
you drive, the further north you get." Until recently, the panhandle was economically backward
and heavily dependent on the military. As the South has become more prosperous, the shore has
attracted vacationing and retiring Southerners to its vast, fine-grained white sand beaches and
its pleasant inlet-dotted bays. It also has become a leading spring break destination for college
students and the site of a large annual gay Memorial Day weekend party. The region has long been
culturally and economically conservative, with a strong pro-military bent.

The 1st Congressional District of Florida is so far west, it's in the Central time zone. The district's shoreline runs from Pensacola, adjoining the Alabama border, through Fort Walton Beach
to the west side of Destin. Inland, the 1st stretches farther east, taking in rural Walton, Holmes
and Washington counties. The population here has grown steadily, with young civilians, not just
military retirees, moving in and shifting attention to education and quality-of-life issues. In 2004,
four massive hurricanes roared through the region, with devastating effect. In Pensacola alone,
45,000 homes were deemed unlivable. In 2005, Hurricane Katrina also left its mark here. With the
most military veterans of any district in the nation, the 1st District is strongly Republican. It voted
69%-31% for George W. Bush in 2000 and 72%-28% in 2004, his best numbers in the state. John
McCain, likewise, had his best Florida showing in this district, with a 67%-32% lead over Barack
Obama.

Jeff Miller (R)

The congressman from the 1st District is Jeff Miller, a Republican who won a special election in
October 2001. The scion of a pioneer farm family that settled in central Florida in the mid-1800s,
Miller grew up in Levy County, where his parents raised cattle. He graduated from the University
of Florida and became an aide to the state's longtime agriculture commissioner, Democrat Doyle
Conner. In 1998, he moved to Santa Rosa County, his wife's family's home, and began to sell real
estate. Also in 1998, a year after he switched to the Republican Party, he ran his first political
campaign, challenging a Republican state representative who had received some negative press
after an altercation with a state trooper. Miller won 53%-47%. Not long afterward, the 1st District
seat came open following the resignation of Republican Rep. Joe Scarborough, who became a talk-
show host on the MSNBC cable network. Miller quickly became the favorite of national party leaders. Sensitive to coastal interests, Miller and the other serious contenders all claimed to be ardent
environmentalists, an unusual twist in a Republican primary. Miller's best-known opponent was

state Rep. Randy Knepper, chief of staff to the district's former Democratic representative, Earl Hutto, who retired in 1994. Scarborough endorsed Miller as "a strong voice for northwest Florida." In the six-candidate contest, Miller got 54% to only 15% for Knepper and 16% for businessman Michael Francisco, a decorated combat pilot. National Democrats made no major effort to win this seat that they had held less than seven years earlier, and Miller won the general election, 66%-28%.

In the House, Miller has compiled a conservative record. His *National Journal* voting score in 2009 was the furthest to the right of any Florida Republican. In contrast to the voluble Scarborough, he gained a reputation for being soft-spoken and a good listener. But he also has a decidedly lower profile. When he arrived in Washington, Miller got seats on the Armed Services and Veterans' Affairs committees, obvious assignments for this district. He made multiple visits to U.S. troops in Afghanistan and Iraq and praised the conduct of the war. He worked to protect local military facilities in the base-closing process. In 2004, when Democrats were seeking to force a House vote on Miller's bill to provide a 100% annuity to surviving military spouses, he persuaded Republican leaders to call up the bill and avoid a partisan conflict; the measure was passed into law. A long-standing foe of oil and gas drilling in the eastern Gulf of Mexico, he relented in 2006, accepting a deal that opened up some offshore drilling but included a ban on drilling rigs in a military training range that extends at least 200 miles south of Fort Walton Beach.

With the Republican takeover of the House in 2011, Miller rose to chairman of Veterans' Affairs. He has vowed to press the Veterans Benefit Administration to reduce its significant backlog of benefit claims. In 2008, he secured in 2008 $54 million for an in-patient center at Eglin Hospital and pushed for a new veterans' hospital near the base to replace one destroyed by Katrina in 2005.

When Democrats still controlled the House, Miller was the ranking Republican on the Armed Services Committee's subcommittee on terrorism and unconventional threats. In that role, he worked with Democrats to increase money for the military's Special Operations Command and for cybersecurity in fiscal 2011. After the BP oil spill disaster in 2010, he introduced a bill to protect affected homeowners from foreclosures and asked the company to provide up to $1 billion for local governments, businesses and residents along the Gulf Coast. An avid gun rights advocate, Miller sponsored a bill in 2007 to give hunters in the District of Columbia in-state rates for licenses in the more open spaces of Maryland or Virginia. He also has sponsored a bill to place the face of Ronald Reagan on the half-dollar coin.

In the 2002 primary, Miller faced a rematch with special election primary runner-up Francisco, who criticized his lack of military experience. Miller won 64%-36%. Since then, Democrats have run only token challengers against him.

SECOND DISTRICT

Steve Southerland (R)

Elected 2010, 1st term; b. Oct. 10, 1965, Nashville, TN; home, Panama City; Troy St. U., B.S. 1987; Jefferson St. Junior Col., A.A. 1989.; Southern Baptist; Married (Susan); 4 children.

Professional Career: Owner, Southerland Family Funeral Homes.

DC Office: 1229 LHOB, 20515, 202-225-5235; Fax: 202-225-5615; Web site: southerland.house.gov.

State Offices: Panama City, 850-785-0812; Tallahassee, 850-561-3979.

Committees: *Agriculture:* Conservation, Energy & Forestry; Nutrition & Horticulture. *Natural Resources:* Fisheries, Wildlife, Oceans & Insular Affairs. *Transportation & Infrastructure:* Aviation; Highways & Transit.

Election Results

2010 general	Steve Southerland (R)	136,371	(54%)	($1,291,071)
	Allen Boyd (D)	105,211	(41%)	($2,690,989)
	Paul McKain (NPA)	7,135	(3%)	($49,931)
	Dianne Berryhill (NPA)	5,705	(2%)	($10,829)
2010 primary	Steve Southerland (R)	28,269	(47%)	
	David Scholl (R)	14,483	(24%)	
	Ron McNeil (R)	6,447	(11%)	
	Eddie Hendry (R)	6,164	(10%)	
	Barbara Olschner (R)	4,965	(8%)	

Population		Race/Ethnicity		Work	
Pop. 2010:	737,519	White:	68.5%	Private:	66.7%
Change since 2000:	Up 15.4%	Black:	21.9%	Government:	27.5%
Urban:	62.1%	Hispanic:	5.5%	Self-employed:	5.6%
Rural:	37.9%	Asian:	1.7%	Blue collar:	17.5%
Area size:	11,143 sq. mi.	Native Am.:	0.4%	White collar:	61.1%
		Hawaiian:	0.0%	Khaki collar:	0.9%
Age		Two+ races:	1.8%	Other:	20.5%
Median age:	35.8 yrs.				
More than 65 yrs:	13.1%	*Ancestry*		Median income:	$42,429
Less than 18 yrs:	21.1%	Irish	10.9%	Median Home Value:	$169,900
		German	9.9%		
Education		English	9.0%	**Military Veterans**	
H.S. grad:	84.8%			% of Pop:	12.8%
College grad:	24.8%				
Grad degree:	9.7%				

Panhandle; Tallahassee

Tallahassee is a small city in the middle of swampy lowlands, the opposite of the image people have of the typical booming Florida city, with endless miles of beach or a Magic Kingdom beckoning vacationing families or snowbirds from elsewhere. So how did Tallahassee become the capital of the nation's fourth-largest state? The answer is, it was chosen back when Florida's modest population lived mostly along the state's northern tier, placing Tallahassee, more or less,

2008 Presidential Vote
John McCain (R) 199,661   (54%)
Barack Obama (D) 163,872   (45%)

2004 Presidential Vote
George Bush (R) 181,300   (54%)
John Kerry (D) 153,164   (46%)

Cook Partisan Voting Index: R+6

at the state's center of gravity. Ralph Waldo Emerson, visiting Tallahassee in the 19th century, called it a "grotesque place, rapidly settled by public officers, land speculators and desperadoes." Today the countryside around Tallahassee is distinctly Dixie: cotton fields, soft pine stands, catfish farms, small towns with big churches. Until recently, Tallahassee was little more than a Spanish-mossed county seat with a pair of universities and a handsome Creole capitol, built in 1845 and preserved opposite its 1977 skyscraper replacement. Since the 1980s, it has spread out and become a middling-sized city, with a tight-knit and sometimes fractious political and legal elite, bringing a taste of newly urbanized Florida to the state's north. Tallahassee has not yet attained the critical mass of Sacramento, Austin or Albany, but perhaps it is on its way as the state continues to expand and diversify. In 2009, Moody's *Economy.com* index ranked the city 79th among 392 U.S. cities in job growth.

The 2nd Congressional District of Florida is centered on Tallahassee, and extends along the Gulf coast west to Destin and east to the Suwannee River, which empties into the Gulf in the only part of Florida where the beach is still undeveloped. Inland, the 2nd runs north to the Alabama and Georgia borders, and far enough east to be within an hour's drive of Jacksonville. Historically, this was Democratic country, as in Jeffersonian and segregationist. Today, it is still mostly Democratic, though for different reasons. More than one in three Tallahassee-area jobs are in city and state government, three times the statewide level. The city's African-American population grew from about 25% into the 1990s to 35% in 2010. The district includes Gadsden County, the state's only black-majority county. Growth is spreading south into Wakulla County, and there is similar growth along the beach areas near Destin, which have attracted affluent families to "new urbanist" communities like Seaside and Rosemary Beach. The opening of an airport in 2010 near Panama City was sure to spur development along the state's pretty and underappreciated northwest beaches. Southwest and Delta immediately announced plans for flights there. For all this recent growth, this remains the part of Florida with the highest percentage of native Floridians.

Tallahassee and Leon County have voted solidly for Democratic presidential nominees in recent elections. Beyond Leon County, which casts about 40% of the district's votes, partisan performance is less predictable. Gadsden County is heavily Democratic, while the Gulf beach areas tend to be Republican. The 2nd District voted twice for George W. Bush and for John McCain in 2008, 54%-45%.

Steve Southerland (R)

The new congressman from Florida's 2nd District is Republican Steve Southerland, who upset seven-term Democrat Allen Boyd in 2010. Southerland grew up in Panama City, Fla. His family has lived in Bay County for five generations, and he is a third-generation funeral director. His grandfather opened the Southerland Family Funeral Home and Crematory in 1955, and he began working there as a child, washing cars with his younger two brothers and a sister. After graduating from Alabama's Troy State University with a bachelor's degree in business administration, he returned to the business, which he now co-owns with his sister. He also owns a timber business with his wife of 23 years, Susan. Over the years, Southerland got involved in civic organizations, including the Early Learning Coalition of Northwest Florida and the Bay County Chamber of Commerce. In 2008, he got actively involved in politics, helping to found the Bay Patriots, a local tea party group. Southerland told the news website *Daily Caller* that his experience in the funeral business prepared him for Congress. "I'm a grief expert," Southerland said. "I know what grief looks like. And when you close your family's business for the last day, send all employees home, when you lose your home, when you can't send your kids to college, (that's) grief."

In August, Southerland topped a crowded Republican primary field that included Air Force veteran David Scholl, getting 47% of the vote, for the right to challenge Boyd, a conservative Blue Dog Democrat who was vulnerable after voting for President Obama's health care insurance overhaul in 2010. Boyd voted against the initial bill, but later voted for the final version. As a result, he got hammered from both the right and the left on an issue that polarized voters in the 2010 election. He drew a primary challenge from state Sen. Al Lawson, who attacked him for his vote against the bill initially. Boyd survived the primary with just 51% of the vote.

The primary depleted much of the $2.5 million war chest that Boyd would have turned on Southerland in the fall campaign. Then he spent much of the campaign on the defensive, this time explaining his decision to switch his vote on the health care bill from no to yes. Southerland, who raised $1 million, campaigned on reducing the deficit and hammering Boyd on the health care vote. He portrayed him as unwilling to stand up to liberal House Speaker Nancy Pelosi, who led the effort to pass the bill. Republican yard signs chided Boyd with the expression: "Blue Dog = Lap Dog." Boyd responded that while the law wasn't perfect, it would "effectively curb the skyrocketing cost of health care." He tried to shore up his conservative credentials by touting endorsements from the National Rifle Association and the U.S. Chamber of Commerce.

He also tried to paint Southerland as a right-wing extremist, saying that his opponent would take Social Security benefits away from orphans and would vote to repeal the 17th Amendment providing for the direct election of senators. At a candidate forum, Southerland said he was "fine with" returning the ability to choose senators to state legislators. A spokesman for his campaign said that Southerland does not want to repeal the amendment, but does want to return to the "founding principles of the Constitution." Southerland won, 54% to 41%.

THIRD DISTRICT

Corrine Brown (D)

Elected 1992, 10th term; b. Nov. 11, 1946, Jacksonville; home, Jacksonville; FL A&M, B.S. 1969, M.S., 1971; Baptist; single; 1 child.

Elected Office: FL House of Reps., 1982–92.

Professional Career: Prof., FL Commun. Col., 1977–82, Guidance counselor, 1982–92.

DC Office: 2336 RHOB, 20515, 202-225-0123; Fax: 202-225-2256; Web site: www.house.gov/corrinebrown.

State Offices: Jacksonville, 904-354-1652; Orlando, 407-290-9031.

Committees: *Transportation & Infrastructure:* Coast Guard & Maritime Transportation; Railroads, Pipelines & Hazardous Materials (RMM); Water Resources & Environment. *Veterans' Affairs:* Health.

Group Ratings

	ACLU	ACU	ADA	CFG	AFS	FRC	LCV	ITIC	NTU	COC
2010	88	0	100	0	100	0	100	67	5	13
2009	–	0	100	0	100	–	93	–	2	40

National Journal Ratings

	2010 LIB	—	2010 CONS	2009 LIB	—	2009 CONS
Economic	76%	—	24%	87%	—	12%
Social	80%	—	18%	80%	—	18%
Foreign	66%	—	29%	69%	—	30%
Composite	75%	—	25%	79%	—	21%

Key Votes of the 111th Congress

1. Overturn Ledbetter	Y	5. Bar federal abortion funds	N	9. Stop detainee transfers	Y
2. Pass $820 billion stimulus	Y	6. Pass health care bill	Y	10. Legalize immigrants' kids	Y
3. Let guns in national parks	N	7. Regulate financial firms	Y	11. Repeal don't ask, tell	Y
4. Pass cap-and-trade	Y	8. Pass tax cuts for some	Y	12. Limit campaign funds	Y

Election Results

2010 general	Corrine Brown (D)	94,744	(63%)	($990,489)
	Michael Yost (R)	50,932	(34%)	($156,856)
	Terry Martin-Back (NPA)	4,625	(3%)	($8,105)
2010 primary	Corrine Brown (D)	35,312	(80%)	
	Scott Fortune (D)	8,718	(20%)	

Prior Winning Percentages: 2008 (100%), 2006 (100%), 2004 (100%), 2002 (59%), 2000 (58%), 1998 (55%), 1996 (61%), 1994 (58%), 1992 (59%)

Population		Race/Ethnicity		Work	
Pop. 2010:	659,055	White:	32.9%	Private:	81.7%
Change since 2000:	Up 3.1%	Black:	51.2%	Government:	14.1%
Urban:	89.7%	Hispanic:	11.3%	Self-employed:	4.2%
Rural:	10.3%	Asian:	1.9%	Blue collar:	24.4%
Area size:	2,097 sq. mi.	Native Am.:	0.3%	White collar:	50.3%
		Hawaiian:	0.1%	Khaki collar:	0.2%
Age		Two+ races:	1.9%	Other:	25.2%
Median age:	33.1 yrs.				
More than 65 yrs:	10.9%	*Ancestry*		Median income:	$33,852
Less than 18 yrs:	25.6%	West Indian	5.6%	Median Home Value:	$138,200
		German	5.5%		
Education		USA	5.5%	**Military Veterans**	
H.S. grad:	78.2%			% of Pop:	10.4%
College grad:	14.4%				
Grad degree:	4.6%				

North Florida; Part Jacksonville

Before the Civil War, most of Florida was still an uncharted watery wilderness, festooned with exotic greenery, inhabited by unusual animals, a part of the United States so far out of the experience of most Americans as to seem foreign. As late as 1940, Florida had the smallest population of any Southern state, and most of the people here lived in classic Dixie rural counties with small courthouse towns, where civic affairs were run by the richest white men, and African-Americans lived in poorly constructed, unpainted shotgun shacks propped up on blocks, with little money and no vote. This was a land of swamps, lakes and orange groves, and of author Marjorie Kinnan Rawlings's Cross Creek, where she wrote the great children's classic *The Yearling*. The broad St. Johns River, one of the few North American rivers that flows (if only sluggishly) north, meanders through orange-grove country to the port of Jacksonville, which was for many years Florida's largest city.

2008 Presidential Vote		
Barack Obama (D)	190,646	(73%)
John McCain (R)	69,099	(27%)
2004 Presidential Vote		
John Kerry (D)	151,466	(65%)
George Bush (R)	81,778	(35%)
Cook Partisan Voting Index:	D+18	

The 3rd Congressional District of Florida occupies much of this swampy terrain. The district was created in 1992 to be north Florida's black-majority seat and has had three sets of boundaries. The district borders five Republican-held districts, each of which was designed to shift as many Democrats as possible to the 3rd to strengthen Republicans elsewhere. In its current form, it follows the St. Johns River upstream from Jacksonville's city center to downtown Orlando, reaching out to pluck additional minority and Democratic voters from Sanford, where Amtrak's Auto Train unloads its Florida-bound travelers, and Gainesville, home of the University of Florida. Along the way, the district takes in smaller black settlements, such as lettuce-producing Zellwood, and Eatonville, home of author Zora Neale Hurston. In time, this relatively unpopulated, lake-filled region may become Florida's next development frontier. In recent years, however, it has struggled along with the rest of Florida: Orlando went from being the 13th strongest economy among U.S. metropolitan areas in 2007 to 27th in 2010, according to an annual report by Policom Corp., while Jacksonville's construction industry went into a sharp decline. The Gallup-Healthways Well-Being Index found in 2010 that the 3rd District had the nation's highest percentage of constituents without health insurance. It is solidly Democratic.

Corrine Brown (D)

The congresswoman from the 3rd District is Corrine Brown, a Democrat first elected in 1992. She grew up in Jacksonville, taught at the community college, was a guidance counselor and in 1982, was elected to the Florida House. With her Jacksonville base, she was the clear favorite in this new district. In the Democratic primary, she faced white talk-radio host Andy Johnson, who called himself "the blackest candidate in the race." Brown led 43%-31% in the primary and won 64%-36% in the runoff. She won the general election 59%-41%.

Brown has compiled a liberal record on most issues. In her district, many voters work at military bases and she tends to support high defense spending and argues that the military can be a source of opportunity. She hailed the Navy's January 2009 decision to create a home port for a nuclear carrier at Jacksonville's Mayport naval station as a local economic boost and "a decision that will make our country safer." On the Veterans' Affairs Committee, she sought additional veteran's cemeteries for Florida, which is the home to more veterans than any other state except California. New cemeteries were approved for Jacksonville and Sarasota in 2003. On the Transportation and Infrastructure Subcommittee, Brown worked on legislation to strengthen security at the ports. A project of hers in the 111th Congress (2009-10) was a high-speed rail line from Tampa to Orlando and Miami.

Her outspoken, partisan views cause her problems from time to time. In 2004, she criticized Bush administration representatives at a briefing on the Haiti crisis, saying that they were "a bunch of white men" who "all look alike to me." After Rep. Henry Bonilla, R-Texas, called her on her remarks, Brown apologized, but she continued to call the White House policy on Haiti racist. In a dispute in 2008 over the seating of convention delegates from Florida, Brown, who had endorsed Hillary Rodham Clinton for president, said, "If we are not seated, then nobody is going to be seated." The problem was resolved after Barack Obama became the certain nominee.

Brown has had spirited campaign opposition, resulting largely from personal issues. Her most difficult contest came in 1998 amid charges of questionable ethical conduct. In June of that year, the *St. Petersburg Times* reported that her daughter had been given a $50,000 Lexus car by agents of African millionaire Foutanga Sissoko. He had been imprisoned in Miami on federal charges of paying an illegal gratuity to a Customs Service officer, and Brown worked furiously to get him released, lobbying Attorney General Janet Reno to have him deported to Africa to continue his humanitarian work. The newspaper also reported that she kept a jazz singer on her payroll as a "congressional outreach specialist" and that the singer occasionally visited the district from her New York City home. Brown reacted with fury, filing a criminal contempt charge against the *Times* reporters with the Capitol Police, claiming they "accosted" her and their questions made her cry. The charges went nowhere.

The Republicans found a credible challenger in Bill Randall, an African-American and a former General Motors manager who had become a minister. He opposed abortion rights and favored local control of schools and government vouchers for private school tuition. He held Brown to 55%, getting 45% of the vote.

A subsequent investigation by the House Committee on Standards of Official Conduct found that Brown "demonstrated, at the least, poor judgment and created substantial concerns regarding both the appearance of impropriety and the reputation of the House." But it dropped the case because, the committee said, it was unable to question key witnesses, including Sissoko.

But the story continued to have political repercussions for Brown. She faced a vigorous re-election challenge in 2000 from Republican Jennifer Carroll, a retired 20-year Navy officer who criticized Brown for a lack of vision and an inability to work with people. She also outspent Brown. Brown called Carroll "a zero" and "a Republican puppet." With a strong grass-roots organization, Brown won 58%-42%. In 2002, Carroll again challenged Brown. But local Republicans were not enthusiastic about her candidacy in this heavily Democratic district. Brown won 59%-41%, again with huge leads in Jacksonville and Orlando. She has been unopposed or won with ease since then. In 2010, former Florida GOP Chairman Tom Slade shared with the *Florida Times-Union* his advice for any would-be challengers: "Don't do it. Go find a tree and beat your head against it. You may find the result more pleasurable."

FOURTH DISTRICT

Ander Crenshaw (R)

Elected 2000, 6th term; b. Sept. 1, 1944, Jacksonville; home, Jacksonville; U. of GA, B.A. 1966, U. of FL, J.D. 1969; Episcopalian; married (Kitty); 2 children.

Elected Office: FL House of Reps., 1972-78; FL Senate 1986-93.

Professional Career: Investment banker, 1980-2000.

DC Office: 440 CHOB, 20515, 202-225-2501; Fax: 202-225-2504; Web site: crenshaw.house.gov.

State Offices: Jacksonville, 904-598-0481; Lake City, 386-365-3316.

Committees: *Appropriations:* Defense; Homeland Security; Legislative Branch (Chmn).

Group Ratings

	ACLU	ACU	ADA	CFG	AFS	FRC	LCV	ITIC	NTU	COC
2010	13	88	5	75	0	93	60	67	84	100
2009	–	84	5	78	22	–	7	–	77	87

National Journal Ratings

	2010 LIB — 2010 CONS		2009 LIB — 2009 CONS	
Economic	33%	67%	25%	74%
Social	0%	85%	36%	64%
Foreign	39%	60%	26%	68%
Composite	27%	73%	30%	70%

Key Votes of the 111th Congress

1. Overturn Ledbetter	N	5. Bar federal abortion funds	Y	9. Stop detainee transfers	Y
2. Pass $820 billion stimulus	N	6. Pass health care bill	N	10. Legalize immigrants' kids	N
3. Let guns in national parks	Y	7. Regulate financial firms	N	11. Repeal don't ask, tell	N
4. Pass cap-and-trade	N	8. Pass tax cuts for some	N	12. Limit campaign funds	N

Election Results

2010 general	Ander Crenshaw (R)	178,238	(77%)	($554,327)
	Troy Stanley (NPA)	52,540	(23%)	($15,779)
2010 primary	Ander Crenshaw (R)	unopposed		

Prior Winning Percentages: 2008 (65%); 2006 (70%), 2004 (100%), 2002 (100%), 2000 (67%)

Population		Race/Ethnicity		Work	
Pop. 2010:	744,418	White:	71.8%	Private:	79.4%
Change since 2000:	Up 16.4%	Black:	14.7%	Government:	16.1%
Urban:	78.2%	Hispanic:	7.1%	Self-employed:	4.3%
Rural:	21.8%	Asian:	3.8%	Blue collar:	19.3%
Area size:	4,369 sq. mi.	Native Am.:	0.3%	White collar:	63.3%
		Hawaiian:	0.1%	Khaki collar:	1.1%
Age		Two+ races:	2.0%	Other:	16.4%
Median age:	36.8 yrs.				
More than 65 yrs:	12.0%	*Ancestry*		Median income:	$54,185
Less than 18 yrs:	23.0%	Irish	11.4%	Median Home Value:	$201,300
		German	10.5%		
Education		English	10.2%	**Military Veterans**	
H.S. grad:	87.8%			% of Pop:	13.3%
College grad:	27.2%				
Grad degree:	9.3%				

North Florida; Part Jacksonville

With a metropolitan area of 1.2 million people, Jacksonville has outgrown its reputation as Florida's overlooked city. Not long ago, it was considered a backwater, dominated by insurance companies and smelly paper mills. It now boasts a National Football League franchise, bold new skyscrapers looming above the St. Johns River, and a shopping mall that overshadows tiny shotgun houses. Wide freeways sidestep primeval wetlands on their way to huge

2008 Presidential Vote
John McCain (R) 229,996 (62%)
Barack Obama (D) 136,777 (37%)

2004 Presidential Vote
George Bush (R) 227,431 (69%)
John Kerry (D) 100,414 (31%)

Cook Partisan Voting Index: R+17

beachfront subdivisions. The harbor has grown as a destination for cargo and passenger operations. With the Mayport Naval Station and the Naval Air Station, Jacksonville has a significant military employment base; the two are the largest metro area employers. Shrewd marketing has lured big-name private-sector companies. Jacksonville is the headquarters of railway giant CSX and also hosts major operations such as Winn-Dixie supermarkets, UPS, and Bank of America. Business leaders are working to make the area into the "Silicon Valley of Logistics"—building on its land, air, and sea transportation facilities—and they have dredged the port for larger ships. The city experienced the same economic downturn as other Florida communities in recent years, but economists say the port—which does about 70% of its business in exports, an unusually large amount—is crucial to its long-term recovery.

The 4th Congressional District of Florida includes much of Jacksonville, minus the African-American neighborhoods, which are in the 3rd District. It takes in a northern tier of counties along the Georgia border that runs all the way west to Tallahassee. This northern tier is sleepy territory punctuated by small towns like White Springs, Lake City, and Raiford (home to a big state prison). It is crisscrossed by Interstates 10 and 75. Some 70% of the population is in Jacksonville and rapidly growing Nassau County. The boosterish Jacksonville civic culture and significant military presence make the 4th a pro-business, pro-military and pro-Republican district. George W. Bush won 66% of the district's vote in 2000 and 69% in 2004; each was his second highest percentage in Florida. John McCain won 62% in 2008.

Ander Crenshaw (R)

The congressman from the 4th District is Ander Crenshaw, a Republican first elected in 2000. He grew up in Jacksonville, where he has family roots dating to the early 20th century. The son of a lawyer, he attended the University of Georgia on a basketball scholarship, and then graduated from the University of Florida law school. His wife's father, Claude Kirk, was a Republican elected governor in 1966, then defeated in 1970. Crenshaw was elected to the state House in 1972 and served for six years, before running unsuccessfully for secretary of state. He then became an investment banker. In 1980, he ran for the U.S. Senate and finished third of six in the 1980 Republican primary, which was won by Paula Hawkins. From 1986 until 1993, he served in the state Senate and in 1992, became the first Republican state Senate president in 118 years. He ran for governor in 1994 but finished fourth in the primary, far behind Jeb Bush, who narrowly lost to Lawton Chiles in November. Crenshaw's opportunity to run for the House came in 2000, when Republican Rep. Tillie Fowler announced that she would honor her promise to serve only four terms. Crenshaw was promptly endorsed by local Republican leaders, which discouraged several potential candidates. He won the primary 70%-30% and the general election 67%-31%. He has won re-election easily since then, though he drew some flak from local Republicans for supporting the 2008 financial industry rescue.

In the House, Crenshaw is a reliable conservative. Although his tall frame makes him hard to miss in a crowd, he has not sought the limelight. He says he adheres to former President Reagan's motto: "There's no limit to what you can do as long as you don't care who gets the credit." He was his freshman class's liaison to the Republican leadership, and he became friends with former Majority Whip Roy Blunt, who later named him to chair a House GOP budget task force. In his second term, Crenshaw won a seat on the Appropriations Committee, where his top priorities are the district's large military and veterans' facilities. In 2008, he slipped a provision into the military construction spending bill telling the Navy to start work on converting Mayport to a nuclear base. The next year, the Pentagon announced that a carrier would be moved from Norfolk to Mayport as early as 2014, despite objections by Virginia officials. He pushed successfully for new veterans' cemeteries in Jacksonville and Sarasota, and he fought for expanded disability coverage for Gulf War veterans. He also has introduced legislation to provide savings accounts for people caring for family members with disabilities. Despite drawing more than 200 cosponsors, it gained little traction in the 111th Congress (2009-10).

Crenshaw made a bid for the senior Republican seat on the Budget Committee, raising nearly $1 million for other Republican candidates in the 2006 election to pay his dues. But the slot went to Paul Ryan of Wisconsin, who had less seniority than Crenshaw. He was not helped by his role in an earlier lobbying scandal that felled former Majority Leader Tom DeLay of Texas: Crenshaw had traveled with DeLay on a trip to South Korea in 2001 that had been paid for by lobbyists close to DeLay. Crenshaw also was on the wrong side of a pitched leadership battle for DeLay's successor; he backed Blunt for the job, but John Boehner of Ohio emerged the winner.

FIFTH DISTRICT

Rich Nugent (R)

Elected 2010, 1st term; b. May 26, 1951, Evergreen Park, IL; home, Spring Hill; Saint Leo Col., B.A. 1990; Troy St. U., M.P.A. 1995.; Methodist; Married (Wendy); 3 children.

Military Career: IL Air Natl. Guard, 1969-75.

Elected Office: Sheriff, Hernando Cnty., 2000-10.

Professional Career: Police officer, Romeoville, IL, 1972-84; operations bureau commander, Hernando Cnty. Sheriff's Office, 1984-2000.

DC Office: 1517 LHOB, 20515, 202-225-1002; Fax: 202-226-6559; Web site: nugent.house.gov.

State Offices: Brooksville, 352-799-8354.

Committees: *House Administration:* Elections; Oversight. *Rules.*

Election Results

2010 general	Rich Nugent (R)	208,815	(67%)	($518,609)
	James Piccillo (D)	100,585	(33%)	($146,686)
2010 primary	Rich Nugent (R)	52,586	(62%)	
	Jason Sager (R)	31,969	(38%)	

Population		Race/Ethnicity		Work	
Pop. 2010:	929,533	White:	79.5%	Private:	80.9%
Change since 2000:	Up 45.4%	Black:	6.0%	Government:	13.1%
Urban:	64.5%	Hispanic:	10.8%	Self-employed:	5.7%
Rural:	35.5%	Asian:	1.7%	Blue collar:	21.9%
Area size:	4,801 sq. mi.	Native Am.:	0.3%	White collar:	58.1%
		Hawaiian:	0.0%	Khaki collar:	0.1%
Age		Two+ races:	1.4%	Other:	20.0%
Median age:	45.3 yrs.				
More than 65 yrs:	23.7%	*Ancestry*		Median income:	$44,628
Less than 18 yrs:	20.4%	German	14.0%	Median Home Value:	$169,100
		Irish	12.2%		
Education		English	9.6%	**Military Veterans**	
H.S. grad:	85.1%			% of Pop:	16.3%
College grad:	18.5%				
Grad degree:	6.0%				

Northwest Florida Coast

Over the past quarter-century, Florida's urban areas have grown in almost every direction, occupying the high ground between the swamps that still take up much of the state's peninsula. The pattern of development is evident in counties to the north and east of St. Petersburg and Tampa, where subdivisions, trailer parks, and shopping centers with Eckerd drugstores and Winn-Dixie supermarkets sprang up in what had been farms and sleepy little towns with low

2008 Presidential Vote
John McCain (R) 255,714   (56%)
Barack Obama (D) 197,613   (43%)

2004 Presidential Vote
George Bush (R) 221,259   (58%)
John Kerry (D) 156,632   (41%)

Cook Partisan Voting Index: R+9

brick buildings baking in the Florida sun. This area—a haven for manatees, the unusual and beloved sea mammal—has seen suburban development run up the spines of U.S. 19, along the Gulf Coast, and along U.S. 41 and Interstate 75. Persistent development, and a few unruly tourists, prompted the federal government in 2010 to declare Kings Bay a restricted manatee refuge. Tourists had been observed chasing, riding and poking the gentle sea cows.

Though there are plenty of working people in this area, it is mainly retirement country. Residents are comfortable, though not usually affluent. One of every four residents is over 65, and Citrus and Hernando counties have high percentages of military veterans. Drawn by the many inland lakes, greenery and the pleasant climate, retirees from Michigan, Indiana and Ohio flocked here by traveling south on Interstate 75 south—a pattern distinct from the retirees who drove Interstate 95 from the Boston-Washington corridor to such destinations as Palm Beach, Fort Lauderdale and Miami. To meet increased demand, the local electric utility plans to open an additional nuclear power plant in 2020.

The 5th Congressional District of Florida occupies much of this rapidly growing area. Between 2000 and 2007 it added 206,000 new residents, more than any other congressional district in the state. The beach areas in Levy, Citrus and Hernando counties are largely undeveloped. The bulk of the population lives inland, in such places as Citrus Springs, Brooksville, Zephyrhills, Land o' Lakes, and Clermont. More than two-thirds of the population is in Pasco, Hernando and Citrus counties. Sumter County, one of the few areas on the Florida peninsula with large tracts of open land, is growing rapidly in part due to a massive "golf cart" retirement community of 75,000 known as The Villages, which is split between the 5th and 6th Districts. In 2009, the district had nearly 273,000 Social Security recipients, more than any other district in the country. Politically, this is marginal territory. The district lines were drawn by Republicans in 2002 to make the district more Republican. In 2008, John McCain ran strongly in these counties and won the district 56%-43%.

Richard Nugent (R)

The new congressman from Florida's 5th District is Richard Nugent, a Republican who succeeded the retiring Ginny Brown-Waite, also a Republican, in 2010. Nugent was born in Evergreen Park, Ill., a Chicago suburb, the youngest of three children. His father worked in a steel mill and his mother was a homemaker. After high school, Nugent served in the Illinois Air National Guard for six years and became a police officer, working his way up to sergeant in the Romeoville, Ill., police department. He adopted Florida as his home after attending Saint Leo University, a Catholic liberal-arts college in St. Leo. He went on to earn a master's degree in public administration from Troy State University. Nugent joined the Hernando County Sheriff's Office in 1984; he was elected to his first term as sheriff in 2000, and was re-elected in 2004 and 2008. He and his wife, Wendy Nugent, have two sons in the Army and a third in the Army Reserve.

Over the years, Nugent presided over a drop in crime. In 2009, Hernando County recorded its lowest violent-crime rate since he took office. The next year, his office took control of operations of the Hernando County Jail, which had been run by the private Corrections Corporation of America. The firm had been criticized for being soft on prisoners. Nugent told the *St. Petersburg Times*, "There's a new sheriff in town. It's not going to be a relaxed, Club Med atmosphere." Nugent canceled weekly "pizza nights" and other advantages enjoyed by Hernando County prisoners. He returned $2 million in unspent funds to the county in 2009.

In April 2010, Brown-Waite announced she would not seek re-election to a fifth term because of health problems. She made the announcement on candidate filing day in Florida, which allowed Nugent to file the necessary legal papers by the deadline. Brown-Waite also issued a statement strongly endorsing Nugent. The arrangement sparked bitter complaints from other Republicans who had been waiting for the opportunity to run for a House seat. Public Service Commission Chair Nancy Argenziano and state Sen. Mike Fasano both said they might have run.

Nugent did draw a primary challenge from Jason Sager, a political neophyte whose father served as his campaign chief. Sager, a former audiovisual technician, was backed by tea party activists, but the upstart campaign never gained traction. In a July debate, Sager attacked Nugent for the succession deal with Brown-Waite. Nugent charged that Sager wanted to end Social Security and Medicare, a political no-no in the retiree-heavy congressional district. Sager countered that he supported a long-term phase-out of Social Security that would not deprive benefits to people who paid into the system. Nugent won the August 24 primary, 62% to 38%.

In the general election, he faced Democrat Jim Piccillo, a 36-year-old business consultant and a former Republican, who had an uphill battle in the GOP-tilting district. Piccillo cast himself as a moderate and a pragmatist who would work to reduce federal spending and regulation on businesses. Piccillo also reprised the issue of Nugent's anointment by Brown-Waite and criticized him for using a picture of his sheriff's badge on his campaign website. For his part, Nugent proposed freezing government spending at 2008 levels and campaigned against the Democrats' $787 billion economic stimulus bill. He portrayed Piccillo in a mailing as the "hand-picked candidate" of liberal House Speaker Nancy Pelosi, prompting Piccillo to call him a "flat out liar." Nugent outraised his opponent is this relatively low-budget affair, $518,000 to $147,000, and won easily, 67% to 33%.

SIXTH DISTRICT

Cliff Stearns (R)

Elected 1988, 12th term; b. April 16, 1941, Washington, DC; home, Ocala; George Washington U., B.S. 1963; Presbyterian; married (Joan); 3 children.

Military Career: Air Force, 1963–67.

Professional Career: Data Control Systems Inc., 1967–68; Negotiator, CBS, 1969–70; Pres., Stearns House Inc., 1972–present.

DC Office: 2306 RHOB, 20515, 202-225-5744; Fax: 202-225-3973; Web site: stearns.house.gov.

State Offices: Gainesville, 352-337-0003; Ocala, 352-351-8777; Orange Park, 904-269-3203.

Committees: *Energy & Commerce:* Commerce, Manufacturing & Trade; Communications & Technology; Oversight & Investigations (Chmn). *Veterans' Affairs:* Health; Oversight & Investigations.

Group Ratings

	ACLU	ACU	ADA	CFG	AFS	FRC	LCV	ITIC	NTU	COC
2010	13	96	0	87	0	100	0	33	89	88
2009	–	96	5	88	22	–	0	–	85	80

National Journal Ratings

	2010 LIB — 2010 CONS		2009 LIB — 2009 CONS	
Economic	15% —	84%	24% —	76%
Social	18% —	77%	13% —	84%
Foreign	12% —	79%	26% —	68%
Composite	18% —	83%	23% —	78%

Key Votes of the 111th Congress

1. Overturn Ledbetter	N	5. Bar federal abortion funds	Y	9. Stop detainee transfers	Y
2. Pass $820 billion stimulus	N	6. Pass health care bill	N	10. Legalize immigrants' kids	N
3. Let guns in national parks	Y	7. Regulate financial firms	N	11. Repeal don't ask, tell	N
4. Pass cap-and-trade	N	8. Pass tax cuts for some	N	12. Limit campaign funds	N

Election Results

2010 general	Cliff Stearns (R)	179,349	(71%)	($771,907)
	Steve Schonberg (NPA)	71,632	(29%)	($10,727)
2010 primary	Cliff Stearns (R)	50,432	(71%)	
	Don Browning (R)	20,111	(29%)	

Prior Winning Percentages: 2008 (61%), 2006 (60%), 2004 (64%), 2002 (65%), 2000 (100%), 1998 (100%), 1996 (67%), 1994 (100%), 1992 (65%), 1990 (59%), 1988 (54%)

Population		Race/Ethnicity		Work	
Pop. 2010:	812,727	White:	71.0%	Private:	74.6%
Change since 2000:	Up 27.1%	Black:	14.4%	Government:	19.5%
Urban:	69.4%	Hispanic:	8.9%	Self-employed:	5.6%
Rural:	30.6%	Asian:	3.2%	Blue collar:	20.2%
Area size:	3,025 sq. mi.	Native Am.:	0.3%	White collar:	60.4%
		Hawaiian:	0.1%	Khaki collar:	0.5%
Age		Two+ races:	1.9%	Other:	19.0%
Median age:	38.2 yrs.				
More than 65 yrs:	16.9%	*Ancestry*		Median income:	$46,349
Less than 18 yrs:	21.7%	German	12.1%	Median Home Value:	$175,800
		Irish	10.5%		
Education		English	9.0%	**Military Veterans**	
H.S. grad:	87.4%			% of Pop:	15.1%
College grad:	23.8%				
Grad degree:	9.4%				

North Central Florida; Jacksonville

The flat grasslands of central Florida, once by-passed by southbound tourists heading for the coastal resorts and cities, have over the past two decades become a prime growth area in this high-growth state. Central Florida's economy once depended on farming, on tourists getting off the interstate, and on state institutions, most notably the University of Florida in Gainesville. Then retirees began settling in places like the bluegrass country around Ocala, one of Ameri-

2008 Presidential Vote

John McCain (R)	226,985	(57%)
Barack Obama (D)	170,173	(43%)

2004 Presidential Vote

George Bush (R)	211,328	(61%)
John Kerry (D)	135,292	(39%)

Cook Partisan Voting Index: R+10

ca's prime horse-breeding grounds, and Leesburg, perched on a narrow spit of land between Lake Griffin and Lake Harris. Initially, these areas were studded with trailer parks, but the 1990s brought more-upscale development, albeit nothing approaching the high-rise apartments and gated communities that line the coasts farther south. At the same time, the large citrus groves have been cut back, victims of booming property values and of environmental changes that have resulted in devastating frosts and more diseases. Some of this development is at the intersection of Lake, Marion and Sumter counties in the sprawling retirement community known as The Villages. This part of central Florida grew by 19% from 2000 to 2007. But the economic downturn hit the region hard, with Ocala's unemployment rate soaring past 14% in 2010 and home foreclosures reaching record levels.

The 6th Congressional District of Florida includes much of central Florida and also part of the Jacksonville metropolitan area, connected by a strip of lightly populated counties. In the south, it includes parts of Marion and Sumter counties, around Ocala, and a corner of Lake County. In the north, it includes the western part of Jacksonville's Duval County and most of Clay County. In between, it includes most of Alachua County except for Gainesville. On balance, this is a Republican district. Alachua is one of the few Florida counties to regularly vote Democratic, but its most heavily Democratic precincts are located in the 3rd District. The country around Ocala and the Villages in the south is Republican. Western Jacksonville and Clay County, with many military retirees, are even more Republican. In the 2008 presidential race, Republican John McCain won 71% of the vote in Clay County, and 57% in the district.

Cliff Stearns (R)

The congressman from the 6th District is Cliff Stearns, a Republican first elected in 1988. The son of a U.S. Justice Department attorney, Stearns grew up and attended public schools in Washington, D.C. After college, he served in the Air Force, where he was a specialist in satellite reconnaissance. In the early 1970s, he saw potential in land development in Florida and moved to Ocala. He ultimately ended up owning five motels, three restaurants and other properties, while also becoming active in community affairs. In 1988, he beat the favored candidate for the district seat, Democratic state House Speaker Jon Mills, 54%-46%. "I was elected to put the federal government on a diet," Stearns said, and went on to compile a mostly conservative voting record. Since losing a low-level leadership contest in 1994, he has been an occasional maverick. He bucked party leaders on free trade in the 1990s and backed the Democratic 2007 minimum-wage increase. Stearns also supports ending automatic cost-of-living increases for members of Congress. He was among the first to join the Tea Party Caucus in 2010.

Stearns has been a productive legislator, particularly on the influential Energy and Commerce Committee, where he has focused on health care and Internet policy. In 2004, he won House passage of a bill to restrict abuses of computer spyware. His Do-Not-Call Implementation Act became law and authorized the Federal Trade Commission to establish a national registry of consumers who opt out of telemarketing calls. He helped to enact the anti-spam law that requires most commercial e-mail to be labeled and to have a valid return address. He was the chief sponsor of the widely debated 2005 legislation that limited lawsuits against the firearms industry when their products are used in crimes. In 2009, he became the ranking Republican on the Subcommittee on Communications, Technology, and the Internet. In that role, he pressed for additional steps to protect personal privacy from corporations using computers to collect vast amounts of information on people. In 2010, he introduced a draft bill with Rick Boucher, D-Va., giving consumers the right to opt out of behavioral targeting for advertising.

With the GOP takeover of the House in 2011, Stearns sought to chair Energy and Commerce, but lost out to Michigan Republican Fred Upton. But he got the gavel of the Oversight and Investigations Subcommittee, a position guaranteed to raise his public profile as Republicans aggressively looked into the activities of the Obama administration. He has also expressed a desire to help rewrite the outdated 1996 Telecommunications Act. On energy policy, Stearns has opposed new drilling in Florida waters. After the 2010 BP oil spill disaster in the Gulf of Mexico, he called for BP America Chairman Lamar McKay to resign.

His legislative setbacks in recent years included the defeat in the House of his proposal for a Federal Boxing Commission, with enforcement of uniform standards, and an unsuccessful amendment to prohibit federal funds for bilingual ballots and language assistance under the Voting Rights Act. He and Del. Madeleine Bardallo, D-Guam, were unable to prevent Defense Secretary Robert Gates in 2009 from transferring the C-27J cargo aircraft program from the Army to the Air Force and cutting its budget by half.

In 2008, Stearns won re-election easily, 61%-39%, over Democratic Ocala attorney Tim Cunha. But Alachua, which produced the second largest vote among the counties in the district, backed the Democrat, 52%-48%. That could signal redistricting changes in 2011. In 2010, Sterns was re-elected with 71.5% of the vote.

SEVENTH DISTRICT

John Mica (R)

Elected 1992, 10th term; b. Jan. 27, 1943, Binghamton, NY; home, Winter Park; Miami-Dade Commun. Col., A.A. 1965, U. of FL, B.A. 1967; Episcopalian; married (Patricia); 2 children.

Elected Office: FL House of Reps., 1976–80.

Professional Career: Exec. dir., Palm Beach & Orange Cnty. Govt. Charter Study Commissions, 1970–74; Pres., MK Development, 1975–92; A.A., U.S. Sen. Paula Hawkins, 1981–85; Partner, Mica, Dudinsky & Assoc., 1985–92.

DC Office: 2187 RHOB, 20515, 202-225-4035; Fax: 202-226-0821; Web site: mica.house.gov.

State Offices: Deltona, 386-860-1499; Maitland, 407-657-8080; Ormond Beach, 386-676-7750; Palatka, 386-328-1622; Palm Coast, 386-246-6042; St. Augustine, 904-810-5048.

Committees: *Oversight & Government Reform:* Health Care, District of Columbia, Census & the National Archives; National Security, Homeland Defense & Foreign Operations. *Transportation & Infrastructure* (Chmn).

Group Ratings

	ACLU	ACU	ADA	CFG	AFS	FRC	LCV	ITIC	NTU	COC
2010	6	96	0	78	0	93	10	33	85	88
2009	–	100	0	81	22	–	7	–	82	80

National Journal Ratings

	2010 LIB	—	2010 CONS	2009 LIB	—	2009 CONS
Economic	24%	—	76%	19%	—	81%
Social	0%	—	85%	13%	—	84%
Foreign	29%	—	68%	0%	—	75%
Composite	21%	—	79%	15%	—	85%

Key Votes of the 111th Congress

1. Overturn Ledbetter	N	5. Bar federal abortion funds	Y
2. Pass $820 billion stimulus	N	6. Pass health care bill	N
3. Let guns in national parks	Y	7. Regulate financial firms	N
4. Pass cap-and-trade	N	8. Pass tax cuts for some	N

9. Stop detainee transfers	Y
10. Legalize immigrants' kids	N
11. Repeal don't ask, tell	N
12. Limit campaign funds	N

Election Results

2010 general	John Mica (R)	185,470	(69%)	($1,205,985)
	Heather Beaven (D)	83,206	(31%)	($239,084)
2010 primary	John Mica (R)	unopposed		

Prior Winning Percentages: 2008 (62%), 2006 (63%), 2004 (100%), 2002 (60%), 2000 (63%), 1998 (100%), 1996 (62%), 1994 (73%), 1992 (56%)

Population		Race/Ethnicity		Work	
Pop. 2010:	812,442	White:	74.7%	Private:	82.0%
Change since 2000:	Up 27.1%	Black:	9.6%	Government:	12.3%
Urban:	86.7%	Hispanic:	11.3%	Self-employed:	5.7%
Rural:	13.3%	Asian:	2.3%	Blue collar:	16.6%
Area size:	2,223 sq. mi.	Native Am.:	0.3%	White collar:	64.8%
		Hawaiian:	0.0%	Khaki collar:	0.2%
Age		Two+ races:	1.6%	Other:	18.4%
Median age:	41.0 yrs.				
More than 65 yrs:	17.2%	*Ancestry*		Median income:	$50,156
Less than 18 yrs:	21.9%	German	12.4%	Median Home Value:	$224,500
		Irish	11.5%		
Education		English	9.2%	**Military Veterans**	
H.S. grad:	89.4%			% of Pop:	13.3%
College grad:	28.0%				
Grad degree:	9.5%				

Northeast Florida; Daytona Beach

In 1513, Spanish explorer Ponce de Leon headed to the New World, hoping to discover the Fountain of Youth. Instead, he found Ponte Vedra Beach, located just south of modern day Jacksonville. A few decades later, Spanish colonists founded St. Augustine, the oldest permanent European settlement in North America—42 years older than Jamestown, Va., and 55 years older than the Plymouth colony in Massachusetts. Much later, John D. Rockefeller wintered

2008 Presidential Vote		
John McCain (R) 218,858	(54%)
Barack Obama (D) 187,417	(46%)
2004 Presidential Vote		
George Bush (R) 204,454	(57%)
John Kerry (D) 155,302	(43%)
Cook Partisan Voting Index: R+7		

in Ormond Beach, and cars have been zooming up and down Daytona's rock-hard beach for decades. Near St. Augustine is a Northrop Grumman aircraft plant and some new communities. St. Johns and Flagler counties, the two coastal counties between Jacksonville and Daytona Beach, were filled with cattle ranches a few decades ago. But St. Johns grew 37% between 2000 and 2007. Flagler County grew 83% from 2000 to 2008, making it the fastest growing county in the nation. But by 2010, its growth rate had slowed as unemployment hit 16% and the mortgage foreclosure crisis increased the supply of vacant housing. In 2010, a three-bedroom, two-bathroom house in Daytona Beach could be had for less than $100,000.

Nearby DeLand has a small-town atmosphere centered around the Stetson University campus, while Heathrow, just off Interstate 4, serves as the home base of the American Automobile Association. Other places are much newer, instant cities: the Palm Coast development on the beach in Flagler County, and Deltona, which was built inland on a drained swamp in Volusia County. Although disappearing, some farm and ranches continue to fill gaps between these growing areas.

The 7th Congressional District of Florida covers the Atlantic coast for nearly 100 miles, from Ponte Vedra Beach to Daytona Beach. Inland it includes affluent, Seminole County suburbs of Orlando as well as the timber center of Palatka. Nearly two-thirds of the population is in the south, around Orlando, Deltona, and Daytona Beach. The political tendencies in this area are mixed. Seminole County and St. Augustine's St. Johns County are affluent and heavily Republican. Palm Coast's Flagler County is marginal. Daytona Beach's Volusia County leans Democratic, but about 40% of it is in the 24th District. On balance, this is a Republican district, but not overwhelmingly so.

John Mica (R)

The congressman from the 7th District is John Mica, a Republican first elected in 1992. Mica (*MY-kah*) grew up in south Florida, in a bipartisan political family originally from upstate New York. His younger brother, Dan Mica, was a Democratic congressman from Palm Beach County from 1978 to 1988, when he lost a primary for the U.S. Senate; he then became a credit union lobbyist. Another brother, David Mica, worked for Democratic Gov. Lawton Chiles and became executive director for the Florida Petroleum Council. John Mica made a small fortune in real estate by developing New Smyrna beachfront. He was elected to the state House in 1976 and served four years. He worked on the staff of U.S. Sen. Paula Hawkins, a Republican, from 1981 to 1985, and then became a lobbyist. He ran for the U.S. House when the district was created after the 1990 census. In the GOP primary, his opponents attacked him as an insider representing special interests, to which Mica responded, "Some of the finest folks I've met are lobbyists." He still managed to win the primary 53%-34%. In the general election, against a liberal Democrat, he won 56%-44%.

Mica has been a consistent conservative but also a brash reformer. After taking office, he led the charge to abolish House select committees and to make public the names of lawmakers who sign petitions to bring bills to the floor for a vote over the objections of congressional leaders. In 1995, Mica became chairman of Government Reform's Civil Service Subcommittee. There he helped pass the White House Accountability Act of 1996, imposing on the White House the laws that are imposed on the private sector. On other issues, Mica has focused on fighting drugs by promoting eradication and interdiction programs. He was the only House member from Florida who voted to lift the moratorium on oil drilling off the coasts of his state.

His chief legislative front has been at the Transportation and Infrastructure Committee, which he now chairs. Over the years, he has worked to build more airplane runways across the nation and to improve security in the post-September 11 era. When the Senate passed a bill that federalized airport screeners, Mica and other House Republicans sought to preserve some role for the private sector. They reached a deal to allow airports to opt out of the federal system after three years if they met certain standards. A few months later, Mica introduced a bill to permit commercial airline pilots to carry guns in the cockpit. The bill was initially opposed by the Bush administration and the Senate, and airlines worried about the risks. But the House voted 310-113 to allow pilots to carry guns. The Senate agreed 87-6, and Bush bowed to popular will. Since then, Mica has raised alarms about gaps in security. He complained in a June 2010 op-ed column that the Transportation Security Administration was a "huge, rudderless agency (that) has lacked leadership for too long and is in need of reevaluation and reorganization."

On local transportation issues, Mica waged a long fight for mass transit in the traffic-clogged Orlando area and ultimately secured a pledge from federal officials of $300 million for a commuter rail project in central Florida. "You can only pave over so much of central Florida," he said. He promised in 2010 to authorize money to extend the line eastward. And even though he joined all other House Republicans in opposing the Democrats' $787 billion economic stimulus bill, he subsequently lauded the inclusion of $8 billion for high-speed rail projects, including the project in his district. Gov. Rick Scott, R-Fla. later rejected federal money for the project, but Mica continued to push for a downsized version of the rail line. Mica has also engaged in some sharp criticism of the Obama administration. In 2010, he pinned the safety failure of the BP oil spill in the Gulf of Mexico on the administration. "I'm not going to point fingers at BP, the private industry, when it's the government's responsibility to set standards to do the inspections," he said.

Part of Mica's anger at the administration stemmed from its refusal to cooperate on a multiyear transportation reauthorization bill. Administration officials balked at the idea partly because of Democratic Rep. James Oberstar's proposal to increase the federal gasoline tax. Mica strongly opposes the tax and called for replacing the per-gallon tax with a percentage sales tax on gasoline, which he said would be a more stable method of augmenting current transportation revenue. He blasted Obama's call in 2010 for investing $50 billion on infrastructure projects, saying it was no substitute for not enacting a full six-year reauthorization.

In 2002, Mica faced a serious challenge at home from Democrat Wayne Hogan, a Jacksonville trial lawyer who spent $2.7 million of his own money on his campaign. Hogan, part of the legal team that won Florida's settlement with the tobacco industry, said he would fight for "ordinary families against powerful interests." Mica responded that Hogan was trying to buy the seat and that his pledge not to take contributions from political action committees was like "Rockefeller saying he won't take food stamps." Mica won comfortably, 60%-40%, carrying all six counties. Since then, he has not been seriously challenged.

EIGHTH DISTRICT

Daniel Webster (R)

Elected 2010, 1st term; b. April 27, 1949, Charleston, WV; home, Orlando; GA Inst. of Technology, B.S. 1971.; Baptist; Married (Sandra Jordan); 6 children.

Elected Office: FL House 1980-98, speaker 1996-98; FL Senate 1998-2008.

Professional Career: Owner, Webster Air Conditioning and Heating.

DC Office: 1039 LHOB, 20515, 202-225-2176; Fax: 202-225-0999; Web site: webster.house.gov.

State Offices: Ocala, 352-629-9160; Tavares, 352-383-3552; Winter Garden, 407-654-5705.

Committees: *Rules.*

Election Results

2010 general	Daniel Webster (R)	123,586	(56%)	($1,821,764)
	Alan Grayson (D)	84,167	(38%)	($6,041,742)
	Peg Dunmire (Tea)	8,337	(4%)	($302,122)
2010 primary	Daniel Webster (R)	24,753	(40%)	
	Todd Long (R)	14,082	(23%)	
	Kurt Kelly (R)	8,311	(13%)	
	Patricia Sullivan (R)	6,507	(11%)	
	Bruce O'Donoghue (R)	4,394	(7%)	

Population		Race/Ethnicity		Work	
Pop. 2010:	805,608	White:	57.0%	Private:	84.7%
Change since 2000:	Up 26.0%	Black:	9.6%	Government:	10.0%
Urban:	91.7%	Hispanic:	26.0%	Self-employed:	5.2%
Rural:	8.3%	Asian:	4.7%	Blue collar:	17.9%
Area size:	1,159 sq. mi.	Native Am.:	0.2%	White collar:	63.9%
		Hawaiian:	0.1%	Khaki collar:	0.1%
Age		Two+ races:	1.8%	Other:	18.1%
Median age:	35.9 yrs.				
More than 65 yrs:	12.9%	*Ancestry*		Median income:	$50,248
Less than 18 yrs:	23.3%	German	10.5%	Median Home Value:	$225,600
		Irish	8.9%		
Education		English	7.6%	**Military Veterans**	
H.S. grad:	88.3%			% of Pop:	10.2%
College grad:	29.0%				
Grad degree:	9.1%				

Central Florida; Orlando

Who would have supposed 40 years ago that the most popular tourist destination in the world would rise amid the swamps and orange groves of central Florida? The answer: Walt Disney, and just about no one else. In the mid-1960s, Disney looked at the map and decided that the intersection of Interstate 4 and Florida's Turnpike, the "crossroads of Florida," just a few miles southwest of Orlando, was the perfect place for the vast theme park he was planning. The spirit

2008 Presidential Vote
Barack Obama (D) 181,151   (52%)
John McCain (R) 165,043   (47%)

2004 Presidential Vote
George Bush (R) 160,722   (55%)
John Kerry (D) 133,328   (45%)

Cook Partisan Voting Index: R+2

of this place was established by a man who never lived here but created something now taken for granted. Disney conceived the first theme park in Orange County, Calif., in 1955, but he perfected it in the 17,000 acres of Florida swamp that his associates stealthily snapped up and where Walt Disney World opened in 1971. With the invention of the theme park, Disney also pioneered sophisticated communications, utility, and waste-disposal methods—all out of sight and underground. Disney World is not just an engineering marvel. It requires some 56,000 people with know-how and earnest cheerfulness to entertain its 40 million-plus visitors annually. But it is hardly the only site that has made Orlando one of the world's great tourist destinations. Other popular theme parks here include Sea World and Universal Studios; Cape Canaveral is less than 40 miles away. The high-tech economy also has moved into Greater Orlando. Defense contractor Lockheed Martin has a big missile facility southwest of the city, with more than 6,000 employees. Continuing growth—of the downtown skyline and in the expanding metropolitan region—has spurred what may be uphill efforts to control the sprawl and congestion in one of the nation's booming areas.

The 8th Congressional District of Florida includes parts of Orlando and surrounding Orange County and most of the enormous Disney complex, including the Disney new-urbanist town of Celebration. It includes most of the southeast and southwest parts of Orlando and adjoining suburbs. Heavily African-American areas of central Orlando are in the 3rd District. More than three-quarters of the district's residents live in Orange County. The rest live in a ribbon of territory to the northwest, past Lake Apopka, in little market towns like Mount Dora and Umatilla in Lake County, which seem insulated from the booming metro area. Around here, turtles, alligators, and river otters go about their lives underneath cypress trees draped with Spanish moss. Nearby is Silver Springs, where tourists can view the world's largest formation of clear artesian springs from glass-bottomed boats—a theme park from an earlier era. Beyond that is the horse farm country of Marion County, around Ocala. In the 1980s, the Orlando area was heavily Republican, but in the 1990s, it moved perceptibly toward national Democrats. The 8th District was designed to be a Republican district, though it's not comfortably so. Some 26% of its residents are Hispanic, most of them not Cubans, but Puerto Ricans and people from elsewhere in Latin America; many work in the tourism industry. The district voted for President George W. Bush by 55% in 2004, but four years later, Barack Obama beat John McCain here 52%-47%.

Daniel Webster (R)

The new congressman from Florida's 8th District is Republican Daniel Webster, who defeated freshman Democrat Alan Grayson in one of 2010's most negative campaigns.

Webster was born in Charleston, W.Va. His family moved to Florida when he was 7 years old because a doctor told them the climate would help cure Webster's sinus problems. He graduated from the Georgia Institute of Technology in 1971 with a degree in electrical engineering, and began working in his family's heating and air conditioning business. In 1972, he married Sandra Jordan, and the couple had six children. Webster eventually took over the family business. He became politically active in 1979, when he led his church's effort to turn a house into a Sunday school, only to be refused a zoning exemption by the county commission.

He won a seat in the state House in 1996, and later became the first Republican speaker of the Florida House in 122 years. He sponsored a bill to ban nude performances in bars and another that would have required the legislature to study the impact of proposed laws on families. In 1998, Webster moved on to the state Senate, where he pushed to decrease the amount of gun control regulation and to restrict abortion rights. He also led legislative efforts to prolong the life of Terri Schiavo, a woman in a persistent vegetative state who became a national cause for conservatives. In 2008, he sponsored a bill requiring women to get an ultrasound and view the results before getting an abortion.

With the backing of national Republicans, he challenged Grayson in 2010. Grayson had become a lightning rod for conservatives because of his harsh rhetoric toward them during his two years in Congress. He once called Republicans "knuckle-dragging Neanderthals," and on another occasion charged that the GOP solution to the health care crisis was for people to "die quickly." His unapologetic liberalism made him a hero to the left, but Webster and Republicans believed him to be a poor fit for the more tempered politics of the district. Webster prevailed in a crowded primary with 40% of the vote. His nearest opponent was lawyer Todd Long, who finished with 23%.

In the fall, things heated up quickly. One of Grayson's television ads dubbed Webster "Taliban Dan," and accused him of proposing to make divorce illegal and believing that women should submit to their husbands. A video clip of Webster in the ad, however, was taken out of context; Webster was actually asserting the opposite, according to the *Orlando Sentinel,* which endorsed Webster in part because of Grayson's negative campaigning. Webster refused to debate Grayson, and to return his attacks in kind, saying, "We're taking the high road. I'm not getting down in the dirt with him." He focused his campaign on his opposition to the size of the federal government and the passage of President Obama's health care law.

Grayson's strategy did manage to energize liberals nationally, and he raked in $6 million for his campaign, way outspending Webster, who raised just $1.8 million. But the district's voters had other ideas; they turned out Grayson decisively, voting for Webster 56% to 38%.

NINTH DISTRICT

Gus Bilirakis (R)

Elected 2006, 3rd term; b. Feb. 8, 1963, Gainesville; home, Palm Harbor; Attended St. Petersburg Jr. Col., U. of FL, B.A. 1986, Stetson U., J.D. 1989; Greek Orthodox; married (Eva Lialios); 4 children.

Elected Office: FL House of Reps., 1998-2006.

Professional Career: Intern, U.S. Pres. Ronald Reagan, 1983; Intern, NRCC, 1984; Aide, U.S. Rep. Don Sundquist, 1985; Teacher, St. Petersburg Col., 1997-2001; Practicing atty., 1989-2006.

DC Office: 407 CHOB, 20515, 202-225-5755; Fax: 202-225-4085; Web site: bilirakis.house.gov.

State Offices: Palm Harbor, 727-773-2871; Plant City, 813-752-9849.

Committees: *Foreign Affairs:* Europe and Eurasia; Middle East & South Asia. *Homeland Security:* Emergency Preparedness, Response & Communications (Chmn); Oversight, Investigations & Management. *Veterans' Affairs* (VChmn): Economic Opportunity; Health.

Group Ratings

	ACLU	ACU	ADA	CFG	AFS	FRC	LCV	ITIC	NTU	COC
2010	6	88	15	75	13	100	30	0	79	75
2009	–	100	5	79	22	–	14	–	77	73

National Journal Ratings

	2010 LIB — 2010 CONS		2009 LIB — 2009 CONS	
Economic	34%	— 65%	27%	— 73%
Social	16%	— 82%	29%	— 68%
Foreign	12%	— 79%	0%	— 75%
Composite	23%	— 77%	23%	— 77%

Key Votes of the 111th Congress

1. Overturn Ledbetter	N	5. Bar federal abortion funds	Y	9. Stop detainee transfers	Y
2. Pass $820 billion stimulus	N	6. Pass health care bill	N	10. Legalize immigrants' kids	N
3. Let guns in national parks	Y	7. Regulate financial firms	N	11. Repeal don't ask, tell	N
4. Pass cap-and-trade	N	8. Pass tax cuts for some	N	12. Limit campaign funds	N

Election Results

2010 general	Gus Bilirakis (R)	165,433	(71%)	($1,088,911)
	Anita dePalma (D)	66,158	(29%)	($13,496)
2010 primary	Gus Bilirakis (R)	unopposed		

Prior Winning Percentages: 2008 (62%), 2006 (56%)

Population		Race/Ethnicity		Work	
Pop. 2010:	753,549	White:	75.6%	Private:	82.5%
Change since 2000:	Up 17.9%	Black:	5.3%	Government:	12.2%
Urban:	93.8%	Hispanic:	13.6%	Self-employed:	5.1%
Rural:	6.2%	Asian:	3.3%	Blue collar:	14.9%
Area size:	800 sq. mi.	Native Am.:	0.2%	White collar:	69.0%
		Hawaiian:	0.0%	Khaki collar:	0.2%
Age		Two+ races:	1.7%	Other:	15.9%
Median age:	41.5 yrs.				
More than 65 yrs:	17.4%	*Ancestry*		Median income:	$50,706
Less than 18 yrs:	22.1%	German	14.0%	Median Home Value:	$203,400
		Irish	12.9%		
Education		English	9.3%	**Military Veterans**	
H.S. grad:	89.1%			% of Pop:	13.2%
College grad:	28.9%				
Grad degree:	9.9%				

West Florida; Tampa Suburbs

Half a century ago, the land north of St. Petersburg and Tampa was scarcely inhabited. Behind
the barrier island of beaches, the land along
the Gulf shore was swampy. Further inland was
dense, semitropical forest spotted with lakes.
Over the years, development has moved up the
coast and inland via the major highways, first
to Clearwater and Tarpon Springs in Pinellas
County and then up the once-empty coast of
Pasco County. Much of this area originally was

2008 Presidential Vote		
John McCain (R)	190,344	(52%)
Barack Obama (D)	169,897	(47%)
2004 Presidential Vote		
George Bush (R)	196,837	(57%)
John Kerry (D)	148,694	(43%)
Cook Partisan Voting Index: R+6		

designed for retirees, offering everything from condominiums to garden apartments to trailer
parks. In 2000, Clearwater, in Pinellas County north of St. Petersburg, had a higher percentage
of senior citizens than any other city over 100,000. It also has the spiritual headquarters of the
Church of Scientology, which has transformed the city's downtown by redeveloping a dozen buildings, turning five waterfront acres into a luxury condominium complex and building a 384,000-
square-foot religious center. There are about 12,000 Scientologists in the city.

Before the recession hit in 2007, businesses were sprouting in northern Pinellas County and
inland off the Interstate 75 corridor. Nearly half of Pasco County's workers commute to jobs in
other counties. The people who settled here in recent decades brought their ancestral political beliefs with them. In the 1950s and 1960s, only white-collar retirees could afford to buy new places
in Florida, and they were heavily Republican. As Florida retirements became more feasible for
people with modest incomes in the 1970s and 1980s, the partisan balance shifted toward Democrats. In the 1990s, young immigrants with professional and technical backgrounds flooded the
area. Their political independence has turned this into one of Florida's politically marginal areas.
In 2004, Republican organizers brought out a lot of new voters, many of them Christian conservatives. Republican President Bush won the district that year with 57%. Four years later, Democrat
Barack Obama's campaign worked to increase turnout in this area, which was vital to his statewide
win in Florida. In Hillsborough, Obama got nearly 59,000 more votes than Democrat John Kerry
had in 2004, while Republican John McCain got 9,000 votes fewer than Bush in 2004. John McCain
narrowly won the district with 52%.

The 9th Congressional District of Florida covers an area north of St. Petersburg and north and
east of Tampa. It includes the string of towns on the coast of Pasco County—Holiday, New Port
Richey, Bayonet Point, and Hudson. In Pinellas County to the south, the 9th includes Clearwater,
Tarpon Springs, an old resort first settled by Greek sponge divers a century ago, the affluent neighborhoods of East Lake, the young commuter families of Oldsmar, and the bayside community of
Safety Harbor. The district also includes the northern Tampa suburbs in Hillsborough County and
much of the eastern part of the county, including part of strawberry-growing Plant City (named
not for plants but for Tampa pioneer Henry B. Plant). The area produces 90% of Florida's strawberry yield. In recent years, the area has been losing retirees without attracting new ones to take
their places. Between 2000 and 2009, Clearwater's population dropped more than 3%. The massive
2010 BP oil spill off the Gulf Coast didn't help economic matters any.

Gus Bilirakis (R)

The congressman from the 9th District is Gus Bilirakis, a Republican first elected in 2006 to succeed his father, 12-term Republican Rep. Michael Bilirakis. Bilirakis *(bil-uh-RACK-iss)* joined Republican Connie Mack in the Florida delegation as a lawmaker who followed a parent into Congress. Bilirakis remembers stuffing envelopes at age 7 for Republican Louis "Skip" Bafalis, who
lost his 1970 bid for governor but was elected to five terms in Congress. In college, Bilirakis interned
in the Reagan White House and went on to earn a law degree from Stetson University. He worked
for former Rep. Don Sundquist, a Republican who went on to become Tennessee's governor, and
later was a probate lawyer and estate planner. In 1998, he was elected to the first of four terms
in the Florida House. Bilirakis' career has always been closely tied to his father's. When Michael
Bilirakis decided not to seek a 13th term, his son was presumed to be the favorite for the seat and
drew only nominal opposition for the Republican nomination. Gus Bilirakis was not shy about running on the family name. He touted the relationship on his web site, appeared on the ballot as
Gus Michael Bilirakis and raised money from many political action committees that supported his
father, who had had a seat on the powerful House Energy and Commerce Committee.

Democrats recruited Phyllis Busansky, a former eight-year member of the Hillsborough County Commission and the first executive director of the state's welfare-to-work program. Busansky played up her background in health care and senior citizens' issues. Bilirakis pointed to his own credentials as a lawyer who specialized in elder law. In the legislature, he had also spearheaded legislation supporting community health care centers that treat the uninsured. Bilirakis' soft-spoken style contrasted with Busansky's assertive personality. She ran television ads portraying Bilirakis as a follower and accused him of relying on his father's reputation. She trailed in the polls for much of the campaign, but gained some momentum in October after criticizing Bilirakis for his "deep and lucrative ties" to GOP leaders who had failed to act on knowledge of sexually explicit emails that were sent by former Republican Rep. Mark Foley of Florida to congressional pages. The national Republican Party did not leave this race to chance. President Bush, Vice President Dick Cheney and Speaker Dennis Hastert all stumped for Bilirakis and helped him raise money. He outspent Busansky $2.6 million to $1.4 million, and won 56%-44%.

In the House, Bilirakis established a voting record placing him near the center of House Republicans. He initially distanced himself from partisan fights and focused on his legislative agenda. Soon after taking office, he voted to increase the minimum wage. And in 2008, he worked with Rep. Lloyd Doggett, a Texas Democrat, to win House passage of a "silver alert" bill to assist states in finding senior citizens who disappear. Bilirakis was spurred by the case of an 86-year-old Largo woman who was found dead in the Intracoastal Waterway after she disappeared from an assisted-living facility. But in 2010 he joined the Tea Party Caucus and showed a sharper rhetorical edge in attacking President Obama's economic initiatives as too costly. He also took the House floor on several occasions to denounce the 2010 health care overhaul as a "government takeover."

From his perch on the Homeland Security Committee, Bilirakis tends to focus on immigration and border security. He has sponsored legislation to expand a program collecting fingerprints of suspected terrorists and illegal immigrants caught at sea. The House has passed the bill twice, but it has languished in the Senate.

In 2008, he has a surprisingly easy re-election against lawyer and former naval submarine Officer Bill Mitchell, who criticized Bilirakis' opposition to the bailout of the financial markets and to a bill extending the renewable energy credit, calling him "a friend of Big Oil." Bilirakis largely ignored the attacks and won handily, 62%-36%. He had even less trouble in 2010, winning more than two-thirds of the vote over Anita de Palma, a retired concert pianist.

TENTH DISTRICT

Bill Young (R)

Elected 1970, 21st term; b. Dec. 16, 1930, Harmarville, PA; home, Indian Shores; St. Petersburg H.S.; Methodist; married (Beverly); 6 children.

Military Career: Army Natl. Guard, 1948-57.

Elected Office: FL Senate, 1960–70, Min. ldr., 1966–70.

Professional Career: Aide, U.S. Rep. William Cramer, 1957–60; Insurance executive.

DC Office: 2407 RHOB, 20515, 202-225-5961; Fax: 202-225-9764; Web site: house.gov/young.

State Offices: Seminole, 727-394-6950.

Committees: *Appropriations:* Defense (Chmn); Military Construction, Veterans Affairs & Related Agencies.

Group Ratings

	ACLU	ACU	ADA	CFG	AFS	FRC	LCV	ITIC	NTU	COC
2010	6	84	10	90	17	87	10	0	80	100
2009	–	92	15	73	38	–	29	–	69	80

National Journal Ratings

	2010 LIB	—	2010 CONS	2009 LIB	—	2009 CONS
Economic	36%	—	64%	33%	—	67%
Social	29%	—	71%	32%	—	68%
Foreign	0%	—	88%	0%	—	75%
Composite	24%	—	76%	26%	—	74%

Key Votes of the 111th Congress

1. Overturn Ledbetter	N	5. Bar federal abortion funds	Y	9. Stop detainee transfers	Y
2. Pass $820 billion stimulus	N	6. Pass health care bill	N	10. Legalize immigrants' kids	N
3. Let guns in national parks	Y	7. Regulate financial firms	N	11. Repeal don't ask, tell	N
4. Pass cap-and-trade	N	8. Pass tax cuts for some	N	12. Limit campaign funds	N

Election Results

2010 general	Bill Young (R)..137,943	(66%)	($697,978)
	Charlie Justice (D)...71,313	(34%)	($321,128)
2010 primary	Bill Young (R)... unopposed		

Prior Winning Percentages: 2008 (61%), 2006 (66%), 2004 (69%), 2002 (100%), 2000 (76%), 1998 (100%), 1996 (67%), 1994 (100%), 1992 (57%), 1990 (100%), 1988 (73%), 1986 (100%), 1984 (80%), 1982 (100%), 1980 (100%), 1978 (79%), 1976 (65%), 1974 (76%), 1972 (76%), 1970 (67%)

Population		Race/Ethnicity		Work	
Pop. 2010:	633,889	White:	81.5%	Private:	82.3%
Change since 2000:	Down 0.8%	Black:	5.4%	Government:	11.7%
Urban:	100.0%	Hispanic:	7.6%	Self-employed:	5.8%
Rural:	0.0%	Asian:	3.3%	Blue collar:	17.4%
Area size:	448 sq. mi.	Native Am.:	0.2%	White collar:	66.3%
		Hawaiian:	0.1%	Khaki collar:	0.2%
Age		Two+ races:	1.7%	Other:	16.2%
Median age:	45.7 yrs.				
More than 65 yrs:	21.3%	*Ancestry*		Median income:	$45,109
Less than 18 yrs:	17.7%	German	15.0%	Median Home Value:	$189,300
		Irish	12.8%		
Education		English	10.5%	**Military Veterans**	
H.S. grad:	88.3%			% of Pop:	13.9%
College grad:	26.5%				
Grad degree:	8.8%				

West Florida; St. Petersburg

St. Petersburg was first settled in the 1870s, it was reached by railroad in 1888, and it got its name in 1892, when, after a coin toss, builder and railway operator Pyotr Dementyev christened it in memory of his native city in Russia. For decades, it was known as the American city with the largest percentage of elderly residents. In the early 1900s, *St. Petersburg Times* editor W. L. Straub sought to reverse the industrialization of the waterfront, establishing the parks

2008 Presidential Vote

Barack Obama (D) 164,148	(52%)
John McCain (R) 150,962	(47%)

2004 Presidential Vote

George Bush (R) 158,082	(51%)
John Kerry (D) 150,761	(49%)

Cook Partisan Voting Index: R+1

that continue to define the city's character. Starting out on the grid streets facing Tampa Bay, St. Petersburg later spread toward the Gulf Coast as the migration of retirees accelerated. Mostly from the North and modestly affluent, the newcomers adapted easily to a city whose civic tone was set by the *St. Petersburg Times* and its longtime owners Nelson and Henrietta Poynter: Sober, good-humored, supportive of clean government and civil rights. More recently, St. Petersburg has become a more conventional central city, with a larger working population, more families and minorities, and more office buildings and civic attractions, such as the Salvador Dali Museum, the Florida International Museum, and the Museum of Fine Arts.

The new balance has brought new politics. In the 1940s and 1950s, white-collar Yankee retirees made St. Petersburg and surrounding Pinellas County the first Republican county in ancestrally Democratic Florida. Then, in the early 1970s, Social Security was vastly increased and indexed to inflation, and St. Petersburg basked in prosperity. As more workers could afford a Florida retirement, the affluent moved farther down the Gulf Coast, and in the 1970s and 1980s, St. Petersburg trended Democratic. The whole of St. Petersburg and Pinellas County are now pretty well built up, with new projects replacing old buildings in downtown St. Pete and elsewhere. In 2008, the area was hit hard by the housing foreclosure crisis, but by the end of 2010, foreclosure filings had tailed off sharply. Crime also was down from a year earlier as well, although unemployment remained above 11% and homelessness was a growing concern.

The 10th Congressional District is the only district in Florida contained entirely within one county. It includes all of Pinellas County south of Clearwater except for heavily African-American precincts in south St. Petersburg, which are part of the Tampa-based 11th District. It includes all the Pinellas County beach communities on the barrier islands facing the Gulf, from Belleair Beach to Mullet Key. North of Clearwater, it includes middle-class Dunedin, pricey Palm Harbor, and the new subdivisions of Largo in the center of the peninsula. In 2004, the district voted 51% for President Bush, but in 2008 it went for Democrat Barack Obama 52%-47%.

Bill Young (R)

The congressman from the 10th District is Bill Young, a courtly and genial Republican first elected in 1970. He is the most senior Republican in the House, and only Michigan Democrats John Dingell and John Conyers have more seniority than he does. He cast his 20,000th floor vote in May 2009.

Young grew up poor in a Pennsylvania coal town. His first home was a shotgun shack that was swept down a river when he was 6 years old. At 16, he was shot in a hunting accident. The family moved to Florida, and Young dropped out of high school to support his ill mother by hauling concrete blocks and mixing mortar. At age 25, he applied for a job as an insurance salesman and ultimately ran a successful insurance agency. In the 1950s, he worked for St. Petersburg's first Republican congressman, William Cramer, and got the politics bug. Young was elected to the state Senate in 1960, at age 29, and back then, was the lone Republican in the body. When Cramer ran for the U.S. Senate in 1970, Young ran for his House seat and won.

Young has a moderate to conservative voting record. He has joined Democrats on legislation to raise the minimum wage and extend unemployment benefits, and championed measures to improve federal responses to oil spills. Early on, he got a seat on the Appropriations Committee, where he, like many Republicans, worked closely with the Democratic chairmen through many years in the minority. When Republicans won control of the House in 1994, Young did not rise to full committee chairman though he had the seniority to do so. Then-Speaker Newt Gingrich passed over him, as well as two more senior Republicans, for being too accommodating to Democrats. With some reason: After 34 years as a minority-party legislator, Young's instincts were bipartisan. "I came into the majority party with this strong conviction that every member of Congress has been elected by their constituents and should be given respect," he said at the time. But he certainly was not left powerless. He assumed the chairmanship of the defense appropriations subcommittee, giving him considerable sway over U.S. defense spending. In that role, he worked to produce bipartisan appropriations bills out of the spotlight.

In 1998, Young considered retiring, but at the end of the year, he finally got the full committee gavel. Three days after the November election, when Republicans suffered stinging losses, Gingrich decided to resign as speaker. In the subsequent leadership reshuffling, Young took over as Appropriations chairman from Bob Livingston of Louisiana. He stayed in the job six years, until 2004, the maximum allowed under GOP rules. During the Bush era, Young was often caught between White House demands to hold down spending and the rank and file's enormous appetite for earmarks, the special projects for home districts. For the most part, he came down on the president's side, but he demurred when the administration tried to get him to end earmarking altogether. An appropriator at heart, he also chafed at various attempts by the Budget Committee to impose caps on spending. Ever the bipartisan conciliator, he refused repeated demands from the Republican leadership to reduce the number of projects for Democratic appropriators.

Young by no means ignored his own district or his own self-interest when it came to earmarking. "I try to make sure things that are needed in the whole state of Florida are taken care of," he once said. But he has also not been immune to the ongoing controversy surrounding earmarks, and in 2008, two of his earmarks dinged his reputation for high ethical standards. The *St. Petersburg Times* reported that he had directed $45 million to defense contractor Science Applications International Corp. after the company hired his 20-year-old son, Patrick, as a security administrator, though Patrick had only a GED and scant work experience. The newspaper also reported that Young had directed $28 million over nine years to another company that had employed another son, Billy Young, 23, for almost a year. The senior Young said that the companies got the earmarks on merit, not because they hired his children. In 2009, Young again came under scrutiny as one of seven lawmakers who steered hundreds of millions in largely no-bid contracts to clients of the lobbying firm PMA Insurance Group while accepting large campaign donations from those companies. The Ethics Committee cleared them of wrongdoing in 2010.

When the Republicans won majority control of the House again in 2010, Young got the chairmanship of the Defense Subcommittee for a second time. In that role, he takes an avid interest in Florida's many military installations. MacDill Air Force Base in Tampa, across the bay from St. Petersburg, is the headquarters of Central Command and Special Operations Command. In recent years, he pushed through a $25 million intelligence and operations center and $78 million for a conference center for SOCOM, as well as $31 million for more family housing. Another of Young's special projects has been the bone-marrow donor program, originated by Dr. Robert Good of All Children's Hospital in St. Petersburg. In 2010, Taxpayers for Common Sense reported that Young received $90.5 million in earmarks that he alone requested, more than any other House member that year.

He also pays close attention to veterans' issues. In the 1970s, he persuaded Congress and President Ford to build the Bay Pines Veterans Medical Center in St. Petersburg, now the second largest veterans' hospital. He worked in 2009 to add $20 million to a war supplemental spending bill to assist a private brain-injury center for U.S. troops. Since the Iraq War began in 2003, Young and his wife, Beverly, have visited wounded soldiers almost every week at military hospitals, including Walter Reed Army Medical Center and Bethesda Naval Hospital. Sometimes they found care lacking—a soldier sitting in a pool of urine, a sergeant's brain surgery delayed because of malfunctioning equipment—and they regularly complained to Gen. Kevin Kiley at Walter Reed and others officers. In 2007, *The Washington Post* published a series of stories about wretched conditions at the facility, which led to reforms.

The trend toward Democrats in Pinellas County for years has not posed a threat to Young. Republican redistricters in 2002 made the district more Republican, so that the party could hold it when he retires. He seriously considered stepping down in 2010, but decided to remain. Young's son, Billy, is sometimes mentioned as a possible successor when his father retires.

ELEVENTH DISTRICT

Kathy Castor (D)

Elected 2006, 3rd term; b. Aug. 20, 1966, Miami; home, Tampa; Emory U., B.A. 1988, FL St. U., J.D. 1991; Presbyterian; married (William Lewis); 2 children.

Elected Office: Hillsborough Cnty. Comm., 2002-06.

Professional Career: Asst. gen. counsel, FL Dept. of Community Affairs, 1991-94; Practicing atty., 1994-2000.

DC Office: 137 CHOB, 20515, 202-225-3376; Fax: 202-225-5652; Web site: castor.house.gov.

State Offices: Tampa, 813-871-2817.

Committees: *Armed Services:* Air & Land Forces; Emerging Threats & Capabilities. *Budget.*

Group Ratings

	ACLU	ACU	ADA	CFG	AFS	FRC	LCV	ITIC	NTU	COC
2010	88	0	95	0	100	0	100	100	7	25
2009	–	0	100	4	100	–	100	–	2	33

National Journal Ratings

	2010 LIB	—	2010 CONS	2009 LIB	—	2009 CONS
Economic	90%	—	0%	88%	—	9%
Social	79%	—	20%	89%	—	0%
Foreign	73%	—	27%	91%	—	0%
Composite	83%	—	18%	93%	—	7%

Key Votes of the 111th Congress

1. Overturn Ledbetter	Y	5. Bar federal abortion funds	N	9. Stop detainee transfers	Y
2. Pass $820 billion stimulus	Y	6. Pass health care bill	Y	10. Legalize immigrants' kids	Y
3. Let guns in national parks	N	7. Regulate financial firms	Y	11. Repeal don't ask, tell	Y
4. Pass cap-and-trade	Y	8. Pass tax cuts for some	Y	12. Limit campaign funds	Y

Election Results

2010 general	Kathy Castor (D)	91,328	(60%)	($887,033)
	Mike Prendergast (R)	61,817	(40%)	($510,417)
2010 primary	Kathy Castor (D)	29,556	(85%)	
	Tim Curtis (D)	5,097	(15%)	

Prior Winning Percentages: 2008 (72%), 2006 (70%)

Population		Race/Ethnicity		Work	
Pop. 2010:	673,799	White:	40.8%	Private:	82.5%
Change since 2000:	Up 5.4%	Black:	26.8%	Government:	12.5%
Urban:	99.6%	Hispanic:	27.5%	Self-employed:	4.8%
Rural:	0.4%	Asian:	2.6%	Blue collar:	19.4%
Area size:	460 sq. mi.	Native Am.:	0.2%	White collar:	59.9%
		Hawaiian:	0.1%	Khaki collar:	0.4%
Age		Two+ races:	1.8%	Other:	20.3%
Median age:	34.5 yrs.				
More than 65 yrs:	11.4%	*Ancestry*		Median income:	$39,370
Less than 18 yrs:	24.1%	German	8.2%	Median Home Value:	$178,200
		Irish	7.0%		
Education		English	5.8%	**Military Veterans**	
H.S. grad:	82.0%			% of Pop:	9.3%
College grad:	24.6%				
Grad degree:	8.3%				

West Florida; Tampa

Tampa's history goes back not much more than a century. Its industrial past can be traced to 1886, when Cuban cigar-makers from Key West settled in the city's Latin Quarter, called Ybor City. Then Tampa became the major embarkation port for U.S. troops in the Spanish-American War of 1898. It also became a major citrus distribution center. The old industrial city developed along the waterfront, with distinctive architectural touches like the 13 minarets on the

2008 Presidential Vote
Barack Obama (D) 179,523   (66%)
John McCain (R) 89,410   (33%)

2004 Presidential Vote
John Kerry (D) 145,831   (58%)
George Bush (R) 103,748   (41%)

Cook Partisan Voting Index: D+11

Arabian-style Tampa Bay Hotel, built by railroad and real estate tycoon Henry B. Plant in the 1890s. The building is now part of the University of Tampa. For a time, Tampa was Florida's only industrial city. Today, it has a diversified economy: a service sector, an academic sector with two universities, and tourism, led by Busch Gardens. Tampa's subdivisions and condominiums, office towers, and low-rise commercial buildings have spread inland across swamps and lowlands. The recession hit especially hard here. In 2010, the Tampa Bay area's unemployment rate topped 12%, the fifth highest among the largest U.S. metropolitan areas. But there were some encouraging signs. In May of that year, the city broke ground on a 30-acre redevelopment project funded in part with $28 million in federal stimulus funds. That same month, the Republican National Committee picked Tampa for its 2012 convention.

Through its history, in contrast to St. Petersburg with its many retirees, Tampa has remained a city of families and young people. Senior citizens account for only about one in eight residents here, an unusually low percentage for Florida. Tampa is an important military center. MacDill Air Force Base, on the south side of the city and jutting into Tampa Bay, is the headquarters of Central Command, which ran the Persian Gulf War and the campaigns in Afghanistan and Iraq. It is also headquarters for Special Operations Command. Generals Norman Schwarzkopf and Tommy Franks retired in the same gated community in Tampa.

The 11th Congressional District of Florida is centered on Tampa, but has irregular boundaries. It includes most of the city and close-in suburbs, the east shore of Tampa Bay, plus two areas across Tampa Bay. One is the heavily African-American and lower-income neighborhoods south of Central Avenue in St. Petersburg. The other is a strip of Manatee County bordering Tampa Bay that includes working-class neighborhoods in Memphis, Palmetto, and Bradenton. Connecting them is the distinctive Sunshine Skyway Bridge, a four-mile span completed in 1987 that has come to symbolize the Tampa Bay area. The district has a population that is 27% black and 28% Hispanic. While Hillsborough County as a whole voted for Republican George W. Bush in 2000 and 2004, the 11th District cast solid majorities for Democrats Al Gore and John Kerry. In 2008, Barack Obama won the district with 66% of the vote.

Kathy Castor (D)

The congresswoman from the 11th District is Kathy Castor, a Democrat first elected in 2006. Castor studied political science at Emory University, earned her law degree from Florida State University and worked as a land-use attorney. Her parents were heavily involved in public service. Her father, Don Castor, sat on the Hillsborough County court for two decades. Her mother, Betty Castor, served in the state Senate, as state education commissioner and as president of the University of South Florida. In 2004, Betty Castor was the Democratic nominee for U.S. Senate, but lost 49%-48% to Republican Mel Martinez. Kathy Castor ran unsuccessfully for the state Senate in 2000, but two years later won a four-year term on the Hillsborough County Commission.

When five-term Democratic Rep. Jim Davis decided to run for governor in 2006, opening up a safe Democratic district, Kathy Castor entered the contest, benefiting from the familiarity of the Castor name from her mother's Senate race. In a district where Democrats enjoy a nearly 2-to-1 advantage over Republicans, Castor faced four opponents in the primary. The most formidable was state Senate Minority Leader Les Miller, a veteran African-American legislator. Although Miller was familiar to voters from his service in the state House and Senate, he proved unable to keep pace with Castor's prolific fundraising. With the support of EMILY's List, Castor raised nearly $1 million before the primary and outspent Miller 3-to-1. Whites make up less than half the district's population, and Miller contended the seat was drawn to elect a minority candidate after the 2000 census, especially since the Tampa-St. Petersburg area has never elected a black representative. Castor trailed Miller in the heavily African-American portion of the Pinellas County, but she defeated him by more than 8,600 votes in Tampa's Hillsborough County. She won 54%-34%.

The outcome of the general election in this comfortably Democratic district was never in doubt. Republican Eddie Adams, an architect, struggled to raise money and was absent from the campaign trail for three weeks in October while recovering from a ruptured appendix. Castor campaigned for expanded health care for low-income families and for stronger ethics and lobbying rules. Both were issues she advocated as a county commissioner. She also advocated a rapid withdrawal of U.S. troops from Iraq. She won the general election 70%-30%.

In the House, Castor has a liberal voting record. From her early days in Congress, she positioned herself for future roles in the Democratic leadership. She asked Democratic Speaker Nancy Pelosi to be appointed as the freshman representative to the Democratic Steering and Policy Committee, which determines committee assignments. Pelosi, surprised because no one had asked her for the position before, promptly gave it to Castor. In 2007, she got choice seats on the Rules and the Armed Services committees. Two years later, she agreed to serve on the ethics panel, and subsequently became chair of the subcommittee looking into California Democrat Maxine Waters' alleged efforts to help get federal bailout money for a bank in which her husband owned stock.

Castor was rewarded in 2009 with a seat on the influential Energy and Commerce Committee, where she was among a group of liberals who insisted that any savings from a government-run public insurance option be used to increase subsidies to low-income people to purchase insurance. She also added an amendment to the Waxman-Markey energy and climate change bill to allow states to set rates for electricity generated from renewable energy under state incentive programs.

Typically a party loyalist, Castor in 2007 was one of only eight House Democrats to oppose the expansion of the State Children's Health Insurance Program, complaining that Senate revisions to the bill made its benefits less favorable for Florida. Many of her constituents were also opposed to a significant hike in the cigar tax in the legislation. Later, Castor, following her loyalist instincts, voted to override President Bush's veto of the bill. When Republicans pushed in 2008 for increased oil production, she insisted on a permanent offshore drilling ban within 125 miles of the Florida coastline. She became a major player on the issue following the BP oil spill in the Gulf of Mexico in 2010, prodding the company and the administration for more research on the extent and impacts of the spill. In recent years, Castor took up the issue of increased trade and travel to Cuba. When the Obama administration also embraced the issue, she became the first member of Florida's House delegation in 2010 to sign on to a bill lifting travel restrictions to Cuba and sought to add Tampa to the list of airports approved to host charter flights to Havana.

In a rematch against Republican Eddie Adams in 2008, she increased her share of the vote from 70% to 72%, winning easily. In 2010 she brushed off a primary challenge from Tim Curtis, a tea party-backed political novice. In the general election, she faced a tougher challenge from Republican Mike Prendergast, a retired Army colonel. She substantially outraised Prendergast and won, providing one of the few bright spots of the night for Florida Democrats, though her winning percentage dipped to 60%.

TWELFTH DISTRICT

Dennis Ross (R)

Elected 2010, 1st term; b. Oct. 18, 1959, Lakeland; home, Lakeland; Auburn U., B.S. 1981; Samford U., J.D. 1987.; Presbyterian; Married (Cindy); 2 children.

Elected Office: FL House, 2001-08.

Professional Career: Practicing atty., 1987-89; cnsl., Walt Disney World, 1989; founder, partner, Ross Vecchio P.A.

DC Office: 404 CHOB, 20515, 202-225-1252; Fax: 202-226-0585; Web site: dennisross.house.gov.

State Offices: Lakeland, 863-644-8215.

Committees: *Education & the Workforce:* Health, Employment, Labor & Pensions; Workforce Protections. *Judiciary:* Courts, Commercial & Administrative Law; Immigration Policy & Enforcement. *Oversight & Government Reform:* Federal Workforce, U.S. Postal Service & Labor Policy (Chmn); TARP, Financial Services & Bailouts of Public & Private Programs.

Election Results

2010 general	Dennis Ross (R)	102,704	(48%)	($1,179,682)
	Lori Edwards (D)	87,769	(41%)	($657,353)
	Randy Wilkinson (Tea)	22,857	(11%)	($46,003)
2010 primary	Dennis Ross (R)	33,212	(69%)	
	John Lindsey (R)	14,936	(31%)	

Population		Race/Ethnicity		Work	
Pop. 2010:	842,199	White:	59.4%	Private:	81.3%
Change since 2000:	Up 31.7%	Black:	15.3%	Government:	13.6%
Urban:	84.3%	Hispanic:	21.2%	Self-employed:	5.0%
Rural:	15.7%	Asian:	1.9%	Blue collar:	22.4%
Area size:	2,098 sq. mi.	Native Am.:	0.3%	White collar:	57.5%
		Hawaiian:	0.1%	Khaki collar:	0.3%
Age		Two+ races:	1.7%	Other:	19.8%
Median age:	37.4 yrs.				
More than 65 yrs:	15.8%	*Ancestry*		Median income:	$45,921
Less than 18 yrs:	25.0%	German	10.3%	Median Home Value:	$163,200
		Irish	9.3%		
Education		English	8.4%	**Military Veterans**	
H.S. grad:	82.6%			% of Pop:	12.4%
College grad:	19.9%				
Grad degree:	6.1%				

Central Florida; Polk County

The heart of central Florida is Polk County, filled with lakes and small-to-medium-sized cities: Lakeland, Bartow, Lake Wales, Winter Haven, Frostproof, and Haines City. It is the part of Florida most dependent on agriculture. Strawberries, cattle, and citrus are economic mainstays, although periodic freezes in recent years have persuaded some orange growers to move south or to switch to tomatoes. Still, Polk County remained the largest citrus producer in the state in 2010. Turpentine distilleries, dependent on the big stands of pine, and phosphate mining businesses can be found as well. Proportionately, there are more manufacturing jobs here than almost anywhere else in Florida (though still not very many). In 1929, retired *Ladies' Home Journal* Editor Edward Bok built the most prominent landmarks here: the 205-foot-tall gothic Bok Tower and the surrounding Mountain Lake Sanctuary and gardens. A remnant of old Florida, this area has not become a major retiree haven. Its population grew 20% between 2000 and 2007—an impressive rate by national standards but not compared with other parts of Florida.

2008 Presidential Vote		
John McCain (R)	168,501	(50%)
Barack Obama (D)	164,732	(49%)

2004 Presidential Vote		
George Bush (R)	167,216	(58%)
John Kerry (D)	119,825	(42%)

Cook Partisan Voting Index: R+6

The 12th Congressional District of Florida includes almost all of Polk County, which holds about 60% of the population. This was the home of Spessard Holland and Lawton Chiles, two legendary Democrats who each served as governor and senator. Even today there are more registered Democrats than Republicans, but Polk County, like most of the Deep South, increasingly votes Republican. The 12th District also includes a sliver of Osceola County and the rapidly growing suburbs east of Tampa in Republican-leaning Hillsborough County—such places as Brandon, home to strip malls and younger, pro-business families. Overall, this district is becoming reliably Republican. It voted 58% for President Bush in 2004. And in the locally hard-fought 2008 campaign, Republican John McCain narrowly beat Democrat Barack Obama 50%-49%.

Dennis Ross (R)

The new congressman from the 12th District in Florida is Dennis Ross, a Republican who in 2010 succeeded GOP Rep. Adam Putnam, who ran for statewide office. Ross grew up in Lakeland, Fla., the youngest of five children. He remembers his mother, Loyola Ross, as a strict parent who preached the virtues of hard work. "She made us self-sufficient and believed in us working to earn our own spending money," Ross told *The Lakeland Ledger* after his mother died in 2006. "In the eighth grade, she had me mowing lawns and she was my accountant." He was active in student government in high school and attended the University of Florida for a year before transferring to Auburn University and graduating in 1981 with a degree in organizational management. He spent a year working as a legislative aide to then-state Rep. Dennis Jones, for a short time had a job installing and selling computers, and then enrolled in law school at Samford University in Birmingham, Ala. He returned to Lakeland and became an in-house counsel for Walt Disney World, handling workers' compensation claims for the company. But he wanted to start his own law practice, so he borrowed $10,000 from a neighbor and opened a firm that eventually grew to seven lawyers and 27 employees. Ross spent three years as chairman of Polk County's Republican Executive Committee. In 2000, he won a seat in the Florida House, where he developed a reputation as a faithful, but not automatic, GOP vote.

When Putnam announced plans in 2008 to leave his seat to run for state commissioner of agriculture, Ross, who had hit his term limit in the legislature, jumped into the race. In the August primary, he trounced fellow Republican John Lindsey, a businessman and political neophyte, winning 69% of the vote.

In the general election, he faced Democrat Lori Edwards, the Polk County supervisor of elections, and tea party nominee Randy Wilkinson, a former Polk County commissioner. Edwards campaigned as a moderate, saying she would fit in with the Blue Dog Coalition of fiscally conservative Democrats in the House. Her main theme was a promise to defend the interests of the middle class against the influence on Congress of from special interests and lobbyists.

Ross called for repeal of the Democrats' health care overhaul and tougher immigration laws. He ran ads tying Edwards to President Obama and liberal House Speaker Nancy Pelosi, while playing up his embrace of Putnam's conservative philosophy, as well as touting his support from former Gov. Jeb Bush and former House Majority Leader Dick Armey, R-Texas. Ross also had an overwhelming financial advantage, raising over $1 million compared to Edwards' $657,000. Ross won convincingly, 48% to 41%, with 11% of the vote going to Wilkinson.

THIRTEENTH DISTRICT

Vern Buchanan (R)

Elected 2006, 3rd term; b. May 8, 1951, Detroit, MI; home, Longboat Key; Cleary U., B.B.A. 1975, U. of Detroit, M.B.A. 1986; Baptist; married (Sandy); 2 children.

Military Career: MI Air Natl. Guard, 1970-76.

Professional Career: Taekwondo instructor, 1971-74; Marketing representative, Burroughs Corp., 1975-76; Founder, Vern Buchanan and Associates, 1976-78; Founder and CEO, American Speedy Printing Centers, 1976-92; Founder and chmn., Buchanan Automotive Group, 1992-2007; Founder and chmn., Buchanan Enterprises, 1992-2007.

DC Office: 221 CHOB, 20515, 202-225-5015; Fax: 202-226-0828; Web site: buchanan.house.gov.

State Offices: Bradenton, 941-747-9081; Sarasota, 941-951-6643.

Committees: *Ways & Means:* Oversight; Trade.

Group Ratings

	ACLU	ACU	ADA	CFG	AFS	FRC	LCV	ITIC	NTU	COC
2010	13	83	0	85	0	93	30	33	84	88
2009	–	88	15	73	33	–	29	–	69	87

National Journal Ratings

	2010 LIB	—	2010 CONS		2009 LIB	—	2009 CONS
Economic	35%	—	64%		35%	—	64%
Social	36%	—	63%		33%	—	65%
Foreign	26%	—	72%		0%	—	75%
Composite	33%	—	67%		27%	—	73%

Key Votes of the 111th Congress

1. Overturn Ledbetter	N	5. Bar federal abortion funds	Y	9. Stop detainee transfers	Y
2. Pass $820 billion stimulus	N	6. Pass health care bill	N	10. Legalize immigrants' kids	N
3. Let guns in national parks	Y	7. Regulate financial firms	N	11. Repeal don't ask, tell	N
4. Pass cap-and-trade	N	8. Pass tax cuts for some	N	12. Limit campaign funds	N

Election Results

2010 general	Vern Buchanan (R)	183,811	(69%)	($2,082,575)
	James Golden (D)	83,123	(31%)	($130,766)
2010 primary	Vern Buchanan (R)	61,517	(83%)	
	Don Baldauf (R)	12,197	(17%)	

Prior Winning Percentages: 2008 (56%), 2006 (50%)

Population		Race/Ethnicity		Work	
Pop. 2010:	757,805	White:	79.9%	Private:	81.5%
Change since 2000:	Up 18.5%	Black:	5.3%	Government:	11.7%
Urban:	89.4%	Hispanic:	12.0%	Self-employed:	6.6%
Rural:	10.6%	Asian:	1.4%	Blue collar:	20.2%
Area size:	2,948 sq. mi.	Native Am.:	0.2%	White collar:	59.2%
		Hawaiian:	0.0%	Khaki collar:	0.1%
Age		Two+ races:	1.2%	Other:	20.5%
Median age:	47.9 yrs.				
More than 65 yrs:	26.5%	*Ancestry*		Median income:	$47,792
Less than 18 yrs:	18.3%	German	15.0%	Median Home Value:	$223,400
		Irish	11.5%		
Education		English	10.8%	**Military Veterans**	
H.S. grad:	87.8%			% of Pop:	14.9%
College grad:	26.6%				
Grad degree:	9.9%				

Southwest Florida; Sarasota

When the Ringling Brothers made a success of the circus they founded in the 1880s, they needed a place for performers and animals to rest during the winter months. They settled on the bayfront village of Sarasota, located behind a barrier island on the Gulf of Mexico. It was just far enough north to be reachable by railroad and just far enough south to be semitropical so the elephants would stay healthy.

2008 Presidential Vote		
John McCain (R)	199,585	(52%)
Barack Obama (D)	178,349	(47%)
2004 Presidential Vote		
George Bush (R)	200,932	(56%)
John Kerry (D)	156,727	(44%)
Cook Partisan Voting Index: R+6		

Here, on the calm Sarasota Bay, John Ringling established the Ringling Museum of Art, a huge sculpture garden, and his own Venetian palace, the Ca'd'Zan. Next door, his brother, Charles, built a pair of neoclassical revival mansions in pink Georgia marble, which are now part of New College of Florida. After World War II, the balmy Gulf Coast attracted new settlers—affluent, well-educated Republicans from upper-crust suburbs in the North. The population exploded. Manatee and Sarasota counties grew from 63,000 people in 1950 to 688,000 in 2009. This part of Florida is no longer a winter community for snowbirds from the North. It has generated its own economy, which is as diverse as the places from which its residents have come. In 2007, *Money* magazine ranked Sarasota as the seventh best city "to retire young." But like many Florida cities experiencing boom times, it was hit hard by the collapse of the housing market. In 2009, one of every 19 homeowners in Manatee and Sarasota counties received a foreclosure notice. The rate slowed in 2010 as the local economy began to recover.

The 13th Congressional District of Florida runs from just below Tampa Bay to Charlotte Harbor, north of Fort Myers. It includes all of Sarasota County, which accounts for just over half the district's population. It takes in all of lightly populated, rural DeSoto and Hardee counties, most of Manatee County to the north and an adjoining sliver of Charlotte County to the south. Idyllic beachfronts beautify the barrier islands, from sleepy Anna Maria down through pricey Longboat Key and Lido Key to more casual Siesta Key.

The bayfront area, along the Intracoastal Waterway, is lined with high-rises and often clogged with traffic from Bradenton to Sarasota. Below that, Venice—established in 1920 as a speculative land venture by the Brotherhood of Locomotive Engineers—sits directly on the Gulf of Mexico. Though some high-tech firms diversify the economy, the district as a whole remains a place of tourists and well-off retirees: 26% of its population is 65 and older, and it has 195,000 Social Security recipients, the second highest level of all congressional districts in Florida. For many years, the 13th District was heavily Republican, and it remains that way in party registration. But like the affluent northern suburbs from which so many of its voters came, it trended toward the Democrats in the 1990s. George W. Bush carried this district, but with just 54% of the vote in 2000 and 56% in 2004. In 2008, Republican John McCain won the district, 52%-47%, over Barack Obama.

Vern Buchanan (R)

The congressman from the 13th District is Vern Buchanan, a Republican first elected in 2006. Buchanan grew up outside of Detroit, the eldest of six children and the son of a factory foreman. He joined the Michigan Air National Guard and worked his way through college as a tae kwon do instructor. He earned a business degree at Cleary University and later an M.B.A. at the University of Detroit. Buchanan founded American Speedy Printing Centers and made his fortune by selling 700 quick-printing franchises before his 40th birthday. In 1990, he moved his family to Florida, where he found new success as an automobile dealer with franchises throughout the Southeast. Buchanan became active in Republican Party politics, serving as a top fundraiser for Gov. Jeb Bush and Sen. Mel Martinez. In 2002, he wanted to run for the 13th District House seat, but stepped aside for then-Florida Secretary of State Katherine Harris, who had become a national Republican figure after her controversial role in the 2000 presidential vote recount.

Buchanan got his chance in 2006, when Harris ran for the Senate. His party connections and personal wealth made him the front-runner. In the primary, he stressed his conservative credentials and challenged his chief rival, former Sarasota Republican Party Chairman Tramm Hudson, for his positions on abortion rights and immigration. Hudson claimed that Buchanan resigned from his printing company just days before it declared bankruptcy. But Hudson stumbled when, in telling a story about his Army days, he asserted that black soldiers were poor swimmers. After spending more than $2 million of his own money, Buchanan won 32% victory in the five-way primary. But the bruising fight left Buchanan little time to recover before the general election.

The Democratic nominee was Christine Jennings, who like Buchanan, was a transplanted Midwesterner and a self-made business success. An Ohio native, she rose from bank teller to bank owner. National Democrats took an interest in the Jennings campaign and pummeled Buchanan through the fall for his business dealings. Buchanan responded by characterizing Jennings as a pro-tax liberal, a charge that was tough to stick on the former Republican with a business background. Despite the Republican advantage in the district, Buchanan was hurt by the attacks on his business dealings, the poor political environment for Republicans and late-breaking revelations about Florida GOP Rep. Mark Foley's sexually explicit e-mails to congressional pages. But he was able to spend over $8 million on his campaign, including $5.5 million of his own money. Jennings spent $3 million, about $2 million out of her own pocket. They made it the most expensive House race in 2006.

Buchanan prevailed on Election Day, but Democrats disputed the results for another year. After a recount, Republican election officials certified Buchanan as the winner by 369 votes out of nearly 240,000 votes cast. Jennings filed a lawsuit alleging there a gross undercount due to voting machine malfunction, but several rounds of testing were inconclusive, and she dropped her lawsuit.

In the House, Buchanan softened his ideological positions. He was one of 19 Republicans who supported most of the Democrats' early legislative agenda when they took control of the House in 2007. He voted for raising the minimum wage, cutting subsidies to industries, and allowing the federal government to negotiate lower drug prices with pharmaceutical companies. "I ran as a conservative, but I also ran as someone who is going to be independent," Buchanan told the *Sarasota Herald-Tribune*. He took stances further to the right on such issues as immigration and terrorism, calling for an English official-language law and using military tribunals instead of civilian courts to try terrorist suspects.

Buchanan worked with Democrats on a bill to clean up the Gulf of Mexico, and on other environmental and consumer issues. After the BP oil spill disaster in 2010, he pushed for a moratorium on all deepwater drilling permits for new and existing oil rigs in the Gulf. The former car dealer voted against the bailout of Detroit automakers in 2008 because, he said, the companies "failed to develop viable restructuring proposals." The industry problems led him to sell several of his dealerships.

In 2008, Jennings came back for a rematch. Though not as costly as the 2006 race, the contest was similarly bitter, with a cross fire of accusations of business fraud, slander, and campaign finance violations. Buchanan emphasized his bipartisanship, and won 56%-37%. A third-party candidate got 6% of the vote. He was mentioned as a possible candidate for senator in 2010, but decided to stay put after newspapers reported that he and his dealerships faced 14 lawsuits accusing them of shady business practices. Buchanan continued to maintain that lawsuits were nothing more than a smear campaign by backers of Jennings. He cruised to re-election over Democrat James Golden with more than two-thirds of the vote.

FOURTEENTH DISTRICT

Connie Mack (R)

Elected 2004, 4th term; b. Aug. 12, 1967, Fort Myers; home, Fort Myers; U. of FL, B.S. 1993; Catholic; married (Mary Bono Mack); 4 children.

Elected Office: FL House, 2000-03.

Professional Career: Marketing consultant, 1994-2004.

DC Office: 115 CHOB, 20515, 202-225-2536; Fax: 202-226-0439; Web site: mack.house.gov.

State Offices: Cape Coral, 239-573-5837; Naples, 239-252-6225.

Committees: *Foreign Affairs:* Middle East & South Asia; Western Hemisphere (Chmn). *Oversight & Government Reform:* Federal Workforce, U.S. Postal Service & Labor Policy; Government Organization, Efficiency & Financial Management (VChmn); Regulatory Affairs, Stimulus Oversight & Government Spending.

Group Ratings

	ACLU	ACU	ADA	CFG	AFS	FRC	LCV	ITIC	NTU	COC
2010	13	96	5	95	0	100	20	0	90	75
2009	–	100	0	92	0	–	7	–	89	73

National Journal Ratings

	2010 LIB	—	2010 CONS	2009 LIB	—	2009 CONS
Economic	15%	—	84%	14%	—	86%
Social	0%	—	85%	18%	—	81%
Foreign	29%	—	71%	0%	—	75%
Composite	17%	—	83%	15%	—	85%

Key Votes of the 111th Congress

1. Overturn Ledbetter	N	5. Bar federal abortion funds	Y	9. Stop detainee transfers	Y
2. Pass $820 billion stimulus	N	6. Pass health care bill	N	10. Legalize immigrants' kids	N
3. Let guns in national parks	Y	7. Regulate financial firms	N	11. Repeal don't ask, tell	N
4. Pass cap-and-trade	N	8. Pass tax cuts for some	N	12. Limit campaign funds	N

Election Results

2010 general	Connie Mack (R)	188,341	(69%)	($963,782)
	James Roach (D)	74,525	(27%)	($65,456)
	William St. Claire (NPA)	11,825	(4%)	
2010 primary	Connie Mack (R)	unopposed		

Prior Winning Percentages: 2008 (59%), 2006 (64%), 2004 (68%)

Population		Race/Ethnicity		Work	
Pop. 2010:	858,956	White:	73.9%	Private:	81.5%
Change since 2000:	Up 34.4%	Black:	6.5%	Government:	11.4%
Urban:	90.7%	Hispanic:	16.7%	Self-employed:	6.8%
Rural:	9.3%	Asian:	1.3%	Blue collar:	20.1%
Area size:	1,719 sq. mi.	Native Am.:	0.2%	White collar:	59.0%
		Hawaiian:	0.0%	Khaki collar:	0.1%
Age		Two+ races:	1.1%	Other:	20.8%
Median age:	46.4 yrs.				
More than 65 yrs:	25.2%	*Ancestry*		Median income:	$51,393
Less than 18 yrs:	19.3%	German	14.0%	Median Home Value:	$238,700
		Irish	10.8%		
Education		English	9.5%	**Military Veterans**	
H.S. grad:	88.1%			% of Pop:	14.8%
College grad:	28.0%				
Grad degree:	10.2%				

Southwest Florida; Cape Coral

The edge of the tropics, in a physical environment once teeming with disease and inhospitable to advanced civilization, Florida's Gulf Coast has evolved into a model for retirement living. Early on, there were only a few white settlements here. One was Fort Myers, built in 1850 as an Army post to pursue the Seminole Indians; in 1858, the last of the natives were driven out. For a century after that, this corner of Florida was mostly deserted. But in time, it became resort country, thanks to its wide, white-sand beaches with gentle breakers. The inlets and broad estuaries are perfect for boating, and the wetlands are graced with exotic birds. Thomas Edison had his winter home in Fort Myers, Henry Ford used to visit here, and tourists were drawn to beaches thick with seashells on nearby Sanibel and Captiva islands. But the local economy could not support many permanent residents, and at the beginning of World War II, there were only 68,000 people living on the Gulf Coast from Bradenton south to Naples.

2008 Presidential Vote		
John McCain (R) 226,818	(57%)
Barack Obama (D) 168,404	(42%)
2004 Presidential Vote		
George Bush (R) 222,234	(62%)
John Kerry (D) 136,049	(38%)
Cook Partisan Voting Index: R+11		

But the climate and environment, and the fact that Florida has no state income or inheritance tax, attracted waves of affluent postwar suburbanites from the Midwest and Northeast. Developers such as Barron Collier, who built the Tamiami Trail across the soggy Everglades and designed Naples with the wealthy in mind, were determined to avoid the high-rise canyons that line the Atlantic from Palm Beach to Miami. Their alternative was to construct low-rise, city-style developments such as Cape Coral, a retirement community. Much of this area was damaged by multiple hurricanes over the past decade, but there was no appreciable slowdown in development until the recession took hold in 2008. That year, land values sank and a large inventory of housing went unsold. The area had the nation's greatest number of housing foreclosures, and they accounted for nearly half of the home sales. Exurban Lehigh Acres became an extreme example of the boom-bust pattern, as housing growth suddenly stopped, and the town was plagued by high crime. In Lee County, the number of students taking free and reduced-cost meals climbed to 70% in 2010, a higher percentage than more urbanized districts around Miami and Fort Lauderdale. Local officials predicted a long, slow recovery.

The 14th Congressional District of Florida occupies the southern half of the habitable Gulf Coast below Tampa Bay. Retirees account for more than one in four residents. The 14th includes a small part of Port Charlotte and Charlotte County; all of Lee County; and the coastal strip of Collier County, including Naples and Marco Island. Two-thirds of the district's residents live in Lee County, in Fort Myers and Bonita Springs and on Sanibel and Captiva islands. In a state where Republican registration rates often understate GOP voting strength, the district in 2008 counted 48% of its electorate as registered Republicans. Just 29% were registered Democrats, the lowest percentage of any Florida congressional district.

Connie Mack (R)

The congressman from the 14th District is Connie Mack, a Republican elected in 2004. His father is also Connie Mack; he held the same seat for three terms in the 1980s and then served two terms in the Senate. His great-grandfather and best-known forebear was the owner and manager of baseball's Philadelphia Athletics for 50 years, Cornelius McGillicuddy, who shortened his name to Connie Mack. His wife is Rep. Mary Bono, a California Republican and the widow of former pop singer and GOP Rep. Sonny Bono. Rep. Mack graduated from the University of Florida after seven years and worked as a marketing consultant. In 2000, he was elected to the state House from a district in Broward and Palm Beach counties. In Tallahassee, he formed the anti-tax Freedom Caucus, which was against increased state spending and in favor of lower taxes and limits on attorneys' fees in personal injury and malpractice cases.

In 2004, after Florida Republican Porter Goss left the House to head the Central Intelligence Agency, Mack resigned from the legislature and moved across the state to Lee County to run for the seat. He raised $1.4 million for the primary, outpacing his nearest Republican rival by more than 2-to-1 and blanketing southwestern Florida with television ads. His three GOP opponents, state Rep. Carole Green, Lee County Commissioner Andy Coy, and Naples physician Frank Schwerin, attacked him as a carpetbagger who hadn't lived in the district since he was a teenager. Mack countered that he was the only candidate born and raised in the district. His opponents claimed that he was an inexperienced lightweight, and editorial writers were dismissive of his business credentials. The four Republicans differed little on the issues: All of them campaigned as conservatives and all backed President Bush's policies. Mack won the primary with 36% of the vote. Green was his closest competitor with 32%. In the November general election, Mack won easily, 68%-32%. Since then, he has not been seriously challenged.

In the House, he has a conservative voting record, but has taken pains to distinguish himself from other Republicans. He was a rare House GOP critic of Arizona's tough 2010 immigration law, comparing its provisions allowing law enforcement to stop suspected illegal immigrants to that of Nazi Germany. He also is more moderate on environmental issues, especially those that threaten his district's tourist trade. He parted with other Florida House members to oppose a compromise to permit oil drilling off the state's coast and was strongly critical of BP in the aftermath of the 2010 Gulf oil spill disaster. On local issues, he worked to secure money to widen Interstate 75. But he also was drawn into the controversy surrounding Rep. Don Young, an Alaska Republican, who in 2005 included a $10 million earmark for the federal purchase of Fort Myers-area property owned by a campaign contributor to both Young and Mack. Mack angrily said he knew nothing about the deal, which became part of a U.S. Justice Department investigation of Young.

In 2011, Mack became the chairman of the Foreign Affairs Committee's Western Hemisphere Subcommittee, where he has been an outspoken critic of Venezuelan President Hugo Chavez. He introduced a bill calling on the administration to designate Venezuela as a state sponsor of terrorism and joined fellow Florida Republican Ileana Ros-Lehtinen in excluding Ecuador from an expiring Andean trade bill, citing its leaders' ties to Chavez. He also said in June 2009 that Iran's growing influence in the region was reminiscent of Russia's relationship with Cuba during the missile crisis era.

After the Republican takeover of the House in the 2010 elections, Mack waged a brief bid to become Republican Policy Committee chairman before dropping out.

FIFTEENTH DISTRICT

Bill Posey (R)

Elected 2008, 2nd term; b. Dec. 18, 1947, Washington, DC; home, Rockledge; Brevard Comm. Col., A.A. 1969.; Methodist; married (Katie Ingram); 2 children.

Elected Office: Rockledge City Cncl., 1976-86; FL House, 1992-2000; FL Senate, 2000-08.

Professional Career: McDonnell Douglas Astronautics Co., 1966-69; Crawford & Co./Gay & Taylor, 1970-74; Founder, Posey & Co. Realtors, 1974-present.

DC Office: 120 CHOB, 20515, 202-225-3671; Fax: 202-225-3516; Web site: posey.house.gov.

State Offices: Melbourne, 321-632-1776.

Committees: *Financial Services:* Capital Markets and Government Sponsored Enterprises; Oversight & Investigations.

Group Ratings

	ACLU	ACU	ADA	CFG	AFS	FRC	LCV	ITIC	NTU	COC
2010	13	83	10	77	13	100	20	33	81	88
2009	–	100	0	88	22	–	7	–	84	93

National Journal Ratings

	2010 LIB	—	2010 CONS		2009 LIB	—	2009 CONS
Economic	33%	—	66%		19%	—	80%
Social	29%	—	69%		13%	—	84%
Foreign	29%	—	68%		0%	—	75%
Composite	31%	—	69%		16%	—	85%

Key Votes of the 111th Congress

1. Overturn Ledbetter	N	5. Bar federal abortion funds	Y	9. Stop detainee transfers	Y
2. Pass $820 billion stimulus	N	6. Pass health care bill	N	10. Legalize immigrants' kids	N
3. Let guns in national parks	Y	7. Regulate financial firms	N	11. Repeal don't ask, tell	N
4. Pass cap-and-trade	N	8. Pass tax cuts for some	N	12. Limit campaign funds	N

Election Results

2010 general	Bill Posey (R)...157,079	(65%)	($1,094,181)	
	Shannon Roberts (D) 85,595	(35%)	($29,681)	
2010 primary	Bill Posey (R).. unopposed			

Prior Winning Percentages: 2008 (53%)

Population		Race/Ethnicity		Work	
Pop. 2010:	813,570	White:	66.3%	Private:	82.2%
Change since 2000:	Up 27.3%	Black:	8.9%	Government:	12.1%
Urban:	89.6%	Hispanic:	20.2%	Self-employed:	5.6%
Rural:	10.4%	Asian:	2.2%	Blue collar:	20.4%
Area size:	3,252 sq. mi.	Native Am.:	0.3%	White collar:	58.2%
		Hawaiian:	0.1%	Khaki collar:	0.2%
Age		Two+ races:	1.8%	Other:	21.2%
Median age:	42.0 yrs.				
More than 65 yrs:	19.3%	*Ancestry*		Median income:	$47,223
Less than 18 yrs:	21.9%	German	12.4%	Median Home Value:	$196,500
		Irish	11.5%		
Education		English	9.0%	**Military Veterans**	
H.S. grad:	88.2%			% of Pop:	14.4%
College grad:	24.9%				
Grad degree:	8.9%				

East Central Florida; Palm Bay

When Cape Canaveral was chosen as the nation's rocket testing site in the 1940s, there were only 20,000 people in all of Brevard County, which stretches along 63 miles of the coast north and south of the Cape. It was reliant economically on fishing and citrus-growing and was chosen because it was on the sunny Atlantic coast. Rockets could be launched eastward so that spent parts fell into the ocean. In 1948, the Brooklyn Dodgers (now the Los Angeles

2008 Presidential Vote
John McCain (R) 199,604   (51%)
Barack Obama (D) 185,314   (48%)

2004 Presidential Vote
George Bush (R) 195,076   (57%)
John Kerry (D) 146,914   (43%)

Cook Partisan Voting Index: R+6

Dodgers) established their spring training home in Vero Beach, 60 miles south of Canaveral in Indian River County. Today, the region has come a long way. Brevard County has 536,000 people, and the Kennedy Space Center attracts 1.5 million visitors annually. The county has no city center but plenty of shopping centers along strip highways, with a white-collar, service economy, knitted together by interest in the space program. Uncertainty exists over the retirement of the space shuttle fleet, a move that could mean the disappearance of as many as 8,000 aerospace jobs. Local officials have begun to look at alternatives, such as nature tourism to draw out-of-towners eager to glimpse the seas of purple, pink and yellow wildflowers in spring. Proximity to Disney World has spawned growth in the cruise line business, and Port Canaveral is the second-largest passenger port in the world. And Vero Beach lost the Dodgers. The team held its last spring training there in 2008 before moving to Glendale, Ariz., in 2009.

The 15th Congressional District of Florida includes much, but not all, of the 72-mile Space Coast; the area code here is 321. Its northern end is at Cape Canaveral itself, but most of the space center facilities, including the visitors' center, are in the 24th District. It runs south along the Atlantic Coast and includes 75% of Brevard County and all of Indian River County. Among the bigger towns are Cocoa Beach, Melbourne, Palm Bay, and Vero Beach. To the west, the district includes all but a small piece of Osceola County; the population there is just south of Disney World and concentrated around Kissimmee and St. Cloud. This is the fastest-growing part of the district, with a rapidly increasing population of Puerto Ricans and other Latinos. The district also includes the northern tip of Polk County. The population there is a mix of young workers and retirees, plus military families stationed at Patrick Air Force Base, home of the 45th Space Wing.

Politically, the district leans Republican. In 2004, the Bush campaign worked intensively on outreach to the new Latino voters in Osceola County and won the county itself, 52%-47%, after losing it four years earlier. Brevard remains Republican too, but it is becoming less so. Republican Charlie Crist got 54% there in his successful 2006 governor's race. Republican John McCain won the district in 2008 with 51% of the vote to Democrat Barack Obama's 48%.

Bill Posey (R)

The congressman from the 15th District is Bill Posey, a Republican who succeeded seven-term GOP Rep. Dave Weldon in 2008. Posey was born in Washington, D.C., but moved several times due to his father's work in the aircraft business. His family landed in Brevard County in 1956, and after graduating from high school, Posey took a job with McDonnell Douglas Astronautics at the Kennedy Space Center. He worked on the Apollo 11 Launch Team and attended Brevard Community College at night. After Apollo 11 successfully put men on the moon, Posey received a congratulatory letter from the director of NASA, and a month later, was laid off. Posey changed careers and went into real estate. He founded Posey & Co. Realtors in 1974 and is still president of the company. Posey is also an accomplished stock car racer, although since an accident at an Orlando speedway in 2004 left him with spinal fractures he has taken a break from racing.

Posey was the first member of his family to register as a Republican, a decision inadvertently inspired by a college professor who lauded the Democratic Party's championing of inflation and deficit spending. "He literally was trying to convince the class that inflation was good because you could buy the things you wanted now and finance them later with cheaper money," Posey recalls. He was elected to the Rockledge City Council in 1976 and served until 1986. Four years later, he won a seat in the Florida House of Representatives, where he authored legislation that set new standards for state government accountability. He also wrote a book entitled *Activity Based Total Accountability* detailing his work on the issue. He served in the state House until 2000, when term limits forced him to resign. He then won a close state Senate race.

After Weldon announced his retirement in January 2008, Posey decided to run for the seat. He got Weldon's endorsement and that of Florida GOP Chairman Jim Greer, who called for the party to unite behind Posey. Veteran state Rep. Stan Mayfield, who had also announced his candidacy, fell in line, withdrew from the race and endorsed Posey.

Florida Democrats were unable to find a strong candidate, and Posey became the clear favorite to win the general election. He won the GOP primary with 77% of the vote, and faced Democrat Stephen Blythe, a Melbourne family physician, in the general election.

Posey made government accountability and reform of the immigration system the central themes of his campaign. It was an amiable contest. The candidates expressed mutual admiration and said that they would vote for each other if they could not vote for themselves. Posey outspent Blythe by almost 9-to-1 and won 53% to 42%.

Once in Washington, Posey almost instantly became controversial for introducing a bill requiring future presidential candidates to provide birth certificates proving they are natural born U.S. citizens. The move came at the height of the 2009 "birther" flap on the far right over whether President Obama was born overseas, and made Posey the target of considerable venom in the liberal blogosphere. He contended his bill had nothing to do with Obama, but even some of his GOP colleagues publicly expressed their distaste with his proposal.

He subsequently joined Republicans in opposing Obama's major legislative initiatives, but showed a willingness to occasionally break with his party. He voted with Democrats on extending unemployment benefits, and joined Florida Democrat Suzanne Kosmas on her bill to double the one-year waiting period before members who leave their seats can lobby ex-colleagues. As a member of the Financial Services Committee, he continued his quest for more accountability in government. He succeeded in getting the committee to post the results of every committee vote on its website within two days. He also introduced bills to require a 72-hour waiting period before legislation could be brought to the House floor and to require state governments to submit fiscal accounting reports as a condition of getting federal money.

Posey coasted to re-election in 2010, receiving 65% in facing Democrat Carolyn "Shannon" Roberts.

SIXTEENTH DISTRICT

Tom Rooney (R)

Elected 2008, 2nd term; b. Nov. 21, 1970, Philadelphia, PA; home, Tequesta; Washington & Jefferson Col., B.A., 1993; U. of FL, M.A., 1996; U. of Miami, J.D., 1999.; Catholic; married (Tara); 3 children.

Military Career: Army JAG, 2000-04; Army Reserves, 2004-07.

Professional Career: FL asst. atty. gen., 2004-05; CEO, Children's Place at HomeSafe, 2005-06.

DC Office: 1529 LHOB, 20515, 202-225-5792; Fax: 202-225-3132; Web site: rooney.house.gov.

State Offices: Fort Pierce, 772-461-3933; Punta Gorda, 941-575-9101; Stuart, 772-288-4668.

Committees: *Agriculture:* Livestock, Dairy & Poultry (Chmn); Nutrition & Horticulture. *Armed Services:* Air & Land Forces; Military Personnel; Oversight & Investigations. *Permanent Select Committee on Intelligence:* Oversight; Terrorism, HUMINT, Analysis & Counterintelligence.

Group Ratings

	ACLU	ACU	ADA	CFG	AFS	FRC	LCV	ITIC	NTU	COC
2010	13	100	0	83	0	93	20	33	88	88
2009	–	96	5	79	22	–	14	–	78	87

National Journal Ratings

	2010 LIB — 2010 CONS		2009 LIB — 2009 CONS	
Economic	23% —	77%	27% —	73%
Social	25% —	71%	29% —	68%
Foreign	12% —	79%	0% —	75%
Composite	22% —	78%	23% —	77%

Key Votes of the 111th Congress

1. Overturn Ledbetter	N	5. Bar federal abortion funds	Y	9. Stop detainee transfers	Y
2. Pass $820 billion stimulus	N	6. Pass health care bill	N	10. Legalize immigrants' kids	N
3. Let guns in national parks	Y	7. Regulate financial firms	N	11. Repeal don't ask, tell	N
4. Pass cap-and-trade	N	8. Pass tax cuts for some	N	12. Limit campaign funds	N

Election Results

2010 general	Tom Rooney (R)	162,285	(67%)	($1,428,128)
	Jim Horn (D)	80,327	(33%)	($50,300)
2010 primary	Tom Rooney (R)	unopposed		

Prior Winning Percentages: 2008 (60%)

Population		Race/Ethnicity		Work	
Pop. 2010:	797,711	White:	71.2%	Private:	80.0%
Change since 2000:	Up 24.8%	Black:	8.9%	Government:	13.5%
Urban:	84.5%	Hispanic:	16.5%	Self-employed:	6.3%
Rural:	15.5%	Asian:	1.5%	Blue collar:	19.7%
Area size:	5,251 sq. mi.	Native Am.:	0.3%	White collar:	56.5%
		Hawaiian:	0.0%	Khaki collar:	0.1%
Age		Two+ races:	1.3%	Other:	23.7%
Median age:	44.9 yrs.				
More than 65 yrs:	23.4%	*Ancestry*		Median income:	$46,958
Less than 18 yrs:	21.1%	German	12.9%	Median Home Value:	$199,300
		Irish	11.3%		
Education		English	8.7%	**Military Veterans**	
H.S. grad:	84.4%			% of Pop:	14.1%
College grad:	21.9%				
Grad degree:	7.7%				

South Florida; Port St. Lucie

Urban Florida has fanned far across the swamplands from its original nuclei in beachfront resort communities. Once, metro Palm Beach was
a narrow stretch along Lake Worth; now it runs
inland almost halfway to Lake Okeechobee,
spreading out from its original locus around the
posh Breakers Hotel. Old beach towns such as
Hobe Sound have become the hub of affluent developments that stretch all the way to Stuart in
Martin County. Farther north, near the old town

2008 Presidential Vote		
John McCain (R) 192,453	(52%)
Barack Obama (D) 175,031	(47%)

2004 Presidential Vote		
George Bush (R) 183,339	(54%)
John Kerry (D) 154,632	(46%)

Cook Partisan Voting Index: R+5

of Fort Pierce, are larger but more modest developments like Port St. Lucie, which lost its image
as a sleepy bedroom community with the $40 million relocation of the Torrey Pines Institute of
Molecular Studies in 2009. But Port St. Lucie was hit hard during the 2008 mortgage meltdown,
resulting in more than 10,000 properties in foreclosure and an unemployment rate above 12%, one
of the highest in Florida. By 2010, foreclosure filings had declined by almost one-third from the
year before, but property values were down 14%.

The 16th Congressional District of Florida stretches from the Atlantic Ocean almost to the
Gulf of Mexico, and is one of the most oddly designed districts in the nation. On the Atlantic coast,
it includes most of Martin County, with its affluent towns of Stuart and Hobe Sound, and also much
of St. Lucie County. Tequesta is its northernmost beach town. By a thin corridor of land, this coastal
area is connected to rural territory north and west of Lake Okeechobee. There, huge farms produce
citrus, tomatoes, and other vegetables, or support large dairy herds. The only population cluster
is around Sebring, with its automobile racetrack. In recent years, encroaching development, hurricanes, and citrus diseases have threatened the viability of the citrus industry, and rising land prices
have tempted farmers to get out of the business. This area is connected by the swamps of eastern
Charlotte County with the Gulf Coast towns of Port Charlotte and Punta Gorda on the wide Peace
River, where it empties into Port Charlotte and the Gulf of Mexico. In recent presidential elections,
the district has voted consistently for Republicans but not by large margins. President Bush won
the district with 54% in 2004, and in 2008, McCain carried it by a similar margin, 52%-47%.

Tom Rooney (R)

The congressman from the 16th District is Tom Rooney, a Republican elected in 2008.

The grandson of Pittsburgh Steelers founding owner Art Rooney, he was born in Philadelphia
and was a water boy for the team. (The Steelers were his largest single campaign contributor between 2008 and 2010.) When he was 14, his father moved to Palm Beach Gardens, Fla., where his
family owned the Palm Beach Kennel Club, a racetrack and gambling business. Rooney briefly
attended Syracuse University, where he earned a spot as a tight end and deep snapper for the
Orangemen. But with no desire for a professional football career, Rooney transferred to the smaller
Washington and Jefferson College just outside Pittsburgh, where he played both football and golf.
He was a staff assistant for former Republican Sen. Connie Mack of Florida for a brief period, and
then got a law degree from the University of Miami, where he met his wife, Tara. After graduation,
Rooney was a special assistant U.S. attorney at Fort Hood in Texas, and later taught constitutional
and criminal law at the U.S. Military Academy at West Point. When Republican Charlie Crist
became the Florida attorney general, he hired Rooney as an assistant attorney general in 2004.
After leaving the attorney general's office, he headed a home for abused children and, in 2006,
entered private law practice in Stuart.

The two occupants of the 16th District seat before Rooney had been forced from office by scandal. In 2006, Democrat Tim Mahoney won the seat after Republican incumbent Mark Foley resigned amid allegations that he had sent sexually explicit messages to male congressional pages.
Then in 2008, Mahoney looked to be headed for an easy re-election until ABC News broke the story
that he had paid a former aide $121,000 to keep quiet about their affair after he ended the relation-
ship and fired her. By that time, Rooney was already in the race and his campaign immediately
picked up momentum as Mahoney's political problems deepened. He became the obvious choice
for scandal-fatigued voters in the district.

In the primary, Rooney had secured endorsements from Mack and Crist, who had since become governor. The governor's endorsement riled the other two candidates, state Rep. Gayle Harrell and former Palm Beach Gardens City Councilman Hal Valeche, who pointed to the campaign
contributions Crist had received from Rooney's family. Rooney won the primary by only 1,011 votes
over Harrell, 36.7%-34.9%. Harrell won pluralities in Martin and St. Lucie counties, but Rooney's
decisive victory in Charlotte County put him over the top.

In the general election campaign, Rooney portrayed Mahoney as too liberal for the district. But Mahoney far outpaced him in fundraising, and was ahead in most polls throughout the fall. The race changed course abruptly when the news of Mahoney's extramarital affair and subsequent offer of hush money broke on Oct. 13. Mahoney then admitted to having "multiple affairs" while in Congress, but asserted he had done nothing to violate his oath of office. Rooney shot up nearly 25 points in the polls. Still, Mahoney declined to end his bid for re-election, even after Democratic House Speaker Nancy Pelosi called for an Ethics Committee investigation into the payment. Mahoney's financial contributions quickly dried up. Rooney won easily won with 60% of the vote.

In the House, Rooney has shown a repeated willingness to cross party lines, joining with fellow freshman Rep. Michael McMahon, a New York Democrat, in taking up the cause of improving mental health in the military. They got a provision into the fiscal 2010 defense authorization bill requiring confidential one-on-one screening for all returning Iraq and Afghanistan veterans. Later that year, they introduced a measure to give participants in the military's Tricare program direct access to mental health counseling without a referral. Rooney also joined with Democrat Rick Larsen of Washington on a bill to increase penalties for violent, gang-related crimes. And he was one of several Judiciary Committee Republicans in 2009 who opposed federal antitrust protections shielding health insurance companies from investigations into price-fixing and other practices.

But Rooney's bipartisanship has its limits. When Judiciary members approved a bill in April 2009 expanding federal hate-crime protections to gays and lesbians, he sought to add military personnel and veterans to the list of protected groups. That led to an angry rebuke from Florida Democrat Debbie Wasserman Schultz, and his amendment was defeated. He joined the Agriculture Committee in mid-2010 and became an outspoken critic of efforts to lift the ban on travel and food sales to Cuba. He has taken a strong stand against illegal immigration and introduced a bill in 2010 to require incarcerated illegal immigrants to be deported as soon as they are released from jail.

In 2010, Democrats initially had high hopes that St. Lucie County Commissioner Chris Craft would make a strong run at Rooney. But Craft dropped out in March, leaving the Democratic race between two entrants without political experience. Democrat Jim Horn, an Army veteran and business consultant, won the August primary. But he could not come close to competing with Rooney, who sailed to re-election with 67% of the vote. Rooney's brother, Brian, had less success in his own bid for the Michigan 7th District seat held by Democrat Mark Schauer; Brian Rooney lost in the GOP primary to former Rep. Tim Walberg, who ultimately reclaimed the seat.

SEVENTEENTH DISTRICT

Frederica Wilson (D)

Elected 2010, 1st term; b. Nov. 5, 1942, Miami; home, Miami; Fisk U., B.A. 1963; U. of Miami, M.Ed. 1972.; Episcopalian; Widowed; 3 children.

Elected Office: FL House 1998-2002; FL Senate 2002-10.

Professional Career: Teacher; principal; asst. principal.

DC Office: 208 CHOB, 20515, 202-225-4506; Fax: 202-226-0777; Web site: wilson.house.gov.

State Offices: Miami Gardens, 305-690-5905.

Committees: *Foreign Affairs:* Asia & the Pacific. *Science, Space and Technology:* Space & Aeronautics; Technology & Innovation.

Election Results

2010 general	Frederica Wilson (D)	106,361	(86%)	($512,381)
	Roderick Vereen (NPA)	17,009	(14%)	($131,728)
2010 primary	Frederica Wilson (D)	17,047	(34%)	
	Rudolph Moise (D)	7,986	(16%)	
	Shirley Gibson (D)	5,900	(12%)	
	Yolly Roberson (D)	5,080	(10%)	
	Phillip Brutus (D)	4,173	(8%)	
	Marleine Bastien (D)	2,967	(6%)	
	Scott Galvin (D)	2,750	(6%)	
	James Bush (D)	2,693	(5%)	

Population		Race/Ethnicity		Work	
Pop. 2010:	655,160	White:	12.3%	Private:	78.1%
Change since 2000:	Up 2.5%	Black:	55.9%	Government:	15.5%
Urban:	100.0%	Hispanic:	28.2%	Self-employed:	6.3%
Rural:	0.0%	Asian:	1.5%	Blue collar:	22.2%
Area size:	99 sq. mi.	Native Am.:	0.2%	White collar:	51.0%
		Hawaiian:	0.0%	Khaki collar:	0.1%
Age		Two+ races:	1.6%	Other:	26.7%
Median age:	33.2 yrs.				
More than 65 yrs:	11.2%	*Ancestry*		Median income:	$36,380
Less than 18 yrs:	26.8%	West Indian	23.0%	Median Home Value:	$213,500
		USA	4.8%		
Education		Italian	2.1%	**Military Veterans**	
H.S. grad:	75.4%			% of Pop:	4.4%
College grad:	17.1%				
Grad degree:	5.5%				

South Florida; Part Miami

North from downtown Miami, alongside Interstate 95, Miami's main north-south artery, is the city's largest African-American community. It stretches from the Miami Arena downtown through Allapattah and Liberty City to the brightly painted minarets and Moorish arches of the city of Opa-Locka. This has been a kind of frontierland in Miami, where hostilities between Miami's blacks and its Cuban-American

2008 Presidential Vote
Barack Obama (D) 209,758   (87%)
John McCain (R) 29,723   (12%)

2004 Presidential Vote
John Kerry (D) 178,605   (83%)
George Bush (R) 35,642   (17%)

Cook Partisan Voting Index: D+34

majority have played out. Many of Miami's African-Americans have resented the economic upward mobility and political strength of the Cubans. There is also tension between the Cubans and the Haitians in Little Haiti as a result of federal policies that give Cubans who reach U.S. shores refugee status while Haitians are treated as any other immigrant group with the potential for deportation. This animosity is reflected in partisan politics. Cuban Americans have been solidly Republican over the years, though somewhat less so recently. South Florida blacks have remained largely Democratic, as has the growing Haitian-American community.

The 17th Congressional District of Florida covers much of northeast Miami-Dade County, including Liberty City and Overtown, Opa-Locka, and Miami Gardens (known as Carol City until it was incorporated in 2003), right up to Biscayne Boulevard. It does not include the affluent enclaves facing Biscayne Bay or the beach towns north of Miami Beach, nor does it include heavily Latino Hialeah to the west. This is the historic heart of Miami's black community. Some 58% of the district's residents are black, the highest percentage of any Florida district; 25% are Hispanic. The district also includes part of Hollywood and other communities in southern Broward County, which are also strongly Democratic.

Frederica Wilson (D)

The new congresswoman from Florida's 17th District is Democrat Frederica Wilson, who succeeded Democrat Kendrick Meek after he gave up the seat to run for the Senate. Wilson's politics were inspired by her father, Thirlee Smith, a native of Timpson, Texas, a town that in his day had an active chapter of the Ku Klux Klan. "He would sit me on his knee and tell me stories of what happened to him in Texas and how people were lynched," she recalled. During a visit to Miami, Smith met Frederica's mother, Beulah Finley; the two wed and settled in South Florida. In Miami, Smith ran a restaurant and a billiard hall but also became active in the civil rights movement, registering voters and pushing for sanitation workers' rights. The couple's three children were sensitized to acts of injustice at a young age. Once, in high school, Wilson spied a new kid in school being teased for wearing torn clothes. Wilson, who weighed about 70 pounds at the time, stepped into the circle of bullies and ordered them to leave the boy alone. She went on to pursue a career in education and eventually politics, and her brother, the late Thirlee Smith Jr., became the first African-American full-time reporter at *The Miami Herald*.

In 1963, Wilson graduated from Fisk University with a bachelor's degree in elementary education. She worked as a teacher for a time and then became an assistant educational coordinator for a Head Start program. After taking a leave of absence to raise her three children, she returned to the field as an assistant principal and eventually became principal of a Miami elementary school. She also served on the Miami-Dade County School Board. During that period, she became more politically active. In 1984, she got involved in a campaign to lobby Congress to remove Haitian refugees from a local detention center. The Haitian women in particular, she said, "had no privacy at all, from guards, from visitors, from INS, from no one. When they would take a shower, they had no curtains. They were treating them like animals." The women were eventually released and allowed to remain in Miami.

Wilson first won a seat in the Florida House in 1998, serving two terms before being elected to the state Senate. In office, she continued her work on immigrants' rights issues, proposing a bill in 2007 banning the term "illegal alien" from state documents. She also focused on education. In 2004, she led a sometimes bitter fight against then-Gov. Jeb Bush to scale back the use of standardized testing in schools, which she claimed had a negative impact on children. Wilson was also known in the legislature for her fondness for large, cowboy-style hats and colorful outfits. Her trademark headgear was inspired by her grandmother, who wore similar hats as part of a cultural tradition in her native Bahamas.

When Meek ran for the Senate, Wilson decided to run for his House seat, continuing a pattern of succession for the two lawmakers: Wilson took Meek's seat when he left the Florida House and his place in the state Senate in 2002 when he ran for Congress. Eight other Democrats got into the August 2010 primary. Wilson won with 34% of the vote, helped by the district's sizable Haitian population splitting its support among the four Haitian-American candidates. Rudy Moise, a Haitian-American lawyer and doctor, came in second.

In the fall, she had no Republican opponent, and her only competition on Election Day was lawyer Roderick Vereen, an underdog independent. Wilson campaigned as a staunch backer of the Obama administration in a district that gave the president 87% of the vote in 2008. Her website sported a photograph of her with first lady Michelle Obama and noted that Wilson was "among the first officials in Florida to endorse Barack Obama." Wilson won with 86% of the vote to 14% for Vereen.

EIGHTEENTH DISTRICT

Ileana Ros-Lehtinen (R)

Elected Aug. 1989, 11th full term; b. July 15, 1952, Havana, Cuba; home, Miami; Miami-Dade Comm. Col., A.A. 1972, FL Intl. U., B.A. 1975, M.S. 1986, U. of Miami, Ed.D.. 2004; Episcopalian; married (Dexter); 4 children.

Elected Office: FL House of Reps., 1982–86; FL Senate, 1986–89.

Professional Career: Teacher, principal & owner, Eastern Academy Elem. Schl., 1978–85.

DC Office: 2206 RHOB, 20515, 202-225-3931; Fax: 202-225-5620; Web site: ros-lehtinen.house.gov.

State Offices: Miami, 305-668-2285; Miami Beach, 305-934-9441; Monroe County, 305-304-7789.

Committees: *Foreign Affairs* (Chmn).

Group Ratings

	ACLU	ACU	ADA	CFG	AFS	FRC	LCV	ITIC	NTU	COC
2010	44	70	30	66	13	62	50	33	79	88
2009	–	72	40	59	56	–	57	–	58	73

National Journal Ratings

	2010 LIB — 2010 CONS		2009 LIB — 2009 CONS	
Economic	35%	— 65%	40%	— 60%
Social	43%	— 57%	43%	— 56%
Foreign	38%	— 61%	0%	— 75%
Composite	39%	— 61%	32%	— 68%

Key Votes of the 111th Congress

1. Overturn Ledbetter	N	5. Bar federal abortion funds	Y	9. Stop detainee transfers	Y
2. Pass $820 billion stimulus	N	6. Pass health care bill	N	10. Legalize immigrants' kids	Y
3. Let guns in national parks	Y	7. Regulate financial firms	N	11. Repeal don't ask, tell	Y
4. Pass cap-and-trade	N	8. Pass tax cuts for some	Y	12. Limit campaign funds	N

Election Results

2010 general	Ileana Ros-Lehtinen (R) 102,360	(69%)	($1,668,779)
	Rolando Banciella (D)..46,235	(31%)	($11,019)
2010 primary	Ileana Ros-Lehtinen (R) .... unopposed		

Prior Winning Percentages: 2008 (58%), 2006 (62%), 2004 (65%), 2002 (69%), 2000 (100%), 1998 (100%), 1996 (100%), 1994 (100%), 1992 (67%), 1990 (60%), 1989 (53%)

Population		Race/Ethnicity		Work	
Pop. 2010:	712,790	White:	24.8%	Private:	78.1%
Change since 2000:	Up 11.5%	Black:	6.0%	Government:	10.0%
Urban:	99.1%	Hispanic:	66.9%	Self-employed:	11.8%
Rural:	0.9%	Asian:	1.3%	Blue collar:	19.8%
Area size:	3,196 sq. mi.	Native Am.:	0.1%	White collar:	58.0%
		Hawaiian:	0.0%	Khaki collar:	0.1%
Age		Two+ races:	0.7%	Other:	22.0%
Median age:	40.2 yrs.				
More than 65 yrs:	17.3%	*Ancestry*		Median income:	$40,706
Less than 18 yrs:	18.8%	German	4.1%	Median Home Value:	$365,600
		Irish	3.4%		
Education		Italian	3.2%	**Military Veterans**	
H.S. grad:	76.8%			% of Pop:	4.3%
College grad:	31.2%				
Grad degree:	12.3%				

South Florida; Miami

A century ago, Miami was a tiny tropical village where the Miami River empties into Biscayne Bay. Today it is a world-class city. The surrealistic high-rises of Brickell Boulevard, the reminders of the 1920s in the pseudo-Spanish Villa Vizcaya, the winding lanes of Coral Gables, and the shimmer of orange and pink neon signs in the hot night air: This is Miami today. It lives on the cusp of two civilizations, North America and Latin America, with different traditions,

2008 Presidential Vote
Barack Obama (D) 129,145   (51%)
John McCain (R) 123,570   (49%)

2004 Presidential Vote
George Bush (R) 127,746   (54%)
John Kerry (D) 107,073   (46%)

Cook Partisan Voting Index: R+3

styles, and sensibilities converging in this one place, with the strength of both despite some friction. Miami is in many ways the commercial and economic capital of Latin America. From Miami, it is easy to fly directly to any part of Latin America where top business and banking services are available to a sophisticated Spanish-speaking (and usually also English-speaking) clientele.

John Quincy Adams believed that Cuba would inevitably become a part of the United States. That never happened, but many of Cuba's people have become U.S. citizens, and the focus of Cuban America has been Miami, ever since the first refugees fled Fidel Castro in 1959. In the 1960s, the tone of Miami civic life was set by the large Jewish community and the liberal voice of the *Miami Herald*. But increasing numbers of Cuban immigrants, implacably opposed to the totalitarian Castro, entered the voting stream as Republicans. Then, Cubans were a noisy minority in the Miami area. Now, they are a dominant voice in a Latino majority in Miami-Dade County (as Dade County was renamed in 1997). In 2009, the population of Miami-Dade was 61% Hispanic and 20% black, leaving Anglo whites a fading but still elite minority, with educational backgrounds and incomes well above the national average. The city has the highest percentage of immigrants of any large city in the world, though the percentage of foreign-born residents in Miami-Dade declined from 51% in 2000 to 49% in 2009, a drop probably due to the recent recession. Most of South Florida's Jewish community has moved north to Broward and Palm Beach counties. Little Havana, centered around Calle Ocho (S.W. 8th Street in English), is now home to many Nicaraguans, Hondurans and Peruvians. Latinos in Miami-Dade tend to go to school at Miami Dade College, the nation's largest community college, or Florida International University, then start businesses or join the professions in Miami's vibrant economy.

Politically, Miami-Dade County is sharply divided, with black neighborhoods north of downtown and the remaining heavily Jewish condominium developments in the northeast heavily Democratic, and the Latino districts in the west and south mostly Republican. Once the most Democratic county in Florida, it delivered relatively small margins for Democratic presidential candidates in the last five elections. Cuban-Americans remain Republican, but less monolithically than in the past. Younger Cubans are less focused on overthrowing the Castro regime, and many opposed the Bush administration's restrictions on travel and remittances to Cuba while still favoring the embargo.

The 18th Congressional District of Florida is one of Miami-Dade's three Hispanic-majority districts. It is 67% Hispanic and 6% African-American. The district includes most of the city of Miami. It follows Calle Ocho west to heavily Hispanic West Miami and Westchester. It includes most of metro Miami's high-income residential areas: Coral Gables, with luxurious streets laid out in the 1920s; Cocoplum, a gated community with huge houses for rich Cuban-Americans and docks for their boats; the postmodern apartment buildings and upscale hotels along Brickell Boulevard; and Key Biscayne, with its high-rise apartments owned mostly by Latin American immigrants and their second-generation offspring.

The district includes parts of Miami Beach: South Beach, where old art-deco hotels are home to the glitziest celebrities of North America, Latin America and Europe. It also takes in the high-rises along Collins Avenue facing the ocean, and the Latino neighborhoods around 63rd Street. Miami Beach was the focus of the Florida land boom of 1925 and the bust of 1926, and in the past few years, boom has turned to bust again. Big apartment buildings on Brickell and in downtown Miami stand mostly empty as speculators default on mortgages. The county had one of the nation's highest foreclosure rates through 2010, and foreclosure sales made up almost 40% of home sales. Condo values have plummeted by as much as 40%.

South of Miami, the district is connected to the Florida Keys by U.S. 1. The highway ends in bustling, tropical Key West, the southernmost city in the continental United States. Key West has attracted famous residents—Ernest Hemingway, Tennessee Williams, Jimmy Buffett—and a large gay population, many living in quaint clapboard bungalows called "conch houses." The gay communities in Key West and Miami Beach are solidly Democratic, and they wield some clout. The 18th was drawn to be a Republican district and voted twice for George W. Bush. But in 2008, it delivered a narrow majority to Barack Obama.

Ileana Ros-Lehtinen (R)

The congresswoman from the 18th District is Ileana Ros-Lehtinen, the first Cuban-American and the first Hispanic woman elected to Congress. With the Republican takeover of the House in 2010, she became chair of the Foreign Affairs Committee.

Ros-Lehtinen (*ross-LAY-teh-nin*) was born in Havana. She came to Miami at the age of 8 not knowing English, and graduated from Miami Dade Community College and Florida International University. She became a teacher, and then was the owner of a private school. In 2004, she got her doctorate in education from the University of Miami. Her dissertation was on U.S. House members' views on national testing for high school students. She was elected to the Florida House in 1982, at age 30, and to the state Senate in 1986. While there, she met her husband, Dexter Lehtinen, who also served in both houses of the legislature and as U.S. attorney in Miami during the first Bush administration. In 1989, Ros-Lehtinen ran for the U.S. House in the special election after the death of Democrat Claude Pepper, one of the most enduring liberals in American politics and a staunch opponent of Castro. At that time, there were no Republicans and no Cuban-Americans representing Miami or Dade County. Democratic nominee Gerald Richman played on suspicions of Cubans and won the votes of 96% of blacks and 88% of non-Hispanic whites. Ninety percent of Hispanics, almost all of them Cuban, voted for Ros-Lehtinen. That was enough to give her a 53%-47% victory. In the years afterward, the district became more Hispanic, and she had no serious challenges until 2008.

Ros-Lehtinen has a mixed voting record: moderate on cultural policy and more conservative on economic and foreign issues. When Republicans won a House majority in 1995, she refused to sign the party's Contract with America policy manifesto and was a harsh critic of Republican attempts to pass English-only legislation, to cut off welfare benefits for legal immigrants—she voted against the 1996 welfare bills—and to reduce the immigration quota for relatives of U.S. citizens. In the 2007 debate over immigration, she pleaded with Republicans not to alienate the growing Hispanic voting bloc. She has been the chief sponsor of a bill to bar the transport of minors across state lines for abortions. The House passed it, but it died in the Senate. But she opposed the military's ban on openly gay troops and in 2008, she opposed the Florida constitutional amendment banning same-sex marriage. She also cosponsored the 2009 Employment Non-Discrimination Act making it illegal for employers to discriminate on the basis of sexual orientation or gender identity. In 2010, she was the only GOP member of the Congressional LGBT (Lesbian, Gay, Bisexual and Transgender) Equality Caucus. Ros-Lehtinen has personal experience with the group's issues: Her daughter, Amanda, is today a transgender man named Rodrigo Lehtinen, who is also active in the LGBT rights movement.

On the Foreign Affairs panel, she strongly backed the 1996 Helms-Burton law that tightened sanctions against Castro, and she has opposed farm-state Republicans who have sought to relax the trade embargo on Cuba in effect since 1961. In February 2008, after Castro stepped down as head of state, she called for his indictment for shooting down two Brothers to the Rescue planes in 1996. She has been a booster of Israel, winning enactment of bills to impose additional economic sanctions on Libya and Iran. In September 2007, after Israel bombed an apparent nuclear installation in Syria, reportedly constructed with help from North Korea, Ros-Lehtinen criticized the Bush administration for its "veil of secrecy" on intelligence about the raid and its willingness to reach agreements with North Korea in light of the Syrian installation. Ros-Lehtinen also supported the Israeli shelling of the Gaza Strip in December 2008. She has also been a strong supporter of the Iraq war. In taking over Foreign Affairs' chairmanship in 2011, she vowed to put Iran at the top of her list, noting that country's "increasingly worrisome" ties to Venezuela.

She and the ranking Democrat on the panel, Rep. Howard Berman of California, have one of the closest relationships among Congress' committee leaders. Berman told the Associated Press in November 2010, "People greatly underestimate her skill and tenaciousness." She and Berman led the House in 2008 in approving a nuclear agreement with India, but with international oversight of civilian nuclear reactors. But the two broke over a 2009 authorization bill for the State Department and related agencies. She unsuccessfully sought to cut almost $3 billion while capping spending increases at State at 3.7% in place of then-Chairman Berman's proposal to hike spending by 8%.

In 2010, her otherwise impressive record on Foreign Affairs was set back when she invited lobbyists to join a newly created advisory council on foreign policy matters and then canceled after it was reported she planned to solicit $2,500 in campaign contributions per person.

As the 2008 election approached, national Democrats thought Ros-Lehtinen might be vulnerable. Democrat Annette Taddeo, owner of the LanguageSpeak translation service, launched a challenge and financed it with $400,000 of her own money. Colombian-born Taddeo favored the embargo but wanted to ease travel restrictions and money transfers. The Democratic Congressional Campaign Committee poured $1.4 million into television ads, and New York Sen. Hillary Rodham Clinton and then-House Speaker Nancy Pelosi campaigned for Taddeo.

Ros-Lehtinen won 58%-42%, even though the district voted 51%-49% for Barack Obama. (The other two Florida districts represented by Cuban-Americans voted 51%-49% and 50%-49% for John McCain.) "If I can make it in this election, I can make it in any election," she told the *Miami Herald*. Obama even called with congratulations, but Ros-Lehtinen, thinking that one of the local radio stations was pulling a prank, hung up on him. She said, "I thought, 'Why would Obama want to call a little slug on the planet like me?'" When White House Chief of Staff Rahm Emanuel called to explain, she hung up on him, too. Then Berman called and persuaded her that the calls were genuine. She took the president's second call, and the two shared a laugh over the episode. The 2010 election marked her return to dominance, as she took 69% of the vote.

NINETEENTH DISTRICT

Ted Deutch (D)

Elected April 2010, 1st full term; b. May 7, 1966, Bethlehem, PA; home, Boca Raton area; U of MI, B.A. 1988, J.D. 1990; Jewish; Married (Jill); 3 children.

Elected Office: FL Senate, 2006-10.

Professional Career: Practicing attny., 1991-2010.

DC Office: 1024 LHOB, 20515, 202-225-3001; Fax: 202-225-5974; Web site: deutch.house.gov.

State Offices: Boca Raton, 561-988-6302; Margate, 954-972-6454.

Committees: *Foreign Affairs:* Europe and Eurasia; Middle East & South Asia. *Judiciary:* Crime, Terrorism & Homeland Security; Intellectual Property, Competition & the Internet.

Group Ratings

	ACLU	ACU	ADA	CFG	AFS	FRC	LCV	ITIC	NTU	COC
2010	75	0	80	0	100	0	86	100	8	20
2009	–	–	–	–	–	–	–	–	–	–

National Journal Ratings

	2010 LIB	—	2010 CONS	2009 LIB	—	2009 CONS
Economic	82%	—	18%	*	—	*
Social	69%	—	30%	*	—	*
Foreign	83%	—	17%	*	—	*
Composite	78%	—	22%	*	—	*

Key Votes of the 111th Congress

1. Overturn Ledbetter	*	5. Bar federal abortion funds	*	9. Stop detainee transfers	N
2. Pass $820 billion stimulus	*	6. Pass health care bill	*	10. Legalize immigrants' kids	Y
3. Let guns in national parks	*	7. Regulate financial firms	Y	11. Repeal don't ask, tell	Y
4. Pass cap-and-trade	*	8. Pass tax cuts for some	Y	12. Limit campaign funds	Y

Election Results

2010 general	Ted Deutch (D)	132,098	(63%)	($2,002,626)
	Joe Budd (R)	78,733	(37%)	($86,340)
2010 primary	Ted Deutch (D)	unopposed		
2010 special	Ted Deutch (D)	43,269	(62%)	
	Edward Lynch (R)	24,549	(35%)	
	Jim McCormick (NPA)	1,905	(3%)	
2010 primary	Ted Deutch (D)	23,959	(85%)	
	Ben Graber (D)	4,151	(15%)	

Population		Race/Ethnicity		Work	
Pop. 2010:	736,419	White:	61.9%	Private:	83.4%
Change since 2000:	Up 15.2%	Black:	12.4%	Government:	11.0%
Urban:	99.6%	Hispanic:	20.6%	Self-employed:	5.5%
Rural:	0.4%	Asian:	3.0%	Blue collar:	16.3%
Area size:	234 sq. mi.	Native Am.:	0.1%	White collar:	64.8%
		Hawaiian:	0.0%	Khaki collar:	0.1%
Age		Two+ races:	1.4%	Other:	18.9%
Median age:	45.4 yrs.				
More than 65 yrs:	26.0%	*Ancestry*		Median income:	$49,409
Less than 18 yrs:	20.2%	Italian	8.7%	Median Home Value:	$222,800
		German	7.8%		
Education		Irish	7.7%	**Military Veterans**	
H.S. grad:	88.9%			% of Pop:	11.6%
College grad:	30.9%				
Grad degree:	11.3%				

South Florida; Part Boca Raton

When the first millionaires came to Palm Beach in the 1920s to winter in their new Addison Mizner pseudo-Mediterranean mansions, there was virtually nothing man-made between Palm Beach and Miami. In 1920, Dade, Broward, and Palm Beach counties boasted a mere 66,000 residents. In 2008, 5.4 million people lived in the five- to 20-mile strip between the Atlantic Ocean and the protected Everglades. The contrast between then and now is especially striking in Boca Raton, where Mizner built the Boca Raton Resort & Club in 1926. Its azure fountains and red-tiled roofs, its pseudo-Moorish columns and pink stucco walls bespeak a vision of a holiday Florida, a bit mannered and antique to today's eye, but still exuberant and benefiting from tasteful refurbishing. The coast from Boca Raton to Palm Beach is fully built up, and over the past 20 years, the area has become home to one of the nation's largest Jewish populations. There are the "condo commandos," the political activists among elderly Jewish retirees from New York and the Northeast, but also young families and middle-aged businessmen. However, since 2005, growth here has stalled, and the area has been hit by many foreclosures and a loss in construction jobs. In Boca Raton, city officials in 2010 faced an $8 million budget gap.

2008 Presidential Vote		
Barack Obama (D) 223,144	(66%)
John McCain (R) 115,719	(34%)
2004 Presidential Vote		
John Kerry (D) 210,695	(66%)
George Bush (R) 107,348	(34%)
Cook Partisan Voting Index:	D+15	

The 19th Congressional District of Florida includes Palm Beach and Broward counties. It does not touch the ocean at all, kept inland by the 22nd and 23rd districts. The boundaries of the 19th District are irregular, obviously drawn for political advantage. The Republicans who controlled the redistricting process were happy to pack heavily Democratic precincts into the 19th. It extends north from Fort Lauderdale to Okeechobee Boulevard in unglamorous West Palm Beach. The district also takes in Margate, Mission Bay, most of Boca Raton, and parts of Boynton Beach and Delray Beach. The district's Jewish percentage is the one of the largest among the 435 congressional districts. A lot of people here are still voting for the party of Franklin D. Roosevelt, and the 19th is solidly Democratic, although neither John Kerry nor Barack Obama was able to duplicate the 73% of the vote that the ticket of Al Gore and Joe Lieberman received here in 2000.

Ted Deutch (D)

The congressman from the 19th District is Democrat Ted Deutch, who won the seat in a special election on April 13, 2010. He replaced Democratic Rep. Robert Wexler, who resigned midterm to become president of the Center for Middle East Peace & Economic Cooperation. Deutch (*Doitch*) is a liberal with a staunchly pro-Israel posture on foreign policy, very much in the mold of Wexler, but without his predecessor's in-your-face style. Deutch has working-class roots in Bethlehem, Pa., where his father ran a small painting contracting company and his mother kept the books. His parents, who met at a "bagel brunch," did not go to college and were determined that their five children would. He excelled in high school and was class president for four years. (He recalls suffering a "bitter loss" for 5th grade class president; he rebounded with victory in the 6th grade and hasn't lost an election since.) The industrious teenaged Deutch also did odd jobs to earn money, once delivering balloons in a rabbit costume. At the University of Michigan, Deutch majored in political science and volunteered in political campaigns during summers, including working for unsuccessful Democratic presidential candidate Joe Biden in 1987. He also caught the eye of an academic advisor who encouraged him to apply for a Harry S. Truman Scholarship, which recognizes college students with potential in public service careers. His involvement in the four-year program reinforced his inclination toward public life, which was seeded by his father. The late Bernard Deutch was forced into an early retirement from his small painting business because of heart disease and he spent a lot of time in front of the television tuned to CNN. When he was in high school, Ted found that sitting next to his dad on the couch discussing events unfolding on the news channel was a good way to spend precious time with an ailing parent.

After law school, Ted Deutch specialized in real estate law in Washington, D.C., at one of the firms hired to sell off government assets in the wake of the savings and loan crisis of the 1980s. He married Jill Weinstock and the couple moved to Cleveland, Ohio, to be closer to his wife's family. Eventually, they moved their growing family (three children) to Boca Raton, Fla., where Ted's older brother, also a lawyer, had opened an office for Broad and Cassel and hired him to handle the firm's real estate business. Deutch got active in Florida politics, including working on issues and raising money for Bill Clinton's two presidential campaigns in the state. He also lobbied for pro-Israel causes. In 2006, he ran successfully for a Florida Senate seat, his first elective office. In a little over three years in the legislature, Deutch authored two signature pieces of legislation: a bill putting a surcharge on tobacco products to help pay for smoking prevention programs and cancer research, and another measure barring the state from investing pension funds in any enterprise that aided Iran's effort to attain nuclear weapons or that indirectly abetted genocide in the Darfur region of the Sudan.

When Wexler announced he would resign his seat in the middle of his term to go to the Middle East think tank, Deutch announced his candidacy for the seat the next day. He seemed a natural successor to Wexler. His liberal, pro-Israel politics appealed to the region's large population of Jewish retirees and he'd represented half the congressional district in the state Senate. West Palm Beach business consultant Ed Lynch gamely took on the job as Deutch's Republican challenger but faced terrible odds in a district where Democrats outnumber Republicans 2-to-1.

Lynch thought his best shot was to make the race a referendum on the Obama administration and its health care overhaul, which had recently been signed into law and was unpopular with conservatives. Lynch joined national Republican leaders in calling for outright repeal. Deutch maintained that the changes would improve access to health care for people without insurance, for those who had been denied insurance because of preexisting medical problems, and for seniors who rely on Medicare for their prescription drugs. The special election was watched nationally as a possible harbinger for the fall elections, particularly if Lynch were successful in snatching a heavily Democratic seat. But Deutch won easily, topping 62% of the vote. Lynch got 35%. Deutch outspent his opponents mightily, raising $1.7 million compared to $117,000 for Lynch. Seven months later, Deutch repeated his accomplishment in the general election, topping Republican Joe Budd to win re-election after raising nearly $2 million to Budd's $75,000.

In Washington, Deutch kept many of Wexler's aides, and made one of them his chief of staff. He focused on economic issues, introducing a bill in July 2010 to create a separate new consumer price index to factor in costs that he said have been undercounted, such as prescriptions and medical equipment. His bill also phased out the $106,800 cap on income subject to the payroll tax. Deutch took over Wexler's seats on the Foreign Affairs and Judiciary Committees, working to strengthen liability claims from the BP Gulf oil spill disaster and requiring U.S. companies to spell out their investments in Iran. He also found time to dabble in music: When former Monkee band member Micky Dolenz came to Capitol Hill in June 2010 to lobby for music royalty legislation, Deutch played keyboards in a band at a reception for Dolenz that included New York Democrat Joseph Crowley on guitar and Florida Republican Tom Rooney on drums.

TWENTIETH DISTRICT

Debbie Wasserman Schultz (D)

Elected 2004, 4th term; b. Sept. 27, 1966, Forest Hills, NY; home, Weston; U. of FL, B.A. 1988, M.A. 1990; Jewish; married (Steve); 3 children.

Elected Office: FL House, 1992-2000; Min. leader pro tem., 1999-2000; FL Sen., 2000-04.

Professional Career: State legislative aide, 1989-1992.

DC Office: 118 CHOB, 20515, 202-225-7931; Fax: 202-226-2052; Web site: wassermanschultz.house.gov.

State Offices: Aventura, 305-936-5724; Pembroke Pines, 954-437-3936.

Committees: *Budget.*

Group Ratings

	ACLU	ACU	ADA	CFG	AFS	FRC	LCV	ITIC	NTU	COC
2010	88	0	90	0	100	0	90	100	4	14
2009	–	0	100	0	100	–	93	–	2	40

National Journal Ratings

	2010 LIB — 2010 CONS		2009 LIB — 2009 CONS	
Economic	82%	17%	82%	14%
Social	87%	12%	84%	11%
Foreign	92%	8%	87%	9%
Composite	87%	13%	87%	14%

Key Votes of the 111th Congress

1. Overturn Ledbetter	Y	5. Bar federal abortion funds	N	9. Stop detainee transfers	N
2. Pass $820 billion stimulus	Y	6. Pass health care bill	Y	10. Legalize immigrants' kids	Y
3. Let guns in national parks	N	7. Regulate financial firms	Y	11. Repeal don't ask, tell	Y
4. Pass cap-and-trade	Y	8. Pass tax cuts for some	Y	12. Limit campaign funds	Y

Election Results

2010 general	Debbie Wasserman Schultz (D)........................100,787	(60%)	($1,930,111)
	Karen Harrington (R)...63,845	(38%)	($376,835)
2010 primary	Debbie Wasserman Schultz (D)...................unopposed		

Prior Winning Percentages: 2008 (77%), 2006 (100%), 2004 (70%)

Population		Race/Ethnicity		Work	
Pop. 2010:	691,727	White:	51.8%	Private:	82.5%
Change since 2000:	Up 8.2%	Black:	11.5%	Government:	11.5%
Urban:	99.7%	Hispanic:	31.3%	Self-employed:	5.9%
Rural:	0.3%	Asian:	3.2%	Blue collar:	13.9%
Area size:	218 sq. mi.	Native Am.:	0.2%	White collar:	70.5%
		Hawaiian:	0.0%	Khaki collar:	0.2%
Age		Two+ races:	1.5%	Other:	15.4%
Median age:	40.3 yrs.				
More than 65 yrs:	15.1%	*Ancestry*		Median income:	$55,775
Less than 18 yrs:	21.8%	Italian	7.9%	Median Home Value:	$278,900
		Irish	7.1%		
Education		German	7.0%	**Military Veterans**	
H.S. grad:	90.2%			% of Pop:	7.7%
College grad:	36.3%				
Grad degree:	14.0%				

South Florida; Part Hollywood

Back when Connie Francis made it famous in the 1960 spring break movie *Where the Boys Are*, Fort Lauderdale was just a small town with a strip of motels along the beach and some nice houses fronting its canals. Now it's the center of a sprawling metropolitan area with resort hotels on the beach but a much larger workaday population inland. It is a center of business and commerce and a major port. In 1950, Fort Lauderdale and the rest of Broward County had

2008 Presidential Vote

Barack Obama (D)	187,054	(63%)
John McCain (R)	106,455	(36%)

2004 Presidential Vote

John Kerry (D)	183,510	(64%)
George Bush (R)	104,039	(36%)

Cook Partisan Voting Index: D+13

183,000 people; in 2009, they had 1.76 million. From the strip of beach along the Atlantic Ocean, west to the Sawgrass Expressway and the Everglades Wildlife Management Area, the land has filled up with subdivisions, shopping centers, office complexes, warehouses, and trucking terminals. As it has grown, the ethnic composition of Broward County has changed. In the 1950s, it was understood that Jews couldn't buy houses or rent hotel rooms this far north of Miami. But from the 1960s through the 1990s, as Cubans and other Latinos moved into the Miami-Dade County area, many Jews moved north, and Broward County became one of the most heavily Jewish parts of the United States. Nearer the coast, especially in the huge high-rises of Hollywood and Hallandale, most of Broward's Jews were retirees from New York and other Northeastern cities. But inland, in towns like booming Davie, Plantation, and Sunrise, many young Jewish parents raised families in communities that prided themselves on fine schools and high property values.

Now Broward County seems to be changing again. Jewish migration over the past 15 years has gone farther north, to Palm Beach County. Broward's population peaked in 2006; then, for the first time in history, it fell, as whites moved out of the county and immigrants moved in. Fort Lauderdale and next-door Wilton Manors have become the home of choice for many gay people, and metro Fort Lauderdale now has a higher percentage of same-sex couples than any other metropolitan areas except San Francisco/Oakland and Seattle. But Fort Lauderdale was one of the nation's hardest-hit cities in the house foreclosure crisis of 2007-08, and property values across the region dropped by more than 10% in 2010. Numerous planned high-rise developments went unbuilt.

The 20th Congressional District of Florida includes much of southeastern Broward County and the northern Biscayne Bay shoreline in Miami-Dade County. Precinct by precinct, its computer-generated borders are drawn to include heavily Democratic areas. It includes much of Fort Lauderdale, Hollywood and Dania Beach on the coast. But its biggest blocks of territory are inland. In Miami-Dade, it includes the shores of Biscayne Bay, both on the Miami and Miami Beach side, with expensive homes and huge high-rises. This is a strongly Democratic district, though in recent years not quite as strong as in 2000, when it cast 69% of its vote for Al Gore and Joe Lieberman.

Debbie Wasserman Schultz (D)

The congresswoman from the 20th District is Debbie Wasserman Schultz, a hard-charging Democrat elected in 2004. With a nod to her considerable skills as a media messenger and fundraiser, she was tapped as chairman of the Democratic National Committee in April 2011. She planned to keep her House seat while heading the DNC, which will have a major role in the 2012 presidential contest.

Like many of her constituents, she was born in Queens. She grew up on Long Island, where she ran for student council every year and always lost. She got bachelor's and master's degrees from the University of Florida. In her last year at school, she sent out 180 resumes to legislators in Florida and New York and got five interviews. Florida State Rep. Peter Deutsch, a Democrat and former New Yorker from Broward County, gave her a summer job, and then appointed her as his legislative aide. In 1992, he ran for the 20th District House seat and urged Wasserman Schultz to run for his seat in the legislature. She did, knocking on doors for six months and finishing far ahead of four opponents in the Democratic primary. At age 26, she became the state's youngest woman ever elected to the state House. She served eight years in the state House, including two years as minority leader, followed by four years in the state Senate. She called herself "a pragmatic liberal," and she sponsored a controversial law to require an equal number of men and women on state boards and a bill that failed to pass requiring that dry cleaners and some other businesses charge the same prices for women as for men.

In 2004, when Deutsch ran for the Democratic nomination for Bob Graham's open Senate seat, Wasserman Schultz moved to again replace Deutsch, this time in Congress. She began laying the groundwork early. More than a year before the primary, she had raised $115,000. By February 2004, she had lined up endorsements from Minority Leader Nancy Pelosi and six of Florida's seven House Democrats. Wasserman Schultz ultimately collected more than $1 million for what turned out to be an uncompetitive race, since no one else filed to run in the decisive Democratic primary. Wasserman Schultz called for repeal of the Bush tax cuts, a reduction in the budget deficit, greater use of diplomacy overseas, improved prescription drug coverage, gay civil rights, and abortion rights. Against a Republican who attacked the "homosexual agenda" in the public schools, she won 70%-30%. She has not faced a serious challenge since, allowing her to channel campaign contributions from a wide spectrum of Democratic interests to her colleagues. In 2009 alone, she raised nearly $5 million for House Democrats, matching the dollars brought in by more senior leaders.

In the House, she has a mostly liberal voting record, though it's more centrist on foreign policy. Within days of arriving in Congress, she was making an impact. In the debate then raging over whether to intervene to retain the feeding tube for severely brain-damaged Terri Schiavo of Florida, Wasserman Schultz argued that Congress would set a dangerous precedent if it attempted to circumvent the courts. She also sponsored a bill, passed by the House in 2007, toughening the Internet Crimes Against Children program by adding hundreds of federal agents at a cost of $1 billion over eight years. She has been one of the Florida delegation's most ardent opponents of offshore oil drilling, declaring after the 2010 BP oil spill disaster in the Gulf of Mexico that "our country needs to run on something other than oil."

In 2006, Wasserman Schultz was appointed co-chairman of the DCCC's "Red to Blue" effort. Working closely with then-Chairman Rahm Emanuel, now Chicago mayor, she became a party spokesperson and a mentor to Democratic recruits. When Democrats won House control that year, she was a prime beneficiary. Majority Whip James Clyburn tapped her as a chief deputy whip. She got a seat on the Appropriations Committee, and immediately became a "cardinal" as chairman of the Legislative Branch Subcommittee. Working with ranking Republican Zach Wamp of Tennessee, she took charge of the Capitol Visitor Center project, which was plagued by cost overruns, and extracted commitments on costs and completion dates. She pushed successfully for a unionization vote at the Government Accountability Office. Wasserman Schultz founded the Cuban Democracy Caucus and was a founding member of the Lesbian, Gay, Bisexual, and Transgender Equality Caucus.

In the 2008 election season, Wasserman Schultz was criticized by liberal bloggers when she refused to campaign against the three Cuban-American Republican members from South Florida as part of her DCCC duties. They were facing unusually strong Democratic challenges, and ultimately all three—Ileana Ros-Lehtinen and brothers Lincoln and Mario Diaz-Balart—were re-elected. She was Hillary Rodham Clinton's co-chair in Florida and nationally.

In late 2008, Wasserman Schultz was interested in becoming vice chairman of the Democratic Caucus if the incumbent, California's Xavier Becerra, a favorite of then-House Speaker Nancy Pelosi, was appointed special trade representative, and she was mentioned as a candidate to succeed Maryland's Chris Van Hollen as DCCC chairman. But Becerra did not accept the job, and Van Hollen was reappointed. Wasserman Schultz was named vice chair of the DCCC's incumbent retention program. A *National Journal* poll of anonymous congressional insiders in 2009 predicted she had the brightest political future of anyone on Capitol Hill.

Her precocious success seemed all the more impressive when she announced in March 2009 that for much of the previous year she had been battling breast cancer. Although her tumor was in early stages, which would typically require only surgery and radiation, she said that she elected to have a double mastectomy after learning that as an Ashkenazi Jew, she had a greater predisposition to recurrence. The mother of three school-aged children, Wasserman Schultz was diagnosed just after turning 40. She talked about her experience on ABC's *Good Morning America* as a way of educating young women about the importance of early diagnosis.

TWENTY-FIRST DISTRICT

Mario Diaz-Balart (R)

Elected 2002, 5th term; b. Sept. 25, 1961, Ft. Lauderdale; home, Miami; U. of S. FL; Catholic; married (Tia); 1 child.

Elected Office: FL House of Reps., 1988-92, 2000-02; FL Senate, 1992-00.

Professional Career: A.A., Miami Mayor Xavier Suarez, 1985-88; Public relations executive.

DC Office: 436 CHOB, 20515, 202-225-4211; Fax: 202-225-8576; Web site: mariodiazbalart.house.gov.

State Offices: Miami, 305-470-8555.

Group Ratings

	ACLU	ACU	ADA	CFG	AFS	FRC	LCV	ITIC	NTU	COC
2010	31	79	20	74	13	81	40	33	79	88
2009	–	72	45	61	56	–	36	–	64	80

National Journal Ratings

	2010 LIB — 2010 CONS		2009 LIB — 2009 CONS	
Economic	36%	— 64%	38%	— 62%
Social	41%	— 59%	38%	— 61%
Foreign	36%	— 63%	0%	— 75%
Composite	38%	— 62%	30%	— 70%

Key Votes of the 111th Congress

1. Overturn Ledbetter	N	5. Bar federal abortion funds	Y	9. Stop detainee transfers	Y
2. Pass $820 billion stimulus	N	6. Pass health care bill	N	10. Legalize immigrants' kids	Y
3. Let guns in national parks	Y	7. Regulate financial firms	N	11. Repeal don't ask, tell	N
4. Pass cap-and-trade	N	8. Pass tax cuts for some	N	12. Limit campaign funds	N

Election Results

2010 general	Mario Diaz-Balart (R)	unopposed	($739,771)
2010 primary	Mario Diaz-Balart (R)	unopposed	

Prior Winning Percentages: 2008 (53%), 2006 (58%), 2004 (100%), 2002 (65%)

Population		Race/Ethnicity		Work	
Pop. 2010:	693,501	White:	13.8%	Private:	81.6%
Change since 2000:	Up 8.5%	Black:	7.3%	Government:	10.7%
Urban:	99.9%	Hispanic:	75.6%	Self-employed:	7.6%
Rural:	0.1%	Asian:	2.4%	Blue collar:	22.4%
Area size:	140 sq. mi.	Native Am.:	0.1%	White collar:	60.7%
		Hawaiian:	0.0%	Khaki collar:	0.2%
Age		Two+ races:	0.7%	Other:	16.8%
Median age:	39.3 yrs.				
More than 65 yrs:	15.5%	*Ancestry*		Median income:	$47,603
Less than 18 yrs:	22.2%	West Indian	3.1%	Median Home Value:	$292,000
		USA	2.4%		
Education		German	2.4%	**Military Veterans**	
H.S. grad:	79.0%			% of Pop:	3.3%
College grad:	27.2%				
Grad degree:	9.2%				

South Florida; Hialeah

Miami's Cuban-American community has been one of America's most dynamic immigrant groups over the past 40 years, growing from 50,000 in 1960, the year after Fidel Castro took over Cuba, to well over 1 million today. Over time, the Cuban-American neighborhoods centered along S.W. 8th Street—Calle Ocho—expanded west to the Florida Turnpike Extension in Weston and Sweetwater, southwest to Kendall and northwest to Hialeah. Starting in the

2008 Presidential Vote
John McCain (R) 127,084   (51%)
Barack Obama (D) 121,805   (49%)

2004 Presidential Vote
George Bush (R) 127,326   (57%)
John Kerry (D) 96,232   (43%)

Cook Partisan Voting Index: R+5

1980s, there was an influx of other Latinos, from Nicaragua, El Salvador, Venezuela, and Colombia. In the process, new communities were built and old ones transformed. Built on swampland, Sweetwater is now probably more Cuban than the old Little Havana on Calle Ocho. Kendall, where the last strawberry field was torn up 30 years ago, is the site of the upscale Dadeland Mall, where Spanish is heard more often than English. Hialeah, famous for its racetrack first opened in 1925, was transformed, as one writer put it, "from redneck to Latino" in just a few years. The racetrack closed in 2001, but unexpectedly reopened in 2009 during the peak of the recession. It lost between $6 million and $7 million that year, but its owner was planning to add slot machines, a hotel and other features to try to save it.

The 21st Congressional District of Florida is an irregular rectangle about 20 miles long and two to six miles wide in Miami-Dade County and southern Broward County. In Miami-Dade, it includes Kendall, Cutler, Westwood Lakes and Sweetwater. It includes raffish Hialeah and nearby Miami Lakes, a planned town developed in the 1960s. In Broward County, the district includes much of Miramar and Pembroke Pines. It includes Florida International University, which opened South Florida's only public medical school in August 2009, and Miami International Airport, which surpassed Orlando as Florida's busiest airport in 2009. Its 16 million international passengers that year made it second to New York's John F. Kennedy for travel abroad among U.S. airports.

The population of the district is 76% Hispanic, the highest of any Florida district, and 44% of residents are of Cuban origin. Cuban voters continue to be heavily Republican. Other Latino voters are less so, but by no means are they overwhelmingly Democratic. Many here do not vote at all: The 21st has the lowest number of registered voters of any Florida district. With relatively few Hispanics, the Broward County portion of the district tends to vote Democratic. Overall, this is a Republican district, but one that sometimes votes for Democrats who support the Cuban community's issues. George W. Bush carried the district twice, but Barack Obama came close to winning it in 2008. He got 48.8% of the vote to John McCain's 50.9%.

Mario Diaz-Balart (R)

The congressman from the 21st District is Mario Diaz-Balart, a Republican first elected in 2002 from the neighboring 25th District. His hold on that district had been increasingly tenuous, and, after an especially close re-election contest in 2008, Diaz-Balart announced in February 2010 that he would not run again in the 25th. Instead, he said he would run for the neighboring 21st District seat being vacated by his brother, Lincoln Diaz-Balart, who announced his plans to retire on the same day. Lincoln's Miami-Dade County district is more heavily Cuban American and more Republican than Mario's old district. Mario said it would be a "natural move" for him considering he represented much of the district in the Florida Legislature.

The Diaz-Balart family history is intertwined with that of Fidel Castro and the rise of communism on the island nation of Cuba. His father, Rafael Lincoln Diaz-Balart, was the majority leader in pre-revolution Cuba's House of Representatives. His uncle and grandfather also served in the Cuban House. His family is sometimes called the "Cuban Kennedys" and seems to have politics in its blood. The Diaz-Balarts fled Cuba in 1959, shortly after Castro took over and after their house was looted and burned while they were vacationing in Paris. His aunt was briefly Castro's wife and is the mother of his only recognized child. Mario Diaz-Balart, unlike Lincoln, was born in the United States after the family had resettled. Another brother is a television news anchorman for Telemundo and a fourth is an investment banker.

Diaz-Balart dropped out of the University of South Florida at age 24 to work for former Miami Mayor Xavier Suarez, a Republican. In 1988, he was elected to the Florida House; four years later, at age 31, he became the youngest person ever elected to the state Senate. Diaz-Balart was named chairman of the Senate Ways and Means Committee, where he was a budget hawk. His 1995 call for state agencies to cut spending by 25% earned him the nickname "The Slasher"—a moniker he wore with pride. The eight-year term limit forced him from the state Senate in 2000, so he again ran for the Florida House and was elected. No ordinary freshman, Diaz-Balart requested and received the chairmanship of the congressional redistricting committee. The resulting plan included a central Florida district tailored to state House Speaker Tom Feeney and a western Miami-Dade district tailored for Diaz-Balart. He coasted to victory over Democratic state Rep. Annie Betancourt, a former social worker and the widow of a Bay of Pigs veteran. Her campaign was underfinanced, and she remained largely unknown. With support from teachers and other unions, Diaz-Balart won the new 25th District, 65%-35%.

In the House, his voting record has generally been more conservative than his brother Lincoln's on economic and foreign policy, and he has been a moderate on cultural issues. He told the *Naples Daily News* in July 2008: "I'm not a laissez-faire Republican. I don't like government. It's bloated, fat, and doesn't work." He co-sponsored a bill in 2007 to ban disaster aid spending on puppet shows, dance lessons, yoga on the beach, and other entertainment. He has opposed oil drilling off Florida's coast in the Gulf of Mexico. He blasted the 2010 health care overhaul as "a bill that will take our country down the path of bankruptcy." A year earlier, he unsuccessfully tried in the Budget Committee to cut new taxes from the fiscal 2010 budget blueprint.

Diaz-Balart organized the Congressional Hispanic Conference, a Republican alternative to the Democrats' Congressional Hispanic Caucus. Diaz-Balart vocally opposed the Democratic proposal to expand the State Children's Health Insurance Program because it was to be financed in part with a $3 tax on cigars. He said the tax would hurt South Florida-based cigar producers, an industry, he said, "that is almost entirely Hispanic." With his brother and GOP Rep. Ileana Ros-Lehtinen, also of South Florida, he supported a bill to allow children of illegal immigrants to qualify for college. During the illegal immigration debate in Congress, he said, "The tone of some Republicans was offensive to the vast majority of Hispanics." Like his older brother, Mario Diaz-Balart favored maintaining the trade embargo on Cuba and the 2004 restrictions on travel and remittances to Cuba.

Heading into the 2008 election season, Democrats believed that Diaz-Balart was vulnerable. Younger Cuban-Americans are less focused on Castro, and many opposed the restrictions on travel and remittances. The number of non-Cuban Hispanics in the area also had been increasing, and the Republican registration advantage fell almost to zero. That year, Diaz-Balart faced a serious challenge from Joe Garcia, the Miami-Dade County Democratic chairman. Garcia opposed the restrictions on travel and remittances to Cuba, and criticized the Diaz-Balart brothers for focusing on Cuba rather than on gas prices and the crisis in housing foreclosures. Diaz-Balart returned the fire and he won, although by a disappointing 53%-47%.

For his 21st District bid in 2010, it was a much different story: Thanks to his family name and backing from local Republicans, he was unopposed in both the primary and the general election. When the GOP took majority control of the House in 2011, Diaz-Balart got a coveted seat on the Appropriations Committee.

TWENTY-SECOND DISTRICT
Allen West (R)

Elected 2010, 1st term; b. Feb. 7, 1961, Atlanta, GA; home, Plantation; U. of TN, B.A. 1983; KS St. U., M.A. 1996; U.S. Army Command and Gen. Staff Officer Col., master of military arts and sciences 1997.; Christian; Married (Angela); 2 children.

Military Career: Army, 1982-2004 (Persian Gulf, Afghanistan, Iraq).

Professional Career: Teacher, 2004-05; military contractor, MPRI, 2005-07.

DC Office: 1708 LHOB, 20515, 202-225-3026; Fax: 202-225-8398; Web site: west.house.gov.

State Offices: Fort Lauderdale, 954-202-6211; West Palm Beach, 561-655-1943.

Committees: *Armed Services:* Emerging Threats & Capabilities; Military Personnel. *Small Business:* Contracting & Workforce; Investigations, Oversight & Regulations.

Election Results

2010 general	Allen West (R)	118,890	(54%)	($6,542,738)
	Ron Klein (D)	99,804	(46%)	($3,776,867)
2010 primary	Allen West (R)	30,024	(77%)	
	David Brady (R)	9,137	(23%)	

Population		Race/Ethnicity		Work	
Pop. 2010:	694,259	White:	72.3%	Private:	83.4%
Change since 2000:	Up 8.6%	Black:	7.0%	Government:	9.1%
Urban:	99.2%	Hispanic:	16.3%	Self-employed:	7.3%
Rural:	0.8%	Asian:	2.5%	Blue collar:	15.0%
Area size:	500 sq. mi.	Native Am.:	0.2%	White collar:	67.5%
		Hawaiian:	0.0%	Khaki collar:	0.0%
Age		Two+ races:	1.3%	Other:	17.4%
Median age:	44.4 yrs.				
More than 65 yrs:	19.5%	*Ancestry*		Median income:	$61,122
Less than 18 yrs:	19.0%	Irish	11.5%	Median Home Value:	$342,500
		German	11.5%		
Education		Italian	9.4%	**Military Veterans**	
H.S. grad:	91.3%			% of Pop:	10.8%
College grad:	38.0%				
Grad degree:	13.5%				

South Florida, Part Fort Lauderdale

The barrier islands of Florida's Gold Coast have been developed in spasms of land speculation frenzy, not just as vacation places and retirement homes but as embodiments of dreams and fantasies. Consider Palm Beach, the great beach resort of the 1920s, where rich WASPs would abandon their snow-covered Tudor or Georgian mansions to live in Addison Mizner's pseudo-Mediterranean confections. Or Boca Raton, where Mizner built the Boca Raton Resort and Club in 1926. Or Fort Lauderdale, a tiny town when Clyde Beatty brought his circus there for the winter in the 1930s (locals complained about the roaring lions). Back in the 1950s, many of these beachfront communities were "restricted," which meant no Jews were allowed. Starting in the 1970s, high-rise condominiums sprouted up and down the Atlantic coast of Broward and Palm Beach counties. Today, they are home to many Jewish retirees from New York and the Northeast generally. But there are also working-age people here and plans to attract more. Florida and Palm Beach County have subsidized the Scripps Research Institute's new center in Jupiter, in hopes of attracting biotechnology businesses.

In recent years, the old town centers have been revived. Palm Beach remains, as it has been since the 1920s, the precinct of the very rich. Conservative talk-show host Rush Limbaugh has his

2008 Presidential Vote		
Barack Obama (D)	175,895	(52%)
John McCain (R)	162,076	(48%)
2004 Presidential Vote		
John Kerry (D)	169,161	(53%)
George Bush (R)	153,265	(48%)
Cook Partisan Voting Index: D+1		

South Florida headquarters there, and it was the favorite playground of swindler Bernard Madoff—and many of his now unhappy clients. Boca Raton now sports the stylish Mizner Park, a collection of upscale stores. Downtown Fort Lauderdale, separated from the beach by miles of canals, is the site of new condominiums, the Museum of Art Fort Lauderdale, the Museum of Discovery and Science, the Broward Center for the Performing Arts, and the International Swimming Hall of Fame. But the housing market collapse hit the area hard, with some of the highest foreclosure rates in Florida. Unemployment topped 12% in the region in 2010, and home prices were not expected to fully recover until 2030, according to Moody's *Economy.com*.

The 22nd Congressional District of Florida covers most of the Atlantic oceanfront in Palm Beach and Broward counties, from Jupiter in Palm Beach County to Fort Lauderdale in Broward County. It is rarely more than a few miles wide, and in some places it is not much wider than the barrier islands separated from the mainland by the Indian River and Lake Worth. But it also has jagged salients that extend several miles inland. The district, a testament to the advances made in redistricting software, was drawn by Republicans in an attempt to provide a safe seat for Republican Rep. Clay Shaw after he barely won re-election in 2000. They removed the Miami-Dade County portion of the district and heavily Democratic Hollywood in Broward County, and they brought in Republican precincts in Plantation and Coral Springs. The resulting district is affluent and elderly, with a large Jewish population that's politically very active in condominium groups. But the intentions of the mapmakers, here as elsewhere, were defeated by changing demographics and changing attitudes. The 22nd District has given Democratic nominees at least 52% of the vote in the past three presidential elections, and in 2006 it ousted Shaw.

Allen West (R)

The congressman from Florida's 22nd District is Allen West, a Republican who upset Democrat Ron Klein in 2010. West grew up in inner-city Atlanta in a military family. His father was a World War II veteran, and West told *The New York Times* that his father encouraged him to join the military because "he felt it was a good place to be for a young black man." West was a commissioned officer by the time he graduated from the University of Tennessee. He received a master's degree in political science from Kansas State University and a master of military arts and sciences from the U.S. Army Command and General Staff Officer College in political theory and military operations. In his 22-year career, he served in Italy and South Korea and fought in the Persian Gulf War, the Iraq war, and Afghanistan.

His service was the subject of some controversy in 2003 after the military reprimanded him for threatening to kill an Iraqi detainee he believed had information about an attack on American soldiers. In August of that year, West, an Army lieutenant colonel serving in Iraq, said he learned of a plot to assassinate him. Soldiers under his command detained an Iraqi police officer named Yehiya Kadoori Hamoodi, whom they believed had relevant information. West threatened to kill Hamoodi and fired a pistol next to his head. Further investigation uncovered no additional evidence of a plot, and Hamoodi later said he gave meaningless information out of fear. The Army decided against holding a court martial; at an administrative hearing, West was fined $5,000 and allowed to retire with full benefits.

He moved to Florida, taught high school history classes for a year, and then began working for a defense contracting firm. In 2008, he made his first foray into politics, challenging Klein. West was unopposed for the Republican nomination but struggled to raise funds, and Klein won, 55% to 45%. Back for a rematch in 2010, West had more money, the support of tea party groups, and a political climate strongly favoring Republicans. In August, West defeated businessman David Brady for the Republican nomination to run against Klein a second time.

He proved to be a much more prodigious fundraiser than before. By October 13, he had raised $5.6 million to Klein's $3.4 million, and he had the endorsement of former Alaska Gov. Sarah Palin. Klein pulled no punches in his attacks. He accused West of being associated with a criminal biker gang, and implied in one ad that West wanted to take up arms against the government. West struck back in kind. In a debate, he called Klein a "mama's boy" for House Speaker Nancy Pelosi and declared his goal to be "destroying the liberal progressive socialist machine and its legislative agenda. Klein is just a stepping-stone to that end."

West had made polarizing comments before. In a 2009 interview with the conservative *Weekly Standard*, he said, "There are three words I hate to hear used. I hate 'big tent.' I hate 'inclusiveness.' And I hate 'outreach.' I think you stand on the principles that make you great, which transcend everybody in America, and people will come to it." At a public forum in March 2010, West claimed that Islam is not a religion, and called it a "very vile and very vicious enemy that we have allowed to come in this country because we ride around with bumper stickers that say 'Coexist.' " In an interview with conservative radio host Michael Savage, West called President Barack Obama "the dumbest person walking around in America right now."

Klein did his best to focus attention to West's edgy personality and rhetoric. Even Obama made an appearance in his behalf. Klein touted his support for continuing the Bush-era tax cuts set to expire and he ran ads depicting West as "too extreme, too dangerous." But the offensive did little to stop West's momentum. He emphasized the area's economic woes under a Democratic administration, which struck a chord with many voters, especially those registering displeasure with Obama in poll after poll. This time, West won by 8 percentage points, beating Klein 54% to 46%.

TWENTY-THIRD DISTRICT

Alcee Hastings (D)

Elected 1992, 10th term; b. Sept. 5, 1936, Altamonte Springs; home, Miramar; Fisk U., B.A. 1958, Howard U., 1958-60, FLA&M, J.D. 1963; Methodist; single; 3 children.

Elected Office: Broward Cnty. Circuit Court judge, 1977–79.

Professional Career: Practicing atty., 1964–77; Federal judge, U.S. District Court, 1979–89.

DC Office: 2353 RHOB, 20515, 202-225-1313; Fax: 202-225-1171; Web site: alceehastings.house.gov.

State Offices: Ft. Lauderdale, 954-733-2800; Mangonia Park, 561-881-9618.

Committees: *Rules.*

Group Ratings

	ACLU	ACU	ADA	CFG	AFS	FRC	LCV	ITIC	NTU	COC
2010	100	5	85	3	100	6	90	50	6	25
2009	–	0	95	0	100	–	79	–	1	36

National Journal Ratings

	2010 LIB	—	2010 CONS	2009 LIB	—	2009 CONS
Economic	75%	—	25%	91%	—	0%
Social	75%	—	25%	89%	—	0%
Foreign	90%	—	9%	83%	—	16%
Composite	80%	—	20%	91%	—	9%

Key Votes of the 111th Congress

1. Overturn Ledbetter	Y	5. Bar federal abortion funds	N	9. Stop detainee transfers	*
2. Pass $820 billion stimulus	Y	6. Pass health care bill	Y	10. Legalize immigrants' kids	Y
3. Let guns in national parks	N	7. Regulate financial firms	Y	11. Repeal don't ask, tell	Y
4. Pass cap-and-trade	*	8. Pass tax cuts for some	*	12. Limit campaign funds	N

Election Results

2010 general	Alcee Hastings (D)	100,066	(79%)	($780,445)
	Bernard Sansaricq (R)	26,414	(21%)	($105,750)
2010 primary	Alcee Hastings (D)	unopposed		

Prior Winning Percentages: 2008 (82%), 2006 (100%), 2004 (100%), 2002 (77%), 2000 (76%), 1998 (100%), 1996 (73%), 1994 (100%), 1992 (59%)

Population		Race/Ethnicity		Work	
Pop. 2010:	684,107	White:	22.6%	Private:	81.6%
Change since 2000:	Up 7.0%	Black:	54.9%	Government:	12.7%
Urban:	97.9%	Hispanic:	18.4%	Self-employed:	5.6%
Rural:	2.1%	Asian:	1.7%	Blue collar:	22.9%
Area size:	3,703 sq. mi.	Native Am.:	0.3%	White collar:	48.2%
		Hawaiian:	0.0%	Khaki collar:	0.1%
Age		Two+ races:	1.7%	Other:	28.8%
Median age:	33.9 yrs.				
More than 65 yrs:	11.1%	*Ancestry*		Median income:	$37,974
Less than 18 yrs:	26.1%	West Indian	19.0%	Median Home Value:	$189,300
		German	4.2%		
Education		Irish	3.8%	**Military Veterans**	
H.S. grad:	74.6%			% of Pop:	6.4%
College grad:	16.9%				
Grad degree:	5.0%				

South Florida; Part Fort Lauderdale

In the morning shadow of the high-rise condo-miniums that line the Atlantic Ocean, behind the quiet waters that separate the barrier islands from the mainland and a few blocks off old U.S. 1, are the African-American neighborhoods of South Florida's Gold Coast. They are gatherings of older stucco homes and commercial storefronts, ranging from upper-middle-class enclaves to rundown slums. These neighborhoods, populated by the working poor and with relatively few seniors, are bypassed by most tourists.

The 23rd Congressional District of Florida gathers together many of South Florida's black neighborhoods in a geographically contrived, but demographically coherent, constituency. Geographically, most of the district is in the Everglades, east and south of Lake Okeechobee. This is a land of swamps and drainage canals, with some farms and citrus groves. Some people live in migrant worker camps, some on the Miccosukee Indian Reservation, and some in places like Southwest Ranches, a community where residents have opposed roads and street lights. The district has four narrow tentacles that extend east from the Everglades and get close to, but never reach, the Atlantic Ocean. The northernmost section stretches into St. Lucie County and takes in black neighborhoods in Fort Pierce. In northern Palm Beach County, a tentacle reaches past high-income Wellington into West Palm Beach, and then continues south along the railroad tracks and U.S. 1 to Delray Beach, which was the site of a civil rights showdown in 1956 and now has a large Haitian community. Census officials say the area is one of the nation's most difficult to accurately count, with heavy concentrations of poor people and immigrants who don't speak English.

The most populated tentacle reaches east into Broward County to take in African-American areas in Lauderhill, Fort Lauderdale, Pompano Beach, and Deerfield Beach. Farther south in Broward County, a smaller tentacle reaches into parts of fast-growing Miramar and Pembroke Pines, home to upwardly mobile Haitians and also to one of the Century Village communities, the retirement development known for its politically powerful, liberal associations led by "condo commandos." But in some parts of Pembroke Pines and Sunrise, Hispanics from Miami-Dade County are replacing Jews. Overall, the population is 55% black and 18% Hispanic. This is a heavily Democratic district, with incoming Cubans providing the only minor countertrend. But it is not uniformly liberal on all issues. In 2008, African-American voters backed a state constitutional amendment banning same-sex marriage by about 2-to-1, enabling it to carry Broward County despite its large gay population.

Alcee Hastings (D)

The congressman from the 23rd District is Alcee Hastings, a Democrat first elected in 1992. Hastings had a relatively wide-ranging upbringing in the segregated America of the post-World War II decades. He grew up in a black suburb of Orlando and moved as a child to Jersey City and New York, where his parents worked as domestic servants for a rich Jewish family. He recalls attending a bar mitzvah as a guest. He also attended a Rosenwald school in Altamonte Springs, one of hundreds established for Southern blacks by Sears executive Julius Rosenwald. He graduated from Fisk University in Nashville and from Florida A&M law school in Tallahassee. From those beginnings, he made a rapid ascent, practicing law in Fort Lauderdale and finishing fourth in the five-candidate Democratic primary when he ran for the U.S. Senate in 1970, at age 34. He became a state judge in Broward County in 1977 and was appointed a federal judge in 1979.

Then his career took a sharp turn downward. He was charged with conspiring with a friend to take a $150,000 bribe and give two convicted swindlers light sentences. A Miami jury acquitted Hastings in 1983, but the friend was convicted. The 11th Circuit Court of Appeals called for impeachment in 1987 and referred the case to Congress. Hastings was impeached by the U.S. House on a vote of 413-3 and convicted by the Senate 69-26. In the House, Democratic Rep. John Conyers of Michigan, senior member of the Congressional Black Caucus, made the case for impeachment. As a footnote, during a 1997 investigation into the Federal Bureau of Investigation crime lab, the Department of Justice found that an agent falsely testified against Hastings. He and Conyers moved to reopen the case, but nothing came of it.

After his removal from the bench, Hastings in 1990 ran an abortive campaign for governor, and then lost in a primary for secretary of state. When the 23rd District was created in 1992, he ran to represent it and led in the primary 28%-27%. In the October runoff, he faced Palm Beach County legislator Lois Frankel, who blasted Hastings for his record. He responded, "The bitch is a racist." Hastings was helped by a ruling by federal Judge Stanley Sporkin that his removal from office was invalid since the full Senate did not hear the charges. The Supreme Court later ruled to the contrary in a case of another convicted federal judge in 1993, but by that time Hastings was in Congress. He won the runoff 58%-42%, with voting closely following racial lines. He won the general election 59%-31%. Since then, he has not had a serious primary or general election challenge.

In the House, Hastings' voting record has been mostly liberal, but toward the center on foreign policy. He opposed the use of force in Iraq, voted against legislation to increase spending for Afghanistan and has been a strong supporter of Israel. Pro-Israel groups are among his most prominent campaign contributors. He told *The Palm Beach Post* in May 2007: "There is a nexus between Jews and blacks by virtue of the Holocaust and by virtue of slavery which, independent of each other, were horrible events that humankind does not want to happen again."

In 2004, with the support of then Republican Speaker Dennis Hastert, he was elected president of the Organization for Security and Cooperation in the pan-European Parliamentary Assembly and served two one-year terms. In 2007, he became chairman of the counterpart U.S. commission. In 2006, the House passed his resolution condemning Iran for hosting a conference on Holocaust denial. The next year, Hastings pressed for the opening of Holocaust archives in Bad Arolsen, Germany, and three weeks later, the archives were opened. As head of the OSC, he monitored the elections in Georgia in January 2008. However, he drew the attention of ethics investigators in 2010 over whether he exceeded foreign travel stipends. He told *The Wall Street Journal* that he was generous in giving money to people he encountered and said: "You are all concerned about nickels and dimes, and I'm not. You know, in a taxicab in Kazakhstan, I don't have time to get a receipt—I don't speak Kazakh."

After the 2006 election, he was seriously considered for chairman of the House Intelligence Committee. He had support from the Congressional Black Caucus but was opposed by the Blue Dogs and others who maintained that his controversial past disqualified him from such an assignment. Hastings attacked his critics as "misinformed fools," but House Speaker Nancy Pelosi nevertheless selected Texas Democrat Silvestre Reyes. However, Hastings does have a seat on the Rules Committee, an influential post that gives him a hand in setting the terms for bringing bills to the floor. He irked conservatives in 2010 for his defense of a controversial "deem and pass" strategy for the health care overhaul that was briefly considered. He paraphrased an expression of Thomas Edison's: "There aren't no rule around here, we're trying to accomplish something."

Hastings made his mark on some issues of local importance. He sponsored a bill to preserve former stops on the Underground Railroad in Florida and elsewhere. His bill to prevent Haitian illegal immigrants from being routinely deported received little support in September 2008, but when hurricanes hit Haiti, he successfully pressed Homeland Security Secretary Michael Chertoff to delay deportations for two months. He pressed the issue again in 2010 following the country's devastating earthquake.

Taking an original stand, Hastings in June 2008 called for a commission to consider expanding the size of the House beyond 435 members. That number, he pointed out, was established by statute in 1929 and can be changed by an act of Congress. He said there were too many constituents in each district for lawmakers to serve them adequately. In recent years he also joined gay activists in calling for an end to the military's "don't ask, don't tell" policy that he considered discriminatory.

TWENTY-FOURTH DISTRICT
Sandy Adams (R)

Elected 2010, 1st full term; b. Dec. 14, 1956, Wyandotte, MI; home, Orlando; Columbia Col., Orlando, B.A. 2000.; Episcopalian; Married (John); 3 children.

Military Career: Air Force, 1974-75.

Elected Office: FL House, 2002-10.

Professional Career: Dep. sheriff, Orange Cnty. Sheriff's Dept., 1985-2002.

DC Office: 216 CHOB, 20515, 202-225-2706; Fax: 202-226-6299; Web site: adams.house.gov.

State Offices: Oviedo, 407-977-7601; Port Orange, 386-756-9798.

Committees: *Judiciary:* Crime, Terrorism & Homeland Security; Intellectual Property, Competition & the Internet. *Science & Technology:* Investigations & Oversight; Space & Aeronautics.

Election Results
2010 general	Sandy Adams (R)	146,129	(60%)	($1,328,778)
	Suzanne Kosmas (D)	98,787	(40%)	($2,540,354)
2010 primary	Sandy Adams (R)	19,898	(30%)	
	Karen Diebel (R)	19,355	(29%)	
	Craig Miller (R)	18,282	(28%)	
	Tom Garcia (R)	6,446	(10%)	

Population		Race/Ethnicity		Work	
Pop. 2010:	799,233	White:	70.1%	Private:	82.1%
Change since 2000:	Up 25.0%	Black:	8.1%	Government:	12.9%
Urban:	91.2%	Hispanic:	16.3%	Self-employed:	4.9%
Rural:	8.8%	Asian:	3.2%	Blue collar:	17.0%
Area size:	1,912 sq. mi.	Native Am.:	0.2%	White collar:	65.0%
		Hawaiian:	0.1%	Khaki collar:	0.1%
Age		Two+ races:	1.8%	Other:	17.8%
Median age:	38.8 yrs.				
More than 65 yrs:	14.7%	Ancestry		Median income:	$54,224
Less than 18 yrs:	21.8%	German	11.8%	Median Home Value:	$223,300
		Irish	10.3%		
Education		English	8.7%	Military Veterans	
H.S. grad:	90.0%			% of Pop:	12.6%
College grad:	28.1%				
Grad degree:	9.3%				

Central Florida; Orlando suburbs

In 1960, central Florida was a sleepy place. Orlando was a small city surrounded by citrus groves. The Atlantic coast from Cape Canaveral north was a quiet winter-vacation spot, with small motels lining U.S. 1 and the beach. Then two outsiders—President John F. Kennedy and Walt Disney—transformed this part of America, making it in two different ways a leader in the world. Kennedy promised in 1961 to put a man on the moon before the end of the decade, and the Kennedy Space Center was built on an island near Cape Canaveral. The Space Coast was created. In 1971, Disney opened Disney World southwest of Orlando, near the intersection of Interstate 4 and Florida's turnpike. Other theme parks followed, and metro Orlando became the nation's No. 1 tourist destination. In the process, the populations of metro Orlando and the Space Coast have more than quadrupled since 1960. People from all over the United States, and more recently, immigrants from Latin America, have come in large numbers; with the aid of ubiquitous air conditioning, they have transformed sleepy backwaters into vibrant metropolitan areas. This part of Florida

2008 Presidential Vote
John McCain (R)	193,808	(51%)
Barack Obama (D)	186,825	(49%)

2004 Presidential Vote
George Bush (R)	188,973	(55%)
John Kerry (D)	153,130	(45%)

Cook Partisan Voting Index: R+4

has attracted many more young families and people in their working years than retirees. With a diversified economy and continuing tourism, metro Orlando has been hit less hard by the recession than other parts of Florida. But Brevard County's economy has been lagging, and the shutdown of the Space Shuttle program, scheduled for 2011, threatened up to 8,000 local aerospace jobs.

The 24th Congressional District of Florida has about half its population in the Orlando area, much of it in affluent Orange and Seminole county suburbs north and northeast of Orlando. It takes in all of Oviedo and parts of Maitland and Altamonte Springs. The other half of the district is on the coast. The 24th covers nearly 80 miles of coastline and encompasses the northern half of Brevard County, including the main grounds of the Space Center, the Canaveral National Seashore, and the county seat of Titusville. The 24th also takes in the southern half of Volusia County, including part of Daytona Beach, where NASCAR is a big employer. Also in the district is New Smyrna Beach. The 24th is as close as Florida gets to a typical suburban district. There are higher than average numbers of homeowners, families with children, working women, and white-collar employees. This was designed by Republican legislators to be a Republican district, but after voting 55% for George W. Bush in 2004, it voted only 51% for John McCain in 2008.

Sandy Adams (R)

The new congresswoman from the 24th District is Sandy Adams, a Republican who defeated freshman Democrat Suzanne Kosmas in 2010. Adams was born in Michigan and grew up in a military household. Her father was a career Navy sailor who served during World War II as a chief petty officer, and her mother was a homemaker. The family moved to Florida in 1964. Her older brother dropped out of high school to join the Army at the height of the Vietnam War; Adams followed in his footsteps, dropping out of school at 17 to join the Air Force and serving as an aircraft electrician. Adams received her high school equivalency degree in 1983, and in 2000, she earned a bachelor's degree in criminal justice administration from Columbia College, a private school based in Missouri that has satellite campuses in Florida. In 1985, Adams joined the Orange County Sheriff's Office, where she was an investigator and deputy sheriff for 17 years. In 1989, her husband, fellow Deputy Sheriff Frank Seton, died in a helicopter accident during a search for a shooting suspect.

After Seton's death, Adams became active in victim's rights groups. Over time, she says, she came to believe that the Florida legislature was not doing enough to protect victims. In 2002, she ran for and won a seat in the state House. (Adams remarried in 2001, to Circuit Court Judge John Adams.) In the legislature, Adams focused on criminal-justice issues, sponsoring a bill to make hiring illegal immigrants more difficult. Adams also co-sponsored a bill that would have allowed Florida voters to decide by ballot whether they wanted to abide by the health care law passed by Congress in 2010. Her bill was overturned in a state court.

In the 2010 election season, she challenged Kosmas, whose election in 2008 was viewed in part as a voter backlash against Republicans in the wake of a corruption scandal involving her predecessor, GOP Rep. Tom Feeney. Adams faced a crowded field in the Republican primary, but with the support of tea party groups, she narrowly defeated businesswoman Karen Diebel and businessman Craig Miller. Her campaign focused on dramatically limiting the size of government, but she also enthusiastically supported federal funds for NASA, which is important to the economy of Central Florida. In an interview with *The Orlando Sentinel*, Adams questioned whether the federal departments of Education, Energy, and the Interior are authorized by the Constitution.

In the general election, Kosmas ran ads calling Adams's views "strange" and "crazy." She charged that Adams wanted to repeal the 17th Amendment providing for the direct election of U.S. senators. Kosmas also ran ads hammering her opponent for supporting a proposed "fair tax," which would replace the federal income tax with a 23% sales tax. The ad failed to mention that the policy would eliminate income taxes and it featured an elderly woman saying of Adams's proposal, "I'll be a dead duck because I won't be able to afford anything."

In turn, Adams attacked Kosmas for supporting President Obama's health care overhaul. But after the bruising primary, her campaign was low on cash and unable to afford to air many commercials. At the end of September, Adams had raised $943,000, less than half of Kosmas' $2.4 million. (Overall, Adams raised $1.3 million for both the primary and general.) Outside groups such as the anti-tax Club for Growth and U.S. Chamber of Commerce stepped in, spending heavily in support of Adams. In an ominous sign for an incumbent, the Democratic Congressional Campaign Committee canceled its spending for Kosmas in mid-October to focus on Democrats with a better chance of winning. Adams trounced Kosmas, 60%-40%.

TWENTY-FIFTH DISTRICT

David Rivera (R)

Elected 2010, 1st full term; b. Sept. 16, 1965, New York, NY; home, Doral; FL Intl. U., B.A. 1986, M.P.A. 1994.; Catholic; Single.

Elected Office: FL House, 2002-10.

Professional Career: Miami-Dade Cnty. dir., Sen. Connie Mack, R-Fla., 1988; public affairs dir., Valladares Foundation; writer, researcher, Cuban American Natl. Foundation; special asst., St. Dept. Office of Cuba Broadcasting, 1991-99; political affairs dir., FL Repub. Party, 1999-2002.

DC Office: 417 CHOB, 20515, 202-225-2778; Fax: 202-226-0346; Web site: rivera.house.gov.

State Offices: Collier County, 239-348-1620; Miami, 305-222-0160.

Committees: *Foreign Affairs:* Oversight & Investigations; Western Hemisphere. *Natural Resources:* Energy & Mineral Resources; National Parks, Forests & Public Lands.

Election Results

2010 general	David Rivera (R)	74,859	(52%)	($1,895,640)
	Joe Garcia (D)	61,138	(43%)	($1,662,117)
	Roly Arrojo (Tea)	4,312	(3%)	
	Craig Porter (FWP)	3,244	(2%)	
2010 primary	David Rivera (R)	19,228	(63%)	
	Paul Crespo (R)	8,158	(27%)	
	Mariana Cancio (R)	3,272	(11%)	

Population		Race/Ethnicity		Work	
Pop. 2010:	807,176	White:	16.8%	Private:	81.5%
Change since 2000:	Up 26.3%	Black:	8.9%	Government:	12.0%
Urban:	94.4%	Hispanic:	71.6%	Self-employed:	6.4%
Rural:	5.6%	Asian:	1.5%	Blue collar:	19.5%
Area size:	4,724 sq. mi.	Native Am.:	0.1%	White collar:	60.5%
		Hawaiian:	0.0%	Khaki collar:	0.1%
Age		Two+ races:	0.8%	Other:	19.9%
Median age:	34.9 yrs.				
More than 65 yrs:	10.3%	*Ancestry*		Median income:	$54,290
Less than 18 yrs:	26.9%	USA	4.1%	Median Home Value:	$286,700
		West Indian	3.8%		
Education		German	3.1%	**Military Veterans**	
H.S. grad:	77.8%			% of Pop:	4.1%
College grad:	24.1%				
Grad degree:	7.8%				

South Florida; Everglades

An interconnected sea of wetlands once covered 8.9 million acres of southern Florida, stretching from present-day Orlando to the peninsula's southern tip. It was once a coherent ecosystem, a "river of grass" in which water moved slowly down a gentle slope to the ocean. It buffered plants and animals from meteorological extremes and provided different micro-environments for flora and fauna based on an inch or two of variation in elevation. It was long a dream of Florida's white settlers to make it more useful, but for decades, this goal proved elusive. It took three attempts between 1915 and the late 1920s to build the Tamiami Trail from Miami to Tampa. To this day, it is one of only two roads that cross the South Florida interior from coast to coast. Over time, people managed to reshape the Everglades. In 1948, Congress approved the Central and South Florida Project, which authorized the construction of 1,000 miles of canals and 720 miles of levees to channel and drain the Everglades. Since then, about half of the original ecosystem has

2008 Presidential Vote

John McCain (R)	130,062	(50%)
Barack Obama (D)	127,910	(49%)

2004 Presidential Vote

George Bush (R)	122,342	(56%)
John Kerry (D)	95,001	(44%)

Cook Partisan Voting Index: R+5

been turned over to agriculture and housing, and the amount of water discharged into the ocean has fallen by 70%.

In recent years, Floridians have had second thoughts about taming the Everglades. In 2000, Congress passed a law to restore the land in 16 counties, authorizing $7.8 billion over 30 years. In 2002, President George W. Bush and his brother Jeb Bush, the governor of Florida, signed an agreement to proceed. After a slow start, initial steps have included a huge storage reservoir and a safety valve to protect Lake Okeechobee and its dikes. In 2008, the South Florida Water Management District approved Republican Gov. Charlie Crist's proposal to buy much of the land owned by U.S. Sugar Corp. around Lake Okeechobee for $1.35 billion, with most farming to be phased out within seven years. That would allow water to pass over land from the lake, through the Everglades, to the Gulf of Mexico. But the recession forced Crist to scale back the project to $533 million, with a 10-year option to buy the remaining acreage.

The 25th Congressional District of Florida sprawls almost all the way across this uninhabitable portion of South Florida, connecting population centers near, but not on, each of Florida's two coasts. About 13% of its residents live in Collier County, in new housing wedged between decidedly upscale and artsy Naples and the wild Everglades, and in the farm town of Immokalee, where an estimated 80% of workers are illegal immigrants. The large majority of the district's residents live on the western and southern edges of metropolitan Miami, mostly close to the swamps. Here one can drive out on roads past the subdivisions and find strawberry, tomato, and citrus farms. The trees thin out, and then the road just ends where the Everglades begin.

The towns in the northern part of Miami-Dade are heavily Cuban and Latino—Hialeah Gardens, Tamiami, Kendale Lakes, South Miami Heights and Cutler Ridge. The county itself is 65% Hispanic. Farther south, the 25th takes in low-income agricultural areas along South Dixie Highway (U.S. 1), like Princeton and Naranja, as well as a few older tourist attractions like the Metrozoo, the Monkey Jungle and Coral Castle. Even farther south is Homestead, which was leveled by Hurricane Andrew in 1992 and has since been redeveloped with housing, shops, hospitals, parks, and schools, plus a Coast Guard base. NASCAR has an annual race at the speedway. By 2007, Homestead was the fastest-growing town in Florida, with large Mexican and Cuban populations. Politically, this area leans Republican, thanks to the allegiance of its many Cuban-Americans, though this is the least Cuban of the three South Florida districts that have Hispanic majorities.

David Rivera (R)

The new congressman from the 25th District is David Rivera, a Republican who succeeded GOP Rep. Mario Diaz-Balart, who vacated the seat to run in the neighboring 21st District. Originally from New York City, Rivera is the second child of Cuban exiles. His mother ran a driving school and his father was a taxi driver. They divorced when Rivera was 2 years old, and he moved to Florida with his mother and sister when he was 9. He considered a career in sportswriting but decided to pursue politics after volunteering for Ronald Reagan's presidential campaign when he was in the ninth grade. He attended Florida International University, where he received an undergraduate degree in political science in 1986 and a master's in public administration in 1994. In college, he played Chino in the musical *West Side Story*.

Rivera began his political career in 1988 as political director for Jack Kemp's presidential campaign. He was a legislative aide to former Sen. Connie Mack, R-Fla., and was political director for Miami-Dade County during Mack's successful 1988 campaign. Rivera came to Washington to serve as a writer and researcher for the Cuban American National Foundation, an organization that seeks to overthrow the government of Fidel Castro. He also worked as public-affairs director for the Valladares Foundation, an international human-rights watch group. When he ran for the House, Rivera was the chairman of the Republican Party of Miami-Dade. He is also a close friend of new GOP Sen. Marco Rubio. In 2002, Rivera won a seat in the Florida House, where he eventually chaired the Appropriations Committee. In office, he pushed to establish a law school and medical school at his alma mater, Florida International University, and supported a sales tax holiday for back-to-school shopping. He also championed a ban on using tax money to fund Florida university students' research trips to Cuba.

The 25th District seat came open when incumbent Rep. Mario Diaz-Balart decided to move to a more GOP-friendly district, the neighboring 21st, which was represented by his older brother, Lincoln Diaz-Balart, who announced his retirement in 2010. Rivera easily won the Republican primary in August to succeed Diaz-Balart, drawing 62% of the vote. In the general election, he had a much tougher time getting by Democrat Joe Garcia, who had come within 6 percentage points of defeating Mario Diaz-Balart two years earlier.

The race devolved into several solid weeks of mudslinging. Garcia honed in on Rivera's personal finances, alleging he falsely claimed on financial disclosure forms that he had worked for the U.S. Agency for International Development. The agency told *The Miami Herald* it had no record of hiring Rivera or any affiliated firms. Rivera explained that he actually had worked for a USAID subcontractor, but provided no evidence of that arrangement. A county judge dismissed a lawsuit by Garcia's allies seeking to remove Rivera from the ballot. Garcia also highlighted a 2002 incident in which Rivera's car forced a truck carrying campaign fliers for a political opponent off the road. Rivera issued a statement saying that the mailers falsely accused him of being the target of a domestic violence complaint, which he said actually involved another man of the same name. *The Herald* interviewed the woman, who confirmed that the incident involved a different David Rivera.

For his part, Rivera called Garcia a Castro sympathizer, a charge that resonated with older Cuban-American voters. Garcia supported increased engagement with Cuba, in line with the thinking of second-generation Cuban-Americans who are not as anti-Castro as their parents and grandparents. Republicans also slammed Garcia for accepting campaign contributions from companies that charter flights to Cuba and would benefit from an easing of U.S. travel and trade restrictions. Both candidates spent heavily on a negative ad war, with Rivera raising $1.9 million and Garcia $1.7 million. On Election Day, Rivera prevailed, 52%-43%.

But his respite from negative headlines was brief. *The Herald* reported in January 2011 that Rivera was under investigation by local and state police agencies for his alleged ties to a company called Millennium Marketing, which was paid $510,000 in 2006 by the Flagler Dog Track to lobby for voter approval for slot machines at dog tracks. Rivera told the Associated Press that Millennium Marketing was owned by his 70-year-old mother and his godmother. He did not disclose income from Millennium or the dog track on financial disclosure forms from 2006 to 2010. Still, Rivera filed new disclosure forms with the House listing a $137,000 loan from Millennium.

★ GEORGIA ★

Metro Atlanta spreads out over the red clay hills of 28 of Georgia's 159 counties, and has been one of America's great boom areas over the last two decades. It has also been the site of one of the great political transformations of the first decade of the 21st century. From 2000 to 2010, Georgia's population grew by 18%, a rate just behind North Carolina and ahead of Florida. Over that decade, it passed New Jersey to become the nation's ninth-largest state, and it is closing in on eighth-ranked Michigan. Metro Atlanta grew by 24% from 2000 to 2010, from 4.24 million to 5.26 million. Growth slowed in the 2007-09 recession, unemployment rose and foreclosures became frequent, but the impact of two decades of rapid growth remains pervasive. Atlanta and Georgia have been in many ways, for many years, the center of the South, at least since Gen. William Tecumseh Sherman marched here in 1864. This is where John Stith Pemberton invented Coca-Cola, where Margaret Mitchell wrote *Gone With the Wind*, where Martin Luther King Jr. grew up, and where most of the civil rights organizations that changed America were headquartered. But in population and reputation, Georgia for decades was outdazzled nationally by other parts of the South—by Texas with its oil wells and high-tech industries, by Florida with Miami Beach and Disney World, and even by North Carolina with its Research Triangle and college basketball champions.

Neither Atlanta's rise to world eminence nor its role as the "capital" of the South was inevitable. Georgia was the last of the seaboard colonies, founded by James Oglethorpe in 1733 as an "asylum of the unfortunate," reserved for debtors and other outcasts from England. Oglethorpe forbade slavery, but the settlers rebelled and repealed his ban in 1750. Atlanta was only a small, though strategic, railroad crossroads when it was burned by Sherman's Union troops on their "march to the sea." Richmond, Charleston, and New Orleans all had stronger claims to being the central focus of the South a century ago. But in the 20th century, two figures imprinted Atlanta on the national imagination. One was Mitchell, whose 1936 novel inspired the 1939 movie of the same name. The other was King, who was based in Atlanta for most of his career and who ultimately led the civil rights revolution that changed the South and the nation. Linking the two was Atlanta's business community, notably Robert Woodruff, who headed Coca-Cola from 1932 to 1960 and made Coke a worldwide enterprise. Perhaps aware that a world company could not indefinitely be associated with racial segregation, Woodruff and William Hartsfield, the city's mayor from 1937 to 1961, cooperated with black leaders and promoted Atlanta as "the city too busy to hate." Hartsfield's successor, Ivan Allen, elected in 1961 and 1965, supported the Civil Rights Act of 1964, as Peachtree Center and the first atriumed Hyatt Regency were going up in downtown Atlanta. It's fitting that Atlanta's airport, the busiest in the world, is named for Hartsfield and Maynard Jackson, Atlanta's first African-American mayor.

This new Atlanta was growing up amid a mostly rural, deeply segregationist Georgia that as late as 1960 cast the second-highest Democratic percentage of any state for president. Hatred of Sherman was still strong 96 years later. Political contests typically matched Atlanta-supported moderates against rural-supported segregationists, and the latter invariably won. Georgia's electoral votes were cast for Barry Goldwater in 1964 and George Wallace in 1968. Then came change in the person of Jimmy Carter, a one-term state senator who was elected governor in 1970 with a rural base as well as conspicuous black support. On taking office, he proclaimed a reconciliation of the races and installed a portrait of King in the state capitol. Carter thus became one of the first politicians from the rural South to celebrate and honor the civil-rights movement, and in the process, set himself on the road to being elected president in 1976.

Since then, Georgia and Atlanta have seen an in-migration of African-Americans. The state's population was 31% black in 2010, a rate higher than any other state except Mississippi and Louisiana. The presence of nine historically black colleges, and of large numbers of prominent black public officials and businessmen have made metro Atlanta in some sense the capital of black America. There has been a major migration of black Americans from the big cities of California, the Northeast and the industrial Midwest to metro Atlanta, which, with its Southern culture, attractive and inexpensive housing and fast-growing suburbs, is a congenial place to live. Georgia has four black Democratic representatives, two from non-black-majority districts, and Andrew Young was elected in a white-majority district as long ago as 1972. Georgia also elected its first black Republican state representative since Reconstruction in 2004. It has been attracting immigrants, and 9% of its residents in 2010 were Hispanic and 3% were Asian—quite a change over the past quarter-century. And it has been attracting significant numbers of internal migrants from the United States: Domestic inflow from 2000 to 2008 was 7% of the 2000 population. These newcomers were attracted

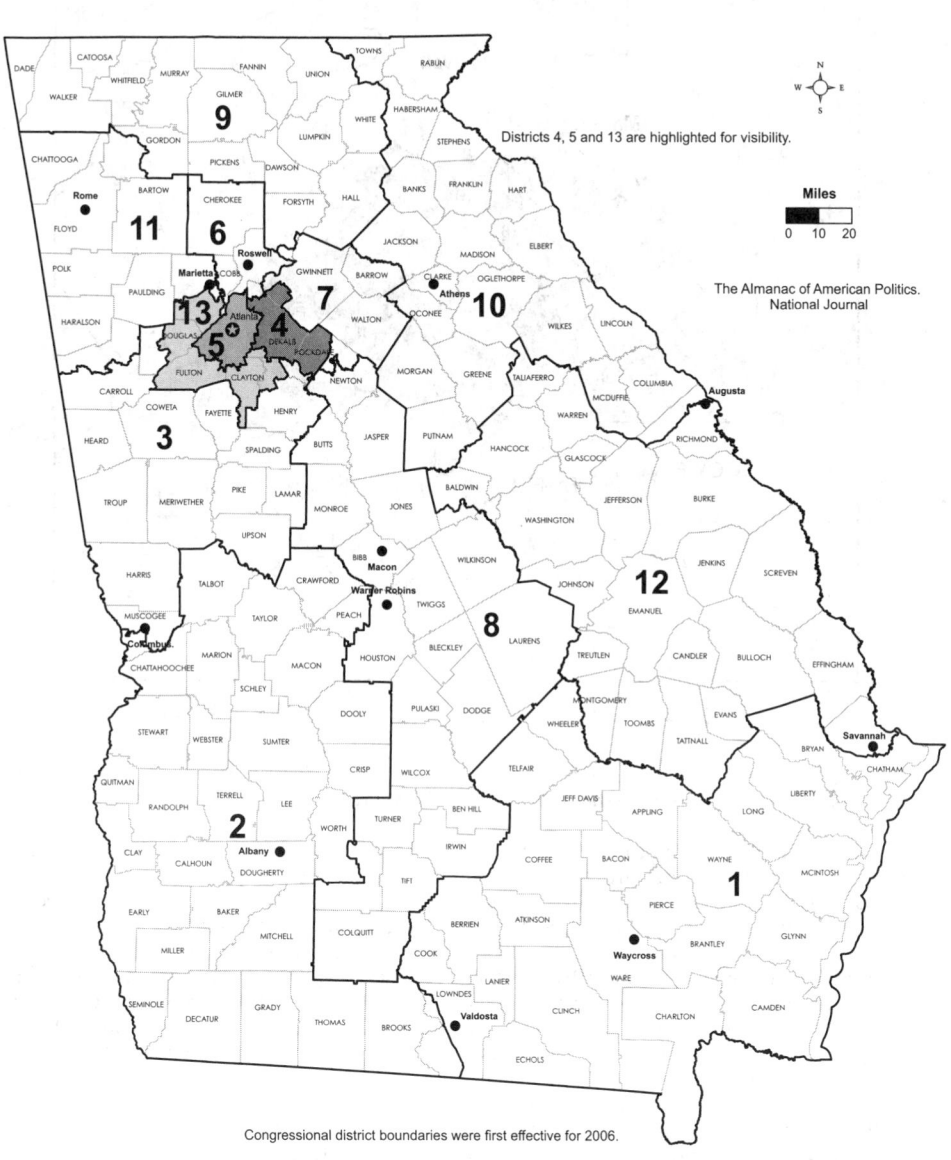

Districts 4, 5 and 13 are highlighted for visibility.

Miles

0   10   20

The Almanac of American Politics.
National Journal

Congressional district boundaries were first effective for 2006.

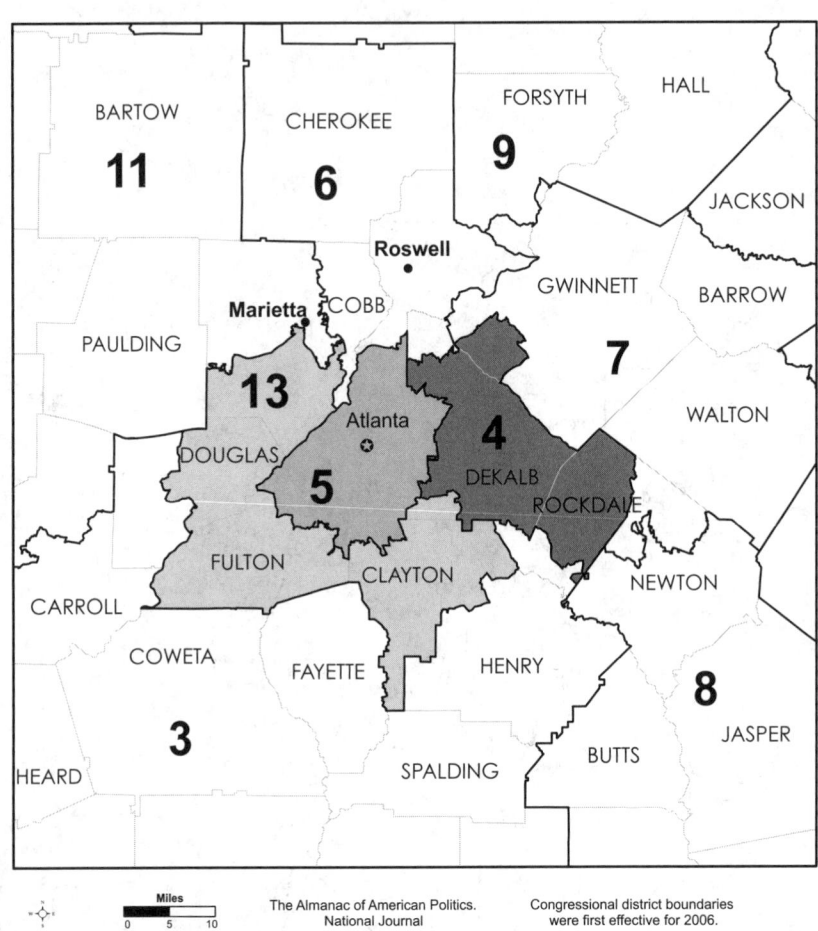

The Almanac of American Politics.
National Journal

Congressional district boundaries
were first effective for 2006.

Miles
0   5   10

by Georgia's vibrant private sector economy. At the same time, few native-born Georgians leave. The proportion of people born in the state who still live there is higher than in any other states but North Carolina and Texas.

Demographic change and economic change in Georgia have been followed by political change, to the point that this once heavily Democratic state now seems to be, despite increasing black voter turnout, solidly Republican. In retrospect, this change was a long time coming. It was delayed by the presence of politically skillful Democrats, from Georgia and other parts of the South, with rural bases: Wallace, who carried the state in 1968; Carter, who sent it in a different direction in 1970 and carried it solidly in 1976 and 1980; Carter's successors as governor, each of whom served for eight years—George Busbee, Joe Frank Harris, and Zell Miller; and Bill Clinton, who carried the state 43.5%-42.9% in 1992 and lost it by only 47%-46% in 1996. The year 2000 signaled a change. George W. Bush carried Georgia by a solid 55%-43%. Bush carried metro Atlanta (which cast 53% of the state's votes) by 52%-45% and the rest of Georgia, historically Democratic, by a resounding 57%-41%. The memory of William Tecumseh Sherman was dead.

The Republican trend has continued in elections since, with a weak Democratic countertrend in 2008. In 2002, incumbent Democratic Gov. Roy Barnes, with a $19 million campaign chest, was beaten by Republican Sonny Perdue, 51%-46%. And incumbent Democratic Sen. Max Cleland, a wounded Vietnam veteran, who had won by 1% six years before, lost to Republican Rep. Saxby Chambliss 53%-46%. The Republican trend continued in 2004, as Democratic Sen. Zell Miller, about to retire from office, denounced his party in his book *A National Party No More*. He endorsed Bush for re-election and gave a rip-roaring speech at the Republican National Convention. Though Georgia was not a target state in 2004, turnout rose 28%, and Bush beat John Kerry 58%-41%. In the Senate contest that year, Republican Johnny Isakson beat Democratic Rep. Denise Majette by an almost identical 58%-40%. Republicans increased their majority in the state Senate to 34-22 and transformed the state House from a 102-77 Democratic majority to a 99-80-1 Republican majority. The reign of Tom Murphy, the House speaker for 30 years and the force behind the 2002 Democratic redistricting plan, was over. The Republican legislature passed a tough law on illegal immigration, requiring employers to consult a federal database when hiring, and required welfare recipients to prove their legal status. They cut income, corporate, and property taxes. And they passed their own partisan districting plan for Georgia's 13 congressional districts.

For many years, Georgia shunned Republican presidential candidates even when states less ravaged by Gen. Sherman's troops, like next-door South Carolina and Alabama, embraced them. It was the second-most Democratic state for John F. Kennedy in 1960, but it also voted for opponents of the Civil Rights Act—Barry Goldwater in 1964 and George Wallace in 1968. It voted heavily Republican only in 1972, 1984, and 1988. Then, in 2000 and 2004, Georgia, both in metro Atlanta and the counties beyond, voted solidly for Bush. The 2008 elections saw Georgia swinging some distance, but not fully, toward the Democrats. It was not exactly a target state in the presidential election, but Democratic nominee Barack Obama's campaign set up 25 offices in the state and worked to turn out rural as well as urban blacks. African-American turnout rose from 25% of the total in 2004 to 30% in 2008. There were particularly sharp increases in turnout in rapidly growing black and Latino suburbs. As a result, Georgia, which had long had one of the nation's lowest voting participation rates, moved up toward the national average.

But even with increased black turnout, Republicans have still carried the state. John McCain won here 52%-47%, with Obama carrying metro Atlanta 51%-48%. Outside metro Atlanta, McCain won 58%-41%, but these 131 counties cast only 43% of the vote, a historic low. Obama carried 98% of black voters; McCain won 76% of white voters. Democratic Senate nominee Jim Martin held Chambliss to a 49.8%-46.8% edge, requiring a runoff. In that December contest, turnout was down 43%, and Chambliss won 57%-43%. In 2010, black turnout remained high, but Republicans won up and down the line. Sen. Johnny Isakson was re-elected 58%-39%, and Republican Nathan Deal, despite ethics questions hovering over him, beat former Gov. Roy Barnes, probably the most formidable possible Democratic candidate, by a 53%-43% margin. Deal carried metro Atlanta by only 50%-46%, but won 58%-39% in the rest of the state. Republicans won all of the other eight statewide offices for the first time, with percentages ranging from 52%-44% to 56%-40%. They defeated 8th District Rep. Jim Marshall, a Democrat, and increased their majorities in the legislature. It doesn't look like Georgia will be a target state in the 2012 presidential election.

Georgia has one rather unique political problem, and it has to do with water. Since 1989, Georgia has been quarreling with Alabama and Florida over the allocation of water from reservoirs

Population		Household Income		Work	
Pop. 2010:	9,687,653	Under $15k:	14.2%	Private:	77.7%
State rank:	9th	$15k to $50k:	36.6%	Government:	16.6%
Change since 2000:	Up 18.3%	$50k to $100k:	30.7%	Self-employed:	5.6%
Urban:	69.6%	$100k to $200k:	14.9%	Unemployment (3-yr. average):	5.7%
Rural:	30.4%	Over $200k:	3.7%	Poverty:	15.3%
Native of state:	55.8%	Median income:	$49,173	Blue collar:	22.7%
Not a citizen:	6.1%			White collar:	60.1%
Area size:	59,425 sq. mi.	**Home Value**		Khaki collar:	0.8%
		Under $100k:	22.7%	Other:	16.4%
Most populous cities		$100k to $300k:	58.3%		
Atlanta	420,003	$300k to $500k:	12.5%	**Age**	
Augusta-Richmond Co.	200,549	$500k to $1 mil:	5.3%	Median age:	34.6 yrs.
Columbus	189,885	Over $1 million:	1.3%	More than 65 yrs:	10.1%
Savannah	136,286	Median:	$165,100	Less than 18 yrs:	26.4%

Race/Ethnicity				Military Veterans		Registered Voters in 2010	
White:	55.9%	*Language*		% of Pop:	9.9%	No Party registration	
Black:	30.0%	English:	87.7%			Voter turnout:	2,622,527
Hispanic:	8.8%	Spanish:	7.2%	*Veterans by Period*		Turnout as % of	
Asian:	3.2%	Asian:	1.9%	WWII and before:	6.6%	voting age:	36.4%
Native Am.:	0.2%	Other European:	2.6%	Korea:	8.3%		
Hawaiian:	0.1%			Vietnam:	32.4%	**Legislature**	
Two+ races:	1.6%	**Education**		Gulf (pre-2001):	16.3%	Senate:	20 D 36 R
		H.S. grad:	83.5%	Gulf (post-2001):	10.5%	House:	66 D 113 R 1 I
Ancestry		College grad:	27.4%	Peace time:	25.8%		
USA	9.3%	Grad degree:	9.7%				
Irish	8.2%						
English	8.0%						

created by federal dams that serve Atlanta and that drain into the other two states. Low rainfall in 2006 and 2007 threatened to dry up lakes Lanier and Allatoona. The three states brought dueling lawsuits, and in April 2008, the Georgia legislature called for restoring the border specified in the act of Congress admitting Tennessee to the Union, which surveyors in 1818 erroneously placed several miles to the south. That would give Georgia access to the waters of the Tennessee River but, as might be expected, Tennessee Gov. Phil Bredesen wants nothing to do with the proposal. In 2009, a federal judge ruled that metro Atlanta has no right to water from lakes Lanier and Allatoona, and gave the state three years to reach agreement with Alabama and Florida.

Presidential politics   Georgia's presidential primary comes early in the cycle and has been of some importance. In 1992, Gov. Zell Miller had it scheduled one week before Super Tuesday in order to help Bill Clinton, and it did: Clinton won solidly to balance losses in Maryland and Colorado the same day. In 1996 and 2000, Georgia was of little importance. In 2004, Democratic hopeful John Edwards of North Carolina visited Georgia five times after the Iowa caucuses and John Kerry only once. But Kerry beat Edwards 47%-41%, making it plain that Edwards had no chance to win the nomination and would be hard-pressed to win other Southern states. He withdrew from the race.

For 2008, Georgia moved up its primary to Feb. 5, Super Tuesday. On the Democratic side, it was no contest once black voters swung behind Obama. He beat Hillary Rodham Clinton 66%-31%, as turnout rose sharply to over 1 million, by far the highest ever. Turnout was almost as high,

2008 Presidential Vote		
John McCain (R) 2,048,759	(52%)
Barack Obama (D) 1,844,123	(47%)

2008 Presidential Primary		
Barack Obama (D) 704,247	(66%)
Hillary Clinton (D)................330,026	(31%)

2008 Presidential Primary		
Mike Huckabee (R)................326,874	(34%)
John McCain (R) 304,751	(32%)
Mitt Romney (R)....................290,707	(30%)

2004 Presidential Vote		
George W. Bush (R)............1,914,254	(58%)
John Kerry (D) 1,366,149	(41%)

964,000, in the Republican primary. This was almost a three-way tie. Arkansas's Mike Huckabee won with 34%, carrying rural counties and exurban metro Atlanta counties. John McCain finished second with 32%, carrying the Savannah River valley and the southwest corner of the state, both areas with big military bases. Mitt Romney was third with 30%, carrying most of metro Atlanta, although McCain ran close behind in the inner counties.

Congressional districting   Democrats, notably longtime House Speaker Tom Murphy, dominated congressional redistricting in Georgia after the 1990 and 2000 censuses, and produced some of the most convoluted boundaries in the nation. The state gained one seat from the 1990 reapportionment and two from the 2000 reapportionment. But in both cases, the plans failed to prevent Republicans from making major gains in the delegation. In March 2004, a court redrew the district lines for state legislative seats, which helped the Republicans increase their Senate margin and gain control of the state House in November. In February 2005, Republicans, moving more deliberately and facing far less Democratic resistance than Republicans encountered in Texas in 2003, passed a congressional redistricting plan that passed the federal review mandatory under the Voting Rights Act and survived a court challenge. It had much more regularly shaped districts than the 2001 Democratic map, and split many fewer counties (19 rather than 34). It strengthened Republican incumbent Phil Gingrey and weakened Democrats Jim Marshall and John Barrow. Republicans quietly worked with some of the African-American congressional Democrats to accommodate their concerns with the new districts. Two Atlanta-area districts are 56% and 53% African-American, while three others have black percentages of 48%, 45%, and 41%. In 2007, Republican Gov. Perdue called for the establishment of an independent commission to draw redistricting plans that can be voted up or down by the legislature. Perdue seemed to be confident that relatively regularly shaped and neutrally drawn districts would leave the party with majorities in Georgia in the 21st century. But the legislature perhaps did not share that confidence, and in 2008 it failed to adopt his plan.

112th Congress Lineup	
8 R	5 D

111th Congress Lineup	
7 R	6 D

Georgia gained one seat from the reapportionment following the 2010 census, giving it a total of 14, the same as Michigan will have. With Republicans firmly in control, it is likely that something resembling the current plan will be adopted, with a new Republican-leaning seat in metro Atlanta.

Governor

Nathan Deal (R)

Elected 2010, term expires Jan. 2015, 1st term; b. Aug. 25, 1942, Millen; home, Atlanta; Mercer U., B.A. 1964, J.D. 1966; Baptist; Married (Sandra); 4 children.

Military Career: U.S. Army, 1966–68.

Elected Office: Hall Cnty. Juvenile Court judge, 1971-72; GA Senate, 1980-92, Pres. pro tem, 1989-90, 1991-92; U.S. House, 1992-2010.

Professional Career: Asst. dist. atty., NE Judicial Circuit, 1970-71; Practicing atty., 1969-92.

Office: 203 State Capitol, 30334, 404-656-1776; Fax: 404-657-7332; Web site: gov.georgia.gov.

Election Results

2010 general	Nathan Deal (R)	1,365,832	(53%)
	Roy Barnes (D)	1,107,011	(43%)
	John Monds (Lib)	103,194	(4%)
2010 primary	Nathan Deal (R)	291,035	(50%)
	Karen Handel (R)	288,516	(50%)
2010 primary	Karen Handel (R)	231,990	(34%)
	Nathan Deal (R)	155,946	(23%)
	Eric Johnson (R)	136,792	(20%)
	John Oxendine (R)	115,421	(17%)

Prior Winning Percentages: House: 2008 (76%); 2006 (77%); 2004 (100%); 2002 (100%); 2000 (75%); 1998 (100%); 1996 (66%); 1994 (58%); 1992 (59%)

Nathan Deal, a Republican, was elected governor of Georgia in 2010. Deal grew up in Gainesville, graduated from Mercer University, and then served in the Army from 1966 to 1968. He returned home to practice "street-level law," always choosing offices located on a ground floor. He was an assistant district attorney, a juvenile court judge, and a county attorney. In 1980, at age 38, he was elected to the state Senate as a Democrat; Jimmy Carter was still president, and the legislature was overwhelmingly Democratic. A capable legislator, Deal was elected Senate president pro tem twice. In 1992, when "Boll Weevil" Democrat Ed Jenkins retired from the U.S. House, Deal ran for his seat and defeated a Republican by winning 59% of the vote. Deal opposed Clinton policies and was seen as a potential party-switcher, but while campaigning in 1994 he said, "If I choose to switch during the term, I think the honest thing to do is resign and have a special election." In early 1995, he worked with other Democrats to offer an alternative to the Republicans' welfare reform package. He expressed unhappiness with his party's opposition to tax cuts and with senior Democrats' criticism of Clean Water Act revisions that he had won on a bipartisan committee vote. On April 10, 1995, back home in Gainesville, Deal announced that he was switching to the Republican Party—but he did not resign and run in a special election. He said the national Democratic Party was unwilling to admit it was "out of touch with mainstream America." Democrats were stunned, and Republican House Speaker Newt Gingrich of Georgia was delighted. Deal's reward was a seat on the powerful Energy and Commerce Committee.

Deal became chairman of the panel's Health Subcommittee and, after Democrats took control of the House in 2007, he was the ranking Republican. In 2005, he assembled $11 billion in Medicaid cuts over five years. In 2007, he sought additional funds for low-income kids in Georgia's PeachCare health insurance system, but opposed Democrats' attempts to expand the State Children's Health Insurance Program by $35 billion in five years. He insisted that already-eligible persons should receive coverage first and that immigrant children wait five years. He also sought to raise the income threshold for eligibility to reduce costs. Deal was a key negotiator at talks with the majority Democrats that ultimately failed to produce a SCHIP bill that year. In March 2009, he and Democrat Henry Waxman of California co-sponsored a bill protecting biologic drugs from generic competition for five years, with brand biologics approved for new conditions getting three years of protection. In 2008, he pressed Congress to require public disclosure of medical costs, saying such transparency is necessary to stop health providers from price-gouging the uninsured, who are often charged more than patients with insurance for the same services. He also called for ending automatic citizenship for the children of illegal aliens born in the United States.

In March 2010, with incumbent Republican Gov. Sonny Perdue term-limited, Deal announced he was running for governor. He resigned his seat immediately, possibly motivated by the fact that he faced an ethics probe into a 20-year business tie with the Georgia state government. The Office of Congressional Ethics found in February 2010 that Deal intervened with state officials to preserve a state program that earned $300,000 a year for the salvaged vehicle business he ran with a business partner. Under the state program, Deal's firm dominated the vehicle inspection business in the Gainesville region. State Revenue Commissioner Bart Graham had proposed opening the program to competition beyond the handful of businesses already doing inspections, which would have threatened Deal's regional monopoly. In a series of meetings, Deal and his chief of staff discouraged the change, and Graham later told ethics investigators that one meeting grew "contentious." The OCE recommended that the House Ethics Committee open an investigation, but Deal left Congress before the panel could act to campaign for governor.

He called the charges a "political witch hunt," and said the business arrangement with the state had been pre-approved by the Ethics Committee. He delayed his resignation from the House from March 8 to March 21, so he could vote against the Democrats' health care bill, after which he promptly resigned. At that point, the House lost jurisdiction over any ethics complaint against him. This was not the only cloud over Deal's campaign concerning his personal finances. It was revealed that he was rendered insolvent by a $2.3 million debt for which he was liable after co-signing a loan for his daughter and son-in-law to start a sporting goods store. The store failed and they went bankrupt, leaving Deal in the position of having to sell his house to pay the debt.

His financial dealings were an issue in the Republican primary. In a seven-way contest, former Georgia Secretary of State Karen Handler, based in metro Atlanta, finished first with 34%, while Deal managed to win second place with 23%, edging out state Senate President Eric Johnson, with 20%, for a spot in the August runoff. The runoff campaign between Handler and Deal was highly negative. Deal accused Handler of being insufficiently conservative on same-sex marriage and abortion rights, while Handler called Deal a "corrupt relic of Washington." Gingrich endorsed Deal, saying he stood for "conservative Georgia values," while former Alaska Gov. Sarah Palin campaigned for Handler and dubbed her one of her "mama grizzlies" of 2010. Deal just narrowly defeated Handler in the runoff, 50.2% to 49.8%, with a popular vote margin of 2,519 out of 579,551 votes cast. Handel's greatest strength was in the affluent north side of Atlanta and Fulton County, but she did not win a wide margin out of metro Atlanta as a whole. Deal benefited from large margins and large turnouts in the counties around his home base of Gainesville; Handel carried most of Georgia south of metro Atlanta.

The Democratic primary was a much quieter affair; former Gov. Roy Barnes won with 66% of the vote to 22% for Attorney General Thurbert Baker. Deal and Barnes tangled over several issues during the fall campaign, and Deal was once again on the defensive over his ethics. Barnes criticized Deal for voting against an increase in the minimum wage, which Deal called a "state's rights" issue. Deal emphasized his longtime opposition to birthright citizenship for the children of illegal immigrants. After remaining mum on birthright citizenship for many weeks, Barnes said he too opposed it but would not support changing the Constitution. In October, WAGA-TV in Atlanta reported that Deal's former chief of staff had used his congressional email to lobby Hall County to take over a private road next to Deal's salvage business. The Barnes campaign dubbed him "one of the most corrupt members of Congress." The Barnes campaign also circulated copies of a lien for $4,000 in taxes Deal had failed to pay the city of Gainesville. "If you cannot pay your own taxes, how can you expect to run a state effectively?" Barnes asked Deal during a candidate debate.

In any other year, Deal's ethical cloud might have tipped the balance against him. But 2010 was a particularly strong year for Republicans among recession-weary voters. Deal overcame the multiple personal issues to win convincingly, 53%-43%. He did not run much ahead in metro Atlanta—50%-46%—but carried the rest of the state by an overwhelming 58%-39%.

Georgia, like many states, entered 2011 with serious fiscal problems. It faced an expected budget shortfall of as much as $1.8 billion, an especially challenging environment for Deal, who promised in his campaign to invest more in public education and cut taxes. He said he would end the practice of saving money by forcing teachers to take days off without pay. In his first major address as governor, he said, "Let me be clear. My budget will end teacher furloughs and keep students in school for a full school year." Deal also had called for an Arizona-style crackdown on illegal immigrants in Georgia, but in his first months in office was coming under pressure from businesses that rely on immigrants as a cheap source of labor.

Senior Senator

Saxby Chambliss (R)

Elected 2002, term expires 2014, 2nd term; b. Nov. 10, 1943, Warrenton, NC; home, Moultrie; U. of GA, B.A. 1966, U. of TN, J.D. 1968; Episcopalian; married (Julianne); 2 children.

Elected Office: U.S. House of Reps., 1994-2002.

Professional Career: Practicing atty., 1968–94.

DC Office: 416 RSOB, 20510, 202-224-3521; Fax: 202-224-0103; Web site: chambliss.senate.gov.

State Offices: Atlanta, 770-763-9090; Augusta, 706-738-0302; Macon, 478-741-1417; Moultrie, 229-985-2112.

Committees: *Aging (Special). Agriculture, Nutrition & Forestry:* Commodities, Markets, Trade & Risk Management (RMM); Conservation, Forestry & Natural Resources; Jobs, Rural Economic Growth & Energy Innovation. *Armed Services:* Emerging Threats & Capabilities; Personnel; Readiness & Management Support. *Intelligence (Select)* (VChmn). *Rules & Administration.*

Group Ratings

	ACLU	ACU	ADA	CFG	AFS	FRC	LCV	ITIC	NTU	COC
2010	7	100	0	92	5	95	0	67	97	100
2009	–	92	10	100	9	–	0	–	90	71

National Journal Ratings

	2010 LIB	—	2010 CONS		2009 LIB	—	2009 CONS
Economic	0%	—	87%		13%	—	86%
Social	0%	—	79%		14%	—	84%
Foreign	0%	—	72%		16%	—	80%
Composite	10%	—	90%		16%	—	85%

Key Votes of the 111th Congress

1. Overturn Ledbetter	N	5. Pass health care bill	N	9. Ratify New START	N
2. Pass $787 billion stimulus	N	6. Regulate financial firms	N	10. Confirm Elena Kagan	N
3. Repeal DC gun laws	Y	7. Pass tax cuts for some	N	11. Stop EPA climate regs	Y
4. Confirm Sonia Sotomayor	N	8. Legalize immigrants' kids	N	12. Repeal don't ask, tell	N

Election Results

2008 runoff	Saxby Chambliss (R)	1,228,033	(57%)	
	Jim Martin (D)	909,923	(43%)	
2008 general	Saxby Chambliss (R)	1,867,097	(50%)	($18,346,273)
	Jim Martin (D)	1,757,393	(47%)	($7,490,201)
	Allen Buckley (Lib)	127,923	(3%)	($28,666)
2008 primary	Saxby Chambliss (R)	unopposed		

Prior Winning Percentages: 2002 (53%); House: 2000 (59%); 1998 (62%); 1996 (53%); 1994 (63%)

Saxby Chambliss, the senior senator from Georgia, was elected in 2002. He earlier served four terms in the House. Chambliss grew up in Shreveport, La., the son of an Episcopalian minister, and graduated from the University of Georgia. He practiced business and agricultural law in Moultrie starting in 1968, working for farmers who grew subsidized crops like peanuts and cotton. In 1992, he ran for the U.S. House and lost the Republican primary. In 1994, he ran again and was the sole Republican candidate. In the general election, he faced Democrat Craig Mathis, the 32-year-old son of Rep. Dawson Mathis (1971-81). Chambliss won 63%-37%. House Speaker Newt Gingrich of Georgia saw that Chambliss got the committee assignments he needed most—Armed Services, to look after Robins Air Force Base, and Agriculture, to protect subsidies for peanut farmers.

When Budget Chairman John Kasich, R-Ohio, announced his retirement in July 1999, Chambliss started a campaign for the post. In July 2000, after Republican Sen. Paul Coverdell died suddenly, Chambliss considered running in the November election to succeed him. House Speaker Dennis Hastert persuaded him to stay in the House, and Chambliss came away feeling he would get the Budget chairmanship. But he had competition from Jim Nussle of Iowa. The Republican leadership ultimately picked Nussle, and as consolation, Chambliss got an Agriculture subcommittee chairmanship. Hastert also made him chairman of the Intelligence Subcommittee on Terrorism and Homeland Security.

Chambliss got a second chance to run for the Senate in 2002. Democratic incumbent Max Cleland had won the seat only narrowly, 49%-48%, in 1996, and Georgia was trending Republican, evident in George W. Bush's 55%-43% victory there in 2000. Chambliss was not an early favorite to win. Cleland had a compelling biography. After college he volunteered for the Army and in 1967 went to Vietnam, where he lost both legs and his right arm in a grenade explosion. He served on the Armed Services Committee and had a moderate voting record. But in 2001 and 2002, he tended to stick with the Democratic Caucus while his new colleague, Georgia Democratic Sen. Zell Miller, dissented vociferously on issues from the Bush tax cuts to the Department of Homeland Security personnel rules. After easily winning the Republican primary 61%-27%, Chambliss set out to convince voters that Cleland was "too liberal for Georgia."

Cleland's two major strengths—his sacrifice in Vietnam and support from the highly popular Miller—seemed formidable. Cleland backers noted that Chambliss had received four student deferments in the 1960s and then was found ineligible for service because of a bad knee. Miller, in ads, told voters of Cleland's "rock-solid Georgia values." But that did not deter Chambliss from sharp attacks. He ran a series of ads mentioning Cleland's opposition to an amendment banning aid for schools that barred the Boy Scouts, his votes against a ban on partial-birth abortion, and his support of school clinics passing out morning-after pills without parental permission—all ending with an astounded announcer asking, "Why would he do that?"

But probably the most important issue was homeland security. Cleland stood with other Senate Democrats in opposing anti-union rules in the new department. The dispute occupied the Senate for much of October 2002 and prevented passage of the bill to create the department. Chambliss ran an ad showing pictures of Al Qaeda leader Osama bin Laden, Iraqi President Saddam Hussein, and Cleland, and saying that Cleland "voted against the president's vital homeland security efforts 11 times." Against this, Cleland's ads attacking Chambliss for opposing an increase in the minimum wage and for cutting student loans were weak stuff. Apparently Cleland's impressive record in Vietnam did not inoculate him against charges that he had given short shrift to homeland security. Chambliss won 53%-46%, a much bigger victory than just about anyone expected. Chambliss carried metro Atlanta 52%-46%, and he carried the rest of Georgia 54%-46%.

In the Senate, Chambliss established a mostly conservative voting record, supporting such proposals as the "Fair Tax," which would replace the income tax with a national sales tax. (He also gained a reputation for a great golf game. He has been rated one of the best golfers in the Senate, with a 6.5 handicap.) During the Republicans' 2003-07 majority, he was the chairman of the immigration subcommittee of Judiciary. Initially, he was favorable to Bush's proposal for a guest worker program, at least for farm workers, but he opposed a controversial provision to give illegal workers a process to achieve citizenship. In the spring of 2007 he and his Georgia GOP colleague Johnny Isakson—the two have known each other since their days as classmates at the University of Georgia—worked together in a bipartisan coalition to fashion a bill. Chambliss argued that Georgia was the No. 1 destination for illegal border crossings and that the state's agricultural industry needed a guest worker program. They got a provision requiring that the border be secured before the guest worker program could begin. When Majority Leader Harry Reid brought the bill to the floor in late June, Chambliss and Isakson opposed allowing the legislation to move forward unless a separate appropriations bill for border security was passed. The two cooperated closely on other issues, co-sponsoring an amendment in 2009 legalizing gun ownership in Washington, D.C. It was tacked on to the bill giving the District of Columbia a seat in the House, and when Democrats objected, the bill stalled. Chambliss also opposed the confirmation of Sonia Sotomayor to the Supreme Court, singling out her decision as dean of Harvard Law School to restrict military recruiters' access to the campus.

On the Armed Services Committee, Chambliss has paid close attention to the needs of Georgia military bases and defense contractors. In 2006, he moved successfully to reverse plans to cut back on procurement of the F-22 Raptor, produced by Lockheed Martin, and he later opposed Defense Secretary Robert Gates' decision to stop F-22 production. He sponsored legislation that reduced the retirement age for National Guard members in proportion with overseas deployments. Chambliss supported the Bush administration on Iraq, but in 2007, he showed his frustration, telling the *Macon Telegraph* there were "a lot of bad decisions" in the conduct of the war. However, he consistently voted against cutting off funding for Bush's troop surge. Though he questioned the legitimacy of the August 2009 election in Afghanistan, Chambliss urged patience and said he would support more troops. Of President Obama's policy in the country, he said in December 2009, "He did a very good job of laying the groundwork, but I strongly disagree with even mentioning the 18 months. That is what the Taliban were hoping to hear, that we're not going to be there for long." In 2010, he questioned the New START pact, saying he feared it would leave the U.S. without missile interceptors until 2020, and he opposed changing the don't-ask-don't-tell policy barring openly gay military personnel.

The senator's other locus of activity is the Agriculture Committee. He resisted demands to impose income caps on wealthy farmers and budget cuts in cotton and other commodity programs important to Georgia. As the ranking Republican on the panel in 2008, he worked on that year's farm bill with Democratic Chairman Tom Harkin of Iowa, striving to keep programs at existing levels. In bipartisan negotiations, he added incentives to the bill for cellulosic ethanol, made from switchgrass and pine trees that are plentiful in south Georgia. He supported the legislation that passed the Senate in December 2007, and later voted to override Bush's veto. In early 2009, he got 19 other Republicans and Montana Democrat Max Baucus to sign a protest of the outgoing Bush administration's limits on government payments to those not "actively engaged" in farming. And the next year, he opposed the Obama administration's proposal to cut farm payments and provide farmers a five-year blueprint for assistance. Chambliss said it was an unfair policy change in "midstream." Also in 2010, while other conservatives criticized first lady Michelle Obama for taking on the issue of childhood obesity, Chambliss publicly backed her. The Agriculture panel has jurisdiction over federally funded school nutrition programs. After a meeting on the issue with the first lady and administration officials in February 2010, Chambliss said, "School cafeterias, gymnasiums and playgrounds are important venues to teach children about healthy eating and exercise."

In 2008, Chambliss had an unexpectedly close race for re-election. Obama's smashing 66%-31% victory in the state's Feb. 5 presidential primary and the high black turnout convinced many Democratic leaders that they had a chance to win the seat. Conservatives were also disgruntled with Chambliss' stands on immigration and the farm bill. In March 2008, Democrat Jim Martin got into the contest. He was little known but had a long résumé: a stint as a military intelligence officer in Vietnam, a former member of the state House, and the head of the state Human Resources Department. He was promptly endorsed by former first lady Rosalynn Carter and former Gov. Roy Barnes, and raised serious money. He won a primary runoff against DeKalb County Chief Executive Officer Vernon Jones with 60% of the vote.

The Obama campaign's registration and turnout efforts gave Democrats confidence that African-Americans would be a higher percentage of the electorate than in the past. Martin linked Chambliss to President George W. Bush's policies, while the incumbent took pains to point out that he differed with Bush on immigration, the Medicare prescription drug bill, and the farm bill. After the financial crisis hit in mid-September, some polls showed the race to be close, with Chambliss well under 50%. When Chambliss and Isakson, operating as usual in tandem, voted for the $700 billion rescue of the financial markets on Oct. 1, Martin responded with ads denouncing their votes. Chambliss ultimately outspent Martin, $16 million to $7.5 million, but the Democratic Senatorial Campaign Committee and other Democratic groups made up much of the difference. Georgia law requires general election candidates to get 50% of the vote to avoid a runoff. When the votes were counted in November, Chambliss led Martin by 110,000 votes, but got just 49.8% of the vote to Martin's 46.8%, falling 9,146 votes short of winning without a runoff. The biggest drop-offs in Chambliss's percentages from 2002 were in metro Atlanta counties with rising black populations—Rockdale, Douglas, Clayton, Henry, and Newton—or growing Latino populations, as in Gwinnett County. African-Americans, who were 28% of voters, voted 93%-4% for Martin. Whites voted 70%-26% for Chambliss.

The runoff came four weeks later, on Dec. 2. The national parties and allied groups pumped in at least $5 million. The Obama campaign kept open its 25 field offices and sent 75 more organizers to help Martin. National Republicans sent in operatives to work for Chambliss as well as their top attractions: John McCain, vice presidential nominee Sarah Palin, Arkansas' Mike Huckabee and Massachusetts' Mitt Romney. Democrats sent in former President Clinton and Obama taped a radio ad and robo-calls.

This was a battle of turnout, and the signs for Democrats were ominous. While 35% of early voters before the November election were black, only 23% of early voters for the December runoff were. Overall, turnout in the runoff was only 57% of that for the general election, and all indications were that the drop-off was greater than average among African-Americans, left-leaning students, and other Democratic constituencies. Only 2.1 million Georgians voted, far fewer than the 3.7 million in November. Chambliss won 57%-43%.

Junior Senator

Johnny Isakson (R)

Elected 2004, term expires 2016, 2nd term; b. Dec. 28, 1944, Atlanta; home, Marietta; U. of GA, B.B.A. 1966; Methodist; married (Dianne); 3 children.

Military Career: GA Air Natl. Guard, 1966-72.

Elected Office: GA House of Reps., 1976-90, Repub. ldr., 1983-90; GA Senate, 1993-96; U.S. House of Reps., 1999-2004.

Professional Career: Northside Realty, 1967-99, Pres., 1979-99; Co-chair, Dole GA presidential campaign, 1988, 1996; Chmn., GA Board of Ed., 1997.

DC Office: 131 RSOB, 20510, 202-224-3643; Fax: 202-228-0724; Web site: isakson.senate.gov.

State Offices: Atlanta, 770-661-0999.

Committees: *Commerce, Science & Transportation:* Aviation Operations, Safety & Security; Communications, Technology & the Internet; Oceans, Atmosphere, Fisheries & Coast Guard; Surface Transportation & Merchant Marine Infrastructure, Safety & Security. *Ethics (Select)* (RMM). *Foreign Relations:* African Affairs (RMM); International Operations & Organizations, Democracy & Global Women's Issues; Near Eastern & South & Central Asian Affairs; Western Hemisphere, Peace Corps & Global Narcotics Affairs. *Health, Education, Labor & Pensions:* Children & Families; Employment & Workplace Safety (RMM); Primary Health & Aging. *Veterans' Affairs.*

Group Ratings

	ACLU	ACU	ADA	CFG	AFS	FRC	LCV	ITIC	NTU	COC
2010	7	91	5	86	2	91	0	67	96	100
2009	–	96	5	99	9	–	18	–	90	86

National Journal Ratings

	2010 LIB — 2010 CONS		2009 LIB — 2009 CONS	
Economic	0%	— 87%	6%	— 91%
Social	0%	— 79%	16%	— 83%
Foreign	33%	— 66%	16%	— 80%
Composite	17%	— 83%	14%	— 86%

Key Votes of the 111th Congress

1. Overturn Ledbetter	N	5. Pass health care bill	N	9. Ratify New START	Y
2. Pass $787 billion stimulus	N	6. Regulate financial firms	N	10. Confirm Elena Kagan	N
3. Repeal DC gun laws	Y	7. Pass tax cuts for some	N	11. Stop EPA climate regs	Y
4. Confirm Sonia Sotomayor	N	8. Legalize immigrants' kids	N	12. Repeal don't ask, tell	N

Election Results

2010 general	Johnny Isakson (R)	1,489,904	(58%)	($9,671,128)
	Michael Thurmond (D)	996,516	(39%)	($336,907)
	Chuck Donovan (Lib)	68,750	(3%)	
2010 primary	Johnny Isakson (R)	unopposed		

Prior Winning Percentages: 2004 (58%); House: 2002 (80%); 2000 (75%); 1999 (65%)

Johnny Isakson, a Republican, was first elected Georgia's junior senator in 2004. Isakson grew up outside Atlanta, in south Fulton County. His father drove a Greyhound bus, and his parents bought old houses, renovated them, and sold them for a profit. Isakson graduated from the University of Georgia and served in the Air National Guard. He went to work for Northside Realty in 1967 and eventually became president of the firm. He volunteered for Republican Barry Goldwater's presidential campaign in 1964 and for President Nixon's in 1972. In 1974, he ran for the state House and lost. In 1976, he ran again and won, and in 1983 became minority leader. He ran for governor in 1990, losing 53%-45% to Democrat Zell Miller. Two years later, he was elected to the state Senate. In 1996, he ran statewide again and lost the Republican runoff for U.S. senator to self-financing businessman Guy Millner, who lost in November to Democrat Max Cleland 49%-48%. In December 1996, Gov. Miller appointed Isakson head of the state board of education. His partisan political career seemed over, but it was revived by two timely retirements.

In November 1998, Newt Gingrich of Georgia announced that he was stepping down as speaker of the House and that he would resign his seat in Congress. That opened up a vacancy in the heavily Republican 6th District, which included much of Atlanta's northern suburbs plus the affluent Buckhead neighborhood. Isakson was by far the best-known of the six candidates in the February 1999 nonpartisan election. He raised $1 million and spent $500,000 of his own money. He won the seat with 65% of the vote. In the House, Isakson served on the Transportation and Infrastructure Committee, where he pushed for a rapid transit line for the overburdened Georgia 400 corridor. On the Education and the Workforce Committee, he took a leading role in negotiations on President George W. Bush's signature education law, the No Child Left Behind Act, which tied federal funds for schools to test performance. He added a provision requiring that 25% of technology funds be used for teacher classroom training.

Isakson passed up a chance to run against Cleland in 2002. But the state's other Senate seat came open in 2004 when Zell Miller, who by then had moved from governor to senator, announced he would retire after just one term. Isakson decided to run for the seat. He had two serious competitors in the Republican primary: Herman Cain, who grew up in a black neighborhood in Atlanta and, starting from low-level jobs, became the owner of Omaha-based Godfather's Pizza; and Rep. Mac Collins, whose district included the southern edge of metro Atlanta. Cain and Collins were both solid conservatives and abortion rights opponents, and they made abortion a major issue. Isakson also was an opponent of abortion, but he had voted against a law preventing the use of foreign aid money to fund abortions overseas and had voted for allowing servicewomen to have abortions at their own expense in military hospitals. In the 1996 Senate primary, he had irked religious conservatives by saying, "I will not vote to amend the Constitution to make criminals of women and their doctors. I trust my wife, my daughter, and the women of Georgia to make the right choices." Collins called him "a certified moderate," and Cain, in a television spot, said, "There's a big difference between me and Johnny Isakson. And it's not just the color of our eyes." Cain also backed a consumption tax and private investment accounts in Social Security; Collins criticized Isakson for favoring an extension of the date for the turnover of sovereignty in Iraq. Isakson called for staying the course in Iraq and for tax reform. With his business contacts, Isakson raised $5.5 million for the primary; Cain spent $3 million, much of it his own money, and Collins spent $1.9 million. Many observers thought the race would end with a runoff. But Isakson got 53% of the vote to 26% for Cain and 21% for Collins.

The Democratic race came down to two late-entering candidates, 4th District Rep. Denise Majette and businessman Cliff Oxford. In the primary, Majette had served just one term after her upset victory over Cynthia McKinney in the 2002 primary, and she had a solidly liberal voting record. Oxford was accused of spousal abuse by a former wife. He spent $1 million of his own money. Majette beat Oxford in an August runoff, 59%-41%.

In the general election campaign, Isakson attacked Majette's liberal voting record, including her vote against an $87 billion spending bill for Iraq. Majette criticized Isakson for undercutting Bush's education reforms by not voting to fully fund them. Isakson won 58%-40%, almost the same margin by which Bush beat John Kerry in the state. Majette carried only 19 of 159 counties, including Atlanta's Fulton County and two black-majority counties in metro Atlanta.

Isakson has a conservative voting record in the Senate, though his folksy pragmatism makes him markedly less edgy than other Republicans in Georgia's congressional delegation. He said his experience selling homes taught him the virtues of negotiation and compromise. "If you want to ever learn how to accept rejection, sell real estate for a few years," he told the Associated Press in 2010. On the Health, Education, Labor, and Pensions Committee, he worked actively on pension reform, with the chief goal of advocating the interests of Delta Airlines, which was bankrupt and had huge pension obligations to its workers. In 2005, the Senate passed a pension-reform measure that included Isakson's amendment to give airlines 20 additional years to meet their obligations. Negotiations between the House and Senate dragged on; House Education Committee Chairman John Boehner, R-Ohio, was unhappy with what he called Isakson's "industry-specific relief" in the bill. But in 2006, a final version passed giving Delta and Northwest 17 years to amortize their pension payments, while American and Continental got 10 years.

On many issues, Isakson works closely with Georgia colleague Sen. Saxby Chambliss, a Republican whom he has known since their days as classmates at the University of Georgia. Although Isakson opposed the McCain-Kennedy immigration bill in 2006, he and Chambliss worked with a bipartisan group of senators in 2007 on a bill including a path to legalization for illegal workers, a guest worker program, and tougher enforcement. Isakson sponsored a "trigger" provision that would delay legalization measures until enforcement goals were met. Nonetheless, he and Chambliss were booed by anti-illegal-immigration hardliners at the May 2007 Republican state convention. In June, when Democratic Majority Leader Harry Reid brought the bill to the floor, Isakson and Chambliss said they would vote against allowing it to go forward unless a separate appropriation boosting border security was passed.

Isakson also severely rebuked Republican National Committee Chairman Michael Steele in 2010 when Steele described the Afghanistan conflict as "a war of Obama's choosing." The same year, he joined Democrats on the Foreign Relations Committee in supporting the New START arms-reduction pact with Russia. He and Chambliss stood together in September 2008 in supporting the "Gang of 10" bipartisan energy bill that was opposed by many conservatives. He became entangled in a brief controversy during the 2009 health care debate when conservatives seized on end-of-life counseling provisions, which former Alaska Gov. Sarah Palin derided as "death panels." President Obama responded that one of the leading sponsors of the effort was Isakson, a longtime advocate for end-of-life counseling and assistance in drafting living wills. But Isakson rebutted Obama, saying that he backed a much different policy. The provisions ultimately were dropped from the bill. The flap came several months after Isakson had his own experience with the health-care system: He was rushed to the hospital after having a toxic reaction to bacteria in his blood-stream and was diagnosed with an irregular heartbeat.

With Massachusetts Democrat John Kerry, he co-sponsored a bill to finance interstate high-speed rail projects, specifically supporting such connections on the route from Birmingham to Washington, which runs through Atlanta. In February 2009, the Senate unanimously passed his $15,000 tax credit for home-buyers as part of the economic stimulus bill, and later that year concurred with Isakson's argument that further extension of the credit was needed to boost the weak economy. Also in early 2009, he and Democrat Kent Conrad of North Dakota called for setting up a commission like the 9/11 commission to examine the collapse of the financial system. He introduced another bill that year that would move the annual congressional budgeting process to a two-year cycle, a reform he and other lawmakers say would make budget planning far easier.

In 2010, he breezed to re-election against Democrat Michael Thurmond, Georgia's labor commissioner, who in July had managed to raise just $117,000 compared to Isakson's $7.5 million.

FIRST DISTRICT

Jack Kingston (R)

Elected 1992, 10th term; b. April 24, 1955, Bryan, TX; home, Savannah; U. of GA, B.S. 1977; Episcopalian; married (Libby); 4 children.

Elected Office: GA House of Reps., 1984–92.

Professional Career: Insurance agent, 1979–92.

DC Office: 2372 RHOB, 20515, 202-225-5831; Fax: 202-226-2269; Web site: kingston.house.gov.

State Offices: Baxley, 912-367-7403; Brunswick, 912-265-9010; Savannah, 912-352-0101; Valdosta, 229-247-9188.

Committees: *Appropriations:* Agriculture, Rural Development, FDA & Related Agencies (Chmn); Defense; Labor, HHS, Education & Related Agencies.

Group Ratings

	ACLU	ACU	ADA	CFG	AFS	FRC	LCV	ITIC	NTU	COC
2010	13	100	5	98	0	100	0	0	89	75
2009	–	96	5	89	22	–	0	–	89	73

National Journal Ratings

	2010 LIB — 2010 CONS		2009 LIB — 2009 CONS	
Economic	11%	— 89%	17%	— 82%
Social	18%	— 77%	18%	— 81%
Foreign	26%	— 72%	0%	— 75%
Composite	20%	— 81%	16%	— 84%

Key Votes of the 111th Congress

1. Overturn Ledbetter	N	5. Bar federal abortion funds	Y
2. Pass $820 billion stimulus	N	6. Pass health care bill	N
3. Let guns in national parks	Y	7. Regulate financial firms	N
4. Pass cap-and-trade	N	8. Pass tax cuts for some	N

9. Stop detainee transfers	Y
10. Legalize immigrants' kids	N
11. Repeal don't ask, tell	N
12. Limit campaign funds	N

Election Results

2010 general	Jack Kingston (R)	117,270	(72%)	($1,028,117)
	Oscar Harris (D)	46,449	(28%)	
2010 primary	Jack Kingston (R)	.... unopposed		

Prior Winning Percentages: 2008 (67%), 2006 (69%), 2004 (100%), 2002 (72%), 2000 (69%), 1998 (100%), 1996 (68%), 1994 (77%), 1992 (58%)

Population		Race/Ethnicity		Work	
Pop. 2010:	722,068	White:	65.2%	Private:	69.9%
Change since 2000:	Up 14.7%	Black:	25.0%	Government:	24.0%
Urban:	57.3%	Hispanic:	6.4%	Self-employed:	5.9%
Rural:	42.7%	Asian:	1.2%	Blue collar:	25.6%
Area size:	12,243 sq. mi.	Native Am.:	0.3%	White collar:	52.7%
		Hawaiian:	0.1%	Khaki collar:	2.8%
Age		Two+ races:	1.7%	Other:	18.8%
Median age:	34.5 yrs.				
More than 65 yrs:	11.7%	*Ancestry*		Median income:	$41,424
Less than 18 yrs:	26.0%	English	10.0%	Median Home Value:	$130,500
Education		Irish	9.4%		
		USA	8.6%	**Military Veterans**	
H.S. grad:	82.2%			% of Pop:	13.0%
College grad:	19.8%				
Grad degree:	7.3%				

South Georgia; Savannah Suburbs

Georgia's south Atlantic coast was settled in the 1730s by Englishman James Oglethorpe as a refuge and reformatory for convicts. But before long, the sea islands and lowlands along the wide rivers and inlets were plantation country. It is here that Gen. William Tecumseh Sherman and his troops famously marched from Atlanta in 1864 and, without supplies or lines of communication, burned plantation houses, destroyed crops, and captured the Confederacy's leader.

2008 Presidential Vote
John McCain (R) 166,138   (63%)
Barack Obama (D) 95,451   (36%)

2004 Presidential Vote
George Bush (R) 148,806   (66%)
John Kerry (D) 75,399   (34%)

Cook Partisan Voting Index: R+16

When their march was complete, they left behind memories of property destroyed and slaves freed, which have been handed down as family lore through several generations.

The 1st Congressional District of Georgia includes much of the state's south and southeast. It includes the state's southern Atlantic coast and runs west approximately to Interstate 75 at Valdosta, the largest city in the district. It heads toward the center of the state just short of Vidalia and runs from the Ocmulgee and Altamaha rivers in the north to the Florida border. It takes in almost one-third of Chatham County's population but only a sliver of Savannah, most of which is now in the 12th District. It contains the Sea Islands, with their vibrant resort economy and efforts to preserve the African-American Gullah culture and its eponymous West African-originated Creole language. One of those coastal communities is the historic black settlement of Pin Point, 11 miles southeast of Savannah. Its 300 citizens are mostly descendants of the first slaves in the area. Its most famous son is U.S. Supreme Court Justice Clarence Thomas.

It has a few modest-sized cities, like Brunswick, a World War II shipbuilding center that has been revitalized as the gateway to the Sea Islands, and isolated Waycross, a railroad junction and gateway to the Okefenokee Swamp, the largest swamp in North America. Prior to the abolitionist movement, this swamp-filled area was a site of the Underground Railroad, with trails to north Florida. Much of the district is rural, with cotton and tobacco fields and softwood forests inhabited by wild hogs and bears. Appling County and Berrien County are known for their turpentine and bell peppers. Many popular films have been produced in the region, including *Glory* and *Forrest Gump*. Shipping has grown at the Savannah and Brunswick ports, and Savannah is now the country's fourth-busiest port for container cargo. Even during the 2007-09 recession, the ports were able to sustain jobs and increase their economic impact on the state.

This was Democratic country for a century after Sherman's troops marched through Georgia, but voters here are solidly conservative on most issues. For two decades, this part of south Georgia voted for national Republicans but Georgia Democrats. Since 2000, it has voted solidly Republican for governor and senator as well. Redistricting changes in 2005 increased the black population and reduced George W. Bush's vote in 2004 from 68% to 66%. In 2008, Republican John McCain did nearly that well, with 63%.

Jack Kingston (R)

The congressman from the 1st District is Jack Kingston, an amiable and media-savvy Republican first elected in 1992. The son of a college professor, Kingston grew up in Texas and Georgia, but also spent time in Ethiopia. After college, he moved to Savannah to be a commercial insurance agent. In 1984, at age 29, he was elected to the Georgia House and served eight years. In 1992, when Democratic U.S. Rep. Lindsay Thomas retired, Kingston ran for Congress against Democrat Barbara Christmas, a school principal. He won decisively, 58%-42%, and has not been seriously challenged since.

In the House, Kingston has a mostly conservative voting record but he is not among the hard-liners in the Georgia delegation. He was the only one of the delegation's Republicans in 2006 to support renewing the 1965 Voting Rights Act. He also rebuked former Alaska Gov. Sarah Palin in 2010 for wading into the GOP gubernatorial primary to endorse Karen Handel over former Rep. Nathan Deal, who eventually won the race. In 2005, he joined Rep. Eliot Engel, D-N.Y., in a bipartisan initiative to reduce oil consumption by increasing auto fuel efficiency. "The age of cheap oil and gas is over," Kingston said, a view that proved to be prescient in the late 2000s as gas prices soared.

During the Clinton era, he parted company with Republicans on trade issues, notably the North American Free Trade Agreement and normal trade relations with China. But during a 2007 visit to Cuba, he softened his opposition on trade with that country, at least where the market for Georgia-grown Vidalia onions was concerned. During the Obama administration, he has made several attempts at pleasing the right, calling in September 2009 to cut back the use of White House policy "czars" whose jobs did not require Senate confirmation.

In the 112th Congress (2011-12), he is the chairman of the Appropriations Subcommittee on Agriculture, where he is an advocate of the peanut-warehousing program. He helped play a role in 2009 in overturning a ban on Chinese poultry imports that had led China to file a complaint with the World Trade Organization. In 2008, he helped House Minority Leader John Boehner craft the party's position on earmarking after the practice came under widespread criticism as wasteful government spending. But Kingston also has made it his business to grab his slices of pork. He has brought millions of dollars home to improve the water flow of the Savannah River and to complete the Sidney Lanier drawbridge in Brunswick. "I am convinced there are good earmarks and bad earmarks," he said, while conceding that they got out of control when Republicans ran the House.

Kingston has been a party activist in the House. As head of the Republicans' "theme team," he became a spokesman for the House GOP on television talk shows. He encouraged colleagues to make appearances on Comedy Central and to make more use of blogs. (He himself was the first lawmaker to appear on comedian Stephen Colbert's "Better Know a District" segment.) In 2002, he was elected vice chairman of the Republican Conference. But he was a victim of a desire for change in 2006, after Republicans lost their majority in the House. Kingston fell short in a bid for chairman of the conference, losing to Adam Putnam of Florida on the third ballot.

He considered but turned down opportunities to run for the Senate in 2002 and 2004, when less-senior Republicans prevailed. But long before Republicans regained control of the House in 2010, Kingston began floating his name to take over the top Republican slot on Appropriations. He argued that California Republican Jerry Lewis had served his three full terms under House GOP rules and was required to step aside. Two weeks after the election, he formally announced his bid, stressing his conservatism as well as his media-friendly credentials in communicating the panel's work. But the Appropriations chairmanship went to Harold Rogers of Kentucky.

SECOND DISTRICT

Sanford Bishop (D)

Elected 1992, 10th term; b. Feb. 4, 1947, Mobile, AL; home, Albany; More-house Col., B.A. 1968, Emory U., J.D. 1971; Baptist; married (Vivian Creighton Bishop); 1 child.

Military Career: Army, 1970–71.

Elected Office: GA House of Reps., 1976–90; GA Senate, 1990–92.

Professional Career: Practicing atty., 1971–92.

DC Office: 2429 RHOB, 20515, 202-225-3631; Fax: 202-225-2203; Web site: www.house.gov/bishop.

State Offices: Albany, 229-439-8067; Columbus, 706-320-9477.

Committees: *Appropriations:* Agriculture, Rural Development, FDA & Related Agencies; Legislative Branch; Military Construction, Veterans Affairs & Related Agencies (RMM).

Group Ratings

	ACLU	ACU	ADA	CFG	AFS	FRC	LCV	ITIC	NTU	COC
2010	81	4	75	8	100	18	90	100	9	38
2009	–	8	95	2	100	–	93	–	4	53

National Journal Ratings

	2010 LIB	—	2010 CONS	2009 LIB	—	2009 CONS
Economic	73%	—	25%	64%	—	34%
Social	48%	—	51%	58%	—	41%
Foreign	56%	—	38%	58%	—	41%
Composite	61%	—	40%	61%	—	39%

Key Votes of the 111th Congress

1. Overturn Ledbetter	Y	5. Bar federal abortion funds	Y
2. Pass $820 billion stimulus	Y	6. Pass health care bill	Y
3. Let guns in national parks	Y	7. Regulate financial firms	Y
4. Pass cap-and-trade	Y	8. Pass tax cuts for some	Y

9. Stop detainee transfers	Y
10. Legalize immigrants' kids	Y
11. Repeal don't ask, tell	Y
12. Limit campaign funds	N

Election Results

2010 general	Sanford Bishop (D)..86,520	(51%)	($1,485,600)
	Mike Keown (R) 81,673	(49%)	($1,213,707)
2010 primary	Sanford Bishop (D)..................................... unopposed		

Prior Winning Percentages: 2008 (69%), 2006 (68%), 2004 (67%), 2002 (100%), 2000 (54%), 1998 (57%), 1996 (54%), 1994 (66%), 1992 (64%)

Population		Race/Ethnicity		Work	
Pop. 2010:	631,973	White:	44.9%	Private:	68.5%
Change since 2000:	Up 0.4%	Black:	48.1%	Government:	26.0%
Urban:	58.1%	Hispanic:	4.6%	Self-employed:	5.3%
Rural:	41.9%	Asian:	0.8%	Blue collar:	25.4%
Area size:	11,001 sq. mi.	Native Am.:	0.3%	White collar:	49.2%
		Hawaiian:	0.1%	Khaki collar:	5.3%
Age		Two+ races:	1.2%	Other:	20.2%
Median age:	34.9 yrs.				
More than 65 yrs:	12.3%	*Ancestry*		Median income:	$33,905
Less than 18 yrs:	25.8%	USA	8.3%	Median Home Value:	$95,100
		Irish	7.1%		
Education		English	5.9%	**Military Veterans**	
H.S. grad:	77.3%			% of Pop:	10.4%
College grad:	14.8%				
Grad degree:	5.5%				

Southwest Georgia; Part Columbus

Before the Civil War, the southwest corner of Georgia was plantation country. This is where the Confederate Army ran the Andersonville military prison, which killed about 13,000 of the 45,000 Union soldiers confined there. They are remembered at the National Prisoner of War Museum at Andersonville, which is dedicated to all Americans who have endured wartime captivity. Today, the U.S. military is a strong presence, and bases in the area have been largely

2008 Presidential Vote
Barack Obama (D) 131,408   (54%)
John McCain (R) 108,818   (45%)

2004 Presidential Vote
George Bush (R)...................104,014   (50%)
John Kerry (D) 103,163   (50%)

Cook Partisan Voting Index: D+1

unscathed by several rounds of closings in recent years. Fort Benning is the Army's third largest installation, home of the Army Infantry School and the Army Armor Center and School. Benning can train as many as 16,000 soldiers at a time. As a boost to the otherwise gloomy local economy, its workforce in 2013 is expected to be 41,600, including transfers as a result of the military's overseas downsizing.

But the region is mostly farmland: Cotton and peanuts are major crops, and pecans are also grown here. In fall 2010, peanut growers experienced their most severe documented outbreak of damage from burrower bugs. Near the Florida border is Cairo, the birthplace of baseball's black pioneer Jackie Robinson; Plantation Trace, near Thomasville, is where rich Northerners have come to shoot quail and ducks in winter since the 1880s. A bit to the north is Albany, with several factories, a civil rights museum and the site of Martin Luther King Jr.'s least successful civil rights protests in the 1960s. Not far from Albany, between upland pine stands and bottomland habitats, lies the Chickasawatchee Swamp, one of the Southeast's largest freshwater swamps and home to rare plant species such as the needle palm and the green fly orchid. Two counties north is the village of Plains, the home since childhood of former President Jimmy Carter, who has said he wants to be buried in his front yard. Plains now has a major biofuels factory. This is still hardscrabble country: As recently as World War II, most rural residents lived in clapboard cabins without power or running water, eking a living out of over-tilled soil. The area's economic struggles continue today. Unemployment in Albany was above 10% in 2010, a higher level than in most of Georgia's other cities.

This is Georgia's 2nd Congressional District. In the 2005 redistricting, it lost virtually all of Valdosta, but increased to two-thirds its share of Columbus and Muscogee County. Eight rural counties between Columbus and Macon were added. The net effect was to raise the African-American population in the district from 45% to 48%. President George W. Bush won here in 2004, but with only 50.02%. In 2008, Barack Obama took Muscogee County 60%-40%, and the district as a whole voted for Obama 54%-45%.

Sanford Bishop (D)

The congressman from the 2nd District is Sanford Bishop, a Democrat first elected in 1992. Bishop grew up in Mobile, Ala., where his father was a college president. He went to Morehouse College in Atlanta, where he was student body president in 1968 and sang at Martin Luther King Jr.'s funeral. "I resolved, after his death, that I would try to follow in his footsteps," he told the *Columbus Ledger-Enquirer* years later. He went to Emory Law School, then served in the Army. After a year in New York, he settled in Columbus to practice law. He was elected to the state legislature in 1976 at age 29. He served there until 1990, when he was elected to the Georgia Senate. In 1992, he ran for the U.S. House against Democratic Rep. Charles Hatcher, who, with more than 800 check overdrafts, was tarred by the House bank scandal that year. Bishop defeated Hatcher in the runoff 53%-47% and won the general election 64%-36%.

Bishop is a moderate Democrat who calls himself a "traditionalist" on cultural issues. His voting record is among the most conservative in the Congressional Black Caucus, though he was significantly more loyal in recent years when his party held the majority. He is also a member of the conservative Blue Dog Democrats and over the years supported a balanced budget, school prayer, a ban on flag burning and a proposed constitutional amendment to prohibit same-sex marriage. He refused to back liberal Nancy Pelosi for Democratic leader after their party lost control of the House in 2010, saying that having her at the helm would make it difficult to recruit candidates in the South and Republican-leaning states.

In 2003, Bishop won a long-sought seat on the Appropriations Committee. He has worked to safeguard and deliver funds to his district's military facilities. Bishop also has been active on farm issues. He worked with the Republican House majority in 1996 on the Freedom to Farm Act to fashion a "market-oriented, no-net cost" program for peanuts. In 2002, he helped to craft the scaled-back program for peanut support, which was based on phasing out quotas and price guarantees. On the 2008 farm bill, he again was focused on the peanut farmers in his district. He helped design the peanut-rotation program, which he said encourages "a cleaner, greener method of planting while ensuring an affordable and accessible supply to the markets that rely on U.S.-grown peanuts." When Transportation Secretary Ray LaHood in June 2010 proposed banning peanuts on airplanes to protect passengers with allergies, Bishop pointedly asked why the agency didn't also seek to ban milk, eggs, and traveling dogs and cats.

After the Democrats won control of the House in 2006, Bishop was considered for the chairmanship of the Intelligence Committee, but it ultimately went to Rep. Silvestre Reyes, D-Texas. Instead, Bishop gained seats on the constituent-friendly Agriculture, Defense and Military Construction subcommittees at Appropriations. In 2008, he won passage of an amendment to the defense spending bill that provided 180 days of health care for military members who transition from active to reserve status.

In 2000, Bishop faced serious re-election competition from Dylan Glenn, a former aide to George H.W. Bush. The contest between two African-Americans in a rural, then majority-white district was unprecedented, but race was not an issue in the campaign. Bishop largely ignored the challenger and ran on his record, while Glenn offered the perspective of a new generation focusing on economic growth. Bishop won 54%-46%. Bishop contemplated a run in 2008 against GOP Sen. Saxby Chambliss, but decided to stay in the House, where his seniority gave him growing influence.

However, Bishop found himself in the race of his life in 2010, as Republicans targeted him for what they called excessive fealty to Pelosi. His opponent was Mike Keown, a white state representative who highlighted Bishop's support of the Democrats' health care overhaul. In the year's anti-incumbent climate, Keown also got a strong boost from news reports that Black Caucus Foundation scholarships had gone to Bishop's stepdaughter and his wife's niece. Bishop said the scholarships were awarded before rules barring such awards were enacted.

He attacked Keown for lacking much of a political record, and got a break of his own when a strategist for Keown was indicted in a vote-buying case in Alabama. Their battle went down to the wire, with the Associated Press calling the race for Keown on Election Night. But thousands of votes from Muscogee County had not yet been counted, and within a few hours, Bishop had a nearly 5,000-vote lead, prompting the AP to retract its announcement. He eventually prevailed with 51.4% to Keown's 48.6%. He and fellow Georgia Democrat John Barrow remain vulnerable to GOP-led redistricting efforts.

THIRD DISTRICT

Lynn Westmoreland (R)

Elected 2004, 4th term; b. April 2, 1950, Atlanta; home, Grantville; Attended GA State U., 1969-71; Baptist; married (Joan); 3 children.

Elected Office: GA House of Reps., 1992-2004; Min. ldr. 2000-03.

Professional Career: Real estate developer; Owner, L.A.W. Builders, 1982-present.

DC Office: 2433 RHOB, 20515, 202-225-5901; Fax: 202-225-2515; Web site: westmoreland.house.gov.

State Offices: Newnan, 770-683-2033.

Committees: *Financial Services:* Financial Institutions & Consumer Credit; Insurance, Housing & Community Opportunity. *Permanent Select Committee on Intelligence:* Oversight (Chmn).

Group Ratings

	ACLU	ACU	ADA	CFG	AFS	FRC	LCV	ITIC	NTU	COC
2010	13	100	0	89	0	100	0	33	92	88
2009	–	100	0	96	0	–	0	–	91	71

National Journal Ratings

	2010 LIB	—	2010 CONS	2009 LIB	—	2009 CONS
Economic	0%	—	97%	11%	—	88%
Social	0%	—	85%	0%	—	93%
Foreign	23%	—	76%	0%	—	75%
Composite	11%	—	89%	9%	—	91%

Key Votes of the 111th Congress

1. Overturn Ledbetter	N	5. Bar federal abortion funds	Y	9. Stop detainee transfers	Y
2. Pass $820 billion stimulus	N	6. Pass health care bill	N	10. Legalize immigrants' kids	N
3. Let guns in national parks	Y	7. Regulate financial firms	N	11. Repeal don't ask, tell	N
4. Pass cap-and-trade	N	8. Pass tax cuts for some	N	12. Limit campaign funds	N

Election Results

2010 general	Lynn Westmoreland (R)	168,304	(69%)	($843,044)
	Frank Saunders (D)	73,932	(31%)	($44,112)
2010 primary	Lynn Westmoreland (R)	unopposed		

Prior Winning Percentages: 2008 (66%), 2006 (68%), 2004 (76%)

Population		Race/Ethnicity		Work	
Pop. 2010:	817,247	White:	66.8%	Private:	76.3%
Change since 2000:	Up 29.8%	Black:	24.2%	Government:	18.1%
Urban:	56.4%	Hispanic:	4.9%	Self-employed:	5.3%
Rural:	43.6%	Asian:	2.0%	Blue collar:	24.2%
Area size:	4,182 sq. mi.	Native Am.:	0.2%	White collar:	60.3%
		Hawaiian:	0.1%	Khaki collar:	0.7%
Age		Two+ races:	1.6%	Other:	14.8%
Median age:	36.5 yrs.				
More than 65 yrs:	10.9%	*Ancestry*		Median income:	$55,964
Less than 18 yrs:	27.4%	USA	12.8%	Median Home Value:	$172,600
		Irish	9.7%		
Education		English	9.1%	**Military Veterans**	
H.S. grad:	85.1%			% of Pop:	12.4%
College grad:	24.5%				
Grad degree:	8.7%				

Central Georgia; Atlanta Suburbs

South of Atlanta, Henry County is among the
fastest growing areas in the United States, with
a leap in population of 64% from 2000 to 2009.
The county's flourishing residential, commercial
and industrial development took root near its
seven Interstate 75 interchanges and has benefited from the proximity to Hartsfield-Jackson
Atlanta International Airport. West of Henry
County is the old courthouse town of Fayetteville, whose Holliday-Dorsey-Fife House is

2008 Presidential Vote		
John McCain (R)	233,197	(65%)
Barack Obama (D)	125,087	(35%)
2004 Presidential Vote		
George Bush (R)	207,252	(70%)
John Kerry (D)	86,361	(29%)
Cook Partisan Voting Index:	R+19	

thought to have inspired the columned architecture of Tara in author Margaret Mitchell's
Gone With the Wind. The town is now engulfed by suburban subdivisions spreading out from
Atlanta. Sprawl has reached Newnan and Carrollton, and spread farther south to Thomaston.
In the old textile town of West Point in Troup County, along the Alabama border, South Korean
automaker Kia built a $1.2 billion plant that opened in 2009 and, with its supplier companies,
brought 3,000 jobs to the area. Several other companies, including NCR Corp., also have set up
shop or expanded in recent years.

Much of this territory is within the 3rd Congressional District of Georgia. In the 2005 redistricting, it replaced the old 8th District. It includes roughly one-third of the small industrial city of
Columbus (the rest is in the 2nd District, which also contains most of Fort Benning), but Fayette
County is the largest population center. And the ring of five counties that are closest to Atlanta
include roughly half of the district's population. This is conservative country, with young tradition-
minded families and a large share of military families. People here are upwardly mobile, but aren't
necessarily at the upper end of the income scale. The ancestral politics of most of this area was
Democratic, but that is as much a part of history now as Tara. This is one of the most heavily Republican congressional districts in Georgia. President Bush won 70% here in 2004, and Republican
candidate John McCain won 65% in 2008.

Lynn Westmoreland (R)

The congressman from the 3rd District is Lynn Westmoreland, a Republican first elected in 2004.
Westmoreland grew up in the Atlanta area, left Georgia State University after two years and became a real estate broker and homebuilder in Fayette County. After losing two races for the state
Senate, Westmoreland was elected in 1992 to the Georgia House, where he founded the Conservative Policy Caucus, a group of fiscally conservative, anti-tax lawmakers. He got under the skin of
the Democratic establishment to say the least; longtime Democratic House Speaker Tom Murphy
once called him "a braying jackass." In 2000, he was elected House minority leader and in that
position refused to agree to tax increases, even when it meant defying newly elected Republican
Gov. Sonny Perdue.

In 2004, Republican Rep. Mac Collins ran for the Senate, and Westmoreland faced a choice
between staying in the Georgia Legislature, where he stood to become speaker if Republicans won
a majority in the state House, or running for a safe Republican open seat in the U.S. House. He
chose the latter and ran on an anti-spending platform. The primary race was a contest between
Westmoreland and Dylan Glenn, a former staffer for Perdue and George H.W. Bush. Glenn, an
African-American from Columbus, had run twice unsuccessfully in the 2nd District. He was endorsed by former House Speaker Newt Gingrich of Georgia, who argued that a Glenn victory would
help the party appeal to black voters. Republican Sen. Saxby Chambliss endorsed Westmoreland.
In the primary, he beat Glenn 46%-38%. During the three weeks between the primary and the
August runoff, Glenn accused Westmoreland of taking gifts from lobbyists, and Westmoreland
labeled Glenn a "Washington insider." Westmoreland won 55%-45%, carrying 12 of the 18 counties.

In the House, Westmoreland has a conservative voting record and was among the first members to join the Tea Party Caucus in 2010. He was a deputy whip in the 111th Congress (2009-10)
as well as one of five vice chairs for the National Republican Congressional Committee, helping to
recruit and raise money for GOP candidates in the South. He focused on districts where McCain
outpolled Obama. After the Republican takeover of the House in the 2010 elections, he landed a
seat on the Financial Services Committee. In public, he has shown a hard edge that has sometimes
drawn controversy. At a 2007 House Oversight hearing to discuss security contractor Blackwater
USA, which had been accused of killing 11 Iraqis a month earlier, Westmoreland praised the company and said Democrats were investigating it because their party "does not like companies who
show a profit." Following Hurricane Katrina in 2005, he worked with other conservatives to propose "Operation Offset," an attempt to limit the cost of the relief and reconstruction efforts in Gulf

Coast states. In 2008, he helped to organize a month-long protest on the House floor of Speaker Nancy Pelosi's refusal to bring up for a vote energy legislation allowing more oil exploration.

Westmoreland was outspoken in his opposition to the extension of the Voting Rights Act, citing the "great progress" Georgia made since enactment of the law in 1965. When the House debated the bill in 2006, he offered an amendment to make it easier for states to opt out of the law's requirements, but lost. He also opposed the bill giving the majority-black District of Columbia a full vote in the House, and in 2007, he was one of two House members who voted against a resolution setting up special divisions in the Justice Department to investigate murders during the civil rights era. His views have led to rocky relationships with leading African-American politicians. During the 2008 presidential campaign, he called Democratic candidate Barack Obama "uppity." He said he was surprised to learn it was a racially loaded term.

Shortly after he took office, Westmoreland worked intensively with the new Republican majority in the state legislature to redraw congressional district lines to create more compact districts, with the not unintended benefit of making a Republican incumbent safer and jeopardizing two incumbent Democrats. In March 2005, the legislature passed a new map designed by a 23-year-old legislative aide to Westmoreland. In recognition of his service, House Republican leaders put Westmoreland in charge of monitoring states' efforts to redraw congressional districts following the 2010 census. In his re-election bids, he has won with only token opposition.

FOURTH DISTRICT

Hank Johnson (D)

Elected 2006, 3rd term; b. Oct. 2, 1954, Washington, D.C.; home, Lithonia; Clark Atlanta U., B.A. 1976, Texas S. U., J.D. 1979; Buddhist; married (Mereda Davis); 2 children.

Elected Office: DeKalb Cnty. comm., 2001-06.

Professional Career: Practicing atty., 1980-2006; Associate judge, DeKalb Cnty. Magistrate Court, 1989-2006.

DC Office: 1427 LHOB, 20515, 202-225-1605; Fax: 202-226-0691; Web site: hankjohnson.house.gov.

State Offices: Lithonia, 770-987-2291.

Committees: *Armed Services:* Emerging Threats & Capabilities; Seapower & Projection Forces. *Judiciary:* Courts, Commercial & Administrative Law; Crime, Terrorism & Homeland Security.

Group Ratings

	ACLU	ACU	ADA	CFG	AFS	FRC	LCV	ITIC	NTU	COC
2010	94	0	90	0	100	0	100	100	8	25
2009	–	0	95	0	100	–	93	–	2	33

National Journal Ratings

	2010 LIB —	2010 CONS	2009 LIB —	2009 CONS
Economic	67%	32%	87%	12%
Social	77%	21%	69%	30%
Foreign	73%	24%	77%	23%
Composite	73%	27%	78%	22%

Key Votes of the 111th Congress

1. Overturn Ledbetter	Y	5. Bar federal abortion funds	N	9. Stop detainee transfers	Y
2. Pass $820 billion stimulus	Y	6. Pass health care bill	Y	10. Legalize immigrants' kids	Y
3. Let guns in national parks	Y	7. Regulate financial firms	Y	11. Repeal don't ask, tell	Y
4. Pass cap-and-trade	Y	8. Pass tax cuts for some	Y	12. Limit campaign funds	Y

Election Results

2010 general	Hank Johnson (D)	131,760	(75%)	($581,545)
	Lisbeth Carter (R)	44,707	(25%)	($121,425)
2010 primary	Hank Johnson (D)	28,095	(55%)	
	Vernon Jones (D)	13,407	(26%)	
	Connie Stokes (D)	9,411	(18%)	

Prior Winning Percentages: 2008 (100%), 2006 (75%)

Population		Race/Ethnicity		Work	
Pop. 2010:	665,541	White:	21.2%	Private:	80.6%
Change since 2000:	Up 5.7%	Black:	55.2%	Government:	14.3%
Urban:	98.5%	Hispanic:	16.1%	Self-employed:	4.8%
Rural:	1.5%	Asian:	5.3%	Blue collar:	23.8%
Area size:	333 sq. mi.	Native Am.:	0.2%	White collar:	59.5%
		Hawaiian:	0.0%	Khaki collar:	0.1%
Age		Two+ races:	1.6%	Other:	16.6%
Median age:	33.1 yrs.				
More than 65 yrs:	7.2%	*Ancestry*		Median income:	$47,605
Less than 18 yrs:	26.2%	English	3.9%	Median Home Value:	$167,200
		Subsaharan	3.8%		
Education		Irish	3.7%	**Military Veterans**	
H.S. grad:	83.9%			% of Pop:	7.6%
College grad:	29.1%				
Grad degree:	10.4%				

Atlanta Suburbs; DeKalb County

In 1920, when Gutzom Borglum began sculpting Jefferson Davis, Robert E. Lee, and Stonewall Jackson into the side of Stone Mountain, the huge outcropping of granite—the largest single piece of sculpture in the world—was a day's drive into the country from central Atlanta and was soon to become a rallying point for the Ku Klux Klan. Even when the memorial was completed in 1972, suburban development barely reached this far. But today, after three decades

2008 Presidential Vote
Barack Obama (D) 219,046   (79%)
John McCain (R) 55,378   (20%)

2004 Presidential Vote
John Kerry (D) 167,666   (71%)
George Bush (R) 67,040   (29%)

Cook Partisan Voting Index: D+24

of some of the most explosive metropolitan growth in the country, DeKalb (pronounced *dee-KAB* by locals) County is part of the Atlanta metropolitan area, and this monument to the Confederacy sits among one of the most cosmopolitan and liberal constituencies in the South.

In north DeKalb County are affluent suburbs, including much of Atlanta's Jewish community, with voting habits much more liberal than in other suburbs. South DeKalb County has been transformed from mostly rural territory in the 1970s into one of the nation's largest collections of affluent African-American neighborhoods, rivaled only by Prince George's County in Maryland. The county was a prime destination for evacuees from New Orleans following Hurricane Katrina in 2005. DeKalb's population grew by 22% in the 1990s, and by 12% from 2000 to 2009. The demographic changes have moved its politics well to the left. It was a Republican county when rural Georgia was almost all Democratic in the 1960s. Now it is the most heavily Democratic major county in Georgia. In 2004, DeKalb voted 73%-27% for Democrat John Kerry, his best percentage in the state, except for one tiny rural county. In 2008, Democrat Barack Obama won DeKalb, 79%-20%.

The 4th Congressional District of Georgia consists of more than two-thirds of DeKalb County, a corner of the more Republican Gwinnett County and much of Rockdale County, including Conyers. In 2008, Rockdale elected its first black county commission chairman. About 75% of the population of the district now is in DeKalb. The 4th and the next-door 5th District, both with African-American majorities, are the most Democratic in Georgia.

Hank Johnson (D)

The congressman from the 4th District is Hank Johnson, a Democrat who won the seat in 2006. He was born in Washington, D.C., where his father was director of classifications and paroles for the Bureau of Prisons and his mother was a schoolteacher. He practiced law as a civil and criminal litigator, served 12 years as a magistrate judge in DeKalb County and then five years on the DeKalb County Commission. He resigned from the commission to run for Congress. Although his immediate family members are Presbyterians, he has been a Buddhist since the 1970s; he and Rep. Mazie Hirono, D-Hawaii, are the first practicing Buddhists in Congress. "If you could say what drives me, it's the middle ground, the middle way," he told *The Atlanta Journal-Constitution* in 2009, invoking a Buddhist principle.

Johnson ousted Democratic Rep. Cynthia McKinney in the primary. McKinney had served five terms in the House before losing her seat to Denise Majette in the 2002 Democratic primary. But she won it back two years later, after Majette vacated it to run for the Senate. She was a controversial incumbent, once suggesting that President Bush might have had prior knowledge of the

September 11 terrorist attacks but did not act on it because a war on terrorism would boost defense stocks held by his father's friends. Her own party lost patience with her after she struck a Capitol police officer who had stopped her at a security checkpoint.

In the July 18 primary, McKinney led Johnson, 47%-44%, but her failure to break the 50% threshold in the three-candidate field forced a runoff three weeks later. Johnson gained additional momentum after the primary. His fundraising suddenly picked up, donors, including former Democratic Gov. Roy Barnes, weighed in against McKinney. She responded by criticizing Johnson's past financial troubles, which included declaring bankruptcy in the late 1980s. But in the runoff, turnout was up and Johnson beat McKinney easily, 59%-41%. He won 57%-43% in McKinney's stronghold of DeKalb. Johnson breezed to victory in the general election against minor opposition.

In the House, Johnson has a solidly liberal voting record and a reputation as a thoughtful lawmaker. Republicans, however, have taken him to task for what they consider his embarrassing verbal gaffes. After South Carolina Republican Rep. Joe Wilson shouted, "You lie!" at President Obama during a September 2009 address to Congress, Johnson suggested racial tensions would be inflamed and said, "We'll have folks putting on white hoods and white uniforms again" if no disciplinary action was taken against Wilson. At an Armed Services Committee hearing in 2010, he expressed concern that the island of Guam "will become so overly populated that it will tip over and capsize." He sought to explain that he was "using a metaphor" to describe how adding more military personnel to Guam could hamper its ecosystem and infrastructure.

On the Judiciary Committee, Johnson questioned political hirings and firings at the Justice Department during the Bush administration and sponsored a resolution calling for the impeachment of Vice President Cheney. He also called for an investigation of the use of waterboarding, a form of coercion that simulates drowning that has been used on suspected terrorists. He backed relief for people facing housing foreclosures and sought protections against predatory lending. In 2009, he became chairman of the revamped Judiciary Subcommittee on Courts and Competition Policy, and he took a step in the direction of getting on a leadership track by joining the House Democratic whip organization in 2009.

Johnson won re-election in 2008 without major party opposition, the first such outcome in 52 years in the 4th District. McKinney considered a rematch with Johnson, but then decided to run for president as the nominee of the Green Party. In 2009, Johnson announced that he had battled Hepatitis C, an incurable blood-borne liver disease, for more than a decade. Two Democrats lined up to challenge him in the 2010 primary, and one of them, former DeKalb County head Vernon Jones, openly questioned his missing a series of debates. Johnson, however, insisted his health was fine and unveiled an endorsement from Obama, who said the congressman "has done an outstanding job." He won the July primary with 55% to Jones' 26% and former DeKalb County Commissioner Connie Stokes' 18%, then trampled Atlanta business consultant Liz Carter in the general election with 75% of the vote.

FIFTH DISTRICT

John Lewis (D)

Elected 1986, 13th term; b. Feb. 21, 1940, Troy, AL; home, Atlanta; Amer. Baptist Theol. Seminary, B.A. 1961, Fisk U., B.A. 1963; Baptist; married (Lillian); 1 child.

Elected Office: Atlanta City Cncl., 1981–86.

Professional Career: Chmn., Student Nonviolent Coord. Cmte., 1963–66; Field Foundation, 1966–67; Community organization dir., Southern Regional Cncl., 1967–70; Exec. dir., Voter Educ. Project, 1970–76; Assoc. dir., ACTION, 1977–80; Community affairs dir., Natl. Coop. Bank, 1980–82.

DC Office: 343 CHOB, 20515, 202-225-3801; Fax: 202-225-0351; Web site: johnlewis.house.gov.

State Offices: Atlanta, 404-659-0116.

Committees: *Ways & Means:* Human Resources; Oversight (RMM).

Group Ratings

	ACLU	ACU	ADA	CFG	AFS	FRC	LCV	ITIC	NTU	COC
2010	93	0	100	0	100	0	100	67	7	13
2009	–	0	85	4	100	–	79	–	3	43

National Journal Ratings

	2010 LIB	—	2010 CONS		2009 LIB	—	2009 CONS
Economic	90%	—	0%		91%	—	0%
Social	93%	—	0%		89%	—	0%
Foreign	97%	—	0%		*	—	*
Composite	97%	—	3%		*	—	*

Key Votes of the 111th Congress

1. Overturn Ledbetter	Y	5. Bar federal abortion funds	N	9. Stop detainee transfers	N
2. Pass $820 billion stimulus	Y	6. Pass health care bill	Y	10. Legalize immigrants' kids	Y
3. Let guns in national parks	N	7. Regulate financial firms	Y	11. Repeal don't ask, tell	Y
4. Pass cap-and-trade	Y	8. Pass tax cuts for some	Y	12. Limit campaign funds	Y

Election Results

2010 general	John Lewis (D)	130,782	(74%)	($1,013,992)
	Fenn Little (R)	46,622	(26%)	($115,223)
2010 primary	John Lewis (D)	unopposed		

Prior Winning Percentages: 2008 (100%), 2006 (100%), 2004 (100%), 2002 (100%), 2000 (77%), 1998 (79%), 1996 (100%), 1994 (69%), 1992 (72%), 1990 (76%), 1988 (78%), 1986 (75%)

Population		Race/Ethnicity		Work	
Pop. 2010:	630,462	White:	36.9%	Private:	81.7%
Change since 2000:	Up 0.1%	Black:	49.7%	Government:	12.7%
Urban:	99.7%	Hispanic:	8.0%	Self-employed:	5.6%
Rural:	0.3%	Asian:	3.4%	Blue collar:	12.7%
Area size:	247 sq. mi.	Native Am.:	0.2%	White collar:	70.5%
		Hawaiian:	0.0%	Khaki collar:	0.1%
Age		Two+ races:	1.6%	Other:	16.7%
Median age:	33.9 yrs.				
More than 65 yrs:	8.5%	*Ancestry*		Median income:	$51,599
Less than 18 yrs:	21.5%	English	7.3%	Median Home Value:	$258,400
		German	6.1%		
Education		USA	5.6%	**Military Veterans**	
H.S. grad:	86.5%			% of Pop:	6.4%
College grad:	45.8%				
Grad degree:	18.4%				

Atlanta

Venture out of the quiet of the Ebenezer Baptist Church or the shade of the Rev. Martin Luther King Jr.'s boyhood home two blocks away and into the steamy heat of the Georgia sun, and one can see, a mile away, downtown Atlanta's atrium skyscrapers. They are evidence of the wealth and vibrant growth of the commercial capital of the South, the metropolis that has grown up where there was little more than a railroad junction at the time of the Civil War. But

2008 Presidential Vote		
Barack Obama (D) 231,893	(80%)
John McCain (R) 57,213	(20%)

2004 Presidential Vote		
John Kerry (D) 179,576	(74%)
George Bush (R) 62,351	(26%)

Cook Partisan Voting Index: D+26

the human achievement that is downtown Atlanta is overshadowed by the revolution started in large part by a man who grew up on Auburn Avenue. Atlanta's white establishment, led by Mayors William Hartsfield and Ivan Allen and Coca-Cola's Robert Woodruff, deserve credit for abandoning segregation, but it was King and other civil rights leaders who took the risks that led them to do so. Atlanta's city fathers acted out of good will, but also with an eye for the economic growth of the city, which they knew would be hurt by violent resistance.

Today, Atlanta is the center of the nation's ninth-largest metropolitan area. From Auburn Avenue, it spreads into two dozen counties of northern Georgia. Its Hartsfield-Jackson Atlanta Airport is the busiest in the world, with 88 million passengers in 2009, nearly 1 million takeoffs and landings and an expansion of its international terminal under way. It has helped make the city the nation's fourth busiest hospitality hub, and by mid-2010, at least six new hotels had opened. Atlanta also has vibrant office centers, in downtown, midtown and Buckhead to the north. Modern stadiums and sports facilities were built for the 1996 Summer Olympics. Unemployment in metropolitan Atlanta climbed above 10% in 2010, but was beginning to decline. Coca-Cola's skyscraper headquarters stands as a symbol of Atlanta's most successful worldwide business. In 2006, Coca-Cola donated a $10 million parcel of land near Centennial Park for a $100 million civil rights museum to house the Martin Luther King Jr. papers.

The 5th Congressional District of Georgia includes all of the city of Atlanta, down to the suburb of East Point to the south. It occupies most of the land inside the Interstate 285 ring road—the city of Atlanta, including posh and Republican Buckhead, the westernmost part of DeKalb County, and the northern edge of Clayton County, including the airport. The 5th District is overwhelmingly Democratic.

John Lewis (D)

The congressman from the 5th District is John Lewis, first elected in 1986. Lewis made history as a leader of the civil rights movement, an experience he recounted in his 1998 autobiography, *Walking With the Wind*. A sharecropper's son from Troy, Ala., he was seized by religious fervor as a child, preaching in the barnyard, determined to be a minister. Lewis was the first in his family to finish high school. He wrote to activist Ralph Abernathy for help in suing for the right to enter Troy State College, and he met King when he was 18. In 1959, at age 19, he helped organize the first lunch counter sit-in, which was received with open hostility. In 1960, the day after John F. Kennedy was elected president, Lewis sat in the Krystal Diner in Nashville, where a waitress poured cleansing powder down his back and water over his food to get him to leave. The restaurant manager then turned a fumigating machine on him.

In May 1961, he was on the first of the Freedom Rides, in which protesters of segregation rode buses through the South and were attacked as they went. Lewis was viciously beaten in Rock Hill, S.C., and Montgomery, Ala. He spoke at the 1963 March on Washington, criticizing Kennedy liberals for inaction on civil rights and calling for massive help for the poor. In 1964, he helped coordinate the Mississippi Freedom Project. And in March 1965, he led the Selma-to-Montgomery march to petition for voting rights. During that historic event, he was beaten by policemen, who fractured his skull. Quietly maintaining his poise and sound judgment under harsh circumstances, Lewis was one of the people who risked their lives to make the civil rights revolution happen. He worked for Robert Kennedy's campaign for president in 1968 and was with him in Indianapolis when they heard King had been shot. Today, his activism is inspired by other causes. He was among five members of Congress arrested in April 2009 outside the Sudanese embassy in protest of that country's decision to remove aid agencies from the Darfur region.

Lewis' first foray into electoral politics was unsuccessful. He ran in 1977 to succeed Democratic Rep. Andrew Young in the House and was soundly beaten by Democrat Wyche Fowler in a special election. After winning a seat on the Atlanta Council in 1981, Lewis ran again for Congress in 1986 and trailed Julian Bond 47%-35% in the primary. Even though Bond won more than 60% of the black vote, Lewis won the runoff by assembling a coalition of poor blacks and affluent whites. "Vote for the tugboat, not the showboat" was his slogan, stressing his work on local issues. He has been re-elected easily ever since.

Lewis has been a strong partisan, with a firmly liberal voting record. Usually quiet, he can speak in the forceful cadences reminiscent of black civil rights-era preachers, as he did in opposition to the Gulf War resolution in January 1991 and to the impeachment of President Clinton in December 1998. At the dramatic finale of the health care legislation in March 2010, Lewis linked arms with House Speaker Nancy Pelosi and walked to the Capitol through a gauntlet of taunting anti-health care reform protestors. "I think I will remember the walk across the street with John Lewis for the rest of my life," Rep. Brad Miller, D-N.C., said later.

Lewis is the senior chief deputy whip in the Democratic leadership, and also the ranking Democrat on the Oversight Subcommittee of the Ways and Means Committee. In 2009, the ethics travails of Ways and Means Chairman Charles Rangel, D-N.Y., fueled speculation that Lewis could be an acceptable alternative if Rangel were forced to step down, even though Lewis was only the fifth-ranking Democrat on the panel. But he ultimately ceded the job to Rep. Sander Levin, D-Mich. Only occasionally does he defect from his party, as when he opposed the 1994 crime bill because of his disapproval of capital punishment and when he voted against the Iraq supplemental spending bill in 2007 because it contained funds for continued military action.

Lewis has worked to commemorate the civil rights revolution in which he played such a large part. He got a federal building in Atlanta named for King and won historic-trail designation for the demonstrators' route from Selma to Montgomery. Since 1998, he has led members of Congress on pilgrimages to civil rights sites. Lewis has stoutly defended racial quotas and preferences. He strongly championed the reauthorization of the Voting Rights Act, and his support helped ensure it carried by a large majority over the objections of critics, who claimed it was no longer necessary. In June 2007, he won House passage of his bill funding new offices in the FBI and the Justice Department to investigate old civil rights cases that have languished.

The 2008 presidential campaign was a difficult experience for Lewis. Following extensive pressure from various camps, he endorsed Hillary Rodham Clinton in 2007 as "a strong leader," and he defended her from attacks by other civil rights leaders. When Barack Obama won the Georgia primary, Lewis came under local and national pressure to switch. Some of the pressure came from two challengers in the July primary, which Lewis eventually won, with 69% of the vote. In late February, he endorsed Obama "following a long, hard, difficult struggle" and spoke of Obama's candidacy as a transformational moment. "Something's happening in America, something some of us did not see coming," Lewis said. "It's a movement. It's a spiritual event."

Obama welcomed the switch, and Lewis became an outspoken advocate, sometimes excessively so, as in an October statement when he compared the campaign rhetoric of Republican nominee John McCain to that of former segregationist presidential candidate George Wallace of Alabama. McCain called the comparison "beyond the pale." At the Democratic convention in August, where he was treated as an iconic hero, Lewis broke down in tears as he spoke of Obama's historic candidacy and the 45th anniversary of King's famous "I Have a Dream" speech. In a dramatic epilogue to Lewis' involvement in the presidential campaign, in February 2009, Elwin Wilson of Rock Hill, S.C., apologized on national television for slugging Lewis in the Freedom Ride attack, saying, "I am ashamed." Seated next to him, Lewis embraced the 68-year-old man, and said, "I forgive you." Lewis called the apology "amazing, unreal, unbelievable" and said that it showed the "power of reconciliation."

SIXTH DISTRICT

Tom Price (R)

Elected 2004, 4th term; b. Oct. 8, 1954, Lansing, MI; home, Roswell; U. of MI, B.A. 1976, M.D. 1979; Presbyterian; married (Betty); 1 child.

Elected Office: GA Senate, 1996-2004; Maj. ldr., 2002-03.

Professional Career: Practicing orthopedic surgeon, 1979-2002; Asst. prof., Emory U., 2002-present.

DC Office: 403 CHOB, 20515, 202-225-4501; Fax: 202-225-4656; Web site: tomprice.house.gov.

State Offices: Canton, 678-493-6176; Marietta, 770-565-4990.

Committees: *Budget. Ways & Means:* Health; Human Resources.

Group Ratings

	ACLU	ACU	ADA	CFG	AFS	FRC	LCV	ITIC	NTU	COC
2010	13	100	0	100	0	93	0	33	93	88
2009	–	100	0	100	0	–	0	–	93	73

National Journal Ratings

	2010 LIB	—	2010 CONS	2009 LIB	—	2009 CONS
Economic	8%	—	91%	9%	—	89%
Social	0%	—	85%	17%	—	82%
Foreign	0%	—	88%	0%	—	75%
Composite	7%	—	93%	13%	—	87%

Key Votes of the 111th Congress

1. Overturn Ledbetter	N	5. Bar federal abortion funds	Y	9. Stop detainee transfers	Y
2. Pass $820 billion stimulus	N	6. Pass health care bill	N	10. Legalize immigrants' kids	N
3. Let guns in national parks	Y	7. Regulate financial firms	N	11. Repeal don't ask, tell	N
4. Pass cap-and-trade	N	8. Pass tax cuts for some	N	12. Limit campaign funds	N

Election Results

2010 general	Tom Price (R) .... unopposed	($2,105,230)
2010 primary	Tom Price (R) .... unopposed	

Prior Winning Percentages: 2008 (68%), 2006 (72%), 2004 (100%)

Population		Race/Ethnicity		Work	
Pop. 2010:	767,798	White:	70.7%	Private:	84.5%
Change since 2000:	Up 21.9%	Black:	10.0%	Government:	8.7%
Urban:	93.5%	Hispanic:	9.3%	Self-employed:	6.6%
Rural:	6.5%	Asian:	7.6%	Blue collar:	12.0%
Area size:	695 sq. mi.	Native Am.:	0.2%	White collar:	75.6%
		Hawaiian:	0.0%	Khaki collar:	0.0%
Age		Two+ races:	1.8%	Other:	12.3%
Median age:	36.0 yrs.				
More than 65 yrs:	8.4%	*Ancestry*		Median income:	$79,139
Less than 18 yrs:	27.7%	German	10.5%	Median Home Value:	$285,500
		English	10.5%		
Education		Irish	10.0%	**Military Veterans**	
H.S. grad:	92.8%			% of Pop:	8.3%
College grad:	51.2%				
Grad degree:	16.8%				

North Atlanta Suburbs

In the red clay north of Atlanta, an almost wholly new metropolitan quarter has grown up over the past four decades, as affluent Atlanta has spread out past the Interstate 285 Perimeter into territory that was once farms, small towns, and modest factory cities. Where there were perhaps 100,000 people in the 1950s, there are more than 1 million today. No longer is downtown Atlanta the only focus. The edge cities of Perimeter Center and the area near Cumberland Mall are not

2008 Presidential Vote		
John McCain (R) 226,456	(65%)
Barack Obama (D) 120,093	(34%)
2004 Presidential Vote		
George Bush (R) 215,437	(70%)
John Kerry (D) 90,348	(29%)
Cook Partisan Voting Index: R+19		

just for shopping. They are major office centers, exceeding downtown Atlanta in square footage. Along the usually jammed Georgia 400 Highway, in the fast-growing northern part of Fulton County, are the affluent suburbs of Sandy Springs, Roswell, and Alpharetta. At the tip of the county, near the Chattahoochee River, the new cities of Johns Creek and Milton were incorporated in 2006 to free residents of county government. Cobb County is the headquarters of the Weather Channel. Home Depot, the nation's second-largest retailer, is based in Sandy Springs.

Farther out in Cherokee County, where the population has more than doubled since 1990, the big issue has been the proposed Northern Arc highway. Commuters on congested roads have ached for relief. For all this economic and demographic change, this Golden Crescent north of the Perimeter and between Interstate 75 in Cobb County and Interstate 85 strives to keep at least some reminders of old rural Georgia. The buildings are tree-shaded, and lush foliage and large-lot requirements have given most of the communities a woodsy look. Local officials expect the growth that stalled during the recession will continue, albeit at a much slower pace. Eastern Cobb County will see more infill development and smaller homes to accommodate the expected numbers of senior citizens arriving over the next 20 years.

The 6th Congressional District of Georgia occupies a large portion of this suburban area north of Atlanta, including the eastern slice of Cobb County, much of northern Fulton, the northwest tip of DeKalb, and all of Cherokee County. It contains affluent Alpharetta, fast-growing Canton, and historic Roswell. This seat was created after the 1990 census, and its boundaries have twice been reshaped by redistricting. It ranks among the nation's richest and most educated congressional districts. It is also a heavily Republican district, and the political tension here tends to be between economic and cultural conservatives. In 2004, President Bush defeated Democrat John Kerry 70%-29%. In 2008, Democrat Barack Obama trimmed the Republican lead for John McCain here to 65%-34%.

Tom Price (R)

The congressman from the 6th District is Tom Price, a Republican first elected in 2004 who has become one of the leading spokesmen for his party's conservative message. Price grew up in Michigan and graduated from the University of Michigan and its medical school. His father and grandfather were both physicians. He did his residency in orthopedic surgery at Emory Medical School and then moved to Roswell, where he was involved in civic affairs and was president of the Rotary Club. Working closely with the Medical Association of Georgia, he campaigned locally against President Clinton's health care plan in the early 1990s. When a seat opened in the state Senate in 1996, he was elected, and quickly moved up the leadership ranks to become majority leader when Republicans captured the Senate in 2002 for the first time since Reconstruction.

When Republican U.S. Rep. Johnny Isakson announced he was running for the Senate seat being vacated by Democrat Zell Miller, the contest for this heavily Republican open seat was hard-fought and big-spending. Three state senators ran—Price from Fulton County, and Robert Lamutt and Chuck Clay from Cobb County. Price spent $499,000 of his own money and contrasted his work in medicine with the legal and business careers of his two main opponents. He highlighted his fiscal conservatism and strong support for limiting jury awards in malpractice suits, a position that won him considerable support from the medical community. Calling the federal income tax "broken," he supported a national retail sales tax. He said that he had "a surgeon's mentality.... I get things done."

Price led the first round of the primary with 35% of the vote; Lamutt made it into the runoff with 28%. Lamutt, who gave $1.5 million to his campaign, criticized Price as a "special interest" candidate because he raised large sums from fellow doctors. He also attacked Price's 2003 support for a 25-cent tax increase on cigarettes. Price defended his vote as a tool to reduce local property taxes, and claimed Lamutt helped cigarette makers at the expense of everyday people. In the run-off, Price got 79% in Fulton County and held Lamutt to 59% in Cobb. With the small vote in Chero-kee County split nearly evenly, Price won 54%-46%.

In the House, Price's voting record is among the most conservative. As a member of the Finan-cial Services Committee, he has dealt contentiously on housing and other issues with liberal Rep. Barney Frank, D-Mass. When Democrats sought to extend unemployment benefits in 2010, Price cited economists who warned of a "moral hazard" in doing so. On health care, he opposed govern-ment intervention to negotiate Medicare drug prices, which he said were being reduced by market forces. He also countered the Democratic health care reform bill with his own legislation focused on creating tax incentives for consumers to purchase insurance on the individual market. As one of 13 physicians in the House in 2009, he helped to create the Medical and Dental Doctors in Congress Caucus to try to establish a unified Republican message on health care.

Price also has been a fierce partisan. In 2009, he became chairman of the Republican Study Committee, which promotes conservative ideas and legislation. He helped create an "Official Truth Squad" to highlight statements and positions of Democrats that he thinks might be unpopular with the public. *The Washington Post* wrote in 2007: "The bookish physician has transformed himself into a Republican guerrilla warrior, a near-constant presence on the House floor, gumming up the works with parliamentary objections, verbal volleys, and partisan maneuvering."

He was a leading organizer of the House Republicans' protest in the House chamber during the August 2008 recess, which was aimed at pressuring Democratic Speaker Nancy Pelosi to bring to the floor a bill allowing offshore oil exploration in America's coastal waters. He found an addi-tional foil in President Obama, frequently sending out YouTube videos and appearing on television news shows and writing op-ed columns to blast the president and promote "fundamental American principles," including low taxes and limited government. Democrats brushed him off as an ideologi-cal irritant, but his energy—he told *The Atlanta Journal-Constitution* he gets in before 7:30 a.m. and leaves at 10:30 or 11 p.m.—and his enthusiasm for playing political hardball impressed his GOP colleagues.

In 2010, Price took a step up in leadership to become chairman of the House Republican Policy Committee, the party's in-house idea factory. Rep. Connie Mack of Florida initially considered chal-lenging him for the position, but dropped out. "Now we must begin earning back the public's trust," Price said after winning the post.

Georgia's redistricting in 2005 served the Fulton County-based Price's interest by reducing opportunities for GOP primary challengers from Cobb County. That county is now divided between the 6th, 11th, and 13th districts. He has been re-elected with only minor opposition and ran unop-posed in 2010. He did get some negative attention 2010, when it was revealed he was among eight lawmakers under investigation by the Office of Congressional Ethics for holding fundraisers or receiving donations shortly from businesses shortly before voting on a Wall Street regulation bill.

SEVENTH DISTRICT

Rob Woodall (R)

Elected 2010, 1st term; b. Feb. 11, 1970, Athens; home, Lawrenceville; Furman U., B.A. 1992; U. of GA, J.D. 1997.; Methodist; Single.

Professional Career: Law clerk, private firm, 1993-94; chief of staff, legis. aide, Rep. John Linder, R-Ga., 1994-2010.

DC Office: 1725 LHOB, 20515, 202-225-4272; Fax: 202-225-4696; Web site: woodall.house.gov.

State Offices: Lawrenceville, 770-232-3005.

Committees: *Budget. Rules.*

Election Results

2010 general	Rob Woodall (R)	160,898	(67%)	($399,086)
	Doug Heckman (D)	78,996	(33%)	($81,220)
2010 primary	Rob Woodall (R)	39,987	(56%)	
	Jody Hice (R)	31,426	(44%)	
2010 primary	Rob Woodall (R)	27,634	(36%)	
	Jody Hice (R)	20,034	(26%)	
	Clay Cox (R)	15,249	(20%)	
	Jef Fincher (R)	4,608	(6%)	

Population		Race/Ethnicity		Work	
Pop. 2010:	903,191	White:	53.9%	Private:	82.3%
Change since 2000:	Up 43.4%	Black:	21.8%	Government:	11.8%
Urban:	86.8%	Hispanic:	13.2%	Self-employed:	5.7%
Rural:	13.2%	Asian:	8.7%	Blue collar:	19.1%
Area size:	978 sq. mi.	Native Am.:	0.2%	White collar:	67.3%
		Hawaiian:	0.0%	Khaki collar:	0.1%
Age		Two+ races:	1.9%	Other:	13.5%
Median age:	34.0 yrs.				
More than 65 yrs:	7.5%	*Ancestry*		Median income:	$63,661
Less than 18 yrs:	29.9%	Irish	8.6%	Median Home Value:	$197,600
		German	8.4%		
Education		USA	7.9%	**Military Veterans**	
H.S. grad:	88.0%			% of Pop:	8.8%
College grad:	33.7%				
Grad degree:	10.9%				

East Atlanta Suburbs

In the last two decades, greater Atlanta has grown out in every direction: south past the airport, west over the Chattahoochee River, north past the Perimeter Center, and east and northeast past Stone Mountain. The outer suburbs north of Atlanta have grown fastest of all. Gwinnett County features more-mature neighborhoods of affluent professionals and entrepreneurs. The closer-in portions of Gwinnett, near Interstate 85, with their older shopping districts, have been attracting Georgia's largest concentration of Hispanics and also middle-class blacks. The county's rapidly growing school system boasts that its students speak more than 100 languages. Farther out in Lawrenceville, Duluth, and Buford, downtown Atlanta seems very far away, both physically—it is 30 to 50 miles, and more than an hour of clogged rush-hour driving, to Peachtree Street—and in state of mind. For many, Atlanta is something that whizzes by on the way to Hartsfield-Jackson Atlanta International Airport.

The growth here and its diversity are hard to overstate. Gwinnett County cast 21,000 votes in 1972 and 291,000 in 2008. By contrast, Fulton County, which includes central Atlanta, cast

2008 Presidential Vote
John McCain (R) 211,493   (60%)
Barack Obama (D) 139,259   (39%)

2004 Presidential Vote
George Bush (R) 199,492   (70%)
John Kerry (D) 85,472   (30%)

Cook Partisan Voting Index: R+16

405,000, and DeKalb County cast 322,000. Gwinnett's population grew 37% from 2000 to 2010, to more than 805,000. Rapid growth in the area took a noticeable pause during the 2007-09 recession and the collapse of the national housing finance market, which all but killed residential and commercial development in Atlanta's northern suburbs. Like other metro Atlanta counties, the non-Hispanic white population has been dropping in the schools, while the overall numbers soar. There is some international flavor here: Mexicans in Norcross, Koreans in Duluth, and Bosnians in Lawrenceville. Beyond Gwinnett County, pre-recession growth was equally robust in Barrow, Walton, and Newton counties. These were once rural, low-income, and heavily Democratic areas. Now they are full of strivers and achievers, with many religious conservatives and many economic conservatives, and relatively few liberals and Democrats.

The 7th Congressional District of Georgia owes its existence to the rapid growth here since the early 1990s. Redistricting in 2005 gave it a more compact shape and recentered the district in Gwinnett, which has 78% of the population, compared to 58% previously. In addition to all of Barrow and Walton counties, the 7th includes thin slices of Forsyth and Newton counties. The changes increased the African-American population and had the effect of reducing the 2004 vote here for President Bush from 76% to 70%. In 2008, Republican John McCain beat Democrat Barack Obama in the district 60%-39%.

Rob Woodall (R)

The new congressman from Georgia's 7th District is Republican Rob Woodall, who succeeded the retiring Rep. John Linder after working for Linder as an aide for 16 years.

Woodall was born in Athens, Ga., the college town where his parents were finishing their studies at the University of Georgia. The family later moved to Avondale, Ga. His father was an entomologist who would take Rob and his older sister on expeditions to collect bugs in swampy areas. His parents now own his grandparents' farm, where they raise organic beef. Woodall calls his father a "rock" who still "throws hay and wrestles goats." The family was of modest means, shopped at Goodwill stores, and drove used cars. "Nobody squeezes a nickel harder than I do," Woodall said. He went to college on a ROTC scholarship and worked summers to pay his expenses, including a stint on the assembly line at an RC Cola bottling plant. While in law school, he clerked for a firm in Washington, where he worked on issues related to President Clinton's energy policy and then first lady Hillary Rodham Clinton's health care initiative. He fell in love with being on the frontlines of national policymaking, and worked out a deal with the dean of the University of Georgia School of Law to allow him to finish his degree in Washington. In 1994, Woodall left his job at the law firm and took a 50% pay cut to go to work as a legislative aide for Linder. He rose to chief of staff in 2000.

He became a candidate for the House after Linder announced his retirement in February 2010 after 18 years of service. Eight candidates entered the GOP primary in July. Woodall and radio talk-show host Jody Hice received the most votes, but neither attained the 50% threshold necessary to avoid a runoff.

In the runoff campaign, Hice was able to self-fund his campaign and had more money to spend than Woodall. Both candidates courted support from tea party groups. Woodall embraced the tea party movement's principles of limited government, strict constitutional constructionism and fiscal responsibility. "Uniting around those three principles so appeals to me," he said, adding that adherents get a bum rap for being uncaring. "Just because we don't want the government to do something doesn't mean that it shouldn't be done," he said. He also advocated shifting some of the federal government's powers to the states, repealing President Obama's health care overhaul and creating tougher measures to deal with immigration, including "sealing" the border with Mexico to stem the flow of illegal immigrants and drugs. Yet, he didn't get endorsements from most of the local tea party groups. They backed Hice after he bought billboards sporting a Soviet-era hammer and sickle and depicting Obama as a socialist. Woodall was endorsed by Linder and former Arkansas Gov. Mike Huckabee.

He won the August runoff election, 56% to 44%. In the general election, he had little trouble dispatching his Democratic opponent, financial services manager Douglas Heckman. Woodall won, 67% to 33%.

Like Linder, Woodall's main issue is the current tax code. He calls it "a monstrosity" that should be done away with and replaced with a national sales tax, which conservatives refer to as the "fair tax." Woodall contributed to the book that Linder and Neal Boortz published called *The FairTax Book*, which was a *New York Times*' best seller in 2005. Woodall said that the tax code punishes productivity and encourages debt, and that a national sales tax would boost the rate of personal savings and shift the country from its position as the largest consumer in the world to the largest producer in the world. Studies show that a national sales tax would have to be around 23% to produce the same revenue as current federal taxes.

EIGHTH DISTRICT

Austin Scott (R)

Elected 2010, 1st term; b. Dec. 10, 1969, Augusta; home, Ashburn; U. of GA, B.B.A. 1992.; Baptist; Married (Vivien); 1 child.

Elected Office: GA House, 1997-2010.

Professional Career: Owner, Southern Group; agent, Principal Financial Group, 1993-2010.

DC Office: 516 CHOB, 20515, 202-225-6531; Fax: 202-225-3013; Web site: austinscott.house.gov.

State Offices: Tifton, 229-396-5175; Warner Robins, 478-971-1776.

Committees: *Agriculture:* General Farm Commodities & Risk Management; Rural Development, Research, Biotechnology & Foreign Agriculture. *Armed Services:* Military Personnel; Readiness; Strategic Forces.

Election Results

2010 general	Austin Scott (R)	102,770	(53%)	($1,035,300)
	Jim Marshall (D)	92,250	(47%)	($1,496,152)
2010 primary	Austin Scott (R)	22,191	(52%)	
	Ken Deloach (R)	13,228	(31%)	
	Diane Vann (R)	6,959	(16%)	

Population		Race/Ethnicity		Work	
Pop. 2010:	715,599	White:	57.5%	Private:	73.0%
Change since 2000:	Up 13.6%	Black:	34.7%	Government:	21.7%
Urban:	56.6%	Hispanic:	4.9%	Self-employed:	5.2%
Rural:	43.4%	Asian:	1.2%	Blue collar:	26.0%
Area size:	7,237 sq. mi.	Native Am.:	0.2%	White collar:	54.7%
		Hawaiian:	0.0%	Khaki collar:	0.7%
Age		Two+ races:	1.3%	Other:	18.7%
Median age:	35.6 yrs.				
More than 65 yrs:	12.3%	*Ancestry*		Median income:	$42,127
Less than 18 yrs:	26.3%	USA	11.5%	Median Home Value:	$117,600
		English	8.7%		
Education		Irish	7.7%	**Military Veterans**	
H.S. grad:	79.7%			% of Pop:	11.4%
College grad:	18.3%				
Grad degree:	7.0%				

Central Georgia; Macon

The hub of central Georgia, Macon is a city proud of its restored houses and its Japanese cherry trees, which it shows off during its annual International Cherry Blossom Festival. It has been the home of music legends Otis Redding, James Brown, Little Richard, and the Allman Brothers, and of the Harriet Tubman African-American Museum. Surrounding Macon are the farm and forest lands of central Georgia. Much of this land was the site of Gen. William Tecumseh Sher-

2008 Presidential Vote		
John McCain (R)	161,027	(56%)
Barack Obama (D)	123,712	(43%)
2004 Presidential Vote		
George Bush (R)	147,729	(61%)
John Kerry (D)	93,875	(39%)
Cook Partisan Voting Index: R+10		

man's 1864 march from Atlanta to the sea. Twiggs and Wilkinson counties have been among the world's major sources of kaolin, a clay used for china and ceramics. A short drive north on Interstate 75 is Juliette, an old mill town that's too small for most maps. Many scenes in the movie *Fried Green Tomatoes* were filmed there. In the 2007-09 recession, the area suffered from major job losses in manufacturing and health care services, and construction of a new tire plant was delayed.

The 8th Congressional District of Georgia includes all of Macon and Bibb County and stretches about 200 miles north and south, from Newton County in metro Atlanta to Colquitt County nearly at the Florida border. About one-half of its votes are cast in the five-county Macon metro area. With its Air Logistics Center and testing and repair site for the F-22 Raptor, Robins Air Force Base and the surrounding city of Warner Robins have grown significantly in recent years.

The sprawling base has an annual payroll of $1.6 billion, which has a big impact on the local economy.

This was Democratic country from the time of Gen. Sherman's march until the civil-rights revolution of the 1960s. Today, the political balance is different. More than 70% of whites usually vote Republican. About 90% of blacks usually vote Democratic. So the political leanings of any district in this part of Georgia depend on the racial percentages. Redistricters in 2005 significantly changed the district with the goal of electing a Republican. It was renumbered from the 3rd to the 8th, and its shape was elongated to add new Republican territory. Slightly more than half of the population was new to the district in the 2006 election, and the new lines reduced the black population from 40% to 33%. President Bush's 2004 performance in this district was 61%, up from 55% four years earlier. In 2008, Republican John McCain won the district 56%-43%.

Austin Scott (R)

The new congressman from the 8th Congressional District is Austin Scott, a Republican who upset four-term incumbent Democrat Jim Marshall in 2010. Scott was born in Augusta, Ga. His father was an orthopedic surgeon and his mother was a teacher. He graduated from the University of Georgia with a degree in risk management and insurance in 1992. After college, Scott opened an insurance brokerage firm, which he continues to operate today. Scott had a child with his first wife, but they divorced in 2001. He remarried and now lives with his son and second wife, Vivien Scott.

Scott first won election to the state House at 26. He sponsored a bill to provide better funding for the state's trauma-care system. He also championed the expansion of charter schools and allowing students to express their religious beliefs in schools. In January 2009, Scott got into the Georgia governor's race. To boost awareness of his campaign, he went on a 1,000-mile walk around the state, talking to voters. He made his 64-day journey in the height of summer, losing 7 pounds in the process. But his campaign failed to gain traction, and after briefly considering running for lieutenant governor, he decided to challenge Marshall. Scott won the July GOP primary with little trouble.

Although Marshall ranked as one of the most conservative Democrats in Congress, and voted against President Obama's health care bill, he was vulnerable in 2010 simply because he was a Democrat. In his campaign against Marshall, Scott promised to reduce the deficit, and he attacked the incumbent for voting for Obama's $787 billion economic stimulus bill, which Scott claimed paid to create jobs in China. Marshall was difficult to paint as a traditional liberal. He was endorsed by the U.S. Chamber of Commerce and the National Rifle Association. In one ad, Marshall showed his driver's license to prove that he wasn't House Speaker Nancy Pelosi, who became a Republican symbol of the reviled Democratic agenda in Congress. Still, he lost the seat to Scott, who got 53% of the vote to 47% for Marshall.

When he got to Washington, Scott's leadership qualities were apparent to his fellow GOP freshmen, who chose him as their class president.

NINTH DISTRICT

Tom Graves (R)

Elected June 2010, 1st full term; b. Feb. 3, 1970, St. Petersburg, FL; home, Ranger; U. of GA, B.B.A. 1993.; Baptist; Married (Julie); 3 children.

Elected Office: GA House, 2002-10.

Professional Career: Owner, Southern Vision; real estate developer.

DC Office: 1113 LHOB, 20515, 202-225-5211; Fax: 202-225-8272; Web site: tomgraves.house.gov.

State Offices: Dalton, 706-226-5320; Gainesville, 770-535-2592.

Committees: *Appropriations:* Agriculture, Rural Development, FDA & Related Agencies; Commerce, Justice, Science & Related Agencies; Financial Services & General Government.

Election Results

2010 general	Tom Graves (R)	unopposed		
2010 prim. runoff	Tom Graves (R)	41,787	(55%)	($1,312,938)
	Lee Hawkins (R)	33,975	(45%)	($1,042,707)
2010 primary	Tom Graves (R)	38,851	(49%)	
	Lee Hawkins (R)	20,957	(27%)	
	Steve Tarvin (R)	11,529	(15%)	
	Chris Cates (R)	5,051	(6%)	

Prior Winning Percentages: 2010 special: 56%

Population		Race/Ethnicity		Work	
Pop. 2010:	823,583	White:	80.0%	Private:	81.2%
Change since 2000:	Up 30.8%	Black:	3.2%	Government:	12.3%
Urban:	47.3%	Hispanic:	13.5%	Self-employed:	6.2%
Rural:	52.7%	Asian:	1.7%	Blue collar:	30.3%
Area size:	4,417 sq. mi.	Native Am.:	0.3%	White collar:	54.6%
		Hawaiian:	0.0%	Khaki collar:	0.1%
Age		Two+ races:	1.1%	Other:	14.9%
Median age:	36.3 yrs.				
More than 65 yrs:	11.9%	*Ancestry*		Median income:	$48,048
Less than 18 yrs:	26.6%	USA	14.6%	Median Home Value:	$168,600
		Irish	11.5%		
Education		English	9.4%	**Military Veterans**	
H.S. grad:	78.0%			% of Pop:	9.8%
College grad:	20.7%				
Grad degree:	6.8%				

North Georgia

At the end of the 20th century, the hills and mountains of north Georgia suddenly became one of the boom areas of the South. It was a sharp turn in the region's history. Since the early 19th century, when settlers drove out the Cherokee Indians, this was poor country, where small farmers scratched out a living on rocky land. Gen. William Tecumseh Sherman's march through Georgia during the Civil War devastated the area, and many of its young men who

2008 Presidential Vote

John McCain (R)	227,063	(75%)
Barack Obama (D)	70,718	(24%)

2004 Presidential Vote

George Bush (R)	196,023	(77%)
John Kerry (D)	58,530	(23%)

Cook Partisan Voting Index: R+28

left to fight for the Confederacy never returned. After the war, not much changed for a long time. Most communities lived in isolation. Roads with hairpin curves led to remote hills where moonshine stills were more common than summer cabins. James Dickey's 1970 novel *Deliverance* was a thinly disguised portrait of life along the Coosawattee River in Gilmer and Murray counties (although the movie was filmed on the Chattooga River in Rabun County). Eventually, textile mills began springing up along the railroads; poultry production became a big business around Gainesville; and in Dalton, the traditional craft of tufted bedspread handiwork was transformed into a carpet industry so large that at its height it produced 60% of the world's tufted carpet. But these were low-wage industries populated by poor whites.

Since the 1980s, north Georgia has seen a rush of change. Interstate highways have brought it within easy range of Atlanta. Small manufacturing is thriving, with higher-skill workplaces replacing low-tech mills. Vacation and retirement communities have sprung up in the mountains and around the lakes. Agribusiness remains important, with huge poultry processors in Hall County around Gainesville. The carpet industry, more high-tech now than before, still plays a key economic role because the area is vulnerable to fluctuations in new construction. Once-rural counties are now part of the boom encircling Atlanta. The area around Lake Sidney Lanier, named for the 19th-century poet who wrote "The Song of the Chattahoochee," is filled with vacation houses and second homes. Tens of thousands of Latinos from Mexico and other countries came to the Dalton and Gainesville areas to snap up jobs before the 2007-09 recession. This area, 1,200 miles from the Mexican border, is now home to almost four times as many Hispanics as blacks, and the surge of illegal immigrants that rescued the carpet industry has strained local services. Whitfield County, where Dalton is located, is now 32% Hispanic, and Gainesville's Hall County is 26% Hispanic.

The 9th Congressional District covers most of northwest Georgia. Its northern tier of counties borders North Carolina, Tennessee, and Alabama, and those counties are in the Chattanooga media market. The district extends south to the outer reaches of metro Atlanta to include most of Forsyth County, which grew robustly in the last decade. Today this region has mostly forgotten its Democratic history, and it is solidly Republican in national and state elections. In the 2004 presidential election, the 9th gave George W. Bush won his biggest margin of victory in the state: He won 77% of the district's support. In 2008, Republican John McCain beat Democrat Barack Obama, 75%-24%.

Tom Graves (R)

The congressman from the 9th District is Tom Graves, a Republican elected in a June 2010 special election to replace 17-year incumbent Nathan Deal, also a Republican, who resigned his seat in March to run for governor. Graves is from the small town of Ranger, with fewer than 100 people, where he still lives with his wife, Julie Graves, and their three children on a farm. He sold off his last bull during his election to Congress, but maintains a variety of animals, including horses. Growing up, he lived in a single-wide trailer on a tar and gravel road, the son of a Georgia Power laborer who told him to "dream big and then work hard." In high school, he wasn't a top student, but he excelled in math and played both offensive guard and defensive linebacker on the football team. Graves took out loans and worked to pay for college, becoming the first in his family to earn a degree. After graduation, Graves worked for Federated Department Stores, now Macy's, as an asset recovery specialist. He saved his money, and, in 1995, bought a small landscaping business. Graves eventually sold off portions of the company to begin investing in real estate.

He met his future wife at Roswell Street Baptist Church, and she was instrumental in getting him involved in the anti-abortion movement. He says he opposes abortion "without exception," including cases in which the mother's life is at stake. In 2001, he and Julie, the founding president of the Gordon County Right to Life chapter, successfully opposed the construction of an abortion clinic in the area. The campaign propelled Graves to a seat on the county board and later in the Georgia Assembly, where he served more than seven years. While a state legislator, he advocated for abortion restrictions and lower taxes, including a successful 2009 business tax cut bill. Of his political philosophy, he says, "There is a spectrum of conservatism from fiscal to social....And I'm a conservative all the way across the board." He said former President Ronald Reagan is the figure he admires most in politics.

In the special election to succeed Deal, Graves bested Republican state Sen. Lee Hawkins, 56% to 44%, in a June 2010 runoff for the remainder of Deal's term. Then, the two faced off again in the primary for a full term.

During the primary campaign, Graves called for abolition of the departments of Education and Energy and the Environmental Protection Agency. He supported constitutional amendments to balance the budget and to give the president line-item veto power over spending bills. He also opposed amnesty for illegal immigrants and called for stricter enforcement of current immigration laws. Graves and Hawkins staked out similar positions. Both supported the "Fair Tax," a conservative proposal to replace the income tax with a national sales tax. Both called for the repeal of President Obama's health care overhaul and railed against the $787 billion economic stimulus package. Hawkins cast Graves as "out of touch" and attacked him for a bank loan that had gone into default. But he could not overcome Graves' backing from national Republican organizations, House Minority Leader John Boehner and local tea party groups. Graves also outraised Hawkins,

$1.3 million to $1 million. Graves won the August primary runoff, 55% to 45%, earning the Republican nomination to run in the general election, which was a pro forma affair with no Democratic opposition.

In Washington, Graves joined the congressional Tea Party Caucus. His first bill was a proposal to deny funding to implement the 2010 health care law.

TENTH DISTRICT

Paul Broun (R)

Elected July 2007, 2nd full term; b. May 14, 1946, Atlanta; home, Athens; U. of GA, B.S.1967; Medical Col. of GA, M.D. 1971; Baptist; married (Niki Bronson); 3 children.

Military Career: Marine Corps Reserves, 1964-1967; Naval Reserves, 1967-1973; GA Air Natl. Guard, 1972-1973; Air Force Reserves, 1973-1988.

Professional Career: Owner, Travel and Adventure, 1985-92; Practicing physician, 1971-present.

DC Office: 325 CHOB, 20515, 202-225-4101; Fax: 202-226-0776; Web site: broun.house.gov.

State Offices: Athens, 706-549-9588; Augusta/Evans, 706-447-3857; Toccoa, 706-886-1008.

Committees: *Homeland Security:* Border & Maritime Security; Counterterrorism & Intelligence (VChmn). *Natural Resources:* Energy & Mineral Resources; National Parks, Forests & Public Lands. *Science & Technology:* Energy & Environment; Investigations & Oversight (Chmn).

Group Ratings

	ACLU	ACU	ADA	CFG	AFS	FRC	LCV	ITIC	NTU	COC
2010	13	100	5	100	0	100	0	0	94	75
2009	–	100	0	100	0	–	0	–	96	73

National Journal Ratings

	2010 LIB	—	2010 CONS		2009 LIB	—	2009 CONS
Economic	10%	—	90%		9%	—	89%
Social	0%	—	85%		0%	—	93%
Foreign	0%	—	88%		26%	—	68%
Composite	8%	—	92%		14%	—	86%

Key Votes of the 111th Congress

1. Overturn Ledbetter	N	5. Bar federal abortion funds	Y	9. Stop detainee transfers	Y
2. Pass $820 billion stimulus	N	6. Pass health care bill	N	10. Legalize immigrants' kids	N
3. Let guns in national parks	Y	7. Regulate financial firms	N	11. Repeal don't ask, tell	N
4. Pass cap-and-trade	N	8. Pass tax cuts for some	N	12. Limit campaign funds	N

Election Results

2010 general	Paul Broun (R)	138,062	(67%)	($2,047,417)
	Russell Edwards (D)	66,905	(33%)	($220,662)
2010 primary	Paul Broun (R)	unopposed		

Prior Winning Percentages: 2008 (61%), 2007 (50%)

Population		Race/Ethnicity		Work	
Pop. 2010:	738,248	White:	70.7%	Private:	70.7%
Change since 2000:	Up 17.2%	Black:	19.2%	Government:	22.3%
Urban:	50.4%	Hispanic:	6.0%	Self-employed:	6.8%
Rural:	49.6%	Asian:	2.2%	Blue collar:	23.7%
Area size:	6,061 sq. mi.	Native Am.:	0.2%	White collar:	56.5%
		Hawaiian:	0.1%	Khaki collar:	1.5%
Age		Two+ races:	1.5%	Other:	18.3%
Median age:	35.4 yrs.				
More than 65 yrs:	12.9%	*Ancestry*		Median income:	$41,888
Less than 18 yrs:	23.8%	USA	12.8%	Median Home Value:	$154,800
		English	9.1%		
Education		Irish	8.9%	**Military Veterans**	
H.S. grad:	81.5%			% of Pop:	10.4%
College grad:	24.7%				
Grad degree:	10.3%				

Northeast Georgia; Athens

Northeastern Georgia is a land where the coastal plains and cotton fields yield to gently rolling hills and, near the North Carolina border, to the Appalachian Mountains. For most of its history, this was quiet, rural country, with courthouse towns and a few small cities, mostly forgotten by national elites, bypassed even by Union soldiers on their march to the sea. But in the last two decades, economic growth has radiated outward from Atlanta and spread across much of the region. The effects can be seen as far away as the old city of Augusta, on the Savannah River across from South Carolina. Founded in 1735, it is rich in history, with an old Cotton Exchange and mansions untouched by General Sherman. It is also a center for newer industries that are replacing the paper industry, though the city retains a large share of low-income people. The Medical College of Georgia, which is based there, has been undergoing an expansion and changed its name in 2011 to Georgia Health Sciences University. Unemployment in the Augusta area climbed to 10% in 2009 but by late 2010 was below 9%. The Brookings Institution's quarterly Metro-Monitor rankings have cited it as one of the most resilient metropolitan economies. Augusta is best known as the home of the Augusta National Golf Club, the site of the Masters Tournament every year, its entrance barely visible off four-lane Washington Road. The city also houses the Fort Gordon Army base and has become a site for Hollywood film production.

2008 Presidential Vote		
John McCain (R)	191,401	(62%)
Barack Obama (D)	113,210	(37%)
2004 Presidential Vote		
George Bush (R)	168,831	(65%)
John Kerry (D)	90,304	(35%)
Cook Partisan Voting Index:	R+15	

The 10th Congressional District of Georgia takes in much of the northeast corner of the state. It includes about 40% of Augusta in Richmond County, but not the city's heavily black precincts. The 2005 redistricting added Clarke County and the liberal enclave of Athens, home of the University of Georgia, graceful Greek Revival mansions, boxwood gardens, and magnolias—and also, incidentally, rock bands R.E.M. and the B-52s. State planners have discussed a "brain train" to connect Athens to Atlanta. Clarke and Richmond counties are now the two largest population centers here. Columbia County, next to Augusta, and Oconee County, next to Athens, are particularly affluent and also rapidly growing. The Lake Oconee area has more than 100 subdivisions, including gated communities and golf courses that beckon to second-home buyers and retirees. Voters here prefer traditional ways: Several counties recently rejected ballot propositions to end a prohibition of alcohol. The redistricting changes increased the African-American population from 14% to 20%, but this remains a solidly Republican district in national politics. In 2008, John McCain led Democrat Barack Obama here, 62%-37%.

Paul Broun (R)

The congressman from the 10th District is Paul Broun, a Republican who was the surprise winner of a special election in 2007 after the death of GOP incumbent Charlie Norwood. Born in Atlanta, Broun is a lifelong Georgia resident who got his bachelor's degree from the University of Georgia and his medical degree from the Medical College of Georgia in Augusta. His father, Paul Broun Sr., served as a moderate Democratic state senator from Athens for 38 years. The younger Broun was also active in politics, though he has said that he was "far, far apart on the issues" from his father. He served as president of the Georgia Sport Shooting Association, an affiliate of the National Rifle Association, and as vice president of political action for Safari Club International, a national advocacy group for hunters. (His Capitol Hill office is jammed with stuffed sheep, bears and other trophies.)

He first ran for the House in 1990 but lost against Democratic incumbent Richard Ray in the old 3rd District, which was then based in west-central Georgia. After redistricting two years later, Broun ran in the revamped and more Republican 3rd District south of Atlanta, and lost the primary to Mac Collins, who held the seat for 12 years. In 1996, Broun closed his medical practice to campaign full-time for a year for Georgia's open Senate seat. He was vastly outspent, and finished a distant fourth in the primary with an anemic 3%.

There was little doubt that a Republican would succeed Norwood in this conservative district, but few predicted it would be Broun. State Sen. Jim Whitehead was the early front-runner. Whitehead attended the University of Georgia, where he was a star offensive lineman. He later opened a tire and auto shop in the Augusta area, served seven years on the Columbia County Commission—the final two as chairman—and won a state Senate seat in 2004. He was endorsed by Norwood's widow, Gloria.

The seat seemed to be Whitehead's to lose, which is exactly what he did. He avoided debates and committed several gaffes, including a 2004 comment that dismissed the University of Georgia as a "bunch of liberals" who, except for the football team, ought to be bombed. In the June 19 special election, he won 44%, ahead of Broun's 21%, but not enough to avoid a runoff. The race turned into a contest between candidates representing the district's two population centers, Augusta, Whitehead's turf, and Athens, Broun's home base.

Broun touted his medical background, claiming he was perhaps the only physician in Georgia who regularly made house calls. "I've got an old-fashioned medical bag," he said. "My office is my GMC Yukon." Broun said he opposed any steps to permit illegal immigrants to gain legal status, highlighted his connections to Christian conservatives on social issues, and also reached out to African-Americans and other Democrats, especially in Athens. Whitehead talked up his Augusta-area roots and complained about his Athens-based opposition. Whitehead had a considerable advantage in campaign dollars. Still, Broun won with 50.4%, just 394 votes ahead of Whitehead, with 49.6%. Broun carried Athens's Clarke County with a remarkable 90%, while holding Whitehead to 73% in Columbia County. He also won 12 other counties.

In the House, Broun has cultivated his religious conservative base while becoming a favorite of the tea party movement. "I wasn't supposed to be here," he told anti-abortion protesters in January 2008. "I believe in my heart the Holy Spirit called me to run for Congress." He introduced a bill in 2009 to designate a "Year of the Bible." He also has become an inviting target for bloggers and opinion writers on the left. *Salon.com*'s Joe Conason dubbed him "the new stupidest member of Congress" in 2010 for boasting that he returned his federal census form without filling in any of the questions. The first bill he introduced would ban all abortions, and he called for a national sales tax to replace the income tax. He also called for a ban on the sales of *Playboy* and *Penthouse* magazines at military installments, no doubt getting thousands of soldiers stationed at Georgia's bases to snap to attention. With a flourish for colorful quotes, he said of his opposition to the financial market bailout bill in 2008: "This is a huge cow patty with a piece of marshmallow stuck in the middle of it, and I am not going to eat that cow patty." In May 2009, he and Rep. Phil Gingrey, R-Ga., objected to spending $1.5 million in a defense supplemental bill to develop an H1N1 flu vaccine. "We are stealing our grandchildren's future by borrowing and spending," he said.

After Democrat Barack Obama's historic election as the first African-American president, Broun described Obama's agenda as "Marxist" and criticized Republican nominee John McCain's campaign as "inept." He ultimately backed away from those remarks. But his management of his office seemed to be no smoother than his political discourse. Broun spent almost all of the annual allotment that lawmakers receive to run their offices in the first half of 2008, prompting staff members to quit, the *Atlanta Journal-Constitution* reported. After reducing office staff, he succeeded in staying within his budget in 2009. But he later encountered a different financial problem: A bank that was partly owned by him and two brothers failed and was taken over by the federal government in March 2010.

Broun had another competitive primary in 2008, this time against former state House Majority Whip Barry Fleming, who was Augusta-based and sought to play down tensions with Athens. Fleming criticized Broun's opposition to federal spending for economic development and law enforcement. But Broun was helped by the endorsement of the anti-tax group Club for Growth and by other Republicans in the Georgia delegation. Broun won the primary with unexpected ease, 71%-29, leading in every county. In the general election against Bobby Saxon, an Iraq war veteran and gun-rights advocate, Broun won 61%-39%. He increased his percentage to 67% in 2010.

ELEVENTH DISTRICT

Phil Gingrey (R)

Elected 2002, 5th term; b. July 10, 1942, Augusta; home, Marietta; GA Inst. of Tech., B.S. 1965, Med. Col. of GA, M.D. 1969; Catholic; married (Billie); 4 children.

Elected Office: Marietta Schl. Bd., 1993-97; GA Senate, 1998-2002.

Professional Career: Practicing obstetrician, 1976-present.

DC Office: 442 CHOB, 20515, 202-225-2931; Fax: 202-225-2944; Web site: gingrey.house.gov.

State Offices: Marietta, 770-429-1776; Rome, 706-290-1776.

Committees: *Energy & Commerce:* Communications & Technology; Health; Oversight & Investigations. *House Administration:* Oversight (Chmn).

Group Ratings

	ACLU	ACU	ADA	CFG	AFS	FRC	LCV	ITIC	NTU	COC
2010	14	100	5	89	0	100	0	0	91	75
2009	–	96	5	90	11	–	0	–	88	73

National Journal Ratings

	2010 LIB — 2010 CONS	2009 LIB — 2009 CONS
Economic	6% — 94%	15% — 84%
Social	0% — 85%	13% — 87%
Foreign	12% — 79%	0% — 75%
Composite	10% — 90%	14% — 86%

Key Votes of the 111th Congress

1. Overturn Ledbetter	N	5. Bar federal abortion funds	Y
2. Pass $820 billion stimulus	N	6. Pass health care bill	N
3. Let guns in national parks	Y	7. Regulate financial firms	N
4. Pass cap-and-trade	N	8. Pass tax cuts for some	N

9. Stop detainee transfers	Y
10. Legalize immigrants' kids	*
11. Repeal don't ask, tell	N
12. Limit campaign funds	N

Election Results

2010 general	Phil Gingrey (R).. unopposed	($1,421,266)
2010 primary	Phil Gingrey (R).. unopposed	

Prior Winning Percentages: 2008 (68%), 2006 (71%), 2004 (57%), 2002 (52%)

Population		Race/Ethnicity		Work	
Pop. 2010:	794,969	White:	72.1%	Private:	80.7%
Change since 2000:	Up 26.2%	Black:	15.3%	Government:	14.1%
Urban:	70.4%	Hispanic:	8.6%	Self-employed:	5.1%
Rural:	29.6%	Asian:	1.9%	Blue collar:	24.9%
Area size:	2,718 sq. mi.	Native Am.:	0.2%	White collar:	59.8%
		Hawaiian:	0.0%	Khaki collar:	0.2%
Age		Two+ races:	1.7%	Other:	15.1%
Median age:	34.4 yrs.				
More than 65 yrs:	10.2%	*Ancestry*		Median income:	$52,216
Less than 18 yrs:	27.3%	USA	12.7%	Median Home Value:	$162,600
		Irish	10.0%		
Education		English	9.7%	**Military Veterans**	
H.S. grad:	82.7%			% of Pop:	9.7%
College grad:	25.1%				
Grad degree:	8.1%				

Northwest Georgia; Marietta

Northwest Georgia was long the home of the Cherokee Nation before the tribe was sent west in the 1830s on the Trail of Tears. It has been manufacturing country for the last century. Hundreds of textile mills and dozens of carpet mills once clustered near the supply of natural cotton and along the railroad lines heading southwest at the base of the southern Appala-chian chain. The late 19th-century propagand-ists of the New South hailed factories as the van-

2008 Presidential Vote		
John McCain (R) 207,298	(66%)
Barack Obama (D) 102,493	(33%)
2004 Presidential Vote		
George Bush (R) 183,750	(71%)
John Kerry (D) 74,268	(29%)
Cook Partisan Voting Index: R+20		

guard of technological progress, and in fact the plants produced a higher standard of living than farms on this stubborn land. But the mills put scant premium on education or the cultivation of civic virtues and did little to bring in higher-skilled work. All-white hiring practices maintained racial segregation in mostly white north Georgia. Today, this area is developing a different kind of economy, as metro Atlanta spreads out along highways to the north and to the west. There are sprawling subdivisions in what once were mill towns. Floyd County is home to an auto parts manu-facturing cluster, in addition to the carpet mills of Rome, where Latino immigrants have become a major part of the workforce.

The 11th Congressional District of Georgia includes much of this part of the state, taking in small industrial towns, rural areas producing cotton, poultry, and cattle, and a cluster of older suburbs around Atlanta. It stretches from Rome in the north to suburban Marietta, which is where Lockheed Martin builds the F-22 jet fighter and the C-130 cargo plane. The F-22 in 2009 became the first casualty of the Obama administration's decision to cut what it considered unnecessary weapons programs. But the Marietta plant has remained busy: It is a major contributor to the production of the F-35 Lightning II stealth fighter and has other work as well. West of Atlanta is Carrollton, once the home of Newt Gingrich, who went on to become U.S. House speaker.

The 2005 redistricting made the 11th significantly more compact (it is more than 1,000 square miles smaller than the previous version) and more Republican, by moving boundaries to include the northern part of Cobb County, all of exurban Bartow County and all of Paulding County, which had a 67% increase in population between 2000 and 2009. The changes also shifted many African-American precincts of Cobb County to the 13th District and reduced the black share in the new 11th. The result considerably altered the partisan composition, changing this from a somewhat competitive seat to one that seems out of reach for Democrats.

Phil Gingrey (R)

The congressman from the 11th District is Republican Phil Gingrey, an obstetrician first elected in 2002. Gingrey grew up in Augusta, graduated from Georgia Tech, and returned home to attend the Medical College of Georgia. After training in Georgia hospitals, he settled in Marietta, where he set up an obstetrics and gynecology practice. He also chaired the local school board. In 1998, he was elected to the state Senate, where he had a reputation as a staunch social conservative who could work with Democrats on other issues. Gingrey says the book that most influenced his political thinking is Barry Goldwater's classic *The Conscience of a Conservative*. In the contest for the U.S. House seat, Gingrey faced tough competition in both the primary and general election. The issue differences were small among the three candidates in the Republican primary. Gingrey styled him-self as the only native Georgian. Cecil Staton, an ordained Baptist minister, vowed to view all legis-lation from the perspective of the traditional family. Gingrey won 40% of the vote to 32% for Staton and 28% for Bob Herriott, a pilot for Delta Airlines.

The bitter September runoff revolved around allegations by Staton that Gingrey supported homosexual causes. Voters who knew Gingrey from his state Senate tenure didn't buy it. He won 64%-36%, carrying every county. The Democrats, meanwhile, nominated Roger Kahn, a million-aire beer distributor who spent $2.8 million from his own pocket. Gingrey spent $600,000 of his own money. With a boost from the Georgia Republican tide that year, Gingrey won 52%-48%.

In the House, Gingrey has a very conservative voting record and was among the first to join the Tea Party Caucus in 2010. But he is less rhetorically provocative than his Georgia GOP col-leagues Tom Price and Paul Broun. So he quite unexpectedly found himself on the wrong side of some of the nation's best known conservatives in 2009 when he told *Politico* in offhand remarks: "It's easy if you're Sean Hannity or Rush Limbaugh or even sometimes Newt Gingrich to stand back and throw rocks." His sentiments may have resonated with other office-holders, but he wound up apologizing to the pundits the next day, praising Limbaugh as a "conservative giant," and adding, "I regret those stupid comments." He drew more national notice in early 2011 when, after touring the U.S.-Mexico border, he said: "If I had to choose from immigrants across the globe, my favorite alien would be our Hispanic and Latino residents coming from across the Southern border."

In 2005, Gingrey tried but failed to get a seat on the powerful Ways and Means Committee. Instead, he got a seat on the Rules Committee, an influential panel that writes the rules for bringing bills to the floor. The following year, Gingrey lost a bid for the chairmanship of the Republican Policy Committee, part of the GOP leadership.

When Democrats took control of the House in 2007, he had to give up his seat on Rules, and he shifted his focus to the Armed Services Committee, where he has been an avid booster of Lockheed's Marietta plant. In 2009, he got a seat on the influential Energy and Commerce Committee, where he can work more effectively on health care issues, including shifting the industry toward electronic record-keeping and limiting damages in malpractice lawsuits. During the panel's drafting of the health care bill in 2009, he tried to address one of conservatives' biggest concerns by offering an unsuccessful amendment to bar any federal worker or political appointee from interfering in relationships between doctors and patients. Gingrey has taken up the cause of business interests on other legislation before the committee. In October 2009, he unsuccessfully tried to amend a bill ending the use of mercury in the production of chlorine by giving plants until at least 2018 to abandon mercury. But he hasn't always seen eye-to-eye with other conservatives: He was among 92 House Republicans who voted with Democrats to reject an extra $22 billion in budget cuts.

Democrats claimed they would seriously contest Gingrey's seat in 2004, but he had an easier than expected re-election. He raised $2.3 million, much of it from the medical community. His opponent, conservative Democrat Rick Crawford, failed to impress national Democrats. Gingrey won 57%-43%, and has not had a problem getting re-elected since. He was unopposed in 2010.

TWELFTH DISTRICT

John Barrow (D)

Elected 2004, 4th term; b. Oct. 31, 1955, Athens; home, Savannah; U. of GA, B.A. 1976, Harvard U., J.D. 1979; Baptist; Divorced; 2 children.

Elected Office: Athens-Clarke City-Co. comm., 1990-2004.

Professional Career: Practicing atty, 1981-2004.

DC Office: 2202 RHOB, 20515, 202-225-2823; Fax: 202-225-3377; Web site: barrow.house.gov.

State Offices: Augusta, 706-722-4494; Sandersville, 478-553-1923; Savannah, 912-354-7282; Vidalia, 912-537-9301.

Committees: *Energy & Commerce:* Communications & Technology; Environment & the Economy. *Veterans' Affairs:* Disability Assistance & Memorial Affairs; Oversight & Investigations.

Group Ratings

	ACLU	ACU	ADA	CFG	AFS	FRC	LCV	ITIC	NTU	COC
2010	63	17	65	25	88	37	90	100	32	75
2009	–	17	75	35	89	–	79	–	18	64

National Journal Ratings

	2010 LIB — 2010 CONS	2009 LIB — 2009 CONS
Economic	55% — 44%	52% — 48%
Social	42% — 57%	47% — 52%
Foreign	49% — 49%	42% — 57%
Composite	49% — 51%	47% — 53%

Key Votes of the 111th Congress

1. Overturn Ledbetter	Y	5. Bar federal abortion funds		9. Stop detainee transfers	Y
2. Pass $820 billion stimulus	Y	6. Pass health care bill	N	10. Legalize immigrants' kids	N
3. Let guns in national parks	Y	7. Regulate financial firms	Y	11. Repeal don't ask, tell	Y
4. Pass cap-and-trade	N	8. Pass tax cuts for some	Y	12. Limit campaign funds	N

Election Results

2010 general	John Barrow (D)	92,459	(57%)	($1,951,721)
	Raymond McKinney (R)......................................	70,938	(43%)	($250,534)
2010 primary	John Barrow (D)	19,505	(58%)	
	Regina Thomas (D)	14,201	(42%)	

Prior Winning Percentages: 2008 (66%), 2006 (50%), 2004 (52%)

Population		Race/Ethnicity		Work	
Pop. 2010:	692,529	White:	49.6%	Private:	73.3%
Change since 2000:	Up 10.0%	Black:	42.9%	Government:	21.2%
Urban:	59.9%	Hispanic:	4.6%	Self-employed:	5.3%
Rural:	40.1%	Asian:	1.2%	Blue collar:	27.3%
Area size:	8,734 sq. mi.	Native Am.:	0.2%	White collar:	51.3%
		Hawaiian:	0.1%	Khaki collar:	0.8%
Age		Two+ races:	1.4%	Other:	20.7%
Median age:	33.2 yrs.				
More than 65 yrs:	11.4%	*Ancestry*		Median income:	$36,000
Less than 18 yrs:	25.0%	USA	8.9%	Median Home Value:	$107,900
		Irish	7.9%		
Education		English	7.3%	**Military Veterans**	
H.S. grad:	79.6%			% of Pop:	10.9%
College grad:	16.4%				
Grad degree:	5.9%				

Augusta, Savannah

In Georgia, the focus is usually on Atlanta. But the state also has some urbane smaller cities with deep roots in the past. One is Savannah, the state's first capital, which by the 1830s was one of America's booming cotton ports. It languished after the Civil War, and lived off paper mills and chemical plants in the 20th century, while impoverished blacks on the islands a few miles offshore still spoke Gullah dialects. Then, a few decades ago, preservationists started restoring houses and churches on a street grid punctuated by 24 squares that James Oglethorpe had laid out more than 200 years before. Today, Savannah is one of the most graciously preserved cities in the country and a major tourism destination. Tourism remained vibrant even during the recent recession. Local officials, however, want to bolster trade by deepening the port of Savannah to attract the next generation of large container ships. In 2007, Savannah acquired a different sort of notoriety when the local Episcopal Church parted ways with the national diocese over the main church's decision to affirm an openly gay bishop. The city actively competes with neighboring, and equally well-preserved, Charleston, S.C., not only for tourists but also for shipping. Another such city is Augusta, upriver on the Savannah. Founded in 1735 as a fur-trading post, it has been home to the Medical College of Georgia since 1835. It has become home to such manufacturers as Procter & Gamble, Solo Cup and International Paper. Georgia State University reported in 2010 that Augusta had the strongest economy in the state and was the only Georgia metro area adding jobs.

2008 Presidential Vote		
Barack Obama (D)	145,107	(55%)
John McCain (R)	116,072	(44%)
2004 Presidential Vote		
George Bush (R)	112,735	(50%)
John Kerry (D)	110,192	(49%)
Cook Partisan Voting Index:	D+1	

The 12th Congressional District of Georgia runs along the Savannah River and comprises almost all of Savannah and some of its suburbs and about 60% of Augusta. It contains the Depression-racked farm country near Augusta that Erskine Caldwell chronicled in his scandalous bestseller, *Tobacco Road*. The titular dirt thoroughfare, which led to a small port on the Savannah River, is now paved and runs through a nondescript mix of residential and commercial areas. In 2008, the district voted for Democrat Barack Obama over Republican John McCain, 55%-44%.

John Barrow (D)

The congressman from the 12th District is Democrat John Barrow, whose family has been rooted in Georgia for seven generations. Of the nine House Democrats representing states in the Deep South, he is the only one left who is white. His father handled school desegregation cases as a lawyer and as a Superior Court judge in the Athens area. A graduate of the University of Georgia and Harvard Law School, Barrow became a trial lawyer and made his name in local politics by winning four terms as an Athens-Clarke city-county commissioner. In 2004, he decided to run against Republican Rep. Max Burns, who had won the 12th District seat in an upset in 2002.

Although most Democratic voters in the district are African-American, all four candidates in the Democratic primary were white. Barrow raised more than $700,000 and, with the endorsements of former Sen. Max Cleland, the Sierra Club, and the Georgia AFL-CIO, extended his appeal beyond his home base. He won 51% of the vote and all 14 counties, enough to avoid a runoff. In the general election, Barrow distanced himself from Democratic presidential nominee John Kerry and the national party. He focused on Burns' support of a national retail sales tax to replace the income tax, attacking the proposal as anti-family and labeling it "the Max Tax." Burns accused Barrow of distorting his proposal and called his opponent a "liberal trial attorney" controlled by "Atlanta party bosses." Burns ran well in rural areas, but Barrow won big margins among African-American voters in the three counties that cast two-thirds of the district's votes—62% in Richmond, 58% in Chatham, and 58% in Clarke. Overall, Barrow won 52%-48%.

In the House, Barrow ranks among the most conservative Democrats. He is a member of the fiscally conservative Blue Dog Democrats, and supported fellow Blue Dog Heath Shuler of North Carolina over liberal Nancy Pelosi for Democratic leader after their party lost its majority in 2010. He voted against the 2010 health care overhaul, contending it would cost too much and fail to halt abuses by insurance companies. He took a hard line against illegal immigrants and cast votes in 2007 against proposals to limit war funding in Iraq. Also in 2007, Democratic leaders gave him a leading role in pushing for an increase in the minimum wage, and he secured a seat on the powerful Energy and Commerce Committee. But he declined to back the 2009 energy and climate change bill, which, with health care, was the other major measure to emerge from Energy and Commerce in the 111th Congress (2009-10). He complained that the national renewable energy mandate was too high. Although bill sponsors agreed to weaken the standard, Barrow still voted against it. In 2008, after an explosion at a sugar refinery near Savannah, Barrow won House passage of his bill to force the Occupational Safety and Health Administration to tighten rules on industrial dust.

Barrow's political life was made more difficult by the 2005 redistricting, which moved his Clarke County base into the heavily Republican 10th District. He said he would run in the new district that included the largest part of his former district, which turned out to be the 12th. Barrow moved his residence to Savannah and emphasized his independence. "No boss, no leader, no caucus can tell me how to vote. And none of them has," he declared. Burns ran against him and got fundraising help from national Republicans. The outcome was even closer this time, 50.3%-49.7%. Barrow won only eight of 22 counties, but he captured 62% of the vote in Chatham and 65% in Richmond, the two largest counties.

In 2008, Barrow faced state Sen. Regina Thomas, an African-American, in the Democratic primary. Although a liberal group ran ads criticizing Barrow for supporting President George W. Bush on tax cuts and the Iraq war, he won 76%-24%. In November, he won re-election easily, 66%-34%, against Republican John Stone. Two years later, angered by Barrow's vote against the health care overhaul, Thomas returned for a rematch. However, she again had little success raising money to compete with Barrow, who won the 2010 primary with 60%. Barrow's general election opponent was Ray McKinney, a Republican nuclear engineer and a favorite of tea party activists. He drew from the GOP playbook by trying to tie Barrow to Pelosi, but the lawmaker cited his record of independence. Even so, he left nothing to chance. The *Savannah Morning News* reported that he sent mailers to some voters boasting of working "hand-in-hand" with President Obama and a different one to others saying he "stood up to Nancy Pelosi and the Democrats in Washington." He won with 58%, escaping the fate of many other Blue Dogs that year. But he is considered vulnerable to a Republican-orchestrated redistricting effort in 2012.

THIRTEENTH DISTRICT

David Scott (D)

Elected 2002, 5th term; b. June 27, 1946, Aynor, SC; home, Atlanta; FL A&M U., B.A. 1967, U. of PA, M.B.A. 1969; Baptist; married (Alfredia); 2 children.

Elected Office: GA House of Reps., 1974-82; GA Senate, 1982-2002.

Professional Career: Founder and pres., Dayn-Mark Advertising, 1979-2002.

DC Office: 225 CHOB, 20515, 202-225-2939; Fax: 202-225-4628; Web site: davidscott.house.gov.

State Offices: Jonesboro, 770-210-5073; Smyrna, 770-432-5405.

Committees: *Agriculture:* General Farm Commodities & Risk Management; Livestock, Dairy & Poultry. *Financial Services:* Financial Institutions & Consumer Credit; International Monetary Policy & Trade.

Group Ratings

	ACLU	ACU	ADA	CFG	AFS	FRC	LCV	ITIC	NTU	COC
2010	81	0	90	0	100	6	100	100	5	25
2009	–	0	95	4	100	–	93	–	2	47

National Journal Ratings

	2010 LIB — 2010 CONS		2009 LIB — 2009 CONS	
Economic	69% —	30%	71% —	28%
Social	71% —	25%	67% —	31%
Foreign	66% —	29%	57% —	42%
Composite	70% —	30%	66% —	34%

Key Votes of the 111th Congress

1. Overturn Ledbetter	Y	5. Bar federal abortion funds	N	9. Stop detainee transfers	N
2. Pass $820 billion stimulus	Y	6. Pass health care bill	Y	10. Legalize immigrants' kids	Y
3. Let guns in national parks	N	7. Regulate financial firms	Y	11. Repeal don't ask, tell	Y
4. Pass cap-and-trade	Y	8. Pass tax cuts for some	Y	12. Limit campaign funds	Y

Election Results

2010 general	David Scott (D)	140,294	(69%)	($862,262)
	Mike Crane (R)	61,771	(31%)	($147,199)
2010 primary	David Scott (D)	34,374	(76%)	
	Mike Murphy (D)	7,556	(17%)	
	Michael Frisbee (D)	3,229	(7%)	

Prior Winning Percentages: 2008 (69%), 2006 (69%), 2004 (100%), 2002 (60%)

Population		Race/Ethnicity		Work	
Pop. 2010:	784,445	White:	25.8%	Private:	79.4%
Change since 2000:	Up 24.6%	Black:	56.0%	Government:	15.9%
Urban:	96.6%	Hispanic:	12.7%	Self-employed:	4.6%
Rural:	3.4%	Asian:	3.2%	Blue collar:	24.5%
Area size:	577 sq. mi.	Native Am.:	0.2%	White collar:	58.6%
		Hawaiian:	0.0%	Khaki collar:	0.4%
Age		Two+ races:	1.8%	Other:	16.6%
Median age:	32.5 yrs.				
More than 65 yrs:	7.5%	*Ancestry*		Median income:	$50,463
Less than 18 yrs:	28.4%	USA	5.7%	Median Home Value:	$153,500
		Irish	4.9%		
Education		Subsaharan	4.8%	**Military Veterans**	
H.S. grad:	85.3%			% of Pop:	10.3%
College grad:	25.5%				
Grad degree:	8.2%				

Atlanta Suburbs

Many of the great landmarks of the civil-rights movement, and the headquarters of many of its leading organizations, are in the central city of Atlanta. The city's cohesive African-American community, more than any other, provided the leadership and inspiration for the struggle that transformed the United States. In the 1960s, Atlanta's blacks were clustered in ghetto neighborhoods on the south and west sides of the city. The north side and the suburbs in every direction were heavily or entirely white. Today, metro Atlanta's thriving black middle class has moved outward in almost every direction in one of the nation's fastest-growing metro areas—to southern DeKalb County to the east, to Clayton County directly south of the city, to southwest Fulton County, to eastern and southern Cobb and Douglas counties to the west. Cobb has made national news in recent years for its aggressive approach to immigration. It was the first county in the state to be certified for a federal program giving state and local enforcement the authority to arrest illegal immigrants. The program has been hailed as a success, but it also has driven away immigrants seeking friendlier territory.

2008 Presidential Vote		
Barack Obama (D) 226,700	(72%)
John McCain (R) 87,228	(28%)
2004 Presidential Vote		
John Kerry (D) 144,870	(60%)
George Bush (R).....................96,393	(40%)
Cook Partisan Voting Index: D+15		

The 13th Congressional District of Georgia is a collection of suburban areas that have attracted Atlanta's African-American middle class. It is a majority-black district with a nucleus in Clayton County, which is heavily dependent economically on the airport. Its unemployment rate topped 12% in 2010. The biggest change in the 2005 redistricting was the addition of Cobb County. Cobb and Clayton counties each contain about one-third of the district's population, and the rest is parceled out across DeKalb, Douglas, Fulton, and Henry counties. The district is heavily Democratic.

David Scott (D)

The congressman from the 13th District is David Scott, a Democrat first elected in 2002. Born in rural South Carolina, Scott is the son of a minister and grandson of a deacon. During his middle-school years, his family moved to tony Scarsdale, N.Y., where his parents took jobs as a chauffeur and housekeeper for a wealthy family. Scott was the only African-American in his otherwise all-white school. He later graduated from Florida A&M University, and then did an internship at the U.S. Labor Department in Washington. There he met George Taylor, an authority in labor-management relations who encouraged the bright young man to apply to the prestigious Wharton School at the University of Pennsylvania, which Scott did, eventually earning his M.B.A. He moved to Atlanta in the early 1970s, and in 1974, he was elected to the Georgia House. In 1982, he won election to the state Senate, where he chaired the Rules Committee. From 1979 to 2002, he owned Dayn-Mark Advertising, which creates and places radio, television, and print ads. The firm is now operated by his wife and two daughters.

In 2002, Scott made a bid for the newly created 13th District seat. It was obvious that the primary would be decisive in this heavily Democratic district. Four other Democrats ran, the best known of whom was former state party Chairman David Worley, who had nearly defeated Republican Rep. Newt Gingrich in 1990. Scott, however, was familiar to many voters after more than a quarter-century in the state legislature. And if they didn't know Scott, they certainly knew of his campaign co-chairman: Hank Aaron, the Hall of Fame slugger and Atlanta-area icon, who is Scott's brother-in-law. Scott brought his advertising expertise to the campaign, plastering the interstate highways with eye-catching billboards. His chief competitors, Worley and state Sen. Greg Hecht of Clayton County, both white, ran ads attacking each other. Scott won the primary with 54% of the vote. He won the general election 60%-40%.

In the House, Scott's voting record is centrist for a Democrat, especially on foreign policy. He joined both the liberal Congressional Black Caucus and the conservative Blue Dog Democrats, and has had no reluctance about going his own way. In 2003, he was one of seven House Democrats to vote for final passage of President Bush's tax cut and one of 16 to vote for the new Republican prescription drug benefit under Medicare. He split with most of his party by voting for the constitutional amendment to ban same-sex marriage. But after Democrats took control of the House in 2007, he was a more faithful party vote. Though usually reserved, he drew national attention in 2009 when he engaged in a heated give-and-take with town hall audience members over health care reform. He ended up receiving threatening phone calls and hate mail, and a swastika was painted outside his Smyrna office. "There are people out there that...don't want to see the president succeed," he told CNN.

On the Financial Services Committee, Scott criticized predatory lenders that exploit would-be homeowners in poor communities, but he was reluctant to pass measures to eliminate favorable interest deals. He spoke out strongly for extension of the Voting Rights Act and against claims by Georgia Republicans that the law was no longer necessary. He initially opposed the bailout of the financial markets, but after Chairman Barney Frank, D-Mass., promised to address the Black Caucus' call for additional protections for homeowners facing foreclosure, Scott switched his vote in support of a revised version. He also served on the Agriculture Committee, and chaired the livestock, dairy and poultry subcommittee before Democrats lost the majority. He accused Agriculture Department officials in 2010 of an "end-run around Congress" in writing a rule on the marketing of livestock and poultry that did not have enough support to make it into the 2008 farm bill.

In 2006, Scott faced a primary challenge from Donzella James, who served 10 years in the state Senate and criticized Scott for living outside the district. Scott won 67%-33%. In the general election, he was opposed by first-time candidate Deborah Honeycutt, a family physician who surprisingly raised $1.3 million. But she had little name recognition and lost 69%-31%.

Before the 2008 election, Scott was the subject of several unflattering stories about back taxes he owed on his home and business, and about payments out of his campaign fund to family members and Dayn-Mark Advertising. Since his first congressional race in 2002, Scott's campaign had paid a total of $643,000 to his family and to Dayn-Mark and its employees. An attorney for Scott said that the transactions were legal under campaign finance law.

Nonetheless, Scott attracted both primary and general election challenges in 2008 and 2010. In the 2008 Democratic primary, James again challenged Scott and attacked him for backing President Bush on the war in Iraq, for favoring the GOP prescription drug benefit, and for opposing increases in education funding. Scott won 64%-36%. In a November rematch, Honeycutt upped the stakes considerably by spending $5.2 million to try to defeat Scott, who spent far less, $1.4 million. Despite the negative news stories about his finances, Scott swamped Honeycutt, 69%-31%. Two years later, he easily fended off two Republicans-turned-Democrats in the primary, then trounced Republican Mike Crane, who had edged out Honeycutt in the GOP primary. He was re-elected easily with 69% of the vote.

★ HAWAII ★

Geographically the most isolated archipelago in the world and geologically some of the youngest land on Earth, Hawaii is continuing to undergo transformations. Humans settled these islands only about 1,000 years ago, when Polynesians paddled across vast Pacific expanses in small outrigger canoes. When Capt. James Cook arrived in 1776, he found that his Maori interpreter from New Zealand could understand Hawaiian. On this subtropical land, teeming with food and seldom inconvenienced by bad weather, Hawaiians built a fierce yet wondrous civilization of harsh taboos and cannibalism as well as alluring music and dance. The islands were united politically in 1779 by King Kamehameha I, who ate one of his rivals and maintained the old culture. In 1819, within a year of his death, his consort Kaahumanu outlawed the Hawaiian religious taboos and welcomed the American missionary Hiram Bingham. New England missionaries and their trader cousins came, while British and Russian ships occasionally put into port, and established the dominant culture. Starting in the 1850s, laborers from China, Japan, Portugal, and the Philippines streamed in to work the sugar and pineapple plantations. American planters and businessmen bridled at the caprices of the royal family and, in January 1893, with the help of the U.S. Marines, ousted Queen Liliuokalani from the Iolani Palace and called on the United States to annex Hawaii. President Grover Cleveland demurred, and Hawaii for five years was a republic until President William McKinley annexed it in July 1898. This history is a source of regret for some. An *Onipa'a* ceremony remembering Liliuokalani's overthrow was staged by John Waihee, the first governor of Native Hawaiian descent, in January 1993, with the American flag conspicuously absent. Later that year, Congress passed and President Bill Clinton signed an apology for the overthrow of Liliuokalani 100 years before. In 2010, Hawaii staged a commemoration, not a celebration, of the 50th anniversary of statehood.

For many years, Hawaii created a better life for its citizens than almost any other Pacific island. Its people did not wall themselves off in ethnic blocs and have been mixing for the last century. Each group has made worthy contributions. The Asian migrant laborers brought traditions of hard work, family loyalty, and group solidarity that found expression most vividly in the performance of the 442nd "Go for Broke" Regimental Combat Team, which was made up mostly of sons of Japanese immigrants and became the most decorated unit in U.S. military history. The Yankee spirit has been evident in Hawaii's commercial success and in its attachment to the rule of Anglo-American law. The Hawaiian spirit is apparent in the vitality of the *aloha* ambience, the welcoming of others despite their differences, and a willingness to absorb the teachings of others while maintaining a certain Polynesian attitude toward life. It was Hawaii's tolerance that inspired segregationist Southern Democrats to block its admission to the Union for years. Today's Hawaiians can take pride in their ethnic heritage—or heritages: About half of the married couples in Hawaii are, like President Obama's parents, interracial. In the 2010 Census, 24% of Hawaiians identified themselves as being of two races; 23% described themselves as at least partly Native Hawaiian or Pacific Islander, 42% as at least partly white, 58% as at least partly Asian (with about equal numbers of Japanese and Filipino) and 3% as partly black.

Politically, Hawaii as a territory was Republican. John Kennedy carried it in 1960 by just 115 votes. But from 1962 to 2002, its politics was dominated by a Democratic machine that had its beginning in the 1950s. At that time, World War II veterans such as Daniel Inouye, Spark Matsunaga, and George Ariyoshi joined forces with former mainlander John Burns, who as a police officer during the war helped prevent persecution of Japanese-Americans. They allied themselves with the then-powerful International Longshoremen's and Warehousemen's Union, which represented sugar and pineapple plantation hands as well as dock workers, and cemented the allegiance of Japanese-American voters. The Burns-Inouye alliance built on the grievances against the *haole* (the Hawaiian word for white) owners of the big companies, and triumphed. Inouye was elected the territorial delegate to the U.S. House in 1954, and later was elected as a full-fledged congressman and then as a senator. Burns was elected governor in 1962, and for 40 years the office was passed down in lineal succession to George Ariyoshi, John Waihee, and Benjamin Cayetano. Over the years, this machine has built a large government. Hawaii has high taxes and by far the highest number of state and local employees per capita. This is centralized government: Hawaii has five counties (and one, Honolulu, has 70% of the population), one school district, and one statewide health care plan. Landholdings are centralized too. The state and federal governments are the largest landowners in Hawaii. The Bishop Estate—founded by descendants of Kamehameha I—now called the Kamehameha Schools Bishop Estate, owns a significant share of land.

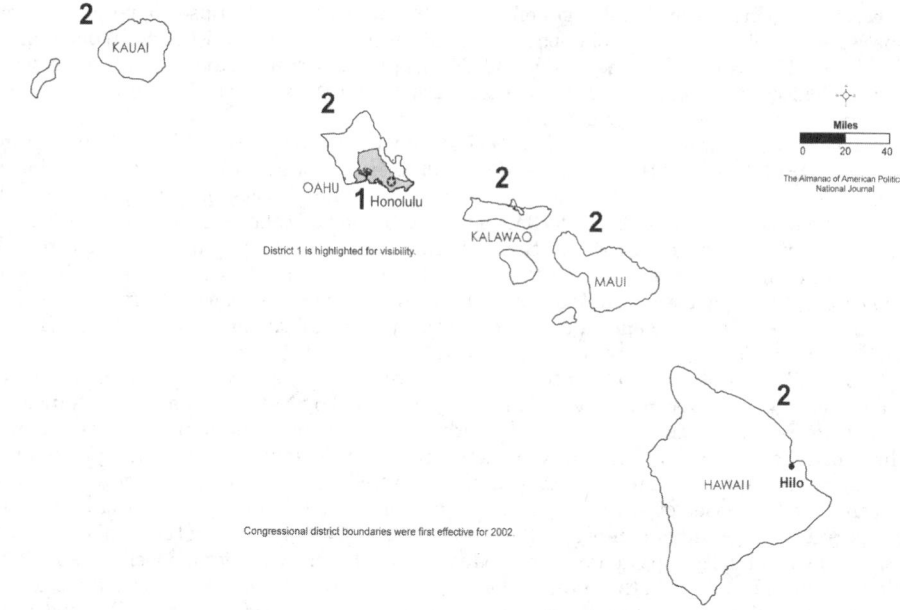

District 1 is highlighted for visibility.

Congressional district boundaries were first effective for 2002.

During the 50 years of Democratic dominance, Hawaii's economy was transformed. By the 1960s, tourism edged out agriculture—mainly pineapples and sugar—as Hawaii's No. 1 industry. (With more than 100 military installations of varying size, the state's No. 2 industry is the military.) Pineapple acreage declined from 77,000 to 10,000, and Del Monte closed its last pineapple operations in 2006. Sugar production declined 67% in the 1990s, and most of the sugar produced is now processed into biofuel. Hawaii's agriculture today is dedicated to specialty crops whose high cost of production can be recovered in local, national, or international markets: flowers, wasabi, macadamia nuts, Kona coffee, bananas, avocados, papayas, and genetically engineered seeds. As big agriculture shriveled, the ILWU has become overshadowed by the 44,000-member Hawaii Government Employees Association. Voting long tended to follow ethnic lines. Japanese-Americans, used to working in organizations in unions and government, were the heart of the Democratic Party. Whites, with relatively high incomes, have tended toward Republicans. Filipinos, often in menial jobs, are heavily Democratic, and Chinese, somewhat less so. Native Hawaiians are heavily Democratic.

As it changed, Hawaii found its vulnerabilities. It imports 90% of its food, and has only one-week's supply available at any given time. Expanded production is impractical because farm worker wages are not high enough to afford Hawaii's expensive housing. Tourism has been vulnerable to slumps in the business cycle. Tourism was robust until the September 11 attacks; it bounced back from 2004 to 2007, and then crashed again with the U.S. recession in 2008 and 2009. For the locals, housing prices are bid up by luxury buyers who have made their money elsewhere. The median home price in Maui in 2010 was $440,000—out of reach for many. Hawaii has a low rate of homeownership and many properties are held on 99-year leases. Also, lawsuits and political requirements have held up sales of 1.2 million acres of "ceded lands," subject to Native Hawaiian claims. The combination of high housing prices and an economy that is not generating as many high-paying jobs for young people has prompted more migration of Hawaiians to the mainland. Obama, who has chronicled his anxiety growing up black in the seemingly tolerant Hawaii of the 1970s, is the first president born and raised in the state. But he chose to be educated in California, New York, and Massachusetts, and to make his career in Illinois.

This economic turbulence has been accompanied by some political turbulence. Hawaii's Democratic machine faced challenges over the years, in primaries and from third-party candidacies, and from Republican Linda Lingle, who was the mayor of Maui and the Hawaii governor from 2003 to 2010. Lingle was unable, however, to persuade the heavily Democratic legislature to pass many of her policies. It even passed a tax increase over her veto, creating a top income tax rate of 11%. Her acrimonious fights with public employee unions resulted in spending cuts, furloughs, and delayed tax refunds when the state faced huge deficits in 2009 and 2010. And she raised some hackles when she vetoed a civil unions law. Union-backed Democrats made gains in legislative elections, and as Lingle left office, Hawaii had the most lopsided legislative majorities in the nation. The election of former Democratic Rep. Neil Abercrombie as governor in 2010 installed an energetic liberal in the governor's office. He won decisively, 58%-41%.

The "king of Hawaii," as *The Washington Post* dubbed him, remains Sen. Inouye. That became crystal clear in the May 2010 special election to fill Abercrombie's seat in the U.S. House. Inouye opposed the choice of national Democrats and the Obama White House, former Rep. Ed Case, who made an enemy of Inouye in 2006 by challenging his friend and colleague, Sen. Daniel Akaka, in the 2006 primary. Inouye backed state Sen. Colleen Hanabusa in the race, which resulted in a split Democratic vote and an easy ride for Republican Charles Djou to the seat with 40% of the vote. Inouye eventually got his way. In the contest the following November for a full term, Case declined to run, and in the ensuing one-on-one match with Djou, Hanabusa prevailed, 53%-47%. Inouye himself was re-elected to a ninth term by a 75%-21% margin at age 86.

Hawaii's reputation for tolerance has been marred by controversy over the status of Native Hawaiians and by occasional attacks on military personnel by Native Hawaiians. A Native Hawaiian protest movement grew in the 1990s, with demonstrations on the anniversaries of the overthrow of Queen Liliuokalani and the U.S. annexation of the islands. A state sovereignty commission sponsored a referendum on electing delegates to create a Native Hawaiian government. All of this raised the issue of just who is a Native Hawaiian, since almost no one is of pure native ancestry any longer. Advocates of special treatment for Natives argued that they ranked below all other Hawaii ethnic groups in income and education, and some called for independence from the United States. But some in the movement strongly disagreed with drastic action. Native activist Haunani-Kay Trask said, "As a nationalist, I hate the United States of America. But (independence) doesn't live in the political-military world we live in, with 26 military bases in Hawaii and 7 million tourists a year." She has also said, "Our native people have been essentially confined to a servant class."

In 2000, the U.S. Supreme Court declared unconstitutional the 1978 Hawaii state constitutional amendment setting up Native-Hawaiian-only elections for the Office of Hawaiian Affairs, which administers a $400 million trust fund. That decision casts doubt on other provisions of the 1978 amendment, including the Hawaiian Homes Commission and the recognition of Native gathering rights on private property. Sen. Akaka has responded with bills granting Native Hawaiians sovereignty. They would authorize a separate, sovereign Native Hawaiian government, with apparently no territorial jurisdiction, but with potential custody of the $400 million trust monies held in the Office of Hawaiian Affairs. He has repeatedly since 2000 tried to get the bill through Congress without success. After the 2008 election, Akaka felt his bill would have a better chance with Obama in the White House. But in December 2009, negotiations between Akaka and the Obama administration produced a version opposed by Gov. Lingle. The Senate Indian Affairs Committee passed it, followed by the full House in March 2010 on a mostly party-line vote of 245-164. But it died in the Senate, and with more Republican senators elected in 2010, its prospects seemed dim.

Hawaii, so far removed from any other land, has a particularly fragile ecology, with a profusion of bird and plant species that are vulnerable to invasive predators. Airliners' wheel housings are routinely inspected for the brown tree snakes that have killed off most of the birds in Guam. The oceans around the islands are vulnerable too, and a source of controversy. In 2006, President George W. Bush issued an order dedicating the Northwestern Hawaiian Islands Marine National Monument, which covers an expanse of ocean plus a few uninhabited islands that is 1,400 miles long and 100 miles wide. The area contains 70% of the nation's tropical, shallow-water coral reefs, some 7,000 marine species (one-quarter found nowhere else), the endangered Hawaiian monk seal population, and threatened species of predatory fish (sharks, groupers, jacks). Concerns were raised on Kauai and Maui when an 866-passenger, 286-vehicle ferry between Oahu and those islands started operating in August 2007. Until then, Hawaii was the world's only archipelago without ferry service. Kauai protesters claimed it would bring heavy traffic and despoil fish stocks and habitats. The ferry was shut down in March 2009, when the Hawaii Supreme Court ruled it needed an environmental impact statement; the company went bankrupt two months later. Meanwhile, Hawaii, with great potential for wind and geothermal energy, is still 90% dependent on imported oil, although a recent law requires 40% to come from renewable sources. But nature is not always benign. The Kilauea volcano on the Big Island started erupting in 1983 and hasn't stopped, and it is threatening hundreds of houses insured by a state program instituted in 1993. There is always at least a little trouble in paradise.

Population		Household Income		Work	
Pop. 2010:	1,360,301	Under $15k:	9.4%	Private:	67.1%
State rank:	40th	$15k to $50k:	28.0%	Government:	25.3%
Change since 2000:	Up 12.3%	$50k to $100k:	34.8%	Self-employed:	7.4%
Urban:	90.8%	$100k to $200k:	22.9%	Unemployment (3-yr. average):	3.5%
Rural:	9.2%	Over $200k:	5.0%	Poverty:	9.3%
Native of state:	53.5%	Median income:	$65,305	Blue collar:	17.8%
Not a citizen:	7.8%			White collar:	56.7%
Area size:	10,932 sq. mi.	**Home Value**		Khaki collar:	3.6%
		Under $100k:	2.7%	Other:	21.8%
Most populous cities		$100k to $300k:	14.8%		
Urban Honolulu	337,256	$300k to $500k:	26.8%	**Age**	
East Honolulu	49,914	$500k to $1 mil:	46.0%	Median age:	37.6 yrs.
Pearl City CDP	47,698	Over $1 million:	9.6%	More than 65 yrs:	14.3%
Hilo CDP	43,263	Median:	$543,600	Less than 18 yrs:	22.6%

Race/Ethnicity				Military Veterans		Registered Voters in 2010	
White:	22.7%	*Language*		% of Pop:	11.2%	No Party registration	
Black:	1.5%	English:	74.6%			Voter turnout:	385,464
Hispanic:	8.9%	Spanish:	2.3%	*Veterans by Period*		Turnout as % of	
Asian:	37.7%	Asian:	21.3%	WWII and before:	9.1%	voting age:	36.5%
Native Am.:	0.2%	Other European:	1.6%	Korea:	9.8%		
Hawaiian:	9.4%			Vietnam:	32.0%	**Legislature**	
Two+ races:	19.4%	**Education**		Gulf (pre-2001):	10.9%	Senate:	24 D 1 R
		H.S. grad:	90.1%	Gulf (post-2001):	16.2%	House:	43 D 8 R
Ancestry		College grad:	29.3%	Peace time:	22.0%		
German	6.1%	Grad degree:	9.9%				
Irish	4.6%						
English	4.0%						

Presidential politics Hawaii's presidential voting over the years has been the product of two sometimes countervailing forces. One is the state's historic preference for the Democratic Party. The other is an inclination to support incumbents in a state that takes patriotism seriously, in part because the patriotism of so many of its citizens was once unjustly questioned and in part because of the large presence of the military. This helps explain why Hawaii supported Ronald Reagan solidly in 1984, although it wasn't enough to help George H.W. Bush in 1992; Democrat Bill Clinton carried Hawaii 48%-37%. In 1996 and 2000, both those forces were moving in the same direction, and Hawaii voted 57%-32% for Clinton and 56%-37% for Al Gore, respectively.

2008 Presidential Vote
Barack Obama (D) 325,871 (72%)
John McCain (R) 120,566 (27%)

2004 Presidential Vote
John Kerry (D) 231,708 (54%)
George W. Bush (R)..............194,191 (45%)

In 2004, the two countervailing forces were in tension. October polls showed the contest a dead heat and suggested that Filipino- and Japanese-Americans, ordinarily Democratic, were leaning toward Bush, the commander-in-chief. Vice President Cheney flew 8,270 miles to appear in Honolulu at 10 p.m. on the Sunday night before the election and left two hours later—the first national nominee to campaign in Hawaii since 1960, when Republican Richard Nixon fulfilled his pledge to campaign in all 50 states. But Hawaii's Democratic preference prevailed, and John Kerry won 54%-45%. In 2008, the Democratic presidential candidate was, for the first time for any party in America's history, a native of Hawaii. Barack Obama vacationed in Hawaii for a week before the Democratic National Convention, and returned to the state just before the election to see his ailing grandmother, who died two days before the election. He carried Hawaii 72%-27%, winning in almost every precinct, his best showing in any state. Whites voted 70% for him, Asians 68%, and "others" (presumably mostly Native Hawaiians) 80% for him.

Hawaii chooses presidential delegates by caucus. Sometimes insurgent candidates have been able to swamp thinly attended meetings and win, as Democrat Michael Dukakis and Republican Pat Robertson did in 1988. In 2008, Hawaii Democrats held their caucuses on February 19, and more than 37,000 voters turned out, compared with just 4,000 in 2004. The Obama campaign stressed the candidate's Hawaiian heritage. Hillary Rodham Clinton sent daughter Chelsea in to campaign for a couple of days. Obama's 76%-24% win was one of the string of victories in February that propelled him to the nomination. The Republican caucuses took place on May 17, long after Arizona's John McCain had clinched the party's nomination.

Congressional districting

Hawaii has two congressional districts: The 1st includes urban Honolulu and extends westward to Pearl Harbor and the rural area beyond. The 2nd includes the rest of Oahu and the Neighbor Islands. The 1st District elected a Republican in 1986 and 1988. The 2nd District has elected only Democrats since it was created in 1970. Before that, Hawaii elected one Democrat at large in 1959 and 1960 and two Democrats at large from 1962 to 1968. The Democratic Legislature made minor and politically insignificant changes in the district lines in 2002 and seems likely to do the same by 2012.

Governor

Neil Abercrombie (D)

Elected 2010, term expires Dec. 2014, 1st term; b. June 26, 1938, Buffalo, NY; home, Honolulu; Union Col., B.A. 1959, U. of HI, Manoa, M.A. 1964, Ph.D. 1974; No religious affiliation; Married (Nancie Caraway).

Elected Office: HI House of Reps., 1974–78; HI Senate, 1978–86; U.S. House of Reps., 1986–87; Honolulu City Cncl., 1988–90; U.S. House, 1990–2010.

Professional Career: College prof., 1959–63; Probation officer, Marin Cnty., CA, 1964–67; Sociologist, 1967–74; Asst. prof., HI Loa Col., 1979–80; Consultant, 1983–87, 1989–90; Asst., HI Superintendent of Educ., 1987–88.

Office: Executive Chambers, State Capitol, 96813, 808-586-0034; Fax: 808-586-0006.

Election Results

2010 general	Neil Abercrombie (D)	222,724	(58%)
	J. 'Duke' Aiona (R)	157,311	(41%)
2010 primary	Neil Abercrombie (D)	142,304	(60%)
	Mufi Hannemann (D)	90,590	(38%)

Prior Winning Percentages: House: 2008 (77%); 2006 (69%); 2004 (63%); 2002 (73%); 2000 (69%); 1998 (62%); 1996 (50%); 1994 (54%); 1992 (73%); 1990 (60%); 1986 (30%)

The new governor of Hawaii is Democrat Neil Abercrombie, who represented the state's 1st District for 10 terms before easily winning election as governor in 2010. With his graying beard and sometimes ponytail, he was affectionately referred to as the aging hippie of Capitol Hill. He was also known for an aggressive and bombastic debating style that was often tempered by enthusiasm and good humor. After college in upstate New York, Abercrombie taught school, moved to Hawaii, earned a Ph.D. in American studies, and at various times worked as a waiter, custodian, and probation officer. In those years, Abercrombie, now in his 70s, got to know Barack Obama's parents and knew their son as "Little Barry." He was elected to the Hawaii legislature in 1974 and served 12 years. He first came to Congress in 1986, when he won a special election, and served only three months. He lost the primary for the full term to Democrat Mufi Hanneman (now mayor of Honolulu), who then lost to Republican Pat Saiki. When Saiki ran for the U.S. Senate in 1990, Abercrombie won a three-way primary for her House seat and won the general election easily.

As a House member, Abercrombie's voting record was mostly liberal, though a bit less so on economic issues. He served on the Armed Services Committee and saw no contradiction between his protests of the Iraq war and his votes for military spending for Hawaii and elsewhere. When Republicans controlled Congress, he and Ohio liberal Rep. Dennis Kucinich were the lead sponsors of a resolution calling for a date-certain withdrawal of U.S. troops from Iraq. Abercrombie also was a vocal opponent of the Bush administration's "surge" proposal for adding more combat troops. "This is the craziest, dumbest plan I've ever seen or heard of in my life," he told Joint Chiefs of Staff Chairman Gen. Peter Pace during a 2007 hearing. That year, the House passed the bill he sponsored with Democratic Rep. John Tanner of Tennessee requiring the Bush administration to report every 90 days on its plans to withdraw troops from Iraq; the bill died in the Senate.

Once Democrats took the majority in 2007, Abercrombie chaired the Tactical Air and Land Forces Subcommittee. He worked to assure adequate funding for Micronesia and the Marshall Islands 2,500 miles to the southwest in the Pacific, and he pressed the Army to explain the dumping of 8,000 tons of chemical munitions off Oahu after World War II. In 2007, he backed an $867 million cut in technology-based Future Combat Systems, the Army's main modernization program, after continual delays in testing the new systems. In his usual colorful way, Abercrombie described his frustration with the Army: "The problem with FCS is, they're waiting for Dumbledore or someone to come in and say, 'Harry, this is the magic incantation. Say this and, believe me, the Dark Lord will be vanquished'—the Dark Lord of schedule and testing and delays. They're looking for Harry Potter!" In the 2008 defense bill, Abercrombie added 15 C-17 transports and 20 F-22 fighters that the Pentagon did not request. The watchdog group Citizens Against Government Waste listed him in 2008 as the fourth-highest House recipient of local earmarks, mostly for military projects. Abercrombie consistently backed Hawaii Democratic Sen. Daniel Akaka's bill to recognize Native Hawaiians as an indigenous people with a right to self-determination.

The 1st District is usually solidly Democratic, but in 1994 Abercrombie had serious competition from Orson Swindle, a Marine Corps pilot, a Vietnam-era prisoner of war, and a national leader of Ross Perot's United We Stand America. Swindle charged that Abercrombie was too dovish, but Abercrombie outraised him, and won 54%-43%. Swindle ran again in 1996, labeled Abercrombie a far-left hippie, and called for big spending cuts. Abercrombie narrowly outspent him, and won 50%-46%. After that, he was re-elected by overwhelming margins.

In March 2009, Abercrombie announced he would run for governor in 2010, when Republican Gov. Linda Lingle was term-limited. His Democratic primary opponent was Honolulu Mayor Mufi Hanneman. The primary between the two men was unusually negative by Aloha State standards. Calling himself an "agent of change," Abercrombie stressed education and jobs, also expressing support for a civil unions bill that Lingle vetoed in 2010. He accused Hanneman of politicizing work on Honolulu's planned 20-mile commuter rail system, a charge the mayor angrily denied. Hanneman made a bid for the state's non-white majority by playing up his island roots, also noting that Abercrombie had been in office for 40 years and did not represent the change that the state needed. His supporters, meanwhile, aired a radio ad claiming Abercrombie did not hold "traditional Christian values." Hanneman held a slight edge in fundraising through the campaign's final months, but Abercrombie won the endorsement of unions, whose members were most likely to vote in the primary. He beat Hanneman with 60% of the vote, setting up a general election race with Republican Lt. Gov. James "Duke" Aiona.

Abercrombie continued to focus on education, pledging to create a state Department of Early Childhood and restore funding for the Healthy Start child abuse prevention program. He also vowed not to raise the state's general excise tax. Aiona, who trailed badly in early polls, made the race competitive in the final weeks by portraying his opponent's two decades in Congress as largely ineffective. But Abercrombie got a boost when hugely popular native son Obama recorded a TV spot proclaiming his old friend an "inspiring leader." He and his running mate for lieutenant governor, Brian Schatz, outraised Aiona's campaign 2-to-1. With Aiona unable to pick up the moderate voters that had propelled Lingle into office, Abercrombie won by a 17-point margin, a figure that surprised many Hawaii political observers.

Senior Senator

Daniel Inouye (D)

Elected 1962, term expires 2016, 9th term; b. Sept. 7, 1924, Honolulu; home, Honolulu; U. of HI, B.A. 1950, George Washington U., J.D. 1952; United Methodist; married (Irene Hirano); 1 child.

Military Career: Army, 1943–47 (WWII).

Elected Office: HI House of Reps., 1954–58; HI Senate, 1958–59; U.S. House of Reps., 1959–62.

Professional Career: Honolulu dpty. public prosecutor, 1953–54.

DC Office: 722 HSOB, 20510, 202-224-3934; Fax: 202-224-6747; Web site: inouye.senate.gov.

State Offices: Hilo, 808-935-0844; Honolulu, 808-541-2542; Kauai, 808-245-4611; Kona, 808-935-0844; Maui, 808-242-9702; Molokai, 808-642-0203; West Oahu, 808-623-8334.

Committees: *Appropriations* (Chmn): Commerce, Justice, Science & Related Agencies; Defense (Chmn); Department of State, Foreign Operations & Related Programs; Homeland Security; Labor, Health & Human Services, Education & Related Agencies; Military Construction, Veterans Affairs & Related Agencies. *Commerce, Science & Transportation:* Aviation Operations, Safety & Security; Communications, Technology & the Internet; Oceans, Atmosphere, Fisheries & Coast Guard; Science & Space; Surface Transportation & Merchant Marine Infrastructure, Safety & Security. *Indian Affairs. Rules & Administration.*

Group Ratings

	ACLU	ACU	ADA	CFG	AFS	FRC	LCV	ITIC	NTU	COC
2010	93	0	80	0	94	0	86	67	7	27
2009	–	0	95	3	100	–	100	–	5	43

National Journal Ratings

	2010 LIB — 2010 CONS		2009 LIB — 2009 CONS	
Economic	75%	— 22%	81%	— 15%
Social	65%	— 0%	85%	— 0%
Foreign	47%	— 0%	55%	— 0%
Composite	78%	— 23%	84%	— 16%

Key Votes of the 111th Congress

1. Overturn Ledbetter	Y	5. Pass health care bill	Y	9. Ratify New START	Y
2. Pass $787 billion stimulus	Y	6. Regulate financial firms	Y	10. Confirm Elena Kagan	Y
3. Repeal DC gun laws	N	7. Pass tax cuts for some	Y	11. Stop EPA climate regs	N
4. Confirm Sonia Sotomayor	Y	8. Legalize immigrants' kids	Y	12. Repeal don't ask, tell	Y

Election Results

2010 general	Daniel Inouye (D)..277,228	(75%)	($5, 216,102)
	Cam Cavasso (R)..79,939	(22%)	($266,398)
	Jim Brewer (Green) 7,762	(2%)	
2010 primary	Daniel Inouye (D)...198,711	(88%)	
	Andrew Woerner (D)..26,411	(12%)	

Prior Winning Percentages: 2004 (76%); 1998 (79%); 1992 (57%); 1986 (74%); 1980 (78%); 1974 (83%); 1968 (83%); 1962 (69%); House: 1960 (74%); 1959 (68%)

The largest figure in Hawaii's public life remains Democrat Daniel Inouye, the state's senior senator, who has held various elective offices since before Hawaii attained statehood in 1959. The son of Japanese immigrants, Inouye (*in-NO-ay*) grew up in Honolulu. His ambition was to become a surgeon. At age 17, he was teaching a first aid course when Pearl Harbor was attacked. He tended the wounded for a week, and then went on to serve in the 442nd Regimental Combat Team in France and Italy, eventually earning 15 medals and citations. Just as the war was ending, he lost his right arm in combat. Recovering in a Michigan veterans' hospital, he asked a fellow veteran from Kansas, whose right arm had been shattered, what his plans were. The soldier said he planned to go to law school, run for the state legislature, and eventually get elected to Congress. He was Bob Dole, who was also wounded in Italy, exactly one week before Inouye, and who went on to become a senator and the Republican nominee for president in 1996. Inouye took a similar path. He graduated from the University of Hawaii and George Washington University Law School, then became a leader of a group of young veterans who took over Hawaii's creaking Democratic Party. Inouye was elected to the state legislature in 1954, and five years later, he was elected to the U.S. House. In 1962, he was elected to the Senate. In June 2010, he passed former Sen. Strom Thurmond, R-S.C. to become the second-longest serving senator in history. He is on track to beat the late Robert Byrd's record as the longest-serving member of Congress in 2016. Currently, Inouye is the most senior member of the Senate. Inouye was elected Senate president pro tem after Byrd's death in July 2010; he is third in line for the presidency. Other Inouye milestones: He was a member of the Senate Watergate Committee in 1973-74 and the first chairman of the Senate Intelligence Committee in 1976. In 2000, he was awarded the Congressional Medal of Honor for his heroism in World War II.

In 2009, Inouye rose to the chairmanship of the powerful Appropriations Committee. He replaced the chronically ill Byrd, who was pressed by Senate Majority Leader Harry Reid to step down from the demanding job after the 2008 election. Byrd called Inouye a friend and "genuine American hero," and predicted he would be a "skillful and fair" replacement. Inouye has said that he would not alter the committee's handling of lawmakers' pet projects, in spite of recent controversies over congressional earmarks, but he and then-House Chairman David Obey said that members must make public on their website their earmark requests and explanations for the requests. He found himself completely at odds with the Hawaii-raised President Obama over spending issues. When Obama in 2010 backed legislation giving the president rescission authority over spending bills, Inouye said, "I have long defended the congressional power of the purse, and as chairman of the Appropriations Committee, I have no intention of ceding that authority to the executive branch."

Inouye has long used his seat on Appropriations to fund projects he finds worthy, from his alma mater of George Washington University to Native Hawaiian education to the Maui Space Surveillance System. In the 2009 defense bill alone, he sponsored 37 earmarks worth $198 million. In 2008, his defense spending bill gave nearly full funding to the Bush administration's requests for new combat systems, national missile defense, and shipbuilding. During the Obama administration, he has been willing to buck the Pentagon. Inouye backed the alternate engine for the F-35 Joint Strike Fighter, a program that the administration held up as an example of wasteful spending. Because of opposition to the program within the Senate, Inouye ultimately gave up on funding the engine in the Defense Appropriations bill. In October 2009, he supported Gen. Stanley McChrystal's counterinsurgency strategy in Afghanistan. In November 2009, he accepted the administration's decision to withdraw missile defense facilities from Eastern Europe. The funds were transferred to a Hawaii test facility for the Navy's Aegis weapons system. Inouye and ranking Republican Thad Cochran of Mississippi in May 2010 worked to bar substantive amendments to the defense supplemental to obtain quick passage, and it was passed that month with only a few amendments.

Inouye chaired the Indian Affairs Committee from 1989-94 and again in 2001-03. He saw many analogies between the condition of mainland American Indians and Native Hawaiians, and generally erred on the side of Native Americans in disputes with the federal government. In 2006, he removed from a lobbying regulation bill a provision that would require Indian tribes to report contributions to the Federal Election Commission. He also sponsored a measure, defeated 6-6, to give tribes the right to appeal a rejection by the states of their bids for casinos. At one point, he refused contact with companies that hired disgraced lobbyist Jack Abramoff, who was accused of swindling tribes. "I took it personally. He was ripping off Indians," Inouye told *The Washington Post*. He was also a co-sponsor of the 1993 bill in which the United States apologized for overthrowing the Hawaiian monarchy. On the issue of Native Hawaiian sovereignty, some activists consider him lukewarm, especially in comparison to the junior senator from Hawaii, Daniel Akaka, who has sponsored legislation for years that would recognize Native Hawaiians as an indigenous people with a right to self-determination and establish a process for formation of a Native Hawaiian governing body that would have, as many Indian tribes do, a government-to-government relationship with the United States. For many years, Inouye sought pension benefits for Filipino veterans who served in the American military during World War II, and he got $198 million for that purpose in the 2009 economic stimulus bill.

On the Commerce, Science, and Transportation Committee, which Inouye chaired from 2007 to 2008, he has been deeply involved in communications issues. He was not enthusiastic about Republican Ted Stevens' far-ranging rewrite of the 1996 telecommunications act, and when Inouye took over the chairmanship in 2007, he indicated that he was not interested in such sweeping legislation. Instead he pushed more modest measures, like one setting criteria for Commerce Department grants to strengthen emergency communications, and a 2008 bill to crack down on online predators. Also that year, Congress passed Inouye's Broadband Data Improvement Act, aimed at identifying areas of the nation that have fallen behind in high-speed Internet access. He opposed a permanent ban on Internet taxes because "we don't know what the future holds."

He also took an active interest in the cause of Japanese-Americans interned during World War II. Inouye sponsored a 2006 law granting $38 million to research and restore sites where internments took place, and in 2007, he sponsored a bill to investigate the cases of people of Japanese origin in Latin America who were deported from countries there and sent to the United States, evidently to be exchanged for American prisoners of war held by Japan. He objected to House-passed legislation that year to call on Japan to apologize for its use of sex slaves during the war. Six Japanese prime ministers already had apologized, he said, while noting the U.S. government's improper war-time internment of Japanese-Americans.

During the hard-fought Democratic 2008 primary contest, Inouye endorsed Hillary Rodham Clinton for president, saying native-son Obama needed more experience. He was forced to issue an apology after suggesting during the primaries that Obama attended an elitist high school in Hawaii. "Shame on Danny for trying to pull that stunt," Obama told a local interviewer. "I went to Punahou [School] on a scholarship."

Although he by and large has avoided ethics issues during his long tenure, Inouye in 2009 came under fire in *The Washington Post* and *The New York Times* for asking bank regulators about the status of a request from Central Pacific Financial for government bailout funds. Inouye has the bulk of his wealth invested in the bank, which he co-founded. Its stock price dropped dramatically during the financial crisis, and Treasury eventually gave the bank $135 million in bailout funds.

As the informal dean of Hawaii's Democratic politics, he took a lead role in the May 2010 special election for the 1st Congressional District seat to fill the vacancy created when Neil Abercrombie resigned to campaign for governor. Inouye strongly backed state Sen. Colleen Hanabusa, who also had support from traditional state Democrats. He actively opposed the candidacy of former Democratic Rep. Ed Case, who had run against Democratic Sen. Daniel Akaka in the 2006 primary. But under state law, this was a multiparty contest in which the top finisher would win, and Republican Charles Djou, a member of the Honolulu City Council, ended up with 40% of the vote after Hanabusa and Case split the Democratic vote. However, Democrats were united later. Case did not run in November for the full term, and Hanabusa was nominated easily against a little known opponent. She went on to unseat Djou 53%-47%.

Inouye himself was nominated for re-election with 88% of the vote in the September 2010 primary and prevailed 75%-22% over his Republican opponent in November.

Junior Senator

Daniel Akaka (D)

Appointed May 1990, term expires 2012, 3rd full term; b. Sept. 11, 1924, Honolulu; home, Honolulu; U. of HI, B.Ed. 1952, M.A. 1966; Congregationalist; married (Mary Mildred); 5 children.

Military Career: Army Corps of Engineers, 1945–47 (WWII).

Elected Office: U.S. House of Reps., 1976–90.

Professional Career: Public schl. teacher, principal & admin., 1953–71; Dir., HI Office of Econ. Oppor., 1971–74; Asst., HI Gov. Ariyoshi, 1975–76; Dir., Progressive Neighborhoods Program, 1975–76.

DC Office: 141 HSOB, 20510, 202-224-6361; Fax: 202-224-2126; Web site: akaka.senate.gov.

State Offices: Hilo, 808-935-1114; Honolulu, 808-522-8970.

Committees: *Armed Services:* Personnel; Readiness & Management Support; Seapower. *Banking, Housing & Urban Affairs:* Financial Institutions & Consumer Protection; Housing, Transportation & Community Development; Securities, Insurance & Investment. *Homeland Security & Governmental Affairs:* Disaster Recovery & Intergovernmental Affairs (Ad Hoc); Federal Financial Management, Government Information, Federal Services & International Security; Oversight of Government Management, the Federal Workforce & the District of Columbia (Chmn). *Indian Affairs* (Chmn). *Veterans' Affairs.*

Group Ratings

	ACLU	ACU	ADA	CFG	AFS	FRC	LCV	ITIC	NTU	COC
2010	93	0	85	5	98	0	86	67	7	27
2009	–	0	95	3	100	–	100	–	6	43

National Journal Ratings

	2010 LIB	—	2010 CONS	2009 LIB	—	2009 CONS
Economic	75%	—	22%	81%	—	15%
Social	65%	—	0%	85%	—	0%
Foreign	47%	—	0%	55%	—	0%
Composite	78%	—	23%	84%	—	16%

Key Votes of the 111th Congress

1. Overturn Ledbetter	Y	5. Pass health care bill	Y	9. Ratify New START	Y
2. Pass $787 billion stimulus	Y	6. Regulate financial firms	Y	10. Confirm Elena Kagan	Y
3. Repeal DC gun laws	N	7. Pass tax cuts for some	Y	11. Stop EPA climate regs	N
4. Confirm Sonia Sotomayor	Y	8. Legalize immigrants' kids	Y	12. Repeal don't ask, tell	Y

Election Results

2006 general	Daniel Akaka (D)	210,330	(61%)	($2, 692, 645)
	Cynthia Thielen (R)	126,097	(37%)	($336,209)
2006 primary	Daniel Akaka (D)	129,158	(55%)	
	Ed Case (D)	107,163	(45%)	

Prior Winning Percentages: 2000 (73%); 1994 (72%); 1990 (54%); House: 1988 (89%); 1986 (76%); 1984 (82%); 1982 (89%); 1980 (90%); 1978 (86%); 1976 (80%)

Democrat Daniel Akaka is the first senator of Native Hawaiian descent. Born four days after fellow Democratic Sen. Daniel Inouye, he graduated from the Kamehameha School for Boys and served in the Army Corps of Engineers from 1943 to 1947, then became a public school teacher and principal. In 1971, he was the director of the Hawaii anti-poverty program, and in 1975, he became an assistant to Democratic Gov. George Ariyoshi. The next year, when both of Hawaii's representatives ran for the Senate, he was elected to the House, where he served quietly on the Appropriations Committee. In May 1990, after the death of Democratic Sen. Spark Matsunaga, Democratic Gov. John Waihee appointed Akaka to the Senate. He has thus been an integral part of the dominant Democratic organization, and a quiet but diligent worker on Hawaii issues, for more than 30 years. But after all of his time in Congress, Akaka is not well known nationally. He was stung in particular by a 2006 *Time* magazine article that called him "affectionate and earnest" but one of the five worst senators in terms of effectiveness. "I was taught not to be a show horse but a workhorse," he told *The Honolulu Advertiser* then. "So, in a way, it's been a part of me not to brag."

Still, after the article, Akaka began to raise his profile on Capitol Hill. Beginning in 2007, when he became chairman of the Veterans' Affairs Committee, he set for himself an ambitious agenda.

He sought more health care funding for "invisible wounds" such as post-traumatic stress disorder and brain injuries for veterans. In 2009, he got through Congress a bill aimed at changing the budgeting processes at the Veterans Affairs Department to get benefits to veterans more quickly. The law was a response to the often long delays in services by the department's unwieldy bureaucracy. His bill passed both houses unanimously and was signed into law by President Obama in October 2009. The following year, Akaka pushed through a significant expansion in benefits to veterans, particularly the thousands not located near a VA health facility. His legislation provides federal assistance to care-givers who often take on the responsibility of home care for disabled vets. He got the five-year, $3.7 billion bill through the Senate over the objections of conservative Sen. Tom Coburn of Oklahoma, who demanded that its costs be offset by cuts elsewhere in the federal budget. The bill was signed into law in May 2010.

Akaka likely would have become chairman of the Homeland Security and Governmental Affairs Committee in 2009 if Senate Democrats had been successful in ousting Chairman Joe Lieberman, the Connecticut independent who fell out of favor with his party after actively supporting Republican John McCain in the 2008 presidential contest. But Lieberman held on, with support from Obama. In 2009, Akaka introduced a bill, approved by Homeland Security Secretary Janet Napolitano, to repeal the Real ID Act, a Bush-era law requiring the states by 2010 to issue driver's licenses only to people who could prove their immigration status. Governors had widely panned Real ID as impractical to execute. In 2006, he was one of nine Senate Democrats who voted against renewing the USA PATRIOT Act, the Bush administration's antiterrorism law that expanded law enforcement powers.

On other issues, Akaka recently demonstrated an interest in creating a more user-friendly federal government. In a move that anyone who has ever read a government document would applaud, he introduced a bill banishing bureaucratic language from government letters, forms, and other public documents. Dubbed the "Writing Act," it passed in 2010 and was signed into law. He also sponsored a successful bill requiring government agencies to establish flexible policies allowing employees to "telework" from home when practical.

Akaka has waged a long campaign in the Senate to pass legislation recognizing Native Hawaiian sovereignty. He was the sponsor of the 1993 Apology Resolution, signed by President Clinton, in which the United States acknowledged as illegal the overthrow of the Kingdom of Hawaii in 1893 and the denial of Native Hawaiians' right to self-determination. Akaka in 2000 introduced a bill to recognize Native Hawaiians as an indigenous people with a right to self-determination and establish a process for formation of a Native Hawaiian governing body that would have, as many Indian tribes do, a government-to-government relationship with the United States. Many Hawaiians believe they need the law to allow them to negotiate more forcefully with the federal government over land use issues. A companion bill passed the House that year but died in the Senate. Akaka brought the bill up again in 2001, but it stalled after some Native Hawaiians argued it would make them wards of the government. He tried but failed again in 2004. Sen. Jon Kyl of Arizona said then: "Persons of different races, who live together in the same society, would be subject to different legal codes....It is a recipe for permanent racial conflict."

After Democrats won control of Congress in 2006, the House passed a version of his bill in October 2007, and Akaka secured a commitment from Senate Majority Leader Harry Reid of Nevada to bring it to the floor, but Reid never did so. When Obama was elected president, Akaka said he was "ecstatic" that the native-son president was supportive. In 2009, after negotiations between Akaka and the Obama White House, the Senate Indian Affairs Committee approved the bill. It passed the House in March 2010, on a mostly party-line 245-164 vote, but it failed to pass the Senate. A furious Akaka said the legislation fell victim to a "misinformation" campaign by opponents, who claimed it would have allowed Native Hawaiians to secede, private lands to be taken, and gambling to be permitted.

Akaka has supported oil drilling in the Arctic National Wildlife Refuge, perhaps in part out of solidarity with colleagues from Alaska, who like Hawaiians often feel resentment that policy is made by mainlanders who have little knowledge or understanding of the unique needs of their states. "To some of my colleagues, the debate about the Arctic National Wildlife Refuge is about energy. To others, it is about the environment," Akaka said. "To me, the (issue) is really about whether or not the indigenous people who are directly impacted have a voice about the use of their lands." Another of Akaka's legislative causes was passage of a law making permanent the waiver of visa requirements from some countries, including Japan, which sends 2 million visitors a year to Hawaii.

Since his initial 54%-45% victory in 1990 against Republican Rep. Pat Saiki, Akaka has won re-election by large margins. But in 2006, at the age of 82, he faced a competitive primary challenge from 2nd District Democratic Rep. Ed Case. This was a remarkable election for Hawaii, where the Democratic establishment headed by Democratic Sen. Daniel Inouye has dominated elections for most of the past 50 years and no Democratic member of Congress has ever been defeated for re-election. Akaka was the establishment candidate, strongly supported by labor unions, Inouye, and Hawaii's other Democratic representative and now governor, Neil Abercrombie. Case was an arch-enemy of the establishment after challenging its candidate in the 2002 primary for governor. The 54-year-old Case argued that Hawaii, with its two octogenarian senators, needed to begin preparing for the inevitable transition by electing a more youthful Democrat who could begin accumulating seniority.

In most other states, Case would have had ample ammunition, given Akaka's low profile in Washington. But in Hawaii, Akaka is revered for his gentleness and modesty, and there were limits on how far Case could go in criticizing him. Akaka played up his vote against authorizing the use of force in Iraq and his close relationship with Inouye, and suggested that Case was not a real Democrat. He won 55%-45%. Akaka carried Oahu, where 69% of the votes were cast, 53%-47%; he won larger margins elsewhere. In the general election, Akaka was re-elected 61%-37%, a solid margin but his smallest in a Senate election since he first won the seat with 54% of the vote in 1990. Akaka has announced that he will not seek re-election in 2012.

FIRST DISTRICT

Colleen Hanabusa (D)

Elected 2010, 1st term; b. May 4, 1951, Honolulu; home, Wai'anae; U. of HI, B.A. 1973, M.A. 1975, J.D. 1977.; Buddhist; Married (John Souza).

Elected Office: HI Senate, 1998-2010.

Professional Career: Labor atty., 1978-2010.

DC Office: 238 CHOB, 20515, 202-225-2726; Fax: 202-225-0688; Web site: hanabusa.house.gov.

State Offices: Honolulu, 808-541-2570.

Committees: *Armed Services:* Oversight & Investigations; Readiness. *Natural Resources:* Fisheries, Wildlife, Oceans & Insular Affairs; Indian & Alaska Native Affairs.

Election Results

2010 general	Colleen Hanabusa (D)	94,140	(53%)	($2,447,129)
	Charles Djou (R)	82,723	(47%)	($2,698,779)
2010 primary	Colleen Hanabusa (D)	85,732	(79%)	
	Rafael Del Castillo (D)	22,874	(21%)	

Population		Race/Ethnicity		Work	
Pop. 2010:	658,672	White:	16.6%	Private:	66.9%
Change since 2000:	Up 8.6%	Black:	1.8%	Government:	27.3%
Urban:	99.3%	Hispanic:	6.8%	Self-employed:	5.7%
Rural:	0.7%	Asian:	51.4%	Blue collar:	16.4%
Area size:	326 sq. mi.	Native Am.:	0.1%	White collar:	59.0%
		Hawaiian:	7.3%	Khaki collar:	4.2%
Age		Two+ races:	15.9%	Other:	20.4%
Median age:	38.7 yrs.				
More than 65 yrs:	16.2%	*Ancestry*		Median income:	$65,553
Less than 18 yrs:	20.8%	German	4.7%	Median Home Value:	$561,200
		Irish	3.7%		
Education		English	2.9%	**Military Veterans**	
H.S. grad:	90.0%			% of Pop:	11.3%
College grad:	32.1%				
Grad degree:	11.1%				

Honolulu

The landmarks for visitors to Honolulu are the Pearl Harbor Hickam Air Force Base, the USS *Arizona* monument in Pearl Harbor, the downtown area, with its wondrously Victorian Iolani Palace, and, of course, Waikiki, with its 40-story hotels rising within a few feet of each other. This part of Hawaii is tightly packed with people living between the 3,000-foot Koolau Range and the beaches and harbor, where tropical bungalows and garden apartments house Hawaiians

2008 Presidential Vote		
Barack Obama (D) 152,990	(70%)
John McCain (R) 61,116	(28%)

2004 Presidential Vote		
John Kerry (D) 110,702	(53%)
George Bush (R) 99,256	(47%)

Cook Partisan Voting Index: D+11

of all incomes. Hawaii's largest shopping centers and its state university are located here. Neighborhoods where the rich overlook the ocean are wedged next to poor enclaves where residents are crammed onto clogged streets. Hawaii's topography jams cars onto just a few freeways and avenues, where traffic slows during rush hour and the *aloha* spirit is sorely tested. High taxes and high land and utility costs have limited growth. And although tourism remains brisk, the recession hit here early, resulting in declining hotel occupancy. Homelessness grew, and Aloha Airlines went bankrupt, ending its passenger service in 2008. But the Honolulu area also weathered the recession better than most other U.S. cities. Its unemployment rate in March 2010 was only 5.6%, one of the best in the nation and far lower than the 9% to 10% rates of many American cities at that time. The military remains an important presence on Oahu. Hickam is home to eight C-17 Air Force cargo carriers that can transport 20-ton armored Stryker vehicles.

All of these areas are in the 1st Congressional District of Hawaii. It is an area of well-established neighborhoods, and with little land left to develop, it is growing less rapidly than the rest of the state. Politically, the neighborhoods around Honolulu's downtown and the university campus are middle and lower income and usually Democratic. To the west, around the harbor, are many military families in modest neighborhoods who may vote for Democrats but can be attracted to Republicans. To the east, past Waikiki, around Diamond Head, and out to the Kahala and Koko Head beach areas, is higher-income territory that often votes Republican. Asians are 60% of the population in the Honolulu metro area. Favorite-son Barack Obama, who was photographed bodysurfing at Sandy Beach during his presidential campaign, reigned supreme here in 2008, when he got 70% of the vote in Honolulu County.

Colleen Hanabusa (D)

The new congresswoman from the 1st District of Hawaii is Colleen Hanabusa, a Democrat who won the seat in 2010. Hanabusa is a Yonsei, a fourth-generation American of Japanese ancestry. Both of her grandfathers were among the more than 100,000 Japanese-Americans forcibly relocated and interned after Japan's attack on Pearl Harbor during World War II. She was raised on a sugar plantation by her maternal grandmother while her parents worked long hours running a gas station in Waianae. She learned the value of hard work, she said, adding that "chipping in to get people through a hard time is very much a part of the plantation lifestyle." While young, she learned ikebana, the Japanese art of flower and plant arrangement that has a strong spiritual component. In ikebana, she says, if the core piece isn't well placed and balanced, the arrangement falls apart. "What I learned from that has always stuck with me," Hanabusa says. She graduated from the University of Hawaii with a bachelor's degree in economics and sociology and a master's degree in sociology, and went on to get a law degree from the William S. Richardson School of Law.

Elected to the Hawaii Senate in 1998, Hanabusa served for 12 years, rising in 2007 to Senate president and becoming the first woman to lead either house of Hawaii's legislature. One of her signature issues was education, including the creation of charter schools for underserved children and improving special-education programs. Hanabusa, who regularly joins Republican colleagues on a local conservative talk radio show, says that her legislative experience "taught me cooperation and the ability to collaborate."

When 10-term Rep. Neil Abercrombie left Congress to run for governor in 2010, Hanabusa was the early favorite of the state's Democratic establishment in the May special election. But former Rep. Ed Case also jumped in, disrupting the plans of kingmaker Sens. Daniel Inouye and Daniel Akaka, both Democrats who backed Hanabusa and held a grudge against Case for challenging Akaka in the Senate primary in 2006. With Case siphoning off Democratic votes, Hanabusa finished second to Djou. He won 40% to Hanabusa's 31% and Case's 28%.

Djou had to run again in November to earn a full, two-year term. Hanabusa came back for a rematch, and this time, Case stayed out. Hanabusa sailed to an easy victory in the primary, and then had a one-on-one shot at Djou in the general election. Both she and Djou were well financed, with about $1.7 million each. Hanabusa was a stand-up supporter of Obama's policies while many other Democrats in tough contests distanced themselves. She was a robust defender of the health care overhaul that Democrats pushed through Congress, calling health care a "right" and the legislation a first step toward universal health insurance. Obama's $787 billion economic stimulus bill worked, she said, and "kept people working and put money in people's pockets."

Her positions stood in sharp contrast to Djou's. He attacked "wasteful" federal spending and supported a constitutional amendment to require a balanced budget. He also said he would seek a moratorium on congressional earmarks. He is more moderate on social issues, and was one of only five House Republicans to back repeal of the "don't ask, don't tell" legislation barring openly gay men and women from the military. The *Honolulu Star-Advertiser* pointed out that there have been only two Republicans to represent Hawaii on Capitol Hill since statehood—Rep. Pat Saiki and the late Sen. Hiram Fong—and both were moderates. This time, Hanabusa won, 53% to 47%.

SECOND DISTRICT

Mazie Hirono (D)

Elected 2006, 3rd term; b. Nov. 3, 1947, Fukushima, Japan; home, Honolulu; U. of HI, B.A. 1970, Georgetown U., J.D. 1978; Buddhist; married (Leighton Kim Oshima); 1 child.

Elected Office: HI House of Reps., 1980-94, HI lt. gov. 1994-2002.

Professional Career: Dep. atty. gen., 1978-80; Practicing atty., 1984-88.

DC Office: 1410 LHOB, 20515, 202-225-4906; Fax: 202-225-4987; Web site: hirono.house.gov.

State Offices: Honolulu, 808-541-1986.

Committees: *Education & the Workforce:* Early Childhood, Elementary & Secondary Education; Workforce Protections. *Ethics. Transportation & Infrastructure:* Aviation; Coast Guard & Maritime Transportation; Highways & Transit; Water Resources & Environment.

Group Ratings

	ACLU	ACU	ADA	CFG	AFS	FRC	LCV	ITIC	NTU	COC
2010	94	0	95	0	100	6	100	67	6	13
2009	–	0	100	0	100	–	100	–	1	33

National Journal Ratings

	2010 LIB	—	2010 CONS	2009 LIB	—	2009 CONS
Economic	90%	—	0%	91%	—	0%
Social	89%	—	7%	70%	—	29%
Foreign	84%	—	11%	87%	—	9%
Composite	91%	—	9%	85%	—	15%

Key Votes of the 111th Congress

1. Overturn Ledbetter	Y	5. Bar federal abortion funds	N	9. Stop detainee transfers	N
2. Pass $820 billion stimulus	Y	6. Pass health care bill	Y	10. Legalize immigrants' kids	Y
3. Let guns in national parks	N	7. Regulate financial firms	Y	11. Repeal don't ask, tell	Y
4. Pass cap-and-trade	Y	8. Pass tax cuts for some	Y	12. Limit campaign funds	Y

Election Results

2010 general	Mazie Hirono (D)	132,290	(72%)	($992,526)
	John Willoughby (R)	46,404	(25%)	($30,738)
2010 primary	Mazie Hirono (D)	unopposed		

Prior Winning Percentages: 2008 (76%), 2006 (61%)

Population		Race/Ethnicity		Work	
Pop. 2010:	701,629	White:	28.5%	Private:	67.3%
Change since 2000:	Up 16.0%	Black:	1.2%	Government:	23.2%
Urban:	83.8%	Hispanic:	10.9%	Self-employed:	9.2%
Rural:	16.2%	Asian:	24.9%	Blue collar:	19.3%
Area size:	10,606 sq. mi.	Native Am.:	0.3%	White collar:	54.4%
		Hawaiian:	11.4%	Khaki collar:	3.0%
Age		Two+ races:	22.7%	Other:	23.3%
Median age:	36.3 yrs.				
More than 65 yrs:	12.4%	*Ancestry*		Median income:	$65,036
Less than 18 yrs:	24.3%	German	7.4%	Median Home Value:	$524,900
		Irish	5.4%		
Education		Portuguese	5.3%	**Military Veterans**	
H.S. grad:	90.2%			% of Pop:	11.1%
College grad:	26.4%				
Grad degree:	8.5%				

Outer Oahu, Other Islands

The 2nd District encompasses all of the islands in the Hawaii archipelago, including most of Oahu's acreage beyond Honolulu, which belongs to the state's other congressional district. It takes in Wheeler Army Airfield and the farmlands north of Pearl Harbor, between two jagged chains of mountains that lift the island out of the sea. Over the mountains to the west on Oahu is the Leeward Coast—calm, sultry, and lightly populated. Over the mountains to the northeast

2008 Presidential Vote
Barack Obama (D) 172,881   (73%)
John McCain (R) 59,450   (25%)

2004 Presidential Vote
John Kerry (D) 120,633   (56%)
George Bush (R) 94,860   (44%)

Cook Partisan Voting Index: D+14

is the Windward Coast, with many prosperous, Republican-leaning subdivisions in and around Kaneohe and Kailua. The 137 islands have distinct personalities. Hawaii, the Big Island, is the size of Connecticut and boasts huge cattle ranches; the active volcano Kilauea, which started erupting in 1983 and has not stopped since; and Mauna Kea, the highest mountain in the world if the count begins at its base far under the ocean. Tourists are told that it is bad luck to take pieces of lava home. On the north shore, with heavy rainfall and tropical foliage, is the old port of Hilo and Hawaii's macadamia nut industry; this is a blue-collar Democratic area in a natural wonderland. On the Kona Coast, where there is little rainfall and the landscape is dominated by lava flows, there are retirement condominiums and a higher-income, more Republican population.

Tourism dropped sharply on the island during the recession of 2007-09, but by mid-2010, the out-of-town visitors had returned in increasing numbers, with arrivals to Oahu making the biggest jump. The local housing market remained volatile, however, making Hawaii one of the top 10 states for foreclosure activity in 2010. Energy prices are among the highest in the nation, and "vog" emissions from volcanoes are a growing health concern. The island of Maui, favored more by North American than Asian tourists, has dozens of luxury condominiums and upscale resorts. Hawaii long was the world's only archipelago without ferry service. Then in 2007, a new $300 million ferry service between the islands went into operation. Residents on Maui and Kauai feared it would bring heavy traffic and despoil fish stocks and habitats. In March 2009, the private company was ordered to stop service by the Hawaii Supreme Court, which ruled that the legislature erred in exempting the firm from an environmental impact statement. The company went bankrupt, and the islands were again ferry-less.

Workers on the islands are employed chiefly in tourism, the military, social services, and agriculture. In recent years there has been a push to grow crops and algae for use as biofuels. Kauai, much of which was devastated by Hurricane Iniki in 1992, is the least developed and most agricultural of the main islands. Parts of it have the nation's highest rainfall, while others seldom get wet. Its large farm workforce—a reminder of what most of Hawaii was like a century ago—makes it the most Democratic of the islands. Overall, the district is Democratic.

Mazie Hirono (D)

The congresswoman from the 2nd District is Mazie Hirono, a Democrat elected in 2006. Hirono was born in Fukushima, Japan, and immigrated to Hawaii in 1955 just before her eighth birthday with her mother, who fled an abusive husband with alcohol and gambling problems. As a child, she shared a single bed in a boardinghouse room with her mother and older brother, and at age 10 was sent to work to help support the family. These childhood struggles with poverty and the adjustment to a new country shaped her liberal politics. "I know what it feels like to be discriminated against, to feel powerless, to have landlords who threaten to kick you out, and not having a place to go," she told *The Honolulu Star-Advertiser*. Hirono mastered English in the public schools and became a naturalized citizen in 1959, the same year Hawaii became a state. After graduating from the University of Hawaii, she ran for a seat in the state House and lost, then earned a law degree from Georgetown University and worked in the Hawaii attorney general's office. She ran again for the state House in 1980 and won; she held the seat for 14 years. In 1994, she was elected to the first of two terms as lieutenant governor. In 2002, she defeated Democrat Ed Case, who was then a state representative, in the gubernatorial primary. After that, her poorly organized campaign struggled to gain momentum, and she was undermined by Democratic corruption scandals, budget woes, and an acrimonious teachers' strike. She lost the general election 52%-47% to Linda Lingle, the first Republican to win the office since 1959.

Hirono's defeat was a painful setback for her, but not a career-ender. She formed the Patsy Mink political action committee (named for the late Hawaii representative) to assist state-level Democratic women who support abortion rights. When then-U.S. Rep. Case decided to challenge Sen. Daniel Akaka in the Democratic Senate primary in 2006, Hirono was one of 10 Democrats and two Republicans who wanted to succeed him. The field included experienced campaigners such as state Sens. Colleen Hanabusa and Clayton Hee, and former state Sen. Matt Matsunaga, the son of the late U.S. Sen. Spark Matsunaga. Hirono entered the race in April 2006 and was endorsed by the abortion rights fundraising group EMILY's List. She had more money and name recognition than the other candidates and was considered a front-runner. She ran radio ads that highlighted her efforts on early-childhood education, land reform, and workers' compensation. Hirono faced lingering doubts about the strength of her candidacy in the wake of her 2002 gubernatorial defeat. But she narrowly won the splintered September primary with 22% of the vote and finished 844 votes ahead of Hanabusa, who got 21%. Matsunaga was third with 14%.

After clinching the Democratic nomination, Hirono had a much easier time winning the general election in a district that had never elected a Republican. Republican state Sen. Bob Hogue, a former sportscaster, depicted Hirono as too liberal even for Hawaii, and Republicans mocked her as a "big-government peacenik" for her support for liberal presidential candidate Dennis Kucinich's proposal to create a federal Department of Peace. Hirono emphasized her experience and raised serious money, winning the general election 61%-39%.

In the House, Hirono has had a solidly liberal voting record and kept a relatively low profile. She worked with other delegation members to protect Hawaii's state-based health care system as part of the 2010 overhaul of the national health insurance system. Like her Democratic colleague Sen. Daniel Inouye, she has been an unabashed proponent of earmarking, and in fiscal 2010 ranked third among all House members, with more than $116 million in solo and combined earmarks, according to Taxpayers for Common Sense.

On the Education and Labor Committee, she pushed to add $1 billion over five years for preschool education. The House passed her bill to create a memorial on Kalaupapa Peninsula in Hawaii for the 8,000 people with leprosy forcibly exiled there from 1866 to 1969. She also introduced a bill in 2010 calling for improved transportation on federal lands, noting that if the national park system were counted as a state, it would rank 13th for road fatalities and injuries. In October 2008, she reversed her earlier opposition to the $700 billion bailout of the financial and insurance industries after getting a call from Democratic presidential nominee Barack Obama, who was raised in Hawaii. Hirono was re-elected easily in 2008 and 2010.

★ IDAHO ★

One of the American success stories of the last two decades has been the state of Idaho. Tucked off near the northwest edge of the country, far from any major metro area, it was ignored by coastal elites except for those who jetted in to Sun Valley. From 1990 to 2010 the state's population grew 57%, from 1 million to 1.57 million, thanks to technological progress and economic creativity. That was the fourth highest rate of growth of any state, ahead of all but Nevada, Arizona, and Utah. It has spawned some awesomely large businesses. Mining is less important here than potatoes, of which Idaho produces one-third of the nation's total. And it processes them: Back in 1953, J. R. Simplot perfected the process of freezing French fries; his company got a contract with a relatively new enterprise called McDonald's and grew to be one of the biggest potato processors in the world, selling 3 billion pounds a year. Idahoans complain about the Atkins diet, and they bellyached when then-Republican Gov. Dirk Kempthorne put the peregrine falcon and not the potato on the Idaho quarter. The potato business continues to thrive nonetheless. In the 1970s Simplot put up $1 million to finance Micron Technology, which spawned a booming high-tech sector including Hewlett-Packard's laser-jet printers. Micron grew to a peak workforce of 9,000 people in Idaho by 2008, although the recent recession reduced that number to 5,000 workers. A decade ago, Idaho produced more patents per worker than any other state and in 2009 was No. 3, far above average in per-capita research and development and IPOs (initial public offering).

Idaho is big: Montpelier, in the southeast, is closer to Farmington, N.M., than to Bonner Springs in the northern panhandle. And the wilderness is never far away. Towering over the state Capitol in Boise is the vast peak of Shafer Butte, and not far away are the impassable mountains of the Frank Church River of No Return Wilderness, the largest U.S. wilderness area outside Alaska, and the Salmon River, at 425 miles the longest undammed river in the lower 48 states. Idaho was the last North American area that European fur traders set eyes on. In the 1840s, New England Yankees led by ministers made their way west on the Oregon Trail through southern Idaho. Idaho's northern panhandle, an extension of Washington's Columbia River Valley, was first settled by miners seeking gold and silver, then by loggers seeking timber. Mormons moved north from Utah and settled in eastern Idaho. Federal water reclamation projects first authorized in 1894 attracted the most settlers; they transformed the barren Snake River Valley into some of the nation's best volcanic, soil-enriched farmland, which along with warm days and cool nights, proved ideal for the Burbank russet potato and, more recently, for a fledgling wine industry. Still fresh in family lore are the people who pioneered this state, built the first towns and farms, established the first churches and schools, and became its community leaders. Some major businesses got their start in Idaho—the Albertsons supermarket chain, the construction giant Morrison-Knudsen, and of course Simplot and Micron.

Idaho's economic vitality attracted many newcomers over the past 20 years. A few highly publicized liberal entertainment personalities and investment bankers have moved to Sun Valley or over the state line from Jackson Hole, Wyo., and some liberal professionals are appearing in Boise. But a much larger number of conservative engineers and entrepreneurs have come, from California and all over, for a fresh environment and a fresh start, clean air and sparse crowds, and few cumbersome or expensive regulations. As Republican Gov. James Risch said in 2006, "People are coming not because they want to change Idaho, but because they like what they see." As a result, Idaho has been transformed from a state of farms and small towns, where Boise, the pleasant state capital, was just the largest of them. Today, nearly 60% of its people live in just five counties in and around Boise, Idaho Falls, Coeur d'Alene, and Pocatello, and all but the last are growing rapidly. About 40% of Idahoans live in Treasure Valley around Boise, which accounted for most of the state's population growth in the last decade. Large influxes of people have come from California and from Mexico and other parts of Latin America. Idaho's Hispanic population is now 11% of the total; African-Americans (0.6%) are outnumbered by American Indians (1%) and Asians (1.2%). The state gives driver's license exams in English, Spanish, Serbo-Croatian, Russian, Arabic, and Vietnamese. Overall, the political trend has been toward the Republican Party. Many newcomers are from Orange County, Calif., looking for a good environment in which to raise children.

Even in the prosperous years before the 2008 recession, small counties that depended on mining and grazing were hurting. But people there see themselves as pioneering entrepreneurs who, rather than seek federal help, want to get a bloated, bossy federal government off their backs. The U.S. government owns 62% of Idaho's land, and most Idahoans strongly opposed federal policies that block road-building on one-third of national forestland, limit grazing on public lands, and to

Congressional district boundaries were first effective for 2002.

breach Snake River dams to protect salmon (in the process, depriving potato farmers of water). Such policies made a Republican state more Republican, and George W. Bush carried it by 67%-28% in 2000 and 68%-30% in 2004. John Kerry carried only one county, the richest by far in the state, where his wife, Teresa Heinz, owns a house near Sun Valley. In 2008, John McCain carried the state 62% to 36% over Barack Obama.

But as memories of the 1990s grow dim, Idaho may have inched a little toward the Democratic Party. Republican Kempthorne was re-elected governor by just 56%-42% in 2002. His successor as governor, Republican James Risch, won the nomination for U.S. senator in 2008 in the open seat that was, prudently, vacated by Larry Craig after the revelation of his arrest on suspicion of soliciting sex in a men's room in the Minneapolis-St. Paul airport. Risch beat former Democratic Rep. Larry LaRocco, 58%-34%. Freshman Republican Rep. Bill Sali, a narrow winner in 2006, managed to lose in 2008 to Walt Minnick in 2008, the first Democrat Idahoans have elected to Congress since 1992. But the recession and the collapse of housing prices—down as much as 50% in Ada and Canyon Counties west of Boise—did not push Idaho voters to Democrats. The Idaho economy continued to flounder in late 2010, with unemployment rising toward the national average and nearly 40% of mortgage-holders under water. The February 2009 federal economic stimulus sent $468 million to the Idaho National Laboratory, one of the state's largest employers, for nuclear waste cleanup. But Republicans nevertheless swept the state in November. Sen. Mike Crapo won 71%-25%, carrying every county, and Butch Otter was re-elected governor 59%-33%, carrying all but three counties. Republicans increased their margin in the state House.

Population		Household Income		Work	
Pop. 2010:	1,567,582	Under $15k:	12.2%	Private:	76.1%
State rank:	39th	$15k to $50k:	41.6%	Government:	15.8%
Change since 2000:	Up 21.1%	$50k to $100k:	32.7%	Self-employed:	7.9%
Urban:	64.9%	$100k to $200k:	11.3%	Unemployment (3-yr. average):	4.5%
Rural:	35.1%	Over $200k:	2.2%	Poverty:	13.3%
Native of state:	46.2%	Median income:	$46,327	Blue collar:	23.5%
Not a citizen:	4.0%			White collar:	57.2%
Area size:	83,569 sq. mi.	**Home Value**		Khaki collar:	0.3%
		Under $100k:	17.1%	Other:	19.0%
Most populous cities		$100k to $300k:	62.6%		
Boise City	205,671	$300k to $500k:	13.8%	**Age**	
Nampa	81,557	$500k to $1 mil:	5.0%	Median age:	34.1 yrs.
Meridian	75,092	Over $1 million:	1.6%	More than 65 yrs:	11.9%
Idaho Falls	56,813	Median:	$177,400	Less than 18 yrs:	27.2%

Race/Ethnicity				Military Veterans		Registered Voters in 2010	
White:	84.0%	*Language*		% of Pop:	11.7%	No Party registration	
Black:	0.6%	English:	90.0%			Voter turnout:	459,079
Hispanic:	11.2%	Spanish:	7.4%	*Veterans by Period*		Turnout as % of	
Asian:	1.2%	Asian:	0.8%	WWII and before:	9.7%	voting age:	40.3%
Native Am.:	1.1%	Other European:	1.5%	Korea:	10.3%		
Hawaiian:	0.1%			Vietnam:	34.0%	**Legislature**	
Two+ races:	1.7%	**Education**		Gulf (pre-2001):	12.6%	Senate:	7 D 28 R
		H.S. grad:	88.1%	Gulf (post-2001):	9.5%	House:	13 D 57 R
Ancestry		College grad:	24.0%	Peace time:	23.9%		
German	15.8%	Grad degree:	7.5%				
English	13.4%						
Irish	8.4%						

Presidential politics Idaho is one of the most Republican states in presidential politics. No Democratic nominee has come close to carrying it since 1964, and Bill Clinton came within 1% of finishing third behind Ross Perot and George H.W. Bush in 1992. Despite his victories in both caucuses and primary here, Barack Obama was not in contention in Idaho and carried just three counties, two of them populated by wealthy expatriates from New York and California and one of them the home of the University of Idaho. John McCain carried the state 62%-36%.

Idaho has held its presidential primary in late May, long after the action in most recent presidential contests, and McCain's victory over Texas Rep. Ron Paul here was little noticed. But Democrats decided to select their delegates in caucuses, with the first round held on Super Tuesday, Feb. 5. Few of the presidential campaigns paid much heed, but Obama's team did, setting up a state headquarters and organizing supporters around the state. Some 20,200 Idahoans participated, and Obama led Hillary Rodham Clinton 80%-17%. This was a far bigger victory than the 56%-38% Obama win in the May 27 primary, in which 42,800 Idahoans voted. Obama's success in this and other caucus states, mostly in the Midwest and West, provided his margin of victory over Clinton, who won more votes and more delegates than her rival in Democratic primaries.

2008 Presidential Vote		
John McCain (R)	403,012	(62%)
Barack Obama (D)	236,440	(36%)
2008 Presidential Primary		
John McCain (R)	87,460	(70%)
Ron Paul (R)	29,785	(24%)
2004 Presidential Vote		
George W. Bush (R)	409,235	(68%)
John Kerry (D)	181,098	(30%)

Congressional districting Idaho has two congressional districts, which split Boise between them. After the 2000 census, a bipartisan commission drew new boundaries, moving the dividing line in Boise about a mile to the west, along Cole Road, a minor and uncontroversial change. If Idaho ever gets a third district, redistricting should be a cinch. Most of the Boise area would become one district, and eastern Idaho and northern Idaho would get one each. But Idaho came in shy of winning a third district in the reapportionment following the 2010 census, and chances are that the boundary will be shifted a few miles again.

112th Congress Lineup
2 R
111th Congress Lineup
1 R   1 D

Governor

C.L. 'Butch' Otter (R)

Elected 2006, term expires Jan. 2015, 2nd term; b. May 3, 1942, Caldwell; home, Star; Col. of ID, B.A. 1967; Catholic; married (Lori Easley); 4 children.

Military Career: ID Natl. Guard, 1967-73.

Elected Office: ID House of Reps., 1972-76; ID lt. gov., 1986-2000; U.S. House of Reps., 2000-06.

Professional Career: Rancher; Dir., Food Products Div., Pres., Simplot Livestock, Pres., Simplot Intl., 1963-1993.

Office: P.O. Box 83720, Boise, 83720, 208-334-2100; Fax: 208-334-3454; Web site: http://gov.idaho.gov.

Election Results

2010 general	C.L. 'Butch' Otter (R)	267,483	(59%)
	Keith Allred (D)	148,680	(33%)
	Jana Kemp (I)	26,655	(6%)
2010 primary	C.L. 'Butch' Otter (R)	89,117	(55%)
	Rex Rammell (R)	42,436	(26%)
	Sharon Ullman (R)	13,749	(8%)
	Ron Peterson (R)	8,402	(5%)

Prior Winning Percentages: 2006 (53%); House: 2004 (70%); 2002 (59%); 2000 (65%)

Clement Leroy "Butch" Otter is the Republican governor of Idaho. He was elected in 2006 and re-elected in 2010. Otter was the sixth of nine children and the first in his family to get a college degree. His father was a journeyman electrician and carpenter and a lifelong Democrat. After high school, Otter entered an abbey to pursue the priesthood but quickly decided that was not his calling. In 1967, at the age of 25, he graduated from the College of Idaho, now known as Albertson College of Idaho. He went to work for his father-in-law, billionaire J.R. Simplot, at the J.R. Simplot Company, one of the largest potato processors in the world and owner of the largest feedlot in the nation. In 1972, Otter won the first of two terms in the state House. He ran for governor in 1978, finishing third in the Republican primary, and in 1986, he was elected lieutenant governor. His career advancement was temporarily halted by a drunk-driving arrest. Otter unsuccessfully tried to talk the police officer out of charging him by explaining that he had not been drinking, but chewing tobacco soaked in Jack Daniels whiskey. The officer didn't buy it. Otter was convicted in 1993 of drunk driving, dashing his hopes of running for governor the following year. Still, he went on to be re-elected lieutenant governor and held the post longer than anyone in Idaho history. He served under three governors before he was elected to Congress in 2000.

As part of his libertarian political philosophy, Otter is a big supporter of gun ownership and property rights. But he is not the social conservative that other Idaho Republicans have been. (In 1992, he won the "Mr. Tight Jeans" contest at the Rockin' Rodeo bar in Boise.) During his tenure in the state Legislature, Otter voted against an anti-pornography bill by responding "Hell no!" during the roll call. He also questioned the government's right to restrict marijuana use. In Congress, where he served three terms, he sought to check the power of the federal government. Having become a ranch owner after his 1993 divorce, he was acquainted with the government's reach. The Environmental Protection Agency had charged him three times with violating the Clean Water Act. In 2001, after fighting the agency for two years, he paid a fine of $50,000 for dredging and filling wetlands without a permit. In Congress, Otter was one of three House Republicans to vote against the USA PATRIOT Act, a tough anti-terrorism enforcement law, because of potential intrusions on privacy and civil liberties. In 2004, he sponsored an amendment with independent Bernie Sanders of Vermont to prevent authorities from using the act to demand information on book buyers or library users. He lost on a tie vote after Republican leaders held the roll call open for 23 extra minutes to turn the outcome their way.

In December 2004, Otter announced his intention to run for governor, giving him an organizational and fundraising head start over then-Lt. Gov. Jim Risch, a Republican who was also considering running. In November 2005, Risch decided to run for re-election as lieutenant governor (later briefly becoming governor when Republican Gov. Dirk Kempthorne left office in 2006 to serve as President Bush's Interior secretary). Without competition from Risch, Otter easily outdistanced three opponents in the May 2006 primary, winning with 70%.

He then faced Democrat Jerry Brady, a former publisher of the Idaho Falls *Post Register* making his second consecutive bid for governor. In heavily Republican Idaho, which hadn't elected a Democratic governor since 1990, Otter began as the front-runner. But Brady, who highlighted environmental issues and compared himself to former Democratic Gov. Cecil Andrus, gained momentum by criticizing Otter's co-sponsorship of a bill that would have sold millions of acres of federal land in Idaho and the western United States to raise money for Hurricane Katrina relief. Otter eventually rescinded his support for the bill. Brady also attacked Otter for accepting $6,000 from a company attempting to build a coal-fired power plant in Idaho. Otter countered by highlighting controversial editorials written by Brady's newspaper, the second largest in Idaho, including one that called for breaching Snake River dams to protect endangered salmon.

Otter ran a Rose Garden campaign, avoiding the traditional Idaho public-television debate and initially refusing to take a position on Proposition 2, a controversial property-rights initiative that required state and local governments to compensate property owners when the value of their land was reduced by land-use regulations. Otter later came out against the ballot measure. In August, he found time to get married to a former Miss Idaho, whom he had first met at a Fourth of July parade in 1991. Brady proved to be a more energetic candidate and remained competitive. Polls taken a week before the election showed him within striking distance. Despite national discontent with the Republican Party and a lackluster campaign, Otter won, 53%-44%. In heavily Mormon eastern Idaho, where Otter's libertarian stands and lifestyle had hurt him in prior statewide elections, he lost just two counties: Bannock, home to Pocatello and Idaho State University, and Teton County, which shares a border with Wyoming's wealthy Teton County, where Jackson Hole and its ski resort are located.

Soon after taking office, Otter caused a minor controversy by halting construction on a $130 million statehouse expansion that the Republican-controlled legislature had approved the previous year. He objected to the project's cost and the fact that it represented an expansion of government. Negotiations with the legislature produced a compromise that reduced the size of the new addition by half and cut out construction of new offices for legislators, though it was unclear if the changes would lessen the project's total cost.

Otter supported removing gray wolves from the federal government's Endangered Species List and allowing public hunting of the animals in Idaho. In January 2007, he got national media attention when he stood on the Idaho statehouse steps and proclaimed, "I'm prepared to bid for that first ticket to shoot a wolf." He later softened his stance by backing a plan to let the Idaho Department of Fish and Game manage the state's wolf population.

Otter's ability to attract media attention did not translate into legislative success. In 2007, he proposed increasing the state's grocery tax credit for the lowest-income Idahoans to $90 a year. Idaho gives people a credit on their taxes as reimbursement for sales taxes they've paid on their groceries. The legislature agreed to increase the credit to $40 for all Idahoans and to $60 for senior citizens; Otter vetoed the bill because it didn't target the lowest-income groups. The legislature did pass a highway bill that approved $250 million in borrowing power—Otter originally wanted $264 million—and gave the Idaho Transportation Board the authority to earmark money for road projects, a practice Otter hoped would take politics out of the earmarking process.

In 2008, Otter also had difficulty getting many of his proposals through the Legislature, even though he had Republican majorities in both chambers. He proposed an 11% increase in the state's budget, a 5% pay raise for state employees, and an increase in vehicle registration fees to fund road repairs, all of which the legislature either modified or rejected outright. As the session came to a close, he criticized legislators publicly for rejecting his proposals, and they in turn accused him of refusing to compromise. Yet Otter did sign grocery tax legislation that was similar to the bill he'd vetoed the year before.

Otter's priority for the 2009 session was providing money for road and bridge construction and maintenance. Despite reservations about increased government spending, he decided to accept $1.2 billion in economic stimulus money from the federal government. Over the course of what became the second-longest legislative session in state history, he and Republican legislators hammered out a deal. Otter had sought a 6-cent increase in Idaho's gasoline tax, but lawmakers adamantly ruled it out. The governor had sought $174.5 million, but eventually had to settle for $54 million. The 2010 session was shorter and less messy, but still offered controversy. With Republicans disgusted with President Obama's agenda, GOP lawmakers offered a series of initiatives aimed at protecting state sovereignty. As the health care overhaul neared passage in the U.S. Congress, Otter signed into law a bill blocking any individual mandate to secure health insurance. *Idaho Statesman* columnist Dan Popkey lamented Otter's failure to address some of the state's critical problems and said the governor was "showing signs of losing touch."

In 2010, Otter drew a challenge to his re-election from Keith Allred, a professional mediator and founder of a bipartisan citizens' group called The Common Interest. During the legislative session, Allred frequently showed up at the Capitol to criticize Otter's "irrational pessimism" on low-balling the budget, something he said hurt public schools. He had a well-earned reputation for being nonpartisan, and his decision to run as a Democrat surprised observers, although he said he considered himself an independent. He proposed restoring education funding, eliminating tax exemptions to reduce the overall tax rate and starting a scholarship program for at-risk youths. He also said Idaho should adopt its own health care law rather than accept the federal one.

Allread outraised Otter during the early months of 2010, and steadily chipped away at the governor's lead. Otter touted his ability to balance the budget without raising taxes and said his real-world experience in running a government outshone his opponent's ideas. "You can't operate a state on theory, folks. You have to operate a state with real decisions," he said during one debate. In the end, Idaho's staunch Republicanism gave him the edge, and he won re-election with 59% to Allred's 33%. Three minor-party candidates—including one who legally changed his name to "Pro-Life"—split the remainder of the vote.

Senior Senator

Mike Crapo (R)

Elected 1998, term expires 2016, 3rd term; b. May 20, 1951, Idaho Falls; home, Idaho Falls; Brigham Young U., B.A. 1973, Harvard U., J.D. 1977; Mormon; married (Susan); 5 children.

Elected Office: ID Senate, 1984–92, Senate ldr., 1988-92; U.S. House of Reps., 1992-98.

Professional Career: Practicing atty., 1977–92.

DC Office: 239 DSOB, 20510, 202-224-6142; Fax: 202-228-1375; Web site: crapo.senate.gov.

State Offices: Boise, 208-334-1776; Caldwell, 208-455-0360; Coeur D'Alene, 208-664-5490; Idaho Falls, 208-522-9779; Lewiston, 208-743-1492; Pocatello, 208-236-6775; Twin Falls, 208-734-2515.

Committees: *Banking, Housing & Urban Affairs:* Financial Institutions & Consumer Protection; Housing, Transportation & Community Development; Securities, Insurance & Investment (RMM). *Budget. Environment & Public Works:* Superfund, Toxics & Environmental Health (RMM); Transportation & Infrastructure; Water & Wildlife. *Finance:* Fiscal Responsibility & Economic Growth (RMM); International Trade, Customs & Global Competitiveness; Taxation & IRS Oversight. *Indian Affairs.*

Group Ratings

	ACLU	ACU	ADA	CFG	AFS	FRC	LCV	ITIC	NTU	COC
2010	13	100	0	87	1	95	14	67	99	100
2009	–	92	10	83	0	–	18	–	86	71

National Journal Ratings

	2010 LIB	—	2010 CONS		2009 LIB	—	2009 CONS
Economic	0%	—	87%		22%	—	76%
Social	0%	—	79%		10%	—	87%
Foreign	0%	—	72%		0%	—	84%
Composite	10%	—	90%		14%	—	86%

Key Votes of the 111th Congress

1. Overturn Ledbetter	N	5. Pass health care bill	N	9. Ratify New START	N
2. Pass $787 billion stimulus	N	6. Regulate financial firms	N	10. Confirm Elena Kagan	N
3. Repeal DC gun laws	Y	7. Pass tax cuts for some	N	11. Stop EPA climate regs	Y
4. Confirm Sonia Sotomayor	N	8. Legalize immigrants' kids	N	12. Repeal don't ask, tell	N

Election Results

2010 general	Mike Crapo (R)	319,953	(71%)	($5,098,869)
	P. Tom Sullivan (D)	112,057	(25%)	($93,490)
	Randy Bergquist (C)	17,429	(4%)	
2010 primary	Mike Crapo (R)	127,332	(79%)	
	Claude Davis (R)	33,150	(21%)	

Prior Winning Percentages: 2004 (99%); 1998 (70%); House: 1996 (69%); 1994 (75%); 1992 (61%)

Mike Crapo is a Republican first elected to the House in 1992 and to the Senate in 1998. He grew up in Idaho Falls. His father ran the local post office, and his mother stayed home to care for their six children. The couple also farmed on 200 acres, growing potatoes and grain. Crapo (*CRAY-po*) graduated from Brigham Young University and Harvard Law School. A devout Mormon, he was named a bishop in the church at age 31. A former congressional intern, he was elected to the state Senate at 33 in 1984, two years after leukemia took his older brother Terry's life. Terry Crapo had been state House majority leader and a rising star in state politics. The two brothers were close, and Mike Crapo decided to follow his brother's path to the legislature. He became state Senate leader in 1988. Four years later, he ran for Congress, campaigning against tax increases and in favor of spending cuts, a balanced-budget amendment, and the line-item veto. He won the primary 68%-32%. "Cowboy Democrat" J.D. Williams, the state controller, ran on a "Put America First" platform on industrial policy and trade. Crapo won 61%-35%.

With a self-professed "passion for reform," Crapo became a Republican freshman class leader and championed institutional reforms, advocating more power for rank-and-file members to bring bills to the floor and calling for more open voting. Like many Republicans then, Crapo favored hard-and-fast rules in the budget process to force tough decisions: He favored a balanced budget and across-the-board discretionary spending cuts, excluding Social Security. He sponsored the deficit-reduction bill that passed the House in 1995. His overall voting record in the House was very conservative, with some exceptions on economics. He opposed the North American Free Trade Agreement in 1993 but supported normalizing trade relations with China in 2000. He criticized some trade agreements for accepting limits on U.S. agricultural exports as leverage for opening up access for other products.

In 1997, Crapo, who prides himself on returning to Idaho Falls to be with his family every weekend, faced a career choice. Republican Gov. Phil Batt announced his retirement, and GOP Sen. Dirk Kempthorne said he would run for governor. Within days, Crapo announced he would run for the Senate seat the following year, and he was unopposed in the Republican primary. His opponent was Bill Mauk, a former Democratic state chairman and Boise trial lawyer. Idaho, one-quarter Mormon, had never elected a Mormon to the Senate, but this time it did. Crapo led in polls by a wide margin and won 70%-28%, carrying every county.

In his first years in the Senate, Crapo was active in the effort to fix the financially troubled Superfund program and other environment-related issues. He sponsored the Senate version of the Bush-era Healthy Forests Restoration Act, aimed at cutting dense forest land after widespread fires in 2002. He has worked over the years on altering the Endangered Species Act, and he is among the Republicans calling for greater incentives for nuclear power. In 2010, President Obama signed into law his bill regulating formaldehyde in wood products.

Despite a uniformly conservative voting record, Crapo has developed a reputation for diligence in trying to forge consensus legislation. Oregon Democrat Ron Wyden said, "He is not a showboat. He is somebody who, day in and day out, is always a constructive force for sensible public policy." Senate Democratic leader Harry Reid in 2005 suggested Crapo as one of three GOP senators who would make "outstanding" Supreme Court justices. At the same time, his stock has risen among Republican leaders. In 2009, he was tapped as a deputy whip and made chairman of the GOP caucus panel charged with committee assignments. He also was named in 2010 to the bipartisan debt commission. He joined fellow commission members and GOP senators Tom Coburn of Oklahoma and Judd Gregg of New Hampshire along with eight others in backing its recommendations, which fell short of the 14 supporters needed for Senate floor consideration.

From his seat on the powerful Finance Committee, which he secured in 2005, Crapo has worked quietly and productively. He secured a permanent tax break for state colleges by attaching it to a pension bill, while separately heading off a proposed cut in food stamps. Crapo also urged the Internal Revenue Service to implement a tax break that would help the country's short-line railroads, one of the largest of which is used by Idaho farmers to move crops and equipment. Crapo and Montana Democrat Max Baucus, the Finance Committee chairman, co-sponsored bills to relax restrictions on agricultural sales to Cuba. During the 2009 health care debate, Crapo sought to amend the bill in committee to seek to prevent individuals making $200,000 annually and families earning $250,000 a year or less from being taxed to pay for the policy changes in the bill; it was defeated after Baucus called it a "killer amendment" that would deprive the legislation of needed revenue. In 2007, Crapo was named to the Senate Republican task force on earmarks, where he supported increased transparency but not a moratorium on spending earmarks.

From his seat on the Banking Committee, Crapo won passage in 2006 of a bill that would ease outdated regulation of the banking industry. Four years later, he worked on the Dodd-Frank financial industry overhaul legislation but said he was disappointed with the result, citing its creation of a new consumer protection bureau and its requirement for commercial banks to spin off most of their derivatives trading operations. He also expressed frustration that the bill would not revamp troubled mortgage giants Fannie Mae and Freddie Mac.

For several years, Crapo worked to forge a consensus on the Owyhee Canyonlands wilderness proposal with local officials, landowners, cattlemen, environmental groups, and the Shoshone-Paiute tribe. The agreement that was ultimately reached opened 199,000 acres formerly off limits to fence-building and pipelines; set aside 517,000 acres as wilderness; and protected 316 miles of rivers. The habitat of the California bighorn sheep and sage grouse were protected. His measure was included in the lands bill enacted in early 2009.

Though he had expressed interest in a federal District Court judgeship, Crapo sought re-election in 2004. He had no Democratic opponent and won with 99% of the vote. In 2010, he won handily against Democratic financial consultant Tom Sullivan, 71%-25%.

Junior Senator

James Risch (R)

Elected 2008, term expires 2014, 1st term; b. May 2, 1943, Milwaukee, WI; home, Boise; U. of ID, B.S. 1965, J.D., 1968.; Catholic; married (Vicki); 3 children.

Elected Office: Ada Co. prosecuting atty., 1970-74; ID Senate, 1974-89, 1995-2003; ID lt. gov., 2003-2006, 2007-09; ID gov., 2006.

Professional Career: Partner, Risch, Goss, Insinger, 1975-08; Rancher.

DC Office: 483 RSOB, 20510, 202-224-2752; Fax: 202-224-2573; Web site: risch.senate.gov.

State Offices: Boise, 208-342-7986; Coeur d'Alene, 208-667-6130; Idaho Falls, 208-523-5541; Lewiston, 208-743-0792; Pocatello, 208-236-6817; Twin Falls, 208-734-6780.

Committees: *Energy & Natural Resources:* Energy (RMM); Public Lands & Forests; Water & Power. *Ethics (Select). Foreign Relations:* East Asian & Pacific Affairs; European Affairs; International Development & Foreign Assistance, Economic Affairs & International Environmental Protection; Near Eastern & South & Central Asian Affairs (RMM). *Intelligence (Select). Small Business & Entrepreneurship.*

Group Ratings

	ACLU	ACU	ADA	CFG	AFS	FRC	LCV	ITIC	NTU	COC
2010	7	100	0	92	0	100	14	67	99	100
2009	–	96	10	94	0	–	18	–	87	71

National Journal Ratings

	2010 LIB	—	2010 CONS	2009 LIB	—	2009 CONS
Economic	0%	—	87%	14%	—	81%
Social	0%	—	79%	0%	—	94%
Foreign	0%	—	72%	0%	—	84%
Composite	10%	—	90%	9%	—	91%

Key Votes of the 111th Congress

1. Overturn Ledbetter	N	5. Pass health care bill	N	9. Ratify New START	N
2. Pass $787 billion stimulus	N	6. Regulate financial firms	N	10. Confirm Elena Kagan	N
3. Repeal DC gun laws	Y	7. Pass tax cuts for some	N	11. Stop EPA climate regs	Y
4. Confirm Sonia Sotomayor	N	8. Legalize immigrants' kids	N	12. Repeal don't ask, tell	N

Election Results

2008 general	James Risch (R)	371,744	(58%)	($3,114,815)
	Larry LaRocco (D)	219,903	(34%)	($1,424,818)
	Rex Rammell (I)	34,510	(5%)	
2008 primary	James Risch (R)	80,743	(65%)	
	Scott Syme (R)	16,660	(13%)	
	Richard Phenneger (R)	6,532	(5%)	

James Risch, who has been Idaho's lieutenant governor and governor, was elected to the U.S. Senate in 2008. During his first year in the Senate, he kept at the entrance to his Washington office a large plaque identifying him not as a senator but as governor, and his wife as first lady. He succeeded Republican Sen. Larry Craig, who declined to seek re-election after he was arrested the previous year in a solicitation-for-sex sting. Risch (*RISH, like wish*) grew up in Wisconsin and moved to the West to study forestry. He earned a law degree at the University of Idaho. In 1970, at age 27, Risch was elected Ada County prosecutor—a high-profile position in the state's capital and largest city, Boise. He went after the illicit drug trade so aggressively that his enemies tried to plant a bomb in his car. After that incident, Risch and his wife and political confidant, Vicki, put a piece of tape on the hood of their car every night so they could detect any tampering. In 1974, Risch was elected to the state Senate, where he served longer than anyone else in Idaho history. He earned a reputation as an ambitious and determined legislator. He always carried an index card in his back pocket, one side listing bills that he wanted to pass and the other listing bills he was determined to kill. Immediately gunning for a leadership position, he became majority leader after the 1976 election, defeating a young colleague named Larry Craig for the position. Although popular with some of his colleagues, Risch was known as a bully to a number of the younger senators whom he pressured to vote his way.

He was brought back down to earth by a Democratic challenger who beat him in the 1988 election. He ran again in 1990, but this time he was defeated in the GOP primary. Five years later, he was appointed to fill a state Senate vacancy. Less confrontational this time around, Risch moved back into the ranks of leadership as assistant Republican floor leader. He became one of the driving forces in the Idaho Republican Party even as the state elected a string of Democratic governors. In 2002, Risch ran for lieutenant governor and won by a comfortable margin. He served in the shadow of Republican Gov. Dirk Kempthorne for three years and finally assumed the top job when Kempthorne became President George W. Bush's Interior secretary.

Risch had just seven months in what he considered his dream job, and he was determined to make the most of it. Within two weeks of taking office, Gov. Risch ordered a reorganization of Idaho's Health and Welfare Department. He created the position of state drug czar to counter the growth in the illicit methamphetamine market in the state. Displeased that the legislature failed to provide property tax relief in its regular session, he called the first special session in 14 years. One day in August, the heavily Republican legislature obediently passed bills cutting local property taxes by $260 million, raising the sales tax from 5% to 6% (which generated $219 million), and cutting state spending by $50 million. The voters approved the tax changes 72%-28%. After wide consultation, he prepared a roadless-areas plan for 9 million acres of national forest that was approved by U.S. Agriculture Secretary Mike Johanns and was generally accepted by environmental groups. Risch moved to protect the Boulder-White Clouds and Owyhee Canyonlands wilderness areas. To prevent mercury contamination, he effectively barred construction of pulverized coal plants in the state.

When November rolled around, Risch beat former Democratic Rep. Larry LaRocco for lieutenant governor 58%-39%. But another goal beckoned: the U.S. Senate seat first won by his old rival Craig in 1990. Craig was arrested in a Minneapolis airport men's room in 2007 for soliciting sex from an undercover police officer and pleaded guilty to disorderly conduct. Craig resisted immense pressure from his Senate colleagues to resign immediately, but then decided against seeking re-election in 2008. Risch announced his intention to run.

He had little competition for the Republican nomination. His Democratic opponent was, once again, LaRocco, who had been elected to the House in 1990 and 1992, but was defeated in the Republican sweep of 1994. Another opponent was Democrat Rex Rammell, a rancher who had lost 160 of his elk herd after they escaped from his land and were ordered shot by then-Gov. Risch. Rammell ran as an independent. Risch raised more than twice as much money as LaRocco, and the national Democratic Party never targeted the race. He won the election 58%-34%, with 5% for Rammell.

Risch entered the Senate at age 65, after an extensive political career as well as years in business as owner of a trailer company and property management firm, which made him one of the Senate's wealthiest members. After spending decades in control in Republican-dominated Idaho, he joined a relatively powerless minority in the Senate. He immediately became an aggressive conservative ally of his more mild-mannered Idaho Senate colleague Mike Crapo. During the 2009 debate over President Obama's economic stimulus bill, Risch accused Democratic House Speaker Nancy Pelosi of taking $50 million from the bill to save a species of mouse found only in her district, a claim that turned out to be wrong. He opposed most of Obama's spending initiatives, including a Senate-passed, $35 billion jobs bill in February 2010 that he complained cost too much. "I ran for this office as a deficit hawk, and now that I am here I have moved even further in that direction," he told *The Idaho Statesman*. On the Energy and Natural Resources Committee, he worked to add provisions increasing the roles for biomass and geothermal energy in the 2009 energy bill. He wound up voting against the final bill because, he said, it didn't go far enough to reduce U.S. dependence on foreign oil and did too little to encourage expansion of nuclear power.

Risch also decided to try his hand at national security and foreign policy matters, joining the Foreign Relations and Select Intelligence committees. He complained to Defense Secretary Robert Gates in December 2009 about the lack of "a sense of urgency" in Afghanistan. When the Foreign Relations panel sought to take up the New START arms control treaty with Russia in September 2010, Risch tried to stop the vote, citing new intelligence that he said he couldn't reveal in open session that led him to question Russia's intentions. And when the full Senate took up the pact in December 2010, he again unsuccessfully demanded a delay, noting that Russian troops reportedly had stolen five U.S. Humvees used in military exercises. "They are serial cheaters," he said.

FIRST DISTRICT

Raul Labrador (R)

Elected 2010, 1st term; b. Dec. 8, 1967, Carolina, PR; home, Eagle; Brigham Young U., B.A. 1992; U. of WA, J.D. 1995.; Mormon; Married (Rebecca); 5 children.

Elected Office: ID House, 2006-10.

Professional Career: Law clerk, U.S. Atty., WA St., 1994; practicing atty., 1994-96; law clerk, U.S. District Court, District of ID, 1996-98; practicing atty., 1998-2010.

DC Office: 1523 LHOB, 20515, 202-225-6611; Fax: 202-225-3029.

State Offices: Caldwell, 208-454-5518; Coeur d'Alene, 208-667-0127; Lewiston, 208-743-1388; Meridian, 208-888-3188.

Committees: *Natural Resources:* Indian & Alaska Native Affairs; National Parks, Forests & Public Lands; Water & Power. *Oversight & Government Reform:* National Security, Homeland Defense & Foreign Operations (VChmn); Regulatory Affairs, Stimulus Oversight & Government Spending; Technology, Information Policy, Intergovernmental Relations & Procurement Reform.

Election Results

2010 general	Raul Labrador (R)	126,231	(51%)	($811,288)
	Walt Minnick (D)	102,135	(41%)	($2,659,979)
	Dave Olson (I)	14,365	(6%)	
2010 primary	Raul Labrador (R)	38,711	(48%)	
	Vaughn Ward (R)	31,582	(39%)	
	Michael Chadwick (R)	5,356	(7%)	

Population		Race/Ethnicity		Work	
Pop. 2010:	841,930	White:	85.3%	Private:	76.1%
Change since 2000:	Up 29.8%	Black:	0.5%	Government:	15.4%
Urban:	65.8%	Hispanic:	9.9%	Self-employed:	8.3%
Rural:	34.2%	Asian:	1.1%	Blue collar:	23.4%
Area size:	39,971 sq. mi.	Native Am.:	1.1%	White collar:	58.1%
		Hawaiian:	0.1%	Khaki collar:	0.2%
Age		Two+ races:	1.9%	Other:	18.3%
Median age:	35.7 yrs.				
More than 65 yrs:	12.4%	*Ancestry*		Median income:	$47,520
Less than 18 yrs:	27.0%	German	17.3%	Median Home Value:	$192,800
		English	11.2%		
Education		Irish	9.4%	**Military Veterans**	
H.S. grad:	88.3%			% of Pop:	12.6%
College grad:	22.9%				
Grad degree:	6.7%				

West Idaho; Part Boise, Nampa

The 1st District of Idaho stretches from the Nevada border to Canada and includes some of usually Republican Boise and all of the panhandle, which is historically Democratic but more recently has been leaning Republican. It encompasses two of Idaho's big growth areas, the western suburbs of Boise and the Coeur d'Alene area in Kootenai County. High-tech businesses and tourism have fueled the economy. Boise is home to Micron Technology, which has led the nation

2008 Presidential Vote
John McCain (R) 220,787   (62%)
Barack Obama (D) 128,134   (36%)

2004 Presidential Vote
George Bush (R) 215,069   (69%)
John Kerry (D) 94,915   (30%)

Cook Partisan Voting Index: R+18

in patents. In 2007, *Forbes* named Boise the third-best city in the country for business, citing the region's low unemployment rate. In Nampa—whose population nearly doubled in the 1990s, allowing it to replace Pocatello as Idaho's second-largest city—commercial developers have taken over land that not long ago grew wheat and alfalfa. Subdivisions are being constructed in nearby Meridian, the fastest-growing city in Idaho, with over 27,000 new residents since 2000. Valley County, just north of Boise, has seen a 14% spike in population in that period. The once sleepy Harrison has gotten a pump of adrenaline with an invasion of bicycle enthusiasts seeking to experience a 72-mile trail that was created by converting old Union Pacific railroad lines. Bike shop owner John Kolbe told the *Lewiston Morning Tribune* in 2009, "The whole place feels like a support system for bikers."

The growth is turning these once-rural areas into urban centers, but that has reinforced, rather than altered, the political landscape. Newcomers routinely say they moved to conservative Idaho to escape from city life. Some old-timers worry that their communities may become new versions of San Jose or Orange County. Politically, the 1st District is overwhelmingly Republican. Kootenai County, once a Democratic stronghold, is now as likely to cast as many Republican votes as conservative Canyon County. Northern mining counties were once the district's Democratic base; now it is the university town of Moscow in Latah County, one of only two in Idaho to vote against a 2006 constitutional amendment outlawing same-sex marriage. Every county in the district voted for George W. Bush in 2000 and 2004. In 2008, Latah County went for Democrat Barack Obama, but the district as a whole voted for Republican John McCain, giving him 62%.

Raul Labrador (R)

The new congressman from Idaho's 1st District is Republican Raul Labrador, who unseated Democratic Rep. Walt Minnick in the GOP tidal wave of 2010. Labrador is the first Hispanic elected to Congress from Idaho.

He was born in Puerto Rico and raised by his mother, Ana Pastor, who was unmarried. His father, who was married and had five other children, saw Raul once a year on his birthday, according to a story in *The Idaho Statesman*. Pastor, a sales representative for the Mars candy company in Puerto Rico, moved to Las Vegas for a new start when Raul was a young teenager, taking a job as a change girl in a casino. She joined the city's Mormon church, which provided help during lean times. A church official became a surrogate father for Labrador, helping pay his way to Brigham Young University, where he earned a bachelor's degree in Spanish and philosophy. He went on to get a law degree from the University of Washington. With the exception of a couple of stints as a law clerk for government offices, Labrador spent his career in private practice. Before he came to Washington, he was the managing partner of Labrador Law Offices in Nampa, Idaho, which specializes in immigration law.

Labrador stepped into the political arena in 2006 when he won a seat in the state House. He quickly made a name for himself as a steadfast conservative, standing up to GOP Gov. Butch Otter on his plan to raise fuel taxes to pay for new roads. Labrador also had a hand in legislation to restore gun rights to those deemed mentally defective by the courts and to exempt Idaho from the federal health care law.

He got into the contest for the Republican nomination to challenge Minnick after Ken Roberts, the Republican caucus chairman in the Idaho House, withdrew for health reasons. He saw Minnick as vulnerable as a Democrat in Idaho even though Minnick had voted against major elements of President Obama's agenda, including the economic stimulus, the overhaul of health care, and the cap-and-trade energy bill.

In the primary, Labrador lagged behind Marine Maj. Vaughn Ward, a decorated Iraq war veteran, who had a 3-to-1 fundraising advantage and the backing of the state and national party establishment. Former Alaska Gov. Sarah Palin also came to Boise to boost Ward, who had been the Nevada director for John McCain and Palin in the 2008 presidential contest. But Ward made a series of gaffes that left him vulnerable, including violating Pentagon rules prohibiting the use of military uniforms in campaign ads, and failing to disclose his wife's assets. She worked for mortgage giant Fannie Mae, which received $76 billion in federal rescue funds. Labrador beat Ward in the May primary, 47.6% to 39%.

In his fall campaign against the Democratic incumbent, Labrador made an issue of Minnick's vote to elect California liberal Nancy Pelosi as speaker of the House in 2009. He called for large cuts in federal spending and repeal of the Democratic health care law. Minnick, with $2.5 million in the bank and a 5-to-1 money edge, let loose a barrage of attacks, including one that showed a former U.S. marshal criticizing Labrador for running a website that "offers advice to illegal immigrants seeking amnesty." Labrador responded that he in fact advises illegal immigrants to return to their home countries and reapply for admission to the United States through proper channels. None of the attacks were enough to save Minnick, who had been elected just two years earlier with 51% of the vote. Labrador defeated Minnick, 51% to 41%.

SECOND DISTRICT

Mike Simpson (R)

Elected 1998, 7th term; b. Sept. 8, 1950, Burley; home, Blackfoot; UT St. U., 1968-72; Washington U., D.D.S. 1977; Mormon; married (Kathy).

Elected Office: Blackfoot City Cncl., 1980-84; ID House of Reps., 1984-98, Speaker, 1993-98.

Professional Career: Practicing dentist, 1977-98.

DC Office: 2312 RHOB, 20515, 202-225-5531; Fax: 202-225-8216; Web site: simpson.house.gov.

State Offices: Boise, 208-334-1953; Idaho Falls, 208-523-6701; Pocatello, 208-233-2222; Twin Falls, 208-734-7219.

Committees: *Appropriations:* Energy & Water Development; Interior, Environment & Related Agencies (Chmn); Labor, HHS, Education & Related Agencies. *Budget.*

Group Ratings

	ACLU	ACU	ADA	CFG	AFS	FRC	LCV	ITIC	NTU	COC
2010	6	96	5	87	0	100	10	0	83	75
2009	–	84	10	72	33	–	21	–	72	80

National Journal Ratings

	2010 LIB	—	2010 CONS	2009 LIB	—	2009 CONS
Economic	27%	—	72%	30%	—	69%
Social	31%	—	67%	35%	—	65%
Foreign	33%	—	65%	33%	—	63%
Composite	31%	—	69%	34%	—	67%

Key Votes of the 111th Congress

1. Overturn Ledbetter	N	5. Bar federal abortion funds	Y	9. Stop detainee transfers	Y
2. Pass $820 billion stimulus	N	6. Pass health care bill	N	10. Legalize immigrants' kids	N
3. Let guns in national parks	Y	7. Regulate financial firms	N	11. Repeal don't ask, tell	N
4. Pass cap-and-trade	N	8. Pass tax cuts for some	N	12. Limit campaign funds	N

Election Results

2010 general	Mike Simpson (R)	137,468	(69%)	($792,074)
	Mike Crawford (D)	48,749	(24%)	(no FEC report)
	Brian Schad (I)	13,500	(7%)	
2010 primary	Mike Simpson (R)	45,148	(58%)	
	M. C. 'Chick' Heileson (R)	18,644	(24%)	
	Russell Mathews (R)	7,452	(10%)	
	Katherine Burton (R)	6,214	(8%)	

Prior Winning Percentages: 2008 (71%), 2006 (62%), 2004 (71%), 2002 (68%), 2000 (71%), 1998 (53%)

Population		Race/Ethnicity		Work	
Pop. 2010:	725,652	White:	82.5%	Private:	76.0%
Change since 2000:	Up 12.5%	Black:	0.7%	Government:	16.2%
Urban:	67.0%	Hispanic:	12.8%	Self-employed:	7.5%
Rural:	33.0%	Asian:	1.2%	Blue collar:	23.6%
Area size:	43,598 sq. mi.	Native Am.:	1.1%	White collar:	56.1%
		Hawaiian:	0.1%	Khaki collar:	0.4%
Age		Two+ races:	1.5%	Other:	19.8%
Median age:	32.0 yrs.				
More than 65 yrs:	11.2%	*Ancestry*		Median income:	$45,061
Less than 18 yrs:	27.5%	English	16.1%	Median Home Value:	$161,400
		German	14.0%		
Education		Irish	7.3%	**Military Veterans**	
H.S. grad:	88.0%			% of Pop:	10.7%
College grad:	25.3%				
Grad degree:	8.4%				

East Idaho; Part Boise, Pocatello

The 2nd District of Idaho, from central Boise east to the Wyoming border, is one of America's most picturesque, with thick forests, mountain ranges, broad river valleys, and vacant expanses. It was settled from the east by overland pioneers who stopped in Idaho's farmlands, and from the south by Mormons moving up from Utah to Franklin, Bear Lake, and Caribou counties. It has one of the largest concentrations of Mormons among congressional districts. Poca-

2008 Presidential Vote		
John McCain (R)	182,225	(61%)
Barack Obama (D)	108,306	(36%)
2004 Presidential Vote		
George Bush (R)	194,166	(69%)
John Kerry (D)	86,183	(30%)
Cook Partisan Voting Index:	R+17	

tello began as a railroad town, with unionized railroad workers. Fifty miles north on Interstate 15, Idaho Falls serves as the metropolis for a vast region stretching from West Yellowstone, Mont., to the Salmon River Mountains. Near Idaho Falls, on a windswept, desolate range, is Idaho National Laboratory, known locally as "The Site," one of the Energy Department's 10 national laboratories. DOE's leading laboratory for civilian nuclear energy research, development, and demonstration, the facility covers 890 square miles and employs more than 7,000 workers, making it the third-largest employer in the state. It has kept the area's economy fairly stable, thanks in part to $468 million in federal economic stimulus money in 2009 to speed up its work cleaning up Cold War-era nuclear plants. In addition, the French nuclear company Areva in May 2010 won a $2 billion loan guarantee from the Energy Department to build a uranium enrichment plant nearby.

West of the laboratory campus, amid the mountains, are Sun Valley and the nearby town of Ketchum. Sun Valley was established as a ski resort in 1936 by Averell Harriman before he began his political career. Ketchum attracted writer Ernest Hemingway in 1939, and various movie stars followed. In recent years, Blaine County, which includes both Sun Valley and Ketchum, has attracted rich expatriates from the East and West coasts, who have made it the most Democratic county in Idaho. It stands in vivid contrast to the Idaho Falls area, the Mormon country, and the farmland along the Snake River, which are among the most Republican areas in the nation. The 2nd District also includes the east side of Boise, which leans Republican but has some Democratic precincts.

Mike Simpson (R)

The congressman from the 2nd District is Mike Simpson, a Republican first elected in 1998. Simpson grew up in Blackfoot, became a dentist, and joined his father's dental practice. He was elected to the City Council in 1980 and to the state House in 1984. He didn't declare himself as a Republican until then, and was opposed by the local Republican party. In 1993, he became speaker of the Idaho House, but he kept up his dental practice as well. In the legislature, he was known as a moderate in a predominately conservative chamber, affable and able to get differing sides together. When Republican Gov. Phil Batt announced he would retire in 1998, Simpson wanted to run, but GOP Sen. Dirk Kempthorne's decision to seek the office closed that option. GOP Rep. Mike Crapo decided to run for Kempthorne's Senate seat, thus opening up the House race for Simpson.

The seat was hotly contested. In the Republican primary, state Rep. Mark Stubbs called for lower payroll taxes. He had opposed nuclear programs at the INL, while Simpson wanted more work at the facility. But the big issue was term limits. Simpson refused to take a pledge to serve only three terms, while the other candidates did. Term-limit advocates spent large sums against Simpson. Angry at the ads, Batt endorsed Simpson five days before the election. Simpson ran ads against "out-of-state folk" interfering with Idaho's elections. Simpson beat Stubbs 47%-41%.

The Democratic nominee was Richard Stallings, a former history professor elected to the U.S. House in 1984 and re-elected three times. In 1992, he ran against Kempthorne for the Senate and lost 57%-43%. Stallings emphasized his conservative voting record in the House, called for more education spending, and said he would act to fix falling farm commodity prices. Simpson called for a smaller federal role in education. He favored tax cuts and the creation of personal investment accounts in Social Security. Simpson won 53%-45%, losing the most well-known parts of the district—Pocatello, Sun Valley, Boise—but carrying just about everything else.

In the House, Simpson posted a moderate record, particularly for a Western Republican. He has reached out to Democrats on economic and social issues, and he helped establish a bipartisan caucus to talk about the trade-related needs of farmers and ranchers. Simpson voted against the Central American Free Trade Agreement in 2005 because of its potential impact on Idaho's sugar beet industry. "When I came to Congress, I was a free-trader. But we don't live in an ideal world, and

I've come to understand that more and more. I'm starting to become one of those people I disagreed with a few years ago," he said in 2007. He once joined the American Civil Liberties Union because he wanted to learn more about the left-leaning group. In 2010, he refused to take the state Republican Party's oath endorsing the party platform. His open-mindedness led *Esquire* magazine to call him one of the 10 best members of Congress in 2008, saying he "lives by the philosophy that democratic representation is a matter of finding not advantageous positions but common ground."

In 2003, Simpson showed his skills as a party insider when he got a seat on the Appropriations Committee, a post he has used to secure funding for the Idaho National Laboratory, the Bureau of Reclamation, and the Army Corps of Engineers. Simpson became a leading defender of appropriations earmarks; he opposed restricting earmarks but supported greater transparency in the process. After Democrats took control of the House in 2007, Simpson called incoming Appropriations Chairman David Obey, a Wisconsin liberal, one of Congress' most honest members. When Simpson lost his seat on the Energy and Water Appropriations Subcommittee, which oversees nuclear energy spending, he pleaded with Obey, and Obey obliged by adding one Democratic and one Republican seat—Simpson's—to the subcommittee. Obey said of Simpson, "He works with people on both sides and he's a good, solid legislator."

In 2008, Simpson was the only member of the Idaho congressional delegation to support the $700 billion bailout of the financial markets. "We got into this mess because of failure of government oversight," he said. "Consequently, I think there's a role for government to play in trying to get us out of this, as much as I don't like it." When President Obama took office, he supported Democratic bills to rein in credit card companies and predatory housing lenders. But he stuck with his party on most major fiscal legislation. He unsuccessfully sought in the Appropriations Committee to impose pay-as-you-go rules requiring offsets for spending in the economic stimulus bill. In reaction to the Democrats' restricted rules on offering floor amendments to spending bills, he introduced a resolution in July 2009 calling for regular order on the bills; all but six Democrats voted to table his measure.

Simpson has said he would "die trying" to create a Boulder-White Cloud Management Area and he has spent years negotiating the plan with opposing constituencies. In 2006, he came up with a plan to preserve 312,000 acres in the central Idaho mountains and to transfer federal land in the Sawtooth National Recreation Area, a winter range for elk, to the city of Stanley and to Custer County to bolster their tax bases. To placate motorized-recreation advocates, he included a new 960-acre motorized park south of the Boise airport. To woo environmental groups, which were divided over the plan, Simpson added 630 acres of state land along the Salmon River and proposed to turn over federal land in eastern Idaho for a new state park. Simpson got his bill added to a sure-to-pass tax-cut bill in 2006, and secured a promise from Idaho Sen. Larry Craig, a Republican who opposed it, not to stand in the way. But the bill was dropped in last-minute tinkering by congressional leaders, and Simpson has continued to push versions of it since without success. In the 111th Congress (2009-10), he could not overcome opposition from two influential fellow Republicans—Idaho Gov. C.L. "Butch" Otter and Sen. James Risch.

Simpson won re-election three times with better than 2-to-1 ratios, but his lead slipped to 62%-34% in 2006, when he faced former Democratic state Rep. Jim Hansen, the son of former Republican Rep. Orval Hansen, who represented the district from 1969 to 1975. Simpson was back on his game in 2008, winning re-election with 71% of the vote. In 2010, however, his support for the Wall Street bailout and his other independent stances drew two primary opponents, state Rep. Russ Mathews and tea party-backed Chick Heileson, a retired heating contractor. They held Simpson to 58%, his worst primary showing since 1998. He received 69% in the general election against Democrat Mike Crawford.

★ ILLINOIS ★

Illinois and the giant city that dominates it, Chicago, have been experiencing the best and the worst of times. The best of times came in November 2008, when a crowd of 1 million people thronged to Chicago's lakefront Grant Park to cheer Barack Obama on election night. Downtown Chicago was festooned with posters in the style favored by the Obama campaign, hailing the election of Chicago's own as president of the United States. Contrast the joy and grandeur of that scene with the crowd gathered in October 2009 in Daley Plaza, where the Picasso sculpture stands across the street from Chicago City Hall. They were there to hail the city's selection as the site for the 2016 Olympics, seen as a fitting capstone to Obama's second term and to the career of Richard M. Daley, who with his father Richard J. Daley, had held the mayor's office for 41 of the last 54 years. But despite Obama's appearance before the Olympic committee in Copenhagen, it was not to be. To the shock of the crowd, Chicago was eliminated in the first round of voting.

That rejection was just one of several shocks—cultural, economic and political—that Chicago and Illinois suffered following the election of the first president from Illinois since Abraham Lincoln and Ulysses S. Grant (Ronald Reagan hailed from Illinois, but his political career was launched in California). Lincoln and Grant, like Obama, came from elsewhere—Lincoln heading west toward Springfield when his father moved east to Indiana, Grant living in the boom town of Galena just before the Civil War, Obama heading to Chicago to work as a community organizer and, when he found that less than satisfying, in politics. It's a perilous trade in a state and city given to spasms of public corruption, with a political culture that has little use for people who aren't "from here" but that bestows great rewards on those who can navigate the political rapids.

Illinois has come a long way since May 1860, when Abraham Lincoln was nominated at the Republican National Convention in the 10,000-seat Wigwam in Chicago, less than a mile from Grant Park. Chicago had just 112,000 people then, but it was the nation's boom city in the next three-quarters of a century, growing to a population of 1.4 million by the time it hosted the Columbian Exposition in 1893. "Make no little plans," Chicago architect Daniel Burnham exhorted. And the city made vast plans, building grand parks on the lakefront, erecting America's first downtown of skyscrapers, lining its boulevards with retail palaces, creating a great university from scratch on the Exposition's Midway Plaisance, and housing union agitators as well as corporate leaders. Chicago hosted the Democratic Convention of 1896 that nominated 36-year-old William Jennings Bryan after his "cross of gold" speech, and was the headquarters of the brilliant campaign Mark Hanna waged for William McKinley, who beat Bryan in the fall. Chicago started with the advantage of a great location, where the Great Lakes meet the prairies of the vast Mississippi Valley, and the city's entrepreneurs made it the hub of the nation's railroad network and the center of U.S. trade in lumber, grain, and meat.

A century later, Chicago is the nation's third-largest metropolis. Although often overshadowed by coastal New York and Los Angeles, it is still a creative, world-class city, the center of a metropolitan area of 9.7 million people. In commerce, Chicago has been a prime producer and processor of food products, a major manufacturing center, and the strongest service economy between the coasts. In finance, it is the home of the world's greatest commodities exchanges and futures markets. O'Hare Airport, promoted and nurtured for half a century by both Mayor Daleys, is one of the world's great hubs of commerce. Chicago was settled by Yankee pioneers from New England and upstate New York, by immigrant Irishmen who dug the first canal connecting Lake Michigan to the Illinois River, by railroad promoters who saw its potential as the great connecting point between East and West. Its factories were built where iron ore from Great Lakes freighters and coal from inland hills came together. Today, many of the old factories have been closed or demolished, and some of the Chicago area's biggest corporations have had problems. The years from 1997 to 2007 produced only minimal job growth. Manufacturing has visibly declined, and while some factory sites have been gracefully gentrified, others lie fallow and underused. Finance and commodities were hit by the economic collapse of fall 2008; unemployment shot up above the national average in 2009 and 2010. As Illinois raises taxes while nearby states move in the other direction, it's not clear that Chicago can keep its competitive edge even with its neighbors, much less with its rivals on the coasts.

Illinois emerged from the Civil War as a solidly Republican state, with fast-growing Chicago and the northern counties settled by Yankees decisively outvoting the southern-origin folk from Springfield down to Cairo, which is closer to Mississippi than to Chicago. Then, waves of immigrants thronged to Chicago, which has attracted immigrants more than any other Midwestern

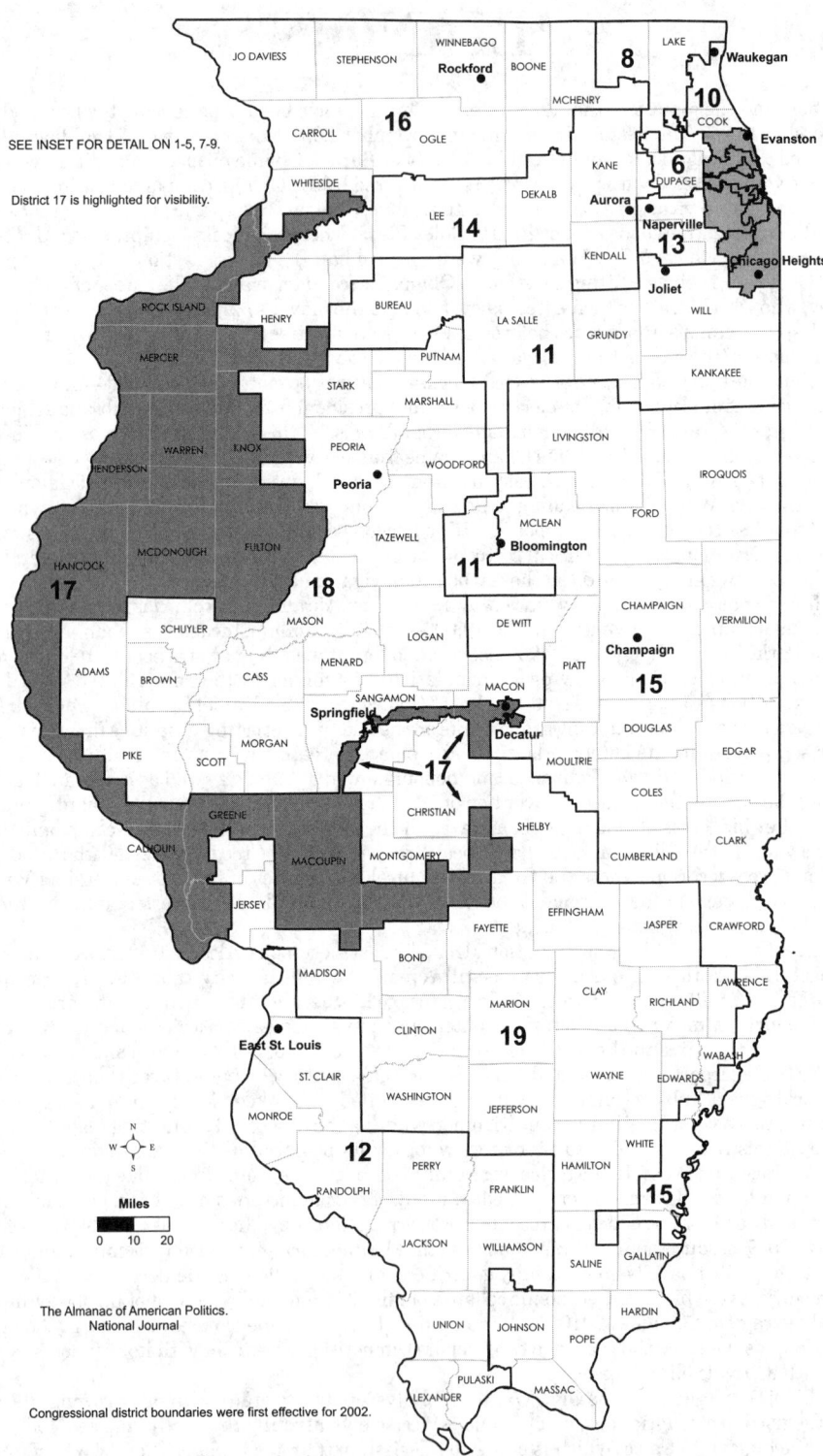

SEE INSET FOR DETAIL ON 1-5, 7-9.

District 17 is highlighted for visibility.

The Almanac of American Politics.
National Journal

Congressional district boundaries were first effective for 2002.

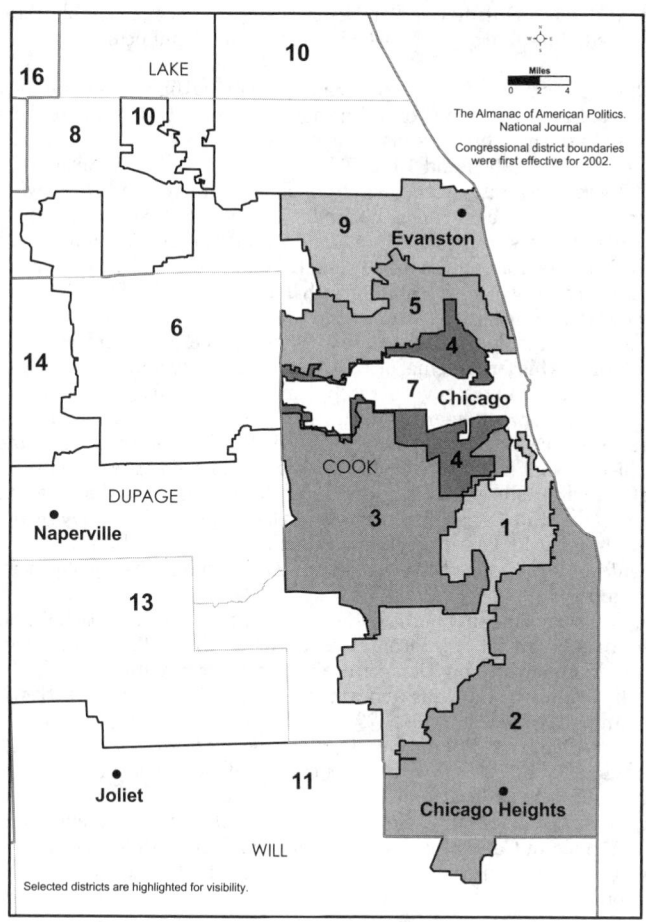

The Almanac of American Politics.
National Journal

Congressional district boundaries
were first effective for 2002.

Selected districts are highlighted for visibility.

metro area, to the point that Illinois' population is 16% Hispanic (and 4% Asian) as well as 14% black. Illinois' mixture of blacks and whites and Hispanics, immigrants and pioneers, city-dwellers and suburbanites and farmers, the affluent and the impoverished, heavy industry and high-technology, long made it a rough proxy for the nation. For a century, Illinois was a political bellwether, voting only twice for losing presidential candidates between 1896 and 1996—in 1916 and 1976, when it went Republican while the nation went Democratic. But in the 1990s, Illinois became steadily more Democratic than the nation. In 2000, it was one of Al Gore's best states. In 2004, it voted a solid 55%-44% for John Kerry, with Kerry leading in metro Chicago 60%-39% and George W. Bush leading downstate 55%-45%. In 2008 with favorite son Obama on the ballot, Illinois was not even close. Obama carried the state 62%-37%, metro Chicago 68%-31%, and he won formerly rock-ribbed Republican DuPage and McHenry counties. He carried downstate as well by a more modest 51%-47%.

Illinois has produced important political figures—Charles Dawes, Calvin Coolidge's vice president; Chicago lawyer Harold Ickes, a Bull Moose Republican who was Franklin Roosevelt's Interior secretary; Republican Speaker Joseph Cannon and Senate Minority Leader Everett Dirksen; and Governor and Democratic presidential nominee Adlai Stevenson. But perhaps more than any other state, Illinois has a history of machine politics and more than occasional political corruption. Lincoln was no stranger to the Republican machine of his day, which rallied thousands of partisans to cheer him at his debates with Stephen Douglas in 1858 and packed the Wigwam convention hall for him in 1860. Machine politics continued through the Gilded Age, as politicians in a closely divided state competed for public jobs and as politicians of both parties courted the immigrants streaming into Chicago. Both the city and downstate had thriving two-party politics in the early 20th century. It was a Republican mayor, Big Bill Thompson, who threatened to punch King George V "in the snoot" if he came to Chicago and who looked the other way as Al Capone's goons controlled the speakeasies. During the Depression, Chicago became reliably Democratic. In the decades that followed, the suburbs, wary of Chicago, became Republican and developed machines of their own

In the past half century, the state's most prominent political figure, and the one most formative of political attitudes, has been the mayor of Chicago. Richard J. Daley, mayor from 1955 to 1976, turned out the vote in the city, but as a machine politician, turned off suburbanites and the state trended Republican in the 1960s and 1970s. Harold Washington, the African-American mayor from 1983 to 1987, aroused great enthusiasm from blacks but opposition from white ethnic politicians and their constituents. Obama's original ambition was to follow Washington into the mayor's office. But the senior Daley's son, Richard M. Daley, had a lock on the mayor's office from 1989 until he retired in 2011. He was popular among lakefront liberals, ethnic whites and affluent suburbanites, and managed to stay in good standing with blacks as well. He forged the kind of consensus politics under the Democratic banner that Obama was able to capitalize on while running for the Senate in 2004 and as a presidential candidate in 2008. Democrat Rahm Emanuel, with close ties to Daley and to Obama as his former chief of staff, was elected mayor in April 2011 to succeed Daley.

Republicans held the Illinois governorship from 1976 to 2002, but the last GOP governor, George Ryan, went to jail for racketeering and fraud. Ryan's disgrace opened the way for Democrat Rod Blagojevich, who was elected governor in 2002 and 2006. But he had a fast and sure fall from power after disclosures that he tried to profit personally and politically from his power to appoint President-elect Obama's replacement in the Senate. He was impeached by the Illinois House, removed from office by the state Senate and, in August 2010, was convicted of lying to federal investigators. He was replaced by Lt. Gov. Pat Quinn, a Democrat and something of a maverick in Illinois politics, who spent much of the next two years trying to persuade the legislature to raise Illinois' 3% state income tax.

In 2010, Republicans suddenly had a better chance at the top of the ticket than they'd had in a dozen years. Quinn's advocacy of the income tax increase and his difficulty in working with Illinois Speaker Michael Madigan, a fellow Democrat, made him seem vulnerable. GOP state Sen. Bill Brady, who was little known statewide and won the March primary only narrowly, led Quinn in polls during the campaign and lost by just 47%-46%. The GOP also saw promise in the open Senate seat being vacated by Democrat Roland Burris, Blagojevich's tainted appointee. Obama had been elected to the seat in 2004 by 70%-27%, the most one-sided Senate victory in Illinois history, after a serious contender, Jack Ryan, was forced to withdraw amid allegations that he pressured his ex-wife to go to sex clubs. But before that, Republican Peter Fitzgerald had held it for one term after ousting one-term Democrat Carol Moseley Braun in 1998. Fitzgerald's decision to give up the seat opened the way for Obama to jump from the Illinois Senate to the U.S. Senate.

National Republicans were delighted when U.S. Rep. Mark Kirk, who represented a North Shore swing district, decided to run. His moderate record seemed likely to appeal in the once heavily Republican suburbs, where Democrats had been gaining ground on cultural issues since the Clinton years. The Democratic nominee, state Treasurer Alexi Giannoulias, had excellent political connections and political moves, but also had a record as an officer of a family-owned bank that had made large loans to mob figures and convicted Chicago fixer Tony Rezko. Despite Giannoulias' weaknesses, Kirk won narrowly, 48%-46%. Democrats lost four U.S. House seats, but they retained their majorities in the Illinois General Assembly.

In both the governor and U.S. senator races, Democrats won only four counties out of 102—the two containing East St. Louis and Cairo, with their large black populations; one containing Southern Illinois University; and Cook County, which contains Chicago and its inner suburbs and casts

Population		Household Income		Work	
Pop. 2010:	12,830,632	Under $15k:	12.0%	Private:	82.1%
State rank:	5th	$15k to $50k:	33.5%	Government:	12.7%
Change since 2000:	Up 3.3%	$50k to $100k:	32.0%	Self-employed:	5.0%
Urban:	86.6%	$100k to $200k:	17.8%	Unemployment (3-yr. average):	5.6%
Rural:	13.4%	Over $200k:	4.7%	Poverty:	12.6%
Native of state:	66.8%	Median income:	$55,095	Blue collar:	21.8%
Not a citizen:	7.5%			White collar:	61.3%
Area size:	57,914 sq. mi.	**Home Value**		Khaki collar:	0.2%
		Under $100k:	19.8%	Other:	16.7%
Most populous cities		$100k to $300k:	50.4%		
Chicago	2,695,598	$300k to $500k:	20.1%	**Age**	
Aurora	197,899	$500k to $1 mil:	7.9%	Median age:	36.0 yrs.
Rockford	152,871	Over $1 million:	1.8%	More than 65 yrs:	12.2%
Joliet	147,433	Median:	$207,300	Less than 18 yrs:	24.8%

Race/Ethnicity				Military Veterans		Registered Voters in 2010	
White:	63.7%	*Language*		% of Pop:	8.1%	No Party registration	
Black:	14.3%	English:	78.5%			Voter turnout:	3,792,770
Hispanic:	15.8%	Spanish:	12.5%	*Veterans by Period*		Turnout as % of	
Asian:	4.5%	Asian:	2.5%	WWII and before:	12.2%	voting age:	39.1%
Native Am.:	0.1%	Other European:	5.6%	Korea:	12.5%		
Hawaiian:	0.0%			Vietnam:	32.8%	**Legislature**	
Two+ races:	1.4%	**Education**		Gulf (pre-2001):	9.9%	Senate:	35 D 24 R
		H.S. grad:	86.1%	Gulf (post-2001):	6.9%	House:	64 D 54 R
Ancestry		College grad:	30.2%	Peace time:	25.7%		
German	16.5%	Grad degree:	11.4%				
Irish	10.4%						
Polish	6.2%						

38% of the state's popular votes. The lopsided Democratic margins in Cook County are due in part to 90% support from African-Americans and more than 60% support from Latinos, but they also owe much to changes in the Cook County suburbs, which for many years were as solidly Republican as the city was Democratic. In the past 20 years, the northern suburbs have trended Democratic on cultural issues and the southern suburbs have become increasingly black, as middle-income blacks move south from Chicago rather than north or west in the city. The western suburbs have an increasing population of immigrants, especially Latinos. At the same time, the collar Counties just beyond Cook County, which used to vote 2-1 or more Republican, have now taken to giving Republicans small majorities or, as in the 2008 presidential race, voting Democratic.

Presidential politics Illinois' presidential primary, for years held fittingly on or around St. Patrick's Day, clinched the nominations for Republican victors Gerald Ford in 1976, Ronald Reagan in 1980 and George Bush in 1988, and Democratic victors Jimmy Carter in 1980, Walter Mondale in 1984 and Bill Clinton in 1992. As more states have moved their primaries to earlier dates, Illinois has voted too late to decide a nomination. In 2007, the legislature moved the primary to Feb. 5, 2008 to help Obama. Some 2 million people turned out to vote in the Democratic primary, many more than the 1.1 million who voted in 2004 or the record 1.66 million in 1984. Obama beat Hillary Rodham Clinton 65%-33%, losing only a few downstate counties. There was little campaigning on the Republican side, and only 893,000 Republican votes were cast, well below the record 1.1 million in 1980, when Illinois native Reagan and U.S. Rep. John Anderson of Illinois were on the ballot. John McCain won the primary with 47% of the vote, to 29% for Mitt Romney and 16% for Mike Huckabee.

2008 Presidential Vote
Barack Obama (D) 3,419,348   (62%)
John McCain (R) 2,031,179   (37%)

2008 Presidential Primary
Barack Obama (D) 1,318,234   (65%)
Hillary Clinton (D)................667,930   (33%)

2008 Presidential Primary
John McCain (R) 426,777   (47%)
Mitt Romney (R)....................257,265   (29%)
Mike Huckabee (R)...............148,053   (16%)
Ron Paul (R) 45,055   (5%)

2004 Presidential Vote
John Kerry (D) 2,891,550   (55%)
George W. Bush (R)...........2,345,946   (44%)

In the 1990s, as Republican margins in the suburban collar counties dwindled, Illinois became a solidly Democratic state in presidential politics. It was not seriously contested in 2000 or 2004, much less in 2008, when favorite son Obama carried it by 62%-37%.

Congressional districting Illinois, with its sluggish population growth, lost a House seat in Congress after the 2000 census and is slated to lose another one as a result of the 2010 census. After the 2000 census, control of redistricting was split between the Democratic state House and the Republican state Senate and governor. In similar circumstances, the 1980s and 1990s redistricting plans had been drawn by courts, with results that were politically unpredictable and unpalatable to incumbents. In 1992, four incumbents lost their primaries. Things worked differently in 2001. U.S. House Speaker Dennis Hastert of Illinois, a Republican, and 3rd District Democratic Rep. Bill Lipinski started negotiating early to produce an incumbent-protection plan that would pass both houses of the legislature. Before the census data came in, it was assumed that the

112th Congress Lineup
11 R   8 D
111th Congress Lineup
12 D   7 R

5th District would be eliminated, since Democratic incumbent Blagojevich had announced his bid for governor. But the census figures showed that the 5th District and adjacent districts in Chicago, bursting with new immigrants, had gained population, while rural Southern Illinois had lost population. Mayor Daley let it be known that he would not like to see Chicago lose a seat.

So Hastert and Lipinski concocted a new plan taking a district away from Southern Illinois. The victim was 19th District Democrat David Phelps, a former professional gospel singer with little seniority and a somewhat conservative voting record. Phelps had no clout in Congress, and the Hastert-Lipinski plan became law in May 2001. Why were Lipinski, Daley and Speaker Michael Madigan willing to sacrifice a fellow Democrat and lose their party's 10-10 parity in the House delegation? Because Phelps could do little for them in the House, while Hastert had been generous in using his powers as speaker to aid Daley, Lipinski, and other Chicago Democrats on Chicago issues and projects. Maintaining a Republican majority that would keep Hastert in the speakership was in the interest of Chicago Democrats.

For 2012, Democrats control the redistricting process, and the key player is likely to be House Speaker Madigan. Republicans now hold every district south of metro Chicago except for the 12th District centered on the St. Louis suburbs. Presumably, at least one of those GOP incumbents will be targeted for political extinction. In addition, Democrats may well target one of the suburban districts now held by Republicans—the 10th, 8th, 6th and 13th—for elimination or absorption into a Democratic district.

Governor

Pat Quinn (D)

Assumed office Jan. 2009, term expires Jan. 2015, 1st full term; b. Dec. 16, 1948, Chicago; home, Chicago; Georgetown U., B.A., 1971; Northwestern U., J.D. 1980.; Catholic; divorced; 2 children.

Elected Office: Commissioner, Cook Cnty. Bd. of Tax Appeals, 1982-86; IL treasurer, 1991-95; Lt. gov., 2003-09.

Professional Career: Chicago revenue dir., 1986-87; Practicing atty., 1994-2002; Author.

Office: Office of the Governor, 207 State House, Springfield, 62706, 217-782-0244; Fax: 217-524-4049; Web site: http://www.illinois.gov/gov/.

Election Results

2010 general	Pat Quinn (D)	1,745,219	(47%)
	Bill Brady (R)	1,713,385	(46%)
	Scott Cohen (I)	135,705	(4%)
	Rich Whitney (Green)	100,756	(3%)
2010 primary	Pat Quinn (D)	462,049	(50%)
	Daniel Hynes (D)	453,677	(50%)

Democrat Pat Quinn became governor of Illinois on Jan. 29, 2009, after the impeachment and removal from office of Gov. Rod Blagojevich. He was elected to a full term in 2010. Quinn's grandfather was an Irish immigrant and his father rose to become the public-relations director of Catholic Cemeteries in the Chicago archdiocese. Pat Quinn grew up in the affluent Chicago suburb of Hinsdale, attended Catholic schools and graduated from Georgetown University. In 1972, a year out of college, he signed up as a volunteer for the anti-machine Democratic candidate for Illinois governor, Daniel Walker. When Walker won, Quinn got a job in state government, working on patronage appointments and transferring state workplace safety operations to the federal Occupational Safety and Health Administration. In 1975, he left state government to attend Northwestern Law School—and to engage in politics, in his own way.

Walker, defeated for renomination in 1976 and later jailed for defrauding a savings and loan, could be of no help. And with his suburban upbringing, Quinn acquired none of the connections that are usually essential to the rise of Democratic politicians in Illinois. "It's not exactly an easy path I had," he told the *Chicago Tribune* in February 2009. "I had no political patrons or ward committeemen backing me for any job." Young and idealistic, Quinn launched the Coalition for Political Honesty, which operated out of an Oak Park basement, and got enough signatures for a 1976 referendum to stop legislators from collecting their entire salaries on the first day of their terms. In 1980, he got enough signatures for a "cutback" initiative to reduce the size of the state House from 177 to 118 members. Previously, each district elected three legislators, with each party allowed only two candidates. This gave minority parties representation, but in some Chicago wards, the nominal Republicans were obedient to Chicago machine politicians. The measure passed, with help from what became a Quinn trademark—Sunday morning press conferences that took advantage of local reporters' thirst for news on a slow day. Some labeled Quinn a political gadfly; others saw him as a political reformer.

In 1982, Quinn was elected to the Cook County Board of Tax Appeals, which handled property tax appeals. In 1983, he created the Citizens Utility Board, a group that challenged utility and phone rate increases. CUB became a well-known consumer organization and established Quinn's reputation statewide. In 1986, he ran for state treasurer and lost in the Democratic primary. Chicago Mayor Harold Washington appointed him city revenue director, but he lost the job after a falling-out with other officials in the administration and some internal grumbling about his penchant for seeking publicity. He began practicing law, specializing in property tax appeals, and wrote a book called *How to Appeal Your Property Taxes Without a Lawyer*. He was also the lead attorney in a case, decided by the U.S. Supreme Court in 1990, that banned political considerations in state and local hiring.

In 1990, Quinn was elected state treasurer. He claimed to have made $848 million in investment income for taxpayers, but in the Republican year of 1994, he lost a contest for secretary of state to incumbent George Ryan. Throughout his career in state politics, a reputation for over-the-top self-promotion followed Quinn from post to post. His successor as treasurer, Republican Judy Baar Topinka said that on taking office she found "Quinn for Governor" bumper stickers in the desk. In 1996, he ran for U.S. senator and lost in the primary, 65%-30%, to downstate U.S. Rep. Richard Durbin. In 1998, Quinn ran for lieutenant governor, narrowly losing the Democratic primary to Kane County Coroner Mary Lou Kearns. He continued to practice law and to attract public attention, notably by walking across Illinois from the Mississippi River to Lake Michigan to highlight the need for decent health care.

In 2002, he ran for lieutenant governor again, and this time won the Democratic primary, with 42% of the vote to 32% for Chicago hospital executive Joyce Washington and 25% for downstate college teacher Mike Kelleher. He ran 849 votes behind Washington in Cook County, 150 votes ahead of Kelleher downstate, and carried the collar county suburbs with 50% of the vote, to 28% for Washington and 22% for Kelleher. It was a rare example of a Democrat winning an Illinois primary by sweeping the suburbs. Success in the primary put Quinn on the ticket in November with U.S. Rep. Rod Blagojevich, whose political career began to thrive after he married the daughter of powerful 33rd Ward Committeeman and Alderman Dick Mell. Quinn had not been the choice of most Chicago insiders, and his relations with Blagojevich were never warm, but the ticket won 52%-45%.

Gov. Blagojevich spent most of his time in Chicago, taking the state plane to Springfield when the legislature was meeting. Quinn lived mostly in Springfield, and frugally, never accepting his $32-a-day meal allowance and proudly showing off his Super 8 Motel preferred customer card. He pushed a relief act for aid to families of National Guardsmen and reservists called to active duty and a law to prevent disruptive protests at service members' funerals. He carried a beat-up, 28-year-old briefcase he called Betsy and eschewed a laptop in favor of scribbling notes on scraps of paper. In 2006, as he and Blagojevich ran for second terms, he supported the incumbent governor without reservation, despite the fact that Blagojevich was under federal investigation. Quinn told the *Tribune* he found the governor to be "an honest person." The Blagojevich-Quinn ticket prevailed 50%-39%.

In Blagojevich's second term, Quinn became more critical of the governor. He was not alone. Blagojevich was at odds with legislators of both parties, especially Michael Madigan, the Illinois House speaker. At one point, the House rejected the governor's budget by a unanimous vote. Later that year, he called on Blagojevich to urge the legislature to pass an ethics bill. By April 2008, he was telling reporters he was "disappointed" in Blagojevich, blaming him for a "disintegration of comity in Springfield."

Then in December 2008, as Chicago was celebrating Obama's election as president, the city was stunned by the news that Blagojevich had been arrested by federal marshals and charged with attempting to trade the appointment to Obama's Senate seat for personal or political favors. Quinn initially called for a special election to fill the Senate seat in the light of the taint of a Blagojevich appointment, but he quickly backed down under pressure from other Democrats, who evidently feared a Republican might win such a contest. Quinn called for Blagojevich's resignation, as did several other prominent Illinois Democrats, but the governor proclaimed his innocence and refused to budge. On Dec. 30, even as the possibility of impeachment loomed, Blagojevich went forward and appointed former state Attorney General Roland Burris to the Senate. Senate Democrats at first refused to seat him, then acquiesced. In the meantime, the Illinois House voted 114-1 to impeach Blagojevich, and on Jan. 29, 2009, the Illinois Senate voted 59-0 to remove him from office. The erstwhile gadfly Pat Quinn was suddenly governor of Illinois.

In February, Burris admitted he had more contacts with Blagojevich associates about the Senate appointment than he had disclosed, and Quinn called on him to resign the Senate seat and compete in a special election. When black Chicago politicians objected, Quinn said he feared a revival of an era of racial polarization in the city like the 1980s, when African-American Mayor Washington was opposed by powerful white aldermen. He backed down from his call for Burris' resignation.

Overshadowing this political tussling was the fact that state government faced a parlous fiscal situation. It needed another $3 billion to get through the fiscal year. State workers' health care bills were delinquent, school districts were scrambling for cash, and doctors and hospitals were going unpaid. On Feb. 4, 2009, Comptroller Dan Hynes said the state faced a $9 billion budget deficit. Quinn ordered cuts in travel, contracts, and hiring, but opposed raising highway tolls (a significant expense for Chicago suburbanites). Then in March, he proposed raising the state income tax from 3%, where it has been since 1989, to 4.5%, cushioning the blow by raising the personal exemption from $2,000 to $6,000. The legislature resisted, and in July 2009, Quinn was forced to repeatedly cut spending.

Quinn had political problems as well. He had opposition in the February 2010 Democratic primary from Hynes, a member of a politically connected Chicago family, who curiously campaigned as an outsider. Both sought support from black voters. One of Hynes' ads show the late Mayor Washington calling Quinn "undisciplined" as his revenue director. Quinn struck back with allegations that as comptroller, Hynes ignored abuses at an all-black cemetery, where profiteers allegedly exhumed human remains and reburied them in mass graves in order to resell the burial plots. Quinn won 50%-49%, with a popular vote margin of 8,372 out of 920,000 votes cast. Quinn carried Cook County, which cast 62% of the Democratic votes, by 53%-46%; Hynes narrowly carried the collar county suburbs and won downstate.

The Republicans had an even closer, seven-candidate primary, in which state Sen. Bill Brady beat state Sen. Kirk Dillard 20.26%-20.24%, a popular vote margin of 193 votes. Brady won only 5% of the votes in Cook County and 6% in the collar counties, but he had a big 37%-21% lead over Dillard in downstate Illinois, which cast 46% of the Republican votes.

Early in the general election campaign, the media disclosed that the Democratic nominee for lieutenant governor, pawnshop owner Scott Lee Cohen, had been arrested for domestic battery against a prostitute girlfriend in 2005 and also owed $54,000 in child support to his ex-wife. The disclosures hurt Quinn, even though the governor and lieutenant governor are nominated separately in Illinois. In the general election, they run as a team. Pressure mounted, and five days after the primary, Cohen resigned his nomination. In March, Democratic leaders chose law professor Sheila Simon, daughter of the late U.S. Sen. Paul Simon, as their lieutenant governor nominee. Brady, an executive in a family construction business, was embarrassed as well by disclosure that he had not recently paid income taxes because of significant business losses.

The candidates had clear differences on issues. Quinn called for increasing the income tax from 3% to 4%, and also proposed a tax on iTunes purchases and a nickel tax on shopping bags. Brady opposed all tax increases and called for "deconstructing" the state budget. He said he would replace state-guaranteed pensions (which Illinois was far short of funding) with contributions to 401(k) accounts. But he generated controversy when he vowed to cut the state budget by 10%. Quinn claimed that Brady's cuts in education spending would sacrifice a generation of children. Quinn was criticized for an early-release prison program he backed to lower prison costs after more than 50 former inmates violated parole or committed crimes.

Brady led in most polls, but when the results came in, Quinn won 47%-46%, with 4% voting for independent Scott Lee Cohen. Brady carried 98 counties, while Quinn carried only four—one of them being Cook County, which cast 38% of the state's votes. Whites voted 60% for Brady; blacks and Latinos voted 90% and 62%, respectively, for Quinn. Democrats lost two seats in the state Senate and six in the state House, although still maintained large majorities, leaving Illinois one of only two states between West Virginia and the West Coast with state government controlled by Democrats. The other was Arkansas. And in vivid contrast to most states, Quinn and the legislature opted to increase taxes in response to enormous fiscal problems, finally raising the income tax from 3% to 5%.

Senior Senator

Richard Durbin (D)

Elected 1996, term expires 2014, 3rd term; b. Nov. 21, 1944, E. St. Louis; home, Springfield; Georgetown U., B.S. 1966, J.D. 1969; Catholic; married (Loretta); 3 children (1 deceased).

Elected Office: U.S. House of Reps., 1982–96.

Professional Career: Staff, Lt. Gov. Paul Simon, 1969–72; Legal cnsl., IL Sen. Judiciary Cmte., 1972–82; Prof., S. IL Schl. of Medicine, 1978–82.

DC Office: 711 HSOB, 20510, 202-224-2152; Fax: 202-228-0400; Web site: durbin.senate.gov.

State Offices: Chicago, 312-353-4952; Carbondale, 618-351-1122; Rock Island, 309-786-5173; Springfield, 217-492-4062.

Committees: *Appropriations:* Defense; Department of State, Foreign Operations & Related Programs; Energy & Water Development; Financial Services & General Government (Chmn); Labor, Health & Human Services, Education & Related Agencies; Transportation, HUD & Related Agencies. *Foreign Relations:* African Affairs; European Affairs; International Development & Foreign Assistance, Economic Affairs & International Environmental Protection; International Operations & Organizations, Democracy & Global Women's Issues. *Judiciary:* Constitution, Civil Rights & Human Rights (Chmn); Crime & Terrorism; Immigration, Refugees & Border Security. *Rules & Administration.*

Group Ratings

	ACLU	ACU	ADA	CFG	AFS	FRC	LCV	ITIC	NTU	COC
2010	93	0	95	0	98	0	100	67	6	18
2009	–	0	95	3	100	–	100	–	4	43

National Journal Ratings

	2010 LIB	—	2010 CONS	2009 LIB	—	2009 CONS
Economic	75%	—	22%	88%	—	0%
Social	65%	—	0%	82%	—	15%
Foreign	47%	—	0%	55%	—	0%
Composite	78%	—	23%	85%	—	15%

Key Votes of the 111th Congress

1. Overturn Ledbetter	Y	5. Pass health care bill	Y	9. Ratify New START	Y
2. Pass $787 billion stimulus	Y	6. Regulate financial firms	Y	10. Confirm Elena Kagan	Y
3. Repeal DC gun laws	N	7. Pass tax cuts for some	Y	11. Stop EPA climate regs	N
4. Confirm Sonia Sotomayor	Y	8. Legalize immigrants' kids	Y	12. Repeal don't ask, tell	Y

Election Results

2008 general	Richard Durbin (D)	3,615,844	(68%)	($11,317,550)
	Steve Sauerberg (R)	1,520,621	(29%)	($1,117,161)
	Kathy Cummings (Green)	119,135	(2%)	
2008 primary	Richard Durbin (D)	unopposed		

Prior Winning Percentages: 2002 (60%); 1996 (56%); House: 1994 (55%); 1992 (57%); 1990 (66%); 1988 (69%); 1986 (68%); 1984 (61%); 1982 (50%)

The senior senator from Illinois is Richard Durbin, a Democrat first elected to the House in 1982 and to the Senate in 1996. He is the Democratic whip and assistant majority leader, making him the second most powerful senator after Majority Leader Harry Reid. Durbin grew up in East St. Louis, the youngest of three brothers. His father, a railroad night watchman, died of lung cancer when Durbin was 14. He graduated from Georgetown University and its law school, and then returned to Illinois with an ambition for politics. He joined Democrat Paul Simon's staff when Simon was the lieutenant governor (1969-73), then was a state Senate staffer in the 1970s. Durbin lost races for the state Senate in 1976 and for lieutenant governor in 1978. But in 1982 he won the nomination to oppose Republican U.S. Rep. Paul Findley, who had characterized himself as Palestinian leader Yasser Arafat's best friend in Congress. Durbin had no trouble raising money from well-heeled Israel supporters. Durbin won the race.

In the House, he got a seat on the Appropriations Committee, where in 1993, he became chairman of the Agriculture subcommittee. Durbin's centerpiece legislation in the House was the 1988 ban on smoking on domestic airline flights, a battle inspired by the death of his chain-smoking father. He followed that up by trying to limit tobacco subsidies and to give the Food and Drug Administration authority to regulate tobacco as a health hazard—both accomplished after years of effort. "I didn't realize it would trigger a change in America," he later said of the airline smoking ban, but indeed it led to smoking bans in many more settings. After his onetime boss Paul Simon announced his retirement from the Senate in 1996, Durbin ran for the seat. Raising more than $1 million, he outspent former state Treasurer (now governor) Pat Quinn in the March 1996 primary and won 65%-30%. In the general, he faced trial lawyer and abortion opponent Al Salvi and won 56%-41%.

In the Senate, Durbin has compiled a largely liberal voting record, though he supported welfare reform in the 1990s and has always supported the death penalty. While in the House, Durbin favored restrictions on abortion, but has opposed most legislation to restrict abortion since coming to the Senate. (In 2004, the Catholic priest at his home church in Springfield said that he wouldn't give him communion as a consequence of his position.) On other domestic issues, Durbin has had a strong pro-union voting record, but split with labor on trade, supporting the North American Free Trade Agreement and normal trade relations with China: Illinois is a big exporter. But in 2006 Durbin said he felt "betrayed" by the results of NAFTA and has opposed more recent trade agreements. In 2001, Democratic Leader Tom Daschle appointed Durbin assistant floor leader. After Daschle's defeat in 2004 and the elevation of Reid as minority leader, Durbin became minority whip, and then majority whip in 2007, after Democrats won their Senate majority.

On the Judiciary Committee, Durbin strongly opposed many Bush administration judicial nominees, including John Roberts and Samuel Alito to the Supreme Court, and strongly supported Obama administration nominees, including Supreme Court justices Sonia Sotomayor and Elena Kagan. In July 2010, after listening to Republican Sen. Lindsey Graham's speech supporting Kagan's nomination, Durbin said, "I reflected on some of the things that I have said and how I have voted in the past, and thought that perhaps his statement suggested a better course."

In 2003, Durbin was the Democrats' point man on efforts to limit damages in medical malpractice lawsuits, and he successfully blocked action on the legislation. He also took a lead role on asbestos legislation that year. He negotiated with Judiciary Committee Chairman Orrin Hatch, a Utah Republican, on a bill that established quick recovery for injured plaintiffs and reduced the burden on businesses only tangentially connected with asbestos. But the two failed to produce a compromise bill. In 2006, he helped defeat the asbestos trust fund sponsored by Pennsylvania Republican Arlen Specter, which would have replaced a multitude of lawsuits against the asbestos industry with a $140 billion trust fund to compensate victims. Durbin strongly opposed taking the matter out of the courts, although he conceded the need for "significant changes in the existing tort system."

In 2007, Durbin was also the chief sponsor of the DREAM Act, a bill to allow high school graduates who are illegal immigrants to go to U.S. colleges. He was unable to get a filibuster-proof majority for the bill, however, and the bill failed in December 2010. In September 2008, when the Senate was considering the $700-billion rescue of the financial industry, Durbin voted in favor though he expressed reservations, saying, "I'm not sure what the right thing is." In 2008 and 2009, as the housing crisis deepened, Durbin pushed for his "cram-down" bill allowing bankruptcy judges to modify the terms of distressed mortgages on primary residences in bankruptcy cases. The Senate voted 51-45 against the bill, with 12 Democrats joining all the Republicans—the first big loss by Democrats in the 111th Congress. When the Senate was considering the financial regulation bill in May 2010, Durbin worked with his colleagues on a successful amendment giving the Federal Reserve authority to reduce the fees banks charge merchants for processing debit card transactions.

Durbin voted against the Gulf War resolution in 1991 and the Iraq war resolution in 2002, though he supported the use of force in Iraq under President Clinton in February 1998. In 2005, Durbin was at the center of a storm over remarks he made from the Senate floor concerning detainees at Guantanamo Bay, Cuba. Citing an FBI report that described the mistreatment of some prisoners, Durbin likened the American interrogators to "Nazis, Soviets in their gulags, or some mad regime—Pol Pot or others—that had no concern for human beings." His comments dominated the news for days. Durbin at first said he regretted the misunderstanding of his remarks, but after then-Chicago Mayor Richard M. Daley criticized them, he issued an emotional apology from the Senate floor. In 2007, he voted with 92 other senators for a resolution opposing the transfer of Guantanamo detainees to the continental United States. But he supported the Obama administration's policy of closing Guantanamo and supported transfer of detainees to the former state prison in Thomson, Ill.

Durbin was voted the most admired senator in *National Journal*'s poll of Democratic congressional insiders in late 2009. And as whip, he has worked hard on the floor to advance Democratic bills. He gave up a Judiciary subcommittee chairmanship to Arlen Specter when Specter switched parties in April 2009. In early 2010, Durbin worked with then-Sen. Byron Dorgan, D-N.D., to put together a Democratic jobs bill—an effort frustrated by the election of Massachusetts Republican Scott Brown—and he led the push against Kentucky Republican Jim Bunning's filibuster of extended unemployment benefits.

Nonetheless, there were signs of tension with his Democratic colleague Chuck Schumer of New York, who was elevated to a newly created No. 3 leadership position after his successes in ensuring a Democratic majority in 2006 and 2008, when he ran the Senate Democrats' election committee. In 2009 and 2010, when it seemed likely or at least possible that Harry Reid would be defeated in a tough re-election contest in Nevada, there was speculation that Durbin and Schumer would both seek to succeed Reid. Widely admired for his liberal convictions, Durbin has had less contact with the Washington lobbying community than Schumer has, and while much more active on the floor, he is seen in some quarters as more ingenuous. As one longtime Democratic staffer told *Politico*, "He's a great guy. But he thinks with his heart, not his head. He's great at communicating ideas, but not at thinking strategically."

Durbin's leadership position enables him to work effectively on local issues. He has had a hand in securing funding for the Metra and CTA mass transit systems in the Chicago region, for Mississippi River locks and dams, and for O'Hare Airport expansion. He has worked for ethanol tax incentives and pushed for an ethanol research pilot plant at Southern Illinois University at Edwardsville. On the Appropriations Committee, he keeps an eye out for Chicago's commodities exchanges, opposing new fees on the exchanges and in 2008, working behind the scenes to soften the impact of proposed controls on speculators in the oil futures market as gas prices soared. Durbin is also a champion of the $4.6 billion FutureGen clean-coal project in Mattoon, which critics have derided as "the biggest earmark in history." The Bush Energy Department declined to build FutureGen, but Durbin renewed the push in 2009 with the more supportive Obama administration. When it comes to his home state, he's also loyal. After former Illinois Republican Gov. George Ryan was imprisoned for racketeering and fraud, Durbin, who had worked with Ryan on projects for the state, urged President George W. Bush to pardon him in 2008.

In a backdrop of many clashing egos in the Senate, many senators have tense relationships with home-state colleagues, but Durbin had a warm relationship with Obama after he was elected in 2004. Rather than chafing at Obama's quick rise and celebrity, Durbin in 2006 urged him to run for president. He endorsed Obama when he announced his candidacy in February 2007. When Obama was elected, Durbin said, "To have a president of the United States who is a close, personal friend and has the opportunity to lead this nation and change the world is a dream come true for me in public life." Obama has called Durbin "a terrific partner." (Durbin did not join Obama at the election night celebration in Chicago's Grant Park because his 40-year-old daughter had died three days before.)

By contrast, Durbin did not have a close relationship with former Democratic Gov. Rod Blagojevich, who was driven from office after he was wiretapped saying he expected to profit either personally or politically from his power to appoint a Senate successor after Obama was elected president in 2008. Before he was impeached, Blagojevich denied wrongdoing and went ahead and appointed former Illinois Attorney General Roland Burris to the Senate in December 2008. Durbin encouraged Burris not to accept, and then raised the possibility the Senate would refuse to seat him. In February 2009, when it was reported that Burris had had more contacts with Blagojevich's brother than he had earlier indicated, Durbin advised Burris to resign, but then drew back after Rep. Bobby Rush, an African-American Democrat from Chicago, suggested Burris was being treated badly because of his race. Durbin then encouraged state Treasurer Alexi Giannoulias to run. In February 2010, Giannoulias kicked off his campaign at Durbin's Springfield home, although he ultimately lost the election to Republican Mark Kirk.

Durbin was mentioned briefly in 2000 as a possible vice presidential nominee, but he ultimately withdrew his name from consideration. In 2004, he was not much mentioned as a vice presidential nominee and played only a small role at the Democratic National Convention. In his 2008 re-election campaign, Durbin was opposed by physician Steven Sauerberg, who loaned his campaign $1.7 million and spent only $1 million, while Durbin spent $13 million. Sauerberg criticized Durbin for his 2005 "Nazis" statement, but the issue proved to have little traction. Durbin won 68%-29%.

Junior Senator

Mark Kirk (R)

Elected Nov. 2010, term expires 2016, 1st full term; b. Sept. 15, 1959, Champaign; home, Highland Park; Universidad Nacional Autonoma de Mexico, 1977-78, Cornell U., B.A. 1981, London Sch. of Econ., M.Sc. 1982; Georgetown U., J.D. 1992; Congregationalist; divorced.

Military Career: U.S. Naval Reserve, 1989-present.

Elected Office: U.S. House, 2000-10

Professional Career: Parliamentary aide, British House of Commons, 1981-83; A.A., U.S. Rep. John E. Porter, 1984-89; staffer, World Bank, 1990-91; spec. asst., U.S. Dept. of State, 1991-93; practicing atty., 1993-95; counsel, U.S. House Cmte. on Intl. Relations, 1995-2000.

DC Office: 524 HSOB, 20510, 202-224-2854; Fax: 202-228-4611; Web site: kirk.senate.gov.

State Offices: Chicago, 312-886-3506; Springfield, 217-492-5089.

Committees: *Aging (Special). Appropriations:* Department of State, Foreign Operations & Related Programs; Financial Services & General Government; Labor, Health & Human Services, Education & Related Agencies; Military Construction, Veterans Affairs & Related Agencies (RMM); Transportation, HUD & Related Agencies. *Banking, Housing & Urban Affairs:* Housing, Transportation & Community Development; Securities, Insurance & Investment; Security & International Trade & Finance. *Health, Education, Labor & Pensions:* Children & Families; Employment & Workplace Safety.

Group Ratings (House)

	ACLU	ACU	ADA	CFG	AFS	FRC	LCV	ITIC	NTU	COC
2010	21	63	10	66	33	62	70	–	–	100
2009	–	72	35	58	38	–	71	–	60	87

National Journal Ratings (House)

	2010 LIB	—	2010 CONS	2009 LIB	—	2009 CONS
Economic	40%	—	60%	37%	—	63%
Social	39%	—	61%	42%	—	58%
Foreign	38%	—	61%	39%	—	61%
Composite	39%	—	61%	39%	—	61%

Key Votes of the 111th Congress (House)

1. Overturn Ledbetter	N	5. Bar federal abortion funds	Y	9. Stop detainee transfers	Y
2. Pass $820 billion stimulus	N	6. Pass health care bill	N	10. Legalize immigrants' kids	*
3. Let guns in national parks	N	7. Regulate financial firms	N	11. Repeal don't ask, tell	*
4. Pass cap-and-trade	Y	8. Pass tax cuts for some	*	12. Limit campaign funds	N

Election Results

2010 general	Mark Kirk (R)	1,778,698	(48%)	($14,305,287)
	Alexander Giannoulias (D)	1,719,478	(46%)	($9,923,570)
	LeAlan Jones (Green)	117,914	(3%)	
	Mike Labno (Lib)	87,247	(2%)	
2010 primary	Mark Kirk (R)	420,373	(57%)	
	Patrick Hughes (R)	142,928	(19%)	
	Donald Lowery (R)	66,357	(9%)	
	Kathleen Thomas (R)	54,038	(7%)	
	Andy Martin (R)	37,480	(5%)	

Prior Winning Percentages: Special Senate: 2010 (47%); House: 2008 (53%); 2006 (53%); 2004 (64%); 2002 (69%); 2000 (51%)

The junior senator from Illinois is Republican Mark Kirk, who dealt President Obama one of the worst blows of the punishing 2010 election by winning the president's former Senate seat for the GOP. Kirk defeated Democrat Alexi Giannoulias, the state treasurer who got strong backing from Obama.

Kirk was born in downstate Illinois, but grew up mostly in Kenilworth, a wealthy suburb north of Chicago, along Lake Michigan. The son of a telephone company executive, he graduated from Cornell University and the London School of Economics. He got a job in the Washington office of Rep. John Porter, R-Ill., and rose to chief of staff in three years. Kirk left staff work on Capitol Hill in 1989 but stayed in Washington, doing stints first at the World Bank and then as a State

Department aide working on the Central American peace process, while earning a law degree at Georgetown University. After two years of international law practice, he served for five years as counsel to the House International Relations Committee. He is also a commander in the Naval Reserves.

In 1999, when Porter announced his retirement, Kirk returned home to the suburban 10th District, where he was one of 11 competitors in the Republican primary. This contest included six multi-millionaires who spent nearly $4 million of their own money. Kirk did not spend nearly as much, but he had great advantages: the endorsement of the popular Porter, his positioning as the only candidate with moderate views on cultural issues, and his greater experience in government. He won the primary with 31%, ahead of Shawn Margaret Donnelley, an R.R. Donnelley & Sons printing company heiress, who got 15%, and suburban Northbrook Mayor Mark Damisch, who got 14%.

Democrats nominated state Rep. Lauren Beth Gash. Kirk and Gash campaigned as candidates in the Porter mold, promising to carry on his fiscally conservative, culturally moderate record. Gash touted her legislative experience while talking about the need for action on Social Security solvency and affordable prescription drugs. But Kirk won 51%-49%.

After a few easy elections, Kirk held on by narrower margins in 2006 and 2008 as his centrist district broke strongly toward the Democrats. In those elections, he was twice challenged by Democrat Dan Seals, a marketing specialist who built well-financed grassroots campaigns. In 2006, the war in Iraq was a central issue. Kirk, while largely maintaining his support for the war, distanced himself from President George W. Bush and his handling of the conflict. The Democratic Congressional Campaign Committee did some last-minute spending for Seals, including a mailing in which Bush had his arm around Kirk. But it wasn't enough. Kirk won 53%-47%.

Seals ran again in 2008, a tough year for Republicans, especially those from the home state of Democratic presidential nominee Obama. Kirk kept his distance from the national GOP, and slammed John McCain's choice of Alaska Gov. Sarah Palin as his running mate by saying he would not have chosen her. The DCCC ran ads depicting Kirk as a rubber stamp for Bush. Kirk cited his independence and campaigned more aggressively this time, calling Seals a carpetbagger without a steady job. He raised $5.4 million to Seals' $3.5 million, and won by the same margin as 2006, 53% to 47%.

In the House, Kirk compiled a centrist voting record that leaned liberal on social issues and conservative on foreign policy. He supported abortion rights, and while he voted in 2009 against ending the "don't ask, don't tell" policy that bars homosexuals from serving openly in the military, he was generally supportive of gay rights. He received good marks from environmental groups and teamed with then-Democratic Rep. Rahm Emanuel of Illinois in 2005 to push through a sweeping bill to clean up the Great Lakes. He was one of eight Republicans to vote for the Democrats' 2009 energy bill putting limits on industrial carbon emissions, but later reversed positions in his Senate campaign. He supported Obama's troop increase in Afghanistan, but opposed the president's timetable for withdrawal.

Kirk decided to run for the Senate in 2010, after the seat was vacated by Democrat Roland Burris, who had been appointed by then Illinois Gov. Rod Blagojevich to fill Obama's unexpired term after he won the 2008 presidential election. Burris was soon neck-deep in the pay-to-play scandal that ended Blagojevich's political career. The Democratic governor was impeached by the Illinois General Assembly amid allegations he attempted to profit politically and personally from his power to make the Senate appointment. He was later convicted of lying to federal investigators. In the course of the scandal, Burris conceded to having several conversations with the governor's associates while the appointment was pending. His reputation badly damaged, Burris decided against seeking election to the seat in 2010.

As a fiscal conservative and foreign policy hawk, Kirk was the only socially moderate Republican with a chance of winning a Senate seat in 2010, the year of the tea party. In the February primary, he did not face a credible challenge from his right and avoided a tough primary challenge. Meanwhile, Giannoulias emerged from the Democratic primary bloodied, facing questions about his role in his family bank's loans to criminals and high-risk decisions that had put the bank in trouble. Federal regulators seized Broadway Bank in April 2010 after it became financially insolvent, and from then on, Giannoulias was unable to escape questions about his role in the bank's failure. He was a vice president of the bank from 2002 until he ran for state treasurer and won in 2006. Republican dubbed him the "mob banker."

National Democrats pulled out all the stops for Giannoulias, including two appearances by Obama, a friend who included Giannoulias in his pickup basketball games. A parade of administration officials and Democratic senators campaigned with Giannoulias or helped him raise money. He spent a cool $10 million, but Kirk still managed to top that with $14 million.

However, Kirk faced his own character issue. During the campaign, he was caught telling voters he had been previously named the Navy's intelligence officer of the year, which wasn't true. He also exaggerated other aspects of his military record. And he was on the defensive for some of his votes, including his support of the Wall Street bailout in 2008 and of the Democrats' cap-and-trade bill to curb carbon emissions associated with global warming. During the campaign, he said he no longer supported cap and trade because of its potential harm to businesses in the state. He told *National Journal*, "I didn't back away a little. I backed away entirely."

Television ads from both sides reflected the battle over character. Democrats' spots called Kirk a liar, while Republicans highlighted Giannoulias' connection to reputed organized crime figures. Polling in the contest see-sawed between the two candidates. Giannoulias benefited from a Democratic registration advantage and the outpouring of support from the White House, but he struggled to close the deal. Polls in the final weeks showed a large segment of the electorate, roughly 15%, still undecided. On Election Day, Kirk eked out a 48% to 46% victory.

Kirk said in the *National Journal* interview that in the Senate, he would look to work with "the people who are not in favor of new taxes but do not bring a strong social agenda to the table."

FIRST DISTRICT

Bobby Rush (D)

Elected 1992, 10th term; b. Nov. 23, 1946, Albany, GA; home, Chicago; Roosevelt U., B.A. 1973, U. of IL, M.A. 1994, McCormick Seminary, M.A. 1998; Baptist; married (Carolyn); 6 children (1 deceased).

Military Career: Army, 1963–68.

Elected Office: Chicago city alderman, 1983–92; 2nd ward committeeman, 1984–present.

Professional Career: Member, Student Non–Violent Coord. Cmte., 1966–68; Co–founder, IL Black Panther Party, 1968; Med. clinic dir., 1970-1973; Insurance agent, 1978-83.

DC Office: 2268 RHOB, 20515, 202-225-4372; Fax: 202-226-0333; Web site: house.gov/rush.

State Offices: Chicago, 773-224-6500; Midlothian, 708-385-9550.

Committees: *Energy & Commerce:* Commerce, Manufacturing & Trade; Communications & Technology; Energy & Power (RMM).

Group Ratings

	ACLU	ACU	ADA	CFG	AFS	FRC	LCV	ITIC	NTU	COC
2010	94	9	85	3	100	6	80	67	7	14
2009	–	0	100	2	100	–	100	–	2	47

National Journal Ratings

	2010 LIB	—	2010 CONS		2009 LIB	—	2009 CONS
Economic	65%	—	35%		70%	—	30%
Social	60%	—	39%		89%	—	0%
Foreign	72%	—	27%		66%	—	34%
Composite	66%	—	34%		77%	—	23%

Key Votes of the 111th Congress

1. Overturn Ledbetter	Y	5. Bar federal abortion funds	N	9. Stop detainee transfers	N
2. Pass $820 billion stimulus	Y	6. Pass health care bill	Y	10. Legalize immigrants' kids	Y
3. Let guns in national parks	N	7. Regulate financial firms	Y	11. Repeal don't ask, tell	Y
4. Pass cap-and-trade	Y	8. Pass tax cuts for some	Y	12. Limit campaign funds	N

Election Results

2010 general	Bobby Rush (D)	148,170	(80%)	($532,447)
	Raymond Wardingley (R)	29,253	(16%)	
	Jeff Adams (Green)	6,963	(4%)	
2010 primary	Bobby Rush (D)	68,585	(80%)	
	Joanne Guillemette (D)	8,035	(9%)	
	Fred Smith (D)	5,203	(6%)	

Prior Winning Percentages: 2008 (86%), 2006 (84%), 2004 (85%), 2002 (81%), 2000 (88%), 1998 (87%), 1996 (86%), 1994 (76%), 1992 (83%)

Population		Race/Ethnicity		Work	
Pop. 2010:	587,596	White:	25.8%	Private:	78.0%
Change since 2000:	Down 10.1%	Black:	62.2%	Government:	17.8%
Urban:	100.0%	Hispanic:	8.8%	Self-employed:	4.1%
Rural:	0.0%	Asian:	1.8%	Blue collar:	20.1%
Area size:	98 sq. mi.	Native Am.:	0.1%	White collar:	58.9%
		Hawaiian:	0.0%	Khaki collar:	0.0%
Age		Two+ races:	1.2%	Other:	20.9%
Median age:	35.1 yrs.				
More than 65 yrs:	12.9%	*Ancestry*		Median income:	$41,139
Less than 18 yrs:	26.1%	Irish	6.9%	Median Home Value:	$199,000
		German	6.2%		
Education		Polish	4.8%	**Military Veterans**	
H.S. grad:	83.8%			% of Pop:	7.9%
College grad:	21.4%				
Grad degree:	8.6%				

Chicago; South Side

The South Side of Chicago has been home to a large urban black community for nearly a century, which is one of the reasons why the city has the third largest African-American population in the nation, after New York and Atlanta. A hundred years ago, there were just a few blocks where black families from the South could settle. But the ghetto grew rapidly with the first influx of blacks from the Mississippi Delta in the 1910s. By the 1920s, the South Side was well

2008 Presidential Vote
Barack Obama (D) 251,102   (87%)
John McCain (R) 37,472   (13%)

2004 Presidential Vote
John Kerry (D) 234,086   (83%)
George Bush (R) 47,533   (17%)

Cook Partisan Voting Index: D+34

established, a center of black-owned businesses and of music, from blues to jazz. Politically, the South Side was a heavily Republican constituency throughout those years. The comfortable, white Protestants who settled in solid brick houses here believed in the party of Yankee propriety, while the blacks had faith in the party of Lincoln. This was a Republican Party heartland, represented in the House in the 1920s by Appropriations Chairman Martin Madden. After Madden died in the Appropriations Committee room in 1928, the 1st District elected Republican Oscar DePriest, the first African-American elected to the House in the 20th century. Blacks remained faithful to the party of Lincoln even during the Depression, voting for Herbert Hoover and DePriest in 1932.

The New Deal and the racial liberalism of New Dealers like Eleanor Roosevelt and Interior Secretary Harold Ickes, both former Republicans themselves, attracted blacks to the Democratic Party, and black Democrat Arthur Mitchell beat DePriest in 1934. The South Side has been Democratic ever since. For 40 years, it was a cooperative part of Chicago's Democratic machine. Then, after the death of longtime Rep. William Dawson, it rebelled against Mayor Richard J. Daley. The South Side seemed to take over the city when Rep. Harold Washington was elected mayor in 1983 and 1987. After he died in November 1987, other black South Side politicians were bogged down by infighting, though Chicago's black electorate peaked at about 40%.

The 1st Congressional District of Illinois includes about half of Chicago's African-American community on the South Side, plus many suburbs beyond the city boundaries. It is nearly two-thirds black. The 1st has a northern salient that includes some of Chicago's first black neighborhoods as well as the Gothic spires of the University of Chicago and the mansions of Kenwood, once the home of Chicago's Jewish aristocracy and now a more eclectic and racially integrated mix of well-to-do inhabitants. Kenwood is home to President Obama and first lady Michelle Obama. Bronzeville, once a destination point for thousands of black families from the South, lately has become popular with upscale professionals of diverse backgrounds, who reside in condos and townhouses. The Illinois Institute of Technology has attracted dozens of high-tech growth companies by building a research institute and business center. The district includes most of the South Side, from Stony Island west almost to the city limit and from 60th Street to 95th—miles and miles of bungalow neighborhoods, where single-family houses line arrow-straight streets. For 20 years, Barack Obama attended church at Trinity United Church of Christ, where the pastor was Jeremiah Wright; Wright's racially inflamed remarks later became controversial during Obama's quest for the White House.

In neighborhoods such as Englewood, once the city's second busiest shopping district before losing half of its population after 1970, thousands of private residential homes have been built with federal support in recent years in hopes of creating a new black middle-class community; some have been placed on vacant land or in abandoned buildings that had housed gangs. Illinois Gov. Pat Quinn in 2009 signed a tax credit for auto manufacturers, enabling Ford Motor Co. to bring jobs to the company's South Side assembly plant. A narrow neck of urban geography connects the city part of the 1st with a still mostly white collection of suburbs, starting with Blue Island and fanning southwest to Palos Heights, Orland Park, and Oak Forest. The district is overwhelmingly Democratic. Just 17% of people here voted for George W. Bush in 2004. Obama beat McCain in 2008, 87% to 13%.

Bobby Rush (D)

The congressman from the 1st District is Bobby Rush, a man who has gone through several transformations. He grew up on the North Side, a Boy Scout whose mother was a Republican precinct captain. While in the Army, he became involved in the Student Non-Violent Coordinating Committee in the South, then became disillusioned with the military and went AWOL in 1968. That year, he founded the Illinois Black Panthers, with its "Power to the People" slogan, and recruited Fred Hampton, who became chairman of the organization but was later killed by police in a 1969 raid. The next day, police raided Rush's family's apartment, but he wasn't there. Rush served six months in prison for illegal possession of firearms, but also during his time with the Black Panthers he ran a program providing free breakfasts to children and a medical clinic that developed the nation's first mass sickle-cell-anemia testing program. "I don't repudiate any of my involvement in the Panther party. It was part of my maturing," Rush later said. Lately, he has commemorated the anniversary of the raid by holding a job fair to promote the future. In 1983, he was elected the 2nd Ward alderman on the Chicago City Council and became a strong supporter of Harold Washington, who became mayor. As he built a career in politics, Rush went back to school and earned master's degrees in political science and theological studies. In 1992, he challenged Democratic Rep. Charles Hayes, an older-generation politician with a union background. Just before the primary, it was revealed that Hayes had 716 overdrafts on the House bank, a practice among lawmakers that blossomed into a national scandal. Rush won 42%-39%.

In the House, Rush has a liberal voting record. His rhetoric has softened over the years, and his more deliberate style contrasts sharply with his days as a Panther. Gun violence caused great pain to Rush in 1999, when his son Huey Rich, who was born three weeks before the 1969 police raid, was murdered by a man wielding a handgun as he returned to his South Side home with his fiancée. Ordained as a Baptist minister, Rush founded a church in 2002 in the depressed Englewood community, but it struggled financially. Legislatively, he has focused on children's health and the nursing shortage.

In recent years, he has devoted much of his time to the Energy and Commerce Committee, where he was chairman of the Commerce, Trade and Consumer Protection Subcommittee until Democrats lost control of the House in 2011. He is now the ranking Democrat on the Energy and Power Subcommittee. In the 111th Congress (2009-10), he worked on measures to protect companies' private information against data security breaches, to add protections to consumers' personal information and to ensure that tax-exempt hospitals treat patients without insurance. He also got an unexpected audience with Cuban leader Fidel Castro during an April 2009 visit to Havana. Rush told the *Chicago Tribune* that Castro said he respected his involvement with the Black Panthers because of its attitudes toward human rights.

Rush waged a quixotic campaign in 1999 against Richard M. Daley's iron grip on the mayor's office. Rush was a frequent Daley critic, and during the campaign he attacked the mayor for tolerating police brutality, inadequate mass transit service, and cronyism in city government. Only three of the 50 aldermen endorsed him, and although Rush tried to build a multiracial coalition, his only chance was with black voters. Daley was popular, and his financial advantage overwhelming. The incumbent won the primary 72%-28%, with nearly 45% of the African-American vote and the support of many prominent black ministers.

After that pounding, Rush found himself challenged in his own re-election primary in 2000 by two state senators—Donne Trotter and the then little-known Barack Obama. Obama waged an aggressive campaign, saying at the time that Rush "exemplifies a politics that is reactive, that waits for crises to happen then holds a press conference, and hasn't been particularly effective at building broad-based coalitions." But Obama came under attack for being absent from the legislature for two months and missing a vote on a gun control bill while on a family trip to Hawaii, where he was raised. "It was a race in which everything that could go wrong did go wrong," Obama later wrote in his book *The Audacity of Hope.* Rush was also helped by an endorsement from President Clinton and beat Obama 61%-30%. Surely not by coincidence, redistricting in 2002 shifted Obama's

Hyde Park home two blocks outside the new lines and removed the 19th Ward that he had carried. Rush has been routinely re-elected since then.

When Obama ran for the U.S. Senate in 2004, Rush backed Democrat Blair Hull, who finished third in the primary. Afterward, he endorsed Obama. During Obama's pitched battle with Hillary Rodham Clinton in the presidential primary four years later, Rush again endorsed Obama, calling it "one of the most difficult decisions I've had to make in politics."

In other political machinations in recent years, Rush in 2008 pushed to ensure that President-elect Obama's vacant Senate seat went to an African-American. He applauded Illinois Gov. Rod Blagojevich's appointment of Roland Burris, and then, when Burris declined to run for re-election in 2010, he backed former Chicago Urban League President Cheryle Robinson Jackson. After Jackson finished third in the Senate primary, Rush declined for months to endorse the winner, state Treasurer Alexi Giannoulias, who is white. He finally did so in October. After Daley announced he wouldn't run for re-election as mayor, Rush in early 2011 joined other black Democratic leaders in backing former U.S. Sen. Carol Moseley Braun. The job ultimately went to former Obama White House chief of staff Rahm Emanuel.

Rush had a brush with cancer in 2008. He was absent from Capitol Hill for much of the year recovering from salivary gland cancer and surgery to remove a tumor near his jaw. Doctors in August ruled him cancer free.

SECOND DISTRICT

Jesse Jackson, Jr. (D)

Elected Dec. 1995, 8th term; b. March 11, 1965, Greenville, SC; home, Chicago; NC A&T, B.S. 1987, Chicago Theological Seminary, M.A. 1990, U. of IL, J.D. 1993; Baptist; married (Sandi); 2 children.

Professional Career: Civil rights activist; Pres., Keep Hope Alive PAC, 1989–90; V.P., Operation PUSH, 1991–95; Field dir., Natl. Rainbow Coalition, 1993–95.

DC Office: 2419 RHOB, 20515, 202-225-0773; Fax: 202-225-0899; Web site: jackson.house.gov.

State Offices: Chicago, 773-734-9660; Homewood, 708-798-6000.

Committees: *Appropriations:* Labor, HHS, Education & Related Agencies; State, Foreign Operations & Related Programs.

Group Ratings

	ACLU	ACU	ADA	CFG	AFS	FRC	LCV	ITIC	NTU	COC
2010	88	0	100	0	100	6	100	67	7	13
2009	–	0	90	0	100	–	86	–	2	36

National Journal Ratings

	2010 LIB	—	2010 CONS	2009 LIB	—	2009 CONS
Economic	73%	—	25%	91%	—	0%
Social	82%	—	14%	89%	—	0%
Foreign	78%	—	17%	87%	—	9%
Composite	80%	—	21%	93%	—	7%

Key Votes of the 111th Congress

1. Overturn Ledbetter	Y	5. Bar federal abortion funds	N	9. Stop detainee transfers	Y
2. Pass $820 billion stimulus	Y	6. Pass health care bill	Y	10. Legalize immigrants' kids	Y
3. Let guns in national parks	N	7. Regulate financial firms	Y	11. Repeal don't ask, tell	Y
4. Pass cap-and-trade	Y	8. Pass tax cuts for some	Y	12. Limit campaign funds	Y

Election Results

2010 general	Jesse Jackson, Jr. (D)	150,666	(81%)	($795,723)
	Isaac Hayes (R)	25,883	(14%)	($74,664)
	Anthony Williams (Green)	10,564	(6%)	
2010 primary	Jesse Jackson, Jr. (D) .... unopposed			

Prior Winning Percentages: 2008 (89%), 2006 (85%), 2004 (88%), 2002 (82%), 2000 (90%), 1998 (89%), 1996 (94%), 1995 (76%)

Population		Race/Ethnicity		Work	
Pop. 2010:	602,758	White:	16.1%	Private:	79.3%
Change since 2000:	Down 7.8%	Black:	68.8%	Government:	17.2%
Urban:	99.9%	Hispanic:	13.0%	Self-employed:	3.4%
Rural:	0.1%	Asian:	0.6%	Blue collar:	22.9%
Area size:	192 sq. mi.	Native Am.:	0.2%	White collar:	56.0%
		Hawaiian:	0.0%	Khaki collar:	0.1%
Age		Two+ races:	1.3%	Other:	21.0%
Median age:	34.9 yrs.				
More than 65 yrs:	12.3%	*Ancestry*		Median income:	$44,225
Less than 18 yrs:	27.9%	German	4.7%	Median Home Value:	$155,900
		Irish	3.7%		
Education		Polish	3.3%	**Military Veterans**	
H.S. grad:	83.9%			% of Pop:	8.6%
College grad:	21.0%				
Grad degree:	7.6%				

Chicago; South Side

Chicago is a great center of both commerce and industry, and if the city's white-collar offices are heavily concentrated in the Loop, its blue-collar heavy industries are most visible on the far South Side. This part of Chicago, diminished in economic importance today, is historically significant and, with the remnants of its great, hulking factories around Lake Calumet and the nearby rail yards, has a certain, undeniable majesty. Thomas Geoghegan wrote in his book,

2008 Presidential Vote		
Barack Obama (D) 262,750	(90%)
John McCain (R) 28,748	(10%)
2004 Presidential Vote		
John Kerry (D) 230,613	(84%)
George Bush (R) 43,822	(16%)
Cook Partisan Voting Index: D+36		

Which Side Are You On?, of the fights to win benefits for the workers of shuttered steel mills and of the decline of the labor movement in a place where it got much of its inspiration. This is where the Pullman strike of 1894 was broken by federal troops and where policemen killed 10 union supporters in the Little Steel strike of 1937. Over the years, Chicago grew around the tight ethnic neighborhoods where workers went home at shift break each afternoon or midnight. Today, those workplaces are mostly empty buildings that suburbanites speed past on the Calumet and Dan Ryan expressways. The Hulett Iron Ore Unloaders, built in 1912 and resembling a giant praying mantis, have inspired local attempts at preservation.

The 2nd Congressional District of Illinois includes much of Chicago's old South Side industrial area; U.S. Cellular Field, the new home of the White Sox baseball team near the site of the old Comiskey Park; and several Cook County suburbs to the south. The district reaches north to include Jackson Park, where the Columbian Exposition of 1893 was held, and south to take in the South Shore, a once heavily Jewish neighborhood and now home to middle-class blacks. The district includes all of Chicago south of 95th Street and east of Interstate 57, including the old industrial area around Lake Calumet. Over the last two decades, the lake and the Calumet River have become popular angling spots, drawing a dozen or more bass fishing tournaments every summer.

The Chicago portion of the 2nd is overwhelmingly black, though many African-Americans, especially young parents fleeing Chicago public schools, are moving into suburbs directly to the south—Harvey, Dolton, Markham, Hazel Crest, and Lynwood. Farther south are economically revitalized Homewood and Flossmoor, with significant Jewish populations; high-income Olympia Fields; and the still vibrant Park Forest, the post World War planned town where William H. Whyte's *The Organization Man* was set. In the south end of the district is struggling Ford Heights, where a quarter of the households are single women with children, many of whom live in public housing. The 2nd District now has more people in the suburbs than in Chicago. Only 40% of the 2008 vote was cast in Chicago precincts. The district remains one of the most Democratic in the nation.

Jesse Jackson, Jr. (D)

The congressman from the 2nd District is Jesse Jackson Jr., a Democrat first elected at age 30 in 1995 and the son of civil rights leader Jesse Jackson, who ran for president in 1984 and 1988. Jesse Jackson Jr. was born in Greenville, S.C., while his father was marching to Selma. But he spent much of his early life in Washington, D.C., and attended the prestigious St. Albans School. He went to North Carolina A&T, his father's alma mater, earned a master's degree at Chicago Theological Seminary and a law degree at the University of Illinois. He spent his 21st birthday in a Washington, D.C., jail for protesting apartheid at the South African embassy. Jackson worked for his father's Rainbow Coalition and did not run for office until Democratic Rep. Mel Reynolds was driven from office in a sex scandal. In a 1995 special election, Jackson had serious competition from Democrat Emil Jones, then a state legislator for 23 years and later the state Senate President, who had the support of Mayor Richard M. Daley. Jones emphasized his clout and political experience. Jackson said being his father's son was a lifetime of political experience. He talked of bringing dollars to the South Side and, quoting longtime Illinois Democratic Rep. Dan Rostenkowski, said, "The only way one grows into leadership in Congress is to get elected young enough that you become speaker of the House or chairman of the Ways and Means Committee." Jackson won the primary 46%-37% and easily won the special election in December.

In the House, Jackson has combined liberal advocacy with careful attention to the interests of his constituents and to the steady advancement of his own influence. In 2001, he helped to create the National Center on Minority Health and Health Disparities at the National Institutes of Health. In recent years, he has sponsored few legislative bills, but nine constitutional amendments creating new rights, such as a right to "health care of equal high quality," to "decent, safe, sanitary, and affordable housing" and to "full employment and balanced economic growth." He plans to keep introducing his amendments "as long as I am alive and in Congress," he says. None have passed or are likely to, given the high hurdles to changing the Constitution. Topping Jackson's list of parochial projects is a long-standing proposal for a third Chicago-area airport in Peotone, 45 miles south of the Loop and just south of the district. He endorsed Gov. Pat Quinn for re-election in 2010 partly because of Quinn's support of the project. The fight has pitted him against fellow Democrats, whose priority has been expansion of O'Hare Airport. Jackson's allies have included Republicans from the northern suburbs who are worried about an increase in noise levels in neighborhoods around O'Hare.

Jackson has had a seat on the powerful Appropriations Committee for nearly a decade. After years of flirting with a race for mayor of Chicago, he seems content to remain in the House. Jackson has been careful not to exploit his high degree of name recognition, and, as an early and enthusiastic supporter of Barack Obama for president, he criticized as "reckless" his father's off-color gibes at Obama. At the same time, he has had his share of disagreements with the president, joining Congressional Black Caucus members in 2010 in complaining that the White House wasn't listening to their concerns. The movement of middle-class blacks to the far suburbs continues to diminish his core constituency, but Jackson's connection to the city's politics is still strong. In 2007, his wife, Sandi Jackson, a deputy political director of the Democratic National Committee, was elected alderman of Chicago's 7th Ward. Jackson received a Federal Election Commission advisory opinion in 2001 allowing him to pay her for consulting work without breaking rules on personal use of political donations. Since then, Jackson has hired his wife's chief of staff as a part-time "special assistant" to him while she earns a city salary. And Sandi Jackson's political committee paid for a statewide poll showing her husband as "the favorite" to replace Obama in the Senate.

After Obama's election in 2008, Jackson was caught up in the behind-the-scenes campaign for Obama's open Senate seat that led to the downfall of Illinois Gov. Rod Blagojevich, who was charged with trying to profit personally and politically from his power to appoint a successor. Jackson was "Senate Candidate Five" in the transcripts of prosecutors' wiretapped conversations, in which fundraising for Blagojevich was discussed. In comments aimed at persuading the public to "give me my name back," Jackson said: "I did not initiate or authorize anyone at any time to promise anything to Governor Blagojevich on my behalf....I thought, mistakenly, that the process was fair, aboveboard, and on the merits. I thought, mistakenly, that the governor was evaluating me and other Senate hopefuls based upon our credentials and qualifications."

Before the scandal broke, the *Chicago Sun-Times* endorsed Jackson as "a thoughtful, committed legislator" for the seat. But Senate Majority Leader Harry Reid quietly opposed his selection, reportedly because he did not believe Jackson could win a statewide election. Other events that year did not help Jackson's political future. The *Sun-Times* reported that fundraiser Raghuveer Nayak told federal authorities that Jackson had instructed him to approach then-Gov. Blagojevich with a campaign cash offer in exchange for the Senate seat. Though Jackson denied the allegation, he acknowledged another detail—his relationship with a nightclub hostess whom he had called a "social acquaintance." The revelations led him to avoid making public appearances around the district for much of his re-election campaign. He later told the Associated Press: "Every one of us has erred in their personal lives, and while I don't claim to be a perfect servant, I'm a public servant."

A House ethics investigation into the matter was delayed because the Justice Department planned to re-try Blagojevich, who was convicted in 2010 of just one of the 24 counts in his corruption case. Meanwhile, when Daley abruptly announced he would not seek re-election in 2011, Jackson helped broker a deal to have Rep. Danny Davis step aside in favor of former Sen. Carol Moseley Braun, so that black leaders could unite around one consensus candidate in the Democratic primary.

THIRD DISTRICT

Dan Lipinski (D)

Elected 2004, 4th term; b. July 15, 1966, Chicago; home, Western Springs; Northwestern U., B.S. 1988, Stanford U., M.A. 1989, Duke U., Ph.D. 1998; Catholic; married (Judy).

Professional Career: Asst. professor, U. of TN, 2001-04.

DC Office: 1717 LHOB, 20515, 202-225-5701; Fax: 202-225-1012; Web site: lipinski.house.gov.

State Offices: Chicago, 312-886-0481; LaGrange, 708-352-0524; Oak Lawn, 708-424-0853.

Committees: *Science & Technology:* Research & Science Education (RMM); Technology & Innovation. *Transportation & Infrastructure:* Aviation; Railroads, Pipelines & Hazardous Materials.

Group Ratings

	ACLU	ACU	ADA	CFG	AFS	FRC	LCV	ITIC	NTU	COC
2010	50	8	65	20	100	62	100	100	19	25
2009	–	8	90	6	100	–	86	–	8	43

National Journal Ratings

	2010 LIB — 2010 CONS		2009 LIB — 2009 CONS	
Economic	58% —	42%	57% —	42%
Social	44% —	55%	45% —	55%
Foreign	42% —	57%	53% —	44%
Composite	48% —	52%	52% —	48%

Key Votes of the 111th Congress

1. Overturn Ledbetter	Y	5. Bar federal abortion funds		9. Stop detainee transfers	Y
2. Pass $820 billion stimulus	Y	6. Pass health care bill	Y	10. Legalize immigrants' kids	N
3. Let guns in national parks	N	7. Regulate financial firms	Y	11. Repeal don't ask, tell	Y
4. Pass cap-and-trade	Y	8. Pass tax cuts for some	Y	12. Limit campaign funds	Y

Election Results

2010 general	Dan Lipinski (D)	116,120	(70%)	($752,199)
	Michael Bendas (R)	40,479	(24%)	($28,807)
	Laurel Schmidt (Green)	10,028	(6%)	
2010 primary	Dan Lipinski (D)	57,684	(78%)	
	Jorge Mujica (D)	16,372	(22%)	

Prior Winning Percentages: 2008 (73%), 2006 (77%), 2004 (73%)

Population		Race/Ethnicity		Work	
Pop. 2010:	663,381	White:	54.5%	Private:	82.2%
Change since 2000:	Up 1.5%	Black:	6.8%	Government:	13.7%
Urban:	100.0%	Hispanic:	34.0%	Self-employed:	4.0%
Rural:	0.0%	Asian:	3.5%	Blue collar:	26.4%
Area size:	126 sq. mi.	Native Am.:	0.1%	White collar:	55.2%
		Hawaiian:	0.0%	Khaki collar:	0.0%
Age		Two+ races:	1.0%	Other:	18.4%
Median age:	35.8 yrs.				
More than 65 yrs:	12.4%	*Ancestry*		Median income:	$55,815
Less than 18 yrs:	26.4%	Irish	13.3%	Median Home Value:	$253,000
		Polish	12.4%		
Education		German	10.2%	**Military Veterans**	
H.S. grad:	80.6%			% of Pop:	7.0%
College grad:	23.8%				
Grad degree:	8.9%				

West and South Chicago Suburbs

A century ago, humorist Finley Peter Dunne's fictional Mr. Dooley pontificated on matters political in a saloon on Archery Road. This was Archer Avenue on the South Side of Chicago, one of the radial streets that cut across what was once open prairie near the Loop and along the Chicago River. Archer Avenue was one of the paths of outward migration and upward mobility for the children and grandchildren of Chicago's ethnic and cultural groups, and still is. Even today,

2008 Presidential Vote		
Barack Obama (D) 158,161	(64%)
John McCain (R) 86,406	(35%)
2004 Presidential Vote		
John Kerry (D) 144,657	(59%)
George Bush (R) 100,257	(41%)
Cook Partisan Voting Index: D+11		

in Archer Heights, you can scarcely go a block without hearing someone speaking Polish. Italians from the river wards along the Chicago and Sanitary Ship Canal moved west, the South Side Irish moved west and south along Cicero Avenue toward Oak Lawn, and the Bohemians (as they were called then; now Czechs) were heavily concentrated in the neat bungalows of industrial suburbs like Berwyn. Today, Latinos are driving these same avenues, up before dawn to arrive at factory jobs, or taking CTA "El" trains to the Loop or to "edge city" jobs along the expressways. Midway Airport, Chicago's main airport from 1927 until O'Hare Airport opened in 1955, is now a busy discount-airline hub. It has been renovating and expanding its congested terminals and parking lots, all squeezed into the heart of a busy commercial area on the Southwest Side.

The 3rd Congressional District of Illinois consists of much of this territory, crisscrossed by grid-pattern streets, the canal, the railroad lines, and the switching yards so common in this, the center of the nation's rail network. It is part of Chicago's bungalow belt, with one after another of the ubiquitous peaked brick houses neatly lining every street like Monopoly pieces, the handiwork of Swedish, Italian, and Polish masons. The 3rd also includes the far southwest edge of Chicago, most of the suburbs of Berwyn and Riverside, with its early-20th-century prairie-style houses, and a few older, affluent suburbs like Western Springs and the more recent and middle-income expanses of Oak Lawn and Palos Hills.

In the Archer Avenue city neighborhoods, Poles cling to their heritage, with more than 20 weekend schools teaching Polish to local kids and adults. A narrow corridor extends to the famed Bridgeport neighborhood, the lifetime home of the late Mayor Richard J. Daley, father of former Mayor Richard M. Daley, and the storied Irish stronghold that produced four other Chicago mayors. In recent years, Bridgeport has diversified, as Hispanics and Asians have moved in along with artists taking studio space in old warehouses. But it still attracts few African-American families, wary of Bridgeport's history of racial hostility and violence. The district's overall Hispanic population increased to 34% in 2010, making it the second largest in the state. Politically, this has been marginal territory: ancestrally Democratic, culturally conservative, multiethnic and viscerally patriotic. Of the seven congressional districts that include parts of Chicago, the 3rd has cast the highest percentages for Republican presidential candidates, though the GOP vote has fallen well short of a majority.

Dan Lipinski (D)

The congressman from the 3rd District is Democrat Dan Lipinski, first elected in 2004 and the son of Rep. Bill Lipinski, who represented the district for 22 years. Dan Lipinski grew up in Chicago, in the city's 23rd Ward, and first served as a campaign volunteer for his father in 1979. He got engineering degrees from Northwestern and Stanford universities before switching to political science with his doctorate at Duke. He worked on the staffs of four House Democrats from Illinois, though not on his father's, and was an American Political Science Association congressional fellow for the House Democratic Policy Committee. He wrote his doctoral thesis on the topic of congressional newsletters (*Congressional Communication,* published by the University of Michigan Press). At the beginning of 2004, he was an assistant professor of political science at the University of Tennessee in Knoxville.

The process behind Lipinski's nomination to run for his father's seat is a case study in Chicago's still thriving backroom politics. In the summer of 2004, Bill Lipinski denied widespread rumors that he was going to give up his seat. Then on Aug. 13, he abruptly announced he would not seek re-election in November because he wanted to return to Chicago and "spend more time with my wife." (Not *that* much time as it turns out, because he later became a transportation lobbyist.) His announcement came just 13 days before the Aug. 26 deadline to replace a withdrawing candidate. A meeting was scheduled for Aug. 17 for the 19 ward and township Democratic committeemen in the 3rd District. The group was to choose the new nominee by weighted vote and consisted of a *Who's Who* of connected Chicago politicians, including John Daley, the 11th Ward committeeman and brother of then-Mayor Richard M. Daley; Michael Madigan, the 13th Ward committeeman and speaker of the Illinois House; Edward Burke, the 14th Ward committeeman and husband of an Illinois Appeals Court judge; and, apparently not feeling the need for a pretense of objectivity, Bill Lipinski, the 23rd Ward committeeman. At the meeting, Lipinski offered for consideration the name of the most qualified person he could think of, his son, Dan, and shortly afterward, he was nominated without opposition.

The nominee was not briefed quite as well by the political pros in the room as he perhaps should have been. At his first press conference, Lipinski, who had not lived in Illinois for 15 years, made the politically unconscionable assertion that he had for many years been a fan of the Chicago Cubs, Chicago's North Side baseball team. The White Sox are the hands-down favorite team of the 3rd District's South Side neighborhoods and suburbs. A state lawmaker at the back of the room signaled Lipinski to wrap up his remarks before further damage could be done. Luckily for Lipinski, a Democratic nomination, even one decided by a group of longtime political pals getting together in a room, is tantamount to election in the 3rd District, and he sailed to victory in November. The Republican nominee was Ryan Chlada, a 26-year-old bar owner who won the GOP nomination unopposed. Chlada avoided publicity, had no website, and filed no federal campaign reports, which is legal if a candidate does not raise much money. Lipinski won, 73%-25%.

In the House, Dan Lipinski has kept his pledge to be "not really that different from my father," who was the most conservative Democrat in the Illinois delegation. He opposes same-sex marriage and abortion rights except when the mother's life is at stake. He was among the Democrats who declined to vote for California liberal Nancy Pelosi in 2011 as their party's leader in the House; he cast his vote for Rep. Marcy Kaptur, an Ohioan who is the House's most senior woman. A year earlier, he declined to support the Democrats' health care overhaul, saying that its provision banning federal funds for abortions wasn't strong enough even as other anti-abortion Democrats expressed satisfaction with it. As a member of the Science and Technology Committee, he worked on reauthorizing the National Science Foundation in 2010. The same year, he won House passage of a measure setting up a national manufacturing strategy; the measure died in the Senate.

Also like his father, Lipinski has focused on local transportation projects, especially helping Midway Airport, which generates more jobs than any other employer in the district, and on improving Chicago's rail infrastructure. In his second term, he played a key role on two pieces of that year's massive energy bill: cash incentives for progress toward hydrogen-based energy and a mandate requiring high-efficiency light bulbs in federal buildings. He has drawn attention in recent years for introducing unsuccessful bills to set a standard limit on the size of carry-on baggage for airplanes, a cause his father also backed. The decision is currently left to each airline.

Lipinski drew significant primary opposition in his first two re-election bids. In 2006, John Sullivan, an assistant Cook County state's attorney, made an issue of Lipinski getting the seat in "a backroom deal." Financial planner John Kelly used "no tricks, no fix" as a campaign slogan. Lipinski won with 54%, to 26% for Kelly and 20% for Sullivan. In the 2008 primary, Lipinski faced Cook County Assistant State's Attorney Mark Pera, an abortion rights supporter who criticized Lipinski's support for the war in Iraq and questioned his campaign payments to his father for consulting work. Liberal interest groups, local reformers, and others contributed to Pera, who spent $770,000. But Lipinski prevailed, 54%-25%.

In 2010, however, his only primary challenger was little-known immigration activist Jorge Mujica, and Lipinski got nearly 78% of the vote. Even so, the district's fast-growing Hispanic population could spell electoral worries in the future.

FOURTH DISTRICT

Luis Gutierrez (D)

Elected 1992, 10th term; b. Dec. 10, 1953, Chicago; home, Chicago; NE IL U., B.A. 1975; Catholic; married (Soraida); 2 children.

Elected Office: Chicago city alderman, 1986–92, Pres. pro tem, 1989–92.

Professional Career: Teacher, Puerto Rico, 1977–78; Social wkr., Chicago Dept. of Children & Family Svcs., 1979–83; Advisor, Chicago Mayor Harold Washington, 1984–86.

DC Office: 2266 RHOB, 20515, 202-225-8203; Fax: 202-225-7810; Web site: gutierrez.house.gov.

State Offices: Chicago, 312-342-0774.

Committees: *Financial Services:* Financial Institutions & Consumer Credit; Insurance, Housing & Community Opportunity (RMM). *Permanent Select Committee on Intelligence:* Terrorism, HUMINT, Analysis & Counterintelligence.

Group Ratings

	ACLU	ACU	ADA	CFG	AFS	FRC	LCV	ITIC	NTU	COC
2010	87	0	90	0	100	0	70	100	7	14
2009	–	0	100	0	100	–	100	–	3	33

National Journal Ratings

	2010 LIB — 2010 CONS		2009 LIB — 2009 CONS	
Economic	90%	— 0%	91%	— 0%
Social	71%	— 25%	80%	— 20%
Foreign	73%	— 27%	91%	— 0%
Composite	80%	— 20%	90%	— 10%

Key Votes of the 111th Congress

1. Overturn Ledbetter	Y	5. Bar federal abortion funds	N	9. Stop detainee transfers	N
2. Pass $820 billion stimulus	Y	6. Pass health care bill	Y	10. Legalize immigrants' kids	Y
3. Let guns in national parks	N	7. Regulate financial firms	Y	11. Repeal don't ask, tell	Y
4. Pass cap-and-trade	Y	8. Pass tax cuts for some	Y	12. Limit campaign funds	Y

Election Results

2010 general	Luis Gutierrez (D)	63,273	(77%)	($512,939)
	Israel Vasquez (R)	11,711	(14%)	
	Robert Burns (Green)	6,808	(8%)	
2010 primary	Luis Gutierrez (D)	34,000	(99%)	

Prior Winning Percentages: 2008 (81%), 2006 (86%), 2004 (84%), 2002 (80%), 2000 (89%), 1998 (82%), 1996 (94%), 1994 (75%), 1992 (78%)

Population		Race/Ethnicity		Work	
Pop. 2010:	601,156	White:	18.9%	Private:	88.3%
Change since 2000:	Down 8.0%	Black:	4.2%	Government:	7.9%
Urban:	100.0%	Hispanic:	73.5%	Self-employed:	3.8%
Rural:	0.0%	Asian:	2.3%	Blue collar:	32.3%
Area size:	40 sq. mi.	Native Am.:	0.1%	White collar:	46.2%
		Hawaiian:	0.0%	Khaki collar:	0.1%
Age		Two+ races:	0.8%	Other:	21.4%
Median age:	29.7 yrs.				
More than 65 yrs:	6.6%	*Ancestry*		Median income:	$42,452
Less than 18 yrs:	28.3%	German	4.9%	Median Home Value:	$293,000
		Irish	4.3%		
Education		Polish	4.1%	**Military Veterans**	
H.S. grad:	64.7%			% of Pop:	2.7%
College grad:	22.4%				
Grad degree:	7.4%				

Chicago; North and Southwest Sides

Just west of the Loop, the Chicago River splits into the North and South Branches, both penetrating the heart of old neighborhoods where immigrants got their start. The South Branch is the guts of Chicago, the site of one of Western civilization's astonishing engineering feats. In 1900, the course of the river was reversed so that sewage flowed downstate through a canal rather than out into Lake Michigan. Just blocks away was Maxwell Street, then thronged with market

2008 Presidential Vote		
Barack Obama (D)	126,399	(85%)
John McCain (R)	19,777	(13%)
2004 Presidential Vote		
John Kerry (D)	105,419	(79%)
George Bush (R)	27,684	(21%)
Cook Partisan Voting Index:	D+32	

stalls and long the arrival point for Chicago-bound Jews. Not far away in an Italian-American neighborhood on Halsted Street was Jane Addams's Hull House, the original settlement house, where social workers instructed new immigrants on adapting to American life. To the south were Pilsen, arrival neighborhood for the Bohemians (Czechs), and the Irish neighborhoods along Archer Avenue. To the north was Milwaukee Avenue, the main street of Polish-Americans and Ukrainian-Americans.

Today, many of these places are arrival neighborhoods again, mostly for Chicago's wide variety of Hispanic immigrants. On the South Side, in the old river wards, is Chicago's Mexican-American community, extending west into Pilsen and into the once Bohemian suburb of Cicero, famous as a haven for Al Capone's mobsters in the 1920s. This is the largest community of Mexican-Americans in the nation outside California. There are also many Mexicans, plus Puerto Ricans and other Hispanics, on the edges of the gentrifying North Side. This is by far the largest Latino concentration north of Texas and Florida and between the two coasts.

The 4th Congressional District of Illinois is a Hispanic-majority district, first created after the 1990 census. With the South Side Mexican-American areas and the smaller North Side Puerto Rican communities separated by the West Side black ghetto, the solution was the creation of one of the most bizarrely shaped congressional districts in the country. Essentially these two Latino communities, defined by careful boundaries to maximize the district's Hispanic percentage, are connected by a thin line of territory stretching around the black-majority 7th District to meet at the Cook-DuPage County line. The district is sandwiched between the 5th District to the north and the 3rd District to the south. It is shaped something like a pair of earmuffs. More than 95% of the votes are in Chicago or Cicero. In 2010, the population was 74% Hispanic, with Mexicans (56%) far outnumbering Puerto Ricans (9%) and other Hispanics (6%). The proportions of voters are different, since all Puerto Ricans and most non-Hispanics in the district are U.S. citizens, while some 29% of district residents, the large majority of them Mexican, are not.

Luis Gutierrez (D)

The congressman from the 4th District is Luis Gutierrez, a Democrat and the first Hispanic member of Congress from Illinois. He has represented the district since it was created in 1992. Gutierrez (*goo-tee-AIR-ez*) is of Puerto Rican descent and grew up in Chicago. As a student at Northeastern Illinois University in the 1970s, he joined a protest of the lack of basic English classes for students from other countries, which ended up with the protesters taking over an administration building. Gutierrez worked as a teacher for two years in Puerto Rico after college. When he returned to Chicago, he worked as a cab driver and social worker. In 1983, he ran for 32nd Ward committeeman against Democratic U.S. Rep. Dan Rostenkowski and lost decisively. Then he became a staffer for Mayor Harold Washington, the city's first black mayor. He ran for alderman in 1984 and lost. In 1986, he ran again and won in one of two new Hispanic-majority wards. After Washington died, Gutierrez backed Richard M. Daley in the 1989 election. Backing winners is a formula that works in Chicago politics. In the 1992 primary, for the new House seat, rival Alderman Juan Solis called Gutierrez a machine candidate. Gutierrez won, 60%-40%. Since easily winning a rematch in 1994, Gutierrez has not had serious competition.

In the House, Gutierrez has staked out liberal positions, and is known for his feisty, blunt style. As a freshman, his outspoken opposition to congressional pay raises, including labeling the House "the belly of the beast" in a television interview, got him into hot water with Democratic leaders. "I've gotten my rear end kicked around here," Gutierrez told *The Washington Post*. Gutierrez was denied seats on choice committees, and he has stayed on the Financial Services Committee, which may have seemed a backwater then, before the financial crisis. Now the panel is at the center of major economic debates. Gutierrez chaired the Financial Institutions and Consumer Credit Subcommittee when Democrats controlled the House and now is the ranking minority member on the Subcommittee on Insurance, Housing, and Community Opportunity. In 2009, he proposed higher FDIC charges for big banks and lower fees for community banks. He also sponsored the $200 billion receivership fund (later reduced to $150 billion) for banks, which was included in the financial regulation bill of 2010. "This is not a bailout fund," he said. "This is a dissolution fund."

His major effort in recent years has been pushing for a comprehensive immigration bill. Over the years, he has pushed to restore food stamp eligibility to legal immigrants, to grant automatic citizenship to immigrants in military combat, and legal status to immigrants without documentation who make major contributions in the United States. "I want to be a spokesperson for people that are new to this country," he has said. In 2005, he was the lead Democratic sponsor of the House version of an overhaul in immigration policy, which passed the Senate in 2006 but died in the Republican-controlled House. In the 110th Congress (2007-08), he revived the bill with a provision to allow illegal immigrants who had been employed in the U.S. before June 1, 2006, to apply for "conditional non-immigrant status." After an appearance on MSNBC to debate the immigration issue, Gutierrez got into a shoving match with then-Rep. Tom Tancredo of Colorado, a Republican known for his tough, anti-illegal immigrant positions. Gutierrez said afterward, "It wasn't my best moment."

In March 2010, Gutierrez said he would vote against the Democrats' sweeping health care bill because it barred illegal immigrants from the proposed insurance exchanges; two days before the vote, he switched and said he would vote yes. For much of the 111th Congress (2009-10), he pressed the Obama White House and the House Democratic leadership to advance comprehensive immigration legislation, to no avail. When Arizona Gov. Jan Brewer signed a bill authorizing immigration status checks of people stopped by police, Gutierrez in April 2010 called for federal intervention, and the next month, was arrested in a demonstration outside the White House.

Gutierrez has weighed in on Puerto Rican issues. He stoutly opposed the Democratic leadership's bill mandating a referendum on the current commonwealth status in Puerto Rico, and, if that were rejected, giving Puerto Rican voters a choice between the current status and independence. "This bill is not the product of consensus. It does not provide for true self-determination. The two-step process in the bill is designed to craft an artificial majority for statehood," he argued. The House passed the bill 223-169 in April 2010, but it died in the Senate.

In 2008, Gutierrez was the subject of unflattering news coverage about real estate deals with local developers. The *Chicago Tribune* reported that starting in 2002, Gutierrez had made about $421,000 by investing in half a dozen real estate deals with campaign supporters and then exiting a short time later. Gutierrez told the newspaper that he had made a profit in five of the deals but lost money on the sixth. Developer Calvin Boender, who loaned him $200,000 in a 2004 real estate deal, was convicted on bribery charges in March 2010. During the trial, there was testimony that Gutierrez helped Boender get a zoning change for a development on the West Side of Chicago.

Though he often plays the rebel, Gutierrez has been capable of building bridges as well. In the past, he has brought together Chicago's fractious Democratic politicians to maximize Latino influence. He considered running for mayor of Chicago, but decided against challenging Mayor Richard Daley after Democrats regained the House majority in 2006. In early 2009, he announced he would retire from Congress but reversed that decision in time for the candidate filing deadline. In the February 2011 mayoral election, he endorsed Chicago schools chief Gery Chico. Had he chosen Emanuel, he would have backed a winner.

FIFTH DISTRICT

Mike Quigley (D)

Elected April 2009, 2nd full term; b. Oct. 17, 1958, Indianapolis, IN; home, Chicago; Roosevelt U., B.A. 1981; U. of Chicago, M.P.P. 1985; Loyola U., J.D. 1989.; married (Barbara); 2 children.

Elected Office: Cook Cnty. commissioner, 1998-2009.

Professional Career: Cook Co. aldermanic aide, 1983-89; Adjct. prof., Roosevelt U., 2006-07; Adjct. prof. in political science, Loyola U. Chicago, 2002-09; Practicing atty., 1990-present.

DC Office: 1124 LHOB, 20515, 202-225-4061; Fax: 202-225-5603; Web site: quigley.house.gov.

State Offices: Chicago, 773-267-5926.

Committees: *Judiciary:* Constitution; Courts, Commercial & Administrative Law; Crime, Terrorism & Homeland Security. *Oversight & Government Reform:* National Security, Homeland Defense & Foreign Operations; TARP, Financial Services & Bailouts of Public & Private Programs (RMM).

Group Ratings

	ACLU	ACU	ADA	CFG	AFS	FRC	LCV	ITIC	NTU	COC
2010	83	4	95	0	100	0	100	100	7	29
2009	–	0	–	13	80	–	100	–	6	42

National Journal Ratings

	2010 LIB — 2010 CONS		2009 LIB — 2009 CONS	
Economic	71%	— 29%	62%	— 38%
Social	82%	— 14%	64%	— 36%
Foreign	84%	— 11%	91%	— 0%
Composite	81%	— 20%	74%	— 26%

Key Votes of the 111th Congress

1. Overturn Ledbetter	*	5. Bar federal abortion funds	N	9. Stop detainee transfers	N
2. Pass $820 billion stimulus	*	6. Pass health care bill	Y	10. Legalize immigrants' kids	Y
3. Let guns in national parks	N	7. Regulate financial firms	Y	11. Repeal don't ask, tell	Y
4. Pass cap-and-trade	Y	8. Pass tax cuts for some	Y	12. Limit campaign funds	Y

Election Results

2010 general	Mike Quigley (D)	108,360	(71%)	($1,301,374)
	David Ratowitz (R)	38,935	(25%)	($65,556)
	Matthew Reichel (Green)	6,140	(4%)	
2010 primary	Mike Quigley (D)	unopposed		

Prior Winning Percentages: 2009 special (69%)

Population		Race/Ethnicity		Work	
Pop. 2010:	648,610	White:	60.0%	Private:	84.7%
Change since 2000:	Down 0.8%	Black:	2.7%	Government:	10.1%
Urban:	100.0%	Hispanic:	28.8%	Self-employed:	5.1%
Rural:	0.0%	Asian:	6.6%	Blue collar:	18.6%
Area size:	58 sq. mi.	Native Am.:	0.2%	White collar:	64.7%
		Hawaiian:	0.0%	Khaki collar:	0.1%
Age		Two+ races:	1.6%	Other:	16.7%
Median age:	34.0 yrs.				
More than 65 yrs:	10.4%	*Ancestry*		Median income:	$59,915
Less than 18 yrs:	20.5%	Polish	12.2%	Median Home Value:	$348,800
		German	11.8%		
Education		Irish	10.5%	**Military Veterans**	
H.S. grad:	84.8%			% of Pop:	4.5%
College grad:	40.6%				
Grad degree:	15.8%				

Chicago; North Side

Few places in America today have more ethnic and cultural variety than the North Side of Chicago. This has been the destination of one immigrant group after another and its neighborhoods harbor all manner of successful, middle-class people. Wooden workingmen's cottages from the late 19th century give way to sturdy brick houses from the early 1900s, and then to the prairie bungalows of the 1920s and the white-shuttered, orange-brick colonials of the 1950s. Chi-

2008 Presidential Vote		
Barack Obama (D) 181,458	(73%)
John McCain (R) 63,733	(26%)

2004 Presidential Vote		
John Kerry (D) 161,348	(67%)
George Bush (R) 79,349	(33%)

Cook Partisan Voting Index: D+19

cago was America's top immigrant destination for Poles, Lithuanians, Czechs, Slovaks, Ukrainians, and Romanians. Something about the heavy, dull clouds of the long winters, the short, hot summers, and a climate suited to potatoes and cabbage and other hardy vegetables, may have reminded them of central and eastern Europe. By the late 1980s, upwardly mobile immigrants from Mexico and Guatemala, Korea, and the Philippines were moving in. The 1990s witnessed new rounds of immigrants from Poland and Ukraine, and also from Pakistan, India, and Bosnia. Family ties, webs of acquaintances that reach back to ancestral villages, have made the North Side of Chicago a natural port of entry for Eastern bloc migrants, even as other newcomers arrive with relationships extending to Latin America and Southeast Asia.

The 5th Congressional District covers an oddly shaped swath across Chicago's North Side, running from the lakefront to the suburbs directly south of O'Hare Airport. The 5th includes Chicago's most glamorous lakefront apartments facing the Oak Street Beach and the gentrified neighborhoods of Old Town, where Crate & Barrel was founded in 1962 and where old houses and factories are being converted into upscale condominiums, often over the objections of preservationists. Nearby Lincoln Park abounds with boutiques. It also features clubs and restaurants and had the highest median household income of Chicago's 77 community areas in a DePaul University study of 2000 census data. The district is home to baseball's famed Wrigley Field, which opened in 1914 and is a protected landmark that has defied the teardown trend in ballparks and endured the heartbreak of the Cubs. After taking over as the Cubs' new owner in 2009, businessman Tom Ricketts unveiled a renovation plan costing upward of $200 million to remodel and update the ballpark, but state officials and the public balked at the initial outlines.

The district takes in the Polish-American and Ukrainian-American neighborhoods, with their own museums around Milwaukee Avenue, and the old Italian neighborhoods running west on Grand Avenue. A couple of blocks from the Chicago River is the grand, old St. Stanislaus Kostka Church, a traditional center of the Polish community since the 19th century that now conducts Masses in Spanish. With the increase of Hispanic population to 29% in 2010, a language other than English is spoken in 46% of the district's households. The district's politics are vintage Chicago. Longtime political consultant Don Rose says, "The 5th is the second-toughest machine-controlled Democratic congressional district in Chicago. It differs slightly from the conservative 3rd District because of a handful of independent-liberal lakefront precincts comprising 18 percent of the vote." This is a solidly Democratic district. In 2008, Barack Obama won here 73%-26%.

Mike Quigley (D)

The congressman from the 5th District is Mike Quigley, a Democrat who won a special election in April 2009 to succeed Democratic Rep. Rahm Emanuel after Emanuel was named President Obama's White House chief of staff. Quigley grew up in the working-class suburb of Carol Stream in DuPage County. He graduated from Roosevelt University, got his law degree from Loyola University in Chicago, and practiced criminal law. He also taught political science part-time at Loyola. He started his career in politics as an aide to Ald. Bernard Hansen while studying for a master's degree in public policy from the University of Chicago. He got involved in a community battle to stop the addition of lights for night games at Wrigley Field, which is in the heart of an old, gentrified neighborhood. In 1998, Quigley was elected to the Cook County Board, where he became an independent voice and a frequent nemesis of board President John Stroger. He pushed reforms such as ending patronage jobs at the Cook County Forest Preserve District, promoted environmental action, and sponsored a proposal to allow gay and lesbian couples to register as domestic partners. In 2005, Quigley decided to challenge Stroger for board president, but later dropped out and backed Forrest Claypool, saying the two would have split the anti-incumbent vote if they had both remained in the race. Claypool repaid the favor by endorsing Quigley for the House seat.

After Obama plucked Emanuel from the House, a long list of candidates jumped into the wide-open Democratic primary. State Rep. Sara Feigenholtz was endorsed by EMILY's List. Ald. Patrick O'Connor and state Rep. John Fritchey had local party machine support. The appointment of Roland Burris to the Senate by impeached Democratic Gov. Rod Blagojevich became a campaign issue, with candidates seeking to burnish their credentials as reformers and attacking their opponents for having been associated with the disgraced governor. Fritchey suffered from having defended Burris at a legislative hearing in January 2009. Quigley ran a late ad comparing Feigenholtz to President Nixon, saying she had resorted to unfair campaign charges. That may have extinguished any lingering friendship between Quigley and Feigenholtz, who had dated briefly years earlier.

Quigley received key newspaper endorsements from the *Chicago Sun-Times* and the *Chicago Tribune,* the latter praising him for an "outstanding record of independent, reform-minded performance in office." In a low-turnout event on March 3, Quigley won with 20% of the vote to 17% for Fritchey and 15% for Feigenholtz. He ran especially well in the "lakefront liberal" wards. Fritchey's support from organization bosses and Feigenholtz's backing by women's groups failed to deliver. Quigley then breezed to victory in the April 7 general election against Republican Rosanna Pulido.

In the House, Quigley has sought to establish himself as a reform-minded Democrat who is unafraid to ruffle feathers. Shortly after taking office, he supported Arizona Republican Rep. Jeff Flake's push for an ethics investigation of then-Rep. John Murtha, D-Pa. and other senior appropriators. He co-founded the Congressional Transparency Caucus and introduced legislation requiring lobbyists to disclose the name of each affected executive branch official and the office of each member of Congress and staff with whom they meet. He also sponsored a bill requiring lawmakers to file financial disclosure forms electronically. He joined fellow Oversight and Government Reform Committee member Paul Hodes, D-N.H., in October 2009 in calling for a formal investigation of Countrywide Financial's "VIP" mortgage program that allegedly offered favorable deals to federal officials.

On the Judiciary Committee, Quigley joined Republicans in November 2009 to support retaining a section of the USA Patriot Act making it easier for investigators to monitor phone calls of suspected "lone wolf" terrorists. In 2010, he complained about the Democratic leadership's decision to move a campaign finance bill that exempted the National Rifle Association from disclosing its membership rolls and the donors behind its political ads.

Quigley coasted to re-election in 2010 with 71% of the vote. In the weeks leading up to the election, he toyed with the idea of running in 2011 to succeed retiring Chicago Mayor Richard M. Daley but decided not to join the crowded field that included Emanuel among the aspirants. In the end, Emanuel was elected Chicago mayor.

SIXTH DISTRICT

Peter Roskam (R)

Elected 2006, 3rd term; b. Sept. 13, 1961, Hinsdale; home, Wheaton; U. of IL, B.A. 1983, Chicago-Kent Col. of Law, J.D. 1989; Anglican; married (Elizabeth); 4 children.

Elected Office: IL House, 1992-98; IL Senate, 2000-06, Min. Whip, 2003-06.

Professional Career: Aide, U.S. Rep. Tom DeLay, 1985-86, U.S. Rep. Henry Hyde, 1986-87; High school teacher, 1983-85; Exec. Dir., Educational Assistance Ltd., 1987-1993; Practicing atty., 1994-2006.

DC Office: 227 CHOB, 20515, 202-225-4561; Fax: 202-225-1166; Web site: roskam.house.gov.

State Offices: Bloomingdale, 630-893-9670.

Committees: *Ways & Means:* Health; Select Revenue Measures.

Group Ratings

	ACLU	ACU	ADA	CFG	AFS	FRC	LCV	ITIC	NTU	COC
2010	13	100	5	75	0	100	0	33	89	86
2009	–	100	0	88	11	–	29	–	84	80

National Journal Ratings

	2010 LIB	—	2010 CONS		2009 LIB	—	2009 CONS
Economic	20%	—	80%		17%	—	82%
Social	0%	—	85%		24%	—	73%
Foreign	12%	—	79%		26%	—	68%
Composite	15%	—	85%		24%	—	76%

Key Votes of the 111th Congress

1. Overturn Ledbetter	N	5. Bar federal abortion funds	Y	9. Stop detainee transfers	Y
2. Pass $820 billion stimulus	N	6. Pass health care bill	N	10. Legalize immigrants' kids	N
3. Let guns in national parks	Y	7. Regulate financial firms	N	11. Repeal don't ask, tell	N
4. Pass cap-and-trade	N	8. Pass tax cuts for some	N	12. Limit campaign funds	N

Election Results

2010 general	Peter Roskam (R)	114,456	(64%)	($2,381,858)
	Benjamin Lowe (D)	65,379	(36%)	($66,632)
2010 primary	Peter Roskam (R)	unopposed		

Prior Winning Percentages: 2008 (58%), 2006 (51%)

Population		Race/Ethnicity		Work	
Pop. 2010:	657,131	White:	66.5%	Private:	86.8%
Change since 2000:	Up 0.5%	Black:	3.6%	Government:	8.8%
Urban:	100.0%	Hispanic:	18.2%	Self-employed:	4.3%
Rural:	0.0%	Asian:	10.1%	Blue collar:	19.5%
Area size:	215 sq. mi.	Native Am.:	0.1%	White collar:	67.6%
		Hawaiian:	0.0%	Khaki collar:	0.0%
Age		Two+ races:	1.4%	Other:	12.9%
Median age:	37.1 yrs.				
More than 65 yrs:	11.6%	*Ancestry*		Median income:	$70,667
Less than 18 yrs:	24.9%	German	17.1%	Median Home Value:	$298,000
		Irish	11.7%		
Education		Polish	9.7%	**Military Veterans**	
H.S. grad:	89.2%			% of Pop:	7.0%
College grad:	37.8%				
Grad degree:	12.9%				

North and West Chicago Suburbs

During World War II, the largest troop and cargo airplane, the Douglas C-54, was built at a military airstrip called Orchard Field, just northwest of Chicago. Today, Orchard Field is known as O'Hare International Airport, the nation's second-busiest. (O'Hare's three-letter code, ORD, borrows three letters from the word "orchard.") In the 1940s, Chicago politicians in search of a new airport site annexed Orchard Field, along with thousands of adjacent acres,

2008 Presidential Vote		
Barack Obama (D)	152,127	(56%)
John McCain (R)	115,339	(43%)
2004 Presidential Vote		
George Bush (R)	139,028	(53%)
John Kerry (D)	121,344	(47%)
Cook Partisan Voting Index: EVEN		

and renamed it for a Navy flyer who lost his life in the war and hailed from Chicago, Lt. Edward O'Hare. Mayor Richard J. Daley opened O'Hare in 1955 and aggressively promoted its development, correctly concluding that a great airport in the 20th century could do for Chicago what railroad stations and rail yards did for the city in the 19th century. For years, O'Hare has vied with Atlanta's Hartsfield-Jackson as America's No. 1 or No. 2 airport, and it has done much to maintain Chicago as the most vibrant center of commerce in the Midwest.

Today, with O'Hare operating close to capacity, the city has plans to reconfigure the runways and expand the airport, all aimed at maintaining its pre-eminence. By late 2010, the city had built a new north runway and extended others, and was trying to enlist United and American airlines to help pay for a new western terminal. However, expansion is highly unpopular in the densely packed suburbs that surround O'Hare. Politically, these suburbs were for many years solidly Republican, convinced that civic virtues could best be realized by opposing the party of City Hall in Chicago, and that economic growth could best be assured by opposing the party that backed stifling government regulation. But in the 1990s, they became less Republican, as voters here recoiled from the national party's cultural conservatism.

The 6th Congressional District of Illinois includes O'Hare and much of the suburban area to its west. Most of the district is in DuPage County, the second most populous county in Illinois after Cook County. It includes the string of long-settled suburbs due west of the Loop: Elmhurst, Villa Park, Lombard, Glen Ellyn, and Wheaton. It takes in other suburbs along Interstate 290: Bensenville, Addison, Wood Dale, and Bloomingdale. Economically, this remains high-income territory; culturally, it is now moderate or even liberal. In 1988, George H.W. Bush carried DuPage by 124,000 votes, with 68% of the vote, but in 2004, his son carried it by only 39,000 votes, for a total of 54%—which tells you in a nutshell why the elder Bush carried Illinois in 1988 and the younger Bush twice wrote it off. In 2008, Illinois was a lost cause for Republicans opposed to favorite-son Democrat Barack Obama. John McCain lost DuPage by 45,000 votes.

Peter Roskam (R)

The congressman from the 6th District is Peter Roskam, a Republican elected in 2006 to succeed the iconic Henry Hyde, who retired after 32 years. He is considered one of the GOP's bright young stars and was named chief deputy House whip in the 112th Congress (2011-12).

A native of DuPage County, Roskam was a varsity gymnast in high school, graduated from the University of Illinois, and got his law degree while directing a charitable organization that used corporate resources to fund college scholarships. During law school, he was part of a team that won a national mock trial competition. As a young man, he also once worked as an aide to Hyde. Roskam served six years in the state House, and six years in the state Senate, where he was the Republican whip and floor leader. Between those legislative stints, he ran unsuccessfully in 1998 for the open congressional seat in the neighboring 13th District, losing 45%-40% against state House colleague Judy Biggert in the Republican primary. In 2006, Hyde, one of the most widely respected conservatives on Capitol Hill, stepped down. Roskam raised nearly $400,000 in two months, and managed to scare off potentially competitive Republican challengers. He ran unopposed for the GOP nomination, conserving his money for the general election.

In the general election campaign, his Democratic opponent was Tammy Duckworth, a former manager for Rotary International and an Iraq war veteran. She was famous as a Black Hawk helicopter pilot who served with the Illinois National Guard and lost both legs in Iraq after her helicopter was hit by a rocket-propelled grenade and crashed. As part of an effort to nominate military veterans for Congress, then-Rep. Rahm Emanuel, from the neighboring 5th District and chairman of the Democratic Congressional Campaign Committee, hand-picked Duckworth. Her high profile made this one of the nation's most closely watched House races, and one of the most expensive. First, she faced a competitive primary from technology consultant Christine Cegelis, who ran against Hyde in 2004 and held him to a 56%-44% win, his smallest margin since he was first elected. She benefited from a wave of favorable news coverage for her compelling personal story. Duckworth won the primary with 44% to 40% for Cegelis and 16% for a third candidate.

The two nominees sparred over tax cuts, earmarks, the Iraq war, and immigration policy. They also clashed over abortion rights, federal funding for embryonic stem cell research, and expansion of O'Hare, all of which Roskam opposed. Duckworth criticized Roskam as "a rubber stamp" for the Bush administration, and referred to the scandal-plagued House GOP Leader Tom DeLay of Texas as Roskam's "mentor." While Roskam was climbing a political ladder with DeLay, her campaign said, "Tammy Duckworth was climbing into helicopters and serving her country." Former President Bill Clinton and actor Michael J. Fox made campaign appearances for her. Roskam disparaged Duckworth as the "candidate from the Chicago Democratic machine" because of her ties to the well-connected Emanuel. He also sought to portray her as a carpetbagger. In one of the few Republican successes in a competitive House contest that year, Roskam won with 51%-49%. Duckworth got 53% of the vote in Cook County, but Cook cast only 20% of the total vote. Roskam won 52%-48% in DuPage—sufficient, though not overwhelming.

In the House, Roskam votes near the center of the Republican Party, aligning with GOP colleagues to oppose Democrats' economic proposals while acknowledging his moderate constituency on social issues. He backed bills in 2009 to tighten food safety, impose more stringent regulations on credit card companies, and to give the Food and Drug Administration authority to regulate some tobacco products. In May 2007, the House, by a 173-245 vote, defeated his amendment to limit contributions to the affordable housing trust fund when the government is running a deficit. With Rep. John Shimkus, R-Ill., he unveiled in 2008 an energy independence plan that was based on aggressive domestic production, conservation, and alternative fuels. That year, he also voted against the government bailout of the financial markets because, he said, it was not tough enough on Wall Street executives and "places too great a burden on taxpayers with no guarantee of success." As a constituent outreach technique, he encouraged participation in his "There Oughta Be a Law" campaign soliciting proposals for new laws from residents of his district. It was the prototype for the House Republican leadership's "America Speaking Out" outreach project on which Roskam served as a deputy chairman.

In 2009, his solid freshman year and his friendship with party leaders got him a seat on the powerful Ways and Means Committee. During the health care overhaul debate, he parlayed his connections with President Obama—the two served together in the state Senate—into talks with White House officials about cutting waste, fraud, and abuse in Medicare. At a 2010 summit on the issue, he called on the president to work with Republicans, who he complained had been "stiff-armed by Speaker [Nancy] Pelosi." When Ways and Means approved a $15 billion package of small-business tax breaks in 2010, Roskam unsuccessfully sought to index individual tax rates to reflect not only inflation but increases in federal spending. He said the change would enable household income to grow with federal spending without incurring a tax increase.

Illinois Democratic Sen. Dick Durbin vowed that Democrats would give Roskam a strong challenge in 2008, but in July 2007 Duckworth, the party's top prospect, decided to stay in her job as head of the Illinois Veterans' Affairs Department. Instead, Democrats nominated another Iraq war veteran, retired Army Col. Jill Morgenthaler, who was the Army spokeswoman during the Abu Ghraib prison scandal. She campaigned on her support for President Bush's troop surge in Iraq, and accused Roskam of having "extreme" views on abortion, health care, and the economy. Despite early Democratic hopes that Obama's coattails would reach across Illinois, the national party gave little help to Morgenthaler. Roskam handily won a second term, 58%-42%. He got 52% in the Cook County suburbs and 59% in DuPage. With far more pressing concerns two years later, Democrats essentially gave up on the race and Roskam won easily with 64%. He is the only current member of Congress who served with Obama in the state Senate.

SEVENTH DISTRICT

Danny Davis (D)

Elected 1996, 8th term; b. Sept. 6, 1941, Parkdale, AR; home, Chicago; AR AM&N Col., B.A. 1961, Chicago St. U., M.S. 1968, Union Inst., Ph.D. 1977; Baptist; married (Vera); 2 children.

Elected Office: Chicago city alderman, 1979–90; Cook Cnty. commissioner, 1990–96.

Professional Career: Teacher, Chicago Public Schls., 1962–69; Health Care Planner, 1969–79.

DC Office: 2159 RHOB, 20515, 202-225-5006; Fax: 202-225-5641; Web site: davis.house.gov.

State Offices: Broadview, 708-345-6857; Chicago, 773-533-7520.

Committees: *Homeland Security:* Oversight, Investigations & Management; Transportation Security. *Oversight & Government Reform:* Federal Workforce, U.S. Postal Service & Labor Policy; Health Care, District of Columbia, Census & the National Archives (RMM).

Group Ratings

	ACLU	ACU	ADA	CFG	AFS	FRC	LCV	ITIC	NTU	COC
2010	94	4	85	3	100	6	90	100	8	29
2009	–	0	95	0	100	–	100	–	1	40

National Journal Ratings

	2010 LIB	—	2010 CONS		2009 LIB	—	2009 CONS
Economic	76%	—	23%		87%	—	12%
Social	70%	—	30%		89%	—	0%
Foreign	84%	—	11%		86%	—	13%
Composite	78%	—	22%		90%	—	11%

Key Votes of the 111th Congress

1. Overturn Ledbetter	Y	5. Bar federal abortion funds	N	9. Stop detainee transfers	N
2. Pass $820 billion stimulus	Y	6. Pass health care bill	Y	10. Legalize immigrants' kids	Y
3. Let guns in national parks	N	7. Regulate financial firms	Y	11. Repeal don't ask, tell	Y
4. Pass cap-and-trade	Y	8. Pass tax cuts for some	Y	12. Limit campaign funds	N

Election Results

2010 general	Danny Davis (D)	149,846	(82%)	($593,861)
	Mark Weiman (R)	29,575	(16%)	
	Clarence Clemons (I)	4,428	(2%)	
2010 primary	Danny Davis (D)	52,728	(67%)	
	Sharon Dixon (D)	10,851	(14%)	
	Darlena Williams-Burnett (D)	10,173	(13%)	
	Jim Ascot (D)	5,221	(7%)	

Prior Winning Percentages: 2008 (85%), 2006 (87%), 2004 (86%), 2002 (83%), 2000 (86%), 1998 (93%), 1996 (83%)

Population		Race/Ethnicity		Work	
Pop. 2010:	638,105	White:	32.1%	Private:	82.5%
Change since 2000:	Down 2.4%	Black:	50.6%	Government:	13.0%
Urban:	100.0%	Hispanic:	9.0%	Self-employed:	4.4%
Rural:	0.0%	Asian:	6.5%	Blue collar:	13.1%
Area size:	59 sq. mi.	Native Am.:	0.1%	White collar:	71.5%
		Hawaiian:	0.0%	Khaki collar:	0.0%
Age		Two+ races:	1.5%	Other:	15.4%
Median age:	33.9 yrs.				
More than 65 yrs:	10.7%	*Ancestry*		Median income:	$51,053
Less than 18 yrs:	21.6%	German	7.3%	Median Home Value:	$313,700
		Irish	6.7%		
Education		Italian	3.6%	**Military Veterans**	
H.S. grad:	84.2%			% of Pop:	5.7%
College grad:	40.0%				
Grad degree:	18.4%				

Chicago; Downtown, West Side

An airplane passenger on a cloudless day can get a clear view of the biggest man-made cityscape between the Atlantic and Pacific oceans: Chicago's Loop. Its high-rises and parks along Lake Michigan were pioneered a century ago, and the downtown district was named in 1897 for the quadrilateral shape the elevated train forms around the city's center. International School modernists built their most impressive collection of buildings here and along Lake Shore

2008 Presidential Vote		
Barack Obama (D) 260,925	(88%)
John McCain (R) 34,481	(12%)

2004 Presidential Vote		
John Kerry (D) 227,018	(83%)
George Bush (R) 45,071	(17%)

Cook Partisan Voting Index: D+35

Drive in the years after World War II. The Loop now spreads beyond the elevated train, or the "El" as it's known locally. It reaches west beyond the financial exchanges to the 110-story Sears Tower—once the world's tallest building, now seventh—situated near the Chicago River. (However, one of the Loop's major office towers flirted with foreclosure in 2010, the first time in 11 years that had occurred with such a building.) The Loop reaches north and stops at the Gold Coast, the wondrous shopping district along North Michigan Avenue. West of the Gold Coast is the River North neighborhood, which has become one of the city's most vibrant. This is the face Chicago likes to present to the world: giant structures rising where the prairies meet the inland sea, a vast concentration of brains and muscle, the nerve center of the nation's commodities markets.

Just west of the lakefront neighborhoods are the muscle and sinew, gristle and fat of the city. Houses and apartment buildings are abandoned, commercial space stands empty and vandalized, and public housing projects are crime racked. The West Side of Chicago, the vast acres directly west of the Loop, for years was a grimy and dangerous slum, with some areas almost completely abandoned. The decay spread west to the Austin neighborhood, almost to the city border with upper-income and racially integrated Oak Park. Many factories that made Chicago the chocolate and candy center of the nation were shuttered, and production went mostly overseas. In the 1990s, there was some revival. The United Center, the erstwhile home court of Michael Jordan, sparked commercial development of the West Side, and lower crime rates raised land values. Former meat-packing buildings have been turned into art galleries. A massive new downtown dormitory houses students from nearby DePaul University, Roosevelt University, and Columbia College. A 2009 study said the area essentially has become a vibrant college town, pumping more than $4 billion a year into the economy.

The 7th Congressional District of Illinois contains the Loop and most of the North Michigan corridor and the Near North Side, where the infamous Cabrini-Green housing project has been replaced by new, mixed-market housing. It goes south, past landmark museums, Soldier Field, and 19th-century mansions along Prairie Avenue to take in a few South Side neighborhoods chronicled in the groundbreaking 1945 book *Black Metropolis*. Its heart, demographically and spiritually, is the predominately African-American West Side, which is more depopulated and socially disorganized than the predominately black South Side. To the west, just outside city limits, are Oak Park, the boyhood home of writer Ernest Hemingway and the location of architect Frank Lloyd Wright's home and museum and many of his prairie style houses. There is also well-heeled River Forest; more modest Maywood, which is a black-majority suburb; and Broadview and Hillside. African-Americans make up 51% of the district's population.

Danny Davis (D)

The congressman from the 7th District is Danny Davis, a Democrat first elected in 1996. Davis grew up on a cotton farm in Arkansas, graduated from college in that state, then moved to Chicago and worked as a teacher, assistant principal, and guidance counselor in Chicago public schools. For 10 years, he ran a community health project on the West Side. He was elected alderman in the 29th Ward in 1979, and supported Mayor Harold Washington, the city's first black mayor, in his notorious 1980s battles with white machine aldermen dubbed the "Council Wars." In 1990, Davis was elected a Cook County commissioner and a year later, made a quixotic run for mayor against Richard M. Daley. In 1996, when Democratic Rep. Cardiss Collins retired after nearly 24 years in the House, Davis decided to run for the seat. His major opponents were 3rd Ward Alderman Dorothy Tillman, a Daley ally, and 28th Ward Alderman Ed Smith. Davis campaigned as a big-government liberal, calling for a $7.60 minimum wage, affirmative-action programs, and a nationalized health care plan. Davis won with 33%. He went on to win the general election with ease and has not faced a serious challenge since. However, he lost his 29th Ward committeeman post to a Daley-backed challenger in 2000.

In the House, Davis has a liberal voting record, though he's moved closer to the center on economic issues in recent years. He has opposed income tax cuts, even when advocated by Democratic President Bill Clinton. He opposed the sugar program as corporate welfare (Chicago remains the nation's leading candy manufacturer). On the Oversight and Government Reform Committee, he was a champion of organized labor as he worked with a bipartisan coalition that in 2006 enacted major changes in the Postal Service. With his wife, Vera Davis, who was then president of the West Side NAACP, Davis advocated a local program to increase the low share of black home ownership in his district by offering credit counseling and innovative forms of mortgage financing. His devotion to issues affecting the poor has won him respect even among Republicans. With the view that everybody deserves a second chance, Davis has taken a deep interest in the problems of former convicts seeking to transition to the mainstream. He teamed with Rep. Mark Souder, a conservative Republican from Indiana, on a bill creating tax credits to encourage transitional housing and job training for former prisoners. It evolved into his Second Chance Act, which President George W. Bush signed into law in 2008.

Davis is eager for political advancement and in recent years has signaled his readiness to leave the House, but repeatedly has stopped short. In 2006, he sought to become Cook County Board president when incumbent John Stroger suffered a serious stroke. But Democratic committeemen overwhelmingly supported Stroger's son, Todd, for the nomination, and Davis was a distant second. After the 2008 election, he campaigned publicly to win the support of Democratic Gov. Rod Blagojevich to fill the Senate seat vacated by President-elect Obama. Blagojevich later was charged with trying to gain politically and personally from his power to make the appointment. The disgraced governor decided to go ahead and make the appointment anyway and called Davis his top choice. But Davis turned down what was bound to be viewed as a tainted appointment. Blagojevich then appointed former Illinois Attorney General Roland Burris to the seat. As a significant consolation prize, the Democratic House leadership gave Davis a seat on the Ways and Means Committee. He was an outspoken defender of the committee's chairman, black New York Democrat Charles B. Rangel, during Rangel's ethics scandal, and called the health care overhaul "good for black America." Davis lost his seat on Ways and Means when Republicans took control of the House in 2011.

In 2009, Davis weighed another bid for the Cook County board and filed to run for the job concurrently with filing for re-election, only to back out at the last minute. After Daley announced abruptly in 2010 he would not seek re-election as mayor, Davis jumped into the race, collecting endorsements from 15 African-American aldermen. But with pressure mounting to settle on a single black candidate in early January, he endorsed former U.S. Sen. Carol Moseley Braun, who had stressed her fundraising advantages over Davis. She eventually lost to former Obama White House staff chief Rahm Emanuel, who is white.

EIGHTH DISTRICT

Joe Walsh (R)

Elected 2010, 1st term; b. Dec. 27, 1961, Barrington; home, McHenry; U. of IA, B.A. 1985; U. of Chicago, M.A. 1991.; Catholic; Married (Helene Miller); 5 children.

Professional Career: Mgr., Youth Job Center, 1992-93; devel. assoc., Heartland Inst., 1994-96; exec. dir., Daniel Murphy Scholarship Foundation, 1997-2001; develop. dir., American Education Reform Cncl., 2002-04; fundraiser, Milton and Rose Friedman Foundation, 2004-05; V.P., Advantage Futures, 2005-08; investment advisor, Ravenswood Advisors, 2007; develop. dir., Fabretto Children's Foundation, 2006-10.

DC Office: 432 CHOB, 20515, 202-255-3711; Fax: 202-225-7830; Web site: walsh.house.gov.

State Offices: Fox Lake, 847-973-9341.

Committees: *Homeland Security:* Counterterrorism & Intelligence; Emergency Preparedness, Response & Communications; Transportation Security (VChmn). *Oversight & Government Reform:* Health Care, District of Columbia, Census & the National Archives; TARP, Financial Services & Bailouts of Public & Private Programs. *Small Business:* Economic Growth, Tax and Capital Access (Chmn); Healthcare & Technology; Investigations, Oversight & Regulations.

Election Results

2010 general	Joe Walsh (R)	98,115	(48.47%)	($646,794)
	Melissa Bean (D)	97,825	(48.32%)	($2,292,879)
	Bill Scheurer (Green)	6,495	(3%)	
2010 primary	Joe Walsh (R)	16,162	(34%)	
	Dirk Beveridge (R)	11,708	(25%)	
	Maria Rodriquez (R)	9,803	(21%)	
	Christopher Geissler (R)	4,267	(9%)	
	John Dawson (R)	3,921	(8%)	

Population		Race/Ethnicity		Work	
Pop. 2010:	738,840	White:	69.0%	Private:	84.6%
Change since 2000:	Up 13.0%	Black:	4.1%	Government:	11.1%
Urban:	96.1%	Hispanic:	16.9%	Self-employed:	4.0%
Rural:	3.9%	Asian:	8.1%	Blue collar:	19.4%
Area size:	646 sq. mi.	Native Am.:	0.1%	White collar:	66.8%
		Hawaiian:	0.0%	Khaki collar:	0.2%
Age		Two+ races:	1.6%	Other:	13.6%
Median age:	36.0 yrs.				
More than 65 yrs:	9.3%	*Ancestry*		Median income:	$73,689
Less than 18 yrs:	27.0%	German	19.0%	Median Home Value:	$257,600
		Irish	11.8%		
Education		Polish	9.3%	**Military Veterans**	
H.S. grad:	89.9%			% of Pop:	7.4%
College grad:	35.9%				
Grad degree:	12.7%				

Chicago Suburbs; Schaumburg

Schaumburg may not be nationally known, but it is one of America's major corporate headquarters cities. It has the second largest economy in Illinois, after Chicago. Sixty years ago, this suburb northwest of Chicago was farmland. Today, Schaumburg—near the intersection of the Northwest Tollway and Interstate 290—is the site of the headquarters of Motorola and Zurich North America insurance. Nearby are the headquarters of Sears and Kemper Insurance, as well as the gargantuan Woodfield Mall and subdivisions as far as the eye can see. Schaumburg has built a performing arts center, formed an orchestra for young people, and built from

2008 Presidential Vote
Barack Obama (D) 170,333 (56%)
John McCain (R) 130,384 (43%)

2004 Presidential Vote
George Bush (R) 153,245 (56%)
John Kerry (D) 121,710 (44%)

Cook Partisan Voting Index: R+1

scratch a traditional downtown district. Lately, civic endeavors are taking a backseat to concerns about the recession, which hit here early. Motorola lost 4,000 jobs worldwide in 2008 alone. And for the first time in its 54-year history, Schaumburg in 2010 levied a property tax on homeowners and businesses in order to close a budget gap. Before that, the city had been able to rely almost exclusively on sales taxes.

The 8th Congressional District of Illinois is made up of Schaumburg and dozens of similar communities north and northwest of Chicago. A short drive from Schaumburg is Palatine and country-manor Barrington Hills. The district includes the western half of Lake County, with little lake communities being surrounded by new suburbs like Deer Park and Volo. It also includes the Lake Michigan town of Zion at the Wisconsin border. To the west, the 8th includes about half of McHenry County, where Democrats have begun to show some life. The area lacks a regional identity, other than the "northwest suburbs." The local newspaper, the *Daily Herald* based in Arlington Heights, tried valiantly for a few years to give it a sense of place with a billboard campaign that dubbed it "Herald City." It didn't quite stick.

The tone of life is not elite, but people here are affluent. Culturally, it has more in common with the great rural Midwest than it does yeasty, lusty Chicago. Economically, its suspicion of government and trade restrictions has declined, as Motorola has become the victim of overseas competition. Historically, this was one of the most Republican places in the nation. In the past decade, like other Chicago suburbs, it moved toward the Democrats. If the 8th is still one of Illinois's most Republican districts, as measured by its 56% support of George W. Bush in both 2000 and 2004, it has become far less Republican than districts with similar demographics in Texas and Georgia. Like most of the Chicago metropolitan area, the district voted for Barack Obama in 2008. Obama won 56% here compared to John McCain's 43%.

Joe Walsh (R)

The new congressman from the 8th District is Republican Joe Walsh, who pulled off one of the biggest upsets of 2010 by defeating well-respected Democratic Rep. Melissa Bean.

Walsh grew up in the suburb of Barrington, Ill., the middle of nine children in a Roman Catholic family. His father was a mortgage banker and real estate appraiser, and his mother was a special education teacher. His mother sparked his passion for politics at an early age. She had volunteered for Richard Nixon's 1960 presidential campaign and often discussed history and politics with her children. In high school, Walsh was president of his senior class and played football, basketball, and baseball. He started college at Grinnell, a small liberal arts school in Iowa, but yearned to be part of a larger environment, especially when Ronald Reagan ran for president in 1980 and Walsh, an enthusiastic Reagan supporter, found himself relatively isolated at the predominately liberal campus. (Walsh did manage to persuade some of his fellow athletes to root for the new president.) In 1982, he transferred to the University of Iowa. Walsh took a semester off to study acting in Los Angeles, and after graduating with a degree in English, continued his theater studies at the Lee Strasberg Theatre and Film Institute in New York City. He later got parts in commercials and small theater productions.

After Walsh married, the couple moved to Chicago, where he worked for a nonprofit organization, teaching reading, math, and job skills to inner-city youths. He also earned a master's degree in public policy at the University of Chicago. "The policy area that most interested me was, why are our urban public schools in such horrific shape and what do we do about urban poverty?" Walsh told *National Journal*. He developed a preference for free-market solutions to social problems, and, after getting his degree, worked for nonprofit organizations and think tanks specializing in education issues, including the Daniel Murphy Scholarship Fund, which gives money to low-income students to attend private high schools.

In 1996, Walsh ran for Congress against Rep. Sidney Yates in Illinois's 9th District and handily lost to the veteran Democrat. Two years later, he ran for a seat in the state House, focusing his campaign on maintaining local control over schools, but he lost to the Democratic incumbent. When his first marriage fell apart, the couple divorced. In 2006, he married again, and about the same time, Walsh switched careers. He joined Ravenswood Advisors, a Chicago-based investment banking firm. "I wanted to try to make money for the first time in my life," he said. He retained an interest in politics, however, and in late 2009 decided to try again for a House seat.

With the support of tea party groups, Walsh entered a crowded Republican primary to challenge Bean, a three-term representative who was re-elected in 2008 with more than 60% of the vote. He blamed both parties for the country's problems and called himself a "tea party conservative first and a Republican second." Walsh won the February primary with 34% of the vote, topping businessman Dirk Beveridge and Long Grove Mayor Maria Rodriguez.

Even national Republicans gave Walsh little chance of winning against Bean and ignored his campaign throughout most of the fall campaign season. But with the backing of tea party groups and a widespread voter backlash against incumbent Democrats, Walsh made quiet and steady progress. He had setbacks for sure. Soon after the primary, the local newspaper, the *Daily Herald*, reported that Walsh lost his condominium to foreclosure in October 2009 after he had failed to pay his mortgage. He blamed his divorce and the recession for his money troubles, and said the experience showed that he understood the financial struggles of average people. His campaign manager quit and sued for nonpayment, and the former Eagles guitarist Joe Walsh threatened to sue him for copyright infringement for using one of the band's songs.

Bean had a formidable financial advantage. She raised nearly $2 million by mid-October, compared with Walsh's $466,000. Bean aired ads portraying Walsh as a political extremist, and he attacked her for backing President Barack Obama's health care overhaul and $787 billion economic stimulus bill. The National Republican Congressional Committee did not spend any money on Walsh's behalf, a decision that he said frustrated him but left him with no lasting resentment toward GOP leaders.

Early election results showed Walsh with a narrow lead, and he declared victory. But Bean did not concede until all the ballots were counted two weeks later after Election Day. She trailed by just 290 votes out of more than 202,000 cast. Walsh got 98,115 votes to Bean's 97,825. A third candidate won 6,495 votes. In Washington, Walsh said he would focus on cutting taxes and reducing spending.

NINTH DISTRICT

Jan Schakowsky (D)

Elected 1998, 7th term; b. May 26, 1944, Chicago; home, Evanston; U. of IL, B.S. 1965; Jewish; married (Robert Creamer); 3 children.

Elected Office: IL House of Reps., 1990-98.

Professional Career: Founder, Natl. Consumers Unite, 1969-73; Prog. dir., IL Public Action, 1976-85; Exec. dir., IL State Cncl. of Sr. Citizens, 1985-90.

DC Office: 2367 RHOB, 20515, 202-225-2111; Fax: 202-226-6890; Web site: schakowsky.house.gov.

State Offices: Chicago, 773-506-7100; Evanston, 847-328-3409.

Committees: *Energy & Commerce:* Commerce, Manufacturing & Trade; Health; Oversight & Investigations. *Permanent Select Committee on Intelligence:* Oversight (RMM).

Group Ratings

	ACLU	ACU	ADA	CFG	AFS	FRC	LCV	ITIC	NTU	COC
2010	88	0	95	0	100	0	100	100	5	25
2009	–	0	100	0	100	–	100	–	2	33

National Journal Ratings

	2010 LIB	—	2010 CONS	2009 LIB	—	2009 CONS
Economic	90%	—	0%	91%	—	0%
Social	93%	—	0%	89%	—	0%
Foreign	97%	—	0%	91%	—	0%
Composite	97%	—	3%	95%	—	5%

Key Votes of the 111th Congress

1. Overturn Ledbetter	Y	5. Bar federal abortion funds	N	9. Stop detainee transfers	N
2. Pass $820 billion stimulus	Y	6. Pass health care bill	Y	10. Legalize immigrants' kids	Y
3. Let guns in national parks	N	7. Regulate financial firms	Y	11. Repeal don't ask, tell	Y
4. Pass cap-and-trade	Y	8. Pass tax cuts for some	Y	12. Limit campaign funds	Y

Election Results

2010 general	Jan Schakowsky (D)	117,553	(66%)	($1,520,106)
	Joel Pollak (R)	55,182	(31%)	($677,066)
	Simon Ribeiro (Green)	4,472	(3%)	
2010 primary	Jan Schakowsky (D) .... unopposed			

Prior Winning Percentages: 2008 (75%), 2006 (75%), 2004 (76%), 2002 (70%), 2000 (76%), 1998 (75%)

Population		Race/Ethnicity		Work	
Pop. 2010:	628,859	White:	60.2%	Private:	84.2%
Change since 2000:	Down 3.8%	Black:	10.0%	Government:	9.6%
Urban:	100.0%	Hispanic:	12.7%	Self-employed:	6.1%
Rural:	0.0%	Asian:	14.3%	Blue collar:	15.0%
Area size:	78 sq. mi.	Native Am.:	0.2%	White collar:	68.8%
		Hawaiian:	0.0%	Khaki collar:	0.0%
Age		Two+ races:	2.3%	Other:	16.2%
Median age:	37.8 yrs.				
More than 65 yrs:	14.4%	Ancestry		Median income:	$55,413
Less than 18 yrs:	20.3%	German	11.2%	Median Home Value:	$337,900
		Irish	9.3%		
Education		Polish	9.2%	Military Veterans	
H.S. grad:	87.8%			% of Pop:	5.3%
College grad:	44.0%				
Grad degree:	18.4%				

Chicago, Suburbs; Evanston

"Make no little plans," architect Daniel Burnham once said, and he made no small plans for the Chicago lakefront. The glorious parks he designed are among America's urban jewels, and the row of high-rise apartment buildings—some austere works of masters of the International style, some in traditional styles evocative of some other place and time, some sleek Art Deco works of the 1920s and 1930s—is a splendid accompaniment. Beyond the lakefront is all the

2008 Presidential Vote
Barack Obama (D) 189,497 (72%)
John McCain (R) 69,081 (26%)

2004 Presidential Vote
John Kerry (D) 175,288 (68%)
George Bush (R) 81,138 (32%)

Cook Partisan Voting Index: D+20

diversity of Chicago. In sturdy brick houses, with scarcely a shoehorn's space between them, or in stubby apartment buildings, are ethnic and racial groups of every sort, from Argentineans to Slavs, from Poles to Plains Indians. In the 1970s, the neighborhoods behind the lakefront seemed to be getting seedier and tipping downhill. But since the late 1980s, they have been gentrifying, as young couples and gays, professionals and entrepreneurs renovate old houses and open new businesses. Today, this part of Chicago has as much urban energy and lively diversity as any place in America.

The lakefront has long been the most heavily Jewish part of Chicago. The local Jewish community, prominent for more than a century, has never been as much a force as it is in New York, or connected to a glamorous industry as in Los Angeles. Yet these Jewish voters' liberal impulses have been strong: the 19th century impulse to resist state authority and the imposition of cultural uniformity, and the 20th century impulse to increase state responsibility for individuals' lives. Chicago's North Side Jews have been a solidly Democratic voting bloc, involved with—but always keeping at arm's length—the old Democratic machine. In city politics since the 1980s, Jewish voters and lakefront liberals of all backgrounds have been a key swing group.

The 9th Congressional District of Illinois covers most of Chicago's lakefront, from just north of Diversey Harbor past the thriving Asian and orthodox Jewish communities in West Rogers Park and on to Evanston. The home of Northwestern University, Evanston has moved gracefully from historic Yankee Republicanism to trendy, postgraduate Democratic and is even getting its own 35-story skyscraper. From Evanston and nearby Wilmette (which is shared with the 10th), the 9th presses inland through heavily Jewish Skokie to Morton Grove and Niles and includes most of Des Plaines. Skokie made national headlines when Nazi sympathizers got court permission to march there in 1977. Skokie's residents settled the score with the opening in 2009 of the Illinois Holocaust Museum and Education Center; former President Clinton and Nobel Prize-winning author Elie Wiesel attended. These bustling inner-ring suburbs have become the center of Chicagoland's job base. With its financial markets and the professionals that support them, the city once known as the hog butcher of the world has evolved into the hog belly trader of the world. The district extends west to once-rock-solid Republican territory—Park Ridge, with its characteristic Chicago brick houses in orderly rows, where Hillary Rodham Clinton grew up at 235 Wisner, and the cluster of office buildings and interchanges in Rosemont, next to O'Hare International Airport. The district is 10% black, 13% Hispanic, and 14% Asian, and is overwhelmingly Democratic.

Jan Schakowsky (D)

The congresswoman from the 9th District is Jan Schakowsky, a Democrat elected in 1998 and an outspoken progressive. She grew up in Rogers Park and worked for two years as a teacher. In 1969, she formed National Consumers Unite to fight for date-of-freshness labels on dairy products and other food. Later she joined Illinois Public Action, a consumer group. In 1985, she became executive director of the Illinois State Council of Senior Citizens, where she organized the pivotal 1989 protest of Democratic Rep. Dan Rostenkowski's Medicare catastrophic health care law for seniors. Television news images of the powerful Rostenkowski fleeing an angry crowd of old people led Congress to repeal the benefit, which many said did not provide adequate coverage. In 1990, Schakowsky was elected to the state House from Evanston and Skokie, and served as Democratic floor leader.

In 1998, Schakowsky was selected in the Democratic primary to replace Sidney Yates, a liberal Democrat who had represented the lakefront in Congress for 48 years. Her strategy was to run from the left—"I don't think I can be defined as too far left in a district like this"—and to build a volunteer organization. With ads in college papers, she hired young field organizers to set about identifying Schakowsky voters. She raised $1.4 million, with help from the women's abortion rights fundraising group EMILY's List. Her opponent was state Sen. Howard Carroll, who had the support of most Democratic ward committeemen and attacked Schakowsky for her opposition to the death penalty. Schakowsky's 1,500 workers, 250 of them from labor unions, helped her to a 45%-34% win. She easily won the general election.

Schakowsky has one of the most liberal voting records in the House and regularly scores perfect ratings from liberal interest groups. A close ally of Democratic Leader Nancy Pelosi, Schakowsky has worked with Democratic leaders on electoral strategy, including heading a training program for political organizers. She was an early supporter of Pelosi for party whip when Pelosi was getting her start in leadership, and Pelosi rewarded her with the chief deputy whip post. After Democrats won House control in November 2006, Schakowsky seconded the nomination of Pelosi for speaker, calling her "my treasured friend." Her contacts with national liberal groups have helped Schakowsky become a major party fundraiser.

In early 2006, she sought a higher leadership post as vice chairman of the Democratic Caucus, which would put her on a track to become caucus chairman, the No. 3 leadership job. With support from Pelosi, Schakowsky was the early front-runner against New York's Joe Crowley and Connecticut's John Larson. But on the first ballot, she finished third behind Crowley and Larson. Schakowsky threw her support to Larson, another Pelosi ally. With Schakowsky's former supporters on board, Larson prevailed. Some Democrats speculated that Schakowsky was hurt by the timing of the contest, which occurred soon after her husband, Robert Creamer, the longtime head of Illinois Public Action Fund, pleaded guilty in August 2005 to bank fraud in a check-kiting scheme. Schakowsky said that her husband had "made mistakes," but that she was unaware of his financial problems and was "proud of who Bob is.... He has been a constant crusader." After Fox News host Glenn Beck criticized Creamer's attendance at a White House dinner in November 2009, Creamer called Beck part of a "new McCarthyist movement of the far right."

Schakowsky briefly considered a run for the Senate in 2004 but decided against it, and later, in 2008, she was interested in being appointed to the remainder of President-elect Barack Obama's Senate term until the scandal broke out over Democratic Gov. Rod Blagojevich's alleged attempts to profit personally and politically from his power to make the appointment. She was an early backer of Obama for president, giving cover to other prominent Democratic women who may have wanted to support him but felt obliged to support then-New York Sen. Hillary Clinton.

In 2009, she was a strong supporter and co-sponsor of legislation creating a federally-run insurance option in the Democrats' health care bill. But the public option provision ultimately was dropped because of opposition from party moderates. A fierce opponent of military action in Iraq, Schakowsky hailed Obama's June 2009 speech, saying, "The president's brave speech in Cairo convinced me he deserves my support—and at least the benefit of the doubt when it comes to extracting us from Iraq and Afghanistan."

As chairman of the oversight subcommittee of the Intelligence Committee, Schakowsky in July 2009 backed Pelosi's claim that she had not been informed of the use by U.S. interrogators of water boarding, as Central Intelligence Agency Director Leon Panetta had maintained. In May 2010, she co-sponsored an amendment giving the Government Accountability Office power to investigate intelligence agencies.

On the Energy and Commerce Committee, Schakowsky was a player in the enactment in 2008 of the child product safety bill, which toughened regulations. More recently, she sponsored a bill to give chemical plants two years to stop using mercury in manufacturing chlorine. And with Sen.

Dianne Feinstein, D-Calif., she introduced a bill in 2010 with tougher restrictions on cosmetics after findings that many included mercury. Pelosi appointed Schakowsky to a newly created commission on the national debt in March 2010, where she opposed ending federal economic stimulus spending and argued that safety-net spending for the poor should be exempt from budget cuts.

Schakowsky has been re-elected without difficulty. Illinois is one of the few states where Democrats control redistricting, so she seems safe in her heavily Democratic, lakefront district.

TENTH DISTRICT

Robert Dold (R)

Elected 2010, 1st term; b. June 23, 1969, Evanston; home, Kenilworth; Denison U., B.A. 1991; IN U., J.D. 1996; Northwestern U., M.B.A. 2000.; Christian; Married (Danielle); 3 children.

Professional Career: Aide, White House, 1991-93; investigative cnsl., House Cmte. on Oversight and Government Reform, 1997-99; mgr., Exodus Communications, 2000-03; pres., Rose Pest Solutions, 2007-10.

DC Office: 212 CHOB, 20515, 202-225-4835; Fax: 202-225-0837; Web site: dold.house.gov.

State Offices: Northbrook, 847-940-0202.

Committees: *Financial Services:* Financial Institutions & Consumer Credit; Insurance, Housing & Community Opportunity; International Monetary Policy & Trade (VChmn).

Election Results

2010 general	Robert Dold (R)	109,941	(51%)	($2,985,088)
	Daniel Seals (D)	105,290	(49%)	($2,935,602)
2010 primary	Robert Dold (R)	19,691	(38%)	
	Elizabeth Coulson (R)	16,149	(31%)	
	Dick Green (R)	7,595	(15%)	
	Arie Friedman (R)	7,260	(14%)	

Population		Race/Ethnicity		Work	
Pop. 2010:	650,425	White:	69.5%	Private:	82.4%
Change since 2000:	Down 0.5%	Black:	4.7%	Government:	11.7%
Urban:	99.6%	Hispanic:	15.6%	Self-employed:	5.7%
Rural:	0.4%	Asian:	8.5%	Blue collar:	14.6%
Area size:	252 sq. mi.	Native Am.:	0.1%	White collar:	71.6%
		Hawaiian:	0.0%	Khaki collar:	1.7%
Age		Two+ races:	1.3%	Other:	12.1%
Median age:	39.3 yrs.				
More than 65 yrs:	13.9%	*Ancestry*		Median income:	$83,686
Less than 18 yrs:	26.2%	German	14.4%	Median Home Value:	$410,400
		Irish	9.6%		
Education		Polish	7.8%	**Military Veterans**	
H.S. grad:	90.0%			% of Pop:	7.3%
College grad:	50.7%				
Grad degree:	21.8%				

North Shore

Since 1855, when the Chicago & Northwestern opened the railroad line from downtown Chicago north along the lakeshore, the North Shore suburbs along Lake Michigan have been home to Chicago's elite. The North Shore starts in Evanston, goes north through Wilmette, Winnetka, and Glencoe, then leaves Cook County and crosses into the eastern Lake County towns of Highland Park and Lake Forest. Each burg has a slightly different personality, each is long established and mightily prosperous, and each exudes a patina of age. These are communities of affluent, well-educated people living in an environment whose natural beauty—the vistas over

2008 Presidential Vote
Barack Obama (D)	181,071	(61%)
John McCain (R)	114,035	(38%)

2004 Presidential Vote
John Kerry (D)	150,267	(53%)
George Bush (R)	134,536	(47%)

Cook Partisan Voting Index: D+6

Lake Michigan, the gentle rolling terrain, and the old trees—is carefully disciplined. Corporate headquarters fit comfortably here, including Baxter Healthcare, Abbott Laboratories, and Allstate Insurance. The North Shore suburbs were the setting for the 1980s films *Risky Business, Sixteen Candles,* and *Ferris Bueller's Day Off,* which depicted teen angst and lust for adventure among the pampered offspring of the rich. The median home price in tony Lake Forest, situated on Lake Michigan, was $1 million in 2008. The one exception to the atmosphere of gracious high living is the area around the Great Lakes Naval Training Center, where income is lower, to say the least.

The 10th Congressional District of Illinois is the North Shore district, starting on the lakefront in Wilmette and running north all the way to the blue-collar city of Waukegan and almost to the Wisconsin border. The district goes inland to Northbrook and Deerfield through what for many years were cornfields. Farther inland are suburbs like Arlington Heights, developed in the 1950s and 1960s on the Northwestern railroad line, and Wheeling, developed in the 1970s. To the north is Libertyville, near where the Adlai Stevensons, the governor and three-time presidential candidate and his son the former senator, owned a farm. After the family home on the property was donated to Lake County, it was restored as the Adlai Stevenson Center on Democracy in 2008. With the big movement toward Democrats in the Chicago suburbs in the 1990s, this establishment Republican district voted narrowly for Al Gore in 2000 and by a slightly larger margin for John Kerry in 2004. Barack Obama ran strongly here in 2008, getting 61% of the vote to John McCain's 38%.

Robert Dold (R)

The new congressman from the 10th District is Republican Robert Dold, elected in 2010 to succeed GOP Rep. Mark Kirk, who ran successfully for the Senate that year. Dold was born in the suburb of Evanston and raised with three sisters in affluent Winnetka, one of the towns that make up Chicago's northern lakefront suburbs. His father ran Rose Pest Solutions, the family business, and his mother was an English teacher. Being exposed to the management side of a small business fundamentally shaped Dold's future. "I knew I was eventually going to go into business...and being part of a small business and a family business—we learn to work hard," he told *National Journal.* In high school, Dold played sports and got involved in student government. He went to Denison University, where he earned a degree in political science. After graduation, he landed a job as an aide in the White House during the George H.W. Bush administration. He got a law degree and spent two years on the staff of the House Government Reform Committee, where he was on the team of Republican lawyers investigating President Bill Clinton's and Vice President Al Gore's fundraising practices during the 1996 campaign. Dold returned to school to get a master's degree in business from Northwestern University. He was a manager for several years with the Internet service provider Exodus Communications before settling in at the family business. In 2007, he became president of Rose Pest Solutions. In his free time, he was the scoutmaster for the same troop in which he became an Eagle Scout. "My scoutmaster, with the exception of my parents, probably had one of the greatest impacts on my life," Dold said.

When Kirk, a friend of Dold's, announced his decision to run for the Senate, Dold decided to enter the House contest. Dold handily clinched the GOP nomination against four challengers, but then faced a much tougher battle against business consultant Dan Seals, who had solid name recognition from previous runs for the House in 2006 and 2008 and from his father, George Seals, a former lineman for the Chicago Bears. Seals and Dold were neck-and-neck in fundraising, with each raking in $2.5 million by mid-October.

In one of the most closely watched races in the country, Dold campaigned on his business experience and moderate policy positions, defying the odds in a district that had voted Democratic in the past three presidential elections. He called himself "pro-choice, pro-stem cell research, pro-environment." That prompted the Illinois Federation for Right to Life to rescind its testimonial for Dold. But he secured endorsements from Kirk, the U.S. Chamber of Commerce, and former New York City Mayor Rudy Giuliani.

Seals accused Dold of being a conservative in disguise who was pandering to the district's culturally moderate votes. But Seals also had to be wary of appearing to be too liberal in a year voters nationally were rejecting the Democratic brand. He abandoned his past support of President Obama's view that the Bush-era tax cuts should be discontinued for upper income-earners. He also said he disagreed with Obama's desire to increase the tax on capital gains, which would affect many of the district's wealthy inhabitants. "I think you don't raise taxes on anybody until the economy is better," Seals told the *Chicago Sun-Times.* But Seals did support the president's health care overhaul, which by then had become unpopular in some quarters. Dold opposed the legislation.

The polls showed the contest to be a tossup until Election Day. Dold eked out a 51% to 49% victory over Seals.

ELEVENTH DISTRICT

Adam Kinzinger (R)

Elected 2010, 1st term; b. Feb. 27, 1978, Kankakee; home, Bloomington; IL St. U., B.S. 2000.; Protestant; Single.

Military Career: Air Natl. Guard, 2003-present (Iraq, Afghanistan).

Elected Office: McLean Cnty. Bd., 1998-2003.

Professional Career: Partner, sales rep., STL Technology, 2000-03.

DC Office: 1218 LHOB, 20515, 202-225-3635; Fax: 202-225-3521; Web site: kinzinger.house.gov.

State Offices: Joliet, 815-729-2308.

Committees: *Energy & Commerce:* Commerce, Manufacturing & Trade; Communications & Technology.

Election Results

2010 general	Adam Kinzinger (R)	129,108	(57%)	($1,881,629)
	Debbie Halvorson (D)	96,019	(43%)	($2,702,605)
2010 primary	Adam Kinzinger (R)	32,233	(64%)	
	Dave White (R)	5,257	(10%)	
	David McAloon (R)	4,880	(10%)	
	Henry Meers (R)	4,555	(9%)	
	Darrel Miller (R)	3,701	(7%)	

Population		Race/Ethnicity		Work	
Pop. 2010:	759,445	White:	77.5%	Private:	82.4%
Change since 2000:	Up 16.2%	Black:	8.4%	Government:	13.0%
Urban:	78.2%	Hispanic:	11.4%	Self-employed:	4.4%
Rural:	21.8%	Asian:	1.1%	Blue collar:	26.6%
Area size:	4,285 sq. mi.	Native Am.:	0.1%	White collar:	55.7%
		Hawaiian:	0.0%	Khaki collar:	0.0%
Age		Two+ races:	1.3%	Other:	17.7%
Median age:	35.4 yrs.				
More than 65 yrs:	11.3%	*Ancestry*		Median income:	$58,183
Less than 18 yrs:	26.0%	German	19.6%	Median Home Value:	$181,100
		Irish	13.2%		
Education		Italian	7.1%	**Military Veterans**	
H.S. grad:	88.2%			% of Pop:	9.0%
College grad:	21.7%				
Grad degree:	7.4%				

Chicago Exurbs; Joliet

The low-lying land west and south of Chicago, where sluggishly flowing rivers run circles around industrial sites, is a great divide over which French explorers portaged the easiest path from the Great Lakes to the Mississippi River valley. Today there is still a kind of borderland here, as the factories and shopping centers and subdivisions stop somewhere past the Cook County line and downstate prairies begin, cornfields bisected by highways and railroads radiating out from the Loop, and the rail yards of the nation's transportation hub. Politically, this is a borderland as well, between the traditionally Democratic Chicago area, with its hard-bitten politics, and heavily Republican downstate Illinois.

The 11th Congressional District of Illinois covers much of this borderland. It includes most of Will County, which, before the recession hit, was the fastest-growing of the large suburban Chicago counties. Its population jumped from about 500,000 in 2000 to 677,560 in 2010, and the number of Hispanic residents nearly doubled. But its growth spurt was interrupted by the collapse of the housing finance market and a spike in unemployment to 10% in 2009. The county seat, Joliet, had

2008 Presidential Vote		
Barack Obama (D)	175,808	(53%)
John McCain (R)	148,600	(45%)
2004 Presidential Vote		
George Bush (R)	162,779	(54%)
John Kerry (D)	140,619	(46%)
Cook Partisan Voting Index: R+1		

a foreclosure rate of over 7%, among the highest in the Chicago area. Once a canal boat town, and later the producer of one-third of America's wallpaper, Joliet was home to the famed Joliet Correctional Center, the prison featured in the movie *The Blues Brothers*, until it closed in 2002. Joliet is also the location of a 75,000-seat NASCAR racetrack.

Farther west, on bluffs above the Illinois River, are the factory towns of Ottawa, LaSalle, and Streator. South of Joliet is Kankakee, a county seat amid rich prairie earth on the Illinois Central main line. This is Republican territory. It has two ungainly-looking appendages. One goes west to rural Bureau County; the other heads south at the intersection of Interstates 80 and 39 and includes most of Bloomington in McLean County. The district includes Peotone, where residents are in a pitched battle against Democratic Gov. Pat Quinn and a plan to build a third Chicago-area airport there. The 2001 redistricting made this district more Republican than its 1990s incarnation, but it's been trending Democratic. It is politically marginal territory. President Bush won here with 54% in 2004, but in 2008, Democrat Barack Obama took 53% to Republican John McCain's 45%.

Adam Kinzinger (R)

The new congressman from the 11th District is Republican Adam Kinzinger, who dispatched first-term Democratic Rep. Debbie Halvorson in 2010. At age 32, the former Air Force pilot is among the youngest members of Congress.

Kinzinger was born in Kankakee, Ill., but spent the majority of his life in Bloomington, 70 miles to the southwest. He attributes his interest in public service to his father, who ran a nonprofit homeless shelter, and his mother, a public school teacher. He says that growing up in a middle-class family with two siblings taught him to spend money prudently. Wanting to stay near home, he attended Illinois State University and graduated with a bachelor's degree in political science in 2000. His first foray into politics came before that: In 1998, as a college sophomore, he took seriously a joking suggestion that he run for the McLean County Board. He did, defeating an incumbent and serving until 2003. When the September 11 terrorist attacks occurred, "that's when I basically woke up," he recalled. A month later, he joined the Air Force. But he began working in the private sector for STL Technology Partners until he could begin officer and pilot training. He eventually served three tours in Iraq from 2007 to 2009 and a tour in Afghanistan.

In the summer of 2006, Kinzinger was returning from the border of Mexico as part of his mission when he saw an attempted murder. Seeing a woman whose throat had been slashed running from her knife-wielding aggressor, he wrestled the man to the ground until police arrived. As a result, he was awarded the National Guard's Valley Forge Cross for heroism. "During that whole thing, I thought I was going to die," he told *National Journal*. "It really was a life-changing moment about sacrificing yourself for others."

In May 2009, after returning from his final tour in Iraq, Kinzinger began to campaign for the 11th District seat. Touting his military service, he beat four opponents in the 2010 Republican primary, getting 64% of the vote. In the fall, he was up against Halvorson, who had racked up an impressive 58% of the vote in 2008. But Kinzinger went into the contest with important backing from local tea party activists.

Halvorson attacked Kinzinger's stance on free trade and depicted him as inexperienced, running a campaign ad with a senior citizen scolding, "Young man, you have no idea what you're doing." Kinzinger countered with endorsements from former Alaska Gov. Sarah Palin and former Massachusetts Gov. Mitt Romney. He also won the support of the U.S. Chamber of Commerce and the National Federation of Independent Business over Halvorson, a blow to an incumbent who had been known in Washington for her advocacy of small-business issues. He also picked up an endorsement from the *Chicago Sun-Times*, which often backs Democrats. The newspaper called him "a compassionate young man who will let reason and a humanitarian impulse drive his decisions."

Kinzinger won convincingly, with 57% of the vote to 43% for Halvorson. He beat her in every county in the district, including Will, where he won 55% of the vote.

When he got to Washington, Kinzinger declined to join the newly formed Tea Party Caucus led by Minnesota GOP Rep. Michele Bachmann. "I was supported by the tea party," Kinzinger told *National Journal*. "But I don't consider myself a tea partier because I'm representing the entire 11th District." He had his first brush with the national news media when *The New York Times* took him to task in a December 2010 editorial after Kinzinger held a $5,000-a-head breakfast at the Capitol Hill Club to raise money for his campaign debt, which the editorial said smacked of "business as usual" for a lawmaker who had promised to be different.

TWELFTH DISTRICT

Jerry Costello (D)

Elected Aug. 1988, 12th full term; b. Sept. 25, 1949, E. St. Louis; home, Belleville; Belleville Area Col., A.A. 1971, Maryville Col., B.A. 1973; Catholic; married (Georgia); 3 children.

Elected Office: Chmn., St. Clair Cnty. Bd. of Supervisors, 1980–88.

Professional Career: Dir., IL Court Svcs. & Probation, 1973–80; Chmn., Region's Cncl. of Govts., 1980–84.

DC Office: 2408 RHOB, 20515, 202-225-5661; Fax: 202-225-0285; Web site: costello.house.gov.

State Offices: Belleville, 618-233-8026; Carbondale, 618-529-3791; Chester, 618-826-3043; E. St. Louis, 618-397-8833; Granite City, 618-451-7065; West Frankfort, 618-937-6402.

Committees: *Science, Space & Technology:* Space & Aeronautics. *Transportation & Infrastructure:* Aviation (RMM); Railroads, Pipelines & Hazardous Materials; Water Resources & Environment.

Group Ratings

	ACLU	ACU	ADA	CFG	AFS	FRC	LCV	ITIC	NTU	COC
2010	50	13	70	13	100	56	60	67	10	0
2009	–	12	85	15	100	–	86	–	12	50

National Journal Ratings

	2010 LIB — 2010 CONS		2009 LIB — 2009 CONS	
Economic	63%	— 36%	57%	— 42%
Social	43%	— 56%	45%	— 53%
Foreign	40%	— 59%	52%	— 48%
Composite	49%	— 51%	52%	— 48%

Key Votes of the 111th Congress

1. Overturn Ledbetter	Y	5. Bar federal abortion funds	Y	9. Stop detainee transfers	Y
2. Pass $820 billion stimulus	Y	6. Pass health care bill	Y	10. Legalize immigrants' kids	N
3. Let guns in national parks	Y	7. Regulate financial firms	Y	11. Repeal don't ask, tell	Y
4. Pass cap-and-trade	N	8. Pass tax cuts for some	Y	12. Limit campaign funds	Y

Election Results

2010 general	Jerry Costello (D)	121,272	(60%)	($1,351,182)
	Teri Newman (R)	74,046	(37%)	
	Rodger Jennings (Green)	7,387	(4%)	($445)
2010 primary	Jerry Costello (D)	unopposed		

Prior Winning Percentages: 2008 (71%), 2006 (100%), 2004 (69%), 2002 (69%), 2000 (100%), 1998 (60%), 1996 (72%), 1994 (66%), 1992 (71%), 1990 (66%), 1988 (53%), Special: 1988 (51%)

Population		Race/Ethnicity		Work	
Pop. 2010:	666,459	White:	76.4%	Private:	76.4%
Change since 2000:	Up 2.0%	Black:	17.5%	Government:	18.0%
Urban:	76.7%	Hispanic:	3.0%	Self-employed:	5.6%
Rural:	23.3%	Asian:	1.0%	Blue collar:	22.4%
Area size:	4,557 sq. mi.	Native Am.:	0.2%	White collar:	56.8%
		Hawaiian:	0.0%	Khaki collar:	0.6%
Age		Two+ races:	1.7%	Other:	20.2%
Median age:	37.2 yrs.				
More than 65 yrs:	14.2%	*Ancestry*		Median income:	$41,771
Less than 18 yrs:	23.5%	German	22.7%	Median Home Value:	$97,200
		Irish	11.0%		
Education		English	7.7%	**Military Veterans**	
H.S. grad:	86.1%			% of Pop:	12.4%
College grad:	20.3%				
Grad degree:	7.7%				

Southwest Illinois; Belleville

Their waters roiling together, the nation's two mightiest rivers, the Mississippi and Missouri, join just a few miles below Alton, Ill. Its 19th-century buildings recall its turbulent history, when it was the home of the antislavery agitator Elijah Lovejoy, who was murdered by a mob. More recently, it was the longtime home of conservative crusader and columnist Phyllis Schlafly. Nearby in Hartford, Lewis and Clark

2008 Presidential Vote		
Barack Obama (D) 170,391	(56%)
John McCain (R) 131,443	(43%)
2004 Presidential Vote		
John Kerry (D) 152,055	(52%)
George Bush (R) 139,710	(48%)
Cook Partisan Voting Index: D+3		

spent five months preparing their team and collecting supplies for their journey westward. Farther south along the Mississippi is East St. Louis, situated on the Illinois side of the river, with a view of the Gateway Arch in the city of St. Louis on the Missouri side. It is a terminus for dozens of rail lines and highways that funnel into bridges over the river. Once a rail and stockyard center second only to Chicago, East St. Louis is now one of America's poorest and most troubled cities, a half-abandoned slum with one of the nation's highest crime rates and a rapidly declining tax base. It is dependent on a riverboat casino and an adjacent waterfront hotel for local revenue, but casino taxes have increased and revenues have dipped, leaving the future of gambling in Illinois in question. After peaking at 82,000 in 1960, its population is now less than 29,000 and almost entirely African-American. When cash-strapped city officials announced plans in July 2010 to lay off 37 workers, including one-third of its police officers, the move sparked an angry public outcry. East St. Louis is in St. Clair County, long heavily Democratic. Alton is in Madison County, which is politically more marginal. A new amphitheater and federal funds for high-speed rail have bolstered its economy.

South of East St. Louis and the industrial area around Belleville, the river counties are lightly inhabited. This was the site of the French Kaskaskia settlement that became Illinois's first capital in 1818, but repeated flooding turned it into an island and reduced its population to nine people and many more egrets. Farther south, the river abuts coal country and is not far from Carbondale, once a coal center but now, as the home of Southern Illinois University, bustling with students. In 2006, Maytag shut its plant and eliminated 1,000 jobs in nearby Herrin. The land here is sometimes known as Little Egypt, the southern end of Illinois where the Ohio River meets the Mississippi: flat, fertile farmland, protected by giant constructed levees because it is susceptible to yearly floods. The marshy landscape has created the Sinkhole Plain, with more than 10,000 sinkholes. There is more than a touch of Dixie here: The unofficial capital of Little Egypt, Cairo (pronounced *KAY-roh*), is a declining town closer to Memphis than to Chicago. A more enticing locale not far from Cairo is the Shawnee National Forest, which has preserved Native American sites that are 10,000 years old. The Cherokee Nation left here in the 1830s on its devastating, forced march to Oklahoma, which became known as the Trail of Tears.

The 12th District of Illinois covers all of this Mississippi riverfront from Alton south to Cairo, with some inland territory as well. Most of its population is in the Metro East area in St. Clair and Madison counties. The largest employer in Southern Illinois is Scott Air Force Base near Belleville, which has a workforce of 14,000 and is home of the 932nd Airlift Wing. George W. Bush lost this district twice. John McCain lost it to Barack Obama, 56%-43% in 2008.

Jerry Costello (D)

The congressman from the 12th District is Jerry Costello, a Democrat first elected in 1988. He grew up in a St. Clair County political family—his father was the county sheriff. He graduated from high school in East St. Louis, and then the family moved to Belleville. As a young man, Costello went to work for the county as a court bailiff, and eventually worked his way up to administrator of the county court system. He was elected to the St. Clair County Board of Supervisors and became chairman. He waited with some impatience for the retirement of Democratic U.S. Rep. Mel Price, who was first elected in 1944 and served for more than 40 years. Price died in office in April 1988. Experienced, well-connected, supported by organized labor, Costello was the obvious successor. He received 51% of the votes in the special election and 53% for a full term.

Costello is a practical-minded, low-profile politician with a centrist voting record that is a bit more liberal on economics than on cultural issues. He was among the anti-abortion Democrats who joined Michigan's Bart Stupak in demanding concessions on the final 2010 health care overhaul, and later that year opposed repealing the "don't ask, don't tell" policy barring openly gay soldiers from serving. Seniority has moved him toward top posts on both the Science and Technology and the Transportation and Infrastructure committees, where he chaired the Aviation Subcommittee until the GOP takeover of the House in 2011. He wants the federal government to make a much larger contribution to modernize the air traffic control system.

In 2008, the Transportation Committee approved his proposal to ban cell phone use on planes. He considered becoming the Science, Space and Technology Committee's top Democrat in 2011. But after his ally Transportation and Infrastructure Chairman James Oberstar's startling 2010 defeat and Republicans reassumed control of the House, he decided instead to focus on that panel's work.

In his district work, Costello is attempting to revive his district's largely dormant high-sulfur coal mines with incentives for clean-coal research and development and has been successful in including several provisions in recent energy bills. He opposed the 2009 cap-and-trade bill to fight greenhouses gases blamed for global warming out of concern for the measure's effect on coal. Costello also tries to get as much federal money as he can for infrastructure improvements for downtrodden East St. Louis. Despite setbacks, Costello finally won approval of a new Mississippi River bridge north of the current congested bridge on Interstates 70, 64, and 55. In 2008, Costello received Ethics Committee approval to continue seeking spending earmarks for Southwestern Illinois College after his wife, Georgia, was named president of the college.

Costello usually draws no serious challenges at election time. But in 1998, he faced Bill Price, an orthopedic surgeon and son of Mel Price, who switched parties and ran as a Republican. At the time, Costello had been weakened by disclosures at the trial of his former business partner, who ultimately was convicted of trying to obstruct a federal investigation. The trial brought out testimony that Costello was a silent partner in casino deals at a time when he was working on legislation to help an Indian tribe that owned the land for the proposed casinos. Despite an opponent with a well-known and respected name locally, Costello won by a solid 60%-40%. Since then, he has been easily re-elected every two years.

THIRTEENTH DISTRICT

Judy Biggert (R)

Elected 1998, 7th term; b. Aug. 15, 1937, Chicago; home, Hinsdale; Stanford U., B.A. 1959, Northwestern U., J.D. 1963; Episcopalian; married (Rody); 4 children.

Elected Office: Hinsdale Bd. of Ed., 1982-85; IL House of Reps., 1992-98.

Professional Career: Clerk, U.S. Ct. of Appeals, 1963-64; Practicing atty., 1975-98.

DC Office: 2113 RHOB, 20515, 202-225-3515; Fax: 202-225-9420; Web site: judybiggert.house.gov.

State Offices: Willowbrook, 630-655-2052.

Committees: *Education & the Workforce:* Early Childhood, Elementary & Secondary Education; Higher Education & Workforce Training. *Financial Services:* Capital Markets and Government Sponsored Enterprises; Insurance, Housing & Community Opportunity (Chmn). *Science & Technology:* Energy & Environment; Technology & Innovation.

Group Ratings

	ACLU	ACU	ADA	CFG	AFS	FRC	LCV	ITIC	NTU	COC
2010	31	71	20	72	0	62	50	67	77	100
2009	–	80	20	77	22	–	29	–	73	93

National Journal Ratings

	2010 LIB	—	2010 CONS	2009 LIB	—	2009 CONS
Economic	37%	—	63%	33%	—	67%
Social	36%	—	63%	42%	—	57%
Foreign	36%	—	63%	39%	—	60%
Composite	37%	—	63%	38%	—	62%

Key Votes of the 111th Congress

1. Overturn Ledbetter	N	5. Bar federal abortion funds	Y	9. Stop detainee transfers	Y
2. Pass $820 billion stimulus	N	6. Pass health care bill	N	10. Legalize immigrants' kids	N
3. Let guns in national parks	Y	7. Regulate financial firms	N	11. Repeal don't ask, tell	Y
4. Pass cap-and-trade	N	8. Pass tax cuts for some	N	12. Limit campaign funds	N

Election Results

2010 general	Judy Biggert (R)..152,132	(64%)	($1,584,517)
	Scott Harper (D)...86,281	(36%)	($648,365)
2010 primary	Judy Biggert (R).. unopposed		

Prior Winning Percentages: 2008 (54%), 2006 (58%), 2004 (65%), 2002 (70%), 2000 (66%), 1998 (61%)

Population		Race/Ethnicity		Work	
Pop. 2010:	773,095	White:	71.2%	Private:	85.1%
Change since 2000:	Up 18.3%	Black:	6.8%	Government:	10.3%
Urban:	98.8%	Hispanic:	10.7%	Self-employed:	4.4%
Rural:	1.2%	Asian:	9.4%	Blue collar:	15.0%
Area size:	362 sq. mi.	Native Am.:	0.1%	White collar:	72.3%
		Hawaiian:	0.0%	Khaki collar:	0.0%
Age		Two+ races:	1.6%	Other:	12.7%
Median age:	36.7 yrs.				
More than 65 yrs:	10.3%	*Ancestry*		Median income:	$81,365
Less than 18 yrs:	26.9%	German	16.1%	Median Home Value:	$317,800
		Irish	13.4%		
Education		Polish	11.0%	**Military Veterans**	
H.S. grad:	93.1%			% of Pop:	7.1%
College grad:	45.4%				
Grad degree:	18.0%				

Chicago Suburbs; Naperville

Most residents of Chicagoland now live not in the city but in the suburbs, and increasingly not even in Cook County, but in the collar counties all around Cook. DuPage County, straight west of Chicago, had 103,000 residents in 1940; in 2009, there were 932,000, with new subdivisions still springing up at the western edges. This is not a one-trick county of bedroom suburbs. Since 1970, DuPage has generated nearly half of the new jobs in metropolitan Chicago. In Oak Brook

2008 Presidential Vote		
Barack Obama (D) 191,306	(54%)
John McCain (R) 156,695	(45%)
2004 Presidential Vote		
George Bush (R) 175,705	(55%)
John Kerry (D) 142,397	(45%)
Cook Partisan Voting Index: R+1		

are the headquarters of Ace Hardware, Federal Signal, and most famously, McDonald's and its Hamburger University, an 80-acre campus where more than 80,000 trainees have received bachelor of hamburgerology degrees since it was founded in 1961. Nearby are graceful, old railroad-commuter towns like Hinsdale and Downers Grove, but also Naperville, once a country village, now an edge city, with a school district that is top-ranked globally in science. The Argonne National Laboratory, which conducts basic and applied research in disciplines that range from high energy physics to biotechnology, has sparked numerous private research firms. Argonne received attention in 2010 and 2011 for technology developed there that could enable electric cars to travel twice the distance before recharging.

The 13th Congressional District of Illinois includes the southern part of DuPage County, including Oak Brook, Downers Grove, and Naperville; a small section of the southwest corner of Cook County; and a northern slice of Will County, including Bolingbrook, Romeoville, and Lockport. *Money* magazine rated Naperville No. 2 among the best places to live in the United States in 2006. But by mid-2010, three pawnshops opened there within a mile of each other in a year, a sign of the recession's effect on residents willing to sell expensive items. Politically, this has been a heavily Republican area, suspicious of the motives and operations of Chicago Democrats, devoted to free enterprise, and hostile to higher taxes. George W. Bush twice won the district with 55% of the vote. Barack Obama nearly reversed Bush's numbers, winning 54% to 45%.

Judy Biggert (R)

The congresswoman from the 13th District is Judy Biggert, a Republican first elected in 1998. She grew up in affluent Kenilworth on the North Shore, graduated from New Trier Township High School, Stanford University, and Northwestern Law School, and then clerked for a federal appeals judge. She raised four children in Hinsdale, practicing estate and real estate law out of her home. She served on the Hinsdale Township Board of Education and in 1992, was elected to the state House, where she was a member of the leadership. Biggert started running for the U.S. House in

1997, when incumbent Republican moderate Harris Fawell announced his retirement. He endorsed her as his successor. In the campaign, she portrayed herself as a "former car pool mom and assistant soccer coach." She supported abortion rights and opposed most gun control measures. She had primary opposition from state Rep. Peter Roskam, who moved to the district to run (and now holds the 6th District seat). Biggert put in $402,000 of her own money and got support from Planned Parenthood and the gay rights group Human Rights Campaign. She won the primary 45% to 40% for Roskam and the general election 61%-39%.

In the House, Biggert has a moderate voting record, especially on cultural issues. "As a moderate, you work across the aisle, and some of the more conservative members don't understand that," she told *Esquire* magazine in 2010. She was one of just 15 House Republicans in 2010 to support repeal of the military's "don't ask, don't tell" policy barring openly gay service members. In 2008, after a five-year campaign by Biggert, Congress passed her bill barring employers and insurers from denying a job or a health insurance policy on the basis of genetic tests. After Hurricane Katrina in 2005, she strongly opposed a proposed school voucher program for evacuees. In 2007, Congress enacted her proposal to ensure that homeless youth have equivalent access to student aid. Two years later, she won House passage of her bill to expand the availability of self sufficiency programs offered in connection with the Housing and Urban Development Department's Section 8 low-income housing program. She founded a Congressional Caucus on Homelessness with several Democrats in 2010.

Biggert has been a strong supporter of the Argonne Lab. On the Science Committee, she has sponsored bills authorizing hundreds of millions of dollars for university nuclear science and engineering programs. In 2004, she sponsored a successful bill authorizing the Energy Department to spend $165 million to build a supercomputer. Her challenge in the 111th Congress (2009-10) was trying to persuade appropriators to sustain a high level of funding for research during the recession. The funding was needed, she said, to avert a "brain drain" at the national labs. Another area of interest for Biggert is public education. She has sponsored bills to ensure that homeless children get schooling, to help children with eating disorders and to finance school construction. She contemplated seeking the top Republican slot on the Education and Labor Committee in 2009, but bowed out in favor of the more conservative John Kline of Minnesota.

In 2009, Biggert became the ranking Republican on the Financial Services Subcommittee on Oversight and Investigations. She worked with Democrats Paul Kanjorski, D-Pa., and Jackie Speier, D-Calif., in 2009 to create a new Federal Insurance Office within the Treasury Department to offer advice on non-health related insurance policy issues. She was unsuccessful, though, in amending the financial overhaul bill to have a new financial institutions regulator oversee consumer protection as an alternative to Democrats' push to form a new agency for that purpose. After the GOP takeover of the House in 2010, she was named to chair the Financial Services' Subcommittee on Insurance, Housing, and Community Opportunity. At the local level, Biggert has worked to secure funding for electric fish barriers on the Chicago Sanitary and Ship Canal to keep the huge Asian carp from invading the Great Lakes.

Biggert has ambitions to get into the Republican leadership in the House, but has been left behind as her caucus has moved to the right. In 2000 and 2001, she lost contests for secretary of the Republican Conference to more conservative lawmakers. For years, she was not seriously challenged for re-election, even though in 1999 she abandoned her pledge to serve only three terms.

But in 2008, she faced former health care marketing executive Scott Harper, who criticized her as too friendly to corporate interests and out of touch with voters' economic anxieties. He was competitive financially, raising over $1 million, and criticized her for being "asleep at the wheel" for initially voting against the financial markets bailout. She later voted to support the legislation. She won 54%-44%, getting 54% in DuPage County and 60% in the Cook County suburbs, but only 50% in the outlying Will County suburbs. Harper came back for a rematch in 2010, but had a more difficult time raising money and lacked Obama's candidacy to lure Democrats to the polls. Biggert raised more than $1.5 million and won easily with 64%.

FOURTEENTH DISTRICT

Randy Hultgren (R)

Elected 2010, 1st term; b. March 1, 1966, Park Ridge; home, Winfield; Bethel U., B.A. 1988; IL Inst. of Technology, J.D. 1993.; Christian; Married (Christy); 4 children.

Elected Office: DuPage Cnty. Bd., 1994-98; IL House, 1998-2006; IL Senate, 2006-10.

Professional Career: Office mgr., Rep. Dennis Hastert, R-Ill., 1988-90; V.P., Trust Investment Advisors, 1995-2010; practicing atty., 1993-2010.

DC Office: 427 CHOB, 20515, 202-225-2976; Fax: 202-225-0697; Web site: hultgren.house.gov.

State Offices: Dixon, 815-288-1174; Geneva, 630-232-7104.

Committees: *Agriculture:* Conservation, Energy & Forestry; General Farm Commodities & Risk Management; Rural Development, Research, Biotechnology & Foreign Agriculture. *Science & Technology:* Investigations & Oversight; Research & Science Education; Technology & Innovation. *Transportation & Infrastructure:* Aviation; Economic Development, Public Buildings & Emergency Management; Railroads, Pipelines & Hazardous Materials.

Election Results

2010 general	Randy Hultgren (R)	112,369	(51%)	($1,601,719)
	Bill Foster (D)	98,645	(45%)	($3,910,302)
	Daniel Kairis (Green)	7,949	(4%)	
2010 primary	Randy Hultgren (R)	34,833	(55%)	
	Ethan Hastert (R)	28,840	(45%)	

Population		Race/Ethnicity		Work	
Pop. 2010:	840,956	White:	65.6%	Private:	84.0%
Change since 2000:	Up 28.7%	Black:	5.2%	Government:	11.5%
Urban:	86.2%	Hispanic:	24.5%	Self-employed:	4.4%
Rural:	13.8%	Asian:	3.2%	Blue collar:	24.6%
Area size:	2,866 sq. mi.	Native Am.:	0.1%	White collar:	60.7%
		Hawaiian:	0.0%	Khaki collar:	0.0%
Age		Two+ races:	1.2%	Other:	14.6%
Median age:	33.7 yrs.				
More than 65 yrs:	9.1%	*Ancestry*		Median income:	$66,125
Less than 18 yrs:	28.1%	German	19.9%	Median Home Value:	$236,300
		Irish	10.8%		
Education		Polish	5.9%	**Military Veterans**	
H.S. grad:	85.1%			% of Pop:	7.6%
College grad:	30.4%				
Grad degree:	10.3%				

North Central Illinois; Aurora

Downstate Illinois, as it is known locally, is a misnomer. Although it certainly does refer to the territory south of Chicago, and therefore "down the state" from Chicago, it also means everything north and west of the nation's third-largest city. In the vernacular, downstate Illinois is everything that is not Chicago or its suburbs, just as upstate New York is everything that is not New York City. The 14th Congressional District is where downstate Illinois begins, at least

2008 Presidential Vote

Barack Obama (D)	181,329	(55%)
John McCain (R)	145,345	(44%)

2004 Presidential Vote

George Bush (R)	158,428	(55%)
John Kerry (D)	125,269	(44%)

Cook Partisan Voting Index: R+1

where it begins in the westerly direction from the city. Where the densely packed suburban areas leave off, the district begins in western DuPage County. It is home to two great Illinois landmarks: Cantigny, the estate of Col. Robert McCormick, longtime publisher of the *Chicago Tribune*, and Fermilab, which houses the world's second-fastest particle accelerator, which takes 2,000 people to operate. The 14th also contains the Fox River Valley and its industrial cities, Elgin and Aurora.

Before the recent recession, Aurora's population grew 19% from 2000 to 2006, with a large influx of Hispanics. In contrast, there is urbane St. Charles, a small city bisected by the Fox River that is filled with antique stores and restaurants and sponsors the well-attended annual Scarecrow Festival.

The district also includes Kendall County, rated the fastest-growing large county in the nation by the U.S. Census Bureau in 2010. It went from a population of 54,500 in 2000 to nearly 105,000 in 2009, as urban flight brought in families interested in its affordable housing, good schools, and low crime rates, all located near job centers in suburban DuPage and Kane counties. In effect, Kendall became a suburb of the suburbs. The downside of the rapid growth became evident during the collapse of the housing finance market, when Kendall posted the highest foreclosure rate in the state.

Farther west, the 14th passes through DeKalb County, long the world's leading manufacturer of barbed wire, and goes on to Lee County, to take in Ronald Reagan's boyhood home in Dixon. This was traditionally some of the most heavily Republican territory in the country. Northern Illinois was settled when Chicago was just a frontier village, by Yankees from Ohio, Indiana, upstate New York, and New England, and by Germans emigrating after the failed revolutions of 1848. They were the heart of the Republican Party from its founding in 1854, and the core of the Grand Army of the Republic a few years later. Their descendants remain mostly Republican today.

Randy Hultgren (R)

The new congressman from Illinois' 14th District is Randy Hultgren, a Republican who ousted Democratic Rep. Bill Foster in 2010. Hultgren was raised in Wheaton, a suburb west of Chicago. He was the youngest of three children who lived above their family's funeral home. His penchant for politics developed early. In the eighth grade, Hultgren found he liked his government class, especially when the teacher organized the students into a mini model Congress. In high school, he got involved in student government, as well as in choir and musical theater. The grandson of a Baptist pastor, Hultgren became the third generation in his family to attend Bethel College (now Bethel University) in Minnesota. After graduation, he headed to Washington, and in 1988, was hired on the staff of Rep. Dennis Hastert, R-Ill, who eventually became House speaker. Hultgren progressed quickly from intern to office manager for Hastert, and the work persuaded him to return to his hometown to pursue a degree from Chicago-Kent College of Law.

After graduation, Hultgren practiced with a local firm for a while, and in the mid-1990s, opened his own firm. During that time, he got a stock broker's license so he could also do investment work, a practice he continued until his election to Congress. This period was also formative in his political career. In 1990, he was elected as a Republican precinct committee member for Milton Township, and, four years later, Hultgren won a seat on the DuPage County Board, a governing body for several densely populated western suburbs.

In 1998, when Hultgren caught wind that a personal friend, state Rep. Peter Roskam, was planning a bid for Congress, he moved quickly to get into position to run for Roskam's Illinois House seat, which he won. Following that pattern in 2006, he was elected to succeed Roskam in the state Senate after Roskam ran for Congress.

In the summer of 2009, Hultgren decided to take on Foster, a Democrat, who had won Hastert's former seat in a March 2008 special election. But Hultgren wasn't the only one who sensed possibilities in a district that, before Foster came along, had been in GOP hands since the Great Depression. Hultgren had to compete for the nomination with Ethan Hastert, the son of his former political mentor. "It certainly wasn't anything personal," Hultgren told *National Journal.* "But I felt pretty strongly that it hadn't worked very well for Republicans' kids to take their parents' spots here in Illinois. I just felt like we needed someone who had run for office before to be able to win the seat back."

In an upset, Hultgren overcame Hastert's high name recognition and political pedigree to win the February primary by a comfortable 10 percentage points. Afterward, Hastert endorsed Hultgren in his contest with Foster. Hultgren also won backing from tea party activists, the National Federation of Independent Business, and the U.S. Chamber of Commerce.

During the general election campaign, he portrayed Foster as a liberal out of touch with the exurban district, and he made frequent references to liberal House Speaker Nancy Pelosi of California. Hultgren said he would not have voted for the $787 billion economic stimulus bill or the health care overhaul, both of which Foster supported. A Harvard-trained physicist, Foster decreed Hultgren to be too "far right" for the district. He also raised significantly more money than Hultgren, and conspicuously did not mention his party affiliation. On Election Day, Hultgren won with 51% of the vote to Foster's 45%. Green Party candidate Daniel Kairis got nearly 4%. Foster won only one population center—DeKalb County, home to the liberal-leaning academic community of Northern Illinois University. Hultgren won the largest county, Kane, 51%-46%; and he also won Kendall County, 53% to 44%.

FIFTEENTH DISTRICT
Tim Johnson (R)

Elected 2000, 6th term; b. July 23, 1946, Champaign; home, Urbana; U. of IL, B.A. 1969, U. of IL, J.D. 1972; Christian; divorced; 9 children.

Elected Office: Urbana City Council, 1971-76; IL House of Reps., 1976-2000.

Professional Career: Practicing atty., Johnson, Frank, Frederick & Walsh.

DC Office: 1207 LHOB, 20515, 202-225-2371; Fax: 202-226-0791; Web site: timjohnson.house.gov.

State Offices: Bloomington, 309-663-7049; Champaign, 217-403-4690; Charleston, 217-348-6759; Mt. Carmel, 618-262-8719.

Committees: *Agriculture:* Department Operations, Oversight & Credit; Rural Development, Research, Biotechnology & Foreign Agriculture (Chmn). *Transportation & Infrastructure:* Economic Development, Public Buildings & Emergency Management; Highways & Transit; Water Resources & Environment.

Group Ratings

	ACLU	ACU	ADA	CFG	AFS	FRC	LCV	ITIC	NTU	COC
2010	38	79	25	75	25	100	80	67	78	88
2009	–	80	15	79	44	–	43	–	79	87

National Journal Ratings

	2010 LIB — 2010 CONS		2009 LIB — 2009 CONS	
Economic	39%	— 60%	35%	— 65%
Social	36%	— 64%	36%	— 63%
Foreign	39%	— 61%	40%	— 60%
Composite	38%	— 62%	37%	— 63%

Key Votes of the 111th Congress

1. Overturn Ledbetter	N	5. Bar federal abortion funds	
2. Pass $820 billion stimulus	N	6. Pass health care bill	
3. Let guns in national parks	Y	7. Regulate financial firms	
4. Pass cap-and-trade	N	8. Pass tax cuts for some	N

9. Stop detainee transfers	Y
10. Legalize immigrants' kids	N
11. Repeal don't ask, tell	N
12. Limit campaign funds	N

Election Results

2010 general	Tim Johnson (R)	136,915	(64%)	($342,063)
	David Gill (D)	75,948	(36%)	($145,099)
2010 primary	Tim Johnson (R)	unopposed		

Prior Winning Percentages: 2008 (64%), 2006 (58%), 2004 (61%), 2002 (65%), 2000 (53%)

Population		Race/Ethnicity		Work	
Pop. 2010:	681,580	White:	84.0%	Private:	74.4%
Change since 2000:	Up 4.3%	Black:	6.6%	Government:	19.0%
Urban:	64.2%	Hispanic:	3.7%	Self-employed:	6.4%
Rural:	35.8%	Asian:	3.8%	Blue collar:	24.1%
Area size:	10,123 sq. mi.	Native Am.:	0.2%	White collar:	58.4%
		Hawaiian:	0.0%	Khaki collar:	0.1%
Age		Two+ races:	1.6%	Other:	17.4%
Median age:	35.7 yrs.				
More than 65 yrs:	14.0%	*Ancestry*		Median income:	$45,432
Less than 18 yrs:	21.8%	German	21.3%	Median Home Value:	$108,500
		Irish	10.6%		
Education		USA	10.5%	**Military Veterans**	
H.S. grad:	89.4%			% of Pop:	9.9%
College grad:	26.1%				
Grad degree:	10.2%				

East Illinois; Champaign, Urbana

South of Chicago, the Illinois Central Railroad heads to the city of New Orleans on a railbed elevated a few feet above the rich, black soil of the Illinois prairie, topsoil reaching down not just inches but feet. This land dazzled its first settlers, who were accustomed to land that had to be cleared of trees and stumps before it could be plowed. This treeless prairie could be cultivated almost immediately, and with bounteous results.

2008 Presidential Vote		
John McCain (R)	152,222	(51%)
Barack Obama (D)	143,965	(48%)
2004 Presidential Vote		
George Bush (R)	174,928	(59%)
John Kerry (D)	121,814	(41%)
Cook Partisan Voting Index: R+6		

Today, the region is still farming country, made up not of small family farms, but of large and profitable commercial operations, typically of 1,000 acres or more. The chief crops are corn and soybeans. The prairie landscape of rural, Eastern Illinois is marked by only a few towns, the largest of which are the sites of universities: the University of Illinois in Champaign-Urbana, Illinois State University in Bloomington-Normal, Illinois Wesleyan, also in Bloomington. Politically, these prairie lands incline much more to the party of former House Speaker Joseph Cannon, a Republican from the manufacturing city of Danville, east of Urbana, than to the party of Vice President Adlai Stevenson, a Democrat from Bloomington, who was the grandfather of the Adlai Stevenson nominated by Democrats for president in 1952 and 1956.

The 15th Congressional District of Illinois occupies much of this prairie, beginning in Iroquois County and covering some 130 miles south to the old National Road and U.S. 40, traditionally the line between northern Republican and southern Democratic downstate Illinois. The biggest city here is Champaign-Urbana and the district includes parts of Normal and next-door Bloomington. Downtown Normal and Illinois State University are in the 11th District, while southern Normal and eastern Bloomington are in the 15th. The area did far better than most other parts of Illinois in coping with the recession, thanks to an insurance industry that, with its related support industries, employs nearly one-quarter of the workforce. The district also features a narrow corridor of land extending more than 100 miles along the Wabash River border with Indiana as far south as the Ohio River, with an extension to the town of Eldorado. The university towns are somewhat liberal, but the prairie counties have long been Republican, and on balance, this is a Republican-oriented district.

Tim Johnson (R)

The congressman from the 15th District is Tim Johnson, a Republican first elected in 2000. Johnson was born in Champaign, grew up in Urbana, and graduated from the University of Illinois and its law school. He was elected to the Urbana City Council while still in law school and served four years before winning election to the state House in 1976. In the legislature, Johnson worked his way up to deputy majority leader. He was a trial lawyer and managed a small farm operation until he sold it in 2005.

Johnson ran for Congress after Republican Rep. Tom Ewing retired. Ewing had delayed his retirement announcement until his 29-year-old son, Sam, could move back to the district from Texas to launch his candidacy to succeed his father. That angered then GOP House Speaker Dennis Hastert, who endorsed state Rep. Bill Brady, the scion of a prominent real estate family from Bloomington. Johnson had more political experience than either of the other Republican candidates and was a ferocious campaigner. The primary results broke along regional lines. Brady won his base of McLean County with 62% of the vote, while in Champaign, Johnson led Brady with 61%. Johnson carried seven of the 11 counties, winning 44% of the vote, to 36% for Brady and 17% for Ewing. In the general election against Illinois State University instructor Mike Kelleher, the voting pattern was similar. Kelleher narrowly won his home of McLean County, while Johnson secured Champaign and nine of the 11 counties, winning 53%-47% overall.

In the House, Johnson has compiled a moderate voting record, though his reputation for quirkiness has overshadowed his legislative work. He talks by phone daily to between 100 and 200 of his constituents, a reflection of his belief that lawmakers talk to each other more than the people they represent. He told the Associated Press in 2010 that his one-day call record was nearly 1,000 while vacationing in Hawaii—"I had nothing to do except lay on the beach." Johnson says he sometimes gets ideas for legislation from his phone conversations, such as a measure increasing disclosure of congressional travel. An avid fitness buff who can be seen walking everywhere on Capitol Hill, he owns two treadmills, multiple gym memberships, and an indoor swimming pool.

Johnson has been more inclined to side with his party in recent years but still has maverick tendencies. He was the only House Republican in November 2009 to oppose the GOP's alternative health care plan, although he did not endorse the Democrats' proposal either. He exercised notable independence from Hastert while Republicans were still in the majority, and was given only modest committee assignments. But he found other routes to influence. He took issue with the Bush administration's environmental record and voted against opening the Alaska National Wildlife Refuge to oil drilling, winning him a re-election endorsement from the League of Conservation Voters. In 2005, he was one of 14 House Republicans who voted against $50 billion in proposed domestic spending cuts.

Johnson also bucked the Republican administration on the war in Iraq. In February 2007, he was one of 17 House Republicans who voted for a resolution opposing President Bush's troop "surge" plan. However, Johnson later opposed Democratic proposals calling for a timetable to withdraw troops. He also took issue with President Obama's decision in 2009 to increase troops in Afghanistan, calling military operations "a folly of a war we cannot afford and a mission that has no endgame." In June 2008, he cited the impact on civil liberties when he was the only Republican to vote against renewal of the law to permit a secret court to approve intelligence surveillance, which the House passed 293-129. He serves on the Agriculture Committee and after the House GOP takeover in 2010, was named chairman of its rural development subcommittee. He has joined Democratic efforts to expand agricultural exports to Cuba. Believing that Congress has grown too partisan, he and New York Democrat Steve Israel formed the bipartisan Center Aisle Caucus in 2005.

Johnson reneged on his term-limits pledge in October 2002. In subsequent bids for re-election, in 2004 and 2006, emergency-room physician David Gill challenged Johnson as the Democratic nominee, promoting universal health care as his prime issue. But Johnson prevailed by solid margins. In 2008, he breezed to a 64%-36% re-election—a result he duplicated against Gill in a rematch two years later.

SIXTEENTH DISTRICT

Don Manzullo (R)

Elected 1992, 10th term; b. March 24, 1944, Rockford; home, Egan; American U., B.A. 1967, Marquette U., J.D. 1970; Baptist; married (Freda); 3 children.

Professional Career: Practicing atty., 1970–92; author.

DC Office: 2228 RHOB, 20515, 202-225-5676; Fax: 202-225-5284; Web site: manzullo.house.gov.

State Offices: Crystal Lake, 815-356-9800; Rockford, 815-394-1231.

Committees: *Financial Services:* Capital Markets and Government Sponsored Enterprises; Financial Institutions & Consumer Credit; International Monetary Policy & Trade. *Foreign Affairs:* Asia & the Pacific (Chmn); Middle East & South Asia.

Group Ratings

	ACLU	ACU	ADA	CFG	AFS	FRC	LCV	ITIC	NTU	COC
2010	13	92	10	82	13	93	10	33	84	88
2009	–	96	5	85	11	–	0	–	86	73

National Journal Ratings

	2010 LIB — 2010 CONS		2009 LIB — 2009 CONS	
Economic	29% —	71%	16% —	83%
Social	0% —	85%	17% —	82%
Foreign	12% —	79%	0% —	75%
Composite	18% —	82%	16% —	85%

Key Votes of the 111th Congress

1. Overturn Ledbetter	N	5. Bar federal abortion funds	Y	9. Stop detainee transfers	Y
2. Pass $820 billion stimulus	N	6. Pass health care bill	N	10. Legalize immigrants' kids	N
3. Let guns in national parks	Y	7. Regulate financial firms	N	11. Repeal don't ask, tell	N
4. Pass cap-and-trade	N	8. Pass tax cuts for some	N	12. Limit campaign funds	N

Election Results

2010 general	Don Manzullo (R)..138,299	(65%)	($1,160,685)
	George Gaulrapp (D)...66,037	(31%)	($73,357)
	Terry Campbell (Green)..8,425	(4%)	
2010 primary	Don Manzullo (R).. unopposed		

Prior Winning Percentages: 2008 (61%), 2006 (64%), 2004 (69%), 2002 (71%), 2000 (67%), 1998 (100%), 1996 (60%), 1994 (71%), 1992 (56%)

Population		Race/Ethnicity		Work	
Pop. 2010:	718,791	White:	79.8%	Private:	83.9%
Change since 2000:	Up 10.0%	Black:	6.1%	Government:	10.1%
Urban:	78.4%	Hispanic:	10.4%	Self-employed:	5.9%
Rural:	21.6%	Asian:	2.0%	Blue collar:	25.8%
Area size:	4,158 sq. mi.	Native Am.:	0.2%	White collar:	58.1%
		Hawaiian:	0.0%	Khaki collar:	0.0%
Age		Two+ races:	1.5%	Other:	16.1%
Median age:	38.1 yrs.				
More than 65 yrs:	12.9%	*Ancestry*		Median income:	$55,819
Less than 18 yrs:	26.1%	German	23.3%	Median Home Value:	$165,200
		Irish	11.3%		
Education		English	6.4%	**Military Veterans**	
H.S. grad:	87.4%			% of Pop:	9.9%
College grad:	24.2%				
Grad degree:	8.1%				

Northern Illinois, Rockford

The far northwest corner of Illinois is one of the heartlands of the Republican Party. In the town square of Freeport, some 15,000 people came to hear Abraham Lincoln and Stephen Douglas in one of their seven debates in 1858. Settled by New England Yankees, northern Illinois was one of the strongest Republican constituencies in 1860 and for years after. Not far away, on a little river once navigable by Mississippi River steamboats, is Galena, one of the earliest settle-

2008 Presidential Vote
Barack Obama (D) 168,503   (53%)
John McCain (R) 145,795   (46%)

2004 Presidential Vote
George Bush (R) 168,303   (55%)
John Kerry (D) 133,701   (44%)

Cook Partisan Voting Index: R+2

ments in northern Illinois and the home of Ulysses S. Grant. Once larger than Chicago, Galena is now a tourist attraction. The second largest city in Illinois is Rockford, on the Rock River, settled by Swedes as well as Yankees, and one of America's leading furniture manufacturers at one time. It is the nation's leading manufacturer of fasteners, and there is a big Chrysler plant a few miles east in Belvidere. But the city's manufacturing base steadily declined after World War II, and by the 1980s, Rockford had a serious unemployment problem. It rebounded as it moved toward becoming a center for professional services and high technology, but then the recession hit with brutal force. The area's unemployment rate was the state's highest during much of 2009 and climbed to nearly 20% in early 2010 before creeping downward. To create jobs in the region, President Obama ordered the purchase of a state-owned prison in Thomson, west of Rockford, as part of a plan to move terrorist detainees out of the Guantanamo Bay, Cuba, facility. The move became bogged down in politics when Illinois Republican Sen. Mark Kirk in December 2010 threatened to put a hold on the fiscal 2011 defense authorization bill unless the plan was dropped. Meanwhile, a conflict between state and federal laws thwarted the federal Bureau of Prisons' efforts to buy the site from the state.

The 16th Congressional District of Illinois consists of much of the northwest part of the state. It includes the hilly, almost mountainous country around Galena and the Mississippi River, and the flatter plains in the farming counties to the east and south. The fastest-growing part of the district is in the east, in McHenry County and in Boone and Winnebago counties. Politically, Northern Illinois, perhaps in stubborn opposition to Democratic Chicago, remained steadfastly Republican for many years. It backed Herbert Hoover in 1932, Barry Goldwater in 1964, and George H. W. Bush in 1992 when the rest of Illinois was going the other way. But in recent years, the trend has reversed. In 2004, George W. Bush ran far behind his father's 1988 percentages in metro Chicago and in almost every one of the state's northern counties. In 2008, Barack Obama won eight of the nine counties in this district, winning 53% of the vote.

Don Manzullo (R)

The congressman from the 16th District is Donald Manzullo, a Republican first elected in 1992. He grew up in Rockford, where his father ran a grocery store and Manzullo's Famous Italian Restaurant, from 1953 until it closed in 2004. While in college in Washington, D.C., in the mid-1960s, Manzullo worked for Republican candidates and then practiced law in Illinois. For 20 years, he was a small-town lawyer in Oregon, Ill. He hosted a radio talk show for a while and wrote books on constitutional law. An ardent social conservative and passionate abortion rights foe, Manzullo early in his career started the Northern Illinois Crisis Pregnancy Center. Later, he and his wife, a microbiologist, home-schooled their three children until the eighth grade. Manzullo ran for Congress in 1990 and lost the primary to a moderate Republican. Democrat John Cox won the seat, but was weakened when heavily Republican McHenry County was added during redistricting. Two years later, Manzullo ran again and, with support from conservative Christians, beat a moderate Republican in the primary, 56%-44%. In the general election, Cox campaigned for higher taxes; Manzullo for a 10% across-the-board income tax cut. Manzullo won with 56% of the vote. He has not been seriously challenged for re-election since.

Manzullo has a generally conservative voting record. He came to Congress as a market conservative and a strong supporter of free trade. He co-chairs the House Manufacturing Caucus and has worked to exclude products like tool-grade steel from steel tariffs.

He has been dismayed by local job losses in manufacturing, which he attributes to Chinese competition, some of it in violation of international trade rules. He has worked to encourage a revival of manufacturing in America and has called for tax cuts for businesses that create jobs in the United States, an end to Chinese currency manipulation, and enforcement of Buy American laws. He also wants China to tighten and enforce its intellectual property laws while the United States modernizes its export-control laws. He said in 2009 that legislation to limit greenhouse gas emissions blamed on global warming without similar action by China, India, and other developing countries was "nothing less than unilateral surrender." From 2001 to 2006, as chairman of the Small Business Committee, he went to war with the Bush administration over funding cuts for the Small Business Administration and its guaranteed loan program. When the White House insisted on funding the program with higher fees on borrowers and lenders, Manzullo in 2004 got the House to add $79 million to the SBA budget.

From his seat on the Financial Services Committee, Manzullo has worked recently to try to accelerate tax breaks for domestic manufacturers. He was one of 32 House Republicans who voted for the bailout of the Big Three automakers in December 2008, after urging the companies to purchase U.S.-made supplies. He enthusiastically supported the "Cash for Clunkers" program, calling for it to be extended to all Americans buying new cars. He and Michael Michaud, D-Maine, led a bipartisan group of lawmakers in opposition to efforts to overhaul patent laws. Among his concerns in 2009 was a provision awarding a patent to the first person to file instead of the individual inventing the product, a move he said could disadvantage universities and small inventors. When the committee approved a bill in 2009 creating a new Consumer Financial Protection Agency, Manzullo unsuccessfully sought to amend the bill to sunset the agency after five years unless Congress reauthorized it.

On issues back home, Manzullo helped secure $12 million for Rockford's EIGERlab, a city-state-university center for the study of advanced manufacturing technologies like micromachining. He also has obtained money in recent years for Northern Illinois University's technology program. Of the many bills he's taken the lead on over the years, Manzullo has said he is most proud of the 2001 law ordering the Veterans Affairs Department to recognize Gulf War syndrome.

SEVENTEENTH DISTRICT

Bobby Schilling (R)

Elected 2010, 1st full term; b. Jan. 23, 1964, Rock Island; home, Colona; Black Hawk Col., attended 1982-83.; Catholic; Married (Christie); 10 children.

Professional Career: Machine operator, Container Corp. of America, 1983-87; salesman, Prudential Insurance, 1987-95; owner, Saint Giuseppe's Heavenly Pizza, 1996-present.

DC Office: 507 CHOB, 20515, 202-225-5905; Fax: 202-225-5396; Web site: schilling.house.gov.

State Offices: Galesburg, 309-343-1194; Moline, 309-757-7630.

Committees: *Agriculture:* General Farm Commodities & Risk Management; Rural Development, Research, Biotechnology & Foreign Agriculture. *Armed Services:* Emerging Threats & Capabilities; Readiness.

Election Results

2010 general	Bobby Schilling (R)	104,583	(53%)	($1,127,490)
	Phil Hare (D)	85,454	(43%)	($1,364,578)
	Roger Davis (Green)	8,861	(4%)	
2010 primary	Bobby Schilling (R)	unopposed		

Population		Race/Ethnicity		Work	
Pop. 2010:	634,792	White:	83.5%	Private:	79.3%
Change since 2000:	Down 2.9%	Black:	8.3%	Government:	14.3%
Urban:	71.1%	Hispanic:	5.4%	Self-employed:	6.2%
Rural:	28.9%	Asian:	0.8%	Blue collar:	26.9%
Area size:	8,288 sq. mi.	Native Am.:	0.2%	White collar:	52.9%
		Hawaiian:	0.0%	Khaki collar:	0.1%
Age		Two+ races:	1.7%	Other:	20.0%
Median age:	39.3 yrs.				
More than 65 yrs:	16.3%	*Ancestry*		Median income:	$40,742
Less than 18 yrs:	22.3%	German	21.4%	Median Home Value:	$89,900
		Irish	10.8%		
Education		English	8.1%	**Military Veterans**	
H.S. grad:	85.5%			% of Pop:	11.6%
College grad:	18.0%				
Grad degree:	6.1%				

Moline, Part Decatur

Illinois' western prairies are some of America's richest agricultural land. They were first settled by Yankees coming overland from northern Indiana and Ohio and upstate New York. After 1848, Germans left their homeland in search of better opportunities and settled in a place that in many ways resembled the flat, orderly plains of northern Germany. These migrants farmed quarter-sections and built small towns, with banks and stores, community churches and

2008 Presidential Vote
Barack Obama (D) 160,104 (57%)
John McCain (R) 118,163 (42%)

2004 Presidential Vote
John Kerry (D) 148,562 (51%)
George Bush (R) 139,251 (48%)

Cook Partisan Voting Index: D+3

libraries. As farming expanded, so did the need for agricultural equipment. Entrepreneurs and investors built farm-machinery factories, and the Quad Cities of the Mississippi—Davenport and Bettendorf in Iowa, and Rock Island and Moline in Illinois—became one of the nation's biggest agricultural equipment-manufacturing centers. The plants were unionized in the 1930s and 1940s, and in post-World War II America wages went up as the demand for more sophisticated machines increased on Midwest farms, many of them reliant on government subsidies. But eventually the cost of subsidies rose too high, and the market had its revenge. In the early 1980s, farm profits vanished, land values declined, and orders for new machinery and equipment dried up. The result was a depression in western Illinois and neighboring Iowa, and a political swing toward the Democrats and away from the Republicans, who had been the ancestral party in most of this area. The Democratic tide has receded a bit, but this was still one of the few parts of rural America carried by Al Gore in 2000, John Kerry in 2004, and Barack Obama in 2008. Recent job losses and wildly oscillating farm prices have helped Democrats maintain majorities here. From 2000 to 2010, population in the region declined, with Rock Island County down 1.4% and East Moline down about 1%.

The 17th Congressional District includes the Illinois portion of the Quad Cities plus several rural counties to the south. It takes in the entire Mississippi River border with Iowa almost to St. Louis. From there, the geography gets more imaginative. A thin strip of land along the Mississippi River and the lower Illinois River connects the district to an extension that includes rural Macoupin County and some parts east of there. Then another thin reed sprouts north from Macoupin to include central Springfield (but not the state Capitol building), and then reaches some 40 miles farther east to take in a portion of the city of Decatur.

Decatur is home to politically influential Archer Daniels Midland, the world's largest agricultural processor and a key champion of ethanol. It would be fairly easy to drive directly from any part of the 17th District to another, but only if you crossed over into the 18th or 19th districts. There is, of course, a political explanation for this weird configuration. By removing the Republican counties east and north of the Quad Cities during the post-2000 redistricting, the 17th District was made more safely Democratic, and neighboring districts were reinforced for Republicans. Macoupin County is historically Democratic, as are central Springfield and Decatur.

Bobby Schilling (R)

The new congressman from the 17th Congressional District of Illinois is Republican Bobby Schilling, who upset Democratic Rep. Phil Hare in 2010. Schilling was raised in Rock Island. His parents ran a restaurant, where he and his four siblings helped out by washing dishes. In high school, he lettered in football and track, and was crowned homecoming king. With an interest in math and an aspiration to become an accountant, he attended Black Hawk College in nearby Moline, but did not graduate. He left early to find work, which he did at the Container Corporation of America. During his five years with the company, he became steward of Local 191 of the United Paperworkers International Union. His union involvement continued when he moved on to work for Prudential Insurance; he served as treasurer for the United Food and Commercial Workers Union for eight years. Schilling married his wife, Christie, in 1986; they have 10 children. In 1996, the couple opened Saint Giuseppe's Heavenly Pizza in Moline. "Having the restaurant background as a kid...I thought I would open one up and every night just back the truck up and get the money out, but it didn't tend to work that way," Schilling told *National Journal*.

The ups and downs of owning a small business, he said, played a role in his decision to run for office. In February 2009, he announced his candidacy for the 17th District seat, launching a "Bob's for Jobs" campaign that focused on conservative approaches to spending and lowering unemployment. Schilling has cited his decision not to take a family vacation in 14 years as proof that he understands the country's financial crisis on both political and personal levels, and he criticized the Democratic "job-crushing" bills, such as the 2009 House-passed energy legislation to reduce greenhouse gas emissions.

With local and national Republicans expecting Hare to hold the seat, Schilling ran unopposed in the GOP primary. He won the endorsement of the *Chicago Tribune*, which described him as "a smart, independent conservative." Hare was slow to realize the threat, but ultimately spent $1.8 million to fight back. No slouch in fundraising himself, Schilling spent $1.1 million. Hare made an issue of the fact that his opponent's home was located about a mile outside the 17th District boundary, which he said demonstrated that Schilling was unfamiliar with the district. The Schilling campaign maintained that the house fell out of the district only after state Democrats redrew its lines after the 2000 census.

With the help of tea party activists, Schilling won decisively, 53% to 43%. Green Party candidate Roger Davis got 4%. Although Schilling and Hare more or less split the biggest population center in the district, Rock Island County (23,000 votes for Schilling to 22,000 for Hare), Schilling got substantial majorities in some of the smaller towns, including Quincy in Adams County and Decatur in Macon County.

EIGHTEENTH DISTRICT

Aaron Schock (R)

Elected 2008, 2nd term; b. May 28, 1981, Morris, MN; home, Peoria; Bradley U., B.S. 2001; Baptist; single.

Elected Office: Peoria Bd. Of Education, 2001-05, V.P., 2003-04, Pres., 2004-05; IL House, 2005-08.

Professional Career: Founder, GarageTek, 2001-03; Dir. of devel. & construction, Petersen Co., 2007; Real estate investor/developer, 2001-present.

DC Office: 328 CHOB, 20515, 202-225-6201; Fax: 202-225-9249; Web site: schock.house.gov.

State Offices: Jacksonville, 217-245-1431; Peoria, 309-671-7027; Springfield, 217-670-1653.

Committees: *House Administration:* Elections; Oversight. *Ways & Means:* Oversight; Social Security; Trade.

Group Ratings

	ACLU	ACU	ADA	CFG	AFS	FRC	LCV	ITIC	NTU	COC
2010	13	88	0	72	0	100	10	33	84	100
2009	–	92	5	72	22	–	29	–	70	93

National Journal Ratings

	2010 LIB	—	2010 CONS	2009 LIB	—	2009 CONS
Economic	30%	—	70%	31%	—	68%
Social	33%	—	66%	29%	—	68%
Foreign	36%	—	63%	0%	—	75%
Composite	33%	—	67%	25%	—	75%

Key Votes of the 111th Congress

1. Overturn Ledbetter	N	5. Bar federal abortion funds	Y
2. Pass $820 billion stimulus	N	6. Pass health care bill	N
3. Let guns in national parks	Y	7. Regulate financial firms	N
4. Pass cap-and-trade	N	8. Pass tax cuts for some	N

9. Stop detainee transfers	Y
10. Legalize immigrants' kids	N
11. Repeal don't ask, tell	N
12. Limit campaign funds	N

Election Results

2010 general	Aaron Schock (R)	152,868	(69%)	($2,408,587)
	Deirdre Hirner (D)	57,046	(26%)	($138,081)
	Sheldon Schafer (Green)	11,256	(5%)	($4,055)
2010 primary	Aaron Schock (R)	unopposed		

Prior Winning Percentages: 2008 (59%)

Population		Race/Ethnicity		Work	
Pop. 2010:	665,723	White:	86.5%	Private:	80.5%
Change since 2000:	Up 1.8%	Black:	7.4%	Government:	13.7%
Urban:	68.0%	Hispanic:	2.8%	Self-employed:	5.7%
Rural:	32.0%	Asian:	1.5%	Blue collar:	22.3%
Area size:	8,302 sq. mi.	Native Am.:	0.2%	White collar:	59.9%
		Hawaiian:	0.0%	Khaki collar:	0.1%
Age		Two+ races:	1.5%	Other:	17.7%
Median age:	39.3 yrs.				
More than 65 yrs:	15.4%	*Ancestry*		Median income:	$50,914
Less than 18 yrs:	23.0%	German	25.0%	Median Home Value:	$114,400
		Irish	11.4%		
Education		USA	9.3%	**Military Veterans**	
H.S. grad:	89.1%			% of Pop:	11.2%
College grad:	24.3%				
Grad degree:	8.0%				

Central Illinois; Peoria

Old vaudeville bookers, presented with a new act, used to ask, "Will it play in Peoria?" The implication was that if an act went over in this small city on the bluffs above the Illinois River, 154 miles from Chicago and 171 miles from St. Louis, it would go over just about anywhere. In the first half of the 20th century, Peoria did seem pretty typical of America. If its citizens were mostly of British or German descent, with a small percentage of African-Americans, that

2008 Presidential Vote		
John McCain (R)	156,898	(50%)
Barack Obama (D)	151,687	(48%)
2004 Presidential Vote		
George Bush (R)	181,058	(58%)
John Kerry (D)	130,669	(42%)
Cook Partisan Voting Index:	R+6	

was the image of ordinary America that prevailed through the 1960s, despite the great immigrations of 1880-1924 and the northward, urban migrations of Southern rural blacks of 1940-1965. But Peoria's economy has changed, much as America's has changed. This is still a heavy manufacturing town, dominated by big plants that produce farm machinery and earth-moving equipment. Its biggest employer is Caterpillar, which was founded in 1910 with 12 employees, and a century later was the world's leading producer of earth-moving and construction equipment, and one of America's major exporters. There are more than just memories here of the sharp divide between blue collar and white collar, union and management, Democrat and Republican—the basis of the class warfare politics that was the norm in heavy industrial metropolises of the Great Lakes region starting with the sit-down strikes of the late 1930s.

But the blue-collar workers now are not as numerous and the unions not as strong. The Peoria area went through terrible times in the 1980s, as big farm machinery plants laid off workers and even closed down. Then Caterpillar, struck by the United Auto Workers in 1992, hired replacement workers and continued to operate—not without some friction and inefficiency, but profitably—something unheard of a decade or more earlier. Not until 1998 did union members approve a settlement, pretty much on the company's terms. Memories of those hard times were revived by the 2007-09 recession. Caterpillar laid off 22,000 employees in the months up to February 2009, when Obama came to Peoria to stump for his economic stimulus bill. Although Obama said Caterpillar had promised to recall workers if the stimulus bill passed, the company laid off 900 more people in March. There were recent signs of hope for the manufacturing giant. As China and other countries rebounded economically, Caterpillar's sales revived in late 2010 and workers were re-hired.

The 18th Congressional District of Illinois, variously configured, has been the Peoria district since the 1940s. It includes all 11 counties that President Abraham Lincoln represented during his one term in Congress, 1847-49. It has been represented by two national Republican leaders: from 1933-49 by Everett McKinley Dirksen, who was the Senate Republican leader from 1959-69, and Robert Michel, a House member from 1957-95 and House minority leader from 1981-95. The 18th's boundaries currently extend through rich farmland south along the Illinois River and east to include half of Springfield, including the state Capitol, and west within a few miles of Iowa. It is the home of Eureka College, which dedicated the Ronald Reagan Peace Garden in honor of its 1932 graduate and the end of the Cold War that he helped to achieve. George W. Bush won this district in 2004 with 58% of the vote, but in 2008 Republican John McCain eked out a win with 50% to Democrat Barack Obama's 48%.

Aaron Schock (R)

The congressman from the 18th District is Republican Aaron Schock, who is the first member of Congress born in the 1980s. Schock was elected in 2008 to succeed Republican Rep. Ray LaHood, who became President Obama's Transportation secretary.

Ambitious as a child—Schock started his own Individual Retirement Account at 14 and amassed $18,000 working in a gravel pit in high school—he graduated from Bradley University with a finance degree in just two years. While still in college, Schock decided to challenge the sitting Peoria school board president because the board had refused to let him graduate early. The incumbent challenged Schock's petition signatures, and he was disqualified. Undeterred, Schock staged a write-in campaign and went door-to-door to campaign. On Election Day, he won with 60% of the vote. After two years, he was elected vice president of the board, and the following year, at 23, was unanimously elected school board president. Schock didn't stop at local politics. In 2004, he mounted a campaign against eight-year incumbent Democratic state Rep. Ricca Slone, in a district rated as 60% Democratic. He argued that her liberal votes stopped jobs from coming to the district.

Schock was outspent but, relying on the same grassroots outreach that had made his school board campaigns successful, won again.

In the Illinois General Assembly, Schock passed several bills in his first five months in office, including reforms in disability testing for students in elementary schools and a change in the way colleges report eligibility of transfer courses. Schock also worked on identity theft, prescription drug affordability, and road construction issues. He was also an outspoken opponent of Democratic Gov. Rod Blagojevich's economic policies.

When LaHood announced his retirement in July 2007 after seven terms, Schock quickly made plans to run for the open seat. He met with LaHood in mid-August to seek his support, and LaHood gave him the names of county chairmen to contact. Shortly afterward, LaHood learned his son was considering running for the seat, and so he called the chairmen to ask that they stay neutral, only to learn Schock had already received 11 endorsements. LaHood's son decided not to run. During the campaign, Schock made some missteps. In November 2007 he called for China to impose sanctions on Iran in an effort to stop its nuclear program and, if it refused, for the United States to sell nuclear weapons to Taiwan. His two opponents in the Republican primary criticized him sharply and LaHood said the remark showed immaturity. Schock later said that his statement was meant to underscore China's importance in dealing with Iran. In any case, he won the February 2008 primary with 71% of the vote.

In the general election, he did not shy away from President George W. Bush, as many other Republicans were that year, and even invited him to a summer fundraiser that brought in $700,000. Former House Speaker Dennis Hastert, from the neighboring 14th District, endorsed Schock as "the embodiment of the kind of candidates the Republican Party needs to win again." His general election opponent, former television news reporter Colleen Callahan, was selected by the state Democratic Party to run after the withdrawal of primary winner Dick Versace, the former Bradley University men's basketball coach. Schock raised $2.6 million to Callahan's $600,000. Callahan ran ads criticizing Schock after he was investigated for possibly backdating tax documents when serving as a notary public for his father. Two weeks before the election, the Peoria County state's attorney dropped the case. Schock won 59%-38%, losing only one county.

Schock arrived in Washington with near-instant celebrity as the new "Generation Y" congressman, parlaying his youth into positive stories in the media and television appearances. Attractive and unmarried, the liberal blog *The Huffington Post* named him the "Hottest Freshman" of the 111th Congress (2009-10). He was featured in a four-page fashion spread in the September 2009 *GQ* and was grilled about his abs on the *Colbert Report* comedy show. But one high profile admirer was rebuffed. On his February 2009 trip to Peoria to promote his massive economic stimulus bill, President Obama invited Schock to ride with him on Air Force One and then, during his speech, praised him as "a very talented young man" who would support his recovery plan. But like all of his House Republican colleagues, Schock voted no.

His legislative work included a 2009 bill to allot $310 million for courses in energy efficiency and green technology, which was approved unanimously by the Small Business Committee. He promoted an increase in the ethanol blend limits from 10% to 15% (although he'd like to see 20% eventually), and he supported the innovative efforts in the private sector to develop biodiesel fuel. On the Oversight and Government Reform Committee, he stirred Democratic opposition in February 2010 with his proposal for a bipartisan commission with power to abolish agencies and programs that fail to achieve goals or are duplicative.

Schock was re-elected easily in 2010. His political challenge in 2012 will likely be redistricting, controlled by Democrats in Illinois. Republicans in 2010 captured the adjacent 11th, 14th, and 17th districts.

NINETEENTH DISTRICT

John Shimkus (R)

Elected 1996, 8th term; b. Feb. 21, 1958, East St. Louis; home, Collinsville; West Point Military Acad., B.S. 1980, Christ Col., Teaching Cert., 1990, S. IL U., M.B.A. 1997.; Lutheran; married (Karen); 3 children.

Military Career: Army 1980–85; Army Reserves, 1985-2008..

Elected Office: Collinsville Township trustee, 1989-93; Madison Cnty. treas., 1990–96.

Professional Career: High schl. teacher, 1986–90.

DC Office: 2452 RHOB, 20515, 202-225-5271; Fax: 202-225-5880; Web site: shimkus.house.gov.

State Offices: Centralia, 618-532-9676; Collinsville, 618-344-3065; Harrisburg, 618-252-8271; Olney, 618-392-7737; Springfield, 217-492-5090.

Committees: *Energy & Commerce:* Communications & Technology; Energy & Power; Environment & the Economy (Chmn); Health.

Group Ratings

	ACLU	ACU	ADA	CFG	AFS	FRC	LCV	ITIC	NTU	COC
2010	13	96	0	84	0	93	10	33	87	88
2009	–	92	5	86	13	–	7	–	81	73

National Journal Ratings

	2010 LIB	—	2010 CONS	2009 LIB	—	2009 CONS
Economic	24%	—	76%	27%	—	72%
Social	25%	—	71%	32%	—	67%
Foreign	12%	—	79%	0%	—	75%
Composite	23%	—	78%	24%	—	76%

Key Votes of the 111th Congress

1. Overturn Ledbetter	N	5. Bar federal abortion funds	Y	9. Stop detainee transfers	Y
2. Pass $820 billion stimulus	N	6. Pass health care bill	N	10. Legalize immigrants' kids	N
3. Let guns in national parks	Y	7. Regulate financial firms	N	11. Repeal don't ask, tell	N
4. Pass cap-and-trade	N	8. Pass tax cuts for some	N	12. Limit campaign funds	N

Election Results

2010 general	John Shimkus (R)	166,166	(71%)	($1,845,128)
	Tim Bagwell (D)	67,132	(29%)	($17,763)
2010 primary	John Shimkus (R)	48,680	(85%)	
	Michael Firsching (R)	8,363	(15%)	

Prior Winning Percentages: 2008 (64%), 2006 (61%), 2004 (69%), 2002 (55%), 2000 (63%), 1998 (61%), 1996 (50%)

Population		Race/Ethnicity		Work	
Pop. 2010:	672,930	White:	92.3%	Private:	77.5%
Change since 2000:	Up 3.0%	Black:	3.8%	Government:	15.6%
Urban:	52.2%	Hispanic:	1.8%	Self-employed:	6.7%
Rural:	47.8%	Asian:	0.7%	Blue collar:	25.7%
Area size:	11,645 sq. mi.	Native Am.:	0.2%	White collar:	56.5%
		Hawaiian:	0.0%	Khaki collar:	0.2%
Age		Two+ races:	1.2%	Other:	17.6%
Median age:	40.1 yrs.				
More than 65 yrs:	15.8%	*Ancestry*		Median income:	$48,473
Less than 18 yrs:	22.5%	German	26.3%	Median Home Value:	$105,900
		Irish	11.2%		
Education		English	8.9%	**Military Veterans**	
H.S. grad:	87.6%			% of Pop:	12.0%
College grad:	20.7%				
Grad degree:	7.1%				

Southern Illinois; Part Springfield

Much of Southern Illinois is a land of prairies, of flat, treeless land sloping imperceptibly down to the Ohio and Mississippi rivers. It was settled almost entirely from the south by farmers coming overland from Kentucky, such as Abraham Lincoln's family. Just beyond the Ohio River, they found hilly terrain, some of which turned out to have coal deposits. As they traveled farther north, they must have been astonished, after miles of thick forest, to see the great American prairie stretch before them, a vast sea of empty land extending past the horizon. The prairie lands proved wondrously rich and were soon crisscrossed by rail lines taking their produce away and bringing in industrial products from St. Louis, Chicago, and points east. About the same time, vast coal deposits were found in southern Illinois, and several mining towns sprouted. This was the home turf of John L. Lewis, the imperious leader of the United Mine Workers for half a century and, in the late 1930s and early 1940s, one of the most powerful and eloquent figures in American public life.

2008 Presidential Vote		
John McCain (R)	176,342	(54%)
Barack Obama (D)	142,316	(44%)
2004 Presidential Vote		
George Bush (R)	192,678	(61%)
John Kerry (D)	123,172	(39%)
Cook Partisan Voting Index:	R+9	

The 19th Congressional District of Illinois, the largest in the state, extends more than 200 miles up, down, and across. It covers all or part of 30 counties in the rich heartland of southern Illinois—most of the land area south of Springfield, from the Ohio River to the Mississippi. Much of it is south of the old National Road, which became U.S. 40 and is paralleled by Interstate 70, the traditional boundary between the part of downstate Illinois settled by Southerners and the part settled by Yankees. The city of Effingham, which straddles that line, is where corn and soybean fields give way to hills and valleys with orchards and woodlands. Racial diversity is nonexistent here; in 2008, the district was nearly 99 percent white.

The boundaries of the 19th are jagged, but there is a rational political explanation for them. The biggest voting blocs are in Madison, Clinton and Washington counties, part of the St. Louis metropolitan area, and the Sangamon County suburbs of Springfield, the state capital. Unemployment in Madison County surged above 12% in early 2010, but dropped sharply as the year progressed. The district includes the coal-mining area around Mount Vernon, sparsely settled areas along the Ohio River, and some prairie counties along U.S. 40. Traditional Democrats have become harder to find here. George W. Bush won 61% of the vote in 2004, his best performance in the state. In 2008, John McCain won 26 of the 30 counties in the district.

John Shimkus (R)

The congressman from the 19th District is John Shimkus, a Republican first elected in 1996. Shimkus grew up in Collinsville, in Madison County. His father was an installer for Illinois Bell, and his mother a township trustee. He is of Lithuanian descent, as is his predecessor in the seat, Democratic Sen. Richard Durbin. Shimkus graduated from West Point, trained in the Army as a Ranger and paratrooper, went to college in California, then came back to Collinsville to teach high school. Almost immediately, he began running for local office. In 1988, he ran for the Madison County Board and lost. The very next year, however, he was elected a Collinsville Township trustee. In 1990, at age 32, he beat a 12-year incumbent to become Madison County treasurer. He challenged then-U.S. Rep. Durbin in 1992 and lost 57%-43%, a closer margin for Durbin than in his previous campaigns.

In 1996, when Durbin ran for the Senate, Shimkus easily won the Republican primary, with 51% against seven other candidates. In the general election, he faced state Rep. Jay Hoffman. Both were anti-abortion rights, anti-gun control, and pro-balanced budget amendment. Hoffman raised more money and had the benefit of support and financial backing from the AFL-CIO, but Shimkus won, 50.3% to 49.7%.

In the House, Shimkus' voting record is generally conservative, particularly on foreign policy. He told *Esquire* magazine in 2010 that he believes President Obama's world view "is of government control, of government solving the inequities of society. And that means big government and higher taxes....It's just not what makes this country great." When Obama addressed Congress on health care in September 2009, Shimkus walked out before the speech's end. "It was the same old malarkey," he said later.

From his seat on the Energy and Commerce Committee, Shimkus has been an aggressive supporter of business and a fierce critic of regulations he considers overly burdensome. His ardor can sometimes give way to hyperbole that triggers criticism on the left. When Democrats issued a draft plan to regulate greenhouse gas emissions in April 2009, he called it the "largest assault on democracy and freedom in this country that I've ever witnessed." Around the same time, he drew attention for arguing that carbon dioxide—the leading greenhouse gas—is valuable "plant food" that did not need to be reduced. The floods that scientists warn could result from a rapidly changing climate won't happen, Shimkus said, because God promised the Earth would not be destroyed by a flood. He has been especially vocal in supporting nuclear power, extending tax credits for ethanol, and giving incentives to coal-to-liquid refineries to help coal-producing areas. In 2010, after Republicans won control of the House, he vied to become the full committee chairman, but lost out to Michigan's Fred Upton. Shimkus was named chairman of a new subcommittee on environment and economy that enables him to closely monitor the Obama administration's regulatory activities.

As a former high school teacher, Shimkus took what seemed to be a routine assignment as chairman of the House page board and imposed stricter review procedures for applicants. But five weeks before the 2006 election, revelations that Republican Rep. Mark Foley had sent inappropriate and sexually explicit e-mails to former male pages was a political bombshell for the party, including for Shimkus and then GOP Speaker Dennis Hastert of Illinois. Both men had known of questionable contacts Foley had with pages and failed to launch an investigation. The Committee on Standards of Official Conduct later found that Shimkus should have shared the information with other House members on the page board and should have demanded copies of all of Foley's e-mails. But the committee called for no sanctions against him. Shimkus said he wished that he had done more to investigate the allegations about Foley, and he stepped down from the board.

In 2001, when the state's redistricting plan eliminated the seat held by Rep. David Phelps, a conservative Democrat, Phelps decided to run against Shimkus in the new 19th District. After a spirited contest, in which organized labor spent more than $1.5 million trying to dislodge Shimkus, he won 55%-45%. Since then, he has been re-elected easily. When he first ran for the seat, Shimkus said he would limit himself to six terms. But Shimkus reconsidered and in September 2005 called his earlier pledge "a mistake." He said, "Unless everyone plays by the same rules, term limits don't make sense."

★ INDIANA ★

Indiana, a state named for inhabitants who are mostly gone, nonetheless has a culture and even a nickname that are distinctive. The Hoosier State is on display every Memorial Day for the Indianapolis 500 auto race, a combination of sports and manufacturing that is symbolic of Indiana's historic strengths. Indiana's industrial base and sports heritage sometimes seem as antique as the bricks that originally paved the Indianapolis Speedway, where all but one yard at the start-finish line has long since been asphalted. The Speedway is literally at the center of American manufacturing: Almost half of the country's manufacturing jobs are east of Indiana and the other half are west, almost half are north and half are south. Indiana has the nation's highest percentage of workers in manufacturing—19% in 2010—and the highest percentage of gross product attributable to manufacturing of any state. It is the No. 2 steel producer in the country, with giant, heavily automated steel mills on the south shore of Lake Michigan and mini-mills scattered across the state. Indiana leads the nation in making elevators, refrigerators, engines, engine-electrical equipment, recreational vehicles, mobile homes, and truck and bus bodies. It gives the world canned pork and beans, tomato juice, Coca-Cola bottles, Coffee-Mate, and Alka-Seltzer. It has big General Motors and Chrysler plants and newer Toyota, Subaru, and Honda plants.

The downside of a manufacturing economy, apparent in the 2007-09 recession, is that it is prone to sharp contraction when the economy is in decline. Indiana's economy did relatively well before the recession, increasing its manufacturing output 20% in the decade up to 2008 while Michigan's went down 12%. Growth was strong in metro Indianapolis, which with about one-quarter of the state's population accounted for nearly two-thirds of its population growth from 2000 to 2007. Cummins and American Commercial Lines opened new factories in 2007, and Honda's plant in Greensburg opened in 2008. But manufacturing is increasingly capital-intensive. Indiana continues to churn out huge tonnages of steel to meet Chinese demands, but with less than 20,000 workers. The recession hit especially hard in a state that ranks third nationally in auto-related manufacturing. Unemployment skyrocketed in late 2008 with General Motors and Chrysler headed toward bankruptcy, and Elkhart, which bills itself as the RV capital of the world, posted the nation's highest unemployment after high gas prices slashed RV sales. Auto employment peaked at 140,000 in 2004 and temporarily fell below 100,000 during the recession. The bright spot for Indiana is its other industries, especially life sciences. Biopharmaceutical development was under way at Indianapolis-based Eli Lilly, which has a $1.5 billion payroll in the state; prosthetics, orthopedics, and biofuels were also growing—to the point that life sciences produced a quarter of Indiana's new jobs in the years before the recession.

Culturally, Indiana is like an earlier America. It retains some of the old norms that in the 1920s and 1930s attracted sociologists Robert and Helen Lynd in their search for the typical American place to "Middletown" (actually Muncie). Ethnically, Indiana seems like an earlier America too. Except for the steel area around Gary—really an extension of the Chicago metropolitan area—Indiana has relatively few descendants from the 1840-1924 wave of immigration and only a small flow of recent Hispanic or Asian immigrants. But it does have religious diversity: with 109 denominations, according to the Glenmary Center, only six states have more. The major metropolitan area, Indianapolis, now has 1.6 million people. It has one of the nation's largest foundations, the Lilly Endowment, which gives much of its money locally, and a willingness to create and innovate. In the 1980s, the Lilly Endowment urged Indianapolis to make itself a sports center. The city attracted the Colts professional football team, and in the late 1990s Indianapolis's downtown filled with construction projects: the professional basketball Pacers' Conseco Fieldhouse, the new National Collegiate Athletic Association headquarters, a conservatory, and the Indiana State Museum. To cap it off, Indianapolis is scheduled to host the 2012 Super Bowl.

The partisan patterns in Indiana state politics sometimes seem typical of an older America, too, with preferences anchored in the Civil War era and the union-organizing days of the 1930s. It was a crucial target state from the Civil War to the New Deal in the struggles between Republicans and Democrats. Party identification was handed down like religious affiliation—the Lynd research team noted that Presbyterians had little to do with Methodists, but that was nothing next to divisions between Republicans and Democrats. The people of Indiana, by and large, are descendants of its original settlers, Yankees from Ohio and New England, and "Butternuts," as they were called in the Civil War years, from Kentucky and the South. Most Yankees became Republicans and most Butternuts became Democrats, and that split has persisted over generations and been a factor in elections for state office from New Deal times until today. Those enduring traditions

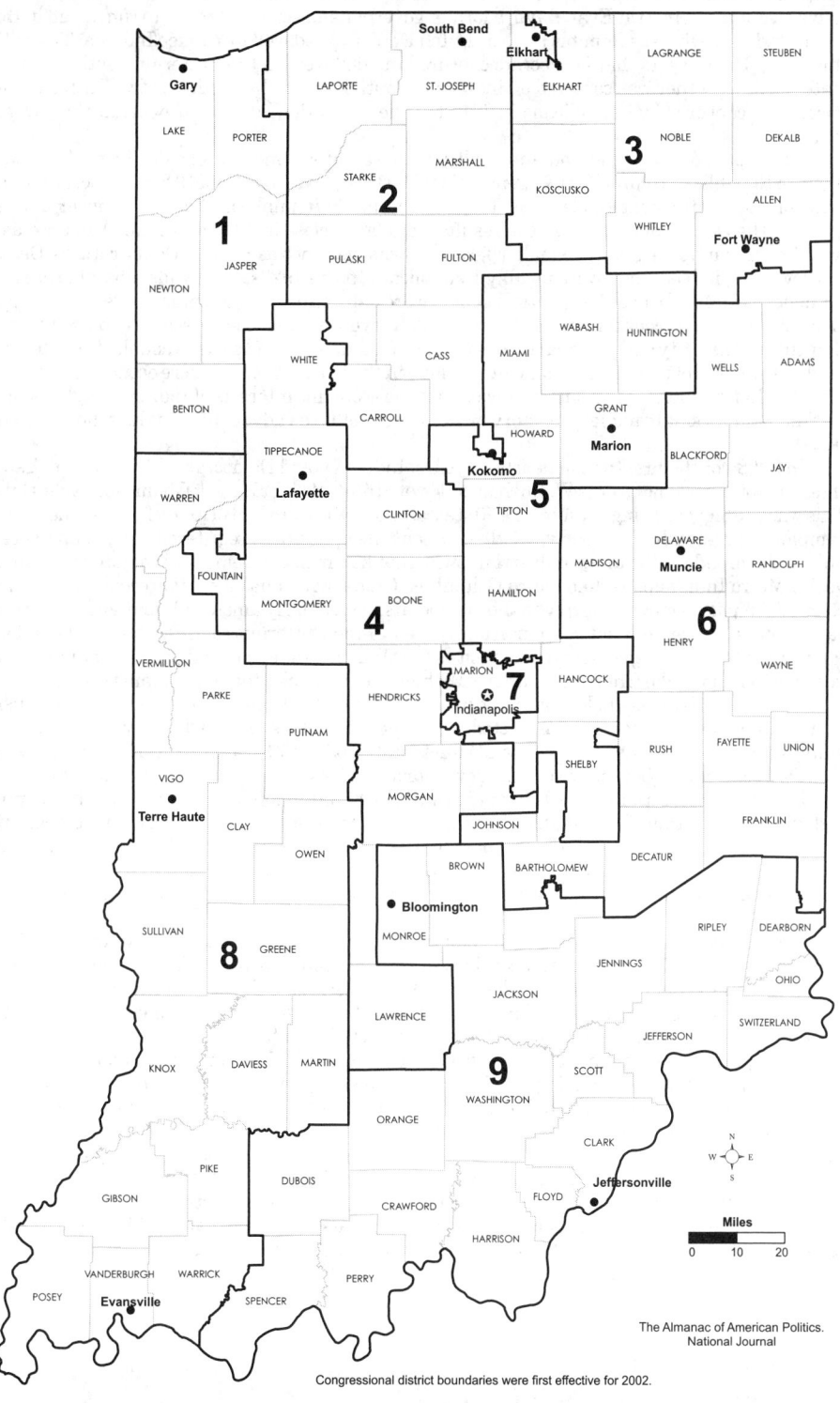

The Almanac of American Politics.
National Journal

Congressional district boundaries were first effective for 2002.

enabled Democrats to hold the governorship from 1988 to 2004 and to be competitive in state legislative elections. Democrat Evan Bayh, a former governor and senator, tended to run ahead in Butternut Indiana, whereas Republican Gov. Mitch Daniels fared well in Yankee Indiana. Two of the three U.S. House seats that Democrats captured in 2006 were in the Butternut south end of the state, while the other was centered on industrial South Bend in the north; the two Butternut districts were captured by Republicans in 2010 but the South Bend district stayed narrowly Democratic.

At the presidential level, Indiana's cultural conservatism and lack of a dovish tradition kept it in the Republican column for two generations. In 1964, it voted 56%-43% for Democrat Lyndon Johnson. But in the next 10 elections it was so resolutely Republican that it was never a target state for the Democrats, although the results were fairly close in 1976 and 1996. A main reason was that Indianapolis and the smaller factory towns were not as heavily Democratic as Detroit or Cleveland; indeed, they were usually Republican. In the 1920s, the Lynds, liberal academics influenced by Marx's idea that political beliefs were determined by economic interests, were puzzled why the factory workers in "Middletown" didn't vote against the bosses. One reason may be that cultural identity and personal values tend to be permanent and so have usually been the critical determinants of political allegiance, especially in the United States, where economic status can often be changeable. Another factor may be that the economic interests of Indiana's highly skilled workers and its small and large factory owners may not be as adversarial as the academics supposed.

In 2008, for the first time in nearly 45 years, Indiana voted Democratic for president. A state that went 60%-39% for George W. Bush in 2004 voted 50%-49% for Barack Obama four years later. This was the biggest swing in any of the 50 states, and was the product of many factors. The Obama campaign targeted Indiana early, vastly outspent the opposition, registered new, young voters, and made inroads in the ailing industrial towns that had resisted Democratic nominees for many years. Metro Indianapolis, like metro Columbus, Ohio—which has a similar economic base and Republican past—moved sharply to the Democrats, particularly among affluent and better-educated voters. Obama did not run particularly well in the Butternut counties, but made up for it farther north in auto-dependent towns such as Fort Wayne, Anderson, and Muncie. Indiana began voting much more like Ohio and southern Michigan and less like the Great Plains states.

However, this did not hold true all the way down the ballot. Daniels, who was George W. Bush's first-term budget director, was re-elected by a solid 58%-40% even as Obama was carrying the state, a considerably bigger victory than Daniels' initial 53%-45% win in 2004. The victory was all the more remarkable because two of the governor's policies were hugely controversial: the leasing for 75 years of the North Indiana Toll Road to an Australian-Spanish consortium and the adoption of daylight saving time. Indiana straddles the Eastern and Central time zones, with most counties in the Eastern time zone choosing not to observe daylight saving. Few issues impinge so drastically on personal lives, and several counties ended up outside their preferred time zone under Daniels' policy. Democrats put up an outcry, and in 2006 and 2008 the party won narrow majorities in the state House.

Daniels' popularity increased as he emphasized his Indiana Economic Development Corp., which committed $700 million in incentives to bring a promised 75,000 jobs to the state, and a property-tax law that increased the sales tax by 1% but decreased the burden on local government. Once re-elected, he made substantial budget cuts and used reserve funds to keep the budget in balance as revenues flagged. Beyond Indiana, he attracted attention as a possible presidential candidate despite earlier statements that he would not run. To visiting journalists and in speeches in Washington, he insisted that rising entitlement costs meant permanent budget deficits or economically disastrous tax increases, and that if he did run nationally, he would push proposals to address the problem. A June 2010 *Weekly Standard* article quoted him as saying that the nation needed a "truce" in the culture wars. When religious conservatives objected, Daniels said his point was that the fiscal issues demanded full attention and a united approach.

The 2010 election results were favorable to his party. Evan Bayh's retirement from the Senate left the way open for his predecessor, Republican Dan Coats, to win the seat handily, while Republicans also picked up the 8th and 9th district House seats. Republicans gained 59-40 control of the state House to go with their lopsided margin in the state Senate.

Population		Household Income		Work	
Pop. 2010:	6,483,802	Under $15k:	13.1%	Private:	83.3%
State rank:	15th	$15k to $50k:	39.5%	Government:	11.5%
Change since 2000:	Up 6.6%	$50k to $100k:	32.4%	Self-employed:	5.0%
Urban:	69.0%	$100k to $200k:	12.7%	Unemployment (3-yr. average):	5.5%
Rural:	31.0%	Over $200k:	2.2%	Poverty:	13.4%
Native of state:	68.6%	Median income:	$47,135	Blue collar:	27.3%
Not a citizen:	2.7%			White collar:	55.9%
Area size:	36,420 sq. mi.	**Home Value**		Khaki collar:	0.1%
		Under $100k:	36.9%	Other:	16.8%
Most populous cities		$100k to $300k:	54.9%		
Indianapolis	829,718	$300k to $500k:	5.8%	**Age**	
Fort Wayne	253,691	$500k to $1 mil:	1.9%	Median age:	36.6 yrs.
Evansville	117,429	Over $1 million:	0.5%	More than 65 yrs:	12.7%
South Bend	101,168	Median:	$122,800	Less than 18 yrs:	24.9%

Race/Ethnicity				Military Veterans		Registered Voters in 2010	
White:	81.5%	*Language*		% of Pop:	10.0%	No Party registration	
Black:	9.0%	English:	92.6%			Voter turnout:	1,786,213
Hispanic:	6.0%	Spanish:	4.1%	*Veterans by Period*		Turnout as % of	
Asian:	1.6%	Asian:	0.9%	WWII and before:	10.6%	voting age:	36.6%
Native Am.:	0.2%	Other European:	2.1%	Korea:	11.5%		
Hawaiian:	0.0%			Vietnam:	33.0%	**Legislature**	
Two+ races:	1.5%	**Education**		Gulf (pre-2001):	11.1%	Senate:	13 D 37 R
		H.S. grad:	86.1%	Gulf (post-2001):	6.1%	House:	40 D 59 R 1 I
Ancestry		College grad:	22.4%	Peace time:	27.6%		
German	21.4%	Grad degree:	8.0%				
Irish	10.6%						
English	7.8%						

Presidential politics   Indiana saw little presidential campaigning between 1968, when Democrats Robert Kennedy and Eugene McCarthy battled in the May primary against Lyndon Johnson's stand-in, Gov. Roger Branigan, and 2008, when Barack Obama contested the state in both the primary and general election. The closest the Democrats came to winning was President Bill Clinton's loss by 5% to GOP presidential nominee Bob Dole in 1996, a year in which Clinton had more than enough electoral votes and did not target Indiana. The 2008 election was different.

Everyone had assumed that both parties' nominees would already be settled by Indiana's May 6 primary. But Democrat Hillary Rodham Clinton was still battling Obama and, after solid victories in Ohio and Pennsylvania, she hoped that a win in Indiana would balance an expected loss in North Carolina on the same day. Clinton had the active support of Sen. Evan Bayh, who

2008 Presidential Vote
Barack Obama (D) 1,374,039   (50%)
John McCain (R) 1,345,648   (49%)

2008 Presidential Primary
Hillary Clinton (D) 646,282   (51%)
Barack Obama (D) 632,073   (49%)

2008 Presidential Primary
John McCain (R) 320,318   (78%)
Mike Huckabee (R)..................41,173   (10%)
Ron Paul (R) 31,612   (8%)

2004 Presidential Vote
George W. Bush (R)............1,479,438   (60%)
John Kerry (D) 969,011   (39%)

had chosen not to run for president himself. And Indiana seemed demographically similar to Ohio and Pennsylvania. But not quite. Indiana's population is a bit younger, its African-American percentage is lower, and metro Indianapolis does not have the racially polarized urban politics that Cleveland and Cincinnati do (with the exception of Gary and Lake County. Moreover, Indiana does not have party registration, as Pennsylvania does. Independents and Republicans could vote in the Democratic primary. And they did.

Only 412,684 people voted in the Republican primary, while nearly 1.3 million voted in the Democratic primary, *four times* as many as the 317,211 that voted in the 2004 Democratic contest. Obama won by huge margins among black and young voters. Clinton carried women, the elderly, and blue-collar voters by much smaller margins. Indianapolis and its suburbs voted heavily for Obama, who also carried the counties that included Gary, South Bend, Elkhart, and Fort Wayne, and the university towns of Lafayette and Bloomington. While Clinton emerged the winner, she was denied the satisfaction of announcing her victory on prime time television because Lake County authorities held back their results, and network analysts, knowing there were many black voters there, refrained from calling her the winner. That was also the night that the late Tim Russert of NBC News declared, accurately, that Obama would ultimately be the Democratic nominee. The Obama campaign's organizational work in the primary paid off in the general election. In a state that had seen no intensive presidential campaigning since the 1940s, the campaign opened 44 offices, hired 210 paid staff, attracted 80,000 volunteers, and had 50,000 people going door to door and making phone calls in the final week. The Obama team outspent Republican John McCain's campaign 5-to-1 in the state. Excitement was intense. Obama attracted a crowd of 30,000 in Indianapolis while McCain's vice presidential nominee, Sarah Palin, could muster a crowd of only 25,000 in suburban Noblesville. Obama carried only 15 of Indiana's 92 counties but racked up big enough margins to win 50% to McCain's 49% statewide.

The exit poll showed that 63% of young voters went for Obama, 61% of the elderly for McCain; 62% of white Protestants and 52% of white Catholics voted for McCain; 73% of whites with no religion and 90% of African-Americans voted for Obama. Turnout was up 11% statewide. The Democrat did not run particularly well in the Butternut counties, but he made major gains in the industrial landscape between Indianapolis, Fort Wayne, and South Bend.

Congressional districting

112th Congress Lineup	
6 R	3 D
111th Congress Lineup	
5 D	4 R

Indiana lost one congressional district in the 2000 census, and that required significant changes in district lines. In charge were Democrats, who then had the governorship and a majority in the state House, though Republicans had a majority in the state Senate. Indiana law provides that if the House and Senate cannot agree, the decision goes to a five-member commission, with the tie-breaking member appointed by the governor. In May 2001, the commission adopted a plan largely identical to that passed by the state House. Democrats hoped to retain the four seats they held and to improve their chances in at least one more. But as often happens with redistricting, the results did not come out as intended. Both parties carried the 2nd, 8th, and 9th districts at different points in the ensuing five elections and after the 2010 election, Republicans had a 6-3 edge in the delegation.

Indiana did not win or lose any seats as a result of the 2010 census. Republicans, with majorities in the legislature and Daniels as governor, have control of the process. Daniels has urged legislators to refrain from a partisan districting plan, but the possibility of making the 2nd District significantly less Democratic by adding Democratic areas to the already safe Democratic 1st District is obvious.

Governor

Mitch Daniels (R)

Elected 2004, term expires Jan. 2013, 2nd term; b. April 7, 1949, Monongahela, PA; home, Indianapolis; Princeton U., B.A. 1971, Georgetown U., J.D.
1979; Presbyterian; married (Cheri); 4 children.

Professional Career: Advisor, mayor of Indianapolis Richard Lugar,
1971-76; Chief of staff, U.S. Sen. Lugar, 1977-83; Exec. dir., NRSC, 1983-84;
Senior adv., White House, 1985-87; CEO, Hudson Institute, 1987-90; Executive, Eli Lilly, 1990-2001; Dir., OMB, 2001-02.

Office: 200 W. Washington St., Room 206, Indianapolis, 46204, 317-232-
1800; Fax: 317-232-3443; Web site: www.in.gov/gov.

Election Results

2008 general	Mitch Daniels (R)...1,563,885	(58%)
	Jill Thompson (D) 1,082,463	(40%)
	Andy Horning (Lib)..57,376	(2%)
2008 primary	Mitch Daniels (R).................................... unopposed	

Prior Winning Percentages: 2004 (53%)

Mitch Daniels has been the Republican governor of Indiana since 2005. He grew up in Indianapolis
and graduated from Princeton University and Georgetown University's law school. He worked as
a staffer for Republican Richard Lugar when Lugar was mayor of Indianapolis in the early 1970s,
and was chief of staff for Lugar from 1977 to 1983 after Lugar moved to the Senate. He was political
director in the Reagan White House. According to journalist Lou Cannon in his *President Reagan:
The Role of a Lifetime*, when unpopular chief of staff Don Regan became regarded as a political
liability, Daniels was the only staffer willing to confront Regan and tell him to resign for President
Reagan's sake. He worked there until 1987, when he returned to Indianapolis to join the Hudson
Institute think tank.

In 1990, Daniels went to work for Eli Lilly, the pharmaceutical giant based in Indianapolis.
He had climbed the ranks to become president of Lilly's North American pharmaceutical operations, but resigned in 2001 to re-enter government, liquidating at least $27 million in stock hold-
ings. He turned down Gov. Robert Orr's offer to appoint him to the Senate in 1988 when Indiana
Republican Dan Quayle was elected vice president. Instead, he became President George W. Bush's
director of the Office of Management and Budget. In that role, he developed a reputation as a committed spending-cutter and for having disdain for members of Congress, whose motto he said
should be "'Don't just stand there, spend something.' This is the only way they feel relevant." Bush
insiders referred to him as "the Blade," and Alaska's Sen. Ted Stevens, a fellow Republican, said
the only way Daniels could fix his relationship with Congress was to "go home to Indiana."

He did go home, but not because Stevens told him to. In 2003, Daniels said he was tired of
commuting between Washington and his family in Indianapolis. But he also saw an opportunity
to run for governor of his home state. Lt. Gov. Joseph Kernan, a Vietnam veteran and prisoner of
war for 11 months and a popular, former three-term mayor of South Bend, was widely assumed to
be the strongest Democrat to succeed the term-limited Frank O'Bannon. But in December 2002,
Kernan shocked just about everyone by announcing that he would not seek the job. Soon after he
returned to Indiana, Daniels announced his candidacy. All but one of the Republicans then running, including 2000 nominee and former U.S. Rep. David McIntosh, left the race and endorsed
him. On a visit to the state, President Bush referred to "my man Mitch," at a time when that was
still a politically advantageous thing to be. Daniels campaigned around the state in plaid shirts
and sweaters, traveling in an RV with supporters' signatures all over it. He went to every one of
Indiana's 92 counties and eventually visited some of them repeatedly. Then, in September 2003,
O'Bannon suffered a major stroke and died within a few days. Kernan was sworn in as acting governor. He handled the tragic transition gracefully and reconsidered his decision not to run in 2004.
In November, he announced his candidacy, and other Democrats ended their campaigns.

From there, it was a two-man race. While his former boss, President Bush, was on the defensive nationally for job losses in the manufacturing sector, Daniels was attacking Kernan and local
Democrats for job losses in manufacturing in Indiana, saying it was time for a "new crew." He called
for tax breaks for new business property investments, new hires, and research and development.

He said he would put more emphasis on winning federal grants, create a state agriculture department, and provide tougher enforcement of child-support obligations. He called for health savings accounts for state employees and credits for employees who stopped smoking and stayed fit. Kernan called for lower property taxes and for tax abatements for new business on a case-by-case basis. He endorsed full-day kindergarten. He criticized Daniels for his budget cuts as OMB director and for signing off on foreign contracts and job outsourcing. He blamed Indiana job losses on federal trade policy.

After enjoying modest leads in polls during most of the campaign, Daniels won 53% to 45%. He carried metro Indianapolis 57%-42%, but ran behind in Northern Indiana and Kernan's home town of South Bend. Republicans increased their margin in the state Senate to 33-17 in 2004, and converted a 51-49 deficit in the state House to a 52-48 majority. It was the first time Republicans had won control of state government since 1986.

Fiscal problems loomed. State government faced a $645 million deficit and owed $710 million in back payments to schools, universities, and local governments. Daniels achieved some notable but controversial successes in his first two years. With the help of business interests, he persuaded lawmakers to enact daylight saving time to stop Indiana from being one of three states that does not go on daylight saving time. And he persuaded the Department of Transportation to allow eight counties to switch to the Central time zone. He created a state economic development corporation and a new inspector general post for ethics. He also got a small funding increase for schools, a voter-identification bill, and a crackdown on methamphetamine production. He signed a bill requiring state vehicles to run on agricultural-based fuels when possible. He reduced the state's property tax relief payments, and in turn sought to give local governments more control over how they raise revenue.

His most controversial plan was "Major Moves," a 10-year transportation plan that aimed to cover shortfalls in the state's transportation budget by privatizing transportation assets rather than raising gasoline taxes or borrowing. The centerpiece was a 75-year deal to lease the Indiana Toll Road, a 157-mile-long span across Northern Indiana that connects Ohio and Illinois, to an Australian-Spanish consortium in exchange for a $3.8 billion lump-sum payment. Daniels sold the plan as a way to raise cash to improve the state's road system and create jobs, while leaving toll collection and highway maintenance to the private sector. Democrats protested that the state would lose control of toll increases and decades of future revenue, while supporters of the plan argued that the highway was losing money. After the Republican legislature approved the deal in 2006, Daniels proposed spending $12 billion on the state's infrastructure over a decade, including the construction of an "Illiana Expressway" to ease traffic congestion between Illinois and Indiana and a privately funded toll beltway around metro Indianapolis.

The toll-road lease program and the switch to daylight saving time proved unpopular. Daniels largely stayed off the campaign trail in 2006, and his political woes contributed to Republican losses in the state, including the ouster of three members of Congress. Democrats won a narrow 51-49 seat majority in the state House.

In 2007, the governor's plans to privatize the Hoosier Lottery were frustrated by Democratic House Speaker Patrick Bauer and a U.S. Justice Department ruling warning that it would violate federal law. But Daniels was able to privatize intake services at the Bureau of Motor Vehicles and at the Family and Social Services Administration. His Indiana Economic Development Corporation committed to $700 million in tax incentives to new businesses and took credit for deals that promised to generate more than 75,000 jobs. Tight fiscal policy resulted in an AA+ credit rating for the state in 2006 and an AAA rating in 2008. In 2007, Daniels proposed a 1% increase in the sales tax in return for a cap on property taxes of 1% of assessed value for homeowners, 2% for apartments and farms, and 3% for businesses. His tax proposal passed in March 2008.

Going into his 2008 re-election campaign, Daniels' job ratings were well under 50%, and Democrats sensed he was vulnerable. Most Democratic leaders supported South Bend architect Jim Schellinger, but Schellinger was upset, 51%-49%, in the May primary by former U.S. Rep. Jill Long Thompson. She attacked Daniels for privatizing the Indiana Toll Road and other government functions and on the switch to daylight saving time. She advanced a Reinvest in Indiana program, with tax changes, business incentives, and tax credits for health care and continuing education. Daniels called for a constitutional amendment making his property tax changes permanent and for giving modest-income students tuition for two years at Ivy Tech Community College or an equivalent amount at another state school, to be funded by borrowing against future lottery proceeds. He outspent Long Thompson 3-to-1 and won 58% to 40%. He was especially strong in metro Indianapolis. He won 56% in Marion County, which Democratic presidential nominee Barack Obama won with 64% in 2008, and he carried affluent, fast-growing Hamilton County, 83%-15%. Democrats gained a seat in the state House and thus kept their majority there.

Daniels' victory, in a state carried by Obama and in a dismal year for Republicans, led some to urge him to consider a run for president. But Daniels seemed reluctant. One of his campaign ads showed him saying, "Here's some good news. This is the last time you'll have to watch me in an ad like this. See, governor is the only office I've run for or ever will."

Nevertheless, as President Obama's popularity sank and political pundits began speculating about challenges in 2012, Daniels' name surfaced repeatedly. He was the subject of an admiring profile in the conservative *Weekly Standard* that described him as the "un-Obama," noting his insistence for staying with local families every night during his campaign and eating catfish with diner patrons. He acknowledged taking former GOP House Speaker Newt Gingrich's advice of not categorically ruling out a presidential run because it gave him a larger forum for his views. He called the health care overhaul a "wasted opportunity," blaming Republicans as well as Democrats, and said the proposed cap-and-trade legislation to reduce greenhouse gas emissions would "cost us dearly in jobs and income." But he enraged social conservatives in June 2010 when he called for a "truce" on social issues such as abortion rights in order to focus on economic recovery. And he drew accusations of hypocrisy from Democrats when he denounced a new $26 billion stimulus bill in August 2010, six months after joining with 41 other governors urging an extension of the original stimulus program's federal match for Medicaid. Daniels ultimately decided against running for president, announcing his decision in May 2011.

At home, Daniels went into his second term forced to cope with the budget crunch affecting Indiana and most other state governments. He announced plans in December 2009 to cut $150 million in higher education and $300 million in elementary education over 18 months. He struggled to push through education reforms, such as changes in teacher seniority rules, that met with fierce opposition from Democrats. He also called for reshaping local government, including merging the state's smallest school districts, eliminating township governments, and creating a single county chief executive to replace commissioners. Those initiatives also ran into obstacles.

Senior Senator

Richard Lugar (R)

Elected 1976, term expires 2012, 6th term; b. April 4, 1932, Indianapolis; home, Indianapolis; Denison U., B.A. 1954, Rhodes Scholar, Oxford U., M.A. 1956; Methodist; married (Charlene); 4 children.

Military Career: Navy, 1957–60.

Elected Office: Indianapolis Bd. of Schl. Commissioners, 1964–67; Indianapolis mayor, 1968–75.

Professional Career: Mgr., family farm; V.P. & treas., Thomas L. Green & Co., 1960–67; Prof., U. of Indianapolis, 1976.

DC Office: 306 HSOB, 20510, 202-224-4814; Fax: 202-228-0360; Web site: lugar.senate.gov.

State Offices: Evansville, 812-465-6313; Ft. Wayne, 260-422-1505; Indianapolis, 317-226-5555; Valparaiso, 219-548-8035.

Committees: *Agriculture, Nutrition & Forestry:* Conservation, Forestry & Natural Resources; Jobs, Rural Economic Growth & Energy Innovation; Nutrition, Specialty Crops, Food & Ag Research (RMM). *Foreign Relations* (RMM).

Group Ratings

	ACLU	ACU	ADA	CFG	AFS	FRC	LCV	ITIC	NTU	COC
2010	13	71	25	70	12	62	0	33	91	100
2009	–	68	35	76	27	–	18	–	76	86

National Journal Ratings

	2010 LIB	—	2010 CONS		2009 LIB	—	2009 CONS
Economic	29%	—	70%		37%	—	62%
Social	35%	—	64%		39%	—	60%
Foreign	41%	—	53%		44%	—	54%
Composite	36%	—	64%		41%	—	59%

Key Votes of the 111th Congress

1. Overturn Ledbetter	N	5. Pass health care bill		9. Ratify New START	Y
2. Pass $787 billion stimulus	N	6. Regulate financial firms	N	10. Confirm Elena Kagan	Y
3. Repeal DC gun laws	N	7. Pass tax cuts for some	N	11. Stop EPA climate regs	Y
4. Confirm Sonia Sotomayor	Y	8. Legalize immigrants' kids	Y	12. Repeal don't ask, tell	N

Election Results

2006 general	Richard Lugar (R) 1,171,553	(87%)	($5,538,844)
	Steve Osborn (Lib) 168,820	(13%)	
2006 primary	Richard Lugar (R) .... unopposed		

Prior Winning Percentages: 2000 (67%); 1994 (67%); 1988 (68%); 1982 (54%); 1976 (59%)

Richard Lugar, the senior senator from Indiana, has had a career in public life stretching back to the late 1950s, when as a young Navy officer he prepared intelligence briefings for Chief of Naval Operations Adm. Arleigh Burke and also briefed President Dwight Eisenhower. He is the first Indiana senator ever elected to fourth, fifth, and sixth terms and has long been a powerful voice on foreign policy. He is the longest serving Republican in the Senate, along with Utah's Orrin Hatch.

Lugar grew up in Indianapolis, near his family's farm and food-machinery firm that dates back to 1893. He was an Eagle Scout, a straight-A student at Denison College, and a Rhodes scholar. After military service, Lugar returned to the family business. He was elected to the Indianapolis school board in 1964, persuaded to run by neighbors who thought their schools were being ignored. He was elected the city's mayor in 1967, at age 35. In office, he consolidated the city and Marion County into Unigov, which brought in tax resources and suburban voters, keeping the city both solvent and Republican. In the late 1960s, Lugar bucked fashion and called for fewer rather than more federal programs, and he became known as President Richard Nixon's favorite mayor. That was not a political asset in the Watergate scandal year of 1974, however, when Lugar challenged Democratic Sen. Birch Bayh. He lost 51%-46%. But in the more favorable climate of 1976 and against a weaker Democratic incumbent, Sen. Vance Hartke, Lugar won his Senate seat, 59%-40%.

Throughout his public life, Lugar's strength has been following his stubborn convictions and letting his considerable intellect guide him, regardless of political risk or reward. Over his long career, he has plenty of accomplishments but also some disappointments. His autonomous course has produced mixed results in the Senate and in the national arena. In 1996, he ran for the Republican nomination for president on his own platform and without any concessions to the political shorthand or television sensibility of the day. Lugar based his campaign on "nuclear security and fiscal sanity"—deterring nuclear terrorism and backing a 17% national sales tax. But he got little media coverage, and after he finished seventh in the Iowa caucuses and fifth in the New Hampshire primary he left the race. Lugar has a mostly conservative voting record with some exceptions, and has lately challenged some of the shibboleths of tea party Republicans.

Lugar's great interest is foreign policy. He chaired the Foreign Relations Committee from 1985 to 1987 and from 2003 to 2007 and has been the ranking Republican on the panel since then. In 1985, he quickly took command over a committee sharply divided between conservative Jesse Helms and liberal Democrats. Lugar was often in the middle, backing aid to the Contra rebels in Nicaragua and favoring sanctions against the apartheid government of South Africa. Helms had allowed Lugar to ascend to Foreign Relations chairman that year, despite Helms' having more seniority, because the North Carolinian had made a campaign promise in the 1984 election to take the chairmanship of the Agriculture Committee. But after Republicans lost their Senate majority in 1986, Helms said he was no longer bound by his promise and invoked seniority. Lugar took the issue to the Republican Conference, but lost a vote there. So Helms was the ranking minority member and chairman for 16 years, while Lugar waited. Helms excluded Lugar from conference committees and seldom communicated with him.

Lugar led the fight to ratify the chemical weapons treaty in 1997, over Helms' opposition, and won. He favored other arms control treaties, including START I in 1992 and START II in 1996, despite opposition from conservatives. Also in the 1990s, Lugar supported expansion of NATO and urged the U.S. to pay its dues to the United Nations. Lugar strongly supported the New START treaty as "a modest treaty that sets the stage for an ongoing relationship with the Russians." With Lugar's help, the treaty got more than the required 67 votes in the December 2010 lame duck session of Congress.

His greatest achievement was the Nunn-Lugar Cooperative Threat Reduction program to pay Russia, Ukraine, Belarus, and Kazakhstan to dismantle and destroy their nuclear weapons as well as some chemical and biological weapons. The goal of the 1991 legislation was to prevent weapons of mass destruction from falling into the hands of hostile powers or terrorists. Since then, Lugar has overseen the program to ensure its effectiveness. As of 2011, Nunn-Lugar has resulted in the destruction or elimination of a multitude of weapons, including 7,600 strategic warheads, 791 intercontinental ballistic missiles, 669 submarine-launched ballistic missiles launchers, 32 nuclear submarines, and 194 nuclear test tunnels. It also has resulted in upgraded security at 24 nuclear weapons storage sites and neutralized 1,395 metric tons of Russian and Albanian chemical weapons agents. All nuclear weapons have been removed from Ukraine, Belarus, and Kazakhstan.

After the September 11 attacks, Lugar called for a Nunn-Lugar approach to prevent chemical and biological weapons throughout the world from falling into the hands of terrorists. In 2004, the George W. Bush administration got $10 billion for the program from the other members of the G-8, establishing the Global Threat Reduction Initiative to secure radioactive materials, ending weapons of mass destruction programs in Libya, and securing a U.N. resolution requiring states to criminalize nuclear proliferation. In 2005, Lugar and then freshman Sen. Barack Obama made a trip to Russia, Ukraine, and Azerbaijan to monitor progress. He and Obama co-sponsored a measure extending the Nunn-Lugar program to target terrorists, and President Bush signed the bill in January 2007.

Lugar kept an eye on Iraq throughout the 1990s. Starting in August 1990, he called for an end to Saddam Hussein's regime and said that U.S. ground troops might have to be sent to Iraq to kill him. But he was not necessarily a team player for the Bush administration. In 2002, he and Joe Biden, then the Democratic chairman of Foreign Relations, conducted hearings on the Iraq war, but the administration declined to send witnesses. That year, Lugar and Biden drafted a use of force resolution to impose geographical limits on the authorization for war and require the administration either to obtain a U.N. resolution supporting the war or to certify to Congress that such efforts at the U.N. failed. Their work was bypassed when House Minority Leader Dick Gephardt and Democratic Sens. Joe Lieberman and Evan Bayh agreed with the administration on a different, less restrictive resolution. Although Democrats accused Republicans of failing to perform oversight while in the majority, Lugar held 40 hearings on Iraq.

In 2009, Lugar and Foreign Relations Chairman John Kerry co-sponsored a bill to provide Pakistan with military aid, especially counterinsurgency weapons, contingent of its meeting specified benchmarks; it also tripled economic development aid to $1.5 billion over five years. It was unanimously approved in committee and became law in 2009. In 2010, Lugar and Kerry sought to create a fund to encourage private sector jobs in Pakistan as was done in Eastern Europe after the fall of the Berlin wall. He also worked with Kerry on a program that reduces Third World debt burdens in return for protection of tropical forests and coral reefs.

Lugar was chairman of the Agriculture Committee from 1995 to 2001. He liked to point out that he was the only working farmer on the committee—he owns 604 acres—and he played a key role in the 1996 passage of the Freedom to Farm Act, which purported to phase out over seven years the farm subsidies of which he had long been a critic. But low crop prices starting in 1998 resulted in disaster-relief payments that kept in place something very much like the old subsidy system. In 2001, Lugar opposed the House farm bill with its big increases for historically subsidized crops, and proposed his own bill, guaranteeing up to 80% of income of qualified farmers, but at far less cost. But with key Senate races coming up in states with historically subsidized farmers, the Senate passed a farm bill similar to the House's, which President Bush signed into law. Lugar took a similar course, with similar results, when the farm bill came up for renewal in 2007. He sponsored an amendment to end almost all crop subsidies in favor of more crop insurance and conservation spending. It was defeated 58-37. In action on the school lunch program, which the committee oversees, Lugar in 2010 sought to get healthier meals in the program and called for cuts in payments to farmers to fund the summer program for school lunch-eligible children.

Another priority issue for Lugar is energy, particularly reducing dependence on oil. He has driven a Toyota Prius since 2005, and he grows carbon-sequestering walnut trees on his farm. In 2002, he voted for oil drilling in the Arctic National Wildlife Refuge, and, despite the importance of auto manufacturing in Indiana, he has voted to raise fuel efficiency standards. He has supported ethanol production, but also sponsored a bill in 2007 to revoke the ethanol tax credit when oil prices rise above $45 a barrel. And he has often called for eliminating the 54% tariff on biofuels, which prevents the importation of cheap Brazilian sugar ethanol. In the 2007 energy bill, Lugar sought higher production of biofuels and stricter efficiency standards for appliances. But in 2009 and 2010, he opposed the cap-and-trade bill aimed at reducing greenhouse gases. He advanced an alternative energy bill to increase fuel efficiency standards on light trucks as well as cars, to encourage use of renewable fuels, and to require the building of more flex-fuel vehicles.

Lugar was one of the 23 Republicans who in May 2006 supported the Senate immigration bill, with its guest worker program and path-to-legalization provisions. In 2009-10, he co-sponsored the DREAM Act providing a path to citizenship for children of illegal immigrants who meet requirements for college attendance or military service.

Lugar was re-elected 68%-32% in 1988, 67%-31% in 1994, and 67%-32% in 2000. In 2006, he had no Democratic opponent. Democratic state Chairman Dan Parker said, "Let's be honest. Richard Lugar is beloved not only by Republicans, but by independents and Democrats." But Lugar's increasing bipartisanship irritated some Hoosier conservatives. He did not object when Democratic presidential candidate Barack Obama frequently mentioned their joint work on nuclear prolifera-tion and used pictures of the Indianan in campaign ads. In the 111th Congress (2009-10), he voted to confirm Obama Supreme Court nominees Sonia Sotomayor and Elena Kagan.

Junior Senator

Dan Coats (R)

Elected 2010, term expires 2016, 2nd full term; b. May 16, 1943, Jackson, MI; home, Fort Wayne; Wheaton Col., B.A. 1965; IN U., J.D. 1971.; Presbyterian; Married (Marsha); 3 children.

Military Career: Army Corps of Engineers, 1966-68.

Elected Office: U.S. House, 1981-89; U.S. Senate, 1989-99.

Professional Career: Asst. v.p., Mutual Security Life Insurance, 1972-76; staffer, Rep. Dan Quayle, R-Ind., 1976-80; lobbyist, Verner, Liipfert, Bernhard, McPherson & Hand, 2000-01; U.S. ambassador to Germany, 2001-05; lobbyist, King & Spalding, 2005-10.

DC Office: B-40E DSOB, 20510, 202-224-5623; Fax: 202-228-1820; Web site: coats.senate.gov.

State Offices: Indianapolis, 317-554-0750.

Committees: *Appropriations:* Defense; Department of State, Foreign Operations & Related Programs; Homeland Security (RMM); Military Construction, Veterans Affairs & Related Agencies; Transportation, HUD & Related Agencies. *Energy & Natural Resources:* Energy; National Parks; Water & Power. *Intelligence (Select). Joint Economic Committee.*

Election Results

2010 general	Dan Coats (R)...952,116	(55%)	($4,396,274)
	Brad Ellsworth (D)..697,775	(40%)	($2,368,351)
	Rebecca Sink-Burris (Lib) 94,330	(5%)	
2010 primary	Dan Coats (R)..217,225	(39%)	
	Marlin Stutzman (R) 160,981	(29%)	
	John Hostettler (R) 124,494	(23%)	

Prior Winning Percentages: 1992 (57%); 1990 (54%); House: 1988 (62%); 1986 (70%); 1984 (61%); 1982 (64%); 1980 (61%)

The junior senator from Indiana is Republican Dan Coats, elected in 2010 to a second stint in the Senate. He had served from 1988 to 1999, and then was a lobbyist and diplomat before running for the seat of retiring Democratic Sen. Evan Bayh.

Coats grew up in Jackson, Mich. When he was 9 years old, his mother, a Swedish immigrant, took him to see President Dwight Eisenhower. Coats still remembers touching the president's sleeve, and cites him, along with Winston Churchill, as his political idol. In college, he considered becoming a doctor, but decided against it. He joined the Army, went to law school, and worked for an insurance company. In 1976, he turned down a job offer from a bank to work for a young, Republican member of Congress named Dan Quayle. Four years later, Coats was elected to succeed Quayle in the House. In 1988, he was appointed to succeed him in the Senate when Quayle was chosen as the GOP vice presidential nominee. Coats was elected in his own right in 1990 to serve the remain-ing two years of Quayle's term, getting 54% of the vote. In 1992, he was elected to a full term with 57%.

One of the causes he championed while in the Senate was the line-item veto, which he said would help curb federal spending. Coats served on the Armed Services Committee, the Labor and Human Resources Committee, and, starting in 1997, the Intelligence Committee. He compiled a conservative voting record. He strongly opposed abortion rights and was a leader on a ban on re-search using fetal tissue. He sponsored a law allowing parents to block the numbers of "dial-a-porn" phone-sex lines and one restricting "indecent or lewd" material on the Internet. Coats did occasionally buck his party. He voted for the assault weapons ban and for the Family and Medical Leave Act, which requires companies to provide paid leave to their employees to care for a newborn child or a sick family member.

In December 1996, he announced he would not seek re-election in 1998. At the time, most polls showed him trailing outgoing Democratic Gov. Bayh, who went on to win the Senate seat. Coats joined the lobbying firm Verner, Liipfert, Bernhard, McPherson & Hand. In 2001, President George W. Bush considered him for Defense secretary before choosing Donald Rumsfeld. But he appointed Coats the U.S. ambassador to Germany. Disagreement over the Iraq war strained U.S.-German relations during Coats' tenure, but in 2005, he told *National Journal* that visits by Bush and Secretary of State Condoleezza Rice had helped to ease tensions. He left that post in 2005 and joined lobbying firm King & Spalding. He tried to help Bush rally Senate support for Supreme Court nominee Harriet Miers, although she withdrew after members of both parties questioned her qualifications.

In early 2010, with public opinion turning against incumbent Democrats, Bayh appeared vulnerable, and Republicans were searching for a top-tier candidate. Just two weeks after Coats announced his candidacy, Bayh declared that he would not seek re-election.

Coats faced a crowded GOP primary field that included former Rep. John Hostettler and state Sen. Marlin Stutzman, both of whom appealed to tea party groups. Coats was the only candidate to go on the air with significant advertising, and national Republicans backed him. He won the primary with 39% of the vote to 29% for Stutzman and 23% for Hostettler. Coats benefited from tea party Republicans splitting their votes between Stutzman and Hostettler.

In the general election, Coats honed a message that he returned to politics to combat President Barack Obama's agenda, and he accused his Democratic opponent, Rep. Brad Ellsworth, of being in lock-step with the national Democratic Party. Democrats, in turn, hammered Coats for his lucrative career as a lobbyist who did the bidding of special interests. They labeled him as a Washington insider, a strategy used widely in 2010 to appeal to recession-battered voters.

Republicans, meanwhile, went after Ellsworth as a rubber stamp for liberal House Speaker Nancy Pelosi and the Democratic agenda, parts of which were unpopular with conservative voters. They criticized his votes in favor the $787 billion economic stimulus bill and the health care overhaul. He also may have fallen out of favor with the anti-abortion rights voters who had been in his camp in the past because he voted for the health care bill even though the abortion restriction they favored had been dropped from the legislation.

In the final weeks before Election Day, Coats maintained a double-digit lead over Ellsworth. But he took no chances. With his coffers running low after the expensive primary, he put $200,000 of his own money into his campaign. Altogether, Coats raised $4.4 million, far more than Ellsworth, who had $2.4 million. Coats won 54.6% to 40%.

FIRST DISTRICT

Peter Visclosky (D)

Elected 1984, 14th term; b. Aug. 13, 1949, Gary; home, Merrillville; IN U. Northwest, B.S. 1970, U. of Notre Dame, J.D. 1973, Georgetown U., LL.M. 1982; Catholic; married (Joanne Royce); 2 children.

Professional Career: Practicing atty., 1973–76, 1983–84; Aide, U.S. Rep. Adam Benjamin, 1976–82.

DC Office: 2256 RHOB, 20515, 202-225-2461; Fax: 202-225-2493; Web site: visclosky.house.gov.

State Offices: Merrillville, 219-795-1844.

Committees: *Appropriations:* Defense; Energy & Water Development (RMM); Financial Services & General Government.

Group Ratings

	ACLU	ACU	ADA	CFG	AFS	FRC	LCV	ITIC	NTU	COC
2010	87	4	95	7	75	0	100	67	8	14
2009	–	8	90	15	100	–	86	–	10	47

National Journal Ratings

	2010 LIB	—	2010 CONS		2009 LIB	—	2009 CONS
Economic	59%	—	41%		58%	—	42%
Social	60%	—	40%		72%	—	28%
Foreign	56%	—	38%		91%	—	0%
Composite	59%	—	41%		75%	—	25%

Key Votes of the 111th Congress

1. Overturn Ledbetter	Y	5. Bar federal abortion funds	N	9. Stop detainee transfers	Y
2. Pass $820 billion stimulus	Y	6. Pass health care bill	Y	10. Legalize immigrants' kids	N
3. Let guns in national parks	N	7. Regulate financial firms	Y	11. Repeal don't ask, tell	Y
4. Pass cap-and-trade	N	8. Pass tax cuts for some	N	12. Limit campaign funds	*

Election Results

2010 general	Peter Visclosky (D) 99,387	(59%)	($891,338)
	Mark Leyva (R) 65,558	(39%)	($17,848)
	Jon Morris (Lib) 4,762	(3%)	
2010 primary	Peter Visclosky (D) .... unopposed		

Prior Winning Percentages: 2008 (71%), 2006 (70%), 2004 (68%), 2002 (67%), 2000 (72%), 1998 (73%), 1996 (69%), 1994 (56%), 1992 (69%), 1990 (66%), 1988 (77%), 1986 (73%), 1984 (71%)

Population		Race/Ethnicity		Work	
Pop. 2010:	705,600	White:	64.8%	Private:	84.8%
Change since 2000:	Up 4.4%	Black:	18.5%	Government:	11.1%
Urban:	87.0%	Hispanic:	14.0%	Self-employed:	4.0%
Rural:	13.0%	Asian:	1.1%	Blue collar:	28.4%
Area size:	2,443 sq. mi.	Native Am.:	0.2%	White collar:	54.3%
		Hawaiian:	0.0%	Khaki collar:	0.1%
Age		Two+ races:	1.2%	Other:	17.2%
Median age:	37.2 yrs.				
More than 65 yrs:	12.9%	*Ancestry*		Median income:	$50,607
Less than 18 yrs:	25.9%	German	15.5%	Median Home Value:	$140,700
		Irish	10.6%		
Education		Polish	7.2%	**Military Veterans**	
H.S. grad:	87.4%			% of Pop:	10.2%
College grad:	19.5%				
Grad degree:	6.4%				

Northwest Indiana: Gary, Hammond

At the southernmost shore of Lake Michigan is a part of America made by steel. Here, in the northwest corner of Indiana, where the water highway of the Great Lakes comes closest to the rail highway of the transcontinental railroads, America's leading capitalists of a century ago identified an ideal site for manufacturing steel. On empty sand dunes, United States Steel, then the nation's largest corporation, founded the city of Gary in 1906 and named it for the company's

2008 Presidential Vote
Barack Obama (D) 184,871   (62%)
John McCain (R) 111,895   (37%)

2004 Presidential Vote
John Kerry (D) 148,698   (55%)
George Bush (R) 118,417   (44%)

Cook Partisan Voting Index: D+8

chairman, Chicago Judge Elbert Gary. For nearly 70 years, the steel mills attracted a diverse workforce, more like Chicago than the rest of Indiana: Irish, Poles, Czechs, Ukrainians, and blacks from the South. Politics here has always been turbulent, from the long and unsuccessful steel strike of 1919 to the racially polarized politics of the 1960s and 1970s. The city has been the setting for other historical events: It is the birthplace of the late pop star Michael Jackson and lent its name to a famous tune in the Broadway musical *The Music Man*. But the tone of public life—the clash between union stewards and management foremen, between African-Americans and Eastern European ethnics, between the stalwarts of different factions vying for control of Gary's massive City Hall—was a clash of steel on steel.

Steel brought sudden growth and sudden depression to northwest Indiana. The massive storefronts built on Gary's aptly named Broadway bear witness to the confidence and exuberance of the 1920s. Today they stand vacant—vandalized, whole blocks burned down—witness to steel layoffs, crime waves, and an acute sense of loss. The steel mills went cold during the Depression of the 1930s, but were again thronged with workers during World War II, and in the years afterward, their massiveness helped create the illusion that a robust economic life in the steel towns of Gary, Hammond, and East Chicago would last forever. But technological advances replaced increasingly expensive workers with increasingly efficient machines. And the efforts to seal off the U.S. steel market from the world inevitably failed.

The oil crunch of 1979 was the catalyst for change, reducing the demand for large-sized autos, the biggest customer for steel. Steel employed 70,000 workers in northwest Indiana in 1979, 35,000 a few years later, and 18,500 in 2007. But with the average pay-and-benefits package exceeding $81,000 a year, the industry remains vital to the local economy. Obsolete mills were closed, old mills modernized, and new ones built that cut the number of man-hours needed by two-thirds. Just-in-time methods were introduced, and management and highly skilled workers cooperated to engineer higher-quality, less-expensive steel to meet market demands. In recent years, Indiana has been the No. 1 or No. 2 steel-producing state.

As the steel industry was shifting and changing, Gary was falling almost into ruins. Nobel Prize-winning economist Joseph Stiglitz in 2006 said the city was saddled with "the same problems facing less developed countries." High crime rates gave Gary the distinction for many years as the "murder capital" of the country, with the most homicides per capita. About half of 2010's 54 violent deaths remain unsolved, which police blame on witnesses refusing to cooperate, even anonymously. White flight to the suburbs has reduced the city's population from a peak of 178,000 in 1960 to 80,000 in 2010. In nearby majority-white Hammond, with many Hispanic immigrants, the population loss was not as dramatic. Like other economically desperate cities in the Midwest, Gary has come to rely on gambling for tax income. But neighboring states have gotten the same idea, and local officials are trying to remain competitive.

Indiana's 1st Congressional District stretches from Gary and Hammond along the Lake Michigan shoreline, east almost to Michigan City. It includes Lake County and Porter County to the east. In Porter is the city of Valparaiso, notable for its annual Popcorn Festivals honoring longtime resident and developer of 300 popcorn hybrids Orville Redenbacher. The district includes three small Republican-leaning counties south of Gary, but nearly three-quarters of the population is in Lake County. This remains the most Democratic district in politically balanced Indiana, as it has been since the United Steelworkers' organizing drives of the late 1930s.

Peter Visclosky (D)

The congressman from the 1st District is Peter Visclosky, a Democrat first elected in 1984. Visclosky grew up in Lake County. His father was mayor of Gary in the early 1960s, and Visclosky went to college there and to law school at the University of Notre Dame. He practiced law and then worked for six years in Washington for 1st District Rep. Adam Benjamin, a Democrat. Benjamin died suddenly of a heart ailment in 1982, and Visclosky returned to Indiana. In 1984, he ran for the seat in the Democratic primary against Katie Hall, a black state senator who had been given the 1982 nomination—and thus the election, in this Democratic district—by Gary Mayor Richard Hatcher, who was also the district's party chairman. In the 1984 contest, she faced a determined Visclosky, who pulled out all the stops to connect with voters since he couldn't rely on the local Democratic establishment, which was backing Hall. He called himself the "Slovak Kid" to connect with the district's many European ethnic groups, and he held hot dog dinners to attract young people and others not usually steeped in local politics. Visclosky narrowly prevailed over Hall with 34% of the vote to her 33%.

Visclosky's voting record has trended moderate, and he concentrates much of his effort on projects to help the local economy, especially the steel industry. He has a solid pro-union voting record. He is a leader of the Congressional Steel Caucus and has been vigilant in monitoring surges in steel imports. When George W. Bush was elected president in 2000 with critical help from steel-producing areas, Visclosky had greater leverage, and Bush did impose steel import quotas. But when the quotas were removed, Visclosky protested that Bush "stabbed the American steelworkers in the back." In 2008 and 2009, he sought to require that federally funded projects use only American-made steel, and he called for increased duties on subsidized steel, especially steel from China. Two years later, he led the Steel Caucus in calling for an investigation into China's investment in an American steel company. He opposed the House-passed bill in 2009 establishing a cap-and-trade system to curb greenhouse gas emissions because it "leaves no margin of error as it relates to jobs in the domestic steel industry."

As the chairman of the Appropriations Subcommittee on Energy and Water Development, Visclosky was one of the powerful "cardinals" of the House. But he was forced to step aside, at least temporarily, in June 2009 after he was subpoenaed as part of a grand jury investigation into possible corruption. The next-in-line in seniority, Democrat Ed Pastor of Arizona, took over the subcommittee for the duration of the investigation, and the following year also oversaw the fiscal 2011 energy and water spending bill. In 2007, *The Indianapolis Star* reported that Visclosky had steered more than $12 million to out-of-state defense companies that contributed to his campaign. Much of that federal money had been secured through the efforts of a lobbying firm, PMA Group, that hired a former top Visclosky aide, Richard Kaelin, the newspaper reported. Visclosky said he expected to be cleared of wrongdoing. "I have always abided by the law and adhered to the rules and code of ethics of the House," he said in a June 2, 2009, statement. The Committee on Standards of Official Conduct (Ethics) formally cleared him and six other Appropriations members in February 2010, but a Justice Department investigation reportedly was still ongoing.

Visclosky has been adept at securing federal funding for projects in his district and doling them out to other lawmakers. One of his efforts was passing an exemption to the federal Johnson Act that made Lake Michigan waters eligible for gambling and thus allowing riverboat casinos for Gary. On broader national issues, Visclosky in 2007 rejected the Bush administration's request for $89 million for a new nuclear warhead, and he slashed from $405 million to $120 million the administration's proposed funding for reprocessing fuel rods in nuclear power plants, which was opposed by environmentalists.

At home, Visclosky appeared secure until he became a target in the corruption probe in early 2009. But Republicans had trouble finding a candidate who could compete in the costly Chicago media market, and the GOP nomination again fell to Mark Leyva, a carpenter who had lost four previous races to Visclosky. All Leyva could do was narrow the margin of victory for Visclosky, who won with 59% of the vote.

SECOND DISTRICT

Joe Donnelly (D)

Elected 2006, 3rd term; b. Sept. 29, 1955, Massapequa, NY; home, Granger; U. of Notre Dame, B.A. 1977, J.D. 1981; Catholic; married (Jill); 2 children.

Elected Office: Mishawaka Marian High School Board, 1997-2001.

Professional Career: Practicing atty., 1981-96; Owner, Marking Solutions, 1996-2006.

DC Office: 1530 LHOB, 20515, 202-225-3915; Fax: 202-225-6798; Web site: donnelly.house.gov.

State Offices: La Porte, 219-326-6808 ext. 2414; Logansport, 574-753-2671; Michigan City, 219-873-1403 ext. 308; South Bend, 574-288-2780.

Committees: *Financial Services:* Capital Markets and Government Sponsored Enterprises; International Monetary Policy & Trade. *Veterans' Affairs:* Health; Oversight & Investigations (RMM).

Group Ratings

	ACLU	ACU	ADA	CFG	AFS	FRC	LCV	ITIC	NTU	COC
2010	44	25	60	8	100	75	70	100	17	63
2009	–	24	70	22	89	–	78	–	21	53

National Journal Ratings

	2010 LIB — 2010 CONS		2009 LIB — 2009 CONS	
Economic	48%	— 51%	47%	— 53%
Social	42%	— 57%	42%	— 57%
Foreign	45%	— 55%	43%	— 56%
Composite	45%	— 55%	44%	— 56%

Key Votes of the 111th Congress

1. Overturn Ledbetter	Y	5. Bar federal abortion funds	Y
2. Pass $820 billion stimulus	Y	6. Pass health care bill	Y
3. Let guns in national parks	Y	7. Regulate financial firms	Y
4. Pass cap-and-trade	N	8. Pass tax cuts for some	Y

9. Stop detainee transfers	Y
10. Legalize immigrants' kids	N
11. Repeal don't ask, tell	Y
12. Limit campaign funds	N

Election Results

2010 general	Joe Donnelly (D)	91,341	(48%)	($1,723,644)
	Jackie Swihart (R)	88,803	(47%)	($1,331,778)
	Mark Vogel (Lib)	9,447	(5%)	
2010 primary	Joe Donnelly (D)	unopposed		

Prior Winning Percentages: 2008 (67%), 2006 (54%)

Population		Race/Ethnicity		Work	
Pop. 2010:	679,254	White:	80.0%	Private:	84.3%
Change since 2000:	Up 0.5%	Black:	8.7%	Government:	10.4%
Urban:	72.8%	Hispanic:	8.0%	Self-employed:	5.2%
Rural:	27.2%	Asian:	1.1%	Blue collar:	31.2%
Area size:	3,720 sq. mi.	Native Am.:	0.3%	White collar:	52.1%
		Hawaiian:	0.0%	Khaki collar:	0.0%
Age		Two+ races:	1.9%	Other:	16.7%
Median age:	36.9 yrs.				
More than 65 yrs:	13.3%	*Ancestry*		Median income:	$43,631
Less than 18 yrs:	25.2%	German	20.7%	Median Home Value:	$110,900
		Irish	10.8%		
Education		English	6.6%	**Military Veterans**	
H.S. grad:	84.2%			% of Pop:	10.4%
College grad:	19.6%				
Grad degree:	7.3%				

North Central Indiana; South Bend

When the University of Notre Dame was founded in 1842, Catholics were still a rarity in most of America and certainly rare on the limestone-bottomed plains of northern Indiana. This was still farm country and South Bend no more than a crossroads on the banks of the St. Joseph River. But by the 1920s, both the school and the town had grown. Notre Dame, thanks to its football team, the Fighting Irish, was the most famous Catholic university in the land,

2008 Presidential Vote
Barack Obama (D) 153,363 (54%)
John McCain (R) 126,796 (45%)

2004 Presidential Vote
George Bush (R) 146,000 (56%)
John Kerry (D) 112,671 (43%)

Cook Partisan Voting Index: R+2

and South Bend was a significant industrial city, home of Studebaker and Bendix and dozens of other factories. In the past 50 years, Notre Dame has grown in size and reputation, but South Bend, like many Rust Belt cities, diminished in size and reputation. In the 1960s, Studebaker went out of business. In the early 1980s, there were massive factory layoffs, and in the early 1990s, there were well-publicized layoffs in nearby Elkhart. But these high-visibility job losses were accompanied by the much less visible creation of jobs in small factories throughout the region. The work in those facilities required more skill than did the old assembly lines, and the products had to be more responsive to just-in-time prime contractors or computer-inventory retailers. In the late 1990s, many employers had trouble filling job openings, and the economic base was more secure than when it depended on the fate of two or three big companies. Notre Dame in 2008 acquired the Midwestern Institute for Nanoelectronics Discovery, which in conjunction with other topflight colleges in the country, is doing research into the building blocks of the next generation of computers.

The 2nd Congressional District of Indiana is centered on South Bend. This is an industrial and ethnic city, with one of the nation's largest percentage of Hungarian-Americans, plus a growing community of Mexican-Americans. It is strongly Democratic, as is LaPorte County around Michigan City. Also in the district is Kokomo, an auto manufacturing center with more than 10 plants. During the 2008 financial crisis in the domestic automobile market, President Barack Obama took on Kokomo as a sort of pet project after making several campaign trips there, which resulted in Kokomo getting $400 million in economic stimulus money. The city's unemployment rate climbed past 20% in 2009, but by late 2010 had improved to 11%.

Elkhart County to the east is heavily Republican and conservative. But it, too, got federal help, including $4 million to build a new 6,000-foot concrete runway at the airport. "You can't drive anywhere in Elkhart and not see the stimulus," Democratic mayor Dick Moore told *The Indianapolis Star* in 2010. The 2nd District also includes several counties on the limestone plains to the south down past the Wabash River. This is an area rural in appearance but with much small manufacturing; politically, it has been part of the Republican heartland since the party was created in the 1850s. Indiana Democrats in 2002 drew the lines of the 2nd to maximize their chance to hold it. Still, it took four years to elect a Democrat, in 2006. In recent presidential contests, George W. Bush won the 2nd District with 53% in 2000 and 56% in 2004. Obama won it with 54% in 2008.

Joe Donnelly (D)

The congressman from the 2nd District is Joe Donnelly, a Democrat first elected in 2006. Donnelly was born in Massapequa, N.Y., and grew up on Long Island's South Shore. He attended the University of Notre Dame, earning an undergraduate degree in government and a law degree in 1981. He practiced law in the area until 1996, when he opened Marking Solutions, a printing and rubber stamp company. Donnelly served on the state election board in 1988 and 1989, but his early bids for public office were disappointing, to say the least. He ran unsuccessfully for the Democratic nomination for state attorney general in 1988, failed in a bid for the state Senate in 1990, and then lost his first attempt at a seat in Congress in 2004. However, he at least came in close in the latter contest, holding Republican Rep. Chris Chocola to 54% to his 45%.

The year 2006 was much more difficult for Republicans like Chocola nationally, and he had some problems at home as well. Republican Gov. Mitch Daniels' move to daylight saving time and the privatization of the Indiana Toll Road, which runs through the district, proved unpopular. This time, the Democratic Congressional Campaign Committee took a much greater interest in the race by installing a campaign manager for Donnelly and elevating the race to its "Red to Blue" program. Donnelly made Bush's handling of the Iraq war an issue, and although Chocola again outspent him 2-to-1, it seemed it was finally Donnelly's year to win. He beat Chocola 54%-46%, carrying five of the district's 12 counties.

In the House, Donnelly has a centrist voting record. An opponent of abortion rights, Donnelly has urged Democratic leaders to advance a moderate agenda in Congress. He also joined the Blue Dogs, a group of conservative Democrats. In the meantime, he went his own way on some issues, and was among 12 Democrats to vote against the budget in 2007. He also opposed the 2009 bill creating a cap-and-trade system for reducing greenhouse gas emissions, which he said contained too many uncertainties for businesses. He backed the House version of the health care overhaul, but was among the anti-abortion Democrats who withheld their support of the final version until President Obama agreed to issue an executive order reaffirming the government's ban on funding abortion-related services. Donnelly also refused to support liberal Nancy Pelosi of California for Democratic leader in 2011.

He has focused on veterans' issues, working with Rep. Fred Upton, R-Mich., to expedite veterans' claims, and got a bill through the House in September 2010 to speed up processing veterans' benefits. On the Financial Services Committee, he backed the fall 2008 bailouts for the financial markets and big automobile companies. On the housing bill in 2007, he added a provision to raise loan limits for manufactured housing, which has a strong presence in Indiana. In 2009, he got the House to include recreational vehicles—many of which are made in his district—to be included in an advanced vehicle technology research bill.

Donnelly had an unexpectedly easy re-election campaign in 2008, after Republicans failed to recruit a strong challenger. He was not so fortunate in 2010. Republicans put up conservative state Rep. Jackie Walorski, a favorite of tea party activists. She bashed Donnelly for his support of the health care bill, while he charged that she would replace the income tax with a regressive national sales tax. Donnelly got just enough support from independent voters to eke out a 48%-47% win. He also benefited from the candidacy of Libertarian Mark Vogel, who in winning 5% probably drew votes away from Walorski. After his district was altered to make it significantly more Republican as part of post-2010 census redistricting, Donnelly announced in May 2011 that he would run for Republican Richard Lugar's Senate seat in 2012.

THIRD DISTRICT

Marlin Stutzman (R)

Elected 2010, 1st term; b. Aug. 31, 1976, Sturgis, MI; home, Howe; Trine U., attended.; Baptist; Married (Christy); 2 children.

Elected Office: IN House, 2002-08; IN Senate, 2008-10.

Professional Career: Co-owner, Stutzman Farms; owner, Stutzman Farms Trucking.

DC Office: 1728 LHOB, 20515, 202-225-4436; Fax: 202-226-9870; Web site: stutzman.house.gov.

State Offices: Fort Wayne, 260-424-3041; Goshen, 574-533-5802; Kendallville, 260-599-0554; Winona Lake, 574-269-1940.

Committees: *Agriculture:* Conservation, Energy & Forestry; Rural Development, Research, Biotechnology & Foreign Agriculture. *Budget. Veterans' Affairs:* Disability Assistance & Memorial Affairs; Economic Opportunity (Chmn).

Election Results

2010 general	Marlin Stutzman (R)	116,140	(63%)	($597,306)
	Thomas Hayhurst (D)	61,267	(33%)	($807,543)
	Scott Wise (Lib)	7,631	(4%)	
2010 primary	Dan Coats (R)	217,225	(39%)	
	Marlin Stutzman (R)	160,981	(29%)	
	John Hostettler (R)	124,494	(23%)	

Population		Race/Ethnicity		Work	
Pop. 2010:	723,633	White:	83.7%	Private:	85.3%
Change since 2000:	Up 7.1%	Black:	5.9%	Government:	8.9%
Urban:	65.1%	Hispanic:	6.8%	Self-employed:	5.6%
Rural:	34.9%	Asian:	1.6%	Blue collar:	31.4%
Area size:	3,293 sq. mi.	Native Am.:	0.2%	White collar:	53.4%
		Hawaiian:	0.0%	Khaki collar:	0.1%
Age		Two+ races:	1.6%	Other:	15.2%
Median age:	35.5 yrs.				
More than 65 yrs:	12.0%	*Ancestry*		Median income:	$48,120
Less than 18 yrs:	27.0%	German	27.4%	Median Home Value:	$121,200
		Irish	8.9%		
Education		USA	7.7%	**Military Veterans**	
H.S. grad:	84.8%			% of Pop:	9.4%
College grad:	21.2%				
Grad degree:	6.8%				

Northeast Indiana; Fort Wayne

The flat northeast corner of Indiana was first settled by people of New England Yankee stock, establishing orderly communities with public schools and even colleges. They were joined by German immigrants, who built tidy farms and their own civic institutions. In the northern part of the state, there are hills and lakes, and the strange swamp that is the central focus of Gene Stratton-Porter's children's classic, *A Girl of the Limberlost.* The one large city here, Fort Wayne,

2008 Presidential Vote
John McCain (R) 162,147   (56%)
Barack Obama (D) 123,558   (43%)

2004 Presidential Vote
George Bush (R) 172,919   (68%)
John Kerry (D) 79,674   (31%)

Cook Partisan Voting Index: R+14

was built on the flat terrain along the Maumee River that flows to Toledo, Ohio. It grew as a factory town, surging ahead and then falling back as large factories, often tied to the auto industry, opened and closed over the years. As much as anything else, this part of Indiana is a place where people make things. Northwest of Fort Wayne on U.S. Route 33, Elkhart County is a manufacturing hub where local companies make everything from pharmaceuticals to musical instruments—oboes, bassoons, and piccolos. The county is best known as the nation's manufacturing center for recreational vehicles, and doesn't much care what the greenies think of that.

But steep rises in gasoline prices, like those in recent years, can have a big impact in Elkhart, where several recent plant closings rippled through the economy to endanger suppliers and other dependent businesses. The onset of recession strangled demand for big-ticket luxury goods like RVs. And from 2007 to 2008, Elkhart's unemployment jumped to 15%, the largest increase of any other metropolitan area in the nation, prompting *The New York Times* to call it "the white-hot center of the meltdown of the American economy." The story noted that the city council passed a law limiting residents to one garage sale per month. The mayor responded that the *Times* article was one-sided and "painted it much worse than it really is." But joblessness in Elkhart continued to be a worry, and even President Obama dropped in for a visit in February 2009, having found no better location to tout his economic recovery plan. Unemployment lingered at a stubborn 13% in Elkhart in 2010.

Neighboring Kosciusko (*Kosh-CHOO-shko*) County is renowned for medical supplies. In Warsaw, the orthopedics manufacturing capital of the world, residents have been making orthopedic devices for more than a century. Manufacturing jobs in the Fort Wayne area dropped significantly in the 2000s, but the area began to revive a bit after Claypool opened a $150 million biodiesel complex, including a soybean processing plant capable of producing 88 million gallons of fuel annually. This is a surprisingly diverse area. Its eclectic population mix includes a concentration of Amish, plus Central Americans, Bosnians, Somalis, and the nation's largest population of Burmese refugees.

The 3rd Congressional District of Indiana consists of most of eight counties in the northeast part of the state. This part of Indiana has been heavily Republican since the Civil War, though it has sometimes veered Democratic in times of economic distress. The seat sends its representatives on to higher positions: Dan Quayle, elected here in 1976, was later a senator and vice president, and Dan Coats, who succeeded Quayle in the Senate seat, was ambassador to Germany before getting elected to the Senate for a second stint in 2010. GOP presidential candidates have won this district handily. In 2008, John McCain carried it with 56% of the vote.

Marlin Stutzman (R)

The new congressman from Indiana's 3rd District is Marlin Stutzman, a Republican elected in 2010 after conservative GOP Rep. Mark Souder confessed publicly to an extramarital affair and gave up the seat.

Stutzman is a fourth-generation farmer who grew up in Howe, Ind. His parents were Mennonites, a denomination of Anabaptists that shares historical roots with the Amish. His father was 19 and his mother 17 when they were married, and neither attended college. Stutzman is the oldest of four children, all of whom worked on the family farm from a young age, driving tractors, feeding livestock, and sorting vegetables. When he was 14, Stutzman started raising his own livestock herd, which reached almost 100 animals before he sold them. He attended Tri-State University (now Trine University) for two years to study accounting, but he dropped out to focus on farming. He married a teacher when he was 23, and converted to her Baptist religion. They had their first child a year later. He co-owned Stutzman Farms with his father and also was the sole owner of a trucking company before his election to Congress. (He estimates that in the past 15 years, he has collected $100,000 in farm subsidies from the federal government. But Stutzman says he favors phasing out subsidies because he views them as unnecessary government interference in the free market and because they increase the federal debt.)

Stutzman says he did not have political ambitions growing up; he formed his early political views by listening to conservative talk radio programs while driving his tractor. He first became involved in local politics out of frustration with navigating state regulations as a small business owner, recalling one incident in which incorrect information from the state Revenue Department regarding the transfer of license plates for his trucking company cost him thousands of dollars. In 2002, when no one registered to challenge a longtime incumbent Democrat in the Indiana House, Stutzman filed papers to run on the last possible day. He won by 249 votes, becoming the youngest member of the House at age 26. In three terms, he helped to pass a tax credit for ethanol producers and authored Indiana's lifetime handgun permit law, which frees gun owners from having to renew their licenses. He was the co-author of the bill that created the Indiana Agriculture Department, which he describes as an advocacy agency rather than a regulatory one. In 2005, he pushed a bill that created tougher regulations for abortion providers. From 2005 to 2008, while still a state representative, Stutzman worked as a special assistant in Souder's district office. In 2008, Stutzman won a seat in the state Senate.

The following year, he announced he would seek the Republican nomination to challenge Democratic Sen. Evan Bayh. Then in February 2010, Bayh said he would not seek re-election, creating an open seat opportunity that generated interest among other Republicans. In the primary, Stutzman faced former Sen. Dan Coats and former Rep. John Hostettler. Although national Republicans recruited Coats for the race, Stutzman had the support of tea party activists and conservative Sen. Jim DeMint, R-S.C., who was attempting to boost the number of conservative candidates around the country. Coats ultimately won the nomination with 39% of the vote, and Stutzman came in second with 29%.

The results raised Stutzman's political profile and helped him win the support of Republican officials when Souder ran into political trouble in the spring of 2010. The incumbent looked to be well on his way to securing a ninth term when he revealed in May that he had engaged in an extramarital affair with one of his aides. Because Souder had already won the GOP primary, party officials chose Stutzman as their new nominee at their June caucus.

In the general election campaign, he was the heavy favorite over his Democratic opponent, former Fort Wayne City Council member Tom Hayhurst, in one of the most Republican districts in Indiana. Although Hayhurst raised an impressive $730,000 for the contest, Stutzman, who raised $1 million, won with ease, with 63% of the vote to Hayhurst's 33%. Stutzman won a double victory on Nov. 2: He was elected to fill the final weeks of Souder's term in the 111th Congress (2009-10) while, at the same time, winning a full two-year term for the 112th Congress (2011-12). He was sworn in on Nov. 16, two months ahead of other newly elected lawmakers, whose terms began in January 2011.

FOURTH DISTRICT

Todd Rokita (R)

Elected 2010, 1st term; b. Feb. 9, 1970, Chicago, IL; home, Indianapolis; Wabash Col., B.A. 1992; IN U., Indianapolis, J.D. 1995.; Catholic; Married (Kathy); 2 children.

Elected Office: IN Secy. of St., 2003-10.

Professional Career: Practicing atty., 1995-97; gen. cnsl., Office of IN Secy. of St., 1997-2000; IN dep. secy. of st., 2000-02.

DC Office: 236 CHOB, 20515, 202-225-5037; Fax: 202-226-0544; Web site: rokita.house.gov.

State Offices: Mitchell, 812-849-9378; Plainfield, 317-838-0404.

Committees: *Budget. Education & the Workforce:* Health, Employment, Labor & Pensions; Workforce Protections. *House Administration:* Elections; Oversight.

Election Results

2010 general	Todd Rokita (R)	138,732	(69%)	($1,095,067)
	David Sanders (D)	53,167	(26%)	($110,434)
	John Duncan (Lib)	10,423	(5%)	
2010 primary	Todd Rokita (R)	36,411	(42%)	
	Brandt Hershman (R)	14,712	(17%)	
	R. Michael Young (R)	6,991	(8%)	
	Eric Wathen (R)	5,493	(6%)	

Population		Race/Ethnicity		Work	
Pop. 2010:	789,835	White:	88.2%	Private:	81.0%
Change since 2000:	Up 16.9%	Black:	3.1%	Government:	13.9%
Urban:	68.2%	Hispanic:	4.6%	Self-employed:	5.0%
Rural:	31.8%	Asian:	2.4%	Blue collar:	25.5%
Area size:	4,033 sq. mi.	Native Am.:	0.2%	White collar:	58.7%
		Hawaiian:	0.0%	Khaki collar:	0.1%
Age		Two+ races:	1.4%	Other:	15.7%
Median age:	35.5 yrs.				
More than 65 yrs:	11.7%	*Ancestry*		Median income:	$53,802
Less than 18 yrs:	24.8%	German	21.0%	Median Home Value:	$137,900
		Irish	11.6%		
Education		English	10.0%	**Military Veterans**	
H.S. grad:	89.1%			% of Pop:	9.9%
College grad:	26.0%				
Grad degree:	9.4%				

West Central Indiana

The landscape of central Indiana is some of the most prosaic in the United States. It is mostly flat, with neat farms and towns of frame bungalows, looking mostly unchanged from many years ago. Across this landscape run some of the nation's chief transportation arteries. The earliest was the old National Road, from Baltimore to St. Louis, which was paralleled by U.S. 40 in the 1930s. The region was also crisscrossed by the great east-west rail lines carrying famed passenger trains like the old *Wabash Cannonball*. There is no *Cannonball* today. People bounce around the Midwest on commuter airlines from small city to hub, and U.S. 40 has been replaced by Interstate 70. The landscape still looks rural, and there are some large farms. But the economy is more industrial, with small factories in crossroads and courthouse towns. This is a part of America with little heritage from the early waves of immigration, relatively few blacks, and only modest numbers of Latino and Asian immigrants.

2008 Presidential Vote		
John McCain (R) 185,843	(56%)
Barack Obama (D) 142,930	(43%)
2004 Presidential Vote		
George Bush (R) 196,010	(69%)
John Kerry (D) 85,179	(30%)
Cook Partisan Voting Index: R+14		

The 4th Congressional District of Indiana covers much of this territory, running from Indiana's northern plains to its southern hills. It includes all or part of 12 counties in western Indiana, including the far western edge of Indianapolis and Marion County. It extends south to Lawrence County, the source of the limestone used to rebuild the Pentagon after the September 11 attacks. The largest city is Lafayette, where the main employer is Purdue University. Growing and prosperous, the city has benefited from a 2006 partnership between Toyota and longtime local manufacturer Subaru to annually produce 100,000 Camry sedans while continuing to produce Subarus. Lafayette ranked sixth on *Forbes* magazine's 2009 list of "smartest small towns in America," and it tends to vote Republican. Even more Republican are the small counties and the suburban territory outside Indianapolis, such as fast-growing Hendricks County, which delivered 73% for George W. Bush in 2004 and 61% for John McCain in 2008.

Todd Rokita (R)

The new congressman from the 4th District is Republican Todd Rokita, elected in 2010 to replace retiring GOP Rep. Steve Buyer. Rokita grew up in Munster, Ind., the oldest of three children. His father was a dentist who owned his own practice, and his mother was a dental hygienist. Rokita was president of his high school student body and won a full scholarship to Wabash College, an all-male liberal arts school. He majored in political science, focusing on political philosophy, and studied for a semester at the University of Essex in England. Rokita told *National Journal* that his semester in Europe reinforced his already conservative political beliefs. Fellow students told him about long lines and poor service in government-run hospitals, and he noticed the high cost of goods because of a value-added tax, a form of consumption tax collected in Europe. On an excursion to Amsterdam, he saw what he described as the dangers and social costs of legalized drugs. His experience abroad was "a good glimpse into what the future of America would and could be with liberalism on the march here," Rokita said.

After earning his law degree at the Indiana University School of Law-Indianapolis, Rokita worked in private practice for several years. A licensed pilot, Rokita focused on aviation law, among other fields. While volunteering on local and state campaigns, he met Indiana's then-Secretary of State Sue Anne Gilroy, who hired him as her general counsel and later made him deputy secretary of state. Rokita also worked for George W. Bush's presidential campaign in 2000, training workers in how to challenge ballots during the historic 2000 Florida recount.

In 2002, Gilroy was term-limited out of office, and Rokita ran for the Republican nomination to succeed her. In Indiana, convention delegates choose the nominees for all statewide offices other than governor. Rokita took a leave of absence from his job, bought a surplus police car, and drove across the state, meeting with delegates in their homes. He estimates that by the time of the convention, he had met 1,500 of the 2,000 delegates. He won the Republican nomination for secretary of state on the third ballot and went on to win the general election.

In office, he fulfilled a campaign pledge to get a bill through the legislature requiring a photo ID at polling places to combat perceived voter fraud. Critics of the 2005 law argued that it disenfranchised poor voters who are less likely to have driver's licenses (and are more likely to vote Democratic). A lawsuit challenging the constitutionality of the law made it all the way to the Supreme Court, which upheld it in 2008. Rokita was embroiled in another controversy with civil rights undercurrents. In a 2007 speech, he questioned why 90% of blacks vote for Democrats. "How can that be?" Rokita said, according to the Associated Press. "Ninety to 10. Who's the master and who's the slave in that relationship? How can that be healthy?" After African-American leaders condemned his remarks, Rokita apologized.

In 2009, he managed to infuriate members of both political parties in the state when he proposed making it a felony for lawmakers to draw legislative districts based on political data such as party registration and where incumbents live. He argued that the current process allows incumbents to draw districts in their own favor instead of trying to keep communities together, and he created a website to raise awareness of his campaign. "I don't think it's his business," the Republican leader in the state Senate told *The Indianapolis Star*. "The secretary of state has overstepped his bounds." Although Rokita later backed off his call to prosecute lawmakers who violate the redistricting rules, he continued to push for reform.

Last year, Rokita considered challenging Democratic Sen. Evan Bayh, but jumped into the congressional race instead when Buyer announced his retirement. His main primary opponent was state Sen. Brandt Hershman, Buyer's district director. With high name recognition and solid fundraising, Rokita won 42% of the vote to Hershman's 17%. There were 11 other candidates in the race, but none of them earned more than 10%. He easily won in November against Purdue University professor David Sanders, the Democratic candidate, 68.5% to 26%. Libertarian John Duncan got 5%.

FIFTH DISTRICT

Dan Burton (R)

Elected 1982, 15th term; b. June 21, 1938, Indianapolis; home, Indianapolis; IN U., 1958-59, Cincinnati Bible Seminary, 1959-60; Protestant; married (Samia); 4 children.

Military Career: Army, 1956–57, Army Reserves, 1957–62.

Elected Office: IN House of Reps., 1966–68, 1976–80; IN Senate, 1968–70, 1980–82.

Professional Career: Real estate broker; Founder, Dan Burton Insurance Agency, 1968.

DC Office: 2308 RHOB, 20515, 202-225-2276; Fax: 202-225-0016; Web site: burton.house.gov.

State Offices: Indianapolis, 317-848-0201; Marion, 765-662-6770.

Committees: *Foreign Affairs:* Asia & the Pacific; Europe and Eurasia (Chmn). *Oversight & Government Reform:* Health Care, District of Columbia, Census & the National Archives; National Security, Homeland Defense & Foreign Operations.

Group Ratings

	ACLU	ACU	ADA	CFG	AFS	FRC	LCV	ITIC	NTU	COC
2010	6	100	0	89	0	100	0	33	90	100
2009	–	96	5	85	11	–	0	–	88	73

National Journal Ratings

	2010 LIB	—	2010 CONS	2009 LIB	—	2009 CONS
Economic	3%	—	97%	19%	—	80%
Social	0%	—	85%	7%	—	90%
Foreign	29%	—	68%	0%	—	75%
Composite	14%	—	86%	14%	—	87%

Key Votes of the 111th Congress

1. Overturn Ledbetter	N	5. Bar federal abortion funds	Y	9. Stop detainee transfers	Y
2. Pass $820 billion stimulus	N	6. Pass health care bill	N	10. Legalize immigrants' kids	N
3. Let guns in national parks	Y	7. Regulate financial firms	N	11. Repeal don't ask, tell	N
4. Pass cap-and-trade	N	8. Pass tax cuts for some	N	12. Limit campaign funds	N

Election Results

2010 general	Dan Burton (R)	146,899	(62%)	($1,131,679)
	Tim Crawford (D)	60,024	(25%)	
	Richard Reid (Lib)	18,266	(8%)	
	Jesse Trueblood (I)	11,218	(5%)	
2010 primary	Dan Burton (R)	32,769	(30%)	
	Luke Messer (R)	30,502	(28%)	
	John McGoff (R)	20,679	(19%)	
	Michael Murphy (R)	9,805	(9%)	
	Brose McVey (R)	9,372	(8%)	

Prior Winning Percentages: 2008 (66%), 2006 (65%), 2004 (72%), 2002 (72%), 2000 (70%), 1998 (72%), 1996 (75%), 1994 (77%), 1992 (72%), 1990 (63%), 1988 (73%), 1986 (68%), 1984 (73%), 1982 (65%)

Population		Race/Ethnicity		Work	
Pop. 2010:	809,107	White:	88.1%	Private:	83.6%
Change since 2000:	Up 19.8%	Black:	4.0%	Government:	11.3%
Urban:	74.5%	Hispanic:	3.4%	Self-employed:	5.0%
Rural:	25.5%	Asian:	2.6%	Blue collar:	19.2%
Area size:	3,291 sq. mi.	Native Am.:	0.2%	White collar:	66.9%
		Hawaiian:	0.0%	Khaki collar:	0.1%
Age		Two+ races:	1.5%	Other:	13.8%
Median age:	37.4 yrs.				
More than 65 yrs:	12.1%	*Ancestry*		Median income:	$60,549
Less than 18 yrs:	25.9%	German	22.7%	Median Home Value:	$156,400
		Irish	11.2%		
Education		English	9.7%	**Military Veterans**	
H.S. grad:	91.6%			% of Pop:	10.1%
College grad:	35.6%				
Grad degree:	12.2%				

Central Indiana; Hamilton County

Indiana's most rapid growth is taking place in the suburban ring counties around Indianapolis, especially in Hamilton County, directly north of the city. This is affluent suburbia, with subdivisions full of spacious houses, shopping centers, and office developments in what were not too long ago farm fields. Hamilton County's population increased from 82,000 in 1980 to 182,000 in 2000 and to an estimated 301,000 in 2010—a 66% jump in a decade, making it one of the fastest growing counties in the Midwest. In 2010, a group of business and civic leaders came up with a mass transit plan that could cause even more growth. Hamilton County is affluent, having drawn many wealthy people from Indianapolis, where they used to be concentrated on the north side of the city. Now they're more likely to be in the former farm communities of Carmel, Fishers, and Noblesville. Hamilton is the most Republican of the large counties in Indiana and is one of the most Republican in the nation. It voted 74%-24% for George W. Bush in 2004 and 61%-38% for John McCain in 2008.

2008 Presidential Vote

John McCain (R)	218,973	(59%)
Barack Obama (D)	149,752	(40%)

2004 Presidential Vote

George Bush (R)	233,215	(71%)
John Kerry (D)	91,955	(28%)

Cook Partisan Voting Index: R+17

Almost half the people of the 5th Congressional District of Indiana live in Hamilton County. The district also includes suburban but less affluent (and less Republican) Hancock County, where the U.S. Lawn Mower Racing Association's championship is held every September. It takes in parts of Shelby and Johnson counties to the south. On its northern end, the district includes quite different parts of Indiana, with small, industrial cities like Marion heavily dependent on the auto industry and suffering from auto-parts industry bankruptcies and layoffs. There is also Miami County, once the winter headquarters for Ringling Brothers and other circuses and now home to the International Circus Hall of Fame. Wabash and Huntington counties are the birthplaces of vice presidents: Democrat Thomas Marshall, Woodrow Wilson's vice president, was from North Manchester in Wabash County, and Republican Dan Quayle, President George H.W. Bush's vice president, spent his high school years and later practiced law in Huntington. The latter town was in a Fort Wayne-based district when Quayle represented it in the House.

Dan Burton (R)

The congressman from the 5th District is Dan Burton, a Republican first elected to the House in 1982 and one of the chamber's most controversial figures. By his own acknowledgement, Burton had a horrific childhood. His father was abusive and left the family; his mother worked as a waitress and bought the kids' clothes at Goodwill. His father ultimately kidnapped his mother and went to jail, and the kids were sent to the county home. "I think part of my aggressive nature is because of my childhood," Burton told author Studs Terkel in an interview for *Hope Dies Last*. "The highest moment of hope in my childhood was when we finally got away from my father. When I was five, six years old, my mother used to stand between me and him when he'd start to beat me and take the blows. I was black and blue from my neck to my ankles." As a teenager, Burton earned money shining shoes and at age 18 enlisted in the Army. He never finished college but was successful as a real estate broker and insurance salesman. He also ran for public office, often losing but not giving up. He was finally elected to the Indiana House in 1966 and to the Indiana Senate in 1968. He lost races for Congress in 1970 and 1972, but won a seat in 1982 when the GOP-controlled legislature created a heavily Republican suburban seat.

For years, Burton was regarded by many as a gadfly, excitedly pursuing lost causes. During the Clinton era, he long insisted that the suicide of White House deputy counsel Vince Foster was a murder, and famously staged a reenactment in his backyard, using a gun and a pumpkin or watermelon–it was never clear which. For years, he has investigated the link between thimerosal, a mercury-based vaccine preservative, and autism, firm in his belief that his grandson's autism was caused by thimerosal even though the Institutes of Medicine reported finding no link between the drug and autism. His position puts him at odds with one of his district's major employers, Indianapolis-based Eli Lilly, the company that developed thimerosal. Some 5,000 Lilly employees live in the district, and he has received no contributions from Lilly's political action committee since 2002.

But Burton is nothing if not fearless and often goes his own way in the face of pressure from GOP leaders to toe the line. He is an enthusiastic supporter of alternative medicine, and he favors importation of prescription drugs from Canada. In 2007, Burton sided with Democrats to support giving the government power to negotiate lower drug prices with the pharmaceutical industry, a proposal staunchly opposed by most Republicans and by Eli Lilly. Some of his views on health care policy have evolved from his personal experience: Burton's wife died of cancer in 2002, and four years later, he married her doctor. On other issues, Burton has for years called for encasing the House visitors' galleries in Plexiglas for security reasons. The idea has been taken more seriously since the January 2011 shooting of Rep. Gabrielle Giffords, D-Ariz., at a constituent event.

Burton has had some significant legislative successes, but his biggest achievement was the Helms-Burton Act of 1996. Drafted in response to the Cuban Air Force's downing of American planes, it stated that foreign companies could be sued in U.S. courts if, as part of business deals with former Cuba Leader Fidel Castro's regime, they took over property expropriated from American owners. The low point of his congressional career was probably the tumultuous hearings he conducted into campaign finance irregularities by President Bill Clinton's presidential campaign from 1997 to 2000. Burton was then chairman of the Government Reform Committee, and he promised bipartisan hearings. But they were actually highly partisan, an impression sealed by Burton himself when he described Clinton to *The Indianapolis Star* in 1998 as "a scumbag."

Because of Republican term limits on chairmen, Burton had to relinquish the Government Reform chairmanship in January 2003. He turned his focus to the Foreign Affairs Committee, where he had enough seniority to become chairman of the South Asia Subcommittee. Republican leaders judged Burton too compromised by his staunch support for Pakistan and denied him the gavel. Four years later, in 2007, Burton was in line to become chairman of the full committee, but leaders passed him over for the less senior Ileana Ros-Lehtinen, R-Fla. When Republicans recaptured the House in 2010, Burton got the chairmanship of the Europe and Eurasia Subcommittee.

For all the negative press he has generated over his career in Congress, Burton has won mostly without difficulty—even after it was revealed in 1998 that he had fathered an illegitimate son some 15 years earlier. At the time of the revelations, Burton was being highly critical of Clinton's extramarital dalliances. The woman had not notified Burton at the time of the child's birth. When he found out, he took a blood test to confirm paternity and began to pay child support.

In 2008, he faced a serious primary challenger in John McGoff, a former Air Force flight surgeon in Iraq and Afghanistan and the Marion County coroner. McGoff slammed Burton's decision to skip 19 House votes to play in a Palm Springs golf tournament in 2007, and ran as a reformer, promising to make public all of his meetings with special interest groups. Burton apologized for his missed votes and blamed the news media for his problems. He spent $1.5 million to McGoff's $473,000 and won 52% to 45%. He defeated a token opponent in the general election, 66%-34%.

The result left Burton vulnerable to another primary challenge in 2010, and an unprecedented six Republicans jumped in, including Luke Messer, a former state representative and executive director of the Indiana Republican Party. But Messer and the others ended up splitting the anti-incumbent vote, and Burton survived by winning barely one-third of the ballots cast. After that he had no trouble dispatching Democrat Tim Crawford.

SIXTH DISTRICT

Mike Pence (R)

Elected 2000, 6th term; b. June 7, 1959, Columbus; home, Columbus; Hanover Col., B.A. 1981, IN U., J.D. 1986; Protestant; married (Karen); 3 children.

Professional Career: Practicing atty., 1986-91; Pres., IN Policy Review Fndt., 1991-93; Radio broadcaster, Network Indiana, 1992-99; Host, pub. affairs TV, UPN-23, 1995-99.

DC Office: 100 CHOB, 20515, 202-225-3021; Fax: 202-225-3382; Web site: mikepence.house.gov.

State Offices: Anderson, 765-640-2919; Muncie, 765-747-5566; Richmond, 765-962-2883.

Committees: *Foreign Affairs:* Middle East & South Asia (VChmn). *Judiciary:* Constitution (VChmn); Intellectual Property, Competition & the Internet.

Group Ratings

	ACLU	ACU	ADA	CFG	AFS	FRC	LCV	ITIC	NTU	COC
2010	7	100	5	100	0	81	0	0	89	71
2009	–	100	0	99	11	–	0	–	92	73

National Journal Ratings

	2010 LIB — 2010 CONS	2009 LIB — 2009 CONS
Economic	4% — 96%	5% — 95%
Social	0% — 85%	0% — 93%
Foreign	26% — 72%	0% — 75%
Composite	13% — 87%	7% — 93%

Key Votes of the 111th Congress

1. Overturn Ledbetter	N	5. Bar federal abortion funds	Y	9. Stop detainee transfers	Y
2. Pass $820 billion stimulus	N	6. Pass health care bill	N	10. Legalize immigrants' kids	N
3. Let guns in national parks	Y	7. Regulate financial firms	N	11. Repeal don't ask, tell	N
4. Pass cap-and-trade	N	8. Pass tax cuts for some	N	12. Limit campaign funds	*

Election Results

2010 general	Mike Pence (R)	126,027	(67%)	($2,684,316)
	Barry Welsh (D)	56,647	(30%)	($115)
	Talmadge Thompson (Lib)	6,635	(4%)	
2010 primary	Mike Pence (R)	unopposed		

Prior Winning Percentages: 2008 (64%), 2006 (60%), 2004 (67%), 2002 (64%), 2000 (51%)

Population		Race/Ethnicity		Work	
Pop. 2010:	676,548	White:	91.2%	Private:	82.4%
Change since 2000:	Up 0.1%	Black:	3.9%	Government:	11.7%
Urban:	59.3%	Hispanic:	2.5%	Self-employed:	5.6%
Rural:	40.7%	Asian:	0.8%	Blue collar:	29.5%
Area size:	5,572 sq. mi.	Native Am.:	0.2%	White collar:	52.0%
		Hawaiian:	0.0%	Khaki collar:	0.1%
Age		Two+ races:	1.3%	Other:	18.5%
Median age:	38.7 yrs.				
More than 65 yrs:	14.8%	*Ancestry*		Median income:	$43,199
Less than 18 yrs:	23.6%	German	22.5%	Median Home Value:	$103,200
		Irish	10.0%		
Education		USA	9.3%	**Military Veterans**	
H.S. grad:	85.1%			% of Pop:	10.5%
College grad:	16.5%				
Grad degree:	6.3%				

East Indiana; Muncie

Muncie, Indiana, became famous as the "Middletown" where sociologists Robert and Helen Lynd lived and did research for their report in 1924 and 1925. The Lynds were attracted to Muncie because it was typical of "every small city from Maine to California," as *Life* magazine put it. But it wasn't exactly. Muncie was a factory town in a country still almost 50% rural in the 1920s, and it was almost entirely Protestant and Northern in a country that was one-fifth

2008 Presidential Vote		
John McCain (R)	151,601	(52%)
Barack Obama (D)	133,461	(46%)
2004 Presidential Vote		
George Bush (R)	177,214	(64%)
John Kerry (D)	97,781	(35%)
Cook Partisan Voting Index:	R+10	

Catholic and one-third Southern. Muncie was more typical in that it was culturally homogeneous but economically riven. In the 1920s, when General Motors opened a plant in Muncie, the city celebrated its common values and was loath to admit its economic disparities. In the 1930s, those differences were exposed when Muncie, like much of the industrial Midwest, was unionized, a process that sometimes led to violent clashes. Workers who were joining CIO unions and voting for Democrats fiercely opposed the business elite—local bankers, merchants, GM executives, and the Ball family's glass company. Partisan politics took on the sharp, bitter tone of a struggle for wealth between two rival classes whose claims seemed irreconcilable. Echoes of such class-warfare politics grew louder at times of economic distress, such as when Ball moved its headquarters to Colorado in 1998.

When in 2006 Muncie was ranked ninth nationwide in poverty rates among cities its size or larger, local officials downplayed the situation as not unexpected in a small city with a large student population. That year, GM closed its manual transmission plant, which once employed 3,000 workers. That loss was tempered by Honda's decision to build a car assembly plant on farmland in Greensburg, about 60 miles south of Muncie. The Honda plant opened in 2008 with about 2,000 workers and by 2010 was producing the Civic GX powered by compressed natural gas and Civics for export to Mexico and Latin America. It boasts of its status as a zero waste-to-landfill facility.

The 2007-09 recession hit central Indiana hard, but the political response was not the Democratic trend visible in recession years of yore like 1958 or 1970. Voters here instead continued to embrace a political consensus for tax cuts, tight budgets, and traditional cultural values. Unions were once strong here, but the different fates of UAW-organized GM and non-union Honda seem to have undercut their appeal. Basketball is the civic religion here: Indiana has nine of the nation's 10 largest high school gyms. The Fieldhouse, in New Castle near the Indiana Basketball Hall of Fame, is No. 1 in size. Not far away, in Richmond, is Tom Raper Inc., the nation's largest RV dealer.

The 6th Congressional District of Indiana covers most of the east-central part of the state. It includes Muncie and Anderson in the north as well as Richmond, founded by a major branch of American Quakers and home to their Earlham College. In the north and south are suburban fringes of Fort Wayne and Cincinnati. The 6th is solidly Republican in presidential politics but has been a swing district in some state races. Barack Obama carried Delaware County, which includes Muncie, 57%-42%, but John McCain won the district 52%-46%.

Mike Pence (R)

The congressman from the 6th District is Mike Pence, a Republican first elected in 2000. He grew up in Columbus, Ind., as a John F. Kennedy-admiring Catholic, and graduated from Hanover College as a Republican and evangelical Christian. He got his law degree from Indiana University, and then went into practice and within two years he ran for Congress. He was the Republican nominee in 1988 and 1990 against longtime incumbent Philip Sharp. Afterward, he wrote "Confessions of a Negative Campaigner," an article in which he apologized for running negative ads. He was president of the conservative Indiana Policy Review Foundation, a think tank based in Fort Wayne, and then in 1994 began broadcasting *The Mike Pence Show*, a conservative talk-radio program that was syndicated statewide.

In 2000, when Republican Rep. David McIntosh retired from Congress to run for governor, Pence ran for the House again. He won a six-candidate Republican primary and then faced Robert Rock, son of former Lt. Gov. Robert Rock. Also in the contest was Bill Frazier, a former Republican state senator who ran as an independent. All three candidates opposed abortion rights and gun control, and supported increased military spending. Rock, a former Marine, attacked Pence for not serving in the military, although Pence was only 13 when the draft was abolished and U.S. troops left Vietnam. Rock called for tax cuts for middle-income families, while Pence wanted across-the-board tax cuts and reform of Medicare financing. Pence got 51% of the vote to 39% for Rock and 9% for Frazier. He has since won re-election easily.

Pence quickly established himself as one of the House's outspoken conservatives. As the only House member to become a plaintiff in the lawsuit challenging the constitutionality of the McCain-Feingold campaign finance law, Pence said that Arizona Republican Sen. John McCain was "so deep in bed with the Democrats that his feet are coming out of the bottom of the sheets." He was one of 33 House Republicans to vote against President George W. Bush's "No Child Left Behind" education bill in 2001, and one of just 25 to oppose Republicans' Medicare prescription drug bill in 2003, calling it too costly. He did vote for the big-spending farm bill in 2002, conceding, "I don't have clean hands," and later voiced regret about his vote.

Pence did not forget his work as a talk-radio host. He was the chief House sponsor of a media shield law, to allow journalists to refuse to testify in federal cases with certain exceptions. "As a conservative who believes in limited government, I believe the only check on government in real time is the freedom of the press," he said. The measure passed the House in 2007 and again in 2009, but it died in the Senate.

In 2005, Pence became chairman of the Republican Study Committee, a group of conservative House Republicans. "We win as conservatives when we communicate. If you can't communicate, you can't govern," he said, calling himself "Rush Limbaugh on decaf." Under his stewardship, the RSC worked with Majority Whip Roy Blunt and Budget Committee Chairman Jim Nussle to impose procedural roadblocks on appropriations bills that exceeded annual spending limits. Although some House insiders dismissed the outcome as a "fig leaf," Pence contended that the changes toughened budget discipline. When Majority Leader Tom DeLay in 2005 said that it would be difficult to offset the costs of cleaning up the damage from Hurricane Katrina because Republicans had already cut most of the waste in government, Pence held a televised press conference to document billions of dollars in possible spending cuts. Republican leaders were miffed at the stunt, but the conservative publication *Human Events* named Pence its "Man of the Year" in 2005.

In 2006, Pence's career took some unexpected twists. On immigration, he teamed with Republican Sen. Kay Bailey Hutchison of Texas on what they hoped would be a compromise bill to break the deadlock between the hard-line approach of House Republicans and the bipartisan proposal in the Senate. Their plan called for strengthening security along the border with Mexico and for sending illegal immigrants home, although it also permitted most of them to return and become eligible for citizenship. But Congress failed to agree on comprehensive immigration reform that year. Republicans suffered big losses in the 2006 election, prompting Pence to challenge John Boehner of Ohio for the party's top leadership job in the House. "We didn't just lose our majority," he said. "I believe we lost our way." But Boehner distanced himself from former Speaker Dennis Hastert and his team, and Pence won just 27 votes to Boehner's 168. After the 2008 election, when Republicans lost more seats, Pence was elected chairman of the Republican Conference with support from Boehner and with no opposition.

In the minority, Pence served as the ranking Republican on the Middle East and South Asia Subcommittee of the Foreign Affairs Committee. During an April 2008 visit to Iraq, he drew flak back home after saying that the Baghdad market was like "a normal outdoor market in Indiana in the summertime." In 2009, he and Democratic Committee Chairman Howard Berman sponsored a resolution condemning the Iranian regime's crackdown on green movement protesters, and in 2010, he defended Israel's blockade of Gaza. He also opposed U.S. participation of the International Monetary Fund and in the European Union's bailout fund to help members like Greece and Portugal.

On domestic issues, he was an outspoken opponent of the $700 billion bailout of the financial industry in 2008, saying, "Economic freedom means the freedom to succeed and the freedom to fail." He worked on an alternative with loan guarantees, rather than outright grants. As head of a House Republican task force on energy in 2009, he called for the building of 100 new nuclear power plants, with safe storage and fuel recycling. He also championed drilling for oil in the Arctic National Wildlife Refuge, tax incentives for plug-in and hybrid vehicles, and restrictions on environmental lawsuits. He was a leader of the spontaneous move by House Republicans to keep the House chamber open in August 2009 after Democratic Speaker Nancy Pelosi called for a recess without first allowing a vote on a bill to step up oil exploration as a response to soaring gas prices. Pence is also a co-sponsor of a proposed constitutional amendment to limit federal spending to 20% of gross domestic product, except after a declaration of war or a two-thirds vote by Congress.

Pence was quick to join the House Tea Party Caucus when it formed in 2010, and campaigned assiduously for Republicans in Indiana and across the country. His trips to Iowa and South Carolina triggered speculation that he might be a presidential candidate, as did his decision to relinquish the Republican Conference chairmanship after the 2010 election. "I have no plans to run for president," he said. In May 2011, Pence announced that he would run for governor in 2012.

SEVENTH DISTRICT

André Carson (D)

Elected March 2008, 2nd full term; b. Oct. 16, 1974, Indianapolis; home, Indianapolis; Concordia U., B.A., 2003, IN Wesleyan U., M.S., 2005; Muslim; married (Mariama); 1 child.

Elected Office: Indianapolis/Marion City-Cnty. Cncl., 2007-08.

Professional Career: Investigator, IN State Excise Police, 1996-2005, Investigator, IN Dept. of Homeland Security, 2006-08.

DC Office: 425 CHOB, 20515, 202-225-4011; Fax: 202-225-5633; Web site: carson.house.gov.

State Offices: Indianapolis, 317-283-6516.

Committees: *Financial Services:* Capital Markets and Government Sponsored Enterprises; International Monetary Policy & Trade.

Group Ratings

	ACLU	ACU	ADA	CFG	AFS	FRC	LCV	ITIC	NTU	COC
2010	88	0	90	0	100	0	100	100	4	25
2009	–	0	100	0	100	–	100	–	1	33

National Journal Ratings

	2010 LIB — 2010 CONS	2009 LIB — 2009 CONS
Economic	85% — 14%	91% — 0%
Social	71% — 25%	84% — 11%
Foreign	56% — 38%	87% — 9%
Composite	73% — 28%	90% — 10%

Key Votes of the 111th Congress

1. Overturn Ledbetter	Y	5. Bar federal abortion funds	N	9. Stop detainee transfers	Y
2. Pass $820 billion stimulus	Y	6. Pass health care bill	Y	10. Legalize immigrants' kids	Y
3. Let guns in national parks	N	7. Regulate financial firms	Y	11. Repeal don't ask, tell	Y
4. Pass cap-and-trade	Y	8. Pass tax cuts for some	Y	12. Limit campaign funds	Y

Election Results

2010 general	André Carson (D)	86,011	(59%)	($951,790)
	Marvin Scott (R)	55,213	(38%)	($228,901)
	Dav Wilson (Lib)	4,815	(3%)	
2010 primary	André Carson (D)	26,364	(89%)	
	Bob Kern (D)	2,150	(7%)	

Prior Winning Percentages: 2008 (65%)

Population		Race/Ethnicity		Work	
Pop. 2010:	676,351	White:	52.5%	Private:	85.0%
Change since 2000:	Up 0.1%	Black:	32.3%	Government:	10.8%
Urban:	99.7%	Hispanic:	10.6%	Self-employed:	4.1%
Rural:	0.3%	Asian:	1.7%	Blue collar:	23.1%
Area size:	265 sq. mi.	Native Am.:	0.2%	White collar:	57.8%
		Hawaiian:	0.0%	Khaki collar:	0.1%
Age		Two+ races:	2.3%	Other:	19.1%
Median age:	33.0 yrs.				
More than 65 yrs:	10.5%	*Ancestry*		Median income:	$37,950
Less than 18 yrs:	25.6%	German	14.2%	Median Home Value:	$108,000
		Irish	9.2%		
Education		English	6.1%	**Military Veterans**	
H.S. grad:	80.9%			% of Pop:	8.8%
College grad:	23.9%				
Grad degree:	8.1%				

Indianapolis

Indianapolis, radiating outward from the soldiers and sailors statue in Monument Circle, is
precisely at the center of Indiana and is the largest, and most dominant, city in the state. What
residents once disparaged as "Nap Town" has
become a thriving metropolis, including the
downtown district. The city is the political and
governmental capital, industrial and financial
center, and the intellectual center of Indiana as

2008 Presidential Vote		
Barack Obama (D) 191,381	(71%)
John McCain (R) 76,530	(28%)
2004 Presidential Vote		
John Kerry (D) 130,779	(58%)
George Bush (R) 93,347	(42%)
Cook Partisan Voting Index: D+14		

well. It is symmetrically laid out: Just to the west
of the circle is the state Capitol, to the north is the American Legion headquarters, to the east is
the City-County building, and to the south is the Circle Centre mall and Lucas Oil Stadium. Farther out are some classic and some new Indianapolis institutions: the Indiana University Medical
Center; the Convention Center; the Eiteljorg Museum of American Indians and Western Art; Conseco Fieldhouse; and the NCAA's headquarters. Indianapolis has become the nation's amateur
sports capital, especially for basketball, and it is a popular place for religious conventions. City
officials in 2010 persuaded the Indiana Pacers basketball team to stay in the city. With its strong
service economy, Indianapolis did better than most cities during the recession, with its downtown
experiencing a multibillion-dollar construction boom. The city grew 12% from 2000 to 2008, faster
than the national rate of 7.8%.

Politically, Indianapolis has long had robust competition in local and national races. Republicans held the mayor's office from 1967, when Richard Lugar won it, until 1999. Lugar expanded
Indianapolis' city limits to include all of Marion County in a new entity called UniGov, which made
it a solidly Republican constituency. But more recently, affluent young people have been moving
to counties farther out, and Marion County has been trending Democratic. In 2004, the county
voted for John Kerry by 51%-49%, even as seven surrounding suburban counties gave Bush 70%
to 75% of the vote. Barack Obama took Marion County by a stunning 64%-35%.

Indiana's 7th Congressional District includes all of Indianapolis and most of Marion County.
It also takes in Center Township, a Democratic stronghold with a large African-American population and a gentrified middle class. But it excludes the affluent, Republican northern edge of the
county. The district extends west to include Speedway, where the Indianapolis 500 has been held
on a 2.5-mile track since 1911, southward and east to modest neighborhoods, and it includes Amtrak's largest repair yard, which is in Beech Grove. The Mexican population nearly tripled in size
during the 1990s and is the newest immigrant community. In 2010, the Hispanic share of the district's population was nearly 11%. The 7th District leans Democratic, and it gave solid majorities
to recent Democratic presidential nominees.

André Carson (D)

The congressman from the 7th District is André Carson, who won the seat in a March 2008 special
election to succeed his grandmother, Julia Carson, who died in office after representing the district
for nearly 11 years. He is only the second Muslim to be elected to Congress; the other is Rep. Keith
Ellison, a Minnesota Democrat.

As a child, André Carson was interested in the priesthood, and he studied religion. He also
had an artistic side. He wrote poetry as a young man and performed as a rap artist. But his career
took him into law enforcement. He got a bachelor's degree in criminal justice management from
Concordia University and a master's degree in business management from Indiana Wesleyan. Carson spent nine years as a plainclothes officer of the Indiana State Excise Police, which enforces
alcohol and tobacco laws. "I loved law enforcement," he told *Esquire* magazine in 2010. "But this
job sure beats sitting and waiting for something bad to go down at three in the morning." He recalled
that his political interest began in 1984, at age 10, when he attended the Democratic convention
in San Francisco. There, he heard civil-rights leader Jesse Jackson speak. Carson said that his
thinking was transformed by reading *The Autobiography of Malcolm X,* and he attended Louis
Farrakhan's Million Man March in 1995. In August 2007, at age 32, he won a seat on the Indianapolis City Council, his first elected office.

After Julia Carson died in December 2007 following multiple and lengthy illnesses, her grandson faced significant opposition for the Democratic nomination in the special election to fill the
remainder of Carson's term. At the January 2008 Democratic caucus, he won 223 of the 439 votes;
state Rep. David Orentlicher, a lawyer and doctor, got 123 votes; and Marion County Treasurer

Michael Rodman came in third with 27 votes. Against Republican state Rep. Jon Elrod, a young lawyer, Carson received extensive assistance from the Democratic Congressional Campaign Committee. On issues, he called for withdrawing U.S. troops from Iraq, endorsed tax cuts for working families, and said that companies should have incentives to keep them from sending jobs overseas. Elrod emphasized aid to small businesses and tougher enforcement of immigration laws, and he called for an end to federal spending earmarks. Carson won, 54%-43%.

Meanwhile, Carson had to continue campaigning for a May primary to determine the winner of a full term. That field included Orentlicher, former state Health Commissioner Woodrow Myers, and state Rep. Carolene Mays. Running as the incumbent this time and with an endorsement from presidential candidate Barack Obama, Carson won the primary with 47% of the vote to 24% for Myers, 20% for Orentlicher, and 8% for Mays. In the contest for a full term, Elrod won the GOP nomination. But he soon withdrew and ran unsuccessfully to retain his seat in the state House. Carson faced minimal opposition then and again in 2010.

In the House, Carson has established a liberal voting record. But one of his role models is Indiana Republican Sen. Richard Lugar, and he tries to occasionally lunch with conservative GOP Rep. Mike Pence. One year after taking office, *The Indianapolis Star* described him as "relentlessly positive and seriously hardworking...a solid U.S. representative." He got a seat on the Financial Services Committee and soon found himself embroiled in the debate over the $700 billion bailout of the financial markets in fall 2008. After initially opposing the bailout bill, he switched his position to vote in favor after Obama encouraged him to support it.

In 2009, Carson included a provision in a predatory lending bill to ensure information on foreclosure rules is provided to low-income, elderly, and minority home owners. He also introduced a bill letting newly released prisoners have their disability and Medicaid benefits reinstated and another measure to require post-bankruptcy carmakers to cover all current and future claims over defective vehicles. Before the final vote on the health care overhaul in March 2010, he drew national attention by contending that angry protesters outside the Capitol hurled racial epithets at him and Rep. John Lewis, D-Ga., a leader of the civil rights movement. At home, he worked with Sen. Evan Bayh, D-Ind., to have the Housing and Urban Development Department block the sale of a notorious and deteriorating Indianapolis apartment complex from one out-of-state owner to another.

EIGHTH DISTRICT

Larry Bucshon (R)

Elected 2010, 1st term; b. May 31, 1962, Kincaid, IL; home, Newburgh; U. of IL, Urbana-Champaign, B.A. 1984; U. of IL, Chicago, M.D. 1988.; Lutheran; Married (Kathryn); 4 children.

Military Career: Navy Reserve, 1989-98

Professional Career: Private medical practice, 1995-98; Ohio Valley HeartCare, 1998-2010, president, 2003-10.

DC Office: 1123 LHOB, 20515, 202-225-4636; Fax: 202-225-3284; Web site: bucshon.house.gov.

State Offices: Evansville, 812-465-6484; Terre Haute, 812-232-0523.

Committees: *Education & the Workforce:* Health, Employment, Labor & Pensions; Higher Education & Workforce Training; Workforce Protections. *Science, Space & Technology:* Investigations & Oversight; Research & Science Education. *Transportation & Infrastructure:* Highways & Transit; Railroads, Pipelines & Hazardous Materials; Water Resources & Environment.

Election Results

2010 general	Larry Bucshon (R)..117,259	(57%)	($1,098,071)
	William VanHaaften (D)....................................76,265	(38%)	($762,359)
	John Cunningham (Lib) 10,240	(5%)	
2010 primary	Larry Bucshon (R)..16,262	(33%)	
	Kristi Risk (R)..14,273	(29%)	
	John Smith (R)..4,715	(9%)	
	Dan Stockton (R)..4,697	(9%)	
	Steve Westell (R)..4,324	(9%)	
	John Snyder (R) 2,523	(5%)	

Population		Race/Ethnicity		Work	
Pop. 2010:	694,398	White:	91.3%	Private:	81.9%
Change since 2000:	Up 2.8%	Black:	4.2%	Government:	12.4%
Urban:	58.1%	Hispanic:	1.8%	Self-employed:	5.6%
Rural:	41.9%	Asian:	0.9%	Blue collar:	29.2%
Area size:	7,133 sq. mi.	Native Am.:	0.2%	White collar:	52.1%
		Hawaiian:	0.0%	Khaki collar:	0.1%
Age		Two+ races:	1.4%	Other:	18.6%
Median age:	38.3 yrs.				
More than 65 yrs:	14.4%	*Ancestry*		Median income:	$43,657
Less than 18 yrs:	22.8%	German	23.5%	Median Home Value:	$99,800
		USA	14.4%		
Education		Irish	10.6%	**Military Veterans**	
H.S. grad:	85.8%			% of Pop:	11.2%
College grad:	17.5%				
Grad degree:	6.5%				

West Indiana; Evansville

"Evansville," wrote John Bartlow Martin in 1947, "is the capital of a tri-state area comprising the neglected tag ends of Indiana, Kentucky, and Illinois." It was a factory town then, making car parts and refrigerators, drawing workers from Kentucky, Tennessee, and the picturesque but not very fertile hills of Southern Indiana. Today, Evansville has become the headquarters for a number of midsize companies that offer many high-paying, skilled jobs. Car parts still get

2008 Presidential Vote
John McCain (R) 151,570   (51%)
Barack Obama (D) 140,063   (47%)

2004 Presidential Vote
George Bush (R) 170,390   (62%)
John Kerry (D) 104,625   (38%)

Cook Partisan Voting Index: R+8

made here, though it is auto assembly that helps anchor the local manufacturing economy. Toyota in 1998 opened a plant in nearby Princeton that builds SUVs and minivans, employing approximately 4,500 workers who take home as much as $28 an hour. In 2009, the company announced plans to spend $500 million outfitting the plant to build Highlander SUVs. The auto industry helped Evansville weather the recession; its unemployment rate was 8% in 2010, among the lowest in Indiana and not bad for an economy reliant on manufacturing.

Evansville is one of two major centers of the 8th Congressional District, which covers most of southwest and west-central Indiana. The other, in Vigo County, is Terre Haute, an old manufacturing town and the boyhood home of socialist Eugene Debs. It hosts a maximum-security penitentiary, which includes the only federal death chamber; Oklahoma City bomber Timothy McVeigh was executed there in 2001. In 2008, Pfizer closed a local plant that had employed about 800 workers producing the insulin drug Exubera. The district also takes in Vincennes, now a small town on the banks of the Wabash River but once a major metropolis. Downstream is New Harmony, established by Welsh philanthropist and visionary Robert Owen. His son was the first congressman from the area, elected in 1842 and 1844. Southern Indiana is ancestrally Democratic, just as northern Indiana is ancestrally Republican. These southern counties were hostile to the Union during the Civil War. In New Deal times, workers in Evansville again moved toward the Democrats.

The result has been a very close political balance, and this district has become known as the "Bloody 8th" for its tight congressional races. At one point in the 1970s, it sent four different members to the House in four successive elections. In 1984, the state certified the Republican as the winner by exactly 34 votes. The Democratic majority in the U.S. House overturned the result, however, in a fight that left many Republican members bitterly aggrieved. Since then, the district has been as fiercely contested as ever. The trend in presidential politics, however, is away from national Democrats. Bill Clinton twice carried the 8th by a 2% margin, George W. Bush won it with 56% in 2000, and again in 2004 with 62%. After campaigning there vigorously, Barack Obama won Vanderburgh and Vigo counties, but he narrowly lost the district, 51%-47%.

Larry Bucshon (R)

The new congressman from the 8th District is Larry Bucshon, a Republican elected in 2010 to the seat of Democratic Rep. Brad Ellsworth, who ran unsuccessfully for the Senate that year. Bucshon (*Boo-SHON*) was raised in the rural town of Kincaid, Ill., southeast of Springfield. His mother was a nurse and his father a coal miner; both tended to vote Democratic. Bucshon developed his own ideology as an undergraduate at the University of Illinois, however, where he says that meeting people from other parts of the country "made me realize my personal values were more conservative than my parents." His rightward beliefs were solidified during the 1980s, when he became enamored of President Ronald Reagan. While still in high school, Bucshon decided on a career in medicine, inspired by the surgeons he met at the hospital where his mother worked. After college, he enrolled in medical school at the University of Illinois at Chicago. He went on to complete a residency at the Medical College of Wisconsin and landed a fellowship there specializing in cardiothoracic surgery. It was during his residency that he met his wife, Kathryn, a medical student at the time. Bucshon then enlisted with the Naval Reserve, serving for nearly a decade. After spending three years in private practice in Wichita, Kan., in 1998 he joined Ohio Valley HeartCare, one of the largest cardiology and cardiovascular surgery practices in the tri-state region. Five years later, he became its president.

Having harbored desires to run for national office for years, Bucshon took advantage of the open seat left by Ellsworth's Senate bid, announcing his candidacy in October 2009. "I didn't feel like [Ellsworth] was representing our district, which leans conservative," Bucshon said. With help from the National Republican Congressional Committee, he prevailed over seven other candidates in the May GOP primary with 33% of the vote, edging out second-place finisher Kristi Risk, a tea party-backed candidate, by 4 percentage points.

In the general election campaign, he faced Democratic state Rep. Trent Van Haaften, who fit Ellsworth's mold, and who was regarded as an ideal Democratic candidate for the Republican-leaning district. He was a prosecutor in rural Posey County for several years and was praised there for his work fighting a regional methamphetamine epidemic. In the campaign, he emphasized his law-and-order background over his legislative experience to avoid being tagged an "insider." Bucshon campaigned on curbing spending and repeal of the national Democrats' health care overhaul. Republicans targeted Van Haaften for opposing a property tax cap proposal in the legislature and Democrats accused Bucshon of favoring privatizing Social Security.

Bucshon raised and spent $1 million, compared to $762,000 for Van Haaften. He won with 57.5% of the vote to Van Haaften's 37%.

NINTH DISTRICT

Todd Young (R)

Elected 2010, 1st term; b. Aug. 24, 1972, Lancaster, PA; home, Bloomington; U.S. Naval Academy, B.S. 1995; U. of Chicago, M.B.A. 2000; U. of London, M.A. 2001; IN U., J.D. 2006.; Christian; Married (Jennifer Tucker); 4 children.

Military Career: Marine Corps, 1996-2000.

Professional Career: Staff, Heritage Foundation, 2001; legis. asst., Sen. Richard Lugar, R-Ind., 2001-03; adviser, Gov. Mitch Daniels, R-Ind., 2004; management consultant, 2004-06; dep. prosecutor, Orange Cnty., 2007-10.

DC Office: 1721 LHOB, 20515, 202-225-5315; Fax: 202-226-6866; Web site: toddyoung.house.gov.

State Offices: Bloomington, 812-336-3000; Jeffersonville, 812-288-3999.

Committees: *Armed Services:* Oversight & Investigations; Seapower & Projection Forces. *Budget.*

Election Results

2010 general	Todd Young (R)	118,040	(52%)	($1,964,852)
	Baron Hill (D)	95,353	(42%)	($2,172,449)
	Greg Knott (Lib)	12,070	(5%)	($6,093)
2010 primary	Todd Young (R)	19,141	(35%)	
	Travis Hankins (R)	17,909	(32%)	
	Mike Sodrel (R)	16,868	(30%)	

Population		Race/Ethnicity		Work	
Pop. 2010:	729,076	White:	91.1%	Private:	82.2%
Change since 2000:	Up 7.9%	Black:	2.6%	Government:	12.7%
Urban:	52.3%	Hispanic:	3.1%	Self-employed:	5.1%
Rural:	47.7%	Asian:	1.5%	Blue collar:	29.9%
Area size:	6,672 sq. mi.	Native Am.:	0.2%	White collar:	52.8%
		Hawaiian:	0.0%	Khaki collar:	0.1%
Age		Two+ races:	1.3%	Other:	17.3%
Median age:	36.8 yrs.				
More than 65 yrs:	13.0%	*Ancestry*		Median income:	$44,574
Less than 18 yrs:	23.0%	German	24.5%	Median Home Value:	$123,400
		Irish	11.8%		
Education		USA	9.4%	**Military Veterans**	
H.S. grad:	84.9%			% of Pop:	9.9%
College grad:	19.2%				
Grad degree:	7.9%				

Southeast Indiana; Bloomington

The southeastern corner of Indiana swelled with new settlers in the early 19th century as Southerners, or "Butternuts," came across the Ohio River from Kentucky or over the mountains from Virginia. They built the first large Indiana settlements. Today, you can see their work in the marvelous old buildings of Madison, now a quiet hamlet but once one of the busiest ports on the river. Its landmark Broadway Fountain first appeared at the 1876 Centennial Exposition in Philadelphia. It arrived in Madison in 1886, thanks to the Independent Order of Odd Fellows, which had purchased it after the exposition. Farther down the river is Corydon, which was the state capital from 1816 to 1825. Its early 19th-century buildings are well preserved. These small towns were bypassed first by the railroads, then by U.S. routes and interstate highways, and they are remote from today's major airports. The river remains an artery of commerce, although utilitarian barges have replaced all of the old steamers, except for riverboat casinos.

> **2008 Presidential Vote**
> John McCain (R) 160,248 (50%)
> Barack Obama (D) 154,629 (49%)
>
> **2004 Presidential Vote**
> George Bush (R) 171,926 (59%)
> John Kerry (D) 117,647 (40%)
>
> **Cook Partisan Voting Index:** R+6

Butternut Indiana retained its affection for all things Southern into the Civil War and beyond. In 1851, the state denied blacks the right to vote or serve in the militia. In 1862, the U.S. Senate expelled local politician Jesse Bright for "supporting the rebellion." The people who live in the hills along the Ohio River have typically voted Democratic, but the Clark County suburbs of Louisville have trended Republican. This part of Indiana is now filling up with migrants from Cincinnati, which was a Yankee and German abolitionist bastion in Bright's time but is an overwhelmingly Republican stronghold in ours.

The 9th Congressional District of Indiana comprises most of the state's Ohio River counties. It includes tiny Milan, home to the championship high school of *Hoosiers* movie fame, and Indiana University in Democratic-leaning Bloomington, the largest city in the district. To the east of Milan is Batesville, home of the Batesville Casket Co., which makes the coffins for U.S. military personnel who die in the line of duty. To the west of Batesville is French Lick, a former rural resort town, well known to basketball fans as the hometown of former Boston Celtics star Larry Bird. Most of the district is culturally conservative, but the area is highly competitive politically, both in local and national elections. George W. Bush won this district 59%-40% in 2004, but John McCain won it by the much narrower margin of 50%-48.5%. Barack Obama won Monroe County and Bloomington 66%-33%.

Todd Young (R)

The new congressman from Indiana's 9th District is Republican Todd Young, who unseated Democratic Rep. Baron Hill in 2010. Born in Lancaster, Pa., Young spent the first 13 years of his life outside Indiana, but his family has deep ties to the Hoosier State stretching back five generations. His father is a small business owner who sells heating, ventilation, and air-conditioning equipment. His mother is a registered nurse. He went to high school in Hamilton County, Ind., where his prowess on the soccer field helped his school win a state championship. When he graduated in 1990, he enlisted in the Navy and a year later received an appointment to the U.S. Naval Academy, where he played on the school's Division I soccer team. When he graduated, he joined the Marine Corps because of its reputation for toughness. "If I was going to be in the military, I wanted to be in the warrior class," he told *National Journal*. In the Marines, he worked with unmanned aerial vehicles doing reconnaissance work, which included a stint aiding government anti-narcotics efforts in the Caribbean. In 1998, he was transferred to Chicago, where he managed Marine recruiting in the area.

An avid reader, Young attended the University of Chicago's business school at night, in large part to gain a better understanding of the stories he found in *The Wall Street Journal* and the *Financial Times*. "It was that economic knowledge that I really desired," he said. Young became a fan of free-market economist Friedrich von Hayek. Young applied to the University of London's Institute of United States Studies, where he wrote a thesis on the economic history of Midwest agriculture. Shortly after graduating, Young moved to Washington, where he worked first at the conservative Heritage Foundation and later for Republican Indiana Sen. Richard Lugar as his legislative assistant for energy policy. In 2004, Young returned to Indiana to help craft energy and veterans' affairs policies for the gubernatorial campaign of Republican Mitch Daniels. He also earned a law degree at the University of Indiana, where he met his wife, Jennifer, who is now a practicing attorney and a leader in the local Republican Party.

In the GOP primary for the right to challenge Hill, Young narrowly won a contest with former Rep. Mike Sodrel, a trucking company owner who briefly held the House seat from 2005 to 2006. (Hill first won the seat in 1998 and held it until he was defeated in 2004 by Sodrel, and then won it back in the pro-Democratic year of 2006.)

In the general election campaign, Young portrayed Hill as a rubber stamp for the Obama administration and Democratic congressional leadership, hammering Hill for his votes in favor of the $787 billion economic stimulus bill, the health care overhaul, and an energy bill setting limits on carbon emissions. Hill emphasized his Hoosier roots as a former high school basketball star, while characterizing Young as a wealthy, out-of-touch lawyer who had spent much of his career outside the state. Hill also slammed Young for comments at a town hall meeting referring to Social Security as a "Ponzi scheme." Young said that his comments were taken out of context and that he does not endorse privatizing the program.

The candidates raised and spent about the same amount of money, Hill with $2 million and Young with $1.9 million. Young was also the beneficiary of $437,000 in independent expenditures from the National Republican Congressional Committee and more than $250,000 from the conservative American Future Fund. He won with 52% of the vote to 42% for Hill. Libertarian candidate Greg Knott got 5%.

★ IOWA ★

In the great westward movement of the 1840s, young Yankee and German farmers crossed the Mississippi River and streamed into Iowa. Wagon trains headed to the Oregon Trail, and the thousands of Mormons mustered by Brigham Young traveled across Iowa's rolling hills to Council Bluffs on the Missouri River, and then to points further west. Iowa was young and proud of its hundreds of schools and dozens of colleges, sending more than its share of young men back East to fight for the Union. After that war, Iowans built a solid civilization based on farming, farm-machine manufacturing, and meat processing that resisted the blandishments of William Jennings Bryan's populism and cheap money. Iowa became one of the most solidly Republican states in the nation.

But starting around 1900, Iowa's model society stopped attracting new transplants. "If you build it, they will come" was the theme from the movie Field of Dreams, set in Iowa. Yet during the 20th century, very few people came. The region's commercial and financial center remained the railroad hub of Chicago, Iowa's economy failed to diversify and develop the dense manufacturing base of the Great Lakes states, and its young people started to move east or west to make their fortunes. The state's population, which increased from 674,000 in 1860 to 2.2 million in 1900, did not reach 3 million until 2008. In 1900, Iowa had 11 congressional districts and California had seven. In 2012, Iowa will have four and California 53. Iowa's solid Capitol, a memorial to its Civil War dead, its courthouses, and its sturdy but mostly old housing stock give testimony to Iowa's strengths but also suggest a lack of dynamism. Its great economic achievement has been the development of high-tech and ever more productive, but also less labor intensive, agriculture. Iowa is the nation's leading producer of pork, corn, and soybeans, yet it remains near the bottom in population growth.

Iowa had a particularly tough time in the 1980s. The number of Iowans whose principal occupation was farming dropped from 86,000 in 1982 to 56,000 in 1997, and the state's population dropped by 4.7% between 1980 and 1990, down to the 1960 level. Most of the next two decades were a big improvement. Iowa's high level of literacy and good work habits produced white-collar and high-tech growth in and around its pleasant small cities, especially Des Moines and Cedar Rapids. Even as many old factories closed, some Iowa emigrants to big cities like Chicago were persuaded to come home, and Mexican immigrants moved to small towns with meatpacking plants, to Des Moines and to the old industrial cities of Sioux City and Waterloo. Jobs and small-town life also attracted Bosnians and Liberians as well as Congolese, Sudanese and Somali refugees. Ethanol has boosted the Iowa economy since 1998, when Sen. Charles Grassley got the ethanol tax credit extended. Today, Iowa produces almost one-fourth of the nation's ethanol, and the renewable fuel industry generates nearly 49,000 jobs in the state. Demand for ethanol has helped raise corn prices, and therefore farmland prices. Soybean prices boomed as well. Some factory jobs have disappeared. But the state lost far fewer jobs in the recent recession than it did in the early 1980s. The housing bubble wasn't big here, financial institutions remained strong, and unemployment, while uncomfortably high, has remained well below the national average.

For much of the 20th century, Iowa was a culturally and politically countercyclical state, headed in the opposite direction of the rest of the nation—determinedly, with confidence in its own chipper rectitude, unabashedly out of step. In the industrial New Deal era, it stayed mostly agricultural and Republican, even as Davenport and Des Moines radio announcer Ronald Reagan became an enthusiastic Roosevelt Democrat and headed to Hollywood. Iowa was dovish during the Vietnam War and afterward. In the 1980s, when Reagan, by then a conservative Republican, was president, Iowa's economy was hit hard and self-pity became the dominant note of Iowa's politics, as voters sought protection from the vagaries of the market. In the 1988 caucuses, Iowa Republicans voted against Reagan's vice president, George H.W. Bush, and Iowa Democrats voted for populist Dick Gephardt of Missouri. In the fall, it gave Democrat Michael Dukakis his second highest vote percentage of any state.

Since then, Iowa and the nation have converged politically. It voted twice for Bill Clinton and went for Al Gore by 4,144 votes in 2000 and for George W. Bush by 10,059 votes in 2004. It gave Barack Obama a decisive boost in its 2008 precinct caucuses and then voted 55%-44% for him in November. It has had one Republican and one Democratic U.S. senator, and the same ones, since 1984. After 30 years of Republican governors, Iowa elected Democrats three times, starting in 1998 and then went Republican again in 2010. Republicans won majorities in the legislature in the 1990s, lost them in 2004 and regained a state House majority in 2010. Collectively, these results

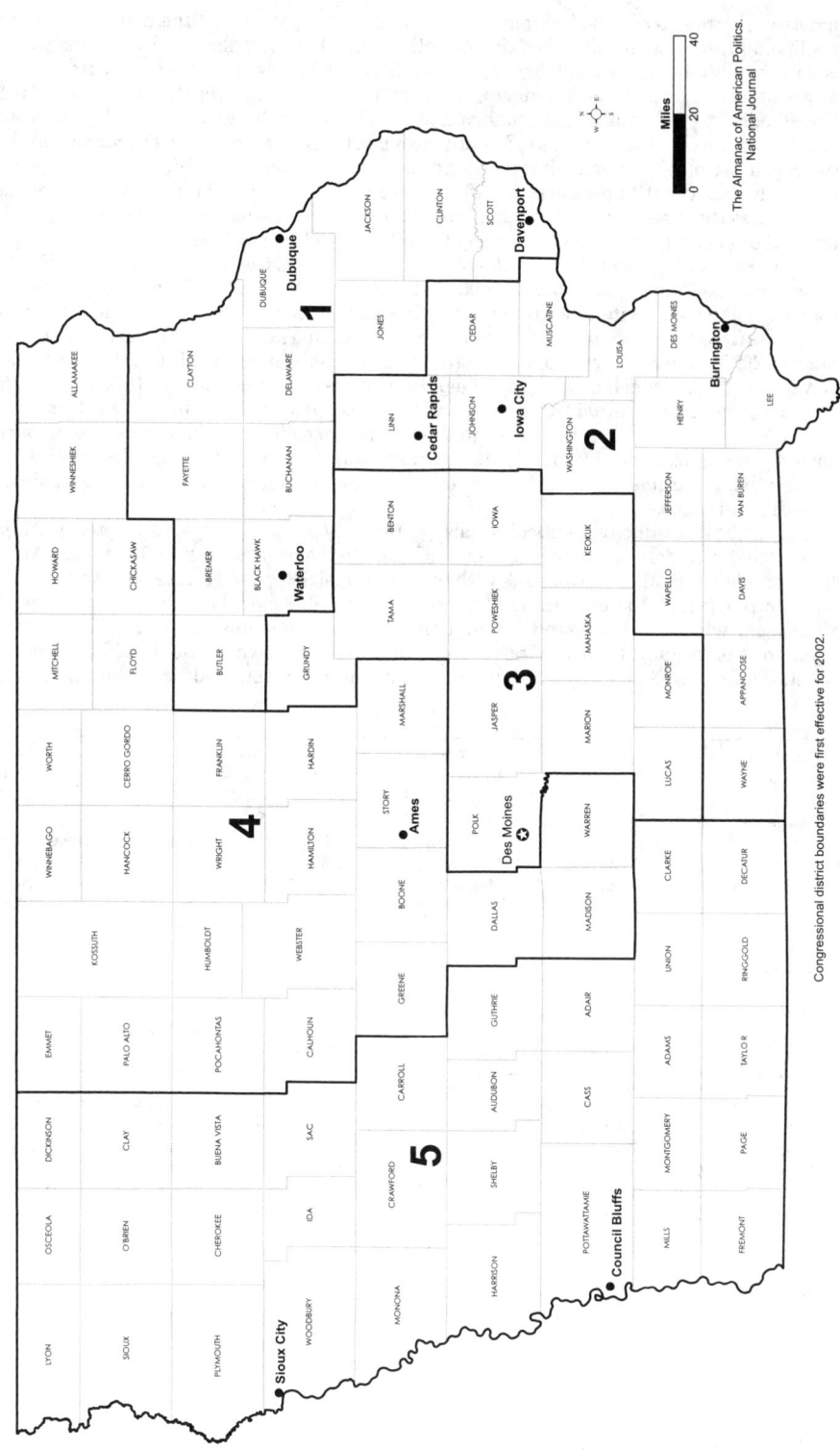

The Almanac of American Politics.
National Journal

Congressional district boundaries were first effective for 2002.

indicate a sort of steady moderation, a desire to accept the verdict of the markets and to honor traditional values, with a little hedging on both counts. Iowa remains quirky in some respects. It is still probably one of the most dovish, isolationist-prone states, and at the same time very much aware of its role as an international exporter. Its delegation voted for the 1993 North American Free Trade Agreement and for normalizing trade relations with China in 1999 (Mexicans eat lots of corn and the Chinese like pork). Eastern Iowa has become increasingly Democratic in the past two decades, metro Des Moines has trended a bit toward Republicans, while western Iowa remains heavily Republican. But the partisan differences are not nearly as wide as in many larger states.

Iowa is thrift-minded, seeing a balanced budget more as a badge of moral rectitude than as prudent economic policy. It pioneered legal riverboat gambling in 1989, but also has a large anti-abortion rights movement. Iowans like to think of themselves as tolerant and in April 2009, the state Supreme Court unanimously ruled that the state's limitation of marriage to opposite-sex couples violated the state constitution. Only in Massachusetts, Connecticut and California had high state courts reached similar conclusions, and California's decision was overturned by referendum in 2008. Many in Iowa applauded the decision, but others called it judicial overreach. In November 2010, voters had their say when three of the Supreme Court justices came up for approval. Ordinarily approval is routine, but all three were defeated, two by a 54%-46% margin and one, 55%-45%—closer than responses to the exit poll question on whether same-sex marriages should be recognized, which showed 57%-38% disapproval. The voting seems to have followed party lines, with big margins for the justices in counties with universities and big margins against them in most rural counties.

Iowa has its distinctive political rituals, particularly the first-in-the-nation precinct caucuses. Prospective candidates come in a year or two before to the Iowa State Fair, held every August on the east side of Des Moines, complete with the traditional 600-pound butter cow. And Republicans hold a straw poll on the Iowa State University campus in Ames the August before the primary season, one which has winnowed out more than one candidate in a crowded field and may do so again in 2011. Finally, there are the precinct caucuses themselves, usually held on a cold winter night, the first occasion in which ordinary Americans cast a vote to decide who will be the next president.

Population		Household Income		Work	
Pop. 2010:	3,046,355	Under $15k:	12.4%	Private:	79.0%
State rank:	30th	$15k to $50k:	39.1%	Government:	13.7%
Change since 2000:	Up 4.1%	$50k to $100k:	33.6%	Self-employed:	7.1%
Urban:	60.3%	$100k to $200k:	12.6%	Unemployment (3-yr. average):	3.4%
Rural:	39.7%	Over $200k:	2.3%	Poverty:	11.5%
Native of state:	72.6%	Median income:	$48,457	Blue collar:	24.9%
Not a citizen:	2.5%			White collar:	57.7%
Area size:	56,273 sq. mi.	**Home Value**		Khaki collar:	0.1%
		Under $100k:	39.3%	Other:	17.3%
Most populous cities		$100k to $300k:	53.4%		
Des Moines	203,433	$300k to $500k:	5.3%	**Age**	
Cedar Rapids	126,326	$500k to $1 mil:	1.6%	Median age:	38.0 yrs.
Davenport	99,685	Over $1 million:	0.4%	More than 65 yrs:	14.7%
Sioux City	82,684	Median:	$120,100	Less than 18 yrs:	23.7%

Race/Ethnicity				Military Veterans		Registered Voters in 2010	
White:	88.7%	*Language*		% of Pop:	10.6%	Democrats:	663,215
Black:	2.9%	English:	93.5%			Republicans:	618,614
Hispanic:	5.0%	Spanish:	3.6%	*Veterans by Period*		Ind./other:	703,166
Asian:	1.7%	Asian:	1.1%	WWII and before:	12.1%	Voter turnout:	1,133,434
Native Am.:	0.3%	Other European:	1.5%	Korea:	14.3%	Turnout as % of	
Hawaiian:	0.1%			Vietnam:	33.1%	voting age:	48.9%
Two+ races:	1.4%	**Education**		Gulf (pre-2001):	9.8%		
		H.S. grad:	90.2%	Gulf (post-2001):	6.7%	**Legislature**	
Ancestry		College grad:	24.5%	Peace time:	24.0%	Senate:	26 D 24 R
German	30.1%	Grad degree:	7.4%			House:	40 D 60 R
Irish	11.7%						
English	7.4%						

Presidential politics Every four years, tens of thousands of Iowans troop to caucuses in nearly 2,000 precincts to begin the formal process of electing a president. The precinct caucuses were scheduled early in the 1972 cycle by Democratic doves who wanted more leverage for their views, and that year, they started George McGovern on his way to the Democratic nomination. But the caucuses have had other, unanticipated consequences. In 1976, Jimmy Carter strategist Hamilton Jordan determined that intensive campaigning could produce a surprise victory that could make a little-known candidate a national

2008 Presidential Vote		
Barack Obama (D) 828,940	(54%)
John McCain (R) 682,379	(44%)
2004 Presidential Vote		
George W. Bush (R)...............751,957	(50%)
John Kerry (D) 741,898	(49%)

contender: Without Iowa and the next-up New Hampshire primary, Carter would not have become president.

Over the next 20 years, the Iowa caucuses were less decisive. In 1980, George H.W. Bush's intensive campaigning gave him a victory among Republicans, while Carter, still profiting from his 1976 contacts, trounced Edward Kennedy. But Bush lost the nomination to Ronald Reagan, and Carter lost in November. In 1984, Democratic favorite Walter Mondale won 49% of the "delegate strength" (Democrats don't compute the actual number of votes), but the momentum went to the 17% second-place finisher Gary Hart, though Mondale did win the nomination. In 1988, Iowa failed to pick the winners on either side. Dick Gephardt capitalized on Iowa's economic woes to win among Democrats; among Republicans, George H.W. Bush finished in third place behind Kansas' Bob Dole and televangelist Pat Robertson, a harbinger of an era of political activism by Christian conservatives in the party. But Gephardt and Dole lost in New Hampshire, and neither was nominated. In 1992, Iowa went dark. No Democrat challenged Iowa's Tom Harkin here, and Pat Buchanan began his campaign against Bush in New Hampshire. In 1996, Dole had the support of leading Republicans, led by Gov. Terry Branstad and Sen. Chuck Grassley, and he had farm-state roots as well. Dole's very narrow victory was an omen of the weakness of his candidacy.

In 2000, the Iowa caucuses became decisive again, for both parties, and remained so for Democrats in 2004 and 2008. In 2000, George W. Bush won the 25,000-strong August 1999 Republican straw poll at Ames, after which Dan Quayle, Lamar Alexander and Elizabeth Dole dropped out, and Pat Buchanan left the Republican Party altogether. Bush continued to build his organizational strength and won the caucus straw poll with 41% of the vote to Steve Forbes' 30%. Alan Keyes was third with 14%. On the Democratic side, the race was between Al Gore and Bill Bradley. In his 1988 campaign, Gore had skipped what he called the "madness" in "the small state of Iowa," but a decade later, he was proclaiming, "I love Iowa." With the help of Iowa's labor unions, Gore won in "delegate strength" with 63% to Bradley's 35%. That gave Gore momentum in New Hampshire, which he won eight days later, though only 50%-46%. With five weeks to the next Democratic contest, Bradley dropped out, and Gore became the nominee.

Iowa was dispositive in 2004 as well. With President Bush unopposed for the nomination, this was the Democrats' show. The leader in Iowa polls in late 2003 and early 2004 was Howard Dean. His opposition to the war in Iraq was popular among the state's overwhelmingly dovish caucusgoers. His thousands of out-of-state volunteers built the best turnout organization. But as the year opened, Democrats suddenly confronted the possibility that they could actually defeat Bush, and the question for many became not who could most stridently criticize the president and his policies but who could defeat him. Dean's comment that the December 13 capture of Iraqi Leader Saddam Hussein "has not made America safer" raised doubts about his electability. Dean's irritated outshouting of a 68-year-old Republican questioner in Oelwein on Jan. 11, 2004 was a breach of Iowa manners. His poll numbers started to fall. Gephardt, supported by labor unions and veterans of his campaign 16 years earlier, failed to gather new adherents. John Edwards, endorsed by the *Des Moines Register*, had only a few chipper out-of-staters organizing things. John Kerry, who mortgaged his Boston house for $6.4 million and put all of his effort into Iowa, had the superior organization; the endorsement of Christie Vilsack, the wife of the technically neutral Democratic Gov. Tom Vilsack; and a strong message. Joined in Iowa by a Green Beret he had rescued in the waters of Vietnam, Kerry proclaimed that he could stand up to Bush on Iraq because of his heroism in the Vietnam War.

On caucus night, Howard Dean's 3,500 orange-stocking-capped Perfect Stormers were swarming in the streets of Des Moines, but Kerry got the votes. Under Iowa Democrats' procedures, the supporters of candidates who fail to meet a 15% threshold of the votes in any precinct can choose to caucus for another candidate. Entry polls at the caucuses showed Kerry well ahead, with Edwards, Dean, and Gephardt trailing. But Edwards had shrewdly targeted supporters of Dennis Kucinich, and their second-choice support for Edwards helped swell his numbers in the final standings, while Dean and Gephardt, failing to make the threshold in many precincts, saw their numbers dwindle below the entry poll. The final results in "delegate strength" were Kerry 38%, Edwards 32%, Dean 18%, and Gephardt 11%. Gephardt soon left the race. Dean was effectively finished even before he emitted his famous scream that night. Kerry clinched the nomination six weeks and one day later. But it was Iowa Democrats—some 122,000 of them—who gave him his head start.

In 2008, both parties had candidates competing in the Iowa caucuses, but the Democratic contest was much more vigorous. In late 2006, outgoing Gov. Vilsack announced he was running, but his entry still left other Democrats competitive in the polls; in February 2007, he withdrew and endorsed Hillary Rodham Clinton. By the end of the year, Democratic candidates had more than 500 paid staffers in Iowa, while Republicans had fewer than 100. John Edwards had never really stopped visiting Iowa after the 2004 campaign, and by November 2007, he had made appearances in all 99 counties. Taking advantage of the propinquity of his home in Chicago, Barack Obama was in the state often. Joe Biden and Christopher Dodd took time off from their duties as chairmen of the Senate Foreign Relations and Banking committees, respectively, to campaign frequently in the state. And in November, Dodd moved his family to Iowa and enrolled his daughter in a Des Moines kindergarten. Clinton visited often, and in the spring, a staffer's memo recommending she skip Iowa leaked to the press. She led in initial polls, but her vote for the 2002 Iraq war resolution and her refusal to apologize for it (as Edwards did in 2005) hurt her with dovish Iowa Democrats. Her support of ethanol subsidies, a reversal of her previous opposition to them, did not seem to help much. But in the fall, she stepped up her Iowa campaign. The chief event of the Democratic race was the Jefferson-Jackson Day Dinner on November 10. All of the candidates had fans in the crowd, but the highlight was an electrifying speech by Obama. His campaign shrewdly distributed tapes of the almost entirely white crowd cheering their candidate to African-American Democrats in South Carolina and other states.

Republican candidates attracted less attention. Mitt Romney outspent all other Republicans combined and had many more staffers in the state. He started running television ads in the spring and leapt to a lead in the polls. But Mike Huckabee built a network made up largely of evangelical Christians, and on the stump, the former Baptist minister displayed an appealing sense of humor and knowledge of popular culture. At the Ames straw poll in August 2007, Romney finished first and Huckabee an impressive second. But turnout was only 14,300, about 10,000 less than in 1999. Fred Thompson trailed. Rudy Giuliani and John McCain, with unpopular positions on abortion and immigration, respectively, did not show up.

About 239,000 people participated in the Democratic caucuses, more than double the record set in 2004. Obama won 38% of "state delegates," a clear lead. He had big leads in the counties with universities: Johnson (Iowa City), Story (Ames), Polk (Des Moines), Linn (Cedar Rapids), and Scott (Davenport). He won especially large margins among independents, liberals, unmarried voters and affluent voters. Edwards, carrying mainly small, rural counties, finished second with 30% "delegate strength," just ahead of Clinton, with 29%. She carried western Iowa, the most conservative part of the state, but did not roll up big numbers in industrial counties as Gore had in 2000. The 15% threshold essentially eliminated the rest of the field from the race: Bill Richardson, Biden, and Dodd. Obama's victory in a state with a 3% black population was decisive. Through December 2007, polls showed that he had been splitting the black vote with Clinton in South Carolina and in other states. After Iowa, his support from black voters skyrocketed. Had Clinton won, she might have clinched the nomination on or before Super Tuesday. Her victory in the New Hampshire primary five days later was the beginning of a long, close race. Edwards fell to the wayside after his poor third-place showing in South Carolina, adjacent to his home state of North Carolina. In retrospect, it's hard to see how Obama could have become president without winning the Iowa caucuses.

The result on the Republican side was far less decisive. Caucus turnout was 119,000, a little higher than the Republican record set in 1980 but only about half the level of the Democrats. Some 60% of caucus attendees told entrance poll-takers that they were evangelical or born-again Christians; 46% of them voted for Huckabee, who won with 35% of the vote. Romney, for all his campaigning and spending, finished second with 25%. Trailing were Thompson (13%), McCain (13%), Ron Paul (10%) and Giuliani (4%). Romney carried the eastern and western ends of the state. Paul carried Jefferson County, the home of Maharishi University. "Tonight we proved that American politics is still in the hands of ordinary folks like you," Huckabee proclaimed on caucus night. But in the primaries to come, he was not able to expand his appeal substantially beyond evangelical and born-again Christians, who made up a larger percentage of Iowa caucus-goers than of primary voters in almost any other state. Romney, defeated here and in New Hampshire, lost crucial primaries by narrow margins to McCain, who effectively clinched the nomination on Super Tuesday. He was the first Republican presidential nominee to have finished below third in Iowa.

In 2000 and 2004, Iowa was one of the closest states in presidential elections. It was one of only three that switched between the two elections, giving Gore a narrow victory in 2000 but voting for Bush in 2004. In 2008, it proved not to be such a close contest. Most polls throughout the year showed Obama well ahead of McCain, and the balance of enthusiasm, as demonstrated in caucus turnout, was on Obama's side. He returned to the state on May 20, so that the glow of his caucus victories would overshadow what was expected to be a tough evening of primary returns. (He lost Kentucky by a wide margin, and his victory in Oregon was not reported until most Americans had gone to bed.) In October, McCain and running mate Sarah Palin stumped half a dozen times in Iowa, though perhaps only because other potential target states looked farther out of reach. Obama carried Iowa 54%-44%, winning four of the five congressional districts. He was especially strong in eastern Iowa. He won 61%-36% among young voters. White evangelical Protestants voted 65%-33% for McCain, but Catholics, traditionally Democratic in Iowa, voted 59%-41% for Obama.

Iowa's first-in-the-nation status has been under attack, but was preserved against challenges at the 2004 Republican National Convention and by the rules adopted by the Democratic National Committee in 2006. Provoked by a complaint from Michigan Sen. Carl Levin and others that Iowa and New Hampshire lack racial diversity (Iowa is 3% black and 4% Hispanic), Democrats staged a second early caucus in Nevada and, after the New Hampshire primary, a second early primary in South Carolina. At their 2008 national conventions, both parties reaffirmed New Hampshire's first-in-the-nation-primary status but were silent on the Iowa caucuses. Iowa politicians of both parties will surely try to maintain it. As David Yepsen, the longtime dean of Iowa political reporters, wrote in September 2008, "Defending the caucuses is a never-ending battle and a never-ending responsibility of political leaders in both parties in Iowa."

Congressional districting   Iowa's congressional district lines are drawn by the nonpartisan Legislative Services Bureau and then approved by the governor and legislature, a process that is often praised by many critics of partisan gerrymandering. But it is not entirely apolitical. The bureau is not supposed to take past voting patterns or a legislator's place of residence into account, and in good Iowa fashion, they

112th Congress Lineup	
3 D	2 R
111th Congress Lineup	
3 D	2 R

don't. But the governor and legislators can and do. In 2001, the Iowa Senate rejected the bureau's first plan after Republicans said the population disparities were too large. Its second plan placed Republican Reps. Jim Nussle and Jim Leach in the same district and separated Des Moines from suburban Dallas and Warren counties. Indeed, with the exception of the 5th District in western Iowa, all the districts combined quite disparate parts of Iowa. Nevertheless, Vilsack and the Republican legislature approved the plan. Leach moved into the 2nd District, most of which he had been representing, and Democrat Leonard Boswell moved into Des Moines in the new 3rd District, whose incumbent, Republican Greg Ganske, was running for the Senate.

The Iowa plan has produced more strenuous competition than has been seen in most states. In 2002, four of the five districts were contested seriously by both parties, and the 5th District had a spirited Republican primary. In 2004, only one district was seriously contested, and four of the five incumbents improved their vote percentages. But in 2006, Nussle, who was running for governor, was replaced by a Democrat in the 1st District and Leach, after 30 years in the House, was defeated in the 2nd District. Two years later, all five incumbents easily held their seats, but in 2010, Republicans gave all three Democrats tough races.

Iowa lost a House seat in the reapportionment following the 2010 census, and there is no telling who will be the victim—or victims—of the next round of redistricting by the bureau and the governor and legislature. Both parties will have a say. Gov. Terry Branstad is a Republican, and his party controls the state House, but Democrats have a majority in the Senate.

Governor

Terry Branstad (R)

Elected 2010, term expires Jan. 2015, 5th term; b. Nov. 17, 1946, Leland; home, Des Moines; U. of IA, B.A. 1969; Drake U., J.D. 1974; Catholic; married (Chris); 3 children.

Military Career: U.S. Army, 1969-71.

Elected Office: IA House, 1972-78; IA lt. gov., 1978-82; IA gov., 1982-98.

Professional Career: Practicing atty. and farmer, 1974-82; Pres., Des Moines U., 2003-09.

Office: State Capitol, 1007 East Grand Avenue, 50319, 515-281-5211; Web site: www.governor.iowa.gov/.

Election Results

2010 general	Terry Branstad (R)	592,494	(53%)
	Chet Culver (D)	484,798	(43%)
2010 primary	Terry Branstad (R)	114,450	(50%)
	Bob Vander Plaats (R)	93,058	(41%)
	Rod Roberts (R)	19,896	(9%)

Prior Winning Percentages: 1994 (57%); 1990 (61%); 1986 (52%); 1982 (53%)

Terry Branstad, a Republican, was elected the governor of Iowa for the fifth time in 2010. He was previously elected in 1982, 1986, 1990 and 1994. During his last term he was the most senior governor in the nation, although he now lags behind Democrat Jerry Brown of California, elected in 1974, 1978 and 2010.

Branstad was born on a farm in Northern Iowa. He calls himself "a country kid" who learned hard work through farming and has never claimed to be an intellectual. But he likes to note that he has been running for office, and winning, since the eighth grade. He grew up in a Democratic family, but was converted by reading Barry Goldwater's *Conscience of a Conservative*. He was a conservative at the left-leaning University of Iowa in the late 1960s, and then spent two years in the Army in the military police. He returned to his Lake Mills farm, started a family and graduated from law school. Branstad was elected to the state House in 1972, at age 25, and served three terms. In 1978, he was elected Iowa lieutenant governor, winning the primary with conservative support and coasting into office on the ticket with moderate Republican Bob Ray, who had been in office for a decade. In 1982, when Ray retired as governor, Branstad ran and defeated a Democrat who had legally avoided paying state taxes.

Branstad's strengths in his four terms were persistence, a clear set of convictions and the capacity for flexibility in rough political patches. He visited all 99 Iowa counties once a year and was "a safe conservative manager," in one Democrat's words. Des Moines-based journalist Thomas Fogarty wrote he had a "total absence of flashiness in a state where most voters seem to think that bland is beautiful." Despite his anti-tax and anti-gambling leanings, he increased the sales tax 1% in 1983 and approved a lottery in 1985. He went along with legalizing riverboat casinos, with limited stakes, in 1989, then eliminated the betting limits and legalized slot machines at racetracks in 1994. And his conservatism did not prevent him from approving some active government programs, such as Community Economic Betterment Account business subsidies in 1985, a groundwater protection act in 1987, and regulation of livestock feedlots in 1995. He has said he is proudest of the Iowa Communications Network, set up to connect all Iowa schools to fiber optic cable in 1989. He approved another penny increase in the sales tax in 1992, but income taxes were significantly lowered during his tenure.

Branstad had some tough races. He was re-elected with only 52% of the vote in 1986, when national Republicans were highly unpopular in Iowa. He survived a primary challenge from Rep. Fred Grandy 52%-48% in 1994. He won that fall, 57%-42%. Branstad retired from office in 1998 and, living on 17 acres in the city of Boone, became a consultant and joined a law firm. From 2003 to 2009, he was president of Des Moines University, an osteopathic medical school.

From 1999 to 2007, Democratic Gov. Tom Vilsack served two terms and generally had high job ratings. After Vilsack came Democrat Chet Culver, a two-term secretary of state and the son of former Sen. John Culver. Elected governor in 2006, he was not faring well in the polls in 2009 as the state government began to experience serious budget problems during the national recession. With five other Republicans mulling a challenge to Culver, Branstad announced in fall 2009 that he was resigning from the university to run for governor again, 28 years after his first gubernatorial race.

In the primary, his major opponent was Sioux City business consultant Bob Vander Plaats, the 2006 Republican nominee for lieutenant governor. Branstad raised substantially more money than Vander Plaats and had wide support across the state. He went on a charm offensive, deploying his gift for remembering names and faces. Still, many conservatives had long memories of Branstad raising sales taxes twice, although he countered that he had lowered income taxes and the overall tax burden. Vander Plaats won high profile endorsements from actor Chuck Norris and Focus on the Family's James Dobson, but Branstad got a shout-out from former Alaska Gov. Sarah Palin on her Facebook page.

Branstad won the primary 50%-41%. He declined to name Vander Plaats as his running mate, as 2006 nominee Jim Nussle had, and Vander Plaats refused to endorse Branstad. Branstad's choice for lieutenant governor, state Sen. Kim Reynolds, was approved 56%-44% over Vander Plaats by delegates at the Republican state convention.

In the general election campaign, Branstad led Culver in the polls. He promised to cut government spending by 15% over five years, restructure state employee salaries and sell the state's vehicle fleet. He opposed Culver's program of free preschool for all and favored instead aid to those who couldn't afford preschools. Branstad also opposed the state Supreme Court's unanimous decision in April 2009 legalizing same-sex marriage, which he called "a tragic mistake." He also called for a state constitutional amendment reinstating the opposite-sex marriage law he had signed in 1998.

Branstad raised more money than Culver, and was helped by a June 2010 audit report that said Culver misspent federal election funds as secretary of state. Branstad attacked Culver for using federal economic stimulus dollars to increase spending. The Republican pledged to join other states in lawsuits challenging the constitutionality of the national Democrats' health care law, and he voiced support for Republican Gov. Jan Brewer of Arizona and a new law in that state letting police check the immigration status of people stopped for other reasons. Culver responded by pointing to Branstad's record of raising taxes and said, "Terry Branstad has been a serial promise-maker and a habitual promise-breaker." There was an element of presidential politics in the contest as well. With a Republican contest looming in Iowa's 2012 precinct caucuses, potential presidential candidates—Mitt Romney of Massachusetts, Tim Pawlenty of Minnesota, and Haley Barbour of Mississippi—swooped into Iowa to campaign for Branstad.

The election wasn't close. Branstad beat Culver 53%-43%, carrying 90 of 99 counties. It was the first time an Iowa governor had been defeated for re-election since 1962. Republicans made significant gains in the state legislature, winning a 60-40 majority in the state House and falling just short of a majority in the state Senate. And as Branstad had urged, voters denied three of the seven members of the Supreme Court new terms, two by margins of 54%-46%, and one, 55%-45%, signaling clear though narrow disapproval of the court's same-sex marriage ruling. Branstad's call for a state constitutional amendment to overturn the decision seemed likely to be stymied by the Democratic majority in the Senate, led by Majority Leader Mike Gronstal.

Senior Senator

Charles Grassley (R)

Elected 1980, term expires 2016, 6th term; b. Sept. 17, 1933, New Hartford; home, New Hartford; U. of N. IA, B.A. 1955, M.A. 1956, U. of IA, 1957-58; Baptist; married (Barbara); 5 children.

Elected Office: IA House of Reps., 1958–74; U.S. House of Reps., 1974–80.

Professional Career: Farmer.

DC Office: 135 HSOB, 20510, 202-224-3744; Fax: 202-224-6020; Web site: grassley.senate.gov.

State Offices: Cedar Rapids, 319-363-6832; Council Bluffs, 712-322-7103; Davenport, 563-322-4331; Des Moines, 515-288-1145; Sioux City, 712-233-1860; Waterloo, 319-232-6657.

Committees: *Agriculture, Nutrition & Forestry:* Jobs, Rural Economic Growth & Energy Innovation; Livestock, Dairy, Poultry, Marketing & Ag Research. *Budget. Finance:* Energy, Natural Resources & Infrastructure; Health Care; International Trade, Customs & Global Competitiveness. *Joint Committee on Taxation. Judiciary* (RMM): Administrative Oversight & the Courts; Antitrust, Competition Policy & Consumer Rights; Immigration, Refugees & Border Security.

Group Ratings

	ACLU	ACU	ADA	CFG	AFS	FRC	LCV	ITIC	NTU	COC
2010	7	88	10	76	11	100	0	67	93	91
2009	–	96	20	91	9	–	0	–	88	71

National Journal Ratings

	2010 LIB	—	2010 CONS		2009 LIB	—	2009 CONS
Economic	34%	—	65%		22%	—	76%
Social	21%	—	74%		24%	—	73%
Foreign	0%	—	72%		29%	—	69%
Composite	24%	—	76%		26%	—	74%

Key Votes of the 111th Congress

1. Overturn Ledbetter	N	5. Pass health care bill	N	9. Ratify New START	N
2. Pass $787 billion stimulus	N	6. Regulate financial firms	Y	10. Confirm Elena Kagan	N
3. Repeal DC gun laws	Y	7. Pass tax cuts for some	N	11. Stop EPA climate regs	Y
4. Confirm Sonia Sotomayor	N	8. Legalize immigrants' kids	N	12. Repeal don't ask, tell	N

Election Results

2010 general	Charles Grassley (R)	718,215	(64%)	($7,701,183)
	Roxanne Conlin (D)	371,686	(33%)	($3,152,122)
	John Heiderscheit (Lib)	25,290	(2%)	
2010 primary	Charles Grassley (R)	unopposed		

Prior Winning Percentages: 2004 (70%); 1998 (68%); 1992 (70%); 1986 (66%); 1980 (54%); House: 1978 (75%); 1976 (57%); 1974 (51%)

Charles Grassley, the senior senator from Iowa, was first elected to the House in 1974 and to the Senate in 1980. He grew up on a farm in Butler County near Waterloo. His parents switched to the Republican Party when Franklin Roosevelt ran for a third term in 1940. Grassley received his bachelor's degree from the University of Northern Iowa, and while in graduate school, he ran for the state House in 1956, losing by only 70-some votes. Two years later, he ran again and was elected at age 25. While he was in the state legislature, he worked as a sheet metal shearer and on an assembly line. He won an open U.S. House seat in 1974, the hugely successful post-Watergate year for the Democrats, and six years later, he won his Senate seat by beating incumbent Democratic Sen. John Culver, the father of future Gov. Chet Culver. Sen. Culver was an uncompromising liberal who came under fire from religious conservatives in 1980. Grassley was a conservative who had built up strong loyalty in his north central Iowa House district, which gave him nearly half his statewide lead over Culver. In his other career as a part-time farmer, Grassley runs an 80-acre farm that he inherited in 1960 and has added to it over the years. It's now a 710-acre concern that produces corn and soybeans. Grassley's son manages the farm, but the senator likes to go back to help out in the fields on weekends, sometimes conducting congressional business on the cell phone that he keeps tucked under his cap. He stays in touch with his state in other ways, too. He has held meetings in each of the state's 99 counties every year that he has served in the Senate.

Though he's a steady conservative on social issues—he opposes abortion rights and most gun control initiatives—Grassley is also a populist in the American agrarian tradition. He has distinguished himself in Congress as a defender of government whistle-blowers and other underdogs, and he has made oversight of bloated, indifferent or corrupt government agencies a focal point of his Senate career. To the chagrin of his party, Grassley also takes on well-heeled political contributors when they raise his ire, as many a pharmaceutical executive can attest. Throughout the George W. Bush era, Grassley repeatedly went after Food and Drug Administration officials who he thought were too cozy with the industries they were supposed to regulate. In the mid-1980s, Grassley's first major legislative achievement was passage of the Federal False Claims Act, which authorized lawsuits for fraud on behalf of the government; he says it has since brought the taxpayers more than $17 billion.

Over the years, Grassley has conducted intensive oversight of the FBI, the Homeland Security Department, the Centers for Medicare and Medicaid Services, and the FDA. He has long advocated that Congress follow the same laws it imposes on citizens, and he was the chief Senate sponsor of the sweeping Congressional Accountability Act of 1995. At his urging, the Senate in late 2010 passed a whistleblower protection bill for federal employees. Although it left out Grassley's specific provision protecting whistleblowers in the intelligence community, he was happy with the outcome. "Whistleblowers know where the skeletons are, deep in the closets of the federal bureaucracy," he said. "The bill restores the congressional intent behind a number of key whistleblower laws."

Grassley has shown an inclination to challenge Wall Street. He was one of four Republicans who voted for the initial Senate financial services package in May 2010, although he voted against the final version later in July. "There's no question this bill has flaws, but a message needs to be sent to Wall Street that business-as-usual is over," Grassley said. He also was the only Republican to vote with Democrats on the Senate Agriculture Committee for sweeping reform of the derivatives market in April 2010. And his support for whistleblower rights led him to co-sponsor with Sen. Ben Cardin, D-Md. an amendment in May 2010 that extended whistleblower protections to employees of credit rating agencies, such as Standard & Poor's, which have been criticized for not providing accurate credit ratings for high risk securities. Grassley voted for the government rescue of the financial industry during the final months of the Bush administration and faced criticism from Iowa conservatives in early 2009. Grassley won Senate approval of an amendment co-sponsored with Baucus that required companies accepting tax dollars from the Troubled Asset Relief Program to cooperate with requests for information from the Government Accountability Office.

As a farmer, Grassley supported both the Republicans' 1996 Freedom to Farm law that attempted to phase out government subsidies and the subsequent disaster payments to farmers when they suffered financially under the law. He opposed the 2002 farm bill, drafted by Iowa Democratic Sen. Tom Harkin, on the grounds that it allowed a higher limit on subsidies than the $275,000 that Grassley had persuaded the Senate to vote for. He has consistently argued that high payments to individual farmers put the whole program in political jeopardy. A July 2007 Government Accountability Office report that Grassley requested revealed that the Agriculture Department had given more than $1 billion to deceased farmers from 1999 to 2005. Grassley pushed an amendment to the 2008 budget to cap payments to farmers at $250,000.

Grassley has served two stints as chairman of the powerful Senate Finance Committee, in the first half of 2001 and from 2003 to 2007. With Democrats in control of the Senate, Grassley is now the ranking Republican on the committee. Over the years, he has had close relations and weekly meetings with his Democratic counterpart, Max Baucus of Montana, often to the dismay of conservative Republicans who think Grassley is too accommodating of Baucus. But the working relationship between the two was crucial to many of the GOP initiatives during the Bush era. Grassley and Baucus rounded up bipartisan support for the massive tax cuts early in Bush's first term. And Grassley was one of the leaders in creating the prescription drug benefit under Medicare in 2003. After the bill passed, he defended it against continuing Democratic attacks, and in 2007, he helped halt Democratic efforts to pass a measure that Republicans had expressly kept out of the earlier bill: to allow the government to negotiate drug prices with pharmaceutical companies. The industry balked at the greatly enhanced powers the bill would give the government in setting prices, and Grassley threatened to filibuster any such bill that came to the floor. Also in 2007, Grassley worked with Baucus to secure Senate support to expand the federal Children's Health Insurance Program.

When President Obama in 2009 proposed a far-reaching bill to bring more people into the health insurance market, Grassley was one of the Senate negotiators trying to broker a deal. Some

Democrats were skeptical that Grassley would ever sign on to an Obama-backed bill. He was also under pressure from his own party leadership for negotiating on health care with Democrats. In August 2009, Grassley told *National Journal:* "Wouldn't you rather have a conservative Republican at the table than have nobody at the table?" In the end, Grassley voted against the legislation, complaining that it would cut funding for Medicare and would neither hold down taxes nor contain health care costs. When critics charged that the legislation created so-called "death panels" to selectively dole out care, Grassley helped fan the flames when he said, "[You] should not have a government-run plan to decide when to pull the plug on Grandma."

With his populist bent, he has for years pursued "fairness" in the tax code. He sought a charitable deduction for non-itemizers and tighter rules for foundations, with tougher penalties. He led the committee to tighten the rules on partial gifts of art, which allowed donors to retain possession while receiving tax deductions. "Call it what it is, a subsidy for millionaires to buy art," he said. "Where I come from, the word 'giving' doesn't mean 'keeping.'" In 2007, Grassley joined Baucus in backing a bill to repeal the alternative minimum tax, which has been ensnaring an increasing number of middle-income taxpayers in addition to the wealthy itemizers it was designed to catch. But Grassley also said it would be unfair to raise other taxes to repeal the AMT.

Corn-based ethanol is an important product of Iowa's agribusiness, and Grassley has used his influence on the committee to win advantageous tax treatment of ethanol. He has also sought tax incentives for biodiesel, made with soybean oil or recycled cooking oil. The United States is a major exporter of agricultural products, and Grassley has been a supporter of free trade, backing the North American Free Trade Agreement in 1993, normal trade relations with China and the Central America Free Trade Agreement.

Grassley also serves on the Judiciary Committee, where for years he was the chief sponsor of the bankruptcy law overhaul bill that finally passed and was signed into law in 2005. He took special care to see that Chapter 12, which applies to farmers, would allow them to reorganize their debt without creditors' consent. Grassley's vote against the Supreme Court nomination of Sonia Sotomayor was the first time he ever opposed a nominee for the high court. "I question if Judge Sotomayor will be able to set aside personal biases and prejudices to decide cases in an impartial manner and in accordance with the Constitution," Grassley said in a statement. He voiced displeasure with her views on property rights and gun ownership rights.

In January 2011, Grassley won passage of a binding resolution requiring senators to make the holds they put on legislation and nominees public. The use of so-called "secret holds," unique to the Senate, had allowed individual senators to delay or stop action by the Senate anonymously, and it has been a major obstacle to getting judicial nominees confirmed. Grassley won a 92-4 vote forcing senators to put their objections in writing and submit them for publication in The Congressional Record no longer than two days after the holds are made.

For more than two decades, Grassley has been the most popular politician in Iowa. "I commune with Iowans on a regular basis, and I think they know that. They appreciate it, and they don't feel like Washington has gone to my head. I suppose if I don't get smug and overconfident, I'll be re-elected," he said in 2004, shortly before he was returned to the Senate by a vote of 70%-28%. In 1986, he became the first Iowa senator to win re-election in 20 years, with a record 66% of the vote. He has not had a tough race since 1974, when he won his House seat with 51% of the vote. He won re-election in 2010 with 64% of the vote against Democrat Roxanne Conlin, a Des Moines attorney, who got 33%.

Junior Senator

Tom Harkin (D)

Elected 1984, term expires 2014, 5th term; b. Nov. 19, 1939, Cumming; home, Cumming; IA St. U., B.S. 1962, Catholic U., J.D. 1972; Catholic; married (Ruth); 2 children.

Military Career: Navy, 1962–67; Naval Reserves, 1969–72.

Elected Office: U.S. House of Reps., 1974–84.

Professional Career: Practicing atty., 1972–74; Staff aide, House Select Cmte. on U.S. Involvement in SE Asia, 1973–74.

DC Office: 731 HSOB, 20510, 202-224-3254; Fax: 202-224-9369; Web site: harkin.senate.gov.

State Offices: Cedar Rapids, 319-365-4504; Davenport, 563-322-1338; Des Moines, 515-284-4574; Dubuque, 563-582-2130; Sioux City, 712-252-1550.

Committees: *Agriculture, Nutrition & Forestry:* Conservation, Forestry & Natural Resources; Jobs, Rural Economic Growth & Energy Innovation; Nutrition, Specialty Crops, Food & Ag Research. *Appropriations:* Agriculture, Rural Development, Food and Drug Administration & Related Agencies; Defense; Department of State, Foreign Operations & Related Programs; Energy & Water Development; Labor, Health & Human Services, Education & Related Agencies (Chmn); Transportation, HUD & Related Agencies. *Health, Education, Labor & Pensions* (Chmn). *Small Business & Entrepreneurship.*

Group Ratings

	ACLU	ACU	ADA	CFG	AFS	FRC	LCV	ITIC	NTU	COC
2010	92	0	100	0	94	0	86	33	5	9
2009	–	0	100	3	100	–	100	–	4	43

National Journal Ratings

	2010 LIB	—	2010 CONS	2009 LIB	—	2009 CONS
Economic	73%	—	26%	80%	—	19%
Social	65%	—	0%	85%	—	0%
Foreign	47%	—	0%	55%	—	0%
Composite	77%	—	24%	84%	—	17%

Key Votes of the 111th Congress

1. Overturn Ledbetter	Y	5. Pass health care bill	Y	9. Ratify New START	Y
2. Pass $787 billion stimulus	Y	6. Regulate financial firms	Y	10. Confirm Elena Kagan	Y
3. Repeal DC gun laws	N	7. Pass tax cuts for some	Y	11. Stop EPA climate regs	N
4. Confirm Sonia Sotomayor	Y	8. Legalize immigrants' kids	Y	12. Repeal don't ask, tell	Y

Election Results

2008 general	Tom Harkin (D)...	941,665	(63%)	($9,179,122)
	Christopher Reed (R)...	560,006	(37%)	($59,087)
2008 primary	Tom Harkin (D)...	90,785	(99%)	

Prior Winning Percentages: 2002 (54%); 1996 (52%); 1990 (54%); 1984 (55%); House: 1982 (59%); 1980 (60%); 1978 (59%); 1976 (65%); 1974 (51%)

Tom Harkin, a Democrat first elected to the House in 1974 and the Senate in 1984, is an accomplished veteran of Capitol Hill who brings the attitude of the aggrieved outsider to his work. Harkin grew up poor in a rural town; his father was a coal miner, and his mother, a Slovenian immigrant, died when he was just 10. He worked his way through college and law school before spending five years in the Navy during the 1960s ferrying planes out of Vietnam for repair. In 1970, as an aide to Democratic Rep. Neal Smith of Iowa, Harkin returned to Vietnam and discovered the infamous "tiger cages." America's allies, the South Vietnamese, used these underground cells to hold and torture prisoners of war. (A young Harkin slipped past prison guards on a guided tour to confirm the existence of the secret cells.)

Two years later, Harkin ran for a House seat and lost narrowly; he tried again in 1974 and won. In that campaign, he invented "work days," a concept widely imitated since: He spent a day working at each of a dozen local jobs to better understand people's experiences. He held the seat with solid percentages in four re-election contests. In 1984, he challenged Republican Sen. Roger Jepsen in the midst of a farm depression in Iowa. Harkin's support of subsidies for farmers contrasted Jepsen's advocacy of free market solutions to economic woes. Jepsen was also vulnerable going into his first re-election. He had voted in favor of selling Airborne Warning and Control System aircraft to Saudi Arabia after professing loyalty to Israel, which staunchly opposed the sale. He also came across as arrogant for claiming special privileges as a senator after being stopped for driving alone in high-occupancy vehicle lanes on the highway. Harkin won with 55% of the vote.

In September 2009, Harkin took over the reins of the Senate Health, Education, Labor and Pensions Committee after the death in late August of longtime committee Chairman Edward Kennedy, D-Mass. The move gave Harkin substantial impact on health policy and the Obama administration's health care initiative. He also chairs the Appropriations Subcommittee on Labor, Health and Education, giving him enormous power over both the policy and purse strings of a sizeable segment of the government.

Harkin long has had a hand in health care issues. Two of his sisters died from breast cancer and one brother died from thyroid cancer; another brother became deaf at age 9. Harkin was a key player in shaping the Americans with Disabilities Act of 1990, a major achievement and one that required a bipartisan coalition to overcome resistance to the cost and qualms about the real-world fallout of the regulations. On Appropriations, Harkin worked with his then Republican counterpart, Arlen Specter of Pennsylvania, to double the budget for the National Institutes of Health over five years. He has been a prominent supporter of alternative medicine, prompted by his own experience taking bee-pollen capsules to successfully cure his allergies. He was instrumental in establishing an Office of Alternative Medicine at the National Institutes of Health in 1992. He also strongly backs preventative medicine, and added a provision to the 2010 health care overhaul for a new interagency council to develop a national strategy for such efforts while boosting doctor training and insurance coverage of preventive services.

Harkin was chairman of the Agriculture Committee from June 2001 to January 2003, an advantageous assignment for a senator from a farm state. He regained the post in January 2007 when Democrats took control of the Senate (although he gave it up to take over the HELP Committee). In both stints, Harkin controlled the gavel during reauthorization of the all-important farm bill. He steered to passage the 2002 farm measure, a considerable achievement because he fashioned a bill to restore subsidies phased out by the Republicans' 1996 Freedom to Farm Act. The legislation ultimately increased but limited subsidies for grain and cotton, and doubled the money for conservation over 10 years. Farm exports are important to Iowa, and Harkin, despite his warm feelings for labor unions, voted for the North American Free Trade Agreement in 1993 and for normalizing trade relations with China in 2000. Unions generally oppose free trade agreements as a threat to domestic jobs.

Democratic victories at the polls in 2006 made Harkin chairman again as the farm bill came up for reauthorization in 2007. In an unusual twist, key negotiations shifted to farm-state members of the Senate Finance Committee, led by Democrats Max Baucus of Montana and Kent Conrad of North Dakota and Republican Sen. Charles Grassley of Iowa. Harkin's critics said he was too protective of his pet programs. But eventually most of his programs were included in the bill: federal support for ethanol, more money for nutrition programs, modest caps on subsidies, and a renamed Conservation Stewardship Program. Two-thirds of the funds in the five-year, $300-billion bill were for food stamps and other nutrition programs. Harkin said his work on the complex legislation was "like giving birth to a porcupine."

Throughout this decade, Harkin has been the Senate's leading advocate of better nutrition and fitness for children, and he is a crusader against childhood obesity. A bill he sponsored in 2006 would have removed candy bars, french fries, ice cream bars, and non-diet soft drinks from schools. He achieved many of his goals in 2010 with the enactment into law of a child nutrition bill that gave the Agriculture Department authority to set nutrition standards for foods sold in school vending machines as well as at snack bars and cafeterias. During the 2010 lame-duck session, he also played a central role in getting into law a food safety bill that some supporters had abandoned any hope of passing. Harkin and Sen. Richard Durbin, D-Ill., won admiration from consumer activists for steering the measure around a variety of Republican objections and parliamentary obstacles.

Harkin has had more difficulty with another of his leading priorities—the Employee Free Choice Act, the so-called "card check" bill to require an employer to recognize a union if a majority of workers sign union authorization cards in place of holding secret ballot elections. He devoted much of 2009 and 2010 trying in vain to win the support of skeptical centrist Democrats. At the same time, he invested energy in another cause that had trouble picking up bipartisan support—reforming the Senate's filibuster rules. He first took on the idea in 1995, and in 2010 joined New Hampshire Democrat Jeanne Shaheen on a resolution to set diminishing vote benchmarks to end filibusters until the level finally hits a simple majority of 51. In 2011, he joined New Mexico Democrat Tom Udall and Oregon Democrat Jeff Merkley in proposing a series of proposed changes that included requiring senators to actually talk at length on the floor if they filibuster rather than the current practice of simply threatening to filibuster.

On foreign policy, Harkin's views have been shaped by the Vietnam War. He was a vocal opponent of aid to the Nicaraguan Contras in the 1980s and of the Persian Gulf War resolution in 1991. But he voted to authorize the use of force in Iraq in 1998, when President Clinton sought it and again in 2002, when President George W. Bush requested congressional approval to use force against Iraq. But as the violence continued, Harkin said in 2003, it "may not be Vietnam, but, boy, it sure smells like it." In 2004, he said abuses of prisoners at Abu Ghraib in Iraq reminded him of the tiger cages in Vietnam, and concluded, "It's time to fire the secretary of Defense." When GOP Vice President Cheney in 2004 criticized presidential candidate John Kerry's Vietnam service, Harkin said, "When I hear this coming from Dick Cheney, who was a coward, who would not serve during the Vietnam War, it makes my blood boil. He'll be tough, but he'll be tough with someone else's kid's blood." In 2008, Harkin was one of only two senators who opposed the nomination of Gen. David Petraeus to take over the U.S. Central Command. He was also one of just 18 senators to back Wisconsin Democrat Russ Feingold's ill-fated attempt in May 2010 to require President Barack Obama to submit a timetable for withdrawing troops from Afghanistan.

As an appropriator, Harkin is generous to Iowa and defends spending earmarks. As he said in November 2006, "I happen to be a supporter of earmarks, unabashedly. But I don't call them earmarks. It is 'congressional directed spending.'" In 2010, according to watchdog groups, Harkin ranked fifth among senators in winning earmarks, procuring or helping to procure more than $267 million for his state. One of his initiatives drew attention in March 2009 when several Republicans complained about $1.7 million for swine odor and manure management research at Iowa State University. Harkin invited one of the Republicans, Oklahoma's Tom Coburn, to visit Iowa farms to smell the problem firsthand.

Harkin has been a major force in Iowa politics. He takes advantage of his state's critical role in presidential elections, hosting an annual steak fry that is a required stop for Democratic candidates for all the national media attention it commands. His fervent stands on issues and his hard-edged campaigning give him a large base of loyal supporters as well as strong detractors. In his career, he has beaten no fewer than five members of Congress while rarely topping 55% of the vote. He ran for president in 1992. With Trumanesque zest, Harkin preached that incumbent President George H.W. Bush and the Republicans helped only the rich and that government must get involved to help the poor and middle class. Organized labor withheld an early endorsement despite his 90%-plus AFL-CIO voting record—a great tactical victory for rival Bill Clinton, then the Arkansas governor. Harkin's sweep of the Iowa caucuses on Feb.10 was mostly discounted as a home-field advantage. He finished with only 10% of the vote in the New Hampshire primary, and when he got just 7% in South Carolina on March 7, he quit the race.

In 2002, Harkin faced a serious challenge from Rep. Greg Ganske, a Des Moines plastic surgeon and Republican who had upset 36-year incumbent Neal Smith for a House seat in 1994. Ganske argued that his work in the House regulating health maintenance organizations showed that he could find bipartisan solutions to problems. Harkin attacked Ganske for supporting Republican proposals to partially privatize the Social Security fund and touted passage of the farm bill. Polls showed the race fairly close in the summer. Harkin had far more money and, for the first time, the endorsement of the Iowa Farm Bureau Federation. He won 54%-44%.

He breezed to re-election in 2008. Despite early speculation, Iowa's two Republican House members, Tom Latham and Steve King, declined to challenge Harkin. Instead, he ran against political neophyte Christopher Reed, a small-business owner who raised little money and had scant name recognition. Harkin won 63%-37%.

FIRST DISTRICT

Bruce Braley (D)

Elected 2006, 3rd term; b. Oct. 30, 1957, Grinnell; home, Waterloo; IA St. U., B.A. 1980, U. of IA, J.D. 1983; Presbyterian; married (Carolyn); 3 children.

Professional Career: Practicing atty., 1983-2006.

DC Office: 1727 LHOB, 20515, 202-225-2911; Fax: 202-225-6666; Web site: braley.house.gov.

State Offices: Davenport, 563-323-5988; Dubuque, 563-557-7789; Waterloo, 319-287-3233.

Committees: *Oversight & Government Reform:* National Security, Homeland Defense & Foreign Operations; Regulatory Affairs, Stimulus Oversight & Government Spending. *Veterans' Affairs:* Economic Opportunity (RMM).

Group Ratings

	ACLU	ACU	ADA	CFG	AFS	FRC	LCV	ITIC	NTU	COC
2010	94	0	100	0	100	0	100	67	4	13
2009	–	0	95	1	89	–	100	–	2	40

National Journal Ratings

	2010 LIB	—	2010 CONS		2009 LIB	—	2009 CONS
Economic	88%	—	10%		68%	—	32%
Social	66%	—	33%		82%	—	17%
Foreign	84%	—	11%		91%	—	0%
Composite	81%	—	19%		82%	—	18%

Key Votes of the 111th Congress

1. Overturn Ledbetter	Y	5. Bar federal abortion funds	N	9. Stop detainee transfers	N
2. Pass $820 billion stimulus	Y	6. Pass health care bill	Y	10. Legalize immigrants' kids	Y
3. Let guns in national parks	*	7. Regulate financial firms	Y	11. Repeal don't ask, tell	Y
4. Pass cap-and-trade	Y	8. Pass tax cuts for some	Y	12. Limit campaign funds	Y

Election Results

2010 general	Bruce Braley (D)	104,428	(50%)	($2,098,471)
	Benjamin Lange (R)	100,219	(48%)	($519,505)
2010 primary	Bruce Braley (D)	unopposed		

Prior Winning Percentages: 2008 (65%), 2006 (55%)

Population		Race/Ethnicity		Work	
Pop. 2010:	596,443	White:	89.1%	Private:	81.3%
Change since 2000:	Up 1.9%	Black:	4.6%	Government:	12.3%
Urban:	66.3%	Hispanic:	3.2%	Self-employed:	6.2%
Rural:	33.7%	Asian:	1.1%	Blue collar:	26.4%
Area size:	7,292 sq. mi.	Native Am.:	0.2%	White collar:	55.9%
		Hawaiian:	0.1%	Khaki collar:	0.1%
Age		Two+ races:	1.6%	Other:	17.7%
Median age:	38.3 yrs.				
More than 65 yrs:	14.9%	*Ancestry*		Median income:	$47,020
Less than 18 yrs:	23.7%	German	35.8%	Median Home Value:	$121,700
		Irish	12.4%		
Education		English	6.3%	**Military Veterans**	
H.S. grad:	90.1%			% of Pop:	11.0%
College grad:	23.4%				
Grad degree:	7.3%				

East Iowa; Davenport, Waterloo

Northeast Iowa, along the Mississippi River and westward, has some of the loveliest landscape in America. Here the Mississippi flows past green bluffs, then broadens out in great quiet pools alongside picturesque towns. A century and a half ago, as settlers surged west of the Mississippi, Germans stopped at the river bluffs reminiscent of their native land and built neat farmhouses and substantial towns. Inland, on the rolling hills portrayed with surprisingly little

2008 Presidential Vote		
Barack Obama (D)	175,394	(58%)
John McCain (R)	122,629	(41%)
2004 Presidential Vote		
John Kerry (D)	157,380	(53%)
George Bush (R)	138,073	(46%)
Cook Partisan Voting Index:	D+5	

exaggeration in the paintings of Iowa's Grant Wood, and in the more open territory to the west, New England Yankees and Midwesterners built their characteristic farmhouses, barns, town halls, church spires, and small colleges. Railroad companies, headquartered in Chicago, extended their networks of steel rails over the plains and rivers. Davenport, on the hills over the Mississippi, still has the look of the city where Ronald Reagan got his first radio job. German Catholics settled Dubuque, whose giant Victorian courthouse looks down on the river. Home to a giant John Deere facility that sells tractors worldwide, it is a self-styled green city that has other large factories but is also proud of its waterfront-generated tourism. *Forbes* magazine in 2010 named Dubuque the best small city in America in which to raise a family. Farther west is Waterloo, which grew rapidly after 1900 as its John Deere tractor factory expanded and the eight-floor Rath factory became the largest meat-packing plant in the world. Rath closed in 1984 and Deere has laid off thousands, but Waterloo has rebounded somewhat with new industries, from telemarketing to a high-tech Iowa Beef Processors factory, acquired by Tyson Foods in 2001. In June 2010, Deere announced it would invest about $100 million to modernize its Waterloo foundry over the next four to five years.

The 1st Congressional District covers much of northeast Iowa, including the Mississippi riverfront, from the antiques town of McGregor south to Davenport, Iowa's part of the Quad Cities. From the river, it spans west 100 miles to Butler County. There is considerable political variation here. Davenport and next-door Bettendorf were historically Republican, but in 2000 and 2004, like much of eastern Iowa, they voted narrowly for Al Gore and John Kerry. In 2008, as Iowa began to look favorably on Barack Obama, these areas helped lead the way. Dubuque, heavily German Catholic, was for years Iowa's most Democratic city, and still is unless abortion is the issue. But the rural counties along the river and farther west—more German Protestant, Scandinavian, and Yankee—were traditionally Republican. Waterloo and Cedar Falls, originally Republican, trended sharply Democratic in the 1980s. Overall, this district is pretty evenly balanced and has become a key battleground in presidential contests. Bush lost the district by 7 percentage points each time, and Obama won it by 17 percentage points in 2008.

Bruce Braley (D)

The congressman from the 1st District is Bruce Braley, a Democrat from Waterloo elected in 2006. Braley is a native of Brooklyn, Iowa. His mother was a teacher, and his father was a farmer who died of injuries sustained in a fall down a grain elevator. The family struggled financially for years as a result. Braley graduated from Iowa State University and got his law degree from the University of Iowa. He was a trial lawyer and is a former president of the Iowa Trial Lawyers Association. His candidacy for Congress drew considerable financial support from the Association of Trial Lawyers of America and many of its members and officers, connections that made him the target of lawyer-bashing. National Republicans disparaged him as "a trial lawyer's trial lawyer." In the June primary, Braley overcame two competitive opponents: former state Rep. Rick Dickinson, an economic development official in Dubuque, and Bill Gluba, a real estate agent in Davenport. Although Braley was making his first run for office, he had a distinct fundraising advantage and the support of the Iowa AFL-CIO. He won 36% to 34% for Dickinson and 26% for Gluba. Meanwhile, Republicans nominated Mike Whalen, a Harvard Law School graduate, wealthy entrepreneur, and owner of the Machine Shed Restaurant chain.

From the start, Republicans knew it would be a tough contest. In his eight terms, outgoing Rep. Jim Nussle (who vacated the seat to run for governor in 2006) never got more than 57% of the vote despite his prominence as the chairman of the House Budget Committee from 2001 to 2006. The candidates disagreed on many issues, including the Iraq war, tort reform, international trade deals, and abortion rights. Braley portrayed Whalen as an out-of-touch millionaire. He attacked Whalen's opposition to raising the hourly minimum wage. When Whalen insisted that all his employees were paid more than the federal minimum wage, Braley produced a Machine Shed waitress who claimed that, even with tips, she and her co-workers earned only the minimum wage. For his part, Whalen charged that Braley's litigious occupation contributed to higher health care costs and the medical liability crisis. Although the National Republican Congressional Committee spent heavily on direct mail and television ads against Braley, it wasn't enough. Braley won surprisingly easily, 55%-43%. He took each of the 12 counties, except for two rural counties. As expected, he ran strongly in Waterloo's Black Hawk County, with 59%; but he also took Whalen's Quad Cities base in Scott County, with 53%.

Braley was among the more active members of his freshman class. He won House passage of a bill to require federal agencies to write in plain English, a longtime interest from his days practicing law. He took up the cause of veterans who had been neglected in government hospitals. The 2008 farm bill included his provision to fund advanced technology education centers to train technicians in renewable energy. His success led to an appointment to the influential Energy and Commerce Committee in 2008. He also founded the Populist Caucus, a group of about 30 House Democrats focusing on economic issues affecting the middle class. During the 2009 health care debate, he sharply rebuked what he called Iowa GOP Sen. Charles Grassley's "scare tactics" about end-of-life counseling provisions in the House bill. He also promoted tax credits for biodiesel and won House passage of a bill in September 2010 requiring federally bought American flags to be entirely American-made.

Braley was re-elected easily in 2008. He appeared headed for a similar fate in 2010 until an outside conservative group, the American Future Fund, put him in its sights. The group, which was founded by a former Nussle political aide, spent more than $570,000 on anti-Braley ads, including one that falsely accused him of "supporting" a mosque and Islamic cultural center proposed for construction two blocks from New York's Ground Zero. The U.S. Chamber of Commerce chimed in with $250,000 of its own for attack ads, and as a result, Braley struggled to maintain his lead against Republican attorney Benjamin Lange. But unlike other endangered Democrats who distanced themselves from their votes on health care and other controversial topics, he gave a full-throated defense of his positions and managed to eke out a slim victory over Lange, 49.5%-47.5%. He could not win Scott County this time, but held on to his base in Black Hawk and Dubuque counties. Some local Democrats have mentioned Braley as a possible contender if one of Iowa's veteran senators retires.

SECOND DISTRICT

Dave Loebsack (D)

Elected 2006, 3rd term; b. Dec. 23, 1952, Sioux City; home, Mt. Vernon; IA St. U., B.S. 1974, M.A. 1976, U. of CA, Ph.D., 1985; Methodist; married (Teresa); 4 children.

Professional Career: Professor, Cornell Col., 1982-2006.

DC Office: 1527 LHOB, 20515, 202-225-6576; Fax: 202-226-0757; Web site: loebsack.house.gov.

State Offices: Cedar Rapids, 319-364-2288; Iowa City, 319-351-0789.

Committees: *Armed Services:* Military Personnel; Readiness. *Education & the Workforce:* Health, Employment, Labor & Pensions; Higher Education & Workforce Training.

Group Ratings

	ACLU	ACU	ADA	CFG	AFS	FRC	LCV	ITIC	NTU	COC
2010	94	4	95	0	100	0	90	100	6	25
2009	–	0	95	0	100	–	100	–	2	36

National Journal Ratings

	2010 LIB	—	2010 CONS		2009 LIB	—	2009 CONS
Economic	80%	—	20%		80%	—	20%
Social	67%	—	31%		57%	—	42%
Foreign	78%	—	17%		91%	—	0%
Composite	76%	—	24%		78%	—	22%

Key Votes of the 111th Congress

1. Overturn Ledbetter	Y	5. Bar federal abortion funds	N	9. Stop detainee transfers	N
2. Pass $820 billion stimulus	Y	6. Pass health care bill	Y	10. Legalize immigrants' kids	Y
3. Let guns in national parks	N	7. Regulate financial firms	Y	11. Repeal don't ask, tell	Y
4. Pass cap-and-trade	Y	8. Pass tax cuts for some	Y	12. Limit campaign funds	Y

Election Results

2010 general	Dave Loebsack (D) 115,839	(51%)	($1,122,051)
	Mariannette Miller-Meeks (R) 104,319	(46%)	($1,196,436)
2010 primary	Dave Loebsack (D) .... unopposed		

Prior Winning Percentages: 2008 (57%), 2006 (51%)

Population		Race/Ethnicity		Work	
Pop. 2010:	620,856	White:	88.0%	Private:	78.0%
Change since 2000:	Up 6.1%	Black:	3.1%	Government:	15.6%
Urban:	66.0%	Hispanic:	4.6%	Self-employed:	6.2%
Rural:	34.0%	Asian:	2.2%	Blue collar:	24.4%
Area size:	7,684 sq. mi.	Native Am.:	0.2%	White collar:	58.0%
		Hawaiian:	0.1%	Khaki collar:	0.1%
Age		Two+ races:	1.6%	Other:	17.5%
Median age:	36.4 yrs.				
More than 65 yrs:	13.3%	*Ancestry*		Median income:	$48,133
Less than 18 yrs:	23.0%	German	28.2%	Median Home Value:	$124,700
		Irish	12.7%		
Education		English	7.8%	**Military Veterans**	
H.S. grad:	91.1%			% of Pop:	10.1%
College grad:	27.6%				
Grad degree:	9.4%				

Southeast Iowa; Cedar Rapids

Eastern Iowa is little known to outsiders. It is a land of rolling hills and deep river valleys, of undulant farm fields and big skies, of prosperous small towns and grain elevators and factories. Even political writers, who come to Iowa by the thousands for the quadrennial precinct caucuses, tend to hang out in Des Moines and do their reporting there or in the counties within an hour's drive of the city. The drive from Des Moines east to the second-largest city, Cedar Rapids, takes more than two hours. The biggest metropolis in these parts, Cedar Rapids has high-tech employers and contemporary office buildings. Unlike in most of Iowa, population boomed here in the past decade, and per capita income rose. The production of ethanol and other biofuels in Cedar Rapids and elsewhere helped the state deal with the recession.

2008 Presidential Vote
Barack Obama (D) 190,973 (60%)
John McCain (R) 122,395 (38%)

2004 Presidential Vote
John Kerry (D) 171,561 (55%)
George Bush (R) 135,991 (44%)

Cook Partisan Voting Index: D+7

Yet traditional industries are still a mainstay: Go down by the river and you can't miss the smell of cooking oats coming from the Quaker Oats and General Mills factories. The town suffered a major setback in the summer of 2008, when record floods caused $3.5 billion in damage, with the downtown area described as a "war zone." But disaster losses were offset in part by $2.4 billion in federal aid. Iowa City, just to the south, is a university town dotted with trendy bookstores and vegetarian eateries. The University of Iowa is known for its Writers' Workshop, which produced the nation's first creative writing degree program and some of its most gifted young authors. *The Advocate*, a magazine for the gay community, in February 2010 ranked Iowa City as the nation's third most gay-friendly city, behind Atlanta and Burlington, Vt. Conesville, in Muscatine County near the Mississippi River, is the only city in Iowa with a Hispanic majority, a legacy of an abundance of farm work in the area and, more recently, of the availability of jobs at the Iowa Beef Processors plant in nearby Columbus Junction.

Farther afield, Iowa's 2nd Congressional District offers up some offbeat claims to fame. Bentonsport, in Van Buren County near the Missouri border, is an artists' and craftsmen's colony. Anamosa, in Jones County just east of Cedar Rapids, is the site of the house depicted by Anamosa native Grant Wood in his famous *American Gothic* painting—the models for the two figures were his dentist and Wood's own sister, who died in 1990. Iowa's newest city, incorporated in 2001, is Maharishi Vedic City, in Jefferson County, where followers of the Maharishi Mahesh Yogi built

Maharishi University in 1973 and made the town a magnet for believers in transcendental meditation. The 2nd is by most measures Iowa's most Democratic congressional district, thanks in large part to big Democratic majorities in Iowa City and Johnson County. Cedar Rapids and Linn County have also been inclined toward the Democrats in recent years.

Dave Loebsack (D)

The congressman from the 2nd District is Dave Loebsack (*LOBE sak*), a Democrat elected in a stunning 2006 upset. He defeated 15-term Rep. Jim Leach, a Republican who often was out of step with his party but who held views that seemed well-connected to this district. A native of Sioux City, Loebsack lived as a child in poverty with his mother, grandmother, and three siblings in a two-bedroom house and worked as a high school janitor to pay for college. He got a master's degree at Iowa State University and went on to the University of California (Davis) to earn a Ph.D. in political science. From 1982 until his election to Congress, he was a professor of international relations at Cornell College in Mount Vernon, a few miles from Cedar Rapids. He had been active in local politics for several years, including a stint as fundraising chairman for Linn County Democrats.

When Loebsack decided to challenge Leach in 2006, he insisted that his campaign was not an attack on Leach's three decades in Congress but rather on the GOP leadership in Congress; he called Leach, a moderate Republican, an "enabler" for his party leaders. The two had enjoyed a friendly relationship before the contest. A prominent member of the House Foreign Affairs Committee, Leach had lectured to Loebsack's classes on several occasions.

The war in Iraq was a pivotal issue from the start of this contest. And although Leach was the only member of the Iowa delegation to oppose the war, Loebsack sought to tie him to President Bush's defense secretary, Donald Rumsfeld, on the basis that Leach had been an aide to Rumsfeld when Rumsfeld was a House member from Illinois in the late 1960s. Leach refused to disparage his former boss, calling him a friend and insisting that his ouster would not change the administration's policy in Iraq. The campaign remained civil, with Leach emphasizing the need to promote ethanol and Loebsack calling for national health insurance.

But Leach may have underestimated the hostility toward the war in the district's population centers, especially in the university communities that welcomed Loebsack's anti-Iraq war message. Loebsack raised $522,000, which ordinarily would have not been nearly enough for a competitive House race, and he had little support from the Democratic Congressional Campaign Committee. But Leach unwittingly helped Loebsack overcome those obstacles. Leach eschewed modern campaign practices, particularly negative campaigning, and was a notoriously reluctant fundraiser. When the Iowa Republican Party sent out negative mailers targeting Loebsack, Leach told them to stop. He refused to accept contributions from political action committees or from sources outside the district, and raised only $491,000. Leach did earn the endorsement of the district's major newspapers, but it wasn't enough. Loebsack beat him, 51%-49%. Of the district's 15 counties, Leach carried 10. Loebsack won by 367 votes in Linn County (Cedar Rapids), the largest county in the district. The election hinged on the second-largest county, Johnson (Iowa City), where Loebsack got 58%, a margin of 8,525 votes.

In Washington, one of Loebsack's first official actions was to sponsor a measure to name the federal building in Davenport, Iowa, the James A. Leach Federal Building; it passed the House in May 2007. He spoke out against the war in Iraq and voiced frustration with the Democrats' failure to change Bush administration policy. However, after noting progress being made by U.S. forces during a 2007 visit to Anbar province, Loebsack abandoned his goal of removing all U.S. troops within one year.

Loebsack has a consistently liberal voting record. He belongs to the Center Aisle Caucus, an informal group of around 40 House members seeking to establish greater civility between the parties. He has introduced legislation to expand the school lunch program and to help children eat more nutritious meals at school. Mostly, he tended the home fires in his first term, focusing on securing $28 million in earmarks, the often-criticized special provisions in appropriations bills added by individual lawmakers, to help his flood-stricken district. The House in May 2009 passed his "green schools" bill authorizing $6.4 billion for modernizing and making environmental improvements to schools. The following year, it passed his legislation to offer competitive grants for community colleges and local business working together to help train workers.

In 2008, Loebsack won a comfortable re-election, 57%-39%, against political neophyte Mariannette Miller-Meeks, a Republican ophthalmologist. Miller-Meeks returned for a rematch in 2010, hoping the national political climate favoring her party would give her a boost. She criticized Loebsack's support for the health care overhaul and called for reforming the tax code. She was able to remain roughly even with Loebsack on fundraising, and some polls showed her ahead in the closing weeks. But Loebsack's work on behalf of flood-stricken communities helped offset his support of President Obama's policies. The *Gazette*, which had endorsed Miller-Meeks in 2008, backed Loebsack, calling him "a thoughtful legislator who remembers his roots." He won, 51%-46%.

THIRD DISTRICT

Leonard Boswell (D)

Elected 1996, 8th term; b. Jan. 10, 1934, Harrison Cnty., MO; home, Davis City; Graceland Col., B.A. 1969; Community of Christ; married (Dody); 3 children.

Military Career: Army, 1956–76 (Vietnam).

Elected Office: IA Senate, 1984–96, Pres., 1992–96.

Professional Career: Farmer.

DC Office: 1026 LHOB, 20515, 202-225-3806; Fax: 202-225-5608; Web site: boswell.house.gov.

State Offices: Des Moines, 515-282-1909.

Committees: *Agriculture:* General Farm Commodities & Risk Management (RMM); Livestock, Dairy & Poultry. *Transportation & Infrastructure:* Aviation; Highways & Transit.

Group Ratings

	ACLU	ACU	ADA	CFG	AFS	FRC	LCV	ITIC	NTU	COC
2010	80	0	90	5	100	6	80	100	7	25
2009	–	0	95	1	89	–	93	–	4	47

National Journal Ratings

	2010 LIB	—	2010 CONS	2009 LIB	—	2009 CONS
Economic	68%	—	31%	61%	—	39%
Social	61%	—	35%	58%	—	42%
Foreign	66%	—	29%	91%	—	0%
Composite	67%	—	33%	72%	—	29%

Key Votes of the 111th Congress

1. Overturn Ledbetter	Y	5. Bar federal abortion funds	N	9. Stop detainee transfers	Y
2. Pass $820 billion stimulus	Y	6. Pass health care bill	Y	10. Legalize immigrants' kids	Y
3. Let guns in national parks	Y	7. Regulate financial firms	Y	11. Repeal don't ask, tell	Y
4. Pass cap-and-trade	Y	8. Pass tax cuts for some	Y	12. Limit campaign funds	Y

Election Results

2010 general	Leonard Boswell (D)	122,147	(51%)	($1,519,582)
	Brad Zaun (R)	111,925	(46%)	($682,761)
	Rebecca Williamson (I)	6,258	(3%)	
2010 primary	Leonard Boswell (D)	unopposed		

Prior Winning Percentages: 2008 (56%), 2006 (52%), 2004 (55%), 2002 (53%), 2000 (63%), 1998 (57%), 1996 (49%)

Population		Race/Ethnicity		Work	
Pop. 2010:	642,116	White:	85.5%	Private:	81.5%
Change since 2000:	Up 9.7%	Black:	4.2%	Government:	12.5%
Urban:	73.1%	Hispanic:	5.7%	Self-employed:	5.8%
Rural:	26.9%	Asian:	2.6%	Blue collar:	21.1%
Area size:	7,033 sq. mi.	Native Am.:	0.4%	White collar:	62.8%
		Hawaiian:	0.0%	Khaki collar:	0.1%
Age		Two+ races:	1.5%	Other:	16.0%
Median age:	36.5 yrs.				
More than 65 yrs:	13.0%	*Ancestry*		Median income:	$53,225
Less than 18 yrs:	24.9%	German	25.1%	Median Home Value:	$140,600
		Irish	11.8%		
Education		English	8.2%	**Military Veterans**	
H.S. grad:	91.0%			% of Pop:	9.8%
College grad:	28.8%				
Grad degree:	8.1%				

Central Iowa; Des Moines

Iowa, which today seems very much in the middle of the country, was once part of the West. It was not only the home of sober farmers and pious burghers, but also the eastern terminus of the first transcontinental railroad, a way station for people in a hurry to get across the Great Plains to the Rockies and the Pacific Northwest. Those who stayed behind used the wealth accumulated by methodical husbandry of their fertile farmlands to implant firmly the glories of

2008 Presidential Vote		
Barack Obama (D)	173,932	(54%)
John McCain (R)	143,771	(44%)
2004 Presidential Vote		
George Bush (R)	154,919	(50%)
John Kerry (D)	154,652	(50%)
Cook Partisan Voting Index:	D+1	

Western civilization. One can feel that impulse today in Des Moines, looking across the river from downtown to the Victorian capitol, its gold dome above a Corinthian pediment. Terrace Hill, the beautifully restored governor's mansion, sits atop a hill overlooking the Raccoon River. Nearby Living History Farms, which recreates Indian villages, frontier towns, and turn-of-the-century farms, shows off the efforts of the early settlers.

The 3rd Congressional District covers 12 counties in central Iowa, including Des Moines' Polk County, and it extends mostly to the east. It is the most urbanized district in Iowa and the only one that does not border another state or a major river on the east or west. Some 65% of its votes are cast in Polk County. However, it does not include rapidly growing Dallas or Warren counties in the Des Moines metropolitan area. The city itself remains classically Middle American, even as it gains a livelier downtown and spreads into the countryside. *Forbes* in 2010 named Des Moines the top spot in the country for business and careers, and *Newsweek* cited it as one of 10 cities poised for recovery. The area has become a sanctuary for people from outside of Iowa looking for a family-friendly urban lifestyle. And, more than 12,000 Bosnians have settled in Des Moines, where the climate reminds them of home. Insurance, agricultural supply, and printing and service businesses are expanding in office centers downtown and at freeway interchanges. Kemin Industries Inc., which makes nutritional ingredients, announced a $30 million expansion in 2010.

The remainder of the district is largely rural, with no city larger than 30,000. But these towns house some giant manufacturing plants. Pella (pop. 10,207) is home to the Pella window and door maker, which employs 3,000. The famed Amana colonies, with seven quaint villages, were founded in 1855 by the Community of True Inspiration, German pietists who have retained many of their old customs. In 2008, Newton (pop. 15,254) became the site of a fiberglass wind turbine plant that drew a visit from President Obama in April 2009. Polk County has historically voted Democratic, but has become more Republican as white-collar businesses overtake blue-collar ones. The district's other rural counties have mostly been Republican in the past. The result is a district about as evenly divided as any in the nation: It went 49%-48% for Al Gore in 2000 and 49.7%-49.6% for George W. Bush in 2004. In 2008, though, it favored Obama 54%-44%.

Leonard Boswell (D)

The congressman from the 3rd Congressional District is Leonard Boswell, a Democrat first elected in 1996. Boswell grew up on farms in Ringgold and Decatur counties, near the Missouri border. He was drafted in 1956, at age 22, and was a private in the Army. He re-enlisted as an officer, graduated first in his class in both fixed-wing and helicopter flying school, served two years in Vietnam, and retired as a lieutenant colonel in 1976. He then taught at the Army command college at Fort Leavenworth, Kansas. Boswell settled down on his Decatur County farm and became head of the local farmers' co-op, which he managed to keep out of bankruptcy during the farm depression of the 1980s.

In 1984, he was elected state senator from a six-county Republican district, served as chairman of the Appropriations Committee and, after 1992, Senate president. Boswell was also the Democratic nominee for lieutenant governor in 1994. In 1996, he ran for an open seat in the old 3rd District, which was largely rural and extended across the state's southern tier. Boswell flew his four-seater Piper Comanche 250 across the district, campaigning for a balanced federal budget, higher education spending, and fewer Medicare reductions, all to be financed with Pentagon cuts and eliminating waste in Medicare. Poweshiek County attorney Mike Mahaffey ran as a moderate Republican. Boswell was endorsed by the Farm Bureau, which usually backs Republicans. He raised more money than Mahaffey and, like other Democrats, ran ads attacking GOP House Speaker Newt Gingrich of Georgia and cuts in Medicare. The result was a 49%-48% victory for Boswell.

A member of the Blue Dog Coalition, he has a voting record in the most conservative quadrant of House Democrats, though he has demonstrated more loyalty to his party in recent years. When President Obama took office, Boswell joined the majority of his party in backing the president's economic stimulus bill, his health care overhaul and the Democrats' cap-and-trade bill to regulate greenhouse gas emissions.

From his seat on the Agriculture Committee, Boswell has supported normal trade relations with China, the world's biggest market for pork, a major Iowa commodity. He had a hand in writing the 2008 farm bill as chairman of the Subcommittee on Livestock, Dairy, and Poultry. Boswell added provisions to the House bill that gave pricing benefits to food processors, and changed the dairy price support so that it was based on all dairy products, not just milk. On the Intelligence Committee, his military background and his security clearance made him well-positioned to investigate the nation's response to terrorism. He voted to authorize military action in Iraq, but later criticized the Bush administration for not spending enough money on counter-terrorism. In 2007, he won enactment of a bill for a suicide prevention program for veterans of the wars in Iraq and Afghanistan.

The nonpartisan redistricting plan after the 2000 census created enormous political problems for Boswell. Only seven of the 27 counties and 24% of the population in his former district were moved to the new 3rd District. Decatur County, where he continued to operate his family farm, was one of eight counties moved to western Iowa's new, heavily Republican 5th District. His only other option was to move to the new 2nd District, which leans Democratic but where he would have faced a tough contest against then-Rep. Jim Leach, R-Iowa. Boswell decided to move to Des Moines and run in the newly redrawn 3rd District in 2002. His Republican challenger was Stan Thompson, a Des Moines lawyer who worked for George W. Bush in the 2000 Iowa caucuses. Thompson argued that Boswell was out of step with the new district's philosophy. He won several important endorsements, including a joint designation with Boswell from the Iowa Farm Bureau. Boswell won, 53%-45%. Thompson came back two years later for a rematch. In that contest, the *Des Moines Register* complained that Boswell had become "almost so low-key he is no longer heard." But he still won 55%-45%, and carried Polk County 57%-43%.

Nonetheless, in 2006, Boswell faced yet another tough challenge—from state Senate Co-President Jeff Lamberti, scion of a family-owned chain of convenience stores and gas stations. Lamberti got help from national Republicans and highlighted his differences with Boswell on taxes, spending, and border control. In a strongly Democratic year, Boswell won by only 52%-46%. In 2008, Boswell spent more than $1 million to defeat a primary challenge from Ed Fallon, a former state legislator, 61%-39%. Fallon, who suggested that Boswell might soon retire, was backed by the *Register*, which called Boswell "out of touch" and criticized him for a relatively light record of accomplishments. In the general election, Boswell attracted a politically savvy but little-known GOP challenger, lawyer Kim Schmett, and prevailed with 56% of the vote.

Early in the 2010 election season, when a *Register* poll pointed to a highly anti-incumbent mood in the district, Republicans again took an interest in dislodging Boswell. The GOP primary attracted seven candidates, including former Iowa State University wrestling coach Jim Gibbons, who later became a Wells Fargo vice president. Gibbons got support from some House Republican leaders, but the eventual nominee was Brad Zaun, a GOP state senator and former mayor of Urbandale. He called for tax cuts and lower government spending, and sharply rebuked Boswell for saying that the economy was improving. But the Republican was hit by a swarm of negative publicity—a nine-year-old report showed that police had once warned him to stay away from an ex-girlfriend, who had accused him of harassment, plus subsequent news articles about unpaid medical bills, missed mortgage payments and a federal tax lien against him. The race, which had been a tossup, swung in Boswell's favor in the closing weeks, and he won 51%-46%, with Socialist Rebecca Williamson getting 3%.

FOURTH DISTRICT

Tom Latham (R)

Elected 1994, 9th term; b. July 14, 1948, Hampton; home, Ames; Wartburg Col., 1966-67, IA St. U., 1967-70; Lutheran; married (Kathy); 3 children.

Professional Career: Farmer; Bank teller/bookkeeper, 1970–72; Independent Insurance agent, 1972–74; Hartford Insurance mktg. rep., 1974–76; Co–owner, Latham Seed Co., 1976–present.

DC Office: 2217 RHOB, 20515, 202-225-5476; Fax: 202-225-3301; Web site: tomlatham.house.gov.

State Offices: Ames, 515-232-2885; Clear Lake, 641-357-5225; Fort Dodge, 515-573-2738.

Committees: *Appropriations:* Agriculture, Rural Development, FDA & Related Agencies; Homeland Security; Transportation, HUD & Related Agencies (Chmn).

Group Ratings

	ACLU	ACU	ADA	CFG	AFS	FRC	LCV	ITIC	NTU	COC
2010	6	91	0	90	13	100	30	33	84	88
2009	–	80	5	74	22	–	0	–	72	80

National Journal Ratings

	2010 LIB — 2010 CONS		2009 LIB — 2009 CONS	
Economic	30%	70%	31%	68%
Social	25%	71%	29%	68%
Foreign	29%	68%	0%	75%
Composite	29%	71%	25%	75%

Key Votes of the 111th Congress

1. Overturn Ledbetter	N	5. Bar federal abortion funds	Y	9. Stop detainee transfers	Y
2. Pass $820 billion stimulus	N	6. Pass health care bill	N	10. Legalize immigrants' kids	N
3. Let guns in national parks	Y	7. Regulate financial firms	N	11. Repeal don't ask, tell	N
4. Pass cap-and-trade	N	8. Pass tax cuts for some	N	12. Limit campaign funds	N

Election Results

2010 general	Tom Latham (R)	152,588	(66%)	($1,329,211)
	Bill Maske (D)	74,300	(32%)	($142,869)
	Dan Lensing (I)	5,499	(2%)	
2010 primary	Tom Latham (R)	unopposed		

Prior Winning Percentages: 2008 (61%), 2006 (57%), 2004 (61%), 2002 (55%), 2000 (69%), 1998 (100%), 1996 (65%), 1994 (61%)

Population		Race/Ethnicity		Work	
Pop. 2010:	609,487	White:	91.5%	Private:	76.2%
Change since 2000:	Up 4.1%	Black:	1.2%	Government:	15.6%
Urban:	50.5%	Hispanic:	4.5%	Self-employed:	7.9%
Rural:	49.5%	Asian:	1.6%	Blue collar:	25.5%
Area size:	15,833 sq. mi.	Native Am.:	0.2%	White collar:	57.0%
		Hawaiian:	0.0%	Khaki collar:	0.1%
Age		Two+ races:	1.0%	Other:	17.4%
Median age:	38.7 yrs.				
More than 65 yrs:	15.8%	*Ancestry*		Median income:	$48,367
Less than 18 yrs:	22.9%	German	30.9%	Median Home Value:	$112,700
		Irish	10.7%		
Education		Norwegian	8.6%	**Military Veterans**	
H.S. grad:	90.6%			% of Pop:	10.7%
College grad:	23.9%				
Grad degree:	7.2%				

North and Central Iowa; Ames

Central Iowa is where the Great Plains begins—farmlands marked off by straight highways and punctuated by occasional crossroads towns and grain elevators; the landscape rolls slightly upward to the west, topped by a sky that seems to fill the eyes. Pioneers coming here in the 1840s and 1850s found prairie grass with roots two feet thick, and girded trees with grubbing machines to cut off their roots below-ground. Central Iowa has some of the world's

2008 Presidential Vote		
Barack Obama (D) 166,104	(53%)
John McCain (R) 142,396	(45%)
2004 Presidential Vote		
George Bush (R) 155,587	(51%)
John Kerry (D) 148,331	(48%)
Cook Partisan Voting Index: EVEN		

most productive soil, and also some of its most creative agricultural scientists and farmers. A monument to one of them is the 12-foot statue of Norman Borlaug, a scientist who worked on increasing crop yield and ending hunger, in Borlaug's hometown of Cresco, near the Minnesota border. This is long-settled land now, and Iowans' productivity means that there are fewer people living on farms than there were a century ago.

But its towns and small cities remain centers of creativity. One is Ames, in Story County, home of Iowa State University and the host of the Iowa Republican straw poll, which has launched several GOP nomination contests. Ames is part of the growth zone around Des Moines, one county south. Directly west of the city and its most affluent suburbs is fast-growing Dallas County. To the south is Madison County, famous for the wooden covered bridges that gave their name to a best-selling novel and movie; in 2002, one of the bridges caught fire and burned, leaving just five. To the north is Mason City, the boyhood home of *The Music Man* author Meredith Wilson. In Winnebago County is Winnebago Industries, which manufactures motor homes and recreational vehicles on computer-controlled assembly lines with robotic equipment; the main factory in Forest City employs 3,200, though increased gas prices and the recession have badly hurt sales. The first tractors were manufactured in Charles City.

The 4th Congressional District includes all these parts of central and northern Iowa, and covers 28 counties. It does not include Des Moines, but counties around Des Moines cast more than one-third of its votes. Like Iowa, the 4th District is closely divided politically: George W. Bush carried the district 49%-48% in 2000 and 51%-48% in 2004; Barack Obama won it in 2008, 53%-45%.

Tom Latham (R)

The congressman from the 4th District is Tom Latham, a Republican first elected in 1994. Latham grew up on a farm in Franklin County, near Alexander (pop. 162), where his family has owned a seed company since 1947. For years, Latham was active in Republican politics, attending the national convention and serving as a farm adviser to Rep. Fred Grandy. In 1994 Grandy unsuccessfully challenged Gov. Terry Branstad in the primary, and Latham ran for the House. In the general election, he beat a Democrat who had served on an advisory panel for Hillary Clinton's health care proposals, 61%-39%.

In the House, Latham has a moderately conservative record. He is a close confidant of Speaker John Boehner of Ohio, and worked to help elect him to the party leadership, despite their differences on some issues. (Boehner does not seek earmarks for his district or state while Latham is an energetic earmarker.) In recent years, perhaps because of his alliance with Boehner, Latham has been more outspoken on national issues. He fiercely opposed the $787 billion economic stimulus bill in 2009, which he called "out-of-control spending." And he criticized Democratic leaders for failing to include previously agreed-to changes in Medicare reimbursement rates in their 2009 health care legislation.

With a seat on the Appropriations Committee, Latham long has been a defender of earmarks, working to fund local programs from disaster relief to farm research, including the National Animal Disease Center in Ames. He criticized Iowa's Democratic Sen. Tom Harkin for not persuading his Appropriations colleagues to complete the center, which he described as essential to "agro-terrorism" prevention. In 2007, after a local Navy officer died in Iraq, Latham pushed to passage a law to permit grandparents and other family members to get the military death benefit if they assume custody of a dead soldier's children. Earlier, he worked with Senate Republicans to give Reserve and National Guard soldiers the same health benefits as regular military personnel.

As the ranking Republican on the Transportation and Housing Appropriations Subcommittee, Latham offered an amendment in 2009 to reduce the amount of money a borrower can take out of their home under the federal reverse mortgage program. The committee adopted the amendment, but Democrats altered it to ensure that any money saved would go toward the Housing and Urban Development Department's Section 8 low-income housing program. Another amendment he offered to transfer $3 billion from high-speed rail to the highway trust fund was defeated. In 2009, he tried unsuccessfully to get a ban on Environmental Protection Agency rulemaking on manure into an appropriations bill.

The congressional districts adopted after the 2000 census in Iowa made Latham's district more competitive, and he had serious opposition in 2002 from John Norris, former chief of staff to Democratic Gov. Tom Vilsack. Norris attacked Latham for supporting Republican positions on taxes and health care and raised more than $1 million. But Latham won by a relatively comfortable 55%-43% vote, carrying all 28 counties.

Latham won by increasing margins in the Democratic years of 2006 and 2008 and by more than 2-1 in 2010. In the 2010 election season, he raised over $1 million but spent only $326,000. That gives him a reserve if he faces an unfavorable redistricting plan in 2011 and 2012. Iowa lost a House seat in the reapportionment following the 2010 census, which means that if all five incumbents run, at least two will be thrown into the same district. The Republican state House will presumably reject any plan that places the two Republicans together— Latham and Steve King, from adjacent districts. But Latham could face a contest against Democratic incumbent Leonard Boswell if a new district is centered on Des Moines. Ironically, both originally come from small rural counties rather than from metro Des Moines. Congressional redistricting in Iowa is done by a non-partisan commission, whose plans may be rejected by the legislature and governor.

FIFTH DISTRICT

Steve King (R)

Elected 2002, 5th term; b. May 28, 1949, Storm Lake; home, Kiron; NW MO St. U., 1967-70; Catholic; married (Marilyn); 3 children.

Elected Office: IA Senate, 1996-2002.

Professional Career: King Construction Co. owner, 1975-2002.

DC Office: 1131 LHOB, 20515, 202-225-4426; Fax: 202-225-3193; Web site: steveking.house.gov.

State Offices: Council Bluffs, 712-325-1404; Creston, 641-782-2495; Sioux City, 712-224-4692; Spencer, 712-580-7754; Storm Lake, 712-732-4197.

Committees: *Agriculture:* Department Operations, Oversight & Credit; General Farm Commodities & Risk Management; Livestock, Dairy & Poultry; Nutrition & Horticulture. *Judiciary:* Constitution; Immigration Policy & Enforcement. *Small Business:* Agriculture, Energy & Trade; Contracting & Workforce; Economic Growth, Tax and Capital Access; Healthcare & Technology.

Group Ratings

	ACLU	ACU	ADA	CFG	AFS	FRC	LCV	ITIC	NTU	COC
2010	13	96	5	100	0	93	10	0	89	75
2009	–	96	0	98	0	–	0	–	92	73

National Journal Ratings

	2010 LIB	—	2010 CONS	2009 LIB	—	2009 CONS
Economic	18%	—	81%	5%	—	94%
Social	0%	—	85%	0%	—	93%
Foreign	0%	—	88%	0%	—	75%
Composite	11%	—	89%	7%	—	93%

Key Votes of the 111th Congress

1. Overturn Ledbetter	N	5. Bar federal abortion funds	Y	9. Stop detainee transfers	Y
2. Pass $820 billion stimulus	N	6. Pass health care bill	N	10. Legalize immigrants' kids	N
3. Let guns in national parks	Y	7. Regulate financial firms	N	11. Repeal don't ask, tell	N
4. Pass cap-and-trade	N	8. Pass tax cuts for some	N	12. Limit campaign funds	N

Election Results

2010 general	Steve King (R)	128,363	(66%)	($1,015,039)
	Matthew Campbell (D)	63,160	(32%)	($269,164)
2010 primary	Steve King (R)	unopposed		

Prior Winning Percentages: 2008 (60%), 2006 (59%), 2004 (63%), 2002 (62%)

Population		Race/Ethnicity		Work	
Pop. 2010:	577,453	White:	89.5%	Private:	77.8%
Change since 2000:	Down 1.3%	Black:	1.0%	Government:	12.2%
Urban:	49.4%	Hispanic:	6.9%	Self-employed:	9.7%
Rural:	50.6%	Asian:	1.0%	Blue collar:	27.9%
Area size:	18,431 sq. mi.	Native Am.:	0.5%	White collar:	53.9%
		Hawaiian:	0.1%	Khaki collar:	0.1%
Age		Two+ races:	1.1%	Other:	18.2%
Median age:	40.4 yrs.				
More than 65 yrs:	16.9%	*Ancestry*		Median income:	$45,307
Less than 18 yrs:	24.3%	German	31.0%	Median Home Value:	$98,900
		Irish	11.0%		
Education		English	7.0%	**Military Veterans**	
H.S. grad:	87.8%			% of Pop:	11.5%
College grad:	18.4%				
Grad degree:	5.1%				

West Iowa; Sioux City

Sioux City, one of the oldest market towns on the Great Plains, is nestled in the loess bluffs above the Missouri River. Although still the largest city on the Plains west of Des Moines and north of Omaha, Sioux City has not grown much in the past half-century, and unemployment in the area climbed past 7% during 2010, higher than Iowa's other cities. Its original economic base has become obsolete: The waterfront, once rau-cous with boatmen and stockyard workers, is

2008 Presidential Vote
John McCain (R) 151,188   (54%)
Barack Obama (D) 122,537   (44%)

2004 Presidential Vote
George Bush (R) 167,387   (60%)
John Kerry (D) 109,974   (39%)

Cook Partisan Voting Index: R+9

now quiet. Downtown stores have been replaced by shopping malls at the edge of town, where people spend a day doing a season's shopping and then drive for hours to get home. The stockyards, which employed thousands and slaughtered millions of hogs during their peak years in the 1920s, are shuttered. But there are still many hogs in western Iowa. Instead of meeting sellers in the markets of the Sioux City stockyard, packers now contract directly with large farms and build their modern slaughterhouses nearby. Tyson Foods has facilities in Buena Vista and Crawford counties. Meanwhile, wind farming has grown. Iowa is among the top states generating electricity from wind, over objections from some farmers to the noise and the hazard to birds. All of this helped Sioux City rank 14th on Forbes' 2010 list of best small places for business and careers.

Sioux City is the largest city in the 5th Congressional District, which covers the western part of the state from Minnesota to Missouri and borders South Dakota and Nebraska to the west. This is the state's largest congressional district geographically, the one with the most 4-H members, and the nation's chief hog- and pig-producing district. In recent years, outside investors moved into the district's small towns for large-scale ethanol production. Council Bluffs is home to the man-sion of General Grenville Dodge, who in 1859 lobbied Illinois lawyer Abraham Lincoln on the need for a transcontinental railroad. Lincoln got it through Congress in 1863, Dodge became its chief engineer, and Council Bluffs became its eastern terminus when it was completed in 1869. Sur-rounded by beef grazing territory, Council Bluffs looks west across the Missouri River to Omaha, taking on the culturally more conservative tone of Nebraska and the conservative politics of the *Omaha World-Herald,* despite the presence of three Nevada-style casinos in the city. But Council Bluffs is also developing an economically hip side with Google's opening of a data facility there. This is by far the most Republican district in Iowa, and George W. Bush twice carried it by wide margins. In 2008, McCain won it 54%-44%.

Steve King (R)

The congressman from the 5th District is Steve King, a Republican who first won the seat in 2002. He was born in Storm Lake, in western Iowa, and attended Northwest Missouri State University, though he didn't graduate. In 1975, he founded the King Construction Company. After building up his business, he launched his political career in 1996, at age 47, with his election to the state Senate, where he quickly gained a reputation as an ultraconservative. He opposed abortion rights, racial quotas and preferences, and same-sex marriage. He sponsored Iowa's "God and Country" bill, which required Iowa schools to recognize that the United States "has derived its strength from biblical values," and he was a driving force behind the state's English-only law. On economic matters, King supported repeal of the state's inheritance tax, and backed a 15% state income tax cut and a national right-to-work law.

When the U.S. House seat came open in 2002, there were four main contenders in the Republican primary. King ran as a strong conservative and as the only rural candidate, and called for limiting federal control of local schools. King led in the June primary with 30% of the vote. Because no one candidate received the required 35% of the vote, the nomination was determined by a special party convention three weeks later. The 533 voting delegates needed three ballots to select a winner. King led on each ballot and defeated House Speaker Brent Siegrist of Council Bluffs, 272-253, in the final round. The general election outcome was never in doubt. Democrat Paul Shomshor attempted to paint King as too conservative for the district, and won the endorsement of the *Omaha World-Herald,* but fell far short, 62%-38%. The conservative *National Review* magazine heralded King as the "Great Right Hope."

In the House, King has not been shy about sharing his hyper-partisan views, and gets a fair amount of national press for controversial remarks. Together with Minnesota Republican Michele Bachmann, who has called King her best friend in Congress, he is one of the most vilified conservatives among liberals. He also makes some Republicans uneasy. When King said in June 2010 that President Obama "has a default mechanism in him that breaks down the side of race on the side that favors the black person," Colorado GOP congressional candidate Cory Gardner canceled a fundraiser at which the congressman was to speak.

King has been an outspoken proponent of tougher immigration laws. The House has twice passed his amendment to enforce a 1996 law that forbids localities from standing in the way if police officers want to report immigration information to the federal government. He advocates English as the official language of the United States. In April 2008, an Iowa district court judge ruled in favor of King's challenge to state officials who had placed bilingual voting forms on state websites. A Carroll, Iowa *Daily Times Herald* columnist who assembled some of King's quotes into a book, *King Kong Krazy,* calls him "maniacally nationalistic." King makes no apologies for his style. "We've got to shoot from the hip sometimes," he said of himself and Bachmann. "It's not always 'Ready, aim, fire.' Sometimes it's just time to fire. And you'd better have good instincts so that you can shoot, and it might look later like you didn't shoot from the hip but you took careful aim."

In 2007, King became the ranking Republican on the Judiciary Immigration Subcommittee, which put him in the middle of the high profile debate. He built a model fence on the House floor to show how simple it would be to construct a 2,000-mile fence on the border, and criticized Democrats who voted for the fence while they backed lawsuits to thwart its construction. When the subcommittee passed a bill to permit foreign fashion models into the country for a photo shoot, King called it the "Ugly American Bill" because he said it implied that attractive Americans could not be found for the work. As soon as Republicans formally took control of the House in 2011, King introduced a bill to end birthright citizenship, a controversial idea that had gained currency in conservative circles the previous year but was widely unpopular among Hispanics. "Steve King is positioning our party for disaster," the Latino group Somos Republicans said in a statement. With Republicans in the majority, King was positioned to rise from ranking member to chairman of the Immigration Subcommittee, but the gavel went instead to the less bombastic Elton Gallegly of California. King blamed Speaker John Boehner, whom he said "isn't very aggressive on immigration."

On local issues, King has called for expansion of "value-added agriculture," including biotechnology and ethanol production, to strengthen the local economy. He successfully promoted an expanded tax credit for small ethanol and biodiesel producers as part of the 2005 energy law.

In his re-election bid in 2004, King carried all but one small county and won 63%-37% over Democrat Joyce Schulte. She ran again in 2006, accused him of "racist remarks" on immigration, and lost again, 59%-36%. King refused to debate her, saying that most voters already knew his views. After endorsing Republican Fred Thompson for president in 2008, he said in March that "radical Islamists and their supporters will be dancing in the streets" if Barack Obama won. John McCain's campaign condemned those remarks, but King declined to apologize. His constituents haven't minded his boisterousness, continuing to re-elect him comfortably. He briefly considered a bid for Iowa governor in 2010 and appears likely to explore higher office in the future, if only to get a bigger megaphone for his views.

★ KANSAS ★

The flat land of Kansas seems to invite the sort of storms that uprooted Dorothy's life in the children's classic *The Wonderful Wizard of Oz*. In May 2007, a 205-mile-per-hour tornado—rated EF-5, the most dangerous category—destroyed the town of Greensburg, killing 10 people and prompting Democratic Gov. Kathleen Sebelius to complain that desperately needed National Guard equipment was tied up in Iraq. In this tragedy, there is an echo of Kansas's chief claim to literary fame; in the 1939 film, based on L. Frank Baum's 1900 novel, the Kansas from which Dorothy and Toto are swept by a tornado is shown in dreary black-and-white, in contrast to the brilliant Technicolor of Oz. Thomas Frank, author of the best-selling *What's the Matter With Kansas?*, seemed to get it right when he said, "Kansas may be the land of averageness, but it is a freaky, militant, outraged averageness." For the history of seemingly placid Kansas—it actually is flatter than a pancake, geographers announced in 2004 after comparing its topography to an IHOP product—has been punctuated by uprisings, intellectual and violent, by episodes of anger and rage sweeping through the tall sheaves like a tornado wind. The state's history began in a moment of violence, the Bleeding Kansas of the 1850s that led proximately to the terrible war that split the entire nation. The trigger was the Kansas-Nebraska Act of 1854, which left to local settlers the question of whether this new Kansas Territory would be a free or slave state. Pro-slavery "bushwhackers" rode over the line from Missouri, stealing elections and writing a pro-slavery constitution. But much larger numbers of free-soil "jayhawkers," from New England and the New England-Yankee-settled Great Lakes states, put down roots and, despite the massacres of the mad John Brown, prevailed and established their own law and order. This was a civil war before the Civil War, and, as Wichita State University historian Charles Miner points out, one conducted by literate people who produced mountains of documents that have not been fully mined by historians.

Kansas's effect on national politics was tumultuous. The Democratic Party was split on the slavery issue, the Republican Party was created, and the nation was plunged into civil war. The ultimate effect on Kansas was calming: The antislavery majority bent the soil to the plow and built small towns with sturdy networks of schools, churches, and colleges. But the rebellious impulse did not totally die out. Kansans' livelihoods were always at risk: Hailstorms, grasshopper invasions, dry seasons or a drop in world farm prices could mean disaster for thousands of families. The high rainfall of the 1880s attracted hundreds of thousands of new settlers to Kansas. The low rainfall of the 1890s produced a bust and a populist rebellion. "What you farmers should do," said orator Mary Ellen Lease, "is to raise less corn and more hell." For a few years in the 1890s, and then in the farm rebellions of the 1930s, 1950s and 1970s, Kansans did, but afterwards, the state always returned to jayhawker Republicanism.

Kansas remains mostly Republican in the 21st century, but not in quite the same old way. Russell, the home town of its most famous recent politician, Bob Dole, is a small county seat way out on the plains. But Kansas' population is increasingly metropolitan. Two-thirds of Kansans live in just 10 of the state's 105 counties, and they include the population centers of Kansas City, Lawrence, Topeka, and Wichita. A majority of Kansans live in or within easy reach of metropolitan Kansas City, which has a diverse economy that is by no means dependent on farming.

At the same time, some small towns on the plains are suffering, their city halls and post offices sometimes padlocked and their high schools closed because of low enrollment. Some towns have bought land to be distributed free to homesteaders. The state promotes agritourism at buffalo ranches and the wild Tallgrass Prairie. But new office complexes and corporate headquarters are rising amidst the affluent suburbs of Johnson County. The smaller metropolitan area of Wichita, while less diversified, has an economy built on its role as the world's leading producer of small airplanes. Many World War II planes were built in Wichita, and today Cessna, Bombardier Learjet, Gulfstream, Spirit and other firms make more than half the general aviation aircraft in the world, though during the recession, they got competition from Honda Aircraft Company and Brazil's Embraer. Hispanics have been flocking to work in meatpacking factories in towns like Dodge City, Garden City, and Liberal. Kansas' population is now nearly 11% Hispanic and in some meatpacking towns, almost all the schoolchildren are from Latino homes.

These demographic shifts have had political consequences. Some 40% of Kansas' votes in 2010 were cast in the mostly suburban counties from Kansas City west to Topeka and another 26% in Wichita's Sedgwick County. If rural Kansas once produced farm rebellions, these urban and suburban Kansans have produced their own kind of commotion. For most of the last two decades, Kansas had in effect three-party politics—conservative Republicans versus moderate Republicans

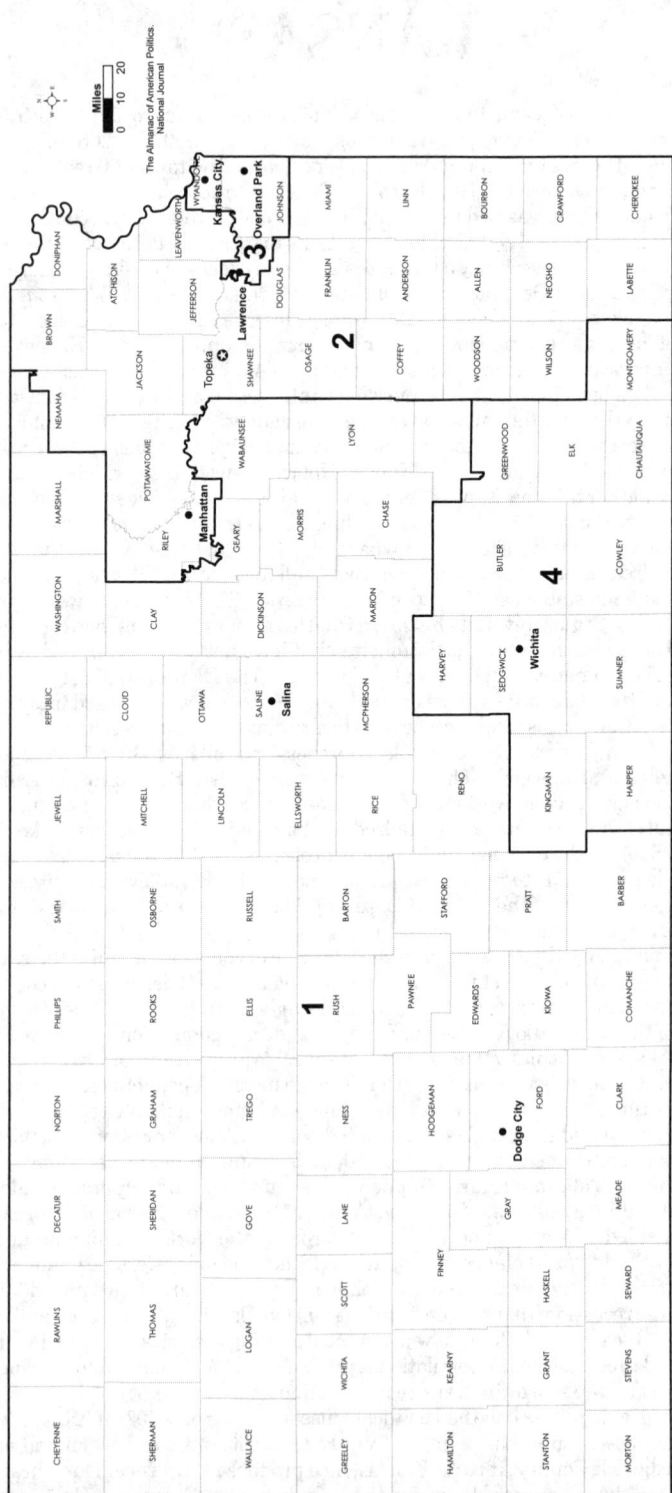

The Almanac of American Politics.
National Journal

Congressional district boundaries were first effective for 2002.

versus Democrats—and fought a kind of culture war over abortion rights and the teaching of evolution in the schools. Moderate Republican Bill Graves, pro-abortion rights and pro-gun control, was elected governor in 1994 and 1998, but conservative Republicans won a majority on the state Board of Education and in 1999 issued guidelines that treated evolution as a theory. There was a national uproar and for a time elections to this once obscure board featured fierce fights, mostly in Republican primaries. In February 2007, the board repealed the guidelines. The Republican family battles created opportunities for Democrats, who captured the 3rd Congressional District seat in 1998 by beating a conservative who'd alienated suburban moderates, and won the governorship in 2002 when Democratic Insurance Commissioner Kathleen Sebelius beat conservative Treasurer Tim Shallenburger.

But elections have rarely succeeded in settling the ideological warfare. In office, Sebelius vetoed plans to build coal-fired power plants in southwestern Kansas, out of concern for climate change, and Republicans tried but failed to override her veto. Her battle with state Republicans over abortion rights was the fiercest of all, and the bitter divisions over the issue in Kansas had tragic unintended consequences. Sebelius vetoed a bill for stricter regulation of abortion clinics, while Republican Attorney General Phillip Kline sought the records from Dr. George Tiller, a Wichita physician who performed late-term abortions. In 2006, Sebelius recruited former Republican state Chairman Mark Parkinson to be her running mate and won 58%-40%, while Kline lost 59%-41% to a former Republican, Johnson County District Attorney Paul Morrison, who switched parties. Kline, appointed Johnson County District Attorney, sought to bring charges against Tiller for performing late-term abortions without a sign-off from a second doctor with no common financial interests, but a grand jury declined to bring an indictment. Kline lost in the August 2008 Republican primary. Tiller was murdered in May 2009 by an anti-abortion activist, who shot him in the head while Tiller attended church services.

In March 2009, President Obama appointed Sebelius as his secretary of Health and Human Services. Parkinson stepped up to fill the remainder of her term, but made it clear he would not run for a full term. After their advances in the previous decade, Kansas' Democrats and moderate Republicans were no match for the GOP wave of 2010. Sen. Sam Brownback, a cultural conservative who ran briefly for president in 2008, was the Republican nominee. No serious opponent appeared in the GOP primary or general election, and he won 63%-32%. The contest for Brownback's Senate seat was between two Republican House members: western Kansas' Jerry Moran beat Wichita's Todd Tiahrt 50%-45%. Kansas hasn't elected a Democratic U.S. senator since 1932—the

Population		Household Income		Work	
Pop. 2010:	2,853,118	Under $15k:	12.2%	Private:	75.8%
State rank:	33rd	$15k to $50k:	39.0%	Government:	17.2%
Change since 2000:	Up 6.1%	$50k to $100k:	32.0%	Self-employed:	6.8%
Urban:	71.0%	$100k to $200k:	13.9%	Unemployment (3-yr. average):	3.9%
Rural:	29.0%	Over $200k:	2.9%	Poverty:	12.1%
Native of state:	58.8%	Median income:	$48,767	Blue collar:	22.9%
Not a citizen:	4.0%			White collar:	59.7%
Area size:	82,278 sq. mi.	**Home Value**		Khaki collar:	0.6%
		Under $100k:	40.1%	Other:	16.8%
Most populous cities		$100k to $300k:	51.0%		
Wichita	382,368	$300k to $500k:	6.5%	**Age**	
Overland Park	173,372	$500k to $1 mil:	2.0%	Median age:	35.9 yrs.
Kansas City	145,786	Over $1 million:	0.5%	More than 65 yrs:	13.0%
Topeka	127,473	Median:	$123,600	Less than 18 yrs:	25.0%

Race/Ethnicity				Military Veterans		Registered Voters in 2010	
White:	78.2%	*Language*		% of Pop:	10.8%	Democrats:	460,318
Black:	5.7%	English:	90.0%			Republicans:	744,975
Hispanic:	10.5%	Spanish:	6.6%	*Veterans by Period*		Ind./other:	501,505
Asian:	2.3%	Asian:	1.5%	WWII and before:	10.9%	Voter turnout:	857,658
Native Am.:	0.8%	Other European:	1.5%	Korea:	10.9%	Turnout as % of	
Hawaiian:	0.1%			Vietnam:	33.7%	voting age:	40.3%
Two+ races:	2.3%	**Education**		Gulf (pre-2001):	12.1%		
		H.S. grad:	89.4%	Gulf (post-2001):	9.5%	**Legislature**	
Ancestry		College grad:	29.3%	Peace time:	22.9%	Senate:	8 D 32 R
German	24.2%	Grad degree:	10.0%			House:	33 D 92 R
Irish	11.0%						
English	8.7%						

longest such period of any state—and it didn't this time. Moran won the general election 70%-26%, carrying 103 of 105 counties. Republican Lynn Jenkins ousted a Democrat from the 2nd District seat in 2008, and Republican Kevin Yoder won the seat of retiring 3rd District Rep. Dennis Moore in 2010, 58%-39%. Also that year, Republicans won all of the statewide offices and increased their already large margins in both houses of the legislature.

Author Frank argues that Kansas voters have been hornswoggled into voting against their economic interests by big business operatives. That's not an entirely accurate picture. His hometown, which he cites as evidence of economic decline, is in booming Johnson County. Kansas' unemployment rate has been well below the national average; its economy, with large agriculture, energy and aircraft sectors, withstood the recession far better than those in many other states. Anyway, lots of other voters—liberals on the Upper East Side of New York, for example—sometimes vote against their short-term economic interests, because cultural issues are more important to them. Kansas voters in 2010 seemed far less fixated on cultural issues than in past years, and strongly united in their opposition to the policies of Obama and the Democratic Congress.

Presidential politics   Except for 1964, when it narrowly favored Lyndon Johnson over Barry Goldwater, Kansas has voted Republican for president for three-quarters of a century. In 2000 and 2004, George W. Bush carried 103 of its 105 counties, losing only those containing the old industrial city of Kansas City and the university town of Lawrence. Some polls showed the 2008 race could be closer, especially if Gov. Sebelius were the Democratic vice presidential nominee. John McCain won by a solid but not overwhelming 57%-42% margin, carrying 102 of 105 counties. He lost the two that had gone for John Kerry, plus Crawford County in the southeast. In 1996, the state legislature voted to cancel the April presidential primary, and none has been held since.

2008 Presidential Vote		
John McCain (R) 699,655	(57%)
Barack Obama (D) 514,765	(42%)

2008 Presidential Primary		
Mike Huckabee (R)..................11,627	(60%)
John McCain (R) 4,587	(24%)
Ron Paul (R) 2,182	(11%)

2008 Presidential Primary		
Barack Obama (D) 27,172	(74%)
Hillary Clinton (D)....................9,462	(26%)

2004 Presidential Vote		
George W. Bush (R)...............736,456	(62%)
John Kerry (D) 434,993	(37%)

Congressional districting   In 2002, Republicans had full control of redistricting in Kansas for the first time since the 1960s, but did not use it to partisan advantage. Why? As one legislator put it, "What's ground zero with reapportionment? I'd say it's Lawrence." In the previous plan, Lawrence, midway between Kansas City and Topeka and home of the University of Kansas, was in the 3rd District captured by Democrat Dennis Moore in 1998 and held by him in 2000. The 3rd District had to shed 61,000 people, and the obvious partisan move was to remove Lawrence, which Moore carried by wide margins, and place it in the heavily Republican 2nd District, where incumbent Republican Jim Ryun was thought to be unbeatable. But Lawrence civic leaders insisted that Lawrence be kept together in the 3rd District—they wanted the university to be in the same district as its hospital in Kansas City—and Republicans in the state House in March 2002 passed a plan splitting the city but keeping most of it, including the university, in the 3rd. The state Senate in April 2002 passed a different plan, promoted by national Republicans, which extended the western 1st District all the way to the southeast corner of the state. But the House's plan prevailed and was adopted in June.

112th Congress Lineup	
4 R	0 D
111th Congress Lineup	
3 R	1 D

After the 2010 census, Republicans again have control of the redistricting process. Three of the state's four Republican congressmen are freshman; the other is Jenkins, who captured the 2nd District from Democrat Nancy Boyda in 2008. The question is, will Lawrence once again demand to be united with Kansas City in a 3rd District dominated by Johnson County?

Governor

Sam Brownback (R)

Elected 2010, term expires Jan. 2015, 1st term; b. Sept. 12, 1956, Garnett; home, Topeka; KS St. U., B.S. 1978, U. of KS, J.D. 1982; Catholic; Married (Mary); 5 children.

Elected Office: U.S. House of Reps., 1994–96; U.S. Senate, 1997-2010.

Professional Career: Radio broadcaster, KKSU, 1978–79; Practicing atty., 1982–86, 1993; Prof., KS St. U. Law Schl., 1982–86; Ogden & Leonardville City Atty., 1983–86; KS secy. of agriculture, 1986–93; White House Fellow, Office of USTR, 1990–91.

Office: Capitol, 300 S.W. 10th Ave., Ste. 241S, 66612-1590, 877-579-6757; Fax: 785-368-8788; Web site: governor.ks.gov/home.

Election Results

2010 general	Sam Brownback (R)	530,760	(63%)
	Tom Holland (D)	270,166	(32%)
	Andrew Gray (Lib)	22,460	(3%)
2010 primary	Sam Brownback (R)	263,920	(82%)
	Joan Heffington (R)	57,160	(18%)

Prior Winning Percentages: Senate: 2004 (69%); 1998 (65%); 1996 (54%); House: 1994 (66%)

The governor of Kansas is Sam Brownback, a Republican elected in 2010 after spending two years in the U.S. House and 12 in the Senate.

Brownback grew up on a farm in Anderson County, some 50 miles south of Kansas City; he has family roots in Osawatomie, a center of evangelical abolitionism in Kansas in the 1850s. He was state president of Future Farmers of America while in high school and student body president at Kansas State University. He worked briefly as a farm broadcaster before graduating from law school at the University of Kansas. He practiced law for four years in Manhattan, Kan., and then was appointed secretary of the state Board of Agriculture in 1986, serving until it was abolished in 1993. Brownback was a White House fellow, working from 1990 to 1991 for Special Trade Representative Carla Hills. In March 1994, when 2nd District Rep. Jim Slattery, a Democrat, ran for governor, Brownback announced his candidacy for the seat, condemning "a welfare system that discourages the work ethic and encourages the disintegration of families, and a government that can't say no to spending or yes to reform." He won the primary 48%-35% over Bob Bennie, who campaigned as a strong opponent of abortion rights. In the general election, Brownback defeated John Carlin, who was governor from 1978 to '86, by carrying every county in a 66%-34% win.

Brownback was among the "revolutionary" Republican freshmen in 1995 who tried to shake up Congress. He headed a group called the "New Federalists," which sought to abolish three Cabinet departments, and he denounced "influence peddling" in Washington. As the immigration issue heated up, he played a key role in separating the debate over illegal immigration from discussion of legal immigration, which led to passage of a tough measure against illegal immigrants but no major reductions in the number of legal immigrants. In 1995, he had a melanoma removed, and this brush with a fatal disease led him toward a deeper faith. "I did a lot of internal examination. My conclusion was that if this were to be terminal, at that point in time I would not be satisfied with how I had lived life," he told *The Weekly Standard* magazine. An evangelical Christian, Brownback later converted to Catholicism, with Sen. Rick Santorum of Pennsylvania as his sponsor; on Sundays in Topeka he attends both Catholic mass and a service at the Topeka Bible Church. Brownback believes that the nation has "re-engaged with its faith" in a spiritual revival. At a prayer breakfast, he apologized to Sen. Hillary Rodham Clinton of New York for having despised her and her husband years earlier when President Bill Clinton was in office. He also described washing the feet of a staffer at a farewell party to demonstrate respect and humility.

In May 1996, Republican Bob Dole of Kansas, in the midst of his presidential campaign, made the surprise announcement that he would resign from the Senate that June. Two days later, Brownback said he would seek the seat. But Republican Gov. Bill Graves chose a fellow moderate, Lt. Gov. Sheila Frahm, to fill the vacancy until the election, setting up a primary contest between Frahm and conservative Brownback. There were strong differences between the two: She favored abortion rights; he did not. Brownback accused her of voting as a state legislator to raise taxes by

$500 million; she criticized his "slash-and-burn" approach to federal spending. Brownback won the August primary, 55%-42%.

In the fall race for the remaining two years of Dole's term, Brownback faced Democrat Jill Docking, a Wichita stockbroker and the wife of a former lieutenant governor whose father and grandfather both served as governor. Docking promised "Kansas common sense" and likened herself to Nancy Landon Kassebaum, a prominent moderate Republican who represented Kansas in the Senate for nearly 20 years. Brownback campaigned on the three R's: "Reduce, reform, and return. Reduce the size and scope of the federal government. Reform the Congress. Return to the basic values that built the country: Work and family and the recognition of a higher moral authority." He promised to serve only two terms. Both candidates spent liberally, and some fall polls showed the race to be close. But Brownback won by a convincing 54%-43%.

Brownback had a mostly conservative voting record. He sponsored bills to require doctors to tell women seeking abortions that fetuses can feel pain and to bar doctors from prescribing controlled drugs for use in assisted suicides. In 2005, after the Janet Jackson "wardrobe malfunction" at the Super Bowl, the Senate passed his bill raising the maximum fine on broadcasters for indecency from $32,500 to $325,000. With Rep. John Lewis, D-Ga., he worked to authorize the African-American museum on the National Mall, and with Sen. Byron Dorgan, D-N.D., he sponsored a resolution apologizing to American Indians for past government misdeeds. To the dismay of many conservatives, Brownback was a leading co-sponsor of the immigration bill that passed in the Senate in 2006 and established a guest worker program.

On foreign policy issues, he led the fight to bring attention to the Sudanese civil war, called for $100 million to promote democracy in Iran and pushed for action to combat AIDS and malaria in Africa. Brownback supported the Bush administration on the Iraq war until he made a trip there in early 2007. "I do not believe that sending more troops to Iraq is the answer," he said. "Iraq requires a political rather than a military solution." After meeting with Iraqi officials and U.S. military leaders, he called for Iraq to be divided into three relatively autonomous zones.

Brownback was elected to a full, six-year term in 1998 on a 65%-32% vote after well-known Democrats declined to run. In 2004, Democrats again had a hard time finding a candidate to run against him, and he was re-elected 69%-27%, carrying 104 of Kansas's 105 counties.

After that election, conservatives encouraged Brownback to run for president. He made several trips to Iowa, where, he hoped, his background in agriculture and his strong religious convictions would resonate with Republican caucus-goers. He eventually waded into the 2008 contest, offering himself as "a full-scale, Ronald Reagan conservative....My positions are at the heart of where the Republican Party is." His platform included Social Security privatization and support for the development of alternative fuel vehicles. But, lagging in the polls and in fundraising, he was unable to break out of the pack of Republican candidates. Brownback's moment of truth came at the Iowa straw poll in August 2007, when he finished third with 15% behind former Arkansas Gov. Mike Huckabee. *National Review* editor Rich Lowry wrote that Brownback's candidacy had reached the point of "extreme pointlessness," and he withdrew, later endorsing Sen. John McCain of Arizona, who became the nominee.

In the 111th Congress (2009-10), Brownback was the ranking Republican on the Joint Economic Committee, where he was a staunch critic of Obama's spending policies, blasting the president's creation in 2010 of a national debt commission as "mere political window dressing." On the Energy Committee, he agreed in 2009 to support a comprehensive energy bill crafted by Democratic Chairman Jeff Bingaman of New Mexico that included a renewable electricity mandate opposed by other Republicans. His work on the Foreign Relations Committee drew criticism when, in the summer of 2010, he held up Frank Ricciardone's nomination as ambassador to Turkey, complaining about his human rights record in Iraq and Egypt. Obama eventually gave Ricciardone a recess appointment.

During that period, Brownback was also preoccupied with thoughts of running for Kansas governor. At the time, Mark Parkinson held the post. He was a Republican-turned-Democrat who switched parties in 2006 to run for lieutenant governor as Democratic Gov. Kathleen Sebelius' running mate. He rose to governor when she was appointed Obama's secretary of Health and Human Services in April 2009. But Parkinson had decided not to run for governor in 2010 when Sebelius' original term expired. Once Brownback got into the contest in early 2009, no prominent Democrat emerged to challenge him. The task fell to state Sen. Tom Holland, an information technology consultant.

Brownback first trounced businesswoman Joan Heffington in the August 2010 GOP primary, 82%-18%, and then turned his focus to the general election. He consistently maintained a healthy lead in name recognition, polling and fundraising. He campaigned on a platform of economic growth, with fewer regulations and lower taxes. "We are not creating jobs in this state the way we need to," he said. "Coming out of this recession, if you are not pro-growth, then God help you, because people and businesses are going to move." He proposed creating a new State Office of the Repealer charged with disposing of needless regulations and he promised to revamp the school finance formula.

Holland sought to portray Brownback opponent as a "career Washington politician" with ties to the energy conglomerate Koch Industries of Wichita, a leading financial backer of conservative candidates and causes. But the Republican wave, already a longtime fixture over the Jayhawk State, proved overpowering. Brownback won 63%-32%, with two minor-party candidates splitting the remainder, to become the state's first conservative governor in half a century. He chose as his running mate conservative state Sen. Jeff Colyer, an old friend he had known since their days together as White House fellows.

Senior Senator

Pat Roberts (R)

Elected 1996, term expires 2014, 3rd term; b. April 20, 1936, Topeka; home, Dodge City; KS St. U., B.A. 1958; United Methodist; married (Franki); 3 children.

Military Career: Marine Corps, 1958–62.

Elected Office: U.S. House of Reps., 1980–96.

Professional Career: Co–owner & editor, *The Westsider* (AZ newspaper) 1962–67; A.A., U.S. Sen. Frank Carlson, 1967–68; A.A., U.S. Rep. Keith Sebelius, 1968–80.

DC Office: 109 HSOB, 20510, 202-224-4774; Fax: 202-224-3514; Web site: roberts.senate.gov.

State Offices: Dodge City, 620-227-2244; Overland Park, 913-451-9343; Topeka, 785-295-2745; Wichita, 316-263-0416.

Committees: *Agriculture, Nutrition & Forestry* (RMM). *Ethics (Select). Finance:* Energy, Natural Resources & Infrastructure; Health Care; International Trade, Customs & Global Competitiveness; Taxation & IRS Oversight. *Health, Education, Labor & Pensions:* Children & Families. *Rules & Administration.*

Group Ratings

	ACLU	ACU	ADA	CFG	AFS	FRC	LCV	ITIC	NTU	COC
2010	7	96	0	93	3	95	0	67	97	100
2009	–	96	5	93	0	–	18	–	84	67

National Journal Ratings

	2010 LIB	—	2010 CONS	2009 LIB	—	2009 CONS
Economic	18%	—	81%	11%	—	87%
Social	0%	—	79%	17%	—	81%
Foreign	0%	—	72%	0%	—	84%
Composite	14%	—	86%	13%	—	87%

Key Votes of the 111th Congress

1. Overturn Ledbetter	N	5. Pass health care bill	N	9. Ratify New START	N
2. Pass $787 billion stimulus	N	6. Regulate financial firms	N	10. Confirm Elena Kagan	N
3. Repeal DC gun laws	Y	7. Pass tax cuts for some	N	11. Stop EPA climate regs	Y
4. Confirm Sonia Sotomayor	N	8. Legalize immigrants' kids	N	12. Repeal don't ask, tell	N

Election Results

2008 general	Pat Roberts (R)	727,121	(60%)	($6,506,851)
	Jim Slattery (D)	441,399	(36%)	($1,677,905)
	Randall Hodgkinson (Lib)	25,727	(2%)	
2008 primary	Pat Roberts (R)	unopposed		

Prior Winning Percentages: 2002 (83%); 1996 (62%); House: 1994 (77%); 1992 (68%); 1990 (63%); 1988 (100%); 1986 (75%); 1984 (76%); 1982 (68%); 1980 (62%)

Republican Pat Roberts is the state's senior senator, first elected in 1996. His abolitionist great-grandfather "arrived in Kansas with a flat-bed press, a six-gun and a Bible" and founded Kansas' second-oldest newspaper, the *Oskaloosa Independent*. His father, Wes Roberts, was briefly Republican National Committee chairman during the Eisenhower years. Pat Roberts graduated from

Kansas State University with a journalism degree. He served four years in the Marine Corps, then spent five years running a weekly newspaper in the suburbs of Phoenix. Starting in 1967, he worked for two years as an aide to Sen. Frank Carlson, R-Kan. and then 12 years as chief aide to 1st District Rep. Keith Sebelius, R-Kan., the father-in-law of Health and Human Services Secretary and former Gov. Kathleen Sebelius. When Keith Sebelius retired in 1980, Roberts won the make-or-break GOP primary with 56% of the vote in a three-way contest, and then went on to easily win the general election. For 14 years, he was in the minority party in the House. He concentrated on farm issues, learning their intricacies and minutiae, and traveling in a van to keep in touch with constituents in a district so large it took two weeks to visit every county seat. His voting record was moderate, and he looked after Kansas' interests.

In 1995, after Republicans won majority control of Congress for the first time in 40 years, Roberts became chairman of the House Agriculture Committee. He had long believed that the huge subsidies of the early 1980s would never return. Faced with tight Republican budget parameters, Roberts drafted the so-called Freedom to Farm bill designed to phase out subsidies over seven years. In September 1995, his bill failed in committee when Southern Republicans, eager to protect cotton, rice and peanut subsidies, voted against it. Two months later, Roberts persuaded Agriculture conferees to include most of his bill in the 1996 budget reconciliation bill, which President Bill Clinton vetoed. To attract more support, Roberts agreed to maintain cotton and rice marketing loans and managed to preserve the popular Conservation Reserve Program. But overall, his legislation was the biggest change in agriculture policy since the New Deal of 1933. Roberts' revised bill passed the Agriculture Committee 29-17 in January 1996, the full House in February, and became law in April.

A Senate seat came open when in November 1995 Republican Nancy Landon Kassebaum announced her retirement. Although Roberts enjoyed considerable power as a committee chairman, the Republicans had imposed term limits on chairmen, and the Freedom to Farm law diminished the Agriculture Committee's portfolio. In early 1996, Roberts announced his candidacy and went on to win the August primary with an overwhelming 78% of the vote in a four-way race. In the general election, he faced Democratic state Treasurer Sally Thompson and won easily, 62%-34%. Thus Roberts became the first House member to give up a committee chairmanship to run for the Senate since Lister Hill in 1938 (and Hill got appointed to his Senate seat).

In the Senate, Roberts got on the Agriculture Committee and continued his focus on farm issues. The Freedom to Farm Act worked well in 1997, and farmers seemed to do fine with a much diminished government role in their businesses. But in 1998, crop prices plunged—in line with a long trend of falling prices for basic commodities—and some farmers demanded a return to the old system. Roberts resisted, and bills were passed to accelerate $4.5 billion in payments and to give farmers an extra $4 billion in disaster assistance. In 2000, the pattern continued. Roberts argued that increased subsidies for crop insurance would mean less need for yearly assistance and that limiting production would not raise prices because the U.S. accounts for less than one-fifth of world production. The problem seemed intractable. The number of family farmers continued to fall in places like western Kansas, where farm communities were disappearing, yet prices were not sufficient to maintain many operations.

Freedom to Farm came up for reauthorization in 2002, and this time, Democrats were in control of the Senate. Roberts was not chairman but the fifth-ranking member of the minority on the committee. He admitted that the Freedom to Farm Act "didn't work out as anybody would have hoped" and, with Mississippi Republican Thad Cochran, he pushed for farm savings accounts. But their proposal was rejected in favor of Chairman Tom Harkin's approach: Revival of countercyclical subsidies when crop prices are low, plus a larger Conservation Reserve Program, which paid farmers not to farm their land in order to protect environmentally sensitive areas. Harkin prevailed on the Senate floor 58-40 in February 2002. Roberts wasn't even on the conference committee. "This policy fails farmers," he said. He argued that it would provide no aid when production was low and crop prices rose, which is exactly what happened when drought struck the Great Plains in the summer of 2002.

Roberts has tried to encourage farm exports in many ways, opposing cargo preferences and urging expanded powers for the president to negotiate trade deals and replenishment of International Monetary Fund funds. He was a lead sponsor of the 2000 law to end the embargo on food to Cuba, and he and fellow Kansas Sen. Sam Brownback sponsored the 1999 law allowing the president to lift the embargo on India and Pakistan. Roberts supported normalizing trade relations with China. When the farm bill came up for reauthorization in 2007, Roberts pressed for maintaining protections against losses from weather and market fluctuations for producers of major commodities—wheat, corn and soybeans. "Somebody has to press the case for production agriculture. They are the people who are really responsible for our food supply," he told the *Topeka Capital-Journal*, not those in "Walden Pond agriculture," a reference to competing bids for government subsidies from fruit- and vegetable-growing states. Roberts moved successfully in committee to amend one farm program in a way that prevented corn growers from getting reductions in crop insurance at the expense of wheat growers in Kansas and other states.

In the early 2000s, Roberts gave up the ranking minority position on Agriculture to be the top Republican on the Intelligence Committee. But he remained active in farm policy. He once quipped, "When you're from Kansas, you're not appointed to (the Agriculture Committee). You're sentenced to it." In the 112th Congress (2011-12), he is again the ranking Republican on the committee.

Roberts' other major sphere of influence is national security. In 1999, as the new chairman of the Emerging Threats and Capabilities Subcommittee on Armed Services, he held hearings probing the nation's vulnerability to terrorists and he presciently asserted that targets would be "selected for their symbolic value, like the World Trade Center in the heart of Manhattan." He was particularly immersed in the issue of intelligence gathering as the Intelligence chairman when Republicans controlled the Senate. But the panel grew increasingly partisan and therefore less productive. In 2003, Roberts resisted Democratic calls for an investigation of how Bush administration officials used intelligence on Iraq, prompting Democrats to try to circumvent him in the release of pre-war intelligence data

But over time, both sides on the committee arrived at the conclusion that pre-war intelligence was deeply flawed. In the summer of 2004, committee members led by Roberts unanimously criticized intelligence-gathering on Iraq and concluded that the Central Intelligence Agency had not seriously considered the possibility that Iraqi leader Saddam Hussein had no weapons of mass destruction. Roberts proposed that the Intelligence panel take over from the Armed Services Committee oversight of Defense Department intelligence operations, but the proposal was predictably resisted. Later, a bipartisan reorganization of intelligence operations was undertaken by the Senate Governmental Affairs Committee.

The New York Times touched off another partisan battle in the committee when it reported in December 2005 that the National Security Agency was secretly monitoring contacts between al Qaeda suspects abroad and people in the United States. Democrats led by Sen. Jay Rockefeller of West Virginia sought a committee investigation, while Roberts insisted that the program was not only within the president's constitutional powers but "legal, necessary and reasonable." In March 2006, the committee voted along party lines not to conduct an investigation into the domestic surveillance program but to establish a seven-member panel charged with that responsibility. Roberts complained that some Democrats "believe the gravest threat we face is not Osama bin Laden and al Qaeda, but rather the president of the United States." Roberts rotated off the committee in early 2007.

After President Obama took office, Roberts staunchly opposed sending detainees at Guantanamo Bay, Cuba to Fort Leavenworth in Kansas. "Not in our backyard. Not in Kansas. Not on my watch," he said in May 2009. He and Brownback placed holds on executive branch appointees to the Defense and Justice departments to pressure the Pentagon to block the proposed transfers, and the idea eventually died.

Roberts has worked with Democrats on some issues. In recent years, he worked with Harkin and Edward Kennedy of Massachusetts to limit consumer advertising on risky prescription drugs. He opposed Republican-inspired cuts in Medicare reimbursement rates for doctors, and told Treasury Secretary Henry Paulson in February 2008 that Medicare cuts were "just not gonna happen." He also co-sponsored a bill with Harkin in 2009 to increase special education funding.

The Democrats' health care bill in 2009 and 2010 was another story. In the Finance Committee, Roberts said, "All indications are that this bill will be pulled increasingly toward more cost, more regulations and more rationing as it continues through this process." When HHS Secretary Sebelius said she would have "zero tolerance" for insurers claiming costs were increased by the bill, Roberts was livid. "She is threatening to shut down private companies for exercising their First Amendment right to free speech," he said. "And she is keeping a list. Some have called this 'gangster government.' As a former newspaperman, I am shocked." In the 111th Congress (2009-10), he also opposed Democrat Christopher Dodd's financial regulation bill because he considered it a bailout of failing Wall Street firms.

Roberts' famously edgy rhetoric was aimed at President Obama in May 2010 after a meeting with GOP senators. "The more he talked, the more he got upset. He needs to take a valium before he comes in and talks to Republicans, and just calm down, and don't take anything so seriously," the senator said. "If you disagree with someone, it doesn't mean you're attacking their motives."

Immersion in the issues of the day gets you only so far at home, and Roberts is too savvy and seasoned to neglect the home front. He frequently promotes science and technology projects in

Kansas, including a $450 million national biological defense facility at Kansas State University. After visiting Greensburg just after the town was destroyed by a tornado in 2007, Roberts phoned President George W. Bush and got him to declare Kansas eligible for federal disaster aid. In 2005, he helped make sure that Fort Riley came out of the base-closing process not only still operating, but with additional forces, including the 1st Infantry Division, which moved from Germany to Kansas. He and Brownback got the Senate to agree in October 2009 to $3.5 million for the town of Treece, which was severely contaminated by a lead and zinc mine.

Around Washington, Roberts is known for his caustic but also dead-on sense of humor. He often makes the list of "funniest senators" in *Washingtonian's* biennial poll of congressional staffers. He once complained that he wasn't satisfied with the distinction. "I was lobbying for the 'hottie of the year,' but I can't even get to lukewarm," said the 70-something, utterly bald Roberts. He has compiled a "bucket list" of things to do before he dies. So far, he has succeeded in conducting the Kansas symphony orchestra, and riding, very briefly, a rodeo bull. But he has not yet been able to meet actress Sophia Loren, despite trips to Italy. "She just doesn't answer my calls," he complained.

Roberts had no Democratic opponent in 2002. The next time around, former Rep. Jim Slattery, who had been working as a Washington lawyer and lobbyist since losing a race for governor in 1994, returned to the state to challenge Roberts in 2008. Slattery ran a vigorous campaign, but Roberts, who routinely visits all 105 Kansas counties, spent nearly $7 million and called Slattery a lobbyist, "Gucci loafers and all." He won 60%-36%, running ahead of GOP presidential nominee John McCain in the state. Slattery carried just three counties: Wyandotte (industrial Kansas City), Douglas (the University of Kansas) and Atchison.

Junior Senator

Jerry Moran (R)

Elected 2010, term expires 2016, 1st term; b. May 29, 1954, Great Bend; home, Hays; U. of KS, B.S. 1976, J.D. 1981; Methodist; married (Robba); 2 children.

Elected Office: KS Senate, 1988–96, majority ldr., 1995–96; U.S. House, 1997-2010.

Professional Career: Operations officer, Consolidated State Bank, 1975–77; mgr., Farmers State Bank & Trust Co., 1977–78; practicing atty., 1981–96; instructor, Ft. Hays St. U., 1986.

DC Office: C4-RSOB, 20510, 202-224-6521; Fax: 202-228-6966; Web site: moran.senate.gov.

State Offices: Hays, 785-628-6401; Olathe, 913-393-0711; Topeka, 785-232-2605; Wichita, 316-631-1410.

Committees: *Aging (Special). Appropriations:* Agriculture, Rural Development, Food and Drug Administration & Related Agencies; Financial Services & General Government (RMM); Homeland Security; Labor, Health & Human Services, Education & Related Agencies; Transportation, HUD & Related Agencies. *Banking, Housing & Urban Affairs:* Financial Institutions & Consumer Protection; Housing, Transportation & Community Development; Securities, Insurance & Investment. *Small Business & Entrepreneurship. Veterans' Affairs.*

Group Ratings (House)

	ACLU	ACU	ADA	CFG	AFS	FRC	LCV	ITIC	NTU	COC
2010	13	100	5	88	0	100	0	0	90	71
2009	–	96	5	85	13	–	0	–	84	80

National Journal Ratings (House)

	2010 LIB — 2010 CONS		2009 LIB — 2009 CONS	
Economic	14%	— 86%	24%	— 75%
Social	0%	— 85%	10%	— 90%
Foreign	25%	— 75%	0%	— 75%
Composite	16%	— 85%	16%	— 84%

Key Votes of the 111th Congress (House)

1. Overturn Ledbetter	N	5. Bar federal abortion funds	Y	9. Stop detainee transfers	Y
2. Pass $820 billion stimulus	N	6. Pass health care bill	N	10. Legalize immigrants' kids	N
3. Let guns in national parks	Y	7. Regulate financial firms	N	11. Repeal don't ask, tell	N
4. Pass cap-and-trade	N	8. Pass tax cuts for some	N	12. Limit campaign funds	N

Election Results

2010 general	Jerry Moran (R) 587,175	(70%)	($4,154,081)
	Lisa Johnston (D)..220,971	(26%)	($32,017)
	Michael Dann (Lib)..17,922	(2%)	
2010 primary	Jerry Moran (R) 163,483	(50%)	
	Todd Tiahrt (R) 146,702	(45%)	

Prior Winning Percentages: House: 2008 (82%); 2006 (79%); 2004 (91%); 2002 (91%); 2000 (89%); 1998 (81%); 1996 (73%)

The junior senator from Kansas is Republican Jerry Moran, who won the seat in 2010 after nearly 15 years in the U.S. House. Moran grew up in the tiny town of Plainville on the western plains of Kansas, the son of an oil-field worker and a secretary at the local electric utility. He was known in high school as an ambitious student with a potentially bright future in politics. "I sat in government class and knew that this guy was going to do something," Bonnie Staab, one of his classmates, told *The Hays Daily News* in August. In college, Moran worked as a summer intern for then-Rep. Keith Sebelius, R-Kan., whose son later married current Health and Human Services Secretary Kathleen Sebelius, a former Kansas governor. The job enabled Moran to have a seat at the 1974 impeachment hearings of President Richard Nixon. After graduating with a bachelor's degree in economics, Moran spent four years as a banker. He returned to the University of Kansas to get a law degree, and then practiced law in the town of Hays for 15 years. He also got involved in politics, winning election in 1988 as a state senator and rising to become Senate majority leader in 1995. When 1st District Rep. Pat Roberts, a Republican, ran for the Senate in 1996, Moran stepped into the House race to succeed him. With the help of GOP leaders, he avoided serious primary competition and won with 76% of the vote, which was tantamount to election.

In the House, Moran developed a reputation as a moderate, although he says he sees himself as a traditional Republican. He has sometimes gone his own way on major issues that split the two parties. To the dismay of GOP Speaker Dennis Hastert, he was one of 25 House Republicans who opposed the 2003 GOP Medicare prescription drug bill. Moran said the bill did not do enough to lower prescription drug prices, and he favored a Democratic proposal to give federal officials negotiating authority to lower drug costs. He later joined Democrats in backing an expansion of the Children's Health Insurance Program. He has called for easing restrictions on trade with Cuba, which he said would benefit Kansas's farmers. In 2007, Moran's amendment to ease restrictions on shipments of food and medicine to Cuba passed the House, though it was removed from the final legislation to avoid a veto from President Bush.

As a member of the House Agriculture Committee, he was a defender of the U.S. system of farm subsidies, which brought billions of federal dollars to his district. During the debate over the 2008 farm bill, Moran argued that the legislation was diverting too much money from farm subsidies for nutrition programs and other uses. He also said urban legislators had too much say in the process. "More and more of the farm bill is being written to satisfy the desires of urban constituencies—not by those of us who represent the nation's farmers and ranchers," he said. He voted against the final bill because it contained cuts to federal subsidies for farmers.

Moran also became known for his devotion to meeting with constituents. Each year, he has logged about 50,000 miles visiting every county in the district—no minor task considering that the 66 counties cover an area roughly the size of Illinois. He was re-elected in 1998 with 81% of the vote and did not face another Democratic challenger until 2006, when he got 79%. He resisted state party leaders' pressure to challenge popular Gov. Sebelius in 2006, but decided to run for the Senate when Republican Sam Brownback announced that he would step aside to run for governor.

But he had to first get by Rep. Todd Tiahrt, another Republican House member who wanted the seat. Tiahrt preceded Moran in the House by two years. The two waged a nasty and costly primary race, with their campaigns spending nearly $7 million combined. Tiahrt sought to turn the contest into a referendum on which of them was more conservative, and the candidates battled over endorsements. Former Alaska Gov. Sarah Palin was in Tiahrt's camp and recorded a phone message for him. He also drew the support of former Sen. Rick Santorum of Pennsylvania and Fox News personality Sean Hannity. Moran secured the backing of Sens. John McCain of Arizona, Tom Coburn of Oklahoma, and Jim DeMint of South Carolina, and received most of the major newspaper endorsements. Moran won the contest with 50% of the vote to 45% for Tiahrt, prevailing on the strength of his home base in the state's most Republican district.

The general election was uneventful. Moran faced Democrat Lisa Johnston, an assistant dean at Baker University and a newcomer to politics. Kansas has not elected a Democrat to the Senate since 1932, so Moran had little to fear. He won 70%-26%.

Moran refused to debate Johnston, giving her no opportunity to raise her profile or to be seen as a credible challenger. He spent $6.5 million on his campaign; she was able to raise just $32,000. During the campaign, Moran highlighted his vote against President Obama's $787 billion economic stimulus bill and called for extending the Bush-era tax cuts for all taxpayers. Johnston said the stimulus was working. She took the position that the Bush tax cuts "just aren't sustainable," and said she favored a return to Clinton-era tax rates. Moran also called for repeal of Obama's health care overhaul, while Johnston said she would tinker with it, but leave most of the legislation intact.

One of Moran's first acts as a senator was to join the Senate Tea Party Caucus. The group was formed to capitalize on the momentum of tea party activists during campaigns around the country in 2010. The caucus initially attracted four members: Moran, DeMint, Rand Paul of Kentucky and Mike Lee of Utah.

FIRST DISTRICT

Tim Huelskamp (R)

Elected 2010, 1st term; b. Nov. 11, 1968, Fowler; home, Fowler; Col. of Santa Fe, B.A. 1991; American U., Ph.D. 1995.; Catholic; Married (Angela); 4 children.

Elected Office: KS Senate, 1997-2010.

Professional Career: Farmer, rancher.

DC Office: 126 CHOB, 20515, 202-225-2715; Fax: 202-225-5124; Web site: huelskamp.house.gov.

State Offices: Dodge City, 620-225-0172; Hutchinson, 620-665-6138; Salina, 785-309-0572.

Committees: *Agriculture:* Conservation, Energy & Forestry; General Farm Commodities & Risk Management; Livestock, Dairy & Poultry. *Budget. Veterans' Affairs:* Economic Opportunity.

Election Results

2010 general	Tim Huelskamp (R)	142,281	(74%)	($1,185,350)
	Alan Jilka (D)	44,068	(23%)	($162,130)
	Jack Warner (Lib)	6,537	(3%)	
2010 primary	Tim Huelskamp (R)	34,819	(35%)	
	Jim Barnett (R)	25,047	(25%)	
	Tracey Mann (R)	21,161	(21%)	
	Rob Wasinger (R)	9,296	(9%)	
	Sue Boldra (R)	7,892	(8%)	

Population		Race/Ethnicity		Work	
Pop. 2010:	655,310	White:	79.8%	Private:	71.7%
Change since 2000:	Down 2.5%	Black:	2.2%	Government:	18.4%
Urban:	52.4%	Hispanic:	14.8%	Self-employed:	9.7%
Rural:	47.6%	Asian:	1.1%	Blue collar:	27.1%
Area size:	57,577 sq. mi.	Native Am.:	0.4%	White collar:	53.2%
		Hawaiian:	0.1%	Khaki collar:	0.7%
Age		Two+ races:	1.5%	Other:	19.0%
Median age:	38.6 yrs.				
More than 65 yrs:	16.1%	*Ancestry*		Median income:	$43,017
Less than 18 yrs:	24.4%	German	29.0%	Median Home Value:	$84,100
		Irish	9.0%		
Education		English	8.1%	**Military Veterans**	
H.S. grad:	85.7%			% of Pop:	11.0%
College grad:	19.8%				
Grad degree:	6.2%				

Western Kansas; Salina

"A prairie is not any old piece of flatland in the Midwest," writes Kansas-born reporter Dennis Farney. "No, a prairie is wine-colored grass, dancing in the wind. A prairie is a sun-splashed hillside, bright with wild flowers. A prairie is a fleeting cloud shadow, the song of the meadowlark. It is the wild land that has never felt the slash of the plow." The prairie Farney describes once covered almost all of Kansas. Now only a little virgin prairie can still be found, in the Flint

2008 Presidential Vote		
John McCain (R)	...184,501	(69%)
Barack Obama (D)	...79,638	(30%)

2004 Presidential Vote		
George Bush (R)	...199,554	(72%)
John Kerry (D)	...73,309	(27%)

Cook Partisan Voting Index: R+23

Hills region west and south of Topeka, where you can see 30 miles on a clear day and a waist-deep sea of grass waves in the wind as it did when pioneers on the Santa Fe Trail passed through some 150 years ago. (With such vast expanses, it's little surprise that numerous UFO sightings were reported here in the 1970s.) The 11,000-acre Tallgrass Prairie National Preserve was created in 1996 to protect this unique landscape, and it is the largest privately owned parcel of land in the National Park system. "The Flint Hills do not take your breath away," wrote western folklorist Jim Hoy. "They give you a chance to catch it." Much of the area was grazing land, first for buffalo, then for the cattle driven to Kansas railheads like Abilene and Dodge City in the 1870s and 1880s. This brief moment in history has been recaptured in the Boot Hill Museum of kitschy Dodge City, where Main Street is called Wyatt Earp Boulevard.

After the harsh winter of 1886-87 wiped out the cattle herds, farmers moved in with plows and barbed wire (commemorated in Lacrosse's Barbed Wire Museum), which enabled farmers to keep livestock out of their wheat fields. The farmers also brought Yankee civilization to this vacant landscape—schools and churches and some foreign traditions as well, like the Cathedral of the Plains built by German Catholics. Today, the area's farm-dependent economy is changing as the average age of Kansas farmers approaches 60. Big meatpacking plants in Dodge City, Garden City and Liberal (the "Golden Triangle of meatpacking") have attracted large numbers of Hispanic immigrants, many living in trailer parks. Nearly two-thirds of the schoolchildren in these counties are Hispanic, and Spanish-language radio is prominent. The dairy industry has made something of a comeback, enticed by inexpensive land and labor and abundant feedstocks. Wind farms have grown on prairie land, though some worry that they may disturb the prairie ecosystem.

The 1st Congressional District consists of most of this expanse of Kansas, almost everything west of the Flint Hills and Abilene, the boyhood home of President Dwight Eisenhower. It contains 66 full counties and parts of three others; only the Nebraska's 3rd District has more counties. The "Big First," which stretches 350 miles east from the Colorado border, is roughly the size of Illinois. Population increased from 76,000 people in 1870 to 570,000 in 1890, but it has not grown much since then. Census Bureau figures in 2011 showed it had the smallest population of the four Kansas districts, 655,310 compared to the others, which were all over 700,000. From 1995 to 2009, the district received the second-highest percentage of federal farm subsidies of any congressional district behind North Dakota. Politically, the 1st District is solidly Republican. It voted for George W. Bush by nearly 3-to-1 in 2004, and it voted for John McCain by better than 2-to-1 in 2008. It voted narrowly for Democratic Gov. Kathleen Sebelius, whose late father-in-law, Republican Keith Sebelius, represented the district in the House for 12 years. In the 2010 governor's race, it reverted to form and went heavily for Republican Sam Brownback.

Tim Huelskamp (R)

The new congressman from the 1st District is Tim Huelskamp, a Republican who won the seat of retiring GOP Rep. Jerry Moran. Huelskamp (*HYUELS-kamp*) was born in Fowler, Kan., and from an early age worked on the farm that his grandparents founded in 1925. He was valedictorian of his high school graduating class and was active in 4-H and Future Farmers of America. He said that his "first political realization" was President Carter's imposition of a grain embargo against the Soviet Union in January 1980, when Huelskamp was 11 years old. "I realized that what happens in Washington impacts the prices that we received" as farmers, he recalled. He became enamored of Carter's successor, Ronald Reagan. "He had a way of communicating basic American principles and concerns in a way that people really got it," Huelskamp said. He briefly attended a seminary in Santa Fe, N.M., and later graduated from the College of Santa Fe, working part-time as a budget and legislative analyst for the state government while still in school. He decided to further his studies in government and graduated from American University in Washington in four years with a doctorate in political science, specializing in agricultural policy. He then went back to Fowler to work on the family farm.

In 1996, Huelskamp won a seat in the state Senate, becoming the youngest member there in 20 years. He authored the state's anti-gay marriage amendment that voters passed in 2005, and was active on anti-abortion rights issues. In 2009, Huelskamp called for legislation to deny federal funding used by Planned Parenthood for family planning programs in Kansas. His maverick ways got him in hot water with the Republican leadership, and in 2003, he lost his seat on the Ways and Means Committee; Huelskamp said it was because he opposed wasteful spending, but two state Republican leaders told *The Topeka Capital-Journal* in 2010 he was booted off because he would not work with the leadership.

He initially considered running for the 1st District seat in 2005, but Republican Rep. Jerry Moran decided to run for re-election, and Huelskamp awaited his next chance. That came in 2010, when Moran decided to challenge GOP Sen. Sam Brownback, after Brownback announced he would run for governor.

Huelskamp faced five challengers in the GOP primary, including state Sen. Jim Barnett, who lost the 2008 governor's race to Democrat Kathleen Sebelius; Tracey Mann, a Salina real estate agent; and Rob Wasinger, a former chief of staff to Brownback. The candidates differed little in their conservative message, but Huelskamp distinguished himself by picking up endorsements from the National Rifle Association and former Arkansas Gov. Mike Huckabee. One of his television ads boasted, "He's not one of those weak-kneed Republicans." Huelskamp won with 35% of the vote. Barnett drew 25% and Mann received 21%, while the others were in single digits.

His general election opponent was Democrat Alan Jilka, a former Salina mayor who campaigned as a pragmatic problem-solver. But Huelskamp held a commanding lead in fundraising. He took in more than $1.2 million compared to Jilka's $162,000. The district's conservative tilt assured Huelskamp an easy 74%-23% victory.

In Washington, Huelskamp joined the Tea Party Caucus and landed a seat on the Budget Committee, a rare plum for a freshman and a good platform for his strong views on the need to slash federal spending. "The debt crisis cannot be overstated," he said at a February 2011 town hall meeting. "We're at a crossroads....We need to make some tough decisions on real reform." He also joined the budget task force of the Republican Study Committee, a group of the most conservative House members. Huelskamp voted against a short-term resolution to fund the government in March 2011 while Democrats and Republicans sought to negotiate a budget deal for the rest of the fiscal year. In addition to spending concerns, Huelskamp said he opposed the bill because it failed to specifically rule out money for Planned Parenthood. At least one prominent conservative activist, Grover Norquist of Americans for Tax Reform, questioned whether it was appropriate for the GOP to add such policy questions to a spending fight.

Meanwhile, Huelskamp also raised eyebrows for hiring as his chief of staff a conservative Denver talk show host who lacked Capitol Hill experience but who had worked as an organizer against gay marriage and abortion.

SECOND DISTRICT

Lynn Jenkins (R)

Elected 2008, 2nd term; b. June 10, 1963, Holton; home, Topeka; KS St. U., A.S. 1985; Weber St. U., B.S., 1985; Methodist; divorced; 2 children.

Elected Office: KS House, 1999-2001; KS Senate, 2001-03; KS treasurer, 2003-08.

Professional Career: C.P.A., 1984-98.

DC Office: 1122 LHOB, 20515, 202-225-6601; Fax: 202-225-7986; Web site: jenkins.house.gov.

State Offices: Pittsburg, 620-231-5966; Topeka, 785-234-5966.

Committees: *Ways & Means:* Oversight; Trade.

Group Ratings

	ACLU	ACU	ADA	CFG	AFS	FRC	LCV	ITIC	NTU	COC
2010	19	100	0	100	0	87	0	33	90	88
2009	–	92	5	87	0	–	7	–	82	87

National Journal Ratings

	2010 LIB	—	2010 CONS	2009 LIB	—	2009 CONS
Economic	22%	—	77%	23%	—	76%
Social	0%	—	85%	24%	—	73%
Foreign	0%	—	88%	25%	—	74%
Composite	12%	—	88%	25%	—	75%

Key Votes of the 111th Congress

1. Overturn Ledbetter	N	5. Bar federal abortion funds Y	9. Stop detainee transfers Y
2. Pass $820 billion stimulus	N	6. Pass health care bill N	10. Legalize immigrants' kids N
3. Let guns in national parks	Y	7. Regulate financial firms N	11. Repeal don't ask, tell N
4. Pass cap-and-trade	N	8. Pass tax cuts for some N	12. Limit campaign funds N

Election Results

2010 general	Lynn Jenkins (R)	130,034	(63%)	($1,471,057)
	Cheryl Hudspeth (D)	66,588	(32%)	($29,209)
	Robert Garrard (Lib)	9,353	(5%)	
2010 primary	Lynn Jenkins (R)	41,458	(57%)	
	Dennis Pyle (R)	31,085	(43%)	

Prior Winning Percentages: 2008 (51%)

Population		Race/Ethnicity		Work	
Pop. 2010:	710,047	White:	84.4%	Private:	69.6%
Change since 2000:	Up 5.6%	Black:	4.7%	Government:	23.7%
Urban:	59.8%	Hispanic:	5.8%	Self-employed:	6.5%
Rural:	40.2%	Asian:	1.3%	Blue collar:	23.6%
Area size:	14,318 sq. mi.	Native Am.:	1.2%	White collar:	57.3%
		Hawaiian:	0.1%	Khaki collar:	1.6%
Age		Two+ races:	2.5%	Other:	17.5%
Median age:	36.0 yrs.				
More than 65 yrs:	13.3%	*Ancestry*		Median income:	$45,263
Less than 18 yrs:	23.8%	German	24.8%	Median Home Value:	$116,700
		Irish	12.0%		
Education		English	8.4%	**Military Veterans**	
H.S. grad:	90.5%			% of Pop:	11.9%
College grad:	26.9%				
Grad degree:	9.8%				

East Kansas; Topeka

The green plains of eastern Kansas have seen more than their share of American history. In 1827, on bluffs above the Missouri River, settlers built Fort Leavenworth, famous in later years for its war college and military prison and now the oldest U.S. fort west of the Mississippi. In the 1850s, newly founded towns along the Kansas River and along the Missouri border were the centers of Bleeding Kansas, the name the state took after pro-slavery bushwhackers set up a

2008 Presidential Vote		
John McCain (R)	170,885	(55%)
Barack Obama (D)	134,747	(43%)
2004 Presidential Vote		
George Bush (R)	176,764	(59%)
John Kerry (D)	117,924	(40%)
Cook Partisan Voting Index: R+9		

state capital in tiny Lecompton and anti-slavery New Englanders established their stronghold down the river at Lawrence.

Farther up the river is Manhattan, home of Kansas State University, and Fort Riley, once an outpost against Indians, then a major Army base. In 2005, the Pentagon designated Fort Riley the headquarters of the 1st Infantry Division—the "Big Red One." Like some other towns near military bases, it had above-average rising incomes from 2000 to 2008. Topeka, the state capital, sits on a low bluff above the river and has had some success attracting corporate headquarters, including Payless ShoeSource and Hill's Pet Nutrition. In an earlier era, Topeka's system of legal segregation prompted the 1954 landmark case *Brown v. Board of Education*. Farther south, on the Missouri border, are the hills called "the Balkans," where coal miners of Eastern European origin lived in and near towns such as Pittsburg and Girard that were once a center of American socialism. Clarence Darrow and Upton Sinclair made pilgrimages to the area, and the local paper, *Appeal to Reason*, had a circulation of 750,000 across the nation. Population loss is not as great here as in western Kansas. The area around Lawrence has been growing as, in effect, the perimeter of metropolitan Kansas City. Coal-bed methane gas wells have provided an economic boost to southeast Kansas.

These disparate areas, Topeka and Manhattan, Fort Riley and Fort Leavenworth, the wheat-growing counties and the Balkans—most of eastern Kansas except the Kansas City metropolitan area—make up the 2nd Congressional District. The heritage of most of this area has been Republican ever since the jayhawkers defeated the bushwhackers once the votes were counted honestly in the 1850s. Yet in recent decades, Democrats have been competitive in state races, especially in Topeka. For 20 of the years from 1970 to 1994, Democrats held the 2nd District seat. In the following dozen years, it voted for conservative Republicans, usually by comfortable margins.

Lynn Jenkins (R)

The congresswoman from the 2nd District is Lynn Jenkins, a Republican who won the seat by defeating one-term Democrat Nancy Boyda in 2008. Jenkins was born in Topeka and grew up in the rural town of Holton on a dairy farm. After graduating from college, she worked for close to 15 years as an accountant. She was elected to the state House in 1998 and served one term there and one in the state Senate. In 2002, Jenkins was elected Kansas treasurer and four years later, even as Democratic Gov. Kathleen Sebelius won a second term, she was re-elected. She next set her sights on the 2nd District House seat. In 2006, Boyda had pulled off one of that year's biggest upsets by unseating Republican Jim Ryun, but she was up against the district's Republican tilt.

In the GOP primary Jenkins faced Ryun, who had held the seat for five terms and wanted it back. Many leading Republicans saw Ryun's loss as an anomaly that would be easily corrected in a rematch with Boyda. The contest also fell along the divide between the two long-warring wings of the state Republican party. Ryun was a staunch conservative, while Jenkins had a profile as a pro-business and pro-abortion-rights moderate. Ryun called on Jenkins to sign a "clean campaign pledge," and after she declined, he attacked her for voting to raise taxes in the legislature. But Jenkins effectively turned Ryun's arguments against him. Calling him her "friend" all the way through the primary, she countered that Ryun had run up a large tab in Congress by adding earmarks for special projects to spending bills, and she promised to limit the number of earmarks she sought for the district. Although heavily outspent by Ryun, she eked out a win by just over 1,300 votes. Eager to quash any bitterness from the contest, Ryun heartily endorsed her.

Jenkins still faced an uphill battle in the general election. Boyda had carefully crafted a voting record mostly in line with her constituents' views. The incumbent also sought to distance herself from her party in July 2008 by publicly renouncing the support of the Democratic Congressional Campaign Committee. But Jenkins tied Boyda to liberal House Speaker Nancy Pelosi every chance she got and accused her of supporting tax increases by voting for Democratic budgets that phased out the Bush era tax cuts for high income earners. The strategy paid off. Jenkins won 51%-46%, turning the come-from-behind winner in 2006 into one of the rare Democratic losers of 2008.

Jenkins had a bumpy first term. After criticizing federal spending earmarks during the campaign, Jenkins in April 2009 submitted requests for 23 earmarked projects totaling $68 million to the Appropriations Committee, including $1.5 million for the Great Plains Sorghum Improvement and Utilization Center at Kansas State and $1.3 million for wheat genetics research. The conservative group Club for Growth removed her from its "Sworn Off Earmarks" list. She responded that her pledge "only set rigorous standards for how a congressional member must go about requesting those earmarks," and that she wouldn't seek an earmark without a specific federal purpose. In August 2009, she got more negative publicity at a town hall meeting in Hiawatha. Discussing possible Republican candidates' future prospects, Jenkins said, "Republicans are struggling right now to find the great white hope." She later apologized and said she did not realize the phrase had a negative connotation. She said she was referring to GOP House leaders, not the Republican field of challengers to President Obama in 2012.

Jenkins had an easier time of it when Republican leaders chose her in early 2009 to deliver the party's response to Obama's radio message and specifically his massive economic stimulus bill. Jenkins said that the legislation "was supposed to be about jobs, but it's gone off the rails in practically no time at all, and millions of your tax dollars are being wasted."

Back home, some conservatives were unhappy with Jenkins' record. State Sen. Dennis Pyle challenged her in the 2010 primary, and although he didn't spend a lot of money, he held Jenkins to a 57%-43% win, not a strong percentage for an incumbent in her party's primary. She won the general election easily against Democrat Cheryl Hudspeth, 63% to 32%.

THIRD DISTRICT

Kevin Yoder (R)

Elected 2010, 1st term; b. Jan. 8, 1976, Hutchinson; home, Overland Park; U. of KS, B.A. 1999, J.D. 2002.; Methodist; Married (Brooke).

Elected Office: KS House, 2002-10.

Professional Career: Practicing atty., 2002-10.

DC Office: 214 CHOB, 20515, 202-225-2865; Fax: 202-225-2807; Web site: yoder.house.gov.

State Offices: Kansas City, 913-621-0832.

Committees: *Appropriations:* Commerce, Justice, Science & Related Agencies; Financial Services & General Government; Military Construction, Veterans Affairs & Related Agencies.

Election Results

2010 general	Kevin Yoder (R)	136,246	(58%)	($1,972,243)
	Stephene Moore (D)	90,193	(39%)	($965,853)
	Jasmin Talbert (Lib)	6,846	(3%)	
2010 primary	Kevin Yoder (R)	32,210	(44%)	
	Patricia Lightner (R)	26,695	(37%)	

Population		Race/Ethnicity		Work	
Pop. 2010:	767,569	White:	73.8%	Private:	81.3%
Change since 2000:	Up 14.2%	Black:	8.4%	Government:	13.2%
Urban:	94.7%	Hispanic:	11.0%	Self-employed:	5.4%
Rural:	5.3%	Asian:	3.8%	Blue collar:	15.6%
Area size:	787 sq. mi.	Native Am.:	0.6%	White collar:	69.4%
		Hawaiian:	0.1%	Khaki collar:	0.1%
Age		Two+ races:	2.2%	Other:	14.9%
Median age:	34.4 yrs.				
More than 65 yrs:	10.3%	*Ancestry*		Median income:	$62,170
Less than 18 yrs:	25.3%	German	21.5%	Median Home Value:	$189,700
		Irish	12.0%		
Education		English	9.2%	**Military Veterans**	
H.S. grad:	92.1%			% of Pop:	9.0%
College grad:	43.1%				
Grad degree:	15.0%				

Kansas City

Though its central core is in Missouri, about 40% of metropolitan Kansas City's residents lived west of the state line in Kansas. Some are in Kansas City, Kan., or KCK as it is sometimes called, where the low-lying land near the Missouri River used to house one of the nation's largest stockyards. This is still a working-class town with lots of modest frame houses, new Latino neighborhoods, a large African-American community and a Catholic ethnic neighborhood.

2008 Presidential Vote		
Barack Obama (D)	186,962	(51%)
John McCain (R)	177,564	(48%)
2004 Presidential Vote		
George Bush (R)	186,476	(55%)
John Kerry (D)	150,598	(44%)
Cook Partisan Voting Index: R+3		

Kansas City's Wyandotte County has lost 35,000 people since the 1970s, and is 27% black and 22% Hispanic. South of Kansas City and Wyandotte is Johnson County, which is much more affluent and more than three times the size of Wyandotte. The newer neighborhoods are arrayed along the interstates, as subdivisions have replaced croplands. They have grown to the point that Overland Park, Olathe, Shawnee and Lenexa are among the largest cities in the state. These suburbs are not just residential. The Applebee's restaurant chain is headquartered in Lenexa, and Sprint Nextel is headquartered in Overland Park. Politically, Wyandotte County has an old Democratic-machine style of politics, though its influence has been tempered by the consolidation of city and county governments. Johnson County has long been heavily Republican, but with plenty of moderate and even liberal voters on cultural issues. It has also been a battleground for the fierce fights between the moderate and conservative wings of the Kansas Republican Party, which sometimes benefits the Democrats.

The 3rd Congressional District of Kansas consists of Johnson County, Wyandotte County and a section of Douglas County to the west, including the portion of Lawrence that is home to the University of Kansas campus. The university gets consistently high ratings from *U.S. News and World Report*'s annual survey of colleges. And in 2010, Lawrence was ranked one of the top 10 college communities by the American Institute for Economic Research. With its liberal-leaning academic community, Douglas County was the only one of Kansas' 105 counties to oppose a 2005 state constitutional amendment banning same-sex marriage. The majority of the district residents live in Johnson County, which is expected to become the largest county in metropolitan Kansas City by 2023. This is an affluent metropolitan district in a historically rural state.

Kevin Yoder (R)

The new congressman from the 3rd District in Kansas is Kevin Yoder, a Republican who won the seat in 2010 by defeating Democrat Stephene Moore, the wife of retiring incumbent Dennis Moore, also a Democrat.

Yoder grew up on a farm in the aptly named town of Yoder, founded in 1907 by an Amish settler. His family has been there since the 1880s, and hundreds of Yoders live in the area. His father's farm produces grains, soybeans, corn, and meat. His maternal grandfather, William Alexander, who grew up as a poor farmer, was the Republican mayor of Wilmette, Ill., and president of the Chicago Bar Association. As a child, Yoder recalls visits to his grandfather in downtown Chicago, drawing inspiration from him. Yoder studied English and political science at the University of Kansas, where he was student body president. He was a registered Democrat before undergoing what he calls his own "personal maturation and growth" and switching to become a Republican. During his senior year in college and into law school, he volunteered in campaigns and interned at the state legislature. He worked as a law clerk at the Pentagon in Washington doing counternarcotics work. He left a month before the September 11, 2001, terrorist attacks, an event that inspired him to get more involved with politics. Yoder was elected to the Kansas House in 2002 at age 26, and got a seat on the Appropriations Committee, where he had interned in college. He eventually chaired the committee.

Yoder takes a conventional conservative approach on economic issues, pushing to scale back the government and to cut spending. During the campaign, he called for President George W. Bush's 2001 and 2003 tax cuts to be extended. On cultural issues, he is more moderate, and backs abortion rights. When Dennis Moore announced he would not seek another term, Yoder jumped into the race. His state legislative district, which includes some of Overland Park and the headquarters of Sprint, gave him access to a large donor base, and his acumen at fundraising—more than $800,000 by summer 2010—forced the early GOP front-runner, state Sen. Nick Jordan, the 2008 House nominee, out of the race. Yoder's primary opponents pointed to his party switch as evidence of flip-flopping on issues. But Yoder managed to win the nine-person contest with 44% of the vote. The candidate running hardest to the right, former state Rep. Patricia Lightner, took 37%.

In the fall, both candidates stressed the economy and the federal deficit. Stephene Moore, a nurse, supported President Obama's health care bill while Yoder opposed it. He also came out against reinstating the estate tax, which affects many family farms, while Moore said she favored an estate tax on large inheritances but at lower rates than before. She supported the congressional Democrats' cap-and-trade bill to lower greenhouse gases, while Yoder said it would put the brakes on economic recovery.

Moore also seized on a *Topeka Capital-Journal* report that Yoder refused to take a preliminary breath test during a 2009 traffic stop. Yoder pleaded guilty to refusing a law enforcement officer's request and was fined $165. His campaign said that he wasn't intoxicated and that he refused the test because he had passed a field sobriety test. Moore, meanwhile, was criticized for going too far in running an ad comparing Yoder to celebrities Lindsay Lohan and Mel Gibson. *The Kansas City Star* endorsed Yoder, calling him "quick-witted and thoughtful," and saying he "could be a force in Congress." He won 58% to 39% for Moore.

FOURTH DISTRICT

Mike Pompeo (R)

Elected 2010, 1st term; b. Dec. 30, 1963, Orange, CA; home, Wichita; U.S. Military Academy, B.S. 1986; Harvard U., J.D. 1994.; Presbyterian; Married (Susan); 1 child.

Military Career: Army, 1986-91.

Professional Career: Practicing atty., 1994-96; CEO, Thayer Aerospace, 1996-2006; pres., Sentry Intl., 2006-10.

DC Office: 107 CHOB, 20515, 202-225-6216; Fax: 202-225-3489; Web site: pompeo.house.gov.

State Offices: Wichita, 316-262-8992.

Committees: *Energy & Commerce:* Commerce, Manufacturing & Trade; Energy & Power.

Election Results

2010 general	Mike Pompeo (R)	119,575	(59%)	($2,261,023)
	Raj Goyle (D)	74,143	(36%)	($1,891,733)
	Susan Ducey (Ref)	5,041	(2%)	
	Shawn Smith (Lib)	4,624	(2%)	
2010 primary	Mike Pompeo (R)	31,180	(39%)	
	Jean Schodorf (R)	19,099	(24%)	
	Wink Hartman (R)	18,365	(23%)	
	Jim Anderson (R)	10,294	(13%)	

Population		Race/Ethnicity		Work	
Pop. 2010:	720,192	White:	75.2%	Private:	79.8%
Change since 2000:	Up 7.2%	Black:	6.9%	Government:	14.1%
Urban:	78.8%	Hispanic:	10.8%	Self-employed:	5.8%
Rural:	21.2%	Asian:	3.0%	Blue collar:	26.7%
Area size:	9,596 sq. mi.	Native Am.:	1.0%	White collar:	56.9%
		Hawaiian:	0.1%	Khaki collar:	0.2%
Age		Two+ races:	2.8%	Other:	16.1%
Median age:	35.7 yrs.				
More than 65 yrs:	12.8%	*Ancestry*		Median income:	$47,356
Less than 18 yrs:	26.5%	German	22.3%	Median Home Value:	$109,800
		Irish	10.8%		
Education		English	8.9%	**Military Veterans**	
H.S. grad:	88.8%			% of Pop:	11.5%
College grad:	25.7%				
Grad degree:	8.2%				

Southern Kansas; Wichita

With about 380,000 people, Wichita may be smaller than 2 million-plus metro Kansas City, but it is a Great Plains metropolis of the magnitude of Omaha or Tulsa and still growing. It began as a farm market town and grew with local oil and gas discoveries in the 1920s. But its real impetus came during World War II and the years just afterward, when aircraft factories sprouted up on the Kansas plains, and Wichita suddenly became the nation's major producer of

2008 Presidential Vote		
John McCain (R) 166,674	(58%)
Barack Obama (D) 113,412	(40%)

2004 Presidential Vote		
George Bush (R) 173,643	(64%)
John Kerry (D) 93,129	(34%)

Cook Partisan Voting Index: R+14

small planes. Today the big four—Cessna, Raytheon, Boeing, Bombardier—are all located in Wichita. In the early 1990s, the general aviation industry was hurt by the recession and by lawsuits that held manufacturers liable for planes they had produced years earlier. Later in the decade, the demand for small planes was robust, and a federal limit on liability enlivened the industry. The September 11 attacks were a severe blow to the airline industry, with the loss of some 15,000 jobs in Wichita. The Navy gave the area a boost in 2004 with a contract for 100 modified 737s to be used to hunt submarines. Boeing, the area's largest employer, sold its commercial airplane operations in Kansas, but its military division remained strong. The 2007-09 recession sparked another wave of layoffs in the industry, with Cessna and Hawker Beechcraft idling over 1,000 workers in 2010 alone. But the aviation industry is just one facet of the local economy: Wichita also has become a regional health-care center in the Great Plains, as people from miles around come to the metropolis for treatment.

Kansas' 4th Congressional District is centered around Wichita, covering wheat-growing areas to the east and west, but with most of its people in Wichita and Sedgwick County. Politically, it has voted Republican in federal elections but has voted Democratic occasionally in state contests. The city elected its first African-American mayor, Democrat Carl Brewer, in April 2007.

Mike Pompeo (R)

The new congressman the 4th District is Republican Mike Pompeo, elected in 2010 to take the place of GOP Rep. Todd Tiahrt, who left to run for the Senate. Pompeo's mother met his father over the phone while she was working as a purchasing clerk for Boeing in Wichita, Kan., and he was selling parts to the company from Southern California. They married in Wichita and moved to Santa Ana, Calif., in the heart of conservative Orange County, where Pompeo was born, raised, and attended high school. He graduated first in his class from West Point, and served as a tank platoon leader, cavalry troop executive officer, and squadron maintenance officer in Germany. Pompeo left the Army with the rank of captain. He went on to Harvard Law School, and after graduation, moved to Washington D.C. to join the prestigious Williams & Connolly firm, specializing in tax law. He also volunteered to represent a group of Arkansas residents who were enmeshed in an ultimately unsuccessful effort to uphold term limits for members of Congress.

Pompeo moved to Kansas in 1996, at the invitation of a friend, to start the company Thayer Aerospace. The company later opened a factory in Mexicali, Mexico, which became an issue in the primary campaign. His opponents argued that it was evidence that he was willing to outsource jobs from Kansas. Pompeo said in response that a contract he won for the factory created 40 jobs at his Kansas site.

Pompeo had been active in Republican politics, working on Sen. Sam Brownback's campaigns and ultimately serving as a GOP national committeeman. When Tiahrt decided to run for the Senate seat Brownback vacated to run for governor, Pompeo saw an opportunity to bring his pro-business, limited-government philosophy to Congress. The passage of the Democratic health care overhaul in March, he said, "proves political elites have lost their way." In the Republican primary, Pompeo faced competition from state Sen. Jean Schodorf, as well as from businessmen Wink Hartman and Jim Anderson. Hartman was initially seen as the front-runner and spent more than $1.6 million on the race, but he ran into trouble after Pompeo's campaign charged that he had taken up residency in Florida for tax purposes. The moderate Schodorf, meanwhile, faced a series of negative ads in the final days of the campaign from outside groups supporting Pompeo; one of them featured a man seeking a hunting license to "bag a RINO"—a reference to "Republican in Name Only," a pejorative term conservatives often use to describe moderates.

Pompeo won the August primary with 39% of the vote, with Schodorf taking 24%, Hartman receiving 23%, and Anderson getting 13%. Both Schodorf and Hartman told *The Wichita Eagle* that they were dismayed by the campaign that Pompeo had run, and Hartman briefly considered running in the general election as a Libertarian before dropping the idea.

Pompeo's Democratic opponent in the general election, state Rep. Raj Goyle, sought to emphasize his commitment to helping workers victimized by layoffs in Wichita's aircraft industry. Pompeo took a commanding early lead in fundraising, although Goyle stayed competitive. He raised $1.9 million to Pompeo's $2.2 million. Goyle also made an issue of a billboard ad erected by a Pompeo supporter that read, "Vote American. Vote for Pompeo." Goyle, whose parents are from India, called the ad "bigoted," and the Pompeo supporter took it down. Goyle could not overcome the district's GOP leanings, however, and Pompeo won 59% to 36%.

★ KENTUCKY ★

Kentucky, the first state west of the Appalachian chain to be admitted to the union, in many ways remains close to its beginnings. This is, literally, a Jeffersonian commonwealth: It is one of four commonwealths—the others are Massachusetts, Pennsylvania, and Virginia—and when the first settlers came here, in the years when Thomas Jefferson was writing his *Notes on the State of Virginia*, this region was part of his state. Kentucky was admitted to the union in 1792, when Jefferson was secretary of state. Aroused by the Federalists' anti-sedition acts, Jefferson ghost-wrote the Kentucky Resolutions, a defense of self-governance by the states, in 1798. Kentucky's largest county is named after Jefferson, and its largest city after the monarch to whom he was credentialed as ambassador to France, Louis XVI. To this day, Kentucky has a constitution informed by a Jeffersonian suspicion of concentrating power. Its one-term limit on governors was raised to two only in 1992. It limited its state legislature to one 60-day session every two years until 2001, so much important business was done in special sessions. Every governor must swear that he or she has not participated in a duel (remember what Jefferson thought of Aaron Burr).

Kentucky long favored the Democratic Party, which can trace its ancestry at least tenuously back to Jefferson. But here too there has been change recently. The state voted for George W. Bush twice, after twice voting, by diminishing margins, for Bill Clinton. In 2008, Kentucky remained immune to the charms of Barack Obama, who campaigned scarcely at all here and lost both the Democratic primary and the general election by wide margins. Both of Kentucky's senators and four of its six House members are Republicans, but Democrats still have a lead in party registration. They recaptured the governorship in 2007 and have held onto a majority in the state House.

The agrarian Jefferson might approve of Kentucky's current demography, which is still quite rural, with well under half the population living in the big metropolitan areas of Louisville, Lexington, and the Northern Kentucky counties across the Ohio River from Cincinnati. And the tobacco planters, who once presided over what one historian called "the alcoholic republic," might not entirely disapprove of a Kentucky economy that remained for years heavily dependent on such century-old industries as whiskey (Bourbon County is where that liquor was invented in the 18th century), tobacco (Kentucky has long been the nation's number No. 2 producer after North Carolina), and coal. But change is coming. Kentucky has ranked No. 1 in percentage of smokers, but the Lexington Urban County Council voted a ban on smoking in public places. Employment is down sharply in the coal and tobacco industries, although Kentucky still has big plants producing appliances, Toyotas, Ford trucks, and Lexmark printers. The state is also home to Humana health services and Ashland Inc., a chemical and plastics company. And if its economy has not sparkled in recent decades and suffered higher than average unemployment in the recession, it has not been hit, as many other states have, by sharp collapses in its manufacturing industries or housing prices.

Many of the buildings here are old: the small-town 19th-century courthouses, the cabins in the coal-mining Appalachians, the unpainted houses in the soggy lowlands beneath the levees by the Mississippi River. Kentucky is the home of some of the nation's oldest traditions, from bourbon to bluegrass music to religious revivals; the Disciples of Christ got their start in the enormous revival at Cane Ridge in 1801. Mother's Day was invented here in 1887, and a Louisville restaurant claims credit for inventing the cheeseburger. Some things have changed. Satellite dishes and four-lane highways have brought modern civilization into hollows and lowland farms that lacked indoor plumbing and electricity within living memory, and farmers once dependent on crops like burley tobacco have begun to diversify their crops. Eastern Kentucky farmers raise goats for meat production, and the state touts its vineyards and fruit orchards. But Kentuckians still have a strong attachment to place and family. Kentucky's population grew just 43% over the past 50 years, while the nation's almost doubled. Few outsiders have moved in, so most of today's residents are descendants of settlers who poured over the mountains in the 40 years after Daniel Boone made his way through the Cumberland Gap in 1775.

Kentucky has seen hearty, though lopsided, political competition, with most of the 120 counties still voting in many recent elections as they did in the Civil War era. The eastern mountains were pro-Union and remain Republican, except for counties where coal miners were organized by the United Mine Workers in the 1930s. Even so, coal country voted heavily against Barack Obama in 2008. The Bluegrass region and the western end of the state were slaveholding territory and voted Democratic. Louisville, with many German immigrants, was an anti-slavery town, and for years flirted with Republicans, but the city and surrounding Jefferson County has been conspicuously more Democratic than the state as a whole over the last decade. For years, all of this meant

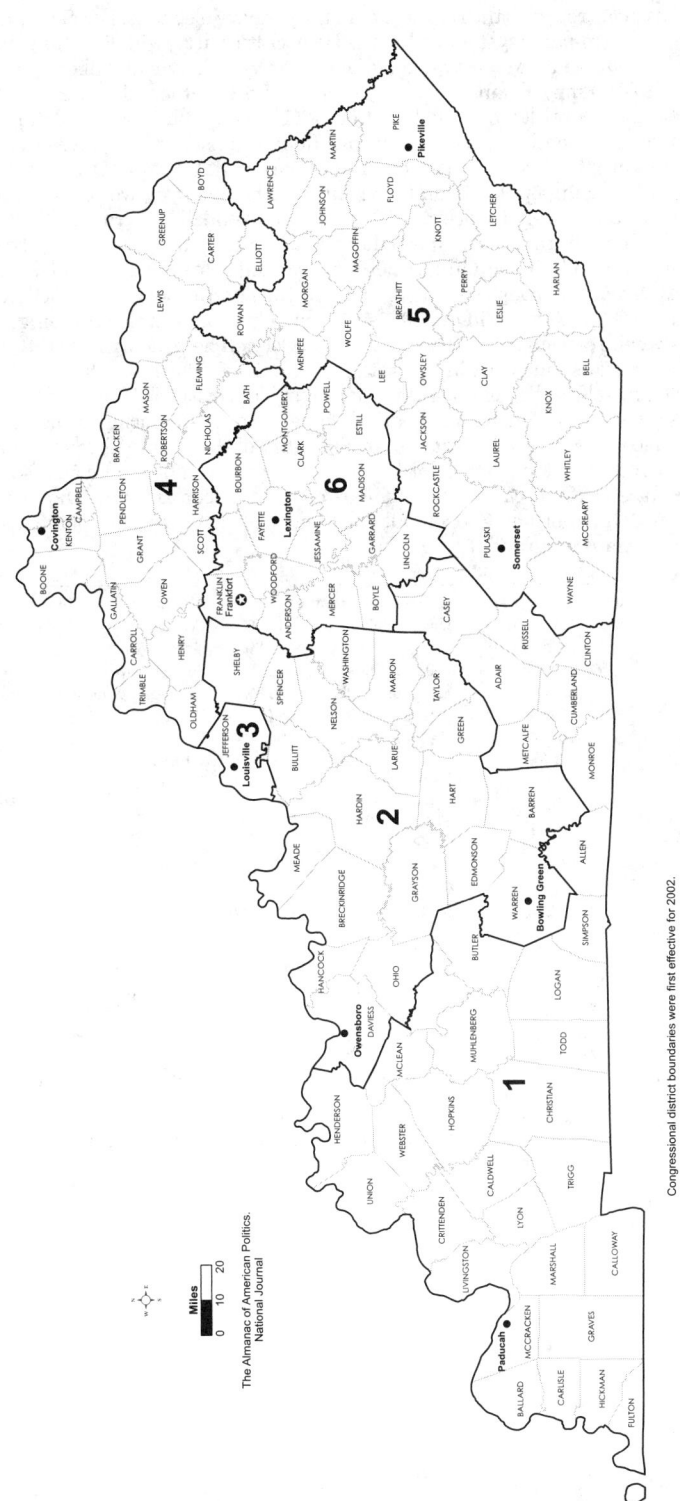

The Almanac of American Politics.
National Journal

Miles
0 10 20

Congressional district boundaries were first effective for 2002.

Democratic Party control, with the real battles in the primary elections. For nearly half a century, there was almost a two-party system within the Democratic party, with factions going back to the 1938 primary, when Senate Majority Leader (and later Vice President) Alben Barkley was challenged by Gov. A.B. (Happy) Chandler, who was later a U.S. senator and commissioner of baseball. Barkley's faction was later led by Gov. Bert Combs (1959-63) and Gov. Wendell Ford (1971-74). Since then, partisan competition has been sharper. Republicans were competitive for the governorship in 1995 and won it in 2003. They lost it by a wide margin in 2007, with Democrat Steve Beshear winning 59%-41% over unpopular incumbent Ernie Fletcher, but they won other statewide offices. They have not lost a U.S. Senate race since the last time Wendell Ford ran, in 1992.

Much of the Republican trend has been the work of Sen. Mitch McConnell, first elected in 1984 and Senate minority leader since January 2007. McConnell helped line up candidates who carried three formerly Democratic congressional districts in 1994 and 1996. He provided key support for Sen. Jim Bunning's 6,766-vote win in 1998, and then helped orchestrate Bunning's exit when he looked to be a weak re-election prospect in 2010. McConnell helped engineer the party switches which gave Republicans a majority in the state Senate in 1999, which they have maintained since. But McConnell himself, while holding the fort for President George W. Bush in the Senate in 2007 and 2008, was put on the defensive and nearly defeated by a self-financing Democrat in 2008. And in 2010, his choice for Bunning's Senate seat, Secretary of State Trey Grayson, was rejected by primary voters in favor of tea party favorite Rand Paul, who won by a solid 56%-44%. McConnell has earned a place in Kentucky politics similar to that of Alben Barkley, Happy Chandler and Republican Sen. John Sherman Cooper, but like them, he has had to learn not to take the trust of his fellow Kentuckians for granted.

Population		Household Income		Work	
Pop. 2010:	4,339,367	Under $15k:	18.5%	Private:	77.9%
State rank:	26th	$15k to $50k:	40.3%	Government:	15.9%
Change since 2000:	Up 7.4%	$50k to $100k:	28.3%	Self-employed:	5.9%
Urban:	55.0%	$100k to $200k:	10.8%	Unemployment (3-yr. average):	4.8%
Rural:	45.0%	Over $200k:	2.0%	Poverty:	18.0%
Native of state:	70.8%	Median income:	$40,807	Blue collar:	26.4%
Not a citizen:	1.9%			White collar:	56.0%
Area size:	40,408 sq. mi.	**Home Value**		Khaki collar:	0.5%
		Under $100k:	41.9%	Other:	17.0%
Most populous cities		$100k to $300k:	49.4%		
Louisville/Jefferson*	741,096	$300k to $500k:	6.2%	**Age**	
Lexington-Fayette	295,803	$500k to $1 mil:	2.0%	Median age:	37.5 yrs.
Bowling Green	58,067	Over $1 million:	0.5%	More than 65 yrs:	13.0%
Owensboro	57,265	Median:	$116,800	Less than 18 yrs:	23.7%

Race/Ethnicity				Military Veterans		Registered Voters in 2010	
White:	86.3%	*Language*		% of Pop:	10.0%	Democrats:	1,624,360
Black:	7.7%	English:	95.6%			Republicans:	1,067,537
Hispanic:	3.1%	Spanish:	2.3%	*Veterans by Period*		Ind./other:	193,877
Asian:	1.1%	Asian:	0.7%	WWII and before:	9.6%	Voter turnout:	1,417,995
Native Am.:	0.2%	Other European:	1.2%	Korea:	10.8%	Turnout as % of	
Hawaiian:	0.0%			Vietnam:	33.7%	voting age:	42.8%
Two+ races:	1.5%	**Education**		Gulf (pre-2001):	12.7%		
		H.S. grad:	81.0%	Gulf (post-2001):	8.1%	**Legislature**	
Ancestry		College grad:	20.4%	Peace time:	25.2%	Senate:	15 D 22 R 1 I
USA	16.3%	Grad degree:	8.2%			House:	58 D 42 R
German	13.4%						
Irish	11.7%						

Presidential politics For many years, Kentucky was a competitive state when Democrats ran a Southerner or two on their ticket, as in such widely separated years as 1952, 1976, 1980, 1992, and 1996. In 2000, Al Gore initially targeted Kentucky, which is just north of his home state of Tennessee and which the Clinton-Gore ticket carried twice. But Kentucky was part of the rural trend away from Clinton Democrats and toward Republicans in the 1990s, and Gore had taken stands seen as hostile to the state's leading industries—tobacco, coal, and automobiles. Bush swept the state, 57%-41%. In 2004, Kentucky was never on anyone's list of battleground states, and Bush won 60%-40%. He lost Jefferson County 50%-49%, but carried 108 of the 119 other counties. John Kerry carried just Jefferson and 11 counties in the eastern mountains.

In the 2008 presidential election, Kentucky was a battleground state of sorts—not a target state but something in the nature of a killing field for the otherwise spectacularly successful Barack Obama. The state's May primary had not been critical in living memory, but the Democratic race was still undecided at that point, and Kentucky, voting on May 20, was coming on strong for Hillary Rodham Clinton. As early as February 12, when the Virginia primary returns came in, it was apparent that Clinton was very strong or Obama was very weak—or both—in the great Appalachian chain settled by Scots-Irish who streamed southwest and over the mountains in the 18th and 19th centuries. These are fighting peoples, as Virginia Sen. Jim Webb has memorialized in his book *Born Fighting*, and they were the constituency least attracted to Obama in the primaries and most inclined to abandon him in the general election. Democratic registration in Kentucky spiked upward before the primary, but this did not benefit Obama as similar trends did in other states.

Clinton campaigned hard in the state, while Obama made only one appearance after August 2007, in the week before the primary. Clinton's ads portrayed her as a fighter for the people; Obama ran a few ads stressing his Christian faith—a response, perhaps, to polls that showed his long association with the controversial Rev. Jeremiah Wright hurting him with Kentucky voters. Clinton beat Obama 65%-30%. He carried Louisville's Jefferson County and Lexington's Fayette County, and lost the other 118 counties; in 19 counties he won less than 10% of the vote. Twenty percent of voters said that race was important in their vote, and 80% of those voters went for Clinton. But Obama, with his professorial demeanor and his promise to sit down without preconditions with the leaders of enemy states, was also out of sync with the martial traditions of the Scots-Irish Andrew Jackson and the Kentucky war hawk Henry Clay. Kentucky turned out to be Obama's third-weakest primary state, after Arkansas and West Virginia.

Obama did not target Kentucky in the general election; the state has a much smaller black population than either Virginia or North Carolina, which he targeted successfully, and fewer upscale whites than Indiana, which he also targeted successfully. An increase in Democratic registration did not help Obama. The exit poll showed that he won only 69% of the vote from self-identified Democrats, far lower than in almost any other state. Without much effort, John McCain carried Kentucky 57%-41%, the same as George W. Bush's victory in 2000.

Of those who said they favored Clinton for the Democratic nomination, only 54% voted for Obama; 45% voted for McCain. Obama ran behind John Kerry's 2004 percentage in 63 of 120 counties, particularly in the Appalachian coal-mining counties in the east and south-central portions of the state, and in the far western area known historically as the Jackson Purchase. He carried only eight counties altogether. The exit poll showed that he carried young voters by only a 51%-48% margin and those with postgraduate degrees by just 52%-48%.

2008 Presidential Vote		
John McCain (R)	1,048,462	(57%)
Barack Obama (D)	751,985	(41%)
2008 Presidential Primary		
Hillary Clinton (D)	459,511	(65%)
Barack Obama (D)	209,954	(30%)
2008 Presidential Primary		
John McCain (R)	142,918	(72%)
Mike Huckabee (R)	16,388	(8%)
Ron Paul (R)	13,427	(7%)
2004 Presidential Vote		
George W. Bush (R)	1,069,439	(60%)
John Kerry (D)	712,733	(40%)

Congressional districting   Kentucky's 1991 redistricting plan, drawn by Democrats after the state lost one U.S. House seat in the 1990 census, was intended to protect Democratic incumbents but instead produced a delegation that was 5-1 Republican by 1996. Party control of the state legislature in 2001 was split. House Democrats prepared a plan that would have made re-election more difficult for Republican Rep. Ed Whitfield, while state Senate Republicans backed a plan to add heavily Republican Oldham County to the 3rd District to strengthen Rep. Anne Northup. The impasse continued through January 2002, delaying the January 29 filing deadline for candidates. On February 1, the legislature finally adopted a compromise plan that changed the lines very little, with one important exception: It removed increasingly Republican suburban Shelby County from the 4th District and added three and a half traditionally Democratic counties.

112th Congress Lineup
4 R   2 D
111th Congress Lineup
4 R   2 D

Kentucky did not lose a House seat in the reapportionment following the 2010 census. Neither party has control of the process, so the likely result is only a minor alteration of district boundaries.

Governor

Steve Beshear (D)

Elected 2007, term expires Dec. 2011, 1st term; b. Sept. 21, 1944, Dawson Springs; home, Clark County; U. of KY, B.A., 1966, U. of KY, J.D., 1968; Baptist; married (Jane); 2 children.

Military Career: U.S. Army Reserves, 1969-75.

Elected Office: KY Gen. Assembly, 1974-79, KY atty. gen., 1980-84, Lt. gov., 1984-88.

Professional Career: Attorney, 1968-71, 1989-2006.

Office: State Capitol, 700 Capitol Ave., Frankfort, 40601, 502-564-2611; Fax: 502-564-2517; Web site: gov.state.ky.us.

Election Results

2007 general	Steve Beshear (D)	619,552	(59%)
	Ernie Fletcher (R)	435,773	(41%)
2007 primary	Steve Beshear (D)	142,838	(41%)
	Bruce Lunsford (D)	74,578	(21%)
	Steve Henry (D)	60,893	(18%)
	Jody Richards (D)	45,433	(13%)
	Gatewood Galbraith (D)	20,704	(6%)

Kentucky's governor is Democrat Steve Beshear, elected in November 2007. The governor wields extraordinary authority in Kentucky, including broad appointment powers. Until the passage of a constitutional amendment in 2000, the legislature met in regular session for only 60 days in even-numbered years. Beginning in 2001, it began meeting for 30 days in odd-numbered years as well. But the governor retains the power to shift around line items in the state budget and to call special sessions. Beshear defeated Republican Gov. Ernie Fletcher, whose administration was mired in a political hiring scandal.

The son and grandson of Baptist ministers, Beshear grew up in Dawson Springs, a small western Kentucky town with a population of less than 3,000. He has strong ties to the city—his father was also a funeral director and served as mayor. Valedictorian of his high school class, Beshear was able to attend the University of Kentucky thanks to a second mortgage on the family's home. He was elected student body president in his junior year and went on to earn a law degree from the school, graduating with honors. In a moot court national competition in New York City, Beshear impressed the judges with a skillful performance, and he was invited to interview with two international law firms. Offered a job by both, Beshear accepted a position with the Wall Street firm White & Case, and during that time, he joined an Army Reserve unit in the Bronx, serving as an intelligence analyst. But after three years in the Big Apple, Beshear was ready to return home to the Bluegrass State. He and his wife, Jane, whom he had met in college, settled in Lexington, where he took a job with a smaller firm. In 1973, he launched his first campaign for state representative to succeed a retiring member. Winning easily, Beshear went on to serve three terms in Frankfort, where he gained a reputation for supporting proposals to stimulate job growth and attract businesses to the state. But he was also in the minority among his peers for his support of abortion rights and his opposition to measures to stop school integration.

In 1979, Beshear made his first successful bid for statewide office, winning a race for attorney general at age 35. During his term, he took several stands that were unpopular in the conservative state. In 1982, he declared that a state law restricting abortion was unconstitutional. Then he announced that his interpretation of a U.S. Supreme Court decision meant that copies of the Ten Commandments had to be removed from Kentucky classrooms. His decision prompted thousands of calls to the governor's office and letters to newspapers. A billboard that said "Keep The 10 Commandments, Remove Steve Beshear" went up in Lexington. In 1983, then-Lt. Gov. Martha Layne Collins captured the Democratic nomination for governor and selected Beshear as her running mate. The two defeated the Republican challenger, Jim Bunning (later a U.S. senator), by 10 percentage points and more than 100,000 votes, making Collins the first and only female governor in the commonwealth's history.

In 1987, Beshear sought his party's nomination for governor. But the primary drew two other high-profile choices: KFC millionaire and former Gov. John Brown and wealthy bookstore businessman Wallace Wilkinson, who ended up winning. Beshear finished a distant third. In 1996, Beshear challenged Republican Sen. Mitch McConnell, who was seeking a third term. McConnell had more than a 2-to-1 fundraising advantage and won handily, 55%-43%. Following his second loss, Beshear went back to private law practice in Lexington. While Democrats had once been dominant in the state, by the mid-1990s, the congressional delegation and state offices were shifting toward Republicans, helped by the aggressive efforts of McConnell.

But in 2006, Democratic fortunes were on the rise everywhere. The party took control of Congress. John Yarmuth defeated GOP Rep. Anne Northup, a perennial Democratic target, in the state's 3rd District and GOP Rep. Ron Lewis had to fight to hang on to his seat in the 2nd District. In the race for the governor, always held in odd-numbered years, the time seemed ripe for Democrats to defeat Fletcher. In May 2006, a grand jury indicted Fletcher on misdemeanor charges of criminal conspiracy, official misconduct, and political discrimination after a 15-month investigation into political patronage. But in August 2006, a judge ruled that Fletcher had immunity from prosecution for official acts and could not be tried unless he was out of office. The case was settled, and Fletcher was cleared of the charges. But politically, he was damaged goods. His approval ratings had sunk below 30%, and a majority of voters supported his resignation. Republicans tried to use the scandal as evidence that Fletcher was unelectable, but he beat back primary challenges from Northup and his former finance chairman, Billy Harper, to win by 13 percentage points.

In seeking the Democratic nomination to take on Fletcher, Beshear called for expanded gambling in the state. Citing the huge sums Kentuckians were already spending at casinos across the border in Illinois, Indiana, and West Virginia, Beshear argued that legalized gambling could provide money for education reform and expanded health care. He won the May 2007 primary relatively easily, 41%-21%, beating hospital executive Bruce Lunsford and narrowly avoiding a runoff. In the five months leading up to the general election, Fletcher condemned Beshear's gambling proposal in an attempt to rally social conservatives to his side. He also emphasized Beshear's past support of abortion rights and his position on the Ten Commandments display. But the indictment and investigation had taken a toll. Beshear won, 59%-41%.

As governor, Beshear pressed to put his casino proposal before the voters, but the legislature was slow to move. He also made waves among lawmakers for vetoing their $3.8 billion, two-year highway-improvement plan. Senate President David Williams, a Republican, said that the bill would fund needed road projects and bridges, and that Beshear's veto was unconstitutional because it came the day after the last legal day for issuing vetoes in the legislative session. In 2008, he filed a lawsuit against Beshear, alleging that the veto was invalid. A circuit judge later ruled that the Beshear's version of the plan was valid.

In the 2009 session, Beshear and state lawmakers struggled to come up with ways to deal with the faltering economy, as the state's unemployment rate climbed past 9%, its highest level in 25 years. But the session ended with lawmakers spurning his request to take up several high profile measures, including tax credits to lure a NASCAR race to the Kentucky Speedway. Beshear called a special session in June. Legislators succeeded in addressing the state's projected $1 billion shortfall, but also added a series of tax breaks that the governor warned would bring deeper cuts than anticipated to most state agencies. He sought approval of a measure allowing Kentucky's financially ailing horse race tracks to operate video slot casinos, but it failed to get out of committee. Williams declared the idea dead for the 2010 session as well, angering Beshear. The governor's troubles didn't end there: A recording surfaced on the Internet of Lt. Gov. Daniel Mongiardo criticizing his boss in a profanity-laced tirade as the state's "worst" governor. Two other anonymous tapes surfaced, which Beshear dismissed as "political shenanigans" and said he thought Mongiardo's words were edited out of context.

Beshear sought to revive gambling as a means of economic development in the 2010 legislative session, but Williams and other Republicans remained steadfast. The state resorted to other methods of raising money, including selling a Covington parking facility. The legislature struggled to produce a budget, and reconvened in a special session. The $17.3 billion budget that was ultimately approved "is not what I wanted, and not what I originally proposed," Beshear said, and he used his line item veto on 19 provisions. He announced a six-day unpaid furlough of most executive branch employees, saying it would avert layoffs of 400 workers.

Despite the state's economic troubles and the national tide turning against Democrats, Beshear looked to be in reasonably good shape in early 2011 to secure a second term later in the year. A November 2010 Public Policy Polling survey gave him a 44%-35% lead on Williams as well as a 45%-26% advantage over Louisville businessman Phil Moffett, a favorite of tea party activists. In July 2009, he announced Louisville Mayor Jerry Abramson as his running mate to replace Mongiardo, who unsuccessfully sought the Democratic nomination for U.S. Senate in 2010. Beshear's campaign in January 2011 reported raising more than $3.5 million, more than four times that of Williams.

Senior Senator

Mitch McConnell (R)

Elected 1984, term expires 2014, 5th term; b. Feb. 20, 1942, Sheffield, AL; home, Louisville; U. of Louisville, B.A. 1964, U. of KY, J.D. 1967; Baptist; married (Elaine Chao); 3 children.

Elected Office: Jefferson Cnty. judge exec., 1978–85.

Professional Career: Chief legis. asst., U.S. Sen. Marlow Cook, 1968–70; Dpty. asst. U.S. atty. gen., 1974–75.

DC Office: 317 RSOB, 20510, 202-224-2541; Fax: 202-224-2499; Web site: mcconnell.senate.gov.

State Offices: Bowling Green, 270-781-1673; Ft. Wright, 859-578-0188; Lexington, 859-224-8286; London, 606-864-2026; Louisville, 502-582-6304; Paducah, 270-442-4554.

Committees: *Agriculture, Nutrition & Forestry:* Conservation, Forestry & Natural Resources; Livestock, Dairy, Poultry, Marketing & Ag Research; Nutrition, Specialty Crops, Food & Ag Research. *Appropriations:* Agriculture, Rural Development, Food and Drug Administration & Related Agencies; Commerce, Justice, Science & Related Agencies; Defense; Department of State, Foreign Operations & Related Programs; Energy & Water Development; Military Construction, Veterans Affairs & Related Agencies. *Rules & Administration.*

Group Ratings

	ACLU	ACU	ADA	CFG	AFS	FRC	LCV	ITIC	NTU	COC
2010	7	96	0	90	8	100	0	67	97	100
2009	–	96	10	95	9	–	9	–	88	71

National Journal Ratings

	2010 LIB	—	2010 CONS	2009 LIB	—	2009 CONS
Economic	22%	—	76%	14%	—	81%
Social	0%	—	79%	6%	—	92%
Foreign	0%	—	72%	0%	—	84%
Composite	16%	—	84%	11%	—	90%

Key Votes of the 111th Congress

1. Overturn Ledbetter	N	5. Pass health care bill	N	9. Ratify New START	N
2. Pass $787 billion stimulus	N	6. Regulate financial firms	N	10. Confirm Elena Kagan	N
3. Repeal DC gun laws	Y	7. Pass tax cuts for some	N	11. Stop EPA climate regs	Y
4. Confirm Sonia Sotomayor	N	8. Legalize immigrants' kids	N	12. Repeal don't ask, tell	N

Election Results

2008 general	Mitch McConnell (R)	953,816	(53%)	($20,991,678)
	Bruce Lunsford (D)	847,005	(47%)	($10,883,172)
2008 primary	Mitch McConnell (R)	168,127	(86%)	
	Daniel Essek (R)	27,170	(14%)	

Prior Winning Percentages: 2002 (65%); 1996 (55%); 1990 (52%); 1984 (50%)

Mitch McConnell, the senior senator from Kentucky, is the Senate minority leader. First elected in 1984, he is known as a tough, thick-skinned leader who does not shrink from a fight. As a Republican in Kentucky, he has been used to frequently coming up on the losing side, but has perservered with considerable success nonetheless.

McConnell grew up in Alabama, where he overcame polio, and at age 13, moved to Louisville. He has been in politics for most of his adult life. Between college and law school at the University of Louisville, he was an intern for Republican Sen. John Sherman Cooper of Kentucky. Soon after graduating from law school, he became chief legislative assistant to Kentucky Sen. Marlow Cook. He served in the Ford administration Justice Department and then moved back to Louisville. In 1977, at age 35, McConnell won the office that had been Cook's political stepping-stone, Jefferson County judge-executive. In 1981, he was re-elected, and in 1984, he ran for the Senate against incumbent Democrat Walter (Dee) Huddleston. McConnell ran a clever ad showing bloodhounds sniffing for Huddleston in vacation locales where Huddleston had collected fees for speeches while the Senate was in session. McConnell won by 5,169 votes out of 1.2 million cast. Part of a Washington power couple, he is married to former Bush administration Labor Secretary Elaine Chao.

McConnell began his Senate career with a seat on the Foreign Relations Committee. In 1992, he won a seat on the powerful Appropriations Committee and then moved up to become chairman of the Foreign Operations Subcommittee. In that role, he has worked since the early 1990s in opposing Burmese dictators who imprisoned Nobel Prize winner Aung San Suu Kyi. With Dianne Feinstein, he sponsored bills imposing trade sanctions on the regime. McConnell has long been a strong supporter of Israel and an advocate for human rights in Cambodia, Egypt, and other nations. But he also took care of Kentucky. He frequently used his seat on Appropriations to channel aid to his home state, and he was particularly active on issues affecting the tobacco industry. In 2003, he forged an agreement for a buyout of tobacco quotas from farmers with the trade-off that the industry accept some Food and Drug Administration oversight of tobacco. But House Republican conservatives balked at FDA regulation, and in 2004, the Senate backed the tobacco buyout without it, passing it as part of the corporate tax bill 69-17.

Another major area of interest for McConnell has been campaign finance law. He became the Senate's leading opponent of efforts to curb political action committees and soft money, the large, unregulated contributions to political parties. He argued that such restrictions were unconstitutional infringements of free speech. In October 1999, with more than 40 senators on his side, he killed a version of the McCain-Feingold campaign finance bill. In early 2001 John McCain brought the bill forward again, and despite McConnell's efforts, it passed. But it excluded many provisions from previous McCain-Feingold bills, including public subsidies for candidates and voluntary spending limits. McCain's bill was also amended with a provision to double the limit on individual contributions, which McConnell supported. When he was challenged about the potential inconsistency between his opposition to campaign finance regulation and his vote for amending the Constitution to allow the banning of flag-burning, another form of free expression, McConnell switched his position and became one of the few Republicans to consistently vote against measures to ban the burning of the American flag.

After the campaign finance law was enacted, McConnell filed a lawsuit challenging its constitutionality. "There won't be any less speech or money spent. Dramatically more will be spent, just in a different way," McConnell predicted, and warned that unregulated fundraising groups called 527s would raise and spend huge amounts of money, as indeed they did in the 2004 cycle. The lower courts upheld most provisions of the law. But in January 2010, the Supreme Court, reversing earlier precedents, struck down a key reform when it ruled that curbs on political spending by corporations are an unconstitutional infringement on free speech. The law banned the broadcast, cable, or satellite transmission of election messages paid for by corporations or labor unions from their general funds in the 30 days before a presidential primary and in the 60 days before the general elections.

In 1990, McConnell began to climb the leadership ladder. He ran for chairman of the National Republican Senatorial Committee, but lost to Phil Gramm of Texas. He tried again in 1996 and won. But he was unable to get Republican senators to contribute as much to the campaigns of fellow Republicans as the Democrats gave to their campaigns, and Republicans gained no seats in 1998. In the 2000 cycle, he had even tougher sledding. Republicans lost most of the close Senate contests, and the outcome was a 50-50 split that put Democrats in position to gain a majority a few months later, when Jim Jeffords left the Republican Party in May 2001 to become an independent affiliated with the Democrats.

In 2002, when Don Nickles of Oklahoma stepped down as Republican whip, McConnell campaigned for months among colleagues, and his only opponent, Larry Craig of Idaho, dropped out several days before the contest. Then in December, Republican Leader Trent Lott of Mississippi came under a storm of criticism when he spoke favorably of Strom Thurmond's segregationist campaign for president in 1948 at an event honoring Thurmond on his 100th birthday. McConnell was Lott's strongest public defender, threatening retaliation against Democrats if they moved to censure him. But on Dec. 20, as the controversy showed no sign of abating, he privately recommended to Lott that he "step down as soon as possible." Ordinarily, McConnell might have been in line for the leader's position at that point, but he did not challenge Tennessee's Bill Frist when Frist ran for Lott's post. So Frist became Senate majority leader and McConnell majority whip and a key adviser to Frist, who was relatively unversed in Senate procedures. While others complained about heightened divisiveness in Congress, McConnell declined to join the lament. "I'm amazed at all the hand-wringing over the level of discourse and partisanship. It leads me to believe that nobody has read any history. The level of divisiveness now is really quite mild when it's compared with numerous periods in our history," he said.

McConnell showed considerable mastery of Senate rules and, when Frist retired from the Senate in 2006, he ran for majority leader. It was a behind-the-scenes campaign, as described by his ally, Utah's Robert Bennett. "Brick by brick, he built a firewall. So whenever somebody decided they wanted to run, all we had to do was sit down and say to them, 'This is what you're going to have to deal with.' One by one potential opponents said, 'Wait a minute, I don't want to run and lose,'" Bennett said, later describing the campaign to the Associated Press. Republicans ended up losing their Senate majority at the polls in 2006, so McConnell became minority leader instead of majority leader, but he did so without opposition. Making a comeback in leadership, Lott narrowly beat Lamar Alexander for minority whip. "There will be nothing here (the Democrats) can do without some degree of cooperation from a very robust 49-vote minority," McConnell told *The New York Times* soon after the 2006 election. "The question is, Are you going to work together and try to do good things for the country or not?"

There was some bipartisan cooperation at first. Appropriations bills left over from the previous Congress were passed in early 2007, and agreement on a minimum wage increase was reached after Democrats agreed to Republicans' demand for tax cuts for small businesses. But harmony did not last long. In February, Majority Leader Harry Reid introduced a resolution, supported by some Republicans, opposing President Bush's strategy for a troop surge in Iraq. McConnell announced that he would block debate on Reid's resolution unless Republicans got votes on their resolutions setting 11 goals for the Iraqi government. On this, as on other issues throughout the next two years, McConnell was able to hold 41 or more Republicans together to get Reid to meet their demands, as Republicans conducted a record number of filibusters. McConnell observed that he lived by "an 80/20 rule." He spent 80% of his time trying to coax 20% of Republican senators to stick with the party.

On Iraq, he succeeded, although Bush later wrote in his memoir that McConnell was not sure he would. By the summer of 2007, even some Republicans admitted to doubts about the war, but McConnell was able to hold enough of them to prevent passage of the Democrats' timetable for troop withdrawals or a funding cutoff. By September, there were signs the troop surge was having an impact, and by the end of the year, Democrats had abandoned their drive for withdrawal timetables.

On another issue, immigration, McConnell faced a deeply divided Republican Conference. He supported the attempts of Arizona Republican Jon Kyl to fashion a comprehensive bill that included a guest worker program and a legalization process for illegal immigrants currently in the country. But most Republicans opposed the bill. It failed to survive a vote to end a filibuster against it, and an alternative was offered later in June 2007. McConnell, recognizing its unpopularity in Kentucky (a state with a very small immigrant population), this time opposed it.

In maneuverings on the budget in 2007, McConnell insisted Democrats hold down spending to the levels proposed by the Bush administration and provide funding for the Iraq war without strings attached, and he prevailed. He forced the Democrats to back down on a tax increase they wanted to pay for an adjustment in the alternative minimum tax to prevent the tax from hitting middle-income taxpayers. He opposed a bill by John Warner of Virginia and Joe Lieberman of Connecticut to regulate reductions in carbon emissions on the grounds that it would impose "a stealth and giant tax on virtually every aspect of industrial consumer life." Still, McConnell worked on a bipartisan basis on some issues. He cut an early deal with Reid that paved the way for Senate passage of the $700 billion Wall Street rescue that the Bush administration sought in the fall of 2008. He also supported the loan package that year for the Detroit automakers; General Motors and Ford as well as Toyota have big plants in Kentucky.

McConnell has seldom had an easy time of it in his re-election bids, and 2008 was no exception. Since 1984, he had won re-election three times, but always after spirited competition, from former

Louisville Mayor Harvey Sloane in 1990; from now Gov. Steve Beshear in 1996; and from Lois Combs Weinberg in 2002. Sloane and Beshear held McConnell to 52% and 55% of the vote, respectively. He did much better against Weinberg, winning 65%-35%. But in 2008, Democrats, still smarting from former Majority Leader Tom Daschle's defeat in 2004, were determined to put up a tough opponent against McConnell. They found Bruce Lunsford, a hospital and nursing home operator and multimillionaire who ran for governor in 2007 but lost the Democratic primary to Beshear. Lunsford spent some $10.8 million, more than $7 million of it his own money, and ran a string of negative ads against McConnell, including one showing dogs chasing the senator—a take-off on McConnell's 1984 bloodhound ads—and another criticizing McConnell for supporting the financial industry bailout.

McConnell seemed unfazed by the political peril. He raised $21 million from 2003 to 2008 and ultimately spent it all. His ads compared himself to Kentucky's long-serving Democratic Sen. Alben Barkley, who was Senate majority leader and later Harry Truman's vice president, and reminded voters of the money and projects he had brought home. In the last two weeks of the campaign, he embarked on a 4,000-mile statewide bus tour with 62 stops in 55 counties. On Nov. 1, just before the election, he announced that the Veterans Affairs Department had approved $75 million for a veterans' hospital in Louisville.

McConnell won 53%-47%, running behind GOP presidential candidate John McCain's 57% in Kentucky. McConnell lost the state's two largest urban counties, Jefferson and Fayette, where the Louisville and Lexington newspapers have long opposed him. He also lost some traditionally Democratic counties in the eastern mountains and in the western part of the state. He won 13% among African-Americans, more than McCain, and 44% among voters under 30. Interestingly, given his yeoman work to prevent Bush's troop surge from being undermined by withdrawal timetables, he won only 57% among voters for whom Iraq was the most important issue.

The victory made McConnell the longest-serving senator in Kentucky history—and a Senate minority leader facing difficult challenges. Barack Obama restored the Democrats' hold on the White House, and Democrats emerged from the election with a larger majority in the House and with 58 seats in the Senate, leaving them just short of the 60 votes needed to defeat a filibuster. McConnell later told *National Journal*, "In January of 2009, I looked at a lot of poll data, and the ray of hope that I could give my members was that the independents that wiped us out in '06 and '08 held similar views, ones that I knew most of my members had, on spending and national security. I thought we could regain their confidence on spending and national security." But it was essential to hold the 41 Republicans together. He was not entirely successful at first. In February 2009, the Senate approved Obama's $787 billion economic stimulus bill 61-37 with three Republican votes. "Pushing back these efforts to basically Europeanize America will not be easy," McConnell told a conservative audience that month. Then came significantly more bad news for McConnell. Arlen Specter of Pennsylvania, trailing his 2004 Republican primary opponent Pat Toomey in polls, announced in late April 2009 that he would switch parties and join the Democrats. In July, when Democrat Al Franken was seated in Minnesota after a recount, the Democrats got to the magic 60, a theoretically filibuster-proof majority.

As with Iraq, McConnell may have had his doubts about holding his caucus together, but he plugged ahead anyway. In May 2009, sensing dissent among Democrats, he got the Senate to deny the administration $80 million to close the detention facility at Guantanamo Bay, Cuba. He opposed the Democrats' health care proposals as a government takeover of health care, and with Republicans united and Democrats divided, he took aim at the option in the bill for a federally run insurance provider. He encouraged the Senate's two physicians, Tom Coburn of Oklahoma and John Barrasso of Wyoming, to speak out against the Democrats' plans. The so-called public option was eventually dropped from the legislation when it passed in 2010. Throughout work on the bill, McConnell deepened his working relationship with the Republican leader in the House, John Boehner of Ohio. "I have found him absolutely delightful to work with," he told *National Journal* in March 2010, "and philosophically we tend to see things the same way. I think he understands the Senate and I understand the House and we both see the differences."

In April and May 2010, McConnell made efforts to stop the Democrats from passing their version of the financial regulation bill, but, like health care, it ultimately passed. He also fought President Obama's nominations of Sonia Sotomayor and Elena Kagan to the Supreme Court without success. In July 2009, he reversed his previous opposition to filibusters of high court nominees, claiming that the Democrats had changed the rules of the game. When he was speaking on the floor against Kagan in August, Sen. Al Franken, a former comedian, was presiding in the chair and at one point rolled his eyes. McConnell later admonished the freshman senator, saying, "This isn't *Saturday Night Live*, Al."

McConnell's ability to hold his caucus together paid off at some critical moments. After the election, Obama hoped to strike a deal with congressional Republicans to extend the Bush-era tax cuts for two more years for all taxpayers except those earning over $200,000 a year. But Senate Republicans led by McConnell rejected any proposal that did not extend the tax cuts for everyone, and Obama was forced to go along. Congress approved a bill extending the tax cuts for all taxpayers. The Senate also stopped in its tracks the Democrats' bill to impose a cap-and-trade system of emissions swaps on industry. It passed the House in 2009, but never came up for a vote in the Senate in the 111th Congress (2009-10).

In March 2010, McConnell spoke about GOP efforts in the House and Senate to repair the party's brand. "Unified opposition has been the single most important thing that occurred this past year," he told *National Journal.* "That turned the political environment literally upside down from where it was 12 months ago and let the public know that there was a genuine debate up here over principle." In August 2010, after McConnell had his first one-on-one meeting with President Obama, he showed no sign of finding common ground with the president and his party. Asked whether there was too much obstruction in the Senate, McConnell said, "I think the Senate is operating largely like our founding fathers anticipated it would."

In the November 2010 election, Republicans gained six Senate seats, leaving McConnell with 47 GOP votes and Democrats far short of a filibuster-proof majority. But Congress-watchers speculated that McConnell might have difficulty in working with the strong independent-minded conservatives who gained power in the elections, including Sen. Jim DeMint of South Carolina, who went over the head of GOP establishment leaders and backed several primary candidates who were more conservative and plugged in to the tea party movement than establishment-backed candidates. The most dramatic case was the contest for Kentucky's other Senate seat.

After helping Republican Jim Bunning win the seat in 1998, McConnell had lost faith in Bunning's political skills and ability to hold the seat, especially after he was re-elected in the Republican year of 2004 by only 51%-49%. Going into the 2010 election, McConnell made it clear Bunning should not run again. The incumbent was livid. He called McConnell a "control freak," and blamed him when he managed to raise only $300,000 in the first quarter of 2009. "Leaders of the Republican Party in the Senate have done everything in their power to dry up my fundraising," Bunning said.

The consensus choice of McConnell and other Kentucky Republicans to replace Bunning was state Secretary of State Trey Grayson. But also running was Rand Paul, a Bowling Green ophthalmologist and the son of 2008 libertarian presidential candidate Ron Paul, a House member from Texas. Bunning and DeMint endorsed Paul, who also had support from tea party groups. In the May 2010 primary, Paul beat Grayson, 59%-35%. McConnell appeared at a victory rally for Paul in a conciliatory gesture. And Paul reciprocated by saying he would support McConnell's re-election as Senate GOP leader. But the presence of Paul, DeMint and other activist conservatives in the Senate introduced a new political dynamic that was bound to present McConnell with management challenges well into the 112th Congress (2011-12).

Junior Senator

Rand Paul (R)

Elected 2010, term expires 2016, 1st term; b. Jan. 7, 1963, Lake Jackson, TX; home, Bowling Green; Baylor U., attended 1981-84; Duke U., M.D. 1988.; Presbyterian; Married (Kelley); 3 children.

Professional Career: Ophthalmologist, 1993-2010.

DC Office: C5 RSOB, 20510, 202-224-4343; Fax: 202-228-6917; Web site: paul.senate.gov.

State Offices: Bowling Green, 270-782-8303; Crescent Springs, 859-426-0015; Hazard, 606-435-2390; Hopkinsville, 270-885-1212; Lexington, 859-219-2239; Louisville, 502-582-5341; Owensboro, 270-689-9085.

Committees: *Energy & Natural Resources:* Energy; National Parks; Public Lands & Forests. *Health, Education, Labor & Pensions:* Children & Families; Primary Health & Aging (RMM). *Homeland Security & Governmental Affairs:* Contracting Oversight (Ad Hoc); Disaster Recovery & Intergovernmental Affairs (Ad Hoc); Investigations (Permanent). *Small Business & Entrepreneurship.*

Election Results

2010 general	Rand Paul (R)	755,411	(56%)	($7,809,324)
	Jack Conway (D)	599,843	(44%)	($5,905,455)
2010 primary	Rand Paul (R)	206,986	(59%)	
	C. M. 'Trey' Grayson (R)	124,864	(35%)	

Rand Paul, a Republican elected in 2010, is Kentucky's junior senator. He is the son of Rep. Ron Paul, R-Texas, a libertarian and 2008 and 2012 presidential candidate who has a devoted following among strict adherents of limited government. The younger Paul was born in Lake Jackson, Texas. He attended Baylor University, where he was an active member of the Young Conservatives of Texas. Although he failed to get an undergraduate degree at Baylor, Paul chose to follow in his father's footsteps to become a doctor. He got a high score on the medical entrance exam and was admitted to Duke University, where he got his medical degree.

His schooling and residency finished, Paul moved to Bowling Green, Ky., near his wife's home town, and opened an ophthalmology practice. Paul also established an eye clinic to treat low-income patients. Paul mulled entering politics for some time, writing newspaper columns, helping with his father's campaigns, and founding an anti-tax watchdog group called Kentucky Taxpayers United. His father's denunciation of the Federal Reserve and espousal of free market principles in the 2008 presidential campaign attracted a cult-like following and showed the potential of an unconventional candidate to raise large sums online. When Rand Paul gave a speech on April 15, 2009—Tax Day—to a tea party group, the energy of the crowd persuaded him that "something enormous was going on," as he later told the *Bowling Green Daily News*. He decided to run for the Senate.

The seat was held by two-term Republican incumbent Jim Bunning, who had a solid conservative record but had been only barely re-elected in 2004 and was being pressed by Sen. Mitch McConnell of Kentucky, the powerful Senate Republican leader, not to run. In July 2009, Bunning announced he would retire, and the favorite for the Republican nomination was state Secretary of State Trey Grayson, who had the backing of McConnell and much of the state GOP establishment. But Paul had his father's name and access to his vast network of contributors. His backers eagerly embraced his outspoken views that government should stick to the functions outlined in the Constitution, that some agencies such as the Environmental Protection Agency and the Education Department should be abolished, and that the powers of the Federal Reserve should be drastically curbed.

McConnell appeared in television ads for Grayson, and Grayson ran spots charging Paul was weak on national security. But Paul ended up winning the primary in a rout, 59%-35%, carrying 109 of 120 counties. McConnell made a point of appearing at a victory rally for Paul and complimenting his campaign. Paul, who had previously declined to say whether he would vote for McConnell for Senate minority leader, said there was virtually no scenario where he wouldn't support him. On the Democratic side, the primary was much closer: Attorney General Jack Conway beat Lt. Gov. Dan Mongiardo by 44%-43%.

Paul's decisive upset was quickly overshadowed by an appearance on MSNBC's *Rachel Maddow Show*. When the liberal host challenged him on his beliefs, he indicated his opposition in principle to the Civil Rights Act of 1964, arguing that the federal government shouldn't interfere with private businesses. The remarks caused a furor, even after Paul issued a statement saying he did not support repealing the landmark law barring discrimination against minority groups. After that, he limited his media appearances and subsequently traveled to Washington to meet with Republicans and interest groups that had viewed him with suspicion. But his Democratic opponent, Conway, hammered him for that and other public statements, such as a claim that imposing a $2,000 deductible on Medicare beneficiaries would solve the financial problems of the behemoth government medical insurance program. Paul said that the idea was just an option under consideration and that he did not endorse it.

One of the two nominees was arguably too conservative and the other too liberal for the median Kentucky voter, and both tried to take advantage of that. Conway seized on Paul's support for raising the Social Security retirement age and opposing federal involvement in drug enforcement. Paul had plenty of material to work with, however, in his attempt to paint Conway as too liberal. Conway supported abortion rights, the Democrats' health care bill, repeal of the ban on open gays in the military, and a pro-union bill effectively abolishing the secret ballot in unionization elections. Conway may also have hurt himself with an ad that political operatives considered over the top. In the ad, the narrator says, "Why was Rand Paul a member of a secret society that called the Holy Bible a 'hoax'?...Why did Rand Paul once tie a woman up, tell her to bow down before a false idol, and say...god was Aqua Buddha?" The charges mostly referred to pranks during Paul's college years. *GQ* magazine had reported that Paul once belonged to a secret society called the NoZe Brotherhood, which often taunted the school's administration; he and a friend were once accused of blindfolding a female acquaintance and trying to get her to smoke marijuana.

Paul won by 56%-44%, a slightly smaller margin than John McCain's in 2008 in Kentucky, but nonetheless decisive. He did not carry Louisville's Jefferson County or Lexington's Fayette County, but ran strongly in the Northern Kentucky counties across the Ohio River from Cincinnati.

His victory was counted as one of the major triumphs for the tea party movement, although on some issues, notably defense, he seemed closer to his father's views than those of most tea party supporters. As soon as he got to Washington, Paul established a Tea Party Caucus in the Senate. And he showed no sign of giving up his penchant for sending up rhetorical flares. In May 2011, Paul accused President Barack Obama of trying to block Boeing from creating jobs in the South, saying he suspected Obama kept an "enemies list."

FIRST DISTRICT

Ed Whitfield (R)

Elected 1994, 9th term; b. May 25, 1943, Hopkinsville; home, Hopkinsville; U. of KY, B.S. 1965, J.D. 1969; Methodist; married (Connie); 1 child.

Military Career: Army Reserves, 1967–73.

Elected Office: KY House of Reps., 1974–75.

Professional Career: Practicing atty., 1969–79; Owner, Rhodes Oil Co., 1975–79; Cnsl., Seaboard System Railroad, 1979–83; V.P., CSX, 1983–91; Cnsl., Interstate Commerce Comm., 1991–93.

DC Office: 2368 RHOB, 20515, 202-225-3115; Fax: 202-225-3547; Web site: whitfield.house.gov.

State Offices: Henderson, 270-826-4180; Hopkinsville, 270-885-8079; Paducah, 270-442-6901; Tompkinsville, 270-487-9509.

Committees: *Energy & Commerce:* Energy & Power (Chmn); Environment & the Economy; Health.

Group Ratings

	ACLU	ACU	ADA	CFG	AFS	FRC	LCV	ITIC	NTU	COC
2010	25	77	15	68	13	100	30	50	78	88
2009	–	88	0	72	33	–	29	–	74	93

National Journal Ratings

	2010 LIB	—	2010 CONS	2009 LIB	—	2009 CONS
Economic	32%	—	68%	30%	—	70%
Social	33%	—	66%	28%	—	71%
Foreign	12%	—	79%	37%	—	62%
Composite	27%	—	73%	32%	—	68%

Key Votes of the 111th Congress

1. Overturn Ledbetter	Y	5. Bar federal abortion funds	Y	9. Stop detainee transfers	Y
2. Pass $820 billion stimulus	N	6. Pass health care bill	N	10. Legalize immigrants' kids	N
3. Let guns in national parks	Y	7. Regulate financial firms	N	11. Repeal don't ask, tell	N
4. Pass cap-and-trade	N	8. Pass tax cuts for some	N	12. Limit campaign funds	N

Election Results

2010 general	Ed Whitfield (R)	 153,519	(71%)	($1,254,885)
	Charles Hatchett (D)	 61,960	(29%)	
2010 primary	Ed Whitfield (R)	.... unopposed		

Prior Winning Percentages: 2008 (64%), 2006 (60%), 2004 (67%), 2002 (65%), 2000 (58%), 1998 (55%), 1996 (54%), 1994 (51%)

Population		Race/Ethnicity		Work	
Pop. 2010:	686,989	White:	88.3%	Private:	74.0%
Change since 2000:	Up 2.0%	Black:	6.8%	Government:	17.8%
Urban:	36.5%	Hispanic:	2.6%	Self-employed:	7.9%
Rural:	63.5%	Asian:	0.5%	Blue collar:	31.4%
Area size:	12,058 sq. mi.	Native Am.:	0.2%	White collar:	49.2%
		Hawaiian:	0.1%	Khaki collar:	1.4%
Age		Two+ races:	1.4%	Other:	18.0%
Median age:	38.8 yrs.				
More than 65 yrs:	15.1%	*Ancestry*		Median income:	$36,363
Less than 18 yrs:	23.4%	USA	15.4%	Median Home Value:	$86,400
		English	10.9%		
Education		German	10.3%	**Military Veterans**	
H.S. grad:	78.8%			% of Pop:	10.7%
College grad:	13.9%				
Grad degree:	5.8%				

West Kentucky; Hopkinsville

The point where the Ohio River flows into the Mississippi—the intersection Huckleberry Finn and Jim missed in the fog—must have struck early settlers as a site for a great city. But no Pittsburgh or St. Louis grew up on this fertile black soil. Instead, the Kentucky land west of the dammed-up Tennessee and Cumberland rivers, bought from the Chickasaw Indians by Gen. Andrew Jackson and Gov. Isaac Shelby in 1818—the Jackson Purchase—was settled by

2008 Presidential Vote		
John McCain (R)	 176,807	(62%)
Barack Obama (D)	 104,626	(37%)
2004 Presidential Vote		
George Bush (R)	 180,446	(63%)
John Kerry (D)	 102,346	(36%)
Cook Partisan Voting Index:	R+15	

farmers. Most people here today are the descendants of these farmers, with memories of earlier generations living in family lore. Just to the east of the Tennessee and the Cumberland rivers is the Pennyrile (after pennyroyal, a common variety of local wild mint), a land of low hills, small farms, and the west Kentucky coalfields. There is Lyon County, founded by Matthew "Spitting" Lyon, who represented western Kentucky in the U.S. House from 1803 to 1811 and earned his epithet as a congressman for spitting in the face of a fellow member of Congress. The Land Between the Lakes, the boating and recreational haven created by the damming of the Tennessee and Cumberland rivers just before the debouch into the Ohio, is the fastest-growing area in these parts, as the Jackson Purchase and the Pennyrile struggle economically. A uranium enrichment plant operated by the company USEC in Paducah has been under federal cleanup since 1988 and has been slated to close in May 2012. In the meantime, the government has been slow to compensate workers stricken with radiation-related sickness.

The 1st Congressional District of Kentucky is made up of the Jackson Purchase and much of the Pennyrile, plus a line of counties stretching some 200 miles east of the Mississippi in the mountains along the Tennessee border and then north toward the center of the state. There is a distinctive Southern atmosphere here—in the crops that are grown, in the historically low wages, and in the fact that the big city with the most influence locally is Nashville, not Louisville. Paducah on the Ohio River has made some strides to reinvent itself with an artist relocation program that has boosted development. Turkey hunting also has become a draw for outsiders. The Army base at Fort Campbell is home to the 101st Airborne Division, which has deployed multiple times over the last decade.

The Jackson Purchase and the Pennyrile are ancestrally Democratic. Paducah produced one of the most enduring Democratic politicians of this century: Alben Barkley, whose career from 1912 to 1956 included 14 years in the House, 24 in the Senate and four as vice president. But the hills far from the Mississippi are Republican country, and this, combined with the Republican trend that reached north from Dixie to Paducah, has made the 1st District seriously contested territory in state elections—and one of the longtime Democratic rural areas that went solidly for George W. Bush in 2000 (58%) and 2004 (63%). In 2008, John McCain won the district with 62% of the vote.

Ed Whitfield (R)

The congressman from the 1st District is Ed Whitfield, a Republican elected in 1994. Whitfield grew up in Hopkinsville and Madisonville, in a family with Pennyrile roots going back to before 1800. He served in the Army Reserve, practiced law in Hopkinsville, and was elected to the state legislature in 1973 as a Democrat. After one term in Frankfort, Whitfield ran an oil distributorship in the west Kentucky coalfields, and then in 1979, moved to Washington, D.C., to become an executive for the Seaboard and CSX railroads. He was legal counsel to the chairman of the Interstate Commerce Commission from 1991 to 1993, and then returned to west Kentucky to run for Congress. The district had been represented by quiet, long-serving, conservative Democrats. But the one-term incumbent, Tom Barlow, was a free-spirited supporter of the Clinton administration. Encouraged by Sen. Mitch McConnell, Whitfield ran as a Republican, turned aside criticism that he was a carpetbagger, and concentrated on attacking Barlow's vote for Clinton's first-term budget and tax increase. With help from the mountain counties and running strongly in the Pennyrile, Whitfield won 51%-49% in the big Republican sweep of 1994.

In the House, Whitfield has a moderate-to-conservative voting record. He generally takes his party's side on major votes, but occasionally shows his independence. He supported the Lilly Ledbetter Fair Pay Act extending the statute of limitations in equal pay lawsuits in 2009 and voted for the minimum wage hike two years earlier.

With the Republicans assuming the majority in 2011, Whitfield became chairman of the Energy and Power Subcommittee of the main Energy and Commerce Committee. The job put him at the helm of Republican efforts to fight Obama administration environmental efforts, including the Environmental Protection Agency's climate regulations, which took effect in January 2011 after legislation to regulate greenhouse gas emissions stalled in the Senate. Whitfield also vowed to reexamine the 1970 Clean Air Act, the first federal law to control lead, mercury and other pollutants that endanger human health. EPA determined in 2009 that carbon dioxide, the main greenhouse gas, is among those pollutants. "Ever since I've been in Congress, various groups on the business side—those entities that are creating jobs out there—have felt that the Clean Air Act (has) all sorts of presumptions in favor of the environmentalists," Whitfield told *National Journal* in January 2011. In addition, he said he would scrutinize the rise in oil and gasoline prices and the need for offshore drilling in the wake of the BP oil spill disaster. He is a strong proponent of "clean coal" technology as well as sequestration research that some experts say could someday store underground carbon captured in the atmosphere.

On health issues before the committee, Whitfield authored a successful 2005 law to discourage "doctor shopping" by prescription-drugs addicts. It established an electronic database that states can use to monitor people who cross state lines to buy pharmaceuticals. He got a bill through the House in 2010 fostering the establishment of state-administered monitoring systems for dangerous drugs.

Whitfield has used his seat on the influential panel to tend to local concerns. He worked to secure federal aid for workers exposed to radiation at the uranium plant in Paducah. He overcame objections from the Bush administration to cleaning up the site, which is projected to cost more than $3 billion and last until around 2030. A thoroughbred owner, Whitfield co-sponsored legislation in 2006 to ban the killing of horses for meat. The House overwhelmingly passed the bill, but it died in the Senate. He also has encouraged industry leaders to restrict performance-enhancing drugs given to racehorses.

Whitfield has entrenched himself to the point that he is no longer much of a Democratic target. In 1996, when lawyer Dennis Null opposed him, Whitfield carried 18 of the district's 31 counties and won re-election 54%-46%. In 1998, former Rep. Tom Barlow ran again, and Whitfield won 55%-45%. Since then, he has won easily. He defeated Barlow a third time in 2006, increasing his winning margin to 60%-40%. And in 2008, he beat anti-war protester Heather Ryan 64%-36%. There was speculation in 2009 that he would run for the Senate, but he decided instead to seek a ninth term. This longtime Democratic stronghold now seems to be a safe Republican seat.

SECOND DISTRICT

Brett Guthrie (R)

Elected 2008, 2nd term; b. Feb. 18, 1964, Florence, AL; home, Bowling Green; U.S. Military Academy, B.S. 1987; Yale U., M.A. 1997.; Church of Christ; married (Beth); 3 children.

Military Career: Army, 1987-2001

Elected Office: KY Senate, 1998-2008.

Professional Career: V.P., Trace Die Cast, 2001-08.

DC Office: 308 CHOB, 20515, 202-225-3501; Fax: 202-226-2019; Web site: guthrie.house.gov.

State Offices: Bowling Green, 270-842-9896.

Committees: *Energy & Commerce:* Commerce, Manufacturing & Trade; Communications & Technology; Health.

Group Ratings

	ACLU	ACU	ADA	CFG	AFS	FRC	LCV	ITIC	NTU	COC
2010	13	95	0	84	0	93	0	33	85	88
2009	–	88	10	78	22	–	7	–	79	80

National Journal Ratings

	2010 LIB	—	2010 CONS	2009 LIB	—	2009 CONS
Economic	16%	—	83%	23%	—	76%
Social	18%	—	77%	29%	—	68%
Foreign	12%	—	79%	0%	—	75%
Composite	18%	—	82%	22%	—	78%

Key Votes of the 111th Congress

1. Overturn Ledbetter	N	5. Bar federal abortion funds	Y	9. Stop detainee transfers	Y
2. Pass $820 billion stimulus	N	6. Pass health care bill	N	10. Legalize immigrants' kids	N
3. Let guns in national parks	Y	7. Regulate financial firms	N	11. Repeal don't ask, tell	N
4. Pass cap-and-trade	N	8. Pass tax cuts for some	N	12. Limit campaign funds	N

Election Results

2010 general	Brett Guthrie (R) 155,906	(68%)	($1,233,573)
	Ed Marksberry (D)... 73,749	(32%)	
2010 primary	Brett Guthrie (R) .... unopposed		

Prior Winning Percentages: 2008 (53%)

Population		Race/Ethnicity		Work	
Pop. 2010:	760,032	White:	87.9%	Private:	76.6%
Change since 2000:	Up 12.9%	Black:	5.6%	Government:	17.0%
Urban:	47.2%	Hispanic:	3.3%	Self-employed:	6.1%
Rural:	52.8%	Asian:	1.0%	Blue collar:	31.1%
Area size:	7,669 sq. mi.	Native Am.:	0.2%	White collar:	51.0%
		Hawaiian:	0.1%	Khaki collar:	1.3%
Age		Two+ races:	1.6%	Other:	16.6%
Median age:	37.3 yrs.				
More than 65 yrs:	12.4%	*Ancestry*		Median income:	$43,075
Less than 18 yrs:	24.5%	USA	17.8%	Median Home Value:	$117,800
		German	12.2%		
Education		Irish	11.2%	**Military Veterans**	
H.S. grad:	82.3%			% of Pop:	11.4%
College grad:	16.2%				
Grad degree:	6.7%				

Central Kentucky; Owensboro

In the 1770s and 1780s, Americans began settling the limestone-soil country of central Kentucky, staking out towns like Bardstown and
Elizabethtown and starting academies and colleges. They were well settled when Stephen Foster wrote "My Old Kentucky Home" just before
the Civil War. The war tore deeply here. This
part of Kentucky gave birth to Abraham Lincoln,
and during the conflict, it lost thousands of soldiers, both Union and Confederate. The area is

2008 Presidential Vote		
John McCain (R) 188,955	(61%)
Barack Obama (D) 118,700	(38%)
2004 Presidential Vote		
George Bush (R) 190,612	(65%)
John Kerry (D) 100,580	(34%)
Cook Partisan Voting Index: R+15		

the home of several Kentucky landmarks—Fort Knox, the nation's gold depository; some of the
nation's largest bourbon distilleries; and Mammoth Cave, the world's largest accessible cavern,
near Bowling Green.

The 2nd Congressional District of Kentucky consists of much of the territory south and
southwest of Louisville, starting with Spencer County and proceeding south to Bowling Green.
That city did better than the rest of Kentucky in coping with the recession: It is the headquarters
of apparel giant Fruit of the Loom, which added around 600 jobs in 2010, and it has a bustling
General Motors Corvette assembly plant. The district continues west along the Ohio River to Owensboro, a port with warehouses that receive aluminum alloys to make lightweight engine parts.
The city has aggressively and successfully courted new economic development in recent years, and
in 2010 U.S. Bank Home Mortgage announced plans to add 500 jobs to its more than 1,000 employees there. It also hosts an annual international barbecue festival where mutton, a throwback to
Welsh shepherds who settled in western Kentucky, remains a favorite.

Much of the district is rural and small-town country, where people have family roots that go
back generations and a connection with the past not often found in metropolitan areas. Civil War
loyalties are reflected in the election returns here. Kentucky was deeply split on secession, with
some counties pro-South and others pro-Union. For many years, the balance of opinion here favored
the Democrats. But in the 1990s, it moved toward the Republican Party, which better matched
its conservative cultural leanings. In 2000 and 2004, this was George W. Bush's best district in
Kentucky. In 2008, Republican nominee John McCain did well here, winning the district 61%-38%
over Democrat Barack Obama.

Brett Guthrie (R)

The congressman from the 2nd District is Brett Guthrie, a Republican elected in 2008 to succeed
retiring GOP Rep. Ron Lewis. A graduate of West Point, Guthrie served 14 years in the U.S. Army,
first in the Reserve, then as a field artillery officer with the 101st Airborne division at Fort Campbell. After his discharge, Guthrie joined the family business in Bowling Green, Ky., Trace Die Cast,
Inc., a leading supplier of aluminum castings for the automobile industry with a workforce of more
than 500. His father had started the business with his savings and just five employees in the 1980s.
Guthrie eventually became vice president. In 1998, Guthrie was elected to the state Senate, where
he focused on education issues and became chairman of the Transportation Committee, helping
the state develop its highway budget. Republicans expected him to eventually join the leadership
ranks, but Guthrie had his sights set on Congress.

After Lewis announced his retirement, his longtime chief of staff, Daniel London, jumped into
the race to succeed him. But leading local Republicans criticized Lewis and London, saying they'd
set up a succession plan: Lewis had waited until just before the filing deadline to announce his
retirement, leaving little time for candidates other than London to file. London apologized and
withdrew from the race. Guthrie avoided a contested primary and marshaled his resources for the
contested general election.

The Democratic nominee was state Sen. David Boswell, a 30-year veteran of Kentucky politics
and a former Agriculture commissioner. He ran as a conservative Democrat, and the two contenders were virtually indistinguishable on the issues. Both opposed abortion rights and supported gun
ownership, and both spoke out against the massive bailout for the financial industry passed by
Congress that fall.

National Democrats sensed they might be able to pick up a Republican House seat and made
the contest one of their top priorities of 2008. Guthrie found himself neck-and-neck with Boswell
in a district that had been held by a Republican for 15 years. He ran ads tying Boswell to liberal
congressional Democrats and their opposition to offshore drilling. And he emphasized his military

background to the district's sizable active and retired military population. The Democratic Congressional Campaign Committee ran an ad claiming that Trace Die Cast had sent jobs to Mexico. Former President Bill Clinton stumped for Boswell in the district; and first lady Laura Bush put in an appearance for Guthrie. Guthrie proved more adept at fundraising, with a war chest of nearly $1.3 million; Boswell's barely topped $900,000. Guthrie won 53%-47%.

Once in the House, Guthrie proved to be a loyal Republican vote. He joined other GOP colleagues in angrily accusing Democrats of rushing major legislation to passage, and he co-sponsored legislation that required a 72-hour waiting period before a floor vote. He complained that the House-passed health care overhaul "raises taxes for just about everyone," although supporters noted it imposed a surtax on only the top 0.3% of households. When the House passed a bill in September 2009 with major changes in the student lending system and establishing the government as the only provider of loans, Guthrie unsuccessfully sought a study for a new private-sector model for lending.

Guthrie sailed to re-election in 2010 with 69% of the vote over Democrat Ed Marksberry, who didn't bother to submit reports that showed him raising any money. He was rewarded with a plum seat on the Energy and Commerce Committee, enabling him to work with fellow Kentucky Republican Ed Whitfield on assisting their state's coal and oil industries.

THIRD DISTRICT

John Yarmuth (D)

Elected 2006, 3rd term; b. Nov. 4, 1947, Louisville; home, Louisville; Yale U., B.A. 1969, attended Georgetown, 1972-74, attended U. of Louisville, 1975; Jewish; married (Catherine); 1 child.

Professional Career: Stockbroker, 1969-71; Sr. aide, U.S. Sen. Marlow Cook, 1971-74; Publisher, Louisville Today magazine, 1976-82; Asst. vp of university relations, U. of Louisville, 1983-86; VP, Caretenders, 1986-90; Owner, columnist & executive editor, Louisville Eccentric Observer, 1990-2002; Co-host, Yarmuth & Ziegler, 2003; Commentator, Hot Button, 2004-05.

DC Office: 435 CHOB, 20515, 202-225-5401; Fax: 202-225-5776; Web site: yarmuth.house.gov.

State Offices: Romano Mazzoli Federal Building, 502-582-5129; Southwest Government Center, 502-935-6934.

Committees: *Budget. Ethics. Oversight & Government Reform:* National Security, Homeland Defense & Foreign Operations; TARP, Financial Services & Bailouts of Public & Private Programs.

Group Ratings

	ACLU	ACU	ADA	CFG	AFS	FRC	LCV	ITIC	NTU	COC
2010	88	0	100	0	100	0	90	67	3	13
2009	–	0	100	4	100	–	100	–	2	40

National Journal Ratings

	2010 LIB — 2010 CONS		2009 LIB — 2009 CONS	
Economic	77%	— 22%	68%	— 30%
Social	80%	— 18%	72%	— 26%
Foreign	84%	— 16%	78%	— 17%
Composite	81%	— 19%	74%	— 26%

Key Votes of the 111th Congress

1. Overturn Ledbetter	Y	5. Bar federal abortion funds	N	9. Stop detainee transfers	N
2. Pass $820 billion stimulus	Y	6. Pass health care bill	Y	10. Legalize immigrants' kids	Y
3. Let guns in national parks	N	7. Regulate financial firms	Y	11. Repeal don't ask, tell	Y
4. Pass cap-and-trade	Y	8. Pass tax cuts for some	Y	12. Limit campaign funds	Y

Election Results

2010 general	John Yarmuth (D)	139,940	(55%)	($1,537,401)
	Todd Lally (R)	112,627	(44%)	($855,434)
2010 primary	John Yarmuth (D)	unopposed		

Prior Winning Percentages: 2008 (59%), 2006 (51%)

Population		Race/Ethnicity		Work	
Pop. 2010:	721,626	White:	70.3%	Private:	83.8%
Change since 2000:	Up 7.1%	Black:	20.9%	Government:	11.6%
Urban:	98.3%	Hispanic:	4.3%	Self-employed:	4.5%
Rural:	1.7%	Asian:	2.2%	Blue collar:	21.1%
Area size:	379 sq. mi.	Native Am.:	0.2%	White collar:	62.1%
		Hawaiian:	0.1%	Khaki collar:	0.1%
Age		Two+ races:	1.9%	Other:	16.7%
Median age:	37.5 yrs.				
More than 65 yrs:	13.5%	*Ancestry*		Median income:	$45,332
Less than 18 yrs:	23.6%	German	16.3%	Median Home Value:	$149,100
		Irish	11.8%		
Education		USA	9.0%	**Military Veterans**	
H.S. grad:	87.7%			% of Pop:	10.6%
College grad:	29.4%				
Grad degree:	11.6%				

Louisville Area

At the falls of the Ohio River, Americans more than 200 years ago founded one of their first inland metropolises, the river port and industrial city of Louisville. Established by George Rogers Clark in 1778, the city has always retained an air of the South. When Kentucky decided not to secede from the union in 1861, the decision was not unanimous, and the culture of tidewater Virginia is still evident in the Louisville lawn party. Mint juleps are served on the verandas of

2008 Presidential Vote
Barack Obama (D) 193,260   (56%)
John McCain (R) 150,552   (43%)

2004 Presidential Vote
John Kerry (D) 167,440   (51%)
George Bush (R) 160,772   (49%)

Cook Partisan Voting Index: D+2

mansions, especially (but not only) during Kentucky Derby week in May; horse racing is a preoccupation throughout the year. Although the Ohio River is crossed by many bridges and the accent across the river in Indiana may sound the same to outsiders, Louisville partakes of the Cavalier culture that second sons of big landowners from England brought to Virginia in the 17th century, and their heirs brought over the Appalachians to the valleys of Kentucky in the 18th century.

With an estimated 784,000 people in 2010, Louisville is Kentucky's largest city, surpassing Lexington in 2003 after Louisville voters decided to consolidate the city and surrounding Jefferson County. Louisville has not been growing as rapidly as many other Southern and Midwestern cities. Its economy is in many ways pre-postindustrial: It produces cigarettes and whiskey, large appliances and Ford automobiles. The unemployment rate climbed past 12% in 2010 before it began to improve. However, Louisville is also the headquarters of Humana health services and of Yum! Brands, which owns KFC, Pizza Hut, Taco Bell and Long John Silver's. Its downtown hosts a new medical services center, the Muhammad Ali Center and the Owsley Brown Frazier Historical Arms Museum. The long-term health care facility operator Signature HealthCARE relocated its national headquarters here from Florida in 2010. But the pace of growth in Louisville-Jefferson County is still slower than in the counties that ring it and in the counties across the river in Indiana. This regional growth has fueled plans to build two massive bridges over the Ohio River, at an estimated cost of more than $4 billion and a scheduled completion date of 2024.

The 3rd Congressional District of Kentucky includes all but a dozen or so precincts of Louisville-Jefferson County. There is a large black population in the West End of Louisville and just south of the old city limits, and a lower-income white population along the strip highway that leads to Fort Knox. The suburbs to the east tend to be affluent. Small, elite neighborhoods—Mockingbird Valley, Glenview, Ten Broeck—are nestled in the hills above the Ohio River. Louisville has long been an odd duck in Kentucky politics. If its elite were Virginia Cavaliers, many of its burghers were Germans and Pennsylvanians who made this river town a Republican and anti-slavery island in a secessionist and pro-slavery sea. That tradition helps explain why Republican Mitch McConnell was able to get elected as Jefferson County judge-executive in 1977 and 1981, when the state was electing Democrats to most other offices. Since the 1990s, Louisville, like many metro areas, has trended toward the Democrats, even as the rest of Kentucky trended Republican. The 3rd District voted by narrow margins for Al Gore in 2000 and John Kerry in 2004, while the state's other five districts all voted twice for George W. Bush. In 2008, the district voted for Barack Obama even as the rest of Kentucky went solidly for John McCain.

John Yarmuth (D)

The congressman from the 3rd District is Democrat John Yarmuth, who won the district in 2006 by defeating five-term Republican Anne Northup. Yarmuth never held elected office before, but had spent four years as a Senate aide and more than two decades as a newspaper editor, publisher, and columnist. He told *Esquire* in 2010 that he had trouble making the adjustment: "I never had to compromise on my opinion in the column. Suddenly you have to swallow all sorts of compromises, and that's not easy at all." He comes from a wealthy family. His father, Stanley Yarmuth, founded National Industries, a conglomerate that started as a used car business; his maternal grandfather, Samuel Klein, ran the Bank of Louisville. John Yarmuth grew up in Louisville and went to Atherton High School, where he was elected student government president. After graduating from Yale University in 1969, he worked briefly as a stockbroker and then as an aide to Republican Sen. Marlow Cook. Yarmuth attended two years of law school but didn't finish his degree.

In 1976, he founded *Louisville Today* magazine, and served as publisher until 1982. He ran unsuccessfully for Louisville alderman in 1975, and for county commissioner in 1981. He worked in public relations from 1983 to 1990 for the University of Louisville and for a health care company. Unhappy with the policies of President Ronald Reagan and the Republican Party, Yarmuth switched his party affiliation to Democrat in 1985. (He says he first registered as a Republican as a favor to his father, who was a fundraiser for President Richard Nixon.) In 1990, Yarmuth founded the *Louisville Eccentric Observer*, a free newsweekly popularly known as LEO, and for the next 15 years, penned a column called "Hot Coals" that promoted his mostly liberal views. He sold the publication in 2003, but continued his column and also did political commentary on television.

In 2006, Northup was again vulnerable in this Democratic-leaning district, which she'd fought hard to keep by bringing in millions of dollars in federal funds from her perch on the House Appropriations Committee. The Democratic Congressional Campaign Committee touted attorney Andrew Horne, an Iraq war veteran and first-time candidate. But Yarmuth raised more money and proved a more formidable candidate than Horne, winning the four-way primary 54%-32%. He called for an immediate pullout of troops from Iraq and referred to Northup as a "rubber stamp" for President George W. Bush. Northup campaigned on the Republican tax cuts and her work for the district. Yarmuth ran on his support for universal health coverage, a minimum-wage increase and revamping the Bush administration's No Child Left Behind education law.

The mother of six children, Northup suffered a wrenching personal tragedy during the campaign when her son died of an undiagnosed heart condition. She suspended her campaign for six weeks before returning to campaigning at the end of the summer. Then she unleashed a radio, television and Internet offensive that blasted Yarmuth for his liberal writings, saying he supported removing the phrase "under God" from the Pledge of Allegiance and legalizing marijuana. Northup raised nearly $3.4 million to Yarmuth's $2.3 million, which included $700,000 of his own money. Northup, who carried the district while Bush lost it in 2000 and 2004, could not overcome a national tide against Republicans that year, an environment made worse locally by a patronage scandal surrounding Republican Gov. Ernie Fletcher. Yarmuth won 51%-48%.

In the House, Yarmuth is generally a moderate Democrat. He was loyal enough to snare a seat on the powerful Ways and Means Committee in the 111th Congress (2009-10). He introduced a bill to cut the capital gains tax on investment property to shore up the ailing commercial real estate market. He also pushed a bill giving the Small Business Administration $20 billion to lend directly to businesses instead of going through banks. And in a nod to his state's horse-racing industry, he sponsored legislation to automatically withhold federal taxes on 25% of racetrack winnings above $5,000 if the odds on the bets are at least 300-1. Yarmuth lost the seat on the panel after Republicans won a House majority in the 2010 election.

With his journalism background, Yarmuth joined a "messaging" group that advised Speaker Nancy Pelosi and other Democratic leaders on media strategy. He also served as Pelosi's strategic communications adviser on the health care overhaul, a task he later said was made difficult by the Senate's changes to the measure. "We couldn't really go to the average American citizen and say, 'Here's what it means to you,'" he told a Louisville radio station.

Northup came back for a rematch in 2008, after losing a primary challenge to Fletcher for governor. She criticized Yarmuth for supporting the $700 billion bailout for the financial markets in 2008, and also attacked his "present" vote on a resolution honoring Christmas, asserting he had lost touch with his constituents. (Yarmuth is Jewish.) Even though Northup raised more money than Yarmuth, he had a much easier time than in 2006, winning 59%-41%. In 2010, he drew a far less well-known opponent in Todd Lally, a United Parcel Service pilot with tea party backing. With Republicans focused on trying to topple 6th District Democrat Ben Chandler, Yarmuth held back the Republican wave with 55% of the vote.

A scratch golfer who once played as many as 100 rounds of golf a year, Yarmuth says that the demands of Congress prompted him to scale back his plans to spend a month every year at a home he recently built near a golf course in Ireland.

FOURTH DISTRICT

Geoff Davis (R)

Elected 2004, 4th term; b. Oct. 26, 1958, Montreal, Canada; home, Hebron; U.S.M.A., B.S. 1981; Christian; married (Pat); 6 children.

Military Career: Army, 1976-87.

Professional Career: Technology consultant, 1989-2004; Owner, Republic Consulting, 1992-2004.

DC Office: 1119 LHOB, 20515, 202-225-3465; Fax: 202-225-0003; Web site: geoffdavis.house.gov.

State Offices: Ashland, 606-324-9898; Fort Mitchell, 859-426-0080; LaGrange, 502-222-2233; Maysville, 606-564-6004; Williamstown, 859-824-3320.

Committees: *Ways & Means:* Human Resources (Chmn); Trade.

Group Ratings

	ACLU	ACU	ADA	CFG	AFS	FRC	LCV	ITIC	NTU	COC
2010	13	96	0	84	0	87	0	50	87	86
2009	–	92	5	81	22	–	7	–	83	87

National Journal Ratings

	2010 LIB — 2010 CONS		2009 LIB — 2009 CONS	
Economic	18%	— 82%	22%	— 77%
Social	0%	— 85%	20%	— 78%
Foreign	24%	— 75%	26%	— 68%
Composite	17%	— 83%	24%	— 76%

Key Votes of the 111th Congress

1. Overturn Ledbetter	N	5. Bar federal abortion funds	Y	9. Stop detainee transfers	*
2. Pass $820 billion stimulus	N	6. Pass health care bill	N	10. Legalize immigrants' kids	N
3. Let guns in national parks	Y	7. Regulate financial firms	N	11. Repeal don't ask, tell	N
4. Pass cap-and-trade	N	8. Pass tax cuts for some	N	12. Limit campaign funds	N

Election Results

2010 general	Geoff Davis (R)	151,774	(69%)	($1,676,564)
	John Waltz (D)	66,675	(31%)	($444,682)
2010 primary	Geoff Davis (R)	unopposed		

Prior Winning Percentages: 2008 (63%), 2006 (52%), 2004 (54%)

Population		Race/Ethnicity		Work	
Pop. 2010:	741,464	White:	92.4%	Private:	81.1%
Change since 2000:	Up 10.1%	Black:	2.7%	Government:	13.3%
Urban:	59.7%	Hispanic:	2.4%	Self-employed:	5.5%
Rural:	40.3%	Asian:	0.9%	Blue collar:	25.1%
Area size:	5,770 sq. mi.	Native Am.:	0.2%	White collar:	59.2%
		Hawaiian:	0.0%	Khaki collar:	0.1%
Age		Two+ races:	1.3%	Other:	15.7%
Median age:	37.7 yrs.				
More than 65 yrs:	12.1%	*Ancestry*		Median income:	$48,727
Less than 18 yrs:	24.8%	German	21.7%	Median Home Value:	$134,100
		Irish	14.7%		
Education		USA	10.6%	**Military Veterans**	
H.S. grad:	83.8%			% of Pop:	9.9%
College grad:	22.4%				
Grad degree:	8.1%				

North Kentucky; Covington

Along the Ohio River are some very different parts of Kentucky. Ashland, near the West Virginia border, is industrial, the former home of Ashland Inc.; the river here is bound in by tight hills that hold smoke and soot close in the air. Farther down the river, the country is more bucolic. This is where Eliza fled across the ice floes in Harriet Beecher Stowe's *Uncle Tom's Cabin.* Farther west, between Louisville and Cincinnati, are counties that look like they're still in

2008 Presidential Vote		
John McCain (R) 189,008	(60%)
Barack Obama (D) 118,773	(38%)
2004 Presidential Vote		
George Bush (R)...................195,055	(63%)
John Kerry (D) 111,049	(36%)
Cook Partisan Voting Index: R+14		

the 19th century. But metropolitan growth obtrudes. Oldham County, just upriver from Louisville, has some of Kentucky's oldest homes, and is by far the most affluent county in the state. The three Northern Kentucky counties across the river from Cincinnati—Campbell, Kenton and fast-growing Boone—are urban and suburban. Overlooking the suspension bridge built by John Roebling are new buildings on the Covington waterfront, and new subdivisions are rising on the hills in Boone County, above the river and near the Cincinnati-Northern Kentucky International Airport. Newport, with its panoramic view of the Cincinnati skyline plus its nightlife, has become a regional hot spot.

But, as in other parts of the region, this area suffered during the recession, losing more than 4,000 private-sector jobs between June 2009 and June 2010. Home sales in Northern Kentucky declined in 2010 for the sixth straight year. But by year's end there were some encouraging signs: United Dairy Farmers announced a 100,000-square foot addition to its refrigerated warehouse in Erlanger, and ZF Steering Systems, which makes steering components for cars and SUVs, said it would invest $96 million over three years at its facility in Florence.

The 4th Congressional District of Kentucky is the northernmost district in the state. It includes the counties along the Ohio and also lightly populated counties just inland. Economically, it runs the gamut from coal mining towns to rich suburbs. Politically, it has some of the most Democratic counties in America, like mountain-bound Elliott County, which voted 61%-36% for Barack Obama in 2008, his strongest county in Kentucky, and 70%-30% for John Kerry in 2004. It also has some of the most Republican territory in Kentucky, like Oldham County, which voted 65%-34% for John McCain in 2008 and 69%-30% for George W. Bush in 2004. The three northern Kentucky counties across the river from Cincinnati cast nearly half the district's votes, and they too are heavily Republican. Overall, this is a Republican district.

Geoff Davis (R)

The congressman from the 4th District is Geoff Davis, a Republican elected in 2004. He grew up in Pittsburgh and worked as a janitor in high school to help the family pay the bills. He was the victim of an abusive, alcoholic stepfather and left home right after high school to join the Army. His life turned around after he received an appointment to attend the prestigious U.S. Military Academy at West Point. He studied Arabic and Asian and European cultures, focusing his studies on national security and international affairs. In the service, Davis was an assault helicopter flight commander in the 82nd Airborne Division, and later ran U.S. Army aviation oversight on the Israel-Egypt border. After 11 years in the military, he moved to Fort Worth, Texas, then to Northern Kentucky, where in 1992 he started a consulting firm that advised companies on how to streamline manufacturing technology.

In 2002, he ran against Rep. Ken Lucas, a conservative Democrat first elected in 1998, but lost 51%-48% after receiving very little assistance from the national party. Lucas decided to honor his pledge to serve only three terms and announced his retirement in 2003. Davis became the front-runner in this heavily Republican district in 2004, but he still faced a formidable challenge from Democrat Nick Clooney, a locally famous newspaper columnist and television commentator, and the father of actor George Clooney. Through his son, Clooney got checks from movie stars Paul Newman, Kevin Costner and Catherine Zeta-Jones. Davis charged that his opponent had more in common with the people of Southern California than in Northern Kentucky.

Billing himself as a moderate, Clooney said he supported President George W. Bush's tax cuts and opposed same-sex marriage and abortion rights. The Davis campaign unearthed columns Clooney had written over a period of 15 years, including one in which he criticized gun ownership. Davis touted his lifetime membership in the National Rifle Association. Despite Clooney's help from Hollywood, Davis had a big fundraising advantage; he spent $2.6 million to Clooney's

$1.5 million. Clooney won rural and mining areas in the eastern end of the district, but Davis carried the three Cincinnati-area suburban counties and won the race, 54%-44%.

In the House, Davis established a solidly conservative voting record, especially on foreign policy. In 2006, Bush signed into law Davis's bill to protect military personnel from being sold overpriced insurance and investment products. As a member of the Financial Services Committee, Davis pushed for a cap on interest rates on "payday" loans to members of the military. In early 2009, he secured a coveted seat on the Ways and Means Committee. He called Democratic dealmaking on the health care overhaul bill that year "the worst of Congress on full display." At a raucous rally outside the Capitol shortly before the bill passed in March 2010, Davis and Bill Posey, R-Fla., waved the yellow "Don't Tread On Me" flag of the tea party movement. David sponsored a measure in 2009 requiring congressional approval of any major rule promulgated by federal agencies, a cause he shares with conservative kingpin Sen. Jim DeMint, R-S.C. The same year, he joined with Sander Levin of Michigan, Ways and Means' ranking Democrat, on a bill to expand and make permanent a tax break on charitable food donations.

In 2006, national Democrats decided to challenge Davis by recruiting Lucas, a conservative who opposed abortion, same-sex marriage and gun control and who had held the district for three terms. Davis, usually a reliable vote for Bush administration policies, distanced himself from Bush by saying he strongly disagreed with the White House on immigration and on the partial privatization of Social Security. Lucas had difficulty tapping into national anti-Republican sentiment or disenchantment with the Iraq war. He had voted for the Iraq invasion, which he later said he regretted. Davis won 52%-43%.

In 2008, he easily won re-election against Democrat Michael Kelley, an Oldham County physician. But he was blasted after he referred to Democratic presidential candidate Barack Obama as a "boy" during a political dinner in April. Talking about Obama's lack of military experience, he said, "That boy's finger does not need to be on the button." Davis quickly made a public apology to Obama. He had no trouble holding onto the seat in 2010.

FIFTH DISTRICT

Harold Rogers (R)

Elected 1980, 16th term; b. Dec. 31, 1937, Barrier; home, Somerset; U. of KY, B.A. 1962, J.D. 1964; Baptist; married (Cynthia); 3 children.

Military Career: Army Natl. Guard, 1957–64.

Professional Career: Practicing atty., 1964–69; Pulaski–Rockcastle Commonwealth's Atty., 1969–80.

DC Office: 2406 RHOB, 20515, 202-225-4601; Fax: 202-225-0940; Web site: halrogers.house.gov.

State Offices: Hazard, 606-439-0794; Prestonburg, 606-886-0844; Somerset, 606-679-8346.

Committees: *Appropriations* (Chmn).

Group Ratings

	ACLU	ACU	ADA	CFG	AFS	FRC	LCV	ITIC	NTU	COC
2010	6	96	0	84	0	100	0	33	85	88
2009	–	88	0	76	22	–	21	–	75	87

National Journal Ratings

	2010 LIB	—	2010 CONS	2009 LIB	—	2009 CONS
Economic	21%	—	79%	23%	—	76%
Social	29%	—	69%	29%	—	68%
Foreign	12%	—	79%	0%	—	75%
Composite	23%	—	78%	22%	—	78%

Key Votes of the 111th Congress

1. Overturn Ledbetter	N	5. Bar federal abortion funds	Y	9. Stop detainee transfers	Y
2. Pass $820 billion stimulus	N	6. Pass health care bill	N	10. Legalize immigrants' kids	N
3. Let guns in national parks	Y	7. Regulate financial firms	N	11. Repeal don't ask, tell	N
4. Pass cap-and-trade	N	8. Pass tax cuts for some	N	12. Limit campaign funds	N

Election Results

2010 general	Harold Rogers (R) 151,019	(77%)	($895,671)
	James Holbert (D)...44,034	(23%)	($13,012)
2010 primary	Harold Rogers (R) .... unopposed		

Prior Winning Percentages: 2008 (84%), 2006 (74%), 2004 (100%), 2002 (78%), 2000 (74%), 1998 (78%), 1996 (100%), 1994 (79%), 1992 (55%), 1990 (100%), 1988 (100%), 1986 (100%), 1984 (76%), 1982 (65%), 1980 (67%)

Population		Race/Ethnicity		Work	
Pop. 2010:	670,051	White:	96.3%	Private:	74.3%
Change since 2000:	Down 0.5%	Black:	1.3%	Government:	19.1%
Urban:	21.3%	Hispanic:	1.1%	Self-employed:	6.3%
Rural:	78.7%	Asian:	0.3%	Blue collar:	30.6%
Area size:	10,757 sq. mi.	Native Am.:	0.2%	White collar:	51.7%
		Hawaiian:	0.0%	Khaki collar:	0.1%
Age		Two+ races:	0.8%	Other:	17.6%
Median age:	38.6 yrs.				
More than 65 yrs:	13.6%	*Ancestry*		Median income:	$27,110
Less than 18 yrs:	23.1%	USA	30.7%	Median Home Value:	$66,600
		Irish	10.2%		
Education		English	9.7%	**Military Veterans**	
H.S. grad:	68.4%			% of Pop:	8.0%
College grad:	11.4%				
Grad degree:	5.3%				

Eastern Kentucky

Mountainous eastern Kentucky has been a unique place since Daniel Boone came through the Cumberland Gap in 1775. As Virginians poured through and created their version of a Tidewater civilization in the Bluegrass country, the people brought their assertive egalitarianism, loyalty to family and community, and passionate willingness to defend honor by feuds or violence. Most of the inhabitants of the mountains today are Scots-Irish—descendants of the

2008 Presidential Vote
John McCain (R) 162,614   (67%)
Barack Obama (D) 75,815   (31%)

2004 Presidential Vote
George Bush (R) 159,489   (61%)
John Kerry (D) 102,142   (39%)

Cook Partisan Voting Index: R+16

Ulster Protestant and Border Scot families who settled there in the two or three generations after Boone. Handed down were living memories of the old ways of doing things from an era when there was little contact with the outside world. The first agent of change here was the Civil War; the second was the great United Mine Workers organizing drives in the coal mines in the 1930s. The Civil War made the mountains and the Cumberland Plateau a stronghold of the Republican Party. This was never slave territory—hardly any blacks have ever lived here—yet communities and families were riven by the rebellion of the South. Today, the counties around Somerset and Corbin in south central Kentucky cast some of the highest Republican percentages in the nation, election after election.

Early in the 20th century, vast seams of coal were discovered under the Kentucky mountains. Representatives of eastern capitalists (including the young Franklin D. Roosevelt) began prowling these hills, hiring town lawyers to buy up mineral rights from unsuspecting farmers, building industrial slum towns in hollows and creek beds beneath glowering, heavily forested mountains. Coal mining was harsh and deadly work. Mine accidents, black lung disease, and simple exhaustion killed tens of thousands of miners, while low wages and company stores kept them poor. Then John L. Lewis's United Mine Workers came in, and open warfare followed, with neither mine operators nor union organizers reluctant to use violence and threats. The union mostly won in eastern Kentucky and in the short run raised wages and built hospitals for miners and their families. In the longer run, the impact of the UMW was a phasing out of many jobs in the mines in return for job security and health benefits, as use of oil expanded. Today, there are just over 500 mines in Kentucky, compared with 25 years ago, when there were 2,000. Politically, the UMW counties in the eastern part of the state became heavily Democratic.

In the mid-1960s, Lyndon B. Johnson came to eastern Kentucky and cited the poverty here in pushing for his Appalachian and anti-poverty bills. The high energy prices of the 1970s sparked strip mining, and eastern Kentucky's economy moved upward. High coal prices in 2004 stepped up the pace at existing mines, but the big mining companies that increasingly controlled production were wary of opening new mines. Mountaintop mining has become common, requiring huge machines and few workers. Most eastern coal counties have lost population since 1980, and counties far from the interstate highways have a hard time attracting new businesses. But life here today is much closer to the ordinary American standard of living than it was in Johnson's time. Income levels are low, not much over 50% of the national average, but so is the cost of living. Religion remains important here. The Pulaski County Fiscal Court in 2008 voted to appeal the ruling of a federal judge who had tried to stop the county's display of the Ten Commandments. And this part of Kentucky has produced stars in that quintessentially American medium, country music—Loretta Lynn, Ricky Skaggs, Dwight Yoakam, Crystal Gayle. The Hillbilly Days Festival draws 100,000 people every year to Pikeville.

The 5th Congressional District of Kentucky includes much of the Cumberland Plateau and most of the eastern mountains, a mixture of heavily Republican and heavily Democratic territories. There are huge political differences here between counties separated by just a mountain ridge or two, evidence of the depth of Civil War and United Mine Workers political loyalties, and only somewhat modulated by the recent trend toward Republicans in the coal country. But overall this is a solidly Republican district—it voted 61% for George W. Bush in 2004 and 67% for John McCain in 2008.

Harold Rogers (R)

The congressman from the 5th District is Harold Rogers, a Republican first elected in 1980, and now chairman of the House Appropriations Committee.

Rogers grew up in Wayne County, graduated from the University of Kentucky, served in the National Guard, and then practiced law in Somerset before buying the Citizens National Bank in Somerset. In 1969, at age 34, he was elected Pulaski-Rockcastle Commonwealth attorney. In 1979, he was the Republican nominee for lieutenant governor. The following year, when the 5th District congressman retired, Rogers was one of 11 Republicans in the primary. He got the nomination with 23% of the vote (Kentucky has no runoff except in gubernatorial races) and then easily won in November. His toughest race came in 1992, after redistricting. At first, his likely opponent was 7th District incumbent Rep. Chris Perkins, a Democrat and the son of longtime Rep. Carl Perkins. But then Perkins suddenly retired from Congress, just before it was revealed that he had 514 overdrafts at the House bank when such overdrafts were developing into a major Washington scandal. Rogers ended up facing state Sen. John Doug Hays of Pike County. Rogers won with 55% of the vote.

Rogers rose to chairman of Appropriations in 2011 after Republicans won control of the House. He had first sought the post after the 2004 election, but the GOP leadership chose the more senior Jerry Lewis of California. After the 2010 election, Lewis sought a waiver of the Republicans' three-term limit on chairman and ranking member positions, but the Republican Steering Committee did not agree and named Rogers as chairman.

His voting record is mostly, but not always, conservative. His district has long been hungry for federal aid, and Rogers often has found it difficult to maintain an impeccably conservative record on spending issues. In Republicans' earlier stint in the majority (1995-2007), he supported zeroing out many domestic programs, but not those important to his district—the Appalachian Regional Commission and the Legal Services Corporation. Over the years, he secured $162 million to protect the solvency of the United Mine Workers Combined Benefit Fund, $15 million for a 760-seat theater near Somerset, and $341 million for a massive concrete wall to close off leaks at Wolf Creek Dam at Lake Cumberland after the lowering of lake water levels caused a drop in tourism. When he chaired the Appropriations Transportation Subcommittee in 2001, Kentucky became the fourth-highest state in transportation funding per capita. The Daniel Boone Parkway, from London to Hazard, has been renamed the Hal Rogers Parkway. "The rate of return on highway spending far exceeds most other investments and is a proven engine," Rogers once wrote when he was criticized for his earmarked spending. The *Lexington Herald-Leader* dubbed him "the Prince of Pork."

In recent years, controversy over earmarks, the special provisions that lawmakers slip into spending bills for their districts and states, put an unaccustomed spotlight on Rogers and other powerful appropriators, who for years were used to going about their business quietly on Capitol Hill. When he was criticized for fighting to keep the Transportation Worker Identification Credential program in Corbin, he replied that it was one of only three government facilities with sufficient security to produce the cards. Rogers has continued raising significant sums of political cash from firms that have won homeland security contracts. He responded, "I've had a lot of fundraisers.

Campaign contributions mean nothing on my watch." Rogers says that he has created 15,000 jobs in his district and brought his constituents "peace of mind."

But Rogers rose to Appropriations chairman just as most House Republicans, especially the 87 freshmen, were determined to end the practice of earmarking. Despite his work over the years funding projects at home, he went along with the GOP leadership's moratorium on earmarks in November 2010. "We are at a crossroads, with the most serious fiscal crisis staring us in the face," Rogers said. "Now is the time to fix a broken system and demonstrate to the American people that we are listening. We will rein in spending and get this economy back on track."

On national issues, Rogers over the years has focused on homeland security. Even before the September 11 attacks, he lamented that most airport screeners were not U.S. citizens, and after Congress voted to federalize airport screeners, he kept a close watch on the new agency. In 2006, he took Homeland Security Secretary Michael Chertoff to task for a proposed budget that Rogers insisted was way short of meeting the country's needs. His bill out of the Homeland Security Appropriations Subcommittee that year was $1.8 billion above the administration's request. Rogers also demanded that the agency rearrange some of its priorities more to his liking.

More recently, he questioned in March 2010 the Obama administration's proposals for airport body scanners because, he said, it was unclear whether such a costly and manpower-intensive approach would get results. In June 2009, he criticized the Homeland Security Department for delaying a requirement that federal contractors use the E-Verify system to confirm the immigration status of new employees. Rogers also questioned the Immigration and Customs Enforcement agency's policy of giving work permits to apprehended illegal immigrants who testify against their employers. The Obama administration, he complained, had practically given up deporting illegal immigrants arrested at work sites in favor of what he derisively called "virtual amnesty."

Rogers has been re-elected by overwhelming margins, carrying even the most Democratic counties, and has never received less than 65% of the vote. Many Republicans urged him to run for governor in 2003, but he said he felt he could do more for the state in Congress. He was re-elected without Democratic opposition in 2008 and won 77%-23% in 2010.

SIXTH DISTRICT

Ben Chandler (D)

Elected Feb. 2004, 4th full term; b. Sept. 12, 1959, Versailles; home, Versailles; U. of KY, B.A. 1983, J.D. 1986; Presbyterian; married (Jennifer); 3 children.

Elected Office: KY auditor, 1991-95; KY atty. gen. 1995-2004.

Professional Career: Practicing atty., 1986-95.

DC Office: 1504 LHOB, 20515, 202-225-4706; Fax: 202-225-2122; Web site: chandler.house.gov.

State Offices: Lexington, 859-219-1366.

Committees: *Foreign Affairs:* Middle East & South Asia. *Permanent Select Committee on Intelligence:* Technical & Tactical Intelligence.

Group Ratings

	ACLU	ACU	ADA	CFG	AFS	FRC	LCV	ITIC	NTU	COC
2010	56	17	65	30	75	31	100	100	32	63
2009	–	20	80	20	89	–	93	–	13	69

National Journal Ratings

	2010 LIB	—	2010 CONS	2009 LIB	—	2009 CONS
Economic	50%	—	49%	54%	—	45%
Social	47%	—	52%	51%	—	48%
Foreign	51%	—	48%	53%	—	44%
Composite	50%	—	50%	54%	—	47%

Key Votes of the 111th Congress

1. Overturn Ledbetter	Y	5. Bar federal abortion funds	Y	9. Stop detainee transfers	Y
2. Pass $820 billion stimulus	Y	6. Pass health care bill	N	10. Legalize immigrants' kids	N
3. Let guns in national parks	Y	7. Regulate financial firms	N	11. Repeal don't ask, tell	Y
4. Pass cap-and-trade	Y	8. Pass tax cuts for some	Y	12. Limit campaign funds	Y

Election Results

2010 general	Ben Chandler (D)...119,812	(50.1%)	($1,674,100)
	Garland Barr (R)...119,165	(49.8%)	($1,580,018)
2010 primary	Ben Chandler (D)....................................... unopposed		

Prior Winning Percentages: 2008 (65%), 2006 (85%), 2004 (59%), Special: 2004 (55%)

Population		Race/Ethnicity		Work	
Pop. 2010:	759,205	White:	83.4%	Private:	76.2%
Change since 2000:	Up 12.7%	Black:	8.4%	Government:	17.8%
Urban:	71.3%	Hispanic:	4.5%	Self-employed:	5.8%
Rural:	28.7%	Asian:	1.7%	Blue collar:	21.9%
Area size:	3,777 sq. mi.	Native Am.:	0.2%	White collar:	60.1%
		Hawaiian:	0.0%	Khaki collar:	0.1%
Age		Two+ races:	1.7%	Other:	17.9%
Median age:	35.6 yrs.				
More than 65 yrs:	11.7%	*Ancestry*		Median income:	$44,605
Less than 18 yrs:	22.7%	USA	16.4%	Median Home Value:	$144,200
		German	12.0%		
Education		Irish	11.9%	**Military Veterans**	
H.S. grad:	84.6%			% of Pop:	9.4%
College grad:	28.3%				
Grad degree:	11.6%				

Central Kentucky; Lexington

With its white picket fences, horse farms and small towns, the rolling plateau of Bluegrass in central Kentucky is the part of interior America longest settled by English speakers: Lexington was founded in 1775; the town of Hopewell was renamed Paris in 1789 out of gratitude for French help during the American Revolution and in recognition of the French Revolution. To-bacco farming started here in the 1770s, horse racing in 1787, and the first whiskey distillery, in Bourbon County, was built in 1790. Tobacco, whiskey and racehorses remained the staples of the Bluegrass economy for six generations, until 1956, when IBM built its typewriter plant in Lex-ington. The personal computer eventually outclassed the typewriter, and the IBM plant was put on the block. The big employer here became Lexmark International, an independent IBM spinoff that makes inkjet and laser printers. Another mainstay is the Toyota plant that produces 500,000 cars annually in Georgetown, a town with early-19th-century houses and lush countryside just one county north of the city. Lexington, which includes all of Fayette County, grew by a sprightly 31% between 1990 and 2009. It is the second-largest metropolitan area in the state, after Louisville-Jefferson County.

2008 Presidential Vote		
John McCain (R) 180,526	(55%)
Barack Obama (D) 140,811	(43%)

2004 Presidential Vote		
George Bush (R) 182,787	(58%)
John Kerry (D) 128,967	(41%)

Cook Partisan Voting Index: R+9

The 6th Congressional District of Kentucky includes Lexington and the surrounding coun-ties—a natural unit, unlike some other Kentucky districts. Lexington casts 40% of the votes. In the 1990s, the area became more Republican, and George W. Bush carried the district in 2000 and 2004. John McCain won the district in 2008, 55% to 43%. Lexington voters in 2010 elected construction executive Jim Gray as mayor, making it the third-largest U.S. city with an openly gay chief executive.

Ben Chandler (D)

The congressman from the 6th District is Ben Chandler, a Democrat who won a special election in February 2004 and who, after coasting in his next three elections, barely squeaked by in 2010.

He grew up in Versailles, in the horse country west of Lexington, the grandson of A.B. "Happy" Chandler, the former governor, senator, and commissioner of baseball. His father owned a local newspaper. Ben Chandler got his bachelor's degree and law degree from the University of Ken-tucky and practiced law for five years. In 1991, he was elected state auditor and in 1995 attorney general. In that job, he made a name for himself by prosecuting corrupt politicians. In 2003, Chan-dler ran for the Democratic nomination for governor and beat Speaker Jody Richards in the pri-mary 50%-47%. But he lost the general election to 6th District Rep. Ernie Fletcher, 55%-45%.

Chandler decided that if he could not defeat Fletcher, he would try to succeed him. He won the Democratic nomination for Fletcher's House seat without opposition and faced Republican state Sen. Alice Forgy Kerr in the general election. Both candidates supported the Iraq war and a constitutional amendment to ban same-sex marriage, and opposed amnesty for illegal aliens. National Democrats strongly backed Chandler, who carefully kept his distance from liberal Democratic House Leader Nancy Pelosi. Chandler scored an unexpectedly easy victory, 55%-43%, marking the first time since 1991 that Democrats captured a Republican seat in a special election. In the next regularly scheduled election, in November 2004, Chandler defeated state Sen. Tom Buford, 59%-40%.

In the House, Chandler has a moderate voting record, though it is more liberal on economic issues. A former member of the Science Committee, he had been a main proponent of legislation to authorize billions of dollars for "green" school renovation and energy-efficient modernization projects. His bill got through the House in 2008 and 2009 over Republican objections about the loss of local authority for school districts. He still shows evidence of his background as a former attorney general, introducing bills in 2009 barring parole for violent sex offenders and those convicted of crimes involving children and the elderly.

After Democrats won the majority in 2006, he secured a plum seat on the House Appropriations Committee. He worked to get $9 million into the 2009 economic stimulus bill for green schools in his district. He was among the fiscally conservative Blue Dog Democrats who refused to back the 2010 health care overhaul, which he said did not go far enough to address "the real problem"—the cost escalation of health care services. But he did support the 2009 energy bill creating a cap-and-trade program to reduce greenhouse gas emissions, a risky vote for a lawmaker from a coal-dependent state.

Chandler was his party's consensus favorite to run for governor in 2007, but after winning reelection with 85% of the vote in 2006 and after Democrats won control of the House, Chandler decided to remain in Congress. He was mentioned as a possible challenger to Republican Sen. Jim Bunning in 2010, but his endorsement of Democratic presidential candidate Barack Obama prior to the Kentucky primary generated considerable local opposition.

As it turned out, Chandler had to struggle to keep his House seat in the GOP wave of 2010. His Republican opponent was Andy Barr, a Lexington lawyer and former deputy general counsel to Fletcher. He distanced himself from the by-then unpopular governor while Chandler and his backers sought to play up those ties, as well as Barr's membership in an exclusive country club that until 2009 had never admitted a black member. Chandler opened with the early lead in fundraising, but Barr became competitive as the race picked up steam. Outside groups got involved, including Americans for Tax Reform, which spent nearly $300,000 in September on attack ads, one of which cited five House votes Chandler cast that falsely contended that he raised constituents' taxes. The race became a tossup, and returns on Election Night showed Chandler with about a 600-vote edge. Barr hoped a recheck of voting machines would narrow the gap, but decided against a recount, conceding 10 days later when Chandler's lead held firm.

With the Republican takeover of the House, Chandler lost his seat on Appropriations, and got heat back home for backing Pelosi for minority leader in the 112th Congress (2011-12).

★ LOUISIANA ★

Afflicted by Hurricane Katrina in 2005 and the Gulf oil spill in 2010, Louisiana has suffered greatly, but has also gotten a chance to wipe the slate clean and start anew. To many, this state long seemed to be America's banana republic, with its charm and inefficiency, its communities interlaced by family ties and its public sector sometimes laced with corruption, with its own indigenous culture and its tradition of fine distinctions of class and caste. It has been a state with an economy uncomfortably like that of an underdeveloped country, based on pumping minerals out of soggy ground or under the Gulf and shipping grain produced in the vast hinterland drained by its great river, an economy increasingly dependent on tourism and gambling. Its politics, too, has had its own peculiar election laws and a heritage of no-holds-barred conflict and demagoguery no other state can match: What other state has produced the likes of Huey Long or Edwin Edwards? Louisiana has a hereditary rich class and a large, low-wage working class. It has conservative cultural attitudes. Louisiana and Utah have the most restrictive abortion laws in the United States, and Louisiana in 1997 became the first state to offer covenant marriages, in which spouses agree not to be covered by no-fault divorce laws. But Louisiana also has a lazy tolerance of rule-breaking, and feels more like the Caribbean or the Mediterranean than the North Atlantic or the Pacific Rim. This is not an entirely original observation. Architect Andres Duany once noted, "New Orleans is not among the most haphazard, poorest, or misgoverned American cities, but rather the most organized, wealthiest, cleanest, and competently governed of the Caribbean cities."

It was also the state least equipped states to handle the aftermath of a Category 5 hurricane. On August 29, 2005, Hurricane Katrina raged in the Gulf waters off Louisiana and then slammed the coastline, resulting in flooding that devastated most of New Orleans and sent hundreds of thousands of evacuees to shelter on higher ground. One of the costliest natural disasters in the nation's history, Katrina destroyed large parts of Louisiana and, in the process, laid bare its political and economic frailties. New Orleans mostly withstood the initial winds and storm surge. But then the levees broke, submerging much of the city under water as water sought its level. The 17th Street Canal sprang a 200-foot gash through which came much of the water inundating 80% of New Orleans. Levees along the Industrial Canal, in the poverty-stricken 9th Ward, likewise failed to hold back water driven by a wave surge that reached 30 feet. The Mississippi River Gulf Outlet, built by the Army Corps of Engineers as a shipping channel (though precious few ships ever used it), funneled waters and winds into St. Bernard Parish east of the city and the lowlands of New Orleans, devastating all in its wake. More than half of the 270 miles of federally constructed levees and flood walls in Louisiana were breached or heavily damaged by winds and flood waters.

Just five years later, disaster struck again, when BP's Deepwater Horizon oil rig exploded on April 20, 2010 and began spewing oil into the Gulf of Mexico—estimated first at a rate of 1,000 barrels a day but later thought to be closer to 60,000 barrels a day. Offshore drilling, underway since 1947, had become a major part of Louisiana's economy, with the oil industry employing 58,000 people in the state with an average salary of $95,000. By late April, the oil slick had spread from the drilling site southeast of the mouth of the Mississippi River to the Mississippi delta and was threatening the state's oyster beds and shrimp fisheries. Volunteers streamed in to tend oil-stained pelicans and herons, while attempts to plug the leak failed. Congress held hearings in May and June, with BP chief Tony Hayward performing badly, and President Obama visited the state four times. On May 27, Interior Secretary Ken Salazar ordered a six-month moratorium on all offshore drilling, a decision that was ruled invalid by a federal trial judge and a federal appeals court. BP promised to pay all damages, and Obama set up a federally administered fund. Finally, after several unsuccessful attempts to seal off the well, a procedure called "static kill" was tried and declared a success on August 4. But in 107 days, an estimated 205 million gallons of oil flowed into the Gulf.

The things that made Louisiana vulnerable to Katrina and the Gulf oil spill were a product of its history. Its position on the Gulf of Mexico inspired the French in 1718 to found New Orleans and declare the Mississippi Valley the colony of Louisiana. Even then, it was known that most of the land in and around New Orleans, beyond the two ridges piled high by the silt coming down the Mississippi River, was below sea level. But the city's strategic position made it so important to the United States that President Thomas Jefferson concluded that any nation that controlled the mouth of the Mississippi was the young republic's greatest enemy. For that reason, his envoys quickly accepted Napoleon's offer of the Louisiana Purchase. Louisiana, despite its large French and small Spanish population, was admitted to the Union in 1812, and by the outbreak of the Civil

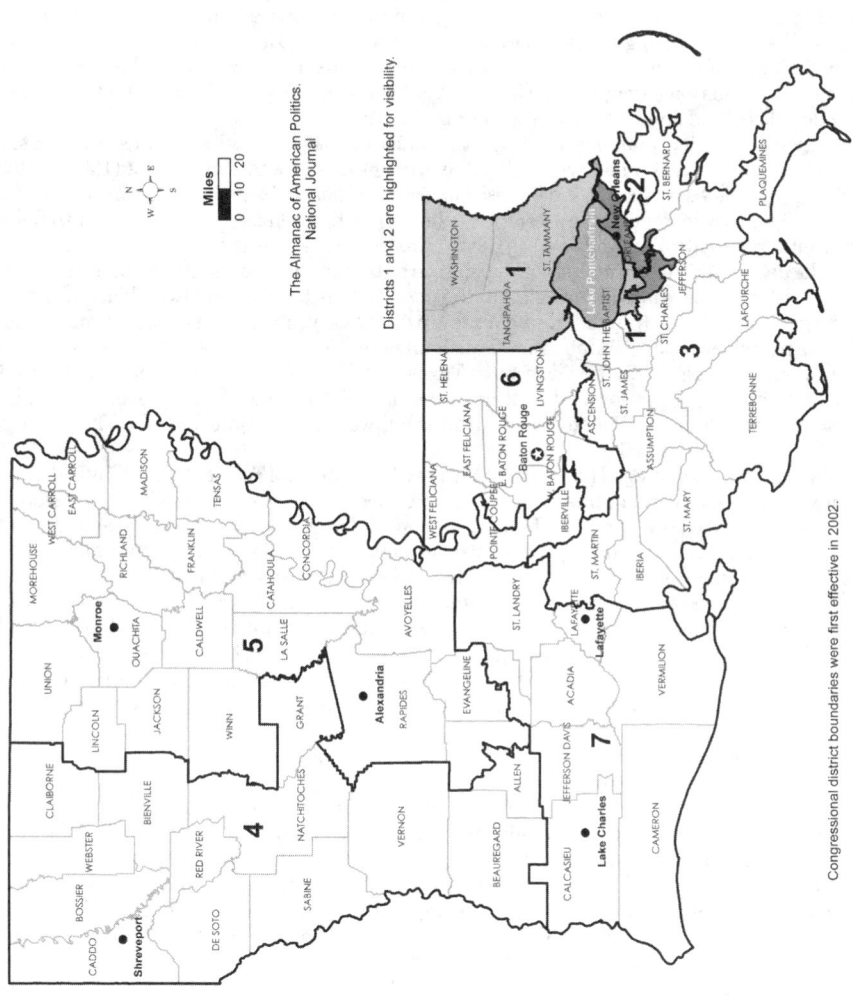

The Almanac of American Politics.
National Journal

Districts 1 and 2 are highlighted for visibility.

Congressional district boundaries were first effective in 2002.

War, New Orleans was the nation's fifth largest city—and the only substantial city in the Confederate South.

The very things that made New Orleans distinctive—the look and feel of a French and Spanish outpost in the New World—were linked also to traditions of dirigiste centralized control and easygoing corruption. Louisiana is the only state whose law is based not on the common law of England but on the Napoleonic Code of France; the concept of civil liberties has shallower roots in Louisiana than in the other 49 states. Its economy has always been based on the export of raw materials—sugar, rice, and cotton in the 19th century; oil and gas in the 20th and 21st centuries. Antebellum Louisiana's agricultural abundance generated the wealth that built grand plantation houses. Oil, discovered in 1901 at the dawn of the automobile age, has generated much of its wealth since. In 1921, Democratic Gov. John Parker and a young Public Service Commission chairman, Huey Long, got the idea of putting a severance tax on oil. In the 1970s, Democratic Gov. Edwin Edwards, a man similar in many ways to Long, changed it from a tax on amount of production to a tax on market value. Thus, oil money gushed into the Louisiana treasury and financed state government for six decades—and found its way into other pockets as well.

The most enduringly famous politician here, and by far the most talented, was Democrat Huey Long, who in less than a single term each as governor (1928-32) and U.S. senator (1932-35) left an imprint on the state's public life and imposed an organization on its politics that faded into history less than a generation ago. Long's genius was not that he promised to tax the rich to help the poor—hundreds of idealists and demagogues in America have done that—but that, to an amazing extent, he delivered. He dominated the legislature so thoroughly that, as governor, he roamed the floors of both chambers at will, bringing to the podium bills he insisted lawmakers pass without changing a comma—and they did. He was ready to use bribery, intimidation, and physical violence. He built a new skyscraper Capitol, a new Louisiana State University, and more miles of roads than any other state but rich New York and huge Texas had. He also built a national following and, by 1935, was planning to run for president on a platform of "Share the wealth, every man a king." That year, Long was assassinated at age 42 in the hallway of the Capitol he built. The bullet holes can still be seen in the marble walls.

His impact was lasting. The Long threat may have moved President Franklin D. Roosevelt to embrace the liberal programs—the Wagner Labor Act, Social Security, steeply graduated taxes—of the second New Deal. For Louisiana, Long delivered a political structure that revolved around him even after he was dead—and a class of political leaders who, lacking his talents, treated the state as Long's incompetent doctors had treated his fatal wound, leaving Louisiana with neither a fully developed economy nor a fully competent public sector. For 50 years, until Huey's son, Democratic Sen. Russell Long, retired in 1986, Longs and Long protégés held high political office in Louisiana and elections were run along pro- and anti-Long lines. The Long experience strengthened Louisiana's already strong predispositions—tolerance of corruption, disinterest in abstract reform, and a taste for colorful extremists regardless of their short-term means or long-term ends. In a way, that helps explain the rise and fall of such unlikely politicians as the four-term Gov. Edwards and the onetime Ku Klux Klan leader and state legislator David Duke, both of whom by 2003 were spending time in jail.

It also helps to explain the state's lack of economic dynamism. It has been a state with low incomes and workforce participation and low levels of education, with income disparities greater than almost anywhere else in the United States. New Orleans' elite class, like many of their counterparts in Latin America, have been notoriously tight-knit, not venturesome, and determined to hold on to their wealth against the grasp of the impecunious and unlearned masses. This has made a huge difference over time. Metro New Orleans in 1940 had a population of 564,000; it was about the same size then as metro Houston (610,000) and metro Dallas (624,000). But in 2004, just before Katrina struck, metro Houston had 5.1 million people, metro Dallas 5.8 million, and New Orleans just 1.3 million.

The oil shocks of 1973 and 1979 did for Louisiana what they did for Saudi Arabia, Nigeria, and Venezuela: They made it suddenly hugely richer. Louisiana incomes reached national levels and 500,000 new jobs were generated between 1972 and 1981. But oil prices plummeted in the 1980s, Louisiana's rig count dropped by two-thirds, the state lost 150,000 jobs, and energy taxes fell from 41% of state revenues in 1982 to 9% in 1996. The state's economy has never regained much forward momentum. Gambling, legalized in 1991, produced less revenue than expected and nothing like the boom that some had promised. People have been leaving the state. From 1980 to 2005, Louisiana increased in population only 7%, far less than any other Southern state and less than any state nationally except two in the Great Plains and the industrial triangle of Ohio, Pennsylvania, and West Virginia. Then, as evacuees left New Orleans after Katrina, its population fell by some

250,000, according to census estimates. It rebounded as people returned, but the 2010 census showed the city with 140,000 fewer people than it had in 2000. Suburban Jefferson and St. Bernard parishes lost 54,000 people. Yet, St. Tammany Parish across Lake Pontchartrain from the city grew by 42,000 people, and the four parishes in and around the state capital of Baton Rouge had 96,000 more people in 2010. In Lafayette Parish, the center of the offshore oil drilling industry, there was a jump up of 31,000. These growth areas represent an acceleration of the long-term trend of Louisianans withdrawing from the lowland silt brought down over the centuries by the Mississippi River and relocating to higher ground. And despite the focus on those fleeing New Orleans's impoverished and predominately black 9th Ward, two-thirds of those who left the state were white, which is about the same proportion of whites in the state's population. The 2010 census showed that African-Americans were 32% of the state's population, the same as in 2000.

Louisiana has long had natural political divides. One is by religion. Catholic Cajun parishes cast about 30% of the state's vote; the New Orleans area casts 25%, down from 30% before Katrina; and Protestant parishes from Baton Rouge on north cast about 45%. White Protestants for years have wanted nothing to do with national Democrats, while Cajuns sometimes supported them. Another divide is by race. Louisiana's black percentage is second only to Mississippi's, and African-Americans vote overwhelmingly Democratic, while whites have been split in seriously contested state elections. A third divide is by income. Low- and high-income whites have voted very differently and are much less influenced than voters in most other states by candidates' cultural values, marital status, lifestyles, and the like. As a result, Louisiana politics since Huey P. Long's time has often been a struggle between reformist and conservative forces on one side and roguish populists on the other, a struggle waged in lavishly financed campaigns with grandiloquent rhetoric.

For a quarter-century, the lead role was played by Edwards as the roguish populist, with a number of rivals as reformist conservatives. Edwards was elected governor in 1971 and 1975, sat out 1979 because he was ineligible to run, and then in 1983 won a third term. While in office, he faced corruption charges and was acquitted by a jury in 1986. He lost a bid for re-election in 1987 but ran again in 1991. In Louisiana's (since altered) all-party system, he won 34% of the vote to 32% for Duke, the onetime Nazi sympathizer and Klansman who had won a special election to the legislature as a Republican in 1989. Duke was repudiated by Republican National Chairman Lee Atwater and President George H.W. Bush as well as Louisiana Republicans. Bumper stickers read, "Vote for the crook—it's important," and Edwards won 61%-39%. He was convicted on corruption charges in May 2000 and went to prison.

In the years since, Louisiana has become increasingly Republican. It voted for Bill Clinton in 1992 and 1996, but it cast increasing percentages for Republican candidates in the four presidential elections from 1996 to 2008. Democratic Sen. Mary Landrieu has been elected to three terms starting in 1996, but never with more than 52% of the vote; Republican Sen. David Vitter was elected in 2004 with 51% under Louisiana's old system of multiparty primaries, and despite scandal in his personal life, was re-elected 57%-38% in 2010. Republican Bobby Jindal, defeated for governor 52%-48% by Democrat Kathleen Blanco in 2003, came back in 2007 and won the multi-party primary with 54% of the vote. The legislature, long heavily Democratic, has changed hands, as voters gave Republicans a majority in the state House in 2010 and party switches gave them a majority in the state Senate in February 2011. There have been some variations in the vote: Jindal has run stronger than other Republicans in metro New Orleans and weaker in the Cajun country and Protestant northern Louisiana, and Landrieu has run especially strong in and around New Orleans, where her father Moon Landrieu was mayor in 1970-78 and her brother Mitch Landrieu was elected mayor in 2010. But overall, Louisiana must be counted, for the first time since blacks briefly voted during Reconstruction, a Republican-leaning state.

The twin disasters of the hurricane and oil spill have probably reinforced that tendency. In the aftermath of Katrina, Gov. Blanco's dithering surely made many Louisianans wish that the fast-talking, detail-driven Jindal had been elected instead; she retired rather than run for re-election in 2007. The haplessness of New Orleans Mayor Ray Nagin and his re-election in 2006 after making a racial appeal surely did not help Democrats beyond the city limits. President George W. Bush's performance on Katrina, widely disparaged nationally, was perhaps not as badly thought of in Louisiana, where many were aware that the Coast Guard rescued some 20,000 people from the floodwaters. Barack Obama, with near-unanimous support from black voters, was able to beat Hillary Clinton in Louisiana's presidential primary, but he won the votes of only 14% of whites in November (with a near-identical 11% among white Protestants and 12% among white Catholics).

Katrina gave New Orleans the chance to rebuild. The question is whether that process will be slowed down or halted by the oil spill and the resulting moratorium on offshore drilling. New ethics and tax legislation passed by the legislature on Jindal's watch may be transforming the civic cul-

Population		Household Income		Work	
Pop. 2010:	4,533,372	Under $15k:	17.8%	Private:	76.8%
State rank:	25th	$15k to $50k:	38.9%	Government:	16.8%
Change since 2000:	Up 1.4%	$50k to $100k:	27.7%	Self-employed:	6.2%
Urban:	70.2%	$100k to $200k:	13.0%	Unemployment (3-yr. average):	4.4%
Rural:	29.8%	Over $200k:	2.6%	Poverty:	17.9%
Native of state:	79.1%	Median income:	$42,438	Blue collar:	25.1%
Not a citizen:	1.8%			White collar:	56.1%
Area size:	52,378 sq. mi.	**Home Value**		Khaki collar:	0.4%
		Under $100k:	37.6%	Other:	18.3%
Most populous cities		$100k to $300k:	51.6%		
New Orleans	343,829	$300k to $500k:	7.9%	**Age**	
Baton Rouge	229,493	$500k to $1 mil:	2.3%	Median age:	35.6 yrs.
Shreveport	199,311	Over $1 million:	0.6%	More than 65 yrs:	12.2%
Metairie CDP	138,481	Median:	$131,800	Less than 18 yrs:	25.1%

Race/Ethnicity				Military Veterans		Registered Voters in 2010	
White:	60.3%	*Language*		% of Pop:	9.4%	Democrats:	1,485,385
Black:	31.8%	English:	91.7%			Republicans:	768,163
Hispanic:	4.2%	Spanish:	3.0%	*Veterans by Period*		Ind./other:	679,207
Asian:	1.5%	Asian:	1.1%	WWII and before:	9.6%	Voter turnout:	1,297,150
Native Am.:	0.6%	Other European:	3.9%	Korea:	10.3%	Turnout as % of	
Hawaiian:	0.0%			Vietnam:	33.4%	voting age:	38.0%
Two+ races:	1.3%	**Education**		Gulf (pre-2001):	13.2%		
		H.S. grad:	81.1%	Gulf (post-2001):	10.0%	**Legislature**	
Ancestry		College grad:	20.8%	Peace time:	23.5%	Senate:	19 D 20 R
French	12.9%	Grad degree:	6.7%			House:	49 D 52 R 4 I
USA	7.7%						
German	7.5%						

ture. New Orleans public schools have improved, with most students enrolled in charter schools. Louisiana's Road Home program has financed many new homes, and the state had no housing bubble either before or after Katrina so largely sat out the housing crisis in 2007-09. Nearly half of the hurricane recovery money has gone for infrastructure like roads and bridges, and it appears that the canals and levees have been strengthened as they should have been many years ago. Louisiana's unemployment rate remained below the national average during the recession. And finally, Tulane University, which was shut down after Katrina, received 44,000 applications in 2010, more than any other private university in the nation—an indication that New Orleans and Louisiana have not lost their historic charm.

Presidential politics   In recent years, Louisiana's presidential politics have been racially polarized, and the trend continued in 2008, when Republican nominee John McCain won 59%-40% over Democrat Barack Obama, the first African-American to be nominated by a major party. In 2004, whites voted 75%-24% for Republican President George W. Bush and African-Americans voted 90%-9% for Democrat John Kerry. Four years later, the difference was even starker. Whites voted 84%-14% for McCain, and blacks voted 94%-4% for Obama. Even young whites voted 81% for McCain, as did 60% of white Democrats. Those who indicated that race was an important factor in their voting split almost evenly, which is to say, more in Obama's favor than the state's electorate as a whole. As a result, Louisiana was one of the few states that trended Republican in 2008, despite a significant increase in black registration and turnout. The exodus of African-Americans from New Orleans after the hurricane was one reason, but

2008 Presidential Vote
John McCain (R) 1,148,275   (59%)
Barack Obama (D) 782,989   (40%)

2008 Presidential Primary
Barack Obama (D) 220,632   (57%)
Hillary Clinton (D) 136,925   (36%)

2008 Presidential Primary
Mike Huckabee (R)..................69,594   (43%)
John McCain (R) 67,551   (42%)
Mitt Romney (R).....................10,222   (6%)
Ron Paul (R) 8,590   (5%)

2004 Presidential Vote
George W. Bush (R)............1,102,169   (57%)
John Kerry (D) 820,299   (42%)

only a minor one. In terms of percentages, an exodus of whites from Republican St. Bernard Parish was even greater. And the metro New Orleans vote changed only marginally, from 50%-49% Republican in 2004 to 52%-46% Republican in 2008.

The biggest drops in Democratic percentage came in Cajun parishes—perhaps Kerry's Catholicism had some appeal there—and in the two heavily Cajun congressional districts, the 3rd and the 7th. The Democratic percentage rose in Baton Rouge and Shreveport and in rural parishes with large black populations. But the pattern was mixed, as might be expected in a state that was not targeted by either party in either election and in which the Obama campaign had far less occasion to organize than it did in target states such as Florida, North Carolina, and Virginia.

Louisiana has seldom played a significant role in presidential primaries and caucuses, with one odd exception. That was 1996, when Republican allies of candidate Phil Gramm of Texas set up a pre-Iowa and pre-New Hampshire caucus in Louisiana on February 6. The aim was to jump-start Gramm's campaign. Instead, the caucuses killed it. Only 20,000 Republicans showed up at 42 voting sites (compared with 100,000 at 2,000 sites later in Iowa), and conservative commentator Pat Buchanan won more votes than Gramm and took 13 of the 21 delegates. Gramm left the race before the New Hampshire primary. The 2000 and 2004 primaries were held in March, after both parties' nominees had been chosen.

Louisiana did make at least a little bit of difference in 2008. Legislators chose to hold the primary in early February, but not on Super Tuesday, Feb. 5, because that was Mardi Gras, when it was unthinkable to hold an election. Instead, the voting was set for the next Saturday, a day on which Louisiana has often held state elections. The decision left Louisiana at risk of irrelevance if both parties' nominations were settled on Super Tuesday, but they weren't. Obama came in and held a rally at Tulane University, and Bill Clinton spent Friday campaigning around the state for his wife. In retrospect, the outcome should have been no surprise. As recently as 2000, the body of registered Democrats in Louisiana was 58% white and 40% African-American, but in 2008, after a big rush in registration, blacks made up nearly half of the state's registered Democrats. Democratic turnout in the primary was 384,000—roughly double what is was in 2004 and 2000. Obama won 57% of the vote (and about 80% of the African-American vote), and Clinton got 36%.

There was less enthusiasm on the Republican side because it was pretty clear after Super Tuesday that McCain would be nominated. Nonetheless, evangelical Christians and others set up telephone networks for Arkansas's Mike Huckabee. With a turnout of 161,000 voters, half the Democratic level but the highest Republican turnout in Louisiana ever, Huckabee won 43% of the vote to 42% for McCain. McCain carried metro New Orleans big and ran about even in the heavily Catholic Cajun country. Huckabee won large majorities in heavily Protestant northern Louisiana. But it didn't matter. A candidate must win 50% of the vote in Louisiana's Republican primary to win any delegates. A few days later, party insiders awarded 44 of the 47 delegates to McCain.

Congressional districting

112th Congress Lineup	
6 R	1 D
111th Congress Lineup	
6 R	1 D

Louisiana redrew its congressional districts three times in the 1990s. The first two plans created two black-majority districts, and in each case one of them was highly irregular in shape. They were declared unconstitutional in federal court in 1993 and 1994. In January 1996, a federal court came up with a plan, adopted by the legislature, that cut through few parish boundaries and had much more regular lines. And it had only one black-majority district, centered in New Orleans. The plan was upheld by the Supreme Court in June 1996.

During the 2000 reapportionment, six of the seven House incumbents (one was running for the Senate) submitted a plan to the legislature. Republican Gov. Mike Foster called a special session for redistricting in October 2001, and the legislators made minor tweaks in the House incumbents' plan. It was opposed by the Black Legislative Caucus, which drew up a plan with a second black-majority district stretching from Lafayette and Baton Rouge along the Mississippi River to the Arkansas border. But the legislature rejected it by solid margins. Foster signed the new plan in October, and the Justice Department approved it in April 2002. Generally, it has favored Republicans, but five of the seven districts have elected members of both parties in the elections from 2002 to 2008. The black-majority 2nd district even elected Republican Joseph Cao in 2008 over a scandal-tarred incumbent. He made a game effort in 2010, but was unable to repeat his unlikely triumph.

Louisiana's big population loss after Katrina made it clear that the state would lose one House seat after the 2010 census, as it might well have done anyway given the state's sluggish pre-Katrina growth. Demographically, the 2nd District, centered in New Orleans, suffered the greatest population loss by far. But Voting Rights Act jurisprudence forbids the elimination of the state's one black-majority district and practically commands the now Republican legislature to create an African-American majority seat, perhaps by connecting part of New Orleans with part of Baton Rouge through a corridor running up the Mississippi River. That would leave a heavily Republican suburban New Orleans seat and four more districts in territory currently represented by five Republicans.

Governor

Bobby Jindal (R)

Elected 2007, term expires Jan. 2012, 1st term; b. June 10, 1971, Baton Rouge; home, Kenner; Brown U., B.A. 1991, Oxford U., M.Lit. 1994; Catholic; married (Supriya); 3 children.

Elected Office: U.S. House of Reps., 2004-2007.

Professional Career: Secy., LA Dept. of Health and Hospitals, 1996-98; Exec. dir., Natl. Bipartisan Comm. on the Future of Medicare, 1998-99; Pres., U. of LA System, 1999-2001; Asst. sec., U.S. Dept. of HHS, 2001-03.

Office: Office of the Governor, P.O. Box 94004, Baton Rouge, 70804-9004, 225-342-7015; Fax: 225-342-7099; Web site: gov.state.la.us.

Election Results

2007 general	Bobby Jindal (R)	699,275	(54%)
	Walter Boasso (D)	226,476	(17%)

Prior Winning Percentages: House: 2006 (88%); 2004 (78%)

The governor of Louisiana is Bobby Jindal, a Republican elected in October 2007 who is considered one of his party's young stars with a presumed future in presidential politics. Jindal (*JIN-dil*) grew up in Baton Rouge, the son of immigrants from India who came to the United States so his mother could do graduate work at Louisiana State University. His given name was Piyush, but as a boy he insisted on being called Bobby, after his favorite character in the television series *The Brady Bunch*. As a teenager, he converted from Hinduism to Catholicism. He was an honors student at Baton Rouge High School, went on to graduate from Brown University with degrees in biology and public policy, then studied at Oxford as a Rhodes Scholar.

After college, Jindal worked briefly for McKinsey & Co. in Washington, D.C., and then landed his first job in politics as an intern for 4th District Rep. Jim McCrery, a Republican. He quickly built an impressive resume. When McCrery assigned him to work on health policy, Jindal holed himself up in the Library of Congress for two weeks to master the complexities of the Medicare program. He eventually plopped on McCrery's desk a thick report spelling out possible solutions to the financial problems confounding the gigantic government-run medical program for the elderly. A few years later, Jindal, at age 24, set his sights on becoming the new head of Louisiana's Department of Health and Hospitals and asked McCrery to introduce him to the governor, Republican Mike Foster. "Bobby knocked their socks off," McCrery told the Baton Rouge *Advocate*. Foster gave Jindal the job of running a 13,000-employee agency that accounted for about 40% of the state budget. Jindal managed to erase a $400 million deficit within two years. He returned to Washington and, at age 27, became executive director of the National Bipartisan Commission on the Future of Medicare. In 2001, he became assistant secretary for planning and evaluation at the U.S. Health and Human Services Department.

In 2003, Jindal ran for governor, his first race for elective office. He campaigned as a policy expert with ideas for restructuring government. He attracted national attention and his candidacy was front-page news in India. In the October 2003 primary, he ran first, with 33% of the vote, ahead of three Democrats: Lt. Gov. Kathleen Blanco, with 18%; Attorney General Richard Ieyoub, with 16%; and former U.S. Rep. Buddy Leach, with 14%. Between the primary and the runoff, Blanco ran ads raising doubts about Jindal's success running the state health department, to which Jindal failed to respond forcefully. In the November runoff, he lost to Blanco 52%-48%, but he carried the New Orleans, Baton Rouge, Shreveport and Monroe metro areas. Blanco carried her home area, the Cajun country, by a wide margin; Jindal carried only one of the northern parishes that most Republicans have won in other statewide races.

In 2004, when U.S. Rep. David Vitter decided to run for the Senate seat of retiring Democrat John Breaux, Jindal ran for Vitter's House seat, ideally situated in a congressional district where Jindal's wife's family lived and where he had won 68% of the vote in his campaign for governor. Republican state Rep. Steve Scalise abandoned his campaign in August after trailing badly in fundraising and the polls, and Jindal was endorsed by state GOP leaders. He won 78% of the vote in November and was elected without a runoff. He was the first Indian-American elected to Congress since Democrat Dalip Saund won in the 29th District of California in 1956.

In the House, Jindal's voting record was moderate to conservative. He was elected president of the Republican freshman class and spoke out early for the GOP proposal to create private retirement accounts in the Social Security program. Following the devastation of Louisiana and other Gulf states by Hurricane Katrina in 2005, Jindal worked on revamping the Federal Emergency Management Agency, the federal flood-insurance program and financial aid to state and local school boards. Perhaps his most significant achievement was enactment in December 2006 of a bill that opened more than 8 million acres in the Gulf of Mexico to offshore drilling, and mandated that a substantial portion of the revenues go to Louisiana and other Gulf states with Katrina damage.

Jindal never stopped thinking about running again for governor. He kept a campaign-style schedule during congressional recesses, traveling around the state to give speeches and hold fundraisers. Blanco had been widely criticized for her response to Katrina, and her job rating was low. In March 2007, when she announced she would not seek another term, Jindal was ready. Other prominent Louisiana politicians stayed out of the race for various reasons. Breaux considered running, but he had established residence in the Maryland suburbs outside Washington, and Jindal supporters made it clear they would challenge his eligibility to run.

Three serious opponents did enter the race. Democratic state Sen. Walter Boasso spent personal money liberally and argued that he had worked to reduce patronage politics at levee boards. Businessman John Georges also spent millions and ran as a nonpartisan political unifier. Public Service Commissioner Foster Campbell, a Democrat, ran on a proposal to replace the state income tax with a levy on oil and gas producers. Jindal stressed his work in Congress on post-Katrina aid and promised to clean up the state's famously corrupt politics and rejuvenate Louisiana's economy. "We need a plan that won't just rebuild things the way they were, where we were 50th in health care and 50th in the best places to do business. We need to move to the top of those lists and others," he said. Jindal led in polls throughout the campaign and won 54% of the vote, more than the 50% required to avoid a runoff. Boasso won 17% of the vote, Georges 14%, and Campbell 12%.

Taking office, Jindal called a special session of the legislature in February 2008 and won passage, with only minor changes, of ethics bills requiring elected and appointed officials to disclose their personal finances and banning them from doing business with the state. He called a second special session in March to "eliminate unorthodox business taxes that are holding Louisiana's economy back." The legislature voted to accelerate $367 million in tax phase-outs on utilities, machinery purchases and corporate debt and to pass $20 million in tuition and home schooling tax credits. In addition, he persuaded the legislature to spend much of the $1.1 billion budget surplus on repairs to public university buildings and on infrastructure—roads, bridges, ports and hurricane protection.

In the regular session that followed, the legislature did not always ratify Jindal's initiatives. The state House cut health and education funds in his budget and declined to pass his proposal for merit pay for teachers. He was dogged as well by his campaign's failure to report $100,000 in financial aid from the state Republican Party and by newspaper stories that one of the businesses benefiting from his Terrebonne Parish port expansion was a big contributor to his campaign. Jindal in turn vetoed $16 million of legislators' special projects. But his biggest misstep involved a raise in legislators' pay, stuck at $16,800 to $37,500 for many years. During his campaign, he had pledged to oppose a pay increase. On June 16, 2008, after the legislature passed a pay raise, he said he would allow it to become law without his signature. There was widespread protest, and on June 27, papers were filed for a recall petition. Jindal responded by vetoing the pay raise.

Jindal's early successes brought him into the national spotlight. He spent Memorial Day weekend at Republican presidential candidate John McCain's home in Sedona, Ariz., together with former Massachusetts Gov. Mitt Romney and Florida Gov. Charlie Crist. The next month, "Jindal for VP" bumper stickers were circulating in Baton Rouge. But he was not a finalist for the job. When Hurricane Gustav bore down on New Orleans in September, he was determined to do a better job than Blanco had during Katrina. He canceled a speaking date at the Republican National Convention and ordered the evacuation of 1.9 million people from coastal parishes. Jindal gave frequent press conferences, rattling off wind speeds, shelter populations, damage descriptions, phone numbers and websites, seemingly in total command of the state response. Later in the month, he traveled to Washington to lobby Congress for relief.

Jindal's trip to Iowa to deliver two speeches after the 2008 election stimulated talk of a presidential candidacy, though he declared he had no thoughts of running. GOP leaders in Washington chose him to deliver the rebuttal to President Obama's address to Congress in February 2009. In a speech he wrote himself, he talked about his immigrant heritage and attacked high government spending. But his delivery was uninspiring, and the critical postgame analysis was almost entirely negative. Still, he retained a wide audience of admirers. *Washington Post* columnist Kathleen Parker called him "the intellectual equivalent of a nuclear power plant."

In 2009, Jindal, like most other governors, faced a serious budget shortfall amid a deepening national recession. In March 2009, he presented a $26 billion budget that cut spending on health care and higher education and eliminated hundreds of state jobs. It included nearly $1 billion in federal economic stimulus funds. Jindal also called for redesigning the health care system, with Medicaid being administered through private insurance companies. After weeks of often stormy negotiations, he got most of what he wanted. The legislature reduced spending while putting $210 million of one-time money into health care, education and other programs. Jindal also was able to thwart several tax-related measures he objected to, including a hike in tobacco taxes and a freeze on income tax deductions to benefit colleges and schools. He fell short in other areas, such as a bill he had sought to allow cuts to specially protected funds when the state runs a deficit.

In 2010, the devastating BP oil spill in the Gulf further elevated Jindal's national profile. Unlike most governors in the region, he was fiercely and openly critical of the Obama administration's handling of the issue. He made repeated visits to afflicted areas—drawing reams of news coverage that largely cast him as a bold leader—and proposed building a protective line of sand booms, or islands, using mud dredged from the Gulf. In the months after the oil company capped the damaged well, he proceeded with plans to build the sand barriers, aided by the Obama administration's agreements that BP should foot the $360 million cost.

His energetic efforts following the spill led many in Louisiana to agree that Jindal had vanquished the political doubts from his lackluster State of the Union response. But his absences touched off grumbling from state lawmakers who said they complicated efforts at progress in the 2010 legislative session. Numerous pieces of his agenda did not pick up support that year, including his budget-cutting proposals to eliminate the lieutenant governor's office and consolidate higher education boards and his plan to make it easier to draw on the state's rainy day fund during a fiscal crisis. But he got much of his education proposals into law, including a controversial plan to let local schools seek waivers from a variety of state rules and regulations. Teachers' unions denounced the measure as unconstitutional. Another controversial bill he signed into law allowing guns to be carried into churches drew nationwide criticism from gun control advocates.

Jindal's re-election in 2011 was all but assured. In December 2010, a Public Policy Polling Survey gave him an approval rating of 58%, the highest among U.S. governors facing re-election. He had more than $7 million for his campaign. Even if Jindal passes on a presidential run in 2012, he will be only 45 years old in November 2016.

Senior Senator

Mary Landrieu (D)

Elected 1996, term expires 2014, 3rd term; b. Nov. 23, 1955, Arlington, VA; home, New Orleans; LA St. U., B.A. 1977; Catholic; married (Frank Snellings); 2 children.

Elected Office: LA House of Reps., 1980–88; LA treasurer, 1988–96.

DC Office: 431 DSOB, 20510, 202-224-5824; Fax: 202-224-9735; Web site: landrieu.senate.gov.

State Offices: Baton Rouge, 225-389-0395; Lake Charles, 337-436-6650; New Orleans, 504-589-2427; Shreveport, 318-676-3085.

Committees: *Appropriations:* Department of State, Foreign Operations & Related Programs; Energy & Water Development; Homeland Security (Chmn); Interior, Environment & Related Agencies; Labor, Health & Human Services, Education & Related Agencies; Military Construction, Veterans Affairs & Related Agencies. *Energy & Natural Resources:* Energy; National Parks; Public Lands & Forests. *Homeland Security & Governmental Affairs:* Disaster Recovery & Intergovernmental Affairs (Ad Hoc); Investigations (Permanent); Oversight of Government Management, the Federal Workforce & the District of Columbia. *Small Business & Entrepreneurship* (Chmn).

Group Ratings

	ACLU	ACU	ADA	CFG	AFS	FRC	LCV	ITIC	NTU	COC
2010	87	8	75	4	85	0	29	67	11	36
2009	–	16	90	14	91	–	91	–	10	60

National Journal Ratings

	2010 LIB	—	2010 CONS	2009 LIB	—	2009 CONS
Economic	60%	—	39%	51%	—	48%
Social	57%	—	42%	53%	—	45%
Foreign	47%	—	0%	55%	—	0%
Composite	64%	—	36%	61%	—	39%

Key Votes of the 111th Congress

1. Overturn Ledbetter	Y	5. Pass health care bill	Y	9. Ratify New START	Y
2. Pass $787 billion stimulus	Y	6. Regulate financial firms	Y	10. Confirm Elena Kagan	Y
3. Repeal DC gun laws	Y	7. Pass tax cuts for some	Y	11. Stop EPA climate regs	Y
4. Confirm Sonia Sotomayor	Y	8. Legalize immigrants' kids	Y	12. Repeal don't ask, tell	Y

Election Results

2008 general	Mary Landrieu (D)	988,298	(52%)	($11,304,952)
	John Kennedy (R)	867,177	(46%)	($4,828,982)
2008 primary	Mary Landrieu (D)	unopposed		

Prior Winning Percentages: 2002 (52%); 1996 (50%)

Mary Landrieu, the state's senior senator, is a Democrat elected in 1996. Landrieu (*LAN-drew*) has Louisiana politics in her blood and has proven that she can withstand her Republican-dominated state's rough-and-tumble politics as one of the Senate's few remaining Southern Democrats. She grew up in New Orleans, the oldest of nine children of Moon Landrieu, the Democratic mayor of New Orleans from 1970 to 1978 and Housing and Urban Development secretary in the Carter administration. Her brother is Mitch Landrieu, Louisiana's former lieutenant governor and now New Orleans mayor. She was educated at Ursuline Academy and Louisiana State University. In 1979, at age 23, she became the youngest woman ever elected to the Louisiana Legislature. In 1987, she was elected state treasurer. A sharp critic of Democratic Gov. Edwin Edwards, she was re-elected in 1991. In 1995, she ran for governor and in the September primary finished third. Democrats lost the governor's mansion that year to Republican Mike Foster.

   Landrieu immediately started running for the Senate seat held by Democrat Bennett Johnston, who was retiring after 24 years in office. She had a well-known name and a moderate platform—she supported the proposed balanced budget amendment and capital gains tax cuts and promised to make education a top priority. Her competition was Attorney General Richard Ieyoub, also a Democrat, and Woody Jenkins, a 25-year state legislator and strong abortion opponent who had run twice unsuccessfully for the Senate as a Democrat and now was running as a Republican. Jenkins led the September primary with 26% to 22% for Landrieu and 20% for Ieyoub; former Ku Klux Klan member David Duke got 12%.

Going into the runoff, Jenkins looked like the favorite. But he had little money left, and Landrieu, who ultimately outspent him, ran ads attacking him as an extremist. The result was an exceedingly close election. The official results showed Landrieu ahead by 5,788 votes, 50.2% to 49.8% for Jenkins. He sued, claiming vote fraud, but withdrew the lawsuit and submitted his claim to the Senate. In October 1997, the Senate Rules Committee concluded that while "isolated instances" of voter fraud did occur, there was no evidence to prove a "widespread effort to illegally affect the outcome of this election" or that Landrieu was involved in the violation of election laws. Landrieu finally claimed the seat.

In the Senate, Landrieu's voting record places her among the more conservative Democrats, particularly on energy and national security matters. She voted for the Iraq war resolution in 2002 and for a 2007 measure giving U.S. spy agencies expanded power to eavesdrop on foreign suspects without a court order. Her first bill was for a $5 million block grant for adoption services; her two children are adopted. She backs adoption tax credits and wants better tax breaks for those who adopt special needs or foster children. She was the lead co-sponsor of the law providing for speedy citizenship for foreign-born children adopted by U.S. citizens. When it went into effect, it created the largest number of new U.S. citizens ever on a single day.

All the while she was running hard for re-election in 2002. She was an obvious Republican target, because of her small margin of victory in 1996 and because of President George W. Bush's popularity in Louisiana at the time. In 2001, 5th District Rep. John Cooksey, a Republican and a north Louisiana ophthalmologist, launched a challenge. But his candidacy was undone by one word: diaper. On September 18, 2001, a week after the September 11 attacks, Cooksey said in a radio interview in Louisiana, "If I see someone comes in that's got a diaper on his head and a fan belt wrapped around the diaper on his head, the guy needs to be pulled over." The National Republican Senatorial Committee encouraged other Republicans to run and ultimately backed Elections Commissioner Suzanne Haik Terrell. State Rep. Tony Perkins, a sponsor of a school-prayer bill, also got into the contest.

Republicans compared Landrieu's voting record with then-New York Sen. Hillary Rodham Clinton's. Terrell, a New Orleans Catholic, was better positioned than Cooksey or Perkins, both northern Louisiana Protestants, to take votes away from Landrieu in the New Orleans area. In mid-October, Landrieu started running anti-Terrell ads, charging that taxes and spending went up in New Orleans when she was on the City Council. Perkins attacked Landrieu for living in a "Washington mansion." On Nov. 5, Landrieu failed to clinch a victory. She won 46% of the vote, to 27% for Terrell, 14% for Cooksey and 10% for Perkins. The three Republicans together led Landrieu 51%-46%.

In the runoff, there was discontent on the Democratic side among black leaders about Landrieu's ads touting her support for many of President Bush's policies. In debates the two candidates tangled over abortion. In one case, on leaving the television studio, Landrieu said to Terrell, "This is your last campaign." Terrell, taken aback, said, "She threatened me." The candidates argued about tax cuts, personnel rules for the Department of Homeland Security and privatizing government jobs. Then, a Democratic opposition researcher made a propitious find—an article in the Mexican center-left newspaper *Reforma* reporting that the Bush administration had agreed with the Mexican government to double the amount of sugar that could be imported from Mexico, bad news for a major domestic sugar-producing state like Louisiana. The Office of Special Trade Representative and the State Department denied that any such agreement had been made. But Landrieu trumpeted the claim in ads and promised to do everything she could to stop any such agreement. It was a fine issue for Landrieu to use to document her claim that Terrell would be a "rubber stamp" for Bush, even though Terrell said she too opposed any deal. Landrieu met with trade and State Department officials in January 2003 and reported that she'd been assured there had not been a sugar deal with Mexico. The incident may have changed enough votes to give Landrieu her 52%-48% victory.

In her second term, Landrieu stepped into more national issues and into the limelight. As the ranking Democrat on the District of Columbia Appropriations Subcommittee, she insisted on restrictions on a program allowing D.C. parents to send their children to private schools on government vouchers. Voucher supporters ran an ad in the New Orleans newspaper saying, "My mom wants you to know that Sen. Mary Landrieu doesn't want me to go to the same school where her children go."

She supported oil drilling in the Arctic National Wildlife Refuge and, when it passed in March 2005, was one of three Democrats voting for it. (The others were the two senators from Hawaii.) In 2004, she won passage of an amendment eliminating the reduction in veterans' widows' pensions when they became eligible for Social Security. And she wasn't shy about putting holds on legislation or threatening to filibuster bills to force action on her issues. In 2004, she filibustered a corporate tax bill for three days in support of an amendment to give tax credits to employers who make up lost pay for reservists and National Guard troops called to active duty. She ultimately accepted a compromise limiting the tax credit to companies with 50 or fewer workers.

In the 2004 campaign she endorsed neither of the two well-known Democrats running for retiring Democratic Sen. John Breaux's seat, but campaigned extensively around the state against Republican David Vitter. "Don't send me a puppet to work with, send me a partner," she said over and over. On Election Night, she had an abrupt conversation with Vitter, who, against expectations, won the seat with 51% of the vote. She called Vitter to tell him the second-place finisher, Democrat Chris John, was not conceding, kicking off a rocky working relationship between Louisiana's two senators.

The following year, Hurricane Katrina forced them to grudgingly work together and put the outspoken Landrieu in the national spotlight as advocate for her state. Three of her siblings lost their homes to Katrina. In response to the post-hurricane comment by President Bush that nobody "anticipated the breach of the levees," she said tartly, "Everybody anticipated the breach of the levees, Mr. President." In early September, Landrieu said on national television that if anyone, including Bush, criticized the state and local government response to Katrina, "I might likely have to punch him. Literally."

Six weeks after the catastrophe, she objected that Louisiana was being treated less sympathetically than had other states during emergencies. Vitter disagreed with her protest. But the criticism did not deter Landrieu. In April 2006, she said that she would block every presidential nomination until Bush agreed to $6 billion for repair of Louisiana levees. When the Senate approved that money and more a few weeks later, Landrieu backed off her general threat, but vowed to block nominees at the Energy and Interior departments until there was agreement on using royalties from offshore oil and gas production to pay for coastal restoration and additional hurricane protection. She played a major role when that bill finally was enacted in December 2006.

In the closely divided Senate in 2007 and 2008, Landrieu cast some key votes. She was one of two Democrats to vote in March 2008 to reduce the estate tax, and she voted for Vitter's amendment to cut community policing funds for cities that refuse to enforce immigration laws. She cast the deciding vote in December 2007 against eliminating a tax deduction for oil companies and directing the money to alternative fuels, calling it "one-sided policymaking" that left "Louisiana industry footing the bill."

Going into the 2008 election season, Republican strategists targeted Landrieu, but had difficulty finding a top-tier candidate. Rep. Richard Baker declined to run, as did Louisiana Secretary of State Jay Dardenne. Then in August 2007, state Treasurer John Kennedy, who had run third, with 15% of the vote, in the 2004 Senate race, switched from the Democratic to the Republican Party and announced he would challenge Landrieu in November.

Landrieu had been busy fundraising, which enabled her to maintain a significant cash advantage. Kennedy criticized her for voting against ending the moratorium on oil shale development. She called him a "confused politician" and said he'd mismanaged the treasurer's office. She got endorsements from Republican local officials in St. Tammany and Jefferson parishes and from former Republican Gov. David Treen. Landrieu won 52%-46%. She had 96% support from African-Americans, 33% from whites and 42% from white independents, while Democratic presidential nominee Barack Obama won only 14% of whites and 21% of white independents. Landrieu won Orleans Parish with 84%. Her work on recovery issues evidently more than offset the decline in the number of black voters there. She won 52% in metro Baton Rouge, and 52% in the rest of the state.

In January 2009, Landrieu became the chairman of the Small Business Committee. Continuing her heavy involvement in hurricane recovery, she threatened in March 2009 to stop federal housing spending in New Orleans unless Democratic Mayor Ray Nagin accounted for millions of dollars in unspent and expiring federal grants. She criticized President Obama's proposed fiscal 2010 budget's taxes on oil and gas revenues, which she said would drive Louisiana into recession. She opposed a comprehensive energy bill in 2009, partly because it contained a renewable energy mandate that she and other Southern senators said their states would have difficulty meeting. She also took a skeptical view of proposed cap-and-trade legislation to reduce greenhouse gas emissions, and was one of six Democrats in June 2010 to support a failed GOP resolution attempting to block the Environmental Protection Agency from regulating the issue on its own.

As part of negotiations on the health care overhaul, Landrieu won a commitment of $300 million for Louisiana's Medicaid program to help make up for a shrinking federal split with the state following Katrina. Republican critics dubbed the deal "the Louisiana Purchase," and said it represented an example of secret, special-interest bargaining in the legislation. Landrieu was unrepentant, saying the arrangement was made openly and with Republican support. She forcefully offered to debate anyone who questioned her. "Being in office takes more than being smart or having a fancy resume," said. "It takes guts." And maybe a security detail—Landrieu in 2010 was a target of James O'Keefe, a conservative activist known for his political pranks, who was charged with three others of plotting to tamper with the telephone system in her New Orleans office.

Following the massive BP oil spill in the Gulf in the spring of 2010, Landrieu pressed the Obama administration to allow a revenue-sharing plan directing more offshore royalty payments to coastal states to go into effect immediately instead of 2017. She later introduced a bill containing that provision as well as one lifting the moratorium on deep-water drilling. In protest of the moratorium, she put a legislative "hold" for six weeks on the nomination of Jacob Lew to be director of Obama's Office of Management and Budget.

Junior Senator

David Vitter (R)

Elected 2004, term expires 2016, 2nd term; b. May 3, 1961, New Orleans; home, Metairie; Harvard U., A.B. 1983, Rhodes Scholar, Oxford U., B.A. 1985, Tulane Law Schl., J.D. 1988; Catholic; married (Wendy); 4 children.

Elected Office: LA House of Reps., 1991-99; U.S. House of Reps., 1999-2004.

Professional Career: Practicing atty., 1988-99; Adjunct law prof., Tulane U. & Loyola U., 1995-98.

DC Office: 516 HSOB, 20510, 202-224-4623; Fax: 202-228-5061; Web site: vitter.senate.gov.

State Offices: Alexandria, 318-448-0169; Baton Rouge, 225-383-0331; Lafayette, 337-262-6898; Lake Charles, 337-436-0453; Metairie, 504-589-2753; Monroe, 318-325-8120; Shreveport, 318-861-0437.

Committees: *Armed Services:* Airland; Personnel; Strategic Forces. *Banking, Housing & Urban Affairs:* Economic Policy (RMM); Financial Institutions & Consumer Protection; Securities, Insurance & Investment. *Environment & Public Works:* Children's Health & Environmental Responsibility; Clean Air & Nuclear Safety; Transportation & Infrastructure (RMM); Water & Wildlife. *Small Business & Entrepreneurship.*

Group Ratings

	ACLU	ACU	ADA	CFG	AFS	FRC	LCV	ITIC	NTU	COC
2010	13	95	5	89	0	95	0	67	95	100
2009	–	100	10	90	0	–	9	–	88	86

National Journal Ratings

	2010 LIB — 2010 CONS		2009 LIB — 2009 CONS	
Economic	26%	— 73%	19%	— 80%
Social	0%	— 79%	0%	— 94%
Foreign	0%	— 72%	21%	— 74%
Composite	17%	— 83%	15%	— 85%

Key Votes of the 111th Congress

1. Overturn Ledbetter	N	5. Pass health care bill	N	9. Ratify New START	N
2. Pass $787 billion stimulus	N	6. Regulate financial firms	N	10. Confirm Elena Kagan	N
3. Repeal DC gun laws	Y	7. Pass tax cuts for some	N	11. Stop EPA climate regs	Y
4. Confirm Sonia Sotomayor	N	8. Legalize immigrants' kids	N	12. Repeal don't ask, tell	N

Election Results

2010 general	David Vitter (R)	715,415	(57%)	($12,560,392)
	Charlie Melancon (D)	476,572	(38%)	($3,957,917)
2010 primary	David Vitter (R)	85,225	(88%)	
	Chet Traylor (R)	6,841	(7%)	
	Nick Accardo (R)	5,232	(5%)	

Prior Winning Percentages: 2004 (51%); House: 2002 (81%); 2000 (80%); 1999 (51%)

Louisiana's junior senator is David Vitter, a Republican elected in 2004. He grew up in the New Orleans area, the son of a Chevron petroleum engineer. He graduated from Harvard University and Tulane University's law school and was a Rhodes Scholar. He was a business attorney and taught law at Tulane and Loyola. In 1991, Vitter was elected to the state House from the district that had been represented by former Ku Klux Klansman David Duke. There he passed a term-limits bill through a reluctant state Legislature and was noted for his ability to irritate other politicians. Many of them held grudges because of his crusade for term limits; others were put off by his crusades for ethics in government. Vitter led the effort to recall Democratic Gov. Edwin Edwards, who ultimately went to prison for racketeering. A popular sheriff sued Vitter three times after Vitter criticized his ethics.

Vitter ran for Congress and won in a May 1999 special election to replace Republican Bob Livingston, the Speaker-designate who announced in late 1998 that he would resign after confessing that he had had extramarital affairs. Many Republicans jumped into the race, and many Louisiana and national Republicans feared that Duke would run and embarrass the party by making it into the runoff. The establishment choice was David Treen, 70, who had served four terms in the House starting in 1972 and had been elected governor in 1979. Vitter argued, in effect, that Treen was too old, saying, "We need a younger congressman like me, so we can start building up the seniority we lost when Bob Livingston resigned." The top two vote-getters in the initial balloting were Treen, with 25%, and Vitter, with 22%. The two advanced to the runoff under the system then in use. Duke, unnervingly close to making the runoff, finished third with 19%. Low turnout was probably a factor in deciding the runoff, as Vitter rallied his troops and won 51%-49%.

Vitter had one of the most conservative voting records in the House and the most conservative in the delegation. He twice won re-election in his heavily Republican, suburban New Orleans district with at least 80% of the vote.

In December 2003, Democratic Sen. John Breaux announced that he would not seek a fourth term, and two days later, Vitter jumped into the contest. Wooden in manner, a self-described loner and highly conservative, Vitter was the stylistic opposite of Breaux, a gregarious dealmaker and respected centrist from Cajun country who had been a major force for reform of entitlements and health care. But the state party and national Republicans worked hard to clear the field for Vitter, viewing him as the strongest possible candidate, thanks to his suburban political base and his habit of traveling the state to announce projects secured from his perch on the Appropriations Committee. He was also familiar in Cajun country after his well-publicized opposition to an Indian casino in southwestern Louisiana.

On the Democratic side, three serious candidates joined the race: U.S. Rep. Chris John, two-term state Treasurer John Kennedy; and state Rep. Arthur Morrell, an African-American from New Orleans. There was little doubt that Vitter would win the state's unique Election Day primary against a divided Democratic field; the real issue for Democrats was holding him below the 50%-plus-one threshold necessary to avoid a December runoff. Vitter ran as a strong supporter of President George W. Bush and called for making Bush's tax cuts permanent, new job creation and medical malpractice lawsuit restrictions. He opposed abortion rights, same-sex marriage and gun-ownership restrictions. He said he best represented "mainstream Louisiana values" and painted John as an out-of-touch Washington liberal who was close to John Kerry, the 2004 Democratic presidential nominee. John, the Democratic front-runner who had Breaux's endorsement, responded by referring to Vitter as a Republican Party puppet and strove to distance himself from Kerry's presidential campaign—a wise move in a state that Bush wound up carrying with 57% that November.

Sugar was an important issue. Louisiana is the prime cane sugar-producing state, and producers worry about being undercut by cheap imports. Vitter broke with the Bush administration over the Central American Free Trade Agreement, opposing it because it did not exempt sugar imports from the deal. Vitter ran some of the most creative television ads of the election cycle, making light of his image as a stiff politician with humorous commercials featuring his daughter's home movies. Meanwhile, John failed to gain momentum and was caught in the crossfire between Vitter on the right and Kennedy and Morrell on the left.

With Vitter leading in the polls going into November, the Democratic candidates began scrambling to keep him below the 50% threshold. The Democratic Senatorial Campaign Committee spent more than $1.5 million in ads criticizing Vitter's positions on prescription drug reimportation and Social Security. It wasn't enough. Vitter won the race outright with 51%, becoming the first Republican in 121 years to represent Louisiana in the Senate. John was the leading Democratic vote-getter, with 29% to 15% for Kennedy and 3% for Morrell. Bush's strong performance helped Vitter, but he ran well on his own, winning Mississippi River parishes that Bush lost, carrying nearly all of Louisiana north of Baton Rouge, and posting large margins in the New Orleans suburbs. In populous St. Tammany Parish, which he had represented in Congress, Vitter won by more than 5-to-1. His 60,000-vote margin there was more than enough to erase John's 25,000-vote advantage in New Orleans.

In the Senate, Vitter has compiled a relatively conservative voting record with maverick touches. In January 2007, during the Senate's debate of the lobbying reform bill, he won passage of his amendments to increase criminal sanctions for willful violations. He sought to prohibit lobbying by spouses of senators. He also advocated for a lost cause in the Senate: a constitutional amendment to limit members of the House and Senate to 12 years of service. But Vitter continued to be a thorn in the side of lawmakers who preferred business as usual. In March 2009, he sponsored an amendment to require a vote on any annual congressional pay raise before it could take effect. Although the amendment was defeated, the move pressured Democratic Senate Majority Leader Harry Reid to put the pay raise to a stand-alone vote. It passed.

After Democrat Barack Obama's election as president in 2008, Vitter was not inspired to try to make friends across the aisle. He cast one of the two votes against confirming New York Democrat Hillary Rodham Clinton as secretary of state, although her qualifications for the job were not an issue. Vitter has opposed much of the Obama administration agenda. He not only voted against the $787 billion economic stimulus bill in February 2009, he continually pushed a conservative "No Cost Stimulus Act," focused on domestic oil and gas production and regulatory relief for business. Vitter also attached an amendment to a September 2009 Interior appropriations bill that would have blocked funds for any policy initiated by White House climate change and energy adviser Carol Browner. The amendment was defeated. On the Senate Banking, Housing and Urban Affairs Committee, Vitter opposed Ben Bernanke's second term as Federal Reserve chairman in early 2010, complaining that the Fed had doled out trillions of dollars and "worsened our economic crisis by making 'too big to fail' a permanent government policy." He formed an unlikely alliance with socialist Sen. Bernie Sanders, I-Vt. in placing a hold on Bernanke's nomination, and Vitter ultimately voted against Bernanke's confirmation.

Some of his legislative guerrilla tactics for conservative causes have enjoyed more success. In 2007, Vitter's amendment to bar funding of organizations advocating international gun control policies passed 81-10. In 2008, the Senate passed his amendment giving inspectors general more access to documents on the Global Fund to Fight AIDS, Tuberculosis and Malaria. Vitter is particularly interested in law-and-order issues. In February 2010, he co-sponsored with Sen. Amy Klobuchar, D-Minn., a bill giving administrative subpoena authority to the Marshals Service, the Bureau of Immigration and Customs Enforcement, and the Postal Inspection Service in cases of child exploitation. He also sponsored a bill to require the states to collect DNA samples from convicted felons.

Home-state issues have been especially challenging for Vitter and other members of Congress from the disaster-prone Gulf region. At a Senate hearing two months before Hurricane Katrina struck in 2005, Vitter predicted that someday a huge storm would smash the city and leave it under water: "It's not a question of if. It's a question of when," he said. After the catastrophe, he criticized the U.S. Army Corps of Engineers for failing to provide flood protection for the city. And he worked with Louisiana's Democratic senator, Mary Landrieu, in pressing for federal recovery funds, though the two famously don't get along personally. In September 2007, Vitter pushed Majority Leader Reid to call a vote on a water resources bill that authorized nearly $2 billion for Louisiana coastal restoration and $886 million for a 72-mile system of levees and floodwalls for low-lying Terrebonne and Lafourche parishes. The next month, Vitter got 22 Republican senators to sign a letter urging President George W. Bush to abandon his threat to veto the bill. Bush refused, but his veto was ultimately overridden by Congress.

The deadly April 2010 explosion of the BP-operated Deepwater Horizon oil rig off the coast of Louisiana sparked outrage from fisherman and residents throughout the Bayou State. BP became the focus of considerable public criticism. Vitter's campaigns had received more than $450,000 from the oil and gas industry in the preceding five years, putting him in a tough position politically. Along with Landrieu, Vitter called on the Obama administration to support a state proposal to create barrier islands to protect the land from oil spills. After the administration announced a six-month moratorium on all deep-water drilling operations in the Gulf of Mexico, Vitter wrote to Obama warning that the drilling moratorium would result in the loss of 20,000 jobs in the state within a year. He advocated that drilling operations be shut down only if specific safety problems were identified during rig inspections. As a member of the Environment and Public Works Committee, he also opposed Democratic efforts to eliminate the cap on liability for oil companies after a spill.

Vitter's political career was dealt a major blow in July 2007, when it was revealed that between 1999 and 2001 his phone number had appeared on the call list of "D.C. Madam" Deborah Jeane Palfrey. A week later he appeared with his wife, Wendy, at his side and issued a public apology, saying he had committed "a very serious sin." The same year, the Senate Ethics Committee debated whether to punish Vitter, but ruled that the conduct in question had occurred before he entered the Senate. Vitter tried to use his campaign funds to pay $160,000 in legal fees in the case, but the Federal Election Commission would not permit it. In another round of negative publicity, in March 2009, the Transportation Security Administration looked into an incident in which Vitter allegedly opened a security gate to try to board a flight at Dulles Airport after the flight had been boarded and the doors locked. The attempt set off alarms. Vitter later claimed he had mistakenly gone through the wrong door at the gate, and the TSA ruled that he had not posed a security threat. Trouble for Vitter continued with an ABC News report in 2010 that a longtime Vitter aide had had repeated brushes with the law, including a knife-wielding incident with an ex-girlfriend. The staff member was kept on board two years after the episode, during which he worked on women's issues for the senator. The aide resigned in late June.

Considering the well-publicized scandals, Vitter did remarkably well in his bid for a second term in 2010. He won re-election 57% to 38% over Democratic Rep. Charlie Melancon. In anticipation of a tough contest and a rehash of the prostitution story, Vitter raised over $12.6 million to Melancon's $4 million. Indeed, Melancon made an issue of Vitter's "sin," but in running a predominately anti-Vitter campaign, he failed to define himself, Louisiana political analysts said. Vitter did that for him by portraying Melancon as an Obama administration yes-man, slamming him for his vote for the president's $787 billion economic stimulus bill. The message resonated in a year voters were less focused on personal characteristics than on their worries about their household finances and the economy.

Melancon also missed opportunities to separate himself from Obama by highlighting his votes against the health care overhaul and the cap-and-trade energy bill that imposed new regulations on industry, which naturally would find a receptive audience in an energy-dependent state. To counter the attacks about his use of prostitutes, Vitter ran a negative ad critical of overseas trips Melancon took at taxpayers' expense, including one to Paris with his wife, which Melancon called a fact-finding mission to learn about the energy policies of U.S. NATO allies. But Vitter also came under fire for an ad that depicted illegal Mexican immigrants sneaking through a fence. The Hispanic Chamber of Commerce denounced the ad as racist. Vitter accused his critics of "ridiculous political correctness," saying the ad revealed "a fact and not a stereotype."

The election seemed to liberate Vitter, who had kept a low profile in the months after the scandal broke. Once back in Washington, he joined newly elected Sen. Rand Paul of Kentucky, one of 2010's tea party Republicans, in a proposal to amend the Constitution to end birthright citizenship. It would provide automatic citizenship to children born in the United States only if one parent is a U.S. citizen, a legal immigrant or an active member of the U.S. military. In February 2011, Vitter put a hold on Obama's appointment of a Fish and Wildlife Service director to force the Interior Department to approve offshore drilling permits.

FIRST DISTRICT

Steve Scalise (R)

Elected May 2008, 2nd full term; b. Oct. 6, 1965, New Orleans; home, Jefferson; LA St. U., B.S., 1989; Catholic; married (Jennifer); 2 children.

Elected Office: LA Legislature, 1996-2007, LA Senate, 2008.

Professional Career: Systems engineer, Diamond Data Systems, eVenture Technologies.

DC Office: 429 CHOB, 20515, 202-225-3015; Fax: 202-226-0386; Web site: scalise.house.gov.

State Offices: Hammond, 985-340-2185; Mandeville, 985-893-9064; Metarie, 504-837-1259.

Committees: *Energy & Commerce:* Communications & Technology; Energy & Power; Oversight & Investigations.

Group Ratings

	ACLU	ACU	ADA	CFG	AFS	FRC	LCV	ITIC	NTU	COC
2010	13	96	0	98	0	100	20	33	89	88
2009	–	100	0	92	11	–	0	–	89	80

National Journal Ratings

	2010 LIB — 2010 CONS		2009 LIB — 2009 CONS	
Economic	25%	74%	6%	93%
Social	0%	85%	18%	81%
Foreign	0%	88%	0%	75%
Composite	13%	87%	13%	88%

Key Votes of the 111th Congress

1. Overturn Ledbetter	N	5. Bar federal abortion funds	Y	9. Stop detainee transfers	Y
2. Pass $820 billion stimulus	N	6. Pass health care bill	N	10. Legalize immigrants' kids	N
3. Let guns in national parks	Y	7. Regulate financial firms	N	11. Repeal don't ask, tell	N
4. Pass cap-and-trade	N	8. Pass tax cuts for some	N	12. Limit campaign funds	N

Election Results

2010 general	Steve Scalise (R)	157,182	(79%)	($1,358,024)
	Myron Katz (D)	38,416	(19%)	($64,420)
	Arden Wells (I)	4,578	(2%)	
2010 primary	Steve Scalise (R)	unopposed		

Prior Winning Percentages: 2008 (66%); 2008 Special (75%)

Population		Race/Ethnicity		Work	
Pop. 2010:	686,961	White:	73.0%	Private:	78.7%
Change since 2000:	Up 7.6%	Black:	15.8%	Government:	14.4%
Urban:	79.6%	Hispanic:	7.6%	Self-employed:	6.8%
Rural:	20.4%	Asian:	1.9%	Blue collar:	20.8%
Area size:	2,840 sq. mi.	Native Am.:	0.3%	White collar:	63.4%
		Hawaiian:	0.0%	Khaki collar:	0.3%
Age		Two+ races:	1.2%	Other:	15.5%
Median age:	38.5 yrs.				
More than 65 yrs:	13.5%	*Ancestry*		Median income:	$50,810
Less than 18 yrs:	23.4%	French	14.3%	Median Home Value:	$191,900
		German	12.7%		
Education		Italian	10.6%	**Military Veterans**	
H.S. grad:	86.3%			% of Pop:	10.3%
College grad:	28.8%				
Grad degree:	9.4%				

New Orleans and Suburbs

Founded in 1718 and the nation's fifth largest city at the outbreak of the Civil War, New Orleans is ancient for an American metropolis. It is still closely girded by the peculiar wilderness of the mushy Delta lands of the sluggish Mississippi River. For decades, you could climb a levee overlooking the Mississippi and see an expanse of water with untidy clumps of trees and disorganized-looking, seemingly abandoned docks

2008 Presidential Vote		
John McCain (R) 222,090	(73%)
Barack Obama (D) 79,326	(26%)
2004 Presidential Vote		
George Bush (R) 215,538	(71%)
John Kerry (D) 87,009	(29%)
Cook Partisan Voting Index: R+24		

what Mark Twain had in his mind's eye while writing *Life on the Mississippi* in the 1870s. For years, the river funneled the products of half a continent down to a single port with an international heritage and flair. The New Orleans metropolitan area has lived off that geography and history, with an inward-looking elite preoccupied with who is in which Mardi Gras krewe and interested more in the genealogy of old families than in the geography of the Oil Patch. The old buildings of New Orleans are finely proportioned and its old neighborhoods charming, like those in France. Its early-20th century improvements, like Olmstead's City Park, were grand. But its late-20th century streetscapes and subdivisions were without ornament or charm, utilitarian works that were part of an attempt to master the below-sea-level environment. After Hurricane Katrina struck with Category Four force on Aug. 29, 2005, many of those details changed dramatically. The city's population plummeted, housing stock was destroyed, some levees were breached and others were no longer reliable. The last act of nature to have wreaked so much damage on an American city was the San Francisco earthquake of 1906.

The 1st Congressional District of Louisiana encompasses some of the places hardest hit by Katrina. About half of its people live south of Lake Pontchartrain in affluent white neighborhoods, in the Uptown area and west of City Park, and in mostly white neighborhoods on the West Bank of the Mississippi. The district takes in the vast suburb of Metairie in Jefferson Parish and also part of suburbanizing St. Charles Parish. Jefferson is a leader in business and population; with more than 443,000 residents in July 2009—down about 8,300 from four years earlier—it was still one of the state's most populous.

The percentage of African-Americans in the 1st District (16%) is the lowest of any Louisiana district. The 1st extends across the 26-mile Lake Pontchartrain Causeway to include St. Tammany Parish, with its old towns lush with trees and clusters of new growth around giant intersections. After the BP Gulf oil spill disaster in 2010, parish officials complained that the oil company's maps were not accurately showing the location of giant oil slicks. By July, balls of tar were spotted in the Rigolets, one of two passes connecting Lake Pontchartrain with the Gulf. As in other parts of the state, coastal erosion is a longstanding concern; every 38 minutes, an area of wetlands about the size of a football field is lost.

Nearly 75% of the homes in St. Tammany were damaged to some degree by Katrina, but much of the parish, with the notable exception of Slidell, was spared from the worst effects. As a result, St. Tammany neighborhoods recovered more quickly, and many evacuees found their way to its higher ground in the ensuing months. The local real estate market surged, and the population grew by about 23% in the first year after Katrina. The 1st District also includes, to the north and west, Washington and Tangipahoa parishes, still mostly rural

This is the most upscale, affluent, highly educated district in Louisiana, and easily the most Republican, supportive of political reformers and against economic redistribution. George W. Bush got 71% of the vote here in 2004, by far his best performance in the state. John McCain bested Barack Obama 76%-22% in St. Tammany, and took the district 73%-26%.

Steve Scalise (R)

The congressman from the 1st District is Steve Scalise, a Republican who won a special election in May 2008 to succeed GOP Rep. Bobby Jindal, who became governor. A native of New Orleans, Scalise (*sca-LEEZ*) grew up in Metairie. When his parents gave their son a battery-powered microphone, he played town crier on his neighborhood street, decorating his bicycle in red, white and blue and calling people to the polls—the start of a political career. He majored in computer science at Louisiana State University, where he was speaker of the student assembly. After college, he settled in Jefferson Parish as a systems engineer. In 1995, when he was 30, he was elected to the state House, where he served 12 years before winning a state Senate seat in 2007. He pushed legislation to give incentives to the motion picture industry to produce films in Louisiana, and he helped pass a bill that made Louisiana the first state to bar cities from suing gun manufacturers for the actions of criminals. Scalise had considered running for the open seat in the 1st District in 1999 and 2004, but deferred first to David Vitter, now a U.S. senator, then to Jindal.

In the special election to replace Jindal, the key contest was the April 5 Republican runoff between Scalise and state Rep. Tim Burns of Mandeville in St. Tammany. Burns cited Scalise's opposition to a bill banning smoking in restaurants and tried to tie him to special interests. Scalise called for limits on "out-of-control spending" and said he had "the experience to hit the ground running from Day One." Scalise won 58%-42%, capturing 83% of the Jefferson Parish vote.

The May 3 contest against Democrat Gilda Reed, a college instructor and political neophyte, was never in doubt. Scalise won 75%-23%. But the following November, when Scalise had to defend the seat in regularly scheduled congressional election, he faced a bigger challenge. Democrat Jim Harlan, a venture capitalist, sank $1.8 million of his own money into the race and was not shy about throwing mud. In one television ad, he tried to tie Scalise to a local scandal involving a federal investigation of the abuse of tax credits by the Louisiana Institute of Film Technology because Scalise had been a sponsor of the tax credit program in the legislature. Scalise cited his opponent's support of presidential candidate Barack Obama as evidence that Harlan was too liberal for the district. Scalise coasted to a 66%-34% win for a full two-year term, taking 71% in Jefferson Parish and 68% in St. Tammany, which together accounted for 71% of the total vote. He coasted to re-election in 2010 with 79%.

Scalise is a down-the-line Republican and "has emerged as one of the GOP's most full-throttled conservatives," *The Times-Picayune* said in 2010. His rhetorical edge is sharper than that of his predecessors, Republicans Jindal and former Appropriations Committee Chairman Bob Livingston. He has railed against what he calls Obama's "radical agenda." He joined the Tea Party Caucus and in 2011 became head of communications for the Republican Study Committee, a group of the House's most conservative members. But Scalise is also known for his sense of humor, and is friendly with many Democrats. He and liberal Henry Waxman of California regularly talk about their children and grandchildren, and he plays basketball with 2nd District Democrat Cedric Richmond, an old friend from their days in Baton Rouge.

In 2009, Scalise joined the powerful Energy and Commerce Committee, a useful assignment for this district. He called for more energy production, including offshore drilling. "Our country's demand for energy increases every year," he told *Esquire* in 2010. "How are you going to meet those needs? Domestic oil, natural gas, clean coal, solar, wind, nuclear power—let's use everything." After the BP spill, he shepherded colleagues down to the region to see the disaster for themselves and was incensed by Obama's moratorium on offshore drilling, calling it "reckless." He supports allowing other states to allow drilling without regulatory encumbrances.

He was a staunch opponent of the Democrats' cap-and-trade bill to allow industries to trade emissions credits in an effort to reduce greenhouse gas emissions. At an April 2009 committee hearing, he accused former Vice President Al Gore of standing to benefit financially from the bill. And Scalise got a provision into a committee-passed bill that year to require a Government Accountability Office study after implementation to assess the legislation's impact on small businesses.

SECOND DISTRICT

Cedric Richmond (D)

Elected 2010, 1st term; b. Sept. 13, 1973, New Orleans; Morehouse Col., B.A. 1995; Tulane U., J.D. 1998.; Baptist; Single.

Elected Office: LA House, 2000-10.

Professional Career: Practicing atty., 1998-2010.

DC Office: 415 CHOB, 20515, 202-225-6636; Fax: 202-225-1988; Web site: richmond.house.gov.

State Offices: Gretna, 504-365-0390; New Orleans, 504-288-3777.

Committees: *Homeland Security:* Cybersecurity, Infrastructure Protection & Security Technologies; Transportation Security. *Small Business:* Contracting & Workforce; Healthcare & Technology (RMM).

Election Results

2010 general	Cedric Richmond (D)	83,705	(65%)	($1,139,879)
	Anh 'Joseph' Cao (R)	43,378	(33%)	($2,079,915)
2010 primary	Cedric Richmond (D)	14,678	(61%)	
	Juan LaFonta (D)	5,171	(21%)	
	Eugene Green (D)	2,500	(10%)	
	Gary Johnson (D)	1,914	(8%)	

Population		Race/Ethnicity		Work	
Pop. 2010:	493,352	White:	29.1%	Private:	77.8%
Change since 2000:	Down 22.7%	Black:	58.2%	Government:	15.3%
Urban:	99.4%	Hispanic:	7.3%	Self-employed:	6.5%
Rural:	0.6%	Asian:	3.5%	Blue collar:	23.7%
Area size:	444 sq. mi.	Native Am.:	0.3%	White collar:	54.4%
		Hawaiian:	0.0%	Khaki collar:	0.2%
Age		Two+ races:	1.3%	Other:	21.7%
Median age:	35.9 yrs.				
More than 65 yrs:	11.0%	*Ancestry*		Median income:	$37,755
Less than 18 yrs:	23.5%	French	8.4%	Median Home Value:	$161,700
		German	5.4%		
Education		Italian	3.8%	**Military Veterans**	
H.S. grad:	79.5%			% of Pop:	8.1%
College grad:	21.0%				
Grad degree:	8.1%				

New Orleans

Founded by the French in 1718, ruled by the Spanish from 1763 until it was sold to the United States in 1803, New Orleans was a Creole city—part French, a bit Spanish, more than a touch Caribbean—when the American flag was raised over what is now Jackson Square. The statue of Andrew Jackson still seems an intrusion in a square set off by a French Market, the Cabildo, the Presbytere, the Pontalba apartments and Cathedral St. Louis. New Orleans

2008 Presidential Vote
Barack Obama (D) 150,191   (75%)
John McCain (R) 46,666   (23%)

2004 Presidential Vote
John Kerry (D) 183,928   (75%)
George Bush (R) 58,855   (24%)

Cook Partisan Voting Index: D+25

was the fifth largest American city from 1840 until the Civil War and the only sizable city in the South. Yet, even as it was sending Southern cotton to the mills of Lancashire, it was an alien cultural force in both the nation and region. Urbanized, yet poor, New Orleans had yellow fever epidemics late in the 19th century, even as it was installing electric lights. It had a riot in which Italian immigrants were massacred, even as it was laying streetcar tracks and telephone lines. This was one of the most corrupt American cities during Reconstruction and the Gilded Age, when its votes were regularly bid for and bought. Like other Southern cities, it became rigidly segregated after 1890.

For a time during the 1970s oil boom, New Orleans seemed to be a fast-growing Sun Belt city. It suffered more economically through the 1980s, when it lost substantial port business—oil to

Houston and Latin American trade to Miami—though it still shipped large amounts of grain. By the 1990s, New Orleans was humming again. Crime rates fell, and no longer depressed tourism. Visitors wanted to see the gaudy bars of Bourbon Street, the graceful restored houses in the Garden District and the Mardi Gras parade. They wanted to dine in the storied restaurants, with a cuisine all New Orleans' own, spicy and rich and unaffected by trends in low-fat food. Incomes went up, and home ownership increased, among blacks as well as whites.

But the nation has since acquired other images of New Orleans. As Hurricane Katrina made landfall early on a Monday morning, Aug. 29, 2005, more than 20,000 people huddled at the downtown Superdome, the shelter of last resort. Although they were told to bring food, water and medicine, many did not. The scene inside was nightmarish, with no power and provisions; conditions worsened when the storm ripped two holes in the roof. A few days later, city officials began to load people on buses for transport to cities that were better positioned to provide services. The breach of the city's levees led to a surge that churned through the low-income 9th Ward, while the French Quarter, on higher ground, was largely untouched by the floodwaters. Still, 80% of the city flooded.

During the months following the devastation, it became clear that New Orleans was in for a very long recovery. Thousands of government trailers became semi-permanent homes. City residents who had fled the floodwaters only slowly trickled back. It took years to restore regular utility service. Expectations repeatedly were downsized. Then in 2008, the last government trailer parks closed, and the restaurants in the French Quarter were back in business. By 2010, the city's population was 344,000, 29% smaller than it was in 2000, according to the Census Bureau. But it was still growing at an impressive rate: by 17% in 2008 and by 5% in 2009. Post-recession wages and median household income in the city and suburbs were also on the rise (although New Orleans was a relatively poor city before the hurricane and remains so; half its residents are classified as low income). "It's very clear we're going to have a much smaller, very different New Orleans," retired Brown University geographer Robert Kates told *USA Today*.

The city's post-hurricane recovery lost some momentum with a second disaster that struck in April 2010. BP's Deepwater Horizon offshore rig exploded and began spewing oil into the Gulf of Mexico at an estimated rate of 60,000 barrels a day. Despite efforts to contain it, the oil slick spread from the drilling site southeast of the mouth of the Mississippi River to the Mississippi Delta, posing a major threat to the area's oyster beds and shrimp fisheries. A federally mandated moratorium on offshore drilling put thousands of oil industry jobs in the region at risk as well, although it was lifted in October 2010 under pressure from local and state officials and the Louisiana congressional delegation. The fragile regional economy took another serious blow in July 2010, when the Avondale shipyard announced it would shut down by 2013, eliminating 5,000 jobs, representing fully 1% of the 520,000 jobs in the greater New Orleans area.

The 2nd Congressional District of Louisiana includes almost all of the city of New Orleans, everything except a few affluent white neighborhoods. It has nearly half of Jefferson Parish, African-American neighborhoods in Metairie and Kenner, and the West Bank towns of Harvey, Marrero, and Westwego. In the French Quarter—the *Vieux Carre* as it was originally called—are the 19th-century-row houses decked out in their island pastels and ornate wrought-iron railings. At street level are restaurants, art galleries and jazz and blues clubs, and the narrow sidewalks fill up nightly with diners, revelers, and patrons of the tiny voodoo establishments found only in New Orleans. South of the quarter is the downtown district, with its skyscrapers and the Superdome, and to the east is the old slum known as the Irish Channel, a reminder that New Orleans had more foreign immigrants than any other part of the South. Up St. Charles Avenue from the Vieux Carre is the Garden District, with the graceful intact homes of the rich early American settlers. The district is solidly Democratic. John Kerry won 75% of the vote here in 2004 and Barack Obama got 75% in 2008.

Cedric Richmond (D)

The new congressman from Louisana's 2nd District is Cedric Richmond, a Democrat who reclaimed the seat for his party in 2010 after it was held for one term by Republican Anh "Joseph" Cao.

Richmond grew up in eastern New Orleans. His father died when he was 7 years old, and he was raised by his mother, a public school teacher. In his youth, life revolved around an urban park where he loved to play sports and later, while in high school, coached teams of younger boys. He graduated from Atlanta's Morehouse College, the nation's only all-male historically black college, and returned to his hometown to earn a law degree from Tulane University.

In 2000, Richmond was elected to the state House of Representatives at age 26, becoming the youngest lawmaker in Baton Rouge. He pushed initiatives such as a redevelopment tax credit for weather-damaged areas, funding for playgrounds, and a ban on assault weapons. He also came out strongly against a proposed legislative pay raise in 2008. Richmond ran for New Orleans City Council in 2005, but was ejected from the race for falsifying his qualifying papers when it was determined in court that he didn't meet the residency requirement to represent the district as he had attested. His law license was later briefly suspended as a result. Despite the controversy, Richmond was re-elected to the legislature in 2007.

Dismayed with New Orleans' slow recovery from Katrina, he decided to run for Congress in 2008. He also made an issue of the district's scandal-plagued incumbent, Rep. William Jefferson, a Democrat who had been stripped of his committee assignments after being indicted on federal corruption charges. Richmond was one of six Democrats who filed to challenge the incumbent, but the divided field split the anti-Jefferson vote. Finishing third, Richmond failed to qualify for the runoff, which Jefferson won. Cao then eked out a narrow general-election victory over Jefferson, who was subsequently sentenced to 13 years in jail for bribery.

In his two years in office, Cao tried to hold onto the seat by establishing one of the most independent voting records among House Republicans. While he stuck with his party in opposing President Obama's economic stimulus bill and a measure to limit carbon emissions, he was the lone Republican to join Democrats in supporting the president's health care legislation in 2009. But when the midterm election rolled around, Cao was viewed as extremely vulnerable given the heavily Democratic makeup of the district.

In the August 2010 primary, Richmond beat three other Democrats, taking 60% of the vote. He garnered two-thirds of the ballots cast in heavily black precincts as well as nearly half of those in heavily white areas. On the campaign trail, he reminded voters of Cao's votes against the $787 billion stimulus and the final version of the health care bill in 2010. His central message was that he would be a more dependable supporter of Obama's agenda than Cao, and he was bolstered in September by a public endorsement from Obama, who called him "a leader on hurricane recovery and a fighter for the people of New Orleans." The Democratic Congressional Campaign Committee put Richmond in its "Red to Blue" program, enabling him to tap more campaign funds to catch up to Cao.

Richmond, however, had several problems of his own. In addition to the fallout from his 2005 City Council filing offense, a political group called Louisiana Truth PAC launched a website that attacked him on several fronts during the primary, including a misdemeanor charge stemming from his involvement in a 2007 bar fight. Richmond's response was that he was only trying to defend himself in the fight. Still, Richmond won easily, 65% to 33%.

THIRD DISTRICT

Jeff Landry (R)

Elected 2010, 1st term; b. Dec. 23, 1970, St. Martinville; home, New Iberia.

Military Career: LA Army Natl. Guard, 1987-98.

Professional Career: Police officer, Village of Parks, 1991; deputy, St. Martinville Sheriff's Office, 1993; practicing atty., 2006-10; owner, UST Environmental Svcs.

DC Office: 206 CHOB, 20515, 202-225-4031; Fax: 202-226-3944; Web site: landry.house.gov.

State Offices: Houma, 985-879-2300; New Iberia, 337-359-9080.

Committees: *Natural Resources:* Energy & Mineral Resources; Fisheries, Wildlife, Oceans & Insular Affairs. *Small Business:* Agriculture, Energy & Trade; Contracting & Workforce; Investigations, Oversight & Regulations. *Transportation & Infrastructure:* Coast Guard & Maritime Transportation (VChmn); Railroads, Pipelines & Hazardous Materials; Water Resources & Environment.

Election Results

2010 general	Jeff Landry (R)...108,963	(64%)	($1,421,922)
	Ravi Sangisetty (D)...61,914	(36%)	($828,014)
2010 primary	Jeff Landry (R)...19,657	(65%)	
	'Hunt' Downer (R)..10,549	(35%)	
2010 primary	Jeff Landry (R)...10,396	(50%)	
	'Hunt' Downer (R)..7,570	(36%)	
	Kristian Magar (R) 2,987	(14%)	

Population		Race/Ethnicity		Work	
Pop. 2010:	637,371	White:	64.1%	Private:	78.9%
Change since 2000:	Down 0.1%	Black:	27.3%	Government:	14.3%
Urban:	73.0%	Hispanic:	4.1%	Self-employed:	6.6%
Rural:	27.0%	Asian:	1.2%	Blue collar:	31.9%
Area size:	13,206 sq. mi.	Native Am.:	1.8%	White collar:	51.3%
		Hawaiian:	0.0%	Khaki collar:	0.2%
Age		Two+ races:	1.4%	Other:	16.7%
Median age:	35.4 yrs.				
More than 65 yrs:	11.4%	*Ancestry*		Median income:	$45,456
Less than 18 yrs:	26.8%	French	20.1%	Median Home Value:	$119,300
		USA	9.4%		
Education		German	6.9%	**Military Veterans**	
H.S. grad:	76.2%			% of Pop:	8.4%
College grad:	13.7%				
Grad degree:	3.9%				

Southeast Louisiana; New Iberia

Below sea level, veined with bayous and creeks and crossed by only an occasional road or railroad, the wetlands of southern Louisiana are one of America's unique landscapes. Technically, most of this waterlogged land rests on islands in a broad river mouth, through which the waters of the Mississippi and its tributaries drain into the Gulf of Mexico. It is rich with animal life: herons and egrets, shrimp and crawfish, muskrats and alligators. Its people live in sturdy small

2008 Presidential Vote		
John McCain (R) 167,046	(61%)
Barack Obama (D) 101,427	(37%)
2004 Presidential Vote		
George Bush (R)....................162,269	(58%)
John Kerry (D) 115,011	(41%)
Cook Partisan Voting Index: R+12		

towns with shopping malls on high ground and in bayou towns, where Cajun French remains the primary language. Here and there, jutting out of the swampy land, are huge elaborate metal sculptures—petrochemical plants and refineries, processing the oil and natural gas trapped under the wetlands and the shallow continental shelf of the Gulf. In the 1960s and 1970s, the oil industry, by providing well-paid jobs for young people, helped preserve Cajun culture and nurtured a Cajun pride that was seldom articulated a generation earlier.

Then, oil payrolls plummeted and the wetlands were threatened by coastal erosion, a series of hurricanes, and worst of all, the man-made disaster known as the BP Deepwater Horizon oil spill. The rig exploded on April 20, 2010 and spewed more than 200 million gallons of crude oil into the Gulf over three months. Shrimp fishermen, whose profits were already under pressure from aquaculture-raised Asian and Latin American shrimp, were idled as BP and the federal government struggled to seal off the underwater leak. Once the well was finally stemmed in July, the hardest part was yet to come: Cleaning up from the largest marine oil spill in U.S. history, one that caused extensive damage to wildlife and habitats, not to mention Louisiana's coastal economy. About 600 miles of shoreline were affected; thousands of dead marine animals and birds were found and many more were suspected to be contaminated. BP set up a compensation fund that by the fall of 2010 had paid out $1.5 billion to fishermen and other businesses hurt by the spill. Gradually, some areas were reopened for fishing, but some were also being sporadically closed again as tar balls and other toxins were discovered in shrimp catches. When the federal government responded to the spill with a moratorium on offshore drilling, it put thousands of oil industry jobs in the region at risk as well. The moratorium was lifted in October 2010.

The BP disaster struck just as the area was beginning to recover from Hurricane Katrina, which made a direct hit on this district, inflicting widespread damage in August 2005. Plaquemines and St. Bernard parishes were ravaged by high winds and floodwaters, and most people fled. By 2010, St. Bernard's population of 36,000 was only about half of what it was in 2000. One sign of the continuing difficulties was the absence of a local hospital. The parish's one hospital was destroyed by the flood. The state finally issued $76 million in bonds to build a replacement hospital in January 2011.

The 3rd Congressional District of Louisiana includes about half of Cajun country. It includes most of Louisiana's swamplands, covering Houma, where seven bayous converge. It takes in the parishes of St. Charles, St. John the Baptist, St. James, and Ascension on both sides of the Mississippi. Roughneck Morgan City services offshore oil rigs. Iberia Parish is the home of McIlhenny's Tabasco sauce. The district also has St. Bernard and Plaquemines parishes, downriver from New Orleans. Behind the Mississippi's western levee, hunkered side by side in Vacherie, are twin reminders of the region's grandeur and pain: the stately Oak Alley plantation and the slave cabins of Laura Plantation, believed to be the original home of the famous Br'er Rabbit stories. The ancestral politics in the district are Democratic, though a very conservative brand of Democratic. George W. Bush won 58% here in 2004, and John McCain took the district with 61% in 2008. Given the regional upheaval in population from consecutive disasters, the 3rd District is at risk of being eliminated in the 2012 redistricting after the 2010 census.

Jeff Landry (R)

The new congressman from the 3rd District is Republican Jeff Landry, who picked up the seat of retiring Democratic Rep. Charlie Melancon in the 2010 election.

Landry was born in St. Martinville, La., and speaks with a heavy Cajun accent. His father, who was the first in his family to attend college, was an architect, and his mother was a high school English and French teacher and basketball coach. Landry was the oldest of four children, and his parents also raised his aunt's three children. After high school, he worked as a farmhand in sugarcane fields. He registered as a Republican when he turned 18 because of his admiration for President Reagan, a decision that raised some eyebrows in a region that was conservative but dominated by Democrats. "They gave me grief when I registered to vote in the courthouse when I was registering as a Republican," Landry told *National Journal*. "They told me I had made a mistake."

In 1987, Landry joined the Louisiana National Guard. He attended the University of Southwestern Louisiana (now the University of Louisiana at Lafayette), where he did not have to pay tuition because of his Guard status. He worked part-time as a police officer to pay for room and board, and he studied environmental science at the recommendation of his father, who told him it was an up-and-coming field. In 1995, he founded UST Environmental Services, an environmental compliance business that advised petroleum companies. Frustration with the legal system led Landry to go on to law school. He recalled thinking at the time, "Next time I go into business, I'd like to be able to know what the law is, fight my own battles." Landry graduated from Loyola University's law school in 2004 and two years later went to work for a defense litigation firm.

He got involved with politics through his friend, former state Sen. Craig Romero, who ran unsuccessfully for the 3rd District seat in 2006 and 2008, losing both times to Melancon. Landry assisted in his campaigns, including a stint as his campaign manager. In 2007, when Romero was term-limited out of his state Senate seat, Landry ran to replace him but lost.

The 3rd District seat came open when Melancon ran for the Senate in 2010. In the Republican primary, Landry faced former state House Speaker Hunt Downer and businessman Kristian Magar. Downer was the favorite of the Republican establishment, but Landry raised and spent more money and attracted the support of tea party activists. Landry ran as a political outsider and attacked Downer, who had won several legislative terms as a Democrat before switching parties, as a "liberal in a conservative's clothing." In the August primary, Downer won just enough votes to force a runoff, which Landry easily won in October with 70% of the vote to Downer's 30%.

In the general election, Landry faced Ravi Sangisetty, a lawyer who billed himself as a "pro-life, pro-gun conservative Democrat." Landry ran against President Obama and the Democratic Congress, promising to cut government spending and repeal the Obama-backed health care overhaul signed into law in 2010. He also called for an overhaul of the government's big entitlement programs, including Social Security, Medicare and Medicaid, though he offered few specifics. Sangisetty gamely took on Landry, claiming Landry exaggerated his military service and even running an ad that questioned Landry's role in the cocaine arrest of a former roommate 17 years earlier. Local police later confirmed Landry was not involved. But Landry was heavily favored in this conservative district, and he won 64% to 36%.

FOURTH DISTRICT

John Fleming (R)

Elected 2008, 2nd term; b. July 5, 1951, Meridian, MS; home, Minden; U. of MA, B.S. 1973, M.D. 1976; Baptist; married (Cindy); 4 children.

Military Career: Navy, 1976-82

Elected Office: Webster Parish coroner, 1996-2000

Professional Career: Physician; Businessman

DC Office: 416 CHOB, 20515, 202-225-2777; Fax: 202-225-8039; Web site: fleming.house.gov.

State Offices: Bossier City, 318-549-1712; Leesville, 337-238-0778; Shreveport, 318-798-2254.

Committees: *Armed Services:* Air & Land Forces; Strategic Forces. *Natural Resources:* Energy & Mineral Resources; Fisheries, Wildlife, Oceans & Insular Affairs (Chmn).

Group Ratings

	ACLU	ACU	ADA	CFG	AFS	FRC	LCV	ITIC	NTU	COC
2010	6	96	5	100	0	100	20	0	88	75
2009	–	100	0	91	11	–	0	–	86	80

National Journal Ratings

	2010 LIB — 2010 CONS		2009 LIB — 2009 CONS	
Economic	16% —	83%	12% —	88%
Social	0% —	85%	20% —	78%
Foreign	0% —	88%	0% —	75%
Composite	10% —	90%	15% —	85%

Key Votes of the 111th Congress

1. Overturn Ledbetter	N	5. Bar federal abortion funds	Y	9. Stop detainee transfers	Y
2. Pass $820 billion stimulus	N	6. Pass health care bill	N	10. Legalize immigrants' kids	N
3. Let guns in national parks	Y	7. Regulate financial firms	N	11. Repeal don't ask, tell	N
4. Pass cap-and-trade	N	8. Pass tax cuts for some	N	12. Limit campaign funds	N

Election Results

2010 general	John Fleming (R)	105,223	(62%)	($1,448,369)
	David Melville (D)	54,609	(32%)	($229,079)
	Artis Cash (I)	8,962	(5%)	($350)
2010 primary	John Fleming (R)	unopposed		

Prior Winning Percentages: 2008 (48%)

Population		Race/Ethnicity		Work	
Pop. 2010:	667,109	White:	59.4%	Private:	72.1%
Change since 2000:	Up 4.5%	Black:	33.7%	Government:	21.9%
Urban:	59.3%	Hispanic:	3.4%	Self-employed:	5.8%
Rural:	40.7%	Asian:	0.9%	Blue collar:	25.7%
Area size:	11,151 sq. mi.	Native Am.:	0.8%	White collar:	52.3%
		Hawaiian:	0.1%	Khaki collar:	2.2%
Age		Two+ races:	1.6%	Other:	19.8%
Median age:	35.4 yrs.				
More than 65 yrs:	13.4%	*Ancestry*		Median income:	$39,023
Less than 18 yrs:	25.3%	Irish	8.9%	Median Home Value:	$97,800
		USA	8.6%		
Education		German	6.9%	**Military Veterans**	
H.S. grad:	82.9%			% of Pop:	12.3%
College grad:	18.7%				
Grad degree:	6.1%				

Northwest Louisiana; Shreveport

Northwestern Louisiana, south of Arkansas and just east of Texas, is part of the Deep South. The overwhelming majority of people here are Protestants, not Catholics, and they are often tradition-minded, with names that are English or Scottish, not French. The tone is set not by wide-open New Orleans—which was not easily accessible by interstate until 1996, when the last chunk of Interstate 49 was completed—but by the smaller Shreveport, which could be just an-

2008 Presidential Vote
John McCain (R) 162,198   (59%)
Barack Obama (D) 108,273   (40%)

2004 Presidential Vote
George Bush (R) 156,298   (59%)
John Kerry (D) 105,962   (40%)

Cook Partisan Voting Index: R+11

other East Texas oil-patch town, albeit one that has its own, comparatively sedate, Mardi Gras. The countryside is agricultural, though there are some vestiges of large riverfront plantations. Roots go back here a long way. Natchitoches is the oldest town in Louisiana, founded by Louis Antoine Juchereay de St. Denis in 1714, and Shreveport was founded in the 1830s.

Oil provided the basis for much of the economic growth of the 20th century, but natural gas took off in the 21st century, helping to sustain the region during the recession. Gas was discovered in 1870, and the nation's first gas pipeline was built from Caddo Field to Shreveport in 1908. However, it wasn't economical to drill until gas prices zoomed upward in 2000. In addition to natural gas, riverboat gambling and the Port of Shreveport-Bossier helped keep the area viable during the recession. There are defense installations nearby, notably Barksdale Air Force Base in Bossier City, one of the nation's largest airfields, where George W. Bush landed on Sept. 11, 2001, and spoke briefly to the nation. Politically, Northern Louisiana, for more than 100 years, have been voting against cosmopolitan New Orleans and the Catholic Cajun south, sometimes for rip-roaring populists and more often recently for market-oriented Republicans.

The 4th Congressional District of Louisiana consists of the northwest corner of the state. More than half of the votes here are cast in Caddo and suburban Bossier parishes in the far corner around Shreveport, with the rest scattered around rural areas. This area seemed to be trending Republican in the 1980s, but in the middle 1990s, it went the other way. Both Bill Clinton and Sen. Mary Landrieu carried the district in 1996, a critical factor in Landrieu's narrow, 5,788-vote statewide victory that year. In 2000, George W. Bush carried the area by a comfortable 55%, and in 2004, by 59%. John McCain won the district easily in 2008.

John Fleming (R)

The congressman from the 4th District is Republican John Fleming. He grew up in Meridian, Miss., the son of a utility substation operator who worked two or three jobs to make ends meet. His father died of a heart attack just before Fleming finished high school. His mother was disabled and so relied on Social Security to support Fleming and two younger siblings. After undergraduate and medical school at the University of Mississippi, he spent six years in the Navy, where he did his medical residency. He later opened a family medical practice in Minden, La., and in the 1990s served as coroner of Webster Parish. He had another sideline: Fleming operated 30 Subway restaurants in the state and had a stake in 130 UPS stores, from Mississippi to Texas. He also wrote a book called *Preventing Addiction: What Parents Must Know to Immunize Their Kids Against Drug and Alcohol Addiction.*

The House seat came open when influential Rep. Jim McCrery, the ranking Republican on the Ways and Means Committee, announced his retirement in December 2007. The early front-runners for the GOP nomination were trucking-company executive Chris Gorman and Bossier Chamber of Commerce President Jeff Thompson, who was supported by McCrery and the National Republican Congressional Committee. In the first round of voting, Fleming led with 35%, to 34% for Gorman and 31% for Thompson. Next came a runoff campaign with Gorman. Both men held similar, conservative views, emphasizing the need to reduce federal spending and taxes, and both spent heavily. Fleming spent over $1 million, much of it his own money, while Gorman spent $1.8 million. Fleming captured the nomination 56%-44%.

Meanwhile, Democrats lined up behind Paul Carmouche, a 30-year Caddo Parish district attorney who styled himself as a centrist Blue Dog Democrat and ran an anti-abortion rights and anti-crime campaign. Fleming emphasized his own conservative credentials, calling himself a Ronald Reagan Republican. He called for abolishing the Internal Revenue Service and replacing the current income tax with a national sales tax. And he said he favored tough measures against illegal immigrants, decrying an "invasion by illegal aliens." Fleming out-raised Carmouche $1.4 million to $1.2 million and got a big helping hand from the NRCC.

The election was held on Dec. 6, 2008, after being delayed a month by the threat from Hurricane Gustav. Fleming won by 350 votes. Carmouche led 57%-39% in Caddo Parish, which cast 43% of the vote. He also took four rural parishes outside Shreveport, but Fleming ran strongly in the southern part of the district and in Bossier.

In the House, Fleming established himself as an unyielding conservative. His fondness for fiery rhetoric has drawn admiration from those on the far right, but even some members of his party have come to regard him as a loose cannon. One of the first Republicans to join the Tea Party Caucus, he regularly took to the House floor to make speeches bashing President Obama. In one newspaper column, he accused the president of "undermining this country's national defense on purpose." During the health care overhaul debate, he sponsored a resolution requiring lawmakers who backed a federally backed insurance plan to enroll in one and said, "How dare Congress force government-run health care down the throats of our fellow Americans?" Fleming also drew scorn from progressives when he publicly supported a Florida urologist's decision to deny care to patients who supported Obama, saying it was that doctor's "First Amendment right."

Democrats acutely missed having a candidate as formidable as Carmouche to take on Fleming in 2010. The party's nominee was David Melville, a Methodist minister who sought to portray the congressman as too partisan. Fleming did raise some eyebrows with an August appearance at a forum in which he cast the election as a choice between godlessness and Christianity. But with Republican Sen. David Vitter powering his way to re-election that fall, Fleming had no trouble winning comfortably with 62% of the vote.

FIFTH DISTRICT

Rodney Alexander (R)

Elected 2002, 5th term; b. Dec. 5, 1946, Quitman; home, Quitman; attended LA Tech. U., 1965; Baptist; married (Nancy); 3 children.

Military Career: Air Force Reserves, 1965-71.

Elected Office: Jackson Parish Police Jury, 1972-87; President, 1980-87; LA House of Reps., 1988-2002.

Professional Career: Insurance agent, 1990-93; Contractor, 1993-present.

DC Office: 316 CHOB, 20515, 202-225-8490; Fax: 202-225-5639; Web site: alexander.house.gov.

State Offices: Alexandria, 318-445-0818; Monroe, 318-322-3500.

Committees: *Appropriations:* Energy & Water Development; Financial Services & General Government; Labor, HHS, Education & Related Agencies (VChmn).

Group Ratings

	ACLU	ACU	ADA	CFG	AFS	FRC	LCV	ITIC	NTU	COC
2010	13	100	5	100	0	100	20	33	89	88
2009	–	88	0	85	22	–	14	–	81	80

National Journal Ratings

	2010 LIB	—	2010 CONS	2009 LIB	—	2009 CONS
Economic	12%	—	87%	20%	—	79%
Social	0%	—	85%	20%	—	78%
Foreign	29%	—	68%	0%	—	75%
Composite	17%	—	83%	18%	—	82%

Key Votes of the 111th Congress

1. Overturn Ledbetter	N	5. Bar federal abortion funds	Y	9. Stop detainee transfers	Y
2. Pass $820 billion stimulus	N	6. Pass health care bill	N	10. Legalize immigrants' kids	N
3. Let guns in national parks	Y	7. Regulate financial firms	N	11. Repeal don't ask, tell	N
4. Pass cap-and-trade	N	8. Pass tax cuts for some	N	12. Limit campaign funds	N

Election Results

2010 general	Rodney Alexander (R)	122,033	(79%)	($1,263,055)
	Tom Gibbs (I)	33,279	(21%)	
2010 primary	Rodney Alexander (R)	14,031	(89%)	
	Todd Slavant (R)	1,744	(11%)	

Prior Winning Percentages: 2008 (100%), 2006 (68%), 2004 (59%), 2002 (50%)

Population		Race/Ethnicity		Work	
Pop. 2010:	644,296	White:	61.1%	Private:	74.8%
Change since 2000:	Up 0.9%	Black:	34.6%	Government:	19.2%
Urban:	52.9%	Hispanic:	1.9%	Self-employed:	5.8%
Rural:	47.1%	Asian:	0.7%	Blue collar:	24.7%
Area size:	14,225 sq. mi.	Native Am.:	0.5%	White collar:	53.8%
		Hawaiian:	0.0%	Khaki collar:	0.1%
Age		Two+ races:	1.0%	Other:	21.3%
Median age:	36.0 yrs.				
More than 65 yrs:	13.5%	*Ancestry*		Median income:	$35,889
Less than 18 yrs:	25.2%	USA	13.7%	Median Home Value:	$88,100
		French	8.7%		
Education		Irish	8.3%	**Military Veterans**	
H.S. grad:	78.2%			% of Pop:	9.0%
College grad:	17.1%				
Grad degree:	5.5%				

Northeast Louisiana; Monroe

Northeast Louisiana is perhaps the least known part of the state. Along the Mississippi River and the Red River and their dozens of tributaries, it was plantation country before the Civil War, and there are African-American majorities today in many parishes. Away from the rivers, in the hill country, small farmers scratched out a living on land connected to parish courthouses by dusty lanes. Such was Winn Parish, where Huey P. Long, the pivotal figure in modern Louisiana

2008 Presidential Vote		
John McCain (R) 177,344	(62%)
Barack Obama (D) 106,026	(37%)

2004 Presidential Vote		
George Bush (R) 168,484	(62%)
John Kerry (D) 100,511	(37%)

Cook Partisan Voting Index: R+14

politics, was born in 1893 and from which he began his meteoric political career. Elected governor in 1928 and senator in 1930, he was a national figure threatening both parties when he was assassinated in 1935 in the new high-rise Capitol he built in Baton Rouge.

The 5th Congressional District of Louisiana contains much of this country, from the river parishes to the hills of Winn Parish. The biggest urban areas here, with about 50,000 people each, are Monroe in the north and Alexandria in the south. Alexandria, in Rapides Parish, sits at the northernmost extension of Cajun, Catholic Louisiana and is majority black. The federal government stunned local officials there in 2010 by determining that the Red River's levees were no longer certified, which would put much of the area in a flood zone and require property owners to buy flood insurance.

Monroe in Ouachita Parish is heavily Protestant. There are some Cajun areas in Allen and Evangeline parishes and black precincts in Pointe Coupee and Iberville parishes, all Democratic. Overall, population has been declining in this area. More than 23% of the district's households report annual incomes of less than $15,000. The Gallup-Healthways Well-Being Index found in 2010 that the district had the country's highest obesity rate, as many residents lack health insurance and access to affordable fruit and vegetables. Except for the parishes along the river, Republicans have run strongly in this district. George W. Bush increased his vote here from 57% in 2000 to 62% in 2004, his second best showing in the state. John McCain won the district 62%-37%.

Rodney Alexander (R)

The congressman from the 5th District is Rodney Alexander, who was elected as a Democrat in 2002 and switched parties to become a Republican in 2004. He attended Louisiana Tech and won election to the Jackson Parish police jury in 1972 at the age of 25. In 1988, he was elected to the state House, where he chaired the Health and Welfare Committee. Although he was a Democrat then, he was pro-gun rights and anti-abortion rights, and he favored prayer in the public schools. When the 5th District seat opened, the primary turned out to be a regional contest. Alexander led with 29% of the vote, carrying three hill counties in his legislative district and five African-American parishes along the Mississippi. Republican Lee Fletcher, outgoing Rep. John Cooksey's chief of staff for five years, was second with 25%, carrying Monroe's Ouachita Parish and three nearby parishes. Close behind, with 23%, was Republican Clyde Holloway, a former congressman from the old 8th District. Alexander attacked Fletcher as a Washington insider and contrasted his "blue jeans" supporters with Fletcher's "blue blood" contributors. Alexander squeaked by with a 50.3%-49.7% victory, a margin of 974 votes. He carried two hill parishes, all of the Mississippi River parishes and all but one of the parishes in the southern end of the district.

In the House, Alexander was a Democratic maverick who voted for the Republican's prescription drug bill in 2003 and co-sponsored legislation to prohibit desecration of the flag and to bar gay marriages. Still, Democratic leaders worked to keep Alexander in the fold and helped him to raise money for his re-election. Alexander repaid these kindnesses by waiting until the last minute before the 2004 election filing deadline to switch parties, declaring himself a Republican. He claimed that had he remained a Democrat, the candidacy of Democrat Zelma Blakes, an African-American and a political neophyte, would draw votes away from him and leave him vulnerable to attacks from both the left and the right. His erstwhile Democratic friends were not sympathetic. "I've seen some cowardly things in my career, but this is the worst," said Louisiana Sen. Mary Landrieu. Louisiana Democrats filed suit to reopen the qualifying period, but the state appeals court rejected their case. Alexander promised to return campaign contributions from Democratic colleagues, but failed to do so until the donors complained.

National Republicans quickly embraced Alexander. Democrats, meanwhile, coalesced around Blakes. But the election turned out to be an afterthought for both parties. It was overshadowed by other major happenings in Louisiana politics that year, including two hotly contested open seat House races and a serious contest for the Senate seat of retiring Democrat John Breaux. Alexander won 59% of the vote, to 25% for Blakes and 16% for former state Rep. Jock Scott, a Republican. He carried all of the parishes except for two on the riverfront near Baton Rouge.

Although Alexander and House Republican leaders insisted that they had made no deal before his switch, as soon as he arrived back in Washington as a Republican in January 2005 he got seats on the sought-after Appropriations Committee and its Agriculture Subcommittee, where he quickly secured funding for several road projects and a transportation and parking facility for the University of Louisiana at Monroe. He said that his views remained the same, but his voting record became markedly more conservative. He was among the first lawmakers to join the House Tea Party Caucus in 2010.

Alexander has bucked Republican conservatives trying to end the use of earmarks in appropriation bills. He continued to secure money for the low-income areas of his district, including rural development grants. "I don't want my voters to be neglected," he said. In 2010, according to watchdog groups, he secured more than $65 million in solo and collaborative earmarks—the most in his state's delegation and 29th overall among House members. Alexander opposed President Obama's $787 billion economic stimulus bill in 2009, not because it spent too much as other Republicans charged, but because it didn't contain enough for transportation infrastructure. And he only reluctantly supported the House Republican earmark ban in the 112th Congress (2011-12).

Alexander improved his relationship with Landrieu, a fellow appropriator, when they worked together on the Next Autoworks project in Monroe. Also in recent years, Alexander has lobbied to end the trade embargo of Cuba, which could benefit Louisiana rice farmers.

In 2008, Alexander ran for re-election unopposed and in 2010 won with 79% of the vote. The increase in the district's African-American population to 35% could pose some redistricting jeopardy for Alexander, who is white, though having key state lawmakers from his region overseeing the redistricting process should help.

SIXTH DISTRICT

Bill Cassidy (R)

Elected 2008, 2nd term; b. Sept. 28, 1957, Chicago, IL; home, Baton Rouge; LA St. U., B.S. 1979; M.D., 1983.; Christian; married (Laura); 3 children.

Elected Office: LA Senate, 2006-08.

Professional Career: Internist and hepatologist, Cigna Med. Cntr, Los Angeles, CA, 1989-90; LA St. U., Asst. Prof. of Medicine, 1990-96; Assoc. prof. of medicine, 1996-present.

DC Office: 1535 LHOB, 20515, 202-225-3901; Fax: 202-225-7313; Web site: cassidy.house.gov.

State Offices: Baton Rouge, 225-929-7711; Livingston, 225-686-4413.

Committees: *Energy & Commerce:* Commerce, Manufacturing & Trade; Environment & the Economy; Health.

Group Ratings

	ACLU	ACU	ADA	CFG	AFS	FRC	LCV	ITIC	NTU	COC
2010	25	91	5	82	0	81	40	33	85	100
2009	–	88	20	89	22	–	21	–	81	87

National Journal Ratings

	2010 LIB	—	2010 CONS		2009 LIB	—	2009 CONS
Economic	32%	—	68%		29%	—	71%
Social	33%	—	66%		38%	—	62%
Foreign	33%	—	65%		26%	—	68%
Composite	33%	—	67%		32%	—	68%

Key Votes of the 111th Congress

1. Overturn Ledbetter	N	5. Bar federal abortion funds	Y	9. Stop detainee transfers	Y
2. Pass $820 billion stimulus	N	6. Pass health care bill	N	10. Legalize immigrants' kids	N
3. Let guns in national parks	Y	7. Regulate financial firms	N	11. Repeal don't ask, tell	N
4. Pass cap-and-trade	N	8. Pass tax cuts for some	N	12. Limit campaign funds	N

Election Results

2010 general	Bill Cassidy (R) 138,607	(66%)	($1,584,256)
	Merritt McDonald (D)..72,577	(34%)	
2010 primary	Bill Cassidy (R) .... unopposed		

Prior Winning Percentages: 2008 (48%)

Population		Race/Ethnicity		Work	
Pop. 2010:	727,498	White:	58.4%	Private:	76.1%
Change since 2000:	Up 14.0%	Black:	34.9%	Government:	18.1%
Urban:	75.5%	Hispanic:	3.4%	Self-employed:	5.6%
Rural:	24.5%	Asian:	1.9%	Blue collar:	23.1%
Area size:	3,210 sq. mi.	Native Am.:	0.2%	White collar:	59.6%
		Hawaiian:	0.0%	Khaki collar:	0.1%
Age		Two+ races:	1.0%	Other:	17.2%
Median age:	33.1 yrs.				
More than 65 yrs:	10.4%	*Ancestry*		Median income:	$47,660
Less than 18 yrs:	25.0%	French	11.5%	Median Home Value:	$154,500
		USA	7.8%		
Education		English	7.3%	**Military Veterans**	
H.S. grad:	84.8%			% of Pop:	8.6%
College grad:	26.3%				
Grad degree:	8.7%				

Baton Rouge

Baton Rouge is the central node of Louisiana, on the boundary between the French-speaking, Catholic Cajun country and the heavily Baptist region. Its skyscraper Capitol and Exxon refinery sit just beyond the levees that line the Mississippi River. Historically, it was part of the Florida parishes, the territory west of the Mississippi River and north of Lake Pontchartrain that was not included in the Louisiana Purchase in 1803.

2008 Presidential Vote		
John McCain (R) 184,355	(57%)
Barack Obama (D) 132,627	(41%)
2004 Presidential Vote		
George Bush (R) 172,080	(59%)
John Kerry (D) 117,255	(40%)
Cook Partisan Voting Index: R+10		

It still belonged to Spain, until the locals rebelled and declared their own Republic of West Florida in 1810. Then it quickly became part of Louisiana and the United States. When the man who dominated Louisiana politics for decades, Huey P. Long, became governor at age 36 in the old (and still-standing) Gothic Capitol, Baton Rouge had only 30,000 people. He built the 34-story Art Deco Capitol next door to the Governor's Mansion, which he also built. Long also died in the capitol, the victim of an assassin in 1935. To the south, are the buildings of Louisiana State University, many of which he built as well.

Today, Baton Rouge is the center of a metropolitan area of nearly 800,000 people that sits on the east bank of the Mississippi and reaches far inland to Livingston Parish. This is one of the faster-growing parts of Louisiana, and did well in coping with the recession. Baton Rouge ranked second on *Forbes'* list of best mid-sized cities for jobs in 2010. The city grew in the weeks and months after Hurricane Katrina as evacuees moved into motel rooms, spare rooms in people's houses, dorm rooms in LSU and Southern University. The city's population may have momentarily doubled; certainly the traffic jams suggested it had. Many people have moved on since then, and the growth has subsided. New Orleans was long the state's largest city, but Baton Rouge, with 229,000 people, now rivals the reduced, post-Katrina New Orleans in size.

The 6th Congressional District of Louisiana includes just about all of metropolitan Baton Rouge, plus three small, mostly rural parishes to the north. Overall, the district is 35% African-American, and historically it was Democratic. In the 1980s, the Baton Rouge area moved toward the Republicans, and in the 1990s, it was fairly closely balanced. In 2004, East Baton Rouge Parish voted 54% for George W. Bush, and Livingston Parish voted 77% for Bush; overall the 6th District voted 59% for Bush. In 2008, the shift was notable. Barack Obama won East Baton Rouge 50%-48%. The only other Democrat to have won the parish since 1964 was Bill Clinton, in 1996. But John McCain won Livingston Parish 85%-13%. McCain won the district 57%-41%.

Bill Cassidy (R)

The Congressman from the 6th District is Republican Bill Cassidy, one of only five Republicans to defeat a House Democratic incumbent in the Democratic year of 2008. The son of a life-insurance salesman, Cassidy grew up in Baton Rouge and went to college at Louisiana State University. He went on to graduate from LSU's medical school, and during his medical training, he met his wife, Laura, who is also a physician and former chief of surgery at Earl K. Long Hospital. Cassidy was an associate professor of medicine at LSU and taught at the same hospital. He went on to cofound the Greater Baton Rouge Community Clinic, which provides free dental and health care to the working uninsured. He developed a school-based hepatitis B vaccination program that has immunized more than 36,000 public, private, and parochial schoolchildren at no cost to parents or schools.

Cassidy had a defining moment when Hurricane Katrina hit in 2005. With the help of several other physicians, he created a makeshift field hospital in an abandoned Kmart store. In a PBS documentary, he recalled entering the store after the storm to find complete ruin: grease all over the floor, no electricity and no phone lines. In two days, he and the others transformed the space to be ready to receive patients. Cassidy won a December 2006 special election to the state Senate and was re-elected in 2007. He sponsored several bills to improve health standards in Louisiana, including one to overhaul the children's mental health system and another to expand Medicaid coverage to patients at new organ-transplant centers.

When GOP Rep. Richard Baker resigned his seat to head a Washington trade group, Cassidy passed on the opportunity to compete in the May 2008 special election. But after state Rep. Don Cazayoux defeated social conservative Woody Jenkins 49%-46%, with a big boost from the Democratic Congressional Campaign Committee, to win the seat in the special election, Cassidy vowed to take the district back for the Republicans in the regularly scheduled congressional election in November 2008.

In the campaign, Cassidy described himself as a "pro-life, pro-gun-rights" social conservative in favor of free enterprise, limited government, and lower taxes. He made the economy his focus, highlighting his record in the state Senate of voting against spending bills and cutting taxes for businesses and for parents with children in private schools. He also criticized Cazayoux for supporting Democratic presidential nominee Barack Obama's tax plan. Cazayoux ran an ad criticizing Cassidy for supporting the idea of private savings accounts in the Social Security program. State Rep. Michael Jackson, who is African-American, ran as an independent, due partly to his unhappiness over the national Democrats' early support for Cazayoux in the special election.

Cassidy won comfortably, with 48% to 40% for Cazayoux and 12% for Jackson. In East Baton Rouge, which cast 62% of the total vote, Cassidy won 44%-42%. His margin of victory came in Livingston and Ascension parishes, which he won by more than 27,000 votes. Two years later, without an opponent as strong as Cazayoux and in a far better year for the GOP, Cassidy coasted to re-election with 66% of the vote.

In the House, Cassidy is a reliable conservative vote and was made a part of the GOP leadership's whip team to help round up votes. He backed the House Republican earmark ban and did not request any earmarks for himself in 2009, citing a lack of transparency in the process. Instead, he and Rep. Jackie Speier, D-Calif., introduced a bill seeking to put all earmarks in a searchable, public database. He was one of four Republicans on the Agriculture Committee to support a proposal in 2010 to end the ban on American travel to Cuba and ease regulations on sales of U.S. agricultural products there. Like the rest of his state's delegation, Cassidy has been an ardent advocate of the oil and gas industry. When the Natural Resources Committee approved a 2010 measure to overhaul federal management of energy as a response to the BP oil spill, Cassidy unsuccessfully tried to amend the bill to push back the effective date of most of the legislation until the Interior secretary certified it would not result in higher energy costs or increased unemployment.

As a physician, Cassidy regularly criticized Democratic approaches to health care and said government should step out of the way of patients. "The key to expanding access is lowering costs," he wrote in one op-ed column. "The key to lowering costs is empowering patients." After the House GOP takeover in November 2010, he expressed interest in emulating the 1996 welfare law for the Medicaid program, which he said offers "the appearance of coverage without the power of access."

SEVENTH DISTRICT

Charles Boustany (R)

Elected 2004, 4th term; b. Feb. 21, 1956, New Orleans; home, Lafayette; U. of SW LA, B.S. 1978, LA St. U., M.D. 1982; Episcopalian; married (Bridget); 2 children.

Professional Career: Practicing surgeon, 1982-2004.

DC Office: 1431 LHOB, 20515, 202-225-2031; Fax: 202-225-5724; Web site: boustany.house.gov.

State Offices: Lafayette, 337-235-6322; Lake Charles, 337-433-1747.

Committees: *Ways & Means:* Human Resources; Oversight (Chmn); Select Revenue Measures.

Group Ratings

	ACLU	ACU	ADA	CFG	AFS	FRC	LCV	ITIC	NTU	COC
2010	6	100	0	93	0	100	20	33	89	88
2009	–	96	5	90	22	–	7	–	88	80

National Journal Ratings

	2010 LIB	—	2010 CONS	2009 LIB	—	2009 CONS
Economic	29%	—	71%	14%	—	85%
Social	18%	—	77%	22%	—	77%
Foreign	0%	—	88%	0%	—	75%
Composite	19%	—	82%	17%	—	84%

Key Votes of the 111th Congress

1. Overturn Ledbetter	N	5. Bar federal abortion funds	Y	9. Stop detainee transfers	Y
2. Pass $820 billion stimulus	N	6. Pass health care bill	N	10. Legalize immigrants' kids	N
3. Let guns in national parks	Y	7. Regulate financial firms	N	11. Repeal don't ask, tell	N
4. Pass cap-and-trade	N	8. Pass tax cuts for some	N	12. Limit campaign funds	N

Election Results

2010 general	Charles Boustany (R).................................... unopposed	($1,679,995)
2010 primary	Charles Boustany (R).................................... unopposed	

Prior Winning Percentages: 2008 (62%), 2006 (71%), 2004 (55%)

Population		Race/Ethnicity		Work	
Pop. 2010:	676,785	White:	69.0%	Private:	79.1%
Change since 2000:	Up 6.0%	Black:	25.3%	Government:	14.1%
Urban:	68.9%	Hispanic:	2.8%	Self-employed:	6.5%
Rural:	31.1%	Asian:	1.0%	Blue collar:	26.6%
Area size:	7,302 sq. mi.	Native Am.:	0.3%	White collar:	55.6%
		Hawaiian:	0.0%	Khaki collar:	0.1%
Age		Two+ races:	1.4%	Other:	17.8%
Median age:	34.6 yrs.				
More than 65 yrs:	12.2%	*Ancestry*		Median income:	$41,784
Less than 18 yrs:	26.2%	French	20.6%	Median Home Value:	$111,800
		German	7.3%		
Education		USA	6.0%	**Military Veterans**	
H.S. grad:	78.9%			% of Pop:	9.2%
College grad:	18.8%				
Grad degree:	5.2%				

Southwest Louisiana; Lafayette

More than 200 years ago, French-speaking settlers in Canada were forced to leave their land
of Acadie, which the British had taken over and
renamed Nova Scotia. They made their way to
the wetlands of southern Louisiana. Here, without much notice, they built steep-roofed houses
to slough off nonexistent snow and adapted
French cuisine to the crawfish and muskrat
they found in abundance in the pelican-tended
swamps. They are the Cajuns, and the heart of

2008 Presidential Vote		
John McCain (R) 188,576	(63%)
Barack Obama (D) 105,118	(35%)
2004 Presidential Vote		
George Bush (R) 168,645	(60%)
John Kerry (D) 110,623	(39%)
Cook Partisan Voting Index: R+14		

their adopted homeland is around Lafayette, just west of the Atchafalaya Basin, where Mississippi
waters pour through bayous and canals. A 30-mile section of Interstate 10 was built on elevated
stilts. Cajun country thrived, thanks to the oil and gas plentiful here and just offshore in the Gulf
of Mexico. Oil rigs are common, and every once in a while the swampy foliage parts to reveal a giant
refinery or petrochemical plant.

Cajun French is surviving decades of efforts to eliminate it. Cajun music—and its black-influ-
enced variant, zydeco—are popular here and nationally; spicy Cajun cooking attracts food lovers,
who learn its secrets and then carry it off, in understated form, to other parts of the United States.
About 45% of the people in Acadiana speak French as a second language. Lafayette, with its Aca-
dian Village and plethora of oil exploration firms, features an annual *Festivals Acadiens* to celebrate music, food and crafts. Unlike New Orleans, its Mardi Gras reveries are still segregated affairs, with an all-white (and sometimes all-male) parade and an all-black parade. Cockfighting
remains locally popular. Louisiana was the only state that still permitted cockfighting until it was
finally banned in 2008.

The oil price crash of the middle 1980s hit Cajun country hard. In 2005, Hurricane Rita, not
Katrina, was the natural disaster with the most devastating local impact. With winds of 120 miles
per hour and a storm surge of up to 15 feet, Rita left a path of destruction 300 miles to the west of
New Orleans. It virtually erased some coastal communities, especially in Cameron Parish. While
the nation was spellbound by every development in New Orleans, local residents and officials complained that they were the victims of "Rita amnesia." All told, Lafayette gained an estimated 5,000
permanent residents in the year following Katrina and Rita. The city ranked 11th on the Milken
Institute's Best Performing Cities Index for creating and sustaining jobs in 2010. In September
2008, Hurricane Ike hit the area, although with much less devastation, thanks in part to new,
stricter building codes.

The 7th Congressional District of Louisiana covers much of the Cajun country, from Lafayette
and the Atchafalaya west along Interstate 10 to Lake Charles and the Texas border. Refineries
and oil field support industries provide many jobs, as do rice and crawfish farming. Some 27% of
the population claims either French or French-Canadian ancestry. Politically, Cajun country once
gravitated to the Democrats, though it disapproves of the party's cultural liberalism, so at odds
with the Cajun tradition of respecting the authority of the church while tolerating a certain amount
of *laissez les bons temps rouler* spirit. The district voted for Bill Clinton in 1992 and 1996, as it had
voted for Louisiana's foremost Cajun politician, Edwin Edwards, who was elected governor four
times. But it gave George W. Bush solid majorities in 2000 and 2004, and gave John McCain 63%
of the vote in 2008.

Charles Boustany (R)

The congressman from the 7th District is Charles Boustany, who in 2004 became the first Republican elected from this area since 1884. Of Lebanese ancestry, Boustany (*Boo STON nee*) grew up
in Lafayette, where his father was parish coroner. He is a cousin of Victoria Reggie Kennedy, widow
of the late Sen. Edward Kennedy, D-Mass. He graduated from the University of Southwestern
Louisiana and from Louisiana State University's medical school. He worked as a cardio-thoracic
surgeon and was active in civic and political affairs.

In 2004, when Democrat Chris John ran for the Senate, Boustany was one of five candidates
running to succeed him. The other Republican was David Thibodaux of Lafayette, who had run
unsuccessfully for the seat three times. But he raised little money, some party leaders viewed him
as too conservative and Boustany quickly became the Republican favorite. The Democratic front-
runners were two state senators: Don Cravins, who was seeking to become the first African-American to hold this seat, and state Sen. Willie Mount. Boustany raised plenty of money early and cam-

paigned on his "prescription for prosperity"—expansion of health savings accounts, high-speed Internet access for local small businesses and opposition to the Central American Free Trade Agreement. The National Republican Congressional Committee ran ads attacking Mount's support for higher taxes in the legislature, presumably because it saw Cravins as a weaker candidate in a runoff. Boustany led the November primary with 39% of the vote, to 25.2% for Mount, 24.6% for Cravins, and 10% for Thibodaux. In the December runoff, Cravins refused to endorse Mount, still angry over the state Democratic Party's "unity ballot" sent to black voters, which included Mount's name and not his. Cravins' neutrality hurt Mount in the Lafayette area. She pointed to her legislative experience, while Boustany emphasized his "values" agenda. Boustany won 55%-45%. Mount won 60% in Lake Charles's Calcasieu Parish, which cast 32% of the vote. But Boustany trumped that with 70% in Lafayette Parish, which cast 30% of the vote.

In the House, Boustany's voting record has been relatively moderate for a Southern Republican, though he sticks with his party on major legislation. On the Education and the Workforce Committee, he was an active proponent of legislation to permit small businesses to join together in associations to pay less for health insurance. He also sought increased federal support for computerizing health records, which he said remain "trapped in the 20th century." His local priorities included more federal funding to restore Louisiana's eroding coastline and to complete Interstate 49 from Shreveport to Lafayette. After Hurricanes Katrina and Rita, he enacted initiatives to provide special rules for disaster relief employment for individuals displaced by the storms and to assist the disabled. He pledged that southwest Louisiana would not be "a stepchild" to New Orleans in hurricane recovery. He pushed for expedited assistance payments from the Federal Emergency Management Agency and criticized the slow cleanup of debris in Cameron Parish.

In recent years, Boustany developed a close relationship with Republican Leader John Boehner, which proved helpful to him in early 2009, when he secured a seat on the powerful tax-writing House Ways and Means Committee. As that panel's only physician in the 111th Congress (2009-10), he took on a prominent role during the health care debate. With his soft-spoken yet authoritative manner, he became a popular television news guest. He was tapped to give the Republican response to President Obama's September 2009 address to Congress on health care, and used the opportunity to talk up GOP ideas such as allowing people to cross state lines to buy insurance. He had initially expressed hope that any overhaul could be bipartisan, and persuaded Boehner and other leaders to let him work with Ways and Means colleague Xavier Becerra, D-Calif. He later became an adviser to other Republican physicians seeking House seats in 2010, appearing at some of their campaign events and further elevating his national profile.

After the 2010 BP spill in the Gulf of Mexico, Boustany and Rep. Gene Green, D-Texas, pressed for allowing new drilling in shallower Gulf waters. He also worked with Democrats in 2009 on reducing tax penalties on small businesses that employ tax shelters. Boustany has shifted positions on trade matters depending on how he perceives its impact on his state. He opposed the 2005 Central American Free Trade Agreement, but backed later pacts with Colombia and Peru. He took over the chairmanship of the oversight subcommittee in the 112th Congress (2011-12), promising to look at tax code reform to spur economic growth.

The Democratic Congressional Campaign Committee tried to recruit Chris John to run for his old seat in 2006, but he declined. With John out of the running, Boustany had an easy race against Democrat Mike Stagg, and won 71%-29%. In 2008, when state Sen. Don Cravins Jr., the son of Boustany's 2004 opponent, decided to challenge him, some Democrats were hopeful. But Cravins' pro-gun ownership, anti-abortion rights stances discouraged national party support. Boustany won 62%-34%, carrying each parish except for Evangeline, which he narrowly lost. He ran unopposed in 2010.

★ MAINE ★

Maine possesses a distinctive personality—ornery, contrary-minded, almost bullheaded, rough-hewn. It is the state geographically closest to Europe, but it was not heavily settled until the mid-19th century, by people migrating from the south and the west—not the east-west migration typical of the rest of the country. Maine grew in a rush, and then mostly stopped. There were 600,000 people here in 1860, but the population dipped after the Civil War—many soldiers did not return—and it did not top 1 million until the 1970s. In the urbanizing and rapidly changing country of the early 20th century, Maine was famous for its pointed firs and steady habits, with a few dozen small factory towns and paper mill towns but nothing like a major metropolis. Eventually the tremors of the New England high-technology booms of the 1980s and 1990s reverberated up Interstate 95 and reached Maine. The simple, back-to-nature Yankee style came into vogue. The antique dockside buildings on Portland's waterfront were restored and an old-style Public Market was constructed. The Maine Mall expanded and office parks sprang up nearby, a miniature edge city. Real estate prices rose dramatically, not just in vacation coves, but also in Portland and small towns that had never considered themselves picturesque. The L. L. Bean headquarters in Freeport, open 24 hours a day, 365 days a year, symbolized the boom. The name suggested Down East Yankees, the 24-hour-a-day schedule reflected the hard work needed to eke out a living from the cold waters of the North Atlantic, and, the commercial success of the enterprise became a prime example of Maine's unexpected boom. Something like the Maine slogan: "The way life should be."

Over the past 30 years, Maine has lost jobs in shoes, chicken processing, papermaking, leather processing, and timber, but gained them in tourism, call centers, high technology, and biotechnology. The Grand Banks have been overfished and fishing seasons shortened, but there's a new market among Northern Europeans for Maine shrimp. The lobster industry has been thriving, as populations expanded for mysterious reasons, causing falling prices but far more sales. Scratching small Maine boiling potatoes out of the soil of Aroostook County has gotten harder. The nation's top potato producer 50 years ago, Maine fell to eighth place in the 1990s. Georgia-Pacific closed its paper mill in Old Town, near Bangor. But Loring Air Force Base, shuttered in 1994, has been redeveloped and is generating jobs in food manufacturing, aircraft disassembly and storage, telemarketing, and state government. Maine exports not just paper and lumber and seafood, but also computer and aircraft parts. Tourism continues to be the biggest business. Bath Iron Works, long the state's largest private employer, has a long-term contract to build 21 *Arleigh Burke* Class Naval destroyers. Maine, its economic development director still insists, has "the best workforce on the planet."

Now, in effect, there are two Maines—humming coastal Maine and declining interior Maine, one symbolized by the lobster and the other by the moose. Growth is greatest in York County and along the coast east of Portland to the Penobscot River. Population is stable in the North Woods and declining in the northern and eastern edges of the state. A slow-growth economy has some advantages: Maine didn't have much of a housing bubble in this decade and so has not had a housing bust like many other states. Its unemployment rate has tracked the national average. Demographically, Maine is like Western Europe, with an aging population, and the highest median age and lowest birth rate of any state. It looks more like neighboring New Brunswick than the rest of the United States. The country as a whole grew by 24% from 1990 to 2010, but Maine grew by just 8%; there was net domestic migration into the state but almost as many deaths as births. An aging population has its advantages—Maine has the nation's lowest incarceration rate. But it also has disadvantages—health care costs are high, and the percentage of people with employer-provided health insurance is low. Maine has the highest high school graduation rate in the country, but its high schools and colleges have not been providing enough graduates to fill its job openings. There has been little foreign immigration here and Maine is the whitest state in the nation. It is 1% black, 1% Hispanic, 1% American Indian and 1% Asian. It treasures what diversity it has, however. French-Canadian immigrant children were once chided when they spoke French. Now the legislature has a French-American day each year, when business is conducted in French and the Pledge of Allegiance recited in French.

In politics, Maine is contrary. Until 1958, it held state elections in September, a date originally chosen because it followed the state's early harvest. Starting in 1840, long before the advent of public opinion polls, the election results were taken as a gauge of national sentiment—hence the saying, "As Maine goes, so goes the nation." Actually, Maine didn't vote like the rest of the country most of the time. In September 1936, Maine voted 56% for a Republican for governor (Lewis Barrows) and in November, only Maine and Vermont voted for Republican Alf Landon over Democrat Franklin D. Roosevelt, prompting Roosevelt's campaign manager to observe, "As Maine goes, so

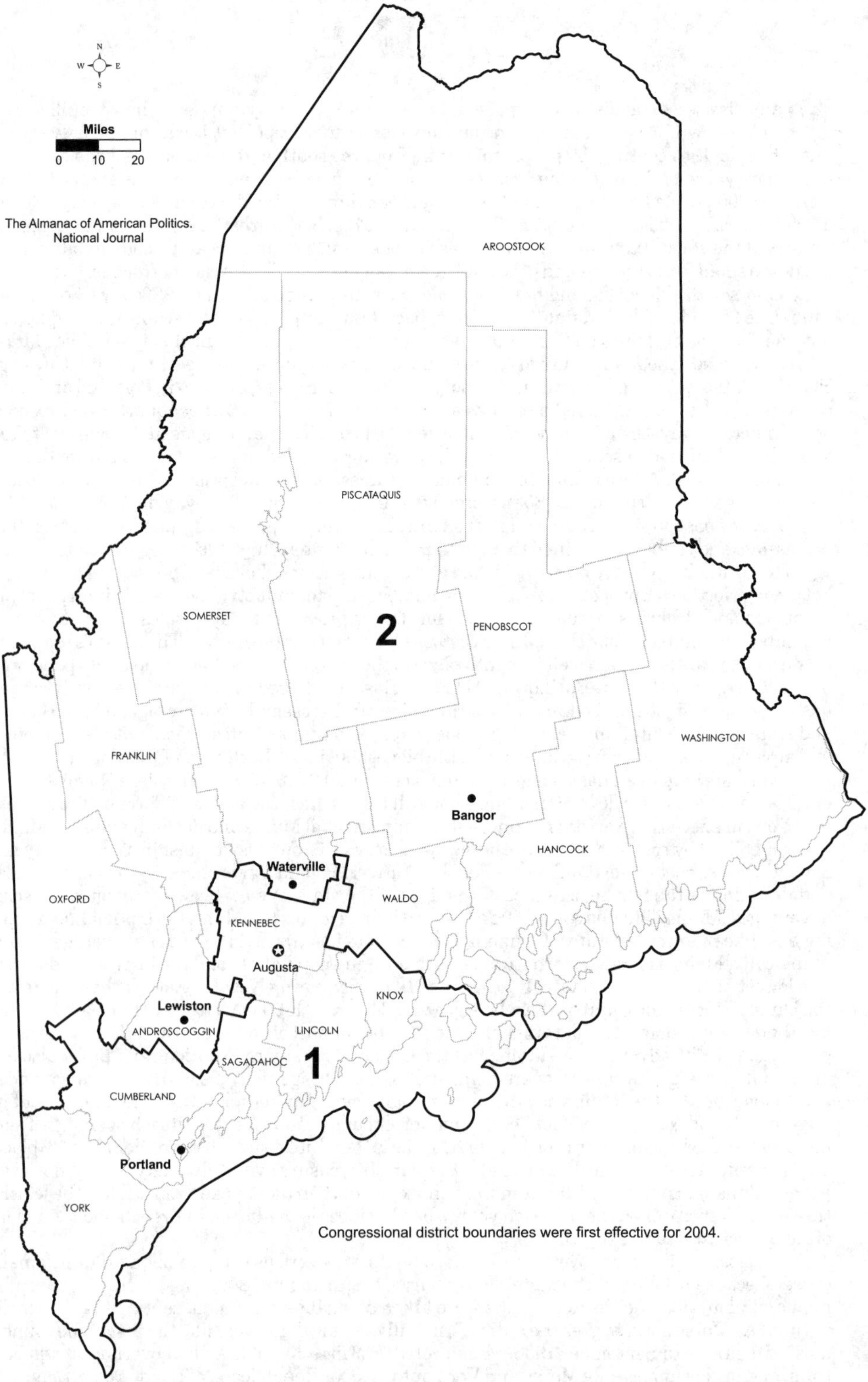

N
W — E
S

Miles
0   10   20

The Almanac of American Politics.
National Journal

AROOSTOOK

PISCATAQUIS

SOMERSET

PENOBSCOT

2

FRANKLIN

WASHINGTON

Bangor

Waterville

HANCOCK

OXFORD

KENNEBEC

WALDO

Augusta

KNOX

Lewiston

ANDROSCOGGIN

LINCOLN

SAGADAHOC

1

CUMBERLAND

Portland

YORK

Congressional district boundaries were first effective for 2004.

goes Vermont." Maine's adherence to flinty Yankee Republicanism and Prohibition was echoed almost nowhere else in the nation. Since then, it has voted for the loser in the close presidential elections of 1948, 1960, 1968, 1976, 2000, and 2004—a record equaled by no other state. Maine cast the nation's highest percentages for third-party presidential candidate Ross Perot, 30% in 1992 and 14% in 1996. In 1994 and 1998, it elected Angus King, an independent and former Democrat, as governor, as it had elected independent and former Republican James Longley in 1974. In 2010, it came close to electing independent Eliot Cutler, who might have won except that early voting allowed many votes to be cast before it was apparent that support for the Democratic nominee was plummeting. The beneficiary was Republican Paul LePage, who eked out a victory with 38% to Cutler's 36%. In the past nine gubernatorial elections, Maine voted three times for Republicans, four times for Democrats, and twice for independents.

If Maine's tradition-minded Yankees kept the state Republican long after the nation embraced the New Deal, the sons and daughters of its ethnic citizens—the Irish, French Canadian, Greek, and Arab immigrants have come to equal the numbers of WASPs—made the Democrats competitive here in the 1980s even as they were losing ground in the rest of the nation. But there are exceptions. Maine has voted Democratic for president five times starting in 1992 and hasn't elected a Republican to the U.S. House since 1994. But it hasn't elected a Democratic U.S. senator since 1988, and only once since then has a Republican Senate candidate won less than 58% of the vote, as moderate Republicans Olympia Snowe and Susan Collins have wielded considerable clout in the Senate.

There are limits to Maine voters' liberalism. In 2009, the legislature approved a bill sanctioning same-sex marriage—the Senate voted 21-13 in favor, the House 89-57—and Democratic Gov. John Baldacci signed the bill. But opponents put the issue on the November 2009 ballot where, despite favorable poll results, the same sex marriage law was rejected 53%-47%. Counties on the coast supported same-sex marriage 53%-47%; those in the interior opposed it 61%-39%. In addition to Republican LePage's victory as governor, Republicans gained five seats in the state Senate and 23 in the state House to capture majorities in both chambers. But these were not necessarily the result of vast changes in opinion. LePage's 38% of the vote was 2% less than John McCain had in 2008. And Maine has more partisan turnover in its legislature than just about any other state. In its small legislative districts—the average population of a state House district is 8,797—Mainers apparently often vote for the person, not the party. Vestiges of Maine's ethnic divides remain: Protestants voted for Republican George W. Bush in 2004 and John McCain in 2008, while Catholics cast bigger percentage margins for Democrats John Kerry and Barack Obama. But young Mainers seem more volatile: Bush carried them in 2004; Obama won 71% of them in 2008.

As the economy changed, Maine moved toward a consensus on how to balance economic growth and preserve the environment. But disagreement rages about the North Woods. The big paper companies, long the largest landowners in Maine, have been selling off millions of acres since 1998. As Conservation Commissioner Patrick McGowan put it, "For generations, the paper companies sort of managed everything for us up here. They gave sportsmen pretty much free rein, and in turn helped up here helped out as stewards of the land. But with all of these new buyers, nobody quite knows what will happen now, and people are getting nervous." Local Mainers want to keep using the land for hunting, trapping, and snowmobiling. But a Concord, Mass., group called Restore the North Woods, with backing from Hollywood movie stars, wants to create a huge national park, bigger than Yellowstone and Yosemite combined. Mainers reacted angrily to advocates "from away," as they say; when he was governor, Baldacci called the national park proposal a "nonstarter."

Population		Household Income		Work	
Pop. 2010:	1,328,361	Under $15k:	13.7%	Private:	76.5%
State rank:	41st	$15k to $50k:	39.9%	Government:	14.1%
Change since 2000:	Up 4.2%	$50k to $100k:	32.3%	Self-employed:	9.3%
Urban:	40.7%	$100k to $200k:	11.9%	Unemployment (3-yr. average):	4.2%
Rural:	59.3%	Over $200k:	2.1%	Poverty:	12.4%
Native of state:	63.7%	Median income:	$46,428	Blue collar:	22.4%
Not a citizen:	1.5%			White collar:	58.1%
Area size:	35,380 sq. mi.	**Home Value**		Khaki collar:	0.1%
		Under $100k:	22.0%	Other:	19.4%
Most populous cities		$100k to $300k:	58.0%		
Portland	66,194	$300k to $500k:	14.0%	**Age**	
Lewiston	36,592	$500k to $1 mil:	4.9%	Median age:	41.9 yrs.
Bangor	33,039	Over $1 million:	1.1%	More than 65 yrs:	15.2%
South Portland	25,002	Median:	$178,100	Less than 18 yrs:	20.9%

Race/Ethnicity			Military Veterans		Registered Voters in 2010	
White:	94.4%	*Language*	% of Pop:	13.1%	Democrats:	324,498
Black:	1.1%	English:	92.8%		Republicans:	276,059
Hispanic:	1.3%	Spanish:	1.1%	*Veterans by Period*	Ind./other:	387,554
Asian:	1.0%	Asian:	0.7%	WWII and before:	10.2%	Voter turnout:	580,538
Native Am.:	0.6%	Other European:	5.0%	Korea:	11.7%	Turnout as % of	
Hawaiian:	0.0%			Vietnam:	34.1%	voting age:	55.1%
Two+ races:	1.4%	**Education**		Gulf (pre-2001):	10.6%		
		H.S. grad:	89.8%	Gulf (post-2001):	6.6%	**Legislature**	
Ancestry		College grad:	26.4%	Peace time:	26.7%	Senate:	14 D 20 R 1 I
English	17.2%	Grad degree:	9.3%			House:	72 D 78 R 1 I
Irish	13.4%						
French	12.9%						

Presidential politics   Maine has been a hard state to predict in recent presidential politics. It gave majorities to Republican George H.W. Bush in 1988 and Democrat Bill Clinton in 1996. In between, the 1992 race was very nearly a three-way tie, with Clinton in first place, Ross Perot in second, and Bush, who spent nearly every summer of his life in Maine, in third. In 2000, Democrat Al Gore won 49%-44%, with 6% for Ralph Nader. The trend since then has been Democratic. Maine was on the campaigns' target lists in 2004, but Democrat John Kerry ended up carrying it 54%-45%. In 2008, GOP vice presidential nominee Sarah Palin campaigned in Hermon, Presque Isle, and Bangor after polls showed a close race. Maine is one of two states (Nebraska is the other) that gives two electors to the statewide winner and one elector to the winner in each congressional district. The John McCain campaign thought it might win the electoral vote of the northern 2nd District. But Barack Obama's lead widened even while Palin was on the

2008 Presidential Vote		
Barack Obama (D)	421,923	(58%)
John McCain (R)	295,273	(40%)

2008 Presidential Primary		
Barack Obama (D)	2,079	(59%)
Hillary Clinton (D)	1,397	(40%)

2008 Presidential Primary		
Mitt Romney (R)	2,826	(52%)
John McCain (R)	1,144	(21%)
Ron Paul (R)	997	(18%)
Mike Huckabee (R)	312	(6%)

2004 Presidential Vote		
John Kerry (D)	396,842	(54%)
George W. Bush (R)	330,201	(45%)

stump, and McCain lost the 2nd District 55%-43%. He did carry Piscataquis County, deep in the woods, with 51% of the vote—the only county he carried in New England. Statewide, Obama won 58%-40%, with his biggest percentages in metro Portland.

Maine held its first-ever presidential primary on March 5, 1996, in an attempt to attract the candidates' early attention. But the ploy didn't work, and the state abolished its presidential primary for 2004. In 2008, the parties held caucuses on different dates in early February. When Republicans voted on Feb. 1, 2, and 3, some 5,000 people turned out. Olympia Snowe and Susan Collins endorsed McCain early on, but that didn't make much difference. Mitt Romney won 52% of the Republican caucus vote, just days before his campaign was ended by the Super Tuesday results. McCain got 21% and Ron Paul got 18%. Democrats voted on Feb. 10 when their race was still very much contested. Gov. Baldacci endorsed Hillary Clinton, and in the week after Super Tuesday she campaigned in the mill town of Lewiston and at the University of Maine in Orono, while Obama campaigned in Bangor. Caucus turnout was only 3,500 people, and Obama won 59%-40%. Clinton carried Lewiston and three northern counties. Obama was strongest along the coast.

Congressional districting   District lines in Maine are drawn by a 15-member, bipartisan Legislative Apportionment Committee. The legislature may amend the plan and must approve it by a two-thirds vote. The governor has a veto, though presumably that's academic since there would be a two-thirds majority to override it. Under state law, the committee sent its last plan to the legislature in spring 2003. This arguably violates the Constitution, since the 2002 elections were based on the congressional districts drawn from 1990, rather than 2000, census results. But no one has challenged the law, for the good reason that it makes no practical difference. There has been little change in the boundary between the two House districts since Maine lost its third seat after the 1960 census. In the 2003 session, however, the legislature failed to adopt a map. On July 2, 2003, the state Supreme Court adopted a plan for the 2004 election, and it stayed in place. It seems likely that an almost identical plan will be adopted again, if not for 2012 then for 2014.

112th Congress Lineup
2 D

111th Congress Lineup
2 D

Governor

Paul LePage (R)

Elected 2010, term expires Jan. 2015, 1st term; b. Oct. 9, 1948, Lewiston; home, Augusta; Husson U., B.S. 1971; U. of Maine, M.B.A. 1975; Catholic; married (Ann); 4 children.

Elected Office: Waterville mayor, 2003-11.

Professional Career: LePage and Kasevich Consulting, 1983-96; Gen. mgr., Marden's Surplus and Salvage, 1996-2011.

Office: #1 State House Station, 04333-0001, 207-287-3531; Fax: 207-287-1034; Web site: www.maine.gov/governor/lepage/.

Election Results

2010 general	Paul LePage (R)	218,065	(38%)
	Eliot Cutler (I)	208,270	(36%)
	Elizabeth Mitchell (D)	109,387	(19%)
	Shawn Moody (I)	28,756	(5%)
2010 primary	Paul LePage (R)	49,126	(37%)
	Leslie Otten (R)	22,945	(17%)
	S. Peter Mills (R)	19,271	(15%)
	Steven Abbott (R)	17,209	(13%)
	William Beardsley (R)	12,061	(9%)

The new governor of Maine is Paul LePage, a conservative Republican elected in 2010 to succeed Democrat John Baldacci, who served the maximum two terms under state law. LePage became the state's first Republican chief executive in 16 years, as well as the first in almost half a century who enjoys the advantage of both a Republican-controlled state House and Senate.

LePage has a compelling rags-to-riches story. He was the oldest son of 18 children in a poverty-stricken, dysfunctional family. After being beaten by his father at age 11, he left home and spent two years living on the streets of Lewiston, supporting himself by shining shoes and cleaning horse stables. He slept in hallways, cars and even a strip joint. "Some of those strippers were like surrogate moms," he told *Forbes* magazine in 2010. When he was 13, two families jointly adopted him, and he earned money hauling boxes and washing dishes. He eventually befriended Peter Snowe, a state legislator who later married future Maine Republican Sen. Olympia Snowe. Peter Snowe persuaded officials at Husson University to let LePage take the SAT test in French after LePage, who had been raised speaking French in Lewiston's "Little Canada," struggled with the verbal section of the test. LePage was admitted and went on to earn a degree in business administration, followed by an M.B.A. from the University of Maine. He worked in forestry and as a consultant before becoming general manager of Marden's Surplus and Salvage, a Maine-based discount store chain, in 1996. The store prospered and he won several business awards.

LePage entered politics in 1998, when he decided to run for the City Council in Waterville, a town of about 15,000 between Augusta and Bangor in the middle of the state. He served two terms, then ran for mayor in 2003 and won. During his gubernatorial race, he boasted that he lowered taxes 13% in six years, improved the city's credit rating and increased its rainy day fund from $1 million to $10 million—all without cutting services and while working with a solidly Democratic council. When he couldn't get Democrats to agree on his ideas, he would make his case to the people through the news media, which earned him the nickname "Front Page LePage."

When LePage entered the Maine governor's race, he was part of a crowded seven-candidate Republican field. He cast himself as a solid fiscal and social conservative who agreed with the principles of the tea party, which was ascendant in Maine as in the rest of the country in 2010. He promised to cut every dollar of state spending he considered wasteful, and used his life story of overcoming challenges to illustrate how that approach could succeed in a Democratic-leaning state. "All my life, I've been told what I can't do," he said at the state Republican convention. "They were wrong every single time, and they'll be wrong again in November." He was the surprise winner of the June GOP primary with 37% of the vote, even though he spent less money than all but one other candidate.

His victory set up a battle with Democratic state Senate president Libby Mitchell and attorney Eliot Cutler, a former associate director of the Office of Management and Budget under Jimmy Carter running as an independent. Though LePage started out with a lead, his campaign ran into obstacles that stemmed in part from his blunt, take-no-prisoners style. He proposed a five-year limit on welfare benefits and said, "At the end of five years, if you still need welfare, I will personally buy (you) a ticket to Massachusetts so (you) can start over." When reporters questioned at a news conference why his wife had claimed a homestead exemption in Florida, he angrily stormed out of the room. He also drew criticism when he said at a September forum, "As your governor, you're going to be seeing a lot of me on the front page saying, 'Governor LePage tells Obama to go to hell.'" Cutler picked up several newspaper endorsements, and he narrowed LePage's lead. But he appeared to run out of time, and LePage eked out a victory with 38% to Cutler's 36%. Mitchell finished a distant third with 19%.

LePage promised to hold town hall meetings in each of Maine's 16 counties. He also vowed to rectify the state's budget problems, which included a revenue shortfall estimated at $1 billion. Fulfilling a campaign pledge, he unveiled a budget revision that paid down a portion of the state's debt to hospitals. But he continued to show his penchant for controversial remarks. When the NAACP criticized him for declining to take part in Martin Luther King Day events, he said: "Tell them to kiss my butt. If they want, they can look at my family picture. My son happens to be black, so they can do whatever they'd like about it." In the furor that ensued, the media reported that Devon Raymond Jr., the "son" to whom LePage was referring, was not technically his adopted son, but had moved in with the family in 2002. A spokesman for the governor said that while adoption paperwork had never been filed, LePage "is like a father" to Raymond.

Senior Senator

Olympia Snowe (R)

Elected 1994, term expires 2012, 3rd term; b. Feb. 21, 1947, Augusta; home, Falmouth; U. of ME, B.A. 1969; Greek Orthodox; married (John McKernan).

Elected Office: ME House of Reps., 1973–76; ME Senate, 1976–78; U.S. House of Reps., 1978–94.

Professional Career: Dir., Superior Concrete Co., 1969-78; Auburn Bd. of Voter Registration, 1971–73.

DC Office: 154 RSOB, 20510, 202-224-5344; Fax: 202-224-1946; Web site: snowe.senate.gov.

State Offices: Auburn, 207-786-2451; Augusta, 207-622-8292; Bangor, 207-945-0432; Biddeford, 207-282-4144; Portland, 207-874-0883; Presque Isle, 207-764-5124.

Committees: *Commerce, Science & Transportation:* Communications, Technology & the Internet; Oceans, Atmosphere, Fisheries & Coast Guard (RMM). *Finance:* Taxation & IRS Oversight. *Intelligence (Select). Small Business & Entrepreneurship* (RMM).

Group Ratings

	ACLU	ACU	ADA	CFG	AFS	FRC	LCV	ITIC	NTU	COC
2010	67	64	40	49	40	29	0	67	74	82
2009	–	48	65	53	55	–	73	–	51	86

National Journal Ratings

	2010 LIB — 2010 CONS		2009 LIB — 2009 CONS	
Economic	39%	60%	40%	59%
Social	38%	60%	46%	52%
Foreign	30%	67%	35%	63%
Composite	37%	63%	41%	59%

Key Votes of the 111th Congress

1. Overturn Ledbetter	Y	5. Pass health care bill	N	9. Ratify New START	Y
2. Pass $787 billion stimulus	Y	6. Regulate financial firms	Y	10. Confirm Elena Kagan	Y
3. Repeal DC gun laws	Y	7. Pass tax cuts for some	N	11. Stop EPA climate regs	Y
4. Confirm Sonia Sotomayor	Y	8. Legalize immigrants' kids	N	12. Repeal don't ask, tell	Y

Election Results

2006 general	Olympia Snowe (R)	402,598	(74%)	($3,788,139)
	Jean Hay Bright (D)	111,984	(21%)	($127,267)
	William Slavick (I)	29,220	(5%)	
2006 primary	Olympia Snowe (R)	unopposed		

Prior Winning Percentages: 2000 (69%); 1994 (60%); House: 1992 (49%); 1990 (51%); 1988 (66%); 1986 (77%); 1984 (76%); 1982 (67%); 1980 (79%); 1978 (51%)

Olympia Snowe, Maine's senior senator, is a Republican who was first elected to the House in 1978 and to the Senate in 1994. She is the first woman to serve in both houses of a state legislature and both houses of Congress. And as an influential, well-liked centrist, Snowe is a pivotal swing vote in the Senate.

After losing her mother to breast cancer when she was 8 years old and her father to heart disease at age 9, Snowe grew up with her aunt and uncle in Auburn. She worked her way through the University of Maine and took a job as a legislative staffer after college. Tragedy visited here again in 1973, when she lost her young husband, Peter Snowe, then a member of the Maine legislature, in an auto accident. She was then elected to his seat. In 1978, when Rep. William Cohen ran for the Senate, she made a bid for his U.S. House seat in the northern 2nd District and won. She maintained a moderate voting record, winning re-election by large margins throughout the 1980s but tighter ones in the 1990s. In 1989, she married Republican Gov. John McKernan. When Sen. George Mitchell announced his retirement in 1994, Snowe decided instantly to run for his seat. She went on the offense against her obvious Democratic opponent, 1st District Rep. Tom Andrews, attacking him for voting for the bill that closed Loring Air Force Base in northern Maine and for opposing the balanced budget amendment. She won 60%-36%.

In the Senate, Snowe has been a moderate Republican. She often casts decisive votes when the Senate is closely divided, as it has been frequently in recent years. Her voting record puts her near the middle of the Senate, although with increasing polarization in the Senate, her record has been more conservative than that of any Democrat. She supports abortion rights and has voted with Democrats on many cultural issues and on some economic issues. For example, she led the move to make the child care tax credit refundable in 2001 and called for applying pay-as-you-go rules to tax cuts as well as to spending increases in 2004. She and Maine colleague Susan Collins, also a moderate Republican, were part of the "Gang of 14" in 2005 that diffused a showdown over President George W. Bush's judicial nominees and preserved the Democrats' ability to filibuster. Later, Snowe voted to confirm Obama appointees Sonia Sotomayor and Elena Kagan to the Supreme Court. "It is true that being a Republican moderate sometimes feels like being a cast member of *Survivor*," she told *The New York Times* in 2009. "You are presented with multiple challenges, and you often get the distinct feeling you're no longer welcome in the tribe."

Snowe was widely expected to play a key role on health care legislation in 2009. She had taken previous initiatives on related issues, supporting legislation to allow the government to negotiate drug prices with pharmaceutical companies and taking a lead role on many women's health issues, pushing for more money for women's health research, more screening for osteoporosis, and gender analysis in Food and Drug Administration clinical trials. With Massachusetts liberal Edward Kennedy and Wyoming conservative Mike Enzi, she co-sponsored a 2008 bill to bar insurance companies from using genetic information in setting premiums. In the first half of 2009, she was in discussions with Finance Committee Democrats and White House staffers to see if they could reach agreement on an overhaul of the health insurance system in order to cover the many millions of uninsured Americans. Snowe said in June that she favored market-oriented reforms, with a government-sponsored insurance option as a safety net. After intense negotiations, she voted for the bill reported out of the Senate Finance Committee, the only Republican to do so, in October 2009. "Is this bill all that I would want? Far from it. But when history calls, history calls," she said. But she also noted, "My vote today is my vote today. It doesn't forecast what my vote will be tomorrow."

Snowe's position on the bill was widely reported and debated: She would not support a bill with a public option, but would support one with a trigger mechanism that would establish a government-run option only if the private market produced insufficient coverage for the uninsured. Criticism rained in from all sides. Liberals who supported the public option maintained that Democrats, with 60 votes in the Senate, were foolish to concede to Snowe's conditions. Conservatives were unhappy that she was considering voting for a public option under any circumstances. Ultimately, the public option, a cornerstone of the House-passed bill, was dropped from the Senate version, and with it, Snowe's trigger plan. She told *Maine Today*: If "you build a real consensus then you can bring people across. And that has just not been their (the Democrats') impetus." Snowe voted against the Senate bill when it passed with 60 Democratic votes in December 2009.

On other economic issues, Snowe has sometimes taken positions contrary to those of most Republicans. She opposed using payroll taxes for private investment accounts in Social Security in 2005. She voted against a $70 billion tax cut and opposed repeal of the estate tax in 2006. She opposed the Australia and Colombia Free Trade Agreements, because of concern over dairy imports from Australia and the failure to prosecute the killers of union leaders in Colombia. She and Oregon Democrat Ron Wyden sought a ban on bonus payments to employees of financial institutions that got federal rescue funds in 2009, but it was left out of the final bill at the insistence of the Obama administration.

With Collins and Massachusetts Republican Scott Brown, she provided the votes necessary to pass the Dodd-Frank financial regulation bill in July 2010, which she said would protect Americans "from the greedy and reckless Wall Street practices that contributed to this epic economic downturn." She and Collins also cast decisive votes in August 2010 for a bill providing $16 billion more in Medicaid funding and $10 billion for teacher pay, which was passed by the Senate as part of an emergency jobs bill. On the major energy issue of the 111th Congress (2009-10), Snowe supported legislation to limit carbon emissions. In summer 2010, she worked with Jeff Bingaman, D-N.M., on a cap-and-trade bill to limit carbon emissions that would apply only to electric utilities, but like other cap-and-trade bills, it failed to progress in the Senate.

As chairman or ranking member of the Small Business Committee since 2003, Snowe sought a one-year delay for small businesses to comply with the Sarbanes-Oxley law's strict reporting requirements, and sought to change the Small Business Administration procurement rules in economically distressed areas. Snowe sponsored a bill endorsed by both business leaders and labor unions to allow small businesses in different states to join together to buy health insurance as a way of reducing prohibitively high premiums.

Snowe's role on the Oceans, Atmosphere, Fisheries, and Coast Guard Subcommittee of the Commerce, Science, and Transportation Committee gives her opportunities to shine for constituents. She helped pass the reauthorization of the Magnuson-Stevens fishery law in 2006. In 2008, she declared that regulations had reduced fishing days by more than half and lamented that the government might "regulate our nation's first fishery out of existence." On other Commerce committee issues, Snowe and Democrat Maria Cantwell of Washington sponsored a measure to regulate foreign exchanges that trade in U.S. commodities; it passed as part of the 2008 farm bill. Snowe's provision to monitor electronic energy markets also got into the bill.

From her seat on the Finance Committee, Snowe has tinkered with legislation to include tax deferrals for military shipbuilding yards, which would benefit Maine's Bath Iron Works. She also worked on income averaging for fishermen, favorable accounting provisions for reforestation, and favorable treatment for energy plants that burn wood chips. She and Collins worked together in 2007 to get empowerment-zone designation for Aroostook County and in 2006, Snowe guided a bill through the Senate designating $1 billion for the Low Income Home Energy Assistance Program, an important federal program in the cold Northeast.

Snowe has enjoyed high job ratings in Maine. She was re-elected 69%-31% in 2000. Six years later, she easily turned back charges of being a "Bush enabler" to win re-election, 74%-21%.

Junior Senator

Susan Collins (R)

Elected 1996, term expires 2014, 3rd term; b. Dec. 7, 1952, Caribou; home, Bangor; St. Lawrence U., B.A. 1975; Catholic; single.

Professional Career: Legis. aide, U.S. Sen. Bill Cohen, 1975–87, Staff dir., Oversight of Gov. Mgmt. Subcmte., 1981–87; Professional & Financial Regulation Comm., 1987–92; New England regional dir., U.S. Small Business Admin., 1992; ME dpty. treas., 1993; Exec. dir., Ctr. for Family Business, Husson Col., 1994–96.

DC Office: 413 DSOB, 20510, 202-224-2523; Fax: 202-224-2693; Web site: collins.senate.gov.

State Offices: Augusta, 207-622-8414; Bangor, 207-945-0417; Biddeford, 207-283-1101; Caribou, 207-493-7873; Lewiston, 207-784-6969; Portland, 207-780-3575.

Committees: *Aging (Special). Appropriations:* Agriculture, Rural Development, Food and Drug Administration & Related Agencies; Commerce, Justice, Science & Related Agencies; Defense; Energy & Water Development; Interior, Environment & Related Agencies; Transportation, HUD & Related Agencies (RMM). *Armed Services:* Personnel; Readiness & Management Support; Seapower. *Homeland Security & Governmental Affairs* (RMM): Contracting Oversight (Ad Hoc); Investigations (Permanent).

Group Ratings

	ACLU	ACU	ADA	CFG	AFS	FRC	LCV	ITIC	NTU	COC
2010	47	64	40	51	36	29	0	67	72	82
2009	–	48	65	60	45	–	64	–	50	86

National Journal Ratings

	2010 LIB	—	2010 CONS		2009 LIB	—	2009 CONS
Economic	40%	—	59%		39%	—	60%
Social	38%	—	60%		43%	—	56%
Foreign	34%	—	65%		35%	—	63%
Composite	38%	—	62%		40%	—	60%

Key Votes of the 111th Congress

1. Overturn Ledbetter	Y	5. Pass health care bill	N	9. Ratify New START	Y
2. Pass $787 billion stimulus	Y	6. Regulate financial firms	Y	10. Confirm Elena Kagan	Y
3. Repeal DC gun laws	Y	7. Pass tax cuts for some	Y	11. Stop EPA climate regs	Y
4. Confirm Sonia Sotomayor	Y	8. Legalize immigrants' kids	N	12. Repeal don't ask, tell	Y

Election Results

2008 general	Susan Collins (R)	444,300	(61%)	($8,039,750)
	Tom Allen (D)	279,510	(39%)	($5,988,773)
2008 primary	Susan Collins (R)	unopposed		

Prior Winning Percentages: 2002 (58%); 1996 (49%)

Susan Collins, Maine's junior senator, is a Republican first elected in 1996. She grew up in Caribou, in potato-growing Aroostook County, about as far northeast as you can get in the United States, closer to the capitals of New Brunswick and Quebec than to the capital of Maine. Her family has been in the lumber business since 1844 and has also long been involved in politics. Her father was a state senator, he and her mother served as mayor, and her uncle was a state Supreme Court justice. She recalls that as a high school senior, she visited Washington as part of a Senate youth program, and home-state Sen. Margaret Chase Smith talked with her for nearly two hours in her office. Right after college, she got a job as an intern with Republican William Cohen, then the 2nd District House congressman and a member of the Judiciary Committee who had voted to impeach President Richard Nixon. Cohen hired Collins, and she remained on his staff for 12 years. She was staff director for the Senate Governmental Affairs Subcommittee on Oversight of Government Management, which Cohen chaired from 1981 to 1987. After Republicans lost their Senate majority, Collins returned to Maine to work for five years for GOP Gov. John McKernan as a financial regulation commissioner. In 1992, she was New England administrator of the Small Business Administration, and in 1994, she ran for governor. It was a disastrous campaign: She won the Republican nomination but was overshadowed by independent Angus King and ran third, with only 23% of the vote.

Two years later, Cohen announced his retirement from the Senate. Collins wanted to run, and indeed there was a precedent in Maine for a third-place gubernatorial finisher to be elected senator: Republican George Mitchell was similarly humiliated in 1974, and then, after being appointed senator in 1980, won smashing victories in 1982 and 1988. In the Republican primary, Collins played up her resemblance to Sen. Olympia Snowe and Cohen on issues and called for a balanced budget amendment, the presidential line item veto, and term limits. She pledged to serve no more than two terms. Collins won with 56% of the vote. In the general election, she was opposed by former Gov. Joseph Brennan. Brennan attacked Collins on economic issues and gun control, but Collins raised much more money and won 49%-44%.

Collins has compiled a centrist voting record, and in recent years, has been a pivotal swing vote on issues that divide the two major parties. As she told the *Waterville Morning Sentinel* in August 2010, "I enjoy playing a key role in the U.S. Senate, but it's been very difficult to be in a pivotal position on every single major issue, on every single vote. The excessive partisanship has eroded the trust among members, and that is corrosive and destructive. There's fault on both sides." Collins has joined Democrats on issues including tax cuts, the partial birth abortion ban and campaign finance regulation. In the latter debate, she sponsored amendments to reduce the advantages of self-financing candidates and to require that a candidate's face appear on negative ads that he or she runs. In 2009, Collins and Ben Nelson, D-Neb., used their pivotal votes to reduce the price tag of the economic stimulus bill from $900 billion to $787 billion before voting for it. She told *Maine Today*, "I knew that those provisions, that funding, would translate into real jobs for real people in Maine." Collins has been the lead Senate Republican sponsor of a bill to ban discrimination on the basis of sexual orientation. On a major financial regulation bill in 2010, she, Snowe and Massachusetts Sen. Scott Brown were the three Republicans who provided votes to pass the bill. In earlier legislative battles, she has called for reducing the size of the Bush tax cuts and for applying the pay-as-you-go rules to tax cuts as well as spending increase. In 2005, Collins joined the bipartisan "Gang of 14" to preserve the possibility but reduce the likelihood of filibusters against Supreme Court nominees.

Since 2003, Collins has been the chairman or the ranking Republican on the Homeland Security and Governmental Affairs Committee, where she once worked as a staffer. There, she has worked very closely with her counterpart, Joe Lieberman of Connecticut, a Democrat turned independent. They collaborated in 2004 on reorganization of the intelligence community, creating the Office of the Director of National Intelligence and a new counter-terrorism center, and together they defeated amendments that would have kept secret the total amount of intelligence spending. Collins and Lieberman also moved legislation that would classify security threats at chemical facilities and require the operators to implement security measures. She and Lieberman in 2009 and 2011 introduced a cyber security bill to allow the Department of Homeland Security to share information on vulnerability with private companies. It was approved in committee. And in early 2011, they issued a blistering report on the military's total inattention to the threat posed by Nidal Hasan, the Fort Hood shooter.

With Washington state Democrat Patty Murray, Collins sponsored a 2006 bill requiring radiation screening of all cargo entering U.S. ports. Also that year, Collins and Democrat Thomas Carper of Delaware moved a Postal Service reorganization bill through the Senate that pegged postal increases to inflation. She has also sponsored bills to strengthen the protection of whistle-blowers, increase competition in government procurement, and reduce the number of political appointees by one-third.

Collins has been front-and-center on energy policy in recent years. She supported raising fuel-efficiency standards for cars to 35 miles per gallon by 2019 and requiring carbon dioxide emissions to be lowered to 1990 levels by 2020. In December 2009, she and Democrat Maria Cantwell of Washington state introduced a "cap-and-dividend" bill to address carbon emissions. Companies would buy carbon shares in auctions, passing on costs to consumers, with 75% of the fund paid as dividends to citizens and 25% devoted to clean energy research and development. They pressed their bill as an alternative to the Democrats' cap-and-trade legislation to no avail.

As a member of the Armed Services Committee, Collins voted for the Iraq war resolution in 2002 and in 2007, opposed a Democratic attempt to set a timetable for withdrawing troops. In May 2010, she was the only Republican on the committee to vote to repeal the ban on openly gay people in the military.

On local issues, Collins in 2006 won approval of a bill that allows minor league athletes and professional ice skaters to apply for P-1 immigration visas, making life easier for the many Canadian hockey players who skate for the former Lewiston MAINEiacs. Collins won protection for financially ailing fishermen under the Bankruptcy Act, and she and Snowe also sought $125 million to offset the "digital cliff effect," to finance building of digital translators to make sure digital TV signals reach remote rural areas.

In her 2002 re-election campaign, Collins was challenged by former state Senate Majority Leader Chellie Pingree, the chief sponsor of the state law allowing government negotiations with pharmaceutical companies as a way of lowering prescription drug costs. Pingree ran ads saying that Collins was "siding with the big drug companies." But Collins cited a successful amendment she sponsored to make prescription drugs cheaper. Both candidates spent about $2 million each. Collins won by a solid 58%-42%.

Six years later, Collins was challenged by 1st District Rep. Tom Allen, a Democrat who made the Iraq war a central issue. She highlighted her opposition to oil drilling in the Arctic National Wildlife Refuge and her work getting emergency equipment for the Monmouth Fire Department and P-1 visas for the MAINEiacs. The war became a less salient issue as the success of President Bush's troop surge strategy became evident. Collins maintained double-digit leads in the polls throughout the campaign and won 61%-39%. She even achieved what she described as "my political dream" of carrying heavily Democratic Lewiston, as well as all 16 counties.

FIRST DISTRICT

Chellie Pingree (D)

Elected 2008, 2nd term; b. April 4, 1955, Minneapolis, MN; home, Northaven; Col. of the Atlantic, B.A., 1979; Lutheran; divorced; 3 children.

Elected Office: ME Senate, 1992-2000, Majority ldr., 1996-2001.

Professional Career: Farmer, 1977-1980; Founder & pres., N. Island Designs Co., 1981-92; Pres. & CEO, Common Cause, 2003-07.

DC Office: 1318 LHOB, 20515, 202-225-6116; Fax: 202-225-5590; Web site: pingree.house.gov.

State Offices: Portland, 207-774-5019.

Committees: *Agriculture:* Conservation, Energy & Forestry; Nutrition & Horticulture. *Armed Services:* Military Personnel; Seapower & Projection Forces.

Group Ratings

	ACLU	ACU	ADA	CFG	AFS	FRC	LCV	ITIC	NTU	COC
2010	94	0	100	0	100	0	100	67	7	13
2009	–	0	100	0	100	–	100	–	4	33

National Journal Ratings

	2010 LIB — 2010 CONS		2009 LIB — 2009 CONS	
Economic	90%	— 0%	82%	— 14%
Social	80%	— 18%	75%	— 20%
Foreign	97%	— 0%	78%	— 17%
Composite	92%	— 9%	81%	— 19%

Key Votes of the 111th Congress

1. Overturn Ledbetter	Y	5. Bar federal abortion funds	N	9. Stop detainee transfers	N
2. Pass $820 billion stimulus	Y	6. Pass health care bill	Y	10. Legalize immigrants' kids	Y
3. Let guns in national parks	N	7. Regulate financial firms	Y	11. Repeal don't ask, tell	Y
4. Pass cap-and-trade	Y	8. Pass tax cuts for some	Y	12. Limit campaign funds	Y

Election Results

2010 general	Chellie Pingree (D)	169,114	(57%)	($1,283,175)
	Dean Scontras (R)	128,501	(43%)	($494,034)
2010 primary	Chellie Pingree (D)	unopposed		

Prior Winning Percentages: 2008 (55%)

Population		Race/Ethnicity		Work	
Pop. 2010:	668,515	White:	94.1%	Private:	77.1%
Change since 2000:	Up 4.9%	Black:	1.3%	Government:	13.8%
Urban:	49.4%	Hispanic:	1.4%	Self-employed:	8.9%
Rural:	50.6%	Asian:	1.3%	Blue collar:	20.1%
Area size:	5,400 sq. mi.	Native Am.:	0.3%	White collar:	61.4%
		Hawaiian:	0.0%	Khaki collar:	0.2%
Age		Two+ races:	1.4%	Other:	18.3%
Median age:	41.9 yrs.				
More than 65 yrs:	14.9%	*Ancestry*		Median income:	$52,424
Less than 18 yrs:	21.0%	English	17.6%	Median Home Value:	$227,300
		Irish	14.5%		
Education		French	12.2%	**Military Veterans**	
H.S. grad:	91.9%			% of Pop:	12.8%
College grad:	32.1%				
Grad degree:	11.5%				

Southern Maine; Portland

The 1st District of Maine stretches from south-ernmost Kittery and nearby Kennebunkport to the craggy-shored ancestrally Republican counties to the east. The historic center is Port-land, Maine's largest city, home to the yuppies and lawyers who have revived and renovated its downtown landmarks. Portland's antique charm, mostly booming economy and tolerant lifestyle have made it a haven for singles and

gays. Maine legalized gay marriage in 2009, but opponents pushed for a referendum and voters rejected the proposal at the polls that November. L.L.Bean is not far away in Freeport. Former farm towns have been transformed into suburbia, and old mill towns like Biddeford and Sanford have been redeveloped. The 2005 base-closing com-mission spared Portsmouth Naval Shipyard at Kittery, the nation's oldest continually operating naval shipyard, and in 2009, Portsmouth announced the hiring of 400 more civilian workers. But the commission voted to close down the Brunswick Naval Air Station in 2011, costing the area $211 million in annual wages and military contracts. Redevelopment authorities faced decisions about what to do with the station's 3,200 acres of real estate, two runways, and 700 empty housing units.

Most voters in the 1st District live within a couple hours drive of the Maine Mall, which is just off the Maine Turnpike and Interstate 295 and is the state's heaviest concentration of retail and office space. But in a lifestyle more reminiscent of the Alaska wilderness, those who live on the district's remote islands depend on ferries and Cessna aircraft as their lifeline to the mainland. In the summer, the air traffic includes the families of *Fortune* 500 executives traveling to their estates. In the winter, lobstermen and local business owners board most flights. Lobsters are not just a tradition here but also an economic resource. Around 6,000 licensed lobstermen in the state hauled in an estimated 100 million pounds in 2010. The industry experienced a boom for several years, but the recession badly hurt sales. Politically, the 1st District votes very much like the state as a whole: quirkily, often for independents, and splitting tickets with abandon. In 2008, every county voted not only for Democratic presidential nominee Barack Obama but also for Republican Sen. Susan Collins. Obama won 61%-38%. From 1968 to 1996, Maine elected three Democrats and three Republicans to the House, with each party holding the seat for 14 years.

Chellie Pingree (D)

The congresswoman from the 1st District is Chellie Pingree, a Democrat elected in 2008. She suc-ceeded Democratic Rep. Tom Allen, who unsuccessfully challenged Republican Sen. Susan Collins that year. Although Maine has a long history of electing women to office, Pingree is the first Demo-cratic woman from Maine elected to Congress.

A veteran of the state Senate, Pingree was already an experienced legislator before coming to Washington, but her path to elected office was hardly conventional. She grew up in Minnesota, the granddaughter of Scandinavian immigrants who came to work as dairy farmers. Her parents moved to Minneapolis, where her father was an accountant and her mother a nurse. The city's anti-war activism during the Vietnam era had a profound influence on Pingree, and she left high school early for alternative education programs on the East Coast. At one program in Worcester, Mass., she met her future husband and followed him to Maine, where they settled on remote North Haven Island in Penobscot Bay. As disciples of the "back to the land" movement, they lived for years in a cabin without running water or electricity and made their living as organic farmers. Although the couple later divorced, Pingree thrived on the island, both politically and professionally. In 1981, she started her own business selling knitting kits. At its peak, the company, the North Island Designs Company, distributed 100,000 mail-order catalogs. She started her political career in local offices on the island, including serving as tax assessor and on the planning and school boards.

In 1991, she took her daughter to a local speech by then-Rep. Patricia Schroeder of Colorado, who briefly sought the Democratic presidential nomination in 1988. The speech inspired Pingree to take her friends seriously when they suggested that she run for an open seat in the state Senate. She went door-to-door in the traditionally Republican district in Knox County and won. Pingree rose to majority leader in 1996. As leader, she fought back a challenge from pharmaceutical companies and persuaded reluctant parties to agree to a law allowing the state to negotiate prescription drug prices, the first such law in the country.

Pingree left the state Senate in 2001, barred by term limits from seeking re-election. She ran unsuccessfully against Collins in 2002. Shortly after her loss, she received an offer to become president of Common Cause, the Washington, D.C., government and campaign watchdog group. She took the reins of the nonprofit organization just as it had been thrust into the national spotlight by the push to overhaul the nation's campaign finance laws. That fight was not an easy one. She recalls an often strained relationship with Sen. John McCain of Arizona, a Republican who accused her of injecting partisanship into her work. As president, Pingree also directed Common Cause to lobby against media consolidation in the hands of a few powerful companies.

She left the job in early 2007 to run for the House seat that Allen gave up to campaign for the Senate. Although she had worked for years to limit the influence of money in politics, Pingree had no trouble raising far more of it than any of her five rivals for the Democratic nomination. She mostly eschewed money from political action committees but enjoyed the backing of EMILY's List, which funds women candidates who support abortion rights. Pingree won the primary with 44% of the vote. In the general election, she had a decisive fundraising advantage, bringing in $2.2 million compared with her Republican opponent, state Sen. Charles Summers, who raised about $645,000. Pingree won 55%-45%.

Pingree has been a consistently loyal Democrat. She was named to the Rules Committee, a prime assignment for a freshman. Drawing on her background at Common Cause, Pingree supported a bill creating a voluntary system for candidates to refuse political contributions from lobbyists and political action committees. During the health care debate, she ardently backed a government-run public option and criticized provisions that were added to appease anti-abortion Democrats. She took a strong interest in environmental issues, helping to form the House Sustainable Energy and Environmental Coalition and introducing a bill forcing BP to pay royalties on the oil from its massive Gulf spill in 2010.

In her 2010 re-election campaign, Pingree's opponent was alternative energy company owner Dean Scontras, who got support from tea party activists. The Maine Republican Party ran ads accusing Pingree of taking trips on the corporate jet of her fiancée, hedge-fund billionaire Donald Sussman, an arrangement they said made the former Common Cause leader appear hypocritical. Scontras also sought to tie her to liberal House Speaker Nancy Pelosi. The nation's anti-incumbent sentiment helped him close the gap, even with far less money than Pingree. But her longtime familiarity with the district's voters helped her pull off a win with 57% of the vote.

SECOND DISTRICT

Michael Michaud (D)

Elected 2002, 5th term; b. Jan. 18, 1955, Millinocket; home, East Millinocket; Schenck H.S., 1973; Catholic; single.

Elected Office: ME House, 1980-94; ME Senate, 1994-2001, Pres., 2001.

Professional Career: Mill worker, Great Northern Paper, 1973-2002.

DC Office: 1724 LHOB, 20515, 202-225-6306; Fax: 202-225-2943; Web site: michaud.house.gov.

State Offices: Bangor, 207-942-6935; Lewiston, 207-782-3704; Presque Isle, 207-764-1036; Waterville, 207-873-5713.

Committees: *Transportation & Infrastructure:* Coast Guard & Maritime Transportation; Economic Development, Public Buildings & Emergency Management; Highways & Transit; Railroads, Pipelines & Hazardous Materials. *Veterans' Affairs:* Disability Assistance & Memorial Affairs; Health (RMM).

Group Ratings

	ACLU	ACU	ADA	CFG	AFS	FRC	LCV	ITIC	NTU	COC
2010	88	0	90	4	100	25	100	67	12	13
2009	–	8	90	5	100	–	100	–	9	40

National Journal Ratings

	2010 LIB — 2010 CONS		2009 LIB — 2009 CONS	
Economic	60%	— 40%	64%	— 34%
Social	77%	— 21%	54%	— 43%
Foreign	92%	— 3%	53%	— 44%
Composite	78%	— 23%	58%	— 42%

Key Votes of the 111th Congress

1. Overturn Ledbetter	Y	5. Bar federal abortion funds	Y	9. Stop detainee transfers	N
2. Pass $820 billion stimulus	Y	6. Pass health care bill	Y	10. Legalize immigrants' kids	Y
3. Let guns in national parks	Y	7. Regulate financial firms	Y	11. Repeal don't ask, tell	Y
4. Pass cap-and-trade	Y	8. Pass tax cuts for some	Y	12. Limit campaign funds	Y

Election Results

2010 general	Michael Michaud (D)	147,042	(55%)	($1,044,372)
	Jason Levesque (R)	119,669	(45%)	($542,626)
2010 primary	Michael Michaud (D)	unopposed		

Prior Winning Percentages: 2008 (67%), 2006 (71%), 2004 (58%), 2002 (52%)

Population		Race/Ethnicity		Work	
Pop. 2010:	659,846	White:	94.7%	Private:	75.8%
Change since 2000:	Up 3.5%	Black:	1.0%	Government:	14.4%
Urban:	31.0%	Hispanic:	1.1%	Self-employed:	9.6%
Rural:	69.0%	Asian:	0.7%	Blue collar:	24.9%
Area size:	29,979 sq. mi.	Native Am.:	0.9%	White collar:	54.3%
		Hawaiian:	0.0%	Khaki collar:	0.1%
Age		Two+ races:	1.4%	Other:	20.7%
Median age:	41.9 yrs.				
More than 65 yrs:	15.6%	*Ancestry*		Median income:	$40,499
Less than 18 yrs:	20.8%	English	16.8%	Median Home Value:	$135,700
		French	13.8%		
Education		Irish	12.3%	**Military Veterans**	
H.S. grad:	87.6%			% of Pop:	13.4%
College grad:	20.3%				
Grad degree:	6.9%				

Northern Maine; Lewiston

The 2nd District of Maine is heavily forested, rough-hewn, and enormous. It covers the north-ern three-quarters of the state, and is the largest congressional district east of the Mississippi River, larger than the states of New Hampshire, Vermont, and Massachusetts combined. The population is not evenly distributed. The district dips south to include the heavily Democratic mill town of Lewiston and also includes Eastport. At Belfast on Penobscot Bay, art galleries and bou-

2008 Presidential Vote		
Barack Obama (D) 189,778	(55%)
John McCain (R) 150,669	(43%)
2004 Presidential Vote		
John Kerry (D) 185,139	(52%)
George Bush (R) 164,377	(46%)
Cook Partisan Voting Index: D+3		

tiques have replaced fish-processing plants. There are several different Maines represented here: The bays of coastal Maine, with their small fishing towns; the potato fields of far northern Aroos-took County; and the mill towns on the fast-running streams of western Maine. Some valleys have more moose than people. This was one of America's frontiers in the 1850s, when Bangor, on the Penobscot River, was the lumber capital of the world. Today, tiny Bangor is the second-largest city in the district after Lewiston.

This part of Maine has had its economic troubles, losing 22,000 jobs to neighboring Canada and other foreign markets after the 1993 passage of the North American Free Trade Agreement. Potato production is only half of what it was in 1980. A once-thriving sardine-canning business ended with the closing of the last cannery in 2010. Logging, long the largest industry in Maine, has suffered job cutbacks as big paper companies sell off acreage and shut down mills. A movement to set aside yet more acreage in a proposed Maine North Woods National Park, which would be larger than the Yellowstone and Yosemite parks combined, has sparked protests. Bumper stickers around the state read: "If you don't like cutting trees, try using plastic toilet paper." But there are also signs of life. Loring Air Force Base was closed in 1994, but new businesses, from aircraft repair to telemarketing, have replaced its civilian jobs and then some. And some long-standing industries are still humming. Washington County's sandy soil plains produce more than 90% of the nation's wild blueberry crop. Politically, the district is iconoclastic and permanently enamored of neither major political party. This was Ross Perot's strongest congressional district in the United States in 1992 and 1996. Al Gore narrowly carried it in 2000 and John Kerry did only slightly better in 2004. Barack Obama won here, but by a closer margin than in Maine's other district.

Mike Michaud (D)

The congressman from the 2nd District is Mike Michaud *(mee-SHOO)*, a Democrat first elected in 2002. Michaud grew up in East Millinocket in the North Woods. He comes from a blue-collar family and is one of the few members of Congress who did not attend college. For 29 years, he was a mill worker and union member at Great Northern Paper, and still proudly displays in his office the lunch bucket he used to carry to work. "I know what it's like to work the day shift, the midnight shift. I've been on strike. I know what it's like to worry about whether you will have a job or not," Michaud says. In 1980, he was elected to the state House and in 1994 to the state Senate, where he chaired the Appropriations Committee and became Senate president. Michaud has an eclectic mix of political views, which seem to be a throwback to earlier Democratic days. He is staunchly pro-labor, but opposes abortion rights. He opposes drilling for oil in the Arctic National Wildlife Refuge, but strongly supports gun ownership. "He's not afraid to go up to leadership," then-Rep. Phil Hare, D-Ill., told the *Portland Press Herald* in 2008. "He's tenacious."

When Democrat John Baldacci left his 2nd District seat to run for governor in 2002, six Demo-crats lined up for the primary. Michaud's chief opponent was state Sen. Susan Longley of Lewiston, the daughter of former independent Gov. James Longley and sister of the 1st District's former Republican congressman, James Longley Jr. She emphasized her support for abortion rights. With strong support from organized labor, Michaud got 31% to Longley's 28%. It was a regional contest: Michaud carried the five most rural counties, and won 66% of the vote in Aroostook. Longley carried six counties chiefly in the southern part of the district, and won 59% in trendy coastal Waldo County.

In the general election, Michaud faced Kevin Raye, the chief of staff to Republican Sen. Olym-pia Snowe. Michaud attempted to turn Raye's experience into a liability. His campaign slogan was, "I'm One of Us, Working for Us," contrasting his blue-collar background with Raye's white-collar job in Washington. Hoping to appeal to feminists despite his opposition to abortion, Michaud set out a 10-point "women's equity agenda," including support for family planning, increased child care aid, breast cancer research, and equal pay for equal work. Michaud defeated Raye 52%-48%. He ran better than most Democrats in rural areas, winning 53% in the seven northern counties, where unions conducted a voter-turnout drive in the mill towns.

In the House, Michaud's voting record has been moderate for a Democrat. He is among the few New Englanders in the fiscally conservative Blue Dog Coalition, and voted against a June 2010 bill extending unemployment insurance by sharply questioning why Democratic leaders would tie jobless aid with help for catfish farmers and Hawaiian sugar cane growers. "Using the plight of the jobless as a way to lard up bills for pet issues represents the worst of the political process and is the height of irresponsibility," he said. He was skeptical about the health care overhaul bill in 2009, but agreed to back it after getting a personal pitch from Obama. He displayed his independence in January 2011 by backing Heath Shuler of North Carolina, a fellow Blue Dog, over liberal Nancy Pelosi for Democratic leader.

Michaud has worked to unite workers and environmentalists on trade and other issues, and has emerged as a power broker on the issue. Michaud co-founded the House Trade Working Group, whose members are highly skeptical of trade agreements. He sponsored a bill in 2009 calling for a review of all existing trade agreements and for halting new ones, which attracted 148 co-sponsors, more than half of the House Democratic caucus. He helped sideline trade pacts with Colombia and Panama. Pro-trade U.S. corporations, he said in 2009, are "looking out for their own interests, not the best interests of security here in the United States or for jobs here in the United States." He also led an effort in March 2010 to have the Obama administration address China's undervalued currency by applying countervailing duties on Chinese exports.

After Democrats won a House majority in 2006, Michaud vied to become chairman of the Veterans' Affairs Committee. But California Rep. Bob Filner had more seniority, and although he worried some Democrats with occasional outbursts of bad temper, he won a vote in the Democratic Caucus, 112-69.

In 2004, Michaud faced Brian Hamel, a Republican with a record of job creation as the president of the Loring Development Authority. National Republicans took an early interest in the race. But Hamel, who had never held elected office, had trouble getting noticed in this sprawling district. Michaud was re-elected 58%-39%. With continued strong support from organized labor, he expanded his margin in 2006 and defeated Republican eye care technician Laurence D'Amboise, 71%-29%. He faced a bit more difficulty in the anti-incumbent environment of 2010, when his opponent was Republican marketing company owner Jason Levesque, a political newcomer and staunch conservative. But Michaud campaigned hard, making regular trips home through the fall, and won with 55% of the vote.

★ MARYLAND ★

Situated at the midpoint of the Atlantic coast, south of the Mason-Dixon Line but just north of the line between the Union and the Confederacy, Maryland is the crossroads state, with claims to both the North and South, and to both industrial and rural influences. This was the only one of the 13 colonies founded by Roman Catholics—the Calvert family—and its embrace of religious tolerance came less from high-minded ideals than from the Calverts' desire to protect their property from Protestant monarchs: a harbinger of Maryland's practical-mindedness. Similarly, although hot-blooded Baltimoreans wanted to secede from the Union in 1861 (the state song, "Maryland, My Maryland," is based on a poem condemning Abraham Lincoln's suppression of pro-Confederate rioters), cooler heads prevailed.

The Puritan impulse was never lively here. Prohibition was enforced only laxly in Baltimore, to the delight of its great journalist-cum-lexicographer H.L. Mencken, who called it Charm City. Slot machines were legal for years in the rural counties of the Eastern Shore and, after years of controversy and pleas from racetrack owners, were legalized statewide in 2008. An old state law guaranteeing blacks equal access to public accommodations specifically excluded the Eastern Shore. By not pursuing any one course rigorously, Maryland could be many things at once—Northern as well as Southern, moralistic as well as libertine, citified but also reliant on nature—mostly leaving people to their own devices. Perhaps as a result, much of Maryland's political history reads like a chronicle of rogues, the latest episode being Baltimore Mayor Sheila Dixon's 2009 conviction for embezzling $500 in gift cards donated for the city's poor. Maryland's genial tolerance may have given it a little too savory a history, but this state cherishes its sense of uniqueness. The Chesapeake Bay is the nation's largest estuary, with water saltier than a river but fresher than the ocean and with distinctive watermen and shellfish. Pollution and years of overharvesting drastically reduced its yield, and the terrapin and Chesapeake oyster are rare today. But an ongoing statewide save-the-bay movement is having an impact. From 2008 to 2010, the population of Chesapeake blue crabs more than doubled, and the state has launched a program to seed oyster beds.

Maryland has reason to be proud of the economy, or economies, it has built over the years. Half a century ago, half the state's population lived in the city of Baltimore and only one-fifth in the suburbs. Now the proportions are the other way around, and then some: 11% live in Baltimore, and 76% in counties classified as suburbs. The Census Bureau defines Washington-Baltimore as a single metropolitan area, the nation's fourth largest, with 8 million people. But Baltimore and Washington are not fraternal twins like Dallas and Fort Worth or Minneapolis and St. Paul, but two quite separate cities, with different economic bases and different attitudes. Washington is a one-industry, white-collar capital city, while Baltimore started off as a port and an industrial city. Baltimore managed to stay diversified and successful as it spread out into the countryside from its new central core at the Inner Harbor and the solidly built edifices of its downtown streets. With its large suburban population, Maryland ranked third in 2010 in median household income, after similarly suburban New Jersey and Connecticut. It is home to the Baltimore Orioles baseball team and their popular Oriole Park at Camden Yards (the first of the new-old ballparks of the 1990s) and to Johns Hopkins University with its Georgian buildings along the affluent corridor that runs directly north from downtown all the way to the developing edge city of Hunt Valley. But with its relatively high tax rates, Maryland started to see net domestic out-migration in mid-decade, in contrast to the continuing domestic in-migration into neighboring Virginia, Delaware and suburban Philadelphia. And the long-term shrinking of the manufacturing workforce continues: Bethlehem Steel's Sparrows Point plant, which employed 30,000 in the 1950s, succumbed to bankruptcy, was bought by a Russian company steelmaker in 2008 and now employs 6,000.

Baltimore remains the focus of Maryland's public life. Nearly half of Marylanders live in its metropolitan area, and its influence is far greater than Washington's on the Eastern Shore and in western Maryland. For years, most of Maryland's successful statewide politicians came from Baltimore. For more than two decades, its U.S. senators have lived there and commuted to Washington. Baltimore has a long Democratic tradition, and most of its voters are registered Democrats. Democrats currently hold more than two-thirds of the seats in both chambers of the legislature, and they outnumber Republicans 6-2 in the state's U.S. House delegation. They have lost the governorship only once since 1966: in 2002, when Republican Bob Ehrlich, capitalizing on the unpopularity of incumbent Parris Glendening, beat Democrat Kathleen Kennedy Townsend 52%-48%. But Democratic legislators battled Ehrlich ferociously, and he lost to Baltimore Mayor Martin O'Malley 53%-46% in 2006. He came back for a rematch in 2010 and lost again, 56%-42%.

In national politics, Maryland for many years was a marginal state. It voted Republican for president as recently as 1988. But now it has become one of the most Democratic states in national

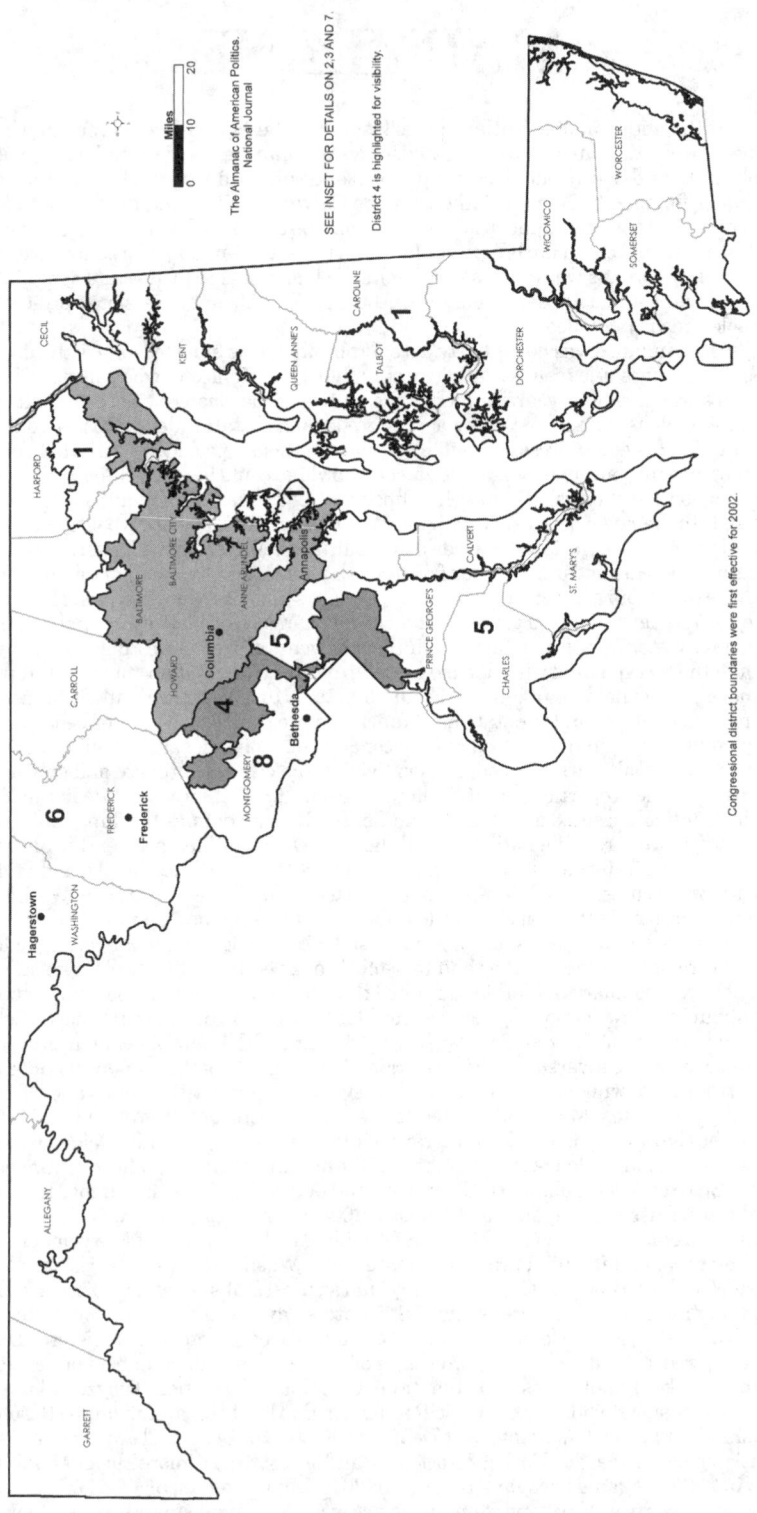

Miles
0   10   20

The Almanac of American Politics.
National Journal

SEE INSET FOR DETAILS ON 2,3 AND 7.

District 4 is highlighted for visibility.

Congressional district boundaries were first effective for 2002.

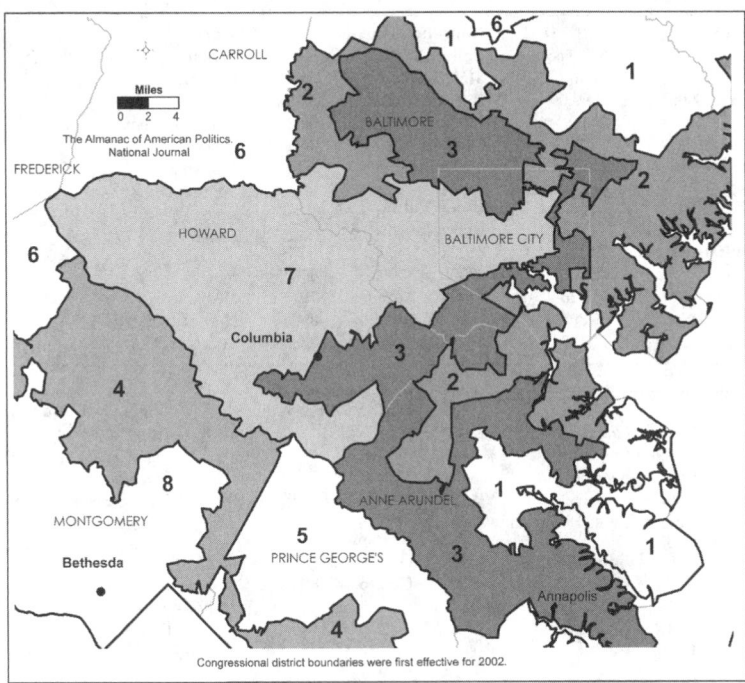

Congressional district boundaries were first effective for 2002.

politics, for two reasons. Some 31% of Marylanders are African-American, many of them, especially in Prince George's County, college-educated and economically upscale. But they vote if anything more heavily Democratic than more downscale blacks. That was even the case in 2006, when the Republican candidate for an open U.S. Senate seat was Lt. Gov. Michael Steele, an African-American from Prince George's County. Steele made some inroads among black voters, but not enough. He got 25% of African-American voters statewide and 50% of white voters; he won 23% in Baltimore city and 24% in Prince George's, not much above George W. Bush's 17% there in 2004. He lost the contest to Democrat Ben Cardin 54%-44%, and went on to become Republican National Committee chairman for two tempestuous years after the 2008 election. In the primary, Cardin had defeated former congressman and NAACP President Kweisi Mfume by a narrow 44%-41%.

The other reason for Maryland's Democratic strength is the increasing Democratic percentages in Montgomery and Prince George's counties, the two that are closest to Washington and that cast almost a third of the state's votes. In 1980, Montgomery and Prince George's weren't more Democratic than the rest of the state. Indeed, in the presidential race that year, they were slightly less so. But over a generation in which Republicans have backed smaller government and taken conservative cultural stands, Montgomery and Prince George's, like all of metro Washington, have become more Democratic than the rest of Maryland and the nation as a whole. In presidential elections from 1984 through 1996, Montgomery and Prince George's were about 10% more Democratic than the rest of Maryland. In the presidential elections of 2000 and 2004, with George W. Bush on the ballot, they were about 15% more Democratic than the rest of Maryland. In 2008, with Barack Obama on the ballot, and with his strong appeal to both black and high-income voters, Montgomery and Prince George's were 25% more Democratic than the rest of Maryland. To look at it another way, Maryland, excluding Montgomery and Prince George's counties, was in 1980 and is today not much more Democratic than the nation generally. This rest of Maryland gave Ronald Reagan and George H.W. Bush comfortable margins in 1984 and 1988; voted by about the national average for Bill Clinton in 1992 and 1996; gave small majorities to Al Gore in 2000 and George W. Bush in 2004; and voted 54%-44%—not much more than the national average—for Obama in 2008. This area voted solidly for Bob Ehrlich in 2002, 2006 and 2010.

Maryland's strong Democratic preferences have helped its members of Congress wield major influence over important issues, though it is often quietly exercised. Paul Sarbanes retired in 2006 after 30 years in the Senate; he was chief sponsor and shaper of the 2002 Sarbanes-Oxley Act, the wide-reaching crackdown on corporate accounting abuses. Barbara Mikulski was elected to the House in 1976 and the Senate in 1986; she was easily re-elected to a fifth term in 2010 and will

Population		Household Income		Work	
Pop. 2010:	5,773,552	Under $15k:	8.4%	Private:	72.2%
State rank:	19th	$15k to $50k:	26.9%	Government:	22.6%
Change since 2000:	Up 9.0%	$50k to $100k:	32.5%	Self-employed:	5.1%
Urban:	84.9%	$100k to $200k:	25.2%	Unemployment (3-yr. average):	4.5%
Rural:	15.1%	Over $200k:	7.0%	Poverty:	8.4%
Native of state:	48.0%	Median income:	$69,695	Blue collar:	16.3%
Not a citizen:	6.9%			White collar:	67.1%
Area size:	12,406 sq. mi.	**Home Value**		Khaki collar:	0.4%
		Under $100k:	5.8%	Other:	16.1%
Most populous cities		$100k to $300k:	36.4%		
Baltimore	620,961	$300k to $500k:	35.3%	**Age**	
Columbia CDP	99,615	$500k to $1 mil:	19.0%	Median age:	37.5 yrs.
Germantown CDP	86,395	Over $1 million:	3.4%	More than 65 yrs:	11.9%
Silver Spring CDP	71,452	Median:	$335,100	Less than 18 yrs:	24.0%

Race/Ethnicity				Military Veterans		Registered Voters in 2010	
White:	54.7%	*Language*		% of Pop:	10.4%	Democrats:	1,957,279
Black:	29.0%	English:	84.8%			Republicans:	925,614
Hispanic:	8.2%	Spanish:	5.9%	*Veterans by Period*		Ind./other:	585,392
Asian:	5.5%	Asian:	3.3%	WWII and before:	9.2%	Voter turnout:	1,873,541
Native Am.:	0.2%	Other European:	4.3%	Korea:	9.2%	Turnout as % of	
Hawaiian:	0.0%			Vietnam:	29.7%	voting age:	42.4%
Two+ races:	2.2%	**Education**		Gulf (pre-2001):	13.7%		
		H.S. grad:	87.8%	Gulf (post-2001):	12.6%	**Legislature**	
Ancestry		College grad:	35.4%	Peace time:	25.7%	Senate:	35 D 12 R
German	13.4%	Grad degree:	15.7%			House:	98 D 43 R
Irish	10.2%						
English	7.3%						

become the longest-serving woman ever in Congress in March 2012. Ben Cardin was elected to Sarbanes' seat in 2006 and had served for 20 years in the House before that. Maryland has two House members in the Democratic leadership. One is Steny Hoyer, a House member since 1981 and a former leader in the Maryland Legislature. Hoyer lost races for minority leader to Nancy Pelosi, a Maryland native whose father, Thomas D'Alessandro, was a U.S. congressman and mayor of Baltimore. The two rivals once served together as interns in the office of Sen. Daniel Brewster of Maryland. Hoyer was an effective House majority leader for four years and resisted attempts by James Clyburn of South Carolina to edge him out of the minority whip position after Democrats lost their majority in 2010 and Pelosi said she wanted to be minority leader. The other is Chris Van Hollen, elected in 2002, who headed the House Democrats' campaign committee in 2008 and 2010.

Presidential politics   With its large black population, most prominently in Baltimore City and Prince George's County but also in other suburban counties, and with the increasing Democratic strength in the Washington suburbs of Montgomery County, Maryland has become one of the most Democratic states in presidential elections. It was Bill Clinton's third-best state in 1992 and fifth-best in 1996. It was Al Gore's fourth-best in 2000, John Kerry's fifth-best in 2004, and Barack Obama's sixth-best in 2008. Obama carried Maryland by a whopping 62%-36% (in only five other states did he win by a bigger margin). He won 94% of the votes from blacks and lost whites to John McCain by only 49%-47%. Turnout increased most in Charles County, which has had a large African-American migration from Prince George's, and in majority-black Prince George's and Baltimore City. The Democratic percentage was up most in Charles and Frederick counties, both with many new residents from closer-in Washington suburbs.

2008 Presidential Vote
Barack Obama (D) 1,629,467   (62%)
John McCain (R) 959,862   (36%)

2008 Presidential Primary
Barack Obama (D) 532,665   (61%)
Hillary Clinton (D) 314,211   (36%)

2008 Presidential Primary
John McCain (R) 176,046   (55%)
Mike Huckabee (R)................91,608   (29%)
Mitt Romney (R)......................22,426   (7%)
Ron Paul (R) 19,196   (6%)

2004 Presidential Vote
John Kerry (D) 1,334,493   (56%)
George W. Bush (R)...........1,024,703   (43%)

From 1992 to 2004, Maryland held its presidential primaries a week before Super Tuesday to try to get noticed, with limited success. The one significant result came in 1992, when Paul Tsongas beat Clinton 41%-33%, with all of his margin and more coming from suburban Baltimore and Montgomery County. In 2008, the primary was held on Feb. 12, the same day that Virginia and the District of Columbia held their primaries. This was the single best day in the nomination contest for Obama. He won Virginia 64%-35%, D.C. 75%-24%, and Maryland 61%-36%. He won 79% in Prince George's County and 74% in Baltimore City and carried all of Maryland's major suburban counties as well. His lowest percentages there were 55% in Montgomery County and 56% in Baltimore County.

Congressional districting

112th Congress Lineup	
6 D	2 R
111th Congress Lineup	
7 D	1 R

Maryland was the scene of the Democrats' most successful partisan gerrymandering in the 2002 cycle. The convoluted shapes of the districts in the Baltimore area would have made Elbridge Gerry blush. The goal of the plan was to protect all four Democratic incumbents and to draw districts that would be impossible for 2nd District Republican Bob Ehrlich and 8th District Republican Connie Morella to win. The Bush 2000 percentage in the 2nd fell from 55% to 41%, and in the 8th from 36% to 31%. Ehrlich ran for governor and had his revenge, though as it turned out, for only four years. The 8th District attracted three Democratic challengers, each arguably a stronger candidate than any Morella had faced before, and she ended up losing narrowly to state Sen. Chris Van Hollen. The four Democratic incumbents had no problems. The two other districts, the 1st, based in the Eastern Shore, and the 6th, based in western Maryland, snake into the Baltimore suburbs to take in heavily Republican precincts and seemed to be safely Republican. But in 2008, after Republican state Sen. Andy Harris beat moderate Republican Wayne Gilchrest in the 1st District primary, the Queen Anne's County state's attorney, Democrat Frank Kratovil, managed to win a narrow victory in the general election—a result Harris reversed, by a wider margin, in 2010.

Governor

Martin O'Malley (D)

Elected 2006, term expires Jan. 2015, 2nd term; b. Jan. 18, 1963, Washington, D.C.; home, Baltimore; Catholic U., B.A. 1985, U. of MD, J.D. 1988; Catholic; married (Katie); 4 children.

Elected Office: Baltimore City Cncl., 1992-99; Baltimore mayor, 1999-2006.

Professional Career: Field dir., pres. candidate Gary Hart, 1982-84, Sen. Barbara Mikulski, 1986-88; Baltimore asst. state's atty., 1988-90; Practicing atty., 1991-99.

Office: 100 State Circle, Annapolis, 21401, 410-974-3901; Fax: 410-974-3275; Web site: www.gov.state.md.us.

Election Results

2010 general	Martin O'Malley (D)	1,044,961	(56%)
	Robert Erhlich (R)	776,319	(42%)
2010 primary	Martin O'Malley (D)	414,595	(86%)
	J. P. Cusick (D)	46,411	(10%)

Prior Winning Percentages: 2006 (53%)

Martin O'Malley, a Democrat, was elected governor in 2006 and re-elected with surprising ease in 2010, fueling considerable speculation about his future political ambitions.

He was born in Washington, D.C., grew up in the Maryland suburbs, and was truly a child of politics. His parents met at the Democratic National Committee headquarters. His father was a trial lawyer active in Montgomery County politics; his mother worked as a receptionist for Democratic Sen. Barbara Mikulski. Young O'Malley attended Gonzaga College High School in Washington, a private Jesuit academy in the shadow of the Capitol that also produced such illustrious graduates as political commentator Pat Buchanan and former Secretary of Education William Bennett. O'Malley went on to get a degree from Catholic University of America and the University of Maryland law school. O'Malley worked as a field organizer for Colorado Sen. Gary Hart's 1984 and 1988 presidential campaigns, and in between worked for Mikulski's 1986 run for Senate, where he met his future wife, Katie, the daughter of Joseph Curran, the longest-serving attorney general in Maryland history.

After law school, O'Malley was a city prosecutor for two years, and then made his first bid for elected office, narrowly losing a state Senate race. In 1991, he won a seat on the Baltimore City Council. He spent eight years as a city councilman, during which time he became known for his energy, ambition, and penchant for headlines. In 1999, at the age of 36, he ran for mayor with a reform message and won the first of two terms as a white mayor in a majority-black city.

O'Malley was the kind of mayor who rides on snowplows and fire engines and seemed to be everywhere. He approached the job with a sense of urgency, calling for zero-tolerance policing and demanding accountability from city officials. Baltimore's high crime, drug use, and murder rates were a priority. He drew national acclaim for a reduction in crime, and he instituted a computerized system called CitiStat to track the performance of municipal government and to make agencies and department heads more efficient. During this time, O'Malley cultivated a national image, appearing on the cover of *Esquire* magazine in 2002 as the "best young mayor in America" and securing a prime speaking role at the 2004 Democratic National Convention. The character of Baltimore Mayor Tommy Carcetti on HBO's popular TV series "The Wire" was in part inspired by O'Malley.

O'Malley had ambitions beyond City Hall, and in 2002 he considered running for governor but decided not to. In 2003, when he sought re-election to a second term, both his Democratic opponents in Baltimore and the state Republican Party groused that he was using the mayor's office as a stepping-stone to the governorship. In September 2005, O'Malley, as expected, announced he would run against Bob Ehrlich, Maryland's first Republican governor since Spiro Agnew in the 1960s. Like O'Malley, Ehrlich had a sterling résumé in Maryland politics. He was raised in the Baltimore suburbs, served in the state House of Delegates, and was a U.S. House member before his 52%-48% victory over Democratic Lt. Gov. Kathleen Kennedy Townsend in 2002. Ehrlich had decent approval ratings, but he had a stormy relationship with the *Baltimore Sun* and clashed with the legislature frequently. He entered the 2006 campaign as one of the most vulnerable governors in the nation. O'Malley did not have a clear path to the Democratic nomination at first; Montgomery County Executive Doug Duncan also entered the race. But in June 2006, Duncan, trailing O'Malley in both fundraising and in the polls, bowed out, citing a recent diagnosis of depression.

In a state where registered Democrats outnumbered Republicans by 2-to-1 and where O'Malley led in the polls for virtually the entire campaign, Ehrlich nevertheless chose to run what he called a "non-campaign." He touted his record of tackling budget deficits and his initiatives to clean up the Chesapeake Bay, but otherwise insisted that the election was about governing, not promises. O'Malley offered a detailed agenda that called for, among other proposals, more funds for school construction, an affordable-housing trust fund, a $1 increase in the hourly minimum wage, and tax incentives for small businesses to join health insurance purchasing pools. The two candidates spent freely—together they spent more than $46 million—and did not pull punches. Ehrlich questioned O'Malley's record as mayor, pointing to Baltimore's high level of violent crime and troubled school system, while O'Malley referred to the governor as "$3 billion Bob," a reference to what his campaign said was the cumulative effect of the state property tax increase and various other fees during Ehrlich's tenure. O'Malley and state Democrats also sought to link Ehrlich to the unpopular Bush administration at every opportunity, referring to him as "the George Bush Mini-Me of Maryland."

O'Malley won 53%-46%. Ehrlich, the only incumbent Republican governor to lose in 2006, carried the Eastern Shore and Western Maryland, but O'Malley won by a landslide in Baltimore city (75%-23%) and in the populous Washington, D.C., suburban counties, Montgomery (62%-37%) and Prince George's (79%-21%).

His first legislative session was marked by a cordial relationship with Democratic legislative leaders who had harried Ehrlich at every turn. He signed a formal apology for Maryland's role in slavery, a freeze on in-state tuition at public universities, legislation to impose tighter automobile emission standards, and the nation's first statewide "living wage" law, requiring state contractors to pay employees more than the minimum wage. He also signed a law giving felons the right to vote as soon as they complete their prison terms. And Maryland became the first state to attempt to circumvent the Electoral College by agreeing to deliver its electoral votes to the winner of the national popular vote. It would not take effect until states that cumulatively hold 270 electoral votes, the number needed to win a presidential election, pass similar laws.

In October 2007, O'Malley called a special session of the legislature, against the advice of legislative leaders, to try to resolve a $1.7 billion budget shortfall by raising taxes and increasing revenue by legalizing slot-machine gambling. A tax increase was needed, he said, to preserve "the very quality of life we all care about." O'Malley also said, "I did not put myself or my family through the meat grinder of public service to preside over decline." He sought to raise the state's income tax rate of 4.75% to 6.5% for high earners, as well as increase taxes on corporate income, tobacco, and vehicle titles. Without the increases, he said, the state would have to lay off 10% of its workforce, close state parks, and freeze education spending. The Senate agreed to a top tax rate of 5.5%, but the legislature otherwise passed most of O'Malley's increases. It also authorized a November 2008 referendum on legalizing slot machines at racetracks. The issue had been heating up since neighboring Delaware legalized slots, and the Maryland horse-racing industry argued that slots were necessary to prevent their financial ruin. Ehrlich had supported slots, but was stymied by House of Delegates Speaker Michael Busch. O'Malley persuaded the legislature to authorize the referendum, and despite the vocal opposition of state Comptroller Peter Franchot, it was approved 59%-41% in November 2008, carrying every county.

Like many other governors, O'Malley was actively engaged in the energy issue as gas prices soared. He signed a bill mandating a 15% reduction in electricity usage by 2015, and he supported the building of a new nuclear power plant at Calvert Cliffs. Amid the housing foreclosure crisis in 2008, the legislature passed a bill extending the foreclosure timetable from 15 to 150 days and making mortgage fraud a crime. On a series of law-and-order measures, the legislature agreed to expand the state's DNA database to include samples from persons arrested as well as those convicted of crimes.

After the passage of his $1.4 billion tax increase, O'Malley's job approval ratings declined but then rebounded somewhat in 2008. The following year, the governor vowed to abolish capital punishment in Maryland, calling it "outdated, expensive and utterly ineffective." In the face of tough opposition, senators decided to shelve the repeal issue and instead limit the circumstances under which the death penalty would be applicable. The resulting law allowed it to be used only in cases with a videotaped confession, or DNA or videotape showing conclusive evidence of a murder. O'Malley also ran into objections from employers over his plans to crack down on Medicaid fraud and to re-regulate the state's electricity market. But in a harsh budget climate, he notched a few successes, including toughened laws with regard to guns and protective court orders. Federal economic stimulus money helped avert up to 700 layoffs and softened cuts to public education. The economy continued to constrain O'Malley in 2010. Nevertheless, that year he managed to get the Assembly to largely adopt his plan to close a $1.9 billion shortfall through a combination of spending cuts, borrowing, transfers and other one-time budget adjustments. He got other bills through as well, including a measure to require lifetime supervision of sexual predators.

During much of this time, Ehrlich, who had launched a radio talk show, barraged the airwaves with criticism of O'Malley. The two squared off in November 2010 for a rematch, this time with Ehrlich in the role of outsider aggressively challenging the incumbent on problems left unaddressed. Ehrlich campaigned on a pledge to roll back a 20% hike in the state sales tax and a small business bill of rights. O'Malley responded by calling Ehrlich a "failed" governor who did not have to cope with an economic recession. He touted his pro-business measures, such as a $5,000 tax credit for businesses hiring unemployed workers.

Polls gave O'Malley an early edge, and as much of the rest of the country turned its back on Democratic incumbents in 2010, Maryland voters bucked the tide. He won re-election 56%-42%, providing one of his party's few bright spots on Election Night. As expected, Ehrlich carried most rural counties, but O'Malley fought Ehrlich to a statistical tie in Baltimore County, which had helped carry the Republican to victory in 2002. The incumbent dominated the Washington, D.C., suburbs, taking Montgomery County by a 2-to-1 margin and nearly 9 out of every 10 votes in Prince George's County.

O'Malley entered 2011 in a strong political position. His job approval rating was at a record 58% in January, and he assumed the chairmanship of the Democratic Governors Association, a high-profile post that other former state chief executives have used to lay the groundwork for White House bids.

Senior Senator

Barbara Mikulski (D)

Elected 1986, term expires 2016, 5th term; b. July 20, 1936, Baltimore; home, Baltimore; Mt. St. Agnes Col., B.A. 1958, U. of MD, M.S.W. 1965; Catholic; single.

Elected Office: Baltimore City Cncl., 1971–76; U.S. House of Reps., 1976–86.

Professional Career: Social worker, Baltimore Dept. of Social Svcs., 1965–70; Chmn., DNC Delegate Selection Comm., 1972; Adjunct prof., Loyola Col., 1972–76.

DC Office: 503 HSOB, 20510, 202-224-4654; Fax: 202-224-8858; Web site: mikulski.senate.gov.

State Offices: Annapolis, 410-263-1805; Baltimore, 410-962-4510; Greenbelt, 301-345-5517; Hagerstown, 301-797-2826; Salisbury, 410-546-7711.

Committees: *Appropriations:* Commerce, Justice, Science & Related Agencies (Chmn); Defense; Department of State, Foreign Operations & Related Programs; Interior, Environment & Related Agencies; Labor, Health & Human Services, Education & Related Agencies; Transportation, HUD & Related Agencies. *Health, Education, Labor & Pensions:* Children & Families (Chmn); Primary Health & Aging. *Intelligence (Select).*

Group Ratings

	ACLU	ACU	ADA	CFG	AFS	FRC	LCV	ITIC	NTU	COC
2010	93	0	90	0	97	0	100	67	6	27
2009	–	0	95	3	100	–	100	–	5	43

National Journal Ratings

	2010 LIB — 2010 CONS		2009 LIB — 2009 CONS	
Economic	88%	— 0%	85%	— 14%
Social	65%	— 0%	85%	— 0%
Foreign	47%	— 0%	55%	— 0%
Composite	83%	— 17%	85%	— 15%

Key Votes of the 111th Congress

1. Overturn Ledbetter	Y	5. Pass health care bill	Y	9. Ratify New START	Y
2. Pass $787 billion stimulus	Y	6. Regulate financial firms	Y	10. Confirm Elena Kagan	Y
3. Repeal DC gun laws	N	7. Pass tax cuts for some	Y	11. Stop EPA climate regs	N
4. Confirm Sonia Sotomayor	Y	8. Legalize immigrants' kids	Y	12. Repeal don't ask, tell	Y

Election Results

2010 general	Barbara Mikulski (D)	1,140,531	(62%)	($5,508,300)
	Eric Wargotz (R)	655,666	(36%)	($932,526)
2010 primary	Barbara Mikulski (D)	396,252	(82%)	
	Christopher Garner (D)	36,194	(8%)	

Prior Winning Percentages: 2004 (65%); 1998 (71%); 1992 (71%); 1986 (61%); House: 1984 (68%); 1982 (74%); 1980 (76%); 1978 (100%); 1976 (75%)

Barbara Mikulski, Maryland's senior senator, was first elected to the House in 1976 and to the Senate in 1986. At the start of the 112th Congress in 2011, she surpassed Maine Republican Margaret Chase Smith to become the longest-serving woman in Senate history, and she is in line to become longest-serving woman in Congress in March 2012.

She has deep roots in immigrant, urban America and a fascination for the new technology and jobs growing in edge cities and beyond. She doesn't look or sound like a traditional politician—just shy of 5 feet and stocky, she has a gruff and unpolished manner. In *Washingtonian* magazine's survey of Capitol Hill staffers, she is frequently voted "meanest senator." But she is a savvy Senate insider; the same magazine named her one of its "Washingtonians of the Year" in 2010. Her roots are in East Baltimore, where her Polish immigrant grandparents ran a bakery, and her father had a grocery store. She attended the Institute of Notre Dame—the same high school that produced House Democratic leader Nancy Pelosi—graduated from Mount St. Agnes College and earned a social work degree at the University of Maryland. She got a job as a social worker, helping at-risk children and educating seniors about Medicare.

She entered politics by organizing a grassroots effort to stop a highway from going through the Highlandtown neighborhood where she grew up. She won, saving the now thriving Inner Harbor, and went on to win a seat on the Baltimore City Council in 1971. She ran for the Senate in 1974, and got a respectable 43% against Republican incumbent Charles Mathias. When Democratic Rep. Paul Sarbanes ran for the other Senate seat in 1976, Mikulski made a bid for his 3rd District House seat and won. Ten years later, when Mathias retired, she gave up her safe seat for what seemed like a chancy Senate race. She won handily, with 50% in the primary to 31% for Democratic Rep. Michael Barnes, and 14% for Gov. Harry Hughes. In the general election, she beat Republican Linda Chavez, a Reagan-era Civil Rights Commission official, 61%-39%. Mikulski still lives in Baltimore and commutes to Washington. Her Baltimore office is in Fells Point, the city's original port area. She has a sideline writing mystery novels. She coauthored *Capitol Offense* and *Capitol Venture,* stories featuring the character Eleanor "Norie" Gorzack, a freshman senator from Pennsylvania.

Mikulski was the first woman elected to the Senate whose husband or father did not serve in high office. She is fond of calling herself "a social worker...with power." In her early years, the only other woman in the Senate was Republican Nancy Kassebaum of Kansas. Every two years since 1992, Mikulski has held workshops for new women senators to help them quickly learn the ropes in what is still a male-dominated realm. Mikulski is one of just 17 women in the Senate, and she takes seriously her role as dean of the women. "When I came...we were a bit of a novelty in the Senate," she said. "I think what we see now is that we're not viewed as a novelty. We're not viewed as celebrities. We're viewed as senators." Mikulski's policy agenda includes many initiatives aimed at women, such as establishing mammography clinic standards and homemaker Individual Retirement Accounts. She got an amendment added to the health care overhaul in 2010 requiring mammograms and other preventative services for women with no copayment—a swipe at a Republican argument that restricting mammograms would be the first step in the Democrats' plan to ration health care. "For many insurance companies, simply being a woman is a pre-existing condition," she said during debate on the measure.

In her first term, Mikulski won a seat on the Appropriations Committee, and within two years, she was chairman of a subcommittee handling housing, space, and veterans' programs. Now she chairs the revamped Commerce, Justice, and Science Subcommittee, which also includes NASA. Mikulski has been one of the Senate's chief advocates of the space program and an enthusiast for space exploration. She has paid close attention to funding for the Goddard Space Center, the Wallops Flight Facility, and Johns Hopkins' Applied Science Lab in Maryland. In 2004, she and Texas Republican Kay Bailey Hutchison moved to add $800 million to NASA's appropriation to repair the space shuttle fleet and service the Hubble Space Telescope. In 2006, she won a big victory when the new NASA Administrator, Michael Griffin, announced that the agency could repair and upgrade Hubble safely and within budget. Since then, she has pressed NASA to move more quickly and cheaply in proceeding with the James Webb Space Telescope, Hubble's more powerful but over-budget successor.

Her other work on the commerce subcommittee has been directed at funding for Maryland highways, homeland security at the Port of Baltimore, cleanup of the Chesapeake Bay, and research on oyster-bed reseeding in the bay. As a member of the Select Intelligence Committee, she keeps a sharp eye out for the National Security Agency, the eavesdropping arm of the spy community headquartered at Fort Meade north of Washington. She also led the effort to get the Intelligence Advanced Research Projects program established at the University of Maryland in 2009. On another local issue, she fought to extend a visa program to permit more seasonal foreign workers to assist Maryland's seafood processors.

On domestic policy, Mikulski is a strong advocate of abortion rights and a solid liberal, although she sometimes votes for Republican initiatives, such as the bipartisan Welfare Reform Act of 1996. On the Health, Education, Labor, and Pensions Committee, she has taken a special interest in elder abuse and neglect and long-term care. She considers one of her proudest achievements the Spousal Anti-Impoverishment Act, a 1988 law helping seniors stay afloat financially while coping with the costs of nursing home care for spouses. She has also been a leader in opposing Republican efforts to contract out government work to private firms.

After voting for many years against higher fuel-efficiency standards—Maryland is home to auto assembly plants—Mikulski concluded in 2007, "It is time for a change." She supported the first major increase in fuel-efficiency standards in three decades. Two years later, she got a provision into the stimulus law making car sales and excise taxes deductible from federal income taxes. A national co-chair of Hillary Rodham Clinton's presidential campaign, she has been lukewarm toward President Obama. She disagreed with his administration's proposal to allow offshore oil drilling in Maryland and in May 2010 expressed dissatisfaction with the federal government's protection of its computer networks. "We don't know who the hell is in charge," she groused at a budget hearing.

Mikulski's toughest Senate election was her first, which she won against strong competition. Since then, she has not had a serious contest. In 2004, she faced Republican state Sen. E.J. Pipkin, a Dundalk native who made millions as a Wall Street bond trader and returned to live on Maryland's Eastern Shore. He put $1 million of his own money into the race and argued that Mikulski's voting record was too far to the left, and that she had not done enough to preserve the health of the Chesapeake Bay. Mikulski managed to outspend him 2-1 and won 65%-34%.

In 1995, Mikulski was mugged near her Fells Point townhouse, and subsequently moved to a more secure condominium building in Baltimore. In 2005, she was briefly hospitalized for an irregular heartbeat. Some Maryland Democrats speculated that she might retire in 2010, at age 74, setting off a wide-open Democratic primary similar to 2006 when Sarbanes retired. Former GOP Gov. Robert Ehrlich indicated that he was mulling a possible challenge. But he backed off, deciding instead to run against Gov. Martin O'Malley, and Mikulski easily won a fifth term with 62% of the vote.

Junior Senator

Ben Cardin (D)

Elected 2006, term expires 2012, 1st term; b. Oct. 5, 1943, Baltimore; home, Baltimore; U. of Pittsburgh, B.A. 1964, U. of MD, LL.B., J.D. 1967; Jewish; married (Myrna); 2 children (1 deceased).

Elected Office: MD House of Delegates, 1966–86, Speaker, 1979–86; U.S. House of Reps., 1986-2006.

Professional Career: Practicing atty., 1967–86; Ways & Means Committee, MD, 1974-79; Chmn., MD Legal Services Corp., 1988-95.

DC Office: 509 HSOB, 20510, 202-224-4524; Fax: 202-224-1651; Web site: cardin.senate.gov.

State Offices: Baltimore, 410-962-4436; Bowie, 301-860-0414; Cumberland, 301-777-2957; Salisbury, 410-546-4250.

Committees: *Budget. Environment & Public Works:* Clean Air & Nuclear Safety; Oversight; Transportation & Infrastructure; Water & Wildlife (Chmn). *Finance:* Health Care; Social Security, Pensions & Family Policy; Taxation & IRS Oversight. *Foreign Relations:* African Affairs; European Affairs; International Development & Foreign Assistance, Economic Affairs & International Environmental Protection (Chmn); Near Eastern & South & Central Asian Affairs. *Small Business & Entrepreneurship.*

Group Ratings

	ACLU	ACU	ADA	CFG	AFS	FRC	LCV	ITIC	NTU	COC
2010	93	0	90	0	100	0	100	67	5	27
2009	–	0	95	3	100	–	100	–	5	43

National Journal Ratings

	2010 LIB	—	2010 CONS		2009 LIB	—	2009 CONS
Economic	88%	—	0%		88%	—	0%
Social	65%	—	0%		85%	—	0%
Foreign	47%	—	0%		55%	—	0%
Composite	83%	—	17%		88%	—	12%

Key Votes of the 111th Congress

1. Overturn Ledbetter	Y	5. Pass health care bill	Y	9. Ratify New START	Y
2. Pass $787 billion stimulus	Y	6. Regulate financial firms	Y	10. Confirm Elena Kagan	Y
3. Repeal DC gun laws	N	7. Pass tax cuts for some	Y	11. Stop EPA climate regs	N
4. Confirm Sonia Sotomayor	Y	8. Legalize immigrants' kids	Y	12. Repeal don't ask, tell	Y

Election Results

2006 general	Ben Cardin (D)	965,477	(54%)	($8,739,737)
	Michael Steele (R)	787,182	(44%)	($8,430,196)
2006 primary	Ben Cardin (D)	257,545	(44%)	
	Kweisi Mfume (D)	283,957	(41%)	
	Josh Rales (D)	30,737	(5%)	

Prior Winning Percentages: House: 2004 (63%); 2002 (66%); 2000 (76%); 1998 (78%); 1996 (67%); 1994 (71%); 1992 (74%); 1990 (70%); 1988 (73%); 1986 (79%)

The junior senator from Maryland is Ben Cardin, a Democrat elected in 2006 who is one of the Senate's workhorses. An unabashed wonk with an agreeable personality, he evinces curiosity about a wide range of legislative topics.

Cardin is one of the many bright politicos who came from the Jewish neighborhoods of northwest Baltimore, the son and nephew of state legislators, a man who was elected to the state House at the age of 23—as soon as he was eligible to run. After serving four years as Ways and Means chairman in Annapolis, he became House speaker in 1979, at age 35. He had an interest in running for governor; but when Barbara Mikulski, now Maryland's senior senator, left her 3rd District House seat to run for the Senate in 1986, Cardin jumped into that race and was easily elected. In his second term in the House, Cardin got a seat on the Ways and Means Committee, where he was able to be a productive and creative legislator. He supported the 1993 North American Free Trade Agreement despite strong union opposition, backed a cap on medical-malpractice damages despite trial lawyers' opposition, and voted for normal trade relations with China after securing a rider designed to crack down on international dumping of subsidized steel in U.S. markets.

More than any other Democrat on the powerful tax-writing committee, he worked skillfully on bipartisan legislation at a time when few were sufficiently clever or independent enough to pursue such initiatives. *The Baltimore Sun* called him a "master of bipartisan lawmaking." Along with then-Rep. Rob Portman, R-Ohio, Cardin co-sponsored the 1998 Internal Revenue Service reform law and the 2000 bipartisan legislation to expand 401(k) savings and other retirement plans. In 2001, when Congress enacted the Bush tax cut, it included Cardin's provision to increase the limits for maximum IRA and 401(k) contributions.

Maryland Senate seats don't come open very often, so when one did, Cardin and 17 other Democrats filed to run. An experienced campaigner and fundraiser, Cardin began as the front-runner even though his earnest, somewhat bland demeanor raised questions about his viability as a statewide candidate. His toughest primary opponents were former Democratic Rep. Kweisi Mfume, who resigned his House seat in 1996 to chair the NAACP, and millionaire businessman Joshua Rales. Mfume and Cardin were friends—they were both elected to Congress in 1986—but Mfume and other black leaders warned that the state Democratic establishment's support for Cardin could breed resentment among African-American voters. The primary was expensive: Cardin, Rales, and Mfume together spent more than $12 million. Cardin outspent Mfume by nearly 4-to-1, but Mfume had a compelling life story and loads of charisma, especially compared with the low-key Cardin. Rales spent heavily from his own pocket but barely registered in the polls. Cardin won 44%-41%, carrying all but two counties and Baltimore City. The win was powered in part by Cardin's nearly 2-1 advantage over Mfume in suburban Washington's Montgomery County, the state's most populous county.

The Republican nominee was Lt. Gov. Michael Steele, the first African-American statewide officeholder in Maryland and a candidate exceptionally well-positioned to exploit Cardin's weaknesses. Steele combined his talent for retail politicking with quirky, unconventional ads designed to highlight his outsider status. Democrats, including Mfume, coalesced around Cardin and portrayed Steele as an inexperienced lightweight. Republicans criticized Cardin as a career pol who was closely tied to big-money special-interest groups. Without a legislative record, Steele made for an elusive target, so Cardin sought to link him to President Bush and criticized Steele for his support for the Iraq war. Cardin won 54%-44%, in what was a tough year for Maryland Republicans. Steele won 18 of 23 counties, carrying the Eastern Shore and Western Maryland, but Cardin carried all of the key suburban counties: 52%-47% in Baltimore County (which doesn't include the city); 54%-45% in Howard; 67%-32% in Montgomery. African-Americans voted overwhelmingly for Cardin. Two years later, in early 2009, Steele became the first African-American chairman of the Republican National Committee, where he became known for several well-publicized gaffes until his ouster in 2011.

A rock-solid Democrat, Cardin was tied for most-liberal senator in *National Journal's* 2010 vote rankings. In 2008, he unsuccessfully called for ending the use of a secret court—which gave President Bush broader surveillance powers in cases involving suspected terrorists—by sponsoring legislation that would allow the Foreign Intelligence Surveillance Act to "sunset" in four years instead of six. Many in Congress believed that the secret surveillance constituted a threat to civil liberties. Based on his recent campaign experience, Cardin sought to make it a crime for candidates to use misleading tactics against opponents. His priorities included incentives for teachers at poorly performing schools, and Chesapeake Bay cleanup, a tried-and-true issue for Maryland lawmakers. During the final weeks of the 2008 presidential campaign, Cardin made numerous appearances for Barack Obama in Jewish neighborhoods in battleground states, where he had strong credibility as a Jewish U.S. senator with a solid record of support for Israel.

With a seat on the influential Finance Committee, Cardin was at the center of the big legislative battles shaping up in the 112th Congress (2011-12). He introduced a bill with Chairman Max Baucus in January 2011 to repeal the so-called "1099" provision to the health care law, which called for businesses to submit forms to the Internal Revenue Service for all purchases above $600, a requirement that many agree was overly burdensome for small businesses. During the 111th Congress (2009-10), Cardin was able to get a guaranteed dental benefit included in the expansion of the State Children's Health Insurance Program. He included an $8,000 tax credit for first-time homebuyers in the massive economic stimulus law of 2009.

Cardin had less success in getting a Chesapeake Bay cleanup bill passed that would expand the Environmental Protection Agency's authority over fertilizer and animal-waste runoff. He also struck out in going to bat for the beleaguered newspaper industry, introducing a measure in 2009 that would treat newspapers as 501(c)(3) nonprofits that could accept charitable contributions. Industry officials expressed fears about the measure leading to government control of the news. He has worked on expanding mass transit in the Washington-Baltimore region, especially as Maryland stood to gain an influx of employees at several military facilities in 2011 as a result of the 2005 BRAC base-closure process.

Cardin's prodigious appetite for work extends to foreign policy. He co-chairs the U.S. arm of the Commission on Security and Cooperation in Europe, known as the Helsinki Commission, which monitors human rights issues. Cardin in April 2010 urged the State Department to block visas for 60 Russians who reportedly were linked to the death in jail of a lawyer for what was once the country's top equity fund. He later introduced a bill to impose financial sanctions as well as visa bans on the officials. "My name is well-known in Russia, some places better than in Maryland," he said.

With Maryland an overwhelmingly Democratic state, Cardin is likely to face little trouble getting re-elected in 2012. A Public Policy Polling survey in late 2010 showed that his disapproval rating was just 28%, lower than any other incumbent senator.

FIRST DISTRICT

Andy Harris (R)

Elected 2010, 1st full term; b. Jan. 25, 1957, Brooklyn, NY; home, Cockeysville; Johns Hopkins U., B.S. 1977; M.D. 1980; M.H.S. 1995.; Catholic; Married (Sylvia); 5 children.

Military Career:　Naval Reserve, 1988-94.

Elected Office:　MD Senate, 1998-2010.

Professional Career:　Anesthesiologist, Johns Hopkins Hospital, 1980-2010; assoc. prof., Johns Hopkins Medical Schl., 1984-2010.

DC Office:　506 CHOB, 20515, 202-225-5311; Fax: 202-225-0254; Web site: harris.house.gov.

State Offices:　Bel Air, 410-588-5670; Kent Island, 410-643-5425; Salisbury, 443-944-8624.

Committees:　*Natural Resources:* Fisheries, Wildlife, Oceans & Insular Affairs. *Science, Space & Technology:* Energy & Environment (Chmn); Research & Science Education. *Transportation & Infrastructure:* Coast Guard & Maritime Transportation; Highways & Transit; Water Resources & Environment.

Election Results

2010 general	Andy Harris (R)	155,118	(54%)	($2,359,142)
	Frank Kratovil (D)	120,400	(42%)	($2,642,384)
	Richard Davis (Lib)	10,876	(4%)	
2010 primary	Andy Harris (R)	46,227	(67%)	
	Rob Fisher (R)	22,409	(33%)	

Population		Race/Ethnicity		Work	
Pop. 2010:	744,275	White:	81.0%	Private:	74.9%
Change since 2000:	Up 12.4%	Black:	11.4%	Government:	18.8%
Urban:	64.2%	Hispanic:	3.5%	Self-employed:	6.1%
Rural:	35.8%	Asian:	2.1%	Blue collar:	19.6%
Area size:	3,701 sq. mi.	Native Am.:	0.2%	White collar:	64.3%
		Hawaiian:	0.0%	Khaki collar:	0.2%
Age		Two+ races:	1.6%	Other:	15.9%
Median age:	40.9 yrs.				
More than 65 yrs:	14.7%	*Ancestry*		Median income:	$68,776
Less than 18 yrs:	23.2%	German	17.8%	Median Home Value:	$315,800
		Irish	14.6%		
Education		English	11.3%	**Military Veterans**	
H.S. grad:	88.9%			% of Pop:	12.3%
College grad:	30.6%				
Grad degree:	12.4%				

Eastern Shore

Chesapeake Bay is technically not a bay but an estuary. It was the central focus of the most thickly settled of the 13 colonies and today remains a central focus for much of modern Maryland. The first British here were amazed at the Chesapeake's oysters and terrapin turtles and crabs and rockfish. This was an estuary civilization in colonial days, with every little hamlet tied together by the highways of bays and creeks and inlets off the Chesapeake. The streets and docks

2008 Presidential Vote
John McCain (R) 216,896   (59%)
Barack Obama (D) 148,029   (40%)

2004 Presidential Vote
George Bush (R) 213,144   (63%)
John Kerry (D) 124,163   (36%)

Cook Partisan Voting Index: R+13

of Chestertown, Oxford, St. Michaels and Cambridge still look something like they did when George Washington slept there.

In post-colonial times, when most Americans were caught up in the romance of westward movement, these estuaries and peninsulas were mostly forgotten, located too far off the main lines of railroads and highways. In the 160 years between 1790 and 1950, the Eastern Shore counties of Maryland only doubled in population. Over the past half-century, much of the Chesapeake has changed beyond recognition, as the Eastern Shore has grown vigorously, with second-home buyers, retirees and commuters crossing the Chesapeake Bay Bridge. Now, this is a land of genteel estates fronting the water and of Frank Perdue's thriving chicken empire around Salisbury, of Easton's Waterfowl Festival and St. Michaels's Oysterfest, and of the swarms of motorboats and sailing ships making their way up and down the inlets or under the twin spans of the Bay Bridge. This growth has forced people along the Bay to confront issues that once would have been unimaginable here, such as high-rise condominiums obscuring the sunrise in an old fishing village like Crisfield.

But more threatening is pollution. Agricultural and suburban runoff have vastly depleted marine populations, and only a few watermen still make their living bringing crabs and oysters to shore. Since 1990, the blue crab harvest has dropped by two-thirds. Various attempts at cleanup by governmental agencies over the years have been helpful but not entirely successful. In early 2009, the Chesapeake Bay Foundation filed a lawsuit seeking to force the Environmental Protection Agency to enforce limits on pollution entering the bay. The EPA had committed to getting the bay off the nation's list of dirtiest bodies of water by 2010, but had conceded it will miss that deadline.

The 1st Congressional District of Maryland includes all nine counties of the Eastern Shore. It extends across the bay and grabs parts of Harford, Baltimore and Anne Arundel counties for their Republican strongholds. The Baltimore and Harford county suburbs north of Baltimore are as solidly Republican as any part of Maryland. Although it is hard to avoid thinking of this district as the Eastern Shore district, nearly half the votes are cast on the west side of the bay. This was one of only two districts in the state that twice voted for Republican George W. Bush—and comfortably. In 2008, it was one of two Maryland districts that voted for Republican presidential nominee John McCain, giving him 59%-40% over Democrat Barack Obama.

Andy Harris (R)

The new congressman from Maryland's 1st District is Andy Harris, a Republican who defeated freshman Democrat Frank Kratovil in 2010. Harris, a Johns Hopkins University anesthesiologist and professor, was born in Brooklyn, N.Y., to immigrants from Eastern Europe. His father, a Hungarian anti-communist activist, had been jailed in a Siberian gulag for a year and a half for his political views before meeting Harris's mother, who had fled Ukraine, at a displaced persons camp in Austria. Harris credits his parents' escape from communism and the spirited dinner-table conversations they encouraged among their four sons with fostering his fiercely held beliefs in the ills of big government and the sanctity of the private sector. After Harris completed his medical studies at Johns Hopkins, he began to practice and teach there. He and his wife, Sylvia, have five children and live in a suburb north of Baltimore.

Harris was elected to the state Senate to represent Baltimore County in 1998. In Annapolis, he was one of the most conservative members, and he served as the chamber's minority whip from 2003 to 2007. He picked up a reputation for his artful filibusters—during a fight against a stem cell research bill, he read from a biology textbook on DNA.

In 2008, Harris challenged 1st District Rep. Wayne Gilchrest, a moderate Republican, in a bloody GOP primary battle. When Harris defeated him, Gilchrest refused to concede the race to Harris and then endorsed Kratovil, the Democratic candidate, for the seat. In the general election campaign, Kratovil continued Gilchrest's primary strategy of portraying Harris as too far right for the district and he edged Harris out by fewer than 3,000 votes. Harris did not concede until a week later.

In 2010, Harris came back for a rematch. He cast Kratovil as a puppet for President Obama in a year when anti-incumbent anger was on the rise and voters were deeply divided over the president's overhaul of the health insurance system. Running on vows not to raise taxes and to repeal the health care overhaul, Harris connected with angry Republicans in a district that gave Sen. John McCain, R-Ariz., nearly 60% of the vote in the 2008 presidential race. In September, Harris also secured the endorsement of 2012 GOP presidential hopeful and former Massachusetts Gov. Mitt Romney.

Harris, one of 18 physicians running for a House seat that year, received more campaign contributions from medical professionals, including fellow anesthesiologists, than any other contender, according to the Center for Responsive Politics. Kratovil, meanwhile, secured donations from nurse anesthetists, who have been engaged in a long-running turf war with anesthesiologists. Ultimately, both candidates were hearty fundraisers. Harris raised $2.4 million while Kratovil brought in about $2.6 million. Since he first ran in 2008, Harris also had started to practice medicine a few days a week on the Eastern Shore, a decision some political analysts attributed to an effort to deflect criticism he received in 2008 for running in an area where he had spent little time.

Kratovil also attacked Harris for his support of a conservative proposal to replace the income tax with a national sales tax of 23% on goods and services. At the same time, Kratovil highlighted his differences with Obama over extending the Bush-era tax cuts, saying he favored an across-the-board extension while the president had said he would let them expire for the wealthiest 2 percent of Americans. But after just one term in office, Kratovil got swept away by 2010's Republican tide, losing to Harris, 54% to 42%.

Harris made national news soon after the election, but probably not in the way he preferred. At an orientation session for incoming lawmakers, Harris complained that his government-subsidized health plan would take a whole month to kick in, remarks that were widely circulated and paired with his staunch opposition to a government-run health care plan for low-income people priced out of the private insurance market.

SECOND DISTRICT

Dutch Ruppersberger (D)

Elected 2002, 5th term; b. Jan. 31, 1946, Baltimore; home, Cockeysville; U. of MD, 1963-67, U of Baltimore, J.D. 1970; Methodist; married (Kay); 2 children.

Elected Office: Baltimore Cnty. Cncl. 1986-94; Baltimore Cnty. exec., 1994-2002.

Professional Career: Prosecutor, Baltimore Cnty. State's Atty. Office, 1970-75.

DC Office: 2453 RHOB, 20515, 202-225-3061; Fax: 202-225-3094; Web site: dutch.house.gov.

State Offices: Timonium, 410-628-2701.

Committees: *Armed Services:* Emerging Threats & Capabilities; Strategic Forces. *Permanent Select Committee on Intelligence* (RMM).

Group Ratings

	ACLU	ACU	ADA	CFG	AFS	FRC	LCV	ITIC	NTU	COC
2010	86	0	80	5	100	0	80	100	6	25
2009	–	4	90	8	100	–	86	–	5	40

National Journal Ratings

	2010 LIB	—	2010 CONS	2009 LIB	—	2009 CONS
Economic	65%	—	34%	67%	—	32%
Social	61%	—	35%	63%	—	36%
Foreign	56%	—	38%	69%	—	31%
Composite	63%	—	38%	67%	—	33%

Key Votes of the 111th Congress

1. Overturn Ledbetter	Y	5. Bar federal abortion funds	N	9. Stop detainee transfers	Y
2. Pass $820 billion stimulus	Y	6. Pass health care bill	Y	10. Legalize immigrants' kids	Y
3. Let guns in national parks	N	7. Regulate financial firms	Y	11. Repeal don't ask, tell	Y
4. Pass cap-and-trade	Y	8. Pass tax cuts for some	Y	12. Limit campaign funds	Y

Election Results

2010 general	Dutch Ruppersberger (D)	134,133	(64%)	($1,137,058)
	Marcelo Cardarelli (R)	69,523	(33%)	($219,333)
	Lorenzo Gaztanaga (Lib)	5,090	(2%)	
2010 primary	Dutch Ruppersberger (D)	42,262	(74%)	
	Raymond Atkins (D)	7,405	(13%)	
	Jeff Morris (D)	3,841	(7%)	
	Christopher Boardman (D)	3,575	(6%)	

Prior Winning Percentages: 2008 (72%), 2006 (69%), 2004 (67%), 2002 (54%)

Population		Race/Ethnicity		Work	
Pop. 2010:	700,893	White:	55.2%	Private:	75.5%
Change since 2000:	Up 5.9%	Black:	33.1%	Government:	20.7%
Urban:	98.3%	Hispanic:	5.0%	Self-employed:	3.7%
Rural:	1.7%	Asian:	3.7%	Blue collar:	19.4%
Area size:	359 sq. mi.	Native Am.:	0.3%	White collar:	63.0%
		Hawaiian:	0.1%	Khaki collar:	0.9%
Age		Two+ races:	2.4%	Other:	16.7%
Median age:	35.8 yrs.				
More than 65 yrs:	11.8%	*Ancestry*		Median income:	$56,911
Less than 18 yrs:	23.9%	German	16.4%	Median Home Value:	$243,000
		Irish	11.4%		
Education		English	6.0%	**Military Veterans**	
H.S. grad:	85.9%			% of Pop:	11.6%
College grad:	24.3%				
Grad degree:	8.9%				

Part Baltimore, Suburbs

The spokes of Baltimore's avenues spread out in all directions from the downtown district on the Inner Harbor, connecting the central city with the suburbs, where most residents of metropolitan Baltimore now live. The streets reach east to Dundalk and Essex, industrial suburbs where the tone of life was set for years by the giant Sparrows Point steel mill, long the biggest in the country. Northeastward, they extend to Havre de Grace and the oldest lighthouse in continuous

2008 Presidential Vote		
Barack Obama (D) 176,198	(60%)
John McCain (R) 111,909	(38%)
2004 Presidential Vote		
John Kerry (D) 144,090	(54%)
George Bush (R) 118,429	(45%)
Cook Partisan Voting Index: D+7		

use on the East Coast, as well as modest working-class suburbs in Harford County. The Aberdeen Proving Ground has generated both military and civilian job growth, but the locale is now better known for its Ripken Stadium, home of the Aberdeen IronBirds, a Class A baseball team owned by hometown hero Cal Ripken, the baseball legend who played 2,632 consecutive games for the Baltimore Orioles. In an arc north of downtown are middle-income towns from Randallstown to White Marsh. A couple of miles northwest of the county seat of Towson is Timonium, the site of the annual Maryland State Fair.

The 2nd Congressional District of Maryland is an irregularly shaped hodgepodge that includes much of this territory. Most of the district is not far from the Chesapeake Bay, running south from Havre de Grace past the Aberdeen Proving Ground and the bustling Port of Baltimore. To the south is the busy Baltimore/Washington International Airport, a major hub for low-cost airlines. Close by is Fort Meade, the large Army post that houses the National Security Agency and stands to gain more than 20,000 jobs from the realignment of military bases in recent years. The growth includes the Defense Information Systems Agency, Defense Media Activity and Defense Adjudication Activity. Fort Meade also was named the center of U.S. cyber defense operations in 2010.

The district angles inland to include some Baltimore County suburbs, residential neighborhoods in northeast Baltimore, and an industrial pocket in far southeast Baltimore. At that point, the district crosses the Harbor Tunnel to capture the row houses of Brooklyn and Curtis Bay, whose residents are mainly descendants of German and East European immigrants who moved there to work on the docks and in the factories along the Patapsco River and the harbor. About 60% of the district's population is in Baltimore County, with the remainder divided roughly equally among Anne Arundel and Harford counties and Baltimore city. The inclusion of Baltimore neighborhoods helped raise the percentage of African-Americans in the district from 8% to 27% and it had grown to 33% by 2008.

Dutch Ruppersberger (D)

The congressman from the 2nd District is Dutch Ruppersberger, a Democrat elected in 2002 in a district drawn specifically for him. Ruppersberger grew up in Baltimore, attended the University of Maryland, and graduated from the University of Baltimore Law School. Working as a Baltimore County assistant state's attorney, Ruppersberger had a near-fatal car accident in 1975 while investigating a drug-trafficking case. When he asked his doctors at the University of Maryland's Shock Trauma Center how he could thank them, he said, they urged him to run for office so he could fund their facility. In 1986, he won a seat on the Baltimore County Council and made good on his promise to help the hospital. In 1994, he was elected Baltimore County executive, a position once held by Republican Vice President Spiro Agnew.

Barred from seeking a third term in 2002, Ruppersberger seriously considered running for governor. But he was dissuaded by state party leaders who felt he was too politically vulnerable at the time. In 2000, he had backed a plan to give him the power of eminent domain to redevelop large pieces of the county, but in a resounding rebuke, voters rejected it 2-to-1 in a referendum. Compounding the situation for Ruppersberger was a damaging story in *The Baltimore Sun* saying that he had given county work to a firm to which he had financial ties. Kathleen Kennedy Townsend, the daughter of the late Robert F. Kennedy, became the gubernatorial candidate, while Ruppersberger got a favorable district for a House run when Democrats redrew the congressional map.

However, he was still weakened politically and faced a primary fight. His little-known opponent, investment banker Osman Bengur, spent more than $500,000 of his own money. But the state's Democratic establishment lined up behind Ruppersberger, and he won 50%-36%. The fall campaign was not much easier. The open seat attracted former Republican Rep. Helen Delich Bentley, who held the 2nd District seat for a decade until she ran, unsuccessfully, for governor in 1994. With a strong record of constituent service and cross-party popularity, she had a chance to overcome the new district's Democratic leanings. Both candidates supported additional dredging of shipping channels in the Chesapeake Bay plus increased port security. Ruppersberger won, 54%-46%. His popular-vote margin was more than 13,000 in the small part of the district in Baltimore city, which he carried 79%-21%, and only 3,000 in the rest of the district.

In the House, Ruppersberger has had the least liberal voting record among Democrats from Maryland. With the help of Baltimore native and House Speaker Nancy Pelosi, he became the first freshman appointed to the Intelligence Committee, where he called for expanded oversight of the intelligence agencies and for shifting resources from the Iraq war to terrorist "safe havens" in Afghanistan. Pelosi in January 2011 named him the panel's ranking Democrat over several other lawmakers, including her close friend Anna Eshoo of California.

Ruppersberger has not hesitated to criticize the Obama administration—he said in April 2009 that he had not been adequately consulted on its ambitious plan to buy and launch spy satellites, and worked to add language to the fiscal 2010 intelligence authorization bill to ensure better oversight of satellite programs. In early 2010, he threw his support behind a House-passed bill to strengthen cyber security, an area he said had been neglected under Obama. He is a frequent participant at events held by "the Cockroaches," a group of several hundred current and former intelligence officials, contractors and others in the spy world that meets for periodic off-the-record dinners.

In other areas, Ruppersberger initiated Operation Hero Miles to facilitate the use of frequent-flyer miles to assist U.S. troops in Iraq traveling home on civilian airlines during the Christmas season, and made the program permanent by including it in the Defense Department spending bill. Concerned about the potential sale of shipping operations at the Port of Baltimore to the United Arab Emirates, he helped to enact port-security legislation.

Ruppersberger has been re-elected easily. His earlier statewide ambitions have dimmed with the election of other Baltimore-area Democrats to vacant seats for governor and the Senate.

THIRD DISTRICT

John Sarbanes (D)

Elected 2006, 3rd term; b. May 22, 1962, Baltimore; home, Towson; Princeton, B.A. 1984, Harvard, J.D. 1988; Greek Orthodox; married (Dina); 3 children.

Professional Career: Clerk, Judge Fred Motz, 1988; Practicing atty., 1988-2006; Asst., MD Schls. Superintendent, 1998-2006.

DC Office: 2444 RHOB, 20515, 202-225-4016; Fax: 202-225-9219; Web site: sarbanes.house.gov.

State Offices: Annapolis, 410-295-1679; Towson, 410-832-8890.

Committees: *Natural Resources:* Energy & Mineral Resources; National Parks, Forests & Public Lands. *Science, Space & Technology:* Research & Science Education; Technology & Innovation.

Group Ratings

	ACLU	ACU	ADA	CFG	AFS	FRC	LCV	ITIC	NTU	COC
2010	94	0	95	0	100	0	100	100	4	25
2009	–	0	100	0	100	–	100	–	2	33

National Journal Ratings

	2010 LIB	—	2010 CONS	2009 LIB	—	2009 CONS
Economic	87%	—	12%	88%	—	9%
Social	88%	—	11%	84%	—	11%
Foreign	78%	—	17%	91%	—	0%
Composite	86%	—	15%	91%	—	10%

Key Votes of the 111th Congress

1. Overturn Ledbetter	Y	5. Bar federal abortion funds	N	9. Stop detainee transfers	N
2. Pass $820 billion stimulus	Y	6. Pass health care bill	Y	10. Legalize immigrants' kids	Y
3. Let guns in national parks	N	7. Regulate financial firms	Y	11. Repeal don't ask, tell	Y
4. Pass cap-and-trade	Y	8. Pass tax cuts for some	Y	12. Limit campaign funds	Y

Election Results

2010 general	John Sarbanes (D) 147,448	(61%)	($908,856)
	Jim Wilhelm (R)..86,947	(36%)	($45,015)
	Jerry McKinley (Lib) 5,212	(2%)	
2010 primary	John Sarbanes (D) 54,710	(83%)	
	Michael Miller (D)..5,456	(8%)	

Prior Winning Percentages: 2008 (70%), 2006 (64%)

Population		Race/Ethnicity		Work	
Pop. 2010:	719,856	White:	65.2%	Private:	75.1%
Change since 2000:	Up 8.7%	Black:	20.0%	Government:	20.3%
Urban:	98.6%	Hispanic:	6.8%	Self-employed:	4.5%
Rural:	1.4%	Asian:	5.2%	Blue collar:	13.7%
Area size:	293 sq. mi.	Native Am.:	0.2%	White collar:	71.8%
		Hawaiian:	0.1%	Khaki collar:	0.6%
Age		Two+ races:	2.3%	Other:	14.0%
Median age:	36.7 yrs.				
More than 65 yrs:	12.2%	*Ancestry*		Median income:	$71,247
Less than 18 yrs:	21.8%	German	15.0%	Median Home Value:	$317,500
		Irish	11.8%		
Education		English	7.5%	**Military Veterans**	
H.S. grad:	88.4%			% of Pop:	10.6%
College grad:	42.6%				
Grad degree:	19.2%				

Part Baltimore, Part Annapolis

Baltimore, one of America's major cities since the Revolution, has been transformed into one of America's star cities. Its Inner Harbor redevelopment, with a spectacular, multilevel aquarium on the water, and its ballpark at Camden Yards are national models. The local cuisine—crab cakes and steamed crabs spiced in a certain way—are known well beyond the watershed of the Chesapeake Bay. In 2009, *Forbes* named it America's eighth most livable city, and that

2008 Presidential Vote

Barack Obama (D) 194,575	(59%)
John McCain (R) 128,342	(39%)

2004 Presidential Vote

John Kerry (D) 163,088	(54%)
George Bush (R) 136,672	(45%)

Cook Partisan Voting Index: D+6

same year, about half of the city became one of 49 National Heritage Areas, a designation expected to help boost tourism and economic development. The central city of Baltimore has had terrible urban problems—high crime, abandoned neighborhoods, poor schools—but the greater Baltimore area that has grown far beyond the city and county lines fares better and retains a distinctive character. To the south, Annapolis was laid out as a capital in 1694, with one circle planned for the Statehouse and one for the Church. The marble-halled Statehouse, built in 1772, is where the Continental Congress ratified the Treaty of Paris and is the oldest state capitol in continuous use. Annapolis is also the home of the U.S. Naval Academy, and the city's gentrified waterfront is both a waterman's and yachter's port.

The 3rd Congressional District of Maryland consists of three oddly disjointed pieces of geography that extend from the locus of the Inner Harbor area. Its boundaries were designed by Democrats with politics in mind: The 3rd borders the majority-black 7th District on three sides. One spoke extends northeast from black city neighborhoods into mostly white suburbs. Another extends north and west from the city to the Baltimore County seat of Towson and the heavily Jewish suburbs of Pikesville and Owings Mills, past the array of temples and synagogues on Park Heights Avenue in Baltimore city. The largest bloc of voters is in the crooked spoke that extends southwest, past the old row house neighborhoods overlooking Fort McHenry and out past blue-collar Arbutus into Linthicum in Anne Arundel County and continuing to Annapolis. Just over one-third of the district population resides in Anne Arundel, including all of Annapolis; a quarter resides within Baltimore city, in such neighborhoods as Roland Park, and among the restaurants and bars of Little Italy and Fell's Point. Another small slice of the 3rd consists of parts of Elkridge and Columbia in Howard County. Redistricting left the new 3rd District less Democratic than it had been; Bush's percentage of the vote increased from 34% in 2000 to 45% in 2004. But the district remains safely Democratic.

John Sarbanes (D)

The congressman from the 3rd District is Democrat John Sarbanes, the son of the former longtime senator from Maryland. Sarbanes graduated from Princeton University and Harvard Law School, following the academic route taken by his dad, Democrat Paul Sarbanes, who retired in 2006 after more than 35 years in Congress. The younger Sarbanes returned to Baltimore to clerk for a federal District Court judge, and then joined the Venable law firm, where he chaired the health care practice and represented nonprofit hospitals and senior-living providers. He also spent seven years as special assistant to the Maryland superintendent of schools, serving as the liaison to the Baltimore schools.

Though his 2006 campaign was his first bid for public office, Sarbanes enjoyed a considerable advantage because of his name recognition. But the primary race was no cakewalk. Openings in the Maryland congressional delegation are rare, so when Democratic Rep. Ben Cardin announced he was giving up his seat to run for the Senate, eight candidates filed for the September primary. Contenders included veteran state Sen. Paula Hollinger and former Baltimore Health Commissioner Peter Beilenson, the son of former Democratic Rep. Anthony Beilenson of California. Sarbanes issued lengthy, detailed proposals on health care and education, which he called his top two legislative priorities. Beilenson emphasized his experience managing a large government budget. Hollinger was endorsed by the teachers association, and had been an active state lawmaker. Sarbanes, who had a small fundraising advantage, won the Democratic primary with 32% to 25% for runner-up Beilenson and 21% for Hollinger. Sarbanes acknowledged that he benefited from his name identification. He ran strongest in Anne Arundel County, which cast the most votes, trouncing Beilenson 40%-18%. In the general election, Republican nominee John White, the founder and CEO of a marketing company, spent nearly a half-million dollars, most of it from his own pocket, but got little attention and lost the general election to Sarbanes, 64%-34%.

In the House, Sarbanes has a solidly liberal voting record, though it's a bit to the center on economic issues. He became an advocate of cleaning up pollution in the Chesapeake Bay as a member of the Natural Resources Committee. With the thousands of federal workers in his district in mind, Sarbanes worked on a House-passed bill to allow qualified federal employees to telecommute at least 20% of their work hours. The bill failed to get the two-thirds majority needed for passage in May 2010, and many Republicans complained about its $30 million cost. From his seat on the Education and Labor Committee, Sarbanes won approval of amendments to bolster instruction in the schools on protecting the environment and to give local school officials more specific guidelines on the objectives of the Bush-era No Child Left Behind education law. He also got a bill signed into law enabling college graduates to erase student loan debts after 10 years of work in public service or the non-profit sector.

Sarbanes was re-elected easily in 2008 and 2010. In the 111th Congress (2009-10), he got the seat he wanted on the Energy and Commerce Committee, giving up posts on Education and Labor and the Oversight and Government Reform Committee. In 2010, he got a provision in an auto safety bill to fund research into new technologies to prevent drunk-driving accidents. Mothers Against Drunk Driving strongly backed the idea, but the American Beverage Institute and some Republicans complained it went too far. After the GOP takeover of the House in 2011, Sarbanes was forced off Energy and Commerce and went to the Science, Space and Technology Committee.

FOURTH DISTRICT

Donna Edwards (D)

Elected June 2008, 2nd full term; b. June 28, 1958, Yanceyville, NC; home, Fort Washington; Wake Forest U., B.A., 1980, Franklin Pierce Law Center, J.D., 1989; Baptist; Divorced; 1 child.

Professional Career: Lockheed Engineering, 1982-86; Lobbyist, Public Citizen and Congress Watch, 1992-94; Executive director, Center for a New Democracy, 1994-96; Co-founder and executive director, National Network to End Domestic Violence, 1996-99; Executive director, The Arca Foundation, 2000-present.

DC Office: 318 CHOB, 20515, 202-225-8699; Fax: 202-225-8714; Web site: donnaedwards.house.gov.

State Offices: Silver Spring, 301-562-7960; Suitland , 301-516-7601.

Committees: *Ethics. Science, Space & Technology:* Investigations & Oversight (RMM); Space & Aeronautics. *Transportation & Infrastructure:* Economic Development, Public Buildings & Emergency Management; Highways & Transit; Water Resources & Environment.

Group Ratings

	ACLU	ACU	ADA	CFG	AFS	FRC	LCV	ITIC	NTU	COC
2010	100	5	95	3	100	6	90	67	7	25
2009	–	0	100	0	100	–	100	–	3	33

National Journal Ratings

	2010 LIB	—	2010 CONS		2009 LIB	—	2009 CONS
Economic	78%	—	20%		91%	—	0%
Social	77%	—	21%		89%	—	0%
Foreign	97%	—	0%		78%	—	17%
Composite	85%	—	15%		90%	—	10%

Key Votes of the 111th Congress

1. Overturn Ledbetter	Y	5. Bar federal abortion funds	N	9. Stop detainee transfers	N
2. Pass $820 billion stimulus	Y	6. Pass health care bill	Y	10. Legalize immigrants' kids	Y
3. Let guns in national parks	N	7. Regulate financial firms	Y	11. Repeal don't ask, tell	Y
4. Pass cap-and-trade	Y	8. Pass tax cuts for some	Y	12. Limit campaign funds	N

Election Results

2010 general	Donna Edwards (D)	160,228	(83%)	($672,650)
	Robert Broadus (R)	31,467	(16%)	($8,861)
2010 primary	Donna Edwards (D)	56,737	(84%)	
	Herman Taylor (D)	5,972	(9%)	

Prior Winning Percentages: 2008 (86%); 2008 special (81%)

Population		Race/Ethnicity		Work	
Pop. 2010:	714,316	White:	20.6%	Private:	68.3%
Change since 2000:	Up 7.9%	Black:	55.7%	Government:	27.0%
Urban:	97.9%	Hispanic:	14.2%	Self-employed:	4.6%
Rural:	2.1%	Asian:	6.9%	Blue collar:	15.4%
Area size:	318 sq. mi.	Native Am.:	0.2%	White collar:	66.6%
		Hawaiian:	0.0%	Khaki collar:	0.3%
Age		Two+ races:	2.2%	Other:	17.7%
Median age:	35.7 yrs.				
More than 65 yrs:	8.9%	*Ancestry*		Median income:	$73,053
Less than 18 yrs:	26.0%	Subsaharan	5.5%	Median Home Value:	$360,300
		German	5.2%		
Education		Irish	4.6%	**Military Veterans**	
H.S. grad:	87.6%			% of Pop:	8.7%
College grad:	35.6%				
Grad degree:	15.4%				

Prince George's County

In 1696, the proprietors of the colony of Maryland created a new county between the Potomac
and Patuxent rivers and named it after the husband of the heir to the throne, Prince George of
Denmark. During its 300 years, Prince George's
County has not often won national fame, maybe
only briefly when investigators chased the plotters of Abraham Lincoln's murder here. With a
population that is nearly two-thirds African-
American, Prince George's is the home of Ameri-

2008 Presidential Vote		
Barack Obama (D) 267,790	(85%)
John McCain (R) 44,996	(14%)
2004 Presidential Vote		
John Kerry (D) 217,549	(78%)
George Bush (R) 58,170	(21%)
Cook Partisan Voting Index: D+31		

ca's largest black middle class. It is also the wealthiest county with a majority black population.
Historically, Prince George's was tobacco country, dotted by slave plantations and pretty much
controlled by its white property owners. A hundred years after the Civil War, the population grew
as middle-class blacks moved out of neighboring Washington, D.C., into modest suburbs at the
county's edge and affluent subdivisions farther to the east. In the 1960s, this was one of the nation's
fastest-growing suburban counties. Its African-American population increased from 14% in 1970,
to 37% in 1980, to 66% in 2009, as the county's total population also grew. Prince George's is affluent
by national standards, and 70% of women here work outside the home, one of the highest percentages in the nation.

The county's median household income of more than $71,000 is far above the national median
of about $48,000 and is double the national median for black households. "The county ranks in the
top 2 percent in the nation in income level, and in people who are employed in executive jobs,"
Ebony magazine reported. Yet amid this success, considerable problems remain: Prince George's
homicide rates and frequency of other crimes tends to be high for a suburban county. The county
also suffered a black eye when outgoing County Executive Jack B. Johnson, his wife, Leslie, and
nine others were arrested in November 2010 as part of a wide-ranging political corruption investigation. When FBI agents showed up at their home with a search warrant, Leslie Johnson allegedly
flushed a $100,000 check down a toilet and tried to hide $79,600 in cash in her bra.

The 4th Congressional District of Maryland includes most of Prince George's County inside
the Capital Beltway that rings Washington. It also includes a large portion of Montgomery County
that is mostly outside the Beltway, starting in Silver Spring, heading up Georgia Avenue and covering a sizable rural area all the way to Clarksburg at the Frederick County line. This Montgomery
County area is heavily Democratic; Barack Obama won Prince George's by an extraordinary 89%-
10% in 2008. Overall, this is the most Democratic district in Maryland. The biggest industry is
government. It has the highest percentage of federal employees of any congressional district in the
nation. Suitland, inside the Beltway, is the home of the Census Bureau.

Donna Edwards (D)

The congresswoman from the 4th District is Donna Edwards, who won a special election in June
2008 to succeed Albert Wynn. She is the first black woman to represent Maryland in Congress.

Edwards was born in North Carolina, the second of six children. The family moved frequently
as a result of her father's career in the Air Force. Edwards says she learned adaptability from her
mother, and, as she told *The Washington Post*, "There's not a room I go in where I feel like a
stranger." She was president of her high school class in New Mexico, and returned to her home
state for college at Wake Forest University, where she was one of six African-American women in
her class. She went to work for Lockheed at the Goddard Space Flight Center in Greenbelt, Md.,
and after the 1986 explosion of the space shuttle *Challenger,* she decided to attend law school. At
Franklin Pierce Law Center in New Hampshire, she focused on public-interest law. She settled in
Fort Washington, Md., and clerked for a District of Columbia Superior Court judge. Later, she co-
founded and was the first executive director of the National Network to End Domestic Violence.
Edwards earned national recognition for her work on behalf of battered women. She was also executive director of the Center for a New Democracy, where she focused on campaign finance reform.
In 2000, she became executive director of The Arca Foundation in Washington, which focuses on
social equity and justice. After separating from her husband, she briefly was homeless and then
lived with her young son in a room in her mother's home.

In 2006, Edwards challenged seven-term Wynn in the Democratic primary and surprised him
with a well-funded and late-blossoming campaign. She ran to his left ideologically, benefited from
strong local opposition to the Iraq war, which Wynn backed, and attacked the incumbent's close

ties to business interests. Wynn accused Edwards of distorting his record. *The Washington Post* endorsed Edwards, writing, "Too often Wynn's votes have been at odds with good government and the interests of his constituents." Wynn won, but by a hair, 49.7%-46.4%. Wynn took his home Prince George's County, 57%-40%. In Montgomery, which cast 32% of the vote, Edwards led 60%-35%. Following that contest, Wynn increased his visibility in the district and co-sponsored a resolution to impeach Vice President Dick Cheney. But Edwards almost immediately began preparing for a rematch in two years.

In 2008, she benefited in the primary from the support of MoveOn.org, the liberal grassroots group, and EMILY's List, the women's fundraising powerhouse. She did not take money from political action committees, and she criticized Wynn for his reliance on special interest money. Still, she was able to raise and spend $1 million to get her message to voters. The outcome this time was not close. Boosted by heavy turnout from the presidential primary, Edwards won the primary contest with Wynn, 59%-37%. She led 55%-41% in Prince George's, and 67%-27% in Montgomery County. Six weeks later, but before the general election, Wynn unexpectedly announced he was quitting Congress to join the Washington law firm of Dickstein Shapiro. That decision gave Edwards a chance to take the seat early and have at least some seniority over other freshmen in the upcoming election. Wynn formally resigned on June 1, 2008. Democratic Gov. Martin O'Malley scheduled a special election for June 17; Edwards won 81%-18% over Republican Peter James, a technology developer, in a low-turnout event. She has been politically untouchable ever since.

Edwards is an extremely loyal Democrat. She got some attention when she was among the House members who initially voted against the $700 billion rescue of the financial industry, but then switched their votes to yes. Edwards said she voted for the revised version of the bill after a phone call from Obama urging her support. She has criticized the Obama administration's efforts in Afghanistan and co-sponsored Ohio Democrat Dennis Kucinich's failed proposal in March 2010 to withdraw U.S. forces there. She also was one of five lawmakers arrested at an April 2009 demonstration protesting the expulsion of aid groups in Darfur. On the Science, Space and Technology Committee, she has worked for greater tracking of minorities' participation in science and math programs. To show her concern for climate change, she plunged into the icy Potomac River in January 2011 with 200 local activists at an event sponsored by the Chesapeake Climate Action Network.

FIFTH DISTRICT

Steny Hoyer (D)

Elected May 1981, 15th full term; b. June 14, 1939, New York, NY; home, Mechanicsville; U. of MD, B.S. 1963, Georgetown U., J.D. 1966; Baptist; widowed; 3 children.

Elected Office: MD Senate, 1966–78, Pres., 1975–78.

Professional Career: Practicing atty., 1966–80; MD Bd. of Higher Educ., 1978–81.

DC Office: 1705 LHOB, 20515, 202-225-4131; Fax: 202-225-4300; Web site: hoyer.house.gov.

State Offices: Greenbelt, 301-474-0119; Waldorf, 301-843-1577.

Group Ratings

	ACLU	ACU	ADA	CFG	AFS	FRC	LCV	ITIC	NTU	COC
2010	88	0	90	0	100	0	100	100	5	14
2009	–	0	100	4	100	–	86	–	2	40

National Journal Ratings

	2010 LIB	—	2010 CONS	2009 LIB	—	2009 CONS
Economic	88%	—	10%	82%	—	14%
Social	71%	—	25%	83%	—	16%
Foreign	66%	—	29%	78%	—	17%
Composite	77%	—	23%	83%	—	17%

Key Votes of the 111th Congress

1. Overturn Ledbetter	Y	5. Bar federal abortion funds	N	9. Stop detainee transfers	N
2. Pass $820 billion stimulus	Y	6. Pass health care bill	Y	10. Legalize immigrants' kids	Y
3. Let guns in national parks	N	7. Regulate financial firms	Y	11. Repeal don't ask, tell	Y
4. Pass cap-and-trade	Y	8. Pass tax cuts for some	Y	12. Limit campaign funds	Y

Election Results

2010 general	Steny Hoyer (D)	155,110	(64%)	($4,511,873)
	Charles Lollar (R)	83,575	(35%)	($585,295)
2010 primary	Steny Hoyer (D)	58,717	(86%)	
	Andrew Gall (D)	6,682	(10%)	

Prior Winning Percentages: 2008 (74%), 2006 (83%), 2004 (69%), 2002 (69%), 2000 (65%), 1998 (65%), 1996 (57%), 1994 (59%), 1992 (53%), 1990 (81%), 1988 (79%), 1986 (82%), 1984 (72%), 1982 (80%), 1981 special (55%)

Population		Race/Ethnicity		Work	
Pop. 2010:	767,369	White:	48.0%	Private:	64.8%
Change since 2000:	Up 15.9%	Black:	36.7%	Government:	30.6%
Urban:	75.2%	Hispanic:	7.9%	Self-employed:	4.5%
Rural:	24.8%	Asian:	4.2%	Blue collar:	18.1%
Area size:	1,505 sq. mi.	Native Am.:	0.3%	White collar:	66.4%
		Hawaiian:	0.0%	Khaki collar:	0.8%
Age		Two+ races:	2.6%	Other:	14.7%
Median age:	36.5 yrs.				
More than 65 yrs:	9.8%	*Ancestry*		Median income:	$83,398
Less than 18 yrs:	25.4%	German	10.2%	Median Home Value:	$367,400
		Irish	9.4%		
Education		English	7.8%	**Military Veterans**	
H.S. grad:	90.2%			% of Pop:	13.0%
College grad:	32.5%				
Grad degree:	13.1%				

Southern Maryland

Southern Maryland was established as a colony of the British Lords Baltimore, who were seeking a refuge for English Catholics in the New World. The Lords Baltimore, first George and then Cecil Calvert, founded St. Mary's in 1634, not long after the founding of Jamestown and Plymouth Rock. Maryland became one of the two great Chesapeake tobacco colonies, with plantation houses on every inlet off the broad Potomac and Patuxent rivers. For years the towns of southern Maryland grew slowly, and even today many of their residents are directly descended from the old families. This area produced John Hanson, the first president of the United States chosen by the Continental Congress in 1781.

2008 Presidential Vote		
Barack Obama (D)	233,930	(66%)
John McCain (R)	118,547	(33%)

2004 Presidential Vote		
John Kerry (D)	177,035	(57%)
George Bush (R)	128,861	(42%)

Cook Partisan Voting Index: D+11

The region was never Puritan country. Liquor flowed even during Prohibition, and for years, Maryland law specifically allowed slot machines. But tobacco farming is nearing an end, even if the area hasn't completely renounced its tobacco heritage. The highlight of the annual Charles County fair remains the crowning of Queen Nicotina, a local high school senior. The area's economic base has owed much to government installations: the Civil War Point Lookout prisoner-of-war camp; the Navy's Patuxent River complex, where many astronauts began their training; and the Naval Air Warfare Center. Today, metro Washington and Baltimore are spreading into Southern Maryland, with rapid growth radiating outward: St. Mary's, Charles and Calvert counties were the three fastest-growing counties in Maryland between 2000 and 2010. Charles County in particular has become the home of many African-American families fleeing crime and troubled schools in Prince George's County. Today, most of Charles County's schoolchildren are black, while median incomes shot up to $89,000, one of the highest levels in the nation. In 2008, minor league baseball arrived here when the Southern Maryland Blue Crabs took up residence in a new stadium in Waldorf.

The 5th Congressional District of Maryland comprises Calvert, Charles, and St. Mary's counties, plus most of Prince George's County outside of the Capital Beltway. Its lines were drawn to ensure a large African-American percentage in the adjacent 4th District, but blacks—both new suburbanites and descendants of old Southern Maryland families—made up 37% of the district's population in 2010. The district takes in College Park, home of the University of Maryland, and nearby Hyattsville, Greenbelt, Beltsville, Laurel, and Bowie. It is chock full of federal facilities: Patuxent Naval Air Station, the Indian Head Naval Surface War Center, the Beltsville Agricultural Research Center and NASA's Goddard Space Flight Center. Historically, this is a Democratic area. Whites in the rural areas have trended Republican, but incoming blacks raised Charles County's voter turnout 19% between 2004 and 2008 and increased its Democratic percentage from 50% to 62%.

Steny Hoyer (D)

The congressman from the 5th District is Steny Hoyer, the House minority whip. He was first elected to the seat in 1981, and in June 2007, he became the longest-serving member of Congress from Maryland.

Hoyer is of Danish descent. His first name, he says, was his parents' adaptation of the Danish name Steen. He grew up in New York City, but moved from place to place with his mother and stepfather, who was in the Air Force and, when Steny was in high school, was transferred from Florida to Andrews Air Force Base in Maryland. Hoyer graduated from the University of Maryland, where in 1959 he listened to Democratic presidential candidate John F. Kennedy deliver a campaign speech that inspired him to switch his major from public relations to political science. While working on his law degree at Georgetown University in Washington, Hoyer interned one summer with Maryland Sen. Daniel Brewster. Another intern in Brewster's office that summer was Nancy D'Alesandro, daughter of the mayor of Baltimore and now, House Minority Leader Nancy Pelosi. In 1966, just after graduating from law school, Hoyer was elected to the Maryland Senate, at age 27. He was Senate president from 1975 to 1978, the youngest person to hold that post in Maryland history. In 1978 he ran for lieutenant governor on a losing ticket. In 1981, after incumbent Gladys Spellman was incapacitated by a heart attack, the 5th District seat was declared vacant. Hoyer won the special election, edging out Spellman's husband and several other Democrats in the primary and beating a well-financed Republican in the general. The district then was entirely in Prince George's County.

Hoyer has fine political instincts, works hard, and can speak in an old-fashioned, patriotic style that is genuinely moving. A fast riser in Maryland politics, he was also a fast riser in Congress. He excelled at constituency service and won a seat on the Appropriations Committee, where he worked with Republicans and became a champion for the Washington metro area. He has been an advocate of more spending for education programs and better pay and benefits for federal workers. He was the chief House sponsor of the Americans with Disabilities Act of 1990, which outlawed discrimination against people with diabilities. Hoyer also took the lead in crafting bipartisan election reform legislation and in enhancing security in the Capitol complex. When the political parties in the House became more polarized in the late 1990s, Hoyer initiated monthly lunches with Roy Blunt, R-Mo., who was then the chief deputy whip for the Republican majority. On September 11, 2001, it was Hoyer's idea to have lawmakers gather in front of the Capitol in a show of strength. The group spontaneously sang "God Bless America," an image captured vividly on television on a dark day in U.S. history.

His voting record is relatively moderate among Democrats, especially on foreign policy issues. He broke with the party by supporting the balanced budget amendment in 1995; he backed many of the free-trade initiatives of recent years that organized labor opposed, including the 1993 North American Free Trade Agreement. In 2002, he voted to authorize military action in Iraq and later complained that President Bush "under resourced" the war. He is a former chairman of the Helsinki Commission and has been a champion of human rights around the world. On the district front, Hoyer has pushed for funding for Chesapeake Bay cleanup and for dredging the bay for Baltimore Harbor. He has worked shrewdly to maintain and increase the number of jobs at the Goddard Space Flight Center in Greenbelt, at Patuxent River Naval Air Station, and at the Naval Surface Warfare Center at Indian Head. Another of his projects was getting the National Center for Weather and Climate Prediction based in College Park.

In 1989, Hoyer won his first leadership post as chairman of the Democratic Caucus. When he tried to move up to the job of majority whip in 1991, he lost, 160-109, to David Bonior of Michigan, who had the support of liberals and the committee chairmen. Hoyer became chairman of the Democratic Steering Committee and has been the parliamentarian at four Democratic conventions. In 2001, Bonior, faced with unfavorable redistricting changes at home, decided to run for Michigan governor. Both Hoyer and Pelosi sought to replace him as minority whip. Hoyer argued that he had greater experience in leadership positions and could do a better job of unifying the caucus.

Pelosi had more publicly committed votes going into the October 2001 Democratic Caucus election, and she won 118-95. (Both did less well than predicted, as usually happens in secret-ballot leadership contests.)

Although he was a two-time loser of leadership contests, Hoyer was undeterred when Dick Gephardt stepped down as minority leader in 2002. With Pelosi running to succeed Gephardt as leader, Hoyer ran for minority whip, the No. 2 position in the Democratic leadership. He collected commitments for months and was elected unanimously. In that position, it was his job to be partisan, and he often was. In the majority, both House Democrats and Republicans have taken a dim view of members of their party who buck their leadership on procedural issues. As Hoyer said in 2010, as he was being criticized by Republicans, "I think both parties have acted defensively in some respects when they were in the majority."

In the pivotal 2006 campaign, Hoyer worked closely with Illinois Democratic Rep. Rahm Emanuel, who chaired the effort to elect a Democratic majority. In the campaign season, Hoyer made 316 campaign stops in 80 districts in 33 states and raised more than $8 million. His September 2006 prediction that Democrats would gain 30 seats turned out to be right on the money. Many of the freshmen subsequently credited the help that Hoyer provided, especially those from swing districts where liberal Democratic leaders are not always welcome.

Even so, when it came time to elect leaders to the new Democratic House in late 2006, Hoyer had to fight for the position of majority leader against Pennsylvania Rep. John Murtha, who had the backing of incoming House Speaker Pelosi. In spite of their years working together in the leadership, Pelosi and Hoyer still viewed each other with suspicion. A defense hawk, Murtha had become an outspoken opponent of the Iraq war, while Hoyer supported the war effort, and Murtha contended that he could work better with Pelosi. Hoyer had little choice but to speak positively about his long-standing relationship with her—he called her a "favorite daughter" of Maryland—and their success in largely unifying an often-unruly party. But he left no doubt about his dismay over her arm-twisting on Murtha's behalf. In spite of Pelosi's efforts for Murtha, Hoyer prevailed 149-86, a powerful endorsement for him, for majority leader, the No. 2 role in the new leadership lineup. Democrats responded to his "ability, patience, know-how, and experience," said a Democratic lobbyist. Even more impressive, Hoyer won the support of many California Democrats who previously had been unified behind Pelosi and of numerous prospective committee chairmen who doubted Murtha's ability to do the job. "Nancy thought she could put these people away because of pressure," former California Rep. Tony Coelho told *The New York Times*. Hoyer "has a tremendous capacity for friendship, and when you have that, people don't flake off on you," Coelho said.

As majority leader, Hoyer assumed responsibility for determining the floor schedule, helping guide Democratic initiatives to passage, and holding weekly press briefings. He described his recipe for holding together what had historically been a fissiparous caucus this way: "First of all work very hard on communications, find out what people can do and can't do. Secondly, put together a consensus that, while it may not be the first choice of everybody, it is a choice they can live with." And for the most part, the record justifies his boast that House Democrats, in their first two years in the majority, were "the most unified the Democratic Party has been in over half a century." Hoyer also kept communications open with the enemy. He stayed in close touch with Blunt, and they maintained one of the best cross-party relationships on Capitol Hill. When Democrats lost their majority in 2010, Hoyer became Democratic whip, the No. 2 position in the minority leadership, while Pelosi took the top slot as minority leader.

In recent years, Hoyer has found himself at odds with the majority of Democrats on some issues. He voted for military funding in Iraq and consistently against linking war funding to a timetable for withdrawing U.S. troops, earning him criticism from the liberal MoveOn.org. And, he worked on the negotiations on changes in the Foreign Intelligence Surveillance Act, which is a law enforcement tool in catching terrorists, and he backed the version of the legislation releasing telecommunications companies from legal liability for complying with government requests for warrantless surveillance of U.S. citizens' communications. Many Democrats did not want to let the companies off the hook. His toughest moment in the 110th Congress (2007-08) came in August 2007, when he urged Democratic Rep. Michael McNulty of New York, who was presiding over the House, to end a vote on limiting aid to illegal immigrants, when Democrats were ahead in the vote count. McNulty declared that the Democrats had prevailed, even though the voting machine lights showed otherwise. The incident was the subject of hearings in May 2008, during which McNulty and Hoyer admitted error. But Hoyer later maintained that the House rule against holding votes open beyond stated time limits was unenforceable.

On domestic issues, Hoyer was a strong supporter of the pay-go rule, which requires that spending increases and tax cuts be "paid for" by corresponding spending decreases or tax increases. He spoke out for maintaining the rule even as many Democrats favored dropping it to give middle-income taxpayers some relief from the alternative minimum tax. In early 2009, working with Pelosi, Hoyer steered to passage the $787 billion economic stimulus legislation, the first major initiative of the Obama administration. Only 11 House Democrats voted against it, and all of the Republicans opposed it. Weeks earlier, Hoyer strongly supported the bailout bill for the financial services industry although he expressed misgivings about the legislation. He also had a hand in the Democrats' successful efforts to increase the hourly minimum wage and in the adoption of most of the 9/11 commission's recommendations.

In the past, Hoyer has been among the top 10 House members in securing spending earmarks for his district. In 2010, he ranked 26th among all House members, according to the Center for Responsive Politics and Taxpayers for Common Sense. He calls earmarks "congressional initiatives," but he hailed what he termed House Democrats' "substantial progress" in limiting them. More inclined to defer to committee chairs and hew to regular order than Pelosi, he supported doing away with term limits for committee chairs, which the Republicans imposed when they were in the majority. Pelosi left term limits in place during the first two years of Democratic rule. (Term limits work to the advantage of the leadership because they make committee chairs less autonomous and therefore less powerful.) At Hoyer's urging, Pelosi agreed to repeal term limits in late 2008. "I am not for term limits for chairmen," Hoyer said. "It puts intellect on hold."

On local issues, he worked with Republican Rep. Tom Davis of Virginia and D.C. Democratic Delegate Eleanor Holmes Norton to pass a bill giving the District of Columbia a voting seat in the House. He sponsored bills allowing more government employees to work four-day weeks, granting eight weeks of paid parental leave, and raising the government contribution to federal employees' health care premiums. In the bitterly fought 2008 Democratic presidential primary, Hoyer stayed neutral even after the Maryland primary, which Illinois Sen. Barack Obama won. Obama carried Prince George's and Charles counties in Hoyer's district, but he ran only slightly ahead of New York Sen. Hillary Rodham Clinton in St. Mary's and Calvert counties.

The last time Hoyer had serious competition in a general election was in 1992, the first election after the district was reconfigured to extend beyond Prince George's County. He has won easily since then, and he has demonstrated an ability to win the loyalty of African-American voters in Democratic primaries.

SIXTH DISTRICT

Roscoe Bartlett (R)

Elected 1992, 10th term; b. June 3, 1926, Moreland, KY; home, Frederick; Columbia Union Col., B.A. 1947, U. of MD, M.S. 1949, Ph.D. 1952; Seventh Day Adventist; married (Ellen); 10 children.

Professional Career: Farmer; Prof., U. of MD, 1948–52; Asst. prof., Loma Linda Schl. of Medicine, 1952–54; Asst. prof., Howard U. Medical Schl., 1954–56; Research scientist, N.I.H., 1956–58; Research scientist, U.S. Naval Aerospace Medical Inst., 1958–62; Research scientist, Johns Hopkins U., 1962–67; Research mgr., IBM, 1967–74; Pres., Roscoe Bartlett & Assoc., 1974–86.

DC Office: 2412 RHOB, 20515, 202-225-2721; Fax: 202-225-2193; Web site: bartlett.house.gov.

State Offices: Cumberland, 301-724-3105; Frederick, 301-694-3030; Hagerstown, 301-797-6043; Westminster, 410-857-1115.

Committees: *Armed Services:* Tactical Air & Land Forces (Chmn); Seapower & Projection Forces. *Science, Space & Technology:* Energy & Environment; Research & Science Education. *Small Business:* Agriculture, Energy & Trade.

Group Ratings

	ACLU	ACU	ADA	CFG	AFS	FRC	LCV	ITIC	NTU	COC
2010	25	92	0	94	0	100	10	67	86	100
2009	–	96	5	90	11	–	14	–	86	93

National Journal Ratings

	2010 LIB	—	2010 CONS	2009 LIB	—	2009 CONS
Economic	28%	—	71%	20%	—	79%
Social	15%	—	84%	18%	—	81%
Foreign	33%	—	65%	26%	—	68%
Composite	26%	—	74%	23%	—	77%

Key Votes of the 111th Congress

1. Overturn Ledbetter	N	5. Bar federal abortion funds	Y	9. Stop detainee transfers	Y
2. Pass $820 billion stimulus	N	6. Pass health care bill	N	10. Legalize immigrants' kids	N
3. Let guns in national parks	Y	7. Regulate financial firms	N	11. Repeal don't ask, tell	N
4. Pass cap-and-trade	N	8. Pass tax cuts for some	N	12. Limit campaign funds	N

Election Results

2010 general	Roscoe Bartlett (R)	148,820	(61%)	($283,046)
	Andrew Duck (D)	80,455	(33%)	($45,905)
	Dan Massey (Lib)	6,816	(3%)	
	Michael Reed (CNP)	5,907	(2%)	
2010 primary	Roscoe Bartlett (R)	49,056	(70%)	
	Joseph Krysztoforski (R)	11,124	(16%)	
	Steve Taylor (R)	4,822	(7%)	
	Seth Wilson (R)	3,860	(6%)	

Prior Winning Percentages: 2008 (58%), 2006 (59%), 2004 (67%), 2002 (66%), 2000 (61%), 1998 (63%), 1996 (57%), 1994 (66%), 1992 (54%)

Population		Race/Ethnicity		Work	
Pop. 2010:	738,943	White:	85.0%	Private:	75.9%
Change since 2000:	Up 11.6%	Black:	6.4%	Government:	18.2%
Urban:	60.5%	Hispanic:	4.2%	Self-employed:	5.7%
Rural:	39.5%	Asian:	2.2%	Blue collar:	19.5%
Area size:	3,097 sq. mi.	Native Am.:	0.2%	White collar:	64.3%
		Hawaiian:	0.0%	Khaki collar:	0.2%
Age		Two+ races:	1.8%	Other:	16.0%
Median age:	39.2 yrs.				
More than 65 yrs:	12.8%	*Ancestry*		Median income:	$67,463
Less than 18 yrs:	24.3%	German	22.8%	Median Home Value:	$316,200
		Irish	13.1%		
Education		English	9.6%	**Military Veterans**	
H.S. grad:	88.6%			% of Pop:	10.9%
College grad:	28.3%				
Grad degree:	10.8%				

Northwest Maryland; Frederick

One of America's first frontiers was Western
Maryland, where the Appalachian ridges that
cross the state diagonally from northeast to
southwest cut through long sloping fields. The
land was settled by Pennsylvania Dutch and
Scots-Irish hill people, not Chesapeake Bay tobacco growers. Maryland is where the 19th century's great paths to the interior were staked out:
The National Road; the nation's first combined
freight and passenger railroad, the Baltimore &

2008 Presidential Vote		
John McCain (R) 200,652	(58%)
Barack Obama (D) 139,421	(40%)

2004 Presidential Vote		
George Bush (R) 209,764	(65%)
John Kerry (D) 110,821	(34%)

Cook Partisan Voting Index: R+13

Ohio, which crossed the wide valleys of bounteous farms and climbed over the Catoctin Mountains;
and the Chesapeake and Ohio Canal, which began operating in 1828, primarily to haul coal from
Western Maryland to the port of Georgetown in Washington. Towns grew up with narrow streets
of row houses that today are overhung with telephone wires. They planted themselves among cornfields, pastureland, and ancient mountains. Across this placid land moved vast armies during the
Civil War. In Frederick, city officials paid the Confederates $200,000 not to burn the town, and
near Sharpsburg, blue- and-gray-clad soldiers fought the Battle of Antietam, on the bloodiest day
in American military history. A century later, on the steps of City Hall in Cumberland, near the
coal-laced hills of Appalachia, President Lyndon Johnson declared his War on Poverty. Poverty
did fall here in the 1970s, but conditions worsened in the 1980s with the closure of several large
factories. Hard-pressed as it is, Western Maryland is trying to preserve its natural wonders of small
mountains and thick, deciduous forests. Cumberland has attempted to refashion itself as an arts
community, with dozens of studios cropping up. To the east, Carroll County in metro Baltimore,
and Frederick County in metro Washington, have grown rapidly in recent years and have become
new hubs for outward expansion.

The 6th Congressional District includes all of Western Maryland, takes in a small part of
northern Montgomery County, and runs eastward across the northern farmlands and hunt country of Baltimore and Harford counties all the way to the Susquehanna River. The political tradition
in most of this area, unlike the rest of Maryland, is Republican. This was Union country during
the Civil War and has been predominantly Republican ever since. The new rush of settlement—which has made this the fastest growing district in Maryland—is mostly made up of young
families of modest incomes seeking respite from urban life, which is strengthening the area's already conservative leanings. However, Frederick County and Washington County also have seen
the two highest increases in the state in Hispanics since 2000. Only seven of Maryland's 24 counties
have more registered Republican voters than Democrats, and five of them are in this district.

Roscoe Bartlett (R)

The congressman from the 6th District is Roscoe Bartlett, a Republican first elected in 1992. In his
mid-80s, Bartlett is the second-oldest member of the House after Republican Ralph Hall of Texas.

Bartlett is a descendant of a signer of the Declaration of Independence and a Seventh Day
Adventist. He and his wife have 10 children (each had four children from previous marriages). He
was born in Kentucky and grew up in poverty in Western Pennsylvania, where his father was
a tenant farmer. After getting a bachelor's degree in theology and biology, he earned a Ph.D. in
physiology at the University of Maryland, where he also taught and wrote more than 100 scientific
articles. Over the years, he has also operated a 145-acre dairy farm, where he still milks goats. He
was awarded 20 patents for inventing life support equipment for pilots, astronauts, firefighters,
and respiratory patients. In 1999, the American Institute of Aeronautics and Astronautics gave
him an award for his career contributions to the advancement of medical knowledge and technologies. When Bartlett first ran for the House, he was a 65-year-old retired professor who seemed to
have no chance of winning. Democrat Beverly Byron had represented the district for 14 years and
had a conservative voting record. Bartlett lost to her in 1982, 74%-26%. But in 1992, Byron was
upset in the primary by a liberal who favored national health insurance and abortion rights. Bartlett's conservative views and his attacks on his opponent's record in the state Legislature drove
him to a 54%-46% victory.

Bartlett has proved a surprisingly durable, if quirky, politician. "Some people look at things
straight on," California GOP Rep. Buck McKeon told *The Washington Post* in January 2011. "He
kind of comes at things from different angles." Bartlett is one of two Republicans in the state's
congressional delegation and was among the first to join the Tea Party Caucus in 2010. His conserv-

ative views have not always followed Republican orthodoxy. "I'm not interested in politics," he says. "I am a conservative who wants to help restore the limited federal government envisioned and established in the Constitution by our nation's founders." He sometimes objects to his party's big spending, including President Bush George W. Bush's No Child Left Behind education law that mandated testing in public schools as a requisite for continued federal funding. But Bartlett voted for the 2003 bill creating a prescription drug benefit in the Medicare program. He also voted against renewal of the Bush administration's USA PATRIOT Act because he saw the anti-terrorism law as a threat to civil liberties. He was one of 33 House Republicans to oppose renewal of the Voting Rights Act.

The first member of Congress to drive a hybrid car, Bartlett purchased a Toyota Prius in 2000. He has been a passionate advocate of alternative energy sources, and he powers his home with solar energy and a wood stove. He has given dozens of floor speeches on what he calls the world's excessive reliance on fossil fuels. When fellow Republicans voiced skepticism about former Vice President Al Gore's warnings about climate change, Bartlett chided them, saying, "It's possible to be a conservative without appearing to be an idiot." He was one of just 36 Republicans in 2007 to support a Democratic energy bill repealing tax breaks to oil and gas companies and funding renewable programs.

On the Armed Services Committee, Bartlett's iconoclastic views have impeded his advancement. He has long warned of the threat of an electromagnetic pulse attack—a massive radiation burst that could render the U.S. electricity grid inoperable. He got a bill into law creating a congressional commission to study the issue, which some experts say has been greatly exaggerated. He introduced a bill in 1997 to ban mixed-sex military training, saying that he did not think a "powder puff" military would be effective. He sought the committee's ranking member slot in 2009 when GOP Rep. John McHugh became Army secretary, but was beaten out by McKeon, who had less seniority but far closer ties to Minority Leader John Boehner.

In the 112th Congress (2011-12), he took over the chairmanship of the Tactical Air and Land Forces Subcommittee. In stark contrast to most conservatives, he indicated his willingness to consider Defense Secretary Robert M. Gates' assertion that tens of billions of dollars of Pentagon spending could be eliminated.

Bartlett has been re-elected by solid margins. In 2004, he faced an unusual primary challenge from Frederick County State's Attorney Scott Rolle, who criticized Bartlett for not supporting the Bush administration strongly enough. Bartlett responded by getting Vice President Dick Cheney to make an appearance in his behalf in Hagerstown just four days before the election. Bartlett won 70%-30% and carried Rolle's Frederick County base, 60%-40%. In 2008, against modestly funded Frederick Mayor Jennifer Dougherty, a Democrat, Bartlett won 58%-39%, one of his lowest percentages since his first election. But he won all eight counties, including 52%-44% in his opponent's home area. Maryland Democrats seem unlikely to take this final Republican outpost any time soon. In 2008, *Slate* magazine named him one of "America's silver lions," a list of the country's most influential people over the age of 80.

SEVENTH DISTRICT

Elijah Cummings (D)

Elected April 1996, 8th full term; b. Jan. 18, 1951, Baltimore; home, Baltimore; Howard U., B.S. 1973, U. of MD, J.D. 1976; Baptist; married (Maya Rockeymoore).

Elected Office: MD House of Delegates, 1982–96, Speaker pro tem, 1995–96.

Professional Career: Practicing atty., 1976–96.

DC Office: 2235 RHOB, 20515, 202-225-4741; Fax: 202-225-3178; Web site: cummings.house.gov.

State Offices: Baltimore, 410-685-9199; Catonsville, 410-719-8777; Ellicott City, 410-465-8259.

Committees: *Joint Economic Committee. Oversight & Government Reform* (RMM). *Transportation & Infrastructure:* Coast Guard & Maritime Transportation; Highways & Transit.

Group Ratings

	ACLU	ACU	ADA	CFG	AFS	FRC	LCV	ITIC	NTU	COC
2010	94	0	95	0	100	0	100	67	5	13
2009	–	0	100	0	100	–	100	–	1	40

National Journal Ratings

	2010 LIB — 2010 CONS		2009 LIB — 2009 CONS	
Economic	90%	— 0%	88%	— 9%
Social	89%	— 7%	89%	— 0%
Foreign	84%	— 11%	70%	— 24%
Composite	91%	— 9%	86%	— 14%

Key Votes of the 111th Congress

1. Overturn Ledbetter	Y	5. Bar federal abortion funds	N	9. Stop detainee transfers	N
2. Pass $820 billion stimulus	Y	6. Pass health care bill	Y	10. Legalize immigrants' kids	Y
3. Let guns in national parks	N	7. Regulate financial firms	Y	11. Repeal don't ask, tell	Y
4. Pass cap-and-trade	Y	8. Pass tax cuts for some	Y	12. Limit campaign funds	Y

Election Results

2010 general	Elijah Cummings (D)	152,669	(75%)	($796,200)
	Frank Mirabile (R)	46,375	(23%)	($12,353)
2010 primary	Elijah Cummings (D)	59,649	(91%)	
	Charles Smith (D)	5,884	(9%)	

Prior Winning Percentages: 2008 (80%), 2006 (100%), 2004 (73%), 2002 (74%), 2000 (87%), 1998 (86%), 1996 (83%), 1996 special (81%)

Population		Race/Ethnicity		Work	
Pop. 2010:	659,776	White:	31.6%	Private:	71.8%
Change since 2000:	Down 0.3%	Black:	55.7%	Government:	23.7%
Urban:	94.9%	Hispanic:	3.5%	Self-employed:	4.4%
Rural:	5.1%	Asian:	6.7%	Blue collar:	13.6%
Area size:	296 sq. mi.	Native Am.:	0.2%	White collar:	67.3%
		Hawaiian:	0.0%	Khaki collar:	0.3%
Age		Two+ races:	2.1%	Other:	18.9%
Median age:	36.7 yrs.				
More than 65 yrs:	12.1%	*Ancestry*		Median income:	$51,821
Less than 18 yrs:	23.3%	German	8.5%	Median Home Value:	$273,500
		Irish	6.8%		
Education		English	4.8%	**Military Veterans**	
H.S. grad:	83.4%			% of Pop:	9.0%
College grad:	33.0%				
Grad degree:	15.1%				

West Baltimore, Suburbs

At the junction of North and South, Baltimore is a product of both European immigration and the migration of African-Americans from the South. Its black community has a rich history. The *Afro-American* newspaper has been published here for more than 100 years, and there was once a black symphony orchestra. Eubie Blake, one of the founders of ragtime music, grew up here and now has a museum in his honor on Charles Street. Jazz great Billie Holiday was born here, as was Cab Calloway, the 1930s and 1940s big band leader, and Thurgood Marshall, the country's first African-American Supreme Court justice. Near downtown on the west side is the childhood home of slugger Babe Ruth and the home of writer H.L. Mencken. For years, this side of town had a biracial, bipartisan politics in which Democrats like Gov. Albert Ritchie and Republicans such as Gov. Theodore McKeldin competed zestfully for black and white votes. Baltimore has been a black majority city since the late 1970s, and most of its west-side neighborhoods are heavily African-American.

2008 Presidential Vote		
Barack Obama (D)	234,123	(79%)
John McCain (R)	60,134	(20%)
2004 Presidential Vote		
John Kerry (D)	192,081	(73%)
George Bush (R)	69,545	(26%)
Cook Partisan Voting Index:	D+25	

In the 1990s, Baltimore was hit by a terrible crime wave, with open drug markets on both the west and east sides. Democratic Mayor Martin O'Malley, elected in 1999, promised to build "a new Baltimore" with zero tolerance of crime. But many of the city's problems remained, with almost 20% of its residential areas classified as distressed. The city's gritty side was vividly depicted in HBO's acclaimed crime drama *"The Wire,"* which President Obama has called his favorite TV show.

Maryland's 7th Congressional District includes most of Baltimore's west side, plus the heavily African-American suburbs west of the city and extending to Catonsville along the old Baltimore National Pike. It also includes most of suburban Howard County. About 40% of the district's votes are cast in Baltimore city's precincts, largely north of Pratt Street, in places like Druid Heights; Harlem Park; Charles Village, which is home to Johns Hopkins University and poverty-stricken Sandtown-Winchester. Howard County is quite a different area. It grew 32% in the 1990s, and its largest community, Columbia, is a planned town that attracts a culturally liberal population that tends to vote Democratic. With Howard County's growth slowing in the 2000s, planners are seeking to convert it to a less urban and more suburban style of development. There is a sharp socioeconomic contrast between these two parts of the district. Howard County is predominately white, has the third-highest median household income of all counties in the nation. In Baltimore city, only 4 % of households earn more than $100,000 and 40% of children are poor.

Elijah Cummings (D)

The congressman from the 7th District is Elijah Cummings, who won a 1996 special election after Kweisi Mfume resigned to become president of the NAACP. Cummings is the son of sharecroppers from South Carolina who moved north for a better life for their seven children. He grew up in Baltimore, graduated Phi Beta Kappa from Howard University, and then got a law degree from the University of Maryland. He practiced law for a time in Baltimore, and then in 1982, at age 31, he ran successfully for the Maryland House of Delegates, where he served 16 years and rose through the ranks to become speaker pro tem. When he ran for the U.S. House, his main competition was the Rev. Frank Reid III, stepbrother of Baltimore Mayor Kurt Schmoke, who raised $255,000. Cummings had support from local businesses and community-development organizations, and raised $450,000. He won with 37% of the vote to 24% for Reid. He has not been seriously challenged in a primary or general election since then.

Cummings lives in troubled west Baltimore, and he is a crusader against drug abuse and for stricter gun control. His voting record has been mostly liberal, and he can be blunt in defending his party. In the fall campaign season of 2010, when some Democrats were de-emphasizing their support of the health care overhaul, he said he was doing just the opposite. "I know the media wants us to apologize for being Democrats," he said at one rally. "They want us to apologize for health care. Why? Because the Democratic Party is the humane party." But Cummings also has a pragmatic streak that allows him to work with Republicans in legislative coalitions. He worked with Indiana conservative Republican Mark Souder to reauthorize the White House drug control office and to establish federal policy to combat rapidly multiplying methamphetamine labs. When Democrats won the majority in 2006, he became chairman of the Coast Guard and Maritime Transportation Subcommittee at Transportation and Infrastructure, a useful niche for his port-dependent district. The House unanimously passed his bill in July 2009 to reform Coast Guard acquisition practices, and a year later he helped get an authorization bill for the agency into law that included some acquisition reforms as well as other changes.

On the Oversight and Government Reform Committee, he worked closely with Democratic Chairman Henry Waxman of California on the investigation of performance-enhancing steroids in baseball, and emphasized the detrimental effect steroid use was having on young people who look up to successful athletes. "You're one of my heroes, but it's hard to believe you, sir," Cummings told former star pitcher Roger Clemens at a 2008 hearing. When Waxman in November 2008 was chosen to chair the Energy and Commerce Committee, some Democrats urged Cummings to challenge the more senior Rep. Edolphus Towns, D-N.Y., to replace Waxman as chairman of Oversight. But Cummings did not run, partly to avoid conflict within the seniority-sensitive Congressional Black Caucus, an influential group that Cummings chaired in 2003 and 2004.

The issue of Cummings challenging Towns for Oversight's top Democratic slot resurfaced in 2010 after the Republicans regained control of the House. Many Democrats worried that Towns could not be a tough enough foil to Darrell Issa, the California Republican who took over as chairman and who pledged numerous aggressive inquisitions into the Obama administration. Towns agreed to step aside, and Cummings took over the job after beating New York's Carolyn Maloney by a 119-61 vote. "The Democratic Caucus must not cede to the new House majority that wishes to move our nation backward," he said. He enlisted Waxman's help in attracting top-notch investigators and quickly showed his willingness to tussle with Issa. In January 2011, Cummings complained that Democrats were being repeatedly denied access to committee records and asked committee Republicans to publicly commit to a bipartisan policy on issuing subpoenas.

Cummings usually wins re-election by landslide margins, and in 2006 he was unopposed. He backed Mfume in the Democratic primary for the open Senate seat that year, and then played a constructive role in coalescing Democrats behind the eventual nominee, former Rep. Ben Cardin. In 2007, he bucked most of the Maryland Democratic establishment by announcing his early support of Barack Obama in the Democratic primary, and went on to serve as co-chairman of Obama's campaign in Maryland. Cummings suffered a personal tragedy in June 2011, when his nephew, Christopher Cummings, was fatally shot near Old Dominion University in Norfolk, Va., where the young man was a student.

EIGHTH DISTRICT

Chris Van Hollen (D)

Elected 2002, 5th term; b. Jan. 10, 1959, Karachi, Pakistan; home, Kensington; Swarthmore Col., B.A. 1982, Harvard U., M.P.P. 1985, Georgetown U., J.D. 1990; Protestant; married (Katherine); 3 children.

Elected Office: MD House of Delegates, 1990-94; MD Senate, 1994-2002.

DC Office: 1707 LHOB, 20515, 202-225-5341; Fax: 202-225-0375; Web site: vanhollen.house.gov.

State Offices: Hyattsville, 301-891-6982; Rockville, 301-424-3501.

Committees: *Budget* (RMM).

Group Ratings

	ACLU	ACU	ADA	CFG	AFS	FRC	LCV	ITIC	NTU	COC
2010	88	0	100	0	100	0	100	100	4	13
2009	—	0	100	4	100	—	100	—	2	33

National Journal Ratings

	2010 LIB	—	2010 CONS	2009 LIB	—	2009 CONS
Economic	86%	—	13%	82%	—	14%
Social	82%	—	14%	75%	—	20%
Foreign	77%	—	22%	78%	—	17%
Composite	83%	—	17%	81%	—	19%

Key Votes of the 111th Congress

1. Overturn Ledbetter	Y	5. Bar federal abortion funds	N	9. Stop detainee transfers	N
2. Pass $820 billion stimulus	Y	6. Pass health care bill	Y	10. Legalize immigrants' kids	Y
3. Let guns in national parks	N	7. Regulate financial firms	Y	11. Repeal don't ask, tell	Y
4. Pass cap-and-trade	Y	8. Pass tax cuts for some	Y	12. Limit campaign funds	Y

Election Results

2010 general	Chris Van Hollen (D) 153,613	(73%)	($1,903,106)
	Michael Phillips (R) 52,421	(25%)	($192,617)
2010 primary	Chris Van Hollen (D) 57,847	(93%)	
	Robert Long (D)..4,392	(7%)	

Prior Winning Percentages: 2008 (75%), 2006 (77%), 2004 (75%), 2002 (52%)

Population		Race/Ethnicity		Work	
Pop. 2010:	728,124	White:	47.5%	Private:	71.9%
Change since 2000:	Up 10.0%	Black:	16.3%	Government:	21.1%
Urban:	98.8%	Hispanic:	20.0%	Self-employed:	6.9%
Rural:	1.2%	Asian:	13.2%	Blue collar:	11.0%
Area size:	307 sq. mi.	Native Am.:	0.2%	White collar:	73.0%
		Hawaiian:	0.0%	Khaki collar:	0.3%
Age		Two+ races:	2.5%	Other:	15.7%
Median age:	38.1 yrs.				
More than 65 yrs:	13.2%	*Ancestry*		Median income:	$88,889
Less than 18 yrs:	23.9%	German	8.0%	Median Home Value:	$490,100
		Irish	7.6%		
Education		English	6.3%	**Military Veterans**	
H.S. grad:	88.8%			% of Pop:	7.2%
College grad:	55.3%				
Grad degree:	29.9%				

Montgomery County; Bethesda

Colonial farmers once rolled barrels of tobacco to the port of Georgetown in Maryland, along an old road that is today the commercial spine of one of America's most affluent and best-educated areas. Wisconsin Avenue begins at the Potomac River in Washington, D.C., traverses the city, and then becomes Rockville Pike after it passes under the Capital Beltway in Montgomery County. The foundation of the economy here is the federal government, with its huge facili-

2008 Presidential Vote		
Barack Obama (D) 234,927	(74%)
John McCain (R) 78,223	(25%)
2004 Presidential Vote		
John Kerry (D) 205,660	(69%)
George Bush (R) 90,108	(30%)
Cook Partisan Voting Index: D+21		

ties—Bethesda Naval Hospital (merged with and renamed for the Army's Walter Reed), the National Institutes of Health, the Food and Drug Administration, and the National Institute of Standards and Technology. Montgomery is one of the centers of America's biotech industry, the home of firms such as Celera and Human Genome Sciences which, in parallel with the Human Genome Project, pioneered the study of the human genetic code. From about the 1960s through the 1980s, Montgomery County ranked at or near the top among counties nationwide in income and education. That changed gradually over the last two decades as the county became a magnet for immigrants attracted by the region's strong and stable economy. Today, Montgomery has a minority majority and has been overtaken in affluence regionally by suburban Loudoun, Fairfax and Arlington counties in Virginia and Howard County in Maryland. Along with very upscale neighborhoods, Montgomery now has large Latino communities in neighborhoods from Wheaton northwest to Gaithersburg. The county's population in 2010 was 17% Hispanic, 17% African-American and 14% Asian. County law enforcement has had difficulty coping with youth gangs, and crime is significantly higher than in Fairfax County, which also has a large immigrant population.

Downtown Bethesda, once a low-rise node amid 1950s and 1960s single-family subdivisions, is now a glitzy and popular entertainment destination, with high-rise apartment buildings. A few decades ago, Montgomery County was the home of earnest civil servants, sympathetic to liberal Democrats, but open to voting for liberal Republicans as well. Its private-sector economy has grown, but it is one tightly interlaced with government, and the county's current population, with the nation's second highest percentage of adults with graduate school degrees, is thoroughly liberal on cultural issues and increasingly loyal to the Democratic Party.

The 8th Congressional District of Maryland includes most of the heavily populated parts of Montgomery County, plus a small slice of strongly Democratic territory in Prince George's County added in 2002 redistricting. Perhaps its most unique precinct is Leisure World in Silver Spring, with its 6,000-plus senior citizens and an extraordinarily high voter-turnout rate. Democratic candidates practically camp out there during the primary season.

Chris Van Hollen (D)

The congressman from the 8th District is Chris Van Hollen, first elected in 2002 and one of the House's most influential Democrats. Wonky, self-assured, and telegenic, Van Hollen earned a prominent role in the Democratic House leadership after helping the party secure its majority in the chamber in 2006. He chaired the Democratic Congressional Campaign Committee in 2008 and 2010; *The Washington Post* dubbed him the party's "Mr. Fix-It."

The son of a Foreign Service officer, Van Hollen was born in Pakistan, and grew up around the globe, living in several countries including Sri Lanka, where his father was the U.S. ambassador. He graduated from Swarthmore College, and got a master's degree from Harvard University and a law degree from Georgetown University. In the 1980s, he worked for the Senate Foreign Relations Committee, where he co-authored a report on Iraq's use of chemical weapons. In 1990, he was elected to the Maryland House of Delegates and in 1994 to the state Senate. In 2002, Van Hollen ran for the 8th District House seat held by liberal Republican Connie Morella since 1986. Maryland's Democratic legislature had changed the district, removing affluent Republican precincts in Potomac and adding heavily Democratic territory to the east. Van Hollen's chief opponent in the Democratic primary was state Del. Mark Shriver, son of Sargent and Eunice Shriver, who had extensive labor support. Bolstered by the endorsement of *The Washington Post*, Van Hollen defeated Shriver 43%-41%, with former trade official Ira Shapiro getting 13%.

Van Hollen then had only eight weeks to campaign against Morella, a hard-working and congenial Republican with a liberal voting record suited to the district's many Democrats. Morella had voted against the Iraq war resolution and often opposed the conservative House GOP leadership. Van Hollen did not directly attack Morella, but argued that she was an enabler of the Republican majority, and that her vote to organize the House with Republicans kept in power conservatives who were out of sync with most district voters. Morella criticized Van Hollen's record in Annapolis, including his decision to quit a Senate subcommittee over proposed budget cuts. The *Post* endorsed Morella, but it wasn't enough. In a race in which the two candidates together spent nearly $6 million, Van Hollen won 52%-47%. Redistricting probably determined the result. Nearly half of Van Hollen's popular vote margin came from the small part of the district in Prince George's County, where he won 78%-21%.

In the House, Van Hollen won an early legislative victory when he got a majority, including 26 Republicans, to approve his amendment to limit a plan to outsource more federal jobs. In 2005, he was appointed by DCCC Chairman Rahm Emanuel of Illinois to manage candidate recruitment and execution of the committee's "Red to Blue" campaign plan. Working closely with the hard-driving Emanuel, the low-key and genial Van Hollen traveled to many battleground districts for hands-on candidate mentoring.

When Democrats won a majority in 2006, Van Hollen was rewarded with a seat on the powerful Ways and Means Committee. He focused on revisions to the Alternative Minimum Tax, which threatened many of his affluent constituents, changes to make prescription drugs more affordable for low-income consumers, and legislation to curb speculation and market manipulation in oil markets. On other issues, he worked with Emanuel to require lobbyists to make additional disclosure of campaign contributions. He sought more money for the region's Metro transit system and for initiatives to clean up the Chesapeake Bay.

House Speaker Nancy Pelosi showed her confidence in Van Hollen by appointing him to head the DCCC after Emanuel stepped down. He worked closely with her on campaign strategy in both the 2008 and 2010 political seasons. Unlike Emanuel, he developed a harmonious relationship with Democratic National Committee Chairman Howard Dean. His goal was to try to reverse historical forces that generally produced losses for a winning party after a wave election like the one in 2006. He helped Democrats win special elections in unlikely territory—downstate Illinois, Baton Rouge, Louisiana and northeast Mississippi. He ran a skillful in-house research operation and expanded the field program. He also performed well in the most important function for any DCCC chairman—raising money. The committee took in $176 million in the 2008 election cycle, compared with $118 million for its counterpart NRCC. Early and aggressive challenges to veteran members helped persuade 26 Republican incumbents not to seek re-election that year. Van Hollen successfully identified pickup possibilities in unlikely districts in Alabama and Idaho. Overall, Democrats gained 21 seats in November 2008, many in traditionally Republican areas, and Van Hollen and the DCCC got much of the credit. Only four freshman Democrats, all in Republican-leaning areas, were defeated out of a class of 33.

After his 2008 electoral success, Van Hollen contemplated a challenge to Caucus Chairman John Larson of Connecticut, a step up the leadership ladder. But Pelosi persuaded him to stay on as DCCC chairman for the 2010 election and also gave him a new leadership post, assistant to the speaker. He remained involved on substantive issues in the 111th Congress (2009-10). In April 2009, he introduced a cap-and-dividend bill, an alternative to the Democrats' cap-and-trade legislation that would impose a carbon tax on coal, oil and gas producers and distribute the proceeds as dividends to citizens. He was concerned about the effect the stricter cap-and-trade bill would have on members in coal states. The energy bill ultimately died in the Senate. During another major debate, on the health care insurance market overhaul, Van Hollen co-sponsored a successful amendment allowing children up to age 26 to stay on their parents' health insurance—a major talking point for Democrats defending the bill in the 2010 campaign. He also sponsored a similar provision for the Federal Employees Health Benefits Plan.

When the U.S. Supreme Court in January 2010 overturned many federal restrictions on corporate involvement in campaign advertising, Van Hollen introduced a bill providing for increased disclosure requirements for corporations. When the powerful National Rifle Association came out in opposition in May, he fashioned an amendment exempting the NRA. When the Congressional Black Caucus and many liberals objected, Van Hollen expanded the exemption to the Sierra Club, the Humane Society and AARP. The bill passed the House in June 219-206. Van Hollen also has a strong interest in foreign policy. In June 2009, he sponsored a successful amendment to a Pakistan aid bill with a provision providing for duty-free entry to goods produced in reconstruction zones in Afghanistan and Pakistan.

But much of Van Hollen's time was necessarily spent on the DCCC's mandate to hold or increase the Democratic majority in 2010. Sensing the national mood turning against incumbents, he said in February 2009 that his job was to "hold the line" and that there would be no "third wave." He worked to give freshman Democrats the lead role on popular amendments. He identified 41 "endangered species" members and worked to give those with conservative districts leeway to vote against the leadership on the budget. Once again, he was successful in special elections, holding one seat in upstate New York and holding the late John Murtha's seat in coal country Pennsylvania. But he was unable to bridge the deep schism in the Hawaii Democratic party, and the party lost Hawaii's 1st District seat as a result.

His job grew increasingly difficult as poll results rolled in showing an increasing number of Democratic incumbents trailing little-known Republican challengers. In August 2010, he warned that Democrats were in for "a very tough campaign season." He said, "We're obviously working closely to protect those who did not prepare themselves." He contributed $1.6 million of his own campaign money to others, but he admitted after the election that he had cut off nine incumbents who could not be saved from further DCCC funding, sending $12 million to districts where Democrats still had hopes of winning in the final days. Van Hollen told *The New York Times*, "Just on the triage side, we believe we saved 15-20 seats." Even so, Democrats lost 63 seats—more than either party had lost since the 1948 election. "It was obviously a brutal night for Democrats," Van Hollen told the *Times*.

With Democrats in the minority in 2011, Van Hollen was no longer assistant to the speaker and he told Pelosi he did not want another term as DCCC chairman. He instead got a plum committee assignment as the ranking Democrat on the Budget Committee, replacing John Spratt of South Carolina, who lost his seat in 2010.

At home, Van Hollen is almost invulnerable to challenge. When Maryland Sen. Paul Sarbanes announced his retirement in early 2005, Van Hollen gave serious thought to jumping into the multicandidate Democratic primary. But with the likely prospect of his advancement in the House, he decided against it.

★ MASSACHUSETTS ★

It would be a city upon a hill, John Winthrop wrote of the Massachusetts Bay Colony that he and his fellow Puritans were building, an example to the entire world. And Massachusetts, in the nearly four centuries since, has always assumed that it has a lot to teach others. The Puritans' austere creed taught that only the elect would be saved and that they must extirpate the forces of Satan—Indians, Papists, tolerationists. For 150 years, New England was partial to learning, but it also was insular, hostile to outsiders, and economically stagnant. Then, after the American Revolution, the war between royal Britain and revolutionary and Napoleonic France allowed New England's ship owners to cross enemy lines to become the world's leading merchants. They made vast profits and invested the money in textile mills, then railroads, then coal mines and steel mills, providing much of the capital that made industrial America.

Massachusetts remade the country in other ways. Intellectually, New England flowered in the 19th century, more than 200 years after Plymouth Rock. Writers from Boston, Cambridge, and Concord—Ralph Waldo Emerson, Henry Wadsworth Longfellow, Henry David Thoreau, John Greenleaf Whittier, Nathaniel Hawthorne—created an American literature and popularized an American philosophy. Demographically, New England Yankees surged across the continent. Long blocked from upstate New York by mountains and the British-Iroquois alliance, they only reached Syracuse in the 1820s. By the 1850s, they were in Iowa, Kansas, and Oregon's Willamette Valley, and by the 1870s, in Los Angeles. They helped found the Republican Party and did much to start—and win—the Civil War. They planted their economic system and their values, articulated in the *McGuffey Readers*, across the continent.

In the meantime, Massachusetts itself and Boston, the "Hub of the Universe," were being remade. The Irish potato famine of the 1840s and an imploding economy sent Irish immigrants across the Atlantic, and many came to Boston, looking for work in the mills, docks, and factories of Massachusetts. Yankee Protestants had seen Catholics as their great political and cultural enemy since the 17th century, and they felt that their commonwealth was under siege. As Catholics became a majority, first in Boston and then statewide, Protestants feared that the Irish would use their political clout to ladle out government jobs and benefits to their own—and the Irish had a much better flair for politics than an instinct for commerce. But they encountered such bigotry and rejection by the Yankees that even as successful an Irish Catholic as Joseph Kennedy abandoned Boston for New York in 1927. Politics in Massachusetts for years was a kind of culture war between Yankee Republicans and Irish Democrats, an argument not so much over the distribution of income or the provision of services as over whose vision of Massachusetts should be honored, and whose version of history should be taught—an argument not unlike the battles being fought between cultural liberals and conservatives today.

Sometimes, the stakes were concrete—control of patronage, command of the Boston Police Department—but more often they were symbolic. Yankee Republicans tended to back activist government programs: public works and protective tariffs to help business; the Civil War and Reconstruction to help suitably distant oppressed people such as Southern blacks; uplifting (and productivity-enhancing) social movements such as temperance. The Irish found the 19th-century Democratic Party and its philosophy of laissez-faire more congenial. The Irish had come from a place where the government was the enemy, and they didn't want government spending money to help the rich or to stimulate commerce. They also didn't want government to restrict immigration, to advance blacks (potential competitors in the labor market), or to ban alcohol.

The Irish and Catholic percentages rose slowly over the years. Yankees had smaller families, moved west, intermarried with people of immigrant stock, and lost their Yankee identity. The Irish mostly stayed put, raised large families, and maintained their identity. Slowly but surely, Massachusetts moved from being one of the most Republican states to one of the most Democratic. Economically, early-20th-century Massachusetts progressed little. The descendants of the Yankees who had been so venturesome in the early 19th century became cautious investors in the early 20th. The predominance of the textile mills in their home state meant that for a century beginning in the 1820s, Massachusetts imported low-skill labor and exported high-skill people. As textile mills started moving south in the 1920s, Massachusetts started exporting low-skill people as well. From the waning of Yankee authority until the national rise of the Kennedys, Massachusetts seemed to run out of things to teach the rest of the nation. The state's Yankee Republicans were backward looking, out of power in Washington, on the defensive at home, and without a cause to champion. The Irish Democrats, not least Joseph P. Kennedy, were hostile to Franklin Roosevelt's

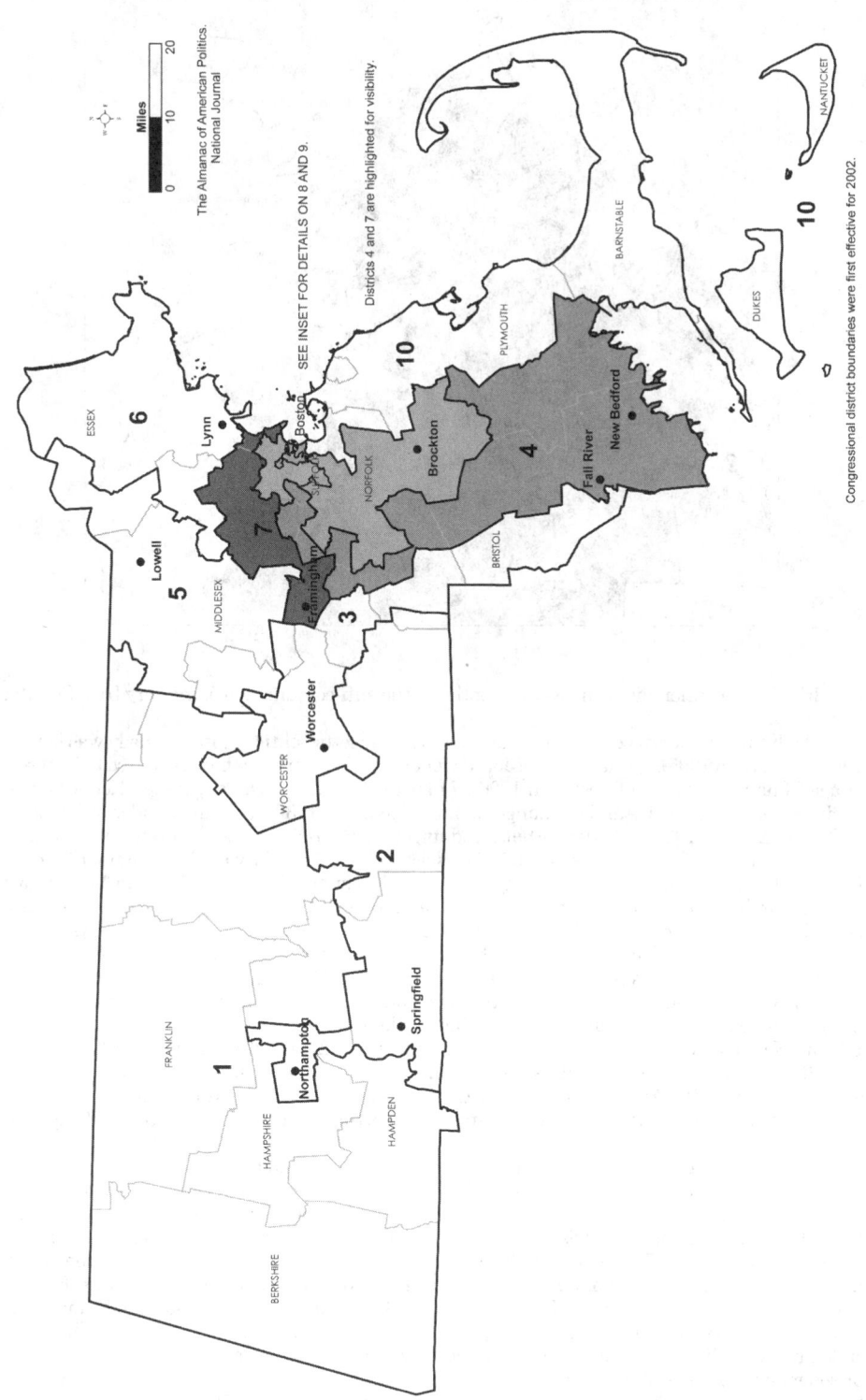

The Almanac of American Politics.
National Journal

SEE INSET FOR DETAILS ON 8 AND 9.

Districts 4 and 7 are highlighted for visibility.

Congressional district boundaries were first effective for 2002.

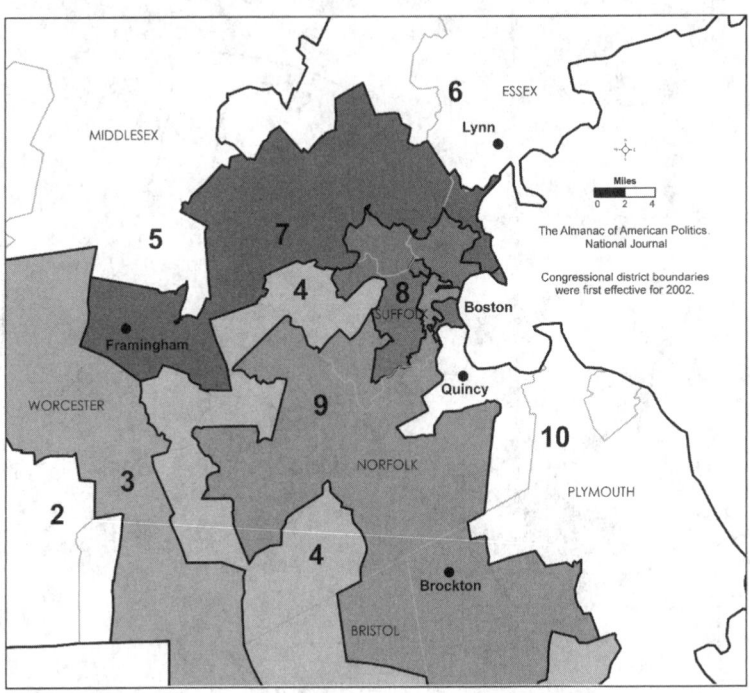

pro-British internationalism and were receptive to the anti-communism of the very Irish Sen. Joe McCarthy.

The Kennedys occupied a unique place in Massachusetts politics. Rose Kennedy was born in 1890 (and died in 1995), the daughter of John "Honey Fitz" Fitzgerald, who was elected to Congress at age 31 and was mayor of Boston in 1906-07 and 1910-14. Her husband, Joseph Kennedy, was chairman of the Securities and Exchange Commission in the 1930s and ambassador to the Court of St. James from 1937 to 1940. Catholic and uncommonly rich, he was a shrewd and ruthless political operator. Their only residence in Massachusetts after 1927 was their summer home in Hyannis Port. In 1946, Joseph Kennedy moved his oldest surviving son, John, to Boston, and helped steer his election to the U.S. House that year, to the U.S. Senate in 1952, and to the presidency in 1960. With their elegant manners, charm, and great achievements, the Kennedys seemed like royalty to the Irish Catholics of Massachusetts. And Catholics across the country, 78% of whom voted for John Kennedy, greeted the Democrat's election in 1960 with great pride. Joseph and John Kennedy were, on many issues, conservative or skeptical. But JFK's administration was increasingly, even before his untimely death, identified as liberal. His example and that of his brother Edward Kennedy, who was elected to the U.S. Senate in 1962, moved Massachusetts Catholics to the left. At the same time, the leftward direction of the state's elite campuses in the 1960s influenced Massachusetts Protestants. The universities also provided the basis for a surging high-tech economy, to the point that Massachusetts started importing high-skill people even as it exported those with low skills.

In the 1970s and 1980s, Massachusetts, with one interval, had the most liberal governance and outlook on national politics of any state in the country. It was the only state to vote for Democratic presidential nominee George McGovern in 1972 and, although it voted twice for Republican Ronald Reagan, the son of an Irish Catholic, its Democratic percentage in presidential contests from 1968 to 1988 was 53%, just 0.4% behind Rhode Island and well ahead of every other state. During that span, its U.S. senators were Edward Kennedy, liberal Republican Edward Brooke, and Democrats Paul Tsongas and John Kerry. Liberal governors such as Republican Francis Sargent and Democrat Michael Dukakis vastly increased spending and endorsed policies that helped sink Dukakis' 1988 presidential campaign, notably the law that granted weekend furloughs to prisoners sentenced to life without parole. As historian David Hackett Fischer points out in *Albion's Seed*, the mind-set of the settlers remains strong even when the ethnicity of current residents is far different, and the spirit of the Puritans, the faith that they had much to teach the rest of the world, is strong in Massachusetts liberals: in the smug liberalism of Michael Dukakis, the hearty liberalism of Edward Kennedy, and the combative liberalism of John Kerry.

Then, in the early 1990s, Massachusetts had a momentary political revolution. The 1980s "Massachusetts miracle" had turned into a curse, as the state's economy sagged badly, as defense cutbacks sent unemployment rising, and as high-tech firms like Wang and Digital withered and Cambridge-based Lotus' software was eclipsed by Microsoft's. The Northeast real estate bubble burst, and Massachusetts banks foundered. The state government essentially went bankrupt. In 1990, as Dukakis retired as governor, voters embraced big tax cuts and elected Republican William Weld in his place.

Four different Republicans held the governorship for the next 16 years. Weld favored a government that taxed and spent lightly, that was friendly to gay rights, that exerted some effort to protect the environment, and that was tough on crime. Referenda limiting taxes and Weld's sharp spending cuts reduced the burden of government, and the state's private economy began recovering. Re-elected with 71% of the vote in 1994, Weld later left the state, but his basic approach prevailed, with variations, under his successors—Paul Cellucci, who took office in 1997 when Weld resigned; Jane Swift, who took office in 2001 when Cellucci resigned; and Mitt Romney, who was elected in 2002. But they were able to reduce the cost of government only so far. The biggest policy innovation was the health care plan passed by the legislature and supported by Romney in 2006. It required all residents to buy health insurance, levied taxes on employers who do not provide it, and subsidized it for low-wage earners. Romney argued that universal coverage would reduce the need to provide free care to the uninsured. Romney's plan became the model for the national health care overhaul embraced by President Barack Obama and passed by Congress in 2010. The fierce conservative backlash that followed caused problems for Romney well into 2011 as he geared up for the Republican presidential primaries.

The Massachusetts economy sagged noticeably after 2000. The state held its own in competition for high-tech and defense industries, but it showed little growth even as the nation's economy surged. Its economy perked up in 2006 and 2007, only to be smacked down by the national recession in 2008. Most who left were young, many were professionals, and many were unable to afford Massachusetts' high housing costs. They have been only partly replaced by immigrants, about half of them Brazilians; Massachusetts has many descendants of Portuguese and Azorean immigrants, and the Brazilians have evidently been attracted to the most Lusophone part of the United States.

At the same time, the cultural liberalism that Weld championed has prevailed. Weld was one of America's first politicians to endorse gay rights, and he appointed Supreme Judicial Court Chief Justice Margaret Marshall, who pushed through the 4-3 decisions in November 2003 requiring the legislature to give gays equal marriage rights. When the legislature declined, the judge in 2004 declared that same-sex couples have the right to marry. A short-lived stampede of same-sex couples to clerks' offices began: Some 2,500 same-sex marriages occurred the week after the court's decision.

But Romney opposed the decision, and urged the legislature to send to the voters a constitutional amendment banning same-sex marriage and endorsing civil unions. Democrats in the state House resisted, and over the next two years, public opinion seemed to accept a change that was already occurring without notable disruption. In 2006, the state House voted 151-45 against the amendment, five votes shy of the 50 needed to place the measure on the ballot. Once again, there were lessons to be learned from the Massachusetts experience. Courts in Connecticut, New Hampshire, and Iowa, as well as the Vermont Legislature had legalized same-sex marriage by 2011. The California legislature and the New York Assembly also voted to do so. However, more than 40 states, stunned by the Massachusetts court's decision on same-sex marriage, went the other way and passed statutes or constitutional amendments barring same-sex marriage (as California did in 2008).

The continuing allegiance of Catholic voters (still a majority, according to the 2008 exit poll), the cultural liberalism of the Yankees and university elites, and the out-migration of Bay State natives who are not similarly minded has made Massachusetts one of the nation's most Democratic states. Deval Patrick's 56%-35% victory in 2006 over Romney's lieutenant governor, Kerry Healey, had returned the governorship to the Democrats, and they held all six statewide offices and all 12 U.S. House and Senate seats.

In May 2008, Edward Kennedy was diagnosed with a brain tumor. This tragedy occurred at the peak of his political success. His endorsed candidate, Barack Obama of Illinois, was poised to win the Democratic nomination for president. In Congress, Democrats held supermajorities and were on the verge of enacting the kind of health care legislation that had been Kennedy's major legislative goal for years. Kennedy soldiered on in the Senate, and succumbed in August 2009. He was the fourth longest-serving senator in U.S. history and one with very substantial legislative achievements. It was widely assumed that his seat would be filled by another Democrat. Gov. Patrick appointed Paul Kirk, a longtime Kennedy aide and Democratic National chairman in the 1980s, to fill the vacancy. Primaries were held in December 2009, and when Attorney General Martha Coakley won the Democratic nomination over 8th District Rep. Michael Capuano by a 47%-28%, she seemed well on her way to the Senate. Little notice was paid to state Sen. Scott Brown of Wrentham, who won the low-turnout Republican primary with 89% of the vote.

But the Jan. 19, 2010, special election turned into a real barn burner, one that foreshadowed great changes to come in the national elections later in the year. Coakley started out well ahead, but on Jan. 5, the first post-holidays poll by Rasmussen showed her leading Brown by only 50%-41%. Brown got considerable attention when, in response to a question at a televised debate about how he would fill the Kennedy seat, he said: "With all due respect, it's not the Kennedys' seat, it's not the Democrats' seat; it's the people's seat."

Brown campaigned assiduously throughout the state, driving a pickup truck and stopping especially often in the traditional Irish redoubt of South Boston, a campaign work ethic that was a marked contrast to Coakley's. She held a last-week-of-the-campaign fundraiser in a wine bar in Washington, D.C. Democrats ridiculed Brown's truck as a gimmick and Coakley scoffed at the idea of shaking hands out in the cold. Brown promised to be the 41st vote against the Democrats' health care bills, while Coakley indicated she would support Democrats on virtually all issues. Brown's candidacy caught fire with tea party activists opposed to the Obama agenda, which helped him generate grassroots enthusiasm. President Obama swooped in during the final week of campaigning to try to help Coakley, to no avail. Brown won 52%-47%. However, Democrats still dominated when the regular election rolled around in November. All 10 House seats stayed Democratic and Republicans barely dented the Democrats' supermajorities in the legislature.

Population		Household Income		Work	
Pop. 2010:	6,547,629	Under $15k:	11.7%	Private:	80.5%
State rank:	14th	$15k to $50k:	27.6%	Government:	13.0%
Change since 2000:	Up 3.1%	$50k to $100k:	30.8%	Self-employed:	6.4%
Urban:	90.8%	$100k to $200k:	23.2%	Unemployment (3-yr. average):	4.9%
Rural:	9.2%	Over $200k:	6.6%	Poverty:	10.1%
Native of state:	63.6%	Median income:	$64,722	Blue collar:	16.2%
Not a citizen:	7.3%			White collar:	66.9%
Area size:	10,554 sq. mi.	**Home Value**		Khaki collar:	0.1%
		Under $100k:	2.8%	Other:	16.8%
Most populous cities		$100k to $300k:	34.0%		
Boston	617,594	$300k to $500k:	40.3%	**Age**	
Worcester	181,045	$500k to $1 mil:	19.3%	Median age:	38.8 yrs.
Springfield	153,060	Over $1 million:	3.7%	More than 65 yrs:	13.4%
Lowell	106,519	Median:	$352,400	Less than 18 yrs:	22.0%

Race/Ethnicity				Military Veterans		Registered Voters in 2010	
White:	76.1%	*Language*		% of Pop:	8.4%	Democrats:	1,528,974
Black:	6.0%	English:	79.4%			Republicans:	474,798
Hispanic:	9.6%	Spanish:	7.2%	*Veterans by Period*		Ind./other:	2,187,135
Asian:	5.3%	Asian:	3.5%	WWII and before:	14.9%	Voter turnout:	2,319,963
Native Am.:	0.2%	Other European:	8.9%	Korea:	14.0%	Turnout as % of	
Hawaiian:	0.0%			Vietnam:	31.3%	voting age:	45.2%
Two+ races:	1.9%	**Education**		Gulf (pre-2001):	7.8%		
		H.S. grad:	88.7%	Gulf (post-2001):	5.9%	**Legislature**	
Ancestry		College grad:	38.2%	Peace time:	26.2%	Senate:	36 D 4 R
Irish	17.8%	Grad degree:	16.3%			House:	128 D 31 R 1 V
Italian	10.6%						
English	8.8%						

Presidential politics Over the last 11 presidential elections, Massachusetts has been the most Democratic state, giving Democratic nominees on average 56% of the vote. It was Bill Clinton's best state in 1996, Al Gore's second best state in 2000, John Kerry's best in 2004, and Barack Obama's sixth best in 2008 (after Hawaii and Vermont, and barely behind New York, Rhode Island, and Illinois). What is also striking about Massachusetts is how many serious presidential candidates it has produced over the last three decades: Edward Kennedy in 1980, Michael Dukakis in 1988, Paul Tsongas in 1992, Kerry in 2004, and Mitt Romney in 2008. Only California and Texas have produced more serious candidates over that period, but they are the No. 1 and No. 2 states in population, respectively, while Massachusetts is now No. 15, having recently fallen behind Washington and Arizona. Some credit must be given to New Hampshire, which

2008 Presidential Vote		
Barack Obama (D) 1,904,097	(62%)
John McCain (R) 1,108,854	(36%)

2008 Presidential Primary		
Hillary Clinton (D)................705,185	(56%)
Barack Obama (D) 511,680	(41%)

2008 Presidential Primary		
Mitt Romney (R)....................255,892	(51%)
John McCain (R) 204,779	(41%)

2004 Presidential Vote		
John Kerry (D) 1,803,800	(62%)
George W. Bush (R)...........1,071,109	(37%)

holds the nation's first primary: The state is just north of Massachusetts and most of its residents receive Boston television stations. But even more credit must go to the hyper political culture of Boston. Only Chicago seems as preoccupied by its local political figures.

In 2008, Obama received 61.8% of the vote in Massachusetts—slightly trailing Kerry's 61.9%, which is understandable given the latter's home-state status. Obama did particularly well among young voters (78%) and women (68%; Massachusetts has a big gender gap). There's evidence in the exit poll of the split between the university elite and the private-sector affluent, which proved decisive in the January 2010 special Senate election. Obama carried those earning more than $100,000 by only 50%-47%, while he won those with postgraduate degrees 69%-29%. Married voters with children voted 58% for Obama, but they made up only one-third of the electorate; the others voted 70% for Obama.

Massachusetts' presidential primary has long been held in early March and was once the scene of great commotion. It produced victories for native sons Dukakis, Tsongas, Kerry and others. In 2000 it voted solidly for Democrat Gore and Republican John McCain, as many independents reregistered as Republicans.

Massachusetts voted on Super Tuesday, Feb. 5, and it was one of the few states where polls showed close races in both parties. Obama was endorsed by Patrick, Kerry, and U.S. Reps. Michael Capuano and Bill Delahunt. Sen. Kennedy gave a rousing welcome to Obama at a rally the night before the primary in Boston's Faneuil Hall. But Hillary Rodham Clinton also had her Massachusetts supporters, including Boston Mayor Thomas Menino and Reps. Richard Neal, Jim McGovern, Barney Frank, and Stephen Lynch. And, as in New Hampshire, she had the support of downscale Democrats. While Obama carried the university towns, she carried the mill towns. She won majorities from Latino and Jewish voters, in a state where each of those groups outnumbers black voters, who overwhelmingly backed Obama. Clinton won 56%-41% in a turnout of 1.2 million voters.

Far fewer people, 500,000, voted in the Republican primary. Many Massachusetts Republicans are liberal on cultural issues, and Romney's turn to the right on those issues earlier in the election season may have produced a backlash. His two predecessors as governor, Paul Cellucci and Jane Swift, endorsed John McCain. Romney won by just 51%-41%. And because Massachusetts Republicans, unlike those in many other states, didn't have a winner-take-all rule, his delegate haul was minimal, while McCain on the same day was harvesting delegates in winner-take-all states such as New York, New Jersey, Missouri, and California.

Congressional districting Massachusetts' convoluted congressional district lines deserve their own biographer, someone with a sure political instinct and a touch of whimsy. This is, after all, the state whose Gov. Elbridge Gerry gave his name to the term "gerrymander" in the early 19th century. The state lost two seats in the 1960 census, and one each in 1980 and 1990.

112th Congress Lineup
10 D
111th Congress Lineup
10 D

It survived the 2000 census without losing another seat, but it lost one in the reapportionment following the 2010 census. Since it has an all-Democratic House delegation, that means the loss of a Democratic seat in 2012. Demographics suggest that western Massachusetts, where population growth has been minimal or negative, will lose a seat, but the final decision will likely be a battle royal. The two most senior members of the delegation, Edward Markey and Frank, hold important committee positions that the state would not want to lose. The permutations and combinations—and the machinations of Beacon Hill politics—make predictions hazardous.

Governor

Deval Patrick (D)

Elected 2006, term expires Jan. 2015, 2nd term; b. July 31, 1956, Chicago, IL; home, Milton; Harvard U., A.B. 1978, J.D. 1982; Presbyterian; married (Diane); 2 children.

Professional Career: Michael Clark Rockefeller Memorial Traveling Fellow, Sudan, 1978-79; Law clerk, 9th Circuit Court of Appeals, 1982-83; Practicing atty., 1983-94, 1997-99; Asst. U.S. Atty. Gen. for Civil Rights, 1994-97; Vice president and general counsel, Texaco, 1999-2001; Executive vice president and general counsel, Coca-Cola, 2001-04; ACC Capital Holdings, 2004-06.

Office: State House, Rm. 280, Boston, 2133, 617-725-4005; Fax: 617-727-9725; Web site: www.mass.gov/gov.

State Offices: Springfield, 413-784-1200.

Election Results

2010 general	Deval Patrick (D)	1,112,283	(48%)
	Charles Baker (R)	964,866	(42%)
	Timothy Cahill (I)	184,395	(8%)
2010 primary	Deval Patrick (D)	345,764	(97%)

Prior Winning Percentages: 2006 (56%)

Deval Patrick, elected in 2006 and re-elected in 2010, is the state's first African-American governor and only the nation's second black governor. Virginia's Douglas Wilder was the first in 1989. Patrick grew up in a tough South Side Chicago neighborhood, and lived in an apartment where he shared a single room with his mother and sister; his father, a saxophone player, left the family when he was a child. He showed tremendous promise in elementary school, and a teacher recommended him to A Better Chance, an organization that sends gifted minority students to college preparatory schools. Patrick received a scholarship to the tony Milton Academy in Massachusetts. "(It) was like coming to a different planet," Patrick recalled. He went on to graduate from Harvard College and then spent a year working in Africa on a United Nations youth training project in the Darfur region of Sudan. When he returned, he graduated from Harvard Law School and clerked for a federal appeals court judge in Los Angeles. In 1983, he joined the NAACP Legal Defense Fund in New York, and in 1986 he went into private law practice. During the Clinton administration, he was the assistant attorney general for civil rights. He returned to private practice in Boston in 1997, and later was general counsel for Texaco and Coca-Cola. Since Democrat Michael Dukakis left office in 1990, Massachusetts has had four Republican governors, the latest of which was Mitt Romney. Romney, elected in 2002, faced large Democratic majorities in the statehouse, and after a single term, decided not to seek re-election but instead to run for president. The open governor's race attracted a formidable Democratic primary field that included Attorney General Thomas Reilly and venture capitalist Christopher Gabrieli. Patrick was a long shot in his first-ever run for elected office, but his grassroots campaign quickly built support among liberal activists who liked his outsider message and his criticism of the state's "backroom" political culture. He won the nomination decisively in the Sept. 19 primary. Despite speculation that, as the most liberal of the three candidates, he would prove to be the weakest nominee, Patrick won 50% to Gabrieli's 27% and Reilly's 23%. The Republican nominee was Lt. Gov. Kerry Healey. Also running was Christy Mihos, a wealthy businessman and former director of the Massachusetts Turnpike Authority, who left the Republican Party to run as an independent. Mihos never gained traction, and Healey struggled to generate enthusiasm for her campaign. One reason was Romney, who was no asset in Healey's bid to succeed him. He had failed to build the state party in his four years, and his frequent out-of-state travel and the jibes he directed at Massachusetts while preparing to run for president left him with low job-approval ratings. Patrick consistently referred to the "Romney-Healey administration," and ran television ads featuring photos of Romney and Healey.

Healey called Patrick soft on crime and insisted he would raise taxes and increase state spending. Patrick pointed to his credentials as a Justice Department prosecutor and highlighted his executive-level experience at two *Fortune* 500 companies as evidence of his business-friendly background. Late in the campaign, Healey's campaign ran tough ads criticizing him for his advocacy on behalf of convicted rapist Benjamin LaGuer. One ad, which featured a woman walking alone in a parking garage, was viewed as going too far and it backfired. The ensuing publicity surrounding the negative ads, muted the charges that Patrick would weaken criminal justice laws. He won a sweeping 56%-35% victory, with 7% for Mihos. Patrick became the first Democrat in 20 years to win the Massachusetts governor's office. In office, he set about unraveling Romney's initiatives. He restored $384 million in budget cuts, rescinded an agreement with the federal government that empowered the state police to arrest illegal immigrants, and cut funding for abstinence-only sex education. But his honeymoon period ended quickly with a series of missteps. Lavish spending on his official state car, helicopter travel, a renovation of the governor's office that included $12,000 drapes and the hiring of a $72,000-a-year chief of staff for his wife led to weeks of bad press. Patrick acknowledged making a telephone call to Robert Rubin of Citigroup, which has significant business interests in the state, on behalf of the subprime mortgage lender Ameriquest, on whose board Patrick served from 2004 to 2006. The state Republican Party filed a complaint with the Massachusetts Ethics Commission, but the commission decided against reprimanding Patrick. Then he scaled back his public appearances after his wife, a prominent local lawyer, was revealed to be suffering from exhaustion and depression.

Patrick forged ahead, advancing big-ticket and bold new policies. He called for $1 billion in investment in biotechnology, which was passed by the legislature in 2008. He called for major transportation projects, including a commuter rail service from Boston to New Bedford. His corporate tax reductions also passed. In January 2008, he proposed a $28 billion budget, with a $368 million increase for education, making possible longer school days and universal pre-kindergarten. He also called for tuition-free community colleges and in-state college tuition for children of illegal immigrants. He risked the wrath of teacher unions by proposing "readiness schools" modeled on charter schools and free from union, school district, and state regulations. But revenues came in lower than expected, and in January 2009 Patrick engineered widespread cuts in planned spending. In March, he proposed a 19-cent gas tax increase, which was defeated, but as a compromise lawmakers agreed to a 25% hike in the state sales tax.

Ever since the state Supreme Judicial Court legalized same-sex marriage in a 4-3 decision in 2004, opponents had sought a vote on a constitutional amendment reversing the decision. To achieve that, they needed the votes of 50 of the state's 200 legislators in two successive legislatures, which they succeeded in getting in 2005. The issue came to a head in 2007. Patrick lobbied legislators heavily to vote against putting the issue on the ballot (although opinion had moved to the point that same-sex marriage might well have been approved), and in intense negotiations, switched 11 votes. The vote was 151-45 against a referendum, with same-sex marriage opponents five votes short of the required 50. Patrick also pressed successfully for repeal of a 1913 law banning out-of-state couples from marrying in Massachusetts if their own state's laws prohibited the union.

Patrick had less luck with a casino gambling proposal in which the state would have sold licenses for three resort casinos and possibly a fourth. He argued that gambling was an old tradition in Massachusetts: Historic Faneuil Hall in Boston had been financed by lotteries. But Democratic Speaker Salvatore DiMasi was strongly opposed to the plan, and in March 2008, the House defeated it 108-46.

In the hotly contested 2008 Democratic primary, Patrick endorsed Sen. Barack Obama of Illinois in October 2007 and spoke at a rally of 10,000 Obama supporters in Boston Common. Obama's chief strategist, David Axelrod, was a consultant on Patrick's 2006 campaign. Even so, Sen. Hillary Rodham Clinton of New York won the Massachusetts presidential primary. Patrick's close ties to Obama would end up proving useful as he ran for re-election in 2010. A *Boston Globe* poll in July 2009 found him with an approval rating of just 36% and an unfavorable rating of 52%, and the surprise election seven months later of Republican Scott Brown to replace the late Sen. Edward Kennedy seemed to indicate further trouble ahead.

Mihos returned for another shot at the governorship, and the state's Republican establishment backed Charles Baker, the former chief executive officer of Harvard Pilgrim Healthcare who had been a well-respected budget aide to GOP Govs. William Weld and Paul Cellucci. Baker's campaign sought to pull off a repeat of Weld's successful 1990 race in which he ran as a social liberal who blamed Democrats for high taxes and overspending. But Baker lacked the political temperament to tap into voter anger, and failed to energize the tea party activists who had helped propel Brown to the Senate. As Baker attacked Patrick for fiscal recklessness, the governor cast his opponent as responsible for a financing plan for the hugely over-budget Big Dig highway project. Baker faced another significant obstacle—state Treasurer Timothy Cahill, who left the Democratic Party to run as an independent. The two men squabbled for months as each sought to attract fiscally conservative voters. Cahill also filed an acrimonious lawsuit accusing former members of his campaign, the Republican Governors Association and Baker of colluding to destroy his candidacy. The uproar overshadowed any debate over Patrick's record. Meanwhile, Obama rushed to his old friend's aid. He again put his political advisers at Patrick's disposal, raised money for the governor and told a Boston crowd of 15,000 two weeks before the election that the governor has "been there for me as a friend" and "continues to inspire me as a leader."

Patrick ended up winning with 49% of the vote to Baker's 42% and Cahill's 8%. The governor did well in the state's cities, drawing 70% in Boston, 63% in Springfield and 60% in Worcester, to offset Baker's stronger showings in suburban and rural areas. As he was sworn in for a second term, Patrick invoked themes that were similar to those Obama would outline a few weeks later in his State of the Union address, including improving public education for the sake of future generations. "What is at stake is the American dream," Patrick said.

Senior Senator

John Kerry (D)

Elected 1984, term expires 2014, 5th term; b. Dec. 11, 1943, Aurora, CO; home, Boston; Yale U., A.B. 1966, Boston Col., LL.B. 1976; Catholic; married (Teresa Heinz); 5 children.

Military Career: Navy, 1966–70 (Vietnam), Naval Reserves, 1970–78.

Elected Office: MA lt. gov., 1982–84.

Professional Career: Organizer, Vietnam Veterans Against the War; Asst. Dist. Atty., Middlesex Cnty., 1976–81; Practicing atty., 1981–82.

DC Office: 218 RSOB, 20510, 202-224-2742; Fax: 202-224-8525; Web site: kerry.senate.gov.

State Offices: Boston, 617-565-8519; Fall River, 508-677-0522; Springfield, 413-785-4610.

Committees: *Commerce, Science & Transportation:* Communications, Technology & the Internet (Chmn); Competitiveness, Innovation & Export Promotion; Consumer Protection, Product Safety & Insurance; Oceans, Atmosphere, Fisheries & Coast Guard; Science & Space; Surface Transportation & Merchant Marine Infrastructure, Safety & Security. *Finance:* Energy, Natural Resources & Infrastructure; Health Care; International Trade, Customs & Global Competitiveness; Taxation & IRS Oversight. *Foreign Relations* (Chmn). *Small Business & Entrepreneurship.*

Group Ratings

	ACLU	ACU	ADA	CFG	AFS	FRC	LCV	ITIC	NTU	COC
2010	93	0	85	0	95	0	86	67	6	27
2009	–	0	95	3	100	–	100	–	4	33

National Journal Ratings

	2010 LIB	—	2010 CONS	2009 LIB	—	2009 CONS
Economic	66%	—	33%	86%	—	12%
Social	65%	—	0%	85%	—	0%
Foreign	47%	—	0%	55%	—	0%
Composite	74%	—	26%	86%	—	14%

Key Votes of the 111th Congress

1. Overturn Ledbetter	Y	5. Pass health care bill	Y	9. Ratify New START	Y
2. Pass $787 billion stimulus	Y	6. Regulate financial firms	Y	10. Confirm Elena Kagan	Y
3. Repeal DC gun laws	N	7. Pass tax cuts for some	Y	11. Stop EPA climate regs	N
4. Confirm Sonia Sotomayor	Y	8. Legalize immigrants' kids	Y	12. Repeal don't ask, tell	Y

Election Results

2008 general	John Kerry (D)	1,971,974	(66%)	($11,105,663)
	Jeffrey Beatty (R)	926,044	(31%)	($2,072,027)
	Robert Underwood (Lib)	93,713	(3%)	
2008 primary	John Kerry (D)	342,446	(69%)	
	Edward O'Reilly (D)	154,395	(31%)	

Prior Winning Percentages: 2002 (80%); 1996 (52%); 1990 (57%); 1984 (55%)

John Kerry, Massachusetts' senior senator, has been a figure in national politics since 1971. He is the chairman of the Senate Foreign Relations Committee, and in 2004 he was the Democratic nominee for president.

The son of a Foreign Service officer, he grew up all over the world and attended boarding school in Switzerland and New Hampshire. He graduated from Yale in 1966 and, after exploring alternatives, enlisted in the Navy. He served on a swift boat in Vietnam—hazardous duty—and was awarded a Silver Star and three Purple Hearts. Once home, Kerry's disillusionment with America's role in the war led to a period of activism, and in the early 1970s, he became one of the leaders of Vietnam Veterans Against the War. He attracted much attention for his eloquence and for his cosmopolitan background, unusual for a Vietnam veteran. Testifying before the Senate Foreign Relations Committee in April 1971, he famously stated: "How do you ask a man to be the last to die for a mistake?" He condemned "war crimes committed in Southeast Asia," which, he said, were "not isolated incidents but crimes committed on a day-to-day basis with the full awareness of officers at all levels of command." Kerry became familiar enough to be featured in *Doonesbury* and plunged quickly into politics. He moved to Lowell, Mass., and ran for a U.S. House seat in 1972, but lost. Chastened, he went to Boston College law school and became an assistant district attorney for Middlesex County. He was elected lieutenant governor on a ticket with Democrat Michael Dukakis in 1982, and he ran for the U.S. Senate in 1984. In both races, he upset a favored rival for the Democratic nomination.

Kerry came to the Senate with a reputation as a strong liberal and has had a mostly liberal voting record. For some years, Kerry seemed respectful of economic free markets and more inclined to support an expansive U.S. foreign and military policy. In his first 20 years in the Senate, Kerry was not a visibly active legislator; the website *factcheck.org* reported during the 2004 presidential campaign that only 11 of his bills became law. He was arguably more influential behind the scenes. One reason was that the late Edward Kennedy, the Democratic senior senator from Massachusetts since 1967, took the lead in many legislative areas and also in many Massachusetts issues and did not welcome junior colleagues to share his turf.

Kerry made his name as an investigator, spending some time up blind alleys but also producing some important discoveries. As the chairman of the Foreign Relations Subcommittee on the Western Hemisphere, Peace Corps, Narcotics, and Terrorism, he investigated the infamous Bank of Credit and Commerce International scandal. Kerry's other prominent investigation was as chairman of the Select Committee on POW/MIA Affairs, which probed whether Americans were left behind in Vietnam. Kerry and New Hampshire Republican Bob Smith went to Vietnam to do their own investigation, and ultimately concluded that there was "no compelling evidence that any American remains alive in captivity in Southeast Asia." By May 1995, Kerry and fellow Vietnam veteran John McCain, R-Ariz., were convinced that Hanoi was fully cooperating and, aware they had standing on the issue, persuaded President Clinton to normalize relations with Vietnam.

When Clinton was president, Kerry took some interesting positions on issues that put him at odds with Democratic interest groups. He supported the balanced-budget amendment and voted for the welfare overhaul of 1996. In 1998, he decried the "implosion" of public education and said it was caused not just by overcrowded classrooms but also by the "stifling bureaucracy" of school systems. His list of reforms, co-sponsored with Oregon Republican Gordon Smith, included proposals strongly opposed by teachers unions—important Democratic allies—such as ending teacher tenure. He favored normalizing trade relations with China and led the floor fight against an amendment that would have required review of China's human rights practices.

After George W. Bush became president, Kerry turned to sharp-edged opposition to administration policy. The 2001 Bush tax cut, he said, was "unfair, unaffordable, and unquestionably ineffective in growing our economy." He was one of the most outspoken opponents of oil drilling in the Arctic National Wildlife Refuge and threatened to filibuster the bill. He criticized the administration for its rejection of the Kyoto Protocol on climate change, although he was one of 95 senators who voted in 1997 to reject Kyoto as long as it exempted developing nations like China and India, a main feature of the treaty. He criticized the administration for letting Afghan troops take the lead in Tora Bora in late 2001, and said that may have allowed al-Qaida and Taliban leaders to escape. Despite considerable criticism of administration policy on Iraq, he voted for the Iraq war resolution in October 2002.

Kerry wanted to run for president in 2000, but with Clinton obviously smoothing the way for his vice president, Al Gore, Kerry announced he would not run. There were no such obstacles in his way in 2004. He had an additional advantage: money. His wife, Teresa Heinz Kerry, inherited $600 million when her first husband, Pennsylvania Republican Sen. John Heinz, died in a 1991 plane crash. Her net worth has been estimated at up to $1 billion, making Kerry one of the richest members of Congress.

In early 2003, Kerry entered the presidential race as the favorite to win the nomination. But by July, he was trailing in the polls far behind Howard Dean of Vermont, whose outspoken opposition to the Iraq war appealed to the left and whose innovative use of the Internet generated an unprecedented number of small contributions. Kerry, who had voted for the war, began to criticize Bush's conduct of it, often in harsh terms. Then, in mid-January 2004, Dean's poll numbers in Iowa and New Hampshire started dropping. Well-organized in Iowa and well-known in New Hampshire, Kerry was the Democrat best positioned to fill the vacuum. His record in Vietnam, he suggested, would protect him against criticisms that he was too soft on foreign and military policy. "Bring it on!" he said at the end of his speeches. He won a solid though not overwhelming victory in the Iowa caucuses and, eight days later, an impressive victory in New Hampshire. Kerry won all the primaries but three and clinched the Democratic nomination on March 2, exactly eight months before the general election.

As early as May, pollster John Zogby said the election was "Kerry's to lose." The Kerry campaign raised far more money than anyone expected, and was helped as well by outside organizations that spent more than $200 million to defeat Bush. Bush's job approval hovered under 50%, and he trailed Kerry in polls for much of the seven-month campaign. Kerry performed well in debates, being judged the winner in snap polls in all three. Yet he lost. One reason may have been encapsulated by his March 16 defense of his 2003 vote against the supplemental appropriations bill for Iraq: "I actually did vote for the $87 billion before I voted against it." The Bush campaign painted Kerry as a flip-flopper, and in fact he has had a propensity, common in politicians, to try to please those on all sides of an issue. More important, he was trying to rally a Democratic Party split between fiercely anti-war Bush haters and moderate Democrats who hoped for the best in Iraq but preferred a Democrat to Bush on most issues. Second, the credential that the Kerry campaign emphasized at the Democratic National Convention, his decorated service in Vietnam, was undermined by the ads and book sponsored by Swift Boat Veterans for Truth. Kerry had claimed—in the *Boston Herald* in 1979, on the Senate floor in 1986, and to the Associated Press in 1992—to have served on secret missions in Cambodia in the Christmas season of 1968. But those claims were withdrawn by his campaign in August, and no one, including the boat mates who supported him, came forward to corroborate his additional claim to have served in Cambodia in later months.

Finally, Kerry was vulnerable to attack as a Massachusetts liberal. The Bush campaign highlighted his rating by *National Journal* as the No. 1 liberal in the Senate in 2003—arguably unfairly, since he skipped many roll-call votes that year while campaigning for president. However, *National Journal* had ranked him as the 11th-most-liberal senator in the course of his career, well to the left of the midpoint. Democratic voter-turnout efforts were successful. Kerry won 59 million votes, 16% more than Gore and then the second-highest total in American history. But Republican voter turnout efforts were even better. Bush won 62 million votes, 23% more than he had four years earlier, and won the popular vote 51%-48%.

Kerry's disappointment at losing was matched only by that of the many Massachusetts politicians who were longing to run for the Senate. The state has not had an open Senate seat since Kerry secured his 1984, and before that, since 1966.

So in 2005, Kerry became the first senator to return to Congress as a defeated presidential nominee since South Dakota Democrat George McGovern in 1973. He proceeded to stake out stands on important issues. He proposed a Kids First bill, to provide health insurance for every child. Kennedy, to whom he had usually deferred on health care issues, agreed to be the lead cosponsor. He followed up with a proposal that would require all Americans to have health insurance by 2012. In 2006, he called for reducing oil consumption by 2.5 million barrels a day by 2015, and for sharp decreases in carbon dioxide emissions. Kerry supported the Bush administration on one foreign policy issue during that period: the agreement on India's civilian nuclear program, provided it pushed India to agree to international standards for safeguarding civilian nuclear plants. But he increasingly opposed the administration's course in Iraq. In June 2006, as the Senate considered an amendment calling for redeployments from Iraq with no set date, Kerry and Democrat Russell Feingold of Wisconsin insisted on bringing up an amendment to withdraw all combat forces by July 2007. It was defeated 86-13.

Kerry's course during 2005 and 2006—his continued sharp criticisms of the administration, his new proposals on major issues, his heavy travel and fundraising schedule in support of Democratic candidates—suggested he was interested in running for president again in 2008. Criticized by some Democrats for having left $15 million in his presidential account long after the 2004 election was over, he contributed more than $1 million to Democratic candidates and the national Democratic campaign committees. Of his 2002 vote for the Iraq resolution, he wrote on the *Huffington Post* blog, "There's nothing—nothing—in my life in public service I regret more, nothing even close."

Then, on October 30, 2006, at Pasadena City College, he told a crowd of students, "Education: If you make the most of it, you study hard, you do your homework, and you make an effort to be smart, you can do well. If you don't, you get stuck in Iraq." The remark was interpreted as a disparaging comment about American military troops, and to some it was reminiscent of his 1971 Foreign Relations Committee testimony. In Seattle the next day, Kerry refused to apologize and blamed Bush adviser Karl Rove for instigating demands that he do so. When criticism continued, and Democratic candidates began to ask Kerry to skip scheduled campaign appearances, Kerry and his staffers maintained that the comment was "a botched joke," and that he had meant to say that "you get us stuck in Iraq". The explanation did not prevent the cancellation of all his appearances for Democratic candidates in the last week of the midterm congressional contests. Kerry had no public events in the seven weeks after the election, and on January 24, 2007, he announced he was not running for president in 2008.

No longer a presidential candidate, Kerry turned his focus to the Senate, especially to the foreign policy issues that interest him. At the World Economic Forum in Davos, Switzerland, in January 2007, he proclaimed that under Bush the United States had become "a sort of international pariah." Later that year, he called for sending 5,000 more troops to Afghanistan. By then, many other Democrats had caught up with his thinking on Iraq and were demanding a timetable for the withdrawal of U.S. troops, similar to the position expressed in the Kerry-Feingold amendment of 2006.

On domestic issues, he was arguably more involved than he was before he ran for president. Kerry staked out issues ranging from insurance coverage for mental illness to better access to sports programming for everyday people. With Kennedy, he pushed for mental health parity in the State Children's Health Insurance Program, which would require the health system to cover treatment for mental illness the same as for physical illnesses. He also sought to reverse the policy barring HIV-positive people from immigrating to the United States. With the publication of *This Moment on Earth*, a book he co-authored with his wife, he renewed his activism on global warming. He attended the United Nations climate-change talks and in December 2007, again criticized the Bush administration for opposing the Kyoto Protocol. With Maine Republican Olympia Snowe, he sponsored a bill to reduce carbon emissions 65% below 1990 levels by 2050. Kerry also proposed legislation to set speed limits on ships in Massachusetts waters to protect whales.

Kerry enjoyed good working relationships with both candidates in the hard-fought Democratic presidential primary in 2008, but he ultimately endorsed Barack Obama over Hillary Rodham Clinton. Kerry had effectively launched Obama's national career by giving the then Illinois state senator the keynote spot at the 2004 Democratic National Convention. He campaigned heavily for Obama in 2008, gave him his 2004 e-mail list for fundraising, and delivered a stirring speech for him at the party's convention in Denver. After the election, it was made known that Kerry would be pleased to be nominated to be secretary of State, but the job went to Clinton. But Joe Biden's election as vice president meant that Kerry became chairman of the Senate Foreign Relations Committee, the same body before which he had entered public consciousness with his testimony 38 years before.

With friends in the White House, Kerry was in a much different position in 2009 than he had been during the Bush administration. He took some initiatives of his own, visiting Damascus to see Bashir Assad in February 2009, foreshadowing the administration's resumption of closer relations a year later. He held hearings with Afghanistan veterans in April 2009, but distinguished that conflict from Vietnam: "In Vietnam there was no threat to the United States in any direct form whatsoever," he said. Kerry worked closely with ranking Republican Richard Lugar of Indiana on several issues. He and Lugar strongly supported the New START treaty with Russia and launched a drive for ratification in September 2010, which, despite considerable Republican opposition, resulted in the necessary two-thirds vote. He persuaded Afghan President Hamid Karzai to agree to a runoff election, although that later proved unfeasible. Kerry pushed for increased development aid to Pakistan and was embarrassed by leaks in July 2010 that elements in the Pakistani government were aiding the Taliban. He called for the United States to establish a no-fly zone in Libya in March 2011, which was ultimately backed by the Obama administration and adopted by the United Nations.

Kerry stepped forward in fall 2009 to play a leading role in the push for legislation to reduce carbon emissions blamed for global warming. In October, he unveiled a 900-page bill with California Democrat Barbara Boxer, chairman of the Environment and Public Works Committee, to create a cap-and-trade system of emissions swapping aimed at reducing the overall level of allowable carbon emissions. The bill passed Boxer's committee with no Republican support. Kerry initiated bipartisan talks with Joe Lieberman, a Connecticut independent, and Lindsey Graham, a South

Carolina Republican, to try to hammer out a version of the bill that could get 60 votes in the Senate. But the efforts bogged down in election-year politics in the spring of 2010. Facing a difficult re-election in Nevada, Majority Leader Harry Reid said an immigration bill would take precedence over the energy bill. That infuriated Graham, who bailed out of the bipartisan negotiations with Kerry. Kerry and Lieberman eventually brought forth a bill, but Reid was still unwilling to bring it to a vote, and the legislation died before the August recess.

No Democratic senator from Massachusetts has been defeated for re-election since 1946, when isolationist Democrat David Walsh was defeated by internationalist Republican Henry Cabot Lodge Jr. Kerry's toughest re-election race was in 1996, when he was opposed by popular. William Weld. They held eight debates, and spent liberally—Kerry, $12.6 million, Weld, $8 million—and attracted more national media attention than any other Senate race that year. But Democratic Massachusetts voted 52%-45% for its junior senator. In 2008, Kerry had primary opposition from Gloucester lawyer Edward O'Reilly, who got 31% of the vote. But he had no problems in the general election and won 66%-31%.

Junior Senator

Scott Brown (R)

Elected Jan. 2010, term expires 2012; b. Sept. 12, 1959, Wakefield, MA; home, Wrentham, MA; Tufts U., B.A. 1981; Boston Coll., J.D. 1985; Reformed Christian; Married (Gail Huff); 2 children.

Military Career: Army National Guard, JAG Corps

Elected Office: Wrentham town assessor; Wrentham town selectman; MA House, 1999-2004; MA Senate, 2004-present

Professional Career: Practicing attorney, 1985-present

DC Office: 314 RSOB, 20510, 202-224-4543; Fax: 202-228-2646; Web site: scottbrown.senate.gov.

State Offices: Boston, 617-565-3170.

Committees: *Armed Services:* Airland (RMM); Emerging Threats & Capabilities; Personnel. *Homeland Security & Governmental Affairs:* Disaster Recovery & Intergovernmental Affairs (Ad Hoc); Federal Financial Management, Government Information, Federal Services & International Security (RMM); Investigations (Permanent). *Small Business & Entrepreneurship. Veterans' Affairs.*

Group Ratings

	ACLU	ACU	ADA	CFG	AFS	FRC	LCV	ITIC	NTU	COC
2010	50	74	20	62	13	100	0	100	84	82
2009	–	–	–	–	–	–	–	–	–	–

National Journal Ratings

	2010 LIB	—	2010 CONS	2009 LIB	—	2009 CONS
Economic	37%	—	62%	*	—	*
Social	36%	—	63%	*	—	*
Foreign	30%	—	67%	*	—	*
Composite	35%	—	65%	*	—	*

Key Votes of the 111th Congress

1. Overturn Ledbetter	*	5. Pass health care bill	*	9. Ratify New START	Y
2. Pass $787 billion stimulus	*	6. Regulate financial firms	Y	10. Confirm Elena Kagan	N
3. Repeal DC gun laws	*	7. Pass tax cuts for some	N	11. Stop EPA climate regs	Y
4. Confirm Sonia Sotomayor	*	8. Legalize immigrants' kids	N	12. Repeal don't ask, tell	Y

Election Results

2010 special	Scott Brown (R)	1,168,178	(52%)	($15,533,145)
	Martha Coakley (D)	1,060,861	(47%)	($9,613,423)
2010 primary	Scott Brown (R)	146,057	(89%)	
	Jack Robinson (R)	17,344	(11%)	

Republican Scott Brown is the junior senator from Massachusetts. He won a special election in January 2010 to succeed the late Democratic Sen. Edward Kennedy, a revered figure in Massachusetts and national politics until he died in office after more than 45 years in the Senate.

Brown is a triathlete, a former fashion model and a Boston College-educated lawyer, but that image belies a turbulent early life growing up in Wakefield, Mass. His parents divorced when Brown was a year old. His mother went on welfare for a short period, and he sometimes lived with his grandparents and an aunt. At age 12, Brown was caught shoplifting music records, an experience that he describes as transformational. "I was a jerk. I had some issues," Brown told *The Boston Globe*. A local judge ordered him to set a better example for his siblings, and Brown went on to be a basketball standout and team co-captain at Wakefield High School. He continued his hoops career at Tufts University, where his he was known as "Downtown Scotty Brown" for his three-point shots.

During his college years, Brown joined the Army National Guard and, after law school, served in the Judge Advocate General's Corps (JAG) as a defense lawyer. Another sidelight of those years was a stint in modeling and filming commercials, which helped him pay for his schooling and also led to a $1,000-gig posing nude for *Cosmopolitan* magazine. ("You don't see anything. It's *Cosmo*, not *Playgirl*," Brown told *The Boston Herald* after the photographs, taken when he was 22, surfaced during the Senate campaign.) His moonlighting also led to love. Brown met and married fellow model Gail Huff after she asked him for help recouping fees from an agent who refused to pay her for a job. Huff is now a news reporter with WCVB-TV. The Browns have two college-age daughters, Ayla, an aspiring singer who competed on television's *American Idol*, and Arianna.

Brown began his political career as town assessor and town selectman for Wrentham, Mass. From there, he ran successfully for the Massachusetts House in 1998. Six years later, he won a special election for a state Senate seat vacated by Democrat Cheryl Jacques, who was taking over as president of the Human Rights Campaign, a national advocacy group for gays and lesbians. Brown sparked criticism from gay rights activists with a remark that it was "not natural" for Jacques and her partner to be parents. Brown opposes same-sex marriage and as a legislator voted in favor of a constitutional amendment defining marriage as a male and female union. That helped establish Brown as one of the most conservative lawmakers in the Massachusetts Senate, where he was one of only five Republicans out of 40 senators. However, Brown supports abortion rights, with the caveat that he favors strict parental consent laws.

When he launched his bid for the U.S. Senate, Brown was universally viewed as a long shot, although the *Boston Globe* called him "the GOP's most attractive Senate candidate since Mitt Romney lost to Kennedy 15 years ago." His victory in the Republican primary was little noticed amid the clamor in the other party, where Coakley had to compete against three other Democrats vying to succeed Kennedy, who died in August 2009 of cancer. She won a Dec. 8, 2009, primary with 47% of the vote, with her closest challenger, U.S. Rep. Michael Capuano, getting 28%. Civic activist Alan Khazei got 13%, and Boston Celtics co-owner Stephen Pagliuca received 12%.

Coakley entered the abbreviated special election season far and away the favorite to win in a state where Democrats outnumber Republicans 3-to-1 and where a Republican had not been elected to the U.S. Senate since 1972. But as in other parts of the country, the growing independent sector of the electorate was in flux, and the two candidates presented stark choices on the issues. Liberal Coakley represented a continuation of Kennedy's philosophy. She called for a robust government option as part of health care reform, and was in line with the national party in supporting cap-and-trade legislation to curb greenhouse gases with a system of emissions credit-swapping and for changes in law giving illegal immigrants a path to citizenship. Brown opposed cap-and-trade legislation and any form of immigration amnesty. He drew the sharpest differences with his opponent on health care. He staunchly opposed the Democrats' bill in Congress, saying it would unfairly force Massachusetts, which already has a universal care law, to pay for health care for other states. He told the *Boston Herald*, "I believe all Americans deserve health care, but we shouldn't have to create a new government option to provide it."

Brown made the issue central to his campaign, striking a chord with voters harboring doubts about the Obama administration's health care and economic stimulus initiatives. He also emphasized lower taxes and smaller government at a time of vigorous government expansion under Obama and Democrats in control of Congress. His theme, and his underdog status, captured the enthusiasm of anti-tax tea party activists, who rushed in to help with voter canvassing and fundraising. Brown also proved to be far more engaged than Coakley on the stump, knocking on countless doors and racking up thousands of miles on his GMC truck, a handy campaign prop in working-class areas. He met voters at diners, pubs and shopping malls. Syndicated columnist Kathleen Parker was among the observers to sound a warning to Democrats, pointing to polls showing Brown leading with independent voters 3-to-1. "Who the heck is Scott Brown?" Parker wrote in early January. "Start with this: He's Joe Six-Pack with a law degree and 30 years in the National Guard."

Coakley did not seem to recognize the threat until the final weeks of the campaign. She took time off over the holidays in December, in contrast to Brown, who manned a Salvation Army collection pot, ringing a bell and introducing himself to shoppers. "I treated this campaign like a sprint triathlon. You have to be good at everything, 18, 19 hours a day. We were just out there cranking," he later told *The New York Times*. Coakley even scoffed at Brown for standing outside in bitterly cold weather to shake hands with hockey fans leaving Fenway Park, which in most playbooks is just good politicking. She was hampered by the mistakes of others —three consecutive Democratic House speakers in Massachusetts have resigned amid scandal—and by mistakes of her own. Asked by a reporter about her experience in international affairs, Coakley suffered a Sarah Palin moment, replying that she has a sister living overseas. In another widely reported episode in sports-crazy Boston, Coakley could not readily identify the Red Sox's Curt Schilling in a radio interview. Although she started out with a fundraising advantage, including considerable help from the national group EMILY's List, Brown became competitive as Republican activists outside the state took notice. Both sides were on the air with negative ads in the final two weeks.

As Coakley's 20-something-point lead evaporated in the polls, fellow Democrats bemoaned Brown's ability to define himself and the contest better than Coakley was able to do. "It's me against the machine," Brown crowed, and chastised Democrats for treating Kennedy's Senate seat as something they expected to have passed to them like the family silver. The *Globe* wrote in the final days of the campaign: "Massachusetts came to exemplify the nation's political divide in recent weeks, as Brown caught fire with voters, including many independents, who are either disenchanted with the Democratic leadership nationally or not sold on the Democratic nominee."

On Jan. 5, pollster Scott Rasmussen reported that Coakley was leading Brown by only 50%-41% among likely voters—a dangerously low lead for a Democrat in a state Barack Obama had carried with 62% of the vote. The Brown campaign announced an online "money bomb" for Jan. 12, a week before the election, seeking $500,000. It raised $1.3 million, and he eventually took in $15.5 million. President Obama paid a hurried visit to Massachusetts on the final weekend, and said derisively of Brown's campaigning, "Anybody can buy a truck."

On Jan. 19, Brown won 52%-47%. He carried most of the cities and towns of Massachusetts. Coakley carried western Massachusetts, a left-leaning area like neighboring Vermont, and rolled up huge margins in college towns and suburbs heavy with academics. She carried heavily Jewish Brookline and Newton by wide margins; she won black neighborhoods in Boston, though turnout there was low. But Brown carried South Boston and the commuter corridors out by I-93 and I-95 to the north of Boston and I-95 and U.S. 3 to the south. He won or nearly won the old textile and shoe mill towns that had once delivered huge percentages to John F. Kennedy in 1952 and 1960. Coakley won the top and bottom of the income and education scales, but Brown carried by a wide margin the vast middle-class in between.

In February, Brown was sworn in and the Democrats' 60-vote supermajority ended. Brown became a key senator in the remaining months of the 111th Congress (2009-10). He voted with Republicans on most issues, but not all. He voted to repeal the ban on gays in the military. He supported a resolution to block the Environmental Protection Agency from regulating carbon emissions after the Democrats' cap-and-trade bill to reduce carbon emissions died in the Senate. In 2010, Brown voted for the financial industry regulation bill after securing a provision exempting Massachusetts mutual funds and insurance companies from a rule barring financial institutions from owning private equity funds. But he was not willing to give Democrats carte blanche. Brown and Maine GOP moderates Olympia Snowe and Susan Collins came out against a recess appointment for the new head of the independent Bureau of Consumer Financial Protection, which effectively blocked the appointment of Harvard Law professor Elizabeth Warren. Brown also opposed the DREAM Act, which would have provided a path to citizenship for undocumented children after completion of a college degree or military service.

No Republican senator from Massachusetts can be considered to have a safe seat. Edward Brooke, elected in 1966 and 1972, was defeated by Democrat Paul Tsongas in 1978 despite a voting record considerably more liberal than Brown's. The last Republican senator to retire undefeated was Leverett Saltonstall in 1966, who was born in 1892, when Massachusetts was still a Yankee Protestant Republican commonwealth. But throughout 2010, Brown's job approval remained the highest of any major Massachusetts politician.

FIRST DISTRICT

John Olver (D)

Elected June 1991, 10th full term; b. Sept. 3, 1936, Honesdale, PA; home, Amherst; Rensselaer Polytechnic Inst., B.S. 1955, Tufts U., M.A. 1956, M.I.T., Ph.D. 1961; no religious affiliation; married (Rose); 1 child.

Elected Office: MA House of Reps., 1968–72; MA Senate, 1972–91.

Professional Career: Chemistry prof., U. of MA, Amherst, 1961–69.

DC Office: 1111 LHOB, 20515, 202-225-5335; Fax: 202-226-1224; Web site: olver.house.gov.

State Offices: Fitchburg, 978-342-8722; Holyoke, 413-532-7010; Pittsfield, 413-442-0946.

Committees: *Appropriations:* Energy & Water Development; Homeland Security; Transportation, HUD & Related Agencies (RMM).

Group Ratings

	ACLU	ACU	ADA	CFG	AFS	FRC	LCV	ITIC	NTU	COC
2010	88	0	100	0	100	6	100	67	6	13
2009	–	0	100	0	100	–	100	–	1	33

National Journal Ratings

	2010 LIB — 2010 CONS		2009 LIB — 2009 CONS	
Economic	90%	0%	91%	0%
Social	93%	0%	89%	0%
Foreign	97%	0%	91%	0%
Composite	97%	3%	95%	5%

Key Votes of the 111th Congress

1. Overturn Ledbetter	Y	5. Bar federal abortion funds	N	9. Stop detainee transfers	N
2. Pass $820 billion stimulus	Y	6. Pass health care bill	Y	10. Legalize immigrants' kids	Y
3. Let guns in national parks	N	7. Regulate financial firms	Y	11. Repeal don't ask, tell	Y
4. Pass cap-and-trade	Y	8. Pass tax cuts for some	Y	12. Limit campaign funds	Y

Election Results

2010 general	John Olver (D)..128,011	(60%)	($863,992)
	William Gunn (R)...74,418	(35%)	($60,342)
	Michael Engle (I)...10,880	(5%)	
2010 primary	John Olver (D)... unopposed		

Prior Winning Percentages: 2008 (73%), 2006 (76%), 2004 (100%), 2002 (68%), 2000 (68%), 1998 (72%), 1996 (53%), 1994 (100%), 1992 (52%), 1991 special (50%)

Population		Race/Ethnicity		Work	
Pop. 2010:	644,956	White:	85.2%	Private:	76.1%
Change since 2000:	Up 1.7%	Black:	2.1%	Government:	16.3%
Urban:	69.3%	Hispanic:	8.6%	Self-employed:	7.3%
Rural:	30.7%	Asian:	2.1%	Blue collar:	20.8%
Area size:	3,191 sq. mi.	Native Am.:	0.2%	White collar:	60.7%
		Hawaiian:	0.0%	Khaki collar:	0.1%
Age		Two+ races:	1.6%	Other:	18.4%
Median age:	40.0 yrs.				
More than 65 yrs:	14.0%	*Ancestry*		Median income:	$53,706
Less than 18 yrs:	21.5%	Irish	15.1%	Median Home Value:	$237,300
		French	11.3%		
Education		English	10.0%	**Military Veterans**	
H.S. grad:	88.9%			% of Pop:	10.2%
College grad:	29.1%				
Grad degree:	11.8%				

Western Massachusetts; Pittsfield

The stony hills and green mountains of western Massachusetts, where more trees dot the landscape today than when Henry David Thoreau was writing in the 1840s and where stone fencing once bounded one working farm from another, look a lot like they did 300 years ago. This was the frontier in the 17th century, where Puritan preachers founded towns in the wilderness, farmed the rocky soil, and preached against declension. This was Yankee New England's west-

2008 Presidential Vote		
Barack Obama (D) 196,565	(64%)
John McCain (R) 102,645	(33%)
2004 Presidential Vote		
John Kerry (D) 185,377	(63%)
George Bush (R) 103,990	(35%)
Cook Partisan Voting Index: D+14		

ern frontier for nearly 200 years. In the 19th century, the area was the home of writers and artists: Emily Dickinson lived quietly in Amherst, Edith Wharton grandly on her estate in Lenox. Herman Melville struck up a friendship with Nathaniel Hawthorne after purchasing a farm near Hawthorne's Pittsfield home, not far from where the Boston Symphony plays at the Tanglewood Festival each summer. Mill towns were here as well, jammed into valleys or along the wide Connecticut River.

As the 20th century progressed, and trees grew on stony land once farmed, western Massachusetts came to look less settled. The exceptions were areas near giant factories like General Electric's now-closed electric transformer plant in Pittsfield and the Crane paper factory in Dalton, which since 1879 has been the only company to print money for the U.S. Treasury. Armed guards protect the facility's secret plating process, which is the benchmark for producing currency and preventing counterfeiting. *Financial Times* dubbed Pittsfield "the Brooklyn of the Berkshires" for its success in drawing people and businesses from ritzier areas in much the same way that the bridge-crossed New York borough has attracted Manhattanites. That influx has helped keep unemployment lower than nearby Leominster (pronounced *LEMON-stir*) a western outpost of the Boston suburbs. The region's rolling hills and charming New England towns support a thriving tourist trade, featuring attractions such as Tanglewood and Jacob's Pillow, the only dance institution to be named a National Historic Landmark. There are year-round, weekend, and vacation homes throughout the Berkshires. Democratic Gov. Deval Patrick has a weekend home there.

Western Massachusetts has changed politically. For many years, it was a heartland of the Republican Party—flinty, thrifty, and chilly, just like the area's most famous politician, Calvin Coolidge. But the area now contains some of the most liberal parts of the United States. Progressive MSNBC host Rachel Maddow has a home here with her partner, Susan Mikula. "We kind of forget we're gay," Mikula told *New York* magazine in 2008. "We live in western Mass and New York, and it's very accommodating." Stockbridge attracted liberal artist Norman Rockwell, and Alice's Restaurant in Great Barrington was immortalized by folk singer Arlo Guthrie in his anti-war song of the same name. The concentration of colleges and universities in the Pioneer Valley brought together a critical mass of liberal scholars and graduate students; the University of Massachusetts in Amherst is the largest of these, and it continues to expand on former farmland.

The 1st Congressional District is the state's largest congressional district geographically. It covers most of western Massachusetts—all of Berkshire and Franklin counties and their small towns; most of Hampshire County; Holyoke and West Springfield on the Connecticut River; and the more-working-class areas of northern Worcester County. It extends east to Pepperell in Middlesex County, about 40 miles from Boston. It borders four states and covers about 40% of the land area of Massachusetts. Over time, the solidly Democratic voting base has shifted from low-income mill workers in places like Holyoke and Pittsfield to liberal academics in the college towns. In 2008, the district voted solidly for Barack Obama over John McCain, 64% to 33%.

John Olver (D)

The congressman from the 1st District is John Olver, a Democrat who won a June 1991 special election after the death of longtime Republican Rep. Silvio Conte. After graduating from high school when he was just 15, Olver was educated at Tufts University and MIT. At age 25, he was a chemistry professor at the University of Massachusetts. His wife, Rose, is a professor of psychology and women's and gender studies at Amherst College. In 1968, he began a 22-year career in the state legislature. In the special election to replace Conte, his Pioneer Valley base helped him win 31% in the fragmented Democratic primary. In the general, he faced Steven Pierce, the former state House Republican leader and Gov. William Weld's conservative opponent in the 1990 primary. With Massachusetts liberalism in disrepute after Gov. Michael Dukakis lost the 1988 presidential campaign, the contest was close. Weld made certain to schedule it after students' summer vacation began, when the area had emptied out of liberal voters. Olver nevertheless pulled off a close 50%-48% win, becoming the first Democrat to hold the seat since the Spanish-American War.

Olver has one of the most liberal voting records in the House. He has voted against international trade deals, and he favors conversion to a Canadian-style single-payer health care system. He is the top Democrat on the Appropriations Subcommittee on Transportation, Housing and Urban Development, and Related Agencies, where he has sought to expand Amtrak train service and subsidies in the Northeast Corridor. He can expound at length to audiences at home on the benefits of expanded rail service—as well as on other things. As he wryly noted on his campaign Web site, "I generally like to answer and inform in a somewhat long-winded style." In recent years, he has helped increase funding for housing vouchers, public transit, and community development block grants. Olver has also advocated increased federal support for bicycling, recreation and transportation. In July 2010, he refuted criticism from Republicans who groused that the fiscal 2011 transportation-housing appropriations bill would add to the federal government's fiscal woes. A $3.9 billion increase above the Obama administration's request for the Federal Highway Administration, he said, would create more than 140,000 jobs. Later that year, he was among the House Democrats to complain that the compromise that Obama struck with Republicans to extend the Bush-era tax cuts represented an "astronomical sum" that would be better used toward reducing the deficit.

He was a persistent critic of the Bush administration, and even co-sponsored a resolution calling for an impeachment investigation of President George W. Bush and Vice President Dick Cheney—a popular idea in this district. But he later back down and voted in 2007 against an impeachment resolution by liberal Rep. Dennis Kucinich of Ohio because, he said, it would be a "totally destructive" move that would divide Democrats. Outside of his Appropriations work, Olver helped to organize the House bipartisan Climate Change Caucus and sponsored legislation to cap greenhouse gas emissions. On the housing mortgage bailout bills in 2008, he worked with Financial Services Committee Chairman Barney Frank of Massachusetts to increase aid for owners of foreclosed properties.

Olver is not a natural politician; he is notably shy, dislikes fundraising, and is ambivalent about the media limelight. He prefers to rock climb, a solitary endeavor. An exception was his April 2006 arrest with four other House Democrats; all were handcuffed and briefly jailed for protesting the violence in Darfur at the Sudanese Embassy in Washington.

Olver has had only one close contest for re-election. In 1996, he beat Republican Jane Swift, then a state representative and later governor, 53%-47%. In 2008, Stockbridge lawyer Robert Feuer challenged Olver in the primary for his inaction on impeaching Bush; Olver won 79%-21%. With Massachusetts likely to lose a seat in 2010's reapportionment, Olver has acknowledged that his rambling district is an obvious target for Boston-area pols. He declared his candidacy for 2012 almost immediately after the 2010 election, the better to avoid questions about whether his seat might be subject to post-census redistricting. Because he is the only lawmaker to represent far-western Massachusetts, it would be difficult—though not impossible—to draw a district that eliminates him.

SECOND DISTRICT

Richard Neal (D)

Elected 1988, 12th term; b. Feb. 14, 1949, Springfield; home, Springfield; Amer. Intl. Col., B.A. 1972, U. of Hartford, M.A. 1976; Catholic; married (Maureen).

Elected Office: Springfield City Cncl., 1978–83; Springfield mayor, 1984–88.

Professional Career: Staff asst., Springfield Mayor William C. Sullivan, 1973–78; High schl. & col. teacher, 1978–83.

DC Office: 2208 RHOB, 20515, 202-225-5601; Fax: 202-225-8112; Web site: neal.house.gov.

State Offices: Milford, 508-634-8198; Springfield, 413-785-0325.

Committees: *Ways & Means:* Select Revenue Measures (RMM); Trade.

Group Ratings

	ACLU	ACU	ADA	CFG	AFS	FRC	LCV	ITIC	NTU	COC
2010	88	0	95	0	100	6	100	67	6	0
2009	–	4	95	6	100	–	93	–	3	40

National Journal Ratings

	2010 LIB	—	2010 CONS		2009 LIB	—	2009 CONS
Economic	90%	—	0%		68%	—	30%
Social	82%	—	14%		67%	—	33%
Foreign	92%	—	3%		91%	—	0%
Composite	91%	—	9%		77%	—	23%

Key Votes of the 111th Congress

1. Overturn Ledbetter	Y	5. Bar federal abortion funds	Y
2. Pass $820 billion stimulus	Y	6. Pass health care bill	Y
3. Let guns in national parks	N	7. Regulate financial firms	Y
4. Pass cap-and-trade	Y	8. Pass tax cuts for some	Y

9. Stop detainee transfers	N
10. Legalize immigrants' kids	Y
11. Repeal don't ask, tell	Y
12. Limit campaign funds	Y

Election Results

2010 general	Richard Neal (D)	122,751	(57%)	($2,273,405)
	Thomas Wesley (R)	91,209	(43%)	($146,857)
2010 primary	Richard Neal (D)	unopposed		

Prior Winning Percentages: 2008 (98%), 2006 (100%), 2004 (100%), 2002 (100%), 2000 (100%), 1998 (100%), 1996 (72%), 1994 (59%), 1992 (53%), 1990 (100%), 1988 (80%)

Population		Race/Ethnicity		Work	
Pop. 2010:	661,045	White:	77.1%	Private:	80.0%
Change since 2000:	Up 4.2%	Black:	5.7%	Government:	14.2%
Urban:	84.8%	Hispanic:	13.2%	Self-employed:	5.7%
Rural:	15.2%	Asian:	2.1%	Blue collar:	20.7%
Area size:	952 sq. mi.	Native Am.:	0.2%	White collar:	61.8%
		Hawaiian:	0.0%	Khaki collar:	0.1%
Age		Two+ races:	1.5%	Other:	17.4%
Median age:	39.0 yrs.				
More than 65 yrs:	13.0%	*Ancestry*		Median income:	$57,918
Less than 18 yrs:	23.8%	Irish	14.8%	Median Home Value:	$243,900
		French	11.5%		
Education		Italian	9.8%	**Military Veterans**	
H.S. grad:	86.1%			% of Pop:	10.0%
College grad:	26.8%				
Grad degree:	10.4%				

Springfield

It's the place where basketball was invented, the city where the Webster's unabridged dictionaries (2nd and 3rd editions) were edited and published, and the site of the armory where unhappy soldiers mounted the Shays' Rebellion in 1786-87. This is Springfield, Mass., the third-largest city in the Bay State, far from Boston but with its own historical cache. An American city founded by Puritans in the 17th Century, it is usually overshadowed by Hartford as the center

2008 Presidential Vote		
Barack Obama (D) 179,466	(59%)
John McCain (R) 117,742	(39%)
2004 Presidential Vote		
John Kerry (D) 169,460	(59%)
George Bush (R) 113,284	(40%)
Cook Partisan Voting Index: D+9		

of the Connecticut River Valley. Immigrants from a dozen countries have worked their way up here. Blacks and Hispanics account for more than half of its population. Like other New England city centers, Springfield's downtown has emptied and its tax base has shrunk. Business leaders have tried to revive it, in part with the expansion of the Basketball Hall of Fame. But the once-powerful city has suffered from corruption and serious crime, and in 2004, it was forced to submit to state control in a financial bailout. For five years until June 2009, the state board reorganized city government and set up a college aid program for high school graduates. But the city has continued to face difficulties. It had more foreclosures than any other city in Massachusetts for much of 2010. Also that year, *NewGeography.com* ranked it the Northeast's worst medium-sized city for job growth. About 27% of its residents live in poverty, more than double the level for the state as a whole.

Springfield is the largest city in the 2nd Congressional District of Massachusetts, which stretches east from Springfield to a point 30 miles southwest of Boston. Its irregular boundaries travel north to South Hadley and Northampton ("Hamp" to locals; "NoHo" to the younger, artsy crowd) and take in Mount Holyoke and Smith colleges. To the east, the district stretches across stony hills and beyond Worcester to the antique center of Brimfield and the factory towns of the Blackstone Valley just north of Woonsocket, R.I. This was a Yankee Republican district for much of the 20th century, then a solidly Catholic Democratic district. Now it is more diverse culturally and even more solidly Democratic.

Richard Neal (D)

The congressman from the 2nd District is Richard Neal, a 12-term Democrat who has sought to establish himself as one of his party's pro-business leaders on economic policy. Neal grew up in Springfield amid the acute racial tensions of the mid-1960s. His parents died when he was a teenager, and Neal and his younger sisters received monthly Social Security survivor benefits while being raised by their grandmother and aunt. He graduated from American International College and earned a master's degree in public administration from the University of Hartford. In Springfield, he worked for the mayor; and in 1978, while teaching high school and college history, he was elected to the City Council. As mayor from 1984 to 1988, Neal worked to rehabilitate the downtown area and revitalize neighborhoods. His congressional predecessor, 36-year incumbent Edward Boland, a longtime pal of former Democratic House Speaker Thomas (Tip) O'Neill, essentially bequeathed him the House seat. Boland announced his retirement just before the filing deadline, and after Neal had traveled the district for a year. Unopposed in the Democratic primary, Neal won the general election with 80% of the vote.

Neal has a generally liberal voting record but has favored enough moderate initiatives to separate himself from more-liberal Massachusetts colleagues. He has close ties to the insurance and investment industries, which are his leading sources of campaign funds. Having depended on Social Security after the death of his parents, he reveres the legacy of President Franklin D. Roosevelt. He voted for the 1996 welfare overhaul and a federal prohibition on same-sex marriages. Neal serves on the influential Ways and Means Committee. He supported both the North American Free Trade Agreement and normalization of trade relations with China, although organized labor opposed the pacts. He also sponsored legislation to drop the requirement that 401(k) plans offer at least one low-cost index fund. In October 2008, he helped to enact expanded tax credits for alternative forms of energy, but the Senate prevailed in blocking the bill.

Neal is rising in seniority at Ways and Means, and in the 111th Congress (2009-10), he chaired the Select Revenue Measures Subcommittee, which handles many tax and tariff bills. He has tried to simplify the tax code and has crusaded for repeal of the alternative minimum tax, which was designed to ensure that the wealthy pay a fair share of taxes but which has been increasingly ensnaring middle-income taxpayers. He proposed in mid-2010 that the expiration of President George W. Bush's tax cuts for the wealthy be used to finance the wars in Iraq and Afghanistan. He took the lead for House Democrats on a popular proposal to clamp down on companies that incorporate in Bermuda and other offshore havens to avoid U.S. taxes. Neal also has spent several years trying without success to change tax policy on foreign insurance firms, and introduced a bill in 2009 limiting insurers' ability to receive U.S. tax deductions on some reinsurance premiums that they send to foreign-based affiliates. President Barack Obama included a related measure in his fiscal 2011 budget. With the administration's backing, Neal also proposed an automatic individual retirement account enrollment measure aimed at helping young and low-income workers lacking employer-based pension and retirement plans.

When Democrat Charles Rangel of New York was forced to step down as Ways and Means' chairman in March 2010 while battling ethics problems, Neal was mentioned as a possible replacement, but the gavel went to the more senior Sander Levin of Michigan. Neal vigorously continued to push for the job, arguing that the party needed to shelve its traditional customs of seniority in favor of a better spokesman. He contended he would be a more business-friendly alternative to Levin, who is strongly pro-labor, and could work more closely with Republicans to get bills passed. Neal raised substantial sums for endangered Democratic incumbents in the 2010 election—always a good way to get the leadership to take you seriously for a chairmanship. After the November elections, he won a 23-22 vote of the Democratic Steering Committee. But he lost to Levin on a vote of the full caucus, 109-78, as many Democrats indicated they were not ready to upend the seniority system.

Like many other Irish Catholic politicians over the years, Neal has encouraged American attempts at reconciliation in Northern Ireland. He chairs the Friends of Ireland Committee, and he traveled to Ireland in 2007 to reaffirm support for the peace process as the power-sharing agreement was signed. The following year, outgoing Prime Minister Bertie Ahern praised Neal in a speech before a joint session of Congress.

On local issues, Neal has focused on the economic problems of Springfield. In 2007, he was instrumental in securing a $22 million grant for renovation of its Union Station, as well as $121 million in 2010 for high-speed rail service in the region.

Neal had serious primary challenges in 1990 and 1992, but won re-election by satisfactory margins. He ran unopposed in four successive elections before facing a challenge in 2010 from Republican business executive Thomas Wesley. Neal campaigned aggressively, getting Education Secretary Arne Duncan to appear with him on opening day of school in Springfield, and he won easily with 57%. Like his Democratic colleague John Olver, he has been the object of speculation about redistricting following the 2010 census, and he announced his 2012 candidacy early to try to ward off such talk.

THIRD DISTRICT

Jim McGovern (D)

Elected 1996, 8th term; b. Nov. 20, 1959, Worcester; home, Worcester; American U., B.A. 1981, M.P.A. 1984; Catholic; married (Lisa); 2 children.

Professional Career: Aide, U.S. Sen. George McGovern, 1977-80; Sr. aide, U.S. Rep. Joseph Moakley, 1982–96.

DC Office: 438 CHOB, 20515, 202-225-6101; Fax: 202-225-5759; Web site: mcgovern.house.gov.

State Offices: Attleboro, 508-431-8025; Fall River, 508-677-0140; Marlborough, 508-460-9292; Worcester, 508-831-7356.

Committees: *Agriculture:* Department Operations, Oversight & Credit; General Farm Commodities & Risk Management. *Rules.*

Group Ratings

	ACLU	ACU	ADA	CFG	AFS	FRC	LCV	ITIC	NTU	COC
2010	94	0	100	0	100	0	100	67	5	13
2009	–	0	100	0	100	–	100	–	2	33

National Journal Ratings

	2010 LIB — 2010 CONS		2009 LIB — 2009 CONS	
Economic	90%	— 0%	91%	— 0%
Social	93%	— 0%	80%	— 18%
Foreign	92%	— 3%	78%	— 17%
Composite	95%	— 5%	86%	— 14%

Key Votes of the 111th Congress

1. Overturn Ledbetter	Y	5. Bar federal abortion funds	N	9. Stop detainee transfers	N
2. Pass $820 billion stimulus	Y	6. Pass health care bill	Y	10. Legalize immigrants' kids	Y
3. Let guns in national parks	N	7. Regulate financial firms	Y	11. Repeal don't ask, tell	Y
4. Pass cap-and-trade	Y	8. Pass tax cuts for some	Y	12. Limit campaign funds	Y

Election Results

2010 general	Jim McGovern (D)	122,708	(56%)	($1,839,052)
	Martin Lamb (R)	85,124	(39%)	($129,237)
	Patrick Barron (I)	9,388	(4%)	($3,167)
2010 primary	Jim McGovern (D)	unopposed		

Prior Winning Percentages: 2008 (98%), 2006 (100%), 2004 (71%), 2002 (100%), 2000 (100%), 1998 (57%), 1996 (53%)

Population		Race/Ethnicity		Work	
Pop. 2010:	664,919	White:	79.3%	Private:	82.2%
Change since 2000:	Up 4.8%	Black:	4.1%	Government:	12.6%
Urban:	93.4%	Hispanic:	8.9%	Self-employed:	5.1%
Rural:	6.6%	Asian:	5.1%	Blue collar:	17.1%
Area size:	612 sq. mi.	Native Am.:	0.2%	White collar:	66.2%
		Hawaiian:	0.0%	Khaki collar:	0.1%
Age		Two+ races:	1.7%	Other:	16.6%
Median age:	38.6 yrs.				
More than 65 yrs:	12.6%	*Ancestry*		Median income:	$64,637
Less than 18 yrs:	23.8%	Irish	17.0%	Median Home Value:	$320,400
		Italian	10.4%		
Education		English	8.6%	**Military Veterans**	
H.S. grad:	87.2%			% of Pop:	8.6%
College grad:	36.3%				
Grad degree:	14.1%				

Central Massachusetts; Worcester

Worcester is still pronounced with a particularly pungent Massachusetts accent making it sound as though it has no *r*'s. For more than 200 years, it has been one of the nation's centers of tinkering, contriving, and inventing, even though it is one of the few active industrial cities not located on a river, lake, or seacoast. In the mid-19th century, the city won renown as the valentine-making capital of the United States for its production of lavish valentines and other greeting cards. In

2008 Presidential Vote		
Barack Obama (D) 175,951	(59%)
John McCain (R) 117,862	(39%)
2004 Presidential Vote		
John Kerry (D) 167,402	(59%)
George Bush (R) 112,957	(40%)
Cook Partisan Voting Index: D+9		

the past, its biggest industries were wire-making, textiles, grinding wheels, and envelopes. It is where the birth control pill was invented and where Worcester native and Clark University professor Robert Goddard shot off experimental rockets before relieved locals saw him off to New Mexico.

In the 1970s and 1980s, electronics and computer firms sprouted along Interstate 495—the circumferential highway 20 miles east of Worcester—just as they had earlier around Route 128, closer to Boston. The high-tech boom brought prosperity, labor shortages, new residents, and higher housing prices to central Massachusetts. Then, in the early 1990s, the minicomputer industry slumped, bringing a recession. But Worcester's ingenious entrepreneurs and skilled labor force hustled, and local leaders set up a Biotechnology Research Institute to draw on the city's nine colleges and the University of Massachusetts Medical School to steer the city back on course. Holy Cross College offered free tuition to students of local families earning less than $50,000 annually. Other communities followed suit, with Shrewsbury developing its own business park and announcing plans for a 600-job expansion in 2010. Just as the city's economy has changed, so has its face, with steep increases in Asians and Hispanics, mainly from Puerto Rico, in the 1990s. Overall, population declined 20% mid-century, but then increased 7% from 1980 to 2000 and an additional 6% since then, as the area attracted Hmong, Albanians, and Africans, many thousands of whom had fled the civil war in Liberia. The local cable television station airs Latino programming. That rebound contrasts with nearby Springfield and Hartford, and enabled Worcester to pass Providence as New England's second-largest city, behind Boston. Since 2000, Worcester County has led the state in growth.

The 3rd Congressional District of Massachusetts has Worcester as its largest city but not its geographic center. A little more than half of its residents live in Worcester and a cluster of adjacent towns. The other population cluster is 60 miles away, in and around the old textile mill town of Fall River, east of Rhode Island. The two are connected by a string of towns that reaches almost to Buzzards Bay. In national elections since 1992, this district has been solidly Democratic. In recent gubernatorial elections, however, the 3rd has been mixed. Worcester and Fall River (only a portion of which is in the district) voted for Democrat Shannon O'Brien in 2002 while the Interstate 495 corridor voted for Republican Mitt Romney. In 2006, Democrat Deval Patrick won by almost 3-1 ratios in Worcester and Fall River and lost only a handful of towns here.

Jim McGovern (D)

The congressman from the 3rd District is Jim McGovern, a Democrat first elected in 1996. McGovern grew up in Worcester, where his parents owned a liquor store. He attended American University in Washington, and, while in graduate school, he worked in the office of then-Sen. George McGovern (no relation), a South Dakota Democrat. He ran McGovern's 1984 campaign in the Massachusetts presidential primary, where the senator finished third with 21% of the vote. He went to work as an aide to Boston-area Rep. Joe Moakley's office and became chief of staff just as Moakley ascended to chairman of the Rules Committee. McGovern got into the spotlight himself, leading a 1989 investigation of the murders of six Jesuits and two lay women in El Salvador, which led to a cutoff of U.S. aid to the country. In 1994, he ran for the House and lost in the Democratic primary, 38%-30%. In 1996, he ran again, this time with no primary opposition. In the general election, two-term Republican Rep. Peter Blute stressed his independence from then-Speaker Newt Gingrich and the rest of the conservative Republican leadership in the House and attacked McGovern for liberal stands on abortion rights and Cuba. McGovern ran a humorous spot that asked, "If you wouldn't vote for Newt, why would you ever vote for Blute?" At age 36, McGovern won, 53%-45%.

With deft maneuvers reflecting his Capitol Hill experience, McGovern positioned himself to become a power broker in the Democratic caucus. In 2001, the dying Moakley personally asked

Democratic Leader Dick Gephardt to help McGovern get a seat on Rules, which schedules most legislation for the House floor. As it turned out, the next seat went to Florida's Alcee Hastings, a member of the Congressional Black Caucus, but McGovern got a commitment for the next available Democratic seat, with seniority over Hastings. He also has a senior job on Minority Whip Steny Hoyer's whip organization.

On Rules, McGovern started with the advantage of already being versed in House procedures. With GOP lawmakers dominating the panel, he showed a sharp partisan edge as he embraced parliamentary maneuvers that led to cries of outrage from House Republicans. When Louise Slaughter of New York—now her 80s—retires, McGovern is in position to assume the top Democratic spot on Rules. With his considerable leverage, he became a party leader on Iraq war policy, sponsoring a 2007 bill to withdraw U.S. troops from Iraq in six months that was defeated on a 255-171 vote. Later that year, he proposed a war surtax, but Democratic leaders rejected it. In 2008, McGovern called for the United Nations to replace U.S. forces in Iraq.

McGovern has a solidly liberal voting record and has urged President Obama to embrace a more progressive agenda. He was among the lawmakers arrested at an April 2009 Darfur protest at the Sudanese embassy and later recalled, "It was really a privilege to be in the same cell as John Lewis," the Georgia lawmaker and civil rights icon. McGovern was among those who pushed for a government-run public option in the health care overhaul bill, but he backed it anyway when the public option was dropped under pressure from Democratic moderates. He is a member of the Cuba Working Group, which has called for easing sanctions against the Castro regime. He contends that the U.S. embargo has not achieved its goal of improving human rights and the economic situation in Cuba, and that only a change in policy, not continued sanctions, will improve living conditions and foment democratic reforms there. Citing human rights violations, he was a leading opponent of the U.S. free-trade deal with Colombia.

McGovern chairs the Congressional Hunger Center, and in 2007 he participated in a one-week "food stamp challenge" in which he spent no more than $21 on food. He has pushed for more spending on international nutrition and for less support of biofuels, which he says have driven up food costs. He agreed to support a $4.5 billion child nutrition bill in late 2010 after getting assurances from the White House that it would try to restore $2.2 billion taken from future funding for food stamp programs.

On issues affecting his district, McGovern led opposition to a proposed liquefied natural gas plant on the Taunton River. The Coast Guard ruled that the river was not safe for LNG tankers and blocked construction. Although Republicans held this seat not long ago, they have all but given up on it. McGovern was unopposed in four of the past five congressional elections, and won easily with 57% in the anti-incumbent environment of 2010. Less than a week later, he was treated for thyroid cancer and given a promising prognosis.

FOURTH DISTRICT

Barney Frank (D)

Elected 1980, 16th term; b. March 31, 1940, Bayonne, NJ; home, Newton; Harvard U., B.A. 1962, J.D. 1977; Jewish; single.

Elected Office: MA House of Reps., 1972–80.

Professional Career: Exec. asst., Boston Mayor Kevin White, 1967–71; A.A., U.S. Rep. Michael Harrington, 1971–72; Teaching fellow, Harvard JFK Schl. of Govt., 1978–80.

DC Office: 2252 RHOB, 20515, 202-225-5931; Fax: 202-225-0182; Web site: www.house.gov/frank.

State Offices: New Bedford, 508-999-6462; Newton, 617-332-3920; Taunton, 508-822-4796.

Committees: *Financial Services* (RMM).

Group Ratings

	ACLU	ACU	ADA	CFG	AFS	FRC	LCV	ITIC	NTU	COC
2010	88	0	100	0	100	0	80	67	4	13
2009	–	0	100	4	100	–	100	–	2	33

National Journal Ratings

	2010 LIB — 2010 CONS		2009 LIB — 2009 CONS	
Economic	90%	— 0%	91%	— 0%
Social	93%	— 0%	83%	— 16%
Foreign	84%	— 11%	91%	— 0%
Composite	93%	— 7%	92%	— 9%

Key Votes of the 111th Congress

1. Overturn Ledbetter	Y	5. Bar federal abortion funds	N	9. Stop detainee transfers	N
2. Pass $820 billion stimulus	Y	6. Pass health care bill	Y	10. Legalize immigrants' kids	Y
3. Let guns in national parks	N	7. Regulate financial firms	Y	11. Repeal don't ask, tell	Y
4. Pass cap-and-trade	Y	8. Pass tax cuts for some	Y	12. Limit campaign funds	Y

Election Results

2010 general	Barney Frank (D)	126,194	(54%)	($4,152,944)
	Sean Bielat (R)	101,517	(43%)	($2,458,132)
2010 primary	Barney Frank (D)	39,974	(80%)	
	Rachel Brown (D)	10,289	(20%)	

Prior Winning Percentages: 2008 (68%), 2006 (100%), 2004 (78%), 2002 (100%), 2000 (75%), 1998 (100%), 1996 (72%), 1994 (100%), 1992 (68%), 1990 (66%), 1988 (70%), 1986 (89%), 1984 (74%), 1982 (60%), 1980 (52%)

Population		Race/Ethnicity		Work	
Pop. 2010:	656,083	White:	83.7%	Private:	80.9%
Change since 2000:	Up 3.4%	Black:	2.9%	Government:	12.2%
Urban:	88.2%	Hispanic:	5.2%	Self-employed:	6.9%
Rural:	11.8%	Asian:	4.6%	Blue collar:	16.8%
Area size:	844 sq. mi.	Native Am.:	0.2%	White collar:	67.8%
		Hawaiian:	0.0%	Khaki collar:	0.0%
Age		Two+ races:	2.2%	Other:	15.4%
Median age:	39.2 yrs.				
More than 65 yrs:	13.7%	*Ancestry*		Median income:	$69,473
Less than 18 yrs:	22.7%	Irish	14.8%	Median Home Value:	$373,700
		Portuguese	14.1%		
Education		English	9.1%	**Military Veterans**	
H.S. grad:	86.5%			% of Pop:	7.9%
College grad:	39.6%				
Grad degree:	19.4%				

Southeast Mass.; New Bedford

The political transformation of Massachusetts is nowhere better illustrated than in the Boston suburbs of Brookline and Newton. These were Yankee enclaves a century ago, with avenues built to resemble the sweep of Haussmann's Grand Boulevards in Paris and villages of giant clapboard houses clustered within a few blocks of commuter rail stations. Brookline was where the Country Club (the very first one) was established in 1882, and where Joseph Kennedy, an

2008 Presidential Vote		
Barack Obama (D) 198,079	(63%)
John McCain (R) 107,758	(35%)
2004 Presidential Vote		
John Kerry (D) 194,914	(65%)
George Bush (R) 99,878	(34%)
Cook Partisan Voting Index: D+14		

Irish Catholic, 20-something banker seeking respectability, moved his family in 1914. Brookline and Newton then were solidly Republican in politics, the base of such leading politicians as Christian Herter, the governor of Massachusetts and U.S. secretary of State in the 1950s. As late as 1960, Brookline, Newton, and adjacent wards of Boston were electing a Republican to Congress. Then came the transformation, personified by the election in 1962 of Michael Dukakis at age 29 to the Great and General Court (the legislature). As Massachusetts' university-educated classes became more liberal, as Brookline's and Newton's Jewish populations grew, and as young, liberal-minded families refurbished the graceful old houses, these towns became Democratic bastions. Now there are an increasing number of Russian Jews and of Orthodox and Hasidic synagogues. Brookline and Newton are part of the liberal heart of Massachusetts.

The 4th Congressional District of Massachusetts includes Brookline and Newton. Anchoring the hook-like northern tip of the district, they account for less than one-quarter of the district's votes. The shape results from successive redistrictings. New Bedford and Fall River are close to the ocean, and New Bedford is proud of the Greek revival architecture of its great whaling days, when it was one of the richest cities in the country. It stages a daylong reading of *Moby Dick* every Jan. 3, the day that Ishmael and his friend Queequeg sailed out under the command of Captain Ahab. Today, it still lives off the ocean. The local fishing industry is dominated these days by Portuguese-Americans, together with some recent Brazilian immigrants; 14% of 4th District residents identify their ancestry as Portuguese. A budding industry here is wind power: a marine terminal for offshore wind turbines is going up in New Bedford.

The northern and southern end of the districts are very different sociologically and economically—affluent Boston suburbs suffered relatively little in the 2007-09 recession, Fall River quite a lot—but in recent decades have both voted heavily Democratic. Connecting the two is a corridor that in some places is less than a mile wide but with a considerable variety of towns—Foxborough with its Patriots football stadium; Wellesley with its college and high-income residents; Dover, the home of some old-time Boston Brahmins; and Sharon with its Orthodox Jews. Politically, these areas were historically mostly Republican but in recent decades they have been, like most of middle-income Massachusetts, Democratic. Barack Obama carried the 4th District by 63%-34% in 2008. But in January 2010, the district voted for Republican Scott Brown in the special Senate election over Democrat Martha Coakley. Brown won only narrowly and was helped because his home town of Wrentham is close to the district; he in fact represented some of its towns in the state Senate.

Barney Frank (D)

The congressman from the 4th District is Barney Frank, an influential Democrat elected to the House in 1980. He was chairman of the Financial Services Committee from 2007 until the Democrats lost their House majority in 2011. He is a savvy legislator known for his keen intelligence and sharp tongue.

Frank grew up in Bayonne, N.J. His father ran a truck stop on the New Jersey Turnpike and loved to talk politics. All four of his children went on to careers in government service and politics. Barney distinguished himself as a student and was accepted at Harvard, where he got to know local politicians as well as political scientists. In 1967, he took a job as an aide to newly elected Boston Mayor Kevin White, and four years later, he arrived in Washington as an aide to Democratic Rep. Michael Harrington of Massachusetts. In 1972, Frank was elected to the Massachusetts House from Boston's Back Bay, which was transitioning from a staid Republican bastion to a liberal singles neighborhood. In 1980, when Democratic Rep. Robert Drinan retired after Pope John Paul II commanded Jesuits to leave elective office, Frank moved to Brookline and ran in the 4th District. With a strong base in Brookline and Newton, he won. After redistricting threw him in with Republican Rep. Margaret Heckler in 1982, he defeated her 60%-40%. He has been re-elected by wide margins since.

In the House, Frank quickly gained a reputation for his smarts and debating skills. He has a distinct, rapid-fire style that leaves opponents tongue-tied. David Shribman, the former longtime Washington Bureau chief of the *Boston Globe*, once called Frank "cranky, impatient, rude —and utterly brilliant." In *Washingtonian* magazine's annual poll of congressional staffers, he is frequently voted "brainiest." He is admired even by Republicans for his intellectual rigor and honesty. At the same time, he is a wily political operator. He does not profess to be a political theoretician, though few in the House exceed him as such. Frank once said, "My job is to be the mediator between people who have policy ideas and public policy. My strength is to be able to understand policy ideas and decide how best to implement them. I am about the political process. I know the rules of the House as much as anybody. I am a wonk about how to get things done, more than about what to do." In his early years in the House, he often worked behind the scenes on substantive issues. After Republicans won control of Congress in 1994, Frank started spending much more time on the floor, pouncing on the new majority's mistakes, criticizing its policies, and taking it to task when he felt its treatment of the minority was unfair.

Much of his focus in recent years has been on issues involving the House Financial Services Committee. He became the panel's ranking minority member in 2003 and its chairman in 2007, after Democrats won a House majority. The committee has not been as partisan as many in Congress, and Frank has frequently cooperated with Republicans, including the current chairman, Spencer Bachus, R-Ala. He mastered the complex subjects covered by the committee: securities, corporate governance, accounting issues, and insurance. The regulatory matters that come before the committee are heavily lobbied, the negative effects of bad decisions can be long-lasting, and many issues do not break down along party lines.

Unlike previous Democrats who have chaired this committee—notably Wright Patman of Texas in the 1960s and 1970s—Frank believes in the efficiency and productivity of markets. "I think people may misunderstand what being a liberal means. I really do believe in the free market. You need inequality in the capitalist system, but we are at a point now where we are getting more inequality than is necessary for efficiency or socially helpful. The role of government should put some limits on that inequality, through raising the minimum wage, encouraging unions, providing public-sector programs that help people go to college," he says. Frank says there is a need for a "grand bargain" between business and liberals. Such pro-growth policies as free-trade agreements and tax cuts, in his view, have tended to widen economic inequality. His grand bargain would have Republicans accept a hike in the minimum wage, a tax increase on high-income earners, and union certification based on the signatures of a majority of workers rather than a secret-ballot election. It would have Democrats accept free-trade agreements with labor and environmental measures that meet "minimal standards of civility," while accepting foreign direct investment in the United States without restriction. "I want to get the people who have been concerned about equity to support growth policies and the people who have been chafing that we aren't doing enough for growth to support policies that provide equity," Frank says. He can claim that he has been carrying out his side of the bargain: He has supported many free-trade agreements and has trenchantly criticized farm subsidies backed by most Democrats. He argues that "employer-paid health care is a mistake" that "depresses wages"—a point that former President George W. Bush was fond of making.

In the majority, Frank initially focused on the credit crunch for housing, and then moved on to even more difficult challenges in the real estate and banking industries and in the overall economy. As the nation headed toward recession in September 2007, he won House approval of a bill designed to expand homeownership by easing loan rates to borrowers who were suffering from the meltdown in the subprime mortgage market. The next month, Frank won passage, with Republican support, of a bill to create an affordable-housing trust fund for low-income families, with the goal of producing 1.5 million housing units in the next decade. After the collapse of the investment bank Bear Stearns in March 2008, Frank moved a bill requiring investment banking houses to hold larger capital reserves similar to commercial banks. Major damage to the financial system "was done by inadequate regulation," he said. In July 2008, as federal mortgage giants Fannie Mae and Freddie Mac faced major capital losses, Frank moved to increase their credit lines and to give regulators broader oversight of the two housing banks. But Frank's counterpart in the Senate, Christopher Dodd of Connecticut, chairman of the Banking Committee, was off campaigning for president in Iowa, and the Senate did not act until the middle of 2008. The legislation did increase their credit lines and provide for more supervision. But it was too late for tougher regulation to take hold, and the government placed Fannie and Freddie into conservatorship in September 2008.

Within days, Lehman Brothers collapsed and the financial markets reeled. Frank survived a major legislative test after Treasury Secretary Henry Paulson Jr. and Federal Reserve Board Chairman Ben Bernanke told congressional leaders in a dramatic late-night session in Speaker Nancy Pelosi's office that swift congressional action was needed to prevent several large financial firms from going under. The two recommended a plan for the government to purchase the bad assets of the financial institutions. Frank predicted quick agreement on the proposal, initially estimated to cost $700 billion. "It will be bipartisan, bicameral, bi-everything," he vowed. The subsequent discussions proved harrowing, with a toxic mix of presidential campaign politics, congressional pre-election jitters in both parties, a roller-coaster ride (mostly down) on Wall Street, and spreading fears of financial panic.

While Frank played a central role in crafting the bailout, he warned Republicans of the need for bipartisan support. "This is a Bush administration initiative," he said. To Frank's embarrassment and dismay, 95 Democrats voted against the deal on Sept. 29 and it collapsed, 205-228, in a rank-and-file rebuke of leaders of both parties. The Dow Jones industrial average dropped 777 points that day, its worst single-day point loss ever. Frank and the other negotiators went back to work on the bill and agreed to add $150 billion in tax cuts that the Senate favored. Democratic presidential nominee Barack Obama telephoned recalcitrant House Democrats to urge their support. Four days later, the House passed the bailout legislation, with only 63 Democrats voting no. A veteran House Democrat later complained that one of the problems with the initial bill had been Frank trying to run "a one-man show."

By early 2009, Frank had taken such criticism to heart. He launched his committee on a mission to pass the most sweeping overhaul of banking and financial industry regulation since the Great Depression. The legislation was aimed at averting the kind of abuse-fueled meltdown that led to the government bailout. Frank led months of endless give-and-take sessions between liberals who wanted more sweeping reforms and Democratic conservatives who supported a lesser governmental role. He also had to overcome the objections of powerful financial firms and their many friends on the committee For example, he worked out a compromise with conservatives over more stringent regulation on the trading of so-called derivatives, the risky financial instruments that played a role in the economic crisis. In December 2009, Frank brought to the floor an overhaul bill that passed 223-202, although without a single Republican vote.

The legislation, 1,300 pages in length, created a new agency to protect consumers from unfair and abusive lending practices, gave the government more power to break up reeling financial firms thought to be "too big to fail," and also required companies to set aside certain amounts in capital reserves. Like many Democrats, Frank was dismayed at the widening gap between executives' and workers' compensation, but he opposed having the government set limits. The legislation incorporated his idea of giving shareholders an advisory vote on executive compensation, and also banned "imprudently risky" pay incentives. House passage of the bill was a major achievement for Frank.

After the Senate passed its version in May 2010, Frank chaired the conference committee that ironed out the differences between the two chambers. Included in the final bill was creation of a Consumer Financial Protection Agency, to be financed partly by Federal Reserve funds and partly by appropriations. Agreement was reached on debit card fees, on derivatives regulation and on imposing a fiduciary duty on broker-dealers selling annuities. Frank declared that the final bill was tougher than his House version. The conference committee's bill passed both houses and became law in July 2010. It did not, however, address the issue of Fannie and Freddie, which Frank said would have to be tackled in the 112th Congress (2011-12). "I believe the remedy is abolishing Fannie Mae and Freddie Mac in their present form and coming up with a whole new system of housing finance," he said. In October 2010, he reflected on his previous stands on the mortgage giants and told *The Washington Post*, "I was too late to see they were a problem. I did see them as an important source of rental housing. I did not foresee the extent to which bad decisions . . . were causing problems."

As one of the House's most productive chairmen and a trusted confidant of Speaker Pelosi, Frank was constantly at her side in meetings with top officials of the Bush and Obama administrations. "They understand each other and have similar political backgrounds. Urban, ethnic, political," said a House insider who knows both members. "With that common background, they can communicate well, and they share the same values. Plus, humor helps."

For all his professional accomplishments, Frank's personal life once threatened to end his career. In 1987, in a seemingly casual answer to a reporter's question, Frank disclosed that he is gay. Then in 1989, *The Washington Times* newspaper reported that Frank had employed as a personal aide a male prostitute and convicted drug user, Steve Gobie, who was also living in Frank's apartment. He admitted paying Gobie but said he was careful never to use official or campaign funds. He also said he had ejected Gobie from his apartment. Frank voluntarily submitted to an investigation by the House Standards of Official Conduct (Ethics) Committee, which resulted in two minor charges. The committee recommended a reprimand but not censure. Frank made a contrite appearance before the House in July 1990, and the chamber voted 287-141 against censure. The vote for reprimand was 408-18. "I think members will agree that I have always had a reputation for honesty, not always tact or tolerance," Frank said in his remarks to the House. Today, Frank is a leading House legislator on gay-rights issues and the sponsor of a bill to allow benefits for same-sex partners of federal employees.

From 1984 to 2008, Frank had no difficulty winning re-election. Like others in the Massachusetts House delegation, he was alert to the possibility of a Senate vacancy if John Kerry had been elected president in 2004, but that possibility never arose. Busy with financial reform and nearing 70, he showed no interest in running for the Senate after the death of Sen. Edward Kennedy in August 2009. But the election of Republican Scott Brown to Kennedy's seat in January 2010—and the fact that Brown narrowly carried the 4th District—was a sign that Frank might face serious opposition in November 2010, and he did.

Republican Sean Bielat, a Brookline management consultant and Marine reservist, did not attract much attention when he won the September primary with 60% of the vote. But a *Boston Globe* poll showed Frank under the 50% support mark, leading by 46%-33%. In the first two weeks of his campaign, Bielat received $600,000 from around the country. Former President Bill Clinton came to Taunton to campaign with Frank in late September, and Frank, used to sending his campaign funds to Democrats in trouble elsewhere, focused on his own campaign, telling *Politico* that he didn't intend to be ambushed by "the kind of right wing smears that assailed John Kerry in 2004 and that led to the defeat this year of responsible Republican members of Congress whose records were badly distorted by tea party-backed candidates." Bielat criticized "bailout Barney" for his work on the financial industry rescue, and one of his ads said, "He supported policies that caused the economy to crumble."

In the end, Frank won 53%-43%, running 7% to 11% ahead of Martha Coakley in cities and towns in the southern and central part of the district. The well-educated voters of Brookline, Newton and Wellesley split almost exactly as they had in the Brown-Coakley contest, suggesting strong party loyalties of both the liberal majority and the conservative minority. It was Frank's lowest percentage since he first won the seat 52%-48% in 1980.

The reapportionment following the 2010 Census deprived Massachusetts of one House seat, and in early 2011, it was unclear which of the all-Democratic members of the delegation would find themselves in the same district. Frank's strategy in the past was to insist that he would run in whatever district Brookline ended up in, which was aimed at preventing others from stealing this heavily Democratic town. In late 2009, Frank became one of the few members of Congress to generate sufficient interest to warrant a biography. Author Stuart Weisberg published *Barney Frank: The Story of America's Only Left-Handed, Gay, Jewish Congressman.*

FIFTH DISTRICT

Niki Tsongas (D)

Elected Oct. 2007, 2nd full term; b. April 26, 1946, Chico, CA; home, Lowell; Attended MI St. U., Smith Col., B.A. 1968, Boston U., J.D. 1988; Episcopalian; widowed; 3 children.

Professional Career: Social worker; Practicing attorney; Dean of external affairs, Middlesex Comm. Col., 1997-2007.

DC Office: 1607 LHOB, 20515, 202-225-3411; Fax: 202-226-0771; Web site: tsongas.house.gov.

State Offices: Acton, 978-263-1951; Lawrence, 978-681-6200; Lowell, 978-459-0101.

Committees: *Armed Services:* Air & Land Forces; Military Personnel. *Natural Resources:* Energy & Mineral Resources; National Parks, Forests & Public Lands.

Group Ratings

	ACLU	ACU	ADA	CFG	AFS	FRC	LCV	ITIC	NTU	COC
2010	88	0	95	0	100	0	100	100	6	25
2009	–	0	95	4	100	–	100	–	4	29

National Journal Ratings

	2010 LIB — 2010 CONS		2009 LIB — 2009 CONS	
Economic	90%	— 0%	82%	— 14%
Social	87%	— 12%	89%	— 0%
Foreign	97%	— 0%	77%	— 23%
Composite	94%	— 6%	85%	— 15%

Key Votes of the 111th Congress

1. Overturn Ledbetter	Y	5. Bar federal abortion funds	N	9. Stop detainee transfers	N
2. Pass $820 billion stimulus	Y	6. Pass health care bill	Y	10. Legalize immigrants' kids	Y
3. Let guns in national parks	N	7. Regulate financial firms	Y	11. Repeal don't ask, tell	Y
4. Pass cap-and-trade	Y	8. Pass tax cuts for some	Y	12. Limit campaign funds	Y

Election Results

2010 general	Niki Tsongas (D)	122,858	(55%)	($1,950,422)
	Jonathan Golnik (R)	94,646	(42%)	($401,986)
2010 primary	Niki Tsongas (D)	unopposed		

Prior Winning Percentages: 2008 (99%); 2007 special (51%)

Population		Race/Ethnicity		Work	
Pop. 2010:	662,269	White:	72.3%	Private:	80.9%
Change since 2000:	Up 4.2%	Black:	2.5%	Government:	12.7%
Urban:	93.5%	Hispanic:	15.6%	Self-employed:	6.3%
Rural:	6.5%	Asian:	7.6%	Blue collar:	17.7%
Area size:	582 sq. mi.	Native Am.:	0.1%	White collar:	66.9%
		Hawaiian:	0.0%	Khaki collar:	0.1%
Age		Two+ races:	1.4%	Other:	15.4%
Median age:	38.8 yrs.				
More than 65 yrs:	11.8%	*Ancestry*		Median income:	$71,380
Less than 18 yrs:	25.4%	Irish	17.2%	Median Home Value:	$356,700
		Italian	10.2%		
Education		English	9.2%	**Military Veterans**	
H.S. grad:	87.4%			% of Pop:	8.0%
College grad:	38.0%				
Grad degree:	16.2%				

Northern Massachusetts; Lowell

The Merrimack River Valley at the northern edge of Massachusetts has had an erratic history: High-tech boom, bust, boom, bust, boom, bust. When Massachusetts was a kind of maritime republic in the 19th century, with its farmers struggling to scratch out a living from the stony soil, a few clever Yankees used their profits from the sea trade to try to tame the rapidly flowing Merrimack and build cotton-spinning mills.

2008 Presidential Vote		
Barack Obama (D)	176,547	(59%)
John McCain (R)	117,877	(39%)
2004 Presidential Vote		
John Kerry (D)	158,455	(57%)
George Bush (R)	114,874	(42%)
Cook Partisan Voting Index:	D+8	

Creating the cities of Lowell and Lawrence, they built model dormitories and recreation programs for their female workers. This was the center of America's textile industry for more than a century, long after the maritime industry faded. But in the 1920s, the price of labor rose and newly built mills in the Carolinas, much closer to the cotton supply, decimated the industry that Lawrence and Lowell built. Many residents, by then rather elderly, waited forlornly for an upturn in the local economy.

It came eventually, largely from an unexpected source. High-tech industry drove the growth, beginning in the 1960s around the Massachusetts Institute of Technology, and then moving out to the Route 128 ring road and eventually to Interstate 495, which passes through Lowell and Lawrence. Wang, headquartered in Lowell, grew spectacularly, and Democratic Sen. Paul Tsongas—the local kid who made it big before his early death to cancer—spearheaded a national historic restoration of the old mill area. This was the Massachusetts miracle of the 1980s. Then came the bust: Sales of Wang's word processors and minicomputers slumped as businesses purchased personal computers and linked them together in networks. But Lowell revived again. Its new immigrants provided vitality and entrepreneurial creativity. Cambodians own many small businesses and are nearly one-quarter of the local population, making Lowell second only to Long Beach, Calif., as a home for transplanted Cambodians in the United States. The first Spanish-language daily newspaper in New England began here in September 2008. The old Wang buildings have been replaced with health care, banking, telecommunications, and Internet companies, plus fledgling green-energy industries. Old mills have been converted to artists' lofts and upscale condos. The Tsongas Arena is home to a professional hockey team. The recent recession took its toll, though. Unemployment in Lowell climbed above 12% in 2009, but job growth in the information technology and financial sectors brought it down around 10% by year's end.

The 5th Congressional District of Massachusetts includes Lawrence and Lowell, which, along with a handful of nearby towns, account for about two-thirds of the district's population. The remainder of the district is the high-tech corridor south along I-495. The district also includes the tony suburbs near the Revolutionary War battleground of Concord, where the Minutemen stood their ground in 1775; the mountains along the New Hampshire state line; and the small towns west of Lowell. Except for Lowell and Lawrence, the district is ancestrally Yankee Republican. It is culturally liberal, with pockets of big wealth, and it trended Democratic in the early 1970s. Back then, the 5th District produced two Democratic candidates who would later run for president: Tsongas and John Kerry. In the 1980s and early 1990s, amid the high-tech boom, it went Republican in national and some statewide elections. In 1992, it gave Bill Clinton his lowest percentage in the state, while a big portion of the vote went to high-tech pioneer Ross Perot, the Texan who formed his own political party. But its cultural liberalism has moved it toward the Democrats, though not as far as in some Massachusetts districts: Al Gore carried the 5th District 57%-36% in 2000, Kerry 57%-41% in 2004, and Barack Obama 59%-39% in 2008. Democrats hold a 3-to-1 registration advantage over Republicans, but more than half the district's voters are independents.

Niki Tsongas (D)

The congresswoman from the 5th District is Niki Tsongas, a Democrat who won the seat in a 2007 special election. She is the widow of Paul Tsongas and a political force in her own right. Growing up in an Air Force family, Niki Tsongas (*SONG-us*) never had a place to call home thanks to her father's frequent moves. While interning in Washington, D.C., during college, she was invited to a party where she met her future husband, who was an intern for 5th District Republican Rep. Brad Morse. On one of their early dates, he told her of his plans to get involved in electoral politics by running for the Lowell City Council. Inspired by his vision and vigor for local politics, Niki followed him to Lowell in 1968 to help with his successful campaign for city councilor. They were married soon after. Tsongas stumped for her husband several times during his various campaigns for office. "I couldn't have run for office if I hadn't spent time campaigning on my own," she said. Paul Tsongas was first elected to the U.S. House in 1974 and to the U.S. Senate four years later. After retiring in 1984 with non-Hodgkin's lymphoma, he regained his health and launched a campaign for the 1992 Democratic presidential nomination. Although he won the New Hampshire primary, then-Arkansas Gov. Clinton's surprise second-place finish in the Granite State gave him the momentum to overtake Tsongas, who withdrew in March after defeats in the Illinois and Michigan primaries. The Tsongases moved back to Lowell, and soon thereafter Paul's cancer returned. He succumbed to the disease in 1997.

While acting as a political adviser to her husband, Tsongas started the first all-woman law firm in Lowell, raised their three daughters, and eventually took a job at Middlesex Community College as the dean of external affairs. When Democratic Rep. Marty Meehan retired in July 2007 to become chancellor of the University of Massachusetts (Lowell), Tsongas decided to run for the seat. Noting that Massachusetts had not had a female House member in more than 25 years, Tsongas was also motivated by what she saw as the need for change in Washington and her strong disagreement with the Bush administration on the Iraq war. Facing four other Democrats in a September primary, she was the early favorite and had endorsements from influential Democratic Rep. Barney Frank and Kitty Dukakis, the wife of former Democratic presidential nominee Michael Dukakis. Her most formidable challenge came from former Lowell Mayor Eileen Donoghue. Tsongas drew heavily on her ties to Lowell and emphasized her husband's years representing the district, but she erred during a debate in saying she spent 10 years in Washington representing the 5th District, a statement that actually described her husband's career. Tsongas's opponents seized on the comment to highlight her lack of elective experience and criticized her for moving away from Lowell to nearby Charlestown. Tsongas said she moved to be closer to her daughters, who were attending college in Boston. Tsongas edged out Donoghue, 36% to 31%. Tsongas lost nearly 2-to-1 in Lowell but won most of the other towns.

In the general election, Tsongas faced a Republican with an intensely personal story and a recognizable name in the district. Retired Air Force Lt. Col. Jim Ogonowski's brother, John, was the pilot of the first plane to hit the World Trade Center on September 11. Each candidate sought to wrap the George W. Bush administration around the other. Ogonowski criticized Tsongas for supporting a path to citizenship for illegal immigrants, which Bush favored. Tsongas attacked Ogonowski for not supporting the expansion of the State Children's Health Insurance Program, then up for renewal in Congress. Both national parties spent heavily on the race, and EMILY's List got involved for Tsongas. Former President Clinton drew a crowd of several thousand during a campaign stop in her behalf. Tsongas's victory was surprisingly close, 51%-45%. Ogonowski won 11 towns, mostly in the northern part of the district. Tsongas handily took Lowell and Lawrence, plus the area closer to Boston.

In the House, Tsongas has kept a low profile, especially compared with the rest of the Massachusetts delegation. She has been a staunch liberal who has backed her party on all major votes. But she also ardently backs pay-as-you-go legislation requiring new spending to be offset, calling it a "critical first step" toward addressing the deficit. On the Armed Services Committee, she pushed for reductions of U.S. forces in Iraq and demanded a better-defined strategy for Afghanistan. She got provisions into the fiscal 2011 defense authorization bill speeding up development of lightweight body armor and protecting the legal rights of sexual assault victims. As a member of the Natural Resources Committee, she introduced a bill in 2010 aimed at strengthening the Groundwork USA program providing federal funding for "green-space" projects.

After her tough contests a year earlier, Tsongas was re-elected in 2008 without opposition. The 2010 election was a far different story. After the surprise victory of Republican Sen. Scott Brown showed that the Democrats' hold on Massachusetts had its limits, Tsongas drew seven Republican and four independent challengers. The eventual GOP nominee was Jon Golnik, a former Wall Street currency trader who enjoyed tea party backing. Golnik invoked standard tea party themes of individual power over government control while blasting Tsongas' votes on President Obama's health care bill and other legislation. But he had to compete with a higher-profile gubernatorial election as well as the incumbent's overwhelming financial advantage—he raised $400,000 while Tsongas collected more than $1.9 million. She won with nearly 55% of the vote.

SIXTH DISTRICT

John Tierney (D)

Elected 1996, 8th term; b. Sept. 18, 1951, Salem; home, Salem; Salem St. Col., B.A. 1973, Suffolk U., J.D. 1976; no religious affiliation; married (Patrice).

Professional Career: Practicing atty., 1976–96.

DC Office: 2238 RHOB, 20515, 202-225-8020; Fax: 202-225-5915; Web site: tierney.house.gov.

State Offices: Lynn, 781-595-7375; Peabody, 978-531-1669.

Committees: *Education & the Workforce:* Health, Employment, Labor & Pensions; Higher Education & Workforce Training. *Oversight & Government Reform:* National Security, Homeland Defense & Foreign Operations (RMM).

Group Ratings

	ACLU	ACU	ADA	CFG	AFS	FRC	LCV	ITIC	NTU	COC
2010	94	0	95	0	100	0	90	67	6	13
2009	–	0	95	2	100	–	100	–	5	33

National Journal Ratings

	2010 LIB — 2010 CONS		2009 LIB — 2009 CONS	
Economic	84%	— 16%	75%	— 21%
Social	93%	— 0%	72%	— 26%
Foreign	92%	— 3%	78%	— 17%
Composite	92%	— 8%	77%	— 23%

Key Votes of the 111th Congress

1. Overturn Ledbetter	Y	5. Bar federal abortion funds	N	9. Stop detainee transfers	N
2. Pass $820 billion stimulus	Y	6. Pass health care bill	Y	10. Legalize immigrants' kids	Y
3. Let guns in national parks	N	7. Regulate financial firms	Y	11. Repeal don't ask, tell	Y
4. Pass cap-and-trade	Y	8. Pass tax cuts for some	Y	12. Limit campaign funds	Y

Election Results

2010 general	John Tierney (D)	142,732	(57%)	($901,893)
	Bill Hudak (R)	107,930	(43%)	($827,877)
2010 primary	John Tierney (D)	unopposed		

Prior Winning Percentages: 2008 (70%), 2006 (70%), 2004 (70%), 2002 (68%), 2000 (71%), 1998 (55%), 1996 (48%)

Population		Race/Ethnicity		Work	
Pop. 2010:	650,161	White:	84.5%	Private:	79.9%
Change since 2000:	Up 2.1%	Black:	2.6%	Government:	12.7%
Urban:	94.9%	Hispanic:	7.7%	Self-employed:	7.3%
Rural:	5.1%	Asian:	3.4%	Blue collar:	15.4%
Area size:	805 sq. mi.	Native Am.:	0.1%	White collar:	69.4%
		Hawaiian:	0.0%	Khaki collar:	0.1%
Age		Two+ races:	1.3%	Other:	15.1%
Median age:	41.5 yrs.				
More than 65 yrs:	14.8%	*Ancestry*		Median income:	$72,768
Less than 18 yrs:	22.6%	Irish	19.8%	Median Home Value:	$400,500
		Italian	14.5%		
Education		English	10.8%	**Military Veterans**	
H.S. grad:	91.5%			% of Pop:	9.2%
College grad:	40.7%				
Grad degree:	16.2%				

North Shore; Lynn, Peabody

The North Shore of Massachusetts Bay has often been at the leading edge of the nation's economy. In 1640, the Saugus Iron Works was built here—the beginning of American heavy industry. When Europe's great powers were convulsed in international war from 1792 to 1815, American ship owners suddenly became the richest in the world, and traders from Boston and Salem accumulated the capital needed to build textile mills and railroads and to finance

2008 Presidential Vote		
Barack Obama (D) 192,995	(57%)
John McCain (R) 136,116	(41%)
2004 Presidential Vote		
John Keary (D)......................185,264	(58%)
George Bush (R)....................130,924	(41%)
Cook Partisan Voting Index: D+7		

much of the American Industrial Revolution. From the small port of Salem, ships left for China, bringing back porcelain and artifacts, which helped change American styles forever. Salem, first settled by Europeans in 1626, had the nation's first millionaire, Elias Hasket Derby. In 1900, it was the richest city per capita in the nation.

Today, the North Shore is a quiet place. From Boston Harbor north to the mouth of the Merrimack River, it is a collection of ethnic factory towns from Lynn to Peabody (once one of the world's great leather producers with more than 100 tanneries) to the former shipbuilding Newburyport. There are a few high-income enclaves, such as Marblehead with its yachts, Beverly with its estates, and artsy Rockport. Salem's House of the Seven Gables is a popular tourist site. Built in 1668, it inspired the novel by Nathaniel Hawthorne and is the oldest surviving wooden mansion in New England. The Salem witch trials are probably the town's most famous legacy, and local officials have capitalized on them—its Halloween festivities contribute around $9 million to Salem's $65 million annual tourism industry. Some of the area's economic hopes are tied to a proposed marine research institute and a cruise terminal that opened in 2007. Lynn is the district's largest city, and its General Electric jet engine plant has been the largest employer, although it has only a fraction of the jobs that it had at its peak of 13,000 in the late 1970s.

The 6th Congressional District includes the North Shore from Saugus and Lynn northward, plus towns and cities inland west to Burlington, and the Hanscom Air Force Base in Bedford. Its high-income Yankee towns were historically liberal Republican, while Lynn, Salem, Peabody, and the Merrimack mill towns are still Irish working-class Democratic. The 6th has been a Democratic district since the 1960s, though only marginally so in the 1980s and in the early 1990s. While this district is the site of the original gerrymander—named after Elbridge Gerry—the current 6th boundaries are hardly grotesque by contemporary standards.

John Tierney (D)

The congressman from the 6th District is John Tierney, a Democrat elected in 1996. Tierney grew up in Salem in modest circumstances. He worked his way through Salem State College and Suffolk University Law School as a janitor on the night shift and as a clerk at a Boston law firm. For nearly 20 years, he practiced law in Salem. In 1994, he spied a political opening and ran for Congress. The incumbent, Peter Torkildsen, was a Republican elected in 1992 by beating veteran Democrat Nicholas Mavroules, who had been indicted on tax evasion and bribery charges. But in a year highly favorable to Republicans as 1994 was, Torkildsen managed to defeat Tierney by only 51%-47%. In 1996, Tierney ran again. His ads, along with the AFL-CIO's, assailed GOP House Speaker Newt Gingrich and cutbacks in Medicare. He called for health care insurance for children and criticized Torkildsen for not bringing enough defense dollars to the district. Torkildsen spent $1.1 million, while keeping his promise to accept no political action committee money. Tierney had $776,000 to spend, and he concentrated it on a blitz close to the election. The result was one of the closest races in the country. After several recounts, which stretched into December, Tierney won by 371 votes.

In the House, Tierney has been a solid ally of labor unions on the Education and Labor Committee and a consistently liberal vote. His work on that panel has included support for alternative paths to teaching, gang- and drug-free schools, and strengthened vocational education. In the 2008 higher education bill, Tierney won an amendment to penalize states that fail to meet budget benchmarks for college aid. He has unsuccessfully sought for years to advance his sweeping "Clean Money, Clean Elections" legislation, which would require public financing of elections and free broadcast time for candidates. He also joined Rep. Louise Slaughter, D-N.Y., in 2009 on legislation to set a 16% cap on credit interest rates and limit other fees

In the 111th Congress (2009-10), Tierney was the chairman of the National Security and Foreign Affairs Subcommittee of the Oversight and Government Reform Committee, where he has joined Senate Foreign Relations Chairman John Kerry in calling for tighter controls on U.S. aid to Pakistan. Tierney's panel issued a little-noticed but scathing report in 2010 about the use of Afghan warlords to safeguard shipments of supplies to U.S. and NATO troops. "This contract has fueled warlordism, extortion, corruption, and maybe even funded the enemy," he said. "U.S. taxpayer dollars are feeding a protection racket in Afghanistan that would make Tony Soprano proud." In April 2008, he also questioned the growing sales of military equipment on eBay and other websites. But he is not reflexively against military spending—he supports developing a controversial backup engine for the F-35 Joint Strike Fighter in competition with Connecticut's Pratt & Whitney as a way to lower costs. The engine is being built at the GE plant in Lynn. Tierney is well connected to Democratic Leader Nancy Pelosi, whose daughter, Christine, once worked as his top aide.

Torkildsen challenged Tierney in a 1998 rubber match, but Tierney won 55%-42%. He faced only token opposition until 2010, when he had to defend against a scandal involving his wife, Patrice. She pleaded guilty in October to four counts of aiding and abetting the filing of false tax returns for her brother, a federal fugitive under indictment for illegal gambling and money laundering. She was later sentenced to 30 days in jail. The congressman insisted he knew of no wrongdoing, and posted a detailed explanation on his website. But his Republican opponent, lawyer Bill Hudak, saw an opening. He blasted Tierney for being ignorant of any illegalities, leading Tierney, during one angry debate between the two men, to criticize Hudak for a lawn sign he put up in 2008 likening Barack Obama to Osama bin Laden. Tierney also said Hudak urged a reporter to examine whether Obama was born in the United States. Hudak said the lawn sign was satire and denied being part of the so-called "birther" movement. Voters gave Tierney the benefit of the doubt, and he won with 57%.

SEVENTH DISTRICT

Edward Markey (D)

Elected Nov. 1976, 18th full term; b. July 11, 1946, Malden; home, Malden; Boston Col., B.A. 1968, J.D. 1972; Catholic; married (Susan Blumenthal).

Military Career: Army Reserves, 1968–73.

Elected Office: MA House of Reps., 1973–76.

DC Office: 2108 RHOB, 20515, 202-225-2836; Fax: 202-226-0092; Web site: markey.house.gov.

State Offices: Framingham, 508-875-2900; Medford, 781-396-2900.

Committees: *Energy & Commerce:* Communications & Technology; Energy & Power; Oversight & Investigations. *Natural Resources* (RMM).

Group Ratings

	ACLU	ACU	ADA	CFG	AFS	FRC	LCV	ITIC	NTU	COC
2010	94	0	100	0	100	0	100	67	3	13
2009	–	0	100	4	100	–	100	–	2	33

National Journal Ratings

	2010 LIB — 2010 CONS		2009 LIB — 2009 CONS	
Economic	90% —	0%	73% —	25%
Social	93% —	0%	89% —	0%
Foreign	92% —	3%	91% —	0%
Composite	95% —	5%	88% —	12%

Key Votes of the 111th Congress

1. Overturn Ledbetter	Y	5. Bar federal abortion funds	N	9. Stop detainee transfers	N
2. Pass $820 billion stimulus	Y	6. Pass health care bill	Y	10. Legalize immigrants' kids	Y
3. Let guns in national parks	N	7. Regulate financial firms	Y	11. Repeal don't ask, tell	Y
4. Pass cap-and-trade	Y	8. Pass tax cuts for some	Y	12. Limit campaign funds	Y

Election Results

2010 general	Edward Markey (D)	145,696	(66%)	($1,535,340)
	Gerry Dembrowski (R)	73,467	(33%)	($48,817)
2010 primary	Edward Markey (D)	unopposed		

Prior Winning Percentages: 2008 (76%), 2006 (100%), 2004 (74%), 2002 (100%), 2000 (100%), 1998 (71%), 1996 (70%), 1994 (64%), 1992 (62%), 1990 (100%), 1988 (100%), 1986 (100%), 1984 (71%), 1982 (78%), 1980 (100%), 1978 (85%), 1976 special/general combined (77%)

Population		Race/Ethnicity		Work	
Pop. 2010:	648,162	White:	73.1%	Private:	81.9%
Change since 2000:	Up 2.2%	Black:	5.4%	Government:	11.3%
Urban:	99.5%	Hispanic:	8.8%	Self-employed:	6.6%
Rural:	0.5%	Asian:	8.7%	Blue collar:	13.6%
Area size:	188 sq. mi.	Native Am.:	0.1%	White collar:	70.5%
		Hawaiian:	0.0%	Khaki collar:	0.2%
Age		Two+ races:	2.2%	Other:	15.7%
Median age:	38.9 yrs.				
More than 65 yrs:	14.3%	*Ancestry*		Median income:	$71,032
Less than 18 yrs:	20.5%	Irish	18.3%	Median Home Value:	$424,600
		Italian	16.1%		
Education		English	7.2%	**Military Veterans**	
H.S. grad:	90.1%			% of Pop:	7.0%
College grad:	44.4%				
Grad degree:	20.8%				

Boston Suburbs; Framingham

The Yankee Protestants and Irish Catholics who settled Massachusetts arrived by boat, the Yankees to a cold, stony land with a few Indians, the Irish to a crowded city with Yankees who seemed no more welcoming. The Yankees whose ancestors once farmed the soil had, by the early 20th century, founded suburbs filled with solid brick and white frame houses. As the years went on, their local public schools emptied as young people with children moved out, and attendance at Protestant churches fell. The Irish, for decades heavily concentrated in the crowded wards of Boston, started moving out into the suburbs after World War II. There were other ethnic groups here and there (Jews, Italians, French-Canadians), but the major conflict—fought out in neighborhood playgrounds, in school committee meetings, and not least in political campaigns—was between Protestant Yankee Republicans and Catholic Irish Democrats.

2008 Presidential Vote
Barack Obama (D) 193,130   (65%)
John McCain (R) 99,062   (33%)

2004 Presidential Vote
John Kerry (D) 192,133   (66%)
George Bush (R) 96,374   (33%)

Cook Partisan Voting Index: D+15

The 7th Congressional District of Massachusetts is made up of northern and western Boston suburbs, where vestiges of this conflict can still be seen. Geographically, the district forms an arc around Boston, starting with the clapboard beach towns of Winthrop and Revere just beyond Logan Airport, going north as far as working-class Woburn (where Charles Goodyear developed the art of vulcanizing rubber), and west along Route 9, and reaching modest-income Natick and Framingham, the headquarters town of Staples and TJX (T.J.Maxx, Marshalls, HomeGoods). The 7th also includes university towns—Medford, home of Tufts University, and Waltham, home of Brandeis University. It includes the patriot town of Lexington, where minutemen fired the shots heard 'round the world in 1775, and high-income Lincoln and Weston. Some 18% of district residents say they are of Irish descent and 16% report Italian ancestry, much larger numbers than its percentages of African-Americans (5%), Hispanics (9%) and Asians (9%). Many of these towns were Yankee Republican through the 1950s, but by the late 1960s, they were solidly Democratic. Politically, the district's suburbanites tend to lean Democratic; Mitt Romney carried the district 51%-49% in 2002, but Scott Brown lost it to Democrat Martha Coakley in the January 2010 Senate special election, 54%-46%.

Edward Markey (D)

The congressman in the 7th District is Democrat Edward Markey, first elected in 1976 at age 30, and now dean of the Massachusetts delegation, and indeed the delegations from the rest of New England. He grew up in Malden, where his father was a milkman. He graduated from Malden Catholic High, Boston College, and Boston College law school, then immediately was elected to the state House, at age 26. In 1976, he ran for the U.S. House and won a 12-candidate primary with 22% of the vote. Now he ranks ninth in House seniority.

In his first years in the House, Markey made his name as a fierce opponent of nuclear power plants and as a crusader for the nuclear freeze (a popular idea among progressives in the early 1980s). Speaker Tip O'Neill put him in a position to be a serious legislator in the House from early on, with a seat on the Energy and Commerce Committee, and he has long since become one of the House's most legislatively productive and creative members. Impressed by the high-tech boom around Route 128, he joined the communications subcommittee early. In 1985, after only eight years in the House, he became chairman of the Energy Conservation and Power Subcommittee. In 1987, with help from Chairman John Dingell, D-Mich., who liked aggressive and loyal younger Democrats, Markey became chairman of the telecommunications subcommittee. This is one of the plum positions in the House, with lucrative possibilities for fundraising, and with subject matter that is intellectually more demanding (and, in lobbying terms, more fiercely contested) than almost anything else in Congress.

Markey has been an important shaper of public policy, often working with Republicans, often coming up with original initiatives, knowledgeable about the workings of the industries he oversees, and often inclined toward deregulation, though he can just as often be found siding with consumers. In 1992, he shrewdly produced the cable television regulation bill with enough support that Congress was able to override President George H.W. Bush's veto—the only bill passed over his veto. Markey's influence was not greatly reduced when he became ranking minority member in 1995; bills in these areas are hard to pass without bipartisan consensus. He was a major player in the passage of the landmark Telecommunications Act of 1996. He has been an impetus as well behind the transition to digital television. He and Dingell pressed in 2005 to have the government pay for the converter boxes that would be required on old sets after digital television became universal in 2009. In 2007, he called on the Federal Communications Commission to regulate children's program advertising for unhealthy foods.

On the big telecom issues during the Bush administration, Markey favored allowing regional Bell and satellite companies to compete with cable companies locally (and cable companies compete with others nationally) in providing broadband and other Internet services, but only with a requirement that new entrants serve all video customers in a geographic area. He has been a booster of so-called "net neutrality," which would prohibit Internet carriers from charging higher fees to big-volume users like Google and Yahoo. "If we don't protect the openness of the Internet for entrepreneurial activity, we're ruining a wonderful model for low-barrier entry, innovation, and job creation," Markey said. In 2010, he sought to have the Federal Communications Commission national broadband plan accommodate those with disabilities using Internet TV and questioned whether Google's collection of information from private WiFi networks and its Street View feature, which allows close-up views of specific streets and buildings, violated privacy laws.

In 2007, House Speaker Nancy Pelosi picked Markey to be chairman of a Select Committee on Energy Independence and Global Warming. This was an attempt to get around Dingell, who as chairman of the Energy Committee, had resisted efforts to toughen auto emissions standards. When Dingell strenuously objected, she announced the select committee would not have authority to propose legislation, but she gave Markey free rein to hold hearings and travel widely—often with Pelosi—to make the case for a far-reaching bill to curb global warming. In 2007, Markey, working closely with Pelosi, proposed an increase in fuel-efficiency standards to 35 miles per gallon by 2018. The domestic auto industry and the United Auto Workers union criticized the plan as extreme and said that it would impose a far lower burden on foreign companies. Their allies backed a 2022 deadline and more-flexible terms. Dingell's resistance to including the provision in that year's energy bill led to extended negotiations. The bill that was passed and signed by President George W. Bush set the 35 miles per gallon standard for 2020, the first increase in the fuel-efficiency standards since 1975. Markey has long opposed oil drilling in the Arctic National Wildlife Refuge and has sought to declare it a wilderness area. When gasoline prices surged in 2008, he unsuccessfully urged the Bush administration to release oil from the Strategic Petroleum Reserve. He has long been a proponent of tougher regulation of nuclear power, and proposed a ban on radioactive materials used in dirty bombs in 2009. Markey criticized the 2008 U.S.-India nuclear cooperation deal as a "historic mistake."

After the 2008 election, California Democrat Henry Waxman defeated Dingell for the chairmanship of the full Energy and Commerce Committee, and Markey became chairman of the Energy and Environment Subcommittee while retaining the select committee gavel. Now Pelosi had the people she needed in place to achieve the Democrats' goal of an 85% cut in greenhouse gas emissions by 2050, along with a cap-and-trade program that would allow companies to buy and sell emissions credits with the overall goal of reducing emissions. "The stars are aligned for great change," Markey told the *Boston Globe* in January 2009.

But bringing about that change meant imposing higher costs on regions dependent on coal-generated electricity and Markey, working closely with Waxman, strove to propitiate adverse interests. The original Obama budget counted on revenues from carbon emission permits, but Waxman and Markey agreed that 85% of them would in early years be provided free to coal-using utilities and others. Markey worked with Agriculture Chairman Collin Peterson, D-Minn., on provisions affecting farmers and biofuel producers; he worked with oil and gas interests, with the auto industry, and with manufacturers generally to gain their support, or at least, reduce their level of opposition. The Congressional Budget Office said that the bill would cost average households less than $200 a year, which helped blunt Republicans' characterization of the bill as "cap-and-tax." He got support from leading corporations—Nike, Starbucks, Exelon, Symantec, and PG&E. After fierce negotiations, the bill came to the floor in June 2009 and passed 219-212. Markey said that passage of the bill showed the power in bringing business and consumer interests together "to create a pathway that works for both."

He also gamely predicted that the Senate would pass a bill. But it was not to be. In the Senate, many Democrats had reservations about the bill, and the only Republicans pursuing bipartisan alternatives, Lindsey Graham of South Carolina and Susan Collins of Maine, were pushing very different approaches. Majority Leader Harry Reid first said he would schedule cap-and-trade and then reneged. Markey's energy bill died for the remainder of the 111th Congress (2009-10).

But Markey continued to be productive legislatively on other fronts. He and Peter Welch, D-Vt., were able to pass a bill with tax rebates for energy-efficient home improvements, dubbed "cash for caulkers." In response to the massive BP oil spill in the Gulf of Mexico in April 2010, he repeatedly pressed BP and the Obama administration for specifics on how much oil was leaking. In June, he proposed a new commission with power to subpoena BP's internal records and he held a subcommittee hearing that month in which he excoriated top executives of five oil companies, noting that four of them had response plans that detailed steps to deal with walruses, which are not found in the Gulf of Mexico. Closer to home, he backed the Cape Wind project, a wind farm proposed off the coast of Cape Cod that has stirred protests from the cape's wealthy second-homeowners.

From his seat on the Homeland Security Committee, Markey has worked on air cargo security issues. In 2003, his proposal to require screening of all air cargo passed the House easily, but it was opposed by the Bush administration and went nowhere in the Senate. He claimed victory late in 2007 when President Bush signed a bill requiring inspection of all freight on commercial passenger planes. And he continued to push for mandatory inspections of all-cargo aircraft.

For many years, Markey coveted a Senate seat. In 1984, he wanted to run for the seat vacated by Democrat Paul Tsongas but deferred to then-Lt. Gov. John Kerry, who went on to win the seat. In 2004, he was again disappointed when Kerry lost the presidential contest and remained in the Senate. In September 2009, after the death of Democratic Sen. Edward Kennedy produced the first vacant Massachusetts Senate seat in 25 years, he declined to run, and the Democratic nomination went to state Attorney General Martha Coakley. Markey has been re-elected in the 7th District without difficulty.

EIGHTH DISTRICT

Michael Capuano (D)

Elected 1998, 7th term; b. Jan. 9, 1952, Somerville; home, Somerville; Dartmouth Col., B.A. 1973, Boston Col., J.D. 1977; Catholic; married (Barbara); 2 children.

Elected Office: Somerville alderman Ward 5, 1977-79; Somerville alderman-at-large, 1985-89; Somerville mayor, 1989-98.

Professional Career: Chief legal cnsl., MA Legislature Taxation Cmte., 1978-84; Practicing atty., 1984-90.

DC Office: 1414 LHOB, 20515, 202-225-5111; Fax: 202-225-9322; Web site: www.house.gov/capuano.

State Offices: Cambridge, 617-621-6208.

Committees: *Financial Services:* Insurance, Housing & Community Opportunity; Oversight & Investigations (RMM). *Transportation & Infrastructure:* Aviation; Highways & Transit; Water Resources & Environment.

Group Ratings

	ACLU	ACU	ADA	CFG	AFS	FRC	LCV	ITIC	NTU	COC
2010	93	0	95	0	100	0	100	67	7	13
2009	–	0	95	0	100	–	93	–	2	29

National Journal Ratings

	2010 LIB	—	2010 CONS	2009 LIB	—	2009 CONS
Economic	73%	—	25%	91%	—	0%
Social	93%	—	0%	89%	—	0%
Foreign	73%	—	24%	76%	—	24%
Composite	82%	—	18%	89%	—	11%

Key Votes of the 111th Congress

1. Overturn Ledbetter	Y	5. Bar federal abortion funds	N	9. Stop detainee transfers	N
2. Pass $820 billion stimulus	Y	6. Pass health care bill	Y	10. Legalize immigrants' kids	Y
3. Let guns in national parks	N	7. Regulate financial firms	Y	11. Repeal don't ask, tell	Y
4. Pass cap-and-trade	Y	8. Pass tax cuts for some	Y	12. Limit campaign funds	Y

Election Results

2010 general	Michael Capuano (D)	134,974	(98%)	($943,592)
2010 primary	Michael Capuano (D)	unopposed		

Prior Winning Percentages: 2008 (99%), 2006 (91%), 2004 (100%), 2002 (100%), 2000 (100%), 1998 (82%)

Population		Race/Ethnicity		Work	
Pop. 2010:	660,414	White:	46.9%	Private:	84.8%
Change since 2000:	Up 4.0%	Black:	19.8%	Government:	10.5%
Urban:	100.0%	Hispanic:	18.8%	Self-employed:	4.7%
Rural:	0.0%	Asian:	9.9%	Blue collar:	10.0%
Area size:	92 sq. mi.	Native Am.:	0.2%	White collar:	69.8%
		Hawaiian:	0.0%	Khaki collar:	0.2%
Age		Two+ races:	2.7%	Other:	20.0%
Median age:	30.9 yrs.				
More than 65 yrs:	9.3%	*Ancestry*		Median income:	$52,909
Less than 18 yrs:	16.4%	Irish	10.7%	Median Home Value:	$433,100
		Italian	7.3%		
Education		English	5.0%	**Military Veterans**	
H.S. grad:	84.2%			% of Pop:	3.5%
College grad:	47.4%				
Grad degree:	23.0%				

Part Boston, Suburbs; Cambridge

The "Hub of the Solar System" is what the elder Oliver Wendell Holmes called the Massachusetts State House in the 19th century, though over time, his statement has come to be remembered as referring to Boston as the "Hub of the Universe." Either way, this most political of cities has often been the focal point of essential moments in American history. On its streets, originally laid out as 17th-century cowpaths, Samuel

2008 Presidential Vote		
Barack Obama (D) 205,113	(85%)
John McCain (R) 33,104	(14%)
2004 Presidential Vote		
John Kerry (D) 168,264	(79%)
George Bush (R) 40,885	(19%)
Cook Partisan Voting Index: D+32		

Adams and Paul Revere plotted revolution, the abolitionist movement helped ignite the Civil War, and various Kennedys opened their campaign headquarters. Today's Boston is different from the Boston of John F. Kennedy's time. Then it was a gray city with no new buildings and dust on every windowsill. The sky was dark with pollution, and the air was thick with ancient Yankee and Irish animosity. The old office buildings were full of Yankees seeking safe investments for their antique family fortunes. The State House and City Hall were full of Irishmen, scampering after good patronage jobs and regaling one another with political battle stories. These days, that Boston is mostly gone. The new skyscrapers are full of well-educated venture capitalists, lawyers, and management consultants, many working for high-tech companies radiating from Cambridge out into the countryside. Boston ranks 8th among large U.S. cities in the share of residents with college degrees or some college-level study, ahead of college towns like Madison, Wis., and just behind Silicon Valley's No. 7-ranked San Jose, according to the business news website *Portfolio.com*. Boston's neighborhoods, full of large Irish families when the city reached its peak population of 801,000 in 1950, are now different, with young singles in rowhouse apartments, professionals in waterfront apartment towers and African-Americans in old triple-deckers.

A generation ago, students from suburbs across the country who were exploring Boston from their dormitories and campuses felt as if they were pawing through the living remnants of 1920s America, a quaint town where the locals call traffic circles "rotaries" and milk shakes "frappes." But Massachusetts has evolved, and nowhere more than in Boston and Cambridge. As universities and high tech and biotech have become driving forces of economic growth, Cambridge has gone glitzy, with restaurants and high-priced hotels, trendy boutiques and upscale condominiums. The Harvard University campus now has more land in Boston than in Cambridge. Greater Boston may well have a larger concentration of graduate students and post-graduate hangers-on than any other major American city, and this graduate student community's world is centered on Cambridge, with outposts in lower-income Somerville and in the neighborhoods of tony Back Bay, Fenway, Allston and Brighton.

These communities are all part of Massachusetts' 8th Congressional District, a region rich with historical sites, from the Paul Revere house in the North End to the frigate USS *Constitution* in the Charlestown docks. And with MIT and the software concentration in Cambridge's once-downscale Lechmere Square, the district is one of the high-tech capitals of America. The 8th includes all of Cambridge, Somerville, economically revived Chelsea, and many Boston neighborhoods—newly upscale and diverse East Boston around Logan Airport, Brighton and the Back Bay, Fenway, Mattapan, Mission Hill, and the South End. Some 18% of its residents are college or graduate students and 57% of its residents over age 15 are not married—both figures among the highest of any congressional district. This is by far the most Democratic district in Democratic Massachusetts.

Michael Capuano (D)

The congressman from the 8th District is Michael Capuano, the winner of a 10-candidate brawl in the 1998 Democratic primary who has been safe ever since. Over the past 70 years, this district has been represented alternately by townies and Kennedys: James Michael Curley, the scampish five-term mayor of Boston and one-term governor was followed by John F. Kennedy in 1946. Then, from 1952, the seat belonged to Tip O'Neill of North Cambridge and Boston College, who rose to become speaker of the House. After he retired in 1986, the seat went to Joe Kennedy, son of Robert Kennedy. Then came Capuano, who was born and raised in Somerville. His paternal grandfather emigrated from Italy, and his father was the first Italian-American elected official in Somerville. His mother is the granddaughter of Irish immigrants. Capuano graduated from Dartmouth and Boston College Law School.

He returned to Somerville to raise his family, practice law, and enter politics. By day, he worked for the legislature's Joint Committee on Taxation and practiced law. In off-hours, he served as alderman of the 5th Ward, as his father had. He then won election five times as Somerville mayor. For decades an Irish and Italian town, Somerville now has many graduate students and young couples. Capuano seems to have been the right politician for this mix, with deep Somerville roots and a penchant for innovation and reform. He had a solid base of support to run for the 8th District seat when Joe Kennedy declined to seek re-election. In a 10-candidate field, Capuano led with 23%, with former Boston Mayor Ray Flynn (1983-93) the runner-up at 17%.

In the House, Capuano is well to the left on the political spectrum. He has supported same-sex marriage and he harshly criticized the Bush administration's handling of the war in Iraq. On the Financial Services Committee, he has worked closely with Massachusetts neighbor and fellow Democrat Barney Frank, pressing in 2010 for an amendment to the financial regulation bill requiring annual shareholder approval of corporate political spending. When some Catholic bishops said in 2004 that they would deny communion to presidential candidate John Kerry of Massachusetts because of his support for abortion rights, Capuano was out front with a public reply that Catholics should be able to vote their conscience.

Capuano is close to House Minority Leader Nancy Pelosi, who grew up in Baltimore as the daughter of a congressman and shares with Capuano an urban, ethnic political background. After Democrats won the majority in 2006, Pelosi put Capuano in charge of the transition. Tasked with helping to revise party caucus rules and ethics guidelines, Capuano emphasized inclusion and reform. In March 2008, the House passed his chief proposal, creating an Office of Congressional Ethics, an independent board that for the first time allowed non-lawmakers to review possible ethics violations by House members. Capuano also chaired the House Administration Committee's Capitol Security Subcommittee, in charge of the Capitol Police force and other internal operations of Congress, and the Commission on Mailing Standards, which supervises franked mail, another sensitive insider task that requires the trust of House leaders. Republicans groused about possible free speech violations in a Capuano proposal to require House approval of members' postings on outside websites, but he responded that the criticism was "laughably inaccurate."

Despite his close proximity to the leadership, Capuano has a penchant for pugnacious commentary. In February 2009, he told the corporate titans of eight banks that took a government bailout: "All or most of you engaged in all or some of the activities that created this crisis. You come here today on your bicycles after buying Girl Scout cookies and helping out Mother Teresa. You're saying, 'We're sorry. We didn't mean it. We won't do it again. Trust us.' America doesn't trust you any more." In September 2010, before his party was swamped in the election that year, Capuano complained openly about President Barack Obama and his top advisers to *The Daily Beast* website: "They're too disconnected from the grass roots and members of the House close to the grass roots," he said. "If they don't change, we'll probably be stuck in the same situation in two years, and then they'll be on the ballot." After Democrats lost their House majority in the election, despite his alliance with Pelosi, he said that the entire leadership team should step down, and told *Politico*, "If the Red Sox came in and lost every game of the year and they kept the manager at the end of the year, that's a problem. That's what we seem to be on the verge of doing." But he nonetheless supported Pelosi for minority leader when she announced she would seek the post.

After the death of Democratic Sen. Edward Kennedy, Capuano entered the special election race to fill the remainder of his term. Pelosi endorsed him and came to his defense when Democratic candidate Martha Coakley, the state attorney general, criticized his vote in 2009 for the health care overhaul that included an amendment banning coverage for abortions in insurance plans receiving federal funds. He emphasized his vote against the USA PATRIOT Act and its provision authorizing roving wiretaps. But Coakley had superior name recognition and won the Dec. 8, 2009, primary 47%-28%. Capuano carried Boston, Cambridge, Chelsea and Somerville in his district plus seven small towns in western Massachusetts; in two others he was tied with Coakley. But he lost just about everywhere else. Coakley went on to lose the general election to Republican Scott Brown.

Capuano has been re-elected by wide margins. He faces a potential problem in post 2010 census redistricting. Massachusetts will lose a House seat, which means that unless one of its 10-member Democratic delegation retires, at least two of them will be facing each other in a primary.

NINTH DISTRICT

Stephen Lynch (D)

Elected Oct. 2001, 5th full term; b. March 31, 1955, Boston; home, South Boston; Wentworth Inst., B.S. 1988, Boston Col. Schl. of Law, J.D. 1991, Harvard U. JFK Schl. of Gov., M.A. 1998.

Elected Office: MA House of Reps., 1994-96; MA Senate, 1996-2001.

Professional Career: Structural ironworker, 1973-91; Practicing atty., 1991-2001.

DC Office: 2348 RHOB, 20515, 202-225-8273; Fax: 202-225-3984; Web site: lynch.house.gov.

State Offices: Boston, 617-428-2000; Brockton, 508-586-5555.

Committees: *Financial Services:* Capital Markets and Government Sponsored Enterprises; Financial Institutions & Consumer Credit; Oversight & Investigations. *Oversight & Government Reform:* Federal Workforce, U.S. Postal Service & Labor Policy; National Security, Homeland Defense & Foreign Operations; Technology, Information Policy, Intergovernmental Relations & Procurement Reform.

Group Ratings

	ACLU	ACU	ADA	CFG	AFS	FRC	LCV	ITIC	NTU	COC
2010	80	0	95	15	100	18	100	67	12	13
2009	–	4	90	0	100	–	93	–	3	36

National Journal Ratings

	2010 LIB	—	2010 CONS	2009 LIB	—	2009 CONS
Economic	59%	—	40%	70%	—	29%
Social	71%	—	25%	67%	—	31%
Foreign	65%	—	35%	62%	—	35%
Composite	66%	—	34%	67%	—	33%

Key Votes of the 111th Congress

1. Overturn Ledbetter	Y	5. Bar federal abortion funds	Y	9. Stop detainee transfers	Y
2. Pass $820 billion stimulus	Y	6. Pass health care bill	Y	10. Legalize immigrants' kids	Y
3. Let guns in national parks	N	7. Regulate financial firms	Y	11. Repeal don't ask, tell	Y
4. Pass cap-and-trade	Y	8. Pass tax cuts for some	Y	12. Limit campaign funds	Y

Election Results

2010 general	Stephen Lynch (D)	157,071	(68%)	($1,000,091)
	Vernon Harrison (R)	59,965	(26%)	($26,499)
	Philip Dunkelbarger (I)	12,572	(5%)	($13,285)
2010 primary	Stephen Lynch (D)	42,527	(65%)	
	MacDonald D'Alessandro (D)	23,109	(35%)	

Prior Winning Percentages: 2008 (99%), 2006 (78%), 2004 (100%), 2002 (100%), 2001 special (66%)

Population		Race/Ethnicity		Work	
Pop. 2010:	650,381	White:	71.3%	Private:	80.8%
Change since 2000:	Up 2.6%	Black:	12.6%	Government:	14.1%
Urban:	98.4%	Hispanic:	6.6%	Self-employed:	5.0%
Rural:	1.6%	Asian:	5.1%	Blue collar:	14.2%
Area size:	319 sq. mi.	Native Am.:	0.2%	White collar:	69.2%
		Hawaiian:	0.0%	Khaki collar:	0.0%
Age		Two+ races:	2.3%	Other:	16.5%
Median age:	38.7 yrs.				
More than 65 yrs:	13.6%	*Ancestry*		Median income:	$71,908
Less than 18 yrs:	22.6%	Irish	24.4%	Median Home Value:	$374,600
		Italian	10.5%		
Education		English	7.4%	**Military Veterans**	
H.S. grad:	90.5%			% of Pop:	8.2%
College grad:	39.3%				
Grad degree:	16.0%				

Part Boston, Suburbs; Brockton

The Irish remain the dominant political tribe in Boston and in Massachusetts, though even in South Boston, long the center of Irish Boston, vestiges of the old neighborhoods are starting to gentrify. Southie's influence endures in the memory of two Irish Democrats who represented the area for all but two years from the Great Depression to the start of the 21st century. The first was John McCormack, an old-style backroom deal-maker who served as House

2008 Presidential Vote		
Barack Obama (D) 188,887	(60%)
John McCain (R) 120,394	(38%)
2004 Presidential Vote		
John Kerry (D) 188,439	(63%)
George Bush (R) 106,734	(36%)
Cook Partisan Voting Index: D+11		

speaker during the 1960s; the second was Joe Moakley, a close pal of Thomas (Tip) O'Neill's, who chaired the influential Rules Committee before Democrats lost the House majority in 1994.

The 9th Congressional District, historically anchored in Boston, has followed the move of the Irish to the suburbs. Today, fewer than one-third of its residents are in Boston, mostly in the still-Irish areas of South Boston, Hyde Park (shared with the 8th District), and West Roxbury. Completion of the transformational Big Dig highway construction project, with a tunnel under Boston Harbor, has spurred economic development along the waterfront, including office buildings, hotels, condominiums, the John Joseph Moakley Courthouse, and a huge convention center. One mega-project called for more than 200 condos, a 300-room hotel and 640,000 square feet of retail space before being scaled back because of the weak economy. The movie business has followed as well—in recent years the crime dramas *The Town*, *Gone Baby Gone* and *The Departed* were filmed in South Boston. The development has reduced some of the parochialism but has increased complaints of gentrification and of pricing the working class out of old neighborhoods.

Now that the ugly Central Artery, the north-south expressway that for five decades divided the city, has been moved underground, traffic flows far more efficiently (though progress came at a price: huge cost overruns drove the Big Dig bill to $15 billion, and the collapse of ceiling tile in a tunnel in July 2006 killed a woman). The 9th District also takes in much of Beacon Hill, including the gold-domed State House facing Boston Common. From there, the 9th heads west to the comfortable suburbs of Needham and Medfield, and southeast to Braintree, ancestral home of the presidential Adamses, and Brockton, the once-bustling shoe manufacturing town that is now lined with stretches of empty buildings and has had Massachusetts' highest foreclosure rate. Ethnically, this remains a heavily Irish congressional district, with Southie as home to an annual St. Patrick's Day parade preceded by a political breakfast and roast that is a must-attend for state politicians. Only the neighboring 10th District has more residents of Irish ancestry—further evidence of the Irish move out of Boston to the far suburbs.

Stephen Lynch (D)

The congressman from the 9th District is Democrat Stephen Lynch, who won a special election in October 2001 to succeed the late Joe Moakley. Lynch grew up in Boston's housing projects and took pride in making good by following the old ethnic precepts of hard work, family loyalty, and personal determination. After graduating from South Boston High School, he joined his father as a full-time ironworker while attending the Wentworth Institute. Eventually, he became the youngest president in the history of the 2,000-member Local 7 of the Ironworkers union. After a fall on the job cut short his ironworking career, he graduated from Boston College Law School and opened a legal practice representing working people. In 1994, he was elected to the state House. Fourteen months later, he won a special election for a seat in the state Senate.

Lynch built a political base in South Boston and had strong union ties, advantages that led him to pursue the seat when Moakley announced in February 2001 that he would not seek re-election. The ailing Moakley, who was beloved by many House Democrats as a link between the party's old and new generations, died in May of that year. Lynch was one of several Democrats who had expressed interest in the race. The most prominent was Max Kennedy, son of Robert and Ethel Kennedy, but his campaign never gained traction. Lynch became the front-runner. He stumbled after *The Boston Globe* revealed his student loan defaults years earlier, plus a tax lien that was resolved in 1998. He had also been arrested twice two decades earlier, for striking an anti-American student demonstrator and for smoking marijuana at a concert.

Three other state senators opposed Lynch, and the strongest among them was Cheryl Jacques, who is openly gay and had support from EMILY's List and other national feminist groups that criticized Lynch's anti-abortion-rights views. But her switch in opposition to capital punishment stirred controversy. Moakley's two brothers, who wielded much influence, endorsed Lynch. Primary Election Day was September 11, 2001, but Republican Gov. Jane Swift decided not to postpone the vote despite the terrorist attacks. Lynch bested Jacques, 39% to 29%. In the anti-climactic general election five weeks later, he defeated another state senator, Jo Ann Sprague, 66%-33%.

In the House, Lynch falls roughly in the middle of the Democratic Caucus, and he has had the most conservative voting record in the Massachusetts delegation, especially on cultural issues. "That's like being called the slowest of the Kenyans in the marathon," he once quipped to the *Boston Herald.* He backed building a fence on the U.S.-Mexico border and was one of three Massachusetts House members to vote for the Iraq war resolution. He showed unexpected support for gay rights causes, developing a political alliance with home-state colleague Barney Frank, an openly gay Democrat. To help the financially strapped Postal Service, which overpaid tens of billions of dollars into the Civil Service Retirement System, he sponsored a measure in 2010 to recalculate the retirement system obligations under a new formula. Lynch was much engaged in the congressional investigations into steroid use in professional baseball. When former Red Sox star pitcher Roger Clemens testified in February 2008 that he had not used steroids, Lynch said he doubted that Clemens was telling the truth and called for prosecuting players who use steroids.

His occasional departures from the party line were tolerated by the leadership, but Lynch went too far when he voted against the final health care overhaul bill in 2010. He was one of five Democrats to switch their votes after having backed the initial House version, and not even a last-minute appeal from Sen. Edward Kennedy's widow, Victoria Kennedy, could change his mind. He cited the Senate's decision to strip out an antitrust exemption for insurance companies and the elimination of the government-run public option to compete with insurers. "In the end, we allowed the insurance companies to prevail," he said. He did side with his party against House Republicans' legislation to repeal the law in January 2011.

Lynch has been re-elected without difficulty. He was unopposed in 2008, but his opposition to the health care bill prompted a primary challenge on the left in 2010 from Mac D'Alessandro, a former regional political director for the Service Employees International Union. D'Alessandro also attacked Lynch's support for the USA PATRIOT Act, and drew support from MoveOn.org and other progressive groups. But Lynch stressed his independence to voters, out-raised his opponent by more than 2-to-1, and won handily, 66%-34%. From there, he had an effortless ride to re-election, winning with 68%.

TENTH DISTRICT

Bill Keating (D)

Elected 2010, 1st term; b. Sept. 6, 1952, Norwood; home, Quincy; Boston Col., B.A. 1974; M.B.A. 1982; Suffolk U., J.D. 1985; Catholic; Married (Tevis); 2 children.

Elected Office: MA House, 1977-84; MA Senate, 1985-98; Norfolk Cnty. district atty., 1999-2010.

Professional Career: Practicing atty., 1999-2010.

DC Office: 315 CHOB, 20515, 202-225-3111; Fax: 202-225-5658; Web site: keating.house.gov.

State Offices: Hyannis, 508-771-0666; Quincy, 617-770-3700.

Committees: *Foreign Affairs:* Middle East & South Asia. *Homeland Security:* Cybersecurity, Infrastructure Protection & Security Technologies; Oversight, Investigations & Management (RMM). *Small Business:* Agriculture, Energy & Trade.

Election Results

2010 general	Bill Keating (D)	132,743	(47%)	($1,508,869)
	Jeffrey Perry (R)	120,029	(42%)	($1,297,757)
	Maryanne Lewis (I)	16,705	(6%)	($85,144)
	James Sheets (I)	10,445	(4%)	($47,940)
2010 primary	Bill Keating (D)	29,953	(51%)	
	Robert O'Leary (D)	28,656	(49%)	

Population		Race/Ethnicity		Work	
Pop. 2010:	649,239	White:	88.3%	Private:	77.2%
Change since 2000:	Up 2.1%	Black:	2.1%	Government:	13.5%
Urban:	92.2%	Hispanic:	2.2%	Self-employed:	9.2%
Rural:	7.8%	Asian:	4.5%	Blue collar:	16.8%
Area size:	2,969 sq. mi.	Native Am.:	0.3%	White collar:	66.2%
		Hawaiian:	0.0%	Khaki collar:	0.1%
Age		Two+ races:	1.6%	Other:	16.8%
Median age:	43.5 yrs.				
More than 65 yrs:	17.6%	*Ancestry*		Median income:	$67,466
Less than 18 yrs:	20.8%	Irish	25.2%	Median Home Value:	$391,900
		English	12.3%		
Education		Italian	10.4%	**Military Veterans**	
H.S. grad:	93.8%			% of Pop:	11.5%
College grad:	39.4%				
Grad degree:	14.5%				

South Shore; Cape Cod, Quincy

The South Shore of Massachusetts Bay, from Boston southward to Plymouth and then down Cape Cod (there is a lot of dispute about which way is up and down on the Cape), is Massachusetts's oldest settled territory. The Pilgrims landed here at Plymouth Rock in 1620. This stony land was farmed by John Adams' father, who was anything but the aristocrat some later members of the Adams family would have had you believe. Daniel Webster lived in the South Shore town of Marshfield, today a high-income suburb of Boston far out on the usually clogged Southeast Expressway. Joseph P. Kennedy used to summer with his young family on Nantasket Beach in Hull, before moving out of Massachusetts when the Yankees wouldn't let them into their beach club in Cohasset in the 1920s. But the Kennedys continue to summer at their Hyannis Port compound on the Cape. Provincetown, at the tip of the Cape, is still a fishing port, one of the major gay vacation areas in the country. The islands of Martha's Vineyard and Nantucket, rich whaling ports in the early 19th century, are favored summer resorts for the liberal rich of Boston, New York, and Washington. Half the nation's cranberry growers are clustered among the bogs along Cape Cod Bay. But the Cape is also filled with retirees who enjoy the beauty and quiet pace.

2008 Presidential Vote		
Barack Obama (D)	197,365	(55%)
John McCain (R)	156,294	(43%)
2004 Presidential Vote		
John Kerry (D)	194,092	(56%)
George Bush (R)	151,209	(43%)
Cook Partisan Voting Index:	D+5	

The 10th Congressional District of Massachusetts follows the South Shore from Quincy, with its large Asian population, to the Cape. It juts inland almost, but not quite, to Brockton and includes Martha's Vineyard and Nantucket, where the glitterati have generated a "not in my backyard" fury over a proposed windmill farm in the nearby channel waters. With the loss of blue-collar jobs, business growth in the South Shore has been slower than elsewhere in the Boston area. The South Shore and the Cape were once exclusively Protestant and Yankee, but in the Massachusetts way, they have changed over the years, with Irish and Italian surnames as common as Yankee ones (this is the nation's most heavily Irish congressional district), and the descendants of Portuguese-Azorean fishermen have fanned out into the countryside. Liberal politics, well established on the Vineyard and Nantucket, have spread inland as well. Although Republican Mitt Romney carried the area in 2002, the South Shore is generally Democratic territory.

Bill Keating (D)

The new congressman from the 10th District is Democrat Bill Keating, who won the open seat of retiring Democratic Rep. Bill Delahunt in 2010.

Keating's father was a police officer and later a veterans' services agent who assisted former soldiers with service-related disabilities. Keating put himself through Boston College by working at a post office. In 1977, at the age of 23, he was elected to the Massachusetts House. One of the first things Keating did was work on a law requiring smoke detectors in houses after a fire in a nearby town killed a family living in a house without detectors. In 1985, Keating was elected to the state Senate, eventually becoming chairman of the Judiciary Committee and the Committee on Taxation. He also was involved in environmental issues, sponsoring a bill to safeguard lakes and streams from pollutants by banning phosphates in household cleaners.

Keating was elected district attorney for Norfolk County in 1998. Four years later, his office became the first in the state to win a murder conviction in the absence of a victim's body. In that case, DNA evidence taken from a saw helped to convict Joseph D. Romano Jr. of murdering and dismembering his wife. Keating also worked to curb bullying in schools, a hot-button issue in the state after a teenage girl in western Massachusetts committed suicide after being bullied. He also set up facilities for veterans suffering from post-traumatic stress disorder, an issue that hit close to home; one of Keating's uncles suffered from PTSD after World War II. And he helped create the Norfolk Advocates for Children, an organization for children who have been victimized by sexual assault.

Keating decided to run for Congress after Delahunt announced he would step down after seven terms. The district has been in Democratic hands for more than 30 years, but it is relatively conservative for Massachusetts. It gave Republican Sen. Scott Brown 60% of the vote in his upset victory over Democratic Attorney General Martha Coakley in the 2010 special election to fill the late Democratic Sen. Edward Kennedy's seat. Keating faced tea party-backed Republican Jeff Perry, a member of the state House.

Keating actively supported the Democrats' health care overhaul, and he got help from Kennedy's widow, Victoria Reggie Kennedy, who said that Keating shared her husband's commitment to universal health care. Keating also was generally supportive of President Barack Obama's $787 billion economic-stimulus bill, although he said he would have done it differently, doling out money "more slowly" and in a "more targeted" way. In contrast, Perry campaigned on a tea party platform calling for smaller government and smaller federal budgets. Part of Keating's campaign strategy was to paint Perry, a police officer, as having a "troubled relationship with the truth," pointing to a case in the 1990s in which an officer under Perry's command was involved in illegal strip searches of teenage girls. Perry said he did not know about the searches at the time. In response to the attack ad, Perry's campaign released a video of Wareham Police Chief Tom Joyce saying Perry was a good police officer.

Keating provided Democrats a rare moment of triumph on an otherwise dismal Election Night. He won with 45.6% of the vote to Perry's 41.3%. Three other candidates divided the remaining votes.

★ MICHIGAN ★

When the French aristocrat Alexis de Tocqueville on his travels to America in 1831 wanted to visit the frontier, he boarded a boat and steamed across Lake Erie to visit the Michigan Territory. Tocqueville was not the first Frenchman to travel there. Two centuries before, French explorers and missionaries sailed the Great Lakes and slapped their version of Indian names on the landscape, which is why Michigan's *ch* is pronounced like *sh* and why Mackinac is pronounced with a silent final *c*. (But Michiganders don't carry it to extremes: Detroit ends with a robust English *oit*.) Michigan was not effectively occupied by the United States until 1796, and was bypassed in the initial westward rush into Ohio, Indiana and Illinois. Tocqueville was still able to travel through virgin woods occupied by Indian tribes, but only barely. In the 1830s Michigan was settled in a rush by Yankee migrants from upstate New York and New England, who cut down trees and built farms and orderly towns complete with schools and colleges. Politically, Michigan was full of Yankee reformers who hated slavery, manned the Underground Railroad, promoted temperance and in 1855 gave Michigan a constitution that banned (as it does to this day) capital punishment. Michigan was one of the birthplaces of the Republican Party, which held its first official meeting in Jackson in 1854. (The party held its first informal meeting in Ripon, Wis.) Until 1929, Michigan was one of the most Republican states in the nation.

After the Civil War, Michigan developed an industrial economy. Its Lower Peninsula was mostly covered with trees, and lumber was the first boom industry on which Michigan over-relied. Forests were clear-cut or swept by blazes like the 1881 fire that burned out half of Michigan's geographic "Thumb." In the late 1800s, huge copper deposits were discovered on the Keweenaw Peninsula, which juts from the Upper Peninsula into icy Lake Superior. Immigrants from Italy and Finland, Cornwall and Croatia came to work in the mines. Then came the auto industry. A combination of accident and shrewdness—the prickly genius of Henry Ford and the willingness of local bankers to finance auto start-ups—ensured that America's fastest-growing industry for the first 30 years of the 20th century was centered in Michigan. Detroit became a boomtown, the nation's fastest-growing major metropolitan area after Los Angeles. The three-county Detroit metro area zoomed from a population of 426,000 in 1900 to 2.2 million in 1930, and in 2010, it had 4 million. The auto industry drew labor from outstate Michigan, from southern Ontario and from the farms of Ohio and Indiana. It attracted Poles and Italians, Hungarians and Belgians, Greeks and Jews. During World War II and after, it brought whites from the Kentucky and Tennessee mountains and blacks from Alabama and Mississippi.

This influx of a polyglot proletariat eventually changed Michigan's politics. The catalyst was the Great Depression of the 1930s and company managers' desire to use machines efficiently, treating employees as extensions of machines and with great distrust. That culminated in the 1937 sit-down strikes organized by the new United Auto Workers (UAW). Management and labor fought, sometimes literally, for pieces of what both sides feared was a shrinking pie. The UAW won and organized most of the companies after Democratic Gov. Frank Murphy refused to send in troops to break the illegal strikes. In the years that followed, autoworkers became a heavily Democratic voting bloc.

Michigan politics became a kind of class warfare, conducted with a bitterness that split families and neighbors. The union mostly won, because demographics benefited the Democrats: Autoworkers and post-1900 immigrants produced more children than did outstate Yankees or management. After Walter Reuther's election as UAW president in 1947, voters elected young, liberal G. Mennen Williams as governor in 1948. By 1954, the Democrats, closely tied to the UAW, seemed to have become the natural majority in the state. As growth continued, economic issues became less bitter. By the early 1960s, class warfare had dissipated; in 1964, Henry Ford II joined Reuther in backing Democrat Lyndon Johnson for president. Republicans George Romney, the former American Motors president elected governor in 1962, and his successor, William Milliken, accepted the welfare state policies endorsed by the UAW leadership and the Democrats. The state government was one of the nation's most generous, and not just to the poor and the unemployed. It supported one of the nation's most distinguished and extensive higher-education systems, built state parks and recreation areas, and pioneered efforts to end racial discrimination.

Michigan grew faster than the nation as a whole from 1910 to 1970. Successive censuses and reapportionments increased its U.S. House delegation from 12 to 19. But in the four decades from 1970 to 2010, Michigan grew less than one-quarter as fast as the nation, and its House delegation will fall back to 14 in 2012. A key turning point may have been the changes in the domestic auto

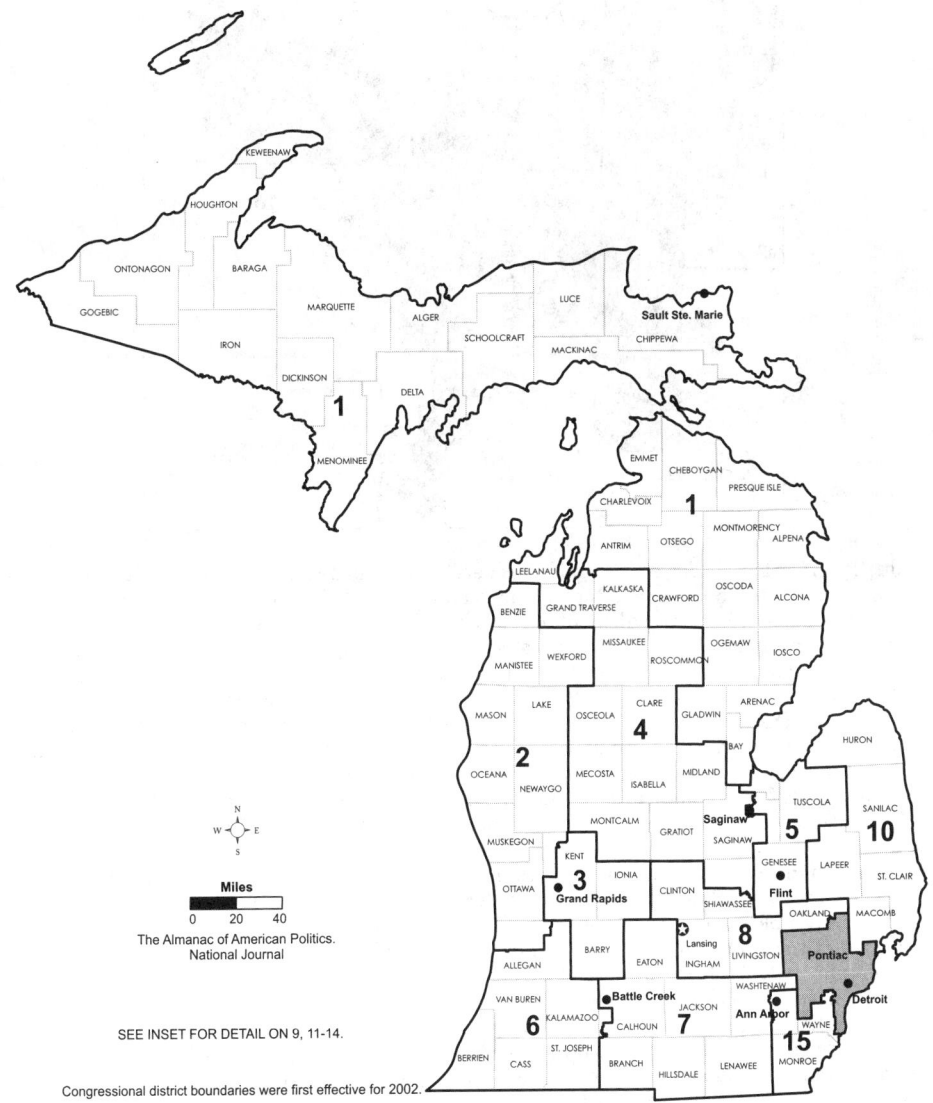

The Almanac of American Politics.
National Journal

Miles
0   20   40

SEE INSET FOR DETAIL ON 9, 11-14.

Congressional district boundaries were first effective for 2002.

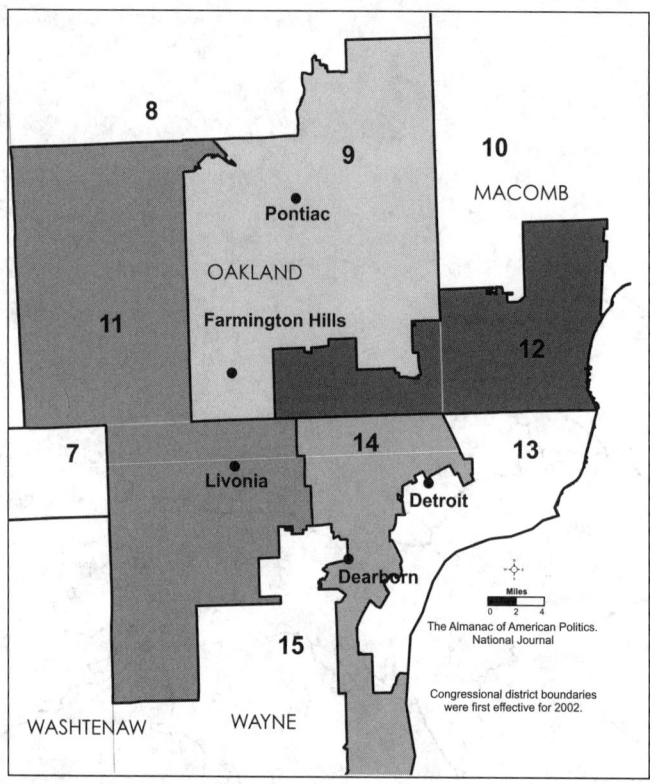

industry. After the UAW's strike against General Motors in 1970, the union won its central demand: "30 and out," retirement after 30 years on the assembly line. That, in turn, led to demands
for generous retiree health care benefits on top of those negotiated for active workers. The assumption was that the Big Three—General Motors, Ford and Chrysler—would continue to dominate
the U.S. auto market as they had for decades and could afford top-shelf benefits. The reality turned
out to be different. Foreign competitors started producing better and cheaper cars that were more
responsive to changes in gas prices and consumer preference, first in Europe and Japan and then
in nonunion U.S. plants. The adversarial system that pitted union shop stewards against company
foremen and enforced 5,000 pages of work rules throttled innovation and prevented the Big Three
from matching foreign-based firms in quality. Auto sales plummeted in the oil shock and recession
of 1979-82, and Chrysler was saved from bankruptcy by a federal bailout, while GM and Ford
foundered.

Politicians woke up to the need for change before the Big Three management or the UAW
leaders. Gov. James Blanchard, a Democrat elected in 1982, tried to stimulate high-skill, capital-
intensive, flexible manufacturing and used $750 million of state pension funds as venture capital
for manufacturers of items ranging from tape drives for microcomputers to fiberglass coffins. Gov.
John Engler, a Republican elected in 1990 and re-elected twice, cut taxes more than 30 times and
slashed welfare rolls by more than two-thirds. He pressed for public school choice and charter
schools, and changed state pensions from defined benefits to defined contributions. For a time,
Michigan's economy boomed. The auto industry became more high-tech, with fewer unionized
workers and higher skill requirements. Just-in-time production methods encouraged subcontrac-
tors to stay in Michigan near big assembly plants and the state boasted the nation's highest per
capita concentration of engineers. Michigan's population grew 7% in the 1990s and unemployment
stayed below the national average. Grand Rapids, the vacation area around Traverse City, and the
northern and western Detroit suburbs seemed to be booming. The great exception was the city of
Detroit, whose population fell from 1.8 million in 1950 to 713,777 in 2010. Starting with the riots
of 1967, crime rates in Detroit were enormously high for 25 years, and much of the city simply
vanished—houses were abandoned or burned down, commercial frontage had nearly 100% vacancy rates, and the downtown was a beleaguered fortress surrounded by blasted-out square miles.

The DNC objected and asked presidential candidates to withdraw their names from the ballot. Barack Obama, John Edwards, Joe Biden and Bill Richardson did so in October. Hillary Rodham Clinton and Christopher Dodd did not (Dennis Kucinich did not file the right paperwork to withdraw and remained on the ballot). Two lower courts ruled against the primary law, but the state Supreme Court upheld it on Nov. 21. Then on Dec. 1, the DNC voted to strip Michigan of all of its delegates for holding its primary too early. The Republican National Committee, in contrast, stripped Michigan of only half its delegates, and its candidates did campaign in the state.

Only 600,000 people voted in the Democratic primary, compared with 869,000 in the Republican primary and 1.3 million in the Republican primary in 2000 (when exit polls showed that 17% of those voters were self-identified Democrats, by far the largest such number that year). On the Democratic side, Clinton ran ahead of "uncommitted" 55%–40%. She carried all but two of the 83 counties, and 13 of the 15 congressional districts. "Uncommitted" ran ahead in heavily black precincts and in the university towns; obviously these were mostly votes for Obama, who had won the Iowa caucuses 12 days earlier.

On the Republican side, Mitt Romney beat John McCain 39%–30%, with 16% going to Mike Huckabee. McCain had hoped to duplicate his Michigan victory in 2000, when he won among self-identified Democrats and independents and lost to George W. Bush among self-identified Republicans. But with at least a semblance of a contest on the Democratic side, there were fewer crossover voters this time. Romney grew up in Michigan, and his father, George Romney, was elected governor three times in the 1960s. He promised to restore the American auto industry, while McCain said that some jobs that had been lost would never be recovered. Romney ran strongest in metro Detroit and in affluent areas like the Traverse Bay area. McCain ran strongest in small-town western Michigan and in the Upper Peninsula.

The Michigan result was accepted by national Republicans, and no one was much troubled by the state losing half its delegates. As it turned out, the Republicans' winner-take-all delegate allocation rules enabled McCain to essentially clinch the party's nomination by winning several close victories between Jan. 15 and Super Tuesday on Feb. 5. In contrast, the Democrats' proportional-representation delegate allocation rules, and the closeness of the race between Clinton and Obama, made Michigan (and Florida, which held its primary Jan. 29), a continuing issue. Dingell and other Michigan Democratic leaders tried to schedule a rerun primary, but got no cooperation from the Republican-controlled state Senate. Michigan Democrats and the Clinton campaign sought some representation for Michigan, but the Obama campaign decried that as unfair. Pundits argued whether the Michigan and Florida numbers should be included wholly or partially when calculating which candidate had won the most popular votes. On May 31, the DNC met and voted to seat half the Michigan delegates, allocating 69 delegates to Clinton and 59 to Obama—a ratio more favorable to Obama than the election results.

In early 2011, Michigan was once again seeking to schedule a primary earlier than the dates allowed by agreement of the Democratic and Republican National Committees. This will probably not be a problem for Democrats if Obama has no serious primary opposition. Republicans, as they showed in 2008, tend to take a more lenient approach to enforcement of the rules.

Congressional districting   Michigan has now lost five seats in the last four censuses—one after the 1980 census, two after the 1990 census and one each after the 2000 and 2010 censuses.

112th Congress Lineup
9 R   6 D
111th Congress Lineup
8 D   7 R

In 2001, for the first time since the 1930s, redistricting was controlled by Republicans, with GOP majorities in both houses of the legislature and with Gov. John Engler determined to use the power to shift the Democrats' 9-7 edge to a 9-6 Republican edge. He succeeded. There was no pretense of bipartisanship: Bills were introduced in the House and Senate abruptly in June 2001 and passed on near party-line votes. The plan ended the 26-year congressional career of House Democratic Whip David Bonior and put two pairs of Democratic incumbents in the same districts. Jim Barcia of the 5th District decided to return to the state Senate, where he used to serve, while John Dingell, the dean of the House, beat liberal (and Nancy Pelosi-endorsed) Democrat Lynn Rivers in the new 15th District. A new Republican district was created in western Wayne and Oakland counties, and shaky Republican incumbents Mike Rogers and Joe Knollenberg were strengthened.

For a time, this was arguably the most successful partisan redistricting plan in the nation. But as is often the case, when the tide of opinion shifts, the partisan intentions of even the cleverest boundary drawers can be thwarted. In 2002, 2004 and 2006, Republicans won a 9-6 edge in the House delegation. But in 2008 they lost two seats—Knollenberg's in suburban Oakland County by a wide margin, and the seat of conservative freshman Tim Walberg, in south-central Michigan, by a narrow margin. Democrats emerged with an 8-7 edge in the House delegation.

In 2010, the partisan pendulum swung the other way. Walberg regained the 7th District seat and, after Democratic Rep. Bart Stupak retired, Republican Dan Benishek won the 1st District by a solid margin.

Republicans will control redistricting in 2011. And, while Snyder does not seem as partisan as Engler, the legislature is likely to pass at least something of a partisan plan. But demographics do not suggest an easy route to Republican gains, and legislators may want to strengthen leading legislators of both parties. The two black-majority districts will presumably be retained, despite continuing population loss in Detroit. And there are enough Democratic votes in the suburbs to fashion safe Democratic districts for John Dingell, the longest-serving member of the House in history and still a power on the Energy and Commerce Committee, and Sander Levin, the ranking Democrat on the powerful Ways and Means Committee. On the Republican side, safe seats likely will be carved out for outstater Dave Camp, the new chairman of Ways and Means; Fred Upton, the Energy and Commerce chairman; and Mike Rogers, the Intelligence Committee chairman. Sharply partisan Republicans might try to eliminate the Flint-Saginaw-Bay City 5th District seat held by Democrat Dale Kildee since 1976. But more-cautious strategists will probably not want to put so much heavily Democratic territory into Republican-held districts. So the member most in peril would seem to be the Democrat Gary Peters in the 9th District. He won a second term only narrowly in 2010.

Governor

Rick Snyder (R)

Elected 2010, term expires Jan. 2015, 1st term; b. Aug. 19, 1958, Battle Creek; home, Ann Arbor; U. of MI, B.A. 1977, M.B.A. 1979, J.D. 1982; Presbyterian; Married (Sue); 3 children.

Professional Career: Adjct. asst. prof., U. of MI, 1982-84; Employee and partner, Coopers & Lybrand, 1982-91; Exec. V.P., Gateway Inc., 1991-96; Pres. and chief operating officer, Gateway Inc., 1996-97; Founder and pres., Avalon Investments Inc., 1997-2000; Founder and chmn., CEO, Ardesta, 2000-10.

Office: P.O. Box 30013, 48909, 517-373-3400; Fax: 517-335-6863; Web site: www.michigan.gov/snyder.

State Offices: Marquette, 906-228-2850.

Election Results

2010 general	Rick Snyder (R)	1,874,834	(58%)
	Virg Bernero (D)	1,287,320	(40%)
2010 primary	Rick Snyder (R)	381,588	(36%)
	Pete Hoekstra (R)	281,695	(27%)
	Mike Cox (R)	240,677	(23%)
	Mike Bouchard (R)	127,422	(12%)

Rick Snyder, a Republican, was elected governor of Michigan in 2010 in his first foray into electoral politics. Snyder grew up in Battle Creek and graduated from the University of Michigan and both its law and business schools. He went to work for the accounting firm of Coopers & Lybrand, first in Detroit and then in Chicago. In 1991, he joined Gateway, the direct sales personal computer firm co-founded by Ted Waitt on a farm outside Sioux City, Iowa. Gateway capitalized on its countrified image by shipping computers with Holstein cow-like black spots and was wildly successful in the 1990s, rising to No. 194 on the *Fortune* 500 list. Snyder became president and chief operating officer in 1996, and in 1997, he left active management but remained on the board of directors. Gateway stock sold for $3.75 in its initial public offering in 1993 and reached $84 in 1999 at the peak of the technology boom. Snyder exercised options on 2 million shares of stock between 1995 and 2001, which made him, by the time he turned 40, a very rich man.

Snyder could have moved to a warm climate, as Gateway did when it relocated to San Diego County. Instead, in 1997, he moved back to Ann Arbor, and with $100 million of his own and investors' money, established Avalon Investments. This venture capital fund had some great successes: Esperion Therapeutics in Plymouth, Mich., and HealthMedia in Ann Arbor. In 2000, he started another $100 million venture capital firm, Ardesta, to invest in micromechanical technologies and

Senior Senator

Carl Levin (D)

Elected 1978, term expires 2014, 6th term; b. June 28, 1934, Detroit; home, Detroit; Swarthmore Col., B.A. 1956, Harvard U., J.D. 1959; Jewish; married (Barbara); 3 children.

Elected Office: Detroit City Cncl., 1969–77, Pres., 1973–77.

Professional Career: Practicing atty., 1959–64, 1971–73, 1978–79; MI asst. atty. gen. & gen. cnsl., MI Civil Rights Comm., 1964–67; Detroit chief appellate defender, 1967–69.

DC Office: 269 RSOB, 20510, 202-224-6221; Fax: 202-224-1388; Web site: levin.senate.gov.

State Offices: Detroit, 313-226-6020; Escanaba, 906-789-0052; Grand Rapids, 616-456-2531; Lansing, 517-377-1508; Saginaw, 989-754-2494; Traverse City, 231-947-9569; Warren, 586-573-9145.

Committees: *Armed Services* (Chmn). *Homeland Security & Governmental Affairs:* Federal Financial Management, Government Information, Federal Services & International Security; Investigations (Permanent) (Chmn); Oversight of Government Management, the Federal Workforce & the District of Columbia. *Small Business & Entrepreneurship.*

Group Ratings

	ACLU	ACU	ADA	CFG	AFS	FRC	LCV	ITIC	NTU	COC
2010	93	0	95	0	95	0	100	33	2	9
2009	–	0	95	3	100	–	100	–	6	43

National Journal Ratings

	2010 LIB	—	2010 CONS	2009 LIB	—	2009 CONS
Economic	88%	—	0%	81%	—	15%
Social	65%	—	0%	85%	—	0%
Foreign	47%	—	0%	55%	—	0%
Composite	83%	—	17%	84%	—	16%

Key Votes of the 111th Congress

1. Overturn Ledbetter	Y	5. Pass health care bill	Y	9. Ratify New START	Y
2. Pass $787 billion stimulus	Y	6. Regulate financial firms	Y	10. Confirm Elena Kagan	Y
3. Repeal DC gun laws	N	7. Pass tax cuts for some	Y	11. Stop EPA climate regs	N
4. Confirm Sonia Sotomayor	Y	8. Legalize immigrants' kids	Y	12. Repeal don't ask, tell	Y

Election Results

2008 general	Carl Levin (D)	3,038,386	(63%)	($8,632,073)
	Jack Hoogendyk (R)	1,641,070	(34%)	($297,747)
2008 primary	Carl Levin (D)	unopposed		

Prior Winning Percentages: 2002 (61%); 1996 (58%); 1990 (57%); 1984 (52%); 1978 (52%)

Democrat Carl Levin, first elected in 1978, is a member of one of Michigan's most respected political families and the longest-serving U.S. senator in the state's history. He is the chairman of the Senate Armed Services Committee. His older brother, Democrat Sander Levin, is Michigan's 12th District representative. Compared to Senate colleagues, Levin is often rumpled and a bit tardy with a haircut, but also compared to many of the rest, he is articulate without political artifice, and he takes unpopular stands on issues.

Levin grew up in Detroit, graduated from Swarthmore College and Harvard Law School, and then went to work as counsel for the state Civil Rights Commission in the turbulent 1960s. After a stint as a public defender, Levin was elected to the Detroit City Council in 1969 with substantial support from both blacks and whites. In 1978, he ran for the U.S. Senate and was helped when Republican incumbent Robert Griffin got out of the race and then back in. Levin won 52%-48%. In 1984, he won his first re-election by a similar margin, and since then, he has returned four times by wide margins. He cast his 11,000th vote in May 2009, which made him No. 20 on the all-time list.

Levin was chairman of the Armed Services Committee in 2001-03, and has been serving a second stint as chair since January 2007. He has the skepticism of large-scale defense spending and military involvements common among Democrats in the 1970s and has built up an impressive expertise in military affairs. Levin was very dubious about the need for military action in Iraq in 2002 and argued fervently that any action should be multilateral. He also argued that military action was not necessary because Iraqi leader Saddam Hussein could be deterred from using weapons of mass destruction if he had them. He offered an alternative resolution calling on the Bush administration to get the United Nations to adopt a more vigorous weapons inspection program before any military action was taken. It was defeated 75-24. In 2004, Levin issued a report charging that Pentagon official Douglas Feith deliberately exaggerated ties between Hussein and the terrorist group al-Qaida, and ignored corrections requested by the Central Intelligence Agency.

In June 2006, Levin and Jack Reed, D-R.I., sponsored an amendment calling for a "phased redeployment" of U.S. troops in Iraq in six months, with no deadline for withdrawal; it also called for U.S. forces to transition to training Iraqi security forces. A more stringent alternative, John Kerry's amendment calling for withdrawal by July 2007, was defeated 86-13; the Levin-Reed amendment lost 60-39. In late 2006, Levin described the situation in Iraq as "a low-grade civil war" and called for a bipartisan resolution supporting phased redeployment. Despite his disagreements with administration policy, he voted to confirm the nomination of Defense Secretary Robert Gates, saying Gates was a "welcome break of honest, candid realism."

Levin has been a sharp-eyed overseer of the Pentagon, joining with John McCain, R-Ariz., in strongly questioning the Pentagon's leasing, rather than purchase, of KC-767 refueling tankers from Boeing. After e-mails obtained by McCain revealed improper negotiations between the Air Force and Boeing, Levin, McCain and John Warner, R-Va., won approval in 2003 of a proposal to lease only 20 of the aircraft and purchase 80 others to keep the total cost down. During hearings in 2004, Levin said that the Army was stretched too thin, that there were not enough soldiers and protective gear in Iraq, that too many personnel were held in the service by stop-loss orders and that the Army was not adequately replacing old equipment. Levin has been the Senate's most persistent critic of efforts over the years to build a missile defense system.

When President Barack Obama began reconsidering U.S. strategy in Afghanistan in September 2009, Levin argued against sending in more U.S. troops until an acceleration of training and equipping Afghan security forces took place, putting him in opposition to Joint Chiefs Chairman Mike Mullen. He also argued against a total pullout. Just before Obama announced his decision to send more troops in December, Levin questioned how that would increase the size of Afghan security forces. When Obama relieved Gen. Stanley McChrystal of his duties in command of Afghanistan after he and his aides were quoted criticizing administration officials in a June 2010 *Rolling Stone* article, Levin scheduled expedited hearings and endorsed Gen. David Petraeus as his successor. Also that summer, Levin called for more- aggressive airstrikes within Pakistan and for a terrorist designation for the Haqqani network operating over the Pakistan-Afghanistan border. In July 2010, he said that the United States was on track to meet Obama's July 2011 date for the beginning of troop withdrawals, but added a note of caution, saying, "The speed of reductions and the location of reductions, by the way, is going to be based on conditions at the time."

Levin had long opposed the ban on openly gay people serving in the military enacted in 1993 and signed by President Bill Clinton. He put forces in motion in 2010 that led to repeal of the so-called "don't ask, don't tell" policy. Levin included a repeal measure in the 2010 defense authorization bill. McCain, the committee's ranking Republican, blocked the bill from coming to the floor in September. Ultimately, the repeal was dropped from the defense bill but was passed as a free-standing bill on a vote of 65-31. The House approved a similar measure and the policy was repealed.

Levin has also weighed in on intelligence matters. He objected to the National Security Agency surveillance of communications between Qaida suspects abroad and people in the United States. And in April 2009, Levin said that independent investigators, rather than the Justice Department, should determine whether CIA interrogators and Bush administration officials should face charges for the use of enhanced interrogation techniques. Although he supported closing the U.S. detention center at Guantanamo Bay, Cuba, where the United States has detained suspected terrorists, he conceded in June 2010 that it would probably remain open for the foreseeable future.

Levin generally has one of the most liberal records in the Senate, with some Michigan accents. He opposed the 1993 North American Free Trade Agreement, which the powerful labor unions in Michigan were fighting, and over the years, he has called for crackdowns on tax avoidance by foreign automakers and on Chinese and Japanese currency manipulation. He also supported the 2008 loan guarantees and government help for General Motors and Chrysler when they were on the brink of bankruptcy. He also has stood in the way of Democratic efforts to significantly raise fuel efficiency standards for cars and trucks. In 2007, he opposed the increase in fuel standards to 35 miles per gallon by 2020 under consideration in the Senate, and his resistance increased the leverage of House Energy and Commerce Committee Chairman John Dingell, the Michigan Democrat, in gaining some concessions for the automobile industry in the bill, which eventually passed. As alternative-fuel vehicles have taken off in popularity and availability, Levin in 2010 called for separate standards for plug-in hybrid cars, all-electric vehicles and fuel-cell vehicles. A one-size-fits-all

though her performance was limited. Other senior Senate Democrats quietly discussed replacing her after the 2006 election. Ultimately, they reached an agreement: Stabenow got a seat on the Finance Committee and became chair of the Democratic Steering and Outreach Committee, a liaison to grassroots groups across the nation, while Washington state Sen. Patty Murray became conference secretary. In the 112th Congress (2011-12), she returned to the leadership as vice chair of the Democratic Policy Committee.

She also became chairman of the Agriculture Committee in early 2011, after Iowa's Tom Harkin left the post to chair the Health, Education, Labor and Pensions Committee. (On the HELP Committee, Harkin replaced Edward Kennedy of Massachusetts, who died in office in August 2009.) The post has national importance because the $289 billion farm bill, passed in 2008, expires in 2012. Traditionally, farm bills have favored crops such as corn and wheat that receive big subsidies of various kinds. But Michigan mostly produces so-called specialty crops like cherries, blueberries and apples. Stabenow can be expected to tilt farm legislation in the direction of specialty crops, which may put her at odds with her House counterpart, Frank Lucas, a conservative Republican from Oklahoma. In addition, Stabenow has been interested in nutrition issues since her service in the Michigan Legislature. Federal nutrition programs fall under the Agriculture committees.

During the Bush era, Stabenow was a leading foe of the Republican president's international trade agenda, insisting on protections for American workers who lose their jobs to foreign competition. With Kentucky Republican Jim Bunning she sponsored a proposal to make it easier for U.S. manufacturers to show currency manipulation by other nations, a measure directed at China. With other rust-belt Democrats, she successfully fought Senate action on climate change legislation in recent years, and she opposed tougher fuel economy standards for the auto industry, which ultimately passed the Senate.

In 2009, with Democrats in control of the executive and legislative branches and enjoying a 60-vote supermajority in the Senate, Stabenow had more leeway to legislate. She strongly supported loan guarantees for the Detroit Three automakers and the government acquisition of General Motors and Chrysler. In November 2010, after GM's successful initial public offering, she told Bloomberg News, "This is an example of America partnering with our industry just as every other country around the world partners with their industry."

When the Senate passed the "Cash for Clunkers" program providing government reimbursements for trading in old cars for more fuel-efficient models in 2009, Stabenow successfully fended off a proposal by Democratic Sen. Dianne Feinstein of California for higher mileage standards. She also pushed the move to transfer $2 billion of economic stimulus funds into the clunkers program, and criticized Japan and Korea for rules that excluded American-made cars from their similar programs. In October 2010, the Senate passed Stabenow's small-business bill with a $30 billion lending fund that she said could generate a $300 billion pool of capital. With Republican Rep. Dave Camp of Michigan, Stabenow in January 2010 sponsored a bill to close the Chicago area locks and dams to prevent the invasive Asian carp from getting into the Great Lakes. Later that year, she called for poisoning the carp in Chicago's Lake Calumet, where they were breeding in great numbers.

In 2006, when Stabenow came up for re-election, Republicans were unable to recruit House members Candice Miller and Mike Rogers to run, and her opponent was Oakland County Sheriff Mike Bouchard. Stabenow won easily, 57%-41%.

FIRST DISTRICT

Dan Benishek (R)

Elected 2010, 1st term; b. April 20, 1952, Iron River; home, Crystal Falls; U. of MI, B.S. 1974; Wayne St. U., M.D. 1978; Catholic; Married (Judy); 5 children.

Professional Career: Gen. surgeon, Dickinson Cnty. Memorial Hospital, 1983-2010; gen. surgeon, V.A. Medical Center, 1990-2010.

DC Office: 514 CHOB, 20515, 202-225-4735; Fax: 202-225-4744; Web site: benishek.house.gov.

State Offices: Gaylord, 989-448-8811; Iron Mountain, 906-828-1581; Marquette, 906-273-1661; Petoskey, 231-348-0657.

Committees: *Natural Resources:* Energy & Mineral Resources; Indian & Alaska Native Affairs. *Science, Space & Technology:* Investigations & Oversight; Research & Science Education. *Veterans' Affairs:* Health; Oversight & Investigations.

Election Results

2010 general	Dan Benishek (R)	120,523	(52%)	($1,388,629)
	Gary McDowell (D)	94,824	(41%)	($838,208)
	Glenn Wilson (NPA)	7,847	(3%)	($127,237)
2010 primary	Dan Benishek (R)	27,077	(38%)	
	Jason Allen (R)	27,062	(38%)	
	Tom Stillings (R)	5,418	(8%)	
	Linda Goldthorpe (R)	4,980	(7%)	
	Don Hooper (R)	3,969	(6%)	

Population		Race/Ethnicity		Work	
Pop. 2010:	650,222	White:	92.5%	Private:	76.4%
Change since 2000:	Down 1.9%	Black:	1.2%	Government:	15.9%
Urban:	33.4%	Hispanic:	1.2%	Self-employed:	7.4%
Rural:	66.6%	Asian:	0.5%	Blue collar:	25.0%
Area size:	27,809 sq. mi.	Native Am.:	2.7%	White collar:	52.4%
		Hawaiian:	0.0%	Khaki collar:	0.1%
Age		Two+ races:	1.7%	Other:	22.5%
Median age:	44.3 yrs.				
More than 65 yrs:	18.7%	*Ancestry*		Median income:	$39,759
Less than 18 yrs:	20.1%	German	19.2%	Median Home Value:	$114,000
		Irish	9.0%		
Education		English	8.8%	**Military Veterans**	
H.S. grad:	88.2%			% of Pop:	13.7%
College grad:	18.1%				
Grad degree:	6.4%				

Upper Peninsula

Michigan's Upper Peninsula, commonly known as the U.P., is a land apart. Surrounded on three sides by frigid Lakes Superior, Huron, and Michigan, the U.P. is no farther north than Montreal or Seattle, but there are places here that have some of the coldest climates in settled parts of North America. The area surrounding Keweenaw County, which juts into Lake Superior, often ranks high in the nation's heaviest snowfall. The first snow is often in October, and the

2008 Presidential Vote		
Barack Obama (D)	166,185	(50%)
John McCain (R)	160,142	(48%)
2004 Presidential Vote		
George Bush (R)	177,315	(53%)
John Kerry (D)	151,450	(46%)
Cook Partisan Voting Index: R+3		

last, eight months later. Far away from any major city, with ground too frozen and stony and a growing season too short for most crops, the Upper Peninsula was explored by French voyagers and missionaries more than 300 years ago, but was never thickly settled until prospectors found rich veins of ore here. The mineral veins of the Keweenaw Peninsula produced 13.3 billion pounds of copper. The Marquette, Menominee, and Gogebic iron ranges produced more than 1 billion tons of iron ore. Starting in the 1840s, immigrants flocked here to work the mines: Irish, Italians, Swedes, Norwegians, miners' sons from Wales and Cornwall, and most prominently, Finns, who must have found this cold land with its lakes and hills much like home. Many were Roman Catholic, and their descendants are predominantly anti-abortion. Before 1900, the U.P. was a northern industrial belt, with a few bosses, some absentee overlords, and a workforce disposed to radical ideas and union movements.

A major strike in 1913-14 and falling ore prices after World War I—events that would be long forgotten elsewhere—are recalled in the U.P. as accelerating the copper decline. The accessible copper veins were mostly depleted by then, mining iron ore became less labor intensive, and lumber and farming provided only a few thousand jobs. Other industries have grown since then: Marinette Marine, which builds Coast Guard cutters and military ships just across the state border in Wisconsin, is important to Menominee County. Enstrom Helicopter, founded in Menominee in the 1950s by a lumberman who wanted a helicopter suited for the rugged U.P., sells models that are popular overseas and with law enforcement. The region's natural beauty—90% of the U.P. is forested—has made tourism the leading economic driver today. And its remote location have made "Yoopers," as the locals call themselves, into laptop junkies; the federal government's decision in 2010 to spend $100 million in economic stimulus funds to expand broadband access in the northern reaches of the state made headlines here. In the last half-century, there was a migration out of the U.P. to Detroit for auto jobs, and to the West for mining. Its population peaked at 332,000 in 1920. In 2010, there were 311,000 Yoopers, many of whom remain devoted to their land. "The U.P. is really a place of slow, steady economic decline. We actually find it kind of charming," says local writer Don Hunt.

The 1st Congressional District of Michigan includes the Upper Peninsula and 16 northern counties in the Lower Peninsula, geographically, almost half of all Michigan. Nearly half the people in the district live in the U.P., in small towns spread across heavily forested distances. Often-snow-bound Marquette, with 21,300 people, is the largest city in the district, followed by the "Soo," the more vibrant Sault Ste. Marie, with 14,100. The other half lives south of the breathtaking Mackinac Bridge, which connects the two peninsulas. This is a vast area, in sheer size the second-largest district east of the Mississippi, after Maine's 2nd District, and it has the most shoreline of any district. On the Lower Peninsula, along Lake Michigan, are affluent resort areas around Petoskey and Charlevoix, long summer places for people from Chicago (this is Ernest Hemingway's "Up in Michigan").

Politically, the U.P. has long been Democratic, some parts more than others, but it can be contrarian. This is one part of Michigan that has not liked many national Democrats' environmental and gun control stands. The Lake Michigan shore of the Lower Peninsula is growing fast and is heavily Republican; the sunrise side is growing more slowly and is politically marginal. The 1st District voted solidly for Bush in 2000 and 2004, and 50% for Barack Obama in 2008.

Dan Benishek (R)

The new congressman from Michigan's 1st District is Republican Dan Benishek, who won the seat of retiring Democratic Rep. Bart Stupak. Benishek was born in Stambaugh, Mich., on the rural Upper Peninsula. He and his brother, Tim, were raised by their mother and grandparents after their father died in a mining accident when Dan was 5 years old. As a teenager, he made beds, cooked, cleaned, and hauled beer at his grandparents' hotel and bar, earning $10 a week—money that would later help put him through college. In 1970, Benishek took a bus to Ann Arbor to enroll as a freshman at the University of Michigan, the first time he had crossed the Mackinac Bridge that separates the U.P. from the rest of the state. He studied first to be an engineer, but took an uncle's suggestion and switched to medicine on the assumption that a medical degree would allow him to work wherever he wanted. After medical school, he did a stint as a resident practicing family medicine in Flint, and then opted to become a surgeon. In four years, he returned to the U.P. and joined a private practice in Iron Mountain that had been created to serve Ford Motor workers.

Benishek and his friends were discussing their unhappiness with Democratic policies in Washington during an ice-fishing excursion; one of them suggested that Benishek make a bid to unseat Stupak. "And I said, 'Maybe I will,'" he recalled. At the time, Stupak had put himself at the center of the national health care debate by insisting on an amendment to prevent federal funding for abortions. Stupak ultimately backed off and voted for the health care overhaul, angering anti-abortion Republicans, who began donating money to Benishek. He ultimately raised $1.4 million for his campaign. "The phone didn't stop ringing for a week," he said. After the health care debate was over, Stupak announced in April 2010 he would not seek re-election.

In the GOP primary in August, Benishek faced state Sen. Jason Allen, who had moved from his hometown of Traverse City in the 4th District one county over to run in the 1st District. With tea party support, Benishek edged out Allen for the nomination by just 15 votes out of nearly 99,000 cast.

In the general election campaign, Benishek's competition was Democratic state Rep. Gary McDowell, a Teamsters Union member who drove a United Parcel Service truck for over 30 years, was a county commissioner and then a member of the Michigan House. He sought to paint Benishek as an extremist by highlighting his comments in favor of privatizing Social Security. McDowell supported the Democrats' health care overhaul and called for withholding tax breaks for companies that take jobs offshore. He raised a respectable $838,000, but GOP groups stepped in and outspent their Democratic rivals 4-to-1 in the district.

Benishek wooed voters with tea party themes of less spending and lower taxes, and vowed he would not seek appropriations earmarks for the district. He called for repeal of the heath care bill, and got some national attention when he slammed President Barack Obama's "socialist agenda." He was also endorsed by former Alaska Gov. Sarah Palin. He won 52% to 41%, breaking the Democrats' two-decade hold on the seat.

SECOND DISTRICT

Bill Huizenga (R)

Elected 2010, 1st term; b. Jan. 31, 1969, Holland; home, Zeeland; Calvin Col., B.A. 1991. ; Christian Reformed; Married (Natalie); 5 children.

Elected Office: MI House, 2002-08.

Professional Career: Realtor, 1991-96; aide, Rep. Pete Hoekstra, R-Mich., 1997-2002; admin., Zeeland Christian Schools, 2009-10; owner, Huizenga Gravel.

DC Office: 1217 LHOB, 20515, 202-225-4401; Fax: 202-226-0779; Web site: huizenga.house.gov.

State Offices: Cadillac, 231-775-0050; Holland, 616-395-0030; Muskegon, 231-722-8386.

Committees: *Financial Services:* Domestic Monetary Policy & Technology; Financial Institutions & Consumer Credit; International Monetary Policy & Trade.

Election Results

2010 general	Bill Huizenga (R)	148,864	(65%)	($709,347)
	Fred Johnson (D)	72,118	(32%)	($125,674)
2010 primary	Bill Huizenga (R)	27,041	(25%)	
	Jay Riemersma (R)	26,378	(25%)	
	Wayne Kuipers (R)	23,226	(22%)	
	Bill Cooper (R)	20,584	(19%)	

Population		Race/Ethnicity		Work	
Pop. 2010:	698,831	White:	85.3%	Private:	83.5%
Change since 2000:	Up 5.5%	Black:	4.6%	Government:	10.3%
Urban:	56.2%	Hispanic:	6.6%	Self-employed:	5.9%
Rural:	43.8%	Asian:	1.2%	Blue collar:	29.1%
Area size:	5,508 sq. mi.	Native Am.:	0.6%	White collar:	52.9%
		Hawaiian:	0.0%	Khaki collar:	0.1%
Age		Two+ races:	1.6%	Other:	18.0%
Median age:	37.5 yrs.				
More than 65 yrs:	13.3%	*Ancestry*		Median income:	$46,063
Less than 18 yrs:	25.0%	German	17.7%	Median Home Value:	$140,800
		Dutch	15.1%		
Education		Irish	8.3%	**Military Veterans**	
H.S. grad:	88.1%			% of Pop:	10.4%
College grad:	21.2%				
Grad degree:	7.1%				

Western Michigan; Muskegon

Lining the eastern shore of Lake Michigan, where the lake winds temper the frigid Michigan winters, are some of the nation's longest and highest sand dunes. In the late 19th century, this shoreline was America's lumber country. The river ports were choked with logs and full of lumbermen from Norway and Sweden, Ireland and Scotland, Quebec and New England. During the timber boom, the shoreline just to the south was the locus of the country's largest migration

2008 Presidential Vote		
John McCain (R) 179,427	(51%)
Barack Obama (D) 167,607	(48%)
2004 Presidential Vote		
George Bush (R) 203,051	(60%)
John Kerry (D) 131,552	(39%)
Cook Partisan Voting Index: R+7		

from the Netherlands and today still has the nation's largest concentration of Dutch-Americans. Wooden shoes are now seen only at the Tulip Festival in Holland, but conscientious Dutch work habits have produced many highly skilled workers, and this is a busy manufacturing area, with products ranging from baby food at Gerber in Fremont to self-dimming car mirrors at Gentex in Zeeland. It is also the center of the American office furniture industry, with Herman Miller in Zeeland, Haworth in Holland and Steelcase in Grand Rapids. But the 2007-09 recession had an impact, for sure. Pfizer shut down a factory in Holland. And unemployment lingered at 14% in Muskegon County, one of the region's most populous, in 2010. Territory away from the shore is fruit-growing country, with some of the nation's largest cherry orchards to the north and blueberry patches to the south.

The 2nd Congressional District of Michigan occupies the Lake Michigan shoreline counties, plus a tier of inland counties, including a small part of Grand Rapids' Kent County. It stretches from the lumber country around Manistee south to Holland and the wealthy resort town of Saugatuck. For years, Dutch-American voters have been as strongly Republican as Cuban-Americans have been as an ethnically identifiable group, and the 2nd and 3rd Districts centered on Grand Rapids are the two most Republican districts in Michigan. Ottawa County voted 72% for George W. Bush in 2004, and 61% for John McCain in 2008.

Bill Huizenga (R)

The new congressman from the 2nd District of Michigan is Bill Huizenga, a Republican who succeeded his friend and former boss, Rep. Pete Hoekstra. Huizenga (*Hi-ZEN-guh*) grew up in Zeeland, Mich., and minus a few short absences, he has lived there all of his life. His grandparents were farmers who bought a gravel business by selling the leftover sand and stone that was lying around the farm. Huizenga's father did combat duty during World War II and, after the war, went to college on the GI Bill. He started his own ready-mix concrete business during the postwar building boom years. In high school, Huizenga was an inattentive student who ultimately transferred to vocational school. But his instructors told him he had academic potential and advised him to finish his studies and go on to college. Huizenga took the advice, studying political science at Calvin College. Between his freshman and sophomore years, he made his first real estate investment. With money he had saved from working in his father's gravel pit, he became the junior stakeholder with his father and two other investors in a 19-unit housing development. Also while attending Calvin, he met his future wife. As a young adult, Huizenga also indulged his love of travel, taking trips around the world. Once, during anti-government unrest just before the fall of the Berlin Wall, he was chased by riot police and dogs at a pro-democracy rally in Prague.

After college, Huizenga worked for a local real estate firm and took over as co-owner in the family business, Huizenga Gravel. Hoekstra offered him a job in his district office, and he became Hoekstra's director of public policy. After six years, he decided to run for public office himself, winning a seat in the Michigan House in 2002. He was re-elected twice, and served a term as chairman of the Commerce Committee. He was forced to retire in 2008 because of term limits.

When Hoekstra decided to run for Michigan governor in 2010, the real contest for his House seat in this Republican-leaning district was the GOP primary. In the seven-way race, former pro-football tight end Jay Riemersma, also of Zeeland, began as the front-runner. Riemersma raised $850,000 to Huizenga's $553,000. Huizenga touted his conservative credentials, saying he supported conservative proposals for a "flat tax," which would replace the income tax with a 23% sales tax on goods and services, and to create private Social Security accounts. He opposed abortion rights and is a longtime member of Michigan Right to Life. Riemersma, the former regional director for the Family Research Council, also ran as an anti-abortion and fiscal conservative. He tried to weaken Huizenga's claims by attacking him for voting for the Michigan Business Tax in 2007.

Still, Huizenga managed to eke out a victory with a better political organization, built largely on the many contacts he had made among local political and business leaders during his six years on Hoekstra's staff. He prevailed by just 663 votes out of about 106,000 cast.

In the general election, he faced nominal Democratic opposition from history professor Fred Johnson. The seat has been in Republican hands since 1967, and the district has voted for every Republican presidential candidate since Richard Nixon in 1968.

THIRD DISTRICT

Justin Amash (R)

Elected 2010, 1st term; b. April 18, 1980, Grand Rapids; home, Cascade Charter Township; U. of MI, A.B. 2002; J.D. 2005; Christian; Married (Kara); 3 children.

Elected Office: MI House, 2008-10.

Professional Career: Practicing atty., 2006-07; consultant, MI Industrial Tools, 2005-10.

DC Office: 114 CHOB, 20515, 202-225-3831; Fax: 202-225-5144; Web site: amash.house.gov.

State Offices: Grand Rapids, 616-451-8383.

Committees: *Budget. Joint Economic Committee. Oversight & Government Reform:* Federal Workforce, U.S. Postal Service & Labor Policy (VChmn); Government Organization, Efficiency & Financial Management; TARP, Financial Services & Bailouts of Public & Private Programs.

Election Results

2010 general	Justin Amash (R)	133,714	(60%)	($1,103,513)
	Pat Miles (D)	83,953	(37%)	($990,599)
2010 primary	Justin Amash (R)	38,569	(40%)	
	Steve Heacock (R)	25,157	(26%)	
	William Hardiman (R)	22,715	(24%)	
	Robert Overbeek (R)	5,133	(5%)	

Population		Race/Ethnicity		Work	
Pop. 2010:	694,695	White:	78.4%	Private:	85.9%
Change since 2000:	Up 4.8%	Black:	8.4%	Government:	8.9%
Urban:	77.1%	Hispanic:	8.6%	Self-employed:	5.1%
Rural:	22.9%	Asian:	2.0%	Blue collar:	24.5%
Area size:	1,897 sq. mi.	Native Am.:	0.4%	White collar:	58.1%
		Hawaiian:	0.0%	Khaki collar:	0.0%
Age		Two+ races:	2.0%	Other:	17.3%
Median age:	34.8 yrs.				
More than 65 yrs:	10.9%	*Ancestry*		Median income:	$49,866
Less than 18 yrs:	25.8%	German	17.1%	Median Home Value:	$147,100
		Dutch	13.6%		
Education		Irish	9.3%	**Military Veterans**	
H.S. grad:	88.1%			% of Pop:	8.5%
College grad:	27.5%				
Grad degree:	9.0%				

Central Michigan; Grand Rapids

Grand Rapids is Michigan's second-largest city and the center of its most prosperous metropolitan area. The city's roots are in trees: It grew as a center for processing and turning into furniture the hardwood forests of northern Michigan. By the early 20th century, Grand Rapids was the leading furniture manufacturer in the nation. The Depression knocked the bottom out of the residential furniture market, and many manufacturers moved to North Carolina, where labor was cheaper. So Grand Rapids had to reinvent itself. It went into office furniture, and today three

2008 Presidential Vote		
John McCain (R)	171,255	(49%)
Barack Obama (D)	169,183	(49%)
2004 Presidential Vote		
George Bush (R)	197,493	(59%)
John Kerry (D)	133,460	(40%)
Cook Partisan Voting Index:	R+6	

of the nation's largest office furniture manufacturers—Steelcase, Haworth, and Herman Miller—are located here or nearby. It also capitalized on a knack for sales. Rich DeVos and Jay Van Andel started Amway, the direct sales empire, which now has half of its sales abroad, and Frederik and Hendrik Meijer started Meijer's Thrifty Acres, combining supermarkets with discount stores in a way that even Wal-Mart has not been able to equal. Grand Rapids is also the center of a machine tool empire; the home of Wolverine World Wide, maker of Hush Puppies shoes; and the headquarters of Bissell and its carpet sweepers. Fifty years ago, Grand Rapids and its up-and-coming businesses were outshined by Detroit and the auto industry. Today, while Detroit's Big Three struggle to stay afloat, Grand Rapids chugs along.

One ingredient in Grand Rapids' success is its unique ethnic mix. It was founded by New England Yankees, but much of its character was set by the Dutch immigrants who began arriving in western Michigan in the 1870s, and are still coming today; 14% of people here claim Dutch ancestry (probably no other American city has such a high proportion of "V" pages in the phone book). The Dutch brought with them a piety witnessed in their Reform and Christian Reform churches, and a culture of hard work and precision craftsmanship. Their cultural conservatism and belief in market economics run deep. Dutch tradition and entrepreneurial success have been the ingredients of a civic activism that has given Grand Rapids a host of creative civic institutions. In 2007, the city opened the first certified "green" museum in the world, the new Grand Rapids Art Museum, with triple the space of the old, as well as a new hotel and medical buildings. Years ago, Grand Rapids commissioned an Alexander Calder sculpture for the plaza outside its city hall, and now it has others by Calder, Andy Goldsworthy, and Maya Lin. Other draws for outsiders are the Gerald R. Ford Presidential Library and Museum and the outdoor Meijer Gardens.

Politically, Grand Rapids has been the center of Michigan Republicanism for much of the last century. It has also produced national Republican leaders. Arthur Vandenberg, originally a newspaper editor, was a U.S. senator from 1928 to 1951; he provided key support for the internationalist foreign policies of Franklin D. Roosevelt and Harry Truman. Another was Gerald Ford, who rose to House Republican leader in 1965, vice president in 1973, and then president after Richard Nixon resigned in 1974. The 3rd Congressional District of Michigan includes Grand Rapids and almost all of Kent County, plus Ionia and Barry counties to the east and south. Although it is one of the two most Republican districts in Michigan, it voted only narrowly for John McCain in 2008. He won the 3rd with 49.4% of the vote to Barack Obama's 48.8%.

Justin Amash (R)

The new congressman from the 3rd District is Justin Amash, a Republican who succeeded retiring GOP Rep Vernon Ehlers in the 2010 election. Amash was born in Grand Rapids in 1980, the son of a wealthy Palestinian tool importer who immigrated to the United States with the sponsorship of a Christian church. He began high school at the time of the Republican tidal wave of 1994, and graduated as class valedictorian. He then went on to graduate magna cum laude with a degree in economics from the University of Michigan and earned a degree from its law school in 2005. He counts himself as an admirer of both the 19th-century author Frederic Bastiat, who argued against taxing people to pay for schools or roads, and the 20th-century writer Friedrich Hayek, a favorite of the tea party movement who strongly opposed government intervention in the economy. Amash kept Hayek's portrait on the wall of his congressional campaign offices.

After graduating from college, he became a consultant to his family's tool-import business. He also served as a corporate lawyer for a year before running for a House seat in the Michigan Legislature in 2008. As a legislator, Amash fought to eliminate state taxes on businesses. A proponent of states' rights, he proposed an amendment to the state constitution that would prevent the implementation of President Barack Obama's health care law. *The Grand Rapids Press* reported in July 2010 that Amash was the only "no" vote on 59 bills in his first term, including measures toughening penalties for human trafficking and allowing military members to get out of cell-phone contracts if deployed overseas. He said he refuses to vote in favor of bills that he has not had the chance to read.

Amash entered the 3rd District race, he said, because he was fed up with eight-term incumbent Ehlers's moderate voting record. But then, Ehlers announced his retirement. That opened the door for other Republican candidates, including former Kent County Commissioner Steve Heacock, whom Ehlers personally asked to run. In the primary race, Amash out-raised both Heacock and state Sen. Bill Hardiman, and he also won the backing of the anti-tax group Club for Growth. He won the August primary, getting 40% of the vote to Heacock's 26% and Hardiman's 24%.

His victory set up a general election race against Democratic lawyer Pat Miles, a former Harvard Law School classmate of Obama's. Miles accused Amash of exporting jobs to China through his ownership of Dynamic Source International, a Chinese company that supplies industrial tools to his father's tool-import business. "Instead of making American-made products made by American workers, Justin Amash has chosen Chinese workers to make products, which he then sells in America," Miles campaign manager Lonny Paris told *The Press*. To dispel concerns he might be too liberal for the district, Miles said in October that he would not back liberal Democrat Nancy Pelosi to remain House speaker if his party retained control of the House in 2010.

Amash held a lead in fundraising and a small lead in the polls through October. In his ads, he accused Miles of supporting taxpayer-funded abortions because he backed the Democrats' health care overhaul. Amash got a boost when *Time* magazine named him to its recent "40 under 40" list of civic leaders. He won 60% of the vote to 37% for Miles. Amash is one of two Arab-Americans in the 2010 class. The other is Rep. Richard Hanna, R-N.Y.

FOURTH DISTRICT

Dave Camp (R)

Elected 1990, 11th term; b. July 9, 1953, Midland; home, Midland; Albion Col., B.A. 1975, U. of San Diego, J.D. 1978; Catholic; married (Nancy); 3 children.

Elected Office: MI House of Reps., 1988–90.

Professional Career: Practicing atty., 1978–90; MI special asst. atty. gen., 1980–84; A.A., U.S. Rep. Bill Schuette, 1984–87.

DC Office: 341 CHOB, 20515, 202-225-3561; Fax: 202-225-9679; Web site: camp.house.gov.

State Offices: Midland, 989-631-2552; Traverse City, 231-929-4711.

Committees: *Joint Committee on Taxation* (Chmn). *Ways & Means* (Chmn).

Group Ratings

	ACLU	ACU	ADA	CFG	AFS	FRC	LCV	ITIC	NTU	COC
2010	13	92	0	82	0	100	0	33	88	100
2009	–	88	15	78	13	–	21	–	76	93

National Journal Ratings

	2010 LIB	—	2010 CONS	2009 LIB	—	2009 CONS
Economic	24%	—	76%	32%	—	68%
Social	16%	—	82%	24%	—	73%
Foreign	21%	—	79%	26%	—	68%
Composite	21%	—	79%	29%	—	71%

Key Votes of the 111th Congress

1. Overturn Ledbetter	N	5. Bar federal abortion funds	Y	9. Stop detainee transfers	Y
2. Pass $820 billion stimulus	N	6. Pass health care bill	N	10. Legalize immigrants' kids	N
3. Let guns in national parks	Y	7. Regulate financial firms	N	11. Repeal don't ask, tell	N
4. Pass cap-and-trade	N	8. Pass tax cuts for some	N	12. Limit campaign funds	N

Election Results

2010 general	Dave Camp (R)	148,531	(66%)	($3,051,808)
	Jerry Campbell (D)	68,458	(31%)	($15,881)
2010 primary	Dave Camp (R)	unopposed		

Prior Winning Percentages: 2008 (62%), 2006 (61%), 2004 (64%), 2002 (68%), 2000 (68%), 1998 (91%), 1996 (65%), 1994 (73%), 1992 (63%), 1990 (65%)

Population		Race/Ethnicity		Work	
Pop. 2010:	686,378	White:	91.0%	Private:	79.5%
Change since 2000:	Up 3.6%	Black:	2.6%	Government:	13.2%
Urban:	41.4%	Hispanic:	3.1%	Self-employed:	7.1%
Rural:	58.6%	Asian:	0.9%	Blue collar:	23.9%
Area size:	8,053 sq. mi.	Native Am.:	0.9%	White collar:	54.8%
		Hawaiian:	0.0%	Khaki collar:	0.1%
Age		Two+ races:	1.4%	Other:	21.2%
Median age:	39.7 yrs.				
More than 65 yrs:	15.1%	*Ancestry*		Median income:	$42,394
Less than 18 yrs:	21.9%	German	23.2%	Median Home Value:	$128,300
		Irish	10.3%		
Education		English	10.0%	**Military Veterans**	
H.S. grad:	88.6%			% of Pop:	10.8%
College grad:	20.9%				
Grad degree:	7.8%				

Central Michigan; Midland

Flat and treeless for miles, the central reaches of Michigan's Lower Peninsula are farm country, exposed to bitter winds and snowdrifts in winter and shining sun for precious weeks in summer. Like the steppes of Eastern Europe, these are farmlands that produce hearty crops: potatoes, navy beans, sugar beets. The little cities here are often small factory towns, with neat tree-lined streets that end at bare fields. Each city has some distinction. Midland in 1891 was a declin-

2008 Presidential Vote		
Barack Obama (D)	170,251	(50%)
John McCain (R)	163,855	(48%)

2004 Presidential Vote		
George Bush (R)	181,314	(55%)
John Kerry (D)	145,774	(44%)

Cook Partisan Voting Index: R+3

ing lumber town when Herbert Dow perfected an electrolytic process to extract chemicals from northern Michigan's extensive brine wells. That was the start of Dow Chemical, still headquartered in this now upscale town and today a large producer of pesticides and agricultural biotech products. Owosso in 1902 was the birthplace of Thomas E. Dewey, later New York governor and the Republican nominee for president in 1944 and 1948. It was also the home of novelist James Oliver Curwood and his Curwood Castle writing studio. As recently as the 1970s, Indian tribes in the area clashed with sportsmen over land and water use. A historic agreement in 2007 restored many Indian rights and allowed tribes to oversee their own hunters and anglers. Mount Pleasant, to the north, is the home of Central Michigan University, which is opening a new medical school in 2012.

The 4th Congressional District of Michigan, geographically the state's second-largest, includes much of this territory north of Lansing and Grand Rapids and west of Flint and Saginaw. It stretches north up the freeways, hemmed in by U.S. 131 to the west and Interstate 75 to the east. Thousands of people drive up the routes in the fall to hunt and in the winter to ski. The rolling country around Houghton Lake was once lumber country and is now a retirement and resort area, with condominiums and knotty-pine cottages clustered around icy green lakes. The 4th has more farms than any other district in Michigan. The district reaches Traverse City, which has the world's largest concentration of red tart cherry orchards as well as numerous vacation homes, resorts and more than two-dozen wineries. The recession did not hit here with as much force as in the rest of Michigan, but still had an effect. In February 2009, home prices hit their lowest levels in 15 years. Politically, the district remains mostly Republican territory, especially in the Midland and Traverse City areas, though some counties vote Democratic on occasion. George W. Bush won 54% here in 2000 and 55% in 2004. In 2008, Barack Obama won 50%-48%.

Dave Camp (R)

The congressman from the 4th District is Dave Camp, a Republican who through diligent work and prolific fundraising is now chairman of the powerful Ways and Means Committee. His low-key, consensus-building style stands in sharp contrast to that of several recent Ways and Means chairmen, as well as more openly partisan senior Republicans. "I don't think you need to bang the gavel, pound your fists or shout to be effective," he told *The Wall Street Journal* in November 2010. Camp grew up in Midland and returned there after school to practice law. In 1984, he managed the successful congressional campaign of his boyhood friend, Bill Schuette. In 1990, Schuette unsuccessfully ran against Democratic Sen. Carl Levin, Camp, with two years in the state House under his belt, ran for the vacated House seat. His key victory was in the Republican primary, where he beat Al Cropsey, a former legislator who was allied with evangelical conservatives, 33%-30%.

Camp is a member of the moderate Republican Main Street Partnership but has a generally conservative voting record, especially on fiscal issues. He also has a bipartisan streak. In recent years, he joined with Democrats in the House to expand tax credits for education costs and to boost federal Hope scholarships for low-income students. He has been a champion of free trade on the committee, while also trying to expand trade-adjustment assistance for workers. Camp was a guiding hand behind some of the major initiatives from the era of Republican control of the House, 1995 to 2006. Camp played a key role in passing the welfare overhaul in 1996, and he defended the party's signature 2003 Medicare prescription drug bill against Democratic attacks. He championed the cause of making President George W. Bush's 2001 tax cuts permanent, as well as Bush's failed plan to create private savings accounts in the Social Security program.

When Louisiana Republican Rep. Jim McCrery announced that he would not seek re-election in 2008, Rep. Wally Herger of California had more seniority than Camp and was positioned to succeed McCrery in the ranking minority slot, the most powerful post for the minority party on a committee. Camp did the requisite networking on the K Street lobbying corridor, and, in the most important test—who could raise more money for Republicans in tough election battles—Camp was far and away Herger's superior, bringing in over $2 million for the party, while Herger raised about half that amount. Camp also had better ties to Republican leaders. In 1998, he ran Illinois Republican Dennis Hastert's successful campaign for House speaker. He also served on the leadership-driven Steering Committee, which makes committee assignments.

Camp loyally toed the Republican line during President Barack Obama's first two years in office. He advocated for tax cuts and criticized the idea of spending billions of dollars in the name of lowering health care costs. "If you are shopping for a car, even I have to admit that a Ferrari looks pretty good next to a Ford—until you see the price tag," he said in June 2009. He kept a close eye on corporations that backed Obama's agenda, rebuking lobbyists for Wal-Mart after the retail giant contributed more money to Democrats than Republicans. But in a nod to his economically struggling state, he was among just six Republicans in March 2010 to support a House-passed jobs bill that included tax incentives for businesses hiring unemployed workers. He has an inclusive style on Ways and Means, bringing Republicans together in small groups to hear from experts about complex economic matters—something that helped earn the gratitude of junior members.

Assuming the helm of Ways and Means in 2011, Camp pressed the Obama administration for swift action on pending free-trade deals with Panama, Colombia and South Korea. He also tackled the formidable challenge of overhauling the tax code and lessening the burden for corporations in favor of having more contributors pay less, an approach he called "broadening the base." He stressed that such a task must be bipartisan and pledged to work with fellow Michigander Sander Levin, the Ways and Means pro-labor ranking Democrat. Camp and Levin have known each other for decades, but are not close.

An important pet issue for Camp is adoption law. In 2000, he helped win enactment of the International Adoption Act, which designates the State Department to help adoptive parents in dealing with officials in other nations. Two years later, Congress passed his bill to create financial incentives for domestic adoptions. On an issue of interest to his home state, Camp introduced a bill in 2010 to speed research into stopping invasive Asian carp that threaten the Great Lakes fishing industry.

Camp has had minimal opposition in the 4th District. He keeps in close touch with the district by signing every constituent letter sent from his office, often with a personal note—roughly 30,000 each year.

FIFTH DISTRICT

Dale Kildee (D)

Elected 1976, 18th term; b. Sept. 16, 1929, Flint; home, Flint; Sacred Heart Seminary, B.A. 1952, U. of MI, M.A. 1961, Rotary Fellow, U. of Peshawar, Pakistan; Catholic; married (Gayle); 3 children.

Elected Office: MI House of Reps., 1964–74; MI Senate, 1974–75.

Professional Career: H.S. teacher, 1954–64.

DC Office: 2107 RHOB, 20515, 202-225-3611; Fax: 202-225-6393; Web site: kildee.house.gov.

State Offices: Bay City, 989-891-0990; Flint, 810-239-1437; Saginaw, 989-755-8904.

Committees: *Education & the Workforce:* Early Childhood, Elementary & Secondary Education (RMM); Health, Employment, Labor & Pensions. *Natural Resources:* Indian & Alaska Native Affairs; National Parks, Forests & Public Lands.

Group Ratings

	ACLU	ACU	ADA	CFG	AFS	FRC	LCV	ITIC	NTU	COC
2010	81	0	95	0	100	18	100	100	5	25
2009	–	4	90	0	100	–	100	–	3	33

National Journal Ratings

	2010 LIB	—	2010 CONS	2009 LIB	—	2009 CONS
Economic	80%	—	18%	75%	—	21%
Social	61%	—	35%	57%	—	42%
Foreign	78%	—	17%	70%	—	24%
Composite	75%	—	25%	69%	—	31%

Key Votes of the 111th Congress

1. Overturn Ledbetter	Y	5. Bar federal abortion funds	Y	9. Stop detainee transfers	N
2. Pass $820 billion stimulus	Y	6. Pass health care bill	Y	10. Legalize immigrants' kids	Y
3. Let guns in national parks	N	7. Regulate financial firms	Y	11. Repeal don't ask, tell	Y
4. Pass cap-and-trade	Y	8. Pass tax cuts for some	Y	12. Limit campaign funds	Y

Election Results

2010 general	Dale Kildee (D)	107,286	(53%)	($622,561)
	John Kupiec (R)	89,680	(44%)	($356,589)
2010 primary	Dale Kildee (D)	34,902	(78%)	
	Scott Withers (D)	9,596	(22%)	

Prior Winning Percentages: 2008 (70%), 2006 (73%), 2004 (67%), 2002 (92%), 2000 (61%), 1998 (56%), 1996 (59%), 1994 (51%), 1992 (54%), 1990 (68%), 1988 (76%), 1986 (80%), 1984 (93%), 1982 (75%), 1980 (93%), 1978 (77%), 1976 (70%)

Population		Race/Ethnicity		Work	
Pop. 2010:	635,129	White:	73.7%	Private:	83.0%
Change since 2000:	Down 4.1%	Black:	18.6%	Government:	11.5%
Urban:	79.4%	Hispanic:	4.3%	Self-employed:	5.3%
Rural:	20.6%	Asian:	0.7%	Blue collar:	24.0%
Area size:	1,780 sq. mi.	Native Am.:	0.4%	White collar:	55.0%
		Hawaiian:	0.0%	Khaki collar:	0.1%
Age		Two+ races:	2.1%	Other:	20.9%
Median age:	38.0 yrs.				
More than 65 yrs:	13.6%	*Ancestry*		Median income:	$41,365
Less than 18 yrs:	25.1%	German	16.9%	Median Home Value:	$111,300
		Irish	8.8%		
Education		English	7.7%	**Military Veterans**	
H.S. grad:	86.6%			% of Pop:	10.2%
College grad:	17.5%				
Grad degree:	5.9%				

East Michigan; Flint

The flat plains south of Saginaw Bay, the inlet of Lake Huron that separates Michigan's Thumb (people really call it that) from the mitten of the Lower Peninsula, was once one of the nation's top industrial areas. Some 130 years ago, it was the nation's premier lumber country, with huge stands of virgin trees feeding 36 sawmills in Bay City and with logs piled high along both banks of the Saginaw River. When the trees were gone, farmers took over, and the land was sown with

2008 Presidential Vote		
Barack Obama (D) 207,522	(64%)
John McCain (R) 112,965	(35%)
2004 Presidential Vote		
John Kerry (D) 187,671	(59%)
George Bush (R) 129,457	(41%)
Cook Partisan Voting Index: D+11		

beans and sugar beets. A century ago, heavy industry followed. Flint, a small town on a minor branch of the Saginaw River, was the home base of W.C. Durant, the investor who merged several young auto firms to form General Motors. GM put its Chevrolet and Buick factories in Flint and its power-steering facility in Saginaw, chosen because it was already a center of precision machinery manufacturing. From 1910 through the 1960s, Flint grew lustily as it built Chevys and Buicks, attracting workers from the mountains of Kentucky and Tennessee and the Black Belt of Alabama. Country music, blues and soul, and Southern accents became common in an area originally settled by New England Yankees. There was turmoil, too. Flint was the scene in January 1937 of the great sit-down strike that forced GM to recognize the United Auto Workers as the bargaining agent for all its workers. The UAW-GM contracts produced the world's highest wages for industrial workers along with fringe benefits like a generous health care plan.

Economic disaster struck with the energy crisis of the 1970s. Imports, especially from Japan, that were higher quality and lower priced than American cars, took an increasing share of the market. In 1979, GM employed more than 70,000 workers in its Flint plants, a huge share of the labor force in a metropolitan area of 430,000 people. Eventually, thousands left Flint as GM closed 13 of its 15 factories. By the late 2000s, the GM payroll had fallen below 12,000, and total local employment had dropped about 60%. In June 2009, the company filed for bankruptcy.

Today, a third of Flint households are in poverty, and many skilled workers have fled what *Forbes* magazine calls one of "America's fastest-dying cities." Only two other U.S. cities—Cleveland and Detroit—lost more people in 2009. Michael Moore, the liberal filmmaker, has used his hometown of Flint as the locale for much of his work about deteriorating life in America. Amid the crushing recent recession, Flint's economy saw some faint signs of hope. As General Motors emerged from its government takeover in 2010, it announced plans to keep open a Flint engine plant and to add a third shift at its truck assembly facility. Some restaurants and other businesses have taken advantage of city loan programs to open downtown, while industrial space has been turned into lofts. Genesee County's unemployment rate, which soared above 16% in March 2010, dropped several points by year's end. Gritty Saginaw also suffered, with huge cutbacks by Delphi, its largest employer. But again, there are some modest positive developments. In the Saginaw area, small manufacturing operations requiring highly skilled workers have grown up in old factory buildings once considered worthless. Outgoing Gov. Jennifer Granholm in December 2010 announced an agreement for large-scale production of wind turbines for electric utilities in nearby Buena Vista Township.

The 5th Congressional District of Michigan includes Flint and surrounding Genesee County, Saginaw and eastern Saginaw County, Bay City and eastern Bay County, and rural Tuscola County. Flint, evenly divided between the parties when the sit-down strikes divided the community in the 1930s, is now heavily Democratic, Saginaw and Bay City somewhat less so. Tuscola continues to vote Republican.

Dale Kildee (D)

The congressman from the 5th District is Dale Kildee, a Democrat first elected in 1976. He is a soft-spoken liberal who is admired for his conscientiousness; he timed his knee-replacement surgery around Congress' spring break in 2009 so he wouldn't have to miss votes. When he cast his 20,000th vote in February 2010, Republican Leader John Boehner said he knew of "no kinder, more decent" House member.

Kildee grew up in Flint, the son of an autoworker. He studied for the priesthood, and then taught at a Catholic high school in Detroit and at Flint Central High School. Door-to-door campaigning got him elected to a state legislative seat in 1964, at age 35, and enabled him to beat a 26-year veteran of the state Senate in 1974. Two years later, he ran successfully for the U.S. House seat. Kildee has an intensity of conviction derived from the liberal tradition lively in the American Catholic Church, a tradition with little regard for market economics, a strong sense of obligation to the needy, and a cultural conservatism. He is almost always pro-union and requires his employees to drive to work in cars built by the UAW. He opposes abortion rights and is a stickler on ethics. On the Education and Labor Committee, he is a strong ally of teachers unions, a backer of increased federal aid for education and an opponent of school choice. He backed the original House health care overhaul bill in 2009, but joined fellow Michigan Democrat Bart Stupak in holding out for a tougher anti-abortion provision in the final version before agreeing to support it. As chairman of the Subcommittee on Early Childhood, Elementary and Secondary Education at Education and Labor, he conducted extensive oversight of the Bush administration's No Child Left Behind education policy, while demanding adequate funding for its mandates on schools.

Kildee was a leader in efforts to bail out the state's ailing automakers and defended the Obama administration against criticism when it intervened on behalf of General Motors and Chrysler. When GM made its initial public offering of stock in November 2010, more than halving the government's share in the company, Kildee said it was further evidence of "a smart investment of taxpayer money." He was the first House member to argue that imported minivans should be subject not to the 2.5% tariff for cars but to the 25% tariff for trucks. The truck tariff became a sticking point in U.S. negotiations with several countries, which led to Kildee's fierce opposition to a bilateral trade deal with Thailand. On the Resources Committee, he is a strong advocate for American Indians, influenced by his grandparents' friendships with Indians living on a reservation near their home in northern Michigan. His efforts to clean up the Great Lakes have produced commendations by environmentalists.

In 2002, redistricting put Kildee in the same heavily Democratic district as Bay City Democrat Jim Barcia, a conservative Democrat who also opposed abortion rights. Barcia opted to run for the state Senate rather than battle Kildee for the seat. In 2010, Kildee faced Republican John Kupiec, who picked up the endorsement of the Michigan Right to Life after its members were unsatisfied with Kildee's support of health care reform. Even so, Kildee won an 18th term with 53% of the vote.

SIXTH DISTRICT

Fred Upton (R)

Elected 1986, 13th term; b. April 23, 1953, St. Joseph; home, St. Joseph; U. of MI, B.A. 1975; Protestant; married (Amey); 2 children.

Professional Career: Project coord., U.S. Rep. David Stockman, 1975–80; Legis. affairs, O.M.B., 1981–83, Dir., 1984–85.

DC Office: 2183 RHOB, 20515, 202-225-3761; Fax: 202-225-4986; Web site: upton.house.gov.

State Offices: Kalamazoo, 269-385-0039; St. Joseph, 269-982-1986.

Committees: *Energy & Commerce* (Chmn): Commerce, Manufacturing & Trade; Communications & Technology; Energy & Power; Environment & the Economy; Health; Oversight & Investigations.

Group Ratings

	ACLU	ACU	ADA	CFG	AFS	FRC	LCV	ITIC	NTU	COC
2010	19	92	10	85	13	87	0	33	86	88
2009	–	72	30	64	44	–	36	–	61	93

National Journal Ratings

	2010 LIB — 2010 CONS		2009 LIB — 2009 CONS	
Economic	27%	— 72%	39%	— 61%
Social	25%	— 71%	39%	— 60%
Foreign	12%	— 79%	38%	— 62%
Composite	24%	— 76%	39%	— 61%

Key Votes of the 111th Congress

1. Overturn Ledbetter	N	5. Bar federal abortion funds	Y	9. Stop detainee transfers	Y
2. Pass $820 billion stimulus	N	6. Pass health care bill	N	10. Legalize immigrants' kids	N
3. Let guns in national parks	Y	7. Regulate financial firms	N	11. Repeal don't ask, tell	N
4. Pass cap-and-trade	N	8. Pass tax cuts for some	N	12. Limit campaign funds	N

Election Results

2010 general	Fred Upton (R)	123,142	(62%)	($2,014,321)
	Don Cooney (D)	66,729	(34%)	($62,447)
2010 primary	Fred Upton (R)	42,182	(57%)	
	Jack Hoogendyk (R)	31,660	(43%)	

Prior Winning Percentages: 2008 (59%), 2006 (61%), 2004 (65%), 2002 (69%), 2000 (68%), 1998 (70%), 1996 (68%), 1994 (73%), 1992 (62%), 1990 (58%), 1988 (71%), 1986 (62%)

Population		Race/Ethnicity		Work	
Pop. 2010:	671,883	White:	81.9%	Private:	83.9%
Change since 2000:	Up 1.4%	Black:	8.7%	Government:	10.1%
Urban:	58.3%	Hispanic:	5.2%	Self-employed:	5.9%
Rural:	41.7%	Asian:	1.3%	Blue collar:	25.7%
Area size:	3,420 sq. mi.	Native Am.:	0.5%	White collar:	55.5%
		Hawaiian:	0.0%	Khaki collar:	0.0%
Age		Two+ races:	2.3%	Other:	18.7%
Median age:	37.5 yrs.				
More than 65 yrs:	13.4%	*Ancestry*		Median income:	$43,799
Less than 18 yrs:	23.9%	German	21.3%	Median Home Value:	$138,700
		Irish	10.1%		
Education		English	9.3%	**Military Veterans**	
H.S. grad:	88.2%			% of Pop:	10.0%
College grad:	23.9%				
Grad degree:	9.0%				

Southwest Michigan; Kalamazoo

The southwest corner of Michigan was settled by New England Yankees and Upstate New Yorkers in the 1830s and 1840s. They built small towns with schools and churches and colleges, supported temperance and opposed capital punishment. And in 1854, they started the Republican Party. There are towns in southwest Michigan that still recall proudly their past as termini of the Underground Railroad, and there are black families whose ancestors made their way

2008 Presidential Vote		
Barack Obama (D)	177,497	(54%)
John McCain (R)	145,045	(44%)
2004 Presidential Vote		
George Bush (R)	164,595	(53%)
John Kerry (D)	143,906	(46%)
Cook Partisan Voting Index: EVEN		

north out of slavery to freedom. Later, big industries transformed some of the small towns into significant cities. Kalamazoo, started by Dutch-Americans who introduced celery to this country, became the home of Upjohn pharmaceuticals, which is now part of Pfizer. Predominantly black and struggling Benton Harbor and predominantly white and prosperous St. Joseph, twin towns on Lake Michigan, were originally known for cherry and peach orchards, but now the dominant local fruit is the blueberry, and Benton Harbor is best known as the headquarters for Whirlpool.

But many other local companies and other famous industrial names have moved out, along with their thousands of jobs. Like many other jurisdictions, the region is increasingly turning to casinos for an economic shot in the arm. Kalamazoo has had some success keeping its young people in school with the Kalamazoo Promise program, funded by anonymous philanthropists, that pays college tuition for all public high school students who graduate; it has stabilized enrollment and racial balance and has resulted in higher test scores. The recession hit this area hard, with damages compounded by an oil spill that polluted the Kalamazoo River. Michigan's southwest corner is also heavily influenced by Chicago; people here watch Chicago television and root for the Cubs or White Sox baseball teams rather than the Detroit Tigers.

The 6th Congressional District of Michigan occupies the southwest corner of the state, with Kalamazoo and Benton Harbor-St. Joseph its two major urban areas. It takes in three smaller counties and parts of two others. It was for many years arch-Republican territory, represented by a succession of conservative congressmen who deplored federal spending and welfare-state measures: New Deal opponent Clare Hoffman (1935-63), Nixon defender Edward Hutchinson (1963-77), and Reagan-era Office of Management and Budget Director David Stockman (1977-81). In the 1990s, Kalamazoo trended toward the Democrats, and the 6th District cast small pluralities for Bill Clinton. George W. Bush carried the district twice but lost Kalamazoo County in 2000 and 2004, thanks in part to the influence of the Western Michigan University community. In 2008, Barack Obama carried the district 54%-44%.

Fred Upton (R)

The congressman from the 6th District is Fred Upton, a Republican first elected in 1986 and now chairman of the House Energy and Commerce Committee.

The grandson of one of the founders of Whirlpool, Upton grew up in St. Joseph, attended the University of Michigan and worked for David Stockman, first on Stockman's congressional staff, then at the White House in OMB from 1981 to 1985. Upton returned home and ran in the 1986 Republican primary against Rep. Mark Siljander, a conservative and evangelical Christian, and won 55%-45%, going on to win the seat handily in the general election.

Early in his House career, Upton was known for his amendments to force across-the-board cuts in appropriations. But he developed a moderate voting record over time, and he freely exercised his independence when his party controlled the House from 1995 to 2006. He sought, with limited success, to use his leverage to reduce the size of the tax cuts of the Bush era. He backed increases in the minimum wage, increased funding for Amtrak, and Democratic measures to expand medical insurance for poor children. He also voted with Democrats to preserve the Endangered Species Act and to fund embryonic stem cell research. In 2007, he broke with his party to oppose the Bush administration's troop surge in Iraq, but later backed Bush's veto of Democratic proposals to restrict spending on the war.

On Energy and Commerce, Upton chaired the Telecommunications Subcommittee for six years. He supported a bill to allow regional telephone companies to provide broadband service more easily, and he pushed for higher fines against broadcasters for indecent programming. He also criticized the recording industry for inadequate parental advisory labels on music that contains sex, violence or strong language, but took the view that the First Amendment bars Congress from regulating the content. Bush signed his bill to create a "safe playground for kids" on the Internet, free of pornography and other inappropriate material.

He has strongly opposed so-called net neutrality, which requires that telephone and cable operators controlling the nation's broadband networks provide equal access to rivals and small, independent websites. On other initiatives by the Democratic majority in 2009-10, Upton sharply opposed the cap-and-trade bill to reduce carbon emissions, saying it would cripple the Midwest and send jobs overseas. But not surprisingly, he favored the "Cash for Clunkers" program providing government reimbursements for trading in old cars for more fuel-efficient models, which was a boost for the ailing domestic auto industry.

As opposition to the Obama administration grew and the tea party movement advanced, Upton's moderate record, and the fact that he was next in line to be the ranking Republican on Energy and Commerce, made him a target for conservatives. In spring 2010, former state Rep. Jack Hoogendyk ran against him in the GOP primary, criticizing Upton for voting for the $787 billion bailout of the financial industry, increases in the State Children's Health Insurance Program and the Republicans' Medicare prescription drug bill in 2003. "I see government growing well beyond its intended borders in Washington, and I see that our congressman has participated in this unabated growth of government," said Hoogendyk, who was vastly outspent by the incumbent. Upton won 57%-43%, not a robust outcome for a longtime incumbent. He went on to win 62%-34% in November's general election.

With Republicans poised to capture control of the House in the election, GOP Rep. Joe Barton of Texas asked the Republican Steering Committee to waive term limits so that he could become the chairman of Energy and Commerce. But Barton had opposed John Boehner in the race for Republican minority leader in 2006, and his public apology to BP during the June 2010 hearings on the massive oil spill in the Gulf of Mexico made him a political liability in the minds of some of the GOP rank and file. Two less-senior members of the committee, Cliff Stearns of Florida and John Shimkus of Illinois, were also running in the hope that Upton would be rejected as too moderate. Upton launched an aggressive bid for the chairmanship, contributing thousands of dollars to Republican challengers and setting out a proposed agenda for the committee that included such conservative hobby horses as fighting regulations on power plants and on ozone limits. He said his goal would be "cutting spending, removing regulatory burden, restoring freedom, [and] keeping government accountable through rigorous oversight." He also promised to work with Republicans to seek repeal of the Democrats' 2010 health care overhaul.

The contest for the chairmanship heated up when conservative talk radio host Rush Limbaugh came out against Upton and pundit Glenn Beck called him "all socialist." The League of Conservation Voters did him no favors when they pointed out their lifetime vote rating for Upton of 39% versus Barton's 2%. Nevertheless, the GOP Steering Committee, heavily influenced by Boehner, chose Upton in December 2010 as chairman. Upton named Barton as chairman emeritus, the same title Democrat Henry Waxman of California created for John Dingell of Michigan after he ousted him as chairman in 2008. Shimkus and Stearns got subcommittee chairmanships.

SEVENTH DISTRICT

Tim Walberg (R)

Elected 2010, 2nd term; b. April 12, 1951, Chicago, IL; home, Tipton; Fort Wayne Bible Col., B.S. 1975; Wheaton Col., M.A. 1978; Christian; Married (Sue); 3 children.

Elected Office: MI House, 1982-98; U.S. House, 2007-09.

Professional Career: Minister, 1973-82; pres., Warren Reuther Center, 1999-2000; division mgr., Moody Bible Inst., 2000-05.

DC Office: 418 CHOB, 20515, 202-225-6276; Fax: 202-225-6281; Web site: walberg.house.gov.

State Offices: Jackson, 517-780-9075.

Committees: *Education & the Workforce:* Health, Employment, Labor & Pensions; Workforce Protections (Chmn). *Homeland Security:* Cybersecurity, Infrastructure Protection & Security Technologies (VChmn); Transportation Security. *Oversight & Government Reform:* Federal Workforce, U.S. Postal Service & Labor Policy; Technology, Information Policy, Intergovernmental Relations & Procurement Reform.

Election Results

2010 general	Tim Walberg (R)	113,185	(50%)	($1,678,049)
	Mark Schauer (D)	102,402	(45%)	($3,271,862)
2010 primary	Tim Walberg (R)	41,784	(57%)	
	Brian Rooney (R)	23,505	(32%)	
	Marvin Carlson (R)	7,413	(10%)	

Prior Winning Percentages: 2006 (50%)

Population		Race/Ethnicity		Work	
Pop. 2010:	676,899	White:	86.3%	Private:	79.8%
Change since 2000:	Up 2.2%	Black:	5.8%	Government:	14.0%
Urban:	54.0%	Hispanic:	4.2%	Self-employed:	5.9%
Rural:	46.0%	Asian:	1.2%	Blue collar:	26.4%
Area size:	4,366 sq. mi.	Native Am.:	0.4%	White collar:	55.7%
		Hawaiian:	0.0%	Khaki collar:	0.1%
Age		Two+ races:	2.0%	Other:	17.8%
Median age:	39.5 yrs.				
More than 65 yrs:	13.5%	*Ancestry*		Median income:	$48,846
Less than 18 yrs:	23.7%	German	21.2%	Median Home Value:	$142,500
		English	11.9%		
Education		Irish	10.7%	**Military Veterans**	
H.S. grad:	89.2%			% of Pop:	10.6%
College grad:	22.3%				
Grad degree:	8.2%				

Southern Michigan; Battle Creek

The small cities and towns spotting the farmland counties of south central Michigan have been incubators of innovation since they were settled by Yankees from New England 150 years ago. The state's public school system was established by two politicians from Marshall. A few miles away, in Battle Creek, sanitarium operator W.K. Kellogg invented cornflakes as a health food; he and his onetime patient, C.W. Post, both established factories in the late 19th century and created the American breakfast cereal industry. To the south is Hillsdale, where conservative Hillsdale College has been proudly admitting African-Americans and women since the 1850s and refusing all federal aid. Although the area today is politically marginal, it gave birth to the Republican Party. In 1854, the party was founded in the manufacturing and prison town of Jackson as a

2008 Presidential Vote

Barack Obama (D)	171,566	(52%)
John McCain (R)	154,222	(47%)

2004 Presidential Vote

George Bush (R)	176,624	(54%)
John Kerry (D)	145,979	(45%)

Cook Partisan Voting Index: R+2

kind of reformist institution, growing out of the same activist impulse that produced support for women's rights and Prohibition and opposition to the death penalty. Southern Michigan mostly rejected New Deal tinkering and was hostile to the United Auto Workers union, but the people here were receptive to moral claims made by later 20th-century reformers challenging racial segregation, the Vietnam War, and the Watergate cover-up.

Recently, this region has suffered from debilitating economic woes, largely due to the decline of the automobile industry and heavy manufacturing. Unemployment and poverty rates here have nearly doubled since 2000, with unemployment reaching double digits by 2007, even before the lowest ebb of the national recession. Jackson County, with a population of 150,000, saw 1,400 home foreclosures in 2008 alone, although the local economy has begun inching upward. In May 2009 *Forbes* magazine ranked the cities of Jackson and Battle Creek as two of the four worst small cities for job-seekers.

The 7th Congressional District takes in all of five counties in southern Michigan plus parts of two others. Although Battle Creek retains strong Republican enclaves and the area is still culturally conservative, Democrats have gained ground by focusing on economic issues. Democrat Bill Clinton carried the district by small pluralities in 1992 and 1996, and although Republican George W. Bush won it with 51% in 2000 and 54% in 2004, Democrat Barack Obama took 52% of the district's vote in 2008.

Tim Walberg (R)

The new congressman from the 7th District of Michigan is Tim Walberg, who reclaimed the district in 2010 after losing it narrowly to Democrat Mark Schauer in 2008. Walberg was born in Chicago, growing up on the city's South Side. He worked in a steel mill to get through college and ultimately got degrees from Fort Wayne Bible College and Wheaton College. He was a minister for 10 years before running for office for the first time. In 1982, he won a seat in the Michigan House by beating a moderate GOP incumbent. In his 16 years as a state legislator, Walberg had a reputation as a tireless advocate for gun rights, an opponent of abortion rights, and a staunch fiscal conservative. He belonged to a group dubbed the "No" caucus for its unflinching opposition to tax hikes and increased spending. Term limits put an end to his tenure, and from 1998 to 2005, he was president of a conservative education foundation and a division manager for the Moody Bible Institute of Chicago.

In 2004, Walberg made a bid for the 7th District seat when Republican Rep. Nick Smith retired after 12 years. He came in third in a GOP primary field crowded with other conservatives, and moderate Republican Joe Schwarz went on to win the general election. Two years later, Walberg tried again. In a primary challenge reminiscent of this year's tea party-fueled campaigns, he ran on a record of having never once voted for a tax increase in the legislature. The well-funded anti-tax Club for Growth took notice and poured $500,000 into television ads attacking Schwarz. The national GOP backed the incumbent, and Schwarz had a spending advantage of 2-to-1. Walberg nevertheless prevailed and went on to defeat a weak Democratic opponent, 49% to 46%. He became a prime target for Democrats in 2008.

That year, Democrats nominated Schauer, the Michigan Senate's minority leader and a former community organizer. With unemployment rising, Schauer focused on the economy and secured an endorsement from Republican Schwarz. Schauer also benefited from the favorable national environment for Democrats and the enthusiasm generated by Illinois Sen. Barack Obama's campaign for president. The Club for Growth again spent heavily for Walberg, but Schauer had strong union support and eked out a win, 48.8% to 46.5%.

Walberg came back for a rematch in 2010 in a much more favorable climate for his party. In August, he won a three-way Republican primary with 57% of the vote. In the general election, Walberg and his allies attacked Schauer for his vote for Obama's $787 billion economic stimulus bill, saying that he was part of the problem of deficit spending in Washington. Schauer and his backers portrayed Walberg as too far right for the district, highlighting such positions as his support for privatizing Social Security. They also spotlighted a September radio interview in which Walberg said he didn't know whether Obama is an American citizen. "We don't have enough information about this president," he said. By day's end, he reversed course and acknowledged that Obama is "certainly an American citizen."

Outside groups and both national parties showered money on the race. The National Republican Congressional Committee committed nearly $1 million, and the conservative American Future Fund spent another $500,000 to help Walberg. The Democratic Congressional Campaign Committee invested $500,000, and Schauer received strong financial backing from two major labor groups, the American Federation of State, County, and Municipal Employees, and the Service Employees International Union, which together spent more than $1 million. On Election Day, Walberg won the seat back, 50% to 45%.

EIGHTH DISTRICT

Mike Rogers (R)

Elected 2000, 6th term; b. June 2, 1963, Livingston Cnty.; home, Brighton; Adrian Col., B.A. 1985; Methodist; Married (Diane); 2 children.

Military Career: Army, 1985-88.

Elected Office: MI Senate, 1995-2000, Maj. floor ldr., 1999-2000.

Professional Career: Co-founder, E.B.I. Builders, 1985; FBI spec. agent, 1988-94.

DC Office: 133 CHOB, 20515, 202-225-4872; Fax: 202-225-5820; Web site: mikerogers.house.gov.

State Offices: Lansing, 517-702-8000.

Committees: *Energy & Commerce:* Communications & Technology; Health. *Permanent Select Committee on Intelligence* (Chmn).

Group Ratings

	ACLU	ACU	ADA	CFG	AFS	FRC	LCV	ITIC	NTU	COC
2010	6	91	10	81	13	100	20	33	85	86
2009	–	92	10	82	25	–	21	–	81	93

National Journal Ratings

	2010 LIB	—	2010 CONS	2009 LIB	—	2009 CONS
Economic	29%	—	70%	31%	—	69%
Social	25%	—	71%	24%	—	73%
Foreign	21%	—	77%	0%	—	75%
Composite	26%	—	74%	23%	—	77%

Key Votes of the 111th Congress

1. Overturn Ledbetter	N	5. Bar federal abortion funds	Y	9. Stop detainee transfers	Y
2. Pass $820 billion stimulus	N	6. Pass health care bill	N	10. Legalize immigrants' kids	N
3. Let guns in national parks	Y	7. Regulate financial firms	N	11. Repeal don't ask, tell	N
4. Pass cap-and-trade	N	8. Pass tax cuts for some	N	12. Limit campaign funds	N

Election Results

2010 general	Mike Rogers (R)	156,931	(64%)	($1,778,687)
	Lance Enderle (D)	84,069	(34%)	($12,539)
2010 primary	Mike Rogers (R)	unopposed		

Prior Winning Percentages: 2008 (57%), 2006 (55%), 2004 (61%), 2002 (68%), 2000 (49%)

Population		Race/Ethnicity		Work	
Pop. 2010:	707,572	White:	85.1%	Private:	78.8%
Change since 2000:	Up 6.8%	Black:	5.2%	Government:	15.7%
Urban:	70.0%	Hispanic:	4.6%	Self-employed:	5.4%
Rural:	30.0%	Asian:	2.7%	Blue collar:	19.1%
Area size:	2,287 sq. mi.	Native Am.:	0.4%	White collar:	63.7%
		Hawaiian:	0.0%	Khaki collar:	0.1%
Age		Two+ races:	2.0%	Other:	17.1%
Median age:	36.9 yrs.				
More than 65 yrs:	10.7%	*Ancestry*		Median income:	$57,613
Less than 18 yrs:	23.9%	German	19.5%	Median Home Value:	$179,900
		Irish	11.3%		
Education		English	10.3%	**Military Veterans**	
H.S. grad:	92.3%			% of Pop:	8.7%
College grad:	31.8%				
Grad degree:	12.1%				

Central Michigan; Lansing

Lansing is Michigan's state capital, chosen in 1847 because of its geographic position halfway between Lake Huron and Lake Michigan—and away from the border with Canada and the threat of invasion by British forces. The only drawback was fewer days with sunshine than anyplace else in the state. But it is a tidy and pleasant city with more than its share of amenities. It has a beautifully restored Capitol and a fine state history museum and is neighbor to

2008 Presidential Vote		
Barack Obama (D) 198,206	(53%)
John McCain (R) 172,344	(46%)
2004 Presidential Vote		
George Bush (R) 191,287	(54%)
John Kerry (D) 161,282	(45%)
Cook Partisan Voting Index: R+2		

Michigan State University in East Lansing, started in 1855 as America's first land grant college. Its Oldsmobile plant stimulated growth in the first half of the 20th century, and state government did the same in the second half. GM closed its Olds line and two other Lansing plants in 2004, but two new highly efficient GM assembly plants have been constructed in the Lansing area. The Oldsmobile name also remains alive at two local museums and at the baseball stadium where the Lansing Lugnuts play. Historically, the Lansing area voted Republican up through the 1960s. But as public employee unions have grown in membership and strength, Lansing, like some other state capitals, has become heavily Democratic, as is the affluent university town East Lansing.

Just east of Lansing's Ingham County is quite another part of Michigan, Livingston County. (Most of the counties in these parts were named for members of President Andrew Jackson's Cabinet: Livingston was secretary of State and Ingham secretary of the Treasury.) Forty years ago, Livingston County was mostly rural, known mainly for its many lakes. But over the years, thousands of Detroit area residents have driven out Interstate 96 to Brighton and Howell, and other Livingston townships. Subdivisions, schools and shopping malls sprouted up. Most of these people are conservatives, happy to leave the urban problems of Detroit behind, angry at high taxes and hewing to traditional religious faiths. They have made Livingston Michigan's fastest-growing county—its population rose 57% from 1990 to 2010—and one of its most Republican. Meanwhile, Lansing's population has been slowly declining. In 1970, Livingston had 58,000 people to Ingham's 261,000; in 2010, Livingston had 181,000 people to Ingham's 281,000. So as Ingham has grown more Democratic, Livingston has been casting bigger Republican margins. Ingham County was hurting in the recession, though the 2009 federal economic stimulus spending helped keep state employment up. Livingston County, almost alone in Michigan, still seemed to prosper, with a county government that cut payroll 23% but still delivered services and ran a surplus.

The 8th Congressional District of Michigan includes all of Ingham and Livingston counties, Shiawassee County south of Owosso (the birthplace of Republican almost-president Thomas E. Dewey), plus Clinton County, directly north of Lansing. It also takes in heavily Republican exurban townships in northern Oakland County.

Mike Rogers (R)

The congressman from the 8th District is Mike Rogers, a Republican first elected in 2000 and the chairman of the House Intelligence Committee. (He is one of two Republican Mike Rogers in the House; the other one is from Alabama.)

Rogers grew up in Brighton, in Livingston County, and graduated from Adrian College in southeastern Michigan. He graduated from the FBI Academy and focused on public corruption cases as an FBI special agent in Chicago for six years. In 1994, he returned to Michigan, started a home construction business and was elected to the state Senate, where in 1999 he became majority floor leader. In 2000, when Democrat Debbie Stabenow gave up the 8th District seat to run successfully for the Senate, Rogers and Democrat Dianne Byrum, a fellow state senator, both ran for the seat. Each candidate raised about $2 million, and it turned into the closest race in the country that year. It took six weeks to count the final tally, and Rogers won by 111 votes.

He has described his political philosophy as a version of "compassionate conservatism," with a bit more conservatism on cultural issues than on the economy. With his law enforcement and legislative backgrounds, Rogers made an impression on colleagues with his sound advice in the aftermath of the September 11 attacks. He provided expertise on the high-technology tools used to track terrorists and on the use of wiretaps, and he urged that airport screeners have federal supervision.

Well-respected by the Republican leadership, Rogers in 2010 was named the new chairman of the intelligence panel after the GOP won a majority in the House. The position gives him a perch from which he could play a key role in challenging the Obama administration on national security and anti-terrorism issues. As a member of the committee in recent years, he called on the Obama administration to stick to its September 2009 deadline for the Iranian regime to agree to negotiations over its nuclear program or be subject to sanctions. He also criticized the Justice Department for administering Miranda warnings to the Christmas Day 2009 bomber in the Detroit airport who had not even legally entered the United States for his failed attempt to blow up a passenger airplane. "We don't need to treat terrorists like U.S. citizens," he told MSNBC. "We need to treat them like terrorists."

He also has been an active member of the Energy and Commerce Committee. The House passed his bill to eliminate state food safety warnings that are stronger than comparable federal warnings. He also sponsored a 2007 bill to give Michigan more authority to limit its flow of trash from other states and Canada. "We love our Canadian neighbors. We love their trade. But you don't throw your trash in your neighbor's yard," he said when the House passed the bill.

In the waning years of the Republican majority, Rogers sought a post in the party leadership. He positioned himself to run for whip in 2006, but the Republicans lost the majority that year and there were fewer leadership positions to go around; Missouri Rep. Roy Blunt got the whip job. In the 2010 election, Rogers was called on to help the National Republican Congressional Committee as chairman of incumbent retention. Borrowing from the Democrats' successful campaign tactics, Rogers sat down with incumbent Republicans and discussed ways they could shore up their support before the election and pressuring delinquent incumbents to step up their fundraising, both for their own campaigns and for the party overall.

Rogers can be overtly partisan. In May 2007, Rogers stood up to a threat by then-Rep. John Murtha, D-Pa., chairman of the Defense Appropriations Subcommittee and confidant of then-Speaker Nancy Pelosi, when he challenged a $23 million earmark for Murtha's district. Rogers failed to cut the earmark from the bill, and maintained that Murtha came over to him afterward and said, loudly: "I hope you don't have any earmarks in the defense appropriations bill, because they are gone, and you will not get any earmarks, now and forever." Rogers said that he replied, "Is that supposed to make me afraid of you?" Republicans tried to reprimand Murtha and, though that move was tabled, Murtha apologized. Later, in 2009, Rogers' spirited speech against the Democrats' health care overhaul got more than 5 million hits on YouTube.

Less frequently, Rogers can also be bipartisan, especially when he wants something for his constituents. He persuaded the Republican leadership not to strongly oppose the Democrats' 2009 "Cash for Clunkers" program, which helped Michigan's automakers by offering government reimbursements for replacing old cars with new fuel-efficient models. In August 2009, he voted to extend jobless benefits by 13 weeks, an important issue in Michigan's many pockets of high unemployment. He also co-sponsored with Democrat Edolphus Towns of New York a bill to provide relocation assistance to families of federal law enforcement officers killed in the line of duty; it became law in 2010.

Rogers won re-election with 55% and 57% of the vote in 2006 and 2008, respectively, which were difficult years for a Michigan Republican. In 2010, he had only nominal competition from Lance Enderle, a former football coach and Michigan State University graduate student. Rogers won, 64%-34%.

NINTH DISTRICT

Gary Peters (D)

Elected 2008, 2nd term; b. Dec. 1, 1958, Pontiac; home, Bloomfield Township; Alma Col., B.A. 1980; U. of Detroit, M.B.A. 1984; Wayne St. U., J.D. 1989; MI St. U., M.A. 2007; Episcopalian; married (Colleen); 3 children.

Military Career: Naval Reserve, 1993-2005.

Elected Office: Rochester Hills Cty. Cncl, 1991-93; MI Senate, 1995-2002.

Professional Career: Merril Lynch, asst. v.p., 1980-89; UBS/Paine Webber, v.p., 1989-2003; Michigan Lottery commissioner, 2003-07; Central MI U., professor 2007-08.

DC Office: 1609 LHOB, 20515, 202-225-5802; Fax: 202-226-2356; Web site: peters.house.gov.

State Offices: Troy, 248-273-4227.

Committees: *Financial Services:* Capital Markets and Government Sponsored Enterprises; Domestic Monetary Policy & Technology. *Small Business:* Economic Growth, Tax and Capital Access; Healthcare & Technology.

Group Ratings

	ACLU	ACU	ADA	CFG	AFS	FRC	LCV	ITIC	NTU	COC
2010	88	8	90	6	100	0	100	100	16	25
2009	–	8	95	4	89	–	100	–	11	40

National Journal Ratings

	2010 LIB	—	2010 CONS		2009 LIB	—	2009 CONS
Economic	51%	—	49%		56%	—	44%
Social	58%	—	42%		64%	—	34%
Foreign	55%	—	45%		50%	—	48%
Composite	55%	—	45%		57%	—	43%

Key Votes of the 111th Congress

1. Overturn Ledbetter	Y	5. Bar federal abortion funds	N	9. Stop detainee transfers	Y
2. Pass $820 billion stimulus	Y	6. Pass health care bill	Y	10. Legalize immigrants' kids	Y
3. Let guns in national parks	N	7. Regulate financial firms	Y	11. Repeal don't ask, tell	Y
4. Pass cap-and-trade	Y	8. Pass tax cuts for some	Y	12. Limit campaign funds	Y

Election Results

2010 general	Gary Peters (D)	125,730	(50%)	($3,285,646)
	Rocky Raczkowski (R)	119,325	(47%)	($2,038,244)
2010 primary	Gary Peters (D)	unopposed		

Prior Winning Percentages: 2008 (52%)

Population		Race/Ethnicity		Work	
Pop. 2010:	657,590	White:	74.6%	Private:	85.6%
Change since 2000:	Down 0.8%	Black:	11.4%	Government:	8.9%
Urban:	99.3%	Hispanic:	4.1%	Self-employed:	5.3%
Rural:	0.7%	Asian:	7.6%	Blue collar:	12.2%
Area size:	323 sq. mi.	Native Am.:	0.2%	White collar:	73.9%
		Hawaiian:	0.0%	Khaki collar:	0.1%
Age		Two+ races:	1.9%	Other:	13.8%
Median age:	40.0 yrs.				
More than 65 yrs:	13.7%	*Ancestry*		Median income:	$68,521
Less than 18 yrs:	22.9%	German	14.7%	Median Home Value:	$222,900
		Irish	9.5%		
Education		English	8.1%	**Military Veterans**	
H.S. grad:	92.5%			% of Pop:	7.7%
College grad:	47.0%				
Grad degree:	20.8%				

Detroit Suburbs; Oakland County

Oakland County, long considered just a suburban adjunct of Detroit, is now the center of a sprawling and mostly affluent urban area. It is only minutes on the Lodge or Chrysler Freeways from inner-city Detroit. North of Eight Mile Road, the terrain changes from Detroit's worn-out, abandoned neighborhoods to giant office buildings and expensive houses on large lots. There is one shopping mall after another, education levels are high, and crime rates are low.

2008 Presidential Vote		
Barack Obama (D)	202,341	(56%)
John McCain (R)	155,193	(43%)
2004 Presidential Vote		
George Bush (R)	180,073	(51%)
John Kerry (D)	174,078	(49%)
Cook Partisan Voting Index: D+2		

Even physically, the two areas are distinct: Detroit is on almost perfectly flat land, while much of Oakland County lies on a line of hills and lakes that marks the southernmost advance of an Ice Age glacier. Birmingham and Royal Oak, little suburbs set among farm fields half a century ago, are now upscale gentrified nodes amid a vast suburban expanse. Bloomfield Hills is metro Detroit's wealthiest community, and there are large corporate office centers in Auburn Hills. West Bloomfield is increasingly the focus of metro Detroit's Jewish community and also has a large number of Asians, many from India and Pakistan; there are also Chaldeans, descended from Iraqi Catholics. Oakland County has become the population center of metro Detroit. In 1950, the city of Detroit had 1.8 million people, and Oakland County had 396,000. In 2009, Detroit had 822,000 people, and Oakland had 1.2 million.

But parts of the county have suffered economically in reverberations from the Detroit-based automakers' dire financial condition. Unemployment surged past 14% in 2009. The nerve center of auto-company suppliers and manufacturers along Interstate 75 took a big hit in 2008 and 2009 when General Motors and Chrysler closed several factories. The old factory town of Pontiac has had major economic struggles in the wake of 1,500 layoffs at a GM plant and the company's decision to cancel the town's namesake brand. The city in November 2009 auctioned off its Silverdome stadium—built in 1975 for $55.7 million—to a Toronto businessman for just $583,000. GM also suspended operations in Orion, furloughing another 3,400. Some signs of life emerged in 2010. GM, the United Auto Workers and local leaders negotiated a revamping of the Orion plant to produce smaller cars, and GM announced in October 2010 it would invest $145 million and create 350 jobs there to make the Buick Verano, a new compact sedan, and a new Chevrolet small car.

The 9th Congressional District of Michigan includes a little more than half the population of Oakland County. It does not include Southfield, Oak Park, Ferndale, Hazel Park or Madison Heights in the southeast—all heavily Democratic and part of the 12th District. It does include almost all of Royal Oak, all of Birmingham and Bloomfield Hills, Rochester Hills and Auburn Hills, Farmington Hills (you begin to see the prestige value of hills to people who grew up in the flatlands of Detroit) and West Bloomfield, Pontiac and Waterford Township. It is Michigan's most affluent congressional district.

The district trended toward the Democrats because of cultural issues in the 1990s. This has created problems for Republicans; there is a strong Right to Life movement in Michigan, and as anti-abortion rights activists have gained power, voters have moved toward Democrats. Republicans no longer win huge majorities in Birmingham and Bloomfield Township, and they run no better in fast-growing Troy and Rochester Hills. Royal Oak, Farmington Hills and West Bloomfield, once solidly Republican, now lean Democratic, though Waterford Township, with a more working-class population, leans Republican. Republican George W. Bush carried the 9th District by only 51%-49% in 2004, and Democrat Barack Obama won it 56%-43% in 2008.

Gary Peters (D)

The congressman from the 9th District is Gary Peters, a Democrat elected in 2008. A fifth-generation Oakland County native, Peters grew up in Pontiac. He had early success in his business career. He was vice president of investments for Paine Webber from 1989 to 2003, and before that, he was an executive with Merrill Lynch for nine years. At age 34, Peters became a lieutenant commander in the Naval Reserves, training as a sharpshooter and ultimately spending a dozen years in the Reserves. In the early 1990s, he got involved in politics, landing a seat on the Rochester Hills City Council, where he helped unearth an overcharge to the city that saved taxpayers $400,000. In 1995, he was elected to the state Senate, where he pushed legislation to cut taxes for the middle class and to improve access to children's health insurance. He also led an effort to ban oil drilling in the Great Lakes. In 2002, Peters became the state's lottery commissioner. The *Detroit Free Press* later praised him for increasing lottery sales.

In the 2008 election, Peters challenged eight-term Republican Rep. Joe Knollenberg. A fiscal conservative, Peters talked about middle-class tax cuts during the campaign, but didn't swear off raising taxes on the wealthy, a group that includes many of his district's constituents. Knollenberg criticized him for that stance. Peters attacked the incumbent for voting against legislation to expand the State Children's Health Insurance Program. Knollenberg had faced some difficult races during the previous 16 years, but none that challenged him on nearly every front. He started out with a financial edge, but with the help of the national Democratic Party, Peters was able to bridge the gap. GOP presidential nominee John McCain pulled out of Michigan, making a tough political environment for Michigan Republicans even worse. Knollenberg also lost the endorsement of the powerful United Auto Workers, which backed Peters, despite Knollenberg's leadership in securing a $25 billion bailout for the industry.

A crowded field in the general election favored Knollenberg. The three other candidates, including the assisted-suicide advocate Dr. Jack Kevorkian, were expected to pull votes away from Peters. But the affluent district was mired in an economic downturn, which fueled anti-Republican sentiment. Peters defeated Knollenberg 52% to 43%; Kevorkian received 3% of the vote.

Peters has been a fairly loyal Democrat, backing his party on major votes but showing his independence at times. He joined three other junior House Democrats in 2010 to propose major cuts in defense, energy and other areas. He also came out early in support of the Republicans' push to extend the expiring 2001 and 2003 tax cuts for all taxpayers, including the wealthiest.

With his background at Merrill Lynch, he was an obvious choice for the Financial Services Committee. In March 2009, he introduced legislation to place a surtax on bonuses paid to employees of insurance giant AIG, which was bailed out by the government. Later that year, during debate on requiring private pools of capital to register with the Securities and Exchange Commission, he got a provision through the committee that exempted firms with less than $150 million in assets. In a surprise move, he was put on the 2010 conference committee on the financial services overhaul as a way of boosting his prospects at election time. Peters was able to add a provision to the bill that helped automakers' financing businesses.

On the Science and Technology Committee, he got a bill through the House in September 2009 authorizing $2.9 billion for research on advanced and environmentally friendly vehicle technologies at the Energy Department. Another bill he sponsored, with California Republican Elton Gallegly, to outlaw videos depicting animal torture, became law in 2010.

With Michigan's economy in such dire straits, an aggressive challenge to Peters was inevitable in 2010. But he was fortunate in some ways to draw as an opponent former state Rep. Andrew "Rocky" Raczkowski, a former Army reservist. Raczkowski first had to win a four-way GOP primary in which his opponents raised concerns about a business fraud lawsuit filed against him. Raczkowski's troubles mounted when a video clip aired of him questioning President Obama's citizenship and when Phyllis Schlafly, founder of the conservative Eagle Forum, contended at a Raczkowski fundraiser that unmarried women voted for Obama because they wanted government benefits. Raczkowski also could not keep pace with Peters in fundraising. Bucking the Republican tide that year, Peters won 50%-47%, and four minor-party candidates split the remainder.

Michigan is to lose one of its congressional seats in 2012 because of its declining population, and many political experts think the GOP-led process will force Peters into a district in which he must face a more experienced Democrat in a primary.

TENTH DISTRICT

Candice Miller (R)

Elected 2002, 5th term; b. May 7, 1954, Detroit; home, Harrison Twnshp.; Macomb Cnty. Community Col., 1973-74, Northwood U.; Presbyterian; married (Donald); 1 child.

Elected Office: Trustee, Harrison Twnshp. Bd., 1979-80; Harrison Twnshp. supervisor, 1980-92; Macomb Cnty. treasurer, 1992-94; MI secy. of state, 1994-2002.

Professional Career: Secy.-Treas., D.B. Snider Inc. marina, 1972-79

DC Office: 1034 LHOB, 20515, 202-225-2106; Fax: 202-226-1169; Web site: candicemiller.house.gov.

State Offices: Shelby Twnshp., 586-997-5010.

Committees: *Homeland Security:* Border & Maritime Security (Chmn). *Transportation & Infrastructure:* Highways & Transit; Railroads, Pipelines & Hazardous Materials; Water Resources & Environment.

Group Ratings

	ACLU	ACU	ADA	CFG	AFS	FRC	LCV	ITIC	NTU	COC
2010	6	88	5	89	13	93	0	33	84	88
2009	–	80	25	60	33	–	50	–	61	93

National Journal Ratings

	2010 LIB	—	2010 CONS	2009 LIB	—	2009 CONS
Economic	31%	—	69%	38%	—	62%
Social	18%	—	77%	33%	—	65%
Foreign	12%	—	79%	37%	—	63%
Composite	23%	—	77%	36%	—	64%

Key Votes of the 111th Congress

1. Overturn Ledbetter	N	5. Bar federal abortion funds	Y
2. Pass $820 billion stimulus	N	6. Pass health care bill	N
3. Let guns in national parks	Y	7. Regulate financial firms	N
4. Pass cap-and-trade	N	8. Pass tax cuts for some	N

9. Stop detainee transfers	Y
10. Legalize immigrants' kids	N
11. Repeal don't ask, tell	N
12. Limit campaign funds	N

Election Results

2010 general	Candice Miller (R)	168,364	(72%)	($761,649)
	Henry Yanez (D)	58,530	(25%)	
2010 primary	Candice Miller (R)	unopposed		

Prior Winning Percentages: 2008 (66%), 2006 (66%), 2004 (69%), 2002 (63%)

Population		Race/Ethnicity		Work	
Pop. 2010:	719,712	White:	90.7%	Private:	84.1%
Change since 2000:	Up 8.6%	Black:	2.9%	Government:	10.3%
Urban:	66.0%	Hispanic:	2.8%	Self-employed:	5.4%
Rural:	34.0%	Asian:	1.8%	Blue collar:	25.6%
Area size:	3,663 sq. mi.	Native Am.:	0.3%	White collar:	58.0%
		Hawaiian:	0.0%	Khaki collar:	0.1%
Age		Two+ races:	1.5%	Other:	16.4%
Median age:	39.5 yrs.				
More than 65 yrs:	13.1%	*Ancestry*		Median income:	$55,873
Less than 18 yrs:	24.3%	German	20.7%	Median Home Value:	$173,700
		Polish	11.6%		
Education		Irish	9.4%	**Military Veterans**	
H.S. grad:	88.4%			% of Pop:	10.0%
College grad:	21.0%				
Grad degree:	7.6%				

Eastern Michigan; Macomb County

Macomb County, on the shore of Lake St. Clair just northeast of Detroit, has been one of the nation's most closely watched political battlegrounds, a place where it once seemed the electoral fate of Michigan and even the entire country might be determined. It owes much of that to its reputation as blue-collar suburbia, but that is no longer quite accurate: More people hold white-collar jobs than blue-collar jobs these

2008 Presidential Vote		
John McCain (R) 179,768	(50%)
Barack Obama (D) 173,920	(48%)
2004 Presidential Vote		
George Bush (R) 193,727	(57%)
John Kerry (D) 147,288	(43%)
Cook Partisan Voting Index: R+5		

days, and there is far less work in auto plants than in earlier generations. There are plenty of affluent subdivisions now, and boat ownership is close to the highest in the country. Macomb County is the product of the post-World War II boom. In 2009, Macomb had 831,000 people, as farms continued to convert to subdivisions. Many people came here from the east side of Detroit. These new suburbanites were heavily Catholic, often blue collar, at least modestly affluent, and ancestrally Democratic. They accepted the New Deal as part of their natural heritage, but resented the efforts of Detroit politicians to tax them to pay for welfare programs and they were fearful of the city's crime rates. The recent recession hit Macomb every bit as hard as Detroit—between 2007 and 2009, the number of people in poverty jumped nearly one-third in the county. In response, local officials visited China to try to lure students and manufacturing firms. One bright spot was an expansion at Warren's Tank-automotive and Armaments Command (TACOM), one of the Army's largest weapon systems research organizations.

In 1960, Macomb County was the most Democratic major suburban county in the United States, voting 63% for America's first Catholic president, John F. Kennedy. Over the next three decades, Macomb moved away from national Democrats. From 1976 to 1992, no Democratic presidential candidate got more than 40% of the vote here. In 1996, after great effort and with the advice of pollster Stan Greenberg, who had studied Macomb closely, Bill Clinton carried Macomb County 49%-39%. But the Democratic tide has receded a little. Central and northern Macomb County have been filling up with fast-growing and expensive subdivisions that are not as culturally liberal as the affluent parts of Oakland County. In 2004, President Bush carried Macomb 50%-49%. Four years later, Barack Obama defeated John McCain handily in Macomb, 53%-45%. But the recession swung the county back in the Republicans' favor in 2010; GOP gubernatorial candidate Rick Snyder trounced Democrat Virg Bernero there, 61%-36%.

The 10th Congressional District of Michigan includes the northern two-thirds of Macomb County. It also includes Lapeer County, where once-rapid exurban growth has slowed. Also in the district are St. Clair County, with Port Huron and its Blue Water Bridge to Canada, and two rural counties in Michigan's "Thumb." Northern Macomb has become increasingly Republican, Lapeer and St. Clair have long been fairly Republican, and the Thumb has long been very Republican. Overall this district has voted Republican in recent presidential elections—57% for Bush in 2004, and 50% for John McCain in 2008.

Candice Miller (R)

The congresswoman from the 10th District is Candice Miller, a Republican elected in 2002. Miller grew up in Macomb County. Her family ran a marina, and Miller was engaged in life on the water from an early age. She was on the crew team in high school, and later was a member of the first all-woman team to sail the prestigious Bayview Mackinac Boat Race, one of the longest fresh water regattas. In 1979, at age 25, she was elected Harrison Township trustee. A year later, she was elected as the youngest and first woman supervisor of the township.

In 1992, she won an upset bid to become Macomb County treasurer. And two years later, she defeated 24-year incumbent Richard Austin to become the Michigan secretary of state, the first woman to hold the post. Prevented from running for re-election by term limits, Miller was the favorite to succeed Democratic Rep. David Bonior, who ran for governor in 2002, in a district that had been redrawn to make it more Republican. Still, Democrats were enthusiastic about Macomb County Prosecutor Carl Marlinga, who had been in office for 20 years. But Marlinga could not keep pace with Miller's fundraising. He also called himself a "Hubert Humphrey Democrat"—not a big advantage in the redrawn 10th—while Miller called herself a "George W. Bush Republican." She opposed abortion rights, supported free trade agreements, and favored making the Bush tax cuts permanent—all positions opposite of Marlinga's. Both candidates supported gun rights. Citing her daughter's membership in the United Auto Workers, Miller reached out to unions and was endorsed by the Teamsters, but not the AFL-CIO. She won handily, 63%-36%, carrying Macomb County 61%-37%. She has been re-elected easily ever since.

In the House, Miller has a moderate-to-conservative voting record. She supported the 2007 minimum wage increase and the 2009 expansion of the State Children's Health Insurance Program. She and Ohio Democrat Betty Sutton co-sponsored the bill creating the popular 2009 "Cash for Clunkers" program in which the government gave people money for trading in old cars for new fuel-efficient models. She embraced her party's call for fiscal responsibility in 2010, abandoning her practice of seeking earmarks for her district.

In 2011, she became the chairman of the Homeland Security Subcommittee on Border and Maritime Security, giving her a new platform for her tough illegal immigration stance. She is the sponsor of a proposed constitutional amendment to exclude illegal aliens from the decennial congressional reapportionment process, calling it "absolutely outrageous" that non-citizens have "a profound impact on our political system." She also promised to address the U.S.-Canadian border in 2011 after a Government Accountability Office report said that just 32 miles of that 4,000-mile span has adequate security. Miller takes seriously her district's proximity to the natural assets of the Great Lakes, and has warned that the lakes can't be relied on "to solve the nation's water problems."

Miller is also preoccupied with issues that affect auto manufacturing, a mainstay of her state's economy. She has criticized advocates of tougher fuel-efficiency standards for seeking "to bankrupt Detroit." In 2009, she lobbied to keep open a Chrysler plant that employs 1,400 in Sterling Heights in her district after the company announced plans to close it while maintaining a plant in Mexico with similar production abilities. Chrysler decided to keep it open after securing business tax credits of $1.3 billion from the state.

In her congressional career, Miller had one encounter with the House Ethics Committee. The panel admonished her for attempting to influence the vote of Republican Rep. Nick Smith of Michigan in 2003, when he opposed a major Republican initiative to create a prescription drug bill in Medicare. The committee concluded that Miller tried to intimidate Smith to vote for the legislation. Miller told the *Detroit Free Press:* "If a black belt can be intimidated by an overweight, middle-age woman, that's too bad."

In 2008, Miller chaired recruitment for the National Republican Congressional Committee in what turned out to be a dismal election year for her party. Michigan Republicans are likely to protect her from massive changes stemming from post-2010 census redistricting, when Michigan will lose a House seat.

ELEVENTH DISTRICT

Thaddeus McCotter (R)

Elected 2002, 5th term; b. Aug. 22, 1965, Detroit; home, Livonia; U. of Detroit, B.A. 1987, J.D. 1990; Catholic; married (Rita); 3 children.

Elected Office: Schoolcraft Community Col. Trustees Bd., 1989-92; Wayne Cnty. Commission, 1992-98; MI Senate, 1998-2002.

DC Office: 2243 RHOB, 20515, 202-225-8171; Fax: 202-225-2667; Web site: mccotter.house.gov.

State Offices: Livonia, 734-632-0314; Milford, 248-685-9495.

Committees: *Financial Services:* Capital Markets and Government Sponsored Enterprises; Financial Institutions & Consumer Credit; International Monetary Policy & Trade.

Group Ratings

	ACLU	ACU	ADA	CFG	AFS	FRC	LCV	ITIC	NTU	COC
2010	13	86	15	71	13	93	10	0	78	75
2009	–	84	20	63	33	–	36	–	71	93

National Journal Ratings

	2010 LIB	—	2010 CONS	2009 LIB	—	2009 CONS
Economic	34%	—	66%	36%	—	64%
Social	31%	—	67%	29%	—	68%
Foreign	12%	—	79%	26%	—	68%
Composite	28%	—	73%	32%	—	68%

Key Votes of the 111th Congress

1. Overturn Ledbetter	N	5. Bar federal abortion funds	Y	9. Stop detainee transfers	Y
2. Pass $820 billion stimulus	N	6. Pass health care bill	N	10. Legalize immigrants' kids	N
3. Let guns in national parks	Y	7. Regulate financial firms	N	11. Repeal don't ask, tell	N
4. Pass cap-and-trade	N	8. Pass tax cuts for some	N	12. Limit campaign funds	N

Election Results

2010 general	Thaddeus McCotter (R)	141,224	(59%)	($1,195,301)
	Natalie Mosher (D)	91,710	(38%)	($319,881)
	John Tatar (Lib)	5,353	(2%)	
2010 primary	Thaddeus McCotter (R)	unopposed		

Prior Winning Percentages: 2008 (51%), 2006 (54%), 2004 (57%), 2002 (57%)

Population		Race/Ethnicity		Work	
Pop. 2010:	695,888	White:	80.4%	Private:	86.6%
Change since 2000:	Up 5.0%	Black:	9.2%	Government:	9.1%
Urban:	97.0%	Hispanic:	3.0%	Self-employed:	4.2%
Rural:	3.0%	Asian:	5.1%	Blue collar:	18.5%
Area size:	413 sq. mi.	Native Am.:	0.3%	White collar:	66.3%
		Hawaiian:	0.0%	Khaki collar:	0.0%
Age		Two+ races:	1.8%	Other:	15.2%
Median age:	38.8 yrs.				
More than 65 yrs:	12.1%	*Ancestry*		Median income:	$64,835
Less than 18 yrs:	24.4%	German	16.2%	Median Home Value:	$180,400
		Irish	10.8%		
Education		Polish	9.9%	**Military Veterans**	
H.S. grad:	91.0%			% of Pop:	8.9%
College grad:	33.7%				
Grad degree:	12.5%				

Southeast Michigan; Livonia

The inexorable pattern of growth and its conse-quences are plain to see in the western suburbs of Wayne County, 15 miles from downtown De-troit. Just west of northwest Detroit is Livonia. Sixty years ago, the 36 square miles of Livonia had 17,000 people. In 2010, there were 97,000. Similar growth was taking place just to the south in Westland. Around the old towns of Plymouth and Northville, affluent subdivisions sprang up. To the southwest, Canton Township

2008 Presidential Vote

Barack Obama (D)	197,791	(54%)
John McCain (R)	164,043	(45%)

2004 Presidential Vote

George Bush (R)	183,835	(53%)
John Kerry (D)	164,037	(47%)

Cook Partisan Voting Index: EVEN

grew 34% with more modest subdivisions. To the northwest, Novi, in Oakland County, is one of the metro area's highest income suburbs. Although General Motors closed an engine plant here in 2010, these suburbs all have been faring much better than troubled Detroit. Battery maker A123 Systems Inc. opened a large lithium-ion factory in Livonia in September 2010, and Ford is produc-ing its all-electric Transit Connect van there. A University of Michigan-Dearborn study in October 2010 ranked the city among the state's top communities for fostering business development and local entrepreneurship. Tying them together is Interstate 275, which runs along the western edge of Livonia and Westland and provides easy access to Metro Airport.

Livonia was originally the political base of longtime Wayne County Executive Ed McNamara (1986-2002), an old-style political boss who built the beautiful new midfield terminal at Metro Air-port, which is named after him. Livonia, originally settled by Detroiters, was long closely divided between the two major parties, but the recent affluent influx into western Wayne County has made those areas more Republican. Racial minorities have become a majority in Wayne County, due partly to the rapid growth of Hispanics and Asian-Americans.

The 11th Congressional District of Michigan covers much of the territory in western Wayne and Oakland counties—Livonia and Redford Township just to the east, Westland and Canton Township, Northville and Plymouth, Novi and several fast-growing townships to the north and west. The lines were carefully drawn to produce a district that voted 51% for George W. Bush in 2000 and with the clear intention of electing a Republican representative. But like nearby districts, Republican allegiance here has been slipping. Barack Obama won the district 54%-45% in 2008.

Thaddeus McCotter (R)

The congressman from the 11th District is Thaddeus McCotter, a Republican elected in 2002. He grew up in Livonia, where his mother was city clerk. He graduated from Detroit's Catholic Central High School, where he was a first-team all-Catholic football player, and from the University of Detroit and its law school. He was elected to the Wayne County Commission in 1992, at age 27, and became the driving force to change the county's charter to require a vote of two-thirds of the commission plus 60% of the voters in a referendum to pass a tax increase.

In 1998, he was elected to the state Senate, where he became vice chairman of the Senate's reapportionment committee. After the 2000 census, he helped design the new 11th District, which included his entire Senate district, and so made him the early front-runner for the 2002 election. He won the primary, 69%-31%. But McCotter did not win the seat without a contest. In the general election, he faced Democrat Kevin Kelley, the Redford Township supervisor. Kelley called himself a "centrist Democrat," and both candidates supported the Bush tax cuts and authorization of military force in Iraq, and both opposed creating individual investment accounts in Social Security. McCotter defined himself as a conservative who opposed abortion rights and gun control. Kelley supported abortion rights and restrictions on gun ownership. Kelley hoped to benefit from Democratic gubernatorial candidate Jennifer Granholm's local popularity. McCotter raised more money, much of it at a mid-October fundraiser with Bush. His 57%-40% victory was larger than expected.

In the House, McCotter established a moderate-to-conservative voting record, with streaks of independence. His district's union presence sometimes leads him to support labor-related bills, and he has joined Democrats on Great Lakes environmental initiatives. In 2007, he was one of 13 Republicans to vote for House passage of organized labor's bill to expedite union organization.

He is an avid rock-and-roll fan, with a quirky sense of humor, prone to quoting song lyrics. In a Fox News interview in March 2009, he compared the Republican Party's task of reestablishing itself to the intricately coiffed 1980s new-wave band Flock of Seagulls: "We'd say that looks in disarray, but there was a lot of work that went into sculpting that." He has a large poster of Beatles legend John Lennon on the wall in his congressional office. McCotter plays guitar and, with four other House members, he is part of the Second Amendments, a bipartisan rock and country band that performed for U.S. forces in Iraq and Afghanistan. McCotter drew substantial publicity in October 2009 for introducing a bill to let pet owners deduct as much as $3,500 from their annual tax returns. "We've had reports about people having to turn in pets because of the economic recession," he told the YouTube channel DoggyTV, adding that pets make people more humane.

McCotter was an early supporter of John Boehner of Ohio for majority leader in 2006 and was welcomed into his inner circle. That may have helped him defeat California Republican Rep. Darrell Issa in a November 2006 contest for chairman of the Republican Policy Committee, a rung on the leadership ladder. In that role, McCotter advocated that Republicans should be less centralized and do a better job of engaging rank-and-file members. He took some innovative steps, such as opening committee membership to any House Republican who wants to participate. But in mid-2010, he proposed shutting down the Policy Committee and using its $360,000 budget to reduce the deficit. He told colleagues that the group had completed most of its work for the year and that it had become largely redundant. The move provoked an internal GOP squabble. GOP Whip Eric Cantor effectively stopped the plan and the committee continued. Georgia's Tom Price—a sometime Boehner antagonist—took over the chairmanship.

In this competitive district, McCotter has been blessed by weak opposition. He has won re-election by unimpressive margins against underfinanced opponents. In 2006, he won 54%-43% against Tony Trupiano, an outspoken syndicated radio talk show host. While Democrats captured two adjacent districts in 2008, attorney Joseph Larkin ran a below-the-radar challenge to McCotter in 2008, and McCotter prevailed 51%-45%. Democrats initially put him on their list of top targets in 2010, but he easily beat Democratic nonprofit consultant Natalie Mosher with 59%. He did put his humorous stamp on the campaign by running an ad in which he flatly declared, "Washington's nuts." Michigan Republicans will likely seek to protect him in the redistricting process.

TWELFTH DISTRICT

Sander Levin (D)

Elected 1982, 15th term; b. Sept. 6, 1931, Detroit; home, Royal Oak; U. of Chicago, B.A. 1952, Columbia U., M.A. 1954, Harvard U., LL.B. 1957; Jewish; widowed; 4 children.

Elected Office: Oakland Bd. of Supervisors, 1961–64; MI Senate, 1964–70.

Professional Career: Practicing atty., 1957–64, 1970–76; Fellow, Harvard JFK Schl. of Govt., 1975; A.A., Agency for Intl. Devel., 1977–81.

DC Office: 1236 LHOB, 20515, 202-225-4961; Fax: 202-226-1033; Web site: www.house.gov/levin.

State Offices: Roseville, 586-498-7122.

Committees: *Joint Committee on Taxation. Ways & Means* (RMM).

Group Ratings

	ACLU	ACU	ADA	CFG	AFS	FRC	LCV	ITIC	NTU	COC
2010	88	0	90	0	100	6	100	100	4	25
2009	–	0	90	4	100	–	100	–	3	43

National Journal Ratings

	2010 LIB	—	2010 CONS	2009 LIB	—	2009 CONS
Economic	88%	—	10%	80%	—	20%
Social	82%	—	14%	72%	—	26%
Foreign	66%	—	29%	78%	—	17%
Composite	81%	—	20%	78%	—	22%

Key Votes of the 111th Congress

1. Overturn Ledbetter	Y	5. Bar federal abortion funds	N	9. Stop detainee transfers	N
2. Pass $820 billion stimulus	Y	6. Pass health care bill	Y	10. Legalize immigrants' kids	Y
3. Let guns in national parks	N	7. Regulate financial firms	Y	11. Repeal don't ask, tell	Y
4. Pass cap-and-trade	Y	8. Pass tax cuts for some	Y	12. Limit campaign funds	Y

Election Results

2010 general	Sander Levin (D)	124,671	(61%)	($2,345,155)
	Don Volaric (R)	71,372	(35%)	($62,174)
2010 primary	Sander Levin (D)	42,732	(76%)	
	Michael Switalski (D)	13,480	(24%)	

Prior Winning Percentages: 2008 (72%), 2006 (70%), 2004 (69%), 2002 (68%), 2000 (64%), 1998 (56%), 1996 (57%), 1994 (52%), 1992 (53%), 1990 (70%), 1988 (70%), 1986 (76%), 1984 (100%), 1982 (67%)

Population		Race/Ethnicity		Work	
Pop. 2010:	636,601	White:	71.5%	Private:	84.9%
Change since 2000:	Down 3.9%	Black:	21.0%	Government:	10.1%
Urban:	100.0%	Hispanic:	2.0%	Self-employed:	4.8%
Rural:	0.0%	Asian:	2.8%	Blue collar:	21.7%
Area size:	160 sq. mi.	Native Am.:	0.3%	White collar:	59.8%
		Hawaiian:	0.0%	Khaki collar:	0.1%
Age		Two+ races:	2.3%	Other:	18.4%
Median age:	39.1 yrs.				
More than 65 yrs:	14.9%	*Ancestry*		Median income:	$47,629
Less than 18 yrs:	21.9%	German	14.6%	Median Home Value:	$138,100
		Polish	11.6%		
Education		Irish	8.2%	**Military Veterans**	
H.S. grad:	86.8%			% of Pop:	9.2%
College grad:	22.5%				
Grad degree:	8.0%				

Detroit Suburbs; Warren, Clinton

The flat expanse of land just north of Eight Mile
Road, Detroit's northern city limit, was mostly
vacant in the years just after World War II. A
string of suburbs in Oakland County ran along
Woodward Avenue from the Detroit city limits to
the National Shrine of the Little Flower Catholic
Church in Royal Oak, where Father Charles
Coughlin in the 1930s made his radio broadcasts
opposing Franklin D. Roosevelt and denouncing
bankers and Jews. In the 1950s and 1960s,

2008 Presidential Vote		
Barack Obama (D) 212,850	(65%)
John McCain (R) 108,752	(33%)

2004 Presidential Vote		
John Kerry (D) 193,894	(61%)
George Bush (R) 125,460	(39%)

Cook Partisan Voting Index: D+12

Woodward was one of America's greatest cruising highways, where teenagers drove big Detroit
cars up and down the eight lanes and where the lights were timed at 42 miles per hour. (Since
1994, the Woodward Dream Cruise of old cars has commemorated that era with a mega-celebration
drawing more than 1 million spectators.) To the east, in Macomb County, was some industrial
development along rail lines, but this was mostly empty land, too. Then Polish-Americans began
marching out Van Dyke from Hamtramck to Warren. Italian-Americans headed out Gratiot from
Detroit's east side to Roseville and Clinton Township. Belgian-Americans from the Mack corridor
moved out farther to St. Clair Shores. Today, these areas are well-settled suburbs, long since built
up; a few neighborhoods are edging toward seediness, while many others are continually renovated. Today, half of metro Detroit's population is now north of Eight Mile, as African-Americans
have joined whites in moving to the suburbs. In 2010, 14% of Oakland County residents and 9% of
Macomb County residents were black.

The 12th Congressional District of Michigan is in this suburban territory, with two-thirds of
its population in Macomb County. On the Oakland County side are the southern part of Royal Oak
and Ferndale, which have been economically revitalized, attracting singles and gays as well as
traditional families; Royal Oak's 1920s downtown is spruced up and Ferndale's downtown, spanning the 10 lanes of Woodward, features a blues festival and annual pub crawl. Oak Park, heavily
Jewish in the 1950s, now also has sizable numbers of Arabs and blacks. Hazel Park and Madison
Heights are mostly peopled with descendants of the Appalachian migrants of a few decades ago.
Southfield, Michigan's largest office-space center (far ahead of Detroit), has a black middle-class
majority. On the Macomb side are the county's more Democratic neighborhoods: Warren and the
southern part of Sterling Heights, site of the General Motors Technical Center, a big Chrysler plant
and the M-1 tank plant, which helps make metro Detroit a major defense manufacturer. Farther
east are blue-collar communities of Macomb: Eastpointe (formerly known as East Detroit, it voted
to change its name to make it sound less like Detroit and more like tony Grosse Pointe), Roseville,
St. Clair Shores, Clinton Township and Mount Clemens. The district's population is 21% African-
American, 2% Hispanic and 3% Asian. Politically, it is solidly Democratic.

Sander Levin (D)

The congressman from the 12th District is Sander Levin, a Democrat first elected in 1982 and
the ranking Democrat on the House Ways and Means Committee. He was the chairman of the
committee from March 2010 to January 2011, when Republicans took majority control. He is the
older brother of Sen. Carl Levin, also a Democrat.

Sander Levin grew up in Detroit and got degrees from the University of Chicago, Columbia
University and Harvard Law School. He settled in the Woodward Avenue suburb of Berkley after
school and was elected state senator in 1964. In 1970 and 1974, he ran for governor and lost narrowly each time to Republican William Milliken. During the Carter administration, he was a top
appointee at the Agency for International Development. In 1982, a House seat suddenly opened
up after redistricting when two incumbents retired. Levin won a spirited primary and has held the
seat without difficulty. The 1992 redistricting moved him east, into Macomb County, and placed
him in the same district with Democrat Dennis Hertel, who decided to retire. Levin had serious
competition in the next two elections from retired Army Col. John Pappageorge, and won by just
53%-46% in 1992 and 52%-47% in 1994. Since then, he has won easily.

Levin is a hard worker and a details man, willing to spend endless hours with others working
out solutions. On the Ways and Means Committee, he has played an important role on significant
issues in recent years. On welfare reform, Levin opposed the 1995 bills passed by Republicans but
helped shape the one enacted the following year that overhauled the program by introducing more
work requirements. In 2005, as the ranking Democrat on the Social Security Subcommittee, his

outspoken opposition to personal retirement accounts in Social Security put Republicans on the defensive and helped prevent any legislative changes.

In 2007, Levin became chairman of the Trade Subcommittee. For years, he has been at the center of trade debates, seeking ways, as he has put it, to shape globalization. He favored the 1980s free-trade agreement with Canada, which helped the auto industry. But he was critical of Japanese trade barriers and pushed unsuccessfully for stringent measures on Japanese minivans. He was a strong opponent of the North American Free Trade Agreement in 1993, but supported normal trade relations with China, playing an instrumental role in crafting details with the Clinton administration. He opposed giving the president fast-track powers to negotiate trade agreements in both the Clinton and Bush years.

With many union leaders, Levin has pushed for trade agreements to contain provisions on workers' rights, fair ways of settling workers' disagreements and environmental protection provisions. He got the Bush administration to make changes in labor and environmental protections in the Peru free trade agreement, which was then approved. He also insisted on changes in agreements negotiated with South Korea, Colombia and Panama. During the years of the Democratic House majority (2007-2010), Speaker Nancy Pelosi and Ways and Means Chairman Charles Rangel tended to defer to Levin as support for free trade pacts in the Democratic Caucus declined dramatically. Levin has pressed hard for China to allow its currency to rise in value and introduced a bill to authorize the Commerce Department to decide whether an undervalued currency is an export subsidy; it passed the House 348-79 in September 2010.

On the House Democrats' cap-and-trade energy bill to reduce carbon emissions, Levin reached agreement with Energy and Commerce Committee Chairman Henry Waxman on requiring taxes in 2020 on China, India and other developing countries if they failed to similarly curb carbon emissions. (The cap-and-trade bill ultimately died in the Senate.) He also worked with Senate Finance Committee Chairman Max Baucus, D-Mont., on multiple issues in a 2010 tax bill to extend unemployment benefits, boost oil company payments for oil spills, and create a tax credit for electric vehicle technology development.

While Democrats were still in power, Levin got the gavel at Ways and Means after Rangel became mired in an ethics scandal. In March 2010, Rangel, facing charges he had failed to pay taxes, resigned the chairmanship. For a day, the leadership installed the next most senior Democrat, Pete Stark of California, to the post. But prominent Democrats privately expressed concerns to the leadership about the potential impact on 2010 elections of having the flamboyant Stark at the helm, given his propensity for controversial remarks. In addition, Stark had voted no on the cap-and-trade bill, and so was not in favor with leaders at the time. Next in line in seniority after Stark was the level-headed Levin, who was deemed an acceptable replacement. His first, arguably astute move was to arrange for politically endangered Earl Pomeroy of North Dakota to take over at the trade subcommittee, giving Pomeroy a big promotion just before he faced voters. On assuming the chairmanship of one of the most powerful committees in Congress, Levin told Associated Press, "Every human being is different. I think what I will try to combine is organization, collegiality and making tough decisions."

Still, after the 2010 election, he was challenged for the ranking minority position by Richard Neal, D-Mass. The Democratic Steering Committee voted 23-22 for Neal. Levin, having paid some dues by giving $570,000 to other Democrats during the election season, took his case to the full Democratic Caucus and prevailed over Neal on a 109-78 vote. That put him in the top Democratic job on the committee, opposite the new chairman, Republican Dave Camp, also from Michigan.

Redistricting could be a problem for Levin. Michigan lost one House seat in the 2010 census, which will come out of metro Detroit. Republicans control the legislature and governorship, and are likely to eliminate a metro district and will probably put black-majority Southfield into one of the black-majority, Detroit-based seats, which have suffered huge population losses. That means that Levin may be put into the same district as 9th District Democrat Gary Peters or into a district with considerably more Republican territory. But his importance to Michigan on the Ways and Means Committee could save him.

THIRTEENTH DISTRICT

Hansen Clarke (D)

Elected 2010, 1st term; b. March 2, 1957, Detriot; home, Detroit; Cornell U., B.F.A. 1984; Georgetown U., J.D. 1987; Catholic; Married (Choi Palms-Cohen).

Elected Office: MI House, 1990-92; 1998-2002; MI Senate, 2002-10.

Professional Career: Chief of staff, Rep. John Conyers, D-Mich., 1989-90; admin., Wayne Cnty., 1993-98; practicing atty., 1988-2010.

DC Office: 1319 LHOB, 20515, 202-225-2261; Fax: 202-225-5730; Web site: hansenclarke.house.gov.

State Offices: Detroit, 313-962-7700.

Committees: *Homeland Security:* Border & Maritime Security; Emergency Preparedness, Response & Communications. *Science, Space & Technology:* Research & Science Education.

Election Results

2010 general	Hansen Clarke (D)	100,885	(79%)	($637,049)
	John Hauler (R)	23,462	(18%)	($33,160)
2010 primary	Hansen Clarke (D)	22,573	(47%)	
	Carolyn Cheeks Kilpatrick (D)	19,507	(41%)	

Population		Race/Ethnicity		Work	
Pop. 2010:	519,570	White:	27.6%	Private:	81.9%
Change since 2000:	Down 21.6%	Black:	58.5%	Government:	12.9%
Urban:	100.0%	Hispanic:	10.5%	Self-employed:	5.0%
Rural:	0.0%	Asian:	1.2%	Blue collar:	23.7%
Area size:	108 sq. mi.	Native Am.:	0.3%	White collar:	50.5%
		Hawaiian:	0.0%	Khaki collar:	0.0%
Age		Two+ races:	1.8%	Other:	25.8%
Median age:	34.7 yrs.				
More than 65 yrs:	10.4%	*Ancestry*		Median income:	$30,319
Less than 18 yrs:	27.4%	German	5.8%	Median Home Value:	$86,800
		Irish	4.8%		
Education		Polish	4.4%	**Military Veterans**	
H.S. grad:	75.7%			% of Pop:	7.3%
College grad:	15.1%				
Grad degree:	6.4%				

East Detroit

Few central cities in America were as vibrant in the 20th century as Detroit, or ever as diminished as Detroit is now. This was America's first automobile city, not just because it manufactured so many cars, but also because it was built to automobile scale. Detroit started the century as a city about the size of Milwaukee, with less than half a million people and extending no farther than four or five miles out from the site where the French built Fort Pontchartrain on

2008 Presidential Vote		
Barack Obama (D)	195,150	(84%)
John McCain (R)	36,712	(16%)
2004 Presidential Vote		
John Kerry (D)	188,555	(81%)
George Bush (R)	45,019	(19%)
Cook Partisan Voting Index:	D+31	

the Detroit River in 1701. As the Motor City boomed, it grew outward along wide avenues and, starting in the 1950s, along freeways. The auto companies put their factories and headquarters near the edge of urban settlement. As early as 1954, the nation's first big suburban shopping center, with parking for 10,000 cars, was drawing retail trade from downtown. Metro Detroit expanded to 4 million people, each generation moving out the roadways rapidly in many directions, leaving behind the previous generation's neighborhoods and civic institutions.

Today, large parts of Detroit are literally empty. The central city had nearly 1.85 million people in 1950, dropped below 1 million in 2000, and stood at 714,000 in 2010. Formerly iconic buildings in the downtown area have been torn down, and others are all but empty, while officials struggle to create new population centers and reestablish a business district. Crime is a major problem. For 30 years, Detroit had a murder rate drastically higher than its suburbs, and those who could afford to leave did so. Only 32% of students graduate from high school in four years. General Motors and Ford have been losing billions of dollars each year. (Chrysler went private and closed its finances to public inspection.)

On the positive side, GM bought for $72 million the 70-story Renaissance Center, built in the 1970s for $350 million, and the company moved several thousand employees there. Quicken agreed to move in from the suburbs. Beyond downtown, some of the city's jewels have been maintained: the Detroit Institute of Arts, the hospital center, and the old Fox Theater. New baseball and football stadiums have opened just north of downtown. But beyond these well-policed enclaves lie acres of vacant fields and half-empty blocks where there were once five-story apartments or brick houses.

Detroit's fate is all the more tragic because the city's liberal reformers once hoped to create model anti-poverty and anti-discrimination programs here. Democrat Coleman Young, Detroit's mayor from 1973 to 1993, spent his energy courting the Big Three automakers to boost the number of jobs. Democrat Dennis Archer, who served the next eight years, was able to lower crime and add jobs in the beginning of a thriving private sector. In 2001, Democrat Kwame Kilpatrick, a former state legislator, brought young blood when he was elected mayor at age 31, the self-styled "America's first hip-hop mayor." But his tenure came to an ignominious end in 2008, when he resigned after pleading guilty to obstruction of justice for lying under oath about an affair with his chief of staff. In its appraisal, the *Detroit Free Press* credited the mayor with presiding over the continued revival of parts of downtown, but noted that city services had continued to decline, along with the number of residents and businesses. "At his best, Kilpatrick called to mind an energetic, young Detroit. At his worst, he stood for a corrupt rust-belt city that seems to be running out of luck and time," the newspaper said. In 2009, former steel supply executive and professional basketball star Dave Bing took over as mayor with a promise to lift the city from despair. He slashed $180 million from a $330 million city budget while also managing to make a dent in violent crime. "We are a work in progress," Bing said in early 2011. "Detroit is at a crossroads."

The 13th Congressional District of Michigan includes more than half of Detroit, plus a few adjacent suburbs, from the affluent Grosse Pointe, with nearly 50,000 people, to the down-river industrial towns of River Rouge, Ecorse, Lincoln Park and Wyandotte. It includes practically all of the east side of Detroit and the west side up to about five miles north of the Detroit River—the entire riverfront and downtown, the old General Motors and Fisher buildings, and most of Detroit's auto factories. At 108 square miles, this is the smallest district in the state, with the biggest problems. It has Michigan's highest rates of poverty and unemployment and the highest percentage of residents on public assistance. Politically, this is one of Michigan's two black-majority seats and one of the safest Democratic districts.

Hansen Clarke (D)

The new congressman from Michigan's 13th District is Democrat Hansen Clarke, a former state senator who won the seat in 2010 after defeating 14-year incumbent Carolyn Cheeks Kilpatrick in the Democratic primary. She had been weakened by the storm of negative publicity surrounding her son, former Detroit Mayor Kwame Kilpatrick.

Clarke grew up in a rough inner-city Detroit neighborhood. His father died when he was 8, and when he was 9, he witnessed a slaying. His mother, Thelma, scraped by with jobs as a school crossing guard and a housekeeper, and she pushed her son to excel in school. Recognizing that he was gifted artistically, she got him into classes at the Detroit Institute of Arts when he was in the third grade. Clarke later was accepted at Phillips Exeter preparatory school in New Hampshire on a scholarship. But he didn't adjust well and returned to a public high school in Detroit, where he eventually was expelled for lack of attendance.

Clarke earned his high school equivalency degree through an adult-education program, and was accepted at Governor's Academy near Boston, another elite school, which his mother thought would help him get into a better college. This time, he worked hard at his studies, and his mother paid his tuition out of lottery winnings. Clarke's skills in portraiture earned him a scholarship to Cornell University, where he studied painting. But in his first semester, his mother died unexpectedly, affecting him profoundly. He dropped out of school and went back to Detroit. In an interview, Clarke described this period as the lowest in his life, when he had "no hope at all." He lost his scholarship and his car; he was unemployed and surviving on public assistance. Eventually, a close friend of his mother's rescued him—warning him over dinner one night that he was going to end up living on the streets.

Clarke found a job through the federal Comprehensive Employment and Training Act, and he asked the chairman of Cornell's art department for a second chance. To put himself through school, he worked as a librarian and took out student loans. When the university considered cutting back needs-based scholarship programs, Clarke got his first taste of politics. He ran for the student seat on Cornell's governing board, beating a young Ann Coulter, who went on to become a well-known conservative pundit. Clarke argued to the board that scholarships were "how guys like me got a chance." Later, while getting his law degree at Georgetown University in Washington, Clarke helped raise money for Missouri Democrat Dick Gephardt's 1988 presidential campaign. He eventually became chief of staff for Rep. John Conyers, D-Mich.

In 1990, Clarke ran for the first of three terms in the Michigan House. He went on to serve two terms in the state Senate. In office, he fought for legislation to help Detroit's public schools, including bills providing higher pay for teachers and rewarding students for good grades. He also worked to lower automobile and home insurance premiums for Detroit residents and to help stem the flood of home foreclosures in 2008.

In the 2010 election season, Clarke initially weighed a race for governor but opted instead to challenge Kilpatrick. Her political capital had been depleted by several months of scandal involving her son, who was indicted for fraud and jailed for violating probation. Kilpatrick highlighted the federal money she had brought to the district during her years on the Appropriations Committee. Her campaign raised $636,000 to Clarke's $375,000. Still, Clarke won 47% to 41%, and in the general election easily defeated Republican business owner John Hauler. Hansen launched a series of meetings with federal agency officials in a position to help the city's tattered economy.

FOURTEENTH DISTRICT

John Conyers (D)

Elected 1964, 24th term; b. May 16, 1929, Detroit; home, Detroit; Wayne St. U., B.A. 1957, LL.B. 1958; Baptist; married (Monica); 2 children.

Military Career: National Guard, 1948-50; Army, 1950–54 (Korea), Army Reserves, 1954-57.

Professional Career: Legis. asst., U.S. Rep. John Dingell, 1958–61; Practicing atty., 1959–61; Referee, MI Workmen's Comp. Dept., 1961–63.

DC Office: 2426 RHOB, 20515, 202-225-5126; Fax: 202-225-0072; Web site: conyers.house.gov.

State Offices: Detroit, 313-961-5670; Trenton, 734-675-4084.

Committees: *Judiciary* (RMM): Constitution; Intellectual Property, Competition & the Internet.

Group Ratings

	ACLU	ACU	ADA	CFG	AFS	FRC	LCV	ITIC	NTU	COC
2010	87	0	90	0	100	6	100	67	8	13
2009	–	0	85	0	100	–	93	–	5	33

National Journal Ratings

	2010 LIB — 2010 CONS		2009 LIB — 2009 CONS	
Economic	71%	— 28%	86%	— 14%
Social	77%	— 21%	82%	— 17%
Foreign	90%	— 9%	57%	— 43%
Composite	80%	— 20%	75%	— 25%

Key Votes of the 111th Congress

1. Overturn Ledbetter	Y	5. Bar federal abortion funds	N	9. Stop detainee transfers	N
2. Pass $820 billion stimulus	Y	6. Pass health care bill	Y	10. Legalize immigrants' kids	Y
3. Let guns in national parks	N	7. Regulate financial firms	Y	11. Repeal don't ask, tell	Y
4. Pass cap-and-trade	Y	8. Pass tax cuts for some	Y	12. Limit campaign funds	Y

Election Results

2010 general	John Conyers (D)	115,511	(77%)	($1,137,010)
	Don Ukrainec (R)	29,902	(20%)	($17,649)
	Marc Sosnowski (CNP)	3,206	(2%)	
2010 primary	John Conyers (D)	unopposed		

Prior Winning Percentages: 2008 (92%), 2006 (85%), 2004 (84%), 2002 (83%), 2000 (89%), 1998 (87%), 1996 (86%), 1994 (82%), 1992 (82%), 1990 (89%), 1988 (91%), 1986 (89%), 1984 (89%), 1982 (97%), 1980 (95%), 1978 (93%), 1976 (92%), 1974 (91%), 1972 (88%), 1970 (88%), 1968 (100%), 1966 (84%), 1964 (84%)

Population		Race/Ethnicity		Work	
Pop. 2010:	550,465	White:	34.1%	Private:	81.9%
Change since 2000:	Down 16.9%	Black:	58.9%	Government:	13.9%
Urban:	100.0%	Hispanic:	2.7%	Self-employed:	4.0%
Rural:	0.0%	Asian:	1.8%	Blue collar:	22.8%
Area size:	123 sq. mi.	Native Am.:	0.3%	White collar:	52.4%
		Hawaiian:	0.0%	Khaki collar:	0.0%
Age		Two+ races:	2.1%	Other:	24.9%
Median age:	36.3 yrs.				
More than 65 yrs:	12.9%	*Ancestry*		Median income:	$34,559
Less than 18 yrs:	26.7%	Arab	6.5%	Median Home Value:	$100,600
		German	5.7%		
Education		Polish	4.4%	**Military Veterans**	
H.S. grad:	80.8%			% of Pop:	8.3%
College grad:	15.7%				
Grad degree:	6.2%				

West Detroit, Dearborn

Detroit's early auto factories—Packard, Hudson, Ford Highland Park, Dodge Main, Briggs, Ford Rouge, Cadillac, Kelsey-Hayes, Chrysler, Plymouth, DeSoto—were built between 1905 and 1925 about five miles from the city's center and at the edge of urban development. Almost instantly the flat farmlands all around were platted in grid streets and filled with wooden bungalows and brick prairie-style houses. Detroit's neighborhoods filled up with factory work-

2008 Presidential Vote		
Barack Obama (D)	236,521	(87%)
John McCain (R)	33,872	(12%)
2004 Presidential Vote		
John Kerry (D)	219,075	(83%)
George Bush (R)	46,240	(17%)
Cook Partisan Voting Index:	D+34	

ers and civil servants, professionals and maintenance men, corner-store owners and management personnel, Catholics and Protestants and Jews: a middle-class melting pot. With one exception—Detroit in those days had few blacks; they did not begin their big migration here from Alabama and the rest of the South until around 1940, when defense plants began hiring African-Americans in large numbers.

The history of black Detroit is one of conflict and uplift, inspiration and tragedy. The wartime mixture of Appalachian mountain whites and Deep South blacks in Detroit proved volatile, resulting in a violent race riot in June 1943. During the war years, blacks were pent up in a few severely overcrowded neighborhoods like the Black Bottom, most of it now covered by the Chrysler Freeway. After 1945, when African-Americans began moving outward, real estate agents played on racial fears, and in the 1950s, whole square miles of Detroit changed racial composition in a matter of months. In the 1960s, there was hope that the civil rights movement, encouraged by Walter Reuther's United Auto Workers union, would improve matters, and in fact, many black Detroiters found good jobs and made good incomes. Then came the riots of July 1967, followed by extensive white flight and steep increases in crime. Detroit's first African-American mayor, Democrat Coleman Young, elected in 1973, pressured major employers like the Big Three auto companies to build facilities in Detroit and raised taxes to support expanded city services. But economic conditions continued to deteriorate and violent crime became a part of everyday life in the city.

Detroit took on a garrison atmosphere. Crime reduced the value of residential real estate to near zero, and the city's population dropped from 1.7 million in 1960 to 714,000 in 2010. The public sector took a larger share of residents' income than almost anywhere else in the country, and served citizens poorly. Turnaround came agonizingly late in the 1990s, when Democratic Mayor Dennis Archer, elected in 1993, worked to fight crime and encourage private sector growth. Incomes rose, and the median housing value doubled from $32,000 to $63,000. But the city has remained in decline by almost any measure, from the high rate of home foreclosures to the low achievement rates in the public schools. It has made some small progress under Mayor Dave Bing, a former basketball star for the Detroit Pistons. Detroit ranked seventh among U.S. cities for economic recovery between 2009 and 2010, according to the Brookings Institution. The auto industry's fortunes have brightened since a government takeover of General Motors and Chrysler in March 2009, and violent crime in the city fell nearly 8% during the first six months of 2010 while homicides dropped 28% during that period.

The 14th Congressional District of Michigan consists of nearly half of Detroit, with the exception of the downtown area and some disparate suburbs. Its share of Detroit is north and west of where the old auto plants were built and is mostly residential—square mile after square mile of grid streets, some working class, some middle class, and a few upscale, such as Palmer Woods, Sherwood Forest, and Rosedale Park. In most of them, abandoned houses and empty lots are commonplace, and yet in many neighborhoods, residents struggle to maintain their houses and patrol their streets.

The suburbs of the 14th are diverse. Highland Park is like much of Detroit; Hamtramck still retains the flavor of its original Polish immigrants (on Fat Tuesday, this is where to find the best paczki). The district includes most of Dearborn, including the Ford headquarters, the Ford Rouge plant and Henry Ford's Greenfield Village. It is today the home of the nation's largest Arab-American community, with 30% of residents claiming Arab ancestry, among them Lebanese, Iraqis and Yemenis. From Dearborn, the district extends south, to take in the working-class suburbs of Melvindale, Allen Park, Southgate, Riverview, Trenton, and Gibraltar. Politically, this is one of the most Democratic districts in the United States.

John Conyers (D)

The congressman from the 14th District is John Conyers, the ranking Democrat on the Judiciary Committee and the second most senior member of the House behind fellow Michigan Democrat John Dingell. He was the first African-American to chair the committee, and remains a soft-spoken yet stubborn counterweight to the panel's numerous conservatives. First elected in 1964, he was a founder of the Congressional Black Caucus and has been among the most liberal members of the House.

The son of a UAW operative, he grew up in Detroit. He played cornet at Northwestern and Cass Technical High Schools and watched jazz greats at Baker's Keyboard Lounge. He served in the Army in Korea, practiced law and then worked on the staff of a young John Dingell. Conyers was one of six African-Americans in the House when he was first elected in 1964. Conyers won his primary, in which 60,000 votes were cast, by 108 votes. Civil rights heroine Rosa Parks, who by then had moved to Detroit, worked on his 1964 campaign and then in his Detroit office until her retirement in 1988. When she died, Conyers sponsored the resolution paving the way for her to lie in state in the Capitol Rotunda, the first woman so honored. He sponsored the original Martin Luther King Jr. holiday bill just days after the civil rights leader was assassinated in 1968, and he persevered until it passed in 1983. Since 1989, he has sponsored legislation to establish a commission to examine slavery and its lingering effects, and to consider whether reparations should be paid to descendants of slaves. He opposed the most controversial elements of the crime bills of the past three decades and the welfare changes of the 1990s.

In the early part of this decade, Conyers, as Judiciary's ranking member, worked hand-in-hand with the Republican chairman, Jim Sensenbrenner of Wisconsin, on anti-terrorism legislation in the tense weeks after the September 11 attacks. They agreed that the government could detain immigrants suspected of terrorism without bringing charges, but only for seven days, and they introduced the anti-terrorism bill together. In April 2002, Sensenbrenner got Conyers' support for splitting the Immigration and Naturalization Service into two agencies. Over time, Conyers displayed an ability to work with Sensenbrenner on a number of issues, despite the extreme ideological differences between the liberal Conyers and the conservative chairman. In 2006, they passed through committee an amendment to prohibit telecommunications and cable companies from blocking or degrading Internet services. Conyers does not enjoy the same close relationship with Sensenbrenner's successor, Judiciary Chairman Lamar Smith of Texas, though they did work together on patent overhaul legislation in 2009 and 2010.

Conyers has the distinction of having been involved in two presidential impeachments: the 1974 proceedings against Republican President Richard Nixon and the 1998 impeachment of Democratic President Bill Clinton. For all of his earlier criticisms of Clinton, Conyers rallied the committee behind him and managed to craft an alternative investigation resolution that gave Clinton supporters a rallying point.

Conyers ascended to Judiciary chairman in 2007, after Democrats won control of the House. He favored bringing a censure motion against President George W. Bush and Vice President Dick Cheney for misleading Congress and the American people on the rationale for invading Iraq. He called for creation of a special committee to investigate. But House Speaker Nancy Pelosi, in an effort to calm partisan tensions after the 2006 elections, ruled out any such investigation. Still, Conyers examined the Bush presidency, including alleged abuse of presidential signing statements that went beyond the terms of the legislation. He pushed contempt charges against Bush White House Chief of Staff Joshua Bolten and former Counsel Harriet Miers after they refused to give sworn testimony about the firings of U.S. attorneys across the country for alleged political reasons. During heated debate to extend the Foreign Intelligence Surveillance Act, which some feared was being used by the government to eavesdrop on innocent Americans, Conyers sought measures to curb secret surveillance. He also sponsored a bill to end racial profiling.

Taking a hand in the huge government bailout of the financial sector in 2008, Conyers pushed to allow bankruptcy judges to lower mortgage rates or the principal for homeowners who go bankrupt. He achieved one of his longtime goals in 2010 when he got signed into law a bill reducing the sentencing disparities between crack and powder cocaine, something he and other civil rights activists had argued for years was unfair to African-Americans. But he was unable to advance another priority, requiring radio stations to pay performers a fee for playing their music on air.

Over the years, Conyers—described by The *Detroit News* as "part showman, part junkyard dog, part evangelist"—has been re-elected mostly without difficulty. He made two runs for mayor of Detroit, in 1989 and 1993. But he ran a desultory campaign the first time and almost no campaign the second, and he came in far behind. During his long congressional tenure, he had two serious primary opponents in the 1994 House race, but finished well ahead of both, with 51% of the vote. He was an early supporter of Barack Obama for president, but has had his differences with Obama since then. He accused the president in a November 2009 radio interview of "bowing down" to "nutty right-wing" proposals on the health care overhaul, and also said that the president was "getting bad advice from...clowns" on Afghanistan.

Conyers announced in January 2011 that he would seek a 25th House term, and although his district is likely to remain staunchly Democratic after redistricting, he could face a younger primary challenger. In recent years, he has been the subject of negative news stories at home. In 2003, the *Detroit Free Press* reported that Conyers assigned his congressional staff to work on his political campaigns and also made them run personal errands and babysit his two children. In 2006, the House Ethics Committee concluded an investigation of the allegations by saying Conyers must take "a number of additional, significant steps to ensure that his office complies with all rules and standards regarding campaign and personal work by congressional staff." Then in June 2009, his wife, Detroit City Council President Pro Tem Monica Conyers, pleaded guilty to taking bribes for helping a company called Synagro Technologies get a sludge-hauling contract with the city. She was sentenced in 2010 to three years in prison.

FIFTEENTH DISTRICT

John Dingell (D)

Elected Dec. 1955, 28th full term; b. July 8, 1926, Colorado Springs, CO; home, Dearborn; Georgetown U., B.S. 1949, J.D. 1952; Catholic; married (Deborah); 4 children.

Military Career: Army, 1944–46 (WWII).

Professional Career: Summer Park Ranger, 1947-52; Practicing atty., 1953–55; Wayne Cnty. asst. prosecuting atty., 1954–55.

DC Office: 2328 RHOB, 20515, 202-225-4071; Fax: 202-226-0371; Web site: dingell.house.gov.

State Offices: Dearborn, 313-278-2936; Monroe, 734-243-1849; Ypsilanti, 734-481-1100.

Committees: *Energy & Commerce:* Commerce, Manufacturing & Trade; Communications & Technology; Energy & Power; Environment & the Economy; Health; Oversight & Investigations.

Group Ratings

	ACLU	ACU	ADA	CFG	AFS	FRC	LCV	ITIC	NTU	COC
2010	88	0	85	0	100	6	90	100	4	25
2009	–	0	95	0	100	–	93	–	3	33

National Journal Ratings

	2010 LIB	—	2010 CONS	2009 LIB	—	2009 CONS
Economic	88%	—	10%	73%	—	25%
Social	76%	—	24%	67%	—	31%
Foreign	71%	—	29%	59%	—	39%
Composite	79%	—	21%	67%	—	33%

Key Votes of the 111th Congress

1. Overturn Ledbetter	Y	5. Bar federal abortion funds	N	9. Stop detainee transfers	N
2. Pass $820 billion stimulus	Y	6. Pass health care bill	Y	10. Legalize immigrants' kids	Y
3. Let guns in national parks	Y	7. Regulate financial firms	Y	11. Repeal don't ask, tell	Y
4. Pass cap-and-trade	Y	8. Pass tax cuts for some	Y	12. Limit campaign funds	Y

Election Results

2010 general	John Dingell (D)..118,336	(57%)	($1,960,195)
	Rob Steele (R)..83,488	(40%)	($1,133,250)
2010 primary	John Dingell (D).. unopposed		

Prior Winning Percentages: 2008 (71%), 2006 (88%), 2004 (71%), 2002 (72%), 2000 (71%), 1998 (67%), 1996 (62%), 1994 (59%), 1992 (65%), 1990 (67%), 1988 (97%), 1986 (78%), 1984 (64%), 1982 (74%), 1980 (70%), 1978 (77%), 1976 (76%), 1974 (78%), 1972 (68%), 1970 (79%), 1968 (74%), 1966 (63%), 1964 (73%), 1962 (83%), 1960 (79%), 1958 (79%), 1956 (74%), 1955 special (76%)

Population		Race/Ethnicity		Work	
Pop. 2010:	682,205	White:	74.8%	Private:	80.9%
Change since 2000:	Up 3.0%	Black:	13.6%	Government:	15.1%
Urban:	87.7%	Hispanic:	4.1%	Self-employed:	4.0%
Rural:	12.3%	Asian:	4.5%	Blue collar:	22.0%
Area size:	981 sq. mi.	Native Am.:	0.3%	White collar:	59.9%
		Hawaiian:	0.0%	Khaki collar:	0.1%
Age		Two+ races:	2.5%	Other:	18.0%
Median age:	35.4 yrs.				
More than 65 yrs:	10.8%	*Ancestry*		Median income:	$51,898
Less than 18 yrs:	22.4%	German	16.7%	Median Home Value:	$160,600
		Irish	9.6%		
Education		English	7.4%	**Military Veterans**	
H.S. grad:	88.4%			% of Pop:	8.7%
College grad:	28.6%				
Grad degree:	13.6%				

Southeast Michigan; Ann Arbor

Compared with points further north in "the mitten," the southeast corner of Michigan is elevation challenged. Its flat marshlands along the shore of Lake Erie give way to flat farmlands, with rivers flowing lazily in summer and flashing with ice in winter. Here and there are power plants with giant smokestacks and factories. On the northern horizon is the sprawl of metro Detroit and of the great auto and steel and chemical plants along the Detroit River.

2008 Presidential Vote		
Barack Obama (D) 225,993	(66%)
John McCain (R) 111,041	(32%)
2004 Presidential Vote		
John Kerry (D) 191,091	(62%)
George Bush (R) 118,217	(38%)
Cook Partisan Voting Index: D+13		

The 15th Congressional District of Michigan includes much of the southeastern corner of the state and owes its shape to Republican redistricters, who in 2001 devised one of the most partisan plans of the decennial cycle. In Wayne County, the district takes in parts of Dearborn and most of Dearborn Heights. The most heavily Arab-American parts of Dearborn were put in the 14th District, and these are more middle-class, even affluent, areas. All of Monroe County is in the district, as are Ypsilanti and Ann Arbor, home to the University of Michigan, in Washtenaw County.

There are several working-class Detroit suburbs: Taylor, Romulus (home of Detroit's Metro Airport), and Woodhaven, site of a big Ford plant. Flat Rock is home to a joint Ford-Mazda auto plant, one of the few Japanese plants in Michigan. Monroe County has a statue of Gen. George Armstrong Custer, who grew up there. Once agricultural, the county now is predominantly industrial, and the southern part is in many ways an extension of Toledo, Ohio. (Michigan and Ohio almost went to war over the Toledo land in the 1830s; Ohio got Toledo and Michigan got the Upper Peninsula as recompense.) Ann Arbor is one of the nation's largest university towns, oriented to the university but also home to auto executives and young families who like a town with plenty of bookstores, coffeehouses and liberal neighbors. In 2004 the city voted 74% to legalize medical marijuana. In 2006, it landed the headquarters of Google's AdWords unit, which operates the company's "pay-per-click" advertising method, Google's main revenue source. The company planned to have a workforce of 1,000 in Ann Arbor by 2012.

Ypsilanti, though it also has a university, Eastern Michigan, is less bookish and more industrial. With the decline of the auto industry, hard times have affected the entire district and infected other industries, including pharmaceuticals; in 2007 Pfizer announced the closing of a research plant in Ann Arbor. Unemployment peaked at 16% in Monroe County and 10% in Washtenaw County. All of these areas tend to vote Democratic, though Monroe is often marginal. But they are different kinds of Democrats. In Wayne County, union operatives have dominated Democratic Party politics for 50 years. In Ann Arbor, the party is dominated by leftist peace activists, environmentalists and feminists. Democratic presidential candidates have won this area overwhelmingly.

John Dingell (D)

The congressman from the 15th District is Democrat John Dingell, the dean of the House. He is the longest-serving member of the House and hit a historic milestone in February 2009 by becoming the longest-serving U.S. representative in history. (In combined House and Senate years, the late Democratic Sen. Robert Byrd of West Virginia holds the record for total congressional service, which Dingell will break if he serves until July 2013.)

Dingell's father, John Dingell, Sr., was first elected to the House in 1932, from a district created as a result of the Detroit area's auto boom. The first Rep. Dingell was one of the most productive urban liberals of his day, a sponsor of the Social Security program and, starting in 1943, of national health insurance. His son has been around Capitol Hill almost as long. He was a House page from 1938-43, and then served in the Army in World War II. He graduated from Georgetown University in Washington, D.C., and its law school, helping to pay his way by working as a Capitol elevator operator. He practiced law in Detroit and served as an assistant prosecutor in Wayne County. After his father died, in September 1955, Dingell was elected to succeed him the following December. He was 29, and back then, he represented a district entirely within Detroit with large Polish, African-American and Jewish populations. He still uses his father's office furniture and every session continues to introduce as H.R. 15—the national health insurance bill his father co-sponsored in 1943. Then-House Speaker Nancy Pelosi borrowed Dingell's gavel when the House passed the Democrats' heath care bill in March 2010, the same gavel Dingell used when he presided over the passage of Medicare in 1965. "A good piece of wood doesn't wear out with one great event," Dingell said. He sat next to President Barack Obama when the president signed the bill.

It is a measure of his seniority that the second most senior member of the House, Democrat John Conyers of Michigan, once served on Dingell's staff. His personal life is also wrapped in his political career. He married, had children, but then divorced and was remarried in 1981 to a granddaughter of one of General Motors' Fisher brothers. Debbie Dingell was vice chairman of the General Motors Foundation until 2009 and is a Democratic national committeewoman. She headed the Michigan campaigns for Al Gore in 2000 and John Kerry in 2004, and helped each win 51% of the vote in this battleground state. In 2008 she played a key role in scheduling Michigan's early presidential primary and defending it against the Democratic National Committee's objections.

For 16 years, John Dingell was chairman of the powerful Energy and Commerce Committee, from 1981 to 1995 and from 2007 to 2009. He was also chairman of its Oversight and Investigations Subcommittee. During that time, he established his reputation as was one of the most powerful and effective committee chairmen ever. He grew his jurisdiction to the point that his committee handled up to 40% of all House bills; he had the largest budget and staff of any House committee. And as institutions will, the committee took on the character of its leader: bright, determined and domineering. Dingell, dubbed "the Truck," and his committee superintended the breakup of AT&T and the sale of Conrail by public offering. His 1992 cable reregulation bill was the only one on which Congress overrode President George H.W. Bush's veto. He was a key player in the legislation creating the Medicare program for the elderly in 1965. He had a hand in writing the Endangered Species Act, and after a decade of sparring over clean air legislation, Dingell worked with Democrat Henry Waxman of California to produce the 1990 Clean Air Act.

On other issues, Dingell backed organized labor's agenda against the 1993 North American Free Trade Agreement and other agreements that followed. An avid outdoorsman and a hunter of deer, elk, caribou and moose, he long opposed gun control but voted for the 1994 crime bill and resigned from the National Rifle Association board. One of his proudest accomplishments is the creation in 2001 of the Detroit River International Wildlife Refuge, on both sides of the river, from Zug Island in River Rouge south to Lake Erie. Dingell worked to get donations of land or easements from private landowners, land preservation groups and the Army Corps of Engineers, and the refuge grew from 394 acres to over 5,000. In many ways, he is an old-fashioned Franklin D. Roosevelt Democrat, supporting big government and strenuous regulation, taking a conservative line on some cultural issues and backing an assertive foreign policy. He was the only Michigan Democrat to vote for the Gulf War resolution in January 1991. But he voted against the Iraq war resolution of 2002.

When the Republican majority took over in 1995, Dingell, as the senior House member, swore in Republican Newt Gingrich as speaker and then occasionally cooperated with Republicans to produce legislation. He developed a productive working relationship with Joe Barton, the Energy and Commerce chairman from 2004 to 2007. For years, Dingell opposed raising fuel economy standards for cars and trucks. He sprang into action whenever Michigan's interests were threatened. In 2003, the city of Toronto started transporting its trash—180 truckloads a day—to a landfill in southwest Wayne County in his district. Dingell and Sen. Debbie Stabenow insisted that the Environmental Protection Agency enforce a 1992 treaty that they said required Canada to give notice of each shipment and allowed the United States to reject them. Trash shipments from Canada have since abated but not stopped altogether.

After Democrats won the House majority in 2006, Dingell took over as Energy and Commerce chairman again. Asked about his priorities after 12 years of Republican policies, Dingell said, "We will kill the closest snake first." But while Dingell still had considerable power, it did not compare to his earlier reign as chairman. He no longer also chaired the investigative subcommittee that had been so effective in its heyday at putting top government officials on the hot seat. Moreover, the Energy and Commerce jurisdiction was diminished during the era of Republican control, with securities and insurance legislation reassigned to the Financial Services Committee. Despite a promise from Dingell that he would hold hearings on carbon emissions in spite of his close ties to the big automakers, then-Speaker Nancy Pelosi went around him and created a select committee on global warming to consider legislation on carbon emissions—over Dingell's strenuous objections. "These (select) committees," he sniffed, "are as relevant and useful as feathers on a fish." He called the new panel, headed by Edward Markey, D-Mass., "the Committee on World Travel and Junkets."

In the 110th Congress (2007-08), energy legislation was Dingell's chief priority. After the Senate passed new fuel efficiency standards for cars and trucks, Dingell moved to try to find a compromise that would be easier on Detroit automakers. Negotiating chiefly with Pelosi, he argued for differences between cars and light trucks, and for additional time for the industry to comply. The result, he said, was "a strong bill that (auto companies) will hate but with which they can live." The final bill set a 35-miles-per-gallon fleetwide standard for cars and light trucks. On other issues, Dingell worked with Pelosi to expand the State Children's Health Insurance Program. The bill was supported by some Republicans, but not enough to override a Bush veto. Dingell succeeded in enacting a bipartisan bill to strengthen product safety regulation, however.

The 2008 election ended on an unexpectedly jarring note for Dingell. The morning after the Democrats' victory, Waxman called to tell him he planned to challenge him for the Energy and Commerce chairmanship. Dingell had suffered from health problems in recent years, undergoing two heart operations and the installation of an artificial hip, and he was recovering from knee surgery. Waxman said that with the election of Obama, Democrats had "a narrow window to act" on health and energy issues. But it was widely believed that his chief goal was to push Dingell aside so that he could fashion an energy bill imposing limits on carbon emissions. Dingell was caught off guard and scrambled to put together a two-week campaign to defend his turf as the party organized for the 111th Congress (2009-10).

He was backed by the centrist Blue Dogs, who defended his record and raised alarms about the liberal Waxman, whom Dingell called "an anti-manufacturing, left-wing Democrat." Speaker Pelosi was officially neutral, but Waxman would not have made his move had she disapproved, and, her closest allies backed Waxman. The vote in the Democratic Caucus was close, but Dingell lost 137-122. Waxman gave Dingell the new post of chairman emeritus, with seats on every subcommittee, but no actual subcommittee chairmanship.

Despite his diminished status, Dingell was instrumental in crafting in December 2008 the federal bailout of $13.4 billion in short-term loans for the auto industry, which President George W. Bush approved. And he kept his hand in a variety of issues. In 2009, he added an amendment to the Democrats' cap-and-trade bill that restricted aid for electric cars to those developed and produced in the United States. Also in 2009, he was a lead sponsor of a major food safety bill that passed both houses of Congress and established more frequent inspections of food processors and gave the Food and Drug Administration more power in food recalls.

During the biggest debate of the 111th Congress (2009-10), on the health care insurance overhaul, Dingell stepped in to negotiate with conservative Blue Dog Democrats when they objected to the legislation. During a major telecommunications fight, Dingell successfully opposed a mandate for broadband providers to open their networks to competitors at regulated rates. During this period, Dingell also proved he hadn't lost his old powers as an interrogator. He sharply questioned Toyota executives over charges that their cars' accelerators were malfunctioning and causing accidents. With Waxman, he sponsored a bill to require additional safety features.

Until 2010, Dingell had only two serious challenges in elections, both in Democratic primaries after redistricting plans threw him into a district with another incumbent. In 1964, he ran in a district mostly new to him against John Lesinski of Dearborn, the only northern Democrat to vote against the Civil Rights Act of 1964. With strong support from the UAW, Dingell won 54%-46%.

In 2001, the Republican legislature put him in the same district with Lynn Rivers, an Ann Arbor liberal first elected in 1994. Dingell campaigned as a veteran congressman who had gotten things done. Dingell posed the question to audiences: "Are you going to replace one of the most effective members of the House of Representatives with one of the least effective members?" Rivers emphasized their differences on abortion rights and gun control. Dingell parried by pointing to the women's issues he had worked on—breast and cervical cancer screening and minimum hospital stays after childbirth. This was Michigan's most expensive House primary ever. Dingell spent $2.5 million to Rivers' $1.5 million. Pelosi, then the House minority whip, took the unusual step of stepping in the middle of a family fight by endorsing Rivers. Dingell won the 2002 primary 59%-41%. In the general election, he won easily in this solidly Democratic district.

As the campaign season opened in 2010, Dingell was taken aback by the vehemence of the opposition to the health care legislation voiced by constituents during the August 2009 recess. In June 2010, he told the *Detroit Free Press* that the mood was similar to 1994, when Republicans made big gains and captured a House majority. "It's not only eerie in its similarity...but it's the avowed platform of the Republican Party today to see that nothing happens, so they can take over the House again."

Four Republicans ran in the August 2010 primary, and Ann Arbor area cardiologist Rob Steele emerged the winner with 51% of the vote. In September, Dingell sent out an appeal to his supporters warning that a tea party-backed opponent was determined to defeat him. The incumbent might have also noticed that Republican Scott Brown had carried districts just about as Democratic as his in the January 2010 special Senate election.

Steele ran on his opposition to the Democrats' health care bill. Dingell allies responded with ads depicting Steele as a rich man whose "five-car garage is not big enough to hold all of his nine luxury cars." Dingell told *The New York Times* in October, "This is probably the nastiest climate I've ever seen." A Republican poll showed Steele ahead 44%-39% in October, but media polls continued to show Dingell with a significant lead. Former President Bill Clinton came to Ann Arbor to campaign with Dingell in late October. And the next month, he won 57%-40%. Dingell won only 41% of the vote in Monroe County and 56% in Wayne County. He owed most of his margin to Ann Arbor's Washtenaw County, which had voted more than 2-1 against him in the 2002 Democratic primary; in 2010 he carried it 67%-31%. He had large margins only in Ann Arbor, Ypsilanti and heavily black suburbs in western Wayne County.

Redistricting could be a problem for Dingell again in 2012. His determination to continue serving seems undiminished. He told one interviewer that his model is John Quincy Adams, who, after four years as president, served 17 years in the House and died on a couch in the Capitol at age 80. Republicans control the redistricting process, and the big population loss in Detroit means that the one House seat Michigan must lose will come out of the Detroit metro area. Redistricters will be aware that the state's major economic interests favor Dingell staying in the House. So his prospects for a favorable district are reasonably good, though far from assured.

★ MINNESOTA ★

Minnesota, far up in America's frozen North, is a distinctive commonwealth, a state that in commerce, culture, and politics has set itself apart. It is the node of the transcontinental railroads that linked the winter wheat fields of the northern prairies to Minneapolis, the great grain-milling center, and to the bustling Pacific ports of Puget Sound. It is also the birthplace of Scotch tape, Betty Crocker, Target, and the Mall of America, and the home of dyspeptic chroniclers of small-town America from Sinclair Lewis to Garrison Keillor. Politically, Minnesota for much of the 20th century provided the nation with some of its most articulate and honorable leaders—Harold Stassen, Hubert Humphrey, Eugene McCarthy, Walter Mondale—and with traditions of probity, civic-mindedness, and innovation that are second to none.

Minnesota's distinctiveness derives from its history. The far northern states were ignored by most Yankee migrants, who headed straight west into Iowa, Nebraska, and Kansas. But others saw opportunity in Minnesota's icy lakes and ferocious winters. James J. Hill, the builder of the Great Northern Railroad, once said, "You can't interest me in any proposition in any place where it doesn't snow." He and other entrepreneurs operating out of Minneapolis and St. Paul—already twin cities by 1860—worked to attract Norwegian, Swedish, and German migrants who would find the terrain and climate congenial. By 1890, the Twin Cities—rivals that year in a census competition—were the nerve center of a sprawling and rich agricultural empire stretching west from Minnesota through the Dakotas into Montana and beyond. Minneapolis and St. Paul became the termini of this empire's rail lines and the site of its grain-milling companies.

The Twin Cities also became the center of a three-party politics and an economic radicalism reminiscent of Scandinavia. (American regions do seem to mirror the geography of Europe, with the East Coast resembling the British Isles and France; the industrial Midwest reminiscent of Germany and Poland; the relatively poor and always hawkish South suggesting a Baptist Mediterranean; and the Upper Midwest of Minnesota, Wisconsin, and North Dakota as North American versions of Scandinavia.) One can get lutefisk—smelly, lye-soaked cod—around Christmastime in Minneapolis restaurants. In politics, these Upper Midwestern commonwealths pioneered this country's welfare states and shaped national public policy far out of proportion to their numbers. Alarmed by the unprecedented concentration of economic power and wealth in the hands of a few identifiable millionaires who lived on St. Paul's Summit Avenue or on the hill above Minneapolis's Hennepin Avenue, the immigrants from Scandinavia drew on their native traditions of cooperative activity and bureaucratic socialism.

As in Wisconsin and North Dakota, a strong third political party developed here in the years after the Populist era. This Farmer-Labor Party elected senators in the 1920s and dominated state politics in the 1930s. Hurt by their ties to communists, the Farmer-Laborites were beaten by Gov. Harold Stassen's Republicans in 1938. But this was still a New Deal state, and by 1944, the bedraggled local Democrats were merged with the anti-communist faction of Farmer-Laborites to form the Democratic-Farmer-Labor Party. Hubert Humphrey, the mayor of Minneapolis in 1945 and the dazzling advocate of the civil rights plank at the 1948 Democratic National Convention, played a key role. Humphrey's DFL—clean, idealistic, closely tied to labor, backed by many farmers—attracted dozens of talented politicians, including Eugene McCarthy, Orville Freeman, and Walter Mondale. Humphrey's convention speech helped put the Democrats on record for civil rights, and he was elected to the Senate at age 37.

In the years that followed, the DFL dominated Minnesota politics while a series of progressive businesses led the development of a strong, diversified economy. The DFL stood for a generous, compassionate government, for strong labor unions and high wages, for an expansionist fiscal policy to encourage consumer-led economic growth, for civil rights, and for an anti-communist, but not bombastic, foreign policy. Its base was among blue-collar workers in the Twin Cities, in Duluth and the Iron Range, and among farmers of Scandinavian origin. Minnesota's business leaders were politically conservative and professionally innovative. Over the years, with a pause during the Great Depression, Minnesota's economy mostly hummed along, growing robustly in prosperous years and not falling far behind in recessions. It was news, when in one month of the 2007-09 recession, the state's unemployment rate rose above the national average for the first time in 30 years. But mostly, Minnesota avoided the housing boom and bust that afflicted faster-growing states and the collapse of manufacturing employment that plagued many of its Midwestern neighbors.

Minnesota has low levels of crime, divorce, and aberrant behavior. Workforce participation has been high, with women streaming into the workforce more than in almost any other state.

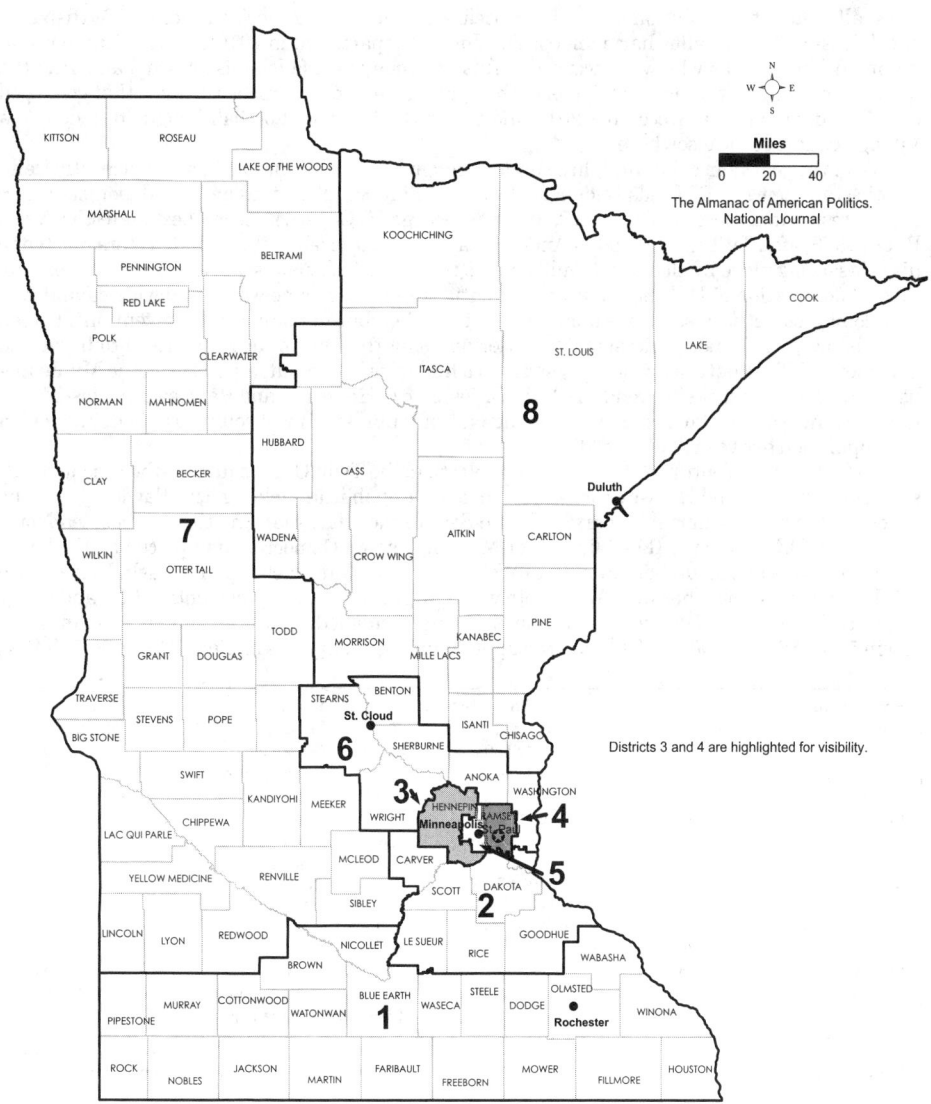

Districts 3 and 4 are highlighted for visibility.

Congressional district boundaries were first effective for 2002.

Minnesota has more social connectedness than any other large state, political scientist Robert Putnam noted in *Bowling Alone,* and this spirit of civic participation is echoed in everything from hockey to the party precinct caucuses and conventions. The 2008 DFL and Republican presidential precinct caucuses attracted 214,000 and 62,000 voters, respectively, more than in any other caucus state. Minnesota has led the Midwest in population growth in recent decades, though it was edged out by low-tax South Dakota in the past decade. The state has attracted an interesting array of immigrants: Hmong and Vietnamese in the 1980s and 1990s, and Somalis since 2000. Once pretty much all white, its population is now 5% African-American, 1% American Indian, 5% Hispanic, and 4% Asian. Yet not all is harmonious. The Justice Department in 2010 indicted Somali immigrants in Minneapolis who were accused of raising money for the Islamist Al-Shabaab. And the weather is always a threat, from floods in the springtime to the 17 inches of snow that collapsed the Metrodome's roof in December 2010 and forced the National Football League to schedule a Vikings-Giants game elsewhere.

Over the years since the Humphrey breakthrough in 1948, Minnesota has been a mostly Democratic state, but the DFL has seldom had total dominance. The state has voted Democratic in every presidential election since 1972, and was George McGovern's second best state that year. But in 1978, after DFL Gov. Wendell Anderson appointed himself to the Senate, voters reacted to his self-serving move by electing Republicans to the two U.S. Senate seats and the governorship. Liberal domination of DFL nominating conventions produced some weak statewide candidates, and, combined with conservative domination of the Republican nominating conventions, helped open the way for former professional wrestler and suburban mayor Jesse Ventura to be elected governor in 1998. Ventura's candidacy sparked a huge rise in turnout, especially in the Minneapolis-St. Paul media market beyond the Twin Cities' core of Hennepin and Ramsey counties. This is family country and by far the fastest growing part of Minnesota; most counties outside the region lost population between 2000 and 2010.

In 2002, when Ventura did not run for re-election, the Twin Cities exurbs—the area just outside the Hennepin and Ramsey core—went heavily Republican, helping Tim Pawlenty win the governorship by a comfortable margin. In the Senate race that year, the tilt also boosted Norm Coleman, a DFLer-turned-Republican over Mondale, whom Democrats had placed on the ballot after two-term DFL incumbent Sen. Paul Wellstone died in an October plane crash. In 2004, the tide began to turn the other way. Minnesota was a target state in the presidential race, and heavy Democratic turnout in Hennepin and Ramsey counties enabled Democratic nominee John Kerry to win 51%-48%. In 2006, the DFL had the upper hand. Pawlenty was re-elected by only 47%-46%,

Population		Household Income		Work	
Pop. 2010:	5,303,925	Under $15k:	10.6%	Private:	81.5%
State rank:	21st	$15k to $50k:	33.3%	Government:	12.0%
Change since 2000:	Up 7.8%	$50k to $100k:	34.5%	Self-employed:	6.3%
Urban:	69.2%	$100k to $200k:	17.6%	Unemployment (3-yr. average):	4.4%
Rural:	30.8%	Over $200k:	4.0%	Poverty:	10.2%
Native of state:	68.9%	Median income:	$56,704	Blue collar:	20.8%
Not a citizen:	3.8%			White collar:	62.7%
Area size:	86,936 sq. mi.	**Home Value**		Khaki collar:	0.1%
		Under $100k:	14.1%	Other:	16.4%
Most populous cities		$100k to $300k:	61.1%		
Minneapolis	382,578	$300k to $500k:	17.7%	**Age**	
St. Paul	285,068	$500k to $1 mil:	6.0%	Median age:	37.2 yrs.
Rochester	106,769	Over $1 million:	1.1%	More than 65 yrs:	12.6%
Duluth	86,265	Median:	$209,900	Less than 18 yrs:	24.1%

Race/Ethnicity				Military Veterans		Registered Voters in 2010	
White:	83.1%	*Language*		% of Pop:	9.9%	No Party registration	
Black:	5.1%	English:	90.2%			Voter turnout:	2,123,369
Hispanic:	4.7%	Spanish:	3.5%	*Veterans by Period*		Turnout as % of	
Asian:	4.0%	Asian:	2.6%	WWII and before:	11.3%	voting age:	52.8%
Native Am.:	1.0%	Other European:	2.2%	Korea:	12.6%		
Hawaiian:	0.0%			Vietnam:	35.2%	**Legislature**	
Two+ races:	1.9%	**Education**		Gulf (pre-2001):	8.9%	Senate:	30 D 37 R
		H.S. grad:	91.4%	Gulf (post-2001):	6.0%	House:	62 D 72 R
Ancestry		College grad:	31.5%	Peace time:	25.9%		
German	26.9%	Grad degree:	10.1%				
Norwegian	11.8%						
Irish	8.3%						

and the DFL's Amy Klobuchar won an open Senate seat by a huge margin. Already in control of the state Senate, the DFL gained control of the House and picked up a U.S. House seat in the 1st Congressional District as well. That trend continued in 2008. Democrat Barack Obama won comfortably in the presidential contest, and DFL nominee Al Franken held Coleman to a 42%-42% tie. After eight months of ballot recounts and court challenges, Franken was certified as the winner in July 2009.

Voter preferences moved in the other direction in 2010, to equipoise between the parties. Former DFL Sen. Mark Dayton won the governorship, after another recount, over Republican Tom Emmer by 43.6%-43.2%. This was a race between a very conservative Republican and a Democrat who called for the nation's highest income tax on high earners. DFL candidates won the other three statewide offices. But DFL Rep. James Oberstar was upset by Republican newcomer Chip Cravaack in the Duluth-Iron Range 8th District, which the DFL had held since 1946. There was massive turnover in the legislature. The state Senate (the largest in the nation, with 67 members) switched from 46-21 DFL to 37-30 Republican. The state House switched from 87-47 DFL to 72-62 Republican. The DFL led in the popular vote for the U.S. House by only 48%-46%, and Republicans led in the popular vote for the state Senate 49.6%-49% and the state House by 52%-47%. Third parties prevented the major parties from breaking the 50% barrier in most races; only DFL Attorney General Lori Swanson and state House Republicans got absolute majorities.

Presidential politics Minnesota has the longest consecutive streak of voting Democratic for president of any state. The last time Minnesota voted Republican was in 1972, and even then, it gave Richard Nixon his lowest percentage margin over McGovern. But in 2000 and 2004, Minnesota was seriously contested, and voters gave Al Gore and John Kerry victories of only 48%-46% and 51%-48%, respectively. In 2008, Barack Obama won 54%-44%, as John McCain carried the Twin Cities exurbs by only 51%-49%. Obama ran way ahead among young voters, and the Humphrey generation also went to Obama. The

2008 Presidential Vote		
Barack Obama (D) 1,573,354	(54%)
John McCain (R) 1,275,409	(44%)

2004 Presidential Vote		
John Kerry (D) 1,445,014	(51%)
George W. Bush (R)............1,346,695	(48%)

DFL base, formerly blue collar workers in factory neighborhoods and the Iron Range, is now the cultural liberals who cluster in comfortable neighborhoods in Minneapolis and St. Paul.

Minnesota has a tradition of selecting national convention delegates in caucuses. The DFL tried to attract more voters to its March 2000 caucuses by moving them from Tuesday night to Saturday and holding a presidential preference vote, with national convention delegates assigned proportionately. But by the time Minnesotans caucused, Gore had already clinched the nomination. Pawlenty tried but failed in 2003 to move the caucus date to February. In 2004, Minnesota was one of 10 states holding contests on March 2. Kerry carried 51% of the 55,000 votes cast in the presidential preference vote, John Edwards took 27%, and Dennis Kucinich finished third with 17%. In 2008, the caucuses were held on Feb. 5, Super Tuesday, and DFL turnout was a thumping 214,000. Obama beat Hillary Rodham Clinton 66%-32% in a contest in which more than half the votes were cast in Hennepin and Ramsey counties. Republican turnout was much lower, at 62,828. Despite Pawlenty's early endorsement of McCain, Mitt Romney beat him 41%-22%, with 20% for Mike Huckabee and 16% for Ron Paul.

Minnesota competed to host the 2008 national political conventions, and as it turned out, the Republicans picked St. Paul's Xcel Energy Center, a hockey arena that was a key project of Norm Coleman when he was mayor of St. Paul. Minneapolis Mayor R. T. Rybak and St. Paul Mayor Chris Coleman, both staunch DFLers, and their townspeople gave the Republicans a "Minnesota Nice" reception, although a few radicals attempted to bomb the convention.

Congressional districting After the 2000 census, it never seemed likely that Minnesota's Republican House, DFL Senate, and Independence Party governor would agree on congressional redistricting, and they didn't. The new plan was drawn by a special panel of five judges. The Republicans wanted to combine Minneapolis and St. Paul into one heavily Democratic district, in the hope of winning three of four suburban districts. Democrats designed a plan that would continue the long-standing pattern of predominantly rural districts anchored in each corner of the state, two districts dominated by Minneapolis and St. Paul, and two in the Twin Cities' suburbs.

112th Congress Lineup	
4 D	4 R
111th Congress Lineup	
5 D	3 R

Gov. Ventura submitted a plan with two urban, three suburban, and three rural districts, one of which stretched along the western side of the state from Iowa to Canada.

The special panel drew its own map, and, when Republicans, Democrats, and Ventura couldn't agree by the March 19, 2002, deadline, that plan went into effect. Minneapolis and St. Paul each continued to dominate a district. The map created three suburban and three rural districts, one running along the southern end of the state from Wisconsin to South Dakota.

Minnesota was to be on the cusp of losing a House seat in the reapportionment following the 2010 census, but under the statutory formula, it qualified for the 435th seat by a margin of about 9,000 people. It edged out North Carolina, which gained a 13th seat in the 2000 census but just missed a 14th this time. After the 2010 election, with DFLer Dayton as governor and Republicans with solid majorities in the state Senate and House, the congressional districts may have to be drawn by a court, as they have been since the 1970s.

But there is at least basis for bipartisan agreement. The Minneapolis-based 5th District and the St. Paul-based 4th have to expand to meet the equal population standard. They could do so by adding DFL territory from the edges of the suburban 2nd and 6th districts, held now by Republicans John Kline and Michele Bachmann, respectively. DFLers would love to get rid of the flamboyant Bachmann, a tea party favorite, but her district was the most Republican one in the state in 2008 and 2010.

The three outer districts could be expanded slightly without much in the way of political repercussions: The 1st and 8th districts changed party hands in 2006 and 2010 and are likely to be seriously contested again in the coming decade. The 7th District is held by Democrat Collin Peterson, who chaired the Agriculture Committee from 2007 to 2011 and habitually runs well ahead of his party. DFLers might be satisfied by the prospect that Peterson could hold onto the seat for some time, while Republicans might be satisfied by the prospect that they would have a good chance of winning it when he retires.

Governor

Mark Dayton (D)

Elected 2010, term expires Jan. 2015, 1st term; b. Jan. 26, 1947, Minneapolis; home, St. Paul; Yale U., B.A. 1969; Presbyterian; Divorced; 2 children.

Elected Office: MN Auditor, 1990-94; U.S. Senate, 2001-07.

Professional Career: Teacher, NYC public schl., 1969-71; Counselor & admin., social service agency, Boston, MA, 1971-75; Legis. asst., U.S. Sen. Walter Mondale, D-Minn., 1975-76; Aide, MN Gov. Rudy Perpich, 1977-78; MN Comm. of Econ. Devel., 1978-82; MN Comm. of Energy and Econ. Devel., 1983-86; Founder and pres., Vermillion Investment Co., 1987-90, 1995-97.

Office: 130 State Capitol, 75 Rev. Dr. Martin Luther King Jr. Blvd. , 55155, 651-201-3400; Fax: 651-797-1850; Web site: mn.gov/governor/.

Election Results

2010 general	Mark Dayton (DFL)	919,232	(44%)
	Tom Emmer (R)	910,462	(43%)
	Tom Horner (Ind)	251,487	(12%)
2010 primary	Mark Dayton (DFL)	182,738	(41%)
	Margaret Kelliher (DFL)	175,767	(40%)
	Matt Entenza (DFL)	80,509	(18%)

Prior Winning Percentages: Senate 2000 (49%)

Mark Dayton, of the Democratic-Farmer-Labor Party, was elected governor of Minnesota in 2010, after a hard-fought campaign and a long political career. Dayton grew up in Minnesota, the son of Bruce Dayton, longtime head of the department store chain Dayton Hudson (now Target). Mark Dayton graduated from Yale University in 1969 and taught ninth grade science in a New York school in the Bowery for two years. He next worked as a counselor and administrator for a Boston crisis center for teenage runaways. He was a conscientious objector and was active in the anti-Vietnam war movement and his name found its way—presumably because of the prominence of his family and that of his then-wife, a Rockefeller—onto President Richard Nixon's enemies list. In 1975 and 1976, he worked for Democratic Sen. Walter Mondale. Dayton then returned to Minnesota to work for DFL Gov. Rudy Perpich. In 1979, after Perpich lost, Dayton spent $400,000 funding a nonprofit agency to spur development in rural Minnesota.

In 1982, Dayton ran for the Senate and spent the then enormous sum of $7 million of his own money. He beat former Sen. Eugene McCarthy's quixotic campaign 69%-24% in the DFL primary, but lost the general election 53%-47% to Republican incumbent David Durenberger. But Perpich was returned to the governorship, and from 1983 to 1986, Dayton was his commissioner of Energy and Economic Development. In 1990, he was elected state auditor. In 1998, he ran in the DFL primary for governor, spending $2 million of his own money, but he finished fourth, far behind the winner, Skip Humphrey, with 18% of the vote.

In 2000, Dayton stepped up to run against Sen. Rod Grams, the most obviously vulnerable Republican senator up that year. Grams' very conservative voting record—as different from his colleague Paul Wellstone's as those of any two senators from the same state in half a century—was out of line with Minnesota opinion on many issues, and he had no signal legislative accomplishments. Grams attracted seven DFL opponents. To call attention to the issue of high prescription drug prices, Dayton accompanied busloads of senior citizens to Canada to buy medicine at lower prices than in the United States. His "Rx Express" got plenty of media attention. He also set up a Health Care Helpline for people having disputes with their HMOs, which were common in Minnesota. He performed menial jobs around the state—the "workday" strategy pioneered by Democratic Sen. Tom Harkin of Iowa in his 1974 House race. Dayton spent his own money liberally and won the primary with 41% of the vote, to 22% for lawyer Mike Ciresi, 21% for state Sen. Jerry Janezich, owner of a bar in the Iron Range who had the DFL endorsement, and 15% for construction company executive Rebecca Yanisch.

Dayton presented voters with a clear contrast to Grams' conservative record. He favored universal government-run health insurance, called for the federal government to lower prescription drug prices and advocated doubling the $500 per child tax credit. He spent $11.6 million, almost all of it his own money, doubling the previous Minnesota record, set by him 18 years earlier. Grams had $6 million. Dayton was also helped by publicity about the two arrests of Grams' 22-year-old son and by rumors that Grams was having an affair with a woman on his staff. (They married the weekend after the election.) Dayton won 49%-43%, with 6% for Jim Gibson, the candidate of Gov. Jesse Ventura's Independence Party.

The prime legislative achievement of Dayton's first two years was the passage in 2002 of an amendment giving Congress the right to a separate vote on any trade agreement provision weakening U.S. anti-dumping laws. In 2003, the Senate adopted his amendment requiring members of Congress to get the same prescription drug benefit as Medicare recipients, though it was later dropped in conference committee. Dayton voted for authorizing military action in Afghanistan in 2001 but opposed the 2002 Iraq war resolution. In the Armed Services Committee, he harshly criticized the Bush administration's course in Iraq, although he supported the $87 billion supplemental appropriation for the war in 2003.

In October 2004, after Congress had recessed for the election, Dayton attracted national attention when he announced that he was closing his Washington office because of security threats. No other member took such action, and he was ridiculed by Democrats as well as Republicans. Washington, D.C. Mayor Anthony Williams was particularly scathing, and the *Minneapolis Star Tribune* ran a critical editorial. "In staking out this Cassandra position, Dayton has added considerably to unfortunate aspects of his reputation: loner, loose cannon, flake." Dayton responded, "I still believe in my soul I made the necessary and wise decision to protect my staff and constituents who might visit my office."

Dayton's action resulted in low poll showings and raised doubts about his ability to win re-election in 2006, well before it was clear that it would be a strong Democratic year. In June 2004, he reported his net worth as between $5 million and $15 million—not enough to enable him to spend as liberally as he had in the past. In February 2005, he announced he would not run again and issued a brief statement. "Everything I've worked for, and everything I believe in, depends on this Senate seat remaining in the Democratic Caucus in 2007. I do not believe I am the best candidate to lead the party to victory next year." DFL nominee Amy Klobuchar, the prosecuting attorney in Hennepin County, went on to win the seat against Republican Rep. Mark Kennedy in November 2006 by 58%-38%.

After reaching the pinnacle of most politicians' ambitions and then falling off, Dayton still was not ready to retire from public life. He decided to run for governor again in 2010, on a promise to reverse the policies of two-term Republican Gov. Tim Pawlenty, who had fought with considerable success against the DFL legislators who controlled one house during his first term and both houses during his second. Pawlenty blocked DFL plans for tax increases, except on cigarettes, and tried to advance his conservative cultural views. By 2010, Pawlenty was focused on a budding campaign for the presidency in 2012. The large legislative majorities held by the DFL after the 2008 elections suggested that a DFL governor would be able to advance progressive taxation and generous spending policies of the sort Dayton favored.

But he had some personal baggage going into the election. In December 2009, two days after Christmas, he told the *Star Tribune* that he was a recovering alcoholic who had a lapse late in his term as a senator and that he had entered a treatment program in February 2007, a month after his Senate term expired. In addition, he said that he had been treated for mild depression during most of his adult life, but was able to control it with diet, exercise and medication. Still, none of the other candidates of either party had his degree of name recognition or statewide electoral experience.

As in 2000, Dayton declined to compete in the DFL precinct caucuses or state convention, making it clear that he would run in the primary against the party-endorsed candidate. In May 2010, he signaled his strategy by naming as his candidate for lieutenant governor state Sen. Yvonne Prettner Solon, who represented a blue-collar Duluth and Iron Range district. His platform was to increase taxes on high-income earners, beginning at $130,000 a year, plus increased property taxes on homes worth $1 million or more. In the August primary, his opponents were House Speaker Margaret Anderson Kelliher, who was endorsed by the DFL convention, and former House Minority Leader Matt Entenza, who spent $5 million of his family money on his campaign and cast himself as a centrist.

Dayton spent $3 million of his own money, aiming his campaign especially at Duluth and the Iron Range, at rural areas generally, and at elderly voters. He was endorsed by the United Steelworkers and by Minnesota teacher unions. Dayton beat Kelliher by just 41%-40%, with 18% of the vote going to Entenza. Kelliher carried the Twin Cities metro area by wide margins, but Dayton ran well over 50% in Duluth and the Iron Range, and he carried many rural counties and places with large numbers of elderly voters.

Public affairs consultant and public radio commentator Tom Horner won the Independence Party nomination with 64% of the vote. The Republican winner, with 82% of the primary vote, was state Rep. Tom Emmer, an earnest conservative. State Republicans immediately ran an ad decrying Dayton's "erratic behavior" and saying, "Dayton is too risky for Minnesota." The contrast was sharp. Dayton called for higher taxes on the wealthy and more spending on education. "Taxes, I believe, are the lubricant for the machinery of our democracy," he told the *St. Paul Pioneer Press*. Emmer called for lower taxes, less regulation and reducing the size of state government. "If we kill job creators with tax increases, we kill jobs in Minnesota," he told the newspaper.

Polls showed a close race right into Election Day. President Barack Obama came in to campaign for Dayton in late October, and former Republican House Speaker Newt Gingrich dropped in for Emmer. Drawing heavily on his personal money, Dayton outspent Emmer nearly 2-to-1. When the results came in, Dayton led Emmer by 8,770 votes, 43.6% to 43.2%, with 12% for Horner. It was a result eerily similar to the near-deadlock between Democrat Al Franken and Republican Norm Coleman in the 2008 Senate race. But the margin was just a bit larger, and the recount process, instead of stretching into months as the Senate recount had, was concluded on Dec. 7, 2010, and Emmer conceded. Dayton became the first DFL governor elected since 1986, the year of the final victory of his onetime boss Gov. Perpich.

When he entered the race, Dayton like most Minnesota political observers assumed he would have a DFL legislature to work with if he won. Instead, he faced a legislature with unexpectedly solid Republican margins—37-30 in the Senate, 72-62 in the House. Dayton continued to call for higher taxes on high earners, arguing that it was morally wrong to cut services, while Republican legislative leaders insisted that they would back no tax increase. He vetoed the first budget sent to him in February 2011, but indicated that he would be willing to meet the legislature halfway.

Senior Senator

Amy Klobuchar (D)

Elected 2006, term expires 2012, 1st term; b. May 25, 1960, Plymouth; home, Minneapolis; Yale U., B.A. 1982, U. of Chicago, J.D. 1985; Protestant; married (John Bessler); 1 child.

Elected Office: Hennepin Cnty. atty., 1998-2006.

Professional Career: Practicing atty., 1985-98.

DC Office: 302 HSOB, 20510, 202-224-3244; Fax: 202-228-2186; Web site: klobuchar.senate.gov.

State Offices: Minneapolis, 612-727-5220; Moorhead, 218-287-2219; Rochester, 507-288-5321; Virginia, 218-741-9690.

Committees: *Agriculture, Nutrition & Forestry:* Conservation, Forestry & Natural Resources; Jobs, Rural Economic Growth & Energy Innovation; Livestock, Dairy, Poultry, Marketing & Ag Research. *Commerce, Science & Transportation:* Aviation Operations, Safety & Security; Communications, Technology & the Internet; Competitiveness, Innovation & Export Promotion (Chmn); Consumer Protection, Product Safety & Insurance; Oceans, Atmosphere, Fisheries & Coast Guard; Surface Transportation & Merchant Marine Infrastructure, Safety & Security. *Joint Economic Committee. Judiciary:* Administrative Oversight & the Courts (Chmn); Antitrust, Competition Policy & Consumer Rights; Crime & Terrorism.

Group Ratings

	ACLU	ACU	ADA	CFG	AFS	FRC	LCV	ITIC	NTU	COC
2010	87	4	90	2	100	0	86	67	15	36
2009	–	12	100	8	100	–	100	–	12	43

National Journal Ratings

	2010 LIB — 2010 CONS		2009 LIB — 2009 CONS	
Economic	62%	— 36%	58%	— 41%
Social	58%	— 41%	53%	— 45%
Foreign	47%	— 0%	49%	— 45%
Composite	65%	— 35%	55%	— 45%

Key Votes of the 111th Congress

1. Overturn Ledbetter	Y	5. Pass health care bill	Y	9. Ratify New START	Y
2. Pass $787 billion stimulus	Y	6. Regulate financial firms	Y	10. Confirm Elena Kagan	Y
3. Repeal DC gun laws	N	7. Pass tax cuts for some	Y	11. Stop EPA climate regs	N
4. Confirm Sonia Sotomayor	Y	8. Legalize immigrants' kids	Y	12. Repeal don't ask, tell	Y

Election Results

2006 general	Amy Klobuchar (DFL)	1,278,849	(58%)	($9,202,052)
	Mark Kennedy (R)	835,653	(38%)	($9,741,224)
2006 primary	Amy Klobuchar (DFL)	294,671	(93%)	
	Darryl Stanton (DR)	23,872	(7%)	

Amy Klobuchar, a Democrat elected in 2006, is Minnesota's senior senator and the fourth occupant of this Senate seat in as many elections. Klobuchar (*KLO-bu-shar*) was born in the Minneapolis suburb of Plymouth, the daughter of longtime Minneapolis *Star Tribune* columnist Jim Klobuchar. She graduated from Yale, where she wrote a senior paper on the machinations behind the building of the Hubert H. Humphrey Metrodome. She went on to get a law degree from the University of Chicago. Returning home, she worked as a lawyer and a lobbyist. In 1998, Klobuchar ran for Hennepin County attorney and defeated the sister of 3rd District U.S. Rep. Jim Ramstad, a Republican, in the general election. She served two terms as county attorney, was president of the Minnesota County Attorneys Association, and took credit for spearheading a crackdown on gun crimes and for securing nearly 300 homicide convictions.

Minneapolis's Hennepin County is the center of a media market that includes most of Minnesota's population, providing Klobuchar an excellent springboard to run for the Senate in 2006 after Mark Dayton announced he would not seek re-election. Quickly, 6th District Republican Rep. Mark Kennedy made it clear he was running. He was fresh from defeating well-known and well-financed Democratic challenger Patty Wetterling; Sen. Norm Coleman and other Minnesota Republicans quickly united behind his candidacy.

The Democratic-Farmer-Labor Party field took time to shake out. Klobuchar was the first to formally announce her candidacy in April. Several other prominent DLFers decided against running, including former Vice President Walter Mondale and radio talk-show host Al Franken. Wetterling pondered the race but decided to run in the open 6th District instead. Minnesota Heart Institute Research Foundation President Ford Bell did run but dropped out after Klobuchar received the party endorsement at the DFL state convention in June.

Kennedy sought to distance himself from the Iraq war and President George W. Bush, by then an unpopular Republican president. He ran an ad listing issues on which he voted against the Bush administration and promised to be independent. He tried to portray Klobuchar as another ineffective liberal, questioning the number of cases she actually prosecuted and highlighting the increasing rate of violent crime in Minneapolis. But all this was unavailing in what turned out to be a heavily Democratic year. Klobuchar called Kennedy a "rubber stamp for President Bush" and called for middle-class tax relief and an increase in the minimum wage. She emphasized her tough-on-crime credentials as a prosecutor. Klobuchar consistently led in polls and won 58%-38%, the biggest Minnesota Senate victory since 1978—only twice did Hubert Humphrey win by a margin that big. She swept the Iron Range, won 2-to-1 in the Twin Cities core counties and carried suburban Dakota, Anoka and Washington Counties handily.

Klobuchar launched her Senate term by announcing she would not accept gifts, meals, or trips from private groups or individuals, regardless of whether congressional rules allow them—an attempt to set herself apart from recent congressional scandals. She instituted "Minnesota Mornings," to meet every Thursday the Senate is in session with visiting Minnesotans for coffee and *potica*, a traditional Slovenian holiday nut roll, a reminder of her ethnic heritage and Iron Range roots.

Her top issue was product safety. In 2007, after a 6-year-old sustained serious injuries from a swimming pool drain in St. Louis Park, Klobuchar and 3rd District Republican Jim Ramstad sponsored a bill banning swimming pool covers that fail to meet entrapment safety standards and requiring automatic drain shutoffs. It was signed into law in December. After news stories described the discovery of lead in children's toys made in China, she sponsored provisions in the Senate child safety bill that banned lead in children's products including clothes and a requirement that toys contain batch numbers to make recalls easier. She served on the conference committee that negotiated the final version, which raised the age for which products were regulated from 7 to 12 years old and became law in 2008. Klobuchar also sponsored a bill to prosecute online stalkers and to require schools to have anti-bullying policies. To the dismay of her teenage daughter, she sponsored a bill requiring states driver's license laws to allow learner's permits at 16, restrictions on the number of passengers at 17 and full licenses only at 18.

With a seat on the Agriculture Committee, Klobuchar had a role in drafting the 2008 farm bill. She got into the final version a provision creating incentives for farmers to switch from carbohydrate-based crops like corn to cellulosic crops like switch grass to make ethanol. She pushed for a transition from the ethanol blender's tax credit to an ethanol producer's tax credit, with a reduction of the import tariff from 54 cents to 36 cents. With Wyoming Republican Mike Enzi, she co-sponsored an easing of restrictions on travel to Cuba. After gasoline prices spiked in May 2008, she backed a windfall profits tax on oil companies and in September, joined a bipartisan group pushing to permit states to allow offshore oil drilling along their coasts. On the financial industry regulation overhaul that passed in 2010, she and Texas Republican Kay Bailey Hutchison successfully moved to maintain regional Federal Reserve banks' supervision of community banks.

With West Virginia Democrat Jay Rockefeller, Klobuchar co-sponsored a bill requiring cell phone companies to allow free termination of contracts within 30 days and prorated termination fees after that. "Sometimes I feel as if I work for these companies because I know all the dead spots on Interstate 35," she said. "If I know, the companies should know. And they should provide this information to consumers before they enter into a contract." Within six months, the companies announced they would prorate termination fees. She continued to complain about early termination fees on "smart" phone contracts, and expressed concern that Google's collection of data from unsecured wireless networks violated consumers' privacy.

Klobuchar has developed a reputation as a resident wit in Washington. She was a hit as a speaker at a national press dinner in 2009, joking that while she held the Senate record for raising money from ex-boyfriends, the House record belonged to Barney Frank. (The Massachusetts Democrat is openly gay.) She kidded about her status as Minnesota's only senator from January to July 2009 and the state's notoriously cold climate: While litigation continued over the outcome of the nail-biter 2008 Senate race, she predicted, wrongly, that it would be settled by the time the ice was out of Minnesota's Lake Minnetonka in April. She extended that prediction to when the ice cracks on Rainy Lake in May.

After the Democrats' drubbing at the polls in 2010, Klobuchar offered her analysis in *The Washington Post*. "The people of this country want more bipartisanship. They want the government to run better," she said. "They want us to help the private sector create jobs. That was the message out of the election, and we'd better heed it." She is up for re-election in 2012. A December 2010 poll showed her with a 59%-29% favorable-to-unfavorable rating.

Junior Senator

Al Franken (D)

Elected 2008, term expires 2014, 1st term; b. May 21, 1951, New York City, NY; home, Minneapolis; Harvard U., B.A.1973; Jewish; married (Franni); 2 children.

Professional Career: Writer, network comedy show; Radio talk show host

DC Office: 309 HSOB, 20510, 202-224-5641; Fax: 202-224-0044; Web site: franken.senate.gov.

State Offices: Duluth, 218-722-2390; St. Cloud, 320-251-2721; St. Paul, 651-221-1016; St. Peter, 507-931-5813.

Committees: *Energy & Natural Resources:* Energy; National Parks; Public Lands & Forests. *Health, Education, Labor & Pensions:* Children & Families; Employment & Workplace Safety. *Indian Affairs. Judiciary:* Antitrust, Competition Policy & Consumer Rights; Constitution, Civil Rights & Human Rights; Immigration, Refugees & Border Security; Privacy, Technology & the Law (Chmn).

Group Ratings

	ACLU	ACU	ADA	CFG	AFS	FRC	LCV	ITIC	NTU	COC
2010	91	0	90	0	100	0	86	100	5	18
2009	–	0	–	–	100	–	100	–	3	50

National Journal Ratings

	2010 LIB	—	2010 CONS	2009 LIB	—	2009 CONS
Economic	80%	—	17%	*	—	*
Social	65%	—	0%	*	—	*
Foreign	47%	—	0%	*	—	*
Composite	79%	—	21%	*	—	*

Key Votes of the 111th Congress

1. Overturn Ledbetter	*	5. Pass health care bill	Y	9. Ratify New START	Y
2. Pass $787 billion stimulus	*	6. Regulate financial firms	Y	10. Confirm Elena Kagan	Y
3. Repeal DC gun laws	*	7. Pass tax cuts for some	Y	11. Stop EPA climate regs	N
4. Confirm Sonia Sotomayor	Y	8. Legalize immigrants' kids	Y	12. Repeal don't ask, tell	Y

Election Results

2008 general	Al Franken (D)	1,212,629	(42%)	($22,502,124)
	Norm Coleman (R)	1,212,317	(42%)	($23,673,308)
	Dean Barkley (Ind)	437,505	(15%)	($163,358)
2008 primary	Al Franken (D)	164,136	(65%)	
	Priscilla Faris (D)	74,655	(30%)	

Al Franken, a Democrat, was sworn in as U.S. senator from Minnesota in July 2009 after the dispute over the result of the extremely close November 2008 election between him and incumbent Norm Coleman was settled. The Minnesota Supreme Court ruled 5-0 in the former comedian's favor on June 30, and Republican Gov. Tim Pawlenty signed the certificate of election declaring Franken the winner by 312 votes. Franken became the 60th Democrat in the Senate, giving the party a filibuster-proof majority that lasted until Republican Scott Brown was seated as the junior senator from Massachusetts in February 2010.

Franken was born in New York City and moved at age 4 to Minnesota, where the family settled in the heavily Jewish suburb of St. Louis Park, just west of Minneapolis. Franken's father was a printing salesman and his mother was a real estate agent. From a young age, Franken reconciled his competing political and comedic impulses by combining them. As a seventh grader, he ran for class president as "Honest Al" and hung posters in the hallways picturing him with a fake beard and a stovepipe hat. Franken graduated from Harvard and took a writing job in New York for the then-new *Saturday Night Live*. For most of the next 20 years, Franken helped to define the program's sense of humor as it evolved from a fledgling variety show into a pop culture mainstay.

Franken also frequently appeared on the program, most memorably as Stuart Smalley, an obnoxious self-help guru.

Franken left *Saturday Night Live* in 1995 and began working as a political commentator. After the Republicans swept to victory in Congress in 1994, he wrote four books, including *Rush Limbaugh Is a Big Fat Idiot*. In 2004, he joined the new liberal Air America Radio network with a daily, three-hour show opposite Limbaugh's program. Franken spent the next three years excoriating conservatives of every stripe, from Bush administration officials to Fox News personality Bill O'Reilly. Franken began thinking about returning to Minnesota to run for the Senate after Democratic Sen. Paul Wellstone died in a plane crash in October 2002 while running for re-election against former St. Paul Mayor Coleman. Democrats chose former Vice President Walter Mondale to replace Wellstone on the ballot, and despite Mondale's prominence and long political history in the state, Coleman won 50%-47%.

In 2006, Franken moved his radio talk show from New York to Minneapolis, and in February 2007, he announced he would run for the Senate. Republicans immediately drew attention to Franken's liberal on-air commentary. His defenders noted that his program often featured in-depth interviews with policy experts. He appeared to have a clear shot at Coleman when lawyer Mike Ciresi dropped out of the race for the Democratic-Farmer-Labor nomination in March 2008. But damaging revelations on the eve of the DFL endorsement convention in June threatened Franken's nomination. A sexually explicit satirical article that he wrote for *Playboy* in 2000 about a virtual sex institute diminished enthusiasm for him among feminist groups. He apologized for the article and won the party's endorsement. But polling showed him looking increasingly weak against Coleman.

Franken slowly won over skeptical Democrats and kept pace with Coleman in fundraising. The dynamics of the race shifted considerably in July, when former Sen. Dean Barkley entered the race as the Independence Party candidate. Throughout October, Barkley consistently drew about 20% in polls. Franken attacked Coleman for reportedly receiving free suits and below-market rent in Washington from political benefactors. But Franken was embarrassed by disclosures that he owed $70,000 in back taxes, and he paid a $25,000 fine to New York state for failing to carry workmen's compensation insurance for his employees. This was an expensive contest; the candidates each spent more than $19 million. As the returns came in on Election Night, they showed the race to be exceedingly tight, with 42% for both Coleman and Franken and 15% for Barkley.

On Nov. 18, the State Canvassing Board showed Coleman with a 206-vote lead. A recount began the next day, and the board ultimately concluded Franken was 225 votes ahead. Coleman contended that 133 ballots were missing in the recount and contested the results. On March 31, a three-judge court issued an order designating 400 absentee ballots for review; 351 of them were opened and counted. And on April 13, the judges ruled that Franken had received the highest number of votes by a margin of 312. Coleman appealed to the state Supreme Court, and his lawyers suggested that he might appeal an adverse ruling to the U.S. Supreme Court on the grounds that different counties had used varying standards in determining the validity of absentee ballots. But after the state Supreme Court ruled, Coleman called Franken to congratulate him and said he had decided against further challenges. By then, each candidate had spent $6 million on the recount process. Franken was sworn in on July 7.

With his arrival in the Senate, Democrats had the 60 votes they needed to prevent Republicans from using the filibuster to block bills. As a new senator who had achieved celebrity in another role, Franken, like Hillary Rodham Clinton of New York, set out to work hard and stay out of the limelight. He refused to talk to the national press and spent the August recess on a strenuous schedule in Minnesota. His first bill, to provide 200 service dogs for wounded veterans, was co-sponsored by three Republicans and passed into law. He worked with GOP moderate Olympia Snowe of Maine to let women in the military have access to emergency contraception. And he joined Indiana Republican Richard Lugar on funding for diabetes prevention.

But he also showed asperity on occasion. His Republican Senate colleagues took umbrage when the liberal MoveOn.org and state Democratic chairmen accused them on being soft on rape because they voted against Franken's amendment to bar defense contracts to firms that required arbitration for claims of workplace discrimination including sexual assault; the Republicans felt that Franken encouraged such attacks. While presiding over the Senate, he cut off independent Sen. Joe Lieberman of Connecticut with an objection of his own, and later made faces while Republican Leader Mitch McConnell of Kentucky was speaking. Franken apologized to McConnell. At a White House meeting in February 2010, he excoriated top Obama aide David Axelrod for failing to set a clear course on health care.

Legislatively, Franken often took a liberal approach. He sought unsuccessfully to amend the health care bill in October 2009 with a provision eliminating the tax deduction for pharmaceutical firms' advertising, a change estimated to save the government $37 billion. That month, he also sponsored a bill for country-of-origin labeling of dairy products. And in May 2010, the Senate voted 64-35 in favor of his amendment requiring the Securities and Exchange Commission to appoint an investor-led board to select securities ratings firms on a rotating basis.

On most issues, Franken supported the Obama administration, although sometimes reluctantly. In January 2010, after a trip to Afghanistan (where he had entertained troops with comic routines), he told the *St. Paul Pioneer Press*, "I think the president's plan, it's probably the best of a series of options that weren't so great. But, you know, I will support him on this." After Obama agreed in December 2010 to extend the Bush-era tax cuts for everyone, not just lower- and middle-class taxpayers as Democrats preferred, Franken said he would vote for it only reluctantly.

Polling in Minnesota indicated that Franken continued to polarize voters; he received roughly equal numbers of favorable and unfavorable ratings. Senate Democratic leaders asked Franken, a magnet for Democratic donors, to head their campaign committee for the 2012 election. But he declined, saying he needed to stay focused on Minnesota issues.

FIRST DISTRICT

Tim Walz (D)

Elected 2006, 3rd term; b. April 6, 1964, West Point, NE; home, Mankato; Chadron St. Col., B.S. 1989, MN St. U., M.S. 2001; Lutheran; married (Gwen); 2 children.

Military Career: Army Natl. Guard, 1981-2005.

Professional Career: Teacher, Pine Ridge Indian Reservation, SD, 1984; Teacher, People's Republic of China, 1989-90; Founder, Educational Travel Adventures, 1991-2006; High school teacher, 1989-2006.

DC Office: 1722 LHOB, 20515, 202-225-2472; Web site: walz.house.gov.

State Offices: Mankato, 507-388-2149; Rochester, 507-206-0643.

Committees: *Agriculture:* Conservation, Energy & Forestry; General Farm Commodities & Risk Management. *Transportation & Infrastructure:* Economic Development, Public Buildings & Emergency Management; Highways & Transit; Railroads, Pipelines & Hazardous Materials. *Veterans' Affairs:* Disability Assistance & Memorial Affairs; Economic Opportunity.

Group Ratings

	ACLU	ACU	ADA	CFG	AFS	FRC	LCV	ITIC	NTU	COC
2010	88	4	90	5	100	0	90	100	9	25
2009	–	4	100	4	100	–	93	–	6	47

National Journal Ratings

	2010 LIB — 2010 CONS		2009 LIB — 2009 CONS	
Economic	64%	— 35%	62%	— 36%
Social	61%	— 35%	54%	— 43%
Foreign	66%	— 29%	70%	— 24%
Composite	65%	— 35%	64%	— 36%

Key Votes of the 111th Congress

1. Overturn Ledbetter	Y	5. Bar federal abortion funds	N
2. Pass $820 billion stimulus	Y	6. Pass health care bill	Y
3. Let guns in national parks	Y	7. Regulate financial firms	Y
4. Pass cap-and-trade	Y	8. Pass tax cuts for some	Y

9. Stop detainee transfers	Y
10. Legalize immigrants' kids	Y
11. Repeal don't ask, tell	Y
12. Limit campaign funds	Y

Election Results

2010 general	Tim Walz (DFL)	122,365	(49%)	($2,163,759)
	Randy Demmer (R)	109,242	(44%)	($939,331)
	Steven Wilson (Ind)	13,242	(5%)	($25,332)
2010 primary	Tim Walz (DFL)	unopposed		

Prior Winning Percentages: 2008 (63%), 2006 (53%)

Population		Race/Ethnicity		Work	
Pop. 2010:	644,787	White:	89.0%	Private:	80.8%
Change since 2000:	Up 4.9%	Black:	2.1%	Government:	10.7%
Urban:	56.5%	Hispanic:	5.2%	Self-employed:	8.3%
Rural:	43.5%	Asian:	2.2%	Blue collar:	25.0%
Area size:	13,520 sq. mi.	Native Am.:	0.2%	White collar:	56.6%
		Hawaiian:	0.0%	Khaki collar:	0.1%
Age		Two+ races:	1.2%	Other:	18.3%
Median age:	38.4 yrs.				
More than 65 yrs:	15.3%	*Ancestry*		Median income:	$50,420
Less than 18 yrs:	23.5%	German	34.2%	Median Home Value:	$147,800
		Norwegian	14.1%		
Education		Irish	7.8%	**Military Veterans**	
H.S. grad:	89.9%			% of Pop:	10.4%
College grad:	25.1%				
Grad degree:	8.6%				

Southern Minnesota; Rochester

The Mississippi River flows majestically south-east from Minneapolis and St. Paul, cutting through rolling hills and, where it widens, forming calm lakes lapping at the bottomlands. It is one of the finest river landscapes of North America, exemplified by the river towns of Wabasha and Winona, with their 19th century stone store-fronts and mountain-like rock outcroppings above the river. This far north, the westward tide of Yankee migrants thinned out. After the Civil War, most settlers following the railroads on the floodplains west of the river were Germans and Scandinavians, bringing their families to a terrain much like the Rhineland and to the rolling uplands beyond, which resemble the northern European plain.

2008 Presidential Vote
Barack Obama (D) 173,884 (51%)
John McCain (R) 158,967 (47%)

2004 Presidential Vote
George Bush (R) 171,952 (51%)
John Kerry (D) 159,776 (47%)

Cook Partisan Voting Index: R+1

Southern Minnesota is a borderland between Yankee and German settlements. Along the Mississippi River, tourism spiked upward (from a nearly nonexistent base) after the old St. Paul and Milwaukee Railroad was converted to a hiker-biker nature trail in the 1990s. "Historic" Bluff Country now draws sufficient visitors to support two upscale bed-and-breakfasts, former jails converted to new use with Minnesota practicality. A little to the west is Rochester, home to the Mayo Clinic, founded in 1863 when English-born physician William Mayo set up a practice to examine inductees into the Union Army. Rochester, with more than 31,000 employed at Mayo, is prosperous and was the fastest-growing of Minnesota's metropolitan areas in 2010. It made news for something other than Mayo in August 2010, when two women were arrested there and charged with raising money for Al-Shabaab, an Islamist terrorist group in Somalia.

Austin, a county away, is the headquarters of the Hormel meatpacking firm, which was the site of a bitter strike in the 1980s. The huge plant produces "miracle meat" Spam, Hormel chili, Dinty Moore stew and, say critics, too much ammonia-loaded waste. This is one place where class-conscious politics survives, with some tensions over the recent influx of Hispanic workers. The farther west you go, the more frequently you find communities with a German heritage, like New Ulm, where the "Hermann the German" monument guards the town. Farther south is dairy country, with a sprinkling of small industries. In tiny Ormsby, North County Seed breeds soybeans to match the wishes of its international customers.

The 1st Congressional District of Minnesota includes the state's two southern tiers of counties, running along Interstate 90 just north of the Iowa border. It stretches 280 miles from the South Dakota border at Sioux Falls to the Wisconsin border at LaCrosse. Historically, this was a political borderland, with Civil War Republicans in the east and Farmer-Laborites more common in the west. Rochester had long been a Republican stronghold, though like many communities with large numbers of professionals, it has been trending toward the Democrats. In the 2010 governor's race, Republican Tom Emmer won Olmsted County, which includes Rochester, 46%-38% over Democrat Mark Dayton. With its working-class tradition, Austin has long been solidly Democratic-Farmer-Labor. To the west, the population-losing farm counties between Mankato and the South Dakota border continue to vote solidly Republican. The district swung to Democratic presidential nominee Barack Obama in 2008, 51%-47%.

Tim Walz (D)

The congressman from the 1st District is Tim Walz, a Democrat first elected in 2006. Walz grew up in Nebraska and joined the Army National Guard when he was 17. When he retired from the military 24 years later, in 2005, he held the rank of command sergeant major. Walz earned his teaching degree in Nebraska, taught school in China for a year through a Harvard University program, and later established an educational travel company that helped high school students study in China. He and his wife moved to Minnesota in 1996 to take teaching jobs in Mankato. There, he taught high school geography and coached the high school football team to two state championships.

Walz got into politics relatively late in life—he was 42 when he ran for Congress. In 2004, President George W. Bush made an appearance in the area as part of his re-election campaign. Walz took two students to the event, where campaign staffers demanded to know whether he supported the president and barred the students from entering after discovering one had a sticker for Democratic candidate John Kerry on his wallet. Walz suggested that it might be bad PR for the Bush campaign to arrest an Army veteran, and he and the students were allowed in. Walz said the experience sparked his interest in politics, first as a volunteer for the Kerry campaign and then as a congressional candidate. "I don't know if I'd necessarily call it an epiphany, but it was definitely one of those things that pushed me into" politics, Walz said.

In 2006, Walz challenged six-term Republican Rep. Gil Gutknecht, an affable conservative who won re-election two years earlier with 60%. The district had sent Republicans to Washington for 100 of the previous 114 years, and Gutknecht was not considered especially vulnerable. Walz was not a polished campaigner. His speaking style was didactic compared to the ease with which Gutknecht, a former auctioneer, handled a crowd. But he struck a chord with his message of declining middle-class wages, tax cuts for the wealthy and Congress' failure to hold Bush accountable on the Iraq war. He ran as a political outsider and painted Gutknecht as too closely tied to Bush.

By October, Republicans began to take the threat against Gutknecht seriously. The incumbent sought to halt his slide by characterizing Walz as a liberal who was out of sync with this socially conservative district. Walz's support for abortion rights and his opposition to a constitutional amendment against same-sex marriage fell outside district norms, but his military experience and football coaching gave an aura of authenticity to his campaign that made him harder to attack. On Election Day, Walz defeated Gutknecht 53%-47%. Walz carried Democratic areas around Mankato and Austin and won Rochester's Olmsted County by more than 1,800 votes (52%-48%). He became the highest-ranking enlisted soldier ever to serve in Congress.

Arriving in the House, Walz was chosen by his peers to share the freshman class presidency with Rep. Paul Hodes, a New Hampshire Democrat. Walz established a mostly centrist voting record. He signed as a co-sponsor of antiwar Massachusetts Rep. Jim McGovern's 2009 bill calling for Obama to devise an "exit strategy" for removing troops from Afghanistan. He opposed the creation of the Troubled Assets Relief Program to assist the financial services industry because he said it didn't do enough to protect homeowners from foreclosure. His championing of gun owners' rights earned him the National Rifle Association's endorsement in 2010. But he backed most of President Obama's major initiatives, including health care reform and the cap-and-trade bill to reduce carbon emissions thought responsible for global warming.

With a seat on the Agriculture Committee, Walz secured increased access to credit and conservation opportunities for farmers in the 2008 farm bill. His district had been among the leading recipients of federal largesse through the farm program. On another local issue, Walz lobbied to have a high-speed train route from the Twin Cities to Chicago go through Rochester. He also got a bill through the House in September 2010 broadening the definition of a veteran to include those serving at least 20 years in the National Guard or Reserve but who did not spend at least 180 consecutive days called up on federal status.

Walz was initially a top target for Republicans in the 2008 election. But the party's preferred contenders decided not to run. National Republicans turned their focus to keeping their existing seats. Walz breezed to a 63%-33% victory, winning all of the counties. Two years later, he faced a much tougher race. His Republican opponent was state Rep. Randy Demmer, a Republican farmer who slammed Walz's support of the Democratic agenda and drew financial help from outside Republican groups. But Walz enjoyed a huge financial advantage, thanks in part to money raised from Mayo Clinic employees. He also highlighted a video of his opponent seeming receptive to the idea of partially privatizing Social Security. Demmer denied the charge, but had trouble persuading voters that Walz was too liberal. Walz won 49%-44%, with two other candidates drawing the remaining votes.

SECOND DISTRICT

John Kline (R)

Elected 2002, 5th term; b. Sept. 6, 1947, Allentown, PA; home, Lakeville; Rice U., B.A. 1969, Shippensburg U., M.P.A. 1988; Christian; married (Vicky); 2 children.

Military Career: Marine Corps, 1969-94 (Vietnam).

Professional Career: V.P., Cntr. of the American Experiment, 2001-02.

DC Office: 2439 RHOB, 20515, 202-225-2271; Fax: 202-225-2595; Web site: kline.house.gov.

State Offices: Burnsville, 952-808-1213.

Committees: *Armed Services:* Emerging Threats & Capabilities. *Education & the Workforce* (Chmn): Early Childhood, Elementary & Secondary Education; Higher Education & Workforce Training; Workforce Protections.

Group Ratings

	ACLU	ACU	ADA	CFG	AFS	FRC	LCV	ITIC	NTU	COC
2010	13	96	0	100	0	100	20	33	88	88
2009	–	100	5	92	0	–	0	–	89	80

National Journal Ratings

	2010 LIB	—	2010 CONS	2009 LIB	—	2009 CONS
Economic	21%	—	79%	12%	—	88%
Social	18%	—	77%	7%	—	90%
Foreign	26%	—	72%	0%	—	75%
Composite	23%	—	77%	11%	—	89%

Key Votes of the 111th Congress

1. Overturn Ledbetter	N	5. Bar federal abortion funds	Y	9. Stop detainee transfers	Y
2. Pass $820 billion stimulus	N	6. Pass health care bill	N	10. Legalize immigrants' kids	N
3. Let guns in national parks	Y	7. Regulate financial firms	N	11. Repeal don't ask, tell	N
4. Pass cap-and-trade	N	8. Pass tax cuts for some	N	12. Limit campaign funds	N

Election Results

2010 general	John Kline (R)	181,341	(63%)	($1,552,172)
	Shelley Madore (DFL)	104,809	(37%)	($88,818)
2010 primary	John Kline (R)	unopposed		

Prior Winning Percentages: 2008 (57%), 2006 (56%), 2004 (56%), 2002 (53%)

Population		Race/Ethnicity		Work	
Pop. 2010:	732,515	White:	85.5%	Private:	83.9%
Change since 2000:	Up 19.1%	Black:	3.2%	Government:	11.1%
Urban:	80.1%	Hispanic:	4.8%	Self-employed:	4.9%
Rural:	19.9%	Asian:	4.0%	Blue collar:	19.6%
Area size:	3,153 sq. mi.	Native Am.:	0.4%	White collar:	65.5%
		Hawaiian:	0.0%	Khaki collar:	0.1%
Age		Two+ races:	1.8%	Other:	14.8%
Median age:	35.7 yrs.				
More than 65 yrs:	8.7%	*Ancestry*		Median income:	$72,902
Less than 18 yrs:	27.2%	German	29.1%	Median Home Value:	$247,200
		Norwegian	11.2%		
Education		Irish	9.8%	**Military Veterans**	
H.S. grad:	93.8%			% of Pop:	9.5%
College grad:	35.6%				
Grad degree:	10.2%				

Twin Cities Suburbs; Eagan

Drive south from the Twin Cities and one encounters big-box-store parking lots and new housing developments inhabited by youngish families working in managerial, business and technical careers. Many come from elsewhere, attracted by Minnesota's strong economy and pleasant living, and tolerant of its cold winters. They have turned places such as Eagan, Lakeville, Apple Valley, Mendota Heights and Burnsville in Dakota County into fast-growing "mall"

2008 Presidential Vote		
John McCain (R)	198,960	(50%)
Barack Obama (D)	193,213	(48%)
2004 Presidential Vote		
George Bush (R)	203,538	(54%)
John Kerry (D)	169,704	(45%)
Cook Partisan Voting Index: R+4		

suburbs. Unemployment here is relatively low, but the local economy was dealt a blow in November 2010 when Lockheed Martin announced plans to close its Eagan plant by 2013, eliminating or moving 1,000 jobs. More upscale are the suburbs of Scott and Carver counties; Scott County grew by an impressive 45% from 2000 to 2010. In recent years, these suburban areas have begun to see an influx of lower-income residents, attracted by the same good schools and low crime rates that attracted the earlier population. Drive farther south on Interstate 35—a little farther every year—and suddenly one is in farm country. There are also modest-sized towns such as Northfield, the idyllic home of Carleton College and its late professor-turned-liberal senator, Paul Wellstone. Northfield is 40 miles from Minneapolis and St. Paul, and some people there commute to the Twin Cities core on I-35.

These 'burbs and hamlets make up the 2nd Congressional District of Minnesota. Dakota County, just south of St. Paul, casts nearly half the votes in the district and historically was marginally Democratic, while the other counties were fairly heavily Republican. As the suburbs have continued growing, Ventura country has become more Republican. George W. Bush narrowly carried Dakota County in 2000 and 2004. In the 2010 governor's race, Republican Tom Emmer carried it 47%-39% over Democrat and eventual winner Mark Dayton. But in 2006, Democrat Amy Klobuchar showed that Democrats can still compete in Dakota County, capturing 56% there. The only remaining Democratic-Farmer-Labor strongholds here are Rice County, home of Northfield, and Washington County. Republican presidential candidate John McCain won the district overall, 49.8%-48.3%.

John Kline (R)

The congressman from the 2nd District is John Kline, a Republican first elected in 2002. A no-nonsense conservative ally of House Speaker John Boehner, Kline has risen in a relatively short time to chair the House Education and the Workforce Committee (formerly Education and Labor), a panel that Boehner himself once headed.

Kline grew up in Corpus Christi, Texas, where his father owned a small hometown newspaper and his mother managed the Corpus Christi Symphony Orchestra for more than 40 years. After graduating from Rice University, he served for 25 years in the Marine Corps. During the Vietnam War, he commanded Marine aviation forces in Somalia, where his duties included responsibility for the Corps' $50 billion program-objective memorandum, a budget and planning analysis. Later, he was assigned to the White House and carried the so-called "football"—the package containing the nuclear launch codes—for presidents Jimmy Carter and Ronald Reagan; he surely has had more face time with presidents than most other members of Congress. When he retired in 1994, he settled in Lakeville, in Dakota County, where he managed his wife's family farm.

In 1998, Kline challenged Democratic Rep. Bill Luther in the old Minnesota 6th District, after Luther had had several expensive and fierce campaigns to keep the seat. Kline favored tax cuts, more military spending and the resignation of President Bill Clinton in that year's impeachment proceedings. He also opposed abortion rights. He spent only $283,000; Luther, who raised $1 million, spent only $412,000. That might have been a mistake. Luther won by only 50%-46%. Kline hardly stopped running. More experienced and better financed in 2000, he made his rematch with Luther one of the nation's high-profile House contests. The result was closer across the board, but Luther survived 50%-48%, and Kline said he was unlikely to run again.

Then the unexpected happened. The redistricting plan ordered into effect by the state Supreme Court in March 2002 placed Kline's home in a new 2nd District that included the home of no incumbent. State GOP leaders urged Kline to run again. But Luther's home was in his old 6th District, which was considerably more Republican after the redistricting. He decided to take on Kline in the 2nd District. The acrimonious campaign resumed where it had left off in 2000. Luther called Kline an extremist who held "Texas values." Luther's campaign manager encouraged Sam Garst, a Sierra Club activist and Luther supporter, to enter the race as a candidate of a new "No New Taxes" party—a purposefully deceptive banner designed to siphon votes from the Republican. At first, the Luther campaign denied all connection with Garst, but Luther had to admit he did not discourage the action, and the local media harshly criticized the scheme as "un-Minnesotan." It turned out to be no contest. Kline won 53%-42%.

In the House, Kline's voting record has put him among the chamber's most conservative members. He proposed legislation to replace Ulysses S. Grant with former President Ronald Reagan on the $50 bill. He later became a trusted deputy of Boehner and was given responsibilities at the National Republican Congressional Committee, the campaign arm of House Republicans.

On the Armed Services Committee, Kline made frequent trips to Iraq and expressed "grave concerns" about the Obama administration's proposals in early 2011 to cut tens of thousands of troops' positions from the budget once the U.S. presence in Iraq and Afghanistan was reduced. On Education and Labor, Kline was a conferee on pension legislation signed into law in 2006. He worked to include relief for struggling airlines, including Minnesota-based Northwest Airlines, by giving them more time to make contributions to employee pensions. The House also passed a Kline bill that would require states to prevent schools from forcing parents to medicate children with behavioral problems.

In 2009, when the ranking Republican slot on Education and Labor came open, House Republicans wanted a tough counterweight to liberal panel Chairman George Miller of California. Kline leapfrogged over several more senior Republicans while also fending off a challenge from the more junior Cathy McMorris Rodgers, another Boehner loyalist.

As it became clearer that Republicans would reclaim the House majority in 2010, Kline was equally tough on conservatives who were campaigning on a pledge to abolish the Education Department as a way to save money. "That's simply not going to get done," he said. However, he did promise to seek to eliminate or consolidate up to 60 of the agency's programs that he said were ineffective. And he said he would seek to increase funding for others, including special education. For all of his conservatism, he forged a good working relationship with Education Secretary Arne Duncan, and both expressed hope that a deal could be struck on revamping the Bush-era No Child Left Behind education law. Both shared an interest in promoting more parental choice and more charter schools.

In 2006, Democrats appeared to have found a strong candidate in Colleen Rowley, a retired Federal Bureau of Investigation agent who was one of *Time* magazine's three "Persons of the Year" in 2002 for going public with the FBI's decision to ignore recommendations to investigate Zacarias Moussaoui, a figure in the September 11 attacks. But as a first-time candidate, Rowley struggled to find her footing, and the party lost interest in her campaign. While other Republicans distanced themselves from Bush and the Iraq war, Kline was forthright about his support for the war, emphasizing his background as a former Marine and as the father of a young Army Blackhawk helicopter pilot (son John Daniel Kline) who did a tour of duty in Iraq. Kline won re-election 56%-40% over Rowley. In 2008 and 2010, he won re-election easily.

THIRD DISTRICT

Erik Paulsen (R)

Elected 2008, 2nd term; b. May 14, 1965, Bakersfield, CA; home, Eden Prairie; Olaf Col., B.A. 1987; Lutheran; married (Kelly); 4 children.

Elected Office: MN House, 1995-2008, Majority ldr., 2002-06.

Professional Career: Marketing analyst, Target Corp.

DC Office: 127 CHOB, 20515, 202-225-2871; Fax: 202-225-6351; Web site: paulsen.house.gov.

State Offices: Eden Prairie, 952-405-8501.

Committees: *Ways & Means:* Human Resources; Select Revenue Measures; Social Security.

Group Ratings

	ACLU	*ACU*	*ADA*	*CFG*	*AFS*	*FRC*	*LCV*	*ITIC*	*NTU*	*COC*
2010	6	92	0	92	0	93	40	33	89	88
2009	–	88	10	72	22	–	21	–	76	87

National Journal Ratings

	2010 LIB	—	*2010 CONS*		*2009 LIB*	—	*2009 CONS*
Economic	30%	—	69%		29%	—	70%
Social	31%	—	67%		33%	—	65%
Foreign	29%	—	68%		26%	—	68%
Composite	31%	—	69%		31%	—	69%

Key Votes of the 111th Congress

1. Overturn Ledbetter	N	5. Bar federal abortion funds	Y	9. Stop detainee transfers	Y
2. Pass $820 billion stimulus	N	6. Pass health care bill	N	10. Legalize immigrants' kids	N
3. Let guns in national parks	Y	7. Regulate financial firms	N	11. Repeal don't ask, tell	N
4. Pass cap-and-trade	N	8. Pass tax cuts for some	N	12. Limit campaign funds	N

Election Results

2010 general	Erik Paulsen (R)	161,177	(59%)	($2,688,948)
	Jim Meffert (DFL)	100,240	(37%)	($529,369)
	Jon Oleson (Ind)	12,508	(5%)	($18,866)
2010 primary	Erik Paulsen (R) .... unopposed			

Prior Winning Percentages: 2008 (48%)

Population		**Race/Ethnicity**		**Work**	
Pop. 2010:	650,185	White:	78.8%	Private:	85.6%
Change since 2000:	Up 5.7%	Black:	7.7%	Government:	9.0%
Urban:	95.8%	Hispanic:	4.0%	Self-employed:	5.3%
Rural:	4.2%	Asian:	6.7%	Blue collar:	14.9%
Area size:	513 sq. mi.	Native Am.:	0.3%	White collar:	72.3%
		Hawaiian:	0.0%	Khaki collar:	0.0%
Age		Two+ races:	2.2%	Other:	12.7%
Median age:	38.4 yrs.				
More than 65 yrs:	11.6%	*Ancestry*		Median income:	$74,664
Less than 18 yrs:	25.3%	German	23.1%	Median Home Value:	$270,700
		Norwegian	11.0%		
Education		Irish	8.4%	**Military Veterans**	
H.S. grad:	94.3%			% of Pop:	8.9%
College grad:	43.2%				
Grad degree:	13.5%				

Twin Cities Suburbs; Bloomington

Over the past half century, Minnesota's twin metropolis has spread out from the neat streets inside the city limits of Minneapolis and St. Paul into the countryside all around. People have sorted themselves out geographically. In the lower lands along the Mississippi and Minnesota rivers, where rail lines fan out from the Twin Cities, are the blue-collar suburbs, with modest houses on grid streets and warehouses and factories near the tracks. Inland, around the

2008 Presidential Vote		
Barack Obama (D)	200,240	(52%)
John McCain (R)	175,728	(46%)
2004 Presidential Vote		
George Bush (R)	190,339	(51%)
John Kerry (D)	179,488	(48%)
Cook Partisan Voting Index: EVEN		

lakes Minnesota is so proud of, in subdivisions with curved streets hugging the hills, are more affluent neighborhoods, quiet and unflashy in the Minnesota way, but comfortable whether blanketed with snow or with a nearby lake glinting in the summer sun. At the edge of Lake Minnetonka is Wayzata, the monied suburb that is the top ZIP code in Minnesota for political donations. In between are the freeway interchanges where some of the Twin Cities' great innovations can be seen—Southdale Shopping Center in Edina, the first enclosed mall; huge indoor water parks; and the giant Mall of America, with its 4.2 million square feet, 520-plus stores, 86 eating options, 14 theaters, eight nightclubs and 11,000 year-round employees. In the works is a 500-room Radisson hotel. The mall attracts 40 million people annually. To the west is Eden Prairie, which *Money* magazine in 2010 named the best medium-sized U.S. city to live in.

The 3rd Congressional District of Minnesota takes in Hennepin County suburbs north, south and west of Minneapolis. On the north side of the district is working-class Brooklyn Park, long a Democratic-Farmer-Labor Party stronghold but more famous now for its former mayor, Jesse Ventura, the celebrity wrestler-turned-governor. On the south is middle-income Bloomington, home of the Mall of America. To the west are Edina, Plymouth, Wayzata and other towns around Lake Minnetonka, all traditionally Republican. It is the district's largest lake, and these are the most affluent communities in the Twin Cities area. The district is home to the headquarters of such diverse companies as Cargill and Radisson Hotels, and has large biotech facilities in Brooklyn Park and Maple Grove. This area trended Democratic in the 1990s, when Bill Clinton twice won pluralities here. The 3rd may be the home of Minnesota's traditional Republican establishment, but it voted just 51% for George W. Bush in 2004. In 2008, it flipped to the Democrats, voting for Barack Obama 52%-46%.

Erik Paulsen (R)

The congressman from the 3rd District is Erik Paulsen, a Republican first elected in 2008 to succeed his retiring former boss, Republican Rep. Jim Ramstad. Raised in the Twin City suburbs, Paulsen was the oldest of four children. He attended nearby St. Olaf College, where he met his wife, Kelly, in a math class. After graduation, Paulsen followed a lifelong dream to work a summer in Yellowstone National Park, and then returned to the Twin Cities to begin a career in marketing. He later took a job in Ramstad's Washington office, where he worked for a year and a half before returning to Minnesota as the director of Ramstad's district office. In 1995, he was elected to the Minnesota House of Representatives, rising to majority leader in 2003. He was a leading supporter of Republican Gov. Tim Pawlenty's no-new-taxes policy. While in the legislature, Paulsen also worked as a business analyst for the Minneapolis-based Target Corp.

Paulsen announced his candidacy for Ramstad's seat in January 2008. He faced no competition for the nomination and got an early fundraising lead. Democratic newcomer Ashwin Madia, an Iraq war veteran, was his opponent in the general election. Madia had upset better-known state Sen. Terri Bonoff to secure the Democratic-Farmer-Labor Party nomination, and he soon pulled even with Paulsen in the polls, making it a very competitive contest. At the Republican National Convention in September in Minneapolis-St. Paul, Paulsen was given a speaking role to help raise his profile. In his remarks, he emphasized fiscal discipline and called himself "one of a new generation of Republican reformers." On the stump, he emphasized his differences with Madia on taxes, contrasting his support for making the Bush-era tax cuts permanent with Madia's position allowing them to expire for people with annual incomes over $250,000.

The campaign turned highly negative. The Democrats ran ads that attempted to link Paulsen to a Republican fundraiser at a Las Vegas strip club. Paulsen parried with ads accusing Madia of lying about his voting record and suggesting he would raise taxes. Republicans ran an ad in the final days of the campaign that the Madia camp said deliberately depicted Madia's skin tone as darker than it is. Madia is of Indian descent. The two candidates were neck and neck in fundraising, each raising $2.7 million. A third candidate, businessman David Dillon, ran as an independent.

The race was tight, but Paulsen emerged the winner, with 48% to Madia's 41%. Dillon picked up a respectable 11%, drawing support in areas where Madia should have been strong. Even as Obama won the district that fall by 6 percentage points, Paulsen got strong support in Bloomington and Coon Rapids to ward off the national Democratic wave.

Paulsen was appointed to the House Financial Services Committee, where he established himself as a serious-minded, business-friendly Republican who, unlike his 6th District colleague Michele Bachmann, avoided partisan rhetoric. He tried without success in November 2009 to get the committee to strip the Treasury Department of the power to extend the Wall Street bailout program for another year. He got an amendment added to a small-business financing bill that passed the House in October 2009 to help medical technology startup companies, which he said face steep initial costs. He showed some independence by joining with Democrats on expanding the State Children's Health Insurance Program, a credit card overhaul bill and a measure giving the Food and Drug Administration oversight over tobacco products. He also backed a measure adding sexual orientation and gender identity to the federal government's hate crimes statutes.

But Paulsen was loyal enough to his party to snag a prized seat on the Ways and Means Committee in 2011. He quickly introduced a bill to repeal the medical device tax that was passed as part of the 2010 health care overhaul. A devout free trade enthusiast, he co-chairs an informal GOP working group on trade with Korea.

Heading into the 2010 election, Paulsen leveraged his numerous business connections to raise more than $2.6 million, with his former employer Target leading the way in donations. He easily beat Democrat Jim Meffert with 59% of the vote.

FOURTH DISTRICT

Betty McCollum (D)

Elected 2000, 6th term; b. July 12, 1954, Minneapolis; home, St. Paul; Inver Hills Comm. Col., A.A. 1980, Col. of St. Catherine, B.A. 1987; Catholic; divorced; 2 children.

Elected Office: N. St. Paul City Cncl., 1986-92; MN House of Reps., 1992-2000.

Professional Career: Teacher; Retail sales & management.

DC Office: 1714 LHOB, 20515, 202-225-6631; Fax: 202-225-1968; Web site: mccollum.house.gov.

State Offices: St. Paul, 651-224-9191.

Committees: *Appropriations:* Interior, Environment & Related Agencies; Military Construction, Veterans Affairs & Related Agencies. *Budget.*

Group Ratings

	ACLU	ACU	ADA	CFG	AFS	FRC	LCV	ITIC	NTU	COC
2010	94	0	100	0	100	0	100	67	6	13
2009	–	0	100	2	100	–	100	–	3	33

National Journal Ratings

	2010 LIB	—	2010 CONS		2009 LIB	—	2009 CONS
Economic	72%	—	27%		81%	—	18%
Social	89%	—	7%		89%	—	0%
Foreign	84%	—	11%		91%	—	0%
Composite	83%	—	17%		91%	—	10%

Key Votes of the 111th Congress

1. Overturn Ledbetter	Y	5. Bar federal abortion funds	N	9. Stop detainee transfers	N
2. Pass $820 billion stimulus	Y	6. Pass health care bill	Y	10. Legalize immigrants' kids	Y
3. Let guns in national parks	N	7. Regulate financial firms	Y	11. Repeal don't ask, tell	Y
4. Pass cap-and-trade	Y	8. Pass tax cuts for some	Y	12. Limit campaign funds	Y

Election Results

2010 general	Betty McCollum (DFL)	136,746	(59%)	($844,301)
	Teresa Collett (R)	80,141	(35%)	($216,532)
	Steve Carlson (Ind)	14,207	(6%)	
2010 primary	Betty McCollum (DFL)	55,491	(87%)	
	Diana Longrie (DFL)	8,622	(13%)	

Prior Winning Percentages: 2008 (68%), 2006 (70%), 2004 (57%), 2002 (62%), 2000 (48%)

Population		Race/Ethnicity		Work	
Pop. 2010:	614,624	White:	69.1%	Private:	81.5%
Change since 2000:	Down 0.1%	Black:	9.7%	Government:	13.8%
Urban:	99.9%	Hispanic:	7.6%	Self-employed:	4.6%
Rural:	0.1%	Asian:	10.2%	Blue collar:	17.0%
Area size:	220 sq. mi.	Native Am.:	0.6%	White collar:	66.6%
		Hawaiian:	0.0%	Khaki collar:	0.1%
Age		Two+ races:	2.6%	Other:	16.3%
Median age:	35.7 yrs.				
More than 65 yrs:	12.8%	*Ancestry*		Median income:	$52,917
Less than 18 yrs:	23.3%	German	22.5%	Median Home Value:	$226,000
		Irish	10.2%		
Education		Norwegian	8.2%	**Military Veterans**	
H.S. grad:	90.5%			% of Pop:	9.0%
College grad:	37.4%				
Grad degree:	14.1%				

St. Paul, Suburbs

Above the Mississippi River bluffs stand the two landmarks of St. Paul: the Minnesota Capitol and Archbishop Ireland's Cathedral. This is the older and smaller of the Twin Cities, settled mainly by Catholic Irish and German immigrants in the 1850s, while Minneapolis was attracting Protestant Swedes and Yankees. St. Paul became a major transportation hub, a railroad center and river port, while Minneapolis,

2008 Presidential Vote		
Barack Obama (D)	217,984	(64%)
John McCain (R)	113,600	(34%)
2004 Presidential Vote		
John Kerry (D)	205,467	(62%)
George Bush (R)	123,313	(37%)
Cook Partisan Voting Index: D+13		

farther upriver at the Falls of St. Anthony, became the nation's largest grain milling center. Both industries stoked the ire of farmers in the Dakotas who had no choice but to deal with them to make a living. Beneath the Capitol and the cathedral, the city's skywalk-linked downtown is home to the Ordway Music Theater, the headquarters of Minnesota Public Radio and an active pop music industry.

Beyond the cathedral is Summit Avenue, on which capitalists like the Great Northern Railway's James J. Hill built grandiose Romanesque houses. With Monument Avenue in Richmond and Meridian Street in Indianapolis, it remains one of America's grand 19th century residential boulevards. The parallel Grand Avenue is home to a pleasant commercial strip with a walkable, urban feel; more modest neighborhoods elsewhere are notable for their grid streets lined with sturdy houses. In recent years, St. Paul has had a mixed bag of results in economic development. It scored a major coup by landing the 2008 Republican National Convention at its state-of-the-art Xcel Energy Center. But its fading industrial base took a blow when Ford Motor Co. announced that it would close its local light-truck plant in 2011, at a cost of nearly 1,000 jobs. St. Paul will get a boost with the long-awaited Central Corridor light-rail project linking the city with Minneapolis. Work on the project got under way in 2010.

Minnesota's 4th Congressional District is made up of St. Paul, the Ramsey County suburbs to the north, and the southern suburbs of West St. Paul and South St. Paul. Even before the Democratic-Farmer-Labor Party was formed in 1944, St. Paul was one of the most Democratic parts of Minnesota and it remained proudly DFL for a half-century. It voted to re-elect Mayor Norm Coleman in 1997 after he switched to the Republican Party, but he failed to carry a single precinct in the city when he ran successfully for the Senate in 2002, and he lost Ramsey County 60% to 40% in his 2008 re-election bid. In the 2010 governor's race, Democrat Mark Dayton beat Republican Tom Emmer here 55%-32%. The area has become home to more than 24,000 Hmong immigrants, the largest concentration in any American city. A spacious new indoor marketplace on St. Paul's east side called Hmong Village caters to their shopping preferences. The Hmong had been recruited by the Central Intelligence Agency and U.S. Special Forces during the Vietnam War and resettled here after Laos fell to the Communists in 1975. Another 5,000 refugees arrived from Thailand in 2004 and 2005.

Betty McCollum (D)

The congresswoman from the 4th District is Betty McCollum, a Democrat first elected in 2000. The daughter of a military intelligence officer, she grew up in North St. Paul and graduated from the College of St. Catherine. For 11 years, she taught high school social studies and then was a retail sales manager for 14 years at Dayton's department store. She was also raising two children. After one of them was hurt on a slide in a city park, McCollum tried without success to get the city of North St. Paul to make immediate repairs. So in 1986, she ran for the North St. Paul City Council and was elected. She served until 1992, when she was elected to the state House of Representatives after defeating incumbents in both the primary and general elections.

In February 2000, Democratic Rep. Bruce Vento announced that he had malignant mesothelioma and would not seek re-election. He died on October 10, 2000. McCollum was endorsed by the Democratic-Farmer-Labor Party in the September primary. She faced three opponents, but with the DFL's endorsement, McCollum won easily, with 50% to 23% for state Sen. Steve Novak. Republicans nominated state Sen. Linda Runbeck, a vigorously anti-abortion candidate. McCollum backed prescription drug coverage under Medicare and opposed tax cuts before Congress paid down the debt. Runbeck, who opposed gun control and took conservative positions on health care and education, attacked McCollum and her Democratic allies for running "hateful, vicious attack ads" that distorted her positions on guns. This was a three-way race, thanks to the candidacy of former Ramsey County prosecutor Tom Foley, a longtime DFLer who ran on the ticket of Gov. Jesse Ventura's Independence Party. Once again, McCollum won unexpectedly easily, 48%-31%, with 21% for Foley.

In the House, McCollum has a consistently liberal voting record. She is an ally of Minority Leader Nancy Pelosi, whom she calls a mentor, and delivered the speech formally nominating Pelosi as party whip in October 2001. With Pelosi's help, McCollum has secured some plums, including a seat on the House Democratic Steering and Policy Committee and in 2006, the Appropriations Committee seat that had been held by former Rep. Martin Sabo, a Minnesota Democrat. In the 111th Congress (2009-10), McCollum was given a seat on the Budget Committee.

Recently McCollum has taken an interest in the role that charities play in the U.S. economy and has sought to help political and nonprofit leaders better coordinate. She introduced a bill in 2010 to set up a national nonprofit council to delve into the issue, which attracted bipartisan support, but did not move. She also has led efforts to change lawmakers' thinking about the World Bank, and founded a caucus advocating more dialogue with the global financier. She has noted that Congress and the bank are involved in many of the same overseas efforts, including fighting poverty and AIDS. Earlier, McCollum worked on the Bush administration's No Child Left Behind education bill as a member of the Education and Labor panel and backed the House version of the bill. Later, she joined the opposing camp because she said the administration had not put sufficient money into the program to make it work. She also sponsored legislation that would crack down on diploma mills that sell worthless degrees. On the Foreign Affairs Committee, McCollum was a vocal critic of the war in Iraq.

An important local project for McCollum has been the Central Corridor, an 11-mile, light-rail link between downtown St. Paul and Minneapolis. She had secured an initial $2 million for the project and was incensed when conservative Republicans targeted proposed additional funding as pork barrel spending. She and Republican Gov. Tim Pawlenty clashed over her insistence that he sign a statement supporting congressional funding for the project. When Pawlenty vetoed a companion state funding plan in 2008, the project seemed dead; McCollum helped to keep it alive, securing $20 million in the omnibus fiscal 2010 spending bill to cover the final design work. She said Republicans' effort to ban earmarks could endanger the project's future.

McCollum has been re-elected easily. She is sometimes mentioned as a possible statewide candidate but has declined opportunities to run.

In 2008, McCollum voiced unusually tough criticism of Democrat Al Franken in his campaign to unseat Republican Sen. Coleman. She called some of the comedian's written work, which had appeared in *Playboy* and other publications, "pornographic writings that are indefensible." Then in August, McCollum, reverting to form as a party loyalist, endorsed Franken and said she would vote for him.

FIFTH DISTRICT

Keith Ellison (D)

Elected 2006, 3rd term; b. Aug. 4, 1963, Detroit, MI; home, Minneapolis; Wayne St. U., B.A. 1985, U. of MN, J.D. 1990; Muslim; married (Kim); 4 children.

Elected Office: MN House of Reps., 2002-06.

Professional Career: Practicing atty., 1990-2002.

DC Office: 1027 LHOB, 20515, 202-225-4755; Fax: 202-225-4886; Web site: ellison.house.gov.

State Offices: Minneapolis, 612-522-1212.

Committees: *Financial Services:* Capital Markets and Government Sponsored Enterprises; Oversight & Investigations.

Group Ratings

	ACLU	ACU	ADA	CFG	AFS	FRC	LCV	ITIC	NTU	COC
2010	94	0	100	0	100	6	90	67	6	13
2009	–	0	95	0	100	–	93	–	4	40

National Journal Ratings

	2010 LIB — 2010 CONS		2009 LIB — 2009 CONS	
Economic	90%	— 0%	91%	— 0%
Social	93%	— 0%	89%	— 0%
Foreign	84%	— 11%	69%	— 31%
Composite	93%	— 7%	86%	— 14%

Key Votes of the 111th Congress

1. Overturn Ledbetter	Y	5. Bar federal abortion funds	N	9. Stop detainee transfers	N
2. Pass $820 billion stimulus	Y	6. Pass health care bill	Y	10. Legalize immigrants' kids	Y
3. Let guns in national parks	N	7. Regulate financial firms	Y	11. Repeal don't ask, tell	Y
4. Pass cap-and-trade	Y	8. Pass tax cuts for some	Y	12. Limit campaign funds	Y

Election Results

2010 general	Keith Ellison (DFL)	154,833	(68%)	($1,397,497)
	Joel Demos (R)	55,222	(24%)	($95,235)
	Lynne Torgerson (I)	8,548	(4%)	($60,717)
	Tom Schrunk (Ind)	7,446	(3%)	
2010 primary	Keith Ellison (DFL)	55,424	(82%)	
	Barb White (DFL)	7,963	(12%)	
	Gregg Iverson (DFL)	4,575	(7%)	

Prior Winning Percentages: 2008 (71%), 2006 (56%)

Population		Race/Ethnicity		Work	
Pop. 2010:	616,482	White:	65.3%	Private:	83.1%
Change since 2000:	Up 0.3%	Black:	15.2%	Government:	11.6%
Urban:	100.0%	Hispanic:	9.5%	Self-employed:	5.2%
Rural:	0.0%	Asian:	5.3%	Blue collar:	15.2%
Area size:	130 sq. mi.	Native Am.:	1.3%	White collar:	67.7%
		Hawaiian:	0.0%	Khaki collar:	0.0%
Age		Two+ races:	3.2%	Other:	17.0%
Median age:	33.9 yrs.				
More than 65 yrs:	10.8%	*Ancestry*		Median income:	$49,842
Less than 18 yrs:	20.1%	German	19.4%	Median Home Value:	$226,600
		Norwegian	8.9%		
Education		Irish	8.4%	**Military Veterans**	
H.S. grad:	89.2%			% of Pop:	7.6%
College grad:	41.5%				
Grad degree:	14.5%				

Minneapolis, Suburbs

From almost nowhere in Minneapolis today can you see the geographic feature that created the city: the Falls of St. Anthony, the head of navigation on the Mississippi River, where waters rush in rapids beneath low downtown bridges. In olden days, every riverboat had to stop here, and the waterpower generated by the falls was the energy source first for the pioneers' grist mills and then for the giant grain mills that processed northern Great Plains wheat into food for the

2008 Presidential Vote		
Barack Obama (D) 254,796	(74%)
John McCain (R) 81,757	(24%)
2004 Presidential Vote		
John Kerry (D) 237,418	(71%)
George Bush (R) 92,797	(28%)
Cook Partisan Voting Index: D+23		

United States. By 1890, Minneapolis and St. Paul made up one of America's largest urban areas, living mainly off grain. Today, Minneapolis is a center of high-technology industry, banking and finance. It is the heart of an economic region that extends almost 1,000 miles to the Rocky Mountains in Montana. It had one of the best-performing economies during the 2007-09 recession— sixth in the United States, according to the Brookings Institution. *Forbes* magazine also ranked it as the nation's third best market for young professionals in June 2010.

The city of Minneapolis, plus a few of its older, adjoining suburbs, make up the 5th Congressional District. In the southwest corner are the affluent neighborhoods around Lake Calhoun and Lake Harriet—long built-up and proudly maintained, amidst trees that turn beautifully golden in early autumn. Not far away are Minneapolis's skywalk-laced downtown skyscrapers, the museum quarter on the hill above Hennepin Avenue, and the Hubert H. Humphrey Metrodome, where the inflatable roof collapsed in December 2010 after a snowstorm, forcing the embarrassing postponement of a Minnesota Vikings game and prompting talk of the need for a new stadium. Straddling the Mississippi River is the University of Minnesota, which has fostered the area's cutting-edge biotechnology research and medical innovations, and nearby Dinkytown, a student area where Robert Zimmerman discovered folk music and reinvented himself as Bob Dylan. Most of the 5th District is low on the income scale. Many of the working-class neighborhoods of small frame houses and ample parks are now kept up by new immigrants.

For a place often thought of as monochromatically white and Scandinavian, the city is surprisingly diverse. To the northeast, behind the railroad and warehouse district along the Mississippi, are many Hmong from Laos. Hennepin County is home to the largest number of African immigrants in the state. The Jewish community here has increased with immigrants from the former Soviet Union. Ticket machines on the new Hiawatha Avenue light-rail line, from downtown to the airport and the Mall of America, do business in four languages—English, Spanish, Hmong and Somali. The 5th is the most heavily Democratic district in the state. Minneapolis's political liberalism is drawn from the Yankee tradition of clean government, the Scandinavian tradition of cooperative enterprise and the industrial-labor tradition of economic redistribution. Democratic presidential candidates Al Gore and John Kerry carried this district by more than 2-to-1 in 2000 and 2004 respectively. Barack Obama did better yet, with 74% to Republican John McCain's 24%. In the 2010 governor's race, Democrat Mark Dayton beat Republican Tom Emmer in Hennepin County 51%-36%.

Keith Ellison (D)

The congressman from the 5th District is Keith Ellison, a Democrat first elected in 2006. Ellison, previously a relatively unknown state legislator, garnered international attention when he became the first Muslim to serve in Congress and the first black representative from Minnesota. Today, he is one of two Muslims in Congress; the other is Democrat Andre Carson of Indiana.

Ellison was raised Catholic in Detroit, the son of a psychiatrist and the third of five boys. (Four became lawyers and the fifth a doctor.) Ellison studied economics at Wayne State University, and it was there that he converted to Sunni Islam. He moved to Minnesota in 1987 to study law at the University of Minnesota, worked in private practice, and ran a nonprofit criminal defense firm while also hosting a public affairs radio show. Ellison won the first of two terms in the state House in 2002.

The retirement of Democratic Rep. Martin Olav Sabo, who had held the seat since 1978, unleashed a torrent of pent-up political ambition. Nearly a dozen Democrats sought the party endorsement at the May 2006 Democratic-Farmer-Labor district convention. But the main contenders were Ellison, former DFL chairman and longtime Sabo aide Mike Erlandson, and former state Sen. Ember Reichgott Junge. Ellison, who strongly opposed the war in Iraq, attracted support from war opponents and key backers of the late Democratic Sen. Paul Wellstone. "I have the passion of a Wellstone and the practicality of a Sabo," he told convention activists. Ellison easily won the DFL endorsement, but Erlandson and Reichgott Junge competed anyway for the Democratic nomination in a seven-way September 12 primary.

Ellison campaigned on his opposition to the war and support for government-funded universal health care. But he had to overcome a number of unhelpful personal revelations: Unpaid parking tickets and moving violations that led to multiple suspensions of his driver's license and $25,000 he once owed in back taxes. Most damaging were his ties to the controversial Nation of Islam leader Louis Farrakhan and Farrakhan's anti-Semitic pronouncements. Ellison said his association with the group was limited to the 18 months he spent helping organize the 1995 Million Man March in Washington, D.C., although his writings about Farrakhan were traced back to his law school days. Ellison reached out to local Jewish leaders, insisting that he'd been unaware of the group's anti-Semitic views. Despite the personal baggage, Ellison won the primary with 41%, followed by Erlandson with 31% and Reichgott Junge with 21%.

Heavily favored in the general election, Ellison faced two third-party candidates and Republican Alan Fine, who described Ellison as "an embarrassment to our district, our state, our country, and our world." But Ellison won with 56% of vote, while Fine and Independence Party candidate Tammy Lee each won 21%. Controversy followed Ellison after the election. A conservative commentator stirred up opposition to Ellison's plan to take the oath of office with the Quran, rather than the Bible. In a politically adept move, Ellison borrowed a Quran from the Library of Congress that was once owned by Thomas Jefferson.

Ellison quickly established a strongly liberal voting record and was elected co-chair of the Congressional Progressive Caucus in 2010. He has continued to be a frequent target for conservatives. Judson Phillips, founder of the Nashville-based Tea Party Nation, called for his defeat in 2010 because of his religious beliefs. Freshman Republican Allen West of Florida in January 2011 called Ellison "the antithesis of the principles upon which this country was established." But Ellison also has won recognition for his legislative work. In *Washingtonian* magazine's anonymous 2010 survey of Capitol Hill staffers, he took third in the "surprise standout" category.

On the Financial Services Committee, Ellison has challenged predatory lending practices and foreclosures by credit card and mortgage companies, which he said "have torn holes in the fabric of neighborhoods" in Minneapolis and elsewhere. In 2007, the House passed the Anti-Predatory Lending Act, which included provisions he helped craft. He also added to the 2009 credit card overhaul bill a provision to stop companies from raising rates on people with unrelated debt problems.

When new Homeland Security Chairman Peter King, R-N.Y., announced plans to explore al-Qaida's attempts to radicalize American Muslims in 2011, Ellison approached King and offered to show that Muslims had thwarted several plots by reporting them to law enforcement officials. In March 2011, he broke into tears as he testified before the King panel, recounting the death of a Muslim-American firefighter on September 11. "The best defense against extreme ideologies is social inclusion and civic engagement," Ellison said. "I fear these hearings may undermine our efforts in this direction."

In January 2009, he was one of 22 House members, all Democrats, who voted "present" on a resolution recognizing Israel's right to defend itself against attacks from Gaza. In December 2008, he became the first member of Congress to make the Hajj pilgrimage to the Muslim holy city of Mecca, later describing it as a "transformative" experience. He has expressed interest in promoting economic ties between his state and Saudi Arabia as a means of creating jobs at home. When President Obama called for a new beginning in relations between the United States and the Muslim world in June 2009, Ellison described it as a positive first step.

In 2008 and 2010, Ellison was re-elected easily.

SIXTH DISTRICT

Michele Bachmann (R)

Elected 2006, 3rd term; b. April 6, 1956, Waterloo, IA; home, Stillwater; Winona State U., B.A. 1978, Oral Roberts U., J.D. 1986, Col. of William and Mary, LL.M. 1988; Lutheran; married (Marcus); 5 children.

Elected Office: MN Senate, 2000-06.

Professional Career: Practicing atty., 1995-2000.

DC Office: 103 CHOB, 20515, 202-225-2331; Fax: 202-225-6475; Web site: bachmann.house.gov.

State Offices: Waite Park, 320-253-5931; Woodbury, 651-731-5400.

Committees: *Financial Services:* International Monetary Policy & Trade; Oversight & Investigations. *Permanent Select Committee on Intelligence:* Oversight; Technical & Tactical Intelligence.

Group Ratings

	ACLU	ACU	ADA	CFG	AFS	FRC	LCV	ITIC	NTU	COC
2010	13	100	5	100	0	100	10	0	87	75
2009	–	100	0	88	0	–	0	–	88	73

National Journal Ratings

	2010 LIB — 2010 CONS	2009 LIB — 2009 CONS
Economic	10% — 90%	7% — 92%
Social	0% — 85%	10% — 89%
Foreign	0% — 88%	0% — 75%
Composite	8% — 92%	10% — 90%

Key Votes of the 111th Congress

1. Overturn Ledbetter	N	5. Bar federal abortion funds	Y	9. Stop detainee transfers	Y
2. Pass $820 billion stimulus	N	6. Pass health care bill	N	10. Legalize immigrants' kids	N
3. Let guns in national parks	*	7. Regulate financial firms	N	11. Repeal don't ask, tell	N
4. Pass cap-and-trade	N	8. Pass tax cuts for some	*	12. Limit campaign funds	N

Election Results

2010 general	Michele Bachmann (R)	159,476	(53%)	($13,567,811)
	Tarryl Clark (DFL)	120,846	(40%)	($4,719,970)
	Bob Anderson (Ind)	17,698	(6%)	($440)
2010 primary	Michele Bachmann (R)	unopposed		

Prior Winning Percentages: 2008 (46%), 2006 (50%)

Population		Race/Ethnicity		Work	
Pop. 2010:	759,478	White:	90.3%	Private:	82.9%
Change since 2000:	Up 23.5%	Black:	2.4%	Government:	11.3%
Urban:	63.8%	Hispanic:	2.4%	Self-employed:	5.6%
Rural:	36.2%	Asian:	2.8%	Blue collar:	23.0%
Area size:	3,237 sq. mi.	Native Am.:	0.4%	White collar:	62.4%
		Hawaiian:	0.0%	Khaki collar:	0.1%
Age		Two+ races:	1.6%	Other:	14.6%
Median age:	35.1 yrs.				
More than 65 yrs:	9.0%	*Ancestry*		Median income:	$68,739
Less than 18 yrs:	26.7%	German	30.9%	Median Home Value:	$234,800
		Norwegian	10.5%		
Education		Irish	8.2%	**Military Veterans**	
H.S. grad:	93.7%			% of Pop:	9.7%
College grad:	28.8%				
Grad degree:	8.6%				

Twin Cities Suburbs; St. Cloud

The earliest settlers of the Twin Cities of Minneapolis and St. Paul came up the Mississippi River or up the rail lines that were soon built on the bottomlands beside it. They lived within walking distance of the mills and factories and rail yards. As the first streetcars and then automobiles allowed them to live farther from work, they spread out in St. Paul and Minneapolis and then all around the lake-strewn countryside.

2008 Presidential Vote		
John McCain (R) 219,936	(53%)
Barack Obama (D) 183,950	(45%)
2004 Presidential Vote		
George Bush (R) 216,574	(57%)
John Kerry (D) 161,601	(42%)
Cook Partisan Voting Index: R+7		

The flatlands are bleak here when the winter sun struggles to shine through gray clouds. The lakes are often surrounded by, and sometimes indistinguishable from, swamps. Stillwater, an old lumber-mill town built by pioneers on the hills above the St. Croix River, once nearly became Minnesota's capital, but later turned into an economic backwater, its Victorian structures ill-tended. Even so, the creativity and productivity of Minnesotans have turned this grim countryside into some of the nation's most pleasant suburbs. Taking maximum advantage of their lakes, they refurbished old towns and farmhouses and built comfortable homes in new subdivisions.

The 6th Congressional District of Minnesota is a suburban and exurban district north of St. Paul and Minneapolis. It dips as far south and east as Stillwater, with new riverfront housing developments along the St. Croix overlooking Wisconsin. It spreads north over Washington and Anoka counties, with a mix of upscale and working-class suburbs. To the northwest, along the Mississippi River, are Wright, Sherburne and Benton counties, which have grown rapidly from a combined total of 141,000 people in 1990 to 251,000 in 2010. The state built a commuter rail line from Target Field in Minneapolis to Big Lake in Sherburne County, but ridership has been lower than projected and an extension to St. Cloud was shelved. Young voters, usually from ancestrally Democratic-Farmer-Labor Party families, have become the key swing voters. Farther to the northwest, the district also includes the eastern half of St. Cloud-based Stearns County, a heavily German-Catholic area and a stronghold of anti-abortion rights sentiment. The 1990s saw an influx of Vietnamese, Chinese and Japanese into St. Cloud. And since 2000, several thousand Somalis have moved in and started businesses. In 2004 and 2008, this was the Minnesota district with the largest margins for George W. Bush and John McCain.

Michele Bachmann (R)

The congresswoman for the 6th District is Michele Bachmann, a Republican first elected in 2006. Bachmann grew up in cities across the Midwest and attended Winona State University, where she met her husband while working on Democrat Jimmy Carter's 1976 presidential campaign. She became disillusioned with Carter and his party's position on abortion rights and gravitated toward Ronald Reagan and the Republican Party in 1980. Bachmann and her husband, Marcus, both born-again Christians, moved to Tulsa, where she earned a degree at Coburn Law School at Oral Roberts University. After studying tax law at the College of William and Mary, Bachmann landed a job as a U.S. Treasury Department attorney in St. Paul, arguing criminal and civil tax cases. She and her husband raised five children and provided a home for 23 foster children. Bachmann's political career began in 1999, with a losing bid for the Stillwater school board. A year later, she won a seat in the state Senate by defeating a moderate Republican incumbent in the primary. In 2002, she defeated a 10-year Democratic incumbent when redistricting put them in the same state Senate district. In the legislature, Bachmann sought to protect private property rights, limit government spending and cut taxes. She was a prominent abortion rights opponent and gained publicity in 2004 for leading an unsuccessful fight for a state constitutional amendment to ban same-sex marriage.

In 2006, 6th District Republican Mark Kennedy ran for the U.S. Senate. With support from cultural conservatives, Bachmann defeated three other candidates at the Republican nominating convention and no one challenged her in the primary. There were clear ideological differences between Bachmann and Democratic nominee Patty Wetterling, who became a nationally recognized advocate for missing children after her 11-year-old son, Jacob, was abducted in 1989 and never found. Wetterling's support for abortion rights, her call for the withdrawal of U.S. troops from Iraq and her opposition to a constitutional amendment outlawing same-sex marriage prompted Republicans to portray her as too liberal for the district. President George W. Bush helped Bachmann raise money, and Wetterling got help from EMILY's List.

Wetterling spent $3.2 million to Bachmann's $2.7 million. Bachmann downplayed cultural issues and emphasized her opposition to taxes and led in the polls. Wetterling received a burst of positive publicity in October, when her background in child advocacy prompted Democrats to make her a spokesman during a scandal involving a Republican lawmaker's sexual overtures to congressional pages. But Bachmann's experience as a foster parent and her bill to establish a task force on Internet crimes against juveniles gave her credence as well. Polls showed Wetterling surging ahead after the scandal broke, but her lead was fleeting. In a difficult year for Republicans, Bachmann won a decisive 50%-42% victory.

In the House, Bachmann established a strongly conservative voting record and a reputation for sometimes controversial statements. In a 2008 appearance on MSNBC, she said that President Barack Obama "may have anti-American views" and suggested that the news media investigate all members of Congress to find who might be "anti-American." Democrats accused her of McCarthyism, and $2 million flowed into the campaign of her Democratic challenger that year, Elwyn Tinklenberg. Bachmann responded, "I have strong views," and charged that liberal bloggers perpetuated the story because they hate her. Conservative donors filled Bachmann's coffers, and she outspent Tinklenberg $3.6 million to $2.5 million. She won 46%-43%, with 10% of the vote going to Independence Party candidate Bob Anderson.

In her second term, Bachmann emerged as one of the most outspoken opponents of the Obama administration and the most identifiable leader in Congress of the tea party. She is a founder of the 50-member congressional Tea Party Caucus. "We are headed down the lane of economic Marxism," she said on Sean Hannity's talk radio program in March 2009. "It's like Thomas Jefferson said, a revolution every now and then is a good thing." She says she considers her role in Washington as that of "a foreign correspondent behind enemy lines." To live up to her message, she stoutly refused to engage in earmarked spending for her district. Bachmann also got a spate of national attention when she told the *Washington Times* that she would report on her census form only the number of people in her household because, she said, that is all the Constitution requires.

But Bachmann has a tendency to jumble her facts, which has brought her less than desirable media scrutiny at times. During the swine flu scare in 2009, Bachmann seemed to suggest that the pandemic was the Democrats' fault. She told the conservative *Pajamas Media*, "I find it interesting that it was back in the 1970s that the swine flu broke out then under Democrat President Jimmy Carter." The 1970s flu outbreak happened during Republican Gerald Ford's presidency. Bachmann also accused Democratic House Speaker Nancy Pelosi of accumulating a $100,000 "bar tab" flying on military aircraft, when in fact the figure was for all in-flight costs. Estimating air travel costs seems to be a particular weakness of Bachmann's: She asserted that Obama's trip to India would cost $200 million a day, a gross overestimate.

Nevertheless, Bachmann in just a short time became a wildly popular national figure among conservative and tea party voters. She often describes a vision of government shared by the tea party that limits government to a strict reading of its constitutional obligations. "This is insanity economics, insanity government," she told a tea party rally outside the Capitol in November 2010. "And it's not representative of who we are and this rich, beautiful legacy of 234 years." She sponsored seminars at the Capitol for "studying and learning the Declaration, the Constitution and the Bill of Rights," to which she invited all House members. The first, in December 2010, featured Supreme Court Justice Antonin Scalia.

Amid all this, Bachmann did some legislating. In 2009, she won amendments to the financial regulation overhaul that prohibit elected officials from receiving money from an entity they voted to create, and that bar organizations indicted for vote fraud from eligibility for housing counseling or legal assistance grants. Bachmann also successfully sponsored amendments to the Internet gambling bill that year, which revoked licenses of operators targeting ads to minors and barred fathers delinquent on child support payments from Internet gambling.

In 2010, she was again a magnet for Democratic activists, who funneled money into the district to help her opponent, DFL state Sen. Tarryl Clark. Bachmann raised $13.6 million, while Clark raised $4.7 million. Former Alaska Gov. Sarah Palin and former Minnesota Gov. Tim Pawlenty campaigned for Bachmann, while Obama and former President Bill Clinton dropped into the district for Clark. Her opponent criticized Bachmann for her out-of-state travels and accused her of wanting to privatize Social Security, while Bachmann criticized Clark for voting to raise taxes on high income-earners and to increase the sales tax. Bachmann won 53%-40%, with 6% for the Independence Party's Anderson, who ran again. It was a solid victory, but no higher than McCain's 2008 showing in the district.

The political threat at home did little to discourage Bachmann's pursuit of a higher profile and deeper involvement in national politics. In August 2010, she set up a leadership political action committee to raise money for other Republicans, and said she planned to endorse candidates in GOP primaries in 2012 the way that Republican Sen. Jim DeMint of South Carolina did in the 2010 election. She also ran for chairman of the Republican Conference, the No. 4 post in the Republican majority leadership. But Texas Republican Jeb Hensarling bid for the post, too. Although the two of them had few differences on issues, Hensarling was endorsed by GOP Whip Eric Cantor, Budget Committee Chairman Paul Ryan and other top House Republicans—a sign that party leaders were wary of Bachmann's penchant for sometimes hard-to-defend statements. Bachmann's support came from conservative Steve King of Iowa, also known for the occasional incendiary remark, and the three Minnesota Republicans in the state's House delegation. Bachmann withdrew from the race before the vote.

GOP Speaker-designate John Boehner appointed her to a seat on the Intelligence Committee, a plum assignment. But she opposed the Republicans' tax cut deal with the Obama administration extending the 2001 and 2003 tax cuts for two years, which was not a stance appreciated by the leadership.

In 2011, some Minnesota Republicans were urging Bachmann to challenge Democratic Sen. Amy Klobuchar in 2012. But Bachmann set her sights higher. In June 2011, she announced her candidacy for president in 2012.

SEVENTH DISTRICT

Collin Peterson (D)

Elected 1990, 11th term; b. June 29, 1944, Fargo, ND; home, Detroit Lakes; Moorhead St. U., B.A. 1966; Lutheran; divorced; 3 children.

Military Career: Army Natl. Guard, 1963–69.

Elected Office: MN Senate, 1976–86.

Professional Career: Accountant, 1966–90.

DC Office: 2211 RHOB, 20515, 202-225-2165; Fax: 202-225-1593; Web site: collinpeterson.house.gov.

State Offices: Detroit Lakes, 218-847-5056; Marshall, 507-537-2299; Montevideo, 320-235-1061; Red Lake Falls, 218-253-4356; Redwood Falls, 507-637-2270; Willmar, 320-235-1061.

Committees: *Agriculture* (RMM).

Group Ratings

	ACLU	ACU	ADA	CFG	AFS	FRC	LCV	ITIC	NTU	COC
2010	31	21	40	44	63	93	80	67	41	88
2009	–	24	55	30	67	–	79	–	25	40

National Journal Ratings

	2010 LIB	—	2010 CONS	2009 LIB	—	2009 CONS
Economic	43%	—	57%	44%	—	56%
Social	41%	—	59%	43%	—	57%
Foreign	52%	—	46%	48%	—	51%
Composite	46%	—	54%	45%	—	55%

Key Votes of the 111th Congress

1. Overturn Ledbetter	Y	5. Bar federal abortion funds	Y	9. Stop detainee transfers	Y
2. Pass $820 billion stimulus	N	6. Pass health care bill	N	10. Legalize immigrants' kids	N
3. Let guns in national parks	Y	7. Regulate financial firms	Y	11. Repeal don't ask, tell	N
4. Pass cap-and-trade	Y	8. Pass tax cuts for some	N	12. Limit campaign funds	N

Election Results

2010 general	Collin Peterson (DFL)	133,096	(55%)	($1,174,500)
	Lee Byberg (R)	90,652	(38%)	($402,707)
	Gene Waldorf (I)	9,317	(4%)	($62,351)
	Glen Menze (Ind)	7,839	(3%)	($13,965)
2010 primary	Collin Peterson (DFL)	unopposed		

Prior Winning Percentages: 2008 (72%), 2006 (70%), 2004 (66%), 2002 (65%), 2000 (69%), 1998 (72%), 1996 (68%), 1994 (51%), 1992 (51%), 1990 (54%)

Population		Race/Ethnicity		Work	
Pop. 2010:	625,512	White:	90.5%	Private:	75.5%
Change since 2000:	Up 1.7%	Black:	0.8%	Government:	14.2%
Urban:	34.0%	Hispanic:	3.8%	Self-employed:	10.0%
Rural:	66.0%	Asian:	0.8%	Blue collar:	27.1%
Area size:	33,745 sq. mi.	Native Am.:	2.7%	White collar:	53.7%
		Hawaiian:	0.0%	Khaki collar:	0.0%
Age		Two+ races:	1.4%	Other:	19.2%
Median age:	40.8 yrs.				
More than 65 yrs:	17.1%	*Ancestry*		Median income:	$45,738
Less than 18 yrs:	23.3%	German	30.8%	Median Home Value:	$135,800
		Norwegian	19.8%	**Military Veterans**	
Education		Swedish	7.2%	% of Pop:	11.3%
H.S. grad:	88.2%				
College grad:	19.6%				
Grad degree:	5.3%				

Western Minnesota; Moorhead

The fabled Mississippi River begins modestly in Minnesota's Itasca State Park, 2,552 miles from the Gulf of Mexico. At that point it can be crossed by foot on stepping-stones. The lake-strewn country in which the river begins has made its own contributions to American literature. More than a century ago, Sinclair Lewis grew up in the town of Sauk Centre, which provided grist for his critical but affectionate portrayals of small-town America in *Main Street* and *Babbitt*. In

2008 Presidential Vote
John McCain (R) 162,941   (50%)
Barack Obama (D) 154,140   (47%)

2004 Presidential Vote
George Bush (R) 180,743   (55%)
John Kerry (D) 140,332   (43%)

Cook Partisan Voting Index: R+5

those years, this seemingly placid country was seething with rage, as WASP nationalists banned German from schools, renamed sauerkraut "liberty cabbage," and boycotted German-American businesses. This fed the bitter isolationism of the 1930s and 1940s, led by Charles Lindbergh, who grew up in Little Falls the son of an isolationist congressman who opposed declaring war on Germany in 1917. This part of Minnesota is probably also the home of the fictional Lake Wobegon. Public radio host Garrison Keillor says he was inspired by small towns in Stearns County that were evenly divided between German Catholics and Norwegian Lutherans.

Farther south, where the plains rise above the river-cut gorges, is great farming country, settled more than 100 years ago by Germans and Scandinavians. Even today farmers toil against the elements to make a profitable living, so productively that their lands are slowly but surely depopulating; 100,000 acres of farmland in the Minnesota River watershed has been taken out of production by the federal Conservation Reserve Program. This area is the nation's leading producer of sugar beets and a leading supplier of turkeys. It also produces wheat, soybeans and oilseeds. On the shores of Plum Creek, near Walnut Grove, is where Laura Ingalls Wilder's family came on the way west to the *Little House on the Prairie* in South Dakota. After all their struggles, Wilder's family left the farm for town as soon as they could. Their pain would be all too familiar to contemporary residents along the Red River of the North, which overflowed its banks in April 1997, inundating Grand Forks, North Dakota, and East Grand Forks, Minnesota, and dislocating 50,000 people—America's largest mass evacuation between the Civil War and Hurricane Katrina.

The 7th Congressional District of Minnesota covers almost all of the western part of the state. Its southeastern end is 30 miles from Minneapolis, just beyond the zone of rapid exurban growth. It takes in the wheat-farming plains adjoining North Dakota as well as the German Catholic areas, with their farm villages named for saints. Farmers have been increasingly turning to corn and soybeans, which have a greater variety of markets and uses. Many political traditions coexist here. Some of the wheat counties are heavily Democratic-Farmer-Labor Party, while heavily Norwegian Otter Tail County leans Republican. The 7th's political history reads like something out of *Lake Wobegon Days*. Back in 1958, DFL Rep. Coya Knutson was defeated for re-election when her husband, Andy, issued a plaintive statement urging her to come home from Washington and make his breakfast again. She was the only incumbent Democrat to lose in that heavily Democratic year. For the next three decades, this was one of America's prime marginal districts. In 2000, the unpopularity of Clinton administration environmental and gun control policies produced a 54%-40% victory for George W. Bush, his best showing in a Minnesota district. In 2004, Bush won the district 55%-43%. In 2008, John McCain won this district by only 50%-47%, as ancestral DFL loyalties resurfaced.

Collin Peterson (D)

The congressman from the 7th District is Collin Peterson, a Democrat first elected in 1990 and the former chairman of the House Agriculture Committee.

Peterson grew up on a farm in Baker, just across the Red River of the North from Fargo, N.D. He graduated from Moorhead State College, and then started a certified public accounting business in Detroit Lakes. In 1976, he was elected to the state Senate. In 1982, he ran for the U.S. House but lost in the DFL caucus and then set out to prove that he's nothing if not persistent. He tried three more times, losing to Republican Arlan Stangeland in 1984 and 1986 (by only 121 votes that year) and losing a DFL primary in 1988. But in 1990, when the *St. Cloud Times* reported that Stangeland made 341 credit card calls to a woman who was not his wife, Peterson won with a robust 54% of the vote.

In office, he has been known as a free spirit, wearing cowboy boots and playing guitar in a band called the Second Amendments (the other four members are Republicans). He acted as his own campaign consultant and his own pilot, flying his Beechcraft Bonanza to stops around the district. He has a small staff of community economic development professionals rather than Washington policy wonks. He opposes abortion rights and gun control. He backs farm subsidies and labor unions, he voted for the Iraq war resolution in 2002 and for extending the Bush tax cuts. (Later, in 2006, he called his vote on Iraq "a mistake," but said withdrawal would be "dangerous," and voted against war spending bills that carried withdrawal timetables.)

Peterson's political fortune was bolstered by the Republican takeover of Congress in 1995, which made him a visibly different kind of Democrat. While voting for parts of the Republicans' Contract with America, he founded, with California Democrat Gary Condit, the Blue Dog Coalition, a group of conservative Democrats for "common sense legislation that embraces the ideas and values of mainstream America." He was one of 16 Democrats to vote for the GOP's Medicare prescription drug bill in 2003. He opposed giving the president broad powers to negotiate free trade agreements and said that local farmers were furious about the Bush administration's trade deals. However, Peterson has supported lifting trade restrictions on Cuba, a move favored by farmers eager for another export market. On environmental issues, Peterson takes the view of his constituents, who hunt and fish as a way of life and often see environmentalists' policies as hindrances.

When Democrat Charles Stenholm of Texas was defeated in 2004, Peterson was next in line to be the ranking minority member on the Agriculture Committee. But the Democratic leadership demanded that he pay $70,000 in back dues to the Democratic Congressional Campaign Committee. He agreed to be more of a team player and to raise money for other Democrats, although he said: "We have a lot of very liberal people in our caucus. They're misguided, in my opinion, in a lot of areas." But he supported Minority Leader Nancy Pelosi on the theory, he said, that only a liberal can tell liberals what to do. Pelosi accepted Peterson's invitation to attend Farmfest in Redwood County in August 2006, where she ate pork chops on a stick and got a warm reception. On several issues, he agreed with her: He supported raising the minimum wage and pay-as-you-go rules requiring that tax cuts be offset with spending decreases. After the Democrats won a House majority in 2006, there was no question about his becoming chairman.

Peterson brought to the chairmanship several firm principles, which mostly reflected the views of his constituents. He expressed reservations that the Republicans' 1996 Freedom to Farm Act would cause low prices and joined the bipartisan majority on the committee in restoring market controls when the farm program was renewed in 2002. In the mid-2000s, Peterson called for extending the Conservation Reserve Program to keep millions of additional acres of farmland idle to produce switch grass and plant waste that could be used to make ethanol. With a ready supply of raw material, Peterson predicted, cellulosic ethanol plants would prove to be profitable.

Peterson worked with then-ranking Republican Bob Goodlatte of Virginia to achieve many of his goals on the farm bill enacted in May 2008. It was not easy. It took six short-term extensions of the bill and two votes to override President George W. Bush's veto of the legislation. Peterson sought an income limit of $900,000 annually for subsidy payments, and the final deal set a ceiling of $750,000 for farmers receiving direct payments. It also barred payments to persons with more than $500,000 in nonfarm income. He finally got his permanent disaster fund so that farmers could get their aid more quickly following a drought or flood. Peterson boosted the subsidy for cellulosic ethanol to $1 per gallon, while reducing the subsidy for corn ethanol from 51 cents to 45 cents per gallon.

With demands for new acreage, especially from the large fruit and vegetable states of Florida and California, the committee reduced the Conservation Reserve Program from 39 million acres to 32 million acres. Peterson, the former accountant, proved adept at figuring the costs of various commodity programs, and he established a solid working relationship with Senate Budget Chairman Kent Conrad of North Dakota, who was the chief Senate negotiator on the bill. Peterson accommodated lawmakers from urban areas by directing to the food stamp program an additional $10 billion over five years. "We have a bill that covers all of the interests in the country," Peterson said.

Looking ahead to a 2012 farm bill, Peterson, now the ranking minority member on the committee, said in June 2010 he wanted to shift from direct farm payments to an expanded crop insurance plan, getting rid of payment limitations and the perennial arguments over them. His other goals, he said, were to get funding for biomass energy studies transferred from the Energy Department to the Agriculture Department's Rural Development Agency; to make sure all states, including California, are covered by the milk marketing program; and to get $50 million a year for flood mitigation for the Red River of the North.

On other issues, Peterson has gone his own way even as Pelosi increasingly used tough tactics to keep her troops in line. He voted against President Barack Obama's economic stimulus bill in 2009, explaining to the *Food & Fiber Letter* that he voted no "for the same reasons I voted against the initial bailout package for the banks, because I knew it would not work....None of this is paid for and I don't want to have China keep funding our debt." Peterson also committed party apostasy by voting against the health care overhaul in 2009 and 2010. He said Obama's legislation tackled the right problems in the wrong way.

On some big issues, Peterson was more cooperative, but generally only after extracting legislative concessions acceptable to the Blue Dog Democrats. In May 2009, he said the Democrats' cap-and-trade bill to limit carbon emissions was "an urban-dominated bill" that catered to the environmental lobby. In June, he reached agreement with Energy and Commerce Committee Chairman Henry Waxman, D-Calif., who, without Peterson and other Blue Dogs, would have been unable to muster a majority for the bill. As part of the deal, Peterson insisted that the Agriculture Department, rather than the Environmental Protection Agency, oversee the carbon emissions offset program for farmers. In addition, Peterson got changes in the ethanol program. The bill passed the House, but it died in the Senate in the 111th Congress (2009-10). When the EPA announced it would move on its own to begin regulating carbon emissions under the Clean Air Act, Peterson co-sponsored a bill to block the move.

When the House was at work in 2010 on a major financial industry regulation bill, Peterson struck an agreement with Financial Services Chairman Barney Frank, D-Mass., that preserved for the Commodities Futures Trading Commission, which reports to the Agriculture committees, some jurisdiction for oversight of agricultural commodities trading; the deal stopped Frank's committee from taking over jurisdiction.

Peterson typically wins re-election easily every two years. He had a close call in the heavily Republican year of 1994, when he retained his seat by just 51%-49%. In 2010, despite the Republican trend that swept away his 8th District, DFL neighbor, James Oberstar, Peterson was re-elected by 55%-38%.

Peterson has shown he can survive in this Republican-leaning district. But redistricting ahead of the 2012 election could change things. If the GOP-controlled legislature takes the Iron Range and Duluth out of the 8th district and puts them into Peterson's 7th, it could help shore up Republican freshman Chip Cravaack by making the 8th more Republican. At the same time, Peterson would get a much more Democratic district. It might, however, reduce his leverage with the Democratic leadership, which has tolerated his "no" votes and let him retain his chairmanship in light of the threat that if he retired, he would be replaced by a Republican.

EIGHTH DISTRICT

Chip Cravaack (R)

Elected 2010, 1st term; b. Jan. 29, 1959, Charleston, WV; home, Lindstrom; U.S. Naval Academy, B.S. 1981; U. of West FL, M.Ed. 1989; Catholic; Married (Traci).

Military Career: Navy, 1981-2005.

Professional Career: Pilot, Northwest Airlines, 1999-2007.

DC Office: 508 CHOB, 20515, 202-225-6211; Fax: 202-225-0699; Web site: cravaack.house.gov.

State Offices: North Branch, 651-237-8220.

Committees: *Homeland Security:* Counterterrorism & Intelligence; Transportation Security. *Science, Space & Technology:* Technology & Innovation. *Transportation & Infrastructure:* Aviation (VChmn); Coast Guard & Maritime Transportation; Water Resources & Environment.

Election Results

2010 general	Chip Cravaack (R)	133,490	(48%)	($659,648)
	James Oberstar (DFL)	129,091	(47%)	($1,757,326)
	Timothy Olson (Ind)	11,876	(4%)	($3,538)
2010 primary	Chip Cravaack (R)	unopposed		

Population		Race/Ethnicity		Work	
Pop. 2010:	660,342	White:	92.9%	Private:	77.1%
Change since 2000:	Up 7.4%	Black:	0.9%	Government:	15.3%
Urban:	37.4%	Hispanic:	1.3%	Self-employed:	7.5%
Rural:	62.6%	Asian:	0.6%	Blue collar:	25.5%
Area size:	32,418 sq. mi.	Native Am.:	2.6%	White collar:	54.4%
		Hawaiian:	0.0%	Khaki collar:	0.2%
Age		Two+ races:	1.7%	Other:	19.9%
Median age:	41.7 yrs.				
More than 65 yrs:	16.4%	*Ancestry*		Median income:	$45,885
Less than 18 yrs:	22.1%	German	23.6%	Median Home Value:	$167,600
		Norwegian	11.4%		
Education		Swedish	9.7%	**Military Veterans**	
H.S. grad:	90.7%			% of Pop:	12.8%
College grad:	20.5%				
Grad degree:	6.5%				

Northeastern Minnesota; Duluth

In the 1860s, prospectors in Minnesota's Arrowhead region, northwest of Lake Superior in the low hills of the Mesabi Range, happened upon one of the nation's largest veins of iron ore. They moved on, looking for gold. But in the 1880s, Duluth banker George Stone and Philadelphia financier Charlemagne Tower started mining the Iron Range and created the northern end of the lifeline of American heavy industry. Rail lines ran south from the Range to the port of Duluth, nestled on dramatic bluffs over the always-cold and, for long months every winter, frozen waters of Lake Superior—one of the most beautiful settings for a city in North America, though also one of the most isolated. Duluth was a grain shipping rival of Chicago and the premier iron ore port. Its city plan was drawn up by architect Daniel Burnham, who also planned Chicago, and its splendid turn-of-the-century buildings still celebrate the triumph of technology and civilization over wilderness and the elements. Millions of tons of ore have been dug out of the Range and loaded into railcars for the ride to Duluth, and into Great Lakes freighters for shipment to Chicago, Gary, Detroit, Cleveland, Pittsburgh, and Buffalo.

For most of the 20th century, in this land where the Arctic winds blow down over the Canadian Shield's thousands of inland lakes, about 100,000 people lived on the Iron Range and another 100,000 in Duluth, most of them descendants of America's 1880-1924 wave of immigration: Ital-

2008 Presidential Vote

Barack Obama (D)	195,147	(53%)
John McCain (R)	163,520	(45%)

2004 Presidential Vote

John Kerry (D)	191,228	(53%)
George Bush (R)	167,439	(46%)

Cook Partisan Voting Index: D+3

ians, Poles, Serbs and Croats, Jews, Swedes, and Finns. In this punishing environment, they built solid houses with staunch central heating, and wore layers of warm clothing to survive the brutal winter, which can be as extreme as 50 degrees below zero. Life was rough. The work was hard, the hours long, and the pay low. The churches, a separate one for each ethnic group, were the main community institutions. Living conditions improved vastly in the decades of great economic growth after World War II, but life remains rough-hewn today, and there is still economic distress. As iron mines and steel factories got more efficient, they needed fewer workers, and employment is now well below its 1970s peak.

In 2010, Duluth's population was down to 86,400. Economic growth was sporadic. In the 1990s, Northwest Airlines built a large repair facility in Duluth and a reservations center in the Iron Range, and the call center survived the 2008 merger with Delta Airlines. The port of Duluth still ships large quantities of grain, and in the late 1990s, a new taconite and steelmaking factory was built—the first big new plant in more than 20 years. Automakers test their new models' performance under extreme winter conditions at International Falls in Koochiching County. A new sports competition is the winter ultramarathon, a 135-mile endurance contest of walking, running, cycling, or skiing from International Falls to Tower.

The 8th Congressional District of Minnesota includes Duluth and the Iron Range, plus much of the north woods and lake country to the west and south. It extends all the way south to the boundaries of the Twin Cities metro area, to Isanti and Chisago counties, where young families are building new homes in pleasant old lakeside towns. This district has been a bulwark of Minnesota's Democratic-Farmer-Labor Party since the DFL was formed in 1944, and has been considered safely Democratic for years. But there are signs of change. The fast-growing counties in the south and west have trended Republican, while Duluth and the Iron Range remain Democratic. However, issues like gun control and environmental regulation have sometimes moved those areas toward the Republicans. In 2004, John Kerry won here 53%-46% over President Bush. Four years later, Barack Obama had a similar 53%-45% win over John McCain.

Chip Cravaack (R)

The new congressman from the 8th District of Michigan is Republican Chip Cravaack, who pulled off one of the biggest upsets of 2010 when he defeated 36-year Democratic incumbent James Oberstar, the dean of the state's congressional delegation. The district had not been in GOP hands since President Truman's administration in the 1940s.

Born in Charleston, W.Va., Cravaack (*kruh-VACK*) grew up outside Cincinnati and attended the U.S. Naval Academy. After several years as a naval aviator, he became a pilot for Northwest Airlines, eventually retiring to Chisago County northeast of Minneapolis. He is a decorated member of the Navy Reserve, and boasts a long list of awards and citations, including a Joint Service Commendation Medal and two Navy Commendation Medals. He holds a master's degree in education from the University of West Florida.

Cravaack decided to run against Oberstar after Democrats passed the health care overhaul, which he adamantly opposed. He went to Oberstar's local office with about two dozen other residents and asked for a town hall meeting on the topic. When the request was denied, he called his friend, the mayor of Lindstrom, the town of 3,000 where he lives, and said, "I want to run for Congress. What do I do?" His key campaign theme became repeal of the health care law. At one debate, Cravaack said that it was "going to be a job killer. It's going to put a bureaucrat between us and our doctor." He faced no primary opposition in August.

Oberstar told Minnesota Public Radio that he "anticipated a difficult year from the very outset." Unlike other endangered Democrats, he mounted a vigorous defense of President Obama's initiatives, including the health care overhaul. But he faced boos and shouts at his debate with Cravaack, and he eventually decided to launch the first attack ad of his career, which refuted Cravaack's suggestion that Malaysia's streamlined business culture could be a model for the United States. Oberstar's ad said that Malaysia's weak regulations had helped lead to deforestation. He was one of several committee chairmen—including Armed Services' Ike Skelton of Missouri and Budget's John Spratt of South Carolina—who became punching bags for frustrated voters.

Former Bush adviser Karl Rove's group Crossroads Grassroots Policy Strategies ran an ad in the district saying, "Minnesota's economy is reeling, and Congressman Jim Oberstar is making it worse." Cravaack also picked up the endorsement of the *Duluth News Tribune*, which cited his fiscal conservatism. But he was mightily outspent by Oberstar. Cravaack raised just $660,000 to Oberstar's $1.8 million, and the incumbent was regarded as a substantial favorite as late as mid-October. Even Minnesota Republicans were shocked on election night when Cravaack won, albeit narrowly, 48% to 47%. Cravaack told his supporters, "It's a miracle what we've done."

★ MISSISSIPPI ★

Mississippi, burdened with a tragic history, has long lagged behind the other states in just about every leading indicator. But now, half a century after the height of the civil rights movement, the state has in many ways entered the American mainstream while keeping some of its benign regional character. This green land was settled in a rush in Jacksonian America, mostly by small farmers heading west from Georgia and south from Tennessee, and also by a few big planters who made, and sometimes lost, vast fortunes, built grand mansions, imported hundreds of slaves and sent their sons to fight in the Civil War. For a century afterward, as planters and engineers drained the Delta lands, Mississippi, with its racial segregation, subsistence farmers and sharecroppers, and low wages, lived apart from most of America. William Faulkner's Mississippi never knew the Homestead Act, giant factories, the rushes of immigration, or the burgeoning of the suburbs that characterized much of 20th-century America. Mississippi never developed great cities: The two commercial metropolises that power it—Memphis and New Orleans—lie just outside its borders.

But if the state did not excel at commerce, it did produce great art. Mississippi gave us the blues and Elvis Presley. It produced writers like Faulkner and Eudora Welty, Walker Percy and Shelby Foote. The state with the lowest literacy rate has also produced the most Pulitzer Prize winners for literature. Their work was informed by a sense of the tragic that is missing or forgotten in most of America, where life is a triumphant sales pitch or a labor-saving invention. For years, no other state had such a painful contrast between image and reality, between an ideal sincerely strived for and the tawdry facts of everyday life. Magnolia trees on the lawns of antebellum mansions, golden-haired women in white dresses on the veranda, faithful black servants and retainers. This was once the ideal. And behind it stood loose-jointed frame houses and unpainted back-country stores, cabins without plumbing and poor white crossroads. As David Sansing wrote, "We at one time have the scent of magnolias and the smell of burning crosses."

Today, Mississippi still ranks 49th or 50th on many quality-of-life scales, but the gulf between the state and the rest of America has narrowed enormously. In 1940, Mississippi had an economy based on low-wage, subsistence or sharecropper agriculture and a system of racial segregation often enforced by violence. If history is, as Sir Henry Maine wrote, the story of the progress from status to contract, then old Mississippi was still starting off, for status—race—meant just about everything. In the years since, Mississippi has moved, not always willingly, from status to contract in its economy and in its race relations. Per capita income in Mississippi was 36% of the national average in 1940; in 1990, it was 67% and in 2010, it was 76%, still well below average but, given the lower cost of living here, a level recognizably American. Unlike New Orleans in neighboring Louisiana, the state quickly got up off the ground and started rebuilding after Hurricane Katrina in 2005. Mississippians of 50 years ago would be astonished by the physical comforts and mechanical marvels their grandchildren take for granted: Nearly every classroom in the state is air-conditioned and is being wired for the Internet.

The elder generation would be astonished as well by relations between whites and blacks, who make up 37% of the population, the highest percentage in any state. As Mississippi native and columnist William Raspberry wrote in *The Washington Post*, "There is an easiness to relationships, a mutual respect and a willingness to move beyond race that, quite frankly, didn't exist during my years in the state. Mississippi is finally a good place to be." Forty years ago, blacks held no public offices in Mississippi. Now the state has more black elected officials than any other, with lots of African-American chairmen of state legislative committees. An African-American state senator from Tishomingo County in the far northeast part of the state was elected from a rural district that is 87% white. Voters have elected black mayors in Vicksburg, Jackson, Hattiesburg, Greenville, and Natchez. That's not to say the race issue has disappeared. It is still uncomfortably present in some Mississippi elections. A decade ago, in 2001, 65% of voters chose to retain the Confederate battle cross—a symbol offensive to many—in the state flag. Yet Mississippi seems intent on moving forward rather than backward. Prosecutors have hunted down the Ku Klux Klan members who killed civil rights activists in the 1960s. One was convicted in 2005 and another charged in 2007. Republican Gov. Haley Barbour signed bills authorizing a civil rights curriculum in public schools and a civil rights museum in Jackson. The Jackson airport is named for movement leader Medgar Evers. In 2008, Ole Miss, which was integrated under force of arms in 1962, hosted Barack Obama, an African-American Democrat, and John McCain, a Republican who has Mississippi ancestors, for a presidential debate.

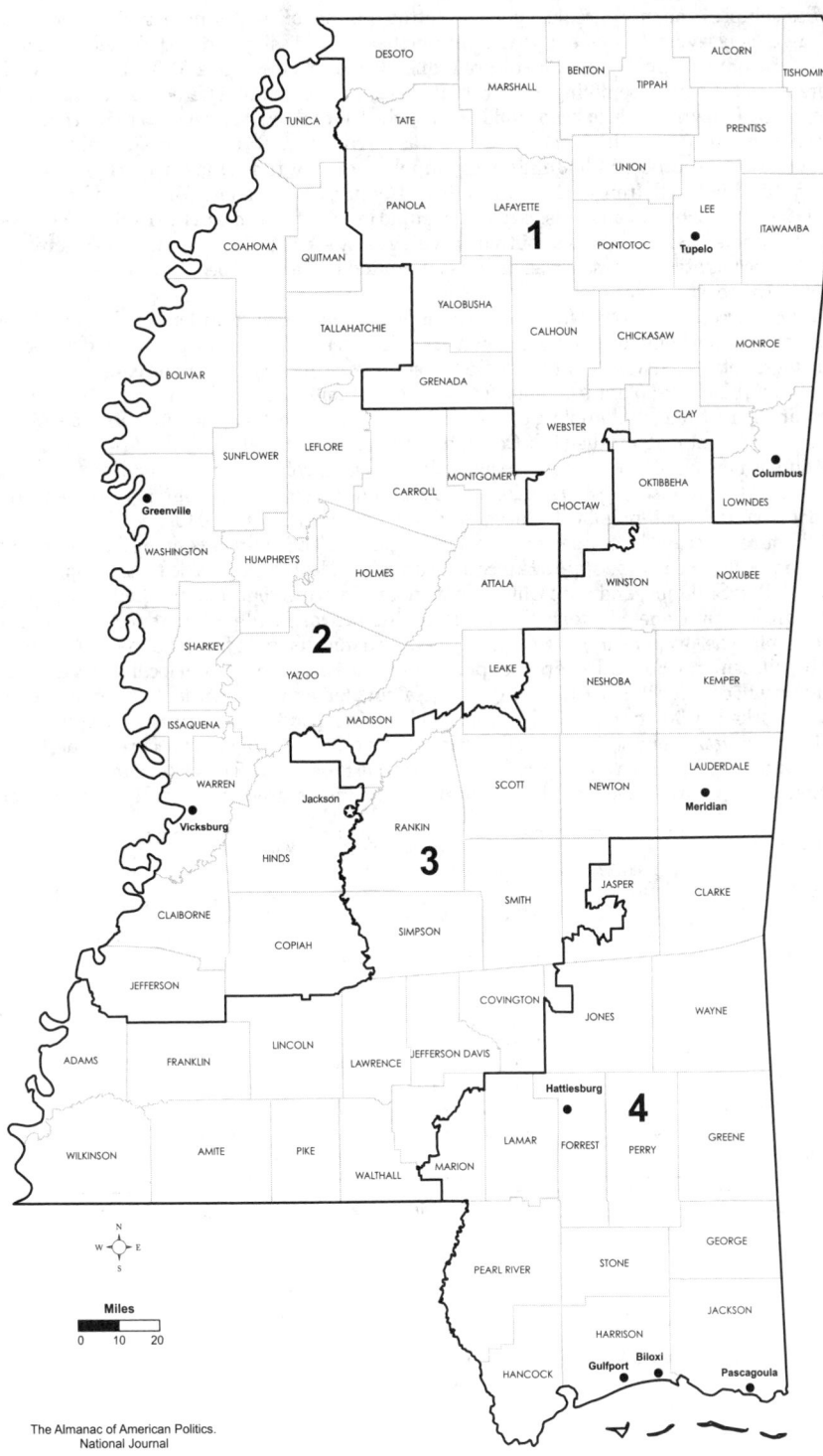

The Almanac of American Politics.
National Journal

Congressional district boundaries were first effective for 2002.

Mississippi's economy once depended on cotton, but no longer. Manufacturing jobs have declined here as elsewhere in recent years, but northeast Mississippi around Tupelo remains the center of the nation's upholstered furniture industry and is the site of a $1.3 billion plant where workers were to begin assembling Prius cars in 2011, after the state offered Toyota $296 million in incentives. Growth has also been rapid around the $1.4 billion Nissan auto plant that opened in 2003 in Canton, just north of Jackson, which was lured with $363 million in state aid and incentives. Its workforce numbers 4,000 and nearby suppliers employ thousands more. Highland Colony Parkway, heading north from Jackson in Madison County, and Lakeland Drive, heading east into Rankin County, anchor boom areas. Even more rapid growth has come in the DeSoto County suburbs of Memphis, just a few miles south of Elvis Presley's estate Graceland. Population growth has been concentrated in these areas and also in inland counties as people, after Katrina, drove them from the coast.

Other sources of growth: Northrop Grumman's huge shipyard in former Senate Majority Leader Trent Lott's hometown of Pascagoula; the Richton salt dome, which is being developed for the Strategic Petroleum Reserve at a cost of $1 billion; General Electric's engine plant in Batesville; and a $175 million steel plant in Amory. Then there is gambling. Mississippi approved gambling in 1990, and since then, big gambling companies have built some 29 casinos, nine in once-impoverished Tunica County, 12 on the Gulf Coast, and the rest scattered along the Mississippi River. Mississippi is now No. 4 among states in gambling revenue, behind Nevada and New Jersey. The industry has produced some $320 million in state revenues a year. But, contrary to expectations, it has not been recession-proof, with revenues down 13% from 2008 to 2010.

To be sure, Katrina was a huge setback for Mississippi. The main force of the August 29, 2005, hurricane was directed at the state's Hancock County, not New Orleans. The Mississippi towns of Waveland, Bay St. Louis, and Pass Christian were totally wiped out. In a few hours, waves up to 55 feet high destroyed one-quarter of the structures in Biloxi and Gulfport. Lott's century-old home in Pascagoula was swept away, as were many houses a quarter-mile from the coast. Floodwaters swept 10 miles inland. Federal emergency plans rest on the assumption that local officials and first responders will cope for the first three days, but Katrina left city halls without power and roads to hospitals blocked by fallen trees. Still, Mississippi's first responders went to work in spite of those obstacles, pulling 24-hour shifts. The Mississippi congressional delegation secured generous federal money to help with the recovery; it did not hurt that Republican Thad Cochran was chairman of the Senate Appropriations Committee. And Barbour administered grants and low-interest loans

Population		Household Income		Work	
Pop. 2010:	2,967,297	Under $15k:	20.8%	Private:	74.0%
State rank:	31st	$15k to $50k:	41.6%	Government:	19.6%
Change since 2000:	Up 4.3%	$50k to $100k:	26.1%	Self-employed:	6.2%
Urban:	46.9%	$100k to $200k:	9.6%	Unemployment (3-yr. average):	5.5%
Rural:	53.1%	Over $200k:	1.8%	Poverty:	21.4%
Native of state:	71.6%	Median income:	$37,034	Blue collar:	27.6%
Not a citizen:	1.4%			White collar:	53.9%
Area size:	48,432 sq. mi.	**Home Value**		Khaki collar:	0.4%
		Under $100k:	51.3%	Other:	18.1%
Most populous cities		$100k to $300k:	41.7%		
Jackson	173,514	$300k to $500k:	5.1%	**Age**	
Gulfport	67,793	$500k to $1 mil:	1.5%	Median age:	35.1 yrs.
Southaven	48,982	Over $1 million:	0.5%	More than 65 yrs:	12.6%
Hattiesburg	45,989	Median:	$97,300	Less than 18 yrs:	26.1%

Race/Ethnicity				Military Veterans		Registered Voters in 2010	
White:	58.0%	*Language*		% of Pop:	9.7%	No Party registration	
Black:	36.9%	English:	96.2%			Voter turnout:	788,549
Hispanic:	2.7%	Spanish:	2.2%	*Veterans by Period*		Turnout as % of	
Asian:	0.9%	Asian:	0.6%	WWII and before:	9.2%	voting age:	35.7%
Native Am.:	0.5%	Other European:	0.7%	Korea:	10.3%		
Hawaiian:	0.0%			Vietnam:	31.2%	**Legislature**	
Two+ races:	0.9%	**Education**		Gulf (pre-2001):	14.1%	Senate:	25 D 27 R
		H.S. grad:	79.6%	Gulf (post-2001):	11.0%	House:	72 D 50 R
Ancestry		College grad:	19.4%	Peace time:	24.2%		
USA	10.3%	Grad degree:	6.8%				
Irish	8.8%						
English	7.6%						

to home and business owners who suffered uninsured losses. Just as the Gulf Coast was getting up and running again, the 2007-09 recession hit. The state never had much of a housing bubble, and so did not see mass foreclosures as other states did, but unemployment rose above 10% and some factories closed.

Politically, Mississippi is increasingly a Republican state, carried by Republicans in the last seven presidential elections. But Democrats have shown some ability to compete. Republicans have held both U.S. Senate seats since the retirement of John Stennis in 1988. But after Barbour appointed GOP Rep. Roger Wicker to fill Lott's seat, Democrat Travis Childers won the May 2008 special election to fill Wicker's 1st District House seat. That left Mississippi with a 3-1 Democratic House delegation, with Bennie Thompson safe in the black-majority 2nd District and conservative Democrat Gene Taylor holding on to the heavily Republican Gulf Coast district he first won in 1989. But the Democrats' momentum was slowed considerably by the Obama administration's agenda, which proved unpopular in Mississippi. Wicker won the remainder of Lott's term in 2008, 55%-45%, over former Gov. Ronnie Musgrove, and in 2010, both Childers and Taylor were swept under by the tea party tide. Now Thompson is the sole Democrat in the state's delegation.

At the state level, the pattern is mixed. In 2003, Musgrove lost his re-election bid to Barbour, who returned to Yazoo City from a Washington lobbying practice and a stint as Republican national chairman. Barbour's sure-footed response to Katrina, in contrast with that of Louisiana Gov. Kathleen Blanco, a Democrat, boosted his poll ratings. Going into the 2007 election, Barbour took credit for converting a $700 million deficit to a $70 million surplus and for boosting test scores in Mississippi public schools. He beat Democrat John Arthur Eaves by a solid 58%-42%. Republicans Phil Bryant and Delbert Hosemann were elected lieutenant governor and secretary of state, respectively, by similar margins. By early 2011, off-year elections and party switches produced a 27-25 Republican margin in the state Senate and reduced Democrats' edge in the state House to 72-50. Barbour, in his last year in office, lost 20 pounds and seemed to be preparing a presidential bid. But in April 2011 he announced that he would not run for president.

Presidential politics   Mississippi voted 56%-43% for John McCain in 2008—a slight downtick from Republican George W. Bush's 58% in 2000 and 59% in 2004. There was some racial polarization in the electorate. Whites voted 88%-11% for McCain over Democratic nominee Barack Obama, while African-Americans voted 98%-2% for Obama—both wider margins than four years before, when both presidential candidates were white. African-Americans accounted for 33% of turnout, not much less than their share of adult population. White evangelical or born-again Protestants made up 46% of the electorate and voted 94%-6% for McCain. Young voters overall voted for Obama, although young whites voted 81% for McCain. It should be noted, however, that few Mississippi whites yearn for a return to racial segregation. They line up with Republicans on a raft of other issues—defense, crime, cultural attitudes, taxes—just as most

2008 Presidential Vote		
John McCain (R) 724,597	(56%)
Barack Obama (D) 554,662	(43%)

2008 Presidential Primary		
Barack Obama (D) 265,502	(61%)
Hillary Clinton (D)...............159,221	(37%)

2008 Presidential Primary		
John McCain (R) 113,074	(79%)
Mike Huckabee (R)..................17,943	(13%)

2004 Presidential Vote		
George W. Bush (R)...............684,981	(59%)
John Kerry (D) 457,766	(40%)

African-Americans line up with Democrats on the same issues. And on some issues, blacks and whites in Mississippi are on the same page: 89% of whites and 77% of blacks voted for a constitutional amendment banning same-sex marriage in 2004.

Mississippi has held a presidential primary in the second week of March since 1988, too late to have made a difference in 2000 and 2004. That was the case again for Republicans in 2008, as Mike Huckabee withdrew from the contest the week before Mississippi voted. Only 145,000 voted in the Republican primary—fewer than in 1988, 1992, and 1996—with 79% of voters supporting McCain. On the Democratic side, the race was still on, and turnout was 434,000, topping the record of 359,000 in 1988. With voting along racial lines, Obama beat Hillary Rodham Clinton 61%-37%, his biggest primary margin anywhere except for Virginia, Georgia, and the District of Columbia.

Congressional districting

Mississippi lost one of its five House districts in the reapportionment following the 2000 census, marking the first time the state had just four representatives since the 1840s. In 2001, Democrats held the governorship and both houses of the legislature, and one might have expected that they would draw a plan ousting one of the state's two Republican congressmen. But a November 2001 special session of the legislature failed to come up with a plan that everyone could agree on. Ultimately, a federal court ordered a plan drawn with a 30% black district that put Republican Chip Pickering and Democrat Ronnie Shows in the same district. Pickering won the 2002 election by a solid margin and when he retired was succeeded by another Republican. Mississippi kept all four of its seats in the reapportionment following the 2010 census. With Republicans currently holding the three majority-white districts and Democrat Bennie Thompson holding the black-majority 2nd district, redistricting is likely to be a much simpler matter than it was ten years before. African-Americans are so widely dispersed throughout the state that the Democratic state House would find it hard to draw a second black-majority district and it is unlikely that the Republican state Senate and Barbour would seek to weaken Thompson.

Governor

Haley Barbour (R)

Elected 2003, term expires Jan. 2012, 2nd term; b. Oct. 22, 1947, Yazoo City; home, Yazoo City; Attended U. of MS; U. of MS, J.D. 1973; Presbyterian; married (Marsha); 2 children.

Professional Career: State dir., U.S. Census Bureau, 1969-70; RNC Committeeman, 1984-98; Dir., White House Office of Political Affairs, 1985-87; CEO & founder, Barbour, Griffith & Rogers, 1991-present; Chmn., RNC, 1993-97.

Office: State Capitol, P.O. Box 139, Jackson, 39205, 601-359-3150; Fax: 601-359-3741; Web site: www.governorbarbour.com/.

Election Results

2007 general	Haley Barbour (R)	430,807	(58%)
	John Eaves (D)	313,232	(42%)
2007 primary	Haley Barbour (R)	184,036	(93%)
	Frederick Jones (R)	13,611	(7%)

Prior Winning Percentages: 2003 (53%)

Republican Haley Barbour was elected governor of Mississippi in 2003 and re-elected in 2007. Barbour grew up in Yazoo City in the Mississippi Delta. His father was a lawyer who died of a heart attack when Haley was 2 years old, leaving his 31-year-old mother to raise the three Barbour boys. A star athlete and class valedictorian, Barbour was voted Mr. Yazoo High School and won a scholarship to attend Ole Miss. But he left during his senior year to take a job on Republican Richard Nixon's 1968 presidential campaign. Barbour returned to Ole Miss and graduated from the university's law school in 1973. Three years later, he ran Republican Gerald Ford's presidential campaign in the Southeast, and he has been actively involved in Republican politics ever since. In 1980, Barbour worked on John Connally's presidential campaign.

In 1982 he challenged Sen. John Stennis, longtime Democratic chairman of the Armed Services Committee. Stennis had not faced a serious challenge since 1947. But by then he was in his 80s, and many expected him to retire. When he ran for re-election, Barbour approached the issue of Stennis' age gingerly, but still lost 64%-36%. Barbour carried only two counties. But at 35, Barbour already showed a sophisticated understanding of the nexus between money and politics. In what was then the most expensive race in state history, he raised and spent more than $1 million at a time when that amount could buy a great deal of attention in Mississippi.

It also got Barbour noticed in Washington, where he became Ronald Reagan's White House political director in 1985. (His boss was Mitch Daniels, now governor of Indiana.) He later was an adviser to George H.W. Bush's presidential campaign. In 1991, he took advantage of his connections and hung out his shingle, founding Barbour Griffith & Rogers, now BGR Group, one of Washington's powerhouse lobbying firms. From 1993 to 1997, Barbour was chairman of the Republican National Committee, heading the party when it won a congressional majority for the first time in 40 years in 1994 and earning some of the credit. He raised record sums, and worked closely with Rep. Newt Gingrich of Georgia when few shared his confidence that Republicans could win a majority in the House. When Barbour left the RNC and returned to his firm, he was positioned as one of Washington's most influential lobbyists, well connected to key members of the House and Senate and much sought after by big corporate clients with interests before the Republican Congress. In his years in Washington, Barbour maintained his ties back home. He served as a Republican national committeeman from 1984 until 1998, and regularly traveled to Yazoo City, where his wife and sons lived.

In 2002, he announced he would challenge Democratic Gov. Ronnie Musgrove, who, after winning just a 49.5% plurality in 1999, had been elected by the Mississippi House of Representatives. Much of Musgrove's term was taken up with controversy over the state flag, which had the Confederate battle cross in the upper-left-hand corner. The state Supreme Court ruled the flag illegal, but the new flag endorsed by Musgrove was rejected by voters in 2001 by 65%-35%.

Barbour's main campaign issue was an overhaul of tort law. Mississippi had had seven product liability judgments of $100 million or more in six years, and medical malpractice lawsuits were driving doctors out of an already underserved state. Musgrove got the legislature to place limits on tort suits in 2002, but Barbour said they didn't go far enough. Barbour also accused him of mismanaging the state economy. Musgrove said, "I've put Mississippi first. Haley Barbour has spent the last 20 years in Washington, D.C., putting special interests first." He criticized Barbour for representing tobacco and pharmaceutical companies and lobbying for the North American Free Trade Agreement, which, Musgrove said, cost Mississippi 41,000 jobs. By contrast, he claimed credit for attracting a Nissan plant to Madison County.

Barbour raised $10.6 million to Musgrove's $8.5 million, setting another state record for campaign spending. Barbour won 53%-46%. He carried 51 of 82 counties and won big margins in key Republican counties such as fast-growing DeSoto County, just south of Memphis, and suburban Rankin County east of Jackson. That offset high African-American turnout, which Democrats had counted on because of the presence of two black statewide nominees in down-ballot races. Exit polls showed that blacks voted 94% for Musgrove and white voters went 77% for Barbour.

Barbour took office with Democratic majorities in the state House and Senate. Still, in 2004 he won approval of his bill to cap pain-and-suffering tort damages generally at $1 million and at $500,000 in medical malpractice cases. The legislation also limited lawsuit forum-shopping and protected "innocent sellers" of faulty products. It approved a tax increase on nursing home beds to help fund the state's ailing Medicaid program, and Barbour and the legislature ultimately restored the program to solvency by borrowing $240 million from Mississippi's health care trust fund and instituting tighter restrictions on the number of prescriptions, emergency room visits, and home health care visits.

Hurricane Katrina slammed into the Gulf Coast on Barbour's watch, on Aug. 29, 2005. He described its aftermath along the Mississippi coast as "nuclear destruction." The main force of the hurricane struck Hancock County, and the towns of Waveland, Bay St. Louis, and Pass Christian were totally wiped out. The shrimping and shipbuilding industries were hurt by extensive damage to the state's 90-mile coastline, and casinos were severely damaged, costing the state $500,000 a day in revenue. Barbour quickly took charge and drew national notice for his decisive leadership, particularly in contrast to the muddled reaction of Louisiana leaders. He appointed a commission to coordinate the recovery, led by former Netscape CEO Jim Barksdale. The state's recovery was assisted by federal money secured by the Mississippi congressional delegation; it did not hurt that Republican Thad Cochran was chairman of the Senate Appropriations Committee. Soon $5 billion was authorized for Mississippi, $3 billion of it for housing. Barbour administered grants and low-interest loans to home and business owners who suffered uninsured losses, and the federal government shelled out $2.4 billion for National Flood Insurance Program claims. The state House and Senate changed the gambling law to allow casinos to be built on land within 800 feet of the shore, and casino owners moved in rapidly to rebuild. By June 2006, the state had gained 30,000 jobs over 2005, wages were up, and developers were gentrifying what were once low-income Gulf Coast neighborhoods. Barbour's connections in Washington paid off, as D.C. lobbyists and friends sent supplies in the first days following the hurricane and later held fundraising events for Barbour's Mississippi Hurricane Recovery Fund.

In July 2006, touting his job-creation efforts and fiscal restraint, Barbour announced the state's first budget surplus in years. He rebuffed efforts by Democrats to lower the grocery tax and raise the cigarette tax, saying that a lower grocery tax would have minimal impact on the poor because the state's 450,000 food stamp recipients were not subject to the tax. His credibility on economic development got a big boost when Toyota announced it had chosen a site near Tupelo for a new 2,000-job assembly plant. In his 2007 State of the State address, Barbour told lawmakers, "There's no doubt in my mind that the future of Mississippi is brighter than it's ever been in our history.... As strange as it might seem, that awful catastrophe Katrina is part of the reason."

He started his campaign for re-election in 2007 as governor with $3.5 million. Democratic nominee John Arthur Eaves, a personal injury lawyer from Madison County, called for cutting the grocery tax while Barbour promised an unspecified tax cut. Barbour also called for spending $125 million over five years to reduce school dropout rates and to raise pay for teachers with 25 years of service. Eaves emphasized prayers and faith and, to Barbour's irritation, pressed for details of Barbour's blind trust. Barbour was helped by endorsements from some prominent Democrats, including former Agriculture Secretary Mike Espy and former Gov. Bill Waller. He won handily, 58%-42%.

Opening his second term, Barbour set his focus on a neglected part of the state, the Delta and southwest Mississippi, which was not sharing in Mississippi's economic rebirth. He said he wanted to improve education and workforce skills, and to "combat and reduce the scourge of illegitimacy." In 2008, he got full funding of the Mississippi Adequate Education Program for the first time in a non-election year. But the state, like the nation, was set on its heels by the 2007-09 recession. Revenues came in 9% under projections, and Barbour demanded that legislators change the Medicaid law to eliminate a $90 million shortfall, threatening to make cuts in the program if they didn't. He trimmed the overall state budget by $42 million. Barbour at first said he might not accept the federal government's economic stimulus money, but as the budget problems worsened, he announced in March 2009 he would accept all but $50 million of the $2.3 billion for Mississippi.

When he and legislative leaders could not agree on several key budget items, Barbour cut spending three times between in the latter half of 2009. After initially resisting demands from legislators to dip into the state's "rainy day" fund, Barbour agreed in April 2010 to take $300 million from reserves. Later that year, Barbour proposed rolling back Medicare reimbursement rates, freezing K-12 teacher pay, and cutting spending another 8%, except for corrections and the Mississippi Development Authority. In 2011, Barbour had a more slightly GOP-friendly legislature: Republicans had 27-25 control of the Senate and Democrats controlled the House, 72-50.

Throughout his tenure as governor, Barbour remained an important voice in national Republican politics. After GOP losses at the polls in 2008, he said, "The fact of the matter is, we brought a lot of this on ourselves, a lot of it by not being faithful to what we told people that we believed in and not adhering to what people thought they had voted for." His views in opposition to the Democratic White House also got attention. In May 2009, he told *Politico*, "Obama has given up on capitalism. . . . He is expanding the size of government beyond anything that anyone previously dreamed of."

In 2009, Barbour was chosen to head the Republican Governors Association after South Carolina Gov. Mark Sanford quit while battling the fallout from an extramarital affair. In that role, Barbour signaled impatience with the all-or-nothing strain of conservative ideology that emerged in 2010 campaigns. "Purity in politics is about losing," Barbour told *The Washington Post*. "Politics is about addition and multiplication; purity is about subtraction and division. . . . You have to remember that now is the time to have the most open of doors." At the same time, he embraced tea party activists, who were a force in campaigns across the country, He told *National Journal*, "I see the tea party people as very similar to the (Ross) Perot people. Their principal concern is outrageously excessive government spending and running up debt. They're for lower taxes and smaller government. And while they may not consider themselves Republicans, they've got a lot more in common with Republicans than they do with Democrats."

Barbour raised over $100 million for GOP candidates in the election, in effect compensating for the weak fundraising of the controversy-prone Michael Steele at the Republican National Committee. In September 2010, the RGA effectively took over the voter turnout efforts previously run by the RNC. Republicans won 23 of the 37 governorships up that year, 11 of which had previously been held by Democrats, giving Republicans a 29-20-1 edge. In addition, the RGA did much to help Republicans gain over 700 seats in state legislatures, and appeared to be in control of the congressional redistricting process in several major states, including Texas, Florida, Pennsylvania, Ohio, Michigan, Georgia, and North Carolina.

Mississippi governors are limited to two terms, and Barbour is scheduled to leave office in January 2012. As the field began to take shape in 2011, he was on the list of possible presidential candidates in 2012. Always the smart political operative, Barbour was upfront about his negatives. He conceded in interviews that an overweight, ex-governor from a small Southern state, who spent years as a lobbyist, may not be the ideal candidate. "What you see is what you get," he said on the TV program *Uncommon Knowledge*. "I am from Mississippi. I do have a Southern accent." Still, he said, the country by then might be looking for "the anti-Obama." But by April 2011, Barbour had perhaps decided that selling himself to a national audience would be too difficult, even for a master salesman. He announced he would not seek the presidency.

His brief exposure to the presidential spotlight was not entirely encouraging. Discussing the violent Mississippi summer of 1964, when three civil-rights workers were killed in Neshoba County, Barbour told the *Weekly Standard*, there was no violence in Yazoo City, where he grew up, "Because the business community wouldn't stand for it. You heard of the Citizens Councils? Up north they think it was like the KKK. Where I come from, it was an organization of town leaders. In Yazoo City, they passed a resolution that said anybody who started a chapter of the Klan would get their ass run out of town. If you had a job, you'd lose it. If you had a store, they'd see nobody shopped there. We didn't have a problem with the Klan in Yazoo City."

His comments evoked a flurry of criticism from civil rights proponents who pointed out that the Citizens Councils also strongly resisted desegregation. In response, Barbour issued a statement to try to clarify his remarks, which said, "My point was, my town rejected the Ku Klux Klan, but nobody should construe that to mean I think the town leadership were saints either. Their vehicle, called the Citizens Council, is totally indefensible, as is segregation. It was a difficult and painful era in Mississippi, the rest of the country, and especially for African-Americans who were persecuted in that time."

Senior Senator

Thad Cochran (R)

Elected 1978, term expires 2014, 6th term; b. Dec. 7, 1937, Pontotoc; home, Jackson; U. of MS, B.A. 1959, J.D. 1965, Rotary Fellow, Trinity Col., Ireland, 1963-64; Baptist; married (Rose); 2 children.

Military Career: Navy, 1959-61.

Elected Office: U.S. House of Reps., 1972–78.

Professional Career: Practicing atty., 1965–72.

DC Office: 113 DSOB, 20510, 202-224-5054; Fax: 202-224-9450; Web site: cochran.senate.gov.

State Offices: Gulfport, 228-867-9710; Jackson, 601-965-4459; Oxford, 662-236-1018.

Committees: *Agriculture, Nutrition & Forestry:* Commodities, Markets, Trade & Risk Management; Conservation, Forestry & Natural Resources; Nutrition, Specialty Crops, Food & Ag Research. *Appropriations* (RMM): Agriculture, Rural Development, Food and Drug Administration & Related Agencies; Defense (RMM); Energy & Water Development; Homeland Security; Interior, Environment & Related Agencies; Labor, Health & Human Services, Education & Related Agencies. *Rules & Administration.*

Group Ratings

	ACLU	ACU	ADA	CFG	AFS	FRC	LCV	ITIC	NTU	COC
2010	7	88	5	81	11	87	0	67	90	100
2009	–	84	10	84	18	–	27	–	72	86

National Journal Ratings

	2010 LIB	—	2010 CONS	2009 LIB	—	2009 CONS
Economic	27%	—	71%	28%	—	71%
Social	0%	—	79%	19%	—	80%
Foreign	30%	—	67%	34%	—	65%
Composite	23%	—	77%	28%	—	73%

Key Votes of the 111th Congress

1. Overturn Ledbetter	N	5. Pass health care bill	
2. Pass $787 billion stimulus	N	6. Regulate financial firms	
3. Repeal DC gun laws	Y	7. Pass tax cuts for some	
4. Confirm Sonia Sotomayor	N	8. Legalize immigrants' kids	N

9. Ratify New START	Y
10. Confirm Elena Kagan	N
11. Stop EPA climate regs	Y
12. Repeal don't ask, tell	N

Election Results

2008 general	Thad Cochran (R)..766,111	(61%)	($2,723,398)
	Erik Fleming (D)...480,915	(39%)	
2008 primary	Thad Cochran (R).. unopposed		

Prior Winning Percentages: 2002 (85%); 1996 (71%); 1990 (100%); 1984 (61%); 1978 (45%); House: 1976 (76%); 1974 (70%); 1972 (48%)

Republican Thad Cochran, Mississippi's senior senator, was elected to the House in 1972 and the Senate in 1978, where he sits at Jefferson Davis's old desk. He has come to personify a vanishing breed of Southern Republican—amiable to all, conservative but not rigidly so, a devoted institutionalist, and a proficient procurer of funding earmarks for his poor, rural state.

Cochran grew up in small towns in northern Mississippi and near Jackson, the son of a principal and a mathematics teacher. Cochran was extremely athletic in high school and lettered in football, basketball, and baseball. He was also valedictorian of his senior class and a talented musician. (He still sometimes plays the baby grand piano in his Senate office for relaxation.) Cochran continued to excel academically at Ole Miss, where he was a cheerleader, which was not uncommon for men at that time and was in fact considered an honor. Cochran went on to get a law school degree from Ole Miss. He served in the Navy, spent a year abroad, and then practiced law in Jackson.

In 1968, he worked on the Nixon-Agnew presidential campaign in Mississippi, where Richard Nixon ran third. Four years later, when President Nixon was sweeping Mississippi, Cochran ran for Congress and was elected as a Republican from the Jackson-area district with a plurality against a white Democrat and a black independent. When segregationist Sen. James Eastland, a Democrat, retired, Cochran jumped into the race and once again won with a plurality over a white Democrat and a black independent. In the House and in the Senate, he has managed to amass a generally conservative record with little controversy or acrimony. His patrician demeanor, his refusal to engage in racial politics, and his Republican Party label—in a state where most whites have been voting Republican for president for three decades—have made him broadly acceptable to voters at home. His toughest race came in 1984, when he was opposed by popular former Democratic Gov. William Winter. Winter could make a case for himself but not against Cochran. Cochran outraised him $2.7 million to $738,000, and won 61%-39%.

Cochran is the ranking minority member on the Appropriations Committee, and was chairman from 2005 to 2007 when Republicans controlled the Senate. He has also been the ranking member since July 2008 on the Defense Appropriations Subcommittee, where he has been a key proponent of missile defense, and has worked to fund projects big and small for Mississippi. Timely amendments to appropriations bills that make major policy are a Cochran specialty.

When he first became chairman, Cochran promised to get appropriations bills passed on time, rather than rolling multiple bills into large "omnibus" measures, which had become practice as Congress grew more partisan and unable to agree on individual spending bills. Cochran also said, "We're not going to have runaway spending on the Appropriations Committee when I'm chairman. I won't tolerate it." In spite of those assurances, earmarks and runaway discretionary spending were to remain major issues during his stewardship. Hurricane Katrina struck on Aug. 29, 2005, causing massive damage in Mississippi, and suddenly keeping tight controls on spending was not the chairman's prime concern. Cochran viewed the devastation by helicopter on Aug. 31, and then persuaded the Senate to immediately vote for $10.5 billion in disaster relief. A week later, he persuaded it to vote for $52 billion more. In late October, President George W. Bush called for an additional $17 billion. Cochran, working closely with Republican Gov. Haley Barbour and others in the Mississippi and Louisiana delegations, pushed for $35 billion, with community development block grants available for homeowners and business owners with uninsured losses. This was a new policy, and one not included in the administration request. On Dec. 21, Congress passed a $29 billion bill, with $11.5 billion for community development block grants. Mississippi received $5.1 billion of the CDBG funds. In the meantime, work on the regular appropriations bills bogged down, and Cochran and House Appropriations Chairman Jerry Lewis, R-Calif., resigned themselves to a continuing resolution for nine appropriations bills they couldn't get passed.

The following year, 2006, brought more vagaries in the appropriations process in the form of the Bush administration's request for large amounts of additional money for the war in Iraq. The president asked for a supplemental Iraq funding bill, a proposal sweetened with nearly $20 billion in additional funds for hurricane recovery. Cochran drafted a bill that included some controversial provisions: $700 million for building a CSX rail line inland, to replace the line on the Gulf Coast; $500 million for Northrop Grumman, which was in litigation with the insurers of its Pascagoula shipyard; and $1 billion for Katrina housing. Cochran's fellow Republicans were among his biggest critics. Speaker Dennis Hastert and House Majority Leader John Boehner called his bill a "special-interest shopping cart," and conservative Republican Sen. Tom Coburn of Oklahoma tried to kill it. But Cochran prevailed on the Senate floor 50-47. Ultimately, Congress agreed to supplemental spending for Iraq and to $20 billion for Katrina recovery, although it rejected the railroad line.

As Cochran resumed trying to pass the regular appropriations bills on time, earmarked spending came increasingly under fire as more conservatives took issue with Congress's long-standing practice of approving special projects for individual lawmakers, projects that often were not requested by any government agency. Cochran and Lewis managed to get through both chambers just two of the 12 spending bills in 2006, those for defense and homeland-security appropriations. Budget hawks raised objections to earmarks in the remaining 10 bills, and GOP Majority Leader Bill Frist declined to bring them to the floor before the November election. When Democrats won majorities in both houses, Congress passed a temporary measure to keep the government running, and work ceased on the remaining spending bills. Cochran lost his chairmanship.

In 2007, the first year of the Democratic majorities in Congress, the appropriations bills became magnets for anti-war lawmakers. Cochran opposed Democrats' attempts to set timetables for troop withdrawals in the 2007 Iraq war supplemental spending bill. In subsequent years, however, he has become more inclined to abandon his party on floor votes. He was one of just 11 Republicans to support a $17 billion Democratic jobs bill in 2010, and joined Democrats that year in backing the New START arms reduction treaty with Russia. He also has worked with Democrats on legislation to enhance national service and to promote geography literacy among students.

Cochran regularly incenses watchdog groups with his additions to spending bills for Mississippi projects. He had the highest total of earmarks in fiscal years 2008, 2009, and 2010, with more than $497 million in fiscal 2010 alone, according to Taxpayers for Common Sense. He takes a particular interest in his state universities' research needs and casts a wide net—in the fiscal 2009 omnibus spending bill he earmarked $3.5 million to the University of Mississippi's National Center for Natural Products Research, at the time the country's legal producer of marijuana for medical research. (The center is housed in a building that bears his name.) As younger, more conservative Republicans sought to halt the practice, Cochran continued to wholeheartedly defend earmarks. "Analyses of how the executive branch spends discretionary federal dollars when left to its own devices show that rural states like Mississippi, states that often have a great deal of need, are largely ignored. This is why our Founding Fathers gave Congress the explicit power to direct spending, so that those who are elected by the people, not bureaucrats, decide how funds are spent," he said. However, when Republicans announced an earmark moratorium for the 112th Congress (2011-12), he reluctantly went along. "I remain unconvinced that fiscal prudence is effectively advanced by ceding to the Obama administration our constitutional authority," he said.

The other area of interest for Cochran is farm legislation. On the Agriculture Committee, he played an important role in shaping the very different 1996, 2002, and 2008 farm bills. In 1996, he supported the Republican initiative to phase out most crop subsidies, although he insisted on maintaining the cotton marketing loan plan that he largely wrote in 1985. In 2002, he supported the strategy of reviving annual crop payments and of vastly increasing the Conservation Reserve Program. In 2005, Cochran defeated on the Senate floor, 53-46, Iowa Republican Charles Grassley's move to cap subsidies to individual farmers at $250,000. In 2006, he opposed Bush's proposed 5% cut in farm subsidies. And in 2008, he supported the farm bill that passed over Bush's veto. The president said the bill was too costly and did not go far enough to curb subsidies.

Also in late 2007, Cochran got a new Mississippi partner in the Senate with the arrival of newly appointed Sen. Roger Wicker, a Republican. The two quickly teamed up to try to compel Congress to allow federal flood insurance policyholders to add wind coverage to protect themselves financially against future hurricanes. A former U.S. House member, Wicker was appointed by Barbour to replace GOP Sen. Trent Lott, who resigned from Congress. It was a welcome change for Cochran, who had competed with Lott over the years to advance in the leadership and usually wound up losing to him. In 1990, Cochran was elected to the chairmanship of the Senate Republican Conference, the No. 3 position. Although he had less seniority than Cochran, Lott set his sights higher. Rather than wait his turn to move up, Lott challenged Wyoming's Alan Simpson for majority whip, the No. 2 position. Cochran pointedly endorsed Simpson, but Lott won anyway, with the support of junior Senate conservatives, and leapfrogged over Cochran to the higher-ranking post of whip. Then in 1996, the top job of Senate majority leader came open when Kansas Republican Bob Dole ran for president. Cochran and Lott both entered the race. Lott was able to sew up a majority of votes quickly. Cochran stayed in the contest and lost 44-8.

Some political observers wondered whether Cochran would run for re-election in 2008. But he did and his challenger wound up being a former state representative with little money and no paid staff. Cochran spent $2.8 million and won 61%-39%, his closest margin since 1984.

Though Cochran has steered clear of scandal, in March 2009 one of his former longtime aides pleaded guilty to swapping legislative favors for event tickets and other gifts from disgraced lobbyist Jack Abramoff's firm. During the presidential contest in 2008, his unflattering remarks about Arizona Sen. John McCain were widely quoted in the media. Cochran told the *Boston Globe*, "The thought of his being president sends a cold chill down my spine. He's erratic. He's hotheaded. He loses his temper, and he worries me." When McCain ultimately became the party's nominee, Cochran was conciliatory and called his earlier appraisal of McCain "ill advised." He added, "I didn't think he was going to win the nomination either."

After Democrat Barack Obama defeated McCain, Cochran said, "There are a lot of people coming in with a lot of enthusiasm. We need some people with a little gray hair to help be a calming influence. That is the role I will play."

Junior Senator

Roger Wicker (R)

Appointed Dec. 2007, term expires 2012, 1st term; b. July 5, 1951, Pontotoc; home, Tupelo; U. of MS, B.A. 1973, J.D. 1975; Baptist; married (Gayle); 3 children.

Military Career: Air Force, 1976–80; Air Force Reserve, 1980–2004.

Elected Office: Tupelo city judge pro tem, 1986–87; MS Senate, 1987–94., U.S. Rep., 1995-2007.

Professional Career: Staff, U.S. House Rules Cmte., 1980–82; Practicing atty., 1982–94; Lee Cnty. public defender, 1984–87; Bd. of Visitors, U.S. Naval Academy, 2005.

DC Office: 555 DSOB, 20515, 202-224-6253; Fax: 202-228-0378; Web site: wicker.senate.gov.

State Offices: Gulfport, 228-604-2383; Hernando, 662-429-1002; Jackson, 601-965-4644; Pascagoula , 228-762-5400; Tupelo, 662-844-5010.

Committees: *Armed Services:* Airland; Seapower (RMM); Strategic Forces. *Banking, Housing & Urban Affairs:* Economic Policy; Housing, Transportation & Community Development; Securities, Insurance & Investment. *Commerce, Science & Transportation:* Aviation Operations, Safety & Security; Communications, Technology & the Internet; Consumer Protection, Product Safety & Insurance (RMM); Oceans, Atmosphere, Fisheries & Coast Guard; Science & Space; Surface Transportation & Merchant Marine Infrastructure, Safety & Security. *Veterans' Affairs.*

Group Ratings

	ACLU	ACU	ADA	CFG	AFS	FRC	LCV	ITIC	NTU	COC
2010	7	96	0	85	4	100	0	67	94	100
2009	–	88	15	92	9	–	18	–	82	86

National Journal Ratings

	2010 LIB	—	2010 CONS		2009 LIB	—	2009 CONS
Economic	14%	—	84%		26%	—	73%
Social	0%	—	79%		13%	—	86%
Foreign	0%	—	72%		28%	—	71%
Composite	13%	—	87%		23%	—	77%

Key Votes of the 111th Congress

1. Overturn Ledbetter	N	5. Pass health care bill	N	9. Ratify New START	N
2. Pass $787 billion stimulus	N	6. Regulate financial firms	N	10. Confirm Elena Kagan	N
3. Repeal DC gun laws	Y	7. Pass tax cuts for some	N	11. Stop EPA climate regs	Y
4. Confirm Sonia Sotomayor	N	8. Legalize immigrants' kids	N	12. Repeal don't ask, tell	N

Election Results

2008 general	Roger Wicker (R)..683,409	(55%)	($5,969,342)
	Ronnie Musgrove (D).....................................560,064	(45%)	($2,686,206)
2008 primary	Roger Wicker (R)... unopposed		

Prior Winning Percentages: House: 2006 (66%); 2004 (79%); 2002 (71%); 2000 (70%); 1998 (67%); 1996 (68%); 1994 (63%)

Roger Wicker was appointed to the U.S. Senate in late 2007 by Republican Gov. Haley Barbour to fill the vacancy created by the resignation of Trent Lott, a powerful Mississippian who served as both majority and minority leader of the Senate. Wicker, a Republican member of the U.S. House at the time of the appointment, went on to win election to the seat in November 2008.

Wicker grew up in Pontotoc, the same north Mississippi town where his senior colleague in the Senate, Republican Thad Cochran, spent part of his childhood. Wicker's father was a conservative Democrat, a state senator, and a circuit judge. He attended public schools and as a teenager became interested in Republican politics. From then on, his career was intertwined with the two more senior and well-established Mississippians, Lott and Cochran. He was a page in the U.S. House and campaigned door to door for Cochran in his first race for Congress, in 1972. At Ole Miss, where both Lott and Cochran went to school, Wicker was associated student body president, and went on to get his law degree there. He then served for four years in the Air Force and remained in the Reserve until 2004. In 1980, he went to work for Lott on the House Rules Committee when Lott was still in the House. Wicker returned to Mississippi in 1982, set up a law practice, and was the county public defender in his wife's hometown of Tupelo. In 1987, at age 36, he was elected to the state Senate, the first Republican elected in north Mississippi since Reconstruction. In the legislature, Wicker helped draft the state's strict abortion law and was also a leading advocate of government-sponsored vouchers for private school tuition.

In 1994, longtime U.S. Rep. Jamie Whitten, a Democrat, momentously retired after becoming the longest-serving member of the House in history. His record of 53 years and 62 days was broken by Michigan Democrat John Dingell in February 2009. The retirement of the powerful Whitten, the chairman of the Appropriations Committee, left large shoes to fill in Mississippi's 1st District. Pent-up demand produced a crowded primary field in both major parties. Six Republicans, including Wicker, and three Democrats lined up to run.

Carrying his home base around Tupelo, Wicker led the GOP primary 27%-19% over Grant Fox, a young former aide to Cochran. In the runoff, Wicker campaigned as a conservative, but Fox hammered him for voting to override Republican Gov. Kirk Fordice's veto of a sales tax increase. Wicker won, 53%-47%. Meanwhile, state Rep. Bill Wheeler, the Democratic nominee, had racked up support from African-Americans, labor unions, and teachers—an advantage in his party's primary but not necessarily in the general election in the conservative 1st District. The result wasn't even close. A district that had been held for five decades by a leading Democrat voted 63%-37% for the Republican.

Wicker got off to a fast start in the House, elected president of the large, 73-member House freshman class that year. The incoming Republicans were by and large a feisty brand of conservatives who had nationalized the election of 1994, capitalized on public discontent with 40 years of Democratic control, and followed GOP firebrand Newt Gingrich to power. Wicker compiled a solidly conservative voting record. He got a seat on Appropriations, an unusual prize for a freshman. Appropriators tend to operate in an atmosphere of bipartisan cooperation, and Wicker worked quietly in subcommittees to get funding for Yalobusha River flood control and an interstate highway through DeSoto County. He delivered research dollars to Mississippi universities, and he worked with Lott, by then a senator, to attract defense technology firms to the state.

Although north Mississippi was not badly hurt by Hurricane Katrina in August 2005, Wicker worked the House for Cochran as Cochran, the newly installed Senate Appropriations chairman, tried to direct federal aid to coastal Mississippi. Wicker's job was to convince his conservative Republican colleagues in the House that the state faced a genuine emergency. He sided with fellow appropriators and against conservatives in his party who tried to limit earmarked spending. For that, he earned the dubious distinction of No. 1 earmarker in the House by the watchdog group Citizens Against Government Waste. His achievement was securing $176 million in projects, most of it for his district. "I am a fiscal conservative, and I believe in keeping spending low," Wicker said in 2008. "But once the national budget is set, I think it is only fair to fight for our fair share for Mississippi." He did, however, join Cochran in reluctantly supporting the GOP's earmark ban in the 112th Congress (2011-12).

In November 2007, Lott announced that he would retire from the Senate before the end of the year, after serving 19 years there and 16 in the House. Wicker wanted the seat, but so did 3rd District GOP Rep. Chip Pickering and Netscape founder and Mississippi native James Barksdale. On Dec. 31, 2007, Barbour appointed Wicker and set the election for the remaining years of Lott's term on Nov. 4, 2008. Attorney General Jim Hood, a Democrat, argued that state law required a special election within 100 days of Lott's resignation and filed a lawsuit against Barbour. Democrats assumed they would fare better in a special election than with the wider electorate in November. And in fact, Democrat Travis Childers won Wicker's House seat—a district that had voted

62% for President George W. Bush in 2004—in the special election in May. On Feb. 6, 2008, the state Supreme Court upheld Barbour 7-2.

Wicker was sworn in and got seats on the Armed Services, Veterans' Affairs, and Commerce committees. He continued to support Bush on the war in Iraq and to oppose timetables for a troop withdrawal. He supported Northrop Grumman and Airbus in their struggle against Boeing to get the Air Force's tanker contract. Airbus's big assembly plant was planned for Mobile, Ala., near the Gulf Coast of Mississippi. He worked closely with Cochran, who had often been at odds with Lott, in backing local projects and co-sponsoring bills. (Citizens Against Government Waste labeled Cochran and Wicker No. 1 and No. 3 Senate earmarkers respectively for 2008 and 2010 in combined solo and joint efforts. They were also first and second in 2009.)

Wicker also worked with Democrats to protect Mississippi's interests. With Democratic Rep. Gene Taylor, he pushed amendments allowing purchasers of federal flood insurance to add wind coverage to their policies, helpful to a hurricane-prone state. After Taylor got his bill passed in the House, Wicker tried to overcome resistance in the Senate from Banking Chairman Christopher Dodd of Connecticut, a state where many of the major insurers are headquartered. Wicker, Cochran, and the two Louisiana senators placed a hold on the flood insurance bill in 2008. But they were eventually defeated, 74-19.

With President Barack Obama's election, Wicker became part of the core of Senate Republicans implacably opposed to most of the administration's initiatives. He called the health care overhaul the "great fight for the rest of this term, maybe our lifetimes," and later introduced a bill to enable state officials to challenge the law. In the interest of protecting gun owners, he amended a fiscal 2010 transportation spending bill to allow Amtrak passengers to carry firearms and ammunition in checked baggage. He was sharply critical of Federal Communications Commission Chairman Julius Genachowski's efforts to regulate broadband Internet services, saying it would undermine the competiveness of small businesses. And when the 112th Congress got under way in 2011, Wicker was named to the Senate Republicans' whip team and re-introduced his bill to overturn *Roe v. Wade.* Wicker had been re-elected easily in the 1st District, but he spent his first year in the Senate facing a serious challenge in the upcoming November 2008 election. Mississippi Democrats had not seriously contested a Senate race in 20 years, but President Bush's low poll ratings, enthusiasm among African-American voters for Democratic presidential nominee Obama, and Childers' victory in Wicker's old district gave them reason to believe they might beat Wicker. He started the year little known outside his congressional district. The Democratic nominee was widely known: former Gov. Ronnie Musgrove, who was defeated for re-election by Barbour in 2003 and had good poll ratings. It was a battle between old friends: Wicker and Musgrove had both been elected to the state Senate for the first time in 1987 and roomed together in an apartment in Jackson.

But Musgrove started out on the attack. He criticized Wicker for his support of earmarks and called him a "poster child" for a moratorium on pork-barrel spending. Musgrove also criticized him for opposing increases in the minimum wage. Wicker said, "The people of Mississippi are tired of politicians like Mr. Musgrove and their negative attacks, and I don't think they're going to stand for his brand of politics." Musgrove even hinted at ethical misconduct, criticizing Wicker for securing a $6 million earmark, not sought by the Pentagon, for Aurora Flight Sciences to build unmanned aerial vehicles in north Mississippi, while company executives contributed $17,000 to his campaign and hired Wicker's former chief of staff to lobby for the project. Wicker said the effort was all about bringing high-paying jobs to Mississippi.

The tables turned on Musgrove after the indictment of three executives of a Georgia company that defaulted on a state government guaranteed loan of $54 million. They had contributed $59,000 to Musgrove's 2003 campaign. Wicker continued to make news on Katrina issues, notably his support of multi-peril insurance. He traveled extensively around the state, often with Cochran, who was up for re-election and was considered sure to win overwhelmingly. Wicker outspent Musgrove, $6.2 million to $5.3 million. But the Democratic Senatorial Campaign Committee pumped in more than enough money to compensate for Wicker's advantage. Wicker won 55%-45%. Eighty-two percent of whites backed Wicker, while 92% of blacks backed Musgrove.

FIRST DISTRICT

Alan Nunnelee (R)

Elected 2010, 1st term; b. Oct. 9, 1958, Tupelo; home, Tupelo; MS St. U., B.S. 1980.; Baptist; Married (Tori); 3 children.

Elected Office: MS Senate, 1994-2010.

Professional Career: V.P., American Funeral Assn. Insurance Co., 1981-94; founder, Allied Funeral Associates.

DC Office: 1432 LHOB, 20515, 202-225-4306; Fax: 202-225-3549; Web site: nunnelee.house.gov.

State Offices: Hernando, 662-449-3090; Tupelo, 662-841-8808; Columbus, 662-327-0748.

Committees: *Appropriations:* Agriculture, Rural Development, FDA & Related Agencies; Energy & Water Development; Military Construction, Veterans Affairs & Related Agencies.

Election Results

2010 general	Alan Nunnelee (R)	121,074	(55%)	($1,739,384)
	Travis Childers (D)	89,388	(41%)	($1,817,037)
2010 primary	Alan Nunnelee (R)	20,236	(52%)	
	Henry Ross (R)	12,894	(33%)	
	Angela McGlowan (R)	5,924	(15%)	

Population		Race/Ethnicity		Work	
Pop. 2010:	788,095	White:	68.0%	Private:	78.1%
Change since 2000:	Up 10.8%	Black:	27.3%	Government:	15.8%
Urban:	38.5%	Hispanic:	3.0%	Self-employed:	6.0%
Rural:	61.5%	Asian:	0.6%	Blue collar:	31.7%
Area size:	11,647 sq. mi.	Native Am.:	0.2%	White collar:	52.5%
		Hawaiian:	0.0%	Khaki collar:	0.2%
Age		Two+ races:	0.9%	Other:	15.6%
Median age:	36.0 yrs.				
More than 65 yrs:	13.0%	*Ancestry*		Median income:	$38,568
Less than 18 yrs:	25.9%	USA	11.5%	Median Home Value:	$96,700
		Irish	11.1%		
Education		English	8.6%	**Military Veterans**	
H.S. grad:	78.2%			% of Pop:	9.2%
College grad:	17.4%				
Grad degree:	6.0%				

Northern Mississippi; Tupelo

The university town of Oxford—the "Jefferson" of William Faulkner's fictional Yoknapatawpha County—sits on a divide between the hill country of Mississippi and the flat farmlands of the Mississippi Delta. Named for Oxford, England, it is the home of the Center for the Study of Southern Culture and of the University of Mississippi, where violence broke out in 1962 when James Meredith became the school's first black student. Ole Miss, as it is known, now houses

2008 Presidential Vote
John McCain (R) 213,479   (62%)
Barack Obama (D) 129,940   (38%)

2004 Presidential Vote
George Bush (R) 187,979   (62%)
John Kerry (D) 111,509   (37%)

Cook Partisan Voting Index: R+14

Meredith's papers in its library. In 1962, Republican Sen. Thad Cochran was a student at the Ole Miss law school, and former Senate Majority Leader Trent Lott of Mississippi was a senior. To the west is the Delta, with a large African-American majority, and also DeSoto County, just south of Memphis and Mississippi's fastest-growing county and one of its most affluent. East of Oxford is the hill country, which stretches up to where the Tennessee River nicks the northeast corner of Tishomingo County. The Tennessee Valley Authority brought electricity here, the Tennessee-Tombigbee Waterway provided construction jobs for years, and a shipping canal was completed in 1985. The Tenn-Tom is the largest water resource project built in the United States. This was traditional farming country, but it is now more engaged in small manufacturing.

The Golden Triangle in the Starkville area has become a center for aerospace research, including work on unmanned air vehicle designs for improved surveillance and communications. The biggest town here is Tupelo. It is home to an upholstered furniture industry that is the largest manufacturing sector in the state and has survived more prosperously than furniture centers elsewhere. Donald Wildmon's American Family Association, based in Tupelo, is a prominent Christian conservative organization. Elvis Presley was born in Tupelo in 1935, in a two-room house that is open to visitors, and the Elvis Presley Museum has a modest collection of the rock 'n' roll idol's memorabilia. The Tupelo region got a big economic boost when Toyota in 2010 started hiring at a newly built auto plant, where it planned a workforce of 2,000 producing 150,000 vehicles a year. Toyota suppliers have sprung up nearby, with expectations of eventually employing another 2,000 people.

The 1st Congressional District of Mississippi includes Oxford, Tupelo, most of the hill country, and DeSoto County. This is the descendant of the district represented by Jamie Whitten, the long-time Democratic chairman of the Appropriations Committee and formerly the longest-serving House member. He served 53 years and 62 days, ending in January 1995; Democratic Rep. John Dingell of Michigan surpassed his mark in February 2009. Historically this was conservative Democrat territory. The district voted solidly for Democratic Gov. Ronnie Musgrove in 1999, but in 2003 favored his Republican successor, Haley Barbour. In national politics, it is solidly Republican, voting 59% for George W. Bush in 2000 and 62% in 2004. Similarly, the district voted 62% for John McCain in 2008.

Alan Nunnelee (R)

The new congressman from Mississippi's 1st District is Republican Alan Nunnelee, who returned it to the GOP fold with his defeat of freshman Democrat Travis Childers. Nunnelee was born in Tupelo, the first of four children. His mother was just 17 when he was born; his father 19. But the couple began to save for their children's college education from the time they were babies. His father became a successful insurance agent and his mother returned to community college to become a pediatric nurse when Nunnelee was in middle school. "When I think about a young couple doing without so their children would have the opportunities that they didn't have, that overwhelms me," Nunnelee said. His parents were devout Christians, he said. "Church was very much a part of my life, and I think that laid the foundation of my political beliefs."

When he was in college, a congenital disease caused Nunnelee's eyesight to deteriorate until he went blind during his junior year. Determined to continue his studies, he bought his textbooks on tape, recorded his lectures, and arranged for friends to drive him to classes. His vision problems once resulted in a job offer being retracted. But he said the disability also taught him to be self-reliant. In 1980, Nunnelee received his bachelor's degree in marketing from Mississippi State University. Shortly after graduating, Nunnelee underwent cornea transplants on both eyes to restore his vision, which were made possible by the family of an organ donor around his age. "All I know is that there was a family of a 20-something-year-old man or woman, and on the very worst day of their life—when they had lost a child, a brother or a sister—they thought of someone other than themselves," he said. "I see today because of their generosity."

Around the same time, friends set him up on a date with a girl he had known since high school—"a real blind date," Nunnelee jokes. Their romance blossomed, and Nunnelee married Tori in 1982. He followed his father into the insurance industry, working at the American Funeral Association Insurance Co. from 1981 to 1994, until "the merger from hell" prompted him to leave and start his own company, Allied Funeral Associates, where he is still vice president and director. He and his wife have three grown children and are now grandparents.

One of Nunnelee's first experiences in politics was working for 1st District Rep. Roger Wicker's 1994 campaign for the House. When Wicker won, local Republicans urged Nunnelee to run for Wicker's vacated seat in the state Senate, which he won. Over the course of a 16-year career in the legislature, Nunnelee championed conservative causes and wielded considerable control over the state budget as chairman of the Appropriations Committee. In 2001, he helped pass legislation that placed the motto "In God We Trust" in every classroom in Mississippi, helping to raise money for the effort with GOP Lt. Gov. Amy Tuck to avoid using tax dollars. In 2003, he headed a successful effort to amend the state constitution to ban same-sex marriage. Nunnelee says that his proudest accomplishment was passing a statutory rape law increasing the age of consent for sex from 13 to 16.

In 2010, he challenged Childers, who had won the seat in a special election in 2008 to replace Wicker after Wicker was appointed to the Senate. Republicans had been targeting him for defeat from almost the moment he won in a low-turnout affair against Greg Davis, the mayor of Southaven.

In his campaign to unseat Childers, Nunnelee tried to tie him to President Barack Obama and liberal House Speaker Nancy Pelosi, casting himself as the only "true conservative" in the contest. Childers, a member of the Blue Dog Coalition of conservative House Democrats, highlighted his endorsements from the National Rifle Association and the National Right to Life organization. He also opposed abortion rights. Nunnelee kept close to Childers in fundraising, with Childers raising $1.3 million and spending nearly $400,000 by the fall. Nunnelee raised almost $900,000 and spent about $660,000. He won 55% to 41%.

SECOND DISTRICT

Bennie Thompson (D)

Elected April 1993, 9th full term; b. Jan. 28, 1948, Bolton; home, Bolton; Tougaloo Col., B.A. 1968, Jackson St. U., M.S. 1972; Methodist; married (London); 1 child.

Elected Office: Bolton Bd. of Aldermen, 1969–73; Bolton mayor, 1973–79; Hinds Cnty. Supervisor, 1980–93.

DC Office: 2466 RHOB, 20515, 202-225-5876; Fax: 202-225-5898; Web site: benniethompson.house.gov.

State Offices: Bolton, 601-866-9003; Greenville, 662-335-9003; Greenwood, 662-455-9003; Jackson, 601-946-9003; Marks, 662-326-9003; Mound Bayou, 662-741-9003.

Committees: *Homeland Security* (RMM).

Group Ratings

	ACLU	ACU	ADA	CFG	AFS	FRC	LCV	ITIC	NTU	COC
2010	88	4	95	3	100	6	100	67	5	25
2009	–	0	95	0	100	–	100	–	1	43

National Journal Ratings

	2010 LIB	—	2010 CONS	2009 LIB	—	2009 CONS
Economic	80%	—	18%	91%	—	0%
Social	67%	—	31%	74%	—	25%
Foreign	84%	—	11%	62%	—	35%
Composite	79%	—	22%	78%	—	22%

Key Votes of the 111th Congress

1. Overturn Ledbetter	Y	5. Bar federal abortion funds	N	9. Stop detainee transfers	N
2. Pass $820 billion stimulus	Y	6. Pass health care bill	Y	10. Legalize immigrants' kids	Y
3. Let guns in national parks	Y	7. Regulate financial firms	Y	11. Repeal don't ask, tell	Y
4. Pass cap-and-trade	Y	8. Pass tax cuts for some	Y	12. Limit campaign funds	N

Election Results

2010 general	Bennie Thompson (D) 105,327	(61%)	($1,808,681)
	Bill Marcy (R)...64,499	(38%)	($47,933)
2010 primary	Bennie Thompson (D) .... unopposed		

Prior Winning Percentages: 2008 (69%), 2006 (64%), 2004 (58%), 2002 (55%), 2000 (65%), 1998 (71%), 1996 (60%), 1994 (54%), 1993 Special (55%)

Population		Race/Ethnicity		Work	
Pop. 2010:	668,263	White:	30.4%	Private:	71.8%
Change since 2000:	Down 6.0%	Black:	66.2%	Government:	22.3%
Urban:	62.8%	Hispanic:	1.9%	Self-employed:	5.7%
Rural:	37.2%	Asian:	0.6%	Blue collar:	25.4%
Area size:	13,936 sq. mi.	Native Am.:	0.2%	White collar:	51.7%
		Hawaiian:	0.0%	Khaki collar:	0.2%
Age		Two+ races:	0.6%	Other:	22.7%
Median age:	33.2 yrs.				
More than 65 yrs:	11.7%	*Ancestry*		Median income:	$29,779
Less than 18 yrs:	27.7%	USA	6.5%	Median Home Value:	$78,000
		Irish	4.8%		
Education		English	4.6%	**Military Veterans**	
H.S. grad:	76.2%			% of Pop:	7.6%
College grad:	18.6%				
Grad degree:	6.3%				

Western Mississippi; Jackson

"The Mississippi Delta," wrote Delta native David Cohn, "begins in the lobby of the Peabody Hotel in Memphis and ends on Catfish Row in Vicksburg." For centuries, the flooding Mississippi and Yazoo rivers left their sediments here, producing a fertile, dark soil. Ironically, what may well be America's richest agricultural land has been home for more than a century to many of its poorest people. Crisscrossed by rivers and

2008 Presidential Vote		
Barack Obama (D)	196,444	(66%)
John McCain (R)	99,548	(33%)
2004 Presidential Vote		
John Kerry (D)	153,786	(59%)
George Bush (R)	104,749	(40%)
Cook Partisan Voting Index:	D+12	

famously disease-ridden, the Delta wasn't much settled until after the Civil War. Then, Reconstruction-era profit-seeking operators used late-19th-century technology to drain the land, line the river with levees, and build railroads on tracks above the rise of the river. Black sharecroppers and field hands worked here in conditions almost of bondage. From this episode of industrial farming came both great misery and great art: Clarksdale in Coahoma County was the real birthplace of blues music, the home of W.C. Handy and Muddy Waters, John Lee Hooker, Ike Turner, and Sam Cooke. Greenville on the Mississippi has produced writers of the caliber of Walker Percy and Shelby Foote. Yazoo City produced author Willie Morris and bluesman Skip James. Today, Vicksburg's antebellum mansions and battlefield monuments attract 1.5 million tourists annually.

Twentieth-century technology changed life in the Delta. The mechanical cotton-picking machine, invented in 1944, came along just as Northern factories were seeking low-wage workers. The great exodus to Chicago and other cities in the North began, and the Delta's population has been declining ever since. Income levels remain very low, poverty is over 50% in some areas, and infant mortality is at Third World levels. Crime and drugs from Chicago have been brought to the area by Delta migrants returning home. Yet there are signs of hope. Soybeans have become a big-dollar crop here and poultry farms have become a major enterprise. The Delta produces most of the nation's catfish, although in 2010, catfish acreage in the state was at its lowest level since the mid-1980s. Excessive summer heat drove up production costs, and farmers had to pump more groundwater because of high evaporation rates and reduced rainfall. The Mississippi Delta Strategic Compact, a nonprofit group of Delta residents, was formed in 2010 to identify strategies for improving economic conditions.

Tunica County is, by some measures, the nation's poorest county, and the best it could do economically in recent years was to attract gambling businesses. It has nine casinos, and runways at the regional airport have been extended to accommodate jets bearing tourists and tournament poker players. The casinos have increased local per capita income, but there is still a gulf between rich and poor. Just north of the fast-growing and affluent suburbs of Jackson, Nissan operates a 5,000-employee factory in Canton, historically a heavily African-American area. The plant underwent an expansion to begin building Nissan's new light commercial vehicle, the NV2500, in January 2011. One consequence was the tripling of land values, as thousands more jobs were created for suppliers, and property moved from agriculture to residential or commercial use.

The 2nd Congressional District of Mississippi includes the entire Delta, indeed the whole Mississippi riverfront from Tunica almost to Natchez. It includes most of heavily African-American Jackson and surrounding Hinds County except for the affluent Belhaven neighborhood. This is Mississippi's one black-majority district. It includes a few counties in the east that are majority white and vote Republican, but the political tone of the district is set by the African-American neighborhoods in Jackson and the counties of the Delta. Before the Voting Rights Act of 1965, these were run politically by segregationists like Democratic Sen. James Eastland, a Delta cotton plantation owner and Senate Judiciary Committee chairman from 1955 to 1979. In 1986, the district elected its first black congressman since Reconstruction, Democrat Mike Espy, whose grandfather and father were among the biggest landowners in the state. In 2008, the 2nd was the only Mississippi district to vote for Barack Obama, who got 66% of the vote here.

Bennie Thompson (D)

The congressman from the 2nd District is Democrat Bennie Thompson, who was elected in April 1993. He grew up in Bolton, in Hinds County outside Jackson, and graduated from Tougaloo College and Jackson State University. He was elected alderman in Bolton in 1969, at age 21, and elected mayor four years later. He got a street named after the Rev. Martin Luther King Jr. A volunteer firefighter for much of his adult life, he got the first fire engine for Bolton, too. In 1980, he became a Hinds County supervisor. A lifelong grass-roots activist and labor organizer, he successfully encouraged other African-Americans to run for office. After Espy resigned from Congress in 1993 to become President Bill Clinton's Agriculture secretary, Thompson ran for the seat in an all-party primary. He came out ahead of Henry Espy, Mike Espy's brother and mayor of Clarksdale, 28%-20%. Republican Hayes Dent, an aide to Gov. Kirk Fordice, led with 34%. Voting in the runoff was mostly along racial lines, and Thompson won 55%-45%, with his margin coming mostly from Hinds County.

Thompson has a solidly liberal voting record, though his loyalty to the Congressional Black Caucus occasionally leads him to part company from the mainstream of his party. He was one of 15 House Democrats in April 2010 to vote against blocking an automatic pay raise for lawmakers, a proposal that some caucus members complained was unfair. He initially made no particular attempt to win white votes in his district, making almost as few concessions across the racial divide as Eastland had. In time, he moderated his votes and reached out to whites, including some of the district's large farmers.

The locus of his legislative activity is the Homeland Security Committee, where he has been both the ranking minority member and the chairman in recent years and where he has focused on the needs of first responders. When he first arrived on the committee in 2005, he caused some turmoil by firing some staffers, cutting the pay of others, and hiring more minority aides. But he also began a sometimes-productive working relationship with the top Republican on the committee, Peter King of New York.

After Hurricane Katrina struck Louisiana and Mississippi in August 2005, revealing the weaknesses in the Federal Emergency Management Agency's ability to respond to a disaster of that magnitude, Thompson worked with King to restructure FEMA. House Republicans wanted it to become an entirely independent agency. Thompson and King called for keeping it within the Department of Homeland Security, but with the kind of autonomy the Coast Guard has. They came to an agreement, but when Thompson demanded an additional $3 billion to improve state and local governments' communications capability, King declined and the deal foundered.

Taking over as chairman in January 2007, Thompson shepherded through the House one of the new Democratic majority's "first 100 hours" bills, which was to adopt the recommendations of the 9/11 commission. It included a requirement to screen all passenger jet and ship cargo, and became law in 2007. Thompson's priorities included encouraging awards of contracts to minority firms, making sure that contractors hired minorities, and ensuring that border security and Transportation Security Administration officers didn't single out travelers because of race or ethnicity. In the 111th Congress (2009-10), Thompson pushed to centralize oversight of the Homeland Security Department under his committee, ending the current practice of spreading jurisdiction among several committees. He persuaded the Democratic Caucus to adopt rules ensuring more bills would be referred to his committee, but failed in stopping the numerous inter-committee turf battles that many security experts say have thwarted attempts to pass more comprehensive legislation and conduct successful oversight. He was able to work with King in getting Homeland Security authorization bills through the House each year, only to have the Senate ignore them. After Republicans regained control of the House in 2011 and Thompson returned to the ranking slot, he sought to expand King's planned hearings on the radicalization of American Muslims, which drew widespread concern among Muslims. Thompson suggested the panel also look at neo-Nazis and other domestic extremist groups.

Thompson's sometimes confrontational politics have brought him opposition in the 2nd District. In 2002, he was re-elected by a less than impressive 55%-43% against Republican challenger Clinton LeSueur, a consultant to the Yazoo Community Action Agency. LeSueur ran again in 2004 and spent three times the money he had before, but Thompson increased his victory to 58%-41%. In 2006, state Rep. Chuck Espy, nephew of the former representative, challenged him in the primary, but Thompson prevailed 64%-35%. He also cruised to re-election in 2008 and 2010.

In 2009, Thompson came under fire from local Republicans after the *Jackson Clarion-Ledger* reported on trips he took to vacation destinations that were paid for by special-interest groups. The AFL-CIO labor union paid for him to travel to Las Vegas, the International Longshoremen's Association sent him to Fort Lauderdale, Fla., and the Carib News Foundation, which publishes a newspaper on Caribbean issues, funded a trip to the island of St. Maarten in the Caribbean. Thompson defended the trips as necessary to learn firsthand about homeland security issues, and said they were approved by the House Ethics Committee. *The Washington Post* reported in December 2009 that Thompson used his committee's consideration of expensive new rules on credit card companies to extract $15,000 in campaign donations from the companies. His staff denied the charge, as well as a claim that the committee's former policy director was fired after complaining about a lobbyist's improper requests of staffers.

THIRD DISTRICT

Gregg Harper (R)

Elected 2008, 2nd term; b. June 1, 1956, Jackson; home, Pearl; MS Col., B.S. 1978; U. of MS, J.D. 1981.; Baptist; married (Sidney); 2 children.

Professional Career: Practicing atty.

DC Office: 307 CHOB, 20515, 202-225-5031; Fax: 202-225-5759; Web site: harper.house.gov.

State Offices: Brookhaven, 601-823-3400; Meridian, 601-693-6681; Pearl , 601-932-2410; Starkville, 662-324-0007.

Committees: *Energy & Commerce:* Commerce, Manufacturing & Trade; Environment & the Economy. *Ethics. House Administration:* Elections (Chmn). *Joint Committee on the Library* (VChmn). *Joint Committee on Printing* (Chmn).

Group Ratings

	ACLU	ACU	ADA	CFG	AFS	FRC	LCV	ITIC	NTU	COC
2010	13	96	0	84	0	100	0	33	88	88
2009	–	96	0	90	13	–	7	–	85	80

National Journal Ratings

	2010 LIB	—	2010 CONS	2009 LIB	—	2009 CONS
Economic	7%	—	92%	11%	—	89%
Social	29%	—	69%	22%	—	77%
Foreign	12%	—	79%	0%	—	75%
Composite	18%	—	82%	15%	—	85%

Key Votes of the 111th Congress

1. Overturn Ledbetter	N	5. Bar federal abortion funds	Y	9. Stop detainee transfers	Y
2. Pass $820 billion stimulus	N	6. Pass health care bill	N	10. Legalize immigrants' kids	N
3. Let guns in national parks	Y	7. Regulate financial firms	N	11. Repeal don't ask, tell	N
4. Pass cap-and-trade	N	8. Pass tax cuts for some	N	12. Limit campaign funds	N

Election Results

2010 general	Gregg Harper (R)	132,393	(68%)	($715,014)
	Joel Gill (D)	60,737	(31%)	
2010 primary	Gregg Harper (R)	unopposed		

Prior Winning Percentages: 2008 (63%)

Population		Race/Ethnicity		Work	
Pop. 2010:	756,924	White:	60.2%	Private:	72.0%
Change since 2000:	Up 6.4%	Black:	34.7%	Government:	21.2%
Urban:	40.3%	Hispanic:	2.3%	Self-employed:	6.6%
Rural:	59.7%	Asian:	0.8%	Blue collar:	24.9%
Area size:	13,312 sq. mi.	Native Am.:	1.1%	White collar:	58.5%
		Hawaiian:	0.0%	Khaki collar:	0.4%
Age		Two+ races:	0.8%	Other:	16.2%
Median age:	35.5 yrs.				
More than 65 yrs:	13.1%	*Ancestry*		Median income:	$38,316
Less than 18 yrs:	25.5%	USA	12.0%	Median Home Value:	$99,100
		Irish	9.0%		
Education		English	8.9%	**Military Veterans**	
H.S. grad:	81.3%			% of Pop:	9.1%
College grad:	23.0%				
Grad degree:	8.3%				

Central Mississippi; Jackson Area

The Neshoba County fair has been held every August since 1889 in the town of Philadelphia. What started as a farmer's picnic has become the traditional place where Mississippi politicians announce their candidacies, with the crowds watching to take their measure. The crowds are also there to watch the races on the state's only legal horse track. But nationally, Philadelphia and Neshoba County are known for something

2008 Presidential Vote		
John McCain (R)	213,025	(61%)
Barack Obama (D)	134,878	(39%)
2004 Presidential Vote		
George Bush (R)	203,376	(65%)
John Kerry (D)	106,455	(34%)
Cook Partisan Voting Index: R+15		

else. There is no memorial, except engraved stones at two African-American churches, to mark the events of the summer of 1964, when three civil rights workers, two white and one black, were murdered for the crime of urging black American citizens to register to vote. It wasn't until June 2005 that a jury of nine whites and three blacks convicted Edgar Ray Killen, an 80-year-old preacher and sawmill operator, of manslaughter. He was sentenced to three life sentences.

Some 80 miles away, in Rankin and Madison counties, east and north of Jackson, subdivisions, shopping centers, and office complexes are sprouting up in the countryside. A big Nissan plant operating in Canton since 2003 employs more than 5,000 workers. Even as other areas of the state were feeling the effects of the nationwide recession, Rankin County had the lowest unemployment rate in Mississippi—just 6 percent in 2010, more than two-thirds below that of some hard-hit nearby counties.

The 3rd Congressional District of Mississippi includes the Jackson suburbs in Rankin County and south Madison County, plus the affluent neighborhoods of northeast Jackson in Hinds County. It stretches north to Starkville, home of Mississippi State University, and south almost to Laurel. In the southwest, it reaches over to include Natchez, where 600 antebellum mansions and other properties with live oaks sit atop bluffs overlooking the Mississippi River. The small town of Macon was the scene in 2007 of a first-ever Justice Department lawsuit against a black Democratic Party official for discriminating against the voting rights of minority whites. In the middle of the district are Neshoba County and Meridian, home of Peavey Electronics Corp., whose electric guitars and powerful amplifiers are popular with rock stars. The district's political tradition had been Democratic for many years, but its preference now is strongly Republican. In 2008, John McCain had no problem winning the district, 61%-39%.

Gregg Harper (R)

The congressman from the 3rd District is Gregg Harper, a Republican elected in 2008 to succeed the retiring Chip Pickering, also a Republican. Harper was born in Jackson, where his father was a petroleum engineer and his mother was a homemaker. The family moved frequently because of his father's job, but always came back home to Mississippi. By the time he'd finished high school, Harper had attended 10 different schools. Harper became a Christian after attending a youth rally in high school, and later met his wife, Sidney, at a church function. They have a daughter, Maggie, and a son, Livingston, who suffers from a developmental disorder called fragile X syndrome.

Harper has long experience in politics. He was the chairman of the Rankin County Republican Party and worked on several local and state campaigns. As a young man, he campaigned for Pickering's father when he ran for the state Senate. Harper was also a delegate to the 2000 and 2008 national Republican conventions. When the 2000 presidential election was in limbo and hinged on results in Florida, Harper volunteered as a legal observer for George W. Bush's recount efforts. Until his election, he was the prosecuting attorney for the cities of Brandon and Richland.

He jumped into the primary contest for the House seat as soon as Pickering announced his retirement. Harper's toughest Republican competitors were state Sen. Charlie Ross, considered the early favorite, and wealthy businessman David Landrum. On the Democratic side, popular former Rep. Ronnie Shows pondered a run but ultimately decided against it.

Ross shored up endorsements from local leaders and national groups such as the anti-tax Club for Growth, and both he and Landrum outspent Harper. But Harper rallied a hardworking core of young volunteers and family members, and focused on door-to-door campaigning. He also got one important endorsement, from former U.S. Senate Republican Leader Trent Lott of Mississippi, who appeared at a January fundraiser for him. In the March 2008 primary, Ross emerged as the top vote-getter with 33%, and Harper finished second with 28%. Because no candidate won more than 50%, the contest went to a runoff in April. In the runoff campaign, Ross portrayed Harper as too inexperienced for the job, but Harper emphasized his conservative stances against abortion rights and same-sex marriage in an appeal to the district's small-town voters. He won with 57% of the vote to Ross's 43%. Ross narrowly edged Harper in pivotal Meridian and Lauderdale County by 128 votes, but Harper won 63%-37% in Ross' native Rankin, the district's largest county.

In the November general election, Harper faced Democrat Joel Gill, a rancher and a Pickens alderman. Gill ran folksy ads that referred to him as "Joel the Cattleman." Still, a catchy ad was not enough in this Republican district, and Harper easily won with 63% of the vote. He had even less trouble in a 2010 rematch with Gill, drawing 68%.

In Washington, Harper has been a dependable conservative vote and has impressed Republican leaders. He was the only freshman elected to serve on the Republican Steering Committee in 2009, and was the only first-term lawmaker appointed to the House Administration Committee. After the 2010 election, he joined the Tea Party Caucus, and joined that group's members in frequently blasting Democratic policies.

But with his son in mind, he is bipartisan on governmental efforts to help children with special needs. Harper worked with Democrats to secure $1.9 million for fragile X syndrome research at the Centers for Disease Control and Prevention, and he also got the disorder added to the list eligible for Defense Department medical research.

After the Republican takeover in 2010, Harper became chairman of House Administration's elections panel. He introduced a bill to eliminate the Election Assistance Commission, a nine-year-old group setting voluntary voting system guidelines for states as well as distributing funds to update voting equipment. He said the move would save $14 million annually. He also landed a plum spot on the Energy and Commerce Committee.

FOURTH DISTRICT

Steven Palazzo (R)

Elected 2010, 1st term; b. Feb. 21, 1970, Gulfport; home, Biloxi; U. of Southern MS, B.S. 1994, M.A. 1996.; Catholic; Married (Lisa); 3 children.

Military Career: Marine Corps Reserve, 1988-96 (Persian Gulf); MS Army Natl. Guard, 1997-present.

Elected Office: MS House, 2007-10.

Professional Career: CFO, Biloxi Housing Authority; owner, Palazzo & Co. PLLC.

DC Office: 331 CHOB, 20515, 202-225-5772; Fax: 202-225-7074; Web site: palazzo.house.gov.

State Offices: Gulfport, 228-864-7670; Hattiesburg, 601-582-3246.

Committees: *Armed Services:* Readiness; Seapower & Projection Forces. *Science & Technology:* Research & Science Education; Space & Aeronautics (Chmn).

Election Results

2010 general	Steven Palazzo (R) 105,613	(52%)	($1,111,453)
	Gene Taylor (D)...95,243	(47%)	($855,983)
2010 primary	Steven Palazzo (R) 15,556	(57%)	
	Joe Tegerdine (R) 11,663	(43%)	

Population		Race/Ethnicity		Work	
Pop. 2010:	754,015	White:	70.0%	Private:	73.6%
Change since 2000:	Up 6.0%	Black:	23.0%	Government:	19.8%
Urban:	53.7%	Hispanic:	3.7%	Self-employed:	6.5%
Rural:	46.3%	Asian:	1.4%	Blue collar:	27.7%
Area size:	9,536 sq. mi.	Native Am.:	0.3%	White collar:	52.6%
		Hawaiian:	0.1%	Khaki collar:	0.8%
Age		Two+ races:	1.4%	Other:	18.8%
Median age:	35.6 yrs.				
More than 65 yrs:	12.5%	*Ancestry*		Median income:	$41,223
Less than 18 yrs:	25.4%	USA	10.6%	Median Home Value:	$120,300
		Irish	9.7%		
Education		English	7.8%	**Military Veterans**	
H.S. grad:	82.2%			% of Pop:	12.6%
College grad:	18.4%				
Grad degree:	6.7%				

Southeast Mississippi; Gulf Coast

Coastal Mississippi has gone through several transformations in its history. French explorers founded Biloxi in 1699, before New Orleans or St. Louis, and made it the capital of an empire extending to what is now Yellowstone National Park. Two hundred years later, rich people from New Orleans came to this section of the Gulf Coast in summer to get away from yellow fever and to rest on Victorian verandas. Six American presidents have vacationed here, and Pasca-

2008 Presidential Vote		
John McCain (R)	198,545	(67%)
Barack Obama (D)	93,399	(32%)
2004 Presidential Vote		
George Bush (R)	188,880	(68%)
John Kerry (D)	86,010	(31%)
Cook Partisan Voting Index:	R+20	

goula is the birthplace of the original beach bum, singer Jimmy Buffett. The Gulf Coast grew more than any other major part of Mississippi in recent years. Along much of the shoreline, new 1,000-room hotels rose as part of the boom, and about 50,000 jobs were created. There is also a military flavor to the Gulf Coast. Biloxi's Keesler Air Force Base employs 11,000 and in 2009, was chosen for a new cyberspace training facility. Pascagoula is home to more than 12,000 employees at Ingalls Shipyard, whose gray, hangar-like buildings and skeletons of ships under construction loom over the landscape.

But the region's economic growth was put on hold for several years after these coastal communities took a direct hit from Hurricane Katrina on Aug. 29, 2005. From Waveland to Pascagoula, about 80 miles were obliterated: Beachfront cottages, fishing villages, hotel casinos, oil-drilling platforms, and refineries all were either cruelly swamped or swept away. Status meant nothing. The homes of Confederate President Jefferson Davis in Biloxi and former Senate Majority Leader Trent Lott, R-Miss., in Pascagoula were destroyed. The eye of the monster storm passed over the area, and in an instant, the storm ruined countless livelihoods, caused losses in the tens of billions of dollars, and laid waste to a way of life.

If there was a saving grace, many of these communities were left with a clean slate to restart development, with more control over the building of high rises and strip malls that had started to overwhelm more distinctive properties. It helped to have Haley Barbour, a well-connected national Republican insider, as governor and Mississippi Sen. Thad Cochran as chairman of the Senate Appropriations Committee. Even while the cleanup continued, important decisions were made, especially in Biloxi. Condominium projects were more carefully managed; shrimp boaters got docks for their boats and places to sell their catch; casinos were permitted to be built on land, instead of the barges they were restricted to in the past. The state used $600 million in hurricane recovery money for a $1.6 billion expansion of the Port of Gulfport, which, when completed, will be the largest container terminal in the United States, capable of handling the more numerous and wider ships that are expected to sail through an upgraded, broadened Panama Canal in coming years. In the spring of 2010, the Gulf areas suffered another setback from the massive BP oil spill, although beach tourism was on the rebound a year later.

This is the heart of the 4th Congressional District of Mississippi. Prior to Katrina, half of its people lived on the Gulf Coast. The rest were inland, in farm counties or around Hattiesburg and Laurel. This was mostly scrubland, not much good for plantations. It has long been Republican territory. In close to its current form, it gave Republican President Richard Nixon his highest percentage of any congressional district in 1972; it voted five times against fellow Southerners Jimmy Carter, Bill Clinton, and Al Gore, and it was represented for 16 years in the House by Lott, until he was elected to the Senate in 1988. In 2008, the district gave GOP presidential nominee John McCain his highest percentage in the Magnolia State, 67%, to Democrat Barack Obama's 32%.

Steven Palazzo (R)

The new congressman from the 4th District is Republican Steven Palazzo, who upset 21-year incumbent Democrat Gene Taylor in 2010. Palazzo was born and raised in Gulfport, where his family has deep roots: Five generations have called South Mississippi home. He describes his community as characterized by "God-fearing men and women" who believe in faith and personal responsibility. After graduating from high school and enrolling for a semester at his local community college, Palazzo enlisted in the Marines, inspired by his grandfather, who served in the Pacific during World War II. From 1988 to 1996, Palazzo served with the 3rd Force Reconnaissance Company, gathering intelligence and doing tours of duty in Kuwait and Saudi Arabia during the Persian Gulf War. "The Marine Corps breaks you down and builds you back up," Palazzo said. "The traditions and the warrior spirit—those things are still instilled in me." He has remained active in the military in later life, joining the Mississippi National Guard in 1997 and spending a year supporting base operations at Camp Shelby for Operation Iraqi Freedom.

After he returned from the Persian Gulf War, Palazzo went back to school, earning bachelor's and master's degrees in accounting from the University of Southern Mississippi. It was also while in college that he met his future wife, Lisa Belvin. Palazzo worked in accounting positions at various firms throughout the late 1990s, primarily in the construction industry. In 2001, he and his wife began the accounting practice Palazzo & Co., targeting as clients Americans working abroad. The business, started out of their home, has since grown into an international firm specializing in doing individual income-tax returns for expatriates. Palazzo has highlighted his experience as an entrepreneur on the campaign trail: "As a small-business owner, you learn real quick that most things that can destroy your business come from government action," he said.

In 2007, he ran in a special election for the state House and won handily. Two years later, he decided to challenge Taylor for his congressional seat, although Taylor was almost a folk hero in coastal Mississippi—Taylor lost his home to Katrina, was in good stead with the National Rifle Association, had one of the most conservative voting records among House Democrats, and had spoken out against many of his party's major initiatives, including health care reform.

But even Taylor, once thought of as one of the safest Democrats in the House, had reason to sweat in the anti-incumbent environment of 2010, when recession-weary voters were in the mood for change. Even though it was difficult for Palazzo to pick apart Taylor's quite conservative voting record, he portrayed him as an enabler of the Democratic agenda for his vote for liberal California Democrat Nancy Pelosi as House speaker, thereby promoting, he said, a "liberal socialist agenda." And Taylor couldn't count on much help from national Democrats, whom he had frequently bucked over the years. Taylor touted his conservative positions, and even boasted to his local newspaper that he voted for Republican John McCain for president in 2008. It wasn't enough, not in 2010. Palazzo won 52% to 47%.

★ MISSOURI ★

St. Louis, established by French frontiersmen and acquired by the United States as part of the Louisiana Purchase, was the place where Meriwether Lewis and William Clark set out on their expedition to the Pacific in May 1804. On high ground just below the point where the Missouri River swirls into the Mississippi, St. Louis was then the one well-established city in America's interior, with an aristocracy of French merchants, a brawling bourgeoisie of Yankee and Southern frontiersmen and fur traders, and a proletariat of black slaves. Several years later, in 1821, the city was part of the new state of Missouri, and for decades St. Louis and Missouri were the gateways to the frontier. West of St. Louis, Daniel Boone finally found elbow room; St. Joseph was the eastern terminus of the Pony Express; Westport, now part of Kansas City, was the starting point of the Santa Fe Trail. The Mississippi River steamboats celebrated by Mark Twain linked North and South before the Civil War; afterward, railroads reached across the continent, connecting the farmers on the prairies with their markets.

Missouri was not just the gateway to the frontier; it was also a focus of the furious battle over slavery. Missouri was the northernmost slave state in 1850. Missouri ruffians rode across the border and killed antislavery settlers in the Kansas Territory—acts that led proximately to the Civil War. The state had its own bloody civil war in the hilly counties along the Missouri River and in the southwest. After the war, in 1874, the Eads Bridge opened, one of the very few spans on the Mississippi; St. Louis's Cupples Station was then the largest rail hub in the world. At the turn of the 20th century, Missouri was the fifth-largest state and St. Louis was the fourth-largest city, site of the 1904 World's Fair and one of the few cities with two Major League Baseball teams, the Cardinals and the Browns. Missouri was also the national center of the mule trade (Harry Truman's father's line of work), an important business at a time when half of Americans lived on farms and motorized tractors had not been invented. After the 1900 census, Missouri had 16 congressional districts, compared with the nine it had in 2010.

Today, Missouri does not loom as large in the national consciousness, yet it is in some ways still central. In the 20th century, Americans increasingly headed toward the coasts, to the big cities of the East and West, and eventually to Florida and Texas. (Like the baseball Browns, who moved to Baltimore in the 1950s, and the football Cardinals, who moved to Phoenix in the 1980s.) Missouri has had below-average population growth since 1900, and today it is the 17th-largest state. But Missouri was the geographic center of the nation's population in the 2010 census: An imaginary, flat map of the United States population, if everyone weighed the same, would balance in Texas County, Missouri. The state started perking up demographically in the 1990s, as dozens of rural counties that had been losing population for most of the 20th century started regaining it. The Lake of the Ozarks region in central and southwest Missouri, around the country music center of Branson, have been attracting modest-income retirees looking for traditional lifestyles and inexpensive recreation. Missouri, outside its two big metro areas, St. Louis and Kansas City, grew at near the national average over the last two decades and the Missouri portion of metro Kansas City just about kept pace (as its Kansas portion grew even more). Metro St. Louis lagged somewhat behind. Major companies based there—McDonnell Douglas, TWA, Ralston Purina, May Department Stores, Monsanto, Anheuser-Busch—were acquired by outside firms. St. Louis City, inside its narrow 19th century boundaries, hemorrhaged population and so did the inner suburban ring in St. Louis County.

Culturally, Missouri remains more conservative than most of the bigger states. Its relatively slow-growing metro areas have not overwhelmed the countryside, a land of farms and small towns thick with churches and modest shopping centers and laced with artificial lakes and boat launches. Only one city outside the two big metro areas, Springfield, has a population over 150,000, and in the state's 103 rural counties, life—and politics—seems not to have changed much over the past half-century. Missouri has some tough immigration laws, even though it has attracted relatively few immigrants. Local police agencies have seized many methamphetamine labs, but the state has one of the nation's few declining prison populations.

For a century, Missouri was one of America's political bellwether states. It voted for every presidential winner but one in the century from 1904 to 2004; the exception was when it narrowly backed Adlai Stevenson in 1956. From the 1960s to the 1990s, it mirrored national trends by moving its congressional politics from fairly solidly Democratic to leaning Republican. Missouri was not only a mixture of urban and rural, but its Civil War political divisions still held: Democrats dominated in Little Dixie in the northeast, first settled by Virginians, and in the northwest, settled

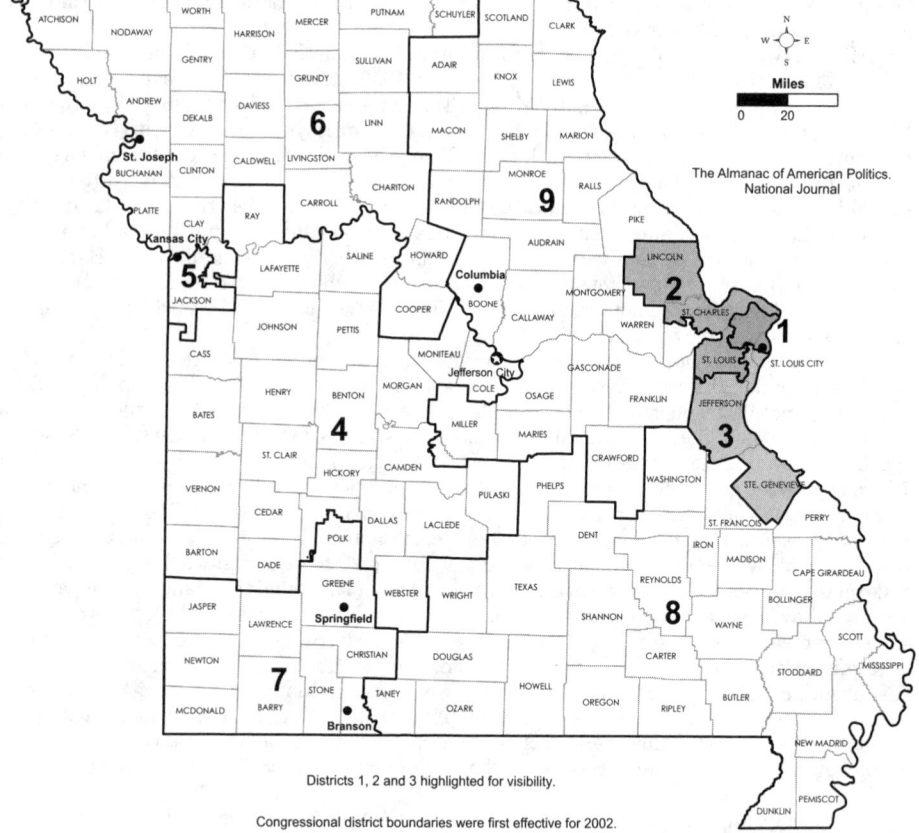

Districts 1, 2 and 3 highlighted for visibility.

Congressional district boundaries were first effective for 2002.

The Almanac of American Politics.
National Journal

by Southerners. Republicans held sway in the Ozarks in the southwest, which was pro-Union, and the southeast was split, like next-door downstate Illinois. By 2000, however, historic patterns were being overridden. The large metro areas, with significant black populations, became more Democratic and the remainder of the state more Republican as Civil War loyalties gave way to cultural conservatism. The result was equipoise. In the state's 10 contests for president, senator, and governor between 2000 and 2008, only two were decided by wide margins: Republican Sen. Christopher (Kit) Bond's re-election in 2004 and Democratic Gov. Jay Nixon's election in 2008. In the eight other contests, Republicans got between 47% and 53% of the vote, Democrats between 46% and 50%. In the 2008 presidential contest, the two large metro areas voted Democratic and the rest of the state, by wider percentages, Republican. Barack Obama got big margins in St. Louis City, St. Louis County and Kansas City's Jackson County, but carried only six of the other 113 counties.

In 2010, Missouri like much of the nation moved toward the Republicans. Gov. Nixon forged compromises with the legislature's Republican majorities and went on to cut spending between sessions. But that did little for his party. A referendum on the August 2010 primary ballot resulted in 71%-29% approval of a ban on the kind of health care insurance mandate contained in national Democrats' health care legislation. Republican Rep. Roy Blunt beat Democratic Secretary of State Robin Carnahan, the daughter of a governor and a U.S. senator, by 54%-41%. Republicans carried the popular vote for the House 57%-38%, and beat 34-year incumbent Democratic Rep. Ike Skelton. Republicans increased their legislative majorities to 26-8 in the state Senate and 106-57 in the state House—their largest margins in history. In the state Senate Democrats were left with the two seats in St. Louis City, two majority-black seats in St. Louis County, three seats in Kansas City and, by a narrow margin, one seat in Jefferson County just south of St. Louis. Republicans won some seats only narrowly, and the political tides will likely shift around as the years go on, but Missouri Democrats at least in 2010 were stuck with the image of an urban party in a state that is increasingly non-urban. And one that is in one unique way divided: this is the only state whose name is pronounced two ways, depending on the region. In metro St. Louis, they say "Mizzuree." In the rest of the state, it's "Mizzuruh."

Population		Household Income		Work	
Pop. 2010:	5,988,927	Under $15k:	14.3%	Private:	80.1%
State rank:	18th	$15k to $50k:	39.5%	Government:	13.5%
Change since 2000:	Up 7.0%	$50k to $100k:	31.1%	Self-employed:	6.2%
Urban:	68.2%	$100k to $200k:	12.7%	Unemployment (3-yr. average):	4.8%
Rural:	31.8%	Over $200k:	2.4%	Poverty:	13.8%
Native of state:	66.4%	Median income:	$46,109	Blue collar:	23.0%
Not a citizen:	2.1%			White collar:	59.2%
Area size:	69,707 sq. mi.	**Home Value**		Khaki collar:	0.3%
		Under $100k:	32.1%	Other:	17.4%
Most populous cities		$100k to $300k:	56.4%		
Kansas City	459,787	$300k to $500k:	8.1%	**Age**	
St. Louis	319,294	$500k to $1 mil:	2.7%	Median age:	37.5 yrs.
Springfield	159,498	Over $1 million:	0.7%	More than 65 yrs:	13.6%
Independence	116,830	Median:	$139,700	Less than 18 yrs:	24.1%

Race/Ethnicity				Military Veterans		Registered Voters in 2010	
White:	81.0%	*Language*		% of Pop:	11.2%	No Party registration	
Black:	11.5%	English:	94.2%			Voter turnout:	1,943,898
Hispanic:	3.5%	Spanish:	2.7%	*Veterans by Period*		Turnout as % of	
Asian:	1.6%	Asian:	1.0%	WWII and before:	10.5%	voting age:	42.6%
Native Am.:	0.4%	Other European:	1.8%	Korea:	12.0%		
Hawaiian:	0.1%			Vietnam:	33.9%	**Legislature**	
Two+ races:	1.8%	**Education**		Gulf (pre-2001):	10.6%	Senate:	8 D 26 R
		H.S. grad:	86.2%	Gulf (post-2001):	7.2%	House:	57 D 106 R
Ancestry		College grad:	25.0%	Peace time:	25.8%		
German	21.5%	Grad degree:	9.2%				
Irish	11.9%						
English	8.0%						

Presidential politics   In 2008, Missouri departed from its pattern as a bellwether state by preferring McCain. But in this race, and in both the Democratic and Republican presidential primaries, Missouri was the site of some of the closest contests in the nation. On Feb. 5, Obama won the Democratic primary over Hillary Rodham Clinton, 49.3%-47.9%. McCain won the Republican primary over Mike Huckabee, 33%-31.5%, with Mitt Romney capturing 29.3% of the vote. On Nov. 4, McCain carried Missouri with 49.4% to 49.2% for Obama. Altogether, these three contests were decided by popular-vote margins totaling 24,046 votes out of 4.3 million cast.

All three elections showed similar patterns. Obama benefited in both the Democratic primary and general election by winning huge margins in St. Louis City (49% black in 2010), St. Louis County (23% black) and Jackson County, which includes most of the central city of Kansas City and some of its suburbs. In the primary, he also carried the counties including the state capital (Cole), the University of Missouri (Boone), and Northwest Missouri State University (Nodaway). In the general election, he carried Jefferson County south of St. Louis, Washington and Iron counties (old mining territory), Boone County, and Buchanan County (St. Joseph).

The pattern was a little more complicated in the three-way Republican primary. Romney, with his heavy television advertising and his appeal to high-income voters, carried most of the Kansas City media market plus Boone and Cole counties, St. Charles County (St. Louis exurbs), and Cape Girardeau County (Rush Limbaugh's home town). McCain carried St. Louis City and St. Louis County, Jefferson and Franklin counties to the south and west, and a swath of counties in north-central Missouri. Huckabee, riding his strong appeal to evangelical conservatives, carried southwest Missouri by a wide margin and Little Dixie counties in the northeast.

Missouri joined the Super Tuesday multi-state primary for 1988, returned to multi-tiered caucuses to elect delegates in 1992 and 1996, and then rejoined Super Tuesday in 2000. Expected victories for Missouri natives did not result. Both Bill Bradley in 2000 and Dick Gephardt in 2004 were effectively out of the race before Missourians got to vote. In 2008, Obama's narrow victory over Clinton did not cost her much momentum, thanks to the Democrats' proportional representation delegate-allocation rules. But McCain's narrow victory, with less than one-third of the total votes, gave him all 58 of Missouri's GOP delegates thanks to the party's winner-take-all rules. That narrow victory played a key role in forcing Romney out of the race for the Republican nomination immediately; he was joined a few weeks later by Huckabee.

2008 Presidential Vote		
John McCain (R)	1,445,814	(49%)
Barack Obama (D)	1,441,911	(49%)

2008 Presidential Primary		
Barack Obama (D)	406,917	(49%)
Hillary Clinton (D)	395,185	(48%)

2008 Presidential Primary		
John McCain (R)	194,053	(33%)
Mike Huckabee (R)	185,642	(31%)
Mitt Romney (R)	172,329	(29%)

2004 Presidential Vote		
George W. Bush (R)	1,455,713	(53%)
John Kerry (D)	1,259,171	(46%)

Congressional districting   Missouri did not lose any seats in the 2000 census, and control of redistricting was split between the parties: Democrats held the governorship and had a majority in the state House, while Republicans controlled the state Senate. The main problem was how to adjust for the declining population of St. Louis. Back in 1950, the city had 856,000 residents, enough for almost three congressional districts. By 2000, it had 348,000, not enough for half a district. But it is heavily Democratic, and in early 2001, 1st District Rep. William Lacy Clay was demanding more of the city, to keep the black percentage in his district above 50%. That was resisted by 3rd District Rep. Gephardt because the Democrat didn't want his district moved farther out into Republican suburbs. In April, Gephardt and Clay met at the St. Louis Labor Central headquarters and cut a deal that roughly divided the city along Interstate 44. After negotiations, the House and Senate agreed on a plan that gave Gephardt and Deal most of what each of them wanted, and protected GOP incumbents as well. Republican Todd Akin of the 2nd District, who lost some turf in the deal, was the only incumbent who wasn't happy. It was a success for Republicans, considering that their sole leverage was a two-seat margin in the state Senate.

112th Congress Lineup	
6 R	3 D

111th Congress Lineup	
5 R	4 D

Missouri was not so fortunate in the 2010 census. Its population came in 31,000 short of getting the 435th seat under the reapportionment formula, and so its House delegation was reduced from nine to eight. Control over redistricting is split between the parties. Republicans have sufficient seats in the state Senate, but not in the House, to override a veto by Democratic Gov. Nixon. Historically, metro St. Louis has shared most of three districts and metro Kansas City has shared most of two. But sluggish growth in metro St. Louis has left it far short of the population required for three districts and Jackson County in metro Kansas City is 74,000 short of the population required for a single district.

In spring 2011, the Republican-controlled legislature approved a new map that eliminated Democratic Rep. Russ Carnahan's 3rd District, merging much of it into the heavily black 1st District represented by Democrat William Lacy Clay. Nixon vetoed the map, but the legislature overrode his veto.

Governor

Jay Nixon (D)

Elected 2008, term expires Jan. 2013, 1st term; b. Feb. 13, 1956, DeSoto; home, Jefferson City; U. of MO, B.A., 1978; J.D., 1981; Methodist; married (Georganne); 2 children.

Elected Office: MO Senate, 1986-1992; MO atty. gen., 1992-2008.

Professional Career: Practicing atty., 1981-1992.

Office: P.O. Box 720, 65102, 573-751-3222; Fax: 573-751-1495; Web site: gov.mo.gov.

Election Results

2008 general	Jay Nixon (D)	1,680,611	(58%)
	Kenny Hulshof (R)	1,136,364	(39%)
2008 primary	Jay Nixon (D)	304,181	(85%)
	Daniel Carroll (D)	53,835	(15%)

Jay Nixon, the Democratic governor of Missouri, was elected in 2008 after a 15-year stint as Missouri's attorney general and two unsuccessful tries for the U.S. Senate. An astute centrist, he has remained popular even as his state has moved rightward. Nixon grew up in DeSoto, in Jefferson County, 47 miles southwest of St. Louis. His mother was president of the DeSoto school board and his father was mayor of DeSoto when *Look* magazine named it an "All-America City." Jay Nixon graduated from the University of Missouri and its law school and then practiced in Jefferson County. In 1986, when a state senator retired, he ran for the seat and won. In 1988, at age 32, he ran against U.S. Sen. John Danforth, a Republican who had held statewide office in Missouri for 20 years. It was not a deft campaign. His "Nixon '88" signs evoked memories of the disgraced former president, and his attacks on Danforth for running for a third term fell flat. He was trounced 68%-32%, carrying St. Louis city proper by an unimpressive margin and losing all 115 counties.

Nixon did not have to give up his state Senate seat, however, nor his ambition for statewide office. He made a name for himself by investigating a scandal at the State Agency for Surplus Property. In 1992, Nixon ran for attorney general, an office that Republicans had held for 24 straight years, and beat David Steelman. In four terms as attorney general, Nixon developed innovative programs such as No Call, which created a do-not-call list off limits to telemarketers. He established the Agriculture and Environment Division to enforce Missouri's environmental laws. And in a landmark victory, Nixon argued before the U.S. Supreme Court to reinstate Missouri's campaign contribution limits. The decision was a catalyst for national campaign finance reform. He worked to end the protracted school desegregation cases in St. Louis and Kansas City, eventually reaching settlements.

In 1998, Nixon ran for the U.S. Senate again, against two-term incumbent Christopher (Kit) Bond. But Nixon was criticized by many black leaders for his stands in the school desegregation cases and got lukewarm support from Kansas City Mayor Emanuel Cleaver, a prominent African-American who is now a House member. Bond, who had worked on housing and other issues, clearly cut into the Democratic Party's normally near-unanimous African-American vote and ended up winning 53%-44%.

As in his first U.S. Senate race, Nixon was in the middle of a four-year term and did not have to give up his state office. He was re-elected attorney general by wide margins in 2000 and 2004.

In his second term as attorney general, he launched a political challenge to first-term Republican Gov. Matt Blunt. He criticized Blunt for cuts in Medicaid that removed 100,000 people from the rolls and for the sale of assets of the Missouri Higher Education Loan Authority. He also attacked Blunt's cuts in the First Steps program for children with autism and other problems and opposed the governor's limits on damages in lawsuits. Meanwhile, Nixon was ordered to reimburse the state $47,000 for the use of state vehicles to attend fundraisers.

Both candidates raised large sums—$6 million for Blunt and $3 million for Nixon. But then the state Supreme Court ruled that the law that had increased campaign fundraising limits was invalid; both Blunt and Nixon had to refund amounts over the limits, leaving them about equal in November 2007, with Blunt at $1.5 million and Nixon at $1.4 million. At this point, Blunt had low job-approval ratings, and the loss of his financial advantage made Nixon the favorite to win.

Then, in a surprise move, Blunt announced in January 2008 that he would not run for a second term, saying he had accomplished most of what he had set out to do. Republicans scrambled for a nominee. Peter Kinder, the lieutenant governor, decided to run for re-election, and so the two leading GOP candidates were state Treasurer Sarah Steelman and 9th District Rep. Kenny Hulshof. Hulshof was backed by Kinder and Bond, and won the primary 49%-45%. The result set up a contest between two old friends, Nixon and Hulshof, who had worked in the attorney general's office as a roving prosecutor handling murder and other difficult cases. When he became attorney general, Nixon kept Hulshof on, despite his Republican affiliation, and the two men adopted a habit of lunchtime basketball games.

Nixon entered the fall campaign with great advantages. He had good job-approval ratings and a big fundraising lead. Hulshof was short of money after the primary, and Steelman did not endorse him heartily. Nixon called for rescinding Blunt's Medicaid cuts, for expanding college scholarships for families with incomes under $80,000, and for regulation of payday loans. He cast Hulshof as a Washington insider and attacked him for voting for tax breaks for oil companies. He also criticized Hulshof for supporting tax credits for scholarships to private schools. Hulshof characterized Nixon as "old way Jay" and criticized him for seeking a contribution from a utility while investigating the collapse of one of its reservoirs. Hulshof called for using the state's "rainy day fund" to finance job-creating businesses and for bonuses for math and science teachers.

Nixon was the front-runner through most of the campaign season and won 58%-39%. He carried not only the cities but also 66 of the state's 115 counties, losing only in Hulshof's 9th Congressional District, in solidly Republican southwest Missouri, and in counties in the far southeast and northwest corners of the state.

Nixon came into office facing declining revenues but with a budget surplus. He also faced a legislature with significant Republican majorities in both houses and a Republican lieutenant governor, his longtime critic Kinder, who had eked out a 50%-47% win. He worked with Republicans to pass a comprehensive jobs bill as well as an initiative to get colleges to graduate hundreds of additional workers in high-demand health care fields. But he also ran into budget problems as a result of the recession, and in June 2009 announced he would cut $430 million in planned spending, most of it from capital projects that the legislature had sought to finance with federal funds. In January 2010, he introduced a budget with a new fund to help bring businesses to the state modeled after a program in neighboring Kansas. But he soon realized he needed to retrench as a result of the sustained recession. He called for consolidating departments, cutting 1,000 jobs, slashing tax credits and eliminating some holidays for state employees, including Harry Truman's birthday. The governor got some of what he wanted, including the reduction in jobs, but could not persuade lawmakers to cut the holidays or reduce tax credits. Nixon startled political observers in January 2011 when he commuted the sentence of a murderer on death row to life imprisonment, a decision that some called a dangerous move politically.

In 2009, Nixon ran into criticism when *The Kansas City Star* reported that his Department of Natural Resources had withheld a report showing elevated E. coli bacteria in the Lake of the Ozarks in order to protect the lake's tourism season. He contended that his office had nothing to do with the decision and was unaware of the report until late June. But the controversy continued to dog him, and in September he suspended Natural Resources Director Mark Templeton for two weeks without pay. Then, in a bizarre September 2010 episode, a mentally unstable student at Metropolitan Community College-Penn Valley stabbed one of the college's deans in the neck, mistakenly thinking that he was attacking Nixon. The official survived the stabbing.

Senior Senator

Claire McCaskill (D)

Elected 2006, term expires 2012, 1st term; b. July 24, 1953, Rolla; home, St. Louis; U. of MO, B.S. 1975, J.D. 1978; Catholic; married (Joseph Shepard); 7 children.

Elected Office: MO House of Reps., 1982-88; Jackson Cnty. legislature, 1990-92; Jackson Cnty. prosecutor, 1992-98; MO auditor, 1998-2006.

Professional Career: Law clerk, MO Court of Appeals, 1978; Asst. Jackson Cnty. prosecutor, 1978-82; Practicing atty., 1983-92.

DC Office: 506 HSOB, 20510, 202-224-6154; Fax: 202-228-6326; Web site: mccaskill.senate.gov.

State Offices: Cape Girardeau, 573-651-0964; Columbia, 573-442-7130; Kansas City, 816-421-1639; Springfield, 417-868-8745; St. Louis, 314-367-1364.

Committees: *Aging (Special). Armed Services:* Airland; Personnel; Readiness & Management Support (Chmn). *Commerce, Science & Transportation:* Communications, Technology & the Internet; Consumer Protection, Product Safety & Insurance; Surface Transportation & Merchant Marine Infrastructure, Safety & Security. *Homeland Security & Governmental Affairs:* Contracting Oversight (Ad Hoc) (Chmn); Federal Financial Management, Government Information, Federal Services & International Security; Investigations (Permanent).

Group Ratings

	ACLU	ACU	ADA	CFG	AFS	FRC	LCV	ITIC	NTU	COC
2010	87	17	90	18	97	4	43	67	24	27
2009	–	28	95	17	91	–	91	–	25	43

National Journal Ratings

	2010 LIB	—	2010 CONS	2009 LIB	—	2009 CONS
Economic	46%	—	53%	45%	—	54%
Social	48%	—	49%	56%	—	43%
Foreign	47%	—	0%	55%	—	0%
Composite	57%	—	44%	60%	—	40%

Key Votes of the 111th Congress

1. Overturn Ledbetter	Y	5. Pass health care bill	Y	9. Ratify New START	Y
2. Pass $787 billion stimulus	Y	6. Regulate financial firms	Y	10. Confirm Elena Kagan	Y
3. Repeal DC gun laws	Y	7. Pass tax cuts for some	N	11. Stop EPA climate regs	N
4. Confirm Sonia Sotomayor	Y	8. Legalize immigrants' kids	Y	12. Repeal don't ask, tell	Y

Election Results

2006 general	Claire McCaskill (D)	1,055,255	(50%)	($11,412,117)
	Jim Talent (R)	1,006,941	(47%)	($23,765,577)
2006 primary	Claire McCaskill (D)	282,767	(81%)	
	Bill Young (D)	67,173	(19%)	

Claire McCaskill, a Democrat, is Missouri's senior senator. A straight-talking centrist, she was elected in 2006. She is close to President Barack Obama and was the subject of speculation as a possible running mate.

McCaskill was born in Rolla, about halfway between St. Louis and Springfield, and grew up in the Missouri towns of Houston, Lebanon, and Columbia. She hails from a political family. Her father served for a time as state insurance commissioner, and her mother was the first female city council member in the university town of Columbia. McCaskill earned degrees from the University of Missouri and its law school, clerked for the state Court of Appeals in Kansas City, and worked as an assistant prosecutor. In 1982, at the age of 29, she was elected to the Missouri House, where she was the first sitting member to have a baby. Ten years later, she became Jackson County prosecutor. And in 1998, she decided to run statewide and was elected state auditor.

In 2004, halfway through her second term as auditor, McCaskill challenged incumbent Gov. Bob Holden in the Democratic primary. Holden's administration had started off on the wrong foot, holding a $1 million inaugural, the largest in state history, and winding up $417,000 in debt. Things didn't get much better as a tough economic climate necessitated deep spending cuts and Holden battled with the legislature over education funding. Despite roots in the Ozarks, he was also hurt in outstate Missouri by his 2003 veto of a concealed-carry gun law. Democrats worried that they needed a stronger candidate to survive a Republican challenge in November. In stepped McCaskill, who defeated Holden 52%-45%. The state's major labor unions, which backed Holden, quickly united behind her against Republican Secretary of State Matt Blunt, the 33-year-old son of Sen. Roy Blunt. This was not the first contest between the McCaskills and Blunts: Blunt's grandfather, Leroy Blunt, had been elected to the Missouri House in 1978 by defeating McCaskill's mother, Betty McCaskill.

In the general election campaign, Blunt promised to make state government more accountable and efficient. He supported concealed-carry legislation and the constitutional amendment banning same-sex marriage, and he opposed abortion rights. McCaskill supported abortion rights, though she opposed late-term abortions, with an exception for the life of the mother. She opposed the concealed-carry gun law and the same-sex marriage ban. McCaskill sought to take advantage of Blunt's youth and relative inexperience in state government, noting that she would not need on-the-job training. She lost 51%-48%. McCaskill easily carried the Kansas City and St. Louis metropolitan areas but lost big in outstate Missouri, where Blunt won 90 of the 97 counties outside the two metro areas.

Despite the narrow loss, with three previous statewide races, McCaskill was a prize Senate recruit for the national party in 2006. She would be running for a seat that had changed partisan hands in both 2000 and 2002. In 2000, Republican John Ashcroft had lost 51%-48% to Mel Carnahan, the sitting governor whose name remained on the ballot after his death 22 days before the election. Carnahan's wife, Jean Carnahan, was appointed to the vacancy. In the 2002 election for the remaining four years of the term, she lost 50%-49% to Republican Jim Talent. In most election years, Talent would have been well positioned for re-election. But the war in Iraq and the unpopularity of the Bush administration were not helpful to a politician elected to the Senate with a thin 21,000-vote margin.

McCaskill announced her candidacy in August 2005 on the steps of the feed mill where her father once worked—a backdrop that telegraphed her focus on the rural counties that cost her the governor's election. She promised to "never forget rural Missouri." She denounced tax breaks for oil companies, called for an increase in the minimum wage, and said she would push tax credits for first-time home purchases, child care, and college education. Throughout the campaign, McCaskill linked Talent to President George W. Bush. But the issue of embryonic stem cell research generated the most attention. A controversial proposed constitutional amendment forced both candidates to address whether they supported more government funding for the research, which uses surplus embryos from in vitro fertilization procedures. McCaskill supported it, and Talent was against it. Missouri Republicans were split: State business leaders backed the proposal in hopes of attracting biomedical research to the state, while religious conservatives opposed it, considering the destruction of embryos tantamount to abortion.

In October, Talent flayed McCaskill over her family's personal finances and demanded that she release the tax returns of her husband, Joseph Shepard, a developer of low-income housing financed by government loans, who filed his taxes separately from her. Talent also suggested that they hadn't paid all of their taxes and accused McCaskill's husband of owning an offshore tax shelter. Through late October, polls showed the race to be a dead heat. On Election Day, McCaskill won 50%-47%, a difference of just 48,000 votes out of 2.1 million cast. It was the third consecutive election for the seat decided by fewer than 50,000 votes. Just as in the 2004 governor's race, McCaskill won big margins in the Kansas City and St. Louis metro areas, but unlike 2004, she held her own in outstate Missouri and carried 11 counties that she lost earlier.

In her first term in the Senate, McCaskill has emphasized her independence, voting against her party more often than most non-Southern Democrats. She was the first Democrat to back Arizona Republican Sen. John McCain's 2007 proposal blocking bills containing spending earmarks. In December 2010, after incumbent Democrats across the country were portrayed as pork-barrel spenders in the midterm elections, McCaskill joined with conservative Sen. Tom Coburn of Oklahoma to resurrect the ban on earmarks, forcing Senate Majority Leader Harry Reid to bring their bill to a vote. Their proposal, unlike previous measures, would have been binding, not voluntary. The practice of earmarking began in earnest only in the 1970s, so claims that a ban would impede Congress's constitutional "power of the purse" are "horseradish," said McCaskill, in the folksy vernacular that has become a trademark. The measure failed on a procedural vote. However, Appropriations Committee Chairman Daniel Inouye, D-Hawaii, in February 2011 announced a two-year earmark moratorium.

McCaskill has departed from the Democratic line on a host of other issues. In 2010, she joined other moderates in questioning the party's support for continual extensions of unemployment benefits. "At some point, it starts to look like another entitlement program," she said. In the past, she has also joined Republicans in calling for a freeze on federal spending and in attempting to trim the size of President Obama's $787 billion economic stimulus bill. Unlike most Senate Democrats, McCaskill voted against measures to cut off military funding in Iraq and to set timetables to withdraw U.S. troops. She opposed the 2007 immigration bill that created a guest-worker program and a path to citizenship for illegal immigrants. In 2008, she declined to commit to Democratic Sen. Barbara Boxer's bill tightening restrictions on greenhouse gases.

McCaskill also has established herself as a proponent of government reform. With Virginia Democrat Jim Webb, she established a bipartisan commission to look into wartime profiteering, similar to the committee Missouri Sen. Harry Truman chaired during World War II. And she has been a persistent critic of the practice of Senate "holds," in which a single senator can, without explanation, anonymously prevent consideration of a bill or a nomination. With Republican Susan Collins of Maine, McCaskill sponsored a successful 2008 bill to make inspectors general more independent, giving them seven-year terms and their own legal counsel.

McCaskill's image as an ethics watchdog, however, suffered a blow in 2011 with news reports in March saying she had spent $76,000 in taxpayer funds to fly on a private plane that she co-owned with her husband. She sought to quickly extinguish the controversy by contending it was a small oversight and reimbursing the Treasury for the expense. But the situation became worse when the senator acknowledged that she had failed to pay more than $287,000 in personal property taxes on the plane. She had been regarded as a favorite for re-election in 2012, but the turbulence gave Republicans added confidence they could unseat her in a politically marginal state for Democrats.

Her independence from Democratic orthodoxy should help McCaskill. It will give her some separation, if she needs it, from the president, who considers her a good friend from his Senate days. McCaskill was among the early centrists to endorse Obama for president in January 2008, after the New Hampshire primary and at the urging of her 18-year-old daughter. She spoke frequently on Obama's behalf during his primary campaign against then-New York Sen. Hillary Rodham Clinton. Missouri was one of the few states where the margin in the presidential primary, and in the general election, was exquisitely close. Obama won the Missouri primary over Clinton 49.3%-47.9%, carrying just five counties and St. Louis City.

McCaskill is one of Congress' most avid users of Twitter, and has attracted well over 50,000 followers by regularly tweeting both interesting political and personal tidbits. In one such message in late 2010, her followers learned of a potential rematch in 2012 with her old nemesis. "Just ran into Jim Talent at Lambert," she tweeted. "Nice friendly conversation. Asked him if it was gonna be a rematch. He said he 'was working through it.'"

Junior Senator

Roy Blunt (R)

Elected 2010, term expires 2016, 1st term; b. Jan. 10, 1950, Niangua; home, Strafford; SW Baptist U., B.A. 1970, SW MO St. U., M.A. 1972; Baptist; married (Abigail Blunt); 4 children.

Elected Office: MO secy. of state, 1984–93; U.S. House, 1997-2011.

Professional Career: H.S. teacher, 1970–73; Greene Cnty. clerk, 1973–85; Adjunct instructor, Drury Col., 1976–82; Pres., SW Baptist U., 1993–96.

DC Office: 260 RSOB, 20510, 202-224-5721; Fax: 202-225-5604; Web site: blunt.senate.gov.

State Offices: Springfield, 417-887-7814; Kansas City, 816-471-7141; Clayton, 314-725-4484; Cape Girardeau, 573-334-7044; Jefferson City, 573-634-2488; Columbia, 573-442-8151.

Committees: *Appropriations:* Agriculture, Rural Development, Food and Drug Administration & Related Agencies (RMM); Department of State, Foreign Operations & Related Programs; Interior, Environment & Related Agencies; Military Construction, Veterans Affairs & Related Agencies; Transportation, HUD & Related Agencies. *Commerce, Science & Transportation:* Aviation Operations, Safety & Security; Communications, Technology & the Internet; Competitiveness, Innovation & Export Promotion (RMM); Surface Transportation & Merchant Marine Infrastructure, Safety & Security. *Intelligence (Select). Rules & Administration.*

Group Ratings (House)

	ACLU	ACU	ADA	CFG	AFS	FRC	LCV	ITIC	NTU	COC
2010	7	100	0	93	0	93	0	33	88	80
2009	–	92	5	88	11	–	0	–	85	87

National Journal Ratings (House)

	2010 LIB — 2010 CONS		2009 LIB — 2009 CONS	
Economic	15%	— 85%	24%	— 76%
Social	0%	— 85%	13%	— 87%
Foreign	0%	— 88%	32%	— 68%
Composite	10%	— 91%	23%	— 77%

Key Votes of the 111th Congress (House)

1. Overturn Ledbetter	N	5. Bar federal abortion funds	Y	9. Stop detainee transfers	Y
2. Pass $820 billion stimulus	N	6. Pass health care bill	N	10. Legalize immigrants' kids	*
3. Let guns in national parks	Y	7. Regulate financial firms	N	11. Repeal don't ask, tell	N
4. Pass cap-and-trade	N	8. Pass tax cuts for some	N	12. Limit campaign funds	*

Election Results

2010 general	Roy Blunt (R)	1,054,160	(54%)	($11,932,403)
	Robin Carnahan (D)	789,736	(41%)	($10,331,090)
	Jonathan Dine (Lib)	58,663	(3%)	
	Jerry Beck (CNP)	41,309	(2%)	
2010 primary	Roy Blunt (R)	411,040	(71%)	
	Chuck Purgason (R)	75,663	(13%)	
	Kristi Nichols (R)	40,744	(7%)	

Prior Winning Percentages: House: 2008 (68%); 2006 (67%); 2004 (70%); 2002 (75%); 2000 (74%); 1998 (73%); 1996 (65%)

Republican Roy Blunt is the junior senator from Missouri. He was elected in 2010 to replace retiring Sen. Christopher (Kit) Bond, also a Republican. Blunt grew up on a dairy farm near Springfield, Mo. His father was a state representative, who won election in 1978 by defeating the mother of Sen. Claire McCaskill, D-Mo. In 1970, Blunt graduated from Southwest Baptist University, 25 miles north of Springfield. He later taught history and government at the high school and college levels. He got his start in politics in 1972, when he volunteered for Republican John Ashcroft's unsuccessful campaign for Congress. In 1973, then GOP Gov. Bond named the 23-year-old Blunt to be Greene County clerk.

In 1980, Republican Sen. John Danforth asked him to run for lieutenant governor, but Blunt lost. In 1984, he was elected Missouri secretary of state, the first Republican to win that office in half a century; he was re-elected in 1988. In 1992, he ran for governor and lost the Republican primary to William Webster, 44%-39%. Blunt then became president of Southwest Baptist University, his alma mater. In 1996, when Rep. Mel Hancock, R-Mo., retired, Blunt ran for the open House seat and won with 65% of the vote, carrying every county in the district. He was re-elected easily every two years after that, and then ran for the Senate in 2010.

In the House, Blunt had a solidly conservative voting record, with intermittent moves toward the center on social issues. In 2006, he won passage of his Combat Meth Act, the first comprehensive approach to fighting the supply of methamphetamine. With then-Sen. Barack Obama, D-Ill., Blunt sponsored a measure creating an Internet database of federal spending. His greater impact was in his leadership roles in the House, which gave him a say in shaping the major legislation produced in the period that Republicans were in the majority, from 1995 to 2006. For much of that time, Blunt had senior jobs in the whip operation, and from 2003 to 2008, he was the Republican whip. In 1999, Blunt was one of the 10 original members of then Texas Gov. George W. Bush's presidential exploratory committee. Bush called him "a leader who knows how to raise his sights and lower his voice."

At the suggestion of Majority Whip Tom DeLay, R-Texas, Blunt ran for and won the freshman spot on the Republican Steering Committee, a leadership-driven panel that makes recommendations for committee assignments. Then, in January 1999, DeLay plucked him from the ranks of 48 deputy whips and appointed him his chief deputy whip, an important leadership stepping stone. On a number of issues, Blunt's job was to make certain that bills the leadership hoped to pass were palatable to conservatives, who often objected to compromises aimed at giving legislation broader appeal.

Blunt spent a good deal of time meeting with lobbyists and organizing groups around issues such as trade, taxes and energy. He had a reputation as a good listener with a light touch, and he paid attention to party moderates, who were a larger share of the GOP Conference then. Blunt mediated disputes between Republicans and went after votes on critical issues. He also raised substantial sums for GOP candidates. When Majority Leader Dick Armey announced that he would retire in 2002, DeLay moved up to replace him, which left the post of whip available for Blunt. Ray LaHood of Illinois (now Transportation secretary), a moderate Republican, announced that he, too, was running for whip. Within weeks, however, he bowed out after concluding that Blunt had locked up support not only from most conservatives but from many moderates as well.

For the most part, Blunt was successful as whip. He met his toughest challenge in passing the 2003 bill to create a prescription drug benefit as part of the Medicare program. He assembled a solid Republican bloc of support for the bill and brought along a few Democrats, as well. Still, in November, when GOP leaders took the final version to the floor, they were still short of the necessary 218 votes. The roll call started at 3 a.m. and lasted a record two hours and 53 minutes. Finally, two conservative Republicans who had opposed the legislation because of its cost were persuaded to switch their votes, and the bill passed, 220-215, just before dawn. It was a big victory for Blunt and his vote-whipping operation. He ran into a couple of low points in this tenure as well. In 2002, the leadership was embarrassed by disclosures that Blunt had quietly inserted into a homeland security bill a provision benefiting Philip Morris, a tobacco giant with strong political ties to the whip. Still, Blunt's name often surfaced on lists of potential speakers of the House.

His star dimmed over time, in part because of his overweening ambition and in part because of events outside his control, mainly the political immolation of his old mentor, DeLay. In September 2005, a Texas grand jury indicted DeLay and he was forced to step down as majority leader. Blunt persuaded Speaker Hastert to let him keep his post as whip while also assuming the majority leader's job temporarily. It was too heavy a burden, especially because the House was dealing with the devastating impact of Hurricane Katrina in the South. During the next three months, Republicans struggled to pass bills in the House. In January 2006, after DeLay announced that he would permanently give up his post as leader, Blunt positioned himself to take over and, after a week of lobbying his colleagues, claimed that he had the votes to win. His assertion proved to be a bluff. John Boehner of Ohio was aggressively campaigning against him, and the multiple DeLay controversies involving well-heeled lobbyists had indirectly hurt Blunt, who was viewed as being too cozy with Washington's vaunted K Street. In a dramatic showdown, Boehner prevailed, 122-109, over Blunt, who suffered the double indignity of losing his bid and looking like a whip who couldn't count his votes.

However, Blunt remained in the leadership as whip and developed a smooth working relationship with Boehner. When House Republicans lost their majority in November 2006, he faced a new test. Republican Rep. John Shadegg of Arizona challenged him for the downsized post of minority whip. Blunt prevailed by an unexpectedly wide margin, winning 137-57. In the minority, he became more outspoken when criticizing the Democrats' management of the House and, with Boehner, fought the new majority on most issues. One exception was extension of the Foreign Intelligence Surveillance Act; for months, Blunt worked closely with Majority Leader Steny Hoyer,

D-Md., on a compromise bill. In September 2008, Boehner gave him the thankless job of negotiating the $700 billion financial bailout bill, which proved to be wildly unpopular with his fellow Republicans.

After Republicans suffered big electoral losses in 2008, Blunt stepped down from his whip position in favor of Rep. Eric Cantor, R-Va. The following year, he began to focus on a Senate campaign in earnest after Bond announced in February he would not seek re-election to a fifth term. In the spring, he won the primary without breaking a sweat after potentially competitive opponents Sarah Steelman, the former state treasurer, and Thomas Schweich, a Washington University law professor who had Danforth's backing, decided against getting into the race. State Sen. Chuck Purgason did run, and tried to create momentum with an appeal to tea party activists. But Blunt easily prevailed in the August primary with 71% of the vote. Danforth and Schweich both endorsed Blunt, unifying Missouri Republicans for the battle ahead.

The fall campaign was the real contest. Blunt faced Secretary of State Robin Carnahan, the daughter of a former senator and a governor who had instant name recognition. Blunt did his best to tie Carnahan to President Barack Obama and the Democratic policies unpopular with conservative voters. "I thought the Democrats would overreach," he told the *St. Louis Post-Dispatch* in August. "But I never thought they'd overreach so far that the fight would be among Democrats against their own agenda." His opposition to the Obama-backed health care overhaul played well for him on the campaign trail, and his ads featured images of Carnahan with Obama at a Kansas City fundraiser. Carnahan tried to paint Blunt as the insider in the race, but her family ties—her grandfather was in Congress, her father was governor, and her brother, Russ, currently serves in the House—made it difficult for her to be seen as an outsider.

Blunt has had his own family and lobbying connections to defend. Carnahan ran an ad with a Fox News clip in which anchor Chris Wallace mentioned Blunt inserting a favorable provision into a bill that favored tobacco companies while dating tobacco lobbyist Abigail Perlman, whom he later married. It appeared to have mattered little to Missouri voters in a year in which Obama's popularity sharply dropped. The race began as a close contest, but Carnahan fell further and further behind. On Election Night, Blunt won 54% to 41%.

FIRST DISTRICT

William Lacy Clay (D)

Elected 2000, 6th term; b. July 27, 1956, St. Louis; home, St. Louis; U. of MD, B.S. 1983; Catholic; divorced; 2 children.

Elected Office: MO House of Reps., 1983-90; MO Senate, 1991-2000.

Professional Career: Asst. doorkeeper, U.S. House of Reps., 1976-83; Paralegal, 1982-2000; Real estate agent, 1986-2000.

DC Office: 2418 RHOB, 20515, 202-225-2406; Fax: 202-226-3717; Web site: lacyclay.house.gov.

State Offices: St. Louis, 314-367-1970; St. Louis County, 314-383-5240.

Committees: *Financial Services:* Domestic Monetary Policy & Technology (RMM); Insurance, Housing & Community Opportunity. *Oversight & Government Reform:* Health Care, District of Columbia, Census & the National Archives.

Group Ratings

	ACLU	ACU	ADA	CFG	AFS	FRC	LCV	ITIC	NTU	COC
2010	88	0	85	5	100	0	80	100	8	25
2009	–	4	100	2	100	–	100	–	3	33

National Journal Ratings

	2010 LIB	—	2010 CONS	2009 LIB	—	2009 CONS
Economic	67%	—	33%	64%	—	34%
Social	80%	—	18%	84%	—	11%
Foreign	84%	—	16%	87%	—	9%
Composite	77%	—	23%	80%	—	20%

Key Votes of the 111th Congress

1. Overturn Ledbetter	Y	5. Bar federal abortion funds	N	9. Stop detainee transfers	N
2. Pass $820 billion stimulus	Y	6. Pass health care bill	Y	10. Legalize immigrants' kids	Y
3. Let guns in national parks	N	7. Regulate financial firms	Y	11. Repeal don't ask, tell	Y
4. Pass cap-and-trade	Y	8. Pass tax cuts for some	Y	12. Limit campaign funds	Y

Election Results

2010 general	William Lacy Clay (D)	135,907	(74%)	($693,370)
	Robyn Hamlin (R)	43,649	(24%)	($24,076)
	Julie Stone (Lib)	5,223	(3%)	
2010 primary	William Lacy Clay (D)	37,041	(81%)	
	Candice Britton (D)	8,546	(19%)	

Prior Winning Percentages: 2008 (87%), 2006 (73%), 2004 (75%), 2002 (70%), 2000 (75%)

Population		Race/Ethnicity		Work	
Pop. 2010:	587,069	White:	37.5%	Private:	83.6%
Change since 2000:	Down 5.6%	Black:	55.3%	Government:	12.6%
Urban:	99.2%	Hispanic:	2.4%	Self-employed:	3.8%
Rural:	0.8%	Asian:	2.5%	Blue collar:	19.1%
Area size:	227 sq. mi.	Native Am.:	0.2%	White collar:	60.0%
		Hawaiian:	0.0%	Khaki collar:	0.1%
Age		Two+ races:	1.8%	Other:	20.8%
Median age:	36.4 yrs.				
More than 65 yrs:	13.4%	*Ancestry*		Median income:	$41,009
Less than 18 yrs:	24.5%	German	13.3%	Median Home Value:	$120,000
		Irish	7.7%		
Education		English	4.4%	**Military Veterans**	
H.S. grad:	84.3%			% of Pop:	10.3%
College grad:	25.0%				
Grad degree:	10.0%				

North St. Louis, Suburbs

For a century or more, St. Louis seemed the center of America: the starting point for the Lewis and Clark expedition in 1804, the locus half a century later of the *Dred Scott* slavery case, and the site of the 1904 World's Fair, which introduced the hotdog and the ice cream cone and got 19 million people to *Meet Me in St. Louis*. Its 630-foot-high Gateway Arch is just below the point where the waters of the Missouri surge into the Mississippi, about halfway between New Orleans and Lake Superior, between the Atlantic and the Pacific. This was the first major American city west of the Mississippi River, the final resting place of Daniel Boone and for many years, Chicago's rival as the transportation hub of America. This was a heavily German city, with a Teutonic solidity and orderliness that distinguished it from the surrounding Southern-accented rural terrain. And from *Mitteleuropa* came the founders of St. Louis's great businesses—the Anheuser-Busch brewery, May Company department stores, Joseph Pulitzer's *St. Louis Post-Dispatch*—and its first great politician, Carl Schurz, the senator and Interior secretary. There is almost a European aura to Forest Park, the site of the 1904 fair, and the dozen mansion-lined private streets nearby.

2008 Presidential Vote		
Barack Obama (D)	246,448	(80%)
John McCain (R)	59,910	(20%)

2004 Presidential Vote		
John Kerry (D)	216,372	(75%)
George Bush (R)	71,367	(25%)

Cook Partisan Voting Index: D+27

St. Louis is still one of the nation's 20 largest metro areas, but today it does not occupy as central a place in the national consciousness, and the central city itself has largely emptied out. The German order that made so many people comfortable living in close quarters and commuting by streetcar has yielded to an American desire for suburban spaces and the less restrictive automobile. St. Louis' population peaked at 856,000 in 1950; it was down to 319,000 in 2010, a more than 8% decrease from 2000. Downtown St. Louis has been spruced up: A new Busch Stadium opened in 2006 with a panoramic view of the Arch and downtown, part of more than $4.5 billion that has been spent on a variety of projects there since 1999. But most of St. Louis' old factories have closed, and many of its once tight neighborhoods are only a memory. In 2008, local icon Anheuser-Busch was taken over by Belgium-based InBev.

Missouri's congressional districts have followed the people out of St. Louis, where the Democratic organization has been weakened by the loss of patronage and by state approval of term limits. The 1st District has been historically based on the north side of the city, but now three-fourths of its residents live in suburban St. Louis County. The district includes St. Louis City north of Interstate 44, and the northern and some central portions of St. Louis County. It takes in all of the predominantly African-American suburbs north of the city, including Bellefontaine Neighbors,

Ferguson, Spanish Lake, and Black Jack. It also includes working-class St. Ann and Bridgeton and, west of the city, parts of the affluent suburbs of University City, Ladue and Creve Coeur. The district is half African-American, but blacks account for far more than half the votes in Democratic primaries. Barack Obama in November 2008 won the city 84%-16%. He won St. Louis County, with more than triple the turnout, 60%-40%. In 2004, John Kerry won the county, 54%-45%.

William Lacy Clay (D)

The congressman from the 1st District is William Lacy Clay, a Democrat first elected in 2000 to the seat that his father, Bill Clay, held for 32 years. Born in St. Louis, he moved to the Washington, D.C., area at age 12 after his father's election to the House in 1968. He attended public schools in suburban Silver Spring, Md., and then the University of Maryland, studying by night for seven years while he worked as a House staffer by day. He had started law classes at Howard University in 1983, when a special election for the state House drew him back to St. Louis. Party leaders appointed him the Democratic nominee. Eight years later, he was again chosen by party leaders to run in a special election for a safely Democratic state Senate seat.

Then in 1999, his father decided to retire from Congress, after helping to enact many labor and education laws he had fought for. Clay wanted to take his father's place, but he had a serious primary contest. St. Louis Councilman Charlie Dooley raised nearly $400,000 and was an African-American with a base of support in the mostly white suburbs of St. Louis County. Dooley campaigned that the office should not be "inherited," and he attacked what he called Clay's old-style tactics of political threats and bossism. The St. Louis Labor Council and Missouri AFL-CIO, long allied with Bill Clay, declined to endorse his son, but more than 30 locals endorsed him. William Lacy Clay played up his father's name and revved up the still reliable machine. He won the primary 61%-28% over Dooley, winning St. Louis City 76%-12% and St. Louis County, where twice as many votes were cast, 49%-39%. In the general election, Clay won 75%-22%, and since then has won re-election by comparable margins.

In the House, Clay has had a mostly liberal voting record. He is a member of the House Democrats' whip organization and is active in the Congressional Black Caucus. He has worked to protect voting rights for blacks and the reliability of electronic voting equipment. A member of the Oversight and Government Reform Committee, Clay formerly chaired the Information Policy, Census and National Archives Subcommittee, with jurisdiction ranging from the Freedom of Information Act to the Census Bureau. He succeeded in pushing the bureau in 2010 to not automatically count prison inmates—who tend to be urban African-Americans or Latinos—as residents of the rural, mainly white communities that host prisons.

In 2007, he helped enact a rewrite of the Freedom of Information Act to expedite requests and the handling of disputes; he also foiled an attempt by the Bush Administration to eliminate a Census Bureau program that provides information on the effect that federal programs have on the poor. He has promoted efforts to make low-income public housing more energy efficient and to establish a National Civil Rights Trail that would include several stops in the St. Louis area. On foreign policy, he called for the withdrawal of U.S. troops from Iraq in 2006 and famously described President Bush as an "incompetent chicken hawk." The following year, he cosponsored a bill to impeach Vice President Dick Cheney. Clay also led opposition to the request of Rep. Stephen Cohen, a white Democrat from Tennessee, to join the Congressional Black Caucus. "It's an unwritten rule" that only African-Americans can belong, he said.

Upheaval in his personal life caused a minor controversy in May 2009, when Clay's wife, Ivie, accused him of not telling her or their children about his divorce filing before it hit the news media. He responded that he and his wife had been discussing the breakup for months and that the divorce "should not have come as a surprise to anyone." A future concern for him is the declining population in his district and its effect on redistricting.

SECOND DISTRICT

Todd Akin (R)

Elected 2000, 6th term; b. July 5, 1947, New York, NY; home, Town and Country; Worcester Polytech Inst. (MA), B.S. 1971, Covenant Theological Seminary (MO), M. Div. 1985; Presbyterian; married (Lulli); 6 children.

Military Career: Army Reserves 1972-80.

Elected Office: MO House of Reps., 1988-2000.

Professional Career: Marketing mgr., IBM, 1974-78; Mgmt. dir., Laclede Steel, 1977-80.

DC Office: 117 CHOB, 20515, 202-225-2561; Fax: 202-225-2563; Web site: akin.house.gov.

State Offices: St. Charles, 636-949-6826; St. Louis, 314-590-0029.

Committees: *Armed Services:* Air & Land Forces; Seapower & Projection Forces (Chmn). *Budget. Science & Technology:* Energy & Environment; Space & Aeronautics.

Group Ratings

	ACLU	ACU	ADA	CFG	AFS	FRC	LCV	ITIC	NTU	COC
2010	6	100	0	85	0	100	0	33	89	86
2009	–	100	0	97	0	–	0	–	91	73

National Journal Ratings

	2010 LIB	—	2010 CONS	2009 LIB	—	2009 CONS
Economic	0%	—	97%	6%	—	93%
Social	0%	—	85%	0%	—	93%
Foreign	23%	—	77%	0%	—	75%
Composite	11%	—	89%	8%	—	93%

Key Votes of the 111th Congress

1. Overturn Ledbetter	N	5. Bar federal abortion funds	Y	9. Stop detainee transfers	Y
2. Pass $820 billion stimulus	N	6. Pass health care bill	N	10. Legalize immigrants' kids	N
3. Let guns in national parks	Y	7. Regulate financial firms	N	11. Repeal don't ask, tell	N
4. Pass cap-and-trade	N	8. Pass tax cuts for some	N	12. Limit campaign funds	N

Election Results

2010 general	Todd Akin (R)	180,481	(68%)	($767,798)
	Arthur Lieber (D)	77,467	(29%)	($50,504)
	Steve Mosbacher (Lib)	7,677	(3%)	
2010 primary	Todd Akin (R)	72,269	(85%)	
	William Haas (R)	9,494	(11%)	

Prior Winning Percentages: 2008 (62%), 2006 (61%), 2004 (65%), 2002 (67%), 2000 (55%)

Population		Race/Ethnicity		Work	
Pop. 2010:	706,622	White:	89.2%	Private:	86.7%
Change since 2000:	Up 13.7%	Black:	3.2%	Government:	8.5%
Urban:	91.7%	Hispanic:	2.5%	Self-employed:	4.7%
Rural:	8.4%	Asian:	3.3%	Blue collar:	14.8%
Area size:	1,289 sq. mi.	Native Am.:	0.2%	White collar:	71.8%
		Hawaiian:	0.0%	Khaki collar:	0.1%
Age		Two+ races:	1.5%	Other:	13.3%
Median age:	38.8 yrs.				
More than 65 yrs:	12.7%	*Ancestry*		Median income:	$72,994
Less than 18 yrs:	25.2%	German	29.1%	Median Home Value:	$221,400
		Irish	14.4%		
Education		English	8.8%	**Military Veterans**	
H.S. grad:	93.3%			% of Pop:	10.5%
College grad:	41.8%				
Grad degree:	15.5%				

West St. Louis County; St. Charles

Just as the geographic center of the U.S. population has moved west from St. Louis to rural Phelps County, so has the center of metropolitan St. Louis moved farther west from the Gateway Arch on the Mississippi River. Now the midpoint is suburban St. Louis County, established in 1876 when the city, tired of paying for dusty back roads, separated itself from the sticks. That year, there were 350,000 people in the city and 31,000 in the county. In 2010, there were

2008 Presidential Vote
John McCain (R) 215,450   (55%)
Barack Obama (D) 172,169   (44%)

2004 Presidential Vote
George Bush (R) 215,123   (60%)
John Kerry (D) 142,824   (40%)

Cook Partisan Voting Index: R+9

319,000 in the city and just under 1 million in St. Louis County. By the 1960s, the center of office employment moved from downtown across the county line to Clayton. Now, the focus is fast moving out along the Daniel Boone Expressway (U.S. 40) to Chesterfield.

The 2nd Congressional District of Missouri consists of central and western St. Louis County, most of St. Charles County northwest across the Missouri River, and rural Lincoln County to the north. Along the expressway, in the center of St. Louis County, are long-settled suburbs: Kirkwood; most of high-income Town and Country and Ladue; Chesterfield, where Monsanto in 2010 acquired a sprawling research center from Pfizer; and Sunset Hills to the south. They are all Republican areas, more so in newer family-oriented subdivisions than in the leafy precincts of the older enclaves. St. Charles County, where the supply of available land and affordable housing is tight, now casts more votes than the city of St. Louis and is the most Republican suburban county in Missouri. O'Fallon is growing with relocating companies from St. Louis County, such as Fireman's Fund Insurance in 2009, though the boom lessened slightly during the recent recession. This conservative district voted 55% for John McCain in 2008, including 54%-45% in St. Charles County.

Todd Akin (R)

The congressman from the 2nd District is Todd Akin, a strongly conservative Republican first elected in 2000. He still lives in his boyhood home, a 60-year-old farmhouse in an upscale neighborhood in Town and Country. He graduated from Worcester Polytechnic Institute and earned a divinity degree at Covenant Seminary. After service as an Army combat engineer, he worked for IBM in the Boston area and then at Laclede Steel in Alton, Ill. The steel company was founded by his great-grandfather and his father once worked there, too. Akin was elected to the state House in 1988. An avid student and teacher of American history and the Constitution, Akin lectures at various public and private institutions. His religious beliefs are also a guiding force in his life, and Akin enjoys strumming gospel tunes on his guitar. While a state legislator, he sold standardized tests to parents who homeschool their children; he and his wife homeschooled their six children. He also filed a lawsuit to stop the state's approval of riverboat gambling but was ultimately unsuccessful.

When U.S. Rep. Jim Talent, a Republican, launched his bid for governor in 1999, Akin ran for his House seat. He started off as the underdog to Gene McNary, a former Bush administration Immigration and Naturalization Service commissioner, well known locally from his 15 years as St. Louis County executive. Akin emphasized he had never voted to raise taxes and had strong support from religious conservatives. In a low-turnout, rainy-day primary, Akin rallied his committed voters to win the five-candidate contest by 56 votes over McNary. In the general election against Democratic state Sen. Ted House, Akin focused on their differences on taxes. House, whose television ads did not identify himself as a Democrat, depicted Akin as an extreme ideologue and an ineffective legislator. Akin carried St. Louis County 57%-40% and won overall, 55%-42%.

In the House, Akin was among the first House members to join the Tea Party Caucus in 2010 and is known for his doggedness in pursuing social legislation. After a federal appeals court in California ruled that the reference to "one nation under God" in the Pledge of Allegiance was unconstitutional, Akin twice successfully ushered through a bill to strip lower courts of jurisdiction over challenges to the Pledge. But it went nowhere in the Senate. He has repeatedly sponsored the Parent's Right to Know Act, which bars funding to family planning projects that provide contraceptive drugs and devices to minors without parental consent. When "Bodies...The Exhibition," a science exhibit displaying dissected and preserved cadavers, announced plans to come to St. Louis in fall 2010, Akin sought to block it on the grounds that the corpses came from Chinese police, and that the exhibitors could not guarantee the bodies hadn't been subjected to human rights abuses. The organizers eventually agreed to put up a disclaimer. In 2003, Akin burned some bridges with

Republican leaders when he voted against their bill creating a prescription drug benefit under Medicare, saying the new program would be a "budget buster" and attract more illegal immigrants to the country.

On the Armed Services Committee, Akin has emphasized special operation forces, which he considers essential in the fight against terrorism. One of his sons was a Marine in Iraq. He is also a defender of Boeing, a major presence in his district. In May 2008, the House defeated his amendment to restore $193 million for the Army's Future Combat Systems, a Boeing project. In 2009, he opposed the Senate's addition of an anti-hate crimes provision in the Defense authorization bill, drawing a sharp rebuke from his normally mild-mannered Missouri colleague Ike Skelton, then the chairman of Armed Services. But Akin with was unyielding. "They're the enemy," he said of the senators backing the provision.

Akin took over as chairman of Armed Services' Seapower and Projection Forces Subcommittee in 2011 after the GOP won a House majority, and pledged to fight the Pentagon's decision to cancel the $2.3 billion Expeditionary Fighting Vehicle (EFV), a landing craft used to move Marines from ocean to land. He also was given a seat on the Budget Committee, and suggested that spending cuts to Medicare should be examined.

Back home, Akin has been easily re-elected.

THIRD DISTRICT

Russ Carnahan (D)

Elected 2004, 4th term; b. July 10, 1958, Columbia; home, St. Louis; U. of MO, B.S. 1979, J.D. 1983; Methodist; married (Debra); 2 children.

Elected Office: MO House of Reps., 2000-04.

Professional Career: Practicing atty, 1988-96; Consultant, BJC HealthCare, 1996-2004.

DC Office: 1710 LHOB, 20515, 202-225-2671; Fax: 202-225-7452; Web site: carnahan.house.gov.

State Offices: Crystal City, 636-937-8039; St. Louis, 314-962-1523.

Committees: *Foreign Affairs:* Africa, Global Health & Human Rights; Oversight & Investigations. *Transportation & Infrastructure:* Aviation; Economic Development, Public Buildings & Emergency Management; Water Resources & Environment. *Veterans' Affairs:* Health.

Group Ratings

	ACLU	ACU	ADA	CFG	AFS	FRC	LCV	ITIC	NTU	COC
2010	81	0	95	0	100	0	90	100	6	25
2009	–	0	100	2	100	–	100	–	3	40

National Journal Ratings

	2010 LIB	—	2010 CONS	2009 LIB	—	2009 CONS
Economic	69%	—	30%	75%	—	21%
Social	61%	—	35%	75%	—	20%
Foreign	66%	—	29%	67%	—	31%
Composite	67%	—	33%	74%	—	26%

Key Votes of the 111th Congress

1. Overturn Ledbetter	Y	5. Bar federal abortion funds	N	9. Stop detainee transfers	Y
2. Pass $820 billion stimulus	Y	6. Pass health care bill	Y	10. Legalize immigrants' kids	Y
3. Let guns in national parks	N	7. Regulate financial firms	Y	11. Repeal don't ask, tell	Y
4. Pass cap-and-trade	Y	8. Pass tax cuts for some	Y	12. Limit campaign funds	Y

Election Results

2010 general	Russ Carnahan (D)	99,398	(49%)	($2,127,173)
	Ed Martin (R)	94,757	(47%)	($1,539,980)
	Steven Hedrick (Lib)	5,772	(3%)	
2010 primary	Russ Carnahan (D)	36,976	(80%)	
	David Arnold (D)	6,467	(14%)	
	Edward Crim (D)	2,697	(6%)	

Prior Winning Percentages: 2008 (66%), 2006 (66%), 2004 (53%)

Population		Race/Ethnicity		Work	
Pop. 2010:	625,251	White:	83.8%	Private:	85.0%
Change since 2000:	Up 0.6%	Black:	9.1%	Government:	10.2%
Urban:	86.7%	Hispanic:	2.8%	Self-employed:	4.6%
Rural:	13.3%	Asian:	2.3%	Blue collar:	21.6%
Area size:	1,263 sq. mi.	Native Am.:	0.2%	White collar:	61.1%
		Hawaiian:	0.0%	Khaki collar:	0.1%
Age		Two+ races:	1.7%	Other:	17.2%
Median age:	37.3 yrs.				
More than 65 yrs:	12.2%	*Ancestry*		Median income:	$50,741
Less than 18 yrs:	22.6%	German	26.1%	Median Home Value:	$159,400
		Irish	13.2%		
Education		English	6.8%	**Military Veterans**	
H.S. grad:	86.6%			% of Pop:	10.0%
College grad:	28.0%				
Grad degree:	11.0%				

South St. Louis, Suburbs

Middle America, it could be said, lies somewhere on the south side of metropolitan St. Louis. The geographical center of the country's population was here in 1980, just south of St. Louis in Jefferson County. While that point has moved further southwest, St. Louis is still the metro area nearest the demographic midpoint of the country. Geographically, this is a node where some of the nation's main arteries come together. The Missouri River flows into the Mississippi a few miles

2008 Presidential Vote
Barack Obama (D) ....189,727　(60%)
John McCain (R) ....124,536　(39%)

2004 Presidential Vote
John Kerry (D) ....168,740　(57%)
George Bush (R) ....127,668　(43%)

Cook Partisan Voting Index:　D+7

north of St. Louis's Gateway Arch. The National Road and its successors, U.S. 40 and Interstate 70, cross the Mississippi just below the Arch. And the great tides of Southerners migrating west up the Mississippi and of Germans migrating overland met here to create one of the nation's largest and most bustling cities. The south side of St. Louis is famous for its pleasant parks and tight-knit, neat neighborhoods, including "Little Bosnia" in the Bevo Mill section. Its most famous symbols are the Anheuser-Busch brewery south of downtown and Grant's Farm, where Ulysses S. Grant lived in the 1850s and where Anheuser-Busch bred the Budweiser Clydesdales. But many more people now live in the suburbs.

The 3rd Congressional District of Missouri consists of the south side of St. Louis, part of suburban St. Louis County and, to the south, Jefferson County and rural Ste. Genevieve County, the site of Missouri's oldest permanent settlement. Ste. Genevieve County also has the nation's largest cement plant, which opened in 2009 and sparked a welcome mini-economic boom. Jefferson and Ste. Genevieve are also agricultural, producing soybeans, corn and wine. The district's St. Louis County portions are mostly suburbs close to the St. Louis City line—Clayton, Maplewood, Richmond Heights, Webster Groves, Affton, Lemay, and Oakville. This is the descendant of districts dominated by St. Louis voters, but today the city casts less than 25% of its votes; almost half are cast in St. Louis County. Ethnically, this has been a heavily German-American area since the mid-19th century. Politically, it has been Democratic since the New Deal of the 1930s. The district voted 57% for John Kerry in 2004 and 60% for Barack Obama in 2008. Obama carried each of its counties.

Russ Carnahan (D)

The congressman from the 3rd District is Russ Carnahan, a Democrat elected in 2004. He succeeded Richard Gephardt, a Democrat who rose to party leader in the House and who twice unsuccessfully sought the Democratic nomination for president.

Carnahan is the son of the late Democratic Gov. Mel Carnahan and former Sen. Jean Carnahan, who was appointed to the Senate seat her husband had won shortly after he died in an airplane crash in October 2000. His sister, Robin Carnahan, is Missouri's secretary of state and waged an unsuccessful challenge to Roy Blunt for the Senate in 2010. Russ Carnahan grew up in Rolla and graduated from the University of Missouri and its law school. He practiced law with his wife, Debra, until 1996, when he took a job as a lobbyist and consultant with BJC HealthCare, which operates several nursing homes and hospitals. In 1990, he ran unsuccessfully against Republican Rep. Bill Emerson in the old 10th Congressional District in southeast Missouri. In 2000, he was elected to the state House, and after the 2002 election, became chairman of the House Democratic Caucus. Two years later, he ran to succeed Gephardt, who was running for president.

Carnahan was among four current or former state legislators in the primary. Opponents ganged up on him, claiming he had a thin legislative record and was trading on his family name. His toughest opponent was Jeff Smith, a youthful political science instructor at Washington University in St. Louis. Gephardt remained neutral, but many of his allies backed state Sen. Steve Stoll, who supported gun rights and opposed abortion. It turned out to be a very close race. Carnahan won with 23% of the vote; Smith finished second with 21%, and Stoll had 18%.

In the general election, Carnahan faced Republican author Bill Federer, who spent heavily and ran on a platform of opposing abortion in all circumstances and most gun control laws, including a ban on assault weapons, which Carnahan supported. Carnahan called for increased funding for education and said that he would "retarget" Bush's tax cuts to the middle class. Carnahan won 53%-45%. Federer led 50%-48% in Jefferson County, but Carnahan carried St. Louis County, 52%-46%, and St. Louis City, 61%-36%.

In the House, Carnahan has voted near the center of his party, and typically votes with his party on major legislation. He took over in 2011 as co-chairman of the Center Aisle Caucus, an informal group of lawmakers disenchanted with growing partisanship.

Carnahan was among the Midwestern Democrats from blue-collar districts to back cap-and-trade legislation to limit carbon emissions, contending it would add clean energy jobs. He also has taken an interest in energy issues as a way of bolstering the St. Louis area's position as an alternative energy research hub, and got a bill into law in December 2010 to cut electricity usage in federal buildings. To reduce gasoline consumption and increase walking, biking and public transit, he co-sponsored a 2009 bill calling for a long-term, energy efficient transportation strategy.

Carnahan's wife has served on the national board of Planned Parenthood, and he has pushed for increased funding for contraceptives in developing nations. In 2006, Carnahan helped to whip up support for a 2006 bill to provide federal funding for embryonic stem cell research. On an issue with local impact, he worked with colleagues to enact the Combat Meth Act, with tough restrictions on production of methamphetamine, a major problem in Jefferson County.

Carnahan had two initial easy re-elections before 2010. He had hoped to get some mileage out of his sister's appearance on the ballot that year, but she ended up losing by nearly 14 percentage points. His GOP opponent was Ed Martin, a former executive director of Missouri's anti-tax Club for Growth chapter and chief of staff for former GOP Gov. Matt Blunt—Roy Blunt's son. Martin ran an incendiary campaign in which he warned that Carnahan and other Democrats are taking away Americans' right to "find the Lord." He later asserted that "Russ Carnahan, Nancy Pelosi and President Obama are contemptuous of liberty as we know it." Carnahan, along with his sister, also came under harsh attack from Republicans who pointed to their brother, Tom, receiving $107 million in federal stimulus money for a wind energy project. But Carnahan dug in, raising more than $1.8 million, and avoided his sister's fate with a narrow 49%-47% victory. Martin won rural areas and outer-ring suburbs by large margins, but Carnahan carried the city of St. Louis by more than 2-to-1.

But by mid-2011, his future was again uncertain. After Missouri lost a seat in the 2010 reapportionment, the Republican-controlled legislature drew a new map that eliminated the 3rd District, merging much of it into the heavily black 1st District represented by Democrat William Lacy Clay. Democratic Gov. Jay Nixon vetoed the map, but the legislature overrode his veto.

FOURTH DISTRICT

Vicky Hartzler (R)

Elected 2010, 1st term; b. Oct. 13, 1960, Archie; home, Harrisonville; U. of MO, B.S. 1983; U. of Central MO, M.S. 1992; Christian; Married (Lowell); 1 child.

Elected Office: MO House 1995-2001.

Professional Career: Teacher, 1983-94; spokeswoman, Coalition to Protect Marriage, 2004; appointee, MO Women's Cncl., 2005-2010; owner, Hartzler Equipment Co.

DC Office: 1023 LHOB, 20515, 202-225-2876; Fax: 202-225-0148; Web site: hartzler.house.gov.

State Offices: Harrisonville, 816-884-3411; Jefferson City, 573-634-4884; Lebanon, 417-532-5582; Sedalia, 573-634-4884.

Committees: *Agriculture:* General Farm Commodities & Risk Management; Rural Development, Research, Biotechnology & Foreign Agriculture. *Armed Services:* Air & Land Forces; Military Personnel; Readiness.

Election Results

2010 general	Vicky Hartzler (R)...113,489	(50%)	($1,478,530)
	Ike Skelton (D)...101,532	(45%)	($2,923,038)
	Jason Braun (Lib)..6,123	(3%)	
2010 primary	Vicky Hartzler (R)..35,860	(40%)	
	Bill Stouffer (R)..26,573	(30%)	
	Jeff Parnell (R)...7,969	(9%)	

Population		Race/Ethnicity		Work	
Pop. 2010:	679,375	White:	90.2%	Private:	69.4%
Change since 2000:	Up 9.3%	Black:	3.4%	Government:	21.6%
Urban:	39.9%	Hispanic:	3.2%	Self-employed:	8.6%
Rural:	60.1%	Asian:	0.7%	Blue collar:	28.4%
Area size:	14,831 sq. mi.	Native Am.:	0.5%	White collar:	51.9%
		Hawaiian:	0.1%	Khaki collar:	2.2%
Age		Two+ races:	1.7%	Other:	17.5%
Median age:	38.1 yrs.				
More than 65 yrs:	14.8%	*Ancestry*		Median income:	$42,219
Less than 18 yrs:	24.2%	German	23.2%	Median Home Value:	$117,500
		Irish	11.5%		
Education		English	9.3%	**Military Veterans**	
H.S. grad:	85.3%			% of Pop:	13.1%
College grad:	17.8%				
Grad degree:	6.1%				

Western Missouri

Missouri was the first state settled west of the Mississippi, and the folks who settled it were a picture of pioneer diversity. Virginians and other Southerners made their way to counties north of the Missouri River, while Germans settled around the small capital, Jefferson City. A taste of that diversity can be found in the Capitol, with its mural by Thomas Hart Benton, great-grandnephew of one of Missouri's first senators, who championed hard money and westward ex-

2008 Presidential Vote
John McCain (R) 187,394   (60%)
Barack Obama (D) 117,978   (38%)

2004 Presidential Vote
George Bush (R) 187,111   (64%)
John Kerry (D) 102,652   (35%)

Cook Partisan Voting Index: R+14

pansion for 30 years and lost his seat for opposing the expansion of slavery. The painting depicts dance hall girls, black coal miners, and a mother diapering an infant.

The 4th Congressional District occupies central west Missouri. It is not so diverse today. The 2010 census found that only 2% of people in the district are foreign-born. The rest are native, and of those, nearly two-thirds were born in Missouri. The district includes part of Blue Springs and Oak Grove in Jackson County east of Kansas City, but the overall atmosphere here is rural and small-town. The rural counties around Kansas City were full of pro-slavery "bushwhackers" who rode across the Kansas line to thwart the anti-slavery Yankee "jayhawkers," and these areas today vote Democratic. The German area around Jefferson City was anti-slavery and remains among the most Republican parts of Missouri. The growing year-round resort areas around the man-made Lake of the Ozarks are mixed. The southern portion of the district, near Springfield, is predominantly Republican. There are two big military bases here: Fort Leonard Wood in Pulaski County, where Marines, sailors, and airmen train in joint exercises with Army troops; and Whiteman Air Force Base, near Knob Noster in Johnson County, from which B-2 bombers flew to drop precision-targeted bombs in Afghanistan.

President Truman was born in Barton County, at the southern end of the district, and lived in Independence, a few miles from Blue Springs. He spent much of Election Night 1948, when just about everyone thought he would lose, in Excelsior Springs. In his long life, Truman spanned the gaps between country and city, South and North. His mother could remember her house being attacked by Yankee soldiers, and she remained pro-Confederate even when her son was in the White House. He got his political start in urban Independence and Kansas City and desegregated the military services.

Vicky Hartzler (R)

The new member of Congress from the 4th District is Vicky Hartzler, a Republican responsible for one of the biggest upsets of 2010. She defeated 17-term Democrat Ike Skelton, the powerful chairman of the Armed Services Committee who had gotten 62% of the vote or better since 1982.

Hartzler has spent her entire life in rural Cass County, where she grew up working alongside her parents and sister on the family farm. Faith was a cornerstone of the household. "As farmers, we prayed for rain and when it rained too much, we relied on prayer to hope that we had a crop that year," she told *National Journal*. In high school, she excelled in athletics, captained the girls' volleyball and basketball teams, and was a member of the track team. She was also editor of the school yearbook and president of the Future Homemakers of America. After getting her bachelor's degree in education, Vicky married Lowell Hartzler, her college sweetheart, and went to work as a high school home economics teacher. She remained in the classroom for 11 years. The trajectory of her career changed in 1994, however, when Hartzler got a phone call from a friend while she was grading papers, urging her to run to be the district's state representative. "He asked me to think about it and pray about it, and I did," she said. "After 30 days, I knew I was supposed to run."

Hartzler served three terms in Missouri's House. She counts overhauling Missouri's outdated adoption statutes among her proudest accomplishments. The changes smoothed the adoption process. "We went through every line, every word, and we passed two major pieces of legislation," she said. In 2000, Hartzler decided not to run for re-election after her daughter, Tiffany, was born. Hartzler and her husband live on a 1,600-acre farm outside of Harrisonville, where they raise corn, soybeans, and cattle, and run the Hartzler Equipment Co., which sells farming equipment.

In 2004, she headed the Coalition to Protect Marriage in Missouri, a campaign to add an amendment to the state's constitution banning same-sex marriage. Despite being outspent 17-to-1 by opposition groups, the amendment passed with 71% of the vote. Hartzler also wrote the book *Running God's Way: Step by Step to a Successful Political Campaign*, a detailed guide for Christian candidates published in 2008.

Hartzler's bid to unseat Skelton in 2010 drew the attention of former Alaska Gov. Sarah Palin, who endorsed her on her Facebook page and generated tea party interest in her candidacy. In this increasingly conservative district, Skelton had relied on crossover GOP voters in the past, but in an election year that went from bad to worse for Democrats, Hartzler's message resonated. She assailed Skelton on his votes with "the liberal leadership" for the $787 billion economic stimulus bill and an energy bill imposing caps on carbon emissions blamed for global warming. "I don't have a 'To Do list'; I have an 'Undo list,'" she said. "We have to undo all these destructive policies."

The 78-year-old incumbent was wise to the threat and ran an aggressive campaign, with a full schedule of appearances allowing him to emphasize his work on behalf of America's military as committee chairman. Hartzler tried to turn his image as a wise legislative elder into a negative, saying in her stump speech, "So many people in Washington (are) removed from rural America. Ike's lost touch." Skelton raised $3 million for the effort and outspent Hartzler 3-to-1. Skelton maintained a steady lead in the polls. But then in late October, Hartzler made gains and the race tightened, a sobering bit of news for Democrats who thought Skelton was probably safe. Hartzler prevailed on Election Night, 50% to 45%, with the remaining votes split by two minor candidates.

FIFTH DISTRICT

Emanuel Cleaver (D)

Elected 2004, 4th term; b. Oct. 26, 1944, Waxahachie, TX; home, Kansas City; Prairie View A&M U., B.S. 1968, St. Paul Schl. of Theology, M.Div. 1974; Methodist; married (Dianne); 4 children.

Elected Office: Kansas City Cncl., 1979-91; Mayor, 1991-99.

Professional Career: Pastor, 1970-present; Radio talk-show host, 2002-04.

DC Office: 1433 LHOB, 20515, 202-225-4535; Fax: 202-225-4403; Web site: www.house.gov/cleaver.

State Offices: Independence, 816-833-4545; Kansas City, 816-842-4545.

Committees: *Financial Services:* Domestic Monetary Policy & Technology; Insurance, Housing & Community Opportunity.

Group Ratings

	ACLU	ACU	ADA	CFG	AFS	FRC	LCV	ITIC	NTU	COC
2010	94	0	100	0	100	0	100	67	4	13
2009	–	0	95	0	100	–	93	–	1	36

National Journal Ratings

	2010 LIB	—	2010 CONS	2009 LIB	—	2009 CONS
Economic	77%	—	22%	91%	—	0%
Social	89%	—	7%	89%	—	0%
Foreign	84%	—	16%	70%	—	24%
Composite	84%	—	16%	88%	—	12%

Key Votes of the 111th Congress

1. Overturn Ledbetter	Y	5. Bar federal abortion funds	N	9. Stop detainee transfers	N
2. Pass $820 billion stimulus	Y	6. Pass health care bill	Y	10. Legalize immigrants' kids	Y
3. Let guns in national parks	N	7. Regulate financial firms	Y	11. Repeal don't ask, tell	Y
4. Pass cap-and-trade	Y	8. Pass tax cuts for some	Y	12. Limit campaign funds	Y

Election Results

2010 general	Emanuel Cleaver (D)	102,076	(53%)	($637,380)
	Jacob Turk (R)	84,578	(44%)	($274,523)
2010 primary	Emanuel Cleaver (D)	unopposed		

Prior Winning Percentages: 2008 (64%), 2006 (64%), 2004 (55%)

Population		Race/Ethnicity		Work	
Pop. 2010:	633,887	White:	61.6%	Private:	81.8%
Change since 2000:	Up 2.0%	Black:	25.0%	Government:	12.8%
Urban:	96.1%	Hispanic:	8.7%	Self-employed:	5.3%
Rural:	3.9%	Asian:	1.6%	Blue collar:	21.7%
Area size:	519 sq. mi.	Native Am.:	0.4%	White collar:	61.3%
		Hawaiian:	0.2%	Khaki collar:	0.1%
Age		Two+ races:	2.4%	Other:	16.9%
Median age:	36.2 yrs.				
More than 65 yrs:	12.7%	*Ancestry*		Median income:	$44,625
Less than 18 yrs:	24.6%	German	15.4%	Median Home Value:	$128,200
		Irish	10.2%		
Education		USA	8.5%	**Military Veterans**	
H.S. grad:	86.5%			% of Pop:	10.5%
College grad:	26.2%				
Grad degree:	9.5%				

Kansas City, Suburbs

Kansas City, named after a state it isn't in and a river it doesn't touch, is the center of one of America's large metro areas, the biggest on the central Great Plains. The first pioneers here started little towns on the bluffs above the Missouri River—Independence, Kansas City, Westport—that coalesced a few decades later. Here, traders on the Santa Fe Trail set out to cross the Sand Hills of Kansas to reach Mexican territory. Kansas City was a rail center and, in the

2008 Presidential Vote		
Barack Obama (D) 201,337	(63%)
John McCain (R) 114,030	(36%)
2004 Presidential Vote		
John Kerry (D) 175,352	(60%)
George Bush (R) 118,915	(40%)
Cook Partisan Voting Index: D+10		

1920s, had one of the largest stockyards in the country, a major commercial center with lean skyscrapers and the Country Club Plaza, the first shopping center in America. The city is famous also for its black community, its National Negro Leagues Baseball Museum, its historic jazz district that has been home to musicians like Scott Joplin, Charlie Parker and Count Basie, and for its much-praised barbecue. The area is also famous as the home of Harry Truman, who grew up on a farm now in the suburb of Grandview and who lived in his wife's family's house in Independence, the old county seat just to the east.

Overall, Kansas City fared better than most cities during the recession. It was bolstered in part by the designation of a 150-block area as a Green Impact Zone in 2009. The idea was to use federal stimulus money and other public funds on roads and other infrastructure, along with a combination of different strategies, to transform the urban core into a national model of green living. The initiative has had some success, but also has drawn criticism from conservatives who contend its benefits do not translate on a wide scale.

The 5th Congressional District of Missouri includes most of Kansas City, the largest city in Missouri, plus Grandview and the bulk of Independence. The more suburban slices of Jackson County to the east have been filled with new subdivisions. It also includes fast-growing Belton and Raymore along U.S. 71 in Cass County just to the south. Most of the metro area's landmarks, including the Truman home, are here but much of the metropolitan area growth is across the state line in Kansas. One-quarter of the district's residents are African-American, the second highest percentage among Missouri districts. Politically, the seat has been solidly Democratic. John Kerry carried it 60%-40% in 2004, and Barack Obama won it 63%-36% in 2008.

Emanuel Cleaver (D)

The congressman from the 5th District is Emanuel Cleaver, a Democrat first elected in 2004 and the current chairman of the Congressional Black Caucus.

He grew up in Waxahachie, Texas, in a three-room shack with no plumbing or electricity. He graduated from Prairie View A&M University, moved to Kansas City and earned a divinity degree, and then became pastor of St. James United Methodist Church. He was elected to the City Council in 1979 and elected mayor in 1991. As mayor, Cleaver voiced support for the Clinton administration's changes in welfare policy, which he described as "corrective surgery." He backed expansion of downtown's Bartle Hall Convention Center and supported the renovation of the deteriorating Liberty Memorial, the country's largest World War I memorial. After leaving office, he hosted a radio talk show.

In December 2003, Democratic Rep. Karen McCarthy announced that she would not run for re-election, and Cleaver was widely expected to succeed her. Few expected just how tough Cleaver's road to Congress would be. In the primary, he faced former National Security Council aide Jamie Metzl, who raised substantial funds. Metzl hammered Cleaver on ethics issues, questioning the propriety of a loan that Cleaver took out to purchase a car wash business and his failure to pay $36,000 in back taxes on the business. Cleaver won the primary by 60%-40%.

In the general election, Cleaver faced Republican businesswoman Jeanne Patterson, who had $3 million of her own money to spend. Like Metzl, she made an issue of Cleaver's ethics, emphasizing bribery and fraud convictions of Cleaver's allies, though there was no evidence that he was involved in any crimes. Cleaver said that Patterson was politically inexperienced and was trying to buy the seat. Cleaver won 55%-42%. In his Kansas City base, which cast 48% of the vote, he led 71%-27%. Patterson took Jackson County 54%-43%.

In the House, Cleaver's voting record is near the center of the Democrats, though he became more loyal in the years his party held the majority. He led Black Caucus members seeking to play a role on environmental issues and got a seat on Speaker Nancy Pelosi's Select Committee on Energy

Independence and Global Warming. She designated Cleaver to act as a liaison with mayors and faith communities on those issues. He proposed changing House rules to require members to lease energy-efficient vehicles in their districts. "The public would rather see a sermon than hear one," said Cleaver, whose own taxpayer-leased car runs on used cooking grease. (He drew criticism in 2009 when it was revealed that the car's $2,900 monthly cost was higher than that of any other House member.) When Republicans opted to kill the global warming panel after reclaiming the majority in 2010, he called the decision a "travesty."

On the Financial Services Committee, he testified for a bill to protect employees against discrimination because of sexual orientation, citing discrimination against his gay cousin. Cleaver initially opposed the creation of the Troubled Assets Relief Program, but backed a revised version in the face of constituents' anger. He also voted in favor of taxing bonuses paid to AIG executives in March 2009, but later acknowledged it was an ill-considered reaction to public outrage. His idea to create a Green Impact Zone in Kansas City became reality in 2009. He has been among those calling for travel and trade sanctions to be lifted on Cuba.

Cleaver continued preaching regularly at his church in Kansas City, but stepped down in 2008 in favor of his son. He has easily won re-election. In November 2010, he also won unanimous approval of the Black Caucus to be its chairman. He promised to work with Obama, whose relations with the group have been tempestuous at times, but also indicated he would not hesitate to part company with the president if the CBC perceived he was more concerned with his political fate. "We may be moving down two separate paths toward 2012," he said.

SIXTH DISTRICT

Sam Graves (R)

Elected 2000, 6th term; b. Nov. 7, 1963, Tarkio; home, Tarkio; U. of MO, B.S. 1986; Baptist; married (Lesley); 3 children.

Elected Office: MO House of Reps., 1992-94; MO Senate 1994-2000.

Professional Career: Farmer.

DC Office: 1415 LHOB, 20515, 202-225-7041; Fax: 202-225-8221; Web site: house.gov/graves.

State Offices: Liberty, 816-792-3976; St. Joseph, 816-233-9818.

Committees: *Small Business* (Chmn). *Transportation & Infrastructure:* Aviation; Highways & Transit; Railroads, Pipelines & Hazardous Materials.

Group Ratings

	ACLU	ACU	ADA	CFG	AFS	FRC	LCV	ITIC	NTU	COC
2010	8	100	0	84	0	87	10	100	89	88
2009	–	96	0	90	22	–	7	–	89	79

National Journal Ratings

	2010 LIB	—	2010 CONS	2009 LIB	—	2009 CONS
Economic	30%	—	70%	13%	—	86%
Social	0%	—	85%	27%	—	72%
Foreign	24%	—	75%	0%	—	75%
Composite	21%	—	79%	18%	—	82%

Key Votes of the 111th Congress

1. Overturn Ledbetter	*	5. Bar federal abortion funds	Y	9. Stop detainee transfers	*
2. Pass $820 billion stimulus	N	6. Pass health care bill	N	10. Legalize immigrants' kids	N
3. Let guns in national parks	Y	7. Regulate financial firms	N	11. Repeal don't ask, tell	N
4. Pass cap-and-trade	N	8. Pass tax cuts for some	N	12. Limit campaign funds	N

Election Results

2010 general	Sam Graves (R)	154,103	(69%)	($1,057,245)
	Clint Hylton (D)	67,762	(31%)	($9,461)
2010 primary	Sam Graves (R)	54,566	(82%)	
	Christopher Ryan (R)	11,608	(18%)	

Prior Winning Percentages: 2008 (59%), 2006 (62%), 2004 (64%), 2002 (63%), 2000 (51%)

Population		Race/Ethnicity		Work	
Pop. 2010:	693,974	White:	87.9%	Private:	79.3%
Change since 2000:	Up 11.6%	Black:	4.2%	Government:	14.1%
Urban:	66.3%	Hispanic:	4.2%	Self-employed:	6.4%
Rural:	33.7%	Asian:	1.3%	Blue collar:	23.7%
Area size:	13,125 sq. mi.	Native Am.:	0.4%	White collar:	59.5%
		Hawaiian:	0.2%	Khaki collar:	0.2%
Age		Two+ races:	1.7%	Other:	16.7%
Median age:	37.5 yrs.				
More than 65 yrs:	13.1%	*Ancestry*		Median income:	$51,635
Less than 18 yrs:	24.4%	German	22.4%	Median Home Value:	$142,500
		Irish	13.3%		
Education		English	9.4%	**Military Veterans**	
H.S. grad:	89.6%			% of Pop:	11.7%
College grad:	25.4%				
Grad degree:	8.4%				

Northwest Missouri; Kansas City

The rolling fields along the Missouri River in northwest Missouri were settled in a rush in the late 19th century, and they lost people for most of the 20th century as fewer hands were needed on farms. In 1940, this area had one of the largest meatpacking operations in the world, and meatpacking is still an economic asset that has drawn many Hispanics to the area. It is one of the fastest-growing Hispanic communities in the nation, with a 60% increase in growth from 2006 to 2009. Barge traffic on the Missouri has all but disappeared, a victim of low water levels that are the result of drought as well as recreational uses upstream and court rulings in favor of environmentalists.

2008 Presidential Vote
John McCain (R) 180,517   (54%)
Barack Obama (D) 150,101   (45%)

2004 Presidential Vote
George Bush (R) 178,669   (57%)
John Kerry (D) 132,007   (42%)

Cook Partisan Voting Index: R+7

Just as Kansas City was the starting place for many wagon trains heading west, the river town of St. Joseph was the starting point for the Pony Express and its roughly 10-day transport of mail to Sacramento. Today, St. Joe is the biggest town north of Kansas City. The city has gotten a few pieces of good economic news—the animal health company Boehringer Ingelheim Vetmedica expanded here in 2009, and in 2010, the Kansas City Chiefs held their first training camp here, bringing thousands of visitors. Biopharming—the use of genetically modified crops, such as rice, to grow medications—has become a growth industry in some of the outlying rural communities. In 2008, Rock Port became the first area town to use only wind energy.

The 6th Congressional District of Missouri takes in all of the counties in northwest Missouri plus part of metro Kansas City—Clay and Platte counties and a small portion of Jackson County east of Independence, including Blue Springs. The Kansas City area casts about half the district's votes. The historic political tradition here was mostly Democratic, but it has been tempered by dislike for national Democrats' cultural liberalism. This was strong Ross Perot country in 1992; Bill Clinton carried it with a plurality in 1992 and 1996. But the rural vote here, as across the nation, has moved toward Republicans. George W. Bush carried the district with 53% in 2000 and 57% in 2004. John McCain won all of the counties north of Kansas City, except for Buchanan, which he lost by 54 votes.

Sam Graves (R)

The congressman from the 6th District is Sam Graves, a Republican first elected in 2000 and the chairman of the Small Business Committee. He is a lifelong resident of Tarkio in the northwest corner of the state. He graduated from the University of Missouri with a degree in agronomy, farmed with his father and brother, and joined the Farm Bureau. He ran for the state House in 1992 and beat a longtime Democratic incumbent. Two years later, he was elected to the state Senate. He attracted attention in 1998 with a five-hour filibuster against a school desegregation bill that he said put rural areas at a disadvantage, but the bill eventually passed.

Graves got his opportunity to run for the U.S. House when Democratic Rep. Pat Danner withdrew from her race for re-election just minutes before the filing deadline. Not by accident, the immediate favorite to succeed her was her son, state Sen. Steve Danner, also a Democrat. Graves entered the race within the short window provided by state law and drew support from national Republicans. Teresa Loar, a moderate Republican on the Kansas City Council, attacked Graves as the darling of extremist and sexist party leaders, but Graves beat her 68%-17%.

In the general election, Danner billed himself as a conservative Democrat and switched from being pro-abortion rights to opposing abortion. In an editorial endorsing Graves, the *Kansas City Star* said that Danner's campaign switch on abortion showed that he "engaged in raw opportunism at the slightest opportunity." Graves won 51%-47%.

In the House, Graves has usually been a party loyalist. He has tended mostly to local issues. In 2005, the House passed his amendment to the transportation bill to preempt state laws governing liability for damages involving rental cars, a measure of interest to St. Louis-based Enterprise Rent-A-Car. In 2007, the House passed his amendment to the farm bill banning anyone found cheating federal farm programs from participating in the future.

He also is known for his hard-line stance against illegal immigration, introducing a bill in 2010 to build an additional 150 miles of border fencing. In 2009, he vociferously opposed the Democrats' cap-and-trade energy legislation to limit carbon emissions, joining two other Republicans in passing out documents purporting to detail how the measure would unfairly target rural Americans. The Center for American Progress, a liberal think tank, said the information in the documents came directly from Peabody Energy, the world's largest coal company.

On the Small Business Committee, Graves has been a critic of the Obama administration's initiatives. He joined most Republicans in opposing the 2010 Small Business Jobs and Credit Act, which he said represented too much government interference in the private sector. He also has backed allowing venture capitalists to tap into two research grant programs that have been reserved for small businesses. Upon taking the chairmanship in 2011, he said he would look for ways to slash spending at the Small Business Administration while overseeing the regulatory burden imposed on private firms by other agencies as well as the impact of health care reform on those businesses.

Graves was the subject of an ethics investigation for allegedly violating House rules for his role in arranging testimony to his committee by a family friend. The matter touched off a rare public squabble between the new Office of Congressional Ethics and the Committee on Standards of Official Conduct; while OCE recommended that the case merited further consideration, the ethics panel found deficiencies in the office's handling of the matter and voted unanimously in October 2009 to clear Graves.

In 2008, national Democrats were excited when former Kansas City Mayor and St. Joseph native Kay Barnes announced she would challenge Graves. But Graves attacked Barnes for "San Francisco values" and supporting "a homosexual agenda" because her picture had appeared in a gay magazine and he won easily, 59%-37%. In February 2011, after much consideration, he declined the opportunity to take on Democratic Sen. Claire McCaskill in 2012. He said his goal instead was to eventually chair the House Transportation and Infrastructure Committee.

SEVENTH DISTRICT

Billy Long (R)

Elected 2010, 1st term; b. Aug. 11, 1955, Springfield; home, Springfield; U. of MO, attended.; Presbyterian; Married (Barbara); 2 children.

Professional Career: Talk show host, 1999-2006; realtor, 1978-2010; owner, Billy Long Auctions.

DC Office: 1541 LHOB, 20515, 202-225-6536; Fax: 202-225-5604; Web site: long.house.gov.

State Offices: Joplin, 417-781-1041; Springfield, 417-889-1800.

Committees: *Homeland Security:* Counterterrorism & Intelligence; Cybersecurity, Infrastructure Protection & Security Technologies; Oversight, Investigations & Management. *Transportation & Infrastructure:* Aviation; Highways & Transit; Railroads, Pipelines & Hazardous Materials.

Election Results

2010 general	Billy Long (R)	141,010	(63%)	($1,302,007)
	Scott Eckersley (D)	67,545	(30%)	($231,883)
	Kevin Craig (Lib)	13,866	(6%)	
2010 primary	Billy Long (R)	38,218	(37%)	
	Jack Goodman (R)	30,401	(29%)	
	Gary Nodler (R)	14,561	(14%)	
	Darrell Moore (R)	9,312	(9%)	

Population		**Race/Ethnicity**		**Work**	
Pop. 2010:	721,754	White:	89.6%	Private:	81.7%
Change since 2000:	Up 16.1%	Black:	1.6%	Government:	10.3%
Urban:	59.1%	Hispanic:	4.4%	Self-employed:	7.9%
Rural:	40.9%	Asian:	1.1%	Blue collar:	25.1%
Area size:	5,555 sq. mi.	Native Am.:	0.9%	White collar:	56.4%
		Hawaiian:	0.2%	Khaki collar:	0.1%
Age		Two+ races:	2.1%	Other:	18.3%
Median age:	36.4 yrs.				
More than 65 yrs:	14.1%	*Ancestry*		Median income:	$40,963
Less than 18 yrs:	24.0%	German	17.1%	Median Home Value:	$121,800
		Irish	11.7%		
Education		USA	10.3%	**Military Veterans**	
H.S. grad:	86.1%			% of Pop:	11.6%
College grad:	22.0%				
Grad degree:	7.3%				

Southwest Missouri; Springfield

One of the biggest tourist destinations in America today is Branson, Mo.—something almost no one would have predicted 30 years ago. Branson has only 8,500 residents, but it thrives thanks to the surging popularity of country and western music. It has more than 40 theaters with 60,000 seats—more than Broadway—and has become a hub for nonstop, low-cost, family-friendly entertainment. Nearby are fishing and boating

2008 Presidential Vote		
John McCain (R)	208,231	(63%)
Barack Obama (D)	116,660	(35%)
2004 Presidential Vote		
George Bush (R)	202,486	(67%)
John Kerry (D)	97,557	(32%)
Cook Partisan Voting Index:	R+17	

and plenty of shopping. These diversions have made southwest Missouri the fastest-growing part of the state in the past 20 years, generating new businesses and attracting retirees as well as vacationers. Branson even got its own privately financed small airport in 2009 to accommodate the 5.4 million visitors a year who travel over 300 miles to get to Branson. The 1907 novel by Harold Bell Wright, *The Shepherd of the Hills*, acquainted readers with the hardy people of the mountains, hills, and meadows of southwest Missouri, just north of Arkansas. When completion of the Ozark Beach Dam created Bull Shoals Lake in 1913, more tourists came, lured by the native bass and stocked trout. In the 1960s, more manmade lakes were added, and entertainers—notably the four Mabe brothers, who as "The Baldknobbers" entertained audiences with comedy and country music, and Boxcar Willie from the Grand

Ole Opry—started performing. Today, Branson is constantly undergoing new construction and hosts more than 8 million visitors a year.

Springfield is the biggest city in southwest Missouri and the self-styled "buckle of the Bible Belt." It is home to more than 200 churches, including the headquarters of the Assemblies of God, one of the nation's largest and fastest-growing Protestant denominations. It is also the headquarters of such Middle American institutions as the Bass Pro Shops Outdoor World, the mega fishing equipment store. Southwest Missouri is also dairy country and home to a growing poultry industry. Latinos have been moving into McDonald County to work in chicken-processing plants. In May 2011, the town of Joplin in Jasper County was devastated by a tornado that killed 125 people and heavily damaged or destroyed 2,000 buildings, including a hospital and schools. The tornado left a swath of destruction six miles long and at least one half-mile wide in the town of 50,150 people.

The 7th Congressional District of Missouri includes Branson and Springfield. Historically, this area has been Republican territory since 1861, when it opposed secession. Pro-union Springfield changed hands several times as Missouri staged its own civil war. Its conservative response to the big-spending government of the 1960s and cultural liberalism of the 1970s reinforced its allegiance to the GOP, and now it is the most Republican part of Missouri. In the 2008 presidential election, John McCain won all of the counties here, many by 2-to-1.

Billy Long (R)

The new congressman from Missouri's 7th District is Republican Billy Long, who took the seat of GOP Rep. Roy Blunt after Blunt ran for the Senate in 2010.

Long grew up in Springfield, Mo., where he developed an interest in Republican politics at an early age. When he was 9 years old, he told the *Springfield News-Leader*, he would ride his bike to pass out bumper stickers for a Greene County sheriff's candidate who was the brother of a family friend. A few years later, he taught his dog a trick: He would ask, "Little Bear, would you rather be a Democrat or a dead dog?" The family pet responded by flopping over and sticking his feet in the air. While still a teenager, Long was given responsibility, along with his sister, for running his family's miniature golf course. After briefly attending the University of Missouri to study business, he became interested in real estate and attended auction school, eventually starting a company that would conduct as many as 200 auctions a year. He moved into radio in 1999, spending six years as a morning-drive talk show host for an AM station covering all of southwest Missouri.

Long initially considered running for Congress in 1996, the year Blunt was elected, but decided he didn't want to raise his two young daughters in Washington. However, after Blunt decided to seek the Senate seat held by retiring GOP incumbent Christopher (Kit) Bond last year, Long entered the race with the slogan "Fed Up." He ran as a plain-talking conservative who would clamp down on federal spending and set Congress straight. And he billed his lack of experience in elected office as a plus. "We have enough political experience in Washington, D.C., to choke a horse," he told the Associated Press. "That's exactly the problem." He prevailed in the GOP primary over seven other candidates, including two veteran state senators, with more than 37% of the vote.

In the fall, Long's Democratic opponent was former gubernatorial aide Scott Eckersley, who sought to make an issue of racist remarks that Long was accused of making at a bar that featured strippers and illegal gambling tables—a claim that Long dismissed as a "flat-out lie" and "slanderous." Long, meanwhile, campaigned in support of a constitutional amendment to limit the federal government's taxation powers and of repeal of the Democrats' health care law. He said he would oppose all earmarks added to spending bills. He wore a cowboy hat and inveighed against "elitist politicians." Long won with 63% of the vote; Eckersley received 30%.

EIGHTH DISTRICT

Jo Ann Emerson (R)

Elected Nov. 1996, 8th full term; b. Sept. 16, 1950, Washington, D.C.; home, Cape Girardeau; Ohio Wesleyan U., B.A. 1972; Presbyterian; married (Ron Gladney); 8 children.

Professional Career: Deputy communications dir., Natl. Repub. Cong. Cmte., 1984–91; Dir., State Relations & Grassroot Programs, Natl. Restaurant Assn., 1991–94; Sr. V.P., Pub. Affairs, American Insurance Assn., 1994–96.

DC Office: 2230 RHOB, 20515, 202-225-4404; Fax: 202-226-0326; Web site: house.gov/emerson.

State Offices: Cape Girardeau, 573-335-0101; Farmington, 573-756-9755; Rolla, 573-364-2455; West Plains, 417-255-1515.

Committees: *Appropriations:* Agriculture, Rural Development, FDA & Related Agencies; Financial Services & General Government (Chmn); Legislative Branch (VChmn).

Group Ratings

	ACLU	ACU	ADA	CFG	AFS	FRC	LCV	ITIC	NTU	COC
2010	19	88	0	73	13	93	0	33	83	88
2009	–	72	10	57	33	–	14	–	68	87

National Journal Ratings

	2010 LIB	—	2010 CONS		2009 LIB	—	2009 CONS
Economic	25%	—	75%		35%	—	65%
Social	29%	—	69%		36%	—	63%
Foreign	12%	—	79%		33%	—	63%
Composite	24%	—	76%		36%	—	65%

Key Votes of the 111th Congress

1. Overturn Ledbetter	N	5. Bar federal abortion funds	Y	9. Stop detainee transfers	Y
2. Pass $820 billion stimulus	N	6. Pass health care bill	N	10. Legalize immigrants' kids	N
3. Let guns in national parks	Y	7. Regulate financial firms	N	11. Repeal don't ask, tell	N
4. Pass cap-and-trade	N	8. Pass tax cuts for some	N	12. Limit campaign funds	N

Election Results

2010 general	Jo Ann Emerson (R)	128,499	(66%)	($2,006,543)
	Tommy Sowers (D)	56,377	(29%)	($1,588,389)
	Larry Bill (I)	7,193	(4%)	($15,630)
	Rick Vandeven (Lib)	3,930	(2%)	
2010 primary	Jo Ann Emerson (R)	47,880	(66%)	
	Bob Parker (R)	25,118	(34%)	

Prior Winning Percentages: 2008 (71%), 2006 (72%), 2004 (72%), 2002 (72%), 2000 (69%), 1998 (63%), 1996 (50%), 1996 special (63%)

Population		Race/Ethnicity		Work	
Pop. 2010:	656,894	White:	90.9%	Private:	75.2%
Change since 2000:	Up 5.7%	Black:	5.0%	Government:	16.2%
Urban:	39.6%	Hispanic:	1.7%	Self-employed:	8.2%
Rural:	60.4%	Asian:	0.6%	Blue collar:	29.9%
Area size:	18,820 sq. mi.	Native Am.:	0.4%	White collar:	49.9%
		Hawaiian:	0.0%	Khaki collar:	0.1%
Age		Two+ races:	1.4%	Other:	20.1%
Median age:	39.4 yrs.				
More than 65 yrs:	16.1%	*Ancestry*		Median income:	$33,807
Less than 18 yrs:	23.7%	German	17.7%	Median Home Value:	$91,200
		Irish	11.5%		
Education		USA	9.9%	**Military Veterans**	
H.S. grad:	77.1%			% of Pop:	12.4%
College grad:	14.1%				
Grad degree:	5.4%				

Southeast Missouri; Cape Girardeau

Mark Twain might not recognize life on the Mississippi below St. Louis today. The Ozark Mountains to the west flatten out, and the river is hidden behind levees, which ordinarily, except during the terrible flood of 1993, screen small towns and river roads from rows of barges tethered together, full of coal and corn and soybeans. The Mississippi today is an industrial waterway. But it was never really all that romantic. Twain's steamboats, as he was at pains to point

2008 Presidential Vote		
John McCain (R) 174,538	(62%)
Barack Obama (D) 102,739	(36%)
2004 Presidential Vote		
George Bush (R) 173,378	(63%)
John Kerry (D) 97,778	(36%)
Cook Partisan Voting Index: R+15		

out, were dangerous, noisy contraptions, forever blowing up or getting embedded in roots and branches in the river currents. This is one of the oldest settled parts of the United States. French pioneers founded such Missouri towns as Cape Girardeau in the late 1700s. The big influx started a few years after the 1811 earthquake at New Madrid. The spongy Mississippi Valley land is seismically very active, and this was the site of one of the most devastating earthquakes in U.S. history.

The southeast quadrant of Missouri—the river valley and the hills to the west, with coal and lead mines, plus the Bootheel that hangs down in the far southeast—has not seemed to change much in half a century. For years, there has been a population outflow from the Bootheel, as machines replaced low-wage farm workers and crops shifted from cotton to rice, corn, and soybeans. Dairy cattle, pigs, apples, and berries, plus some timber, are among the area's other products. But this is also home to Missouri's Lead Belt, a mining region rich in ore minerals such as lead, zinc, copper, silver, and cadmium. Reynolds and Iron counties produce about 80% of the nation's lead; the Environmental Protection Agency ordered a cleanup of massive piles of lead waste in recent years. Doe Run Company, in agreeing to spend $65 million to clean up those sites, announced in October 2010 it would shut its aging lead smelter by the end of 2013. An aluminum smelting plant in New Madrid provides more than 1,000 jobs and in September 2010 unveiled a $38 million expansion to greatly increase production capacity. Still, the only big growth here has been around the retail and medical hub of Cape Girardeau and along Interstate 44. The poverty rate in the Bootheel is the highest in the state—nearly 22% of the 8th Congressional District's residents earn less than $15,000 a year.

The sprawling 8th District, the largest in Missouri, covers the state's southeast corner and is more than twice the size of Maryland. Its political heritage is mixed. The Bootheel was as solidly Democratic as the Mississippi Valley around Memphis once was, and some mining counties show traces of Democratic sentiment. Cape Girardeau is heavily Republican and an incubator of Republican talent: It is the hometown of Rush Limbaugh and Lt. Gov. Peter Kinder. Once a safely Democratic district, it has been represented since 1980 by Republicans. This was one of the rural areas that trended Republican in the Clinton years. George W. Bush won 63% in 2004, and John McCain won 62% in 2008, including 66% in Cape Girardeau.

Jo Ann Emerson (R)

The congresswoman from the 8th District is Jo Ann Emerson, a Republican first elected in 1996 to succeed her husband, Bill Emerson, who died in office that June. Jo Ann Emerson grew up in Bethesda, Md., in a Republican family. Her father was executive director of the Republican National Committee, but her neighborhood was bipartisan. Next door lived Democrats Hale and Lindy Boggs, who served in Congress nearly 50 years. In 1975, she married Republican Bill Emerson, then a Washington lobbyist. In 1979, spotting the vulnerability of the Democratic incumbent in the Bootheel district, he went home to Missouri to run, and won with 55% of the vote. In 1995, he was diagnosed with cancer. After Bill's death, Jo Ann decided to put her considerable political résumé to work by running for his seat. She had worked for the American Insurance Association and the National Restaurant Association, and as a press aide for the National Republican Congressional Committee.

Leading state and national Republicans quickly endorsed her. Missouri law bars reopening the filing deadline if an incumbent dies less than 11 weeks before the primary, so she ran as an independent. Democratic contender Emily Firebaugh, a timber company owner, attacked Emerson as a product of Washington, and spent $831,000, slightly more than Emerson. The Republican nominee, Richard Kline, was less trouble. In 1995, he had used pepper spray to try to place a Veterans Affairs Department doctor under citizen's arrest; his campaign never got off the ground. Bill Emerson's record, Jo Ann Emerson's conservative views, and the poignancy of her situation all worked toward her victory. She won 50%; Firebaugh got 37%; and Kline, 11%.

In the House, Emerson has had a moderate-leaning voting record with sometimes conservative positions on cultural issues. On the Appropriations Committee and its Agriculture Subcommittee, her priority was rescuing falling farm commodity prices. She wrote the Trade Sanctions Reform and Export Enhancement Act of 2000, which partially lifted embargoes on five nations. And she worked with other members from farm districts to open agricultural trade with Cuba. She championed protection of U.S. food aid programs from international trade restrictions and crusaded for hunger relief, an issue that Bill Emerson popularized. She and Democratic Rep. Jim McGovern of Massachusetts lived for one week on a $21 food budget to dramatize the plight of some food stamp recipients and to gain additional funding for nutrition programs. Her bill to remove liability for federal agencies that donate excess food to shelters was enacted in 2008. By 2011, Emerson had accrued enough seniority to chair the Financial Services Subcommittee.

Emerson earned a footnote in history by casting the deciding vote in 2003 on the House version of the Republican bill creating a prescription drug benefit in the Medicare program. She initially opposed the bill, but changed her vote in exchange for a promise from Speaker Dennis Hastert for a subsequent floor vote on her priority bill, which would have allowed consumers to import American drugs from other countries where prices are lower. She got the vote as promised, but the second-ranking GOP leader, Majority Leader Tom DeLay, worked aggressively against it. Emerson won the floor vote, but the bill ultimately failed to pass Congress. Emerson took her revenge a few months later by voting against the final version of the prescription drug bill.

In the four years that Democrats controlled the House, Emerson regularly went her own way. She voted for five of the six bills in the new majority's first "100-hour" agenda in 2007, including one she co-sponsored, to permit the government to negotiate prices with drug companies. She also voted for a Democratic bill to expand the State Children's Health Insurance Program and long-delayed compensation for first responders on September 11. On the major foreign-policy issue of the 110th Congress (2007-08), Emerson reluctantly supported President Bush's to send more troops into Iraq. Emerson, now remarried, has a personal connection to the war. Her stepdaughter served with the 1st Infantry Division in Iraq.

In June 2010, she was elected co-chair of the moderate Tuesday Group. Her independence has not seemed to adversely affect her influence among House Republicans, perhaps because she has been up-front with party leaders about her views. She also has stuck with the GOP on major votes, and in 2010 was among those introducing a resolution to block the Environmental Protection Agency from regulating greenhouse gases blamed for global warming. A year earlier, she introduced proposed constitutional amendments on school prayer and banning flag desecration. She has won re-election without difficulty. She demolished Democrat Tommy Sowers in 2010, 66%-29%, even though he kept pace with her in fundraising for much of the campaign. In early 2011 she considered challenging Democratic Sen. Claire McCaskill in 2012, but opted against it, saying she felt she could have more impact as a senior Republican in the House majority.

NINTH DISTRICT

Blaine Luetkemeyer (R)

Elected 2008, 2nd term; b. May 7, 1952, Jefferson City; home, St. Elizabeth; Lincoln U., B.A. 1974; Catholic; married (Jackie); 3 children.

Elected Office: MO House, 1999-2005.

Professional Career: Loan officer, Bank of St. Elizabeth, 1978-2008; Pres., Luetkemeyer Insurance Agency, 1978-08; Dir., MO division of tourism, 2007-08.

DC Office: 1740 LHOB, 20515, 202-225-2956; Fax: 202-225-5712; Web site: luetkemeyer.house.gov.

State Offices: Columbia, 573-443-1041; Hannibal, 573-231-1012; Washington, 636-239-2276.

Committees: *Financial Services:* Domestic Monetary Policy & Technology; Financial Institutions & Consumer Credit.

Group Ratings

	ACLU	ACU	ADA	CFG	AFS	FRC	LCV	ITIC	NTU	COC
2010	13	100	0	84	0	93	0	33	87	88
2009	–	96	5	90	22	–	7	–	86	80

National Journal Ratings

	2010 LIB	—	2010 CONS	2009 LIB	—	2009 CONS
Economic	11%	—	89%	9%	—	89%
Social	18%	—	77%	24%	—	73%
Foreign	21%	—	77%	0%	—	75%
Composite	18%	—	82%	16%	—	84%

Key Votes of the 111th Congress

1. Overturn Ledbetter	N	5. Bar federal abortion funds	Y	9. Stop detainee transfers	Y
2. Pass $820 billion stimulus	N	6. Pass health care bill	N	10. Legalize immigrants' kids	N
3. Let guns in national parks	Y	7. Regulate financial firms	N	11. Repeal don't ask, tell	N
4. Pass cap-and-trade	N	8. Pass tax cuts for some	N	12. Limit campaign funds	N

Election Results

2010 general	Blaine Luetkemeyer (R) 162,724	(77%)	($1,609,842)
	Christopher Dwyer (Lib) 46,817	(22%)	
2010 primary	Blaine Luetkemeyer (R) 59,684	(83%)	
	James Baker (R) 12,248	(17%)	

Prior Winning Percentages: 2008 (50%)

Population		Race/Ethnicity		Work	
Pop. 2010:	684,101	White:	90.7%	Private:	76.1%
Change since 2000:	Up 10.0%	Black:	4.0%	Government:	16.8%
Urban:	45.8%	Hispanic:	1.9%	Self-employed:	6.9%
Rural:	54.2%	Asian:	1.4%	Blue collar:	24.8%
Area size:	14,079 sq. mi.	Native Am.:	0.3%	White collar:	57.5%
		Hawaiian:	0.0%	Khaki collar:	0.1%
Age		Two+ races:	1.6%	Other:	17.6%
Median age:	36.8 yrs.				
More than 65 yrs:	13.3%	*Ancestry*		Median income:	$44,087
Less than 18 yrs:	23.6%	German	26.5%	Median Home Value:	$131,200
		Irish	11.9%		
Education		English	8.4%	**Military Veterans**	
H.S. grad:	86.1%			% of Pop:	10.8%
College grad:	23.4%				
Grad degree:	9.1%				

Northeast Missouri; Columbia

Little Dixie, the swath of northeast Missouri along the Mississippi River, was settled by Southerners from Kentucky and Virginia. Its most famous native son is Mark Twain, born Samuel Langhorne Clemens in Hannibal, then as now a little town on bluffs overlooking the river. Hannibal was the thinly disguised St. Petersburg of Twain's classics, *The Adventures of Tom Sawyer* and *The Adventures of Huckleberry Finn*. Little Dixie was pro-Confederate during

2008 Presidential Vote		
John McCain (R) 181,181	(55%)
Barack Obama (D) 144,729	(44%)
2004 Presidential Vote		
George Bush (R) 180,362	(59%)
John Kerry (D) 124,965	(41%)
Cook Partisan Voting Index: R+9		

the Civil War, and Callaway County in fact declared its independence from the Union. For many years faithfully Democratic, Little Dixie has reared some notable politicians. One was Clarence Cannon, author of the definitive text on the House's parliamentary procedures and chairman of the House Appropriations Committee from 1941 to 1964, except for four years of Republican control.

The 9th Congressional District of Missouri is the descendant of the Little Dixie districts that elected Clark and Cannon, but slow population growth has expanded it far to the south and into the foothills of the Ozarks. It includes Columbia, home of the University of Missouri and its "Mizzou" Tigers. The university helped the town avoid the recession; Columbia ranked eighth on *Forbes'* 2010 "Best Small Places for Businesses and Careers" list. The district also includes Fulton, home of Westminster College, where former Prime Minister Winston Churchill, accompanied by President Harry Truman, told the world in 1946: "From Stettin in the Baltic to Trieste in the Adriatic, an iron curtain has descended across the Continent." The district includes the western edge of the St. Louis metro area, western St. Charles County, and Franklin County south of the Missouri River. Its grain fields have become a center for ethanol production; a plant in Macon—the first in Missouri—also produces high-protein animal feed and carbon dioxide for soft drinks. Despite its Democratic heritage, the 9th votes mostly Republican now. George W. Bush carried the district with 59% in 2004, and John McCain carried it with 55% in 2008.

Blaine Luetkemeyer (R)

The congressman from the 9th District is Blaine Luetkemeyer, a Republican first elected in 2008 with Missouri roots that stretch back five generations. He grew up in St. Elizabeth, where his father worked as an insurance agent and then owned a bank. Luetkemeyer *(LOOT-ka-myer)* was a star high school baseball player, but his tryouts with the Kansas City Royals and Pittsburgh Pirates were unsuccessful. He graduated from Lincoln University, a historically black college in Jefferson City, with a degree in political science. He and his wife settled on his great-grandfather's farm in St. Elizabeth. In addition to farming, Luetkemeyer became involved in his family's banking operations and founded the Luetkemeyer Insurance Agency.

In 1999, Luetkemeyer was elected to the Missouri House of Representatives, where he developed a reputation as a thoughtful legislator. He campaigned for Missouri treasurer in 2004 but lost in the Republican primary. In 2007, Luetkemeyer was appointed director of the Missouri Division of Tourism. Two years later, the 9th District House seat came open when Republican Rep. Kenny Hulshof decided to run for governor to succeed retiring Republican Gov. Matt Blunt.

Luetkemeyer entered a five-way GOP primary, and was viewed by Republican politicos as the favorite. The conservative anti-tax group Club for Growth endorsed GOP state Rep. Bob Onder, although Luetkemeyer received a critical endorsement from the anti-abortion group Missouri Right to Life. Luetkemeyer trounced the competition with 40% of the vote.

In the general election, he faced state Rep. Judy Baker, a health care consultant from Columbia. Republicans did not think Baker's liberal message would play well in the district's conservative-leaning rural counties. Luetkemeyer ran as a social conservative opposed to abortion rights and same-sex marriage. He emphasized his farming background to the district's largely rural constituency. Luetkemeyer also questioned Baker's health care credentials by pointing out that a private health care company she worked for in 2000 and 2001 lost more than $2 million in that time. Baker countered that she had helped to fix the company's problems. Democratic Sen. Claire McCaskill, who was the state auditor during that period, also defended Baker's record.

Baker criticized Luetkemeyer for sponsoring a bill that would have allowed Missouri insurance companies to refuse to cover mammograms, maternity benefits, or childhood immunizations. She neglected to note that he eventually withdrew those controversial provisions. Luetkemeyer raised $2.8 million, two-thirds of it his own money; Baker raised $1.7 million. In the election, Baker managed to carry populous Boone County, but Luetkemeyer prevailed in the rural counties and those west of St. Louis. He won 50%-47.5%. When Baker passed on a 2010 rematch, any Democratic hopes of victory vanished, and Luetkemeyer coasted to re-election with 77%-22% over Libertarian Christopher Dwyer.

In the House, Luetkemeyer joined the Tea Party Caucus and established himself as a devout social and fiscal conservative. He introduced a bill in July 2009 barring the United States from contributing to the United Nation's Intergovernmental Panel on Climate Change, which he said engaged in "dubious science." Later, he told a tea party rally that most of cable provocateur Glenn Beck's controversial assertions "must be true, because nobody's refuting" them. He dismissed the economic stimulus law as a "large-scale failure," but the liberal think tank Center for American Progress noted that he later called a grant from the program in Frankford as "critical" and joined Missouri lawmakers in requesting $100 million in stimulus money for a road project.

Following the Republican takeover of the House in 2010, Luetkemeyer won a seat on the Financial Services Committee. He had scorned the Democrats' Wall Street reform bill as detrimental to small banks, saying in a *Washington Times* op-ed, "People on Main Street understand that community banks did not cause the financial crisis and that they already carry daunting regulatory burdens." He enthusiastically backed the committee's decision in February 2011 to investigate whether the Federal Deposit Insurance Corp. was being overly aggressive in overseeing such banks.

★ MONTANA ★

In April 1805, Meriwether Lewis and William Clark and their pirogues wended up the Missouri River just past the Yellowstone into what now is Montana. It was wild, open country under a big sky—and most of it still is. To celebrate July 4, 1976, the historian Stephen Ambrose took his family to Lemhi Pass, where Lewis was the first American to cross the Continental Divide. Ambrose noted that the terrain was little changed from when Lewis and Clark passed through. In recent years, many have come to Montana, to see for themselves this vast expanse—buying up ranchlands or condominiums.

Yet American civilization has only lightly encroached on Montana. It is still a land of great empty vistas, with mountains in the west and vast plateaus and plains in the east—the 4th largest state in area and the 44th in population. Almost nowhere in the state is the wilderness out of sight; it has the lower 48's largest population of grizzly bears and buffalo. Montana sits atop the continental United States, spanning the Rockies so that on Interstate 15 one can cross the Continental Divide three times. Lewis and Clark found those mountains a fierce barrier, and Montana has not been much of a crossroads. The first Americans here were itinerant trappers seeking fur and miners seeking gold, silver and copper. They built ramshackle towns and in a few cases gained sudden wealth, which made them kings not of their barren homestead but of the metropolises back east. Then came the workers who built and serviced the Northern Pacific and Great Northern railroads, followed by wheat farmers and ranchers.

Statehood arrived in 1889, less than a century after Lewis and Clark. The mining economy gave Montana a radical, class-warfare political tradition. On one side was the Anaconda Mining Company, which until 1959 owned five of Montana's six daily newspapers, the Montana Power Company and many of its politicians. It had strong allies in the Stockmen's Association and the Farm Bureau. On the other side were progressives like Sen. Thomas Walsh, who exposed the Teapot Dome scandal, and Sen. Burton Wheeler, a New Dealer who broke with Franklin D. Roosevelt over court packing and isolationism. Allied with them were the labor unions (Montana has no right-to-work law and has been the most pro-union Rocky Mountain state), and pork barrel beneficiaries (for a while in the 1930s, Montana received more federal money per capita than almost any other state). The focus of all this was Butte, with its gold and copper mines on "The Richest Hill on Earth," with its gamblers, bootleggers, and millionaires, its company goons and union thugs, IWW organizers and its Socialist mayor. Today, Butte is far smaller. The mines are closed, the ore depleted, and the stone temples of commerce are grim; looming mine heads are being restored to a cleanliness they never enjoyed in the boom days, while the waters in old pits are laced with toxic chemicals.

Butte's population peaked in 1920, mines gradually closed all over the state, and agriculture—wheat growing and cattle grazing—became the mainstays of the economy. Class warfare died down. Other towns grew, though only Billings has topped 100,000. Other growth areas recently have been the university town of Missoula, Kalispell near Flathead Lake, the university and resort town of Bozeman, and the state capital of Helena. The muscular tone of a land settled by ranch hands, miners and railroad workers remains a link with Montanans going back to the mountain men, miners and cowboys who drove herds of Texas longhorns across the open range. And there is still the sense of space. Hunting and fishing opportunities abound; development in the small cities and resort areas has not been enough to drive the game away.

Over the past quarter-century, Big Sky country attracted at first a trickle and then a flood of affluent Americans who purchased second homes here—high-visibility movie stars and billionaires like Ted Turner, but also just ordinary people buying small spreads near Big Sky or McLeod, near Bozeman, or around Flathead Lake or Big Timber or the Big Mountain ski resort in Whitefish. Some newcomers, from California and other urban states, are putting down roots here, as computers, modems and fax machines make it possible for small-business people and entrepreneurs to work in Montana, far from their customers and clients but in an environment they love—and not far from the coffee houses and gambling parlors one finds along every highway. These new Montanans have added a spark of energy and inventiveness to a population that had consisted of those left behind when others moved elsewhere. Montana grew 13% in the 1990s and another 10% between 2000 and 2010. The 2010 census put the total population at 989,000, about 10,000 short of the total that would have given it back the second U.S. House seat it lost in the 1990 Census. Growth has been especially vigorous around Bozeman and Big Sky, in Missoula and Ravalli County to the south, and around Kalispell and Flathead Lake to the north, while most of the eastern plains counties have lost population. The state's economy, fueled by construction and strong

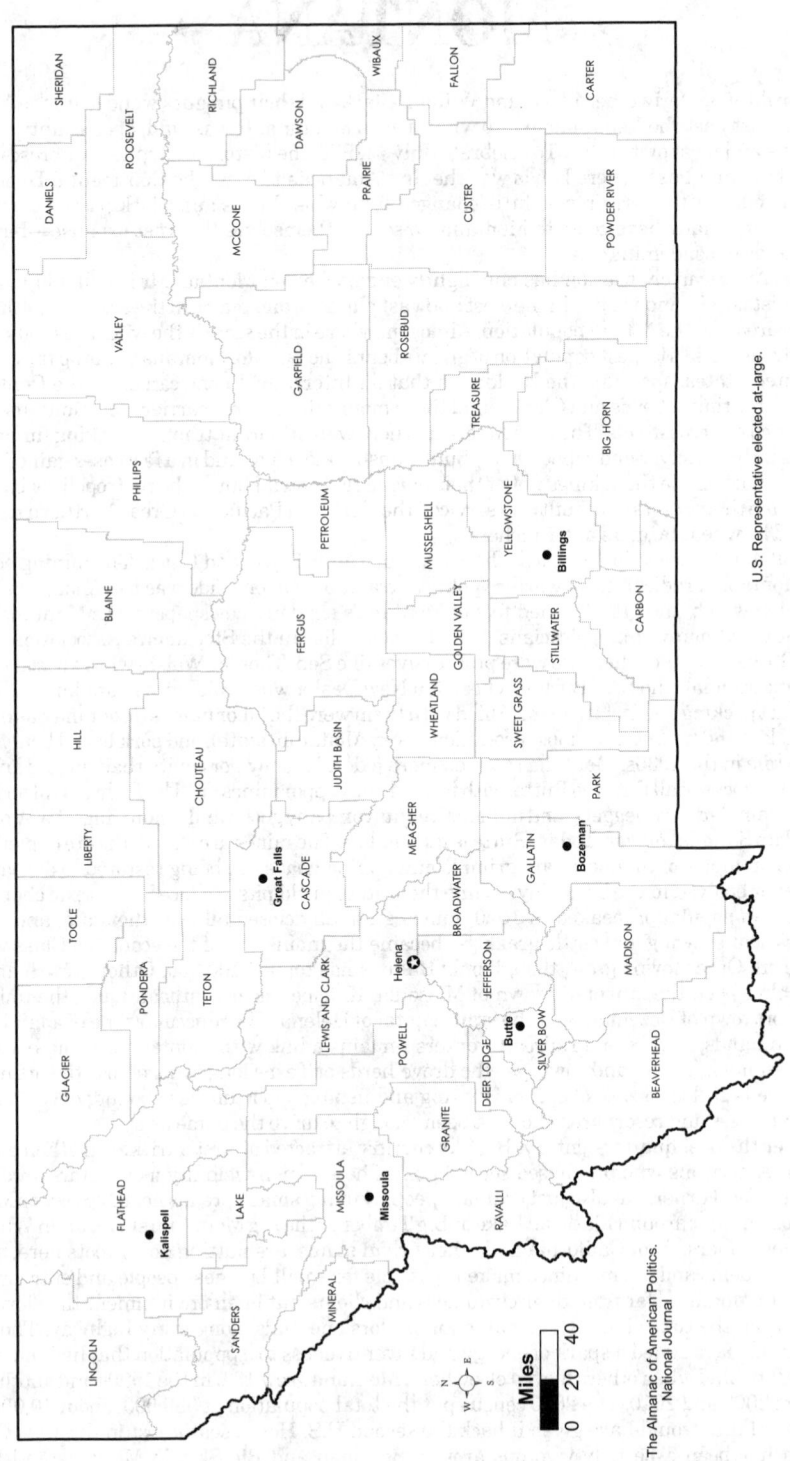

SHERIDAN

RICHLAND

WIBAUX

FALLON

CARTER

ROOSEVELT

DAWSON

DANIELS

MCCONE

PRAIRIE

CUSTER

POWDER RIVER

VALLEY

GARFIELD

ROSEBUD

TREASURE

BIG HORN

PHILLIPS

PETROLEUM

MUSSELSHELL

YELLOWSTONE

● Billings

BLAINE

FERGUS

GOLDEN VALLEY

STILLWATER

CARBON

HILL

WHEATLAND

CHOUTEAU

JUDITH BASIN

SWEET GRASS

LIBERTY

MEAGHER

PARK

GALLATIN

● Bozeman

TOOLE

Great Falls ●

CASCADE

BROADWATER

PONDERA

Helena ✪

JEFFERSON

MADISON

GLACIER

TETON

LEWIS AND CLARK

Butte ●

POWELL

SILVER BOW

DEER LODGE

BEAVERHEAD

GRANITE

FLATHEAD

MISSOULA

RAVALLI

Kalispell ●

LAKE

Missoula ●

LINCOLN

SANDERS

MINERAL

N
W   E
S

Miles

0   20   40

The Almanac of American Politics.
National Journal

U.S. Representative elected at-large.

agricultural commodity and energy prices, grew during the first seven years of the last decade, with unemployment reaching a historic low of 2.8% in 2007. It stayed well below the national average during the recession, helped by the boom in the Bakken shale oil field. Democratic Gov. Brian Schweitzer also successfully pressured Trans-Canada to open its proposed pipeline from Alberta to Oklahoma to Montana oil producers.

Sometimes newcomers are startled by the hardness of Montana life. The DeLorme Montana Road Atlas gives advice on what to do if you should encounter a bear. There are lively political arguments over the grizzly bears and gray wolves reintroduced to Montana in the 1990s. The American Prairie Foundation, funded by Manhattan and Silicon Valley millionaires, is buying up land in the northern plains to create a reserve where buffalo and prairie dogs can roam and to attract tourists and hunters. Buffalo have been released in limited numbers from Yellowstone National Park despite ranchers' fears that they will transmit brucellosis, which causes cows to abort, to their herds.

Montana has had two lively political traditions. One draws on its heritage of class-warfare politics, radical miners and angry labor unions, which made Montana for many years the most Democratic of the Rocky Mountain states. From 1952 to 1984, it elected only Democrats to the U.S. Senate, and since 2006, it has two Democratic senators again. The other, more recent tradition is in line with conservatives' fierce opposition to higher taxes and federal government dictates. Montana has not elected a Democrat to the U.S. House since 1994, and Montana gave George W. Bush big majorities in 2000 and 2004. Barack Obama's campaigning and organization in 2008 held John McCain to a narrow plurality win. The Democratic tradition is strongest in the old mining towns like Butte and Anaconda, on Indian reservations (6% of Montanans are Native Americans), in old railroad towns like Great Falls and Havre, in university towns like Missoula and Bozeman, and in the state capital of Helena. The Republican tradition is strongest in the population-losing eastern plains counties and in fast-growing Flathead and Ravalli Counties in the west.

Republican Denny Rehberg, the state's lone U.S. representative, has won House elections by wide margins, but Democrats won by similarly impressive margins in other races. Rancher Brian Schweitzer, after running a strong race for senator in 2000, was elected governor by 50%-46% in 2004 and was rousingly re-elected, 65%-33%, in 2008. For several years, the legislature was closely divided between the two parties. That changed in 2010 when Republicans won 68-32 control of the state House. In the 2006 Senate race, Democratic state Sen. Jon Tester eked out a 49%-48 victory over incumbent Republican Conrad Burns, who had received more contributions from Indian tribe

Population		Household Income		Work	
Pop. 2010:	989,415	Under $15k:	14.6%	Private:	71.1%
State rank:	44th	$15k to $50k:	42.3%	Government:	18.7%
Change since 2000:	Up 9.7%	$50k to $100k:	30.5%	Self-employed:	9.6%
Urban:	53.6%	$100k to $200k:	10.7%	Unemployment (3-yr. average):	3.8%
Rural:	46.4%	Over $200k:	1.9%	Poverty:	14.9%
Native of state:	54.7%	Median income:	$43,345	Blue collar:	21.2%
Not a citizen:	0.9%			White collar:	57.9%
Area size:	147,040 sq. mi.	**Home Value**		Khaki collar:	0.4%
		Under $100k:	24.8%	Other:	20.6%
Most populous cities		$100k to $300k:	53.6%		
Billings	104,170	$300k to $500k:	14.2%	**Age**	
Missoula	66,788	$500k to $1 mil:	5.3%	Median age:	39.0 yrs.
Great Falls	58,505	Over $1 million:	2.0%	More than 65 yrs:	14.2%
Bozeman	37,280	Median:	$174,900	Less than 18 yrs:	22.8%

Race/Ethnicity				Military Veterans		Registered Voters in 2010	
White:	87.8%	*Language*		% of Pop:	13.3%	No Party registration	
Black:	0.4%	English:	95.4%			Voter turnout:	367,096
Hispanic:	2.9%	Spanish:	1.4%	*Veterans by Period*		Turnout as % of	
Asian:	0.6%	Asian:	0.4%	WWII and before:	9.4%	voting age:	47.9%
Native Am.:	6.1%	Other European:	1.7%	Korea:	11.3%		
Hawaiian:	0.1%			Vietnam:	36.0%	**Legislature**	
Two+ races:	2.2%	**Education**		Gulf (pre-2001):	11.5%	Senate:	22 D 28 R
		H.S. grad:	90.7%	Gulf (post-2001):	8.7%	House:	32 D 68 R
Ancestry		College grad:	27.1%	Peace time:	23.2%		
German	20.9%	Grad degree:	8.4%				
Irish	11.8%						
English	9.5%						

clients of disgraced lobbyist Jack Abramoff than any other member of Congress. This was a key race in giving Democrats a majority in the Senate. In 2008, Democratic Sen. Max Baucus, thought to be in trouble going into the 2002 election season, was re-elected to a sixth term, 73%-27%, the biggest percentage victory in Montana since Mike Mansfield won 76%-24% in 1958. Baucus, as chairman of the Senate Finance Committee, wields more clout on Capitol Hill than any Montanan since Mansfield, the Senate majority leader for 16 years until his retirement in 1976.

Presidential politics   Until very recently Montana, with its three electoral votes, didn't see much of presidential candidates. It holds its presidential primaries in June, at the end of the political primary season, and since 1992 it seemed too heavily Republican to be worth the time it takes to fly here for anyone on a national ticket. But 2008 was different. State Republicans, hoping to be relevant, opted for a Feb. 5 caucus rather than a June primary. But only 1,630 party and local officials participated, giving a win to Mitt Romney, whose campaign was immediately ended by other Super Tuesday results.

Democrats, with more enthusiasm after the successive victories of Brian Schweitzer and Jon Tester, stuck with the June primary, by which time the nomination was still being contested.

2008 Presidential Vote		
John McCain (R) 242,763	(50%)
Barack Obama (D) 231,667	(47%)
Ron Paul (CNP).......................10,638	(2%)

2008 Presidential Primary		
Barack Obama (D) 103,174	(57%)
Hillary Clinton (D).................74,889	(41%)

2004 Presidential Vote		
George W. Bush (R)...............266,063	(59%)
John Kerry (D) 173,710	(39%)

Obama's campaign early on spotted Montana, with its openness to new Democrats and its lack of racially polarized politics, as a state where he could have great appeal. Obama won 57%-41%, balancing Hillary Rodham Clinton's simultaneous win in South Dakota. He scored heavily on the Sioux reservation; in Missoula and Gallatin counties, with their university communities; in Flathead County, with its affluent new migrants; and in Lewis and Clark County, with its state government employees.

After Obama's July 4 visit to Montana, polls showed him competitive with or ahead of McCain, and he put together an impressive and enthusiastic organization. McCain's selection of Sarah Palin as his running mate revived his chances in the state, but after the financial crisis in mid-September, McCain's numbers fell, while the Obama team ran television ads and organized new voters. It was not quite enough, but still impressive. Montana, which had voted 59%-39% for Bush in 2004, voted only 50%-47% for McCain. Obama received 32% more votes than John Kerry had in 2004; McCain got 9 fewer percentage points than Bush had four years earlier—a pattern common to states that were not battlegrounds in 2004 but were targeted by Obama in 2008. Obama had big wins on the Indian reservations in Silver Bow (Butte) and Missoula counties.

Congressional districting   Montana's population has not been growing rapidly enough in the 2000s to make it a contender for a second House seat in the reapportionment following the 2010 census.

Governor

Brian Schweitzer (D)

Elected 2004, term expires Jan. 2013, 2nd term; b. Sept. 4, 1955, Havre; home, Georgetown Lake; CO St. U., B.S. 1978; MT St. U., M.S. 1980; Catholic; married (Nancy); 3 children.

Professional Career: Farm developer, 1980-86; Farmer, rancher, 1986-present; Committee member, Montana Farm Service Agency, 1993-99.

Office: P.O. Box 200801, State Capitol, Helena, 59620, 406-444-3111; Fax: 406-444-5529; Web site: governor.mt.gov.

Election Results

2008 general	Brian Schweitzer (D)	318,670	(65%)
	Roy Brown (R)	158,268	(33%)
	Stan Jones (Lib)	9,796	(2%)
2008 primary	Brian Schweitzer (D)	159,820	(91%)
	William Fischer (D)	9,865	(6%)

Prior Winning Percentages: 2004 (50%)

Brian Schweitzer, a Democrat who was first elected governor of Montana in 2004, has become popular in a strongly Republican state through a combination of political shrewdness and folksy charisma. National Democrats believe he demonstrates how the party can flourish in the rural West.

Schweitzer grew up on his family's ranch in the Judith Basin, east of Great Falls. His Irish grandparents had homesteaded in Hill County, near the Great Northern Railway line. He graduated from Colorado State University with a degree in international agronomy and from Montana State University with a degree in soil science. In the early 1980s, he went off to the Middle East on an agricultural adventure. He developed a 15,000-acre farm in the Sahara in Libya and helped oversee the development of a dairy farm in Saudi Arabia. In 1986, he returned to Montana and bought two farms. He raised cattle and exported bull semen for cattle breeding as well as growing mint and dill. In 1993, when the Clinton administration took office, he was appointed to the three-member, part-time Farm Service Agency that helps distribute federal payments to farmers.

In 1999, with minimal political experience, Schweitzer embarked on a race against two-term U.S. Sen. Conrad Burns, R-Mont. That fall, he organized a bus trip for senior citizens to Canada to buy prescription drugs at low prices, then a popular stunt with politicians making a point about the high cost of drugs. With armed guards, he strode into the Capitol in Helena and poured out $47,000 in cash—the amount, he said, of contributions to Burns from tobacco company political action committees. He attacked Burns for supporting a bill that would limit compensation to people with asbestos-related disease and shut down the giant asbestos tort cases. Burns, who had reneged on a 1988 promise to serve only two terms, outspent Schweitzer by 2-to-1 in the 2000 election but won by only 51% to 47%.

The Senate race made Schweitzer a formidable political figure and an obvious candidate for governor in 2004. The incumbent, Republican Judy Martz, elected in 2000 with only 51% of the vote, had had a rocky tenure. In August 2001, the state House majority leader was killed in a car crash; Martz's chief policy adviser, who was intoxicated, had been driving. She endured months of unfavorable publicity and in August 2003, threatened with a primary challenge, announced she would not run for a second term.

Schweitzer entered the race for governor, and won the primary easily. In the general election, he campaigned against one-party rule—Montana had had Republican governors since 1988—and championed small businesses against out-of-state corporations. Montana had developed into a "salmon economy," he said: "All our young leave the state and then they come home to die." Republicans, he said, were to blame for high property taxes and for the state's low wage levels. He made common cause with both environmental advocates and hunters and fishermen by championing hunting and fishing rights on private lands and opposing the sale of public lands. He called for low-tuition technical colleges to provide training for young Montanans and for creation of pharmacy purchasing pools to buy prescription drugs in Canada. He named Republican state Sen. John Bohlinger as his lieutenant governor candidate and named him head of a Corps of Recovery to come up with $60 million of spending cuts without eliminating services.

The winner of the Republican primary was Bob Brown, who had served 26 years in the legislature and later was a lobbyist for US WEST (now Qwest) and the state university system. Brown, like Schweitzer, declined to take the Americans for Tax Reform pledge not to raise taxes. Brown favored limited oil and gas exploration on the Rocky Mountain Front and the ballot proposition to repeal the state's ban on cyanide mining. Schweitzer took the opposite stand on both issues.

Schweitzer raised more money than Brown, and billed himself as a "pickup-driving, God-fearing, gun-toting, red-meat-eating, take-responsibility-for-my-actions, invest-in-education kind of Democrat." Like Brown, he backed the referendum banning same-sex marriage, which passed with 67% of the vote. Schweitzer won by 50%-46%, even as George W. Bush carried the state by 59%-39%, Democrats also swept to a 27-23 majority in the state Senate and a 50-50 tie in the state House, which under state law, gave the governor's party control. Schweitzer carried the usual Democratic areas around Butte, the Indian reservations, and Missoula but he also won Billings, the state's largest city, and Helena, the capital.

He announced an open-door policy in the governor's office, allowing reporters to come in any time they wanted, and brought his border collie, Jag, there every day. With a projected budget surplus, he and the legislature froze the business equipment tax at 3% and eliminated it for 13,000 businesses that owned $20,000 worth of equipment or less. He signed a bill requiring country-of-origin meat labeling, and helped pass a law requiring public schools to teach American Indian history. He made commencement speeches at high schools with one-student graduating classes.

Schweitzer also unveiled a plan to spend some $31 million on building maintenance, energy programs, and the Indian Education for All program, which passed. In addition, Schweitzer and the legislature put $125 million into the teacher and state employee pension funds, which were figured to be $1.4 billion short because of investment losses and benefit increases. In 2007, again with a surplus, Schweitzer got the legislature to agree to a budget that raised spending 11% a year, with $400 rebates to homeowners.

Schweitzer has emphasized energy issues. In 2005, he persuaded the legislature to pass a bill requiring 10% of motor fuel to be a certain form of ethanol after state ethanol production reaches 55 million gallons a year, and another calling for 15% of electricity to be produced from renewable sources by 2015. Montana—"the Saudi Arabia of coal"—has the nation's largest coal reserves, in deep veins, and Schweitzer has promoted "clean coal" liquefaction, despite opposition from some environmental groups. In 2007, he got the legislature to pass tax breaks for windmill farms, biofuels, and coal liquefaction plants and liquid-fuel pipelines.

Schweitzer has had very high job ratings and shown astute political instincts. As he told *The Washington Post*, "In politics it doesn't matter what the facts are. It matters what the perceptions are. It is the way you frame it." In 2006, he campaigned for Senate candidate Jon Tester, a Democrat who beat incumbent Republican Burns. He also supported two ballot initiatives, an ethics measure that got 76% of the vote and a minimum-wage increase that got 73%. But Democrats, contrary to the national trend, lost seats in both chambers that year: The Senate went from 27-23 Democratic to 25-25, after which a Republican switched parties and made it 26-24. The House went from 50-50 to 49-50, with one Constitution Party member caucusing with Republicans, and a Republican became speaker.

In political circles, there was talk of Schweitzer as a vice presidential nominee in 2008. "I am just a Montana farmer," he said in response. "I don't know if what I say or do is exportable. It is a long way from the Little League to playing for the Yankees." He delivered a spirited speech at the 2008 Democratic National Convention that brought him some national attention, as well as an invitation to headline Iowa Democratic Sen. Tom Harkin's "steak fry," an influential gathering for the party's presidential aspirants.

Schweitzer has his critics at home, and some circulated a YouTube video of a speech in which he bragged about increasing turnout on Indian reservations for Tester in 2006. But he has remained widely popular. In November 2008, he was re-elected by 65%-33% over GOP state Sen. Roy Brown, even as Republican John McCain beat Democrat Barack Obama in Montana, 50%-47%. Republicans gained a 27-23 margin in the state Senate, but they lost ground in the state House, which was tied 50-50.

In his second term, Schweitzer continued to challenge mainstream Democratic orthodoxy. In April 2009, he signed into law a bill that exempted guns made and kept in his state from federal regulation, something he called "another way of demonstrating the sovereignty of the state of Montana." The law provoked a challenge from the U.S. Justice Department, which asserted that federal gun control is "a valid exercise of Congress' commerce power under the Constitution." Other strong gun-rights states followed suit with similar proposals. Schweitzer also showed his willingness to stand up to Republicans. He sent a controversial environmental bill back to lawmakers in April 2009 after weakening GOP provisions that would have made it more difficult for the public to challenge pollution from coal-fired plants.

Schweitzer was credited with keeping Montana in good financial shape during the recession that hammered other states. In May 2010, he touted the more than $400 million it had on hand to pay for general government and fighting wildfires. In keeping with his populist nature, he invited constituents to submit ideas for trimming expenses. The gimmick drew more than 1,000 suggestions. The winning entry called for the state to replace its 15,000 personal computers every five years instead of four, for a savings of about $3 million. "I thought for sure the top idea would be to get rid of the governor and let his dog, who is better-looking and certainly smarter, run the state," he told *The New York Times*.

Senior Senator

Max Baucus (D)

Elected 1978, term expires 2014, 6th term; b. Dec. 11, 1941, Helena; home, Helena; Stanford U., B.A. 1964, LL.B. 1967; Protestant; divorced; 1 child.

Elected Office: MT House of Reps., 1973–74; U.S. House of Reps., 1974–78.

Professional Career: Staff atty., Civil Aeronautics Bd., 1967–69; Legal asst., Securities & Exchange Comm., 1969–71; Practicing atty., 1971–74.

DC Office: 511 HSOB, 20510, 202-224-2651; Fax: 202-224-9412; Web site: baucus.senate.gov.

State Offices: Billings, 406-657-6790; Bozeman, 406-586-6104; Butte, 406-782-8700; Great Falls, 406-761-1574; Helena, 406-449-5480; Kalispell, 406-756-1150; Missoula, 406-329-3123; Glendive, 406-365-7002.

Committees: *Agriculture, Nutrition & Forestry:* Commodities, Markets, Trade & Risk Management; Conservation, Forestry & Natural Resources; Livestock, Dairy, Poultry, Marketing & Ag Research. *Environment & Public Works:* Clean Air & Nuclear Safety; Superfund, Toxics & Environmental Health; Transportation & Infrastructure (Chmn); Water & Wildlife. *Finance* (Chmn): Fiscal Responsibility & Economic Growth; Taxation & IRS Oversight. *Joint Committee on Taxation* (VChmn).

Group Ratings

	ACLU	ACU	ADA	CFG	AFS	FRC	LCV	ITIC	NTU	COC
2010	80	12	85	8	81	0	43	67	9	27
2009	–	20	85	14	91	–	100	–	7	57

National Journal Ratings

	2010 LIB	—	2010 CONS		2009 LIB	—	2009 CONS
Economic	55%	—	44%		57%	—	42%
Social	45%	—	53%		46%	—	52%
Foreign	41%	—	53%		55%	—	0%
Composite	49%	—	52%		61%	—	39%

Key Votes of the 111th Congress

1. Overturn Ledbetter	Y	5. Pass health care bill	Y
2. Pass $787 billion stimulus	Y	6. Regulate financial firms	Y
3. Repeal DC gun laws	Y	7. Pass tax cuts for some	N
4. Confirm Sonia Sotomayor	Y	8. Legalize immigrants' kids	N

9. Ratify New START	Y
10. Confirm Elena Kagan	Y
11. Stop EPA climate regs	N
12. Repeal don't ask, tell	Y

Election Results

2008 general	Max Baucus (D)	348,289	(73%)	($11,602,479)
	Bob Kelleher (R)	129,369	(27%)	
2008 primary	Max Baucus (D)	unopposed		

Prior Winning Percentages: 2002 (63%); 1996 (50%); 1990 (68%); 1984 (57%); 1978 (56%); House: 1976 (66%); 1974 (55%)

Max Baucus, a Democrat first elected in 1978, is the senior senator from Montana. As chairman of the Senate Finance Committee, he is also one of the most influential members of Congress.

Baucus hails from a well-known Montana ranching family. In 1897, his great-grandfather Henry Sieben started the huge Sieben Ranch, including the land in the book and film *A River Runs*

Through It. Baucus grew up on the 125,000-acre (195 square miles) ranch near Helena and graduated from Stanford University and its law school. He then worked four years at the now-abolished Civil Aeronautics Board and at the Securities and Exchange Commission in Washington. Baucus returned to Montana in 1971, and was executive director of the state constitutional convention in 1972. Two years later, at age 32, he won the western House seat (Montana had two U.S. House seats until 1992) by walking 600 miles along highways through the district. He defeated three past or future holders: Democrats Pat Williams and Arnold Olsen in the primary and Republican Richard Shoup in the general election. In 1978, Democratic Sen. Lee Metcalf, first elected in 1960, died in office. Gov. Thomas Judge appointed state Supreme Court Justice Paul Hatfield to succeed Metcalf, but Baucus ran in the Democratic primary and beat Hatfield 65%-19%; he won the general election 56%-44% in a state where no Republican had won a Senate race since 1946. In March 2005, he became the longest-serving senator in Montana history. He has won re-election every six years since; his closest race was in 1996, when he beat back a challenge from Republican Denny Rehberg, now the state's lone representative, 50%-45%.

Baucus got a seat on the Finance Committee early in his Senate career, at age 36. After Democratic Sen. Daniel Patrick Moynihan of New York retired in 2000, Baucus became the ranking minority member on Finance. Then, in June 2001, when Vermont Sen. Jim Jeffords' party switch gave Democrats the majority, Baucus rose to chairman. By the end of his current term in 2014, he will have served as the lead Democrat on Finance longer than anyone except Russell Long of Louisiana, a senator from 1948 to 1987. Finance has jurisdiction over tax, trade, and Social Security, Medicare and Medicaid, making it one of the most important committees in Congress. Under Long and his successors, the committee has tended to operate in bipartisan fashion, on the assumption that it must have a consensus to ultimately get the full Senate to go along, with the proviso that committee members in the process have much to say about specific provisions of tax and trade law that matter to their constituencies. This was clear in the committee's votes creating Medicare in 1965 (12-5), the Reagan tax cuts in 1981 (19-1), Social Security changes in 1983 (18-1), major tax changes in 1986 (18-2) and the balanced budget plan of 1997 (18-2).

Baucus has continued that tradition. It helped that he often found common ground with his Republican counterpart, Charles Grassley of rural Iowa, and that Montana was then trending Republican, as witnessed by Baucus' close race in 1996 and George W. Bush's 58%-33% margin in the state in 2000. In 2001, Baucus and Grassley unveiled a $1.3 trillion tax cut package with specific provisions tailored to moderate Republicans and Democrats on the committee. The bill passed the committee 14-6 and the Senate 62-38 (with 12 Democrats, including Baucus, voting in favor). Key members of the coalition Baucus and Grassley assembled insisted that they would not accept major changes from the Senate bill, so the final version out of the House-Senate conference committee was much like their bill, and the first domestic priority of the Bush administration was passed into law.

Then-Senate Democratic Leader Tom Daschle was reportedly furious that Baucus refused to consult with the Democratic Caucus before the final drafting of the tax bill, and in October, pressure from Daschle may have reined in Baucus when he introduced a $70 billion economic stimulus bill. Although Republicans wanted him to negotiate a compromise with Grassley, Baucus instead called on Bush to step in. Similarly, Baucus was unable to come up with a united Democratic position on welfare that year.

After Republicans won the Senate majority in November 2002, Baucus began working closely again with Grassley on major legislation. The two came up with a corporate tax bill that passed the Senate 92-5 in 2004. Baucus also worked with Grassley in 2003 to draw up a bill creating a prescription drug benefit in the Medicare program, which won a majority in the Finance Committee and in the Senate. Baucus supported provisions, sought mostly by Republicans, for private health insurance to play a larger role in Medicare. However, he got Republicans to make other concessions. In 2005, Grassley and Baucus could not find a way to similarly work out a deal on Bush's proposal for private retirement accounts in Social Security, which Baucus viewed as a threat to achieving Social Security solvency. In 2005, he told the AARP, an advocacy group for older Americans: "I'm the lead guy on this end, the person in charge of preventing privatization, and I love it. I've never had so much fun fighting for something that's right."

Trade issues are important to Baucus and his exporting state. Like other Democrats, he has called for stronger labor and environmental standards in trade agreements, but has generally been more favorable to lowering trade barriers. He was a leading advocate of normal trade relations with China, but in recent years, has been increasingly critical of China for undervaluing its currency. And he has supported an end to the trade embargo on Cuba. After Japan banned U.S. beef in 2003, Baucus negotiated directly with the Japanese to reopen their market, which Japan later did.

As chairman again in 2007, after Democrats regained a narrow majority in the Senate, Baucus continued to work closely with Grassley. "I care about results, and to get results, you have to work together and truly compromise," he said. With solid Democratic backing, they won Senate approval in October 2007 to expand the State Children's Health Insurance Program, and the Senate voted 68-31 vote to override Bush's veto. The two cooperated on the annual fixes to the alternative minimum tax in 2007 and 2008. Also in 2008, Baucus led the committee on the final deal on the farm bill, insisting on additional billions of dollars for disaster assistance, plus tax benefits for biofuels and conservation. Baucus added $500 million in tax credit bonds for the conservation of large tracts of land purchased by the government from Plum Creek Timber, Montana's largest land owner.

Health care legislation was a top priority for Baucus and the committee after the election of Barack Obama as president in 2008. In spring and summer of 2009, Baucus held extended negotiations with Grassley and Republican moderate Olympia Snowe of Maine to come up with a bill that could get bipartisan support. Liberal Democrats chafed, and Grassley charged later that they might have reached agreement except for their resistance. The White House, with 60 Democratic senators after Al Franken of Minnesota was seated in July, insisted Baucus move ahead on a Democratic version. That was the course he took. Baucus' bill did not include the public option allowing for the creation of a government-run health insurance plan. Other features were an excise tax on high-cost health insurance plans and creation of exchanges in each state to run insurance programs in lieu of giving control to the U.S. Health and Human Services Department. It included government subsidies of insurance premiums for low- and middle-earners, and a requirement that employers with 50 or more employees that didn't offer insurance reimburse the government for the subsidies. "My compass is going to be to get a bill that is solid, balanced and fair and doesn't go too far in one direction or another. If it ain't broke, don't fix it," he told *Politico*. In October, the committee passed the bill, 14-9, with the votes of all Democrats plus Snowe. A version of the bill passed the Senate on a party-line vote on Christmas Eve 2009.

Baucus has had a sometimes strained relationship with Senate Majority Leader Harry Reid and the rest of the Democratic leadership. Montana is a major coal producer, and in October 2009, he criticized the Democratic bill creating a cap-and-trade system of reducing carbon emissions, with the aim of a 20% reduction by 2020. He said the bill by liberal Sen. Barbara Boxer of California could achieve no "conceivable consensus on climate change." When Baucus and Grassley announced a jobs bill in February 2010, with an extension of the 2009 Build America Bonds and a one-year extension of the highway bill, Reid immediately killed it, saying it was too favorable to Republican positions. After the 2010 election, Baucus and Grassley with their House counterparts Democrat Sander Levin and Republican Dave Camp, backed an alternative minimum tax fix, which was passed. Baucus had tried unsuccessfully to move a bill extending the Bush-era tax cuts except for high income earners, and he initially came out against the deal negotiated by President Obama with Republicans to reauthorize the 2001 and 2003 tax cuts for all taxpayers. Citing jobs, Baucus ended up voting for it.

Baucus was one of the six senators on Obama's fiscal commission, headed by Erskine Bowles, former Clinton White House chief of staff, and former Republican Sen. Alan Simpson of Wyoming. But he voted against its recommendations, even as the other five senators, including Democrats Richard Durbin of Illinois and Kent Conrad of North Dakota, voted "yes." Baucus said the proposals would paint "a big red target on rural America," by cutting farm programs, military pensions and Social Security and Medicare. In early 2011, Utah Sen. Orrin Hatch replaced Grassley as the ranking Republican on Finance, and it seemed unlikely he would be as inclined toward bipartisanship as Grassley. Hatch is up for re-election in 2012, and he has the recent experience of his former colleague, Utah Sen. Robert Bennett, to keep in mind. Bennett was defeated in the state Republican convention in 2010 for being insufficiently conservative.

Baucus' close call in the 1996 election was not repeated in 2002 or 2008. A Senate Finance Committee chairman can raise enormous sums of campaign cash and many former Baucus staffers are successful lobbyists. In 2002, Baucus attacked his Republican opponent Mike Taylor, owner of a cosmetology school, with an ad slyly suggesting Taylor was gay. It showed 1980s footage of Taylor massaging a man's face while applying facial cream, and asserted that Taylor had failed to refund student loan money when his cosmetology students dropped out. Taylor said the ad played on stereotypes and that his wife had made paperwork errors on their taxes. Baucus spent more than $6 million, while Taylor spent $1 million in personal funds, and won 63%-32%, carrying all but two small counties. In 2008, Baucus' opponent was a former Green Party nominee for governor, and he won easily, 73%-27%, winning all 56 counties even as John McCain was carrying the state.

When he is next up for re-election in 2014, Baucus will be 72. Over the years, he has stayed in excellent physical shape and has made a point of hiking, biking and running in Montana. But he took a bad fall in a 50-mile race in Maryland in 2003 and two months later had surgery to relieve pressure on his brain. In June 2004, he had a pacemaker installed and the following month sustained minor injuries in a motorcycle crash in Montana.

His personal life attracted some unfavorable press coverage in March 2009, when his nominee for U.S. attorney for Montana, Melodee Hanes, withdrew her candidacy for the post and it was later revealed that the two were romantically involved. Both were separated from their spouses. Hanes had been a top Baucus staffer, his state director and senior counsel, and in 2008, he raised her salary by over $13,000. After withdrawing her nomination, she got a position in the Justice Department and the two announced their engagement in early 2011.

Junior Senator

Jon Tester (D)

Elected 2006, term expires 2012, 1st term; b. Aug. 21, 1956, Havre; home, Big Sandy; U. of Great Falls, B.S. 1978; Christian; married (Sharla); 2 children.

Elected Office: Big Sandy Schl. Bd., 1982-92; MT Senate, 1998-2006; MT Senate pres., 2005-06.

Professional Career: Music teacher, Big Sandy Schl. Dist., 1978-80; Custom butcher, T-Bone Farms, 1978-98; Farmer, T-Bone Farms, 1978-present.

DC Office: 724 HSOB, 20510, 202-224-2644; Fax: 202-224-8594; Web site: tester.senate.gov.

State Offices: Billings, 406-252-0550; Bozeman, 406-586-4450; Butte, 406-723-3277; Glendive, 406-365-2391; Great Falls, 406-452-9585; Helena, 406-449-5401; Kalispell, 406-257-3360; Missoula, 406-728-3003.

Committees: *Appropriations:* Energy & Water Development; Homeland Security; Interior, Environment & Related Agencies; Legislative Branch; Military Construction, Veterans Affairs & Related Agencies. *Banking, Housing & Urban Affairs:* Economic Policy (Chmn); Financial Institutions & Consumer Protection; Housing, Transportation & Community Development. *Homeland Security & Governmental Affairs:* Contracting Oversight (Ad Hoc); Disaster Recovery & Intergovernmental Affairs (Ad Hoc); Investigations (Permanent). *Indian Affairs. Veterans' Affairs.*

Group Ratings

	ACLU	ACU	ADA	CFG	AFS	FRC	LCV	ITIC	NTU	COC
2010	80	20	85	9	94	0	57	67	16	36
2009	–	16	90	19	91	–	100	–	10	57

National Journal Ratings

	2010 LIB	—	2010 CONS		2009 LIB	—	2009 CONS
Economic	52%	—	47%		55%	—	44%
Social	45%	—	53%		51%	—	48%
Foreign	41%	—	53%		55%	—	0%
Composite	48%	—	53%		62%	—	39%

Key Votes of the 111th Congress

1. Overturn Ledbetter	Y	5. Pass health care bill	Y	9. Ratify New START	Y
2. Pass $787 billion stimulus	Y	6. Regulate financial firms	Y	10. Confirm Elena Kagan	Y
3. Repeal DC gun laws	Y	7. Pass tax cuts for some	Y	11. Stop EPA climate regs	N
4. Confirm Sonia Sotomayor	Y	8. Legalize immigrants' kids	N	12. Repeal don't ask, tell	Y

Election Results

2006 general	Jon Tester (D)	199,845	(49%)	($5,588,548)
	Conrad Burns (R)	196,283	(48%)	($9,335,274)
2006 primary	Jon Tester (D)	65,757	(61%)	
	John Morrison (D)	38,394	(35%)	

Jon Tester, a Democrat, was elected Montana's junior senator in 2006. He grew up in a farming family, on the same prairie land his grandparents homesteaded almost a century ago near the small town of Big Sandy, home of Big Bud 747, the largest farm tractor in the world. His family ran a custom butcher shop behind their barn; at the age of 9 Tester lost three fingers from his left hand in a meat grinder. The accident, he says, changed him from a saxophone player to a trumpet player. He earned a music degree from the University of Great Falls and later taught music at a local elementary school before devoting himself to farming. He has raised wheat, hay, alfalfa, barley, buckwheat, lentils, millet, and peas and also served on the local Soil Conservation Service Committee. He then switched to organic farming. He told *Esquire*, "I watched neighbor after neighbor sell out, and a fair number of them were bigger than we were. In the eighties, we realized we had to do something to add value to our product, to make it more marketable, to get a better price for it. That's when we made the conversion to organic. It's been a blessing for us. Before we converted, when we sprayed weeds, I just planned on being sick for about a week." He is still at it, spending four days of the August 2010 recess harvesting wheat.

Tester's political career began on the Big Sandy school board, where he served for a decade. In 1998, when his neighbor, a Republican state senator, decided not to run for re-election, Tester ran for the seat and won. In 2002, he was chosen as minority leader and he became Senate president in 2005 after Democrats won a majority. In that role, he helped pass a budget that cut taxes for small businesses and middle-class families while increasing funding for public education. When the 2005 legislative session adjourned, Tester announced he would challenge three-term Republican Sen. Conrad Burns. Tester was one of five Democrats seeking the party nomination; his only real opposition came from two-term state Auditor John Morrison, a former president of the Montana Trial Lawyers Association and the son of a state Supreme Court justice. He outspent Tester nearly 2-to-1. But in a campaign that focused on Burns' ethics, Morrison was weakened by the disclosure that he had an extramarital affair in 1998 with the fiancée of a businessman who was later investigated by the auditor's office. This undercut claims that Morrison was the more electable candidate. Running as an unabashed populist, Tester gained support from Daily Kos and other left-wing Internet activists, and in Montana he assembled a formidable grass roots operation with hundreds of volunteers. He beat Morrison 61%-35%.

Tester was taking on the only Republican senator Montana voters had ever re-elected. But by 2006, the 71-year-old conservative incumbent had two serious problems. The first was his connection to disgraced and later convicted lobbyist Jack Abramoff. He was the largest congressional recipient of campaign donations from Abramoff's clients, and he faced campaign accusations that he "sold his vote" and betrayed Montana's American Indians population by earmarking funds for Abramoff's Indian clients in other states. Tester argued that Burns was not the same down-to-earth Westerner Montanans had sent to Washington 18 years earlier.

Burns' second handicap was a gaffe-prone style, ill-suited for the *YouTube* era. In 2006, while discussing the war on terrorism, he spoke of enemies who "drive taxicabs in the daytime and kill at night." In July, he admonished a group of firefighters for doing a "piss-poor job" of battling a wildfire, and a month later, referred to his handyman as a "nice little Guatemalan man" and joked about the man's immigration status. "I can self-destruct in one sentence," he admitted. "Sometimes in one word." In the past, such blunders might have been overlooked as part of Burns' folksy appeal, but they proved harder to dismiss when memorialized on video. This was a bare-knuckled campaign. Burns spent $8.5 million, $3 million more than Tester, and argued that Tester was too liberal for Montana because of his opposition to the Bush-era PATRIOT anti-terrorism law, his links to "radical environmentalists" and left-wing bloggers. But Tester was not so easily caricatured. His signature $8 flattop haircut, highlighted in a television ad filmed at the Riverview Barbershop in Great Falls, his down-to-earth demeanor (He's fond of saying, "You have two ears and one mouth; act accordingly."), his beefy farmer's build, and his agricultural background worked to temper the criticism. He was helped by popular Democratic Gov. Brian Schweitzer, who taped an ad saying, "Senator Burns and his crooked pals in Washington are lying about my friend Jon Tester."

The race was decided by just 3,562 votes. Burns carried 41 of 56 counties, including Yellowstone County, which includes Billings, the state's largest city. But Tester prevailed in several large counties including Cascade (Great Falls), Lewis and Clark (Helena) and Missoula (home of the University of Montana), carrying the latter nearly 2-1.

In Washington, Democrats hailed Tester's victory as a signal of a new political direction in the Mountain West. His distinctive look—he's tall, barrel-chested, and wears cowboy boots—won him immediate notice in the Senate, as did his practice of prominently posting his daily schedule on the Internet, a Senate first. Arriving in Washington, Tester stressed the importance of transparency and accountability in government, thus distancing himself from the questionable practices that hurt his predecessor. He strongly supported the Senate's 2007 ethics bill and in 2008 he voluntarily asked a retired Montana Supreme Court justice to conduct a comprehensive ethics audit of his office. He also joined a group of senators seeking to ban secret holds on legislation and nominations, a longtime Senate practice, and he co-sponsored a Republican bill to ban former members of Congress from ever lobbying.

Tester voted for Democratic measures seeking to end the Iraq war. He joined Democrats Jim Webb of Virginia and Claire McCaskill of Missouri in an amendment to the defense authorization to establish a bipartisan commission to oversee private contractors in Iraq. President George W. Bush signed the bill into law but attached a signing statement stipulating he felt justified in ignoring the amendment, which did not sit well with Tester. "For the president to say, you know, 'I don't think this is a good idea and I can do that because I'm king,' is a big mistake," he said.

On the Financial Services and General Government Subcommittee, Tester worked on the credit card regulation act signed into law in 2009, banning certain fees and deadlines and providing an extra week for paying bills, and in May 2010, he sponsored a successful amendment requiring large banks to pay higher Federal Deposit Insurance Corporation fees. On other major issues, Tester co-sponsored with Republican Sen. John McCain of Arizona an amendment to repeal the District of Columbia's gun control laws, which effectively stopped legislation to give D.C. a voting representative in Congress. In December 2010, he aroused the ire of left-wing bloggers when he voted against the DREAM Act, which would provide a path for citizenship for the children of illegal immigrants who attend college or serve in the military. Tester said, "Illegal immigration is a critical problem facing our country, but amnesty is not the solution. I do not support legislation that provides a path for citizenship for anyone in this country illegally." The Daily Kos' Markos Moulitsas, a staunch Tester backer in 2006, said he would do whatever he could to defeat him in 2012. Montana has one of the lowest percentages of immigrants, legal or illegal, of any state.

On issues important to Montana, Tester has promoted carbon-capture and sequestration technology as a feasible method of clean-energy production that could lead to the development of the large coal reserves in Montana, "the Saudi Arabia of coal," as he put it. In 2009, he sponsored a bill to designate 660,000 acres of wilderness land, and to allow logging in portions of the Beaverhead-Deerlodge and Kootenai national forests, an unusual combination that he said was suggested by a local coalition of timber companies and environmental groups. But Energy Committee Chairman Jeff Bingaman, D-N.M., opposed the logging provisions as well as others allowing military helicopter landings and motorized vehicles in portions of the proposed wilderness area. Tester drafted a revision, but insisted on the logging allowances, and the bill stalled.

Tester holds one of the 23 Democratic seats up in 2012, and one that Republicans were targeting in early 2011. Republican Denny Rehberg, Montana's sole House member, announced in February 2011 he would run against Tester. Rehberg in 1996 gave Democratic Sen. Max Baucus his closest race ever, losing by just 50%-45%.

REPRESENTATIVE-AT-LARGE

Denny Rehberg (R)

Elected 2000, 6th term; b. Oct. 5, 1955, Billings; home, Billings; WA St. U., B.A. 1977; Episcopalian; married (Jan); 3 children.

Elected Office: MT House of Reps., 1984-90; MT lt. gov., 1991-96

Professional Career: Leg. asst., U.S. Rep. Ron Marlenee, 1979-82; Rancher, 1982-present.

DC Office: 2448 RHOB, 20515, 202-225-3211; Fax: 202-225-5687; Web site: rehberg.house.gov.

State Offices: Billings, 406-256-1019; Great Falls, 406-454-1066; Helena, 406-443-7878; Missoula, 406-543-9550.

Committees: *Appropriations:* Energy & Water Development; Labor, HHS, Education & Related Agencies (Chmn); Legislative Branch.

Group Ratings

	ACLU	ACU	ADA	CFG	AFS	FRC	LCV	ITIC	NTU	COC
2010	13	96	5	84	0	93	10	0	85	75
2009	–	92	15	72	33	–	7	–	77	80

National Journal Ratings

	2010 LIB	—	2010 CONS		2009 LIB	—	2009 CONS
Economic	23%	—	76%		24%	—	75%
Social	16%	—	82%		29%	—	68%
Foreign	12%	—	79%		0%	—	75%
Composite	19%	—	81%		23%	—	78%

Key Votes of the 111th Congress

1. Overturn Ledbetter	N	5. Bar federal abortion funds	Y	9. Stop detainee transfers	Y
2. Pass $820 billion stimulus	N	6. Pass health care bill	N	10. Legalize immigrants' kids	N
3. Let guns in national parks	Y	7. Regulate financial firms	N	11. Repeal don't ask, tell	N
4. Pass cap-and-trade	N	8. Pass tax cuts for some	N	12. Limit campaign funds	N

Election Results

2010 general	Denny Rehberg (R)	217,696	(60%)	($1,384,402)
	Dennis McDonald (D)	121,954	(34%)	($333,295)
	Mike Fellows (Lib)	20,691	(6%)	
2010 primary	Denny Rehberg (R)	96,796	(50%)	
	Mark French (R)	25,344	(13%)	
	Dennis McDonald (D)	24,014	(13%)	
	Tyler Gernant (D)	15,177	(8%)	
	Melinda Gopher (D)	13,170	(7%)	
	Sam Rankin (D)	10,138	(5%)	
	A. J. Otjen (R)	7,461	(4%)	

Prior Winning Percentages: 2008 (64%), 2006 (59%), 2004 (64%), 2002 (65%), 2000 (51%)

Denny Rehberg, a Republican first elected to the House in 2000, is a fifth-generation Montanan and a rancher from Billings who raised cattle and cashmere goats on the same ranch that his great-grandfather homesteaded at the turn of the 20th century. A helicopter pilot, he frequently flies to appointments around the state. Rehberg has been involved in politics most of his life: His father was a state legislator who ran against Democratic Rep. John Melcher in 1970.

After college, Rehberg (*REE-berg*) worked in real estate before moving to Washington so his wife could attend law school. While there, he worked for Republican Rep. Ron Marlenee of Montana. He returned to his home state in 1982 to rebuild and run the family ranch, a third of which—including the house in which Rehberg grew up—had been sold to help pay the inheritance tax levied after his great-grandmother passed away. At 29, Rehberg was elected to the state House. He managed Republican Conrad Burns' first campaign for the U.S. Senate in 1988, and then served as Burns' state director for two years. He was appointed lieutenant governor by Republican Gov. Stan Stephens and was elected to that post on the ticket headed by Marc Racicot in 1992. Four years later, Rehberg ran against Democratic Sen. Max Baucus. Rehberg backed term limits, promised to forgo pay increases, and attacked Baucus for backing the 1993 tax increase and the assault weapons ban. Baucus called Rehberg a "special interest" candidate who would cut taxes for the rich. Rehberg was outspent $4.3 million to $1.4 million, but he made it a serious contest, holding Baucus to 50% of the vote to his 45%.

Rehberg returned to ranching. In 2000, he annexed part of his ranch into the Billings city limits, divided the land into salable lots, and founded Rehberg Ranch Estates. Today, his wife, Jan, manages the company, which contributes significantly to the couple's wealth. In 2009, the watchdog group Center for Responsive Politics listed Rehberg as the 25th richest member of Congress, with an estimated worth of $6.6 million to $56 million.

The opportunity to again run for Congress came in September 1999, when Republican Rep. Rick Hill, re-elected with only 53% of the vote the previous year and facing vigorous opposition from Democratic Superintendent of Public Instruction Nancy Keenan, announced he would not run again because of complications from eye surgery. Rehberg was unopposed for the GOP nomination, and then faced Keenan in the general election, which turned into a classic contest between a conservative Republican and a liberal Democrat.

Rehberg and Keenan agreed on several issues: They both favored gun rights, repeal of the so-called marriage tax penalty, and letting patients sue health maintenance organizations. The race turned on their disagreements—on abortion rights, inheritance taxes, and a prescription drug benefit. Rehberg favored giving the drug benefit to the needy; Keenan favored it for all. The tone got testy as outside groups—the AFL-CIO, the National Education Association and the U.S. Chamber of Commerce all got involved. Rehberg won 51%-46%, almost precisely the same ratio as in the races for governor and senator that year. He was surely helped by George W. Bush's 58%-33% victory over Al Gore in the presidential contest.

As a freshman, Rehberg concentrated on Montana issues. He worked with Sen. Burns in 2002 to put $752 million in drought relief for farmers into the farm bill. He successfully sought repeal of Clinton-era restrictions on snowmobiling in Yellowstone National Park, although it continued to be regulated. In his second term, Rehberg took up the cause of preserving mandatory country-of-origin labeling of meat, a regional issue that pitted Texas cattlemen, who import much of their livestock from Mexico, against their northern counterparts. In 2008, Rehberg backed a provision in that year's farm bill requiring origin labeling, which became law after the House and Senate overrode President Bush's veto by comfortable margins.

Rehberg strongly supported Bush on the Iraq war but went his own way on other issues. He joined Democrats on the House Appropriations Committee in criticizing the level of funding in Bush's budgets for "No Child Left Behind" education mandates. He specifically attacked the amount of money allocated for Impact Aid, a program important to Montana's seven American Indian reservations. During the debate over immigration, Rehberg opposed guest worker and legalization provisions. And he harshly criticized the Endangered Species Act for leading farmers and ranchers to "shoot, shovel, and shut up"—killing endangered animals living on their property rather than reporting the animals' presence and risking their land being confiscated by the government.

During the Obama administration, Rehberg was out front in the Republican opposition to the president's health care overhaul, calling it a "trillion dollar government takeover of health care." After Republicans won majority control of the House in the 2010 election, Rehberg was rewarded with the chairmanship of the health and human services subcommittee on Appropriations, where he vowed to deny funding to implement the new law. On the committee, where he has had a seat since 2005, Rehberg has been an energetic participant in earmarked spending, with some $51 million in spending attributed to him in 2009 by the Center for Responsive Politics. In early 2010, Rehberg said he was swearing off earmarks for one year in a symbolic stance against federal spending.

In 2009, Rehberg was in a serious boating accident. He and two of his aides were in a 22-foot power boat driven by a friend, state Republican Sen. Greg Barkus, when the craft crashed into a rocky shore of Flathead Lake in Montana. Rehberg sustained a broken ankle. His state director, Dustin Frost, suffered a serious brain injury. Barkus' blood alcohol content was above the legal limit, and he was charged in the accident.

Rehberg was re-elected with 65% of the vote in 2002 and 64% in 2004. Then, in 2006, he was opposed by Billings-area state Rep. Monica Lindeen, whose family started Montana's largest Internet service provider. Rehberg was more vulnerable than usual that year after reports that he had accepted $17,000 in contributions from Indian tribes represented by disgraced lobbyist Jack Abramoff. He returned the tribes' money. Lindeen raised $518,000, with notable contributions from Baucus and former Baucus staffers. Rehberg raised $1.2 million. He prevailed 59%-39%.

In 2007, Rehberg declined a repeat run against Baucus for the Senate, although polls suggested that he would be competitive. He won a fifth House term easily in 2008. His Democratic opponent in 2010, Dennis McDonald, tried to make the boating accident an issue in the campaign with an ad suggesting Rehberg had made "bad decisions." Rehberg was a passenger in the boat and not charged in the accident. The ad fell flat, and Rehberg won re-election 60% to 34%.

★ NEBRASKA ★

When the first travelers on the Oregon Trail in the 1840s crossed the Missouri River, they found themselves in "the sea of Nebraska." The Platte River, which is not actually a single river, but a braid of streams that weaves a silver chain around sandbars and islands, flooded the level floor of the great plain, a mile wide, as the saying goes, and six inches deep. The wagons on the Oregon Trail passed through, and Nebraska was largely settled in a single rush in the 1880s, when its population increased from 452,000 to 1 million. It increased to 1.8 million in the next 120 years. In the 1880s, Omaha became a major railroad center, Lincoln the state capital, and farming and food products the main businesses. And for about a century, Nebraska remained pretty much the same. This is not what its founders intended. They hoped that Nebraska would develop a diversified farming, industrial, and commercial economy like that found in Illinois, Missouri and Ohio. But climate is hard to predict. Rains were plentiful in the 1880s, but the 1890s were years of drought, and Nebraska abruptly stopped growing. Many rural counties, and even Omaha, lost population. Nebraska exported people for 100 years: 48% of Nebraskans in 1890 were children; in 2010, only 25% were. For a long time, the creative energies in the American economy seemed to have skipped over the Great Plains and moved west.

The sudden boom of the 1880s and the bust of the 1890s produced the most colorful—and atypical—politics of Nebraska's history: the populist movement and William Jennings Bryan, the "silver-tongued orator of the Platte." Bryan was only 36 when he delivered his Cross of Gold speech at the 1896 Democratic National Convention and was swept to the nomination. He was so radical that Democratic President Grover Cleveland wouldn't support him, but he still won 47% of the popular vote in the first of his three attempts at the presidency. Since Bryan's time, Nebraska's most notable politician has been George Norris, who led the House rebellion against Speaker Joseph Cannon in 1911. In 1934, Norris spurred adoption of the state's unicameral, nonpartisan legislature (in which every bill gets a public hearing where anyone can speak). In Washington, Norris sponsored the Norris-LaGuardia Anti-Injunction Act, the first federal pro-union legislation, and the Tennessee Valley Authority. But most Nebraskans were repelled by the New Deal, which seemed to threaten their way of life. Although it often elects Democratic governors and senators, Nebraska over the past half-century has been the second most Republican state in presidential elections, after Utah.

Since 1990, Nebraska has been growing robustly for the first time in decades. Its population grew 16% between 1990 and 2010, less than the national average of 24% but more than Nebraska has grown since the 1910s. The total population increase during these 20 years was greater than that in the 60 years between 1930 and 1990. The age tilt has changed, too. Nebraska's percentages of old people and children are now within 1% of the national average. The growth has not been even. In 69 of its 93 counties, population declined between 2000 and 2010. In tiny county seats, stores are closing, and across the Plains, farmhouses are shuttered and small school buildings are half-empty. The acreage of irrigated land has been rising, but groundwater irrigation may have peaked during the drought years of 2000-07. Even so, farm incomes have been high, helped by increasing demand for corn because of federal ethanol subsidies, and Nebraska has been exporting more than $2 billion to foreign countries, much of it in food products.

For years, Nebraska's aging population was not producing enough young people to fill its jobs, but for the first time in a century, there has been migration into the state. A hundred years ago, Czechs, Germans, and Danes came to work the factories in Omaha and farms on the Plains—Willa Cather tells the story beautifully in her novels. Now, Hispanics have been coming from Texas and Mexico to work in meatpacking factories, and account for half of the state's population increase. Their share of the population rose from 2% in 1990 to 9% in 2010, and so the population also no longer tilts quite so much to the elderly. Hispanic percentages are highest in the counties around Schuyler (41%), Lexington (32%), South Sioux City (35%), Scottsbluff (21%), and Grand Island (23%). Even so, Nebraska has been hungry for job seekers, and the state's unemployment rate during the recession was the lowest in the nation outside the two Dakotas. Meanwhile, farm counties keep losing population, even though the droughts of 2002 and 2006 have been followed by good weather, and both production and prices have recently been high. Demographically, Nebraska increasingly looks like a Rocky Mountain state, with population concentrated in two cities and several smaller factory towns and relatively few people spread out over farmlands. Every Saturday during the fall, when the 'Huskers (Nebraskans don't say Cornhuskers) play in Lincoln, one out of every 25 Nebraskans is there.

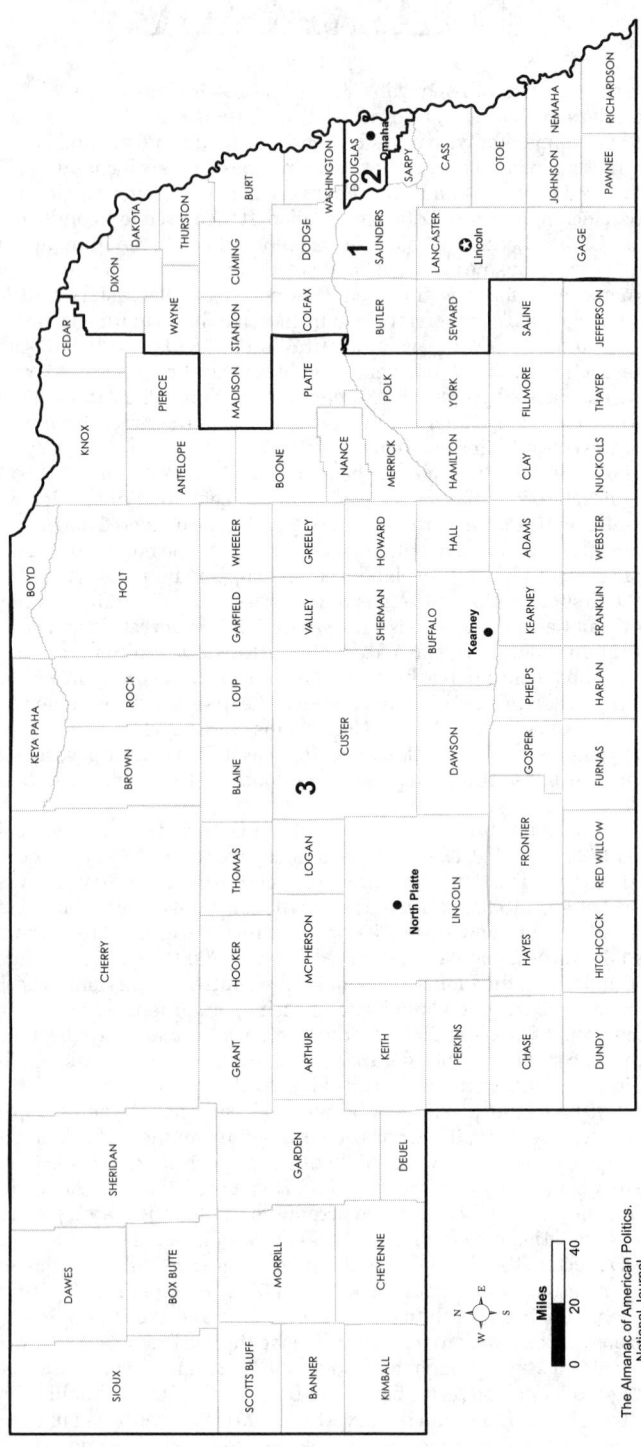

Congressional district boundaries were first effective for 2002.

The Almanac of American Politics.
National Journal

Nebraska may be heavily Republican, but it is also a small enough community that attractive Democrats can win high office. In earlier decades, Democrats winning the governorship then went on to the U.S. Senate—Jim Exon, Bob Kerrey and Ben Nelson. But Nelson, elected senator in 2000 and 2006, had low poll ratings following his support of President Barack Obama's health care plan, even with the infamous "Cornhusker kickback," in which the feds would pay $100 million of Nebraska's Medicaid costs. Nelson first negotiated the provision and then abandoned it. Starting in 1998, Nebraska has elected Republican governors. The first of them, Mike Johanns, did a stint as Agriculture secretary and then won a Senate seat in 2008. His successor, Dave Heineman, compiled a popular enough record that in the 2006 primary, he beat 3rd District Rep. (and former 'Huskers football coach) Tom Osborne by 50%-44% and won the general election 73%-24%.

Republicans hold all five down-ballot statewide offices and have held the state's three House seats since 1994. George W. Bush carried the state 66%-33% in 2004, winning 92 of the state's 93 counties (the exception, Thurston County, is an Indian reservation). John McCain carried the state 57%-42%, but lost four counties, including those that contain Omaha and Lincoln. He also lost the Omaha-based 2nd Congressional District which, under Nebraska law, meant that an electoral vote was cast for Obama, the first time a Nebraska electoral vote was cast for a Democrat since 1964. Omaha Democrats can also count in their ranks one of the country's two richest men, investor Warren Buffett, whose father was a Republican member of Congress in the 1940s and 1950s.

Population		Household Income		Work	
Pop. 2010:	1,826,341	Under $15k:	12.3%	Private:	77.7%
State rank:	38th	$15k to $50k:	39.7%	Government:	14.4%
Change since 2000:	Up 6.7%	$50k to $100k:	33.3%	Self-employed:	7.6%
Urban:	69.3%	$100k to $200k:	12.4%	Unemployment (3-yr. average):	3.5%
Rural:	30.7%	Over $200k:	2.3%	Poverty:	11.7%
Native of state:	65.9%	Median income:	$47,931	Blue collar:	22.5%
Not a citizen:	3.8%			White collar:	59.4%
Area size:	77,348 sq. mi.	**Home Value**		Khaki collar:	0.3%
		Under $100k:	36.6%	Other:	17.8%
Most populous cities		$100k to $300k:	56.3%		
Omaha	408,958	$300k to $500k:	5.2%	**Age**	
Lincoln	258,379	$500k to $1 mil:	1.5%	Median age:	36.0 yrs.
Bellevue	50,137	Over $1 million:	0.3%	More than 65 yrs:	13.4%
Grand Island	48,520	Median:	$122,600	Less than 18 yrs:	25.1%

Race/Ethnicity				Military Veterans		Registered Voters in 2010	
White:	82.1%	*Language*		% of Pop:	11.0%	Democrats:	380,252
Black:	4.4%	English:	90.7%			Republicans:	549,011
Hispanic:	9.2%	Spanish:	6.2%	*Veterans by Period*		Ind./other:	212,794
Asian:	1.7%	Asian:	1.1%	WWII and before:	11.2%	Voter turnout:	497,248
Native Am.:	0.8%	Other European:	1.5%	Korea:	12.9%	Turnout as % of	
Hawaiian:	0.1%			Vietnam:	31.3%	voting age:	36.4%
Two+ races:	1.6%	**Education**		Gulf (pre-2001):	12.6%		
		H.S. grad:	89.8%	Gulf (post-2001):	9.1%	**Legislature**	
Ancestry		College grad:	27.1%	Peace time:	22.9%	49 members; no party labels	
German	30.8%	Grad degree:	8.7%				
Irish	11.2%						
English	7.1%						

Presidential politics   Over the past 50 years, Nebraska has voted more Republican in presidential elections than all but one other state—65% to Utah's 66.5%. It was the last state Democratic President Bill Clinton visited in 1996, and the 2004 exit poll showed that no significant demographic group came close to going Democratic. But 2008 was different. Nebraska Democrats decided to stir up interest by choosing their delegates in a Feb. 9 caucus rather than in the traditional May primary, which hasn't had much significance since Robert Kennedy and Eugene McCarthy contested it in 1968 and Frank Church won a surprise victory in 1976. As in other caucus states, Obama's presidential campaign was enthusiastic and well organized, while Hillary Rodham Clinton's was well-nigh invisible. Obama carried the caucus vote 68%-32%, running up big margins in Lincoln and Omaha and receiving scattered support in the

2008 Presidential Vote		
John McCain (R) 452,979	(57%)
Barack Obama (D) 333,319	(42%)

2008 Presidential Primary		
Barack Obama (D) 46,670	(49%)
Hillary Clinton (D).................43,979	(47%)

2008 Presidential Primary		
John McCain (R) 118,876	(87%)
Ron Paul (R) 17,772	(13%)

2004 Presidential Vote		
George W. Bush (R)..............512,814	(66%)
John Kerry (D) 254,328	(33%)

west (some counties out in the sparsely populated Sand Hills cast one vote). The difference that Obama's organization made in the caucus setting can be gauged by the fact that his margin over Clinton in the admittedly inconsequential May primary was only 49%-47%.

The strength of the Obama organization was evident in the general election as well. Targeting the 2nd District, which includes all of Omaha's Douglas County and most of its Sarpy County suburbs, Obama opened three offices and enlisted some 1,500 volunteers. Showing alarm, the McCain campaign sent in vice presidential nominee Sarah Palin. In the end, Obama carried the district by just 3,370 votes out of 277,809 cast, gaining him one electoral vote. Given his large Electoral College margin, the vote didn't matter. But if, in one scenario that seemed realistic earlier in the campaign, McCain had carried all the states that Bush won in 2004 except Iowa, New Mexico, and Nevada, the 2nd District's single electoral vote would have made the difference between a 270-268 win for Obama and a 269-269 tie.

Congressional districting   Nebraska has had three congressional districts since the 1960 census. Redistricting in 2002 meant only marginal changes in the boundaries. Democrats were angered when traditionally Democratic Saline County was moved from the 1st to the 3rd District. No Democrat has been elected from a Nebraska district since 1992, but Democrats have put up a fight in each of the districts during the past decade. In early 2011, it looked like the legislature might reduce the amount of Sarpy County in the 2nd District and expand the 3rd District to the east. Depending on how the lines are drawn, this could make each of these districts microscopically more Democratic, with consequences more likely to be registered in the Electoral College than in the House of Representatives.

Governor

Dave Heineman (R)

Assumed office Jan. 2005, term expires Jan. 2015, 2nd full term; b. May 12, 1948, Falls City; home, Fremont; U.S. Military Acad., B.S. 1970; Eastern Orthodox; married (Sally Ganem); 1 child.

Military Career: Army Ranger, 1970-75.

Elected Office: Fremont City Cncl., 1990-94; NE treasurer, 1994-2001; Lt. gov., 2003-05.

Professional Career: Ex. dir., NE Republican party, 1979-81; Chief of staff, U.S. Rep. Hal Daub, 1983-88.

Office: P.O. Box 94848, Lincoln, 68509-4848, 402-471-2244; Fax: 402-471-6031; Web site: www.governor.nebraska.gov.

Election Results

2010 general	Dave Heineman (R)	360,645	(74%)
	Mike Meister (D)	127,343	(26%)
2010 primary	Dave Heineman (R)	152,931	(90%)
	Paul Anderson (R)	8,980	(5%)

Prior Winning Percentages: 2006 (73%)

Republican Dave Heineman became governor of Nebraska in January 2005, when Mike Johanns resigned the post to become President Bush's secretary of Agriculture. Heineman, the state's lieutenant governor, moved up to the top job and then ran successfully in 2006 for a full four-year term. He was re-elected easily in 2010, putting him in position to hold office for a record-breaking 10 years. His landslide victory renewed speculation that he would challenge Democratic Sen. Ben Nelson in 2012, but Heineman said in November 2010 that he wouldn't run against his frequent political rival.

Heineman was born in Falls City (pop. 4,375) in the state's southeastern corner, 100 miles equidistant from Omaha and Lincoln. He grew up in a handful of small towns across the state, the son of an itinerant J.C. Penney store manager, before graduating from Wahoo High School. He went east to attend the U.S. Military Academy at West Point and expected to see action in Vietnam, but the war ended first. He served five years in the Army, graduating from Airborne and Ranger schools and rising to the rank of captain. When his tour ended in 1975, Heineman returned to Nebraska and immediately dove into politics as an envelope-stuffing volunteer for the Republican Party in Omaha. He met Hal Daub, the future Omaha mayor and U.S. representative, who became his political mentor. Daub also introduced the 28-year-old to his future wife, Sally Ganem, a Fremont school principal. In 1979, Heineman was named the party's executive director, a job he held for two years; for the rest of the decade, he worked as campaign manager and aide to Daub, as a political consultant, and as the local office manager for then-Rep. Doug Bereuter. Even in those early stages of his career, Heineman harbored an ambition to become governor.

In 1990, he won his first elective office, a seat on the Fremont City Council. He was elected state treasurer in 1994 and re-elected in 1998. Heineman modernized the state's money management system and its methods of returning unclaimed property to residents. In 2002, he ran for lieutenant governor on a ticket with Johanns; they won 69%-28%. As lieutenant governor, Heineman was the state's official lobbyist in Washington, its homeland security director, and chairman of Nebraska's Information Technology Commission; at the commission, he helped to create a telecommunications backbone for state government, state medical facilities, and the University of Nebraska.

When Johanns was appointed to the Bush Cabinet in 2005, Heineman stepped in as governor and then ran for the post the following year as the incumbent, a powerful advantage. On April 11, Heineman signaled his intention to run, and popular GOP Sen. Chuck Hagel endorsed him the same day. From there, Heineman was expected to waltz to election—until Rep. Tom Osborne, one of Nebraska's most popular politicians and a former University of Nebraska football coach, entered the race that spring. After Osborne announced he would give up his seat in Congress to run for governor, national party officials tried to persuade Heineman to change course and challenge Nelson. But Heineman told *The Lincoln Journal Star* in May that his interest in serving in the Senate, on a scale of zero to 100, was "minus-1,000 and dropping."

Heineman moved quickly to cement his hold on the governor's office before the election. That summer, he led a 10-member trade delegation to encourage Cuba to purchase Nebraska-grown products. Despite criticism from several anti-Castro Republican House members from Florida, Heineman met for four hours with Cuban President Fidel Castro and came back with an agreement to sell 5,000 metric tons of dry beans. In August, Heineman signed an agreement with Cuban officials for a total of $30 million in agricultural products from Nebraska.

He also challenged the legislature on a number of controversial issues. Nebraska's unicameral legislature, the Senate (often called the Unicam), has 49 members, who are not grouped by political party as in most other legislatures. In 2006, Heineman vetoed a pay raise for the state's top elected officials, a bill to improve retirement benefits for state workers, and a third measure to allow children of illegal immigrants to qualify for in-state tuition rates at state colleges and universities. The legislature overrode all three vetoes.

The new governor also waded into a highly contentious boundary dispute involving the Omaha public schools. In 2006, the legislature was grappling with a bitter feud touched off by the Omaha school district's attempt to take over 25 schools in suburban Millard and Ralston. The Millard and Ralston school superintendents resisted and were joined in opposition by two other suburban districts. In an attempt to resolve the matter, the legislature passed a bill dividing the Omaha area into three identifiable districts—one largely Latino, one largely black, and one largely white. Heineman signed the bill and then defended it against a barrage of outside criticism that it was state-sanctioned re-segregation. "This bill is far from perfect, and I'll be honest, there are parts that make me less than comfortable and parts that would make me pause as a parent," he said. "It is clear to me that the motivation behind [this] proposal is neither segregation nor separation, but instead the goal of improving student achievement and the responsiveness of schools."

Meanwhile, the May primary showdown was looming. Heineman trailed badly in some 2005 polls, but by April 2006 he had drawn even with Osborne. Omaha businessman David Nabity, who played up his private-sector experience, was a distant third. Heineman's hard-charging approach contrasted with the more sedate campaign style of the 69-year-old Osborne, who had never been seriously challenged in his brief political career. Heineman got key endorsements from the state Farm Bureau, Nebraska Right to Life, and the National Rifle Association. The state employees' and teachers' unions also backed him. Heineman gained traction by criticizing Osborne's support for the in-state college tuition law for illegal immigrants' children; Osborne said he didn't believe that children should be penalized for their parents' actions. For his part, Osborne accused Heineman of embarrassing Nebraska nationally by signing the school boundary bill.

Without a top-tier Democratic candidate in the race, the Republican primary drew heightened interest. As many as 10,000 Nebraskans switched parties so they could vote in the primary. Famed investor and Omaha resident Warren Buffett, a Democrat, said he would change his party affiliation to vote for Osborne. And Osborne said that if he won the governorship, Buffett would oversee a top-to-bottom review of state government operations. But Heineman won 50%-44%, with Nabity finishing third with 5%. Osborne carried the state's two most populous counties, Omaha's Douglas County (47%-44%) and Lincoln's Lancaster County (53%-43%), but not by enough to erase Heineman's margins elsewhere. Heineman's early position in the Omaha schools dispute, in which he sided with suburban schools targeted for takeover by the city, boosted him with suburban voters. He carried the central and eastern parts of the state and also won 54 of the 69 counties in Osborne's western Nebraska-based congressional district.

The general election against Democrat David Hahn, an attorney and Internet entrepreneur from Lincoln, was largely an afterthought. Hahn scoffed at talk of tax cuts and supported abortion rights. He trailed badly in the polls and Heineman won 73%-24%, the largest margin in a Nebraska governor's race since Dwight Griswold won re-election in 1944 with 76% of the vote.

With that boost of voter confidence, Heineman tackled some new initiatives and took pains to close the book on the sensitive schools issue. He signed a bill passed by the legislature that scrapped the old plan and replaced it with one that left school boundaries intact but compelled more-affluent districts to share tax revenues with poorer districts. Heineman also sent to the legislature a get-tough immigration bill to repeal the law making children of illegal immigrants eligible for in-state tuition rates. The measure, which also called for checking the immigration status of anyone applying for government benefits or licenses, stayed bottled up in committee. In mid-2008, with an unexpected rise in state tax revenues of $100 million, Heineman vowed to make tax relief a major push, but the subsequent souring of the national economy late in the year put a crimp in those plans.

With the recession in mind, Heineman in January 2009 called for a bare-bones state budget with only a 1.8% average increase in spending over the next two years, far below the average 7% budget growth in the previous two decades. By November, though, the state's problems had deepened. Heineman called a special session to deal with a $334 million budget shortfall. The governor said he would accept only spending cuts and no tax increases, and after several days and relatively little dissension, the legislature sent him a plan calling for across-the-board cuts to most agency budgets of 2.5% that fiscal year and 5% the following year. As problems continued in 2010, he instituted a wage freeze on most non-union workers and ordered union employees to take two days of unpaid furlough. Even so, Nebraska remained in a far better fiscal environment than most other states.

The budget debate largely overshadowed the rest of Heineman's agenda, which included improving education to close the vast achievement gap between white and black students. But he did draw substantial attention in April 2010 for signing landmark abortion legislation. The law banned the procedure after 20 weeks of pregnancy and required women seeking an abortion to undergo mental health screening. Meanwhile, the health care overhaul bill moving through Congress prompted a public spat between the governor and Nelson. To win Nelson's crucial support for the bill, senators agreed to grant Nebraska full federal funding of expanded Medicaid coverage in lieu of federal-state cost sharing—a controversial arrangement that was dubbed the "Cornhusker Kickback." Heineman refused to support Nelson on the deal, saying that all states should be treated equally, and the provision was dropped.

Heineman was known for his low national profile, but the Cornhusker Kickback flap made him a more frequent guest on television news shows. He remained a highly popular governor at home, thanks in part to his energetic, hands-on style. He often flew to small towns for ribbon-cutting ceremonies and surprised constituents who wrote and emailed his office by calling them at home. A March 2010 Rasmussen IVR poll gave him an astronomical 69% approval rating.

In the election that year, his presumed Democratic opponent was Mark Lakers, an agribusiness investment executive making his first bid for elective office. But Lakers got snarled in a fundraising scandal in May 2010 and dropped out of the race. Democrats turned to attorney Mike Meister. He aggressively criticized Heineman's decision to furlough state workers and accused him of neglecting the poor and elderly. But he had little chance in this solidly Republican state, and Heineman won in a 74%-26% blowout, carrying all 93 counties.

Heineman vowed in 2011 to work on decreasing spending and restructuring the state's Medicaid system.

Senior Senator

Ben Nelson (D)

Elected 2000, term expires 2012, 2nd term; b. May 17, 1941, McCook; home, Omaha; U. of NE, B.A. 1963, M.A. 1965, LL.B. 1970; Methodist; married (Diane); 4 children.

Elected Office: NE Gov., 1991-98.

Professional Career: Gen. cnsl., Central Natl. Group Insurance, 1972–74, Pres. & CEO, 1977–81; NE insurance dir., 1975–76; Exec. V.P., Natl. Assn. of Insurance Commissioners, 1982–85; Practicing atty., 1985–90.

DC Office: 720 HSOB, 20510, 202-224-6551; Fax: 202-228-0012; Web site: bennelson.senate.gov.

State Offices: Kearney, 308-293-5818; Lincoln, 402-441-4600; Omaha, 402-391-3411; Scottsbluff, 308-631-7614; South Sioux City, 402-209-3595.

Committees: *Agriculture, Nutrition & Forestry:* Commodities, Markets, Trade & Risk Management (Chmn); Jobs, Rural Economic Growth & Energy Innovation; Livestock, Dairy, Poultry, Marketing & Ag Research. *Appropriations:* Agriculture, Rural Development, Food and Drug Administration & Related Agencies; Commerce, Justice, Science & Related Agencies; Financial Services & General Government; Interior, Environment & Related Agencies; Legislative Branch (Chmn); Military Construction, Veterans Affairs & Related Agencies. *Armed Services:* Airland; Readiness & Management Support; Strategic Forces (Chmn). *Rules & Administration.*

Group Ratings

	ACLU	ACU	ADA	CFG	AFS	FRC	LCV	ITIC	NTU	COC
2010	53	48	50	50	67	33	0	67	52	73
2009	–	44	70	30	82	–	55	–	27	71

National Journal Ratings

	2010 LIB	—	2010 CONS	2009 LIB	—	2009 CONS
Economic	41%	—	58%	41%	—	58%
Social	41%	—	58%	38%	—	61%
Foreign	41%	—	53%	41%	—	56%
Composite	42%	—	58%	41%	—	59%

Key Votes of the 111th Congress

1. Overturn Ledbetter	Y	5. Pass health care bill	Y	9. Ratify New START	Y
2. Pass $787 billion stimulus	Y	6. Regulate financial firms	Y	10. Confirm Elena Kagan	N
3. Repeal DC gun laws	Y	7. Pass tax cuts for some	N	11. Stop EPA climate regs	Y
4. Confirm Sonia Sotomayor	Y	8. Legalize immigrants' kids	N	12. Repeal don't ask, tell	Y

Election Results

2006 general	Ben Nelson (D)..378,388	(64%)	($7,624,168)
	Pete Rickets (R)...213,928	(36%)	($13,424,896)
2006 primary	Ben Nelson (D)... unopposed		

Prior Winning Percentages: 2000 (51%); Governor: 1994 (73%); 1990 (50%)

Ben Nelson, a former two-term governor of Nebraska, was elected to the Senate in 2000. Though he has resisted entreaties to switch parties, he is the Senate's most conservative Democrat and someone his party cannot take for granted on nearly every major vote.

Nelson grew up in McCook, a small town that is also the birthplace of Willa Cather, whose novels powerfully depict frontier life on the Great Plains. Nelson graduated from the University of Nebraska, practiced law, served as state insurance director, and headed a major insurance company. He is a man of varied avocations. He has collected several hundred clocks, for instance, and is an avid hunter of turkeys and bears. In 1990, Nelson ran for governor, taking on Bill Hoppner, former staff aide to Democratic Sen. Bob Kerrey, in the primary; he won by all of 42 votes. In the general election, he narrowly beat Gov. Kay Orr, 50%-49%. Orr had lost popularity after raising taxes.

As governor, Nelson built prisons, trimmed workers' compensation payments, and reorganized the human services department. He cut property taxes and reduced income and sales taxes. His record won him high job ratings and re-election by 73%-26% in the strongly Republican year of 1994. When Nelson ran for the Senate in 1996, he led in polls most of the way, but then fell behind in October and lost to Republican Chuck Hagel, 56%-42%.

Early in 2000, Nebraska's other Senate seat came open when Sen. Bob Kerrey, one of the Democratic Party's national stars, made the surprise announcement he would not seek re-election. Nelson, then practicing law in Omaha, was the strongest possible Democratic nominee, and he entered the race in February. Attorney General Don Stenberg won the Republican primary, with 50% of the vote against five opponents. Nelson and Stenberg both opposed abortion rights and backed tax cuts. But they had significant differences in style and a long history of clashes. Stenberg ran as part of the "Bush-Hagel-Stenberg Team." Nelson led from the start in the polls, and he raised and spent more money. The popular Kerrey also actively campaigned for his fellow Democrat. Nelson's lead in the polls narrowed in October, but this time he won, 51%-49%.

Second only to Zell Miller of Georgia, Nelson turned out to be the Senate Democrat most likely to support President George W. Bush. He helped to broker the administration's tax cuts of 2001 and 2003. In 2002, Nelson was one of the senators who put together a compromise to permit Bush to cancel collective bargaining rights for homeland security workers, although the measure also allowed future presidents to overturn the decision. Nelson generally supported Bush on the Iraq war, joining Republicans in March 2007 to oppose a plan to start troop withdrawals a year later. With moderate GOP Sen. Susan Collins of Maine, he also authored benchmarks for Iraqi progress. Nelson joined Republicans again to turn back a proposal to restrict funds for Vice President Dick Cheney's office, and shunned his party on global warming by criticizing legislation for setting what he called unrealistic deadlines for new technologies.

His Democratic colleagues tolerated these apostasies. As one said, "He needs to do what he needs to do to keep his seat" in one of the most Republican states in the nation. Nelson has stuck with his party in a few tough fights. He voted against the GOP's Federal Marriage Amendment, for example, arguing that same-sex marriage was a state issue. He also was an early and enthusiastic supporter of Illinois Sen. Barack Obama for president after being impressed by the record audience that Obama drew at a 2006 Nebraska campaign event for Nelson. He often is found in the middle of battles between the extremes of both parties. In 2010, he supported the Democrats' overhaul of financial regulation and repeal of the "don't ask, don't tell" policy prohibiting openly gay service members.

Nelson backed President Obama's $787 billion economic stimulus and the health care reform law, though both issues landed him in controversy. He irked some members of his party when he refused to grant states aid for education as part of the stimulus. Though some education money was included in the final bill, he and Collins were able to trim about $110 billion overall from the measure, disappointing Democrats who had sought more spending. On health care, he was rejected in his bid to add strong anti-abortion language to the original Senate proposal, and indicated he would consider filibustering the bill. After a negotiating session lasting more than 13 hours in December 2009, he agreed to provide the crucial 60th vote. He won new abortion provisions enabling states to opt out of allowing plans to cover the procedure in the insurance exchanges the bill would set up.

More crucially, however, Nelson got an exemption from Nebraska paying its share of Medicaid's expansion in the state, an estimated $100 million cost over the next decade. That provision sparked an uproar, with even Nebraska GOP Gov. Dave Heineman condemning the deal. Calling it the "Cornhusker kickback," angry Republicans held it up as an example of the worst of Democratic backroom negotiating; it was seen as a partial factor in Democrat Martha Coakley's surprise loss in a January 2010 special election for the seat held by the late liberal Sen. Edward Kennedy of Massachusetts. After protesting that he never wanted Nebraska treated differently from other states, Nelson told Senate leaders that month to remove the provision.

Nelson displayed his independent-mindedness on other issues. In July 2010, he held up legislation to restore unemployment benefits for people out of work more than six months, joining Republicans who insisted that at least a portion of the spending be paid for by budget cuts elsewhere. He vowed to oppose a climate change bill containing a cap-and-trade program to limit carbon emissions, helping to scuttle the measure in the Senate. Though he backed Sonia Sotomayor's nomination to the Supreme Court in 2009, he opposed Elena Kagan's 2010 appointment, citing her lack of a judicial record.

During his first Senate term, Republicans tried to persuade Nelson to switch parties. According to the *Omaha World-Herald,* White House strategist Karl Rove in 2004 offered Nelson the job of Agriculture secretary; Nelson considered it for five days before declining. If he had accepted, then-Republican Gov. Johanns would have appointed his successor, allowing the GOP to pick up a Senate seat. Since then, Nelson has tamped down periodic speculation about his becoming a Republican. After the Democrats' drubbing in the 2010 midterm elections, he told Nebraska's KFAB radio: "I'm not looking to leave the party, and that's why the party hasn't left me."

Nelson has focused much of his legislative work on home-state concerns. When the Great Plains were hit by a drought in 2002, he argued that affected areas should get disaster relief, just as states hit by hurricanes and floods do. He has been fighting for such parity ever since. The compensation, he maintains, would be for crops or livestock lost, rather than property destroyed. During debate of the 2008 farm bill, Nelson criticized a reduction in drought assistance and was vocally unhappy that fellow Nebraskan Mike Johanns quit as Agriculture secretary before passage of the bill. (Johanns returned home to run for Hagel's Senate seat.) With Nebraska's farmers in mind, Nelson in 2007 joined a bipartisan farm state group that secured an increase in ethanol production to 15 billion gallons by 2015.

With a seat on the Appropriations Committee, Nelson is able to direct federal dollars to Nebraska. His Senate website boasts of his earmarks for the state in defiance of critics who say that the often narrowly targeted special provisions in spending bills are wasteful. When Obama pledged in January 2011 to veto all legislative earmarks, he said it would hurt his state. "Rural states get hit hardest by the earmark ban. Period," he told Nebraska reporters.

In 2006, Republicans put up Pete Ricketts, an executive with TD Ameritrade and a self-financing multimillionaire, against Nelson. Running on a platform of tax cuts and smaller government, Ricketts sought to appeal to traditional red state values. He supported a guest worker program for immigrants, allowing Nelson to position himself to the right of the Republican by making demands to seal the border. Ricketts supported private savings accounts as a first step in "modernizing" Social Security; Nelson opposed such accounts. Ricketts opposed spending earmarks in the federal budget, but Nelson backed them as vital to Nebraska. Ricketts spent more than $13 million, most of it from his own deep pockets. The combined $20 million-plus spending by the two candidates was roughly three times the previous record for a statewide contest in Nebraska. But the result wasn't close. Nelson won 64%-36%, dominating in Omaha's Douglas County, 65%-35%, and in Lincoln's Lancaster County, 70%-30%. Ricketts won just 13 of 93 counties, all of them sparsely populated and west of the city of North Platte.

Nelson's path to re-election in 2012 in a state that has grown more Republican may be considerably bumpier. His seat was widely viewed as a top target for a Republican takeover.

Junior Senator

Mike Johanns (R)

Elected 2008, term expires 2014, 1st term; b. June 18, 1950, Osage, IA; home, Omaha; St. Mary's Col. (MN), B.A. 1971; Creighton U., J.D. 1974.; Catholic; married (Stephanie); 2 children.

Elected Office: Lancaster Cnty. Bd. of Commissioners, 1983-87; Lincoln City Cncl., 1989-1991; Lincoln mayor, 1991-98; NE gov., 1998-05.

Professional Career: Atty., Cronin and Hannon, 1975-76; Atty., Nelson, Johanns, Morris, Holdeman and Titus, 1976-1991; Clerk, Hon. Hale McCown, NE Supreme Court; U.S. secy. of agriculture, 2005-07.

DC Office: 404 RSOB, 20510, 202-224-4224; Fax: 202-228-0436; Web site: johanns.senate.gov.

State Offices: Kearney, 308-236-7602; Lincoln, 402-476-1400; Omaha, 402-758-8981; Scottsbluff, 308-632-6032.

Committees: *Agriculture, Nutrition & Forestry:* Commodities, Markets, Trade & Risk Management; Livestock, Dairy, Poultry, Marketing & Ag Research (RMM); Nutrition, Specialty Crops, Food & Ag Research. *Banking, Housing & Urban Affairs:* Economic Policy; Financial Institutions & Consumer Protection; Security & International Trade & Finance (RMM). *Environment & Public Works:* Clean Air & Nuclear Safety; Oversight (RMM); Superfund, Toxics & Environmental Health; Transportation & Infrastructure. *Indian Affairs. Veterans' Affairs.*

Group Ratings

	ACLU	ACU	ADA	CFG	AFS	FRC	LCV	ITIC	NTU	COC
2010	7	80	10	87	6	87	0	67	95	100
2009	–	95	15	94	11	–	9	–	87	83

National Journal Ratings

	2010 LIB	—	2010 CONS		2009 LIB	—	2009 CONS
Economic	27%	—	71%		20%	—	79%
Social	29%	—	70%		22%	—	77%
Foreign	28%	—	71%		20%	—	79%
Composite	29%	—	71%		21%	—	79%

Key Votes of the 111th Congress

1. Overturn Ledbetter	N	5. Pass health care bill	N	9. Ratify New START	Y
2. Pass $787 billion stimulus	N	6. Regulate financial firms	N	10. Confirm Elena Kagan	N
3. Repeal DC gun laws	Y	7. Pass tax cuts for some	N	11. Stop EPA climate regs	Y
4. Confirm Sonia Sotomayor	N	8. Legalize immigrants' kids	N	12. Repeal don't ask, tell	N

Election Results

2008 general	Mike Johanns (R)	455,854	(58%)	($3,907,749)
	Scott Kleeb (D)	317,456	(40%)	($1,852,094)
2008 primary	Mike Johanns (R)	112,191	(78%)	
	Pat Flynn (R)	31,560	(22%)	

Prior Winning Percentages: Governor: 2002 (69%); 1998 (54%)

The junior senator from Nebraska is Republican Mike Johanns, a former governor and U.S. secretary of Agriculture in the Bush administration. He was born in Iowa and is of Luxembourgian descent. Johanns grew up on a dairy farm in Osage, Iowa, and started doing chores at age 4. He attended college in Minnesota, earned a law degree at Creighton University in Omaha, and, after clerking for a judge there for a year, settled into a career in Nebraska rather than returning to his native state. He practiced law in O'Neill and got involved in local politics in 1982, when he was elected to the Lancaster County Board of Commissioners. He also served on the Lincoln City Council and was elected mayor of Lincoln in 1991. Johanns was a Democrat until 1988.

Though re-elected mayor of Lincoln in 1995, Johanns began laying the groundwork for a gubernatorial run in 1998 by traveling to each of the state's 93 counties. He faced vigorous competition in the Republican primary. State Auditor John Breslow had a large campaign treasury, and 2nd District House Rep. Jon Christensen had strong support from religious conservatives. A week before the May primary, Christensen distributed fliers accusing Johanns of allowing obscene and racist broadcasts to air on Lincoln's public access cable channel. Johanns maintained that he had, in fact, tried to stop the broadcasts, and the state's nationally respected senator, Republican Chuck Hagel, called the flier "absolute trash." This was a high-spending contest. Breslow spent $3.8 million, Christensen $1.8 million, and Johanns $1.7 million. Johanns prevailed with 40% of the vote to 30% for Breslow and 28% for Christensen. In the general election, Johanns faced Democrat Bill Hoppner, longtime aide to former Sens. James Exon and Bob Kerrey. The campaign was conducted civilly but with major differences on issues. Johanns' solid conservatism was more in step with the Republican leanings of the state and he won, 54% to 46%.

As governor, Johanns' low-key nature belied his strong policy convictions. During his first term, he vetoed 26 bills in five days, the state's strongest use of the veto pen in a decade. He vetoed a moratorium on the death penalty and a bill raising elected officials' salaries and his own salary from the nation's lowest, $65,000 annually. He got passed a $10 million bill for tax credits and entrepreneurship grants to firms that opened businesses in rural areas. In 2001, Nebraska's revenues started coming in below estimates, but Johanns pushed ahead with plans to cut spending by $171 million. "I'm not here to sign tax increases," he said. "Government tends to operate better when it's under pressure." In 2002, state revenues decreased further, but Johanns vetoed temporary increases in the sales, income, and cigarette taxes, though the legislature overrode his vetoes. Johanns was easily re-elected in 2002 without a serious challenge. During his second term, he joined President George W. Bush's Cabinet as Agriculture secretary.

In that role, Johanns more than doubled the number of acres in conservation programs nationwide and focused on opening foreign markets to domestic farm products. By far his biggest undertaking was representing the administration on Capitol Hill as Congress wrote the 2008 bill governing farm and agricultural programs. The administration wanted to reduce farm spending by $88 billion over five years and eliminate government payments to farmers who made more than $200,000 a year, a proposal aimed at complying with international demands to reduce farm subsidies in the United States. Although Johanns and the president were in agreement on the bill, both chambers of Congress opposed it. Top Democrats on the Agriculture committees widely criticized Johanns for leaving the post to run for the Senate in the middle of the negotiations to pass a farm bill, which was set to expire at the end of 2007.

His election to the Senate in 2008 was two years later than some Republicans envisioned. The GOP had heavily courted Johanns to challenge Sen. Ben Nelson, a Democrat who was up for re-election in 2006. Several months later, Johanns apparently saw the opportunity he was waiting for. Hagel announced his retirement in September 2007, leaving an open Senate seat, an easier mark than one inconveniently occupied by an incumbent. Johanns quit his administration job and returned home to campaign.

When jockeying for the Senate began, other prominent Republicans, including Nebraska Attorney General Jon Bruning and Omaha Mayor Hal Daub, were contenders, with Bruning able to raise an impressive $780,000 a year out from the election. But the two men stepped aside as it became increasingly clear that Johanns would win. For the general election, national Democrats aggressively tried to recruit Kerrey, but he opted to remain in his job as president of the New School in New York City. The Democrats turned to rancher and college instructor Scott Kleeb, who in 2006 came within 10 percentage points of winning the open House seat in Nebraska's heavily Republican 3rd District.

Johanns and Kleeb differed on a variety of issues. Johanns advocated increased offshore drilling and exploration in the Arctic National Wildlife Refuge, while Kleeb said he favored more "green" solutions to energy shortages, such as the development of wind energy, ethanol, and biofuels. They also clashed on the seriousness of global warming. Kleeb called the issue a "moral test" for policy leaders, and Johanns took the more typically conservative position that potential fixes should take the costs to industry into account and that reducing carbon emissions to the levels touted by his opponent was unrealistic.

Nelson criticized Johanns for leaving the administration before work on the farm bill was complete. And Kleeb tried mightily to tie Johanns to Bush, by then unpopular in public opinion polls. Johanns responded by saying that he hadn't been in Washington long enough to be defined by the administration he served. "I was in D.C. less time than Barack Obama has been," Johanns was fond of saying on the campaign trail, contrasting himself to the first-term U.S. senator from Illinois then running for the Democratic presidential nomination. It turns out that Johanns' affiliation with Bush hardly resonated in this red state. He won the election with 58%, a percentage point higher than John McCain earned in the state. Kleeb got 40% of the vote. The Democrat prevailed in just seven of 93 counties, including Lancaster County, which is home to Lincoln, the state capital. However, Johanns beat him in most rural counties and in Omaha in Douglas County. Johanns has never lost an election, including six general elections and six primaries.

Putting his Washington experience to use, Johanns quickly became one of the most admired freshmen among his Republican colleagues. He won passage of an amendment on the fiscal 2010 budget resolution preventing the use of the filibuster-proof reconciliation process to advance climate change legislation, something he said would endanger his state's coal-powered agricultural economy. Johanns led the charge in pushing for repeal of the "1099" tax provision in the health care overhaul that imposed what small businesses complained was an unreasonable information burden upon them.

On that measure, as well as on other legislation, he showed that he could work with Democrats. He joined with Alaska Democrat Mark Begich to form a Senate Caucus on General Aviation, an important issue for rural states, that quickly grew to more than two dozen members. He also joined a majority of Democrats in December 2010 in ratifying the New START arms treaty with Russia. He employed a quiet but authoritative manner, often showing a willingness to listen to others. "He doesn't just jump up and pound his views all the time," Minority Leader Mitch McConnell said. But like other ex-governors, he found himself missing the decisiveness of being a chief executive. "You could wake up in the morning as governor and you could get things done," Johanns said.

After Minority Whip Jon Kyl of Arizona announced he would not seek re-election in 2012, Johanns said he would run for Republican Conference chairman to replace Tennessee's Lamar Alexander, who said he would seek the whip's job that year.

FIRST DISTRICT

Jeff Fortenberry (R)

Elected 2004, 4th term; b. Dec. 27, 1960, Baton Rouge, LA; home, Lincoln; LA St. U., 1982, Franciscan U. of Steubenville, M.A. 1985, Georgetown U., M.P.P. 1986; Catholic; married (Celeste); 5 children.

Elected Office: Lincoln City Cncl., 1997-2001.

Professional Career: Staffer, U.S. House Comm. on Ag., 1986; Research assoc., Gulf South Research Inst., 1987-89; Asst. dir., Baton Rouge Downtown Dev. District, 1989-92; Sales rep., Sandhills Publishing, 1995-2004.

DC Office: 1514 LHOB, 20515, 202-225-4806; Fax: 202-225-5686; Web site: fortenberry.house.gov.

State Offices: Fremont, 402-727-0888; Lincoln, 402-438-1598; Norfolk, 402-379-2064.

Committees: *Agriculture:* Department Operations, Oversight & Credit (Chmn). *Foreign Affairs:* Africa, Global Health & Human Rights (VChmn); Middle East & South Asia.

Group Ratings

	ACLU	ACU	ADA	CFG	AFS	FRC	LCV	ITIC	NTU	COC
2010	13	96	15	79	13	100	30	0	80	75
2009	–	88	5	77	22	–	36	–	73	87

National Journal Ratings

	2010 LIB	—	2010 CONS	2009 LIB	—	2009 CONS
Economic	37%	—	63%	32%	—	67%
Social	34%	—	66%	33%	—	65%
Foreign	33%	—	65%	33%	—	63%
Composite	35%	—	65%	34%	—	66%

Key Votes of the 111th Congress

1. Overturn Ledbetter	N	5. Bar federal abortion funds	Y	9. Stop detainee transfers	Y
2. Pass $820 billion stimulus	N	6. Pass health care bill	N	10. Legalize immigrants' kids	N
3. Let guns in national parks	Y	7. Regulate financial firms	N	11. Repeal don't ask, tell	N
4. Pass cap-and-trade	N	8. Pass tax cuts for some	N	12. Limit campaign funds	N

Election Results

2010 general	Jeff Fortenberry (R)	116,871	(71%)	($568,390)
	Ivy Harper (D)	47,106	(29%)	($21,624)
2010 primary	Jeff Fortenberry (R)	57,390	(84%)	
	David Hunt (R)	7,000	(10%)	
	Ralph Bodie (R)	4,053	(6%)	

Prior Winning Percentages: 2008 (70%), 2006 (58%), 2004 (54%)

Population		Race/Ethnicity		Work	
Pop. 2010:	626,092	White:	86.2%	Private:	75.8%
Change since 2000:	Up 9.8%	Black:	2.0%	Government:	16.7%
Urban:	65.1%	Hispanic:	7.0%	Self-employed:	7.2%
Rural:	34.9%	Asian:	1.9%	Blue collar:	22.9%
Area size:	12,034 sq. mi.	Native Am.:	1.2%	White collar:	59.1%
		Hawaiian:	0.0%	Khaki collar:	0.1%
Age		Two+ races:	1.5%	Other:	17.9%
Median age:	35.3 yrs.				
More than 65 yrs:	13.0%	*Ancestry*		Median income:	$49,607
Less than 18 yrs:	24.3%	German	34.6%	Median Home Value:	$129,500
		Irish	10.2%		
Education		English	7.0%	**Military Veterans**	
H.S. grad:	90.5%			% of Pop:	10.5%
College grad:	27.7%				
Grad degree:	8.7%				

Eastern Nebraska; Lincoln

The eastern half of Nebraska, between the Missouri River and the 98th parallel, was laid out in relentless Midwestern mile-square grids and became some of America's prime farmland during the 1880s. The Plains here have completed most of their gentle decline from the Rockies to sea level, and the land has contours just regular enough, and weather just favorable enough, to make farming economically viable. The area was settled by Yankee-descended farmers from the

2008 Presidential Vote
John McCain (R) 148,179 (54%)
Barack Obama (D) 121,411 (44%)

2004 Presidential Vote
George Bush (R) 169,888 (63%)
John Kerry (D) 96,314 (36%)

Cook Partisan Voting Index: R+11

Midwest and immigrants from Germany and other countries. Traces of the immigrant heritage can still be found. Many people from Luxembourg, for example, settled along the Platte River in Butler County, where St. Mary's Presentation Parish still has a statue of Our Lady of Luxembourg. Not far away are villages with names that recall other immigrant groups—Prague (Czechs), Malmo (Swedes), Aloys (Germans). Today, a new wave of immigrants is coming to eastern Nebraska, including Latinos from Mexico and the southwest United States, to work in the region's meatpacking factories. Fremont, a town of 25,000 northwest of Omaha that is about 7% Hispanic, made national news in June 2010 when its voters overwhelmingly approved an ordinance that would mandate an immigration background check for anyone seeking to rent an apartment or house.

The 1st Congressional District of Nebraska comprises 22 full counties and parts of two others in an easternmost slice of the state. It surrounds but does not take in Omaha and most of its suburbs, which are in the 2nd District. It's anchored by Lincoln, the state capital and home of the beloved University of Nebraska Cornhuskers football team. The men's and women's basketball teams get less attention, but voters in May 2010 approved construction of a 16,000-seat arena for them. Lincoln is affluent, with above-national-average incomes and unemployment among the lowest in the United States. It does not have to depend on government or the university—the city is home to more than 100 companies and agencies with 250 or more workers, including a strong manufacturing sector. But it also has a high percentage of people holding down multiple jobs, as well as many with college degrees who consider themselves underemployed. In the smaller towns, there are significant numbers of farm equipment and meatpacking factories. Politically, Lincoln is fond of moderate Democrats but is still, on balance, Republican in national contests. The district voted 63% for George W. Bush in 2004 and 54% for John McCain in 2008.

Jeff Fortenberry (R)

The congressman from the 1st District is Jeff Fortenberry, a Republican elected in 2004. Fortenberry grew up in Baton Rouge, La., where his father was a life insurance salesman and his mother worked as a 4-H Club extension agent. When Fortenberry was 12, his father was killed in a car accident. "It taught me a hard lesson that you wouldn't want to wish on any other child—you have to figure out a lot of things on your own," he told *Esquire* magazine. Fortenberry got the political bug early as a page to a Democratic state senator, but switched to the Republican Party after he graduated from Louisiana State University. He earned one master's degree in theology from

Franciscan University of Steubenville, Ohio, and then another one in public policy from Georgetown University in Washington, D.C. (For a time, he studied for the priesthood but changed his mind.) In 1995, Fortenberry moved to Nebraska to take a public relations position with Sandhills Publishing, a publisher of trade magazines for the trucking, aircraft, and computer industries. He later got into the sales end of the business. Fortenberry's first foray into local politics came in 1997, when he won a seat on the Lincoln City Council. He served for four years, focusing on neighborhood concerns and on increasing the police force.

When U.S. Rep. Doug Bereuter, a Republican, announced he would not run again in 2004, three candidates mounted competitive campaigns for the Republican nomination: Fortenberry; Curt Bromm, the speaker of the state's unicameral legislature; and Greg Ruehle, a former executive vice president of the Nebraska Cattlemen Association. Bromm, a moderate who was endorsed by Bereuter, began as the front-runner. But he quickly lost momentum after a barrage of negative television ads financed by the Club for Growth, a national anti-tax group that supported Ruehle. Fortenberry, a social conservative, drew criticism from his opponents as a single-issue candidate, but his superior grassroots operation and fundraising carried him to victory. He won just seven of the 24 counties, but in Lincoln's Lancaster County, which cast 43% of the votes, he got 52% to 29% for Bromm and 13% for Ruehle. The vote in the rest of the district was closer. Overall, Fortenberry won with 39% of the vote, to 33% for Bromm and 21% for Ruehle.

In November, Fortenberry faced state Sen. Matt Connealy, a farmer from Decatur who sought to exploit Republican divisions—Bromm refused to endorse Fortenberry after the primary—and who characterized Fortenberry as a stranger to Nebraska farm issues, a potent charge in a state where one in four jobs is connected to agriculture. Fortenberry responded by promising to improve trade policies for farmers and to support ethanol development. His main message, however, focused on socially conservative themes: opposition to abortion rights, support of capital punishment and a ban on same-sex marriage. Fortenberry won 54%-43%, losing only two American Indian reservation counties.

In the House, Fortenberry has a reputation as a brainy policy expert who has evolved into a centrist. Teaming with Democratic U.S. Rep. Stephanie Herseth Sandlin of South Dakota, he supported renewable energy sources and pushed for an overhaul of subsidy payments in the 2008 farm bill. In the 111th Congress (2009-10), he joined a minority of Republicans who backed Democrats on such issues as compensating first responders for health problems from the September 11 terrorist attacks, a sweeping overhaul of food safety laws and legislation to reduce lead levels in drinking water. He notes that he and President Barack Obama both won Lincoln in 2008. "People here pride themselves on independence," he told *Esquire*. He was the only member of Nebraska's congressional delegation to oppose the tax cut deal that Obama reached with Republicans in December 2010, calling it "economic rope-a-dope hiding from the hard but necessary fight against overspending and debt."

On the International Relations Committee, Fortenberry supported Bush on the war in Iraq, won House approval of an increase in visas for Iraqi translators, and worked on the deal to promote nuclear cooperation with India. In 2010, he got into law a bill to expedite permanent residency status for Haitian earthquake orphans adopted by Americans. When Republicans regained control of the House that year, he was named chairman of the Agriculture Committee's panel on Agriculture Department operations, oversight and farm credit. He promised to continue to promote alternative fuels and introduced a bill establishing a program to provide no-interest loans for capital costs on biomass energy projects.

In 2006, Fortenberry's first re-election campaign was against former Democratic Lt. Gov. Maxine Moul, who made the Iraq war an issue. Although her fundraising was competitive, Moul's campaign did not catch fire in the district, which has not elected a Democrat since 1964. Fortenberry won 58%-42%. Moul won only in Burt County, where she was born and raised. In 2008 and 2010, Fortenberry had even easier rides to re-election.

SECOND DISTRICT

Lee Terry (R)

Elected 1998, 7th term; b. Jan. 29, 1962, Omaha; home, Omaha; U. of NE at Lincoln, B.A. 1984; Creighton U., J.D. 1987; Protestant; married (Robyn); 3 children.

Elected Office: Omaha City Cncl., 1991-98, Pres., 1995-96.

Professional Career: Practicing atty., 1988-98.

DC Office: 2331 RHOB, 20515, 202-225-4155; Fax: 202-226-5452; Web site: leeterry.house.gov.

State Offices: Omaha, 402-397-9944.

Committees: *Energy & Commerce:* Communications & Technology (VChmn); Energy & Power; Oversight & Investigations.

Group Ratings

	ACLU	ACU	ADA	CFG	AFS	FRC	LCV	ITIC	NTU	COC
2010	13	92	5	79	0	93	10	67	85	88
2009	–	88	15	79	11	–	14	–	77	93

National Journal Ratings

	2010 LIB	—	2010 CONS	2009 LIB	—	2009 CONS
Economic	32%	—	68%	30%	—	70%
Social	25%	—	71%	33%	—	65%
Foreign	12%	—	79%	0%	—	75%
Composite	25%	—	75%	26%	—	75%

Key Votes of the 111th Congress

1. Overturn Ledbetter	N	5. Bar federal abortion funds	Y	9. Stop detainee transfers	Y
2. Pass $820 billion stimulus	N	6. Pass health care bill	N	10. Legalize immigrants' kids	N
3. Let guns in national parks	Y	7. Regulate financial firms	N	11. Repeal don't ask, tell	N
4. Pass cap-and-trade	N	8. Pass tax cuts for some	N	12. Limit campaign funds	N

Election Results

2010 general	Lee Terry (R)	93,840	(61%)	($1,924,726)
	Tom White (D)	60,486	(39%)	($1,051,103)
2010 primary	Lee Terry (R)	18,478	(63%)	
	Matt Sakalosky (R)	10,816	(37%)	

Prior Winning Percentages: 2008 (52%), 2006 (55%), 2004 (61%), 2002 (63%), 2000 (66%), 1998 (66%)

Population		Race/Ethnicity		Work	
Pop. 2010:	638,871	White:	73.7%	Private:	82.7%
Change since 2000:	Up 12.0%	Black:	10.2%	Government:	12.6%
Urban:	97.8%	Hispanic:	10.7%	Self-employed:	4.6%
Rural:	2.2%	Asian:	2.6%	Blue collar:	18.3%
Area size:	421 sq. mi.	Native Am.:	0.5%	White collar:	64.6%
		Hawaiian:	0.1%	Khaki collar:	0.6%
Age		Two+ races:	2.2%	Other:	16.5%
Median age:	33.2 yrs.				
More than 65 yrs:	10.3%	*Ancestry*		Median income:	$51,614
Less than 18 yrs:	26.5%	German	24.2%	Median Home Value:	$141,600
		Irish	13.0%		
Education		English	6.7%	**Military Veterans**	
H.S. grad:	90.4%			% of Pop:	11.2%
College grad:	33.8%				
Grad degree:	11.6%				

Omaha, Suburbs

Omaha is the commercial heart of Nebraska and the largest city on the Great Plains north of Kansas City and west of Minneapolis. It got its start from the government, when President Abraham Lincoln picked it as the eastern terminus of the Union Pacific railroad, from which emerged the stockyards and livestock exchange that made it a thriving town. Over the years, Omaha filled up with cattle hands and European immigrants, especially Germans and Czechs. It developed fine civic institutions, from the Joslyn Art Museum to Boys Town, an orphanage founded by the Rev. Edward Flanagan in 1917 and the subject of a 1938 movie. Today, the facility is a gender-neutral home for troubled youth called Boys and Girls Town.

2008 Presidential Vote		
Barack Obama (D) 138,809	(50%)
John McCain (R) 135,439	(49%)
2004 Presidential Vote		
George Bush (R) 153,041	(60%)
John Kerry (D) 97,858	(39%)
Cook Partisan Voting Index: R+6		

Though a major city by the 1880s, Omaha has remained small enough to be manageable. One doesn't feel distant, physically or psychologically, from the other side of town. The older, less affluent part of Omaha is near Iowa and the Missouri River. Downtown and the riverfront have experienced a construction boom; the Tower at First National Center is the tallest structure between Minneapolis and Denver. To the west, the city has been quietly flourishing with the rise of upscale neighborhoods and new shopping malls. Omaha has also entered into the Wall Street vernacular as the place where investor Warren Buffett—ranked in *Forbes* in 2010 as the world's third richest man—lives and works. The city was largely spared from the recession; unemployment in the area peaked at 6.1% in early 2010 and dropped steadily the rest of the year.

Omaha's economy has been changing. It remains dependent on the overseas trade of meat and is home to many processors of food products, including ConAgra Foods, Omaha Steaks, and Nebraska Beef. ConAgra embarked on an effort to reshape its image in 2009 that included a new logo and a planned statue at its headquarters of Chef Boyardee founder Ettore (Hector) Boiardi. However, the city has also become the nation's telecommunications hub, handling 20 million "800" and "900" calls a day and employing more than 30,000 people in more than three dozen telemarketing centers. The city is also ethnically diverse: About 30% of students in the Omaha public schools are black and about 20% are Hispanic.

The 2nd Congressional District of Nebraska includes most of metropolitan Omaha: Douglas County, which includes Omaha and its western suburbs, and the eastern part of fast-growing Sarpy County, which houses Bellevue and the Offutt Air Force Base, headquarters of the U.S. Strategic Air Command. Politically, Omaha has long had competitive politics, with Democrats strong on the south side around the stockyards and the northeast and Republicans strong on the west side. As Omaha and Nebraska have boomed, they have become more Republican, and increasingly it is the Republican primary that decides elections here. But in 2008, Democratic nominee Barack Obama banked on the district being competitive, and opened three offices and enlisted some 1,500 volunteers. His efforts paid off. He won the district 50%-49%.

Lee Terry (R)

The congressman from the 2nd District is Lee Terry, a Republican first elected in 1998. Terry grew up in Omaha and became interested in politics at age 14 when his father, television anchor Lee Terry Sr., a conservative Republican, ran and lost a race for the House in 1976 against Democrat John Cavanaugh. Terry Sr. remained a prominent local commentator on politics, and his son went off to college and law school, practiced law, and at 29, was elected to the Omaha City Council from an affluent west-side district.

When Republican U.S. Rep. Jon Christensen ran for governor, Terry announced his bid for the House seat. His chief opponents were Brad Kuiper, owner of a pest control business, and Steve Kupka, former chief of staff to Omaha Mayor Hal Daub and an official in President Ronald Reagan's Office of Management and Budget. The contrast among the three was less on issues—all were for lower taxes and against abortion rights—than on style and approach. Kuiper, with less money than the other two, targeted religious conservatives and emphasized cultural issues. Kupka assembled Washington endorsements and, spending the most money, went on the attack, accusing Terry of increasing the city's budget. Terry won 40% to 30% for Kupka and 26% for Kuiper. The general election was anticlimactic. Despite the fact that Democrats had won open seats here in 1976 and 1988, Terry won 66%-34% against Democrat Michael Scott. In April 1999, shortly after taking office, he reneged on his pledge to serve only three terms.

In Washington, Terry has a moderate-to-conservative voting record and occasionally is a consensus-seeker. "I am a policy guy," he said in 2009. "I like to work with Democrats." On the Energy and Commerce Committee, he worked with Democrat Rick Boucher of Virginia to provide federal funds for high-speed Internet service to low-income and rural areas. In 2007, he successfully joined Democrat Baron Hill of Indiana on a bill to increase average fuel efficiency standards to 35 miles per gallon for cars, although he opposed raising the standard to that level for light trucks, widely used by Nebraska farmers. When Democrats controlled the House, he joined a minority of Republicans in supporting the majority's priorities, including a food safety overhaul and a substantial spending boost in federal research agencies in 2010.

But Terry stuck with his party on the two major bills to come before Energy and Commerce—the health care overhaul, which he dubbed a "trillion-dollar tragedy," and energy legislation with a cap-and-trade program to reduce greenhouse gas emissions. When the committee approved legislation in 2010 to mandate "black boxes" in cars to improve safety, he unsuccessfully sought to amend the bill to bar the government from gathering information from those devices for vehicle safety research. After Republicans regained control of the House, he was named vice chair of Energy and Commerce's communications and technology panel.

Terry has survived some well-funded, re-election opponents. In 2004, state Sen. Nancy Thompson ran an aggressive campaign against him, and despite polls indicating a tight contest, Terry won 61%-36%. Two years later, political newcomer Jim Esch, who worked for the Omaha Chamber of Commerce, held him to a 55%-45% win. Terry got only 53% in Douglas County, which cast 82% of the vote. He attributed the closer outcome to discontent over the war in Iraq, which was "deeper than I perceived it to be, honestly."

In 2008, Esch decided to run again, encouraged by Barack Obama's grassroots efforts in the 2nd District, where the presidential candidate and U.S. senator from Illinois was vying for one of three electoral votes that Nebraska awards on the basis of congressional districts. Douglas County Democrats registered a slew of new voters and outnumbered Republicans in total voters for the first time since 1994. Esch linked his candidacy to Obama's and attacked Terry's congressional record, questioning why he had not been elected to a leadership position during a decade in Washington.

Terry hit back by criticizing Esch for accepting $100,000 in agriculture subsidies. Terry was cognizant of Obama's appeal in urban areas. His campaign mailed postcards to independent women urging them to split their ballot by voting Obama-Terry. Terry outraised Esch more than 2-to-1 and went door-to-door asking for support, and both national parties got involved. Two weeks before the election, both national party committees poured money into the state. Terry won with 52% of the vote. He narrowly prevailed in Douglas County, which Obama carried by 51%, but he won by big margins in Republican-leaning Sarpy County.

Two years later, Democrats put up someone they regarded as a strong candidate—Democratic state Sen. Tom White, an anti-abortion rights Catholic. White criticized Terry for not supporting parts of the Obama administration's economic agenda that helped middle-class Nebraskans, such as the economic stimulus bill. Late in the campaign, he also aired an attack ad highlighting a *New York Post* article that claimed Terry flirtatiously asked a female lobbyist, "Why did you get me so drunk?" while at a Capitol Hill club. Terry denounced the charge and worked harder at raising money, eventually pulling in $1.9 million to White's $1 million. He won the *Omaha World-Herald's* endorsement and prevailed easily, 61%-39%.

THIRD DISTRICT

Adrian Smith (R)

Elected 2006, 3rd term; b. Dec. 19, 1970, Scottsbluff; home, Gering; U. of NE, B.S. 1993; Christian; single.

Elected Office: Gering City Council, 1994-98, NE Unicameral, 1998-2006.

Professional Career: Realtor, Buyer Realty, 1997-2006; Owner, My Other Garage, 2003-06.

DC Office: 503 CHOB, 20515, 202-225-6435; Fax: 202-225-0207; Web site: adriansmith.house.gov.

State Offices: Grand Island, 308-384-3900; Scottsbluff, 308-633-6333.

Committees: *Ways & Means:* Human Resources; Social Security; Trade.

Group Ratings

	ACLU	ACU	ADA	CFG	AFS	FRC	LCV	ITIC	NTU	COC
2010	13	100	0	97	0	100	20	33	90	88
2009	–	100	0	93	0	–	0	–	89	80

National Journal Ratings

	2010 LIB — 2010 CONS		2009 LIB — 2009 CONS	
Economic	18% —	81%	5% —	94%
Social	18% —	77%	7% —	90%
Foreign	0% —	88%	0% —	75%
Composite	15% —	85%	9% —	91%

Key Votes of the 111th Congress

1. Overturn Ledbetter	N	5. Bar federal abortion funds	Y
2. Pass $820 billion stimulus	N	6. Pass health care bill	N
3. Let guns in national parks	Y	7. Regulate financial firms	N
4. Pass cap-and-trade	N	8. Pass tax cuts for some	N

9. Stop detainee transfers	Y
10. Legalize immigrants' kids	N
11. Repeal don't ask, tell	N
12. Limit campaign funds	N

Election Results

2010 general	Adrian Smith (R)	117,275	(70%)	($943,619)
	Rebekah Davis (D)	29,932	(18%)	($54,170)
	Dan Hill (Pet)	20,036	(12%)	
2010 primary	Adrian Smith (R)	65,664	(88%)	
	Dennis Parker (R)	8,979	(12%)	

Prior Winning Percentages: 2008 (77%), 2006 (55%)

Population		Race/Ethnicity		Work	
Pop. 2010:	561,378	White:	87.2%	Private:	74.1%
Change since 2000:	Down 1.6%	Black:	0.7%	Government:	13.8%
Urban:	46.1%	Hispanic:	9.8%	Self-employed:	11.6%
Rural:	53.9%	Asian:	0.6%	Blue collar:	26.9%
Area size:	64,893 sq. mi.	Native Am.:	0.8%	White collar:	53.8%
		Hawaiian:	0.0%	Khaki collar:	0.0%
Age		Two+ races:	0.9%	Other:	19.3%
Median age:	40.5 yrs.				
More than 65 yrs:	17.4%	*Ancestry*		Median income:	$42,678
Less than 18 yrs:	24.4%	German	34.4%	Median Home Value:	$90,300
		Irish	10.0%		
Education		English	7.7%	**Military Veterans**	
H.S. grad:	88.6%			% of Pop:	11.4%
College grad:	19.2%				
Grad degree:	5.4%				

Western Nebraska

West of Grand Island, Nebraska is wheat and livestock country. For miles on end you can see nothing but rolling brown fields, sectioned off here and there by barbed wire fences, and in the distance, a grain elevator towering over a tiny town and its miniature railroad depot. The winds, rain and tornadoes that come suddenly out of the sky remind you that the original settlers likened this part of the country to an ocean and thought themselves in their wooden wagons

2008 Presidential Vote		
John McCain (R) 169,361	(68%)
Barack Obama (D) 73,099	(30%)

2004 Presidential Vote		
George Bush (R) 189,885	(75%)
John Kerry (D) 60,156	(24%)

Cook Partisan Voting Index: R+24

almost as helpless as passengers at sea in a rowboat. Settlers passed through here on the Oregon Trail in the 1840s, and then set down roots in the 1880s. But the rain they hoped for fell too unreliably, and wheat lands gave way to pasture and open range. It is a beautiful but hard land, exacting much from its people, as the novels of western Nebraska's Willa Cather make poignantly clear. Chimney Rock—a clay and sandstone spire that marked a good camping spot and offered reliable spring water for travelers and their animals—was the landmark that travelers on the Oregon Trail most frequently mentioned in their journals. This symbol of westward expansion now graces the Nebraska issue of the U.S. quarter.

Dozens of small counties today have fewer people than they did in 1900. Severe droughts in recent years have seemed a kind of end point, as the grasslands turned dry and brown, reservoirs and aquifers began to run dry and ranchers sold off their thinning and sickening herds. But some economic life survives. In North Platte, Bailey Yard is the world's largest railroad classification yard, covering 2,850 acres and handling 10,000 rail cars every 24 hours. The Union Pacific line from North Platte east to Gibbon is the busiest freight rail corridor in the world. Farther west on Interstate 80 is the town of Sidney, home of Cabela's, the world's largest mail order and Internet business for hunting, fishing and camping gear. The area west of North Platte, which includes Lake McConaughy, draws some out-of-state vacationers.

The 3rd Congressional District of Nebraska has one-third of the state's people, 85% of its acreage and exists in two time zones. At nearly 65,000 square miles, it is one of the largest congressional districts—bigger than the state of New York and with more counties. Except along the interstate and around Scottsbluff, the 3rd has been losing population for decades as beef production continues to drop; several of the western ranching counties are among the poorest in the nation. Nebraska's cattle operations began 2010 at their lowest point in 51 years in the number of females with calves. The Census Bureau that year reported a loss of 18,000 residents in the district's population. Still, the 3rd is a major agricultural producer, with the third-highest total in U.S. farm subsidies between 1995 and 2009, according to the Environmental Working Group, a nonprofit group that opposes subsidies. Geographically and politically, the 3rd District is where the Midwest becomes the West. For years people here welcomed farm subsidies even as they angrily opposed federal interference. Politically, it is heavily Republican and sometimes ornery: In 1992, Ross Perot got more votes here than Bill Clinton. The district voted 75% for George W. Bush in 2004 and 68% for John McCain in 2008.

Adrian Smith (R)

The congressman from the 3rd District is Adrian Smith, the youngest of the 13 freshman Republicans elected to the House in 2006. He hails from a politically active family—his father is a former county Republican chairman, and his mother is the state GOP secretary. But the most significant political influence in Smith's life was President Ronald Reagan. When he was in fourth grade, Smith recalls, adults around him were weighing Reagan's attributes against that of Democrat Jimmy Carter's, and it sunk into the boy's head that Reagan favored a strong defense. "It just made sense to me that we needed a strong military," said Smith, whose congressional office is filled with portraits of the former president. In college, Smith served as an intern in the Nebraska governor's office and as a page in the state's unicameral legislature. At 23, shortly after graduating from the University of Nebraska, he won election to the Gering City Council in his hometown. Four years later, he knocked off a Democratic incumbent to win the first of two terms in the legislature. There, Smith devoted his efforts to opposing abortion rights, protecting Nebraskans' right to bear arms, fighting tax increases, and blocking efforts to expand casino gambling. He also worked as a real estate agent and owned a storage business.

In May 2005, two weeks after Rep. Tom Osborne, a Republican, announced his ultimately unsuccessful primary bid for governor, Smith joined the race for Osborne's seat in Congress. The crowded Republican primary field included Grand Island Mayor Jay Vavricek and John Hanson, Osborne's former district director. Smith championed tax incentives to attract new residents and encourage investment in the district. He also promised to expand markets globally for Nebraska farmers. Still, his opponents charged that he betrayed rural Nebraska by accepting more than $300,000 in contributions from members of the Club for Growth, a national anti-tax group that opposes farm subsidies. Smith supports caps on subsidies, which many of his farming constituents do not. He parried by touting his support from the Nebraska Farm Bureau. Smith ultimately carried 39 of the 69 counties to win the nomination with 39%. Hanson finished second with 29% and was strongest in the Republican River valley south of North Platte, while Vavricek's 27% came mainly from the Grand Island area.

In the general election, the Democrats fielded an unusually strong nominee: Yale-educated, cattle rancher Scott Kleeb. He accused Smith of "distorting the truth" about the Club for Growth's opposition to farm subsidies. Smith sought to link Kleeb to Democrats who supported a timetable for the withdrawal of troops from Iraq, and he portrayed Kleeb as a political carpetbagger who grew up overseas on military bases and attended schools in Colorado and Connecticut before settling in Nebraska on a family-owned ranch. Kleeb's retort was, "You don't run as a Democrat in the 3rd District because you thought it would be easy." Kleeb called for changes in farm policy to emphasize niche markets. He was competitive financially and kept the race close in the polls. Still, Smith won 55%-45%.

In Washington, Smith has been much more conservative than his Nebraska colleagues Lee Terry and Jeff Fortenberry, joining the Tea Party Caucus in 2010. He landed a seat on the Agriculture Committee and focused his early efforts on the rewrite of farm policy in 2007, working to expand rural development programs, increase research of biofuels, and open international markets for Nebraska crops.

He stood by President George W. Bush as support for the war in Iraq waned, even turning down the Democrats' offer of billions of dollars in drought relief if he joined them in pushing timetables for withdrawing troops. As co-chairman of the Congressional Rural Caucus, Smith in 2009 pushed President Barack Obama to set up an Office of Rural Affairs, and he pushed to preserve federal grants for tiny airports. The same year, Smith got the House to pass his bill setting up a grant program to relieve veterinarian shortages.

Smith was rewarded for his party loyalty with a coveted assignment to the powerful Ways and Means Committee in 2011. He called for Obama to move more swiftly on pending trade deals. Unlike the budget deficit scoreboard on many Republicans' websites, Smith's site displayed the number of days since the U.S.-Colombia free trade agreement was signed and the estimated tariffs imposed on exports to that country since then.

In the 2008 primary, Smith easily defeated Jeremiah Ellison, an activist supporter of libertarian Rep. Ron Paul of Texas. Kleeb turned down a rematch and instead ran for the U.S. Senate. Two years later, Smith trounced Democrat Rebekah Davis, 70%-18%.

★ NEVADA ★

Boom and bust: That has been the story of Nevada from its very beginnings as a territory. The evidence of the latest boom is apparent as your plane descends for a landing at Las Vegas' McCarren International Airport. You see a pyramid rising from the desert; just across the street from the Sphinx-like lion are New York City-style skyscrapers. Nearby are a fair-sized Eiffel Tower, the gondolas of Venice, the mansard roofs of Paris, and a flaming pirate ship. These surrealistic monuments, and miles of spreading subdivisions, are set in one of North America's most forbidding landscapes, a bowl-shaped desert valley rimmed by barren peaks. "Geologically, Nevada is a gigantic, post-oceanic ditch between the Rockies and the Sierras, filled with rough, secondary mountain ranges that stack and twine across the naked landscape like ranks of FEMA house trailers in a storage lot," writes Las Vegas art critic Dave Hickey.

Prospectors first came to mine silver and gold in Virginia City, on a mountain 6,700 feet above sea level. This is where Mark Twain and Bret Harte documented the heyday of the Comstock Lode, which was discovered in 1859 and produced $500 million worth of silver in the next 20 years. President Abraham Lincoln's Republicans made Nevada a state in 1864, even though it did not meet the population requirement, in order to win three more electoral votes. But that boom went bust, and by 1900, Nevada had only 42,000 residents, down 68% from its 1880 peak. It seemed questionable whether this was a viable state. In the early 1930s, when there were still only 91,000 Nevadans, the state government was about to go bankrupt. So Nevada decided to roll the dice. It reduced its residency requirement for divorce to six weeks and legalized gambling. Catering to what most Americans considered sin—casinos, pawnshops, divorce mills, quick-wedding chapels, and even legal brothels—turned out to be good business. Nevada has been America's fastest-growing state for two decades. Its population more than doubled, from 1.2 million to 2.7 million, from 1990 to 2010.

Las Vegas was a mere dot on the map when gambling was legalized, with only 8,532 people in all of Clark County. In 2010, Clark County had just a shade under 2 million. Reno, once known as "the biggest little city in the world," now has 477,000 in its greater metro area. Gaming—the Nevada word for gambling—generated most of this growth, and gaming, so just about everyone believed, was a recession-proof industry. In early 2011, Las Vegas had nearly 150,000 hotel rooms. Las Vegas' tourists spent more than $33 billion a year and Reno's about $4 billion, and not just in casinos and hotels, but also in increasingly upscale restaurants and shopping malls. They came from all over the United States and from foreign countries, especially Japan. Though at least some form of gambling is now available in 48 states, Las Vegas made itself a destination, with more than twice as much convention exhibit space as its No. 2 competitor Chicago. The 6.75% gambling receipts tax generated enough revenue to make it unnecessary for Nevada to impose income, corporate or inheritance taxes. The cost of living and housing was relatively inexpensive during the peak boom years from 2003 to 2006.

From mining to gambling, Nevada has been a second-chance state, a place for outcasts to succeed and misfits to rebound. Like Alaska, it is one of the few states with more men than women. At 12%, Nevada has the highest percentage of divorced residents in the nation. Only 24% of Nevadans were born in the state, the lowest of any state; in Stateline, on Lake Tahoe, just 5% were born in Nevada. The state has been an avenue of success for ethnic groups who faced roadblocks elsewhere. The four owners of the Comstock Lode—MacKay, Fair, Flood, and O'Brien—were Irishmen. The first big hotel on the Las Vegas strip, the Flamingo, was built in 1946 by Jewish gangster Bugsy Siegel, who was later gunned down in his Beverly Hills home. Most of the big casinos were owned by mobsters until industrialist Howard Hughes—a different kind of outcast—bought them up in the late 1960s. From the 1980s to 2007, Latinos moved here in large numbers, attracted by the strong job market. By 2010, Nevada's population was 27% Hispanic, 8% black, and 7% Asian. Nevadans tend to be nonreligious and not highly educated: According to a 2010 Gallup poll, 30% regularly attend church, the fifth lowest level of any state. A minority of households are made up of married couples, and only 22% of adult Nevadans have college degrees.

The odds seemed to be in favor of Nevada. What could go wrong? But once again, Nevada's boom turned to bust. Gaming, it turns out, is not recession-proof. To the contrary, this time it was a leading indicator of recession. Gaming collections fell off in 2007 for the first time in memory, hotel occupancy fell off sharply, thousands of construction workers were laid off, the Tropicana was headed into bankruptcy, and Starbucks closed 10% of its Las Vegas outlets. Huge projects like City Center were suddenly in danger of collapse. Casino stocks took a nosedive, and much of the fortunes

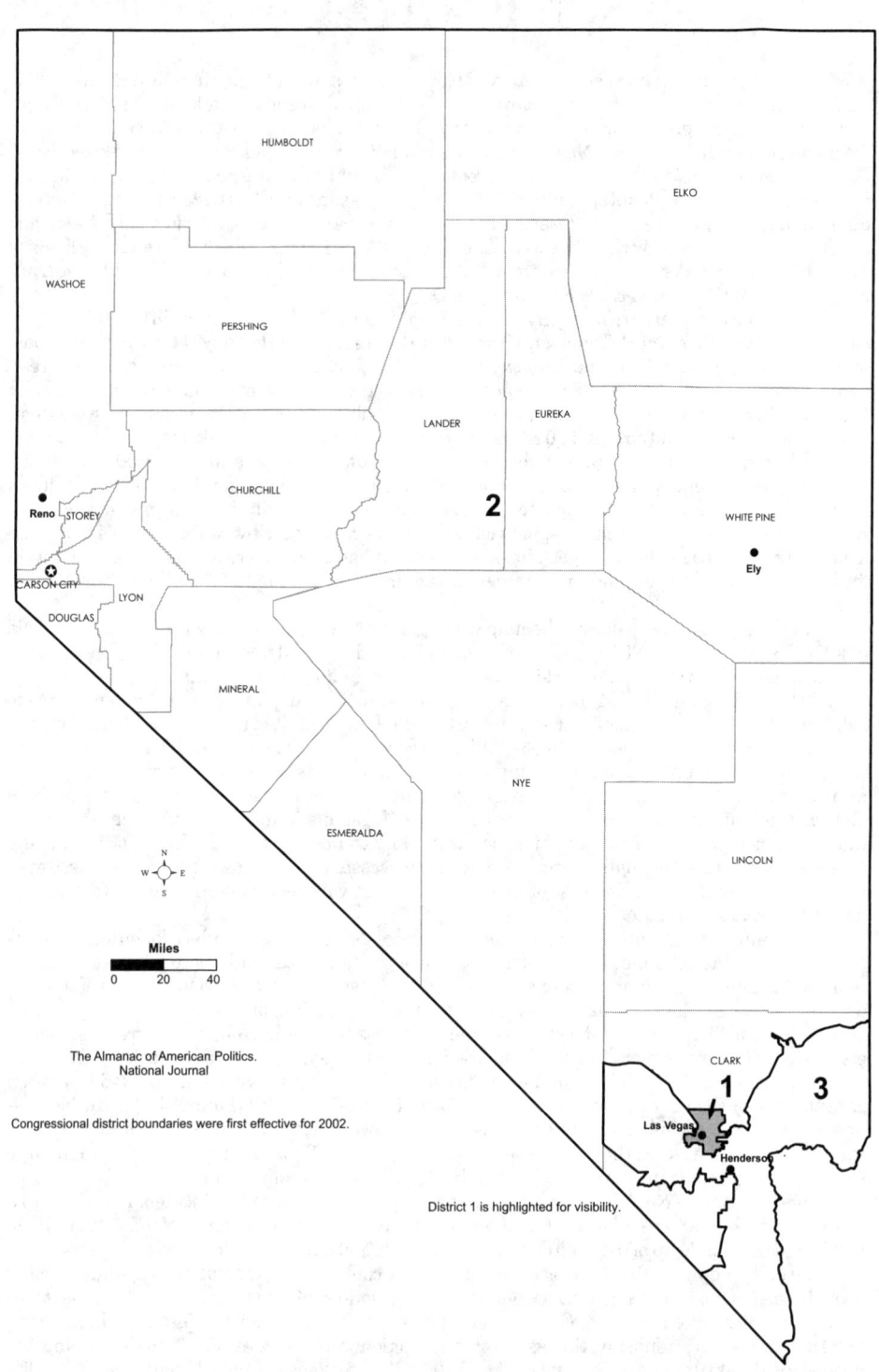

HUMBOLDT

ELKO

WASHOE

PERSHING

LANDER

EUREKA

CHURCHILL

Reno
STOREY

WHITE PINE

CARSON CITY

Ely

LYON

DOUGLAS

MINERAL

NYE

ESMERALDA

LINCOLN

N
W E
S

2

Miles
0   20   40

The Almanac of American Politics.
National Journal

Congressional district boundaries were first effective for 2002.

CLARK

1   **3**

Las Vegas

Henderson

District 1 is highlighted for visibility.

of casino magnates Kirk Kerkorian and Sheldon Adelson vanished. Tax revenues declined nearly 10% in 2007, and the unemployment rate rose above the national average. An economy heavily dependent on construction, finance, and real estate, and entertainment and recreation suddenly stopped new hiring and started laying people off by the thousands. Unemployment rose to a historic high of 15.3% in January 2010, surpassing that of Michigan.

Residential real estate values, which crested in the fourth quarter of 2006, fell off more than 50%. Since then, Nevada has been the No. 1 state for real estate foreclosures, with rates running close to 10% of households; a majority of mortgage holders owed more than their houses were worth. Speculators with adjustable-rate mortgage loans and Hispanic construction workers with sub-prime mortgages suddenly found themselves far underwater in the desert. Las Vegas, with all of its glitter and growth, helped plunge the nation into recession. Immigration plummeted, and for the first time since the 1930s, more Americans left Nevada than moved in.

All of this produced political turmoil in a state that had been a target of both parties in presidential elections from 1992 to 2004. Nevada voted narrowly twice for Bill Clinton and twice for George W. Bush. It had in Harry Reid a Democrat who led his party in the Senate since 2005. Reid won his third term by beating Republican John Ensign by 428 votes in 1998. Reid has been attentive to the interests of the big casino owners, who had in turn provided strong backing for Democratic Gov. Bob Miller (elected in 1990 and 1994) and Republican Gov. Kenny Guinn (elected in 1998 and 2002). Guinn obtained higher taxes—but not an income tax or one on the casinos—to support the public schools serving a burgeoning population heavy with Mexican and Filipino children. In 2006, a Democratic year, Nevada nonetheless elected Republican Jim Gibbons governor. His messy divorce—his wife disputed his right to occupy the governor's mansion—and acerbic style antagonized voters, but he did strive mightily to hold taxes lower than the Democratic legislature wanted.

Gibbons lost the 2010 Republican primary to former Attorney General Brian Sandoval 56%-27% and Sandoval went on to win the general election over Clark County Commission Chairman Rory Reid, son of Harry Reid, by 53%-42%. Interestingly, Sandoval, although he is Hispanic, won a scarcely larger share of the Latino vote than did Sharron Angle, the right-wing Republican nominee against Harry Reid in 2010. Reid had high negative ratings in public opinion polls, but Angle's controversial statements helped Reid overcome her challenge by a 50%-45% margin. One factor was increased Hispanic and Asian turnout (most Asians in Nevada are Filipinos, who tend to vote more Democratic than other Asian groups), spurred initially by the Obama campaign's organizing efforts in 2008. Another factor was the united effort of the gaming interests and the Culinary Union, which represents many casino employees, to keep Reid in the Senate. They remembered that in 1987, when Nevada's two senators had minimal seniority, Congress had voted to store a national nuclear waste repository at Yucca Mountain, a scant 90 miles from Las Vegas. Reid had fought this mightily, and as the Senate majority leader, was well-positioned to block it. The state's other senator, Republican Ensign, had been weakened and eventually resigned in 2011 after revelations that he had an affair with a top staffer's wife and that members of his family had given payments to the woman and her husband. The cavalcade of buses and vans in Las Vegas bringing voters to the polls to cast early votes for Reid were not set in motion by accident or even by revulsion at Angle's right-wing statements. They were the work of hard-headed casino entrepreneurs and forceful union leaders desperate to preserve what they could of their industry in a time of peril.

More should be said about Yucca Mountain. The federal government took responsibility for the nation's nuclear waste in 1982, and the Yucca Mountain site was chosen by Congress in 1987, when Reid was in his first year in the Senate. The plan was to bury the waste deep within the

Population		Household Income		Work	
Pop. 2010:	2,700,551	Under $15k:	9.4%	Private:	82.3%
State rank:	35th	$15k to $50k:	35.1%	Government:	12.9%
Change since 2000:	Up 35.1%	$50k to $100k:	34.9%	Self-employed:	4.7%
Urban:	83.7%	$100k to $200k:	17.2%	Unemployment (3-yr. average):	5.9%
Rural:	16.3%	Over $200k:	3.3%	Poverty:	11.6%
Native of state:	23.6%	Median income:	$55,322	Blue collar:	21.1%
Not a citizen:	11.9%			White collar:	52.7%
Area size:	110,572 sq. mi.	**Home Value**		Khaki collar:	0.3%
		Under $100k:	9.9%	Other:	26.0%
Most populous cities		$100k to $300k:	50.6%		
Las Vegas	583,756	$300k to $500k:	27.0%	**Age**	
Henderson	257,729	$500k to $1 mil:	10.1%	Median age:	35.3 yrs.
Reno	225,221	Over $1 million:	2.3%	More than 65 yrs:	11.3%
Paradise CDP	223,167	Median:	$260,700	Less than 18 yrs:	25.9%

Race/Ethnicity				Military Veterans		Registered Voters in 2010	
White:	54.1%	*Language*		% of Pop:	11.7%	Democrats:	579,108
Black:	7.7%	English:	71.8%			Republicans:	471,819
Hispanic:	26.5%	Spanish:	20.0%	*Veterans by Period*		Ind./other:	288,284
Asian:	7.1%	Asian:	4.8%	WWII and before:	7.5%	Voter turnout:	723,515
Native Am.:	0.9%	Other European:	2.4%	Korea:	10.4%	Turnout as % of	
Hawaiian:	0.6%			Vietnam:	34.5%	voting age:	35.5%
Two+ races:	2.9%	**Education**		Gulf (pre-2001):	12.9%		
		H.S. grad:	83.7%	Gulf (post-2001):	8.5%	**Legislature**	
Ancestry		College grad:	21.7%	Peace time:	26.3%	Senate:	11 D 10 R
German	11.0%	Grad degree:	7.3%			Assembly:	26 D 16 R
Irish	8.5%						
English	7.6%						

mountain, 1,300 feet above the water table, in reinforced steel containers in a 1,400-acre maze with 100 miles of storage tunnels. Many Nevadans argued that rainwater would flush radioactive material out of the repository and into the water table. More recently, Yucca Mountain opponents have charged that the site is geologically flawed and within an earthquake zone, and that transportation of nuclear waste across the country to Yucca Mountain would be hazardous. President Bill Clinton promised to veto a temporary site, but veto-proof majorities in the House approved such a site in Nevada. Reid and then Democratic Sen. Richard Bryan lobbied furiously to get enough votes to prevent a veto override in the Senate and succeeded in 1995, 1997, and 2000. In February 2002, President George W. Bush, on the recommendation of Energy Secretary Spencer Abraham, designated Yucca as the permanent site. The law provided for a veto by the governor, which could be overridden by majorities in both chambers of Congress. In April 2002, with great ceremony, Gov. Guinn issued his veto. In May 2002, the House cast a large majority vote for the Yucca Mountain repository. In the Senate, Reid and Ensign lobbied hard for votes, but the designation was affirmed 60-39. Many Nevadans cheered when the U.S. Court of Appeals for the D.C. Circuit ruled in 2004 that the Environmental Protection Agency's health and safety standards were insufficient. But the court also upheld the selection of the site.

When Reid became majority leader after the Democratic victories in 2006, any legislation furthering Yucca Mountain as the permanent repository seemed doomed. In 2009, thanks to Reid, the Senate's energy bill ordered the shutdown of the site, though the government had spent over $13 billion over 25 years on the project. In his 2008 campaign, Democrat Barack Obama promised to shut the facility down, and his fiscal year 2011 budget zeroed out funding for Yucca Mountain and called for withdrawal of the license. In July 2010, three Nuclear Regulatory Commission administrative judges ruled that the license application couldn't be withdrawn absent affirmative action from Congress, and Congress had not approved Obama's budget. The issue wound up in court. Obama appointed a commission to consider the issue and report by July 2011. So Yucca Mountain, 24 years after Congress designated it as a nuclear waste repository, remained a live issue.

Presidential politics   Nevada was closely divided in the four presidential elections from 1992 to 2004, but in 2008 it went strongly Democratic, which is its historic preference. For years, this sparsely populated desert sent politically shrewd Democrats to Washington and kept them there to protect the interests of a state heavily dependent on the federal government. The most powerful were Key Pittman, chairman of the Senate Foreign Relations Committee, who backed President Franklin Delano Roosevelt's foreign policy only after Roosevelt agreed to buy absurdly large amounts of Nevada silver; and

2008 Presidential Vote		
Barack Obama (D)	533,736	(55%)
John McCain (R)	412,827	(43%)
2004 Presidential Vote		
George W. Bush (R)	418,690	(50%)
John Kerry (D)	397,190	(48%)

Sen. Pat McCarran—author of the repressive McCarran Act—who shamelessly pushed aid for Reno and Las Vegas (where the airport is named for him), and became suddenly solicitous of civil liberties when mobsters and casino owners were called to testify before the Kefauver Committee investigating racketeering.

In the 1980s, Nevada swung heavily Republican. In the 1990s, it twice voted narrowly for Clinton, partly because he promised to stop the nuclear waste site. In 2000 and 2004, it was a target state again, narrowly carried both times by Bush, who arguably would have done better had he taken the same pledge to oppose the repository. In 2006, Nevada again seemed closely divided, electing Republican Gibbons as governor and re-electing Republican Sen. Ensign.

But it changed in 2008 for three reasons. One was presidential politics. The Democratic National Committee, under heavy pressure from Reid, named Nevada as one of its four states allowed to hold early contests, along with Iowa, New Hampshire, and South Carolina. Reid argued that overwhelmingly white Iowa and New Hampshire were not typical of an increasingly diverse nation and that Nevada—with its mix of Hispanics, African-Americans, and Asians—was. Labor leaders pointed out that Nevada, unlike the three other states, has a large number of union members working at the casinos. Other Democrats argued, presciently as it turned out, that Nevada was one of several Western states trending Democratic. So the Democrats held a caucus on Jan. 19, just 16 days after the Iowa caucuses. Hillary Rodham Clinton and Obama both organized in the state; Clinton came out the winner, in the metrics Democrats use, 51%-45%, her only caucus victory all year.

Democrats did not quit organizing after the caucus, which is the second reason for their surge. In 2006, Nevada had 494,000 registered Democrats. But there were plenty of new residents to be signed up, and Democrats got them. The Democratic registration advantage rose to 523,000 to 479,000 for the Republicans by January 2008, and by October 2008, it was a whopping 624,000 to 513,000.

Boosting your lead in registered voters from 12,000 to 111,000 is a great organizational achievement, but the effort was greatly aided by the third reason for Nevada's Democratic trend: the state's sudden economic collapse. Nevada's new Hispanic and Filipino voters, many dependent on the construction and casino industries, found themselves laid off and their subprime mortgages underwater. The Obama campaign was instrumental in getting more than half of the state's voters to cast their ballots early. Obama won 76% of the Hispanic vote (15% of the electorate), 94% of the African-American vote, and lost the white vote by only 51%-47%. Voters younger than 30 cast 67% of their ballots for Obama, and voters 30 to 44 were almost equally supportive, 60%. Voters in union households, nearly a quarter of the electorate, backed him 62%. Obama carried Las Vegas' Clark County by a solid 59%-40% and also won Reno's Washoe County 55%-43%, a real feat considering it had voted Republican for years. John McCain carried the cow counties 58%-38%, but that did not even make it close statewide. Obama carried this heretofore marginal state by an impressive 55%-43%.

Congressional districting

112th Congress Lineup		
1 D	1 R	1 V
111th Congress Lineup		
2 D	1 R	

Nevada gained a second congressional district in the 1980 census, a third district in the 2000 census, and a fourth district in the 2010 census.

After the 2000 census, control of redistricting split between a Republican governor and state Senate and a Democratic Assembly. Clark County, with 69% of the population, was entitled to two of the seats and a small part of the third. In a 2001 special legislative session, agreement was reached on a plan: The inner part of Las Vegas would make up a Democratic 1st District; the 2nd District would comprise all the remaining counties, plus some of outer Clark County, and would be solidly Republican; and the 3rd District would be the outer Las Vegas area, which was just about evenly divided between the two parties. The 3rd proved to be a classic marginal district, won by Republican Jon Porter in 2002, 2004, and 2006, by Democrat Dina Titus in 2008, and by Republican Joe Heck in 2010. By 2010, it was also one of the highest population districts in the nation.

For 2012, control of redistricting is split between Republican Gov. Sandoval and Democratic majorities in both houses of the legislature. One likely response is to maintain the staunchly Democratic 1st and Republican 2nd districts, with minor changes to meet the population standards, and to divide the now huge 3rd District roughly into two new seats. The interest of Republicans, to give Heck a safer seat, and of Democrats, to create a new 4th District more Democratic than the current 3rd, coincide, and so the net result may be a one-seat gain for Democrats. Complicating the issue is the claim by Hispanic organizations for a Hispanic-dominated seat. Latinos are concentrated in the northeast quadrant of metro Las Vegas, but are also widely dispersed in the metro area, and so a Hispanic-majority district would be hard to draw.

Governor

Brian Sandoval (R)

Elected 2010, term expires Jan. 2015, 1st term; b. Aug. 5, 1963, Redding, CA; home, Reno; U. of NV, Reno, B.A. 1986; OH St. U., J.D. 1989; Catholic; married (Kathleen); 3 children.

Elected Office: NV Assembly, 1994-98; Atty. gen., 2002-05.

Professional Career: NV Gaming Commission, 1998-2001; Tahoe Regional Planning Authority, 1998-2001; Judge, U.S. District Court, 2005-09.

Office: 101 North Carson Street, 89701, 775-684-5670; Fax: 775-684-5683; Web site: nv.gov/govsandoval.aspx.

Election Results

2010 general	Brian Sandoval (R)	382,350	(53%)
	Rory Reid (D)	298,171	(42%)
2010 primary	Brian Sandoval (R)	97,201	(56%)
	Jim Gibbons (R)	47,616	(27%)
	Michael Montandon (R)	22,003	(13%)

Republican Brian Sandoval was elected governor of Nevada in 2010, becoming the first Latino to do so. Telegenic and handsome, Sandoval (*SAN-duh-vall*) has been heralded as a trailblazer in Republican circles, having previously been the first Hispanic elected to statewide office as attorney general and the first Hispanic to take the bench as a U.S. District Court judge.

Sandoval was born in Redding, Calif., but his family moved to Fallon, Nev., when he was five, and he grew up in Sparks, just east of Reno. His mother worked as a legal secretary for the U.S. Attorney and for a magistrate judge, and as a teenager, Sandoval had a job at the cafeteria at Reno's federal courthouse. He attended the University of Nevada-Reno and Ohio State University's law school, and then went into private practice. After five years, he ran for a seat in the state Assembly and won. He served two terms, developing a reputation as a moderate. He left office to take over the gaming commission, a powerful post that U.S. Senate Majority Leader Harry Reid had once held. In three years in that job, the commission adopted regulations to limit neighborhood gambling, prohibited child-themed slot machines, and enhanced protections for problem gamblers.

Sandoval quit the commission to run for attorney general in 2002. His Democratic opponent, Las Vegas attorney John Hunt, sought to highlight what he called Sandoval's "very, very limited" legal experience and said he "was groomed to be a legislator—he wasn't groomed to be an attorney." Sandoval retorted that he had litigated about 200 cases. Even though two former Democratic attorneys general formally backed Hunt, they gave Sandoval high marks, and he won with ease, 59%-34%. In the job, he was thrust into the ongoing legal fight over storing nuclear waste from commercial power plants at Yucca Mountain, which was a priority for the Bush administration. He also created the state's first public integrity unit to prosecute corrupt lawmakers. But he became embroiled in a nasty dispute between Republican Gov. Kenny Guinn and the legislature over funding for public schools that led to the governor taking the unprecedented step of filing suit against the lawmakers. The Nevada Supreme Court ruled 6-1 that lawmakers could pass tax increases on a simple majority vote rather than the two-thirds majority required by the legislature. Legal scholars and many Nevada residents blasted the decision, which the state's high court undid several years later.

Just past the midway point in Sandoval's term in office, in 2005, an opening came up on the U.S. District Court in Las Vegas. Reid reached out to Sandoval, and he accepted the offer to become, at 42, one of the youngest federal judges in the country. (The arrangement also removed Sandoval from contention as a potential Senate challenger to Reid in 2010.)

Meanwhile, Nevada GOP Gov. Jim Gibbons, a former U.S. House member, found himself caught in a seemingly unending series of scandals. Before his election in 2006, Gibbons had been the subject of a complaint from a casino cocktail waitress alleging that he had propositioned her and then threatened to sexually assault her in a parking garage after an evening of drinking at a restaurant. Gibbons denied her account, contending that he merely caught her when she tripped. Less than one week before Election Day, *The Wall Street Journal* reported that in 2005 Gibbons took a weeklong Caribbean cruise that was paid for by entrepreneur Warren Trepp, a political contributor whom the congressman had helped to win federal software contracts. Still, Gibbons won the gubernatorial election 48% to 44% over Democrat Dina Titus.

Early in 2007, *The Journal* reported that a federal corruption inquiry into his relations with Trepp had been opened. Gibbons publicly speculated that the newspaper had been paid by Democrats to write the damaging stories. In March, *The Journal* reported that his wife, Dawn Gibbons, had been paid $35,000 in consulting fees by a Sparks, Nev., company that her husband was helping win contracts. In April, she filed for divorce and Gibbons sought a court order to remove her from the governor's mansion. Then it was reported that Gibbons and a state tax official had pressured the Elko County assessor to change the designation of a vacant parcel of land he owned from residential to agricultural, reducing his property taxes from about $5,000 to $15. Nevada residents finally had had enough. Gibbons' job ratings tumbled. At the same time, the collapse of the national housing market and the recession did heavy damage to the economy of what had been the nation's fastest-growing state. Developers had greatly overbuilt, and Nevada clocked the nation's highest home foreclosure rate.

By mid-2008, Gibbons had become radioactive, and Republican John McCain's presidential campaign made sure he was not present at its campaign events around the state. By 2009, the state's projected deficit had ballooned to $3 billion. The governor, preoccupied with his various controversies, had a minimal role in the legislative session that year. Nevada lawmakers passed a series of tax increases, over his veto, aimed at stanching the state's fiscal bleeding. He sent them a budget proposing deep cuts in the Nevada higher education budget and was rebuffed.

When Sandoval decided to challenge Gibbons in the GOP primary in 2010, he had no trouble raising money. Sandoval had the backing of powerful lobbyists as well as state Senate Republican leader Bill Raggio and former Gov. Guinn. But neither Gibbons nor the other GOP aspirant, former North Las Vegas Mayor Mike Montandon, would drop out of the race. With their decision, and with tea party activists gaining strength in Nevada, Sandoval began shifting his emphasis from that of a consensus-builder who could work with Democrats to that of a committed conservative. Despite the state's dire fiscal situation, he vowed not to raise taxes. He backed neighboring Arizona's stringent new immigration law that allowed law enforcement officials to detain those suspected of being in the country illegally—a position that angered Hispanics. And he threatened to file suit to stop the new federal health care overhaul. Sandoval, for his part, said he had remained consistent politically. "People have their perceptions of me," he told the *Las Vegas Sun*. "I've always been a fiscal conservative." Sandoval easily walked away from the June 2010 primary, getting 56% to Gibbons' 27% and Montandon's 13%.

That set up a fall matchup with Rory Reid, a Clark County commissioner and the son of Harry Reid. Sandoval continued to court Hispanic voters, taking to the Spanish-language airwaves to remind voters of the historic nature of his candidacy. But he angered that constituency further when he reportedly said off-camera during a Univision interview that his children wouldn't be stopped by Arizona police because they "don't look Hispanic." He said he didn't recall making the remark, but apologized anyway for it.

But he continued to hold the upper hand against Reid, whose father was locked in an agonizingly close race with tea party favorite Sharron Angle that year. The younger Reid touted his detailed economic plan, which included making Nevada the only energy-independent state, and promised to cut the number of state agencies from 26 to 16. Sandoval, meanwhile, promised to maintain Nevada's low-tax climate, to add as much as $2 million in state spending on economic development, and to privatize some state services. He steered clear of divisive issues such as immigration. Sandoval won a comfortable 54%-42% victory, dominating rural counties while topping his opponent by 7,000 votes on his home turf in Clark County. Taking office, he stuck to themes of "opportunity" and "optimism" in his inaugural address while warning of difficulty ahead. "This will not be easy," he said. "I find no satisfaction in the difficult decisions we must soon make."

Senior Senator

Harry Reid (D)

Elected 1986, term expires 2016, 5th term; b. Dec. 2, 1939, Searchlight; home, Searchlight; S. UT St. Col., A.S. 1959, UT St. U., B.S. 1961, George Washington U., J.D. 1964, U. of NV, 1969-70; Mormon; married (Landra); 5 children.

Elected Office: NV Assembly, 1968–70; NV lt. gov., 1970–74; U.S. House of Reps., 1982–86.

Professional Career: Practicing atty., 1969–82; Henderson City atty., 1964–66; Chmn., NV Gaming Comm., 1977–81.

DC Office: 522 HSOB, 20510, 202-224-3542; Fax: 202-224-7327; Web site: reid.senate.gov.

State Offices: Carson City, 775-882-7343; Las Vegas, 702-388-5020; Reno, 775-686-5750.

Group Ratings

	ACLU	ACU	ADA	CFG	AFS	FRC	LCV	ITIC	NTU	COC
2010	100	0	75	0	92	4	100	67	8	18
2009	–	8	95	3	100	–	100	–	6	43

National Journal Ratings

	2010 LIB — 2010 CONS		2009 LIB — 2009 CONS	
Economic	88% —	0%	88% —	0%
Social	65% —	0%	62% —	37%
Foreign	47% —	0%	55% —	0%
Composite	83% —	17%	78% —	22%

Key Votes of the 111th Congress

1. Overturn Ledbetter	Y	5. Pass health care bill	Y	9. Ratify New START	Y
2. Pass $787 billion stimulus	Y	6. Regulate financial firms	Y	10. Confirm Elena Kagan	Y
3. Repeal DC gun laws	Y	7. Pass tax cuts for some	Y	11. Stop EPA climate regs	N
4. Confirm Sonia Sotomayor	Y	8. Legalize immigrants' kids	Y	12. Repeal don't ask, tell	Y

Election Results

2010 general	Harry Reid (D) 362,785	(50%)	($24,815,104)
	Sharron Angle (R)...321,361	(45%)	($28,162,049)
2010 primary	Harry Reid (D) 87,366	(72%)	
	Alex Miller (D) 9,715	(8%)	

Prior Winning Percentages: 2004 (61%); 1998 (48%); 1992 (51%); 1986 (50%); House: 1984 (56%); 1982 (58%)

Democrat Harry Reid is the Senate majority leader and one of Washington's most accomplished dealmakers, with a record of legislative successes that reflects an astute knowledge of Senate procedure and the psychology of his colleagues. At the same time, though, his lack of political polish and occasionally brusque manner have made him unpopular at home and have contributed to some torturous re-election races, including one in 2010.

Reid was first elected to the Senate in 1986, and before that, he served seven terms in the U.S. House. Reid grew up in Searchlight, Nev., in the scorching desert south of Las Vegas. It was a hard life. His father, a hard-rock miner, was an alcoholic who killed himself at age 58. His mother did laundry for a nearby bordello to keep the family afloat. Reid grew up in a small house without indoor plumbing, and hitchhiked 40 miles to high school in Henderson, where his civics teacher and boxing coach, Mike O'Callaghan, became his political mentor. As a young man, Reid was a middleweight boxer of some local renown, but he aspired to better himself through education. Henderson businessmen helped him pay for college, and he graduated from Southern Utah State, where he and his wife became Mormons. To put himself through law school at George Washington University in Washington, D.C., he worked nights as a Capitol Police officer. He likes to say, "I would rather dance than fight, but I know how to fight." He returned to Henderson to practice law.

At age 28, Reid was elected to the Nevada Assembly. In 1970, his mentor O'Callaghan was elected governor and Reid, running separately, was elected lieutenant governor. In 1974, Reid came within 624 votes of beating Republican Paul Laxalt in the race for senator, and two years later, he ran for mayor of Las Vegas and lost that election too. O'Callaghan named him to head the Nevada Gaming Commission from 1977 to 1981, a sensitive post overseeing the state's top industry at a time when it was controlled by organized crime. Reid later recounted that his life was threatened and his car wired with a bomb. In 1982, when Nevada got two U.S. House seats for the first time and Rep. Jim Santini ran for the Senate, Reid ran in the Las Vegas-based 1st District and won. As Reid was completing his second term in the House, Laxalt retired and Reid tried for the Senate seat again. His opponent turned out to be Santini, who had switched parties at the last minute and ran as a Republican. Reid won 50%-45%.

Over the years, Reid has had a more moderate voting record than many Senate Democrats. He voted for banning partial-birth abortions and against resolutions endorsing *Roe v. Wade,* the Supreme Court ruling legalizing abortion. He co-sponsored the constitutional amendment to outlaw flag-burning. Reid was one of the few Senate Democrats to vote for the Persian Gulf War resolution in 1991, and he voted for the Iraq war resolution in 2002. He has consistently opposed environmental groups on mining issues and blocked attempts to impose higher fees on hard-rock miners. He has opposed most gun-control measures. Reid has steered counter-terrorism money to Nevada and has worked to transform the old Nevada nuclear test site, with its hundreds of underground tunnels, into a $250 million center for training first responders to confront acts of terrorism. He has been a strong supporter of the gambling industry. When President Bill Clinton proposed a 4% gambling tax, Reid vowed, "I will become the most negative, the most irresponsible, the most obnoxious person of anyone in the Senate."

For two decades, a major issue in Nevada has been the proposed nuclear waste repository at Yucca Mountain. In the late 1980s, the federal government named the site as the top candidate for a permanent repository for waste from nuclear reactors that had been piling up at temporary sites in 39 states. Reid has opposed the repository at Yucca Mountain with every parliamentary and political tool at his command while senators from states with temporary sites have pressed hard for it. Clinton carried Nevada by narrow margins in 1992 and 1996 largely because he promised to veto the establishment of even a temporary site at Yucca Mountain. So Reid's task was to assemble sufficient votes to prevent an override of Clinton's veto, which he did consistently through 2000. In 2002, President George W. Bush designated Yucca Mountain as the permanent site. The law provided for a veto by the governor, which could be overridden by majorities in both chambers of Congress. In April 2002, Republican Gov. Kenny Guinn issued his veto. In May 2002, the House cast a large majority for Yucca Mountain. Reid lobbied furiously for Democratic votes, while GOP Sen. John Ensign lobbied for Republican votes. Altogether, he got 34 Democrats and independent James Jeffords to vote his way. With the Bush administration lobbying in the other direction, Ensign could get only two other Republicans. The site was approved, 60-39.

But for Reid, the fight was not over. Lawsuits were filed against the plan, and as the chairman of the Appropriations subcommittee with jurisdiction over the Energy Department, Reid blocked funding for the repository year after year. In November 2004, Reid, now the Senate minority leader, negotiated with the Bush administration over judicial appointments and agreed to approve 175 Bush nominees in return for the appointment of his aide, Gregory Jaczko, to the Nuclear Regulatory Commission, which had to approve the site before it could go forward. He pushed to move up Nevada's presidential primary to January 2008, a move that ended up forcing candidates to take an early stand on waste storage. Then-Democratic candidate Barack Obama obliged in opposing Yucca Mountain and, after taking office, put the repository on hold.

Reid's rise to leader was set in motion when he won the post of minority whip in 1998. For the next six years, he was a constant presence on the floor, advancing his party's causes and maintaining civil relations with GOP leaders. He played a key role in persuading Vermont's Sen. Jeffords to leave the Republican Party in May 2001 and become an independent who caucused with the Democrats; that move effectively put the Democrats in the majority. When Republicans held all-night sessions in November 2003 to protest Democratic filibusters of nominees for Appellate Court judgeships, Reid retaliated by speaking for nine hours, reading from his book about his upbringing in Searchlight. Later, in May 2005, he acquiesced to the agreement of the bipartisan "Gang of 14" to allow some of the nominees to come to a vote.

In 2004, he campaigned for fellow Democrats and contributed generously to their political treasuries. When Democratic Leader Tom Daschle of South Dakota lost his seat in a stunning upset that year, Reid had already lined up the votes he needed to be elected minority leader. (Republicans were back in control of the majority.) Sen. Christopher Dodd of Connecticut was interested in the post but declined to run. Reid was not the Senate's best orator and not much of a policy visionary, but his colleagues knew him as a crafty parliamentarian who would be a scrappy and effective defender of their interests. "I know my limitations," said Reid. "I haven't gotten where I am by my good looks, my athletic ability, my great brain, (or) my oratorical skills."

Reid worked deftly behind the scenes, giving up his committee seats to accommodate other Democrats and pledging to rely on committee chairmen on policy. He blocked non-germane amendments from bills, and he bottled up portions of the Bush agenda that Democrats strongly opposed, such as individual retirement accounts in Social Security. But Reid sometimes undercut himself as a leader by resorting to indecorous comments or insults. He once called Bush a "loser" and a "liar," and Federal Reserve Board Chairman Alan Greenspan "a political hack." He was quoted in a book on the 2008 presidential race as saying he believed Obama could win because he was a "light-skinned" African-American "with no Negro dialect, unless he wanted to have one." Reid acknowledged making the remarks and apologized to Obama.

Reid also has been vulnerable on the ethics front, although he has maintained that none of the issues raised against him over the years have had merit. After a 2003 *Los Angeles Times* story pointed out that his son and a son-in-law were lobbying in Washington for Nevada companies, Reid banned relatives from lobbying his office. From 2003 to 2005, Reid accepted free seats at Las Vegas boxing matches from the Nevada Athletic Commission. But the Senate Ethics Committee determined he had violated no rule because the money came from a state agency. In October 2006, it was reported that Reid had not disclosed a transaction on a land deal that netted him more than $1 million in 2004. Reid said that he had purchased the land in 1998 at market price, then sold it to a friend's corporation in 2001 in return for a stake in that corporation. He got his share of the proceeds in 2004, he said, when the property was sold to a shopping center developer.

In 2006, Democrats won the six seats they needed to regain the Senate majority and Reid ascended to majority leader. After the election, Reid deftly juggled committee and leadership posts, giving Connecticut's Joe Lieberman, whose vote would be crucial to keeping the majority, the chairmanship of the Homeland Security and Governmental Affairs Committee, even though he had been re-elected as an independent. On other issues, Reid was often stymied by the Senate Republicans' constant resort to filibusters. His efforts to place limitations on Bush's handling of the Iraq war mostly fell short of the 60 votes required to shut off debate. And there seemed to be no preventing conservative Oklahoman Tom Coburn from blocking even seemingly acceptable bills from the Senate floor. The contrast to the more lockstep House under Speaker Nancy Pelosi of California was a source of some embarrassment for Senate Democrats.

Reid has sometimes misread the sentiments of his caucus. In April 2009, he smoothed the way for Republican Arlen Specter of Pennsylvania to switch parties, bringing the Democrats within one vote of a filibuster-proof, 60-vote majority. As part of the deal with Reid, Specter said, he would keep his seniority, putting him in line for a subcommittee or full committee chairmanship. But in an embarrassing rebuke to Reid, rank-and-file Senate Democrats refused to go along and stripped Specter of his seniority on committees.

Despite these setbacks, the electoral success of Senate candidates in 2006 and 2008 engendered enormous goodwill for Reid. With a Democratic majority in Congress, and the election of a Democratic president in 2008, he slipped into the role most comfortable for him, that of behind-the-scenes dealmaker. Reid won bipartisan support for tough, new ethics and lobbying rules and expansion of the student loan program. In early 2009, he guided the new administration's $787 billion economic stimulus bill to passage. (The bill happened to include funding for a high-speed bullet train between Las Vegas and Anaheim, Calif., that Reid has championed.) When the $700 billion bailout for the financial industry was in trouble in the House, Reid made several changes to the Senate bill to attract additional votes, including a tweak to the tax code to protect middle-income taxpayers from the alternative minimum tax. That and other modifications were popular with lawmakers in both parties in the House, and the bill ultimately passed. The Senate also approved new financial regulations for Wall Street, credit card reform, and a bill to let the Food and Drug Administration regulate tobacco products. Senators also easily confirmed Obama's two Supreme Court nominees, Sonia Sotomayor and Elena Kagan.

The downside for Reid of Obama's rise to power was the expectation that he would carry water for the new administration even when its policies hurt him politically in his conservative-tilting state. The president's proposed overhaul of the nation's health care delivery system drove that point home like no other. When the responsible Senate committees could not come up with a bill that could attract the requisite 60 votes to deter a Republican filibuster by late in 2009, Reid had to take over or watch Obama's centerpiece domestic initiative die on his watch. (The House had already passed a health care bill.) The legislation had to cover a major share of the nation's uninsured consumers of medical care while adhering to a cost cap of under $900 billion over 10 years. Reid had to navigate the bill around obstacles from the most liberal and most conservative members of his caucus while being unable to count on a single vote from the Senate's 40 Republicans. That meant he needed all 60 Democrats, including two independents who caucused with the Democrats, to pass the bill. In one instance, he agreed to Nebraska Sen. Ben Nelson's insistence that the legislation bar any form of federal support for abortions, a concession that riled liberals. Just before the year ended, Reid was able to pass a health care bill, a great victory for him on the national stage, but a handicap for him at home, where the legislation was far from popular.

Nevada voters are oddly unforgiving when it comes to Reid, given his long tenure in public office. "He's just not a beloved politician," said Eric Herzik, a University of Nevada (Reno) political scientist. "Reid is tough and a backroom politician, which is why a lot of people don't like him. They call him 'Slick Harry' or 'Dirty Harry.' But at the end of the day, they may acknowledge that it might actually benefit Nevada."

Reid has faced two serious challenges to his Senate seat. The first was in 1998, when Republican Rep. John Ensign ran a well-financed campaign against him. Both Reid and Ensign, whose stepfather was head of the Mandalay Resort Group, one of the big Las Vegas casino operations, raised large amounts of money from the gambling industry. Reid spent $4.9 million and Ensign $3.5 million. After a nasty campaign, Reid prevailed by just 428 votes. Two years later, Ensign was elected to Nevada's other Senate seat. Despite the bitterness of the 1998 campaign, Reid and Ensign have worked together on many home-state projects and refrained from public criticism of each other.

Then in the 2010 election, Republicans set out to topple Reid in the same way that Daschle was defeated in 2004 at the pinnacle of his power. He started the race with polls showing him trailing would-be GOP challengers. Yet Republicans had their own problems, including a crowded primary field. Casino executive and former state Sen. Sue Lowden was the putative front-runner, but she committed a series of embarrassing gaffes, including suggesting that people could use chickens as barter to pay their medical bills. She ended up with 26% of the primary vote; former college basketball star and businessman Danny Tarkanian drew 23%. The winner, with 40%, was Sharron Angle, a former state Assembly member and co-founder of a Christian grade school. She ran as a much more conservative alternative to Lowden and Tarkanian, and as a result drew spirited tea party support along with the endorsement of former Alaska Gov. Sarah Palin.

The result gave Reid the matchup he wanted; Lowden had been considered the much stronger general election adversary. He wasted no time in attacking his GOP opponent as being far outside the political mainstream. When a video surfaced of Angle belittling mandates for the treatment of autism, Reid issued six news releases on the matter within a few days, drawing considerable national media coverage. At times, the Reid campaign didn't have to do a thing to raise negative impressions of Angle, because she did it on her own. At a political rally in October, she appeared to agree with a spectator that Dearborn, Mich., had been taken over by its large Arab and Muslim population. "It seems to me there is something fundamentally wrong with allowing a foreign system of law to even take hold in any municipality or government situation in our United States," Angle said. In June, *The Washington Post* reported that Angle once told a radio interviewer: "If this Congress keeps going the way it is, people are really looking toward those Second Amendment remedies and saying, 'My goodness, what can we do to turn this country around?'"

Over the summer, Reid opened up a lead in the polls that was outside the statistical margin of error. But Angle fought back, keeping the race close. She took advantage of widespread anti-government sentiment to outline her conservative philosophy, which called for Washington to be responsible for only those powers enumerated in the Constitution, with the rest turned over to the states or eliminated outright. She also said she backed cutting many domestic programs by 5% annually over the next five years. The relentless mudslinging tarnished both candidates. In a Mason-Dixon poll in August, 52% had a negative opinion of Reid, and Angle's unfavorable rating was 43%.

Yet Reid did not give up easily. He raised $24.8 million, within range of Angle's $28.3 million. (Only the Connecticut Senate race was more expensive in 2010.) He mobilized Hispanics and other parts of the state's Democratic base, including the powerful culinary workers' union. He defeated Angle 50%-45%, a victory made all the more impressive by the fact that an astonishingly large 2.25% of votes were cast for "none of the above." Also impressive was that his triumph came even though his son Rory Reid, a Clark County commissioner, was on the ballot for governor and lost to Republican Brian Sandoval. Angle captured all but one of the state's rural counties, but Reid won where it mattered—he beat Angle 57%-43% in Clark County and 53%-47% in Washoe County.

As if to vindicate his triumph in what was an otherwise brutal year for Democrats, Reid was given ample opportunity to demonstrate his deal-making skills in the lame-duck session of Congress following the election. He played a key role in passing an economic stimulus bill that renewed expiring tax cuts enacted under Bush; a repeal of the military's "don't ask, don't tell" policy barring openly gay service members; and ratification of the New START nuclear arms treaty with Russia. Even Republicans grudgingly acknowledged his legislative acumen. "I don't have people saying, 'he's the greatest speaker,' 'he's handsome,' 'he's a man about town,'" Reid told *The New York Times*. "But I don't really care. I feel very comfortable with my place in history."

Junior Senator

Dean Heller (R)

Appointed May 2011, term expires 2012, 1st term; b. May 10, 1960, Castro Valley, CA; home, Carson City; U. of S. CA, B.A. 1985; Mormon; married (Lynne); 4 children.

Elected Office: NV Assembly, 1990-94, NV sec. of state, 1994-2006; U.S. House, 2007-2011

Professional Career: Stockbroker, 1983-88; Chief deputy state treas., 1988-90; Public funds rep., Bank of America, 1990-95.

DC Office: 125 CHOB, 20515, 202-225-6155; Fax: 202-225-5679; Web site: heller.house.gov.

State Offices: Elko, 775-777-7920; Las Vegas, 702-255-1651; Reno, 775-686-5760.

Committees: *Aging (Special). Commerce, Science & Transportation:* Aviation Operations, Safety & Security; Communications, Technology & the Internet; Competitiveness, Innovation & Export Promotion; Consumer Protection, Product Safety & Insurance; Oceans, Atmosphere, Fisheries & Coast Guard; Science & Space; Surface Transportation & Merchant Marine Infrastructure, Safety & Security. *Energy & Natural Resources:* National Parks; Public Lands & Forests; Water & Power.

Group Ratings (House)

	ACLU	ACU	ADA	CFG	AFS	FRC	LCV	ITIC	NTU	COC
2010	19	88	10	94	13	93	10	33	84	100
2009	–	92	5	77	22	–	7	–	80	87

National Journal Ratings (House)

	2010 LIB	—	2010 CONS	2009 LIB	—	2009 CONS
Economic	26%	—	74%	26%	—	74%
Social	18%	—	77%	24%	—	73%
Foreign	0%	—	88%	0%	—	75%
Composite	18%	—	83%	21%	—	79%

Key Votes of the 111th Congress (House)

1. Overturn Ledbetter	N	5. Bar federal abortion funds	Y
2. Pass $820 billion stimulus	N	6. Pass health care bill	N
3. Let guns in national parks	Y	7. Regulate financial firms	N
4. Pass cap-and-trade	N	8. Pass tax cuts for some	N

9. Stop detainee transfers	Y
10. Legalize immigrants' kids	N
11. Repeal don't ask, tell	N
12. Limit campaign funds	N

Prior Winning Percentages: House: 2010 (63%); 2008 (52%); 2006 (50%)

Republican Dean Heller was appointed to the Senate in May 2011. GOP Gov. Brian Sandoval chose Heller to replace Republican Sen. John Ensign after Ensign resigned in advance of a harshly critical Senate Ethics Committee report on his extramarital affair with the wife of a former aide and allegations of a hush-money scheme. Heller, who was Nevada's 2nd District representative at the time of the appointment, had been planning to run for Ensign's Senate seat in 2012.

Heller was a political fixture in Carson City long before he won his first House contest in 2006. He got a taste of politics during childhood when his newspaper route included deliveries at the state Capitol. He graduated from the University of Southern California in 1985 with a degree in business administration, and then worked as a stockbroker trading on the Pacific Stock Exchange. In 1990, he won the first of two terms in the Nevada House, and in 1994, he was elected to the first of three terms as Nevada secretary of state. During his 12-year tenure, Heller streamlined the corporation registration process, increasing revenues tenfold. He supported more public access to government records and greater transparency in the state campaign finance system. Nevada was seen as a national model in 2004, when it became the first state to create a paper trail for its electronic voting machines.

Heller decided to make a bid for the U.S. House when five-term Republican Jim Gibbons gave up the 2nd District seat to run for governor. Heller faced competition for the Republican nomination from Assemblywoman Sharron Angle and former Assemblywoman Dawn Gibbons, the outgoing congressman's wife. Heller and Gibbons began with the strongest name recognition, but Gibbons' underfunded candidacy never took off. Angle, a Christian conservative, emerged as a serious primary rival after she picked up the endorsement and financial support of the deep-pocketed Club for Growth, a national anti-tax group. Angle ran as the race's true conservative, while Heller campaigned on his record in state office and called for cuts in taxes and government spending. He won the nomination with 36% of the vote, a 421-vote victory over Angle, who got 35%. Gibbons finished third with 25%. Angle went on to give Senate Majority Leader Harry Reid of Nevada the toughest race of his career in 2010.

Heller entered the general election campaign with a depleted campaign treasury to face Democrat Jill Derby, an 18-year veteran of the Nevada Board of Regents. He ran the race as a referendum on President George W. Bush, emphasizing his support for the Iraq war, for making Bush's tax cuts permanent and for creating private Social Security accounts for young workers. While many Republican candidates elsewhere considered Bush a liability in 2006, the president stumped twice for Heller and helped motivate the traditionally Republican-leaning rural vote. Derby emphasized her rural roots, criticized Heller for his stance on the war and framed the election as a chance for voters to reject Republican control in Washington. Heller defeated her 50%-45%.

In selecting Heller to replace Ensign, Sandoval cited the need for an "experienced voice" in Washington. "Too many important issues face our state and our nation to name a caretaker to this important position," the governor said. Nevada was among the states hardest hit by the 2007-09 recession and in March 2011 had an unemployment rate of 13.2%, the nation's highest.

Heller was given seats on the Energy and Natural Resources Committee as well as the Commerce, Science and Transportation Committee. Ensign had served on the latter. Heller said he would seek to lower rising gasoline prices and undo "heavy-handed regulations" that he said were hurting businesses. "If we are going to encourage economic growth, we need to address climbing gas prices, ensure our transportation needs are met and foster a regulatory climate that does not impede interstate commerce," he said.

In the House, Heller broke with conservatives on some issues, but was generally a reliable Republican vote. He was the chamber's 69th most conservative member in 2010, according to *National Journal's* rankings. He supported nuclear energy on the condition that the radioactive waste would be stored where it was produced, not at the Department of Energy's Yucca Mountain project about 100 miles northwest of Las Vegas. Heller also got into an unusual family squabble in 2008, when he criticized what he called the limited impact of the Republican takeover of the House led by Republican Newt Gingrich in 1994. "They came to change Washington, and Washington changed them," he said, adding that he thought it was time for Republicans to clean house.

But Heller was enough of a loyalist to land a coveted seat on the Ways and Means Committee in the 111th Congress (2009-10). He proposed a series of unsuccessful amendments to the health care overhaul, including one requiring members of Congress to take part in a proposed government-run "public option" and another forgiving education loans for doctors and nurses who agree to work in underserved areas. He also had no luck adding a provision to a small business tax bill in March 2010 to allow capital gains exclusion of up to $50,000 for non-primary residences in one of the nation's top 200 high foreclosure areas. Heller teamed with Arizona Democrat Gabrielle Giffords to get a bill through the House in September 2010 to toughen penalties on drug smugglers using ultralight planes. He also backed a bill that year to extend unemployment benefits, but irked liberals when he posed the question, "Is the government now creating hobos?"

Derby and the Democrats tried again for the seat in 2008, but Heller took a comfortable lead in early polls and won the rematch, 52% to 41%. He disappointed Republicans in 2009 when he declined to challenge Reid the following year; he won re-election 63%-33% over Democrat Nancy Price.

In early 2011, Heller was being mentioned as a possible candidate for Ensign's seat. Once seen as a rising star, Ensign's political career had begun to unravel in June 2009, when he publicly admitted to having an extramarital affair with the wife of his top Senate aide. The day after his admission, Ensign resigned his leadership post but said he would remain in the Senate. The following month, Ensign admitted that his parents had paid the woman and former aide $96,000, but he maintained that the money was a gift and not intended to buy her silence. His troubles deepened in October 2009 with a story in *The New York Times* that said Ensign had helped former aide Doug Hampton, his mistress' husband, get a lobbying job and then assisted Hampton in securing clients. E-mail messages that publicly surfaced in March 2010 revealed that Ensign urged a Las Vegas development firm to hire Hampton after the company had approached the senator for help on energy projects.

It initially appeared Ensign might seek to follow the example of Louisiana GOP Sen. David Vitter, who rebounded from an embarrassing prostitution sex scandal to win re-election in 2010. Vitter argued to voters that for all of his personal failings, Democrats could do far less damage with him in office. But in the early months of 2011, Ensign's poll numbers plummeted, with Heller outdistancing him 53%-38% in a potential matchup. The Ethics Committee announced the appointment of a special counsel, a sign that its inquiry was becoming serious. And during a February town hall meeting in Las Vegas, Ensign was asked whether he had "repented to God for your affair"—an ominous indication of questions likely to surface in a re-election campaign.

He announced in March that he would not seek another term, and then a month later said he would resign immediately. The Ethics Committee voted unanimously in May to refer the case to the U.S. Justice Department and the Federal Election Commission to examine whether any laws were broken. Ethics Chairman Barbara Boxer, D-Calif., said that if Ensign had not resigned, the special counsel was prepared to recommend that senators vote on whether to expel him. When Ensign announced his departure, Heller jumped into the race for a successor and immediately was considered the front-runner.

With his subsequent appointment to the Senate, Heller enjoyed some of the advantages of incumbency, such as the ability to communicate with constituents from all parts of the state. He also was likely to get more financial help from national Republicans than if he had remained in the House. But the prospects of Heller retaining the seat in 2012 were by no means a given. Two Democrats—Rep. Shelley Berkley and wealthy businessman Byron Georgiou—were also interested in running, and both were able to raise the money to compete against Heller. Reid also could be counted on to pull out all the stops to try to make the seat a Democratic pickup, drawing from the political network that enabled him to win a brutal re-election battle against Angle in 2010. And because Nevada is a competitive state in presidential politics, President Barack Obama is likely to spend plenty of time there during his 2012 re-election campaign.

FIRST DISTRICT

Shelley Berkley (D)

Elected 1998, 7th term; b. Jan. 20, 1951, Manhattan, NY; home, Las Vegas; UNLV., B.A. 1972; U. of San Diego, J.D. 1976; Jewish; married (Larry Lehrner); 4 children.

Elected Office: NV Assembly, 1982-84; Regent, U. Commun. Col. System of NV, 1990-98.

Professional Career: Cnsl., SW Gas Corp., 1977-82; VP, Sands Hotel, 1989-98; Chair, NV Hotel & Motel Assn., 1994.

DC Office: 405 CHOB, 20515, 202-225-5965; Fax: 202-225-3119; Web site: berkley.house.gov.

State Offices: Las Vegas, 702-220-9823.

Committees: *Ways & Means:* Select Revenue Measures; Social Security.

Group Ratings

	ACLU	ACU	ADA	CFG	AFS	FRC	LCV	ITIC	NTU	COC
2010	88	0	85	5	100	0	90	100	7	38
2009	–	0	100	4	100	–	93	–	4	40

National Journal Ratings

	2010 LIB	—	2010 CONS	2009 LIB	—	2009 CONS
Economic	62%	—	38%	68%	—	30%
Social	71%	—	25%	59%	—	37%
Foreign	65%	—	35%	87%	—	13%
Composite	67%	—	33%	72%	—	28%

Key Votes of the 111th Congress

1. Overturn Ledbetter	Y	5. Bar federal abortion funds	N	9. Stop detainee transfers	Y
2. Pass $820 billion stimulus	Y	6. Pass health care bill	Y	10. Legalize immigrants' kids	Y
3. Let guns in national parks	Y	7. Regulate financial firms	Y	11. Repeal don't ask, tell	Y
4. Pass cap-and-trade	Y	8. Pass tax cuts for some	Y	12. Limit campaign funds	Y

Election Results

2010 general	Shelley Berkley (D)	103,246	(62%)	($2,232,438)
	Kenneth Wegner (R)	58,995	(35%)	($72,946)
2010 primary	Shelley Berkley (D)	unopposed		

Prior Winning Percentages: 2008 (68%), 2006 (65%), 2004 (66%), 2002 (54%), 2000 (52%), 1998 (49%)

Population		Race/Ethnicity		Work	
Pop. 2010:	820,134	White:	39.4%	Private:	85.1%
Change since 2000:	Up 23.1%	Black:	13.3%	Government:	10.9%
Urban:	99.9%	Hispanic:	37.2%	Self-employed:	3.9%
Rural:	0.1%	Asian:	5.9%	Blue collar:	23.1%
Area size:	177 sq. mi.	Native Am.:	0.4%	White collar:	46.6%
		Hawaiian:	0.6%	Khaki collar:	0.4%
Age		Two+ races:	3.0%	Other:	29.9%
Median age:	32.7 yrs.				
More than 65 yrs:	9.4%	*Ancestry*		Median income:	$49,495
Less than 18 yrs:	28.5%	German	8.5%	Median Home Value:	$236,000
		Irish	6.5%		
Education		English	5.1%	**Military Veterans**	
H.S. grad:	77.2%			% of Pop:	10.5%
College grad:	17.2%				
Grad degree:	5.6%				

Las Vegas

Las Vegas, that garish and improbable city, had a fittingly colorful beginning. It began as a Paiute Indian settlement that in the late 1700s served as a watering stop for Spanish priests making the 1,200-mile trek between New Mexico and California. By the 1800s, the Old Spanish Trail, as it came to be known, was used by horse and mule smugglers, by white explorers like John Fremont, and by Mormon emigrants heading west. Las Vegas was still a small crossroads

2008 Presidential Vote		
Barack Obama (D)	158,367	(64%)
John McCain (R)	85,193	(34%)
2004 Presidential Vote		
John Kerry (D)	121,453	(57%)
George Bush (R)	89,800	(42%)
Cook Partisan Voting Index:	D+10	

when Nevada, its mining industry a shambles, legalized gambling in the 1930s. The WPA Guide to Nevada, published in 1940 when the city had 10,000 people, describes a prim Las Vegas: "Relatively little emphasis is placed on the gambling clubs and divorce facilities—though they are attractions to many visitors—and much effort is being made to build up cultural attractions."

All that changed big-time after World War II, when gangster Bugsy Siegel built the Flamingo hotel and casino on what became the Strip south of the city limits. Pseudo-romantic architectural themes became the order of the day (flamingos are found in the waters of Florida, not in the deserts of Nevada), and one casino followed another. Organized crime provided much of the money and muscle for Las Vegas, and investment capital came from Teamsters pension funds. In the late 1960s, eccentric billionaire Howard Hughes moved into the Desert Inn, bought most of the casinos and hired Mormons to run them. After Hughes abruptly left town, most of his hotels eventually were torn down, and other operators built casinos like Caesars Palace, Circus Circus, the Mirage, and Excalibur, the lavish Bellagio, and the Venetian. In the 1970s, the casinos were the haven of flashy high rollers, of Frank Sinatra and girl shows. In the 1990s, diversification became the buzzword. Las Vegas began to produce more family-oriented entertainment, shopping, and even high art, with the Bellagio's museum-quality art collection on view. Las Vegas also built the biggest convention center in the country. But the city has not neglected its core clientele: people who fly in from elsewhere to be entertained, and to be, for a weekend, maybe even a little naughty. "What happens in Vegas stays in Vegas," is how the current saying goes.

The scent of the underworld has not entirely disappeared. The flashy Oscar Goldman, a former mob lawyer, was elected mayor and actively promoted the city. Barred from seeking a fourth term, Goldman announced in February 2011 that his wife, Carolyn, would run to succeed him; she promised to continue his habit of taking scantily clad showgirls along to promotional events. Because of the city's dependence on leisure-time spending, the economic crisis hit hard here in 2008 and persisted long after other areas recovered, with gambling down, joblessness up, and many new homes unsold. The unemployment level climbed above 14% in 2010, higher than in any other metropolitan area. In the third quarter of 2010, homes on average were worth less than half their peak 2006 levels. The Brookings Institution, in surveying the world's 150 largest metropolitan economies coping with the recession in November 2010, ranked Las Vegas 146th. Only Dublin, Dubai, Barcelona, and Thessaloniki, Greece, were worse.

The 1st Congressional District of Nevada consists of the inner core of Las Vegas that visitors are most likely to see. They cross into it as soon as they drive their rental cars out of the lot at McCarran International Airport. On the three-mile Strip, you can find 14 of the nation's 15 largest hotels, each with thousands of rooms. North of Sahara Avenue, Las Vegas Boulevard enters the city of Las Vegas, the older and less glamorous part of town. The district continues north for another dozen miles through the housing developments and scrubland along U.S. 95 and Interstate 15, to include the sizable Hispanic and black communities of North Las Vegas. The 1st District is also home to the University of Nevada-Las Vegas and includes the Clark County Government Center, a circular sandstone complex with Indian-inspired architecture. The district has a high percentage of union members, and more than 80,000 Jewish-Americans live in the area, supporting 18 synagogues and a kosher supermarket. Overall, this is a safely Democratic district.

Shelley Berkley (D)

The congresswoman from the 1st District is Shelley Berkley, a Democrat first elected in 1998. Berkley was born on the Lower East Side of New York and moved to Las Vegas as a child. "I am not a politician who happens to be Jewish. I am a Jew who happens to be in politics," she likes to say. Her parents emigrated from Eastern Europe after World War II. Her mother, an artist, was held in Auschwitz and painted watercolors of Gypsies and other prisoners for Nazi doctor Josef Mengele. Her work saved her from extermination, and she later sought the return of her portraits, which were displayed at the Auschwitz museum in Poland. Berkley's father worked at the Sands and rose to maitre d'. In college, Berkley waited tables and was a keno runner. She was the student body president at the University of Nevada, and then went to law school. She chaired the Nevada Hotel and Motel Association, was government and legal affairs vice president at the Sands and the in-house counsel at Southwest Gas. She was elected to one term in the state House.

After 1st District Rep. John Ensign, a Republican, decided to run for the Senate in the 1998 election, Berkley made a bid for the House seat. Brassy and effusive, she lacked a serious Republican opponent for several weeks and seemed headed for an easy election. But 15 minutes before the filing deadline, Republican Judge Donald Chairez resigned his post to run for the seat. Then came a bombshell that threatened to unravel her campaign. The *Las Vegas Review-Journal* reported the existence of taped 1997 telephone conversations and of a memo in which Berkley seemed to advise Sands owner Sheldon Adelson to make campaign contributions to local judges and to grant concessions to Clark County commissioners as a way of improving chances for approval of his Venetian hotel. Berkley publicly apologized. The Clark County district attorney found no cause for prosecution. But Chairez made his slogan: "Fairness, not favors." With strong support from the gambling industry, Berkley outspent Chairez $1.2 million to $554,000 and won only narrowly, 49%-46%.

In the House, Berkley's voting record has been moderate, especially on foreign issues, but she became a much more loyal Democrat in the years in which her party controlled the House. She voted for the health care overhaul in 2009 and the final version in 2010, although she expressed reservations. Berkley keeps a close watch on the interests of the gambling industry. She led opposition in the House to a proposal by the National Collegiate Athletic Association to bar Nevada casinos from accepting bets on college sports, and in 2009, supported Massachusetts Democrat Barney Frank's bill creating an exemption to a ban on Internet gambling for licensed and regulated businesses. With other Nevada officials, she fought the plan to store nuclear waste at Yucca Mountain.

When Democrats took majority control in the 110th Congress (2007-08), she won a seat on the powerful Ways and Means Committee, where she has fought proposals to tax Internet gambling, saying those decisions should be left to the states. She also pushed for an extension of tax credits for investments in renewable energy sources. She voted against the initial version of the Troubled Assets Relief Fund for the financial services industry in 2008, but supported the second after local business leaders persuaded her. In 2010, she crossed party lines to support a defeated GOP amendment to a $15 billion jobs bill to index individual tax rates to reflect increases in federal spending as well as inflation. Well-known for her outsize personality and candidness, Berkley told colleagues at a 2010 hearing on Ways and Means on bolstering the economy: "What would help me a lot is if you came to Vegas and played and drank like crazy."

Berkley has a strong interest in Middle East affairs and is an advocate for Israel. She forcefully backed President George W. Bush's use of force in Iraq in 2002 and 2003, but later said that she was misled by phony intelligence. She also joined Northeastern Democrats in 2010 urging members to oppose the Obama administration's planned $60 billion arms deal with Saudi Arabia, arguing that the Saudis have been too hostile to Israel. Berkley was also the chief sponsor of a 2009 resolution that pledged an "unwavering commitment" to the Taiwan Relations Act requiring the United States to maintain the capability to defend the island if China attacks.

Berkley initially faced tough re-election contests. In 2000, Republican state Sen. Jon Porter revived the 1998 Sands hotel controversy, but Berkley won 52%-44%. In 2002, Berkley faced Las

Vegas City Council member Lynette Boggs-McDonald, a Republican, but redistricting had removed many suburban precincts favorable to the GOP, and Berkley won with 54%. Since then, she has faced only weak opposition.

SECOND DISTRICT
Vacant

Election Results

2010 general	Dean Heller (R)...169,458	(63%)	($1,487,453)
	Nancy Price (D)..87,421	(33%)	($7,446)
	Russell Best (AMI)..10,829	(4%)	
2010 primary	Dean Heller (R)...72,728	(84%)	
	Patrick Colletti (R)..14,162	(16%)	

Prior Winning Percentages: Heller House: 2010 (63%); 2008 (52%); 2006 (50%)

Population		Race/Ethnicity		Work	
Pop. 2010:	836,562	White:	68.2%	Private:	78.0%
Change since 2000:	Up 25.6%	Black:	2.7%	Government:	16.4%
Urban:	78.5%	Hispanic:	20.4%	Self-employed:	5.5%
Rural:	21.5%	Asian:	3.9%	Blue collar:	23.3%
Area size:	105,641 sq. mi.	Native Am.:	1.8%	White collar:	54.5%
		Hawaiian:	0.4%	Khaki collar:	0.4%
Age		Two+ races:	2.4%	Other:	21.8%
Median age:	37.5 yrs.				
More than 65 yrs:	13.3%	*Ancestry*		Median income:	$54,370
Less than 18 yrs:	24.7%	German	13.6%	Median Home Value:	$255,900
		Irish	10.2%		
Education		English	10.2%	**Military Veterans**	
H.S. grad:	84.9%			% of Pop:	13.6%
College grad:	21.9%				
Grad degree:	7.6%				

Reno, Carson City, "Cow Counties"

Outside of metro Las Vegas, huge, empty, and mountainous Nevada has only one sizable population center, a cluster of small cities and towns near the border with California: the casino cities of Reno and Sparks, the small capital of Carson City, the restored Comstock Lode boomtown of Virginia City, and the resort areas that surround (and endanger) the deep, impossibly blue waters of Lake Tahoe. Reno is so remote from Las Vegas that the only practical way to get there is by air;

2008 Presidential Vote
John McCain (R) 167,920   (49%)
Barack Obama (D) 167,831   (49%)

2004 Presidential Vote
George Bush (R) 172,422   (57%)
John Kerry (D) 123,490   (41%)

Cook Partisan Voting Index: R+5

it takes more than nine hours to drive. Ghost towns that once bustled with miners dot the parched, sand-swept deserts, and in some places, the land is distinctly rutted from the wagon trains that crossed more than 100 years ago. Today, Nevada's small towns survive on mining, ranching, and, in some cases, servicing the human sins of greed and lust: Nevada's legal brothels are generally found in the small, desert counties. Another distinction is the Basque influence. Immigrant Basque shepherds once tended their flocks in remote portions of northern Nevada; Basque festivals, social clubs, and restaurants can still be found in Winnemucca, Ely, and Elko.

The military has vast holdings in the Nevada interior: the Fallon Naval Air Station, home to the Navy Fighter Weapons "Top Gun" School, and the 3-million-acre Nellis Air Force Gunnery Range. Also found there is the Energy Department's Nevada Test Site, where more than 800 underground tests of nuclear weapons were conducted, as well as 100 aboveground tests, before 1962. These explosions have left the Rhode Island-sized facility pockmarked with unstable "subsidence craters" as far as the eye can see. Many places in Nevada are dependent on other federal government programs: the Newlands Irrigation Project near Fallon was among the first of its kind, and Nevada's gold-mining operations, booming since 2000, do not have to pay royalties to the federal government thanks to the Mining Act of 1872.

The recession hit here with as much force as it did Las Vegas—unemployment in the Reno-Sparks area and in Carson City remained above 13% in 2010. Economic diversification is limited to budding solar- and wind-energy enterprises, bio-agriculture, and high-precision technologies. Some 87% of the land in Nevada is owned by the federal government—a constant source of tension with local officials, ranchers, loggers, and miners, whose pursuits, frequently solitary and often ornery, shaped Nevada's culture from its earliest days. On the desolate frontier, speculation runs wild: Art Bell used to broadcast his popular radio show about the paranormal, aliens, and other unexplained phenomena from tiny Pahrump. The federal government's top-secret aviation experiments at places like Area 51 on the Nellis Gunnery Range have stoked UFO lore to the point that adjoining Route 375 was rededicated as the Extraterrestrial Highway in 1996. Anti-establishment views also flourish here in more mainstream ways. Nevada residents have long opposed a nuclear waste repository 1,000 feet beneath Yucca Mountain, 90 miles northwest of Las Vegas. Congress finally approved the project in 2002, but with President Barack Obama's election, it was shelved while a blue ribbon commission explored other waste storage options.

The 2nd Congressional District of Nevada takes in all of this and the vast majority of Nevada's land area. Excluding single-member states, this is the largest congressional district in the nation. Nevada has three congressional districts: Two are contained entirely within Clark County, which had 69% of the state's population; and the 2nd has all the rest, plus small slices of Clark. About one-half of the district's population is in Washoe County, which contains Reno and Sparks. Reno is the state's third-largest city behind Henderson. Its casinos have suffered from competition from Indian casinos in California, and the growth trend gravitates toward Lake Tahoe, to the west. People here are from all over: the Tahoe communities of Stateline, Zephyr Cove, and Incline Village are among the U.S. cities with the smallest percentage of residents born in the state. Historically, Reno has been Republican. In the 1990s, when the federal government was widely viewed as unfriendly to mining, grazing, and timber interests, the "cow counties," as the counties outside Reno and Las Vegas are called, became even more Republican and still are.

Nevada's 2nd District was represented by Republican Dean Heller until May 2011, when he was appointed to the Senate seat formerly held by John Ensign. The Republican senator resigned on May 3 amid an investigation into alleged ethics violations. With Heller succeeding Ensign in the Senate, a special election to fill the remainder of Heller's House term was set for Sept. 13, 2011. The results of the election were not available at press time for the *Almanac*.

The biggest potential name in the race to succeed Heller was former state Rep. Sharron Angle, a Republican who failed in her bid to unseat Majority Leader Harry Reid, a Democrat, in 2010. Angle made headlines with her far-right rhetoric and would have been a long shot to win the support of Republican insiders for the party's nomination. On May 25, 2011, she announced she would not run for the House seat, calling the election process "illegitimate," but she did not rule out running in the general election in 2012. Other possible Republican candidates included state party Chairman Mark Amodei, state Sen. Greg Brower, and former U.S.S. Cole Cmdr. Kirk Lippold. On the Democratic side, potential candidates included state Treasurer Kate Marshall and former education regent Nancy Price.

Ensign resigned after admitting to an extramarital affair with the wife of his top aide. A Senate Ethics Committee investigation concluded that Ensign made false statements to the Federal Election Commission and conspired to help the former aide violate a ban on lobbying the Senate within one year of working there. Ensign said in March 2011 that he would retire at the end of his term, but two months later, resigned. Republican Gov. Brian Sandoval appointed Heller, who had already expressed interest in running for the seat in 2012, when Ensign's term was up.

THIRD DISTRICT

Joe Heck (R)

Elected 2010, 1st term; b. Oct. 30, 1961, Jamaica, NY; home, Henderson; PA St. U., B.S. 1984; Philadelphia Col. of Osteopathic Medicine, D.O. 1988; U.S. Army War Col., M.S.S. 2006.; Catholic; Married (Lisa); 3 children.

Military Career: Army Reserve, 1991-present (Iraq).

Elected Office: NV Senate, 2004-08.

Professional Career: Emergency physician, Southwest Emergency Associates, 1992-98; medical dir., Uniformed Services U. of Health Sciences, 1998-2003; emergency physician, U. Medical Center, 2002-10; president, Specialized Medical Operations Inc., 2002-10.

DC Office: 132 CHOB, 20515, 202-225-3252; Fax: 202-225-2185; Web site: heck.house.gov.

State Offices: Las Vegas, 702-387-4941.

Committees: *Armed Services:* Military Personnel; Readiness. *Education & the Workforce:* Health, Employment, Labor & Pensions; Higher Education & Workforce Training. *Permanent Select Committee on Intelligence:* Technical & Tactical Intelligence (Chmn).

Election Results

2010 general	Joe Heck (R)	128,916	(48%)	($1,563,856)
	Dina Titus (D)	127,168	(47%)	($2,590,868)
	Barry Michaels (I)	6,473	(2%)	
2010 primary	Joe Heck (R)	36,898	(69%)	
	Steven Nohrden (R)	8,853	(17%)	
	Ed Bridges (R)	6,066	(11%)	

Population		Race/Ethnicity		Work	
Pop. 2010:	1,043,855	White:	54.4%	Private:	83.6%
Change since 2000:	Up 56.7%	Black:	7.3%	Government:	11.7%
Urban:	96.3%	Hispanic:	23.0%	Self-employed:	4.6%
Rural:	3.7%	Asian:	10.5%	Blue collar:	17.6%
Area size:	4,754 sq. mi.	Native Am.:	0.5%	White collar:	55.9%
		Hawaiian:	0.7%	Khaki collar:	0.2%
Age		Two+ races:	3.3%	Other:	26.3%
Median age:	35.8 yrs.				
More than 65 yrs:	11.3%	*Ancestry*		Median income:	$60,998
Less than 18 yrs:	24.7%	German	10.7%	Median Home Value:	$283,600
		Irish	8.5%		
Education		English	7.3%	**Military Veterans**	
H.S. grad:	87.7%			% of Pop:	11.0%
College grad:	25.2%				
Grad degree:	8.3%				

Las Vegas Suburbs; Henderson

Las Vegas, "The Meadows" in Spanish, began as a stop along the Old Spanish Trail trading route between Santa Fe and California in the 1830s. Water from artesian wells had created vast grasslands in the area and let traders replenish their supplies. In the early 20th century, Las Vegas was one of the termini of the Las Vegas & Tonopah Railroad, a link to Nevada's silver mines. Even at the end of the 1930s, when gambling was legalized in Nevada, it was still a town

2008 Presidential Vote

Barack Obama (D)	207,439	(55%)
John McCain (R)	159,624	(43%)

2004 Presidential Vote

George Bush (R)	156,335	(50%)
John Kerry (D)	152,150	(49%)

Cook Partisan Voting Index: D+2

of less than 10,000. Then came decades of amazing growth, as Las Vegas became America's destination for gambling and topflight entertainment. From 2000 to 2008, the Las Vegas metropolitan area grew by 36%, to 1.9 million, making it one of the top five fastest-growing metropolitan areas in America. It spread across the desert in every direction from the few blocks around Fremont Street that it occupied in the 1930s, and today it is an exuberant, undisciplined, and chaotic city. But given the fast pace of building in the Las Vegas metro area, it was particularly hard hit by the crisis in the credit markets, and the red-hot real estate market bottomed out. The metro area had the highest foreclosure rate in the nation in 2010, with one in every 110 properties threatened by foreclosure, according to RealtyTrac's annual report.

The 3rd Congressional District is a Y-shaped segment of Nevada's Clark County made up of most of the suburbs of Las Vegas. It includes the south end of the Las Vegas Strip and McCarran International Airport, and spreads west, northeast, and south. It includes active retiree communities, blue-collar towns such as Blue Diamond, and a variety of planned (and often gated) areas like Summerlin, where young families have come for job opportunities and retired baby boomers have purchased vacation homes. Southeast of Las Vegas, the district takes in two additional population hubs: Henderson and Boulder City, originally built for federal workers at Hoover Dam. (Under an old agreement with the federal government, Boulder City is the only place in Nevada where gambling is prohibited.)

The 3rd also includes the Nevada halves of Lake Mead and Lake Mohave on the Arizona border, and the state's southernmost tip, where Searchlight, the hometown of Senate Majority Leader Harry Reid, is found. The district was created after the 2000 census to have an equal number of registered Democrats and Republicans. It gave small pluralities to Al Gore in 2000 and George W. Bush in 2004, and voted for Barack Obama in 2008 by 55%.

Joe Heck (R)

The new congressman from the 3rd District is Joe Heck, a Republican who defeated freshman Democratic Rep. Dina Titus in 2010. Heck was born in Queens, N.Y., and raised in Pennsylvania in a tight-knit family where he says he learned the values of service and giving back. As a young man, he became a volunteer firefighter and ambulance attendant. After graduating from Pennsylvania State University with a degree in health education, he got a doctorate of osteopathy from the Philadelphia College of Osteopathic Medicine, and went on to complete a residency in emergency medicine at the Albert Einstein Medical Center. In 1992, his work took him to southern Nevada. Heck said that his career in emergency medicine put him on the "front lines of health care....I get to see what works and what doesn't work," he told *National Journal*.

A member of the Army Reserve, Heck was called to active duty in 1996 during the Bosnian war and was deployed again in Iraq, where he ran an Army hospital in 2010. "I was militarily inclined as a kid," he said. "I thought about going into the service earlier, but I had decided I wanted to go into medicine and didn't want the military to dictate what my specialty would be." From 1998 to 2003, Heck was the medical director of the casualty care research center of the Uniformed Services University of the Health Sciences in Bethesda, Md. He provided medical support for federal law enforcement agencies, and the experience sparked his interest in the political process. Returning to Nevada, he won a state Senate seat in 2004, and also started a medical consulting business.

Heck considered running for the governorship in Nevada, but decided instead to challenge Titus, a former state Senate colleague, in 2010. With the tea party gaining strength in Nevada, and excited by Sharron Angle's challenge to Senate Democratic Majority Leader Harry Reid of Nevada, Heck tacked to the right during the campaign. He took more conservative, tea party-style positions than he had in the legislature, where he was known as a moderate. He called for the abolition of the U.S. Education Department and the addition of optional private accounts to Social Security. On the stump, Heck described himself as conservative but "a very pragmatic lawmaker, unafraid to cross party lines."

Titus accused him of using "the Republican talking points" and ran an ad calling Heck and Angle "two peas in a pod with the same bad ideas." She also characterized him as dangerous to women for voting against a bill that would have required insurance companies to cover a vaccine for the HPV virus, a precursor to cervical cancer. Her ads featured testimonials from homeowners thanking her for saving their houses from foreclosure.

Heck had substantial help from outside Republican groups, including Americans for Tax Reform, which ran a $600,000 ad for him. But Titus got help from AFSCME and the SEIU unions representing government workers and service industry employees. Heck raised $1.5 million, while Titus raised and spent much more, $2.6 million. Still, Heck won, although only narrowly, 48% to 47.5%, with three minor candidates splitting the rest. Heck's victory margin was 1,748 votes out of about 268,000 cast.

★ NEW HAMPSHIRE ★

With precisely 43 one-hundredths of 1% of the nation's population, New Hampshire every four years becomes the epicenter of the political universe, the place where the contest for the American presidency is temporarily focused, where every vote is avidly sought and where members of the national political press vie for access to candidates and for tables at the season's most fashionable bars and restaurants. New Hampshire has had impact far beyond its miniature size. It gave a huge boost to Republican Dwight Eisenhower's candidacy in 1952, it prompted the retirement of Democrat Lyndon Johnson in 1968. It launched Democrat Jimmy Carter in 1976, Republican Ronald Reagan in 1980 and Republican George H.W. Bush in 1988.

The lever with which this small state has sometimes moved the political world is its first-in-the-nation presidential primary, given that status by Democratic rules writers in the 1970s and exploited by Republicans in the 1980s. Its disproportionate weight in presidential elections is even more impressive considering that its public policies are arguably atypical of the nation and its political terrain is unusual if not eccentric. This is one of the few states that over the past half-century have had more registered Republicans than Democrats, and it was for many years the state with the most antipathy to taxes. Yet in the last two decades, New Hampshire's ability to pick winners and losers has waned. The last three presidents have finished second in the New Hampshire primary. It gave conservative commentator Patrick Buchanan a surprising 37% of the vote in 1992 and a 27% victory in 1996, but he never did as well elsewhere and wound up leaving the Republican Party in 1999. It gave Republican John McCain a thumping victory over George W. Bush in 2000, but that proved to be a harbinger for the Northeast and not the rest of the country. It gave Democrat Hillary Rodham Clinton a surprise victory in 2008, but she still fell short of the nomination. New Hampshire played a key role in nominating Democrats Al Gore in 2000 and John Kerry in 2004, but both lost the general election. However, the big increase in turnout in the 2004 Democratic primary proved prescient, as New Hampshire moved sharply toward the Democrats that fall. Gov. John Lynch, a Democrat elected narrowly in 2004, was re-elected by wide margins in 2006 and 2008. In November 2008, Democrat Barack Obama won a solid 54%-45% victory in a state that had voted 58%, 69% and 62% for Republican presidents in the 1980s, and Jeanne Shaheen became the first Democrat elected U.S. senator from New Hampshire since 1974.

In 2010, New Hampshire moved sharply back in the other direction. Lynch was re-elected governor, but by only 53%-45%, down from 70%-28% in 2008. Republicans won all five executive counselor positions and transformed Democratic majorities in both chambers of the legislature to huge Republican majorities—19-5 in the Senate and 298-102 in the House. Republican Kelly Ayotte was elected to the U.S. Senate by a 60%-37% margin over Democratic Rep. Paul Hodes and Republicans recaptured both U.S. House seats.

New Hampshire has always been distinct. In a country that prides itself on its feistiness and freedom from outside direction, it has always been even feistier and more lightly fettered by authority. Before the Revolutionary War, New Hampshire was almost an outlaw colony, its great fortunes made by poachers in the king's forests and smugglers avoiding taxes. It was the first colony with an independent government and was fighting the British before the Minutemen stood at Lexington and Concord. In this environment, 19th century entrepreneurs built textile mills along fast-flowing rivers. The Amoskeag Mills in Manchester, lining the Merrimack River for a mile, were once the largest cotton mills in the world, employing 17,000 people and producing enough cloth every two months to put a band around the world. Around the mills grew a city of red brick dormitories and three-family frame houses filled with immigrants from Quebec, Ireland, Poland and Greece, set down amid villages of dirt roads and flinty Yankee farmers and mechanics. New Hampshire held to its traditions of local government and little external control, and for years its refusal to join most other states in enacting an income or sales tax, or to provide statewide guidance of schools and social services, seemed to doom it to continued backwardness.

Instead, low taxes proved to be New Hampshire's fortune. From the 1960s to the 1990s, New Hampshire had the fastest growth in the Northeast, attracting businesses from Massachusetts and other high-tax states. It became a location of choice for entrepreneurs and high-tech innovators, attracting an increasing number of people skeptical of government programs. From 1965 to 2000, Massachusetts grew 15%, while New Hampshire grew 83%, from 676,000 to 1.2 million people. The bedraggled New Hampshire of 50 years ago, of poor Yankee farmers and French Canadian mill hands, has largely disappeared, and in its place is one of the nation's most prosperous economic communities. The low taxes that spurred New Hampshire's growth would probably have been

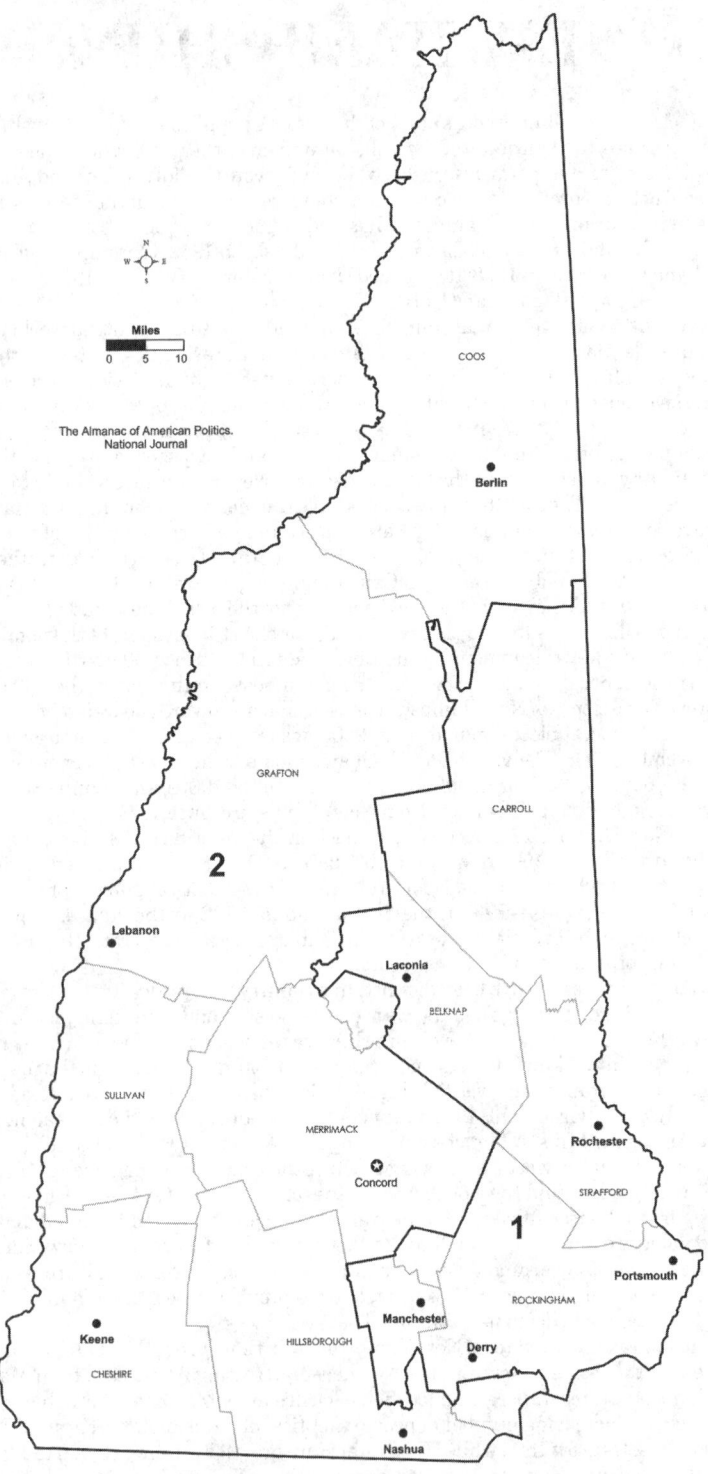

COOS

Berlin

GRAFTON

CARROLL

2

Lebanon

Laconia

BELKNAP

SULLIVAN

MERRIMACK

Rochester

Concord

STRAFFORD

1

Portsmouth

Manchester

ROCKINGHAM

Keene

Derry

HILLSBOROUGH

CHESHIRE

Nashua

The Almanac of American Politics.
National Journal

Miles
0   5   10

Congressional district boundaries were first effective for 2002.

raised in the late 1960s or early 1970s, as they were in so many states at the time, but for the far from gentle advocacy of Manchester's *Union Leader* newspaper and its proprietor William Loeb. *The Union Leader* insisted that governors and legislators "take the pledge" to vote for no sales or income tax and, from 1970 to 1998, almost all did. The two who didn't were defeated. The result was that education and welfare remained local responsibilities. At the same time, New Hampshire boasted the highest SAT scores in the country and had the brainpower to participate fully in New England's high-tech boom. The old Amoskeag Mills were converted to offices, and once-grimy Manchester is now a high-tech center. Fidelity Investment, BAE Systems, Liberty Mutual and Timberland are big employers, and New Hampshire has one of the nation's highest growth rates in information technology jobs and the highest percentage of citizens with Internet access.

This "Nouvelle Hampshire," as *Washington Post* writer Henry Allen dubbed it, has none of the architectural purity of Amoskeag. Its shopping centers and new subdivisions have a slapdash, half-built look, as if there were no time for details in the hurry to build. And, the booming state priced itself out of the growth market. Its giddily high real estate prices in the late 1980s kept out the new workers its businesses needed to continue expanding. The recession of the early 1990s was harsher here than anywhere else, and thousands of jobs disappeared. By the mid-1990s, growth had returned, and during the recessions of 2001-02 and 2007-09, New Hampshire's unemployment stayed low and incomes remained relatively high. There has been less migration to the state in recent years since 2000 and its growth rate fell below the national average, perhaps because Massachusetts and other states have lowered their taxes; the biggest in-migration in the decade was around Concord and the Lake Country. The state has had relatively little foreign immigration, and has virtually no minorities. Its minority population in 2010 was 1% African-American, 3% Hispanic and 2% Asian.

The state's economic ups and downs help to explain the state's political gyrations over the last dozen years. New Hampshire reacted angrily to the recession and the sharp decline in house prices in 1992, holding President George H.W. Bush to an unimpressive 53%-37% win over Buchanan in the Republican primary. It then voted for Democrat Bill Clinton over Bush in November. Like most states dominated by big metropolitan areas, New Hampshire moved toward the Democrats in the 1990s, reassured by economic growth and comfortable with the party's liberal stands on cultural issues. In 1996, Democrat Shaheen was elected to the first of three terms as governor. (New Hampshire and Vermont are the last states to have two-year gubernatorial terms.)

New Hampshire's tax regime came under attack from the state Supreme Court, which in December 1997 ruled the state's school-financing system unconstitutional because it left some dis-

Population			Household Income		Work	
Pop. 2010:	1,316,470		Under $15k:	8.7%	Private:	79.1%
State rank:	42nd		$15k to $50k:	30.9%	Government:	13.0%
Change since 2000:	Up 6.5%		$50k to $100k:	34.3%	Self-employed:	7.8%
Urban:	57.5%		$100k to $200k:	21.7%	Unemployment (3-yr. average):	4.1%
Rural:	42.5%		Over $200k:	4.5%	Poverty:	7.8%
Native of state:	42.1%		Median income:	$62,629	Blue collar:	20.3%
Not a citizen:	2.5%				White collar:	63.6%
Area size:	9,349 sq. mi.		**Home Value**		Khaki collar:	0.1%
			Under $100k:	8.3%	Other:	16.0%
Most populous cities			$100k to $300k:	55.0%		
Manchester	109,565		$300k to $500k:	28.2%	**Age**	
Nashua	86,494		$500k to $1 mil:	7.1%	Median age:	40.0 yrs.
Concord	42,695		Over $1 million:	1.3%	More than 65 yrs:	13.2%
Derry town	33,109		Median:	$257,600	Less than 18 yrs:	22.3%

Race/Ethnicity					Military Veterans		Registered Voters in 2010	
White:	92.3%	*Language*			% of Pop:	11.7%	Democrats:	270,826
Black:	1.0%	English:	92.0%				Republicans:	278,782
Hispanic:	2.8%	Spanish:	2.2%		*Veterans by Period*		Ind./other:	395,733
Asian:	2.1%	Asian:	1.1%		WWII and before:	10.7%	Voter turnout:	461,423
Native Am.:	0.2%	Other European:	4.3%		Korea:	11.3%	Turnout as % of	
Hawaiian:	0.0%				Vietnam:	33.4%	voting age:	44.8%
Two+ races:	1.4%	**Education**			Gulf (pre-2001):	10.1%		
		H.S. grad:	90.8%		Gulf (post-2001):	6.5%	**Legislature**	
Ancestry		College grad:	32.6%		Peace time:	28.0%	Senate:	5 D 19 R
Irish	16.1%	Grad degree:	11.6%				House:	102 D 296 R 2 V
English	13.4%							
French	12.1%							

tricts with fewer taxable resources than others. (At that time, the state provided only 10% of funding, far less than in the 49 other states.) The state got an April 1999 deadline to come up with a new system. The result, after years of struggle, was increased taxes on business, cigarettes, property transfers and rental cars, but no state sales or income tax. That produced a four-fold increase in the state's percentage of school financing. The 2002 election saw a return to Republicans; John Sununu was elected senator and Clark Benson governor. But in 2004, New Hampshire, after narrowly voting for George W. Bush in 2000, voted for John Kerry—the only state to switch to him. Democrat John Lynch, after pledging to oppose a sales or income tax, was elected governor.

The years from 2006 to 2010 were halcyon years for New Hampshire Democrats, who swept the board in 2008 and seemed on the verge of making New Hampshire a safe Democratic state. In 2009, the legislature and the governor legalized same-sex marriage, the first state legislature and governor to do so without being prompted by a court decision. But then came 2010. With much of the rest of the country, New Hampshire shifted Republican. *The Union Leader* responded by calling for a right-to-work law, a ban on public employee union bargaining, elimination of teacher tenure and a loser-pays rule in civil lawsuits. Were the 2010 results an indication that New Hampshire had returned to its 1980s politics? Or, were they just a temporary aberration from what many thought had become the norm in the past decade and a half? The election of 2012 should provide clues.

Presidential politics   Since 1920, New Hampshire had held the first-in-the-nation primary, and since 1952, when candidates' names were first put on the ballot, it has had extraordinary influence on the presidential selection process—a fact that will surely strike 23rd century historians as bizarre. To be sure, there are arguments for having early contests in small states that provide a venue for retail politics, in which candidates meet voters in person, listen to them, exchange ideas and allow citizens to gauge their character. Unlike Iowa, New Hampshire is small enough physically that candidates can efficiently meet voters. Everything except the lightly populated North Country is within an hour's drive of Manchester, and for all the state's abstract dislike of government, New Hampshire does an excellent job of keeping its roads clear of snow. New Hampshire's retail politics offers little-known candidates the ability to propel themselves into the national spotlight, though over the last 35 years, none has gone on to win his party's nomination. The last to do so were Democrats George McGovern and Jimmy Carter in the 1970s.

2008 Presidential Vote		
Barack Obama (D)	384,826	(54%)
John McCain (R)	316,534	(45%)
2008 Presidential Primary		
John McCain (R)	88,713	(37%)
Mitt Romney (R)	75,675	(32%)
Mike Huckabee (R)	26,916	(11%)
Rudy Giuliani (R)	20,344	(8%)
Ron Paul (R)	18,346	(8%)
2008 Presidential Primary		
Hillary Clinton (D)	112,404	(39%)
Barack Obama (D)	104,815	(36%)
John Edwards (D)	48,699	(17%)
Bill Richardson (D)	13,269	(5%)
2004 Presidential Vote		
John Kerry (D)	340,511	(50%)
George W. Bush (R)	331,237	(49%)

In the 1970s, Democrats tried to confine primaries to a "window" period in which New Hampshire would have competition. But New Hampshire, with its outlaw tradition, insisted it would hold its primary before the window if necessary, confident that candidates and reporters would pay it heed even if its tiny delegation was not seated at the national convention as punishment. Republicans made no such rules, but in 1996 let Iowa Gov. Terry Branstad and New Hampshire Gov. Steve Merrill, both Republicans, threaten voter retaliation against candidates who took part in caucuses or primaries held before those in their states or even during the week after their states' events. Democratic Gov. Shaheen continued the tradition in December 1998, demanding that candidates take a pledge not to participate in earlier contests. In 2000, the Democrats imposed a five-week window of no contests after New Hampshire, which made Al Gore's 50%-46% victory here decisive; Bill Bradley's candidacy effectively died of inattention before he could reach Super Tuesday. Fortunately for George W. Bush, the laissez-faire Republicans did not restrict other states as much as the Democrats, and he could recover from his 49%-30% New Hampshire loss to McCain 19 days later in South Carolina.

In 2003, the Michigan Democratic Party, led by U.S. Sen. Carl Levin, attempted to challenge New Hampshire's first-in-the-nation status by moving the 2004 Michigan Democratic caucuses to the same January date as New Hampshire's primary. After a noisy debate, Michigan backed down. But Levin got the national party to promise to convene another commission in 2005 to study the nomination process. In the 2008 election season, Michigan scheduled its primary on Jan. 15 in an attempt to outflank New Hampshire, but in August 2007 the Democratic National Committee commanded the Democratic candidates not to campaign there. In November, after the Michigan Supreme Court upheld the state's January date, New Hampshire Secretary of State William Gardner announced that his state's primary would be held on Jan. 8, five days after the Iowa caucuses, restoring New Hampshire's first-in-the-nation place.

New Hampshire has more registered Republicans than Democrats. Once upon a time, New Hampshire's registered Democrats were mill workers in Manchester and other factory towns, ethnics who rejected the Yankee Republican consensus of the state. Those days are long gone. Democratic turnout is not concentrated in the two largest cities, Manchester and Nashua, which often vote Republican, but in the state capital of Concord and clusters of towns around universities—the area around Durham (the University of New Hampshire) and Dover in southeast New Hampshire, the area around Keene (Keene State College) in the southwest and the area around Hanover (Dartmouth College). The typical Democratic primary voter here now is more likely to be an assistant professor. In 2000, the upscale character of the electorate was already clear. Gore, with strong support from labor unions, had won a wide victory in Iowa. But in New Hampshire, he was fortunate to squeeze out a 50%-46% victory against Bradley, who ran to his right on some economic issues and to his left on cultural issues.

In the 2004 election, New Hampshire was the first venue in which Democrat Howard Dean raced to a lead, far ahead of New Hampshire's Massachusetts neighbor John Kerry. Some voters in the western part of the state were perhaps familiar with Dean's somewhat moderate record as governor of Vermont. But his real appeal—what kept volunteers buzzing at their computers in his crowded Manchester headquarters and his poll numbers above 50% in a multicandidate field—came from his harsh denunciations of President Bush and the war in Iraq. About half of Dean's support evaporated after his third-place showing in Iowa and his infamous election night rant. But he had already set the tone of the campaign and stirred the enthusiasm of New Hampshire Democrats. Kerry argued, as he had in Iowa, that he was the Democrat best able to defeat Bush. New Hampshire gave him 38% of its votes, to 26% for Dean, 12.4% for Wesley Clark, who had skipped Iowa, 12.1% for John Edwards, and 9% for Joe Lieberman, who had also skipped Iowa.

In 2008, campaigning started early in New Hampshire. Despite the Republican registration advantage, there was higher turnout on the Democratic side—a harbinger of the November results. Clinton, who had led in New Hampshire polls most of the year, began to trail Obama after his win in the Iowa caucuses. But shortly before the primary, at a coffeehouse in Portsmouth, Clinton was asked how she was withstanding the rigors of campaigning, and in response she seemed to tear up as she talked about how she felt strongly that the country needed to change. This was the one primary in 2008 in which the result differed from the late polls. Clinton edged Obama 39%-36%; Edwards got just 17%, Bill Richardson 5%. Turnout was 289,000 people, up 30% from 2004 and nearly double that of 2000. Clinton carried Manchester, the southeast and the North Country. She won among women and downscale voters, much as Gore had in 2000. Obama carried Concord and towns in the west, and won among upscale and well-educated voters, much as Bradley had eight years earlier. Clinton's victory ended the possibility that Obama might wrap up the nomination early.

Turnout on the Republican side was 239,000, almost identical to that in 2000. And the winner, as in 2000, was McCain. He edged Mitt Romney 37%-32%; 11% went for Mike Huckabee and 8% for Rudy Giuliani, who had abandoned serious efforts in the state. McCain carried western and northern New Hampshire. Romney carried the southeastern corner of the state, where he was well known from his four years as governor of Massachusetts. That left Romney, who had been considered by many the front-runner and the best-financed Republican, without a victory in either Iowa or New Hampshire. It injected life into the McCain candidacy, which had nearly collapsed just six months before.

Until the 1992 election, political reporters left New Hampshire the day after the primary and never returned in the fall, since it was assumed that the state would go Republican. But Bill Clinton carried New Hampshire twice, and in 2000, the general election contest was close again. Gore unaccountably visited the state just once, yet Bush still carried it by only 48%-47%, with a popular vote margin of 7,211. In 2004, New Hampshire was a target state for both campaigns, and the enthusiasm evoked by the Dean campaign seemed to carry over into the fall. This was the only Bush 2000 state that went for Kerry. Again the vote was close, 50%-49%, with a popular-vote margin of 9,274—without which it would not have mattered whether Bush carried Ohio.

In 2008, New Hampshire was again a target state, but the Democratic tide was rising at a considerable clip. One clue: McCain had won more votes in the 2000 primary than in the 2008 primary. Another indication was that the Obama campaign had 100 organizers in the state, far more than the Republicans. Obama won by a solid 54%-45%. He got 61% of the vote from women and voters under 30.

Congressional districting

112th Congress Lineup
2 R
111th Congress Lineup
2 D

With only slight changes, New Hampshire's two congressional districts basically have had the same boundaries since 1881, neatly separating the Merrimack River mill towns of Manchester and Nashua, the state's largest cities. That was done originally to split the Catholic Democratic vote, but now both cities are high-tech towns. For years, that split helped Republicans hold both districts; it helped Democrats in 2006 and 2008 and Republicans in 2010.

Governor

John Lynch (D)

Elected 2004, term expires Jan. 2013, 4th term; b. Nov. 25, 1952, Waltham, MA; home, Hopkinton; U of NH, B.A. 1974, Harvard U., M.B.A. 1979, Georgetown U., J.D. 1984; Catholic; married (Susan); 3 children.

Professional Career: Ex. Dir., NH Dem. party, 1975-77; Dir. of Admissions, Harvard Bus. Schl., 1982-86; Partner, consulting firm, 1987-94; Pres. and CEO, Knoll Inc., 1994-2001, Pres., Lynch Group, 2001-04.

Office: State House, 107 North Main Street, 3301, 603-271-2121; Fax: 603-271-7640; Web site: www.governor.nh.gov/.

Election Results

2010 general	John Lynch (D)...240,346	(53%)
	John Stephen (R) 205,616	(45%)
	John Babiarz (Lib)..10,089	(2%)
2010 primary	John Lynch (D)..50,348	(88%)
	Timothy Robertson (D) 3,792	(7%)
	Frank Sullivan (D)..3,418	(6%)

Prior Winning Percentages: 2008 (70%); 2006 (74%); 2004 (51%)

John Lynch, a Democrat, was elected governor of New Hampshire in 2004 in his first run for public office and is now the longest-serving governor in more than two centuries. He was re-elected in 2010.

Lynch grew up in Waltham, Mass., the fifth of six children. His father ran a local Boys Club and his mother was a schoolteacher. He graduated from the University of New Hampshire in 1974, got an M.B.A. from Harvard Business School in 1979, and earned a law degree from Georgetown University in 1984. He took an interest in politics in college, interned for Democratic Sen. Tom McIntyre in 1975 and not long after, became executive director of the New Hampshire Democratic State Committee. He left state politics to attend business school. In 1994, he became president and chief executive of Knoll Inc., a Pennsylvania-based office furniture maker. He maintained his New Hampshire political network, however, and commuted from Knoll's headquarters in East Greenville, Pa., to his home in Hopkinton. In the mid-1980s and 1990s, Lynch worked for the Merrimack County Democratic Party, contributing to various campaigns and working to establish a New Hampshire chapter of the centrist Democratic Leadership Council. In 2001, he left Knoll and later opened his own management consulting firm in Manchester. In 2000, Democratic Gov. Jeanne Shaheen appointed Lynch to the University System of New Hampshire's Board of Trustees; he served as chairman from 2001 to 2004, when he resigned to run for governor. Lynch challenged Republican Gov. Craig Benson, who won his first term in 2002 in the state's most expensive gubernatorial race. A high-tech entrepreneur, Benson had the advantage of a GOP-controlled legislature. He had a rough transition to the public sector, however. His brusque and heavy-handed style alienated legislators from both parties. Nonetheless, voters gave him high approval ratings for his call for a constitutional amendment to limit tax increases. But Benson's popularity began to fade after frequent missteps and controversies. Several of his appointees were forced to step down for ethical lapses.

In the Democratic primary, Lynch easily defeated former legislator Paul McEachern, who was making his fourth try for the office. The general election was dominated by two issues: taxes and ethics. In his campaign kickoff speech, Lynch said he would "restore integrity, trust, and a bipartisan spirit" to state government. He highlighted his opposition to a sales or income tax, but he did back an increase in the cigarette tax. He said he would provide targeted aid to schools while phasing out the state property tax adopted in 1999. Benson hewed to a hard anti-tax position and insisted that Lynch's plan to repeal the state property tax would lead to a "back-door income tax." Lynch focused on what he called Benson's "culture of corruption," and pointed out that Benson had been cited twice for having illegal landscaping in front of his beachfront home. The candidates, both multimillionaires, largely self-financed their campaigns. Benson, after spending more than $9 million of his own money in 2002, put up $3.3 million in personal funds, out of a total of $4 million raised. Lynch raised $3 million, $2 million of it his own money. That was enough to keep him competitive through Election Day. He won 51%-49%, results that closely tracked presidential returns that year. Democrat John Kerry ran just 600 votes ahead of Lynch, carrying the state 50%-49% over Republican President George W. Bush. Lynch and Kerry won the same six counties, both carrying western New Hampshire and Concord's Merrimack County and both losing in Manchester's Hillsborough County and Rockingham County. Benson became the first freshman governor in 78 years to be denied a second term.

In Lynch's first act in office, he issued an executive order imposing new ethics rules that required everyone on staff to file a financial disclosure form that detailed their sources of income, loans of $5,000 or more, the location of real estate holdings other than homes, and businesses that they or their spouses were involved in. His mild-mannered and cautious style was in sharp contrast to Benson's and enabled him to work productively with the Republican-controlled legislature. Lynch stressed the importance of bipartisanship. "I was not elected to represent a party," he said.

After severe flooding devastated parts of southwestern New Hampshire in 2005, he flew back from a European trade mission to oversee recovery efforts and surprised homeowners and local officials by handing them laminated cards that included phone numbers of key state and National Guard officials, as well as his own personal cell phone number. Lynch failed to achieve everything he wanted in his first year—he was unable to repeal the statewide property tax, for example—but his work with the state's congressional delegation to help keep the Portsmouth Naval Shipyard open and his response to the flood led to high approval ratings. He was able to establish an ethics commission for the executive branch; he signed a tough law cracking down on child sexual predators; and he pushed through "Michelle's Law," which required health insurers to continue covering severely ill college students who doctors certified were unable to maintain their status as full-time students. The law was named for a cancer-stricken student who had to continue attending classes to keep her insurance benefits.

New Hampshire and Vermont are the last two states with two-year gubernatorial terms. With 70% job-approval ratings, Lynch in 2006 was far ahead of his Republican challenger, state Rep. Jim Coburn. In September 2006, the state Supreme Court ruled that New Hampshire's system of funding education was unconstitutional because its heavy reliance on local property taxes resulted in inequities in per pupil spending. The court set a June 2007 deadline before it would impose its own financing system. Coburn supported a constitutional amendment to remove control of the education financing system from the courts. Lynch argued that the state could fund the public schools without a sales or income tax and said he would consider a narrowly written constitutional amendment designed to give the state more flexibility. Lynch won 74%-26%, the largest victory ever for a gubernatorial candidate in New Hampshire. Democrats also gained 89 seats in the state House to give them a 239-161 majority, along with their 14-10 majority in the state Senate. For the first time since the Civil War era, New Hampshire had a Democratic legislature and governor.

In 2007, the legislature enacted one of Lynch's priorities, raising the legal school dropout age from 16 to 18, and lawmakers also increased the minimum wage and hiked the cigarette tax. The legislature repealed the state's parental notification abortion law, and Lynch also signed a measure that made New Hampshire the fourth state to allow civil unions. But the state House rejected, 253-108, Lynch's fix for school financing. He proposed a constitutional amendment requiring the state to pay for 50% of school funding, up from 7%, as a way to lessen the schools' reliance on local property taxes, which varied widely by locality. Even so, Lynch was able to avoid signing an income or sales tax, and in June 2008, the budget included $80 million in bonds for school construction. The November 2008 election was anticlimactic: Lynch beat state GOP Sen. Joe Kenney 70%-28%, although Republicans reduced Democrats' majority in the House to 225-175.

In Lynch's third term, the recession hit New Hampshire hard, and he laid off hundreds of state workers and closed the Laconia prison, eight district courts, and several state liquor stores. Also in early 2009, the legislature considered passing a mandatory seat belt law, which would end New Hampshire's distinction as the only state without one. The Senate put off action, however. In April, both chambers passed a law legalizing same-sex marriage. Lynch said he would sign the bill provided the legislature added a clause allowing religious organizations to refuse to conduct same-sex weddings if they contradict their beliefs. In June 2009, the legislature approved his condition and Lynch signed the bill. He said he had come to agree with "compelling arguments that a separate system is not an equal system."

Like numerous other states, New Hampshire sought to deal with the recession by considering new forms of gambling for revenue. The Senate, which had approved numerous gambling bills in the past, passed a bill in March 2010 allowing for video slot machines and table games at six sites. But Lynch threatened to veto the bill, and House leaders joined him in insisting that a stronger regulatory structure was needed. As state lawmakers worked to erase most of New Hampshire's projected $300 million budget deficit, the gambling issue became a major sticking point. The final compromise created a seven-member authority to draft gambling regulations. In October 2010, Lynch announced that the state had a $70 million budget surplus.

In 2010, Lynch decided to seek another term as governor although no New Hampshire governor had been elected four times since 1880, and no one had served longer than six years since Federalist John Gilman won 11 one-year terms from 1794 to 1804. Lynch's Republican opponent was John Stephen, a former state Health and Human Services commissioner who had twice run unsuccessfully for Congress. Stephen contended that the federal health care overhaul law would pass significant costs to the state due to the expansion of Medicaid. He also complained about the state's high business tax rates, which he said drove employers elsewhere, and hammered Lynch for signing a law allowing convicted child offenders and other criminals to get a nine-month supervised release before completing their maximum sentence. He got help from outside conservative groups that attacked the governor for signing the law legalizing gay marriage. Though he entered the race as an underdog, Stephen by mid-September was in a statistical dead heat with Lynch.

Lynch struck back hard. His campaign seized on a news report that Stephen had backed a request for a pardon six years earlier from a convicted arsonist who had donated $1,000 to his campaign. Stephen said he saw no conflict with taking the contribution. Lynch's campaign also attacked Stephen for refusing to fire a campaign manager who faced a restraining order for stalking an ex-girlfriend. Lynch regained his lead in the polls and easily won 53%-45%, carrying all but one of the state's counties in a year in which New Hampshire voters elected Republicans to the U.S. Senate and both House seats.

He began his new term in 2011 by proposing a budget that, unlike others in the past, contained no federal stimulus money or other one-time spending to plug shortfalls. He called for eliminating more than 200 state jobs and ending a $150-per-student subsidy for driver's education.

Senior Senator

Jeanne Shaheen (D)

Elected 2008, term expires 2014, 1st term; b. Jan. 28, 1947, St. Charles, MO; home, Madbury; Shippensburg Coll., B.A. 1969, U. of MS, M.A. 1973; Protestant; married (William); 3 children.

Elected Office: NH Senate, 1990–96; NH gov., 1997-2003.

Professional Career: Teacher, 1969–71; A.A., U. of NH, 1973–74, Parents' Assoc. Program Coord., 1982–86; Mgr., seasonal retail business, 1973–76; Campaign mgr., Carter/Mondale NH pres. campaign, 1979–80; Hart NH pres. campaign, 1983–84; McEachern NH gov. campaign, 1986–88.

DC Office: 520 HSOB, 20510, 202-224-2841; Fax: 202-228-3194; Web site: shaheen.senate.gov.

State Offices: Claremont, 603-542-4872; Dover, 603-750-3004; Manchester, 603-647-7500; Nashua, 603-883-0196; Berlin, 603-752-6300.

Committees: *Armed Services:* Emerging Threats & Capabilities; Readiness & Management Support; Strategic Forces. *Energy & Natural Resources:* Energy; Public Lands & Forests; Water & Power (Chmn). *Foreign Relations:* East Asian & Pacific Affairs; European Affairs (Chmn); International Operations & Organizations, Democracy & Global Women's Issues; Western Hemisphere, Peace Corps & Global Narcotics Affairs. *Small Business & Entrepreneurship.*

Group Ratings

	ACLU	ACU	ADA	CFG	AFS	FRC	LCV	ITIC	NTU	COC
2010	93	0	90	0	100	0	71	67	12	18
2009	–	8	100	9	100	–	100	–	8	43

National Journal Ratings

	2010 LIB	—	2010 CONS	2009 LIB	—	2009 CONS
Economic	62%	—	36%	81%	—	15%
Social	65%	—	0%	69%	—	28%
Foreign	47%	—	0%	55%	—	0%
Composite	73%	—	27%	77%	—	23%

Key Votes of the 111th Congress

1. Overturn Ledbetter	Y	5. Pass health care bill	Y	9. Ratify New START	Y
2. Pass $787 billion stimulus	Y	6. Regulate financial firms	Y	10. Confirm Elena Kagan	Y
3. Repeal DC gun laws	N	7. Pass tax cuts for some	Y	11. Stop EPA climate regs	N
4. Confirm Sonia Sotomayor	Y	8. Legalize immigrants' kids	Y	12. Repeal don't ask, tell	Y

Election Results

2008 general	Jeanne Shaheen (D)	358,438	(52%)	($8,342,400)
	John Sununu (R)	314,403	(45%)	($8,879,307)
	Ken Blevens (Lib)	21,516	(3%)	
2008 primary	Jeanne Shaheen (D)	42,968	(88%)	
	Henry Stebbins (D)	5,281	(11%)	

Prior Winning Percentages: Governor: 2000 (49%); 1998 (66%); 1996 (57%)

Jeanne Shaheen, a Democrat elected in 2008, is New Hampshire's senior senator. She is the first woman in U.S. history to be elected both a governor and a senator.

Shaheen grew up in St. Charles County, Mo., north of St. Louis, and graduated from Shippensburg College in Pennsylvania. She got a master's degree at the University of Mississippi. She moved to New Hampshire in 1973, where she worked as a teacher and ran a silver and leather business with her husband, attorney William Shaheen. She worked as a staffer on Democrat Jimmy Carter's successful presidential primary campaigns in New Hampshire in 1976 and 1980, and worked on other Democratic campaigns as well. She managed Democrat Gary Hart's 1984 campaign in the New Hampshire primary, in which he beat Walter Mondale 37%-28%. She also worked for the unsuccessful gubernatorial campaigns of Paul McEachern in 1986 and 1988, when he lost to John Sununu and Judd Gregg, respectively.

In 1990, Shaheen was elected to the state Senate, where she supported expanded health care coverage and term limits on federal and state legislators. In 1996, she ran for governor. She had no serious primary opposition, while the Republicans had a close race between U.S. Rep. Bill Zeliff and Board of Education Chairman Ovide Lamontagne, a strong conservative who won the nomination. Shaheen took a pledge not to support an income or sales tax and won the general election 57%-39%, carrying every county.

As governor, Shaheen won more funding from the legislature for kindergarten programs and signed a bill creating a needle-exchange pilot program. She vetoed bills that would have abolished the estate tax and the death penalty. A 1997 state Supreme Court ruling that outlawed New Hampshire's system of local school financing provided a continual challenge. Shaheen proposed increasing state revenues through slot machine gambling and a hike in the tobacco tax, but the court invalidated her plan in 1998. That same year, when her two-year term was up, Shaheen was reelected by 66%-31%. But she then abandoned her pledge to oppose an income or sales tax and was re-elected in 2000 by only 49%-44%. During that term, the controversy over school funding continued, and the Republican-controlled legislature refused to pass either an income or sales tax.

In 2002, Shaheen ran for the Senate. As in her 1996 race, Republicans had a seriously contested primary in which U.S. Rep. John Sununu, son of the former governor and George H.W. Bush White House chief of staff, defeated the very conservative incumbent, Robert Smith 53%-45%. Shaheen supported President George W. Bush's tax cuts and the authorization of military force in Iraq passed by Congress in October 2002. But her abandonment of the tax pledge came back to haunt her, and Sununu won 51%-46%.

In the 2004 election season, Shaheen was the national chairman of Democrat John Kerry's presidential campaign and helped orchestrate his sudden rise in the polls and his victory in the New Hampshire primary, as competitor Howard Dean's support collapsed. After that election, in 2005, Shaheen became director of the Kennedy School of Government's Institute of Politics at Harvard. She said she had no interest in running for office again. But after the Democratic sweep of November 2006, many local Democrats pressed her to run against Sununu in 2008. Other Democrats were already in the race, including Katrina Swett, wife of former U.S. Rep. Dick Swett and daughter of the late California Rep. Tom Lantos. She raised $1.2 million for the race. A July 2007 poll showed Shaheen far ahead of Sununu in a theoretical matchup, with Swett and other Democrats running behind him. In September, Shaheen quit her job at Harvard and announced that she was running. Swett and others dropped out of the race.

Much of New Hampshire's attention over the next few months was devoted to the presidential race. In December 2007, Shaheen's husband, William, co-chairman of Hillary Rodham Clinton's national and New Hampshire campaigns, told reporters that Republicans would attack Democratic candidate Barack Obama for admitting in his autobiography that he "got into drinking" and experimented with drugs. The next day, Clinton apologized, and Shaheen's husband resigned his position in her campaign.

The Senate campaign was a rematch between two candidates in a very different political atmosphere. In 2002, Shaheen had emphasized areas where she agreed with Bush and congressional Republicans; in 2008, she emphasized her disagreements with them. She attacked Sununu for votes against changing the tax treatment of oil companies and was supported by environmental groups. She also attacked Sununu for supporting the Bush administration's economic policies. Shaheen led in polls throughout the campaign, but Sununu rebounded after gas prices reached $4 a gallon, and he criticized Shaheen's opposition to offshore oil drilling. He also attacked her for doubling state spending in her six years as governor. But he may have lost ground in October 2008, when he voted for the $700 billion government bailout for the financial industry, which Shaheen, like many challenger candidates in both parties, opposed.

It was one of the most closely contested Senate races in the country, and both candidates raised and spent more than $8 million. The outcome was a reversal of 2002. Shaheen won 52%-45%, a spread just slightly greater than Sununu's six years earlier. It was the first Democratic Senate victory in New Hampshire since 1974.

In the Senate, Shaheen has been a reliable Democrat, with some moderate tendencies on economic issues. On the Energy and Natural Resources Committee, she impressed colleagues with her command of issues developed from her days as governor. After the 2010 BP oil spill disaster in the Gulf of Mexico, she called for the abolition of the much-criticized Minerals Management Service—which was subsequently carried out—and introduced a bill creating a new research and development program at the Interior Department to focus on ways to respond to spills. She also sponsored a measure establishing a carbon incentives program to reduce greenhouse gas emissions on private forest land, and another to provide a 30% tax credit for investment in biomass heating systems. When the Obama administration proposed in its fiscal 2012 budget to cut in half the LIHEAP program helping low-income residents pay their energy bills, she was among the Northeastern lawmakers who reacted with outrage. She was given the chairmanship of Energy's water and power subcommittee in 2011 and promised to explore the expansion of hydroelectric power as a renewable energy source.

Shaheen sought to avoid the frustrations many former governors experience in the Senate. Borrowing an idea from her days as a chief executive, she introduced a bill with Georgia Republican Johnny Isakson in January 2011 to move to a two-year budget cycle. She also worked with a bipartisan group that sought to enact many of the recommendations made by President Obama's deficit commission in 2010, and she joined Iowa Democrat Tom Harkin in trying to rein in the number of Senate filibusters, which have contributed to legislative stalemate in recent years. During the health care debate, Shaheen got several provisions in the final bill, including closing a loophole allowing drug companies to avoid competition with generic drugs and launching a pilot program providing follow-up care for hospital patients.

On the Small Business Committee, Shaheen in 2010 raised concerns that federal regulators were wasting taxpayer dollars by funding duplicative broadband infrastructure projects as part of the $7.2 billion broadband stimulus program. In the 112th Congress (2011-12), she picked up a seat on the Armed Services panel, where she can keep an eye on the Portsmouth Naval Shipyard, an important employer in eastern New Hampshire. The Pentagon recommended it be shuttered in 2005, but the independent base closure commission later rejected the idea.

Junior Senator

Kelly Ayotte (R)

Elected 2010, term expires 2016, 1st term; b. June 27, 1968, Nashua; home, Nashua; PA St. U., B.A. 1990; Villanova U., J.D. 1993.; Catholic; Married (Joe Daley); 2 children.

Professional Career: Law clerk, 1993-94; practicing atty., 1994-98; prosecutor, NH Atty. Gen. Office, 1998-2003; legal cnsl., Gov. Craig Benson, R-N.H., 2003; NH dep. atty. gen., 2003-04; NH atty. gen., 2004-09.

DC Office: 144 RSOB, 20510, 202-224-3324; Fax: 202-224-4952; Web site: ayotte.senate.gov.

State Offices: Manchester, 603-622-7979; Nashua, 603-880-3335; Portsmouth, 603-436-7161.

Committees: *Armed Services:* Personnel; Readiness & Management Support (RMM); Seapower. *Commerce, Science & Transportation:* Communications, Technology & the Internet; Competitiveness, Innovation & Export Promotion; Oceans, Atmosphere, Fisheries & Coast Guard; Science & Space; Surface Transportation & Merchant Marine Infrastructure, Safety & Security. *Small Business & Entrepreneurship.*

Election Results

2010 general	Kelly Ayotte (R)	273,218	(60%)	($4,414,291)
	Paul Hodes (D)	167,545	(37%)	($4,939,739)
	Chris Booth (I)	9,194	(2%)	
2010 primary	Kelly Ayotte (R)	53,056	(38%)	
	Ovide Lamontagne (R)	51,397	(37%)	
	Bill Binnie (R)	19,508	(14%)	
	Jim Bender (R)	12,611	(9%)	

The junior senator from New Hampshire is Republican Kelly Ayotte, the former state attorney general who defeated Democrat Paul Hodes in 2010 in an open-seat contest to replace retiring Republican Sen. Judd Gregg.

Ayotte (*AY-aht*) grew up in Nashua, N.H., and studied political science at Pennsylvania State University. She was active in her sorority, Delta Gamma, and skied competitively. She earned a law degree from Villanova, where she was the editor of the Environmental Law Journal. One of her first jobs was a clerkship for state Supreme Court Justice Sherman Horton. In an early legal case, Ayotte was the court-appointed counsel for defendants in a highly publicized murder of two guards in an armored-car robbery in 1994. The experience gave her a taste of trial work, and she sought a job as a prosecutor with the New Hampshire Attorney General's Office. She eventually rose to become head of the homicide division; she says her most challenging case was securing the convictions of two Vermont teenagers in the 2001 murders of Dartmouth College professors Half and Susanne Zantop. Also that year, she married Joseph Daley, of Nashua, a fighter pilot who flew combat missions in Iraq and later opened a landscape design business. They have two young children.

In 2004, Republican Gov. Craig Benson named Ayotte New Hampshire's first female attorney general. In one of her most celebrated cases, she defended the state against numerous court challenges of a law requiring parental notification for minors seeking abortions. In 2005, newly elected Democratic Gov. John Lynch asked her to drop the case and file a brief opposing the law. Ayotte opted instead to defend the law all the way to the U.S. Supreme Court. The high court ruled unanimously that states may require parental notification as long as an exception is allowed for medical emergencies. The state, however, repealed the law in 2007.

Despite Ayotte's differences with the Democratic governor over abortion rights, he nominated her for a second term as attorney general in 2009. Four months later, she resigned to make her first bid for elected office in the Senate race to succeed Gregg.

In a crowded primary field, Ayotte campaigned as a fiscal and social conservative. But tea party activists and Sen. Jim DeMint, R-S.C., a far-right conservative who injected himself into several GOP primaries that year, supported 1996 gubernatorial nominee Ovide Lamontagne. Ayotte also had primary competition from wealthy businessmen Bill Binnie and Jim Bender. But she got a boost from tea party favorite Sarah Palin, the former Republican governor of Alaska, who called her "one tough Granite Grizzly." Lamontagne enjoyed a late surge in the race, but Ayotte beat him, just barely, 38% to 37%, a margin of 1,660 votes out of 139,000 cast.

Meanwhile, Hodes, the U.S. House member from New Hampshire's 2nd District, had the Democratic field pretty much to himself, allowing him to spend his resources getting acquainted with potential general election voters. In his first television ad, he accused Ayotte of failing to investigate a mortgage Ponzi scheme by a firm called Financial Resources Mortgage that cost New Hampshire investors $80 million. Hodes used footage of Ayotte testifying before a state legislative panel that she didn't know about the scheme when she was attorney general. Ayotte countered with ads that portrayed her as a tough prosecutor and highlighted her decision to seek the death penalty for a man who killed a police officer. She also hammered Hodes for his support of President Barack Obama's health care overhaul and said she would vote to repeal it.

In the end, Hodes didn't even keep it close. Ayotte won with 60% of the vote to 37% for Hodes. She carried all 10 counties in the state, and beat Hodes by nearly 2-to-1 in the most populous county of Hillsborough, where Manchester is located. The retiring Gregg, who endorsed Ayotte in the contest, told *The Telegraph* in Nashua that she connected well with voters. Hodes was probably hurt, too, by his association with unpopular items in the Democratic agenda. "Ninety percent of the fight is people liking you and agreeing with your philosophy, and she nailed that from the beginning," Gregg told the newspaper.

FIRST DISTRICT

Frank Guinta (R)

Elected 2010, 1st term; b. Sept. 26, 1970, Edison, NJ; home, Manchester; Assumption Col., B.A. 1993; Franklin Pierce Law Center, M.A. 2000.; Catholic; Married (Morgan); 2 children.

Elected Office: NH House, 2000-02; Manchester alderman, 2001-05; Manchester mayor, 2005-09.

Professional Career: Insurance salesman, 1993-98; legal clerk, NH Insurance Dept., 1999.

DC Office: 1223 LHOB, 20515, 202-225-5456; Fax: 202-225-5822; Web site: guinta.house.gov.

State Offices: Manchester, 603-641-9536.

Committees: *Budget. Oversight & Government Reform:* Government Organization, Efficiency & Financial Management; Regulatory Affairs, Stimulus Oversight & Government Spending; TARP, Financial Services & Bailouts of Public & Private Programs. *Transportation & Infrastructure:* Aviation; Coast Guard & Maritime Transportation; Highways & Transit.

Election Results

2010 general	Frank Guinta (R)	121,655	(54%)	($1,558,556)
	Carol Shea-Porter (D)	95,503	(42%)	($1,647,774)
	Philip Hodson (Lib)	7,966	(4%)	
2010 primary	Frank Guinta (R)	22,237	(32%)	
	Sean Mahoney (R)	19,418	(28%)	
	Richard Ashooh (R)	19,376	(28%)	
	Bob Bestani (R)	5,337	(8%)	

Population		Race/Ethnicity		Work	
Pop. 2010:	657,984	White:	92.3%	Private:	79.9%
Change since 2000:	Up 6.5%	Black:	1.2%	Government:	12.8%
Urban:	66.6%	Hispanic:	2.8%	Self-employed:	7.3%
Rural:	33.4%	Asian:	2.0%	Blue collar:	19.7%
Area size:	2,690 sq. mi.	Native Am.:	0.2%	White collar:	64.0%
		Hawaiian:	0.0%	Khaki collar:	0.1%
Age		Two+ races:	1.4%	Other:	16.2%
Median age:	39.5 yrs.				
More than 65 yrs:	12.6%	*Ancestry*		Median income:	$63,826
Less than 18 yrs:	22.3%	Irish	16.9%	Median Home Value:	$266,300
		English	13.0%		
Education		French	12.5%	**Military Veterans**	
H.S. grad:	90.9%			% of Pop:	11.4%
College grad:	32.5%				
Grad degree:	11.3%				

Eastern New Hampshire; Manchester

The greatest growth in New Hampshire over the past two decades has been in the southeast and south-central parts of the state—the Seacoast and the Manchester area. Manchester was once famous for the Amoskeag Mills, the world's largest textile mill complex. In the first half of the 20th century, it was the quintessential mill town, with a few mansions for mill owners and managers and closely packed neighborhoods of frame houses for mill workers, many of them immigrants—from Quebec, Ireland, and Greece (Manchester has America's largest percentage of Greek-Americans). By the beginning of the 21st century, it was something quite different: a high-tech city, with big shopping malls at freeway interchanges, a spiffy new airport and downtown arena, spruced-up neighborhoods, and growth extending to the wooded suburbs all around. The Seacoast, within easy commuting distance of Massachusetts, is a collection of towns of ancient pedigree and high-tech growth. The biggest city on the coast is Portsmouth, the colonial capital of New Hampshire, with its busy naval shipyard and old seaport with well-preserved houses and a solid local economy that includes many galleries and bars.

2008 Presidential Vote
Barack Obama (D) 186,370   (53%)
John McCain (R) 164,403   (47%)

2004 Presidential Vote
George Bush (R) 171,013   (51%)
John Kerry (D) 163,191   (48%)

Cook Partisan Voting Index: EVEN

Pease Air Force Base, shuttered in 1991, has been successfully redeveloped as the Pease International Tradeport, with office buildings and an airplane runway, resulting in the addition of more than 160 businesses and nearly 10,000 jobs in the Seacoast, as the region along the state's 18-mile coast is known. Not far to the southwest are Stratham, where Swiss chocolate maker Lindt has a major facility, and Exeter, home of Phillips Exeter Academy, the elite boarding school. A quarter of New Hampshire residents claim French or French-Canadian ties; racial minorities are sparse here.

The 1st Congressional District of New Hampshire includes the Manchester area and the Seacoast from Manchester and next-door Bedford, its most affluent suburb, east to Portsmouth. It also extends north to Laconia and gentrifying Lake Winnipesaukee, studded with summer resorts and new mansions, and Ossipee in Carroll County. Politically, this is the slightly more Republican of New Hampshire's two congressional districts. It was the destination of many people fleeing high taxes in Massachusetts. Manchester, the largest city in the state, still has more registered Democrats than Republicans—a relic of its mill town days—but usually votes Republican in general elections. Portsmouth, with its trendy coffee shops, is Democratic, as are Durham, home of the University of New Hampshire, and nearby Dover, once a mill town. Most of the smaller towns in the Seacoast and to the north have been solidly Republican, though that is changing. George W. Bush narrowly carried the district twice, but Barack Obama won it 53%-47% in 2008, despite John McCain's past popularity here.

Frank Guinta (R)

The new congressman from New Hampshire's 1st District is Republican Frank Guinta, who unseated two-term Democratic Rep. Carol Shea-Porter in the 2010 election. Guinta grew up in Montgomery, N.J., one of three children in a household that also served as a base for his parents' small court-stenographer business. His parents hadn't gone to college, and Guinta says that helping them out with their business was a formative experience. By witnessing their work ethic and frustration with taxes, he came to believe in limited government interference in the private sector. Guinta attended a Catholic boarding school in Connecticut before heading to Assumption College in Worcester, Mass., where he met his wife, Morgan. After graduation, the two moved to Boston, where Guinta worked as an insurance claims adjuster and consultant. He bounced from job to job—holding four in a span of five years—before heading back to school.

After getting a master's degree in intellectual property at the Franklin Pierce Law Center in Concord, N.H., in 2000, Guinta decided to settle in New Hampshire. He and his wife loved Manchester's timeworn mill yards and moved into a converted building downtown. Later that year, Guinta, who had been interested in politics since childhood, was elected to the state House. A year later, he became a Manchester alderman and in 2005, was elected mayor of Manchester, a post he held for two terms. As mayor, he cut taxes and lowered the crime rate. He also reduced spending, cutting the amount of borrowed money in the city budget by half. Those feats won him praise from both sides of the fiscally conservative state's political aisle, and his ability to work with the heavily Democratic Board of Aldermen earned him a reputation for bipartisanship.

Guinta played up his mayoral achievements when he decided to run for Congress in 2010. He first had to win a contentious GOP primary battle that sullied his reputation after he failed to disclose a bank account worth between $250,000 and $500,000. Magazine publisher Sean Mahoney attacked Guinta's ethics, while Guinta maintained that he had made a simple paperwork error. In the end, Guinta edged Mahoney and businessman Rich Ashooh by less than 3,000 votes. But Ashooh and Mahoney quickly united behind Guinta after the primary, joining his campaign as co-chairs.

In the fall, Guinta ran on a pledge to reduce the size of government, a popular theme with Republicans in 2010. He called for attacking federal deficits with spending and hiring freezes and extending Bush-era tax cuts to stimulate the economy. Shea-Porter had been a target of National Republican Congressional Committee attack ads since April 2009 over her support for Obama's $787 billion economic stimulus program and other federal spending, and over her outspoken support of liberal U.S. House Speaker Nancy Pelosi. Guinta cast Shea-Porter as a big-spending Democrat; she parried that Guinta wanted to slash vital federal programs like Social Security.

Heading into the final weeks of the campaign, Shea-Porter had raised nearly $1 million and spent about half of it. Guinta had raised nearly the same amount but had depleted most of his reserves battling for the mid-September GOP primary. Several marquee names testing the 2012 presidential waters with trips to New Hampshire stumped for Guinta, including former Massachusetts Gov. Mitt Romney, then Minnesota Gov. Tim Pawlenty, and former House Speaker Newt Gingrich of Georgia. Guinta defeated Shea-Porter, 54% to 42%.

SECOND DISTRICT

Charlie Bass (R)

Elected 2010, 7th term; b. Jan. 8, 1952, Boston, MA; home, Peterborough; Dartmouth Col., A.B. 1974.; Episcopalian; Married (Lisa); 2 children.

Elected Office: NH House, 1982-88; NH Senate, 1988-92; U.S. House, 1995-2007.

Professional Career: Field worker, Rep. William Cohen, R-Maine, 1974; legis. asst., chief of staff, Rep. David Emery, R-Maine, 1975-79; V.P., High Standard Inc., 1980-93; chmn., Columbia Architectural Products, 1980-93.

DC Office: 2350 RHOB, 20515, 202-225-5206; Fax: 202-225-2946; Web site: bass.house.gov.

State Offices: Concord, 603-226-0064; Littleton, 603-444-5505; Nashua, 603-595-7701.

Committees: *Energy & Commerce:* Commerce, Manufacturing & Trade; Communications & Technology; Environment & the Economy.

Election Results

2010 general	Charlie Bass (R)	108,610	(48%)	($1,242,838)
	Ann Kuster (D)	105,060	(47%)	($2,506,615)
	Tim vanBlommesteyn (I)	6,197	(3%)	($24,890)
	Howard Wilson (Lib)	4,796	(2%)	
2010 primary	Charlie Bass (R)	27,457	(42%)	
	Jennifer Horn (R)	22,868	(35%)	
	Robert Giuda (R)	11,145	(17%)	

Population		Race/Ethnicity		Work	
Pop. 2010:	658,486	White:	92.3%	Private:	78.3%
Change since 2000:	Up 6.5%	Black:	0.9%	Government:	13.3%
Urban:	51.7%	Hispanic:	2.8%	Self-employed:	8.3%
Rural:	48.3%	Asian:	2.3%	Blue collar:	20.9%
Area size:	6,659 sq. mi.	Native Am.:	0.2%	White collar:	63.2%
		Hawaiian:	0.0%	Khaki collar:	0.1%
Age		Two+ races:	1.3%	Other:	15.9%
Median age:	40.6 yrs.				
More than 65 yrs:	13.7%	*Ancestry*		Median income:	$61,172
Less than 18 yrs:	22.2%	Irish	15.4%	Median Home Value:	$249,400
		English	13.8%		
Education		French	11.7%	**Military Veterans**	
H.S. grad:	90.8%			% of Pop:	11.9%
College grad:	32.6%				
Grad degree:	11.9%				

Western New Hampshire; Nashua

Political reporters covering New Hampshire's first-in-the-nation primary usually stay in Manchester, the state's largest city and within an hour's drive of the rest of the state except for the North Country. Yet there are other noteworthy cities and towns in New Hampshire. Concord, north of Manchester, is the state capital. On one side of Main Street is the handsome, small, granite Capitol, and on the other you can usually find the headquarters of the two political parties

2008 Presidential Vote

Barack Obama (D)	198,456	(56%)
John McCain (R)	152,131	(43%)

2004 Presidential Vote

John Kerry (D)	177,320	(52%)
George Bush (R)	160,224	(47%)

Cook Partisan Voting Index: D+3

and many candidates: an entire state's politics within 100 yards. Nashua, south of Manchester and on the Massachusetts line, is the state's second-largest city, a high-technology and financial services center that has been mostly booming for three decades.

To the east is prosperous and growing Salem, first chartered in 1750 and the largest of the border suburbs. To the west of Nashua, past the pleasant country around Mount Monadnock, is Keene, the hub of southwest New Hampshire. To the north are the towns along the Connecticut

River; some are mill towns, and some are vacation home enclaves. New Hampshire's prosperity has spread to most of these, just across the river from Vermont. Hanover, home of Dartmouth College, is a tiny, picturesque town set in the mountains. And every political reporter's itinerary has to include a trip, usually by plane, to the little lumber mill city of Berlin in the middle of the North Country, where the last paper mill recently closed, and perhaps also to Dixville Notch in the White Mountains, where the town's 12 voters cast their ballots at a minute past midnight and provide the first reported returns in every presidential election. (Hint for election night analysts: If Dixville Notch doesn't go heavily Republican, the Republicans are in trouble.)

The 2nd Congressional District of New Hampshire includes Concord, Nashua, Salem, Keene, the Connecticut River counties, Hanover, Berlin, and Dixville Notch. It also includes Mount Washington, with its spectacularly violent weather and winds that have measured up to 231 miles per hour; entrepreneurs have been exploring the possibility of wind power parks. The district also takes in the Bretton Woods resort, where the world monetary system was established at a conference in 1944. Politically, this region is mixed, but much of it has been trending Democratic. Nashua is more Democratic than Manchester, Salem more Republican. The area between Mount Monadnock and Keene and the territory running north along the Connecticut River to Hanover and Dartmouth has become very Democratic, much like Vermont across the river. Overall, this is the more Democratic of New Hampshire's two congressional districts; it hasn't been carried by a Republican presidential candidate since 1988.

Charlie Bass (R)

The congressman from the 2nd District is Charlie Bass, first elected in 1994, defeated in 2006 and then elected again in 2010. Bass grew up in Peterborough, in a political family. His grandfather, Robert Bass, was elected governor in 1910 and his father, Perkins Bass, was elected to the U.S. House from the 2nd District in 1954 and served until he ran unsuccessfully for the Senate in 1962. (There were two Basses in the House then, with Perkins Bass known as "Smallmouth Bass" and Ross Bass of Tennessee known as "Bigmouth Bass.") Charlie Bass graduated from Dartmouth and worked for Maine Reps. William Cohen and David Emery in the 1970s. In 1980, when his father's successor, James Cleveland, retired, Bass ran for the House and came in third in a nine-candidate Republican primary, trailing Judd Gregg, later governor and U.S. senator, and state Sen. Susan McLane. Bass then ran an architectural product factory with his two brothers and was elected to the state House in 1982 and the state Senate in 1988. In 1994, he again ran for the House, for the seat then occupied by Democrat Dick Swett, son-in-law of the late California Rep. Tom Lantos. There were 10 candidates in the Republican primary. Bass beat conservative Mike Hammond 29%-24%. In that Republican sweep year, he beat Swett 51%-46%.

In the House, Bass's voting record tended to be conservative on economic issues and moderate on cultural issues, especially on environmental issues. On the Budget Committee, he pushed unsuccessfully for biennial budgeting, which he said would add more stability to government programs. He won re-election five times by respectable margins, once, in 2002, over Dick Swett's wife, Katrina Swett. But in 2006, as Democrats were sweeping New Hampshire, Bass lost 53%-46% to Democrat Paul Hodes. After that, he became head of the Republican Main Street Partnership.

In 2010, Hodes ran for the Senate, and Bass decided to run for the House again. He did not renounce his moderate positions on the environment, but he identified wholeheartedly with the tea party movement, which he called "a grassroots movement in America that is going to save our nation." In a year when many Republicans were suspicious of incumbents, he said, "I was consistently one of the leaders for lower spending and so forth and served on the committee that had jurisdiction of that for eight miserable years."

Of four other Republicans in the primary, his chief opponents were Jennifer Horn, a former radio talk show host who lost 56%-41% to Hodes in 2008, and former state Rep. Robert Giuda. Both ran as strong conservatives, promising to balance the budget and refrain from spending earmarks. Bass won with 43% of the vote to 35% for Horn and 17% for Giuda. Some 64,000 votes were cast in the Republican primary, compared to only 35,000 in the Democratic primary. In that contest, the winner was Ann McLane Kuster, daughter of Bass' 1980 Republican primary opponent. She beat Katrina Swett, 72%-28%.

In the fall campaign, Kuster charged that Bass had supported policies that led to the financial crisis and 2007-09 recession, and said she would bring "Yankee values like fairness, frugality and responsibility" to Washington. Bass emphasized fiscal issues and attacked the Democratic Congress for overspending. Democrats charged that Bass, while serving in the House in 2005, had secured tax rebates for wood-pellet stoves and then invested in New England Wood Pellet. Bass said that his gains on the company's stock did not violate congressional ethics rules because he purchased the stock after he left public office. Kuster raised $2.5 million and spent $2.5 million; Bass raised and spent slightly less than half those amounts. In a year when New Hampshire trended heavily Republican, Bass beat Kuster, 48%-47%. Kuster led in the North Country, had large margins along the Connecticut River and in Concord. But Bass got even larger margins in the towns along the Massachusetts border and just west of Manchester.

In Washington, Bass got a seat on the influential Energy and Commerce Committee. He told *National Journal*, "I'm not in lockstep with the Republican agenda from one end to the other, but when the leadership focuses primarily on the fiscal side, they know they have me with them. I will be a fiscal leader and a deficit hawk. My desk plate says, 'It's the national debt, Stupid.'"

★ NEW JERSEY ★

From modest beginnings New Jersey grew in the 20th century to become one of America's powerhouse states—and in the early 21st century is struggling to retain that status. Benjamin Franklin described New Jersey as "a valley of humility between two mountains of conceit." Even in colonial days, this colony was overshadowed by New York City and Philadelphia. New Jersey was named by King James II, then Duke of York, for the Channel Island on which he was sheltered during the English Civil War. In its early years, New Jersey was plagued by rival claims from its neighbors and, still defensive in the 1980s, went to the U.S. Supreme Court to argue that it and not New York owns the Statue of Liberty and Ellis Island. New Jersey eventually got most of the islands' acreage, but New York got the immigrant museum and the Great Hall, which are built on fill land. New Jersey is "a sort of laboratory in which the best blood is prepared for other communities to thrive on," Woodrow Wilson said when he was governor, just a tad defensively.

For a century after the American Revolution, New Jersey was a modest, slow-growing, even backward state. It became known as the Garden State because of its vegetable farms, which supplied the tomatoes for Campbell's Soup. But its proximity to New York and Philadelphia brought into its empty spaces immigrants and inventors. Jersey City, Newark and Camden grew to be significant cities in their own right. Thomas Edison churned out inventions in his laboratory at Menlo Park and gave birth to General Electric and Bell Labs. On open fields near large labor pools, U.S. automakers built assembly plants in the years after World War II, and the container port on the New Jersey side of New York harbor overshadowed the crumbling, racketeer-plagued docks of Manhattan and Brooklyn. The pharmaceutical industry came to be concentrated here, housing the headquarters of Merck, Johnson & Johnson, Bristol-Myers Squibb, Novartis and Schering-Plough. Connected to Wall Street by Hudson tubes and ferries, New Jersey became the home of finance professionals and lawyers. This economy has given the state a high-income, well-educated workforce and a prosperous middle class, with a relatively high concentration of scientists and engineers. New Jersey has long had the highest or second-highest median household income of any state, although it trails others in per capita income and wealth. This state is the home of high-income Ph.D.s as well as *The Sopranos* and *Jersey Shore*.

Physically, New Jersey has been transformed. The oil tank farms and swamplands of the Meadowlands have become sports palaces and office complexes. The Singer factory in Elizabeth, the Western Electric factory in Kearny and the Ford Motor plant in Mahwah are all gone, replaced by shopping centers and hotels. The General Motors plant in Linden, the state's last auto plant, closed in 2005. The intersection of Interstates 78 and 287 has become a major shopping and office edge city. U.S. 1 north from Princeton to North Brunswick has become one of the nation's high-tech centers. Casting off its suburban image, New Jersey has developed an identity of its own. It is the home of big-league football, basketball, and hockey franchises and of the world's longest expanses of boardwalk, on the Jersey Shore from Cape May to Sandy Hook. New Jersey is also the East Coast's premier gambling getaway. Atlantic City has had gambling revenues second only to Las Vegas—though like Las Vegas it has discovered that gambling is not a recession-proof industry.

Within New Jersey's close boundaries is great diversity: Geographically, from beaches to mountains; demographically, from old Quaker stock to new Hispanic arrivals; economically, from inner-city slums to hunt-country mansions. Although New York writers are inclined to look on New Jersey as a land of 1940s diners and 1970s shopping malls, the state much more closely resembles the rest of America than does Manhattan, although drivers will find some peculiarities: horizontal traffic lights, jug-handle intersections (to make a left turn, you exit to the right and then cross over after the light has changed) and a ban on self-service gas stations. The Jersey City row houses one encounters on emerging from the Holland Tunnel give way within a few miles to the skyscrapers of Newark and its new performing arts center. Farther out are comfortably packed middle-income suburbs and the horse country around Far Hills, the university town of Princeton, old industrial cities such as Paterson and Trenton, and dozens of suburban towns and small factory cities where people work and raise families over generations. Among them are commuter towns such as Middletown, whose commuter trails lead to Lower Manhattan.

Regardless of which state holds legal title to Ellis Island, New Jersey has long been a magnet for immigrants. In its post-World War II years of rapid growth, the state was a quilt pattern of WASPs, Irish, Italians, Jews, and Hungarians (the nation's largest concentration of the latter was in Middlesex County). Small-town-like suburbs centered on Dutch Reform or Episcopal churches

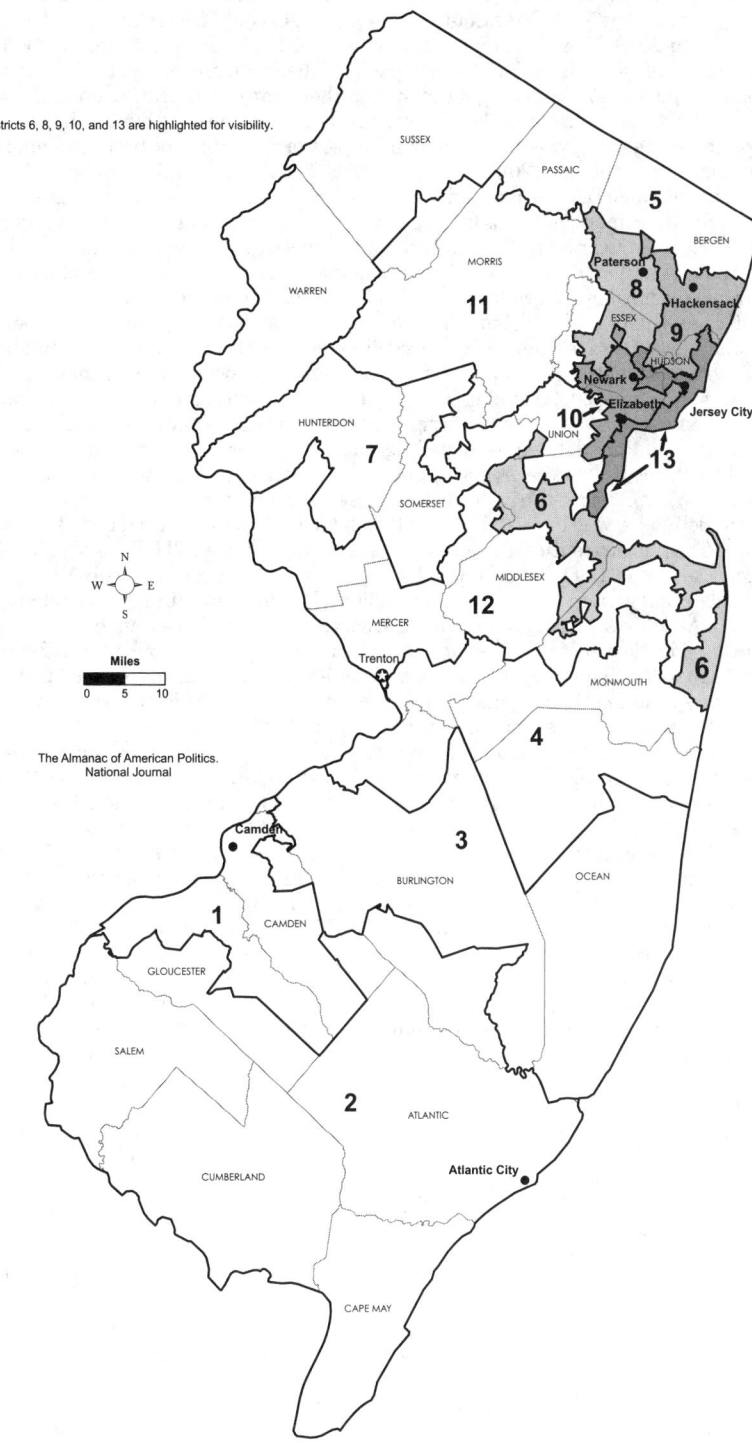

Districts 6, 8, 9, 10, and 13 are highlighted for visibility.

The Almanac of American Politics.
National Journal

Congressional district boundaries were first effective for 2002.

became heavily Catholic or Jewish. Immigrant growth is concentrated in North and Central Jersey, within range of New York City. (South Jersey, as in adjacent Philadelphia, has few immigrant communities.) In 2010, New Jersey's population was 14% African-American, the highest of any state north of the Mason-Dixon line; 18% Hispanic, higher than any other state outside the West, Texas and Florida; and 8% Asian, higher than any other state except Hawaii and California. One-third of New Jersey schoolchildren had immigrant parents. Hudson County, the land along the ridge opposite Manhattan, was the home of hundreds of thousands of Irish, Italian, Polish and Jewish immigrants in the early 20th century, and it is now 42% Hispanic, a grouping that includes Cubans, Puerto Ricans, Dominicans and Mexicans, and 14% Asian. Immigrants are also plentiful in the small middle-American towns of Bergen County: Filipinos in Bergenfield, Guatemalans in Fairview, Koreans in Leonia, Indians in Lodi and Chinese in Palisades Park. The old industrial cities of Elizabeth and Paterson are majority Hispanic and nearly one-quarter of the residents of the area from Woodbridge to New Brunswick in Middlesex County are Asian, primarily from India. Newark still has a black majority, but it includes many of the Portuguese in the Ironbound district.

For all its strengths New Jersey has faced difficulties in the new century. Population growth has slowed to a crawl, with only very small patches of suburban boom. Immigrant inflow from 2000 to 2008 was 4.8% of the 2000 population, but there was an even higher nonimmigrant outflow. Only Ocean County, with its retirement communities, and Gloucester County, on the New Jersey Turnpike outside of Philadelphia, attracted significant numbers of nonimmigrant new residents; to the northwest, people have been moving out past the Delaware River into lower-tax Pennsylvania. New Jersey's emblematic private-sector firms have found themselves in trouble. Lucent, the successor to Bell Labs, was burned in the high-tech bust and was acquired in 2006 by the French firm Alcatel. The pharmaceutical firms have foundered and cut payrolls. The state had 20% of U.S. pharmaceutical jobs in 1990, but only 13% by 2008. Two New Jersey industries that once seemed launched on eternal growth trajectories found themselves in trouble in 2008. Gambling revenues fell steeply in Atlantic City. Banks and financial service firms in distress cut back sharply both on Wall Street and in New Jersey back-office jobs. Unemployment rose from 4.6% in February 2007 to 9.8% in August 2010, equal to the national average and higher than any other state in the Northeast. New Jersey did reap some gains from a 20% tax credit for moviemakers, but the results, at least in *The Wrestler*, were less than flattering to the state's image.

State government has helped build New Jersey's identity, but it also has placed heavy burdens on its private sector. In the 1970s, Democratic Gov. Brendan Byrne started the Meadowlands sports complex and legalized casino gambling in Atlantic City. He also pushed through an income tax in a state that, until that point, had far lower taxes than New York. Republican Gov. Thomas Kean in the 1980s reformed education and promoted the state shamelessly ("New Jersey and you: perfect together"). The revolt against Democratic Gov. Jim Florio's tax increase in 1990 was led by the first all-New Jersey talk radio station and took on national significance with his defeat by Republican Christine Todd Whitman in 1993—a harbinger, as it turned out, of the big Republican congressional victories in 1994. In the 1990s, crime and welfare rolls dropped, but auto insurance and property taxes remained the highest in the nation. Health insurance premiums skyrocketed, thanks to state mandates requiring all policies to cover all manner of treatments. Property taxes kept rising, and under Democratic Govs. Jim McGreevey and Jon Corzine taxes and fees went up. Corzine's proposal to lease the Turnpike and raise tolls for the first time in years would have eliminated one of New Jersey's few bargains. The state legislature voted to spend $270 million on embryonic-stem-cell research, not normally a state government function.

Predominantly suburban New Jersey leaned Republican from the 1940s through the 1980s. But in the last two decades, it has become a Democratic bastion because of a growing immigrant population and the presence of many affluent suburbanites who reject conservative stands on cultural issues. No Republican has won 50% of the state vote for president or for governor since presidential candidate George H.W. Bush in 1988 and Kean in 1985. No Republican has been elected to the U.S. Senate since Clifford Case in 1972. From 2000 to 2008, New Jersey voted between 53% and 57% Democratic and between 42% and 46% Republican for president, senator, and governor. On a map showing election results by city and township, Democrats have carried the spine of the state, on either side of the Amtrak Acela route and through the South Jersey suburbs of Philadelphia. Republicans have carried the outliers, most of the Jersey Shore on the east, and the affluent suburban and exurban areas on the northwest. The Democrats' margins have been augmented by the outflow of modest-income Americans from the formerly middle-class suburbs. In a state where 12% of the voters are African-American, 9% Latino, and 4% Asian, Republicans need to get about 60% of the votes from whites to win.

Several factors beyond demographics have helped Democrats. New Jersey is the third-most expensive political state in the nation, after California and Texas, because candidates have to buy

TV ads in the New York and Philadelphia media markets. That gave a particular advantage to Corzine, who amassed a $300 million fortune when Goldman Sachs went public in the 1990s and who spent well over $100 million on his races for senator in 2000 and for governor in 2005 and 2009. Second, New Jersey's high-earning, relatively well-educated voters tend not to vote in often crucial primaries—nearly half are not registered in either party—and those who do vote tend to defer to the choices of county and city political machines, which are of varying degrees of competence and cronyism. For candidates in both parties, it is a great advantage to have the designation of the local county party on the primary ballot. State law also allows county party organizations to accept contributions 18 times as large as candidate contributions, and as a result, they raise a lot of money and dole it out to favored candidates.

The third factor has been Democrats' willingness to pitch losers aside, and the willingness of the legal and political establishments to go along. In September 2002, Sen. Robert Torricelli, plagued by scandal, was allowed by the state Supreme Court to drop out of his race for re-election and to be replaced by former Sen. Frank Lautenberg. In August 2004, McGreevey, already in trouble because of his ties to a later-convicted fundraiser, announced that he would resign, prompted by the revelation that he had appointed his gay lover as his homeland security adviser. Democratic Senate President Richard Codey stepped in as acting governor and considered running for a full term, but was elbowed aside by Corzine.

But in 2009, none of these factors were enough to elect Corzine to a second term. The Republican nominee was Chris Christie, who as U.S. attorney for New Jersey had secured the convictions of dozens of political figures from both parties. New Jersey government, Christie argued, was bloated and overly expensive, and he promised not to raise taxes. Corzine had a huge financial advantage, spending his own money while Christie was limited to the state's public financing, and he enlisted President Barack Obama in his cause. But Christie stuck to his themes and won 48%-45%, with 6% for independent Christopher Daggett.

In his first year as governor, Christie sought sharp reductions in spending and substantial concessions from public employee unions. He pointed out, in town hall appearances that were replayed on YouTube, that public employee union members were paying far less for health insurance and putting away far less for their generous pensions than the large majority of private-sector employees. He blocked the Democratic legislature from raising taxes and produced a balanced budget, though he did not fully fund the state's depleted pension funds. In October 2010, he turned down $3 billion in federal funds for new New Jersey Transit tunnels to Manhattan, arguing that cost estimates of such projects were unreliable and New Jersey taxpayers would be liable for any

Population		Household Income		Work	
Pop. 2010:	8,791,894	Under $15k:	9.3%	Private:	80.6%
State rank:	11th	$15k to $50k:	27.1%	Government:	14.4%
Change since 2000:	Up 4.5%	$50k to $100k:	30.6%	Self-employed:	4.8%
Urban:	93.6%	$100k to $200k:	25.0%	Unemployment (3-yr. average):	4.9%
Rural:	6.4%	Over $200k:	8.0%	Poverty:	9.0%
Native of state:	52.6%	Median income:	$69,240	Blue collar:	17.9%
Not a citizen:	9.9%			White collar:	65.8%
Area size:	8,723 sq. mi.	**Home Value**		Khaki collar:	0.1%
		Under $100k:	4.2%	Other:	16.1%
Most populous cities		$100k to $300k:	31.8%		
Newark	277,140	$300k to $500k:	38.6%	**Age**	
Jersey City	247,597	$500k to $1 mil:	21.8%	Median age:	38.5 yrs.
Paterson	146,199	Over $1 million:	3.6%	More than 65 yrs:	13.3%
Elizabeth	124,969	Median:	$361,100	Less than 18 yrs:	23.7%

Race/Ethnicity				Military Veterans		Registered Voters in 2010	
White:	59.3%	*Language*		% of Pop:	7.3%	Democrats:	1,755,501
Black:	12.8%	English:	72.0%			Republicans:	1,074,364
Hispanic:	17.7%	Spanish:	14.0%	*Veterans by Period*		Ind./other:	2,444,228
Asian:	8.2%	Asian:	4.3%	WWII and before:	14.9%	Voter turnout:	2,194,192
Native Am.:	0.1%	Other European:	8.4%	Korea:	14.5%	Turnout as % of	
Hawaiian:	0.0%			Vietnam:	31.9%	voting age:	32.6%
Two+ races:	1.5%	**Education**		Gulf (pre-2001):	7.3%		
		H.S. grad:	87.3%	Gulf (post-2001):	5.1%	**Legislature**	
Ancestry		College grad:	34.3%	Peace time:	26.3%	Senate:	24 D 16 R
Italian	13.9%	Grad degree:	12.8%			General As-	47 D 33 R
Irish	12.7%					sembly:	
German	9.9%						

increases. In the process, he became a hero to Republicans and tea party activists around the country. His poll ratings in New Jersey remained positive in early 2011. When his name circulated as a possible presidential candidate, Christie said he would not run in 2012.

Presidential politics   In the second half of the 20th century, New Jersey was a close state in close presidential elections, giving small margins to winners in 1960 and 1968 and to losers in 1948 and 1976. In the 1980s, the vast suburban expanses of New Jersey leaned toward the Republicans. Since the middle 1990s, New Jersey has leaned Democratic. The suburbs, with many secular and Jewish voters and few Christian conservatives, reject Republican positions on cultural issues, and rising immigrant communities have generally voted Democratic, though not by nearly as large a margin as New Jersey's blacks. As a result, New Jersey, which had voted 56%-43% for George H. W. Bush in 1988, voted 54%-36% for Bill Clinton in 1996 and 56%-40% for Al Gore in 2000. In 2004, George W. Bush's campaign strategists kept an eye on New Jersey's polls to see whether September 11 had had enough impact on voters to make the state worth contesting. A few public polls showed the race close or tied, but John Kerry carried the state 53%-46%.

2008 Presidential Vote		
Barack Obama (D) 2,215,422	(57%)
John McCain (R) 1,613,207	(42%)

2008 Presidential Primary		
Hillary Clinton (D)................613,500	(54%)
Barack Obama (D) 501,372	(44%)

2008 Presidential Primary		
John McCain (R) 313,459	(55%)
Mitt Romney (R)...................160,388	(28%)
Mike Huckabee (R)................46,284	(8%)

2004 Presidential Vote		
John Kerry (D) 1,911,430	(53%)
George W. Bush (R)...........1,670,003	(46%)

In 2008, neither party targeted New Jersey. Polls showed the race tightening in the spring and again in early September, but Republicans could not afford to put money into New York television (and even some question whether they could afford Philadelphia), and Democrats saw no need to. Barack Obama carried the state 57%-42%, the best Democratic showing since 1964. Young voters went 67% for Obama, and senior citizens went 53% over John McCain. Whites voted 50%-49% for McCain, blacks 92%-8% for Obama. McCain won 55% from Catholics and 61% from white Protestants, figures that would have carried New Jersey for him in the 1950s. But Obama won about 4-1 among the 17% of voters who were Jewish or secular. A comparison of Obama's and Gore's percentages showed big Democratic gains in North Jersey, with large black and immigrant populations, and Democratic losses in all the Jersey Shore counties, including the largest in fast-growing Ocean County.

For years, New Jersey held its presidential primary in early June, but it was usually overshadowed by the California primary on the same day. In 1996, 2000 and 2004, both parties' nominations were sewn up long before New Jersey voted. In April 2007, the legislature rescheduled the primary for Feb. 5, Super Tuesday. But New Jersey again got lost in the shuffle. Polls showed Hillary Rodham Clinton and John McCain with solid leads here and in New York, which also voted on Super Tuesday. So every campaign decided to save money by not buying New York television. Democratic turnout was 1.1 million, nearly double the previous record, and Clinton beat Obama 54%-44%. She carried Jewish and Latino voters, while Obama carried blacks and did well in high-income suburbs, except those with large Jewish populations. Turnout on the Republican side was only 566,000, more than ever before but only half the number of Democrats who voted. McCain defeated Mitt Romney by a surprisingly large 55%-28%. Romney was unable to duplicate here the appeal he demonstrated in high-income suburbs in several other states. McCain topped 50% in all but two counties.

Congressional districting   New Jersey has a Redistricting Commission, made up of 12 members appointed by the party leaders in the legislature. The members pick an arbiter, and in both 1991 and 2001, they chose professor Alan Rosenthal of the Eagleton Institute at Rutgers University. The 13th member breaks a tie, produces a compromise plan of his own and sees whether a majority will accept it. If not, he forwards the two plans to the state Supreme Court.

112th Congress Lineup	
7 D	6 R
111th Congress Lineup	
8 D	5 R

In 1991, Rosenthal picked the Republican plan, with grotesquely shaped districts. But given the 1990s Democratic trend, by 2000, Republicans held only six of 13 districts.

In 2001, the 13 incumbents agreed on a bipartisan congressional delegation plan and submitted it to the commission. Rosenthal liked the incumbent-protection plan, and in October, the commission adopted it with slight changes. The result is a map with very erose district lines and oddly shaped districts, drawn explicitly to protect incumbents and blessed by an esteemed political scientist. The partisan tilt is plain from the presidential election returns. Within these lines, Bush carried only three of these districts in 2000, when he won 40% of the vote in New Jersey. But in 2004, he carried all six of the districts represented by Republicans. In 2008, McCain carried three of them, while Democrats picked up the open seat in the 3rd District. In 2010, Republicans recaptured it.

During the 2000-10 decade, Georgia and North Carolina passed New Jersey in population and for the first time since the 1910 census, New Jersey is not one of the nation's 10 most populous states. The reapportionment following the 2010 census cost New Jersey one House seat, and so an incumbent-protection redistricting plan is not possible. Any new plan will surely maintain the majority-black 10th District and the heavily Hispanic 13th District (although the latter will have to be renumbered), and the lines are unlikely to be disturbed much in South Jersey, which has grown faster than the rest of the state. Several of the North Jersey districts have convoluted shapes and could easily be divided among their neighbors. Democrats would presumably prefer to divide up the 7th District; Republicans would presumably prefer to divide up the 6th or the 8th, whose Democratic portions could be added to the 9th, 10th, and 13th districts, which will have to be expanded geographically because of low population growth.

Governor

Chris Christie (R)

Elected 2009, term expires Jan. 2014, 1st term; b. Sept. 6, 1962, Newark; home, Mendham; U. of DE, B.A. 1984; Seton Hall U., J.D. 1987; Catholic; married (Mary Pat); 4 children.

Elected Office: Morris County freeholder, 1994-98; Dir. Freeholder Board, 1997.

Professional Career: Practicing attorney, partner, Dughi, Hewit & Palatucci, 1987-2001; U.S. attorney for New Jersey, 2002-08.

Office: 125 W. State St., 8625, 609-292-6000; Fax: 609-292-3454; Web site: www.state.nj.us/governor.

Election Results

2009 general	Chris Christie (R)	1,174,445	(48%)
	Jon Corzine (D)	1,087,731	(45%)
2009 primary	Chris Christie (R)	184,085	(55%)
	Steve Lonegan (R)	140,946	(42%)

Chris Christie, a Republican, was elected governor of New Jersey in 2009. Christie grew up in Livingston, a comfortable suburb 10 miles west of Newark, the son of an accountant who was an ardent Republican, and a Sicilian-American mother who was a lifelong Democrat. He was president of his class throughout middle school and high school and was selected for student leadership programs in Washington. In 1977, when he was 15, he volunteered in Republican Thomas Kean's race for governor, and Kean became his role model. He graduated from the University of Delaware and Seton Hall Law School. After law school, Christie and his wife moved to New Jersey and he joined a law firm in Cranford, where he specialized in corporate securities law and appellate work and became a partner in 1993. His wife, Mary Pat Christie, pursued a career in investment banking. One of Christie's law partners, Bill Palatucci, was state coordinator for George H.W. Bush's campaign in 1992 and the two together raised money in 2000 for his son, George W. Bush. In 1994, Christie was elected as a Republican to the Morris County Board of Chosen Freeholders. In 1995, he ran for the Assembly but lost to candidates favored by the county Republican organization. In 1997, he was defeated in the Republican primary for the freeholder position.

Christie's political work paid off when President George W. Bush appointed him U.S. attorney for New Jersey in 2002. This was a critical position in a state known for its corrupt politics; among others who have held it is Supreme Court Justice Samuel Alito. Ordinarily, U.S. attorneys are chosen by a state's senators, but both were Democrats, and Bush evidently wanted to bypass the county Republican organizations and appoint someone who was not indebted to them. The selection was strongly criticized in the state's legal circles as political patronage; Christie had no experience in criminal law. But he ultimately silenced his critics with a string of successful cases against corrupt public officials, street gangs, child pornographers and terrorists. He hired assistant U.S. attorneys with experience in criminal law, and divided two large divisions into eight separate, specialized divisions aimed at improving prosecutions of commercial crimes, violent crimes, securities fraud and Medicare fraud. In 2007, Christie spearheaded the investigation of a group of foreign-born radical Islamists suspected of plotting to attack soldiers at Fort Dix with assault rifles. He was best known, however, for a crackdown on public corruption in the state that yielded 130 convictions of both Democrats and Republicans, including that of a former state Senate president and a former Newark mayor.

The part of his record that drew criticism was his practice of awarding contracts to law firms to monitor corporations. The companies could avoid indictment for fraud if they paid for a monitor to oversee their practices. One such contract went to former Attorney General John Ashcroft; another went to David Kelley, who as a federal prosecutor in Manhattan had declined to charge Christie's brother, Todd Christie, in a securities fraud investigation. Christie defended the program, saying the contracts were awarded on merit. In June 2009, he stormed out of a hearing of the House Judiciary Committee, which was examining the use of deferred prosecution. Christie said that as an Italian-American, he found offensive a comment from one committee Democrat that the companies were pressured to accept the monitoring fees as a result of Mafia-style offers that they "could not refuse."

In November 2008, Christie resigned as U.S. attorney to run against Gov. Jon Corzine, a former U.S. senator and chief executive officer of Goldman Sachs. This was a formidable challenge. Republicans had not won a statewide race in New Jersey since 1997, when incumbent Gov. Christie Whitman beat Jim McGreevey, 47%-46%. Plus, Corzine had deep pockets, having spent more than $100 million of his own money on his 2000 and 2005 campaigns. But Corzine had problems. He had been unable to fulfill his campaign pledge of lowering property taxes; New Jersey's are the highest in the nation. And his proposal to increase the tolls on the New Jersey Turnpike to provide long-term financing for transportation was rejected by the Democratic legislature. State government faced dizzying budget shortfalls, and the legislature had passed a temporary "millionaire's tax" on people with incomes over $400,000. New Jersey's unemployment rate was the highest in the Northeast, and accordingly, Corzine's job approval was under 40%.

Christie campaigned as a middle-class "Jersey guy," a native of the state, a father of four children under the age of 15, and a Mets baseball fan. He said he played New Jersey native Bruce Springsteen's song "Prove It All Night" to get psyched before press conferences, and in 2003 he attended nine Springsteen concerts. As New Jersey political writer John Martin put it, "He was indisputably the state's most visible law enforcement officer, a finger-wagging prosecutor with Jersey roots who made a name convicting so many corrupt public officials that state GOP leaders practically begged him to ride his white horse into Trenton." Christie was endorsed by most Republican county organizations, but he had primary competition from Steve Lonegan, former mayor of Bogota in Bergen County, who said Christie was insufficiently conservative at a time when the tea party movement was gaining strength. But Christie won the June primary 55%-42%.

In the fall campaign, Christie led Corzine consistently in polls in the months after the primary. He said he would slash state spending down to essentials, take on powerful public employee unions and, finally, cut property tax rates. He called the millionaire's tax "a wet blanket of over-taxation on New Jersey's economy." Corzine criticized Christie for not being specific about his proposed spending cuts and charged that he would ravage the environment and curtail abortion rights. Corzine ultimately spent $27 million of his own money on the campaign, while Christie was limited by New Jersey's public financing law to spending $11 million. Corzine's ads focused on Christie's monitoring contracts, on his failure to report a $46,000 loan to one of his top aides and even on the issue of his weight. One ad depicted the corpulent Christie struggling to emerge from a car with the suggestion that as U.S. attorney, he had "thrown his weight around" during a traffic stop.

By mid-October, Corzine and Christie were running about even in the polls, with Christopher Daggett, a former Republican running as an independent, getting as much as 20%, apparently splitting the anti-Corzine vote. Democratic strategists tried to bolster Corzine, and President Barack Obama came in to campaign for him. Vice President Joe Biden, former President Bill Clinton and Caroline Kennedy put in appearances as well. But celebrity endorsements and a fat campaign chest couldn't save Corzine. Christie beat him 48%-45%, with 6% for Daggett. At his victory celebration, Christie blasted Springsteen's "Born to Run" on the sound system and pledged to immediately begin "the task of fixing our broken state."

The exit poll showed Christie gaining over John McCain's 2008 showing, especially among men, Hispanics and non-college-educated whites. Turnout was down two-thirds from 2008 among young voters, and Christie carried all age groups over 30. He ran especially far ahead of McCain in the central part of the state, with popular vote margins in Monmouth and Ocean counties on the Jersey Shore exceeding Corzine's margins in Hudson and Essex counties (Jersey City and Newark). He carried normally Democratic Middlesex County, including Edison and Woodbridge Townships, which have the nation's largest concentration of Americans born in India. Democrats, however, retained majorities in both houses of the legislature.

When Christie settled into budget-making, the outlook was grim: State government faced a projected deficit of $11 billion. In March 2010, he unveiled a $29 billion budget plan that leaned heavily on spending cuts, including layoffs of 1,300 state workers, a $3 billion reduction in scheduled pension payments, and an $820 million cut in aid to schools. The proposal aimed to save on Medicaid costs by establishing a $350 deductible for beneficiaries. He reneged on a campaign promise to allow a popular property tax rebate scheduled for May 2010 to go through, announcing he was suspending it for a year. Addressing the legislature, Christie said, "We jump off the cliff together to stave off certain fiscal death for the hope of economic salvation tomorrow." Although Democratic Speaker Sheila Oliver called the budget a "disaster for middle-class families," she said her party would be willing to work with Christie on a proposal to cap yearly property tax increases at 2.5%. When the legislature voted to extend the millionaire's tax, Christie immediately vetoed it.

He also took on New Jersey's state employee unions. In early 2010, he issued an executive order limiting their political spending, but it was overturned in court. From there, his relationship with the unions was all downhill. When the head of the New Jersey Education Association came to his office, he told her she must fire the head of the Bergen County branch, who in an e-mail had wished for Christie's death. The NJEA head refused and Christie said she was no longer welcome in the governor's office. In April 2010, Christie charged that teachers union members were "using the students like drug mules" to distribute propaganda to parents. In response to his urgings, twice as many voters came out in the April school elections and rejected proposed property tax increases. Next, Christie picked a fight with the judicial branch. In May 2010, he refused to reappoint Supreme Court Justice John Wallace, as previous governors had routinely done, because of what he called "out of control" activism on the court. Democratic Senate President Stephen Sweeney refused to let the Senate vote on Christie's nominee to fill the post.

Christie challenged other shibboleths. In September 2010, he called for ending the practice of state legislators simultaneously holding local office. (McGreevey had served simultaneously as state senator and mayor of Woodbridge Township, for example.) Among his education reforms, he called for eliminating tenure for ineffective teachers, automatic salary increases for teachers after a certain number of years and increased pay for those with master's degrees. In January 2011, he argued that low-performing school districts be permitted to hire superintendents without education Ph.D.s, as had been done in New York, Chicago and Washington, D.C.

In October 2010, he canceled proposed rail tunnels to Manhattan, turning down $3 billion in federal money on the grounds that estimated costs for the project were rising to $14 billion and that the state would be stuck paying for the cost overruns. "There are new rules of engagement, New Jersey, and here's the most important one—we do not spend money we do not have," he said. But the following month, he said he would consider backing New York Mayor Michael Bloomberg's project to extend seven subway lines to New Jersey since New York would pay for much of it. Yet Christie did not totally cut off relations with New Jersey Democrats. He continued to negotiate with Sweeney and Oliver, and he kept in close and friendly touch with Newark Mayor Cory Booker and Essex County Executive Joseph DiVincenzo. In March 2011, his proposals to cut business taxes passed both houses of the legislature unanimously.

His confrontations with public employee unions helped make him a national political figure. His staff distributed to YouTube dozens of videos produced by hand-held cameras at his town hall meetings. In one of the most often viewed videos, he is shown addressing a complaining teacher: "I stood here and very respectfully listened to you. If what you want to do is put on a show and giggle every time I talk, well then I have no interest in answering your question." On another video, he explained his confrontational style: "I have an Irish father and I had ... a Sicilian mother. For those of you who have been exposed to the combination of Irish and Sicilian, it has made me not unfamiliar with conflict." Suddenly, Christie had an immense following, with his videos getting over 1 million views.

In 2010, he campaigned for Republican gubernatorial candidates in several states, including California, Illinois, Iowa, Massachusetts, New Mexico, Ohio, Pennsylvania and Wisconsin. In October 2010, he won the most votes in a tea party straw poll in Virginia. But Christie said he had no intention whatsoever of running for president in 2012.

Senior Senator

Frank Lautenberg (D)

Elected 2002, term expires 2014, 5th term; b. Jan. 23, 1924, Paterson; home, Cliffside Park; Columbia U., B.S. 1949; Jewish; married (Bonnie); 4 children.

Military Career: Army Signal Corps, 1942–46 (WWII).

Elected Office: U.S. Senate, 1982-2000.

Professional Career: Co–founder, Automatic Data Processing, 1952–82; NY & NJ Port Authority Comm., 1978–82.

DC Office: 324 HSOB, 20510, 202-224-3224; Fax: 202-228-4054; Web site: lautenberg.senate.gov.

State Offices: Camden, 856-338-8922; Newark, 973-639-8700.

Committees: *Appropriations:* Commerce, Justice, Science & Related Agencies; Department of State, Foreign Operations & Related Programs; Energy & Water Development; Financial Services & General Government; Homeland Security; Transportation, HUD & Related Agencies. *Commerce, Science & Transportation:* Aviation Operations, Safety & Security; Communications, Technology & the Internet; Oceans, Atmosphere, Fisheries & Coast Guard; Surface Transportation & Merchant Marine Infrastructure, Safety & Security (Chmn). *Environment & Public Works:* Clean Air & Nuclear Safety; Superfund, Toxics & Environmental Health (Chmn); Transportation & Infrastructure; Water & Wildlife.

Group Ratings

	ACLU	ACU	ADA	CFG	AFS	FRC	LCV	ITIC	NTU	COC
2010	93	0	95	0	100	0	100	33	3	9
2009	–	0	95	3	100	–	100	–	5	43

National Journal Ratings

	2010 LIB	—	2010 CONS		2009 LIB	—	2009 CONS
Economic	83%	—	16%		86%	—	12%
Social	65%	—	0%		85%	—	0%
Foreign	47%	—	0%		55%	—	0%
Composite	80%	—	20%		86%	—	14%

Key Votes of the 111th Congress

1. Overturn Ledbetter	Y	5. Pass health care bill	Y	9. Ratify New START	Y
2. Pass $787 billion stimulus	Y	6. Regulate financial firms	Y	10. Confirm Elena Kagan	Y
3. Repeal DC gun laws	N	7. Pass tax cuts for some	Y	11. Stop EPA climate regs	N
4. Confirm Sonia Sotomayor	Y	8. Legalize immigrants' kids	Y	12. Repeal don't ask, tell	Y

Election Results

2008 general	Frank Lautenberg (D)	1,951,218	(56%)	($9,192,874)
	Dick Zimmer (R)	1,461,025	(42%)	($989,585)
2008 primary	Frank Lautenberg (D)	203,012	(59%)	
	Robert Andrews (D)	121,777	(35%)	
	Donald Cresitello (D)	19,743	(6%)	

Prior Winning Percentages: 2002 (54%); 1994 (50%); 1988 (54%); 1982 (51%)

Democrat Frank Lautenberg is New Jersey's senior senator. He was first elected to the Senate in 1982, retired in 2000, and then returned to run again in October 2002 after Democratic Sen. Robert Torricelli withdrew from his re-election race.

Lautenberg grew up in Paterson, the son of Russian and Polish immigrants. His father, a silk worker who also once ran a tavern, died of cancer while Lautenberg was still in high school, and he worked nights and weekends to help with the family finances. He served in the Army Signal Corps in World War II and says he could not have gone to college without the GI Bill. He graduated from Columbia University and in 1952 he joined a young firm called Automatic Data Processing, which organized information using punch-card machines—the forerunner to computers. In time, ADP was processing the payroll for nearly 10% of the private-sector jobs in the United States. When the company went public in 1961, Lautenberg's stock was valued at $50,000; now, his net worth exceeds $49 million, according to his financial disclosure forms, and ADP is still in business as one of the world's largest providers of outsourced business services. (Lautenberg's charitable foundation, however, lost the $7 million in Bernard Madoff's massive fraud scheme in 2001 and 2002.) Lautenberg was a contributor to Democratic campaigns and landed on President Richard Nixon's "enemies list" after he gave $90,000 to George McGovern's campaign in 1972.

In 1982, Democratic Sen. Harrison Williams resigned after his conviction in the Abscam bribery scandal, and his appointed successor, Republican Nicholas Brady, did not seek a full term. Lautenberg ran for the seat, spending $5 million of his own money and touting his experience in technology. He defeated several more seasoned politicians in the primary. In the general election, he faced U.S. Rep. Millicent Fenwick, an eccentric 72-year-old who was satirized in the *Doonesbury* comic strip. Lautenberg, then still in his 50s, made an issue of Fenwick's age by referring to her as a "national monument" and questioning her "fitness" to do the job. He won 51%-48%.

Lautenberg says he believes that government helped him and others work their way up, and in his first three terms in the Senate he established a solidly liberal voting record. He bucked his party only occasionally. One of his successes then was his battle against smoking in public places. A former smoker himself, Lautenberg got Congress to ban smoking in federal buildings and on airplanes on all domestic flights. In recent years, he has called for stricter labeling of the ingredients in cigarettes and for a ban on electronic cigarettes. He has also been a strong backer of stricter gun laws, and is the author of the 1996 law barring people convicted of domestic abuse from possessing firearms; it was upheld 7-2 by the Supreme Court in 2009. In 1997, Lautenberg was one of the few Democrats to enthusiastically support the balanced-budget deal that President Bill Clinton forged with Republican congressional leaders. His support was key to Clinton's success in getting the measure through the Senate. Lautenberg won re-election relatively easily over retired Gen. Pete Dawkins in 1988 and Assembly Speaker Chuck Haytaian in 1994. In 1998, he seemed primed to run again, and no well-known Republican appeared eager to challenge him. But in February 1999, he announced that he would retire in 2000.

Before long, however, national Democrats were facing a big problem with New Jersey's other Senate seat. The U.S. Attorney's Office in Manhattan was investigating charges that businessman David Chang had given lavish gifts and cash to Torricelli and that Torricelli had worked to advance Chang's business interests in South Korea. Torricelli did give such assistance, but he denied receiving gifts. No charges were brought, but the Senate Ethics Committee "severely admonished" Torricelli for violating a rule against receiving gifts over $50. His Republican opponent, businessman Doug Forrester, made much of Torricelli's problems and Torricelli plummeted in the polls. The following Sunday, Gov. Jim McGreevey, Sen. Jon Corzine (elected in 2000 to succeed Lautenberg) and other New Jersey Democratic leaders met in Trenton, and in a conference call with Senate Majority Leader Tom Daschle, they discussed the need for Torricelli to withdraw from the race. On Monday he did.

New Jersey Democrats were now in need of a well-known candidate to replace Torricelli. Rep. Robert Menendez was seeking a leadership position in the House and was not interested. Rep. Robert Andrews was vetoed by McGreevey, who had narrowly defeated him in the 1997 gubernatorial primary. Lautenberg, well-known and capable of self-financing, let it be known he was available and Democrats quickly agreed on him.

New Jersey law does not contain a provision for substituting a new candidate so late in the campaign unless a candidate has died. Ballots with Torricelli's name had already been printed. But the New Jersey Supreme Court is made up of judicial activists from both parties with a propensity to accommodate party insiders. In October 2002, it quickly approved state Democrats' request to substitute Lautenberg for Torricelli and ordered the state Democratic Party to pay the $800,000 needed to print new ballots. The Lautenberg campaign moved into Torricelli's headquarters and Lautenberg was again a candidate for the Senate, and without having to spend months campaigning. The easiest source of funds proved unavailable: Torricelli, who never liked Lautenberg, said he would not send over a dime from his $5 million campaign treasury.

Republican nominee Forrester suddenly had a more formidable opponent than the weakened Torricelli. He did run a cute ad on cable television showing a kid slamming his hand on his desk and saying, "I can't do this. I quit! If I fail this test, can I have Frank Lautenberg take it for me?" Forrester attacked Lautenberg as soft on defense and terrorism, citing his 1991 vote against the Gulf War resolution, and he questioned whether Lautenberg at 78—six years older than Millicent Fenwick was when Lautenberg questioned her ability to do the job—was too old. Lautenberg hit Forrester on the issues and made a special point of noting his positions against state-paid abortions and gun control. Forrester spent $10 million altogether, including $7.5 million of his own money, but got little help from national Republicans, who did not target the race. Lautenberg spent $1.5 million of his own money and was helped by $1.2 million from national and New Jersey Democrats. He won 54%-44%, a better showing than he'd had in 1994, when the state was significantly less Democratic.

Once back in the Senate, Lautenberg was disappointed when the Democratic Caucus did not give him full credit for his seniority. But he quickly directed his ire toward the Bush administration.

He moved aggressively to stop privatization of the air traffic control system, holding up the Federal Aviation Administration's reauthorization in 2003 until the FAA swore off privatization. He voted against the Republicans' Medicare prescription drug bill that year, even though it was supported by many New Jersey pharmaceutical companies. During 2004, Lautenberg kept up a drumbeat of criticism of the Pentagon for awarding sole-source contracts to Halliburton, which Vice President Dick Cheney's formerly headed. He also opposed the administration on the Iraq war, and he sponsored an amendment to allow the media to photograph the coffins of fallen service personnel being returned to their families through Dover Air Force Base in Delaware. He seemed distinctly more outspoken in his second stint, and his New Jersey colleague in the Senate at the time, Corzine, observed, "He's less risk-averse. I think Frank couldn't care less." Lautenberg said, "I do feel unconstrained."

From his seat on the Commerce Committee, Lautenberg has looked after his state's transportation needs with an emphasis on guarding against terrorist threats. He has pressed for better security at airports, seaports, and railroads. Lautenberg won a seat on the Appropriations Committee in 2007, and inserted provisions in that year's appropriations bills barring federal pre-emption of tougher state chemical safety laws, such as New Jersey's. He sponsored a bill on vessel safety, requiring double hulls on fuel tankers. He and Menendez, now a senator, sponsored a bill, based on the 9/11 commission's recommendations, to require radiation scanning of all shipping cargo containers by 2012. Also in 2007, Lautenberg secured $14.7 million to begin engineering work on the proposed ARC (Access to the Region's Core) twin new rail tunnels from northern New Jersey to Manhattan.

In 2008, in contrast to eight years before, Lautenberg showed no hesitancy in seeking another term. "There is a lot that remains to be done," he told the Bergen *Record*. "The people respect what I do. They know I'm straightforward in my efforts for my state. And I want to continue doing it." He started fundraising early. And when all three Republican candidates for the seat in February 2008 opposed Gov. Corzine's plan to lease the New Jersey Turnpike and raise tolls, Lautenberg came out against it too, despite his close relationship with Corzine. In April, Democratic Rep. Robert Andrews announced he was running in the June Democratic primary. There was an obvious contrast in their ages—Lautenberg was 84, Andrews was 50—and in their political bases. Andrews is from Camden County in South Jersey, and in his previous statewide primary, for governor in 1997, he had won big margins in the Philadelphia media market. Lautenberg had already won the backing of all 21 county party organizations, usually decisive in New Jersey's light-voting primaries, but Andrews accumulated some endorsements, including prominent state legislators from Union and Middlesex counties, as well as from Assembly Speaker Joseph Roberts from Camden County.

Lautenberg campaigned aggressively. "Age has nothing to do with it," he argued. "It's about effectiveness, and I've been effective in office." He ran an ad attacking Andrews for his support for the Iraq war resolution in October 2002, with pictures of President George W. Bush and Cheney. (At the time, Lautenberg issued statements generally supporting military action but, being out of office, did not vote on the resolution.) Andrews countered that he would be a more vigorous senator. His supporters noted that Lautenberg's wife was registered to vote on Park Avenue in New York City. Lautenberg spent $5.7 million, lending his campaign $1.65 million, while Andrews spent $3 million. The voting ran along regional lines. Andrews won 71% of the votes in South Jersey and Lautenberg won 75% in North Jersey. Unfortunately for Andrews, three-quarters of the votes were cast in North Jersey, and Lautenberg won 59%-35%. But Andrews managed a soft landing by figuring out a way to save his place in the House. He had his wife put her name on the ballot in the election for his House seat, so when he lost the Senate race, all he had to do was substitute as the Democratic nominee, which he did.

In the general election, Lautenberg faced former Rep. Dick Zimmer, who had lost to Torricelli 53%-43% in 1996. Zimmer criticized Lautenberg for sponsoring spending earmarks and for supporting the $700 billion rescue of the financial industry in 2008. Lautenberg said that the measure "isn't perfect, but it is real action when we need it," and he defended the earmarks as worthwhile for New Jersey and the country. Zimmer spent only $945,000 and national Republicans, on the defensive in many other states, did not target the race. Lautenberg won 56%-42% and became the first New Jersey senator in history to be elected to a fifth term.

In the 111th Congress (2009-10), Lautenberg was at the forefront to impose some restrictions on guns. He sponsored a bill to require background checks for purchases at gun shows and voted against allowing guns into national parks and wildlife refuges. In 2010, he called for restrictions on gun purchases by persons on the government's terrorist watch list, and objected when Democratic leaders agreed to a provision exempting the National Rifle Association from the DISCLOSE Act, requiring more transparency in campaign financing. In January 2011, he sought to ban high-capacity magazines like those used in the shooting of Arizona Democratic Rep. Gabrielle Giffords and others at a Tucson supermarket.

On fiscal issues, Lautenberg in December 2010 was one of 19 senators who voted against the deal hammered out by President Barack Obama and Republican congressional leaders extending the 2001 and 2003 Bush tax cuts, including those for high-income earners, for two years. He told *The Star-Ledger* newspaper, "Because of a good business career, I made some money and the last thing I need is a tax cut. I'd rather have a strong country than a tax cut." He also continued to earmark funds for New Jersey projects, including $206 million for the ARC tunnels in July 2010.

On the Homeland Security Appropriations Subcommittee, Lautenberg had hoped to become chairman after the 2010 election, claiming that former Senate Majority Leader Daschle had promised him the chairmanship when inducing him to run again in 2002. But current Senate Majority Leader Harry Reid and party leaders gave the gavel to Mary Landrieu of Louisiana, who had more seniority. In memory of the 38 people from New Jersey who died in the 1988 bombing of Pan Am flight 103 engineered by Libyan dictator Muammar Gaddafi, Lautenberg spoke at a rally in Englewood to prevent Gaddafi from staying at Libyan property there. Prompted by the suicide of a New Jersey soldier, he and Rep. Rush Holt, D-N.J., sought to bolster mental health services for National Guard and Reserve personnel. Lautenberg was moved to tears while attending a memorial service in 2010 for Rutgers student Tyler Clementi, who killed himself after fellow students posted a video of him in an intimate, and thought to be private, encounter with another man.

Lautenberg's relations with New Jersey colleagues are sometimes frosty, though the level of hostilities has not risen to the level he had with Torricelli. He and Andrews did not speak for some time after the 2008 election. He reacted angrily, and threatened to hold hearings, when Republican Gov. Chris Christie canceled the ARC tunnels project in October 2010, citing cost overruns. "Killing the ARC tunnel will go down as one of the biggest public policy blunders in New Jersey's history," Lautenberg said. "Without increased transportation options into Manhattan, New Jersey's economy will eventually be crippled."

Asked during the 2008 campaign whether he would serve the full six-year term, Lautenberg, then 84, said, "Yeah. Why not?" On his 86th birthday, his wife took him to a Lady Gaga concert. In February 2010, Lautenberg was diagnosed with B-cell lymphoma of the stomach, a cancer readily treatable by chemotherapy. His seat comes up in 2014, when he turns 90.

Junior Senator

Robert Menendez (D)

Appointed Jan. 2006, term expires 2012, 1st full term; b. Jan. 1, 1954, New York, NY; home, Union City; St. Peter's Col., B.A. 1976, Rutgers Law Schl., J.D. 1979; Catholic; married (Jane Jacobsen-Menendez); 2 children.

Elected Office: Union City Bd. of Ed., 1974–82; Union City mayor, 1986–92; NJ Assembly, 1987–91; NJ Senate, 1991–92; U.S. House of Reps., 1992-2006.

Professional Career: Practicing atty., 1980-92.

DC Office: 528 HSOB, 20510, 202-224-4744; Fax: 202-228-2197; Web site: menendez.senate.gov.

State Offices: Barrington , 856-757-5353; Newark, 973-645-3030.

Committees: *Banking, Housing & Urban Affairs:* Financial Institutions & Consumer Protection; Housing, Transportation & Community Development; Securities, Insurance & Investment. *Finance:* Health Care; International Trade, Customs & Global Competitiveness; Taxation & IRS Oversight. *Foreign Relations:* International Development & Foreign Assistance, Economic Affairs & International Environmental Protection; International Operations & Organizations, Democracy & Global Women's Issues; Near Eastern & South & Central Asian Affairs; Western Hemisphere, Peace Corps & Global Narcotics Affairs (Chmn).

Group Ratings

	ACLU	ACU	ADA	CFG	AFS	FRC	LCV	ITIC	NTU	COC
2010	93	0	90	1	100	0	100	67	7	36
2009	–	0	90	3	100	–	100	–	5	43

National Journal Ratings

	2010 LIB — 2010 CONS		2009 LIB — 2009 CONS	
Economic	84%	— 15%	72%	— 24%
Social	65%	— 0%	85%	— 0%
Foreign	47%	— 0%	55%	— 0%
Composite	80%	— 20%	81%	— 19%

Key Votes of the 111th Congress

1. Overturn Ledbetter	Y	5. Pass health care bill	Y	9. Ratify New START	Y
2. Pass $787 billion stimulus	Y	6. Regulate financial firms	Y	10. Confirm Elena Kagan	Y
3. Repeal DC gun laws	N	7. Pass tax cuts for some	Y	11. Stop EPA climate regs	N
4. Confirm Sonia Sotomayor	Y	8. Legalize immigrants' kids	Y	12. Repeal don't ask, tell	Y

Election Results

2006 general	Robert Menendez (D)	1,200,843	(53%)	($11,950,586)
	Thomas Kean, Jr. (R)	997,775	(44%)	($7,635,186)
2006 primary	Robert Menendez (D)	159,604	(84%)	
	James Kelly (D)	30,340	(16%)	

Prior Winning Percentages: House: 2004 (76%); 2002 (78%); 2000 (79%); 1998 (80%); 1996 (79%); 1994 (71%); 1992 (64%)

Robert Menendez, New Jersey's junior senator, was appointed by Democratic Gov. Jon Corzine in January 2006, and won election to a full term 10 months later. His ascension to the Senate was no lucky break, but rather the culmination of a career marked by an ability to adapt to and thrive in bruising political arenas. Ambitious and hard-driving, he is admired—if not warmly regarded—for his strategic savvy and prodigious fundraising skills. Menendez managed to emerge from what was a disastrous 2010 election for his party with a measure of respect for his work to ensure that the Senate stayed in Democratic hands.

Menendez is of Cuban descent and grew up in Union City, getting into politics early. He was elected to the school board in 1974, at age 20. He worked for Union City Mayor William Musto in the 1970s, but quit and testified against Musto in a corruption trial, wearing a bulletproof vest for protection because of death threats. Menendez was elected mayor in 1986, and elected to the Assembly in 1987 and Senate in 1991; he served both as mayor and legislator, which had been a common practice in New Jersey, until his 1992 election to Congress. Menendez was the first New Jersey Latino in the state legislature and in Congress. When new district lines were created and incumbent Frank Guarini retired, Menendez won the 1992 primary 68%-32% and the general election 64%-31%. As head of the Democratic Party organization in Hudson County, which has the highest number of registered Democrats of any county in the state, he was for many years a major player in state politics.

In the House, Menendez was a strong supporter of anti-Castro legislation, including the 1996 trade embargo. He sponsored a bill in 2004 to put illegal immigrants on the path to permanent worker status and citizenship. Noting the increasing importance of the financial services industry in Hudson County, his home base, he broke with many Democrats to support the 2005 bankruptcy bill and financial services deregulation.

By the late 1990s, Menendez was on track to a possible Senate candidacy. When Democratic Sen. Frank Lautenberg announced his retirement in 1999, Menendez was widely expected to run for the seat, but support was not forthcoming from New Jersey Sen. Bob Torricelli, the Democratic Senatorial Campaign Committee chairman, who preferred Jon Corzine, a wealthy former investment banker who could self-finance his campaign. Minority Leader Dick Gephardt urged Menendez to stay in the House, arguing that as a leader of a Democratic majority—Democrats came within a few seats of winning a majority in November 2000—he would soon have more influence. Menendez busied himself raising more than $4 million for fellow Democrats and traveled around the country campaigning. His Hispanic background was an asset, and not just within the 20-member Hispanic Caucus. "There are 50 to 60 members who are not Hispanic but have significant Hispanic communities in their districts," he said.

When Democrat David Bonior left the House to run for Michigan governor in 2002, Democrats picked California's Nancy Pelosi over Maryland's Steny Hoyer to succeed Bonior as party whip. Menendez announced he would run for caucus chairman, the No. 3 leadership position, against Rosa DeLauro of Connecticut. Pelosi endorsed DeLauro, and Hoyer endorsed Menendez. On the secret ballot, Menendez won 104-103. As caucus chairman, he continued to raise large sums for the party in the 2003-04 election season.

Then on Aug. 12, New Jersey Gov. Jim McGreevey announced that he had had an affair with a man he'd hired as his homeland security chief and would resign. Senate President Richard Codey became the acting Democratic governor for 14 months, and Corzine, then a Democratic U.S. senator, decided to run for governor. Menendez made it known that if Corzine were elected, he would run for Corzine's Senate seat. He had amassed more than $4 million for a statewide campaign, far more than two potential Democratic rivals—U.S. Reps. Robert Andrews and Frank Pallone. Still, Menendez, Pallone and Andrews all actively campaigned for Corzine's gubernatorial bid, while at the same time positioning themselves for a Senate campaign. Democrats worried about Menendez's Hudson County political baggage, and had questions about his relationship with former aide Kay LiCausi and his efforts to steer lobbying and consulting work her way. Nonetheless, after Corzine was elected governor, he appointed Menendez to his Senate seat in January 2006. Menendez joined Sens. Mel Martinez of Florida and Ken Salazar of Colorado as the chamber's Hispanic members.

Still, he had an upcoming election to worry about. Andrews and Pallone each decided they probably couldn't compete with Menendez and declined to challenge him in the primary, leaving Menendez free to focus on his Republican opponent, state Sen. Tom Kean Jr., son and namesake of popular former Republican Gov. Thomas Kean. Menendez campaigned against the Iraq war, while Kean said he would have voted for the Iraq war resolution and opposed a timetable for withdrawing U.S. troops. Kean reminded voters of Menendez's influence in Hudson County.

In September 2006, U.S. Attorney Chris Christie subpoenaed records from a lease arrangement between Menendez and an anti-poverty group for which he had sought federal funding and that paid him some $300,000 in rent on a building he owned in Union City. Republicans spread rumors that Menendez might drop out. But Menendez responded with an attack ad linking Kean to contributors with ethics problems. Then it was revealed that the Kean campaign's opposition researchers had contacted former Hudson County Executive Robert Janiszewski, who was serving time in federal prison on corruption charges. Menendez struck back with a television ad accusing Kean of a smear campaign: "Federal prisoner 25038-050. He's Tom Kean Jr.'s newest adviser." Polls late in the season showed Menendez with only a slight lead, and for a moment it seemed Republicans had one of the few opportunities to contest a Democrat-held seat in 2006. But Menendez held on to win 53%-44%.

In the Senate, Menendez took part in bipartisan discussions aimed at coming up with a comprehensive immigration bill, but walked out in May 2007, arguing that Democratic Sen. Edward Kennedy of Massachusetts had made too many concessions to Republicans and that the bill would "tear at the fabric of family reunification." The proposed $19,000 fees required for legalization for a family of four, he said, were "punitive" and "impractical," he said. Menendez sponsored his own unsuccessful amendment to make green-card holders eligible for legalization from May 2005 to

January 2007. He continued to speak out on immigration after the bill died in 2007. He later defended tax rebates to illegal immigrants in the 2008 economic stimulus bill. "This new dimension about whether that person is undocumented or not—if in fact they paid taxes, then it seems to me that they are also going to continue to stimulate the economy," he said.

He introduced comprehensive immigration legislation in September 2010, but the measure fell victim to a crowded election-year calendar. One of its components—the DREAM Act, which offered the children of illegal immigrants a path of citizenship in return for college or military service—ran into Democratic as well as GOP opposition in the 2010 lame-duck session, and Menendez acknowledged that a broader bill was unlikely to fare any better.

Menendez won a coveted slot on the Finance Committee in 2009. In that role, he backed two attempts in the committee to add a government-run "public option" to the health care bill, but both failed. His stance on that issue, as well as on immigration and other Democratic priorities, incensed New Jersey tea party activists, and in early 2010, they launched an effort to recall him. Menendez dismissed the recall as a "political stunt" and in April appealed to the state Supreme Court to stop their actions, calling them an "attack on the Constitution" because the document forbids the recall of a sitting U.S. senator. Seven months after hearing arguments in May, the court issued a 4-2 decision in agreement.

On the committee, Menendez in January 2009 succeeded in adding a one-year fix to the alternative minimum tax to the economic stimulus bill, which would protect middle-income taxpayers from having to pay a tax originally aimed at wealthy taxpayers who sheltered their earnings. In March 2009, he placed a hold on two of President Barack Obama's nominees to administration jobs to protest a provision easing travel restrictions to Cuba that was included in an appropriations bill. "It's a horrid process to start going down the road on. It means a handful of members can change the foreign policy of the United States," Menendez said of mixing Cuba policy with appropriations legislation. His refusal to vote for the spending bill prevented it from getting the needed 60 votes until he was offered assurances by the administration that the Cuba rider would have little impact.

As a member of the Energy and Natural Resources Committee, Menendez raised his profile on energy and environment issues. When the panel approved a wide-ranging bipartisan energy bill in June 2009, Menendez refused to support it, saying that a renewable energy mandate needed to be stronger and objecting to a provision allowing oil drilling within 45 miles of coastlines. A year later, following the BP oil spill disaster in the Gulf of Mexico, Menendez was a central figure on the contentious issue of liability caps on legal damages that companies would face for the BP spill and future spills. He introduced a bill proposing to eliminate the $75 million cap, but the measure ran into strong opposition from Republicans as well as fellow Democrats Mark Begich of Alaska and Mary Landrieu of Louisiana. Landrieu accused him of trying to put oil companies "out of business." Nevertheless, she, Begich and Menendez sought to work out a compromise, and though they ran out of time in the 111th Congress (2009-10), they renewed their efforts in 2011.

Menendez got some negative attention for blocking a promotion for a prosecutor investigating Puerto Rican Gov. Anibal Acevedo-Vila, a friend of his, who, as the nonvoting delegate from Puerto Rico in the House, had cast a decisive vote for Menendez in the caucus chairman race. The prosecutor was in line to become the U.S. attorney in Puerto Rico and, at the time, was investigating Acevedo-Vila's fundraising practices. The prosecutor got the appointment in the end, and Acevedo-Vila was indicted for violating campaign finance and tax laws in March 2008; he was defeated for reelection in November 2008.

In the 2008 election season, Menendez was the deputy director of the Democratic Senatorial Campaign Committee, helping to raise money for Senate campaigns. He took over the chairmanship in the 2010 election cycle, attaining the fourth-ranking leadership position in the Senate Democratic majority. In February 2009, Menendez indicated that he would target Republican-held seats in Florida, Kansas, Kentucky, Louisiana, Missouri, New Hampshire, North Carolina, Ohio, and Pennsylvania. His low-key, disciplined approach contrasted sharply with that of his frenetic and publicity-driven predecessor, New York Democrat Chuck Schumer. But the economic downturn and the public's discontent with Democrats' health care bill worked heavily against him, and his party was shocked by Republican Scott Brown's upset win in Massachusetts in the January 2010 special election. After that embarrassment, Menendez reportedly urged his party's candidates at a private meeting to "run scared." He ordered a review of their campaigns to ensure they could adjust to the demands of a "volatile" electorate.

As Republicans inched closer to gaining majority control of the House that fall, speculation mounted that the Senate too would fall to the GOP. But under Menendez, the DSCC outraised its Republican counterpart, $130 million to $115 million. Even though Democrats lost six Senate seats, many in the party were relieved that the damage wasn't worse. Several vulnerable incumbents, including Majority Leader Harry Reid of Nevada and Colorado's Michael Bennet, hung on to win, marking the first time in 80 years that the party in charge of the House lost control but the Senate did not. When Menendez arrived at the first post-election meeting with colleagues, he was greeted with a standing ovation. "The windstorm he was walking into, it wasn't just 30 miles per hour winds with gusts up to 40 miles per hour; it was a hurricane," Reid told *The Record* newspaper of Hackensack. Reid's victory was attributed partly to Hispanic voter turnout that Menendez helped to bolster. Other senators said they were impressed given the handicap Menendez had stemming from the Supreme Court's *Citizens United v. Federal Election Commission* ruling that enabled corporations and special-interest groups to donate unlimited amounts of money to Republicans. "People understand the huge challenges he faced," said Sen. Jack Reed of Rhode Island.

For 2012, Menendez declined to stay on as DSCC chairman to concentrate on his own re-election. Menendez was in a strong political position in early 2011, but Republicans were targeting him.

FIRST DISTRICT

Robert Andrews (D)

Elected Nov. 1990, 11th full term; b. Aug. 4, 1957, Camden; home, Haddon Heights; Bucknell U., B.A. 1979, Cornell U., J.D. 1982; Episcopalian; married (Camille); 2 children.

Elected Office: Camden Cnty. Bd. of Chosen Freeholders, 1987–90.

Professional Career: Practicing atty., 1982–90; Adjunct prof., Rutgers Law Schl., 1985–86, 1989–90.

DC Office: 2265 RHOB, 20515, 202-225-6501; Fax: 202-225-6583; Web site: house.gov/andrews.

State Offices: Haddon Heights, 856-546-5100; Woodbury, 856-848-3900.

Committees: *Armed Services:* Emerging Threats & Capabilities; Oversight & Investigations. *Education & the Workforce:* Health, Employment, Labor & Pensions (RMM); Higher Education & Workforce Training.

Group Ratings

	ACLU	ACU	ADA	CFG	AFS	FRC	LCV	ITIC	NTU	COC
2010	81	0	90	0	100	0	100	100	5	25
2009	–	0	100	0	100	–	100	–	2	33

National Journal Ratings

	2010 LIB	—	2010 CONS	2009 LIB	—	2009 CONS
Economic	71%	—	28%	82%	—	14%
Social	86%	—	13%	84%	—	11%
Foreign	62%	—	38%	70%	—	24%
Composite	73%	—	27%	81%	—	19%

Key Votes of the 111th Congress

1. Overturn Ledbetter	Y	5. Bar federal abortion funds	N	9. Stop detainee transfers	Y
2. Pass $820 billion stimulus	Y	6. Pass health care bill	Y	10. Legalize immigrants' kids	Y
3. Let guns in national parks	N	7. Regulate financial firms	Y	11. Repeal don't ask, tell	Y
4. Pass cap-and-trade	Y	8. Pass tax cuts for some	Y	12. Limit campaign funds	Y

Election Results

2010 general	Robert Andrews (D)	106,334	(63%)	($1,455,172)
	Dale Glading (R)	58,562	(35%)	($65,687)
2010 primary	Robert Andrews (D)	14,695	(87%)	
	John Caramanna (D)	2,262	(13%)	

Prior Winning Percentages: 2008 (72%), 2006 (100%), 2004 (75%), 2002 (93%), 2000 (76%), 1998 (73%), 1996 (76%), 1994 (72%), 1992 (67%), 1990 (54%), 1990 special (55%)

Population		Race/Ethnicity		Work	
Pop. 2010:	669,169	White:	65.0%	Private:	81.0%
Change since 2000:	Up 3.4%	Black:	17.2%	Government:	14.9%
Urban:	98.6%	Hispanic:	12.1%	Self-employed:	3.9%
Rural:	1.4%	Asian:	3.7%	Blue collar:	19.8%
Area size:	352 sq. mi.	Native Am.:	0.2%	White collar:	63.5%
		Hawaiian:	0.0%	Khaki collar:	0.1%
Age		Two+ races:	1.7%	Other:	16.6%
Median age:	36.9 yrs.				
More than 65 yrs:	12.3%	*Ancestry*		Median income:	$60,169
Less than 18 yrs:	24.1%	Irish	18.1%	Median Home Value:	$222,100
		Italian	14.9%		
Education		German	13.6%	**Military Veterans**	
H.S. grad:	85.8%			% of Pop:	9.2%
College grad:	24.8%				
Grad degree:	8.0%				

Camden

The closely built streets of Camden, across the Delaware River from Philadelphia, have seen a fair amount of history. This was where the poet Walt Whitman lived when he wrote some of the versions of his *Leaves of Grass*. It was an immigrant-jammed industrial city then, with tinkerers and inventors. In 1894, a Camden machinist named Eldridge Johnson produced the Victor Talking Machine, the birth of the recorded music industry and a company that became RCA

2008 Presidential Vote		
Barack Obama (D)	198,194	(65%)
John McCain (R)	103,994	(34%)
2004 Presidential Vote		
John Kerry (D)	170,786	(61%)
George Bush (R)	111,073	(39%)
Cook Partisan Voting Index:	D+12	

Victor in 1929. A few years later, the new Campbell Soup Company began producing condensed soups. Camden remained for years a major industrial locus on the New Jersey side of the Delaware River, not the broadest and certainly not the most picturesque of Atlantic estuaries, but probably the East Coast's premier industrial waterway, with a concentration of steel factories, chemical plants, and oil tank farms equal to any in the country. The flatlands all around, mostly ignored in the 19th century, had easy access to cheap water transportation and plenty of skilled labor from the Philadelphia area. For a quarter-century starting in the 1940s, this was one of the country's fastest-growing industrial areas.

In the 1980s and 1990s, Camden emptied out. Many of its factories had closed, and fewer than 10,000 manufacturing jobs remained. Its neighborhoods were beset by crime, its mostly minority residents were heavily dependent on public assistance, and its mayor was convicted of doing favors for Philadelphia's organized crime leaders. Camden continues to struggle today. Thirty-eight percent of its population lived in poverty in 2010. From 2002 to 2010, the state controlled its finances and government. It was ranked the second-most-violent city in the nation behind St. Louis, and in January 2011, the mayor laid off almost half of the police department, citing a $26.5 million deficit. The bright spots are a redeveloped riverfront park, the New Jersey aquarium, and a state-of-the-art amphitheater. Campbell's in 2010 opened an addition to its world headquarters. The port of Camden has rebounded, spurred by Del Monte's large fruit-processing plant, plus large imports of foreign steel and exports of scrap metal. Camden and two surrounding counties lost 1,500 jobs a month in the late 2000s, but by 2010, they were adding 1,000 jobs a month.

The 1st Congressional District is, more or less, greater Camden, the Delaware riverfront from Riverton south to a point across from the Delaware state line, and the suburbs running southeast to the flat vegetable fields of South Jersey. The district is traversed by Black Horse Pike and White Horse Pike, which connect Philadelphia to its South Jersey suburbs. Many of these boroughs and townships developed over the past half-century as a result of flight from Camden. The district includes a growing number of Hispanics, who now make up more than 40% of Camden's population. Politically, this area has a Democratic heritage.

Robert Andrews (D)

The 1st District is represented by Robert Andrews, a Democrat first elected in 1990 who is known for his wide-ranging interest in policy as well as his ambition for statewide office. He grew up in Bellmawr, the son of a shipyard worker. At age 14, he got a job with the Suburban Newspaper

Group, dreaming of covering basketball games and becoming a sportswriter. But his editor had other ideas. Assigned to cover city halls, police departments, and zoning boards, Andrews developed an interest in the machinations of government and politics. He excelled in college, became the first in his family to get a degree, and went on to law school. While still in his 20s, he was elected to the Camden County Board of Chosen Freeholders, with the help of then-Democratic U.S. Rep. Jim Florio. When Florio left Congress to become governor in 1990, he postponed the special election for a successor until November and supported Andrews for the post. Andrews had other help. His Republican opponent switched positions on abortion rights and lied about his college attendance, helping Andrews to a 54%-43% victory.

Andrews has a mostly moderate voting record, particularly on foreign policy, but he has been much more inclined to side with his party in recent years. When Democrats regained the majority in 2007, Andrews became chairman of the Health, Employment, Labor, and Pensions Subcommittee. With full committee Chairman George Miller, D-Calif., he spearheaded House approval of the controversial labor-backed Employee Free Choice Act, which would make it easier for unions to organize by gathering the signatures of more than half of the employees in a bargaining unit. The legislation went nowhere in the Senate.

In 2008, Andrews lost an ambitious bid to unseat fellow Democrat Frank Lautenberg in the Senate primary, but he came back from that disappointment to have a productive two years in the House. As the chairman of the subcommittee, he had a role in drafting the landmark health care bill that was signed into law by President Obama in March 2010. It raised taxes on wealthy Americans to help pay for expanded coverage, which was a tough sell in Congress but something Andrews considered necessary for achieving "the right, equitable mix of policy and politics to get this done." In the course of the months-long process, Andrews became a top health care adviser to then-Democratic Speaker Nancy Pelosi, who called on him repeatedly to explain intricate details to colleagues, douse fires and even twist arms in the hours before the final vote on House passage. Andrews was also at the center of a successful effort in the House to reverse a Supreme Court ruling that restricted workers' ability to win pay discrimination lawsuits.

From his seat on the Armed Services Committee, Andrews was called on to carry water for the administration on its controversial plan to transfer suspected terrorists from the U.S. military detention center at Guantanamo Bay, Cuba, to facilities on U.S. soil. He was also one of the primary sponsors of legislation signed into law in May 2009 aimed at curbing an estimated $300 billion in cost overruns in major weapons programs in the Defense Department. He was a longtime ardent proponent of the use of force in Iraq. And in 2007, he opposed President George W. Bush's troop "surge" in Iraq. But he backed Obama's decision to send additional troops to Afghanistan.

Andrews has been re-elected by overwhelming margins and has continued to live with his family in Haddon Heights, commuting by train to Washington. After supporting Obama's $787 billion economic recovery bill, Andrews in 2009 got out front in promoting federally backed projects that flowed from the legislation to South Jersey, including $116 million in transportation projects for the region. He also has remained active in a campaign to stop the Army Corps of Engineers from deepening the Delaware River, which local and state officials believe will dump tons of dredged sludge into New Jersey.

But Andrews has been frustrated in his efforts to attain higher office. He ran for governor in 1997, but was defeated in the primary by then-state Sen. James McGreevey. When McGreevey announced his resignation as governor in 2004, Andrews was interested in running again but stood little chance after Democratic Sen. Jon Corzine announced his candidacy.

In the 2008 election season, he surprised and angered many local Democrats when he challenged Lautenberg in the primary. An Andrews ad called for change in "stale, tired, old politics," an allusion to the 84-year-old Lautenberg's age. Lautenberg shot back, calling Andrews "an enabler" for the Bush administration, especially on the Iraq war. Lautenberg benefited from a fundraising advantage, and won the primary, 59%-35%.

Andrews had said that if he lost the contest for Senate, he would not run again for the House. But political insiders questioned whether he in fact maneuvered to keep the seat warm in case things didn't work out for him in the Senate race: Andrews' wife, Camille, ran for the Democratic nomination for his House seat in the primary and secured it. Then, on Sept. 4, 2008, after Andrews lost the Senate primary, he said he would run for his former House seat after all. Camille Andrews bowed out, allowing the local Democratic committee to designate her husband as the new nominee. Although Andrews called the turnabout a simple change of heart, he in effect circumvented a prohibition on candidates running simultaneously for the Senate and the House. Republican challenger Dale Glading, a minister, accused Andrews of lying to his constituents. Still, he was handily elected, 72%-26%. Glading returned for a rematch in 2010, saying the political climate for Republicans had improved. But Andrews again won easily, 63%-35%.

SECOND DISTRICT

Frank LoBiondo (R)

Elected 1994, 9th term; b. May 12, 1946, Rosenhayn; home, Ventnor; St. Joseph's U., B.A. 1968; Catholic; married (Tina); 2 children.

Elected Office: Cumberland Cnty. Bd. of Chosen Freeholders, 1985–88; NJ Assembly, 1987–94.

Professional Career: Operations mgr., LoBiondo Bros. Motor Express Inc., 1968–94.

DC Office: 2427 RHOB, 20515, 202-225-6572; Fax: 202-225-3318; Web site: house.gov/lobiondo.

State Offices: Mays Landing, 609-625-5008.

Committees: *Armed Services:* Air & Land Forces; Readiness. *Permanent Select Committee on Intelligence:* Technical & Tactical Intelligence; Terrorism, HUMINT, Analysis & Counterintelligence. *Transportation & Infrastructure:* Aviation; Coast Guard & Maritime Transportation (Chmn); Highways & Transit.

Group Ratings

	ACLU	ACU	ADA	CFG	AFS	FRC	LCV	ITIC	NTU	COC
2010	13	67	15	64	25	87	40	67	71	88
2009	–	60	35	52	44	–	79	–	48	87

National Journal Ratings

	2010 LIB — 2010 CONS		2009 LIB — 2009 CONS	
Economic	37% —	62%	40% —	59%
Social	35% —	65%	36% —	63%
Foreign	12% —	79%	26% —	68%
Composite	30% —	70%	35% —	65%

Key Votes of the 111th Congress

1. Overturn Ledbetter	N	5. Bar federal abortion funds	Y	9. Stop detainee transfers	Y
2. Pass $820 billion stimulus	N	6. Pass health care bill	N	10. Legalize immigrants' kids	N
3. Let guns in national parks	Y	7. Regulate financial firms	N	11. Repeal don't ask, tell	N
4. Pass cap-and-trade	Y	8. Pass tax cuts for some	N	12. Limit campaign funds	N

Election Results

2010 general	Frank LoBiondo (R)	109,460	(65%)	($1,253,306)
	Gary Stein (D)	51,690	(31%)	
	Peter Boyce (CNP)	4,120	(2%)	
2010 primary	Frank LoBiondo (R)	19,337	(78%)	
	Linda Biamonte (R)	2,984	(12%)	
	Donna Ward (R)	2,451	(10%)	

Prior Winning Percentages: 2008 (59%), 2006 (62%), 2004 (65%), 2002 (69%), 2000 (66%), 1998 (66%), 1996 (60%), 1994 (65%)

Population		Race/Ethnicity		Work	
Pop. 2010:	692,205	White:	66.3%	Private:	76.7%
Change since 2000:	Up 6.9%	Black:	12.9%	Government:	17.7%
Urban:	79.0%	Hispanic:	14.9%	Self-employed:	5.4%
Rural:	21.0%	Asian:	3.7%	Blue collar:	20.2%
Area size:	2,684 sq. mi.	Native Am.:	0.3%	White collar:	54.3%
		Hawaiian:	0.0%	Khaki collar:	0.2%
Age		Two+ races:	1.7%	Other:	25.3%
Median age:	39.4 yrs.				
More than 65 yrs:	14.0%	**Ancestry**		Median income:	$56,455
Less than 18 yrs:	23.5%	Irish	15.3%	Median Home Value:	$254,700
		Italian	14.4%		
Education		German	13.4%	**Military Veterans**	
H.S. grad:	84.0%			% of Pop:	9.3%
College grad:	22.1%				
Grad degree:	7.2%				

Southern New Jersey; Atlantic City

The builders of the Camden & Atlantic Railroad in 1852 may not have known it, but when they extended their line to the little inlet town of Absecon, they were launching one of America's first beach resorts, Atlantic City. Like all resorts, it was a product of developments elsewhere—of industrialization and spreading affluence, of railroad technology and the conquest of diseases that used to make summer a time of foreboding.

2008 Presidential Vote		
Barack Obama (D)	165,982	(54%)
John McCain (R)	137,440	(45%)
2004 Presidential Vote		
George Bush (R)	141,123	(50%)
John Kerry (D)	138,797	(49%)
Cook Partisan Voting Index:	D+1	

In the years after the Civil War, Atlantic City and the Jersey Shore, from Brigantine to Cape May, became a seaside resort, and Atlantic City developed its characteristic features: the boardwalk in 1870, the amusement pier in 1882, the rolling chair in 1884, salt water taffy in the 1890s, and the Miss America pageant in 1921. (The Atlantic City of the Roaring '20s was recreated in the 2011 HBO series *Boardwalk Empire*.) By 1940, 16 million Americans visited every summer. It declined in the years after World War II, and by the early 1970s, Atlantic City was grim, featuring a bedraggled convention hall (site of the 1964 Democratic National Convention), empty hotels, and bleak streets of Philadelphia-style row houses.

Then in 1977, New Jersey voters legalized casino gambling in Atlantic City, and gleaming new hotels sprang up, big-name entertainers came in, and the resort became more stylish than it had been in 90 years. But it's not that way for all of its residents: Casino and hotel jobs tend to be low-wage, and decrepit neighborhoods begin just feet from the casinos' massive parking lots. For years, its dozen casinos had net annual revenues of more than $5 billion, nearly as much as Las Vegas' casinos. But the recession hit hard here. Revenues fell every year between 2007 and 2010, with a drop of almost 10% in 2010. Employment in the casino industry during that period plummeted from 50,000 jobs to 38,000. The casinos also suffered from the competition of slots parlors in New York and Pennsylvania, with slot revenues from the latter surpassing Atlantic City's for the first time in 2009. To protect the region's economic engine, Republican Gov. Chris Christie in February 2011 signed legislation into law streamlining regulatory oversight of the casinos, which angered watchdog groups that said it was unfair to single out gambling for special treatment during the state's budget crunch.

Other beach resorts lie south of Atlantic City. There is the old Methodist town of Ocean City, where Gay Talese grew up the son of Italian immigrants, a story he told movingly in *Unto the Sons*. There is Wildwood, with its refurbished 1950s motels, and also Cape May, with its lovingly preserved Victorian houses. West of the Shore are swamps and flatlands, the Pine Barrens and vegetable fields that gave New Jersey its "Garden State" nickname. Growth has been slow in these small towns and gas station intersections. Some towns are clustered around low-wage apparel factories or petrochemical plants on the Delaware estuary. The Northeast high-tech and service economy has not reached this far south in Jersey yet.

The 2nd Congressional District covers this part of South Jersey. Politically, it has strong Democratic leanings in the chemical industry towns along the Delaware River and in Vineland and a strong Republican presence in Cape May. Atlantic City often votes Democratic, but it has an antique Republican machine. In 2004, the district voted for President George W. Bush, 50%-49%, but in 2008, Democratic nominee Barack Obama won 54%-45%. A year later, however, Christie completely dominated this region in ousting Democratic Gov. Jon Corzine.

Frank LoBiondo (R)

The congressman from the 2nd District is Frank LoBiondo, a Republican first elected in 1994. He grew up in Vineland, on the vegetable farm his grandparents established after leaving Sicily. LoBiondo's father started transporting his produce to market himself in a used truck, and as Atlantic City boomed in the early 20th century, he found that he could make a good living transporting the produce of other farmers as well. He created LoBiondo Brothers Motor Express, where his son worked when he was young. In 1987, Frank LoBiondo was elected to the New Jersey Assembly; there, he stoutly opposed new taxes and gun control laws. LoBiondo ran against veteran U.S. Rep. William Hughes, a Democrat, in 1992 and lost 56%-41%. After Hughes decided to retire in 1994, LoBiondo ran again. In the primary, he competed with state Sen. William Gormley, whom LoBiondo portrayed as favoring tax increases and gun control laws. LoBiondo won 54%-35%, and then easily won the general election, 65%-35%.

In the House, LoBiondo has compiled a moderate voting record, especially on environmental, economic and labor issues, although he retains his conservative stance on gun control. In the 111th Congress (2009-10), he joined Democrats on backing energy legislation instituting a "cap and trade" system on greenhouse-gas emissions; an expansion of the State Children's Health Insurance Program; compensation for first responders on September 11; and food safety legislation. He also was a cosponsor of the Employee Free Choice Act, the so-called "card check" bill aimed at making it easier for employees to join unions. On the Transportation and Infrastructure Committee, he chairs the Coast Guard and Maritime Transportation Subcommittee, a useful assignment for New Jersey. LoBiondo opposes oil drilling within 125 miles of the Jersey coast, and helped to enact the Delaware River Protection Act, increasing the liability for single-hull oil tankers that pollute.

In 2008, LoBiondo voted against the massive bailout of the financial markets because, he said, taxpayers were not sufficiently protected. A few months later, he opposed President Obama's economic stimulus bill. "You will continue to hear me talk about public-private partnerships as the way to go forward," he said in March 2010. But after his party assumed the majority in 2011, he refused to join with conservatives on a proposal to cut non-security spending to fiscal 2008 levels. On the Armed Services Committee, LoBiondo expressed reservations about the Iraq war, but he opposed efforts to set a timetable for troop withdrawals. With Obama in office, he has lamented that homeland security has become "lost in the mix" of debates on domestic issues and opposed trying terrorists in civilian courts. "These are evil people," he said. "And we're prosecuting Navy officers for not giving these people cookies and singing lullabies to them."

LoBiondo maintains a low profile on Capitol Hill and seems content to climb the seniority ladder at the Transportation and Infrastructure Committee. When he was first elected, LoBiondo promised to serve no more than 12 years but has since broken that pledge. Still, he routinely wins re-election with 60% of the vote or more. In 2008, he was re-elected 59%-39%, the first time that he had fallen short of 60% but still impressive in a competitive district in a Democratic year. Two years later, however, he was back to 66%.

THIRD DISTRICT

Jon Runyan (R)

Elected 2010, 1st term; b. Nov. 27, 1973, Flint, MI; home, Mount Laurel; U. of MI, attended 1992-95 ; Catholic; Married (Loretta); 3 children.

Professional Career: Offensive lineman, NFL, 1996-2010.

DC Office: 1239 LHOB, 20515, 202-225-4765; Fax: 202-225-0778; Web site: runyan.house.gov.

State Offices: Mount Laurel, 856-780-6436.

Committees: *Armed Services:* Tactical Air & Land Forces; Readiness. *Natural Resources:* Fisheries, Wildlife, Oceans & Insular Affairs. *Veterans' Affairs:* Disability Assistance & Memorial Affairs (Chmn); Health.

Election Results

2010 general	Jon Runyan (R)	110,215	(50%)	($1,623,453)
	John Adler (D)	104,252	(47%)	($3,301,321)
2010 primary	Jon Runyan (R)	17,250	(60%)	
	Justin Murphy (R)	11,304	(40%)	

Population		Race/Ethnicity		Work	
Pop. 2010:	680,341	White:	78.4%	Private:	75.9%
Change since 2000:	Up 5.1%	Black:	9.2%	Government:	19.2%
Urban:	96.2%	Hispanic:	6.4%	Self-employed:	4.7%
Rural:	3.8%	Asian:	3.9%	Blue collar:	17.0%
Area size:	1,180 sq. mi.	Native Am.:	0.1%	White collar:	67.6%
		Hawaiian:	0.0%	Khaki collar:	0.5%
Age		Two+ races:	1.7%	Other:	14.8%
Median age:	42.2 yrs.				
More than 65 yrs:	17.5%	*Ancestry*		Median income:	$71,683
Less than 18 yrs:	22.1%	Irish	17.0%	Median Home Value:	$288,100
		Italian	16.4%		
Education		German	14.6%	**Military Veterans**	
H.S. grad:	91.0%			% of Pop:	11.7%
College grad:	31.6%				
Grad degree:	11.3%				

Southern New Jersey; Toms River

The Pine Barrens of New Jersey is one of the last vacant spots on the eastern seaboard—not quite terra incognita, but still not thickly populated. Encroached on by the Philadelphia suburbs of South Jersey on the west and burgeoning retirement developments of the Jersey Shore on the east, the 1 million acres of heavy forest and white sand, with their unusual plant life, are crossed mostly by narrow two-lane roads. For years, the Pine Barrens was seen as a barrier to

2008 Presidential Vote		
Barack Obama (D)	180,999	(52%)
John McCain (R)	162,335	(47%)
2004 Presidential Vote		
George Bush (R)	167,254	(51%)
John Kerry (D)	159,041	(49%)
Cook Partisan Voting Index:	R+1	

development. Only recently have environment-minded Jerseyites come to see the relatively unspoiled area as a natural treasure. There are only a few small towns here, plus Joint Base McGuire-Dix-Lakehurst, the giant amalgamation of an Air Force base, an Army military reservation and a Navy air station that its commander describes as "the economic engine of southern New Jersey."

The 3rd Congressional District of New Jersey spans the Pine Barrens and thousands of acres of farmland. It includes large parts of Burlington and Ocean counties and Cherry Hill in Camden County. Most of its residents live in the South Jersey suburbs of Philadelphia; in spread-out Cherry Hill, with its 1960s-vintage shopping centers; in the older towns, some dating to colonial times, along the Delaware River; or in the newer developments inland toward the Joint Base. This is comfortable, but not affluent, suburban territory, with income levels well above average but only a small proportion over $200,000. Lockheed Martin in Moorestown is a big employer, with its naval electronics and surveillance-system plant. It is the birthplace of the Aegis radar. Politically, it is competitive territory, Democratic along the Delaware River, Republican inland and with big Democratic majorities in majority-black Willingboro (originally the New Jersey version of Levittown).

East of the Pine Barrens is Ocean County, including the barrier islands from Normandy Beach south to Little Egg Harbor, with older communities on the beachfront and larger clusters of new subdivisions and condominiums inland. Here you can find the house in Seaside Heights where two seasons of MTV's *Jersey Shore* were set. Ocean County has been the fastest-growing part of New Jersey, a kind of Frost Belt Florida, with many retirees from New York and North Jersey eager to leave urban crime and high taxes. Racially and ethnically this is a diverse district: 9% black, 6% Hispanic and 4% Asian, and with more than 45% describing their ancestry as Irish, Italian or German. Politically, the district is closely divided. It voted 54%-43% for Al Gore in 2000, 51%-49% for George W. Bush in 2004 and 52%-47% for Barack Obama in 2008.

Jon Runyan (R)

Jon Runyan, a former Philadelphia Eagles offensive lineman, defeated Democrat John Adler to become congressman from the 3rd District in 2010. Runyan grew up in the factory town of Flint, Mich., in a working-class family. His father worked for General Motors for nearly 30 years while his mother raised Runyan and his younger twin brothers. When his father was laid off in the 1980s, Runyan remembers the sacrifices his family made to make ends meet. "Some nights, the only thing on the dinner table was cornbread," he recalled. His father worked odd jobs to keep them afloat. In high school, Runyan excelled at sports, running cross country, playing basketball and football, and becoming a two-time state shot-put champion. Standing at 6 feet 7 inches and weighing 330 pounds, he earned an athletic scholarship to the University of Michigan. He became the first person in his family to attend college, majoring in kinesiology, the science of human movement. Academics, however, were not Runyan's strong suit, and after his first term he was diagnosed with dyslexia. "Battling through that, it was a struggle," he told *National Journal*. "It eventually got easier."

Runyan was drafted in the middle of his senior year by the Houston Oilers in 1996, and stayed with the team as they became the Tennessee Titans in 1997. While with the Oilers, Runyan met his wife of 13 years, Loretta, a Houston police officer. After helping the Titans reach the Super Bowl in 1999, Runyan became a free agent and signed a $30 million, six-year contract with the Philadelphia Eagles, making him the NFL's highest-paid offensive lineman at the time. He played in the 2005 Super Bowl and signed a $12 million three-year contract with the Eagles in 2006; he was sidelined by a knee injury and played his last season in 2009-10 with the San Diego Chargers. A 2006 *Sports Illustrated* poll voted Runyan the second-dirtiest player in the NFL, but he had plenty of fans in the Philadelphia area and had a regular radio show on WPHI-FM. He settled in Mount Laurel, N.J., in Burlington County and took entrepreneurial management classes at the University of Pennsylvania's Wharton School, though he had not graduated from the University of Michigan.

Runyan decided to run for the 3rd District seat against Democrat John Adler, a freshman who had spent 17 years in the New Jersey Senate. He had beat Republican Chris Myers by only 52%-48% in 2008. Adler had much more experience, but Runyan touted his outsider credentials as an asset. "When people question my experience, I ask them a simple question, 'Didn't the people with all this experience get us into this mess in the first place?'" he said. He won the June Republican primary 60%-40% over former Tabernacle Committeeman Justin Murphy. Almost twice as many people voted in the Republican than in the Democratic primary, an early sign that enthusiasm was with the GOP that year.

The general election race was particularly fierce. Democrats attacked Runyan for taking a tax break on his 25-acre estate because he kept donkeys and cut timber on 20 acres of the property. He parried that the arrangement was legal and that he had paid $61,000 in property taxes on the remaining five acres. Republicans accused Democrats of putting up a candidate on a sham New Jersey tea party line to siphon away votes from Runyan. Adler said he had no knowledge of any ploy.

Adler presented himself as knowledgeable and articulate in contrast to political newcomer Runyan. He defended the Democrats' 2009 economic stimulus bill by saying, "My God, how much would it (unemployment) have been if we had not spent the money?" But he noted that he voted against the Democrats' health care bill and in favor of extending the Bush-era tax cuts on capital gains and dividends. In October, with Democratic incumbents in trouble everywhere, Adler distanced himself from liberal Speaker Nancy Pelosi. Though Runyan put $350,000 of his own money into the campaign, Adler spent a total $3.3 million to Runyan's $1.5 million.

Like many Republican challengers in 2010, Runyan ran against the policies of President Barack Obama and the congressional Democrats. Of their health care insurance overhaul, he told *The Philadelphia Inquirer*, "If that was such a great piece of legislation, why did they have to do all the favors to all the people to get them to sign on?" And he argued that the bill's mandate to buy insurance violated the Constitution. He said the 35% corporate tax rate was too high and argued that "loopholes are there for a reason. And they are to avoid people from really paying too many taxes." He opposed raising the retirement age in Social Security, and said he favored repeal of the ban on openly gay personnel in the military.

October polls showed a close race. Runyan won 50%-47%, with the N.J. tea party candidate getting just 1%. Adler carried his home area of Cherry Hill 59%-39%, and edged Runyan 53%-45% in Burlington County. But in Ocean County, where 40% of the votes were cast, Runyan led 59%-37%. In April 2011, Adler died of a heart ailment after leaving Congress.

FOURTH DISTRICT

Chris Smith (R)

Elected 1980, 16th term; b. March 4, 1953, Rahway; home, Hamilton; Trenton St. Col., B.S. 1975; Catholic; married (Marie); 4 children.

Professional Career: Sales exec., family-owned sporting goods business, 1975–80; Exec. dir., NJ Right to Life, 1976–78.

DC Office: 2373 RHOB, 20515, 202-225-3765; Fax: 202-225-7768; Web site: chrissmith.house.gov.

State Offices: Hamilton, 609-585-7878; Whiting, 732-350-2300.

Committees: *Foreign Affairs:* Africa, Global Health & Human Rights (Chmn); Western Hemisphere.

Group Ratings

	ACLU	ACU	ADA	CFG	AFS	FRC	LCV	ITIC	NTU	COC
2010	38	67	15	67	25	100	50	33	70	100
2009	–	64	30	50	67	–	79	–	49	80

National Journal Ratings

	2010 LIB	—	2010 CONS	2009 LIB	—	2009 CONS
Economic	37%	—	62%	40%	—	60%
Social	35%	—	65%	40%	—	59%
Foreign	12%	—	79%	33%	—	63%
Composite	30%	—	70%	39%	—	62%

Key Votes of the 111th Congress

1. Overturn Ledbetter	Y	5. Bar federal abortion funds	Y	9. Stop detainee transfers	Y
2. Pass $820 billion stimulus	N	6. Pass health care bill	N	10. Legalize immigrants' kids	N
3. Let guns in national parks	Y	7. Regulate financial firms	N	11. Repeal don't ask, tell	N
4. Pass cap-and-trade	Y	8. Pass tax cuts for some	N	12. Limit campaign funds	N

Election Results

2010 general	Chris Smith (R)...	129,752	(69%)	($748,363)
	Howard Kleinhendler (D)	52,118	(28%)	($126,020)
2010 primary	Chris Smith (R)...	21,723	(69%)	
	Alan Bateman (R)	9,839	(31%)	

Prior Winning Percentages: 2008 (66%), 2006 (66%), 2004 (67%), 2002 (66%), 2000 (63%), 1998 (62%), 1996 (64%), 1994 (68%), 1992 (62%), 1990 (63%), 1988 (66%), 1986 (61%), 1984 (61%), 1982 (53%), 1980 (57%)

Population		Race/Ethnicity		Work	
Pop. 2010:	724,596	White:	74.7%	Private:	78.2%
Change since 2000:	Up 11.9%	Black:	8.0%	Government:	16.8%
Urban:	93.2%	Hispanic:	12.2%	Self-employed:	4.9%
Rural:	6.8%	Asian:	3.6%	Blue collar:	18.4%
Area size:	762 sq. mi.	Native Am.:	0.1%	White collar:	64.6%
		Hawaiian:	0.0%	Khaki collar:	0.2%
Age		Two+ races:	1.2%	Other:	16.7%
Median age:	39.2 yrs.				
More than 65 yrs:	15.4%	*Ancestry*		Median income:	$68,653
Less than 18 yrs:	24.8%	Italian	16.9%	Median Home Value:	$324,100
		Irish	15.4%		
Education		German	11.9%	**Military Veterans**	
H.S. grad:	88.2%			% of Pop:	9.5%
College grad:	29.4%				
Grad degree:	10.1%				

Central New Jersey; Part Trenton

An invisible and not-well-defined line divides North Jersey and South Jersey. North of the line people watch New York television stations, eat hero sandwiches, and root for the Yankees. South of the line they watch Philadelphia television, eat hoagies, and root for the Phillies. The state capital of Trenton lies south of the line, which passes east somewhere around Six Flags Great Adventure in the Pine Barrens and heads southeast past Lakehurst and Bricktown to the

little village of Mantoloking on the Jersey Shore. But on both sides of the line, a stronger New Jersey identity has developed over the last two decades. The big cities—New York and Philadelphia—are not all that close, particularly when traffic is heavy, which is often. And the economy of central New Jersey has its own character, with big pharmaceutical companies and the consolidated Joint Base McGuire-Dix-Lakehurst. New Jersey politics is also centered in Trenton. The city has been a manufacturing mecca since the 19th century, with the Lenox and Boehm china factories and the old Roebling ironworks, which produced parts for many of the great American bridges. But much of this area is also spanking new, with growing subdivisions just west of the shore and office buildings stretching north from Princeton. Trenton, meanwhile, has been mired in the budget problems afflicting the rest of the state, grappling with a $55 million deficit in 2010.

The 4th Congressional District of New Jersey covers much of the central part of the state. It stretches from the eastern part of Trenton to Mantoloking, Point Pleasant, Sea Girt, and Spring Lake on the shore. The district includes the old colonial town of Burlington on the Delaware River and the new spacious subdivisions of Colts Neck west of the shore, as well as what was Lakehurst Naval Air Station, where the German zeppelin *Hindenburg* exploded while docking in 1937. Population movement has been eastward, away from the old neighborhoods of Trenton and its close-in suburbs and toward the new subdivisions of coastal and exurban Ocean County, which grew 12% from 2000 to 2009. Some towns have curtailed sprawl with laws to preserve farmland and open space. Politically, it is a mixed bag. The Trenton area has long been solidly Democratic, but the Pine Barrens and Jersey Shore have leaned Republican. President George W. Bush won this district 56%-44% in 2004, and John McCain won it four years later with 52% of the vote to Democrat Barack Obama's 47%. In the 2009 governor's race, Mercer County—which includes Trenton—went heavily for Democrat Jon Corzine, while Republican Chris Christie carried both Monmouth and Ocean counties by 2-to-1.

Chris Smith (R)

The congressman from the 4th District is Chris Smith, a Republican first elected in 1980 who combines a vociferous opposition to abortion with an equally passionate commitment to human rights and other normally Democratic priorities. Smith grew up in the Trenton area, worked in his family's sporting goods business, and, after graduating from college, became executive director of the New Jersey Right to Life Committee in 1976. Four years later, he ran for the House in a Trenton-centered 4th District and defeated 26-year Rep. Frank Thompson, a Democrat convicted in the

Abscam bribery scandal. He won passage of 30 bills from 1991 to 2008, the fifth-largest number for any member of Congress during that period. Even during the four years in which Democrats recently controlled the House, Smith still managed to get 11 of his measures passed.

A devout Roman Catholic, Smith is best known for his fight against legalized abortion. He has worked to stop abortions in military hospitals, and he persuaded the Bush administration to reinstate Reagan-era restrictions denying federal funds to family-planning organizations that promote abortions abroad. (In 2009, new Democratic President Barack Obama rescinded the restrictions during his first week in office.) Smith was a prime mover of legislation to ban "partial birth" abortions. He has fought not only Democrats but also the House Republican leadership on the abortion issue. In the 2002 bankruptcy bill, Smith rounded up like-minded Republicans to vote "no" on a major bankruptcy bill to protest a provision preventing abortion protestors from declaring bankruptcy after incurring large civil disobedience fines. The abortion section was ultimately stripped out, and the bill passed the House. After Republicans regained control of the House in 2011, Smith introduced a bill taking away tax benefits from employee-sponsored health insurance plans that offer abortion coverage. He sought to add the word "forcible" to a long-standing exemption for rape, drawing angry criticism from abortion-rights advocates, who said the change could exclude statutory rape or rapes where the victim was drugged or unconscious. He later agreed to remove the word.

Smith has long crusaded for his Unborn Child Pain Awareness Act, which would require doctors to inform pregnant women that some experts say that a fetus can feel pain after 20 weeks of gestation. He also has a bill to revoke the Food and Drug Administration's approval of the abortifacient RU-486, which Smith calls "baby pesticide." He has opposed federal funding for embryonic-stem-cell research, which uses excess embryos from in vitro fertilization, but he has been a champion of other stem cell research. In 2005, Congress enacted his Stem Cell Therapeutic and Research Act, which provides $265 million for research and therapy using umbilical cord stem cells and cells from bone marrow transplants. Disgusted by Obama's policies and appointments, Smith declared in June 2009 that Obama "is on his way to becoming the abortion president."

Smith has brought his strong moral views to his work against human-rights abuses abroad. He has sharply criticized China for its forced sterilizations and abortions, and its persecution of Christians and other religious minorities. As a result, he opposed normalizing trade relations with Beijing. Smith has condemned Russia for barring entry of foreign Catholic priests, and he criticized the Saudis for treating foreign servants as slaves. In 2000, Congress enacted his legislation to combat sex trafficking around the world, including requiring yearly reports on each nation's record. At one point, Smith learned of Ukrainian girls being held against their will in brothels in Montenegro; he personally called the country's prime minister, who ordered a raid on the operation.

After Democrats took over Congress in 2007, Smith became the ranking member of the renamed Africa and Global Health Subcommittee of the Foreign Affairs Committee. On the eve of the Olympics in July 2008, Smith tried to meet human-rights lawyers in Beijing, but they were placed under house arrest, and he unsuccessfully urged President George W. Bush not to attend the Olympic opening ceremonies. In August 2008, he traveled to Tbilisi in the Georgia Republic and helped to rescue two young New Jersey girls who were at risk during the Russian invasion there. Less than a year later, he flew to Brazil to reunite a New Jersey man with his 8-year-old son whose Brazilian mother had taken him out of the United States in defiance of a court order. "I'm a father of four," Smith said in explaining his willingness to help.

Smith is one of the most moderate members of the House GOP. In 2009, he was one of just eight Republicans to support the Waxman-Markey energy bill imposing a cap-and-trade system to limit greenhouse gas emissions blamed for global warming. He also cosponsored the Employee Free Choice Act, the so-called "card check" bill aimed at making it easier for employees to form unions. His tendency to buck his party for the sake of his beliefs was best illustrated by events in 2005, when, as chairman of the Veterans' Affairs Committee, Smith angered budget conservatives by pushing generous benefits for veterans. In 2004, in a major breach of party protocol, he voted for the Democratic spending plan because it contained more money for veterans. In early 2005, the Republican Steering Committee booted Smith from his committee chairmanship and gave it to Steve Buyer of Indiana. Veterans groups expressed outrage, to no avail. But Smith's warnings that veterans programs were being underfunded proved true that June, when Veterans Affairs Secretary Jim Nicholson announced that the department had underestimated the number of returning Iraq war veterans and needed an additional $2.6 billion.

Smith's devotion to principle and his reputation for tending to constituent problems have made him popular in the politically marginal 4th District. Since 1984, he has received at least 61% of the vote in easily winning re-election. In 2008, Democratic challenger Joshua Zeitz, a first-time candidate, accused him of being a resident of Virginia because Smith owns a home there and his daughter paid in-state Virginia tuition. Smith rents a town house in Hamilton Township, N.J. He was re-elected 66%-33%.

FIFTH DISTRICT

Scott Garrett (R)

Elected 2002, 5th term; b. July 9, 1959, Englewood; home, Wantage; Montclair St. U., B.A. 1981, Rutgers U., J.D. 1984; Protestant; married (Mary Ellen); 2 children.

Elected Office: NJ Assembly, 1990-2002.

Professional Career: Practicing atty., 1984-2002.

DC Office: 2244 RHOB, 20515, 202-225-4465; Fax: 202-225-9048; Web site: garrett.house.gov.

State Offices: Glen Rock, 201-444-5454; Newton, 973-300-2000.

Committees: *Budget. Financial Services:* Capital Markets and Government Sponsored Enterprises (Chmn); Insurance, Housing & Community Opportunity.

Group Ratings

	ACLU	ACU	ADA	CFG	AFS	FRC	LCV	ITIC	NTU	COC
2010	13	100	5	100	0	100	0	0	91	71
2009	–	100	0	99	11	–	0	–	93	73

National Journal Ratings

	2010 LIB — 2010 CONS		2009 LIB — 2009 CONS	
Economic	10%	— 90%	12%	— 88%
Social	0%	— 85%	0%	— 93%
Foreign	0%	— 88%	26%	— 68%
Composite	8%	— 92%	15%	— 85%

Key Votes of the 111th Congress

1. Overturn Ledbetter	N	5. Bar federal abortion funds	Y	9. Stop detainee transfers	Y
2. Pass $820 billion stimulus	N	6. Pass health care bill	N	10. Legalize immigrants' kids	N
3. Let guns in national parks	Y	7. Regulate financial firms	N	11. Repeal don't ask, tell	N
4. Pass cap-and-trade	N	8. Pass tax cuts for some	N	12. Limit campaign funds	N

Election Results

2010 general	Scott Garrett (R)	124,030	(65%)	($1,757,865)
	Tod Theise (D)	62,634	(33%)	($25,724)
2010 primary	Scott Garrett (R)	unopposed		

Prior Winning Percentages: 2008 (56%), 2006 (55%), 2004 (58%), 2002 (59%)

Population		Race/Ethnicity		Work	
Pop. 2010:	666,551	White:	79.9%	Private:	79.7%
Change since 2000:	Up 3.0%	Black:	1.9%	Government:	13.1%
Urban:	82.7%	Hispanic:	7.6%	Self-employed:	7.0%
Rural:	17.3%	Asian:	9.0%	Blue collar:	15.2%
Area size:	1,131 sq. mi.	Native Am.:	0.1%	White collar:	72.0%
		Hawaiian:	0.0%	Khaki collar:	0.0%
Age		Two+ races:	1.3%	Other:	12.8%
Median age:	41.6 yrs.				
More than 65 yrs:	13.9%	*Ancestry*		Median income:	$91,702
Less than 18 yrs:	24.7%	Italian	16.9%	Median Home Value:	$454,000
		Irish	16.0%		
Education		German	13.1%	**Military Veterans**	
H.S. grad:	93.0%			% of Pop:	8.0%
College grad:	43.1%				
Grad degree:	15.9%				

Northern New Jersey; West Milford

The northern edge of New Jersey was settled three centuries ago by the Dutch, for whom this plateau of land behind the Hudson River Palisades seemed a natural part of Nieuw Amsterdam. The Dutch influence is seen in old, steep-roofed farmhouses and in many of the place names—Bergen County, Cresskill, Closter. But overall, northernmost New Jersey has the well-settled look of so many northeastern suburbs, with touches of both affluence and small-town

2008 Presidential Vote		
John McCain (R) 179,801	(54%)
Barack Obama (D) 152,544	(46%)
2004 Presidential Vote		
George Bush (R) 184,530	(57%)
John Kerry (D) 137,019	(43%)
Cook Partisan Voting Index: R+7		

hominess, criss-crossed at its edges with limited-access highways and shopping centers. In the late 1950s, Paramus was transformed from celery farms to the site of two of the nation's first large shopping malls—and constant traffic jams. Today, it has five malls and numerous shopping centers that do more than $5 billion a year in retail sales. Not far away are Saddle River and Franklin Lakes, with million-dollar houses on multi-acre lots, and Park Ridge, with office buildings and condominiums. This area may look like WASP suburbia on the surface, but in fact it is home to successful people of all ethnic groups, many of them descended from those who first saw the Statue of Liberty from steerage. Bergenfield, where more than 20% of the population is of Filipino descent, is known as "Little Manila." A curiosity: Asian women in Bergen County have the nation's longest life expectancy, 91 years.

The 5th Congressional District of New Jersey comprises most of northern Bergen County, plus a swath of North Jersey stretching west to the hill-enclosed upper reaches of the Delaware River, crossing one ridge of mountains after another, and then running south to Interstate 78. About 60% of its population is in Bergen County. To the west, little subdivisions set amid the lakes of western Passaic County are filling up with young families. Farther west are once rural, now more or less suburban Sussex and Warren counties. In recent years, the recession took a toll on many of these suburban enclaves as foreclosures and a large inventory of unsold homes sent property values plummeting. But it remains relatively affluent. Politically, this area has long trended Republican. In 2004, George W. Bush won the district 57%-43%, his second-best showing in the state. In 2008, John McCain won it, 54%-46%.

Scott Garrett (R)

The congressman from the 5th District is Scott Garrett, a Republican elected in 2002 and the most conservative member of New Jersey's congressional delegation. Garrett grew up on a farm in Wantage, where his parents grew tomatoes and Christmas trees. The family's main income came from his father's job as a salesman for Uniroyal. A conservative from the start, Garrett questioned his high school administration's spending practices and kept a picture of David Stockman, the father of Reaganomics, at his desk. He graduated from Montclair State College and Rutgers law school, and became a trial lawyer in Sussex County. He is a born-again Christian who meets most Saturday mornings for three hours with a small group that calls itself Joshua Men.

In 1989, he was elected to the New Jersey General Assembly, where he quickly became one of the most conservative members. In 1998 and 2000, he challenged veteran U.S. Rep. Marge Roukema, a moderate Republican, in the primary. He attacked Roukema for supporting abortion rights and gun control laws. She emphasized her conservative votes on economic issues and was backed by the conservative House Republican leadership. Each time, Garrett carried the western part of the district, but Roukema ran strongly in her Bergen County base, winning by 53%-47% in 1998 and 52%-48% in 2000.

Roukema announced that she would not seek another term in 2002, and Garrett ran again. His challenge in the primary was to sell his views in Bergen County, where Sussex County is viewed as a distant province somewhere near Idaho. Two well-known Republicans from Bergen entered the race: state Sen. Gerald Cardinale and Assemblyman David Russo. They argued that nominating Garrett would put the seat at risk. But Garrett won the primary with 41% to 26% for Russo and 25% for Cardinale. Garrett won 81% of the vote in Sussex and 68% in Warren. But he won just 25% in Bergen County, raising Democratic hopes.

The Democratic nominee was Anne Sumers, a former Republican who switched parties in early 2002 and stressed her agreement with Roukema on most issues. With help from the national Democrats, Sumers attacked Garrett as an "extremist," pointing to his support for limited federal aid to education. Garrett pounced on Sumers' failure to vote in local school board elections and her musings on a liberal website, where she characterized American patriotism as "jingoistic." Meanwhile, he soft-pedaled some of his more conservative views. Sumers outspent Garrett, $1.6 million to $1.3 million, including nearly $400,000 of her own money. But national Republicans spent heavily on issue ads on Garrett's behalf. This turned out to be less of a contest than many people expected. Garrett won 59%-38%. In Bergen County, which cast 64% of the total vote, he led 55%-43%.

In the House, Garrett in recent years has rebounded from his vote against the Republicans' Medicare prescription drug bill in 2003, a move that angered GOP leaders and limited his influence in the House. He has long pushed for a resolution that would require all legislation to cite an enumerated power in the Constitution, and he has pushed for to require congressional staff to receive annual training on the document. Because of term limits, he was due to rotate off the Budget Committee in 2011, but incoming Speaker John Boehner appointed him to serve another term. On the Republican Study Committee, the caucus of the House's most conservative members, Garrett chairs the budget task force. He beseeched Boehner in January 2011 to keep the GOP's campaign promise of cutting $100 billion in what remained of the fiscal year. In the November elections, he said in a letter to Boehner, "Voters heard our message of restoring fiscal responsibility, and they decided to give our party one more chance in the majority to get things right."

Even though many of his constituents work on Wall Street, Garret opposed the bailout of the financial markets in 2008, saying he was "wary of using taxpayer dollars to prop up failing businesses." In 2009, he leapfrogged other members and became the ranking Republican on the Financial Services Committee's Subcommittee on Capital Markets, Insurance, and Government-Sponsored Enterprises at the Financial Services Committee, which has authority over the Fannie Mae and Freddie Mac housing finance authorities. He became chairman after the Republican takeover of the House in 2011 and made clear his intention to slow down and de-fund the agencies given new responsibilities for implementing the sweeping financial services overhaul law passed a year earlier.

Garrett has clashed repeatedly with ranking Democrat Barney Frank, of Massachusetts. Frank complained that Garrett and his frequent ally, Jeb Hensarling, R-Texas, set the tone for Republicans' unwillingness to negotiate on the financial services overhaul, and as a result of their intransigence, the two "had no influence on the major parts of the bill," Frank told *The Record* newspaper in July 2010.

Garrett has overcome some serious re-election challenges. In 2006, Paul Aronsohn, a former aide to Democratic Gov. Jim McGreevey, called Garrett "too extreme, too disconnected to the people he represents." He raised nearly $600,000 and cut Garrett's margin in Bergen to 51%-48%. But with more than 60% of the vote in Sussex and Warren counties, Garrett won 55%-44%. He sailed to victory in 2010.

SIXTH DISTRICT

Frank Pallone (D)

Elected 1988, 12th full term; b. Oct. 30, 1951, Long Branch; home, Long Branch; Middlebury Col., B.A. 1973, Fletcher Schl. of Law & Diplomacy, M.A. 1974, Rutgers U., J.D. 1978; Catholic; married (Sarah); 3 children.

Elected Office: Long Branch City Cncl., 1982–88; NJ Senate, 1983–88.

Professional Career: Asst. prof., Rutgers U., 1979–80; Practicing atty., 1981–83; Instructor, Monmouth Col., 1984–86.

DC Office: 237 CHOB, 20515, 202-225-4671; Fax: 202-225-9665; Web site: house.gov/pallone.

State Offices: Monmouth, 732-571-1140; New Brunswick, 732-249-8892.

Committees: *Energy & Commerce:* Communications & Technology; Environment & the Economy; Health (RMM). *Natural Resources:* Fisheries, Wildlife, Oceans & Insular Affairs.

Group Ratings

	ACLU	ACU	ADA	CFG	AFS	FRC	LCV	ITIC	NTU	COC
2010	93	0	95	0	100	0	100	100	7	25
2009	–	0	95	0	100	–	100	–	1	36

National Journal Ratings

	2010 LIB — 2010 CONS		2009 LIB — 2009 CONS	
Economic	90%	0%	86%	13%
Social	87%	12%	70%	29%
Foreign	84%	11%	87%	9%
Composite	90%	10%	82%	18%

Key Votes of the 111th Congress

1. Overturn Ledbetter	Y	5. Bar federal abortion funds	N	9. Stop detainee transfers	N
2. Pass $820 billion stimulus	Y	6. Pass health care bill	Y	10. Legalize immigrants' kids	Y
3. Let guns in national parks	Y	7. Regulate financial firms	Y	11. Repeal don't ask, tell	Y
4. Pass cap-and-trade	Y	8. Pass tax cuts for some	Y	12. Limit campaign funds	Y

Election Results

2010 general	Frank Pallone (D) 81,933	(55%)	($2,235,780)
	Anna Little (R)...65,413	(44%)	($486,065)
2010 primary	Frank Pallone (D) .... unopposed		

Prior Winning Percentages: 2008 (67%), 2006 (69%), 2004 (67%), 2002 (66%), 2000 (68%), 1998 (57%), 1996 (61%), 1994 (60%), 1992 (52%), 1990 (49%), 1988 (52%), 1988 special (52%)

Population		Race/Ethnicity		Work	
Pop. 2010:	668,806	White:	53.5%	Private:	82.1%
Change since 2000:	Up 3.3%	Black:	14.5%	Government:	13.3%
Urban:	99.7%	Hispanic:	17.8%	Self-employed:	4.5%
Rural:	0.3%	Asian:	11.9%	Blue collar:	19.2%
Area size:	388 sq. mi.	Native Am.:	0.1%	White collar:	64.2%
		Hawaiian:	0.0%	Khaki collar:	0.0%
Age		Two+ races:	1.7%	Other:	16.6%
Median age:	36.3 yrs.				
More than 65 yrs:	11.7%	*Ancestry*		Median income:	$68,050
Less than 18 yrs:	22.9%	Italian	13.0%	Median Home Value:	$362,100
		Irish	12.2%		
Education		German	8.1%	**Military Veterans**	
H.S. grad:	87.6%			% of Pop:	7.0%
College grad:	34.0%				
Grad degree:	12.6%				

East New Jersey; New Brunswick

For generations, great transportation arteries
have brought people out of the huge central cities
of New York and Philadelphia and into the flatlands and hills of New Jersey—to vacation, to
raise families, to work toward affluence, and to
build communities. The railroads of the late 19th
century created the towns of the Jersey shore.
After 1874, when the first train from New York
City reached Long Branch, the shore became the
summer home of seven presidents from Grant to

2008 Presidential Vote		
Barack Obama (D) 165,261	(60%)
John McCain (R) 104,932	(38%)
2004 Presidential Vote		
John Kerry (D) 144,105	(57%)
George Bush (R) 109,729	(43%)
Cook Partisan Voting Index: D+8		

Wilson (Garfield, convalescing after he was shot, died there in 1881) and of New York racehorse
owners and socialites. But over time, the ambiance degraded, and the fishing pier and much of the
boardwalk went up in flames in 1987. Only recently have developers sought to revive it. The freight
rail lines in the New York-Philadelphia corridor sparked electrical and chemical industries here.
They built on the inventions of Thomas Edison, many of them produced in his Menlo Park laboratory just off the rail lines, where a 131-foot tower stands as a memorial to the inventor. The same
corridor was the site of America's first cloverleaf intersection, at the junction of U.S. 1 and U.S. 9,
and of the intersection of two of America's post-World War II highways, the New Jersey Turnpike
and the Garden State Parkway. The turnpike, now 12 lanes wide in stretches, roars past oil tank
farms and petrochemical plants, major rail lines, Newark Liberty International Airport, and the
oily waters of Raritan Bay. The parkway links leafy affluent suburbs with the Jersey shore. The
latter has become a cultural icon thanks to the MTV reality series of the same name, which has
become a popular—if not critical—success since it premiered in December 2009.

The 6th Congressional District inelegantly ties together these great transportation nodes, and
the upward mobility and economic progress that have taken place around them. The district is
shaped something like an overturned capital F, with a long string of towns running from Piscata-
way to Sandy Hook, and two appendages running south: one along the Middlesex-Monmouth
county line, the other along the Atlantic Ocean. Middlesex and Monmouth counties account for
90% of the district's population. It includes the central core of Middlesex County: New Brunswick,
Highland Park, Metuchen, Sayreville, and parts of Edison Township and surrounding communities—a heavy industry area that, since the time of Edison, has also housed some of America's great
research and development facilities, plus Rutgers, the state university of New Jersey. In recent
years, Edison Township has seen an influx of immigrants from India, many of them engineers and
doctors.

The 6th also includes Monmouth County territory overlooking Lower New York Bay, with
spacious estates on highlands above little port towns from Sandy Hook, home to the nation's oldest
operating lighthouse (1764), south to the mile-long boardwalk of Belmar. Between them is Asbury
Park, founded as a Christian resort, immortalized by a Bruce Springsteen album, and now plagued
by a high poverty rate; and Ocean Grove, founded in 1869, which has the nation's greatest concentration of Victorian homes. This area also suffered during the recession; the county's Division of
Social Service office began seeing clients dressed in designer clothes who nonetheless are having
trouble making ends meet. "The new client is middle America," intake worker Diane Dowdell told
The Asbury Park Press. The shore has remained a summer vacation area that attracts millions,
but it also hosts year-round communities, with their own upward-striving families. These are comfortable Democratic working-class bastions, wedged between heavily minority urban districts and
upscale suburbia. In 2008, Barack Obama won this district 60%-38%. But the recession and disenchantment with Democrats led Republican Chris Christie to win both Middlesex and Monmouth
counties in the 2009 governor's race.

Frank Pallone (D)

The congressman from the 6th District is Frank Pallone, a Democrat elected in 1988. Pallone is
the son of a disabled Long Branch policeman. He has been an environmentalist since 1969, when
as a Middlebury College freshman in Vermont he worked for that state's first-in-the-nation bottle
deposit law. After getting a master's degree in international relations from Tufts University and
a law degree from Rutgers, he was elected to the Long Branch City Council in 1982, at age 31, and
to the New Jersey Senate a year later. After the death of Democratic U.S. Rep. Jim Howard, Pallone
ran for the House. The district leaned Republican, but residents were angry about untreated
sludge, plastic containers, and medical waste washing up on the beach. Pallone's bumper sticker,

which didn't mention party affiliation, said, "Stop Ocean Dumping." That, combined with his conservative stands on taxes and crime, helped him to win 52% in both the special and general elections.

Pallone started as a political maverick, but has become more loyal to the Democratic Party in recent years. His environmental focus has been on protecting the Jersey shoreline. In 2006, he won passage of a bill to reduce and prevent debris in the marine environment. And two years later, he was the lead sponsor of a bipartisan bill to rebuild American fisheries, in part by requiring a review of factors that lead to over-fishing. After the BP oil spill in the Gulf of Mexico in 2010, Pallone was among several New Jersey Democrats who implored President Barack Obama to reverse his decision to open up waters for drilling off the East Coast.

As chairman of the influential Energy and Commerce Subcommittee on Health in 2009, Pallone helped steer to passage the Democrats' expansion of the State Children's Health Insurance Program, which he called "a down payment to ensuring that all Americans have access to affordable health care." When the Obama administration's economic stimulus bill came up for debate, he backed an increase in the federal matching rate for Medicaid as a step to reduce the program's financial burden on states. During the health care overhaul debate, he shuttled among the various factions of Blue Dogs and progressives to try to get them to be flexible about the plan's contents. When the bill finally became law in 2010, he turned to other issues. He got a bill through the subcommittee that set guidelines for how long student athletes should wait before returning to a sport following a concussion.

In a bow to the many people of Armenian descent in the district, Pallone helped push congressional approval of normalizing trade relations for Armenia. He sponsored the resolution that labeled the 1915 killing of Armenians by Ottoman Turks as genocide. But he agreed in 2007 to defer a vote under pressure from the Turkish government and the Bush administration. Two years later, he joined a bipartisan group of House members who called on Obama to follow up on campaign statements and label the massacre a genocide.

Since 1994, Pallone has usually been re-elected with at least 60% of the vote. In 1998, he faced a tough challenge from 28-year-old Republican Mike Ferguson, an ally of former GOP Gov. Thomas Kean. An insurance group unhappy with Pallone's support for President Bill Clinton's plan to regulate health maintenance organizations spent nearly $2 million on Ferguson's campaign. But Pallone won 57%-40%. In 2010, he drew another formidable opponent in Republican Anna Little, the mayor of Highlands and an immigration lawyer. With strong tea party backing, Little won a stunning GOP primary victory over weekly newspaper publisher Diane Gooch despite having been outraised $433,000-$22,000. Little took strong socially conservative positions and blasted Pallone's efforts to pass the health care bill. Polls showed the race tightening in the campaign's closing days, but Pallone was bolstered by a series of newspaper endorsements and kept his seat with a 55%-44% triumph.

Pallone has long wanted to make a run for the Senate, but the timing and circumstances have not worked out in his favor. When Democratic Sen. Jon Corzine ran for governor in 2005, Pallone endorsed him and said that he would like to have Corzine's Senate seat. Corzine became governor, but he appointed U.S. Rep. Robert Menendez to his Senate seat. During Corzine's re-election bid against Republican Chris Christie, Pallone became an attack dog for the governor, raising questions about Christie's work as U.S. attorney for New Jersey and burnishing his own reputation among state party leaders.

SEVENTH DISTRICT

Leonard Lance (R)

Elected 2008, 2nd term; b. June 25, 1952, Easton, PA; home, Clinton Township; Lehigh U., B.A., 1974; Vanderbilt U., J.D. 1977; Princeton U., M.P.A. 1982; Catholic; married (Heidi Rohrbach); 1 child.

Elected Office: NJ Assembly, 1991-2001; NJ Senate, 2002-08, minority leader 2002-08.

Professional Career: Law clerk, Warren Cnty Court, 1977-78; Asst. cnsl., Gov. Thomas H. Kean, 1983-1990.

DC Office: 426 CHOB, 20515, 202-225-5361; Fax: 202-225-9460; Web site: lance.house.gov.

State Offices: Flemington, 908-789-2869; Westfield, 908-518-7733.

Committees: *Energy & Commerce:* Commerce, Manufacturing & Trade; Health.

Group Ratings

	ACLU	ACU	ADA	CFG	AFS	FRC	LCV	ITIC	NTU	COC
2010	25	88	5	98	13	75	40	33	84	88
2009	–	68	40	57	56	–	71	–	60	87

National Journal Ratings

	2010 LIB	—	2010 CONS	2009 LIB	—	2009 CONS
Economic	36%	—	64%	38%	—	61%
Social	31%	—	67%	39%	—	60%
Foreign	0%	—	88%	33%	—	63%
Composite	25%	—	75%	38%	—	62%

Key Votes of the 111th Congress

1. Overturn Ledbetter	N	5. Bar federal abortion funds	Y
2. Pass $820 billion stimulus	N	6. Pass health care bill	N
3. Let guns in national parks	Y	7. Regulate financial firms	N
4. Pass cap-and-trade	Y	8. Pass tax cuts for some	N

9. Stop detainee transfers	Y
10. Legalize immigrants' kids	N
11. Repeal don't ask, tell	N
12. Limit campaign funds	N

Election Results

2010 general	Leonard Lance (R)	105,084	(59%)	($1,341,109)
	Ed Potosnak (D)	71,902	(41%)	($349,518)
2010 primary	Leonard Lance (R)	17,200	(56%)	
	David Larsen (R)	9,475	(31%)	
	Alonzo Hosford (R)	2,534	(8%)	

Prior Winning Percentages: 2008 (50%)

Population		Race/Ethnicity		Work	
Pop. 2010:	672,885	White:	69.0%	Private:	81.7%
Change since 2000:	Up 4.0%	Black:	5.4%	Government:	12.8%
Urban:	90.4%	Hispanic:	11.2%	Self-employed:	5.2%
Rural:	9.6%	Asian:	12.6%	Blue collar:	14.4%
Area size:	603 sq. mi.	Native Am.:	0.1%	White collar:	73.5%
		Hawaiian:	0.0%	Khaki collar:	0.0%
Age		Two+ races:	1.5%	Other:	12.0%
Median age:	40.2 yrs.				
More than 65 yrs:	13.0%	*Ancestry*		Median income:	$93,739
Less than 18 yrs:	24.6%	Italian	15.0%	Median Home Value:	$440,500
		Irish	13.0%		
Education		German	11.0%	**Military Veterans**	
H.S. grad:	91.9%			% of Pop:	6.8%
College grad:	45.2%				
Grad degree:	18.9%				

Central New Jersey; Part Edison

The transportation arteries beneath the First Watchung Mountain played a large role in New Jersey's development. The rail lines of the late 19th century opened up commuter suburbs. In the 1940s, the four lanes of U.S. 22 made those communities readily accessible by car. And finally, Interstate 78, completed in the mid-1980s, put Newark only an hour's distance from the Pennsylvania line. The interstate stimulated the development of an edge city called Bridge-

2008 Presidential Vote		
Barack Obama (D)	161,497	(50%)
John McCain (R)	159,529	(49%)
2004 Presidential Vote		
George Bush (R)	164,176	(53%)
John Kerry (D)	144,767	(47%)
Cook Partisan Voting Index: R+3		

water Commons halfway between Philadelphia and Manhattan. An enormous shopping mall and office developments, which included the headquarters of AT&T, rose up in the horse country around Far Hills and Bernardsville, where the likes of Malcolm Forbes and Charles Engelhard owned huge estates. (New Jersey claims more horses per square mile than any other state.) These towns are in Somerset County, with a median household income in 2009 of $96,223, the sixth highest among U.S. counties. Celebrity developer Donald Trump opened an exclusive private golf club here in 2004.

The 7th Congressional District of New Jersey, with its contorted boundaries, covers these several generations of suburban development. It ranges across the breadth of the state, from the edge of Pennsylvania's Lehigh Valley in the west almost to Staten Island in the east. It is an agglomeration of places, not a district with a distinct character. Almost half the employed people are in management, professional and related occupations, and more than 40% of its homes are worth more than $500,000. The 7th includes parts of four counties, and parts of Edison, Woodbridge, Bridgewater, Linden and Union. Edison has become a cultural melting pot in recent years, with a majority nonwhite population; it is 36% Asian, 9% African-American and 7% Hispanic.

The district's easternmost points are in Union County, just shy of Newark Liberty International Airport. It includes the suburban communities of Summit, Scotch Plains and North and South Plainfield, but not heavily Democratic Plainfield. It follows I-78 and the Watchung Mountains to western Somerset County. It takes in fast-growing Hunterdon County, where the county seat of Flemington was the site of the "trial of the century" for the kidnapping and murder of the 20-month-old son of aviator Charles Lindbergh. There is, of course, a political imperative behind the weird shape of the district. It was designed as part of a bipartisan incumbent-protection plan, and it put heavily Democratic areas into adjacent districts, while adding Republican areas. President George W. Bush won comfortably here by 53%-47% in 2004, but in 2008, Barack Obama won, though by a much narrower margin, 1,968 votes. Obama got 49.7% to John McCain's 49.1%.

Leonard Lance (R)

The congressman from the 7th District is Leonard Lance, a self-styled "Eisenhower Republican" elected in 2008 to succeed retiring GOP Rep. Mike Ferguson. Lance's English-German ancestors have lived in Hunterdon County for 300 years, and he and his twin brother, James, grew up there in the small town of Glen Gardner. Politics is in Lance's blood. His father, Wesley Lance, was a state senator and eventually rose to Senate president. The younger Lance went to Lehigh University in neighboring Pennsylvania, and then headed south to Vanderbilt University to go to law school. He returned to New Jersey to pursue a master's degree from Princeton University. One of his early jobs was as Republican Gov. Thomas Kean's assistant counsel for county and municipal matters. In 1990, he was elected to the New Jersey legislature, where he made a name for himself as a budget hawk and independent thinker. He opposed a spending plan by GOP Gov. Christie Whitman, a move that cost him the Budget Committee chairmanship. He was known by fellow legislators as a workhorse with a pragmatic streak. In many respects, he is a prototypical Northeastern Republican: fiscally conservative but socially moderate. He supports abortion rights and tends to favor bipartisanship over ideology, which has led political opponents further to the right to label him a "RINO" (Republican in Name Only).

In 2008, Ferguson, facing a rematch against Democratic Assemblywoman Linda Stender, who lost to him by just under 3,000 votes in 2006, did not seek re-election. Well-known in the district, Lance got into the primary race against six other candidates. He was the establishment Republicans' pick, but he faced tough competition from Whitman's daughter, Kate Whitman, who outraised him and questioned his fiscal bona fides. He was forced to spend nearly all of his funds early on, yet he won the primary by a surprisingly large margin, besting Whitman 39%-20%.

Drained by the primary, Lance started the general election campaign seriously outmatched by Stender, who ultimately outspent him 2-to-1. She criticized Lance for opposing her legislation to make it mandatory for pharmacies to fill prescriptions for birth control pills, including emergency contraception. Lance said he voted against the bill because he believed that mom-and-pop pharmacies should have the right to decide whether to fill such prescriptions. Both political parties pulled out all the stops for this seat. President George W. Bush stumped for Lance and helped him raise money. Democratic House Speaker Nancy Pelosi and New York Sen. Hillary Rodham Clinton both came to the district to campaign for Stender. Lance got a boost from the Newark *Star-Ledger* newspaper, which called him "that rarest of birds, an old-fashioned, thrifty, genuinely moderate Republican." Lance did better than expected, winning by 50%-42%.

Once in the House, he regularly showed his willingness to buck his party. He was one of just eight Republicans to support energy legislation that included a cap-and-trade program aimed at reducing greenhouse gas emissions, and one of just three to back the Lilly Ledbetter Fair Pay Act assisting victims of wage discrimination lawsuits. He also was the only freshman Republican to cosponsor a 2009 bill barring employers from discriminating against workers based on sexual orientation. He held firm against most of President Barack Obama's economic agenda, voting against the stimulus bill even as he touted a flood control project in his district that was ready for stimulus money. A member of the Financial Services Committee, he castigated the Dodd-Frank Wall Street reform law, saying he was especially troubled by its reliance on unused government bailout funds.

Lance's moderate stances ensured him a GOP primary challenge in 2010, but he was able to defeat three tea party-inspired challengers with 56% after winning the support of local Republican organizations. He then faced Democrat Ed Potosnak, a former staffer for Rep. Mike Honda, D-Calif., and a former chemistry teacher. Potosnak, who is openly gay, criticized Lance's opposition to repealing the "don't ask, don't tell" policy barring openly gay military service members. He also promised to help small businesses. But Lance outraised him by 4-to-1 and won easily, 59%-41%. For keeping the seat in GOP hands, he was rewarded with a plum spot on the Energy and Commerce Committee. But he is considered to be vulnerable to redistricting.

EIGHTH DISTRICT

Bill Pascrell (D)

Elected 1996, 8th term; b. Jan. 25, 1937, Paterson; home, Paterson; Fordham U., B.A. 1959, M.A. 1961; Catholic; married (Elsie); 3 children.

Military Career: Army, 1961; Army Reserves, 1962–67.

Elected Office: Pres., Paterson Bd. of Ed., 1979–82; NJ Assembly, 1987–97, Minority ldr. pro tem; Paterson mayor, 1990–97.

Professional Career: High Schl. teacher, 1960–74; Dir., Paterson Dept. of Public Works, 1974–77; Dir., Paterson Dept. of Policy, 1977–87.

DC Office: 2370 RHOB, 20515, 202-225-5751; Fax: 202-225-5782; Web site: pascrell.house.gov.

State Offices: Bloomfield, 973-680-1361; Passaic, 973-472-4510; Paterson, 973-523-5152.

Committees: *Budget. Ways & Means: Health.*

Group Ratings

	ACLU	ACU	ADA	CFG	AFS	FRC	LCV	ITIC	NTU	COC
2010	88	4	95	3	100	0	100	100	6	25
2009	–	0	90	4	100	–	93	–	2	36

National Journal Ratings

	2010 LIB — 2010 CONS		2009 LIB — 2009 CONS	
Economic	69%	— 30%	73%	— 27%
Social	71%	— 25%	80%	— 20%
Foreign	78%	— 17%	87%	— 9%
Composite	74%	— 26%	81%	— 19%

Key Votes of the 111th Congress

1. Overturn Ledbetter	Y	5. Bar federal abortion funds	N	9. Stop detainee transfers	N
2. Pass $820 billion stimulus	Y	6. Pass health care bill	Y	10. Legalize immigrants' kids	Y
3. Let guns in national parks	N	7. Regulate financial firms	Y	11. Repeal don't ask, tell	Y
4. Pass cap-and-trade	Y	8. Pass tax cuts for some	Y	12. Limit campaign funds	Y

Election Results

2010 general	Bill Pascrell (D)..88,478	(63%)	($1,499,697)
	Roland Straten (R)...51,023	(36%)	($169,070)
2010 primary	Bill Pascrell (D)... unopposed		

Prior Winning Percentages: 2008 (71%), 2006 (71%), 2004 (69%), 2002 (67%), 2000 (67%), 1998 (62%), 1996 (51%)

Population		Race/Ethnicity		Work	
Pop. 2010:	660,424	White:	45.7%	Private:	83.0%
Change since 2000:	Up 2.0%	Black:	12.7%	Government:	12.4%
Urban:	100.0%	Hispanic:	33.2%	Self-employed:	4.6%
Rural:	0.0%	Asian:	6.5%	Blue collar:	21.5%
Area size:	110 sq. mi.	Native Am.:	0.1%	White collar:	63.3%
		Hawaiian:	0.0%	Khaki collar:	0.0%
Age		Two+ races:	1.5%	Other:	15.2%
Median age:	37.0 yrs.				
More than 65 yrs:	12.8%	*Ancestry*		Median income:	$60,912
Less than 18 yrs:	24.9%	Italian	13.5%	Median Home Value:	$405,800
		Irish	7.5%		
Education		German	5.5%	**Military Veterans**	
H.S. grad:	83.8%			% of Pop:	5.1%
College grad:	32.2%				
Grad degree:	11.4%				

Northeastern New Jersey; Paterson

Paterson is one of the few American cities that have turned out pretty much as planned. It was the brainchild of Alexander Hamilton, who in the 1790s journeyed 20 miles from Manhattan to the Great Falls of the Passaic River in New Jersey. Watching the water surge down 72 feet—the highest falls along the East Coast—he predicted an industrial city would rise on the site. Hamilton formed the Society for Establish-

2008 Presidential Vote		
Barack Obama (D) 163,359	(63%)
John McCain (R) 91,690	(36%)
2004 Presidential Vote		
John Kerry (D) 142,081	(59%)
George Bush (R) 99,239	(41%)
Cook Partisan Voting Index: D+10		

ing Useful Manufactures, and got Pierre L'Enfant, the designer of Washington, D.C., to design Paterson (named after then-Gov. William Paterson). In 1836, Samuel Colt began manufacturing revolvers here. One of the first American locomotives, the Sandusky, was built in Paterson in 1837. Paterson ultimately became America's "Silk City," employing 25,000 silk mill workers before the great strike of 1913 led by the radical Industrial Workers of the World. Throughout, it attracted immigrants from England, Ireland, and, after 1890, Italy and Poland. The city continues to attract immigrants today, even if its economy produces more service jobs than manufacturing jobs. The city has gained a lively artists' community in its postindustrial setting, and downtown's "Little Palestine" reflects the city's sizable Arab community—Turks, Palestinians, Lebanese, Syrians, and Jordanians. The recession lingered here longer than in most other areas—unemployment in both Passaic and Essex counties remained above 10% in 2010.

The 8th Congressional District includes Paterson, its largest city, and much suburban and industrial territory west and south of Paterson and north of Newark. More than half the population lives in Passaic County; the rest are in Essex County. The district includes towns south of Paterson on the Passaic River—Clifton, Nutley, Belleville, Bloomfield, and Passaic, which is majority Hispanic. On higher ground is affluent Montclair, with large populations of well-off African-Americans and Manhattan-oriented Boomers, the most Democratic part of the district outside of Paterson. Over the Watchung Mountain are affluent West Orange and South Orange, both heavily Democratic, and the small Republican towns of Cedar Grove and Verona. In the 1980s, the district leaned Republican; in the 1990s, it became heavily Democratic and remains so.

Bill Pascrell (D)

The 8th District representative is Bill Pascrell, a Democrat with a feisty Jersey-guy demeanor elected in 1996. He grew up in Paterson, the grandson of Italian immigrants. His father worked for the railroad, and Pascrell was the first one in his family to graduate from college. He worked his way through Fordham University, served in the Army, and then taught high school for 14 years. From there Pascrell went into politics, first as director of Paterson's public works department, and then as school board president. In 1987, he was elected to the New Jersey Assembly. In 1990, Pascrell was elected mayor of Paterson but continued to serve in the Assembly—a common practice in New Jersey until the legislature voted in 2007 to stop the practice. In 1996, Pascrell challenged first-term U.S. Rep. Bill Martini, a Republican, whom Pascrell portrayed as the tool of an "extremist" House leadership. His ads showed Martini's face on a puppet being manipulated by Republican House Speaker Newt Gingrich. Despite Martini's support from the Sierra Club and labor unions, Pascrell won 51%-48%. Since then, he has received at least 62% of the vote against weak challengers.

In the House, Pascrell has compiled a liberal record on economics and a more moderate one on cultural and foreign issues. He has voted for some restrictions on abortion, including a ban on partial-birth abortions and a parental notification requirement when a woman under 18 crosses state lines for an abortion. In 2002, he voted to authorize the use of force in Iraq, and, on the Homeland Security Committee, he has been a voice for strengthening homeland defense, calling for improved communications among first responders. "How is it we can talk to people on the moon, but we can't talk one block away?" Pascrell asked. In February 2011, he also succeeded in restoring $510 million in fire department grants that Republicans had proposed to chop.

At home, he endeared himself to Bruce Springsteen fans when he joined them in their gripes against Ticketmaster after the ticket service advertised drastically marked-up seats through a subsidiary's website just minutes after several of the Jersey rocker's shows had sold out. When Russian businessman Mikhail Prokhorov sought to buy the New Jersey Nets basketball team in 2010, Pascrell called for an investigation into Prokhorov's investment bank's ties with Zimbabwe to see if they violated U.S. sanctions. The National Basketball Association called his claims misinformed and approved the sale, a move the congressman called "extremely short-sighted."

Pascrell landed a seat on the powerful House Ways and Means Committee in 2007 after years of lobbying for a spot. He worked with labor and consumer groups to promote "fair trade," and to expand the Trade Adjustment Assistance program for workers who have lost their jobs. Two other pet projects of Pascrell's were successful: A bill to designate Paterson's Great Falls as a 120-acre national park, which was enacted in 2009. When in 2008 a Montclair High School football player died from a brain injury, Pascrell introduced a bill requiring states to pay for neurological testing of student-athletes. The House passed his bill in 2010 calling for development of a new set of concussion-management guidelines for student athletes.

As his party's political fortunes began declining in 2010, Pascrell was among the Democrats who was open in venting his frustrations. When White House spokesman Robert Gibbs speculated that the Democrats' House majority was in doubt in the 2010 election, Pascrell told *The Washington Post*, "What the hell do they think we've been doing the last 12 months? We're the ones who have been taking the tough votes."

He has harbored ambitions for statewide office, and expressed interest in running for governor in 2001. But his support of former Gov. Jim Florio in the 2000 Senate Democratic primary against Jon Corzine left him on the losing side of the state's Democratic establishment. In 2005, he supported Corzine for governor in the hopes of succeeding him in the Senate, but the appointment went to U.S. Rep. Robert Menendez. Having gained a Ways and Means seat, Pascrell is less likely to move elsewhere.

NINTH DISTRICT

Steven Rothman (D)

Elected 1996, 8th term; b. Oct. 14, 1952, Englewood; home, Fair Lawn; Syracuse U., B.A. 1974, Washington U., J.D. 1977; Jewish; Divorced; 2 children.

Elected Office: Englewood mayor, 1983–89; Bergen Cnty. Surrogate Court judge, 1993–96.

Professional Career: Practicing atty., 1978–93.

DC Office: 2303 RHOB, 20515, 202-225-5061; Fax: 202-225-5851; Web site: rothman.house.gov.

State Offices: Hackensack, 201-646-0808; Jersey City, 201-798-1366.

Committees: *Appropriations:* Defense; State, Foreign Operations & Related Programs.

Group Ratings

	ACLU	ACU	ADA	CFG	AFS	FRC	LCV	ITIC	NTU	COC
2010	93	0	90	0	100	0	100	100	4	29
2009	–	0	100	0	100	–	93	–	2	33

National Journal Ratings

	2010 LIB	—	2010 CONS	2009 LIB	—	2009 CONS
Economic	78%	—	20%	82%	—	14%
Social	79%	—	20%	75%	—	20%
Foreign	78%	—	17%	87%	—	9%
Composite	80%	—	20%	84%	—	17%

Key Votes of the 111th Congress

1. Overturn Ledbetter	Y	5. Bar federal abortion funds	N	9. Stop detainee transfers	N
2. Pass $820 billion stimulus	Y	6. Pass health care bill	Y	10. Legalize immigrants' kids	Y
3. Let guns in national parks	N	7. Regulate financial firms	Y	11. Repeal don't ask, tell	Y
4. Pass cap-and-trade	Y	8. Pass tax cuts for some	Y	12. Limit campaign funds	*

Election Results

2010 general	Steven Rothman (D)	83,564	(61%)	($1,085,315)
	Michael Agosta (R)	52,082	(38%)	($197,090)
2010 primary	Steven Rothman (D)	unopposed		

Prior Winning Percentages: 2008 (68%), 2006 (71%), 2004 (68%), 2002 (70%), 2000 (68%), 1998 (65%), 1996 (56%)

Population		Race/Ethnicity		Work	
Pop. 2010:	661,379	White:	50.3%	Private:	82.6%
Change since 2000:	Up 2.2%	Black:	6.9%	Government:	12.6%
Urban:	100.0%	Hispanic:	26.4%	Self-employed:	4.7%
Rural:	0.0%	Asian:	14.3%	Blue collar:	17.8%
Area size:	100 sq. mi.	Native Am.:	0.1%	White collar:	67.1%
		Hawaiian:	0.0%	Khaki collar:	0.1%
Age		Two+ races:	1.5%	Other:	15.1%
Median age:	39.2 yrs.				
More than 65 yrs:	14.1%	*Ancestry*		Median income:	$66,642
Less than 18 yrs:	20.5%	Italian	13.6%	Median Home Value:	$422,000
		Irish	8.1%		
Education		German	6.0%	**Military Veterans**	
H.S. grad:	86.9%			% of Pop:	5.3%
College grad:	37.0%				
Grad degree:	13.2%				

Northeast New Jersey; Jersey City

The George Washington Bridge, one of several wondrous suspension bridges completed in America in the 1930s, strides the Hudson River, its west tower almost up against the green cliffs of New Jersey's Palisades. It is one of the glories of modern engineering, enabling people and goods to be transported through the irregular terrain of metropolitan New York—tidal rivers and cliffs and broad expanses of swamp. For a century, the dramatic

2008 Presidential Vote		
Barack Obama (D) 158,911	(61%)
John McCain (R) 99,129	(38%)

2004 Presidential Vote		
John Kerry (D) 144,723	(59%)
George Bush (R)..................101,229	(41%)

Cook Partisan Voting Index: D+9

beauty of the Palisades contrasted with the sprawl of the Hackensack River Valley and the Jersey Meadowlands not far to the west, which conveyed the image of New Jersey for many—a landscape of gas station signs, oil tank farms, truck terminals, and 12 lanes of New Jersey Turnpike. The Meadowlands, once 8,400 acres of wetlands and home to thousands of species of animals and plants, was developed in the 1970s. The state built the Meadowlands Sports Complex—Giants Stadium, where the Giants and Jets play; the Meadowlands Racetrack; the Brendan Byrne Arena, later Continental Airlines Arena. Private development followed—hotels, warehouses, light industry, shopping centers—in what became a small city. A generation later, the state built a new $1.6 billion stadium at the Meadowlands for the National Football League's Giants and Jets that opened in August 2010. Nearby, the $2 billion Xanadu retail and entertainment center is under construction, although it encountered financing issues in 2009 and stalled. It is now slated to open in 2013 under a new name.

The 9th Congressional District of New Jersey includes much of the Palisades and the Meadowlands and is one of the most densely populated areas in the nation's most densely populated state. The scenery here is familiar to fans of the cable television series *The Sopranos*: Jersey City, Kearny, North Arlington, and Lodi, which is home to the fictitious Bada Bing strip club. The 9th takes in the high-rise towers of Fort Lee, Cliffside Park, and fast-growing Edgewater, where dwellers in luxury apartment houses brag about their views of New York City. It goes west and north to the leafy suburbs of Englewood and Teaneck, and southwest to the high land overlooking the Meadowlands and the Passaic River.

Old towns like Rutherford have enclaves of Polish-, German-, and Italian-Americans. Blue-collar Palisades Park has what has a large concentration of Korean-Americans. Teaneck and Englewood are home to middle-class blacks and young, Orthodox Jewish families. Fairview, Bergenfield, and Hackensack, an old industrial town, are home to growing numbers of Hispanics. Bergen County has about 80% of the district's voters, and ranked 25th among the nation's counties in median household income in 2009. This was a growth area in the 1950s and 1960s, as New Yorkers moved out of the city. It lost population in the next two decades, as young people moved farther out. Now the population is rising because of new immigrants. From 2000 to 2008, the Hispanic population in Bergen County grew more than 47% to 135,000. In 2008, Democratic presidential candidate Barack Obama won 54% of the vote in Bergen, and won the district 61%-38%. A year later, the county narrowly went for Democratic Gov. Jon Corzine, 49%-46%, over his successful GOP challenger Chris Christie.

Steve Rothman (D)

The congressman from the 9th District is Steve Rothman, a Democrat first elected in 1996. Rothman grew up in Englewood and Tenafly, the grandson of Jewish immigrants from Russia, Poland, and Austria. His father was a tool-and-die maker but later found industrial real estate to be more profitable. Rothman went to school at Syracuse University and Washington University law school in St. Louis, and then practiced law. From 1983 to 1989, he was mayor of Englewood. In 1993, he became a judge in the Bergen County Surrogate's Court. When Democrat Bob Torricelli ran for the Senate in 1996, Rothman resigned his judgeship to run for Torricelli's House seat. With the party endorsement, Rothman faced Republican Kathleen Donovan, a former Bergen County clerk, state assemblywoman, and chairwoman of the New York-New Jersey Port Authority. She was endorsed by the New Jersey Education Association. But this part of New Jersey swung sharply to the Democrats after Republicans won control of Congress in 1994. The 9th District voted overwhelmingly for Bill Clinton for president that year, and voted 56%-42% for Rothman.

In the House, Rothman often has been more liberal on economic issues than on foreign policy and defense issues. A staunch supporter of Israel, he voted for the Iraq war resolution in 2002, although he later backed a troop withdrawal deadline. He bonded in 2009 with Michael Oren, Israel's ambassador to the United States, who was raised in nearby West Orange and who knew some of Rothman's favorite local eateries. "We are both Jersey guys," Rothman told *The Record* newspaper. When the Obama administration, in a sharp reversal, reportedly told Arab governments in February 2011 it would support the U.N. Security Council in reaffirming its opposition to continued Israeli settlement activity in the West Bank and East Jerusalem, Rothman was among those reacting with outrage. "Any failure to stand with Israel during these difficult times in the Middle East will only encourage the enemies of America and Israel," he said.

On local issues, his most innovative work has been to limit further development of the Meadowlands and to get protections for environmentally sensitive areas. He secured $5.2 million to help create an 8,400-acre state park in the one-third of the Meadowlands that had not been developed. As a member of the Appropriations Committee, he has been an unabashed defender of earmarking who often boasts that he's gotten more money for his district than anyone who has ever held the seat. In fiscal 2010, he led New Jersey's House delegation in earmarks and was in the top 20 overall, according to Taxpayers for Common Sense. He took a dim view of President Barack Obama's admonition to lawmakers in the 2011 State of the Union address not to send him any earmarked bills. "The subject of congressional earmarks is a decision for Congress to make," he said.

Rothman's district work naturally includes pitching for transportation dollars, including for projects to relieve ever-congested Route 17 and money he secured for commuter rail projects in Bergen County. He also authored a successful bill creating federal grants for better security in public schools, including for metal detectors and security training. He announced his support for same-sex marriage after learning his stepdaughter is a lesbian. Rothman has won re-election by wide margins.

TENTH DISTRICT

Donald Payne (D)

Elected 1988, 12th term; b. July 16, 1934, Newark; home, Newark; Seton Hall, B.A. 1957; Baptist; widowed; 3 children.

Elected Office: Essex Cnty. Bd. of Chosen Freeholders, 1972–78, Dir. 1977–78; Newark Municipal Cncl., 1982–89.

Professional Career: Elem. & high schl. teacher, 1957–64; Exec., Prudential Insurance Co., 1964–72; Pres., YMCAs of the U.S., 1970; V.P., Urban Data Systems Inc., 1975–88.

DC Office: 2310 RHOB, 20515, 202-225-3436; Fax: 202-225-4160; Web site: payne.house.gov.

State Offices: Elizabeth, 908-629-0222; Jersey City, 201-369-0392; Newark, 973-645-3213.

Committees: *Education & the Workforce:* Early Childhood, Elementary & Secondary Education; Workforce Protections. *Foreign Affairs:* Africa, Global Health & Human Rights (RMM); Western Hemisphere.

Group Ratings

	ACLU	ACU	ADA	CFG	AFS	FRC	LCV	ITIC	NTU	COC
2010	100	5	95	3	100	12	100	67	7	25
2009	–	0	100	0	100	–	100	–	3	33

National Journal Ratings

	2010 LIB — 2010 CONS		2009 LIB — 2009 CONS	
Economic	77%	— 23%	91%	— 0%
Social	75%	— 24%	82%	— 17%
Foreign	72%	— 27%	78%	— 17%
Composite	75%	— 25%	86%	— 14%

Key Votes of the 111th Congress

1. Overturn Ledbetter	Y	5. Bar federal abortion funds	N	9. Stop detainee transfers	N
2. Pass $820 billion stimulus	Y	6. Pass health care bill	Y	10. Legalize immigrants' kids	Y
3. Let guns in national parks	N	7. Regulate financial firms	Y	11. Repeal don't ask, tell	Y
4. Pass cap-and-trade	Y	8. Pass tax cuts for some	Y	12. Limit campaign funds	N

Election Results

2010 general	Donald Payne (D)..95,299	(85%)	($617,759)
	Michael Alonso (R)..14,357	(13%)	
2010 primary	Donald Payne (D).. unopposed		

Prior Winning Percentages: 2008 (99%), 2006 (100%), 2004 (97%), 2002 (84%), 2000 (88%), 1998 (84%), 1996 (84%), 1994 (76%), 1992 (78%), 1990 (81%), 1988 (77%)

Population		Race/Ethnicity		Work	
Pop. 2010:	634,343	White:	17.1%	Private:	78.8%
Change since 2000:	Down 2.0%	Black:	55.6%	Government:	17.3%
Urban:	100.0%	Hispanic:	20.4%	Self-employed:	3.7%
Rural:	0.0%	Asian:	4.4%	Blue collar:	21.7%
Area size:	69 sq. mi.	Native Am.:	0.2%	White collar:	56.2%
		Hawaiian:	0.0%	Khaki collar:	0.1%
Age		Two+ races:	1.6%	Other:	21.9%
Median age:	34.2 yrs.				
More than 65 yrs:	10.6%	*Ancestry*		Median income:	$46,296
Less than 18 yrs:	25.8%	West Indian	8.8%	Median Home Value:	$326,300
		Subsaharan	3.7%		
Education		Italian	3.7%	**Military Veterans**	
H.S. grad:	81.2%			% of Pop:	5.0%
College grad:	21.3%				
Grad degree:	7.0%				

Northeastern New Jersey; Newark

Newark was once the heart of New Jersey. All of the main transportation arteries led there, and its corporate headquarters buildings were the tallest in the state. In 1930, 442,000 people lived in Newark, 1 of every 9 in New Jersey. Newark fell on hard times in the latter half of the 20th century. Whole sections of the city were dominated by criminals and deserted by most law-abiding residents. By the year 2000, there were just 273,000 people left in Newark, representing

2008 Presidential Vote
Barack Obama (D) 208,070   (87%)
John McCain (R) 30,395   (13%)

2004 Presidential Vote
John Kerry (D) 167,707   (82%)
George Bush (R) 36,660   (18%)

Cook Partisan Voting Index: D+33

1 in every 30. In recent years, Newark has been attempting a turnaround. Population was up to 277,000 in 2010; new office buildings have joined the Prudential and Public Service Electric & Gas headquarters, and the New Jersey Performing Arts Center has been popular with city-dwellers seeking a less expensive experience than Manhattan. There are new restaurants and trendy bars, and a new downtown arena houses the hockey team the Devils. An assortment of condominium projects are on the drawing board. The young and charismatic mayor, Democrat Cory Booker, brought energy to the city and has declared war on street gangs. But much remains to be done—homicides went up in 2010 for the second year in a row, and with an $80 million budget deficit looming that fall, the city in desperation pushed plans to sell off city-owned office buildings in the hope it could then lease them.

There has been industrial development around Newark Liberty International Airport. The glass- and-aluminum facility has been greatly expanded for international carriers and is prospering as a hub for Continental, the most thriving of the legacy airlines. Port Newark-Elizabeth Marine Terminal is the largest container port on the East Coast and ranks nationally behind only Los Angeles and Long Beach. Old warehouses there have been cleared for more-modern facilities. The question is whether the city's finances will stabilize and Newark can become once again the vital center of New Jersey. Mayor Booker's friendship with President Barack Obama certainly won't hurt. Nor can Facebook founder Mark Zuckerberg's stunning donation in 2010 of $100 million—conditioned on matching grants being raised over the next five years—to remake the city's failing public schools.

The 10th Congressional District of New Jersey is centered in Essex County and is made up of most of Newark—the Central, South, and West wards—plus Irvington, most of the Oranges, and part of Montclair to the west. It also takes in much of Elizabeth, Rahway, and Linden to the south. Its boundary lines wiggle around to include African-Americans in Jersey City, Montclair, and Elizabeth, while leaving Hispanics in the next-door 13th District. Overall the district is 56% black and

North New Jersey; Morris County

Morris County in New Jersey, west of the Watchung Mountains, was one of the first parts of the United States west of the seaboard to be settled. It has long been a place of comparative wealth, the home of skilled craftsmen during the Revolutionary War and plenty of water mills and iron forges by the 19th century. But only in the late 20th century did it come into its own, as one of the most affluent parts of the United States. The county ranked in 2010 as New Jersey's

2008 Presidential Vote		
John McCain (R)	182,731	(54%)
Barack Obama (D)	154,076	(45%)
2004 Presidential Vote		
George Bush (R)	186,993	(58%)
John Kerry (D)	135,578	(42%)
Cook Partisan Voting Index: R+7		

second-wealthiest, behind Hunterdon, and sixth-wealthiest in the nation. It also had the nation's third-lowest poverty rate. But it was not totally immune from the rest of the state's economic problems, as Morris' Office of Temporary Assistance reported a record number of people seeking help in September 2010.

The very rich have lived here for some time, connected to Manhattan by commuter rail lines. But starting in the 1970s, new residents rushed out through the newly completed interstates. Prompted by court-required zoning changes, old farms and woods have been cleared to make way for new subdivisions. This is not just a bedroom community. New Jersey's economic energy, entrepreneurial creativity, and research expertise are found in new office complexes and corporate headquarters. Large forested areas of state parkland remain, including the Wildcat Ridge Wildlife Management Area. The preservation of the state's Highlands region, a 1,000-square-mile forest- and lake-filled stretch from Ringwood southwest to Warren County, has been a priority.

The 11th Congressional District of New Jersey includes all of Morris County plus small slices of Sussex, Passaic, Essex, and Somerset counties. In a 2009 Gallup-Healthways survey, it ranked highest in access to resources deemed necessary to well-being. It is family territory, with relatively few singles, not strongly culturally conservative, but not aggressively liberal, either. It is predominantly white. There is a small community of Hispanics, many of whom arrived as day laborers and some of whom have settled. One of its biggest immigrant populations is of Indians, whose household incomes are double the national average. Politically, it is the most Republican district in New Jersey, and one of the most Republican in the Northeast. President George W. Bush won 58% of the district's vote in 2004, and John McCain won 54% of the vote in 2008.

Rodney Frelinghuysen (R)

The congressman from the 11th District is Rodney Frelinghuysen (*FREE-ling-high-zen*), a Republican first elected in 1994. He is the scion of one of New Jersey's most durable political families. The Frelinghuysens emigrated from Germany near the Dutch border in 1720 and settled in what is now the 11th District. Four Frelinghuysens served as senators from New Jersey, starting in 1793 and as recently as 1923. Theodore Frelinghuysen was the candidate for vice president in 1844 (spawning the memorable chant, "Hurrah! Hurrah! The country's risin,' for Henry Clay and Frelinghuysen"). Frederick Frelinghuysen was President Chester Arthur's secretary of state. Peter Frelinghuysen, Rodney's father, was elected to the House in 1952 and served until his retirement in 1974. History tends to repeat itself, and Frelinghuysens have been involved in every presidential impeachment. Rodney Frelinghuysen's great-great-grandfather Frederick voted to convict Andrew Johnson in 1868, and his father, Peter, after the revelations of July 1974, would have voted to impeach Richard Nixon if the president had not resigned. The current-generation Frelinghuysen voted to impeach Bill Clinton in December 1998.

As a child, Rodney Frelinghuysen lived in the large brick house on Georgetown's N Street that was later owned by former *Washington Post* editor Ben Bradlee and his wife, Sally Quinn. He attended St. Albans preparatory school with the future Democratic vice president, Al Gore. After college, he served in the Army in Vietnam, where he built roads in the Mekong Delta. In 1972, he was an aide to Morris County Freeholder Dean Gallo, who was later elected to Congress from the 11th District. Frelinghuysen was a freeholder himself from 1974 to 1983, and was elected to the state Assembly in 1983. Frelinghuysen ran for Congress in 1990 in what is now the 12th District but lost the primary to Dick Zimmer. In August 1994, Gallo retired from Congress because of illness, and Frelinghuysen was chosen to be the Republican nominee at a September party convention. He was elected with 71% of the vote.

Frelinghuysen has taken moderate and even liberal stands on some issues, but is more conservative on defense and foreign policy. He supported President George W. Bush on the war in

Iraq, and stuck with his party in opposing President Barack Obama's major initiatives in the 111th Congress (2009-10). He refused to join fellow New Jersey moderates Frank LoBiondo, Chris Smith and Leonard Lance in supporting the cap-and-trade bill aimed at reducing greenhouse gas emissions, calling it a "job-killer." He also cited numerous objections to the health care overhaul. But he was one of 92 House Republicans who banded with Democrats in February 2011 to reject the conservative Republican Study Committee's proposed $100 billion in spending cuts on the fiscal 2011 continuing resolution.

He showed his insider skills by winning a seat on the Appropriations Committee while still a freshman, a rarity. Because New Jersey had no senator on the Senate Appropriations Committee between 2000 and 2006, Frelinghuysen became the go-to guy for the entire delegation on projects benefiting New Jersey. He concentrated on big projects: construction of the Hudson-Bergen light rail, dredging of channels in the Port of New York and New Jersey, millions to slow erosion on the Jersey Shore. In 2010, he secured $20 million to improve facilities at two Veterans Affairs hospitals.

As Frelinghuysen has gained seniority, he was able in 2011 to claim the gavel of the Energy and Water Development Subcommittee, making him a critical gatekeeper in Obama's plans to significantly boost clean-energy research. He sounded an ominous note for those plans in February 2011, when he said that in theory, he supported the arm of the Energy Department that conducts such research, but that "I'm not sure in these times I'd find that many members who would agree." During debate on the fiscal 2010 energy and water bill, he expressed concerns about the need to protect and maintain the nuclear weapons stockpile, which the bill also funds.

Frelinghuysen initially opposed the government bailout of the financial markets in 2008, but then voted in favor of it, he said, because Americans needed protection from "economic shockwaves from problems they did not create." He also was among 32 House Republicans to back the bailout of the major automakers that year.

Frelinghuysen is best known nationally as the sponsor of the "Know Your Caller" law, which bars telemarketers from interfering with Caller ID systems of customers seeking to avoid such solicitations. Another of his pet projects is environmental cleanup in his district, which he says has more Superfund sites than any other. He tours the sites annually with environmental and local officials to get updates on cleanup progress. Frelinghuysen has not been seriously challenged for re-election.

TWELFTH DISTRICT

Rush Holt (D)

Elected 1998, 7th term; b. Oct. 15, 1948, Weston, WV; home, Hopewell Township; Carleton Col., B.S. 1970, N.Y.U., PhD. 1981; Protestant; married (Margaret Lancefield); 3 children.

Professional Career: Prof., Swarthmore Col., 1981-89; Asst. Dir., Princeton Plasma Physics Lab., 1989-98.

DC Office: 1214 LHOB, 20515, 202-225-5801; Fax: 202-225-6025; Web site: holt.house.gov.

State Offices: West Windsor, 609-750-9365.

Committees: *Education & the Workforce:* Early Childhood, Elementary & Secondary Education; Health, Employment, Labor & Pensions. *Natural Resources:* Energy & Mineral Resources (RMM); National Parks, Forests & Public Lands.

Group Ratings

	ACLU	ACU	ADA	CFG	AFS	FRC	LCV	ITIC	NTU	COC
2010	94	0	100	0	100	0	100	67	5	13
2009	–	0	100	0	100	–	100	–	1	33

National Journal Ratings

	2010 LIB	—	2010 CONS	2009 LIB	—	2009 CONS
Economic	90%	—	0%	91%	—	0%
Social	93%	—	0%	89%	—	0%
Foreign	84%	—	11%	91%	—	0%
Composite	93%	—	7%	95%	—	5%

Key Votes of the 111th Congress

1. Overturn Ledbetter	Y	5. Bar federal abortion funds	N	9. Stop detainee transfers	N
2. Pass $820 billion stimulus	Y	6. Pass health care bill	Y	10. Legalize immigrants' kids	Y
3. Let guns in national parks	N	7. Regulate financial firms	Y	11. Repeal don't ask, tell	Y
4. Pass cap-and-trade	Y	8. Pass tax cuts for some	Y	12. Limit campaign funds	Y

Election Results

2010 general	Rush Holt (D)	108,214	(53%)	($2,616,604)
	Scott Sipprelle (R)	93,634	(46%)	($2,105,553)
2010 primary	Rush Holt (D)	unopposed		

Prior Winning Percentages: 2008 (63%), 2006 (66%), 2004 (59%), 2002 (61%), 2000 (49%), 1998 (50%)

Population		Race/Ethnicity		Work	
Pop. 2010:	701,881	White:	63.8%	Private:	79.4%
Change since 2000:	Up 8.4%	Black:	11.2%	Government:	15.5%
Urban:	93.2%	Hispanic:	8.0%	Self-employed:	4.9%
Rural:	6.8%	Asian:	15.0%	Blue collar:	11.8%
Area size:	642 sq. mi.	Native Am.:	0.1%	White collar:	75.8%
		Hawaiian:	0.0%	Khaki collar:	0.1%
Age		Two+ races:	1.6%	Other:	12.4%
Median age:	39.9 yrs.				
More than 65 yrs:	13.8%	*Ancestry*		Median income:	$87,014
Less than 18 yrs:	23.7%	Italian	13.8%	Median Home Value:	$407,000
		Irish	12.3%		
Education		German	9.3%	**Military Veterans**	
H.S. grad:	92.2%			% of Pop:	7.0%
College grad:	47.1%				
Grad degree:	21.1%				

Central New Jersey; Part Trenton

It was once the main East Coast arterial highway, carrying the nation's highest volume of truck traffic. Today it is crowded with cars taking high-salaried workers and clerical help to one of the East Coast's thickest concentrations of office buildings in one of the bigger edge cities spawned in the 1980s. U.S. 1, which once just connected the industrial cities of Trenton and New Brunswick on its way from Philadelphia to New York, is better thought of now as connecting

2008 Presidential Vote

Barack Obama (D)	194,988	(58%)
John McCain (R)	136,374	(41%)

2004 Presidential Vote

John Kerry (D)	165,776	(55%)
George Bush (R)	138,454	(46%)

Cook Partisan Voting Index: D+5

the university towns around Princeton and Rutgers, and as a locus of telecommunications and pharmaceutical research. This had been empty bucolic country, to be enjoyed by F. Scott Fitzgerald's undergraduates from their Gothic Princeton towers. Now it is filled with post-modern office campuses, hotels, and restaurants.

The 12th Congressional District of New Jersey meanders across the breadth of central New Jersey, from the Delaware River to the Atlantic Ocean. It extends several dozen miles on either side of U.S. 1 as it slices through Mercer and Middlesex counties. To the west, it takes in some of the rolling country of Hunterdon County. On the other side of U.S. 1, the 12th includes Princeton University and some modest-income suburbs—Franklin in Somerset County, East Brunswick in Middlesex County—and some fast-growing Monmouth County areas, such as Rumson, part of Middletown, and Holmdel. Franklin made *Money* magazine's list of 100 best small cities in 2010. Since 1865, the iconic "Dinky" train has connected the town of Princeton with nearby Princeton Junction, ferrying passengers such as Albert Einstein and Woodrow Wilson. Local planners have proposed replacing it with a light-rail system. Monmouth is undergoing a transition with the Army's closure of the 1,100-acre Fort Monmouth in 2011. The 90-year-old research facility, with 5,000 employees, is in a busy commercial area, and will be redeveloped. The 12th had been represented for most of the 1990s by a Republican, but redistricting earlier this decade made it more Democratic.

Rush Holt (D)

The congressman from the 12th District is Rush Holt, a Democrat first elected in 1998. He is considered one of the smartest members of Congress and has an impressive political pedigree. His father, Rush D. Holt, was a favorite of United Mine Workers leader John Lewis, and was elected as the "boy senator" from West Virginia in 1934 when he was just 29. He had to wait until he turned age 30 in June 1935 to actually take the seat. But he clashed often with President Franklin D. Roosevelt and lost the Democratic primary to Harley Kilgore in 1940. Sen. Holt died when the young Rush was just 6 years old. He grew up in Washington, D.C., where his mother, Helen Holt, who had been West Virginia secretary of state, was an official in the Federal Housing Agency. He went off to Carleton College in Minnesota and to New York University, where he earned advanced degrees in physics and researched alternative energy, eventually becoming assistant director of the Princeton Plasma Physics Laboratory. He later was an arms control specialist for the State Department. Holt is a five-time *Jeopardy!* champion. He demonstrated just how brainy he can be in February 2011, when he defeated the IBM supercomputer "Watson" in a *Jeopardy!*-style contest sponsored by the company. Two of the quiz show's all-time champions had lost to Watson in an earlier matchup.

Holt got into politics in 1996, when he competed for the seat vacated by Republican U.S. Rep. Dick Zimmer when Zimmer ran for the Senate. Holt finished third in the Democratic primary. Conservative Republican Mike Pappas won the general election by only 50%-47%. Two years later, Holt came back for a rematch. It was 1998, the year of the impeachment of President Bill Clinton. New Jersey was pro-Clinton, anti-impeachment territory, and Pappas made the mistake of taking the House floor to recite: "Twinkle, Twinkle Kenneth Starr, now we see how brave you are. We could not see which way to go, if you did not lead us so." His ditty was replayed on network newscasts and incorporated into a Holt ad. It proved a liability, and Holt won 50%-47%.

In Congress, Holt has compiled a solidly liberal voting record. As the second research physicist in the House, he worked with the first, Republican Rep. Vern Ehlers of Michigan, to promote science education and to give science equal standing with reading and math. When House leaders were putting together the research provisions in the economic stimulus bill in 2009, then-Speaker Nancy Pelosi turned to Holt. The final measure included $22 billion for research and other science activities, more than double what was in earlier drafts. He often gets requests to meet with scientists. He once told *The Star-Ledger* of Newark, "The intellectual intricacies of politics are at least as challenging as those of physics, and they count for something in the real world."

Holt is perhaps the House's most prominent crusader on election reform, an interest sparked in part by a belief that his father's close defeat in a bid for West Virginia governor resulted from ballot fraud. "One of my earliest memories is the talk in the family about votes being stolen and ballot boxes being found on the riverbanks," he has said. For the past several years, he has sponsored a bill that would require better paper trails for electronic voting machines. Local election officials have objected to the cost, and his bill has stalled.

On the House Intelligence Committee, Holt in 2007 became chairman of the new Select Intelligence Oversight Panel. Although details of the panel's work mostly remained behind closed doors, Holt has pressed for more vigorous review of intelligence-gathering. He also pushed for an independent review of the FBI's scientific work that concluded Army scientist Bruce Ivins mailed the anthrax-laced letters that killed five people in 2001, a verdict that Ivins' colleagues have questioned. Republicans abolished the oversight panel when they regained control of the House in 2011.

Another of his interests is gun legislation. Holt has sponsored an assortment of gun-control measures, including one to require licensing and registration of all handguns (it attracted no co-sponsors). Locally, he has secured funding for open space and helped to get added protection for the lower Delaware River. He is a fervent opponent of offshore oil drilling and said the BP oil spill disaster in the Gulf of Mexico in 2010 was a signal to increase development of offshore wind power instead.

In his first bid for re-election in 2000, Holt was challenged by Zimmer in what became one of the closest races in the nation that year. Holt won by a bit more than 1,000 votes. In 2001, new congressional district boundaries after the census reduced the number of Republicans in the district and Holt had little trouble in subsequent elections.

But in 2010, he drew a fierce challenge from Republican Scott Sipprelle, a wealthy venture capitalist who accused Holt of being out of touch with constituents. He got some help from an outside pro-Israel group that ran an ad implying the congressman was unsupportive of the Jewish state, a charge that Holt's campaign called a lie. Holt played hardball himself, running an ad saying Sipprelle used his influence on a citizens' panel to receive a better property tax deal for his home, an accusation Sipprelle denied. Holt managed to prevail, 53%-46%.

THIRTEENTH DISTRICT

Albio Sires (D)

Elected Nov. 2006, 3rd full term; b. Jan. 26, 1951, Bejucal, Cuba; home, West New York; St. Peter's Col., B.A. 1974, Middlebury Col., M.A. 1985; Catholic; married (Adrienne); 1 child.

Elected Office: West New York mayor, 1995-2006; NJ Assembly, 1999-2006; NJ Assembly speaker, 2002-06.

Professional Career: High schl. Spanish and ESL teacher, 1975-85; Special asst., NJ Dept. of Community Affairs, 1985; Part-owner, A.M. Title Agency, 1986-2006.

DC Office: 2342 RHOB, 20515, 202-225-7919; Fax: 202-226-0792; Web site: sires.house.gov.

State Offices: Bayonne, 201-823-2900; Carteret, 732-969-9160; Jersey City, 201-222-2828; Perth Amboy, 732-442-0610; West New York, 201-558-0800.

Committees: *Foreign Affairs:* Europe and Eurasia; Western Hemisphere. *Transportation & Infrastructure:* Highways & Transit; Railroads, Pipelines & Hazardous Materials.

Group Ratings

	ACLU	ACU	ADA	CFG	AFS	FRC	LCV	ITIC	NTU	COC
2010	88	0	90	0	100	0	90	100	4	14
2009	–	0	100	4	100	–	86	–	2	33

National Journal Ratings

	2010 LIB — 2010 CONS	2009 LIB — 2009 CONS
Economic	83% — 17%	75% — 21%
Social	80% — 18%	75% — 20%
Foreign	62% — 37%	70% — 24%
Composite	76% — 25%	76% — 24%

Key Votes of the 111th Congress

1. Overturn Ledbetter	Y	5. Bar federal abortion funds	N	9. Stop detainee transfers	Y
2. Pass $820 billion stimulus	Y	6. Pass health care bill	Y	10. Legalize immigrants' kids	Y
3. Let guns in national parks	Y	7. Regulate financial firms	Y	11. Repeal don't ask, tell	Y
4. Pass cap-and-trade	Y	8. Pass tax cuts for some	Y	12. Limit campaign funds	Y

Election Results

2010 general	Albio Sires (D)	62,840	(74%)	($657,768)
	Henrietta Dwyer (R)	19,538	(23%)	($17,526)
2010 primary	Albio Sires (D)	16,022	(87%)	
	Jeff Boss (D)	2,409	(13%)	

Prior Winning Percentages: 2008 (75%), 2006 (78%), 2006 special (97%)

Population		Race/Ethnicity		Work	
Pop. 2010:	684,965	White:	27.4%	Private:	85.0%
Change since 2000:	Up 5.8%	Black:	10.8%	Government:	11.1%
Urban:	100.0%	Hispanic:	50.6%	Self-employed:	3.8%
Rural:	0.0%	Asian:	8.7%	Blue collar:	25.1%
Area size:	74 sq. mi.	Native Am.:	0.1%	White collar:	55.9%
		Hawaiian:	0.0%	Khaki collar:	0.0%
Age		Two+ races:	1.5%	Other:	18.9%
Median age:	33.9 yrs.				
More than 65 yrs:	10.2%	*Ancestry*		Median income:	$49,641
Less than 18 yrs:	22.0%	Italian	6.9%	Median Home Value:	$375,200
		Irish	5.7%		
Education		German	3.5%	**Military Veterans**	
H.S. grad:	74.8%			% of Pop:	3.3%
College grad:	27.5%				
Grad degree:	9.7%				

North New Jersey; Hudson County

Standing in New York Harbor since 1886, the Statue of Liberty has been the symbol of America's receptiveness to immigrants. Actually, the statue is on the New Jersey side of the harbor, and so is, as the U.S. Supreme Court ruled in 1998, most of Ellis Island, where immigrants once were processed. So it's natural that the towns atop the granite and gneiss ridge of Hudson County, overlooking the harbor, became immigrant territory. Many children and grandchil-

2008 Presidential Vote		
Barack Obama (D)	154,219	(75%)
John McCain (R)	50,525	(25%)
2004 Presidential Vote		
John Kerry (D)	127,168	(69%)
George Bush (R)	57,278	(31%)
Cook Partisan Voting Index: D+21		

dren of Irish and Italian immigrants stayed in Hudson County, living in the same neighborhoods, working on the same docks or factories, and voting the dictates of the same political machine. Hudson County was the setting of one of America's classic political machines, undisciplined by any metropolitan elite. From 1917 to 1949, the boss of Hudson County was Frank ("I am the law") Hague. His machine chose governors and U.S. senators, prosecutors and judges, and had influence in the White House of Franklin D. Roosevelt. Hague collected high taxes from industries clustered here, which then passed them on to consumers, and in return, he gave them an orderly city, free of most crime and vice, and a workforce insulated against racketeers and militant unions. Hague's successor, John V. Kenny, was boss from 1949 to 1971—continuous power for 54 years.

But Hudson County began changing. New immigrants were coming in—refugees from Fidel Castro's Cuba and other Latinos and Asians arrived after the 1965 immigration act. Union City became predominantly Cuban; Jersey City neighborhoods became heavily Latino. Starting in the 1980s, huge new condominium and office developments went up in Jersey City, with back-office buildings for big banks and securities firms and, later, Internet content businesses. Upscale young singles looking for lower rents moved into Hoboken's five-story Victorians; they were just a quick commute through the PATH tubes to Wall Street or Greenwich Village. In Hoboken, the home of Frank Sinatra and the Oreo cookie, shopping and apartment complexes have taken up the water-front sites where factories were common (and where the classic movie *On the Waterfront* was filmed).

Bayonne has become a cruise ship port, though its 5,780-foot-long bridge—built in 1931—no longer is tall enough for the latest super-sized container ships to pass beneath. Ferries from Wee-hawken assisted in the miraculous rescue of the US Airways flight that made an emergency landing in the Hudson River in January 2009. Meanwhile, new immigrants continue to arrive. As middle-class Cubans move to Bergen County suburbs, Union City is less Cuban and more Colombian, Ecuadoran, Peruvian, Dominican, and Filipino. Hudson County, which seemed to be dying a generation ago, is now more vibrant. A massive corruption sting in 2009, in which 44 people were arrested—including mayors and rabbis from the area, reinforced New Jersey's image as "the *Soprano* State," the title of a recent book documenting the political disarray.

The 13th Congressional District of New Jersey includes most of Hudson County, plus most of the immigrant entry ports along the water, from West New York and Weehawken, south past Jersey City and Bayonne, where you can still find bocce courts. It extends past the Port of New York and New Jersey to the waterfront areas of Elizabeth, Linden, Carteret (with a large Sikh community), Woodbridge, and Perth Amboy. The district's population is 49% Hispanic and also includes the Ironbound district of Newark, with its Portuguese and Brazilian immigrants and popular restaurants serving hubcap-sized platters of *paella*; working-class Harrison, an aging factory town where European immigrants have been replaced by Hispanic immigrants; and part of industrial Kearny. The 13th is heavily Democratic, giving Barack Obama 75% of the 2008 presidential vote.

Albio Sires (D)

The congressman from the 13th District is Democrat Albio Sires (*SEAR-eez*), who replaced Robert Menendez, also a Democrat, after he was appointed to the Senate in January 2006. Sires, who was born in Cuba, remembers the book burning following the Communist revolution there. His family fled Fidel Castro's regime in 1962 when he was 10. He attended St. Peter's College on a four-year basketball scholarship—he is 6-foot-4-inches—and then earned a master's degree from Middlebury College. He became a high school Spanish teacher. On his fourth try, he was elected mayor of West New York as a Republican in 1995, and held that post until 2006. He focused on the creation of more affordable housing in the small but densely populated town and won praise for merging the fire department with three neighboring departments. He switched parties in 1999 and, with the support of party leaders, defeated a veteran Democratic incumbent in the primary to win a state House seat (dual office-holding was then a common practice in New Jersey). With strong support from newly elected Democratic Gov. Jim McGreevey in 2002, he became speaker of the Assembly.

After newly elected Democratic Gov. Jon Corzine appointed Menendez to replace him in the U.S. Senate, Sires immediately became the front-runner for the House seat. In the primary, Sires faced a fierce challenge from Joe Vas of Perth Amboy, who likewise was a state House member and a mayor. Vas assailed Sires as a puppet of the Hudson County Democratic machine. Sires responded by depicting Vas as soft on crime and won the support of most leading Democrats, except for his longtime rival Menendez, who remained neutral. Although Vas carried his home base of Middlesex County 76%-24%, Sires crushed him 80%-20% in Hudson County, which cast 74% of the total vote. Overall, Sires won 72%-28%. In the general election, Republicans nominated John Guarini, who raised little money and posed no threat. Sires won 78%-19%. He succeeded Menendez as the only Cuban-American House member from a state other than Florida.

In the House, Sires established a liberal voting record that has placed him in the middle of the pack among New Jersey's House Democrats. He allied himself in 2007 with South Florida members who wanted to keep U.S. sanctions on Cuba in place; he joined them again three years later in opposing the Obama administration's proposed loosening of restrictions on travel and economic aid. On the Financial Services Committee, Sires got approval in 2007 of his bill to increase penalties, up to $1 million in some cases, for identity theft. He switched to the Transportation and Infrastructure Committee and prodded the U.S. Army Corps of Engineers to move quickly on solutions to raising the Bayonne Bridge's height to accommodate larger ships. He also introduced legislation to revitalize urban parks and to help commuters find alternative ways to get to work.

In the 2010 election, Sires was one of the vice chairs of the Democratic Congressional Campaign Committee, in charge of member participation and outreach. After Democrats lost their majority, he called for Speaker Nancy Pelosi to step down, though he subsequently backed her bid to become minority leader. He was re-elected easily in 2008 and 2010.

★ NEW MEXICO ★

New Mexico has some of the oldest settlements in America and some of its newest technologies, often in surrealistic proximity to one another. The oldest permanently inhabited city in the United States is not Plymouth or Jamestown or St. Augustine; it is probably Acoma, which apparently thrived in what is now New Mexico long before the Spanish conquistadors arrived in 1540, and has been continuously inhabited for more than 470 years since. While the settlers of Jamestown and Plymouth were building flimsy wood houses, the Indians in New Mexico were living in extensive dwellings hundreds of years old, made with the adobe that is still the characteristic building material here. They used small pebbles as mulch to retain scarce moisture on the rocky desert land. Nearly five centuries later, much of what makes New Mexico distinctive derives from the people found here by the first European explorers—something true of no other state but Hawaii. The cultures in other states are mostly an outgrowth of what early European settlers brought to the land. The native people have mostly disappeared, either killed off by disease or maltreatment, or driven onto reservations. Not so in New Mexico, the northernmost salient of the great Indian-Spanish civilizations of the Cordillera, which extend along the mountain chain through Mexico and Central and South America to the southern end of Chile. The Spanish settled in Santa Fe in 1609, and though their hold on the town was often tenuous, their imprint remains. There are still 19 Indian pueblos in New Mexico today, plus the reservations of the Navajo and the Jicarilla Apache and the Mescalero Apache. A very substantial minority of today's New Mexicans are descendants of those Indians, or the Spanish, or both. New Mexico's population was 46% Hispanic in 2010, the highest percentage of any state, and 9% American Indian. Some 28% of New Mexicans speak Spanish in everyday life, but only 8% have less than a full command of English and only 10% are foreign-born, less than the national average.

Modern New Mexico is also a civilization built on technology. It was to a remote mesa called Los Alamos that Gen. Leslie Groves brought his Manhattan Project scientists during World War II to build a secret town and develop a secret weapon that would, in two explosions, end World War II and change the course of history. Los Alamos is still a government laboratory, and an occasional source of controversy as it was in 1999, when revelations surfaced that Chinese spies had obtained hundreds of computer files from the lab. New Mexico has other high-tech sites as well: the White Sands Missile Range near Alamogordo, where the first atomic bomb was detonated in July 1945; and the Sandia National Laboratories near Albuquerque, run by Lockheed Martin, a non-nuclear weapons research facility with one of the fastest computers in the world, used to simulate nuclear explosions. Near Carlsbad is the federal Waste Isolation Pilot Plant (WIPP), where the U.S. Energy Department deposits transuranic radioactive waste. And at the western edge of White Sands in Sierra County is the Virgin Spaceport America, a project by billionaire Richard Branson to send people on tours of space. Branson started the project in 2005 with a handshake agreement with then Democratic Gov. Bill Richardson, who said, "This sends a message that will be heard around the world, that New Mexico is a state that embraces entrepreneurs, adventurers, and pioneers." Branson plans to launch his SpaceShipTwo crafts from the bellies of airplanes at 55,000 feet and fly them at 2,500 miles per hour on an arc up to 68 miles into space, where passengers can float in glassed-in cabins for six minutes and then glide back down to earth. The state and federal governments financed the runways, over 400 have paid or put down a deposit for a ride. Spaceport opened in October 2010.

New and old New Mexico intermingle in varying proportions in this land of majestically vast vistas. The Hispanic and Indian cultures predominate north and west of Albuquerque, with picturesque old towns and active pueblos, backward Indian reservations and lavish casino resorts. "Little Texas" in the south and east has small cities, plenty of oil wells, vast cattle ranches, and desolate military bases; the region resembles, economically and culturally, the adjacent West Texas high plains. Here, as everywhere in New Mexico, government is a prime employer, accounting for 22% of jobs, one of the highest figures in the country, and often the moving force in the local economy. While New Mexico had neither the housing boom nor the housing bust of next-door neighbor Arizona, its economy sagged in 2009 and 2010 despite its supposedly recession-proof reliance on government jobs.

In the middle of the state is Albuquerque, which, with the arrival of air conditioning, grew from a small desert town of 35,000 in 1940 into a Sun Belt metropolitan area of 887,000 today. The city's economy is heavily based on technology, especially nuclear power, but its people have relatively low income and education levels. New Mexico ranks high among states in the percentage

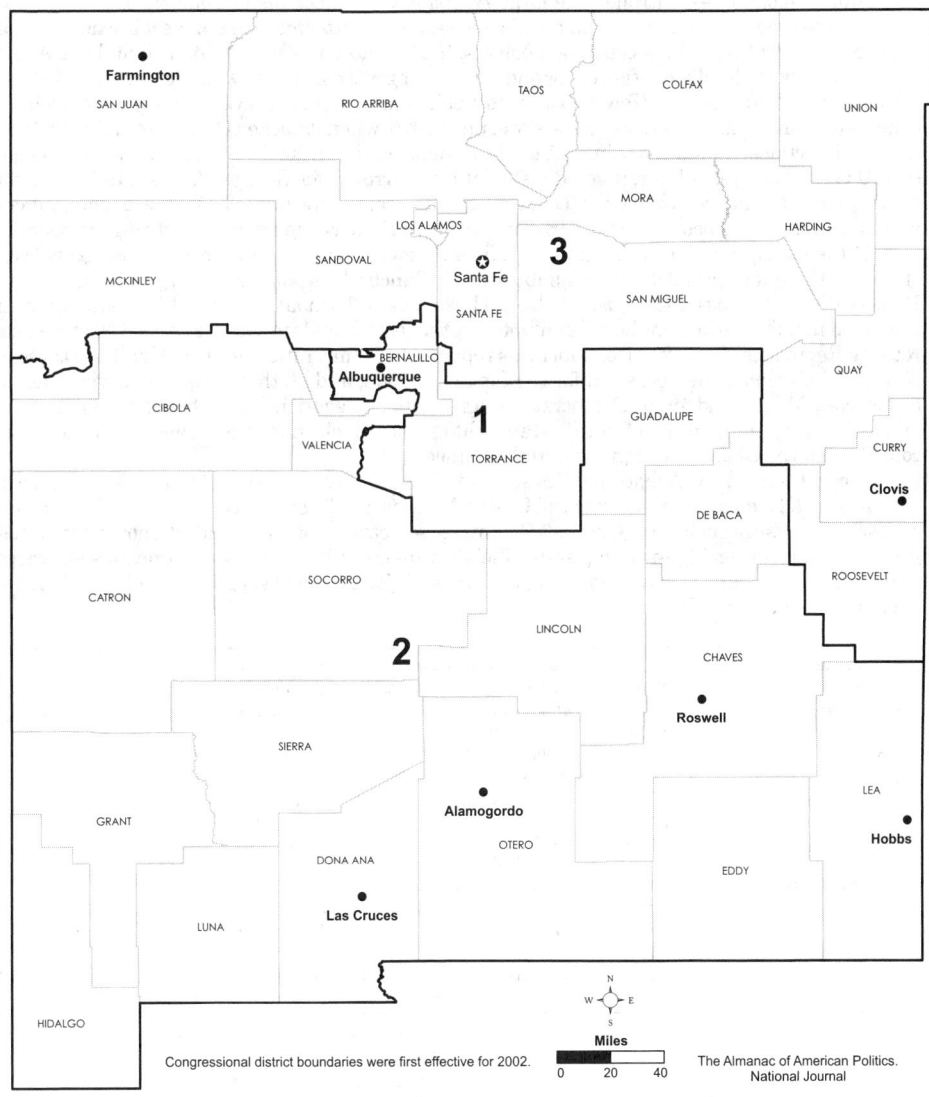

of residents living in poverty. It also has had high rates of drunk driving (and a state law requiring ignition interlocks for DUI offenders), accidental deaths, teenage pregnancies, and drug overdoses. But over the years, its amazing scenery and unique culture have attracted writers such as D.H. Lawrence and painters such as Georgia O'Keeffe. Santa Fe and Taos are magnets today for people with a taste for alternative lifestyles and the trust funds to comfortably finance them. Other migrants are attracted by the 10 or so destination golf courses built by Indian tribes next to their reservation casinos.

For many years New Mexico politics was a somnolent business. Local bosses—first Republican, later Democratic—controlled the large Hispanic vote. Elections in many counties featured irregularities that would have made a Chicago ward committeeman blush. New Mexico had for years another feature of boss-controlled politics: the balanced ticket, one Spanish and one Anglo U.S. senator, with the offices of governor and lieutenant governor split as well. But for all its distinctiveness, in national politics New Mexico was a bellwether, voting for every winning presidential candidate from 1912, when it became a state, until 1976, when it backed Gerald Ford. In the 1988 and 1996 elections, the state was just 1% off the national mark. In 2000, it voted narrowly for Democrat Al Gore. Four years later, it voted just a bit less narrowly for George W. Bush. In 2008, New Mexico moved sharply toward the Democrats, after candidate Barack Obama opened offices around the state and boosted voter turnout sharply in Democratic areas. The strong Democratic base in the north, from Hispanics and from liberal newcomers in Santa Fe and Taos, grew even stronger. Albuquerque and its surging suburb of Rio Rancho, long politically marginal, went solidly Democratic, as did Las Cruces, just north of El Paso, Texas. Turnout sagged in Little Texas, which remained Republican but was heavily outvoted by the rest of the state. Obama carried New Mexico; retiring Republican Sen. Pete Domenici was replaced by Democratic Rep. Tom Udall. All three of New Mexico's House members ran for the Senate in 2008, and all three open seats went Democratic. New Mexico had an all-Democratic congressional delegation for the first time since 1968, and Richardson, the dominant figure in state politics since his election in 2002, was for a time under consideration as Obama's vice presidential nominee.

But just when New Mexico politics seems to have entered a period of stability, it changes. Richardson, a former ambassador to the United Nations and Energy secretary in the Clinton administration, was not chosen as Obama's Commerce secretary though he made it known he wanted the job. About a dozen high-ranking state officials were investigated for corruption, in some cases receiving jail time, and as a consequence, Richardson's job approval sagged. Term-limited, he retired from public life in 2010.

Population		Household Income		Work	
Pop. 2010:	2,059,179	Under $15k:	16.2%	Private:	70.1%
State rank:	36th	$15k to $50k:	40.5%	Government:	22.3%
Change since 2000:	Up 13.2%	$50k to $100k:	28.6%	Self-employed:	7.4%
Urban:	76.3%	$100k to $200k:	12.4%	Unemployment (3-yr. average):	4.3%
Rural:	23.7%	Over $200k:	2.3%	Poverty:	17.8%
Native of state:	51.4%	Median income:	$42,737	Blue collar:	21.9%
Not a citizen:	6.6%			White collar:	57.7%
Area size:	121,590 sq. mi.	**Home Value**		Khaki collar:	0.4%
		Under $100k:	28.9%	Other:	20.0%
Most populous cities		$100k to $300k:	52.8%		
Albuquerque	545,852	$300k to $500k:	12.1%	**Age**	
Las Cruces	97,618	$500k to $1 mil:	5.1%	Median age:	35.7 yrs.
Rio Rancho	87,521	Over $1 million:	1.1%	More than 65 yrs:	12.9%
Santa Fe	67,947	Median:	$160,900	Less than 18 yrs:	25.5%

Race/Ethnicity				Military Veterans		Registered Voters in 2010	
White:	40.5%	*Language*		% of Pop:	11.6%	Democrats:	570,659
Black:	1.7%	English:	64.2%			Republicans:	367,638
Hispanic:	46.3%	Spanish:	28.3%	*Veterans by Period*		Ind./other:	214,620
Asian:	1.3%	Asian:	0.9%	WWII and before:	9.7%	Voter turnout:	607,700
Native Am.:	8.5%	Other European:	1.2%	Korea:	10.8%	Turnout as % of	
Hawaiian:	0.1%			Vietnam:	34.9%	voting age:	39.4%
Two+ races:	1.4%	**Education**		Gulf (pre-2001):	12.1%		
		H.S. grad:	82.6%	Gulf (post-2001):	10.0%	**Legislature**	
Ancestry		College grad:	24.9%	Peace time:	22.6%	Senate:	27 D 15 R
German	9.0%	Grad degree:	10.4%			House:	36 D 33 R 1 I
English	6.8%						
Irish	6.6%						

Elected to succeed him was Republican Susana Martinez, the prosecutor in Dona Ana County (Las Cruces), New Mexico's second-largest population center. Against Democratic Lt. Gov. Diane Denish, who seemed likely to continue Richardson's policies, Martinez won 53%-47%. She carried metro Albuquerque, which has 45% of the state's population and accounted for 73% of its 2000-10 population growth, and made significant inroads in heavily Hispanic counties in northern New Mexico while carrying Little Texas by more than 2-1. Republicans gained eight seats in the state House and recaptured the 2nd Congressional District and came close to recapturing the 1st. The popular vote for the House, 56%-39% Democratic in 2008, was only 52%-48% Democratic in 2010, although Democrats had the advantages of incumbency in all three seats. That leaves an uncertain outlook for 2012, not just in the presidential election but in the contest for the U.S. Senate of retiring Democrat Jeff Bingaman.

Presidential politics   New Mexico has been a battleground state in the last three presidential elections, but the results were very different the third time. In 2000, after some ragged vote counting, the state gave a 365-vote margin to Demo-crat Al Gore. In 2004, it reported a 5,988-vote margin for Republican George W. Bush. Voter rolls and turnout swelled that year, thanks to Richardson's well-publicized efforts to register new Democrats and to the Bush campaign's less-noticed organizational efforts. Overall turnout rose 26% from 2000 to 2004, even though the state's population increased just 5% in that period. High Democratic turnout in Santa Fe and Albuquerque was balanced by high Republican turnout in Little Texas. In addition, Bush won 44% of the Hispanic vote, up from 32% in 2000.

The 2008 contest was another story, with Democrat Barack Obama beating Republican John McCain 57%-42%. As in other states that

2008 Presidential Vote		
Barack Obama (D)	472,422	(57%)
John McCain (R)	346,832	(42%)
2008 Presidential Primary		
John McCain (R)	95,378	(86%)
Ron Paul (R)	15,561	(14%)
2008 Presidential Primary		
Hillary Clinton (D)	73,105	(49%)
Barack Obama (D)	71,396	(48%)
2004 Presidential Vote		
George W. Bush (R)	376,930	(50%)
John Kerry (D)	370,942	(49%)

were targeted in both 2004 and 2008, turnout inched up just marginally, 10%. The Obama campaign opened 39 offices across the state and vastly out-organized the Republicans. But the turnout numbers show that Obama's team shrewdly concentrated its efforts where there were new Democrats. In most counties, turnout rose only 1% to 9%, and in 12 counties it actually dropped. But it rose 7% or more in metro Albuquerque, Santa Fe, and Taos, in heavily Hispanic Rio Arriba County, and in the two heavily Indian counties to the west, and around Las Cruces. Obama won 74% of first-time voters, 71% of young voters, and 83% of young Latino voters. McCain won whites 56%-42%, almost identical to Bush's 56%-43% support from those voters in 2004. But McCain won only 30% of the Latino vote, far below Bush's level and more in line with historic norms.

New Mexico traditionally held its presidential primary in June, long after every major party nomination was clinched from 1984 to 2004. For 2008, with Richardson as a candidate, New Mexico scheduled its Democratic primary for Feb. 5, Super Tuesday. By that time, Richardson had withdrawn, but the race between Obama and Hillary Rodham Clinton was so close it took nine days to count all the votes, including 17,000 provisional ballots. Clinton won 49%-48%, carrying heavily Hispanic counties and Little Texas. Obama carried metro Albuquerque, Santa Fe, Taos, and two rural counties. The Republicans did not hold their primary until June, when no one was paying attention. McCain beat Ron Paul 86%-14%.

Congressional districting   The boundaries of New Mexico's three congressional districts have been substantially the same since 1982. Control of the redistricting process in 2001 was split between the Democratic legislature and Republican Gov. Gary Johnson. From June to September 2001, the legislature passed two plans, one making the 1st District, held by Republican Heather Wilson, more Democratic, and the second making the 2nd District, held by Republican Joe Skeen, more Democratic; Johnson vetoed both of them, and Republicans took the issue to court. In January 2002, state District Judge Frank Allen, a Democrat, imposed his own plan. Reluctant to make major changes, Allen shifted only 22,000 people into different districts. Democrats were disappointed; Republicans were pleased.

112th Congress Lineup	
2 D	1 R
111th Congress Lineup	
3 D	

In 2003, state Senate President Richard Romero, who unsuccessfully challenged Wilson in 2002 and 2004, pressed the legislature to redraw the lines once again. But national Democrats urged caution and Democratic Gov. Richardson seemed uninterested, perhaps because a new plan might have jeopardized his good relations with Republican Sen. Pete Domenici, who would have opposed a plan that hurt Wilson.

New Mexico grew faster than the national average between 2000 and 2010, but fell far short of gaining a fourth House seat. Control of redistricting is once again split between a Republican governor and a Democratic legislature. Most likely a heavily Hispanic and Democratic 3rd District and a more Anglo and Republican 2nd District will emerge. But the boundaries of the 1st District, centered on Albuquerque, may be a subject of great contention, since small changes on the map could make big differences in the election results in a district held, though often tenuously, for 30 years by Republicans and then captured by Democrat Martin Heinrich in 2008.

Governor

Susana Martinez (R)

Elected 2010, term expires Jan. 2015, 1st term; b. July 14, 1959, El Paso, TX; home, Las Cruces; U. of TX at El Paso, B.A. 1981; U. of OK, J.D. 1986; Catholic; married (Chuck Franco); 1 child.

Elected Office: District atty., Dona Ana Cnty., NM, 1996-2010.

Professional Career: Prosecutor, Dona Ana Cnty., NM, 1986-97.

Office: 490 Old Santa Fe Train, Room 400, 87501, 505-476-2200; Web site: www.governor.state.nm.us/.

Election Results

2010 general	Susana Martinez (R)	320,871	(53%)
	Diane Denish (D)	279,888	(47%)
2010 primary	Susana Martinez (R)	62,006	(51%)
	Allen Weh (R)	33,727	(28%)
	Doug Turner (R)	14,166	(12%)
	Pete Domenici, Jr. (R)	8,630	(7%)

The new governor of New Mexico is Susana Martinez, a Republican elected in 2010 to succeed Democrat Bill Richardson, who was term-limited after eight years in office. She is the state's first female governor and the first Hispanic woman in the nation to serve in that post. She handily defeated Richardson's lieutenant governor, Diane Denish, in a campaign in which Martinez promised to end the type of political scandal that made Richardson, a onetime rising star in national Democratic politics, an extremely unpopular figure in the state.

Martinez was born and raised in El Paso, Texas, the daughter of a sheriff's deputy who started a successful security business with his wife. While helping to care for her developmentally disabled older sister, Martinez worked part-time as a security guard while studying for college. After graduating from the University of Texas-El Paso, she attended law school at the University of Oklahoma. After graduation, she joined the Dona Ana County district attorney's office in Las Cruces, 38 miles north of El Paso, and mainly handled prosecutions of crimes against children. In 1996, she decided to run for district attorney. Although she was a registered Democrat, she agreed to meet with local Republicans who hoped to recruit her for their party—an idea she said she initially disdained. "I remember telling my husband, 'We're going to be very polite. We're going to say thank you very much, and we're going to leave,'" she told *The Los Angeles Times*. But she said the meeting influenced her thinking, and recalled her reaction after leaving the meeting: "We got in the car, we looked at each other and said, 'Oh my God, we are Republicans! Now what do we do?'"

Martinez switched parties and did not expect to win in an area where registered Democrats outnumber Republicans by about 3-to-1. But she managed to attract enough support from her old party to capture the office with nearly 60% of the vote. She went on to win re-election three times with ease. As district attorney, she gained a reputation for being driven and meticulous. She went after members of Mexico's drug cartels and prosecuted a number of high-profile child abuse cases herself. She also developed a habit of generously rewarding her staff; the *Albuquerque Journal* reported in August 2010 that she gave out around $477,000 in bonuses from fiscal years 2006 to 2010, more than three times as much as any other district attorney in the state.

Richardson, a former House member, secretary of Energy and United Nations representative, was popular in his early years in office, using his political skills to move a broad variety of environmental, education, and economic development laws through the legislature. He had little trouble winning re-election in 2006. But his decision to run for president in 2008 kept him out of state campaigning for much of 2007. Richardson dropped out after winning just 2% of state delegate equivalents in the Iowa caucuses and 5% of the vote in the New Hampshire primary. Returning to the Capitol, he was unable to persuade lawmakers to pass a universal health care bill and got only pared-down versions of his tax rebate and children's health program. Meanwhile, about a dozen high-ranking state officials were investigated for corruption, in some cases receiving jail time. In addition, there were federal investigations into the governor's own bidding practices. The controversies did not result in any legal action against Richardson directly, but they derailed his bid to serve as President Barack Obama's secretary of Commerce, and cast a political cloud over Denish, who had run the state during his frequent absences.

Martinez announced her candidacy for governor in July 2009, vowing to do things differently. "I have fought corruption and crime, and public safety is my No. 1 priority," she said. "We will remove pay-to-play in this state." She immediately drew the attention of the Republican Governors Association, which saw the merits of having a female Hispanic join its ranks. The organization steered hundreds of thousands of dollars to her campaign and helped line up a coveted endorsement from former Alaska Gov. Sarah Palin. On the campaign trail, Martinez was mindful of New Mexico's general tolerance toward immigrants. She was careful in her attitude toward endorsing neighboring Arizona's stringent new immigration law, which gave law enforcement officials added power to detain those suspected of being in the country illegally. She said only that she "supports the right of any state to ensure the security of its citizens, and today, that means dealing directly with immigration and border concerns." She won the June 1 GOP primary with 51% over four other candidates, including longtime New Mexico Sen. Pete Domenici's son, Pete Domenici Jr., and Allen Weh, a former state Republican chairman.

Her victory set up a battle with Denish, whom Martinez wasted no time linking with the now-unpopular Richardson. She even challenged the outgoing governor to a debate, and ran ads declaring, "Four more years of the same—or bold change." She promised to reverse Richardson's policies on climate change and water pollution, which she claimed had driven away industries. Denish, for her part, frequently pointed out that she had not been the target of any investigation, and tried her best to distance herself from her boss. Her campaign motto was, "A New Way Forward." She also tried to highlight what she called her opponent's own "sweetheart" deals as district attorney, such as paying a former top aide $60,000 without going through a competitive bidding process. But the national Republican tide proved to be an insurmountable obstacle, and Martinez won 54%-46%. In addition to winning her home county of Dona Ana, she edged out Denish in Bernalillo County, the state's most populous, and dominated most of the state's rural areas. Her victory was widely applauded in national Republican circles, with some pundits even holding her up as a possible vice presidential nominee in 2012.

Taking office, Martinez signed executive orders to enhance public access to state records, a sharp contrast to Richardson, whose administration was criticized for invoking executive privilege to deny records requests. She also ordered the sale of the state's jet and terminated two personal chefs at the governor's residence. Her first, $5.4 billion budget provided more money for public school classrooms while cutting spending for colleges, universities, and local education administrators.

Senior Senator

Jeff Bingaman (D)

Elected 1982, term expires 2012, 5th term; b. Oct. 3, 1943, El Paso, TX; home, Santa Fe; Harvard U., B.A. 1965, Stanford U., LL.B. 1968; United Methodist; married (Anne); 1 child.

Military Career: Army Reserves, 1968–74.

Elected Office: NM atty. gen., 1978–82.

Professional Career: NM asst. atty. gen., 1969; Practicing atty., 1970–78.

DC Office: 703 HSOB, 20510, 202-224-5521; Fax: 202-224-2852; Web site: bingaman.senate.gov.

State Offices: Albuquerque, 505-346-6601; Farmington, 505-325-5030; Las Cruces, 575-523-6561; Roswell, 575-622-7113; Santa Fe, 505-988-6647.

Committees: *Energy & Natural Resources* (Chmn). *Finance:* Energy, Natural Resources & Infrastructure (Chmn); Fiscal Responsibility & Economic Growth; Health Care. *Health, Education, Labor & Pensions:* Employment & Workplace Safety; Primary Health & Aging. *Joint Economic Committee.*

Group Ratings

	ACLU	ACU	ADA	CFG	AFS	FRC	LCV	ITIC	NTU	COC
2010	93	4	90	3	93	0	71	33	3	18
2009	–	4	100	11	100	–	100	–	4	43

National Journal Ratings

	2010 LIB — 2010 CONS		2009 LIB — 2009 CONS	
Economic	70%	— 27%	63%	— 36%
Social	65%	— 0%	72%	— 27%
Foreign	47%	— 0%	55%	— 0%
Composite	76%	— 24%	71%	— 29%

Key Votes of the 111th Congress

1. Overturn Ledbetter	Y	5. Pass health care bill	Y	9. Ratify New START	Y
2. Pass $787 billion stimulus	Y	6. Regulate financial firms	Y	10. Confirm Elena Kagan	Y
3. Repeal DC gun laws	N	7. Pass tax cuts for some	Y	11. Stop EPA climate regs	N
4. Confirm Sonia Sotomayor	Y	8. Legalize immigrants' kids	Y	12. Repeal don't ask, tell	Y

Election Results

2006 general	Jeff Bingaman (D)...394,365	(71%)	($4,188,204)
	Allen McCulloch (R)..163,826	(29%)	($559,138)
2006 primary	Jeff Bingaman (D).. unopposed		

Prior Winning Percentages: 2000 (62%); 1994 (54%); 1988 (63%); 1982 (54%)

Jeff Bingaman, a Democrat first elected in 1982, is New Mexico's senior senator. He announced on Feb. 18, 2011, that he would not seek a fifth term. He told *National Journal* that he felt he had spent enough time in Washington, particularly as his 70th birthday neared. "You know, I've been here for 28 years now," he said.

Bingaman was born in Texas but reared in Silver City, a mining town in New Mexico. His father was a professor at Western New Mexico University in Silver City, and his mother was a schoolteacher. His uncle was campaign manager for longtime Democratic Sen. Clinton Anderson (1949-73). Bingaman graduated from Harvard University and Stanford Law School, and then returned to New Mexico. A year out of law school, he was counsel to the state constitutional convention. Later he went into law practice in Santa Fe with former Democratic Gov. Jack Campbell. Bingaman's wife, Anne, started a highly successful law practice of her own that helped finance his first campaigns. She later was assistant attorney general for antitrust in President Bill Clinton's first term. In a small state, bright young people like Jeff Bingaman can rise fast. He ran for attorney general in 1978 and won. In 1982, he ran against Republican Sen. Harrison Schmitt, the former astronaut, also from Silver City, and won with 54%, partly because it was a recession year, but also because Schmitt ran misleading and negative ads.

For years, the taciturn Bingaman followed a course in the Senate much like that of Anderson, who used his influence behind the scenes to great effect but shunned national publicity. Since 1999, Bingaman has been the top-ranking Democrat on the Energy and Natural Resources Committee; he was chairman from 2001 to 2003 and got the gavel again in January 2007 after Democrats won majority control of the Senate. His colleagues have long admired him for his smart and methodical approach as well as his continual avoidance of the spotlight. "Jeff has a sophisticated understanding of the process and timing and when and how to interject," the late Democratic Sen. Paul Wellstone of Minnesota once told the *Albuquerque Journal*.

Bingaman is a longtime proponent of federal support for renewable energy sources. He also is a major advocate of imposing restrictions on greenhouse gases to reduce global warming. In the 110th Congress (2007-08), he led the Senate to passage of a major energy bill that had been in the works for nearly a year. The centerpiece was a boost in vehicle fuel efficiency standards from 25 miles per gallon to 35 miles per gallon by 2020. Bingaman also pushed the Senate to agree to a substantial change in policy that would have forced utilities to generate at least 15% of their electricity from renewable sources such as wind and solar energy by 2020. But Republicans balked, and Bingaman's amendment fell four votes short of passage. Still, Bingaman called the final legislation "the most important energy efficiency legislation that has ever passed in this country." It was the first increase in fuel economy standards for cars and trucks since 1975.

Bingaman planned to try again in 2009 to pass his renewable sources mandate, introducing the bill early in the new Congress. Working with Alaska's Lisa Murkowski, Energy and Natural Resources' top Republican, he managed to get a delicately crafted compromise bill out of the committee in June that drew the backing of four of the panel's Republicans. The legislation called for a 15% renewable emissions standard by 2021—a level that some Democrats considered far too low but that the pragmatic Bingaman said was open to negotiation. His bill also included provisions to expand offshore drilling and to create a division in the Energy Department to help develop and deploy clean technologies. But the legislation became bogged down in the politics of separate "cap and trade" legislation aimed at reducing greenhouse gases linked to global climate change. Some moderate Democrats asked Senate leaders to jettison efforts to pass comprehensive climate change legislation and concentrate on Bingaman's bill, but that did not come to pass.

After the Republican takeover of the House in 2010, President Barack Obama appeared to abandon the idea of cap-and-trade in favor of a broader standard in which 80% of the nation's electricity would come from clean sources by 2035. But he did not spell out many of the details, and the task of uniting lawmakers around it fell to Bingaman. The senator said he planned to seek to define clean energy technology, as well as ensure that the proposal accounts for existing clean energy sources. He also expressed hope that he could separately develop an energy efficiency initiative, offshore drilling regulation, point-of-sale incentives for advanced vehicles, electric grid security and loan guarantees and tax incentives aimed at promoting clean energy technologies.

From 2003 to 2009, Bingaman's New Mexico colleague Pete Domenici was the senior Republican on the committee, the first time in history that the two top members on a Senate committee were from the same state. While they disagreed on some issues, they worked together on many others. In 2005, Bingaman and Domenici made a point of emphasizing areas of agreement during work on the energy bill, and House Republicans agreed to drop a controversial provision to protect oil companies from liability for adding the pollutant MTBE to gasoline. There was also bipartisan agreement on incentives for building more electricity lines to avert major blackouts and for the start-up of advanced design nuclear power plants. The bill passed, and Bingaman praised Domenici's cooperation. The partnership ended when Domenici retired from the Senate in 2008.

Bingaman has been deeply involved in other issues as a member of the Finance and Health, Education, Labor, and Pensions committees. He was a member of the "Gang of Six" senators on Finance that struggled through the summer of 2009 to strike a bipartisan deal on health care legislation. He also said in early 2011 that he wanted to re-examine the accountability provisions in the No Child Left Behind education law as well as work further on pension matters.

In the debate about illegal immigration in 2007, Bingaman sponsored an amendment, supported by labor unions, to reduce the number of permitted guest workers from 400,000 to 200,000 and to eliminate a clause that allowed increases in guest workers in response to economic need. It passed, 74-24. When Arizona Republican Jon Kyl, trying to negotiate a final immigration bill, said that Bingaman's provision could be a deal-breaker, Bingaman said, "I'd say the deal's broken then." In late June, as crucial votes loomed, Bingaman said he was undecided, then voted against the bill although his provision was intact. He argued that other parts of the legislation were ineffective and would have "depressed American wages and encouraged immigrants to overstay their visas." The immigration bill ultimately failed because of disputes over several key provisions.

On local issues, he and Domenici directed $10 million to the descendants of Hispanic homesteaders who had been paid only a few dollars an acre in the 1940s for land that became part of the Los Alamos National Laboratory. The two also shepherded through the Senate in 2006 the Valle Vidal Protection Act, which covered 102,000 acres of Forest Service lands in the Raton Basin of northeast New Mexico. Bingaman was the lead sponsor of the public lands management bill that was signed into law in 2009. It set aside more than 2 million acres in nine states as protected wilderness and 100 miles of wild and scenic rivers. It also included a 5,300-acre national monument to protect Paleozoic fossilized tracks in the Robledo Mountains north of Las Cruces.

Bingaman has been re-elected four times. He faced his most serious challenge in the Republican year of 1994, when Republican Colin McMillan, a rancher and former assistant Defense secretary, spent over $1 million of his own money on his campaign. He attacked Bingaman's vote for Clinton's 1993 tax increase, but Bingaman won 54%-46%. Though he would have been a strong favorite heading into 2012, the reserved Bingaman has always seemed ill at ease on the campaign trail. His decision to retire frees him up to concentrate on legislation without the burdens of traveling or raising money.

Junior Senator

Tom Udall (D)

Elected 2008, term expires 2014, 1st term; b. May 18, 1948, Tucson, AZ; home, Santa Fe; Prescott Col., B.A. 1970; Cambridge U., B.L. 1975; U. of NM, J.D. 1977; Mormon; married (Jill Cooper); 1 child.

Elected Office: NM atty. gen., 1990-98; U.S. House of Reps., 1999-08.

Professional Career: Law clerk, 10th Circuit Court of Appeals, 1977; Asst. U.S. atty, 1978-81; Practicing atty., 1981-83, 1985-90; Chief cnsl., NM Health & Environment Dept., 1983-84.

DC Office: 110 HSOB, 20510, 202-224-6621; Fax: 202-228-3261; Web site: tomudall.senate.gov.

State Offices: Albuquerque, 505-346-6791; Las Cruces, 575-526-5475; Santa Fe, 505-988-6511.

Committees: *Commerce, Science & Transportation:* Aviation Operations, Safety & Security; Communications, Technology & the Internet; Competitiveness, Innovation & Export Promotion; Consumer Protection, Product Safety & Insurance; Surface Transportation & Merchant Marine Infrastructure, Safety & Security. *Environment & Public Works:* Children's Health & Environmental Responsibility (Chmn); Transportation & Infrastructure; Water & Wildlife. *Foreign Relations:* African Affairs; International Development & Foreign Assistance, Economic Affairs & International Environmental Protection; Near Eastern & South & Central Asian Affairs; Western Hemisphere, Peace Corps & Global Narcotics Affairs. *Indian Affairs. Rules & Administration.*

Group Ratings

	ACLU	ACU	ADA	CFG	AFS	FRC	LCV	ITIC	NTU	COC
2010	93	0	95	1	100	0	86	33	5	18
2009	–	8	100	3	100	–	100	–	5	43

National Journal Ratings

	2010 LIB — 2010 CONS		2009 LIB — 2009 CONS	
Economic	80%	— 17%	88%	— 0%
Social	65%	— 0%	64%	— 35%
Foreign	47%	— 0%	55%	— 0%
Composite	79%	— 21%	79%	— 21%

Key Votes of the 111th Congress

1. Overturn Ledbetter	Y	5. Pass health care bill	Y	9. Ratify New START	Y
2. Pass $787 billion stimulus	Y	6. Regulate financial firms	Y	10. Confirm Elena Kagan	Y
3. Repeal DC gun laws	Y	7. Pass tax cuts for some	Y	11. Stop EPA climate regs	N
4. Confirm Sonia Sotomayor	Y	8. Legalize immigrants' kids	Y	12. Repeal don't ask, tell	Y

Election Results

2008 general	Tom Udall (D)	505,128	(61%)	($7,447,684)
	Steve Pearce (R)	318,522	(39%)	($4,690,979)
2008 primary	Tom Udall (D)	unopposed		

Prior Winning Percentages: House: 2006 (75%); 2004 (69%); 2002 (100%); 2000 (67%); 1998 (53%)

Democrat Tom Udall was elected to the House in 1998 and to the Senate in 2008. He belongs to a political clan that is well known in the West and nationally that is sometimes called the "Kennedys of the West." He is the son of Stewart Udall, the Arizona congressman (1955-61) and U.S. Interior secretary (1961-69), and the nephew of Morris "Mo" Udall, an Arizona congressman (1961-91). He is also the first cousin of Sen. Mark Udall of Colorado.

Tom Udall grew up in Tucson and in McLean, Va., a well-to-do Washington, D.C., suburb. He went to Prescott College in Arizona, got a degree at Cambridge University in England and graduated from the University of New Mexico Law School. He worked as a law clerk for a federal judge, then as a lawyer in the New Mexico state government before going into private law practice. Politics was obviously on his mind. He ran for Congress in 1982, when the 3rd District was newly created, and finished last among four candidates, with 13% of the vote. The winner was Democrat Bill Richardson, who went on to become Arizona governor. In 1988, Udall ran in the open, Albuquerque-based 1st District, and won the Democratic nomination, but he lost the general election to Republican Steven Schiff, 51%-47%. In 1990, he was elected state attorney general, and in that role, focused on environmental and consumer protection issues.

In 1997, when Richardson resigned the 3rd District seat, Republican Bill Redmond, an independent Christian minister from Los Alamos, won it in an upset, assisted by a Green Party candidate nominee who won 17%. In 1998, Udall decided he had a shot at the seat, given the district's heavy ratio of Democrats to Republicans. He worked to consolidate the Democratic and leftist vote. Drawing on lawyers, the arts community and friends of the Udall family, he raised daunting sums. The Sierra Club and the League of Conservation Voters criticized Redmond and ran waves of ads against him. As for the third-party threat, Udall said, "I intend to make peace with the Greens." He won with 53% of the vote. Redmond got the same 43% he had won 18 months before, while Green Party nominee Carole Miller saw her 17% evaporate to 4%. Udall won re-election without serious challenges four times.

Udall had a seat on the House Resources Committee, on which his father served and which his uncle chaired. He helped to enact a bill to explore establishment of a national historical park at Los Alamos. With Republican Roscoe Bartlett of Maryland, he formed a bipartisan coalition to seek alternatives to high-priced and finite petroleum resources. Locally, he called for a ban on oil drilling in the Valle Vidal area of the Carson National Forest, which was passed in 2006. He opposed Republican attempts to permit salvage logging in national forests as well. On the 2007 energy bill, he sponsored an amendment requiring 15% of electricity to be generated from renewable sources other than nuclear power by 2020. The Democratic leadership supported this amendment, and the bill passed 220-190. But the Senate refused to accept Udall's proposal, and it was dropped from the legislation that was signed into law.

With a largely liberal voting record, he voted against the Bush administration's USA PATRIOT Act, which gave law enforcement greatly expanded powers to investigate terrorists. He proposed revisions in the act to limit police authority to obtain search warrants and to restore civil liberty protections for libraries and bookstores. Udall opposed the 2002 Iraq war resolution and called "misguided" a bill to restrict illegal immigrants from obtaining driver's licenses.

After Democrats took control of the House in 2007, Udall secured a seat on the powerful Appropriations Committee. He tried unsuccessfully to amend the energy and water appropriations bill to restore $192 million of the $300 million being cut for national laboratories, including Los Alamos National Laboratory in New Mexico. Despite losing that battle, Udall voted for the final bill, unlike New Mexico Republicans Heather Wilson and Steve Pearce, who voted against it. He was criticized at home for his vote, and defended his position as a signal to the labs that their missions needed to change from a focus on nuclear weapons to alternative energy research and other areas. But when the House voted in June 2008 to shut down the plutonium-manufacturing program at Los Alamos, Udall opposed it.

When Republican Sen. Pete Domenici announced he would not run for re-election in 2008, Wilson and Pearce immediately jumped into the race; several Democrats, including moderate Albuquerque Mayor Martin Chavez, considered it as well. This was the first open Senate seat in New Mexico since 1972, and only the second open seat since 1948. Udall at first said he wasn't interested. But Gov. Richardson and Democratic Senatorial Campaign Committee Chairman Charles Schumer of New York urged him to run. On Nov. 10, a little less than a year out from the election, Udall announced his candidacy, which quickly cleared the Democratic field.

Meanwhile, Wilson and Pearce battled for the Republican nomination. Pearce attacked Wilson for supporting the Democrats' expansion of the State Children's Health Insurance Program, which he called "socialized medicine," and for voting to raise taxes. Wilson hit Pearce for votes against additional guards on the U.S. border with Mexico. Domenici endorsed Wilson a few days before the June primary. Still, Pearce still won, 51%-49%.

The primary drained Pearce's war chest, and Udall was able to significantly outspend him, $7.8 million to $4.6 million. Pearce went on the attack, painting Udall as captive to the liberal wing of the Democratic Party and its "hippie" traditions. A former oil industry executive, Pearce also hammered Udall for his opposition to new oil exploration in environmentally sensitive areas. Udall responded that he was for a "do-it-all" approach to energy. It was apparent long before November that this wasn't much of a contest. Udall won 61%-39%. Pearce carried only Little Texas in the southeast and the San Juan Basin in the far northwest corner. Pearce did manage to win back his old House seat in 2010.

In the Senate, Udall joined his cousin Mark Udall, who had just won election to a Colorado Senate seat. Tom Udall has been a bit more faithful Democrat than his cousin, aligning himself largely with the liberal wing of his caucus. In one of his first moves, he succeeded in designating 17,000 acres in San Miguel County as wilderness in a bill that passed in January 2009. A Udall amendment providing tax credits for employers hiring military veterans discharged after 2001 was included in the 2009 economic stimulus bill. On the Environment and Public Works Committee, Udall has pushed for a national renewable energy standard. It failed to pass in 2009, but undaunted, Udall said in March 2011 he would introduce a bill imposing a 25% renewable energy requirement and that it might gain traction as part of President Barack Obama's call for a clean energy standard.

As a member of the Commerce, Science and Transportation Committee, Udall worked on improving rural areas' access to broadband Internet service. He also continued his earlier focus on consumer-related issues. He asked the Federal Trade Commission in 2011 to investigate misleading safety claims in selling football helmets and introduced a 2010 bill requiring new cars to have "black box" data recorders to help investigate crashes. He looked after New Mexico's tribes as a member of the Indian Affairs Committee, working to add a provision to the health care overhaul for improved Indian medical services.

But Udall has drawn the most attention for his efforts to alter how the Senate conducts its business. Like many senators who come over from the House, he found himself dismayed at the frequent use of GOP filibusters to delay or block pending legislation, often resulting in gridlock. At the outset of the 112th Congress (2011-12), he offered a plan that would bar the use of the filibuster on the initial motion to begin debate, but permitting lawmakers to filibuster a final bill if they remain on the floor during debate. His plan also would eliminate secret "holds" used to delay nominations of executive branch officials. The Senate fell 16 votes short of the number needed to adopt Udall's proposed changes. After Majority Leader Harry Reid said he had reached agreement with Republicans informally on several ways to prevent gridlock in the chamber, Udall vowed to push for further improvements, particularly regarding the reduced number of votes needed to cut off a filibuster. "We can do things here in a much better way," he said.

Udall added the Foreign Relations Committee to his workload in 2011, expressing a desire to help ratify the Law of the Sea Treaty defining the international usage of oceans. The treaty has drawn fierce opposition from conservatives concerned about its infringement on U.S. sovereignty.

FIRST DISTRICT

Martin Heinrich (D)

Elected 2008, 2nd term; b. Oct. 17, 1971, Fallon, NV; home, Albuquerque; U. of MO, B.S.E. 1995; Lutheran; married (Julie); 2 children.

Elected Office: Albuquerque City Cncl., 2004-07, Pres., 2006-07.

Professional Career: New Mexico National Resources Trustee

DC Office: 336 CHOB, 20515, 202-225-6316; Fax: 202-225-4975; Web site: heinrich.house.gov.

State Offices: Albuquerque, 505-346-6781; South Valley, 505-877-4069.

Committees: *Armed Services:* Air & Land Forces; Strategic Forces. *Natural Resources:* Energy & Mineral Resources; National Parks, Forests & Public Lands.

Group Ratings

	ACLU	ACU	ADA	CFG	AFS	FRC	LCV	ITIC	NTU	COC
2010	88	0	100	0	100	0	100	67	6	13
2009	–	4	100	2	100	–	100	–	7	40

National Journal Ratings

	2010 LIB — 2010 CONS		2009 LIB — 2009 CONS	
Economic	59% —	41%	68% —	30%
Social	61% —	35%	59% —	37%
Foreign	78% —	17%	62% —	35%
Composite	68% —	33%	65% —	36%

Key Votes of the 111th Congress

1. Overturn Ledbetter	Y	5. Bar federal abortion funds	N	9. Stop detainee transfers	N
2. Pass $820 billion stimulus	Y	6. Pass health care bill	Y	10. Legalize immigrants' kids	Y
3. Let guns in national parks	Y	7. Regulate financial firms	Y	11. Repeal don't ask, tell	Y
4. Pass cap-and-trade	Y	8. Pass tax cuts for some	Y	12. Limit campaign funds	Y

Election Results

2010 general	Martin Heinrich (D)..112,010	(52%)	($2,792,509)
	Jonathan Barela (R) 104,215	(48%)	($1,443,934)
2010 primary	Martin Heinrich (D)....................................unopposed		

Prior Winning Percentages: 2008 (56%)

Population		Race/Ethnicity		Work	
Pop. 2010:	701,939	White:	42.0%	Private:	73.7%
Change since 2000:	Up 15.8%	Black:	2.3%	Government:	20.0%
Urban:	91.3%	Hispanic:	48.4%	Self-employed:	6.2%
Rural:	8.7%	Asian:	2.0%	Blue collar:	19.6%
Area size:	4,721 sq. mi.	Native Am.:	3.4%	White collar:	61.5%
		Hawaiian:	0.1%	Khaki collar:	0.3%
Age		Two+ races:	1.7%	Other:	18.6%
Median age:	35.5 yrs.				
More than 65 yrs:	12.3%	*Ancestry*		Median income:	$45,161
Less than 18 yrs:	24.3%	German	10.0%	Median Home Value:	$185,400
		Irish	7.3%		
Education		English	6.3%	**Military Veterans**	
H.S. grad:	85.4%			% of Pop:	11.8%
College grad:	29.9%				
Grad degree:	13.2%				

Central New Mexico; Albuquerque

New Mexico's past and future come together in its single metropolis, Albuquerque. The city's Spanish and Indian past is memorialized in its name (for a 17th-century Spanish nobleman) and in its age (founded in 1706) and in its quaint Old Town. But Albuquerque's future is decidedly high-tech. For decades, the Sandia National Laboratories, Kirtland Air Force Base and the University of New Mexico have attracted scientists and engineers to Albuquerque and pro-

2008 Presidential Vote		
Barack Obama (D) 180,790	(60%)
John McCain (R) 118,972	(39%)
2004 Presidential Vote		
John Kerry (D) 139,820	(51%)
George Bush (R) 130,946	(48%)
Cook Partisan Voting Index: D+5		

moted private-sector technology growth. The city's minor-league baseball team is the Isotopes, named to honor the area's association with the Atomic Age. When rocket scientist Robert Goddard moved here in 1930 and nuclear scientist J. Robert Oppenheimer reconnoitered the site in 1940, Albuquerque was still a town of 35,000 at the junction of the Rio Grande River and old U.S. 66, which paralleled the Santa Fe Railroad. "A dirty, red sod-hut tortilla desert highway city," novelist Tom Wolfe wrote.

Now, metro Albuquerque, spreading out from Bernalillo County into Sandoval and Valencia counties, has more people— 887,000 in 2010—than all of New Mexico did when the scientists first arrived. Bill Gates founded a little company called Microsoft here in 1975, although the software maker moved its 16 employees to Seattle in 1979. Intel now employs more than 5,000 local residents in an advanced chip-making facility. The city's prosperous neighborhoods have climbed the gently rising heights to the east; poorer residents have spread north and south along the Rio Grande. In the Old Town Plaza, some of the adobe buildings date to the 18th century. Hemmed in by the Sandia Mountains and by federal installations, growth is moving west and north, especially to the new town of Rio Rancho, home of the Intel plant and facilities for Sprint PCS and Victoria's Secret. Despite its cold winters, Albuquerque is part of the Sun Belt. While Albuquerque has seen some growth in tourism—every October, it hosts the International Balloon Fiesta, which features many resident balloonists—it is heavily dependent on federal jobs. Nearly 22% of its workforce is employed by the public sector, up from 19% in 2000. The economic downturn hit here in late 2008, almost a year after the rest of the nation, and caused unemployment to double. But its recession was the mildest among cities in the mountain West region.

The 1st Congressional District of New Mexico includes Albuquerque and some of its suburbs. It is 48% Hispanic and takes in most of Bernalillo County and sparsely populated Torrance County in the desert. But the 1st does not include most of the big-growth suburbs of Corrales and Rio Rancho to the north in Sandoval County or Isleta and Las Lunas to the south in Valencia County. This has been one of the nation's most competitive districts: It voted 51%-48% for John Kerry in 2004—Kerry visited Albuquerque six times during his campaign—and 60%-39% for Barack Obama in 2008. The district had elected a Republican to Congress since its creation in 1969, but the trend ended in 2008. In the 2010 governor's race, Republican Susana Martinez edged out Democratic Lt. Gov. Diane Denish 51%-49% in Bernalillo County.

Martin Heinrich (D)

The congressman from the 1st District is Democrat Martin Heinrich (*HYN-rihk*), first elected in 2008. Heinrich was born in Fallon, Nev., earned a bachelor's degree in engineering from the University of Missouri and moved to New Mexico in 1995. He founded a political consulting business and served as executive director of the Cottonwood Gulch Foundation, which runs adventure programs in the Southwest. In 2003, he was elected to the Albuquerque City Council. His signature issue was increasing New Mexico's minimum wage in 2006; Heinrich worked with the city's business leaders and community activists to produce compromise legislation mandating a gradual increase. He also lobbied for federal protection of the Ojito Wilderness.

Encouraged by Democratic Gov. Bill Richardson, Heinrich announced that he would challenge GOP Rep. Heather Wilson in 2008. National Democrats backed Heinrich's candidacy, and he defeated three other hopefuls in the June 3 primary, including former New Mexico Secretary of State Rebecca Vigil-Giron. In October 2007, Wilson announced her intention to relinquish the seat to run for the Senate. Republicans fielded a strong replacement candidate in Bernalillo County Sheriff Darren White, who had had a long career in New Mexico politics, including two terms as sheriff. Early polls showed he had better name recognition than Heinrich.

But Heinrich made steady gains. He tied White to the unpopular incumbent president by reminding voters that White had served as President George W. Bush's Bernalillo County re-election chairman in 2004. White in turn questioned Heinrich's business practices, saying he had been paid by nonprofit groups for advocacy work without first registering as a lobbyist. Heinrich maintained that the law had not required him to register as a lobbyist when he was a political consultant for the Coalition for New Mexico Wilderness from 2002 to 2005. The campaign took an especially negative turn in the final weeks. Heinrich's campaign ran an ad featuring a group of New Mexico state police officers' wives, who in 1996 accused White of policies they claimed compromised their husbands' safety. White's campaign hit back with an ad in which the mother of a slain Bernalillo County sheriff's deputy referred to Heinrich as "despicable."

Late polls showed a close race. But Heinrich defeated White 56% to 44%, carrying three of the district's five counties. He crushed White by 33,786 votes in populous Bernalillo County, which Wilson had lost by a mere 1,250 votes in 2006. Heinrich out-raised White and was helped by the Democratic wave in 2008.

Before arriving in Washington, Heinrich already generated some inside-the-industry buzz. A poll conducted by the website *Politics1.com* named the handsome Heinrich the "Hottest Man in Politics," ahead of such well-known political heartthrobs as Sen. John Thune of South Dakota. In the House, he is generally a reliable Democratic vote, but a bit more centrist on economic issues. He opposed the December 2010 tax cut deal between Obama and congressional Republicans, saying that the wealthiest Americans did not deserve to be included.

On the Natural Resources Committee, he focused on legislation to make the country energy independent. He supported the House-passed energy bill in June 2009 and added an amendment aimed at making it easier for federal agencies to contract with local clean energy sources. He also amended a spending plan for Sandia and Los Alamos national laboratories enabling them to allocate more money internally to research projects of their own choosing. A year later, he got a provision into the fiscal 2011 defense authorization bill creating a pilot program connecting military bases and the labs to develop energy systems that could be used more widely. On other local issues, he worked to stop the retirement of the New Mexico Air National Guard's 150th Fighter Wing, eventually getting it to merge in 2010 with the 58th Special Operations Wing at Kirtland Air Force Base.

Republicans sought to portray the 2008 election as an aberration in their quest to reclaim the seat two years later. The GOP nominee was Jon Barela, a well-connected former president of the Albuquerque Hispano Chamber of Commerce and former state Republican Party vice chairman. Barela pledged fiscal conservatism to counter Democrats' "unchecked, reckless spending," and said that as a Hispanic, he would have the ability to connect with a broad cross-segment of the population. He got help from the National Republican Congressional Committee, which bought $300,000 of advertising time in October.

Heinrich accused Barela of seeking to privatize Social Security, a charge Barela denied, and defended his support of the economic stimulus and health care overhaul laws. Polls showed a tight race, but Heinrich managed to pull out a 52%-48% re-election win. He lost rural Torrance and Valencia counties as well as the portion of southern Santa Fe County in the district, but came out ahead, 53%-47%, in far more populous Bernalillo County. Heinrich announced in April 2011 his intention to run for the Senate seat of retiring Democrat Jeff Bingaman.

SECOND DISTRICT

Steve Pearce (R)

Elected 2010, 4th term; b. Aug. 24, 1947, Lamesa, TX; home, Hobbs; NM St. U., B.B.A. 1970; Eastern NM U., M.B.A. 1991.; Baptist; Married (Cynthia); 1 child.

Military Career: Air Force, 1970-76 (Vietnam)

Elected Office: NM House, 1996-2000; U.S. House, 2003-09.

Professional Career: Owner, Lea Fishing Tools.

DC Office: 2432 RHOB, 20515, 202-225-2365; Web site: pearce.house.gov.

State Offices: Alamogordo, Hobbs, Las Cruces, Los Lunas, Roswell, Socorro, 855-473-2723.

Committees: *Financial Services:* Capital Markets and Government Sponsored Enterprises; Financial Institutions & Consumer Credit; Oversight & Investigations.

Election Results

2010 general	Steve Pearce (R)	94,053	(55%)	($2,451,279)
	Harry Teague (D)	75,708	(45%)	($2,088,025)
2010 primary	Steve Pearce (R)	33,021	(85%)	
	Cliff Pirtle (R)	5,913	(15%)	

Population		Race/Ethnicity		Work	
Pop. 2010:	663,956	White:	39.8%	Private:	67.8%
Change since 2000:	Up 9.5%	Black:	1.6%	Government:	23.9%
Urban:	71.0%	Hispanic:	51.8%	Self-employed:	7.9%
Rural:	29.0%	Asian:	0.7%	Blue collar:	23.9%
Area size:	69,599 sq. mi.	Native Am.:	4.8%	White collar:	53.0%
		Hawaiian:	0.1%	Khaki collar:	0.5%
Age		Two+ races:	1.1%	Other:	22.6%
Median age:	35.2 yrs.				
More than 65 yrs:	14.1%	*Ancestry*		Median income:	$36,979
Less than 18 yrs:	26.3%	German	8.4%	Median Home Value:	$111,500
		Irish	6.2%		
Education		English	6.0%	**Military Veterans**	
H.S. grad:	78.0%			% of Pop:	12.4%
College grad:	18.7%				
Grad degree:	7.2%				

Southern New Mexico; Las Cruces

Southeastern New Mexico is a disparate landscape: Endless sagebrush-strewn acreage and then, suddenly, 9,000-foot mountain peaks rising along the Continental Divide. The eastern part of this region—places like Clovis and Portales, Lovington and Hobbs—speaks with a Texas twang rather than a northern New Mexico lilt. In Little Texas, as southeastern New Mexico is known, oil has long been the economic mainstay. Cattle ranching is common, and cot-

2008 Presidential Vote

John McCain (R)	118,063	(50%)
Barack Obama (D)	114,928	(49%)

2004 Presidential Vote

George Bush (R)	127,391	(58%)
John Kerry (D)	91,073	(41%)

Cook Partisan Voting Index: R+6

ton is grown on irrigated land. One of the larger towns is Roswell, site of a supposed flying-saucer landing in 1947 and now home of the International UFO Museum and Research Center. Farther west is White Sands National Monument, with its immaculate gypsum dunes and specially evolved animals with white coloration that allows them to elude predators in the harsh environment. Close by is Alamogordo, not far from where the first atomic bomb was exploded at 5:29:45 a.m. Mountain War Time on July 16, 1945. Virgin Galactic, a company started by billionaire Richard Branson, has leased land near White Sands to build the nation's first commercial spaceport. By early 2011, more than 400 people had put down deposits totaling more than $55 million to travel to the edge of space. But the state's struggling economy slowed the plans. New GOP Gov. Susana Martinez said taxpayers had already paid their share and that the facility should be privatized.

As in many places on America's high plains, population here is thinning and old economic pillars are crumbling. Once reliant on potash mining, Carlsbad aggressively sought the Waste Isolation Pilot Plant, a nuclear waste repository, that since 1999 has been burying shipments of plutonium-contaminated garbage from the nation's Energy Department weapons factories. Local officials, undaunted by opposition elsewhere in the state, have lobbied for consideration as a storage site for more types of toxic trash. East of Carlsbad, a uranium enrichment plant was built in Eunice, the first such facility licensed by the Nuclear Regulatory Commission.

In central and western New Mexico, the scrubland shades into desert, and people cram into small cities, protected from summer's burning heat and winter's deathly cold. The Hatch Valley, in the desert adjoining Interstate 25, is home to the world's finest chile peppers—the traditional cornerstone of the Southwest's spicy cuisine and always spelled here with an "e." Places like Silver City and Bayard were built on mining. Now home to miners, artists, ranchers, and outdoor enthusiasts alike, Silver City lacks the polish of Santa Fe or Taos, but locals like to say it offers "the real New Mexico experience."

Las Cruces, New Mexico's second-largest city, has grown at rates well above the statewide average, thanks to migrants from Mexico coming up the Rio Grande. Nearby are the Robledo Mountains, hailed by the Smithsonian Institution as the world's greatest repository of pre-dinosaur-era fossil tracks. For decades, Anglo and Mexican ranchers across the border spoke "the common language of cattle." Communities frequently shared public services with their cross-border neighbors and left the gates open at night for stragglers stuck too late on the wrong side of the border. But rapid development due to the 1993 North American Free Trade Agreement, a surge in illegal immigration, and a sharp uptick in drug trafficking have altered that environment. The mayor and police chief of the tiny border town of Columbus were indicted in March 2011 for allegedly being part of a ring sending firearms illegally to Mexico. Still, the New Mexico portion of the U.S.-Mexico border remains far sleepier than elsewhere, and the border posts that dot New Mexico's largely empty 150-mile frontier apprehend considerably fewer illegal immigrants than those in Arizona.

The 2nd Congressional District of New Mexico covers this southern part of the state, going as far north as the suburb of Las Lunas and the Isleta Pueblo south of Albuquerque and the Acoma Pueblo to the west. Demographically and politically, it is diverse. It includes most of Little Texas—majority Anglo and solidly conservative. It includes the politically marginal Las Cruces and the Democratic mining counties in the southwest corner of the state. And it includes the Indian country around the pueblos, which is strongly Democratic. The district is 52% Hispanic and 6% Indian.

Steve Pearce (R)

The congressman from the 2nd District is Republican Steve Pearce. He won the seat in 2002, abandoned it for an unsuccessful Senate race in 2008, and then reclaimed it two years later in the Republican landslide.

Pearce grew up in Hobbs, near the Texas line, and graduated from New Mexico State University in Las Cruces. He served in the Air Force and flew missions during the Vietnam War. He returned to Hobbs and started an oil-field service company. In 1996, he was elected to the state House. When U.S. Rep. Joe Skeen, a Republican stricken with Parkinson's disease, announced he would not run again, Pearce sought to succeed him. After winning the primary over two competitors, he beat Democratic state Sen. John Arthur Smith by a solid 56%-44% margin in the 2002 election.

In the House, Pearce usually votes with conservatives, though in his earlier House tenure he was a bit more moderate on social issues. In his first floor speech after coming back in January 2011, he made clear his beliefs were firmly rooted on the right. The health care law, he said, needed repeal in part because it "hires 16,000 Internal Revenue Service agents, but does not hire one doctor." (Interest groups backing the law have refuted that assertion, noting the law requires the IRS mostly to hand out tax credits, not collect penalties.) He defended cutting taxes for the wealthy, saying that many people earning more than $250,000 a year are small-business people. And he called for increased logging to bolster the timber industry.

During Pearce's earlier stint, he was the chairman of the National Parks subcommittee and made parks accessibility a priority. He proposed giving states and counties broad authority over rights of way on federal land, but made little progress on the measure before Democrats won majority control of the House in 2006.

When Republican Sen. Pete Domenici announced in 2007 he would not run for re-election in 2008, Pearce jumped into the race along with Rep. Heather Wilson, R-N.M.

Pearce attacked Wilson for supporting the Democrats' expansion of the State Children's Health Insurance Program, which he called "socialized medicine," and for voting to raise taxes. Domenici endorsed her a few days before the June primary, but Pearce still won, 51%-49%. The primary drained Pearce's war chest, and well-liked Democratic Rep. Tom Udall was able to significantly outspend him, $7.8 million to $4.6 million. Udall won 61%-39%.

Harry Teague, meanwhile, took advantage of the national Democratic tide in 2008 to capture Pearce's House seat in a district where Arizona GOP Sen. John McCain narrowly prevailed over Barack Obama. Teague established himself as an extremely conservative Democrat. But his July 2009 vote in favor of the cap-and-trade bill to reduce carbon emissions angered Pearce, who contended the measure would severely impact the region's oil and gas industry.

Pearce also criticized Teague for his vote in support of Obama's $787 billion economic stimulus bill and vowed to push a new strategy "that will reduce job-killing regulations, lower taxes to encourage investment (and) remove mandates that discourage hiring." He also ran advertisements calling Teague "one of the richest men in Congress," neglecting to mention his own personal fortune. He had an average calculated wealth of more than $23 million, the Center for Responsive Politics said in 2011.

The national Republican tide proved too much for Teague, and Pearce won easily, 55%-45%. Less than two months into office, he pondered whether to make another run for the Senate, this time for the seat being vacated in 2013 by retiring Democrat Jeff Bingaman. It would likely mean another primary race against Wilson, who announced her bid in March 2011 within a few weeks of Bingaman's decision. Pearce said he had no desire to repeat the earlier battle, which he said left him "bruised and out of money."

THIRD DISTRICT

Ben Ray Luján (D)

Elected 2008, 2nd term; b. June 7, 1972, Santa Fe; home, Nambè; NM Highlands U., B.B.A., 2007.; Catholic; single.

DC Office: 330 CHOB, 20515, 202-225-6190; Fax: 202-226-1528; Web site: lujan.house.gov.

State Offices: Farmington, 505-324-1005; Gallup, 505-863-0582; Las Vegas, 505-454-3038; Rio Rancho, 505-994-0499; Tucumcari, 575-461-3029.

Committees: *Natural Resources:* Indian & Alaska Native Affairs; Water & Power. *Science & Technology:* Energy & Environment; Technology & Innovation.

Group Ratings

	ACLU	ACU	ADA	CFG	AFS	FRC	LCV	ITIC	NTU	COC
2010	94	0	100	0	100	0	90	67	4	13
2009	–	0	100	2	100	–	100	–	4	40

National Journal Ratings

	2010 LIB	—	2010 CONS	2009 LIB	—	2009 CONS
Economic	80%	—	20%	71%	—	28%
Social	77%	—	21%	80%	—	18%
Foreign	66%	—	29%	87%	—	9%
Composite	76%	—	25%	81%	—	20%

Key Votes of the 111th Congress

1. Overturn Ledbetter	Y	5. Bar federal abortion funds	N	9. Stop detainee transfers	N
2. Pass $820 billion stimulus	Y	6. Pass health care bill	Y	10. Legalize immigrants' kids	Y
3. Let guns in national parks	N	7. Regulate financial firms	Y	11. Repeal don't ask, tell	Y
4. Pass cap-and-trade	Y	8. Pass tax cuts for some	Y	12. Limit campaign funds	Y

Election Results

2010 general	Ben Ray Luján (D)	120,048	(57%)	($1,175,112)
	Tom Mullins (R)	90,617	(43%)	($385,259)
2010 primary	Ben Ray Luján (D)	unopposed		

Prior Winning Percentages: 2008 (57%)

Population		Race/Ethnicity		Work	
Pop. 2010:	693,284	White:	39.6%	Private:	68.1%
Change since 2000:	Up 14.4%	Black:	1.3%	Government:	23.4%
Urban:	62.8%	Hispanic:	39.0%	Self-employed:	8.2%
Rural:	37.2%	Asian:	1.0%	Blue collar:	22.5%
Area size:	47,271 sq. mi.	Native Am.:	17.3%	White collar:	57.9%
		Hawaiian:	0.1%	Khaki collar:	0.3%
Age		Two+ races:	1.6%	Other:	19.4%
Median age:	36.4 yrs.				
More than 65 yrs:	12.2%	*Ancestry*		Median income:	$46,710
Less than 18 yrs:	25.9%	German	8.6%	Median Home Value:	$174,400
		English	8.1%		
Education		Irish	6.2%	**Military Veterans**	
H.S. grad:	84.0%			% of Pop:	10.7%
College grad:	25.7%				
Grad degree:	10.6%				

Northern New Mexico; Santa Fe

"The dancing ground of the sun" is what the Pueblo Indians called the land of northern New Mexico, where the long vistas, dotted with low-lying scrub, are painted in pastel hues in the cold light and clear air. For 100 years, artists have been coming here, attracted by the scenery and by a unique civilization that is part Indian, part Anglo, part Spanish, and a little Mexican. (Northern New Mexico was under Mexican control from 1821-46.) The region's long-surviving

2008 Presidential Vote
Barack Obama (D) 176,704   (61%)
John McCain (R) 109,797   (38%)

2004 Presidential Vote
John Kerry (D) 139,336   (54%)
George Bush (R) 118,350   (46%)

Cook Partisan Voting Index: D+7

traditions, however, mask the instabilities of this blended civilization. The Indians were here first and built adobe pueblos, including some of the world's earliest apartment buildings. The Spanish conquistadors and priests brought the Catholic religion, the baroque architectural accents, and the Spanish language. The Palace of the Governors, built in Santa Fe in 1610, is now a museum on Santa Fe's Plaza and is the nation's oldest extant public building.

Along the back roads in Rio Arriba or Taos counties, one can find a religion that mixes Catholicism with adaptations of Indian festivals, buildings not that much different from the old pueblos and a standard of living reminiscent of the Indian past, although sometimes punctuated by high rates of drug abuse and alcoholism. It's quite a contrast with the ski lodges in the Taos Valley, the high-security research facilities of Los Alamos—long considered to have one of the highest numbers of PhDs per capita in the nation thanks to Los Alamos National Laboratory—and the affluent, bohemian lifestyles of modern-day Santa Fe, where zoning laws vigorously enforce the height and adobe-like appearance of buildings in the downtown historic district.

The 3rd Congressional District of New Mexico contains most of the state's historic Spanish-speaking and Indian parts. At 47,000 square miles, it is larger in size than Pennsylvania. In 2007, Rio Rancho, with 87,000 residents, became the district's most populous city, but trendy state capital Santa Fe, where painter Georgia O'Keeffe was a major cultural force, remains its most dominant. The 3rd runs from the High Plains along the Texas border, past the haunting Sangre de Cristo Mountains, through the vast ridges and isolated buttes in the center, to the windy and dusty desert-like plains. Its Hispanic population is 39%, the lowest of the state's three districts. Another 17% of the district population is Indian, the highest of the state's three districts. Concentrated in and around the Navajo Reservation in the west, the district's Indians live in abject poverty.

The politics of northern New Mexico are unique. For years, debate was conducted and votes bartered in Spanish by Republicans and Democrats, often cynically, sometimes corruptly. Loyalties ran to families and communities more than to principles or parties. Republican territory includes the Little Texas counties to the east, the sprawling Albuquerque suburb of Rio Rancho, the mining and ranching country around Farmington, and the nuclear scientists of Los Alamos, but on the whole, this is a Democratic district. Both Hispanics and Indians are solidly Democratic, and in Santa Fe and Taos, the affluent and hippie migrants have produced a strong leftist tilt. Politically, this is a sharply divided district. Santa Fe, Taos, and San Miguel counties voted more than 70% for John Kerry in 2004 and more than 75% for Barack Obama in 2008. President George W. Bush in 2004 won 65% to 77% in the counties on the Texas border and 66% in Farmington's San Juan County. John McCain's 2008 winning percentages in those counties ranged from 59% to 70%. Overall, the district voted 61%-38% for Obama in 2008.

Ben Ray Luján (D)

The congressman from the 3rd District is Democrat Ben Ray Luján, who was elected in 2008 to the seat vacated when Democrat Tom Udall ran for the Senate. A seventh-generation New Mexican, Luján (*LOO-han*) is the son of state House Speaker Ben Luján. The younger Luján has sometimes been criticized for ascending on the strength of his family connections, and has sought to distinguish himself by focusing on complex topics important to the state, especially energy and technology. He was born in Santa Fe and grew up on his family's farm, where he and his three siblings helped raise cattle, sheep and chickens. Luján's father was a union ironworker who was elected to the New Mexico House in 1975. Luján's mother worked as a secretary for the Pojoaque Valley School District. After graduating from Pojoaque High School, Luján worked as a card dealer in a casino while attending classes at New Mexico Highlands University. In 2002, he became a deputy state treasurer, and a year later, he went to the New Mexico Department of Cultural Affairs as its chief financial officer and director of administrative services.

Luján's first experience with electoral politics was 2004, when he was elected to the New Mexico Public Regulation Commission, which regulates utilities, telecommunications, insurance and transportation in the state. Despite his somewhat sparse credentials, his fellow commissioners elected him chairman. The most pressing issue was the failure of Qwest Communications to invest a promised $788 million in its New Mexico communications network. Under Luján's leadership, the PRC ordered Qwest to invest in infrastructure or refund the money to customers. Qwest refused, and Democratic Gov. Bill Richardson advocated for a settlement. But Luján and the PRC steadfastly rejected Qwest's settlement offer, opting instead to take the company to the New Mexico Supreme Court. In 2006, the court sided with the commission, and Qwest ultimately agreed to spend $270 million in the state over three years.

When Udall gave up his House seat to run for the Senate, Luján courted the local Democratic establishment to get on the ballot. New Mexico developer Donald Wiviott also wanted to run. At the Democratic nominating convention, Luján got 40% of the vote and Wiviott 30%, and since both passed the 20% threshold, their names were on the primary ballot. Also on the ballot was Benny Shendo, former head of the New Mexico Indian Affairs Department.

The primary race quickly turned negative. Wiviott ran ads claiming Luján's father had helped him secure his job as deputy state treasurer. Luján responded with ads claiming that Wiviott's Texas trailer parts company had been charged by the Federal Trade Commission with price-fixing. But Shendo caused the race's biggest controversy when he implied that Luján was gay at a candidate forum. Shendo, who had been gaining traction among the district's liberal voters, drew criticism from local gay rights groups.

Luján picked up endorsements from Gov. Bill Richardson, local labor unions, and the Sierra Club. Wiviott invested almost $1.6 million of his own money in the campaign; Luján spent less than $800,000. Luján won with 42% of the vote to Wiviott's 26%; Shendo got 16%. In the general election, Luján faced Republican Daniel East, a building contractor, and independent Carol Miller. The district's strong Democratic leanings and Luján's aggressive fundraising made the race a foregone conclusion. He won with 57% of the vote. East received 30%, Miller 13%.

Luján has had the most liberal voting record among New Mexico's congressional delegation. He joined the Congressional Progressive Caucus, but unlike some of its members has steered clear of partisan rhetoric and concentrated on state-specific matters.

He serves on the Science, Space and Technology Committee, a relatively obscure panel to which junior lawmakers are often assigned, but its issues overlap with Los Alamos National Laboratory's non-nuclear weapons scientific research. He inserted several provisions into a House-passed bill in May 2010 authorizing federal science research and education programs, including one to help small businesses work with national laboratories. A year earlier, he also got through the House a bill to secure funding for research parks at Los Alamos and other labs. In 2011, he worked with Frank Wolf, R-Va., on starting a bipartisan technology transfer caucus to funnel research from the labs to the private sector. "When you think of high-tech or start-ups, when you think about Silicon Valley or MIT, you should think New Mexico," he said in a speech to the New Mexico Legislature.

On the Natural Resources Committee, Luján has pushed several bills aimed at preserving wilderness areas and settling some high-profile water rights disputes in his state. He also introduced a bill in 2010 authorizing additional money for victims of diseases caused by uranium mining and nuclear tests. Many of the uranium miners were Navajo Indians. He sticks up for the natural gas industry, which has a strong presence in the Four Corners region of the district near the borders of Arizona, Colorado, and Utah.

After his 2008 victory, Luján traveled to his district almost every weekend to engage in the kind of retail politicking that New Mexico voters expect of their lawmakers. Such diligence helped him avoid the pitfalls that some of the state's other Democrats faced in 2010. His Republican opponent was Tom Mullins, a Farmington petroleum engineer seeking office for the first time. Mullins said he was running against a "ruling-class political family," referring to Luján's father, and supported a conservative proposal to replace the income tax with a 23% sales tax, also called a flat tax. But he generated some unwanted headlines when he suggested putting land mines along the U.S. border with Mexico to deter illegal immigrants, and he had trouble drawing national GOP support. Luján won easily, 57%-43%.

★ NEW YORK ★

New York City is America's largest city, its financial capital, its center of arts and letters and media, and its largest immigrant destination. Since September 11, 2001, it also has been a symbol of the country's war on the constant yet unseen threat of terrorism. New York's achievements were not inevitable. They happened because New Yorkers—and not least those who came from elsewhere and opted to become New Yorkers—worked to make them happen. They did it in a city that has a certain enduring character that goes back to its birth as the 17th-century Dutch colony of Nieuw Amsterdam. Simon Schama's *The Embarrassment of Riches* paints a picture of the Old World Amsterdam that speaks to the character of the New World settlers. They came to America from "the richest city in the world; full of people who work hard all day and stay up late at night, smoke too much tobacco and drink too much coffee and gin, but are dazzlingly smart and shrewd; people who know their way around every corner of the globe and can make fine aesthetic discriminations, but are attached to their uncomfortable, crowded, bad-smelling city. They were merchants and manipulators with no aristocratic pedigree, welcoming any religious or ethnic group who can achieve and accumulate and show good taste, cherishing education and culture but indifferent to credentials." Probably fewer than 2% of today's New Yorkers are descended from the Dutch of Nieuw Amsterdam, but the character of the place endures in daily life and in its great institutions, and helps explain its miraculous growth. Combine Amsterdam and America, Dutch character with British-born political freedoms and American military strength, and you have the opportunity to build a city-state that can lead the world—and become the natural target of terrorists who hate that civilization.

New York was not always the nation's leader. In 1776, it was only the seventh most populous colony. Only in the 19th century did the descendants of Dutch patroons, Huguenot refugees, British West Indies traders and Yankee farmers become the nation's most successful merchants and capitalists, forging the first routes to the great American interior through the valleys of the Hudson and the Mohawk and building grand brownstone mansions on broad midtown Manhattan avenues. That early diversity provides one clue to New York's success. If New York has been cynical, ready to cooperate with Loyalists and Revolutionaries, it has also been tolerant, ready to accept anyone smart or rich enough to be counted a success. It has been propelled upward at each stage, forging ahead of London as a financial and manufacturing center by World War I, and staying ahead of surging Chicago and (so far) Los Angeles by incorporating every immigrant wave and consistently rewarding intelligence and hard work, with no concern about preserving hierarchies.

New York state's success has been a product not only of market economics, but also of government—and politics. The English saw New York as a pivotal point in North America, a connecter of its northern and southern colonies and an avenue to the interior. That is why the 30-year-old James, Duke of York, as Lord High Admiral, ordered his fleet to take Nieuw Amsterdam in 1664; the city and state are named for the man who was later King James II. The Iroquois, the most deeply rooted and militarily strong Native Americans, were kept in place for 100 years by an alliance with British troops, and then were driven out of their homelands in upstate New York after the Revolution. New York led the nation in political innovation. Martin Van Buren's Albany Regency was the first state political machine, an ally of New York City's Tammany Hall. Van Buren invented or institutionalized the Democratic Party, the national convention and the inaugural parade. His adversaries, Thurlow Weed and William Seward, formed the Whig Party and ultimately became Republicans. Noting that Van Buren's Democrats were winning large margins from Irish Catholics and other immigrants, the Republicans too made bids for the newcomers' votes. Both parties served the function of mediating between the divergent interests of the New York City masses and upstate New York's farmers and burghers, a conflict still evident in New York between city and country, immigrant and native, Catholic and Protestant, the Big Apple and the apple-knockers.

Both parties also worked to protect New Yorkers against the untrammeled workings of free economic and political markets. Tammany Democrats embarked on an unprecedented, labor-intensive campaign to build infrastructure, the bridges and tunnels that made Greater New York possible. The tradition carried on from the time of Mayor Abram Hewitt, elected in 1886 over the single-taxer Henry George and 27-year-old Theodore Roosevelt, up through the time of Gov. Al Smith in the 1920s and his protégé Robert Moses, who built bridges, tunnels, highways, beaches and World's Fairs in 1939 and 1964. Progressive Republicans, from Theodore Roosevelt through Elihu Root and Henry Stimson, worked to create civil service laws and bureaucratized purchasing

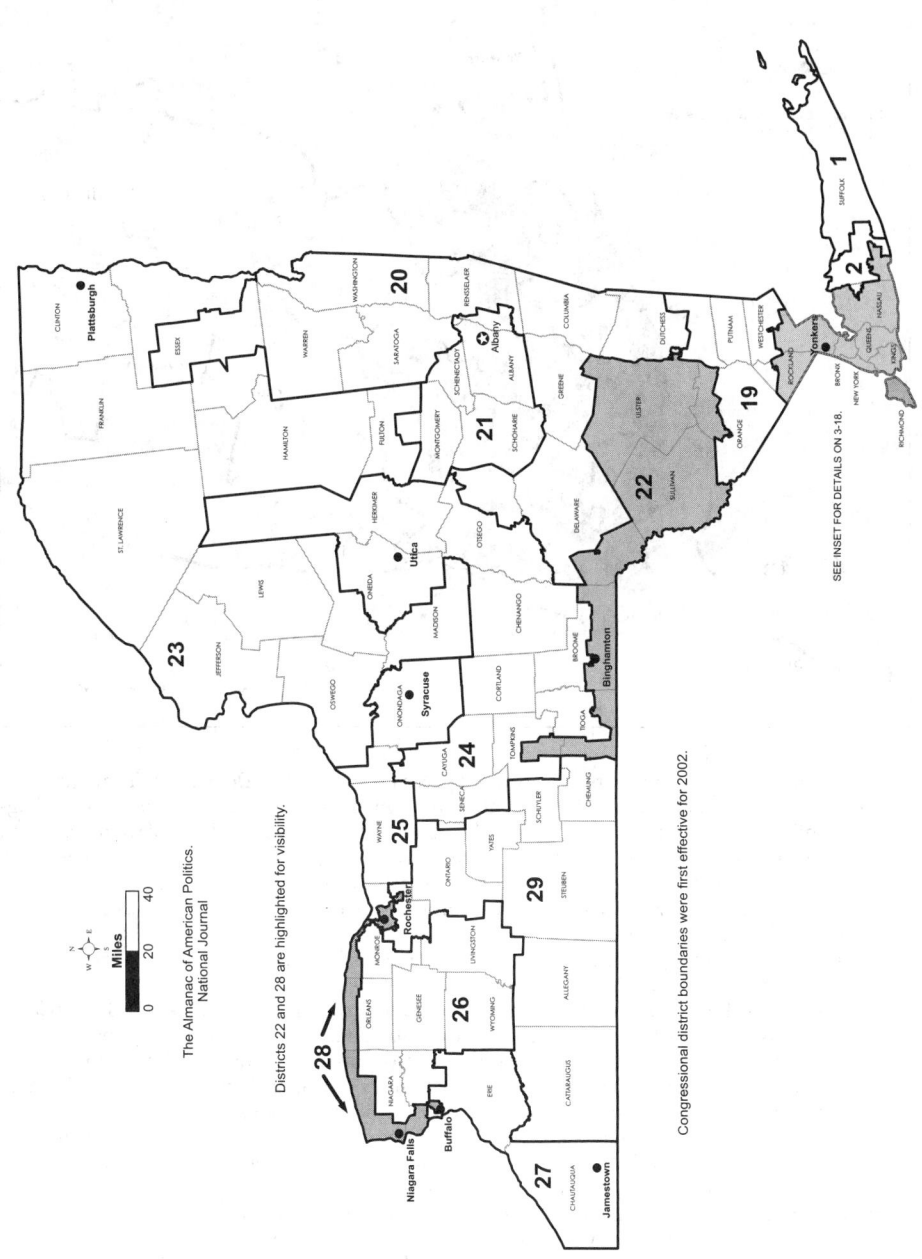

The Almanac of American Politics.
National Journal

Districts 22 and 28 are highlighted for visibility.

Congressional district boundaries were first effective for 2002.

SEE INSET FOR DETAILS ON 3-18.

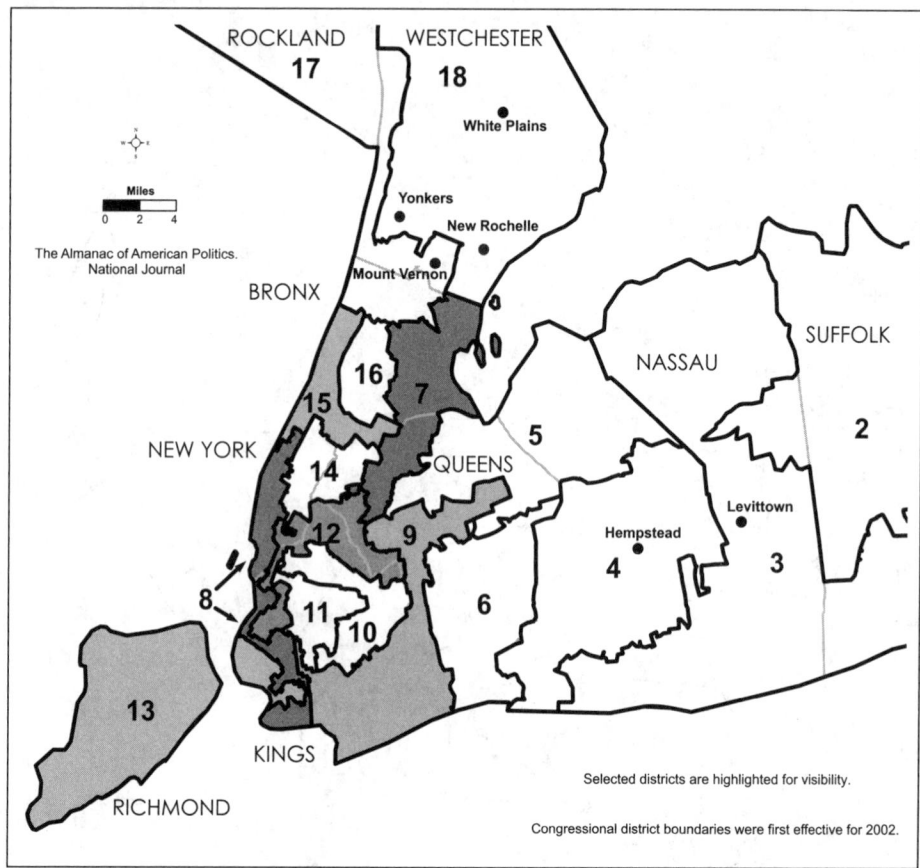

The Almanac of American Politics.
National Journal

Selected districts are highlighted for visibility.

Congressional district boundaries were first effective for 2002.

and spending to protect taxpayers from corrupt party machines. The Democratic Tammany machine led by Charles F. Murphy and the talented young men he advanced, Smith and Robert Wagner, responded to the shocking 1911 Triangle Shirtwaist fire—when hundreds of women jumped 11 floors to their death because fire escapes were blocked—by passing labor and safety laws. The results included minimum wages, maximum work hours, working-condition regulations, encouragement of unions, and state-owned electric utilities—the prototype of the New Deal, 20 years later, and the first American welfare state. In later years, New York pioneered public housing and fair housing laws, industry-wide unions (in the garment trades), rent control and dairy price controls to help both New York City tenants and upstate farmers.

Statewide elections were exceedingly close, with Democrats carrying the New York City Catholic vote and Republicans winning upstate Protestants. Swing votes were cast by the 2 million Jewish immigrants, who supported a generous welfare state but mistrusted the Tammany machine and valued civil rights. The politician who combined these appeals most cannily was Fiorello LaGuardia, a nominal Republican but almost a socialist, an Episcopalian who was half Jewish as well as Italian, and the man who, as mayor of New York City from 1933 to 1945, built much of the public housing and many of the civic monuments that still stand. Incensed that New York had no airport, he built what is now LaGuardia within a year. Both parties produced politicians whose positions appealed to these swing voters, politicians who became nationally prominent and often presidential candidates at a time when the national media was much more concentrated in Manhattan than in Washington, D.C.: Democrats Smith, Wagner, Franklin D. Roosevelt and Averell Harriman; Republicans Thomas Dewey, Wendell Willkie, Nelson Rockefeller and Dwight Eisenhower, who was a New Yorker by virtue of the fact he was president of Columbia University when he was elected president in 1952.

The polity that these men built was productive, generous, tolerant and closely regulated. The country was becoming accustomed to working in big units—being employed by big corporations, represented by big unions, regulated by big government—and in this, New York was a natural leader. The financial dominance of Wall Street and the big banks was protected by federal regulation. The high technology thrust of America in the mid-20th century was directed by big companies headquartered in New York's suburbs or upstate: General Electric and IBM, Eastman Kodak and Xerox. New York took for granted the productivity of its thousands of entrepreneurs and the high skills of its largely immigrant-born, public- and Catholic-school-educated workforce. It was blasé about its own miraculous infrastructure—the bridges and subways, electronic cables and electric wires connecting it better than anyplace else with every corner of the world.

But in the last quarter of the 20th century, New York's public strengths became weaknesses. The state that was clearly the national leader of a big-unit America lost the leadership of a country where growth had shifted to small economic units, where flexibility and adaptability had become more important than centralized planning. The institutions, practices and infrastructure that had helped produce New York's successes became ossified. Welfare state benefits became too expensive, measures meant to protect against corruption stifled innovation, and both failed to achieve their objectives. Ghettos throbbed with the pains of disorganization, and payoffs and rackets remained part of the everyday cost of doing business in New York as in no other place in the country. Rent control kept housing scarce, school bureaucracies and teacher unions stifled good teaching, public hospitals rationed care. The government that intended to aid growth seemed to be cutting it off—not completely, but enough to explain why New York state, which grew 32% in population from 1940 to 1965, grew only 1% from 1965 to 1990, while California grew 67% and Texas grew 64%. From 1990 to 2010, New York grew 8% while California grew 25% and Texas 48%.

People and businesses started voting with their feet, especially during the terms of Mayor John Lindsay, a liberal Republican who caved to municipal unions' demands and borrowed against next year's revenues to pay this year's bills. That brought the city to the brink of bankruptcy in 1975, two years after he left office. In the 1970s, the population of New York, city and state, dropped by 1 million, an unprecedented hemorrhage of talent and productivity. Retrenchment followed, and private financiers and the state government took control of city government, cut spending and negotiated cutbacks in jobs and salaries with public employees' unions. In the 1980s, Wall Street boomed, and Manhattan once again brimmed with confidence. Taxes were cut further under Democratic Mayor Edward Koch (1978-90) and Democratic Gov. Mario Cuomo (1983-95), public employees' unions were for a time reined in, and rational management was installed. But institutional problems remained. New York's legislature remained unusually tightly controlled by the two chambers' leaders, the Democratic Assembly speaker, from New York City, and the Republican state Senate president, from upstate or the suburbs, and these leaders engaged in classic political logrolling, lavishing taxpayers' dollars on each other's pet projects. Public employees' unions reestablished their stranglehold. The mild recession of the early 1990s struck New York with force. Big upstate companies—Xerox, Kodak, IBM—suffered serious reverses, and a private sector that had grown little if at all outside Wall Street could no longer finance the growing demands of the oversized welfare state.

By the end of the 1990s, New York seemed to have adapted and changed. Republican Mayor Rudolph Giuliani, first elected in 1993, cut crime and welfare rolls in half and cut hard deals with the unions. Republican Gov. George Pataki, first elected in 1994, imposed huge tax and spending cuts in 1995. Wall Street and the financial services industry boomed in the late 1990s, to the point that the jobs lost in the 1990-94 recession were replaced. Then came September 11, 2001.

It was a beautiful fall morning, the sunshine lighting a blue sky above the skyscrapers of Manhattan, commuters hurrying through the streets and subways to work. At 8:46 a.m., the first plane hit the North Tower of the World Trade Center. When the second plane hit the South Tower 16 minutes later, it was clear that America was under attack, at war, even as office workers fled the burning buildings and New York firefighters streamed in. The terrorists had chosen to attack a facility in the seat of government in Washington—the Pentagon (and a second target, but they were stopped by the heroes of United Flight 93)—and the seat of commerce in New York, to inflict the maximum possible damage. The people of New York, like those at the Pentagon and on United 93, responded with courage, determination and devotion to duty. Firefighters, police officers and rescue workers risked death to help others. Strangers helped strangers. People who had no experience with disaster figured out how to cope and help others. Millions volunteered to give blood, sent money, and provided food and supplies. The *Wall Street Journal*, headquartered across the street from the World Trade Center, scrambled to put out a newspaper that was distributed at the regular time across the nation the next day. In less than a week, the New York Stock Exchange reopened.

Giuliani and Pataki performed well in the national spotlight. But New York faced an economic downturn and a turn in the course of government. Despite heroic efforts at recovery, Manhattan and New York lost 200,000 jobs in 2001 and 2002. Downtown real estate values tumbled as financial services firms decentralized and sought office space elsewhere. Giuliani was term-limited, and all the leading contestants were well to his left. Media billionaire Michael Bloomberg, long a Democrat, became a Republican and spent $70 million of his own money on the campaign; he beat Public Advocate Mark Green 45.1%-44.5%. Pataki, running for re-election in 2002, made a $1.8 billion deal with the hospital workers' union and ensured that he would be re-elected without serious opposition. Faced with a fiscal crunch in 2002, Bloomberg increased property taxes 18% and raised other taxes as well. In his third term as governor, Pataki tried to hold down spending, but big tax increases, supported by Assembly Democrats and Senate Republicans, were passed over his veto. Nevertheless, the financial industry boomed as never before, generating revenues well beyond expectations. But the boom turned out to be fueled by mortgage-backed securities and other toxic assets, and in September 2008, the financial industry collapsed, with repercussions nationally and internationally, and with grave consequences for New York City and New York State.

In the first decade of the 21st century, New York City's economy grew largely because of the boom (it turned out to be a bubble) in financial services while its population growth was fueled almost entirely by immigration. The city's population grew 2% from 2000 to 2010, to nearly 8.2 million, and the four close-in suburban counties grew 3%. But this small change masked much greater movements. From 2000-09, there was an immigrant inflow of 7.2% and a domestic outflow of 10%. For the most part, the people moving out were the elderly, who headed to Florida and other warmer climes, and middle-income workers and young blue-collar workers, who headed to lower-cost and lower-tax states like the Carolinas, Georgia and Florida. Moving in were immigrants, who streamed into outer borough neighborhoods and created new businesses, churches and neighborhood institutions—Caribbean blacks in Flatbush; Chinese in Flushing, Borough Park and on Staten Island; Colombians and Mexicans in Corona; Pakistanis and Bangladeshis in Jackson Heights; Greeks in Astoria; Russians in Brighton Beach; and Dominicans in Washington Heights and much of the Bronx. The 2010 census showed Hispanics' percentages as 54% in the Bronx, 28% in Queens, 20% in Brooklyn, and 25% in Manhattan. At the same time, the city's black population declined and blacks now are outnumbered by Hispanics in all of these boroughs except Brooklyn. The census also reported that 23% of the people in Queens are Asians, the highest percentage for any county east of the San Francisco Bay area (though nearly equaled in Middlesex County, New Jersey).

Today's immigrants are arriving in a different sort of city. New York has long since lost most of its manufacturing jobs, and many corporate headquarters have moved elsewhere. The financial services industry pays enormous salaries and bonuses to those at the very top and generates service jobs for those who tend to the needs of the rich. But finance was sent reeling by the financial meltdown of 2008, and although it has rebounded, it's not clear whether the cornucopia will be as bounteous as in the days of the housing boom. As historian Fred Siegel points out, the outer boroughs are increasingly dependent on public sector jobs, with one-third of jobs in Brooklyn and half in the Bronx directly dependent on the city or state governments. New York's Medicaid program, designed by Republican Gov. Nelson Rockefeller in 1966 to be far more generous than any other state's, provides a lot of jobs, including many for immigrants. Hospitals are major employers in the outer boroughs and did not cut back during the recession. But they depend ultimately on the now-financially strained federal government. In the meantime, the trend is for an overlarge public sector to squeeze the life out of the private sector. Finance titans can survive drops in the value of their Manhattan co-ops. But immigrants who bought two-family houses in Queens with subprime mortgages have fallen through the cracks.

The suburbs have similar problems, exacerbated by much higher property taxes than those in the city. The immigrant inflow in the four close-in suburban counties of Nassau, Rockland, Suffolk and Westchester is smaller, 3% from 2000 to 2009, with a domestic outflow of 7%. Places like Levittown, buzzing with young families moving from Brooklyn in the 1950s, are aging and losing population. The high property taxes are in effect tuition to good suburban school districts, but become a heavy burden when the kids go off to college. Immigrant communities are coalescing in low-income suburbs whose first residents have departed. But with their high taxes and utility rates, the suburbs are not attractive to new businesses—the hedge-fund sector bloomed across the line in Greenwich, Con.

Upstate New York has even greater problems. Burdened with a state tax system constructed to support New York City's welfare state, it has been at a substantial disadvantage compared with nearby Northeastern states, not to mention the Sun Belt, when it comes to attracting jobs. Medicaid mandates have forced upstate counties to raise property taxes as much as 70%. Large, formerly paternalistic companies have been shedding jobs. IBM has cut back heavily in the Hudson Valley and the Southern Tier. Kodak, hard hit by competition from digital cameras, employed 60,000 people in the Rochester area in 1981 but had cut its workforce in half by 2007. Xerox jobs in the area fell from 16,000 to 8,000. General Electric, which employed 40,000 in Schenectady in the 1950s, cut the payroll there to 3,000 in 2006. Buffalo, once one of the nation's great steel producers, has become a center for the debt collection industry. Overall, upstate New York gained 2% in population in from 2000 to 2010, but the only areas of robust growth were the mid-Hudson Valley, the capital area around Albany and the Finger Lakes. Population fell 2% in the Southern Tier from Binghamton to Chautauqua and 3% in the five counties surrounding Buffalo. An area that had once been one of the nation's economic dynamos now seems to have become a backwater.

In the first half of the 20th century, New York politics was a battle between the Democratic city, then with more than half the state's population, and the Republican upstate. Jewish voters, concentrated in the city and moored to neither party, provided critical swing votes. In the post-World War II period, the suburbs grew and tended to produce small Republican majorities. Today the picture is different. New York voters turned to state and city Republicans amid the economically straitened and crime-ridden early 1990s—Giuliani as mayor, Pataki as governor. But they left no political heirs unless you count Bloomberg, a Democrat who changed his party registration so that he could run for mayor without the inconvenience of going through a left-wing gantlet in a Democratic primary. Bloomberg changed again in 2007, to unaffiliated, and then persuaded the City Council to abolish term limits so he could run for re-election in 2009. But starting with 2004, New York has become solidly Democratic in statewide races. It voted 58%-40% for John Kerry in 2004 and 63%-36% for Barack Obama in 2008. It voted 70% for Gov. Eliot Spitzer in 2006 and 63% for Gov. Andrew Cuomo in 2010. (He lost the Buffalo media market to the eccentric Buffalo-based Republican nominee Carl Paladino.) In U.S. Senate races, it voted 71% for Chuck Schumer in 2004, 67% for Hillary Rodham Clinton in 2006, and 66% for Schumer and 63% for Kirsten Gillibrand (running for the remainder of Clinton's term after being appointed by Gov. David Paterson) in 2010.

There is obviously a pattern here. In the 2008 and 2010 contests, Democrats won between 52% and 59% of the vote in upstate New York and between 55% and 61% in the four suburban counties. All would have won comfortably had not a single vote been cast in New York City. But in those contests, New York City voted between 79% and 82% for the Democrats. The specter of such overwhelming margins have tended to deter strong Republicans like Giuliani from running for office again, and beyond him, the Republicans have no well-known figures. Their state senators are grizzled Albany pros unsuitable for statewide airing; they hold fewer than one-third of the Assembly seats and going into the 2010 elections, they held only three of the state's 29 U.S. House seats.

This does not mean there has not been turnover and turbulence in New York politics. Democrat Eliot Spitzer, elected governor by a record margin in 2006 and vowing to roll over legislative leaders "like a (expletive) steamroller" resigned in March 2008 after he was caught patronizing prostitutes. His successor, Gov. David Paterson, wrestled with budget problems even while divulging more about his personal life than voters perhaps needed to hear. Hillary Rodham Clinton, rousingly re-elected in 2006, set off to run for president and lost by an agonizingly small margin to Barack Obama and then resigned in 2009 to become Obama's secretary of State. Paterson dithered over whether to appoint presidential daughter Caroline Kennedy to Clinton's Senate seat, and then chose upstate Rep. Kirsten Gillibrand instead.

In 2008, Democrats won a majority in the state Senate, controlled by Republicans since 1965, and former Senate Majority Leader Joseph Bruno was facing prosecution on theft of honest services charges. But in June 2009, two Democratic senators announced they were defecting from their party and joining Republicans on organizational issues affecting party control of the chamber. They returned to the fold, but Democratic ranks were depleted by prosecutions, and in 2010 Republicans recaptured control with a 32-30 majority. Any plans Paterson had to run for a full term as governor were scotched by his dismal job approval ratings, and in 2010 Democratic Attorney General Andrew Cuomo cruised to a 63%-33% victory as governor.

In all this there were at least faint echoes of the Republican tide that in 2010 surged across the nation. Republicans reduced the Democrats majority in the Assembly to only 100-48. A second echo came in races for the U.S. House. After the 2008 election, Democrats held a 26-3 lead in the delegation. In the 2010 election, Republicans gained five U.S. House seats in New York. But perhaps the loudest echo was in Cuomo's platform. As a candidate for governor, he sounded more like the George Pataki of 1994 than like his father Mario Cuomo, promising to veto any tax increases and to hold down spending. After winning over the sometimes clownish surprise Republican nominee Paladino, Cuomo delivered on his promises by getting Assembly Speaker Sheldon Silver and Senate Majority Leader Dean Skelos to agree on a budget after less than four months

Population		Household Income		Work	
Pop. 2010:	19,378,102	Under $15k:	13.5%	Private:	77.0%
State rank:	3rd	$15k to $50k:	32.1%	Government:	16.7%
Change since 2000:	Up 2.1%	$50k to $100k:	29.5%	Self-employed:	6.1%
Urban:	87.3%	$100k to $200k:	18.7%	Unemployment (3-yr. average):	4.6%
Rural:	12.7%	Over $200k:	6.2%	Poverty:	13.9%
Native of state:	64.3%	Median income:	$55,353	Blue collar:	17.4%
Not a citizen:	10.3%			White collar:	63.2%
Area size:	54,555 sq. mi.	**Home Value**		Khaki collar:	0.2%
		Under $100k:	18.3%	Other:	19.3%
Most populous cities		$100k to $300k:	30.5%		
New York	8,175,133	$300k to $500k:	23.6%	**Age**	
Buffalo	261,310	$500k to $1 mil:	22.2%	Median age:	37.9 yrs.
Rochester	210,565	Over $1 million:	5.4%	More than 65 yrs:	13.3%
Yonkers	195,976	Median:	$310,100	Less than 18 yrs:	22.9%

Race/Ethnicity				Military Veterans		Registered Voters in 2010	
White:	58.3%	*Language*		% of Pop:	6.8%	Democrats:	5,853,921
Black:	14.4%	English:	71.2%			Republicans:	2,920,366
Hispanic:	17.6%	Spanish:	14.0%	*Veterans by Period*		Ind./other:	3,032,457
Asian:	7.3%	Asian:	4.3%	WWII and before:	14.3%	Voter turnout:	4,763,688
Native Am.:	0.3%	Other European:	9.0%	Korea:	13.9%	Turnout as % of	
Hawaiian:	0.0%			Vietnam:	31.2%	voting age:	31.6%
Two+ races:	1.7%	**Education**		Gulf (pre-2001):	7.9%		
		H.S. grad:	84.4%	Gulf (post-2001):	6.0%	**Legislature**	
Ancestry		College grad:	32.2%	Peace time:	26.7%	Senate:	30 D 32 R
Italian	11.7%	Grad degree:	13.8%			Assembly:	95 D 51 R 4 V
Irish	10.9%						
German	9.4%						

in office. Party discipline is so strong in the New York legislature that such decisions are usually made by "three men in a room"—the governor, Assembly speaker and Senate majority leader—but in this case, Cuomo achieved something Spitzer had failed to accomplish.

Gliding over the turbulent New York political firmament is Sen. Chuck Schumer. His position in New York is impregnable. In two terms as chairman of the Democratic Senatorial Campaign Committee, he helped Democrats gain 14 U.S. Senate seats. (He was not at the helm when seven Senate seats were recaptured by the Republicans in 2010.) Had Senate Majority Leader Harry Reid lost his seat in a close contest in Nevada in 2010, Schumer would have been a serious contender to take over the Senate's top job.

Presidential politics　In the first half of the 20th century, New York was arguably the dominant state in presidential politics. It had the most electoral votes, and of all the large states, it was usually the most evenly divided between the two parties. New York, with 33 electoral votes in 2000, 31 in 2004 and 2008, and most likely 30 in 2012, has come to be the most heavily Democratic large state. In 2008, only Hawaii and Vermont cast higher percentages for Barack Obama. How did this come to pass? One reason is that Jewish voters, who did not identify strongly with either major party in the first half of the 20th century, became strong Democrats in the second. Increases in the percentages of black and Hispanic voters raised the Democratic percentage. White Catholic voters took conservative positions on cultural issues like crime and foreign policy in the 1970s and 1980s, which was one reason that Sen. James Buckley was elected on the Conservative Party line in 1970, that Republican Ronald Reagan won New York's electoral

2008 Presidential Vote
Barack Obama (D-WF) ......4,804,701　(63%)
John McCain (R-Ind-C)......2,752,728　(36%)

2008 Presidential Primary
Hillary Clinton (D).............1,068,496　(57%)
Barack Obama (D) ....751,019　(40%)

2008 Presidential Primary
John McCain (R) ....333,001　(50%)
Mitt Romney (R)...................178,043　(27%)
Mike Huckabee (R).................68,477　(10%)
Ron Paul (R) ....40,113　(6%)

2004 Presidential Vote
John Kerry (D-WF) ....4,314,280　(58%)
George W. Bush (R-C)........2,962,567　(40%)

votes narrowly in 1980 and 1984, and that Republican George H.W. Bush was beaten by only 52%-48% in 1988. But today, these voters, or their descendants, are more likely to take liberal stands on cultural issues salient in the 1990s, such as gun control and abortion rights. In the past four elections, Democratic presidential nominees have won 60%, 60%, 58% and 63% of New York's votes.

The low point for Democrats was 2004, when George W. Bush's percentages rose sharply among Catholics, Latinos and Jews in response to his leadership after September 11. Obama ran weakly among all three groups in New York's presidential primary in February 2008. But in November he won 59% of Catholics and much higher percentages of Latinos and Jews. He carried 36 of 62 counties and 25 of 29 congressional districts, and did not run below 46% of the vote in any of them.

New York Democrats have had presidential primaries since 1980; Republicans voted not for candidates but for slates of delegates through 2000. For 2008, New York scheduled regular primaries for both parties on Feb. 5, Super Tuesday. It was one of more than a dozen states voting that day and got little attention from candidates (except for holding Park Avenue fundraisers) because New York's own, Hillary Clinton and Rudy Giuliani, were well ahead in polls. When Giuliani dropped out after the Florida primary on Jan. 29, he endorsed John McCain. Republican turnout was only 670,000 voters, far fewer than the 2 million who voted for delegate slates in 2000. McCain beat Mitt Romney 50%-27%, carrying every county and congressional district and, with the Republicans' winner-take-all rule, winning all the delegates. Only 12% of Republican primary votes were cast in New York City; 25% came from the suburbs and 63% from upstate counties.

Turnout in the Democratic primary was high, 1.9 million voters, beating the record of 1.5 million set in 1988, when Mayor Koch's endorsement of Al Gore stirred angry talk from Jesse Jackson but did not prevent the victory of Michael Dukakis. In 2008, Clinton beat Obama 57%-40%, carrying 26 of the 29 congressional districts—all but three heavily black districts in Brooklyn and Queens—and 61 of 62 counties, the exception being Tompkins County, home of Cornell University. Blacks tended to vote for Obama, but not unanimously. Jews, Latinos and white ethnics gave about two-thirds of their votes to Clinton. A little under half of all Democratic primary votes were cast in New York City, 18% in the four suburban counties and 30% upstate.

New York law allows third parties to cross-endorse major party candidates, and once upon a time, third parties played a serious role in the state's politics. The Liberal Party and its predecessor, the American Labor Party, were founded to give Jewish garment workers a ballot line on which to vote for Franklin D. Roosevelt for president, but against local Tammany Hall candidates. The Liberal line was a help to Giuliani in the 1993 and 1997 mayoral elections. But in 2002, the Liberals lost their ballot position when their candidate for governor, Andrew Cuomo, received far fewer than the 50,000 votes required. The Conservative Party was formed in the 1960s to oppose Rockefeller Republicans and provided a line on the ballot for William F. Buckley Jr.'s quixotic run for mayor in 1965 and for his brother James Buckley's successful race for the U.S. Senate in 1970. It endorsed Republicans Alfonse D'Amato for the Senate and George Pataki for governor, but has had only spotty influence on local races since. The newest third party is the Working Families Party, which was formed in 1998 by public employee unions and usually endorses Democrats. The most successful recent third-party-line effort was Mayor Michael Bloomberg's creation of an Independent line to support his re-election as mayor in 2009.

Congressional districting

112th Congress Lineup	
22 D	7 R
111th Congress Lineup	
26 D	3 R

When John Kennedy was elected president in 1960, New York elected 43 House members, California 30 and Texas 22. In 2012, New York will elect 27 House members, California 53 and Texas 36. Reapportionment has been carnage time for New York. The state lost five districts in the 1980 census, another three in 1990, two more in 2000 and two again in 2010. In 2002, as in 1992, New York produced a convoluted redistricting plan. New York has more than 200 state legislators, but legislative decisions are made by a small number of stakeholders. In 2002, they were Republican Pataki, Republican state Senate President Joseph Bruno and Democratic Assembly Speaker Sheldon Silver. Party discipline was so strong that Bruno and Silver could always deliver majorities, and Pataki had a veto.

The three political decision-makers decided to target Rochester Democrat Louise Slaughter and Republican Benjamin Gilman. Slaughter said she would run in the primary against Democrat John LaFalce. (She also challenged the map in court to no avail.) But LaFalce announced that he would not run against Slaughter and bowed out. Gilman, who was 79 and serving his 30th year in the House, announced his retirement. All the incumbents running were easily re-elected in 2002, except for 1st District Republican Felix Grucci, who lost for reasons that had nothing to do with redistricting.

New York lost two seats in the reapportionment following the 2010 census and will have to reduce its 29 districts to 27—the lowest number it has had since 1810. The political lineup is again divided, with Speaker Silver still in firm control of the Democratic Assembly and Majority Leader Dean Skelos with a narrow 32-30 margin in the Republican Senate. But the politicians may not be in charge. Cuomo in December 2010 called for an independent commission to draw new legislative and congressional districts and he pledged to "veto any redistricting plan in 2012 that reflects partisan gerrymandering and ensure that the state has set itself on a path to reforming the process itself." The census data make it clear that upstate New York must lose the equivalent of one district; Democrats now hold five districts there and Republicans six. The other district is likely to come out of New York City or its inner suburbs.

Governor

Andrew Cuomo (D)

Elected 2010, term expires Jan. 2015, 1st term; b. Dec. 6, 1957, Queens; home, Albany; Fordham U., B.A. 1979; Albany Law Schl., J.D. 1982; Catholic; Divorced; 3 children.

Elected Office: NY atty. gen., 2006-10.

Professional Career: Asst. district atty., Manhattan, 1984-85; Practicing atty., Blutrich, Falcone & Miller, 1985-88; Founder, Housing Enterprise for the Less Privileged, 1988-93; Asst. secy., Dept. of Housing and Urban Development, 1993-97; Secy., HUD, 1997-2001.

Office: NYS State Capitol Building, 12224, 518-474-8390; Web site: www.governor.ny.gov.

Election Results

2010 general	Andrew Cuomo (D)	2,911,721	(63%)
	Carl Paladino (R)	1,548,184	(33%)
2010 primary	Andrew Cuomo (D)	unopposed	

The governor of New York is Andrew Cuomo, a former state attorney general and secretary of the U.S. Department of Housing and Urban Development in the Clinton administration, as well as the son of former three-term Gov. Mario Cuomo. He was elected in 2010 and succeeded Democrat David Paterson.

Cuomo was born in Queens and grew up in the middle-class neighborhood of Hollis, the second of five siblings. At the time, his father was a lawyer in Brooklyn who assisted journalists such as Pete Hamill, Jimmy Breslin and Jack Newfield in exposing and addressing injustices on city housing policy and other issues. The younger Cuomo showed an early aptitude for repairing and building automobiles. "If Andrew gets a car, it's about (him) making the car," his brother Chris Cuomo, a journalist for ABC News, told *Esquire* in May 2010. "It's really a metaphor for what he does in government—he does it himself, he fixes things." He graduated from Fordham University in 1979, one year after his father was elected lieutenant governor, and from Albany Law School in 1982. He began working for his father's campaign for governor that year and received credit for masterminding his come-from-behind primary victory against popular New York City Mayor Ed Koch. However, some critics said the younger Cuomo was too willing to engage in dirty politics. He spent several years as an aide to his father, working for $1 a year, as the governor's national profile skyrocketed in the wake of his eloquent denunciation of President Ronald Reagan's policies as keynote speaker at the 1984 Democratic National Convention.

After a short stint in the Manhattan district attorney's office, Cuomo in 1986 founded the Housing Enterprise for the Less Privileged (HELP USA), a nonprofit organization dedicated to helping the homeless. He left his private law practice in 1989 to run the group, which became a national model for its formula of offering shelter but also job training, education, drug treatment and other assistance. Two years later, he married Kerry Kennedy, the daughter of Robert F. Kennedy, in a widely-publicized union that was described as a merger of two Democratic political dynasties.

Cuomo's work at HELP caught the attention of Arkansas Gov. Bill Clinton, who asked Cuomo to serve on his transition team after being elected president in 1992 and then as assistant secretary of community planning and development at the HUD. After Clinton's re-election in 1996, Cuomo took over as secretary of the department. He won praise for his energetic efforts in making housing more affordable, but also adopted policies to broaden home ownership for low-income Americans that some later said contributed to the housing crisis a decade later. One of those policies was a dramatic rise in the number of affordable loans that government-sponsored mortgage giants, Fannie Mae and Freddie Mac, were required to buy. HUD also produced rules that explicitly forbade imposing new reporting requirements on the two enterprises. Years later, when questions arose on the campaign trail, his aides blamed policies enacted under Republican President George W. Bush for the mortgage meltdown.

Cuomo returned to New York in 2001 with the intention of running for governor the following year. But he did himself in with some brash and ill-advised remarks. He said that Republican Gov. George Pataki had done little after September 11 other than hold New York Mayor Rudy Giuliani's coat. He also angered African-Americans who had been banking on State Comptroller Carl McCall as their party's candidate. Cuomo dropped out of the race before the primary, and McCall lost to Pataki. Around the same time, Cuomo became engaged in a bitter public divorce and child custody battle with Kennedy.

Cuomo largely disappeared from the public eye for the next several years. In 2006, he came back to run for New York attorney general when the incumbent in that job, Eliot Spitzer, ran for governor. He patched up his differences with Democrats and won the primary with ease, then easily beat the Republican nominee, former Westchester District Attorney Jeanine Pirro, 58%-40%. He conducted investigations of the financial industry's alleged misdeeds, something that had propelled Spitzer's political career. At the same time, he looked into the student loan industry's deceptive marketing practices, uncovered fraud among health insurers and crusaded against online child pornography. He also ended up investigating Spitzer for using the state police to gather information about then-state Senate Majority Leader Joseph Bruno. Cuomo's popularity rose.

When Spitzer resigned in disgrace in 2008 over revelations that he had been the client of an expensive prostitution ring, Paterson took over, becoming the state's first African-American chief executive. But by March 2009, Paterson's job ratings were the lowest in state history. Suburbanites were angry about cuts in school funding, New York City residents were mad about cuts in city aid, and leaders of public employee unions were angry about proposed layoffs and revisions in fringe benefits. The muddy process for appointing Rep. Kirsten Gillibrand to the Senate seat vacated by Hillary Rodham Clinton did not help. Polls showed Cuomo beating Paterson by wide margins in a theoretical Democratic primary and Giuliani leading Paterson in a general election, though running behind Cuomo. Paterson eventually acceded to the demands of the Obama White House, which insisted he should step down rather than become a drag on the entire ticket in New York. That cleared the way for Cuomo to make an unimpeded bid for the Democratic nomination for governor.

In May 2010, Cuomo announced his candidacy, declaring the state had slipped from being a "national model" under his father to a "national disgrace." He unveiled a long list of proposals, from creating more high-tech and energy jobs to a spending cap and salary freeze on state workers. He did not spare Democrats from criticism. The state's corruption, he said, "infects politicians on both sides of the aisle." Accompanying him at the announcement was his girlfriend Sandra Lee, host of a popular cooking show on the Food Network. The only question remaining was who would run against him as the Republican underdog. Former two-term Rep. Rick Lazio sought the GOP nomination, but lost overwhelmingly in the September primary to Carl Paladino, a wealthy real estate executive who self-funded his campaign with support from tea party activists.

Paladino was known for his aggressive and prickly style, and some members of Cuomo's camp wondered if his unpredictability in an anti-establishment climate would work against them. But Paladino hurt no one more than himself, as New York tabloids dubbed him "Crazy Carl." He said that though he did not discriminate against gays, he did not want children "brainwashed into thinking that homosexuality" is acceptable. He accused Cuomo of being unfaithful to his ex-wife, but offered no evidence. And he had to apologize for forwarding racist and sexually explicit e-mails to dozens of associates. Cuomo had little trouble rolling to a landslide 63%-33% victory. Although Paladino won most western New York State counties, Cuomo received more than 75% of the vote in higher-turnout areas such as Queens and the Bronx.

In the early days of his administration, Cuomo sought to dampen expectations that he could correct the state's problems quickly. He warned in his inaugural address that the state was spending too much and receiving too little in return and outlined four broad goals for government: Paying employees for high performance, achieving results rapidly, putting people above special interests and serving as "an icon for integrity." He promised that his fiscal plan would not involve new borrowing or higher taxes on the wealthy, a stand that irked some state lawmakers.

The grumbling among those lawmakers increased dramatically when Cuomo seemed unwilling to produce specifics on how to balance the budget. His administration broke with usual practice in leaving others to fill in the details of almost half of the $8.9 billion in spending cuts it proposed. That strategy was intended to counter the traditional history of governors picking controversial fights with interest groups and the Assembly over programs and almost inevitably losing them. He delegated the task of curbing Medicaid spending to a task force of health industry leaders, which managed to agree on funding cuts in exchange for long-desired limits on malpractice suits. Just days before the March 31 deadline, he was able to strike a deal with the legislature's leaders on a $132.5 billion budget that reduced year-to-year spending by about 2% without imposing taxes. He agreed to add $250 million for schools, education, human services and prescription drugs for the elderly. News of the deal outraged New York City Mayor Michael Bloomberg, who said the cuts would disproportionately affect the city even though it was responsible for generating much of the state's revenue.

Another of Cuomo's proposals, to create an independent nonpartisan redistricting commission, met with resistance. And his efforts to win cooperation from unions—a problem confronting governors in numerous other cash-strapped states—brought strong criticism from labor groups. The public, however, remained solidly in Cuomo's corner. In a March 2011 Siena College poll, he scored an impressive 72% approval rating. He even won praise from Republicans. U.S. Senate Minority Leader Mitch McConnell of Kentucky publicly cited Cuomo and the more bombastic GOP Gov. Chris Christie of New Jersey as "two examples of gubernatorial leadership people ought to look to."

Senior Senator

Charles Schumer (D)

Elected 1998, term expires 2016, 3rd term; b. Nov. 23, 1950, Brooklyn; home, Brooklyn; Harvard U., B.A. 1971, J.D. 1974; Jewish; married (Iris Weinshall); 2 children.

Elected Office: NY Assembly, 1974–80; U.S. House of Reps., 1980-1998.

DC Office: 322 HSOB, 20510, 202-224-6542; Fax: 202-228-3027; Web site: schumer.senate.gov.

State Offices: Albany, 518-431-4070; Binghamton, 607-772-6792; Buffalo, 716-846-4111; Hudson Valley, 914-734-1532; Long Island, 631-753-0978; New York City, 212-486-4430; Rochester, 585-263-5866; Syracuse, 315-423-5471.

Committees: *Banking, Housing & Urban Affairs:* Financial Institutions & Consumer Protection; Housing, Transportation & Community Development; Securities, Insurance & Investment. *Finance:* International Trade, Customs & Global Competitiveness; Social Security, Pensions & Family Policy; Taxation & IRS Oversight. *Judiciary:* Antitrust, Competition Policy & Consumer Rights; Immigration, Refugees & Border Security (Chmn); Privacy, Technology & the Law. *Rules & Administration* (Chmn).

Group Ratings

	ACLU	ACU	ADA	CFG	AFS	FRC	LCV	ITIC	NTU	COC
2010	93	0	95	0	97	0	100	67	5	27
2009	–	0	95	0	100	–	100	–	5	43

National Journal Ratings

	2010 LIB	—	2010 CONS		2009 LIB	—	2009 CONS
Economic	85%	—	12%		88%	—	0%
Social	65%	—	0%		79%	—	19%
Foreign	47%	—	0%		55%	—	0%
Composite	81%	—	19%		84%	—	16%

Key Votes of the 111th Congress

1. Overturn Ledbetter	Y	5. Pass health care bill	Y	9. Ratify New START	Y
2. Pass $787 billion stimulus	Y	6. Regulate financial firms	Y	10. Confirm Elena Kagan	Y
3. Repeal DC gun laws	N	7. Pass tax cuts for some	Y	11. Stop EPA climate regs	N
4. Confirm Sonia Sotomayor	Y	8. Legalize immigrants' kids	Y	12. Repeal don't ask, tell	Y

Election Results

2010 general	Charles Schumer (D) 3,047,880	(66%)	($19,519,748)
	Jay Townsend (R) 1,480,423	(32%)	($218,557)
2010 primary	Charles Schumer (D) .... unopposed		

Prior Winning Percentages: 2004 (71%); 1998 (55%); House: 1996 (75%); 1994 (73%); 1992 (89%); 1990 (80%); 1988 (78%); 1986 (93%); 1984 (72%); 1982 (79%); 1980 (77%)

Charles Schumer, a Democrat first elected in 1998, is New York's senior senator. He grew up in Flatbush, Brooklyn, where his father had a small exterminating business. Schumer graduated first in his class at James Madison High School, the alma mater of Supreme Court Justice Ruth Bader Ginsburg and former Minnesota Sen. Norm Coleman. It's safe to say that Schumer was interested in politics from the start. He graduated from Harvard College and Law School and, with his law degree fresh in hand in June 1974, he ran for an open New York Assembly seat. He won, at age 23, becoming the state's youngest Assembly member since Theodore Roosevelt. In 1980, just before turning 30, he was elected to the U.S. House from an open Brooklyn seat. Through energy, imagination, hard work, and a certain amount of chutzpah, he became a skilled legislator and a politician noted—and sometimes resented—for attracting publicity. (Former Senate GOP Leader Bob Dole of Kansas was one of the first, but not the last, to say that the most dangerous place to be in Washington was between Chuck Schumer and a television camera.)

Schumer got a seat on the Banking Committee, a panel that most talented members lobby to leave. But he stayed on, aware of its importance to New York's financial services industry. He also served on the Judiciary Committee and chaired the Crime Subcommittee. Schumer sponsored the 1994 crime bill that banned assault weapons and shepherded through the House President Bill Clinton's proposal to add 100,000 police officers across the country. The legislation also created "three strikes" mandatory life terms for repeat violent criminals. Schumer was the House sponsor of the Brady bill, which created waiting periods for handgun purchases and was passed over the strong opposition of the National Rifle Association. Schumer also contributed key provisions to the immigration acts in 1986 and 1990.

The idea of running for statewide office was surely never far from his mind. In early 1997 Schumer considered seeking the governorship, but incumbent Republican George Pataki's strong job ratings persuaded Schumer to use his $5 million campaign treasury to run instead against GOP Sen. Alfonse D'Amato. It was by no means obvious that Schumer would win. D'Amato was known for his assiduous constituent service and for his ability to dominate the tabloid wars that are a mainstay of metropolitan New York political campaigns. As the chairman of the Senate Banking Committee, he also excelled at raising money. Schumer started off largely unknown outside his district, and he faced serious primary opposition from Geraldine Ferraro, the 1984 vice presidential nominee, and Mark Green, the New York City public advocate and D'Amato's 1986 opponent. By summer, Schumer was leading in polls and was much better financed than his rivals. In September, he won the primary with 51% of the vote to 26% for Ferraro and 19% for Green.

Schumer immediately launched an attack on D'Amato, saying that the incumbent had told "too many lies for too long," which echoed D'Amato's earlier criticisms of his opponents as "too liberal for too long." Schumer maintained that he was tougher on crime than D'Amato, and he emphasized his support of abortion rights and gun regulation. D'Amato concentrated heavily on Schumer's missed votes while running for the Senate, but the implication that the high-voltage Schumer was lazy was implausible. Still, by mid-October, most of Schumer's poll leads were within the statistical margin of error. Then, in a closed meeting before a Jewish group, D'Amato called Schumer a "putzhead," Yiddish slang for "jerk." When the remark became public, he denied it, before backtracking unconvincingly after his own supporter, former Democratic Mayor Edward Koch, confirmed it. By early November, D'Amato was sagging in the polls. Schumer had announced in October that he would vote against impeaching Clinton, although he said he believed that the president lied under oath about a sexual relationship with a White House intern. Schumer was the beneficiary of two visits from Clinton and no less than four from first lady Hillary Rodham Clinton. (The rousing receptions she got may have encouraged her successful run for the Senate in New York two years later.) Although outspent, Schumer won 55%-44%.

In the Senate, Schumer established a solidly liberal voting record. And he elevated his skills for occupying the limelight to high art. He made a practice of visiting all 62 counties each year and he regularly spent Mondays on upstate swings that got him on Buffalo, Rochester, Syracuse and Albany television. He often held Sunday press conferences to take advantage of the slow news digest that day, a tactic that earned him coverage on the evening news and in the Monday editions of newspapers.

On the Banking Committee, Schumer gladly returned to work on financial services issues. He supported the 1999 Gramm-Bliley-Leach bill eliminating the barriers between banks and investment banks and in 2001 he joined GOP Sen. Phil Gramm of Texas in successfully halving the fees paid by Wall Street firms to the Securities and Exchange Commission. In 2002, Schumer played a key role in scuttling a Republican bankruptcy bill by persuading the Senate to pass an amendment that made fines and penalties for attacking abortion clinics not dischargeable in bankruptcy cases; abortion rights opponents were increasingly declaring bankruptcy to avoid paying such fines. Abortion opponents in the House refused to vote for the bill as long as it contained Schumer's amendment. The bill died, but was revived in 2005. This time, Schumer's abortion amendment was voted down, 53-46, in the Senate, and the bill was ultimately enacted. He has long opposed moves to toughen regulation of the government-sponsored mortgage institutions, Fannie Mae and Freddie Mac, citing the rising rate of homeownership and the possibility of increased interest rates. And Schumer also opposed taxing the carried interest income of hedge fund operators, of vital interest to the city's Financial District.

On the Judiciary Committee, Schumer took the position that senators should reject President George W. Bush's judicial appointees on "purely ideological grounds." Starting with the nomination of Miguel Estrada to the U.S. Court of Appeals, he led the opposition to Bush judicial nominees whom he and liberal lobbying groups judged to be out of the mainstream. Schumer, along with other Democrats, used the filibuster to block the appointment of federal judges who enjoyed majority support, forcing the nominee to earn 60 votes to be confirmed. He took strong exception to Senate Republicans who advocated changing the rules to allow nominations to be considered by majority vote. In 2005, Schumer tried to pin down Supreme Court nominee John Roberts in committee hearings and was one of 22 senators who later voted against him and noted later, "Roberts was quite stealthy, but he was so brilliant he could pull it off." When Bush nominated Samuel Alito in 2005, Schumer said he was "sad that the president felt he had to pick a nominee likely to divide America" and wondered "whether (Alito) would use that seat to reverse much of what Rosa Parks and so many others fought so hard and for so long to put in place." In 2007, Schumer pounced on the Bush administration's firings of seven U.S. attorneys around the country, demanding the resignation of Attorney General Alberto Gonzales.

Schumer played a major role in shepherding recovery money through Congress after the September 11 attacks. On that fateful day in 2001, Schumer's daughter was in school a few blocks from the World Trade Center, although she was unharmed. He immediately requested $20 billion in aid for New York, which Bush readily approved. The Bush administration then turned to Schumer to rally support for its centerpiece anti-domestic terrorism law, the USA PATRIOT Act. Schumer has secured federal grants for all manner of projects for New York, ranging from an ambulance for the volunteer fire department in St. Lawrence County to funding for tritium cleanup at the Brookhaven National Laboratory. He also has gotten along well with New York City Mayor Michael Bloomberg; his wife, Iris Weinshall, was Bloomberg's transportation commissioner from 2002 to 2007.

Schumer has been a prodigious fundraiser since his early days in the House. In 2004, his money skills enabled him to raise nearly $12 million and ward off a serious challenge to his reelection. Constant traveling in upstate New York also made him as well known there as in New York City. Schumer won easily, 71%-24%, exceeding the 67%-31% record set by Daniel Patrick Moynihan in 1988.

Some speculated that Schumer would run for governor in 2006, but that issue was settled when he agreed to accept Democratic Leader Harry Reid's appointment as chairman of the Democratic Senatorial Campaign Committee and got a seat on the Finance Committee to boot. The task ahead looked difficult. The lineup of Senate seats up in 2006 left Republicans with more target seats than Democrats. But Schumer did a brilliant job of persuading Democratic incumbents from states that Bush carried in 2004—Jeff Bingaman of New Mexico, Kent Conrad of North Dakota, Ben Nelson of Nebraska, and Bill Nelson of Florida—not to retire. Then he worked on getting strong challengers to Republican incumbents. In Pennsylvania, he aggressively recruited state Treasurer Robert Casey Jr., son of the late governor known for his strong opposition to abortion rights. Schumer astutely calculated that Casey would make inroads in the culturally conservative base of incumbent Rick Santorum and would be acceptable to abortion rights voters in suburban Philadelphia. Casey won by a wide margin.

Schumer made a pitch over dinner in London to Claire McCaskill to compete in Missouri, where she had shown some strength in her losing 2004 gubernatorial race. She ran and won narrowly. He tried to recruit Rep. Jim Langevin to run in Rhode Island, and although he declined, Democrat Sheldon Whitehouse beat incumbent Lincoln Chafee there anyway. In Montana,

Schumer spent money on ads against incumbent Republican Conrad Burns, reminding voters that he had received more contributions from the clients of disgraced lobbyist Jack Abramoff than any other member of Congress. Democrat Jon Tester won that contest. In Virginia, Schumer backed Jim Webb, a decorated Vietnam veteran who served as President Ronald Reagan's Navy secretary, over liberal lobbyist Harris Miller, and Webb won a narrow victory in the primary and went on in the fall to defeat the heavily favored incumbent, Republican George Allen. During the campaign, Schumer wrote a book, *Positively American: Winning Back the Middle-Class Majority One Family at a Time*, in which he urged Democrats to offer 50% solutions—increase math and reading scores by 50%, cut property taxes by 50%, reduce illegal immigration by 50%, and so forth.

Schumer's success in helping to win a Democratic majority in 2006 led Reid to ask him to head the DSCC again in the 2008 election season. As an inducement, Reid created a leadership position for Schumer as vice chairman of the Democratic Caucus, although the new post did not come with a staff and a detailed portfolio. Schumer effectively became the confidential adviser to the hot-tempered and difficult Reid and the mellifluous and steady Majority Whip Dick Durbin. Once again he played a key role in producing winning candidates at election time. When Pete Domenici announced his retirement in New Mexico and second-tier Democratic candidates emerged, Schumer persuaded Rep. Tom Udall to run, and he won. Late in the election season, Schumer and Reid persuaded Anchorage Mayor Mark Begich to take on 40-year veteran Ted Stevens shortly before Stevens was indicted in July of failure to disclose receiving gifts. Begich won his seat, 48%-47%. In North Carolina, Schumer and former Gov. Jim Hunt pressed state Sen. Kay Hagan to take on incumbent Elizabeth Dole and helped Hagan wage an aggressive campaign that resulted in an impressive victory.

All told, Democrats picked up six seats in 2006 and seven in November 2008 while losing none of theirs. A 45-seat minority became a 58-seat majority. Seldom has one senator made such a difference in the partisan composition of the body. And seldom if ever has the No. 3 person in a party's leadership done as much to determine a major party's policy stands and political positioning in the Senate. As Republican John Cornyn of Texas said ruefully, but with admiration, "In my opinion, his influence is supreme. He's everywhere."

Schumer's position in New York politics is also paramount. When Hillary Rodham Clinton was elected senator in 2000, many thought that she would overshadow Schumer. The earthier Schumer seemed to get along better with Bush, while the more disciplined Clinton seemed to get along better with some Republican senators. And then there are the lifestyle differences. While Clinton held fundraisers in her $2.8 million house off Embassy Row, Schumer shared a spare Capitol Hill townhouse with Durbin and Democratic Reps. Bill Delahunt and George Miller. But Schumer supported Clinton's 2008 presidential campaign, and her appointment as secretary of State in the Obama administration made him indisputably New York's lead senator. When Clinton resigned her Senate seat, and Democratic Gov. David Paterson dithered over choosing a successor, Schumer weighed in on behalf of Rep. Kirsten Gillibrand. He then urged Reid to give her choice committee assignments and put her name on numerous press releases. At a Gillibrand fundraiser that spring, in response to speculation about primary opposition in the 2010 election, he yelled, "There is not going to be a primary!" When former Tennessee Rep. Harold Ford Jr. mulled making the race, Schumer interceded and helped persuade him not to run. As a result Gillibrand, had only desultory primary opposition and won the general election easily.

Schumer entered the 111th Congress (2009-10) in a strong position, having helped in a major way to secure what became, after the 2008 election, a filibuster-proof 60-seat majority, the first time in 30 years that any party had such a large Senate majority. He was heavily engaged in the major issues of the Congress. On President Barack Obama's health care initiative, he supported creating a government-run insurance option, but sensing that it lacked 60 votes, he worked with Republican moderate Olympia Snowe of Maine on a trigger mechanism that would create a public option only if private plans did not meet certain criteria. But those efforts failed to win Republican support and in September 2009, he dropped it. On the major overhaul of financial industry regulation, he pushed provisions to entirely fund the Securities and Exchange Commission through fees and fines rather than congressional appropriations and to give stockholders a non-binding vote on executive compensation.

Schumer has a longstanding interest in immigration policy reform, and although a comprehensive bill was not high on Obama's agenda, he worked in 2009 with Republican Lindsey Graham of South Carolina establishing agreement on concepts for later legislation, including stronger border and workplace enforcement, a guest worker program and a path to legalization for illegal immigrants in the country. After the Supreme Court overturned recent restrictions on campaign donations imposed by Congress in its *Citizens United* decision, Schumer, with Rep. Chris Van Hollen,

D-Md., sponsored the DISCLOSE Act to require disclosure by organizations covered by the decision. The bill passed the House, but in the Senate, Schumer could not satisfy liberals unhappy with the exemption the House carved out for the National Rifle Association, and the bill stalled.

On issues important to New York in recent years, Schumer in February 2010 opposed trying alleged September 11 conspirator Khalid Sheik Mohammed anywhere in New York. "My advice to the president is, with a great deal of respect, take New York off your radar screen. Find another location," he said. He was also the lead sponsor of a bill to compensate September 11 responders for health problems they later encountered.

Though he rarely took a lead position on foreign policy, he did show skepticism about Obama's 2009 troop increase in Afghanistan, telling MSNBC, "It cost us $6 trillion and 4,500 lives, approximately, to bring stability to Iraq. Just in terms of lives lost and treasure, do we want to do the same exercise in Afghanistan?" In May 2010, he was one of 18 senators voting for an amendment requiring a detailed timetable for troop withdrawals in Afghanistan.

Schumer was up for re-election in 2010, but the outcome was never in doubt. He raised $19 million and clobbered Republican Jay Townsend, the owner of a market research firm, 66%-32%. But he probably had his eye just as much on Nevada, where Reid trailed in polls for months. If Reid had lost, there may well have been a battle between Schumer and Durbin, his housemate and the majority whip, for the top leadership post. But Reid won and the issue became moot. Two weeks after the election, Reid assigned Schumer more legislative scheduling and communications duties.

Junior Senator

Kirsten Gillibrand (D)

Appointed Jan. 2009, term expires 2012, 1st full term; b. Dec. 9, 1966, Albany; home, Hudson; Dartmouth Col., A.B. 1988, U.C.L.A., J.D. 1991; Catholic; married (Jonathan); 2 children.

Elected Office: U.S. House of Reps., 2006-09

Professional Career: Practicing atty, 1991-2006; Special counsel, HUD, 2000.

DC Office: 478 RSOB, 20510, 202-224-4451; Fax: 202-228-0282; Web site: gillibrand.senate.gov.

State Offices: Albany, 518-431-0120; Buffalo, 716-854-9725; Hudson Valley, 845-875-4585; Long Island, 631-249-2825; New York City, 212-688-6262; North Country, 315-376-6118; Rochester, 585-263-6250; Syracuse, 315-448-0470; Westchester, 914-725-9294.

Committees: *Aging (Special). Agriculture, Nutrition & Forestry:* Commodities, Markets, Trade & Risk Management; Livestock, Dairy, Poultry, Marketing & Ag Research (Chmn); Nutrition, Specialty Crops, Food & Ag Research. *Armed Services:* Airland; Emerging Threats & Capabilities; Strategic Forces. *Environment & Public Works:* Children's Health & Environmental Responsibility ; Superfund, Toxics & Environmental Health; Water & Wildlife.

Group Ratings

	ACLU	ACU	ADA	CFG	AFS	FRC	LCV	ITIC	NTU	COC
2010	92	0	100	0	100	0	100	33	3	9
2009	–	0	90	3	100	–	100	–	6	50

National Journal Ratings

	2010 LIB	—	2010 CONS	2009 LIB	—	2009 CONS
Economic	85%	—	12%	88%	—	0%
Social	65%	—	0%	81%	—	18%
Foreign	47%	—	0%	55%	—	0%
Composite	81%	—	19%	84%	—	16%

Key Votes of the 111th Congress

1. Overturn Ledbetter	*	5. Pass health care bill	Y	9. Ratify New START	Y
2. Pass $787 billion stimulus	Y	6. Regulate financial firms	Y	10. Confirm Elena Kagan	Y
3. Repeal DC gun laws	N	7. Pass tax cuts for some	Y	11. Stop EPA climate regs	N
4. Confirm Sonia Sotomayor	Y	8. Legalize immigrants' kids	Y	12. Repeal don't ask, tell	Y

Election Results

2010 general	Kirsten Gillibrand (D)	2,837,684	(63%)	($13,418,545)
	Joseph DioGuardi (R)	1,582,693	(35%)	($2,384,584)
2010 primary	Kirsten Gillibrand (D)	464,512	(76%)	
	Gail Goode (D)	145,491	(24%)	

Prior Winning Percentages: House: 2008 (62%); 2006 (53%)

Democrat Kirsten Gillibrand is New York's junior senator. She had been in the House for just one term when Democratic Gov. David Paterson in 2009 appointed her to the Senate seat vacated by Secretary of State Hillary Rodham Clinton. After a bumpy beginning in the job, she began to earn respect for her tenacity, and won a 2010 special election with ease.

Gillibrand (*JILL-uh-brand*) hails from a politically sophisticated family. Her father, Douglas Rutnik, is an attorney and lobbyist who had close ties to Zenia Mucha, a top aide to former Republican Gov. George Pataki. Her grandmother, Polly Noonan, was a prominent Democratic activist in Albany and longtime companion of Albany Mayor Erastus Corning (1942-83). Her grandmother used to bring Gillibrand along with her on the campaign trail. Gillibrand attended the all-girls Emma Willard School in Troy and graduated from Dartmouth College, where she majored in Asian studies and attained fluency in Mandarin Chinese. She traveled widely, worked as a summer intern for Republican Sen. Alfonse D'Amato, graduated from law school at the University of California-Los Angeles, and did a United Nations internship in Vienna, Austria. After law school, Gillibrand clerked for a Reagan-appointed federal Appeals Court judge and served briefly as special counsel for Housing and Urban Development Secretary Andrew Cuomo. She then joined a major New York law firm, Boies, Schiller & Flexner. Gillibrand raised money for Clinton's first Senate campaign in 2000.

In 2005, she launched a quixotic campaign against four-term U.S. Rep. John Sweeney, a rising Republican star with a seat on the Appropriations Committee, who had never faced a serious re-election challenge. With hard work but also a lot of luck, Gillibrand won the seat. Although Sweeney was a strong incumbent, he developed some serious vulnerabilities during the campaign. He missed several weeks of House votes after he was hospitalized in February 2006 for the treatment of vasculitis, an inflammation of the blood vessels. He got negative press about a fundraising event in Utah that included a ski vacation and dinner at the home of a pharmaceutical lobbyist. In April 2006, there were more negative news stories, including accounts of Sweeney's visit to a college fraternity party. The state Democratic Party issued a press release asking, "What is a 50-year-old congressman doing at a frat party at 1 a.m.?"

Still, as late as August, polls showed Sweeney with a solid lead. He called Gillibrand a carpetbagger who lived not in the Hudson Valley-based congressional district but in a Manhattan highrise. He also accused her campaign of making anonymous and intimidating phone calls to his wife. He emphasized his independence from the unpopular Bush administration and contrasted his working-class background with Gillibrand's prep-school pedigree. Gillibrand did plenty of negative campaigning of her own. She demanded that Sweeney release police reports from two arrests in 1977 and 1978 and from a 2001 automobile accident; he called on her to release her income-tax returns. In October, it was revealed that Sweeney had traveled to the Northern Mariana Islands with Tony Rudy, an associate of disgraced lobbyist Jack Abramoff, who pleaded guilty to conspiracy charges in a scandal that involved several congressional junkets to the islands. Then, one week before the election, the Albany *Times Union* reported that Sweeney's wife had called local police in December 2005 to complain that the congressman was "knocking her around." Sweeney's campaign at first insisted that the police report on the incident was "false and concocted by our opposition," but he eventually conceded that state police were called to his home.

Sweeney spent $3.4 million to Gillibrand's $2.6 million. But in a year when Clinton and Democratic Gov. Eliot Spitzer were heading to landslide statewide victories and Republicans were dragged down by Bush, Gillibrand won 53%-47%.

When she arrived in the House, Gillibrand began posting a "Sunlight Report" of her daily schedule, including meetings with lobbyists. She held "office hours" in grocery stores throughout the district. She got the committee seats she wanted—on Agriculture and Armed Services. On the issue of Iraq, she voted for a nonbinding resolution calling for withdrawing troops but also for a bill providing funding for the war without a timetable for troop withdrawal. She cast conservative votes on gun-related issues, compiling a 100% score from the National Rifle Association. Gillibrand said she grew up in a family of hunters and kept two rifles under her bed and that she "always believed in protecting hunters' rights....It's a core value for our region and our state." She opposed driver's licenses for illegal immigrants and voted for a controversial bill granting immunity to telecommunications companies that had cooperated with government requests for warrantless surveillance of U.S. citizens' communications.

Defending the seat for the first time in 2008, Gillibrand did prodigious fundraising and collected $4.6 million. Her opponent was state Republican Chairman Sandy Treadwell, who spent nearly $6 million of his own money on his campaign. But Gillibrand's moderate-to-conservative stands on issues paid off. She won 62%-38%.

When Clinton was named President-elect Barack Obama's choice for secretary of State, Gillibrand was not the first person to spring to mind as a likely Clinton successor. Paterson considered appointing New York Attorney General Andrew Cuomo, which would have removed Cuomo as a possible primary opponent to Paterson in 2010. But Paterson also gave serious thought to appointing Caroline Kennedy, the daughter of the late president. But after Kennedy performed weakly in a series of upstate public appearances and in an interview with *The New York Times,* she withdrew. Two days later, Paterson announced that he was appointing Gillibrand, a surprise pick considering that several more-prominent political figures and more- senior House members were interested. But arguing in Gillibrand's favor was her moderate politics on some issues.

On Jan. 27, 2009, Gillibrand was sworn in as the youngest U.S. senator. She held early meetings with Paterson, Clinton, and Sen. Chuck Schumer, New York's senior senator and a member of the Democratic leadership. Soon afterward, Gillibrand began modifying some of her positions that were out of step with the party, particularly on gun control. "There're a lot of concerns in many of our city communities about gun violence, about keeping our children safe, and keeping guns out of the hands of criminals," she said. Gillibrand subsequently opposed Senate amendments that would have allowed licensed gun owners to carry concealed firearms across state lines and repealed the District of Columbia's tough gun laws.

But she had to contend with a variety of unwanted developments. *The New York Times* published an unflattering front-page article in March 2009 that said Gillibrand, as a lawyer for Philip Morris in 1996, helped defend the tobacco company against allegations that it lied about the existence of internal research on the health effects of smoking. Within weeks of her appointment, news stories began appearing about potential Democratic primary challengers, including Democratic Reps. Carolyn Maloney and Steve Israel and Manhattan Borough President Scott Stringer. By January 2010, an even more prominent possible opponent surfaced—former Tennessee Rep. Harold Ford, who had moved to New York three years earlier to become an adviser to Merrill Lynch after losing a bid for a Senate seat in his home state. A savvy and ambitious centrist, he called on her to drop her support for health care legislation and questioned whether she was independent enough to represent the state.

Gillibrand, however, had two powerful patrons—Schumer and Obama. They personally lobbied would-be challengers to give her a clear path to the nomination. At the same time, Schumer—who was known for being less than thrilled at having to often share the spotlight with Clinton—seemed to delight in taking his new colleague under his wing. He pressed Senate leaders to give her the committee assignments she desired, put her name next to his on project funding announcements in the state and introduced her to deep-pocketed Democratic donors. "He does look after me in a lot of ways," Gillibrand told *The Times* in May 2009.

Ford initially was undaunted by such strong support, saying he would not be "bullied or intimidated" by "party bosses." He and Gillibrand traded barbs in the news media throughout the early months of 2009 while he traveled the state. Nevertheless, in early March, he announced that he, too, would not run. He said he had "examined this race in every possible way," but arrived at the conclusion that a divisive, costly and negative primary would only benefit the Republicans.

Gillibrand turned her full focus to legislating. The reauthorization of the Child Nutrition Act, passed into law in the lame-duck session of 2010, included a number of her proposals, such as banning junk food from schools while establishing nutritional standards for other schools. She worked to win a ban on drop-side cribs that were blamed for causing 32 infant deaths. She joined with several senators to get a bipartisan bill through committee requiring senators to post online their earmark requests for home-state funding projects. Meanwhile, she was able to banish any remaining doubts among Democrats about whether she was a reliable vote. In 2010, according to the *National Journal's* rankings, she was tied with Schumer as the 10th most liberal member of the Senate.

The issue that brought Gillibrand the most attention by far was her call for repeal of the 17-year-old "don't ask, don't tell" policy barring openly gay military service members. She introduced legislation in July 2009 at a time when interest in the issue was lagging—its leading champion, Sen. Edward Kennedy of Massachusetts, was dying of cancer. In subsequent months, she lobbied former House colleagues as well as fellow senators, pushed for hearings and set up a website featuring videos of gay and lesbian veterans telling their stories. "If you care about national security, if you care about our military readiness, then you will repeal this corrosive policy," she said in an emotional floor speech shortly before it passed the Senate. It became law soon thereafter, earning her widespread praise from progressive and gay rights groups.

Gillibrand's poll numbers remained lackluster throughout 2009, giving some Republicans hope for the 2010 special election for the remainder of Clinton's term, which was to be held concurrently with the general election. But by April 2010, Gillibrand had amassed a $6 million war chest, and GOP luminaries like former New York Mayor Rudy Giuliani and former Gov. George Pataki took a pass. She easily dispatched primary challenger Gail Goode, a New York lawyer. In the general election, her opponent was former Rep. Joseph DioGuardi, an accountant from Westchester County. He assailed her support for the economic stimulus bill and other Democratic priorities while blaming her for being unable to prevent the state from losing jobs. But he remained unknown throughout much of the state, and Gillibrand coasted to re-election 63%-35%. She will be on the ballot again in 2012 for a full six-year term.

FIRST DISTRICT

Tim Bishop (D)

Elected 2002, 5th term; b. June 1, 1950, Southampton; home, Southampton; Holy Cross Col., A.B. 1972; Long Island U., M.P.A. 1981; Catholic; married (Kathryn); 2 children.

Professional Career: Admin., Southampton College, 1973-2002.

DC Office: 306 CHOB, 20515, 202-225-3826; Fax: 202-225-3143; Web site: timbishop.house.gov.

State Offices: Coram, 631-696-6500; Southampton, 631-259-8450.

Committees: *Education & the Workforce:* Higher Education & Workforce Training; Workforce Protections. *Transportation & Infrastructure:* Coast Guard & Maritime Transportation; Railroads, Pipelines & Hazardous Materials; Water Resources & Environment (RMM).

Group Ratings

	ACLU	ACU	ADA	CFG	AFS	FRC	LCV	ITIC	NTU	COC
2010	87	0	95	0	100	0	100	100	6	25
2009	–	0	100	4	100	–	100	–	3	33

National Journal Ratings

	2010 LIB — 2010 CONS		2009 LIB — 2009 CONS	
Economic	78%	— 20%	64%	— 34%
Social	76%	— 23%	75%	— 20%
Foreign	63%	— 37%	67%	— 31%
Composite	73%	— 27%	70%	— 30%

Key Votes of the 111th Congress

1. Overturn Ledbetter	Y	5. Bar federal abortion funds	N	9. Stop detainee transfers	Y
2. Pass $820 billion stimulus	Y	6. Pass health care bill	Y	10. Legalize immigrants' kids	Y
3. Let guns in national parks	N	7. Regulate financial firms	Y	11. Repeal don't ask, tell	Y
4. Pass cap-and-trade	Y	8. Pass tax cuts for some	Y	12. Limit campaign funds	Y

Election Results

2010 general	Tim Bishop (D)	98,316	(50.15%)	($3,066,831)
	Randy Altschuler (R)	97,723	(49.85%)	($5,722,691)
2010 primary	Tim Bishop (D)	unopposed		

Prior Winning Percentages: 2008 (58%), 2006 (62%), 2004 (56%), 2002 (50%)

Population		Race/Ethnicity		Work	
Pop. 2010:	705,559	White:	77.9%	Private:	74.5%
Change since 2000:	Up 7.8%	Black:	4.5%	Government:	19.9%
Urban:	94.0%	Hispanic:	12.6%	Self-employed:	5.5%
Rural:	6.0%	Asian:	3.2%	Blue collar:	18.1%
Area size:	1,945 sq. mi.	Native Am.:	0.2%	White collar:	65.2%
		Hawaiian:	0.0%	Khaki collar:	0.1%
Age		Two+ races:	1.3%	Other:	16.6%
Median age:	39.7 yrs.				
More than 65 yrs:	13.4%	*Ancestry*		Median income:	$82,968
Less than 18 yrs:	23.9%	Italian	22.1%	Median Home Value:	$417,800
		Irish	18.6%		
Education		German	13.3%	**Military Veterans**	
H.S. grad:	90.9%			% of Pop:	9.0%
College grad:	32.3%				
Grad degree:	14.9%				

East Long Island; Suffolk County

Long Island—"the Island" to most New Yorkers—is the largest and most populous island in the mainland United States. It stretches 103 miles, from the two-century-old Montauk Point lighthouse on a crumbling bluff to Fort Hamilton at the foot of the Verrazano-Narrows Bridge. Ranging from 12 to 20 miles wide, Long Island is ringed by gentle hills and cliffs above Long Island Sound and sand-spit beaches that front the Atlantic Ocean. Including the populations of

2008 Presidential Vote		
Barack Obama (D)	165,805	(52%)
John McCain (R)	153,419	(48%)

2004 Presidential Vote		
George Bush (R)	154,249	(49%)
John Kerry (D)	152,165	(49%)

Cook Partisan Voting Index: EVEN

Brooklyn and Queens, some 7.5 million people live on Long Island, more than in all but 12 states. Brooklyn, at the island's western end, is urban and thickly settled, while the Hamptons in the east are carefully manicured countryside, preserved as a playground for the New York elite. Demographically, the Hamptons are only a small part of Long Island. More important economically are the suburbs created in the post-World War II migration out of the city.

Developers looking for cheaper land for aircraft factories, shopping centers, subdivisions, and office parks found them first in Nassau County, just east of Queens, and then farther out in Suffolk County. Suffolk attracted young families of Irish and Italian descent looking for more space and less crime. More recently the county has been attracting Latinos, who are now 13% of the population and include Salvadorans and Puerto Ricans in lower-income areas. Over the past 30 years, the island's economy soured as defense plants were decimated by the end of the Cold War, cost overruns on nuclear plants led to electricity rate increases, and young people fled older suburbs for jobs elsewhere. The Long Island Power Authority wants to build wind farms and run underwater cables from Connecticut to bring more energy across Long Island Sound, though it appears unlikely to happen before 2016. High taxes and expensive housing remain endemic problems; nearly a third of the region's homes cost more than $500,000.

The 1st Congressional District of New York consists of the eastern end of Long Island and covers eastern Suffolk County. It runs as far west as Smithtown on the North Shore and Patchogue on the South Shore. It includes Shelter Island, located between the north and south forks of Long Island's "fishtail," and Plum Island, which houses the nation's only animal infection research site, scheduled to be closed in 2015 and replaced by a lab in Kansas. A few farmers remain on Long Island, where they grow sweet corn and pumpkins. There are also more than 35 wineries along one 20-mile stretch. The 1st District includes two areas frequented in the summer by urban sophisticates: the Hamptons, with their extravagant prices, and most of Fire Island National Seashore, the only federal wilderness area in New York state and a magnet for gay vacationers for decades. The district also includes Brookhaven National Laboratory, a physics research lab, and the defense plants in the center of the Island. Suffolk County was long one of the most conservative parts of New York, though not very conservative by today's national standards. Republican voter registration remains robust, despite the district's trending Democratic in recent presidential elections. The district voted solidly for Democrat Al Gore in 2000 but swung narrowly to Republican George W. Bush in 2004—a September 11 effect. It narrowly backed Democratic nominee Barack Obama in 2008.

Tim Bishop (D)

The representative from the 1st District is Tim Bishop, a Democrat first elected in 2002. He grew up in Southampton, the son of a telephone lineman, and graduated from Holy Cross College and Long Island University. He spent his entire professional career at Southampton College, where he began in 1973 as an admissions counselor and by 1986 had become provost. He chaired the town of Southampton's Board of Ethics and was on the board of the Eastern Long Island Coastal Conservation Alliance. Few paid much attention when Bishop announced he would oppose Rep. Felix Grucci, the first-term Republican who had won the seat in 2000 from Mike Forbes, who alienated voters by switching from the Republican Party to become a Democrat. The turn of events allowed Grucci to easily win the general election, 56%-41%.

Grucci seemed headed for re-election in 2002 when, in late September, he ran an ad accusing Bishop of falsifying rape statistics at Southampton College and "turning his back on rape victims." The allegations, based on inaccurate college newspaper stories, were false. Grucci's campaign refused to repudiate the ad, on the ground that no correction had ever appeared in print. National Democrats saw an opportunity to pick up a seat, and soon the airwaves were saturated with ads attacking Grucci both for the rape commercial and in one spot linking the Grucci family's famed fireworks enterprise to chemical contamination of local drinking water. Bishop won 50%-49%.

In the House, Bishop compiled a voting record near the center of House Democrats, becoming more of a loyalist in recent years. After the shooting of Arizona Democrat Gabrielle Giffords in January 2011, he was among the Democrats to quickly cosponsor legislation to limit gun clip sizes to 10 rounds. His initial vote on health care in 2009 enraged some constituents and led him to cancel town hall meetings; after one particularly emotional session, he needed a police escort back to his car. But he still backed the final bill.

With his extensive background in academia, he played a leading role on the Education and Labor Committee in the 2008 higher education bill that enacted spending increases for colleges and universities. And he has championed more federal funding to help schools adapt to the demands of the 2001 No Child Left Behind law. With California Democrat Hilda Solis, he won passage of an amendment in 2005 to bar the Environmental Protection Agency from testing pesticides on humans. And the House passed his bill in April 2010 to implement management plans for 28 estuaries. One of his key issues is adjusting the alternative minimum tax to stop it from ensnaring middle-class taxpayers along with wealthy taxpayers with myriad tax shelters who are its actual target.

On local issues, Bishop successfully fought proposed cutbacks at Brookhaven and sought funds for a third track on the Long Island Railroad. Like other members of Congress representing vacation spots, he has sought to increase seasonal worker visas. Mindful of the high turnover rate in the district in recent years, Bishop has paid close attention to constituent services. In February 2011, he unsuccessfully tried to cancel money for the National Bio and Agro-Defense Facility in Kansas, which is replacing his district's Plum Island animal disease research center. Not surprisingly, the move drew an angry response from Rep. Lynn Jenkins, R-Kan.

Republicans have made Bishop a prime target in the past, but have not succeeded in dislodging him. In 2004, their nominee was Bill Manger, a Southampton village trustee who emphasized his independence from national Republicans and attacked Bishop for opposing tax cuts. But Bishop won handily, 56%-44%. After that, he barely broke a sweat against opponents who were too conservative for the area.

But his 2010 race was among the year's most suspenseful. GOP nominee Randy Altschuler, a wealthy businessman, ran as a stringent fiscal conservative. Bishop accused him of outsourcing jobs overseas, and his negative ratings were higher than nearly any other challenger in the country. One poll in mid-October showed Bishop with a double-digit lead. But Altschuler had the funding to compete, spending more than $4 million of his own money to easily outdistance Bishop's $3.1 million.

On Election Night, Bishop led the race by about 3,500 votes out of more than 180,000 cast. However, underreporting and other serious mistakes were uncovered in almost 40% of election districts, shrinking Bishop's lead to 383 votes. The recount dragged on for weeks, with Altschuler citing voter registration irregularities. More than a month after the election, Bishop maintained a 263-vote edge, and Altschuler finally conceded.

SECOND DISTRICT

Steve Israel (D)

Elected 2000, 6th term; b. May 30, 1958, Brooklyn; home, Dix Hills; George Wash. U., B.A. 1983; Jewish; married (Marlene Budd); 2 children.

Elected Office: Huntington Town Council, 1993-2000, Maj. ldr., 1997-2000.

Professional Career: Legis. asst., U.S. Rep. Richard Ottinger, 1980-83; Fundraising dir., Touro Law Ctr., 1985-88; Pres., Steve Israel Assoc., Inc., 1992-98; Pres. & CEO, Inst. on Holocaust and Law, 1998-2000.

DC Office: 2457 RHOB, 20515, 202-225-3335; Fax: 202-225-4669; Web site: israel.house.gov.

State Offices: Long Island, 631-951-2210.

Group Ratings

	ACLU	ACU	ADA	CFG	AFS	FRC	LCV	ITIC	NTU	COC
2010	88	0	90	0	100	0	100	100	6	25
2009	–	0	95	0	100	–	100	–	2	33

National Journal Ratings

	2010 LIB — 2010 CONS		2009 LIB — 2009 CONS	
Economic	78% —	20%	62% —	36%
Social	71% —	25%	82% —	17%
Foreign	63% —	35%	91% —	0%
Composite	72% —	28%	80% —	20%

Key Votes of the 111th Congress

1. Overturn Ledbetter	Y	5. Bar federal abortion funds	N
2. Pass $820 billion stimulus	Y	6. Pass health care bill	Y
3. Let guns in national parks	N	7. Regulate financial firms	Y
4. Pass cap-and-trade	Y	8. Pass tax cuts for some	Y

9. Stop detainee transfers	Y
10. Legalize immigrants' kids	Y
11. Repeal don't ask, tell	Y
12. Limit campaign funds	Y

Election Results

2010 general	Steve Israel (D)	94,694	(56%)	($2,547,657)
	John Gomez (R)	72,115	(43%)	($404,965)
2010 primary	Steve Israel (D)	unopposed		

Prior Winning Percentages: 2008 (67%), 2006 (70%), 2004 (67%), 2002 (58%), 2000 (48%)

Population		Race/Ethnicity		Work	
Pop. 2010:	679,893	White:	62.9%	Private:	79.1%
Change since 2000:	Up 3.9%	Black:	9.8%	Government:	15.9%
Urban:	99.7%	Hispanic:	21.0%	Self-employed:	4.8%
Rural:	0.3%	Asian:	4.6%	Blue collar:	18.0%
Area size:	330 sq. mi.	Native Am.:	0.2%	White collar:	66.0%
		Hawaiian:	0.0%	Khaki collar:	0.1%
Age		Two+ races:	1.4%	Other:	15.9%
Median age:	39.3 yrs.				
More than 65 yrs:	12.7%	*Ancestry*		Median income:	$91,515
Less than 18 yrs:	25.5%	Italian	19.4%	Median Home Value:	$456,300
		Irish	14.4%		
Education		German	11.0%	**Military Veterans**	
H.S. grad:	88.2%			% of Pop:	7.4%
College grad:	34.2%				
Grad degree:	14.8%				

Central Long Island; Brentwood

Shortly after World War II, hundreds of thousands of New York City residents, many of them young veterans and their families, moved to detached suburban houses built on the former potato fields of central Long Island. Those in the first wave of postwar migration settled in Nassau County, and they included a cross-section of all but the poorest New Yorkers. About half were Catholic, a quarter Protestant, and a quarter Jewish. As Long Island developed its own employment base, another wave moved farther east into Suffolk County. This group was more Catholic, less Jewish, and more blue-collar. Ancestrally Democratic, these voters were culturally conservative, and in the 1970s and 1980s, they tended to vote Republican. Since then, voters in Suffolk County have joined the rest of the New York metro area in shunning the Republican Party as it has increasingly moved to the right.

2008 Presidential Vote		
Barack Obama (D)	164,106	(56%)
John McCain (R)	125,978	(43%)
2004 Presidential Vote		
John Kerry (D)	148,625	(53%)
George Bush (R)	127,626	(45%)
Cook Partisan Voting Index: D+4		

The 2nd Congressional District of New York includes most of western Suffolk County, part of the town of Islip and a small portion of Nassau County—Plainview, Woodbury, and part of Jericho. For the most part, the 2nd is the humbler part of Long Island: farther east than most of the fashionable commuter suburbs, well south of the picturesque North Shore, not as far east as the ritzy Hamptons, and, aside from a handful of ferry-only resort towns on Fire Island, located inland from the southern shore. The area boasts numerous technology companies and is the headquarters for such large firms as Arrow Electronics in Melville and Standard Microsystems in Hauppage. It generally has fared well economically—the unemployment rate in Suffolk was more than 1 percentage point below New York City's in late 2010.

With some of the lowest-priced housing on the island, this area has been attracting minorities and immigrants. Brentwood, settled in 1851 as part of a free-love social experiment that lasted 13 years, is now more than half Hispanic, including Puerto Ricans, Salvadorans, Guatemalans and Mexicans. Illegal immigration has been a divisive issue in Suffolk. Historically Republican, the 2nd District has not voted for a Republican presidential nominee since 1992. In 2008, Democrat Barack Obama won it with 56% of the vote.

Steve Israel (D)

The congressman from the 2nd District is Steve Israel, a Democrat first elected in 2000. Amiable, ambitious and an able fundraiser, he is the current chairman of the Democratic Congressional Campaign Committee, with the formidable challenge of leading his party back to majority status in 2012.

Israel grew up in Wantagh and graduated from George Washington University in 1983. While in college, he worked full-time on Capitol Hill, first doing constituent work for Democratic Rep. Robert Matsui of California, and then as a legislative assistant for Rep. Richard Ottinger of New York, also a Democrat. After college, Israel returned to Long Island, where he was Suffolk director for the American Jewish Congress, fundraising director for Touro Law School, and assistant for intergovernmental relations to Suffolk County Executive Patrick Halpin. Then he started his own public relations and marketing firm and was president of the Institute on the Holocaust and the Law. In 1993, Israel was the only Democrat elected to the Huntington Town Council, where he built a reputation as a bipartisan leader who helped revive the town's finances.

After U.S. Rep. Rick Lazio announced he was running for the Senate, Israel ran for the moderate Republican's seat. He eked out a 45%-41% victory in the Democratic primary. In the general election, he faced Republican Joan Johnson, who had a compelling life story as a 66-year-old who grew up under segregation, moved to New York to become a schoolteacher, and later was elected town clerk of Islip. But despite help from Lazio, Johnson was a disappointing candidate and ran an ad, which she was forced to pull, wrongly attacking Israel for voting to raise taxes. Israel won by a surprisingly easy 48%-35%.

His voting record was moderate in his early years, but more recently he has been a reliable Democrat. In an early sign of his dexterity with House politics, he was elected as the freshman representative to the Democratic Steering Committee, which makes all-important committee assignments. Israel joined the fiscally conservative Blue Dog Coalition and was one of 28 House Democrats who voted for President George W. Bush's tax cuts in 2001. Israel supported the use of force in Iraq but later said that the case for war was based on a "false pretense." After irritating Democratic leaders by voting in 2002 for a Republican prescription drug bill, which increased annual Medicare payments on Long Island, Israel redeemed himself with his party by voting against the GOP's major bill creating a Medicare prescription drug benefit in 2003.

Israel believes that national Democrats can learn something from the successes of centrist Democrats on Long Island. They prevailed locally, he said, by taking positions that protected national security, balanced government budgets, and championed civil and human rights. The party icon, Israel added, should be former Sen. Scoop Jackson of Washington, a defense hawk in the 1960s and 1970s, whose views are hardly in today's Democratic mainstream. In internal party politics, he favored Maryland's Steny Hoyer over California's Nancy Pelosi for minority whip as Pelosi was beginning her climb up the leadership. Pelosi went on to become House speaker, and in the minority, she is the Democratic leader.

In 2007, Israel snagged a seat on the powerful House Appropriations Committee, a sign that he had mended fences with Pelosi. On the committee, he promoted international human rights and pushed for additional funds for renewable energy. Israel joined the select intelligence oversight panel on Appropriations, where he voiced concern about the anti-Israel views of Charles Freeman, who was nominated to chair President Barack Obama's National Intelligence Council. Under pressure, Freeman withdrew. In 2010, Israel called for "a new federalism" through the revival of the U.S. Advisory Commission on Intergovernmental Relations, a bipartisan panel of people from all levels of government that tackled vexing issues until it ended in 1996.

Lazio decided, rather late, against a rematch in 2002. Local Republicans grumbled about his delay in deciding, and quietly threw in the towel. Israel won 58%-40%, and since then, he has become increasingly secure in the seat. After Sen. Hillary Rodham Clinton resigned to become secretary of State in 2009, Israel was among the names discussed as a possible successor. But he did not line up as well in polling as others considered by then Gov. David Paterson, including U.S. Rep. Kirsten Gillibrand, who got the appointment. Disappointed, Israel talked openly about challenging Gillibrand in the 2010 Democratic primary for the Senate seat, but agreed to stay out after a personal appeal from Obama. In the House, he won additional assignments, including as head of candidate recruiting for the DCCC in the 2009-10 election cycle.

After Democrats lost control of the House in November 2010, Pelosi picked Israel for the DCCC chairmanship ahead of other on-the-rise Democrats such as New York's Joe Crowley and Florida's Debbie Wasserman Schultz. The move reflected her confidence in Israel's fundraising skills—he reportedly brought in more than $1.9 million for the committee. With a presidential election in 2012 and about two dozen Democratic-controlled Senate seats up for grabs, the DCCC will have to compete against other party organizations for funding. The committee also had racked up at least $17 million in debts going into 2011. Israel exuded confidence in his early months on the job, noting that if the party could win the 14 districts that went for John Kerry in 2004 and Obama in 2008, it would be more than halfway to majority status. "We have a wind at our back," he told *The Washington Post.* But redistricting in GOP-controlled legislatures is expected to put some Democrats at a serious disadvantage.

THIRD DISTRICT

Pete King (R)

Elected 1992, 10th term; b. April 5, 1944, Manhattan; home, Seaford; St. Francis Col., B.A. 1965, U. of Notre Dame, J.D. 1968; Catholic; married (Rosemary); 2 children.

Military Career: Army Natl. Guard, 1968–73.

Elected Office: Hempstead Town Cncl., 1977–81; Nassau Cnty. comptroller, 1981–92.

Professional Career: Practicing atty., 1968–72, 1978–81; Dep. atty., Nassau Cnty., 1972–74; Exec. asst., Nassau Cnty. exec., 1974–76, Gen. cnsl., comptroller, 1977.

DC Office: 339 CHOB, 20515, 202-225-7896; Fax: 202-226-2279; Web site: peteking.house.gov.

State Offices: Massapequa Park, 516-541-4225; Suffolk County, 631-541-4225.

Committees: *Financial Services:* Capital Markets and Government Sponsored Enterprises; Oversight & Investigations. *Homeland Security* (Chmn). *Permanent Select Committee on Intelligence:* Terrorism, HUMINT, Analysis & Counterintelligence.

Group Ratings

	ACLU	ACU	ADA	CFG	AFS	FRC	LCV	ITIC	NTU	COC
2010	6	92	10	89	13	87	10	33	81	100
2009	–	88	20	67	33	–	36	–	61	93

National Journal Ratings

	2010 LIB	—	2010 CONS	2009 LIB	—	2009 CONS
Economic	33%	—	67%	34%	—	65%
Social	31%	—	67%	33%	—	65%
Foreign	38%	—	61%	37%	—	63%
Composite	35%	—	66%	35%	—	65%

Key Votes of the 111th Congress

1. Overturn Ledbetter	N	5. Bar federal abortion funds	Y	9. Stop detainee transfers	*
2. Pass $820 billion stimulus	N	6. Pass health care bill	N	10. Legalize immigrants' kids	N
3. Let guns in national parks	Y	7. Regulate financial firms	N	11. Repeal don't ask, tell	N
4. Pass cap-and-trade	N	8. Pass tax cuts for some	N	12. Limit campaign funds	N

Election Results

2010 general	Pete King (R)	131,674	(72%)	($1,713,817)
	Howard Kudler (D)	51,346	(28%)	($83,541)
2010 primary	Pete King (R)	21,915	(91%)	
	Robert Previdi (R)	2,231	(9%)	

Prior Winning Percentages: 2008 (64%), 2006 (56%), 2004 (63%), 2002 (72%), 2000 (60%), 1998 (64%), 1996 (55%), 1994 (59%), 1992 (50%)

Population		Race/Ethnicity		Work	
Pop. 2010:	645,508	White:	80.7%	Private:	76.0%
Change since 2000:	Down 1.4%	Black:	2.9%	Government:	18.8%
Urban:	99.6%	Hispanic:	10.1%	Self-employed:	5.0%
Rural:	0.4%	Asian:	4.9%	Blue collar:	14.6%
Area size:	393 sq. mi.	Native Am.:	0.1%	White collar:	70.6%
		Hawaiian:	0.0%	Khaki collar:	0.1%
Age		Two+ races:	1.1%	Other:	14.7%
Median age:	42.6 yrs.				
More than 65 yrs:	15.8%	*Ancestry*		Median income:	$91,458
Less than 18 yrs:	22.5%	Italian	24.1%	Median Home Value:	$472,500
		Irish	18.7%		
Education		German	12.7%	**Military Veterans**	
H.S. grad:	92.4%			% of Pop:	8.3%
College grad:	37.1%				
Grad degree:	15.6%				

Long Island; Nassau County

September 1947 was a pivotal moment in American history: 300 families moved into 750-square-foot houses that sold for $6,990, with no money down for veterans. The location was Levittown—America's first mass-produced suburb, where delivery trucks dropped off piles of prefabricated materials 60 feet apart, to be picked up by roving teams of specialized workers with power tools. By the time the final house was sold for $9,500 in November 1951, Levittown, a former

2008 Presidential Vote		
John McCain (R) 164,682	(52%)
Barack Obama (D) 149,995	(47%)
2004 Presidential Vote		
George Bush (R) 162,181	(52%)
John Kerry (D) 147,317	(47%)
Cook Partisan Voting Index: R+4		

potato field, had become synonymous with instant suburbanization. Southern State Parkway, the road that drew New York City's working- and middle-class families out to Long Island, was originally constructed in the 1920s by the legendary city builder Robert Moses as a way of linking New Yorkers, at least those affluent enough to own a car, with the newly constructed Jones Beach State Park. Three decades later, Moses widened the parkway to accommodate the growing ranks of long-distance commuters who populated Long Island's bedroom communities and worked in New York City. More than a half-century later, aging Nassau County is all but built out and is sometimes referred to as the nation's "first mature suburb." Its population, 450,000 in 1940, zoomed to 1.4 million in 1970. In recent years, it has stabilized at 1.3 million.

As the prototype suburb, Nassau County created what may have been the nation's premier county Republican machine. Among other pols, it produced three-term Sen. Alfonse D'Amato, a former Hempstead supervisor. The GOP-run county government, which was one of the highest-salaried, highest-spending in America, thrived until the late 1990s, when fiscal laxity dropped the county's credit rating to near junk-bond status despite tax rates that were among the highest in the country. Voters rebelled in 1999, by giving Democrats their first-ever majority in the county legislature, and in 2001, by electing Democrat Thomas Suozzi as county executive. He shook up the local government and agreed to abide by the bipartisan legislative majority. But by 2011, the county was back in financial trouble. Even though its malls and retail districts generate about $1 billion annually in sales taxes, and its communities add about $800 million in property taxes, the county was unwilling to cut services or raise taxes. As a result, a state oversight board seized control of Nassau's finances, only to have the county file suit to block the takeover.

The 3rd Congressional District of New York includes roughly half of Nassau County. It covers much of the southern shoreline of Long Island, taking in the old railroad resort of Long Beach, plus Baldwin, Merrick, and Massapequa in Nassau County; and Amityville, Lindenhurst, most of Babylon, Bay Shore, and Islip in Suffolk County. Nearly one-fourth of the district's population lives in Suffolk County. The district runs north all the way to Long Island Sound, where old estates—including Sagamore Hill, the home Theodore Roosevelt built on Cold Spring Harbor in 1885—alternate with more modest homes and newer subdivisions. Most of the people in the district live in towns strung along either side of Sunrise Highway or just off the Southern and Northern State parkways: Levittown, Syosset, Hicksville, which is home to musician Billy Joel, and Bethpage, where a major Northrop Grumman facility was under investigation in 2011 for chemical groundwater contamination. For a district so close to New York City, its minority population remains low—blacks were just 3% of the population in 2010. Although few of Greater New York's wealthiest live in the 3rd District, the overall level of affluence is high. Al Gore carried the district 52%-44% in 2000, but it broke for President George W. Bush in 2004, 52%-47%. In 2008, John McCain beat Barack Obama by an identical 52%-47%.

Peter King (R)

The congressman from the 3rd District is Peter King, a Republican first elected in 1992 who has gone from being known mainly as a loquacious maverick to becoming a serious counterweight to the Obama administration on domestic security matters.

King grew up in Sunnyside, Queens. His parents were Irish immigrants and Democrats, his father a New York City police detective. He went to St. Francis College and law school at the University of Notre Dame, and he clerked one summer at former Republican President Richard Nixon's law firm with a Long Islander named Rudolph Giuliani. After law school, he followed the trek to the suburbs and became part of the Nassau County Republican machine. He worked as a lawyer and staffer in county government beginning in 1972, and in 1981, he became county comptroller. When 22-year Republican Rep. Norman Lent retired in 1992, King ran for the seat and won the

Republican primary. In the general election, King ran as a fiscal conservative, and abortion rights opponent. He won by just 50%-46%, but hasn't had a close re-election since.

King's voting record ranks him near the ideological center of the House. He is more conservative on foreign policy than on economic or social issues, but with distinctive interests. He opposes racial quotas and preferences, bilingual education, and gun regulation. He supports English-only laws and opposes aid to illegal immigrants. He has been an ardent supporter of the Irish Republican Army. Within days of his election in 1992, he flew to Belfast to meet with leaders of Sinn Fein, the IRA's political arm, and he had a role in 1998 peace negotiations, carrying messages between the IRA and the Irish government. His activism on the issue led to an unusually close bipartisan relationship with President Bill Clinton, who helped broker the agreement. But in 2005, after Sinn Fein's suspected involvement in a bank robbery and a highly publicized murder, King called for the IRA to disband.

Over the years, King has been a provocative presence on radio and television chat shows. He also gained attention with three novels about politics and diplomacy in Northern Ireland. In one of them, *Deliver Us From Evil*, a thinly disguised Long Island congressman is the protagonist. "Maybe after I retire from Congress, or get thrown out of Congress, or whatever, I'll be a writer because as I've seen from some newspaper columnists, almost anyone can be a writer," he told the *Long Island Sentinel.*

After the September 11 attacks, in which 160 of his constituents died, King became more of a Republican Party regular and focused on legislation to prevent a repeat of the attacks. In 2005, GOP leaders tapped King to be chairman of the Homeland Security Committee. The following year, he was the first House Republican to attack the Bush administration's plan to give control of six major U.S. ports to a company in Dubai in the United Arab Emirates, and he subsequently helped to enact tighter controls on port security.

In 2009, he bucked his friends in organized labor by opposing their "card-check" bill to facilitate union organizing. King originally supported the controversial bill but cited "the most severe economic crisis in 75 years" to explain his switch. At the same time, he showed his willingness to anger conservatives with his promise to introduce gun safety legislation following the shooting of Arizona Democratic Rep. Gabrielle Giffords in January 2011 at a constituent event in her district.

After President Barack Obama's election, King further sharpened his rhetoric on terrorist threats. He told *Newsday* in December 2009 that the president was not tough enough on Muslim extremists: "Part of his liberal DNA is that he does not want to use the word 'terrorism' unless he absolutely has to," he said. He said excessive concerns about discrimination against Muslims had hamstrung authorities in the case of Army Maj. Nidal Malik Hasan, who allegedly went on a killing rampage at Fort Hood in Texas. When the Homeland Security Department published a report in April 2009 about domestic right-wing extremism, King complained that the agency "has never put out a report talking about 'Look out for mosques.'" The Council on American-Islamic Relations called his remarks "bigoted."

After Republicans regained control of the House in 2010, King decided to pursue hearings on what he described as "the radicalization of the American Muslim community and homegrown terrorism." Islamic leaders said they feared a witch hunt, and King acknowledged that his stance carried risks. "It is controversial," he told *The New York Times.* "But to me, it is something that has to be discussed." The hearings opened in March 2011 amid massive publicity and heightened round-the-clock security for the congressman after reports of threats against him. Some Muslim groups accused him of a double standard in his fervent support of the IRA. King responded, "The fact is, the IRA never attacked the United States. And my loyalty is to the United States."

As one of the few remaining moderate Republicans in Congress, King has occasionally been held up in GOP circles as an example of how the party can make inroads in Democratic territory the Northeast. Freshman Nassau County legislator David Mejias, a Democrat, ran against King in 2006 with an endorsement from the AFL-CIO. In an otherwise dismal year for New York Republicans, King won 56%-44%. He also had easy wins in 2008 and 2010, but national and New York Democrats have publicly vowed to redraw his district following the 2010 census. He considered challenging Democratic Sen. Kirsten Gillibrand in 2010, but said that he would have had a hard time raising enough money to compete with her.

FOURTH DISTRICT

Carolyn McCarthy (D)

Elected 1996, 8th term; b. Jan. 5, 1944, Brooklyn; home, Mineola; Glen Cove Nursing Schl., L.P.N. 1964; Catholic; widowed; 1 child.

Professional Career: Nurse, 1964–93; Gun control activist, 1993–96.

DC Office: 2346 RHOB, 20515, 202-225-5516; Fax: 202-225-5758; Web site: carolynmccarthy.house.gov.

State Offices: Garden City, 516-739-3008.

Committees: *Education & the Workforce:* Early Childhood, Elementary & Secondary Education; Health, Employment, Labor & Pensions. *Financial Services:* Financial Institutions & Consumer Credit; International Monetary Policy & Trade (RMM).

Group Ratings

	ACLU	ACU	ADA	CFG	AFS	FRC	LCV	ITIC	NTU	COC
2010	85	4	80	3	100	6	100	100	5	17
2009	–	0	95	8	100	–	93	–	4	40

National Journal Ratings

	2010 LIB	—	2010 CONS	2009 LIB	—	2009 CONS
Economic	82%	—	17%	66%	—	33%
Social	59%	—	40%	71%	—	29%
Foreign	65%	—	35%	65%	—	34%
Composite	69%	—	31%	68%	—	32%

Key Votes of the 111th Congress

1. Overturn Ledbetter	Y	5. Bar federal abortion funds	N	9. Stop detainee transfers	N
2. Pass $820 billion stimulus	Y	6. Pass health care bill	Y	10. Legalize immigrants' kids	Y
3. Let guns in national parks	N	7. Regulate financial firms	Y	11. Repeal don't ask, tell	*
4. Pass cap-and-trade	Y	8. Pass tax cuts for some	Y	12. Limit campaign funds	N

Election Results

2010 general	Carolyn McCarthy (D)	94,483	(54%)	($1,684,444)
	Francis Becker (R)	81,718	(46%)	($307,510)
2010 primary	Carolyn McCarthy (D)	unopposed		

Prior Winning Percentages: 2008 (64%), 2006 (65%), 2004 (63%), 2002 (56%), 2000 (61%), 1998 (53%), 1996 (57%)

Population		Race/Ethnicity		Work	
Pop. 2010:	663,407	White:	52.3%	Private:	78.2%
Change since 2000:	Up 1.4%	Black:	18.7%	Government:	16.9%
Urban:	100.0%	Hispanic:	20.2%	Self-employed:	4.8%
Rural:	0.0%	Asian:	6.8%	Blue collar:	17.0%
Area size:	103 sq. mi.	Native Am.:	0.1%	White collar:	64.8%
		Hawaiian:	0.0%	Khaki collar:	0.1%
Age		Two+ races:	1.4%	Other:	18.2%
Median age:	38.9 yrs.				
More than 65 yrs:	13.6%	*Ancestry*		Median income:	$86,608
Less than 18 yrs:	24.1%	Italian	16.7%	Median Home Value:	$467,600
		Irish	12.2%		
Education		German	7.3%	**Military Veterans**	
H.S. grad:	86.2%			% of Pop:	6.3%
College grad:	35.5%				
Grad degree:	15.1%				

Southwest Nassau County

By the mid-20th century, Nassau County had changed from being almost entirely rural to being almost entirely suburban. One of its first suburbs was Garden City, founded in 1869 with wide avenues and single-family homes. After World War II, freeways replaced highways, and shopping centers sprang up at intersections. But many of the middle- and upper-income residents there continue to depend on the Long Island Railroad to speed them to jobs in New York City.

2008 Presidential Vote		
Barack Obama (D)	171,346	(58%)
John McCain (R)	122,166	(41%)
2004 Presidential Vote		
John Kerry (D)	153,546	(55%)
George Bush (R)	124,617	(44%)
Cook Partisan Voting Index:	D+6	

Garden City has maintained high real estate prices and is surrounded by some of Nassau County's key institutions: the county seat of Mineola; Hofstra University in Hempstead, where a new medical school was set to open in August 2011; and Roosevelt Field, where Charles Lindbergh took off for Paris (it's now a shopping center). Charles Wang, owner of the New York Islanders hockey team, has proposed developing the area around the Nassau Veterans Memorial Coliseum into a $3.8 billion housing, retail and office complex.

The 4th Congressional District of New York comprises Garden City and the towns around it. The district takes in several suburbs just north of the Jericho Turnpike—New Hyde Park, Mineola, Westbury—as well as a large swath of southern Nassau County east of the Queens County line. This territory includes Hempstead, Uniondale, Rockville Center, and ethnically diverse Valley Stream, as well as the predominantly Jewish "Five Towns"—the railway suburbs of Lawrence, Inwood, Cedarhurst, Hewlett, and Woodmere—many of which have more elementary and high school students in private schools (mostly yeshivas) than in public schools.

Nassau County has traditionally been Republican, and both Garden City and heavily Catholic East Meadow remain that way. But the Five Towns are heavily Democratic, and more than a third of the district's residents are African-Americans or Hispanics who generally vote Democratic. Elmont, near the Queens line and once heavily white, now has a large Caribbean and Latin American population. The traditional Republican heritage in the 4th District appeared to be disappearing, as Democrats controlled the county legislature for a decade and Barack Obama won easily here in 2008. But in 2009, voter unhappiness with the economy enabled Republicans to regain the majority in the legislature.

Carolyn McCarthy (D)

The congresswoman from the 4th District is Carolyn McCarthy, a Democrat first elected in 1996. She was born in Brooklyn, trained as a nurse, and then married and raised a family on Long Island. Originally, she was a Republican, but her life and politics changed dramatically in 1993. That year, her husband, Dennis, a stockbroker, was killed and her adult son, Kevin, was seriously injured in the "Long Island Railroad Massacre." A gunman opened fire on passengers riding a commuter train as it crossed the Nassau County line. McCarthy spoke movingly at the killer's trial, and her strength in tragedy won many admirers. She began campaigning for gun control laws and, in 1995, lobbied her congressman, Republican Daniel Frisa, to vote against repeal of the assault weapons ban. After Frisa voted for repeal, McCarthy inquired about running against him in the GOP primary. When Nassau County Republicans discouraged her, Democrats who had been eyeing the seat for some time recruited her. Initially, McCarthy knew little about politics. But she learned quickly. As the Democratic nominee, she called for stricter gun laws and attacked Frisa as too close to Republican House Speaker Newt Gingrich. Frisa abruptly stopped campaigning the week before the election, did not show up at his election night party, and never made a concession statement. McCarthy won 57%-41%.

In the House, McCarthy has a voting record that mingles strong support for organized labor and abortion rights with occasional conservative stances. She backed the use of force in Iraq in 2002, and in 2006 voted for legislation to build a fence on the U.S.-Mexico border. And in February 2011, she joined Republicans in extending three controversial expiring provisions of the USA PATRIOT anti-terrorism law. One of her closest friends in the House is Republican Jo Ann Emerson of Missouri; they are among a bipartisan group of 20 female House members who meet for dinner once a month at the Monocle, a popular Capitol Hill dining spot for lawmakers.

On guns, however, McCarthy has remained committed to liberal positions. She has called for childproof locks on handguns, fines for parents of children who get possession of handguns, and mandatory jail terms for crimes committed with guns. The House approved her bill to help states gain more access to the federal background check system for gun buyers. The 2002 sniper spree in the Washington, D.C., area gave her the opening to gain approval in the House of her bill to strengthen laws prohibiting the mentally ill from buying guns and requiring states to file records with the national background check system. In 2004, she led an unsuccessful effort to force a House vote on extending the assault weapons ban. McCarthy criticized President George W. Bush for "winking" at the National Rifle Association on the issue, but she also blamed Democrats for their lack of support. After the shooting of her Arizona Democratic colleague Gabrielle Giffords in January 2011, McCarthy unveiled legislation to outlaw high-capacity magazines like the one that was used to shoot Giffords and 20 other people in a matter of seconds.

With only limited success on gun issues, McCarthy has broadened her portfolio, using her experience as a mother and nurse to become active in education and health care. In 2002, Bush signed her bill giving incentives to hospitals to hire more nurses to remedy acute shortages. In March 2009, she sponsored a bill to boost federal support for early child care. Also in 2009, she was the House sponsor of the successful Serve America Act, which had been sponsored in the Senate by the late Democratic Sen. Edward Kennedy of Massachusetts and tripled the number of federally supported volunteers to 250,000. It also established new service corps for clean energy, education, health care, and veterans' services.

McCarthy had a tougher than usual re-election in 2002, when she was challenged by ophthalmologist Marilyn O'Grady, a Republican who took a hard line on terrorism and immigration and opposed abortion rights. Although O'Grady received little party support, she held McCarthy to a 56%-43% victory. In the next three cycles, McCarthy was re-elected easily. She strongly criticized the appointment of Democratic Rep. Kirsten Gillibrand to fill the Senate seat vacated by Secretary of State Hillary Rodham Clinton of New York. She cited Gillibrand's "awful" record on gun control, and indicated that she would challenge Gillibrand in the 2010 primary. She ultimately withdrew for "personal reasons," which she later clarified to *Newsday* involved back surgery that required her to wear a brace for months.

McCarthy's 2010 race ended up becoming her closest in more than a decade. Francis Becker, a former Nassau County GOP legislator, campaigned with an anti-Washington, anti-Obama message that forced McCarthy to compete more vigorously than usual. She ran ads harshly criticizing Becker for several of the stands he took as a county official, and she won 54%-46%.

FIFTH DISTRICT

Gary Ackerman (D)

Elected Mar. 1983, 14th full term; b. Nov. 19, 1942, Brooklyn; home, Roslyn Heights; Queens Col., B.A. 1965; Jewish; married (Rita); 3 children.

Elected Office: NY Senate, 1978–83.

Professional Career: Jr. high schl. teacher, 1966–70; Editor & publisher, *Queens Tribune*, 1970–78; Pres., advertising agcy., 1972–78.

DC Office: 2111 RHOB, 20515, 202-225-2601; Fax: 202-225-1589; Web site: ackerman.house.gov.

State Offices: Bayside, 718-423-2154.

Committees: *Financial Services:* Capital Markets and Government Sponsored Enterprises; Financial Institutions & Consumer Credit. *Foreign Affairs:* Asia & the Pacific; Middle East & South Asia (RMM).

Group Ratings

	ACLU	ACU	ADA	CFG	AFS	FRC	LCV	ITIC	NTU	COC
2010	81	0	90	0	100	0	60	67	2	13
2009	–	0	100	4	100	–	100	–	3	33

National Journal Ratings

	2010 LIB	—	2010 CONS		2009 LIB	—	2009 CONS
Economic	75%	—	25%		71%	—	28%
Social	82%	—	18%		84%	—	11%
Foreign	62%	—	37%		70%	—	24%
Composite	73%	—	27%		77%	—	23%

Key Votes of the 111th Congress

1. Overturn Ledbetter	Y	5. Bar federal abortion funds	N	9. Stop detainee transfers	*
2. Pass $820 billion stimulus	Y	6. Pass health care bill	Y	10. Legalize immigrants' kids	Y
3. Let guns in national parks	N	7. Regulate financial firms	Y	11. Repeal don't ask, tell	Y
4. Pass cap-and-trade	Y	8. Pass tax cuts for some	Y	12. Limit campaign funds	Y

Election Results

2010 general	Gary Ackerman (D)..	72,239	(63%)	($1,109,041)
	James Milano (R)...	41,493	(36%)	($148,624)
2010 primary	Gary Ackerman (D)..	19,394	(76%)	
	Patricia Maher (D)...	6,258	(24%)	

Prior Winning Percentages: 2008 (71%), 2006 (100%), 2004 (71%), 2002 (92%), 2000 (68%), 1998 (65%), 1996 (64%), 1994 (55%), 1992 (52%), 1990 (100%), 1988 (100%), 1986 (77%), 1984 (69%), 1983 special (49%)

Population		Race/Ethnicity		Work	
Pop. 2010:	670,130	White:	35.7%	Private:	80.6%
Change since 2000:	Up 2.4%	Black:	4.0%	Government:	12.3%
Urban:	100.0%	Hispanic:	25.6%	Self-employed:	7.0%
Rural:	0.0%	Asian:	32.6%	Blue collar:	18.0%
Area size:	85 sq. mi.	Native Am.:	0.1%	White collar:	61.9%
		Hawaiian:	0.0%	Khaki collar:	0.0%
Age		Two+ races:	1.6%	Other:	20.2%
Median age:	40.0 yrs.				
More than 65 yrs:	15.1%	*Ancestry*		Median income:	$64,040
Less than 18 yrs:	21.4%	Italian	10.1%	Median Home Value:	$620,800
		Irish	5.5%		
Education		German	3.7%	**Military Veterans**	
H.S. grad:	81.0%			% of Pop:	4.4%
College grad:	36.8%				
Grad degree:	15.2%				

Northeast Queens, Nassau County

Queens is to most Americans the mystery borough, little explored even by many Manhattanites, although it contains both LaGuardia and John F. Kennedy airports. Some of it is almost suburban: Bayside, Douglaston, and Little Neck are upper-middle-income neighborhoods far beyond the subway lines, with detached houses with driveways and views across the water. Other Queens neighborhoods are more modest, with houses crowded together and plain-Jane

2008 Presidential Vote
Barack Obama (D) 128,158   (63%)
John McCain (R) 73,125   (36%)

2004 Presidential Vote
John Kerry (D) 128,252   (63%)
George Bush (R) 74,635   (37%)

Cook Partisan Voting Index: D+12

apartment buildings lining the avenues. In the past two decades, Queens has become the No. 1 immigrant destination in New York City. Corona was once predominantly Italian and African-American (Louis Armstrong, Duke Ellington, and Malcolm X lived here). Today, there is a large Latin American community, with many Dominican immigrants and also many Asians. Flushing, long a modest-income Jewish and white ethnic neighborhood, is now the biggest Asian neighborhood in the city.

West of 138th Street, Queens is dominated by Taiwanese and ethnic Chinese from Malaysia, Vietnam, and Thailand; shops have a more urban "Chinatown" feel and feature an amazing variety of delicacies. (New York City has three Chinatowns—one each in Manhattan and Brooklyn, with the largest in Queens.) East of 138th Street is predominantly Korean, with development following a more suburban pattern. In most of the years since 2004, the area has been represented in the state Assembly by either Chinese businessman Jimmy Meng from Flushing or his daughter, Grace Meng, who drew attention in January 2011 when she demanded that conservative radio personality Rush Limbaugh apologize for what she called a racially insensitive impersonation of Chinese leader Hu Jintao.

Just east of Flushing and its large new condominium development is Flushing Meadow, the huge drainage basin and former dumping ground that hosted two World's Fairs (1939 and 1964) and now is home to the U.S. Open tennis tournament and a new Mets baseball park, Citi Field. Attendance there plunged nearly 19% in 2010 from the stadium's inaugural season, and the team announced it would cut ticket prices by more than 14%.

Just a few miles but a world away is the North Shore of Long Island. For a century it has had an upper-crust ambiance—peninsulas jutting out into Long Island Sound, vast green lawns, and the great capitalist mansions that inspired East Egg and West Egg in *The Great Gatsby*. By the middle of the 20th century, the city had encroached, and the Great Neck and Sands Point peninsulas became affluent, predominantly Jewish suburbs with stately Tudor homes. Lately, many wealthy Asians have moved here.

The 5th Congressional District of New York takes in this territory in Queens and suburban Nassau County. The district includes most of Queens east of Flushing Meadow and north of Union Turnpike—Flushing, Bayside, Douglaston, Little Neck (but not the airports). And it includes the northwest corner of Nassau County—Great Neck, super-rich Sands Point, Lake Success, Port Washington, and Kings Point, home of the U.S. Merchant Marine Academy. The district's population is 33% Asian and 26% Hispanic. Sixty-one percent of the people speak a language other than English at home. Both the Queens and Nassau County portions of the district have long voted heavily Democratic, with Barack Obama getting 63% of the vote in 2008.

Gary Ackerman (D)

The congressman from the 5th District is Gary Ackerman, a Democrat first elected in 1983 and an old-school liberal with a penchant for colorful and tart remarks. Ackerman grew up in Flushing. His father was a cab driver and his mother was a Polish immigrant. As a young man, Ackerman cultivated a variety of interests and careers. He graduated from Queens College, and taught social studies in junior high school. After he and his wife had their first child, Ackerman successfully sued the New York City school district for the right of fathers, as well as mothers, to take time off for a new child. For a time, Ackerman ran an advertising agency, and then started the weekly *Queens Tribune* in 1970, which he sold in 1978. That year, he was elected to the New York Senate.

He won his seat in the U.S. House in a special election from a district that was then centered in the heavily Jewish apartment complexes in central Queens. In Washington, he lives on a houseboat on the Potomac River called the *Unsinkable II*, successor to the *Unsinkable I*, which sank. He hosts an annual "Taste of New York" fundraiser, featuring pastrami sandwiches and stuffed cabbage, with waiters imported from the city. He is a pungent speaker, but with a sense of humor that makes even opponents smile. In admonishing the Securities and Exchange Commission in 2009 for missing financier Bernard Madoff's Ponzi scheme, he said, "You couldn't find your backside with two hands if the lights were on." He always wears a white carnation in his lapel, a habit he started as a teacher to remind his students that "every day is special."

Ackerman has a penchant for taking on worthy but neglected causes. His once solidly liberal voting record has moderated on foreign policy issues. Despite opposition from many constituents, including his wife, Ackerman voted in 2002 to authorize war in Iraq; in 2005 he said he regretted it. He is the ranking Democrat of the Middle East and South Asia Subcommittee on the Foreign Affairs Committee, a panel of great interest to his constituents. He has met frequently with leaders in the region. Between 2006 and 2008, he helped win congressional approval of the nuclear energy deal with India, under which India gained U.S. expertise and nuclear fuel to meet its rapidly rising energy needs in exchange for opening its nuclear facilities to international inspections. A longtime supporter of India—Queens is home to a large Indian-American community—he has been critical of Pakistan, India's leading adversary. In March 2010, Ackerman accused the Pakistani military of tolerating and kowtowing to the Lashkar-e-Taiba, which carried out the November 2008 terrorist attacks on Mumbai. He worked on the measure to stop Iran's nuclear weapons development that became law in June 2010, praising it for including "real sanctions—not 'maybe' sanctions, not 'sorta' sanctions."

Ackerman in 2010 served as president of the International Council of Jewish Parliamentarians, a global group of Jewish lawmakers supporting Israel. He was among the Jewish lawmakers in the House who strongly defended Israel's raid of a Turkish aid flotilla heading for the blockaded Gaza that resulted in 10 deaths and a condemnation from the United Nations. In 2007 and 2008, Ackerman won overwhelming House passage of nonbinding resolutions calling for the release of Israeli soldiers held by the Muslim groups Hamas and Hezbollah and condemning Syria for taking control of the internal affairs of Lebanon. He also pushed a bill to freeze the personal assets of corporate executives whose companies invest in oil in Iran. Peace activists from the group Code Pink protested what they deemed his "provocative" anti-Iran rhetoric by blockading his houseboat with rafts. Ackerman came on deck and discussed the issue with them.

On domestic issues, Ackerman in 1995 helped to pass a bill requiring HIV testing of newborns and disclosure of the results to the mother. The bill also bars insurers from terminating coverage because of HIV/AIDS test results. As one of five New York-area Democrats on the Financial Services Committee, Ackerman worked in 2010 to unite various factions around the Wall Street reform bill even though he did not serve on the conference committee. To deal with the damage caused by Madoff's Ponzi scheme, he sponsored a measure that would provide $100,000 coverage to indirect investors. He also got his bill barring credit card companies from charging customers a fee to pay bills online or by phone as part of the credit card overhaul law. He occasionally stands out as a lonely liberal, such as when he was one of only three House members to vote against a resolution criticizing a federal Appeals Court that ruled unconstitutional the phrase "under God" in the Pledge of Allegiance.

Ackerman twice has survived redistricting, and he takes pride in tending to constituents. He regularly wins re-election by large margins. But redistricting in advance of the 2012 election could prove a problem for him. Population growth in his Nassau County base is stagnant while growing minority communities in Queens seek to wield more clout.

SIXTH DISTRICT

Gregory Meeks (D)

Elected Feb. 1998, 7th full term; b. Sept. 25, 1953, Harlem; home, Far Rockaway; Adelphi U., B.A., 1975, Howard U., J.D., 1978; Baptist; married (Simone-Marie); 3 children.

Elected Office: NY Assembly, 1992–98.

Professional Career: Asst. dist. atty., Queens Co., NY, 1978–84; NY St. Comm. of Investigations, 1984–85; Judge, NY St. Workers Compensation Bd., 1985–92.

DC Office: 2234 RHOB, 20515, 202-225-3461; Fax: 202-226-4169; Web site: www.house.gov/meeks.

State Offices: Far Rockaway, 718-327-9791; Jamaica, 718-725-6000.

Committees: *Financial Services:* Domestic Monetary Policy & Technology; Financial Institutions & Consumer Credit. *Foreign Affairs:* Asia & the Pacific; Europe and Eurasia (RMM).

Group Ratings

	ACLU	ACU	ADA	CFG	AFS	FRC	LCV	ITIC	NTU	COC
2010	94	0	90	0	100	0	100	100	7	25
2009	–	0	100	6	100	–	100	–	2	40

National Journal Ratings

	2010 LIB	—	2010 CONS	2009 LIB	—	2009 CONS
Economic	90%	—	0%	70%	—	29%
Social	93%	—	0%	70%	—	29%
Foreign	65%	—	34%	59%	—	39%
Composite	86%	—	14%	67%	—	33%

Key Votes of the 111th Congress

1. Overturn Ledbetter	Y	5. Bar federal abortion funds	N	9. Stop detainee transfers	N
2. Pass $820 billion stimulus	Y	6. Pass health care bill	Y	10. Legalize immigrants' kids	Y
3. Let guns in national parks	Y	7. Regulate financial firms	Y	11. Repeal don't ask, tell	Y
4. Pass cap-and-trade	Y	8. Pass tax cuts for some	Y	12. Limit campaign funds	Y

Election Results

2010 general	Gregory Meeks (D)	85,096	(88%)	($935,513)
	Asher Taub (R)	11,826	(12%)	($75,142)
2010 primary	Gregory Meeks (D)	unopposed		

Prior Winning Percentages: 2008 (100%), 2006 (100%), 2004 (100%), 2002 (97%), 2000 (100%), 1998 (100%), 1998 (57%)

Population		Race/Ethnicity		Work	
Pop. 2010:	651,764	White:	10.1%	Private:	76.2%
Change since 2000:	Down 0.4%	Black:	49.5%	Government:	18.5%
Urban:	100.0%	Hispanic:	19.0%	Self-employed:	5.1%
Rural:	0.0%	Asian:	13.1%	Blue collar:	19.6%
Area size:	46 sq. mi.	Native Am.:	0.6%	White collar:	55.0%
		Hawaiian:	0.1%	Khaki collar:	0.1%
Age		Two+ races:	4.2%	Other:	25.3%
Median age:	36.1 yrs.				
More than 65 yrs:	11.8%	*Ancestry*		Median income:	$57,057
Less than 18 yrs:	24.3%	West Indian	18.4%	Median Home Value:	$452,500
		Italian	2.9%		
Education		USA	2.8%	**Military Veterans**	
H.S. grad:	79.1%			% of Pop:	4.2%
College grad:	22.7%				
Grad degree:	7.3%				

Southeast Queens

The eastern edge of Queens has been an important transportation hub for New York for almost 250 years. In the 1750s, the British laid out what is now Jamaica Avenue to help them defend Long Island. In the 1830s, the Long Island Rail Road was built. Today, this corner of Queens is sliced by the Belt Parkway and the Van Wyck Expressway—two integral parts of Robert Moses' mid-century highway network. And it is home to John F. Kennedy International Airport, a major hub for air travelers entering the United States. The airport generates around 230,000 jobs in the area, and businesses there reported more activity in late 2010 than in the past—a hopeful sign for New York's economy. The neighborhood of Jamaica is so well situated with transportation links that officials have worked mightily to improve its commercial vitality. The old elevated subway line on Jamaica Avenue has been buried underground, so that shoppers have a less claustrophobic experience. Now, billions of dollars are being spent for a Long Island Rail Road line from Queens to Grand Central Terminal in Manhattan. The need for shoring up the LIRR became apparent in August 2010, when a system of levers and pulleys built in 1913 caught fire and forced employees to switch track manually by hammering switches into place.

2008 Presidential Vote
Barack Obama (D) 185,890   (89%)
John McCain (R) 22,302   (11%)

2004 Presidential Vote
John Kerry (D) 154,468   (84%)
George Bush (R) 27,352   (15%)

Cook Partisan Voting Index: D+36

This part of Queens is home to New York City's largest concentration of middle-class black homeowners, with a median income higher than white households in Queens. A half-century ago, there was a small black community in South Jamaica, and since then, many African-American families have bought houses and raised their families in neighborhoods that fan east from Jamaica. They fought to maintain the relatively spacious streets, relishing the plenitude of natural light, safe schools, and good neighborhood stores. There is block upon block of low-rise, frame and brick houses, built mostly from the 1920s to the 1950s, in the neighborhoods of Springfield Gardens and Laurelton, St. Albans and Rosedale, Cambria Heights and Queens Village. The recent downturn in the housing market hit them disproportionately hard compared with the rest of New York. Many residents were the victims of subprime lenders.

The 6th Congressional District of New York contains all of these southeast Queens neighborhoods, plus others less affluent in southern Queens. It is bounded on the north, more or less, by Jackie Robinson Parkway; on the east by the Nassau County line; and on the west by Cross Bay Boulevard. To the south, it includes part of the Rockaway Peninsula across Jamaica Bay from the rest of Queens. Richmond Hill and Ozone Park, previously white ethnic neighborhoods, now have sizable numbers of Latinos and Asians. South Ozone Park is home to many immigrants from Guyana, Jamaica, Haiti, the Dominican Republic, and Trinidad and Tobago. Despite being just a few blocks from the beach, the Rockaway portions of the district are a relatively undeveloped backwater, leveled by urban renewal in the late 1960s but never completely rebuilt. The 6th District is 50% African-American, 19% Hispanic, and 13% Asian. The common denominator is the amount of time that residents spend on the road: The district is among the nation's worst for commuters, at 46.2 minutes of mean travel time to work. Politically, the district is one of the country's most solidly Democratic.

Gregory Meeks (D)

The congressman from the 6th District is Gregory Meeks, a Democrat first elected in 1998. Meeks grew up in public housing projects in Harlem. He was inspired by his mother, who went back to school when her four children were older and who encouraged community service volunteerism. Meeks's childhood hero was Supreme Court Justice Thurgood Marshall. After graduating from college and law school, Meeks moved to Far Rockaway. He became an assistant district attorney in 1978 and a workers' compensation judge in 1985. After losing a City Council race in 1991, he was elected to the New York state Assembly in 1992. He became an ally of Democratic Rep. Floyd Flake, a minister whose Allen African Methodist Episcopal Church congregation grew from 1,400 members in 1976 to 12,000 in 2000. When Flake retired, Meeks won a majority of Democratic committee members at a January 1998 endorsement meeting and thus became the party's nominee. Democratic state Sen. Alton Waldon and Assemblywoman Barbara Clark ran as independents. With the support of Flake, Rep. Charles Rangel of New York, and civil-rights leaders Al Sharpton and Jesse Jackson, Meeks won with 57% of the vote, to Waldon's 21%, and Clark's 13%. Since then he has had only token opposition.

Meeks has a liberal voting record on social issues, but his stance on economic issues is more pro-business than most other New York City Democrats. He is a member of the commerce-oriented New Democrat Coalition. He backed the 2005 Central American Free Trade Agreement, citing increased traffic for JFK Airport. In 2009, he became chairman of the House Financial Services Committee's International Monetary Policy and Trade Subcommittee and remained as its top Democrat in the 112th Congress (2011-12). He has joined the committee's other African-American members in seeking to ensure that minorities' issues are addressed in Financial Services legislation. He also expressed concerns about the Securities and Exchange Commission's adoption of rules in 2008 to expand its oversight of some fixed indexed annuities that states had been monitoring. Meeks sided with financial companies that want them to remain subject to state oversight, and joined with conservative Rep. Tom Price of Georgia in sponsoring a bill to that effect in 2009.

Meeks has shown a desire to advance within the party. When several House Democratic leadership positions opened up in late 2002, he campaigned for vice chairman of the Democratic Caucus but was bested by Rep. James Clyburn of South Carolina. In 2008, Meeks became chairman of the Congressional Black Caucus's political action committee.

He has sought to bring business deals to Queens by meeting with leaders of other nations, and his many overseas trips have attracted attention. His personal life has caused him some political problems. The Federal Election Commission in 2006 reprimanded him for using more than $6,000 in 2004 campaign funds for a personal trainer and other expenses. He agreed to pay fines totaling $63,000. When his wife, Simone, expressed interest in running for the New York City Council in 2007, Meeks refused to endorse her and she deferred to the candidacy of her husband's aide.

In 2010, his financial ethics became fodder for all of New York's major dailies. *The New York Times* wrote in March that despite acknowledging that he has no more than a few thousand dollars in his savings account, he "lives a life worthy of a jet-setter," staying in luxury hotels, driving a taxpayer-leased $1,000-a-month Lexus and buying a $1 million house built by a developer who was a campaign contributor. He told the newspaper that he observed all campaign finance laws, but "I am not going to raise the money in my district that I need to be a player here in Washington." *The New York Daily News* reported in June that he described his failure to list $55,000 in personal loans as an "oversight." And *The New York Post* found inconsistencies in his political action committee records, including paying $325 in monthly rent on a nonexistent Queens office. He blamed the negative attention on conservative groups out to undermine Democrats.

SEVENTH DISTRICT

Joseph Crowley (D)

Elected 1998, 7th term; b. March 16, 1962, Elmhurst, NY; home, Elmhurst; C.U.N.Y. Queens College, B.A. 1985; Catholic; married (Kasey); 3 children.

Elected Office: NY Assembly, 1986-98.

DC Office: 2404 RHOB, 20515, 202-225-3965; Fax: 202-225-1909; Web site: crowley.house.gov.

State Offices: Bronx, 718-931-1400; Bronx, 718-320-2314; Jackson Heights, 718-779-1400.

Committees: *Ways & Means:* Human Resources; Trade.

Group Ratings

	ACLU	ACU	ADA	CFG	AFS	FRC	LCV	ITIC	NTU	COC
2010	93	0	95	0	100	0	100	100	7	25
2009	–	0	100	4	100	–	100	–	2	40

National Journal Ratings

	2010 LIB	—	2010 CONS	2009 LIB	—	2009 CONS
Economic	90%	—	0%	75%	—	21%
Social	82%	—	14%	89%	—	0%
Foreign	97%	—	0%	91%	—	0%
Composite	93%	—	8%	89%	—	11%

Key Votes of the 111th Congress

1. Overturn Ledbetter	Y	5. Bar federal abortion funds	N	9. Stop detainee transfers	N
2. Pass $820 billion stimulus	Y	6. Pass health care bill	Y	10. Legalize immigrants' kids	Y
3. Let guns in national parks	N	7. Regulate financial firms	Y	11. Repeal don't ask, tell	Y
4. Pass cap-and-trade	Y	8. Pass tax cuts for some	Y	12. Limit campaign funds	Y

Election Results

2010 general	Joseph Crowley (D)	71,247	(81%)	($2,100,428)
	Kenneth Reynolds (R)	16,145	(18%)	($8,029)
2010 primary	Joseph Crowley (D)	unopposed		

Prior Winning Percentages: 2008 (85%), 2006 (84%), 2004 (81%), 2002 (73%), 2000 (72%), 1998 (69%)

Population		Race/Ethnicity		Work	
Pop. 2010:	667,632	White:	20.7%	Private:	77.7%
Change since 2000:	Up 2.0%	Black:	16.4%	Government:	16.8%
Urban:	100.0%	Hispanic:	44.4%	Self-employed:	5.3%
Rural:	0.0%	Asian:	16.1%	Blue collar:	20.9%
Area size:	42 sq. mi.	Native Am.:	0.2%	White collar:	52.9%
		Hawaiian:	0.0%	Khaki collar:	0.0%
Age		Two+ races:	1.6%	Other:	26.2%
Median age:	37.5 yrs.				
More than 65 yrs:	13.2%	*Ancestry*		Median income:	$46,571
Less than 18 yrs:	22.6%	Italian	8.5%	Median Home Value:	$430,500
		Irish	4.6%		
Education		West Indian	4.0%	**Military Veterans**	
H.S. grad:	75.6%			% of Pop:	4.5%
College grad:	23.3%				
Grad degree:	7.8%				

Queens, the Bronx

Over the past two decades, hundreds of thousands of immigrants moved into many of New York City's modest neighborhoods—neighborhoods that had been emptying out as the children of the immigrants who came to New York between 1890 and 1924 died or moved to the suburbs. These are places that affluent New Yorkers and traveling journalists seldom see as they whiz by on freeways to destinations in Manhattan. Rather, these are the neighborhoods that

2008 Presidential Vote		
Barack Obama (D) 148,242	(79%)
John McCain (R) 38,170	(20%)
2004 Presidential Vote		
John Kerry (D) 129,909	(74%)
George Bush (R) 44,607	(25%)
Cook Partisan Voting Index: D+26		

pop star Jennifer Lopez sings about. Most of the housing was built in the decades after 1910, when the subways first started connecting these neighborhoods with job sites in Manhattan. In the East Bronx, off the Bruckner Expressway and near the cluster of highways north of the Bronx-Whitestone Bridge, are such places as Bruckner, Morris Park, Schuylerville, and Throgs Neck. (The Bronx-Whitestone Bridge, opened in 1939, is currently getting a $200 million facelift, to be completed in 2016.) The Hunts Point meat and produce markets supply some of the city's toniest restaurants and are estimated to bring in about 60% of New York City's wholesale produce sales. Vendors have threatened to move to New Jersey, where taxes and rents are lower.

Increasingly, the neighborhoods are filling with Latinos, many from Puerto Rico, but many also from the Dominican Republic and other Caribbean and Latin American countries. Lopez hails from Castle Hill; her *On the 6* album is a reference to the Number 6 subway train that whisked her to Manhattan auditions. Home for many immigrants is one of two massive apartment projects: the Parkchester, built just before World War II by Metropolitan Life Insurance in the center of the Bronx, and the sprawling Co-op City, consisting of 35 buildings that house more than 50,000 residents in 15,000 apartments that were built by a consortium of labor unions in the late 1960s near Eastchester Bay. Out past the bay is City Island, a Cape Cod-like resort area with boat makers and plenty of seafood restaurants; it still looks like it did half a century ago.

Across the bridges in Queens are Jackson Heights, home to Little India and a sizable Latino community; Elmhurst, a place so diverse that one local hospital counted more than 100 different languages and dialects; East Elmhurst; and Woodside, a long-settled enclave with residents from 49 nations. One can find Pakistanis and Peruvians, Koreans and Dominicans, Indians and Filipinos, Mexicans and Bangladeshis.

These Bronx and Queens neighborhoods are all in the 7th Congressional District of New York. The district is a polyglot: In 2010, it was 16% black, 44% Hispanic and 16% Asian. Sixty percent speak a language other than English at home, and 39% are foreign-born. Since 2000, the share of workers and high school graduates has increased and the poverty level has dropped slightly. But a major difference in satisfaction levels separates the residents of the Bronx and Queens. A 2009 report by the Citizens Committee for New York found that among the happiest New Yorkers, 51%, are from Queens, and the least happy, 24%, are from the Bronx. Politically, the 7th District votes heavily Democratic.

Joseph Crowley (D)

The congressman from the 7th District is Joseph Crowley, an ambitious and garrulous Democrat first elected in 1998 who became chairman of the centrist New Democrat Coalition in 2009.

Crowley grew up in Woodside, where his family was involved in politics. His Uncle Walter Crowley was elected to the New York City Council in 1984. When he died in 1985, Joseph Crowley wanted to succeed him, though he was only 23. But Tom Manton, the boss of the efficient Queens County Democratic Party, chose his chief of staff instead. The following year, Assemblyman Ralph Goldstein from Elmhurst died. Fresh from Queens College, Crowley ran and won, with support from Manton. Crowley was interested in Irish affairs and sponsored the law that requires public school students to be taught about the Irish potato famine. He played guitar and sang tenor with the Budget Blues Boys, a group of assemblymen who performed on cold Albany nights. (He still loves to sing, and once did a version of Bruce Springsteen's "Pink Cadillac" at a USO concert with Springsteen's guitarist, Nils Lofgren.) When political boss Manton decided it was time for Crowley to go to Congress, he went.

In 1998, Manton was the 7th District incumbent. He filed for re-election by the July 16 deadline. Then at 11 a.m. on July 21, he convened a meeting of Queens Democratic committeemen, announced that he was retiring, and got them to vote in Crowley as the Democratic nominee. Other potential candidates were not notified beforehand and were naturally miffed, but also resigned to reality. Manton argued that Crowley, at 36, was in a position to accumulate seniority and power in Washington. Crowley was delighted. "What you're hearing is not so much about the process, but sour grapes. What happened here is simply that I was offered an ice cream cone, and I took it." His Republican opponent had no money and no chance. Crowley won in November, 69%-26%.

Once elected, Crowley voted as a centrist Democrat. He was the freshman Democrats' class president that year. Over time, he changed his position from opposing abortion rights to favoring them, a stance in line with the party. He now has a seat on the powerful, tax-writing Ways and Means Committee. His local priorities include aid for city hospitals and adjusting the alternative minimum tax to reduce the number of middle-income taxpayers who are forced to pay it. He also has worked on a range of foreign policy issues, from extending economic sanctions against Burma's military regime to criminalizing the removal of girls from the United States for genital mutilation, a practice common across Africa and parts of the Middle East and Asia.

An active participant in leadership activities, Crowley has had setbacks in seeking a top post. In 2005, he sought the chairmanship of the Democratic Congressional Campaign Committee, highlighting his fundraising connections to Wall Street. But as an ally of Minority Whip Steny Hoyer of Maryland, he was on the wrong side of Democratic Leader Nancy Pelosi, who was then competing with Hoyer to move up the leadership ladder. The DCCC appointment went to Rep. Rahm Emanuel of Illinois, who led Democrats to victory in the next election in 2006. Crowley was named to lead the DCCC's Business Council, a key fundraising post. After that election, Crowley sought to move up to vice chairman of the Democratic Caucus. But Pelosi ally John Larson of Connecticut prevailed, 116-87. Crowley did some bridge-building with Pelosi and her allies, becoming chief deputy whip and DCCC vice chairman for finance. When the caucus vice chairmanship opened again after the 2008 election, he expressed interest but deferred when Pelosi backed Rep. Xavier Becerra of California. He was among those considered for DCCC chairman in 2011 but lost out to fellow New Yorker Steve Israel. After Manton died in July 2006, Crowley became Queens Democratic chairman.

For a time, he also held sway as the head of the New Democrat Coalition, a group of moderate Democrats that had about 40 members in the 111th Congress (2009-10). Crowley sought to work more closely with the leadership than the often-confrontational Blue Dog Coalition, and cited his group's success in reshaping elements of the financial regulatory reform bill that passed the House in 2009 and became law a year later. Their efforts earned them admiration from the industry's lobbyists—an issue that the investigative reporting organization *ProPublica* highlighted in a lengthy October 2010 article detailing the New Democrats' tight connections with K Street. Crowley found himself fighting allegations that he was the object of a lobbyists' fundraiser right before a vote on the financial bill. The Office of Congressional Ethics investigated, and Crowley denied any wrongdoing. The House Ethics Committee ultimately cleared him and two other lawmakers in January 2011. The coalition lost about a third of its members in the November 2010 elections, and with Republicans back in control of the House, its influence has waned.

After the September 11 attacks, Crowley was especially active in homeland security issues. His district lost many firefighters, including his first cousin, who was a battalion chief. He won passage of an amendment to issue the Public Safety Officers Medal of Valor to the 414 first responders who died that day. And in 2007, the House passed his amendment to restore $50 million for homeland security funding in high-threat urban areas. Crowley has worked with Republicans on behalf of business interests to gain approval of bilateral free trade agreements. But when Republicans called for repeal of the Democrats' 2010 health care overhaul, Crowley organized an effort asking GOP lawmakers who backed repeal to forgo their taxpayer-subsidized health insurance as a matter of principle.

Crowley has not faced serious opposition at election time. After the 2000 census, redistricting radically changed his constituency. In the old district, Queens cast 74% of the votes. Now the Bronx casts 62% (Crowley remains a Mets fan, though).

EIGHTH DISTRICT

Jerrold Nadler (D)

Elected Nov. 1992, 10th full term; b. June 13, 1947, Brooklyn; home, Manhattan; Columbia U., B.A. 1970, Fordham U., J.D. 1978; Jewish; married (Joyce Miller); 1 child.

Elected Office: NY Assembly, 1976–92.

Professional Career: Legis. asst., NY Assembly, 1972; Law clerk, 1976.

DC Office: 2334 RHOB, 20515, 202-225-5635; Fax: 202-225-6923; Web site: nadler.house.gov.

State Offices: Brooklyn, 718-373-3198; Manhattan, 212-367-7350.

Committees: *Judiciary:* Constitution (RMM); Intellectual Property, Competition & the Internet. *Transportation & Infrastructure:* Highways & Transit; Railroads, Pipelines & Hazardous Materials.

Group Ratings

	ACLU	ACU	ADA	CFG	AFS	FRC	LCV	ITIC	NTU	COC
2010	93	0	100	0	100	0	100	67	6	14
2009	–	0	95	0	100	–	100	–	2	36

National Journal Ratings

	2010 LIB — 2010 CONS		2009 LIB — 2009 CONS	
Economic	90%	— 0%	81%	— 18%
Social	93%	— 0%	89%	— 0%
Foreign	97%	— 0%	70%	— 24%
Composite	97%	— 3%	83%	— 17%

Key Votes of the 111th Congress

1. Overturn Ledbetter	Y	5. Bar federal abortion funds	N	9. Stop detainee transfers	N
2. Pass $820 billion stimulus	Y	6. Pass health care bill	Y	10. Legalize immigrants' kids	Y
3. Let guns in national parks	N	7. Regulate financial firms	Y	11. Repeal don't ask, tell	Y
4. Pass cap-and-trade	Y	8. Pass tax cuts for some	Y	12. Limit campaign funds	Y

Election Results

2010 general	Jerrold Nadler (D)	98,839	(76%)	($1,304,217)
	Susan Kone (R)	31,996	(24%)	($43,510)
2010 primary	Jerrold Nadler (D)	unopposed		

Prior Winning Percentages: 2008 (80%), 2006 (85%), 2004 (81%), 2002 (76%), 2000 (81%), 1998 (86%), 1996 (82%), 1994 (82%), 1992 (81%), 1992 special (100%)

Population		Race/Ethnicity		Work	
Pop. 2010:	713,512	White:	66.5%	Private:	83.1%
Change since 2000:	Up 9.0%	Black:	4.5%	Government:	7.7%
Urban:	100.0%	Hispanic:	11.8%	Self-employed:	9.1%
Rural:	0.0%	Asian:	15.0%	Blue collar:	9.2%
Area size:	28 sq. mi.	Native Am.:	0.1%	White collar:	79.6%
		Hawaiian:	0.0%	Khaki collar:	0.0%
Age		Two+ races:	1.8%	Other:	11.3%
Median age:	37.3 yrs.				
More than 65 yrs:	13.5%	*Ancestry*		Median income:	$66,172
Less than 18 yrs:	18.4%	Italian	7.8%	Median Home Value:	$760,300
		Russian	7.3%		
Education		Irish	6.2%	**Military Veterans**	
H.S. grad:	86.3%			% of Pop:	3.4%
College grad:	54.3%				
Grad degree:	25.4%				

Lower Manhattan

Over the course of the 20th century, New York City spread so far beyond its original boundaries in Lower Manhattan that, for a while, it became easy to forget how pivotal the southern end of the island had been in making the city what it is today. That all changed in an instant, on the morning of September 11, 2001, when al-Qaida terrorists flew two hijacked jets into the twin towers of the World Trade Center, killing nearly 3,000 people and laying waste to 13 city blocks.

2008 Presidential Vote		
Barack Obama (D) 184,682	(74%)
John McCain (R) 63,769	(26%)

2004 Presidential Vote		
John Kerry (D) 180,080	(72%)
George Bush (R) 66,948	(27%)

Cook Partisan Voting Index: D+22

The terrorists struck the tallest buildings in America's biggest city, toppling a complex whose name embodied the reach of American capitalism.

Lower Manhattan has long been home to Wall Street and the Financial District, but over the years it has represented America's striving spirit in other ways as well. The Brooklyn Bridge, begun in 1867 just a few blocks east of the Twin Towers site and completed in 1883, was half again as long as any bridge then standing and seven times higher than any buildings in the adjoining boroughs. The Holland Tunnel, built in 1927, was the first underwater vehicular tunnel built anywhere in the world. Just offshore are Ellis Island, where members of the great immigration wave first set foot on American soil, and the Statue of Liberty, the symbol of freedom they saw as they sailed in.

The 8th Congressional District of New York includes all of these places. From the Battery, at the very southern tip of Manhattan Island, the 8th spreads north and south. As it moves up the west side of Manhattan, it takes in the Financial District and many of the neighborhoods synonymous with New York: Battery Park City, with its attractive modern apartments and parks; sophisticated TriBeCa, with its artists' lofts; SoHo, the international shoppers' paradise; Greenwich Village; and Chelsea, with its many art galleries. Clinton is the new, economically diverse incarnation of the old slum known as Hell's Kitchen. There is also the economically revived Theater District and the cleaned-up Times Square, where digital screens have replaced neon signs. The Upper West Side is home to Lincoln Center.

South from the Battery, the 8th District crosses into Brooklyn, running along the waterfront before taking in the inland neighborhood of Borough Park and the waterside enclaves of Sea Gate, Brighton Beach and Coney Island, once known as the world's largest playground. Mayor Michael Bloomberg's administration in 2010 unveiled an ambitious waterfront development plan, Vision 2020. In the Financial District, young families and wealthy professionals have filled new condos and hotel rooms despite the economic woes of the city's financial institutions, which have not seemed to have trickled down locally. Total employment rose in 2010 without the industry's help. There also has been substantial progress in redevelopment at Ground Zero. At the site of the former Twin Towers, One World Trade Center hit its halfway mark at 52 stories above ground. The plan to build an Islamic community center and mosque nearby, however, became a topic of fierce national debate in 2010. Although the 8th District has some of the world's biggest concentrations of wealth, nearly one-quarter of its households earn less than $25,000 a year. There are more Asians, 15%, than Hispanics, 12%, and the district is only 5% African-American.

Both parts of the 8th District have a strong Jewish heritage. The city's Dutch founders hailed from a European country that was then most tolerant of Jews. German Jews came to New York in large numbers in the 19th century, and a few of them founded merchant banking, retail and clothing empires. Around 1890, Ashkenazi Jews from Eastern Europe began arriving from Poland, Lithuania, Belarus, Ukraine, Hungary and Romania. In the years after World War I, as many as 400,000 Jews a year debarked at Ellis Island until a 1924 law virtually shut down immigration. Their children moved up faster than those of any new group in memory, despite the incredible odds against them given the widespread prejudice in the professions and in educational institutions. Today, New York has the largest Jewish population behind Tel Aviv. Brighton Beach ("Little Odessa") and Coney Island house the largest concentration of recent Russian Jewish immigrants in New York. Borough Park has one of the nation's largest Orthodox communities, with Yiddish-language ATMs and Russian bathhouses. The political attitudes in these neighborhoods are quite different from those of most American Jews, who are liberal on cultural and economic issues. The Russians, many of whom live close to poverty, are anti-socialist. The Hasidic Jews of Borough Park are conservative and hostile to racial preferences, and they favor tough police treatment of crime. Still, voters in these areas tend to vote Democratic in most elections.

The venerable apartment buildings along Central Park West, West End Avenue and Riverside Drive, and the brownstones on the cross streets, house some of the country's most dedicated liberals. These professional people—satirized on *Seinfeld,* the long-running sitcom that resonated far beyond Manhattan—include a mix of wealthy and less-affluent intellectuals. In the 1950s, West Siders took up the reform banner and eviscerated the old Tammany Hall Democratic machine. In the 1960s, they protested the Vietnam War. Another big voting area is Greenwich Village, which in the 1910s was America's original Bohemia but now has a mix of expensive apartments and cheaper dwellings. Politically, the Village has long had a taste for the radical, though some of its ideas are now mainstream, such as the historic preservation and urbanist policies developed in the Village's successful fight against a proposed Lower Manhattan expressway.

In 2008, the district voted 74%-26% for Democrat Barack Obama over Republican John McCain, although McCain prevailed 55%-44% in the Brooklyn part of the district, which cast 29% of the total vote.

Jerrold Nadler (D)

The congressman from the 8th District is Jerrold Nadler, a West Side Democrat first elected in 1992. Nadler was the House's most liberal member in 2010, according to *National Journal* rankings, with a strong civil libertarian bent.

Nadler was born in Brooklyn and moved around with his family as a child. His parents bought a chicken farm in New Jersey, but the business failed, and they moved back to the city. His father ran a gas station on Long Island and owned an auto parts store. Interested in politics from a young age, Nadler campaigned for Democrat Eugene McCarthy for president while at Columbia University, where he roomed with Dick Morris, who would later become a top adviser to President Bill Clinton. The two were at Columbia during the 1968 campus riots. After getting his law degree from Fordham University, Nadler ran for the New York Assembly in 1976, at age 29. In the primary, he beat Ruth Messinger, the Democratic nominee for mayor in 1997, by 73 votes. In 1992, he was suddenly presented with the opportunity to run for Congress. Ted Weiss, long an Upper West Side icon, died the day before the September primary, which he won posthumously. The nomination was decided by a convention of almost 1,000 county Democratic committee members. Nadler won 62% of the votes to secure the nomination and thus the election. He has not been seriously challenged since.

As the top Democrat on the Constitution, Civil Rights and Civil Liberties Subcommittee of the House Judiciary Committee, Nadler has been a counterweight to lawmakers of both parties seeking expanded police powers to crack down on terrorism. It is not because Nadler, as the representative of the site of the September 11 attacks, is unsympathetic to their cause. But he has worked to narrow the definition of "enemy combatants" and to protect the habeas corpus rights of detainees. In 2008, he sponsored a bill requiring the Federal Bureau of Investigation to surmount higher legal hurdles before being allowed to use "national security letters," which are government demands for information not subject to judicial review. He vigorously opposed the USA PATRIOT Act, the Bush administration's centerpiece anti-terrorism law. Nadler in 2009 moved a bill through the full committee aimed at strengthening the hand of Americans who sue the government to challenge alleged spying or illegal detention

Nadler has little regard for most of the Republican-backed social legislation that makes its way to the Judiciary Committee or for the tea-party conservatives who support reading the Constitution on the House floor. "You are not supposed to worship your constitution; you're supposed to govern your government by it," he told *The Washington Post* in January 2011. He led the fight in the House against conservative proposals to ban same-sex marriage. In early 2009, Nadler held hearings to document what he viewed as the "criminal" abuses of the Bush administration and demanded that former Bush aide Karl Rove testify about the "politicization of the Justice Department" after the firing of several U.S. attorneys around the country allegedly for political reasons.

On foreign policy, Nadler has been a staunch supporter of Israel, but he opposed the Iraq war resolution in 2002. Regarding Afghanistan, he said in July 2010: "An intelligent policy is not to try to remake a country that nobody since Genghis Khan has managed to conquer." He offered an amendment to a spending bill in February 2011 to de-fund military operations there that lost overwhelmingly, 98-331.

For a decade now, Nadler has been involved in post-September 11 issues and concerns in his district. In late 2010, he helped steer into law a long-delayed measure providing more than $4 billion in compensation to first responders suffering health problems—a development he called "without a doubt the proudest moment of my 34-year career in government." Right after the attacks, he helped provide $20 billion for rebuilding, and he spearheaded numerous actions on behalf of affected families and small businesses.

As the Northeast's most senior Democrat on the Transportation and Infrastructure Committee, Nadler has fought to get more rail competition east of the Hudson and to save Amtrak. His biggest project has been a rail-freight tunnel under the Hudson. Lack of a rail-freight line means that New York gets only a tiny share of its freight by rail; a new line could mean cheaper freight and therefore lower consumer prices. Mayor Bloomberg initially sided with neighborhood groups in Queens that object to the plan because it would increase noise, but in 2009, reversed himself and called it "a good long-term solution." Nadler also has been a strong proponent of the Obama administration's commitment to high-speed passenger rail, which many Republicans have rejected as too expensive. "It simply makes no sense to travel by air between New York and D.C. or Boston, or frankly between any cities within a 500-mile radius," he said in February 2011. Nadler also successfully fought developer Donald Trump's attempts to alter the West Side Highway to accommodate his luxury housing project on old rail yards between 59th and 72nd Streets. Trump in turn called Nadler a "hack."

Nadler has been open about his decision to undergo stomach-reduction surgery in 2002 to combat obesity. The 5-foot-4 Nadler weighed as much as 338 pounds before the procedure but lost more than 60 pounds within three months. "I want to live to see my grandchildren grow up," he told *The New York Times*.

NINTH DISTRICT
Vacant

Election Results

2010 general	Anthony Weiner (D)	67,011	(61%)	($1,628,372)
	Robert Turner (R)	43,129	(39%)	($378,863)
2010 primary	Anthony Weiner (D)	unopposed		

Prior Winning Percentages: 2008 (93%), 2006 (100%), 2004 (71%), 2002 (66%), 2000 (68%), 1998 (66%)

Population		Race/Ethnicity		Work	
Pop. 2010:	660,306	White:	57.0%	Private:	77.5%
Change since 2000:	Up 0.9%	Black:	4.4%	Government:	16.6%
Urban:	100.0%	Hispanic:	17.2%	Self-employed:	5.7%
Rural:	0.0%	Asian:	18.6%	Blue collar:	16.5%
Area size:	103 sq. mi.	Native Am.:	0.1%	White collar:	66.3%
		Hawaiian:	0.0%	Khaki collar:	0.0%
Age		Two+ races:	1.9%	Other:	17.2%
Median age:	40.3 yrs.				
More than 65 yrs:	15.7%	*Ancestry*		Median income:	$57,449
Less than 18 yrs:	21.5%	Italian	11.1%	Median Home Value:	$530,500
		Irish	7.1%		
Education		Russian	7.1%	**Military Veterans**	
H.S. grad:	86.2%			% of Pop:	4.4%
College grad:	36.6%				
Grad degree:	13.8%				

Queens, Part Brooklyn

Forty years ago, most of the neighborhoods in New York's outer boroughs were almost all-white. A few were WASPy and high-income Forest Hills in Queens, with its famous tennis stadium and large Tudor houses, was a notable example. But most of them were filled by descendants of the great mass of immigrants who came over from eastern and southern Europe between 1890 and 1924 and from northern Europe earlier—Irish and Italians, Jews and

2008 Presidential Vote
Barack Obama (D) 111,237   (55%)
John McCain (R) 88,307   (44%)

2004 Presidential Vote
John Kerry (D) 111,850   (56%)
George Bush (R) 87,449   (44%)

Cook Partisan Voting Index: D+5

Hungarians, Poles and Czechs and Greeks. The pitched battles of city politics in the 1960s were between John Lindsay, a liberal Manhattan Republican, and his mostly outer-borough opponents. During Lindsay's reign, middle-class New Yorkers fled the city's high taxes and crime-addled neighborhoods. The city lost 1 million people in the 1970s. Some of this neighborhood change would have happened anyway. Neighborhoods settled by immigrants in the 1920s were full of old people, and increasing numbers of African-Americans were bound to move out of the old ghettoes. And after the 1965 changes in immigration law, increasing numbers of new immigrants settled in New York.

The convoluted boundaries of the 9th Congressional District take in parts of Queens and Brooklyn. The district begins in Queens near Fresh Meadows, just inside Nassau County, and runs west through Pomonok and the old rail suburbs of Kew Gardens and Forest Hills, with houses built to resemble English cottages. It continues west to Rego Park ("Regostan"), which has many 1950s high-rise apartments; Middle Village; Glendale; and part of Maspeth. From there, the 9th heads south, taking in Woodhaven, Lindenwood and Howard Beach. It crosses over open parkland to include the shoreline areas of Bergen Beach, Mill Basin, Mill Island, Marine Park and Sheepshead Bay. It takes in Broad Channel, the only inhabited island in Jamaica Bay's Gateway National Recreation Area, where many descendants of the original fishing families still live. In recent years, the U.S. Army Corps of Engineers helped revive dozens of acres of marshland and removed toxic wastes from the bay, and in early 2011 the city began a massive project to improve the bay's water quality.

On the Rockaway Peninsula, the district encompasses the neighborhoods of Seaside, Rockaway Park, Belle Harbor, Roxbury and the tight-knit enclave of Breezy Point, a clannish, white-ethnic, middle-class enclave where the bungalows and brick homes often change hands by word of mouth. While parts of Rockaway have been largely abandoned, parts in the Arverne area have thousands of new housing units. Plans for a liquefied natural gas terminal on a man-made island 15 miles from the peninsula were abandoned after the 2010 BP oil spill disaster in the Gulf of Mexico and opposition from New Jersey Gov. Chris Christie.

The population of the 9th District is only 4% black and 17% Hispanic, and some of its neighborhoods, like the Italian Howard Beach on Jamaica Bay, have remained remarkably parochial and seemingly unaffected by change. But the district's 19% Asian population has added diversity. The district also has a large and diverse Jewish population, with both liberal voters and politically conservative Orthodox voters. This is unquestionably a Democratic district, but conservative by New York City standards: It voted 67%-30% for Democrat Al Gore for president in 2000, but in 2004, after President George W. Bush's response to September 11, it gave Democrat John Kerry only 56%. It was the greatest swing of any congressional district in the nation that year. In 2008, Democrat Barack Obama won with 55%-44% over Republican John McCain. Obama lost the Brooklyn portion of the district, 57%-42%.

Until June 2011, the congressman from the 9th District was Anthony Weiner, a Democrat who was forced to give up the seat amid a sexting scandal. At press time for the *Almanac*, Gov. Andrew Cuomo was expected to set a date for a special election for a new representative.

Weiner (*WEE-ner*) was first elected to Congress in 1998, and he had his sights set on running for mayor of New York City when the scandal broke in late spring 2011. Lewd photos of Weiner surfaced in the media after he sent them to a young woman via his Twitter account in May. Weiner at first denied sending the photo, which was a below-the-waist close-up of a man in underwear with a distinctive bulge. He indignantly claimed his Twitter account had been hacked. But when conservative blogger Andrew Breitbart made good on a threat to publish more suggestive photographs online, a teary-eyed Weiner admitted at a news conference that he had lied about the photo, that it was indeed his, and that he had sent it using the social networking service Twitter accidentally. He also admitted carrying on inappropriate online exchanges with at least six women. Several of the contacts, he said, came after his July 2010 marriage to Huma Abedin, a top aide to Secretary of State Hillary Clinton. "I don't know what I was thinking," he said. "This was a destructive thing to do."

Weiner initially said he would not resign over the scandal, and that his constituents would ultimately decide his fate in November 2012. But Democratic House Leader Nancy Pelosi and many of his House colleagues viewed the nonstop press coverage as an unwelcome distraction from their efforts to focus attention on the Republicans' far-reaching plans for Medicare and cutting the federal budget. Weiner next announced that he would take a leave of absence and seek professional treatment of an unspecified type.

But his attempt to weather the controversy quickly unraveled as new information continued to leak out, including transcripts of sexually themed conversations Weiner had with women online, photographs of a semi-nude Weiner and claims by an exotic dancer that she also had had an online relationship with the congressman. Pelosi, national party Chairman Debbie Wasserman Schultz and other top Democrats demanded publicly on Saturday, June 11 that Weiner step down immediately. Then President Barack Obama also suggested that resignation was Weiner's only option.

On Thursday, June 16, Weiner acquiesced. After meeting at home in New York with his wife, who had been away on an overseas trip with Clinton, Weiner called a press conference and apologized for "the distraction I have caused" the party and his colleagues and resigned the seat.

Weiner, 46, had hoped to finish his seventh term in Congress before running again for New York City mayor in 2013 after a failed 2005 bid. In forcing Weiner out, the Democrats succeeded in containing the damage from the scandal, but they also lost a liberal champion who was unafraid to aggressively take on the conservative right. He was a particularly vocal advocate for a larger government role in health care during the 2009 and 2010 debate about overhauling the health insurance system. It was not only his positions on the issues, but also his New York-style sauciness that catapulted Weiner to the A-list of cable news guests. He routinely appeared on MSNBC, Fox News, and CNN to do battle with Republican colleagues or, on occasion, cable anchors. (Until the sexting scandal, Weiner's best-known TV exploits were with Fox anchor Megyn Kelly— the "cat fights" were popular on YouTube.) Weiner came to the Capitol as an aide to then-Rep. Chuck Schumer and learned from the aggressive and TV-savvy Schumer that few things accumulated power and prestige faster than an elevated media profile.

Weiner grew up in the Park Slope section of Brooklyn, the son of a lawyer and a teacher. He went to college upstate at the State University of New York-Plattsburgh, majored in political science and ran for student government with the slogan "Vote for Weiner. He'll be frank." After graduation, he went to work for Schumer, then in the House. In 1991, Weiner, at age 27, was elected to the New York City Council. In 1997, as Schumer prepared to run for the Senate, Weiner ran for his House seat, narrowly winning the primary 28.1% to 27.5%. He won the general election easily, and was returned to office every two years with at least 66% of the vote.

TENTH DISTRICT

Edolphus Towns (D)

Elected 1982, 15th term; b. July 21, 1934, Chadbourn, NC; home, Brooklyn; NC A&T, B.S. 1956, Adelphi U., M.S.W. 1973; Baptist; married (Gwen); 2 children.

Military Career: Army, 1956–58.

Professional Career: Baptist minister; Social worker; Prof., Medgar Evers Col.; NY public schl. teacher; Dpty. hospital admin., 1965–71; Brooklyn Dpty. Borough Pres., 1976–82.

DC Office: 2232 RHOB, 20515, 202-225-5936; Fax: 202-225-1018; Web site: house.gov/towns.

State Offices: Flatlands Ave., 718-272-1175; Joralemon, 718-855-8018.

Committees: *Energy & Commerce:* Commerce, Manufacturing & Trade; Communications & Technology; Health. *Oversight & Government Reform:* Government Organization, Efficiency & Financial Management (RMM).

Group Ratings

	ACLU	ACU	ADA	CFG	AFS	FRC	LCV	ITIC	NTU	COC
2010	88	0	100	0	100	0	90	67	5	13
2009	–	0	100	4	100	–	100	–	3	40

National Journal Ratings

	2010 LIB	—	2010 CONS	2009 LIB	—	2009 CONS
Economic	76%	—	24%	86%	—	14%
Social	93%	—	0%	89%	—	0%
Foreign	97%	—	0%	87%	—	9%
Composite	90%	—	10%	90%	—	10%

Key Votes of the 111th Congress

1. Overturn Ledbetter	Y	5. Bar federal abortion funds	N	9. Stop detainee transfers	N
2. Pass $820 billion stimulus	Y	6. Pass health care bill	Y	10. Legalize immigrants' kids	Y
3. Let guns in national parks	N	7. Regulate financial firms	Y	11. Repeal don't ask, tell	Y
4. Pass cap-and-trade	Y	8. Pass tax cuts for some	Y	12. Limit campaign funds	Y

Election Results

2010 general	Edolphus Towns (D)..95,485	(91%)	($1,632,842)
	Diana Muniz (R) 7,419	(7%)	
2010 primary	Edolphus Towns (D)....................................unopposed		

Prior Winning Percentages: 2008 (94%), 2006 (92%), 2004 (91%), 2002 (98%), 2000 (90%), 1998 (92%), 1996 (91%), 1994 (89%), 1992 (96%), 1990 (93%), 1988 (89%), 1986 (89%), 1984 (85%), 1982 (84%)

Population		Race/Ethnicity		Work	
Pop. 2010:	677,721	White:	18.3%	Private:	72.8%
Change since 2000:	Up 3.6%	Black:	58.4%	Government:	22.3%
Urban:	100.0%	Hispanic:	17.2%	Self-employed:	4.9%
Rural:	0.0%	Asian:	3.7%	Blue collar:	15.3%
Area size:	18 sq. mi.	Native Am.:	0.3%	White collar:	59.2%
		Hawaiian:	0.0%	Khaki collar:	0.1%
Age		Two+ races:	1.7%	Other:	25.4%
Median age:	32.2 yrs.				
More than 65 yrs:	10.1%	*Ancestry*		Median income:	$39,963
Less than 18 yrs:	27.9%	West Indian	18.3%	Median Home Value:	$522,900
		Subsaharan	3.1%		
Education		USA	2.3%	**Military Veterans**	
H.S. grad:	78.6%			% of Pop:	3.0%
College grad:	24.3%				
Grad degree:	8.8%				

Brooklyn Bedford-Stuyvesant

African-Americans began settling in Brooklyn's Bedford-Stuyvesant neighborhood in the 1930s, with the opening of the subway line that was celebrated in Duke Ellington and Billy Strayhorn's "Take the 'A' Train." After World War II, the pace accelerated, as crime and crowding in Harlem— as well as a large influx of African-Americans from the South—drove black New Yorkers to the aging but solid brownstones of "Bed-Stuy." When job growth slowed, Bed-Stuy faced more

2008 Presidential Vote		
Barack Obama (D) 205,929	(91%)
John McCain (R) 19,677	(9%)
2004 Presidential Vote		
John Kerry (D) 166,840	(86%)
George Bush (R) 25,359	(13%)
Cook Partisan Voting Index: D+38		

than its share of poverty and crime. But after a 1966 visit by New York's two senators, Democrat Robert F. Kennedy and Republican Jacob Javits, Bed-Stuy won a Model Cities designation, which brought federal development funds and the establishment of the Bedford-Stuyvesant Restoration Corporation, the first such community development organization in the United States.

Even as the black community expanded across Brooklyn, Bed-Stuy became almost as powerful a symbol of black New York as Harlem, thanks in part to the films of Spike Lee, a Brooklyn native. His *Do the Right Thing* was shot on Stuyvesant Avenue between Lexington Avenue and Quincy Street, and succinctly captured the racial tensions then brewing in the old neighborhood. The neighborhood also gave birth to rappers Jay-Z and Notorious B.I.G., both of whom had a major impact on the hip-hop scene of the 1990s. By the new century, Bed-Stuy was in better shape than many other areas of Brooklyn. The neighborhood's stately, Hopperesque architecture largely avoided the wrecking ball, and community vigilance kept the streets maintained. The revitalized residential area has developed a Caribbean flavor that, combined with modest prices for handsome brownstones and new shops and galleries, has led to a wave of gentrification. The Bradford, a $45 million retail and housing development serving low- and middle-income families, broke ground in 2010.

The 10th Congressional District of New York takes the shape of a sideways "V" as it zigzags across Brooklyn. It takes in several neighborhoods near, but not on, the East River, including part of affluent Brooklyn Heights; downtown Brooklyn, with Borough Hall and the courthouse complex; Fort Greene, a rising arts area that also has drawn new businesses; and part of Williamsburg (shared with the 12th District), inhabited by large Hasidic families. From there, it runs southeasterly through Bed-Stuy, Clinton Hill and East New York until it hits the Queens border, where it turns to the southwest to take in three communities along Jamaica Bay: Spring Creek, the huge middle-income apartment complex of Starrett City, and Canarsie, the site of Jonathan Rieder's classic sociological study of Jewish and Italian flight from increasingly black neighborhoods.

In the 1990s, Canarsie again experienced significant demographic change, as the neighborhood's black population grew from 10% to 60%, mainly due to an influx of Caribbean immigrants who prized the backyards and single-family homes. The 10th also includes Remsen Village, Flatlands and part of East Flatbush. In East New York, gutted blocks have been torn down and in many cases rebuilt, and talks have been underway for New York City's first Wal-Mart. But crime has hardly disappeared. The district is 58% black—the highest of any New York district—and it is 17% Hispanic. Politically, it is one of the most Democratic districts in the nation. Voter turnout in the 2008 presidential primary, with the first black major-party presidential nominee, was up 17% over 2004, and Democrat Barack Obama won this district with 91% of the vote.

Edolphus Towns (D)

The congressman from the 10th District is Edolphus Towns, a Democrat first elected in 1982. Towns, from East New York, was born in North Carolina, the son of a tobacco sharecropper. He graduated from the historically black North Carolina A&T State University, served two years in the Army and then moved to Brooklyn. He got a job teaching in the public schools and at Medgar Evers College. He became a social worker and hospital administrator, and was active in community affairs. In 1976, he became Brooklyn's deputy borough president, a position he held for six years.

In recent years, Towns' voting record has lost some of its liberal edge, especially on economic issues, where he occasionally sides with business. In November 2008, when Rep. Henry Waxman of California gave up the chairmanship of the Oversight and Reform panel to take over at Energy and Commerce, Towns was the next Democrat in line. Some senior Democrats worried that the low-key Towns would not be aggressive enough in the role. But as Towns made his case in one-on-one conversations and rallied support, opposition quickly dissipated. Towns pledged vigorous oversight of the executive branch, although there naturally would be less of it with a Democratic president than there had been in the previous Congress, when Republican George W. Bush was in the White House.

As chairman, Towns sought to tamp down the panel's rancorous internal dealings. Some Democrats worried that he was giving Republicans too much leeway, but Towns cited President Barack Obama's call for bipartisanship. He established an ambitious schedule of hearings that examined the Marine Corps' controversial MV-22 Osprey hybrid tilt-rotor aircraft, whose reliability had been questioned; the Secret Service's security practices after an uninvited couple found their way into the Obama administration's first state dinner; Toyota vehicles' safety issues; and Countrywide Financial's controversial VIP mortgage program for elected officials. But he repeatedly clashed with California's Darrell Issa, the panel's hard-charging ranking Republican. The committee's Democratic and Republican staffs reportedly had trouble agreeing on issuing subpoenas and planning investigations, and some Democrats privately grumbled that Towns had trouble managing Issa.

After the 2010 elections, when Republicans won majority control, talk of replacing Towns resurfaced. Democrats were keen on having an aggressive foil to counter Issa, who promised vigorous investigations into the Obama administration on several fronts. Towns rallied the support of 14 of the panel's Democrats, who signed a letter affirming their desire to have him remain at the helm. But prominent liberals Dennis Kucinich of Ohio and Carolyn Maloney of New York both made known their interest in the ranking member slot. Faced with the prospect of a divisive matchup, Towns removed himself from consideration, sending a chilly letter to Democratic leader Nancy Pelosi in which he said he made his decision "when you made it clear I did not have your support." He endorsed Maloney. Kucinich bowed out and backed Elijah Cummings of Maryland, who won a 33-18 victory in the Democratic steering committee over Maloney.

In the past, Towns has demonstrated an ability to work effectively across party lines. Working with Republican Mike Rogers of Michigan, he got the House to pass a bill imposing uniform safety rules on food. In 2005, he infuriated Pelosi by breaking ranks to vote for the Central American Free Trade Agreement on a very close roll call vote. She demanded an explanation and threatened to deprive Towns, and a few other maverick Democrats, of their committee seats. When Democrats took over the House in 2007, Towns did not get a subcommittee chairmanship on Energy and Commerce, perhaps as a result of Pelosi's unhappiness over his CAFTA vote. His decision to step down from the top Democratic spot on Oversight enabled him to return to Energy and Commerce in 2011, but he again did not receive a subcommittee ranking position.

Still, he managed to get a few things done while Democrats were in the majority. He won enactment of a bill to permit state and local governments to purchase equipment for homeland security and law enforcement at the discounted prices available to federal agencies. And he won passage of a provision in the higher education bill to aid minority colleges. He introduced bipartisan legislation in 2010 seeking to end the problem of insufficient restroom facilities for women in federal buildings—a measure dubbed "potty parity."

Towns has faced several serious primary challenges. In 1997, after he endorsed Republican Rudolph Giuliani for re-election as mayor of New York, local Democrats recruited Barry Ford, a Harvard-educated Wall Street lawyer, to run against Towns in the primary the following year. But Towns beat Ford 52%-36%. He beat him again two years later in a rematch, 57%-43%.

In 2006, he had to beat back a challenge from Councilman Charles Barron, who said that Towns had been "missing in action for years." But Barron's call for reparations for descendants of slaves was controversial, and Towns won the primary with 47%, to 37% for Barron and 15% for Assemblyman Roger Green. Towns fared better in 2008 against Kevin Powell, a writer and former television reality show participant, whom he beat 68%-32%. There has been speculation that the incumbent would like to pass the district to his son, Darryl Towns, when he retires. The younger Towns has served in the state Assembly and was chosen by Gov. Andrew Cuomo in early 2011 to run the state's housing agency.

ELEVENTH DISTRICT

Yvette Clarke (D)

Elected 2006, 3rd term; b. Nov. 21, 1964, Brooklyn; home, Brooklyn; Attended Oberlin Col.; Christian; single.

Elected Office: NY City Cncl., 2001-06.

Professional Career: Childcare specialist, Erasmus Neighborhood Fed., 1987-89; Leg. aide, state Sen. Velmanette Montgomery, 1989-91; Exec. asst., NY Workers' Compensation Bd., 1992-93; Youth program dir., Hospital League/Local S.E.I.U. 1199 Training and Upgrading Fund, 1993-97; Bus. devel. dir., Bronx Overall Devel. Corp., 1997-2001.

DC Office: 1029 LHOB, 20515, 202-225-6231; Fax: 202-226-0112; Web site: clarke.house.gov.

State Offices: Brooklyn, 718-287-1142.

Committees: *Homeland Security:* Cybersecurity, Infrastructure Protection & Security Technologies (RMM); Oversight, Investigations & Management. *Small Business:* Contracting & Workforce; Economic Growth, Tax and Capital Access.

Group Ratings

	ACLU	ACU	ADA	CFG	AFS	FRC	LCV	ITIC	NTU	COC
2010	100	4	95	3	100	6	100	67	6	25
2009	–	0	100	0	100	–	100	–	1	33

National Journal Ratings

	2010 LIB	—	2010 CONS	2009 LIB	—	2009 CONS
Economic	80%	—	18%	82%	—	14%
Social	70%	—	29%	89%	—	0%
Foreign	92%	—	3%	87%	—	9%
Composite	82%	—	18%	89%	—	11%

Key Votes of the 111th Congress

1. Overturn Ledbetter	Y	5. Bar federal abortion funds	N	9. Stop detainee transfers	N
2. Pass $820 billion stimulus	Y	6. Pass health care bill	Y	10. Legalize immigrants' kids	Y
3. Let guns in national parks	N	7. Regulate financial firms	Y	11. Repeal don't ask, tell	Y
4. Pass cap-and-trade	Y	8. Pass tax cuts for some	Y	12. Limit campaign funds	N

Election Results

2010 general	Yvette Clarke (D)	104,297	(91%)	($732,674)
	Hugh Carr (R)	10,858	(9%)	
2010 primary	Yvette Clarke (D)	unopposed		

Prior Winning Percentages: 2008 (93%), 2006 (90%)

Population		Race/Ethnicity		Work	
Pop. 2010:	632,408	White:	25.6%	Private:	74.5%
Change since 2000:	Down 3.4%	Black:	53.1%	Government:	18.2%
Urban:	100.0%	Hispanic:	13.2%	Self-employed:	7.3%
Rural:	0.0%	Asian:	5.5%	Blue collar:	13.7%
Area size:	12 sq. mi.	Native Am.:	0.2%	White collar:	61.2%
		Hawaiian:	0.0%	Khaki collar:	0.0%
Age		Two+ races:	2.0%	Other:	25.1%
Median age:	34.3 yrs.				
More than 65 yrs:	9.9%	*Ancestry*		Median income:	$45,954
Less than 18 yrs:	24.1%	West Indian	22.5%	Median Home Value:	$587,500
		Subsaharan	5.3%		
Education		USA	3.7%	**Military Veterans**	
H.S. grad:	82.6%			% of Pop:	2.7%
College grad:	33.1%				
Grad degree:	13.8%				

Brooklyn; Flatbush, Crown Heights

Brooklyn. Just saying the word in a comedian's monologue used to elicit laughter. It evoked an accent of twisted English, a raucous, in-your-face style, a sense of humor with an edge, and the chip-on-the-shoulder assertiveness of those sure they will always be in second place. As its name testifies, Brooklyn was a separate community (named after the Dutch town Breukelen) from the 17th century on, and in the 19th century, it was one of the largest cities in the country, with

2008 Presidential Vote
Barack Obama (D) 206,656   (91%)
John McCain (R) 20,709   (9%)

2004 Presidential Vote
John Kerry (D) 172,654   (86%)
George Bush (R) 26,172   (13%)

Cook Partisan Voting Index: D+38

its own celebrities—Henry Ward Beecher, Walt Whitman, John Roebling. By 1898, when the five boroughs were welded into Greater New York, 1 million people lived in Brooklyn, but the Brooklyn of the comedians really came into being as the subways were built in the early 20th century. In 1913, a transit agreement was struck to link the city's then-independent lines and triple the track to 619 miles. The agreement helped Brooklyn expand well beyond its established neighborhoods near the Brooklyn Bridge and into then-rural southwestern Brooklyn.

Suddenly, Manhattan factory workers no longer had to live in the crowded Lower East Side tenements that social reformer Jacob Riis had exposed in the 1890s. They moved in droves into neighborhoods of three- to five-story apartments and four-family houses. Brooklyn grew from 1.1 million in 1900 to 2.6 million in 1930. The old Brooklynites were mostly Protestant—Dutch, Yankee and German, plus some Catholic Irish. The new Brooklynites were heavily Italian and Jewish, and they populated the sports and entertainment businesses for a long generation, making their hometown nationally famous. In 1940, Brooklyn had 2.7 million people: One of every 49 Americans lived in Brooklyn. Around the time Jackie Robinson suited up for the Brooklyn Dodgers in 1947 as the first black player in Major League Baseball, Brooklyn was experiencing an influx of African-Americans into Brownsville and Crown Heights near Ebbets Field. Just as rapid was the flight of ethnic whites, driven away by "blockbusting," in which unscrupulous real estate brokers stoked white fears, then bought their homes cheaply and re-sold high. After "Dem Bums" left for Los Angeles in 1958 and Ebbets Field was knocked down for an apartment complex, Brooklyn's black neighborhoods continued to grow.

By 2010, Brooklyn was done with its growth spurt. It had 2.6 million people, fewer than in 1940. Kings County, which shares its boundaries with the borough of Brooklyn, is New York State's largest county and the nation's seventh largest. Some of its old neighborhoods have been ravaged by crime, but there is also great vitality among upwardly mobile Hispanic, Asian, Caribbean and Russian immigrants, among the hard-working, middle-class blacks, and among new generations of Italians and Jews. A change in zoning laws in 2004 resulted in a burst of new residential and office construction that has reinvigorated Brooklyn's commercial district. It continued to lead the rest of New York City in job creation during the 2007-09 recession.

The 11th Congressional District of New York begins at the edge of downtown Brooklyn and includes some of the borough's jewels: the Grand Army Plaza, the Parisian-style Eastern Parkway (the world's first six-lane parkway), and Prospect Park, home to the Brooklyn Public Library, the Brooklyn Museum and the Brooklyn Botanic Garden, with its Japanese landscaping and placid duck ponds. Park Slope, on Prospect Park's west side, has become increasingly affluent, filling up with young professionals who like the easy commute to downtown Manhattan. On the east side of Prospect Park is Crown Heights, with its mix of modest apartment buildings and nicely restored row houses. Prospect Park South, also adjoining the park, is an affluent neighborhood with artsy yuppies whose stately mansions contrast sharply with the vibrant Caribbean street life just around the corner on Flatbush's Church Avenue and with struggling, depopulated Brownsville to the east.

Most of these neighborhoods have great ethnic diversity. One minute you are in "La Saline," a center of the Haitian community in the East Flatbush-Crown Heights area, nicknamed for the slum district of Port-au-Prince, and the next, you are in "Little Pakistan" in Midwood, home to the largest concentration of Pakistanis in America. The district's population is 53% black and 13% Hispanic. Politically, the district is overwhelmingly Democratic.

Yvette Clarke (D)

The congresswoman from the 11th District is Yvette Clarke, a Democrat elected in 2006. She was born in Brooklyn to immigrant parents from Jamaica. As a young girl, she tagged along to political meetings and events with her mother, Una Clarke, who in 1991 became the first Jamaican elected to the New York City Council. Yvette Clarke attended Oberlin College in Ohio, but fell short of graduating by six credit hours. She returned to New York, helped train child care workers, worked as a state legislative aide and served as business development director for the Bronx Overall Economic Development Corp. In 2001, when term limits forced her mother off the City Council, Clarke defeated four other candidates to succeed her in the predominately Caribbean area of Flatbush and East Flatbush.

Since its creation in 1968 until 2006, the 11th District had been represented by just two people, both Democrats—trailblazer Shirley Chisholm, the first black woman elected to Congress and a 1972 presidential candidate, and Major Owens, who succeeded her in 1982. Owens had announced in 2004 that he would serve just one more term and hoped that his son, Chris, a health industry administrator, would succeed him. But Clarke was also part of a political family that had designs on the seat. Her mother had run unsuccessfully against Owens, an African-American, in the 2000 Democratic primary, a bitter contest that exposed divisions between the local Caribbean-American community and the African-American community. Four years later, Yvette Clarke and fellow City Councilwoman Tracy Boyland challenged Owens in the Democratic primary. The incumbent won the low-turnout primary with an unimpressive 45%, to 29% for Clarke and 22% for Boyland. When Clarke faced re-election to the council in 2005, Owens retaliated by backing, unsuccessfully, her primary opponent.

Clarke ran again in 2006, but first had to navigate a competitive primary field. New York City Councilman David Yassky, who is white, jumped in, only to be called a "colonizer" by Owens for running in a majority-black district that had been created in 1968 in response to a Voting Rights Act lawsuit. The black community feared that the well-financed Yassky, who had moved three blocks into the district to run for the seat, would be the beneficiary if the black vote was splintered among the three prominent black candidates: Clarke, Chris Owens, running as his father had predicted he would, and state Sen. Carl Andrews. By the end of August, Yassky had raised over $1.3 million, more than the other three candidates combined.

But Yassky had an awkward campaign style that made it difficult for him to connect with voters. Clarke's status as the only woman in the contest and her support among Caribbean-Americans were helpful. On the leading local issue, Clarke supported a plan to build an arena for the New Jersey Nets basketball team and other development in Brooklyn, while Owens vigorously opposed it. Clarke stumbled when she was forced to backtrack from her claim that she had graduated from Oberlin. But she picked up the endorsement of the Service Employees International Union's powerful Local 1199, which worked to turn out votes. In the September primary, the only election that mattered in this heavily Democratic district, Clarke defeated Yassky 31%-27%, while Andrews finished third with 23% and Owens last with 19%.

In the House, Clarke has had a solidly liberal voting record, though she is slightly less liberal on social issues than her New York City Democratic colleagues. An active member of the Congressional Black Caucus, she was among those in the group who expressed frustration with President Obama's work on helping minorities. "What we are asking for is that the president use his bully pulpit to look at a more far-reaching, deeper-penetrating jobs initiative...The level of unemployment in our communities is unacceptable," she told National Public Radio in March 2010. She became the CBC's secretary in 2011.

In the 111th Congress (2009-10), she took over the chairmanship of the Homeland Security Committee's panel on emerging threats. In April 2010, after nine months of negotiations with Republicans, she got her bill through the committee to authorize the Homeland Security Department's research and development arm for the first time. Earlier, in June 2008, the House passed her bill to create an appeals process for individuals wrongly denied rights in homeland security investigations. Clarke also worked with other committee members on cyber security legislation, and after Republicans regained control of the House, she became the ranking Democrat on the cyber security subcommittee.

Clarke occasionally goes her own way. In 2007, she voted against a bill to ban workplace discrimination against gays and lesbians because it did not also protect transgender workers. She was one of nine Democrats who voted that year against a resolution recognizing the importance of Christmas.

Clarke ran unopposed in the 2008 Democratic primary and was re-elected with 93% of the vote in November. In April 2010, the New York *Daily News* reported that she had spent more than $3,500 to treat campaign donors to a Broadway show and $5,000 for a Jay-Z concert, and that her campaign was more than $28,000 in debt. But she won easily with 91% of the vote that year. She was also among the five House Democrats who were investigated by the House Ethics Committee in 2010 for accepting Caribbean trips from corporations and later exonerated. She and the other lawmakers said they were unaware of the corporate funding.

TWELFTH DISTRICT

Nydia Velázquez (D)

Elected 1992, 10th term; b. March 28, 1953, Yabucoa, PR; home, Brooklyn; U. of PR, B.A. 1974, N.Y.U., M.A. 1976; Catholic; married (Paul Bader).

Elected Office: NY City Cncl., 1984-86.

Professional Career: Instructor, U. of PR, 1976–81; Adjunct prof., Hunter Col., 1981–83; Special asst., U.S. Rep. Edolphus Towns, 1983; Migration dir., PR Dept. of Labor & Human Resources, 1986–89; Secy., PR Dept. of Community Affairs in the U.S., 1989–92.

DC Office: 2302 RHOB, 20515, 202-225-2361; Fax: 202-226-0327; Web site: velazquez.house.gov.

State Offices: Brooklyn, 718-599-3658; Lower East Side, 212-673-3997; Southwest Brooklyn, 718-222-5819.

Committees: *Financial Services:* Financial Institutions & Consumer Credit; Insurance, Housing & Community Opportunity. *Small Business* (RMM).

Group Ratings

	ACLU	ACU	ADA	CFG	AFS	FRC	LCV	ITIC	NTU	COC
2010	93	0	100	0	100	0	100	67	5	13
2009	–	0	100	2	100	–	93	–	2	33

National Journal Ratings

	2010 LIB — 2010 CONS		2009 LIB — 2009 CONS	
Economic	71%	— 28%	91%	— 0%
Social	93%	— 0%	89%	— 0%
Foreign	84%	— 11%	66%	— 33%
Composite	85%	— 15%	86%	— 15%

Key Votes of the 111th Congress

1. Overturn Ledbetter	Y	5. Bar federal abortion funds	N	9. Stop detainee transfers	N
2. Pass $820 billion stimulus	Y	6. Pass health care bill	Y	10. Legalize immigrants' kids	Y
3. Let guns in national parks	N	7. Regulate financial firms	Y	11. Repeal don't ask, tell	Y
4. Pass cap-and-trade	Y	8. Pass tax cuts for some	Y	12. Limit campaign funds	Y

Election Results

2010 general	Nydia Velázquez (D)	...68,624	(94%)	($838,912)
	Alice Gaffney (C)	...4,482	(6%)	
2010 primary	Nydia Velázquez (D)	...unopposed		

Prior Winning Percentages: 2008 (90%), 2006 (90%), 2004 (86%), 2002 (96%), 2000 (87%), 1998 (84%), 1996 (85%), 1994 (92%), 1992 (77%)

THIRTEENTH DISTRICT

Michael Grimm (R)

Elected 2010, 1st term; b. Feb. 7, 1970, Brooklyn; home, Staten Island; Baruch Col., B.A. 1994; NY Law Schl., J.D. 2002; Catholic; Single.

Military Career: Marine Corps, 1991 (Persian Gulf).

Professional Career: Special agent, FBI, 1997-2006; owner, Healthalicious restaurant, 2006-08; principal, Austin Refuel.

DC Office: 512 CHOB, 20515, 202-225-3371; Fax: 202-226-1272; Web site: grimm.house.gov.

State Offices: Brooklyn, 718-630-5277; Staten Island, 718-351-1062.

Committees: *Financial Services:* Capital Markets and Government Sponsored Enterprises; Financial Institutions and Consumer Credit.

Election Results

2010 general	Michael Grimm (R)	65,024	(51%)	($1,278,332)
	Michael McMahon (D)	60,773	(48%)	($2,728,803)
2010 primary	Michael Grimm (R)	unopposed		

Population		Race/Ethnicity		Work	
Pop. 2010:	686,525	White:	62.3%	Private:	75.7%
Change since 2000:	Up 4.9%	Black:	6.8%	Government:	19.3%
Urban:	100.0%	Hispanic:	16.1%	Self-employed:	4.9%
Rural:	0.0%	Asian:	13.1%	Blue collar:	18.9%
Area size:	113 sq. mi.	Native Am.:	0.1%	White collar:	63.1%
		Hawaiian:	0.0%	Khaki collar:	0.1%
Age		Two+ races:	1.4%	Other:	17.8%
Median age:	38.7 yrs.				
More than 65 yrs:	13.9%	*Ancestry*		Median income:	$62,226
Less than 18 yrs:	22.4%	Italian	27.4%	Median Home Value:	$490,300
		Irish	10.4%		
Education		German	4.2%	**Military Veterans**	
H.S. grad:	83.9%			% of Pop:	5.9%
College grad:	27.8%				
Grad degree:	11.0%				

Staten Island, Brooklyn

Staten Island is part of New York City, yet is a land apart, closer geographically and culturally to New Jersey than to the city's other boroughs. The sixth-largest island in the continental U.S., its inclusion in Greater New York as part of the great 1898 consolidation was something of an afterthought. It was connected to the rest of the city only by ferry or through Bayonne, N.J., until the Verrazano-Narrows Bridge—one of Robert Moses' last and most impressive infrastructure

2008 Presidential Vote		
John McCain (R)	112,491	(51%)
Barack Obama (D)	108,439	(49%)

2004 Presidential Vote		
George Bush (R)	118,370	(55%)
John Kerry (D)	96,474	(45%)

Cook Partisan Voting Index: R+4

achievements—opened to traffic in 1964. Hilly Staten Island (or Richmond County) is the state's southernmost county, one-tenth as densely populated as Manhattan, and that's after it grew 27% between 1990 and 2009, one of the fastest growth rates of any county in New York state. Its rate of home ownership, 64%, is more than double that of the rest of New York City. Ethnically, the 13th District has the highest percentage of residents of Italian ancestry in the nation. The signs on coffee shops read *Caffe* and on delicatessens, *Salumeria*. The Staten Island Ferry docks at St. George, the home of the Staten Island Yankees' ballpark. The north and south shores that spread out from there are notable for their pleasant Victorian homes, while the island's west shore is industrial marshland, with plans for the eventual development of a 2,200-acre park—more than twice as large as Central Park—on top of the now-closed Fresh Kills dump. Staten Island's interior consists of blocks of suburbia alternating with scrubland that's rapidly being turned into suburbia. Population growth, plus a shortage of mass transit, has brought significant traffic congestion to the island, which is more dependent on cars than the other boroughs.

Culturally, Staten Islanders are more conservative than people from the boroughs, particularly the Manhattanites who live a 20-minute ferry ride away. Taking a cue from Fresh Kills, their motto is "Don't dump on us." Not many people here read *The New York Times*; the local paper is the *Staten Island Advance*. Fed up with the city's high income taxes and social programs, Staten Island residents voted in 1993 for secession, but the legislature never acted to carry out their wish. In that same election, Staten Islanders provided the margin of victory for Republican Mayor Rudolph Giuliani, whose agenda of cutting crime and welfare rolls soothed the secessionist fervor. The Giuliani years produced an economic boom, with a new ferry terminal, additional shops and hundreds of new houses near cleaned-up beaches. The biggest victory was the closing of Fresh Kills in 2001, though it opened again temporarily for the cleanup of the World Trade Center site. The crisis on Wall Street in 2008 reverberated strongly in this land of commuters, heavily dependent on jobs off the island. The median household income on Staten Island fell from $74,000 to $66,000 in 2009.

The 13th Congressional District of New York is made up of Staten Island plus Brooklyn neighborhoods with similar demographics. These include heavily Catholic and Italian Bay Ridge, Dyker Heights and Bensonhurst, middle-class enclaves with large single-family brownstones that are nowhere near a subway stop and thus impervious to the gentrification spreading across Brooklyn. Nearly a fourth of all the firefighters who died on September 11 were from Staten Island, which lost a total of 250 people in the terrorist attacks. The entertainment industry has found some memorable characters in these neighborhoods: The Three Stooges (Moe, Curly and Shemp) grew up in Bensonhurst, which also was the home to the fictional Ralph Kramden of *The Honeymooners*. John Travolta danced to fame in the film *Saturday Night Fever* on the streets of Bensonhurst and Bay Ridge. The district also includes Gravesend, with its large population of Sephardic Jews, and Fort Hamilton, the only active-duty military base in New York City and one of the oldest military posts still in operation in the United States.

The 13th is seeing a rising number of immigrants. There are growing numbers of Muslims in Bay Ridge and an influx of newcomers from West Africa, Mexico, South America, Southeast Asia, and Russia in white ethnic neighborhoods near St. George. But Staten Island remains New York's whitest borough and has the fewest immigrants. It was only 7% black and 14% Hispanic in 2009. Voters here solidly backed Republican George Pataki for governor and gave then-Republican Mayor Michael Bloomberg his slim winning margin in 2001. The district voted 52%-44% for Democrat Al Gore in 2000, but snapped back to Republican George W. Bush four years later, 55%-45%. In 2008, it voted for Republican John McCain 51%-49%.

Michael Grimm (R)

The new congressman from the 13th District is Republican Michael Grimm, who unseated freshman Democrat Michael McMahon in 2010. Grimm grew up in Staten Island and left college during his freshman year to join the Marines, serving in the Persian Gulf War. After he left active duty, he joined the FBI, working as a clerk on the midnight shift and taking college classes during the day. Grimm completed the Federal Police Officer Training Program and became a U.S. marshal and uniformed police officer for the FBI. He then got his bachelor's degree in accounting from Baruch College, and returned to the FBI as a special agent, investigating organized crime and financial fraud. He went undercover for two years as a hedge fund manager investigating fraud and stock manipulation as part of a sting operation that resulted in the arrests of more than 30 traders and brokers in 2003. Grimm left the bureau in 2006 to open a health food restaurant in Manhattan. He is also the director of a Texas-based biofuel company.

He was a political novice when he decided to take on McMahon in 2010. He first had to get through a competitive Republican primary against public policy analyst Michael Allegretti, who attacked him for health code violations at his restaurant and for passing out campaign photos of himself sporting ribbons that Allegretti said Grimm did not earn. Grimm responded that he was awarded some ribbons erroneously because of an Army administrative mistake that was discovered only after the photos were taken. Grimm had the support of tea party groups, former Alaska Gov. Sarah Palin, and former New York City Mayor Rudy Giuliani, while Allegretti was backed by the borough Republican Party. Grimm won with a solid 69% of the vote.

In the general election, McMahon had a decisive edge in fundraising. By mid-October, the Democrat had pulled in $2.5 million, compared with Grimm's $925,231. Democrats did not sense danger until it was too late. Democratic gubernatorial candidate Andrew Cuomo endorsed McMahon only the day before the election. Grimm attacked McMahon for his support of President Barack Obama's $787 billion economic stimulus bill and dubbed him "Tax Hike Mike." McMahon focused on his work to help Staten Island, such as seeking federal transportation funds. He also emphasized his independence from the party, touting his votes against the Democrats' health care overhaul and the endorsement of independent Michael Bloomberg, New York's mayor.

Grimm later told the *Staten Island Advance* that he believes momentum turned in his favor after a candidate debate at which McMahon supporters seated Grimm's ex-wife in the front row to "psych him out." Not only did he remain unflustered, he was gracious afterwards, saying his former wife looked as beautiful as the day he met her. With voter sympathy on his side, and a strong Republican tide working in his favor that year, Grimm won 51% to 48%.

FOURTEENTH DISTRICT

Carolyn Maloney (D)

Elected 1992, 10th term; b. Feb. 19, 1946, Greensboro, NC; home, Manhattan; Greensboro Col, A.B. 1968; Presbyterian; widowed; 2 children.

Elected Office: NY City Cncl., 1982–92.

Professional Career: NYC Bd. of Ed., 1970–77; Legis. aide, NY Assembly & NY Senate, 1977–82.

DC Office: 2332 RHOB, 20515, 202-225-7944; Fax: 202-225-4709; Web site: maloney.house.gov.

State Offices: Astoria, 718-932-1804; Manhattan, 212-860-0606.

Committees: *Financial Services:* Capital Markets and Government Sponsored Enterprises; Domestic Monetary Policy & Technology; Financial Institutions & Consumer Credit (RMM). *Joint Economic Committee. Oversight & Government Reform:* TARP, Financial Services & Bailouts of Public & Private Programs.

Group Ratings

	ACLU	ACU	ADA	CFG	AFS	FRC	LCV	ITIC	NTU	COC
2010	94	0	95	0	100	0	90	100	8	25
2009	–	0	95	4	100	–	100	–	2	36

National Journal Ratings

	2010 LIB	—	2010 CONS	2009 LIB	—	2009 CONS
Economic	90%	—	0%	68%	—	30%
Social	77%	—	21%	72%	—	28%
Foreign	78%	—	17%	85%	—	14%
Composite	85%	—	16%	76%	—	25%

Key Votes of the 111th Congress

1. Overturn Ledbetter	Y	5. Bar federal abortion funds	N	9. Stop detainee transfers	Y
2. Pass $820 billion stimulus	Y	6. Pass health care bill	Y	10. Legalize immigrants' kids	Y
3. Let guns in national parks	N	7. Regulate financial firms	Y	11. Repeal don't ask, tell	Y
4. Pass cap-and-trade	Y	8. Pass tax cuts for some	Y	12. Limit campaign funds	Y

Election Results

2010 general	Carolyn Maloney (D)	107,327	(75%)	($3,052,944)
	David Brumberg (R)	32,065	(22%)	($242,401)
2010 primary	Carolyn Maloney (D)	unopposed		

Prior Winning Percentages: 2008 (80%), 2006 (84%), 2004 (81%), 2002 (75%), 2000 (74%), 1998 (77%), 1996 (72%), 1994 (64%), 1992 (50%)

Population		Race/Ethnicity		Work	
Pop. 2010:	652,681	White:	65.7%	Private:	84.7%
Change since 2000:	Down 0.3%	Black:	4.5%	Government:	7.6%
Urban:	100.0%	Hispanic:	13.7%	Self-employed:	7.6%
Rural:	0.0%	Asian:	13.4%	Blue collar:	5.9%
Area size:	15 sq. mi.	Native Am.:	0.1%	White collar:	84.4%
		Hawaiian:	0.0%	Khaki collar:	0.0%
Age		Two+ races:	2.0%	Other:	9.7%
Median age:	37.8 yrs.				
More than 65 yrs:	13.8%	*Ancestry*		Median income:	$81,111
Less than 18 yrs:	13.2%	Irish	8.5%	Median Home Value:	$759,900
		Italian	8.4%		
Education		German	7.0%	**Military Veterans**	
H.S. grad:	91.4%			% of Pop:	4.1%
College grad:	65.9%				
Grad degree:	30.2%				

East Side of Manhattan, Queens

The Upper East Side of Manhattan, the home of people with more accumulated wealth than anywhere else in the world, began as much of New York City did, as farmland. Its eastern border was established at Fifth Avenue when work began on Central Park in 1857, but most of the area was still farmland when the park was completed in 1873. During the 1880s, the avenues—Fifth, Madison, Park, Lexington, Third, Second, First—were paved, and rich New York-

2008 Presidential Vote		
Barack Obama (D) 212,802	(78%)
John McCain (R) 56,946	(21%)
2004 Presidential Vote		
John Kerry (D) 201,782	(74%)
George Bush (R) 66,494	(25%)
Cook Partisan Voting Index: D+26		

ers as well as many who had made their money elsewhere, including Pittsburgh steel baron Andrew Carnegie, built mansions on Fifth Avenue. With its elevated train line, Third Avenue was lined with walk-ups for working- class commuters, while the side streets off Fifth Avenue were filled with massive brownstones shielded from the industrial haze along the East River. The Upper East Side began taking on its present character in 1913, when Grand Central Terminal was opened and the New York Central rail line was buried under Park Avenue. What had been a filthy railroad cut became a broad boulevard lined with grand apartment buildings. The federal income tax, passed the same year, had the unintended consequence of encouraging New York's rich to dispense with grand mansions and live, quietly and out of sight, in apartment buildings where doormen protected their privacy. The Upper East Side remains a world apart from ordinary folks. Even during the recent recession, sales of large apartments in the city costing upwards of $2.5 million swelled in 2009.

The emergence of the modern Upper East Side represented yet another iteration of the pattern noticed by the mid-19th-century New York diarists Philip Hone and George Templeton Strong: On such a compact island, it took only a generation or so before buildings were torn down and rebuilt. Even today, New York is being transformed by gleaming postmodern skyscrapers and high-priced storefronts, though its most enduring landmarks were products of the first half of the 20th century: the Flatiron Building, built in 1901; the Woolworth Building and Grand Central, in 1913; the Chrysler Building, in the 1920s; and the Empire State Building and Rockefeller Center, in the 1930s. The United Nations headquarters, the world's first glass-fronted skyscraper, went up after World War II. This area also holds the more humble distinction of being the site of the first public-housing project in America: The First Houses were built in lower Manhattan in 1935 by Mayor Fiorello LaGuardia.

The 14th Congressional District of New York includes within its irregular borders the Upper East Side and nearly all of these famous buildings. Its median family income, in 2007 inflation-adjusted dollars, was nearly $100,000. It begins at East 96th Street, the historic dividing line between Manhattan's wealthiest and poorest neighborhoods, and runs all the way down to East 9th Street in the East Village. It includes all of Central Park, much of the midtown corporate district, Murray Hill and Gramercy Park. It takes in parts of the East Village, with its pricey lofts and busy nightlife, and the Lower East Side. Midtown Manhattan's skyscrapers and the Garment District are also here, as is Roosevelt Island, a 147-acre expanse in the East River that was transformed in the 1970s from a hospital-and-prison complex into an ethnically diverse residential neighborhood. The 14th also encompasses part of Queens across the East River; blue-collar Long Island City; Steinway, part of historically Irish Sunnyside; and vibrant Greek Astoria, now with many Asians, Latinos and Arabs. The district's cultural landmarks are among the world's finest: the Metropolitan Museum of Art, the Guggenheim, the Whitney Museum of American Art and the Frick Collection, but also a rising arts cluster in Long Island City with the contemporary art gallery P.S. 1 and the American Museum of the Moving Image.

The district has always been dominated by its affluent and highly educated voters, leaders in securities, publishing, advertising, entertainment, broadcasting and communications. Historically, they mistrusted the city's usually Democratic immigrant masses. In the last half century, the attitude of the Manhattan elite was transformed from liberal Republican to leftish Democratic. Recent mayors, Republican Rudolph Giuliani and his successor, Michael Bloomberg, who lives in a town house on East 79th Street, have been cultural liberals on abortion rights, gay rights and gun control. The Upper East Side has been unremittingly hostile to the culturally conservative Republicanism of recent years. The Upper East Side's 10021 zip code was the nation's top zip code for Democratic campaign contributions in 2004, 2008 and 2010. The district voted for Democrat Barack Obama over Republican John McCain 78% to 21% in 2008.

Carolyn Maloney (D)

The congresswoman from the 14th District is Carolyn Maloney, a Democrat elected in 1992. Born and educated in North Carolina, she visited New York in 1970 at the age of 22, loved it and "just stayed." She taught adult-education classes in East Harlem and, from 1977 to 1982, was an influential legislative staffer in Albany. She was elected to the New York City Council in 1982. Redistricting in 1992 made the Silk Stocking district more Democratic, and Maloney ran against incumbent Bill Green, an independent Republican who shared Manhattan's cultural liberalism. But he was poorly positioned to appeal to voters in the outer-borough neighborhoods that had been added to the district, who preferred Republicans to be conservative on cultural issues but liberal on economics. Maloney lost the Manhattan part of the district 50%-44% but carried Queens heavily, winning 50%-48% overall.

Maloney has a mostly liberal voting record. She is one the most prolific legislators in Congress, and has the ancillary distinction of being the first woman in Congress to get a black belt in martial arts. She won new prominence in early 2009 when she became chairman of the Joint Economic Committee, a House and Senate panel that tackles pressing economic issues. She is also a senior member of the Financial Services Committee, where she has been a leading voice on banking issues, but has been overshadowed at times by her well-respected and colorful colleague, Barney Frank of Massachusetts. She worked to win House passage of her bill to promote more transparent practices by credit card companies and to restrict abusive lending practices. She called the bill "a much-needed correction to a market that is out of balance." With a boost from President Barack Obama, the bill was enacted in May 2009. She also had a hand in the Wall Street overhaul bill that became law in 2010, working with Sen. Richard Durbin, D-Ill., to achieve a compromise on interchange fees charged on consumers' debit cards. The fees had been an area of contention between merchants worried about their high rates and the financial industry's worries that lower fees would not cover their costs.

Even though she has many constituents in banking, Maloney had tough rhetoric for bankers who took millions of dollars in bonuses after their firms received federal bailout money in 2008. She did join fellow New York Democrat Michael McMahon in early 2010 in leading the fight against a proposal by Peter DeFazio, D-Ore., to impose a 0.25% tax on stock transactions above $100,000. In earlier years, she worked to keep banks from controlling other businesses, sought more oversight of the Federal Reserve, and added privacy provisions to financial modernization bills. She helped to craft reforms tightening rules for foreign investment. With an eye to her corporate constituents, she voted for normal trade relations with China.

A leader of the Women's Caucus, she demanded that the Food and Drug Administration permit over-the-counter sales of morning-after birth-control pills, and she opposed separating men and women in basic training in the military. She sponsored a bill to create an office within the Internal Revenue Service to prosecute sex traffickers who violate tax laws. In 2007, with Sen. Edward Kennedy, D-Mass., she introduced the Women's Equality Amendment, a latter-day version of the Equal Rights Amendment, which had fallen three states short of constitutional ratification in the 1970s. She reintroduced the measure in 2011. The House passed her 2008 bill to give eight weeks of paid leave to federal employees for the birth or adoption of a child. Also that year, she authored a book, *Rumors of Our Progress Have Been Greatly Exaggerated: Why Women's Lives Aren't Getting Any Easier—And How We Can Make Real Progress for Ourselves and Our Daughters.*

With part of her district in Lower Manhattan and close to Ground Zero, Maloney was heavily involved in the government response to the September 11 attacks. She was among the most outspoken House Democrats urging President George W. Bush to quickly send New York the $20 billion that Congress approved for cleanup and recovery. But her proposal to give a $1,000 tax credit to visitors to the city went nowhere. In the lame-duck session of 2010, she and several other New York lawmakers steered into law a long-delayed measure to compensate Sept. 11 first responders with health problems. "It is so fair, it is so right, it should have passed nine years ago," she said.

Maloney had less success in her bid to become the Oversight and Government Reform Committee's ranking Democrat after her party lost its House majority in 2010. Many Democrats contended that the departing chairman, New York's Edolphus Towns, lacked the aggressiveness to stand up to California's Darrell Issa, the incoming GOP chairman. Towns bowed out of the race and threw his support to Maloney, who campaigned vigorously for the slot. But she lost to the less senior Elijah Cummings of Maryland in a vote of 33-18 in the Democratic Steering Committee and 119-61 in the Democratic caucus. Cummings reportedly had the pivotal backing of Minority Leader Nancy Pelosi.

Maloney has a firm lock on the district. In the Republican year of 1994, City Councilman Charles Millard of Manhattan spent almost $1 million running against her, but Maloney won 64%-35%. Aside from the perils of redistricting, she has not had to worry about re-election since then.

She was bitterly disappointed when Democratic Gov. David Paterson appointed the less-seasoned Rep. Kirsten Gillibrand to the Senate seat vacated by Hillary Rodham Clinton in 2009. Maloney publicly questioned Gillibrand's conservative stance on issues such as gun control and curbing illegal immigration, and she began raising money for a primary challenge in 2010. But after months of groundwork, in August 2009 she heeded the calls of Obama and senior New York Democrats to give Gillibrand a clear path to the nomination. She endured a wrenching personal setback the next month, when her husband, Clifton, died on a mountain-climbing expedition in the Himalayas.

FIFTEENTH DISTRICT

Charles Rangel (D)

Elected 1970, 21st term; b. June 11, 1930, New York City; home, Harlem; N.Y.U., B.S. 1957, St. John's U., LL.B. 1960; Catholic; married (Alma); 2 children.

Military Career: Army, 1948–52 (Korea).

Elected Office: NY Assembly, 1966–70.

Professional Career: Asst. U.S. atty., S. Dist. of NY, 1959-64; Legal cnsl., NYC Housing & Redevel. Bd., Neighborhood Conservation Bureau, 1963–68; Gen. cnsl., Natl. Advisory Comm. on Selective Svc., 1966.

DC Office: 2354 RHOB, 20515, 202-225-4365; Fax: 202-225-0816; Web site: rangel.house.gov.

State Offices: Manhattan, 212-663-3900.

Committees: *Joint Committee on Taxation. Ways & Means.*

Group Ratings

	ACLU	ACU	ADA	CFG	AFS	FRC	LCV	ITIC	NTU	COC
2010	87	0	100	0	100	0	100	67	4	13
2009	–	0	95	4	100	–	100	–	2	43

National Journal Ratings

	2010 LIB — 2010 CONS		2009 LIB — 2009 CONS	
Economic	90%	— 0%	73%	— 25%
Social	87%	— 12%	89%	— 0%
Foreign	91%	— 9%	70%	— 24%
Composite	91%	— 9%	81%	— 20%

Key Votes of the 111th Congress

1. Overturn Ledbetter	Y	5. Bar federal abortion funds	N	9. Stop detainee transfers	N
2. Pass $820 billion stimulus	Y	6. Pass health care bill	Y	10. Legalize immigrants' kids	Y
3. Let guns in national parks	N	7. Regulate financial firms	Y	11. Repeal don't ask, tell	Y
4. Pass cap-and-trade	Y	8. Pass tax cuts for some	Y	12. Limit campaign funds	Y

Election Results

2010 general	Charles Rangel (D)	91,225	(80%)	($2,937,509)
	Michel Faulkner (R)	11,754	(10%)	($223,119)
	Craig Schley (I)	7,803	(7%)	
	Roger Calero (SWP)	2,647	(2%)	
2010 primary	Charles Rangel (D)	unopposed		

Prior Winning Percentages: 2008 (89%), 2006 (94%), 2004 (91%), 2002 (88%), 2000 (92%), 1998 (93%), 1996 (91%), 1994 (97%), 1992 (95%), 1990 (97%), 1988 (97%), 1986 (96%), 1984 (97%), 1982 (97%), 1980 (96%), 1978 (96%), 1976 (97%), 1974 (97%), 1972 (96%), 1970 (87%)

Population		Race/Ethnicity		Work	
Pop. 2010:	639,873	White:	20.9%	Private:	79.1%
Change since 2000:	Down 2.2%	Black:	26.5%	Government:	13.3%
Urban:	100.0%	Hispanic:	46.1%	Self-employed:	7.5%
Rural:	0.0%	Asian:	4.2%	Blue collar:	11.4%
Area size:	16 sq. mi.	Native Am.:	0.2%	White collar:	64.7%
		Hawaiian:	0.0%	Khaki collar:	0.1%
Age		Two+ races:	1.6%	Other:	23.8%
Median age:	34.1 yrs.				
More than 65 yrs:	11.7%	*Ancestry*		Median income:	$38,609
Less than 18 yrs:	20.7%	Irish	3.3%	Median Home Value:	$667,000
		German	3.3%		
Education		West Indian	3.2%	**Military Veterans**	
H.S. grad:	73.3%			% of Pop:	3.3%
College grad:	36.6%				
Grad degree:	17.6%				

North Manhattan; Harlem

Harlem, for many years America's most famous black ghetto, is rebounding from decades of grim times. In the late 19th century, Harlem was a commuter neighborhood for Germans and then Jews and Italians. After the turn of the century, real estate speculators began constructing blocks of impressive brownstones, hoping to capitalize on the impending arrival of the subway. But overbuilding led to high vacancy rates,

2008 Presidential Vote
Barack Obama (D) 226,049   (93%)
John McCain (R) 14,954   (6%)

2004 Presidential Vote
John Kerry (D) 194,186   (90%)
George Bush (R) 20,049   (9%)

Cook Partisan Voting Index: D+41

and some landlords agreed to rent to African-Americans, as long as they were willing to pay a premium. After generations of being shunted from one neighborhood to the next as the city developed, black residents were willing, and the neighborhood soon turned into the locus of New York City's black community. Harlem expanded from its nucleus around Lenox Avenue and 125th Street, while the neighborhood to the east later known as Spanish Harlem grew outward from 116th Street and Pleasant Avenue. Many great black Americans—W. E. B. DuBois, Thurgood Marshall, Ralph Ellison, Joe Louis—lived in northwest Harlem's Sugar Hill.

For a long moment in history, Harlem was a center of writers and professionals and entertainers. The rosters of the Apollo Theater on 125th Street in the 1920s and 1930s were filled with the names of great artists still remembered today. Back then, the *WPA Guide* described Harlem as "the spiritual capital of Black America." But starting with the riot in the summer of 1964, Harlem endured decades of deterioration. Hundreds of brownstones were abandoned or pulled down. As successful black families moved out—to Springfield Gardens in Queens or Williamsbridge in the Bronx or to the Westchester or New Jersey suburbs—Harlem's population shifted increasingly toward welfare dependency and criminal gangs, and it declined by a third between 1970 and 1990.

Starting in the 1990s, Harlem began to recover. The federal government gave $300 million in investment capital, and the huge drop in crime under Republican Mayor Rudolph Giuliani made Harlem real estate valuable again. Brownstones were renovated, vacant city buildings were sold off, neighborhood schools were upgraded, and arts spaces opened. Harlem was made a federal enterprise zone, with favorable federal and state tax treatment, and the Metropolitan Economic Revitalization Fund pumped money into new developments, as did Calvin Butts's Abyssinian Baptist Church. Younger African-Americans are returning, while visitors from overseas, especially Japan and Europe, flock to the area for historical tours, prompting a boomlet in niche hotels and guest houses. The façade of the Apollo Theater has been restored, a new Harlem pier has been constructed, and supermarkets and chain stores have opened. In 2001, former President Bill Clinton opened his post presidential office at 55 W. 125th Street in Harlem. There has been a double-digit percentage increase in median household income in Harlem since 2000. The upward trend abated somewhat in 2008 as Wall Street's problems reduced investment and charitable donations.

Politically, Harlem has been heavily Democratic ever since the 1930s, when black voters switched from the Republican Party of Abraham Lincoln to the Democratic Party of Franklin Roosevelt. Harlem got its own congressional district in 1944 and elected Adam Clayton Powell Jr., minister at the Abyssinian Baptist Church and a brilliant orator. He was the chairman of the Education and Labor Committee when it passed the Great Society programs in 1965, but was excluded from Congress in 1967 (illegally, the Supreme Court later ruled) for refusing to honor a New York decree in a libel case.

Today, the 15th Congressional District of New York includes not just Harlem but all of northern Manhattan, down to 89th Street on the west side and 96th Street on the east side. On the west side, the district's southern reaches include portions of the white, liberal Upper West Side as well as the Morningside Heights precincts around Columbia University. On the east side, at 96th Street, the railroad comes out of the tunnel that runs under Park Avenue to Grand Central Station, and the Upper East Side gives way to Harlem. Spanish Harlem, just to the north, was once Italian (it was Fiorello LaGuardia's political base) and later heavily Puerto Rican. Today, "El Barrio" has fewer Puerto Ricans and more Mexicans and Dominicans along with some gentrifying whites. Still farther north, the district includes Washington Heights and Inwood, both heavily Latino and the center of Dominican life in New York as Dominicans replace Puerto Ricans as New York's most numerous Latino group.

Overall, the district in 2010 was 27% black and 46% Hispanic, figures that testify to decades of black flight from Harlem and the continuing inflow of immigrants from the Western Hemisphere. In 2004, this was the most heavily Democratic congressional district in the nation, voting 90% for John Kerry for president. Democrat Barack Obama won it in 2008 with 93%, his second best in the nation, after New York's adjacent 16th District.

Charles Rangel (D)

The congressman from the 15th District is Democrat Charles Rangel, first elected to the House in 1970. Rangel had wielded considerable power as chairman of the tax-writing House Ways and Means Committee until he was forced to step aside on March 3, 2010 as a result of a House Ethics Committee investigation. Later in the year, Rangel was censured for violations of congressional ethics rules.

Rangel grew up in Harlem and served in the Army in Korea, where he rescued 40 men from behind the lines in Kunu-ri and was awarded the Bronze Star. He graduated from New York University and St. John's University law school, served as legal counsel in several government agencies and was elected to the New York Assembly in 1966. He was part of a group of young black politicians—among them Basil Paterson, Carl McCall, Percy Sutton and Adam Clayton Powell III—who for many years dominated Harlem and greatly influenced New York politics. In 1970, Rangel challenged Powell in the Democratic primary and narrowly won. Remarkably, these two iconic and often controversial figures have been the district's only representatives for two-thirds of a century. Like most Harlem politicians, Rangel has long argued that government aid and racial preferences are needed to solve Harlem's problems.

Aside from some early successes on trade and increasing the minimum wage, Rangel's first two years as chairman in the 110th Congress (2007-08) were stymied by partisan deadlock as his proposals came under veto threat from the Republican White House. In 2009, Rangel said he was eager to "have a head start" in legislative planning for the new administration. "Time is not our friend," he warned in July 2008, describing the multiple challenges on tax policy, health care and entitlements legislation. With Democrat Barack Obama as president, Rangel moved quickly to enact the long-discussed children's health insurance expansion, and he helped craft $348 billion in tax cuts over five years in the administration's $787 billion economic stimulus bill. He also joined other senior House Democrats in extended discussions on health reform. Somewhat less expected was his assertive role on climate change legislation. Environmental legislation traditionally has been under the control of the Energy and Commerce Committee, but Rangel held numerous hearings on a proposed carbon tax.

Rangel's chairmanship was marred by numerous ethics issues uncovered by *The New York Times*. The newspaper raised questions about four rent-controlled apartments that Rangel maintained in Harlem and his failure to report rental income from a villa in the Dominican Republic. Perhaps most damaging, *The Times* reported that Maurice Greenberg, one of the biggest shareholders in financially troubled American International Group, gave a public policy school named for Rangel $5 million in 2007, and that Rangel in early 2008, supported a provision in a tax bill that saved AIG several million dollars a year. Rangel steadfastly denied wrongdoing, and in September 2008, he requested a review by the House Committee on Standards of Official Conduct.

The committee opened an investigation into those allegations. Meanwhile, another issue cropped up: corporate-sponsored trips Rangel took to Antigua, Barbuda and St. Maarten in 2007 and 2008. The panel concluded that Rangel's staff knew that corporations were helping to finance trips, but failed to reveal that fact when they asked the committee to pre-approve them. Rangel was instructed to reimburse the sponsors for the costs of his travel. Several Democrats, including some prominent lawmakers, were prepared to vote in favor of a Republican resolution seeking to remove Rangel as chairman if the measure came to the floor as expected. Rangel said he wanted to save his fellow Democrats from "having to defend me during their elections" in November, and announced in March 2010 he would take a leave of absence from the chairmanship.

After a nearly two-year investigation, the full committee in July 2010 announced 13 allegations against Rangel. They included his acceptance of the rent-stabilized apartments from a Manhattan developer, failure to pay taxes on rental income from the Dominican villa and his acceptance of contributions for his foundations from companies seeking legislative favors. Rangel acknowledged bookkeeping mistakes and said he failed to properly oversee his finances, but argued that he did nothing to personally benefit or enrich himself. Still, in November, the committee ruled there was sufficient evidence to support the allegations. Before the decision, Rangel indignantly walked out of the proceedings claiming he could no longer afford legal representation and that it was unfair to continue. Two days later, the panel voted 9 to 1 in favor of censure, a form of punishment just short of expulsion in which a member is shamed by a public recitation of rules violations on the floor of the House. Rangel's friends and allies, and Rangel himself, lobbied for a milder form of punishment called a reprimand. But on Dec. 2, the House voted 333 to 79 for censure. Rangel stood in the well of the House, his hands clasped behind him, while Speaker Pelosi read a resolution censuring him for bringing discredit to the House. Censure of a member of Congress is rare. The last time it happened was 1983, when Reps. Daniel Crane, R-Ill., and Gerry Studds, D-Mass., were censured for carrying on sexual relationships with congressional pages. After his rebuke, Rangel addressed the chamber briefly, saying, "I know in my heart I am not going to be judged by this Congress. I'll be judged by my life in its entirety."

Rangel's fall from grace was particularly striking given his history as a savvy legislator. When he was on his game, Rangel displayed an effective combination of political shrewdness and personal charm even allowing for his occasional rhetorical extravagance. When a bipartisan majority voted to end racial preferences in broadcasting in 1995, Rangel lashed out in a letter to then-Ways and Means Chairman Bill Archer, R-Texas, saying, "Just like under Hitler, people say they don't mean to blame any particular individuals and groups, but in the U.S. those groups always turn out to be minorities and immigrants." Archer refused to speak to Rangel, then the ranking member of the committee, except in public forums. During the 1990s, Rangel defended President Bill Clinton against impeachment with great vigor, but he did not always get along with Clinton. And he resented it when the administration negotiated directly with Republicans, leaving him and other congressional Democrats out of the loop.

Republican Bill Thomas of California succeeded Archer as chairman. With a notoriously acerbic tongue, Thomas made few if any moves toward a legislative partnership with Rangel. In 2003, a Ways and Means meeting on pension legislation ended in chaos when Democrats led by Rangel walked out in protest, charging they hadn't had time to review a substitute bill the committee was considering. Thomas called the Capitol Police to remove the Democrats from the library where they had gathered, and in their absence, Republicans approved the bill by voice vote. Rangel later offered a resolution to nullify the meeting and chastised Thomas, but dropped the effort after Thomas went to the House floor and made a tearful apology. Yet the committee was never able to work in a bipartisan way. Rangel also protested when Thomas excluded him from the House-Senate conference committee on the 2003 Medicare prescription-drug bill. The only Democrats Thomas allowed in were Senate Finance Committee members Max Baucus of Montana and John Breaux of Louisiana, who favored Thomas's bill.

Rangel has opposed some of the international free-trade agreements of recent years, but has proven open to compromise on others. After becoming chairman in 2007, Rangel moved to have the full committee, not the Ways and Means Trade Subcommittee, handle trade agreements. The subcommittee was chaired by liberal Democrat Sander Levin of Michigan, who has taken a harder line on labor and environmental provisions. In 2000, Rangel worked hard for a bill to cut tariffs on apparel and other imports from sub-Saharan Africa, despite opposition from labor unions, textile interests and other members of the Congressional Black Caucus. During 2004, Rangel did not take a position on the Central American-Dominican Republic Free Trade Agreement, though many Democrats opposed the agreement. There are many Dominican and Central American immigrants in New York. After an earthquake devastated an already destitute Haiti in January 2010, Rangel sponsored a trade bill allowing the country to export more apparel to the United States. The bill passed the House and was signed into law by Obama in May 2010.

One of Rangel's top priorities has been a permanent change in the alternative minimum tax to prevent it from ensnaring middle-class taxpayers. His best chance of getting such a major tax bill through Congress was as chairman of Ways and Means, and that opportunity has passed him by. Over the years, he helped write several bills to help high-poverty areas like Harlem, including the federal empowerment zone law, the low-income housing tax credit and the 1993 increases in the earned income tax credit. Earlier in his House career, Rangel's main emphasis was curbing the illegal drug trade.

On foreign policy, Rangel has long advocated eliminating sanctions on trade with Cuba. He favors allowing Haitian and Dominican immigrants into the United States on the same basis as refugees from Cuba. Rangel voted against the Iraq war resolution in 2002 and the following year called for the resignation of Defense Secretary Donald Rumsfeld. Late in 2002, he called for a revival of the military draft, contending that "a disproportionate number of the poor and members of minority groups make up the enlisted ranks of the military, while the most privileged Americans are underrepresented or absent." He introduced a bill in 2003 to require some form of national service, military or civilian, from Americans ages 18 to 26, and found 13 cosponsors. When House Republican leaders brought it to a vote in October 2004, he called it a "political maneuver to kill rumors of the president's intention to reinstate the draft after the November election" and voted against it, saying it had had no committee hearings. It was voted down 402-2.

Rangel has long been a major player in New York's city and state politics. He strongly backed his old friend, Democrat Carl McCall, for governor in 2002, and in December 2001, he said he would vote for Republican George Pataki if the nomination went to McCall's rival, Democrat Andrew Cuomo. In the 2008 presidential contest, Rangel was an early and vocal supporter of home-state Sen. Hillary Rodham Clinton in her pitched battle with Obama for the Democratic nomination. "This ain't no time for a beginner," he told *The New York Times*, referring to Obama's relative inexperience in the Senate. Despite pressure from many Democrats, including many of his constituents, he stuck with Clinton until she withdrew from the race.

For the most part, Rangel has been easily re-elected every two years. In 1994, he faced primary opposition from the son of his predecessor, New York City Councilman Adam Clayton Powell IV. Rangel spent $1.4 million and won 61%-33%. When he was sorely weakened in 2010 by the ethics case, Powell challenged him again in the Democratic primary, along with four other opponents. The election was a referendum on Rangel's ethics and continued fitness for office, but in the end, the results weren't even close. Rangel won the September primary, which assured his success in the general election, with 51% of the vote to Powell's 23%.

SIXTEENTH DISTRICT

José Serrano (D)

Elected Mar. 1990, 11th full term; b. Oct. 24, 1943, Mayaguez, PR; home, Bronx; Lehman Col.; Catholic; divorced; 5 children.

Military Career: Army Medical Corps, 1964–66.

Elected Office: Dist. 7 Schl. Bd., 1969–74; NY Assembly, 1974–90.

Professional Career: Banker, 1961–69.

DC Office: 2227 RHOB, 20515, 202-225-4361; Fax: 202-225-6001; Web site: serrano.house.gov.

State Offices: Bronx, 718-620-0084.

Committees: *Appropriations:* Commerce, Justice, Science & Related Agencies; Financial Services & General Government (RMM); Interior, Environment & Related Agencies.

Group Ratings

	ACLU	ACU	ADA	CFG	AFS	FRC	LCV	ITIC	NTU	COC
2010	94	0	100	0	100	0	100	50	5	13
2009	–	0	100	0	100	–	100	–	4	33

National Journal Ratings

	2010 LIB	—	2010 CONS	2009 LIB	—	2009 CONS
Economic	90%	—	0%	91%	—	0%
Social	82%	—	14%	89%	—	0%
Foreign	92%	—	3%	78%	—	17%
Composite	91%	—	9%	90%	—	10%

Key Votes of the 111th Congress

1. Overturn Ledbetter	Y	5. Bar federal abortion funds	N	9. Stop detainee transfers	N
2. Pass $820 billion stimulus	Y	6. Pass health care bill	Y	10. Legalize immigrants' kids	Y
3. Let guns in national parks	N	7. Regulate financial firms	Y	11. Repeal don't ask, tell	Y
4. Pass cap-and-trade	Y	8. Pass tax cuts for some	Y	12. Limit campaign funds	Y

Election Results

2010 general	José Serrano (D)..	61,642	(96%)	($373,374)
	Frank Della Valle (R)...	2,758	(4%)	
2010 primary	José Serrano (D)... unopposed			

Prior Winning Percentages: 2008 (97%), 2006 (95%), 2004 (95%), 2002 (92%), 2000 (96%), 1998 (95%), 1996 (96%), 1994 (96%), 1992 (91%), 1990 (93%), 1990 special (92%)

Population		Race/Ethnicity		Work	
Pop. 2010:	693,819	White:	2.4%	Private:	77.9%
Change since 2000:	Up 6.0%	Black:	28.0%	Government:	14.5%
Urban:	100.0%	Hispanic:	66.5%	Self-employed:	7.6%
Rural:	0.0%	Asian:	1.5%	Blue collar:	23.0%
Area size:	13 sq. mi.	Native Am.:	0.2%	White collar:	40.0%
		Hawaiian:	0.0%	Khaki collar:	0.1%
Age		Two+ races:	0.8%	Other:	37.0%
Median age:	29.1 yrs.				
More than 65 yrs:	7.5%	*Ancestry*		Median income:	$23,829
Less than 18 yrs:	31.9%	Subsaharan	5.6%	Median Home Value:	$351,000
		West Indian	4.0%		
Education		Italian	0.9%	**Military Veterans**	
H.S. grad:	59.2%			% of Pop:	2.8%
College grad:	10.7%				
Grad degree:	2.9%				

South Bronx

It may not quite be "the beautiful Bronx," as borough historian Lloyd Ultan calls it, but the Bronx seems to have rebounded from rock bottom. The beautiful days were in the 1930s and 1940s, when Babe Ruth, Lou Gehrig and Joe DiMaggio knocked home runs out of Yankee Stadium, art deco apartment buildings were built along the Grand Concourse, and shoppers thronged Tremont Avenue stores. Bronx County Democratic Chairman Ed Flynn chaired the

2008 Presidential Vote		
Barack Obama (D)	158,671	(95%)
John McCain (R)	8,437	(5%)
2004 Presidential Vote		
John Kerry (D)	130,109	(89%)
George Bush (R)	14,766	(10%)
Cook Partisan Voting Index:	D+41	

Democratic National Committee in the early 1940s. In the 1880s, the Bronx (only recently annexed from Westchester County) had been linked to the level eastern half of Manhattan by elevated steam locomotives. The borough really took off in 1906 with the arrival of the first subway, which allowed the children of immigrants to move from grim Lower East Side tenements to spacious walk-up apartments flooded with light. The Bronx population grew from 200,000 in 1900 to 1.2 million in 1930. Its population peaked at nearly 1.5 million in 1950. Four years later, one of its new residents was now-Supreme Court Justice Sonia Sotomayor, who as an infant lived in a South Bronx tenement before her family moved into the nearby Bronxdale Houses public housing project. After a quarter-century of deterioration, the population had shrunk to 1.2 million by 1990. Now, it's up again, to nearly 1.4 million, as new immigrants revive neighborhoods that had been given up for dead.

The decline of the Bronx began in the mid-1960s, when several factors led to the destruction of neighborhoods. Rent control guaranteed that many owners of low-rent property wouldn't maintain it. Once empty, buildings were torched for the insurance money, sometimes as many as four blocks of buildings a week. At the same time, a drop in low-skill jobs in Manhattan and the Bronx, abetted by high union wages, led to a rise in welfare dependency and crime, and empty building shells became the perfect venue for drug dealing. The 13-year, $250 million effort to build the Cross-Bronx Expressway—a brainchild of Robert Moses that crossed 113 streets and avenues, hundreds of utility mains and ten mass-transit lines—only made things worse. A vicious cycle emerged: Crime drove away jobs, which produced more crime. When Tom Wolfe imagined the "wrong turn" that sank a high-flying Wall Street career in *Bonfire of the Vanities*, he set it in the South Bronx.

Presidents and presidential candidates came in—Democrat Jimmy Carter in 1977, Republican Ronald Reagan in 1980—promising help. The borough's saviors were churches and creative community groups that built single-family, pastel bungalows and small-scale apartment projects for the elderly, for single-parent families and for the homeless. The South Bronx turned a corner. A building spree created the Bronx's first new wave of housing starts since the 1950s, and the first new cluster of private residences since the 1930s. As immigrants from the Dominican Republic, Jamaica, Ecuador, and Central America settled in, the population began to increase. A few corners of the South Bronx, such as Mott Haven, have even seen yuppies and artists colonizing old industrial spaces where gang wars prevailed not long ago. Charlotte Street, which Carter and Reagan visited as the worst of the slums, is now Charlotte Gardens, with owner-occupied houses. After decades of decay, some businesses—warehouses, distribution centers, small industrial parks—have begun to move back in. The new Yankee Stadium, at $1.5 billion the most expensive sports facility ever built in the United States, opened in 2009 and focused attention on the area's economic renewal. But this remains a low-income area, with many people on public assistance, and check-cashing outlets are still easier to find than banks. Unemployment in Bronx County was above 12% for all of 2010.

The 16th Congressional District of New York includes most of the South Bronx. It is bounded by the Harlem River on the west, the East River on the south, the Bronx River and Bronx Park (home of the Bronx Zoo) on the east, and it goes just past Fordham Road on the north. It also includes Belmont, the industrial flatlands of Bruckner Boulevard and Hunts Point (though not the meat and produce markets). The district is 28% black, and it has the highest share of Hispanics—67%—of any New York district. This has long been New York's largest concentration of Puerto Ricans, but about 60% of Hispanics here are now from other parts of Latin America. Measured by median income and percentage of families below poverty status, it ranked in 2010 as the most impoverished congressional district in the nation. The Gallup-Healthways Well-Being Index ranked it dead last among the 435 congressional districts in 2010 for overall health and happiness. This was the most heavily Democratic district in the nation in 2000 (92% for Al Gore) and the second most heavily Democratic in 2004 (89% for John Kerry). In 2008, voter turnout increased 15% with the enthusiasm for Democrat Barack Obama's candidacy, and he won nearly 95% of the vote, his best showing of any congressional district.

José Serrano (D)

The congressman from the 16th District is Democrat José Serrano, who won the seat in a 1990 special election. A native of Mayaguez, Puerto Rico, he grew up in the Mill Brook project in Mott Haven. After serving in the Army, he worked at a bank and as a school administrator. Serrano moved up while other Bronx politicians fell by the wayside because of corruption. He was elected to the New York Assembly in 1974 and chaired its Education Committee. In 1985, he ran for Bronx borough president, bucking the Democratic organization, and nearly won. Then in January 1990, U.S. Rep. Robert García of the South Bronx was convicted of accepting money from the minority contractor Wedtech. His conviction was later reversed, but his resignation paved the way for Serrano's election to the House.

Serrano has one of the most liberal voting records in the House. As a senior member of the Appropriations Committee, he brings as many federal dollars home to his economically strapped district as he can. He chaired its Financial Services subcommittee when the Democrats controlled Congress and is now its ranking Democrat. Among Appropriations members he is known as a jokester, always ready to enliven hearings with a quip. At a June 2010 session on the Federal Communications Commission's budget, he said he was doing his part for technology: "This hearing is online live as we speak. And I sent out a Twitter message. I put it on two Facebook pages and an e-mail. So we should get at least 10 people to watch." He often amiably spars with Rep. Jo Ann Emerson, R-Mo., over his beloved Yankees and her state's St. Louis Cardinals as well as its star slugger Albert Pujols. He told her at a February 2011 hearing, "I just want to know if the Republican (budget) cuts will affect Pujols' contract." Serrano told *National Journal* that humor is useful in a highly polarized House. "We take our work seriously, but we shouldn't always take ourselves so seriously," he said.

Serrano is a critic of outsourcing government services, and in 2007, he moved to end the Internal Revenue Service's use of private debt-collection companies for delinquent taxes. He was the only House member from New York City who voted in 2008 against the federal bailout for banks and other financial services companies. He said he couldn't justify giving money to the wealthy people who'd created the problem. A big local priority for Serrano has been cleaning up the Bronx River, and he delivered about $30 million for the effort. (When the river progressed to the point where it could support wildlife, a beaver appeared and was dubbed "José" in honor of Serrano's work in behalf of the waterway.) He helped secure $10 million in 2010 to rebuild the Fordham transit plaza, one of the city's busiest. He also was able to include illegal immigrants who responded to the September 11 attacks as among those compensated in the long-delayed bill that became law in the 2010 lame-duck session. With Republicans now in control, he said he sees one of his chief goals as "trying to avoid as much harm as possible" on budget cuts and "making sure people understand that cutting can hurt a lot of people."

Another of his issues is statehood for Puerto Rico, which he calls an American "colony." He backs a long-stalled referendum to determine the status of the island, and got a bill through the House in 2010 calling for a two-step process. He also took credit for working with Venezuelan President Hugo Chávez and Citizen Energy Corp. to strike a deal to bring cheaper oil to the South Bronx. He has criticized the reluctance of House Democratic leaders to pass immigration reform, and after Arizona passed the nation's toughest immigration law in 2010, he asked Major League Baseball Commissioner Bud Selig to move the 2011 All-Star Game from Phoenix in protest. Selig rebuffed the idea.

Although he is well-liked by colleagues, Serrano's attempts to join the Democratic leadership have been stymied. In 1997, Democratic Minority Leader Dick Gephardt passed over him and picked the less-senior Robert Menendez of New Jersey, who was a better fundraiser, to be chief deputy whip. In 1998, Serrano ran for Democratic Caucus vice chairman as "the candidate who refuses to raise money to buy your vote for leadership." He again lost out to Menendez, who went on to become a senator. Serrano was among the New York Democrats who briefly toyed with running against newly appointed Sen. Kirsten Gillibrand in the 2010 primary because of concerns over her centrist voting record.

SEVENTEENTH DISTRICT

Eliot Engel (D)

Elected 1988, 12th term; b. Feb. 18, 1947, Bronx; home, Bronx; Hunter-Lehman Col., B.A. 1969, C.U.N.Y., Lehman Col., M.A. 1973, NY Law Schl., J.D. 1987; Jewish; married (Patricia); 3 children.

Elected Office: NY Assembly, 1977–88.

Professional Career: Teacher, guidance counselor, NYC public schl., 1969–77.

DC Office: 2161 RHOB, 20515, 202-225-2464; Fax: 202-225-5513; Web site: engel.house.gov.

State Offices: Bronx, 718-796-9700; Mt. Vernon, 914-699-4100; West Nyack, 845-735-1000.

Committees: *Energy & Commerce:* Energy & Power; Health. *Foreign Affairs:* Europe and Eurasia; Western Hemisphere (RMM).

Group Ratings

	ACLU	ACU	ADA	CFG	AFS	FRC	LCV	ITIC	NTU	COC
2010	94	0	100	0	100	0	100	67	4	13
2009	–	0	100	4	100	–	93	–	1	40

National Journal Ratings

	2010 LIB	—	2010 CONS	2009 LIB	—	2009 CONS
Economic	68%	—	31%	81%	—	19%
Social	89%	—	7%	89%	—	0%
Foreign	73%	—	24%	56%	—	43%
Composite	78%	—	22%	77%	—	23%

Key Votes of the 111th Congress

1. Overturn Ledbetter	Y	5. Bar federal abortion funds	N	9. Stop detainee transfers	Y
2. Pass $820 billion stimulus	Y	6. Pass health care bill	Y	10. Legalize immigrants' kids	Y
3. Let guns in national parks	N	7. Regulate financial firms	Y	11. Repeal don't ask, tell	Y
4. Pass cap-and-trade	Y	8. Pass tax cuts for some	Y	12. Limit campaign funds	Y

Election Results

2010 general	Eliot Engel (D) 95,346	(73%)	($981,834)
	Anthony Mele (R)..29,792	(23%)	($132,898)
	York Kleinhandler (C) 5,661	(4%)	($47,667)
2010 primary	Eliot Engel (D) .... unopposed		

Prior Winning Percentages: 2008 (80%), 2006 (76%), 2004 (76%), 2002 (63%), 2000 (90%), 1998 (88%), 1996 (85%), 1994 (78%), 1992 (80%), 1990 (61%), 1988 (56%)

Population		Race/Ethnicity		Work	
Pop. 2010:	678,558	White:	37.2%	Private:	76.9%
Change since 2000:	Up 3.7%	Black:	30.0%	Government:	17.8%
Urban:	99.9%	Hispanic:	25.6%	Self-employed:	5.1%
Rural:	0.1%	Asian:	4.8%	Blue collar:	15.2%
Area size:	146 sq. mi.	Native Am.:	0.2%	White collar:	62.1%
		Hawaiian:	0.0%	Khaki collar:	0.0%
Age		Two+ races:	1.6%	Other:	22.7%
Median age:	36.1 yrs.				
More than 65 yrs:	13.0%	*Ancestry*		Median income:	$54,628
Less than 18 yrs:	26.4%	West Indian	11.5%	Median Home Value:	$446,400
		Irish	8.5%		
Education		Italian	7.2%	**Military Veterans**	
H.S. grad:	82.0%			% of Pop:	5.2%
College grad:	31.7%				
Grad degree:	13.5%				

North Bronx

The Bronx, settled mostly in the early 20th century, was originally a collection of middle-class neighborhoods clustered around subway stops, places where the children of immigrants left behind Manhattan's gloomy tenements and walkups and basked in the sunlight, wide avenues and hilly vistas. Different ethnic groups collected here: Irish in Kingsbridge, in the valley between Riverdale and the Grand Concourse; well-to-do WASPs and Jews in Riverdale, on the

2008 Presidential Vote

Barack Obama (D) 172,479	(72%)
John McCain (R) 66,027	(28%)

2004 Presidential Vote

John Kerry (D) 149,727	(67%)
George Bush (R) 73,896	(33%)

Cook Partisan Voting Index: D+18

palisades above the Hudson River; and middle-class blacks in Williamsbridge, in the north-central part of the borough. When neighboring areas in the South Bronx began to deteriorate, many of their residents fled to the southern cities of Westchester County. Others drove over the Tappan Zee Bridge to the pleasant suburbs of Rockland County, just north of Bergen County, N.J.

The 17th Congressional District of New York includes the bulk of these Bronx neighborhoods, plus Baychester, Eastchester and Spuyten Duyvil. It has the century-old Van Cortlandt Park, at 1,146 acres, New York City's fourth-largest park. It also includes leafy Woodlawn, still a magnet for Irish immigrants and more like neighboring Westchester County than the Bronx. The district skips around Marble Hill, an African-American and Latino enclave. It extends deep into the suburbs, taking in Yonkers and black-majority Mount Vernon, both of which have dealt with recent economic hardships, and a narrow strip of land running north from Yonkers along the Hudson River. Across the Tappan Zee, the district encompasses the southern half of Rockland County, including Nyack, Orangetown, Suffern, Ramapo and part of Clarkstown. (In 2008, serious discussions began over the possible replacement—not repair—of the 52-year-old Tappan Zee, which AAA in 2009 rated as one of the state's worst bridges.) The minority population of the district is 30% African-American and 26% Hispanic. The Bronx casts 26% of the vote, Rockland casts 37% and Westchester 25%. In 2008, Democrat Barack Obama carried the district, 72% to 28%.

Eliot Engel (D)

The congressman from the 17th District is Eliot Engel, a Democrat elected in 1988. One of the few white lawmakers representing a minority-majority district, he has remained popular by relentlessly staying on top of constituent service and working on issues of interest to its foreign-born and lower-income residents.

Engel is the son of a welder and grew up in the Bronx. As a boy, he was a political junkie who memorized the names of all 100 senators. He graduated from Hunter-Lehman College, got a master's in guidance and counseling from the City University of New York, and then taught in the New York City public schools. He was also a guidance counselor. After 14 years, he went back to school for a law degree from New York Law School. In 1977, at age 30, he was elected to the New York Assembly in a special election to replace a convicted incumbent. He won election to the House in 1988, replacing Democratic Rep. Mario Biaggi, who'd been convicted of bribery.

Engel's once strongly liberal voting record has become more moderate in recent years, especially on foreign policy. On the Foreign Affairs Committee, he made his name as the backer of downtrodden ethnic groups. And he has been a prime sponsor of the resolution to recognize Jerusalem as the capital of Israel, and he has co-chaired the Congressional ad hoc Committee on Irish Affairs to foster the peace process in that country. On many issues he is an ally of Foreign Affairs' Chairman Ileana Ros-Lehtinen, R-Fla. The two worked together during President George W. Bush's administration on legislation to rein in Syria's weapons program and promote human rights there. She has called him "a principled man...an incredible freedom fighter."

Engel is not a 1970s-style dove: He supported the Gulf War resolution in 1990, the bombing of Serbia to get a settlement in Bosnia, and the use of force in Iraq in 2002, though he criticized Bush's handling of that conflict. As chairman of the Western Hemisphere Subcommittee in the 111th Congress (2009-10), he criticized socialist Venezuelan President Hugo Chavez for "provocation" of the United States. He supported continued funding for the war in Afghanistan in 2010, and was one of three lawmakers to participate in a 2011 documentary, *Iranium*, that was intended to sound alarms about Iran's pursuit of nuclear weapons.

On the Energy and Commerce Committee, Engel has pushed for energy conservation and steps to address climate change. With Republican Jack Kingston of Georgia, he worked across the aisle to promote alternative and renewable sources of energy. He also was among a bipartisan group of lawmakers who sponsored a 2009 measure requiring half of all new cars sold in U.S. by 2012 to be flex-fuel vehicles capable of burning any combination of ethanol, methanol and gasoline. The automobile industry fought the measure, and it was not added to the House-passed energy bill that year. He takes an interest in consumer issues, and got passed into law in 2010 a bill making it illegal to use false caller IDs to trick people into revealing personal information. During the 2009 health care debate, he was among the Democrats to engage members of the fiscally conservative Blue Dog Coalition in often-tense negotiations over the scope of the legislation.

Engel has a personal tradition of staking out an aisle seat many hours before the start of the annual State of the Union address so that he can shake the president's hand or occasionally give a hug. In February 2009, CNN anchor Anderson Cooper called Engel "pathetic" for waiting over 12 hours for President Barack Obama's address to Congress. Engel replied that Cooper was "pathetic" for failing to share his enthusiasm.

Given his minority-majority district, Engel can never feel quite secure in his seat. In the 2000 primary, Assemblyman Larry Seabrook argued that the district needed "real leadership" and attacked Engel for living in suburban Maryland. Engel won 50%-41%. After redistricting made his district more suburban in 2002, Engel had vigorous competition from Rockland County Executive Scott Vanderhoef, a Republican who criticized Engel for voting against tax cuts and defense spending. Vanderhoef carried Rockland County by 53%-45%. But Engel won big in Westchester and the Bronx, for a 63%-34% overall victory.

In 2008 and 2010, he had no primary foe and only token Republican opposition. In the months leading up to the latter election, he did face some embarrassing publicity. *The Wall Street Journal* reported that ethics investigators found reason to believe he was one of five members to improperly keep cash intended to cover expenses on overseas trips. He said the amounts were minimal and he had to dig into his own pocket on those trips. The House Ethics Committee declined in January 2011 to pursue the matter.

EIGHTEENTH DISTRICT

Nita Lowey (D)

Elected 1988, 12th term; b. July 5, 1937, Bronx; home, Harrison; Mt. Holyoke Col., B.A. 1959; Jewish; married (Stephen); 3 children.

Professional Career: Asst. for Econ. Devel. & Neighborhood Preservation, NY Secy. of State; Dep. dir., Division of Econ. Opportunity, 1975–85; NY asst. secy. of st., 1985–87.

DC Office: 2365 RHOB, 20515, 202-225-6506; Fax: 202-225-0546; Web site: lowey.house.gov.

State Offices: Rockland, 845-639-3485; White Plains, 914-428-1707.

Committees: *Appropriations:* Homeland Security; Labor, HHS, Education & Related Agencies; State, Foreign Operations & Related Programs (RMM).

Group Ratings

	ACLU	ACU	ADA	CFG	AFS	FRC	LCV	ITIC	NTU	COC
2010	81	0	90	0	100	0	100	100	6	25
2009	–	0	100	4	100	–	100	–	2	33

National Journal Ratings

	2010 LIB	—	2010 CONS	2009 LIB	—	2009 CONS
Economic	88%	—	10%	62%	—	36%
Social	82%	—	14%	75%	—	20%
Foreign	56%	—	38%	70%	—	24%
Composite	77%	—	23%	71%	—	29%

Key Votes of the 111th Congress

1. Overturn Ledbetter	Y	5. Bar federal abortion funds	N
2. Pass $820 billion stimulus	Y	6. Pass health care bill	Y
3. Let guns in national parks	N	7. Regulate financial firms	Y
4. Pass cap-and-trade	Y	8. Pass tax cuts for some	Y

9. Stop detainee transfers	Y
10. Legalize immigrants' kids	Y
11. Repeal don't ask, tell	Y
12. Limit campaign funds	Y

Election Results

2010 general	Nita Lowey (D)	115,619	(62%)	($2,062,770)
	Jim Russell (R)	70,413	(38%)	($30,048)
2010 primary	Nita Lowey (D)	unopposed		

Prior Winning Percentages: 2008 (68%), 2006 (71%), 2004 (70%), 2002 (92%), 2000 (67%), 1998 (83%), 1996 (64%), 1994 (57%), 1992 (56%), 1990 (63%), 1988 (50%)

Population		Race/Ethnicity		Work	
Pop. 2010:	674,825	White:	59.7%	Private:	78.6%
Change since 2000:	Up 3.1%	Black:	9.3%	Government:	14.0%
Urban:	99.3%	Hispanic:	22.6%	Self-employed:	7.2%
Rural:	0.7%	Asian:	6.5%	Blue collar:	13.4%
Area size:	270 sq. mi.	Native Am.:	0.1%	White collar:	70.2%
		Hawaiian:	0.0%	Khaki collar:	0.0%
Age		Two+ races:	1.5%	Other:	16.4%
Median age:	39.9 yrs.				
More than 65 yrs:	14.5%	*Ancestry*		Median income:	$86,040
Less than 18 yrs:	24.2%	Italian	17.2%	Median Home Value:	$594,400
		Irish	11.2%		
Education		German	6.2%	**Military Veterans**	
H.S. grad:	88.0%			% of Pop:	6.1%
College grad:	47.6%				
Grad degree:	24.2%				

Westchester County

The great granite ridges that form the spine of Manhattan and the Bronx move north into lower Westchester County, the thin peninsula of land between Long Island Sound and the Hudson River. American writer Washington Irving sent his headless horseman on a chase for schoolmaster Ichabod Crane through Sleepy Hollow, a fictionalized version of Tarrytown, on the east bank of the Hudson. Blessed with some of America's loveliest scenery and easily accessible from

2008 Presidential Vote		
Barack Obama (D)	184,182	(62%)
John McCain (R)	112,214	(38%)
2004 Presidential Vote		
John Kerry (D)	164,342	(58%)
George Bush (R)	119,981	(42%)
Cook Partisan Voting Index:	D+9	

Manhattan by train since the mid-19th century, this became some of America's first suburban terrain, with grand estates built by great millionaires—Jay Gould's Gothic revival Lyndhurst and John D. Rockefeller's spectacular Kykuit. Today, Westchester still looks suburban, but with the patina of age. It has little commuter railroad stations across from faux Tudor drugstores, soda fountains and cobblestone post offices. But it also has shopping malls and galleries and plenty of corporate headquarters, from IBM and Texaco to PepsiCo, as well as one well-established corporate watchdog: *Consumer Reports* is based in Yonkers. In recent years, Westchester also has been drawing biotech companies; a former Union Carbide site in Tarrytown has become a bustling hub for them. Those firms have helped keep unemployment relatively low—the county's jobless rate was below 7% for much of 2010. Intensive development slows north of White Plains, for Westchester is crossed by the first of several mountain ridges just to the north—the closest the Appalachians come to the ocean. The county does have its share of homeless people and impoverished enclaves. And to the north, in Ossining, on the Hudson River, looms the famed Sing Sing maximum-security prison.

The 18th Congressional District of New York contains the heart of suburban Westchester County and also crosses the Hudson River into Rockland County to Haverstraw. It includes a host of affluent suburbs, many within easy reach of Grand Central via the Metro North rail lines—Bronxville, Tuckahoe, Eastchester, New Rochelle, Scarsdale, White Plains, Larchmont, Mamaroneck, Rye, Harrison, Armonk and Chappaqua, where former President Bill Clinton and Secretary of State Hillary Rodham Clinton have a home. Historically, Westchester was a Republican county, with a successful Republican machine and an electorate of affluent professionals who naturally preferred the political party that opposed the big city political bosses and labor union leaders. But today, Westchester is mostly Democratic, after a heavy influx of Jews who broke down many barriers to residence after World War II. Affluent suburbanites in America's biggest metropolitan area have been strongly on the liberal side of gun control and abortion rights.

Westchester County is more diverse than one might imagine, and the 18th District reflects this: It is 9% black, 23% Hispanic and 7% Asian. Former Republican Gov. George Pataki, who began his political career as mayor of Peekskill in northern Westchester, carried the county by handsome margins in 1998 and 2002. But the county gave strong support to Democrats Al Gore and John Kerry in the presidential elections of 2000 and 2004. Democrat Barack Obama won Westchester, 63%-36%. Two years later, the county gave Democrat Andrew Cuomo 66% of the vote in the governor's race.

Nita Lowey (D)

The congresswoman from the 18th District is Nita Lowey, a Democrat first elected in 1988. She is a formidable insider within the House Democratic caucus—a close and persuasive ally of Minority Leader Nancy Pelosi with a senior position on the Appropriations Committee.

Lowey was born in the Bronx, and after graduating from Mount Holyoke College with a degree in marketing, she moved to Queens, where she became a homemaker raising three children. She first got involved in politics when her neighbor, Mario Cuomo, got Lowey to help out in his campaign for lieutenant governor. He lost that race but was appointed New York secretary of state and hired Lowey as his assistant in 1975. Cuomo later became New York governor. In the 1988 Democratic primary for the House seat, Lowey faced Hamilton Fish III, who was politically well connected but as a former publisher of *The Nation* was considerably to the left of Lowey. She won 44%-36%. In the general election, she challenged two-term Republican Rep. Joseph DioGuardi, who was dogged by charges of illicit contributions. She won 50%-47%. Each spent more than $1 million, with Lowey spending $657,000 of her own money.

In the House, Lowey's voting record is liberal, though she is more moderate on foreign policy. She has been a strong advocate of aid to Israel and voted for the 2002 Iraq war resolution. As the ranking Democrat on Appropriations' State and Foreign Operations Subcommittee, she opposed President George W. Bush's call to increase troop strength in Iraq, but she backed his request for more money for military operations in Afghanistan. However, she became disgusted with corruption in that country and sought in 2010 to dramatically cut aid there. In March 2011, she led the opposition to an unsuccessful GOP proposal to slash U.S. contributions to international financial organizations. She argued that it would impair companies' ability to access foreign markets. After a young Nigerian evaded airport security in Amsterdam and almost blew up a Northwest Airlines flight over American skies, Lowey demanded that airlines submit passenger manifests to the federal government at least 24 hours before a flight's departure to give them more time to catch suspects.

On domestic issues, she has actively supported the National Endowment for the Arts, and also has been a big supporter of biomedical research and helped increase spending on cancer research at the National Institutes of Health. She has become a vigorous crusader against skin cancer after watching two close friends undergo surgeries and chemotherapy for melanoma, calling for better guidelines on sunscreen. Pursuing her interest in feminist issues, she has backed funds for international family planning. And she reportedly played an important behind-the-scenes role in getting the 2010 financial industry overhaul bill to soften proposed regulations on derivatives that would have negatively impacted New York's banking industry.

Since Lowey first won, the boundaries of her district have been radically altered twice by redistricting, but she has been re-elected by wide margins. She thought about a Senate bid in 2000, but deferred to First Lady Hillary Rodham Clinton, and in 2008, she was an enthusiastic supporter of Clinton's presidential campaign. Her party loyalty and avid fundraising led Minority Leader Dick Gephardt to appoint her to chair the Democratic Congressional Campaign Committee for the 2002 election. That year, the GOP's six-seat gain was an acute disappointment to Lowey, who quietly bowed out of the chairmanship. In 2008, she was mentioned as a possible successor to Clinton in the Senate after Clinton became secretary of state, but the plum appointment went to Democratic U.S. Rep. Kirsten Gillibrand of New York.

Lowey's Republican opponent in 2008 and 2010 was Jim Russell, a staunch Christian conservative who proved no match for her. The local GOP in 2010 rescinded its endorsement of Russell after it was exposed that he wrote an anti-integration essay featured on former Ku Klux Klan leader David Duke's web site, and she won 62%-38%.

NINETEENTH DISTRICT

Nan Hayworth (R)

Elected 2010, 1st term; b. Dec. 14, 1959, Chicago, IL; home, Bedford Hills; Princeton U., A.B. 1981; Cornell U. Medical Col., M.D. 1985.; Lutheran; Married (Scott); 2 children.

Professional Career: Ophthalmologist, 1989-96; partner, Mount Kisco Medical Group, 1996-2005.

DC Office: 1440 LHOB, 20515, 202-225-5441; Fax: 202-225-3289; Web site: hayworth.house.gov.

State Offices: Goshen, 845-206-4600; Fishkill, 845-206-4600; Somers, 845-206-4600.

Committees: *Financial Services:* Capital Markets and Government Sponsored Enterprises; Domestic Monetary Policy & Technology; Oversight & Investigations.

Election Results

2010 general	Nan Hayworth (R)	109,956	(53%)	($2,182,668)
	John Hall (D)	98,766	(47%)	($2,173,257)
2010 primary	Nan Hayworth (R)	19,483	(69%)	
	Neil DiCarlo (R)	8,614	(31%)	

Population		Race/Ethnicity		Work	
Pop. 2010:	699,959	White:	76.1%	Private:	73.2%
Change since 2000:	Up 7.0%	Black:	5.8%	Government:	21.1%
Urban:	78.7%	Hispanic:	12.9%	Self-employed:	5.7%
Rural:	21.3%	Asian:	3.2%	Blue collar:	16.4%
Area size:	1,470 sq. mi.	Native Am.:	0.2%	White collar:	65.6%
		Hawaiian:	0.0%	Khaki collar:	1.5%
Age		Two+ races:	1.6%	Other:	16.4%
Median age:	39.2 yrs.				
More than 65 yrs:	11.8%	*Ancestry*		Median income:	$82,068
Less than 18 yrs:	25.3%	Italian	18.0%	Median Home Value:	$382,700
		Irish	16.9%		
Education		German	11.1%	**Military Veterans**	
H.S. grad:	90.4%			% of Pop:	8.5%
College grad:	36.3%				
Grad degree:	16.2%				

Southern Hudson Valley

The great interior of America can be said to begin where the Hudson River squeezes through the series of Appalachian ridges at the Hudson Highlands. This chokepoint became a barrier to British military power during the Revolutionary War, when American forces put a chain across the river to keep the British from sailing north. Benedict Arnold betrayed his country over control of this part of the Hudson, and the new nation built its Military Academy high on the cliffs

2008 Presidential Vote

Barack Obama (D)	160,645	(51%)
John McCain (R)	153,424	(48%)

2004 Presidential Vote

George Bush (R)	162,960	(54%)
John Kerry (D)	137,432	(45%)

Cook Partisan Voting Index: R+3

at West Point. The Hudson was the impetus for the builders of the Erie Canal and the water-level New York Central Railroad, two great projects that made New York City the port of the American interior as well as the port for the builders of the nearby Croton Aqueduct, which provided the water without which New York could not grow. (It also carried the first cockroaches to the city.) Some distant day the great aqueduct may crumble, but the cockroaches will remain.

The 19th Congressional District of New York covers much of the lower Hudson Valley, sprawling across parts of five counties. West of the Hudson, the district takes in much of Orange County, New York's second-fastest-growing county between 2000 and 2010. There, old farming villages like Warwick adjoin mountains, farms and new, middle-income subdivisions on the nation's biggest deposit of muck soil outside the Everglades. Orange County includes Kiryas Joel, a politically controversial Satmar Hasidic settlement where two-thirds of residents live below the poverty line. Its

20,000 residents function almost as a single voting unit, without much regard to partisan affiliation, a fact that has not escaped the notice of the state's top politicians, who regularly court local leaders.

While the district excludes two of Orange County's biggest population centers, Middletown and Newburgh, it takes in portions of northern Rockland County, including Stony Point. The district crosses the Hudson near West Point. East of the river, the district begins in northern Westchester County, including Croton-on-Hudson, Yorktown, Mount Kisco, and Peekskill, where Republican George Pataki was mayor before becoming governor. Farther north, the 19th takes in all of Putnam County and part of Dutchess County, including the suburbs, but not the center city, of Poughkeepsie and Wappingers Falls. Putnam has become popular with first-time home buyers, who make the 80-minute commute to Grand Central Station. The region also has proved attractive to middle- and higher-income public and corporate employees seeking reasonably priced housing in safe areas, a trend that has led to robust growth at a time when other areas of the state are losing population. Overall the district is 6% black, 13% Hispanic and 3% Asian. Politically, this has been a swing area, moving toward Democrats in the 1990s, toward George W. Bush after September 11, to Barack Obama in 2008 and toward Republicans again in November 2009, when Rob Astorino won 57% against the incumbent Democratic Westchester County Executive.

Nan Hayworth (R)

The new member of Congress from the 19th District is Nan Hayworth, a Republican elected in 2010, although she had never run for office, never contributed to a campaign and never even had a political sign on her front lawn. She unseated two-term Democrat John Hall.

Hayworth grew up in Munster, Indiana, south of Gary and southeast of Chicago, and became immersed in politics in high school when she and a group of friends, feeling that individual students were not given enough representation, rewrote their school senate's constitution. She said that her passion for individualism comes from her mother, a World War II veteran of the British army. After the war, Hayworth's mother, supporting herself and her own mother, moved to the United States, where she married Hayworth's father. Hayworth graduated from Princeton, where she met her husband, a pre-med student, and the two attended Cornell Medical School, where Hayworth decided to become an ophthalmologist. After graduating, she began practicing on her own and then with a group practice in Mount Kisco Medical Group. She was an expert consultant for the New York State Department of Health's Office of Professional Medical Conduct.

In 2009, Hayworth said she grew increasingly concerned with the Democratic agenda in Congress. On vacation in Florida, her husband suggested she run for Congress. Friends urged her to do so as well, including Bush White House Press Secretary Ari Fleischer, whose mother was one of her patients and who told her she would have a powerful voice as a female physician. She decided to run, began boning up on policy in her spare time, and won the September 2010 Republican primary 69%-31%.

The incumbent was well-known in the district. Hall had been the front man for the 1970s soft-rock band Orleans, of "Still the One" fame, and had won the seat by upsetting Republican incumbent Sue Kelly in 2006. He was re-elected with 59% of the vote in 2008, and was not on any Republican target list.

Countering those daunting circumstances was a political environment that was turning increasingly sour for Democrats in 2010. In the general election campaign, Hayworth called for maintaining the 2001 and 2003 tax cuts for all taxpayers, a contrast to Democratic proposals that would deny them to the wealthiest taxpayers. She also called for de-funding the Democrats' health care bill and took a hard line on illegal immigration, an issue she said was especially important to her because her mother came into the country legally. Hayworth supported abortion rights, though she backed parental notification laws, and she said she would have voted for repeal of the ban on openly gay service personnel in the military.

Hall defended his support of Democratic programs and said that the party's economic stimulus bill in 2009 helped save jobs. Singer-songwriter Jackson Browne held a benefit concert for him in his district, and singers Bonnie Raitt and Rosanne Cash wrote a letter urging women to back him. Both candidates raised and spent more than $2 million. Hayworth won 53%-47%, trailing in Westchester County but carrying the other four counties.

TWENTIETH DISTRICT

Chris Gibson (R)

Elected 2010, 1st term; b. May 13, 1964, Rockville Centre; home, Kinderhook; Siena Col., B.A. 1986; Cornell U., M.P.A. 1995, Ph.D. 1998; U.S. Army Command and Gen. Staff Col., distinguished honor graduate 2000; Christian; Married (Mary Jo); 3 children.

Military Career: Army Natl. Guard, 1981-86; Army, 1986-2010 (Kosovo, Iraq).

DC Office: 502 CHOB, 20515, 202-225-5614; Fax: 202-225-1168; Web site: gibson.house.gov.

State Offices: Delhi, 607-746-9537; Glen Falls, 518-743-0964; Kinderhook, 518-610-8133; Saratoga Springs, 518-306-5450.

Committees: *Agriculture:* General Farm Commodities & Risk Management; Livestock, Dairy & Poultry. *Armed Services:* Emerging Threats & Capabilities; Readiness.

Election Results

2010 general	Chris Gibson (R)	130,176	(55%)	($1,765,219)
	Scott Murphy (D)	107,077	(45%)	($5,616,128)
2010 primary	Chris Gibson (R)	unopposed		

Population		Race/Ethnicity		Work	
Pop. 2010:	683,198	White:	91.5%	Private:	72.5%
Change since 2000:	Up 4.4%	Black:	2.3%	Government:	19.4%
Urban:	44.9%	Hispanic:	3.2%	Self-employed:	7.8%
Rural:	55.1%	Asian:	1.3%	Blue collar:	20.2%
Area size:	7,200 sq. mi.	Native Am.:	0.2%	White collar:	61.1%
		Hawaiian:	0.0%	Khaki collar:	0.2%
Age		Two+ races:	1.3%	Other:	18.5%
Median age:	41.7 yrs.				
More than 65 yrs:	14.8%	*Ancestry*		Median income:	$56,871
Less than 18 yrs:	21.5%	Irish	16.5%	Median Home Value:	$210,800
		German	13.5%		
Education		Italian	10.8%	**Military Veterans**	
H.S. grad:	89.7%			% of Pop:	11.3%
College grad:	28.6%				
Grad degree:	12.4%				

Northern Hudson Valley

The Hudson River, an avenue of commerce in colonial days and an inspiration to artists in the new federal republic, is still one of America's great sights, though it is no longer central, as it was, to the nation's consciousness and politics. The classic mansions overlooking the river, like Clermont, whose builder Robert Livingston financed Robert Fulton's first steamboat, and Montgomery Place, built by Janet Livingston Montgomery, widow of the general who attacked Quebec in 1775, are reminders of the cool serenity of the 18th century mind and the daring nature of its spirit. Robert Livingston, whose descendants include former first lady Eleanor Roosevelt, former New Jersey Gov. Thomas Kean, and former Rep. Bob Livingston of Louisiana, administered the first oath of office to George Washington in 1789 and helped negotiate the Louisiana Purchase in 1803. On a visit to his land in the 1790s, James Madison and Aaron Burr welded the Virginia-New York alliance that set the course of American political history. The Hudson was also a center of American culture during the Romantic era. From Frederick Church's Moorish mansion, Olana, one can see the still unspoiled river landscape that inspired his art and that of others of the Hudson River School of painters. James Fenimore Cooper lived farther up the river, near the placid shores of Lake George, and his classic work *The Last of the Mohicans* abounds with descriptions of the area. Later, the photographer Alfred Stieglitz and his wife, painter Georgia O'Keeffe, drew inspiration from the same waters, woods and hills.

2008 Presidential Vote		
Barack Obama (D)	167,827	(51%)
John McCain (R)	157,879	(48%)
2004 Presidential Vote		
George Bush (R)	170,307	(54%)
John Kerry (D)	145,289	(46%)
Cook Partisan Voting Index:	R+2	

The Hudson gave birth to America's passionate party politics. Nearby is Kinderhook, home of Ichabod Crane, who was chased by Washington Irving's Headless Horseman, and, more to the political point, the home of Martin Van Buren, the innkeeper's son who in alliance with Andrew Jackson invented the torchlight parade, the national party convention and, some argue, the Democratic Party itself. Later in the 19th century, the Hudson was lined with the palaces of the nation's first great millionaires and the comfortable country homes of New York's gentry. One of the latter, Springwood in Hyde Park, was the birthplace and home of Franklin D. Roosevelt, who, even as president, was most comfortable looking out over his sloping lawn to the river, where he liked to go iceboating in the winter. To the north is the charming town of Rhinebeck, site of the 2010 wedding of Chelsea Clinton and Marc Mezvinsky, the bride the daughter of a former president and the current secretary of State, the groom the son of two former members of the U.S. House, Edward Mezvinsky of Iowa and Marjorie Margolies Mezvinsky of Pennsylvania.

The sprawling 20th Congressional District of New York circles the Albany metropolitan area and includes much of the Hudson Valley. It includes four full counties (Warren, Washington, Columbia, and Greene), most of Saratoga County and parts of five others (Dutchess, Essex, Rensselaer, Delaware, and Otsego). The northern extreme of the 20th extends right up to Lake Placid in the Adirondacks, site of the 1980 Winter Olympics. The southern extreme in Dutchess County is close enough for commuters from New York City. The district extends west just short of Cooperstown, home of the National Baseball Hall of Fame, but it includes Oneonta, home of the less well-known National Soccer Hall of Fame. It also includes Saratoga Springs with its grand racetrack and the nearby battlefield where the British were decisively stopped in 1777 by General Benedict Arnold. Saratoga County was the fastest growing county in New York from 2000 to 2010.

This area had been Republican territory since the Civil War. Indeed, Roosevelt never carried his home territory except when he ran for the state Senate in 1910. The 20th was one of only six New York districts to vote for George W. Bush in 2000 and one of nine to vote for him in 2004. In recent years, the district has trended Democratic, like much of upstate New York. While registered Republicans still outnumber registered Democrats, the district voted for Hillary Clinton and Eliot Spitzer in 2006 and for Barack Obama in 2008.

Chris Gibson (R)

Chris Gibson, a Republican, is the new congressman from the 20th District, elected in 2010. He grew up in Kinderhook, played basketball at Ichabod Crane High School and joined the Army National Guard one day after his 17th birthday. He graduated magna cum laude from Siena College outside Albany and later earned a doctorate from Cornell University. Gibson served 24 years in the Army and was deployed to Kosovo, Haiti and four times to Iraq. He taught American politics at the U.S. Military Academy at West Point, and was a Hoover National Security Affairs fellow at Stanford University. He also was a congressional fellow in the office of Rep. Jerry Lewis, R-Calif., and wrote a 2008 book called *Securing the State*, about civil-military relations in the Defense Department.

In February 2009, Democratic Gov. David Paterson appointed 20th District Rep. Kirsten Gillibrand to the Senate seat vacated by Secretary of State Hillary Clinton. In the special election triggered by the vacancy, the Republican nominee was state Assembly Minority Leader Jim Tedisco and the Democratic nominee was high-tech entrepreneur Scott Murphy, who campaigned as a moderate Democrat with Gillibrand's strong endorsement. The May special election was exceedingly close: Murphy won by a 726-vote margin, 50.2%-49.8%. In the House, Murphy voted against President Barack Obama's health care overhaul in 2009, but later switched and voted for the final bill, because of improvements, he said, in its small-business provisions. That vote and one in favor of the Democrats' cap-and-trade bill to curb carbon emissions made him a target for Republicans running on an anti-Obama theme in 2010.

Gibson focused his campaign on familiar fiscal conservative issues and a tough-on-terrorists national security platform. After a tea party candidate dropped out, he was unopposed in the Republican primary. Not surprisingly, Gibson criticized Murphy for his vote on cap-and-trade and health care. Murphy argued that he had bargained for a reduced tax on medical devices and paper manufacturers, both good for the district.

Gibson called for a property tax cap to encourage economic growth, streamlined regulations and lower health care costs through private sector competition and consumer incentives. On national security, he promised to work to better coordinate efforts to detect terrorist threats. Murphy tried to distance himself from liberal House Speaker Nancy Pelosi and touted his moderate voting record in the mold of Gillibrand and his breaks with Democratic leaders on issues such as gun control. He got some attention with an ad depicting Gibson riding an animated cartoon crocodile that eats a middle-class family, and asserting that his opponent will "feed on the middle class." The day before the election, former President Bill Clinton put in an appearance for Murphy to try to rally Democrats to the polls.

Murphy spent $5.3 million to Gibson's $1.7 million. That was partially offset by Republican-leaning groups that spent $700,000 to help Gibson and Democratic-leaning groups that helped Murphy to the tune of $200,000. Murphy's big cash advantage didn't matter in the end. Gibson won 55%-45%. He carried every county except the district's portion of Essex County in the north.

TWENTY-FIRST DISTRICT

Paul Tonko (D)

Elected 2008, 2nd term; b. June 18, 1949, Amsterdam; home, Amsterdam; Clarkson U., B.S. 1981; Catholic; single.

Elected Office: Montgomery Cnty Bd. of Supervisors, 1974-83, Chmn. 1981; NY Assembly, 1983-2007

Professional Career: NY Dept. of Transportation, 1972-74; NY Dept. of Public Service, 1974-83; Pres. & CEO, NY St. Energy Research & Development Authority, 2007-08

DC Office: 422 CHOB, 20515, 202-225-5076; Fax: 202-225-5077; Web site: tonko.house.gov.

State Offices: Albany, 518-465-0700; Amsterdam, 518-843-3400; Schenectady, 518-374-4547.

Committees: *Budget. Science & Technology:* Energy & Environment; Research & Science Education.

Group Ratings

	ACLU	ACU	ADA	CFG	AFS	FRC	LCV	ITIC	NTU	COC
2010	88	0	100	8	100	0	100	67	4	0
2009	–	0	100	0	100	–	100	–	2	33

National Journal Ratings

	2010 LIB	—	2010 CONS	2009 LIB	—	2009 CONS
Economic	90%	—	0%	82%	—	14%
Social	71%	—	25%	84%	—	11%
Foreign	73%	—	24%	78%	—	17%
Composite	81%	—	19%	84%	—	16%

Key Votes of the 111th Congress

1. Overturn Ledbetter	Y	5. Bar federal abortion funds	N	9. Stop detainee transfers	Y
2. Pass $820 billion stimulus	Y	6. Pass health care bill	Y	10. Legalize immigrants' kids	Y
3. Let guns in national parks	N	7. Regulate financial firms	Y	11. Repeal don't ask, tell	Y
4. Pass cap-and-trade	Y	8. Pass tax cuts for some	Y	12. Limit campaign funds	Y

Election Results

2010 general	Paul Tonko (D)	124,889	(59%)	($987,959)
	Theodore Danz, Jr. (R)	85,752	(41%)	($43,939)
2010 primary	Paul Tonko (D)	unopposed		

Prior Winning Percentages: 2008 (62%)

Population		Race/Ethnicity		Work	
Pop. 2010:	679,193	White:	79.2%	Private:	70.8%
Change since 2000:	Up 3.8%	Black:	9.0%	Government:	24.0%
Urban:	84.3%	Hispanic:	5.4%	Self-employed:	5.1%
Rural:	15.7%	Asian:	3.4%	Blue collar:	16.5%
Area size:	1,962 sq. mi.	Native Am.:	0.2%	White collar:	66.3%
		Hawaiian:	0.0%	Khaki collar:	0.1%
Age		Two+ races:	2.2%	Other:	17.1%
Median age:	39.1 yrs.				
More than 65 yrs:	14.5%	*Ancestry*		Median income:	$52,064
Less than 18 yrs:	21.4%	Irish	16.0%	Median Home Value:	$172,800
		Italian	13.1%		
Education		German	12.5%	**Military Veterans**	
H.S. grad:	88.7%			% of Pop:	9.8%
College grad:	30.0%				
Grad degree:	13.9%				

Albany Metro Area

As readers of its novelist laureate William Kennedy know, Albany is within living memory an antique city. Its solid row houses show its 19th-century prosperity. Its once-teeming lumberyards, railroad car shops, restaurants and hotels have the patina of age and the accumulated grime of decades of coal smoke burned during six-month-long winters. Its history dates to 1624, when the Dutch built Fort Orange on the banks of the Hudson so seagoing ships could

2008 Presidential Vote		
Barack Obama (D) 179,322	(58%)
John McCain (R) 123,378	(40%)
2004 Presidential Vote		
John Kerry (D) 169,693	(55%)
George Bush (R) 133,016	(43%)
Cook Partisan Voting Index: D+6		

dock at the edge of the great, gloomy forests near the confluence of the Hudson and the Mohawk—the natural crossroads of upstate New York even before the building of the Erie Canal and the New York Central Railroad. This was one of America's early industrial centers. A few miles upriver, Troy was a steel town rivaling Pittsburgh in the 1840s. Cohoes, at the junction of the Hudson and the Mohawk, became a leading textile producer. Schenectady, a few miles up the Mohawk, was the site of Charles Steinmetz's fabled General Electric laboratories and long remained a GE town. Albany was one of America's biggest lumber towns in addition to serving as New York's state capital.

In addition to state government, Albany for a while had one of the nation's most famed Democratic political machines, dating to 1921, when Daniel O'Connell and his brothers and local aristocrat Edwin Corning took control of City Hall. The machine was sustained by legions of city and county employees, by a certain creativity when it came to counting votes, and by the raffish atmosphere that was found in the speakeasies of so many cities during Prohibition and lingered in Albany for decades after. Curiously, the machine made possible the transformation of Albany into the shinier metropolis it is today. Mayor Corning and Republican Gov. Nelson Rockefeller collaborated on a smorgasbord of civic improvement projects: the Empire State Plaza with 11,000 employees in 10 government buildings on 98 acres; the distinctive, ovoid performing arts center known as the Egg; and a renovated Union Station.

The 21st Congressional District of New York includes most of the Albany metropolitan area: All of Albany County; Schenectady County, including Schenectady; Montgomery County, including Amsterdam, a carpet-making town until the mills moved south in 1955; rural Schoharie County, and parts of Rensselaer, including the gentrified Troy, with its bustling antique shops. It also takes in Fulton and Saratoga counties. Times have been tough here. The presence of state government has kept unemployment in the region lower than other parts of New York, but in 2010 it still climbed to the highest levels in at least two decades. Recent state government job cuts haven't helped. The area has sought to rebound through green jobs and high-tech manufacturing; GE in 2009 opened a plant producing digital X-ray equipment and built another facility to produce advanced batteries. While the outer counties lean Republican, the Democratic machine vote in Albany makes this a comfortably Democratic district. Even Democrat Carl McCall, who lost every other county in the state outside New York City, beat incumbent Republican Gov. George Pataki in Albany County in 2002. Democrat Barack Obama won 64% of Albany County's vote in 2008—a total that Democrat Andrew Cuomo matched in the 2010 governor's race.

Paul Tonko (D)

The congressman from the 21st District is Paul Tonko, a Democrat elected in 2008. The grandson of Polish immigrants, Tonko was born in the old mill town of Amsterdam, N.Y., where he still lives. His working-class background gave him an appreciation for the "underdog" that remains the underpinning of his political beliefs. Attracted from a young age to public service, he built his career in state government, first at the New York Department of Transportation and then as an engineer at the Department of Public Service, the state's utilities regulator. In 1974, at age 26, he became the youngest person ever elected to the Montgomery County Board of Supervisors. He became board chairman in 1981. Tonko won a seat in the New York Assembly in a 1983 special election, and served for nearly a quarter century. He won passage of a law requiring health insurers to cover most mental illnesses and another requiring social workers to report all cases of suspected child abuse to the state. But he exercised his greatest influence over state energy policy, serving as chairman of the Assembly's energy committee from 1992 to 2007, when he resigned to accept an appointment as head of the state's Energy Research and Development Authority.

Democratic Rep. Michael McNulty decided against seeking an 11th term, and Tonko got into the contest to succeed him in 2008. In the primary, he faced Phil Steck, an Albany County legislator, and Tracey Brooks, a former regional director for New York Democratic Sen. Hillary Rodham Clinton. Both enjoyed a head start raising money. But most of the local Democratic establishment lined up behind Tonko (McNulty remained neutral). Tonko won important union endorsements, as well as the backing of the state's Working Families Party. With few differences between the candidates on major issues, the local support likely made the difference. Outraised and outspent by both Brooks and Steck, Tonko sailed to victory over both.

In the general election Tonko faced Republican Jim Buhrmaster, a Schenectady County legislator who hoped that his appeal to independents might help him overcome the huge registration advantage for Democrats in the district. But Tonko won with 62% of the vote. Buhrmaster received 35%, and Steck, who ran as an independent, received 3%. Two years later, Tonko was re-elected easily over Republican Theodore Danz, 59%-41%.

Tonko is a loyal Democrat who has been particularly liberal on economic issues. He has focused on the issue he knows best, energy policy. He got a bill through the House in September 2009 calling for an $800 million research program in wind energy technologies, which would benefit GE in his district. Another of his bills, which passed two months later, created a research program to improve the efficiency of gas turbines used in power generation systems that convert heat into energy. In 2010, Tonko got a provision in a House-passed oil spill bill following the BP disaster in the Gulf of Mexico to speed up the response to future spills and to involve small businesses in spill research. In 2011, he sponsored an amendment to a fiscal 2011 spending bill seeking to protect the Environmental Protection Agency's authority to regulate carbon emissions.

On other issues, Tonko worked with other lawmakers to expand low-income children's access to healthy meals and to improve engineering education in schools. After the GOP takeover of the House in 2010, he got a seat on the Budget Committee. He was highly critical of expanding the Bush-era tax cuts for high-income earners in December 2010. "The trickle-down effect has not worked," he said.

TWENTY-SECOND DISTRICT

Maurice Hinchey (D)

Elected 1992, 10th term; b. Oct. 27, 1938, New York, NY; home, Saugerties; S.U.N.Y. New Paltz, B.S. 1968, M.A. 1969; Catholic; married (Allison Lee); 3 children.

Military Career: Navy, 1956–59.

Elected Office: NY Assembly, 1974–92.

Professional Career: Cement plant worker, 1959–64; NY St. Thruway toll collector, 1959–68; Analyst, NY St. Dept. of Educ., 1971–74.

DC Office: 2431 RHOB, 20515, 202-225-6335; Fax: 202-226-0774; Web site: hinchey.house.gov.

State Offices: Binghamton, 607-773-2768; Ithaca, 607-273-1388; Kingston, 845-331-4466; Middletown, 845-344-3211; Monticello, 845-791-7116.

Committees: *Appropriations:* Defense; Interior, Environment & Related Agencies. *Joint Economic Committee.*

Group Ratings

	ACLU	ACU	ADA	CFG	AFS	FRC	LCV	ITIC	NTU	COC
2010	94	0	100	8	100	0	100	67	5	13
2009	–	0	100	0	100	–	100	–	2	33

National Journal Ratings

	2010 LIB	—	2010 CONS		2009 LIB	—	2009 CONS
Economic	84%	—	15%		67%	—	33%
Social	80%	—	20%		70%	—	30%
Foreign	91%	—	8%		87%	—	9%
Composite	85%	—	15%		75%	—	25%

Key Votes of the 111th Congress

1. Overturn Ledbetter	Y	5. Bar federal abortion funds	N	9. Stop detainee transfers	N
2. Pass $820 billion stimulus	Y	6. Pass health care bill	Y	10. Legalize immigrants' kids	Y
3. Let guns in national parks	Y	7. Regulate financial firms	Y	11. Repeal don't ask, tell	Y
4. Pass cap-and-trade	Y	8. Pass tax cuts for some	Y	12. Limit campaign funds	Y

Election Results

2010 general	Maurice Hinchey (D)...98,661	(53%)	($1,161,667)
	George Phillips (R)..88,687	(47%)	($607,384)
2010 primary	Maurice Hinchey (D)...................................unopposed		

Prior Winning Percentages: 2008 (66%), 2006 (100%), 2004 (67%), 2002 (64%), 2000 (62%), 1998 (62%), 1996 (55%), 1994 (49%), 1992 (50%)

Population		Race/Ethnicity		Work	
Pop. 2010:	679,297	White:	73.6%	Private:	73.5%
Change since 2000:	Up 3.8%	Black:	8.7%	Government:	19.7%
Urban:	67.8%	Hispanic:	11.9%	Self-employed:	6.6%
Rural:	32.2%	Asian:	3.2%	Blue collar:	19.7%
Area size:	3,333 sq. mi.	Native Am.:	0.2%	White collar:	61.0%
		Hawaiian:	0.0%	Khaki collar:	0.1%
Age		Two+ races:	2.2%	Other:	19.2%
Median age:	37.7 yrs.				
More than 65 yrs:	13.5%	*Ancestry*		Median income:	$50,212
Less than 18 yrs:	21.7%	Irish	14.2%	Median Home Value:	$200,700
		German	12.4%		
Education		Italian	11.7%	**Military Veterans**	
H.S. grad:	87.0%			% of Pop:	9.1%
College grad:	28.0%				
Grad degree:	13.1%				

Southern New York; Binghamton

In colonial days, the Catskills looming over the mid-Hudson River Valley were a mysterious place where Rip Van Winkle was said to have fallen asleep for 20 years after drinking with nine pipe-playing dwarfs and where Indians lurked in the days of James Fenimore Cooper. Eventually, the area became part of a great pathway west, along the Erie Lackawanna and Delaware & Hudson Railroad lines, with engines steaming over giant viaducts and along narrow

2008 Presidential Vote
Barack Obama (D) 170,379   (59%)
John McCain (R) 112,669   (39%)

2004 Presidential Vote
John Kerry (D) 151,890   (54%)
George Bush (R) 127,253   (45%)

Cook Partisan Voting Index: D+6

river valleys through the hills and mountains. Later in the 19th century, huge kosher hotels were built in Sullivan County in the Catskills, the Jewish resort area popularly known as the Borscht Belt. These thrived when Jews were excluded from other resorts, but fell on hard times in the late 20th century, as discrimination against Jews waned. Some survived to cater to Russian-Jewish immigrants and a kosher clientele. Today, the Catskills are no longer on great transportation lines. There is little passenger train service, and the area is bypassed by major airlines.

The sprawling 22nd Congressional District of New York includes all of Sullivan and Ulster counties and most of the Catskills area. It covers part of the Hudson Valley and parts of the counties along the New York-Pennsylvania border. Its two population centers are on its east and west ends. On the east are Newburgh, Poughkeepsie, and Kingston, old towns in the Hudson Valley. Poughkeepsie is the home of Vassar College, and Kingston, in Ulster County, was the political base of George Clinton, the former longtime governor and two-term vice president. This area has been growing relatively rapidly, with new residents from metro New York and a burgeoning technology sector. In the west, connected to the rest of the district by a narrow corridor of southern-tier townships, are Binghamton and Ithaca, where Cornell University sits high above the Cayuga River and is by far the largest employer in Tompkins County. The State University of New York-Binghamton is considered one of the nation's top public colleges and in fall 2010 began work on a $30 million electronics research site.

Ithaca has attracted a number of superlative designations in recent years, including "lesbian-friendliest," "best fly-fishing," one of the "greatest places to retire," and "largest share of commuters who walk or bicycle to work." The district also includes Bethel, site of the 1969 Woodstock music festival, one of the watershed events of the counterculture era. Most of this territory voted Republican for many years, though Sullivan County, with the only large rural Jewish population in the United States, has long been Democratic. Today most of the area is Democratic, especially the university towns of Ithaca, Poughkeepsie, and New Paltz in Ulster County, and the actual Woodstock (not where the festival was held), a favorite country house location for New Yorkers. Democrat Barack Obama won the district in 2008 with 59% of the vote. In the 2010 governor's race, Democrat Andrew Cuomo equaled that percentage in Ulster while getting 55% of the vote in Sullivan.

Maurice Hinchey (D)

The congressman from the 22nd is Maurice Hinchey, a Democrat elected in 1992. Known for his outspoken criticisms of the Bush administration, he has resurrected his fiery rhetoric in a Republican-controlled House.

The son of a cement plant worker, Hinchey grew up in Greenwich Village in humble circumstances. After high school, he enlisted in the Navy at age 18 and served on a destroyer in the Pacific. When he got home, he worked in the cement factory for five years. But Hinchey wanted to go to college, and since his parents couldn't afford to send him, he worked his way through as a New York State Thruway toll collector. After getting his degree, he was an analyst for the state education department. Then, in the Democratic year of 1974, Hinchey was elected as the first Democrat from Ulster County to the New York Assembly since 1912, and served for nine terms. When he ran for Congress, Hinchey called for national health insurance, a repeal of Reagan-Bush tax cuts for upper-income taxpayers and corporations, and "reindustrializing America." His Republican opponent, Bob Moppert, a Binghamton moving company owner, campaigned on reducing government spending and trimming the size of the federal bureaucracy. Hinchey won 50%-47%.

Hinchey has one of the most liberal voting records for a non-urban member in the House. He is frequently the leader of lost causes and can be lacerating in his condemnation of Republicans. In 2008, he co-sponsored a bill calling for Bush's impeachment and the following year accused Bush of "intentionally" letting September 11 mastermind Osama bin Laden escape during a battle in Afghanistan. In February 2011, he called the new House majority's fiscal 2012 budget proposal "a job-crushing budget scheme" and accused the GOP of behaving "like a blindfolded child at a piñata party" for being too indiscriminate in its proposed cuts.

Hinchey has drawn attention for more than just his tough talk. Following an incident at a Rosendale street fair in July 2008, a local official of the National Rifle Association filed harassment charges against Hinchey for allegedly hitting him on the head following a heated exchange. An Ulster County judge dismissed the charges in November 2008. On the campaign trail in October 2010, he told a newspaper reporter to "shut up" while doing a televised interview and then, according to the reporter, later poked him in the chest and put his hands near his throat before backing off. Hinchey issued a statement accusing the reporter, Bill Kemble of the *Kingston Daily Freeman,* of rudely badgering him but expressed regret at not walking away sooner.

With other Democrats, Hinchey has advocated a return of the Federal Communications Commission's Fairness Doctrine requiring equal time for differing political viewpoints. He says that the television networks give disproportionate airtime to conservatives on their Sunday morning talk shows. He tried in 2009 to attach a proposed interest rate cap of 18% to a credit card overhaul bill, accusing companies of raising rates to "levels that would embarrass the Mafia." The proposal was withdrawn over concerns it would complicate passage of the bill, which was signed into law the following year.

On the Appropriations Committee, his focus has been ensuring the independence of the Food and Drug Administration from the pharmaceutical industry, and demanding that owners of oil and gas leases pay "fair market prices." When Republicans in 2008 sought repeal of oil-drilling restrictions, Hinchey countered by seeking increased penalties for gas-price gouging and pressing for more use of renewable fuels. He joined the Defense Subcommittee in 2009, where his focus is seeking money for local defense contractors. He tried without success in 2009 to save a $13 billion plan to develop a new fleet of presidential helicopters manufactured in Oswego that the Obama administration said it did not want. On other local issues, he got a bill through the House in March 2010 calling for a National Park Service study on making the Hudson River Valley part of the national park system.

Early in his House tenure Hinchey was a Republican target, but since the mid-1990s, he has won re-election easily. His opponent in 2008 and 2010 was social studies teacher George Phillips, who in the latter election took advantage of the GOP-allied group American Crossroads' advertising campaign to catch up with Hinchey financially. But Hinchey still managed to win, 53%-47%.

TWENTY-THIRD DISTRICT

Bill Owens (D)

Elected Nov. 2009, 1st full term; b. Jan. 20, 1949, Brooklyn; home, Plattsburgh; Manhattan Col., B.S. 1971; Fordham U., J.D. 1974; Catholic; married (Jane); 3 children.

Military Career: Air Force, 1975-79; Air Force Reserves, 1979-82.

Professional Career: Practicing attorney, 1974-present.

DC Office: 431 CHOB, 20515, 202-225-4611 ; Fax: 202-226-0621 ; Web site: owens.house.gov.

State Offices: Oneida, 315-367-0041; Plattsburgh, 518-563-1406; Watertown, 315-782-3150 .

Committees: *Agriculture:* Conservation, Energy & Forestry; Livestock, Dairy & Poultry. *Armed Services:* Air & Land Forces; Readiness. *Small Business.*

Group Ratings

	ACLU	*ACU*	*ADA*	*CFG*	*AFS*	*FRC*	*LCV*	*ITIC*	*NTU*	*COC*
2010	71	21	70	8	88	25	60	100	17	50
2009	–	14	–	–	100	–	100	–	23	43

National Journal Ratings

	2010 LIB	—	*2010 CONS*	*2009 LIB*	—	*2009 CONS*
Economic	45%	—	55%	*	—	*
Social	42%	—	57%	*	—	*
Foreign	44%	—	55%	*	—	*
Composite	44%	—	56%	*	—	*

Key Votes of the 111th Congress

1. Overturn Ledbetter	*	5. Bar federal abortion funds	N	9. Stop detainee transfers	Y
2. Pass $820 billion stimulus	*	6. Pass health care bill	Y	10. Legalize immigrants' kids	N
3. Let guns in national parks	*	7. Regulate financial firms	N	11. Repeal don't ask, tell	Y
4. Pass cap-and-trade	*	8. Pass tax cuts for some	Y	12. Limit campaign funds	N

Election Results

2010 general	Bill Owens (D)	82,232	(48%)	($2,989,590)
	Matthew Doheny (R)	80,237	(46%)	($3,448,912)
	Doug Hoffman (C)	10,507	(6%)	
2010 primary	Bill Owens (D)	unopposed		

Prior Winning Percentages: 2009 special (48%)

Population

Pop. 2010:	664,245
Change since 2000:	Up 1.5%
Urban:	34.7%
Rural:	65.3%
Area size:	14,737 sq. mi.

Age

Median age:	38.4 yrs.
More than 65 yrs:	13.3%
Less than 18 yrs:	21.7%

Education

H.S. grad:	86.0%
College grad:	18.4%
Grad degree:	7.8%

Race/Ethnicity

White:	91.7%
Black:	2.5%
Hispanic:	2.6%
Asian:	0.8%
Native Am.:	1.0%
Hawaiian:	0.1%
Two+ races:	1.3%

Ancestry

Irish	14.3%
German	12.3%
French	10.4%

Work

Private:	69.4%
Government:	23.2%
Self-employed:	7.3%
Blue collar:	24.3%
White collar:	53.6%
Khaki collar:	1.5%
Other:	20.5%

Median income:	$45,205
Median Home Value:	$100,900

Military Veterans

% of Pop:	11.3%

Northern New York; Watertown

Some early 19th century visionaries believed that the North Country of upstate New York—a battleground in both the Revolutionary War and the War of 1812—was the land of the future. Financier Gouverneur Morris, French slave trader James Leray, and Dutch silver speculator David Parish bought up thousands of acres between the Adirondacks and the St. Lawrence River and tried to unload them on farmers unaware of the shortness of the growing season and

2008 Presidential Vote		
Barack Obama (D)	133,367	(52%)
John McCain (R)	119,944	(47%)
2004 Presidential Vote		
George Bush (R)	134,174	(51%)
John Kerry (D)	123,216	(47%)
Cook Partisan Voting Index: R+1		

the unnavigability of the river. These developers left behind grand mansions, but their hopes for huge profits were frustrated when the Erie Canal turned the stream of settlement westward, and Canadians built their new capital of Ottawa far north of the river. But northern New York was not without its business successes: It was in Watertown in 1878 that 26-year-old Frank Woolworth put a sign over a table of odds and ends that read "Any Article 5 Cents," starting America's first retail chain and inventing the concept of discount stores.

More recently, the North Country has looked to government for help. The St. Lawrence Seaway proved too small for most oceangoing freighters and remains frozen three months of the year. The locks are slow, and icebreakers would wreck the shoreline. The biggest initiative has been the enlargement of Fort Drum, near Watertown and adjacent to Lake Bonaparte, where despite the Army's preference for warm-weather training sites, a 10,000-person light infantry division, the 10th Mountain Division, has been stationed since 1985. (The 10th Mountain has performed valiantly in difficult environs in Afghanistan and Iraq, with some soldiers seeing three and four tours of duty.) The North Country faces a looming housing crunch in spring 2012, when all of Fort Drum's 18,500 soldiers are scheduled to be there instead of deployed overseas. Private developers have built big malls in Watertown and Massena, attracting Canadians, as even New York has lower taxes than Ontario. While the dollar has been cheap, Canadian tourism and shopping here have been strong, notably at the Adirondack State Park.

The 23rd Congressional District of New York covers most of the North Country, starting at Lake Champlain, running westward along the St. Lawrence Seaway and over the Adirondacks Forest Preserve to Lake Ontario. It includes Madison County to the south. The district has only a few population centers, including Plattsburgh on Lake Champlain and Watertown and Oswego on Lake Ontario. Oswego, which occasionally docks oceangoing bulk vessels, bills itself as the first U.S. port of call on the Great Lakes from the Seaway. Geographically it is the largest district in New York State, and one of the largest in the East. Politically, it is ancestrally Republican but more inclined toward moderates than conservatives and increasingly divided in its loyalties to the two parties. It gave Republican George W. Bush a small plurality in 2000 and a small majority in 2004. And it gave Democrat Barack Obama 52% of the vote over Republican John McCain's 47% in 2008. In the 2010 governor's race, Hamilton and Fulton counties in the district's GOP-dominated eastern portion were among the few outside of western New York to back Republican Carl Paladino over the eventual winner, Democrat Andrew Cuomo. But Cuomo handily took the district's remaining counties.

Bill Owens (D)

The congressman from the 23rd District of New York is Democrat Bill Owens, an affable Democrat who has twice eked out victories while preoccupied Republicans fought bloody ideological battles among themselves.

Owens was born in Brooklyn, the only child of a civil engineer and a homemaker. The family moved to Long Island when he was 5 years-old, and later settled in the suburb of Mineola. Owens graduated from Manhattan College, where he joined the Air Force ROTC, and got a deferment to attend law school at Fordham University. When he got his law degree, he was commissioned in the Air Force Judge Advocate General Corps (JAG). He was stationed for two years at Wurtsmith Air Force Base in Michigan and then was transferred to New York's Plattsburgh Air Force Base. Both he and his wife, Jane, whom he had met in college, decided to remain there to raise their family after Owens' military commitment was over. When the Plattsburgh base was shuttered in 1995, Owens helped found the Plattsburgh Airbase Redevelopment Corp., a group that redeveloped it into a commercial center. Owens also went into local private practice, focusing on business and tax law.

In early June 2009, Republican John McHugh, who had represented the 23rd District since 1993, accepted President Barack Obama's offer to become secretary of the Army. There are no primaries for special elections in New York, so candidates for the special election to replace McHugh were chosen by the party chairmen in the 11 counties that make up the district. Republicans nominated six-term Assemblywoman Dede Scozzafava, a moderate similar in her politics to McHugh. She favored abortion rights, supported same-sex marriage and had strong ties to organized labor. Unhappy with the choice, the New York Conservative Party put up its own candidate, Doug Hoffman.

Meanwhile, Democrats, unable to recruit a more experienced candidate, settled on Owens, a political novice with little name recognition. To win over local leaders, Owens stressed his work in the community, particularly on job creation. In lining up behind Owens, Democratic leaders hoped that his independence and military service would remind voters of the moderate McHugh. At the time, Republicans had a registration advantage of about 46,500 voters in the district.

As a possible bellwether for the 2010 midterm elections, the race got the attention of national figures and organizations. Hoffman was helped by the deep pockets of the national anti-tax group Club for Growth, which helped him highlight Scozzafava's liberal social positions and her support for the Democrats' 2009 economic stimulus bill. Scozzafava struggled with fundraising. And in the closing weeks of the campaign, Hoffman won endorsements from Minnesota Gov. Tim Pawlenty, former Alaska Gov. Sarah Palin, a favorite of tea party activists, and former U.S. House Majority Leader Dick Armey. Hoffman's polls numbers rose, and on Oct. 31, Scozzafava announced that she was withdrawing. The National Republican Congressional Committee switched its endorsement to Hoffman, but Scozzafava backed former Democratic rival Owens. On Nov. 3, with Republicans in disarray, Owens eked out a victory of 49% to 46% for Hoffman, with Scozzafava getting 5%. He became the first Democrat to represent the region since 1852.

Owens was sworn in on Nov. 6, 2009, and the next day voted for the House Democrats' health care overhaul. During the campaign, he had stressed expanding coverage to the uninsured and requiring plans to cover pre-existing conditions. A member of the Armed Services Committee, he also joined his party on repealing the "don't ask, don't tell" policy banning openly gay military service members. And he backed additional spending in 2010 to prevent teacher layoffs and extending increased Medicaid payments to states.

But he is the centrist he promised he would be. He opposed the Democrats' financial services industry overhaul and the DREAM Act giving some children of illegal immigrants a path to citizenship. After Democrats lost their majority in the 2010 elections, Owens told the *Adirondack Daily Enterprise* it was "quite possible" he could support Republican John Boehner for speaker over Democratic leader Nancy Pelosi. He didn't follow through on the idea, however.

To show voters back home his seriousness about boosting the area's economy, Owens introduced a slew of economic legislation, including a variety of tax-cutting initiatives and a measure to expand credit for family farmers. He also got a bill into law in January 2011 to develop a strategy to fight drug smuggling between the United States and Canada. Though he backed health care reform, he joined fellow New York Democratic Rep. Scott Murphy in pushing a 2010 bill to repeal a provision to expand 1099 tax reporting for businesses that many small firms complained was overly burdensome.

National Republicans, eyeing a big year in 2010, targeted Owens' seat. Hoffman returned for a rematch, but he struggled to recapture the tea party-fueled enthusiasm for his initial candidacy, and lost in the primary to Republican Matt Doheny, a Wall Street investment banker who put more than $2.2 million of his own money into the race. At first Hoffman stubbornly refused to bow out, vowing to again run on the Conservative Party ticket. Within three weeks, as it became clearer that he could become the spoiler that Scozzafava was a year earlier, he dropped out and threw his support to Doheny. But it apparently was too little, too late. Owens won 48% to Doheny's 46% and Hoffman's 6%. Having established himself, Owens has some breathing room in 2012.

TWENTY-FOURTH DISTRICT

Richard Hanna (R)

Elected 2010, 1st term; b. Jan. 25, 1951, Utica; home, Barneveld; Reed Col., B.A. 1976; Catholic; Married (Kim); 2 children.

Professional Career: President, Hanna Construction; partner, the Gabriel Group, 1992-2010.

DC Office: 319 CHOB, 20515, 202-225-3665; Fax: 202-225-1891; Web site: hanna.house.gov.

State Offices: Auburn, 315-252-6700; Cortland, 607-756-2470; Utica, 315-724-9740.

Committees: *Education & the Workforce:* Early Childhood, Elementary & Secondary Education; Health, Employment, Labor & Pensions; Higher Education & Workforce Training. *Transportation & Infrastructure:* Economic Development, Public Buildings & Emergency Management; Highways & Transit (VChmn); Railroads, Pipelines & Hazardous Materials.

Election Results

2010 general	Richard Hanna (R)..101,599	(53%)	($1,289,710)
	Michael Arcuri (D) 89,809	(47%)	($1,886,555)
2010 primary	Richard Hanna (R).....................................unopposed		

Population		Race/Ethnicity		Work	
Pop. 2010:	657,222	White:	89.5%	Private:	73.2%
Change since 2000:	Up 0.4%	Black:	3.6%	Government:	19.3%
Urban:	50.5%	Hispanic:	3.3%	Self-employed:	7.3%
Rural:	49.5%	Asian:	1.6%	Blue collar:	22.5%
Area size:	6,358 sq. mi.	Native Am.:	0.2%	White collar:	58.3%
		Hawaiian:	0.0%	Khaki collar:	0.1%
Age		Two+ races:	1.5%	Other:	19.1%
Median age:	40.2 yrs.				
More than 65 yrs:	15.3%	*Ancestry*		Median income:	$45,454
Less than 18 yrs:	21.5%	Irish	14.6%	Median Home Value:	$102,900
		German	13.6%		
Education		Italian	11.6%	**Military Veterans**	
H.S. grad:	87.1%			% of Pop:	10.9%
College grad:	22.4%				
Grad degree:	9.2%				

Central New York; Utica, Rome

One of the first American frontiers was the Mohawk River Valley of upstate New York. But from the establishment of Fort Orange in 1624 in what now is Albany until the Revolutionary War, white settlers did not dare move west along the Mohawk. The British used their Iroquois allies as a buffer against the French and in return kept New England Yankees from moving westward. Only after the French were driven from North America in 1759 did the pressures for

2008 Presidential Vote

Barack Obama (D)	139,832	(50%)
John McCain (R)	133,277	(48%)

2004 Presidential Vote

George Bush (R)	147,509	(53%)
John Kerry (D)	130,568	(47%)

Cook Partisan Voting Index: R+2

westward settlement prevail. Once the Revolutionary War started, Iroquois dominion ended. There is little in these rolling hills today to evoke the bloody violence of the conflict or the later digging of the Erie Canal and the building of the New York Central Railroad. The canal was a staggering engineering feat. In 1811, it cost more to ship goods 30 miles inland from New York City than it cost to send them to England. But after eight years of work by 9,000 men, the canal opened in 1825, ahead of schedule and on budget, effectively tying together the nation and guaranteeing the preeminence of New York City in America's economy. Then the New York Central built its water-line route, and the Mohawk Valley became one of the nation's early industrial centers. The little Oneida County hamlets of Utica and Rome, where the canal builders had to dig through the route's highest ground, became sizable factory towns. Even the utopian Oneida Community, with its believers in plural marriage and communal ownership, operated a stainless steel factory. First settled by New England Yankees, these towns attracted a new wave of immigration from the Atlantic coast in the early 20th century, including many Italian- and Polish-Americans.

The 24th Congressional District of New York sprawls through parts of 11 counties in central New York, few of them heavily populated. The biggest towns are Utica and Rome in Oneida County and Auburn in Cayuga County, which sits amid the Finger Lakes. Nearby Seneca Falls was the birthplace of the women's movement in 1848, when Boston transplant Elizabeth Cady Stanton and Lucretia Mott produced a Declaration of Sentiments that initiated the push for women's suffrage. Abolition and temperance were also popular here. Today, this is a part of upstate New York that feels itself bypassed by more recent economic growth. Oneida County lost population from 2000 to 2010. And in a once economically dynamic area, the largest employer today is Oneida Nation's Turning Stone Resort Casino. State government has completed dredging the successor to the Erie Canal in Utica, but barge traffic is not a growth industry. Politically this part of Upstate New York had been Republican since the party came into existence in the 1850s. But in the past two decades, it moved toward the Democrats, and in 2008, the district voted 50%-48% for Barack Obama.

Richard Hanna (R)

The congressman from the 24th District is Richard Hanna, a Republican elected in 2010. Hanna grew up in the district; he was born in Utica and graduated from Whitesboro High School. When his father died in 1971, the 20-year-old Hanna became the main source of income for his mother and four sisters. But he was determined to go to college, and earned enough to put himself through Reed College in Portland, Ore., graduating in 1976. But his money ran out before he could get a master's degree, so he decided to start a business. Since his father had been a carpenter, Hanna started a construction company. For five years he lived in a barn he built, and worked at whatever jobs his fledgling company could pick up. Hanna Construction eventually grew to employ more than 450 people. A licensed pilot, Hanna also volunteered with Angel Flights, a service that provides free transport to the sick and injured in need of long-distance transportation.

In May 2008, Hanna set out to run against freshman Democrat Michael Arcuri, who had won the seat 54%-45% in 2006 after veteran Rep. Sherwood Boehlert, a Republican moderate, retired. Hanna did not get much support from national Republicans, but he held Arcuri to a 52%-48% victory even as Democrat Barack Obama was carrying the district. In 2010, Hanna was back for a rematch, running as a fiscal conservative opposed to government bailouts and, like Boehlert, a moderate on cultural issues. He supported abortion rights and civil unions for gay couples, but dubbed the Democrats' health care legislation "ill-conceived."

Arcuri voted for the Democrats' health care bill in November 2009, but voted against the final version in March 2010. That cost him the ballot line of the union-controlled Working Families Party, so he created his own Moderate Party to give him a second ballot line. On one issue, Hanna ran to Arcuri's left: Arcuri opposed the building of a mosque and Islamic center near Ground Zero in Manhattan, while Hanna issued a statement supporting the developer's right to build it, though he later said it would be "insensitive."

Hanna's business became an issue in the campaign. Arcuri aired an ad questioning Hanna's commitment to restraining government spending, noting his business received $4 million in government contracts, including $1 million that came in while Hanna's uncle was mayor and comptroller of Utica. Arcuri also noted that Hanna's firm has been sued for injuries and was cited 12 times for health and safety violations. Hanna responded that he went through proper avenues when working with his uncle, and that he did not seek favors. Hanna said that any company doing as much construction work as his was bound to accrue some violations and lawsuits.

Arcuri raised and spent $1.9 million, while Hanna raised and spent $1.3 million, $270,000 of it his own money. Hanna won 53%-47%, carrying eight of 11 counties. Hanna was one of two Arab-Americans elected in the large GOP freshman class in 2010; the other was Rep. Justin Amash, R-Mich.

TWENTY-FIFTH DISTRICT

Ann Marie Buerkle (R)

Elected 2010, 1st term; b. May 8, 1951, Auburn; home, Syracuse; St. Joseph's Hospital Schl. of Nursing, R.N. 1972; Le Moyne Col., B.S. 1977; Syracuse U., J.D. 1994; Catholic; Divorced; 6 children.

Elected Office: Syracuse City Cncl., 1994-95.

Professional Career: School nurse, 1977-91; property mgr., 1977-91; NY St. asst. atty. gen., 1997-2010.

DC Office: 1630 LHOB, 20515, 202-225-3701; Fax: 202-225-4042; Web site: buerkle.house.gov.

State Offices: Irondequoit, 585-336-7291; Syracuse, 315-423-5657.

Committees: *Foreign Affairs:* Africa, Global Health & Human Rights; Middle East & South Asia; Terrorism, Nonproliferation & Trade (VChmn). *Oversight & Government Reform:* Regulatory Affairs, Stimulus Oversight & Government Spending; TARP, Financial Services & Bailouts of Public & Private Programs. *Veterans' Affairs:* Disability Assistance & Memorial Affairs; Health (Chmn).

Election Results

2010 general	Ann Marie Buerkle (R)	104,602	(50.15%)	($841,574)
	Dan Maffei (D)	103,954	(49.85%)	($3,192,682)
2010 primary	Ann Marie Buerkle (R)	unopposed		

Population		Race/Ethnicity		Work	
Pop. 2010:	668,869	White:	82.7%	Private:	78.3%
Change since 2000:	Up 2.2%	Black:	8.1%	Government:	16.5%
Urban:	79.0%	Hispanic:	3.9%	Self-employed:	5.1%
Rural:	21.0%	Asian:	2.6%	Blue collar:	18.0%
Area size:	2,559 sq. mi.	Native Am.:	0.6%	White collar:	66.0%
		Hawaiian:	0.0%	Khaki collar:	0.2%
Age		Two+ races:	2.1%	Other:	15.9%
Median age:	39.9 yrs.				
More than 65 yrs:	14.3%	*Ancestry*		Median income:	$52,755
Less than 18 yrs:	23.4%	German	15.8%	Median Home Value:	$124,800
		Irish	15.6%		
Education		Italian	13.2%	**Military Veterans**	
H.S. grad:	89.2%			% of Pop:	10.1%
College grad:	31.4%				
Grad degree:	13.4%				

Central New York; Syracuse

Syracuse is a Middle American city in the middle of upstate New York, halfway between Albany and Buffalo on the Erie Canal and the old New York Central Railroad, which were for years the nation's major east-west transportation routes. Built on a swamp that was a salt spring, Syracuse is the home of many practical-minded inventions—the dental chair, Stickley mission furniture, the drive-in bank teller, the serrated knife, and the foot measuring devices used in shoe stores. It is the site of the New York State Fair, which attracts 1 million visitors annually, and of Syracuse University, which plays basketball inside the Carrier Dome, the largest domed stadium on a college campus. The agricultural hinterland is rich with specialty crops like wine grapes, and its industrial jobs are mostly high-skill. But Onondaga County has been losing population since 1990, with a big loss in the 20-35 age group. Over the decade ending in 2010, it lost about 1% of its population. Manufacturing jobs are being lost, but there are job gains in business services, education, and health care. Because local housing prices increased only modestly during the real estate boom, the area suffered little from the sharp decline in housing prices in 2008 and 2009. *CNN Money* named Syracuse the third most affordable housing market in the nation in 2010, with a median home price of $95,000.

2008 Presidential Vote		
Barack Obama (D)	177,800	(56%)
John McCain (R)	135,941	(43%)
2004 Presidential Vote		
John Kerry (D)	158,063	(50%)
George Bush (R)	150,098	(48%)
Cook Partisan Voting Index:	D+3	

The 25th Congressional District of New York includes all of Syracuse and Onondaga County. West of Syracuse, it includes territory just south of Lake Ontario, northern Cayuga County, and Wayne County, where in the village of Palmyra, Joseph Smith had his vision of the angel Moroni and saw the golden tablets that led him to found the Mormon Church. The district's western end is in the suburbs of Rochester in Monroe County, which is split up between four districts. Historically, Syracuse and Rochester have been heavily Republican, partly out of antipathy to New York City. But in the 1990s, economically ailing upstate New York trended sharply toward national Democrats even as it voted for Republican Gov. George Pataki. This district voted 50% for Democrat John Kerry in 2004 and 56% for Democrat Barack Obama in 2008.

Ann Marie Buerkle (R)

The new member of Congress from the 25th District of New York is Republican Ann Marie Buerkle, who scored one of the biggest upsets of the 2010 election season with her win over freshman Democrat Dan Maffei. Buerkle was raised in Auburn, N.Y., the daughter of first-generation Italian-Americans. "My dad was high school educated, barely," she told *National Journal.* "He scrapped his way, and worked hard, and grew businesses. He was a quintessential entrepreneur." Growing up, Buerkle worked in her parents' grocery store and also frequented the family's roller skating rinks. After high school, Buerkle enrolled at the St. Joseph's Hospital School of Nursing and subsequently worked as a nurse in New York City. When her husband, a lieutenant commander in the Navy, was stationed in Puerto Rico, she volunteered as a nurse there with the Red Cross. She eventually returned to Syracuse, N.Y., to get her undergraduate degree from Le Moyne College in 1977. She worked as a school nurse and in real estate while raising six children. Buerkle also was heavily involved in the anti-abortion movement during the 1980s, working at the non-profit Friends for Life.

In the early 1990s, Buerkle went back to school to get a law degree at Syracuse University. In 1994 and 1995, she was a member of the Syracuse City Council, an appointive post. Two years later, Buerkle was named an assistant attorney general in New York, a position she held for 13 years. That experience and her work as a nurse were major factors in her opposition to the Obama administration's overhaul of the health care system. "Philosophically, I felt that the government should have a limited role in health care," she said, adding that she also didn't think the plan would lower costs as intended. Her frustration influenced her decision to run against Maffei.

In the March primary, Buerkle defeated turkey farm owner Mark Bitz to secure the Republican nomination. Then, in the general-election campaign, Buerkle highlighted the candidates' different approaches to health care and the war in Afghanistan. When Maffei voted against an emergency spending bill in July that included $33 billion for the fighting in Afghanistan, Buerkle accused him of "turning his back on troops at war." During an October debate, Buerkle attacked the health care overhaul and said that it would require 16,000 new employees at the Internal Revenue Service, a charge that Maffei said was fiction. The incumbent, a former House Ways and Means Committee staffer, voted for the health care bill, but he tempered his support by saying that the measure was only a start toward fixing a system headed for disaster.

Buerkle had difficulty getting traction for much of the summer, especially after it was revealed that she owed $46,000 in back taxes on a building she owned. She contended that the tax payments were the responsibility of her tenants. Buerkle trailed by double digits in the polls, and was heavily outspent by Maffei. He raised $2.7 million to her $552,000. But as the GOP's fortunes picked up nationally in the fall, Buerkle began to gain momentum. She was endorsed by former Alaska Gov. Sarah Palin, who dubbed her one of the "mama grizzlies" (female candidates with "common sense," as Palin put it). Buerkle also got help from tea party activists. Her background in the anti-abortion movement set her apart from other tea party candidates, who tended to emphasize reducing taxes and government spending over hot-button social issues.

On election night, Buerkle had a lead of just 659 votes, leaving the contest too close to call. A state judge ruled that the two campaigns could inspect all of the approximately 11,000 absentee ballots. After three weeks of ballot-counting and legal wrangling, Maffei trailed by 567 votes, and he finally conceded the race on Nov. 23. Buerkle raised more money during the recount period than the Democrat did, with cash for her effort flowing in from the likes of former Sen. Alfonse D'Amato, R-N.Y., and billionaire cosmetics heir Ronald Lauder. Buerkle won the race, 50.2% to 49.8%.

TWENTY-SIXTH DISTRICT

Kathy Hochul (D)

Elected May 2011; b. Aug. 27, 1958, Buffalo; home, Hamburg; Syracuse U., B.A. 1980; Catholic U., J.D. 1983; Catholic; Married (William); 2 children.

Elected Office: Clerk, Erie Cnty., 2007-present; Member, Hamburg Town Bd., 1994-2007.

Professional Career: Dep. clerk, Erie Cnty., 2003-07; Founder, Kathleen Mary House, 2006; Cnsl., S M Consulting, 2000-07; Legis. asst., cnsl, Sen. Daniel Patrick Moynihan, D-NY, 1986-88; Legis. asst., cnsl., Rep. John La-Falce, D-NY, 1984-86; Practicing atty., 1983-84; Staff, NY St. Assembly, 1976-80.

DC Office: 1711 LHOB, 20515, 202-225-5265; Fax: 202-225-5910; Web site: hochul.house.gov.

State Offices: Williamsville, 716-634-2324.

Election Results

2011 special	Kathy Hochul (D)	52,713	(47%)	($826,758)
	Jane Corwin (R)	47,187	(42%)	($2,264,860)
	Jack Davis (TEA)	10,029	(9%)	($1,616,820)

Population		Race/Ethnicity		Work	
Pop. 2010:	674,804	White:	89.3%	Private:	78.2%
Change since 2000:	Up 3.1%	Black:	3.8%	Government:	16.4%
Urban:	71.2%	Hispanic:	2.8%	Self-employed:	5.3%
Rural:	28.8%	Asian:	2.3%	Blue collar:	20.8%
Area size:	2,748 sq. mi.	Native Am.:	0.3%	White collar:	62.4%
		Hawaiian:	0.0%	Khaki collar:	0.1%
Age		Two+ races:	1.3%	Other:	16.7%
Median age:	40.6 yrs.				
More than 65 yrs:	14.9%	*Ancestry*		Median income:	$55,093
Less than 18 yrs:	21.7%	German	21.7%	Median Home Value:	$127,300
		Irish	14.0%		
Education		Italian	13.1%	**Military Veterans**	
H.S. grad:	90.1%			% of Pop:	10.0%
College grad:	29.1%				
Grad degree:	13.1%				

West New York; Buffalo Suburbs

The destination of the Erie Canal, the great state engineering project that made New York the Empire State, is Lake Erie. The final 100 miles of the canal passed through the rolling countryside of western New York when it was scarcely settled, except by American Indians. In some ways, the region has a Midwest flavor. People speak not in the pungent accents of New York City but in flat Midwestern tones. The economy, based originally on farming, was dominated by

2008 Presidential Vote
John McCain (R) 166,862   (52%)
Barack Obama (D) 148,577   (46%)

2004 Presidential Vote
George Bush (R) 176,235   (55%)
John Kerry (D) 137,543   (43%)

Cook Partisan Voting Index: R+6

heavy industry by the late 19th century. The land was settled mostly by New England Yankees, with cultural folkways quite different from those of New York City. Later, they were joined by Irish, Italian, and Polish immigrants who came to work in the factories of Buffalo and Rochester. For most of its history, western New York had an economy more prosperous than that of the rest of the country, as you can still see in the solid houses and schools, stores, and factories built to weather the upstate winters. But in the past three decades, economic growth has lagged behind the rest of the nation. Many of Buffalo's factories have closed. Rochester's premier industries, Eastman Kodak and Xerox, have fallen on hard times and laid off thousands of workers. In Rochester, the overall percentage of people employed in manufacturing fell from 19% in 2000 to 12% in 2010, as Kodak cut its workforce 70% during that period. But other entities posted large gains to help offset those losses, including the University of Rochester, which added nearly 5,000 jobs during the decade.

The 26th Congressional District of New York covers much of western New York. About half its people are in the suburbs of Buffalo in Erie and Niagara counties. It extends from the city limits of Buffalo to the city limits of Rochester and includes Rochester's northwestern suburbs. In between is rural and small-town territory. One of them is Attica, scene of a terrible prison uprising in 1970. Politically, this is ancestrally Republican country, based on upstaters' general distrust of Democratic New York City. It was one of six New York districts that voted for Republican George W. Bush in both 2000 and 2004, and it was one of four New York districts that voted for GOP presidential nominee John McCain in 2008. In the 2010 governor's race, Republican and Buffalo native Carl Paladino got his strongest support from this area, beating Democrat Andrew Cuomo 58-38% in Erie County and 65%-32% in Niagara County, even as Cuomo racked up huge margins elsewhere to win in a landslide.

Kathy Hochul (D)

The new congresswoman from the 26th District is Kathy Hochul, a Democrat. She scored a surprising upset in a May 2011 special election to fill the seat of Republican Chris Lee, who abruptly resigned two months earlier following an embarrassing episode in his personal life. Hochul's ability to win in a heavily Republican district—through a campaign that focused on staunchly opposing the House GOP's proposal to overhaul Medicare—raised Democrats' hopes of gaining control of the House in 2012 using similar tactics.

Hochul (*HOE-kul*) grew up in Hamburg, N.Y., one of six children in a family that was known for its social and political activism. Her mother opened a transitional home for victims of domestic violence. As a Syracuse University student in the late 1970s, Hochul led an unsuccessful campaign to name the college's new domed football stadium after football great Ernie Davis—the first African-American to win the Heisman Trophy—instead of a local air-conditioning manufacturer. She went on to obtain a law degree from Catholic University in Washington, D.C., and remained in the city to work as a legal counsel and legislative assistant for two New York Democrats, Rep. John LaFalce and Sen. Daniel Patrick Moynihan. She also started her own law practice representing the computer industry.

Returning to her hometown, Hochul was elected in 1994 to a seat on the Hamburg Town Board. She helped launch an effort to remove toll barriers along the New York Thruway system, and the state did away with the booths in 2003, in a move that reaped her considerable positive publicity. She spent four years as a deputy county clerk in Erie County and was named as the replacement for County Clerk David Swarts in 2007 when Swarts was chosen as state motor vehicles commissioner. She became a highly visible figure in that job, earning a reputation for being aggressive and ambitious. She mobilized other county clerks in 2009 to persuade then-Gov. David Paterson to scrap a plan to raise money by requiring new license plates for drivers. She was elected to her own term in 2010 with 80% of the vote.

The House seat came open when Republican Lee, who had been regarded as a rising GOP star, abruptly resigned in February 2011 after the website *Gawker.com* reported that he had replied to a personal ad on Craigslist from a woman seeking a "financially and emotionally secure" man. Lee sent messages to the woman from his personal account, describing himself as a 39-year-old divorced lobbyist and including a shirtless photo of himself. At the time, Lee was 46 and married with one child. The woman cut off contact with Lee after searching online and finding out he was a congressman.

His departure initially led New York political observers to believe that his district would become the sacrificial lamb to redistricting following the 2010 census. Upstate New York was expected to lose one of the two House seats that New York has to give up in the reapportionment. But that scenario became complicated by the decision of Republican county chairs to nominate GOP Assemblywoman Jane Corwin in the special election. Corwin has closer ties to Albany than any of the delegation's other members. Her family founded the Talking Phone Book, a Buffalo-based publisher of telephone directories and provider of online marketing services. Endorsed by the local tea party and both state Conservative and Independence parties, she initially was considered a strong favorite for the seat.

Hochul jumped into the race even though she did not live in the 26th District; Hamburg is in the adjacent 27th District. She portrayed herself as an independent Democrat, citing her efforts as clerk. "I'm not afraid of telling my own party when they're wrong, or embracing a Republican idea when it's right. I'm not partisan," she told the *Lockport Union-Sun & Journal*. Corwin's campaign, however, sought to portray Hochul as a liberal who would align with House Minority Leader Nancy Pelosi, D-Calif. Corwin had the advantage of being able to self-finance much of her race, with more than three-quarters of the $3.3 million she raised coming from her personal funds, according to the Center for Responsive Politics. Hochul raised just over $1 million.

But national Democrats believed they could exploit the Republicans' support of House Budget Committee Chairman Paul Ryan's controversial budget-balancing blueprint, which passed the House in April 2011 without a single Democratic vote. Ryan's plan called for changing Medicare to a defined-contribution voucher plan, a politically volatile idea from which even some national Republicans sought to distance themselves. The Democratic Congressional Campaign Committee began running ads attacking Corwin for supporting the proposal, helping establish Hochul as an underdog fighting the GOP establishment. Corwin later acknowledged that she was slow to respond to the charges. But she continued to get outside help. The Republican Congressional Campaign Committee and the conservative political action committee American Crossroads together spent more than $1.1 million on the race.

Corwin soon faced another major obstacle—the entry into the race of a prominent third party candidate, wealthy businessman Jack Davis. A Republican-turned-Democrat, Davis had unsuccessfully run for the seat in 2004, 2006 and 2008 as a self-funded candidate, pouring in millions of his own money. After coming in third in the 2008 Democratic primary, he switched his affiliation back to Republican. For the special election, Davis ran under the "Tea Party" banner. A nasty confrontation he had with Corwin's chief of staff made the rounds on YouTube, raising questions about how effectively Corwin was running her campaign. Democrats also painted Corwin as an elitist who drove a Mercedes Benz.

In the final weeks, polls showed Hochul with a slight edge. Republicans blamed the presence of Davis for an artificially close race. But a final Siena College survey showed that while Davis' numbers had plummeted in the last month, those voters weren't moving uniformly to Corwin's camp, and that he was drawing support from both parties. On Election Night, Hochul won with 47% of the vote to Corwin's 42% and Davis' 9%. "Tonight's victory is an achievement many called impossible," Hochul said in her victory speech. "Tonight we showed that many voters are willing to ignore a party label and vote for the person and for the message they believe in."

DCCC Chairman Steve Israel, D-N.Y., said in a statement that the election "served notice to the Republicans that we will fight them anywhere in America when it comes to defending and strengthening Medicare." Republicans were plotting revenge, however, and Hochul will face a tough battle for re-election in November 2012. And with New York required to lose two seats through redistricting, she is not immune to a reshaping of the 26th District, though Democrats expressed hope that her newfound national status would help insulate her.

TWENTY-SEVENTH DISTRICT

Brian Higgins (D)

Elected 2004, 4th term; b. Oct. 6, 1959, Buffalo; home, Buffalo; S.U.N.Y. Buffalo, B.A. 1984, M.A. 1985, Harvard U. M.P.A. 1996; Catholic; married (Mary Jane); 2 children.

Elected Office: Buffalo City Cncl., 1987-93; NY Assembly, 1998-2004.

Professional Career: Chief of staff, Erie Cnty. Leg., 1994-98; Lecturer, Buffalo State College, 2000-03.

DC Office: 2459 RHOB, 20515, 202-225-3306; Fax: 202-226-0347; Web site: higgins.house.gov.

State Offices: Buffalo, 716-852-3501; Jamestown, 716-484-0729.

Committees: *Foreign Affairs:* Middle East & South Asia; Terrorism, Nonproliferation & Trade. *Homeland Security:* Border & Maritime Security; Counterterrorism & Intelligence.

Group Ratings

	ACLU	ACU	ADA	CFG	AFS	FRC	LCV	ITIC	NTU	COC
2010	81	4	90	0	100	0	90	100	4	25
2009	–	0	100	0	100	–	100	–	2	36

National Journal Ratings

	2010 LIB	—	2010 CONS	2009 LIB	—	2009 CONS
Economic	83%	—	17%	82%	—	14%
Social	58%	—	41%	67%	—	31%
Foreign	66%	—	29%	62%	—	35%
Composite	70%	—	30%	72%	—	28%

Key Votes of the 111th Congress

1. Overturn Ledbetter	Y	5. Bar federal abortion funds	N	9. Stop detainee transfers	Y
2. Pass $820 billion stimulus	Y	6. Pass health care bill	Y	10. Legalize immigrants' kids	N
3. Let guns in national parks	Y	7. Regulate financial firms	Y	11. Repeal don't ask, tell	Y
4. Pass cap-and-trade	Y	8. Pass tax cuts for some	Y	12. Limit campaign funds	Y

Election Results

2010 general	Brian Higgins (D)..119,085	(61%)	($1,113,936)
	Leonard Roberto (R) 76,320	(39%)	
2010 primary	Brian Higgins (D).. unopposed		

Prior Winning Percentages: 2008 (74%), 2006 (79%), 2004 (51%)

Population		Race/Ethnicity		Work	
Pop. 2010:	629,271	White:	84.8%	Private:	78.7%
Change since 2000:	Down 3.8%	Black:	5.4%	Government:	16.5%
Urban:	81.5%	Hispanic:	6.2%	Self-employed:	4.6%
Rural:	18.5%	Asian:	1.4%	Blue collar:	22.0%
Area size:	2,444 sq. mi.	Native Am.:	0.7%	White collar:	59.5%
		Hawaiian:	0.0%	Khaki collar:	0.1%
Age		Two+ races:	1.4%	Other:	18.4%
Median age:	40.8 yrs.				
More than 65 yrs:	15.8%	*Ancestry*		Median income:	$44,449
Less than 18 yrs:	21.6%	German	20.2%	Median Home Value:	$103,600
		Polish	14.8%		
Education		Irish	13.7%	**Military Veterans**	
H.S. grad:	86.8%			% of Pop:	10.6%
College grad:	24.1%				
Grad degree:	10.0%				

Western New York; Buffalo

With its massive 1920s City Hall overlooking the Niagara River and Lake Erie, Buffalo declares itself to be a city of substance. But it has gone through some rough times in recent decades. The butt of jokes about the snow from Lake Erie that supposedly keeps it immobilized half the year, Buffalo also can claim credit for building a heavy industrial base in the late 19th and early 20th centuries, as America's No. 1 grain milling center and as a major steel producer. Today,

2008 Presidential Vote

Barack Obama (D) 156,635	(54%)
John McCain (R) 127,249	(44%)

2004 Presidential Vote

John Kerry (D) 158,433	(53%)
George Bush (R) 132,416	(45%)

Cook Partisan Voting Index: D+4

the area still benefits from cheap hydroelectric power, but the Lackawanna steel mills are shuttered, and grain milling waned after the St. Lawrence Seaway opened in the 1950s. Buffalo has been eclipsed economically by the bigger Great Lakes industrial cities of Cleveland, Detroit, and Chicago, and its architecturally bold downtown skyscrapers are overshadowed by the high-rise horizon of Toronto, about 100 miles away.

Buffalo was the nation's 15th-largest city in 1950, when it had a population of 580,000. By 2010, it was 70th-largest, with a population reduced by more than half to about 270,000. The city's unemployment rate, below 6% in 2007, hovered around 10% for much of 2009 and 2010. Right across Buffalo's Peace Bridge is the richest part of Canada, the golden horseshoe from Niagara Falls through Hamilton to Toronto. But Buffalo's hopes of becoming Toronto's back office have faded, and New York taxes are still high enough to leave Buffalo at a serious competitive disadvantage. Local boosters have criticized state capital powerbrokers for lavishing excessive attention on New York City as the state's economic engine. And, to add insult to injury, the Buffalo Bills franchise in the National Football League has moved some of its home games to Toronto. Still, Buffalo retains some considerable assets: a high-skill labor force and inexpensive real estate, including a gentrified and handsome waterfront on a now-cleaner Lake Erie, and some impressive cultural institutions. In 2010, Verizon made plans to expand, enticed by tax breaks and electricity discounts. And *Forbes* magazine that year ranked the area the 10th best place in the nation to raise a family.

The 27th Congressional District of New York consists of the eastern and southern two-thirds of Buffalo, plus most of the Erie County suburbs east and south of the city, from working-class Cheektowaga and Lackawanna to higher-income Hamburg and Orchard Park. It also includes rural Chautauqua County, with its famed summer lecture series dating to 1874. Although some Buffalo suburbs are Republican, this district is solidly Democratic. But as Buffalo struggles, it has become politically volatile. In 1992, Buffalo gave third-party presidential candidate Ross Perot 28% of the vote, his best showing in a central city anywhere. In recent contests for president, Buffalo and Erie County have been solidly Democratic. But the county went decisively for hometown Republican Carl Paladino, over victorious Democrat Andrew Cuomo, 59%-38%, in the 2010 governor's race.

Brian Higgins (D)

The congressman from the 27th District is Brian Higgins, a Democrat elected in 2004. Higgins grew up in Buffalo, the son of a skilled tradesman who was prominent in local politics, serving on the Buffalo City Council and later as commissioner of the New York State Workers Compensation Board. His mother was a schoolteacher. Higgins graduated from Buffalo State College and later got a master's degree from Harvard. A political junkie, he launched his career in government with staff jobs in the Erie County sheriff's office, the state Assembly, and the county legislature. In 1993, after six years on the Buffalo City Council, he ran for county comptroller and lost. In 1998, he was elected to the Assembly and served three terms. In a district crowded with unionized workers, Higgins often reminded voters that his father and uncle were bricklayers and stressed his Irish immigrant heritage.

A House seat unexpectedly opened up in 2004 when Republican Rep. Jack Quinn announced he was retiring after 12 years. Nancy Naples, a former Merrill Lynch executive in Manhattan and a popular local figure with strong name recognition, quickly wrapped up the Republican nomination, while five Democrats battled for their party's nomination. Higgins was the favorite of local and national Democratic leaders, organized labor, and the *Buffalo News*, which called him "an unusually productive member of a largely dysfunctional legislative body" in Albany. He won the primary with 44% of the vote.

In the contentious general election, Higgins reminded voters that Naples supported many of President George W. Bush's policies, and criticized Republicans for shifting the tax burden from the rich to the middle class. He also ran on a platform of making health care more widely available. Naples criticized Higgins for supporting tax increases in Albany. Higgins won 51%-49%, a nearly 3,800-vote victory. Naples got 57% of the vote in Chautauqua County, which cast 20% of the district's votes. Higgins won 53% in Erie County. Naples conceded the race.

In the House, Higgins established a centrist voting record with a liberal bent on economic issues. After spending his first years securing his hold on the seat with an array of mostly successful efforts for his district, he was rewarded with a seat on the powerful Ways and Means Committee in 2009. That year he introduced a bill to enhance renewable energy tax credits for economically distressed cities, as well as a measure to offer tax credits for the production of biogas from landfills and other sources. He initially vowed to oppose the December 2010 deal to extend the expiring Bush-era tax cuts because it would not extend the Renewal Communities program, which had brought $150 million in development to the area. He also criticized Republicans' insistence on including tax cuts for the wealthy. But he said, "The cost of inaction would be far worse for Western New York families and seniors." He eventually voted for the deal.

Since developing skin cancer, Higgins has worked heavily on cancer research, introducing bills to establish a national cancer trust fund and pushing for money for Buffalo's Roswell Park Cancer Institute. Higgins helped to broker an agreement with the New York Power Authority for local financial aid, including waterfront improvements, in exchange for its long-term right to operate the Niagara Power Project. The issue strained his relationship with Democratic Rep. Louise Slaughter in the adjoining district, who disagreed with his strategy. After the Republican takeover of the House in 2011, the number of Democratic seats on Ways and Means was reduced and Higgins was forced off the committee. He took seats on Homeland Security and Foreign Affairs.

On national issues, Higgins' support for the USA PATRIOT Act, which gave law enforcement enhanced powers in terrorism investigations, and his opposition to a deadline for the withdrawal of troops from Iraq led to complaints from some liberals. But those positions may have been a net plus for him in the district. Republicans wanted to try to defeat Higgins in 2006 but couldn't come up with a credible challenger. He appears safe, at least until redistricting, when New York will lose two House seats. He reportedly hired a lobbyist in 2011 to help him on that issue, and donated $18,000 to the New York State Assembly Campaign Committee.

TWENTY-EIGHTH DISTRICT

Louise Slaughter (D)

Elected 1986, 13th term; b. Aug. 14, 1929, Harlan Cnty., KY; home, Fairport; U. of KY, B.S. 1951, M.S. 1953; Episcopalian; married (Robert); 3 children.

Elected Office: Monroe Cnty. Legislature, 1976–79; NY Assembly, 1982–86.

Professional Career: Regional coord., Lt. Gov. Mario Cuomo, 1976–79.

DC Office: 2469 RHOB, 20515, 202-225-3615; Fax: 202-225-7822; Web site: www.louise.house.gov.

State Offices: Buffalo, 716-853-5813; Niagara Falls, 716-282-1274; Rochester, 585-232-4850.

Committees: *Rules* (RMM).

Group Ratings

	ACLU	ACU	ADA	CFG	AFS	FRC	LCV	ITIC	NTU	COC
2010	81	0	100	0	100	0	100	100	4	13
2009	–	4	90	2	100	–	100	–	3	45

National Journal Ratings

	2010 LIB — 2010 CONS		2009 LIB — 2009 CONS	
Economic	90%	— 0%	91%	— 0%
Social	86%	— 13%	89%	— 0%
Foreign	90%	— 10%	91%	— 0%
Composite	91%	— 10%	95%	— 5%

Key Votes of the 111th Congress

1. Overturn Ledbetter	Y	5. Bar federal abortion funds	N	9. Stop detainee transfers	*
2. Pass $820 billion stimulus	Y	6. Pass health care bill	Y	10. Legalize immigrants' kids	Y
3. Let guns in national parks	N	7. Regulate financial firms	Y	11. Repeal don't ask, tell	Y
4. Pass cap-and-trade	Y	8. Pass tax cuts for some	Y	12. Limit campaign funds	Y

Election Results

2010 general	Louise Slaughter (D)	102,514	(65%)	($720,705)
	Jill Rowland (R)	55,392	(35%)	($26,595)
2010 primary	Louise Slaughter (D)	unopposed		

Prior Winning Percentages: 2008 (78%), 2006 (73%), 2004 (73%), 2002 (62%), 2000 (66%), 1998 (65%), 1996 (57%), 1994 (57%), 1992 (55%), 1990 (59%), 1988 (57%), 1986 (51%)

Population		Race/Ethnicity		Work	
Pop. 2010:	611,838	White:	58.1%	Private:	80.7%
Change since 2000:	Down 6.5%	Black:	29.2%	Government:	14.6%
Urban:	93.5%	Hispanic:	7.7%	Self-employed:	4.6%
Rural:	6.5%	Asian:	2.1%	Blue collar:	18.6%
Area size:	2,283 sq. mi.	Native Am.:	0.5%	White collar:	60.5%
		Hawaiian:	0.0%	Khaki collar:	0.1%
Age		Two+ races:	2.2%	Other:	20.8%
Median age:	37.2 yrs.				
More than 65 yrs:	13.8%	*Ancestry*		Median income:	$38,062
Less than 18 yrs:	23.0%	German	14.1%	Median Home Value:	$92,600
		Italian	11.5%		
Education		Irish	10.3%	**Military Veterans**	
H.S. grad:	84.7%			% of Pop:	9.2%
College grad:	24.6%				
Grad degree:	10.4%				

Western New York; Rochester

Rochester, with a metropolitan area of just over 1 million, is one of the major cities of upstate New York. Located where the Erie Canal crosses the Genesee River, Rochester became a major industrial city—the Flour City—in the 1830s, as it milled the wheat produced by western New York farmers. Then, it was one of the early high-tech cities, after a bank clerk named George Eastman marketed the first still camera and film for Thomas Edison's motion picture camera. Later,

2008 Presidential Vote		
Barack Obama (D)	184,209	(69%)
John McCain (R)	81,517	(30%)
2004 Presidential Vote		
John Kerry (D)	162,319	(63%)
George Bush (R)	92,627	(36%)
Cook Partisan Voting Index:	D+15	

Bausch & Lomb developed its lens business in Rochester, and the optics and imaging industry continues to be a significant regional employer. Its industries—Bausch & Lomb, Eastman Kodak, and Xerox, which started here as Haloid—have thrived on technical innovation, precision workmanship, high reliability, and customer service, giving Rochester an affluent and well-educated population as well as fine civic institutions, including the George Eastman House, one of the world's leading repositories of photographic and motion picture history. Rochester was also the home base of women's suffrage leader Susan B. Anthony and abolitionist Frederick Douglass. Unhappily, Rochester's big employers have fallen on hard times, and young professionals have been leaving the area. Kodak, hard hit by competition from digital cameras, employed 60,000 people in the Rochester area in 1981; in 2010, it employed just 7,400 people and posted its third yearly loss as it struggled to build up inkjet printer businesses. Xerox jobs in the area were down to half of what they once were, from 16,000 to 6,900, and in 2010, it announced it would have to eliminate 2% of its overall workforce. The city's population—332,000 in 1950—dropped to around 211,000 in 2010.

Not far west of Rochester is a very different part of upstate New York, the Niagara Frontier—the local name for the Buffalo-Niagara Falls area. The Niagara Frontier was once an armed frontier, between the United States and British-held Upper Canada, where American troops crossed the raging Niagara River during the War of 1812 to fight the Battle of Lundy's Lane. Later in the 19th century, Niagara Falls became a prime vacation spot, a must-see sight for European tourists and American honeymooners. Few tourists today notice the huge water intakes farther up the river or the hydroelectric power lines strung out on giant pylons fanning out in every direction, providing cheap public power for the chemical and steel factories that made the Niagara Frontier one of the heavy industry capitals of America. But the city of Niagara Falls has suffered hard times. It has lost much of its manufacturing since the 1960s and suffered double-digit unemployment and population losses. Changes in regulations requiring Americans to carry passports into Canada helped boost tourism between 8% and 10% during summer 2010.

The 28th Congressional District of New York, created by redistricting in 2002, includes Rochester, Niagara Falls, and part of Buffalo, all connected by a thin strip of land along Lake Ontario and the Niagara River. A bit more than 46% of the district is in Monroe County, and a bit less than 37% is in Erie County. Most of Rochester's suburbs are in three other districts, but the 28th includes Grand Island, Tonawanda, and the northeast quadrant of Buffalo, where it takes in much of the city's downtown and its fine cultural institutions. This is mainly a central city district. Twenty-nine percent of residents are African-American, the highest percentage in any upstate district. Politically, it is solidly Democratic. In the 2010 governor's race, Democrat Andrew Cuomo beat Republican Carl Paladino 62%-35% in Monroe County, while Paladino, a Buffalo native, won Erie and Niagara counties.

Louise Slaughter (D)

The congresswoman from the 28th District is Louise Slaughter, a Democrat elected in 1986. The first woman to chair the powerful Rules Committee, she became its ranking minority member after the Republican takeover of the House, in the process losing much of the power she wielded in setting the ground rules for debate that can make or break a piece of legislation on the House floor.

A coal miner's daughter and a descendant of Daniel Boone, she grew up in Kentucky and still speaks with the accent and distinctive phraseology of the mountains. She wound up in New York in the 1950s when she moved there with her husband. Her involvement in community issues led to a career in government. Slaughter became a staffer for Mario Cuomo when he was lieutenant governor in the 1970s, and she won a seat on the Monroe County Legislature in 1976. She was elected to the New York Assembly in 1982. Four years later, she beat one-term conservative Republican Rep. Fred Eckert, 51%-49%, after charging that he did nothing to free Associated Press reporter Terry Anderson, a Rochester native held hostage in Lebanon. She secured what had been a marginal seat by tending carefully to local problems and by winning the support of area business-men and the local *Democrat & Chronicle* newspaper.

Slaughter has a solidly liberal voting record. She backs feminist causes and is active on health issues. In 2008, she capped a years-long campaign by winning enactment of her bill to bar discri-mination in employment or health insurance based on the use of genetic information. During the 2009 health care debate, she drew criticism among Republicans for shunning town-hall meetings while other lawmakers were going face-to-face with angry constituents. She was a major advocate of including a government-run insurer to compete with private companies, and was sharply critical of the Senate's decision to jettison the public option. But when the final compromise came before the House in March 2010, she prepared a rule to consider the Senate version passed once the House approved a corrections bill making changes to the other body's version. Outraged Republicans dubbed the move the "Slaughter Solution," even as Slaughter noted that the GOP had employed the strategy from time to time in the majority. The idea eventually was scrapped.

As a microbiologist by training, and consistent with the Rochester-area research mindset, Slaughter opposed proposals to ban human cloning and was an outspoken proponent of federal support for embryonic stem cell research. She introduced a bill in 2009 to limit the non-therapeutic use of pharmaceuticals in livestock but not prevent their use when animals are sick. The bill did not move, but hearings on it drew widespread attention. The Food and Drug Administration released guidelines recommending the end of using of antibiotics to promote animal growth, a move Slaugh-ter hailed as a step in the right direction. She reintroduced her bill in 2011. On local issues, Slaugh-ter has been an outspoken advocate of bringing high-speed rail to her region.

As a loyal lieutenant of Democratic leader Nancy Pelosi, Slaughter became an outspoken critic of Republican policies during the 12 years of Republican control ending in early 2007. She accused Republicans of "strong-arm tactics" and a "win-at-all-costs mentality" to move legislation. In Janu-ary 2007, she helped to bring the first legislation to the House floor for the new majority: an over-haul of House rules, largely dictated by Pelosi and her lieutenants. Slaughter hailed the result as "a Congress people can be proud of again." But Republicans quickly cried foul when Democrats next moved to the floor six bills from their campaign agenda, without committee action and with no opportunity for amendments. Her dismissal of procedural objections led to regular flare-ups with ranking Republican David Dreier of California, an astute and partisan master of parliamen-tary procedure. But there also has been occasional Democratic criticism of the committee's strong-arm tactics. Financial Services Committee Chairman Barney Frank, D-Mass., in September 2007 voiced "regret" that the Rules Committee had barred Republican amendments to a flood insurance bill. But she retained the confidence of Pelosi, who once called Slaughter "the best politician that I have ever seen."

Slaughter's ascension to the chairmanship of Rules capped several years of struggle to move up in the Democratic leadership. In 1994, she lost to Barbara Kennelly of Connecticut in the race for vice chairman of the Democratic Caucus, and in 1996 she was defeated by John Spratt of South Carolina for the ranking Democrat post on the Budget Committee. She became the ranking Demo-crat on the Rules Committee in 2005.

In 2002, redistricting was a perils-of-Pauline nightmare for Slaughter. Sluggish population growth meant that upstate New York had to lose one congressional district, and after much political maneuvering, Slaughter was placed in the same district with Democratic Rep. John LaFalce, the party's ranking member on the Banking Committee. Luckily for Slaughter, LaFalce decided to retire. In the general election that year, she campaigned on much new territory, but most of it was Democratic. She won 62%-38% against an inexperienced Republican challenger. She has since won easily.

TWENTY-NINTH DISTRICT

Tom Reed (R)

Elected Nov. 2010, 1st full term; b. Nov. 18, 1971, Joliet, IL; home, Corning; Alfred U., B.A. 1993; OH Northern U., J.D. 1996; Catholic; Married (Jean); 2 children.

Elected Office: Corning mayor, 2008-09.

Professional Career: Law clerk, private firm, 1995; assoc. atty., private firm, 1996-99; owner, Law Office of Thomas W. Reed II.

DC Office: 1037 LHOB, 20515, 202-225-3161; Fax: 202-226-6599; Web site: reed.house.gov.

State Offices: Corning, 607-654-7566; Pittsford, 585-218-0040; Olean, 716-379-8434.

Committees: *Ways & Means:* Human Resources; Oversight.

Election Results

2010 general	Tom Reed (R)	112,314	(57%)	($1,162,565)
	Matthew Zeller (D)	86,099	(43%)	($457,738)
2010 primary	Tom Reed (R)	unopposed		

Population		Race/Ethnicity		Work	
Pop. 2010:	663,727	White:	89.9%	Private:	77.8%
Change since 2000:	Up 1.4%	Black:	3.2%	Government:	15.5%
Urban:	58.4%	Hispanic:	2.3%	Self-employed:	6.6%
Rural:	41.6%	Asian:	2.5%	Blue collar:	21.1%
Area size:	5,762 sq. mi.	Native Am.:	0.5%	White collar:	61.6%
		Hawaiian:	0.0%	Khaki collar:	0.1%
Age		Two+ races:	1.5%	Other:	17.3%
Median age:	40.4 yrs.				
More than 65 yrs:	14.9%	*Ancestry*		Median income:	$50,075
Less than 18 yrs:	22.5%	German	18.5%	Median Home Value:	$113,500
		Irish	14.5%		
Education		English	12.0%	**Military Veterans**	
H.S. grad:	89.7%			% of Pop:	10.9%
College grad:	29.2%				
Grad degree:	13.1%				

Southern Tier; Elmira

The southern tier of New York is one of the nation's forgotten stretches of territory, yet it has an interesting and distinctive history. Elmira was the hometown of Mark Twain's beloved wife, Olivia, and is where Twain is buried. Corning is the headquarters of Corning Glass Works, a company successful over the years not only in manufacturing but also in its artistic distinction, which is showcased at a well-visited glass museum. This area has an Indian presence, with

2008 Presidential Vote

John McCain (R)	153,487	(51%)
Barack Obama (D)	146,758	(48%)

2004 Presidential Vote

George Bush (R)	171,317	(57%)
John Kerry (D)	127,481	(42%)

Cook Partisan Voting Index: R+5

small reservations as well as the Seneca-Iroquois National Museum in Salamanca, plus miles and miles of dairy farms. Sheltered by hills, the lands at the edge of upstate New York's deep lakes constitute the nation's largest grape-growing area outside California and are the headquarters of prime New York wineries. But the region is isolated, and ill-served by air travel or interstate highways. Cattaraugus County, slightly inland from Lake Erie, is actually 110 miles closer to Washington, D.C., than it is to New York City, though getting to either destination requires considerable patience. The cruelest cut was the Internet bust. Corning's prospects grew dramatically when fiber optics and other high-tech components were being installed at a feverish pace, but the reduction in orders following the bust forced the company to lay off more than 1,000 of its local workers in a town of only 11,000 people. In 2007, *Forbes* reported that the company was making a comeback as demand increased for its fiber products, which are key components of the liquid crystal display (LCD) glass used in flat-screen televisions and computers. But the *Fortune* 500 company was increasingly moving jobs overseas, announcing in 2010 it would invest $800 million in a new LCD glass facility not in Corning but in Beijing.

The 29th Congressional District of New York includes much of the state's southern tier, from Elmira to Cattaraugus County. To the north, it includes the westernmost of the Finger Lakes and the southern suburbs of Rochester. Politically, this has been Republican country since the party's founding. The towns and the countryside are no longer homogeneously Protestant, and the trend in upstate New York has been toward national Democrats, but the 29th remains comfortably Republican for now. This was Republican George W. Bush's best congressional district in New York in both 2000 and 2004. And it was one of four New York congressional districts that voted for Republican John McCain in 2008, albeit narrowly. He got 50.5% of the vote.

Tom Reed (R)

The new congressman from the 29th District is Tom Reed, the Republican former mayor of Corning who won the seat in 2010. Reed was born in Joliet, Ill., the youngest of 12 children. His father was an Army veteran and Silver Star recipient who fought in World War II and Korea. When Reed was just 2 years old, his father accidentally died of carbon monoxide poisoning while working on his car. Soon after his father's death, Reed's family moved to Corning, N.Y., where his mother had grown up. She stayed at home to take care of her children, relying on her late husband's military death benefits and Social Security checks for financial support. "We struggled but we never went without, so to speak. We were happy," Reed said in an interview with *National Journal*. As the youngest, Reed said he became used to being the last one to get a bath and to being the one who had to sit on the floor of the family car or the armrest because there weren't enough seats to go around.

In high school, Reed swam competitively and received offers to compete in Division I college athletics programs. He opted to stay close to home, however, attending Alfred University in western New York. He majored in political science with minors in history and literature, and he was captain of the swim team, placing eighth in the Division III College National Championships. When he was a freshman, Reed met his future wife, Jean, who was a senior at the time. They married in 1996. After graduation, Reed considered staying at Alfred as an assistant swim coach, but decided at the last minute to apply to law school at Ohio Northern University College of Law. Reed graduated in 1996 and worked at a law firm in Rochester, N.Y. When his mother died in 1998, he packed up his family to move back to Corning, to the house where he had grown up. In 1999, he founded his own law firm. Reed ran successfully in 2007 for mayor of Corning.

In July 2009, Reed announced that he would run for Congress against Rep. Eric Massa, believing that the Democrat was vulnerable in the conservative-leaning district. Massa, though, had a reputation as a fierce campaigner, and many analysts felt that he had a good chance to hang onto the seat. However, the race was turned on its head in March 2010, when Massa abruptly resigned the seat amid allegations from male staff members that he had inappropriately tickled them during social events. Democratic Gov. David Paterson scheduled a special election to coincide with the general election in November 2010. Potential top-tier candidates such as former Rep. Randy Kuhl, who had been ousted by Massa in 2008, opted not to run, leaving Reed unchallenged for the Republican nomination.

The Democrats chose as their nominee Matthew Zeller, an Afghanistan combat veteran. Zeller argued that he would do a better job of protecting Social Security and creating jobs than would Reed, who focused his message on reducing the deficit and shrinking government. By late in the race, Zeller had raised $346,000, compared with Reed's $941,000. Reed had one slipup in the race. He suggested on Twitter that the district was being shortchanged by the House's failure to vote on the confirmation of Supreme Court Justice Elena Kagan. The Senate votes on judicial confirmations, not the House. But capitalizing on voter angst over excessive spending, Reed won handily, 57% to 43%.

Because there were a few weeks remaining of Massa's term, Reed was sworn in in November for the remainder of the 111th Congress (2009-10) and so took part in the lame-duck session of Congress at the end of 2010. In mid-November 2010, Reed was hospitalized for blood clots in both lungs. In June 2011, Reed got a prized seat on the Ways and Means Committee, which is rare for a freshman House member.

★ NORTH CAROLINA ★

In the first seven years of the 21st century, North Carolina emerged as one of America's leading-edge states, with a fast-growing economy, booming demography and vibrant culture that seemed exemplary. Then, it was struck especially hard by the 2007-09 recession but rallied. By 2010, North Carolina had become the sixth-fastest-growing state over the decade starting in 2000, growing faster than any other state east of Texas and ahead of Georgia and Florida. It also experienced the biggest percentage increase in voter turnout between the 2004 and 2008 presidential elections. Several decades ago, few people would have picked North Carolina as a state that would chart a path to the future. It had no great central city, no Atlanta primed to become another Los Angeles or Chicago, but rather a series of small metropolitan areas spaced out over thickly settled countryside. It did not have what seemed to be cutting-edge industries. The biggest employer was textiles, typically an underdeveloped nation's first industry, and the next two were stolid furniture and soon-to-be-disfavored tobacco. Geographically, it seemed to be off the nation's main lines of commerce, and, meteorologically, it seemed too steamy to be businesslike in the summer and too cold to be a resort in the winter. Yet North Carolina's population nearly doubled from 1970 to 2010, from 5.1 million to 9.5 million, making it the 10th largest state. Its economy has diversified and expanded, while businesses that dominated the state's political dialogue 40 years ago have faded in importance. Textile jobs peaked in 1973. The government's 2004 tobacco buyout, ending tobacco allotments, left in its wake only about 1,800 tobacco farmers and 11,500 tobacco workers. The state agriculture commissioner quit growing tobacco and in another act heavy with symbolism for the state, the legislature in 2009 banned smoking in restaurants and raised the cigarette tax. High Point still hosts annual furniture industry shows, but much production has gone elsewhere, including much of it to China.

In place of farming and furniture, technology and finance have taken root. One key has been the success of Research Triangle Park, established between Raleigh, Durham, and Chapel Hill—and their universities—in 1959. Its first breakthrough was the opening of a big IBM facility in 1965. Now IBM has 10,000 employees in the Triangle and has built a $362 million cloud computing center, complete with green technology. The Triangle today is one of the world's leading biotech, pharmaceutical, medical device, and telecommunications centers, and North Carolina ranks third in biotech employment behind California and Massachusetts. The Triangle's core counties had 536,000 people in 1970 and 1.6 million in 2010. Its success has been echoed farther west in the Piedmont Research Triad between Winston-Salem, Greensboro and High Point. Meanwhile, North Carolina took advantage of its status as one of the first states to allow banks to open branches statewide to become one of the nation's leading banking centers. NCNB became NationsBank, which acquired Bank of America and moved its headquarters from San Francisco to Charlotte. First Union absorbed and took the name of Wachovia, based in Winston-Salem. The financial collapse of September 2008 hit Charlotte's Tryon Street hard. Regulators peddled Wachovia first to Citigroup, then sold it to Wells Fargo, which has moved some functions out but maintains the name and has kept investment banking and capital markets operations in Charlotte. Bank of America was pressured into buying Merrill Lynch, whose huge losses threatened the buyer. It has sent corporate and investment banking to New York. But in the wake of the giants' woes, smaller financial companies proliferated, taking advantage of available human capital. Charlotte still has more bank assets than any American city except New York. The population of metro Charlotte (including adjacent York County, South Carolina) increased from 741,000 in 1970 to 1.76 million in 2010.

Metro Charlotte and the Research Triangle have accounted for just about half of the state's population growth for a generation, and they are now major metropolitan areas, with national sports franchises and huge hub airports. North Carolina has one of the nation's least-unionized workforces, something the state's Democratic politicians have done nothing to change, and it has long been rated one of the best places to relocate a business. "Our biggest advantage over who we compete with—San Diego, San Francisco, Massachusetts, and the Maryland-Virginia area," said former Democratic Gov. Mike Easley, "is that we can do everything they can do, if not more, but we can do it 20% to 25% cheaper when you look at labor and capital investment." The unemployment rate was low enough that thousands of Latinos moved into North Carolina seeking jobs in construction and in meat and chicken factories. The state's Hispanic population rose from 77,000 in 1990 to 800,000 in 2010. Growth continued, albeit at a slower pace, in spite of the recession. North Carolina suffered far lower rates of foreclosures than Georgia or the "sand states" of Florida, Arizona, Nevada and California.

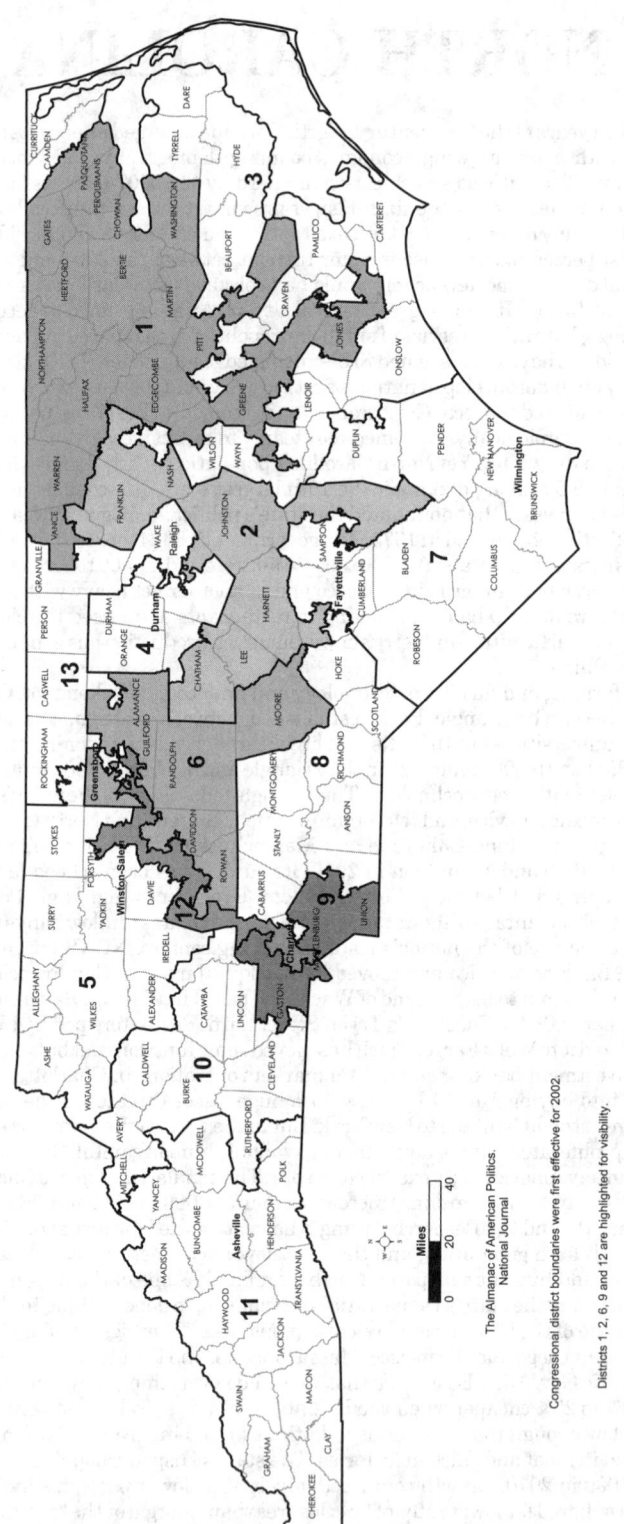

The Almanac of American Politics.
National Journal

Congressional district boundaries were first effective for 2002.

Districts 1, 2, 6, 9 and 12 are highlighted for visibility.

Yet for all its urban development, life in North Carolina has not lost its rural tone. The state is the nation's No. 2 hog producer, with big feedlots and sewage lagoons. The land is so thickly settled that you are never out of sight of others, but there is also plenty of green space and reminders of rural roots, from barbecue stands to country Baptist churches to stock-car tracks.

The forces behind the change are diverse and sometimes even hostile. North Carolina historically had a small and erudite elite, which looked for guidance from the University of North Carolina at Chapel Hill and the liberal editors of the state's newspapers, most prominently the Raleigh *News & Observer* and *The Charlotte Observer*. Quite different attitudes were nurtured by tradition-minded churches in a state where churchgoing is deeply ingrained, reinforced for years by Sunday blue laws and strengthened periodically by religious revivals. North Carolina has grown with the aid of both its progressive and tradition-minded citizens, and in spite of—sometimes because of—the polarized politics that have developed between the two. North Carolina's professionals tend to share progressive values; its businesspeople and conservative Protestants tend to share tradition-minded values. Both groups have contributed to the state's economic dynamism and cultural energy. Liberal progressivism has provided an impetus toward building good schools and universities, as well as highways and amenities like the nation's first state-funded symphony and state high schools for science, mathematics, and the arts. Religious conservatism has provided a communitarian spirit and charitable impulses, and a moral undertone that anchors those who might go astray. Each side also has its excesses: the historic racism that undergirded segregation, and the impulses that led black leaders and university professors to cheer on a rogue prosecutor when he brought a baseless case against three Duke University men's lacrosse players. The three were exonerated.

From these two strands of North Carolina tradition there developed a polarized, increasingly party-line politics, waged partly on economic issues but even more on cultural attitudes. This politics was built on historic partisan patterns. Coastal North Carolina settlers tended to be British Anglicans who became Methodists, and slaveholders who supported the Confederacy and voted Democratic. Piedmont settlers by contrast tended to be Scots-Irish Presbyterians, with a scattering of German sects. They were Union men in 1861 and Republicans ever after. The most effective paladins of both traditions for the last quarter-century, Republican Sen. Jesse Helms and Democratic Gov. Jim Hunt, were each elected to statewide office five times over 25 years, and in 1984 waged what was then the most expensive Senate race in U.S. history. Once bitter rivals, they later reconciled. Helms did not seek re-election in 2002 and died in 2008 at age 86. Hunt left office in 2000 but has remained a driving force in the state Democratic Party.

Over the last four decades Republicans tended to win federal elections in North Carolina, and Democrats tended to do well in state elections. In five elections Helms never got more than 55% of the vote. Republicans carried the state for president in every election from 1968 to 2004, except 1976. George W. Bush won 56%-43% in 2000 and, despite the presence of North Carolinian John Edwards on the Democratic ticket, he won 56%-44% in 2004. At the same time, Democrats have continued to dominate state politics as they have not in other fast-growing Southern states, such as South Carolina, Georgia, Florida, and Virginia. Democrats have held the governorship for 28 of the 40 years from 1970 to 2010, with Hunt elected four times (1976, 1980, 1992, 1996), Easley twice (2000, 2004) and current Gov. Bev Perdue once (2008). But in 2008 and 2010, North Carolina broke some political precedents. In 2008, Democrat Barack Obama won the North Carolina primary 56%-42%, with near-unanimous support from blacks and majorities from upscale professionals. And with brilliant organizational work, he won the state's 15 electoral votes by a 50%-49% margin. As a reward, and at the urging of Duke Energy Chief Executive Officer James Rogers, a

Population		Household Income		Work	
Pop. 2010:	9,535,483	Under $15k:	15.1%	Private:	77.0%
State rank:	10th	$15k to $50k:	39.4%	Government:	16.7%
Change since 2000:	Up 18.5%	$50k to $100k:	29.8%	Self-employed:	6.1%
Urban:	59.3%	$100k to $200k:	12.8%	Unemployment (3-yr. average):	5.4%
Rural:	40.7%	Over $200k:	2.9%	Poverty:	15.2%
Native of state:	58.6%	Median income:	$45,131	Blue collar:	23.9%
Not a citizen:	4.9%			White collar:	58.1%
Area size:	53,819 sq. mi.	**Home Value**		Khaki collar:	1.4%
		Under $100k:	28.2%	Other:	16.6%
Most populous cities		$100k to $300k:	54.6%		
Charlotte	731,424	$300k to $500k:	11.4%	**Age**	
Raleigh	403,892	$500k to $1 mil:	4.7%	Median age:	36.8 yrs.
Greensboro	269,666	Over $1 million:	1.0%	More than 65 yrs:	12.5%
Winston-Salem	229,617	Median:	$151,800	Less than 18 yrs:	24.4%

Race/Ethnicity				Military Veterans		Registered Voters in 2010	
White:	65.3%	*Language*		% of Pop:	10.5%	Democrats:	2,769,324
Black:	21.2%	English:	90.2%			Republicans:	1,958,503
Hispanic:	8.4%	Spanish:	6.5%	*Veterans by Period*		Ind./other:	1,472,876
Asian:	2.2%	Asian:	1.3%	WWII and before:	8.6%	Voter turnout:	2,700,383
Native Am.:	1.1%	Other European:	1.6%	Korea:	9.7%	Turnout as % of	
Hawaiian:	0.1%			Vietnam:	32.6%	voting age:	37.2%
Two+ races:	1.6%	**Education**		Gulf (pre-2001):	14.4%		
		H.S. grad:	83.6%	Gulf (post-2001):	9.4%	**Legislature**	
Ancestry		College grad:	26.2%	Peace time:	25.2%	Senate:	19 D 31 R
German	10.1%	Grad degree:	8.7%			House:	52 D 67 R 1 V
USA	9.7%						
English	9.1%						

proselytizer of green power, Obama awarded the 2012 Democratic National Convention to Charlotte.

Yet Democrats suffered a severe setback in the 2010 election. Republican Sen. Richard Burr was re-elected without demur two years after his Republican colleague, Elizabeth Dole, had been beaten soundly by Democrat Kay Hagan, and Republicans won majorities in both houses of the legislature for the first time since the 1890s. Democrats held on primarily in districts with large percentages of African-Americans or liberal white professionals; rural areas that had been Democratic for years switched parties. Harbinger of the future or just a temporary blip? No one can be sure.

Presidential politics For a quarter-century after 1980, North Carolina was not a competitive state in presidential elections. Democrats hoped to change that in 2004 when John Kerry named Sen. John Edwards of North Carolina as his running mate. But Edwards had won just one election in the state, with 51% of the vote in 1998, and his appeal proved limited. The Kerry-Edwards campaign took its ads off the air in North Carolina in August, and Edwards himself returned to the state only to vote in October.

The 2008 campaign was quite another matter. North Carolina's presidential primary, held on the same day in May as its state primary, had played a serious role in presidential politics only once before, in 1976, when after five straight losses Ronald Reagan started denouncing the Panama Canal Treaty and won his first victory over Gerald Ford in the Republican primary. That kept the Reagan campaign viable until the convention. If it had gone the other way, Reagan

2008 Presidential Vote
Barack Obama (D) 2,142,651 (50%)
John McCain (R) 2,128,474 (49%)

2008 Presidential Primary
Barack Obama (D) 887,391 (56%)
Hillary Clinton (D)...............657,669 (42%)

2008 Presidential Primary
John McCain (R) 383,085 (74%)
Mike Huckabee (R)................63,018 (12%)
Ron Paul (R) 37,260 (7%)

2004 Presidential Vote
George W. Bush (R)...........1,961,166 (56%)
John Kerry (D) 1,525,849 (44%)

might not have been a plausible candidate in 1980. Obama's campaign, quick to spot opportunities, staked out North Carolina as a target, first in the primary and then in the general election. Like Virginia, the state had a large African-American population (21%), much of which had never been politically organized. Its universities and its 2007 state law authorizing same-day-registration, early voting meant that a large student vote could be mobilized. The relatively recent arrival of highly educated outsiders provided another opening.

The results justified Obama's calculations. New registrations in the first three months of 2008 were nearly triple the number in the same months of 2004. Rival Democrat Hillary Rodham Clinton, fresh from March and April victories in Ohio, Texas, and Pennsylvania, was still in the race and was endorsed by then-Gov. Easley. But on May 6, Obama won by a solid 56%-42%, carrying not only the four congressional districts with high black percentages but also two others with affluent white populations in the Research Triangle and Charlotte areas. Clinton carried rural whites in the east and west of the state. Obama's big margin in North Carolina, and Clinton's small margin of victory the same day in Indiana, prompted the late Tim Russert of NBC News to declare that the nomination race was decided, for Obama.

In the fall, Republican John McCain was reluctant to spend resources in North Carolina, where he thought he stood a good shot of winning, and to concentrate on states where he needed to expand his base of support. Organizing for the primary gave the Democrats a head start on the general, and they made good use of it. Early voting was heavy, and overall turnout was up 23% from 2004, the largest percentage gain in any state. Some 36% of early voters, many of them registering the same day, were African-American. McCain got 9% more votes than George W. Bush had four years before. But Obama got 40% more votes than Kerry and Edwards had, with especially large increases in heavily black eastern counties and in the Research Triangle and metro Charlotte. Obama carried the state 49.7%-49.4%. African-American voters went for Obama 95%-5%. But he also got 35% of the votes of whites, up from 27% for Kerry-Edwards. Obama won young voters 74%-26%, and ran behind among voters 30 and over. He carried first-time voters, who were 13% of the total, by 68%-32%.

The 2008 exit poll showed that North Carolina's African-Americans voted heavily for Obama, while white evangelical Protestants voted 74%-25% for McCain. Since blacks formed 23% (down from 26% four years earlier) of those who voted and white evangelical Protestants 44%, they basically canceled each other out—as did the third of voters who did not fit into either category. One question for the future is whether those who came out primarily to vote for Obama will be motivated to vote in the future. Some 140,000 North Carolinians voted for president only and skipped the down-ballot races, more than double the 63,000 people who did so in 2004.

Congressional districting   North Carolina won a 12th House seat in the 1990 census and a 13th seat in the 2000 census. It beat out Utah for the latter by

112th Congress Lineup
7 D   6 R
111th Congress Lineup
8 D   5 R

just 856 people, because its apportionment population includes some 18,000 U.S. troops and diplomats who claim North Carolina as their home. In the 1990s, North Carolina was the epicenter of race-based redistricting litigation, home to a legal controversy that went to the U.S. Supreme Court four times. Democratic legislators created their plans for 2002 with this litigation in mind. Their plan created a 13th District seat in the northern Piedmont, which leaned Democratic and ended up electing Democrat Brad Miller, not coincidentally the chairman of the Senate redistricting committee. The plan significantly weakened 8th District Republican Rep. Robin Hayes, who faced serious challenges in the next four elections and was defeated in 2008. It created six heavily Republican districts and three solidly Democratic districts, with the four other districts tailored to the needs of local Democrats. Republicans filed suit, prevailed in the state courts, but ultimately lost when the U.S. Supreme Court refused to intervene.

In the reapportionment following the 2010 census, North Carolina almost gained a 14th House seat, but its population came in about 16,000 short of what it needed to take the seat away from Minnesota. Before the 2010 election, it was widely assumed that Democrats, with their large margins in the legislature (30-20, 68-52), would control redistricting again. But Republicans shocked even themselves by winning similarly large margins in the legislature (31-19, 67-52-1). Perdue as the Democratic governor is no help to her party because in North Carolina the governor has no veto power in redistricting matters. The one possible restraint on the GOP is that plans are subject to approval by the Justice Department and that North Carolina congressional redistricting cases have regularly been litigated all the way up to the Supreme Court. But it is also in the Republicans' interest to maintain something like the current 1st and 12th districts as black-majority constituencies, since that tends to reduce Democratic percentages in adjacent districts. Republicans picked up only one Democratic district in 2010, despite increasing their share of the statewide popular vote, but they will be looking to capture more in 2012, probably with a particular eye on the 7th and 8th districts.

Governor

Bev Perdue (D)

Elected 2008, term expires Jan. 2013, 1st term; b. Jan. 14, 1947, Grundy, VA; home, New Bern; U. of KY, B.A. 1969; U. of FL., M.Ed. 1974, Ph.D. 1976; Episcopalian; married (Bob Eaves); 2 children.

Elected Office: NC House of Reps., 1986-1990; NC Senate 1990-2000; Lt. gov., 2000-08

Professional Career: Public schl. teacher; Consultant

Office: Office of the Governor, 20301 Mail Service Center, Raleigh, 27699-0301, 919-733-4240; Fax: 919-733-2120; Web site: www.governor.state.nc.us.

Election Results

2008 general	Bev Perdue (D)	2,146,189	(50%)
	Pat McCrory (R)	2,001,168	(47%)
	Michael Munger (Lib)	121,584	(3%)
2008 primary	Bev Perdue (D)	840,342	(56%)
	Richard Moore (D)	594,028	(40%)

Bev Perdue, a Democrat, was elected governor of North Carolina in 2008 as the state's first female chief executive. Initially held up as an example of how Democrats could win statewide office in the South, she is now considered one of the governors whose re-election in 2012 hinges on how effectively she can surmount the voter anger from the recession.

Perdue grew up in the coal-mining town of Grundy in southwest Virginia, near the borders of West Virginia and Kentucky. Her father, Alfred Moore, was a coal miner, and her mother was a homemaker. Neither parent earned a high school diploma, but they were nonetheless an upwardly mobile family. Her father later became a mine owner and utility executive. Beverly Moore became the first college graduate in the family when she got her degree from the University of Kentucky. She taught kindergarten for several years and then went back to school to get advanced degrees in her field of education from the University of Florida. She also took courses in gerontology and volunteered with a local program for senior citizens. In 1975, she and her first husband moved to New Bern, an old colonial town at the confluence of the Neuse and Trent rivers in east North Carolina, where she worked as a geriatric health care consultant at a local hospital.

In 1986, frustration with state government policies affecting senior citizens prompted her to run for the state House. She ran as a Democrat—Republicans seldom won east North Carolina races in those years—and was elected. In 1989, she joined other Democrats and Republicans in favor of ousting House Speaker Liston Ramsey, and then backed out on the morning of the vote. Out of favor in the House, she ran for the state Senate in 1990 and won. In 1995, she sought to become co-chair of the Appropriations Committee, with power over the state budget. Senate President Marc Basnight went to her office to give her the bad news that he was passing her over for the job. But as he listened to her describe her ideas and plans for the committee, he changed his mind and offered her the post. (A decade later Basnight named Kay Hagan to the same post, and she went on to be elected U.S. senator in 2008.) Perdue worked successfully to raise teachers' salaries, which was her top goal, and to pass a children's health insurance program.

In 2000, Perdue ran for lieutenant governor, an office elected separately from governor in North Carolina and one with few explicit duties. She won 64% of the vote in a four-candidate Democratic primary and won in November, 52%-46%, becoming the first female lieutenant governor in state history. She was re-elected 55%-43% in 2004. In the role, she took on assignments from Democratic Gov. Michael Easley, who made her chairman of the Health and Wellness Trust Fund Commission, where she worked to create a prescription drug benefit for seniors and to reduce smoking among young people. She also organized local communities to lobby to maintain North Carolina's military bases.

As many in North Carolina political circles expected, Perdue decided to run for governor in 2008, when incumbent Easley was term-limited. She faced spirited competition in the Democratic primary from state Treasurer Richard Moore. She attacked Moore for investing in what she said were risky hedge funds, for increasing fees to money managers, and for raising $1.5 million in campaign funds from Wall Street. Moore ran an ad criticizing her 1987 vote against a bill authorizing state police to conduct investigations of secret organizations like the Ku Klux Klan—an ad that former Democratic Gov. Jim Hunt, who had appointed Moore head of state law enforcement, said went over the line. Perdue raised some $10 million and spent most of it on the May primary. She won 56%-40%. Republicans nominated Pat McCrory, the mayor of Charlotte since 1995.

In the fall campaign, McCrory, who had developed a long-range transit plan and the LYNX light- rail system in Charlotte, called for a 50-year transportation plan for the state. He attacked Perdue for her "100%" opposition to offshore oil drilling in August, which many North Carolina voters supported. She backed off and said she would appoint a panel to study the issue. Perdue supported increasing the number of college scholarships for North Carolina students, while McCrory emphasized vocational training, saying that four-year college programs did not interest all high school graduates. Endorsed by teachers' unions grateful for her efforts in the legislature, Perdue criticized McCrory's support for government vouchers for private-school tuition.

It was a closely fought election. Perdue won 50%-47%. She clearly benefited from the voter-registration and turnout efforts of Democrat Barack Obama's presidential campaign, which targeted North Carolina. McCrory carried the Charlotte area, though narrowly losing Mecklenburg County. Perdue carried the Research Triangle and Triad areas solidly and ran far ahead on her home turf in eastern North Carolina.

Even in a state that has had a booming economy, Perdue faced serious fiscal problems when she took office in 2009. With the state's unemployment rate above 11% and the government facing a record $4.7 billion budget shortfall, Perdue called for tax increases to avoid deep cuts to public schools. She invoked former Gov. Terry Sanford, a revered figure among the state's liberals, who took a similar step. But her approval rating fell by half—from 60% to 30%—in less than six months. After weeks of wrangling, she reached agreement with lawmakers on a budget raising $990 million in new taxes, most of which came from a 1-cent sales tax increase. She recorded several other achievements, including a Racial Justice Act that allowed defendants to raise statistical evidence of racial bias in their sentencing. Republicans blasted the legislation as a backdoor way to end the death penalty. She also signed into law a measure to shore up the hurricane-prone state's backup coastal insurer while reducing private insurers' liability after a major catastrophe.

With a high-ranking aide to Easley facing federal corruption charges, Perdue vowed to make ethics reform a centerpiece of her 2010 agenda. She ultimately got through a compromise bill that toughened penalties for illegal campaign donations above $10,000 and required members of boards and commissions to report fundraising activities on behalf of the officials who appointed them. Sensitive to the previous year's political fallout over spending, the General Assembly adopted a $19 billion budget without tax increases that was predicated on Congress paying for about $500 million in Medicaid expenses. But Republicans gained control of both chambers of the legislature in the November 2010 elections, marking the first time since 1870 that the GOP had the majority in both houses.

Perdue sought to prepare for the resulting upheaval. She took the initiative on cutting costs by announcing a major reorganization of state government, as well as the unusual step of appearing before the Republican caucus to seek an independent redistricting commission, limits on the length of legislative sessions and changes to make government more transparent. Some GOP lawmakers reacted favorably. "From what I've seen, the governor is proposing basically what some of us got elected on," GOP Sen.-elect William Brent Jackson told the *North Carolina Independent News*.

As Perdue prepared for re-election in 2012, she appeared to be in difficult shape. A February 2011 poll put her approval rating at just 32%. Despite avoiding the ethics problems of her predecessor, her administration was the subject of state and federal investigations into whether she properly reported campaign flights. McCrory prepared for a potential rematch, criticizing her March 2011 veto of a Republican-passed bill to challenge the federal health care law. But she was preparing to make her case to the voters, highlighting a *Site Selection* magazine article naming North Carolina as the best place for business for the ninth time in 10 years. Duke University political scientist Michael Munger, who ran against her as the Libertarian candidate in 2008, told the *Raleigh News & Observer*, "She does a pretty good job of coming across as tough and vulnerable. They (Republicans) can't really play hardball with her, because she looks like your nice grandma.... I think a lot of people underestimate what a good politician she is."

Senior Senator

Richard Burr (R)

Elected 2004, term expires 2016, 2nd term; b. Nov. 30, 1955, Charlottesville, VA; home, Winston-Salem; Wake Forest U., B.A. 1978; Methodist; married (Brooke); 2 children.

Elected Office: U.S. House of Reps., 1994-2004.

Professional Career: Natl. sales mgr., Carswell Distributing, 1978-94.

DC Office: 217 RSOB, 20510, 202-224-3154; Fax: 202-228-2981; Web site: burr.senate.gov.

State Offices: Asheville, 828-350-2437; Gastonia, 704-833-0854; Rocky Mount, 252-977-9522; Wilmington, 910-251-1058; Winston-Salem, 336-631-5125.

Committees: *Finance. Health, Education, Labor & Pensions:* Children & Families (RMM); Primary Health & Aging. *Intelligence (Select). Veterans' Affairs* (RMM).

Group Ratings

	ACLU	ACU	ADA	CFG	AFS	FRC	LCV	ITIC	NTU	COC
2010	13	92	5	90	2	100	0	67	97	100
2009	–	100	10	96	0	–	9	–	92	71

National Journal Ratings

	2010 LIB	—	2010 CONS		2009 LIB	—	2009 CONS
Economic	30%	—	69%		0%	—	97%
Social	28%	—	71%		8%	—	91%
Foreign	0%	—	72%		21%	—	74%
Composite	24%	—	76%		11%	—	89%

Key Votes of the 111th Congress

1. Overturn Ledbetter	N	5. Pass health care bill	N	9. Ratify New START	N
2. Pass $787 billion stimulus	N	6. Regulate financial firms	N	10. Confirm Elena Kagan	N
3. Repeal DC gun laws	Y	7. Pass tax cuts for some	N	11. Stop EPA climate regs	Y
4. Confirm Sonia Sotomayor	N	8. Legalize immigrants' kids	N	12. Repeal don't ask, tell	Y

Election Results

2010 general	Richard Burr (R)	1,458,046	(55%)	($10,868,382)
	Elaine Marshall (D)	1,145,074	(43%)	($2,894,468)
	Michael Beitler (Lib)	55,687	(2%)	
2010 primary	Richard Burr (R)	297,993	(80%)	
	Brad Jones (R)	37,616	(10%)	
	Eddie Burks (R)	22,111	(6%)	

Prior Winning Percentages: 2004 (52%); House: 2002 (70%); 2000 (93%); 1998 (68%); 1996 (62%); 1994 (57%)

Richard Burr, North Carolina's senior senator, was first elected to the Senate in 2004 after serving 10 years in the House. A distant relative of Vice President Aaron Burr, he grew up a minister's son in Winston-Salem, was a star football player at Reynolds High School and Wake Forest University, then worked in sales for national wholesaler Carswell Distributing. In 1992, Burr ran against Rep. Steve Neal, a Democrat first elected in 1974. Although outspent 3-to-1, he lost by a relatively narrow 53%-46%. Neal retired in 1994 and Burr ran again, this time winning a solid 57% of the vote. He did not have a serious challenger in the next four House elections.

In the House, Burr had a mostly conservative voting record. On the Energy and Commerce Committee, his early cause became streamlining the Food and Drug Administration's drug and medical device approval process, which he argued kept lifesaving products from the market. For over two years, he worked with the agency, doctors, patients, consumer groups and the pharmaceutical industry to come up with a consensus. With broad bipartisan support, his FDA Modernization Act became law in 1997. He also helped to set up the National Institute for Biomedical Imaging and Bioengineering at the National Institutes of Health. After the September 11 attacks, he sponsored laws to improve defenses against bioterrorism. He sought a crackdown on illegal textile imports but backed President George W. Bush's call for trade promotion authority after securing promises that the local textile industry would have a seat at the table. He called it a difficult vote but said it could help make U.S. textiles more competitive internationally.

In 2004, a major issue for him was a plan to end the tobacco quota system in place since 1938 by buying out quota holders. The entire North Carolina delegation favored this; tobacco quotas had been cut back in recent years and seemed likely to be again. At issue was whether the buyout should be coupled with FDA regulation of tobacco. The Senate passed a corporate tax bill with both the buyout and FDA regulation. In the House, Burr favored the buyout without FDA regulation, arguing that the toxicity of cigarettes should be regulated by the Centers for Disease Control and Prevention and that package labeling should fall under the Federal Trade Commission. Burr was appointed to the conference committee, where he held out for the buyout without FDA regulation; the Senate yielded and the bill was enacted.

Burr had promised to serve only five terms in the House and by the early 2000s wanted to run for the Senate. In 2002, when GOP Sen. Jesse Helms retired, he deferred to fellow Republican Elizabeth Dole, who had the backing of the Bush White House. Two years later, Democratic Sen. John Edwards was running for president, and Burr had the shot he was waiting for. He had $2 million in his campaign treasury and, this time, had the support of White House political strategist Karl Rove.

He had serious opposition from Erskine Bowles, the White House chief of staff under President Bill Clinton who had had lost the 2002 Senate race 54%-45% to Dole. Bowles had deep roots in North Carolina. His father Hargrove "Skipper" Bowles was the Democratic nominee for governor in 1972, and his wife, Crandall Close, headed Springs Industries, a large textile firm started by her family. As Clinton's top aide, Bowles negotiated the 1997 legislation that helped produce a balanced federal budget for the first time in years. And he had earned the respect of Republican leaders even as they seethed with mistrust of Clinton.

Bowles started running ads in May, and led in polls until September. Burr held back on ads till then and, since both spent about $13 million, had a money advantage in the last two months. Bowles ran on a 10-point economic program and touted his ability to work with both parties while depicting Burr as the king of the special interests, especially the pharmaceutical and tobacco companies. Republicans made much of Burr's role in blocking FDA regulation of tobacco. For his part, Burr linked Bowles to Clinton's policies on tax increases, welfare for immigrants and trade with China.

On Election Day, Bush carried North Carolina 56%-44% in his re-election bid, and Burr beat Bowles 52%-47%. Bowles won big majorities in rural black-majority counties and in the counties with Durham and Chapel Hill. Burr carried almost every rural county in the Piedmont and the mountains. Later, when he co-chaired President Barack Obama's fiscal commission, Bowles said of Burr: "I think by the grace of God we both ended up in the exact right jobs for North Carolina....I can tell you from first hand experience nobody works harder or is smarter than this guy in Washington. I think we are fortunate to have a man like this in the U.S. Senate."

In the Senate, Burr has leaned conservative on cultural issues and toward the center on foreign policy. In 2005, he won enactment of a bill to create the Biomedical Advanced Research and Development Authority to develop vaccines and other countermeasures to biological terrorism or a pandemic, and he co-sponsored reauthorization of the bill in 2009 with the late Edward Kennedy, D-Mass. Opponents criticized the bill for its secret operations and for protecting companies that make ineffective or harmful medicines. Burr responded that the agency would become the "venture capitalist" for private-sector initiatives and would have complete access to their data. Biotech firms applauded the bipartisan deal. In 2005, he amended the defense appropriation with a measure providing liability protection for vaccine manufacturers. And he was an original co-sponsor of the food safety bill that passed in 2010. But Burr continued to oppose FDA regulation of tobacco. In 2009, he tried unsuccessfully to stop a Senate regulation bill from passing.

As the ranking minority member on the Veterans' Affairs Committee, Burr in 2008 sponsored a bill to give transition payments to soldiers moving from active duty to veteran status and also won Senate passage of a bill setting the cost-of-living adjustments for veterans with service-connected disabilities to the same rate as Social Security adjustments. Burr co-sponsored with Republican Sens. Lindsey Graham of South Carolina and John McCain of Arizona a revision of the GI Bill of Rights that would allow veterans to transfer half their benefits to spouses or children after six years and all of them after 12 years. The Senate ultimately passed a bill that went even further, allowing veterans with three years of service to get tuition at the most expensive of their state's public colleges. In 2010, Burr sponsored provisions in a bill raising the level of benefits for veterans with severe brain trauma injuries and veterans with prostheses.

Burr also focused on quality of life issues for the military on the Armed Services Committee. In 2010, he sponsored a successful bill providing relief from the alternative minimum tax on benefits for children or parents of military personnel who die in the line of duty. In December 2010,

Burr surprised his conservative supporters when he voted to end the "don't ask, don't tell" ban on openly gay service personnel. "A majority of Americans have grown up at a time that they don't think exclusion is the right thing for the United States to do," Burr told *The Hill* newspaper. "It is not accepted practice anywhere else in our society, and it only makes sense."

One area where Burr continued to take a strong conservative line was immigration. In 2006, he voted against the Senate immigration overhaul bill because he said it would lead to "blanket amnesty" for illegal immigrants. During negotiations on the compromise bill the following year, Burr supported the "touchback" amendment that would have forced illegal immigrants to return to their home countries before applying for visas. When the amendment was voted down, he voted against allowing the compromise bill to advance.

Burr seems to have a soft spot for animals. He sponsored a bill to bar the National Institutes of Health from recalling chimpanzees from retirement at their haven in Keithville, La., for medical research. And in 2010, he co-sponsored a bill with Democrat Jeff Merkley of Oregon that criminalized so-called animal crush videos, which depict small animals being tortured to death. President Obama signed this bill into law.

During the financial crisis in 2008, Burr voted with many Democrats for the $700 billion government rescue of the financial industry, but later had reservations and opposed release of the second half of the money from the Troubled Asset Relief Program. He also attracted some unfavorable attention during the crisis when he said he had advised his wife to withdraw as much cash as possible out of ATMs.

Burr has an interest in moving up in the Senate leadership. In 2007, he lost a bid for Republican Conference chairman to Lamar Alexander of Tennessee on a 31-16 vote. But in January 2009, he was named chief deputy whip in the GOP leadership.

When he came up for re-election in 2010, there was some speculation that Burr would encounter serious opposition, considering Obama's victory in North Carolina in 2008 and Dole's defeat for re-election to the Senate. There also seemed to be a jinx on the seat. No incumbent had won a second term since Sam Ervin retired in 1974. Moreover, polls showed Burr had a low profile in the state. But the strongest possible Democratic challenger, state Attorney General Roy Cooper, widely respected for his work in the case of three Duke University lacrosse players falsely accused of rape, declined to run. Burr's opponent became Secretary of State Elaine Marshall, holder of statewide office for 14 years. She beat former state Sen. Cal Cunningham, an Iraq war veteran, in a runoff primary, 60%-40%.

Marshall came out of the primary contest with little money and spent $2.8 million altogether. Burr raised and spent $11 million. Marshall hit him for supporting the Wall Street bailout and dubbed him "Bank Run" Burr for his ATM advice to his wife. She attacked him for his support from business political action committees and for boasting of his conservative credentials. But none of this got much traction. Marshall also got no help from the Democratic Senatorial Campaign Committee, which was busy defending a dozen Democratic-held seats that year. Burr won 55%-43%, losing several of the state's largest counties and all its black-majority counties, but carrying virtually everything else.

Junior Senator

Kay Hagan (D)

Elected 2008, term expires 2014, 1st term; b. May 26, 1953, Shelby; home, Greensboro; FL St. U., B.A. 1975; Wake Forest U., J.D. 1978; Presbyterian; married (Chip); 3 children.

Elected Office: NC Senate, 1999-2008

Professional Career: Lawyer; Banker

DC Office: 521 DSOB, 20510, 202-224-6342; Fax: 202-228-2563; Web site: hagan.senate.gov.

State Offices: Greensboro, 336-333-5311; Raleigh, 919-856-4630.

Committees: *Armed Services:* Emerging Threats & Capabilities (Chmn); Personnel; Seapower. *Banking, Housing & Urban Affairs:* Economic Policy; Financial Institutions & Consumer Protection; Securities, Insurance & Investment. *Health, Education, Labor & Pensions:* Children & Families; Primary Health & Aging. *Small Business & Entrepreneurship.*

Group Ratings

	ACLU	ACU	ADA	CFG	AFS	FRC	LCV	ITIC	NTU	COC
2010	80	4	85	6	95	0	43	33	14	18
2009	–	16	95	6	100	–	100	–	8	43

National Journal Ratings

	2010 LIB — 2010 CONS		2009 LIB — 2009 CONS	
Economic	54% —	45%	59% —	39%
Social	53% —	46%	45% —	54%
Foreign	47% —	0%	55% —	0%
Composite	61% —	40%	61% —	39%

Key Votes of the 111th Congress

1. Overturn Ledbetter	Y	5. Pass health care bill	Y
2. Pass $787 billion stimulus	Y	6. Regulate financial firms	Y
3. Repeal DC gun laws	Y	7. Pass tax cuts for some	Y
4. Confirm Sonia Sotomayor	Y	8. Legalize immigrants' kids	N

9. Ratify New START	Y
10. Confirm Elena Kagan	Y
11. Stop EPA climate regs	N
12. Repeal don't ask, tell	Y

Election Results

2008 general	Kay Hagan (D)	2,249,311	(53%)	($8,557,412)
	Elizabeth Dole (R)	1,887,510	(44%)	($19,508,712)
	Christopher Cole (Lib)	133,430	(3%)	
2008 primary	Kay Hagan (D)	801,920	(60%)	
	Jim Neal (D)	239,623	(18%)	
	Marcus Williams (D)	170,970	(13%)	

Kay Hagan is a Democratic centrist and North Carolina's junior senator. She was elected in 2008. Hagan was born in Shelby in Cleveland County, which in the 20th century produced an unusually high proportion of prominent state Democratic politicians. When she was a child, her parents moved to Lakeland, Fla. Her father, Joe Ruthven, worked in the tire business, was a real estate broker, and was elected mayor of Lakeland. There were other political influences in her life. Her uncle was Lawton Chiles, who was a state senator from Lakeland in the 1960s, was elected to the U.S. Senate in 1970, and went on to become Florida governor in 1990. Hagan helped out in Chiles' campaigns, and also interned in his Senate office in the 1970s.

Hagan graduated from Florida State and then went to law school at Wake Forest University in Winston-Salem, where she met her husband, Chip Hagan. After graduation they moved to his hometown, Greensboro, where she worked as an attorney in the trust department at NationsBank (now Bank of America). After their third child was born, she was a stay-at-home mom and got involved in civic affairs—the Greensboro Coliseum, the Greensboro Day School—and Democratic politics. In 1992 and 1996, she was Greensboro chairman for Democratic Gov. Jim Hunt's campaigns. In 1998, Hunt persuaded her to run for the state Senate, convincing her that she could balance her kids' soccer practices and Scout meetings with political life.

With campaign help from Chiles, Hagan defeated an incumbent Republican. Once in Raleigh, Hagan befriended Democratic Senate President Marc Basnight, who became her mentor, giving her important committee posts. Hagan was able to secure money for several projects in her district, including funding for the International Civil Rights Center and Museum, the International Furnishings Market, and Center City Park. As a senator, she cast votes in favor of a state lottery, a two-year moratorium on executions, and financial incentives for corporations to create new jobs.

In 2007, when it looked like GOP Sen. Elizabeth Dole would be re-elected without serious opposition, state and national party leaders got busy looking for a challenger. Former Clinton-era White House Chief of Staff Erskine Bowles, who lost Senate races in 2002 and 2004, declined to run again. Democratic Gov. Michael Easley, though barred from running for a third term, also declined, as did Rep. Brad Miller and Attorney General Roy Cooper. In early October 2007, Hagan announced she would not be a candidate. But Hunt and Democratic Senatorial Campaign Committee Chairman Charles Schumer of New York pressed her hard to run, and later in the month she capitulated. In a five-way May primary, Hagan's chief rival was Chapel Hill investment adviser Jim Neal, who criticized Hagan as too moderate. She was the only candidate to run ads in the May primary and won with 60% of the vote.

Still, Dole was the clear favorite. She had raised nearly $10 million, far more than Hagan. But Dole had also spent much of 2005 and 2006 traveling around the country on behalf of GOP candidates as the chairman of the National Republican Senatorial Committee, and she had spent little time in North Carolina until the May 2008 primary. Hagan seized on this, accusing Dole of being a Washington insider and promising to give her a pair of ruby-red slippers to send her to her husband's home state of Kansas. (Dole is married to former Republican Sen. and presidential candidate Bob Dole of Kansas.) National Democrats also subtly raised the issue of Dole's age with a television ad featuring two elderly men in rocking chairs debating whether Dole was 92, the percentage of her votes in support of Bush administration stands, or 93, her effectiveness ranking in the Senate, according to the website *Congress.org.* At the time, Dole was 72. She attacked Hagan for supporting higher taxes and called Hagan a creature of national Democrats. Dole emphasized her work on North Carolina issues, such as the 2004 tobacco buyout, preserving military bases, and protecting the state's Medicaid funding.

By October, Hagan was consistently leading Dole in polls. With one week to go, Dole ran an ad attacking Hagan for attending a fundraiser in the Massachusetts home of one of the leaders of the Godless Americans Political Action Committee, a group opposed to having Christmas as a national holiday. The announcer said, "Godless Americans and Kay Hagan. She hid from cameras. Took godless money. What did Hagan promise in return?" Hagan, citing her experience as a Sunday school teacher and a Presbyterian elder, said Dole should be "ashamed" of the ad, which she said was "bearing false witness against fellow Christians." Hagan threatened to sue for libel and slander. Some 3,600 people sent in contributions to Hagan.

Some North Carolina analysts said the "godless" ad was the campaign's turning point, and polling evidence suggested it didn't help Dole. Hagan won 53%-44%, running 3 percentage points ahead of Democratic presidential candidate Barack Obama while Dole ran 5 points behind Republican candidate John McCain. Hagan won 71% of voters under 30, while losing narrowly among voters over age 44. Hagan clearly benefited from the huge increase in the number of young and African-American voters that the Obama campaign organization turned out. But she may have prevailed in any case, as she ran ahead of most statewide Democratic candidates.

In the Senate, Hagan supported Obama's economic agenda during her early months in office, but was determined not to be seen as a rubber stamp. She joined a working group of fiscally conservative senators in search of a political middle ground. "We have a Congress now that is kind of divided, and I want to be one of the ones that helps bring people together," she told *National Journal.* She told an audience in April 2009 that Obama's spending path in the face of projected growing deficits was "completely unsustainable and unacceptable." In December 2010, she opposed the tax-cut deal that Obama cut with Republicans because it added $858 billion to the national debt. Hagan broke from her party on other issues as well. She teamed with her Republican North Carolina colleague Richard Burr to oppose efforts to let the Food and Drug Administration regulate tobacco, an important Tar Heel State crop, and joined Republicans in opposing a measure to allow debate on the DREAM Act giving some children of illegal immigrants a potential path to citizenship.

On the Armed Services Committee, Hagan endorsed a commission's recommendation in April 2011 that women be allowed to serve in combat in war zones. She also introduced a bill giving tax credits to companies hiring members of the National Guard and Reserve. On the Health, Education, Labor and Pensions Committee, she added a provision to a food safety bill to compensate farmers who suffer losses from erroneous recalls, and she pushed a bill intended to help senior citizens manage multiple prescription medicines at once. She collaborated with Republicans to ensure that biologic drugs — those derived from proteins, rather than chemicals — could have a longer exclusivity period before generic competition than many Democrats wanted. And on the

Banking Committee, she sought to juggle the pressures of representing the second-biggest banking state with her own support for stronger consumer protection regulation. She helped carve out an exception for USAA—an insurance provider to more than 350,000 military families in North Carolina—from proprietary trading restrictions in the so-called Volcker Rule.

FIRST DISTRICT

G.K. Butterfield (D)

Elected July 2004, 4th full term; b. April 27, 1947, Wilson; home, Wilson; NC Central U., B.A. 1971, J.D. 1974; Baptist; divorced; 2 children.

Military Career: Army, 1968-70.

Elected Office: NC Superior Ct., 1988-2001, 2002-04; NC Supreme Ct., 2001-02.

Professional Career: Practicing atty., 1974-88.

DC Office: 2305 RHOB, 20515, 202-225-3101; Fax: 202-225-3354; Web site: butterfield.house.gov.

State Offices: Weldon, 252-538-4123; Wilson, 252-237-9816.

Committees: *Energy & Commerce:* Commerce, Manufacturing & Trade (RMM); Environment & the Economy.

Group Ratings

	ACLU	ACU	ADA	CFG	AFS	FRC	LCV	ITIC	NTU	COC
2010	87	5	90	3	100	6	100	67	4	25
2009	–	0	95	4	100	–	93	–	2	40

National Journal Ratings

	2010 LIB	—	2010 CONS	2009 LIB	—	2009 CONS
Economic	87%	—	12%	82%	—	14%
Social	66%	—	33%	80%	—	20%
Foreign	65%	—	34%	70%	—	24%
Composite	73%	—	27%	79%	—	21%

Key Votes of the 111th Congress

1. Overturn Ledbetter	Y	5. Bar federal abortion funds	N	9. Stop detainee transfers	N
2. Pass $820 billion stimulus	Y	6. Pass health care bill	Y	10. Legalize immigrants' kids	Y
3. Let guns in national parks	N	7. Regulate financial firms	Y	11. Repeal don't ask, tell	Y
4. Pass cap-and-trade	Y	8. Pass tax cuts for some	Y	12. Limit campaign funds	N

Election Results

2010 general	G.K. Butterfield (D)	103,294	(59%)	($828,117)
	Ashley Woolard (R)	70,867	(41%)	($134,394)
2010 primary	G.K. Butterfield (D)	46,509	(73%)	
	Chad Larkins (D)	17,262	(27%)	

Prior Winning Percentages: 2008 (70%), 2006 (100%), 2004 (64%), 2004 special (71%)

Population		Race/Ethnicity		Work	
Pop. 2010:	635,936	White:	42.6%	Private:	71.0%
Change since 2000:	Up 2.7%	Black:	49.4%	Government:	23.3%
Urban:	47.7%	Hispanic:	5.2%	Self-employed:	5.5%
Rural:	52.3%	Asian:	0.7%	Blue collar:	29.8%
Area size:	7,665 sq. mi.	Native Am.:	0.8%	White collar:	47.8%
		Hawaiian:	0.0%	Khaki collar:	1.3%
Age		Two+ races:	1.3%	Other:	21.2%
Median age:	38.1 yrs.				
More than 65 yrs:	14.7%	*Ancestry*		Median income:	$31,577
Less than 18 yrs:	24.0%	USA	9.3%	Median Home Value:	$94,200
		English	7.7%		
Education		Irish	5.3%	**Military Veterans**	
H.S. grad:	76.4%			% of Pop:	10.5%
College grad:	13.3%				
Grad degree:	4.1%				

Northern Region; Part Goldsboro

In colonial days, the eastern portion of North Carolina was a smaller version of the Chesapeake Bay colonies of Virginia and Maryland, a fertile land laced by rivers and inlets, with tobacco plantations and farms with docks on waterways that were accessible to the ocean and so to London. North Carolina was settled later than the Chesapeake colonies, and was poorer, with smaller landholdings. But vestiges of its 18th-century past can still be seen in New Bern

2008 Presidential Vote		
Barack Obama (D) 179,431	(63%)
John McCain (R) 103,679	(37%)
2004 Presidential Vote		
John Kerry (D) 128,129	(57%)
George Bush (R) 94,738	(42%)
Cook Partisan Voting Index: D+9		

with its Tryon Palace, the governor's house when this was the capital, and in the tiny, well-preserved town of Edenton on Albemarle Sound, where 51 women in 1774 protested the taxing of tea and cloth. It is considered the first women's political protest on these shores.

Today, East Carolina survives with remnants of Tobacco Road, and is still largely inhabited by the descendants of the original white settlers and black slaves of 250 years ago. They live in small towns and cities and in some of the most thickly settled rural land in the United States. Tobacco was a labor-intensive crop that for many years produced yields of $4,000 an acre; a family lucky enough to have a tobacco quota could make a living off 40 acres. In 2004, Congress enacted a $10 billion buyout of quota holders, and many old East Carolina tobacco fields are now planted with cucumbers, sweet potatoes, blueberries, and especially cotton. Food-processing plants increasingly are replacing textile plants; Reser's Fine Foods announced an expansion in 2010 in Halifax County that is expected to bring in 500 jobs. Tobacco's political influence has diminished as well. Hog farming in this area makes North Carolina the second-largest producer behind Iowa. But there have been economic troubles in this region in recent years. Seven counties in northeast North Carolina lost population from 2000 to 2009. Rocky Mount's unemployment rate was above 12% for nearly all of 2010.

The 1st Congressional District of North Carolina covers much of the old tobacco country of East Carolina, touches Albemarle and Pamlico sounds in the east, and juts inland to reach African-American neighborhoods in Greenville and Goldsboro. It includes Halifax County, the state's No. 1 deer-hunting county. The 1st District is among the poorest in the nation. The overall number of families and individuals living in poverty is nearly double the national average, and several rural counties have had high HIV infection rates.

Together, the 1st and the 3rd districts blanket the eastern quarter of the state, with intricately drawn boundaries whose fingers reach deep into each other's territory, like clasped hands. There is a political reason for this. The 1st is 49% percent black, the highest percentage of any district in the state, and solidly though not overwhelmingly Democratic. The 3rd is only 16% African-American and, with retirees and new residents in fast-growing coastal counties, votes Republican.

G.K. Butterfield (D)

The congressman from the 1st District is G.K. (George Kenneth) Butterfield, a Democrat who won a special election in July 2004. Butterfield grew up in Wilson County, where his father was a dentist and the first black elected official in Wilson in the 20th century. His mother was a schoolteacher for 48 years. He got his bachelor's degree and a law degree from North Carolina Central University. A civil-rights lawyer who represented poor people, Butterfield took on many voting rights cases. As a Superior Court judge for 12 years, he handled thousands of civil and criminal cases in 46 counties until February 2001, when Democratic Gov. Michael Easley appointed him to the state Supreme Court. After Butterfield lost election in 2002 to a full term, Easley appointed him as a special Superior Court judge. In the July 2004 special election to replace the retiring Democratic Rep. Frank Ballance, who later pleaded guilty to federal fraud charges in the operation of his antidrug foundation, party caucuses selected the nominees, and the six-week contest in this safe Democratic district received little local or national attention. Butterfield said that his priorities would be strengthening the rural economy and halting U.S. job losses. He won 71%-27% and has not been seriously challenged since.

In the House, Butterfield rarely makes headlines but is considered an important behind-the-scenes strategist for both the Democratic leadership and the Congressional Black Caucus. He has a liberal voting record, particularly on economic matters. One of his issues was settling claims of up to 74,000 African-American farmers who were unfairly discriminated against when applying for Agriculture Department loans and programs between 1983 and 2010. "It brings an end to an unfortunate chapter in our history," he said after the House approved the measure in December 2010. That same month, he and Brad Miller were the only House Democrats from North Carolina to oppose extending the Bush-era tax cuts for high-income earners. He lobbied to include an exhibit in the new Capitol Visitor Center on the slave labor that was employed in building the Capitol and on the careers of the 22 African-Americans who served in Congress during and after Reconstruction. He also pushed for renewal of the Voting Rights Act, noting that his father lost his seat on the local city council in 1957 because of a discriminatory voting law change.

A longtime friend of Democratic Rep. James Clyburn of South Carolina, Butterfield managed his successful campaign for majority whip in 2006. Butterfield subsequently became a chief deputy whip under Clyburn and kept the position in 2011 when Democrats reorganized after losing majority control of the House. In 2009, Butterfield also became secretary of the Black Caucus, an influential faction in the House, and moved up to second vice chair two years later. He has been less confrontational toward Obama than other CBC members, and, along with Clyburn, was one of six in the group who supported the president's 2010 bill to fund the wars in Iraq and Afghanistan.

With his connections to the leadership, Butterfield got a seat in 2007 on the influential Energy and Commerce Committee, where he has worked to prohibit states from passing on their Medicaid costs to counties. In his district, many counties spend more of their property-tax revenues on Medicaid than on public schools. In 2009, he persuaded then-Chairman Henry Waxman, D-Calif., to ensure that more of the revenue from the Democrats' proposed cap-and-trade system of carbon emissions swapping would be used to help low-income areas. However, the bill stalled in the Senate. In early 2011, Butterfield became the ranking Democrat on the Commerce, Manufacturing and Trade Subcommittee. He joined Waxman in pushing back against GOP claims that the Consumer Product Safety Commission was harming manufacturers, citing surveys showing strong public support for the agency.

The independent Office of Congressional Ethics investigated Butterfield and five other House members after *The Wall Street Journal* reported in March 2010 that the members did not return unused portions of their travel allowances. But the House Ethics Committee in January 2011 declined to take any action against the members.

SECOND DISTRICT

Renee Ellmers (R)

Elected 2010, 1st term; b. Feb. 9, 1964, Ironwood, MI; home, Dunn; Oakland U., B.S. 1990; Christian; Married (Brent); 1 child.

Professional Career: Surgical intensive care nurse, Beaumont Hospital; clinical dir., Trinity Wound Care Center, 2007-10.

DC Office: 1533 LHOB, 20515, 202-225-4531; Fax: 202-225-5662; Web site: ellmers.house.gov.

State Offices: Dunn, 910-230-1910.

Committees: *Agriculture:* General Farm Commodities & Risk Management. *Foreign Affairs:* Middle East & South Asia; Terrorism, Nonproliferation & Trade. *Small Business:* Agriculture, Energy & Trade; Contracting & Workforce; Healthcare & Technology (Chmn).

Election Results

2010 general	Renee Ellmers (R)	93,876	(49.47%)	($1,139,876)
	Bob Etheridge (D)	92,393	(48.69%)	($1,414,630)
2010 primary	Renee Ellmers (R)	9,171	(55%)	
	Frank Deatrich (R)	4,280	(26%)	
	Todd Gailas (R)	3,190	(19%)	

Population		Race/Ethnicity		Work	
Pop. 2010:	741,576	White:	55.9%	Private:	70.6%
Change since 2000:	Up 19.8%	Black:	27.9%	Government:	23.8%
Urban:	49.5%	Hispanic:	12.4%	Self-employed:	5.4%
Rural:	50.5%	Asian:	1.1%	Blue collar:	26.6%
Area size:	3,979 sq. mi.	Native Am.:	0.6%	White collar:	51.5%
		Hawaiian:	0.1%	Khaki collar:	5.1%
Age		Two+ races:	1.8%	Other:	16.7%
Median age:	33.3 yrs.				
More than 65 yrs:	10.1%	*Ancestry*		Median income:	$43,011
Less than 18 yrs:	26.0%	USA	9.6%	Median Home Value:	$128,000
		German	8.1%		
Education		English	7.5%	**Military Veterans**	
H.S. grad:	81.0%			% of Pop:	11.0%
College grad:	18.6%				
Grad degree:	5.4%				

Central North Carolina; Raleigh

The coastal plain of North Carolina was long by-passed by history. It was settled after Virginia and South Carolina, and only filled in with English settlers as Scots-Irish families were streaming down the valley of Virginia to the western Piedmont. The coastal plain had long been tobacco country, a high-yield crop that for many years could support a family on 40 acres. Tobacco, an important colonial crop, became even more so after James B. Duke created

2008 Presidential Vote
Barack Obama (D) 158,878   (53%)
John McCain (R) 141,448   (47%)

2004 Presidential Vote
George Bush (R) 128,220   (54%)
John Kerry (D) 107,912   (46%)

Cook Partisan Voting Index: R+2

Lucky Strike cigarettes and founded the American Tobacco Company. But this was long a backward area. Its small farms and little cities were populated mainly by tenant farmers and mill hands, people raising families in thin-walled frame houses, often with no electricity or running water.

In many ways, life here has improved from the residual benefits of its proximity to one of the nation's fastest-growing metropolitan areas, Raleigh-Durham. An example is Johnston County, southeast of Raleigh, site of the Smithfield Tobacco Market and North Carolina's No. 1 tobacco county, producing 26 million pounds in 2007. At mid-century, Johnston County seemed to have a bleak future, and it lost population in the 1950s and 1960s, as young residents sought opportunities in the North. At first, Research Triangle Park, founded in 1959 between Raleigh and Durham 40 miles away, had little effect here. But as the Triangle developed into one of the nation's major centers for biotechnology and computers, it spread far into what had been the countryside. Johnston County grew from 61,000 people to 169,000 and its economy was transformed. Unemployment spiked in the metro area in 2009 and 2010, but the county still kept gaining jobs, including 259 in a new Talecris Biotherapeutics plant and 187 in a Becton-Dickinson distribution center—sophisticated businesses in a place where you can still get plenty of country-baked hams and North Carolina barbecue.

The 2nd Congressional District of North Carolina is an irregular loop south of Raleigh centered on Johnston County, taking in parts of nine counties, including Wake County, which is split among three congressional districts. It includes all of Johnston and parts of hog-producing Sampson County and Cumberland County, and portions of the Army's Fort Bragg and Pope Field. Johnston County in 2010 was 15% black and 13% Hispanic. This is by and large the blue-collar, country music part of the booming Raleigh-Durham metro area, a place where most voters have a Democratic heritage but have gotten into the habit of voting Republican for major offices. The district voted for Republican George W. Bush in 2000 and 2004 but went 53%-47% for Democrat Barack Obama in 2008.

Renee Ellmers (R)

The representative from the 2nd District is Renee Ellmers, a Republican elected in 2010 in a district that was on no one's target list six months before the election. Ellmers grew up in the blue-collar Detroit suburb of Madison Heights, where her father worked in the auto industry. To pay her way through college, she trained as a medical assistant and worked full- and part-time jobs while taking classes. In 1990, she graduated from Oakland University in Rochester, Michigan, with a bachelor's degree in nursing. She worked as a nurse in the surgical intensive care unit at Beaumont Hospital, where she met her husband, surgeon Brent Ellmers. Shortly after the couple had their son, Ben, they took a trip to see family members in Cary, the fast-growing suburb just west of Raleigh, and decided to move to the Tar Heel State—part of a not inconsiderable migration from hard-pressed Michigan to booming North Carolina. They live in Dunn, in Hartnett County south of Raleigh, where Ellmers worked as a nurse in her husband's practice at the Trinity Wound Care Center and got involved in the Dunn chamber of commerce.

State and national Republicans did little to mount a strong challenge to Bob Etheridge, a Democrat first elected in 1996 with a somewhat moderate record in a district that had just voted Democratic for president. North Carolina Democrats thought enough of him to try to talk him into running against Sen. Richard Burr. He was not interested and undoubtedly confident of winning an eighth term in 2010.

Meanwhile, Ellmers in 2009 and 2010 was appalled that her congressman had supported the Democrats' health care legislation wending its way to passage. "So rather than sit at home yelling at the TV set, which I did, I decided I needed to get involved," she told *The Sanford Herald*. Ellmers started going to county GOP meetings and joined the bus tour organized by Americans for Prosperity as it traveled across the country protesting the legislation. Though unnoticed by national Republican strategists, she built enough of an organization to win the May GOP primary with 55% of the vote against two businessmen who got 26% and 19%. She won 70% of the vote in her home county of Harnett, 62% in Lee County next door and 55% in Johnston County. She won more than the 40% needed to win without a runoff in North Carolina in all but one county in the district.

Ellmers cast the general election as a stark choice between the Obama agenda and a different direction for the country. "I'm a mother, wife and nurse, and I never dreamed I'd be running for Congress, but it's time to put a stop to the Obama rubber stamp in Congress and Washington politics as usual," she said, noting that Etheridge had voted with his party over 95% of the time.

In June, she got a break from Etheridge himself. When two young Republican operatives approached the incumbent outside the House office buildings and asked him whether he supported "the Obama agenda," Etheridge asked them repeatedly, in tones of some outrage, who they were, and grabbed one by the wrist and the other, briefly, by the neck. The operatives captured the encounter on videotape and posted it on YouTube. Etheridge quickly apologized, but after the video got 3 million hits, contributions poured into Ellmers' campaign. Republican groups followed up with $360,000 worth of attack ads highlighting the incident. And Ellmers got an endorsement from former Alaska Gov. Sarah Palin.

National Republicans were still skeptical whether she was ready for prime time. In one of her ads, Ellmers claimed that an Islamic center planned for a site near Ground Zero in New York was a "victory mosque." And Etheridge continued to have a huge money advantage. He spent $1.9 million to Ellmers' $890,000.

On Election Day, Ellmers edged out Etheridge 49.5%-48.7%. She won 60% in Harnett County, Etheridge's home as well as hers, 56% in Lee County and 64% in Johnston County, once a reliable Democratic stronghold. Etheridge won 73% in the heavily black portions of Wake County and 75% in heavily black parts of Cumberland County (Fayetteville). Etheridge asked for a recount, but it showed no significant change, and he conceded on Nov.19. In her first month in office, Ellmers attracted some attention when she declined an invitation to the White House.

THIRD DISTRICT

Walter Jones (R)

Elected 1994, 9th term; b. Feb. 10, 1943, Farmville; home, Farmville; NC St. U., 1962-65, Atlantic Christian Col., B.A. 1967; Catholic; married (Joe Anne); 1 child.

Military Career: NC Natl. Guard, 1967-71.

Elected Office: NC House of Reps., 1982-92.

Professional Career: Mgr., Walter B. Jones Office Supply Co., 1967-73; Salesman, Dunn Assoc., 1973-82; Pres., Benefit Reserves Inc., 1989-94; Pres., Judson Co., 1990-94.

DC Office: 2333 RHOB, 20515, 202-225-3415; Fax: 202-225-3286; Web site: jones.house.gov.

State Offices: Greenville, 252-931-1003.

Committees: *Armed Services:* Tactical Air & Land Forces; Military Personnel. *Financial Services:* Domestic Monetary Policy & Technology (VChmn); Financial Institutions & Consumer Credit.

Group Ratings

	ACLU	ACU	ADA	CFG	AFS	FRC	LCV	ITIC	NTU	COC
2010	31	65	30	55	71	93	40	–	71	71
2009	–	83	15	66	25	–	29	–	73	71

National Journal Ratings

	2010 LIB — 2010 CONS		2009 LIB — 2009 CONS	
Economic	40%	— 60%	33%	— 66%
Social	38%	— 62%	27%	— 72%
Foreign	43%	— 57%	41%	— 58%
Composite	40%	— 60%	34%	— 66%

Key Votes of the 111th Congress

1. Overturn Ledbetter	*	5. Bar federal abortion funds	9. Stop detainee transfers	*
2. Pass $820 billion stimulus	N	6. Pass health care bill	N	10. Legalize immigrants' kids	N
3. Let guns in national parks	Y	7. Regulate financial firms	Y	11. Repeal don't ask, tell	N
4. Pass cap-and-trade	N	8. Pass tax cuts for some	Y	12. Limit campaign funds	N

Election Results

2010 general	Walter Jones (R)	143,225	(72%)	($672,357)
	Johnny Rouse (D)	51,317	(26%)	($10,588)
	Darryl Holloman (Lib)	4,762	(2%)	($355)
2010 primary	Walter Jones (R)	21,551	(77%)	
	Bob Cavanaugh (R)	4,221	(15%)	
	Craig Weber (R)	2,261	(8%)	

Prior Winning Percentages: 2008 (66%), 2006 (69%), 2004 (71%), 2002 (91%), 2000 (61%), 1998 (62%), 1996 (63%), 1994 (53%)

Population		Race/Ethnicity		Work	
Pop. 2010:	735,979	White:	72.4%	Private:	61.6%
Change since 2000:	Up 18.9%	Black:	16.4%	Government:	31.6%
Urban:	53.2%	Hispanic:	7.4%	Self-employed:	6.6%
Rural:	46.8%	Asian:	1.2%	Blue collar:	22.8%
Area size:	10,046 sq. mi.	Native Am.:	0.4%	White collar:	53.3%
		Hawaiian:	0.1%	Khaki collar:	7.7%
Age		Two+ races:	1.9%	Other:	16.2%
Median age:	35.3 yrs.				
More than 65 yrs:	12.7%	*Ancestry*		Median income:	$45,605
Less than 18 yrs:	23.2%	English	11.4%	Median Home Value:	$151,900
		Irish	10.3%		
Education		German	9.8%	**Military Veterans**	
H.S. grad:	86.3%			% of Pop:	13.5%
College grad:	22.8%				
Grad degree:	7.3%				

Eastern Region; Jacksonville

Nearly 500 years ago, Giovanni da Verazzano sailed past the Gulf Stream and landed on a sand-spit island he thought was the outer edge of China. It was the Outer Banks of North Carolina. These are probably America's most unstable barrier islands, constantly changing shape and cut by new inlets as they are battered by ocean currents and storm winds. In 2003, 30-foot waves from Hurricane Isabel pounded the beaches, and six years later, Tropical Storm Ida swept away most of the major north-south road on Hatteras Island. The islands were settled early by Europeans. Sir Walter Raleigh's Roanoke colony was founded here in 1587, and then vanished shortly thereafter. Edward Teach, better known as Blackbeard, and other pirates lurked in Pamlico and Albemarle sounds behind the islets.

2008 Presidential Vote		
John McCain (R)	193,564	(62%)
Barack Obama (D)	117,365	(38%)
2004 Presidential Vote		
George Bush (R)	169,674	(68%)
John Kerry (D)	79,936	(32%)
Cook Partisan Voting Index:	R+16	

History is still very much alive on the Outer Banks. An antique form of English is spoken on Ocracoke Island, reachable only by ferry. A pack of wild horses—believed to be the last remaining descendants of late-16th-century Spanish mustangs—roams free in a 12,000-acre sanctuary on Corolla's beaches. The 208-foot lighthouse on Cape Hatteras, America's tallest, looks out on some of the most treacherous currents in the Atlantic. The sands along Kitty Hawk, with their constant winds, brought the Wright brothers to the Outer Banks to undertake mankind's first heavier-than-air flight in December 1903. The Outer Banks are prime vacation and retirement country, with a string of affluent beachfront communities on both the coastal and sound sides.

Inland, amid swamps, is the Marine Corps' Camp Lejeune, home base for one-fifth of the Corps. The base was shaken by government admissions by the government in 2007 that as many as 1 million people consumed tainted water at Camp Lejeune from 1957 to 1987, when the base's drinking wells were contaminated by industrial solvents. By early 2011, more than 60 men with connections to the base had been diagnosed with breast cancer. Many victims have filed health claims against the government, and a documentary about the problem was shown at the 2011 Tribeca Film Festival. Thanks to a massive expansion involving more than $3 billion worth of new facilities, the base has helped give North Carolina's construction industry a much-needed boost. On the other side of the Croatan National Forest is Cherry Point, the world's largest Marine Corps air station. North of the forest is New Bern, the place where Pepsi-Cola was invented. The flatlands of east Carolina have long been tobacco- and peanut-growing country, and are now also hog-raising land.

The 3rd Congressional District of North Carolina covers the Outer Banks and much of the coastal plain of North Carolina, though the northeastern tier moves more in the orbit of Virginia's Hampton Roads than North Carolina's Research Triangle. The 3rd exists in balance with the 1st, with which it shares most of eastern North Carolina. Fingers of the 3rd District reach deeply inland to include mostly white portions of Goldsboro and Greenville, where tobacco farms are fading and a pharmaceutical company is the largest industrial employer. The 3rd is predominantly white and Republican, compared with the 1st, which is half African-American and heavily Democratic. The district voted for Republican George W. Bush by 68%-32% in 2004. And Republican John McCain comfortably won the district with 62% even as he lost the state.

Walter Jones (R)

The congressman from the 3rd District is Walter Jones, a Republican first elected in 1994 and one of his party's leading iconoclasts. An evangelical Christian and devout social conservative, he has become the GOP's most fervently antiwar member. He grew up in eastern North Carolina, attended North Carolina State and Atlantic Christian College, and served in the National Guard. His father, Walter Jones Sr., was a Democratic representative from the old 1st District. The senior Jones served for a quarter-century and chaired the Merchant Marine and Fisheries Committee. The younger Jones, then a Democrat, was elected in 1982 to the state House, where he often broke with party leaders.

In 1992, he ran in the new black-majority 1st District after his father retired. He led the primary with 38% but lost the runoff to Democrat Eva Clayton, an African-American who got 55% to Jones' 45%. In April 1993, Jones switched to the Republican Party and soon announced he was running in the 3rd District. This pitted him against four-term Rep. Martin Lancaster, a Democrat who had worked hard on local projects. But Lancaster voted for President Bill Clinton's budget and tax bills and his crime legislation, while failing to persuade Clinton to drop the cigarette tax from health care legislation. Jones ran an ad showing Lancaster jogging with Clinton, with the voiceover message: "How'd Martin Lancaster get so out of touch? Well, look who he's running around with in Washington." Jones won 53%-47%.

In the House, Jones' voting record began consistently conservative and hawkish, but over the years moderated. He had a remarkable conversion on the issue of the war in Iraq. Jones voted to authorize the use of force in Iraq in 2002, as did all but six House Republicans. He even led the 2003 effort, widely spoofed by late-night comics, to rename the House cafeteria's french fries as "freedom fries" after France declined to support the invasion. But not long afterward, he was profoundly affected by a local marine's funeral, setting the stage for an unlikely conversion from conservative war supporter to passionate critic.

As House Republicans began proposing to cut spending in early 2011, Jones and Rep. Jim McGovern, D-Mass., called for pulling troops out of Afghanistan. "Why do we need to sacrifice more American lives?" they wrote in a *Washington Post* op-ed. "Instead, why aren't we using all our resources to go after the terrorists that murdered so many of our civilians on Sept. 11, 2001?" Around the same time, Jones was part of a group of House and Senate members led by liberal Rep. Barney Frank, D-Mass., to announce a plan to reap nearly $1 trillion in defense savings over the next 10 years to bring down the deficit. And he got the Pentagon to investigate substandard mental health treatment for marines returning from Iraq and Afghanistan to Camp Lejeune.

Earlier, Jones supported Democratic proposals for a timetable for withdrawing troops from Iraq and he opposed President George W. Bush's troop surge plan. But he drew the line at a Democratic plan to attach conditions to future war funding, saying that attempts to "starve" the war to bring it to a close were wrong. Jones also began writing letters to the families of every soldier killed in Iraq and Afghanistan. By March 2011, he had sent almost 10,000 letters, calling them his "mea culpa to my Lord" for voting for the war. He also found time to begin writing a book, *My Daddy's Not Dead Yet*, whose title came from a little boy who feared his Marine father would be killed in Iraq.

Jones was one of only two House Republicans to vote against expanding the scope of the Bush administration's secret surveillance program, and he also supported the closing of the prison at Guantanamo Bay. His independence from his party cost him the top Republican post on the Readiness Subcommittee on Armed Services in 2007. After his punishment at the hands of GOP leaders, Democrats approached Jones about switching parties, but he declined, saying his opposition to abortion rights would make him ill at ease in the party. "I'm a Pat Buchanan American," he told *National Journal* in 2009. "I want to stop trying to take care of the world and fix this country."

In that regard, Jones increasingly takes stands apart from his party on non-defense issues. When his party assumed the majority in 2011, he was the only Republican to vote against a fiscal 2011 bill making billions of dollars in spending cuts. In December 2010, he was one of just three Republicans to support a Democratic bill extending the Bush-era tax cuts for low- and middle-income Americans but not the wealthy. He also was the lone GOP co-sponsor of a bill that year limiting the value of Chinese goods the U.S. government could buy in response to that country's manipulation of its currency, a move that the business community staunchly opposed. After the Supreme Court's controversial *Citizens United* decision on campaign finance, he co-sponsored an Obama White House-backed bill aimed at restricting companies' ability to air campaign ads. He later opposed the bill because of the exemptions granted to the National Rifle Association and other groups.

At home, Jones has generated controversy by intervening in conflicts outside his district. He called for the state school superintendent to remove from an elementary school in Wilmington a book about two gay princes who get married, and opposed full recognition to the Lumbee Indians for fear that they would build a big casino on Interstate 95. Jones, who posted the Ten Commandments in his Capitol Hill office, supported politically active churches with his proposal to permit them to endorse candidates without losing their tax-exempt status. The bill generated lots of traffic on the Internet, but the House defeated it 178-239 in 2002.

His outspoken criticism of the Iraq war brought him a serious primary challenge in 2008 from Onslow County Commissioner Joe McLaughlin, a financial planner and former Army Ranger officer. McLaughlin called Jones "a poster boy for the Left" and said he was "standing shoulder to shoulder with Nancy Pelosi." But Jones seemed to benefit from Iraq fatigue among the public, even among military families. McLaughlin was significantly outspent, and Jones won 59%-41%. He won easily in the fall and has not had a serious challenge since.

FOURTH DISTRICT

David Price (D)

Elected 1996, 12th term; b. Aug. 17, 1940, Erwin, TN; home, Chapel Hill; U. of NC, B.A. 1961, Yale U., B.D. 1964, Ph.D. 1969; Baptist; married (Lisa); 2 children.

Elected Office: U.S. House of Reps., 1986–94.

Professional Career: Legis. aide, U.S. Sen. Bartlett, 1963–67; Prof., Yale U., 1969–73, Duke U., 1973–present; Exec. dir., NC Dem. Party, 1979–80, Chmn., 1983–84; Staff dir., DNC Comm. on Pres. Nominations, 1981–82.

DC Office: 2162 RHOB, 20515, 202-225-1784; Fax: 202-225-2014; Web site: price.house.gov.

State Offices: Chapel Hill, 919-967-7924; Durham, 919-688-3004; Raleigh, 919-859-5999.

Committees: *Appropriations:* Homeland Security (RMM); Legislative Branch; Transportation, HUD & Related Agencies.

Group Ratings

	ACLU	ACU	ADA	CFG	AFS	FRC	LCV	ITIC	NTU	COC
2010	88	0	95	0	100	0	100	100	4	25
2009	–	0	100	4	100	–	100	–	2	33

National Journal Ratings

	2010 LIB	—	2010 CONS	2009 LIB	—	2009 CONS
Economic	87%	—	12%	82%	—	14%
Social	93%	—	0%	84%	—	11%
Foreign	84%	—	11%	91%	—	0%
Composite	90%	—	10%	89%	—	11%

Key Votes of the 111th Congress

1. Overturn Ledbetter	Y	5. Bar federal abortion funds	N	9. Stop detainee transfers	N
2. Pass $820 billion stimulus	Y	6. Pass health care bill	Y	10. Legalize immigrants' kids	Y
3. Let guns in national parks	N	7. Regulate financial firms	Y	11. Repeal don't ask, tell	Y
4. Pass cap-and-trade	Y	8. Pass tax cuts for some	Y	12. Limit campaign funds	Y

Election Results

2010 general	David Price (D)	155,384	(57%)	($994,557)
	William Lawson (R)	116,448	(43%)	($472,914)
2010 primary	David Price (D)	unopposed		

Prior Winning Percentages: 2008 (63%), 2006 (65%), 2004 (64%), 2002 (61%), 2000 (62%), 1998 (57%), 1996 (54%), 1992 (65%), 1990 (58%), 1988 (58%), 1986 (56%)

Population		Race/Ethnicity		Work	
Pop. 2010:	826,878	White:	63.1%	Private:	77.2%
Change since 2000:	Up 33.5%	Black:	19.0%	Government:	17.5%
Urban:	83.2%	Hispanic:	9.1%	Self-employed:	5.1%
Rural:	16.8%	Asian:	6.5%	Blue collar:	12.2%
Area size:	1,297 sq. mi.	Native Am.:	0.3%	White collar:	75.1%
		Hawaiian:	0.0%	Khaki collar:	0.1%
Age		Two+ races:	1.9%	Other:	12.6%
Median age:	34.5 yrs.				
More than 65 yrs:	8.8%	*Ancestry*		Median income:	$64,500
Less than 18 yrs:	25.5%	German	11.1%	Median Home Value:	$240,000
		English	10.6%		
Education		Irish	9.1%	**Military Veterans**	
H.S. grad:	91.4%			% of Pop:	8.4%
College grad:	52.8%				
Grad degree:	22.0%				

Central North Carolina; Durham

Back in the 1950s, few people would have predicted that the countryside around Raleigh and Durham would become one of America's high-tech boom areas. But Democratic Gov. Luther Hodges did, and he started the 6,900-acre Research Triangle Park as a research-and-development industrial park between the musty state capital of Raleigh and the Lucky Strike-manufacturing city of Durham. With the drawing power of three universities—North Carolina

2008 Presidential Vote		
Barack Obama (D)	267,368	(62%)
John McCain (R)	162,591	(37%)
2004 Presidential Vote		
John Kerry (D)	193,126	(55%)
George Bush (R)	154,743	(44%)
Cook Partisan Voting Index:	D+8	

State in Raleigh, Duke in Durham, and the University of North Carolina in Chapel Hill—Research Triangle Park slowly began attracting top R&D organizations, which in turn spawned a dynamic entrepreneurial sector. Today, the big-name employers there include IBM, GlaxoSmithKline, Cisco Systems, Nortel, and RTI International. IBM alone employs about 10,000 people in the area, and announced plans in July 2010 to add 600 more jobs. A sleepy metro area that once trailed the nation in income is now a vibrant, affluent metropolis and the prime engine of North Carolina's growth. During the 2007-09 recession, its population grew faster than that of any major U.S. metropolitan area. The Raleigh-Durham airport, which had four gates in the 1970s, opened a new terminal in January 2011. Local planners are working on a light-rail system for the area and have debated asking voters to approve a half-cent sales tax to pay for it.

Still, the region prides itself on its homier touches, from slow-cooked pit barbecue to a minor-league baseball stadium in Durham that features a smoke-snorting replica of a bull, a prop made famous by the movie set in the region, *Bull Durham*. College basketball makes the headlines here, and UNC, N.C. State, and Duke have fielded more March Madness contenders than any similarly sized area. This combination of upscale and down-home has proved to be a popular draw. From 1990 to 2009, the Raleigh-Durham metro area doubled, from 855,000 to 1.7 million. Many of the new arrivals are from the North; locals joke that the fast-growing town of Cary is an acronym for "Containment Area for Retired Yankees."

The 4th Congressional District of North Carolina covers much of the fast-growing Research Triangle area. It includes Durham County and Chapel Hill's Orange County, part of Chatham County to the south and a little less than half of Wake County. Politics here revolves around cultural issues. The Democratic base is made up of two parts: the black community, with 19% of the district's population, and whites and blacks with postgraduate degrees. This part of the Triangle has one of the highest concentrations of Ph.D.s in the nation, and their livelihoods—in academia, in the sciences, in the social services—tend to depend on government. Durham and Orange counties are heavily Democratic, usually that party's strongest area in North Carolina, except for a few rural counties with large African-American percentages. The burgeoning suburbs of Wake County, like many edge cities, are pretty heavily Republican, and provide some counterweight. On balance, though, this is a district that votes for Democrats, not only local moderates but also liberals like Barack Obama, who got 62% in the district in 2008.

David Price (D)

The congressman from the 4th District is David Price, a Democrat first elected in 1986. He lost the seat in 1994 and regained it in 1996. Since his return, he has distinguished himself as a thoughtful, deliberative voice on anti-terrorism and border security spending in addition to education and science.

Price grew up in east Tennessee, the son of a school principal and an English teacher. He is an interesting blend of political scientist, practical politician, and lay Baptist preacher. He came to Chapel Hill to go to college, worked as a young aide on Capitol Hill, earned a degree in divinity and a doctorate in political science at Yale University and taught there for four years. In 1973, he took a job as a political science professor at Duke. He was executive director of the North Carolina Democratic Party in the 1980 election season and chairman in 1983-84. With Gov. Jim Hunt, Price helped develop North Carolina's robust straight-ticket politics. In 1986, he ran for the House and beat Republican freshman Rep. Bill Cobey. In 1994, Price lost the seat, 50.4%-49.6%, to Fred Heineman, a former New York City police officer and Raleigh police chief in the 1970s. Two years later, Price came back for a rematch and outspent Heineman, winning 54%-44%. Price has written four books, including *The Congressional Experience*, about his observations on Congress. The polarization of the two chambers has made him pessimistic about finding widespread agreement on solving the nation's fiscal problems. "Our capacity to take them on in the bipartisan fashion that history teaches us is almost always necessary is far weaker" than it was in the 1990s, he told *National Journal* in May 2010.

In the House, Price's voting record typically placed him near the center of House Democrats, but he moved sharply leftward during years his party held the majority, 2007-11. A *National Journal* analysis found him to be the House's 31st most liberal lawmaker in 2010, far ahead of the rest of North Carolina's delegation. During his first years, Price helped pass laws increasing the percentage of a home's value the government can insure, aiding technical education at community colleges, and setting up an Advanced Technological Education program at the National Science Foundation. His Education Affordability Act, which he worked on for a dozen years and considers his proudest achievement, was folded into the 1997 Balanced Budget Act and became law. It made interest on student loans tax deductible and allowed penalty-free withdrawals from individual retirement accounts for education expenses.

In January 2007, Price became chairman of the Appropriations Homeland Security Subcommittee, on which he had served quietly under Rep. Harold Rogers, R-Ky., during the years of GOP control of the House. Price pledged to take a bipartisan approach, as he said Rogers had. But he consistently sought higher levels of spending for homeland security measures, like support for first responders, than requested by the Bush administration. In 2007, the House passed Price's bill establishing a code of conduct for private security contractors in Iraq and Afghanistan. A target of the bill was North Carolina-based Blackwater, whose activities in Iraq, including the shooting of 17 people in a Baghdad square, had been extremely controversial.

Price generally has been more in sync with the Obama administration—the fiscal 2010 homeland security bill was about 1% below the administration's request. However, he has been critical of the administration's approach to border security, particularly the problem-plagued SBInet "virtual fence" technology system that ultimately was scrapped in 2011. Price called increased drug trafficking and violence on the border "an emergency" in 2010 and said it merited as much attention as the wars in Afghanistan and Iraq.

Price has also been active in campaign finance law. He sponsored the "stand by your ad" requirement for candidates to appear in the full frame of television ads reading their disclaimers on the air, so they would more likely be held responsible for negative ads. His proposal became part of the campaign reform law in 2002. He wants a similar requirement for Internet ads, and said the Supreme Court's March 2010 *Citizens United* decision allowing unlimited spending by corporations made it important to counter the likely flow of misleading ads. "The least we can do is inform viewers (about) who has bought the ads they are seeing," he said. That same year, he sponsored a bill to make small political donors more important by matching contributions of under $200 to presidential campaigns on a 4-to-1 basis.

In the appropriations process, Price has nurtured local projects, including $272 million for a new Environmental Protection Agency complex in Research Triangle Park as well as a variety of defense- and technology-related programs for colleges in his district.

Since his return to the House in 1996, Price has been re-elected by wide margins. In 2008, he won 63%-37% over a well-funded technology-company executive, B.J. Lawson. In Wake County, the fastest-growing part of the district, responsible for 47% of the total vote, he won just 52%. He ran much better in the areas dominated by universities: 77% in Durham County, 72% in Orange County, and 62% in Chatham County. Lawson returned for a rematch two years later, but managed only to narrow the margin to 57%-43%.

FIFTH DISTRICT

Virginia Foxx (R)

Elected 2004, 4th term; b. June 29, 1943, Bronx, NY; home, Banner Elk; U. of NC, A.B. 1968, M.A.C.T. 1972, U. of NC-Greensboro, Ed.D. 1985; Catholic; married (Thomas); 1 child.

Elected Office: Watauga Bd. of Ed., 1976-88; NC Senate, 1994-2004.

Professional Career: Owner, Grandfather Mountain Nursery, 1976-present; Asst. Dean of General College, Appalachian St. U., 1976-1984; Pres. Mayland CC, 1987-1994.

DC Office: 1230 LHOB, 20515, 202-225-2071; Fax: 202-225-2995; Web site: foxx.house.gov.

State Offices: Boone, 828-265-0240; Clemmons, 336-778-0211.

Committees: *Education & the Workforce:* Early Childhood, Elementary & Secondary Education; Higher Education & Workforce Training (Chmn). *Rules.*

Group Ratings

	ACLU	ACU	ADA	CFG	AFS	FRC	LCV	ITIC	NTU	COC
2010	6	100	5	86	0	100	0	0	88	75
2009	–	100	0	100	0	–	0	–	94	73

National Journal Ratings

	2010 LIB	—	2010 CONS	2009 LIB	—	2009 CONS
Economic	7%	—	92%	9%	—	89%
Social	0%	—	85%	0%	—	93%
Foreign	12%	—	79%	0%	—	75%
Composite	11%	—	90%	9%	—	91%

Key Votes of the 111th Congress

1. Overturn Ledbetter	N	5. Bar federal abortion funds	Y	9. Stop detainee transfers	Y
2. Pass $820 billion stimulus	N	6. Pass health care bill	N	10. Legalize immigrants' kids	N
3. Let guns in national parks	Y	7. Regulate financial firms	N	11. Repeal don't ask, tell	N
4. Pass cap-and-trade	N	8. Pass tax cuts for some	N	12. Limit campaign funds	N

Election Results

2010 general	Virginia Foxx (R)	140,525	(66%)	($853,579)
	Billy Kennedy (D)	72,762	(34%)	($332,361)
2010 primary	Virginia Foxx (R)	38,174	(80%)	
	Keith Gardner (R)	9,639	(20%)	

Prior Winning Percentages: 2008 (58%), 2006 (57%), 2004 (59%)

Population		Race/Ethnicity		Work	
Pop. 2010:	693,414	White:	83.1%	Private:	80.0%
Change since 2000:	Up 12.0%	Black:	7.7%	Government:	12.2%
Urban:	42.9%	Hispanic:	6.5%	Self-employed:	7.5%
Rural:	57.1%	Asian:	1.2%	Blue collar:	27.4%
Area size:	4,424 sq. mi.	Native Am.:	0.2%	White collar:	56.6%
		Hawaiian:	0.0%	Khaki collar:	0.1%
Age		Two+ races:	1.2%	Other:	15.9%
Median age:	40.0 yrs.				
More than 65 yrs:	14.8%	*Ancestry*		Median income:	$44,335
Less than 18 yrs:	22.8%	USA	16.1%	Median Home Value:	$142,000
		German	12.2%		
Education		English	10.1%	**Military Veterans**	
H.S. grad:	82.2%			% of Pop:	9.8%
College grad:	22.7%				
Grad degree:	7.3%				

Northern Region; Winston-Salem

From the Atlantic Ocean, the terrain of North Carolina rises slowly through the Piedmont, a transitional land of modest hills that lies between the coastal plain and the Blue Ridge Mountains. The Blue Ridge, named for the mysterious blue haze that blankets it, provides the headwaters of the New River, which cuts majestic crevasses—alternately lush and mined-out—as it flows north to West Virginia. The lower Piedmont lands of North Carolina were first settled by independent-minded Scots-Irish farmers and by followers of British and German sects like the Moravians. This was hardscrabble farm country before the Civil War, with few slaves. By the late-19th century, it was becoming industrialized, with textile mills alongside streams, furniture factories not far from hardwood forests, and R.J. Reynolds' cigarette factories in Winston-Salem.

2008 Presidential Vote		
John McCain (R)	200,520	(61%)
Barack Obama (D)	126,178	(38%)
2004 Presidential Vote		
George Bush (R)	191,034	(66%)
John Kerry (D)	95,811	(33%)
Cook Partisan Voting Index:	R+15	

Today, the region's pharmaceutical companies, banking institutions, and high-skill Piedmont factories are emerging from a 2007-09 recession, during which much of the region's unemployment level topped 10%. Krispy Kreme Doughnuts and BB&T are headquartered here. The merger of banking giants Wachovia and First Union proved bittersweet for Winston-Salem, Wachovia's home base since 1879. First Union let the new company keep Wachovia's name but shifted its headquarters to Charlotte. Although Dell recently closed operations here, Caterpillar announced in July 2010 construction of a $436 million plant here. Yet large swaths of the region remain rural, from chicken-raising Wilkes County to Appalachian State University in Boone (named for Daniel), a center for resurgent pride in the culture of Appalachia, a region often the target of either pity or condescension.

All of these places lie within the boundaries of the 5th Congressional District. The 5th begins in the heart of the Piedmont: the suburbs of Winston-Salem (though not the city, which is in the 12th District). From there, it drops south just short of the outer fringes of metropolitan Charlotte. It heads west and north to the Tennessee line, taking in mountain communities like Boone. The core of its population base is the Winston-Salem suburbs in Forsyth County, plus small industrial cities in Stokes and Surry counties, including Mount Airy, the model for Mayberry in *The Andy Griffith Show*. That city has been hit hard by the domestic downturn in the textile and apparel business, having lost more than 3,100 jobs since 1999. The district is solidly Republican.

Virginia Foxx (R)

The congresswoman from the 5th District is Virginia Foxx, a Republican first elected in 2004. She graduated from the University of North Carolina and had a diverse professional and political background before winning election to Congress at age 61. She owned a nursery and landscape company, and taught sociology and was assistant dean of the General College at Appalachian State University. Later, she was president of Mayland Community College. She served 12 years on the Board of Education of Watauga County, on the western edge of the district (nearly as close to Knoxville, Tenn., as to Winston-Salem). In 1994, Foxx was elected to the state Senate, where she sponsored a constitutional amendment to ban same-sex marriage and a bill to deny Social Security benefits to illegal aliens. She actively supported gun rights and home schooling, and she opposed abortion rights.

In 2004, Foxx was one of five candidates in a hotly contested Republican primary to succeed Republican Richard Burr, who ran successfully for the Senate that year. Winston-Salem Councilman Vernon Robinson, a retired Air Force officer who campaigned as a staunch conservative and as "the black Jesse Helms," finished first in the primary, with 24% of the vote. Foxx finished second, with 22%, just 511 votes ahead of Ed Broyhill, the son of former Republican Sen. James Broyhill.

In a hard-fought, four-week runoff campaign, Robinson aired several controversial ads targeting his tough position on illegal immigrants. And Foxx warned voters that Robinson's aggressive style would make him a weak general election candidate who would lose the district for the GOP. She won 55%-45%, with between 73% and 82% in her home area in the three mountain counties. Robinson carried Forsyth County, which cast 40% of the vote, but by only 38 votes. In the general election, Foxx won relatively easily, 59%-41%.

In the House, Foxx has become known as one of the House GOP's most incendiary public speakers, with her admirers calling her a passionate conservative voice and her critics dismissing her as a loose cannon. She has a solidly conservative voting record. She said during the health care debate in the 111th Congress (2009-10) that the public had more to fear from the legislation than from terrorists. During debate on a hate-crimes bill named for Matthew Shepard, a Wyoming man tortured and murdered because of his sexual orientation, she said naming the bill for Shepard was "a hoax" because she argued he wasn't gay. (She later apologized.) And when Democrats proposed legislation putting limits on executive bonuses from companies receiving government bailout money, she said: "The Democrats have a tar baby on their hands, and they simply can't get away from it." Democrats called the use of "tar baby" racially loaded and objectionable. A 2010 *Washingtonian* magazine survey of anonymous congressional staffers named her the second-meanest House member, behind Texas Democrat Sheila Jackson Lee. But House Republican leaders saw her as a useful attack dog, putting her on the Rules Committee to regularly object to Democratic-imposed limits on amendments to legislation.

On the Education and the Workforce Committee, she chairs the subcommittee on higher education and workforce training. She has said she believes that the federal Education Department puts overly burdensome regulations on colleges. Foxx is an advocate of for-profit colleges and community colleges and staunchly opposed the 2010 House-passed bill that put the federal government directly in charge of student lending.

Foxx was one of only 11 House members who voted against House passage of the $52 billion relief bill following Hurricane Katrina in 2005 because, she said, there was too little accountability in how the money would be spent. She was more generous with local projects, taking credit for $500,000 for a teapot museum in Sparta, which President George W. Bush later criticized as wasteful spending. After such spending became controversial, Foxx said in 2007 that she would no longer seek earmarks.

Foxx has been re-elected by unimpressive margins against low-profile opponents. The *Winston-Salem Journal*, the largest paper in her district, endorsed her Democratic challenger, Billy Kennedy, in 2010. Though it praised her constituent service work, the newspaper said Foxx had not recorded any great accomplishments for the district and "has angered and embarrassed many" with her rhetoric. But she won 66%-34%.

SIXTH DISTRICT

Howard Coble (R)

Elected 1984, 14th term; b. March 18, 1931, Greensboro; home, Greensboro; Appalachian St. U., 1949-50, Guilford Col., B.A. 1958, U. of NC, J.D. 1962; Presbyterian; single.

Military Career: Coast Guard, 1952-56, 1977-78, Coast Guard Reserves, 1960-81.

Elected Office: NC House of Reps., 1968-70, 1978-84.

Professional Career: Claims rep., State Farm Ins., 1961-67; Asst. Guilford Cnty. atty., 1967-69; Asst. U.S. atty., NC Middle Dist., 1969-73; Secy., NC Dept. of Revenue, 1973-77; Practicing atty., 1979-83.

DC Office: 2188 RHOB, 20515, 202-225-3065; Fax: 202-225-8611; Web site: coble.house.gov.

State Offices: Asheboro, 336-626-3060; Graham, 336-229-0159; Granite Quarry, 704-209-0428; Greensboro, 336-333-5005; High Point, 336-886-5106.

Committees: *Judiciary:* Courts, Commercial & Administrative Law (Chmn); Intellectual Property, Competition & the Internet. *Transportation & Infrastructure:* Aviation; Coast Guard & Maritime Transportation; Highways & Transit.

Group Ratings

	ACLU	ACU	ADA	CFG	AFS	FRC	LCV	ITIC	NTU	COC
2010	13	96	5	88	0	100	0	33	88	100
2009	–	96	5	79	11	–	0	–	85	80

National Journal Ratings

	2010 LIB	—	2010 CONS		2009 LIB	—	2009 CONS
Economic	6%	—	93%		16%	—	83%
Social	0%	—	85%		7%	—	90%
Foreign	29%	—	68%		26%	—	68%
Composite	15%	—	85%		18%	—	82%

Key Votes of the 111th Congress

1. Overturn Ledbetter	N	5. Bar federal abortion funds	Y	9. Stop detainee transfers	Y
2. Pass $820 billion stimulus	N	6. Pass health care bill	N	10. Legalize immigrants' kids	N
3. Let guns in national parks	Y	7. Regulate financial firms	N	11. Repeal don't ask, tell	N
4. Pass cap-and-trade	N	8. Pass tax cuts for some	N	12. Limit campaign funds	N

Election Results

2010 general	Howard Coble (R)..156,252	(75%)	($503,434)
	Sam Turner (D)..51,507	(25%)	($3,775)
2010 primary	Howard Coble (R)..31,663	(63%)	
	Billy Yow (R) 7,929	(16%)	
	James Taylor (R)..7,553	(15%)	

Prior Winning Percentages: 2008 (67%), 2006 (71%), 2004 (73%), 2002 (90%), 2000 (91%), 1998 (89%), 1996 (73%), 1994 (100%), 1992 (71%), 1990 (67%), 1988 (62%), 1986 (50%), 1984 (51%)

Population		Race/Ethnicity		Work	
Pop. 2010:	714,412	White:	79.4%	Private:	80.7%
Change since 2000:	Up 15.4%	Black:	10.1%	Government:	12.9%
Urban:	51.6%	Hispanic:	6.9%	Self-employed:	6.2%
Rural:	48.4%	Asian:	1.8%	Blue collar:	26.6%
Area size:	2,988 sq. mi.	Native Am.:	0.4%	White collar:	58.2%
		Hawaiian:	0.0%	Khaki collar:	0.2%
Age		Two+ races:	1.3%	Other:	15.0%
Median age:	39.8 yrs.				
More than 65 yrs:	14.6%	*Ancestry*		Median income:	$49,140
Less than 18 yrs:	23.7%	German	11.9%	Median Home Value:	$152,100
		English	10.6%		
Education		USA	10.2%	**Military Veterans**	
H.S. grad:	83.7%			% of Pop:	11.1%
College grad:	25.5%				
Grad degree:	8.1%				

Central Region; Part Greensboro

For more than half a century, furniture store managers and owners from all over the country twice a year have converged on the huge Furniture Mart in High Point, the center of the U.S. furniture business. The giant trade show put on by manufacturers now attracts about 80,000 visitors. High Point sits amid rolling farmland originally settled by Quakers. The furniture business grew here early in the 20th century because of the hardwoods in the mountains not far west

2008 Presidential Vote

John McCain (R) 212,548	(63%)
Barack Obama (D) 120,805	(36%)

2004 Presidential Vote

George Bush (R) 200,942	(69%)
John Kerry (D) 87,295	(30%)

Cook Partisan Voting Index: R+18

and the abundance of low-wage labor in the flatlands not far east. For many years, the furniture business has proven more resilient than textiles and tobacco, but lately it has faced serious competition from China, and the area lost 8,000 furniture jobs between 1990 and 2009. By late 2010, according to the Raleigh *News & Observer*, the area had about the same overall number of jobs as it did in March 2001. Some local businesses have been reaching out to China, with increased textile and fabric exports.

The Triad area—Greensboro, High Point, and Winston-Salem—has been forced to scramble for new engines of economic growth to keep pace with booming Raleigh-Durham and Charlotte. In 2009, FedEx opened a hub at Piedmont Triad International Airport, between Winston-Salem and Greensboro, which has led other firms to plan distribution centers to utilize the "aerotropolis." At the same time, the region's Hispanic population is growing. The town of Robbins in Moore County, the childhood home of John Edwards, former Democratic vice presidential candidate and senator, was 49% Hispanic by 2009, as Latinos moved in for jobs in chicken processing and furniture making.

The 6th Congressional District of North Carolina is centered on greater Greensboro and High Point, which collectively cast about one-third of its votes. The Furniture Mart itself is not physically located within the 6th, but the district takes in other parts of High Point, plus Quaker-settled Randolph County. Moore County and its numerous golf courses are in the district, as are parts of furniture-manufacturing Davidson County, most of textile-making Alamance County, much of populous Guilford County (though not central Greensboro), and the eastern half of Rowan County. Many of these areas are historically Republican, and others have moved in that direction in the past generation.

Howard Coble (R)

The congressman from the 6th District is Howard Coble, a Republican first elected in 1984. Older and far more independent-minded than most of his House GOP colleagues, he has been unable to secure a committee chairmanship despite his considerable seniority.

Coble grew up in Guilford County and went to Guilford College. After wrecking his father's car, he fled to the Coast Guard, where he started off collecting garbage and served for five years. He was an insurance claims representative, went to law school, and became an assistant U.S. attorney and the state revenue commissioner. He served in the state House for eight years. Coble was elected to Congress in what was then a swing district. It was the third time the 6th District had changed parties in three elections. Coble won re-election in 1986 by just 79 votes, in a contest that Democrats complained was decided by the Guilford County election board's refusal to hold a recount. But his personal popularity and subsequent redistrictings have made this a safe seat.

Coble is a friendly man who asks visitors if they mind if he smokes his cheap cigars. A true product of his district, he likes bluegrass music and eats pork brains and eggs for breakfast. His voting record is mostly conservative, with interesting twists. He is tightfisted, and since his first term, he has tried to pass legislation to abolish pensions or health coverage for congressional retirees, which he calls "a taxpayer rip-off." He hasn't found many co-sponsors, but he has refused to back down on his pledge to boycott the program himself.

Like many of his constituents, he is leery of free trade. He initially opposed the North American Free Trade Agreement but voted for it in 1993. He has opposed subsequent trade initiatives, including normalizing trade relations with China and the 2005 Central America Free Trade Agreement. He worked with other North Carolina lawmakers to get into law a tariff reduction bill in 2010 aimed at the Glen Raven textile mill in Warren County. The Raleigh *News & Observer* later reported that Glen Raven's president had given Coble more than $7,000 since 2007, including $2,000 two weeks after he first introduced the legislation. Coble responded that there was no link between the donations and his legislation.

In the 112th Congress (2011-12), Coble became the chairman of the Judiciary Subcommittee on Courts, Commercial and Administrative Law. He and Judiciary Chairman Lamar Smith, R-Texas, immediately riled Democrats by introducing a bill aimed at easing small businesses' costs of implementing federal regulations. He co-sponsored another bill that Democrats disliked, a measure to repeal a National Mediation Board rule allowing unions to organize railway and airline workers with less than a majority of employees voting in favor of representation.

"I see my role more as one of keeping bad legislation off the books," Coble once said. Still, he has been legislatively productive on Judiciary, especially in the area of intellectual property. Coble says that industries that depend on copyrights produce more gross domestic product than does manufacturing, and he has supported greater protection for intellectual property. When the Bush administration sought budget cuts from the Patent and Trademark Office, Coble told the appropriators to "keep their grubby paws out of the PTO's coffers." In 2002, he shepherded the enactment of additional changes in the patent law, including the development of an electronic system for the filing and processing of patent and trademark applications. In 2004, the Judiciary Committee approved his bill to protect commercial databases from piracy. Despite his own limitations in operating a computer, Coble is a major cheerleader for the digital revolution and says he has come to appreciate the Internet. In 1997, he was in line to be the ranking Republican on Judiciary, but GOP leaders instead gave the post to Lamar Smith of Texas, a more prolific party fundraiser.

Coble voted in 2002 to authorize the use of force in Iraq, but by 2005 he was raising questions about President George W. Bush's war policy. In 2007, he was one of 17 House Republicans to oppose Bush's troop surge strategy but he would not go along with Democratic proposals for a troop withdrawal deadline. He has been similarly skeptical of President Barack Obama's strategy on Afghanistan. He signed a bipartisan letter to Obama in February 2009 citing Osama bin Laden's vow to "bleed...America to the point of bankruptcy" in that country.

In July 2008, Coble broke James Broyhill's record for the longest tenure in the U.S. House of a Republican from North Carolina. Broyhill served 23 years, from 1963 to 1986. When Coble faces a Democratic opponent, which isn't very often, he typically exceeds 70% of the vote. He faced five Republican challengers in 2010 and dispatched them with ease, drawing 64%; some of them were likely auditioning to replace him when he finally retires. Democrats view this seat as possibly competitive once Coble departs, but that seems a stretch. More likely, the district's future could hinge on redistricting.

SEVENTH DISTRICT

Mike McIntyre (D)

Elected 1996, 8th term; b. Aug. 6, 1956, Lumberton; home, Lumberton; U. of NC, B.A. 1978, J.D. 1981; Presbyterian; married (Dee); 2 children.

Professional Career: Practicing atty., 1981–96.

DC Office: 2133 RHOB, 20515, 202-225-2731; Fax: 202-225-5773; Web site: mcintyre.house.gov.

State Offices: Bolivia, 910-253-0158; Fayetteville, 910-323-0260; Lumberton, 910-735-0610; Wilmington, 910-815-4959.

Committees: *Agriculture:* Conservation, Energy & Forestry; General Farm Commodities & Risk Management. *Armed Services:* Tactical Air & Land Forces; Seapower & Projection Forces (RMM).

Group Ratings

	ACLU	ACU	ADA	CFG	AFS	FRC	LCV	ITIC	NTU	COC
2010	44	38	35	50	50	93	90	100	49	75
2009	–	38	50	35	89	–	79	–	28	80

National Journal Ratings

	2010 LIB	—	2010 CONS	2009 LIB	—	2009 CONS
Economic	44%	—	56%	44%	—	55%
Social	39%	—	60%	41%	—	59%
Foreign	48%	—	51%	44%	—	56%
Composite	44%	—	56%	43%	—	57%

Key Votes of the 111th Congress

1. Overturn Ledbetter	Y	5. Bar federal abortion funds	Y	9. Stop detainee transfers	Y
2. Pass $820 billion stimulus	Y	6. Pass health care bill	N	10. Legalize immigrants' kids	N
3. Let guns in national parks	Y	7. Regulate financial firms	N	11. Repeal don't ask, tell	N
4. Pass cap-and-trade	N	8. Pass tax cuts for some	N	12. Limit campaign funds	N

Election Results

2010 general	Mike McIntyre (D)	113,957	(54%)	($1,320,793)
	Ilario Pantano (R)	98,328	(46%)	($1,235,293)
2010 primary	Mike McIntyre (D)	unopposed		

Prior Winning Percentages: 2008 (69%), 2006 (73%), 2004 (73%), 2002 (71%), 2000 (70%), 1998 (91%), 1996 (53%)

Population		Race/Ethnicity		Work	
Pop. 2010:	742,938	White:	62.1%	Private:	76.2%
Change since 2000:	Up 20.0%	Black:	20.6%	Government:	16.2%
Urban:	45.1%	Hispanic:	6.9%	Self-employed:	7.3%
Rural:	54.9%	Asian:	0.8%	Blue collar:	25.3%
Area size:	6,513 sq. mi.	Native Am.:	7.8%	White collar:	52.8%
		Hawaiian:	0.1%	Khaki collar:	0.7%
Age		Two+ races:	1.7%	Other:	21.2%
Median age:	38.2 yrs.				
More than 65 yrs:	13.8%	*Ancestry*		Median income:	$40,569
Less than 18 yrs:	23.3%	USA	10.2%	Median Home Value:	$150,600
		German	8.7%		
Education		English	8.7%	**Military Veterans**	
H.S. grad:	81.4%			% of Pop:	11.5%
College grad:	21.2%				
Grad degree:	6.9%				

Southern Region; Wilmington

Southernmost North Carolina was long a somnolent part of America. Its one port, Wilmington,
was far overshadowed by Charleston, S.C., and
Norfolk, Va. Its miles of beaches seemed too hot
in the summer and too cold in the winter to attract many tourists. Its inland farmlands were
mainly planted in tobacco. Tobacco was America's first export crop, and one that can be cultivated profitably in only a few places in the world.

2008 Presidential Vote		
John McCain (R) 165,960	(52%)
Barack Obama (D) 151,172	(47%)
2004 Presidential Vote		
George Bush (R) 141,459	(56%)
John Kerry (D) 110,589	(44%)
Cook Partisan Voting Index: R+5		

Under the quota system established in 1938, to-
bacco farmers could make a living off small plots; it probably produced more voters per federally
assisted acre than any other crop. But in recent decades, as smoking declined and tobacco companies were hit by lawsuits, tobacco fell out of favor with the public. Tobacco farmers are diversifying; some have switched to blueberries, pumpkins, and other crops.

Nevertheless, the coastal counties of southern North Carolina, and some inland counties,
have been growing despite hitting a bump in the 2007-09 recession. One reason is the military.
South of Wilmington, the Army runs the 16,000-acre Military Ocean Terminal at Sunny Point,
the largest ammunition port in the United States and the Army's main deep-water port on the East
Coast. Another reason is tourism. Condominiums have sprouted along the beaches north and south
of Wilmington. The region also has some of the busiest American movie- and television-production
facilities outside Los Angeles, with the popular teenage TV drama series *One Tree Hill* among the
projects shot there. In Sampson and Duplin counties, the growth industry is hog farming, which
has been criticized by environmentalists for its enormous output of hog waste. One Smithfield
Foods facility, which is believed to be the largest slaughterhouse in the world, handles 8.5 million
animals a year. The company is among those researching the potential for turning the abundance of
methane gas produced by the hog waste on the farms into a usable source of energy.

The 7th Congressional District of North Carolina covers much of this territory. The district
consists of three main areas: the Wilmington region, with affluent beach dwellers and retiree
sub-divisions reclaimed from timbered-out pinelands; the outskirts of Fayetteville, heavily dependent on Fort Bragg and Pope Field; and economically disadvantaged Robeson County, the home
of the Lumbee Indians. For many years, this was a solidly Democratic district. Robeson
County—with 20% of the district's population, where whites, blacks, and Lumbees each constitute about a third of the population—remains heavily Democratic in both national and state elections. But the Wilmington area and the hog-farming counties are now Republican. The Fayetteville
area and the old tobacco counties are politically marginal. The result is a district that is Republican
in national contests but still Democratic in some state races. George W. Bush twice won the district,
and Republican John McCain also won here in 2008, 52%-47%.

Mike McIntyre (D)

The congressman from the 7th District is Mike McIntyre, a Democrat first elected in 1996. Like
the few remaining white members of his party from the South, he is a centrist and particularly
conservative on cultural issues.

McIntyre grew up in Lumberton, in Robeson County, graduated from college and law school
at Chapel Hill, and practiced law in Lumberton, where his family has been prominent for 200 years.
As an intern for Democratic Rep. Charlie Rose, he witnessed the Watergate hearings and President
Richard Nixon's resignation speech. Afterward, he told his father that he would like to run for
Rose's seat someday. McIntyre finally got that chance in 1995, when Rose decided to retire.

McIntyre's chief opposition in the primary was Rose Marie Lowry-Townsend, a Lumbee and
a liberal who had support from the National Education Association, labor unions, and national
women's groups. Lowry-Townsend led McIntyre 30%-23% in the primary. In the runoff campaign, McIntyre called for smaller government, cited his close ties to the district, and got a boost
from the endorsements of local African-American leaders. He won 52%-48%. In the general election, McIntyre's platform was almost as conservative as that of his Republican opponent, New
Hanover County Commissioner Bill Caster. But McIntyre won 53%-46%.

McIntyre is a member of the fiscally conservative Blue Dog Democrats, and although he has
shown a bit more loyalty to his party in recent years, he remains one of the House Democrats
most likely to break ranks. In the 111th Congress (2009-10), he compiled a more conservative voting record than fellow North Carolina Democrat Heath Shuler. McIntyre came out against most

of his party's other major initiatives, including the health care overhaul and the cap-and-trade bill to reduce greenhouse-gas emissions, both of which he said would result in lost jobs. He also voted against repealing the military's "don't ask, don't tell" policy barring openly gay service members and the DREAM Act giving some children of illegal immigrants a potential path to citizenship. In January 2011, in a supreme act of party heresy, he supported Shuler for minority leader over liberal Nancy Pelosi, who won.

McIntyre did support President Barack Obama's 2009 economic stimulus law, calling it essential to create jobs. And he has supported affirmative action and opposed government vouchers for private-school tuition. He opposed normal trade relations with China, and he sought to impose a higher tariff on new imports of Caribbean Basin footwear. Converse's plant west of Lumberton was once the country's largest shoe factory. On another local issue, McIntyre has sought to break the deadlock in the century-old battle for federal recognition of the Lumbees. In 2011, after earlier attempts failed, he reintroduced his Lumbee Recognition bill, which includes a ban on gambling and gives the state jurisdiction over criminal offenses and civil actions.

In 2011, McIntyre became ranking Democrat on Armed Services' seapower subcommittee, where he vowed to work on bolstering the Navy's fleet and air operations. McIntyre voted to authorize the use of force in Iraq in 2002, but he later criticized the Bush administration for its post-victory planning. More recently, he voted against withdrawing troops in Afghanistan, saying in May 2010 that the plan there "continues to show clear signs of success."

In this swing district, McIntyre did not face a serious challenge until 2010. His Republican opponent, Ilario Pantano, was a Marine veteran of the Gulf War and Iraq war who won national attention for his book, *Warlord: No Better Friend, No Worse Enemy*, about his experience being charged in 2005 with the premeditated murder of two Iraqi prisoners. The case never went to a court martial for lack of evidence. Pantano campaigned as "a hard-core national security hawk" fighting for the "soul of the country." He was backed by tea party groups and the National Republican Congressional Committee. McIntyre touted his endorsements from the National Rifle Association and National Right to Life Committee, and won, 54%-46%. He lost Brunswick County but easily carried Robeson and narrowly came out ahead in Cumberland and New Hanover counties. With North Carolina's legislature in GOP hands, he is a focus of redistricting in 2012.

EIGHTH DISTRICT

Larry Kissell (D)

Elected 2008, 2nd term; b. Jan. 31, 1951, Biscoe; home, Biscoe; Wake Forest U., B.A. 1973; Baptist; married (Tina); 2 children.

Professional Career: Union Carbide, production mgmt., 1973-74; Russell Hosiery, 1974-2001; Social studies teacher, East Montgomery HS, 2001-08

DC Office: 1632 LHOB, 20515, 202-225-3715; Fax: 202-225-4036; Web site: kissell.house.gov.

State Offices: Concord, 704-786-1612; Fayetteville, 910-920-2070; Rockingham, 910-997-2070.

Committees: *Agriculture:* General Farm Commodities & Risk Management; Rural Development, Research, Biotechnology & Foreign Agriculture. *Armed Services:* Tactical Air & Land Forces; Readiness.

Group Ratings

	ACLU	ACU	ADA	CFG	AFS	FRC	LCV	ITIC	NTU	COC
2010	81	8	70	24	88	6	100	100	26	50
2009	–	20	75	31	89	–	79	–	18	60

National Journal Ratings

	2010 LIB	—	2010 CONS	2009 LIB	—	2009 CONS
Economic	53%	—	47%	50%	—	50%
Social	54%	—	42%	52%	—	47%
Foreign	56%	—	38%	50%	—	48%
Composite	56%	—	44%	51%	—	49%

Key Votes of the 111th Congress

1. Overturn Ledbetter	Y	5. Bar federal abortion funds	N	9. Stop detainee transfers	Y
2. Pass $820 billion stimulus	Y	6. Pass health care bill	N	10. Legalize immigrants' kids	N
3. Let guns in national parks	Y	7. Regulate financial firms	Y	11. Repeal don't ask, tell	Y
4. Pass cap-and-trade	N	8. Pass tax cuts for some	Y	12. Limit campaign funds	Y

Election Results

2010 general	Larry Kissell (D)	88,776	(53%)	($1,104,141)
	Harold Johnson (R)	73,129	(44%)	($1,079,623)
	Thomas Hill (Lib)	5,098	(3%)	
2010 primary	Larry Kissell (D)	24,541	(63%)	
	Nancy Shakir (D)	14,600	(37%)	

Prior Winning Percentages: 2008 (55%)

Population		Race/Ethnicity		Work	
Pop. 2010:	709,449	White:	54.3%	Private:	75.4%
Change since 2000:	Up 14.6%	Black:	27.9%	Government:	18.7%
Urban:	69.4%	Hispanic:	11.5%	Self-employed:	5.7%
Rural:	30.6%	Asian:	2.1%	Blue collar:	25.3%
Area size:	3,318 sq. mi.	Native Am.:	1.8%	White collar:	54.1%
		Hawaiian:	0.1%	Khaki collar:	2.4%
Age		Two+ races:	2.1%	Other:	18.2%
Median age:	33.8 yrs.				
More than 65 yrs:	10.8%	*Ancestry*		Median income:	$42,131
Less than 18 yrs:	26.2%	German	9.6%	Median Home Value:	$128,200
		USA	8.3%		
Education		English	7.1%	**Military Veterans**	
H.S. grad:	82.1%			% of Pop:	11.6%
College grad:	19.5%				
Grad degree:	6.3%				

Southern Region; Part Charlotte

In the Carolina Piedmont, from Atlanta to Durham along Interstate 85, lies the thickest concentration of America's once-mighty textile industry. Within North Carolina, I-85 brushes past Concord and Kannapolis, the latter named for its founding company, Cannon Mills. While eastern Carolina was settled by Englishmen, the Piedmont was settled mainly by Scots and diverse groups like Quakers and Moravian sects, coming down the Blue Ridge from Pennsylvania

2008 Presidential Vote
Barack Obama (D)	151,707	(52%)
John McCain (R)	135,607	(47%)

2004 Presidential Vote
George Bush (R)	126,041	(54%)
John Kerry (D)	105,248	(45%)

Cook Partisan Voting Index: R+2

through Virginia. These migratory patterns were reflected in Civil War divisions and continue in current voting habits. The coastal counties all the way up through the Sand Hills were Confederate and are now Democratic. The textile mill towns along the interstate were anti-secession and are now Republican.

Parts of both of these areas are in the 8th Congressional District. The most populous county in the district is Cabarrus County, which includes the southern end of the textile corridor around Kannapolis and Concord. In recent years, Cabarrus, fed by migration from Charlotte, has moved beyond its textile and small-town roots and become an exurban county, growing by 31% from 2000 to 2009. Cabarrus casts one-fourth of the district's votes. Between 2000 and 2009, the number of people in manufacturing jobs plummeted by one-third. The bankruptcy of Pillowtex (formerly Cannon Mills) in 2003 eliminated some 4,000 jobs in Cabarrus and Rowan counties. Six years later, Philip Morris closed its cigarette plant in Concord. As if the region didn't have trouble enough, South Carolina sued in 2007 to try to stop North Carolina from diverting water from the Catawba River basin to Concord and Kannapolis. South Carolina views the river as a recreational resource, while the North Carolina areas rely on it to fill depleted reservoirs and for industrial uses. The two states signed an agreement in December 2010 that sets no concrete limits on water withdrawals, but establishes limits in the amount of water that can be taken during droughts.

The 8th District extends east to include part of Fayetteville's Cumberland County, which casts 20% of the vote, but stops short of the military neighborhoods outside Fort Bragg. It takes in central-city precincts in Charlotte with a mix of African-Americans and white liberals. This split-personality district has usually been carried by Republican presidential candidates and by North Carolina Democrats in close statewide contests. Both parties have long targeted it as a marginal district. Democrat Barack Obama increased the local turnout by nearly 20% over 2004, and won here with 52%.

Larry Kissell (D)

The congressman from the 8th District is Larry Kissell, a Democrat who was elected in 2008 on his second try for the seat and who managed to hold onto it two years later in the face of the Republican wave.

Kissell is a native of Biscoe, at the edge of the Uwharrie National Forest. His mother was a mathematics teacher, and his father was the town's postmaster for many years. After graduating from Wake Forest University, Kissell returned home to work in the local textile mills. He started at Union Carbide, and then joined Russell Hosiery in the town of Star, where he stayed for 27 years. At the time, many of the plants were closing as jobs were shipped overseas, so he switched careers to become a teacher. He says he was inspired by his mother, and also by a recognition that the exodus of factory jobs in the region put a premium on children getting an education. Kissell is a conservative Democrat who espouses smaller government and lower taxes, but says he believes that social issues like abortion rights are matters of individual choice. During the campaign, he said he supported increasing the hourly minimum wage.

He first ran against GOP Rep. Robin Hayes in 2006, and although he lost, he held the four-term incumbent to less than 54% of the vote. Two years later, the Democratic Congressional Campaign Committee had the contest in its sights. Kissell ran an effective grassroots campaign, using a "common man" message in a year voters were feeling anxious about the economy. His small-town upbringing and background as a former mill worker had appeal for many district voters who had not forgiven Hayes, a wealthy hosiery mill owner, for casting a decisive vote in favor of the 2005 Central America Free Trade Agreement after vowing to vote against it. Kissell dubbed the vote Hayes' "CAFTA betrayal," and focused his speeches on job creation in the economically struggling region.

Kissell was outspent $3.8 million to $1.5 million, but the DCCC helped with $2.4 million and he benefited from Obama's aggressive voter registration efforts. Hayes added to his own woes with a controversial remark a few days before the election at a rally for Republican presidential candidate John McCain, saying that "liberals hate real Americans that work and achieve and believe in God." This time, it wasn't close. Kissell won 55%-45%, capturing eight of the 10 counties. Hayes won only the two large suburban counties: 57%-43% in Cabarrus and 62%-38% in Stanly.

In the House, Kissell's first act was to co-sign legislation turning back the pay increase Congress was slated to get in 2009. Shortly thereafter, he got a provision into Obama's economic stimulus bill requiring the Transportation Security Administration to buy U.S.-made uniforms. But his positions became of increasing concern to his district's African-American leaders and other liberals. He voted against energy legislation containing a "cap-and-trade" program to curb greenhouse gas emissions as well as a measure allowing bankruptcy judges to modify troubled primary residence mortgages. The final straw was his decision in November 2009 to join 38 other House Democrats in opposing the health care overhaul. He cited the bill's proposed cuts in Medicare and his campaign promise never to reduce funding for that service. "That's too high a price to pay to get the reform we need," he told the *Charlotte Observer.* Angry local Democrats staged a rally outside his office, waving signs reading "Give Kissell a Big Dismissal."

Kissell, however, has continued to navigate an independent path. He backed many of his party's 2010 priorities, including the financial services industry overhaul and the repeal of the "don't ask, don't tell" policy barring openly gay military service members. But he opposed the DREAM Act providing a path to citizenship for some children of illegal immigrants. And after his party lost its majority in the 2010 elections, he supported fellow North Carolina Democrat Heath Shuler over Nancy Pelosi for minority leader.

By mid-2010, it looked as though Kissell's voting record would inspire challengers from both the left and right. Labor unions collected enough signatures to get Wendell Fant, a former congressional staffer, onto the ballot as an independent. And former Army paratrooper Tim D'Annunzio—who referred on his blog to Obama, Pelosi and Kissell as "Liberal Left God Haters"—appeared ready to spend his way to the GOP nomination. But Fant chose not to run, and D'Annunzio lost the Republican primary to Harold Johnson, a former sportscaster whose less bombastic approach drew broader party backing.

Johnson stayed competitive in fundraising with Kissell, putting more than $600,000 of his own money into the race and getting almost as much from the pro-business outside group, Americans for Job Security. With polls showing a tight race, the DCCC again stepped in to help Kissell, pouring in more than $1.7 million. He won 53%-44%. Johnson won Cabarrus and Stanly counties, but Kissell dominated in Mecklenburg and Cumberland. After redistricting in 2012, Kissell could have another tough fight on his hands.

NINTH DISTRICT

Sue Myrick (R)

Elected 1994, 9th term; b. Aug. 1, 1941, Tiffin, OH; home, Charlotte; Heidelberg Col., 1959-60; Methodist; married (Ed); 5 children.

Elected Office: Charlotte City Cncl., 1983–85; Charlotte mayor, 1987–91.

Professional Career: Pres. & CEO, Myrick Advertising, 1985–94; Pres. & CEO, Myrick Enterprises, 1992–94.

DC Office: 230 CHOB, 20515, 202-225-1976; Fax: 202-225-3389; Web site: myrick.house.gov.

State Offices: Charlotte, 704-362-1060; Gastonia, 704-861-1976.

Committees: *Energy & Commerce:* Health; Oversight & Investigations. *Permanent Select Committee on Intelligence:* Terrorism, HUMINT, Analysis & Counterintelligence (Chmn).

Group Ratings

	ACLU	ACU	ADA	CFG	AFS	FRC	LCV	ITIC	NTU	COC
2010	13	100	0	86	0	100	0	33	90	88
2009	–	96	0	88	11	–	0	–	89	80

National Journal Ratings

	2010 LIB — 2010 CONS	2009 LIB — 2009 CONS
Economic	9% — 91%	18% — 81%
Social	0% — 85%	0% — 93%
Foreign	12% — 79%	0% — 75%
Composite	11% — 89%	12% — 89%

Key Votes of the 111th Congress

1. Overturn Ledbetter	N	5. Bar federal abortion funds	Y
2. Pass $820 billion stimulus	N	6. Pass health care bill	N
3. Let guns in national parks	Y	7. Regulate financial firms	N
4. Pass cap-and-trade	N	8. Pass tax cuts for some	N

9. Stop detainee transfers	Y
10. Legalize immigrants' kids	N
11. Repeal don't ask, tell	N
12. Limit campaign funds	N

Election Results

2010 general	Sue Myrick (R)	158,790	(69%)	($1,038,833)
	Jeff Doctor (D)	71,450	(31%)	($110,132)
2010 primary	Sue Myrick (R)	unopposed		

Prior Winning Percentages: 2008 (62%), 2006 (67%), 2004 (70%), 2002 (72%), 2000 (69%), 1998 (69%), 1996 (63%), 1994 (65%)

Population		Race/Ethnicity		Work	
Pop. 2010:	852,377	White:	71.7%	Private:	85.0%
Change since 2000:	Up 37.7%	Black:	14.8%	Government:	8.7%
Urban:	84.2%	Hispanic:	8.2%	Self-employed:	6.1%
Rural:	15.8%	Asian:	3.2%	Blue collar:	17.1%
Area size:	1,018 sq. mi.	Native Am.:	0.3%	White collar:	70.3%
		Hawaiian:	0.0%	Khaki collar:	0.1%
Age		Two+ races:	1.6%	Other:	12.5%
Median age:	36.2 yrs.				
More than 65 yrs:	10.0%	*Ancestry*		Median income:	$62,528
Less than 18 yrs:	27.1%	German	12.5%	Median Home Value:	$202,600
		English	9.5%		
Education		Irish	9.3%	**Military Veterans**	
H.S. grad:	89.7%			% of Pop:	9.2%
College grad:	39.8%				
Grad degree:	12.2%				

Southern Region; Part Charlotte

"An agreeable village but in a damn rebellious country," recorded British Revolutionary War Gen. Charles Cornwallis when, before the unpleasantness at Yorktown, he visited Charlotte. Settled by Scots-Irish and German colonists who came down from Pennsylvania along the Blue Ridge Mountains, Charlotte is a rapidly growing metropolitan area of some 1.8 million people. It will host the 2012 Democratic National Convention, having been chosen to illus-

2008 Presidential Vote		
John McCain (R) 215,045	(55%)
Barack Obama (D) 174,265	(44%)

2004 Presidential Vote		
George Bush (R) 193,419	(63%)
John Kerry (D) 110,769	(36%)

Cook Partisan Voting Index: R+11

trate President Barack Obama's eagerness to reclaim the South for his party. It will be the party's first convention in the South since 1988. Before the California gold rush, Charlotte was the gold-mining capital of the country; in 1837, the U.S. Mint established a branch here. And the city has continued its preoccupation with the financial sector today. It is headquarters to one of the nation's biggest banks, Bank of America. But it was not immune to the tumult in the financial markets in late 2008. The Charlotte-based Wachovia, which was the area's second-largest employer, was taken over in early 2009 by San Francisco-based Wells Fargo, a move that likely saved Wachovia from failure. Mecklenburg County lost more than 3,000 finance and insurance jobs from 2008 to 2010.

But signs of recovery appeared in 2010. *The Charlotte Observer* reported that more than 20 financial firms had opened, launched satellite offices or expanded in the city in a two-year span. And for a city its size, Charlotte has a respectable share of *Fortune* 500 companies. Nine are head-quartered in the Charlotte area, including Lowe's, Family Dollar Stores, Duke Energy, Sonic Automotive, and Goodrich. Duke Energy announced in January 2011 it would buy Raleigh-based Progress Energy, creating the nation's biggest electric utility. The city is also the center of the nation's biggest textile manufacturing region. Charlotte's metro area is projected to equal Atlanta's by 2030. The downside of this rapid growth is that the city has the worst sprawl of 15 fast-growing metro areas.

The past two decades have brought cultural development to Charlotte worthy of its increasing business stature. It now boasts a $50 million performing arts center across from the 60-story Bank of America tower, and is home to the Carolina Panthers professional football team and the Charlotte Bobcats basketball franchise owned by the legendary former player for the Chicago Bulls, Michael Jordan. The rebelliousness Cornwallis noted can be seen in this region's passion for the stock-car circuit. One of the nation's biggest auto-racing tracks is here, and in 2010, the NASCAR Hall of Fame opened in Charlotte. The city has a booesterish pride in its capacity for accommodation. It is proud that it responded amicably to a busing order approved in a landmark Supreme Court case in 1971, and that it twice elected an African-American Democrat as mayor, Harvey Gantt. (Charlotte can't seem to produce a political star, however. Five mayors have run statewide since 1984, and all have lost—most recently, Pat McCrory in the 2008 race for governor. In the 1990s, Gantt lost two challenges to the late Sen. Jesse Helms, a conservative Republican.)

The 9th Congressional District includes about half of Mecklenburg County. It extends west to include most of Gaston County, long a textile center, and south to take in upscale bedroom communities in Union County, the seventh-fastest-growing county in the nation. Mecklenburg County as a whole is politically competitive, with Obama winning it 62%-38%, but the 9th District overall is Republican. President George W. Bush won here with 63% in 2004, and John McCain won with 55% in 2008.

Sue Myrick (R)

The congresswoman from the 9th District is Sue Myrick, a Republican first elected in 1994. An energetic conservative who was once a rising figure in her party, her ascent has been overshadowed by younger lawmakers with less of a background in government than she has. It also didn't help that she backed Missouri's Roy Blunt over John Boehner for GOP leader in 2006. When Republicans won the House majority in 2010, Boehner became speaker.

Myrick was born on a peach farm in Ohio and graduated from college there. She owned an advertising agency and Amway distributorship in Charlotte, where she also raised her family. In 1983, she was elected to the Charlotte City Council. She ran for mayor and lost in 1985, then beat Harvey Gantt in 1987. In her tenure, Myrick made infrastructure improvements in the city and prevented increases in property taxes. She ran for the U.S. Senate in 1992, but was beaten by Republican Lauch Faircloth in the primary 48%-30%.

In 1994, after Rep. Alex McMillan retired, she ran for his House seat. In the first round of the primary, against state House Minority Leader David Balmer, Myrick led 34%-28%. Before the runoff three weeks later, it was revealed that he had falsely claimed on his résumé to have graduated in the top 20% of his law school class and to have played varsity soccer. Myrick won 68%-32%, and then easily won the general election.

A leader of the brash 1994 Republican freshman class, Myrick served on House Speaker Newt Gingrich's transition team and was the freshman liaison to the leadership. Then in 1997, she joined a group of junior members who had grown disillusioned with Gingrich and wanted to force him to step down as speaker. The plan failed, and with Gingrich still in power, Myrick's influence waned. That year, she lost by 110-65 the leadership post of Republican Conference secretary to Deborah Pryce of Ohio, who had not taken part in the ouster attempt against Gingrich and had the speaker's backing.

Nevertheless, Myrick has remained a reliable conservative who has taken a lead role on many Republican initiatives. She was among the first Republicans to join the Tea Party Caucus in 2010, and maintained a consistent limited-government, business-friendly stance from her seat on the Energy and Commerce Committee. She supports the "FairTax," a plan to replace the income tax with a national sales tax that is popular on the political right. Representing a prosperous and growing district, she once turned down $15 million for Charlotte's freeways because she felt the transportation bill would bust the budget: "I said when I ran for this job, 'If you want somebody to bring home the bacon, don't send me,'" she said.

In 2003, she was chairman of the Republican Study Committee, a group of activist fiscal conservatives. A vocal opponent of illegal immigration, she won House approval in 2005 of a measure to deport illegal immigrants convicted of drunken driving, and more recently advocated slashing federal aid to colleges that knowingly admit illegal immigrants. Also outspoken on antiterrorism issues as a member of the Intelligence Committee, Myrick in April 2008 demanded the revocation of former President Jimmy Carter's passport after he met with Hamas, which the U.S. government considers a terrorist group. She joined three other Republicans in October 2009 in asking the House Sergeant at Arms to investigate the Council on American-Islamic Relations, one of Washington's most visible pro-Islam lobbying groups, for allegedly planting "spies" as interns on Capitol Hill. CAIR rejected the claim and called it racist.

Myrick had surgery and follow-up treatment for breast cancer in 1999, and was later declared cancer-free. But the disease changed her focus. After that, she sponsored the law to provide Medicaid coverage for mammograms and pap smears for low-income women. She also co-sponsored with New York Democrat Nita Lowey a bill to require the National Institutes of Health to explore the connection between environmental pollutants and cancer. On Energy and Commerce, she has focused on health care, including mental health. However, she was an unrelenting critic of the Democrats' health care overhaul. She tried and failed to add an amendment in committee that would automatically enroll the president, vice president and all members of Congress in the government-run "public option" included in the original House bill and later dropped. "By not being allowed to even consider this amendment, we are telling the American people that the rules don't apply to the people who make them," she said.

Myrick has considered but declined to run for the Senate in recent years, and she also turned down a chance to run for governor in 2008. She has won re-election easily. For all of her criticism of Democrats, she was one of just three lawmakers—along with Sen. Joe Lieberman of Connecticut and Virginia Republican Frank Wolf—who agreed to sign a pledge circulated by the Civility Project, a bipartisan group seeking to end harsh partisanship on Capitol Hill.

TENTH DISTRICT

Patrick McHenry (R)

Elected 2004, 4th term; b. Oct. 22, 1975, Charlotte; home, Cherryville; Attended NC St. U., Belmont Abbey Col., B.A. 1999; Catholic; engaged.

Elected Office: NC House of Reps., 2002-04.

Professional Career: Real estate broker, 2000-02.

DC Office: 224 CHOB, 20515, 202-225-2576; Fax: 202-225-0316; Web site: mchenry.house.gov.

State Offices: Hickory, 828-327-6100; Shelby, 704-481-0578; Spruce Pine, 828-765-2729.

Committees: *Financial Services:* Domestic Monetary Policy & Technology; Financial Institutions & Consumer Credit; Insurance, Housing & Community Opportunity. *Oversight & Government Reform:* Health Care, District of Columbia, Census & the National Archives; TARP, Financial Services & Bailouts of Public & Private Programs (Chmn).

Group Ratings

	ACLU	ACU	ADA	CFG	AFS	FRC	LCV	ITIC	NTU	COC
2010	13	96	0	89	0	100	0	33	89	88
2009	–	100	0	94	11	–	0	–	92	73

National Journal Ratings

	2010 LIB	—	2010 CONS	2009 LIB	—	2009 CONS
Economic	4%	—	96%	4%	—	95%
Social	18%	—	77%	7%	—	90%
Foreign	23%	—	76%	0%	—	75%
Composite	16%	—	84%	9%	—	92%

Key Votes of the 111th Congress

1. Overturn Ledbetter	N	5. Bar federal abortion funds	Y	9. Stop detainee transfers	Y
2. Pass $820 billion stimulus	N	6. Pass health care bill	N	10. Legalize immigrants' kids	N
3. Let guns in national parks	Y	7. Regulate financial firms	N	11. Repeal don't ask, tell	N
4. Pass cap-and-trade	N	8. Pass tax cuts for some	N	12. Limit campaign funds	N

Election Results

2010 general	Patrick McHenry (R)	130,813	(71%)	($1,015,155)
	Jeff Gregory (D)	52,972	(29%)	
2010 primary	Patrick McHenry (R)	27,657	(63%)	
	Vance Patterson (R)	11,392	(26%)	
	Scott Keadle (R)	3,604	(8%)	

Prior Winning Percentages: 2008 (58%), 2006 (62%), 2004 (64%)

Population		Race/Ethnicity		Work	
Pop. 2010:	689,468	White:	82.3%	Private:	80.5%
Change since 2000:	Up 11.4%	Black:	8.7%	Government:	13.1%
Urban:	49.9%	Hispanic:	5.5%	Self-employed:	6.3%
Rural:	50.1%	Asian:	1.8%	Blue collar:	32.3%
Area size:	3,362 sq. mi.	Native Am.:	0.2%	White collar:	50.9%
		Hawaiian:	0.0%	Khaki collar:	0.0%
Age		Two+ races:	1.3%	Other:	16.8%
Median age:	39.6 yrs.				
More than 65 yrs:	14.4%	*Ancestry*		Median income:	$41,153
Less than 18 yrs:	23.9%	USA	13.9%	Median Home Value:	$123,500
		German	13.7%		
Education		Irish	9.4%	**Military Veterans**	
H.S. grad:	78.7%			% of Pop:	10.1%
College grad:	16.7%				
Grad degree:	4.9%				

Western North Carolina; Hickory

Steeped in the hues that gave them the name Blue Ridge, the heavily wooded mountains of North Carolina seem placid and ancient. Geologically, they are some of the oldest ranges in the world. In the late-afternoon shadow just east of the Blue Ridge is the hilly country around the Catawba River, the last westward extension of North Carolina's cotton farming. In the early 20th century, this hardscrabble country, around the county seats of Lenoir and Morganton and

2008 Presidential Vote		
John McCain (R)	192,076	(63%)
Barack Obama (D)	108,546	(36%)
2004 Presidential Vote		
George Bush (R)	169,484	(67%)
John Kerry (D)	82,965	(33%)
Cook Partisan Voting Index:	R+17	

the village of Hickory in Catawba County, became a manufacturing area. Textile mill owners moved their operations from New England to western North Carolina for its low-wage workforce. After the collapse of the residential furniture industry in Grand Rapids, Mich., during the Depression, furniture manufacturing took hold in the region because of the abundance of hardwood forests.

But textiles are a low-wage industry that typically is the first stage in industrial development, migrating to cheaper venues when wages rise. And furniture has faced competition from East Asia. So the region has increasingly turned to technology. In the 1990s, the boom industry in the Catawba Valley was fiber optics, with new factories that helped reduce unemployment to near record lows. Unemployment rose above 14% in the Catawba Valley in 2010, a lingering outcome of the recession, but the economy has been kept going by the hosiery business—the area has one-third of U.S. production—and by high tech. Apple announced a $1 billion data center in Catawba County in 2010, after Google built a $600 million data center in Lenoir. The proximity of Charlotte's big airport, about an hour away on freeways, has helped. And the area has also attracted newcomers, including many Hispanics and Laotians; the influx of recent arrivals prompted some anti-immigrant backlash in this previously insular region, including the occasional rejection of school bond proposals on the grounds that they could help immigrants disproportionately.

The 10th Congressional District of North Carolina stretches across the state from Tennessee, where the mountains are high enough to support a modest ski industry, to the South Carolina border. It is composed mostly of small towns, and is 9% black, 6% Hispanic and 2% Asian. It ranks first among 435 congressional districts in the percentage of manufacturing and blue-collar jobs. Its largest population center in the 10th is Hickory in Catawba County, which accounts for just over 6% of the district's population. Despite job losses and worries about international competition, it remains one of North Carolina's most Republican districts. George W. Bush got 67% here in 2004 and John McCain 63% in 2008.

Patrick McHenry (R)

The congressman from the 10th District is Patrick McHenry, a Republican in 2004. He grew up in Cherryville and graduated from Belmont Abbey College, where he was president of the state College Republicans. After school he worked as a real estate broker. As a young staunch conservative, he cut his political teeth on his strenuous opposition to the Clintons. He once dressed up in an Abraham Lincoln costume at a North Carolina appearance by Bill Clinton after Clinton was accused by Republicans of rewarding big contributors with overnight stays in the Lincoln Bedroom in the White House. In 2000, he ran a website, *notHillary.com*, opposing Hillary Clinton's Senate candidacy in New York. McHenry worked on several Republican campaigns in North Carolina, including Rep. Robin Hayes' unsuccessful run for governor in 1996. In 2001 he was appointed to a job in the Labor Department and in 2002 he was elected to the state House.

He ran for Congress after Republican Rep. Cass Ballenger announced he was retiring, leaving an open seat for the first time in 18 years. In the Republican primary, McHenry's chief competition was Catawba County Sheriff David Huffman, and both made conservative Christian values their main issue. Huffman finished first with 35% and McHenry second with 26%. North Carolina allows runoffs when no candidate gets 40% in the primary, and the four-week runoff campaign took a negative turn. Huffman questioned McHenry's record as a businessman and accused him of having noisy all-night parties at his house, which also served as a residence for his campaign staff. McHenry's neighbors said Huffman's claim was untrue. McHenry accused Huffman of campaign finance irregularities. McHenry ran an energetic, door-to-door grassroots campaign, billing himself as a "pro-life, pro-gun, anti-gay-marriage" Christian conservative. He won the runoff by just 85 votes after a recount. Huffman carried Catawba County 59%-41%. But McHenry rolled up huge majorities in the counties south of Interstate 40 and close to his Gaston County home. He easily won the general election.

At age 29, McHenry was the youngest member of the House when he arrived. Instead of keeping a low profile and doing constituent work to sew up his seat, as freshman usually do, he became a noisy partisan. He made repeat appearances on talk shows for his ability to serve up red meat and sound bites. On the House floor, he took on Democrats no matter how powerful or senior. In 2007, he accused Speaker Nancy Pelosi of California of abusing her office by using military jets to fly home to San Francisco during congressional recesses, although former Republican Speaker Dennis Hastert had also used military planes for his Illinois commute. (Current Speaker John Boehner of Ohio flies commercial.) At a private meeting in January 2008, McHenry asked why Republicans "shouldn't be physically ill at the prospects of a President McCain." And in 2009, he briefly joined the notorious "birther" movement by saying at a town hall forum that "I haven't seen evidence one way or the other" of President Barack Obama's U.S. citizenship. He backed away from the comment the next day.

His House colleagues sometimes grow weary of McHenry's hijinks. After he repeatedly took to the floor to criticize other lawmakers' earmarks in spending bills, the House in 2007 voted down, 249-174, one of McHenry's earmarks—$129,000 to expand a Christmas crafts store in Mitchell County.

In 2009, when he was the ranking Republican on the subcommittee overseeing the Census Bureau, McHenry objected strenuously when Obama was reportedly planning to name then-White House Chief of Staff Rahm Emanuel to oversee the bureau, which he and other Republicans called "a naked political power grab." The idea was dropped, and McHenry voiced no complaints when the new census director, statistician Robert Groves, was named. Although fellow conservative Rep. Michele Bachmann of Minnesota complained that some census questions were intrusively personal, McHenry said in September 2009 that every citizen had a "patriotic duty" to fill out census forms.

When Republicans took majority control of the House in January 2011, McHenry became chairman of a new subcommittee specializing in government bailouts, such as the Troubled Asset Relief Program for the financial industry in 2009. He told the *Charlotte Observer* that TARP was "a very uneven response from the federal government," with some banks bailed out and others, notably Charlotte-based Wachovia, forced to merge, producing "a very rich environment for potential oversight hearings." On the Financial Services Committee, he won enactment of his bill allowing financial institutions involved in multiple transactions to combine them into one contract, something helpful to the banking industry in nearby Charlotte.

Given the economic plight of the textile industry, McHenry frequently votes against free-trade deals, as he did in 2005 with a pact proposed with Central America and in 2010 with a Haiti trade relief bill. McHenry attracted some attention in March 2010 when he proposed replacing the image of Ulysses S. Grant on the $50 bill with one of Ronald Reagan. "Every generation needs its own heroes," he said.

He has had little trouble at election time. In 2010, he had two challengers in the Republican primary, but won with 63% of the vote; he then cruised to victory in the general election.

ELEVENTH DISTRICT

Heath Shuler (D)

Elected 2006, 3rd term; b. Dec. 31, 1971, Bryson City; home, Waynesville; U of TN, B.A. 2001; Baptist; married (Nikol); 2 children.

Professional Career: Pro football player, 1994-98; Owner, Heath Shuler Real Estate, 1998-2003; Property development investor.

DC Office: 229 CHOB, 20515, 202-225-6401; Fax: 202-226-6422; Web site: shuler.house.gov.

State Offices: Asheville, 828-252-1651; Murphy, 828-835-4981; Murphy, 828-835-4981; Sylva, 828-586-1962.

Committees: *Budget. Transportation & Infrastructure:* Economic Development, Public Buildings & Emergency Management; Highways & Transit.

Group Ratings

	ACLU	ACU	ADA	CFG	AFS	FRC	LCV	ITIC	NTU	COC
2010	31	22	50	38	75	81	90	50	44	50
2009	–	24	65	27	78	–	86	–	25	53

National Journal Ratings

	2010 LIB	—	2010 CONS	2009 LIB	—	2009 CONS
Economic	47%	—	53%	45%	—	54%
Social	42%	—	58%	40%	—	60%
Foreign	77%	—	23%	50%	—	48%
Composite	55%	—	45%	46%	—	55%

Key Votes of the 111th Congress

1. Overturn Ledbetter	Y	5. Bar federal abortion funds	Y	9. Stop detainee transfers	*
2. Pass $820 billion stimulus	N	6. Pass health care bill	N	10. Legalize immigrants' kids	N
3. Let guns in national parks	Y	7. Regulate financial firms	Y	11. Repeal don't ask, tell	Y
4. Pass cap-and-trade	Y	8. Pass tax cuts for some	Y	12. Limit campaign funds	Y

Election Results

2010 general	Heath Shuler (D)	131,225	(54%)	($1,347,011)
	Jeff Miller (R)	110,246	(46%)	($810,054)
2010 primary	Heath Shuler (D)	26,223	(61%)	
	Aixa Wilson (D)	16,507	(39%)	

Prior Winning Percentages: 2008 (62%), 2006 (54%)

Population		Race/Ethnicity		Work	
Pop. 2010:	703,606	White:	86.5%	Private:	74.8%
Change since 2000:	Up 13.6%	Black:	4.1%	Government:	16.0%
Urban:	43.9%	Hispanic:	5.6%	Self-employed:	9.0%
Rural:	56.1%	Asian:	0.7%	Blue collar:	25.2%
Area size:	6,088 sq. mi.	Native Am.:	1.4%	White collar:	55.3%
		Hawaiian:	0.1%	Khaki collar:	0.1%
Age		Two+ races:	1.5%	Other:	19.4%
Median age:	42.9 yrs.				
More than 65 yrs:	18.7%	*Ancestry*		Median income:	$40,739
Less than 18 yrs:	20.5%	USA	13.0%	Median Home Value:	$169,300
		German	11.8%		
Education		English	11.3%	**Military Veterans**	
H.S. grad:	84.4%			% of Pop:	12.6%
College grad:	24.7%				
Grad degree:	9.0%				

Western North Carolina; Asheville

Western North Carolina, the protrusion of the Tar Heel State deep into the eastern United States' highest and oldest mountains, is a land of long and ornery traditions. First settled not long after the Revolutionary War, it still has Indian communities and hollows where people are descended from the first white settlers. Its biggest city, Asheville, memorialized in Thomas Wolfe's novels, was a retreat for lung patients and the home of the eccentric George Vanderbilt, who built the 255-room Biltmore mansion amid a vast woods where he pioneered scientific forestry. A dozen miles east is Black Mountain College, frequented by such innovators as Buckminster Fuller and minimalist composer John Cage. Asheville's historic structures, from Gothic Revival to Art Deco, remain well preserved and are a magnet for gay couples and tourists, who in turn support a handful of coffeehouses, microbreweries, and artsy cinemas. Asheville's minor league baseball team is called the Tourists. Not far to the west is the Eastern Band of Cherokee's casino, the biggest employer in western North Carolina. Over a ridge is the Great Smoky Mountains National Park, the nation's most heavily visited. Its forested, fog-wisped mountains are 20 degrees cooler in the summer than the lowland towns an hour or so away. The Fraser fir trees grown on farms in the mountains are America's favorite Christmas tree.

2008 Presidential Vote		
John McCain (R) 178,875	(52%)
Barack Obama (D) 159,839	(47%)

2004 Presidential Vote		
George Bush (R) 169,872	(57%)
John Kerry (D) 126,979	(43%)

Cook Partisan Voting Index: R+6

The 11th District of North Carolina is in the western end of the state, including Asheville's Buncombe County, which accounts for one-third of its votes. The orneriness of the mountain country has been manifest in its politics. This part of the state was reluctant to secede in the Civil War. There were few slaves (the district today is 4% black and 6% Hispanic) and many small farmers loyal to the Union. For a time, the 11th was one of the nation's most closely contested districts, throwing out incumbents in five of six elections between 1980 and 1990. Coinciding with an influx of retirees in the mountains south of Asheville, it has tilted Republican in the past few presidential elections, including 2008, when Republican John McCain won it by 52%-47%. But there is a definite liberal trend in Buncombe County, which Democrat Barack Obama carried 56%-47%.

Heath Shuler (D)

The congressman from the 11th District is Heath Shuler, a Democrat first elected in 2006. The son of a mailman, Shuler grew up on Toot Hollow Road in Bryson City, near the entrance to Great Smoky Mountains National Park. He led Swain County High School to three state football championships and starred as quarterback at the University of Tennessee, where he was the 1993 runner-up for the Heisman Trophy. The Washington Redskins picked Shuler, then a college junior, third in the 1994 draft and first among quarterbacks. He played three disappointing seasons before being traded to the New Orleans Saints, where he injured his left foot when a 334-pound defensive tackle fell on him. He attempted a comeback, but was reinjured while playing for the Oakland Raiders. Despite the disappointments in his pro football career, Shuler remained a hero in Swain County and western North Carolina. He started a successful real estate business in Knoxville, Tenn., with his brother and returned to North Carolina with his family in 2003.

Shuler still cuts the figure of a professional athlete, wearing his NFL alumnus ring, and, as in his playing days, refraining from smoking or drinking alcohol or soda. Republicans in 2002 tried to get Shuler to run for public office, but he declined. Democrats aggressively recruited him in 2006 to run for Congress. Rahm Emanuel, then the chairman of the Democratic campaign committee in the U.S. House, allayed Shuler's fears about missing time with his children by calling Shuler on his cell phone each time he dropped his own children off at school or attended their events. Schuler finally agreed.

That year, he challenged eight-term incumbent Charles Taylor, a Republican who was weakened by his business dealings after associates at a bank he controlled pleaded guilty to bank fraud. He was vulnerable on other fronts. Though he later blamed a glitch in the House electronic voting machine, Taylor did not show a recorded vote for the 2005 Central America Free Trade Agreement, which passed only narrowly. This was no small matter in the district, where trade pacts are blamed for the loss of textile jobs. Taylor sought to tie Shuler to national Democrats. "Rookie Heath Shuler is following the playbook of San Francisco liberal Nancy Pelosi," claimed one radio ad.

Shuler was not an easy target. He had no legislative record, and his views seemed in line with the culturally conservative district. He campaigned on "mountain values," opposing abortion rights, gay marriage and gun control. Taylor, an Appropriations subcommittee chairman, campaigned on his ability to bring home federal money. Then, in October, with polls showing Taylor trailing, *The Wall Street Journal* ran a story about spending earmarks sought by Taylor that benefited many of his business interests. Taylor poured $2.5 million of his own money into his race, and spent $4.4 million overall, compared with Shuler's $1.8 million. But Shuler won 54%-46%, an impressive showing for a novice candidate against an incumbent.

In the House, Shuler joined the Blue Dog coalition of conservative Democrats. He has been outspoken for pay-as-you-go budgeting and immigration reform. In 2007 and 2009, he sponsored bills requiring employers to use the E-Verify system and improving border controls. With opposition from most Democrats and the Hispanic Caucus, the bills never made it to the floor. As a freshman, Shuler got the chairmanship of the Small Business Subcommittee on Rural and Urban Entrepreneurship and was able to pass a bill increasing the number of federal contracts for small businesses. Congress also enacted his bill to increase investment in small producers of biofuels and other clean energy sources. But Shuler also attracted some negative publicity in his first term when *The Knoxville News Sentinel* published a story in August 2008 saying that the Tennessee Valley Authority had approved lake access for a development group whose investors included Shuler, who also sits on the committee that oversees the TVA. In November 2009, the House Ethics Committee cleared him of wrongdoing.

Shuler's conservative streak often puts him at odds with his liberal-dominated caucus. Shuler was one of eight Democrats to vote against President Barack Obama's 2009 economic stimulus bill because, he said, it didn't do enough for job growth. Although he supported the Democratic cap-and-trade bill to reduce carbon emissions, he voted against the party's health care initiative. "This legislation fails to control the inefficiencies in health care that could be used to create substantial savings to drive down the bill's overall cost," he said. Shuler in 2010 voted against repealing the ban on openly gay service personnel in the military and heartily backed giving the National Rifle Association an exemption from tougher rules requiring disclosure of campaign donations.

Shuler won re-election easily in 2008. But his independence brought him a challenge in the 2010 Democratic primary from Aixa Wilson, who criticized his votes against the health care legislation. He won by 61%-39%. Then in the general election, Republican opponent Jeff Miller, a dry cleaners owner, criticized him for siding with Democrats on many issues and for the TVA real estate deal. Shuler highlighted his differences with party liberals, and during a campaign debate, went so far as to say he would challenge House Speaker Nancy Pelosi in the election of a speaker for the 112th Congress (2011-2012). Shuler spent over $2 million defending the seat, while Miller spent $800,000. Shuler won 54%-46%.

When Democrats lost their majority in the election, Pelosi ran for minority leader. Shuler called on her to step down in light of the party's drubbing at the polls, and challenged her for the post. He said he did not expect to win— "I can add and subtract pretty well," he said. But he said he wanted to make a point that the party had drifted too far to the left. He lost 150-43. Nevertheless, his bold challenge did not prevent him from winning appointment to the Budget Committee in the new Congress, perhaps because Pelosi was reluctant to further alienate the Blue Dog Democrats, especially one popular with his colleagues.

With an eye on his next election, Shuler in 2011 introduced a bill requiring independent and bipartisan redistricting commissions to draw congressional district boundaries in all states. The process in North Carolina is controlled by the GOP legislature, and Shuler could face changes to his district making it harder for him to win re-election.

TWELFTH DISTRICT

Melvin Watt (D)

Elected 1992, 10th term; b. Aug. 26, 1945, Mecklenburg; home, Charlotte; U. of NC, B.S. 1967, Yale U., J.D. 1970; Presbyterian; married (Eulada); 2 children.

Elected Office: NC Senate, 1984–86.

Professional Career: Practicing atty., 1971–92; Co–owner, East Town Manor nursing home, 1989–2008; Campaign mgr., Harvey Gantt Senate Campaign, 1990.

DC Office: 2304 RHOB, 20515, 202-225-1510; Fax: 202-225-1512; Web site: watt.house.gov.

State Offices: Charlotte, 704-344-9950; Greensboro, 336-275-9950.

Committees: *Financial Services:* Financial Institutions & Consumer Credit; Insurance, Housing & Community Opportunity. *Judiciary:* Courts, Commercial & Administrative Law; Intellectual Property, Competition & the Internet (RMM).

Group Ratings

	ACLU	ACU	ADA	CFG	AFS	FRC	LCV	ITIC	NTU	COC
2010	100	4	85	3	100	12	100	100	11	38
2009	–	0	95	4	100	–	100	–	2	36

National Journal Ratings

	2010 LIB — 2010 CONS		2009 LIB — 2009 CONS	
Economic	78% —	22%	91% —	0%
Social	77% —	21%	89% —	0%
Foreign	78% —	17%	91% —	0%
Composite	79% —	21%	95% —	5%

Key Votes of the 111th Congress

1. Overturn Ledbetter	Y	5. Bar federal abortion funds	N	9. Stop detainee transfers	N
2. Pass $820 billion stimulus	Y	6. Pass health care bill	Y	10. Legalize immigrants' kids	Y
3. Let guns in national parks	N	7. Regulate financial firms	Y	11. Repeal don't ask, tell	Y
4. Pass cap-and-trade	Y	8. Pass tax cuts for some	Y	12. Limit campaign funds	N

Election Results

2010 general	Melvin Watt (D)	103,495	(64%)	($604,719)
	Greg Dority (R)	55,315	(34%)	
2010 primary	Melvin Watt (D)	unopposed		

Prior Winning Percentages: 2008 (72%), 2006 (67%), 2004 (67%), 2002 (65%), 2000 (65%), 1998 (56%), 1996 (71%), 1994 (66%), 1992 (70%)

Population		Race/Ethnicity		Work	
Pop. 2010:	736,346	White:	38.6%	Private:	84.3%
Change since 2000:	Up 18.9%	Black:	43.3%	Government:	11.7%
Urban:	88.5%	Hispanic:	12.4%	Self-employed:	3.9%
Rural:	11.5%	Asian:	3.4%	Blue collar:	26.4%
Area size:	827 sq. mi.	Native Am.:	0.4%	White collar:	55.4%
		Hawaiian:	0.1%	Khaki collar:	0.1%
Age		Two+ races:	1.7%	Other:	18.0%
Median age:	33.6 yrs.				
More than 65 yrs:	10.4%	*Ancestry*		Median income:	$39,633
Less than 18 yrs:	25.5%	German	8.3%	Median Home Value:	$130,700
		Irish	5.4%		
Education		English	5.2%	**Military Veterans**	
H.S. grad:	80.9%			% of Pop:	8.9%
College grad:	23.4%				
Grad degree:	7.0%				

Central Region; Downtown Charlotte

"This is perhaps the Negro's temporary farewell to Congress," said George White, a Tarboro, N.C., lawyer and Republican, in his last days in the House of Representatives in 1901. Segregation was being imposed by law, and blacks informally but effectively were being driven from the voting rolls in the rural South. It was 28 years until another black candidate was elected to Congress (from Chicago), and 72 years until another African-American won in the South (in

2008 Presidential Vote		
Barack Obama (D) 220,586	(71%)
John McCain (R) 88,958	(29%)
2004 Presidential Vote		
John Kerry (D) 149,940	(63%)
George Bush (R) 88,955	(37%)
Cook Partisan Voting Index: D+16		

Atlanta). When White said his farewell, most North Carolina blacks lived on farms or in tiny towns. Through the 20th century, few moved to the textile towns, where most mills hired only whites, but some African-Americans did move to North Carolina's larger cities. In the years after the Voting Rights Act of 1965, they were numerous enough to elect members to the state legislature. And some black candidates were successful with white-majority constituencies, notably Charlotte Mayor Harvey Gantt. But North Carolina blacks were not concentrated in high enough numbers either in the rural areas or in the cities to become the majority of any congressional district, at least not one drawn compactly. No African-American from North Carolina followed White to Congress until the Democratic legislature, after the 1990 census, drew two irregularly shaped black-majority districts. That resulted in the election in 1992 of Eva Clayton in the mostly rural and small-town 1st District, and the election of Melvin Watt in the 12th District.

This 12th Congressional District of North Carolina was the most litigated district in the country during the 1990s, and was the focus of no fewer than four cases that went to the U.S. Supreme Court. It originally was made up of a series of scattered black precincts connected in some places by nothing wider than the lanes of Interstate 85, and it stretched 160 miles from Gastonia all the way to Durham. In the current version, drawn in 2001, the 12th remains a 100-mile-long, snake-like agglomeration that roughly parallels I-85 and includes African-American voters in Charlotte, Winston-Salem, Greensboro, Lexington, Salisbury, and High Point, the international furniture center. A near-majority, 43%, of its residents are black. The Charlotte-area precincts account for a bit more than one-third of the district population, the Greensboro area is slightly more than 20%, and the Winston-Salem portion accounts for a little under 20%. In recent years, Hispanics have increased to 12% of the population in the district.

This is North Carolina's most urban district and includes the major banking center in downtown Charlotte. Politically, it is reliably though not overwhelmingly Democratic. One of the reasons Charlotte was picked to host the 2012 Democratic National Convention is to try to bolster the party's presence here and in Southern places.

Melvin Watt (D)

The congressman from the 12th District is Melvin Watt, a Democrat first elected in 1992. Like Massachusetts' Barney Frank, his frequent ally on the Financial Services Committee, Watt is a strong liberal who is not hostile to the business community.

Watt grew up in a place called Dixie outside Charlotte, in a tin-roofed house with no electricity or running water. His dream was to attend the University of North Carolina, and he was one of the first black students to study there. He had a superb academic record and went on to Yale Law School. He set up a civil-rights law practice in Charlotte. He served one term in the state Senate, and then decided not to seek office again until his sons completed high school. He managed Harvey Gantt's campaigns for city council and mayor in the 1980s and for the U.S. Senate in 1990. In 1992, Watt decided to run for the 12th District seat. The contest turned out to be the kind of friends-and-neighbors Democratic primary common in the South. Watt won 47% in a four-way race. His base in Charlotte was bigger than those of his rivals, and he made inroads in other counties as well. He won the general election easily.

In the House, Watt's voting record is among the most liberal of Southern Democrats, and he's not afraid to go his own way. He reluctantly voted in May 2009 to fund U.S. military activities in Afghanistan and Pakistan, but a year later backed another measure limiting use of new Afghanistan funds to troop withdrawal. In March 2010 he cast one of just 35 Democratic votes against a massive jobs bill that became law because he considered it "woefully inadequate." And he cast the only vote in the House against Megan's Law requiring registration of convicted sex offenders because, he said, individuals ought to be able to get on with their lives once they have paid their debt to society. Watt, whose great-great-grandmother was a Cherokee, threatened to deny housing assistance to the Cherokee Nation after the tribe voted in March 2007 to rescind the tribal citizenship of descendants of African-American slaves.

On Financial Services, Watt has faced a challenge balancing consumer concerns with those of his banker constituents, who have been major contributors to his campaigns. With fellow North Carolina Democrat Brad Miller, he was able to get anti-predatory lending language into the financial services overhaul law in 2010. And he worked with Kansas Democrat Dennis Moore to broker a compromise to allow states to enact tougher rules beyond those of a proposed consumer protection agency. The bill also landed him in an ethics controversy. He withdrew an amendment to include auto dealers under the oversight of the consumer watchdog two days after a fundraiser was held for him at the Democratic National Committee headquarters that included some major players in the auto-financing industry. He said he had done nothing wrong, and several lawmakers came to his defense. The Office of Congressional Ethics looked into whether there was a connection, but closed the case in January 2011.

Watt also serves on the Judiciary Committee, where in 2011 he became ranking member on the panel's subcommittee on intellectual property and the Internet. He previously had focused on voting rights and national security matters on the panel; he was able to work with then-Committee Chairman Jim Sensenbrenner, R-Wis., in 2006 on a bipartisan extension of the Voting Rights Act. Watt has been consistently critical of the USA PATRIOT Act for going too far in the name of preventing domestic terrorism through increased surveillance powers.

In the 109th Congress (2005-06), Watt was the chairman of the Congressional Black Caucus. He showed his independence by voting against a formal challenge by several Black Caucus members to the November 2004 presidential vote count in Ohio. He led the CBC members in an effort to try to open up a legislative dialogue with President George W. Bush, who then included what appeared to be a couple of the CBC's proposals in his State of the Union address. But other than on the broadly backed 25-year extension of the Voting Rights Act, the two sides reached little common ground. Watt also was a sounding board for Sen. Barack Obama of Illinois in his early stages of considering whether to run for the Democratic nomination for president. Watt initially doubted that the nation would elect a black president, and he backed former Sen. John Edwards of North Carolina. He later endorsed Obama prior to the North Carolina primary.

Despite the many twists and turns in the 12th District since he was first elected, Watt has shown the ability to endear himself to voters regardless of their race. His toughest re-election contest came in 1998, when the black share of the district's population had shrunk to 36% and Republicans put up a candidate who attacked him as an "extreme liberal." Watt won 56%-42%, with support from the district's many white liberals. He has not been seriously challenged since. Watt hates fundraising, but he has not needed to do much of it in recent elections.

THIRTEENTH DISTRICT

Brad Miller (D)

Elected 2002, 5th term; b. May 19, 1953, Fayetteville; home, Raleigh; U. of NC, B.A. 1975, London Schl. of Economics, M.S.C. 1978, Columbia U., J.D. 1979; Episcopalian; separated.

Elected Office: NC House of Reps., 1992-94; NC Senate, 1996-2002.

Professional Career: Clerk, Judge J. Dickson Phillips Jr., U.S. Fourth Circuit Ct. of Appeals, Durham, 1979-80; Practicing atty., 1980-2002.

DC Office: 1127 LHOB, 20515, 202-225-3032; Fax: 202-225-0181; Web site: bradmiller.house.gov.

State Offices: Greensboro, 336-574-2909; Raleigh, 919-836-1313.

Committees: *Financial Services:* Capital Markets and Government Sponsored Enterprises; Financial Institutions & Consumer Credit; Oversight & Investigations. *Science & Technology:* Energy & Environment (RMM); Investigations & Oversight.

Group Ratings

	ACLU	ACU	ADA	CFG	AFS	FRC	LCV	ITIC	NTU	COC
2010	88	0	100	0	100	0	100	67	3	13
2009	–	0	100	0	100	–	100	–	3	33

National Journal Ratings

	2010 LIB	—	2010 CONS	2009 LIB	—	2009 CONS
Economic	86%	—	13%	75%	—	21%
Social	71%	—	25%	64%	—	34%
Foreign	65%	—	35%	67%	—	31%
Composite	75%	—	25%	70%	—	30%

Key Votes of the 111th Congress

1. Overturn Ledbetter	Y	5. Bar federal abortion funds	N	9. Stop detainee transfers	Y
2. Pass $820 billion stimulus	Y	6. Pass health care bill	Y	10. Legalize immigrants' kids	Y
3. Let guns in national parks	N	7. Regulate financial firms	Y	11. Repeal don't ask, tell	Y
4. Pass cap-and-trade	Y	8. Pass tax cuts for some	Y	12. Limit campaign funds	Y

Election Results

2010 general	Brad Miller (D)	116,103	(55.5%)	($930,351)
	William Randall (R)	93,099	(45.5%)	($213,449)
2010 primary	Brad Miller (D)	unopposed		

Prior Winning Percentages: 2008 (66%), 2006 (64%), 2004 (59%), 2002 (55%)

Population		Race/Ethnicity		Work	
Pop. 2010:	753,104	White:	56.2%	Private:	79.8%
Change since 2000:	Up 21.6%	Black:	28.1%	Government:	14.8%
Urban:	73.7%	Hispanic:	10.6%	Self-employed:	5.2%
Rural:	26.3%	Asian:	2.7%	Blue collar:	21.3%
Area size:	2,293 sq. mi.	Native Am.:	0.4%	White collar:	62.3%
		Hawaiian:	0.0%	Khaki collar:	0.1%
Age		Two+ races:	1.8%	Other:	16.3%
Median age:	34.9 yrs.				
More than 65 yrs:	10.6%	*Ancestry*		Median income:	$45,822
Less than 18 yrs:	24.1%	English	9.1%	Median Home Value:	$155,500
		USA	8.5%		
Education		German	7.7%	**Military Veterans**	
H.S. grad:	85.1%			% of Pop:	9.1%
College grad:	31.2%				
Grad degree:	9.6%				

Northern Region; Part Raleigh

Metropolitan growth has come to the humble countryside of North Carolina. A generation ago, Raleigh, Durham, Burlington, and Greensboro were a string of small cities connected by Interstate 85 across the central Piedmont, moderately prosperous, with textile, tobacco, and furniture factories, but not very big or showy. Just a few miles from the center of town, farm fields started, dotted by country towns with barbecue restaurants and churches. The counties to the

2008 Presidential Vote		
Barack Obama (D) 206,520	(60%)
John McCain (R) 137,599	(40%)

2004 Presidential Vote		
John Kerry (D) 147,144	(52%)
George Bush (R) 132,581	(47%)

Cook Partisan Voting Index: D+5

north were almost purely rural, with a few factory towns. Today, many of the old tobacco fields are used for growing other crops. And the booming metropolitan areas of North Carolina have spread far beyond the old city and county lines into the adjacent counties. Wake County, which includes Raleigh, grew 44% between 2000 and 2010, reaching a population of more than 900,000. Rural roads are clogged in the morning with commuters headed for jobs in new office parks, and income levels have risen far above what they once were.

Much of this territory makes up the 13th Congressional District of North Carolina, created after the 2000 census. Half of its residents live in Wake County, including the center of Raleigh and its expanding skyline. A tangent goes off to North Carolina State University and much of the northern part of the county, except for the affluent new subdivisions that are mostly in the 4th District. *Portfolio.com* in 2010 ranked Raleigh the nation's third-best city for young job-seekers, after Austin, Tex., and Washington, D.C. Another 16% of district residents live in Guilford County, which has the University of North Carolina's Greensboro campus.

The rest of the district includes all or most of four counties up to the Virginia border—Granville, Person, Caswell, and Rockingham—with fairly large African-American percentages. The district overall is 28% African-American. The district lines were drawn by the Democratic legislature to produce a new Democratic district, one of the few created in the South in recent decades that does not have a majority or near-majority of blacks. But the rural counties have a historical Democratic heritage, and university neighborhoods are heavily Democratic. The district has been closely divided in presidential races. Democrat Barack Obama won it with 59.5% of the vote in 2008. George W. Bush won it narrowly in 2000 and John Kerry won it by a slight margin in 2004. In 2010, GOP Sen. Richard Burr edged out Democrat Elaine Marshall in Wake County, 49.3%-48.3%.

Brad Miller (D)

The congressman from the 13th District is Brad Miller, a Democrat first elected in 2002. He has one of the House's most liberal voting records among white Southerners, and has made his influence felt on housing and mortgage issues.

Born and raised in Fayetteville by his widowed mother, a school cafeteria bookkeeper, Miller graduated from the University of North Carolina. He went on to get a master's degree at the London School of Economics and a law degree from Columbia University. After clerking for a federal appeals court judge, Miller practiced law in Raleigh. In 1992, he was elected to the state House, but was swept away in the Republican year of 1994. He was elected in 1996 to the state Senate where, like many members of the House, he had a hand in drawing his own congressional district as chairman of the Senate's redistricting committee.

Miller drew a district very much in his own political interest, but he couldn't be sure he could get the seat. Utah brought a lawsuit against the Census Bureau, arguing that because the census counted service members overseas with legal residence in North Carolina, it should count Mormon missionaries domiciled in Utah but serving overseas. Such a count would have increased Utah's population enough that it, rather than North Carolina, would have gotten the 435th congressional district that year. Utah lost in federal court, and the Supreme Court affirmed the decision.

Four experienced Democrats, including Miller, launched an 11-week sprint to the September primary, which seemed likely to determine the winner in November. Miller raised the most money and got early endorsements from teachers' and other labor unions, plus the League of Conservation Voters. In the primary, he led with 40%, enough to avoid a runoff. In the general election, Miller faced Carolyn Grant, a commercial real estate broker and former head of the Raleigh Chamber of Commerce. She got little help from national Republicans, and Miller won 55%-42%.

In the House, Miller's relatively liberal record has been especially so on economics. He joined the Financial Services Committee, a useful post for home-state banking interests. In November

2006, the Raleigh *News & Observer* wrote that the shy and soft-spoken Miller "remains somewhat uncomfortable with the rituals of Congress" and often sits alone on the House floor reading memos while colleagues chat up each other in the aisles. "He doesn't make a lot of noise, but he's doing the work," Democratic Rep. Bob Etheridge told the newspaper. His work drew plenty of attention in 2010, as he led a push for a controversial change in bankruptcy laws to permit judges to modify mortgages to avert foreclosures. In addition, he and Massachusetts Democrat William Delahunt championed the idea of an independent consumer agency more than a year before it was made part of the financial overhaul. He also worked with fellow North Carolina Democrat Mel Watt to get an anti-predatory lending provision into the bill.

When Democrats became the majority party in 2007, Miller ascended to chairman of the Science and Technology Subcommittee on Investigations and Oversight, where he explored allegations that the Bush administration politicized scientific research. Then-Gov. Sarah Palin of Alaska, the 2008 GOP vice presidential nominee, criticized Miller for suggesting that polar bears should be classified as an endangered species. In 2011, he moved over to take the ranking Democratic slot on the committee's energy and environment panel, where he vowed to ensure his area's universities received money for alternative energy research. He also introduced a bill in March 2011 to ensure a stable supply of "rare earth" elements used in various technologies after China cut off a supply of those elements to the United States and other countries.

Miller once was regarded as being politically safe, but with Republicans controlling North Carolina's legislature, he was expected to lose Democratic voters from his district as part of redistricting. In 2008, he seriously considered challenging Republican Sen. Elizabeth Dole, and perhaps wishes now that he had. Dole lost the election to the less-seasoned state Sen. Kay Hagan, in one of the biggest upsets of the year. Miller went on to be re-elected easily that year and in 2010.

★ NORTH DAKOTA ★

North Dakota, explored by Americans two centuries ago and settled largely by immigrants a century ago, is now entering a third century with a model for progress that many other states might want to follow. The American story here began in late 1804, when the Lewis and Clark Expedition paddled up the Missouri River and reached what is now North Dakota. The explorers bivouacked for the winter across the river from what is now the state capital of Bismarck and spent 146 nights in North Dakota. On the Lewis and Clark Trail, you can still see much of the pristine landscape that the expeditioners saw—a vast unfenced land where the Indians built a civilization based on the buffalo and, a Spanish import, the horse. Things were starting to change when Theodore Roosevelt came to the Dakota Territory in 1884. Railroads were being constructed across the prairie, the Sioux had been herded onto reservations and T.R. needed perseverance to find a buffalo to shoot.

North Dakota was admitted to the Union in 1889, on the same day as South Dakota (no one knows which got in first), and in the next quarter-century, it shot up to near its present population. Its rolling prairies turned out to be some of the best wheat-growing acreage in the world, and while wheat—mostly spring wheat but also durum (used to make pasta)—is the biggest crop, it is not the only one. North Dakota ranks first in production of sunflowers, barley, dry edible beans, oats, and dry peas; it ranks high in the production of sugar beets and rye. There is also plenty of cattle ranching on the arid plains in the western half of the state. While North Dakota's cold climate discouraged many Americans from coming this far north, it was no deterrent to emigrants from Germany, Norway, Bohemia (now the Czech Republic), Iceland and Russia. There were 190,000 people in North Dakota in 1890 and 632,000 in 1920. Since then, North Dakota's population has oscillated within a narrow range. It peaked at 680,845 in 1930, dropped to 617,792 in 1970, rallied to 652,717 in 1980, fell to 638,800 in 1990, and then headed upward in the last decade to 672,591 in 2010. Behind those numbers are two stories. One is a long story of dependence on an agriculture sector growing ever more productive and efficient, but requiring less labor. The other is a more recent story about the resurgence of a new economy on the plains.

For most of the 20th century, dependence on agriculture shaped North Dakota's politics. Farmers, as much as they like to extol their way of life, are seldom content with the workings of the market. When prices are high, it is often because of low production; when they are low, farmers seek protection. The boosterish optimism of the first settlers was soon followed by cries, reverberating with varying intensity, for government protection against market forces. Since commodity prices tend to fall during periods of economic growth, there was often a countercyclical force at work in North Dakota politics—a tendency to vote against the national trends and a radical strain going back to the 1910s and still lively in recent decades. That strain also owes much to the Scandinavian and German origins of many of the state's early settlers, who produced orderly small towns and grain cooperatives and supported the Nonpartisan League, which operated as an independent force from its founding in 1915 to its alliance with the Democratic Party in 1956.

The NPL appealed to marginal farmers, cut off in many cases from the wider American culture by language barriers and seemingly at the mercy of the grain millers in Minneapolis, the railroads in St. Paul, the banks in New York City and the commodity traders in Chicago. The NPL's program was socialist—government ownership of railroads and grain elevators—and its members, like most North Dakota ethnics, opposed going to war with Germany in 1917 and 1940-41. The NPL often determined the outcome of the usually decisive Republican primary, but sometimes swung its support to the otherwise heavily outnumbered Democrats, instituting reforms and creating a state-owned bank and grain elevator. In the 1950s, the NPL more or less melded into the Democratic Party, a merger symbolized by the election in 1960 of Sen. Quentin Burdick, whose father, Usher Burdick, had served 20 years in the House as an NPL-endorsed Republican. North Dakota's leading Democrats of recent decades, Sens. Kent Conrad and Byron Dorgan and Rep. Earl Pomeroy—allies who worked together for years—championed a politics clearly of NPL lineage: boosterish of government farm programs, wary if not hostile to American military involvement abroad and cheerful championing of the little guy from North Dakota against out-of-state corporations.

One reason Democrats thrived for years while the state steadily voted Republican for president is that politics is personal in a place where everyone knows everyone else. For years, there has been no voter registration because people obviously spot anyone who is not eligible. People live longer here too. The 2000 census reported that North Dakota had the highest proportion of any state of residents ages 85 and older, and tiny McIntosh County had the highest proportion of any

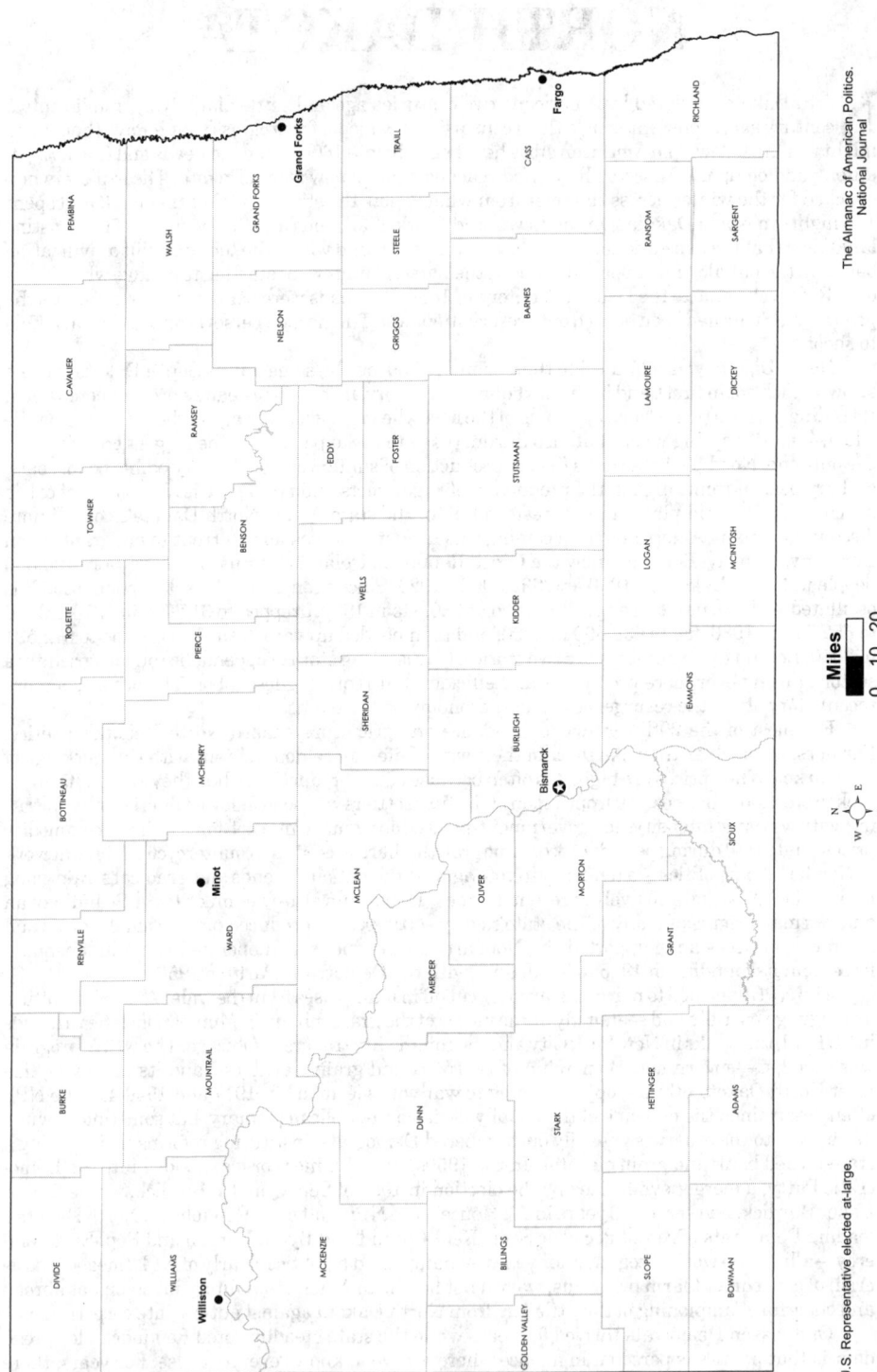

U.S. Representative elected at-large.

county. Communal closeness has produced an innate cultural conservatism in North Dakota. Divorce is as uncommon here as anywhere in the United States, the two-parent family is still very much the norm and abortions are available in just one clinic in the state. North Dakota is noted for its social connectedness and mutual trust. It's a place where you can leave your keys in the car and where others will pitch in and help if they hear that you have a problem. At the same time, in recent years young people were moving to town or, more often, out of state, and the population was increasingly elderly. And its economic future seemed to hinge on the state's location beneath the North American Migration Flyways, which brings in pheasant and duck hunters every season.

Few people could foresee that North Dakota's small cities would become high-technology centers and that the barren lands in the west would turn out to be one of the nation's major sources of coal and gas. North Dakota's four biggest counties, home to Fargo, Grand Forks, Bismarck, and Minot, grew from 134,000 people in 1930 to 359,000 people in 2010, while the state's other 49 counties dropped from 546,000 people to about 313,000 in the same period. This looks very much like the demographics of the Rocky Mountain states, minus the ski resorts, with population concentrated in a few cities and towns. And those small cities are no longer just agricultural trading centers. In 2000, Microsoft bought Great Plains Software for $1.1 billion, and the company's Fargo campus is the headquarters of its business systems division, handling all of Microsoft's U.S. and Canada payroll operations. It is the state's third-largest employer. Alien Technology's Fargo plant produces the tiny radio frequency tags used by Wal-Mart and the military. Grand Forks is the home of the University of North Dakota, with a Center of Excellence in Life Sciences and Advanced Technologies starting up.

North Dakota's public policies, with light taxation and an equally light level of regulation that you might expect in a community with high levels of trust, have made it one of the top-rated states for business start-ups, according to *Fortune* and *Forbes* magazines. Helping things along is the state-owned Bank of North Dakota, a remnant of NPL socialism but also a backer of other banks' small-business loans. North Dakota weathered the 2007-09 recession better than any other state, with job growth continuing to average 2.8% a year and an unemployment rate that never topped 4.3%. It has the nation's third-lowest rate of foreclosures and the lowest rate of credit card defaults. It jumped from 39th in per capita real gross domestic product in 2001 to 13th in 2010.

Aside from technology, North Dakota's economic surge is powered by its growing energy sector. The coal country west of Bismarck supports six electric power plants, and with the world's largest lignite reserves, North Dakota has the potential to build a large coal-gasification industry. The state has six ethanol and three biodiesel plants and can easily grow vast quantities of switch grass to make cellulosic ethanol. The state has enough wind power potential to export plenty of energy, provided that electric transmission lines can be financed and built. Even more important is oil. The giant Bakken formation under much of western North Dakota, discovered in 1951, was estimated to hold the lower 48 states' largest petroleum reserves, but stayed untapped for many years. But in 2006, oil producers began using extended-reach horizontal drilling to reach more deposits and hydraulic fracturing to break up the shale in which the oil is embedded. North Dakota oil production rose from 29 million barrels in 2003 to 113 million barrels in 2010, and it is now the No. 4 petroleum-producing state. Government statisticians have a hard time keeping up with this growth. The Census Bureau's 2009 population estimates for the state were 4% below the 2010 head count, with particularly large underestimates in Fargo and around Minot and Williston in the Bakken region.

To all this development, state government has applied a light touch. State revenues kept pouring in during the national recession, and when Republican Gov. Jack Dalrymple took office in January 2011, he faced the enviable problem of dealing with a $1 billion budget surplus even as most governors were confronting deficits of that magnitude. The likely result: a ratcheting down of tax rates even as the state's economy continues to grow, spending to develop infrastructure in the Bakken region and purchasing electric transmission lines to make wind power commercial. As Republican John Hoeven, governor from 2001 until he was elected to the U.S. Senate in 2010, told *Greenwire,* "Each and every source of energy has some drawbacks, traditional and renewable. We have to be careful in energy policy about picking winners and losers, and instead incentivize states, this country, to develop all of our energy resources and do so in environmentally sound ways."

All of these developments affected the state's political traditions. If the typical elderly North Dakotan is a hardworking retired farmer, with fond memories of NPL agitation and a belief in government programs, the typical young North Dakotan has a family and a college education and is more trusting of markets and the private sector. The 2004 exit poll showed President George W. Bush running stronger among young voters than with the elderly, the opposite of the pattern in most states. While Democrat Barack Obama cut into the young vote here in 2008, the state was certainly not immune to the strong Republican trend in 2010. Democratic Sen. Byron Dorgan retired after 41 years in statewide office and was succeeded by Hoeven, who won an impressive 76%-

Population		Household Income		Work	
Pop. 2010:	672,591	Under $15k:	14.4%	Private:	72.4%
State rank:	48th	$15k to $50k:	39.5%	Government:	18.4%
Change since 2000:	Up 4.7%	$50k to $100k:	32.0%	Self-employed:	9.0%
Urban:	56.3%	$100k to $200k:	11.8%	Unemployment (3-yr. average):	2.3%
Rural:	43.7%	Over $200k:	2.3%	Poverty:	12.2%
Native of state:	69.6%	Median income:	$46,056	Blue collar:	22.7%
Not a citizen:	1.4%			White collar:	57.9%
Area size:	70,698 sq. mi.	**Home Value**		Khaki collar:	0.9%
		Under $100k:	44.1%	Other:	18.5%
Most populous cities		$100k to $300k:	50.1%		
Fargo	105,549	$300k to $500k:	4.2%	**Age**	
Bismarck	61,272	$500k to $1 mil:	1.0%	Median age:	36.6 yrs.
Grand Forks	52,838	Over $1 million:	0.4%	More than 65 yrs:	14.6%
Minot	40,888	Median:	$112,300	Less than 18 yrs:	22.2%

Race/Ethnicity				Military Veterans		Registered Voters in 2010	
White:	88.9%	*Language*		% of Pop:	10.8%	No Party registration	
Black:	1.1%	English:	94.6%			Voter turnout:	240,876
Hispanic:	2.0%	Spanish:	1.4%	*Veterans by Period*		Turnout as % of	
Asian:	1.0%	Asian:	0.5%	WWII and before:	9.6%	voting age:	46.1%
Native Am.:	5.3%	Other European:	2.8%	Korea:	11.5%		
Hawaiian:	0.0%			Vietnam:	32.4%	**Legislature**	
Two+ races:	1.5%	**Education**		Gulf (pre-2001):	10.3%	Senate:	12 D 35 R
		H.S. grad:	89.5%	Gulf (post-2001):	13.6%	House:	25 D 69 R
Ancestry		College grad:	26.1%	Peace time:	22.5%		
German	33.5%	Grad degree:	6.6%				
Norwegian	21.4%						
Irish	5.7%						

22% victory. Democratic Rep. Earl Pomeroy was defeated 55%-45% after 18 years in the House and eight years before that as tax commissioner. Republicans now hold all statewide partisan offices and majorities in both chambers of the legislature, and in early 2011, Democrat Kent Conrad announced that he would retire in 2012 after 26 years in the U.S. Senate

Presidential politics   In 2008, North Dakota was for the first time since 1964 a competitive state in the presidential election. It had given Republican George W. Bush more than 60% of its votes in 2000 and 2004, but by 2008, this historically dovish state was plainly unhappy with the incumbent. And though it has virtually no black residents (and most of them live on military bases), the state was plainly intrigued by Democratic nominee Barack Obama. With North Dakota scheduled to hold caucuses on Super Tuesday, Feb. 5, the Obama campaign moved in early, bought television time and set up offices with paid staff and volunteers in Fargo, Grand Forks, Bismarck and Minot.

2008 Presidential Vote		
John McCain (R)	168,601	(53%)
Barack Obama (D)	141,278	(45%)
2004 Presidential Vote		
George W. Bush (R)	196,651	(63%)
John Kerry (D)	111,052	(35%)

The effort paid off on caucus day. Altogether, 19,012 North Dakotans participated in the Democratic caucuses and only 9,785 in the Republican caucuses. Obama outpolled primary opponent Hillary Rodham Clinton 61%-37%, and got more votes than all of the Republicans put together. On the Republican side, Mitt Romney's 36% of the vote put him ahead of John McCain's 23%, Ron Paul's 21% and Mike Huckabee's 20%. McCain's selection of Alaska Gov. Sarah Palin as a running mate seemed to have had great appeal in this often-snowbound state, at least judging from two post-convention polls showing the Republican ticket far ahead. But after the financial crisis in mid-September, North Dakota became closely contested again. McCain won 53%-45%, doing a little better than late polls suggested but far below Bush's percentages. Obama carried Fargo, Grand Forks and the Indian reservations, but McCain carried Bismarck and Minot by wider margins and most rural counties as well.

Governor

Jack Dalrymple (R)

Assumed office Dec. 2010, term expires Dec. 2012; b. Oct. 16, 1948, Minneapolis, MN; home, Bismarck; Yale U., B.A. 1970; Married (Betsy); 4 children.

Elected Office: ND House, 1985-2000; ND lt. gov, 2000-2010.

Professional Career: Chmn., ND Trade Office; Chmn., Gov. Commission on Education Improvement.

Office: 600 East Boulevard Avenue, 58505-0001, 701-328-2200; Fax: 701-328-2205; Web site: governor.nd.gov.

The new governor of North Dakota is Jack Dalrymple, a Republican who moved up from lieutenant governor in December 2010 to succeed John Hoeven after Hoeven ran for the U.S. Senate. He is serving the final two years of Hoeven's unexpired term.

Dalrymple grew up in Casselton, a farming town of about 2,000 people west of Fargo that has the unique status of also producing three of the state's other governors: Andrew Burke (1891-92), William Langer (1933-34, 1937-38), and George Sinner (1985-92). Dalrymple's family farm was established in 1875 as the state's first large-scale wheat farm. After leaving to get a bachelor's degree from Yale University, he returned to manage its operations. He eventually worked with other farmers to found the Dakota Growers Pasta Co., a mill and processing plant, serving as its initial board chairman. The company is now North America's third-largest pasta manufacturer and was sold in 2010 to a Canadian grain and food processing company. At the same time, he helped establish ShareHouse Inc., a Fargo residential treatment program for alcohol and drug addiction.

Dalrymple entered politics in 1985, when he was elected to a state House seat. He served eight terms, and spent six years chairing the House Appropriations Committee. When economic times were good in the mid-1990s, he pushed Republican Gov. Ed Schafer to put more money aside as a cushion against any future downturns. Dalrymple made two stabs at higher office: In 1988 he made a bid for the U.S. Senate seat held by Democrat Quentin Burdick, but lost in the GOP primary to state House Republican Leader Earl Strinden. Four years later, after Burdick's death, he ran against Democrat Kent Conrad in a December special election to fill the remaining two years of Burdick's term. (At the time, Conrad, elected to the Senate in 1986, was an incumbent who had announced he would not seek re-election in 1992. Democrat Byron Dorgan went on to win the seat that year. But after Burdick died, Conrad had a change of heart about retiring and ran in the special election for Burdick's seat.) Dalrymple attacked Conrad for broken promises, but the senator was more of a known quantity with far more money than Dalrymple. He won easily, 63%-34%. Dalrymple had already run for and won re-election a month earlier to his House seat.

When Hoeven ran for governor in 2000 to replace the retiring Schafer, he came under pressure to choose a woman as his running mate. But Hoeven told the *Grand Forks Herald* that none of the women he approached believed they could balance the task of lieutenant governor with their personal lives, so he turned to Dalrymple. Hoeven said that having a running mate from the state's more populous eastern region helped balance the ticket because he was from the western part. He had little trouble defeating Democrat Heidi Heitkamp, the state's attorney general, 55%-45%. As lieutenant governor, Dalrymple was extremely loyal to his boss. "John Hoeven and I see things in a similar way," he said in November 2010. He was given the task of courting international business for the state, helping in 2009 to arrange a $5 million contract with South Korea for 275,000 bushels of U.S. soybeans. He also worked closely with his former colleagues in the legislature on budget issues, winning praise for his understanding of how to negotiate and cut deals.

As North Dakota's economy thrived, Hoeven became extremely popular, easily winning re-election in 2004 and 2008 and running up record approval ratings. He was considered the logical choice among Republicans to run for the Senate after Dorgan announced he would retire in 2010. Hoeven resigned as governor shortly after winning the election, appointing Dalrymple, the state's longest-serving lieutenant governor, as his successor.

In his first act as governor, Dalrymple appointed Drew Wrigley, a former U.S. attorney for North Dakota and ex-state GOP chairman, as his replacement. The new governor said he would focus on energy and infrastructure issues, saying he wanted to create one central division of state government to focus on developing all of North Dakota's energy sectors. He also expressed interest in setting up a commission to study how the state provides money to its university system. On another matter, he signed into law in March 2011 a bill he supported making the University of North Dakota's sports team name, Fighting Sioux, a matter of state law. The measure came in defiance of the National Collegiate Athletic Association, which opposes the use of Indian names and symbols.

With North Dakota leaning heavily toward the Republicans, Dalrymple has an enviable choice of options heading into 2012. He can either run for another term as governor or seek the open Senate seat held by Conrad that he tried to win two decades earlier.

Senior Senator

Kent Conrad (D)

Elected 1986, term expires 2012, 4th full term; b. March 12, 1948, Bismarck; home, Bismarck; Stanford U., B.A. 1971, George Washington U., M.B.A. 1975; Unitarian; married (Lucy Calautti); 1 child.

Elected Office: ND tax commissioner, 1981–86.

Professional Career: Asst., ND tax commissioner, 1974–80; Dir., mgmt. planning & personnel, ND Tax Dept., 1980.

DC Office: 530 HSOB, 20510, 202-224-2043; Fax: 202-224-7776; Web site: conrad.senate.gov.

State Offices: Bismarck, 701-258-4648; Fargo, 701-232-8030; Grand Forks, 701-775-9601; Minot, 701-852-0703.

Committees: *Agriculture, Nutrition & Forestry:* Commodities, Markets, Trade & Risk Management; Conservation, Forestry & Natural Resources; Jobs, Rural Economic Growth & Energy Innovation. *Budget* (Chmn). *Finance:* Energy, Natural Resources & Infrastructure; Fiscal Responsibility & Economic Growth; Taxation & IRS Oversight (Chmn). *Indian Affairs. Intelligence (Select). Joint Committee on Taxation.*

Group Ratings

	ACLU	ACU	ADA	CFG	AFS	FRC	LCV	ITIC	NTU	COC
2010	73	4	85	1	88	12	57	67	7	36
2009	–	13	95	10	100	–	82	–	10	50

National Journal Ratings

	2010 LIB	—	2010 CONS	2009 LIB	—	2009 CONS
Economic	58%	—	40%	59%	—	39%
Social	65%	—	0%	48%	—	51%
Foreign	47%	—	0%	55%	—	0%
Composite	72%	—	28%	62%	—	38%

Key Votes of the 111th Congress

1. Overturn Ledbetter	Y	5. Pass health care bill	Y	9. Ratify New START	Y
2. Pass $787 billion stimulus	Y	6. Regulate financial firms	Y	10. Confirm Elena Kagan	Y
3. Repeal DC gun laws	Y	7. Pass tax cuts for some	Y	11. Stop EPA climate regs	N
4. Confirm Sonia Sotomayor	Y	8. Legalize immigrants' kids	Y	12. Repeal don't ask, tell	Y

Election Results

2006 general	Kent Conrad (D)	150,146	(69%)	($5,866,380)
	Dwight Grotberg (R)	64,417	(30%)	($187,735)
2006 primary	Kent Conrad (D)	unopposed		

Prior Winning Percentages: 2000 (62%); 1994 (58%); 1992 special (63%); 1986 (50%)

Kent Conrad, North Dakota's senior senator, was first elected to the Senate in 1986. Facing what was likely to be a tough battle for re-election in 2012, the 62-year-old Democrat announced on Jan. 18, 2011, that he would not seek a fifth term. Conrad was considered vulnerable after the state trended Republican in recent elections. In a statement, Conrad said, "There are serious challenges facing our state and nation, like a $14 trillion debt and America's dependence on foreign oil. It is more important I spend my time and energy trying to solve these problems than to be distracted by a campaign for re-election."

Conrad was raised by his grandparents in North Dakota after both his parents were killed in an automobile accident when he was just 5. One of his grandfathers owned a biweekly newspaper in Bismarck and had been the North Dakota chairman for Robert LaFollette's Progressive campaign for president in 1924. His other grandfather was the physician for longtime Republican Gov. and Sen. William Langer. It was a family full of connections in the small world of North Dakota politics. Conrad's first political effort was to lead, in 1968, a campaign to grant voting rights to 19-year-olds. After graduating from Stanford University, he went to work for Democrat Byron Dorgan's unsuccessful 1974 House campaign. Conrad ran for tax commissioner in 1980 and won. When Dorgan declined to run against Republican Sen. Mark Andrews in 1986, Conrad ran and won, 50%-49%. In 1986, he earnestly promised not to run again unless "the federal deficit, the trade deficit and real interest rates will be brought under control." By 1992, the latter two arguably were, and he could claim to have worked to trim the budget deficit. Early 1992 polls showed Conrad well ahead, but in April 1992, shortly after his wife was mugged and dragged down a street near their Capitol Hill home in Washington, D.C., Conrad announced he was retiring because he had not kept his pledge. Dorgan ran successfully for his seat.

Then, in September 1992, the elderly Sen. Quentin Burdick, a Republican and no ally of Dorgan and Conrad, died. State law said a special election had to be held after November but before January. Experiencing a change of heart about leaving the Senate, Conrad ran for Burdick's seat while serving out the last month in his own. He was nominated unanimously at the Democratic state convention. His Republican opponent was Jack Dalrymple, the lieutenant governor (and now governor). Conrad had far more money and won easily, 63%-34%. For a few hours in December 1992, Conrad technically held both of North Dakota's Senate seats: He was sworn in December 14 to fill Burdick's term, and a few hours later, Dorgan was sworn in to fill his. In 1994, Conrad's new Senate seat came up again. Republican Ben Clayburgh, the 70-year-old former head of the state medical association, accused him of voting most of the time with President Bill Clinton. Conrad responded with an ad saying he voted with Republican Leader Bob Dole of Kansas more than half the time. In a Republican year, Conrad won by a reduced 58%-42%.

Conrad is an active dealmaker and the chairman of the Budget Committee. He is proud of his honorary name as a member of the Sioux Tribe, "Never Turns Back." His votes have placed him close to the center of the Senate, especially on economic and cultural issues. Throughout his career, he has decried deficits and focused on trying to force Congress to adopt balanced budgets, often calling for changes in tax laws to increase uncollected taxes owed, to clamp down on tax shelters and havens and, if necessary, to increase tax rates.

When he argues his case on the Senate floor, Conrad often comes equipped with his trademark charts, chock-full of numbers and graphs, familiar to any regular viewer of C-SPAN. In 2001, the Rules Committee informed him he was using more charts than all other senators combined, and provided him with his own printing equipment. Also that year, Conrad lambasted the Bush administration for its tax cut proposals, arguing that lower than expected revenue would lead to deficits. But he did not seek to undo the tax cut. In March 2002, Conrad presented a $2 trillion budget with a $90 billion deficit, which he said would pay down more of the national debt than Bush's budget. His plan passed in committee, but in the 51-49 Senate there were not enough senators willing to constrain appropriators, and Conrad's budget never came to a vote. For the first time since the Budget committees in both chambers were established in 1974, no budget resolution passed Congress that year.

When Republicans held the majority in 2003, Conrad became the ranking minority member on Budget. That year, the Republicans dropped the "pay-go" rule, in place since 1990 and supported by Conrad, that required spending increases and tax cuts to be "paid for" by corresponding spending decreases or tax increases. The change made possible passage of the 2003 Bush tax cuts on dividends and capital gains, and later the extension of various Bush tax cuts. Conrad continued to press, unsuccessfully, for restoration of the pay-go rule. He also tried to focus attention on the surplus in Social Security revenues over benefits, which was reducing the nominal federal budget deficit. But that financial comfort was in jeopardy of disappearing in roughly a decade, when Social Security benefits would begin to exceed revenues. Conrad also complained about Bush's escalating requests for money to pay for the Iraq war without a long-range plan for covering the costs. He told *The Washington Post*: "The president, this is his policy. He's got an obligation to tell us how to pay for it."

When Democrats assumed the majority in 2007, Conrad unveiled a budget resolution that put the budget into balance by 2012, ended the supplemental appropriations strategies used heavily by the Bush administration, and provided for a two-year fix of the alternative minimum tax, which had been designed to ensure that the wealthy paid taxes but in effect had for several years been snaring middle-income taxpayers. His budget called for cutting in half interest rates on student loans, more spending on homeland security, extending the child tax credit and the 10% tax bracket, and eliminating the marriage penalty. Republicans charged that it all amounted to a tax increase, but Democrats envisioned that the Bush tax cuts, set to expire in 2010, would be either allowed to expire or offset at that time. Conrad and House Budget Committee Chairman John Spratt, a South Carolina Democrat, pushed similar bills through the two chambers in April 2007, and they reached a final agreement in May. The next year, when Bush proposed his final budget, Conrad called it "debt on departure" for the lame-duck president. The Senate and House resolved minor differences between the two chambers and adopted a budget, but they postponed major issues until after the 2008 election.

In the 111th Congress (2009-2010), Conrad and Judd Gregg of New Hampshire, the Budget Committee's ranking Republican, concentrated on a proposal to create a bipartisan commission to examine the nation's long-term debt. But the legislation ran into strong opposition. Finance Committee Chairman Max Baucus, a Montana Democrat, said it would undermine lawmakers' power, while Minority Leader Mitch McConnell of Kentucky and other Republicans protested that it would lead to tax increases. Conrad struck a deal with President Barack Obama in January 2010 to form the commission administratively, something he called "the next best option" to a panel created by law. The commission, chaired by former Wyoming GOP Sen. Alan Simpson and former Clinton White House Chief of Staff Erskine Bowles, recommended sharp cuts to military spending, the phase-in of a higher retirement age and a tax hike of nearly $1 trillion by 2020, mainly through eliminating or reducing credits on home mortgage interest and other deductions. Conrad voted to support the panel's plan, along with 10 of its other members. But it still fell three votes short of the number needed for immediate congressional action. Conrad said pieces of the commission's proposal would be considered as part of the 2011 budget process, but he said it would have been far better for Congress to take up its recommendations as a whole.

Conrad also has a seat on the influential Finance Committee, where he voted against the Bush tax cuts and against repeal of the estate tax. But he has been willing to work with Republicans on other issues. He was one of 11 Democratic senators to vote for the 2003 GOP bill creating a prescription drug benefit in the Medicare program. In 2008, he was among the small number of lawmakers who crafted the $700 billion bailout package for wobbling financial markets. He was among the "Gang of Six" senators who worked fruitlessly for months in 2009 to try to reach a compromise on health care overhaul legislation.

Conrad is a big booster of government aid for farmers. On the Agriculture Committee, he helped write a generous 2002 farm bill that abandoned the principles of the 1996 Freedom to Farm Act, which had tried to end farm subsidies. The state received the equivalent of $2,368 per person in payments, more than any other state. During work on the 2008 farm bill, Conrad used his multiple committee posts to significantly influence the details, including passage of a permanent $3.8 billion disaster fund for farmers and a new sugar-subsidy program. When it came time for the final deal-cutting, he worked with Southern senators on commodity programs and largely preempted Agriculture Committee Chairman Tom Harkin of Iowa, who opposed permanent disaster aid.

North Dakota's farm interests, particularly its sugar beet farmers and processors, have been increasingly affected by trade agreements, and Conrad has tried to carve out exemptions for them in the multiple global trade pacts of recent years. On another issue vital to his home state, Conrad in 2007 and 2008 was a major supporter of increased use of ethanol and biodiesel, plus coal liquefaction and tax credits for wind energy. North Dakota produces corn used to make ethanol, has major coal deposits suitable for liquefaction and has more wind-energy potential than any other state. In announcing his retirement, Conrad listed two local issues as being among his top priorities—advancing permanent flood control for the Red River, whose flooding caused major damage in Fargo in 2008 and 2009, and addressing chronic flooding at Devils Lake.

When Conrad came up for re-election in 2006, the Bush White House encouraged popular Republican Gov. John Hoeven to run against him. Conrad ran ads touting his Senate accomplishments, and Hoeven decided not to run. Conrad instead faced a far less serious GOP threat that year in Barnes County farmer Dwight Grotberg. Conrad won 69%-30%, carrying every county. In 2008, he was embarrassed by disclosures that Countrywide loan officers gave him special treatment on a home mortgage, which he claimed was done unknowingly on his part. The Senate Ethics Committee in August 2009 cleared Conrad and Connecticut Democratic Sen. Christopher Dodd of breaking congressional rules by accepting the mortgages, but admonished them for not being more careful to avoid the appearance of a sweetheart deal.

Conrad's announcement of his retirement came just weeks after his two longtime North Dakota Democratic colleagues, Dorgan and Rep. Earl Pomeroy, left Congress. Dorgan retired after three terms in the Senate, while Pomeroy lost his bid for re-election. Conrad met his future wife, Lucy Calautti, when they worked for Dorgan in the state tax commissioner's office, and she later served as Dorgan's chief of staff. Republican state Public Service Commissioner Brian Kalk had already formed an exploratory committee to consider challenging Conrad in two years and other politicians with statewide appeal were also considering the race.

Berg focused his campaign on criticizing Pomeroy's vote in favor of the health care law. He highlighted the law's changes to Medicare, and one of his ads cited a poll finding that 70% of North Dakotans opposed the changes. Pomeroy addressed the issue head-on in his ads, arguing that in supporting the bill, he had made sure that it protected North Dakota hospitals and doctors.

Most of Pomeroy's advertising focused on attacking Berg's 26-year record in the legislature. He accused Berg of supporting GOP proposals to privatize portions of Social Security. A television ad by the Democratic Congressional Campaign Committee called Berg "the Big Banks' best friend" and charged that he tried to allow banks to sell customers' personal information. Pomeroy outpaced Berg in fundraising, hauling in $3 million to Berg's $2 million. But Berg won convincingly, 55% to 45% for the incumbent. Pomeroy later joked that he knew he was in trouble when, while talking with a 102-year-old constituent in his hometown of Valley City, the elderly man confided he would not be voting for Pomeroy. "If the 102-year-olds think you've been around too long, you got a real problem," he said.

★ OHIO ★

O hio, connecting the East with the great interior, bordering the South yet also America's northern frontier on Lake Erie, was the first entirely American state. The original 13 states started as British colonies, and the next three, Vermont, Kentucky and Tennessee, spun off from them. But Ohio sprang Athena-like from the head of Congress, as the first state formed from the Northwest Territory. The Northwest Ordinance of 1787 established 6-mile-square townships, which imposed geometric order on diverse American landscapes west to the Pacific. It set aside one square mile per township for public schools, and the land was soon peppered with schoolhouses and small colleges, the foundation stones of a literate republic. The ordinance prohibited slavery at a time when many Northern states still had it, opening the way for free labor to clear fields, raise crops and build mills and factories. In less than half a century the former wilderness wrested from Indian and British control only in 1796 was one of the most productive parts of the young republic.

In the years after the Civil War, Ohio became one of the great industrial states, the original headquarters of John D. Rockefeller's Standard Oil, the site of major steel mills along the narrow and languidly flowing Cuyahoga and Mahoning rivers, and the location of the biggest soap companies, machine tool makers and tire manufacturers. Dayton was the home of the Wright brothers, who developed the airplane; John Patterson, the inventor and manufacturer of the cash register; and Charles Kettering, the inventor of the automobile starter. Akron was the home of Harvey Firestone, B. F. Goodrich and F. A. Seiberling—the great tire manufacturers. Cincinnati was and is the headquarters of Procter & Gamble. The state was settled by New Englanders in the northeast (in the Western Reserve) and by Virginians in the south, creating a split between the Southern-accented counties south of the National Road and U.S. 40 and the Northern-accented cities and towns to the north. You can see the difference on the map: southern Ohio counties are laid out in irregularly shaped townships, but northern Ohio has the Northwest Ordinance's orderly grid. The state was also similarly split between Butternut and Copperhead territory that didn't want to fight the Civil War and Yankee territory that fiercely prosecuted the war. Southern Ohio was represented by Clement Vallandigham, the Copperhead who rooted for the Confederacy; the Western Reserve in the northeast, settled by Connecticut Yankees, was the most pro-Republican part of the country.

This split heritage made Ohio politically a closely divided state—and a nationally pivotal one. In the 1890s, Ohio produced the candidate and campaign manager who won the presidency in 1896 and 1900: former Rep. and Gov. William McKinley and iron and coal industrialist and Sen. Mark Hanna, respectively. They inaugurated a 34-year period of Republican national majorities. McKinley's Republicans were for high tariffs and hard money and had a friendly regard for workers and even some unions, but they had no patience with large unions. They preached a nationalist Americanism tempered by wariness about making major commitments abroad. Republicans were the majority in this increasingly industrial Ohio, losing rural Butternut counties but carrying the big industrial cities of the north.

Then came the Depression of the 1930s, and Ohio became the scene of class warfare, with sit-down strikes and victories for the CIO industrial unions in autos, steel and tires. CIO cities (Cleveland, Akron, Youngstown, and Toledo) moved sharply toward the Democrats, while places with fewer union members (Cincinnati, Columbus, the dozens of small factory towns dotting the flat limestone plains of northern Ohio) stayed Republican. The political fighting was fierce, and the stakes were high. CIO leaders hoped to organize the entire workforce and build a Scandinavian-style welfare state. Republican leaders like Ohio's Sen. Robert Taft feared union control of business would imperil freedoms and throttle the economy. In the 1930s and 1940s, the unions made great gains, but Taft held them off, reducing union power with the Taft-Hartley Act of 1947 and his own re-election after a hotly contested campaign in 1950.

In the years since, Ohio has oscillated as it has been courted by national campaigns. It has not voted for the loser in a presidential election since 1960. Bill Clinton carried the state twice, but by the narrowest of his margins in any large state—40%-38% in 1992, 47%-41% in 1996. And Al Gore lost here 50%-46% in 2000. In state politics, Republicans held the governorship and the legislature for 16 years starting in 1990, with Gov. George Voinovich re-elected in 1994 by 72%-25%. In the 1990s, both of Ohio's Democratic U.S. senators were replaced by Republicans when they retired, Voinovich and Mike DeWine. Bob Taft was elected governor in 1998, and Republican George W. Bush carried the state by narrow margins in the presidential contests of 2000 and 2004. Republicans then held every statewide office and held large margins in the legislature.

Districts 6, 9 and 13 are highlighted for visibility.

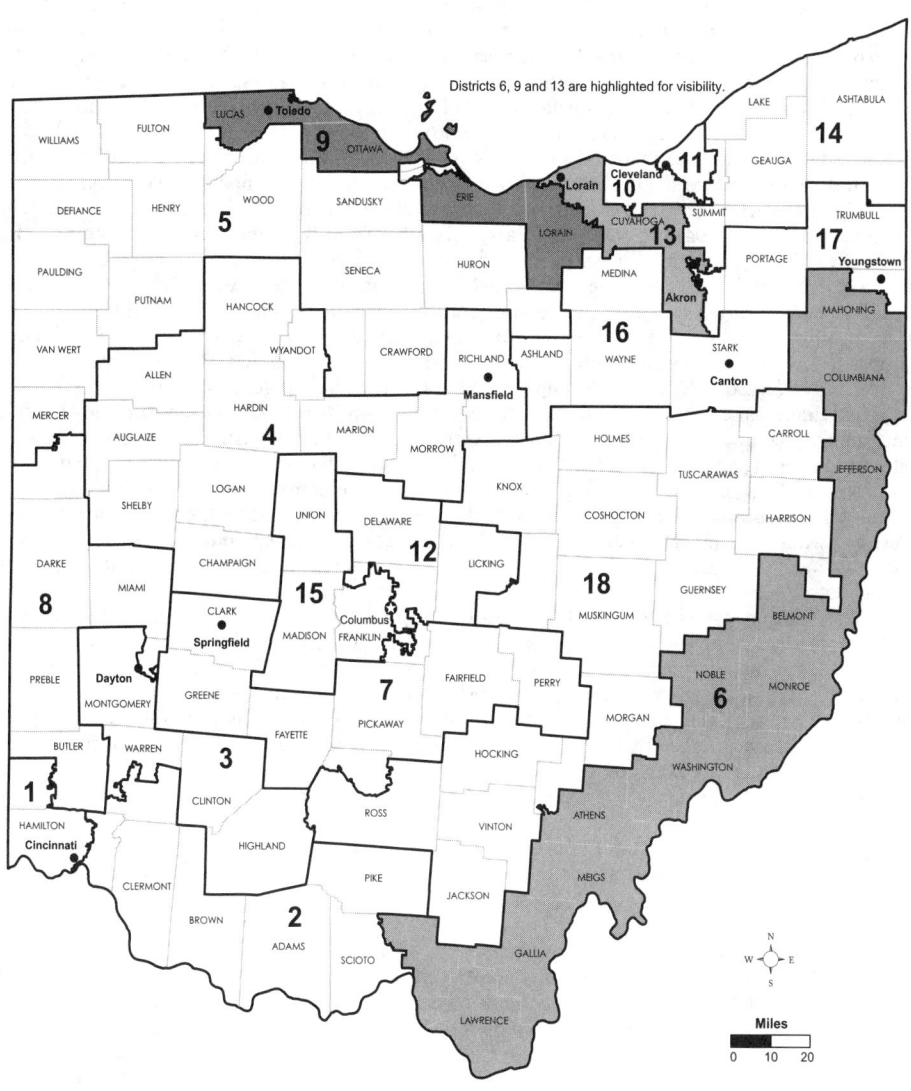

Congressional district boundaries were first effective for 2002.

Then in 2006 came a great turn toward the Democrats. Unused to having one party in control for more than a decade, Ohio recoiled against the Republicans. The state was growing sluggishly even before the 2007-09 recession and Republicans had raised taxes and were beset by scandal. Ohio's state and local tax burden, rated 45th highest in the nation in 1977 by the Tax Foundation, was rated 7th in 2008. Democratic Rep. Ted Strickland, a former minister and prison psychologist, won the governorship in a 61%-37% landslide over Secretary of State Ken Blackwell. Democrats won the offices of attorney general, secretary of state and treasurer and Rep. Sherrod Brown unseated DeWine by a solid 56%-44%. Democrats did not quite sweep the board. Republicans held on to majorities in the legislature. The Democratic trend continued in 2008. Ohio was once again a target state in the presidential contest, with Republicans hoping that Barack Obama would be a weak candidate in a state where he had lost the Democratic primary to Hillary Rodham Clinton, carrying only five of 18 congressional districts. Ohio was the scene of many candidate visits. Republican candidate John McCain introduced Alaska Gov. Sarah Palin as his vice presidential nominee in Dayton, and there were intensive organizational efforts by both campaigns. This was the third campaign in a row in which Ohio was a major target state, and a certain fatigue may have set in. Turnout, up 20% in 2004 despite low population growth, rose only 4% more in 2008. Obama carried the state 52%-47%, a slightly larger margin than either of Bush's. Democrats won a 10-8 majority in the state's U.S. House delegation and a 53-46 margin in the state House.

The 2010 election saw another turnaround. Former U.S. House Budget Chairman John Kasich, after 10 years out of electoral politics, beat Strickland 49%-47%, who was the first incumbent governor to lose since John Gilligan in 1974. Strickland, who carried 72 of 88 counties in 2006, carried only 27 in 2010. The biggest drop-off in Strickland's percentages came in the small counties in his old congressional district along the Ohio River and—quite a different constituency—in affluent suburban counties around Cleveland. His vote held up best among African-Americans in large cities and in northwest Ohio, in traditional Republican small-factory towns afflicted with high unemployment. He won blacks, young voters and those in union households and basically lost everyone else. Republicans won all of the statewide down-ballot offices. And former House member Rob Portman walloped Democrat Lee Fisher 57%-39% in the Senate race. Republicans ousted no fewer than five incumbent House Democrats and won majorities of 23-10 in the state Senate and 59-40 in the state House.

Whether this represented a sustainable shift in opinion was unclear. National politicians will certainly be watching closely in what is still the seventh largest state, with 18 electoral votes (rather than 20, as in the last three elections). It has often been said that Ohio was a great test market, close to the national average in income levels, urban-rural balance, and ethnic mix, as well as presidential percentages. Pivotal, perhaps, but not average. Ohio is still more industrial than post-industrial, a state changed by the immigration of the early 20th century but little touched by the immigration of the late 20th century. Cultural liberalism has a far smaller constituency in Ohio than it does on either coast or even in nearby Illinois and Michigan. Economically and culturally, it is a template perhaps for Indiana or Missouri but not for Colorado or Arizona. Blacks make up 12% of the population, the result of pre-Civil War abolitionist communities as well as the huge 1940-65 migration of Southern blacks to the factory cities of the North. But the population is only 3% Hispanic.

In manufacturing jobs, Ohio trails only California and Texas—which have three and two times as many people, respectively—yet it has 500,000 fewer than it did in the peak year of 1969. From 2000 to 2010, it had a lower rate of population growth than any state other than Rhode Island, Louisiana and Michigan. Like Michigan, Ohio never seemed to recover from the 2001-02 recession. The state has one of the lowest rates of business startups in the nation, according to the Kauffman Foundation, and its income levels have languished as first the steel companies, then the auto sub-contractors and finally the Detroit Three laid off thousands of workers. Honda decided in 2006 not to build a fourth plant in Ohio, but to go to Indiana instead. The state's encouragement of bioscience and high-tech businesses has not generated nearly as many offsetting jobs. Ohio was not actually hit as hard by the 2007-09 recession as some states, including Michigan. The unemployment rate rose from 7% in September 2008 to 9.1% in February 2009 and to 10.6% by early 2010. In January 2010, Michigan's unemployment rate was 13.7%.

Since the political upheavals of the 1930s and 1940s, there have been two politically distinct parts of Ohio. Northeast Ohio—centered on Cleveland and extending westward to Toledo and south and east to the factory towns of Akron and Canton, Youngstown and Warren—has been the state's Democratic heartland, with the highest percentages of union members and black populations in Cleveland and other central cities. In 2008, this area remained Democratic, but there was no significant trend toward Obama except around Toledo, an area hurt by Detroit's troubles. In-

Population		Household Income		Work	
Pop. 2010:	11,536,504	Under $15k:	14.5%	Private:	81.8%
State rank:	7th	$15k to $50k:	38.5%	Government:	12.8%
Change since 2000:	Up 1.6%	$50k to $100k:	31.3%	Self-employed:	5.3%
Urban:	75.7%	$100k to $200k:	13.3%	Unemployment (3-yr. average):	5.6%
Rural:	24.3%	Over $200k:	2.5%	Poverty:	14.0%
Native of state:	75.0%	Median income:	$46,838	Blue collar:	23.9%
Not a citizen:	1.9%			White collar:	58.6%
Area size:	44,826 sq. mi.	**Home Value**		Khaki collar:	0.1%
		Under $100k:	30.2%	Other:	17.5%
Most populous cities		$100k to $300k:	60.3%		
Columbus	787,033	$300k to $500k:	7.0%	**Age**	
Cleveland	396,815	$500k to $1 mil:	2.0%	Median age:	38.2 yrs.
Cincinnati	296,943	Over $1 million:	0.5%	More than 65 yrs:	13.7%
Toledo	287,208	Median:	$136,900	Less than 18 yrs:	23.8%

Race/Ethnicity				Military Veterans		Registered Voters in 2010	
White:	81.1%	*Language*		% of Pop:	10.6%	No Party registration	
Black:	12.0%	English:	93.9%			Voter turnout:	3,956,028
Hispanic:	3.1%	Spanish:	2.1%	*Veterans by Period*		Turnout as % of	
Asian:	1.7%	Asian:	1.0%	WWII and before:	11.6%	voting age:	44.9%
Native Am.:	0.2%	Other European:	2.5%	Korea:	11.8%		
Hawaiian:	0.0%			Vietnam:	33.2%	**Legislature**	
Two+ races:	1.8%	**Education**		Gulf (pre-2001):	10.5%	Senate:	10 D 23 R
		H.S. grad:	87.3%	Gulf (post-2001):	6.0%	House:	40 D 59 R
Ancestry		College grad:	24.0%	Peace time:	26.9%		
German	21.8%	Grad degree:	8.8%				
Irish	11.4%						
English	7.5%						

deed, in Youngstown and Warren, Obama's percentages ran behind those of John Kerry four years earlier, an example of his weakness among white, working-class voters and those of Scots-Irish Appalachian origin. The other part of Ohio—south and west of the industrial belt and including Columbus, Cincinnati and Dayton—was never as heavily unionized and in national elections has tended to vote Republican, much like most of Indiana. This area continued to vote Republican, though Obama carried metro Columbus, the one part of Ohio with significant post-industrial growth, as he did the demographically similar metro Indianapolis. In 2010, Strickland, from southern Ohio himself, fared almost as well in this part of Ohio, but failed to carry Northeast Ohio by a large enough majority to prevail statewide. In the Senate race, Rob Portman actually carried Northeast Ohio narrowly and won the rest of the state 61%-34%.

Presidential politics   From its beginnings, Ohio has been a crucial state in presidential politics, and it has never been more so, with its 20 electoral votes, than in the elections of 2000, 2004 and 2008. Of the large northern states, it has generally been the most Republican, except in 1976, when Jimmy Carter ran well in the Southern-accented counties below U.S. 40 and carried the state by 11,000 votes. (Gerald Ford carried Michigan and Illinois.) No Republican has ever been elected president without carrying Ohio. No Democrat, given recent electoral vote arithmetic, can be sure of winning without it.

Even so, the dynamics of the presidential race in Ohio have been quite different in the past three elections. In 2000, George W. Bush made Ohio a priority state from start to finish, while Al Gore's campaign, looking to opportunities elsewhere, ceased most advertising in mid-October—perhaps its greatest strategic mistake.

2008 Presidential Vote		
Barack Obama (D) 2,940,044	(52%)
John McCain (R) 2,677,820	(47%)

2008 Presidential Primary		
Hillary Clinton (D) 1,259,620	(53%)
Barack Obama (D) 1,055,769	(45%)

2008 Presidential Primary		
John McCain (R) 656,687	(60%)
Mike Huckabee (R)................335,356	(31%)

2004 Presidential Vote		
George W. Bush (R)............2,859,764	(51%)
John Kerry (D) 2,741,165	(49%)

Bush carried Ohio by only 50%-46%. In 2004, both campaigns recognized that Ohio was a major target state. Job losses, especially in manufacturing, seemed to make the atmosphere especially favorable for Democrats. They ran a registration and turnout drive aimed particularly at black neighborhoods in central cities and at university communities. By all measures it was spectacularly successful. The Democratic popular vote margin increased by 60,000 votes in Cleveland's Cuyahoga County, and was up in the counties containing Columbus, Cincinnati, Akron, Toledo, Lorain, Youngstown and Warren and in a five-county cluster around the university town of Athens. But the Bush campaign ran a registration and turnout organization in all 88 counties, which produced a lead of 136,000 votes over John Kerry in the initial count. When the 155,000 provisional ballots were counted, the Bush margin was reduced to 119,000.

In 2008, Ohio was once again a central focus of both campaigns, although Democrat Barack Obama's lead in polls in states like Virginia and Colorado that Bush had won in 2004 made it seem less crucial. Yet both campaign conducted intense organizational efforts. Obama carried the state 52%-47%, winning 198,879 more votes than Kerry had. Republican John McCain got 181,944 fewer votes than Bush, suggesting a decline in Republican turnout and an increase in Democratic turnout compared with 2004. Obama carried union household voters by about the same margin as Kerry had, but he also narrowly won voters in nonunion households. McCain won small margins from both Catholics and Protestants, but not enough to overcome the big Obama margins among those registering no religion. Young voters went 61% for Obama, providing about two-thirds of his popular vote margin. Those with graduate school degrees preferred Obama 54%-44%, a margin much lower than he won among those voters in coastal states.

In 1996, Ohio switched its presidential primary from May to March and voted on the same day as Illinois, Michigan and Wisconsin. But even then, just four weeks after New Hampshire, the race was already over. For the 2000 election, the state legislature voted to move the date to March 7, and Ohio was seriously contested. Bush and Gore won overwhelming victories as they clinched their parties' nominations. In 2004, Ohio held its primary on March 2, with seven other states; Kerry won easily here and elsewhere, and clinched the Democratic nomination nine months before the general election.

In 2008, the Republican contest was effectively over when Ohio voted on March 4. Mike Huckabee remained an active candidate, but McCain beat him 60%-31%, carrying all 88 counties. There was a spirited contest on the Democratic side. Fresh from a series of stunning victories in February, Obama hoped to end Hillary Rodham Clinton's candidacy by beating her in Ohio and Texas. But, casting herself as a fighter for working families, Clinton rallied and won an impressive 53%-45% victory here, which, with a narrower win in Texas, kept her in the race for three more months. Obama carried only five counties, including the central cities of Cleveland, Columbus, Cincinnati and Dayton, and he carried only five of 18 congressional districts. He was particularly weak in white working-class areas—the west side of Cleveland and its close-in suburbs, the Mahoning Valley steel country around Youngstown and Warren, and the Democratic-leaning small industrial counties along the Ohio River. Clinton got as much as 80% of the vote in some counties, evidence of Obama's weakness in Appalachia. That weakness showed up, in muted form, in the general election, when Obama ran behind Kerry's percentages in many of the same areas—not enough to prevent him from carrying Ohio, but enough to prevent him from making the major gains from previous Democratic showings that he did in states like Virginia, North Carolina and Indiana.

Congressional districting

Ohio lost one House seat in the reapportionment following the 2000 census and two seats after the 2010 census, reducing its House delegation to 18 members, the lowest number since the 1820s. In 2001, Republicans had majorities in the legislature and held the governorship, and so had control of the process. It was clear that they could eliminate the seat of 13th District Democratic Rep. Sherrod Brown and imperil the chances of 6th District

112th Congress Lineup	
13 R	5 D
111th Congress Lineup	
10 D	8 R

Democratic Rep. Ted Strickland. But Strickland threatened to run in the 18th District against Republican Rep. Bob Ney, and Brown made it clear that if his seat were eliminated, he would run for governor. Republican Gov. Bob Taft did not want to face a well-financed and politically adept challenger and asked Republican legislators not to target Brown.

The legislature failed to act in 2001, and effectively lost control of the process. Under Ohio law, a statute passed close to the Feb. 21 filing deadline could take effect for the next election only if it got a two-thirds vote in both houses, which meant the Republicans would have to have Democratic votes for their plan. Given the circumstances, the Republicans constructed a pretty ingenious plan. All 11 Republican incumbents got districts very similar to their current ones, as did the two Cleveland Democrats. Every other Democrat got a significantly different district. The incumbent put into the most parlous position was the 17th District's James Traficant. But he was facing trial on bribery charges and had been voting with Republicans on many issues; Democrats were happy to sacrifice him. The 3rd District was made significantly more Republican, but incumbent Democrat Tony Hall was popular enough to win anyway. Strickland was given a district that was much more Democratic, and Brown was left alone. So the Democrats made a deal. They would provide the votes to allow the plan to go into effect immediately and it passed on Jan. 22. After redistricting, the House delegation was 12-6 Republican. Six years later, it was 10-8 Democratic. After the 2010 elections, Republicans had regained the edge with a 13-5 advantage.

In 2011, Republicans were in control of redistricting again. Demographics make it clear that one district must be eliminated in metro Cleveland, and in early 2011, 10th District Democrat Dennis Kucinich was already appealing to his fans nationwide for support in what seemed likely to be a battle with 13th District incumbent Betty Sutton. The Republicans' dilemma was that demographics also make it clear that one of their seats must disappear. They certainly will not want to jeopardize the incumbency of House Speaker John Boehner in the 8th District, and they will presumably want to split the now heavily Democratic central cities of Cincinnati and Columbus in order to avoid creation of a new Democratic district.

Governor

John Kasich (R)

Elected 2010, term expires Jan. 2015, 1st term; b. May 13, 1952, McKees Rocks, PA; home, Westerville; OH St. U., B.A. 1974; Christian; Married (Karen Waldbillig Kasich); 2 children.

Elected Office: OH Senate, 1978-82; U.S. House, 1983-2001.

Professional Career: Admin. asst., OH Sen. Donald Lukens, 1975-77; Managing dir., investment banking division of Lehman Brothers/Barclays Capital, 2001-08; Commentator, FOX News/Heartland with John Kasich, 2001-09; Presidential fellow, OH St. U., 2002-09.

Office: Riffe Center, 30th Floor, 77 South High Street, 43215-6117, 614-466-3555; Web site: governor.ohio.gov/.

Election Results

2010 general	John Kasich (R)	1,889,186	(49%)
	Ted Strickland (D)	1,812,059	(47%)
	Ken Matesz (Lib)	92,116	(2%)
2010 primary	John Kasich (R)	unopposed	

Prior Winning Percentages: House: 1998 (67%); 1996 (64%); 1994 (66%); 1992 (72%); 1990 (72%); 1988 (80%); 1986 (73%); 1984 (70%); 1982 (50%)

The governor of Ohio is John Kasich, a Republican elected in 2010 after defeating incumbent Democratic Gov. Ted Strickland. A former chairman of the U.S. House Budget Committee, Kasich was at the center of his party's budget-balancing confrontations with President Bill Clinton in the 1990s. Shortly after assuming the governorship, he found himself back in the thick of controversy on fiscal matters as he sought to steer Ohio out of recession by calling for drastic reductions in the size and cost of state government.

Kasich (*KAY-sick*) has spent much of his adult life in politics. He grew up the son of a mail carrier in working-class McKees Rocks, Pa., and is of Hungarian, Czech and Croatian ancestry. After graduating from Ohio State University, he worked for a state legislator. In 1978, at age 26, Kasich ran a strenuous door-to-door campaign and a beat a Democratic state senator. He ran for the U.S. House four years later and, with the help of a favorable redistricting plan, ousted Democrat Bob Shamansky. Kasich made his first commotion in the House on the Armed Services Committee, where he was the leading Republican opponent of the B-2 bomber and teamed with California Democrat Ron Dellums in drastically reducing its production. He offended some conservatives by supporting Clinton's assault weapons ban and the 1994 crime bill. He became a devout Christian in 1987 after his parents were killed by a drunk driver and in 1999 wrote a book, *Courage Is Contagious,* profiling Americans who have sought to improve their communities.

Kasich got a seat on the Budget Committee in 1989 and won the ranking Republican spot four years later with the help of Newt Gingrich, R-Ga., then an ascendant figure in the GOP ranks. In that Democratic Congress, he led the Republicans' charge to "cut spending first," which laid the groundwork for the defeat of Clinton's 1993 economic stimulus legislation. He advanced a budget alternative with no tax increases or Social Security cuts, but it did contain means-testing and serious cuts in discretionary spending. In October 1993 and April 1994, he and Democrat Tim Penny of Minnesota put together spending-cut bills that the House narrowly defeated. Kasich did, however, score a few modest wins, including zeroing out the Interstate Commerce Commission. But the serious and detailed work he did then was an indispensable ingredient in his successes in 1995 and 1996 after Republicans regained control of Congress.

Kasich took the Budget chair determined to reduce the size of government and achieved partial success. He scotched the "current services" concept, which assumed that every agency was entitled to past appropriations plus more to serve larger populations plus inflation—a concept that ensured government would always grow faster than the economy. He was determined to start with Republican ideas rather than Clinton administration proposals, and to develop a plan that would plausibly balance the budget in seven years, by 2002. He and other Republicans assumed that Clinton would eventually accept their budgets if they proved stubborn enough, but they underestimated the effectiveness of Clinton's attacks on them for "shutting the government down" for four weeks, including during the holidays. Clinton won the public relations battle in the winter of 1995 and 1996, but Republicans won much of the substance. The final budget for 1996 reduced domestic appropriations by 9%, cutting some $53 billion from discretionary spending over two years. It reduced the deficit to about $100 billion. In 1996, Kasich and the Republicans concentrated on holding ground in the hope of avoiding another budget showdown. Their steadfastness culminated in the Balanced Budget Act of 1997, a sweeping deal that combined tax cuts with reductions in Medicare and Medicaid payments to health care providers, together with added money for higher education assistance and the creation of the State Children's Health Insurance Program for kids living in poverty.

Kasich remained popular in his Columbus-area district, winning re-election eight times. He turned down chances to run for statewide office and to be the GOP vice presidential nominee in 1996. But in 1999, he formed a presidential exploratory committee. "A mailman's kid can change the world," he said ebulliently as he issued an anti-establishment call to return power to the people. But he faced huge obstacles, including fundraising, his often-undisciplined personality and his association with the by-then unpopular Gingrich. He abandoned his bid by July of that year. He left the House in 2001 and took a job as managing director of financial giant Lehman Brothers. He also dabbled in television, hosting a Fox News talk show, *From the Heartland with John Kasich*, until 2007.

But Ohio's dire economic situation during the subsequent recession helped lure Kasich back into politics. Between January 2007 and April 2009, the state lost nearly 300,000 jobs. In June 2009, he announced his challenge to Strickland, who just a year earlier had been popular enough to be considered as a potential running mate for Barack Obama. "We have to face facts: We've drifted in Ohio, and it just hasn't been one political party," Kasich said. He cited the need to balance the state budget as well as cut bureaucracy that he said was hampering business growth, calling Strickland "a nice guy" who lacked the political toughness and skills necessary to "right this ship." With voter unhappiness over the economy particularly high in Ohio, he jumped to an early lead in the polls.

Strickland, however, fought back vigorously. With the help of Bill Clinton, during the spring of 2010 he out-raised not only Kasich but every other Democratic governor facing re-election. The governor and his allies attacked Kasich's congressional voting record, especially his support of free trade agreements that they said had cost the state jobs. They also highlighted his tenure at Lehman Brothers, which had gone bankrupt. News articles described a wealthy lifestyle at odds with Kasich's regular-guy portrayal of himself—his 4,400-square-foot home in suburban Columbus and 2008 tax returns showing an income of $1.4 million, including almost $600,000 from Lehman Brothers. Kasich rebutted such arguments by saying they were evidence of his "hard work." But his lead in the polls shrank by October. In the end, though, he was able to pull out a 49%-47% victory. Strickland took Cuyahoga County, which includes Cleveland, 61%-36%, and Franklin County, which includes Columbus, 53%-44%, along with most of the blue-collar counties in southeastern Ohio that he had earlier represented as a House member. But Kasich prevailed in Hamilton County, which includes Cincinnati, 50%-47%, and dominated the rest of the state.

He immediately made clear his willingness to break with the previous administration. He rejected a passenger rail line through the state that Strickland had pushed, calling it a waste of taxpayer money. He joined other new GOP governors in seeking to curtail the influence of public employee unions, calling for a ban on strikes by teachers and embracing a limit on collective bargaining. But he drew the most controversy with his proposed $55.5 biennial budget, which called for sharing services among agencies, pooling health care costs and reducing prevailing-wage requirements on public construction contracts. It also called for 25% reductions in local government funding in 2012 and 2013. Rather than go on the defensive, an upbeat Kasich sought to sell his approach as being done "with no smoke and mirrors" and promoting growth over the long term. But a litany of Democratic-leaning interest groups attacked him for crippling the state. By mid-March, his approval rating sank to 35%. Polls also showed strong public opposition to his call to limit collective bargaining. With Ohio sure to be a major battleground state in 2012, both parties were watching the unfolding political fallout with great interest.

Senior Senator

Sherrod Brown (D)

Elected 2006, term expires 2012, 1st term; b. Nov. 9, 1952, Mansfield; home, Avon; Yale U., B.A. 1974, OH St. U., M.A. 1979, M.A. 1981; Lutheran; married (Connie Schultz); 4 children.

Elected Office: OH House of Reps., 1974-82; OH secy. of state, 1982-90, U.S. House of Reps., 1993-2007.

Professional Career: Prof., OH St. U. at Mansfield, 1979, 1981, 1991.

DC Office: 713 HSOB, 20510, 202-224-2315; Fax: 202-228-6321; Web site: brown.senate.gov.

State Offices: Cincinnati, 513-684-1021; Cincinnati, 513-684-1021; Cleveland, 216-522-7272; Columbus, 614-469-2083; Columbus, 614-469-2083; Lorain, 440-242-4100; Lorain, 440-242-4100.

Committees: *Agriculture, Nutrition & Forestry:* Commodities, Markets, Trade & Risk Management; Jobs, Rural Economic Growth & Energy Innovation (Chmn); Nutrition, Specialty Crops, Food & Ag Research. *Appropriations:* Agriculture, Rural Development, Food and Drug Administration & Related Agencies; Commerce, Justice, Science & Related Agencies; Department of State, Foreign Operations & Related Programs; Labor, Health & Human Services, Education & Related Agencies; Legislative Branch. *Banking, Housing & Urban Affairs:* Financial Institutions & Consumer Protection (Chmn); Housing, Transportation & Community Development; Security & International Trade & Finance. *Ethics (Select). Veterans' Affairs.*

Group Ratings

	ACLU	ACU	ADA	CFG	AFS	FRC	LCV	ITIC	NTU	COC
2010	93	0	95	0	100	0	100	67	3	9
2009	–	0	100	0	100	–	91	–	4	43

National Journal Ratings

	2010 LIB	—	2010 CONS		2009 LIB	—	2009 CONS
Economic	88%	—	0%		88%	—	0%
Social	65%	—	0%		85%	—	0%
Foreign	47%	—	0%		55%	—	0%
Composite	83%	—	17%		88%	—	12%

Key Votes of the 111th Congress

1. Overturn Ledbetter	Y	5. Pass health care bill	Y	9. Ratify New START	Y
2. Pass $787 billion stimulus	Y	6. Regulate financial firms	Y	10. Confirm Elena Kagan	Y
3. Repeal DC gun laws	N	7. Pass tax cuts for some	Y	11. Stop EPA climate regs	N
4. Confirm Sonia Sotomayor	Y	8. Legalize immigrants' kids	Y	12. Repeal don't ask, tell	Y

Election Results

2006 general	Sherrod Brown (D)	2,257,369	(56%)	($8,937,004)
	Mike DeWine (D)	1,761,037	(47%)	($14,922,228)
2006 primary	Sherrod Brown (D)	583,776	(78%)	
	Merrill Keiser (D)	163,628	(22%)	

Prior Winning Percentages: House: 2004 (67%); 2002 (69%); 2000 (65%); 1998 (62%); 1996 (60%); 1994 (49%); 1992 (53%)

Sherrod Brown is Ohio's senior senator. He is a Democrat first elected to the House in 1992 and to the Senate in 2006. He grew up in Mansfield, the son of a doctor, graduated from Yale in 1974, and won a seat in the state House later that year. Another House member, mistaking the boyish-looking Brown for an intern, gave him a dollar to get her a cup of coffee. He later got master's degrees in education and public administration from the Ohio State University. Brown has spent more than half his life in public office. In 1982, when he was 29, he was elected Ohio secretary of state and worked to increase voter registration and turnout. In 1990, after serving two terms, he lost that office to Republican Bob Taft, who was later elected governor. In 1992, Brown ran for the open 13th District House seat. With solid labor support, he campaigned loud and hard against the North American Free Trade Agreement and championed universal health care. He won 53%-35%.

For many years, Brown has worn a self-designed lapel pin of a canary in a cage, to commemorate underground miners who were at risk back in the days before labor unions and government safety inspections. He had a consistently liberal voting record in the House. On trade, he was one of the most voluble pro-labor and "fair-trade" members from the Great Lakes area, attacking the string of free trade agreements and policies that followed NAFTA in 1993. He sponsored bus trips to Canada for consumers to buy prescription drugs, and he helped to pass the Children's Health Act, which created a new Pediatric Research Institute. In 2003, he helped to secure an increase in Medicaid funding. He urged a ban on the use of antibiotics in farm animals, including penicillin and tetracycline. He called for enforcement of laws against importing goods made with slave labor in China and helped to increase funding for international programs to fight tuberculosis. He has authored the books *Congress From the Inside* and *Myths of Free Trade*. In 2007, his wife, *Cleveland Plain Dealer* columnist Connie Schultz, wrote *And His Lovely Wife: A Memoir From the Woman Beside the Man* about Brown's 2006 campaign for Senate.

Brown long had had his eye on statewide office. In 2005, he at first said he would not challenge two-term Republican Sen. Mike DeWine, which left Iraq War veteran Paul Hackett as the Democratic front-runner. Hackett, who had won some fame after nearly pulling off a major upset in an August 2005 House special election, was an attractive candidate, but there were questions about whether he could raise enough money, and his shoot-from-the-hip style aroused concerns about how he would play statewide. Brown reconsidered and entered the race in October 2005. "The culture of corruption plaguing state and federal government has led our state down the wrong path, and it is time for a change," he said. Although incensed at Brown, Hackett withdrew from the race and Brown breezed to the Democratic nomination.

DeWine, meanwhile, won a lackluster 72% in the GOP primary against two little-known opponents, a reflection of conservative dissatisfaction with his votes on gun control and his role in the bipartisan compromise to end Senate filibusters on federal judicial nominees. DeWine also had the misfortune of running for re-election in an unusually hostile political environment for Ohio Republicans. There was an undertow from various scandals associated with the Republican-controlled state government, though DeWine was not implicated, plus the drag from the unpopular Bush administration. Brown charged that DeWine was a "rubber stamp" for President George W. Bush and tied him to Bush's Iraq policy. He campaigned as a populist progressive, calling for an increase in the minimum wage, denouncing free trade pacts and criticizing the 2003 Medicare prescription drug law as a windfall for the pharmaceutical industry. While Brown sought to nationalize the race, DeWine pursued a more localized approach. He focused on his accomplishments and his ability to work across party lines, hoping to heighten the contrast between himself and the more sharply partisan Brown, whose legislative effectiveness had been limited under Republican rule.

Brown won 56%-44%, dominating nearly all of Ohio's population centers: Cleveland's Cuyahoga County (71%-29%), Toledo's Lucas County (66%-33%), Akron's Summit County (64%-36%), Columbus's Franklin County (59%-41%), and Dayton's Montgomery County (53%-47%). DeWine carried Cincinnati's Hamilton County, but by just 2,000 votes. DeWine carried much of the state west of Interstate 75, where the tone is more Midwestern. Brown carried everything east of Interstate 77, where the coal and steel counties look to Pennsylvania and West Virginia and where his high-profile opposition to free trade resonated.

In the Senate, Brown went on the attack against Bush's troop surge policy in Iraq. "The president calls it a surge, but it's an escalation of the war. It's reprehensible and it's wrong," he told the *Cleveland Jewish News* in 2007. But his major focus has been on trade issues. Early in 2009, Brown fought to include in the Democrats' economic stimulus bill requirements that stimulus money be used on American-made goods. The provision was included in the bill that passed the House and Senate, but it was watered down to allow goods to be purchased from some of America's largest trading partners. "While they call those of us who support labor and environmental standards protectionists, they call it free trade when they protect drug companies and Hollywood films," he said. "Now, I support intellectual-property protections. But if we can protect Hollywood films, we can protect the environment. If we can protect the drug companies, we can protect workers."

He also co-sponsored a bipartisan bill allowing competitors to bring lawsuits against companies that profit from sweatshop goods, and he sought to reinstate the law, repealed in 2006, that allocated penalties in dumping complaints to the complaining companies. In 2009, Brown called on President Barack Obama to take a tougher stance with China on trade, saying the White House should prod the Chinese government to allow its currency to float rather than keep it pegged to the dollar, which would have the effect of raising prices for Chinese goods.

Brown says one of his proudest achievements in the Senate was a bill he passed with the help of the late liberal Sen. Edward Kennedy of Massachusetts. During reauthorization of the Food and Drug Administration in 2009, Brown won passage of an amendment creating incentives for drug companies to produce drugs for diseases common in the developing world. Within weeks of it going into effect, an international aid group reported a flood of new TB drugs on the market.

As a liberal from a coal-producing state—coal provides 90% of Ohio's electricity— Brown is a key swing Democrat on environmental issues. And he was a pivotal player in the 112th Congress (2011-2012) in efforts to regulate carbon emissions thought responsible for climate change. In early 2011, when Obama announced that the Environmental Protection Agency would issue new regulations for carbon emissions, Brown said he would insist on protections for U.S. manufacturers. "I want them to come up with how they're going to do this...and how they're going to, at the same time, make sure it doesn't cause massive job loss and more pollution," Brown told *National Journal*. The new rules would apply mostly to coal-fired plants and oil refineries.

Brown was also a negotiator on the climate change bill that the Senate worked on in 2010 but failed to pass. He was the point man for a bloc of Democrats who dubbed themselves the "Brown Dogs," and refused to support a bill without robust protections for U.S. firms. Brown surprised environmental groups in 2007 when he said nuclear power is safe and should be an option for the country.

On the Banking, Housing and Urban Affairs Committee, Brown worked on the financial industry regulation bill in 2010 and tried unsuccessfully to pass a proposal to limit the size of banks in light of the $700 billion government bailout of financial firms deemed to be "too big to fail." He called for capping banks so they cannot hold more than 2% of the national gross domestic product or 10% of total insured bank deposits nationally. The cap would have affected three large banks: Bank of America, Wells Fargo and JP Morgan Chase. In 2007, he and several other big-state Democrats co-sponsored a bill providing $300 million for housing foreclosure relief.

On another hot issue in 2010, Brown was a proponent for including a government-run insurance option in the Democrats' health care overhaul. When the public option was dropped because it would have sunk the bill, Brown voted for the legislation anyway, saying it at least contained "good insurance reform." Later in the year, he opposed Obama's deal to allow the Bush-era tax cuts to continue even for the top income-earners, but wound up voting for final passage because the legislation also extended unemployment benefits for 13 months. "My principle of not wanting tax cuts for the rich doesn't help an unemployed worker," he told *Politico*.

Brown is up for re-election in 2012, and was being targeted for defeat by Republicans and tea party groups after Ohio Democrats fared poorly in 2010, losing the governor's office, a Senate seat and dropping from 10 to five seats in the U.S. House.

Junior Senator

Rob Portman (R)

Elected 2010, term expires 2016, 1st term; b. Dec. 19, 1955, Cincinnati; home, Terrace Park; Dartmouth Col., B.A. 1979; U. of MI, J.D. 1984; Methodist; Married (Jane); 3 children.

Elected Office: U.S. House, 1993-2005.

Professional Career: U.S. trade rep., 2005-06; dir., Office of Management and Budget, 2006-07; practicing atty., 2007-10.

DC Office: B40D DSOB, 20510, 202-224-3353; Fax: 202-224-9075; Web site: portman.senate.gov.

State Offices: Cincinnati, 513-684-3265; Cleveland, 216-522-7095; Columbus, 614-469-6774, 1-800-205-6446; Toledo, 419-259-3895.

Committees: *Armed Services:* Emerging Threats & Capabilities (RMM); Readiness & Management Support; Strategic Forces. *Budget. Energy & Natural Resources:* Energy; National Parks; Public Lands & Forests. *Homeland Security & Governmental Affairs:* Contracting Oversight (Ad Hoc) (RMM); Federal Financial Management, Government Information, Federal Services & International Security.

Election Results

2010 general	Rob Portman (R)	2,168,742	(57%)	($16,540,629)
	Lee Fisher (D)	1,503,297	(39%)	($6,391,470)
2010 primary	Rob Portman (R)	unopposed		

Prior Winning Percentages: House: 2004 (72%); 2002 (74%); 2000 (74%); 1998 (76%); 1996 (72%); 1994 (77%); 1993 special (70%)

Republican Rob Portman is Ohio's junior senator, elected in 2010 to succeed the retiring George Voinovich, also a Republican. Portman grew up in Cincinnati, where his father in 1960 started a forklift company that eventually employed 300 people. His mother's family owns the Golden Lamb, the oldest inn in Ohio, and his ancestors were Quaker abolitionists active in the Underground Railroad. Portman worked summers at the forklift company, sweeping floors and grinding old paint off trucks. That experience helped convince him that government should provide leeway for the private sector to prosper and create jobs. While at Dartmouth College, Portman took a semester off to work for Cincinnati area Rep. Willis Gradison, a member of the House Ways and Means Committee. After graduating, he worked for Republican George H.W. Bush's 1980 presidential campaign as part of the advance team setting up events—the beginning of a long association with the Bush family. He earned a law degree at the University of Michigan, and then worked for law firms in Washington and Cincinnati.

After Bush was elected president in 1988, Portman went to the White House as a presidential counsel and then was promoted to head the Office of Legislative Affairs. He returned to Cincinnati in 1991, and in January 1993, when Gradison resigned his 2nd District House seat, Portman ran to fill the vacancy. He had help from former first lady Barbara Bush, who made a radio ad for him, and he won the seven-candidate primary with 36% of the vote to 30% for former Rep. Bob McEwen. The special election was anticlimactic; Portman won with 70% of the vote and was easily re-elected from 1994 to 2004.

In the House, he got on the Ways and Means and Budget committees and became known for his fiscal conservatism and his ability to work across the aisle. He co-chaired the National Commission on Restructuring the Internal Revenue Service and won broad support for his repeal of the 3% excise tax on telephone service. He worked with Democrats, notably his current Senate colleague, Ben Cardin of Maryland (then a House member), on issues including pensions, welfare reform, land conservation and drug prevention. He helped revise 401(k) rules to make it easier for small businesses to offer pension plans, but he got nowhere with a 2002 bill to repeal the alternative minimum tax. He also sponsored the bill to create a National Underground Railroad Museum in Cincinnati.

In 2005, President George W. Bush appointed Portman as the U.S. trade representative, in charge of negotiating free trade agreements and representing U.S. interests in global talks on reducing trade barriers. A year later, Bush appointed him director of the Office of Management and Budget, a position that requires immersion in the arcana of federal spending. Portman succeeded in pushing the budget more toward balance and left the agency in 2007. He returned to the Cincinnati area, where he joined a law firm, taught a class at Ohio State University's John Glenn School of Public Affairs, and coached his daughter's soccer team.

Just after Voinovich announced in January 2009 that he would not run for a third term, Portman got into the contest for the seat, saying his focus would be on job creation. The timing of his candidacy did not seem propitious. He had virtually no name recognition beyond the Cincinnati media market. Democratic President Barack Obama had just come to office having carried Ohio and was then widely popular. And soon two Democratic officials with statewide name ID joined the race, Lt. Gov. Lee Fisher and Secretary of State Jennifer Brunner. Polls showed Portman trailing both of them. Unfazed, Portman campaigned around the state in blue jeans and a windbreaker, put out a six-point jobs program and cheerfully opposed the Democrats' $787 billion stimulus bill and their health care overhaul. Portman raised serious money, $16.5 million, and he also profited from the fractious Democratic primary in May 2010, which Fisher won, 56%-44%.

Fisher derided Portman's long friendship with the Bush family, telling *The Columbus Dispatch*, "Rob Portman had his hands on the steering wheel as George W. Bush drove us off the cliff and into the deepest economic ditch in most of our lives." But Fisher had little money—much of the $6.4 million he raised was spent on the primary—and his position as Gov. Ted Strickland's "jobs czar" in 2007 and 2008 proved a liability rather than an asset. Portman asserted that Ohio lost 400,000 jobs while he held the post. Portman called for a one-year suspension of the payroll tax, and he fended off criticism of his work as trade representative by saying he would make enforcement of trade laws a high priority and added it to his six-point economic plan. Portman was not a particular favorite of tea party activists, but they didn't campaign against him.

By October, this race was off everyone's list of competitive contests. Fisher was far behind in the polls and out of money. On Election Day, Portman won 57%-39%. He carried 82 of 88 counties and ran even in usually Democratic northeast Ohio.

FIRST DISTRICT

Steve Chabot (R)

Elected 2010, 8th term; b. Jan. 22, 1953, Cincinnati; home, Cincinnati; Col. of William & Mary, B.A. 1975; Northern KY U., J.D. 1978. ; Catholic; Married (Donna); 2 children.

Elected Office: Cincinnati City Cncl., 1985-90; Hamilton Cnty. Commission, 1990-94; U.S. House, 1995-2009.

Professional Career: Teacher, St. Joseph School, 1975-76; practicing atty., 1978-94.

DC Office: 2351 RHOB, 20515, 202-225-2216; Fax: 202-225-3012; Web site: chabot.house.gov.

State Offices: Cincinnati, 513-684-2723.

Committees: *Foreign Affairs:* Asia & the Pacific; Middle East & South Asia (Chmn). *Judiciary:* Constitution; Intellectual Property, Competition & the Internet. *Small Business:* Economic Growth, Tax and Capital Access.

Election Results

2010 general	Steve Chabot (R)	103,770	(51%)	($2,040,665)
	Steve Driehaus (D)	92,672	(46%)	($1,930,201)
2010 primary	Steve Chabot (R)	unopposed		

Prior Winning Percentages: House: 2006 (52%); 2004 (60%); 2002 (65%); 2000 (53%); 1998 (53%); 1996 (54%); 1994 (56%)

Population		Race/Ethnicity		Work	
Pop. 2010:	598,699	White:	63.4%	Private:	83.2%
Change since 2000:	Down 5.1%	Black:	30.4%	Government:	11.7%
Urban:	94.8%	Hispanic:	2.6%	Self-employed:	5.1%
Rural:	5.2%	Asian:	1.3%	Blue collar:	20.8%
Area size:	420 sq. mi.	Native Am.:	0.2%	White collar:	60.0%
		Hawaiian:	0.1%	Khaki collar:	0.0%
Age		Two+ races:	1.9%	Other:	19.1%
Median age:	36.3 yrs.				
More than 65 yrs:	13.1%	*Ancestry*		Median income:	$42,504
Less than 18 yrs:	24.0%	German	25.0%	Median Home Value:	$134,600
		Irish	10.9%		
Education		English	5.5%	**Military Veterans**	
H.S. grad:	84.5%			% of Pop:	9.2%
College grad:	24.2%				
Grad degree:	8.6%				

Cincinnati Suburbs

From its seven hills, Cincinnati looks down on the curves of the Ohio River. It was Ohio's first major metropolis and a heavily German beehive of riverboats and sausage factories, known in the 1850s as Porkopolis. In the 19th century, Cincinnati was the nation's fourth-largest city and at the outbreak of the Civil War, it was a chief destination for slaves on the Underground Railroad. The city has long given off an air of the recent past. Mark Twain once said he'd like to be there

2008 Presidential Vote		
Barack Obama (D) 165,843	(55%)
John McCain (R) 134,715	(44%)
2004 Presidential Vote		
George Bush (R) 152,441	(51%)
John Kerry (D) 149,180	(49%)
Cook Partisan Voting Index: D+1		

for the apocalypse because everything in Cincinnati is 10 years behind. Growing slowly over many decades, Cincinnati's long-settled good looks and urbanity are somehow consistent with its natural terrain: the bottomlands along the river, the hills and rolling terrain above. In the middle of Cincinnati is Mill Creek, lined with factories. On the hills to the west, above the restored Union Terminal housing several museums, are the modest streetcar suburbs of the 19th century and the early years of the 20th. On Mount Adams and toward the northeast are a string of affluent neighborhoods, with stately mansions like the William Howard Taft house, and the comfortable Tudors and colonials of the 20th century bourgeoisie—Reform Jewish as well as WASP and German. Families have lived for generations in the same neighborhoods, though typically not in ethnic enclaves.

Cincinnati was the site of great innovations: the first iron suspension bridge, built in 1867, which connects Cincinnati to northern Kentucky and was designed by John Roebling, who later built the Brooklyn Bridge; and, the first baseball team, the Red Stockings, who began playing in 1869. It spawned not flashy but solid industries, including America's biggest concentration of machine tool makers, the industry now a fraction of its once-robust size, and the Procter & Gamble soap business, with its twin-towered headquarters at the edge of downtown.

Downtown Cincinnati's spruced-up Fountain Square shows off well-maintained skyscrapers of the past plus a revival of museums, arts institutions and retail shops. Its first-class restaurants still attract a dressy clientele. Old ethnic neighborhoods on the west side, crowded with brick row houses on steep hills, keep their thick local accents and special local foods, from German sauerbrauten to Cincinnati chili. Baseball's career-hitting (and, alas, sports-betting) leader Pete Rose grew up here. Yet the city has faced tough times. Crime is a problem and there has been flight to the suburbs. With fewer recent immigrants than comparable northern cities, Cincinnati saw its population decline in the decade since 2000, falling 10%, to 297,000 people, in 2010. But it's not as reliant on manufacturing as other Midwestern cities, Greater Cincinnati experienced a relatively robust recovery from the 2007-09 recession, thanks to an economy based on consumer products and finance, according to a 2010 Brookings Institution study.

The 1st Congressional District of Ohio includes almost all of Cincinnati, except for parts of its affluent eastern edge, plus most of the middle-class suburbs that cling to the woody hills west of Interstate 71 and south of I-275. It covers the southwest quarter of Butler County plus the western parts of Hamilton County all the way to the Indiana border, including North Bend, the home of President William Henry Harrison. City elections here were for years competitive between oldline Republicans and a combination of Democrats and Charterites (the latter started by Charles Taft, liberal brother of GOP Sen. Robert Taft Sr. and great-uncle of recent Republican Gov. Bob Taft). As its population has declined, Cincinnati has become noticeably more Democratic, but the suburbs, which now cast more votes than the city, remain heavily Republican. This makes the 1st a closely divided district. Republican George W. Bush carried the district with just 51% of the vote in 2000 and 2004 presidential elections and Democratic nominee Barack Obama won it with 55% in 2008.

Steve Chabot (R)

The congressman from the 1st District of Ohio is Republican Steve Chabot, who won his old House seat back by beating Democrat Steve Driehaus in 2010. Driehaus had ousted Chabot in 2008.

Chabot grew up in the Cincinnati area and graduated from La Salle High School, where he says he "got the bug" for politics after serving on the student council. Then came the Watergate scandal. "A lot of people my age got turned off from politics because of all that," Chabot said in an interview with *National Journal.* "I wasn't that way. I thought we needed honest people in government." He went on to earn a degree in history and physical education from the College of William & Mary. He then took night classes at Northern Kentucky University while teaching at an elementary school during the day. Chabot won a seat on the Cincinnati City Council, where he served for four years. He followed that with a four-year stint on the Hamilton County Commission. During that time, Chabot said, he tried to find innovative ways to reduce the cost of government, such as using jail inmates for public service.

In 1994, he was among the conservative Republicans who successfully ran for Congress and ended 40 years of Democratic control of the House. In his 14 years on Capitol Hill, Chabot took principled and politically risky stands opposing federal spending on projects in his district and was a conservative leader on social issues, particularly opposition to abortion rights. In 2003, he helped enact a ban on "partial-birth" abortions, and he also pushed a bill to prevent minors from crossing state lines to get abortions. Chabot was a House manager during the 1998 impeachment of President Bill Clinton. In retrospect, Chabot said, he is most proud of his work in fighting wasteful spending.

Chabot lost his seat in 2008, when Driehaus defeated him by 5 percentage points. He had been spoiling for a rematch since. In the 2010 campaign, Chabot criticized the incumbent for voting with the Democratic majority on President Barack Obama's health care initiative and the $787 billion economic-stimulus package. "I'm for less government, restraining the growth of government and spending. I'm for people having personal control of their own lives," Chabot said. For his part, Driehaus defended the work that Democrats have done during the first two years of the Obama administration, including the health care overhaul, which he called "the right thing" to do. On the stump, he asked voters to give Obama and the Democrats more time to implement change. In one ad, he said: "People are going to work. We're investing in jobs of the future." But Driehaus had trouble generating much voter excitement for his re-election, and in October, the Democratic Congressional Campaign Committee pulled the plug on further spending on television ads for him. Both candidates raised about $2 million each. But Chabot won, 51.5% to 46% for Driehaus.

SECOND DISTRICT

Jean Schmidt (R)

Elected Aug. 2005, 3rd full term; b. Nov. 29, 1951, Cincinnati; home, Miami Township; U. of Cincinnati, B.A. 1974; Catholic; married (Peter); 1 child.

Elected Office: Miami Township Bd. of Trustees, 1989-2000; OH House of Reps., 2000-04.

Professional Career: Branch mgr., Midwest Savings Assoc., 1971-78; Fitness instructor, Elaine Powers, 1984-86; Teacher, 1986-90; President, Right to Life of Greater Cincinnati, 2004-05.

DC Office: 2464 RHOB, 20515, 202-225-3164; Fax: 202-225-1992; Web site: house.gov/schmidt.

State Offices: Cincinnati, 513-791-0381; Portsmouth, 877-354-1440.

Committees: *Agriculture:* General Farm Commodities & Risk Management; Nutrition & Horticulture (Chmn). *Foreign Affairs:* Europe and Eurasia; Western Hemisphere. *Transportation & Infrastructure:* Aviation; Highways & Transit; Railroads, Pipelines & Hazardous Materials.

Group Ratings

	ACLU	ACU	ADA	CFG	AFS	FRC	LCV	ITIC	NTU	COC
2010	13	100	5	100	0	100	0	0	88	75
2009	–	100	0	91	22	–	21	–	86	71

National Journal Ratings

	2010 LIB — 2010 CONS		2009 LIB — 2009 CONS	
Economic	3%	— 97%	20%	— 80%
Social	0%	— 85%	17%	— 83%
Foreign	0%	— 88%	32%	— 67%
Composite	6%	— 95%	23%	— 77%

Key Votes of the 111th Congress

1. Overturn Ledbetter	N	5. Bar federal abortion funds	Y	9. Stop detainee transfers	Y
2. Pass $820 billion stimulus	N	6. Pass health care bill	N	10. Legalize immigrants' kids	N
3. Let guns in national parks	Y	7. Regulate financial firms	N	11. Repeal don't ask, tell	N
4. Pass cap-and-trade	N	8. Pass tax cuts for some	N	12. Limit campaign funds	N

Election Results

2010 general	Jean Schmidt (R)	139,027	(58%)	($1,050,601)
	Surya Yalamanchili (D)	82,431	(35%)	($253,348)
	Marc Johnston (Lib)	16,259	(7%)	
2010 primary	Jean Schmidt (R)	36,214	(62%)	
	C. Michael Kilburn (R)	13,007	(22%)	
	Debbi Alsfelder (R)	5,235	(9%)	
	Tim Martz (R)	4,225	(7%)	

Prior Winning Percentages: 2008 (45%), 2006 (50%), 2005 special (52%)

Population		Race/Ethnicity		Work	
Pop. 2010:	673,873	White:	89.7%	Private:	83.6%
Change since 2000:	Up 6.8%	Black:	4.4%	Government:	10.6%
Urban:	73.0%	Hispanic:	1.8%	Self-employed:	5.7%
Rural:	27.0%	Asian:	2.2%	Blue collar:	19.5%
Area size:	2,632 sq. mi.	Native Am.:	0.2%	White collar:	65.0%
		Hawaiian:	0.0%	Khaki collar:	0.1%
Age		Two+ races:	1.5%	Other:	15.4%
Median age:	38.1 yrs.				
More than 65 yrs:	12.9%	*Ancestry*		Median income:	$56,801
Less than 18 yrs:	24.4%	German	23.8%	Median Home Value:	$167,600
		Irish	13.6%		
Education		English	8.5%	**Military Veterans**	
H.S. grad:	88.4%			% of Pop:	9.7%
College grad:	33.2%				
Grad degree:	12.6%				

East Cincinnati, Suburbs

For a long time, one of the most Republican urban areas in the nation has been the Cincinnati suburbs. Back in the 1850s, when Harriet Beecher Stowe wrote *Uncle Tom's Cabin* there, Cincinnati was an island of German, pro-Union, Republican sentiment in a Southern, Democratic, pro-slavery region. Later, Cincinnati attracted fewer southern and eastern European immigrants than Great Lakes industrial cities like Cleveland, Detroit and Chicago. The city's

2008 Presidential Vote		
John McCain (R)	201,215	(59%)
Barack Obama (D)	137,804	(40%)
2004 Presidential Vote		
George Bush (R)	211,489	(64%)
John Kerry (D)	119,139	(36%)
Cook Partisan Voting Index:	R+13	

ethnic character and political preference, like its physical appearance, remained pretty well fixed until very recently. Many descendents of the Appalachians here are Republicans, from Civil War Republican counties in the hills. Democratic constituencies here never got very large. Economically it was never a strong union town and culturally it is conservative. Cincinnati is the only million-plus-population area that has voted at least 50% Republican in every presidential election since 1992.

Ohio's 2nd Congressional District includes the eastern edge of Cincinnati and the boutiques of Hyde Park Square, a more transient area than the west-side neighborhoods; the mostly affluent suburban subdivisions of eastern Hamilton County; and the fast-growing suburbs of Clermont County and southern Warren County. In once-rural Clermont, Miami Township has become a bedroom community and a center of commercial development along the Interstate 275 Loop. The district also ranges farther east on the Ohio River, all the way to the old industrial city of Portsmouth and the hills of rural Pike County, where the big issue is the ongoing cleanup of the Portsmouth Gaseous Diffusion plant and the uranium enrichment plant in Piketon. These are distinctly different places—"the richest to the poorest, and everything in between," as one area mayor put it. The metropolitan parts of the district, with roughly 80% of the people, are mostly affluent and Republican. The counties farther east are less well off, with most of the old factories gone and with pockets of high unemployment and poverty. They are close to marginal in most elections, and Pike County has a Democratic tradition. Portsmouth, on the district's eastern fringe, has a depressed economy and an Appalachian frame of mind. Overall, this is a very Republican district with a tiny minority population. John McCain carried the 59%-40% in 2008.

Jean Schmidt (R)

The congresswoman from the 2nd District is Jean Schmidt, who won an August 2005 special election after incumbent Rob Portman, now a U.S. senator, resigned to become U.S. trade representative. She grew up on her family's farm in Clermont County. Her father, a well-known local banker, owned a car racing team and she spent time on the racing circuit. "I'd rather smell ethanol than Chanel No. 5," Schmidt once told the *Cincinnati Enquirer*. An avid runner, she has competed in marathons and continues to run in long-distance races. In 2008 and 2009, she finished first among women members of Congress in an annual charity race for lawmakers, executive branch officials and the media. Schmidt graduated from the University of Cincinnati and entered public life as an anti-abortion rights activist. She served 10 years as a Miami Township trustee and two terms in the state House. In 2004, she lost a state Senate primary by 22 votes.

The early favorite in the 2005 special election contest was Pat DeWine, the son of then-U.S. Sen. and current Ohio Attorney General Mike DeWine. He had the highest name identification and the most lavish financing, with the help of his father and the Cincinnati business establishment. But his election the previous November as Hamilton County commissioner led many to believe that he was too eager to move up the political ladder. He had also recently divorced his wife, the mother of their three small children, after having an affair with a business lobbyist. The other leading contenders were former Rep. Bob McEwen, who became a Washington-based lobbyist after he was defeated in 1992, and state Rep. Tom Brinkman. The contest demonstrated the perils of negative campaigning. As DeWine's support dropped, he ran negative ads against McEwen. The Club for Growth ran ads against Schmidt for backing Gov. Bob Taft's tax increases. Conservatives ended up dividing their votes among McEwen, Brinkman and Schmidt. With a strong base in Clermont County, Schmidt was the surprise winner with 31%, to 26% for McEwen and 20% for Brinkman. DeWine was a distant fourth with 12%.

Democrats nominated attorney and Iraq war veteran Paul Hackett for what was expected to be a mere formality given the Republican tilt of the district. Instead it became a harbinger of the 2006 midterm elections nationally. Hackett raised substantial money on the Internet from liberal activists and called President George W. Bush a "chicken hawk" for his failure to serve in the Vietnam War while attacking Bush's decision to invade Iraq. Schmidt squeaked to a 52%-48% victory. Her entire margin of victory came from Clermont County, which cast 26% of the vote and where she led by nearly 5,000 votes. She won just 51% in Republican Hamilton County, which cast 43% of the vote, and 58% in Warren County. It was a wake-up call for Republicans, who went on to lose majority control of Congress that year.

As a junior member of the House, Schmidt gained much attention, not all of it positive. In November 2005, after Marine veteran John Murtha had again called for an end to involvement in Iraq, Schmidt said that a local Marine had advised her to stay there and added, "He also asked me to send Congressman Murtha a message, that cowards cut and run. Marines never do." Across the aisle, Democrats exploded in shouts and boos. Schmidt, who had apparently been oblivious to Murtha's military background, quickly retracted her comments and apologized. She was dubbed "Mean Jean" in the blogosphere and local Democrats drove a "billboard on wheels" across the district reading "Shame on you, Jean Schmidt. Stop attacking veterans." Then, the *Cincinnati Enquirer* reported that two columns Schmidt authored contained passages identical to those in columns written by Ohio colleague Deborah Pryce and by an Ohio highway patrol official.

When the 2006 election rolled around, McEwen ran again in the primary, calling for troop withdrawals in Iraq. Schmidt claimed that McEwen was a resident of Virginia and had voted illegally in Ohio. She won the primary by an unimpressive 48%-43%. Without her 4,000-vote lead in Clermont County, she would have lost. Democrats nominated physician Victoria Wulsin, who was not expected to pose a serious challenge. But Murtha stepped in to campaign for her and Wulsin ran the "cowards" speech in a television ad. Schmidt got more unwelcome attention when she said that it might be a good idea to send nuclear waste from around the world to a storage facility in Pike County. (Later, in May 2007, she introduced a bill to prohibit permanent storage of waste there.) Schmidt won, but only after the three weeks it took to count absentee and provisional ballots. The outcome was 50%-49%. She carried Clermont County by 7,900 votes and Warren County by 5,700 votes, but lost Hamilton County by nearly 5,800 votes.

She faced serious competition in 2008 as well. Wulsin was again the Democratic nominee and Murtha came in again to campaign for her. Four weeks before the election, Schmidt was treated for broken ribs and vertebrae after being struck by a hit-and-run driver while she was out running. With help from national Democrats, Wulsin outspent Schmidt, but the incumbent won 45%-37%, with 18% for independent candidate David Krikorian, who had pressed Schmidt to support a resolution condemning Turks for the genocide of Armenians in the Ottoman Empire.

In the closing days of the race, Krikorian distributed a flier claiming Schmidt accepted "blood money" from the Turkish government for opposing the resolution. Schmidt filed a complaint against him with Ohio's Election Commission, and ultimately, the panel formally reprimanded Krikorian for making false statements. She later filed the defamation lawsuit against Krikorian in state court seeking damages.

In 2010, Krikorian challenged Schmidt, this time as a Democrat, but lost the May primary 41%-37% to Surya Yalamanchili, a Procter & Gamble brand manager. Schmidt raised and spent nearly four times as much as Yalamanchili. In the heavily Republican year, Schmidt won in November 58%-35%.

In January 2011, Schmidt became chairman of the Agriculture Subcommittee on Nutrition and Horticulture, with jurisdiction over food stamps, nutrition, fruits and vegetables, honey and bees, seed adulteration and insect pests.

THIRD DISTRICT

Mike Turner (R)

Elected 2002, 5th term; b. Jan. 11, 1960, Dayton; home, Dayton; OH N. U., B.A. 1982, Case Western Reserve U., J.D. 1985, U. of Dayton, M.B.A. 1992; Protestant; married (Lori); 2 children.

Elected Office: Dayton mayor, 1993-2001.

Professional Career: Practicing atty.

DC Office: 2454 RHOB, 20515, 202-225-6465; Fax: 202-225-6754; Web site: turner.house.gov.

State Offices: Dayton, 937-225-2843; Wilmington, 937-383-8931.

Committees: *Armed Services:* Air & Land Forces; Strategic Forces (Chmn). *Oversight & Government Reform:* National Security, Homeland Defense & Foreign Operations.

Group Ratings

	ACLU	ACU	ADA	CFG	AFS	FRC	LCV	ITIC	NTU	COC
2010	13	82	10	75	13	93	10	33	79	88
2009	–	72	35	63	44	–	43	–	55	80

National Journal Ratings

	2010 LIB	—	2010 CONS		2009 LIB	—	2009 CONS
Economic	33%	—	66%		39%	—	61%
Social	38%	—	62%		33%	—	65%
Foreign	21%	—	77%		26%	—	68%
Composite	31%	—	69%		34%	—	66%

Key Votes of the 111th Congress

1. Overturn Ledbetter	N	5. Bar federal abortion funds	Y	9. Stop detainee transfers	Y
2. Pass $820 billion stimulus	N	6. Pass health care bill	N	10. Legalize immigrants' kids	N
3. Let guns in national parks	Y	7. Regulate financial firms	N	11. Repeal don't ask, tell	N
4. Pass cap-and-trade	N	8. Pass tax cuts for some	N	12. Limit campaign funds	N

Election Results

2010 general	Mike Turner (R)	152,629	(68%)	($764,224)
	Joe Roberts (D)	71,455	(32%)	($7,332)
2010 primary	Mike Turner (R)	50,317	(86%)	
	Rene Oberer (R)	8,267	(14%)	

Prior Winning Percentages: 2008 (63%), 2006 (59%), 2004 (62%), 2002 (59%)

Population		Race/Ethnicity		Work	
Pop. 2010:	640,899	White:	77.6%	Private:	81.6%
Change since 2000:	Up 1.6%	Black:	16.6%	Government:	13.3%
Urban:	84.7%	Hispanic:	1.9%	Self-employed:	4.9%
Rural:	15.3%	Asian:	1.8%	Blue collar:	22.1%
Area size:	1,610 sq. mi.	Native Am.:	0.2%	White collar:	60.3%
		Hawaiian:	0.0%	Khaki collar:	0.2%
Age		Two+ races:	1.8%	Other:	17.4%
Median age:	38.6 yrs.				
More than 65 yrs:	14.3%	*Ancestry*		Median income:	$47,775
Less than 18 yrs:	23.8%	German	20.9%	Median Home Value:	$133,300
		Irish	11.0%		
Education		English	8.0%	**Military Veterans**	
H.S. grad:	88.4%			% of Pop:	11.9%
College grad:	25.5%				
Grad degree:	10.2%				

Southwest Ohio; Dayton, Kettering

The underestimated Dayton can hold its own against bigger cities for fostering creative American genius in commerce. It has strong traditions of tinkering and innovation, practical organization and mechanical dreaming, as well as small-town neighborliness. Just south of the old National Road that spans the Midwest was the home of James Ritty, who in 1879 invented the cash register, that indispensable instrument of mass retail trade that led to the establishment

2008 Presidential Vote
John McCain (R) 170,431 (52%)
Barack Obama (D) 156,611 (47%)

2004 Presidential Vote
George Bush (R) 178,323 (55%)
John Kerry (D) 148,978 (46%)

Cook Partisan Voting Index: R+5

in 1884 of the National Cash Register company. Tom Watson Sr., an employee of NCR owner John Henry Patterson, feuded with Patterson and went off in a huff to found IBM. In Dayton in the 1890s, Wilbur and Orville Wright experimented with kites and gliders and constructed the first wind tunnel in the world and the first heavier-than-air flying machine, which they took to windy Kitty Hawk, N.C., for a test flight in 1903. A few years later, Dayton's Charles Kettering invented the automatic starter for cars and became one of the leaders of the budding automobile industry. More recently, in 1995, Dayton was a most unlikely but effective player on the international stage. It was the site of the international peace negotiations that led to the agreement among countries to stop the bloody fighting in the former Yugoslavia. The 21-day summit took place at nearby Wright-Patterson Air Force Base. "From the time we landed at the airport," wrote U.S. negotiator Richard Holbrooke, "until the time we left, we felt that we were in a community that was literally praying for us. People were lighting candles in their windows, there were signs all over the airport and on the byways. That would never have happened in New York or in Washington."

In the 1970s and 1980s, Dayton's economy sputtered. General Motors, then the area's largest employer, was in trouble and other manufacturing jobs were dwindling. The Wright-Patterson base, where the Air Force analyzes intelligence about foreign aerospace and weapons technology, became the biggest employer. Dayton entered another period of economic gloom in 2008 and 2009 as the national economy soured. DHL closed an air cargo hub at the Wilmington Air Park in Clinton County, costing the region 10,000 jobs. Then, in a major psychological and economic blow for the city, NCR announced in June 2009 that it was leaving after 125 years, taking away Dayton's last *Fortune* 500 company and the 1,300 jobs it provided. The economic picture brightened in 2010, though. General Electric Co. in November announced plans for a $51 million research and development center to develop advanced electric power systems for aircraft, ships and hybrid automobiles.

The 3rd Congressional District of Ohio includes most of Dayton and all but the northeast corner of Montgomery County. It takes in the northern half of fast-growing suburban Warren County, and the mostly rural and small town Clinton and Highland counties. Republican George W. Bush won 55% of the vote in the 2004 presidential election, and GOP nominee John McCain got 52% in 2008. Democratic Gov. Ted Strickland beat Republican John Kasich in Montgomery by just 161 votes in 2010, but Kasich got more than 60% of the vote in Clinton and Highland and more than 68% in Warren.

Mike Turner (R)

The congressman from the 3rd District is Mike Turner, a Republican first elected in 2002. A former Dayton mayor, he has shown a stronger interest in urban issues than most House Republicans while taking a more of a party-line approach on defense and other matters.

Turner grew up in Dayton, where his father worked 42 years for General Motors. He graduated from Ohio Northern University, Case Western law school and the University of Dayton business school and became a corporate lawyer. In 1993, at age 33, he narrowly defeated a scandal-tainted Democratic incumbent to win the first of two terms as Dayton mayor. He narrowly lost a bid for re-election in 2001. Ohio and national Republican leaders recruited him to challenge 3rd District Democratic Rep. Tony Hall, who had served 12 terms but was vulnerable after post-2000 census redistricting made his turf considerably more Republican. In early 2002, Turner announced he was running for Congress, the same day the Ohio Legislature passed their redistricting plan. A week later, President George W. Bush nominated Hall as ambassador to the United Nations' Food and Agriculture Organization in Rome.

In the Republican primary, Turner had fierce opposition from newspaper publisher Roy Brown, grandson and son of former U.S. Reps. Clarence Brown and Clarence Brown Jr., who had represented the neighboring 7th District from 1938 to 1982. Brown spent $1.3 million of his own money in the primary, largely on ads attacking Turner's record on taxes and lambasting him for being insufficiently conservative. Brown owned 10 newspapers in the 3rd District, and Turner contended that Brown's campaign guided his newspapers' coverage of the race. Then, a few days before the primary, the Ohio Election Commission ruled that Brown violated state law with false statements in a televised ad. Voters evidently took the same view. Turner beat Brown 80%-14%. The general election was comparatively sedate. The Democratic nominee was Rick Carne, Hall's chief of staff. He had little support from the national party but he raised nearly $600,000, with help from a local appearance by Dayton native Martin Sheen, who played President Bartlet on popular *The West Wing* television series. Turner won 59%-41%.

In the House, Turner has been generally supportive of his party but is one of the more moderate members of the Ohio delegation. After the GOP takeover of the House in 2010, he became chairman of the Armed Services Committee's Strategic Forces Subcommittee, which oversees the nation's nuclear arsenal, military satellites, the Pentagon's intelligence programs (including Wright-Patterson's center) and missile defense. In 2009, he was strongly critical of the Obama administration's plans to cut funding for missile defense. After the president signed the New START nuclear arms treaty with Russia in February 2011, Turner said he would continue to pursue tougher missile defense options even in the face of potential Russian objections. He also chairs the North Atlantic Treaty Organization (NATO) Parliamentary Assembly, the inter-parliamentary organization of legislators from the countries of the North Atlantic Alliance.

Earlier, he worked successfully to keep Wright-Patterson off the base-closing list and to expand its jobs, including a new center for research on fixed-wing aircraft. Turner also collaborated with Rep. Jane Harman, D-Calif., to review the military's handling of sexual assault charges. To address the nation's budget problems, he told reporters in February 2011 that "everything needs to be on the table," including possible changes to the military's health care program. In 2007, he was successful in getting the Office of the Architect of the Capitol to return the word "God" to the official certificates with flags that are sent to constituents.

Turner formed a caucus of former mayors serving in Congress to focus on urban issues. He has worked on House-passed legislation to accelerate clean-up of polluted brownfields by making it easier for communities to apply for federal grants as well as a separate bill providing business tax credits for cleanups. He also promoted the kind of public-private partnerships that he used for economic development in Dayton. In March 2009, Turner was one of only seven House Republicans to support a bill that would give bankruptcy judges the power to restructure the terms of home mortgages. Then-Minority Leader John Boehner, R-Ohio, called the bill "just the worst idea in the world." That same year, he joined Democrats in backing authorization of the State Children's Health Insurance Program, which covers numerous low-income children in cities, and to overhaul food safety laws.

Turner seems entrenched in what had been a safe Democratic district. In 2008, Ohio Democrats made an issue of the fact that he had not disclosed a five-year business relationship between his wife, Lori Turner, and home builder Tom Peebles, who had contributed to Turner's campaign. Turner asked for a ruling from the House Committee on Standards of Official Conduct and the panel concluded he did not have to disclose the relationship between Peebles and his wife. Turner won 63%-37%. In 2010, he received an all-time best of 69% of the vote.

FOURTH DISTRICT

Jim Jordan (R)

Elected 2006, 3rd term; b. Feb. 17, 1964, Troy; home, Urbana; U. of WI, B.A. 1986, OH St. U., M.Ed. 1991, Capital U., J.D. 2002; Christian; married (Polly); 4 children.

Elected Office: OH House of Reps., 1994-2000; OH Senate, 2000-06.

Professional Career: Asst. wrestling coach, OH St. U., 1987-95; Wrestling camp coach, clinician, 1987-2006.

DC Office: 1524 LHOB, 20515, 202-225-2676; Fax: 202-226-0577; Web site: jordan.house.gov.

State Offices: Findlay, 419-423-3210; Lima, 419-999-6455; Mansfield, 419-522-5757.

Committees: *Judiciary:* Constitution; Intellectual Property, Competition & the Internet. *Oversight & Government Reform:* Federal Workforce, U.S. Postal Service & Labor Policy; Regulatory Affairs, Stimulus Oversight & Government Spending (Chmn).

Group Ratings

	ACLU	ACU	ADA	CFG	AFS	FRC	LCV	ITIC	NTU	COC
2010	13	100	5	100	0	100	0	0	91	75
2009	–	100	0	99	0	–	0	–	93	73

National Journal Ratings

	2010 LIB	—	2010 CONS	2009 LIB	—	2009 CONS
Economic	0%	—	97%	9%	—	89%
Social	0%	—	85%	0%	—	93%
Foreign	0%	—	88%	0%	—	75%
Composite	5%	—	95%	9%	—	91%

Key Votes of the 111th Congress

1. Overturn Ledbetter	N	5. Bar federal abortion funds	Y	9. Stop detainee transfers	Y
2. Pass $820 billion stimulus	N	6. Pass health care bill	N	10. Legalize immigrants' kids	N
3. Let guns in national parks	Y	7. Regulate financial firms	N	11. Repeal don't ask, tell	N
4. Pass cap-and-trade	N	8. Pass tax cuts for some	N	12. Limit campaign funds	N

Election Results

2010 general	Jim Jordan (R)	146,029	(71%)	($850,292)
	Doug Litt (D)	50,533	(25%)	($8,230)
	Donald Kissick (Lib)	7,708	(4%)	
2010 primary	Jim Jordan (R)	unopposed		

Prior Winning Percentages: 2008 (65%), 2006 (60%)

Population		Race/Ethnicity		Work	
Pop. 2010:	632,771	White:	90.3%	Private:	82.6%
Change since 2000:	Up 0.3%	Black:	5.1%	Government:	11.5%
Urban:	58.6%	Hispanic:	2.0%	Self-employed:	5.7%
Rural:	41.4%	Asian:	0.7%	Blue collar:	32.8%
Area size:	4,642 sq. mi.	Native Am.:	0.2%	White collar:	50.2%
		Hawaiian:	0.0%	Khaki collar:	0.0%
Age		Two+ races:	1.6%	Other:	17.0%
Median age:	38.7 yrs.				
More than 65 yrs:	14.4%	*Ancestry*		Median income:	$45,432
Less than 18 yrs:	24.1%	German	28.3%	Median Home Value:	$117,800
		Irish	10.7%		
Education		USA	8.1%	**Military Veterans**	
H.S. grad:	86.9%			% of Pop:	11.2%
College grad:	15.6%				
Grad degree:	5.7%				

Central Ohio; Mansfield, Lima

Central Ohio looks mostly like farmland to the traveler. Yet this is manufacturing country, indeed one of America's premier manufacturing areas, where the economy is based on factories in small towns and on rural highways. These places seem far from anywhere important, yet are on one of the great east-west rail and highway routes that cross the country. They seem old-fashioned and rooted in an older technological time, with some exceptions. Wapakoneta is the hometown of Neil Armstrong, the first man on the moon, and has the Neil Armstrong Air and Space Museum. Politically, this crossroads on the flat limestone plains of northern Ohio is one of the Republican heartlands of the United States. It has been quietly prosperous most of the years since World War II, though it has been hurt by the continuing erosion of the automobile, steel and coal industries and troubled by recent manufacturing job losses, including the closing of a General Motors facility in Mansfield that employed 700 people. In 2009, Siemens closed its plant in Bellefontaine. But considering its old-line economic base, central Ohio seemed to emerge from the recession better than other parts of the state. Calisolar Inc., an alternative energy company, is set to open a facility at the old GM plant. In Shawnee Township, the Joint Systems Manufacturing Center has been building versions of the Abrams tank for 30 years. And, ethanol production is a growth industry in the area.

2008 Presidential Vote		
John McCain (R)	180,255	(60%)
Barack Obama (D)	114,956	(38%)
2004 Presidential Vote		
George Bush (R)	193,875	(65%)
John Kerry (D)	102,332	(34%)
Cook Partisan Voting Index:	R+15	

Much of central Ohio makes up the 4th Congressional District. It includes Lima, where Standard Oil drilled what was once the largest oil field in the nation; Marion, whose prominent citizens include ex-president Warren Harding and Watergate figure John Dean; and Mansfield, home of General William Tecumseh Sherman, who marched his troops through Georgia for the Union. This has been a Republican stronghold since the Civil War. Republican George W. Bush twice carried the district with 62% and 65% of the vote, respectively, in 2000 and 2004. The district was one of the reasons he carried Ohio a second time. Republican presidential nominee John McCain carried the district with 60% in 2008. In the district's three most populous counties, Republican John Kasich beat Gov. Ted Strickland 61%-35% in Hancock County, 58%-39% in Allen County and 55%-40% in Richland County.

Jim Jordan (R)

The congressman from the 4th District is Jim Jordan, a conservative Republican first elected in 2006. Jordan in 2011 took over the chairmanship of the Republican Study Committee, the caucus of the House's most conservative members, and instantly became the public face of his party's efforts to aggressively confront President Barack Obama.

Jordan grew up in Champaign County and graduated from Graham High School in 1982, after earning four state wrestling championships. At the University of Wisconsin, Jordan won two NCAA wrestling championships in the 134-pound weight class and was inducted into the Badger Hall of Fame. After graduating in 1986 with an economics degree, Jordan worked as an assistant wrestling coach at Ohio State University, where he earned a master's degree in education before completing a law degree at Capital University. Within a few years, he began thinking about elected office. "You get married and have kids, and you get sick of having the government take your money and tell you what to do," he told columnist George Will in 2011. He won a state House seat in 1994, won re-election twice, and then won a tough primary in 2000 for the state Senate. During his time in the legislature, Jordan compiled a solidly conservative voting record. He sponsored legislation creating Ohio's "Choose Life" license plates, backed a ban on same-sex marriage, and supported government vouchers for private school tuition.

Jordan announced his bid for Congress after Rep. Michael Oxley, who chaired the House Financial Services Committee, decided to retire after 12 terms. Jordan entered the six-way Republican primary with the most name recognition and had support from the Ohio Right to Life, the National Rifle Association and the national anti-tax group Club for Growth. Findlay real estate developer Frank Guglielmi spent $1.6 million of his own money and saturated the television airwaves with ads. Jordan raised plenty of money but failed to break the $1 million mark before the primary. While money mattered, so did geography. Jordan won with 51%, carrying eight of 11 counties. Guglielmi carried only his home county and one other to finish second with 30%. Kevin Nestor, president of the Mansfield-Richland Area Chamber of Commerce, came in third with 11%.

Despite the tough political environment for Republicans in 2006, Democrats never mounted a competitive campaign for the seat. Jordan beat Lima attorney and Vietnam veteran Rick Siferd 60%-40%.

In the House, Jordan established an unfailingly conservative voting record. He was among the House members who shared the highest conservative score in 2010, according to *National Journal's* ratings. "With the exception of the military, the federal government doesn't do anything very well," he once told the *Mansfield News Journal*. On the Budget Committee, he advocated a commission to reduce government waste. On the Judiciary Committee, he continued his outspoken opponent of abortion and same-sex marriage. Jordan was among just 36 Republicans to oppose the compromise deal that Obama struck with Republicans in December 2010 to extend expiring Bush-era tax cuts, and tried without success to offer an amendment cutting more than $149 billion to offset the bill's $95 billion in increased spending.

With his right-wing bona fides well established, Jordan succeeded Georgia's Tom Price as head of the 170-member Republican Study Committee when Price won a GOP leadership post in late 2010. Jordan had been chairman of the group's budget task force. He beat back a challenge from Texas' Louie Gohmert, who accused him of being a "wing man" for House Speaker-to-be John Boehner, who represents a neighboring Ohio district. But Jordan vowed to be independent of the new House leadership, saying his group would lobby lawmakers just as vigorously as the GOP's formal whip team.

Under Jordan's guidance, the RSC in early 2011 unveiled a budget plan that called for cutting spending by a whopping $2.5 trillion over 10 years. It called for holding fiscal 2011 non-security discretionary spending to fiscal 2008 levels, with such spending frozen at fiscal 2006 levels in the following years. When the House approved a temporary measure in March to keep the government running until April 8 as Republicans and Obama tried to hammer out an agreement on spending cuts, Jordan was openly scornful. "We must do more than cut spending in bite-sized pieces," he said. He denied speculation that his caucus was eager to shut down the government, a move that had disastrous political consequences for Republicans in 1995, and said he was not out to undercut Boehner. But anonymous Republicans and lobbyists told *The Columbus Dispatch* that they were worried about the growing divide between Jordan and Boehner.

Jordan has been re-elected easily.

FIFTH DISTRICT

Bob Latta (R)

Elected Dec. 2007, 2nd full term; b. April 18, 1956, Bluffton; home, Bowling Green; Bowling Green St. U., B.A., 1978, U. of Toledo Col. of Law, J.D., 1981; Catholic; married (Marcie); 2 children.

Elected Office: Wood Cnty. commissioner, 1991-96, Ohio Senate, 1997-2001, Ohio Gen. Assembly, 2001-07.

Professional Career: Attorney, 1981-1991.

DC Office: 1323 LHOB, 20515, 202-225-6405; Fax: 202-225-1985; Web site: latta.house.gov.

State Offices: Bowling Green, 419-354-8700; Defiance, 419-782-1996; Norwalk, 419-668-0206.

Committees: *Energy & Commerce:* Communications & Technology; Environment & the Economy; Health.

Group Ratings

	ACLU	ACU	ADA	CFG	AFS	FRC	LCV	ITIC	NTU	COC
2010	13	100	0	100	0	93	0	50	90	88
2009	–	100	0	97	11	–	0	–	90	80

National Journal Ratings

	2010 LIB	—	2010 CONS	2009 LIB	—	2009 CONS
Economic	4%	—	95%	5%	—	94%
Social	0%	—	85%	11%	—	87%
Foreign	0%	—	88%	0%	—	75%
Composite	6%	—	94%	10%	—	90%

Key Votes of the 111th Congress

1. Overturn Ledbetter	N	5. Bar federal abortion funds	Y	9. Stop detainee transfers		*
2. Pass $820 billion stimulus	N	6. Pass health care bill	N	10. Legalize immigrants' kids		N
3. Let guns in national parks	Y	7. Regulate financial firms	N	11. Repeal don't ask, tell		N
4. Pass cap-and-trade	N	8. Pass tax cuts for some	N	12. Limit campaign funds		N

Election Results

2010 general	Bob Latta (R)..140,703	(68%)	($591,070)
	Caleb Finkenbiner (D)..54,919	(26%)	
	Brian Smith (Lib)..11,831	(6%)	
2010 primary	Bob Latta (R)..42,827	(83%)	
	Robert Wallis (R) 8,754	(17%)	

Prior Winning Percentages: 2008 (64%); 2007 special (57%)

Population		Race/Ethnicity		Work	
Pop. 2010:	627,799	White:	91.6%	Private:	81.6%
Change since 2000:	Down 0.5%	Black:	1.4%	Government:	12.4%
Urban:	48.9%	Hispanic:	5.1%	Self-employed:	5.8%
Rural:	51.1%	Asian:	0.6%	Blue collar:	33.8%
Area size:	6,160 sq. mi.	Native Am.:	0.2%	White collar:	49.3%
		Hawaiian:	0.0%	Khaki collar:	0.1%
Age		Two+ races:	1.1%	Other:	16.8%
Median age:	38.6 yrs.				
More than 65 yrs:	14.2%	*Ancestry*		Median income:	$47,367
Less than 18 yrs:	24.1%	German	34.2%	Median Home Value:	$121,400
		Irish	10.0%		
Education		English	7.5%	**Military Veterans**	
H.S. grad:	88.5%			% of Pop:	10.7%
College grad:	16.7%				
Grad degree:	6.2%				

Northwest Ohio, Bowling Green

Undergirded by limestone, as flat and fertile as any place in America, northwest Ohio was economically productive from the time it was settled. Parts of it were known as the "Firelands," reserved for Connecticut Yankees whose farms were burned in the Revolution, and German Protestants build small towns in the mid-19th century. Northwest Ohio is the beginning of the great corn and hog belt that stretches through Indiana and Illinois into Iowa, and has long been

2008 Presidential Vote

John McCain (R) 165,762	(53%)
Barack Obama (D) 141,321	(45%)

2004 Presidential Vote

George Bush (R) 188,935	(61%)
John Kerry (D) 119,308	(39%)

Cook Partisan Voting Index: R+9

a Republican heartland. Fremont, settled by abstemious Yankees, was the home of President Rutherford B. Hayes, whose wife, Lucy, served only lemonade in the White House. Nearby Sandusky was settled by Germans who built big wineries and breweries.

This is also prime industrial country. Its limestone, rail connections and location near the Great Lakes have spurred the growth of a factory economy that financially is far more important than agriculture. After the first settlement, northwest Ohio grew steadily for many decades, surging ahead in the 1950s and 1960s as its small factories supplied the big auto plants in Detroit and in cities in Ohio. Growth lagged noticeably in the 1980s, when the domestic auto industry collapsed, but rebounded somewhat as small firms sold not only to the Big Three but to foreign customers. That gave this area the highest percentage of blue-collar workers in the state. Honda has dozens of suppliers in the area, though many parts companies continue to cut back with the continuing financial troubles of the domestic auto industry.

The 5th Congressional District of Ohio sweeps across northwest Ohio, from northern Ashland County, almost within the ambit of metro Cleveland, across the limestone plains through Sandusky County and Fremont, past the university town of Bowling Green and the Toledo suburb of Perrysburg, to the towns of Defiance and Napoleon and on to the northwest corner where Ohio borders Michigan and Indiana. Its factories include the aromatic Heinz ketchup plant in Fremont, where 4 million 14-ounce bottles are produced every day, and the largest Whirlpool washing machine plant in Clyde, both in Sandusky County. The company in 2009 announced a $175 million expansion. Bowling Green is the site of the state's first wind turbines, and locals now call it "Blowing Green." Historically, this has been a solidly Republican district since the Civil War. President George W. Bush won it 61%-39% in 2004, and Republican nominee John McCain won it 53%-45% in 2008.

Bob Latta (R)

The congressman from the 5th District is Bob Latta, a Republican who won a special election for the seat in 2007. Latta is the son of Delbert Latta, who held the seat for 30 years, from 1959 to 1989. Bob Latta was born in Ohio but split his early years between his native Bluffton, Ohio and Washington, D.C. Growing up helping in his father's campaigns, Latta says he learned the business of catering to constituents. Young Latta was frequently interrupted during his homework to answer their phone calls and remembers his father following up with federal agencies to try to get results from the vast government bureaucracy. Latta also spent time driving around the district with his dad, going to meetings and events. During college at Bowling Green State University, Latta volunteered in his father's office, where he met his wife, Marcia, who worked for his father. When he graduated from law school at the University of Toledo, his father had one bit of career advice for him: Don't get into politics.

Bob Latta did his best to follow that guidance, and practiced law for several years. But when his father announced his retirement from Congress in 1988, the 31-year-old couldn't pass on the opportunity to try to follow in his footsteps. However, he first had to get by Paul Gillmor, a Republican state senator who had been waiting for a congressional seat to open up during Del Latta's long tenure. In the primary contest with Gillmor, Bob Latta argued that, like his father, he would start out young and eventually gain enough seniority to preside over powerful committees. After a spirited race, Gillmor beat Latta by just 27 votes out of 57,361 cast. With the narrow loss behind him, Latta focused on local politics, first getting elected to the Wood County Commission, and then to the Ohio Legislature, where he served in both the Senate and the state Assembly. One of his major efforts was to repeal the Ohio estate tax, which he succeeded in doing for 78% of Ohioans, although the tax was not eliminated entirely. An avid hunter, Latta also championed conservation issues, including lengthening hunting seasons and expanding wildlife reserves.

On Sept. 5, 2007, Gillmor died at his Washington home, apparently from a fall down stairs. Latta got into the contest for a successor, but had to overcome a brutal Republican primary fight and a Democratic challenger heavily financed by the national party. Latta's major primary opponent was state Sen. Steve Buehrer, who was backed by the national anti-tax group Club for Growth, which ran several ads attacking Latta as an advocate of higher taxes. Latta attacked Buehrer for accepting donations from a former fundraiser for President George W. Bush in Ohio, Tom Noe, a convicted money launderer. But it came to light that Latta had also taken money from Noe. In the end, Latta defeated Buehrer by only 2,542 votes out of 74,191 cast.

Latta's Democratic opponent, Robin Weirauch, a former public administrator who had twice run against Gillmor, had backing from national labor unions and the fundraising group EMILY's list. She also got the endorsements of U.S. Sen. Sherrod Brown and Gov. Ted Strickland, both prominent Ohio Democrats. She attacked Latta on economic issues and on his support for the Iraq war. Still, despite Weirauch's best efforts to capitalize on the anti-incumbent, anti-Washington sentiment that year, she came up short in the solidly Republican district. Latta won 57%-43%. He has subsequently won re-election by much wider margins.

In the House, Latta has been staunchly conservative. He introduced bills in 2011 to eliminate automatic pay raises for lawmakers, to permanently repeal the estate tax and to issue a Ronald Reagan commemorative coin. He took a prized seat on the Energy and Commerce Committee in April 2010, having earlier made energy independence his central issue. He supports new oil refineries, new nuclear power plants and tax incentives for commercial ventures using clean coal, hydrogen, wind, solar and biofuels. His bill calling for increased domestic production and offshore drilling as well as expanded reliance on renewable and alternative sources became one of the GOP's main alternatives to Democratic proposals. Latta dubbed it the "all of the above" strategy to solving the country's energy shortage.

In March 2011, he ardently opposed giving the Environmental Protection Agency the authority to regulate greenhouse gas emissions as well as the Federal Communications Commission's net neutrality rules aimed at preventing phone and cable companies from using their control over broadband connections to dictate where their subscribers go and what they do online. He said both were "bad policy" and that neither agency had the authority to enact such rules.

As vice chairman of the Congressional Sportsmen's Caucus, Latta drew headlines in 2009 for castigating an Obama administration proposal to reclassify pocketknives that can be sprung open with one hand as switchblades. Both chambers passed bills overturning the idea and it was signed into law.

SIXTH DISTRICT

Bill Johnson (R)

Elected 2010, 1st term; b. Nov. 10, 1954, Roseboro, NC; home, Poland; Troy U., B.S. 1979; GA Inst. of Technology, M.S. 1984; U.S. Air Force Squadron Officers Col.; U.S. Air Force Air Command & Staff Col.; Protestant; Married (LeeAnn); 4 children.

Military Career: Air Force, 1973-99.

Professional Career: President, Johnson-Schley Management Group, 1999-2003; owner, J2 Business Solutions, 2003-06; dir., Lockheed Martin, 2005; CIO, Stoneridge Inc., 2006-2010.

DC Office: 317 CHOB, 20515, 202-225-5705; Fax: 202-225-5907; Web site: billjohnson.house.gov.

State Offices: Marietta, 740-376-0868.

Committees: *Foreign Affairs:* Asia & the Pacific; Terrorism, Nonproliferation & Trade. *Natural Resources:* Energy & Mineral Resources; National Parks, Forests & Public Lands. *Veterans' Affairs:* Economic Opportunity; Oversight & Investigations (Chmn).

Election Results

2010 general	Bill Johnson (R)	103,170	(50%)	($700,675)
	Charlie Wilson (D)	92,823	(45%)	($1,057,441)
	Richard Cadle (CNP)	5,077	(2%)	($15,039)
	Martin Elsass (Lib)	4,505	(2%)	
2010 primary	Bill Johnson (R)	14,103	(43%)	
	Donald Allen (R)	12,406	(37%)	
	Richard Stobbs (R)	6,637	(20%)	

Population		Race/Ethnicity		Work	
Pop. 2010:	623,742	White:	94.1%	Private:	79.7%
Change since 2000:	Down 1.1%	Black:	2.5%	Government:	14.6%
Urban:	50.0%	Hispanic:	1.1%	Self-employed:	5.5%
Rural:	50.0%	Asian:	0.7%	Blue collar:	27.7%
Area size:	5,237 sq. mi.	Native Am.:	0.2%	White collar:	53.0%
		Hawaiian:	0.0%	Khaki collar:	0.0%
Age		Two+ races:	1.3%	Other:	19.3%
Median age:	40.5 yrs.				
More than 65 yrs:	15.9%	*Ancestry*		Median income:	$39,302
Less than 18 yrs:	21.4%	German	19.0%	Median Home Value:	$100,900
		Irish	13.3%		
Education		English	8.9%	**Military Veterans**	
H.S. grad:	86.5%			% of Pop:	11.5%
College grad:	16.4%				
Grad degree:	6.0%				

Southeastern Ohio; Boardman

In the years after the American Revolution, the Ohio River was one of the great highways west. From Pittsburgh, where the Allegheny and Monongahela Rivers meet to form the Ohio, the river led south and west toward the Mississippi and the great port of New Orleans. Shipping goods downriver by raft was cheaper than sending them over the Appalachian Mountains, and so the Ohio became a great highway of commerce. For hundreds of miles, the Ohio twisted

2008 Presidential Vote		
John McCain (R)	150,850	(50%)
Barack Obama (D)	142,846	(48%)
2004 Presidential Vote		
George Bush (R)	153,983	(51%)
John Kerry (D)	149,080	(49%)
Cook Partisan Voting Index: R+2		

this way and that through rounded-off mountains and rolling hills, land that marked the boundary between post-Revolutionary Virginia and the Northwest Territory, between slaveholding territory and free soil as determined by the Confederation Congress of 1787. Across this boundary, settlers made their way in those years—Yankees in 1788 to Marietta, Ohio's first town, and, in larger numbers, Virginians. By the late 19th century, the Ohio was an industrial river. Coal was nearby, barge transportation was available and railroads were built in the narrow valleys between the hills. Steel mills went up on the riverfront. This produced prosperity for a while, but it also produced pollution—Steubenville on the Ohio River once had the nation's dirtiest air—and after the old-line steel industry fell on hard times, the Ohio River was lined with some of the least prosperous parts of America. Even with mandates from the Clean Air Act, the pollution in much of this area from coal-fired power plants remains. Construction was scrapped in 2009 on a new $3.9 billion clean coal power plant in Meigs County after the project encountered steep cost overruns and a dip in demand for coal-powered energy.

The 6th Congressional District of Ohio is made up of a string of counties running 325 miles along the Ohio River, plus part of the Mahoning Valley, named after a narrow tributary of the Ohio. In the north, it includes the Youngstown suburbs of Boardman, Canfield and part of Poland in Mahoning County, and East Liverpool and Steubenville on the river. It curves along the lightly populated stretch of the river south from Marietta, past the old industrial town of Ironton and extends to the city limits of Portsmouth, not quite in the Cincinnati metropolitan area. Much of this area is part of poverty-ridden Appalachia. Athens County, with a poverty rate of 35% in 2009, is the state's poorest county. The steel and coal areas in the north became Democratic during the 1930s and the southern counties started trending Republican in the 1960s. This mix makes for a Democratic-leaning district but the cultural conservatism of this region, much like that of West Virginia and eastern Kentucky across the river, put it narrowly in Republican George W. Bush's column, by 49% in 2000 and 51% in 2004. In 2008, the close trend continued with Republican John McCain winning 50%-48%.

Bill Johnson (R)

The new congressman from Ohio's 6th District is Republican Bill Johnson, who beat two-term Democratic Rep. Charlie Wilson in 2010. Johnson was born in Roseboro, N.C., and raised on his family's cotton and tobacco farm. He joined the Air Force when he was just 17. After basic training he went on to graduate with a degree in computer science from Alabama's Troy University. In the military, he was stationed at bases across the country, and, as a director at U.S. Special Operations Command, he briefed congressional and intelligence officials. In 1984, Johnson earned his master's degree in computer science from Georgia Tech. He retired in 1999 as a lieutenant colonel, dealing with communications and computer systems.

After leaving the Air Force, Johnson worked for a number of high-technology companies. He moved to Ohio in 2006, when he began working for Stoneridge, which makes electronic components for automobiles. Upset that shoppers were pouring across the border into Pennsylvania to buy certain goods free of sales taxes, Johnson in 2009 founded an organization called the Ohio Sales Tax Reform Incentive with the goal of creating tax holidays for shoppers.

Initially, Johnson had considered running against Democratic Rep. Tim Ryan in the adjacent 17th District, which includes Johnson's residence close to the district line. But in challenging Wilson, he picked a much more conservative district. In the GOP's May primary, Johnson got 43% of the vote, defeating Donald Allen, a veterinarian, who received 37%, and former Belmont County Sheriff Richard Stobbs, who got 20%.

Johnson tried to characterize Wilson as a puppet of liberal U.S. House Speaker Nancy Pelosi, and as being out of touch with his constituents. In their only debate, Wilson accused Johnson's company of exporting jobs overseas, while Johnson replied that the company actually created jobs in Ohio. The Republican called Wilson's attacks "the desperate act of a career politician who cannot defend his record for his tax-and-spend policies." Wilson was favored to win and had a large fundraising advantage, but the race tightened in the final weeks. In mid-October, the Democratic Congressional Campaign Committee stepped in to buy advertising for Wilson. Meanwhile, Johnson benefited from ads by the U.S. Chamber of Commerce that attacked Wilson as "Party-Line Charlie." In the final days of the campaign, President Barack Obama made a swing through Cleveland, in part to bolster support for Wilson, while House Minority Leader John Boehner of Ohio made an appearance at a Johnson rally.

Still, the Republican trend in 2010 was overpowering, even for a Democrat like Wilson, who cast fiscally conservative votes and backed gun rights. But Wilson had also voted for Obama's overhaul of health care policy and the Democrats' $787 billion economic stimulus bill. Johnson won, 50% to 45%, with two minor candidates splitting the remaining 5%.

SEVENTH DISTRICT

Steve Austria (R)

Elected 2008, 2nd term; b. Oct. 12, 1958, Cincinnati; home, Beavercreek; Marquette U., B.A. 1981; Catholic; married (Eileen); 3 children.

Elected Office: OH House, 1998-2000; OH Senate, 2000-08, Majority whip, 2004-08.

Professional Career: Financial advisor

DC Office: 439 CHOB, 20515, 202-225-4324; Fax: 202-225-1984; Web site: austria.house.gov.

State Offices: Lancaster, 740-654-5149; Springfield, 937-325-0474.

Committees: *Appropriations:* Commerce, Justice, Science & Related Agencies; Military Construction, Veterans Affairs & Related Agencies; State, Foreign Operations & Related Programs.

Group Ratings

	ACLU	ACU	ADA	CFG	AFS	FRC	LCV	ITIC	NTU	COC
2010	13	100	0	87	0	93	10	33	87	88
2009	–	88	15	74	33	–	0	–	77	87

National Journal Ratings

	2010 LIB — 2010 CONS		2009 LIB — 2009 CONS	
Economic	21%	— 79%	28%	— 71%
Social	18%	— 77%	29%	— 68%
Foreign	12%	— 79%	0%	— 75%
Composite	19%	— 81%	24%	— 76%

Key Votes of the 111th Congress

1. Overturn Ledbetter	N	5. Bar federal abortion funds	Y
2. Pass $820 billion stimulus	N	6. Pass health care bill	N
3. Let guns in national parks	Y	7. Regulate financial firms	N
4. Pass cap-and-trade	N	8. Pass tax cuts for some	N

9. Stop detainee transfers	Y
10. Legalize immigrants' kids	N
11. Repeal don't ask, tell	N
12. Limit campaign funds	N

Election Results

2010 general	Steve Austria (R)	135,721	(62%)	($785,806)
	Bill Conner (D)	70,400	(32%)	($29,597)
	John Anderson (Lib)	9,381	(4%)	($157,969)
2010 primary	Steve Austria (R)	46,072	(83%)	
	John Mitchel (R)	9,535	(17%)	

Prior Winning Percentages: 2008 (58%)

Population		Race/Ethnicity		Work	
Pop. 2010:	683,371	White:	83.7%	Private:	77.7%
Change since 2000:	Up 8.3%	Black:	10.1%	Government:	16.8%
Urban:	71.3%	Hispanic:	2.4%	Self-employed:	5.3%
Rural:	28.7%	Asian:	1.3%	Blue collar:	23.6%
Area size:	2,864 sq. mi.	Native Am.:	0.2%	White collar:	58.2%
		Hawaiian:	0.0%	Khaki collar:	0.5%
Age		Two+ races:	2.1%	Other:	17.7%
Median age:	37.2 yrs.				
More than 65 yrs:	12.7%	*Ancestry*		Median income:	$48,936
Less than 18 yrs:	24.3%	German	21.4%	Median Home Value:	$137,500
		Irish	11.2%		
Education		USA	9.7%	**Military Veterans**	
H.S. grad:	87.5%			% of Pop:	12.9%
College grad:	21.2%				
Grad degree:	8.1%				

Central Ohio; Springfield

The hills and plains of central Ohio are dotted with towns and small cities that have been manufacturing centers almost since they were settled in the early 19th century, when the dominant technologies were the waterwheel and the open forge. Later, new technologies—the automobile and the airplane—arrived, and the local manufacturing economy, sometimes in uncomfortable fits and starts, adjusted and advanced.

2008 Presidential Vote		
John McCain (R)	172,647	(54%)
Barack Obama (D)	143,778	(45%)
2004 Presidential Vote		
George Bush (R)	176,365	(57%)
John Kerry (D)	132,124	(43%)
Cook Partisan Voting Index: R+7		

This has been the story of Springfield, often studied as a typical American city. In the early 1980s, International Harvester, the city's largest employer, went bankrupt, downsized dramatically and was renamed Navistar. In 1996, the company cut 3,000 jobs from its Springfield plant, and by 2002, the workforce had been pared down to 2,800. Navistar was on the rebound in 2008 after securing a deal to assemble General Motors medium-duty trucks, but then truck sales hit 50-year lows in the 2007-09 recession. Wright Patterson Air Force Base gained more than 1,000 jobs in 2011 due to the base-closing review of 2005.

The 7th Congressional District of Ohio is made up of a portion of south-central Ohio. It includes Springfield and Clark County and, just to the south, the growing Greene County suburbs of Dayton around Wright Patterson. Clark County was among the recession's leading victims in Ohio, with unemployment climbing past 12% in early 2010 before coming in below 10% by year's end. Other population centers are in Fairfield County, southeast of Columbus, and a slice of Franklin County, including part of the east side of Columbus. Fairfield is home to the 5,200-seat World Harvest Church, where politically active Pastor Rod Parsley is one of the nation's leading evangelicals and a prominent opponent of abortion rights and gay marriage. In the 2008 presidential campaign, Republican candidate John McCain referred to Parsley as "a spiritual guide," but he denounced the pastor's endorsement of his candidacy after Parsley made derogatory comments about the religion of Islam.

Farther east in Perry County, coal mining has revived as the price of oil skyrocketed. The district has always been Republican territory. It backed the policies of Ohio Republican President William McKinley (tariff protection, railroad regulation, antitrust suits against monopolies, discouragement of labor unions) and of Republican Gov. James Rhodes (low taxes, promotion of new businesses and jobs). It is culturally conservative as well. In 2008, Republican presidential nominee John McCain won the district, 54% to 45%. And Republican John Kasich topped that total in most of the district's counties in the 2010 governor's race.

Steve Austria (R)

The congressman from the 7th district is Steve Austria, a protégé of Republican Rep. Dave Hobson, the longtime incumbent whose retirement paved the way for Austria's election in 2008. His father, Dr. Clement Austria, was born in the Philippines but moved to Cincinnati to attend medical school. Austria was born in Cincinnati and grew up in Xenia, Ohio, with eight younger siblings. He graduated from Marquette University with a bachelor's degree in political science, then returned home and founded a financial planning business. He worked for the local GOP, and his wife, Eileen, worked for Hobson as his district director from 1990 to 2007.

In 1998, Austria launched his political career by challenging incumbent state Rep. Marilyn Reid, a fellow Republican embroiled in an ethics scandal. Austria upset Reid in the GOP primary and easily defeated the Democratic candidate in the general election. Two years later, he was elected to the state Senate, where he served two terms as majority whip. In the legislature, Austria focused on law and order issues, sponsoring bills stiffening penalties for soliciting sex from minors over the Internet and toughening penalties for child rapists. In 2003, he won praise for helping to broker a deal on a bill that allowed Ohioans to carry concealed handguns.

When Hobson announced his retirement in October 2007, Austria got into the contest for the seat as the front-runner. Austria had primary competition from former state Rep. Ron Hood, Clark County Republican Party Chairman Dan Harkins and former Air Force officer John Mitchel. Austria was not helped by the *Dayton Daily News*, which editorialized: "What he's most likely to do is settle into a long, long career of keeping people back home happy, while remaining on the congressional back benches." Nevertheless, Austria won, with 55% to Hood's 34%, Harkins's 6% and Mitchel's 5%.

In the general election, Austria faced attorney Sharen Neuhardt. Democrats claimed Neuhardt could run a competitive race, but in spite of help from national Democratic groups, Austria still outraised her $1.2 million to $900,000. A couple months before the election, political blogger Jeff Coryell suggested Austria plagiarized sections of a column he wrote for the *Xenia Gazette* by taking text from a U.S. Department of Labor website. But the negative attention Austria got for that paled in comparison to the flak Neuhardt took a few weeks later, when the *Dayton Daily News* revealed that for six years she had housed a Rwandan refugee who was not legally in the United States. The Rwandan man also had been arrested for disorderly conduct and cited for driving without a license. In the campaign's final stretch, Neuhardt blamed the Republican Party for the job losses in the district, but the message failed to resonate. Austria defeated her 58% to 42%, carrying every county in the district except Franklin.

In the House, Austria has proved to be a loyal Republican. He showed some independence early on, becoming one of 40 Republicans to vote for expanding the State Children's Health Insurance Program in 2009. But he sided with the majority of his party on major votes after that, and was rewarded in 2011 with a slot on the Appropriations Committee. He got a seat on the military construction panel, enabling him to have some say about spending at Wright Patterson. During a February 2009 interview with *The Columbus Dispatch*'s editorial board, Austria compared President Barack Obama's economic-stimulus bill to former President Franklin Roosevelt's economic policies and claimed government spending under Roosevelt caused the Great Depression. A week later, liberal MSNBC's liberal news commentator, Keith Olbermann, ridiculed Austria's take on American history.

Still, Austria won re-election easily in 2010 over Democrat Bill Conner, 62%-32%.

EIGHTH DISTRICT

John Boehner (R)

Elected 1990, 11th term; b. Nov. 17, 1949, Cincinnati; home, West Chester; Xavier U., B.S. 1977; Catholic; married (Debbie); 2 children.

Military Career: Navy, 1969.

Elected Office: Union Township Bd. of Trustees, 1981–85, Pres., 1984; OH House of Reps., 1984–90.

Professional Career: Pres., Nucite Sales Inc., 1976–90.

DC Office: 1011 LHOB, 20515, 202-225-6205; Fax: 202-225-0704; Web site: johnboehner.house.gov.

State Offices: Troy, 937-339-1524; West Chester, 513-779-5400.

Group Ratings

	ACLU	ACU	ADA	CFG	AFS	FRC	LCV	ITIC	NTU	COC
2010	14	100	0	100	0	87	0	33	92	100
2009	–	96	0	86	0	–	0	–	89	80

National Journal Ratings

	2010 LIB — 2010 CONS		2009 LIB — 2009 CONS	
Economic	4%	— 96%	7%	— 92%
Social	0%	— 85%	0%	— 93%
Foreign	0%	— 88%	0%	— 75%
Composite	6%	— 94%	8%	— 92%

Key Votes of the 111th Congress

1. Overturn Ledbetter	N	5. Bar federal abortion funds	Y	9. Stop detainee transfers	Y
2. Pass $820 billion stimulus	N	6. Pass health care bill	N	10. Legalize immigrants' kids	N
3. Let guns in national parks	Y	7. Regulate financial firms	N	11. Repeal don't ask, tell	N
4. Pass cap-and-trade	N	8. Pass tax cuts for some	N	12. Limit campaign funds	N

Election Results

2010 general	John Boehner (R)	142,731	(66%)	($9,796,947)
	Justin Coussoule (D)	65,883	(30%)	($248,141)
	David Harlow (Lib)	5,121	(2%)	
2010 primary	John Boehner (R)	50,555	(85%)	
	Thomas McMasters (R)	6,266	(10%)	

Prior Winning Percentages: 2008 (68%), 2006 (64%), 2004 (69%), 2002 (71%), 2000 (71%), 1998 (71%), 1996 (70%), 1994 (100%), 1992 (74%), 1990 (61%)

Population		Race/Ethnicity		Work	
Pop. 2010:	663,644	White:	86.9%	Private:	82.6%
Change since 2000:	Up 5.2%	Black:	6.0%	Government:	12.1%
Urban:	78.1%	Hispanic:	3.1%	Self-employed:	5.1%
Rural:	21.9%	Asian:	1.8%	Blue collar:	27.1%
Area size:	2,031 sq. mi.	Native Am.:	0.2%	White collar:	56.1%
		Hawaiian:	0.1%	Khaki collar:	0.1%
Age		Two+ races:	1.8%	Other:	16.7%
Median age:	36.7 yrs.				
More than 65 yrs:	12.8%	*Ancestry*		Median income:	$49,192
Less than 18 yrs:	24.7%	German	24.5%	Median Home Value:	$136,400
		Irish	10.9%		
Education		USA	10.2%	**Military Veterans**	
H.S. grad:	85.6%			% of Pop:	11.1%
College grad:	20.2%				
Grad degree:	7.3%				

Western Ohio; Hamilton

Since the early 20th century, the far west end of Ohio—where U.S. 40, the old National Road, heads straight as an arrow in its last miles across Ohio and into Indiana—has been some of the nation's prime industrial country. The Great and Little Miami rivers drain south into the Ohio, and U.S. 40 jogs southward twice to go over the Miami and Stillwater river dams, built after a flood in 1913 that killed 361 people in Dayton and caused $1 billion in damage. The small cities

2008 Presidential Vote		
John McCain (R)	191,639	(61%)
Barack Obama (D)	119,834	(38%)

2004 Presidential Vote		
George Bush (R)	199,265	(65%)
John Kerry (D)	109,374	(35%)

Cook Partisan Voting Index:　R+14

and towns around and between Dayton and Cincinnati were rising industrial country a century ago, and in the years since they have weathered depression and recession and sought to adapt to changing markets and circumstances. Butler County, in between the two cities, was dominated for years by the large factory towns of Hamilton, the county seat founded in 1791, and Middletown. In recent years, major employers, including International Paper, have shut down operations, but other, smaller businesses have started up and the county's population has grown with the outflow of people from the central cities of Cincinnati and Dayton. The center of growth has been West Chester Township, situated on Interstate 75 near a huge Voice of America broadcasting tower and south of Wright-Patterson Air Force Base, which has attracted economic activity, including a new Amylin Pharmaceuticals facility and a new GE Aviation facility.

The 8th Congressional District of Ohio covers much of this territory. It includes all of Butler County except four lightly populated townships. In also takes in two counties to the north on the Indiana line and part of a third. It includes Miami County north of Dayton and the northeastern corner of Montgomery County, including part of Dayton, all of Huber Heights and part of Wright-Patterson AFB. Politically this is very Republican territory. It voted more than 60% Republican in the 2000, 2004 and 2008 presidential elections and has become the most Republican congressional district outside the South and West.

John Boehner (R)

The congressman from the 8th District is John Boehner, a Republican first elected in 1990 and since January 2011, the speaker of the House of Representatives.

Boehner (*BAY-ner*) grew up in Reading, just north of Cincinnati, the second-oldest of 12 children in a home with two bedrooms. His father ran Andy's Café, a neighborhood restaurant and bar. Playing at a much heavier weight than he is now, he was a linebacker for Cincinnati's Archbishop Moeller High School on a team coached by Gerry Faust, before Faust went on to coach at Notre Dame. Boehner worked at various jobs after high school and enlisted in the Navy, from which he was discharged because of a back injury. He spent six years working his way through Xavier University as a janitor, and was the first college graduate in his family. He moved to Butler County, where he worked for the Merrell Dow pharmaceutical firm and met Dave Kessler, owner of Nucite, a small plastic packaging company. Kessler hired Boehner as a salesman and within a year after graduation, he was making $74,000—and complaining about high taxes and government paperwork. Kessler's children were uninterested in the business and he sold it to Boehner, who was also developing an interest in politics. He served on the Union Township Board of Trustees and in 1984, at age 34, was elected to the Ohio House.

In 1990, he ran against Republican incumbent Rep. Donald (Buz) Lukens, who inexplicably sought re-election after he was convicted of having sex with a 16-year-old girl. Also in the Republican primary was former Rep. Tom Kindness, who had run unsuccessfully for the Senate in 1986 and was a lobbyist in Washington. Boehner won the primary with 49%, to 32% for Kindness and 17% for Lukens. The win was tantamount to victory in the heavily Republican district, and Boehner has since been re-elected without difficulty.

In the House, Boehner has a consistently conservative voting record, though he is also pragmatic and more apt to look for compromise on legislation than his more hard-edged, ideological colleagues. In his early years, he was a rabble-rousing reformer. He joined the Gang of Seven, young freshmen Republicans who insisted on naming all 355 members who'd had overdrafts at the House bank, a scandal that revealed that members had routinely abused their tax-subsidized banking privileges. He went on to assail Democrats as well as Republicans who supported a congressional pay raise. Boehner's Gang of Seven infuriated House veterans but struck a chord with the public, and the junior lawmakers earned recognition beyond their years of service. In the process, Boehner became a top ally of Minority Whip Newt Gingrich of Georgia, who was raising money for Republican candidates with the goal of toppling the entrenched Democratic majority in the House. Boehner also managed Gingrich's campaign for Republican leader, though he later would sour on Gingrich and participate in efforts to curb his power.

Boehner worked with Gingrich in putting together the 10-point Contract With America, unveiled in late September 1994 while many political insiders still doubted that Republicans could win a majority in the House, which had been controlled for 40 years by the Democrats. But Gingrich led a national campaign that took advantage of young, outlying Republican talent around the country and gave them positive themes, and plenty of money, to run on. When Republicans defied expectations and won a majority that year, Boehner ran for chairman of the Republican Conference, and with Gingrich's backing, he beat California Rep. Duncan Hunter 122-102. That made Boehner the No. 4 person in the Republican leadership with the responsibility of preparing the party's message and coordinating with GOP-allied outside groups.

The Gingrich years were a turbulent time for Boehner. An ethics investigation of Gingrich instigated by the Democrats placed Boehner in the middle of a legal altercation after a Florida couple taped one of Boehner's cell phone conversations with Republican leaders while he was driving through the state. The tape eventually reached Rep. Jim McDermott of Washington, the senior Democrat on the Ethics Committee, who made the contents available to *The New York Times*. In 1998, Boehner sued McDermott in federal court for invasion of privacy. The two could not agree on a settlement, and the case wound its way through the court system over the course of several years; the Supreme Court denied final review in 2008 and a federal district judge ordered McDermott to pay Boehner more than $1 million in legal fees.

By 1997, many rank-and-file House Republicans had lost confidence in the leadership team, especially the brilliant but erratic Gingrich. Boehner and other high-level members of the leadership team held secret discussions about whether to try to force Gingrich out as speaker. When their plotting became public, the plan dissolved, and the plotters took most of the heat for appearing to be disloyal and self-serving. GOP Whip Tom DeLay of Texas admitted his role and was forgiven. Dick Armey of Texas retained his majority leadership post, even though he had misled members by saying he had nothing to do with the plotting. Boehner did not survive. After the 1998 elections, during which Republicans lost five seats, Gingrich lost power and Boehner also lost the conference chairmanship to J.C. Watts, an African-American from Oklahoma who argued that Republicans needed a more diverse leadership. Watts was backed by DeLay.

Boehner later told *The New Yorker* that he immediately began to plan his comeback. "I just walked out of the room, I looked at Barry"—his longtime aide Barry Jackson—"and I said, 'We're just gonna put our heads down, and we're gonna work our way back.' And we did. I just knew that I was not going to take defeat as an answer." He plunged into his role as a subcommittee chairman on the House Education and the Workforce Committee. In six months, the subcommittee passed eight bills restructuring employer-run health insurance plans. Pleased by Boehner's initiative and dismayed that other committees had not been as effective, Republican Speaker Dennis Hastert adopted many of the subcommittee's bills as part of the Republican health care agenda. After the 2000 election, Boehner secured the chairmanship of the full committee.

When President George W. Bush assumed office in 2001, he made an overhaul of education policy a top priority, putting Boehner in the driver's seat of the new administration's chief domestic initiative. Early on, the new chairman established a working relationship with the chief Democrat on the panel, George Miller of California. Miller believed that current programs weren't helping disadvantaged children keep up with their peers, and Boehner shared his concern. While other committees dissolved into partisan stalemate, Boehner and Miller worked together on the House version of Bush's No Child Left Behind Act, which included the president's mandates for annual testing and increased accountability. It passed the committee and was later overwhelmingly approved by the House, 384-45. Boehner and Miller then worked with their Senate counterparts, Republican Judd Gregg of New Hampshire and Democrat Edward Kennedy of Massachusetts, on a compromise final draft that would be acceptable to both chambers. The House passed the final bill 381-41, with most of the no votes coming from Republicans, and it passed the Senate, 87-10. As a sign of Boehner's enduring partnership with Kennedy, the two sponsored an annual dinner in Washington, D.C., that raised more than $1 million for underfunded Roman Catholic schools in the city and featured motivational speakers, including first lady Laura Bush, and good-natured ribbing between the two hosts.

In January 2005, as bankrupt airlines began ceding their pension obligations to the federal Pension Benefit Guaranty Corporation, Boehner, once again with bipartisan support, pushed for a comprehensive solution to pension problems around the country and then played a leading role in months of painstaking House-Senate negotiations. The legislation, passed in summer 2006, represented a major change in pension law, closing loopholes that had permitted many companies to underfund their plans. It also set deadlines for them to make payments, and created automatic enrollment in 401(k) plans for many workers.

In the fall of 2005, the House Republican leadership was again in turmoil. Majority Leader Tom DeLay was forced to step down after being indicted in Texas for alleged campaign fundraising violations. Speaker Hastert named Majority Whip Roy Blunt to serve as acting leader. Boehner had been quietly planning for a return to the leadership and privately voiced doubts that Republicans could retain their House majority. In January 2006, he announced he would run against Blunt for majority leader and he offered a 37-page campaign manifesto that called for "one big, bold goal" each year and more reliance on the committees to generate legislation. When House Republicans voted, Blunt led with 110 votes to 79 for Boehner and 40 for John Shadegg on the first ballot. On the second ballot, Boehner picked up most of Shadegg's votes and beat Blunt 122-109. Boehner was back, now as the No. 2 leader in the House.

In contrast to the reserved Hastert, Boehner was sociable and adept at the glad-handing side of politics. He regularly held court just off the House floor with reporters and fellow members, puffing on ever-present Barclay cigarettes. As majority leader, he focused on lobbying reform and a crackdown on spending earmarks, which had exploded under Republican control and diminished the party's credibility for fiscal restraint. In October 2006, he campaigned around the country, but Republicans lost 31 seats, and their House majority, to the Democrats. In the wake of that dismal defeat, Hastert announced that he would resign. Boehner ran for minority leader and defeated Indiana's Mike Pence 168-27. "To earn our majority back, House Republicans must rededicate ourselves to the spirit of reform, and we must regain our confidence and courage to tackle the big issues the American people care about," Boehner said after the vote.

At the beginning of the 110th Congress in early 2007, Boehner gracefully handed over the gavel to the new Democratic House speaker, Nancy Pelosi of California. As minority leader, he occasionally cooperated with Democratic leaders, notably on the 2008 economic stimulus bill and Iraq War funding. He also helped deliver votes for the $700 billion government bailout of the financial industry in 2008, despite calling it a "crap sandwich." But under Pelosi (as under Hastert), the minority party played little role in shaping legislation. He led the charge to oust House Ways and Means Committee Chairman Charles Rangel of New York after questions were raised about Rangel's ethics and financial dealings. On immigration reform, he dropped his earlier advocacy of a middle ground and joined Republican hard-liners who emphasized border security and opposed a path to citizenship for illegal aliens.

A low moment for Boehner came in the spring of 2008 with the loss of three longtime Republican-held seats in special elections. Having privately told his members to get off their "dead asses," Boehner had little alternative other than to buck up his party with assurances that November was "not going to be as bad as people think." He turned the focus to the soaring price of oil to spotlight policy differences between the two parties. Then in November, Republicans lost 21 more House seats—including three in Ohio, an abysmal showing and a setback for Boehner, whose only words of encouragement were that it could have been worse, given the party's low public approval and Bush's unpopularity. With Bush gone, Boehner entered the Barack Obama presidency with his best opportunity to try to guide House Republicans back to victory in November 2010.

Boehner's early dealings with Obama did not bode well for future bipartisanship. After a meeting at the White House in January 2009, Obama rejected an alternative economic stimulus plan by Boehner and other GOP leaders, saying, "Elections have consequences," and "I won." Boehner rallied Republicans to oppose the Democrats' $787 billion stimulus bill and all 177 voted against it. He characterized the House Republicans as an "entrepreneurial insurgency" that would oppose Democratic policies through all means at their disposal. He was able to put together solid blocs of GOP opposition to the Democrats' cap-and-trade bill to curb carbon emissions (only eight Republicans voted for it) and their overhaul of health care policy (one Republican voted yes) in 2009, although he was unable to attract a sufficient number of moderate Democrats to stop the bills from passing.

Planning for the 2010 elections began early. In February 2009, Boehner backed National Republican Congressional Committee Chairman Pete Sessions' idea of putting 80 Democratic seats in play. While visiting GOP Rep. Kevin McCarthy's district in Bakersfield, Calif., Boehner was struck by the enthusiasm of tea party activists at a rally on tax day in April 2009 and he embraced their role in the party.

Boehner also vowed that if Republicans won a majority, he would take a different approach from recent speakers of both parties. In a September 2010 speech at the American Enterprise Institute, Boehner said he would avoid omnibus appropriations bills, which had become more frequent as partisan gridlock in Congress made it impossible to pass the regular appropriations bills. He also said he would insist on spending cuts to offset any new increases, that he would post all proposed legislation online, and that he would allow more amendments on major bills. As a former committee chairman, he also said that chairmen should let minority members help shape legislation. "We need to stop writing bills in the speaker's office," he said. "We need to open this place up, let some air in. We have nothing to fear from letting the House work its will, nothing to fear from the battle of ideas. That starts with the committees. The result will be more scrutiny and better legislation."

In November 2010, Republicans gained 63 House seats, more than any party has gained since 1948. Boehner found himself in position to lead a larger Republican majority than Gingrich or Hastert had enjoyed. He called the election a repudiation of Obama's policies of 2009 and 2010. In his first major undertaking as the leader of the new House majority in December 2010, Boehner negotiated with Obama and the Senate on an agreement to continue the 2001 and 2003 Bush-era tax cuts for all taxpayers, including the high income-earners who Obama had wanted to exclude.

Boehner was sworn in as the new speaker of the House on Jan. 5, 2011. When Pelosi handed him the gavel after a laudatory introduction, Boehner said, "Thank you all. It's still just me." The simple remark from the no-frills Midwesterner brought chuckles from his colleagues. He spoke for just 10 minutes, saying, "The American people have humbled us. They have refreshed our memories as to just how temporary the privilege of serving is. They have reminded us that everything here is on loan from them. That includes this gavel." Boehner's wife, his children, and 10 of his 11 siblings were in Washington for the ceremony, and he teared up at points, but avoided the elaborate and extended proceedings with which both Pelosi and Gingrich began their speakerships.

In the early days of his reign, Boehner led the House in a vote to repeal the Democrats' health care legislation, which was largely symbolic considering Democrats still controlled the Senate and the White House. His next task was much harder: Negotiating a budget settlement with the Democrats that would avert a government shutdown, but also mollify the 87 Republican freshmen, many of whom were unfamiliar with, or disinclined toward, the process of cross-party compromise. Many of them wanted the full $100 billion in spending cuts that they had campaigned on, while Obama and the Democrats pushed for far less. Describing his role with the freshmen in the *New Yorker* article, Boehner said, "Hey, I was one myself, I know exactly how this works. . . . You've got to give them room to grow. You've got to give them room to be rebellious from time to time. If you try to tighten down the pressure cooker too much, it's gonna explode." Ultimately, Boehner was able to work out a deal with Obama in April 2011 for $38 billion in spending cuts that was acceptable to most Republicans, a better-than-average start for a House speaker.

NINTH DISTRICT

Marcy Kaptur (D)

Elected 1982, 15th term; b. June 17, 1946, Toledo; home, Toledo; U. of WI, B.A. 1968, U. of MI, M.A. 1974, M.I.T., 1981-82; Catholic; single.

Professional Career: Urban planner, Lucas Cnty. Planning Comm., 1969–75; Urban planning consultant, 1975–77; White House Asst. Dir. for Urban Affairs, 1977–80; Dpty. secy., Natl. Consumer Coop. Bank, 1980–81; Author.

DC Office: 2186 RHOB, 20515, 202-225-4146; Fax: 202-225-7711; Web site: kaptur.house.gov.

State Offices: Toledo, 419-259-7500.

Committees: *Appropriations:* Agriculture, Rural Development, FDA & Related Agencies; Defense; Transportation, HUD & Related Agencies. *Budget.*

Group Ratings

	ACLU	ACU	ADA	CFG	AFS	FRC	LCV	ITIC	NTU	COC
2010	75	8	85	5	88	6	70	67	6	25
2009	–	17	85	10	100	–	100	–	10	40

National Journal Ratings

	2010 LIB	—	2010 CONS	2009 LIB	—	2009 CONS
Economic	68%	—	32%	60%	—	40%
Social	54%	—	42%	67%	—	31%
Foreign	62%	—	37%	56%	—	43%
Composite	62%	—	38%	62%	—	39%

Key Votes of the 111th Congress

1. Overturn Ledbetter	Y	5. Bar federal abortion funds	Y	9. Stop detainee transfers	N
2. Pass $820 billion stimulus	Y	6. Pass health care bill	Y	10. Legalize immigrants' kids	N
3. Let guns in national parks	N	7. Regulate financial firms	N	11. Repeal don't ask, tell	Y
4. Pass cap-and-trade	Y	8. Pass tax cuts for some	Y	12. Limit campaign funds	Y

Election Results

2010 general	Marcy Kaptur (D)	121,819	(59%)	($652,273)
	Rich Iott (R)	83,423	(41%)	($1,976,644)
2010 primary	Marcy Kaptur (D)	33,637	(86%)	
	Dale Terry (D)	5,256	(14%)	

Prior Winning Percentages: 2008 (74%), 2006 (74%), 2004 (68%), 2002 (74%), 2000 (75%), 1998 (81%), 1996 (77%), 1994 (75%), 1992 (74%), 1990 (78%), 1988 (81%), 1986 (78%), 1984 (55%), 1982 (58%)

Population		Race/Ethnicity		Work	
Pop. 2010:	619,010	White:	75.7%	Private:	82.7%
Change since 2000:	Down 1.9%	Black:	15.0%	Government:	12.5%
Urban:	86.0%	Hispanic:	5.4%	Self-employed:	4.8%
Rural:	14.0%	Asian:	1.2%	Blue collar:	25.1%
Area size:	1,244 sq. mi.	Native Am.:	0.2%	White collar:	56.3%
		Hawaiian:	0.0%	Khaki collar:	0.1%
Age		Two+ races:	2.2%	Other:	18.6%
Median age:	38.3 yrs.				
More than 65 yrs:	13.7%	*Ancestry*		Median income:	$43,955
Less than 18 yrs:	23.4%	German	24.8%	Median Home Value:	$130,500
		Irish	10.3%		
Education		English	6.8%	**Military Veterans**	
H.S. grad:	87.0%			% of Pop:	10.3%
College grad:	20.8%				
Grad degree:	7.6%				

Northern Ohio; Toledo

Toledo was one of America's boomtowns in the 1920s. The Willys-Overland plant employed 25,000 workers and turned out an automobile every 30 seconds. The Libbey-Owens-Ford merger made Toledo, with local supplies of natural gas and sand, the nation's largest glass manufacturer. The city built docks for coal and iron ore shipments and later erected an airport that could handle transcontinental flights. Toledo had long been well situated, where the Maumee

2008 Presidential Vote		
Barack Obama (D) 195,240	(62%)
John McCain (R) 113,800	(36%)

2004 Presidential Vote		
John Kerry (D) 181,889	(58%)
George Bush (R) 129,825	(42%)

Cook Partisan Voting Index: D+10

River empties into Lake Erie, where two dozen rail lines connected it with the East Coast, Chicago, and the coal fields of Kentucky and West Virginia. It was well positioned to be a center of the brash auto industry and became a national leader when it first produced the Jeep in the 1940s. But by the early 1980s, the domestic auto industry was overtaken by foreign competitors making lower-maintenance cars that were more economical to drive. And Toledo and other auto-dependent cities went through tough times.

But Toledo's small manufacturers in search of markets showed energy and ingenuity. Sport utility vehicles were invented here, and the city produced one of America's hottest vehicles, the Jeep Cherokee. The old Jeep plant was set to close, but the city offered Chrysler $300 million in incentives to stay, and a new plant was built along Interstate 75. For years, the Jeep Liberty and Jeep Wrangler factories here were barely able to meet demand. Then, with competition and higher gasoline prices, the good times ended. In 2007, Jeep eliminated its third shift and the following year, Chrysler dropped the second shift at the same plant. The continuing loss of auto and other manufacturing jobs took a toll. In 2008, the Milken Institute ranked Toledo 194th among 200 cities in job growth; most of the other bottom cities were in Ohio and Michigan. The Boston economic forecasting firm IHS Global Insight predicted in early 2011 that it would take almost two decades for the area to fully recover from the recession's job losses. But local officials remained somewhat upbeat after General Motors in 2010 invested more than $170 million into its Defiance foundry.

The 9th Congressional District of Ohio is centered on Toledo, spreading east through the flat-lands of Ottawa and Erie counties on the Lake Erie shore and inland to southern Lorain County southwest of Cleveland. It includes Oberlin, home of Oberlin College, founded in 1833 and the first American college to admit women and blacks. Port Clinton, on Lake Erie, bills itself as the "Walleye Capital of the World" and drops a plastic walleye in place of a glittering ball on New Year's Eve. Sandusky is home to the giant Cedar Point amusement park, which was named by the industry newspaper *Amusement Today* as the world's best amusement park in 2010 for the 13th straight year. Not far away is Milan, birthplace of the great inventor and capitalist Thomas Edison. Politically, Toledo has been heavily Democratic since CIO unions organized the plants in the late 1930s. The collapse of the auto industry so unnerved the district it voted for Republican Ronald Reagan in 1980 and elected a Republican congressman, but it switched back to the Democrats in 1982 and has stayed with them in almost every election since. In 2008, the district voted 62% to 36% for Democrat Barack Obama. This region, along with southeast Ohio and the state's other urban areas, was one of Democratic Gov. Ted Strickland's strongholds in his losing 2010 race to Republican John Kasich.

Marcy Kaptur (D)

The congresswoman from the 9th District is Marcy Kaptur, a Democrat first elected in 1982. She is now the most senior woman among Democrats in the House, a distinction not lost on her in her occasional clashes with Minority Leader Nancy Pelosi. Kaptur is a plainspoken, old-fashioned Democrat and a dedicated opponent of free trade who does not always toe the party line.

Kaptur grew up in a blue-collar neighborhood in Toledo, the daughter of Polish-American parents who worked at local auto plants. The family also operated a small grocery store, but her father sold it to get a job with health benefits. "It broke his heart," she said. She has spent almost her entire career in public service. She and her brother, Steve, live in the house where they grew up. She graduated from the University of Wisconsin, the first in her family to attend college, got a master's degree from the University of Michigan, and then spent eight years as an urban planner in Toledo. She worked on urban revitalization in the Jimmy Carter White House, returning home in 1980 with thoughts of running for elected office. That year, Republican Ed Weber defeated 26-year Democratic Rep. Thomas Ashley. In 1982, when no other Democrat would run against Weber for the U.S. House seat, she did and won 58%-39%, despite being outspent 3-to-1.

Kaptur has long been convinced that Toledo and places like it have lost jobs and industry because of unfair trade practices and low-wage competition from countries like Mexico and China. She pressured the Japanese to buy more American auto parts, but has been leery of Japanese investment in the United States. She was featured prominently in controversial liberal filmmaker Michael Moore's 2009 movie *Capitalism: A Love Story*. "I have always said there's a great injustice being done here, because the power rests with a handful of megabanks and millions of Americans are being affected," she told *The Toledo Blade* when the film opened. When the Obama administration sought in November 2010 to close a deal on a free trade pact with South Korea, Kaptur promised to seek alliances with conservative tea party activists to block it.

In earlier decades, Kaptur was probably the most dedicated opponent of the 1993 North American Free Trade Agreement in Congress. She criticized Democratic President Bill Clinton for doing nothing for sagging U.S. industries and for ignoring Democrats opposed to NAFTA. She became something of a national figure in 1995, when she appeared before Texas businessman Ross Perot's United We Stand Party and made a rousing speech on trade that had delegates cheering. Perot, running as a third-party candidate for president in 1996, offered her the vice presidential nomination a year later, but she turned it down. She was a vocal opponent of normal trade relations with China and the 2005 Central American Free Trade Agreement.

Reflecting on those early trade wars years later, Kaptur criticized Pelosi's support of NAFTA. "That's where the real knife was put in the flesh," she said. When Pelosi announced in May 2007 an agreement with Treasury Secretary Hank Paulson on principles for international trade policy, an uninvited Kaptur glared from the back of the room. In 2002, she ran a quixotic, one-day campaign for minority leader against Pelosi but, predictably, got nowhere against the powerful California Democrat. In 2008, Kaptur challenged Pelosi ally Xavier Becerra of California for the leadership post of Democratic Caucus vice chairman and lost badly, 175-67. However, unlike some Democrats who have had issues with Pelosi, Kaptur backed her for minority leader in 2011 when her hold on power within the caucus was at its most tenuous. One of the dissenting Democrats, Daniel Lipinski of Illinois, cast his vote for Kaptur in a symbolic tribute to her as a "strong voice for American workers."

Kaptur has a liberal voting record, but departs from party orthodoxy on abortion—she opposes federal funding for abortion. She is a strong advocate of alternative energy sources such as ethanol and biofuels for Ohio. But again, she made Democrats work to win her vote on energy and climate change legislation in 2009. Energy and Commerce Committee Chairman Henry Waxman, D-Calif., agreed to her demand to establish a new federal power authority with up to $3.5 billion available to lend to alternative energy projects in Ohio and other Midwestern states. Strongly opposed to the war in Iraq, Kaptur and Texas Republican Kay Granger in 2005 became the first women to serve on the Defense Appropriations Subcommittee.

Kaptur keeps close tabs on her district. A constituent gave her the idea to sponsor the legislation that created the World War II Memorial on the Washington Mall. On the Appropriations Committee, she has focused on improvements to bridges, roads, and rail and port facilities in her district. Kaptur is unabashed about working to secure spending earmarks in the appropriations bills for her district, a practice that has come under harsh criticism in recent years. In 2010, she ranked 24th among the top earmark recipients in the House, according to the group Taxpayers for Common Sense. She once challenged Republicans on the committee to limit farm payments, but when they threatened her favorite spending projects, she backed off. "I may be blockheaded sometimes, but I'm not stupid," Kaptur said.

She is proud of her role as a successful woman in what is still a male-dominated realm and wrote a book on women in Congress. She is exceedingly popular in Toledo and is rarely seriously challenged at election time. Her 2010 race made national headlines, but not because she was in grave political danger. Her Republican opponent, Rich Iott, a wealthy supermarket chain executive, came under a barrage of criticism when it was revealed that for years he had worn a German SS uniform and participated in Nazi re-enactments. Kaptur prevailed 59%-41%.

TENTH DISTRICT

Dennis Kucinich (D)

Elected 1996, 8th term; b. Oct. 8, 1946, Cleveland; home, Cleveland; Cleveland St. U., 1967-70, Case Western Reserve U., B.A., M.A., 1973; Catholic; married (Elizabeth Harper); 1 child.

Elected Office: Cleveland City Cncl., 1969–75, 1983–85; Cleveland mayor, 1977–79; OH Senate, 1994–96.

Professional Career: Clerk, municipal courts, 1976–77; Radio talk show host, 1979, 1989; Lecturer, 1980–83; Consultant, 1986–94; TV Reporter, Channel 8, 1989–92.

DC Office: 2445 RHOB, 20515, 202-225-5871; Fax: 202-225-5745; Web site: kucinich.house.gov.

State Offices: Lakewood, 216-228-8850; Parma, 440-845-2707.

Committees: *Education & the Workforce:* Health, Employment, Labor & Pensions; Workforce Protections. *Oversight & Government Reform:* Regulatory Affairs, Stimulus Oversight & Government Spending (RMM).

Group Ratings

	ACLU	ACU	ADA	CFG	AFS	FRC	LCV	ITIC	NTU	COC
2010	94	0	90	4	100	25	100	100	13	25
2009	–	12	75	28	89	–	79	–	21	60

National Journal Ratings

	2010 LIB — 2010 CONS	2009 LIB — 2009 CONS
Economic	73% — 25%	51% — 48%
Social	93% — 0%	89% — 0%
Foreign	55% — 45%	49% — 50%
Composite	75% — 25%	65% — 35%

Key Votes of the 111th Congress

1. Overturn Ledbetter	Y	5. Bar federal abortion funds	N	9. Stop detainee transfers	N
2. Pass $820 billion stimulus	Y	6. Pass health care bill	N	10. Legalize immigrants' kids	Y
3. Let guns in national parks	N	7. Regulate financial firms	Y	11. Repeal don't ask, tell	Y
4. Pass cap-and-trade	N	8. Pass tax cuts for some	Y	12. Limit campaign funds	Y

Election Results

2010 general	Dennis Kucinich (D)	101,343	(53%)	($978,635)
	Peter Corrigan (R)	83,809	(44%)	($420,571)
	Jeff Coggins (Lib)	5,874	(3%)	
2010 primary	Dennis Kucinich (D)	unopposed		

Prior Winning Percentages: 2008 (57%), 2006 (66%), 2004 (60%), 2002 (74%), 2000 (75%), 1998 (67%), 1996 (49%)

Population		Race/Ethnicity		Work	
Pop. 2010:	599,205	White:	80.0%	Private:	83.3%
Change since 2000:	Down 5.0%	Black:	8.3%	Government:	12.3%
Urban:	99.4%	Hispanic:	7.5%	Self-employed:	4.2%
Rural:	0.6%	Asian:	2.2%	Blue collar:	21.9%
Area size:	196 sq. mi.	Native Am.:	0.2%	White collar:	60.2%
		Hawaiian:	0.0%	Khaki collar:	0.0%
Age		Two+ races:	1.7%	Other:	17.9%
Median age:	40.2 yrs.				
More than 65 yrs:	15.4%	*Ancestry*		Median income:	$45,467
Less than 18 yrs:	22.2%	German	17.7%	Median Home Value:	$134,800
		Irish	13.8%		
Education		Polish	8.8%	**Military Veterans**	
H.S. grad:	85.8%			% of Pop:	10.1%
College grad:	24.8%				
Grad degree:	8.7%				

West Cleveland, Suburbs

Cleveland, one of America's great cities at the beginning of the 20th century, faced major hardships in the latter half of the century. It grew up as a center of heavy industry. This was the original base of John D. Rockefeller's Standard Oil. The city's deep, twisting Cuyahoga River was the site of several of the nation's largest steel mills. Great industrial fortunes built civic institutions like the museums in Wade Park, Case Western University and the Cleveland Sym-

2008 Presidential Vote		
Barack Obama (D) 174,598	(59%)
John McCain (R) 115,025	(39%)

2004 Presidential Vote		
John Kerry (D) 175,149	(58%)
George Bush (R) 125,102	(42%)

Cook Partisan Voting Index: D+8

phony, and they financed the campaigns of northeast Ohio Republican Presidents James Garfield and William McKinley. On the old Public Square, designed like a New England town green by the Yankees who settled this Western Reserve (the northeast corner of Ohio) in the early 19th century, the two eccentric Van Sweringen brothers, trolley magnates of the early 20th century, built the Terminal Tower, for many years the highest skyscraper in interior America. As an ethnic city with more than 40 nationalities—Hungarians, Czechs, Serbs, Croatians, Poles, Italians, Germans—and many distinct ethnic neighborhoods, it produced a robust two-party politics. In the 1930s, after CIO unions organized steel factories and auto assembly plants, Cleveland became solidly Democratic, though with some affluent Republican suburbs.

Disgruntled by local taxes, Rockefeller and his corporate operations moved to New York, and Cleveland never led the nation as it had hoped. America's fourth largest city in 1910, it was overtaken in size first by Detroit and eventually by Houston and Dallas. Today, it's not even Ohio's largest metropolis, having fallen behind Columbus and Cincinnati. The metropolitan area lost more people between 2000 and 2009 than any other large metro region except New Orleans and Pittsburgh. As the children who grew up in the tightly packed neighborhoods have made more money and moved to the suburbs, fewer new immigrants have taken their place, although there has been a recent uptick in Asians settling in. The 1970s were a hard decade for Cleveland. Its heavy industries were fast declining, corporate headquarters were departing, Lake Erie and the Cuyahoga River were badly polluted (the river caught fire in June 1969), and the city faced bankruptcy under the youthful Democratic Mayor Dennis Kucinich. The city government was rescued by Republican George Voinovich, elected mayor in 1979. Downtown Cleveland slowly revived, with the theater district center at Playhouse Square, the Jacobs Field baseball stadium, Gund Arena, and the Rock and Roll Hall of Fame. People now swim in a restored Lake Erie. Restaurants and boat docks line the Cuyahoga. In Brook Park, NASA's Glenn Research Center is developing the service module for the next generation of the space shuttle, and Ford Motor Co. added a second shift to its engine plant there in 2010. Cleveland's post-recession recovery ranked 10th among the top 50 U.S. metro areas, the Brookings Institution found.

The 10th Congressional District of Ohio includes most of the west side of Cleveland and the western and southern suburbs in Cuyahoga County. Excluded is one salient area of mostly black Cleveland precincts, which are attached to the 11th District across the river. Suburbs in the 10th include Lakewood, still comfortable middle-class territory, plus Rocky River and Bay Village. Inland is Parma, a creation of the 1950s, when second- and third-generation ethnics moved out to subdivision houses set amid what was once America's densest concentration of bowling alleys. The political tradition is primarily Democratic. In 2008, Democrat Barack Obama won the district with 59% of the vote to 39% for Republican John McCain.

Dennis Kucinich (D)

The congressman from the 10th District is Dennis Kucinich, a Democrat elected in 1996. He was an iconoclastic candidate for president in 2004 and 2008, and once billed himself as "America's most courageous congressman." With his vegan lifestyle, celebrity friendships, and far-left positions, he has come to symbolize the anti-war faction in Congress.

The son of a truck driver who was frequently out of work, Kucinich (*Koo SIN ich*) grew up as the oldest of seven children. The family moved 21 times to various parts of Cleveland and during particularly rough patches slept in the family's car. As the oldest, Kucinich went to work at 12 as a shoe-shine boy. Driven to succeed, he worked to put himself through college. In 1969, at age 23, he was elected to the Cleveland City Council. He saw himself as the champion of the working man and had a confrontational relationship with Cleveland's business establishment.

He was elected mayor in 1977, then the youngest-ever mayor of a major American city. But the city was in dire financial straits, and Kucinich was unwilling or unable to balance the budget and meet fiscal obligations. When bankers demanded that he sell city-owned properties, he refused, and they called in their loans. The public verdict was negative. In 1979, after surviving a recall petition by just 236 votes out of 120,000 cast, Kucinich was defeated. He argued that his primary goal had been to preserve the city-owned Muny Light electric system, and that in succeeding, he had saved residents millions of dollars on their electric bills. "This was a case of the bank blackmailing the city, pure and simple," he once said.

Kucinich was out of politics for a brief period, teaching at Cleveland State and Case Western Reserve universities and hosting a radio talk show. In 1994, he staged a political comeback and was elected to the state Senate. Two years later, he ran for the U.S. House against Republican Rep. Martin Hoke. He campaigned against the North American Free Trade Agreement and as a friend of labor. Many of his former critics rallied around him. The Cleveland City Council named a public power plant for him, and President Bill Clinton campaigned for him in Parma. Kucinich won, but by only 49%-46%.

Kucinich has been a vocal foe of international trade agreements and bars his staff from parking foreign cars in congressional lots. Even in the years Democrats controlled the House, he was largely out of the mainstream. A vegan since before he was elected to Congress, Kucinich has attacked companies that produce genetically modified foods. Active in the Progressive Caucus, his agenda includes a national health care system, universal pre-kindergarten, the abolition of all nuclear weapons, and repeal of the USA PATRIOT Act.

But he is perhaps better known for his non-legislative activities. He became the subject of national headlines in January 2011 when he filed a lawsuit against the congressional cafeteria over an unpitted olive that he said broke a tooth in 2008. (He quickly reached a confidential settlement for his dental expenses.) Four years earlier, he drew more attention when actress and New Age activist Shirley MacLaine—who is godmother to one of the congressman's children—said she hoped his reported sighting of a UFO would force the government to investigate. And in 2005 he drew extensive publicity for marrying his third wife, Elizabeth, who is 31 years his junior. "He has the wisdom of an ancient and the energy of youth," she told *The Plain Dealer,* the Cleveland newspaper.

Since President Barack Obama took office, Kucinich has been both a help and a hindrance to the man he once ran against. The most prominent example of the former was Kucinich's decision in March 2010 to support the final version of the health care overhaul. An outspoken advocate of a government-run, single-payer system, he had resisted previous entreaties from House Democratic leaders. But after Obama came to his district to lobby him personally, Kucinich said he did not want to be the cause of the bill's defeat. But he has remained critical of the president on foreign policy. When the United States joined a NATO coalition in attacking Libyan forces that were quelling a rebel uprising in March 2011, Kucinich angrily told the liberal website *Raw Story* that the move "appeared to be an impeachable offense." But he subsequently backed off that suggestion.

Kucinich has been an active member of the Oversight and Government Reform Committee, having chaired its Domestic Policy Subcommittee. With then-full committee Chairman Henry Waxman of California, he held hearings on high mortgage foreclosure rates in the Cleveland area, the use of taxpayer money for athletic stadiums, and the dealings of U.S. oil companies in Iraq after the fall of Saddam Hussein. Later, he looked into the insurance industry's financial, lobbying and business practices. His chief initiative was a series of resolutions to impeach President George W. Bush and Vice President Dick Cheney for lying to Congress about the justification for invading Iraq. "The war was totally unnecessary, unprovoked and unjustified," Kucinich said in July 2008. Democratic leaders saw the move as an unwelcome distraction and it went nowhere. After Democrats lost their majority in 2010, Kucinich unsuccessfully proposed that he become Oversight and Government Reform's ranking Democrat to counter the aggressive incoming chairman, California Republican Darrell Issa.

Brimming with self-confidence a few years earlier, Kucinich made himself a candidate for the Democratic nomination in the 2004 presidential contest, saying he would be an "FDR Democrat" and "return the Democratic Party to its roots" with strong ties to organized labor. "Miracles occur," he claimed when he announced his candidacy. He spoke to enthusiastic audiences of peace activists. Long an opponent of abortion rights, he changed his position, saying that as president his Supreme Court nominees would have to support the *Roe v. Wade* decision legalizing abortion. Even though he did not come close to winning a single state, trailing far behind Vermont's Howard Dean in winning the support of party leftists, Kucinich remained buoyant and enjoyed the attention. Long after Massachusetts Sen. John Kerry had clinched the nomination, Kucinich continued to campaign.

Running for president again in 2008, Kucinich more than ever marched to his own drummer, and his candidacy was not taken seriously by other Democrats or the news media. He challenged corporate America, emphasized world peace and promised to protect the little guy. "Why should people vote for a Democrat if you can't tell the difference?" he said. Among those endorsing him was country singer Willie Nelson, a friend who shares his anti-war views. Citing his exclusion from national debates, Kucinich ended his campaign in late January 2008 to shift his attention to a competitive primary for his House seat.

He has faced some trouble at home in recent elections. In 2006 the *Plain Dealer* endorsed his primary opponent Barbara Anne Ferris, a former Peace Corps worker, in part because of Kucinich's failure to address local problems. But he won easily, 76%-24%. In 2008, Cleveland City Councilman Joe Cimperman spent more than $600,000 to challenge him in the primary and criticized Kucinich for having little influence in Congress. The *Plain Dealer* endorsed Cimperman and said that Kucinich had ignored his district for "an absolutely hopeless quest for the White House." But Kucinich won 50%-35%. In the general election, he faced Republican Jim Trakas, a former state representative from Independence, who criticized him for "misplaced priorities." Kucinich won 57%-39%. It was much the same story in 2010, as he had to defend his support of health care reform in a strongly anti-incumbent climate. But he campaigned vigorously, outraised Republican businessman Peter Corrigan by more than 2-to-1 and won 53%-44%.

With census figures showing Ohio would lose two congressional seats through GOP-led reapportionment, Kucinich became widely regarded as the state's most vulnerable Democrat. He sought to take the offensive in early 2011, sending an e-mail to supporters titled "My Congressional District May Be Eliminated" and appealing for donations from his national liberal base.

ELEVENTH DISTRICT

Marcia Fudge (D)

Elected Nov. 2008, 2nd full term; b. Oct. 29, 1952, Cleveland; home, Warrensville Heights; OH St. U., B.S. 1975; Cleveland St. U., J.D. 1983; Christian; single.

Elected Office: Warrensville Heights mayor, 2000-08.

Professional Career: Practicting atty.; Aide to U.S. Rep. Stephanie Tubbs Jones, 1991-2000.

DC Office: 1019 LHOB, 20515, 202-225-7032; Fax: 202-225-1339; Web site: fudge.house.gov.

State Offices: Warrensville Heights, 216-522-4900.

Committees: *Agriculture:* Conservation, Energy & Forestry; Department Operations, Oversight & Credit (RMM). *Science, Space & Technology:* Space & Aeronautics.

Group Ratings

	ACLU	ACU	ADA	CFG	AFS	FRC	LCV	ITIC	NTU	COC
2010	100	4	95	3	100	6	100	67	5	25
2009	–	0	100	0	100	–	93	–	1	33

National Journal Ratings

	2010 LIB	—	2010 CONS	2009 LIB	—	2009 CONS
Economic	80%	—	18%	91%	—	0%
Social	71%	—	25%	89%	—	0%
Foreign	92%	—	3%	84%	—	15%
Composite	83%	—	17%	92%	—	9%

Key Votes of the 111th Congress

1. Overturn Ledbetter	Y	5. Bar federal abortion funds	N
2. Pass $820 billion stimulus	Y	6. Pass health care bill	Y
3. Let guns in national parks	N	7. Regulate financial firms	Y
4. Pass cap-and-trade	Y	8. Pass tax cuts for some	Y

9. Stop detainee transfers	N
10. Legalize immigrants' kids	Y
11. Repeal don't ask, tell	Y
12. Limit campaign funds	N

Election Results

2010 general	Marcia Fudge (D)	139,693	(83%)	($566,127)
	Thomas Pekarek (R)	28,754	(17%)	
2010 primary	Marcia Fudge (D)	47,773	(85%)	
	Daniel Reilly (D)	5,385	(10%)	

Prior Winning Percentages: 2008 (85%); 2008 special (100%)

Population		Race/Ethnicity		Work	
Pop. 2010:	540,432	White:	33.6%	Private:	81.2%
Change since 2000:	Down 14.3%	Black:	59.3%	Government:	14.4%
Urban:	100.0%	Hispanic:	2.6%	Self-employed:	4.4%
Rural:	0.0%	Asian:	2.3%	Blue collar:	17.7%
Area size:	135 sq. mi.	Native Am.:	0.2%	White collar:	60.9%
		Hawaiian:	0.0%	Khaki collar:	0.0%
Age		Two+ races:	1.7%	Other:	21.4%
Median age:	37.5 yrs.				
More than 65 yrs:	15.2%	*Ancestry*		Median income:	$34,444
Less than 18 yrs:	24.1%	German	7.0%	Median Home Value:	$115,900
		Irish	5.9%		
Education		Italian	4.8%	**Military Veterans**	
H.S. grad:	83.4%			% of Pop:	9.1%
College grad:	26.0%				
Grad degree:	11.9%				

East Cleveland, Suburbs

Like most great American cities, Cleveland grew in great bursts of migration, during periods when the economy expanded and attracted low-wage workers from around the country and the world. Cleveland's greatest surge of growth started in the 1890s and lasted through the 1920s, as tens of thousands of immigrants from central and southern Europe arrived, looking for jobs in the steel, automobile and other factories.

2008 Presidential Vote		
Barack Obama (D)	245,341	(85%)
John McCain (R)	41,601	(14%)
2004 Presidential Vote		
John Kerry (D)	237,469	(81%)
George Bush (R)	52,372	(18%)
Cook Partisan Voting Index:	D+32	

Bohemians came to the tightly packed neighborhoods along Broadway, Hungarians settled in the northeast, and Jews north of University Circle along East 105th Street. Italians ran produce markets along Mayfield Road. As the nation's heavy industries geared up for World War II and enjoyed years of prosperous growth afterward, a second surge of immigrants came, this time blacks from the South. Starting from Cleveland's old ghetto, south of Carnegie Avenue downtown to East 105th, the rapidly increasing number of African-Americans covered most of the east side by the middle 1960s.

Migration stopped around 1965, but African-Americans continued to move beyond the city limits to the east-side suburbs. These bursts of migration led to political changes. A string of ethnic mayors—Frank Lausche, Anthony Celebrezze, Ralph Locher—was followed by the election in 1967 of Carl Stokes, the nation's first black big-city mayor. Cleveland had racially polarized politics for much of the 1970s. Even so, the west side stayed mostly white, and Cleveland did not have a black majority until the 2000 census, when its declining population was 51% black. The Census Bureau reported in 2010 that Cleveland was second to Detroit as the poorest of the nation's big cities, with more than half of all children living in poverty. Earlier that year, *Forbes* named it America's most miserable city, a distinction that greatly angered local politicians. Its 2010 population of 397,000 was 17% below what it was in 2000.

The 11th Congressional District of Ohio includes most of the east side of Cleveland, plus the suburbs just to the east. Almost one-sixth of the district's households earn less than $10,000 a year. Some of its suburbs—East Cleveland, Warrensville Heights—are mostly black. Some, notably Shaker Heights, have stable black percentages in carefully maintained neighborhoods. Near the campus of Case Western Reserve University on the east side, Severance Hall is one of the nation's grand symphony-orchestra homes. The city's No. 1 employer is health services, and the Cleveland Clinic, with 1,800 doctors, is internationally renowned, especially for cardiac care. The clinic broke ground in 2010 on a new $75 million laboratory. Other suburbs are the destination of African-Americans seeking low-crime neighborhoods and middle-class schools. Still others have attracted Cleveland's relatively few new immigrants, most of them from Eastern Europe—Russians in Mayfield Heights and Serbs in South Euclid. Overall, 58% of the people in the 11th District are African-American. Politically, this is by far the most Democratic district in Ohio.

Marcia Fudge (D)

The congresswoman from the 11th District is Marcia Fudge, a Democrat who succeeded her former mentor and friend, Rep. Stephanie Tubbs Jones, after the five-term Tubbs Jones died on Aug. 20,

2008, from a cerebral aneurysm. Fudge, like many African-Americans of her generation, was greatly influenced by the civil rights movement and got active politically when she was young. She grew up in Cleveland, but her family moved to the suburb of Shaker Heights when she was 12. During high school, Fudge volunteered with "Young Folks for Stokes," a coalition of young people helping to elect Carl Stokes mayor. She helped with get-out-the-vote efforts and with distributing campaign literature. After graduating from the Ohio State University with a degree in business administration, she received her law degree from Cleveland State University. She practiced mainly criminal defense law in the Cleveland area, along with some probate and corporate work, until she went to work for Tubbs Jones. Fudge and Tubbs Jones first met as members of the national Delta Sigma Theta Sorority alumnae association. Fudge later served as national president of the group of predominately African-American women. When Tubbs Jones became the Cuyahoga County prosecutor in 1991, Fudge served as her administrative assistant. When her boss was elected to Congress in 1998, Fudge came with her to Washington as chief of staff.

After a few years, Fudge felt the pull of elected office herself. When the Warrensville Heights mayor resigned after pleading guilty to improper solicitation, she decided to run and won, becoming the first African-American woman to be elected mayor of the city. Fudge focused on economic development and claimed credit for creating 3,000 new jobs and bringing in $500 million for development and infrastructure.

Tubbs Jones died unexpectedly just a few days before the Democratic National Convention in Denver, after winning the Democratic primary for re-election. Members of the district's Democratic Executive Committee were in charge of selecting her replacement on the ballot. Fudge called each member of the committee to explain why she would be the best choice to carry on Tubbs Jones' legacy. The strategy paid off. There were four candidates, and the committee nominated Fudge with 175 votes. Former state Sen. C. J. Prentiss was a distant second, with 64 votes. In the ten-way special primary on October 14 to fill the remainder of Tubbs Jones' term, Fudge cruised to victory with 74%. She won the general election 85%-15% and had no Republican challenger for the Nov. 18 special general election, allowing her to be sworn in before other freshmen members that year.

In the House, Fudge has been a solidly liberal vote. She joined the Congressional Black Caucus and has worked with its other members to decry proposed Republican cuts affecting low-income residents. In urging an extension of unemployment benefits in July 2010, she said on the House floor: "I hope you can't sleep until you understand that our former coworkers, our neighbors, our friends, our family are hurting." She opposed a compromise tax bill in December 2010 because she was skeptical it would put general tax dollars into Social Security to replace lost payroll taxes. She joined other pro-labor Ohio Democrats in March 2011 in seeking to block a pending trade agreement with South Korea because it did not go far enough to help U.S. automakers and auto supply companies.

Some of the attention Fudge drew in the 111th Congress (2009-10) revolved around her proposal to rein in the powers of the independent Office of Congressional Ethics. The OCE found in 2009 that Fudge's chief of staff "improperly influenced" information that a group called Carib News Foundation had given to the House Ethics Committee about an annual Caribbean trip that the group had sponsored for Black Caucus members. Fudge introduced a bill seeking to place limits on the OCE's jurisdiction and to bar "premature publication" of its findings—actions that ethics watchdog groups said would render the OCE ineffectual. Fudge's office said the bill was merely meant to ensure that ethics complaints came from credible sources and did not become media fodder. The bill did not move.

Though redistricting in 2012 is expected to eliminate one of the Cleveland area's two congressional seats, Fudge is considered to be at less risk than fellow Democrat Dennis Kucinich from redistricting. Republicans in charge of the process are mindful of the Voting Rights Act, which helps protect minority-majority districts.

TWELFTH DISTRICT

Pat Tiberi (R)

Elected 2000, 6th term; b. Oct. 21, 1962, Columbus; home, Columbus; OH St. U., B.A. 1985; Catholic; married (Denice); 4 children.

Elected Office: OH House of Reps., 1992-2000, Maj. ldr., 1999-2000.

Professional Career: Staff asst., U.S. Rep. John Kasich, 1984-92; Realtor, ReMax Achievers, 1995-2000.

DC Office: 106 CHOB, 20515, 202-225-5355; Fax: 202-226-4523; Web site: tiberi.house.gov.

State Offices: Columbus, 614-523-2555.

Committees: *Ways & Means:* Select Revenue Measures (Chmn); Social Security.

Group Ratings

	ACLU	ACU	ADA	CFG	AFS	FRC	LCV	ITIC	NTU	COC
2010	13	96	0	79	0	93	20	33	85	88
2009	–	83	15	73	38	–	29	–	74	87

National Journal Ratings

	2010 LIB — 2010 CONS		2009 LIB — 2009 CONS	
Economic	32%	67%	36%	64%
Social	35%	65%	32%	68%
Foreign	33%	65%	0%	75%
Composite	34%	66%	27%	73%

Key Votes of the 111th Congress

1. Overturn Ledbetter	N	5. Bar federal abortion funds	Y
2. Pass $820 billion stimulus	N	6. Pass health care bill	N
3. Let guns in national parks	Y	7. Regulate financial firms	N
4. Pass cap-and-trade	N	8. Pass tax cuts for some	N

9. Stop detainee transfers	Y
10. Legalize immigrants' kids	N
11. Repeal don't ask, tell	N
12. Limit campaign funds	N

Election Results

2010 general	Pat Tiberi (R)	150,163	(56%)	($3,041,995)
	Paula Brooks (D)	110,307	(41%)	($1,447,544)
	Travis Irvine (Lib)	8,710	(3%)	($8,179)
2010 primary	Pat Tiberi (R)	53,632	(86%)	
	Andrew Zukowski (R)	8,442	(14%)	

Prior Winning Percentages: 2008 (55%), 2006 (57%), 2004 (62%), 2002 (64%), 2000 (53%)

Population		Race/Ethnicity		Work	
Pop. 2010:	756,303	White:	68.5%	Private:	80.6%
Change since 2000:	Up 19.9%	Black:	21.7%	Government:	13.7%
Urban:	88.1%	Hispanic:	3.5%	Self-employed:	5.5%
Rural:	11.9%	Asian:	3.6%	Blue collar:	14.4%
Area size:	1,031 sq. mi.	Native Am.:	0.2%	White collar:	70.7%
		Hawaiian:	0.0%	Khaki collar:	0.0%
Age		Two+ races:	2.3%	Other:	14.9%
Median age:	35.2 yrs.				
More than 65 yrs:	10.4%	**Ancestry**		Median income:	$57,258
Less than 18 yrs:	25.8%	German	20.5%	Median Home Value:	$182,800
		Irish	10.8%		
Education		English	8.3%	**Military Veterans**	
H.S. grad:	91.5%			% of Pop:	9.1%
College grad:	38.1%				
Grad degree:	12.8%				

Central Ohio; Columbus, Suburbs

Columbus is on the verge of becoming a major metropolis. With city limits stretching toward farmland at each point of the compass, the central Ohio city had 787,000 people in 2010, far more than Cleveland or Cincinnati. Columbus'

2008 Presidential Vote		
Barack Obama (D) 209,237	(54%)
John McCain (R) 171,448	(45%)
2004 Presidential Vote		
George Bush (R) 178,080	(51%)
John Kerry (D) 171,881	(49%)
Cook Partisan Voting Index: D+1		

Franklin County passed the 1 million mark in the 1990s and was at 1.2 million in 2010. The city is centrally located, not only in the center of Ohio, but also just a one-day truck drive from more than half of the nation's population. It has the advantages of being the state capital, the home of the Ohio State University, and a major white-collar employment town. It is the home of Nationwide Insurance, Wendy's International, and Red Roof Inns. It also is considered to have one of the strongest manufacturing bases in the United States, with companies such as Honda of America and Scotts Miracle-Gro. The city's economic base and civic infrastructure helped it avoid the worst of the 2007-09 recession and have attracted the kind of upscale, enterprising people who have produced much of America's growth in recent years. Its rapidly growing foreign-born population—Latinos, Asians, Ethiopians, Russian Jews, and Somalis—exceeds that of Cleveland or Detroit. But the city also has suffered from traditional big-city problems as well, which has spurred a migration of students from public to private schools.

The politics of Columbus traditionally were Republican. It had few of the Eastern European immigrants and CIO unions that made Cleveland so Democratic. But in 1999, Columbus elected African-American Democrat Michael Coleman as mayor, and in 2000, Franklin County was carried, though just barely, by Democrat Al Gore. In 2004, thanks to out-migration of whites and a vigorous registration drive by Democrats, John Kerry carried the county 54%-45% and Barack Obama won it four years later, 60%-39%.

The 12th Congressional District of Ohio is one of two districts dominated by Columbus and Franklin County. It includes 39% of the city, including most of the east side, plus the affluent suburb of Bexley, site of the Governor's Mansion, and the northeastern suburbs in Franklin County. It also includes Delaware County, directly north of Columbus, which is Ohio's fastest-growing county; it grew 58% from 2000 to 2010. The district takes in most of Licking County east of Columbus, including the small industrial town of Newark and the lovely college town of Granville. With big margins in Delaware and Licking Counties, George W. Bush won here 51%-49% in 2004. But Obama's Ohio victory switched this district to 54%-45% in his favor.

Pat Tiberi (R)

The congressman from the 12th District is Pat Tiberi, a Republican elected in 2000. He is an experienced Ohio politician who is one of Speaker John Boehner's closest allies, and has reaped the benefits of that association by swiftly ascending on the powerful House Ways and Means Committee.

The son of Italian immigrants, Tiberi (*TEE berry*) grew up in Columbus and graduated from the Ohio State University. He worked as a real estate agent and then as an assistant to Republican U.S. Rep. John Kasich (now governor) for eight years. Kasich helped Tiberi win a seat in the state House, where he became majority leader and supported business-friendly legislation and tort law changes. In 1999, Kasich, then chairman of the Budget Committee, announced his retirement from the House. Tiberi won support to replace his mentor from most of the Republican establishment and from the U.S. Chamber of Commerce. He faced a noisy but not very effective primary challenge from state Sen. Gene Watts, who sought to rally conservatives. Tiberi won 73%-21%.

The resounding victory gave him a big boost heading into the general election against Maryellen O'Shaughnessy, a Democratic Columbus City Council member. She had a compelling personal story as the single mother of a 10-year-old son. Tiberi played up his Columbus roots and his membership in the Ohio State marching band and held O'Shaughnessy responsible for negative Democratic Party ads that labeled him a defender of insurance companies on the issue of affordable prescription drugs. This was one of the most-watched House races in the nation. With campaign help from Kasich, Tiberi won 53%-44%.

In the House, Tiberi's record has been conservative on economic and cultural issues but occasionally centrist on defense and foreign policy. He took over the chairmanship of Ways and Means' Select Revenue Subcommittee in 2011 and pledged to work on scrapping the income tax code. His partner in the effort was Sen. Ron Wyden, D-Ore., who has a habit of seeking pragmatic Republicans to work with him on knotty issues. They compared their alliance to President Ronald Reagan working with a Republican Senate and a Democratic House to reform the tax code in 1986.

Tiberi was the campaign manager for Boehner's successful bid for majority leader in early 2006, and he later helped Boehner fix organizational problems at the National Republican Congressional Committee. He typically toes the party line against Democratic proposals on Ways and Means and was a sharp critic of the 2010 health care overhaul, but he supported their bills to expand the State Children's Health Insurance Program. He also supported a Democratic overhaul of food safety laws in 2009 and, at Boehner's urging, backed the final version of the Troubled Asset Relief Program in 2008 after initially opposing it. Tiberi and fellow Ohioan Steve LaTourette were two of only seven Republicans to vote against denying federal funding for National Public Radio in March 2011.

Despite the district's narrow partisan balance, Tiberi has easily won re-election. In 2006, he faced an unusual challenge from 79-year-old Bob Shamansky, a lawyer and real estate investor who held the seat for two years before Kasich defeated him in 1982. Shamansky criticized the Iraq War, but Tiberi distanced himself from President George W. Bush on Iraq, and he won 57%-43%.

In 2008, he was challenged by businessman and environmental advocate David Robinson, a political novice who ran on the need for change in Congress. Tiberi won 55%-42%, although he lost 51%-46% in Franklin County, which cast over half the vote. He drew a serious challenger two years later in Franklin County Commissioner Paula Brooks, who sought to tap into anti-Washington anger. But Tiberi made the most of the fact that Brooks actually lived in the neighboring 15th District, not the 12th. With Kasich leading the GOP wave in Ohio that year, Tiberi won 56%-41%.

THIRTEENTH DISTRICT

Betty Sutton (D)

Elected 2006, 3rd term; b. July 31, 1963, Barberton; home, Copley Township; Kent St. U., B.A. 1985, U. of Akron, J.D. 1990; Methodist; married (Doug Corwon); 2 children.

Elected Office: Barberton City Cncl., 1989-91; Summit Cnty. Cncl., 1991-92; OH House of Reps., 1992-2000.

Professional Career: Practicing atty., 2001-06.

DC Office: 1519 LHOB, 20515, 202-225-3401; Fax: 202-225-2266; Web site: sutton.house.gov.

State Offices: Akron, 330-865-8450; Lorain, 440-245-5350.

Committees: *Armed Services:* Seapower & Projection Forces; Strategic Forces. *Natural Resources:* Energy & Mineral Resources; National Parks, Forests & Public Lands.

Group Ratings

	ACLU	ACU	ADA	CFG	AFS	FRC	LCV	ITIC	NTU	COC
2010	88	0	95	0	100	0	100	100	6	14
2009	–	0	100	0	100	–	100	–	2	33

National Journal Ratings

	2010 LIB — 2010 CONS		2009 LIB — 2009 CONS	
Economic	80%	— 18%	88%	— 9%
Social	61%	— 35%	80%	— 18%
Foreign	66%	— 29%	91%	— 0%
Composite	71%	— 29%	89%	— 11%

Key Votes of the 111th Congress

1. Overturn Ledbetter	Y	5. Bar federal abortion funds	N	9. Stop detainee transfers	Y
2. Pass $820 billion stimulus	Y	6. Pass health care bill	Y	10. Legalize immigrants' kids	Y
3. Let guns in national parks	N	7. Regulate financial firms	Y	11. Repeal don't ask, tell	Y
4. Pass cap-and-trade	Y	8. Pass tax cuts for some	Y	12. Limit campaign funds	Y

Election Results

2010 general	Betty Sutton (D)	118,806	(56%)	($1,799,214)
	Tom Ganley (R)	94,367	(44%)	($8,326,077)
2010 primary	Betty Sutton (D)	37,460	(79%)	
	Justin Wooden (D)	9,706	(21%)	

Prior Winning Percentages: 2008 (65%), 2006 (61%)

Population		Race/Ethnicity		Work	
Pop. 2010:	649,102	White:	79.6%	Private:	83.8%
Change since 2000:	Up 2.9%	Black:	11.8%	Government:	11.7%
Urban:	92.7%	Hispanic:	4.6%	Self-employed:	4.3%
Rural:	7.3%	Asian:	1.7%	Blue collar:	21.8%
Area size:	537 sq. mi.	Native Am.:	0.2%	White collar:	61.3%
		Hawaiian:	0.0%	Khaki collar:	0.1%
Age		Two+ races:	1.9%	Other:	16.8%
Median age:	39.9 yrs.				
More than 65 yrs:	14.0%	*Ancestry*		Median income:	$50,035
Less than 18 yrs:	24.0%	German	18.3%	Median Home Value:	$151,700
		Irish	11.8%		
Education		Italian	7.3%	**Military Veterans**	
H.S. grad:	89.3%			% of Pop:	10.6%
College grad:	26.2%				
Grad degree:	9.6%				

Northeastern Ohio; Part Akron

Fifty years ago, most of the people of metro Cleveland were clustered in the city itself, in tightly packed blocks of houses above the Cuyahoga River valley and its giant steel mills. Around the city were some comfortable suburbs, and beyond them, miles of farm fields before you encountered the nearby industrial cities—Akron, the "Rubber Capital" with its Firestone, B. F. Goodrich and Goodyear tire factories, and Lorain, a sort of mini-Cleveland on Lake Erie

2008 Presidential Vote
Barack Obama (D) 185,742   (57%)
John McCain (R) 137,374   (42%)

2004 Presidential Vote
John Kerry (D) 177,472   (56%)
George Bush (R) 140,908   (44%)

Cook Partisan Voting Index: D+5

with steel mills lining the narrow Black River. Since then, the population of Cleveland has fallen by half, and the metropolitan area has spread out over the northern Ohio countryside. The suburbs now cover an area from Cleveland to Akron without interval. The shoreline from Cleveland to Lorain has been filled in. Medina County, between Lorain and Akron, has also been transformed from farm land to suburbia. Only the Cuyahoga River valley between Cleveland and Akron has been off-limits to development, protected by the creation of the Cuyahoga Valley National Park.

The economy has changed as well. In 1950, Cleveland depended on heavy manufacturing, especially steel, and Akron was reliant on tires. Today, most of the steel mills are shuttered or torn down, most of the old tire factories have been converted to other uses. Lorain has managed to survive as a steel town; U.S. Steel Corp. announced a huge expansion in February 2011 at its plant there to make pipes for natural gas companies. Meanwhile, Akron has promoted itself as the "Polymer Center of America," with 80% of the nation's polymer research and a first-class polymer engineering program at the University of Akron. It ranks second in the nation behind Austin, Texas, in science and engineering students as a percentage of the total workforce. Akron also has produced a number of successful rock musicians, including 1980s new wave legends Devo and Pretenders vocalist Chrissie Hynde, who in 2007 opened a vegan restaurant in the city. (Her song, "My City Was Gone," laments Akron's downfall.) Downtown Akron has been revived by entertainment areas and some upscale housing. Still, the city's population dropped by nearly 10,000 from 2000 to 2009.

The 13th Congressional District of Ohio is made up of much of this metro Cleveland area, though none of the city itself. It includes the west side of Akron and its western suburbs. The lines separating it from the 14th and 17th Districts in Akron's Summit County are absurdly convoluted. The district encompasses the northern and eastern parts of Lorain County, including Lorain and Elyria just to the south; the southern tier of suburban townships in Cleveland's Cuyahoga County—Strongsville, North Royalton, Broadview Heights; and the northern tier of suburban townships in Medina County, including Brunswick. Fifty years ago, this area would have been Republican. Today, as Clevelanders have spread far and wide, it is Democratic, though not overwhelmingly so. Republican George W. Bush twice got 44% of the vote here. In 2008, Democrat Barack Obama won the district with 57%.

Betty Sutton (D)

The congresswoman from the 13th District is Democrat Betty Sutton, first elected in 2006. A strongly pro-labor champion of the middle class, her wildly popular "Cash for Clunkers" car rebate initiative helped her withstand one of the nation's wealthiest Republican challengers in 2010.

Sutton grew up in Barberton as the youngest of six children. Her mother was a library clerk and her father a boilermaker. She graduated from Kent State University and then earned a law degree from the University of Akron. In 1989, while still in law school, Sutton won an at-large seat on the Barberton City Council and in 1991 was elected to the Summit County Council. In 1992, at age 29, she became the youngest woman to win a seat in the state House, where she worked on employment issues like health care and pensions. In 1993, after speaking publicly about an abusive first marriage, she worked to pass legislation to protect women from domestic violence. She fought passage of a Republican bill to cut workers' compensation benefits and then led a referendum to repeal the law. She served in the legislature until term limits forced her out in 2000, and afterward worked as a labor lawyer.

When Democratic Rep. Sherrod Brown announced that he would run for the Senate, Sutton quickly emerged as a leading contender to succeed him. She faced significant opposition in the primary from former eight-term U.S. Rep. Tom Sawyer and from shopping center heiress Capri Cafaro. Sawyer had good name recognition but struggled to raise money and was dogged by his 1993 vote for the North American Free Trade Agreement, which was blamed for sending many of the district's manufacturing jobs overseas. Cafaro, who had run unsuccessfully in 2004 against Republican U.S. Rep. Steven LaTourette, poured more than $2 million of her own money into the primary. Sutton criticized Sawyer for taking privately financed trips and Cafaro for her ties to a federal investigation of former Democratic Rep. James Traficant of Ohio, who had been convicted of bribery in 2002. Cafaro had been an executive of a company run by her father, who pleaded guilty to bribing Traficant. With strong backing from organized labor, Sutton won the eight-way primary with 31%, ahead of Cafaro with 25% and Sawyer with 22%.

In the general election, her Republican opponent was Lorain Mayor Craig Foltin, an accountant who campaigned for sound fiscal management. National Republicans were interested in his candidacy because he had won two races in a Democratic city and had raised an impressive $250,000 for his last mayoral campaign. Democrats attempted to tie Foltin to Republican scandals in Ohio. Sutton raised twice as much as Foltin, including more than $300,000 from EMILY's List donors. The poor political environment for Republicans and the district's large union presence proved too much for Foltin. Sutton won 61%-39%.

In the House, Sutton has been an ardent champion for unions. When Ohio state lawmakers discussed eliminating collective bargaining for public employees in early 2011, as Republicans were doing in other states, she urged her Buckeye State colleagues to stand up to the "unfair, backward-thinking attack." She has been an outspoken foe of free-trade agreements and a leader in pushing for organized labor's "card check" bill, which would bypass the traditional union election process and allow workers to be certified as a bargaining unit if a majority signed cards indicating their support for a union.

In June 2008, the House passed her bill mandating nationwide access to automated external defibrillators, a proposal suggested by an Akron cardiologist. She also has been a key player on other safety issues, working to get into law in December 2010 the broadest-ranging improvements to food safety law since the 1930s. Nothing, however, brought her as much attention as her "Cash for Clunkers" proposal in March 2009 that created vouchers of $3,500 to $4,500 to people trading in old cars for more fuel-efficient vehicles. The bill quickly passed the House Energy and Commerce and gained momentum in late April, when Sutton agreed to drop provisions requiring that cars purchased under the program be made in North America. When an additional $1 billion in rebates was depleted within a week, Congress swiftly put another $2 billion into the program.

Sutton was re-elected easily in 2008, but with Ohio's economy tanking in 2010 Republicans considered her vulnerable. Cleveland-based auto dealer Tom Ganley abandoned his Senate primary bid against former Rep. Rob Portman in February to run against her. Ganley spent $1.7 million of his own money. He raised an astonishing $8.3 million, compared with Sutton's $1.8 million. Ganley also got help from the National Republican Congressional Committee as well as local party organizations. In one flyer sent out by the Medina County GOP, she was urged to get out of the House and back in the kitchen—a comment she called sexist.

Polls showed a tight race. But EMILY's List and other Democratic-leaning groups raced to her aid, and Ganley was hit a month before the election by allegations from a woman who filed a lawsuit alleging that he turned her down for a volunteer job with his campaign because she refused his advances. Just before the election, another woman filed a complaint with police accusing Ganley of grabbing her buttocks while he was showing her a vehicle at his dealership in 2005. Ganley angrily denied the allegations and suggested they were politically motivated. But the damage was done, and Sutton won 56%-44%. With Ohio to lose two House seats in reapportionment in 2012, she must now worry if Republicans try to parcel out her district to two neighboring Democratic seats.

FOURTEENTH DISTRICT

Steven LaTourette (R)

Elected 1994, 9th term; b. July 22, 1954, Cleveland; home, Madison; U. of MI, B.A. 1976, Cleveland St. U., J.D. 1979; Methodist; married (Jennifer Laptook); 5 children.

Elected Office: Lake Cnty. district atty., 1988-94.

Professional Career: Lake Cnty. asst. public defender, 1980–83; Practicing atty., 1983–88.

DC Office: 2371 RHOB, 20515, 202-225-5731; Fax: 202-225-3307; Web site: latourette.house.gov.

State Offices: Painesville, 800-447-0529; Twinsburg, 330-425-9291.

Committees: *Appropriations:* Interior, Environment & Related Agencies; Legislative Branch; Transportation, HUD & Related Agencies (VChmn).

Group Ratings

	ACLU	ACU	ADA	CFG	AFS	FRC	LCV	ITIC	NTU	COC
2010	13	75	10	69	29	81	40	33	71	88
2009	–	68	25	65	44	–	43	–	53	93

National Journal Ratings

	2010 LIB — 2010 CONS		2009 LIB — 2009 CONS	
Economic	39%	— 61%	39%	— 61%
Social	38%	— 62%	36%	— 63%
Foreign	33%	— 65%	38%	— 62%
Composite	37%	— 63%	38%	— 62%

Key Votes of the 111th Congress

1. Overturn Ledbetter	N	5. Bar federal abortion funds	Y
2. Pass $820 billion stimulus	N	6. Pass health care bill	N
3. Let guns in national parks	Y	7. Regulate financial firms	N
4. Pass cap-and-trade	N	8. Pass tax cuts for some	N

9. Stop detainee transfers	Y	
10. Legalize immigrants' kids	N	
11. Repeal don't ask, tell	N	
12. Limit campaign funds	N	

Election Results

2010 general	Steven LaTourette (R)	149,878	(65%)	($1,290,686)
	Bill O'Neill (D)	72,604	(31%)	($137,671)
	John Jelenic (Lib)	8,383	(4%)	
2010 primary	Steven LaTourette (R)	unopposed		

Prior Winning Percentages: 2008 (58%), 2006 (58%), 2004 (63%), 2002 (72%), 2000 (69%), 1998 (66%), 1996 (55%), 1994 (48%)

Population		Race/Ethnicity		Work	
Pop. 2010:	648,128	White:	90.8%	Private:	83.2%
Change since 2000:	Up 2.8%	Black:	3.6%	Government:	10.5%
Urban:	74.1%	Hispanic:	2.3%	Self-employed:	6.1%
Rural:	25.9%	Asian:	1.8%	Blue collar:	22.3%
Area size:	1,818 sq. mi.	Native Am.:	0.1%	White collar:	62.6%
		Hawaiian:	0.0%	Khaki collar:	0.1%
Age		Two+ races:	1.3%	Other:	15.0%
Median age:	41.5 yrs.				
More than 65 yrs:	14.9%	*Ancestry*		Median income:	$58,703
Less than 18 yrs:	24.0%	German	18.4%	Median Home Value:	$177,400
		Irish	12.2%		
Education		Italian	10.2%	**Military Veterans**	
H.S. grad:	91.0%			% of Pop:	10.8%
College grad:	30.6%				
Grad degree:	10.9%				

Northeastern Ohio

The imprint of the westward track of New England Yankee migration is still apparent today on the shores of Lake Erie in northern Ohio. The Yankees, cooped up in New England for 200 years, shot west across the country through upstate New York, across Ohio and Michigan to Chicago, and on to Kansas and Southern California in just two or three generations, providing inspiration, manpower, and technical might for the Union victory in the Civil War and leaving

2008 Presidential Vote		
John McCain (R)	169,495	(49%)
Barack Obama (D)	168,753	(49%)
2004 Presidential Vote		
George Bush (R)	178,510	(53%)
John Kerry (D)	159,929	(47%)
Cook Partisan Voting Index:	R+3	

their imprint along the way. One place they stopped was the Western Reserve, the northeast corner of Ohio, created for the excess population of Connecticut. This area produced some of the nation's strongest opposition to slavery and hardiest support of the Union armies and the Republican Party; Lake Erie ports were prime transit points for the Underground Railroad to Canada. Its thrifty, hardworking, well-educated citizens built communities with fine schools and, with their accumulated savings, invested in what became some of the nation's leading industries. A century ago, that brought great masses of immigrants to Cleveland and the other cities of northeast Ohio. Now, like Connecticut and Massachusetts, it may be moving toward a post-industrial economy. Factory employment has dropped. Chrysler closed its Twinsburg factory, with a Canadian liquidation company snapping up the property in March 2010. Still, total jobs are holding steady in some parts. Small, adaptive business units with highly skilled workers are the growth sectors. Mentor in fall 2010 had the lowest unemployment rate—7.6%—for any Ohio city with more than 50,000 people, and several small manufacturers announced plans to locate or expand there.

The 14th Congressional District of Ohio takes in parts or all of seven counties of northeast Ohio and the old Western Reserve. It includes Lake County, northeast of Cleveland, and Geauga County, with prosperous suburbs amid Western Reserve villages. (The National Park Service considered but rejected designating the Western Reserve as a federal national heritage area in 2011.) Ashtabula, home to 17 covered bridges and several wineries, is in the district, as is the northern part of Trumbull County, which is industrial. The district includes the affluent suburbs of eastern Cuyahoga County, where Cleveland is located, and the comfortable suburbs in northern Summit County and some of Portage County to the east. In the 19th century, the Western Reserve was heavily Republican. The congressman from the area from 1863 to 1880 was James Garfield, a Civil War general who was elected president in 1880 and assassinated the following year. In the 1930s, the area became politically competitive, as Cleveland became heavily Democratic, and it has remained so in most years since. But the district was designed to gather together Republican territory in the Western Reserve, and it voted twice in presidential elections for Republican George W. Bush. In 2008, Republican nominee John McCain won the district but very narrowly, 49.4%-49.2%.

Steven LaTourette (R)

The congressman from the 14th District is Steven LaTourette, a Republican elected in 1994. He grew up in the Cleveland area and went to law school at Cleveland State University. In the 1980s, he worked as a public defender and in 1988, became Lake County district attorney. Well-known, he won a three-candidate Republican primary with 54% of the vote to compete for the House seat. In the general election, he challenged freshman Rep. Eric Fingerhut. LaTourette attacked Fingerhut for backing President Bill Clinton's budget and tax increases and for being soft on crime. He won 48%-43%.

In early 2009, LaTourette got a seat on the coveted Appropriations Committee, though to get the spot, he had to give up his seats on the Financial Services and Transportation and Infrastructure committees.

In the House, LaTourette is a close ally of Speaker John Boehner of Ohio and has the most moderate voting record of Ohio's Republican members. Though he backed his party on most major legislation in the 111th Congress (2009-10), he joined Democrats to expand the State Children's Health Insurance Program, overhaul food safety laws, and allow the Food and Drug Administration to regulate tobacco. After Republicans assumed control of the House in 2011, he and fellow Ohio Republican Pat Tiberi, another Boehner lieutenant, were among just seven GOP members to oppose a bill banning federal funding for National Public Radio. Earlier, LaTourette was an ardent advocate of a minimum wage hike and broke with House Republicans to oppose normalizing trade relations with China, though he did deliver crucial, last-minute support for the Central American Free Trade Agreement. He later said that he regretted that vote.

Adjusting rather unhappily to the new tight-fisted realities of serving on Appropriations, LaTourette in November 2010 led an unsuccessful drive to clarify the definition of an "earmark" when House Republicans voted to adopt a ban on the home-district funding provisions. He secured more than $27 million in earmarks in 2010, according to Taxpayers for Common Sense.

LaTourette was also frustrated in attempts to preserve auto manufacturing jobs in his district in 2009, despite an all-out fight on his part. During discussions of the auto industry bailout, the Obama administration and Chrysler company officials promised LaTourette in May that, despite the company's imminent bankruptcy filing, the plant in his district would remain open and its 1,250 employees would keep their jobs. Days later, after the bankruptcy became official, the company announced that the plant would close. LaTourette accused the administration and Chrysler of lying, and a Chrysler lobbyist called him to apologize. He subsequently took a prominent role in trying to help auto dealers affected by the bankruptcy and bailout of General Motors and Chrysler. His efforts led to the creation of an arbitration process that led automakers to voluntarily reinstate hundreds of dealers.

As a member of the Committee on Standards of Official Conduct in 2004, LaTourette took seriously the responsibility of committee members to render bipartisan decisions and joined in unanimous committee votes to admonish GOP Majority Leader Tom DeLay on three ethics charges. When GOP Speaker Dennis Hastert, without explanation, removed him from the committee in 2005, LaTourette was privately unhappy with his punishment but did not say so publicly. In 2007, he voiced disapproval of attacks on Democratic Rep. William Jefferson of Louisiana, who was a suspect in a federal bribery investigation. The partisan skirmishing over Jefferson, he said, amounted to "the dumbing-down of the House," with both parties to blame.

LaTourette quickly secured the formerly Democratic seat. In 2004, his challenger was Democrat Capri Cafaro, a 26-year-old shopping center heiress who spent nearly $2 million of her own money. But Cafaro struggled with the issues, and LaTourette won easily, 63%-37%. During the campaign, however, he acknowledged an affair with his former chief aide, who had become a lobbyist and whom he later married. LaTourette's ex-wife endorsed Cafaro and complained, "Washington corrupts people." He has breezed to re-election ever since.

FIFTEENTH DISTRICT

Steve Stivers (R)

Elected 2010, 1st term; b. March 24, 1965, Ripley; home, Columbus; OH St. U., B.A. 1989, M.B.A. 1996; United Methodist; Married (Karen).

Military Career: OH Army Natl. Guard, 1988-2008.

Elected Office: OH Senate, 2003-08.

Professional Career: Legis. aide; lobbyist.

DC Office: 1007 LHOB, 20515, 202-225-2015; Fax: 202-225-3529; Web site: stivers.house.gov.

State Offices: Columbus, 614-299-6415.

Committees: *Financial Services:* Capital Markets and Government Sponsored Enterprises; Insurance, Housing & Community Opportunity.

Election Results

2010 general	Steve Stivers (R)	119,471	(54%)	($2,740,058)
	Mary Jo Kilroy (D)	91,077	(41%)	($2,680,124)
	William Kammerer (Lib)	6,116	(3%)	
2010 primary	Steve Stivers (R)	39,963	(82%)	
	John Adams (R)	5,894	(12%)	
	Ralph Applegate (R)	2,708	(6%)	

Population		Race/Ethnicity		Work	
Pop. 2010:	681,557	White:	79.8%	Private:	78.6%
Change since 2000:	Up 8.1%	Black:	9.2%	Government:	16.5%
Urban:	91.3%	Hispanic:	4.5%	Self-employed:	4.8%
Rural:	8.8%	Asian:	3.8%	Blue collar:	18.1%
Area size:	1,182 sq. mi.	Native Am.:	0.2%	White collar:	65.9%
		Hawaiian:	0.1%	Khaki collar:	0.1%
Age		Two+ races:	2.2%	Other:	15.9%
Median age:	33.2 yrs.				
More than 65 yrs:	9.8%	*Ancestry*		Median income:	$50,785
Less than 18 yrs:	22.9%	German	22.2%	Median Home Value:	$160,700
		Irish	12.8%		
Education		English	8.2%	**Military Veterans**	
H.S. grad:	88.4%			% of Pop:	8.3%
College grad:	35.7%				
Grad degree:	12.3%				

Central Ohio; Columbus

Smack in the center of Ohio, Columbus was founded in 1812 as the state capital. Its flat-domed Capitol at Broad and High, with the statue of President William McKinley out front, is surrounded by high rises. The city has grown in all directions into the countryside and is now the center of a 1 million-plus metro area. It is the headquarters of state government and the Ohio State University, which, with 55,000 students, had the second-highest enrollment of any U.S.

2008 Presidential Vote		
Barack Obama (D)	173,526	(54%)
John McCain (R)	143,468	(45%)
2004 Presidential Vote		
George Bush (R)	154,105	(50%)
John Kerry (D)	151,869	(50%)
Cook Partisan Voting Index: D+1		

campus in 2009. (Arizona State University had the highest enrollment.) Columbus is the head-quarters of the Batelle Memorial Institute, the think tank that helped invent compact discs, office copy machines and the Universal Product Code; a major industry here is data retrieval. Multiple annexations have made Columbus Ohio's largest city, with double the population of Cleveland and Cincinnati. More to the point, Columbus is on its way to being Ohio's largest metropolitan area, with 1.8 million people in the 2010 census compared to 2 million for metro Cleveland and 1.6 million for the Ohio portions of metro Cincinnati. Columbus has built civic landmarks—the Center of Science and Industry on the riverfront, the Jerome Schottenstein Center for sports and concerts at OSU, a hockey stadium for the Columbus Blue Jackets and the nation's first stadium built for a professional soccer team, the Columbus Crew, the Major League Soccer champions in 2008. There is residential building downtown in thriving entertainment districts. More than other Ohio cities, Columbus and its suburbs have been attracting young professionals and immigrants alike, and has fared comparatively well in the recession, with unemployment well below the national average.

The 15th Congressional District of Ohio includes all of Columbus except the east side, plus southern and western Franklin County and once-rural Madison and Union counties to the west. Honda has invested $6 billion in Union County since it opened its first plant there, for motorcycles, in 1979. Today, it employs 13,500 Ohioans. The 15th includes white, working-class areas on the south side of the city and in nearby Grove City. Politically, these Democratic areas long were balanced by the heavily Republican suburb of Upper Arlington, across the Olentangy River from Ohio State, and by Republican subdivisions sprouting up in the exurbs. But since 2004, Columbus has been the target of highly successful registration and turnout drives by the Democrats. The 15th District voted 50.3%-49.6% for George W. Bush in 2004 and 54%-45% for Barack Obama in 2008.

Steve Stivers (R)

The congressman from the 15th District is Steve Stivers, a Republican elected in 2010. He grew up in the Cincinnati suburbs, moved to Columbus to attend Ohio State University and never left, except for deployments with the Ohio Army National Guard. For most of his career, he has been associated with the Ohio Legislature. He was a staffer in the state Senate, and then in 1995 began working as a lobbyist for BankOne, which was based in Columbus but later absorbed into Bank of America. He was appointed by the Senate in 2003 to fill the seat of a retiring state senator. Soon afterward, he served tours in Kuwait and Iraq. When his seat came up for election in 2006, he ran his campaign from Iraq and won. Republicans have had large majorities in the Ohio Senate and

Stivers was vice chairman of the Finance Committee, supporting state budgets that cut property taxes and froze tuition at state universities.

Republican Rep. Deborah Pryce decided against running for re-election in the 15th District in 2008. Democrats nominated Franklin County Commissioner Mary Jo Kilroy, who had nearly defeated Pryce 50.2%-49.8% two years earlier. House Minority Leader John Boehner urged Stivers to run, and although he initially declined amid speculation that he wanted to be Ohio Senate president, he got into the contest. He campaigned as a moderate, favoring abortion rights but also emphasizing fiscal discipline and his military experience. The *Columbus Dispatch* lauded Stivers for supporting a two-year federal budget process similar to Ohio's and favoring line-item veto power for the president. Kilroy emphasized her background as a former Columbus school board president, and slammed Stivers for his stint as a bank lobbyist. Stivers portrayed Kilroy as "way outside the mainstream," too liberal for the district, and a captive of big labor. Kilroy won by a narrower than expected 46%-45%.

In her one term in office, Kilroy was a faithful supporter of the majority Democrats' programs, including the economic stimulus bill, the cap-and-trade bill to reduce carbon emissions and the overhaul of the health care system in 2010. Stivers, who continued to run for the seat, called the health care law's mandate to buy insurance "very dangerous" and said the legislation would be a heavy burden on small business. Kilroy portrayed him as a flip-flopper, arguing that he had supported an individual mandate and a carbon emissions bill in the past. She also charged that he had supported a national sales tax to replace the income tax, and she again ran ads attacking him as a lobbyist.

The Kilroy-Stivers rematch in 2010 turned out to be a great disappointment for national Democrats. Stivers and Kilroy raised roughly $2.7 million each, and although they were evenly matched in fundraising, the Democratic Congressional Campaign Committee abandoned the race in October as unwinnable. Stivers prevailed 54%-41%, with a solid majority in Franklin County and overwhelming margins in the other two counties.

In the House, he joined both the Tuesday Group of moderate Republicans and the Republican Study Committee of the most conservative Republicans. He got a seat on the Financial Services Committee.

SIXTEENTH DISTRICT

Jim Renacci (R)

Elected 2010, 1st term; b. Dec. 3, 1958, Monongahela, PA; home, Wadsworth; Indiana U. of PA, B.A. 1980.; Catholic; Married (Tina); 3 children.

Elected Office: Wadsworth City Cncl., 1999-2003; City of Wadsworth mayor, 2004-08.

Professional Career: CEO, LTC Management Svcs., 1985-2003; CEO, LTC Companies Group, 2003-2010.

DC Office: 130 CHOB, 20515, 202-225-3876; Fax: 202-225-3059; Web site: renacci.house.gov.

State Offices: Canton, 330-489-4414.

Committees: *Financial Services:* Financial Institutions & Consumer Credit; Oversight & Investigations.

Election Results

2010 general	Jim Renacci (R)	114,652	(52%)	($2,453,260)
	John Boccieri (D)	90,833	(41%)	($2,071,652)
	Jeffrey Blevins (Lib)	14,585	(7%)	($3,038)
2010 primary	Jim Renacci (R)	30,358	(49%)	
	Matt Miller (R)	24,322	(39%)	
	Paul Schiffer (R)	5,048	(8%)	

Population		Race/Ethnicity		Work	
Pop. 2010:	644,691	White:	90.8%	Private:	83.3%
Change since 2000:	Up 2.2%	Black:	4.9%	Government:	10.7%
Urban:	73.6%	Hispanic:	1.5%	Self-employed:	5.7%
Rural:	26.4%	Asian:	0.7%	Blue collar:	25.2%
Area size:	1,741 sq. mi.	Native Am.:	0.2%	White collar:	56.2%
		Hawaiian:	0.0%	Khaki collar:	0.1%
Age		Two+ races:	1.7%	Other:	18.5%
Median age:	39.7 yrs.				
More than 65 yrs:	14.8%	*Ancestry*		Median income:	$48,080
Less than 18 yrs:	24.0%	German	24.8%	Median Home Value:	$140,300
		Irish	11.1%		
Education		English	8.1%	**Military Veterans**	
H.S. grad:	88.0%			% of Pop:	11.2%
College grad:	22.4%				
Grad degree:	7.5%				

Northeastern Ohio; Canton

A little more than a century ago, Canton, Ohio, was at the center of American politics. It was already an industrial city, but without the huge steel mills of Youngstown or Cleveland. Its high-skill workers were fashioning new kinds of plows and reapers, making watches and, beginning in 1899, roller bearings. Canton did not attract masses of immigrants. Its factories did not run on harsh stopwatch discipline, and the class-warfare politics of other northern Ohio indus-

trial cities did not take root here. Its most famous citizen was Republican President William McKinley, who rose to the rank of major at age 22 in the Civil War, was elected governor, and served in Congress, chairing the House Ways and Means Committee. As the Republican nominee for president in 1896, McKinley campaigned from his front porch in Canton, meeting with delegations brought in by train from around the country. This spectacle, displaying both technological virtuosity and personal modesty, sounded a reverberating note in American politics, as did the McKinley platform—the "full dinner pail," the gold standard, and the enforcement of law and order in labor relations. More than a century later, Canton is a community still based on manufacturing, but one troubled by manufacturing job losses, including those stemming from the crash of the domestic auto industry in 2009. It has become best known as the home of the Professional Football Hall of Fame, with its football-shaped roof.

The 16th Congressional District of Ohio includes all of Canton and Stark County, plus Wayne County to the west and most of Ashland and Medina counties. Wayne County is home to the College of Wooster and the headquarters of Smuckers, which has acquired new brands from other food companies—Jif peanut butter, Hungry Jack pancakes, and Folgers Coffee—and concentrated production in an upgraded plant in Orrville. In the southern part of Wayne County is part of the largest Amish settlement in the world, where people drive horse-drawn tractors, eschew automobiles and electricity (except from their own generators), and quit school after the eighth grade. Tourism has been a growth industry in Amish country, with restaurants, bed-and-breakfasts and gift shops. Ashland is a smaller, non-metropolitan county. Johnny Appleseed once lived on what is now the campus of Ashland University. Medina County, north of Wayne, is part of the Cleveland metropolitan area. Politically, this area is generally Republican, though not always by wide margins. Stark County was the only Ohio county that George W. Bush carried in 2000 but lost in 2004, both times by narrow margins. In 2008, Democrat Barack Obama won the county 52%-46%, but it wasn't enough for him to win the entire district, which voted 50%-48% for Republican John McCain.

Jim Renacci (R)

The congressman from the 16th District is Jim Renacci, a Republican elected in 2010. Renacci (*Ren AY see*) grew up in a working-class family outside Pittsburgh. His mother was a nurse, and his father was a railroad worker who lost his job when Renacci was eight years old. "Very early on, I understood the meaning of balancing a family budget," he said. Renacci graduated from Indiana University of Pennsylvania, the first in his family to graduate from college. He worked for an accounting firm in Pittsburgh with nursing home clients, and in 1984, he moved to Wadsworth, Ohio, in Medina County and soon started his own chain of nursing homes. He also worked in Wadsworth's volunteer fire department. He sold his nursing home chain and formed a company specializing in financial consulting for troubled businesses. Along the way, he accumulated a diverse portfolio of investments, including a share in the Columbus Destroyers, an Arena League football team, a concert promotion firm and several Harley-Davidson dealerships. He was elected to the Wadsworth Council in 1999, and went on to serve as mayor from 2004 to 2008. He says he was able to turn the city's multi-million dollar deficit into a budget surplus without raising taxes by cutting costs.

As the 2010 election approached, Renacci decided to challenge Democrat John Boccieri, who had won the 16th District seat just two years earlier after longtime Republican incumbent Ralph Regula retired. Boccieri had served in the Ohio Legislature, was a former professional baseball player and an Air Force Reservist who served in Iraq and Afghanistan. He had secured the seat with a respectable victory of 55%-45% in 2008, and on the surface, he did not seem an easy incumbent to beat.

But Boccieri had voted for President Barack Obama's $787 billion economic stimulus bill and for the Democrats' cap-and-trade bill to curb carbon emissions. He had initially opposed the health care overhaul bill when it passed the House in November 2009, but when the final version came up for a vote in 2010, he said in a televised appearance with constituents who had health care problems that he would vote for the bill. His record made him vulnerable in what turned out to be a highly favorable year for Republicans and their claims that Democratic policies in Washington were making a bad economy even worse.

With help from national Republicans, Renacci campaigned on a theme that Obama administration policies were killing job creation and stifling the growth of small business. "We have a government that believes we can spend ourselves to prosperity," Renacci said during a debate with Boccieri. "That just isn't going to happen." Democrats referred to Renacci as the "millionaire CEO" who "made his fortune off the government and taxpayers." And they criticized him for a dispute over taxes in 2000 with Ohio authorities in which Renacci accepted a settlement requiring him to pay $1.3 million. Renacci spent $2.4 million on his campaign, but Boccieri remained competitive on that score with $2.1 million.

On Election Day, it wasn't even close. Renacci won 52%-41%, carrying every county; the closest was Stark County where he led 48%-46%. He returned to the GOP column a seat that had been held by only two members, both Republicans, in the 58 years from 1950 to 2008.

SEVENTEENTH DISTRICT

Tim Ryan (D)

Elected 2002, 5th term; b. July 16, 1973, Niles; home, Niles; Bowling Green St. U., B.A. 1995, Franklin Pierce Law Ctr., J.D. 2000; Catholic; divorced.

Elected Office: OH Senate, 2000-02.

Professional Career: Aide, U.S. Rep. Jim Traficant, 1995-97.

DC Office: 1421 LHOB, 20515, 202-225-5261; Fax: 202-225-3719; Web site: timryan.house.gov.

State Offices: Akron, 330-630-7311; Warren, 330-373-0074; Youngstown, 330-740-0193.

Committees: *Armed Services:* Emerging Threats & Capabilities; Readiness. *Budget.*

Group Ratings

	ACLU	ACU	ADA	CFG	AFS	FRC	LCV	ITIC	NTU	COC
2010	81	0	90	0	100	6	100	100	5	38
2009	–	4	95	2	100	–	100	–	3	33

National Journal Ratings

	2010 LIB	—	2010 CONS		2009 LIB	—	2009 CONS
Economic	61%	—	39%		73%	—	25%
Social	77%	—	21%		63%	—	37%
Foreign	73%	—	24%		70%	—	24%
Composite	71%	—	29%		70%	—	30%

Key Votes of the 111th Congress

1. Overturn Ledbetter	Y	5. Bar federal abortion funds	Y	9. Stop detainee transfers	Y
2. Pass $820 billion stimulus	Y	6. Pass health care bill	Y	10. Legalize immigrants' kids	Y
3. Let guns in national parks	Y	7. Regulate financial firms	Y	11. Repeal don't ask, tell	Y
4. Pass cap-and-trade	Y	8. Pass tax cuts for some	Y	12. Limit campaign funds	Y

Election Results

2010 general	Tim Ryan (D)..	102,758	(54%)	($1,071,074)
	Jim Graham (R)...	57,352	(30%)	($71,053)
	James Traficant (I)	30,556	(16%)	
2010 primary	Tim Ryan (D)..	48,750	(79%)	
	Dan Moadus (D)...	7,520	(12%)	
	Robert Crow (D)	5,638	(9%)	

Prior Winning Percentages: 2008 (78%), 2006 (80%), 2004 (77%), 2002 (51%)

Population		Race/Ethnicity		Work	
Pop. 2010:	600,111	White:	82.1%	Private:	83.0%
Change since 2000:	Down 4.9%	Black:	12.0%	Government:	11.8%
Urban:	84.3%	Hispanic:	2.7%	Self-employed:	5.1%
Rural:	15.7%	Asian:	1.0%	Blue collar:	26.8%
Area size:	1,033 sq. mi.	Native Am.:	0.2%	White collar:	53.6%
		Hawaiian:	0.0%	Khaki collar:	0.0%
Age		Two+ races:	1.9%	Other:	19.5%
Median age:	39.6 yrs.				
More than 65 yrs:	15.1%	*Ancestry*		Median income:	$40,242
Less than 18 yrs:	21.7%	German	17.7%	Median Home Value:	$105,400
		Irish	11.8%		
Education		Italian	9.9%	**Military Veterans**	
H.S. grad:	86.6%			% of Pop:	11.4%
College grad:	18.4%				
Grad degree:	6.1%				

Northeastern Ohio; Part Akron

For nearly a century, the Mahoning Valley, between the Lake Erie docks that unload iron ore from Great Lakes freighters and the coalfields of western Pennsylvania and West Virginia, was one of the steel capitals of the United States. The first coal mine opened in 1826, canals followed, and in 1892 the first steel mill was built in Youngstown. The valley soon filled up with mills, converters, and furnaces. Now the steel mills stand empty, smokeless and silent—ex-

2008 Presidential Vote
Barack Obama (D) 183,083   (62%)
John McCain (R) 106,337   (36%)

2004 Presidential Vote
John Kerry (D) 188,531   (63%)
George Bush (R) 111,663   (37%)

Cook Partisan Voting Index: D+12

cept those that have been dynamited or torn down. Big-steel management allowed foreign producers to gain a technological edge in the 1950s and 1960s, and worldwide overcapacity in steel grew as almost every developing country decided it needed its own steel mills. Meanwhile, an agreement between the United Steelworkers and management after a 119-day strike in 1959 boosted wages and fringe benefits to levels that helped price domestic steel out of the market. Import restrictions kept the furnaces hot for a while, but the oil shock of the 1970s produced sharply higher energy prices and a collapse in the U.S. auto and steel markets. Every plant in the Mahoning Valley closed, with a loss of 40,000 jobs. In the early 1980s, Youngstown had one of the nation's highest unemployment rates. From 1990 to 2004, the population of Youngstown's Mahoning County declined by 6% and next-door Trumbull County's by 3%. Steel has since revived, but not here. The high-wage living standard has vanished. Several aluminum plants opened in nearby Warren, but young people looking for opportunities routinely leave. In 2007, Youngstown's population was 74,000, less than half its size in the 1950s. That same year the Census Bureau reported that Youngstown had the lowest median household income in the nation among cities with 65,000 to 250,000 people. Organized crime infiltrated local government, and a federal investigation in the late 1990s led to more than 70 convictions; among those sentenced were a prosecutor, a sheriff and a congressman. Today, Youngstown is struggling to rebound, though it has managed to attract a few high-tech firms, including the fast-growing Turning Technologies software company.

The 17th Congressional District of Ohio encompasses most of the Mahoning Valley industrial area—Youngstown (though not its southern Mahoning County suburbs), Warren, and most of

Trumbull County. It includes nearly all of Portage County to the west and part of eastern Summit County and Akron. It contains two loci of 1970s protest—Kent State University, where four war-protesting students were killed by National Guardsmen, and Lordstown, site of the General Motors plant where workers purposely built shoddy cars to protest the tedium of the assembly line. This is a Democratic district. It voted 63% for John Kerry in 2004, his second-best district in Ohio. In 2008, Democratic nominee Barack Obama did not fare quite as well among the district's mostly white working-class voters, but his 62%-36% victory was comfortable enough.

Tim Ryan (D)

The congressman from the 17th District is Tim Ryan, a Democrat elected in 2002 at age 29. Ryan grew up in Niles, was a star quarterback before a knee injury ended his career, and graduated from Bowling Green State University. His first job was with 17th District Rep. James Traficant, a Democrat later convicted of racketeering and bribery. In 2000, after graduating from Franklin Pierce Law Center, Ryan was elected to the state Senate. His opening to run for Congress came when Traficant was forced to resign in disgrace after his conviction in 2002. For years, Traficant had been a colorful if coarse figure in the House, whose ranting orations ("Beam me up, Scottie" was his expression of incredulity at hearing an opposing viewpoint) and retro haircut ("I do my hair with a weed whacker") were a regular source of fascination for C-SPAN viewers.

Most 17th District insiders thought Akron-based Rep. Tom Sawyer, a Democrat who had been thrown into the district by reapportionment based on the 2000 census, had the inside track to succeed Traficant. And by standard measures, Sawyer should have won easily: He outspent Ryan nearly 6-to-1. But his record on issues gave Ryan an opening. Sawyer had voted for the 1993 North American Free Trade Agreement, and he was one of the few Rust Belt Democrats to vote for normalizing trade relations with China. Ryan hammered on these votes in the Mahoning Valley, where it is gospel that free trade drove the region's high-paying jobs abroad. Ryan also got the endorsement of the National Rifle Association in a district with many hunters. He beat Sawyer 41%-27%. The Republican nominee was state Rep. Ann Womer Benjamin. Ryan slammed her and the Ohio Republican Legislature for votes that had led to higher tuition at state universities. Republicans fired back with ads highlighting several disorderly conduct charges lodged against Ryan while he was in college. The district's Democratic leanings and Ryan's labor support proved decisive. He won 51% of the vote to 34% for Womer Benjamin and 15% for Traficant, who ran as an independent even though he'd been carted off to jail.

Ryan has leaned to the left on economic and foreign policy, while his splits with Democrats on abortion rights and gun control have placed him closer to the center on social issues. With abortion-rights advocate Rosa DeLauro, D-Conn., he sponsored the "Reducing the Need for Abortion and Supporting Parents Act," with federal dollars to fight teen pregnancy, while increasing aid for women who become pregnant; Democratic activists depicted this as a move toward party consensus on a difficult issue. Worried about the loss of local call-center jobs, Ryan was one of just seven House members who voted against the national do-not-call list. For several years, he sponsored the Chinese Currency Act, which sought to counter China's alleged manipulation and undervaluation of its currency.

With the encouragement of then Minority Leader Nancy Pelosi, Ryan and other young Democratic newcomers to the House created the "30-Something Working Group" as a partisan device to reach young C-SPAN viewers with their late-night House speeches. After challenging the Republicans' advocacy of the partial privatization of Social Security in 2005, Ryan said the group noticed that poll numbers were changing among young people. However, Ryan sided with Republicans on some issues, such as repeal of the estate tax and the construction of a security fence along the border with Mexico.

He was a vocal backer of the powerful Pennsylvania Democrat John Murtha in his unsuccessful bid against Maryland's Steny Hoyer for majority leader in 2006, which endeared him to Murtha-backer Pelosi and earned Ryan a coveted seat on the House Appropriations Committee. He immediately went to work securing earmarked projects for his hard-pressed district, including more than $26 million in 2007 alone.

Ryan has not faced serious re-election problems. He considered a run for the Senate in 2006 but decided against it. Democratic Gov. Ted Strickland discussed a shared ticket with Ryan in 2010, but Ryan decided to remain in the House, largely because of his new assignment on Appropriations.

EIGHTEENTH DISTRICT

Bob Gibbs (R)

Elected 2010, 1st term; b. June 14, 1954, Peru, IN; home, Lakeville; OH St. U. Agriculture Technology Inst., A.S. 1974.; Methodist; Married (Jody Cox); 3 children.

Elected Office: OH House, 2003-08; OH Senate, 2008-10.

Professional Career: Technician, OH Agricultural Research and Devel. Center, 1974-78; owner, Hidden Hollow Farms, 1978-2004; owner, Gibbs Enterprises.

DC Office: 329 CHOB, 20515, 202-225-6265; Fax: 202-225-3394; Web site: gibbs.house.gov.

State Offices: Zanesville, 740-452-2279.

Committees: *Agriculture:* Conservation, Energy & Forestry; General Farm Commodities & Risk Management. *Transportation & Infrastructure:* Economic Development; Public Buildings & Emergency Management; Highways & Transit; Water Resources & Environment (Chmn).

Election Results

2010 general	Bob Gibbs (R)	107,426	(54%)	($1,123,244)
	Zackary Space (D)	80,756	(40%)	($2,686,942)
	Lindsey Sutton (CNP)	11,246	(6%)	
2010 primary	Bob Gibbs (R)	11,037	(21%)	
	Fred Dailey (R)	10,881	(21%)	
	Jeannette Moll (R)	10,013	(19%)	
	Ron Hood (R)	8,204	(16%)	
	Dave Daubenmire (R)	6,288	(12%)	
	Hombre Liggett (R)	4,065	(8%)	

Population		Race/Ethnicity		Work	
Pop. 2010:	653,167	White:	94.9%	Private:	79.4%
Change since 2000:	Up 3.6%	Black:	1.9%	Government:	12.9%
Urban:	43.3%	Hispanic:	1.0%	Self-employed:	7.4%
Rural:	56.7%	Asian:	0.3%	Blue collar:	32.0%
Area size:	6,877 sq. mi.	Native Am.:	0.2%	White collar:	48.9%
		Hawaiian:	0.0%	Khaki collar:	0.1%
Age		Two+ races:	1.5%	Other:	19.0%
Median age:	39.0 yrs.				
More than 65 yrs:	14.8%	*Ancestry*		Median income:	$40,270
Less than 18 yrs:	24.2%	German	22.3%	Median Home Value:	$110,900
		Irish	11.4%		
Education		English	8.5%	**Military Veterans**	
H.S. grad:	82.7%			% of Pop:	11.3%
College grad:	12.8%				
Grad degree:	4.8%				

Eastern Ohio; Zanesville

The hills of eastern Ohio are one of those obscure parts of America, seen by most Americans, if at all, from airplanes or speeding cars on the interstates on their way to someplace else. They were settled early on in U.S. history, in the 1790s, mostly by Virginians, and for the most part remained sparsely populated. This was hard land to clear and hard land to farm, better suited for dairy cattle than the plains that lay beyond. In some places near the Ohio River, there was industrial development early on. The local clay was used to make pottery, the coal that lies near the surface was dug up, a green-vitriol works was built, and a nail factory went into operation, all before 1814. In time, the area became dotted with small factory towns and coal mines. Farther south there was little industrial development, and today that landscape has a timeless feel. This region was little affected by the flow of immigrants from Europe in 1880-1924, southern blacks in 1940-1965

2008 Presidential Vote		
John McCain (R)	150,461	(53%)
Barack Obama (D)	128,058	(45%)

2004 Presidential Vote		
George Bush (R)	163,121	(57%)
John Kerry (D)	121,495	(43%)

Cook Partisan Voting Index: R+7

or Latino and Asian immigrants since 1970. Some counties have seen sharp job losses, as coal mines and factories have shut down. Others, despite objections from some local farmers, have benefited from the construction of a gasoline pipeline from the Ohio River to Columbus and beyond to Colorado. As the price of oil and natural gas rose, the coal industry began to rebound, reopening some mines and returning some jobs. The most distinctive people here are the Amish, who drive their horses and buggies over covered bridges in Holmes, Tuscarawas and Wayne counties. They make up the largest concentration of Amish in the world. They run shops now as well as farms, get energy from solar power, and no longer eschew all farm machinery.

The 18th Congressional District of Ohio covers much of this hill country, from Holmes and Tuscarawas counties in the north to Ross and Jackson counties in the south. Geographically, it is the largest district in the state, spanning five media markets, including two in West Virginia. It includes such cities as New Rumley, the birthplace of Gen. George Custer; Zanesville, the birthplace of writer Zane Grey and architect Cass Gilbert; and Chillicothe, the first capital of Ohio, on the Scioto River. Politically, much of this area is ancestrally Democratic, but Republican presidential candidate George W. Bush won 55% of the vote here in 2000 and 57% in 2004. Republican nominee John McCain beat Barack Obama here 53%-45% in 2008.

Bob Gibbs (R)

The new congressman from the 18th District is Bob Gibbs, who ousted two-term Democratic incumbent Zack Space despite being heavily outspent. Gibbs stressed improving the economic climate for small business in addition to scaling back Big Government. "When I talk to employers at all-size businesses every day, it's all about uncertainty," he said.

Gibbs grew up on the west side of Cleveland, "as far away from agriculture as you can get," he says. But he was drawn to farming at a young age. After working in the garden center of his high school, he enrolled in Ohio State University's Agricultural Institute, becoming part of its first graduating class in 1974. He met his wife, Jody, through his best friend, and the couple now has three grown children. After college, Gibbs founded Hidden Hollow Farms and served as president of the Ohio Farm Bureau Federation for two terms starting in 1999. "In agriculture, you have a lot of challenges," Gibbs said. "Every day on the farm, you have chores you have to do. I taught myself how to weld, do electrical work, accounting. There's so much you can do. It's not just the same thing every day." He cites his time on the Ohio Farm Bureau as sparking his interest in politics.

In 2002, Gibbs won a seat in the Ohio House, and he was elected to the Senate in 2008. He focused on agriculture, small-business, and private-property issues. In 2005, he introduced a bill barring the use of eminent-domain takings for private entities, which allows for the transfer of land from one private owner to another to further economic development. He also co-authored legislation to cut Ohio's personal income-tax rates by 21% by 2011.

Gibbs and Space attacked each other on climate change, health care reform, and the "don't ask, don't tell" policy prohibiting gay men and women from serving openly in the military. Republicans also blasted Space for his vote for the 2009 Democratic bill to create a cap-and-trade system to reduce the greenhouse-gas emissions blamed for global warming. Gibbs said he doesn't believe human activity causes climate change. He has also called for repeal of President Obama's health care law; Space, who voted against the final health care reform package, said he would change some elements of it but did not favor repeal. Space ran ads with footage of Gibbs telling an audience, "I'm a free-trader," and tying him to trade deals that have sent Ohio jobs overseas.

★ OKLAHOMA ★

Oklahoma is one of the newest states, the 46th to be admitted to the Union, in 1907. Its Capitol was opened in 1917, but the dome was left unconstructed and was not finally finished until 2002. As that chronology suggests, Oklahoma's history has been a story of sudden stops and starts. It was settled in a rush, first by the Five Civilized Tribes driven west by Andrew Jackson's troops over the Trail of Tears in the 1830s. Then came white settlers one morning in April 1889, when, in the great land rush memorialized by novelist Edna Ferber and half a dozen Hollywood movies, thousands of homesteaders drove their wagons across the territorial line at the sound of a gunshot, the most adventurous or unscrupulous of them literally jumping the gun—the Sooners. In 1905, a convention of the Civilized Nations, as they became known, sought to have eastern Oklahoma admitted as a separate state of Sequoyah. The federal government turned a deaf ear to the Indians and ended the tribal government, combining the Indian and Oklahoma territories as a single state.

The heritage of these hurried settlements is evident today. Oklahoma has the second largest American Indian population of any state, after California—322,000 in the 2010 census—though there is just one reservation and the status of many other tribal entities is often disputed. Some Indian tribes here have unsuccessfully sought a return of native lands. But there has been much intermarriage over the years, and many Oklahomans—and not a few of its politicians—proudly claim Indian blood. Indians own 6% of businesses in Oklahoma, and make up about 9% of the population, although as a group they suffer high unemployment as elsewhere in the United States. There is an ongoing struggle to keep the Cherokee, Choctaw, Chickasaw and Seminole languages from dying out—you can see street signs in the Cherokee alphabet in Tahlequah. The counties with a large Indian heritage in the eastern part of the state have been growing, while the Great Plains farm counties west of Oklahoma City and Tulsa have lost population.

The Rodgers and Hammerstein musical recalled an Oklahoma on the brink of statehood in 1907, at which point the territory rapidly filled up with farmers, rising from 1.5 million people in 1907 to 2.4 million in 1930. Oil helped. The first well was drilled here in 1897, and by 1920, Tulsa was an oil boom town. Then in the 1930s came a decade of bust—or dust—as soil loosened by erosion was whipped into giant swirling clouds: The Dust Bowl. "On a single day, I heard, 50 million tons of soil were blown away," author John Gunther reported later. "People sat in Oklahoma City, with the sky invisible for three days in a row, holding dust masks over their faces and wet towels to protect their mouths at night, while the farms blew by." Okies headed in droves west on U.S. 66 to greener California, and Oklahoma's population steadily declined, falling to 2.2 million in 1950. It did not to reach its 1930 level again until 1970.

Oil brought another boom. As the oil shocks of 1973 and 1979 sent prices up, Oklahoma's population rose from 2.5 million in 1970 to 3 million in 1980. Then, with the collapse of oil prices and of Oklahoma's farm economy as well, it was bust again. A giddy rise was followed by a giddier fall. The rig count went from 882 in 1982 to 232 in 1983 and was just 186 in 2007. The 1990 census reported just 3.1 million Oklahomans. But in the 1990s, Oklahoma began building a more diversified economy, with high-tech employers as well as oil and gas firms. Population rose 10% in the 1990s and 9% from 2000 to 2010, growing to 3.75 million. High oil prices made it worthwhile to squeeze more from marginal wells and horizontal drilling allows more production with the same number of rigs. Oklahoma's natural gas—the state is third in production—has commanded high prices given strong demand. At the same time, Oklahoma has been one of the leading states in developing wind power, with utilities offering customers electricity produced from wind, although at slightly higher-than-ordinary rates. Oklahoma continues to have above-average rates of divorce, teenage pregnancy and crime and a low rate of college graduates. But unemployment has been low, and the housing bust and the 2007-09 recession caused less distress here than in many faster-growing states.

Historically, Oklahoma was a Democratic state, with big Democratic margins in eastern counties and in southeast's Little Dixie. But northwestern Oklahoma, settled by Kansans, has always been Republican, and starting in the 1950s, Tulsa and Oklahoma City leaned Republican too. Today, only vestiges of its Democratic heritage remain. There are still more registered Democrats than Republicans, and Oklahoma elected a popular Democratic governor, Brad Henry, in 2002 and 2006. But Oklahoma has not voted Democratic for president since 1964. And in 2008, it cast a higher percentage for Republican John McCain than any other state. McCain won at least 58% of

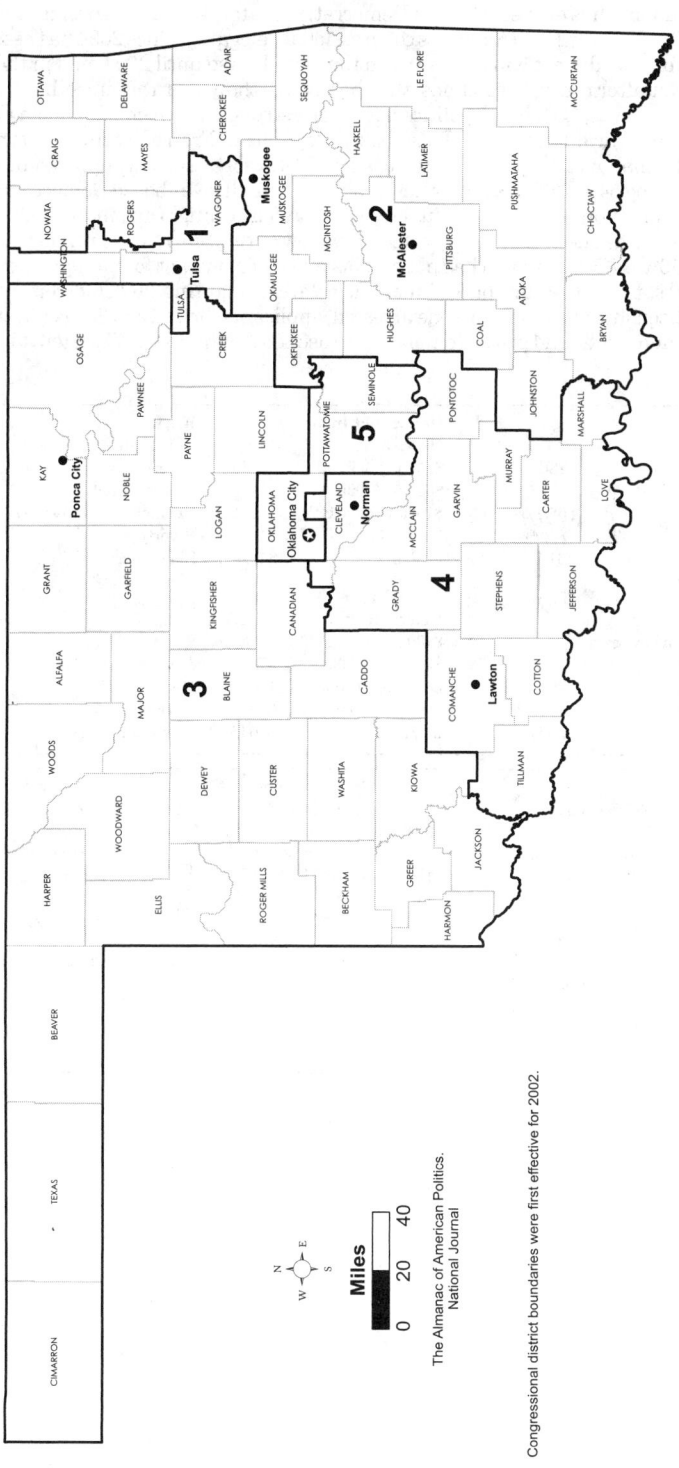

The Almanac of American Politics.
National Journal

Congressional district boundaries were first effective for 2002.

the vote in each of the 77 counties. In 2010, Oklahoma voted 71% to re-elect Republican Sen. Tom Coburn. Oklahoma has elected only one Democratic senator, David Boren, since 1966, and he resigned in 1993. The only Democrat in its congressional delegation since 2004 has been his son, Dan Boren. Republicans did not win a majority in the state House until 2004, and in the state Senate until 2008. But after the 2010 elections, they had better than 2-1 ratios in both.

In some respects, Oklahoma politics has been a struggle between Oklahoma City and Tulsa Republicans and rural Democrats. Tulsa-based Republican Frank Keating, governor from 1995 through 2002, managed to get voters to pass a right-to-work law, long opposed by Democrats in the legislature, by 54%-46% in a 2001 referendum. But small town-based Democrat Henry profited from a referendum on quite a different subject, a ban on cockfighting, in his 2002 gubernatorial run. Oklahoma was one of only three states that allowed this "sport," and urban voters helped the ban to pass 56%-44%. Oklahoma has not been as much of a magnet for immigration as Texas has, but regardless, the legislature passed tough legislation requiring law enforcement personnel to check the citizenship status of everyone arrested, applicants for driver's licenses to establish their legal status, and public and private employers to use the federal E-Verify system to establish legal status.

Population		Household Income		Work	
Pop. 2010:	3,751,351	Under $15k:	15.8%	Private:	74.7%
State rank:	28th	$15k to $50k:	41.4%	Government:	18.0%
Change since 2000:	Up 8.7%	$50k to $100k:	29.5%	Self-employed:	7.1%
Urban:	65.1%	$100k to $200k:	11.2%	Unemployment (3-yr. average):	3.6%
Rural:	34.9%	Over $200k:	2.2%	Poverty:	16.1%
Native of state:	61.1%	Median income:	$42,358	Blue collar:	24.5%
Not a citizen:	3.4%			White collar:	57.0%
Area size:	69,899 sq. mi.	**Home Value**		Khaki collar:	0.9%
		Under $100k:	47.6%	Other:	17.6%
Most populous cities		$100k to $300k:	46.0%		
Oklahoma City	579,999	$300k to $500k:	4.5%	**Age**	
Tulsa	391,906	$500k to $1 mil:	1.4%	Median age:	35.9 yrs.
Norman	110,925	Over $1 million:	0.4%	More than 65 yrs:	13.4%
Broken Arrow	98,850	Median:	$104,900	Less than 18 yrs:	24.9%

Race/Ethnicity				Military Veterans		Registered Voters in 2010	
White:	68.7%	*Language*		% of Pop:	11.6%	Democrats:	999,855
Black:	7.3%	English:	91.6%			Republicans:	813,158
Hispanic:	8.9%	Spanish:	5.6%	*Veterans by Period*		Ind./other:	225,607
Asian:	1.7%	Asian:	1.2%	WWII and before:	9.3%	Voter turnout:	1,034,767
Native Am.:	8.2%	Other European:	1.0%	Korea:	11.1%	Turnout as % of	
Hawaiian:	0.1%			Vietnam:	34.6%	voting age:	36.7%
Two+ races:	5.1%	**Education**		Gulf (pre-2001):	12.7%		
		H.S. grad:	85.3%	Gulf (post-2001):	9.5%	**Legislature**	
Ancestry		College grad:	22.5%	Peace time:	22.9%	Senate:	16 D 32 R
German	13.0%	Grad degree:	7.4%			House:	31 D 70 R
Irish	10.9%						
USA	7.7%						

Presidential politics   Oklahoma has been a solidly Republican state in presidential elections since the 1950s. There are no large blocs of voters here who back national Democrats, and most Oklahomans find national Republicans acceptable. It has been a long time since Oklahoma has been on anyone's list of target states, and seems unlikely to be in the near future. While Tulsa and Oklahoma City were the Republicans' strongholds from the 1950s to the 1990s, now many rural counties are even more Republican. George W. Bush and John McCain carried all 77 counties in 2004 and 2008. This was McCain's best state. He won with 65.6% of the vote, about the same as Bush in 2004. Indeed the two elections were almost carbon copies. McCain got 373 more votes than Bush in 2008, and Democrat Barack Obama got 1,470 fewer votes than Democrat John Kerry did four years earlier. But this was not Obama's worst state. He had lower percentages in Wyoming and Utah, where there were third-party candidates. There was no significant gender gap in Oklahoma and not much of an age gap: Young voters went 60% for McCain. And there are lots of conservative Democrats: 41% of white Democrats voted for McCain.

2008 Presidential Vote		
John McCain (R)	960,165	(66%)
Barack Obama (D)	502,496	(34%)

2008 Presidential Primary		
Hillary Clinton (D)	228,480	(55%)
Barack Obama (D)	130,130	(31%)
John Edwards (D)	42,725	(10%)

2008 Presidential Primary		
John McCain (R)	122,772	(37%)
Mike Huckabee (R)	111,899	(33%)
Mitt Romney (R)	83,030	(25%)

2004 Presidential Vote		
George W. Bush (R)	959,792	(66%)
John Kerry (D)	503,966	(34%)

Oklahoma has had a presidential primary since it joined the Super Tuesday contests in 1988. That year, it voted 37%-35% for Texas neighbor George H.W. Bush over Kansas neighbor Bob Dole in the Republican primary, and it gave Al Gore a solid win in the Democratic primary. In the next three cycles, it was not seriously contested. For 2004, the legislature scheduled the primary for February, a week after New Hampshire. Oklahoma was targeted by Democrats John Edwards and Wesley Clark, both desperate for a win after Kerry's triumphs in Iowa and New Hampshire. Clark won here—his first and only electoral victory—but with just 29.9% to 29.5% for Edwards and 27% for Kerry. Kerry carried the counties including Oklahoma City, Tulsa and Norman (home of the University of Oklahoma) and not much else. Clark got big pluralities in the counties around Fort Sill and Altus Air Force Base, and not much else. Edwards carried most suburban and rural counties, but generally not by big pluralities.

In 2008, Oklahoma was joined by many other states on Super Tuesday on Feb. 5, and did not attract too much attention. In the Democratic primary, Hillary Rodham Clinton was the early favorite here and beat Obama 55%-31%. John Edwards got 10% although he had already dropped out of the race. Obama carried Oklahoma County (Oklahoma City) and Clinton carried the other 76 counties, with very big margins in eastern Oklahoma counties near her longtime home in Arkansas. Edwards finished second in three rural counties. Turnout was 417,000, a record, but not significantly higher than in 1988 or 1992.

The Republican race was much closer. Fresh off victories in New Hampshire and Florida, McCain won with 37% to 33% for Mike Huckabee and 25% for Mitt Romney. Oklahoma's party registration law—and the fact that so many rural conservatives are still registered as Democrats—probably cost Huckabee a victory. He carried the eastern portion of the state, with a high of 58.5% in Adair County, on the border of his home state of Arkansas. McCain ran strongest in the western part of the state, with his best showing, 50%, in rural Ellis County. Turnout was 335,000, a record, and 27% above the previous high in 1996.

Congressional districting   Oklahoma lost one of its six House seats in the reapportionment following the 2000 census, and for months there was a deadlock over redistricting between Republican Gov. Frank Keating and the Democratic legislature. Keating wanted to keep a Tulsa-centered district, especially before the December 2001 special election in which his wife, Cathy Keating, ran for the Tulsa-based 1st District seat vacated by Steve Largent. But she lost the Republican nomination. In 2002, the solution appeared after 3rd District Rep. Wes Watkins announced his retirement. Watkins was a Republican (and a former Democrat) and the 3rd District was centered in Little Dixie; the seat was safe for Watkins, but Democrats carry the area in state elections and would have a good chance to win an open seat contest. The issue went to court, and a county judge ordered the adoption of a plan that eliminated Watkins' district and gave the other incum-

112th Congress Lineup	
4 R	1 D
111th Congress Lineup	
4 R	1 D

bents safe seats. It also had the virtue of creating an Oklahoma City-centered district rather than splitting the city between several districts as it had been since 1981. Democrats, happy that Democratic incumbent Brad Carson got a safe seat, let the matter drop. Carson ran for the Senate in 2004 and lost to Republican Tom Coburn, but Democrat Dan Boren has easily held the seat since. Oklahoma held onto its five seats in the reapportionment following the 2010 census.

Governor

Mary Fallin (R)

Elected 2010, term expires Jan. 2015, 1st term; b. Dec. 9, 1954, Warrensburg, MO; home, Oklahoma City; Attended OK Baptist U., OK St. U., B.S. 1977; attended U. of Central OK; Christian; Married (Wade Christensen); 6 children.

Elected Office: OK House, 1990-94; Lt. Gov., 1994-2006; U.S. House, 2007-11.

Professional Career: OK Dept. of Tourism and Rec., OK Securities Comm., OK Office of Personnel Mgt., 1977-82; Hotel mkting. and mgt., 1983-90.

Office: Oklahoma State Capitol, 2300 N. Lincoln Blvd., Room 212, 73105, 405-521-2342; Fax: 405-521-335; Web site: www.ok.gov/governor/.

Election Results

2010 general	Mary Fallin (R)	625,506	(60%)
	Jari Askins (D)	409,261	(40%)
2010 primary	Mary Fallin (R)	136,477	(55%)
	Randy Brogdon (R)	98,170	(39%)

Prior Winning Percentages: House: 2008 (66%); 2006 (60%)

Oklahoma's new governor is Mary Fallin, a Republican elected in 2010 as the state's first female chief executive. She previously spent two terms in the House representing the Oklahoma City-based 5th District and also served as the state's lieutenant governor.

Fallin was born in Missouri but raised in Tecumseh, Okla. Her mother and father were Democrats and each served as mayor of the town. After graduating from Oklahoma State University, Fallin managed hotel properties and was a commercial real estate broker. In 1990, she was elected to the state House, where she championed victims' rights and health care reform. She became lieutenant governor four years later, making her the first Republican and the first woman to hold the office in Oklahoma. During her three terms as lieutenant governor, she expanded her reach well beyond the office's traditional ribbon-cutting responsibilities. With a focus on economic development, she compiled a pro-business record and played a key role in bringing the right-to-work issue to a successful statewide vote. But in 2005, she failed to get the Democratic-controlled Senate to overhaul the state workers' compensation system. Her star had dimmed a bit in 1998 when, in the course of a bitter divorce, she was accused of having a sexual relationship with a state trooper assigned to her security detail; both of them denied the charge.

In June 2005, Fallin announced that she would seek a fourth term as lieutenant governor. But she changed her mind when GOP Rep. Ernest Istook decided to relinquish his House seat and run for governor. She joined a wide-open primary race for Istook's House seat as one of six Republican candidates. Her chief opponents were state Corporation Commissioner Denise Bode and Oklahoma City Mayor Mick Cornett. Bode's Republican credentials were suspect because she was a former aide to U.S. Sen. David Boren, a Democrat. Cornett had the backing of Christian conservatives, who were pleased that the mayor had removed gay-themed books from the children's section of public libraries. In the initial July balloting, Fallin led with 35% and Cornett's base in Oklahoma City propelled him to a second-place finish with 24%. Bode came in third with 19%. Fallin and Cornett competed in an August runoff. The two candidates had few differences on the issues, but Fallin had a big fundraising advantage. She defeated Cornett, 63%-37%, even though Oklahoma County cast 93% of the vote. In this solidly Republican district, the general election was an afterthought. Against Oklahoma City physician David Hunter, Fallin won 60%-37% to become the first woman sent to Washington by Oklahoma since 1922.

In the House, Fallin quickly established her bona fides as an ardent conservative, and she sought leadership roles as a freshman. In June 2007, she saw her first bill passed in the House: a revamping of federal grants for women's business centers. She joined a group of 38 Republicans who staked out negotiating positions in opposition to the Democrats' proposal to expand the State Children's Health Insurance Program. In July 2008, she was part of a House Republican delegation that traveled to Alaska to try to bolster the case for oil drilling in the Arctic National Wildlife Refuge. Fallin became politically active on the executive committee of the National Republican Congressional Committee, which fellow Oklahoman Tom Cole chaired. In the 2008 presidential contest, she was an enthusiastic backer of Alaska Gov. Sarah Palin as the GOP vice presidential nominee, calling her "an excellent model for other women." And Fallin took a vocal role in defending Palin against attacks by Democrats.

Eager to return to Oklahoma, Fallin announced her candidacy for governor in February 2009, a time when few Republicans had any idea they would reclaim the majority in the House the following year. With two-term Democratic Gov. Brad Henry ineligible to seek a third term, GOP officials were optimistic about her chances, especially when she was able to raise more than $2.4 million before the July 2010 primary. Her main opponent was state Sen. Randy Brogdon of Owasso, who sought to generate tea party support by making an issue of her 2008 vote for the bailout of the financial industry, accusing her in one ad of "compromising" Oklahoma values. Fallin, however, capitalized on her friendship with Palin to get her endorsement and those of several other big-name Republicans, including Minnesota Gov. Tim Pawlenty and Arizona Gov. Jan Brewer. She drew 55% of the primary vote, easily avoiding a runoff, while Brogdon got 39%. Two minor candidates received 3% apiece.

In the general election, Fallin's opponent was Democratic Lt. Gov. Jari Askins, who eked out a come-from-behind primary win over state Attorney General Drew Edmonson. The campaign centered on overcoming the state's financial challenges, with Askins touting a two-year budget plan to improve efficiency in addition to her background as a special county judge and state House member. To stay competitive in fundraising, she loaned her campaign $1.1 million. Fallin stressed job creation through lower taxes as well as reducing excessive workers' compensation and legal fees. She also suggested cutting the number of state agencies from more than 500 to levels similar to those in Oregon and Kansas, which each had around 130.

In October, Fallin suggested she was more qualified than Askins as a result of her experience "being a mother, having children, raising a family." Askins was single and had no children, and argued that her circumstances would make her no less capable a governor. Fallin had recently married a divorced father of four and had two children from an earlier marriage. She said she didn't intend her remarks as an attack on Askins. In any event, the outcome was never in doubt. Fallin won handily, 60%-40%, capturing every county except Askins' home of Stephens County and three nearby south-central Oklahoma counties.

Making good on her campaign promise to cut spending, Fallin asked the legislature to approve a 3% reduction of budgets for core state agencies, such as public safety and education, and a steeper 5% cut for others. She also promised reforms in the state's workers' compensation and tort systems and called for requiring the state to move from paper to electronic billing and payment services. Despite her opposition to President Barack Obama's health care overhaul while in the House, she supported a state House bill to set up a framework for the insurance exchanges called for in the federal legislation. Her position caused grumbling among some Republicans. "The people of Oklahoma do not want Obamacare, but now our executive branch and our legislative branch is trying to shove it down our throats," GOP state Rep. Mike Ritze said. Fallin denied that her support for the bill meant she had changed her position on the issue, saying that doing nothing would leave the state vulnerable to further federal mandates.

Senior Senator

James Inhofe (R)

Elected 1994, term expires 2014, 3rd full term; b. Nov. 17, 1934, Des Moines, IA; home, Tulsa; U. of Tulsa, B.A. 1973; Presbyterian; married (Kay); 4 children.

Military Career: Army, 1957–58.

Elected Office: OK House of Reps., 1966–69; OK Senate, 1969–77, Repub. ldr., 1975–77; Tulsa mayor, 1978–84; U.S. House of Reps., 1987–95.

Professional Career: Businessman, land developer, 1962–86.

DC Office: 205 RSOB, 20510, 202-224-4721; Fax: 202-228-0380; Web site: inhofe.senate.gov.

State Offices: Enid, 580-234-5105; McAlester, 918-426-0933; Oklahoma City, 405-608-4381; Tulsa, 918-748-5111.

Committees: *Armed Services:* Airland; Readiness & Management Support; Strategic Forces. *Environment & Public Works* (RMM). *Foreign Relations:* African Affairs; East Asian & Pacific Affairs (RMM); International Development & Foreign Assistance, Economic Affairs & International Environmental Protection; International Operations & Organizations, Democracy & Global Women's Issues.

Group Ratings

	ACLU	ACU	ADA	CFG	AFS	FRC	LCV	ITIC	NTU	COC
2010	7	96	0	93	2	95	0	67	96	100
2009	–	100	5	100	0	–	0	–	93	71

National Journal Ratings

	2010 LIB	—	2010 CONS	2009 LIB	—	2009 CONS
Economic	25%	—	74%	0%	—	97%
Social	0%	—	79%	0%	—	94%
Foreign	0%	—	72%	0%	—	84%
Composite	17%	—	83%	4%	—	96%

Key Votes of the 111th Congress

1. Overturn Ledbetter	N	5. Pass health care bill	N
2. Pass $787 billion stimulus	N	6. Regulate financial firms	N
3. Repeal DC gun laws	Y	7. Pass tax cuts for some	N
4. Confirm Sonia Sotomayor	N	8. Legalize immigrants' kids	N

9. Ratify New START	N
10. Confirm Elena Kagan	N
11. Stop EPA climate regs	Y
12. Repeal don't ask, tell	N

Election Results

2008 general	James Inhofe (R)	763,375	(57%)	($6,484,560)
	Andrew Rice (D)	527,736	(39%)	($2,869,433)
	Stephen Wallace (I)	55,708	(4%)	
2008 primary	James Inhofe (R)	116,371	(84%)	
	Evelyn Rogers (R)	10,770	(8%)	
	Ted Ryals (R)	7,306	(5%)	

Prior Winning Percentages: 2002 (57%); 1996 (57%); 1994 special (55%); House: 1992 (53%); 1990 (56%); 1988 (53%); 1986 (55%)

James Inhofe, Oklahoma's senior senator, was first elected to the House in 1986 and to the Senate in 1994. He grew up in Tulsa, served in the Army, and worked in real estate and insurance. Inhofe was elected to the Oklahoma House in 1966, at age 31, and to the Oklahoma Senate in 1969. As a state legislator, he worked to promote the balanced budget constitutional amendment championed by Nebraska Sen. Carl Curtis. Inhofe ran for governor in 1974 and lost to David Boren, 64%-36%. In 1976, he ran for the U.S. House against Democrat Jim Jones and lost. From 1979 to 1984, he was mayor of Tulsa. He won the heavily Republican 1st District House seat in 1986, when Jones ran unsuccessfully for the Senate, but held it with uninspiring margins. He was hurt by negative publicity from a family business lawsuit and charges of campaign finance irregularities, often leveled by the liberal-leaning *Tulsa World*. Inhofe's greatest achievement in the House was reforming the arcane discharge petition rule. For years, House rules kept secret the names of signers of petitions to force bills stuck in committees to the floor for action; anonymity allowed lawmakers to claim they had worked to bring legislation to the floor when they in fact had done the opposite. That was changed in 1993, and one of the first bills to benefit from the new rules was an aviation liability reform bill, co-sponsored by flying buff Inhofe and limiting the liability of small airplane manufacturers in lawsuits resulting from crashes.

Inhofe jumped into the 1994 Senate race after Boren, a conservative Democrat, announced he was retiring to become president of the University of Oklahoma with two years left in his Senate term. The Democratic nominee was moderate Dave McCurdy, a congressman from southwest Oklahoma since 1980 who was favored to win. But in Oklahoma in 1994 the burden of Bill Clinton's unpopularity among conservatives was too much for McCurdy, who had voted for the 1993 budget and tax legislation and for the 1994 crime bill with its ban on assault weapons. Inhofe won by a solid 55%-40%. In the Senate, Inhofe was president of the conservative freshman class of 11 senators. In 1996, he was elected to a full six-year term over James Boren, David Boren's cousin, 57%-40%.

Inhofe has a solidly conservative voting record and is blunt, even acerbic, at times. "I'm not afraid of controversy. I'm not afraid to say what's on my mind and what's on a lot of people's minds," he says. He speaks his mind in pungent terms, with his barbs often targeted at his opponents in the green movement. He once accused Clinton Environmental Protection Agency chief Carol Browner of "Gestapo tactics." In recent years, as the most senior Republican on the Environment and Public Works Committee, he has been a leader of those who cast doubt on the claims that carbon dioxide emissions cause catastrophic climate change. In 2003, Inhofe said that the idea that man-made emissions have caused global warming was "the greatest hoax ever perpetrated on the American people." After e-mails in 2009 revealed attempts by some scientists to bolster the case for global warming, he said in March 2010 that "the world's first climate billionaire is running for cover. Yes, I'm talking about Al Gore. He's under siege these days. The credibility of the IPCC (Intergovernmental Panel on Climate Change) is eroding. The EPA's endangerment finding is collapsing. And belief that global warming is leading to catastrophe is evaporating."

When Inhofe chaired the committee from 2003 to 2007, he favored oil drilling in the Arctic National Wildlife Refuge and more oil and gas drilling exploration in the United States generally. He also has low regard for the Endangered Species Act. "America has adopted an attitude that places more value on the life of a critter than on a human being. We want to protect the Arkansas River shiner, a bait fish in Oklahoma, yet we will allow unborn babies to have their brains sucked out in a partial-birth abortion," he once said.

Much of Inhofe's tenure as chairman was devoted to the reauthorization of the highway bill, which is one of the main institutional responsibilities of the committee. By early 2004, Inhofe had hammered out an agreement in the Senate on a $318 billion transportation bill. House Transportation Chairman Don Young was seeking a $375 billion bill, while the Bush administration wanted to cap spending at $256 billion. Inhofe argued that money was needed to maintain the highway system and would be funded entirely by user fees, primarily the gas tax. The Senate passed Inhofe's bill, but the House reduced the size of its version to $275 billion. The political differences were also significant. A goal of Inhofe's bill was to guarantee that every state got 95% of its gas tax money back, but if total spending were decreased, that meant other states would lose projects. So the issue was deferred to 2005. By that time, Republican leaders were eager to cut a final deal with Bush, and Inhofe backed a scaled-down version of a transportation bill at $286 billion.

After Democrats won control of the Senate, Inhofe in January 2007 withstood a backroom challenge from Virginia Republican John Warner to become the ranking minority member on the committee. Prospects for his cooperation with incoming Democratic Chairman Barbara Boxer, a liberal from California, seemed to be nil. He spoke out strongly against her bill to impose a mandatory cap on carbon dioxide emissions. When Boxer's proposal died in the Senate in June 2008, he said that it showed "momentum is going our way." But he insisted their personal relations were good and revealed that they exchanged gag gifts—a mug showing sea levels engulfing California and a stuffed polar bear.

In late 2009, the committee approved Boxer's cap-and-trade carbon emissions bill 11-1, with Montana Democrat Max Baucus voting no and all Republicans not voting. Eventually, Sen. John Kerry, D-Mass., took over from Boxer in attempting to shepherd the cap-and-trade bill through, but it failed to attract sufficient support to succeed on the Senate floor. Inhofe told *Politico*, "I'm for renewables. I'm for geothermal. I'm for everything out there. But if you were to do away with fossil fuels, let's say, next year, how would you generate enough electricity to run the machine called America? And the answer is, we couldn't." In February 2011, Inhofe co-sponsored a bill to stop the EPA from regulating carbon dioxide emissions and also limiting states' authority to do so. After the April 2010 BP oil spill in the Gulf of Mexico, he opposed a Democratic initiative to remove the $75 million cap on damages for offshore drilling accidents and argued there should be some limit.

Inhofe is the second-ranking Republican on the Armed Services Committee after Arizona's John McCain. Inhofe has been a strong supporter of missile defense and was one of the leaders of the successful fight to stop President Bill Clinton's effort to ratify the Comprehensive Test Ban Treaty. He supported the Bush administration on the Iraq war, and later strongly opposed closing the U.S. detention center for suspected terrorists at Guantanamo Bay, Cuba.

Inhofe has also been a leader in the movement to make English the country's official language, and during the 2006 debate on overhauling immigration policy, he got the Senate to pass his amendment. "This is not just about preserving our culture and heritage, but also about bettering the odds for our nation's newest potential citizens," he said. When immigration reform came up in the Senate in 2007, Inhofe again was able to get his language amendment passed. And Inhofe's contrarian streak has not slackened in the least. In June 2009, he refused to meet with Supreme Court nominee Sonia Sotomayor on the grounds that he had decided to oppose her.

In 2002 and 2008, Inhofe was re-elected by almost identical margins, both somewhat smaller than Republican presidential margins in Oklahoma. In 2002, he beat former Gov. David Walters, who had years earlier pleaded guilty to a misdemeanor count of violating campaign finance laws, by 57%-36%. In 2008, he beat state Sen. Andrew Rice, 57%-39%, carrying all but four counties in the Muskogee area.

Inhofe has for years regularly flown airplanes and is one of the few certified commercial pilots in Congress. He flew around the world following the historic route of Wiley Post, the first pilot to fly solo around the globe. But he encountered problems in October 2006 when the small plane he was flying spun out of control and suffered significant damage on landing in Tulsa, though he and an aide escaped injury. His penchant for daredevil stunts in the air is well-known around the Capitol, and few of his aides will take him up on his offers of airplane rides. But in October 2010, his flouting of air safety rules became a serious issue. Inhofe set his six-seat Cessna down on a runway clearly marked closed at a South Texas airport, and just narrowly missed hitting a group of construction workers during an aborted landing attempt. The Federal Aviation Administration ordered him to take remedial flying lessons, but did not take away his pilot's license. Inhofe has a major backer of a bill signed into law by Bush in 2007 that raised the mandatory retirement age for airline pilots from 60 to 65.

Junior Senator

Tom Coburn (R)

Elected 2004, term expires 2016, 2nd term; b. March 14, 1948, Casper, WY; home, Muskogee; OK St. U., B.S. 1970, OK U., M.D. 1983; Southern Baptist; married (Carolyn); 3 children.

Elected Office: U.S. House of Reps., 1995-2001.

Professional Career: Mgr., Coburn Optical Industries, 1970–78; Practicing physician, 1983–present.

DC Office: 172 RSOB, 20510, 202-224-5754; Fax: 202-224-6008; Web site: coburn.senate.gov.

State Offices: Oklahoma City, 405-231-4941; Tulsa, 918-581-7651.

Committees: *Finance:* Fiscal Responsibility & Economic Growth; Health Care; Social Security, Pensions & Family Policy (RMM). *Homeland Security & Governmental Affairs:* Federal Financial Management, Government Information, Federal Services & International Security; Investigations (Permanent) (RMM); Oversight of Government Management, the Federal Workforce & the District of Columbia. *Judiciary:* Administrative Oversight & the Courts; Constitution, Civil Rights & Human Rights; Privacy, Technology & the Law (RMM).

Group Ratings

	ACLU	ACU	ADA	CFG	AFS	FRC	LCV	ITIC	NTU	COC
2010	7	100	5	100	0	91	14	33	96	82
2009	–	100	5	100	0	–	0	–	97	71

National Journal Ratings

	2010 LIB	—	2010 CONS	2009 LIB	—	2009 CONS
Economic	13%	—	86%	0%	—	97%
Social	0%	—	79%	10%	—	87%
Foreign	0%	—	72%	0%	—	84%
Composite	13%	—	87%	7%	—	93%

Key Votes of the 111th Congress

1. Overturn Ledbetter	N	5. Pass health care bill	N	9. Ratify New START	N
2. Pass $787 billion stimulus	N	6. Regulate financial firms	N	10. Confirm Elena Kagan	N
3. Repeal DC gun laws	Y	7. Pass tax cuts for some	N	11. Stop EPA climate regs	Y
4. Confirm Sonia Sotomayor	N	8. Legalize immigrants' kids	N	12. Repeal don't ask, tell	N

Election Results

2010 general	Tom Coburn (R)	718,482	(71%)	($2,644,376)
	Jim Rogers (D)	265,814	(26%)	
	Stephen Wallace (I)	25,048	(2%)	
2010 primary	Tom Coburn (R)	223,997	(90%)	
	Evelyn Rogers (R)	15,093	(6%)	

Prior Winning Percentages: 2004 (53%); House: 1998 (58%); 1996 (55%); 1994 (52%)

Tom Coburn, a Republican who previously served in the House, was elected to the Senate in 2004 and re-elected in 2010. Coburn grew up in Muskogee, where his father started Coburn Optical Services, which became the town's biggest employer. Coburn graduated from Oklahoma State University and, while there, married his childhood sweetheart, who was Miss Oklahoma 1967. His father moved his company to Virginia, and Coburn followed to join the business. These were years of campus and youth rebellions, but not for Coburn. "I was focused on business, kind of driven. I was sort of aloof to the counterculture. I never even heard of marijuana," he says. Coburn took over the lens division of the company and increased sales from $100,000 to $40 million. In 1975, the company was sold to Revlon. After being stricken with melanoma, Coburn decided to go to the University of Oklahoma Medical School. He graduated at age 35, moved back to Muskogee and opened Maternal and Family Practice Associates. In addition to running his practice, he went on medical missions around the world. In 1994, Coburn read in his local newspaper that the area's congressman, Mike Synar, was calling for a greater role for the government in running the health care system, and decided to run against him. Synar's 2nd District, covering northeast Oklahoma outside Tulsa, was traditionally Democratic but increasingly conservative. As it turned out, Synar was beaten in the 1994 Democratic primary by a 71-year-old retired middle school teacher. That left an easier path for Coburn to prevail in the general election, which he did, 52%-48%.

Coburn belonged to the group of conservative agitators who came to power with Republican leader Newt Gingrich and were determined to make big changes. He regularly angered appropriators by opposing their bills and offering multiple amendments. A strong opponent of abortion rights, Coburn sponsored bills requiring AIDS counseling for pregnant women and labels on condoms disclosing that they don't prevent infections that lead to cervical cancer. He became known around the Capitol for conducting graphic slide shows for lawmakers and staff about the effects of sexually transmitted diseases. In time, Coburn and other firebrands in the Class of '94 became disenchanted with Gingrich and attempted to oust him as House speaker in July 1997. The attempt failed, but it marked the beginning of the end of Gingrich's reign, and he resigned from Congress in early 1999. In 2000, Coburn kept his campaign promise to serve only three terms in the House and did not run for re-election. He went home to his medical practice in Muskogee and wrote *Breach of Trust: How Washington Turns Outsiders into Insiders,* in which he called members of Congress "Pharisees" and attacked Republican leaders by name.

In 2003, when Republican Don Nickles announced he would retire after four terms in the Senate, several well-known politicians lined up to run. In the GOP primary were Kirk Humphreys, Oklahoma City mayor, and Bob Anthony, an Oklahoma energy commissioner. Coburn at first stayed out of the contest because he had been recently treated for colon cancer. But after several weeks, he changed his mind, saying he had "an impression in my spiritual life that I was supposed to do this." Humphreys criticized Coburn for attending a Las Vegas fundraiser, prompting Coburn to return contributions from gambling figures, and Humphreys also ran an ad attacking him for voting against intelligence and airport spending bills. Coburn's cultural and fiscal conservatism, his opposition to Washington insiders and his adherence to his House term-limit pledge had earned him fans across the state, and though early polls showed a close race, he won 61% of the vote to 25% for Humphreys and 12% for Anthony.

The Democratic nominee was Brad Carson, who had been elected in the 2nd District to succeed Coburn in 2000. He was part Cherokee and a Southern Baptist, an honors graduate from Baylor and a Rhodes Scholar. He had one of the most moderate voting records of any House Democrat and had supported gun rights, the death penalty and the Iraq war. Carson described himself as a practical-minded lawmaker, and said Coburn was an extremist whose sometimes impolitic public remarks "already made us a laughingstock all across not only the country but the whole globe." With support from national Democrats, he raised more money than Coburn. Coburn presented himself as a part-time lawmaker, determined to uphold principle and willing to take on his own party's leadership, while portraying Carson as an extreme liberal who would be "a vote for Ted Kennedy and Hillary Clinton to run the Senate."

The race was close going into September, when the most incendiary issue was raised. News broke of a lawsuit, long since settled, by a woman who claimed Coburn in 1990 sterilized her without consent when operating on her ectopic pregnancy and then filed a false Medicaid claim. Coburn said the woman gave oral consent and that he'd never sought reimbursement for the sterilization. A Carson ad said Coburn "sterilized an underage girl without her consent," then committed Medicaid fraud "to get paid for the illegal procedure." Coburn charged that Democrats had connived with reporters to raise the issue. Coburn won by a solid 53%-41%. Carson carried all but two of the counties in the 2nd Congressional District and won in some other historically Democratic rural counties. But Coburn won in the major cities, 56%-37% in metro Oklahoma City and 55%-41% in metro Tulsa.

In his first term, Coburn wanted to continue practicing medicine while serving in the Senate, but the Rules Committee found the arrangement to be a conflict of interest. Coburn objected and said it would "make me a better senator" and asked to be allowed to practice, charging just enough to pay malpractice insurance premiums. Coburn got 51 votes from fellow senators, not the required 60 for approval, but he called it "a moral victory."

Early in his Senate career he vowed not to seek earmarks and was quick to criticize those who did. When he tried to delete $453 million for two bridges in Alaska, Republican Sen. Ted Stevens exploded. "If the Senate decides to discriminate against our state ... I will resign from this body," he fumed. Coburn lost on a 82-15 vote, but he continued to challenge other senators' earmarks, making him a less than popular colleague. He also challenged the Bush administration's financing of the Iraq war through supplemental appropriations. And he teamed up with Democratic Sen. Barack Obama of Illinois in 2006 to win enactment of a central database for federal grants and contracts, which Coburn called "a small but significant step toward changing the culture in Washington."

Coburn's constant challenges of Senate operations infuriated Democratic Majority Leader Harry Reid. He proposed multiple amendments to the Democrats' omninus appropriations bill in March 2009 and tried to remove $5.5 billion in what he deemed wasteful projects in the 2009 economic stimulus legislation. With the Senate's other physician, Republican John Barrasso of Wyoming, he opposed the Democrats' health care overhaul bill in 2009. He also attracted considerable attention with an amendment barring federal payments for erectile dysfunction pills to convicted sex offenders.

Coburn insisted that Democratic measures be paid for, and he blocked any he thought were not offset with spending cuts, including a major food safety bill, National Science Foundation grants in political science, home health care for veterans, aid to victims of strife in Uganda, and money for the Federal Emergency Management Agency. "If we don't start paying for things, we'll face a disaster worse than Greece," he told *National Journal*. In February 2010, he objected to an extension of unemployment insurance that was not paid for and in May 2010, he placed holds on eight nominees to the Broadcasting Board of Governors out of concern about waste in the Voice of America. The same year, he revealed that he called $120 billion in spending on 640 duplicative programs and also charged that the federal government had sent out $1 billion in payments to dead people. Not all of these moves were successful, although eventually, many Republicans embraced a crackdown on earmarks. Coburn did more than anyone else to prevent Senate Democrats from passing a $1.1 trillion omnibus appropriation in the December 2010 lame duck session, a failure which left Democrats having to agree on significant budget cuts in early 2011.

In March 2010, Minority Leader Mitch McConnell named Coburn as one of three Senate Republicans to President Obama's commission on the federal debt, co-chaired by former White House Chief of Staff Erskine Bowles and former Sen. Alan Simpson of Wyoming. The panel's recommendations included tax increases, continuation of the 2010 health care legislation and substantial changes in entitlement programs. But they did not get the supermajority Obama required to trigger his support for enacting the recommendations. Coburn joined Senate Republican colleagues Judd Gregg of New Hampshire and Mike Crapo of Idaho in voting for the recommendations, as did Senate Democrats Dick Durbin of Illinois and Kent Conrad of North Dakota. Coburn recognized that most Republicans opposed any tax increase but argued it was a good starting place for discussions between the two parties. "The only thing worse than being for it is being against it," he told *Politico*. In early 2011, Coburn was part of a group of six senators who agreed to continue meeting in an effort to find bipartisan agreement on fiscal policy. Republican Sen. Mike Johanns of Nebraska told *National Journal* that Coburn is one of the senators he most admires: "He really doesn't shoot from the hip. He always does his homework."

Going into the 2010 election, some Democratic strategists thought Coburn might be vulnerable because he admitted counseling his Washington, D.C., housemate and Nevada GOP Sen. John Ensign about an affair Ensign had had with the wife of his chief aide and his efforts to negotiate a financial settlement with the aide. But that apparently had no negative impact in Oklahoma, where he was re-elected in 2010 with ease, 71%-26%.

FIRST DISTRICT

John Sullivan (R)

Elected Jan. 2002, 5th full term; b. Jan. 1, 1965, Tulsa; home, Tulsa; Northeastern St. U., B.B.A., 1992; Catholic; married (Judy); 4 children.

Elected Office: OK House of Reps., 1994-2001.

Professional Career: Trucking salesman, 1988-92; Gas and Fleet sales rep., 1991-98; Realtor, 1997-2002.

DC Office: 434 CHOB, 20515, 202-225-2211; Fax: 202-225-9187; Web site: sullivan.house.gov.

State Offices: Bartlesville, 918-336-6500; Tulsa, 918-749-0014.

Committees: *Energy & Commerce:* Energy & Power (VChmn); Environment & the Economy; Oversight & Investigations.

Group Ratings

	ACLU	ACU	ADA	CFG	AFS	FRC	LCV	ITIC	NTU	COC
2010	8	100	5	100	0	93	0	0	89	75
2009	–	100	0	91	0	–	0	–	88	69

National Journal Ratings

	2010 LIB	—	2010 CONS	2009 LIB	—	2009 CONS
Economic	7%	—	92%	*	—	*
Social	24%	—	75%	*	—	*
Foreign	0%	—	88%	*	—	*
Composite	13%	—	87%	*	—	*

Key Votes of the 111th Congress

1. Overturn Ledbetter	N	5. Bar federal abortion funds	Y	9. Stop detainee transfers	Y
2. Pass $820 billion stimulus	N	6. Pass health care bill	N	10. Legalize immigrants' kids	N
3. Let guns in national parks	Y	7. Regulate financial firms	N	11. Repeal don't ask, tell	N
4. Pass cap-and-trade	*	8. Pass tax cuts for some	N	12. Limit campaign funds	N

Election Results

2010 general	John Sullivan (R)	151,173	(77%)	($940,406)
	Angela O'Dell (I)	45,656	(23%)	
2010 primary	John Sullivan (R)	38,673	(62%)	
	Kenneth Rice (R)	10,394	(17%)	
	Nathan Dahm (R)	8,871	(14%)	

Prior Winning Percentages: 2008 (66%), 2006 (64%), 2004 (60%), 2002 (56%), 2002 special (54%)

Population		Race/Ethnicity		Work	
Pop. 2010:	754,310	White:	67.1%	Private:	83.5%
Change since 2000:	Up 9.3%	Black:	9.0%	Government:	10.1%
Urban:	89.6%	Hispanic:	9.8%	Self-employed:	6.3%
Rural:	10.4%	Asian:	2.1%	Blue collar:	22.5%
Area size:	1,790 sq. mi.	Native Am.:	6.6%	White collar:	61.7%
		Hawaiian:	0.1%	Khaki collar:	0.1%
Age		Two+ races:	5.3%	Other:	15.8%
Median age:	35.5 yrs.				
More than 65 yrs:	12.3%	*Ancestry*		Median income:	$47,761
Less than 18 yrs:	25.8%	German	13.1%	Median Home Value:	$127,400
		Irish	10.4%		
Education		English	8.4%	**Military Veterans**	
H.S. grad:	88.0%			% of Pop:	10.9%
College grad:	27.6%				
Grad degree:	8.5%				

Tulsa, Broken Arrow

The gushers of the 1905 Glenn Pool discovery made Tulsa one of America's oil boomtowns, settled not just by people from the immediate hinterland but also by Midwesterners and New Englanders of Yankee stock. In the 1920s, as its art deco skyscrapers rose on the heights above the Arkansas River, it was still a raw town, but one bent on becoming more cultural. It was optimistic and ready to seek economic change, yet culturally and politically conservative, with a

2008 Presidential Vote		
John McCain (R)	205,482	(64%)
Barack Obama (D)	114,174	(36%)
2004 Presidential Vote		
George Bush (R)	206,744	(65%)
John Kerry (D)	109,486	(35%)
Cook Partisan Voting Index: R+16		

Yankee elite and an American Indian heritage recalled today in one of the nation's best collections of Western art at the Gilcrease Museum—left by oil millionaire Thomas Gilcrease, who was one-eighth Creek Indian. In the decades since, Tulsa has boomed and occasionally busted. The city also is the headquarters of Oral Roberts University and its 60-story City of Faith Hospital. It has remained cosmopolitan but conservative. A travel writer for *The Washington Post* once termed Tulsa "a fine replica of European grandeur." People here do not resent the oil companies or the new rich; they identify with them.

In 2003, voters approved a $900 million investment funded by a one-cent sales tax increase, as part of Tulsa's efforts to diversify from being solely one of America's leading petroleum centers. The initiative has helped pay for everything from Arkansas River protection work to new university buildings to upgrades at city parks and golf courses. After Citgo Petroleum announced that it was moving its corporate headquarters from Tulsa to Houston, local officials persuaded American Airlines to move its maintenance and engineering center and over 7,000 jobs to Tulsa from Kansas City; that move spurred other aerospace-related development in the city. With 28,000 jobs, Tinker Air Force Base is the state's largest single-site employer. The military and aerospace industry helped shield Tulsa from the worst of the recession.

The 1st Congressional District of Oklahoma includes Tulsa, Wagoner, and Washington counties, and slices of Rogers and Creek counties—just about all of the Tulsa metropolitan area. The political tradition here is heavily Republican, strengthened in recent decades by opposition to national Democrats' cultural liberalism. Even during the collapse of oil prices in the 1980s, Tulsa maintained its contagious enthusiasm for new business enterprises and innovations.

John Sullivan (R)

The congressman from the 1st District is John Sullivan, a Republican who won a January 2002 special election to succeed Steve Largent, who resigned to run for governor. Sullivan grew up in Tulsa and graduated from Northeastern Oklahoma State University. In Tulsa, he worked in the transportation, oil and gas, and real estate industries. In 1994, at age 29, he was elected to the state House, where he served as Republican whip. In the December 2001 primary for the 1st District seat, the best-known candidate was Cathy Keating, wife of Republican Gov. Frank Keating, who enthusiastically backed her campaign. She had a big fundraising advantage, but she stumbled in the course of the five-week campaign. Sullivan accused her of being too moderate for the conservative district. Sullivan, meanwhile, built a strong grassroots network among conservative activists. He led the first round of balloting, 46%-30%. Under state law, Sullivan's failure to win 50% entitled Keating to a runoff. But his unexpectedly large lead, plus the unlikelihood that four weeks of additional campaigning would change the outcome, convinced Keating to drop her candidacy. In January, Sullivan faced the Democratic nominee, Doug Dodd, a Tulsa lawyer and former school board member. Dodd ran a spirited campaign and raised money from organized labor. Even though this is a district that George W. Bush carried with more than 60% of the vote in 2000 and 2004, Sullivan only won 54%-44%, and national Democrats may have regretted ignoring the race.

Sullivan voted more conservatively in 2010 than fellow Oklahoma Republicans Frank Lucas and Tom Cole, according to *National Journal* ratings. He was the only member of the state's House delegation to oppose the tax-cut extension deal that his party cut with President Barack Obama in late 2010, citing its added burden on the national debt. In February 2011, however, he joined Cole and Lucas in joining Democrats to defeat an unsuccessful bid by the House's most conservative members to slash $100 billion from the fiscal 2011 budget. And he declined to join an earlier conservative-led campaign to ban earmarks, the special projects that lawmakers insert into spending bills for their districts and states. "I don't want to cut myself off from helping my district," he told the *Tulsa World* in 2008. Two years later, he went along with a House GOP earmark moratorium, saying the process needed reform.

Sullivan won a seat on the Energy and Commerce Committee, where oil and gas issues are often front and center. On behalf of the petroleum industry, he got an amendment added to the fiscal 2011 stopgap spending bill preventing the Environmental Protection Agency from spending money on waivers to use E15—a blend of gasoline and up to 15% ethanol—that it had granted over the past year. The blend can be used in newer cars and trucks as well as flex-fuel vehicles. He won House approval in July 2009 for his bill to spend $150 million to research natural gas-powered vehicles.

He has also pushed for tougher controls on illegal immigration, contending that truckloads of illegal immigrants have been dumped into Tulsa neighborhoods, and he criticized President George W. Bush for failing to take a tougher stand against proposals to establish a path to citizenship for illegal immigrants.

Despite some missteps, Sullivan has become increasingly popular with constituents over the years. In his first rematch against Dodd, Sullivan raised his margin of victory to 56%-42%. In 2004, he faced a primary challenge from Bill Wortman, who was backed by two disgruntled ex-consultants who claimed Sullivan had stiffed them on fees, but Sullivan won 70%-25%. In the fall, in a second rematch with Dodd, he prevailed 60%-38%.

In 2008, Democrat Georgianna Oliver, a Tulsa technology company executive who funded her own campaign, challenged Sullivan's record, charging that he was not attuned to local needs and that he flip-flopped on the massive government bailout for financial institutions. With national Democrats busy elsewhere, Oliver had little help from the party, and Sullivan won easily. He gained attention with some quotable comments, such this quip about New York Sen. Hillary Rodham Clinton's presidential bid: "The Clintons are like cockroaches. They could survive a nuclear holocaust."

Sullivan's alcohol abuse first became an issue in 2004, when it was revealed that he had been arrested or taken into custody for incidents that ranged from public intoxication to hitting a police officer. He told constituents in a June 2009 message that he would take a leave of absence from Congress for help with "my addiction to alcohol." He returned from the Betty Ford Clinic a month and a half later, and though he won just 62% of the 2010 primary vote against a weak field, he coasted in the general election with an all-time high of 77%-23% over independent Angelia O'Dell. No Democrat filed to run against him. Now he is a fitness buff, often espousing the arduous CrossFit strength and conditioning program.

SECOND DISTRICT

Dan Boren (D)

Elected 2004, 4th term; b. Aug. 2, 1973, Shawnee; home, Muskogee; TX Christian U., B.S. 1997, U. of OK, M.B.A. 2000; Methodist; married (Andrea); 1 child.

Elected Office: OK House of Reps., 2002-04.

Professional Career: Aide, OK Corp. Comm., 1997-98; Loan processor, Banc First Corp., 1999-2000; Staffer, U.S. Rep. Wes Watkins 2000-01.

DC Office: 2447 RHOB, 20515, 202-225-2701; Fax: 202-225-3038; Web site: boren.house.gov.

State Offices: Claremore, 918-341-9336; Durant, 580-931-0333; McAlester, 918-423-5951; Muskogee, 918-687-2533.

Committees: *Natural Resources:* Energy & Mineral Resources; Indian & Alaska Native Affairs (RMM). *Permanent Select Committee on Intelligence:* Oversight; Terrorism, HUMINT, Analysis & Counterintelligence.

Group Ratings

	ACLU	ACU	ADA	CFG	AFS	FRC	LCV	ITIC	NTU	COC
2010	20	38	30	60	63	87	60	100	46	100
2009	–	44	40	47	56	–	57	–	30	87

National Journal Ratings

	2010 LIB	—	2010 CONS	2009 LIB	—	2009 CONS
Economic	43%	—	57%	42%	—	57%
Social	41%	—	59%	39%	—	60%
Foreign	48%	—	52%	43%	—	56%
Composite	44%	—	56%	42%	—	58%

Key Votes of the 111th Congress

1. Overturn Ledbetter	N	5. Bar federal abortion funds	Y	9. Stop detainee transfers	*
2. Pass $820 billion stimulus	Y	6. Pass health care bill	N	10. Legalize immigrants' kids	N
3. Let guns in national parks	Y	7. Regulate financial firms	N	11. Repeal don't ask, tell	N
4. Pass cap-and-trade	N	8. Pass tax cuts for some	N	12. Limit campaign funds	N

Election Results

2010 general	Dan Boren (D)..108,203	(57%)	($1,615,296)
	Charles Thompson (R)...................................112,146	(43%)	($112,146)
2010 primary	Dan Boren (D)..66,439	(76%)	
	Jim Wilson (D) 21,496	(24%)	

Prior Winning Percentages: 2008 (70%), 2006 (73%), 2004 (66%)

Population		Race/Ethnicity		Work	
Pop. 2010:	729,887	White:	66.0%	Private:	71.8%
Change since 2000:	Up 5.8%	Black:	3.5%	Government:	19.7%
Urban:	35.6%	Hispanic:	4.1%	Self-employed:	8.2%
Rural:	64.4%	Asian:	0.5%	Blue collar:	30.9%
Area size:	21,226 sq. mi.	Native Am.:	18.4%	White collar:	50.2%
		Hawaiian:	0.1%	Khaki collar:	0.2%
Age		Two+ races:	7.4%	Other:	18.8%
Median age:	38.4 yrs.				
More than 65 yrs:	15.5%	*Ancestry*		Median income:	$35,638
Less than 18 yrs:	24.6%	Irish	11.8%	Median Home Value:	$83,300
		German	11.0%		
Education		USA	8.0%	**Military Veterans**	
H.S. grad:	81.4%			% of Pop:	12.2%
College grad:	14.9%				
Grad degree:	5.0%				

Eastern Oklahoma; Muskogee

The land that is now northeast Oklahoma used to be Indian territory, the place where in the 1830s the Five Civilized Tribes were driven from Georgia and Alabama over the Trail of Tears. Eighteen percent of people here report their race as American Indian, and in some counties, one-third or more say they are part Indian. The Native American identity is highest in the hilly counties just west of the Ozarks of Arkansas, where county names—Cherokee, Osage, Se-

2008 Presidential Vote
John McCain (R) 174,230 (66%)
Barack Obama (D) 91,760 (34%)

2004 Presidential Vote
George Bush (R) 166,826 (59%)
John Kerry (D) 114,113 (41%)

Cook Partisan Voting Index: R+14

quoyah—recall the Civilized Tribes. The street signs in scenic Tahlequah, the Cherokee capital since 1839, are written in both English and Cherokee. The Creek Nation chose its tribal site in Okmulgee in the belief that tornadoes would not strike the area; history has proven the choice correct so far. This pleasant land of gentle hills and man-made lakes recently has grown at a healthy pace with the advent of Indian-owned casinos and a population spread from Tulsa.

South of Indian country is Oklahoma's Little Dixie, settled between 1889 and 1907 by white Southerners, most of them poor. Some of the county names—LeFlore, Pontotoc—are borrowed straight from Mississippi. Interstate highways and turnpikes connect people to jobs in more-vibrant metropolitan areas, while dam-made lakes have spurred resort and retirement communities. Still, traditional cultural attitudes and folkways remain strong. When Oklahoma voted in 2002 to outlaw cockfighting, voters in many Little Dixie towns turned out in large numbers to oppose the ban.

The 2nd Congressional District includes most of the eastern third of Oklahoma, except for metropolitan Tulsa. It includes Muskogee; Claremore, Will Rogers's hometown; and McAlester, former House Speaker Carl Albert's home. McAlester is the site of a massive Army ammunition plant that manufactures non-nuclear bombs. The abandoned Tar Creek lead and zinc mines left a destructive legacy and the region became a Superfund site in the 1980s. A federal buyout of homes and businesses created a ghost town by 2010. This area was ancestrally Democratic, but in the 1980s, it trended Republican on cultural issues. Democrat Al Gore was competitive with a 52%-47% loss to George W. Bush, but Democrat John Kerry lost 59%-41%. In 2008, Republican John McCain defeated Democrat Barack Obama 66%-34%.

Dan Boren (D)

The congressman from the 2nd District is Dan Boren, who was elected in 2004 and hails from one of Oklahoma's prominent political families. He is serving his fourth and final term in Congress. Boren announced in June 2011 that he would not seek re-election in 2012, expressing a desire to spend more time with his wife and two young children and saying he had tired of the "constant campaigning" that has come to define service in the House. Republicans were likely to target Boren in 2012, and after his announcement, were in an even better position to compete for the conservative district.

Boren's grandfather, Lyle Boren, represented southeastern Oklahoma in Congress from 1937 to 1947. His father, David Boren, a Democrat, was elected governor in 1974 and senator in 1978. David Boren was chairman of the Senate Intelligence Committee before he resigned from Congress in 1994 to become president of the University of Oklahoma. Dan Boren grew up in Shawnee and in Longview, Texas, where he lived with his mother and stepfather. He graduated from Texas Christian University and the University of Oklahoma Business School. He worked as a college fundraiser and as a district aide to Republican Rep. Wes Watkins, who represented Little Dixie until he retired in 2002. Based in rural Okfuskee County, Boren ran for the state House in 2002 at age 29, raised $200,000, and unseated a Republican who had switched from the Democratic Party. He became chairman of the Democratic Caucus.

When 2nd District Rep. Brad Carson, announced he was running for the Senate, Boren decided to make a play for Carson's seat. The Democratic primary narrowed to a contest between Boren and former district prosecutor Kalyn Free. Boren had the backing of local business and was the more conservative candidate. While he supported abortion rights, he favored restrictions, such as parental consent for minors. Unlike many other Democrats, Boren opposed repeal of the Bush-era tax cuts, and he said he would have voted to authorize the use of force in Iraq. Several labor unions, environmental groups, and MoveOn.org endorsed Free. EMILY's List poured more than $500,000 into her campaign, but it wasn't enough. Boren won the Democratic primary 58%-36%. In the general election, he won 66%-34% against Republican horse breeder Wayland Smalley.

His voting record is in line with that of many moderate Republicans. He was elected to the National Rifle Association's board of directors in 2008 and in February 2011 amended a GOP spending bill to bar using federal money to require firearm dealers to report multiple sales of assault weapons, something the Obama administration proposed to prevent Mexican drug traffickers from obtaining U.S.-sold guns. A month later, he was one of three Democrats to oppose a Democratic amendment that put the House on record as accepting that climate change is occurring and caused largely by human activities. In January 2011, he supported fellow Blue Dog Democrat Heath Shuler of North Carolina over California liberal Nancy Pelosi for minority leader.

On the Armed Services Committee, Boren sponsored a bill to ban the use of names and images of military members in anti-war commercial enterprises. Although he sometimes disagreed with the tactics in Iraq, he mostly supported the Bush administration's policies there and in Afghanistan and continued to do so under Obama. He persuaded Pelosi to put him on the Intelligence Committee in 2009 and got a provision added to an intelligence authorization bill that expanded a language-training program created by his father. On the Natural Resources Committee, he has strongly advocated for increased domestic drilling. He also has pushed a bill to apologize to American Indians for their mistreatment by the federal government.

Boren has won re-election easily every two years. He has taken advantage of his father's connections; between 2004 and 2010, according to the Center for Responsive Politics, the University of Oklahoma was his second-leading source of campaign contributions. Despite considerable support from other Democrats, he declined to challenge Republican Sen. James Inhofe in 2008.

THIRD DISTRICT

Frank Lucas (R)

Elected May 1994, 9th full term; b. Jan. 6, 1960, Cheyenne; home, Cheyenne; OK St. U., B.S. 1982; Baptist; married (Lynda); 3 children.

Elected Office: OK House of Reps., 1988–94.

Professional Career: Farmer & rancher.

DC Office: 2311 RHOB, 20515, 202-225-5565; Fax: 202-225-8698; Web site: www.house.gov/lucas.

State Offices: Stillwater, 405-624-6407; Woodward, 580-256-5752; Yukon, 405-373-1958.

Committees: *Agriculture* (Chmn). *Financial Services:* Capital Markets and Government Sponsored Enterprises; Domestic Monetary Policy & Technology. *Science & Technology:* Energy & Environment; Space & Aeronautics.

Group Ratings

	ACLU	ACU	ADA	CFG	AFS	FRC	LCV	ITIC	NTU	COC
2010	6	100	0	86	0	87	30	33	86	88
2009	–	91	0	86	0	–	0	–	85	80

National Journal Ratings

	2010 LIB	—	2010 CONS		2009 LIB	—	2009 CONS
Economic	15%	—	84%		13%	—	87%
Social	18%	—	77%		23%	—	76%
Foreign	12%	—	79%		0%	—	75%
Composite	18%	—	83%		16%	—	84%

Key Votes of the 111th Congress

1. Overturn Ledbetter	N	5. Bar federal abortion funds	Y	9. Stop detainee transfers	Y
2. Pass $820 billion stimulus	N	6. Pass health care bill	N	10. Legalize immigrants' kids	N
3. Let guns in national parks	Y	7. Regulate financial firms	N	11. Repeal don't ask, tell	N
4. Pass cap-and-trade	N	8. Pass tax cuts for some	N	12. Limit campaign funds	N

Election Results

2010 general	Frank Lucas (R)	161,927	(78%)	($1,024,225)
	Frankie Robbins (D)	45,689	(22%)	($1,975)
2010 primary	Frank Lucas (R)	unopposed		

Prior Winning Percentages: 2008 (70%), 2006 (67%), 2004 (82%), 2002 (76%), 2000 (59%), 1998 (65%), 1996 (64%), 1994 (70%), 1994 special (54%)

Population		Race/Ethnicity		Work	
Pop. 2010:	732,394	White:	76.7%	Private:	71.4%
Change since 2000:	Up 6.1%	Black:	3.6%	Government:	20.0%
Urban:	50.7%	Hispanic:	8.5%	Self-employed:	8.1%
Rural:	49.3%	Asian:	1.0%	Blue collar:	26.8%
Area size:	34,383 sq. mi.	Native Am.:	6.2%	White collar:	54.3%
		Hawaiian:	0.2%	Khaki collar:	0.4%
Age		Two+ races:	3.8%	Other:	18.5%
Median age:	36.9 yrs.				
More than 65 yrs:	14.2%	*Ancestry*		Median income:	$42,253
Less than 18 yrs:	24.3%	German	15.9%	Median Home Value:	$91,000
		Irish	11.7%		
Education		English	7.9%	**Military Veterans**	
H.S. grad:	85.0%			% of Pop:	11.1%
College grad:	20.1%				
Grad degree:	6.3%				

West Oklahoma; Enid, Stillwater

Settled just a century ago, western Oklahoma is a fertile land forever at the mercy of the elements. The western plains are scorching hot under the summer sun and blown frozen by bitter winter winds. Visitors to the Tallgrass Prairie Preserve, maintained by the Nature Conservancy near Pawhuska, can experience what settlers found when they arrived here: a swaying ocean of 10-foot-high grasses filled with insects emitting a dull, incessant roar. One can still get a

2008 Presidential Vote		
John McCain (R) 210,074	(73%)
Barack Obama (D) 78,426	(27%)

2004 Presidential Vote		
George Bush (R) 209,598	(72%)
John Kerry (D) 82,670	(28%)

Cook Partisan Voting Index: R+24

sense of what the old towns looked like. In 1910, three years after statehood, Oklahoma moved its capital south 25 miles, from Guthrie to Oklahoma City, leaving behind what has become one of the nation's largest historic preservation districts. Many rural counties here are not much more populated than they were 100 years ago. Far fewer people live here than did before the Dust Bowl days in the 1930s, and fewer than during the Anadarko Basin oil and natural gas boom of the 1970s. Today, local entrepreneurs see the possibility of economic revival in another abundant natural resource: the wind. The region is one of the windiest parts of America and is being billed locally as the "Saudi Arabia of wind," and a Kansas company announced plans in October 2010 to build a $200 million wind farm in western Oklahoma. The region is also home to the world's largest plot of switch grass, and there are hopes that it too can be turned into a profitable source of alternative energy at the new cellulosic ethanol production plant near Guymon.

The 3rd Congressional District includes Oklahoma's western plains and nearly half of the state's land, from the Panhandle to the northern fringes of Oklahoma City. It extends to north central Oklahoma, including Ponca City, the university town of Stillwater, and Osage County, site of the state's lone Indian reservation. A few of the southern counties, settled by farmers crossing the Red River from Texas, are ancestrally Democratic. But farmers coming south from Kansas settled most of these plains, and they were heavily Republican. In Kingfisher County, George W. Bush won by more than 3-to-1 in 2004, and John McCain trounced Barack Obama there 84%-16% in 2008. Farther west in the Panhandle is Beaver County, which claims to be the cow-chip-throwing capital of the world, and Texas and Cimarron counties. Few blacks live in this part of Oklahoma, but an increasing number of Hispanics are moving here to work on hog farms and in meatpacking plants. One of the largest of those is Seaboard Corp.'s plant in Guymon, which has more than 3,000 employees. Texas County, on the Panhandle, is now more than 21% Hispanic, by far the highest percentage in the state.

Frank Lucas (R)

The congressman from the 3rd District is Frank Lucas, a Republican who won the seat in a 1994 special election. Soft-spoken and unflashy, he is the chairman of the House Agriculture Committee.

Lucas' family roots in western Oklahoma extend more than 100 years; he owns a farm and cattle ranch in Roger Mills County and was elected to the Oklahoma House in 1988, at age 28. He got his chance to run for Congress when Glenn English, a 19-year conservative Democrat, resigned. Lucas had serious competition in both the primary and the general election. In the initial voting in the primary, he trailed state Sen. Brooks Douglass, who campaigned from his Oklahoma City base, 36%-34%. In the runoff, Lucas ridiculed "some Johnny-come-lately dressed up like a drugstore cowboy" and carried all of the rural areas to win 56%-44%. In the general election, he faced Dan Webber, the 27-year-old press secretary to former U.S. Sen. David Boren. Lucas ran an ad depicting the U.S. Capitol and saying, "This is where Dan Webber has worked his entire adult life." The ad displayed a picture of Oklahoma farmland and said, "This is where Frank Lucas has worked his entire adult life." Lucas won 54%-46%. Since then, he has been re-elected by wide margins.

Lucas' voting record is mostly conservative, but less so on cultural issues. His main focus is the pragmatic work of the Agriculture Committee, where he became the ranking Republican in the 111th Congress (2009-10). After rising to chairman in 2011, he told *The Wall Street Journal* in March that "everything is on the table" for cutting spending and that he regarded farm subsidies ardently championed by rural lawmakers from both parties as part of the discussion. But he said reducing subsidy programs should be done through the farm bill, which is due for completion in 2012. He also promised to work on implementing pending free trade agreements and conducting aggressive oversight of the Environmental Protection Agency. "It seems that every day the EPA is proposing a new regulation, facilitating new litigation or allowing unelected bureaucrats to run wild across the farms and ranches of America," he told the American Farm Bureau Federation's newspaper. He has been sharply critical of President Barack Obama, accusing him in April 2010 of seeking to turn rural areas into "bedroom communities" by proposing to cut the maximum direct payment to farmers, which go to those who have received subsidies in the past even if they are not actively growing crops.

On the committee during the drafting of the 2002 bill, Lucas helped to unravel the 1996 Freedom to Farm Act and its attack on government subsidies, although he had once embraced the law and its conservative philosophical underpinnings. Lucas helped write provisions to control erosion, aid farmers hit by drought, and protect air and water quality. He successfully fought a plan to reduce the number of Farm Service Agency field offices. In the minority party during the work on the 2008 farm bill, Lucas strongly opposed an overhaul of farm programs as "a threat to the nutrition of the whole, entire world," and he mostly succeeded in preserving subsidies for his district, which ranked 14th in subsidies between 1995 and 2009.

Also with an eye on his district, Lucas helped to write the final provisions in the 2005 energy bill governing rural grants and biodiesel tax credits. He remains a proponent of government support for alternative fuels, particularly switch grass. On the Financial Services Committee, Lucas has been a reliable supporter of the banking and insurance industries. The liberal Center for American Progress complained in December 2010 when Lucas hired a former U.S. Chamber of Commerce lobbyist as the senior staffer to oversee the Community Futures Trading Commission, which was charged with implementing the new law cracking down on the financial industry, including provisions on over-the-counter derivatives. The Office of Congressional Ethics in 2010 targeted Lucas as one of eight lawmakers who conducted fundraisers around the time of a vote on the bill, but dropped its inquiry.

Back home, his main challenge is the physical size of the district. From his home in Cheyenne, it extends 80 miles south, 240 miles west to the Panhandle, and 270 miles east to Tulsa's outskirts—more than 34,000 square miles. But the real trouble for the easygoing Lucas seems to be on his ranch, which he operates. He broke his nose years ago when a cow slammed a gate on him, and he lost a tooth while trying to attach an identification tag to a 250-pound heifer.

FOURTH DISTRICT

Tom Cole (R)

Elected 2002, 5th term; b. April 28, 1949, Shreveport, LA; home, Moore; Grinnell Col., B.A. 1971, Yale U., M.A. 1974, U. of OK, Ph.D. 1984; Methodist; married (Ellen); 1 child.

Elected Office: OK Senate, 1988-91.

Professional Career: OK GOP Chmn., 1985-89; Exec. dir. NRCC, 1991-95; OK secy. of state, 1995-99; Pol. consultant, 2000-2002.

DC Office: 2458 RHOB, 20515, 202-225-6165; Fax: 202-225-3512; Web site: cole.house.gov.

State Offices: Ada, 580-436-5375; Lawton, 580-357-2131; Norman, 405-329-6500.

Committees: *Appropriations:* Defense; Interior, Environment & Related Agencies; State, Foreign Operations & Related Programs (VChmn). *Budget.*

Group Ratings

	ACLU	ACU	ADA	CFG	AFS	FRC	LCV	ITIC	NTU	COC
2010	6	96	0	89	13	100	30	33	84	88
2009	–	92	0	87	0	–	7	–	84	80

National Journal Ratings

	2010 LIB — 2010 CONS		2009 LIB — 2009 CONS	
Economic	25%	— 75%	14%	— 86%
Social	34%	— 66%	20%	— 78%
Foreign	36%	— 63%	0%	— 75%
Composite	32%	— 68%	16%	— 84%

Key Votes of the 111th Congress

1. Overturn Ledbetter	N	5. Bar federal abortion funds	Y	9. Stop detainee transfers	Y
2. Pass $820 billion stimulus	N	6. Pass health care bill	N	10. Legalize immigrants' kids	N
3. Let guns in national parks	Y	7. Regulate financial firms	N	11. Repeal don't ask, tell	N
4. Pass cap-and-trade	N	8. Pass tax cuts for some	N	12. Limit campaign funds	N

Election Results

2010 general	Tom Cole (R) .... unopposed		($852,384)
2010 primary	Tom Cole (R) 32,589	(77%)	
	R. J. Harris (R)...9,593	(23%)	

Prior Winning Percentages: 2008 (66%), 2006 (65%), 2004 (78%), 2002 (54%)

Population		Race/Ethnicity		Work	
Pop. 2010:	785,424	White:	73.2%	Private:	69.1%
Change since 2000:	Up 13.8%	Black:	6.4%	Government:	24.4%
Urban:	63.3%	Hispanic:	7.4%	Self-employed:	6.4%
Rural:	36.7%	Asian:	2.2%	Blue collar:	22.5%
Area size:	10,410 sq. mi.	Native Am.:	5.8%	White collar:	57.3%
		Hawaiian:	0.1%	Khaki collar:	3.0%
Age		Two+ races:	4.8%	Other:	17.2%
Median age:	35.0 yrs.				
More than 65 yrs:	12.4%	*Ancestry*		Median income:	$46,315
Less than 18 yrs:	24.5%	German	12.9%	Median Home Value:	$109,800
		USA	11.6%		
Education		Irish	11.3%	**Military Veterans**	
H.S. grad:	87.5%			% of Pop:	12.7%
College grad:	22.4%				
Grad degree:	7.6%				

South Central Oklahoma; Norman

In the years after 1900, the brown hills west of Oklahoma City and north of the Red River suddenly filled up with farmers riding north from Texas, past the quenched green lands of the east toward the bare pasturelands of the west. The first settlers here arrived just as the buffalo were dying out, down from an estimated 60 million animals to no more than 1,000. So in 1901, Republican President William McKinley established the nation's first wildlife preserve in the

2008 Presidential Vote

John McCain (R) 200,353	(67%)
Barack Obama (D) 101,115	(33%)

2004 Presidential Vote

George Bush (R) 194,977	(67%)
John Kerry (D) 96,100	(33%)

Cook Partisan Voting Index: R+18

Wichita Mountains, 25 miles northwest of Lawton. Fifteen bison were donated by the New York Zoological Society and arrived at the preserve via rail in 1907—a major factor in the survival of the species. Today this habitat supports grazing for Rocky Mountain elk, white-tailed deer and Texas longhorn cattle. Government has played a role in the survival of the people, too. Population in southwest Oklahoma clusters around major government institutions: the state capital in Oklahoma City; the University of Oklahoma in Norman, which was the world's first school of petroleum geology; Tinker Air Force Base in southern Oklahoma City; and the Army Field Artillery School at Fort Sill in Lawton. Sill also is the new home of the Army Air Defense Artillery School, which was relocated from Fort Bliss, Texas.

The 4th Congressional District of Oklahoma begins a few miles from the capitol in Oklahoma City, smack dab in the middle of the state, and proceeds south and west to cover half of Oklahoma's Red River Valley. Demographically, this district is becoming more suburban, but the cultural tone remains countrified. That is true even in the Oklahoma City suburbs, where the state's fastest-growing counties are located. One of them, Canadian, grew by nearly one-third from 2000 to 2010. Ancestrally, this is Democratic country, and four counties in the district's western end—Comanche, Stephens, Jefferson and Cotton—were the only ones in the state that Stephens native and Democrat Jari Askins carried in her unsuccessful 2010 race for governor against Republican Mary Fallin. But Norman, Lawton and the Oklahoma City fringe have voted solidly Republican since the 1990s.

Tom Cole (R)

The congressman from the 4th District is Tom Cole, a Republican first elected in 2002 after a long career working for other politicians. With the retirement of Republican Sen. Ben Nighthorse Campbell of Colorado in 2004, Cole became the only American Indian in Congress and a leading defender of Indian interests in Washington.

Cole grew up in Moore, south of Oklahoma City. He is a fifth-generation Oklahoman, and his mother was a state representative and senator. He's also a member of the Chickasaw Nation tribe; more than half of the nation's Chickasaw Indians live in the district. Cole's father served in the Air Force and later worked at Tinker Air Force Base. Cole graduated from Grinnell College, got a master's degree at Yale University and a Ph.D. in British history at the University of Oklahoma, studying for a year at the University of London. From 1985 to 1989, he was the Oklahoma Republican Party chairman. In 1988, he was elected to the state Senate. He moved to Washington in 1991 to become executive director of the National Republican Congressional Committee, then returned to Oklahoma and was appointed secretary of state, becoming the first Republican to hold that office. He went back to Washington to serve as the chief of staff for the Republican National Committee during the 2000 presidential campaign. During much of that period, he was also the president of a polling and political consulting firm in Oklahoma City.

In 2002, when Rep. J.C. Watts announced that he would not seek re-election, Cole moved quickly to run. Despite his party connections and an endorsement from Watts, he faced formidable opposition from attorney Marc Nuttle. The two shared positions on most issues and extensive party connections. Nuttle had been Cole's predecessor at the NRCC, and had worked on Republican Pat Robertson's 1988 presidential campaign. Nuttle and Cole also had worked together to pass an Oklahoma right-to-work law in a 2001 referendum. But in the showdown between the strategists, Cole won 60%-33%. He had tough competition in the general election from former state Senate Majority Leader Darryl Roberts, who appealed to the "yellow dog" Democratic tradition that is particularly strong in the Red River counties. Cole countered by linking Roberts to all of the past Democratic presidential nominees he had supported, and described him as "pro-tax," "pro-abortion" and "pro-lawsuit." Cole won 54%-46%.

In the House, Cole has a mostly conservative voting record. He is a member of the GOP whip team and sits on the Republican Steering Committee, which makes committee assignments.

Cole differs from his younger conservative colleagues in being generally supportive of government spending. From his plum seat on the Appropriations Committee, he tends to the needs of his district's installations and supports federal programs that help his constituents. Among them is the Education Department's Gaining Early Awareness and Readiness for Undergraduate Programs (GEAR UP), which helps disadvantaged students prepare for college and which Cole said has served more than 31,000 Oklahoma students. He joined Oklahoma Republicans John Sullivan and Frank Lucas in defeating an unsuccessful move by Republican Study Committee members in February 2011 to slash $100 billion from the fiscal 2011 budget. A month later, he warned that a government shutdown could "cause panic" in the financial markets.

Cole began his House career on the Armed Services Committee, a seat of obvious importance to the district, before leaving the panel in 2005 to serve on the Rules Committee, which launched him on a career in leadership. He has been actively involved in issues related to American Indians. In the wake of an influence-peddling scandal involving Republican lobbyist Jack Abramoff, who represented several tribes, Cole strongly opposed proposed limits on the right of tribes to contribute to political campaigns. He and Rep. Dan Boren, D-Okla., denounced a call in May 2009 to have the Justice Department investigate whether Oklahoma tribes took steps to strip the descendants of slaves once owned by tribal members of full citizen rights. "The idea of using the Justice Department as a weapon to beat tribes into submission is abhorrent and unfair," he said.

Following the dismal 2006 election for Republicans, Cole was elected by his peers to be chairman of the NRCC, the fifth-ranking GOP leadership job and one that put him in charge of national Republican efforts to regain the party's majority in the House in 2008. Cole defeated Texan Pete Sessions, 102 to 81, to take over the committee, where he'd cut his teeth as a political strategist years before. He vowed to expand the playing field of competitive seats. But his two-year chairmanship was dismal. The party had had a rough transition to the minority after a dozen years in control, the committee was $19 million in debt, and there were an inordinate number of GOP retirements. Cole and the Republicans raised $116 million for 2008 contests, compared to $171 million for the Democrats. On top of all that, the committee had internal problems, notably the discovery that its longtime treasurer had embezzled hundreds of thousands of dollars. Retiring Rep. Tom Davis of Virginia, a former NRCC chairman himself, circulated a memo warning that the party's campaign apparatus was badly broken and its message "stale" and "obsolete." But the biggest obstacle was largely out of Cole's control: President George W. Bush's abysmal public approval ratings, which made re-election an uphill climb for most Republicans, despite their efforts to distance themselves from the president.

Before long, the relationship between Cole and then-Minority Leader John Boehner of Ohio deteriorated, with public sniping and second-guessing over who was to blame for the party's failure to make gains that year. Boehner believed that Cole's top staffers at the NRCC were not sufficiently aggressive at fundraising and candidate recruitment, and created an advisory group to look over Cole's shoulder at the committee. The two had started out with a cool relationship. Cole had defeated Sessions, a Boehner ally, for the post, and earlier, Cole had publicly backed Republican Rep. Roy Blunt of Missouri over Boehner in the bitterly contested race for majority leader in 2006.

The results of the 2008 election were disappointing for Cole, to say the least. Republicans lost rather than gained seats in the House, winding up at a 257-178 disadvantage. Nevertheless, after the election, Cole decided to seek re-election to another two years as NRCC chairman. Once again, Sessions was seeking the post, with the active support of Boehner. Sensing he could well lose the showdown this time when the decision went to a vote by all House Republicans, Cole withdrew. In a gesture of conciliation, Boehner gave Cole a seat on Appropriations in 2009. And Cole subsequently worked himself back into Boehner's good graces through voracious fundraising. Without a general election opponent to divert his attention in 2010, he brought in more than $270,000 through his political action committee and more than $148,000 from his campaign committee on behalf of other Republicans.

FIFTH DISTRICT

James Lankford (R)

Elected 2010, 1st term; b. March 4, 1968, Dallas, TX; home, Edmond; U. of TX, B.S. 1990; Southwestern Theological Baptist Seminary, M.Div. 1994.; Christian; Married (Cindy); 2 children.

Professional Career: Youth dir., Baptist Gen. Convention of TX, 1990-95; youth camp dir., Baptist Gen. Convention of OK, 1995-2009.

DC Office: 509 CHOB, 20515, 202-225-2132; Fax: 202-226-1463; Web site: lankford.house.gov.

State Offices: Oklahoma City, 405-234-9900.

Committees: *Budget. Oversight & Government Reform:* Government Organization, Efficiency & Financial Management; Technology, Information Policy, Intergovernmental Relations & Procurement Reform (Chmn). *Transportation & Infrastructure:* Aviation; Water Resources & Environment.

Election Results

2010 general	James Lankford (R)	123,236	(63%)	($1,245,097)
	Billy Coyle (D)	68,074	(35%)	($393,912)
2010 runoff	James Lankford (R)	29,817	(65%)	
	Kevin Calvey (R)	15,902	(35%)	
2010 primary	James Lankford (R)	18,760	(34%)	
	Kevin Calvey (R)	18,147	(32%)	
	Mike Thompson (R)	10,008	(18%)	
	Shane Jett (R)	5,956	(11%)	

Population		Race/Ethnicity		Work	
Pop. 2010:	749,336	White:	60.2%	Private:	76.7%
Change since 2000:	Up 8.6%	Black:	13.7%	Government:	16.3%
Urban:	87.5%	Hispanic:	14.5%	Self-employed:	6.8%
Rural:	12.5%	Asian:	2.7%	Blue collar:	21.3%
Area size:	2,089 sq. mi.	Native Am.:	4.4%	White collar:	59.8%
		Hawaiian:	0.1%	Khaki collar:	0.4%
Age		Two+ races:	4.3%	Other:	18.4%
Median age:	34.1 yrs.				
More than 65 yrs:	12.7%	*Ancestry*		Median income:	$41,302
Less than 18 yrs:	25.5%	German	12.1%	Median Home Value:	$114,200
		Irish	9.5%		
Education		English	7.2%	**Military Veterans**	
H.S. grad:	84.7%			% of Pop:	11.1%
College grad:	27.5%				
Grad degree:	9.3%				

Oklahoma City

Oklahoma City, like many state capitals, was not the spontaneous creation of commerce but the deliberate creation of government, sited in the geographic center of the state on what turned out to be oil land. Rigs were pumping crude on the grounds of the Capitol until 1989, and a derrick still stands sentinel outside the governor's window. The land here is browner and more eroded by creeks than the rolling Oklahoma farmland farther east. From its center, Okla-

2008 Presidential Vote		
John McCain (R) 170,027	(59%)
Barack Obama (D) 117,019	(41%)

2004 Presidential Vote		
George Bush (R) 181,644	(64%)
John Kerry (D) 101,595	(36%)

Cook Partisan Voting Index: R+13

homa City has grown far out into the countryside, and, as has happened in so many southwestern cities, its limits expanded so that the city now extends into four counties and three congressional districts, and covers 621 square miles. The city's population grew briskly from 2000 to 2010, with a 14.6% increase from 506,000 to 580,000.

The capital captured worldwide attention in April 1995 when a bomb destroyed the Alfred P. Murrah Federal Building, killing 168 people and injuring more than 500. The profound grief here was channeled into the construction of the Oklahoma City National Memorial on the site of the blast, movingly dedicated exactly five years later in April 2000. In 2006, fueled by the oil boom and sales tax revenues, the city moved to rebuild its downtown with condominiums, a baseball stadium, and a canal through the Bricktown area. The revival was set back by the closing of a General Motors assembly plant the same year. But overall, the area's soaring farm commodities prices have helped to keep the economy strong while much of the nation moved toward recession. Local pride spiked in 2008 when the Seattle SuperSonics of the National Basketball Association relocated to the city and became the Oklahoma City Thunder, the state's first major sports franchise.

The 5th Congressional District includes Oklahoma City and all but a small section of Oklahoma County where Midwest City and Tinker Air Force Base are located. It also takes in Pottawatomie and Seminole counties to the east. These two counties partake of the ancestral Democratic leanings of most of Oklahoma. But Oklahoma City is solidly Republican in state and national politics, and Oklahoma County casts about 90% of the district's votes.

James Lankford (R)

The new congressman from Oklahoma's 5th District is James Lankford, a Republican elected in 2010 to succeed two-term GOP Rep. Mary Fallin, who ran successfully for governor.

Lankford grew up impoverished in Dallas. His parents divorced when he was only 4 years old and he, his mother, and his older brother were forced to move into the garage behind his grandparents' house. Lankford says he became a Christian when he was 8 years old, and that his religion has helped him endure tough times since then. When he was 12, his mother, an elementary school librarian, remarried and the family moved to Garland, a Dallas suburb.

Lankford went on to graduate from the University of Texas with a degree in secondary education, specializing in speech and history. He then attended the Southwestern Theological Baptist Seminary in Fort Worth, where he earned a master's degree in divinity. At that time, he began dating his now-wife, Cindy, whom he had known since high school and who was also studying for a master's degree. In 1995, Lankford moved to Oklahoma City and began working for the Baptist General Convention of Oklahoma. A year later, he was made director of the Falls Creek Christian youth summer camp, which touts itself as the largest summer camp in the country. He was in charge of organizing and coordinating activities for more than 50,000 campers each summer. He served there until 2009, when he resigned to run for Congress.

Lankford announced on Facebook that he was running for Fallin's open seat and he used the social-networking site as a messaging tool. In the Republican primary in July, former state Rep. Kevin Calvey had the backing of national Republicans, but Lankford was able to keep pace with him in fundraising. With grassroots support largely among the Christian community, Lankford came out ahead in the initial voting with 34% to Calvey's 32%. In the August runoff, Lankford won a stunning 65%. He benefited in part from an endorsement from *The Oklahoman*, which described him as "a solid conservative but not a reactionary. He doesn't substitute ideology for intelligence."

After the runoff, Lankford made headlines when he began taking a salary out of campaign funds, citing dwindling family resources. Federal regulations permit primary winners to be paid from campaign money if the payments are no more than they received from their jobs in the previous year or no more than the office that they're seeking pays, whichever is less.

Lankford's Democratic opponent was lawyer Billy Coyle, an Oklahoma City attorney and former Marine sergeant. He sought to distance himself from the Obama administration in an attempt to win support in this conservative district, but was badly underfunded. He raised $363,000 to Lankford's $1.2 million. Lankford won easily, 62.5% to 34.5%, with two minor candidates splitting the rest.

★ OREGON ★

Oregon, far removed from where most Americans live, has made its mark on the rest of the nation. It sees itself as an experimental commonwealth and a laboratory of reform, a maker of national trends, from bike trails to Nike sneakers, light-rail trams to Pendleton shirts. In public policy, it was first state to sanction assisted suicide and to adopt mail-in ballot elections. Oregon is an affluent, high-tech civilization where you can still see much of the same land that Lewis and Clark saw in 1805, when they came down the Columbia River gorge, past the Willamette River, to the Pacific Ocean. This land was settled by Americans after John Jacob Astor set up his fur trading post at Astoria in 1811. New England Yankees in the 1840s rode the Oregon Trail and floated down the Columbia to the well-watered Willamette Valley. In this remote spot, nearly 2,000 miles from the Mississippi River frontier and 700 miles from the small Mexican settlements in California, they built an orderly, productive society—a kind of western New England. It grew steadily, with a few booms—in the early 1900s as timber harvesting surged, during the world wars and then again in the 1970s, when home building skyrocketed and Oregon's natural environment began to be widely appreciated. Its Yankee settlers brought town meeting-style government to Oregon. This was the first state to give people direct decision-making via the initiative and referendum. It pioneered recall of elected officials and the election of U.S. senators by popular vote. It was the first state to institute Labor Day.

Oregon grew much faster than the national average in the 1940s, when war industries brought thousands of people to the West Coast, and again in the 1970s, when the pleasant environment attracted so many young people, the state's population shot up 26%. In response, Republican Gov. Tom McCall famously invited people to visit Oregon, but not to stay, and he and other local politicians set about trying to contain growth. At McCall's prodding, the legislature in 1973 passed a law that in many ways limited development, and in the 1990s, the Portland metropolitan area sharply restricted growth and sprawl. These measures were popular in Portland and the university towns of Eugene and Corvallis and to a lesser extent in the suburbs. The lumber industry, which for decades accounted for most of Oregon's exports, was hurt in the Pacific Northwest in the 1990s because of restrictions imposed to protect the threatened spotted owl. Still, Oregon remains the nation's leader in lumber production. Oregon also leads the U.S. in producing Christmas trees, mainly in the counties around Salem, mostly for sale in arid California. In 2001, the Interior Department cut off water to 1,000 farmers in the Klamath Basin to protect the endangered sucker fish. These policies, even as they devastated the economies of some rural areas, attracted environment-minded newcomers to Portland and the university towns. Portland's postmodern skyscrapers are connected to residential areas studded with brew pubs by one of the nation's largest light rail systems.

These developments have made what was once one of the nation's most politically homogeneous states (moderates from both parties dominated elections) to one of the nation's most polarized polities. This despite one of the highest rates of racial homogeneity: In 2010, Oregon's population was only 2% black, 12% Hispanic and 4% Asian. Metro Portland, with its hugely liberal core neighborhoods, is one of America's whitest metropolitan areas. The highest Hispanic percentages are around the state capital of Salem and farming counties far east of the Cascades. Oregon, founded by New England churchmen, has become America's most non-churchgoing state, with the lowest rate of church membership—in the 2008 exit poll, 31% of voters said their religion was "other" or "none"—and large numbers of believers in astrology and New Age spiritualism. This is the core constituency for some of the state's policy innovations over the last two generations, when Oregon passed the nation's first bottle deposit law, decriminalized medical marijuana, legalized most abortions before the U.S. Supreme Court's *Roe v. Wade* decision and backed limits on land development and use of property. It is one of two states (the other is New Jersey) that ban self-service gas. In 2007, the Democratic-controlled legislature imposed limits on smoking, banned discrimination on the basis of sexual orientation and mandated recycling of discarded electronics materials. Oregon legalized assisted suicide, in referenda in 1994 and 1997, to the point that doctors can prescribe, but not administer, lethal drugs, a law upheld by the U.S. Supreme Court in 2006.

Another innovation was Democratic Gov. John Kitzhaber's Oregon Health Plan, under which state Medicaid officials drew up lists of some 700 medical treatments and ranked them by effectiveness and importance to basic health. Then, based on cost estimates, the state decided how many treatments it could afford to subsidize. Sometimes Oregon's liberals have moved faster than the voters. In 2004, Portland's Multnomah County Commission chairwoman ordered clerks to issue

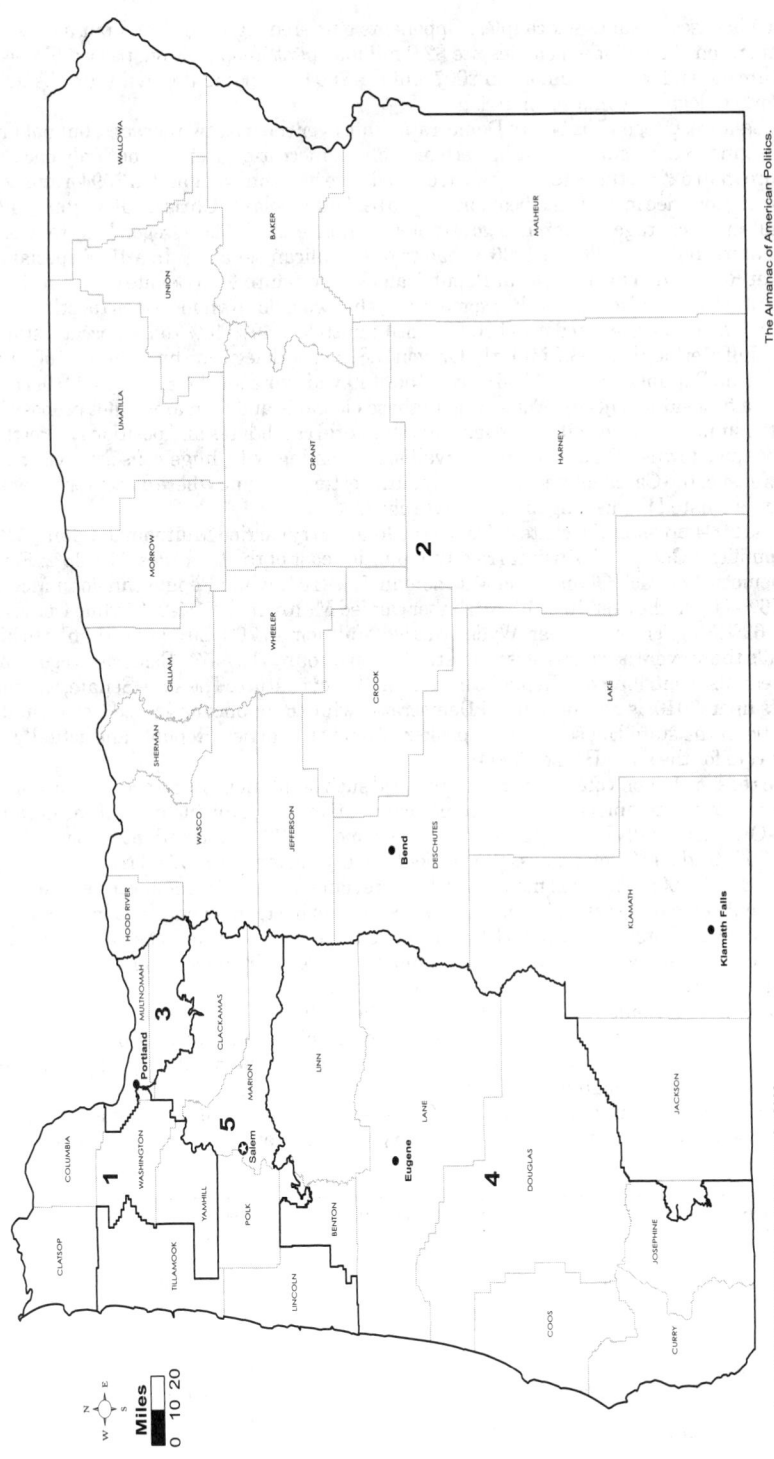

The Almanac of American Politics.
National Journal

Congressional district boundaries were first effective for 2002.

marriage licenses to same-sex couples. Opponents gathered signatures and put a constitutional amendment on the ballot which, despite $2.9 million spent in opposition, passed 57%-43%. The legislature did endorse civil unions in 2007, but the 2004 amendment remains an obstacle to further efforts to legalize same-sex marriage.

On balance, Oregon has been a Democratic state over the past two decades, but not always by wide margins. Starting in 1986, it has elected only Democratic governors but only once, in 1998, with more than 52% of the vote. Kitzhaber, elected governor that year and in 1994, returned as the Democratic nominee in 2010 and beat former pro basketball player Chris Dudley by only 49%-48%, the smallest percentage margin in a governor's race since the 1950s. Oregon has two Democratic U.S. senators, but from 1968 to 1996, it had two Republican senators. In a 1996 special election, Democrat Ron Wyden narrowly beat Republican Gordon Smith for a Senate seat, but then Smith won the other seat in November. For some years, the two held town meetings together across the state, and each was re-elected comfortably until Smith lost 49%-46% to Democratic state House Speaker Jeff Merkley in 2008. Similarly, Oregon U.S. House delegation has consisted of four Democrats and one Republican since 1996, but in the statewide vote for the House in 2010, Democrats won only a 51%-46% majority. The voting in these elections and on many ballot propositions has followed a similar pattern, with huge margins for liberal candidates and positions in Portland and the university towns of Eugene and Corvallis contrasting with huge conservative margins in counties east of the Cascades and in much of southwestern Oregon, where discontent over the policies that decimated the logging industry has raged.

In the 2004 presidential contest, Democrat John Kerry carried Multnomah County 72%-27%, and Republican George W. Bush carried the counties east of the Cascades 63%-36%. Four years later, Democrat Barack Obama won Multnomah 77%-21%, while Republican John McCain prevailed 56%-41% in the east. In 2010, Kitzhaber carried Multnomah 71%-27% while Dudley carried the east 63%-33%. The same year, Wyden carried Multnomah 76%-20% but—thanks to his many town halls there over the years—lost eastern Oregon by only 51%-45%. Eastern Oregon and other rural areas also contributed to Republican gains in the legislature. The state Senate, with only half the seats up in 2010, is now only 16-14 Democratic, while Republicans gained 6 seats and gained a 30-30 tie in the state House, with co-speakers from both parties. Republicans actually won the popular vote for the state House 50%-48%.

One reason Oregon voters may have produced such oscillations is the poor performance of the state's economy. Unemployment rates remained relatively high during most of the decade of the 2000s—Oregon actually led the nation in unemployment in 2002, and had rates above 8% in much of 2002, 2003 and 2004. Joblessness then spiked rapidly during the 2007-09 recession, to a peak of 12.2% in March 2009. That has made for volatile revenues, since Oregon has no sales tax and depends heavily on a progressive income tax, which results in steep revenue declines in a recession. In January 2010, voters approved 54%-46%, along the usual partisan lines, a higher tax rate on people with incomes over $250,000, but that did not prevent Kitzhaber from facing an estimated budget gap of $3.5 billion when he took office in January 2011.

In 1998, Oregonians voted by referendum to hold all elections by mail, so there are no polls open on Election Day. Voters have until the night of the election to get their ballots to an election clerk. Proponents of mail-in ballots argue that they increase the percentage of people who vote, which has always been high in Oregon anyway, and that they give voters time to read over and think about the numerous ballot initiatives. Opponents say mail-in voting increases the possibility of fraud. Because Oregon has no statewide registry, unscrupulous voters could cast ballots in multiple counties.

Population		Household Income		Work	
Pop. 2010:	3,831,074	Under $15k:	12.8%	Private:	77.6%
State rank:	27th	$15k to $50k:	37.7%	Government:	13.8%
Change since 2000:	Up 12.0%	$50k to $100k:	32.1%	Self-employed:	8.4%
Urban:	79.2%	$100k to $200k:	14.4%	Unemployment (3-yr. average):	5.5%
Rural:	20.8%	Over $200k:	2.9%	Poverty:	13.7%
Native of state:	45.7%	Median income:	$49,325	Blue collar:	20.7%
Not a citizen:	6.1%			White collar:	60.1%
Area size:	98,379 sq. mi.	**Home Value**		Khaki collar:	0.1%
		Under $100k:	10.0%	Other:	19.1%
Most populous cities		$100k to $300k:	49.4%		
Portland	583,776	$300k to $500k:	27.2%	**Age**	
Eugene	156,185	$500k to $1 mil:	11.3%	Median age:	37.9 yrs.
Salem	154,637	Over $1 million:	2.1%	More than 65 yrs:	13.3%
Gresham	105,594	Median:	$263,200	Less than 18 yrs:	23.0%

Race/Ethnicity				Military Veterans		Registered Voters in 2010	
White:	78.5%	*Language*		% of Pop:	11.9%	Democrats:	863,322
Black:	1.7%	English:	85.8%			Republicans:	664,123
Hispanic:	11.7%	Spanish:	8.5%	*Veterans by Period*		Ind./other:	541,353
Asian:	3.6%	Asian:	2.7%	WWII and before:	11.4%	Voter turnout:	1,487,210
Native Am.:	1.1%	Other European:	2.5%	Korea:	10.9%	Turnout as % of	
Hawaiian:	0.3%			Vietnam:	36.3%	voting age:	50.2%
Two+ races:	2.9%	**Education**		Gulf (pre-2001):	10.0%		
		H.S. grad:	88.7%	Gulf (post-2001):	5.4%	**Legislature**	
Ancestry		College grad:	28.7%	Peace time:	25.9%	Senate:	16 D 14 R
German	16.8%	Grad degree:	10.3%			House:	30 D 30 R
English	10.4%						
Irish	9.9%						

Presidential politics Oregon was once the most Republican state in the West, the only one voting for Thomas Dewey over Harry Truman in 1948 and voting for other losing Republican nominees in 1960 and 1976. By the late 1980s, it had become one of the most Democratic states, voting for Democrats who lost the race for president in 1988, 2000 and 2004. For a time, the unpopularity of Clinton administration logging policies in much of Oregon threatened to make the state competitive, and Democrat Al Gore carried it by only 47.0%-46.5% in 2000, with 5% for Green Party candidate Ralph Nader. Nader was not on the ballot in 2004, and Democrat John Kerry won here 51%-47%. During most of the 2008 election cycle, Oregon seemed solidly Democratic, though poll results from the first half of September suggested it might be competitive. But after the financial crash of mid-September, Oregon was not seriously contested, and Barack Obama carried the state by a solid 57%-40%.

2008 Presidential Vote
Barack Obama (D) 1,037,291   (57%)
John McCain (R) 738,475   (40%)

2008 Presidential Primary
Barack Obama (D) 375,385   (59%)
Hillary Clinton (D) 259,825   (41%)

2008 Presidential Primary
John McCain (R) 285,881   (81%)
Ron Paul (R) 51,100   (14%)

2004 Presidential Vote
John Kerry (D) 943,163   (51%)
George W. Bush (R)..............866,831   (47%)

Oregon once had an important presidential primary, scheduled in late May. In 1948, Oregon ended Republican Harold Stassen's presidential prospects, when he lost 52%-48% to Dewey. In 1968, Oregon gave Democrat Robert Kennedy the only defeat in his electoral career when it voted 44%-38% for Eugene McCarthy. Oregon in those days was part of a West Coast campaign swing, just before the California primary, at a time when candidates were not used to routinely crisscrossing the country, and like National Football League teams in the 1950s, scheduled West Coast contests together to minimize travel time. For 1992 and 1996, Oregon scheduled its primary for Super Tuesday in March, but it was overshadowed by bigger contests in the South. In 2000 and 2004, the primary was held again in May. That was well after the parties' nominees were determined. But in 2004, Ohio Democrat Dennis Kucinich spent four weeks campaigning in Oregon, hoping to rally a constituency with his New Age ideas, which included a proposed U.S. Department of Peace. He nonetheless lost to Kerry, 79%-16%. In 2008, the primary was again held in May, when the race between Obama and Hillary Rodham Clinton was still raging. Obama carried Oregon, 59%-41%, with especially large margins in Multnomah County and the university towns.

Congressional districting Oregon's current congressional map is the product of a partisan battle between a Republican legislature and a Democratic governor. Republican redistricters wanted to move solidly Democratic western Multnomah County from the arguably marginal 1st District to the hugely Democratic 3rd District. But in June 2001, Kitzhaber vetoed the Republican plan and in the inevitable lawsuit, a Multnomah County judge chose the Democratic alternative, saying it was less disruptive and better preserved communities.

112th Congress Lineup
4 D   1 R
111th Congress Lineup
4 D   1 R

Oregon's population rose 12% from 2000 to 2010, not much more than the national average of 9.7%, and Oregon did not gain a seat from the reapportionment following the 2010 census. Democrats hold the governorship and a 16-14 majority in the state Senate, while the state House is split 30-30, so the likely result is a plan that looks very much like the present one, with an overwhelmingly Republican 2nd District in eastern Oregon and an overwhelmingly Democratic 3rd District anchored in Multnomah County. The current 5th District is relatively marginal and the 4th District might be seriously contested if Democrat Peter DeFazio retires.

Governor

John Kitzhaber (D)

Elected 2010, term expires Jan. 2015, 3rd term; b. March 5, 1947, Colfax, WA; home, Portland; Dartmouth Col., B.S. 1969; U. of OR Medical Schl., M.D. 1973; No religious affiliation; Partner (Cylvia Hayes); 1 child.

Elected Office: OR House, 1979-81; OR Senate, 1981-93; OR gov., 1995-2003.

Professional Career: Emergency room doctor, Roseburg, 1974-88; Founder and dir., Center for Evidence-based Policy, OR Health & Science U., 2003; Pres., Estes Park Inst., 2003; Founder, Archimedes Movement, 2006.

Office: 160 State Capitol, 900 Court Street, Salem, OR, 97301-4047, 503-378-4582; Fax: 503-378-6827; Web site: governor.oregon.gov/.

Election Results

2010 general	John Kitzhaber (D)	716,525	(49%)
	Chris Dudley (R)	694,287	(48%)
2010 primary	John Kitzhaber (D)	242,545	(65%)
	Bill Bradbury (D)	110,298	(29%)

Prior Winning Percentages: 1998 (64%); 1994 (51%)

Democrat John Kitzhaber was elected to a second stint as Oregon's governor in 2010, having served from 1995 to 2003.

Kitzhaber (*KITZ hab er*) was born in Colfax, Wash., and moved to Eugene at age 11. After going east to attend Dartmouth, he returned to Oregon to study medicine at the University of Oregon Medical School—now Oregon Health & Science University—and practiced emergency medicine in Roseburg from 1974 to 1988. He was elected to the state House in 1978 and to the state Senate two years later, serving as Senate president from 1985 to 1993. His manner is Western and unpretentious—he often wears blue jeans and cowboy boots and holds rafting trips as fundraisers. He also disdains the normal ceremony of politics and has been known to duck out early from rallies for visiting politicians, giving him a reputation for aloofness. In January 1994, when one-term Democratic Gov. Barbara Roberts announced she would not run again, Kitzhaber jumped in the race and won the Democratic primary with 88% of the vote. He then beat Republican former congressman Denny Smith 51%-42%. Kitzhaber carried the Portland area and university towns handsomely, but won only a handful of counties in the rest of the state. At the same time, Republicans won control of the legislature.

Kitzhaber's great achievement early in his career was the Oregon Health Plan, which increased Medicaid coverage by rationing treatments. Though initially blocked by Republican President George H.W. Bush's administration, it received a special waiver and went into effect in 1994. The plan drew criticism, especially after a 7-year-old boy with leukemia died because the state wouldn't pay for a bone marrow transplant. But it added health care for 100,000 Oregonians who until then had not had health insurance, and brought Kitzhaber considerable acclaim as an innovator. As governor, he worked on a variety of other initiatives that were known for their cool rationality and reliance on expert judgments. His welfare reform plan used money from food stamps and cash benefits to subsidize employment for nine months, with employers contributing $1 an hour to education accounts. He worked to develop a program of incentives for private landowners to preserve the habitat of coastal coho and steelhead salmon.

But much of his time was spent fighting the legislature on taxing and spending issues. He became known as "Dr. No" because he vetoed so many bills—69 in 1999 when he beat the record established by Gov. Oswald West in 1911. Despite these battles, Kitzhaber brought a high job rating into the 1998 campaign. He ended up with a weak opponent—Bill Sizemore, who spearheaded numerous conservative ballot initiatives, mostly anti-tax ones. Kitzhaber won 64%-30%, carrying all but one county. He was the first Oregon governor to be re-elected since 1982 and the first Democratic governor to be re-elected there since 1906.

His epic battle with the legislature continued, and at one point he famously called the state "ungovernable." Kitzhaber struck a compromise with Republicans on a gas tax in 1999 but was unable to win support for a proposed 1% income tax increase. Kitzhaber vetoed GOP tax cuts, many land use bills, a parental consent abortion bill and the 75 mile-per-hour speed limit. He also kept battling Sizemore, raising $2.5 million from businesses and labor to campaign against his former opponent's anti-tax ballot initiatives. He won on most, but not all. In 2002, Kitzhaber helped launch the Oregon Business Plan, a 12-point proposal for revitalizing the state's economy developed with input from business and community leaders, He was term-limited and could not run for re-election in 2002, and endorsed Democrat Ted Kulongoski, who had been a member of the state Supreme Court as well as state attorney general.

Kulongoski went on to win two terms as governor. But within his own party, there was considerable dissatisfaction with Kulongoski's performance, particularly among labor groups, which resented his efforts to reduce pension benefits of public employees and to freeze state salaries. Meanwhile, Kitzhaber continued to concentrate on health issues, serving as president of the Estes Park Institute, which sponsors conferences on behalf of community hospitals, and founding the Archimedes Movement to encourage more citizen input in solving thorny public problems on health care as well as other issues.

With Oregon's economy mired in a slump—its unemployment rate soared above 11% in early 2009 and stayed there for months—Kitzhaber announced his candidacy for governor in September 2009, calling himself the best person to lead the state to recovery. It was an audacious move. No Oregon governor had ever been elected to a third term, and the only one ever to try a comeback, Republican Tom McCall, lost in the 1978 GOP primary. Kitzhaber talked of making use of the state's "natural advantages" of livability and its reputation for environmental stewardship to create jobs, in part by speeding up the thinning of forests on federal lands and investing in biomass energy operations that could convert timber waste into electricity. He also pointed to the need to increase high school graduation rates and invest in state colleges and universities. Polls showed that he had retained his popularity, and he coasted to victory in the 2010 Democratic primary over Secretary of State Bill Bradbury, 65%-29%.

In the general election, he faced Republican Chris Dudley, a former basketball center with the Portland Trail Blazers. After retiring from the NBA, Dudley set up a foundation in Oregon to improve the lives of diabetic children and became a financial adviser. Even though he had no prior political experience and Democrats had won the last six governor's races in the state, Dudley stressed his outsider credentials in making a case that he could bring change faster and easier. He took moderate stances on most issues and vowed to slash the state's highest-in-the-nation capital gains tax.

With an anti-incumbent attitude enveloping much of the nation, Dudley stayed close in the polls. He also raised an impressive $10.4 million, $3 million more than his opponent. All of this led Kitzhaber to make the uncharacteristic move of airing attack ads. He hammered Dudley for his inexperience and his decision to live in Washington state when he played for Portland. Taking advantage of the state's mail-in balloting system that boosted turnout, as well as Dudley's struggles in their one televised debate to fully explain his positions, he managed to stem the national GOP tide with a narrow 49.4%-47.9% win. Unlike his 1998 re-election, in which he took 35 of Oregon's 36 counties, Kitzhaber won just seven this time. But of those, he took three of the largest ones: Portland-based Multnomah (71%-27%), nearby Washington (50%-48%) and Eugene-based Lane (57%-40%). Dudley won the more blue-collar and conservative Clackamas County south of Portland.

Kitzhaber had hoped to work with a Democratic-controlled legislature, but the party posted heavy losses in both chambers. Though Democrats managed to narrowly remain in control of the state Senate, the House was split 30-30, meaning no legislation could move without at least one member of the opposing party backing it. He unveiled a two-year budget in February 2011 that called for cutting the Oregon Health Plan by 35%, scaling back an energy tax break for businesses, and cutting the number of beds for juvenile offenders by almost half. Despite the number of cuts, the budget won praise from members of both parties.

Senior Senator

Ron Wyden (D)

Elected Jan. 1996, term expires 2016, 3rd full term; b. May 3, 1949, Wichita, KS; home, Portland; Stanford U., B.A. 1971, U. of OR, J.D. 1974; Jewish; married (Nancy Bass); 4 children.

Elected Office: U.S. House of Reps., 1981–96.

Professional Career: Co–dir. & co–founder, OR Gray Panthers, 1974–80; Dir., OR Legal Svcs. for the Elderly, 1977–79; Prof. of Gerontology, U. of OR, 1976, Portland St. U., 1979, U. of Portland, 1980.

DC Office: 223 DSOB, 20510, 202-224-5244; Fax: 202-228-2717; Web site: wyden.senate.gov.

State Offices: Bend, 541-330-9142; Eugene, 541-431-0229; La Grande, 541-962-7691; Medford, 541-858-5122; Portland, 503-326-7525; Salem, 503-589-4555.

Committees: *Aging (Special). Budget. Energy & Natural Resources:* Energy; Public Lands & Forests (Chmn); Water & Power. *Finance:* Health Care; International Trade, Customs & Global Competitiveness (Chmn); Taxation & IRS Oversight. *Intelligence (Select).*

Group Ratings

	ACLU	ACU	ADA	CFG	AFS	FRC	LCV	ITIC	NTU	COC
2010	93	12	100	5	92	0	86	33	5	0
2009	–	4	100	13	100	–	100	–	9	43

National Journal Ratings

	2010 LIB	—	2010 CONS	2009 LIB	—	2009 CONS
Economic	67%	—	31%	71%	—	28%
Social	62%	—	37%	74%	—	23%
Foreign	*	—	*	55%	—	0%
Composite	*	—	*	75%	—	25%

Key Votes of the 111th Congress

1. Overturn Ledbetter	Y	5. Pass health care bill	Y	9. Ratify New START	Y
2. Pass $787 billion stimulus	Y	6. Regulate financial firms	Y	10. Confirm Elena Kagan	Y
3. Repeal DC gun laws	N	7. Pass tax cuts for some	Y	11. Stop EPA climate regs	N
4. Confirm Sonia Sotomayor	Y	8. Legalize immigrants' kids	Y	12. Repeal don't ask, tell	Y

Election Results

2010 general	Ron Wyden (D)	825,507	(57%)	($6,930,089)
	Jim Huffman (R)	566,199	(39%)	($2,375,849)
2010 primary	Ron Wyden (D)	333,652	(90%)	
	Loren Hooker (D)	25,152	(7%)	

Prior Winning Percentages: 2004 (63%); 1998 (61%); 1996 special (48%); House: 1994 (73%); 1992 (77%); 1990 (81%); 1988 (99%); 1986 (86%); 1984 (72%); 1982 (78%); 1980 (72%)

Ron Wyden, Oregon's senior senator, was elected to the Senate in January 1996 after serving in the House. He grew up in California, graduated from Stanford University and moved to Oregon to attend the University of Oregon law school. After graduating in 1974, he founded the Oregon chapter of the Gray Panthers, an advocacy group for the elderly. His first foray into electoral politics was sponsoring a successful referendum reducing the price of dentures. In 1980, at age 31, he boldly launched a primary challenge to Robert Duncan in the 3rd Congressional District, which covers most of Portland, and won 60%-40%. He went on to easily capture the seat in the heavily Democratic district.

Wyden's way to the Senate was opened by the Senate Ethics Committee's decision in September 1995 to expel Republican Sen. Bob Packwood for sexual harassment of former aides and lobbyists. Wyden, who had long been eyeing the seat, decided to run in the special election to replace Packwood—the first election Oregon conducted by mail-in ballot. With his home base in Portland, where the local television broadcasts reach most of the state, Wyden had greater name identification than his competitors. But he had spirited opposition in the Democratic primary from Eugene-based Rep. Peter DeFazio, who carried his own district overwhelmingly, holding Wyden to a 50%-44% win. The Republican nomination went to state Senate President Gordon Smith, a frozen vegetable tycoon from eastern Oregon who spent $2 million of his own money. Most polls had the race in a dead heat, and negative ads flooded the airwaves. Wyden picked up strength the week before the Jan. 30 mail deadline, and won 48%-47%.

Ten months later, Smith won the state's other Senate seat, marking the first time two senators were elected who had run against each other in the same year. With the departure of Packwood and Republican Mark Hatfield, Oregon lost 56 years of Senate seniority and gained two senators who everyone expected would be bitter enemies. Instead they became friends and collaborators, holding dozens of joint town meetings across Oregon and having lunch every Thursday with their chiefs of staff. The bipartisan working alliance between the two ended in 2008, when Smith lost his re-election bid to Democrat Jeff Merkley.

In his years in Washington, Wyden has displayed a genius for coming up with sensible-sounding ideas no one else had thought of and for making the counterintuitive political alliances that prove helpful in passing bills. He says, "My record is based on the proposition that if you want to get anything done, it's got to be bipartisan. But sometimes you have to stand alone." An illustration was Wyden's work with Maine Republican Olympia Snowe in early 2009. Wyden and Snowe astutely predicted that high-dollar bonuses and "golden parachutes" for executives of financial companies being bailed out by American taxpayers would be unpopular with the public. They won passage of a provision in that year's economic stimulus bill to prevent such bonus payments. But the stipulation was left out of the final bill at the insistence of the Obama administration, which said employees might sue to keep their bonuses. In March 2009, there was an outpouring of public anger over bonuses paid to employees of troubled insurance giant AIG, which embarrassed the administration and which would have been prevented by the Wyden-Snowe measure.

Wyden's portfolio of interests is wide, ranging from Senate procedure to new technology. In 1997, he and Iowa Republican Charles Grassley called for disclosure of the names of senators who place holds on legislation, blocking it from consideration. Wyden and Grassley were rebuffed in their efforts for years, but made slow progress. Finally, in January 2011, the Senate voted 92-4 to require public disclosure of holds after two days, ending the ability of a single senator to secretly stop legislation from advancing.

Another Wyden cause has been the Internet. He and former California Republican Rep. Christopher Cox sponsored the three-year ban on Internet taxation that passed in 1998. In 2001, they sought to extend the ban permanently, but also set up a procedure to allow states to tax Internet sales if they adopt uniform sales tax rules and provide a means to remit sales taxes electronically. In 2004, the Senate passed a four-year extension that grandfathered in pre-1998 taxes and permitted states to apply telephone taxes to voice-over-Internet protocol (VOIP) services. Wyden has also worked on Internet privacy issues and on anti-spam legislation, which passed in 2003. As spam purveyors evolved, he moved to restrict spam messages over text-messaging systems and cell phones. In November 2010, he worked to block action on a bill passed by the Judiciary Committee that would allow the government to blacklist websites and bar credit card companies and ad networks from dealing with them in cases of copyright infringement. Wyden told *Wired* that the approach was "like using a bunker-busting cluster bomb when what you really need is a precision-guided missile. The collateral damage of this statute could be American innovation, American jobs and a secure Internet."

Health care has long captured Wyden's interest. He was one of 11 Senate Democrats to vote for the Republican-authored Medicare prescription drug law in 2003 in the face of criticism from fellow Democrats. "It wasn't a bill I would have written. But I thought it was the right thing to do to get started," he said. He won amendments creating a national commission on health care and extending a managed care option for rural Oregon. Later, with Snowe, he sponsored a bill to allow the federal government to negotiate drug prices with pharmaceutical companies. During the debate over health care reform, Wyden joined Republican Robert Bennett of Utah on a bill to replace the tax exclusion for employer-provided health insurance with a tax deduction for individuals to buy insurance from private insurers. They lined up six Democratic and four Republican co-sponsors, and argued in 2009 that their approach would produce a bipartisan health care bill, with universal coverage. But the Obama administration and key Senate committee chairmen disagreed that changes in tax incentives alone would achieve the goal of insuring millions of Americans without health insurance. Wyden presciently predicted that the more government-heavy approach President Barack Obama favored would be a hard sell. He told *The Wall Street Journal*, "People don't want the government in the driver's seat."

Wyden also argued that the Obama administration's initiative did not inject enough competition into the system to improve the performance of health insurers, and that it failed to give consumers more choices of health plans. He sponsored an amendment requiring employers to offer their employees a choice of at least two insurance plans, and also allowing more Americans access to the insurance exchanges—new insurance marketplaces—created by the legislation.

For some years, Wyden has promoted a restructuring of the tax code akin to the reform bill of 1986, including reductions in tax rates and an expansion of the tax base by eliminating tax preferences and deductions. In February 2010, he and Republican Judd Gregg of New Hampshire sponsored a measure with three income tax brackets (15%, 25%, 35%), a lower corporate tax rate and immediate expensing of inventory and equipment for businesses with receipts under $1 million. Wyden reintroduced the bill in April 2011, and argued that President Obama's State of the Union endorsement of tax changes was consistent with his approach. Undaunted by conventional wisdom that Congress is too politically polarized to accomplish major tax reform, Wyden told *The Oregonian* newspaper, "Tax reform is absolutely, totally completely impossible until 15 minutes before it comes together."

Wyden voted against the Iraq war resolution in 2002, and also opposed Obama's plan to add troops in Afghanistan in 2009. He also voted against the $700 billion bailout of the financial industry in 2008, and was one of 13 Democrats who joined with Republicans in trying to end the Troubled Asset Relief Program in January 2010.

Wyden has also been a staunch defender of the state's assisted-suicide law, the only one like it in the nation, and has fought various legislative attempts to nullify the law over the years. He has pushed for federal legislation similar to Oregon's 2006 law making pseudoephedrine, used to make methamphetamines, available only by prescription. He has sponsored the county payments law, in which Oregon counties and rural school districts are paid $250 million a year to compensate for revenues lost due to federal restrictions on logging; it has brought in more than $2 billion to the state. He worked to expand the wilderness area in the Mount Hood National Forest and the Columbia River Gorge, which became law in March 2009.

Wyden's attention to state issues, and to keeping his visibility up at home—he continues to hold open meetings in all 36 counties every year, even in heavily Republican eastern Oregon—has paid off at election time. He won a full term in November 1998 by 61%-34%. In 2004, he won easy re-election against a little known candidate 63%-32%.

In 2010, he was opposed by Lewis and Clark law professor James Huffman. After the May primary, Wyden had $3.7 million and Huffman $224,000. In a heavily Republican year, Wyden won by the reduced margin of 57%-39%. His hard work in eastern Oregon paid off when he lost there by only 51%-46%. Wyden underwent prostate surgery in December 2010, and made a quick recovery, voting on the Senate floor two days later.

Junior Senator

Jeff Merkley (D)

Elected 2008, term expires 2014, 1st term; b. Oct. 24, 1956, Myrtle Creek; home, Portland; Stanford U., B.A. 1979; Princeton U., M.P.P. 1982; Lutheran; married (Mary Sorteberg); 2 children.

Elected Office: OR House, 1999-2008, House Speaker, 2006-08.

Professional Career: Pres. fellow, Office of the Secy. of Defense, 1982-85; Natl. security analyst, CBO, 1985-1989; Exec. dir., Portland Habitat for Humanity, 1991-94; Dir. of housing development, Human Solutions, 1995-96; Pres., World Affairs Cncl. of OR, 1996-2003.

DC Office: 313 HSOB, 20510, 202-224-3753; Fax: 202-228-3997; Web site: merkley.senate.gov.

State Offices: Bend, 541-318-1298; Eugene, 541-465-6750; Medford, 541-608-9102; Pendleton, 541-278-1129; Portland, 503-326-3386; Salem, 503-362-8102.

Committees: *Banking, Housing & Urban Affairs:* Financial Institutions & Consumer Protection; Housing, Transportation & Community Development; Securities, Insurance & Investment. *Budget. Environment & Public Works:* Clean Air & Nuclear Safety; Green Jobs & the New Economy; Superfund, Toxics & Environmental Health. *Health, Education, Labor & Pensions:* Children & Families; Primary Health & Aging.

Group Ratings

	ACLU	ACU	ADA	CFG	AFS	FRC	LCV	ITIC	NTU	COC
2010	93	4	100	2	100	0	100	33	4	0
2009	–	4	100	0	100	–	100	–	6	43

National Journal Ratings

	2010 LIB	—	2010 CONS		2009 LIB	—	2009 CONS
Economic	88%	—	0%		88%	—	0%
Social	63%	—	35%		69%	—	28%
Foreign	47%	—	0%		55%	—	0%
Composite	77%	—	23%		81%	—	19%

Key Votes of the 111th Congress

1. Overturn Ledbetter	Y	5. Pass health care bill	Y	9. Ratify New START	Y
2. Pass $787 billion stimulus	Y	6. Regulate financial firms	Y	10. Confirm Elena Kagan	Y
3. Repeal DC gun laws	N	7. Pass tax cuts for some	Y	11. Stop EPA climate regs	N
4. Confirm Sonia Sotomayor	Y	8. Legalize immigrants' kids	Y	12. Repeal don't ask, tell	Y

Election Results

2008 general	Jeff Merkley (D)	864,392	(49%)	($6,512,321)
	Gordon Smith (R)	805,159	(46%)	($13,297,429)
	Dave Brownlow (CNP)	92,565	(5%)	
2008 primary	Jeff Merkley (D)	246,482	(45%)	
	Steve Novick (D)	230,889	(42%)	
	Candy Neville (D)	38,367	(7%)	

The junior senator from Oregon is first-term Democrat Jeff Merkley, a progressive who was elected to the Senate in 2008. Merkley was born in Myrtle Creek, Ore., to parents who worked at a local sawmill. A declining local economy forced them into career adjustments during Merkley's formative years. The sawmill closed when he was 2 years old, obliging his father to work as a logger and homebuilder in the neighboring town of Roseburg. When those jobs disappeared, the family moved to Portland, where his father took a job as a mechanic. "My parents lived with an ethic of making sure they saved and spent very little money on frills," he says. In high school, Merkley broadened his perspective on economic struggles by spending a summer in Ghana as part of the American Field Service Exchange Program. The first in his family to attend college, Merkley pursued international affairs and travel as an undergraduate at Stanford University. He spent a trimester in Florence, Italy, and a summer hitchhiking around Israel. After graduating with a bachelor's degree in international relations, he took an internship with the Carnegie Endowment for International Peace. In the summer of 1980, Merkley and a fellow intern traveled through war-torn Central America by bus. He earned a master's degree in public policy from Princeton University, landed a presidential fellowship at the Pentagon in 1982, and then worked as an analyst in the Congressional Budget Office.

Merkley moved back to Portland in the early 1990s and took a job as director of the city's Habitat for Humanity chapter, where he concentrated on affordable housing and skills training for at-risk youth and low-income families. In 1998, he was elected to the state House, campaigning on his desire to improve Oregon's school system. As a state legislator, Merkley supported fee increases on deeds and other home purchase filings to increase funding for low-income housing. In 2003, he was chosen by his peers as the Democratic House minority leader, and fellow House members cited his consensus-building ability. But the state House was plagued by bitter partisanship between the two parties, making it difficult to get anything done. Merkley demonstrated a competitive edge by aggressively campaigning on behalf of Democratic House candidates in 2006, including a controversial television ad that accused Republican House Speaker Karen Minnis of covering up suspected sexual misconduct by her brother-in-law. State Republicans condemned the ad as too personal. Yet Democrats won control of the Oregon House for the first time in 16 years, and Merkley was unanimously elected speaker.

During his tenure as speaker, the legislature passed several reforms, including an expanded indoor smoking ban and greater rights for same-sex couples. He also pushed through an ethics bill aimed at curbing gifts and other perks from lobbyists to lawmakers. In 2007, Merkley fought Oregon's payday loan industry with a bill that imposed an interest rate cap of 36% annually on consumer loans of less than $50,000. He also negotiated the establishment of a state rainy-day fund to protect schools and other state services from recessions; an increase in the state's corporate minimum tax paid for the fund. *The Oregonian* newspaper called the session "one of the most successful legislative sessions of recent years."

Merkley got the attention of Democratic Senatorial Campaign Committee Chairman Chuck Schumer of New York, who recruited him to challenge incumbent GOP Sen. Gordon Smith in the 2008 election. National Democrats thought Merkley would appeal to the same voters who had elected the moderate and pragmatic Smith to two Senate terms. Despite the endorsements and financial backing of his national party, Merkley faced stiff primary competition from liberal activist and political consultant Steve Novick, who had opposed Merkley's elevation to House minority leader in 2003. Merkley initially ignored Novick and focused his campaign on Smith. But Novick, who stands just 4 feet, 9 inches tall, built support among liberal voters and ran ads saying he would "stand up for the little guy." He labeled Merkley as pro-war for a vote he cast in favor of a 2003 resolution that praised both President George W. Bush and American troops for courage in the war against Iraq. Merkley narrowly defeated Novick, 45%-42%. Novick won liberal Multnomah County around Portland by 12 percentage points, but Merkley's large victories in rural areas gave him the nomination.

The general election was one of the most expensive and closely watched contests of 2008. In Smith, Merkley faced a moderate Republican who had demonstrated an independent policy streak and a willingness to work across the aisle. Smith had broken with his party by voting for higher automobile mileage standards and against oil drilling in the Arctic National Wildlife Refuge. To combat Smith's centrist appeal, Merkley allied himself with Barack Obama and his presidential campaign theme of change. The message resonated in a state where Bush's approval ratings were below the national average. In late October, Merkley aired a television ad that featured Obama urging voters to bring about "real change" by casting their ballots for Merkley. Smith touted his reputation for bipartisanship, particularly his good relationship with fellow Oregon Sen. Ron Wyden, a Democrat. He attempted to distance himself from Bush, running ads that featured Wyden, Democratic icon Sen. Edward Kennedy of Massachusetts, and even Obama.

On issues, Merkley criticized Smith for supporting the $700 billion government bailout of financial institutions. The two-term senator also faced renewed questions about the legal status of seasonal immigrant workers at his family business, Smith Frozen Foods. Ironically, as House speaker, Merkley had helped kill the bill that would have required Oregon employers to verify the legal status of foreign workers; Smith voted for such legislation in Congress. Smith ran an ad that claimed Merkley had voted to increase state taxes 44 times. An independent review showed that Merkley had voted eight times to directly raise taxes. In one of the campaign season's oddest attack ads, the National Republican Senatorial Committee aired an unflattering clip of Merkley gobbling a hot dog and fielding questions about Russia's invasion of Georgia with his mouth full. In addition to capturing an inelegant moment for Merkley, the ad also caught him uninformed on the issue. Smith later condemned the ad.

Another hurdle for Smith was Constitution Party candidate Dave Brownlow, a libertarian with almost no campaign budget but who threatened to attract conservative voters. On Nov. 4, Merkley defeated Smith 49%-46% with Brownlow getting 5%. Smith out-raised Merkley $13 million to $7 million, but the DSCC and other outside groups poured $11 million into the race. The election gave Oregon two Democrats in the Senate for the first time in 40 years. Smith went on to be named president of the National Association of Broadcasters.

In the Senate, Merkley has been a dependable liberal vote, particularly on economic and social issues. He was granted his request for a seat on the Banking, Housing and Urban Affairs Committee. Merkley was one of just 11 Democrats to oppose Ben Bernanke's confirmation as Federal Reserve chairman in January 2010, contending Bernanke was partly at fault for the recession and was the wrong person to trust with an economic recovery. One month later, Merkley was among a group of Democrats who unsuccessfully pushed for a Senate vote on a government-run "public option" to compete with private insurers as part of the healthcare overhaul. During the debate on the Dodd-Frank financial industry overhaul, he joined forces with Michigan Democrat Carl Levin of Michigan to craft a stringent version of the "Volcker Rule" banning banks from engaging in risky investment practices that may have contributed to the crisis. Their provision remained in the final bill, though in watered-down form to attract Republican support. In April 2011, he was among the cosponsors of the Employment Non-Discrimination Act banning job discrimination based on sexual orientation and gender identity.

On the Environment and Public Works Committee, Merkley supported a permanent ban on offshore drilling on the West Coast and unveiled an energy plan in 2010 that relied on electric cars and increased mass transit to make the United States independent of foreign oil in two decades. He also joined Maine Republican Olympia Snowe on a bill in 2011 to give the president additional emergency authority to reduce gasoline prices. And he worked with Wyden on a measure to extend federal payments to timber-dependent counties.

Like other members of his Democratic freshman class, Merkley has chafed at the Senate's procedures. He told *The New Yorker* in 2010 that he winces when he hears the chamber described as the world's greatest deliberative body, "because the amount of real deliberation, in terms of exchange of ideas, is so limited." He joined Democrats Tom Udall of New Mexico and Amy Klobuchar of Minnesota on a proposal to bar filibustering of motions to proceed to legislation. Their measure also required senators opposing a bill to stay on the Senate floor, limited debate on nominations to two hours, and targeted "secret holds" that permit senators to anonymously block legislation. When Senate leaders announced a bipartisan agreement in January 2011 that retained the filibuster, he expressed skepticism that it would amount to much in terms of change. His proposal to make senators come to the floor to carry out filibusters fell 18 votes short of the amount needed for passage.

FIRST DISTRICT

David Wu (D)

Elected 1998, 7th term; b. April 8, 1955, Hsinchu, Taiwan; home, Portland; Stanford U., B.S. 1977; Harvard Med. Schl., 1978; Yale Law Schl., J.D. 1982; Presbyterian; married (Michelle); 2 children.

Professional Career: Law clerk, 9th Circuit Court of Appeals, 1982-83; Campaign staff, Gary Hart for president, 1984; Practicing atty., 1984-98.

DC Office: 2338 RHOB, 20515, 202-225-0855; Fax: 202-225-9497; Web site: house.gov/wu.

State Offices: Portland, 503-326-2901.

Committees: *Education & the Workforce:* Health, Employment, Labor & Pensions; Higher Education & Workforce Training. *Science, Space & Technology:* Space & Aeronautics; Technology & Innovation (RMM).

Group Ratings

	ACLU	ACU	ADA	CFG	AFS	FRC	LCV	ITIC	NTU	COC
2010	87	0	85	2	100	0	100	67	10	13
2009	–	0	100	0	100	–	100	–	2	33

National Journal Ratings

	2010 LIB	—	2010 CONS	2009 LIB	—	2009 CONS
Economic	59%	—	41%	80%	—	19%
Social	51%	—	48%	72%	—	26%
Foreign	56%	—	38%	62%	—	35%
Composite	57%	—	44%	72%	—	28%

Key Votes of the 111th Congress

1. Overturn Ledbetter	Y	5. Bar federal abortion funds	N	9. Stop detainee transfers	N
2. Pass $820 billion stimulus	Y	6. Pass health care bill	Y	10. Legalize immigrants' kids	*
3. Let guns in national parks	N	7. Regulate financial firms	Y	11. Repeal don't ask, tell	Y
4. Pass cap-and-trade	Y	8. Pass tax cuts for some	Y	12. Limit campaign funds	Y

Election Results

2010 general	David Wu (D)	160,357	(55%)	($1,537,849)
	Rob Cornilles (R)	122,858	(42%)	($1,045,912)
2010 primary	David Wu (D)	61,439	(81%)	
	David Robinson (D)	14,102	(19%)	

Prior Winning Percentages: 2008 (72%), 2006 (63%), 2004 (58%), 2002 (63%), 2000 (58%), 1998 (50%)

Population		Race/Ethnicity		Work	
Pop. 2010:	802,570	White:	74.4%	Private:	82.3%
Change since 2000:	Up 17.3%	Black:	1.5%	Government:	10.9%
Urban:	86.7%	Hispanic:	13.3%	Self-employed:	6.7%
Rural:	13.3%	Asian:	6.5%	Blue collar:	17.2%
Area size:	3,236 sq. mi.	Native Am.:	0.7%	White collar:	66.2%
		Hawaiian:	0.3%	Khaki collar:	0.1%
Age		Two+ races:	3.1%	Other:	16.5%
Median age:	35.9 yrs.				
More than 65 yrs:	10.5%	*Ancestry*		Median income:	$58,251
Less than 18 yrs:	24.1%	German	16.3%	Median Home Value:	$308,300
		English	10.2%		
Education		Irish	9.7%	**Military Veterans**	
H.S. grad:	90.3%			% of Pop:	10.2%
College grad:	37.3%				
Grad degree:	13.7%				

West Portland, Suburbs

Postmodern skyscrapers rising above the riverfront and below a range of hills: This is downtown Portland. The city—which would have been named Boston if a coin toss had gone the other way—started here, along the Willamette River just before it flows into the Columbia. Downtown Portland was built on the narrow strip of land west of the river and below the hills, not on the flat expanse that stretches eastward toward the snow-capped peak of Mount Hood. It

2008 Presidential Vote		
Barack Obama (D)	228,817	(61%)
John McCain (R)	135,975	(36%)
2004 Presidential Vote		
John Kerry (D)	200,489	(55%)
George Bush (R)	161,738	(44%)
Cook Partisan Voting Index:	D+8	

was once a dowdy place, proper in a New England kind of way, with a few formal buildings above the warehouses and factories. But in the last 30 years, there has been an explosion of affluence and creativity here, symbolized by handsome high-rises—the pyramid-crested brick KOIN Tower, the wedge-shaped Justice Center—restored Victorian storefronts, a downtown transit trolley, and a light-rail line known as MAX (for Metropolitan Area Express). There is a free wireless network in Pioneer Courthouse Square, and just across the river is the Oregon Museum of Science and Industry. The well-to-do neighborhoods in the hills overlooking downtown are full of old lumber barons' mansions with splendid views.

Just over the hills are the valleys and interstices between green mountains of suburban Washington County. This was once farm country, with 39,000 people in 1940; now it has 537,000 and is an integral part of metro Portland. Its population zoomed up 73% between 1990 and 2009. And it enjoys a high-tech, healthy-lifestyle affluence. Its towns are cushioned by protected forests and anchored by major employers that include Tektronix, Intel, IBM, Columbia Sportswear, and Adidas. Beaverton has the world headquarters of Nike, housed in 16 buildings spread over 178 acres. Like Silicon Valley, the Silicon Forest has an environment that appeals to a highly skilled workforce: Nestled at the foot of mountains, it is woodsy and even rustic, but it's outfitted with all the comforts of modern life. These companies went through a rough patch in the 2007-09 recession, cutting jobs and sending unemployment in the Portland area well above 10% though 2010.

The 1st Congressional District of Oregon includes downtown Portland and its western hills, and all of suburban Washington County. The 1st also proceeds nearly 100 miles northwest from Portland along the Columbia River to the rain-swept port of Astoria on the Pacific Coast, where

Lewis and Clark spent the winter of 1805-06 at what is now the Fort Clatsop National Memorial. To the southwest is Yamhill County and Beaverton, known for its wineries, and coastal Newport is popular for its oysters. Like Oregon, the 1st District was historically New England Republican, electing only GOP members of Congress from 1892 to 1972. Like New England, it then trended sharply left on cultural issues. Since 1974, it has elected only Democrats. In 2004, John Kerry won the district 55%-44%, and in 2008, Barack Obama won it with 61%. In the 2010 governor's race, Democrat John Kitzhaber's dominance in Portland's Multnomah County, where he got 71% of the vote, was a key factor behind his narrow victory.

David Wu (D)

The congressman from the 1st District is David Wu, a Democrat elected in 1998 and the first Chinese-American to serve in the House. He was born in Taiwan in 1955 and came to the United States with his family to join his father, who was studying at Rensselaer Polytechnic Institute, in 1961. He grew up mostly in Orange County, Calif., graduated from Stanford, started medical school at Harvard, and then switched to law school at Yale. He clerked for a federal judge in Portland and settled there. He worked on Jimmy Carter's presidential campaign in 1980 and Gary Hart's in 1984. He started his own law firm in 1988 and served on the Portland Planning Commission.

When the House seat became available, the Democratic front-runner was Linda Peters, who was well known as the Washington County Board chairwoman and had the financial backing of the abortion rights group EMILY's List. Wu left his law practice and spent $100,000 of his own money. He attacked Peters in ads for taking a personal loan from a developer and accused her of misspending tax dollars while traveling on county business. He won the primary 52%-43%. The Republican nominee was 29-year-old Molly Bordonaro, the daughter of a prominent Portland real estate developer. Wu used his life story to extol America's system of education and to call for more spending on Head Start (his wife was a Head Start teacher) early education and aid to college students. He won 50%-47%.

In the House, Wu joined the New Democrat Coalition and developed a voting record less liberal than that of Oregon's other House Democrats. He has been a generally reliable Democratic vote on education, health care, abortion rights and gun control. As a member of the House Science panel's Subcommittee on Technology and Innovation, Wu has pushed for environmentally friendly transportation and has championed a bill to promote technology innovation. He angered local tech firms by voting against normal trade relations with China because of "the sacrifices of countless families like mine." He was appointed in 2010 to the President's Export Council to advise the White House on trade matters, and he is now the ranking minority member of the subcommittee. In November 2003, he had a rare moment in the national spotlight as one of only 16 House Democrats to vote for the Republican leadership's Medicare prescription drug bill.

Afterward, Wu conceded that he would have to mend fences with Democrats. But when the party took control of the House in 2007, other Oregon Democrats gained influence in the new majority while Wu remained a backbencher, criticized by some back home as increasingly marginalized. Conservative radio host Rush Limbaugh poked fun of Wu's use of metaphors from the television program *Star Trek* to criticize President George W. Bush's policy in Iraq and his tendency to compare Bush administration officials to the show's war-like Klingons.

He drew far more attention in early 2011 during a period of erratic and unexplained personal behavior. An article in *The Oregonian* of Portland in January said at least six staffers and most of Wu's political team had quit over concerns about his mood swings. The newspaper later reported that just before the 2010 election, in which he easily defeated GOP business owner Rob Cornilles 54%-43%, several of his senior staffers implored him to seek psychiatric treatment. They cited his penchant for angry and unpredictable remarks, capped by a bizarre monologue to a Washington County Democratic group that had stunned the staffers. Several of his aides received messages from his private House e-mail address that were purportedly written by his adolescent children in defense of their father. The staffers, however, told the newspaper they were convinced that the congressman wrote the e-mails. He had included a picture of himself wearing a tiger costume for Halloween and grinning broadly—a photo that many labeled an embarrassment when it zoomed across the Internet. Wu said in response that he had gone through a rough period, citing a December 2009 separation from his wife, but that he had sought professional treatment.

As more details emerged, Wu disclosed he had quit drinking the previous summer, but denied that he suffered from alcoholism. He also said he had suffered a "severe episode" of an unspecified pain and that a campaign contributor gave him two tablets that he swallowed, even though he said he wasn't sure what they were. A staffer anonymously told the newspaper the pills were the prescription medication oxycodone. The Eugene *Register-Guard* called for his resignation. Wu, however, wrote in a March message to supporters that he was "in a good place now" and gave no indication that he was thinking of resigning. One poll that month showed constituents were evenly split over the idea, but it also found that if the 2010 election were held again, Cornilles would win.

It was not the first time that Wu's personal behavior had become an issue. In 2004, *The Oregonian* published a lengthy article detailing allegations that Wu had sexually harassed and physically attacked a former girlfriend when they were both Stanford undergraduates. The newspaper reported that he was not arrested and that no criminal charges were filed, but that the university disciplined him and he privately apologized. After the story was published, Wu issued a statement taking responsibility and admitting to "inexcusable behavior." Some Wu supporters questioned the newspaper's decision to run the story so close to the election and just a few days after it had endorsed Republican Goli Ameri, an Iranian-born communications consultant. The story and the extensive coverage that followed appeared to cause little political harm to Wu. He won 58%-38%, carrying Washington County 55%-41%.

By 2006, the incident from his past had disappeared locally. Wu was re-elected 63%-34%, and his victory over state House majority whip and self-styled maverick Derrick Kitts was never in serious doubt. In 2008, Wu was easily re-elected over businessman Joel Haugen, an independent.

SECOND DISTRICT

Greg Walden (R)

Elected 1998, 7th term; b. Jan. 10, 1957, The Dalles; home, Hood River; U. of OR, B.S. 1981; Episcopalian; married (Mylene); 1 child.

Elected Office: OR House of Reps., 1988-94, Majority ldr., 1991-93; OR Senate, 1994-96.

Professional Career: Press secy., U.S. Rep. Denny Smith, 1981-84, Chief of staff, 1984-86; Owner, Columbia Gorge Broadcasters Inc., 1986-2008.

DC Office: 2182 RHOB, 20515, 202-225-6730; Fax: 202-225-5774; Web site: walden.house.gov.

State Offices: Bend, 541-389-4408; La Grande, 541-624-2400; Medford, 541-776-4646.

Committees: *Energy & Commerce:* Communications & Technology (Chmn); Energy & Power.

Group Ratings

	ACLU	ACU	ADA	CFG	AFS	FRC	LCV	ITIC	NTU	COC
2010	19	96	0	90	0	75	10	33	88	88
2009	–	80	15	71	22	–	43	–	70	86

National Journal Ratings

	2010 LIB	—	2010 CONS	2009 LIB	—	2009 CONS
Economic	31%	—	68%	33%	—	67%
Social	25%	—	71%	40%	—	59%
Foreign	26%	—	72%	33%	—	67%
Composite	29%	—	72%	36%	—	65%

Key Votes of the 111th Congress

1. Overturn Ledbetter	N	5. Bar federal abortion funds	Y	9. Stop detainee transfers	Y
2. Pass $820 billion stimulus	N	6. Pass health care bill	N	10. Legalize immigrants' kids	N
3. Let guns in national parks	Y	7. Regulate financial firms	N	11. Repeal don't ask, tell	N
4. Pass cap-and-trade	N	8. Pass tax cuts for some	N	12. Limit campaign funds	N

Election Results

2010 general	Greg Walden (R)	206,245	(74%)	($1,944,720)
	Joyce Segers (D)	72,173	(26%)	($34,448)
2010 primary	Greg Walden (R)	74,970	(99%)	

Prior Winning Percentages: 2008 (70%), 2006 (67%), 2004 (72%), 2002 (72%), 2000 (74%), 1998 (61%)

Population		Race/Ethnicity		Work	
Pop. 2010:	769,987	White:	81.8%	Private:	74.1%
Change since 2000:	Up 12.5%	Black:	0.5%	Government:	14.6%
Urban:	64.2%	Hispanic:	12.3%	Self-employed:	11.0%
Rural:	35.8%	Asian:	0.9%	Blue collar:	22.8%
Area size:	70,225 sq. mi.	Native Am.:	1.9%	White collar:	55.0%
		Hawaiian:	0.2%	Khaki collar:	0.1%
Age		Two+ races:	2.2%	Other:	22.2%
Median age:	40.6 yrs.				
More than 65 yrs:	16.1%	*Ancestry*		Median income:	$44,569
Less than 18 yrs:	23.3%	German	16.5%	Median Home Value:	$235,000
		Irish	10.6%		
Education		English	10.5%	**Military Veterans**	
H.S. grad:	88.0%			% of Pop:	14.4%
College grad:	21.8%				
Grad degree:	7.6%				

Eastern Oregon; Medford, Bend

The Cascade Mountains that wall off eastern Oregon from the rest of the state are a magnificent chain of once (and quite possibly still) active volcanic mountains that drain almost every drop of moisture out of the air blowing in from the Pacific Ocean. They separate green, wet, western Oregon from brown, parched, eastern Oregon. The eastern part has 70% of the state's land, but only around half a million of its 3.8 million people, most of whom still make their living off the

2008 Presidential Vote		
John McCain (R)	193,002	(54%)
Barack Obama (D)	154,848	(43%)
2004 Presidential Vote		
George Bush (R)	218,288	(61%)
John Kerry (D)	135,560	(38%)
Cook Partisan Voting Index:	R+10	

land: beef and dairy cattle, timber and lumber, fish from the Columbia River, and wheat and sugar beets from the irrigated plains. The effect of the Cascades can be felt in the one place they are breached—by the Columbia River Gorge. There, surrounded by brown hills on both sides, funneled winds pound in steadily from the west, making the confluence of the Columbia and Hood rivers the best windsurfing site in the United States. The world's largest wind farm has been planned here for years, but has encountered various obstacles, including the Pentagon's concern that radar signals could reflect off the blades and cause interference.

The 2nd Congressional District of Oregon covers all of the state east of the Cascades and the southernmost valley between the Cascades and the Coast Range. Much of this land is forested and unpopulated: Harney County, with a land area larger than that of nine states, has just 7,422 residents. Population centers are miles apart. Pendleton is a genuine rodeo town amid the northeastern wheat fields. In the town of The Dalles, where the Columbia River Gorge begins, housing prices spiked after Internet giant Google purchased 30 acres of riverfront land for a $600 million, 100-employee data center to be powered by cheap hydroelectricity. Facebook four years later picked Prineville, to the south, for its own data center. In the town of Bend, sawmills have closed but the wilderness and high desert plateau attract lots of outdoor activity, tourism and telecommuters. In the district's southwestern corner, west of the Cascades, is the 1,932-foot-deep Crater Lake, the deepest in the nation, created when the top blew off a huge volcano.

The 2nd District is heavily Republican. This is part of the leave-us-alone Rocky Mountain Basin, not the hipster West Coast. The federal government owns three-quarters of the district's land. Court decisions protecting the spotted owl eviscerated the logging industry here, and the cutoff of water in 2001 from the Klamath Basin to protect the endangered suckerfish threatened to destroy the livelihoods of 1,400 farmers. The flow of water was restored, but logging remains endangered, with a lasting impact. In 2009, rural Jackson County saw its last remaining large sawmill dismantled; it had 91 in its heyday. The district voted 61% for George W. Bush in 2004 and 54% for John McCain in 2008. Republican Chris Dudley did even better in the 2010 governor's race, beating Democrat and eventual winner John Kitzhaber here 70%-26%.

Greg Walden (R)

The representative from the 2nd District is Greg Walden, a Republican elected in 1998. The lone Republican in Oregon's congressional delegation and well-liked by the House GOP leadership, he got a prized Energy and Commerce subcommittee chairmanship overseeing telecommunications policy in 2011.

Walden grew up on an 80-acre cherry orchard near The Dalles in the Columbia Gorge; his father ran radio stations that had been in the family since the 1930s and also served in the state House. Walden followed his father into both pursuits. As a young man, he was a disc jockey and talk show host. Then, he got involved in politics as the press secretary and chief of staff for Republican Rep. Denny Smith from 1981 to 1987. Walden returned to Hood River to run the family's five-station broadcast business, Columbia Gorge Broadcasters. In 1988, he was elected to the state House, eventually becoming majority leader.

When the 2nd District seat opened up in 1998 with the retirement of GOP Rep. Bob Smith, Walden ran and faced substantial primary opposition from Perry Atkinson, a Christian broadcaster who was backed financially by Gary Bauer's Campaign for Working Americans and Americans for Limited Terms. Walden stayed competitive by raising $500,000 and prevailed over Atkinson with 55% of the vote. In the anticlimactic general election against a conservative Democrat, Walden won 61%-35%.

In the House, he is a conservative on fiscal issues but more moderate on cultural issues; he supports abortion rights, but opposes federal funding of abortions. Walden has been an active legislator who has caught the eye of Republican leaders with his political knowledge, knack for forming friendships and devotion to the party agenda. He is close to Pete Sessions, R-Texas, and when Sessions took over the National Republican Congressional Committee chairmanship, he made Walden his deputy. Then in early 2010, Minority Leader John Boehner picked Walden to fill the position of chairman of the Republican leadership, a post that had been vacant since Ohio's Rob Portman left the House five years earlier. When Republicans reclaimed the House majority that fall, Walden became chief operating officer of his party's transition to power, examining issues ranging from rules changes governing debate to finding ways to save money on House operations.

In January 2011, Walden took over as chairman of the Energy and Commerce telecommunications subcommittee. As a fierce critic of Federal Communications Commission Chairman Julius Genachowski, his appointment let the Obama administration know that Republicans would wage a fierce battle against the FCC. Walden vowed to upend the FCC's Internet rules, known as "network neutrality," that prohibit anticompetitive behavior by phone and cable companies and that many Republicans regard as unnecessary regulatory interference. The full committee passed a ban on the rules on a party-line vote in March. He also promised to target another of Obama's main priorities—a $7.2 billion program intended to spur Internet development in rural areas.

In 2007, Walden was a leader of a coalition to stop efforts to restore the Fairness Doctrine in broadcasting, which forced broadcasters to offer views opposing those of their on-air commentators. The rule was abandoned in 1987, and liberals have pushed to revive it to counter the influence of popular conservative talk show hosts such as Rush Limbaugh. Recalling his own days in broadcasting, Walden told *The Oregonian* newspaper that it was difficult to figure out who qualified to offer opposing viewpoints when his father read editorials on the air, so the family stopped airing editorials altogether. Political chatter over the broadcast network tends to be conservative, he said, but that should not matter. "Is it more conservative than liberal? Yeah," Walden told the newspaper. "Are there a lot more country-western stations than polka stations? Yeah. Listeners make these determinations. The marketplace decides."

Walden has focused on another national issue with strong local implications—forest management. He played a central role in 2003 in assembling bipartisan support for the Healthy Forests Restoration Act, which was a legislative response to wildfires raging across the West from unlogged dry timber. He also successfully sought to reopen the flow of water to farmers in the Klamath Basin. The House passed his bill to expand the Mount Hood wilderness area, which became part of a 2009 omnibus public-lands law. Walden has worked to curb regulations under the Endangered Species Act by encouraging a greater role for outside scientists to review government proposals. In recent years, he also has tried to restore timber payments to rural counties, joining forces with homestate Sen. Ron Wyden, a Democrat. He worked with another Oregon Democrat, Kurt Schrader, on a bill in 2009 aimed at thinning woodlands and using the material to meet the demand for renewable fuels.

Walden has been re-elected easily. He has been urged repeatedly to run for governor, but has so far declined.

THIRD DISTRICT

Earl Blumenauer (D)

Elected May 1996, 8th full term; b. Aug. 16, 1948, Portland; home, Portland; Lewis & Clark Col., B.A. 1970, J.D. 1976; no religious affiliation; married (Margaret); 4 children.

Elected Office: OR House of Reps., 1972–78; Multnomah Cnty. Comm., 1978–86; Portland City Cncl., 1986–96.

Professional Career: Asst. to pres., Portland St. U., 1970–77.

DC Office: 1502 LHOB, 20515, 202-225-4811; Fax: 202-225-8941; Web site: blumenauer.house.gov.

State Offices: Portland, 503-231-2300.

Committees: *Budget. Ways & Means:* Health.

Group Ratings

	ACLU	ACU	ADA	CFG	AFS	FRC	LCV	ITIC	NTU	COC
2010	88	5	100	7	100	0	100	67	7	0
2009	–	0	90	6	100	–	100	–	3	40

National Journal Ratings

	2010 LIB — 2010 CONS	2009 LIB — 2009 CONS
Economic	70% — 29%	73% — 25%
Social	93% — 0%	84% — 11%
Foreign	92% — 3%	70% — 24%
Composite	87% — 13%	78% — 22%

Key Votes of the 111th Congress

1. Overturn Ledbetter	Y	5. Bar federal abortion funds	N	9. Stop detainee transfers	N
2. Pass $820 billion stimulus	Y	6. Pass health care bill	Y	10. Legalize immigrants' kids	Y
3. Let guns in national parks	N	7. Regulate financial firms	Y	11. Repeal don't ask, tell	Y
4. Pass cap-and-trade	Y	8. Pass tax cuts for some	Y	12. Limit campaign funds	Y

Election Results

2010 general	Earl Blumenauer (D)	193,104	(70%)	($1,286,059)
	Delia Lopez (R)	67,714	(25%)	($135,851)
	Jeff Lawrence (Lib)	8,380	(3%)	
	Michael Meo (Green)	6,197	(2%)	
2010 primary	Earl Blumenauer (D)	73,962	(91%)	
	John Sweeney (D)	6,774	(8%)	

Prior Winning Percentages: 2008 (75%), 2006 (73%), 2004 (71%), 2002 (67%), 2000 (67%), 1998 (84%), 1996 (67%), 1996 special (68%)

Population		Race/Ethnicity		Work	
Pop. 2010:	762,155	White:	72.4%	Private:	80.2%
Change since 2000:	Up 11.4%	Black:	5.1%	Government:	11.8%
Urban:	93.1%	Hispanic:	11.2%	Self-employed:	7.9%
Rural:	6.9%	Asian:	6.4%	Blue collar:	20.5%
Area size:	1,055 sq. mi.	Native Am.:	0.8%	White collar:	61.6%
		Hawaiian:	0.5%	Khaki collar:	0.0%
Age		Two+ races:	3.5%	Other:	17.9%
Median age:	35.6 yrs.				
More than 65 yrs:	10.4%	*Ancestry*		Median income:	$51,150
Less than 18 yrs:	22.8%	German	15.4%	Median Home Value:	$281,600
		Irish	9.3%		
Education		English	8.6%	**Military Veterans**	
H.S. grad:	88.4%			% of Pop:	9.3%
College grad:	31.6%				
Grad degree:	10.9%				

East Portland, Suburbs

Portland, the Rose City set between Mount Hood and the Tualatin Mountains, spans the Willamette River and keeps its industrial back to the Columbia. For most of its history, Portland was a prosaic city, a blue-collar town that piled Oregon lumber and Oregon pears into freight cars or unloaded machines from back East or automobiles from Japan on its docks. But in the past three decades, Portland has been transformed. Out on the Pacific Rim, it increasingly makes its living on foreign trade with Asia. It has become a home to high-tech industries, particularly in the Silicon Forest suburbs. Government has also produced change. Oregon's land-use act, passed in 1973, required local governments to set geographic limits on growth. Metro, the regional government established in 1979 just as growth was accelerating, is a counterweight against the endless population spread outward into former farmland. With gentrification in the city, old neighborhoods have been revived with new names: "NoPo" refers to north Portland. The city encouraged the development of high-density commercial space and housing around transit stops, and bicycle paths wind throughout the metropolitan area. Portland in fact is the nation's most bicycle-friendly large city, with the highest percentage of bike commuters. Local leaders now are seeking to make Portland the nation's leader for biodiesel and other renewable fuels, while President Barack Obama's secretary of transportation, Ray LaHood, has touted its multimodal approach to getting around as the shining example for other urban areas to follow.

2008 Presidential Vote		
Barack Obama (D)	260,156	(71%)
John McCain (R)	93,934	(26%)

2004 Presidential Vote		
John Kerry (D)	242,075	(67%)
George Bush (R)	118,442	(33%)

Cook Partisan Voting Index: D+19

In the process, the central city of Portland, like San Francisco and Seattle, has attracted political and cultural liberals. And, like those two cities, Portland has its share of traffic congestion and high home prices. The recession arrived relatively late here, but it did arrive—unemployment in the Portland area went from 5.9% to 10.6% between 2008 and 2009, and hovered around 10% for much of 2010.

The 3rd Congressional District of Oregon includes the large part of Portland and Multnomah County east of the Willamette River and some of suburban Clackamas County to the south. It extends over plains and hills to the exquisite scenery of Mount Hood high in the Cascades and Bonneville Dam in the Columbia River Gorge. Politically, it remains dominated by liberals, which sets Portland apart from its suburbs and the rest of Oregon. In 2004, Multnomah County voted 72%-27% for John Kerry over George W. Bush, and in 2008, Barack Obama beat John McCain in Multnomah, 77%-21%. Democrat John Kitzhaber took 71%, by far his best showing statewide, in Multnomah in the 2010 governor's race.

Earl Blumenauer (D)

The congressman from the 3rd District is Earl Blumenauer, who won a special election in May 1996 to replace Ron Wyden, elected to the Senate that year. He is best known for his role as Congress' point person on "smart growth" planning strategies that combat urban sprawl and promote alternatives to driving. He is also known for his fondness for bow ties.

Blumenauer grew up in Portland, and graduated from Lewis and Clark College and its Northwestern Law School. He was inspired by the civil rights and anti-war movements of the 1960s, while in his teens. In 1969 in college, he headed a statewide campaign to lower Oregon's voting age. He has held public office almost all of his adult life. In 1972, at age 23, he was elected to the Oregon House; in 1978, he was elected to the Multnomah County Board of Commissioners. In 1986, he was elected to the Portland City Council. He championed many of the policies that have made Portland distinctive—regional light-rail transit, curbside recycling, and aggressive land-use planning. He encouraged bicycle riding and "regional rail summits," which bring neighborhood residents into the planning for higher densities at transit nodes. Blumenauer has had some setbacks, notably when he lost the 1992 mayoral race. But he was the obvious successor to Wyden and won the special election 68%-25%. His campaign slogan was "Vote Earl, Vote Often." He has never drawn less than 67% of the vote in any election since.

In the House, Blumenauer is the most liberal member of the Oregon delegation. To promote biking as an alternative to driving, he rides his bicycle everywhere he travels around Washington from his Capitol Hill apartment. He formed a Congressional Bike Caucus that boasts over 100 members and fought for showers for bike commuters at the Capitol. Blumenauer was astonished to find that the House subsidized parking for employees, but not mass transit; now, employees can

Peter DeFazio (D)

The congressman from the 4th District is Peter DeFazio (*da-FAH-zee-oh*), a Democrat first elected in 1986. The Republican takeover of the House has returned him to a position he held during the GOP's earlier stint in the majority, as a demonstrative critic of conservative ideas he disdains.

He grew up in Massachusetts, came to Oregon for graduate school, was a bike mechanic, and went to work for 4th District Rep. Jim Weaver, a Democrat. In 1982, DeFazio moved to Springfield and won a seat on the county commission. When Weaver retired in 1986, DeFazio won his House seat in a tight race. He beat Bill Bradbury 34%-33% in the primary and won the general election 54%-46%. DeFazio has compiled a record that seems to satisfy both Eugene and the rest of the district: He's liberal on most issues, and moderate on social issues. An original founder of the loose-knit Progressive Caucus, he has not been shy to express his anger that millions of working Americans suffered during the boom years before 2008. He opposed the Clinton-era North American Free Trade Agreement and later was a leader in the fight to defeat normal trade relations with China.

DeFazio often takes idiosyncratic views. He introduced a bill in 2011 allowing people to opt out of the health care law's individual mandate reviled by Republicans—but only if they waived the right to any government-backed medical help for at least three years. He voted against climate legislation in 2009 putting caps on carbon emissions because he said there were better ways to reduce greenhouse gas emissions, such as a carbon tax. And he introduced a bill calling for a tax on large stock and derivative transactions that drew predictable enmity from Wall Street and business-minded Democrats. He took the lead in the House effort to permit airline pilots to carry guns in the cockpit, and although the Bush administration opposed it, DeFazio won by an astonishing 250-175. The Senate later followed suit.

When Democrats won control of the House in 2006, DeFazio took the influential post of chairman of Transportation and Infrastructure's Highways and Transit Subcommittee. He called for taxing oil companies, rather than imposing a gas tax on consumers, after high gas prices prompted people to drive less, with a resulting falloff in revenues in the highway trust fund. He was the only member of Congress to oppose the final 2009 economic stimulus bill after backing the original House version, saying it did not sufficiently boost transportation spending. When the newly GOP-dominated committee passed a bill in March 2011 to eliminate the requirement for a Clean Water Act permit for some pesticides, he dismissed it as nothing but "great talking points" because environmentalists' ardent opposition would prevent it from becoming law.

Until 2010, DeFazio routinely won re-election by more than 60% in a marginal district. Against former FBI agent Jim Feldkamp, who favored more local control of forests and spent a total of $1 million in back-to-back challenges in 2004 and 2006, DeFazio got 61% and 62%, respectively.

After GOP Sen. Bob Packwood resigned in 1995, DeFazio ran to succeed him. His opposition to gun control and NAFTA provided clear contrasts to Democratic Rep. Ron Wyden, but the better-funded Wyden won the primary 50%-44% and went on to prevail in the general election. In 2002, DeFazio considered running again for the Senate, this time against Republican Gordon Smith, but declined. In 2010, the opponent in his re-election bid was Republican chemist Art Robinson, who got a boost from outside interest groups' ads tying DeFazio to liberal House Speaker Nancy Pelosi. DeFazio won 54%-44%, his poorest showing since his first race.

FIFTH DISTRICT

Kurt Schrader (D)

Elected 2008, 2nd term; b. Oct. 19, 1951, Bridgeport, CT; home, Candy; Cornell U., B.A. 1973; U. of IL, D.V.M. 1977; Christian; married (Martha); 4 children.

Elected Office: OR House, 1997-2003; OR Senate, 2003-08.

Professional Career: Former aide, AK Gov. office; Veterinarian, 1978-2008.

DC Office: 314 CHOB, 20515, 202-225-5711; Fax: 202-225-5699; Web site: schrader.house.gov.

State Offices: Oregon City, 503-557-1324; Salem, 503-588-9100.

Committees: *Agriculture:* Conservation, Energy & Forestry; Livestock, Dairy & Poultry. *Small Business:* Contracting & Workforce; Economic Growth, Tax and Capital Access (RMM); Investigations, Oversight & Regulations.

Group Ratings

	ACLU	ACU	ADA	CFG	AFS	FRC	LCV	ITIC	NTU	COC
2010	75	17	85	15	100	0	80	67	13	13
2009	–	8	80	13	78	–	93	–	10	53

National Journal Ratings

	2010 LIB — 2010 CONS	2009 LIB — 2009 CONS
Economic	57% — 43%	52% — 48%
Social	47% — 52%	66% — 33%
Foreign	73% — 24%	70% — 24%
Composite	60% — 40%	64% — 36%

Key Votes of the 111th Congress

1. Overturn Ledbetter	Y	5. Bar federal abortion funds	N	9. Stop detainee transfers	Y
2. Pass $820 billion stimulus	Y	6. Pass health care bill	Y	10. Legalize immigrants' kids	N
3. Let guns in national parks	Y	7. Regulate financial firms	Y	11. Repeal don't ask, tell	Y
4. Pass cap-and-trade	Y	8. Pass tax cuts for some	Y	12. Limit campaign funds	Y

Election Results

2010 general	Kurt Schrader (D)	145,319	(51%)	($1,872,837)
	Scott Bruun (R)	130,313	(46%)	($1,153,710)
	Chris Lugo (Green)	7,557	(3%)	
2010 primary	Kurt Schrader (D)	57,282	(98%)	

Prior Winning Percentages: 2008 (54%)

Population		Race/Ethnicity		Work	
Pop. 2010:	757,128	White:	77.9%	Private:	75.4%
Change since 2000:	Up 10.6%	Black:	0.8%	Government:	16.7%
Urban:	80.4%	Hispanic:	14.9%	Self-employed:	7.7%
Rural:	19.6%	Asian:	2.3%	Blue collar:	20.6%
Area size:	5,830 sq. mi.	Native Am.:	1.0%	White collar:	59.9%
		Hawaiian:	0.4%	Khaki collar:	0.1%
Age		Two+ races:	2.5%	Other:	19.4%
Median age:	37.8 yrs.				
More than 65 yrs:	13.5%	*Ancestry*		Median income:	$52,041
Less than 18 yrs:	23.7%	German	18.3%	Median Home Value:	$271,500
		English	11.1%		
Education		Irish	9.2%	**Military Veterans**	
H.S. grad:	88.1%			% of Pop:	11.4%
College grad:	28.9%				
Grad degree:	10.3%				

Willamette Valley; Salem

The Willamette Valley was the great Promised Land at the end of the Oregon Trail, shielded from the cold storms of the Pacific by mountains but squeezing most of the moisture out of the clouds in the form of rain, fog, and persistent mist. New England Yankees planted small towns they called Salem and Oregon City, founded schools and colleges, built tall-spired churches and eventually Salem's distinctive Art Deco state capitol. This was one of the few val-

2008 Presidential Vote		
Barack Obama (D) 192,327	(54%)
John McCain (R) 154,485	(43%)
2004 Presidential Vote		
George Bush (R) 181,070	(50%)
John Kerry (D) 176,558	(49%)
Cook Partisan Voting Index: D+1		

leys in the West that settlers found readily suitable for agriculture. The Willamette Valley's soil is fertile, and the plain created by the waters of the Willamette sweeping down from the mountains is broad, but industrial runoff has made the river among the most polluted in the nation. Metro Portland has also intruded on the land, with young people leapfrogging over the parcels protected from development and into Clackamas and Marion counties to the south. Salem and Eugene are battling for the distinction of Oregon's second-largest city. Eugene regained second-largest-city status in 2007, but two years later census figures showed Salem with about 2,000 more people.

The 5th Congressional District of Oregon includes much of the northern Willamette Valley. Like the rest of the state, it has had to cope with the recession, including double-digit unemployment in Salem through the end of 2010. Near Portland is the old pioneer town of Oregon City, which was the end point of the Oregon Trail. The district spreads south to the state capital of Salem, also home of Willamette University, the oldest university west of the Mississippi River. It includes part of Corvallis, home of Oregon State University and its renowned agricultural science department. Then it hops over the Coast Range to take in Lincoln and Tillamook counties, which are fishing and logging and cheese-making communities. The district also includes all of rural Polk County.

Although the area remains one of the nation's chief producers of processed vegetables, its crops of beans and berries have dropped significantly, while nurseries have become a new growth industry. The Willamette Valley is also home to a burgeoning wine industry that produces prize-winning Pinot Noir. In 2007, wine grapes became one of Oregon's top 10 money-producing crops, and vintners have begun expanding sales in Hong Kong and throughout Asia. Historically, the valley was Republican, like the original home of many of its settlers, New England. But like New England, it has been trending Democratic, and now is marginal territory. The Corvallis area is heavily Democratic, the Salem area more likely to be Republican, while Clackamas County is competitive. Republican George W. Bush won this district by fewer than 5,000 votes in both the 2000 and 2004 presidential elections. In 2008, Democrat Barack Obama defeated John McCain 54%-43%.

Kurt Schrader (D)

The congressman from the 5th District is Kurt Schrader, a moderate-to-liberal Democrat elected in the strong Democratic year of 2008 who managed to survive 2010's GOP wave.

Schrader was born in Bridgeport, Conn., the oldest of three children. His father was a chemical engineer. He studied government at Cornell University in Ithaca, N.Y., where he met his wife, Martha, also a Cornell student. Schrader went on to pursue his passion for veterinary medicine at the University of Illinois. After college, the couple wanted to move west, and settled in Oregon. Schrader ran two veterinary clinics in Canby, Ore., and his wife served on the Clackamas County Commission before replacing him in the state Senate. They live on a 60-acre gentleman's farm listed on the National Register of Historic Places. He launched himself into public service as a member of the Canby planning commission for 15 years, assisting in development of the city's land use plan. In 1997, he won a seat in the state House, and six years later, was elected to the state Senate. There, he was co-chairman of the Joint Ways and Means Committee, with jurisdiction over taxation. His major focus was improving public education, and Schrader pushed legislation to tax new construction to pay for schools. He developed a reputation as a conservative Democrat and opposed his party on increasing the minimum wage.

The 5th District seat opened when six-term Democratic Rep. Darlene Hooley announced her retirement in February 2008. Schrader was the first Democrat to file for the race. He lent his campaign $130,000 during the primary and won over 50% of the vote against three opponents. In the general election, he faced Republican shipping entrepreneur Mike Erickson, who had challenged

Hooley two years earlier. In the 2008 Republican primary, Erickson lent his campaign $1.6 million and managed to win in spite of his opponent publicizing allegations that Erickson had impregnated a woman in 2000 and then paid for an abortion. Erickson admitted to the relationship but denied paying for an abortion. The general election was initially considered wide open. This was George W. Bush territory in 2000 and 2004, but the district had experienced a surge in new Democratic voters in the latter half of 2008, giving Democrats their first voter-registration advantage in 12 years.

Erickson was unable to shake the allegations about his earlier romantic relationship, and he limited his public appearances during the campaign. Schrader received endorsements from the Oregon Farm Bureau and several newspapers. He also got financial help from the Democratic Congressional Campaign Committee. Erickson outspent Schrader by over $1 million, but Schrader prevailed 54% to 38%. He carried every county in the district and won 74% of the vote in the liberal stronghold of Multnomah County.

In the House, Schrader has backed his party on most significant measures but also shown a willingness to go his own way. He reluctantly supported a 2009 spending bill to finance the wars in Iraq and Afghanistan, but opposed another a year later because he said he had not seen enough progress in Afghanistan. He criticized the December 2010 tax deal between President Barack Obama and Republicans because he said it would add more debt and wouldn't help the economy. He cast the only vote for Maryland's Steny Hoyer over liberal Nancy Pelosi of California for minority leader in 2011. A month later he became chair of the Blue Dog Coalition's fiscal responsibility task force to seek a middle ground between the Republican majority's heavy spending reductions and the Democratic caucus' desire to shield many programs from drastic cuts. He earned a spot on the Agriculture Committee, a good fit for his agriculture-heavy district.

National Republicans were eager to reclaim Schrader's seat in 2010 and recruited state Rep. Scott Bruun, who had lost overwhelmingly to Democrat Earl Blumenauer in the 3rd District race in 1996. Bruun accused Schrader of not being the fiscal hawk he portrayed himself to be and going "on a world-class spending spree with your money." Schrader parried that Bruun wanted to privatize Social Security, and he out-raised Bruun, $1.8 million to $1.1 million. Schrader won 51%-46%, benefiting from the huge Democratic vote in Multnomah while carrying Benton and Clackamas counties and staying even in Marion County.

★ PENNSYLVANIA ★

Pennsylvania started as the center of America. It was one of the newer colonies, founded 52 years after Massachusetts and 75 years after Virginia. Under the benevolent rule of the Penn family and with its Quaker traditions, Pennsylvania soon became the major settlement in the Middle Colonies. Its tolerance attracted Englishmen of many religious sects and thousands of Germans as well. Bordermen from Scotland, Yorkshire, and Northern Ireland crossed the corduroy ridges of the Appalachians and settled the mountainous interior where Gen. Edward Braddock had been beaten by the French and Indians in 1754. Pennsylvania, in the geometric lines founding father William Penn had obtained from King Charles II, connected two major river systems—the golden triangle where the Allegheny and Monongahela rivers joined to form the Ohio, and the wide Delaware estuary, with its thriving commerce and rich hinterland. Philadelphia was the 13 colonies' largest city when it hosted the Continental Congress in 1776 and the Constitutional Convention in 1787. It seemed destined to become the London of America, the metropolis of government and commerce and culture. Pittsburgh, founded four years after Braddock's defeat, was the frontier metropolis, the gateway to the great interior of North America and the fulcrum point of American expansion.

But Philadelphia—and Pennsylvania—failed to hold the central position the founding fathers expected. As part of a political deal, the young republic's capital was located on a site along the Potomac River. And the Erie Canal built from the Hudson to Lake Erie channeled trade away from Philadelphia to New York. Philadelphia lost its chance to be the nation's financial capital when Andrew Jackson, in righteous rage, vetoed the rechartering of the Second Bank of the United States. Philadelphia's Quaker tradition, tolerant of diversity, was overshadowed in intellectual life by New England's Puritan tradition, morally stern, angrily intolerant, ready to use the state to impose cultural values from abolition to prohibition. Instead, Pennsylvania became America's energy and heavy industry capital. The reason was coal. Northeast Pennsylvania was the nation's primary source of anthracite, the hard coal used for home heating, and western Pennsylvania was laced with bituminous coal, the soft coal used in steel production. Connected with Philadelphia by the Pennsylvania Railroad, Pittsburgh was the center of the nation's steel industry by 1890.

Immigrants poured in from Europe and from the surrounding hills to work in western Pennsylvania's mines and factories. Pittsburgh became synonymous with industrial prosperity. In 1900, Pennsylvania was the nation's second-largest state and growing rapidly. But the boom ended conclusively with the Great Depression of the 1930s, and in parts of Pennsylvania, it has never returned. After World War II, both home heating and industry switched away from coal. Even when coal prices boomed in the 1970s, strip mining created relatively few new jobs. Similarly, Pennsylvania steel began its decline four decades ago, when management decided not to keep up with new technology and agreed to big wage and benefit increases with the mistaken confidence they could always pass the costs along to consumers. Big steel got import quotas as long ago as 1969—Pennsylvania has been a protectionist state since the first Bessemer converter furnaces were lit—but they didn't create jobs. By the time quotas lapsed in the 1990s, the industry had modernized, but mostly in huge new Indiana mills and in small mini-mills scattered far from the factories that once lined the Monongahela. Only the embers remain, or, the fires: The Red Ash colliery fire, ignited in 1915, burns on beneath the hills above Wilkes-Barre, as do 35 other fires in abandoned coal mines.

The result has been the slowest population growth of any major state: There were 9.6 million Pennsylvanians in 1930, and 12.7 million in 2010. Pennsylvania cast 36 electoral votes for Franklin Roosevelt in 1940 and will cast 20 in 2012. It had 30 House members, as many as California and more than Texas, in 1960. In the next Congress, it will have 18 to California's 53 and Texas' 36. Over most of these years, people growing up here have been as likely to leave as to stay, and few outsiders moved in; half of all housing units in the state were built before 1960. But in the last two decades, Pennsylvania has begun to perk up, and may be about to perk up even more. Pennsylvania has held taxes down more than many of its Northeastern neighbors, and there has been significant growth in the counties along its eastern border and in York County north of Baltimore. New Yorkers are moving a couple of miles farther out on Interstate 80 to retire near the Delaware Water Gap, and Hispanics from New York and North Jersey are moving out Interstate 78 to work in Bethlehem, Allentown and Reading. Metro Philly, and even the central city of Philadelphia, grew from 2000 to 2010.

Districts 12 and 18 are highlighted for visibility in the Pittsburgh area.

Districts 1, 2, 6 and 13 are highlighted for visibility in the Philadelphia area.

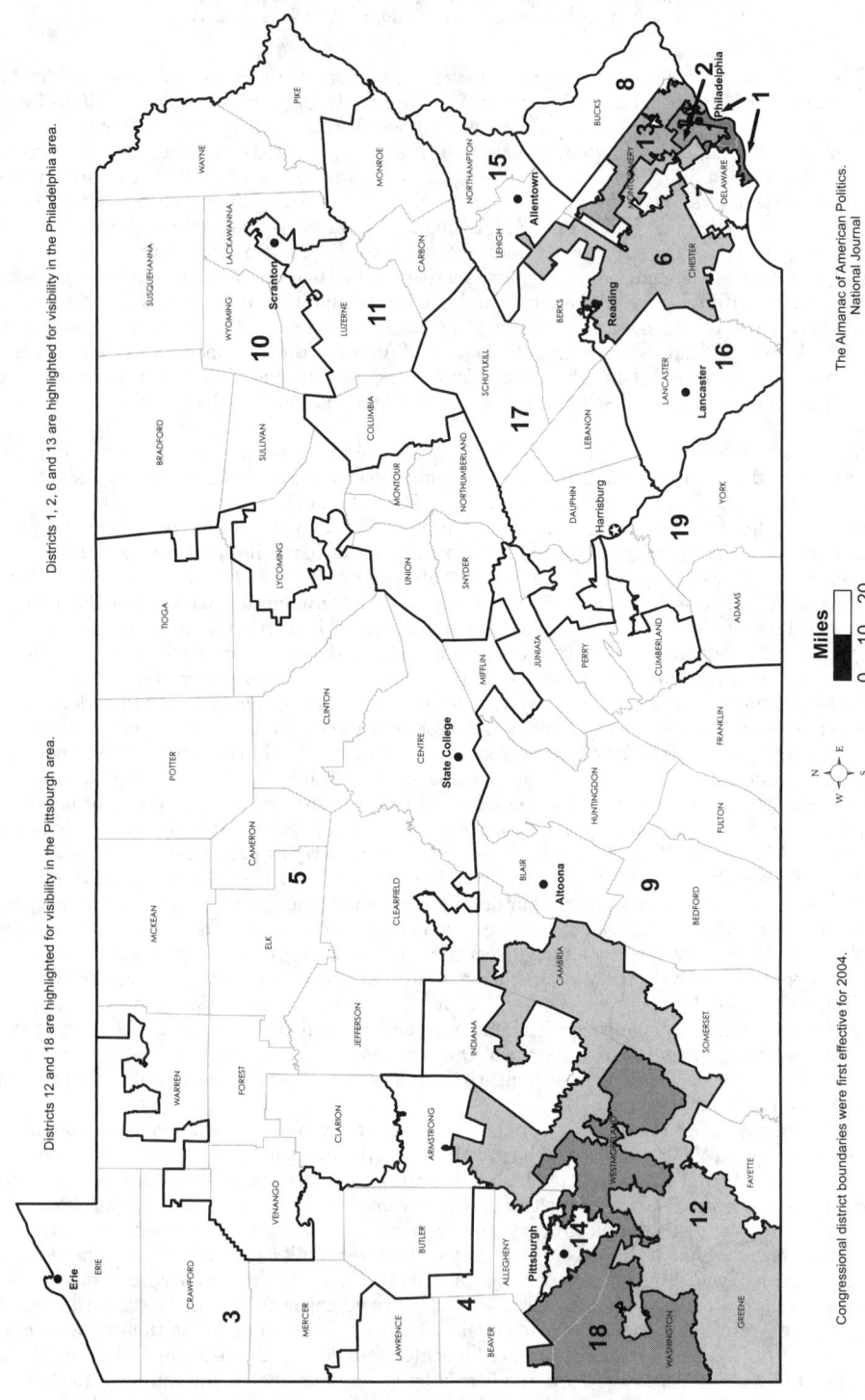

The Almanac of American Politics.
National Journal

Congressional district boundaries were first effective for 2004.

Miles

0 10 20

As for rural Pennsylvania, once the site of the world's first oil well and first commercial nuclear power plant, it is on the brink of being a major energy producer for America again. The Marcellus Shale beneath 60% of Pennsylvania and much of upstate New York contains the nation's largest reserves of natural gas, and it now can be produced commercially by hydraulic fracturing, or "hydro fracking," a technique developed in the last decade in which water under high pressure is injected into the shale, fracturing it and releasing gas previously locked inside. Environmental groups have charged that hydro fracking can pollute drinking water sources, and New York state has limited production. Pennsylvania regulators have encouraged development, with horizontal drilling reducing the impact of forest and farm lands. A Penn State study reported that Marcellus Shale drilling added $3.9 billion to the state's economy in 2009 and created 44,000 jobs, many of them in rural counties that have not seen much growth in decades.

Although Pennsylvania started off as the country's center of government, government has not been central to Pennsylvania for most of its history. During the Civil War, Pennsylvania was the site of the northernmost advance of the Confederate Army, at Carlisle, just north of Gettysburg. For generations afterward, it was the most Republican of the large states, because of Abraham Lincoln and the Union, and because of the steel industry and the high tariff. Its malodorous Republican machines built parties that were not representative of one ethnic segment, but had a place for just about everyone. In 1932, Pennsylvania was the only big state that stuck with Republican Herbert Hoover and voted against Democrat Franklin Roosevelt. But then, the political landscape changed. The New Deal, John L. Lewis' United Mine Workers and the CIO industrial union movement, and a series of bloody strikes, made industrial Pennsylvania almost as Democratic in the 1930s and 1940s as it had been Republican from the 1860s to the 1920s. Even then, parts of Pennsylvania not heavy with big steel factories and coal mines—the northern tier of counties along the New York border, the central part of the state around Altoona, and the Pennsylvania Dutch country around Lancaster—remained the strongest Republican voting bloc in the East. Philadelphia became a heavily Democratic city after the last Republican mayor left office in 1952, but in the suburban counties, the old Republican machines stayed in control. The result was a pivotal, marginal state in presidential elections from the 1950s to the 1990s.

In the 1980s, prosperous eastern Pennsylvania trended Republican and ailing western Pennsylvania trended Democratic. In the 1990s, culturally liberal eastern Pennsylvania trended Democratic and culturally conservative western Pennsylvania trended Republican. The east is larger—metro Philadelphia cast 34% of the state's votes in 2008 and metro Pittsburgh 20%—and the state has mostly gone its way. Pennsylvania voted Republican for president three times in the 1980s and Democratic for president in the five elections from 1992 to 2008. Metro Philadelphia, which voted 50%-49% for Democrat Michael Dukakis in 1988, voted 66%-33% for Democrat Barack Obama in 2008. Metro Pittsburgh, which voted 59%-40% for Dukakis, gave Obama a win of only 51%-48%. In 2010, Republicans Tom Corbett and Pat Toomey got only 40% and 38% in their races for governor and senator in metro Philadelphia. But both carried metro Pittsburgh—Corbett, who grew up in the area, by more than 100,000 votes—and they carried the remainder of Pennsylvania, which cast almost half the state's votes, with 63% and 59%, respectively. Outside metro Philadelphia, Corbett lost only one county and Toomey only four.

This leaves Pennsylvania as politically marginal, but with a balance on cultural issues that is different from any other state's. Since 1950, it has rotated the governorship between the two parties every eight years. In 1986, it elected Democrat Bob Casey, who was a strong opponent of abortion rights. In 1994, it elected pro-abortion-rights Republican Tom Ridge. In 2002, it elected Democrat Ed Rendell, the ebullient former mayor of Philadelphia who had issued bonds to finance

Population		Household Income		Work	
Pop. 2010:	12,702,379	Under $15k:	13.2%	Private:	82.6%
State rank:	6th	$15k to $50k:	36.8%	Government:	11.6%
Change since 2000:	Up 3.4%	$50k to $100k:	31.5%	Self-employed:	5.6%
Urban:	76.6%	$100k to $200k:	15.0%	Unemployment (3-yr. average):	4.5%
Rural:	23.4%	Over $200k:	3.5%	Poverty:	12.1%
Native of state:	74.8%	Median income:	$50,028	Blue collar:	22.5%
Not a citizen:	2.7%			White collar:	60.6%
Area size:	46,054 sq. mi.	**Home Value**		Khaki collar:	0.1%
		Under $100k:	28.5%	Other:	16.8%
Most populous cities		$100k to $300k:	52.3%		
Philadelphia	1,526,006	$300k to $500k:	13.6%	**Age**	
Pittsburgh	305,704	$500k to $1 mil:	4.7%	Median age:	39.7 yrs.
Allentown	118,032	Over $1 million:	1.0%	More than 65 yrs:	15.3%
Erie	101,786	Median:	$161,700	Less than 18 yrs:	22.3%

Race/Ethnicity				Military Veterans		Registered Voters in 2010	
White:	79.5%	*Language*		% of Pop:	10.5%	Democrats:	4,311,203
Black:	10.4%	English:	90.4%			Republicans:	3,132,039
Hispanic:	5.7%	Spanish:	3.9%	*Veterans by Period*		Ind./other:	1,035,267
Asian:	2.7%	Asian:	1.6%	WWII and before:	14.1%	Voter turnout:	3,987,551
Native Am.:	0.1%	Other European:	3.6%	Korea:	13.1%	Turnout as % of	
Hawaiian:	0.0%			Vietnam:	32.0%	voting age:	40.2%
Two+ races:	1.4%	**Education**		Gulf (pre-2001):	8.8%		
		H.S. grad:	87.4%	Gulf (post-2001):	5.8%	**Legislature**	
Ancestry		College grad:	26.3%	Peace time:	26.2%	Senate:	20 D 30 R
German	21.0%	Grad degree:	10.0%			House:	91 D 112 R
Irish	13.5%						
Italian	9.4%						

sports stadiums, museum wings, hospital additions and factory expansions. In 2010, it elected Corbett, who had been state attorney general, a quieter sort who faced a $4 billion budget shortfall upon entering office. For most of the last 40 years, this politically balanced state has had two Republican senators, except after Democrat Harris Wofford won a 1991 special election after the death of Republican John Heinz. Wofford lost in 1994, and for a dozen years Pennsylvania had two very different Republicans, the moderate Arlen Specter and strong cultural conservative Rick Santorum. But in 2006, Santorum lost 59%-41% to Democrat Bob Casey Jr., and in April 2009, Arlen Specter switched parties to become a Democrat after many years as a moderate Republican, saying that he could not possibly win the GOP primary in his re-election bid. That judgment was surely correct: With strong support from President George W. Bush and Santorum, Specter had beaten conservative Rep. Pat Toomey by only 51%-49% in the Republican primary in 2004, and Toomey was running again. But, in spite of the desperate party switch, Specter lost the Democratic primary to Rep. Joe Sestak by 54%-46%. Sestak in turn lost 51%-49% to Toomey in November, and so Pennsylvania has two freshman senators for the first time since the early 1980s, one Democrat and one Republican.

Presidential politics   From 1976 to 2004, Pennsylvania was a seriously contested state in every presidential general election, while its presidential primary had little impact on outcomes. In 2008, that pattern came close to being reversed. Falling six weeks after contests in Ohio and Texas, Pennsylvania's April Democratic primary was an epic battleground in the close contest between Barack Obama and Hillary Rodham Clinton. In the general election, both parties started off targeting Pennsylvania, and all candidates campaigned extensively in the state. But the final result—a 54%-44% Obama victory—made it clear that Pennsylvania was not really in contention.

Pennsylvania was not supposed to be a Democratic primary battleground in 2008. But the caucuses and primaries held in the nine weeks between Jan. 3 and March 4 left the Democrats nearly deadlocked. Obama had a narrow lead in delegates, but Clinton had just won in Ohio and Texas, two of the seven largest states, and Pennsylvania looked, demographically and politically, a lot like Ohio. In contrast, Obama seemed to be headed into hostile territory. Videotapes of divisive, black-versus-white speeches by his longtime pastor the Reverend Jeremiah Wright (who grew up in Philadelphia) were played over and over on cable television, and Obama responded in a widely hailed speech on race relations in Philadelphia.

But he also squandered goodwill with his off-the-cuff comments that people in small towns were "bitter" about their economic straits, and that "they cling to guns or religion." News of his remarks, made at a fundraiser in San Francisco, did not play well in blue-collar Pennsylvania. Moreover, it was plain from earlier results in Ohio, Virginia, Tennessee, and Georgia that he was particularly weak in Jacksonian America, in the Appalachian chain that stretches from Alabama and Georgia in the south to southwestern Pennsylvania, a weakness that some ascribed to racism. But that explanation overlooked the fact that southwest Virginia counties who rejected Obama by

2008 Presidential Vote
Barack Obama (D) 3,276,363   (54%)
John McCain (R) 2,655,885   (44%)

2008 Presidential Primary
Hillary Clinton (D) 1,275,039   (55%)
Barack Obama (D) 1,061,441   (45%)

2008 Presidential Primary
John McCain (R) 595,175   (73%)
Ron Paul (R) 129,323   (16%)
Mike Huckabee (R)................92,430   (11%)

2004 Presidential Vote
John Kerry (D) 2,938,095   (51%)
George W. Bush (R)............2,793,847   (48%)

overwhelming margins had voted for Douglas Wilder, an African-American, for governor in 1989. Obama had the support of Sen. Bob Casey Jr., who hoped to help Obama carry his base around Scranton., an area that was formerly anthracite coal country. But Clinton had the support of Gov. Ed Rendell, who had strong appeal in metro Philadelphia, especially in the suburban counties that Obama hoped to carry.

The battle turned out to be a milestone of the primary season, complete with bowling and cheesesteaks and 2.3 million registered Democrats who voted. More than 130,000 voters switched their party registration to do so. This was far above the 1.3 million-1.5 million turnouts in Democratic primaries from 1972 to 1992, and triple the 700,000-odd turnouts in 2000 and 2004, when Pennsylvania Democrats voted after the contest was long over.

Clinton won a convincing 55%-45% victory. As in earlier contests in other states, she ran strongest among older and downscale voters, and she won among Jewish and Latino voters, enabling her to carry suburban Montgomery and Bucks counties. Obama carried only seven counties—Philadelphia, Delaware, and Dauphin, with large black populations; Chester and Lancaster, relatively affluent areas; and Centre and Union, dominated by Penn State University and Bucknell University. Nonetheless, Obama's huge majority in Philadelphia enabled him to carry the 19 counties of eastern Pennsylvania by 52%-48%. Clinton won 69% to 79% in five counties just southwest of Pittsburgh, and beat Obama 63%-37% in the 48 counties of western Pennsylvania.

As November approached, Obama's apparent weakness among key electoral groups, plus the fact that Democratic presidential candidates Al Gore and John Kerry had carried Pennsylvania with just 51% of the vote in 2000 and 2004, put Pennsylvania on everyone's list of target states. After the Democratic National Convention in August, Obama and running mate Joe Biden headed straight for Beaver County, just northwest of Pittsburgh, to campaign in the old steel country that Obama had lost 69%-30% in the primary. Later in the campaign, Biden campaigned in Scranton, where he had been born and lived for the first years of his life. Republican John McCain sent in running mate Sarah Palin for multiple visits. McCain strategists, having conceded Michigan, had accurately calculated that without Pennsylvania, their candidate had no chance of an electoral vote majority.

Obama won Pennsylvania 54%-44%. He carried the 19 counties of eastern Pennsylvania 59%-40%, running far ahead of Democrats John Kerry in 2004 and Al Gore in 2000. He lost the 48 counties of western Pennsylvania by only 50%-49%. Obama's biggest percentage gains over Kerry in 2004 came not so much in metro Philadelphia, but in fast-growing counties along the state's eastern and southeastern borders. Newcomers leaving high-tax states may have been, if less liberal than voters in the states they left, more liberal than most voters in Pennsylvania.

Young voters preferred Obama 65%-35% and Baby Boomers (age 45-64) preferred him 55%-43%. The rest of the electorate was evenly split. The old anthracite area around Scranton delivered handsome majorities to the Obama-Biden ticket, despite its primary votes, as did Jewish and Latino voters. Southwestern Pennsylvania tended to vote against the Democratic ticket. White Catholics voted 54% for McCain and white Protestants 61% for him, but African-Americans voted 95% for Obama, and voters registering no religion—11% of the total—voted 84% for Obama. Voters with incomes over $150,000, a group heavily concentrated in the Philadelphia suburbs, voted 58% for Obama.

Congressional districting

Pennsylvania lost two seats in the reapportionment following the 2000 census. Republicans held the governorship and majorities in both houses of the legislature and so were in firm control of redistricting. They were determined to redraw the lines to increase their 11-10 advantage in the congressional delegation to 13-6. Demographics suggested eliminating one district each from Philadelphia and the Pittsburgh area. In late 2001, state Senate Republicans unveiled their plan, which put three pairs of Democratic incumbents into the same districts. But state House Majority Leader John Perzel had different ideas about how to draw the map.

112th Congress Lineup	
12 R	7 D
111th Congress Lineup	
12 D	7 R

Then, Perzel got beseeching phone calls from White House political strategist Karl Rove, who told him that Democrats in Georgia had just passed a redistricting plan that seemed likely to cost Republicans seats. He asked Perzel to accept the Senate plan. In January 2002, an agreement was reached. The new plan made adjustments in western Pennsylvania to please Democrat John Murtha, a powerful appropriator, but overall, it eliminated four Democratic seats and created two Republican-leaning seats. Lawsuits were filed in both federal and state courts. Democrats argued that the plan was unconstitutional as a partisan gerrymander. But the U.S. Supreme Court took the position that while it was unconstitutional to draw contorted boundaries for racial reasons, it was permissible to do so for partisan reasons.

The plan achieved most of its partisan aims, but only for a while. Republicans took the new suburban districts, and Murtha won re-election handily. The result was a 12-7 Republican delegation, but the Republicans' hold on several districts was shaky. That was borne out in the 2006 elections, when Democrats gained four House seats and emerged with an 11-8 edge. They captured an additional seat in 2008 for a 12-7 edge. Then in 2010, Republicans captured five seats, giving them a 12-7 edge.

With the 2010 census counts in, Pennsylvania lost one House seat in the reapportionment that followed the census. Republicans once again control the governorship and both houses of the legislature. Because western Pennsylvania lost significant population, it seemed likely to lose a seat. One seat that seemed likely to disappear was the 12th District, created to re-elect the late John Murtha 10 years earlier.

Governor

Tom Corbett (R)

Elected 2010, term expires Jan. 2015, 1st term; b. June 17, 1949, Philadelphia; home, Shaler Township; Lebanon Valley Col., B.A. 1971; St. Mary's U., San Antonio, TX, J.D. 1975; Catholic; married (Susan Manbeck Corbett); 2 children.

Military Career: PA Army Natl. Guard, 1971-84.

Elected Office: PA atty. gen., 2004-10.

Professional Career: Teacher, civics and history, Pine Grove Area schl. district, 1972-73; Asst. district atty., Allegheny Cnty., 1976-80; Asst. U.S. atty., Western District, PA, 1980-83; Practicing atty., 1983-89; U.S. atty., Western district, PA, 1989-93; Aide, Rep. Tom Ridge, R-Pa, 1990; Practicing atty., 1993-95; PA atty. gen., 1995-97; Owner, Thomas Corbett & Associates, 1997-2004; Asst. gen. cnsl., Waste Management, Inc., 1998-2002.

Office: 225 Main Capitol Building, Harrisburg, 17120, 717-787-2500; Fax: 717-772-8284; Web site: www.governor.state.pa.us.

Election Results

2010 general	Tom Corbett (R)	2,172,763	(54%)
	Dan Onorato (D)	1,814,788	(46%)
2010 primary	Tom Corbett (R)	585,571	(69%)
	Samuel Rohrer (R)	266,845	(31%)

The new governor of Pennsylvania is Tom Corbett, a Republican elected in 2010 to replace Democratic Gov. Ed Rendell, who was term-limited after eight years in office. Corbett was a popular two-term attorney general.

Corbett was born in Philadelphia but grew up in Shaler, a Pittsburgh suburb. His father was a lawyer, while his mother battled cancer for years before she died of a heart attack when he was in high school. He attended Lebanon Valley College during the Vietnam War era, joining the Army National Guard and eventually reaching the rank of captain. It was at college that he met his wife, Susan, whom he married while in law school at St. Mary's University in Texas. After a stint as a high school civics and history teacher back in Pennsylvania, he worked as an assistant district attorney for Allegheny County, and then spent three years as an assistant U.S. Attorney for the Western District of Pennsylvania. After a stint in private practice, he was appointed by President George H.W. Bush as U.S. attorney.

Corbett was briefly a policy advisor to Republican Tom Ridge, who was then serving in the U.S. House, and worked on Ridge's successful 1994 gubernatorial campaign. When state Attorney General Ernest Preate was indicted for mail fraud, Ridge appointed Corbett to fill the remaining 15 months of Preate's unexpired term. But Corbett decided against running for re-election the following year, choosing instead to start his own law firm in 1997. He kept the practice running until 2004, during which time he also worked as a counsel to the trash-removal and recycling company Waste Management Inc. of Houston, the largest landfill operator in Pennsylvania.

Corbett ran for attorney general in 2004, touting his experience as a federal and state prosecutor. His Democratic opponent, Jim Eisenhower, proved no pushover and kept the race close. Eisenhower—a distant relative of former President Dwight Eisenhower—sought to make an issue of

Corbett's work with Waste Management, which included defending the company to the media when its trucks were cited for nearly 900 safety and environmental violations. But Republicans had controlled the attorney general's office since it became an elected position in 1980, and Corbett managed a narrow 50%-48% win. During his first term in the job, he launched a wide-ranging investigation into state legislative corruption, which resulted in criminal charges against 12 people with ties to the House Democratic Caucus for allegedly using state resources for campaigns. (Eventually more than two dozen people would be charged, with several convictions and guilty pleas.) The probe, which became known as "Bonusgate," was controversial. Rendell said he didn't understand why only members of his party were charged after two years of investigating. Corbett responded that he first targeted House Democrats because they had given out far more money in bonuses to staffers. Corbett's 2008 re-election essentially became a referendum on the issue, as Democrat John Morganelli picked up the charge of playing politics and called for the appointment of an independent prosecutor. But Corbett withstood those charges and the Democratic electoral sweep across Pennsylvania that year to win another term, 52%-46%.

Corbett's victory established him as the GOP frontrunner for governor, and he entered the race in September 2009. He ran on a pledge to clean up corruption, calling for a ban on all gifts to state officials and eliminating WAMs, or "walking-around money," which lawmakers used as a form of earmarking to help their districts. But most of his focus was on fiscal issues. He said Pennsylvania needed to become more business-friendly, vowed not to raise taxes, and said he would use future federal economic stimulus dollars only for infrastructure needs. In March 2010, he joined a lawsuit seeking to overturn the federal health care law as unconstitutional, a move that Democrats harshly criticized as a sop to the tea party movement. Most activists in that movement, though, cast their lot with Republican Sam Rohrer, a state legislator who waged an insurgent candidacy highlighting issues such as home-schooling and morality. But he proved little match for Corbett, who won the primary 69%-31%.

Awaiting Corbett in the general election was Democrat Dan Onorato, the Allegheny County executive who already had spent millions of dollars in television ads to become acquainted with Eastern Pennsylvania voters. Though Rendell had promised to stay out of the primary, his biggest allies and campaign donors backed Onorato. He sought to depict himself as a solid manager who had brought fiscal discipline to the county, and attacked Corbett for a remark that some unemployed Pennsylvanians would rather collect benefits than work. Corbett responded by criticizing Onorato for advocating a severance tax on natural gas from the Marcellus Shale and other areas, a move he contended would chase away industries. The race tightened by mid-September, but Onorato failed to pick up much ground following a series of October debates. With Pennsylvania joining the national Republican tide, Corbett coasted to a 54%-46% victory. He outraised Onorato, $25.5 million to $21 million. Except for the Philadelphia region and blue-collar Lackawanna County to the north, he dominated the rest of the state, even taking advantage of his Pittsburgh ties to edge out Onorato in Allegheny County.

Taking office, Corbett talked of modeling his administration after that of neighboring New Jersey GOP Gov. Chris Christie, who drew national attention for his hard-nosed stands against labor unions and for making deep budget cuts to state departments. Corbett unveiled his own budget proposing severe reductions, including $1 billion to public schools and a 50% reduction in aid to colleges and universities. During his early months in office, polls showed that voters were willing to trust him to handle such problems, and he was able to avoid the confrontations with unions that ensnared other GOP chief executives, including Christie and Republican Gov. Scott Walker in Wisconsin. But a Franklin & Marshall College survey in March 2011 showed that some key planks of Corbett's agenda were proving increasingly unpopular. In particular, the poll showed strong opposition to his refusal to tax natural gas extraction as well as his proposed cuts in public education. But Corbett was unfazed. To bolster his case, he repeatedly stressed the state's $4.2 billion budget shortfall, which he compared to a stack of $1,000 bills piled 250 miles into the sky.

Senior Senator

Robert Casey, Jr. (D)

Elected 2006, term expires 2012, 1st term; b. April 13, 1960, Scranton; home, Scranton; Col. of the Holy Cross, B.A. 1982, Catholic U., J.D. 1988; Catholic; married (Terese); 4 children.

Elected Office: PA aud. gen., 1996-2004; PA st. treas., 2004-06.

Professional Career: Practicing atty., 1988-96.

DC Office: 393 RSOB, 20510, 202-224-6324; Fax: 202-228-0604; Web site: casey.senate.gov.

State Offices: Bellefonte, 814-357-0314; Erie, 814-874-5080; Harrisburg, 717-231-7540; Lehigh Valley, 610-782-9470; Philadelphia, 215-405-9660; Pittsburgh, 412-803-7370; Scranton, 570-941-0930.

Committees: *Aging (Special). Agriculture, Nutrition & Forestry:* Jobs, Rural Economic Growth & Energy Innovation; Livestock, Dairy, Poultry, Marketing & Ag Research; Nutrition, Specialty Crops, Food & Ag Research (Chmn). *Foreign Relations:* East Asian & Pacific Affairs; European Affairs; International Operations & Organizations, Democracy & Global Women's Issues; Near Eastern & South & Central Asian Affairs (Chmn). *Health, Education, Labor & Pensions:* Children & Families; Primary Health & Aging. *Joint Economic Committee* (Chmn).

Group Ratings

	ACLU	ACU	ADA	CFG	AFS	FRC	LCV	ITIC	NTU	COC
2010	87	0	90	3	100	20	86	67	8	27
2009	–	12	90	3	100	–	100	–	6	43

National Journal Ratings

	2010 LIB	—	2010 CONS	2009 LIB	—	2009 CONS
Economic	80%	—	17%	72%	—	24%
Social	65%	—	0%	42%	—	57%
Foreign	47%	—	0%	49%	—	45%
Composite	79%	—	21%	56%	—	44%

Key Votes of the 111th Congress

1. Overturn Ledbetter	Y	5. Pass health care bill	Y	9. Ratify New START	Y
2. Pass $787 billion stimulus	Y	6. Regulate financial firms	Y	10. Confirm Elena Kagan	Y
3. Repeal DC gun laws	Y	7. Pass tax cuts for some	N	11. Stop EPA climate regs	N
4. Confirm Sonia Sotomayor	Y	8. Legalize immigrants' kids	Y	12. Repeal don't ask, tell	Y

Election Results

2006 general	Robert Casey, Jr. (D)	2,392,984	(59%)	($17,929,395)
	Rick Santorum (R)	1,684,788	(41%)	($28,641,536)
2006 primary	Robert Casey, Jr. (D)	629,271	(85%)	
	Chuck Pennacchio (D)	66,364	(9%)	
	Alan Sandals (D)	48,113	(6%)	

Robert Casey, Jr., a Democrat elected in 2006, is the senior senator from Pennsylvania. With the defeat of his colleague, Arlen Specter, in 2010, he is his state's most powerful Democrat.

Casey was born in the former coal town of Scranton, the oldest son in a large Irish-Catholic political family. He grew up in the Green Ridge neighborhood, the same area of town as the city's other famous politician, Vice President Joe Biden, though Biden moved away two years before Casey's birth. Casey's father, Robert Casey, lost in three Democratic primaries before winning the first of his two terms as governor in 1986. He was a feisty, tradition-minded practitioner of New Deal-style politics, known best nationally as a steadfast opponent of abortion rights. In 1992, he was prevented from speaking at the Democratic National Convention, a decision certainly related to his stance on abortion but also brought on by his skepticism about Bill Clinton as the right candidate. Robert Casey Jr.'s brother, Pat Casey, twice ran unsuccessfully for the House with another Casey brother serving as his campaign manager.

Like his father, Robert Jr. graduated from the College of the Holy Cross in Massachusetts. He taught in an inner-city Philadelphia school for the Jesuit Volunteer Corps and got his law degree from Catholic University in Washington, D.C. He practiced law in Scranton, and then won election as state auditor general in 1996. He was re-elected in 2000. In 2002, running as a cultural conservative with strong labor support, he lost a bitter and expensive primary for governor to former Philadelphia Mayor Ed Rendell. Casey's tightly scripted campaign and negative ads tarnished his image, but he showed some resilience by returning two years later to win the state treasurer's office with 3.4 million votes, more than any other candidate in Pennsylvania history.

In 2005, national Democrats were looking for a strong challenger against Republican Sen. Rick Santorum, a high-profile social conservative with a red-state following and a blue-state constituency. First in the House and then in the Senate, Santorum showed a knack for winning elections against tough odds. But the state's political landscape had shifted considerably since his first election to the Senate in 1994. Democratic Senatorial Campaign Committee Chairman Charles Schumer of New York considered Casey the only prospective heavyweight challenger to Santorum and quickly moved to clear the field to avoid a cash-draining primary. There was one problem: Casey's opposition to abortion rights, which made him anathema to many cultural liberals in the Philadelphia area. But Schumer believed that Casey could make inroads into Santorum's culturally conservative and "pro-life" base, and, as the Democratic alternative to Santorum, also could be acceptable to "pro-choice" voters in suburban Philadelphia. The national party's heavy-handed involvement rankled many Democrats. Resistance to Casey's candidacy faded in the run-up to the election as Casey maintained a steady and sizable lead over Santorum in the polls.

Santorum began the campaign in a difficult position. Though he was mentioned as a potential presidential candidate, his standing at home was tenuous. As early as April 2005, he trailed Casey by double digits in the polls. That summer, he released a book titled, *It Takes a Family: Conservatism and the Common Good*. The year before he stood for re-election was perhaps not the best timing for a frank discourse on some of the most divisive cultural issues of the day. Despite his stature as a member of the Senate Republican leadership, his avid support for the increasingly unpopular Bush administration was unhelpful in 2006. Casey hammered him for voting "98 percent of the time" with President George W. Bush and characterized Santorum as having close ties to the oil, pharmaceutical, and insurance industries. Democrats sought mileage from the issue of Santorum's residence—an issue Santorum had used against his opponent in his first House campaign in 1990—and questioned whether his Virginia home disqualified him from casting a vote in Penn Hills, the Pittsburgh suburb where Santorum owned a home and was registered to vote. Democrats also criticized him for using Penn Hills school district taxpayer dollars to educate his children in a Pennsylvania-based online charter school though they spent much of their time in Virginia.

Santorum did not run like an incumbent nor Casey like a challenger. Santorum, who trailed in the polls from beginning to end, campaigned aggressively across the state while Casey limited his public appearances in the early stages of the campaign. The two candidates clashed over the war in Iraq, Social Security, and immigration. Casey's socially conservative positions—he also opposes gun control and same-sex marriage—helped cut into Santorum's advantage outside the state's metropolitan areas.

Together the two candidates raised $43 million. Santorum outspent Casey by more than $8 million, but it wasn't enough. Casey won 59%-41%, to become the first Pennsylvania Democrat elected to a full Senate term since Joe Clark in 1962, and the first senator elected from Northeastern Pennsylvania. Casey won by huge margins in Pittsburgh's Allegheny County, 65%-35%, and in Philadelphia, 84%-16%, while holding his own in the Republican "T" that stretches from Pennsylvania Dutch country around Lancaster to the northern tier of sparsely populated counties along the New York border. Casey also swept the populous Philadelphia suburbs, winning 62% in Delaware and Montgomery counties, 59% in Bucks County, and 55% in Chester County.

In the Senate, Casey is a reliable supporter of his party's agenda, though his devout Catholicism and his social conservatism occasionally cause him to break ranks. He has voted with President Barack Obama on most major issues. In 2011, he took over as chairman of the Joint Economic Committee, becoming the first of the 10 senators elected in 2006 to take the helm of a full committee. Because it cannot move legislation, it functions as more of a platform for lawmakers' views. Casey promised to hold hearings on the nation's competitiveness, an issue Obama stressed in his January 2011 State of the Union address. He sponsored a bill in March to have the federal government regulate the controversial natural gas drilling technique known as hydraulic fracturing or "hydro fracking," which environmentalists blame for contaminating groundwater in Pennsylvania and elsewhere. He angered some anti-abortion groups in April 2011 when he voted against denying federal funds to Planned Parenthood, saying the group provides many family planning services beyond abortion.

Two of Casey's main causes have been agriculture and expanding access to child care. On the former, after milk prices collapsed in 2009, he called for Congress to explore why processors and retailers kept prices high and joined Specter in introducing legislation to change the amount farmers are paid for milk. Meanwhile, he introduced a bill in 2009 that would create a program to award grants to states establishing or expanding high-quality, full-day pre-kindergarten programs. In

2007 and 2009, he sponsored bills to provide financial aid and counseling to pregnant women. He also was an avid booster of funding for the State Children's Health Insurance Program, similar to a program his father instituted in Pennsylvania in 1992.

From his seat on the Foreign Relations Committee, Casey was strongly critical of Afghanistan leader Hamid Karzai, who he blamed in 2009 for lacking urgency in rooting out corruption. He also pushed Pakistani President Asif Ali Zardari in November 2010 to improve customs enforcement at border crossings after news reports that caravans of Pakistani trucks carrying bomb-making materials were crossing the Afghan border through the Khyber Pass. He joined Republican Richard Burr of North Carolina in forming a new bipartisan caucus in 2009 on weapons of mass destruction and terrorism.

Casey is skeptical about the free-trade policies of the last two decades, and in May 2007, he called for Congress to have the power to terminate future trade agreements that fail to meet benchmarks for creating U.S. jobs, improving U.S. wages, or opening markets to U.S. products. On other issues of strong local interest, Casey opposed the building of high-voltage transmission lines from the Appalachian chain to the East Coast as "federal government arrogance" and in October 2007, threatened to block the reconfirmation of the Federal Energy Regulatory Commission chairman. The Department of Energy had classified 52 of Pennsylvania's 67 counties as a "national interest electric transmission corridor." In January 2011, he introduced a bill mandating that unspent "orphan earmarks" that are more than three years old be turned over to states to use on highway projects in Pennsylvania and elsewhere.

In the 2008 presidential campaign, Casey endorsed fellow Democratic Sen. Obama of Illinois and campaigned hard for Obama in the old coal country around his native Scranton and in the southwest part of the state. But Obama lost the Pennsylvania primary to New York Sen. Hillary Rodham Clinton 55%-45%. Casey spoke about the economy at the Democratic National Convention in Denver and continued to campaign for Obama in the fall.

Republicans would dearly love to unseat Casey in 2012, but several House Republicans in early 2011 declined a challenge. Pennsylvania is likely to be one of the most important battleground states for Obama, and given his past allegiance to the president, Casey is likely to have all the help he needs.

Junior Senator

Pat Toomey (R)

Elected 2010, term expires 2016, 1st term; b. Nov. 17, 1961, Providence, RI; home, Allentown; Harvard U., B.S. 1984; Catholic; Married (Kris); 3 children.

Elected Office: U.S. House, 1999-2005.

Professional Career: Investment banker, Chemical Bank, 1984-86; investment banker, Morgan Grenfell, 1986-90; financial consultant, Springfield Ltd., 1990-91; restaurateur, 1990-2001; pres., Club for Growth, 2005-09.

DC Office: 502 HSOB, 20510, 202-224-4254; Fax: 202-228-0284; Web site: toomey.senate.gov.

State Offices: Allentown/Lehigh Valley, 610-434-1444; Erie, 814-453-3010; Harrisburg, 717-782-3951; Pittsburgh, 412-803-3501.

Committees: *Banking, Housing & Urban Affairs:* Financial Institutions & Consumer Protection; Housing, Transportation & Community Development; Securities, Insurance & Investment. *Budget. Commerce, Science & Transportation:* Aviation Operations, Safety & Security; Communications, Technology & the Internet; Consumer Protection, Product Safety & Insurance; Surface Transportation & Merchant Marine Infrastructure, Safety & Security. *Joint Economic Committee.*

Election Results

2010 general	Pat Toomey (R)	2,028,945	(51%)	($17,155,694)
	Joe Sestak (D)	1,948,716	(49%)	($8,590,124)
2010 primary	Pat Toomey (R)	668,409	(81%)	
	Peg Luksik (R)	151,802	(19%)	

Prior Winning Percentages: House: 2002 (57%); 2000 (53%); 1998 (55%)

Republican Pat Toomey is the junior senator from Pennsylvania. The onetime head of the anti-tax organization Club for Growth and a former U.S. House member, Toomey emerged on top in one of 2010's most competitive Senate races against Democratic Rep. Joe Sestak.

Toomey grew up in Providence, R.I., the third of six children of a union worker and a part-time church secretary. He graduated from Harvard University thanks to scholarship money and earnings from part-time jobs. After college, he worked in investment banking, founding a successful international financial services consulting firm in 1990 and amassing considerable wealth. After six years on Wall Street, Toomey moved to Allentown, Pa., where he joined his brothers to start Rookies Restaurant and Sports Bar, which grew into a chain with outlets across the state. In 1994, he was elected to the Allentown Government Study Commission, where he pushed to lower taxes and to require a supermajority vote by the city council to raise taxes.

In 1998, Toomey ran for the seat of retiring 15th District Rep. Paul McHale, a Democrat. One of six candidates in the Republican primary, he called for individual Social Security investment accounts, creation of a flat tax to replace income taxes, and term limits for members of Congress. He promised to serve only six years. He won the primary with 27% of the vote to 25% for the 1996 nominee, Bob Kilbanks, and 23% for state Sen. Joseph Uliana. In the general election, he beat state Sen. Roy Afflerbach 55%-45%. In the House, Toomey worked primarily on economic issues. He pushed to limit spending and to force Congress to set aside money for debt reduction, which irked some longtime Appropriations Committee members who were not accustomed to having their earmark spending limited. He supported free-trade agreements and criticized President George W. Bush's steel import quotas. He was re-elected 53%-47% in 2000 and 57%-43% in 2002 in a district that has voted Democratic for president since 1992.

Toomey kept his term limit pledge in 2004 and ran for the Senate seat held by then-Republican Arlen Specter. Specter was supported by Bush and by conservative colleague Sen. Rick Santorum and raised far more money. He spotlighted the projects he had obtained for the state over his 24 years in the Senate, and said that Toomey was inattentive to constituents and flip-flopped on issues. Toomey was supported by the Club for Growth and by culturally conservative groups. He criticized Specter's voting record as too liberal and criticized his support from trial lawyers. The result was exceedingly close. Specter won 51%-49%, by 17,000 votes out of over 1 million cast. Specter carried metro Philadelphia with 57%, but Toomey carried metro Pittsburgh with 58% and, thanks to 2-1 support in his home district, came within less than 2,000 votes of leading Specter in the rest of the state.

After he lost the election, Toomey became president of the Club for Growth, a national organization with deep pockets that champions lower taxes and spends generously to support conservative candidates who share its views. It frequently supported conservative candidates in Republican primaries who were opposed by the local party establishment, and in some cases, it opposed incumbent Republicans. Toomey's view was that the GOP was courting political disaster because it had abandoned conservative principles. In the process, Toomey made contacts around the country among conservative activists and major fundraisers.

In January 2010, Toomey said he would not run against Specter and was thinking about running for governor. But after Specter cast one of three Republican votes for the Democrats' economic stimulus bill in February 2009, Toomey changed his mind and announced on April 13 he would run for the Senate. Two weeks later, Specter announced he was switching parties to become a Democrat, saying he did not want to put his service at the mercy of Republican primary voters. For joining the Democrats, Specter was promised support from President Barack Obama, Vice President Joe Biden and Gov. Ed Rendell. But unfortunately for Specter, his path to the Democratic nomination was not clear despite his backing from party heavyweights. Sestak, a retired Navy admiral, was already in the race as a challenger to Specter the Republican, and refused to drop out of the contest now that he joined the same party. Sestak also made headlines when he alleged that an unnamed high-level source in the White House offered him an administration job if he got out of Specter's way. Sestak ran ads that revealed the opportunistic side of Specter's party switch in which the senator was depicted saying, "My change in parties will enable me to be re-elected." Sestak won the Democratic primary, 54%-46%, carrying all but three counties (Philadelphia and those containing Harrisburg and Scranton). Toomey won the Republican primary with 81% of the vote.

The general election presented a clear contrast on issues. Sestak had voted not only for the stimulus bill, but for the Democrats' cap-and-trade bill to limit carbon emissions and their health care overhaul. Toomey called for extending the Bush-era 2001 and 2003 tax cuts for everyone, including the wealthy, and for lower corporate and capital gains tax rates. Toomey said to the McClatchy news service, "I've been out of Congress for six years. Joe's been there the last four years, voting for all the bailouts, the stimulus, all the spending, voting for all those huge deficits and debt." He labeled Sestak a "San Francisco liberal" who voted 100% of the time with liberal House Speaker Nancy Pelosi. For his part, Sestak said of Toomey, "I tell everybody that he isn't a witch"—a reference to the controversial comments of Delaware Republican Senate nominee Christine O'Donnell—"but his politics are scary."

Toomey led in polls during most of the contest. Sestak insisted he would come from behind at the end, as he had against Specter in the Democratic primary. Indeed, his standing did get better in the last weeks, and President Obama came to Pennsylvania twice in October to campaign for him. Toomey raised and spent $17 million; Sestak spent $12 million, much of it in the primary.

In an earlier era, one would have expected Pennsylvania, especially western Pennsylvania, to go Democratic in a recession. But the state's unemployment rate remained below the national average, and western Pennsylvania, with its aging population and contracting workforce, experienced nothing like the anguish it suffered when the domestic steel industry was dying in the late 1970s and early 1980s. Toomey beat Sestak, 51%-49%, even as Republican Tom Corbett was elected governor, 54%-46%. Toomey lost metro Philadelphia, 62%-38%, but he carried metro Pittsburgh, 53%-47%, and in the rest of the state, 59%-41%.

After the election, Toomey immediately joined Democratic Sen. Claire McCaskill of Missouri in signing a letter urging colleagues to abandon earmarks in appropriations bills. He said that Congress should extend unemployment benefits, but offset the cost with spending cuts. He surprised some of his supporters in late 2010 by favoring repeal of the ban on openly gay service personnel in the military. "My highest priority is to have the policy that best enables our armed services to do their job," Toomey told the *The Morning Call* in Allentown. After a trip to Afghanistan, he said that he expected U.S. troops to still be there, in dramatically reduced numbers, in 2017 when his Senate term ends. The first bill he introduced in the Senate would require the U.S. Treasury to pay its debt obligations before any other spending. He said the idea was to block any default on the debt if the debt ceiling was not raised by an act of Congress, but Treasury Secretary Timothy Geithner opposed the legislation.

FIRST DISTRICT

Robert Brady (D)

Elected May 1998, 7th full term; b. April 7, 1945, Philadelphia; home, Philadelphia; St. Thomas More H.S.; Catholic; married (Debra); 2 children.

Elected Office: 34th Ward Dem. exec. cmte. mbr., 1967–present, Ward ldr., 1980.

Professional Career: Carpenter; Real estate salesman; Philadelphia dpty. mayor for labor, 1984-87; Chmn., Philadelphia Dem. Party, 1986; Legis. rep., Metro. Regional Cncl. of Carpenters & Joiners, 1987-98; Lecturer, U. of PA, 1997-present.

DC Office: 102 CHOB, 20515, 202-225-4731; Fax: 202-225-0088; Web site: brady.house.gov.

State Offices: Chester, 610-874-7094; Philadelphia, 215-389-4627; Philadelphia, 215-426-4616; Philadelphia, 267-519-2252.

Committees: *Armed Services:* Military Personnel. *House Administration* (RMM): Elections (RMM).

Group Ratings

	ACLU	ACU	ADA	CFG	AFS	FRC	LCV	ITIC	NTU	COC
2010	88	0	95	0	100	0	100	100	5	25
2009	–	0	100	0	100	–	100	–	1	33

National Journal Ratings

	2010 LIB — 2010 CONS		2009 LIB — 2009 CONS	
Economic	83%	— 16%	91%	— 0%
Social	71%	— 25%	84%	— 11%
Foreign	78%	— 17%	87%	— 9%
Composite	79%	— 21%	90%	— 10%

Key Votes of the 111th Congress

1. Overturn Ledbetter	Y	5. Bar federal abortion funds	N	9. Stop detainee transfers	N
2. Pass $820 billion stimulus	Y	6. Pass health care bill	Y	10. Legalize immigrants' kids	Y
3. Let guns in national parks	N	7. Regulate financial firms	Y	11. Repeal don't ask, tell	Y
4. Pass cap-and-trade	Y	8. Pass tax cuts for some	Y	12. Limit campaign funds	Y

Election Results

2010 general	Robert Brady (D)... unopposed		($904,748)
2010 primary	Robert Brady (D)... unopposed		

Prior Winning Percentages: 2008 (91%), 2006 (100%), 2004 (86%), 2002 (86%), 2000 (88%), 1998 (81%), 1998 special (74%)

Population		Race/Ethnicity		Work	
Pop. 2010:	655,146	White:	25.7%	Private:	82.3%
Change since 2000:	Up 1.4%	Black:	46.4%	Government:	13.0%
Urban:	100.0%	Hispanic:	19.3%	Self-employed:	4.3%
Rural:	0.0%	Asian:	6.4%	Blue collar:	20.2%
Area size:	68 sq. mi.	Native Am.:	0.2%	White collar:	54.8%
		Hawaiian:	0.0%	Khaki collar:	0.1%
Age		Two+ races:	1.7%	Other:	25.0%
Median age:	32.3 yrs.				
More than 65 yrs:	10.9%	*Ancestry*		Median income:	$32,949
Less than 18 yrs:	26.5%	Irish	8.1%	Median Home Value:	$111,000
		Italian	6.5%		
Education		German	4.7%	**Military Veterans**	
H.S. grad:	76.1%			% of Pop:	7.1%
College grad:	18.3%				
Grad degree:	7.3%				

South and Central Philadelphia

Everywhere in Center City Philadelphia, American history is close at hand. The statue of William Penn, who founded the city in 1682, stands 37 feet high atop the ornate, Empire-style City Hall built in the 1880s at Market and Broad. To the east is Independence Hall, where Americans in the 1780s drew up the Constitution, and not far away are the restored townhouses of Society Hill. Penn was a Quaker, a member of one of the 17th century sects that prized reason, and he im-

2008 Presidential Vote		
Barack Obama (D)	256,940	(88%)
John McCain (R)	34,276	(12%)
2004 Presidential Vote		
John Kerry (D)	227,327	(84%)
George Bush (R)	41,509	(15%)
Cook Partisan Voting Index:	D+35	

posed order on his new environment: no cow-path street patterns here, like those in Boston or Charleston, but a grid of numbered and named streets, with precisely spaced open squares. Penn's "City of Brotherly Love" grew to be a commercial and industrial metropolis that spread out over the countryside until it was the young nation's largest city.

For all the grandeur of its City Hall, Philadelphia has seldom had a city government to be proud of. While the city's private economy grew robustly in the 1980s, the city government lurched toward bankruptcy under Democratic Mayor Wilson Goode. Then in 1991, Democrat Ed Rendell was elected mayor, and did well enough to become in 2002 the first former Philadelphia mayor to be elected governor since 1906. Unfortunately, Rendell's push for reform stalled in the mid-1990s. Philadelphia still has an inordinately expensive city government. It is among the cities using unrealistic accounting practices to hide future pension-fund shortages, according to a 2010 Northwestern University-University of Rochester study. And it has crime-ravaged neighborhoods that have emptied out over the years. But there are signs of hope. Center City remains attractive to young professionals, a growing number with families, and the population there has increased 26% over the past two decades. Violent crime citywide dropped 3% in 2010.

The 1st Congressional District of Pennsylvania contains much of Philadelphia east of Broad Street and all of 18th-century Philadelphia: Independence Hall, the U.S. Mint, and Elfreth's Alley, the oldest continually occupied residential block in the country. It also takes in Chinatown, Society Hill, Overbrook, the Northern Liberties village, Penn's Landing, and Philadelphia's four-square-block convention center, the largest in the Northeast. North of Center City, the district includes much of heavily black North Philadelphia, a couple of wards of Northeast Philadelphia (connected to the rest by irregular boundaries), and Kensington and its closely packed 19th-century homes that are increasingly occupied by Hispanic immigrants. The 1st includes once heavily Italian South Philadelphia, where families and their small stores and restaurants have been pressed tightly into narrow streets. Nearby, the district takes in the city's stadium and arena complex. It continues along the Delaware River southwest into Delaware County to impoverished Chester, which has been undergoing a revival that includes a new soccer stadium opened in 2010. And it takes in three wards in heavily black West Philadelphia and a few small adjacent suburbs. Those hard-pressed areas have made the 1st District the poorest in Pennsylvania. The population of the minority-majority district is 46% African-American and 19% Hispanic. Despite growth in Center City, the district's population overall fell by more than 50,000 between 2000 and 2010. This is a heavily Democratic district that gave the party's 2008 nominee, Barack Obama, 88% of the vote.

Robert Brady (D)

The congressman from the 1st District is Robert Brady, a Democrat elected in 1998. He is the personification of Philadelphia's old-fashioned urban politics, and is one of the few remaining white ethnic party bosses in big-city America.

Brady grew up in Overbrook Park in West Philadelphia, with an Irish father who was a policeman and an Italian mother. After high school, he went to work as a carpenter, quickly rose through the ranks of the carpenters' union, and remains a dues-paying member. He entered politics in 1967, at age 22, when the local ward leader wouldn't replace a burnt-out streetlight. Brady was elected to the 34th Ward Democratic Executive Committee, and in 1980 he was elected ward leader. In 1986, he became chairman of the Philadelphia Democratic Party. He depicts himself as a roll-up-your-sleeves guy who represents working-class voters, and says he's proud to be the boss of what he calls the nation's largest big-city machine—or, as he calls it, an "organization." Brady is known for making "arrangements" with others—"They're always arrangements, never deals," he insists—and he has been chairman for a quarter century.

In November 1997, Democratic Rep. Thomas Foglietta, a veteran of South Philly politics, became ambassador to Italy, and Brady ran for the seat. The district's ward leaders determined the Democratic nomination for the special election and they favored Brady. With the endorsement of many black leaders and a strong Election Day organization, he won the special election with 74% of the vote. That same year he married his wife Deb, a former Eagles cheerleader who later took a position on the city's housing authority board.

After his election to the House, Brady's focus remained back home. "Ninety-five percent of my day is not Congress," he once said. He mediated a local teachers' strike in 2000, and he sought common ground between the mayor and City Council on a deal for two new stadiums. In 2009, he helped settle a transit strike that plagued the city's traffic for a week; a year later, he worked to end a 28-day walkout by staffers at Temple University Hospital. His ties to City Hall and to local unions gave him credibility with both sides. Brady worked to resolve local intra-party conflicts. "It's all about ego with a lot of these guys," he told *The Philadelphia Inquirer* in 2010. "I lost mine a long time ago."

Brady has a liberal voting record and keeps a low profile in Washington. For "the most powerful man in Philadelphia," *Philadelphia* magazine once wrote, "Washington gas-bagging is not his thing." His initiatives reflect his local orientation. He boasts of once refusing to take a phone call from President Bill Clinton because he was busy dealing with a woman asking if he could send someone to fix her toilet. He says he decided that he was in favor of abortion rights after asking his mother. His loyalty to unions led him to buck environmentalists and most Democrats to vote for drilling in the Arctic National Wildlife Refuge. In 2007, House Speaker Nancy Pelosi may have found the perfect job for him. Brady became chairman of the House Administration Committee, the so-called "Mayor of Capitol Hill" who oversees operations of the House and doles out favors like choice office space. He got a bill through the House in July 2009 to honor African-Americans who had been slave laborers during the original construction of the building, and the next year joined Pelosi on a House staff diversity initiative. He stayed on as the panel's ranking Democrat when Republicans regained control of the House. After the January 2011 shooting of Arizona Democratic Rep. Gabrielle Giffords at a constituent event, Brady proposed treating potentially threatening language against members of Congress the same way it is handled when it involves the president.

Brady ran for Philadelphia mayor in the May 2007 primary. He joined the field late and had significant opposition, including from three veteran local black officials who had operated largely outside Brady's organization—U.S. Rep. Chaka Fattah, state Rep. Dwight Evans and former City Councilman Michael Nutter. Brady's platform was standard fare, including a call for more open government, safer streets, improved schools, and lower taxes. Democratic ward leaders endorsed him in overwhelming numbers but with varying enthusiasm. And his campaign ran into an unusual stumbling block: a lawsuit seeking to remove Brady from the ballot because he did not include his union pension on a candidate disclosure form. Brady revealed in court that his pension benefits were accruing as though he was working a full work week, a curiosity, given the fact that he was serving in Congress. He paid nearly $20,000 in fines for violating the city's campaign finance laws. And he finished a distant third in the primary, with 15% of the vote.

In Philadelphia's Byzantine politics, Brady's weak performance—he lost even his home ward in Overbrook—raised questions about his political vulnerability. There was talk of a 2008 primary challenge from an African-American candidate, but it never materialized. He was unopposed in

2010 after his would-be GOP challenger, tea party activist Pia Varma, was removed from the ballot when a judge determined she did not submit enough valid signatures on her nominating petitions. She accused Republicans of colluding with Brady to keep her off the ballot, a charge the city GOP chairman denied.

Brady concentrated instead on trying to bolster turnout for Republican-turned-Democratic Sen. Arlen Specter in the May primary, but could not prevent a Specter loss to Rep. Joe Sestak. Nor could his organization help Sestak beat Republican Pat Toomey that fall.

SECOND DISTRICT

Chaka Fattah (D)

Elected 1994, 9th term; b. Nov. 21, 1956, Philadelphia; home, Philadelphia; Community Col. of Philadelphia, U. of PA, M.A. 1986, Harvard U. Kennedy Schl. of Gov., 1984; Baptist; married (Renee Chenault-Fattah); 4 children.

Elected Office: PA House of Reps., 1982–88; PA Senate, 1988–94.

Professional Career: Asst. dir., House of Umoja, 1977-79; City of Philadelphia, Spec. asst. to dir. of Housing & Community Dev., 1980, Spec. asst. to managing director, 1981.

DC Office: 2301 RHOB, 20515, 202-225-4001; Fax: 202-225-5392; Web site: fattah.house.gov.

State Offices: Philadelphia, 215-848-9386; Philadelphia, 215-387-6404.

Committees: *Appropriations:* Commerce, Justice, Science & Related Agencies (RMM); Energy & Water Development.

Group Ratings

	ACLU	ACU	ADA	CFG	AFS	FRC	LCV	ITIC	NTU	COC
2010	88	0	95	0	100	0	100	100	7	25
2009	–	0	100	0	100	–	100	–	1	33

National Journal Ratings

	2010 LIB	—	2010 CONS	2009 LIB	—	2009 CONS
Economic	90%	—	0%	91%	—	0%
Social	71%	—	25%	84%	—	11%
Foreign	84%	—	11%	86%	—	13%
Composite	85%	—	15%	90%	—	11%

Key Votes of the 111th Congress

1. Overturn Ledbetter	Y	5. Bar federal abortion funds	N	9. Stop detainee transfers	N
2. Pass $820 billion stimulus	Y	6. Pass health care bill	Y	10. Legalize immigrants' kids	Y
3. Let guns in national parks	N	7. Regulate financial firms	Y	11. Repeal don't ask, tell	Y
4. Pass cap-and-trade	Y	8. Pass tax cuts for some	Y	12. Limit campaign funds	Y

Election Results

2010 general	Chaka Fattah (D)	182,800	(89%)	($458,055)
	Rick Hellberg (R)	21,907	(11%)	($11,807)
2010 primary	Chaka Fattah (D)	unopposed		

Prior Winning Percentages: 2008 (89%), 2006 (89%), 2004 (88%), 2002 (88%), 2000 (98%), 1998 (87%), 1996 (88%), 1994 (86%)

Population		Race/Ethnicity		Work	
Pop. 2010:	630,277	White:	30.4%	Private:	81.5%
Change since 2000:	Down 2.5%	Black:	56.5%	Government:	14.6%
Urban:	100.0%	Hispanic:	4.8%	Self-employed:	3.8%
Rural:	0.0%	Asian:	5.8%	Blue collar:	14.1%
Area size:	60 sq. mi.	Native Am.:	0.3%	White collar:	65.7%
		Hawaiian:	0.0%	Khaki collar:	0.1%
Age		Two+ races:	2.1%	Other:	20.2%
Median age:	34.1 yrs.				
More than 65 yrs:	12.6%	*Ancestry*		Median income:	$37,498
Less than 18 yrs:	21.6%	Irish	8.2%	Median Home Value:	$143,600
		Italian	6.4%		
Education		German	5.9%	**Military Veterans**	
H.S. grad:	82.8%			% of Pop:	7.4%
College grad:	30.1%				
Grad degree:	14.0%				

West Philadelphia

Looking out over the Schuylkill River north of Center City Philadelphia, you can still see the landscape painted 100 years ago by Philadelphia artist Thomas Eakins: the tightly packed but formidable rowhouses, the old fieldstone houses of Germantown, the gray-blue water flowing past boat houses below the small Greek temples of the Water Works and the larger temple of the Philadelphia Museum of Art. On both sides of this romantic scene are some of Philadelphia's

2008 Presidential Vote		
Barack Obama (D)	298,834	(90%)
John McCain (R)	31,584	(10%)
2004 Presidential Vote		
John Kerry (D)	266,174	(87%)
George Bush (R)	37,811	(12%)
Cook Partisan Voting Index:	D+38	

long-established black neighborhoods: West Philadelphia, across the Schuylkill on either side of Market Street; North Philadelphia, on either side of Broad Street; historic Germantown to the northwest, off the narrow diagonal of Germantown Avenue. Pennsylvania never had slavery, thanks to William Penn and his Quaker legacy, and Philadelphia has been home to a large black community since before the Civil War. That heritage is reflected in places like the John Coltrane House on North 33rd Street, designated a national historic landmark in celebration of the jazz innovator's early years here. Suburban Cheltenham Township includes old, comfortable communities like Cheltenham, Melrose Park, Elkins Park, and Glenside. Some neighborhoods continue to suffer from poverty and blight, and the city had 545,000 fewer people in 2010 than it did in 1950. But in recent years, city officials have made a concerted effort to bring young, affluent people back to the city, and Philadelphia actually grew by 8,500 people from 2000 to 2010, a less than 1% gain.

The 2nd Congressional District of Pennsylvania takes in much of the city of Philadelphia west of Broad Street, plus Cheltenham Township in suburban Montgomery County. It doesn't include the key colonial landmarks—they're in the neighboring 1st District—but it does include most of the skyscrapers of Center City and well-heeled Rittenhouse Square, the Philadelphia Zoo (America's first), the University of Pennsylvania, and Drexel University. It also includes lush Fairmount Park, the largest landscaped urban park in the world, which climaxes at the grand Philadelphia Museum of Art, where a *Rocky*-like run up the steps has become *de rigueur* for tourists. The district takes in West Oak Lane, Strawberry Mansion, and, farther west, the distinguished old neighborhoods of Mount Airy, Chestnut Hill, and East Falls. The 2nd also covers Roxborough and the old mill area of Manayunk, now an artsy enclave. With a 57% African-American population, it is Pennsylvania's only black-majority district. It lost more than 75,000 people between 2000 and 2010, one of the highest losses of any Keystone State district. The district is heavily Democratic, and was Republican nominee John McCain's fifth-worst-performing district in the nation in 2008. He got just 10% of the vote. The bottom four were all in New York.

Chaka Fattah (D)

The congressman from the 2nd District is Chaka Fattah (*SHOCK-ah Fu-TAH*), a Democrat first elected in 1994. Unlike Rep. Robert Brady, the city's other congressman, Fattah's focus is more nationally oriented. "A policy wonk with savvy," *The Philadelphia Inquirer* has called him.

Fattah was born Arthur Davenport, one of six children of a poor single mother in Philadelphia. She changed his name after she married community activist David Fattah; his first name was taken from a Zulu warrior. His parents were both politically active, producing a magazine for African-Americans and opening their home as a neighborhood gathering spot for teens at risk of joining street gangs. Fattah dropped out of high school, but later got an equivalent diploma and went on to earn a master's degree in government administration at the University of Pennsylvania. In 1982, at age 25, was elected to the Pennsylvania General Assembly, at the time its youngest member ever. Six years later, he was elected to the state Senate.

In 1991, Democratic Rep. William Gray, the powerful House majority whip, resigned to become head of the United Negro College Fund. In the special election to succeed him, local Democratic ward leaders nominated Councilman Lucien Blackwell, a former longshoreman and labor union stalwart. Fattah ran under the Consumer Party label while state Welfare Secretary John White ran as an independent. Blackwell won with 39% to 28% for Fattah and 27% for White. In 1994, Fattah ran again, this time taking on the Democratic establishment in the primary. Blackwell relied mostly on ward politicians. Fattah was endorsed by the Black Clergy of Philadelphia and Vicinity. This time Fattah won, 58%-42%. He has had no serious primary or general election challenge since. Fattah's wife, Renee Chenault-Fattah, is a local television news anchor in Philadelphia.

Fattah has a liberal voting record; he just slightly trailed Democrat Mike Doyle as the most liberal member of Pennsylvania's House delegation in the 111th Congress (2009-10). He has focused on education and worked on the "Gear Up" program to prepare low-income students for college, although in 2007, the *Philadelphia Daily News* reported that the program had limited effectiveness for local kids, and the city's schools phased it out. He has advocated eliminating the federal tax code and replacing all individual and corporate taxes with a system that would tax all individual transactions, an idea that generated some interest among Republicans. But most Democrats are leery of anything that looks like a consumption tax. He got a provision into the 2010 financial overhaul law to provide mortgage relief to the unemployed that was based on a program he developed when he was a state Assembly member. Later that year, Fattah broke with the rest of the Congressional Black Caucus to support President Barack Obama's tax-cut extension deal with Republicans, citing its assistance to his poor constituents. Black Caucus members "cannot wait for the 'perfect' solution from an imperfect and divided Washington," he said.

Fattah also has used his post on the Appropriations Committee to secure money to curb witness intimidation in Philadelphia, to combat the use of unsafe blood supplies that transmit HIV/AIDS in Africa and to increase the number of minorities working on defense programs. He sought to become Appropriations' top Democrat in 2010, but lost a 26-18 vote of the leadership-run Democratic Steering Committee to Norm Dicks of Washington, who had more seniority. Fattah settled for the ranking Democratic post on the panel funding the Commerce and Justice departments and science programs.

Fattah ran and lost a campaign for Philadelphia mayor in 2007. The move prompted grumbling among local Democrats planning to run for mayor that he was giving up his clout as an appropriator, and even some threats that Fattah would face a primary challenge for his House seat. Also in the crowded primary race was Brady, of the neighboring 1st District, former City Councilman Michael Nutter, and wealthy businessman Thomas Knox. Fattah began the race as the early frontrunner, but his campaign struggled to raise money and drew criticism over his refusal to release his income tax returns. Nutter was the eventual winner with 37% of the vote, followed by Knox with 25%. Fattah finished fourth with 15%, less than 200 votes behind Brady, who also had 15%.

With Pennsylvania slated to lose a seat to 2012 redistricting, there has been speculation that Fattah could be put in a district with 13th District Democrat Allyson Schwartz. But it would be a risky strategy, as almost all of the districts near Schwartz's are GOP-held swing districts.

THIRD DISTRICT

Mike Kelly (R)

Elected 2010, 1st term; b. May 10, 1948, Pittsburgh; home, Butler; U. of Notre Dame, B.A. 1970.

Elected Office: Butler City Cncl., 2005-09.

Professional Career: Owner, mgr., Kelly Chevrolet-Cadillac Inc.

DC Office: 515 CHOB, 20515, 202-225-5406; Fax: 202-225-3103; Web site: kelly.house.gov.

State Offices: Butler, 724-282-2557; Erie, 814-454-8190; Greenville, 724-885-1113.

Committees: *Education & the Workforce:* Early Childhood, Elementary & Secondary Education; Workforce Protections. *Foreign Affairs:* Asia & the Pacific (VChmn); Oversight & Investigations. *Oversight & Government Reform:* Regulatory Affairs, Stimulus Oversight & Government Spending; Technology, Information Policy, Intergovernmental Relations & Procurement Reform (VChmn).

Election Results

2010 general	Mike Kelly (R)	111,909	(56%)	($1,335,430)
	Kathy Dahlkemper (D)	88,924	(44%)	($2,028,693)
2010 primary	Mike Kelly (R)	15,428	(28%)	
	Paul Huber (R)	14,474	(26%)	
	Clayton Grabb (R)	7,486	(14%)	
	Steven Fisher (R)	6,499	(12%)	
	Ed Franz (R)	5,838	(11%)	
	Martha Moore (R)	5,151	(9%)	

Population		Race/Ethnicity		Work	
Pop. 2010:	640,356	White:	91.6%	Private:	82.1%
Change since 2000:	Down 0.9%	Black:	4.1%	Government:	11.4%
Urban:	58.4%	Hispanic:	2.0%	Self-employed:	6.3%
Rural:	41.6%	Asian:	0.7%	Blue collar:	26.5%
Area size:	4,778 sq. mi.	Native Am.:	0.1%	White collar:	55.0%
		Hawaiian:	0.0%	Khaki collar:	0.1%
Age		Two+ races:	1.3%	Other:	18.4%
Median age:	40.2 yrs.				
More than 65 yrs:	15.9%	*Ancestry*		Median income:	$43,299
Less than 18 yrs:	22.0%	German	25.2%	Median Home Value:	$110,100
		Irish	13.4%		
Education		Italian	8.5%	**Military Veterans**	
H.S. grad:	88.3%			% of Pop:	11.6%
College grad:	20.5%				
Grad degree:	7.1%				

Northwest Pennsylvania; Erie

The best natural harbor on Lake Erie is in Erie, Pennsylvania, protected by the Presque Isle ("almost an island") peninsula—a cowlick-shaped, seven-mile-long sand spit blanketed by mature forest, with a lighthouse dating to 1872. Erie is in Pennsylvania's far northwest corner, only about 100 miles from Cleveland. There is farmland here, and even some woods, but the land between the Great Lakes and the basin of the Ohio River has been prime heavy industry territory for more than a century. The jeep, which Gen. George Marshall called America's greatest contribution to World War II, was invented in Butler County. In the 1990s, under Republican Gov. Tom Ridge, who grew up in Erie, the state invested $100 million in Erie's waterfront to develop a cruise ship terminal, hotel and convention center, a ballpark for the double-A Erie SeaWolves baseball team, and restorations to the Warner Theatre. The effort spruced up a dying downtown, but it didn't buffer Erie from a subsequent economic downturn. International Paper, American Meter, Gunite/EMI, and American Sterilizer laid off employees and closed plants. General Electric Transportation, one of the area's largest employers for much of the 20th century, also had major cutbacks, though it still had 4,200 in the Erie area in 2011.

2008 Presidential Vote		
John McCain (R)	143,433	(49%)
Barack Obama (D)	143,416	(49%)

2004 Presidential Vote		
George Bush (R)	152,473	(53%)
John Kerry (D)	133,764	(47%)

Cook Partisan Voting Index: R+3

The 3rd Congressional District of Pennsylvania occupies this northwest corner of the state—all of Erie County; most of Mercer, Crawford, and Butler counties; and about half of Warren, Venango, and Armstrong counties. Erie County, with 44% of the district's population, declined slightly in population, to 280,600, from 2000 to 2010. Growth has been modest too in Butler County, on the northern edge of the Pittsburgh metropolitan area, while other parts of the district have lost population. Politically, the mix of industrial and rural voters makes for closely balanced territory. Erie and Mercer counties vote Democratic in most national elections, but they have also voted for Republicans with working-class appeal, like Ridge, who is from a Catholic working-class family in Erie. The other counties are culturally conservative and solidly Republican. In 2008, GOP presidential nominee John McCain won the district by a mere 17 votes out of more than 291,000 cast. McCain won all of the outlying counties, but Democrat Barack Obama carried Erie, 59%-39%.

Mike Kelly (R)

The new congressman from Pennsylvania's 3rd District is Republican Mike Kelly, who won this seat in 2010 from Democratic freshman Kathy Dahlkemper. Kelly was born in Pittsburgh in 1948, and his family moved to Butler, Pa., four years later, where his father started a small automobile business in 1953, working seven days a week. "He took the cars off the trains himself, and he serviced them himself. And he built a business, based around a strong work ethic, which was similar to his parents. It's pretty much the story of western Pennsylvania," Kelly told *National Journal*. In high school, Kelly was an all-state football player and was recruited to play at the University of Notre Dame. But he tore up a knee during his freshman year at Notre Dame and dislocated it again in his sophomore season, ending his football career. "It was over very quickly," he recalled. After college, he worked in the family business, Kelly Chevrolet-Cadillac, as a salesman, eventually becoming general manager. He took out a mortgage to buy the dealership from his father in 1995.

"My dad was the kind of guy who believed that unless you have some skin in the game, you wouldn't be on top of things," Kelly said. In 2005, Kelly was elected to the Butler City Council.

As the 2010 midterm election approached, Kelly decided to take on Dahlkemper, who had knocked off seven-term GOP incumbent Phil English only narrowly, 51% to 49%, in 2008. Dahlkemper opposed abortion rights, but she took heat from conservatives for voting for the Democrats' health care reform law, which many anti-abortion activists believed opened the door to taxpayer-funded abortions. Dahlkemper also voted for President Barack Obama's $787 billion economic stimulus bill. Sensing that she was vulnerable, Kelly and five other Republicans jumped into the race.

In the May primary, Kelly's toughest opponent proved to be Paul Huber, former chief executive of Seco/Warwick, a maker of industrial furnaces. Kelly ran an ad accusing Huber of outsourcing jobs. Huber asserted that he never outsourced jobs while running his company. Huber also faced criticism over the fact that he had been a registered Democrat until recently, though he said he often voted Republican. Kelly eked out a victory over Huber by just 954 votes out of 54,000 cast.

In the general election, Dahlkemper outraised and outspent Kelly 2-to-1. Kelly stressed his football background, which was an asset in Western Pennsylvania, a football mecca that has produced Hall of Famers Dan Marino and Joe Montana and current stars such as New York Jet Darrelle Revis. On issues, he promised to cut government spending and curtail government interference with small business. Dahlkemper ran an ad in September playing on populist themes, calling Kelly a multimillionaire who has "millions invested in Wall Street and big gas-and-oil companies." But Kelly described his determination to serve in Congress after the 2008 restructuring of the auto industry resulted in government meddling in his family-owned business. Although his dealership was financially sound, he said that a GM representative told him he could sell Chevrolets but not Cadillacs. With a strong Republican trend in 2010 working in his favor, Kelly won 56% to 44%.

FOURTH DISTRICT

Jason Altmire (D)

Elected 2006, 3rd term; b. March 7, 1968, Kittaning; home, McCandless Township; FL. St. U., B.S. 1990, George Washington U., M.H.A. 1998; Catholic; married (Kelly); 2 children.

Professional Career: Aide, U.S. Rep. Pete Peterson, 1991-96; Asst. VP, Fed. of American Hospitals, 1996-98; VP of Govt. Relations, U. of Pittsburgh Med. Ctr., 1998-2005.

DC Office: 332 CHOB, 20515, 202-225-2565; Fax: 202-226-2274; Web site: altmire.house.gov.

State Offices: Aliquippa, 724-378-0928; Natrona Heights, 724-226-1304.

Committees: *Small Business:* Healthcare & Technology; Investigations, Oversight & Regulations (RMM). *Transportation & Infrastructure:* Highways & Transit; Railroads, Pipelines & Hazardous Materials; Water Resources & Environment.

Group Ratings

	ACLU	ACU	ADA	CFG	AFS	FRC	LCV	ITIC	NTU	COC
2010	63	21	65	25	88	31	80	100	33	50
2009	–	20	70	29	89	–	79	–	25	60

National Journal Ratings

	2010 LIB	—	2010 CONS		2009 LIB	—	2009 CONS
Economic	48%	—	51%		47%	—	52%
Social	46%	—	53%		45%	—	53%
Foreign	42%	—	57%		45%	—	53%
Composite	46%	—	54%		47%	—	54%

Key Votes of the 111th Congress

1. Overturn Ledbetter	Y	5. Bar federal abortion funds	Y	9. Stop detainee transfers	Y
2. Pass $820 billion stimulus	Y	6. Pass health care bill	N	10. Legalize immigrants' kids	N
3. Let guns in national parks	Y	7. Regulate financial firms	Y	11. Repeal don't ask, tell	Y
4. Pass cap-and-trade	N	8. Pass tax cuts for some	Y	12. Limit campaign funds	Y

Election Results

2010 general	Jason Altmire (D)..	120,827	(51%)	($2,503,953)
	Keith Rothfus (R)..	116,958	(49%)	($1,292,104)
2010 primary	Jason Altmire (D).......................................	unopposed		

Prior Winning Percentages: 2008 (56%), 2006 (52%)

Population		Race/Ethnicity		Work	
Pop. 2010:	647,418	White:	92.3%	Private:	84.4%
Change since 2000:	Up 0.1%	Black:	3.5%	Government:	9.9%
Urban:	78.5%	Hispanic:	1.1%	Self-employed:	5.5%
Rural:	21.5%	Asian:	1.7%	Blue collar:	19.1%
Area size:	1,318 sq. mi.	Native Am.:	0.1%	White collar:	65.1%
		Hawaiian:	0.0%	Khaki collar:	0.0%
Age		Two+ races:	1.2%	Other:	15.8%
Median age:	43.2 yrs.				
More than 65 yrs:	17.6%	*Ancestry*		Median income:	$54,376
Less than 18 yrs:	22.0%	German	23.6%	Median Home Value:	$142,500
		Irish	14.2%		
Education		Italian	13.2%	**Military Veterans**	
H.S. grad:	91.9%			% of Pop:	11.2%
College grad:	32.2%				
Grad degree:	12.0%				

Western Region; Pittsburgh Suburbs

For a century, one of America's great industrial zones was near the intersection of the Beaver and Ohio rivers in western Pennsylvania. This was steel country, with mills rising from the bottomlands and filling the narrow river valleys with smoke. Immigrant families lived in small frame houses on hillsides, looking down on riverscapes lined with piles of iron ore, limestone, and coal and littered with cranes, stocks, and furnaces. This was not an environmentalist's idea of perfection, but it was a land of opportunity for thousands whose lives were worse before moving to steel country. One grandchild of a Hungarian immigrant steelworker in Beaver Falls was Joe Namath, one of the many great quarterbacks produced by southwestern Pennsylvania (a few of the others are fellow Hall of Famers Jim Kelly, Joe Montana, and Dan Marino, and more recently, Ohio State star Terrelle Pryor). During the heady years, high union wages and early retirement plans made working in the mills a path to the middle class. But the industry crashed after the oil shock of 1979. Many mills closed and jobs vanished. Today, thousands of workers who long ago exhausted their unemployment benefits have given up and left the Beaver and Ohio valleys.

2008 Presidential Vote		
John McCain (R)	185,052	(55%)
Barack Obama (D)	149,661	(44%)

2004 Presidential Vote		
George Bush (R)	179,855	(54%)
John Kerry (D)	149,070	(45%)

Cook Partisan Voting Index: R+6

The 4th Congressional District of Pennsylvania includes much of steel country and, equally important, a large swath of suburban Pittsburgh. The 4th begins around Farrell in Mercer County, located as close to Erie as to Pittsburgh, then travels south along Route 60 through steel-mill country in Lawrence and Beaver counties. The district then turns to the east, taking in a fast-growing tier of suburban southern Butler County and the longer-established Allegheny County suburbs north of Pittsburgh. It includes old-money Fox Chapel and Sewickley, which is now attracting the region's high-tech wealth, and affluent McCandless and middle-class Ross in the North Hills. It also takes in a tiny portion of Westmoreland County.

The steel mill areas tend to be Democratic, with unions still capable of flexing some muscle. The suburbs of Butler County are tax-averse and strongly Republican, with solid growth in Cranberry and Seven Fields. The older suburbs in Allegheny County, with some of the highest senior-citizen populations in the country, are politically marginal. Overall, the district's heritage is Democratic but it has been trending slightly toward the Republicans. George W. Bush carried this district with 54% of the vote in 2004. Although 2008 Democratic presidential nominee Barack Obama launched his post-convention campaign in Beaver County, Republican John McCain won it with 55% of the vote.

Jason Altmire (D)

The congressman from the 4th District is Jason Altmire, a Democrat elected in 2006. He is a one-time lobbyist and congressional aide whose carefully centrist politics helped him survive the GOP landslide of 2010.

Altmire grew up outside of Pittsburgh, the only child of a single mother who was a school teacher. He was a star high school athlete until he suffered a knee injury. He attended Florida State University, worked to rehabilitate his knee, and made the football team as a walk-on player. He suffered another injury as the team trained to play in the Sugar Bowl. Altmire volunteered for the successful campaign of Florida Democrat Pete Peterson for the U.S. House, and then worked as Peterson's legislative aide for six years, developing expertise in health care issues. Altmire earned a master's degree in health administration at George Washington University while working on Capitol Hill, and at age 25, was appointed to President Bill Clinton's health care task force. Following a short stint with the Federation of American Hospitals, he returned home to western Pennsylvania in 1998 for a job with the University of Pittsburgh Medical Center, eventually becoming vice president for government relations. Sixteen months before the general election in 2006, Altmire quit his $130,000-a-year job and jumped into the race against Republican Rep. Melissa Hart, who had held the seat since 2000.

In the Democratic primary, Altmire defeated businesswoman Georgia Berner, who supported abortion rights while Altmire stressed his opposition to both abortion rights and gun control. He was outspent, but he enjoyed support from key labor groups. He won 55%-45% with strong support from his Allegheny County base, which he carried by nearly 10,000 votes. In the general election campaign, Altmire positioned himself as more socially conservative than the national Democratic Party. Hart outspent Altmire by more than $1 million, but she was fighting an anti-Republican current in a traditionally Democratic district. Altmire won 52%-48%, narrowly losing Allegheny County but winning by large margins in traditionally Democratic Beaver County.

In the House, Altmire's voting record puts him almost precisely at the center of the House. He is a member of the centrist New Democrats and the Blue Dog Coalition of fiscally conservative Democrats. In the 111th Congress (2009-10), he incensed labor unions by opposing the health care overhaul, contending that his constituents weren't ready for such a sweeping change. He also opposed energy legislation creating a cap-and-trade program to reduce carbon emissions, and supported fellow Blue Dog Heath Shuler of North Carolina over liberal Nancy Pelosi of California for minority leader in January 2011.

With his legislative experience, he scored some accomplishments. His proposal to extend education benefits to National Guardsmen who serve domestically became law in 2010. With help from Majority Leader Steny Hoyer, Altmire also won passage of a bill to prevent the military from curtailing bonuses to soldiers who end their service because of serious injury. But he made life difficult for Hoyer in 2009 by insisting on repeal of the District of Columbia's strict gun control laws as a condition for his support for D.C. getting a voting member in the House.

On the Small Business Committee, Altmire tended to his district's technology interests in 2009 by pushing a bill through the House to boost small business research and innovation. He joined Pennsylvania Republican Glenn Thompson on a bill in 2011 to eliminate a competitive bidding program for certain kinds of home medical equipment. Consumer groups and medical providers complained the program is poorly run and has led to numerous delays in obtaining equipment.

Hart sought a rematch in 2008. She blasted Altmire's votes for higher taxes and said that he failed to take action on high gas prices. Altmire said Hart was "wrong then and now." He raised twice as much money as Hart and easily held the seat, 56%-44%.

After labor leaders still angry over his health care vote decided against a 2010 primary challenge, Altmire drew a tough GOP opponent in lawyer Keith Rothfus, who once worked in President George W. Bush's Office of Faith-Based and Community Initiatives. Rothfus trounced former U.S. Attorney Mary Beth Buchanan by a 2-to-1 margin in the primary. In the general election, he called Altmire "an enabler for the Democratic Party," while Altmire labeled Rothfus "a radical right-winger" and accused him of representing a Wall Street bank that took government bailout funds. Rothfus said his firm was not involved in TARP. With tea party support, Rothfus raised nearly $1.3 million, but that was only half of Altmire's take, and the incumbent won 51%-49%. He narrowly lost Allegheny County, just as he did in his initial race, but he carried Beaver County 58%-42% and Lawrence County 55%-45%. But 2012 redistricting could force him into a matchup with Rep. Mark Critz, a similarly centrist Democrat who has support from labor groups.

FIFTH DISTRICT

Glenn Thompson (R)

Elected 2008, 2nd term; b. July 27, 1959, Bellefonte; home, Howard Township; PA St. U., B.S. 1981; Temple U., M.Ed. 1998; Church of Christ; married (Penny); 3 children.

Elected Office: Bald Eagle Area Schl Bd., 1990-96

Professional Career: Therapist, Williamsport Hospital, 1982-1995; Adjct. faculty, Cambria Cnty. Comm. Col, 1997-1999; Mgr., Susquehanna Health Rehabilitation Services, 1995-2008; Centre Cnty. GOP Chmn., 2002-08; Firefighter & EMT

DC Office: 124 CHOB, 20515, 202-225-5121; Fax: 202-225-5796; Web site: thompson.house.gov.

State Offices: Bellefonte, 814-353-0215; Titusville, 814-827-3985.

Committees: *Agriculture:* Conservation, Energy & Forestry (Chmn); Rural Development, Research, Biotechnology & Foreign Agriculture. *Education & the Workforce:* Health, Employment, Labor & Pensions; Higher Education & Workforce Training. *Natural Resources:* Energy & Mineral Resources.

Group Ratings

	ACLU	ACU	ADA	CFG	AFS	FRC	LCV	ITIC	NTU	COC
2010	13	100	0	87	0	100	10	33	86	88
2009	–	88	15	78	33	–	0	–	80	87

National Journal Ratings

	2010 LIB — 2010 CONS		2009 LIB — 2009 CONS	
Economic	26%	— 73%	18%	— 81%
Social	25%	— 71%	29%	— 68%
Foreign	29%	— 68%	0%	— 75%
Composite	28%	— 72%	21%	— 80%

Key Votes of the 111th Congress

1. Overturn Ledbetter	N	5. Bar federal abortion funds	Y	9. Stop detainee transfers	Y
2. Pass $820 billion stimulus	N	6. Pass health care bill	N	10. Legalize immigrants' kids	N
3. Let guns in national parks	Y	7. Regulate financial firms	N	11. Repeal don't ask, tell	N
4. Pass cap-and-trade	N	8. Pass tax cuts for some	N	12. Limit campaign funds	N

Election Results

2010 general	Glenn Thompson (R)	127,427	(68%)	($1,070,715)
	Michael Pipe (D)	52,375	(29%)	($26,394)
	Vernon Etzel (Lib)	5,710	(3%)	($263)
2010 primary	Glenn Thompson (R)	unopposed		

Prior Winning Percentages: 2008 (57%)

Population		Race/Ethnicity		Work	
Pop. 2010:	651,762	White:	94.0%	Private:	78.2%
Change since 2000:	Up 0.8%	Black:	1.8%	Government:	14.5%
Urban:	46.0%	Hispanic:	1.5%	Self-employed:	7.1%
Rural:	54.0%	Asian:	1.5%	Blue collar:	29.2%
Area size:	11,106 sq. mi.	Native Am.:	0.1%	White collar:	51.7%
		Hawaiian:	0.0%	Khaki collar:	0.1%
Age		Two+ races:	0.9%	Other:	19.0%
Median age:	39.5 yrs.				
More than 65 yrs:	16.2%	*Ancestry*		Median income:	$40,252
Less than 18 yrs:	19.9%	German	25.1%	Median Home Value:	$97,700
		Irish	10.7%		
Education		English	7.6%	**Military Veterans**	
H.S. grad:	87.5%			% of Pop:	11.7%
College grad:	19.0%				
Grad degree:	7.5%				

North Central Pennsylvania

North central Pennsylvania, isolated from the rest of the country by mountains and off the main east-west rail and highway lines until the 1970s, is one of those empty spaces that make even the northeastern states seem lightly populated compared to the densely packed terrain of Western Europe or East Asia. Forest County has one of the highest percentages of second homes or cottages of any county in the nation. Pressed tightly by narrow valleys and fast-flowing rivers, roads here are often forced to switch back as they wind their way precariously over the mountains. Tioga County is home to Pine Creek Gorge, known as "Pennsylvania's Grand Canyon." This part of the state is a prime area for hunting, fishing, and snowmobiling. There are wide-open spaces like the Allegheny National Forest, which sprawls across four counties and is a popular recreational area. Neatly preserved Ridgway, just outside the Allegheny National Forest, holds the largest chainsaw carving event in the world. Elk County and the Elk State Forest feature a free-roaming herd of elk, of course, but also are home to a trout hatchery.

2008 Presidential Vote		
John McCain (R)	153,015	(55%)
Barack Obama (D)	123,485	(44%)
2004 Presidential Vote		
George Bush (R)	165,343	(61%)
John Kerry (D)	105,295	(39%)
Cook Partisan Voting Index: R+9		

The downturn in manufacturing in recent years hit this area hard, but the prospect of natural gas deep underground in the Marcellus Shale formation has brought considerable optimism locally. A 2009 Pennsylvania College of Technology report predicted that the number of natural gas-related jobs in the region could more than double by 2013. DuBois in Clearfield County is home to glass production and a powdered metal industry. In Bradford, Zippo manufactures lighters. Punxsutawney in Jefferson County is home of the legendary groundhog Phil, who predicts the arrival of spring every year by looking for his shadow on Gobbler's Knob on Feb. 2. The 1993 movie *Groundhog Day* sparked a tourism boomlet in this town of 6,000, even though the movie was filmed in Woodstock, Ill.

To the southeast is the Nittany Valley, home of State College and Pennsylvania State University, which keep Centre County's unemployment rate among the state's lowest. Penn State has long been known for its powerful football teams coached by iconic Joe Paterno ("JoePa," locally), and the university's cutting-edge facilities have spawned a high-skills job market. Interstate 80 makes this part of Pennsylvania accessible to big markets, and there has been some modest population growth since 1990. The state has sought to turn I-80 into a toll road to raise money, but the federal government has rejected the idea, which many Republicans oppose.

The 5th Congressional District of Pennsylvania is the state's most rural and its largest in land area, and is one of the largest districts east of the Mississippi River. Politically, this area became Republican in the 1850s when the party was founded, and it has remained heavily Republican since. In 2004, President George W. Bush won 61% of the vote here, and in 2008, GOP nominee John McCain did not do as well, but still won with 55%.

Glenn Thompson (R)

The congressman from the 5th District is Republican Glenn Thompson, who won the seat in 2008. A lifelong resident of Centre County, Thompson—whose nickname is "G.T."— was born in Bellefonte, Pa., where he grew up with a sister and two brothers. Staying close to home for college, he attended Penn State in nearby State College. After graduating, he launched his career in health care at Williamsport Hospital, which later consolidated with two other area hospitals to form the community health network Susquehanna Health, where he worked as a rehabilitation services manager. Now a resident of Howard Township, Thompson served as a member of the board of the Bald Eagle Area School District from 1990 to 1996. He ran twice for state representative, both times unsuccessfully, but was elected to three terms as chairman of the Centre County Republican Party.

When GOP Rep. John Peterson announced in early January 2008 that he would not seek re-election, Thompson jumped into the nine-candidate primary. His hopes at first appeared dim against the robust spending by rivals. Businessmen Matt Shaner and Derek Walker financed their own campaigns, and took to the airwaves hoping to reach voters across the geographically expansive district. Thompson instead hit the pavement, crisscrossing the district in a low-key campaign that emphasized his Republican positions and focused on rural issues. He opposed tolling on local Interstate 80 and called for expanding rural Medicare initiatives. He also spoke of the Iraq war in personal terms; his son, Logan, was injured by a landmine in late 2007 while serving there.

Two developments late in the campaign likely allowed Thompson to break out of the pack. Less than two weeks before the primary, Peterson threw his support behind Thompson as the candidate who would follow in his legacy and who best understood rural issues. The following week, the Clearfield County district attorney filed charges against Walker for allegedly breaking into his ex-girlfriend's apartment. Together, Peterson's endorsement and Walker's personal problems allowed Thompson to eke out a small victory. Vastly outspent, he won 19% of the vote to beat Walker by just over 800 votes.

The general election was a breeze by comparison. Thompson's opponent, Clearfield County Commissioner Mark McCracken, did not raise much money and received little help from the Democratic Party. Thompson won 57% to 41%. He had an even easier time in the Republican year of 2010, when he crushed Democrat Michael Pipe, a fast-food restaurant manager, 69%-28%.

In the House, Thompson broke with the majority of House Republicans in January 2009 by voting to expand the State Children's Health Insurance Program. After that, however, he stuck with his party on major votes. He also drew some attention early on for spending more on his staff's salaries than any other freshman; he responded that the pay levels were part of effectively serving his district.

Rural causes have been a priority for Thompson. In 2011, when Republicans took majority control, he got the chairmanship of the Agriculture Committee's panel on Conservation, Energy, and Forestry along with a seat on the Natural Resources Committee, and vowed to push for more natural gas drilling in the Marcellus Shale formation. He dismissed concerns raised in a lengthy *New York Times* investigation and by environmentalists that the gas-drilling technique of hydraulic fracturing or "hydro fracking" is contaminating groundwater. "We've been given the technology not just to access this natural gas, but to do it in a profoundly safe, environmentally safe way," he told *The Daily Item* newspaper in March 2011. He also was highly critical of the Environmental Protection Agency's efforts to protect the Chesapeake Bay from agricultural-related pollution, accusing the EPA of a "quixotic quest to impose unreasonable regulatory mandates."

SIXTH DISTRICT

Jim Gerlach (R)

Elected 2002, 5th term; b. Feb. 25, 1955, Ellwood City; home, Chester Springs; Dickinson Col., B.A. 1977, J.D. 1980; Presbyterian; married (Karen); 6 children.

Elected Office: PA House of Reps., 1990-94; PA Senate, 1994-2002.

Professional Career: Practicing atty., 1980-2002.

DC Office: 2442 RHOB, 20515, 202-225-4315; Fax: 202-225-8440; Web site: gerlach.house.gov.

State Offices: Exton, 610-594-1415; Trappe, 610-409-2780; Wyomissing, 610-376-7630.

Committees: *Ways & Means:* Health; Select Revenue Measures.

Group Ratings

	ACLU	ACU	ADA	CFG	AFS	FRC	LCV	ITIC	NTU	COC
2010	19	67	10	62	38	87	30	67	68	100
2009	–	76	20	63	44	–	43	–	60	87

National Journal Ratings

	2010 LIB	—	2010 CONS	2009 LIB	—	2009 CONS
Economic	39%	—	61%	37%	—	63%
Social	36%	—	63%	40%	—	60%
Foreign	12%	—	79%	26%	—	68%
Composite	31%	—	69%	35%	—	65%

Key Votes of the 111th Congress

1. Overturn Ledbetter	N	5. Bar federal abortion funds	Y	9. Stop detainee transfers	Y
2. Pass $820 billion stimulus	N	6. Pass health care bill	N	10. Legalize immigrants' kids	N
3. Let guns in national parks	Y	7. Regulate financial firms	N	11. Repeal don't ask, tell	N
4. Pass cap-and-trade	N	8. Pass tax cuts for some	N	12. Limit campaign funds	N

Election Results

2010 general	Jim Gerlach (R)	133,770	(57%)	($2,120,901)
	Manan Trivedi (D)	100,493	(43%)	($1,448,024)
2010 primary	Jim Gerlach (R)	35,575	(80%)	
	Patrick Sellers (R)	8,998	(20%)	

Prior Winning Percentages: 2008 (52%), 2006 (51%), 2004 (51%), 2002 (51%)

Population		Race/Ethnicity		Work	
Pop. 2010:	726,465	White:	79.2%	Private:	85.7%
Change since 2000:	Up 12.4%	Black:	7.4%	Government:	8.6%
Urban:	85.8%	Hispanic:	7.8%	Self-employed:	5.6%
Rural:	14.2%	Asian:	3.7%	Blue collar:	17.3%
Area size:	819 sq. mi.	Native Am.:	0.1%	White collar:	69.1%
		Hawaiian:	0.0%	Khaki collar:	0.1%
Age		Two+ races:	1.6%	Other:	13.5%
Median age:	39.0 yrs.				
More than 65 yrs:	13.6%	*Ancestry*		Median income:	$70,585
Less than 18 yrs:	23.6%	German	20.1%	Median Home Value:	$262,800
		Irish	14.5%		
Education		Italian	10.6%	**Military Veterans**	
H.S. grad:	90.3%			% of Pop:	9.3%
College grad:	39.8%				
Grad degree:	15.9%				

Chester and Montgomery Counties

The gentle hills of southeastern Pennsylvania, settled in the 18th century by Quaker townsmen, Welsh farmers, German peasants, and members of pietistic sects who became known as the Pennsylvania Dutch, were America's first polyglot interior. Before and after independence, a diverse lot looking for tolerance in the area above Philadelphia and the Delaware River found a land that yielded riches, first in crops, then in ironworking. Valley Forge is where Gen.

2008 Presidential Vote

Barack Obama (D)	206,593	(58%)
John McCain (R)	147,207	(41%)

2004 Presidential Vote

John Kerry (D)	167,431	(51%)
George Bush (R)	156,634	(48%)

Cook Partisan Voting Index: D+4

George Washington and his men spent the terrible winter and spring of 1777-78, while the British luxuriated in Philadelphia 25 miles away. In Revolutionary times, the area was countryside, a long day's ride from the markets and docks of Philadelphia. Then, rail lines were built from Philadelphia: The Main Line of the Pennsylvania Railroad headed west to industrial Pittsburgh and the Midwest, and the Reading Railroad headed northwest to Reading and the anthracite coalfields beyond. Factories were built in some of the towns here, and many farms continued to thrive, but by the late 19th century, some of the land had become commuter territory.

The most lavish Philadelphia suburbs were built on the Main Line, where in mansions shaded by huge trees, Philadelphia's captains of commerce could get respite from the row houses and narrow streets of the city. This was affluent suburbia for the masses, or a large part of them. Prosperity even came to some of the factory towns. Reading, the decaying industrial town that inspired John Updike's *Rabbit* novels, in the 1970s was the site of the first factory outlet store, when a company called Vanity Fair began selling seconds and overruns of stockings and lingerie at wholesale prices. But it remains an economically challenged area. Berks County posted one of the state's highest unemployment rates in 2010.

The 6th Congressional District of Pennsylvania includes parts of this countryside in Chester County, which has about 40% of the population, and Berks and Montgomery counties, with 30% each. Chester County has the highest median income levels in the region. The boundaries of the 6th District are irregular. Geographically, the main body of the district is northern Chester County, including Coatesville, Downingtown, and Phoenixville, and southern Berks County. The district also includes a salient that runs northward in eastern Berks County, with its rapidly growing exurbs. Another, much more heavily populated, salient reaches into Montgomery County from Pottstown to Lower Merion Township, which is home to some of Philadelphia's wealthiest people. The district includes Valley Forge, with its American Revolution Center; part but not all of Reading; and most of the Main Line suburbs: Ardmore, Bryn Mawr, and part of Paoli. Until the 1990s, the area had been heavily Republican, and the district was drawn for a Republican. The suburbs of Philadelphia, like those in other large metropolitan areas, had been trending to the Democrats since 2000. Democratic presidential nominee John Kerry carried the district 51%-48% in 2004, and Barack Obama won it 58%-41% in 2008. He led comfortably in each of the three counties, illustrative of his strong showing in the Philadelphia suburbs. In the 2010 governor's race, Republican Tom Corbett was able to easily win Chester and Berks counties, while Democrat Dan Onorato took Montgomery County 52%-48%.

Jim Gerlach (R)

The congressman from the 6th District is Jim Gerlach, a moderate Republican elected in 2002. After surviving two of the House's fiercest re-election battles in 2004 and 2006, he abandoned a bid for governor in 2010 and retained his seat with ease. His decision to remain in the House earned him a prized slot on the Ways and Means Committee.

Gerlach grew up in Ellwood City, Pa., midway between Pittsburgh and Youngstown, Ohio. He graduated from Dickinson College and its law school, just west of Harrisburg. He continued moving east, settled in Chester County, and practiced law. He was elected to the state House in 1990 and to the state Senate in 1994. When Republicans in 2002 created a new district in suburban Philadelphia, Gerlach was the obvious intended beneficiary. He had spirited competition from Democrat Dan Wofford, a former adviser to Democratic Gov. Robert Casey. Wofford had not previously run for office, but his name was well known; his father, Harris Wofford, was elected to the Senate in a 1991 special election. Gerlach ran on his legislative accomplishments, including votes to expand Pennsylvania's prescription drug program for low-income seniors. Wofford attacked Gerlach as a career politician. Polls showed the race close, and national Republicans spent more than $1.5 million on ads for Gerlach. The outcome was not clear until the early-morning hours, when Gerlach won 51%-49%.

In the House, Gerlach's voting record is mostly moderate, though it is more conservative on foreign policy. He has become increasingly loyal to his party. After joining Democrats in 2009 on expanding the State Children's Health Insurance Program, a food safety overhaul, and several other social issues, he toed the GOP line on major votes in 2010. Earlier, he was a strong supporter of the Bush-era tax cuts and eliminating the marriage penalty in the tax code, but opposed the Bush administration's proposal to create personal retirement accounts in Social Security. He was one of the deciding "yes" votes on the 2005 Central America Free Trade Agreement, which came days after Bush adviser Karl Rove and first lady Laura Bush each held fundraisers for him. He denied any connection.

On Ways and Means, Gerlach has worked on several measures that generated bipartisan support, such as a proposal to make permanent a tax depreciation for restaurant improvements and a bill he had pushed earlier to require dog breeders in high-volume "puppy mills" to be federally licensed and inspected regularly. In October 2005, his late vote helped Republican leaders to win narrow passage of a bill to facilitate construction of new oil refineries.

With House Republicans seemingly ensconced in the minority in July 2009, Gerlach announced his candidacy for governor, fashioning himself as a fiscal conservative and social moderate in the mold of popular former Gov. Tom Ridge. But Gerlach faced a steep battle in winning over Western Pennsylvania voters, and his poll numbers fell after Ridge threw his support behind Attorney General Tom Corbett. Gerlach withdrew in January 2010, leaving the Republican nomination open to Corbett, who eventually won the post.

After brushing aside a tea party challenger in the Republican primary for his House seat, Gerlach won re-election with ease for the first time that fall, over Democratic physician Manan Trivedi, 57%-43%.

Gerlach previously had been a prime Democratic target. In 2004, he faced Democratic attorney Lois Murphy, who managed Ed Rendell's 2002 gubernatorial campaign in Montgomery County. The well-financed Murphy made it an unexpectedly close contest, but Gerlach won, again by 51%-49%. Two years later, Murphy ran again with strong encouragement from EMILY's List and the Democratic Congressional Campaign Committee. She was better-known and the issues were similar, but the campaign rhetoric was harsher. Gerlach may have benefited from more aggressive attacks by his campaign on alleged inconsistencies in Murphy's agenda. For the third consecutive election, Gerlach won by 51%-49%. In 2008, Gerlach had a more than 3-to-1 fundraising advantage over Democrat Robert Roggio, a retired corporate executive. But he still managed only a 52%-48% win.

SEVENTH DISTRICT

Pat Meehan (R)

Elected 2010, 1st term; b. Oct. 20, 1955, Cheltenham; home, Drexel Hill; Bowdoin Col., B.A. 1978; Temple Law Schl., J.D. 1986.; Catholic; Married (Carolyn); 3 children.

Elected Office: Delaware Cnty. district atty., 1996-2001.

Professional Career: Practicing atty., 1986-91; 2008-10; counsel, Sen. Arlen Specter, R-Pa., 1991-94; campaign aide, Sen. Rick Santorum, R-Pa., 1994; U.S. atty., 2001-08.

DC Office: 513 CHOB, 20515, 202-225-2011; Fax: 202-226-0280; Web site: meehan.house.gov.

State Offices: Springfield, 610-690-7323.

Committees: *Homeland Security:* Counterterrorism & Intelligence (Chmn); Cybersecurity, Infrastructure Protection & Security Technologies. *Oversight & Government Reform:* TARP, Financial Services & Bailouts of Public & Private Programs; Technology, Information Policy, Intergovernmental Relations & Procurement Reform. *Transportation & Infrastructure:* Aviation; Economic Development, Public Buildings & Emergency Management; Railroads, Pipelines & Hazardous Materials.

Election Results

2010 general	Pat Meehan (R)	137,825	(55%)	($3,031,825)
	Bryan Lentz (D)	110,314	(44%)	($1,669,458)
2010 primary	Pat Meehan (R)	unopposed		

Population		Race/Ethnicity		Work	
Pop. 2010:	673,623	White:	80.1%	Private:	85.2%
Change since 2000:	Up 4.2%	Black:	9.7%	Government:	9.6%
Urban:	98.6%	Hispanic:	2.7%	Self-employed:	5.1%
Rural:	1.4%	Asian:	5.7%	Blue collar:	15.1%
Area size:	294 sq. mi.	Native Am.:	0.1%	White collar:	71.7%
		Hawaiian:	0.0%	Khaki collar:	0.0%
Age		Two+ races:	1.5%	Other:	13.2%
Median age:	39.4 yrs.				
More than 65 yrs:	14.7%	*Ancestry*		Median income:	$71,262
Less than 18 yrs:	22.6%	Irish	22.8%	Median Home Value:	$276,000
		Italian	14.9%		
Education		German	14.1%	**Military Veterans**	
H.S. grad:	92.3%			% of Pop:	9.0%
College grad:	41.0%				
Grad degree:	16.9%				

Philadelphia Suburbs

The close-in suburbs of Philadelphia are a mixture of the antique and the high-tech.

A century ago, Delaware County, southwest of Philadelphia, was already filling up, with industrial towns strung out along the rail lines paralleling the Delaware River and bucolic residential suburbs along the inland commuter rail lines. This was at a time when Pennsylvania and Philadelphia were Republican bastions, as devoted to one party as the states of the then-solid Democratic South. Politics in Delaware County in those days was run by a Republican machine headed by state Sen. John McClure of the gritty industrial city of Chester. McClure ran the county Republican Party from 1907 to 1965, and such was his power that in 1960 presidential candidate Richard Nixon stopped by the ailing McClure's home to pay homage. McClure exercised his influence through the War Board, a 15-member panel that decided on all nominations for public office and some less savory business, like making deals with bootleggers during Prohibition, buying votes, and forcing contributions out of public employees. Delaware County even then was multiethnic and multiracial; the black community in Chester predated the Civil War.

2008 Presidential Vote		
Barack Obama (D)	203,407	(56%)
John McCain (R)	157,367	(43%)

2004 Presidential Vote		
John Kerry (D)	184,392	(53%)
George Bush (R)	163,095	(47%)

Cook Partisan Voting Index: D+3

The astonishing thing about this machine was its resilience. The War Board technically went out of business in 1975, but one of its products, Tom Judge, remained county Republican chairman till 2010. Affluent and high-minded suburbs, like Swarthmore, home of the college of that name, were content to let machine Republicans rule, as were blue-collar workers in towns like Chester and Marcus Hook. The current Republican chairman, Andy Reilly, says that the party has been reformed, but it still holds the bulk of offices in the county seat of Media and in most of its 49 municipalities. This despite demographic and political change: Blacks have been moving out of Philadelphia into adjacent Delaware County suburbs in large numbers (they made up 19% of the county's population in 2010), and cultural liberalism in affluent suburbs has led many here to vote Democratic. Delaware County has not gone Republican for president since 1988, when it voted 60%-39% for George H. W. Bush. In 2008, it voted by the identical margin for Democrat Barack Obama. The Republican registration advantage dropped from 63%-28% in 1999 to 46%-43% in 2010.

The 7th District includes almost all of Delaware County, except for a few towns with large African-American populations that are part of Philadelphia's 1st District. The 7th extends north to include a few Montgomery County suburbs, such as modest Conshohocken, an old Schuylkill River factory town that is now the U.S. headquarters for Swedish home furnishings retailer IKEA. It also includes affluent Upper Merion Township and King of Prussia, an edge city where the Schuylkill Expressway intersects the Pennsylvania Turnpike. The 7th takes in southeastern Chester County, including part of the commercial hub of West Chester and a few farther out suburbs such as Malvern and part of Paoli. About 70% of the population is in Delaware County, with the remainder split between Montgomery and Chester counties. The 7th includes the elite small colleges of Haverford and Swarthmore, and the refined farm country of Chadds Ford, home to generations of Wyeth artists. It also includes Boeing's big plant in Ridley Park, where the V-22 Osprey and other military planes are assembled. Its population is above average in income and people here have deep roots in greater Philadelphia—the cheesesteak restaurant Tony Luke's has a branch in the Springfield Mall—although they may rarely venture into Center City.

Patrick Meehan (R)

The new congressman from the 7th district is Patrick Meehan, a Republican elected in 2010 and a former U.S. attorney in Philadelphia. Meehan grew up in Cheltenham Township, in Montgomery County, just north of Philadelphia. His father was a construction worker, his mother a secretary. Neither went to college, but Meehan began saving for college when he was 13, walking more than a mile to caddy at a golf course. He helped pay his tuition at Bowdoin College by working at a rubber factory, where he shoveled rubber pellets into an incinerator. He played hockey in college and between 1979 and 1982, worked as a referee in the National Hockey League, a job that he says was good training for politics. He learned to stand behind controversial calls, to be fair in the public spotlight, and to know when to break up a fight and when to let the players slug it out, Meehan told *National Journal*. And he said that standing up to angry hockey players also made going to law school seem less intimidating.

Meehan graduated from Temple University law school, and then went to work for the large law firm founded by long ago Philadelphia Mayor Richardson Dilworth (1956-62). He left the firm in 1991 to become counsel to then-Republican Sen. Arlen Specter. In 1994, Meehan was the campaign manager for Republican Rick Santorum in his successful Senate race against incumbent Democrat Harris Wofford. With his solid Republican credentials, he was elected district attorney in Delaware County in 1995. In that role, he got substantial publicity for the successful prosecution of millionaire John Eleuthère du Pont for the murder of Olympic wrestler Dave Schultz. He also created a special victims unit that allowed domestic violence cases to be prosecuted without victims having to testify in open court. In 2001, on Specter's recommendation, Meehan was appointed U.S. attorney for the Eastern District of Pennsylvania. He brought several high-profile corruption cases against Philadelphia-area politicians, Republicans as well as Democrats, some resulting from wiretaps in the office of Philadelphia Mayor John Street, who himself was not charged with any crime.

When Democratic Rep. Joe Sestak decided to challenge Specter in 2010, Meehan ran for Sestak's House seat. Though the 7th District was trending Democratic, Meehan was a well-known prosecutor with moderate positions on cultural issues. Relying primarily on his Philadelphia-area contacts, he managed to raise $3 million, almost twice that raised by his Democratic opponent, Bryan Lentz, an Iraq war veteran and two-term state representative from Swarthmore. The two differed on economic issues, with Meehan favoring extension of the 2001 and 2003 tax cuts for all taxpayers, and Lentz saying he would carve out an exception for high-income earners. Meehan was endorsed by the United Aerospace Workers Local 1069, which represents workers at Boeing's

Ridley Park plant. But his campaign took a hit when local newspapers reported that a Republican activist had produced some 39 false signatures on Meehan's candidacy petition.

Meehan criticized Lentz for casting ghost votes—having someone else vote for him—in Harrisburg. Lentz's campaign manager vehemently denied it, but then backtracked when Meehan produced testimony from a witness in the spectator's gallery at the state Capitol. Meehan also charged that Democratic volunteers helped place a third-party conservative on the general election ballot to try to draw votes from him.

Meehan won 55%-44%, carrying all three counties in the district. That was a pretty solid margin in a district that had voted 56%-43% for Democrat Barack Obama for president. In Washington, Meehan was one of three freshmen appointed to the Republican Steering Committee, a leadership-run panel that makes committee assignments.

EIGHTH DISTRICT

Mike Fitzpatrick (R)

Elected 2010, 2nd term; b. June 28, 1963, Philadelphia; home, Levittown; St. Thomas U., B.A. 1985; Dickinson Schl. of Law, J.D. 1988; Catholic; Married (Kathleen); 6 children.

Elected Office: Bucks Cnty. Commission, 1994-2004; U.S. House, 2005-07.

Professional Career: Practicing atty., 2007-10.

DC Office: 1224 LHOB, 20515, 202-225-4276; Fax: 202-225-9511; Web site: fitzpatrick.house.gov.

State Offices: Langhorne, 215-579-8102.

Committees: *Financial Services:* Capital Markets and Government Sponsored Enterprises; Oversight & Investigations (VChmn).

Election Results

2010 general	Mike Fitzpatrick (R)	130,759	(54%)	($2,090,793)
	Patrick Murphy (D)	113,547	(46%)	($4,246,047)
2010 primary	Mike Fitzpatrick (R)	33,671	(77%)	
	Gloria Carlineo (R)	6,529	(15%)	
	Ira Hoffman (R)	2,424	(6%)	

Population		Race/Ethnicity		Work	
Pop. 2010:	672,685	White:	86.5%	Private:	83.1%
Change since 2000:	Up 4.2%	Black:	3.7%	Government:	10.9%
Urban:	90.8%	Hispanic:	4.3%	Self-employed:	5.8%
Rural:	9.2%	Asian:	3.9%	Blue collar:	18.6%
Area size:	634 sq. mi.	Native Am.:	0.1%	White collar:	68.5%
		Hawaiian:	0.0%	Khaki collar:	0.2%
Age		Two+ races:	1.3%	Other:	12.7%
Median age:	41.1 yrs.				
More than 65 yrs:	14.2%	*Ancestry*		Median income:	$73,539
Less than 18 yrs:	23.0%	Irish	19.6%	Median Home Value:	$316,900
		German	19.6%		
Education		Italian	11.6%	**Military Veterans**	
H.S. grad:	91.3%			% of Pop:	9.5%
College grad:	33.1%				
Grad degree:	12.8%				

Philadelphia Suburbs; Bucks County

Bucks County was one of Pennsylvania founding father William Penn's three original settlements and the launching point for George Washington's crossing of the frigid Delaware River to surprise English and Hessian forces on Christmas Day 1776. But it has had a split personality from the start. Upper Bucks County was at once a bucolic paradise of rolling hills and creeks running into the Delaware River and, after Penn's secretary, James Logan, built the Durham Furnace

2008 Presidential Vote		
Barack Obama (D) 192,570	(54%)
John McCain (R) 160,695	(45%)
2004 Presidential Vote		
John Kerry (D) 177,008	(51%)
George Bush (R) 165,239	(48%)
Cook Partisan Voting Index: D+2		

iron works in 1727, it became one of the nation's major industrial sites. In the 1920s, Bucks County's well-settled farmland, old fieldstone houses and covered bridges captured the imagination of writers and artists, attracting the New York theatrical crowd—Oscar Hammerstein, Moss Hart, Dorothy Parker, S. J. Perelman. New Hope remains a popular weekend spot with hip boutiques and restaurants. After World War II, its location between Philadelphia and Trenton, N.J., brought industrial Lower Bucks County to the forefront. The ocean-navigable Delaware River and several rail lines resulted in huge new developments: U.S. Steel's Fairless Works, one of the few big postwar steel plants, and the Levitt organization's second Levittown, in what had been a swamp between U.S. 13 and U.S. 1. The steel mill closed in 1991 and a wind turbine plant on part of the site was the venue for a visit from President Barack Obama in April 2011.

Historically, Bucks County was heavily Republican, but more recently, it has been marginal. This was the home of Republican Sen. Joseph Grundy, longtime head of the Pennsylvania Manufacturers Association, who opposed the 1930 Smoot-Hawley tariff as insufficiently protectionist. Development in Bucks came after the New Deal, unlike other suburban Philadelphia counties, where most blue-collar immigration occurred decades earlier. Lower Bucks around Fairless Works and Levittown, with its tightly packed homes filled with blue-collar workers, became Democratic. Upper Bucks, faster-growing and attracting trendy New Yorkers, has favored Democratic policies such as green space programs to keep developers away.

The 8th Congressional District of Pennsylvania includes all of Bucks County, a tiny finger of Montgomery County and parts of two wards in Northeast Philadelphia. Bucks has a small minority population and the second highest income of any county in the state. The 8th was marginal in elections during the 1980s. Since then, it has moved with other Philadelphia suburban areas toward the Democrats and has voted for Democratic presidential candidates since 1992. Obama won the district 54%-45% in 2008.

Mike Fitzpatrick (R)

The new congressman from the 8th District is Mike Fitzpatrick, a Republican elected in 2004, defeated in 2006, and elected again in 2010. Fitzpatrick grew up in Bucks County's Levittown, one of seven children. He was an Eagle Scout and graduated from St. Thomas University and Dickinson School of Law at Penn State University. From 1994 to 2004, he served on the Bucks County Commission, where he worked on land preservation and had a reputation for supporting environmental causes. The House seat first came open when Rep. Jim Greenwood, a moderate Republican, announced in July 2004 that he would not seek re-election after accepting an offer to head of the Biotechnology Industry Organization. However, Greenwood had already won the Republican primary, so local Republican leaders chose Fitzpatrick to replace him on the general election ballot. He went on to win 55%-43%. In the House, he sponsored a successful bill requiring schools and libraries to restrict minors' access to social networking sites and chat rooms.

In 2006, Fitzpatrick was challenged by Democrat Patrick Murphy, the son of a Philadelphia policeman and an Army lawyer and Iraq war veteran. Murphy favored an end to the war at a time antiwar sentiments were running high. Fitzpatrick tried to distance himself from the Bush administration's policies in Iraq. When Fitzpatrick ran an ad questioning Murphy's claim that he had worked as a Justice Department prosecutor, Murphy declared at a forum, "Mike, you are a liar and a coward." Murphy won 50.3%-49.7%, with a popular vote margin of 1,518 votes out of almost 250,000 votes cast. Fitzpatrick returned to private law practice. He was later diagnosed with colon cancer; after treatment, doctors gave him a clean bill of health in 2010.

That year was shaping up to be a favorable political climate for Republicans, and Fitzpatrick decided to try to get the seat back. In the GOP primary, Fitzpatrick had three opponents and was viewed as the establishment candidate, endorsed by *The Philadelphia Inquirer.* He was embarrassed, however, by a comment he made about primary opponent Gloria Carlineo, whom he called an "immigrant," even though she hails from Puerto Rico. Fitzpatrick later said he meant the comment as a compliment in the sense that she is living the American dream. Fitzpatrick won the primary with 77% of the vote.

In the general election, Fitzpatrick emphasized not the environmental issues he had in the past, but his opposition to the Obama administration. "Cash for clunkers, Obamacare, stimulus—no jobs. We've wasted a lot of money in the last few years," he told *The New York Times*. Like many Democrats in 2010, Murphy emphasized his support for allowing the Bush-era tax cuts to expire for high-income earners while extending them for other taxpayers. Murphy also attacked Fitzpatrick for "Fitzflops"—formerly co-sponsoring and now opposing a bill making it easier to organize labor unions, and formerly bragging of being one of the House's most liberal Republicans but now campaigning as a tea partier.

Murphy was a favorite of many Democratic insiders who hoped that, at age 37, he might someday be a statewide candidate. He had also raised his profile as the leader in the House effort to repeal the ban on openly gay service personnel in the military. Murphy spent $4.3 million, more than twice the $2 million Fitzpatrick spent. Nonetheless Fitzpatrick won by a decisive 54%-46%. After the election, he told the *Bucks County Courier Times*, "This election was a referendum on President Obama's handling of the economy and it was also a referendum on Pat Murphy because Murphy is Obama."

NINTH DISTRICT

Bill Shuster (R)

Elected May 2001, 5th full term; b. Jan. 10, 1961, McKeesport; home, Hollidaysburg; Dickinson Col., B.A. 1983; American U., M.B.A. 1987; Lutheran; married (Rebecca); 2 children.

Professional Career: Mgr., Goodyear Tire & Rubber Co., 1983-87; District mgr., Bandag Inc., 1987-90; Owner & gen. mgr., Shuster Chrysler, 1990-2001.

DC Office: 204 CHOB, 20515, 202-225-2431; Fax: 202-225-2486; Web site: shuster.house.gov.

State Offices: Chambersburg, 717-264-8308; Hollidaysburg, 814-696-6318; Indiana, 724-463-0516; Somerset, 814-443-3918.

Committees: *Armed Services:* Tactical Air & Land Forces; Emerging Threats & Capabilities. *Transportation & Infrastructure:* Highways & Transit; Railroads, Pipelines & Hazardous Materials (Chmn); Water Resources & Environment.

Group Ratings

	ACLU	ACU	ADA	CFG	AFS	FRC	LCV	ITIC	NTU	COC
2010	13	100	0	84	0	100	0	33	88	88
2009	–	88	5	77	22	–	7	–	81	87

National Journal Ratings

	2010 LIB	—	2010 CONS	2009 LIB	—	2009 CONS
Economic	23%	—	77%	23%	—	76%
Social	0%	—	85%	23%	—	77%
Foreign	12%	—	79%	0%	—	75%
Composite	16%	—	84%	20%	—	80%

Key Votes of the 111th Congress

1. Overturn Ledbetter	N	5. Bar federal abortion funds	Y	9. Stop detainee transfers	Y
2. Pass $820 billion stimulus	N	6. Pass health care bill	N	10. Legalize immigrants' kids	N
3. Let guns in national parks	Y	7. Regulate financial firms	N	11. Repeal don't ask, tell	N
4. Pass cap-and-trade	N	8. Pass tax cuts for some	N	12. Limit campaign funds	N

Election Results

2010 general	Bill Shuster (R)	141,904	(73%)	($852,099)
	Tom Conners (D)	52,322	(27%)	
2010 primary	Bill Shuster (R)	unopposed		

Prior Winning Percentages: 2008 (64%), 2006 (60%), 2004 (69%), 2002 (71%), 2001 special (52%)

Population		Race/Ethnicity		Work	
Pop. 2010:	666,810	White:	94.4%	Private:	78.8%
Change since 2000:	Up 3.1%	Black:	2.1%	Government:	13.2%
Urban:	40.5%	Hispanic:	1.9%	Self-employed:	7.7%
Rural:	59.5%	Asian:	0.5%	Blue collar:	31.1%
Area size:	7,200 sq. mi.	Native Am.:	0.1%	White collar:	51.3%
		Hawaiian:	0.0%	Khaki collar:	0.2%
Age		Two+ races:	1.0%	Other:	17.4%
Median age:	41.2 yrs.				
More than 65 yrs:	16.6%	*Ancestry*		Median income:	$43,763
Less than 18 yrs:	21.8%	German	30.3%	Median Home Value:	$122,500
		Irish	12.4%		
Education		English	6.1%	**Military Veterans**	
H.S. grad:	84.8%			% of Pop:	12.1%
College grad:	15.7%				
Grad degree:	5.5%				

South Central Pennsylvania; Altoona

The old towns of south central Pennsylvania look much as they did a century ago: farmhouses and red barns set amidst rolling hills in the shadow of mountain ridges, seemingly isolated from the pulsing rhythms of 21st century America. But this tranquility was shattered on September 11, 2001, when United Airlines Flight 93 crashed into an empty former coalfield near Shanksville in Somerset County, killing all 40 passengers and crew on board. To Americans,

2008 Presidential Vote
John McCain (R) 176,023   (63%)
Barack Obama (D) 98,430   (35%)

2004 Presidential Vote
George Bush (R) 183,717   (67%)
John Kerry (D) 89,208   (33%)
Cook Partisan Voting Index: R+17

the crash site became a symbol of both sadness and pride at the passengers' effort to wrest back control of the plane, initiated by the now-famous cry of "Let's roll!" The National Park Service has been working to complete a permanent memorial to Flight 93 by the 10th anniversary of the attacks. In 2002, Somerset County was struck again by catastrophe when nine miners at the Quecreek coal mine were trapped by rising waters 240 feet underground. As a breathless nation looked on, rescuers strained to dig rescue shafts, and this time, the outcome was happy. After 77 hours in confinement, the miners were lifted one by one to safety.

The Appalachian Mountains run like a series of vertebrae up and down central Pennsylvania, long posing a formidable barrier. During the 18th century, the mountains provided Quaker Pennsylvania with a rampart against Indian attacks, and allowed the Commonwealth to become the richest and most populous of the colonies. But the colonials led by Gen. Edward Braddock to defeat near Pittsburgh in 1754 found the mountains hard-going, despite guidance from George Washington. Nineteenth century pioneers in Conestoga wagons found it not much easier. Later, the mountains proved to be a barrier to commerce, and people flocked to the easier routes through New York: the Erie Canal and the New York Central Railroad.

It took the aggressive capitalists who built the Pennsylvania Railroad to get trains over the ridges. Conquering the mountains near Altoona required the work of several hundred Irish laborers, equipped with hand tools, gunpowder and pack animals. They built Horseshoe Curve between 1851 and 1854, one of the finest examples of railroad engineering anywhere. The local AA baseball team is called the Altoona Curve. Though Pennsylvania's rail links remained important—the Nazis considered them key sabotage targets during World War II—the war-bound nation in 1940 opened the road of the future here: the Pennsylvania Turnpike, the first highway in America that was able to move vehicles dependably at high speeds over long distances. "The Pennsylvania Turnpike is a triumph of engineering," wrote Tom Lewis in *Divided Highways*, a study of the interstate highway system. The road tunnels under the Allegheny Mountains and cuts about five hours off the journey between the cities.

Pennsylvania's 9th Congressional District takes in a wide swath of south and central Pennsylvania, including six full counties and parts of eight others. Most of the 9th is not coal country and was thus spared the boom-bust cycles of northeastern Pennsylvania and West Virginia. But this is a slow-growth, low-income area today. The largest city is Altoona, which withered from 82,000 people in 1930 to 46,000 in 2010 as the once-prosperous Pennsylvania Railroad succumbed to competition from truck traffic. Politically, this part of Pennsylvania has been solidly Republican since 1860, when Mercersburg resident James Buchanan left the White House, and has not come close to electing a Democrat to Congress for decades. George W. Bush won 64% of the vote here in 2000 and 67% in 2004. John McCain won the district with 63% in 2008, his best performance in the Northeast, and Republican gubernatorial winner Tom Corbett drew at least 65% of the vote in each of the district's counties in 2010.

Bill Shuster (R)

The congressman from the 9th District is Bill Shuster, a Republican who won a May 2001 special election to succeed his father, Bud Shuster, the powerful chairman of the Transportation and Infrastructure Committee in the 1990s. The younger Shuster has become an important GOP figure on transportation issues in his own right.

Bill Shuster grew up in the Pittsburgh area, where his father started a successful business. After graduating from Dickinson College and American University's business school, he moved to Blair County, where he took over the family's car dealership, Shuster Chrysler in East Freedom, near Altoona. He sold the business in 2002.

Bud Shuster announced his resignation in January 2001, unhappy that Republican leaders refused him an exemption from term limits on chairmanships. The contest for the House seat was for all practical purposes decided at a district-wide Republican convention. Facing nine other contenders, Shuster, with back-room help from his father, ran an insider campaign that took advantage of his father's name and years of service. Although there was some local grumbling about a Shuster dynasty, opponents failed to coalesce behind a candidate. Shuster won 69 of the 133 votes, two more than the required majority. National Democrats ignored the race in the heavily Republican district, which seemed to them hopeless. But Democrat H. Scott Conklin campaigned vigorously as an opponent of abortion rights and gun control. Shuster won by a closer than expected 52%-44%. National Republicans attributed the narrow margin to residual intra-party ill will over Shuster's nomination.

In the House, Bill Shuster has a solidly conservative voting record. Naturally, he ended up on the Transportation and Infrastructure Committee, and in 2011 took the gavel of the Railroads, Pipelines, and Hazardous Materials Subcommittee. Though he had earlier backed additional funding for the government-run Amtrak rail service, he joined committee Chairman John Mica, R-Fla., in arguing in March 2011 that private investment should supplant federal funding in building future rail service. He added an amendment to an aviation bill that month requiring the Federal Aviation Administration to give more weight to economic factors before adopting safety rules. Safety groups sharply criticized the proposal, but it narrowly passed.

His loyalty to the House GOP agenda has earned him a spot on its whip team and Republican leaders occasionally have called on him for behind-the-scenes jobs, such as reportedly leading an unsuccessful effort to persuade Pennsylvania Democrat Christopher Carney to switch parties in 2009. Shuster does occasionally reach across the aisle, joining with Vermont Democrat Peter Welch in 2011 in an effort to expedite limits on credit-card swipe fees. He said Sheetz Corp. executives told him that such fees were the company's second-largest expense behind labor.

In his father's tradition, Shuster has been an avid practitioner of earmarked spending for his district, a practice that in recent years has been attacked by budget conservatives as wasteful. In 2010, he claimed more than $23 million in earmarks—a figure only slightly below that of his home-state colleague Chaka Fattah, a Democratic member of the Appropriations Committee. But he subsequently went along with House Republicans' push to ban the practice. Democrats lampooned him in March 2009 for taking credit for $9 million to his district from President Barack Obama's economic stimulus bill, even though he had voted against the legislation. He was less amenable to funding for Berkeley, Calif. He tried unsuccessfully to cut $2 million for the city from an appropriations bill in 2008 after Berkeley told Marine recruiters they were unwelcome to set up shop in the city; Shuster called Berkeley "ground zero for radicals and leftist zealots."

Shuster had an unusually strong challenge in the 2004 primary from Michael DelGrosso, a management consultant whose family owns a Blair County tomato sauce company. He said that the district needed a new economic approach. DelGrosso carried Blair County and three nearby counties in the northern part of the district, but Shuster ran strongly elsewhere and squeezed by with a 51%-49% win. He has not been seriously challenged in recent elections.

TENTH DISTRICT

Tom Marino (R)

Elected 2010, 1st term; b. Aug. 15, 1952, Williamsport; home, Cogan Station; Lycoming Col., B.A. 1985; Dickinson Schl. of Law, J.D. 1988; Catholic; Married (Edie); 2 children.

Elected Office: Lycoming Cnty. district atty., 1992-2002.

Professional Career: U.S. atty., 2002-07; practicing atty., 2007-10.

DC Office: 410 CHOB, 20515, 202-225-3731; Fax: 202-225-9594; Web site: marino.house.gov.

State Offices: Tunkhannock, 570-836-8020; Williamsport, 570-322-3961.

Committees: *Foreign Affairs:* Africa, Global Health & Human Rights; Europe and Eurasia; Middle East & South Asia. *Homeland Security:* Cybersecurity, Infrastructure Protection & Security Technologies; Emergency Preparedness, Response & Communications; Oversight, Investigations & Management. *Judiciary:* Crime, Terrorism & Homeland Security; Intellectual Property, Competition & the Internet.

Election Results

2010 general	Tom Marino (R)	110,599	(55%)	($714,385)
	Christopher Carney (D)	89,846	(45%)	($1,617,154)
2010 primary	Tom Marino (R)	24,435	(41%)	
	David Madeira (R)	18,524	(31%)	
	Malcolm Derk (R)	16,690	(28%)	

Population		Race/Ethnicity		Work	
Pop. 2010:	669,257	White:	92.9%	Private:	79.0%
Change since 2000:	Up 3.5%	Black:	2.4%	Government:	13.3%
Urban:	44.6%	Hispanic:	2.7%	Self-employed:	7.5%
Rural:	55.4%	Asian:	0.7%	Blue collar:	28.5%
Area size:	6,663 sq. mi.	Native Am.:	0.2%	White collar:	53.7%
		Hawaiian:	0.0%	Khaki collar:	0.1%
Age		Two+ races:	1.0%	Other:	17.7%
Median age:	42.2 yrs.				
More than 65 yrs:	16.9%	*Ancestry*		Median income:	$44,507
Less than 18 yrs:	21.5%	German	22.3%	Median Home Value:	$141,800
		Irish	13.2%		
Education		Italian	9.0%	**Military Veterans**	
H.S. grad:	87.1%			% of Pop:	12.0%
College grad:	20.3%				
Grad degree:	7.6%				

Northeast Region; Williamsport

The northeast corner of Pennsylvania is a land of crevassed valleys and rugged mountains, crisscrossed by giant viaducts built for the railroads linking the East Coast with the Great Lakes and the mines to the big cities that heated their houses with the region's anthracite coal. Except for a row of anthracite coal cities from Scranton to Wilkes-Barre, this part of Pennsylvania still has a wild look to it. The superstructure of railroads and Interstate 80 pass through

2008 Presidential Vote		
John McCain (R)	155,438	(54%)
Barack Obama (D)	131,168	(45%)
2004 Presidential Vote		
George Bush (R)	170,880	(60%)
John Kerry (D)	112,923	(40%)
Cook Partisan Voting Index:	R+8	

an area that seems otherwise little touched by recent prosperity. The region has numerous long-established small towns, with solidly built courthouses and banks and elderly citizens. It's a part of the Northeast that seems worlds away from the region's huge central cities and growing suburbs. The biggest towns here are Lewisburg, home of Bucknell University and a major federal penitentiary, and Williamsport, home of the Little League World Series. Only at the eastern edge is there significant growth. Pike County on the Delaware River was the state's second-fastest growing county (the first was Forest County) from 2000 to 2010, increasing in population by 24%, in part as a result of people fleeing high taxes in New Jersey and New York. The local Pocono Mountains are a destination for weekenders and, for a few days each November, for bear hunters. In the winter months, hunters in increasing numbers turn to tracking coyote in the fresh snow.

The 10th Congressional District of Pennsylvania includes all of northeast Pennsylvania except for Scranton, Wilkes-Barre and fast-growing Monroe County, which are in the 11th District. The area's most consequential congressman was probably David Wilmot, who in the 1840s introduced the Wilmot Proviso barring slavery from the New Mexico and California Territories acquired in the Mexican War; this raised the issue of slavery in the territories which led proximately to the Civil War. Wilmot was a founder of the Republican Party. Most people in this part of Pennsylvania have been Republicans ever since. John McCain won the district with 54% in 2008, a sizable dip from George W. Bush's 60% win in 2004.

Tom Marino (R)

The new congressman from the 10th District is Republican Tom Marino, who defeated Democratic Rep. Christopher Carney in 2010. Marino was born and raised in Williamsport, Pa. His father was a janitor and a firefighter, and his mother was a homemaker. After high school, Marino held jobs in manufacturing and managed a bakery for several years before deciding to enroll at Williamsport Area Community College at age 30. He went on to earn a law degree from Penn State University's Dickinson School of Law. He started out with a local law firm, McNerney, Page, Vanderlin & Hall. In 1992, he was elected district attorney for Lycoming County, a post he held until 2002. That year, he was appointed as the U.S. attorney for Pennsylvania's Middle District, which includes Scranton and Harrisburg.

One of the cases he was involved in as a federal prosecutor became an issue in his congressional campaign. Marino once served as a reference for Louis DeNaples on an application for a gambling license for the Mount Airy Casino Resort while his office was investigating DeNaples on another matter. After Marino resigned as U.S. attorney in October 2007, he took a job as an in-house counsel for DeNaples on some of his non-casino businesses.

When his role in the application surfaced during the campaign, Marino said that he had received authorization from his employer, the Justice Department, to help DeNaples with the gambling license. But an Associated Press story in September quoted an anonymous Justice Department source as saying there was no record of Marino seeking approval to serve as a personal reference. Marino then said that he never asked for permission to provide the reference but that it was understood at the time to be aboveboard and ethical, as long as he didn't use his job title in the reference. The DeNaples affair proved to be an ongoing distraction for Marino.

There was also negative reaction to a video clip of Marino shouting at protesters outside a campaign event in Williamsport, Pa. "What do you do for a job?" and "What kind of welfare are you on?" he demanded. The clip was widely distributed on the Internet. But Marino received some public sympathy when he was hospitalized after a head-on collision involving a car whose operator was charged with driving under the influence of alcohol.

During the race, Marino and Carney sparred over Social Security, with the incumbent contending that Marino wanted to eliminate the program and the challenger accusing Carney and Democratic leaders of raiding the Social Security trust fund to pay for other government programs. In the Republican primary in May, Marino defeated retired chiropractor David Madeira and Snyder County Commissioner Malcolm Derk. His connection to DeNaples was a factor in his bitterly negative campaign against Carney, who raised questions about his character and trustworthiness. But in a strong Republican year, Marino won, 55% to 45%.

ELEVENTH DISTRICT

Lou Barletta (R)

Elected 2010, 1st term; b. Jan. 28, 1956, Hazleton; home, Hazleton; Blooms-burg U., attended.; Catholic; Married (Mary Grace); 4 children.

Elected Office: Hazleton City Cncl., 1998-2000; Hazleton mayor, 2000-10.

Professional Career: Co-owner, Interstate Road Marketing, 1984-2000.

DC Office: 510 CHOB, 20515, 202-225-6511; Fax: 202-226-6250; Web site: barletta.house.gov.

State Offices: Hazleton, 570-751-0050.

Committees: *Education & the Workforce:* Early Childhood, Elementary & Secondary Education; Health, Employment, Labor & Pensions; Higher Education & Workforce Training. *Small Business:* Agriculture, Energy & Trade; Contracting & Workforce. *Transportation & Infrastructure:* Economic Development, Public Buildings & Emergency Management; Highways & Transit; Railroads, Pipelines & Hazardous Materials.

Election Results

2010 general	Lou Barletta (R)	102,179	(55%)	($1,290,913)
	Paul Kanjorski (D)	84,618	(45%)	($1,877,477)
2010 primary	Lou Barletta (R)	unopposed		

Population		Race/Ethnicity		Work	
Pop. 2010:	687,860	White:	83.8%	Private:	80.5%
Change since 2000:	Up 6.4%	Black:	5.2%	Government:	14.1%
Urban:	72.6%	Hispanic:	8.1%	Self-employed:	5.2%
Rural:	27.4%	Asian:	1.4%	Blue collar:	26.2%
Area size:	2,249 sq. mi.	Native Am.:	0.1%	White collar:	55.8%
		Hawaiian:	0.0%	Khaki collar:	0.1%
Age		Two+ races:	1.3%	Other:	18.0%
Median age:	41.0 yrs.				
More than 65 yrs:	16.5%	*Ancestry*		Median income:	$43,852
Less than 18 yrs:	21.4%	German	16.6%	Median Home Value:	$140,000
		Irish	14.7%		
Education		Italian	13.0%	**Military Veterans**	
H.S. grad:	86.4%			% of Pop:	11.7%
College grad:	19.3%				
Grad degree:	6.8%				

Northeast Pennsylvania; Scranton

"Coal is the theme song of this city in the hills," the *WPA Guide* said of Scranton in 1940, but even as those words were written, the anthracite kingdom around Scranton and Wilkes-Barre was crumbling. In the 19th century, anthracite had become America's main home heating fuel and the valley along the East Branch of the Susquehanna River was the No. 1 source of anthracite. Thousands of immigrants flocked to the valley, settling in a chain of little cities north and

2008 Presidential Vote		
Barack Obama (D)	164,646	(57%)
John McCain (R)	121,916	(42%)
2004 Presidential Vote		
John Kerry (D)	143,205	(53%)
George Bush (R)	127,866	(47%)
Cook Partisan Voting Index:	D+4	

south of Wilkes-Barre, which is named for two backers of the American Revolution, and Scranton, which is named for its founding family. They took jobs with long hours, modest pay, poor working conditions and high death rates—facts of life that made the violently pro-union Molly Maguires popular here and that spawned periodic clashes between workers and the Pinkerton security forces hired by the industrial moguls. While the supply of coal was endless—the area produced 40% of the world's hard coal—demand proved fleeting. Anthracite production peaked in 1917, with long strikes in 1922 and 1925 quickening the conversion to oil and gas. Demand for anthracite began to fall in the 1920s and plummeted in the 1940s. The counties containing Wilkes-Barre and Scranton, Luzerne and Lackawanna, had 755,000 people in 1930 and 535,000 in 2010. As the area's 50 collieries shut down, the once-ubiquitous coal dust vanished. The local ethnic mix—Irish, Polish, Ukrain-

THIRTEENTH DISTRICT

Allyson Schwartz (D)

Elected 2004, 4th term; b. Oct. 3, 1948, Queens, NY; home, Jenkintown; Simmons Col., B.A. 1970, Bryn Mawr Col., M.S.W. 1972; Jewish; married (David); 2 children.

Elected Office: PA Senate, 1990-2004.

Professional Career: Exec. dir., Elizabeth Blackwell Center, 1975-88; Dep. comm., Philadelphia Human Services Dept., 1988-90.

DC Office: 1227 LHOB, 20515, 202-225-6111; Fax: 202-226-0611; Web site: schwartz.house.gov.

State Offices: Jenkintown, 215-517-6572; Philadelphia, 215-335-3355.

Committees: *Budget. Foreign Affairs:* Middle East & South Asia; Terrorism, Nonproliferation & Trade.

Group Ratings

	ACLU	ACU	ADA	CFG	AFS	FRC	LCV	ITIC	NTU	COC
2010	81	0	90	0	100	0	100	100	6	25
2009	–	0	100	6	100	–	100	–	3	40

National Journal Ratings

	2010 LIB	—	2010 CONS	2009 LIB	—	2009 CONS
Economic	68%	—	32%	64%	—	34%
Social	61%	—	35%	75%	—	20%
Foreign	56%	—	38%	57%	—	43%
Composite	63%	—	37%	67%	—	34%

Key Votes of the 111th Congress

1. Overturn Ledbetter	Y	5. Bar federal abortion funds	N	9. Stop detainee transfers	Y
2. Pass $820 billion stimulus	Y	6. Pass health care bill	Y	10. Legalize immigrants' kids	Y
3. Let guns in national parks	N	7. Regulate financial firms	Y	11. Repeal don't ask, tell	Y
4. Pass cap-and-trade	Y	8. Pass tax cuts for some	Y	12. Limit campaign funds	Y

Election Results

2010 general	Allyson Schwartz (D)	118,710	(56%)	($2,906,212)
	Carson Adcock (R)	91,987	(44%)	($935,168)
2010 primary	Allyson Schwartz (D)	unopposed		

Prior Winning Percentages: 2008 (63%), 2006 (66%), 2004 (56%)

Population		Race/Ethnicity		Work	
Pop. 2010:	674,188	White:	74.8%	Private:	83.3%
Change since 2000:	Up 4.1%	Black:	9.8%	Government:	11.7%
Urban:	98.5%	Hispanic:	6.7%	Self-employed:	4.8%
Rural:	1.5%	Asian:	6.7%	Blue collar:	18.0%
Area size:	258 sq. mi.	Native Am.:	0.1%	White collar:	66.6%
		Hawaiian:	0.0%	Khaki collar:	0.1%
Age		Two+ races:	1.6%	Other:	15.2%
Median age:	40.0 yrs.				
More than 65 yrs:	15.5%	*Ancestry*		Median income:	$59,740
Less than 18 yrs:	23.2%	Irish	19.8%	Median Home Value:	$242,000
		German	16.2%		
Education		Italian	10.2%	**Military Veterans**	
H.S. grad:	88.2%			% of Pop:	9.1%
College grad:	32.4%				
Grad degree:	12.6%				

Northeast Philadelphia

Montgomery County is the proximate hinterland of Philadelphia: rolling hills cut on one side by the Schuylkill River and at intervals by the Pennsylvania and Reading Railroad lines radiating outward from Center City. Older suburbs, both rich and modest, grew up around rail stations, with comfortable houses within walking distance for commuters. Farther out are 18th and 19th century villages, once surrounded by farm fields, now encroached by subdivisions where people depend on cars, not rail lines, to get to work. Montgomery County has its shopping malls and office parks, but not many freeways. Most of the traffic here is along roads on the area's diagonal grid or along the old pikes laid out when Pennsylvania was a colony. It is the most populous and second most affluent county, behind Chester, in suburban Philadelphia, with solid job growth prospects. Its unemployment rate, just 3.6% in April 2008, was more than twice that level during most of 2010, with an unusually broad range of people seeking jobs.

2008 Presidential Vote		
Barack Obama (D)	192,968	(59%)
John McCain (R)	133,740	(41%)
2004 Presidential Vote		
John Kerry (D)	182,552	(56%)
George Bush (R)	140,900	(43%)
Cook Partisan Voting Index:	D+7	

Quite a different place, though adjacent to southern Montgomery County, is Northeast Philadelphia. This is relatively new urban territory, with more than half its houses built after 1950. When the alley-wide streets of North and South Philadelphia and the river wards were already teeming with people, and the Main Line suburbs were well-settled, the workers of Philadelphia's docks, factories and offices were just starting to fill up vacant land here. They settled in neighborhoods like Bustleton, Somerton and Torresdale. Many of Philadelphia's Hispanics live in the industrial river wards along the Delaware River, but the other wards of Northeast Philadelphia are still mostly white and ethnic. Outside investors and Hasidic Jews from New York looking for more space and opportunity have bid up residential prices and have revived a vibrant Jewish community. Some white-collar industries have settled here; Teva Pharmaceuticals USA announced in October 2010 it would expand operations here, creating 200 jobs.

The 13th Congressional District of Pennsylvania includes much of southeastern and central Montgomery County and most of Northeast Philadelphia. From 2000 to 2010, the district's population increased more than 4%. Historically, Montgomery was quintessentially Republican, with a style of politics set for years by Ivy-educated Republican men. But the county, like other affluent suburbs in the Boston-Washington corridor, swung toward the Democratic Party in national politics in the 1990s, with abortion rights and other cultural issues usually trumping economic interests. Montgomery voted by large margins for Republicans Ronald Reagan and George H.W. Bush in the 1980s, but has voted strongly for Democratic presidential candidates since then. Northeast Philadelphia has a different political heritage. Its feisty Republican organization has won some elections and shown facility in making deals to get its share of patronage. Republican John McCain's presidential campaign made a big advertising and organizational drive in this area in 2008, but Democrat Barack Obama won 60% of the vote in Northeast Philly and 57% in Montgomery County, for an overall 59%-41% win in the district. In the 2010 governor's race, Democrat Dan Onorato took Montgomery by a narrower 52%-48% over Republican Tom Corbett, the eventual winner.

Allyson Schwartz (D)

The congresswoman from the 13th District is Allyson Schwartz, a Democrat elected in 2004. She leveraged her considerable professional expertise on health-care issues into an influential role in the 2010 health care debate, and also has emerged as a Democratic political strategist.

Schwartz's mother fled Vienna as a teenager in 1938, after the Germans annexed Austria, and traveled alone to the United States, where she was taken in by a Jewish foster home in Philadelphia. Her father was a dentist in Flushing, Queens, where she grew up. A graduate of Simmons College with a master's degree in social work from Bryn Mawr College, Schwartz started a women's health center in 1975 and worked on health care issues as first deputy commissioner for the Philadelphia Department of Human Services. Her husband is a cardiologist. In 1990, Schwartz was elected to the state Senate. In 2000, she ran for the U. S. Senate and finished second in the Democratic primary, with 27% of the vote, behind U.S. Rep. Ron Klink, who had 41%.

The 13th District seat opened when Democratic Rep. Joe Hoeffel ran, unsuccessfully, against then-Republican Sen. Arlen Specter in 2004. Schwartz faced two rounds of serious competition. In the primary, her opponent was Joe Torsella, an aide to then-Philadelphia Mayor Ed Rendell. She was backed by EMILY's List, which spent $170,000 on her behalf and conducted voter outreach. Torsella did well in the city portion of the district, but Schwartz carried Montgomery County with 62%, for an overall win of 52%-48%.

In the general election, Fitzpatrick opponent was Republican Melissa Brown, an ophthalmologist who supported abortion rights. Schwartz called herself a "new Democrat," not a liberal, but Brown labeled her a radical. Schwartz called Brown "sleazy" because of her links to a bankrupt health maintenance organization and a lawsuit that the state insurance department filed against her. "The two opponents proved that women can sling mud as capably as any men," *The Philadelphia Inquirer* observed. Both candidates emphasized health care. Schwartz emphasized her sponsorship of the State Children's Health Insurance Program, which provided health insurance for 133,000 children from low-income families. Brown, a physician with an M.B.A., called for changes in tort law, arguing that it would keep doctors' liability insurance down and lower the cost of health care. Schwartz won 56%-41%, getting 60% of the vote in Northeast Philadelphia and 53% in Montgomery County. Schwartz's 2010 Republican opponent, Carson Dee Adcock, dubbed her "the Nancy Pelosi of the East." But Schwartz had voted frequently with moderate Democrats, and was a vice-chairman of the moderate New Democrat Coalition.

As a member of the Ways and Means Committee in 2009, Schwartz proposed the creation of "Health Care Innovation Zones" to better coordinate care among physicians, hospitals and other providers. During the subsequent health care overhaul debate, she led the efforts to include a provision barring insurance companies from denying coverage to children and adults with pre-existing conditions, as well as ensuring adult children could remain on their parents' coverage until age 26 and eliminating copayments for seniors' preventive care services. She also added an amendment to a House-passed water quality bill in March 2009 calling for a study of how pharmaceuticals can harm the U.S. water supply. In other issues on the committee, Schwartz played a central role in the House's November 2007 passage of the bilateral trade agreement with Peru. As a condition of her support, she secured assurances of environmental and labor protections in that country. She lost her seat on Ways and Means after the GOP takeover slashed the number of Democratic seats, but she remained on the Budget Committee.

Schwartz has been re-elected easily, and has climbed the ranks at the Democratic Congressional Campaign Committee and was put in charge of candidate recruiting for the 2012 election. Her district stands to gain more Democrats in 2012 as Republicans add voters through redistricting to shore up the political fortunes of the Philadelphia area's four suburban Republicans.

FOURTEENTH DISTRICT

Mike Doyle (D)

Elected 1994, 9th term; b. Aug. 5, 1953, Pittsburgh; home, Forest Hills; PA St. U., B.S. 1975; Catholic; married (Susan); 4 children.

Elected Office: Swissvale Borough Cncl., 1977-81.

Professional Career: Insurance agent, 1975–77; Exec. dir., Turtle Creek Valley Citizens Union, 1977–79; Chief of Staff, PA Sen. Frank Pecora, 1978–94; Co–Founder/owner, Eastgate Insurance Agency, 1983–present.

DC Office: 401 CHOB, 20515, 202-225-2135; Fax: 202-225-3084; Web site: doyle.house.gov.

State Offices: Pittsburgh, 412-390-1499.

Committees: *Energy & Commerce:* Communications & Technology; Energy & Power.

Group Ratings

	ACLU	ACU	ADA	CFG	AFS	FRC	LCV	ITIC	NTU	COC
2010	81	0	90	0	100	12	90	–	7	14
2009	–	4	95	0	100	–	93	–	1	33

National Journal Ratings

	2010 LIB — 2010 CONS		2009 LIB — 2009 CONS	
Economic	90% —	0%	91% —	0%
Social	86% —	13%	63% —	37%
Foreign	92% —	3%	87% —	9%
Composite	92% —	8%	83% —	18%

Key Votes of the 111th Congress

1. Overturn Ledbetter	Y	5. Bar federal abortion funds	Y
2. Pass $820 billion stimulus	Y	6. Pass health care bill	Y
3. Let guns in national parks	N	7. Regulate financial firms	Y
4. Pass cap-and-trade	Y	8. Pass tax cuts for some	Y

9. Stop detainee transfers	N
10. Legalize immigrants' kids	Y
11. Repeal don't ask, tell	Y
12. Limit campaign funds	Y

Election Results

2010 general	Mike Doyle (D)	122,073	(69%)	($726,537)
	Melissa Haluszczak (R)	49,997	(28%)	($61,137)
	Ed Bortz (Green)	5,400	(3%)	
2010 primary	Mike Doyle (D)	unopposed		

Prior Winning Percentages: 2008 (91%), 2006 (90%), 2004 (100%), 2002 (100%), 2000 (69%), 1998 (68%), 1996 (56%), 1994 (55%)

Population		Race/Ethnicity		Work	
Pop. 2010:	584,493	White:	68.5%	Private:	84.8%
Change since 2000:	Down 9.5%	Black:	24.3%	Government:	10.9%
Urban:	99.8%	Hispanic:	1.9%	Self-employed:	4.2%
Rural:	0.2%	Asian:	2.7%	Blue collar:	16.0%
Area size:	170 sq. mi.	Native Am.:	0.2%	White collar:	63.2%
		Hawaiian:	0.0%	Khaki collar:	0.1%
Age		Two+ races:	2.3%	Other:	20.7%
Median age:	38.5 yrs.				
More than 65 yrs:	16.3%	*Ancestry*		Median income:	$36,864
Less than 18 yrs:	18.7%	German	17.1%	Median Home Value:	$84,100
Education		Irish	13.3%		
H.S. grad:	89.0%	Italian	10.8%	**Military Veterans**	
College grad:	27.7%			% of Pop:	10.3%
Grad degree:	12.0%				

Pittsburgh Suburbs

The Golden Triangle is the inevitable focus of Pittsburgh, the tip of land where the Allegheny and Monongahela rivers come together to form the Ohio. It has been a strategic site for more than 200 years. During the French and Indian War, British Gen. Edward Braddock's army was heading to Fort Duquesne, with George Washington helping lead the way, when it was ambushed and famously defeated in 1754. A few years later, the first American city west of the

2008 Presidential Vote

Barack Obama (D)	209,749	(70%)
John McCain (R)	86,703	(29%)

2004 Presidential Vote

John Kerry (D)	205,636	(69%)
George Bush (R)	88,316	(30%)

Cook Partisan Voting Index: D+19

Appalachian chain was carved out of the wilderness and named after the English statesman William Pitt. Pittsburgh grew rapidly in the days when most of the nation's commerce moved over water. When railroads became ascendant, Pittsburgh still did nicely, since rail lines tend to run along the riverside rather than scaling mountains. Then Andrew Carnegie, a Scottish immigrant, foresaw that steel would replace iron for railroad bridges. He built a steel factory in Pittsburgh, which was then not much more than a rail junction but one blessed with ready deposits of coal and access to iron ore from the Great Lakes. Carnegie built his capacity to the point that when he sold out in 1901, the resulting U.S. Steel Corporation held a near-monopoly.

The Pittsburgh that Carnegie and his steel men built was one of giant mills in the bottomlands along the rivers and massive buildings downtown, such as H.H. Richardson's classic Allegheny County Courthouse building. Back then, the smog—a word used here long before it was a problem in Los Angeles—was so bad that street lights had to stay on all day downtown. A famous 1947 photograph shows a midnight-like darkness at nine in the morning. But then, an alliance of local elected officials and corporate titans, including the leaders of such local *Fortune* 500 companies as USX, Heinz, Alcoa, and PPG, pushed through a series of forceful and visionary projects designed to improve the city's quality of life. Early on, this model produced tremendous successes. In the 1950s, Mayor David Lawrence and financier Richard King Mellon led efforts to cut air pollution, control river flooding, and construct an advanced network of highways and tunnels. They also turned a derelict industrial zone at the three-rivers confluence into Point State Park, a triangular gem that remains popular with office workers. But as the steel industry and other blue-collar industries contracted over the years, so did Pittsburgh. In 1940, it was the nation's 10th largest city, with 672,000 people. In 2010, it was the 58th largest, with 306,000 people.

Pittsburgh is a city of neighborhoods, built on or beneath vertiginous hills, with more bridges, it is often said, than any other city in the world except Venice. Neighborhoods that are situated right next to each other on the map are in fact quite separate and distinct. There is the uptown neighborhood around Carnegie Mellon University and the University of Pittsburgh. These institutions have helped to spur robust high-technology and medical sectors that have replaced some of the lost manufacturing jobs. The city also has become a banking center. Local universities and hospitals now have far more workers than the downsized U.S. Steel Corporation. Such economic diversity helped Pittsburgh survive the 2007-09 recession better than other Rust Belt cities. Among and atop the hills are neighborhoods as different as the predominantly black Hill District, where playwright August Wilson set most of his chronicles. There are WASPy Shadyside and Jewish Squirrel Hill, with fine mansions and fashionable shops. Along the Monongahela River are small industrial neighborhoods and towns, like Clairton, where the classic movie *The Deer Hunter* was set and filmed.

The 14th Congressional District of Pennsylvania includes all of Pittsburgh and the mostly working class suburbs to the east, south and west. There is some suburbia here, but much of the district is in the Monongahela (or Mon) Valley, where the old steel mills stand, or once stood, and the hills above. More affluent suburbs to the north and south are in the 4th and 18th Districts. This is a heavily Democratic district.

Mike Doyle (D)

The congressman from the 14th District is Mike Doyle, an ardently pro-labor Democrat first elected in 1994 who was the most liberal member of Pennsylvania's House delegation in the 111th Congress (2009-10)

Of Irish and Italian descent, Doyle grew up in the Mon Valley town of Swissvale and worked in steel mills during summers off from Penn State. He became an insurance agent and was elected to the Swissvale Borough Council in 1977, at age 24. In 1978, he became chief of staff to state Sen. Frank Pecora, a Republican. Pecora switched parties in 1992 and briefly gave Democrats control of the state Senate. In 1994, Doyle, who had just switched himself to the Democratic Party, ran for the House seat vacated by Republican Rep. Rick Santorum, who ran successfully for the Senate. Doyle was one of seven Democrats and four Republican candidates. With endorsements from labor unions and community leaders, he won the primary. In the general election, he faced John McCarty, an aide to the late Republican Sen. John Heinz. McCarty was pro-abortion rights and Doyle opposed abortion rights. Doyle also campaigned for sweeping health care changes. In a Republican year, he won 55%-45%.

In the House, Doyle had a mixed voting record, often on the right on cultural issues and on the left on economics. During the years in which his party controlled the House and emphasized the latter, he became much more of a progressive populist. As an anti-abortion Catholic, he helped broker the deal on abortion during the final days of the 2010 health care debate that brought other anti-abortion members of his party on board. Two years earlier, he was among the religious-minded lawmakers living together near the Capitol on C Street who confronted their housemate, Nevada GOP Sen. John Ensign, over his affair with the wife of an aide—a revelation that ultimately led Ensign to resign his seat in 2011.

Doyle rarely seeks attention, nor has he caused much of a ruckus. He has worked to reduce foreign imports, and he pushed a bill to create a national historic site at the former U.S. Steel facilities along the Mon River. On the Energy and Commerce Committee, his focus has been on high-tech initiatives, including increased availability of broadband services in underserved areas. He has been a leading advocate of the "Do Not Call" restrictions on telephone marketers, and won passage in 2008 a bill to make the national list permanent. During the debate over so-called cap and trade legislation, which would cap harmful carbon emissions but allow companies to trade on the right to pollute, he vigorously advocated the interests of steel and other Rust Belt industries, even as he sought to work out a compromise with environmentalists. When Republicans in 2011 voted to slash the Environmental Protection Agency's power to regulate emissions, Doyle accused the GOP of "scaring American people" into wrongly believing that failure to curb EPA's authority would cause gasoline prices to rise further.

Doyle is an avid earmarker of spending projects for his district, a practice that has become increasingly controversial with budget conservatives. In 2010 he secured more than $23 million in earmarks, a figure just slightly behind that of fellow Pennsylvania Democrat Chaka Fattah, who sits on the Appropriations Committee. One of Doyle's favorite beneficiaries is the Doyle Center for Manufacturing Technology in South Oakland, which was started in 2003 by a $1.5 federal million grant he helped secure. He also is active on funding autism research and cracking down on illegal dog-breeding called "puppy mills."

Doyle has been politically untouchable and has little to fear from redistricting, when the state is set to lose a House seat in 2012.

FIFTEENTH DISTRICT

Charlie Dent (R)

Elected 2004, 4th term; b. May 24, 1960, Allentown; home, Allentown; PA St. U., B.A. 1982, Lehigh U., M.P.A. 1993; Presbyterian; married (Pamela); 3 children.

Elected Office: PA House of Reps., 1990-98; PA Senate, 1998-2004.

Professional Career: Development officer, Lehigh U., 1986-90.

DC Office: 1009 LHOB, 20515, 202-225-6411; Fax: 202-226-0778; Web site: dent.house.gov.

State Offices: Bethlehem, 610-861-9734; East Greenville, 215-541-4106.

Committees: *Appropriations:* Homeland Security; State, Foreign Operations & Related Programs; Transportation, HUD & Related Agencies. *Ethics.*

Group Ratings

	ACLU	ACU	ADA	CFG	AFS	FRC	LCV	ITIC	NTU	COC
2010	33	61	25	59	38	62	40	67	68	100
2009	–	72	20	64	44	–	36	–	64	87

National Journal Ratings

	2010 LIB — 2010 CONS		2009 LIB — 2009 CONS	
Economic	40%	— 60%	34%	— 65%
Social	40%	— 60%	42%	— 57%
Foreign	39%	— 61%	33%	— 63%
Composite	40%	— 60%	37%	— 63%

Key Votes of the 111th Congress

1. Overturn Ledbetter	N	5. Bar federal abortion funds Y	9. Stop detainee transfers Y
2. Pass $820 billion stimulus	N	6. Pass health care bill N	10. Legalize immigrants' kids N
3. Let guns in national parks	Y	7. Regulate financial firms N	11. Repeal don't ask, tell Y
4. Pass cap-and-trade	N	8. Pass tax cuts for some N	12. Limit campaign funds N

Election Results

2010 general	Charlie Dent (R)..	109,534	(54%)	($2,415,571)
	John Callahan (D)...	79,766	(39%)	($1,995,389)
	Jake Towne (I)	15,248	(7%)	($59,229)
2010 primary	Charlie Dent (R)..	31,618	(83%)	
	Mat Benol (R)...	6,514	(17%)	

Prior Winning Percentages: 2008 (59%), 2006 (54%), 2004 (59%)

Population		Race/Ethnicity		Work	
Pop. 2010:	721,828	White:	77.3%	Private:	84.8%
Change since 2000:	Up 11.7%	Black:	4.6%	Government:	9.9%
Urban:	87.2%	Hispanic:	13.7%	Self-employed:	5.2%
Rural:	12.8%	Asian:	2.6%	Blue collar:	23.5%
Area size:	851 sq. mi.	Native Am.:	0.1%	White collar:	61.1%
		Hawaiian:	0.0%	Khaki collar:	0.0%
Age		Two+ races:	1.5%	Other:	15.4%
Median age:	39.6 yrs.				
More than 65 yrs:	15.0%	*Ancestry*		Median income:	$57,798
Less than 18 yrs:	23.1%	German	22.4%	Median Home Value:	$221,500
		Irish	10.7%		
Education		Italian	9.2%	**Military Veterans**	
H.S. grad:	86.5%			% of Pop:	10.4%
College grad:	26.7%				
Grad degree:	9.9%				

Lehigh Valley; Allentown

Allentown has long been derided by songwriters, from "42nd Street" back in 1933, in which it was scorned as the polar opposite of Broadway, to Billy Joel's "Allentown" in 1982, with its grim picture of closed factories and joblessness. Though both contain nuggets of truth, neither is an entirely fair portrait of Pennsylvania's Lehigh Valley today. Allentown and next-door Bethlehem did suffer when big employers—Mack Truck in Allentown and Bethlehem Steel

2008 Presidential Vote		
Barack Obama (D) 179,589	(56%)
John McCain (R) 139,396	(43%)
2004 Presidential Vote		
John Kerry (D) 150,939	(50%)
George Bush (R) 150,213	(50%)
Cook Partisan Voting Index: D+2		

in Bethlehem—closed down massive plants in the 1980s. Before the recent recession, the Lehigh Valley around Allentown and Bethlehem in recent years had solid growth and low unemployment, thanks to a mix of regional health care networks, telephone call centers for insurance companies and banks, and long-surviving industries, such as Air Products and Chemicals, energy utility PPL and the remnants of Mack Truck's local operations. The recovery has been slow; the region's unemployment rate was 9.6% at the end of 2010, twice what it was prior to the recession. A September job fair in Allentown drew more than 4,300 people.

If the Lehigh Valley is off the main lines of traffic, it does have several features that make it attractive to people from the big city, which helps to explain why its population increased almost 12% from 2000 to 2010, in contrast to the stagnant growth in the Philadelphia area. Commuters seeking less expensive housing and lower taxes are connected by Interstate 78 to New York and by the Northeast Extension to Philadelphia. It has a cluster of colleges—Lehigh, Muhlenberg, Moravian—and a strong regional newspaper in the Allentown *Morning Call*. It has both Dorney Park, one of the nation's oldest amusement parks, and the child-friendly Crayola Factory in Easton. Easton's old industrial buildings, just across the Delaware River from New Jersey, have become something of a magnet for artists seeking inexpensive loft and warehouse space. Bethlehem's Sands Casino Resort employs over 1,000.

The 15th Congressional District of Pennsylvania consists of the Lehigh Valley plus a small adjoining slice of northern Montgomery County, which has 11% of the district's population. Some 14% of the population here is Hispanic, an increase from 8% in 2000, higher than in any other Pennsylvania metropolitan area and a sure sign that the area is generating new jobs. In Allentown, the Hispanic share is 43%. Politically, this has long been a classic swing area, located at the intersection of heavily Democratic industrial precincts and the Republican farmlands of the Pennsylvania Dutch Country. The valley backed Republican Ronald Reagan twice, Republican George H.W. Bush in 1988 and Democrat Bill Clinton twice. It voted for Democrats Al Gore and John Kerry in 2000 and 2004, respectively, by miniscule margins. In the past seven governors' races, it voted for the winner each time: twice for Democrat Robert Casey, twice for Republican Tom Ridge, twice for Democrat Ed Rendell and for Republican Tom Corbett in 2010. Again reflecting the national vote, the district gave Democratic presidential nominee Barack Obama a 56%-43% win in 2008.

Charlie Dent (R)

The congressman from the 15th District is Charlie Dent, a Republican elected in 2004. He is prominent in the rapidly dwindling ranks of moderate House Republicans, and admired by more conservative colleagues for his political survival skills.

Dent grew up in Allentown, graduated from Penn State University and got a graduate degree at Lehigh, where he later worked as a development officer. In 1990, he was elected to the state House and in 1998 to the state Senate. When Republican Rep. Pat Toomey announced that he would run against Sen. Arlen Specter in the 2004 Republican primary, Dent was the front-runner to succeed him. Dent's lifelong residence in the Lehigh Valley was in sharp contrast to the background of the Democratic nominee, businessman Joe Driscoll. Driscoll grew up in Massachusetts, where he went sailing with the Kennedys and made enough money to spend $2 million on this race. But he lived for years in posh Lower Merion Township in Montgomery County, just outside Philadelphia.

Dent framed the campaign as a contest between a native son and a carpetbagging outsider who thought of the Lehigh Valley as "a speed bump on his way to Congress." Driscoll sought to deflect the residency issue with aggressive criticism of the Bush administration, asserting that a vote for Dent was an endorsement of President George W. Bush's by-then unpopular policies. Dent's moderate record, which included support for abortion rights, made it difficult to tie him to

Bush, and he insisted he would be an independent voice in Washington. Dent won 59%-39%. A few weeks after the election, Driscoll's real estate agent said that he put his townhouse here up for sale and moved back to Lower Merion Township.

In the House, Dent has one of the most liberal voting records among members of his party. He is a co-chairman of the Tuesday Group, a caucus of about 49 GOP moderates in a Republican Conference dominated by conservatives. In the 111th Congress (2009-10), he broke from the majority of Republicans to back such issues as expanding the State Children's Health Insurance Program, allowing the Food and Drug Administration to regulate tobacco and overhauling food safety laws. Earlier, he opposed Bush's plan for partial "privatization" of Social Security.

But he has stuck with the GOP on most major economic votes since Barack Obama became president, even refusing Obama's personal entreaties to support the economic stimulus bill in 2009. When he served on the Homeland Security Committee, Dent took positions aligning him with the mainstream of Republicans, pushing a bill to use the Civil Air Patrol to prevent illegal crossings at the border, as well as measures to deport illegal immigrants convicted of crimes in the United States.

Dent in 2011 was rewarded with a seat on the Appropriations Committee. That post also was an acknowledgment of his willingness two years earlier to serve on the House ethics panel, regarded by most lawmakers as an unpalatable chore.

Democrats tried, but failed, to find a credible opponent to Dent in 2006. Northampton County Councilman Charles Dertinger got on the ballot as a write-in candidate, and criticized Dent for Bush's "culture of corruption." Dent won by a surprisingly narrow 54%-43%. In 2008, Democrats nominated Siobhan "Sam" Bennett, who ran an Allentown charity. She spent $950,000, but lost to Dent 59%-41%.

Two years later, Dent faced his toughest opponent by far in Bethlehem Mayor John Callahan. He was one of the few Democratic challengers that year who was able to raise considerable amounts of money and touted his record of creating jobs. Polls showed the race in a statistical dead heat a month before the election, and former President Bill Clinton and Vice President Joe Biden both made campaign stops for Callahan. But Dent was able to paint Callahan as fiscally irresponsible while portraying himself as a restraint on big government spending. The congressman also seized the high ground after Callahan accused him of ignoring veterans, citing his endorsement from the Veterans of Foreign Wars' political action committee. Dent pulled off a surprisingly easy 54%-39% victory, and said shortly afterward that he would consider challenging Democratic Sen. Robert Casey in 2012.

SIXTEENTH DISTRICT

Joe Pitts (R)

Elected 1996, 8th term; b. Oct. 10, 1939, Lexington, KY; home, Kennett Square; Asbury Col., B.A. 1961, West Chester U., M.Ed. 1972; Protestant; married (Virginia); 3 children.

Military Career: Air Force, 1963–69 (Vietnam).

Elected Office: PA House of Reps., 1972–96.

Professional Career: High schl. teacher, 1969–72; Owner, Landscape & Nursery Co., 1974–90.

DC Office: 420 CHOB, 20515, 202-225-2411; Fax: 202-225-2013; Web site: house.gov/pitts.

State Offices: Lancaster, 717-393-0667; Unionville, 610-444-4581.

Committees: *Energy & Commerce:* Environment & the Economy; Health (Chmn).

Group Ratings

	ACLU	ACU	ADA	CFG	AFS	FRC	LCV	ITIC	NTU	COC
2010	13	100	0	89	0	100	10	33	88	88
2009	–	96	5	88	0	–	0	–	88	87

National Journal Ratings

	2010 LIB	—	2010 CONS	2009 LIB	—	2009 CONS
Economic	11%	—	88%	15%	—	84%
Social	0%	—	85%	7%	—	90%
Foreign	12%	—	79%	0%	—	75%
Composite	12%	—	88%	12%	—	88%

Key Votes of the 111th Congress

1. Overturn Ledbetter	N	5. Bar federal abortion funds	Y	9. Stop detainee transfers	Y
2. Pass $820 billion stimulus	N	6. Pass health care bill	N	10. Legalize immigrants' kids	N
3. Let guns in national parks	Y	7. Regulate financial firms	N	11. Repeal don't ask, tell	N
4. Pass cap-and-trade	N	8. Pass tax cuts for some	N	12. Limit campaign funds	N

Election Results

2010 general	Joe Pitts (R)	134,113	(65%)	($759,218)
	Lois Herr (D)	70,994	(35%)	($409,696)
2010 primary	Joe Pitts (R)	unopposed		

Prior Winning Percentages: 2008 (56%), 2006 (57%), 2004 (64%), 2002 (88%), 2000 (67%), 1998 (71%), 1996 (59%)

Population		Race/Ethnicity		Work	
Pop. 2010:	723,977	White:	79.4%	Private:	84.6%
Change since 2000:	Up 12.0%	Black:	4.1%	Government:	8.5%
Urban:	76.0%	Hispanic:	13.3%	Self-employed:	6.6%
Rural:	24.0%	Asian:	1.8%	Blue collar:	26.6%
Area size:	1,326 sq. mi.	Native Am.:	0.1%	White collar:	57.1%
		Hawaiian:	0.0%	Khaki collar:	0.0%
Age		Two+ races:	1.3%	Other:	16.2%
Median age:	36.7 yrs.				
More than 65 yrs:	13.6%	*Ancestry*		Median income:	$56,141
Less than 18 yrs:	25.8%	German	26.7%	Median Home Value:	$204,600
		Irish	10.2%		
Education		English	6.9%	**Military Veterans**	
H.S. grad:	82.6%			% of Pop:	9.1%
College grad:	26.5%				
Grad degree:	9.2%				

Southeast Pennsylvania; Lancaster

The Pennsylvania Dutch Country, settled by Germans in the 18th century when it was Pennsylvania's frontier, remains a distinctive part of America. These Germans were Amish and Mennonite, pietistic sects seeking religious liberty and determined to farm rich lands in the same intensive way they had in Germany. Today, many of their descendants—the Eisenhower family is the most famous example—have blended into mainstream America. But in the

2008 Presidential Vote		
John McCain (R) 161,844	(51%)
Barack Obama (D) 150,341	(48%)
2004 Presidential Vote		
George Bush (R) 182,856	(61%)
John Kerry (D) 113,193	(38%)
Cook Partisan Voting Index: R+8		

Dutch area around Lancaster, many "Plain People" still live in the old way, though today they are willing to use some modern devices, such as battery-powered electricity. Though larger communities exist in Ohio and Indiana, tourists can still see families of Plain People clad in black, clattering over the back roads in horse-drawn carriages, with scrupulously tended farms set amid rolling hills and barns decorated with hex signs.

Beneath the surface, Amish communities are facing the strains of modernity. In recent years, Amish teens have attracted public attention for using drugs and alcohol while participating in the "rumschpringes," a period when adolescents are freed from their community's rigid rules and mores, before being given the choice of returning to the fold as an adult. Some families have been moving out of the region, drawn by cheaper land in states such as Colorado. Modern-style crime also invades their peaceful lifestyle. In October 2006, five girls were killed and five others seriously wounded by a gunman at their one-room schoolhouse in Nickel Mines. The local Amish community quickly demolished the building and erected a new one six months later. But the community remains robust, and tourism, much of it linked to interest in the Amish, brings in 11million people annually.

Agriculture is the other pillar of the local economy. Farmers here produce some of the highest per-acre yields on earth. (Many do use some farming technology, as well as pesticides.) Within an easy drive from Philadelphia, Baltimore and Washington, the area has also become home to outlet malls, a fitting development given that the first Woolworth's five-and-dime store opened in Lancaster in 1879. Lancaster County and Chester County grew by double-digit rates in the 1990s, but the 2007-09 recession undid some of that growth. Average personal income in Lancaster County dropped 2% in 2009, the largest one-year decrease among the state's metropolitan areas. And during the previous decade, the county's income growth was the third weakest in Pennsylvania. The situation led some Amish to consider taking new and previously unconsidered jobs. One told *USA Today* in September 2010 that he bought a restaurant and potato chip company because he needed another source of income besides the building industry.

The 16th Congressional District of Pennsylvania includes all of Lancaster County, plus parts of southwestern Chester County that adjoin the Maryland and Delaware borders, as well as a small slice of Berks County that reaches to Reading. Outside the regional hub of Lancaster, the 16th is mostly small-town territory, with numerous quaint and quirkily named villages, such as Bird-in-Hand, Blue Ball and Intercourse (the first two named for the posted logos of old pubs, the third for reasons that are obscure, but almost certainly not sexual in nature). Closer to Philadelphia, the district takes in suburbs, including West Chester and Kennett Square. During the 1990s, Reading and Berks County attracted a large number of Hispanics in search of jobs. The district is now the third-most Hispanic in the state, at 13%. Still, this remains a Republican district. In 2008, Republican presidential nominee John McCain won it 51%-48%. He lost in Chester and Berks, and led 55%-44% in Lancaster, which cast 73% of the votes. Two years later, Republican Tom Corbett overwhelmed Democrat Dan Onorato in Lancaster, 71%-29%, and easily took Chester, 56%-44%, en route to becoming governor.

Joe Pitts (R)

The congressman from the 16th District is Joe Pitts, a Republican elected in 1996. One of the Pennsylvania delegation's staunchest conservatives, he now has a prominent platform for his free-market views as chairman of the Energy and Commerce Committee's Health Subcommittee.

Pitts was born in Kentucky, and spent time in the Philippines with his parents, where they served as religious missionaries. He joined the Air Force after college, and served three tours of duty, flying 116 B-52 combat missions in Vietnam. He returned home to become a math and science teacher in Malvern in Chester County, and later owned a nursery near Kennett Square. In 1972, at age 33, he was elected to the Pennsylvania General Assembly. In 1989, he became chairman of the Appropriations Committee, and oversaw the restoration of the Pennsylvania Capitol. Pitts is also an amateur artist. He and his daughter have exhibited their artwork, everything from painting to sculpture and woodwork, at local galleries.

When Republican Rep. Bob Walker, one of the conservative reformers of the Newt Gingrich era in the House, cited the "Pennsylvania Dutch tradition" of not serving over 20 years, Pitts ran to succeed him. In the primary, he ran as a "true conservative," speaking out in favor of home schooling and against gambling. He raised the most money and won with 45% of the vote. The runner-up, a moderate Republican, received 26%. In the general election, Pitts easily defeated newspaper publisher James Blaine, a descendant of James G. Blaine, the Republican presidential nominee in 1884.

In the House, Pitts was the Pennsylvania House delegation's most conservative member in the 111th Congress (2009-10), according to *National Journal*'s rankings. He was especially vocal in his opposition to the health care overhaul. "This unprecedented expansion of government power is only making health care more expensive," he said in September 2010. After taking the helm of Energy and Commerce's Health Subcommittee, he quickly moved a series of bills through the panel in March 2011 aimed at dismantling the law by repealing mandatory funding for state-based exchanges and school-based health center construction. The measures had very little chance of passing the Democratic-controlled Senate. Pitts has been an advocate of increased energy production, including the construction of new oil refineries on closed military bases. He is one of Congress' champions of nuclear power, and introduced a bill in 2009 aimed at reducing the time required for federal approval of new reactors.

Pitts led the Pro-Life Caucus and headed the Republicans' "values action team" that worked with the Christian Coalition and other groups to promote a pro-family agenda. During the health care debate, he was among the anti-abortion lawmakers pushing for a ban on federal funding for insurers that cover abortions. He also was a chief proponent of legislation to ban human cloning. With his appreciation for both human rights and national defense, Pitts founded two diverse groups: the Religious Prisoners Congressional Task Force to plead for human rights around the world, and the Electronic Warfare Working Group, to encourage more congressional support for military technology. In 2008, he urged a boycott of the Olympics in Beijing unless China improved its human rights record.

Pitts originally promised not to serve more than five terms, but later changed his mind. In 2006, he had a tough re-election against former corporate executive Lois Herr who ran on an anti-Iraq war platform. But Pitts won 57%-40%. Herr came back for a rematch in 2010, and this time focused on his legislative record, contending that just three of his bills had passed in 15 years. Pitts waved off the criticism, and won 65%-35%.

SEVENTEENTH DISTRICT

Tim Holden (D)

Elected 1992, 10th term; b. March 5, 1957, Pottsville; home, St. Clair; U. of Richmond, 1976-78, Bloomsburg U., B.A. 1980; Catholic; married (Gwen).

Elected Office: Schuylkill Cnty. sheriff, 1985–92.

Professional Career: Real estate agent; Insurance broker, Holden Insurance Agency, 1980–85; Probation officer, 1980-85.

DC Office: 2417 RHOB, 20515, 202-225-5546; Fax: 202-226-0996; Web site: holden.house.gov.

State Offices: Harrisburg, 717-234-5904; Lebanon, 717-270-1395; Pottsville, 570-622-4212; Temple, 610-921-3502.

Committees: *Agriculture:* Conservation, Energy & Forestry (RMM); Livestock, Dairy & Poultry. *Transportation & Infrastructure:* Aviation; Highways & Transit.

Group Ratings

	ACLU	ACU	ADA	CFG	AFS	FRC	LCV	ITIC	NTU	COC
2010	56	17	55	28	88	43	70	100	35	88
2009	–	16	75	27	89	–	86	–	15	60

National Journal Ratings

	2010 LIB — 2010 CONS		2009 LIB — 2009 CONS	
Economic	50%	— 50%	48%	— 51%
Social	42%	— 58%	49%	— 50%
Foreign	44%	— 55%	48%	— 51%
Composite	46%	— 55%	49%	— 51%

Key Votes of the 111th Congress

1. Overturn Ledbetter	Y	5. Bar federal abortion funds	Y	9. Stop detainee transfers	Y
2. Pass $820 billion stimulus	Y	6. Pass health care bill	N	10. Legalize immigrants' kids	N
3. Let guns in national parks	Y	7. Regulate financial firms	Y	11. Repeal don't ask, tell	Y
4. Pass cap-and-trade	N	8. Pass tax cuts for some	Y	12. Limit campaign funds	N

Election Results

2010 general	Tim Holden (D)	118,486	(56%)	($1,363,850)
	Dave Argall (R)	95,000	(44%)	($374,726)
2010 primary	Tim Holden (D)	30,630	(65%)	
	Sheila Dow-Ford (D)	16,296	(35%)	

Prior Winning Percentages: 2008 (64%), 2006 (65%), 2004 (59%), 2002 (51%), 2000 (66%), 1998 (61%), 1996 (59%), 1994 (57%), 1992 (52%)

Population		Race/Ethnicity		Work	
Pop. 2010:	681,835	White:	82.6%	Private:	80.0%
Change since 2000:	Up 5.5%	Black:	8.0%	Government:	14.6%
Urban:	68.6%	Hispanic:	6.0%	Self-employed:	5.3%
Rural:	31.4%	Asian:	1.7%	Blue collar:	26.2%
Area size:	2,380 sq. mi.	Native Am.:	0.1%	White collar:	57.0%
		Hawaiian:	0.0%	Khaki collar:	0.1%
Age		Two+ races:	1.4%	Other:	16.8%
Median age:	40.6 yrs.				
More than 65 yrs:	15.6%	*Ancestry*		Median income:	$50,105
Less than 18 yrs:	22.1%	German	28.9%	Median Home Value:	$148,600
		Irish	10.8%		
Education		Italian	6.2%	**Military Veterans**	
H.S. grad:	85.4%			% of Pop:	11.6%
College grad:	20.4%				
Grad degree:	7.2%				

With a seat on Energy and Commerce since 2005, Murphy has focused in particular on programs for military veterans with mental illness and on improving security for their medical records. In 2009, he called for creation of a trust fund to pay physicians a few dollars for every patient that converts to an electronic personal health record. "Everybody has a stake in healthcare IT," he said. He worked with Texas Democrat Gene Green to get a bill through the House to address the shortage of doctors in underserved communities. On energy issues, Murphy and Oklahoma Democrat Dan Boren led an effort in January 2011 to convince Interior Secretary Ken Salazar not to impose regulatory burdens on companies using hydraulic fracturing to extract natural gas. The technique has been blamed for increased groundwater contamination.

On other issues, Murphy sought in 2010 to assist domestic manufacturers to seek relief from years of underpriced Chinese imports. He sponsored a bill with Ohio Democrat Tim Ryan that passed the House to permit the Commerce Department to impose countervailing duties on imported goods of countries found to have undervalued their currency. He also has sought federal funding for upgrades at Pittsburgh's airport as well as a study to replace aging lock and dam structures on the Ohio River.

Murphy has not been seriously challenged for re-election.

NINETEENTH DISTRICT

Todd Platts (R)

Elected 2000, 6th term; b. March 5, 1962, York; home, York; Shippensburg U., B.S. 1984, Pepperdine U., J.D. 1991; Episcopalian; married (Leslie); 2 children.

Elected Office: PA House of Reps., 1992-2000.

Professional Career: Practicing atty, 1991-93.

DC Office: 2455 RHOB, 20515, 202-225-5836; Fax: 202-226-1000; Web site: house.gov/platts.

State Offices: Carlisle, 717-249-0190; Gettysburg, 717-338-1919; York, 717-600-1919.

Committees: *Armed Services:* Tactical Air & Land Forces; Seapower & Projection Forces. *Education & the Workforce:* Early Childhood, Elementary & Secondary Education; Higher Education & Workforce Training. *Oversight & Government Reform:* Government Organization, Efficiency & Financial Management (Chmn); National Security, Homeland Defense & Foreign Operations.

Group Ratings

	ACLU	ACU	ADA	CFG	AFS	FRC	LCV	ITIC	NTU	COC
2010	19	67	15	72	38	81	20	33	73	88
2009	–	76	30	62	44	–	36	–	60	93

National Journal Ratings

	2010 LIB	—	2010 CONS	2009 LIB	—	2009 CONS
Economic	37%	—	63%	36%	—	63%
Social	39%	—	60%	40%	—	59%
Foreign	29%	—	68%	26%	—	68%
Composite	36%	—	64%	35%	—	65%

Key Votes of the 111th Congress

1. Overturn Ledbetter	N	5. Bar federal abortion funds	Y	9. Stop detainee transfers	Y
2. Pass $820 billion stimulus	N	6. Pass health care bill	N	10. Legalize immigrants' kids	N
3. Let guns in national parks	Y	7. Regulate financial firms	N	11. Repeal don't ask, tell	Y
4. Pass cap-and-trade	N	8. Pass tax cuts for some	N	12. Limit campaign funds	N

Election Results

2010 general	Todd Platts (R)	165,219	(72%)	($218,611)
	Ryan Sanders (D)	53,549	(23%)	($30,148)
	Joshua Monighan (I)	10,988	(5%)	($3,662)
2010 primary	Todd Platts (R)	51,792	(70%)	
	Michael Smeltzer (R)	22,210	(30%)	

Prior Winning Percentages: 2008 (67%), 2006 (64%), 2004 (91%), 2002 (91%), 2000 (73%)

Population		Race/Ethnicity		Work	
Pop. 2010:	728,630	White:	87.3%	Private:	82.1%
Change since 2000:	Up 12.7%	Black:	4.2%	Government:	12.6%
Urban:	71.4%	Hispanic:	5.0%	Self-employed:	5.2%
Rural:	28.6%	Asian:	1.8%	Blue collar:	25.7%
Area size:	1,666 sq. mi.	Native Am.:	0.1%	White collar:	58.9%
		Hawaiian:	0.0%	Khaki collar:	0.1%
Age		Two+ races:	1.5%	Other:	15.2%
Median age:	39.5 yrs.				
More than 65 yrs:	14.5%	*Ancestry*		Median income:	$57,696
Less than 18 yrs:	22.3%	German	31.5%	Median Home Value:	$182,200
		Irish	10.9%		
Education		English	7.0%	**Military Veterans**	
H.S. grad:	87.7%			% of Pop:	11.5%
College grad:	24.5%				
Grad degree:	8.4%				

South Central Pennsylvania; York

The Mason-Dixon Line, the historic boundary between Maryland and Pennsylvania, runs through some of the country's most pleasant rolling farmlands, west of the Susquehanna River and through the Appalachian Mountains. The area was home to the westernmost capital of the United States during the Revolutionary War: the small city of York, capital from September 1777 to June 1778. York is where the Continental Congress passed the Articles of Confedera-

2008 Presidential Vote
John McCain (R) 187,857   (56%)
Barack Obama (D) 142,398   (43%)

2004 Presidential Vote
George Bush (R) 198,192   (64%)
John Kerry (D) 110,274   (36%)

Cook Partisan Voting Index: R+12

tion, received word from Benjamin Franklin in Paris that the French would help the colonies with money and ships, and issued the first proclamation calling for a national day of thanksgiving. A little more than four score years later, Robert E. Lee's Confederate troops crossed over this invisible line and were repelled in the Battle of Gettysburg in July 1863. Not much today suggests that this region was either a frontier or the object of bloody struggle. This is where former President Dwight D. Eisenhower, of Pennsylvania Dutch stock, chose to quietly spend his retirement years. One of the biggest controversies of recent years has been whether a casino should be built within a half-mile of Gettysburg National Military Park.

The Mason-Dixon Line forms the southern boundary of the 19th Congressional District of Pennsylvania, which includes all of Adams and York counties and part of Cumberland County to the north—relatively fast-growing areas in slow-growing Pennsylvania. The 19th takes in the fruit belt of Adams County, the Harrisburg suburbs across the Susquehanna and part of the old town of Carlisle, with Dickinson College and the U.S. Army War College. Hanover, in York County, is one of the world's snack headquarters, home to Snyder's of Hanover and potato chip giant Utz. The district's biggest city is York, the site of Harley-Davidson's largest manufacturing plant. It once had a workforce of about 2,500, but restructuring plans in 2010 called for eventual reductions to about 1,000. With a 14% population increase from 2000 to 2010, York has been one of the fastest-growing large counties in the Northeast. The city also has a growing Hispanic population. In Gettysburg, many Hispanics work the abundant orchards, which has led local farmers to advocate for increased immigration.

Politically, the 19th is heavily Republican. President George W. Bush won 64% of the vote here in 2004, and John McCain won 56% in 2008. Republican Tom Corbett drew at least 70% in Adams, York and Cumberland counties in the 2010 governor's race.

Todd Platts (R)

The congressman from the 19th District is Todd Platts, a moderate Republican elected in 2000. He has made his reputation as a stickler for good government as a senior member of the Oversight and Government Reform Committee.

Platts grew up in York, graduated from Shippensburg University and Pepperdine University School of Law. In 1992, at age 30, he was elected to the state House, where he served four terms. In 2000, he was the first to announce his candidacy after longtime Republican Rep. Bill Goodling, chairman of the Education and the Workforce Committee, said that he would retire. Platts' chief primary opponents were state Rep. Al Masland, attorney Dick Stewart, who was endorsed by Goodling, and Charlie Gerow, head of the state Citizens Against Government Waste. Platts refused contributions from political action committees and was outspent by his chief Republican rivals, but he campaigned on the theme "Putting People First." He won with 33% of the vote to 29% for Masland and 19% for Stewart, rolling up huge margins in his home base of York County. In the general election, Platts won 73%-26%. He has been re-elected with only minor opposition.

In the House, Platts has a moderate voting record for a Republican, especially on social matters. He sided with his party on the major economic issues of the 111th Congress (2009-10), but joined Democrats in voting to expand the State Children's Health Insurance Program and overhauling food safety laws. He also cosponsored the law enabling the Food and Drug Administration to regulate tobacco as well as the 2009 Employment Non-Discrimination Act barring employers from discriminating against homosexuals. In early 2007, he was one of only three House Republicans who voted in favor of all six bills that the new Democratic majority brought to the floor as part of its "first 100 hours" agenda. Also that year, he was the chief Republican co-sponsor of a successful bill to increase fuel efficiency standards for cars and trucks.

In naming Platts one of the 10 best members of Congress in 2009, *Esquire* magazine observed: "He manages to be straitlaced in the extreme without being a moralist, which is harder than it sounds." He is among the rare lawmakers who refuse PAC contributions. With his party's return to the majority in 2011, he took over the chairmanship of Government Reform's Government Organization, Efficiency & Financial Management panel and vowed to find ways to cut spending through identifying fraud and waste. A year earlier, he and Democrat Henry Cuellar of Texas won unanimous House approval of their bill requiring federal agencies to work with the Office of Management and Budget on developing plans to meet specific performance goals. He also has pushed legislation to require review of all government programs at least once every five years to evaluate their performance, and another bill to overturn a federal court ruling that he said created loopholes in the Whistleblower Protection Act.

Platts has not been afraid to challenge sacred cows in Congress. He sponsored, with Rep. Jim Matheson, D-Utah, a bill to repeal automatic annual pay raises for members of Congress. He supported "real lobbying reform," including an outside Office of Public Integrity to police the behavior of members of Congress. But in 2009, he abandoned a pledge not to accept earmarked spending for his district because, he said, it would be an unfair disadvantage for his constituents. Instead, he created a vetting committee to help him decide which local projects should receive funding.

Platts may hold the title for the longest daily commute to Congress. He drives the roughly 100 miles from his home in York to Washington nearly every day that the House is in session. No matter what happens with 2012 redistricting, he is expected to retain his loyal GOP base there.

★ RHODE ISLAND ★

Rhode Island and Providence Plantations, a tiny state with a mouthful of an official name—and one its voters in 2010 decided by referendum to keep, 78% to 22%—boasts as long and as turbulent a political history as any in the union. It was founded by Roger Williams as a refuge for religious dissenters, "the sewer of New England," as the orthodox Puritan Cotton Mather put it. It has been a successful trading community since the late 17th century and a leader in manufacturing since Samuel Slater replicated from memory an English water-powered cotton textile mill in Pawtucket in 1791. Rhode Island profited from slavery (two-thirds of America's slaves arrived from Africa on ships owned by Rhode Islanders) and war (the state boomed during the Civil War), and carried its tradition of tolerating just about anything into its politics. Rhode Island refused to pay its share for the Revolutionary War, declined to send delegates to the 1787 Constitutional Convention and delayed joining the union until the other 12 states had, prompting George Washington to say, "Rhode Island still perseveres in that impolitic, unjust—and one might add without much impropriety—scandalous conduct, which seems to have marked all her public counsels of late." The new nation's first bank failure occurred here in 1809, when a bank capitalized at $45 issued $800,000 in bank notes. In the 1840s, conflict between hard-money merchants and soft-money farmers resulted in two state governments and a conflict known as Dorr's War, with the outcome determined when merchant Thomas Dorr's two ancient cannons failed to fire.

Then in the 1930s the state had something resembling a political revolution. Thousands of immigrants from Ireland, Italy and French Canada came to Rhode Island to work in textile mills, and this colony founded by dissident Protestants became the most heavily Catholic state in the nation. Yankee Republicans tried to appeal to Catholics by running French Canadians for office. But national events—Catholic Democrat Al Smith's presidential candidacy in 1928 and Franklin Roosevelt's New Deal—moved the Catholics toward the Democrats. Then came the revolution: Although they had won only 20 of the 42 state Senate seats, the Democrats under Gov. Theodore Green refused to seat two Republicans in 1935. With the lieutenant governor's tiebreaker, they voted Democrats into the seats, and proceeded in 14 minutes to declare the state Supreme Court vacant, to abolish state boards that controlled Democratic cities, to increase the power of the governor and to reorganize state government to purge Republicans. This ended the political control of Rhode Island's "Five Families"—the Browns, Metcalfs, Goddards, Lippitts and Chafees—who owned or ran many of the textile mills, the Rhode Island Hospital Trust (long the largest bank), the Providence *Journal-Bulletin*, Brown University, the Rhode Island School of Design and the state Republican Party. Democrats have won most elections ever since, with the lion's share of votes from Rhode Island's Catholic majority, starting with Green's election in 1936, at age 69. From 1940 to 1980, Democrats won every election for U.S. House seats. The state's Democratic percentages in presidential elections from 1968 to 2008 are rivaled only by those of Massachusetts. Republicans have won when they've been able to capitalize on scandal or Democratic disarray, as governors Lincoln Almond and Donald Carcieri did in 1994 and 2002. But even the most durable Republican politician here, the late governor and senator John Chafee, lost elections as well as won them, and his son, Lincoln Chafee, having been defeated in 2006 after one term in the Senate, was elected governor in 2010 by running as an independent.

Rhode Island has gone through a long and often painful economic transformation, from blue collar to white collar, from textiles toward high tech. It suffered economic problems in the early 1990s, as the submarine factory and Navy base at Quonset Point shed thousands of jobs, and employment in costume jewelry, Rhode Island's major manufacturer, fell from 32,500 in 1977 to 6,300 in 2000. Gov. Lincoln Almond, elected in 1994 and 1998, persuaded the overwhelmingly Democratic legislature to gradually cut income taxes and eliminate the car tax, and Providence Mayor Buddy Cianci promoted successful redevelopment in the state's capital and largest city. Its downtown was enlivened with new buildings such as the GTECH tower and events such as the SoundSession music festival and WaterFire, an art fair with 100 bonfires lit along the city's three rivers. After the legislature passed a 25% tax rebate for moviemakers, Disney was given free rein to shoot the *Underdog* film scenes at the statehouse, and all 11 episodes of the *Brotherhood* series were shot in the state. Tourism became Rhode Island's second-largest industry and computer data processing a major part of the economy. The state's population, after hovering around 1 million for decades, started to grow again.

But all was not well. Cianci, caught up in scandal, was disgraced and imprisoned, and investigators honed in on state legislators. The state's population began declining in 2003, even as the nation emerged from recession. High taxes and strong unions weighed on the state's economy even as Massachusetts, with a more educated population and a much bigger high tech sector, surged

Presidential politics Rhode Island is almost always one of the most Democratic states in presidential elections—over the last generation, the most Democratic, though just a bit less so lately. It voted 61%-32% for Al Gore in 2000—his best state in the country—but gave John Kerry from neighboring Massachusetts a somewhat smaller margin of 59%-39% in 2004. In 2008, it voted 63%-35% for Barack Obama, his third best percentage in the nation, after his native Hawaii and liberal Vermont. Turnout was 469,000, well above the records of 437,000 in 2004 and 432,000 in 1980. Rhode Island's Catholic majority is heavily Democratic and, interestingly, favors abortion rights: In states where Catholics are beleaguered minorities, they may stand together and strongly oppose abortion, but in Rhode Island, where they're a strong majority, they oppose the official position of the church.

2008 Presidential Vote		
Barack Obama (D) 296,571	(63%)
John McCain (R) 165,391	(35%)
2008 Presidential Primary		
Hillary Clinton (D)...............108,949	(58%)
Barack Obama (D) 75,316	(40%)
2008 Presidential Primary		
John McCain (R) 17,480	(64%)
Mike Huckabee (R)...................5,847	(21%)
Ron Paul (R) 1,777	(7%)
2004 Presidential Vote		
John Kerry (D) 259,760	(59%)
George W. Bush (R)...............169,046	(39%)

For years, Rhode Island held a presidential primary on the same day as Massachusetts. In 2008, the state voted on March 4, the same day as Vermont, Ohio and Texas. At that point, the Republican contest was effectively decided, although Mike Huckabee remained in the race and lost to John McCain here by a predictably large, 64%-21%. But the Democratic race after Obama's string of victories in February was very much alive, and both his campaign and Hillary Rodham Clinton's opened Rhode Island offices, sent in paid staff and recruited local volunteers. The economic divide seemed fairly apparent in the results. As in Massachusetts, Obama carried upscale towns and city neighborhoods, while Clinton ran much better in blue-collar areas that have not shared in the prosperity. She won the state 58%-40%, and with her narrower victories in Ohio and Texas, could claim to have won the majority of the March 4 primaries. That outcome kept her in the race for three more months.

Congressional districting Redrawing Rhode Island's two congressional districts has not been much of a problem since the state was reduced to two seats in the reapportionment following the 1930s census. Indeed, the two districts have remained pretty much the same since 1842, except for the period from 1912 to 1932, when Rhode Island had three districts. Providence is split and both districts are overwhelmingly Democratic. For the 2002 reapportionment, 14,000 people needed to be moved from the 2nd House District to the 1st House District. Democratic incumbents Patrick Kennedy and Jim Langevin agreed on a change in Providence that gave Kennedy his old state legislative district near Providence College.

112th Congress Lineup
2 D
111th Congress Lineup
2 D

Rhode Island held onto its two districts in the reapportionment following the 2010 census, although not by much. Montana, with only 63,000 fewer people, had to be content with one seat. This means that Rhode Island's two House members will represent fewer people than anyone else in the House elected in 2012. Most likely, the heavily Democratic legislature will give the boundary a slight tweak as it did a decade ago.

Governor

Lincoln Chafee (I)

Elected 2010, term expires Jan. 2015, 1st term; b. March 26, 1953, Providence; home, Warwick; Brown U., B.A. 1975; Episcopalian; Married (Stephanie); 3 children.

Elected Office: Warwick City Cncl., 1986-91; Warwick mayor, 1992-99; U.S. Senate, 1999-2007.

Professional Career: Blacksmith, Harness Racetracks, 1976-83; Manufacturing planner, Electric Boat, Quonset, 1986-90; Exec. dir., Northeast Corridor Initiative, 1990-92; Distinguished visiting fellow, Brown U. Watson Inst. for Intl. Studies, 2007-09.

Office: 222 State House, Providence, 02903-1196, 401-222-2080; Web site: www.governor.ri.gov/.

Election Results

2010 general	Lincoln Chafee (I)	123,571	(36%)
	John Robataille (R)	114,911	(34%)
	Frank Caprio (D)	78,896	(23%)
	Kenneth Block (Mod)	22,146	(6%)

Prior Winning Percentages: Senate: 2000 (57%)

Rhode Island's new governor is Lincoln Chafee, a former U.S. senator who in 2010 became the first independent to serve as the state's chief executive. He won the governorship in unconventional fashion by promising to take the best ideas from both parties while being freed from the normal constraints of party politics.

Chafee is soft-spoken and taciturn to the point of shyness, but he possesses the most powerful name in Rhode Island politics—he is the son of John Chafee, a former moderate Republican governor and senator as well as secretary of the Navy. The younger Chafee grew up on an estate in Warwick, developing a love of horses. He attended the prep school Andover, where one of his classmates was Jeb Bush, later Florida's governor. He returned to the state to go to college at Brown, where he was captain of the wrestling team. Anxious to learn a trade and see more of the world, he went off to horseshoeing school at Montana State University, and then spent seven years working as a blacksmith at racetracks in the United States and Canada. He returned to Rhode Island in 1984, and a year later was elected to the Rhode Island Constitutional Convention, followed by an election to the city council in Warwick, the state's second-largest city. In 1992, he was elected mayor of Warwick by 335 votes, and was re-elected three times. In March 1999, John Chafee announced he would not seek re-election in 2000, and the next day Lincoln said he would run for the seat. The older Chafee was a productive legislator who was greatly beloved in Rhode Island, respected as a member of one of the "Five Families" that dominated the state's business and political landscape until the 1930s.

When the senator died in October, Republican Gov. Lincoln Almond appointed Lincoln Chafee to fill his father's unexpired term. He was only the second son appointed to the Senate to succeed his father, the other being Harry Byrd, Jr., in 1965. He quickly established himself as the heir to his father's philosophy, regularly joining Democrats on social and economic issues. But he said he would not switch parties, explaining, "I'm named after Abraham Lincoln." He was easily elected on his own in 2000 with 57% of the vote over 2nd District Democratic Rep. Robert Weygand. As a moderate Republican in the Senate from 1999 to 2007, Chafee developed a reputation for going to great lengths to dissociate himself from his party as it shifted to the right.

Chafee became greatly disenchanted with the policies of President George W. Bush, and his vote helped defeat the 2003 energy bill. He also opposed Bush's proposal for a prescription drug benefit under Medicare and was the only Senate Republican to vote against the Iraq War resolution in 2002. Then in 2004, he declined to be co-chairman of Bush's re-election campaign in Rhode Island and withdrew his earlier endorsement of the president. Other Republicans in the state declined to challenge him in the GOP primary, but in 2006 he drew an aggressive Democratic opponent in former state Attorney General Sheldon Whitehouse (whose father had roomed with Chafee's father at Yale in the 1940s). Chafee stressed his willingness to cross party lines, but Whitehouse urged voters to vote their party preference, especially as Republicans were in danger of losing their majority in the Senate. He easily beat Chafee, 54%-46%, helping Democrats assume control of the chamber.

Chafee spent the next two years as a visiting fellow at Brown and wrote a book, *Against the Tide: How a Compliant Congress Empowered a Reckless President*, an indictment of Bush's failure to fulfill his campaign pledge to be "a uniter, not a divider." He endorsed his former Senate colleague Barack Obama for president. In January 2010, Chafee entered the race to succeed Republican Gov. Donald Carcieri, who was barred from seeking re-election because of term limits. He formally declared himself an independent at a time when public distrust of both major political parties was peaking. He vowed to right the state's ailing finances not by cutting social programs but by eliminating a series of exemptions to the state sales tax, a proposal amounting to a tax increase that he said would raise more than $100 million. He also promised to help create more jobs by promoting a new transportation hub near the Providence airport.

The goodwill he had earned as a senator put him atop the early polls over Democratic state Treasurer Frank Caprio and Republican John Robitaille. (Caprio had had no Democratic primary opposition, while Robitaille beat former state Rep. Victor Moffitt in the GOP primary, 70%-30%.) Chafee's main competition was Caprio—at least until Caprio, in a radio interview about President Barack Obama's decision not to endorse him on a visit to Rhode Island, responded that Obama could "take his endorsement and really shove it." In a Democratic-dominated state that remained loyal to the president, the effect was instantaneous, and Robitaille surged ahead of Caprio in the polls. Chafee was able to withstand an October scandal—his campaign manager resigned after a report that he was collecting unemployment benefits while on Chafee's payroll—and got campaign help from New York City Mayor Michael Bloomberg. Chafee was able to pull out a close victory, getting 36% to Robitaille's 34%—a difference of about 8,600 votes. Caprio finished with 23%. Chafee won Providence County, by far the largest source of votes, along with Washington County to the south.

Chafee's early moves as governor generated controversy. As his first official act, he rescinded an executive order that cracked down on the hiring of illegal immigrants. State Police superintendent Brendan Doherty resigned in March after clashing with Chafee, though both sides denied that friction played any role. He removed reform-minded members of the state education board and named as its chairman a lobbyist for a gambling parlor. He angered the news media by forbidding top state officials from appearing on talk radio programs and suggested that businesses refrain from advertising on such shows. And some of the state's largest employers, such as toymaker Hasbro Inc. and biotechnology company Amgen Inc., came out strongly against his call to stop corporations from using out-of-state subsidiaries to reduce their Rhode Island state taxes.

Senior Senator

Jack Reed (D)

Elected 1996, term expires 2014, 3rd term; b. Nov. 12, 1949, Providence; home, Jamestown; U.S. Military Acad., West Point, B.S. 1971, Harvard U., M.P.P. 1973, J.D. 1982; Catholic; married (Julia Hart); 1 child.

Military Career: Army, 1967–79; Army Reserves, 1979-91.

Elected Office: RI Senate, 1984–90; U.S. House of Reps., 1991–97.

Professional Career: Assoc. prof., U.S. Military Acad. at West Point, 1978–79; Practicing atty., 1982–90.

DC Office: 728 HSOB, 20510, 202-224-4642; Fax: 202-224-4680; Web site: reed.senate.gov.

State Offices: Cranston, 401-943-3100; Providence, 401-528-5200.

Committees: *Appropriations:* Commerce, Justice, Science & Related Agencies; Defense; Energy & Water Development; Interior, Environment & Related Agencies (Chmn); Labor, Health & Human Services, Education & Related Agencies; Military Construction, Veterans Affairs & Related Agencies. *Armed Services:* Emerging Threats & Capabilities; Seapower (Chmn); Strategic Forces. *Banking, Housing & Urban Affairs:* Financial Institutions & Consumer Protection; Housing, Transportation & Community Development; Securities, Insurance & Investment (Chmn).

Group Ratings

	ACLU	ACU	ADA	CFG	AFS	FRC	LCV	ITIC	NTU	COC
2010	93	0	90	0	99	0	100	67	6	18
2009	–	0	95	3	100	–	100	–	4	43

National Journal Ratings

	2010 LIB — 2010 CONS		2009 LIB — 2009 CONS	
Economic	85%	— 12%	88%	— 0%
Social	65%	— 0%	85%	— 0%
Foreign	47%	— 0%	55%	— 0%
Composite	81%	— 19%	88%	— 12%

Key Votes of the 111th Congress

1. Overturn Ledbetter	Y	5. Pass health care bill	Y	9. Ratify New START	Y
2. Pass $787 billion stimulus	Y	6. Regulate financial firms	Y	10. Confirm Elena Kagan	Y
3. Repeal DC gun laws	N	7. Pass tax cuts for some	Y	11. Stop EPA climate regs	N
4. Confirm Sonia Sotomayor	Y	8. Legalize immigrants' kids	Y	12. Repeal don't ask, tell	Y

Election Results

2008 general	Jack Reed (D)	320,644	(73%)	($4,735,246)
	Robert Tingle (R)	116,174	(27%)	
2008 primary	Jack Reed (D)	48,038	(87%)	
	Christopher Young (D)	7,277	(13%)	

Prior Winning Percentages: 2002 (78%); 1996 (63%); House: 1994 (68%); 1992 (71%); 1990 (59%)

Jack Reed, Rhode Island's senior senator, was first elected to the House in 1990 and the Senate in 1996. He grew up in working-class Cranston, the second of three children of a school custodian and a housewife. Disappointed that she never got to go to college, Mary Reed prepared her children for success in school. She insisted on music and art classes for Jack beginning at age 5. But her son was fascinated by history and World War II as a child, and eventually decided he wanted to go to the U.S. Military Academy. At LaSalle Academy, a Catholic prep school in Providence, he played football, though he was small for the sport. He also ran track, was elected to the student council and worked on the school newspaper. Reed was accepted at West Point, and then went on to serve in the 82nd Airborne as a paratrooper. He also received a master's degree from Harvard's Kennedy School while in the Army, and after retiring from active duty, he graduated from Harvard Law School. Throughout his life, Reed has maintained connections with West Point, teaching there briefly in the late 1970s, serving on the academy's governing board and choosing it as the site of his wedding in April 2005.

In 1984, at 35, Reed won public office for the first time, beating an incumbent in the primary for the state Senate, where he served six years. When Republican Claudine Schneider left the U.S. House to run against Sen. Claiborne Pell in 1990, Reed ran for her seat. He beat former Rep. Edward Beard 49%-27% in the Democratic primary and won the general election 59%-41%. In 1995, when Pell announced his retirement after 36 years, Reed ran for the Senate. Reed had no serious competition for the Democratic nomination and faced state Treasurer Nancy Mayer in the general election. National Republicans spent nearly $1 million on ads attacking Reed as a liberal for opposing bills requiring welfare recipients to work and for supporting labor unions—not especially harmful charges in liberal, heavily unionized Rhode Island. Reed spent $2.7 million to Mayer's $773,000. His biography was his message: Reed launched his campaign in a public school conference room named for his late father, he stressed his bootstraps rise from a working-class background and he called for education spending to help others achieve the same success. He won 63%-35%.

Reed arrived as one of the few senators of his generation with military experience and has been regarded by many colleagues as an authority on defense and military matters. He has served on the Armed Services Committee since January 1999, and he got a waiver from the Democratic leadership to remain on the panel after securing a seat on the Appropriations Committee in 2007.

Reed supported President Bill Clinton's bombing campaigns in Afghanistan and Sudan in 1998, but in October 2002, he opposed the Iraq war resolution. Reed argued that Defense Secretary Donald Rumsfeld grossly underestimated the strength of anti-American insurgents in Iraq and failed to send in adequate troops and equipment. Reed has traveled to Iraq and Afghanistan many frequently, often straying from the safe zones to talk with officers and soldiers on the front lines. In 2005, after his fifth trip to Iraq, he said: "My job is to be critical about what's going on and what needs to be improved. I think my criticism has been accurate, certainly in the operations in this region, in that we didn't organize ourselves for the appropriate occupation and stabilization" after the overthrow of Iraqi leader Saddam Hussein.

In 2006, Reed was at the forefront of Democratic efforts to convince President George W. Bush to redeploy forces in Iraq. With Michigan Democrat Carl Levin, he sponsored a bill calling for a "phased redeployment" in six months, with no deadline for complete withdrawal and with some U.S. forces remaining to transition to training Iraqi security forces. The Levin-Reed amendment lost 60-39. That summer, Reed said that Iraq had deteriorated into a "low-grade civil war," but pointed to gains in training Iraqis. In December 2006, he said the Iraq Study Group's report "may be the last chance to get it right" and noted that its recommendations were "strikingly similar" to the Levin-Reed amendment. After President Bush's successful troop surge in 2007, Reed continued to push for alternatives that would leave only a residual force in Iraq for counter-terrorism, protection of U.S. personnel and logistical support for Iraqi security forces. But most Republicans were opposed, and Reed failed to gain the 60 votes required to force a final vote.

Reed accompanied Democratic presidential candidate Barack Obama on his 2008 trip to Iraq and Afghanistan, and Obama later considered him a potential running mate until Reed ruled himself out. He also was on the short list of possible defense secretaries, but Obama decided to retain Robert Gates. In September 2009, while Obama was mulling strategy in Afghanistan, Reed expressed doubts about sending more troops and said the burden of proof was on commanders to justify a troop increase. After a visit there in July 2010, Reed was cautiously upbeat. Also that year, he told *National Journal*, "I've been to Afghanistan 11 times. I do not just seek out just one opinion. I talk to people in the field, diplomats and soldiers. I go recognizing, frankly, everyone has an institutional agenda. I try to approach all these things with a questioning mind."

Reed has long backed efforts to permanently increase the size of the Army. In 2003, the Senate voted 52-45 for his amendment to add 10,000 troops, but it was dropped in conference with the House. The following year, he and Nebraska GOP Sen. Chuck Hagel called for an increase of 30,000 troops, and the Senate agreed to 20,000. In 2006, Reed worked with the Republican leadership to add $3.7 billion for more soldiers and Marines, and sponsored an amendment to add $10 billion to replace damaged or destroyed equipment.

On most issues, Reed has had a solidly liberal voting record. In February 2009, a *National Journal* examination of roll call votes dating to the 1980s found him to be the most liberal senator, slightly ahead of Barbara Boxer of California and Edward Kennedy of Massachusetts.

He has championed the Low-Income Home Energy Assistance Program popular with members of Congress from the Northeast. In February 2011, he and Republican Olympia Snowe of Maine wrote to White House budget chief Jacob Lew protesting proposed cuts to LIHEAP. Reed was the lead opponent of a bill to prevent victims from suing to hold gun manufacturers liable for crimes committed with their products. He has supported extensions of unemployment benefits and work-share programs, like those in Rhode Island, in which employers reduce the hours of full-time employees in order to avoid lay-offs during financial hard times.

Reed is the second ranking Democrat on the Banking Committee, just behind South Dakota's Tim Johnson, who became chairman after the retirement of Connecticut's Christopher Dodd in

2010. On the committee, Reed pushed for expanding the affordable housing fund and said that federal regulators had been too complacent in overseeing the financial derivatives market. He was assigned by Dodd to work on derivatives provisions of the financial regulation bill of 2010. He also advanced a proposal to require hedge funds, private equity firms and venture capitalists to provide information to the Securities and Exchange Commission, which would determine whether they pose a systemic risk to the financial markets. He sponsored a bill in February 2010 to create a National Institute of Finance to help regulators monitor systemic risk in the system. In June 2010, Senate conferees rejected by a 10-2 vote his amendment requiring that the president of the New York Federal Reserve Bank be appointed by the president and confirmed by the Senate.

In Rhode Island politics, Reed has always been his own man, unentangled with local Democratic Party affairs. He was re-elected 78%-22% in 2002 and 73%-26% in 2008. This is a Senate seat whose members have had long tenures. Theodore Green, elected at age 69, served 24 years; Claiborne Pell, elected at 41, served 36 years. Reed, first elected at 47, has the potential for similarly long service.

Junior Senator

Sheldon Whitehouse (D)

Elected 2006, term expires 2012, 1st term; b. Oct. 20, 1955, New York City; home, Providence; Yale U., B.A. 1978, U. of VA, J.D. 1982; Protestant; married (Sandra); 2 children.

Elected Office: RI Atty. Gen., 1998-2002.

Professional Career: RI spec. asst. atty. gen., 1984-90; Legal counsel, Gov. Bruce Sundlun, 1991; Policy director, Gov. Bruce Sundlun, 1992; Director, RI Dept. of Business Regulation, 1992-1994; U.S. atty. for RI, 1994-1998; Practicing atty., 2003-2006.

DC Office: 717 HSOB, 20510, 202-224-2921; Fax: 202-228-6362; Web site: whitehouse.senate.gov.

State Offices: Providence, 401-453-5294.

Committees: *Aging (Special). Budget. Environment & Public Works:* Children's Health & Environmental Responsibility ; Oversight (Chmn); Transportation & Infrastructure; Water & Wildlife. *Health, Education, Labor & Pensions:* Employment & Workplace Safety; Primary Health & Aging. *Judiciary:* Administrative Oversight & the Courts; Constitution, Civil Rights & Human Rights; Crime & Terrorism (Chmn); Privacy, Technology & the Law.

Group Ratings

	ACLU	ACU	ADA	CFG	AFS	FRC	LCV	ITIC	NTU	COC
2010	93	0	90	0	100	0	100	67	5	18
2009	–	0	95	0	100	–	100	–	4	43

National Journal Ratings

	2010 LIB	—	2010 CONS	2009 LIB	—	2009 CONS
Economic	88%	—	0%	88%	—	0%
Social	65%	—	0%	85%	—	0%
Foreign	47%	—	0%	55%	—	0%
Composite	83%	—	17%	88%	—	12%

Key Votes of the 111th Congress

1. Overturn Ledbetter	Y	5. Pass health care bill	Y	9. Ratify New START	Y
2. Pass $787 billion stimulus	Y	6. Regulate financial firms	Y	10. Confirm Elena Kagan	Y
3. Repeal DC gun laws	N	7. Pass tax cuts for some	Y	11. Stop EPA climate regs	N
4. Confirm Sonia Sotomayor	Y	8. Legalize immigrants' kids	Y	12. Repeal don't ask, tell	Y

Election Results

2006 general	Sheldon Whitehouse (D)	206,043	(54%)	($6,579,757)
	Lincoln Chafee (R)	178,950	(46%)	($5,422,253)
2006 primary	Sheldon Whitehouse (D)	69,290	(82%)	
	Christopher Young (D)	8,739	(10%)	
	Carl Sheeler (D)	6,755	(8%)	

The junior senator from Rhode Island is Sheldon Whitehouse, a Democrat elected in 2006. He is a wealthy descendant of Charles Crocker, one of California's "Big Four" men who built the Central

Pacific Railroad, the eastbound section of railroad that connected with the Union Pacific line at Promontory Summit, Utah, to form the nation's first transcontinental railroad. His grandfather was a diplomat and so was his father, Charles Whitehouse, a World War II Marine Corps pilot who became U.S. ambassador to Laos and Thailand in the 1970s. Sheldon Whitehouse was born in New York City and spent his formative years overseas, including in Cambodia, South Africa, the Philippines and Guinea; as a teenager, he taught English to Vietnamese children in Saigon. He graduated from St. Paul's preparatory school, Yale College and the University of Virginia Law School. Afterward, Whitehouse clerked for an appeals court judge, and then moved to Rhode Island to take a job as an assistant state attorney general. He was appointed a top staffer for Gov. Bruce Sundlun in 1991, and served two years as head of the state's department of business regulation. In 1994, on the recommendation of Democratic Sen. Claiborne Pell, a family friend and former Foreign Service officer himself, Whitehouse was appointed U.S. attorney for Rhode Island. Whitehouse launched an undercover investigation that resulted in the conviction of Providence Mayor Buddy Cianci for public corruption. He also focused on environmental cleanup, leading an investigation that resulted in the largest fine in state history for an oil spill in Narragansett Bay.

Whitehouse ran for state attorney general in 1998. In the three-way Democratic primary, his opponents portrayed him as an inexperienced, fox-hunting patrician trying to buy his way into public office. But Whitehouse was better known in the state than his opponents, and he got the nomination. In the general election, state Treasurer Nancy Mayer forced Whitehouse to concede that he had tried drugs as a student and questioned whether he was tough enough for the job. Whitehouse told *The Providence Journal*, "The book on me was, 'Smart kid, works hard, but, you know, has no common touch, can't relate to people, will be a disaster.' In fact, I got advice from some political types to run sort of a Rose Garden strategy. You know, 'Don't go out, don't let people see you, 'cause if they see you, they're not going to like you. Just mail your resume around, you know, and spend a lot of money on television.'" But the tide began to turn after Mayer ran highly negative ads on the drug issue that backfired in the absence of evidence that the incident was more than a short chapter from Whitehouse's distant past. He won the election, 66.5% to 33%.

By 2002, Whitehouse was widely viewed as a contender for governor. He ran, but lost the Democratic primary by 926 votes to Myrth York, the 1998 nominee and a Federal Hill neighbor in Providence who outspent Whitehouse by more than 2-to-1. York lost in November to Republican Donald Carcieri.

Whitehouse also considered running for the Senate in 1999, when four-term incumbent John Chafee announced he would not seek a fifth term. But then, Chafee, a Yale roommate of Whitehouse's father, died that November and Republican Gov. Lincoln Almond appointed his son, Lincoln Chafee, then mayor of Warwick, to fill the vacancy. The following year, Chafee won a full term by beating 2nd District Democratic Rep. Robert Weygand, 57%-41%. In the Senate, Chafee sided with Democrats often enough that there was frequent speculation that he would switch parties. In 2006, Chafee was opposed in the Republican primary by Cranston Mayor Steve Laffey, a conservative and a sharp-elbowed campaigner who was backed by the national anti-tax group Club for Growth. The National Republican Senatorial Committee vigorously defended Chafee, reasoning that he would be the stronger general election candidate, and he won the September primary, 54%-46%.

Meanwhile, Whitehouse had an easier time in the Democratic primary after Secretary of State Matt Brown dropped out in April amid allegations of campaign finance violations. Chafee had little cash left after the primary fight, while Whitehouse had $1 million. Chafee emphasized his willingness to work across party lines, but Whitehouse urged people to vote their party preference. There was little daylight between the candidates on issues—both backed federal funding of embryonic stem cell research, abortion rights, and gun control—so Whitehouse campaigned against the then-unpopular Bush administration, running ads with the tagline, "Finally, a Whitehouse in Washington you can trust." Whitehouse won 54% to 46%. He won 72% of the vote in Providence, 66% in Pawtucket, 61% in East Providence, 64% in Woonsocket, and 77% in Central Falls. Chafee won 54% in Warwick, he carried Kingston and Westerly's Washington County, and he ran not much better than even in Newport and Bristol counties.

Whitehouse was one of eight new Democratic senators whose election gave the party a majority in the Senate. He got seats on the Environment and Public Works, Budget, Intelligence and Judiciary Committees, where he joked that he was the only WASP among the committee's mostly Catholic and Jewish Democrats. "This is the first time in my life I've brought diversity to a group," he said. On Judiciary, Whitehouse criticized Attorney General Alberto Gonzalez for firing U.S. attorneys for what Democrats alleged were political motivations. After Gonzalez resigned, Whitehouse opposed the nomination of Michael Mukasey for refusing to say whether water boarding was an illegal tactic against terrorism detainees. In response to the Supreme Court's *Citizens United* decision lifting limits on corporate expenditures in campaigns, Whitehouse decried "the activist, corporate-leaning pattern of the Supreme Court's conservative bloc." He was also one of the leaders of the unsuccessful fight to limit filibusters at the beginning of the 112th Congress in 2011.

Whitehouse supported President Barack Obama's $787 billion economic stimulus bill in 2009, and said he'd even like to see a second stimulus bill focused entirely on the nation's infrastructure. Whitehouse sparked controversy when he said on the Senate floor that opposition to Obama's health care reform measure was driven in part by "right-wing militias and Aryan support groups."

Whitehouse sponsored successful 2010 legislation that authorized the Federal Communications Commission to regulate the volume of television ads. And his amendment facilitating prosecution of anyone using lasers to attack airplanes passed the Senate 96-1 in 2011. On other issues, Whitehouse, with Democratic Sen. Richard Durbin of Illinois, co-sponsored a bill in 2009 to free users of credit cards carrying interest rates 15% above Treasury bonds from the obligation to repay in bankruptcy proceedings. He also co-sponsored a bill for a 65% tax on estates over $500 million. After a March 2007 visit to Iraq, Whitehouse toned down his earlier criticism of the Bush administration and pointed to improved security in the country. Similarly, after an October 2010 trip to Afghanistan, he said the counterinsurgency strategy was working.

Whitehouse comes up for re-election in 2012. In heavily Democratic Rhode Island, he entered the campaign season as a clear favorite.

FIRST DISTRICT

David Cicilline (D)

Elected 2010, 1st term; b. July 15, 1961, Providence; home, Providence; Brown U., B.A. 1983; Georgetown U., J.D. 1986; Jewish; Single.

Elected Office: RI House, 1995-2003; Providence mayor, 2003-10.

Professional Career: Public defender, 1986-87.

DC Office: 128 CHOB, 20515, 202-225-4911; Fax: 202-225-3290; Web site: cicilline.house.gov.

State Offices: Pawtucket, 401-729-5600.

Committees: *Foreign Affairs:* Oversight & Investigations; Terrorism, Nonproliferation & Trade. *Small Business:* Agriculture, Energy & Trade; Economic Growth, Tax and Capital Access.

Election Results

2010 general	David Cicilline (D)	81,269	(51%)	($2,054,788)
	John Loughlin (R)	71,542	(45%)	($812,972)
	Kenneth Capalbo (I)	6,424	(4%)	
2010 primary	David Cicilline (D)	21,142	(37%)	
	Anthony Gemma (D)	13,112	(23%)	
	David Segal (D)	11,397	(20%)	
	William Lynch (D)	11,161	(20%)	

Population		Race/Ethnicity		Work	
Pop. 2010:	519,021	White:	76.7%	Private:	82.0%
Change since 2000:	Down 1.0%	Black:	5.4%	Government:	12.4%
Urban:	95.5%	Hispanic:	11.0%	Self-employed:	5.5%
Rural:	4.5%	Asian:	2.5%	Blue collar:	20.1%
Area size:	565 sq. mi.	Native Am.:	0.3%	White collar:	61.4%
		Hawaiian:	0.0%	Khaki collar:	0.6%
Age		Two+ races:	2.7%	Other:	17.9%
Median age:	38.9 yrs.				
More than 65 yrs:	15.0%	*Ancestry*		Median income:	$52,672
Less than 18 yrs:	21.0%	Irish	13.8%	Median Home Value:	$287,000
		Italian	11.2%		
Education		French	10.2%	**Military Veterans**	
H.S. grad:	82.0%			% of Pop:	9.5%
College grad:	30.4%				
Grad degree:	12.3%				

Eastern Rhode Island; Providence

The 1st Congressional District is the eastern half of Rhode Island, divided from the state's only other congressional district by a boundary line that cuts through the state capital of Providence and then proceeds west and north to the Massachusetts-Connecticut border. It includes the eastern coast of Narragansett Bay and the small island chain off Rhode Island's coast. In recent years, once down-on-its-luck Providence has been revived, with a more accessible water-

2008 Presidential Vote		
Barack Obama (D) 148,176	(65%)
John McCain (R) 75,806	(33%)
2004 Presidential Vote		
John Kerry (D) 131,245	(62%)
George Bush (R) 77,480	(36%)
Cook Partisan Voting Index: D+13		

front, active night life, and restoration of neighborhoods around the state capitol. The district takes in much of the city, including the elite East Side and College Hill around Brown University. It also captures all of next-door Pawtucket, whose Slater Mill is known as the birthplace of the American Industrial Revolution. It is also home to Hasbro, the nation's second-largest toy company. Providence hosts an annual G.I. Joe Convention hosted by a collectors' club devoted to America's first action figure. The onetime textile mill towns of the Blackstone Valley, Woonsocket and Central Falls, are also in the 1st District, along with high-income Barrington and Bristol. To the south on the ocean is the old city of Newport, with its restored 18th-century houses and summer "cottages" that are more like mansions. Newport was once home to the America's Cup races and now hosts a popular jazz festival. It is also the site of the oldest synagogue in North America, where George Washington once told a congregation that the United States gives "to bigotry no sanction, to persecution no assistance." Ethnically, this district is the more French Canadian and the less Italian of Rhode Island's two congressional districts. Politically, it is strongly Democratic.

David Cicilline (D)

The new congressman from Rhode Island's 1st District is Democrat David Cicilline, the former mayor of Providence who won the seat of retiring Democratic Rep. Patrick Kennedy.

Cicilline (*sis-ih-LEE-nee*) was born in Providence, the middle of five children. His parents eloped when his mother was 16 and his father 17, which caused some tension between the two families. His mother is Jewish and his father is Catholic, and Cicilline grew up celebrating the traditions of both religions. He now identifies as Jewish. His father was a criminal defense attorney whose clients included suspected members of organized crime. Cicilline told *National Journal*, "My father was very clear about explaining to us that in our country, everyone has a right to representation and our system of justice depends on that." He was interested in politics from a young age. When he was 10, he wrote letters to his elected representatives when he had something on his mind, and at 14, he had his parents drop him off at city council meetings so he could participate in the public comment period. In high school, Cicilline wanted to study Italian, but his school did not offer it. He did some research and discovered an obscure state law requiring schools to offer a language course if eight or more students expressed interest. He submitted a list of interested students to the school board, obliging the school to hire an Italian teacher. In his high school years, he led a successful campaign against development on a parcel of land, even though the developer was his father's friend.

Cicilline attended Brown University, where he majored in political science and founded, along with classmate John F. Kennedy Jr., a chapter of the College Democrats. He was active in student government and worked two jobs waiting tables. Cicilline came out as gay in college and says he was fortunate to have a supportive family. "I had a very different experience than, unfortunately, most LGBT (lesbian, gay, bisexual and transgender) kids have," he said. After getting a law degree from Georgetown University, he remained in Washington to work as a public defender for juveniles. In addition to defending the youths in court, Cicilline sometimes enrolled them in school, substance-abuse treatment, and other support services.

He returned to Rhode Island to campaign for the state Senate. He lost that bid, but ran for the state House two years later and won. In the legislature, he supported a variety of liberal policies. He pushed to raise the legal age to buy a gun from 13 to 18, introduced a bill creating a needle exchange program for drug users, and fought attempts to restrict abortion rights.

After four two-year terms, Cicilline ran for mayor of Providence in 2002. He campaigned as a reformer, promising to clean up the city after the 21-year reign of Buddy Cianci, who was convicted of corruption and resigned. Cicilline beat several other prominent politicians in the Democratic primary with 53% of the vote. He went on to win the general election in a landslide, becoming the first openly gay mayor of a state capital city. In office, Cicilline sought to end cronyism in the police department and expanded after-school programs. But as the city's revenue shriveled in the recession, he laid off nearly 500 city employees and raised property taxes. Cicilline also served as president of the National Conference of Democratic Mayors.

When Kennedy announced he would not seek re-election in 2010, national Democrats were intent on holding the seat, having lost the Senate seat of the late Edward Kennedy, the incumbent's father, in Massachusetts earlier in 2010. In the primary, Cicilline defeated businessman Anthony Gemma, state Rep. David Segal, and former state party Chairman Bill Lynch for the nomination, winning 37% of the vote. In the general-election, Cicilline campaigned as a pragmatist focused on creating jobs. His Republican opponent, state Rep. John Loughlin, emphasized the state's economic condition and said he would balance the budget. Cicilline raised $1.7 million, easily outpacing Loughlin, and won 50.6% to 44.6%, with an independent candidate collecting 4%. It was an unusually close outcome in the heavily Democratic district, and a testament to the strength of the Republican trend in 2010. Kennedy won nearly all of his races by wide margins.

When he took office in January 2011, Cicilline became the fourth openly gay member of Congress.

SECOND DISTRICT

Jim Langevin (D)

Elected 2000, 6th term; b. April 22, 1964, Warwick; home, Warwick; RI Col., B.A. 1990, Harvard U., M.P.A. 1994; Catholic; single.

Elected Office: RI House of Reps., 1988-94; RI sec. of state, 1994-2000.

DC Office: 109 CHOB, 20515, 202-225-2735; Fax: 202-225-5976; Web site: langevin.house.gov.

State Offices: Warwick, 401-732-9400.

Committees: *Armed Services:* Emerging Threats & Capabilities (RMM); Seapower & Projection Forces; Strategic Forces. *Permanent Select Committee on Intelligence:* Technical & Tactical Intelligence.

Group Ratings

	ACLU	ACU	ADA	CFG	AFS	FRC	LCV	ITIC	NTU	COC
2010	81	0	85	4	100	6	100	100	7	25
2009	–	4	95	0	100	–	100	–	3	33

National Journal Ratings

	2010 LIB	—	2010 CONS	2009 LIB	—	2009 CONS
Economic	88%	—	12%	75%	—	21%
Social	71%	—	25%	64%	—	34%
Foreign	56%	—	38%	78%	—	17%
Composite	73%	—	27%	74%	—	26%

Key Votes of the 111th Congress

1. Overturn Ledbetter	Y	5. Bar federal abortion funds	Y	9. Stop detainee transfers	Y
2. Pass $820 billion stimulus	Y	6. Pass health care bill	Y	10. Legalize immigrants' kids	Y
3. Let guns in national parks	N	7. Regulate financial firms	Y	11. Repeal don't ask, tell	Y
4. Pass cap-and-trade	Y	8. Pass tax cuts for some	Y	12. Limit campaign funds	Y

Election Results

2010 general	Jim Langevin (D)	104,442	(60%)	($1,095,292)
	Mark Zaccaria (R)	55,409	(32%)	($185,537)
	John Matson (I)	14,584	(8%)	($2,006)
2010 primary	Jim Langevin (D)	25,603	(57%)	
	Elizabeth Dennigan (D)	15,146	(34%)	
	Ernest Greco (D)	3,833	(9%)	

Prior Winning Percentages: 2008 (70%), 2006 (73%), 2004 (75%), 2002 (76%), 2000 (62%)

★ SOUTH CAROLINA ★

South Carolina stands proud but not untroubled, a state that has made much progress but still has some distance to go. Within living memory, South Carolina looked like an underdeveloped country. Aside from a relatively small pool of very wealthy people, it was among the poorest of states, with income levels less than half the national average and with high levels of illiteracy and disease. The state was founded by planters from Barbados, and even today there are reminders of the West Indies—the semitropical climate, the lush foliage and trademark palmettos, and the billions of dollars in damage from hurricanes. South Carolina started off with a plantation economy built on the swampy Lowcountry below the Fall Line, where 18th and 19th century planters built rice paddies and cultivated exotic crops like indigo in the days before cotton was king. The great wealth of these Lowcountry planters was destroyed by the Civil War, which they, more than any other Southerners, provoked. But their pride and way of life continued, as did that of former slaves. As late as 1940, 43% of South Carolinians were black, most living in conditions inconceivable today. South Carolina's economic growth started in the 1920s, with the low-wage textile industry. Mills were built in the Upstate region northwest of Columbia, hiring poor whites (never blacks) from the hardscrabble farms in the area. Politics remained a rough business, with harsh appeals to racial fear and economic envy, and with limited participation. In 1940, just 99,000 South Carolinians voted for president, 96% of them Democratic, the highest Democratic percentage in the nation. In the 1946 Democratic primary, the year Strom Thurmond was elected governor, only 271,000 people voted in a state of more than 2 million.

In the last half-century, this once underdeveloped state joined the First World, and has moved dramatically ahead in the last 20 years. Personal incomes have risen sharply and are near the national average. Factory productivity rose 59%. Poverty fell sharply. Health standards are as good as those in the rest of the nation. Educational achievement still lags, though not nearly as much as before, with 80% of white adults and 65% of black adults classified as high school graduates. Homeownership is well above the national average. Back in the 1970s, much of South Carolina's economy depended on the military bases clustered around Charleston and on the big textile mills around Greenville and Spartanburg. Then, South Carolina became the most aggressive state in the South in attracting new industry. It advertised its business climate, with the nation's lowest rates of unionization, low taxes and a willingness to splurge on tax incentives. From 1960 to 1990, international investment in the state grew from $80 million to $16.4 trillion. It enticed foreign firms to set up major operations in the Piedmont, starting with Michelin and Fuji Photo and capped by a large BMW facility in Spartanburg. Since production started in 1994, more than 1.5 million vehicles have been produced there, including the X3 sports utility vehicle. With an expanded capacity today of 240,000 vehicles a year, BMW has generated some 23,000 jobs and was adding to its workforce despite the recent economic doldrums in the auto industry.

Navy bases were the mainstay of Charleston's economy during the reign of House Armed Services Chairman Mendel Rivers in the 1970s. The bases closed in the early 1990s, but Charleston has not only survived but thrived, thanks in large part to the creative energy of longtime Mayor Joe Riley Jr., first elected in 1975 and now in his 9th term in office. The city's historic center has become a graceful tourist attraction, while the closed military bases have become a center of aircraft production, first with Vought Aircraft and Alenia Aeronautica and then when Boeing in 2009 chose North Charleston to build a 3,800-worker plant to assemble its 787 Dreamliner. Hilton Head and the Grand Strand around Myrtle Beach bring in millions of tourists every year, along with thousands of new residents, many of them affluent retirees. Economically and culturally, South Carolina has been part of the booming South Atlantic region from Maryland to Florida, filling up with new retirement condominiums, time shares, factories, office buildings and giant shopping centers.

But with the robust growth, problems have emerged. Unemployment spiked in the 2007-09 recession to the highest levels in the South Atlantic. South Carolina's Savannah River Site, once the nation's leading producer of plutonium, is now the site of a massive cleanup operation that is often the subject of dispute. Savannah River received $1.6 billion in 2009 in federal economic stimulus money because it was relatively easy to ramp up the multi-year, multi-billion-dollar cleanup of radioactive nuclear waste. But a dispute between the local contractor and the Energy Department resulted in slowdowns. And some South Carolinians objected when the site's contractor proposed in 2010 to ship spent nuclear fuel from other states for recycling at Savannah River. The proposal raised the possibility that Savannah River would effectively replace Nevada's Yucca Mountain as

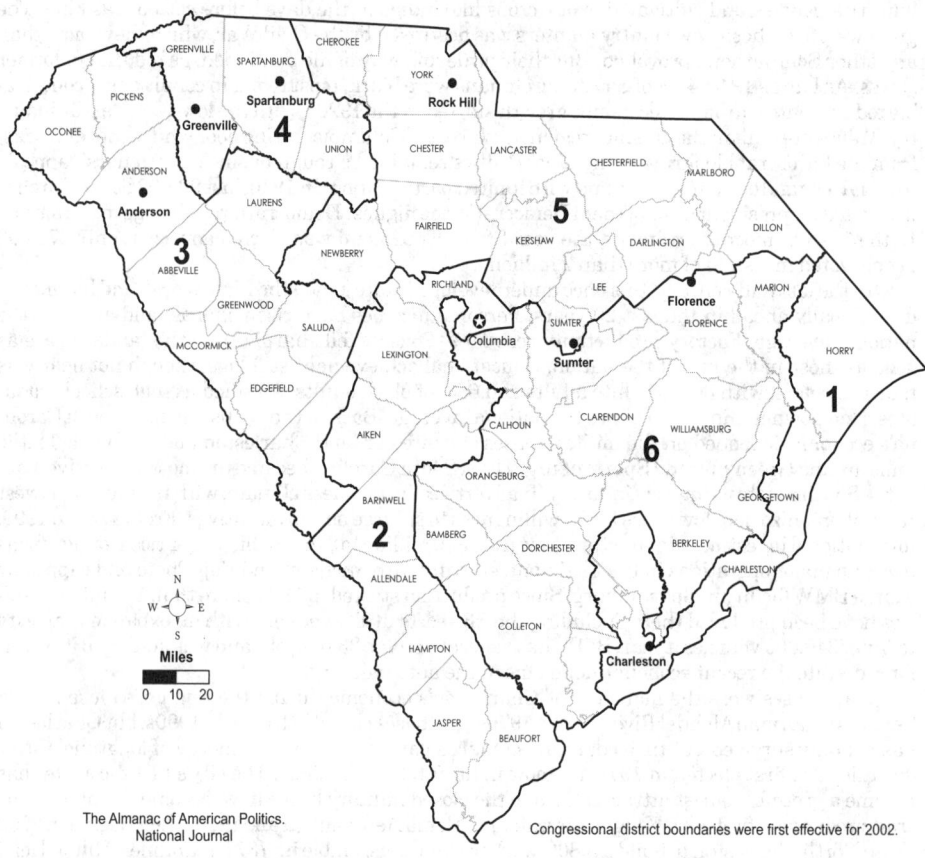

Congressional district boundaries were first effective for 2002.

Governor

Nikki Haley (R)

Elected 2010, term expires Jan. 2015, 1st term; b. Jan. 20, 1972, Bamberg; home, Lexington; Clemson U., B.S. 1994; Methodist; married (Michael); 2 children.

Elected Office: SC House, 2004-10.

Professional Career: Accounting supervisor, FCR Inc., Charlotte, N.C., 1994-96; Chief financial officer, Exotica Intl., Lexington, S.C., 1996-2004.

Office: 1205 Pendleton Street, Columbia, 29201, 803-734-2100; Fax: 803-734-5167; Web site: www.governor.sc.gov.

Election Results

2010 general	Nikki Haley (R)	690,525	(51%)
	Vincent Sheheen (D)	630,534	(47%)
2010 runoff	Nikki Haley (R)	233,733	(65%)
	Gresham Barrett (R)	125,601	(35%)
2010 primary	Nikki Haley (R)	206,326	(49%)
	Gresham Barrett (R)	91,824	(22%)
	Henry McMaster (R)	71,494	(17%)
	Andre Bauer (R)	52,607	(12%)

South Carolina's new governor is Nikki Haley, a conservative, Indian-American Republican elected in 2010. As the first woman and first racial minority to become the deeply conservative state's chief executive, she is at the forefront of the national Republican Party's efforts to tout an image of inclusiveness.

Haley was born Nimrata Nikki Randhawa to Sikh parents who had emigrated from India to Bamberg, S.C. Her father was a biology professor, while her mother started a gift shop in town. Her upbringing in the small, blue-collar community south of Columbia was at times difficult. Although male Sikhs normally do not cut their hair, her brothers had theirs trimmed when they were viciously taunted at school. When she was 5 years old, she and her older sister entered a beauty pageant in which one white winner and one black winner had historically been crowned; the judges disqualified the girls because they were considered neither. Haley worked at her mother's shop and took over the bookkeeping there at age 13, going on to get an accounting degree at Clemson University, where she met her husband, Michael Haley. She said she subsequently converted to Christianity, though later news reports noted that they were wed in two ceremonies, one Sikh and one Methodist. She worked for a waste management and recycling company, and then returned to her mother's business, which had branched out into clothing and jewelry. She helped it grow into a multimillion-dollar company.

Haley decided in 2004 to challenge Republican state Rep. Larry Koon, who had been in office since 1975 and was the chamber's longest-serving member at the time. She was the target of slurs, but brushed them off, saying she wouldn't let them distract her. She ran as a dedicated fiscal conservative who was strongly opposed to raising taxes and managed to hold Koon to less than 50% of the vote, forcing a runoff. She won that matchup with 55% to become the first Indian-American Republican state legislator in the United States. She won re-election in 2006 and 2008 with ease. She developed a reputation as a staunch fiscal conservative and became a loyal ally of Republican Gov. Mark Sanford. She was named majority whip in 2006; she also chaired a subcommittee of the powerful Labor, Commerce and Industry Committee. She sought to lead the full committee in 2009, but angered her party's leaders for seeking to push regulations on the state's payday lending industry and for openly criticizing the House's reluctance to cast recorded votes. She was reassigned to another committee, a move she characterized as punishment.

Haley in May 2009 announced her intention to succeed Sanford, running as an outsider and reformer. "I know what good government can look like," she said. "I'm running for governor so the people of the state will know what it feels like." She said she drew inspiration from Louisiana Gov. Bobby Jindal, who is also Indian-American. She remained a protégé of Sanford's, and though he declined to endorse her, he told *The State* newspaper that she "would make a terrific and inspiring choice as governor." The next month, though, Sanford became a political embarrassment for the state. After disappearing from the state for several days, he admitted to an affair with a woman living in Argentina. His staff's initial explanation that he had been "hiking the Appalachian Trail" quickly entered the lexicon as a euphemism for adultery.

After that, Haley sought to distance herself from Sanford, taking his photographs down from her campaign website. But she endured other challenges in what would become one of the country's ugliest primary battles. She faced three other prominent Republican candidates: Attorney General Henry McMaster, Lt. Gov. Andre Bauer and U.S. Rep. Gresham Barrett. No one, however, was able to emerge as a frontrunner, and Barrett began running an ad calling himself "a Christian family man who won't embarrass us," while Haley was accused of de-emphasizing her upbringing as a Sikh.

In the final weeks of the campaign, a Republican blogger and former Sanford aide claimed he had had "inappropriate sexual contact" with Haley. She denied the charge, and the blogger produced no proof. Several days later, a Republican lobbyist who worked for Bauer said he also had had a sexual encounter with Haley, who again denied the allegations. "This is South Carolina politics at its worst," her spokesman said. Bauer came under suspicion for having started the reports, a charge that he strongly denied. But Haley, appearing to get the benefit of the doubt from voters, started climbing in the polls. Haley also collected the endorsement of former Alaska Gov. Sarah Palin, as well as the support of Jenny Sanford, who had won widespread admiration among South Carolinians for her graceful conduct during her husband's scandal.

A few days before the primary, the race made negative headlines for another reason. GOP state Sen. Jake Knotts said on a radio show, "We already got one raghead in the White House. We don't need another in the governor's mansion." Knotts apologized. And primary voters were wholly unmoved by the display of bigotry. Haley won with 49% of the vote, to 22% for Barrett, 17% for McMaster and 12% for Bauer.

She had little time to bask in her triumph, which, under normal circumstances, would have sealed her general election victory in the overwhelmingly Republican state. Reports surfaced that she had been late in paying income taxes and that her family's clothing business had been hit with liens for failing to pay its taxes. Then, *The State* reported that the foundation arm of a medical center—an entity she had backed in its fight to open a heart-surgery center—had created a fundraising job for her paying more than $100,000 a year. Her Democratic opponent, lawyer and state Sen. Vincent Sheheen, accused her of hypocrisy. But she denied any wrongdoing and continually stuck to her campaign themes, saying that while Sheheen is "talking about the negative ⋯ I have spent all of my time talking about things that are going to create jobs." She also attacked him for voting to regulate payday lenders while being part of a law firm that made money from suing them, saying it was wrong for him to take from "both pots of money."

The barrage of negative publicity Haley received did inflict some damage, but not enough to cost her the governorship. With help from tea party activists, she beat Sheheen 51%-47%, losing populous Charleston County and Richland County—home of state capital Columbia—but dominating the northwestern counties around Greenville, Spartanburg and Anderson as well as the affluent coastal areas in the northeast. Potential Republican presidential candidates wooed her for support, and she agreed to appear at a rally with Minnesota GOP Rep. Michele Bachmann, the tea party's unofficial doyenne in the U.S. House.

Haley's former colleagues welcomed her—a sharp contrast to Sanford, who often clashed with the legislature. "I think the Senate Republican Caucus probably agrees with 85% so far of what she has talked about," GOP state Sen. John Courson told *The Greenville News*. Lawmakers passed a measure that she signed into law, cutting the state's Medicaid spending by 3% as part of a response to the state Health and Human Services' $225 million deficit. In the House, though, lawmakers turned back most of her recommendations, including the proposed elimination of about $1 million for the 2012 GOP primary. In March, she introduced a "report card" that would grade legislators on an A to F scale depending how strongly they backed their agenda, a move that caused even some Republicans to grumble. "Who are they issuing the report card to, my wife or my mom or what?" GOP Rep. Chip Limehouse griped to Reuters.

Meanwhile, Haley's personnel moves drew considerable controversy. *The State* reported in March that almost half the 59 people she had appointed to state boards or commissions had donated to her campaign. And, drawing national publicity, she yanked philanthropist Darla Moore from the University of South Carolina Board of Trustees and replaced her with one of her campaign donors, even though Moore had given more than $70 million to the school. The governor explained that Moore hadn't shown enough interest in the job. "Whether Haley has committed political suicide so early in her promising career—or merely tightened the bolts on her pledge to remake South Carolina as a leader in education and business—remains to be seen," wrote *Washington Post* syndicated conservative columnist Kathleen Parker.

Senior Senator

Lindsey Graham (R)

Elected 2002, term expires 2014, 2nd term; b. July 9, 1955, Central; home, Seneca; U. of SC, B.A. 1977, J.D. 1981; Baptist; single.

Military Career: Air Force, 1982–88; SC Air Natl. Guard, 1989–94 (Operation Desert Storm); Air Force Reserves, 1995–present.

Elected Office: SC House of Reps., 1992–94; U.S. House of Reps., 1995-2003.

Professional Career: U.S. Air Forces Europe Circuit Trial Counsel, 1984–88; Asst. Oconee Cnty. atty., 1988–92; Practicing atty., 1988–94; Judge advocate, McEntire Air Natl. Guard Base, 1989–94; Central SC city atty., 1990–94.

DC Office: 290 RSOB, 20510, 202-224-5972; Fax: 202-224-3808; Web site: lgraham.senate.gov.

State Offices: Columbia, 803-933-0112; Florence, 843-669-1505; Greenville, 864-250-1417; Mt. Pleasant, 843-849-3887; Pendleton, 864-646-4090; Rock Hill, 803-366-2828.

Committees: *Aging (Special). Appropriations:* Commerce, Justice, Science & Related Agencies; Defense; Department of State, Foreign Operations & Related Programs (RMM); Energy & Water Development; Labor, Health & Human Services, Education & Related Agencies; Legislative Branch. *Armed Services:* Emerging Threats & Capabilities; Personnel (RMM); Readiness & Management Support. *Budget. Judiciary:* Constitution, Civil Rights & Human Rights (RMM); Crime & Terrorism; Privacy, Technology & the Law.

Group Ratings

	ACLU	ACU	ADA	CFG	AFS	FRC	LCV	ITIC	NTU	COC
2010	7	92	5	85	6	79	0	33	97	100
2009	–	88	15	81	20	–	9	–	90	86

National Journal Ratings

	2010 LIB	—	2010 CONS	2009 LIB	—	2009 CONS
Economic	21%	—	78%	14%	—	81%
Social	33%	—	66%	30%	—	69%
Foreign	0%	—	72%	21%	—	74%
Composite	23%	—	77%	24%	—	77%

Key Votes of the 111th Congress

1. Overturn Ledbetter	N	5. Pass health care bill	N	9. Ratify New START	N
2. Pass $787 billion stimulus	N	6. Regulate financial firms	N	10. Confirm Elena Kagan	Y
3. Repeal DC gun laws	Y	7. Pass tax cuts for some	N	11. Stop EPA climate regs	Y
4. Confirm Sonia Sotomayor	Y	8. Legalize immigrants' kids	N	12. Repeal don't ask, tell	Y

Election Results

2008 general	Lindsey Graham (R)	1,076,534	(58%)	($9,713,500)
	Bob Conley (D)	790,621	(42%)	($17,105)
2008 primary	Lindsey Graham (R)	187,736	(67%)	
	Buddy Witherspoon (R)	93,125	(33%)	

Prior Winning Percentages: 2002 (54%); House: 2000 (68%); 1998 (100%); 1996 (60%); 1994 (60%)

Lindsey Graham, South Carolina's senior senator, was elected to the House in 1994 and to the Senate in 2002. He has assumed the mantle once occupied by his close friend, Arizona Republican John McCain, as the media-friendly maverick willing to confound conservatives by collaborating with Democrats on high-profile initiatives.

Graham grew up in Pickens County, where his parents owned a tavern in the textile mill town of Central, S.C. Both his parents died young, while Graham was still attending the University of South Carolina, and he became his younger sister's legal guardian. He was the first in his family to graduate from college, and then received a law degree from the University of South Carolina. He was an Air Force prosecutor who worked on assignments overseas, including one case that led to major changes in the service's drug testing program for soldiers. In 1988, he returned home and practiced law in Seneca. In 1992, he was elected to the state House. Graham was called up to active duty and served stateside during the Gulf War, and he has been in the Air Force Reserves since 1995, as a senior instructor in the Air Force's JAG school and also as a reserve judge on the Air Force Court of Criminal Appeals.

In 1994, with the retirement of 20-year Democratic U.S. Rep. Butler Derrick, Graham ran for the House. Both parties had contested primaries, and Graham won the Republican primary without a runoff with 52% of the vote. In the general election, he faced state Sen. Jim Bryan. Graham called for term limits, supported more defense spending and opposed gays in the military. His attitude toward the Clinton administration and the Democratic leadership was unequivocal. He said, "I'm one less vote for an agenda that makes you want to throw up." Graham won 60%-40%, a smashing victory in a district represented only by Democrats since Reconstruction. In the House, Graham had a solidly conservative voting record but did not always support the Republican leadership. In the summer of 1997, he was among a small group of junior House members who plotted with some senior lawmakers to try to oust Speaker Newt Gingrich, who by then had lost the confidence of his Republican troops. But the attempt failed. In a Republican Conference meeting, when Majority Leader Dick Armey of Texas, one of the plotters, asserted that no member of the leadership was involved, Graham challenged that assertion as false.

As a member of the House Judiciary Committee, Graham played a major role in the 1998 impeachment of President Bill Clinton. In the Senate trial, Graham's folksy manner and clear description of Clinton's offenses—"Where I come from, a man who calls someone up at 2:30 in the morning is up to no good"—made him one of the most effective GOP impeachment managers. In 2000, Graham was one of McCain's staunchest supporters in his first bid for the presidency.

Republican Sen. Strom Thurmond, re-elected to his eighth term in 1996, one month before he turned 94, had promised not to run again in 2002. There had not been an open South Carolina Senate seat since 1941. (Both Thurmond and longtime Democratic Sen. Ernest Hollings won their seats by beating incumbent senators appointed to fill vacancies.) Yet in this now heavily Republican state, Graham had no opposition in the Republican primary. His work on impeachment and in the McCain campaign had made him well-known and popular statewide, and he was endorsed by three former governors and Thurmond. Democrats portrayed him as lacking in substance and recruited Alex Sanders, president of the College of Charleston who in 1985 was appointed to the state Court of Appeals.

Sanders was a gifted raconteur, charming and well-connected around the state. He was a solid fundraiser as well, eventually raising $4.2 million, below Graham's $5.8 million, but a considerable achievement for a candidate consistently behind in the polls. He supported the Bush tax cuts and military action in Iraq. But he opposed the death penalty, on religious grounds, and he opposed a constitutional amendment to allow criminalization of flag burning. Graham hammered him on the death penalty and the flag amendment but most of all tried to label him as a liberal, saying Sanders would advance the agenda of Sens. Hillary Rodham Clinton of New York and Edward Kennedy of Massachusetts. Graham won 54%-44% and took the place of a senator first elected in the year before he was born.

He has had a mostly conservative voting record—he was the 24th most conservative senator in 2010, according to *National Journal's* rankings. But he has made some noteworthy breaks with his party, occasionally testing the limits of Republicans' patience. Graham was the only Judiciary Committee Republican to support President Barack Obama's choice of Sonia Sotomayor for the Supreme Court in 2009, saying the president deserved the prerogative to nominate a qualified person of his choice even if the GOP disagreed with her ideology. He took the same position a year later when Obama nominated Solicitor General Elena Kagan for the court. In addition to praising her intellect, he said, "She's funny, and that goes a long way in my book."

Graham also backed Obama's decision to close the U.S. military prison at Cuba's Guantanamo Bay, though he sharply opposed the president's plans to try suspected terrorists in civilian courts instead of military ones. He even defended Treasury secretary nominee Timothy Geithner after it was revealed Geithner had failed to pay back taxes. Although he had supported the Bush administration's Wall Street bailout legislation in 2008, Graham's centrist tendencies ceased when it came to Obama's $787 billion economic stimulus bill in January 2009. He said the legislation "created more government than jobs," and criticized Obama's outreach to Republican colleagues. When Republican Gov. Mark Sanford initially said he would refuse South Carolina's share of the federal stimulus money unless a portion of it could go to pay down the state's debt, Graham said he believed Sanford should accept the money. But on some economic matters, Graham was still the maverick bucking his party. In February 2009, he said he supported a limited nationalization of some banks and Obama's proposal to "stress-test" banks. "I'm not going to be the Herbert Hoover of 2009," saying 'Just let the free market work it out,'" he told the *Charlotte Observer*.

What brought Graham the most attention, however, was his personal negotiations with Democrats on two of the hot button issues in the 111th Congress (2009-10): climate change and immigration. His actions came as McCain was preoccupied with a 2010 primary challenge from the right and sought to burnish his conservative credentials. On climate change, Graham sought to frame the issue as essential toward achieving energy independence: "To me, it is about jobs, not polar bears," he told *The New York Times*. He made clear his disdain with the House-passed bill in 2009 creating a cap-and-trade program limiting greenhouse gas emissions and embarked with Massachusetts Democratic Sen. John Kerry and Connecticut independent Sen. Joe Lieberman on an alternative method of pricing carbon. But Graham angrily pulled out of those discussions in April 2010 when Majority Leader Harry Reid reportedly planned to bring an immigration bill to the Senate floor before taking up the energy and climate change measure. He told his two colleagues that Reid's move was "nothing more than a cynical political ploy" and that the highly charged subject of immigration would muddy the waters for a compromise on climate change. The Senate never took up a climate bill in 2010, and the Republican takeover of the House in 2010 moved the issue to the back burner.

Graham had earlier been working with Democratic Sen. Chuck Schumer of New York on the immigration issue. They came up with a plan that included toughening border security and requiring biometric Social Security cards to ensure illegal immigrants could not get jobs. But the furor over the climate debate ended the Graham-Schumer partnership. Graham later joined conservatives in calling for an end to birthright citizenship, a position that incensed his onetime immigration allies. "He has either taken leave of his senses or of his principles," pro-immigration former Bush speechwriter Michael Gerson wrote in *The Washington Post*. And Graham joined Republicans in opposing the DREAM Act giving the children of illegal immigrants a potential path to citizenship in December 2010.

It was not the first time Graham had waded into the immigration debate. In 2006 and 2007, Graham supported the McCain-Kennedy and Kennedy-Kyl immigration bills, positions that got him in considerable trouble with conservatives who opposed giving illegal immigrants a process to achieve citizenship. Radio talk show host Rush Limbaugh belittled him as "Lindsey Grahamnesty" and the Greenville County Republican party voted to censure him. Graham's public comments suggesting that immigration bill opponents were "bigots" did not help his cause. He tried to rebound in late 2007 by including a $3 billion border security amendment in a defense spending bill. It would fund 700 miles of fence along the U.S.-Mexico border and provide additional vehicle barriers and ground censors, but it was stripped from the final version of the bill by Senate Democrats. In December 2007, Graham joined with Sen. Evan Bayh to support the Indiana Democrat's legislation to impose higher penalties on people found smuggling illegal immigrants across the border, but the amendment never made it out of the Judiciary Committee.

Graham disagreed with the Bush administration on important issues. He voted against the Medicare prescription drug bill in 2003 and against the Republican medical malpractice bill in 2003 and 2004, calling it "one of the worst pieces of legislation I have ever seen." But he co-sponsored a bill requiring that the losing party pays the other side's legal fees in lawsuits between parties from different states. In 2005, he proposed a federal law shielding reporters from having to disclose their sources in court.

Graham was hard on the Bush administration over its increasingly bold techniques in terrorism investigations. He objected to surveillance of communications between al-Qaida suspects abroad and persons in the United States. He was also a critic of the policy of holding unlawful combatants at Guantanamo Bay without offering them an array of rights. When the Bush administration proposed procedures for trying the detainees, Graham criticized them for not allowing detainees to see all the evidence against them and for defying Geneva Conventions, although he agreed that such unlawful combatants were not entitled to full Geneva Conventions. Working with McCain and Armed Services Chairman John Warner, R-Va., Graham marshaled his expertise in military law and procedure to produce a bill allowing aggressive and classified interrogation techniques, defining what is a "grave breach" of the Geneva Conventions and establishing military tribunals allowing defendants to confront the evidence against them. The legislation passed as part of the 2006 defense spending bill.

Since his arrival in the Senate, Graham has been interested in solutions to the Social Security solvency issue. In 2003, he unveiled his own plan: 4% personal retirement accounts, with higher taxes for workers who do not choose them. The proposal was sharply criticized by some conservatives, but Graham persisted. He participated in private meetings with both Democratic and Republican senators, and he insisted that raising the payroll tax limit was necessary if a plan was to get Democratic support.

Comparing his political style to McCain's, Graham told *The New York Times*: "I've never been a Luke Skywalker; I'm a much more calculating guy than that. I understand that you just don't charge into these things based on some moral belief that you're right and the other guy's wrong." Without much of a threat to his own re-election bid, Graham in 2008 traveled the country with

McCain, the Republican presidential nominee. McCain, Graham and Lieberman formed a sort of bipartisan triumvirate on the campaign trail. Graham's support was helpful to McCain in the pivotal January 2008 South Carolina primary, in which McCain redeemed his 2000 loss by winning with 33% of the vote. "There's nobody I trust more than Lindsey Graham," McCain told the Myrtle Beach *Sun News*. Graham was said to be the member of McCain's inner circle who was the most enthusiastic about him tapping Lieberman as his running mate, according to the 2010 book about the campaign, *Game Change*. But McCain settled on Alaska then-Gov. Sarah Palin after Graham began privately floating the idea of Lieberman with social conservatives, enraging Limbaugh and others when word leaked out.

Graham's departures from the party orthodoxy—especially his vote to confirm Kagan—have fueled talk of a primary challenger in 2014. A Public Policy Polling survey in February 2011 found that 52% of regular GOP primary voters said they would back a more conservative choice, with Rep. Joe Wilson—known for shouting "You lie!" at Obama during the president's 2009 health care speech to Congress—leading Graham 43%-41% in a hypothetical matchup. But Graham will be a formidable opponent. In addition to his considerable GOP connections from his association with McCain, he has had a key ally in his South Carolina Senate colleague Jim DeMint, who emerged as a kingmaker for the far right in 2010. And in 2011, Graham sought to mend fences with the tea party, a movement he had once predicted would "die out." He recruited two freshman senators who were tea party favorites, Rand Paul of Kentucky and Mike Lee of Utah, to work with him on Social Security. And he joined new Republican Gov. Nikki Haley in blasting the Democratic health care overhaul.

Junior Senator

Jim DeMint (R)

Elected 2004, term expires 2016, 2nd term; b. Sept. 2, 1951, Greenville; home, Greenville; U. of TN, B.S. 1973, Clemson U., M.B.A. 1981; Presbyterian; married (Debbie); 4 children.

Elected Office: U.S. House of Reps., 1999-2005.

Professional Career: Sales rep., Scott Paper, 1973-75; Acct. rep., Henderson Advertising, 1975-81; V.P., Leslie Advertising, 1981-84; Pres., DeMint Marketing, 1983-98.

DC Office: 167 RSOB, 20510, 202-224-6121; Fax: 202-228-5143; Web site: demint.senate.gov.

State Offices: Charleston, 843-727-4525; Columbia, 803-771-6112; Greenville, 864-233-5366.

Committees: *Banking, Housing & Urban Affairs:* Financial Institutions & Consumer Protection; Housing, Transportation & Community Development (RMM); Securities, Insurance & Investment. *Commerce, Science & Transportation:* Aviation Operations, Safety & Security; Communications, Technology & the Internet (RMM); Competitiveness, Innovation & Export Promotion; Surface Transportation & Merchant Marine Infrastructure, Safety & Security. *Foreign Relations:* European Affairs; International Operations & Organizations, Democracy & Global Women's Issues (RMM); Western Hemisphere, Peace Corps & Global Narcotics Affairs. *Joint Economic Committee.*

Group Ratings

	ACLU	ACU	ADA	CFG	AFS	FRC	LCV	ITIC	NTU	COC
2010	7	100	5	100	0	100	14	33	96	81
2009	–	100	5	100	0	–	0	–	97	71

National Journal Ratings

	2010 LIB — 2010 CONS		2009 LIB — 2009 CONS	
Economic	0%	— 87%	3%	— 95%
Social	0%	— 79%	0%	— 94%
Foreign	0%	— 72%	0%	— 84%
Composite	10%	— 90%	5%	— 95%

Key Votes of the 111th Congress

1. Overturn Ledbetter	N	5. Pass health care bill	N	9. Ratify New START	N
2. Pass $787 billion stimulus	N	6. Regulate financial firms	N	10. Confirm Elena Kagan	N
3. Repeal DC gun laws	Y	7. Pass tax cuts for some	N	11. Stop EPA climate regs	Y
4. Confirm Sonia Sotomayor	N	8. Legalize immigrants' kids	N	12. Repeal don't ask, tell	N

Election Results

2010 general	Jim DeMint (R)	810,771	(61%)	($7,199,774)
	Alvin Greene (D)	364,598	(28%)	
	Tom Clements (Green)	121,472	(9%)	
2010 primary	Jim DeMint (R)	342,464	(83%)	
	Susan Gaddy (R)	70,194	(17%)	

Prior Winning Percentages: 2004 (54%); House: 2002 (69%); 2000 (80%); 1998 (58%)

South Carolina's junior senator is Jim DeMint, a Republican first elected in 2004. DeMint was born in Greenville, where his father was stationed in the Air Force. When his parents divorced, his mother supported the family by establishing a dance school, the DeMint Academy of Dance and Decorum. He graduated from the University of Tennessee and Clemson University's business school and returned to Greenville to work in his father-in-law's advertising business. In 1983, he founded DeMint Marketing, a research firm with businesses, schools, colleges and hospitals as clients. In 1992, he was hired by Republican Bob Inglis in his campaign for the 4th District House seat, helping Inglis hone his message using focus groups and advertising techniques.

In 1998, when Inglis ran unsuccessfully against Democratic Sen. Ernest Hollings, DeMint ran to succeed him. Like Inglis, he pledged to serve only three terms and take no political action committee money. He called for replacing the graduated income tax with a national sales tax, or, flat tax, for individual retirement accounts in Social Security and for a "right-to-life" amendment to the Constitution. In the Republican primary, he faced state Sen. Mike Fair, a former University of South Carolina quarterback who was favored to win. On the first ballot, Fair led with 32% to 23% for DeMint. In the runoff campaign, DeMint labeled Fair a "career politician" and upset him 53%-47%. He won the general election 58%-40%.

In the House, DeMint was elected president of the Republican freshman class and joined other junior Republicans seeking to rein in spending by the appropriators. Resisting pressure from the state's textile industry, he was the only South Carolina House member to vote for normalizing trade relations with China, arguing that the best way to remedy human rights abuses was "to export our products and principles." DeMint opposed President George W. Bush's No Child Left Behind education bill in 2001 and sought to replace it with block grants to states. Bush eventually persuaded DeMint to back down in a meeting in the Oval Office. In 2003, he sponsored unsuccessful legislation to allow people under age 55 to set aside 3% to 8% of their Social Security withholding income in personal investment accounts.

DeMint's trade votes brought him a primary challenger in 2002. Former state Rep. Phil Bradley had the support of textile titan Roger Milliken, long a financer of conservative and protectionist candidates. But DeMint defended his support for free trade as beneficial for international investment in the district and won 62%-38%.

In 2003, DeMint said that he would keep his promise to serve only three House terms, and that he would run for the Senate seat of the retiring Hollings. In the Republican primary, DeMint faced former Gov. David Beasley, former state Attorney General Charlie Condon and Charleston developer Thomas Ravenel. Trade was a major issue. South Carolina had lost nearly 70,000 manufacturing jobs since 1999. DeMint and Ravenel ran as free traders, while Beasley and Condon took protectionist positions. DeMint was backed by the national anti-tax group Club for Growth, and Beasley's biggest contributors were Milliken, other textile executives and PACs. Beasley ran ads featuring an empty textile plant that claimed DeMint advocated trade policies that had cost the state more than 50,000 jobs. A Condon ad singled out DeMint's vote to allow China into the World Trade Organization. DeMint responded with ads featuring BMW's Spartanburg plant and pointed to increased U.S. exports to China. Beasley led the primary with 37%; DeMint came in second with 26%, Ravenel had 25%, and Condon 9%. In the runoff, DeMint benefited from endorsements from Ravenel and Condon and won 59%-41%.

His general election opponent was state schools Superintendent Inez Tenenbaum, a popular Democrat who had twice won statewide election. Tenenbaum ran on her record in education and the improving SAT scores of South Carolina high school students. Her signature outfits were red dresses and suits, and she campaigned around the state aboard the Red Dress Express, a recreational vehicle with an image of her on its sides. She argued that DeMint's House votes cost the state tens of thousands of jobs and she opposed the 2005 Central American Free Trade Agreement. Tenenbaum also claimed that DeMint's advocacy of a national sales tax would result in a 95% tax hike on South Carolina residents.

DeMint defended his record in radio and television ads, and the party's Senate campaign committee weighed in with $1.3 million for DeMint in October. (Tenenbaum got $2.5 million in help from the Democrats.) Overall, DeMint spent $9 million to her $6.2 million. DeMint stirred some controversy when in a debate he said gay people should not be allowed to teach in public schools. "Folks teaching in schools need to represent our values," he said. Still, DeMint won 54%-44%. He lost Charleston County by 100 votes, but won big margins Upstate, 63%-35% in Greenville County and 59%-38% in Spartanburg County. His election gave South Carolina two Republican senators for the first time since 1877.

DeMint has been consistently ranked among the most conservative senators in *National Journal's* annual vote analysis. He opposed the comprehensive immigration legislation backed by fellow South Carolina Republican Sen. Lindsey Graham in 2006 and 2007, and he has stoutly opposed the cap-and-trade legislation to curb carbon emissions in which Graham has taken an interest. DeMint also introduced the Senate to the over-heated partisan rhetoric more common in the House. In touting his support for the war in Iraq, he told a Spartanburg audience in May 2007, "Al-Qaida knows that we've got a lot of wimps in Congress. I believe a lot of the casualties can be laid at the feet of all the talk in Congress about how we've got to get out, we've got to cut and run." He also suggested that Senate Majority Leader Harry Reid should be censured after he declared the war in Iraq was lost.

DeMint joined Sen. Tom Coburn, R-Okla., in efforts to limit earmarked spending in appropriations bills. In 2008, he proposed a one-year moratorium on earmarks, which was supported by all three then-active presidential candidates—Republican John McCain and Democrats Barack Obama and Hillary Rodham Clinton—but was rejected 71-29 by the Senate. He unsuccessfully opposed expansion of Bush's global AIDS program, telling Columbia's *The State* that "for us to attempt to buy friendship around the world by spending $50 billion is just completely irresponsible. There are enough worthy causes around the world to bankrupt us a hundred times over." He has not hesitated to irritate colleagues of both parties. In July 2007, he forced a Saturday vote on a housing bill and then did not show up himself. He also he tried in 2008 to impose term limits on party leadership positions, which was rejected overwhelmingly. His combative tactics probably cost him a seat on the Finance Committee.

After a dismal year for the GOP in 2008, DeMint chastised fellow Republicans, saying, "The election reflects a failure of Republicans to keep their conservative promises." He also was widely quoted saying he would "rather have 30 Republicans in the Senate who believe in the principles of freedom than 60 who don't believe in anything." And DeMint aggressively went on the attack against the new Democratic president. He tried to substitute President Barack Obama's 2009 economic stimulus bill with one containing only tax cuts, and he tried to stop the advance of Obama's health care initiative, famously telling Republicans in July 2009, "If we're able to stop Obama on this, it will be his Waterloo. It will break him." As usual, he had his own plan, which created vouchers in amounts varying according to need and made it possible for individuals to buy health insurance across state lines. It went nowhere. In October 2010, he tried unsuccessfully to cut funding for National Public Radio after it fired commentator Juan Williams for saying that in the current atmosphere of terrorist threats against the United States, he gets worried boarding an airplane if he sees another passenger in "Muslim garb."

As the 2010 election season shaped up, DeMint decided to get personally involved in contests where he found Republicans to be insufficiently conservative. In any other election year, his plan might have been an ego-driven exercise in pointlessness. But DeMint's unyielding views, and his take-no-prisoners style, appealed to disenfranchised conservatives and especially to the tea party groups springing up around the country. DeMint also set up a fundraising operation separate from the National Republican Senatorial Committee. His Senate Conservatives Fund PAC raised some $9.3 million during the campaign season. In March 2010, *Politico* called DeMint "the Washington leader of the tea party movement."

In May 2009, after Florida Gov. Charlie Crist announced he would run for an open Senate seat, he was endorsed by mainstream Senate Republicans and their campaign committee, headed by John Cornyn of Texas. But DeMint backed former state House Speaker Marco Rubio in the primary because Crist had supported Obama's stimulus bill. Rubio later credited DeMint with helping him win the seat. (Crist, on the verge of losing the primary, ran as an independent and lost to Rubio.) "Jim DeMint believed in me when the only people who believed in me lived in my house," Rubio told *The State.*

DeMint also refused to back Republican incumbents Bob Bennett of Utah, John McCain of Arizona and Lisa Murkowski of Alaska in their nomination contests, and he endorsed tea party favorite Rand Paul of Kentucky, who beat Senate Minority Leader Mitch McConnell's endorsed candidate in the May primary. Bennett lost his seat in the primary. McCain won in the primary and went on to be re-elected. Murkowski was defeated in the GOP primary, but went on to pull off a stunning victory as a write-in candidate. Other DeMint picks were: Marlin Stutzman in Indiana, who lost the May Senate primary to Dan Coats but later won the 3rd House District; Ken Buck in Colorado, who won the August primary and narrowly lost the general election to Democrat Michael Bennet; Ovid Lamontagne in New Hampshire, who lost the September primary, and Christine O'Donnell in Delaware, who upset Republican moderate Mike Castle in the September primary and then lost the general election to Christopher Coons.

DeMint's moves stunned some of his Senate colleagues. Maine Republican Susan Collins told *The New York Times*, "It is a new and shocking development to have a member of our conference opposing incumbent Republicans." After the election, there was speculation that successful De-Mint-endorsed candidates like Rubio, Paul and Mike Lee of Utah would form a cohesive tea party bloc in the Senate in the 112th Congress (2011-12). Writing in *The Wall Street Journal* days after the election, DeMint said, "Tea party Republicans were elected to go to Washington and save the country, not to be co-opted by the club. So put on your boxing gloves. The fight begins today." On Nov. 15, 2010, Minority Leader McConnell endorsed DeMint's ban on earmarks, which he had resisted earlier.

Just how much power his small coalition will wield remains to be seen. In December 2010, DeMint adamantly opposed the tax deal that Obama reached with congressional Republicans, but it passed the Senate anyway and was enacted into law. He also had to back down from his effort to require a full reading of the New START treaty, which also passed in December. And his opposi-tion to earmarks spurred considerable criticism in South Carolina.

DeMint had little trouble retaining his seat in 2010. The Democrats' preferred candidate, Vic Rawl, was defeated 59%-41% in the primary by Alvin Greene, an unemployed man living with his parents who had been arrested for soliciting sex with a University of South Carolina student in 2010. Greene evidently borrowed money to pay the $10,440 filing fee, but spent nothing more on his campaign. Democratic Rep. Jim Clyburn, then the House majority whip, suggested Greene was a Republican plant, but no evidence of that emerged in the campaign. Efforts to dump Greene were unsuccessful, further embarrassing the Democrats. DeMint won with 61% of the vote, to 28% for Greene and 9% for Green Party candidate Tom Clements. DeMint won the highest percentage for any South Carolina senator since Republican Strom Thurmond in 1990, who was re-elected with 64% that year.

But DeMint's tendency to take a hard conservative line seems likely to continue to generate controversy back home, as his trade votes did years earlier. In early 2011, South Carolina civic and business leaders were enraged when DeMint refused to sign a letter requesting $400,000 for a federal study of dredging the Port of Charleston as other members of the South Carolina delegation had. (Rep. Joe Wilson, R-S.C., also wouldn't sign.) That prompted Democratic Sen. Byron Dorgan, the Appropriations subcommittee chairman, to deny the funding request. The Port of Charleston, the deepest in the Southeast, has been integral to the operations of big South Carolina firms like Michelin and BMW, making it an important contributor to the state's economic growth. The dredg-ing would enable the port to accommodate larger ships that will be coming through an enlarged Panama Canal after 2014.

DeMint's role in the 2010 Senate campaigns led some to suggest he should run for president. He said he had no intention to run, but still, he delivered a keynote speech in March 2011 at a Des Moines forum for potential Republican candidates. DeMint has also written two books about his ideas, another typical pre-presidential campaign move. His 2008 book is called *Why We Whisper: Restoring Our Right to Say It's Wrong*, and one published in 2009 is titled *Saving Freedom: We Can Stop America's Slide into Socialism*.

FIRST DISTRICT

Tim Scott (R)

Elected 2010, 1st term; b. Sept. 19, 1965, Charleston; home, Charleston; Charleston Southern U., B.S. 1988; Christian; Single.

Elected Office: Charleston Cnty. Cncl., 1995-2008, chmn., 2007-08; SC House, 2008-10.

Professional Career: Partner, real estate firm; owner, Tim Scott Allstate.

DC Office: 1117 LHOB, 20515, 202-225-3176; Fax: 202-225-3407; Web site: timscott.house.gov.

State Offices: Charleston, 843-852-2222; Myrtle Beach, 843-445-6459.

Committees: *Rules.*

Election Results

2010 general	Tim Scott (R)	152,755	(65%)	($1,213,574)
	Ben Frasier (D)	67,008	(29%)	($26,558)
2010 runoff	Tim Scott (R)	46,989	(68%)	
	Paul Thurmond (R)	21,799	(32%)	
2010 primary	Tim Scott (R)	25,457	(31%)	
	Paul Thurmond (R)	13,149	(16%)	
	Carroll Campbell (R)	11,665	(14%)	
	Larry Kobrovsky (R)	8,521	(11%)	
	Stovall Witte (R)	7,192	(9%)	
	Clark Parker (R)	6,769	(8%)	

Population		Race/Ethnicity		Work	
Pop. 2010:	856,956	White:	70.8%	Private:	76.2%
Change since 2000:	Up 28.2%	Black:	19.6%	Government:	17.8%
Urban:	78.4%	Hispanic:	5.8%	Self-employed:	5.9%
Rural:	21.6%	Asian:	1.5%	Blue collar:	20.4%
Area size:	3,418 sq. mi.	Native Am.:	0.4%	White collar:	60.1%
		Hawaiian:	0.1%	Khaki collar:	1.3%
Age		Two+ races:	1.7%	Other:	18.1%
Median age:	37.3 yrs.				
More than 65 yrs:	13.6%	*Ancestry*		Median income:	$49,210
Less than 18 yrs:	22.8%	USA	10.8%	Median Home Value:	$197,300
		German	10.5%		
Education		Irish	9.7%	**Military Veterans**	
H.S. grad:	88.6%			% of Pop:	13.9%
College grad:	28.4%				
Grad degree:	9.9%				

Eastern South Carolina; Charleston

Looking out across the harbor to Fort Sumter are the glorious mansions of the Battery, gazing on the same view that the hot-blooded young swells of Charleston did in April 1861, when they fired the shots that began the Civil War. Today, there are few more beautiful urban scenes in America than the pastel "single houses" of Charleston, built flush with the sidewalk, turning their shoulders to the streets, with open piazzas inside their iron gateways facing south to catch the breeze.

2008 Presidential Vote

John McCain (R)	196,996	(56%)
Barack Obama (D)	148,218	(42%)

2004 Presidential Vote

George Bush (R)	172,836	(61%)
John Kerry (D)	109,790	(39%)

Cook Partisan Voting Index: R+10

Founded in 1670, Charleston was blessed with one of the finest harbors on the Atlantic, at the point where, Charlestonians like to say, the Ashley and Cooper rivers meet to form the Atlantic Ocean. It was one of the South's two leading cities during the Civil War. Cargoes of rice, indigo, cotton and slaves crossed its docks, enriching the white planters and merchants who dominated the state's economic and political life. After the war, Charleston became an economic backwater, enabling the old buildings to survive. The loving restorations of recent years have made the center city look better than ever and have attracted a considerable tourist trade.

Charleston's old society is descended from Barbados planters and French Huguenots, Sephardic Jews and the second sons of English gentry, and was once a leading force in American political life. The hotheads in the gallery disrupted the 1860 Democratic National Convention here so boisterously that it was adjourned and reconvened in Baltimore, while Southern Democrats split off and nominated their own candidate, enabling Abraham Lincoln to win with 38% of the popular vote. The history of black South Carolinians, memorialized in George Gershwin's *Porgy and Bess*, is noteworthy, but the tale of slavery, once hidden under a blanket of politeness, is only now emerging, as many, though not all, plantations near Charleston add programs on the history of slavery to tours once dominated by romantic tales of the old South.

Navy and Air Force bases once accounted for 20% of payrolls in metropolitan Charleston. Many of these bases are now closed, but a vibrant private economy with lots of small companies has emerged, most notably at the 1,600-acre Charleston Naval Weapons Station, where, thanks to concerted efforts by regional officials, thousands of new jobs have been created since the base closed in 1996. The Port of Charleston Harbor is still a major economic force in the region. With the deepest water in the Southeast, the busy facility generates 261,000 jobs in the state and $1.5 billion in tax revenues. The city of Charleston is investing heavily in its future, with plans for over $1 billion in improvements and a new terminal to boost container capacity by 50% by 2018. The importance of the port to the state's economy was evident in a nasty battle that broke out in the South Carolina congressional delegation in early 2011. President Barack Obama withheld a vital $400,000 grant for initial work on deepening the port after Republicans Jim DeMint in the Senate and Joe Wilson in the House declined to sign a delegation letter requesting the money, apparently out of concern they would be seen as taking part in earmarking. Democratic Rep. James Clyburn, of South Carolina's 6th District, blamed the two for jeopardizing the expansion plans.

Ninety miles northeast, Myrtle Beach has witnessed a boom in retirees and vacationers. Myrtle Beach and the 60-mile Grand Strand, with miles of beachfront and golf courses, attract 14 million tourists annually, and the population of Horry County has grown 34% since 2000. But its brisk growth and new construction made it especially vulnerable when the housing market collapsed in 2007. Unemployment in Myrtle Beach shot from 7.5% that year to 22% in 2009.

The 1st Congressional District of South Carolina stretches along the coast from south of Charleston to north of Myrtle Beach, and takes in Murrells Inlet, Pawleys Island and Litchfield Beach. It includes the heavily white Battery and the area west of the Ashley River but not the heavily African-American areas to the north and in North Charleston. But the 1st District is still relatively diverse, with a 20% black population. It also includes the burgeoning suburbs in Berkeley and Dorchester counties. In addition to the dominant tourism industry, the chief sources of local jobs are the port, the military and farming. This is solidly Republican country. It voted 61% for George W. Bush in 2004 and 56% for John McCain in 2008. The conservatism of the Lowcountry—the term for South Carolina's coastal counties, including Charleston—is more economic and less cultural than the conservatism of the Upstate region of South Carolina. Many voters here favor environmental restrictions and efforts to curb sprawl.

Tim Scott (R)

The new congressman from South Carolina's 1st District is Tim Scott, elected in 2010 to succeed the retiring GOP Rep. Henry Brown. Scott is one of two African-American Republicans in Congress and is a freshman-class representative to the GOP leadership. He earlier made history as the first black Republican elected to the South Carolina Legislature since Reconstruction.

Scott and his siblings were raised by a single mother who worked 16-hour days as a nurse's assistant. Scott got his first job at age 13. He was on the verge of flunking out of high school when he met the man who he says changed his life—John Moniz, the owner of the fast-food restaurant next to the movie theater where Scott worked, and where he would regularly buy french fries, the only food he could afford. Moniz, who considered himself a born-again Christian, became a father figure for Scott, teaching him the value of personal discipline and hard work, according to newspaper accounts of Scott's life. Scott finished high school and went on to earn a partial football scholarship to Presbyterian College. He eventually transferred to Charleston Southern University, where he earned a bachelor's degree in political science.

Scott ran an insurance company and owned part of a real-estate agency. His first elected office was a seat on the Charleston County Council in 1995. Just after his election, he received a handwritten note of congratulations from then-Sen. Strom Thurmond, R-S.C., who had run for president on a pro-segregation platform in 1948. Thurmond's past didn't stop Scott from accepting the job as statewide co-chairman of the now-deceased Thurmond's final senatorial campaign in 1996. Asked how an African-American could help Thurmond, Scott told *The New York Times*, "The Strom

Thurmond I knew had nothing to do with that," and noted that Thurmond's views on race had evolved. Scott also said that Thurmond taught him the value of constituent service.

In the GOP primary, Scott faced opposition from candidates with better name recognition, including Carroll Campbell III, son of former South Carolina Gov. Carroll Campbell Jr.; and Paul Thurmond, the former senator's son. But Scott got help from national Republican organizations. He came in first in the primary and Thurmond took second, but neither got the necessary 50% to avoid a runoff. There were few differences between the two, although Thurmond did not share Scott's willingness to abide by term limits and to swear off earmarked spending. Scott claimed that in his 15 years in elected office, he has never voted for a tax increase. His conservative credentials won him praise from prominent Republicans such as former Alaska Gov. Sarah Palin and former House Speaker Newt Gingrich of Georgia. In the runoff election, Scott defeated Thurmond, 68% to 32%. In the general election, he easily beat Democrat Ben Frasier, a retired federal worker, 65% to 29%. His race appeared to be a non-issue for the district's voters, about 70% of whom are white.

Scott opposes many of President Barack Obama's major initiatives that are backed by the liberal Congressional Black Caucus. Scott favors repeal of the health care overhaul and opposes a proposed Democratic bill to limit carbon emissions. He says he will abstain from earmarking funds for his district. Scott supports school choice and government-funded tuition vouchers, and he opposes same-sex marriage. Scott has said he will serve no more than four terms. He has a brother in the Air Force and one in the Army, and takes a strong interest in military issues.

SECOND DISTRICT

Joe Wilson (R)

Elected Dec. 2001, 5th full term; b. July 31, 1947, Charleston; home, Springdale; Washington & Lee U., B.A., 1969, U. of S.C., J.D., 1972; Presbyterian; married (Roxanne); 4 children.

Military Career: Army Reserves, 1972-75; SC Natl. Guard, 1975-2003.

Elected Office: SC Senate, 1985-2001.

Professional Career: Practicing atty., 1972-2001.

DC Office: 2229 RHOB, 20515, 202-225-2452; Fax: 202-225-2455; Web site: joewilson.house.gov.

State Offices: Beaufort, 843-521-2530; West Columbia, 803-939-0041.

Committees: *Armed Services:* Air & Land Forces; Military Personnel (Chmn). *Education & the Workforce:* Health, Employment, Labor & Pensions. *Foreign Affairs:* Middle East & South Asia.

Group Ratings

	ACLU	ACU	ADA	CFG	AFS	FRC	LCV	ITIC	NTU	COC
2010	13	96	5	87	0	100	10	0	86	75
2009	–	96	0	86	11	–	0	–	89	80

National Journal Ratings

	2010 LIB	—	2010 CONS	2009 LIB	—	2009 CONS
Economic	18%	—	81%	9%	—	89%
Social	23%	—	77%	0%	—	93%
Foreign	12%	—	79%	33%	—	63%
Composite	19%	—	81%	16%	—	84%

Key Votes of the 111th Congress

1. Overturn Ledbetter	N	5. Bar federal abortion funds	Y	9. Stop detainee transfers	Y
2. Pass $820 billion stimulus	N	6. Pass health care bill	N	10. Legalize immigrants' kids	N
3. Let guns in national parks	Y	7. Regulate financial firms	N	11. Repeal don't ask, tell	N
4. Pass cap-and-trade	N	8. Pass tax cuts for some	N	12. Limit campaign funds	N

Election Results

2010 general	Joe Wilson (R)	138,861	(53%)	($4,739,095)
	Rob Miller (D)	113,625	(44%)	($3,134,569)
2010 primary	Joe Wilson (R)	64,973	(83%)	
	Phil Black (R)	12,923	(17%)	

Prior Winning Percentages: 2008 (54%), 2006 (63%), 2004 (65%), 2002 (84%), 2001 special (73%)

Population		Race/Ethnicity		Work	
Pop. 2010:	825,324	White:	62.7%	Private:	70.6%
Change since 2000:	Up 23.4%	Black:	26.9%	Government:	23.8%
Urban:	66.0%	Hispanic:	6.9%	Self-employed:	5.5%
Rural:	34.0%	Asian:	1.6%	Blue collar:	19.4%
Area size:	5,237 sq. mi.	Native Am.:	0.3%	White collar:	60.4%
		Hawaiian:	0.1%	Khaki collar:	4.1%
Age		Two+ races:	1.5%	Other:	16.1%
Median age:	36.6 yrs.				
More than 65 yrs:	12.9%	*Ancestry*		Median income:	$51,156
Less than 18 yrs:	24.4%	German	11.3%	Median Home Value:	$158,700
		English	9.1%		
Education		Irish	8.9%	**Military Veterans**	
H.S. grad:	88.3%			% of Pop:	12.5%
College grad:	31.8%				
Grad degree:	11.7%				

Central South Carolina; Columbia

In 1786, soon after the Revolutionary War, the South Carolina Legislature decided to move the state capital away from the Charleston aristocracy and into the Upstate interior, away from a city named after a king to a new city named after a discoverer of America. So began Columbia. The State House was built on high ground above the Congaree River in a town of one-and-a-half story houses with first-floor porticos, dormers and raised brick basements—"Columbia cottages."

2008 Presidential Vote
John McCain (R) 189,874 (54%)
Barack Obama (D) 158,055 (45%)

2004 Presidential Vote
George Bush (R) 174,340 (60%)
John Kerry (D) 114,253 (39%)

Cook Partisan Voting Index: R+9

In 1865, Gen. William Tecumseh Sherman's army burned almost everything here but the Statehouse—something remembered by a local Presbyterian minister's eight-year-old son, whose name was Thomas Woodrow Wilson. Columbia recovered, but grew slowly, with the state government and the state university, the Army's Fort Jackson and local insurance companies providing steady employment. Columbia's politics were personified by Jimmy Byrnes, the Democrat who was first elected to Congress in 1910 and returned from top posts in President Franklin D. Roosevelt's Washington to serve as governor. Byrnes adamantly opposed the *Brown v. Board of Education* decision in 1954. Since then, upwardly mobile white South Carolinians, transplanted from underdeveloped rural areas to comfortable two-car-garage subdivisions, have turned Republican, first in national elections and then at the state and local levels. Metro Columbia leans Republican, although Columbia's Richland County, which was 45% African-American in 2010, votes Democratic. Across the river, Lexington County is heavily Republican.

The 2nd Congressional District of South Carolina includes most of metro Columbia, except for black neighborhoods in northern and western Columbia and the southern and eastern parts of Richland County that are in the black-majority 6th District. It contains the city's affluent white neighborhoods and the spread-out towns and countryside beyond, with their shopping centers, churches and the Army's huge training center, Fort Jackson. The district extends south, taking in Barnwell County and half of the Savannah River Site, which from 1954 to 1991 was one of the nation's nuclear weapons manufacturing complexes. Since then, it has been undergoing a multi-billion-dollar cleanup—ramped up with $1.6 billion from the 2009 economic stimulus bill.

Connected to this territory by several lightly populated, low-income rural counties is fast-growing Beaufort County on the coast, with the old county seat of Beaufort and the carefully manicured developments of Hilton Head Island. The district also takes in the Marine Corps' Parris Island training base and air station, which was chosen in 2010 as the base for five squadrons of the F-35 Joint Strike Fighter. This part of the district distinctively blends old and new. Beaufort's old mansions and evocative Spanish moss provided the backdrop for the prose of novelist Pat Conroy, while the posh condominium developments and golfing resorts around Hilton Head and the Sun City Hilton Head development helped drive up Beaufort County's population. On nearby St. Helena Island, slave owners escaping the heat and the mosquitoes ran largely absentee operations, thus allowing Gullah culture—a fusion of English and African elements—to thrive. President George W. Bush won 60% of the vote in the 2nd District in 2004, and Republican John McCain got 54% in 2008.

Joe Wilson (R)

The congressman from the 2nd District is Joe Wilson, a Republican who won the seat in a December 2001 special election. In Washington, he has a reputation as a staunch conservative, but mostly he is known as the lawmaker who breached congressional decorum in a spectacular way in 2009 by shouting, "You lie," during President Barack Obama's health care address to a joint meeting of Congress.

Wilson grew up in Charleston and graduated from Washington & Lee University and the University of South Carolina law school. He worked as an aide to 2nd District GOP Rep. Floyd Spence and then for Republican Sen. Strom Thurmond. Wilson was deputy general counsel at the Energy Department during the Reagan administration. He practiced law in West Columbia for 25 years and worked on many political campaigns. In 1984, he was elected to the state Senate, where he chaired the Transportation Committee. During this period, he served 31 years as a staff judge advocate in the South Carolina Army National Guard, retiring in 2003. (All four of Wilson's sons have been Eagle Scouts and served in the military, two of them in Iraq.) In 2001, when Spence died after more than 30 years in the House, Wilson became the front-runner to replace his longtime friend and mentor. In his campaign, he pledged to continue Spence's focus on national defense. He won the Republican primary with 76% of the vote, and defeated his Democratic opponent easily, 73%-25%.

In the House, Wilson has had a conservative voting record. With a seat on the Armed Services Committee, he has concentrated, as promised, on military issues. In January 2011, he became chairman of the Military Personnel Subcommittee of Armed Services. He has advocated a closer military relationship with India, and he supported President George W. Bush on the Iraq war, traveling frequently to Iraq and Afghanistan to gauge progress. When Democrats were in the majority in 2010, he opposed Democratic Chairman Ike Skelton's defense authorization bill that included a provision repealing the ban on openly gay service personnel. Wilson was a strong backer of a 1.9% pay raise for the military that year.

Wilson was unknown outside of his district, and barely known in Washington, before his outburst during Obama's September 2009 speech to House members and senators gathered for a joint session of Congress. As Obama was answering what he called critics' "bogus claims" of his health care legislation, Wilson called out, "You lie!" His behavior was the subject of stinging commentary on editorial pages and talk shows around the country. He apologized to Obama in a phone call, but rebuffed Democratic demands for a more public apology from the well of the House. His South Carolina colleague, then-Democratic Majority Whip James Clyburn, alleged there was a taint of racism in Wilson's reaction, noting that no other president in memory had been the target of a similar breach in protocol during a joint session. Democrats pushed for a floor vote to sanction Wilson and the House passed a "resolution of disapproval" on a mostly party-line vote.

Wilson also took some heat at home in 2010, after he refused to sign a letter requesting an appropriations earmark for a $400,000 study of dredging in the Port of Charleston, a project aimed at making the port capable of accommodating larger ships that will be coming through an enlarged Panama Canal after 2014. The letter was submitted to the Appropriations committees from the South Carolina congressional delegation, but Wilson and Sen. Jim DeMint declined to sign based on their objections to the practice of earmarking. Because of the dissension in the delegation, the earmark for the study was refused, enraging civic and business leaders who saw the project as vital to the state's future economic growth.

On other issues with strong local interest, Wilson joined most other South Carolina Republicans in opposing trade promotion authority for presidents, but he voted for the Central America Free Trade Agreement in 2005. In March 2010, he criticized the Obama administration's decision to withhold funding for the Yucca Mountain nuclear waste depository in Nevada, saying the Savannah River Site would be stuck indefinitely holding 7,200 containers of spent nuclear waste.

On the Education and Labor Committee, Wilson in 2003 won House passage of a bill to expand college loan forgiveness for math, science and special education teachers who work in impoverished areas. He also worked with Democrats to make permanent the child adoption tax credit. But Wilson failed in his quest to get the top Republican slot on the committee in 2009, when California Rep. Buck McKeon relinquished the post to become the ranking member on Armed Services. Wilson had more committee seniority than his competitors, but lost out to John Kline of Minnesota.

Over the years, Wilson has made a practice of conducting an annual five-day bus tour across the district, and from 2002 to 2006, he was re-elected by wide margins. In 2008, Democrat Rob Miller, an Iraq veteran, spent $624,000 without any help from the national party, and held Wilson to a 54%-46% victory.

Miller decided to run again in 2010. A Democratic poll showed an even race, but Miller was a disappointing candidate. *The State* newspaper said Miller ran "a stealth campaign, holding few public events and kicking a Columbia TV crew out of a speech to Democrats." Wilson spent $4.7 million and Miller $3.1 million, setting a record for South Carolina House races. But the result was almost identical to 2008: Wilson won 53%-44%, carrying white-majority counties and losing black-majority counties. It was not the Wilson family's only electoral success that year. His son, Alan, won a race for state attorney general, 54%-44%.

THIRD DISTRICT

Jeff Duncan (R)

Elected 2010, 1st term; b. Jan. 7, 1966, Greenville; home, Laurens; Clemson U., B.A. 1988; Southern Baptist; Married (Melody); 3 children.

Elected Office: SC House, 2002-10.

Professional Career: Asst. V.P., M.S. Bailey and Son, 1989-93; asst. V.P., Palmetto Bank, 1993-95; pres., J. Duncan and Associates, 1995-2010.

DC Office: 116 CHOB, 20515, 202-225-5301; Fax: 202-225-3216; Web site: jeffduncan.house.gov.

State Offices: Aiken, 803-649-5571; Anderson, 864-224-7401; Laurens, 864-681-1028.

Committees: *Foreign Affairs:* Asia & the Pacific; Terrorism, Nonproliferation & Trade. *Homeland Security:* Border & Maritime Security; Oversight, Investigations & Management. *Natural Resources:* Energy & Mineral Resources; Fisheries, Wildlife, Oceans & Insular Affairs.

Election Results

2010 general	Jeff Duncan (R)	126,235	(62%)	($935,503)
	Jane Dyer (D)	73,095	(36%)	($272,698)
2010 runoff	Jeff Duncan (R)	37,352	(51%)	
	Richard Cash (R)	35,185	(49%)	
2010 primary	Artis Cash (R)	20,923	(25%)	
	Jeff Duncan (R)	19,051	(23%)	
	Rex Rice (R)	16,071	(19%)	
	Joe Grimaud (R)	15,503	(19%)	
	Neal Collins (R)	6,787	(8%)	
	Frank Vasovski (R)	4,216	(5%)	

Population		Race/Ethnicity		Work	
Pop. 2010:	722,675	White:	74.1%	Private:	77.9%
Change since 2000:	Up 8.1%	Black:	19.4%	Government:	15.5%
Urban:	50.3%	Hispanic:	4.1%	Self-employed:	6.4%
Rural:	49.7%	Asian:	0.8%	Blue collar:	29.4%
Area size:	5,568 sq. mi.	Native Am.:	0.2%	White collar:	53.7%
		Hawaiian:	0.0%	Khaki collar:	0.1%
Age		Two+ races:	1.2%	Other:	16.8%
Median age:	39.2 yrs.				
More than 65 yrs:	15.0%	*Ancestry*		Median income:	$40,998
Less than 18 yrs:	23.1%	USA	14.0%	Median Home Value:	$114,000
		Irish	9.8%		
Education		English	8.8%	**Military Veterans**	
H.S. grad:	80.6%			% of Pop:	11.1%
College grad:	20.1%				
Grad degree:	7.2%				

Western South Carolina; Anderson

The Upstate in South Carolina is many days' travel by wagon from the Lowcountry plantations along the coast. It was first settled by Scots-Irish farmers, including the family of future Vice President John C. Calhoun, around the time of the Revolutionary War. The pioneers wanted to make big plantations of these forests, but the land was too hilly for the labor-intensive rice crops grown in the Lowcountry and sometimes too cold for cotton. So relatively few slaves were

2008 Presidential Vote		
John McCain (R)	188,692	(64%)
Barack Obama (D)	103,804	(35%)

2004 Presidential Vote		
George Bush (R)	169,283	(66%)
John Kerry (D)	86,947	(34%)

Cook Partisan Voting Index: R+17

brought here, and the land became mostly small farms. Today, the racial and cultural tone of the Upstate shows traces of these roots. This is a mostly white part of the South, with a hell-of-a-fella tone to daily life and a tradition-minded slice of Middle America. Yet it is not untouched by change.

Aiken, with its horsey trappings for polo and steeplechase, has long attracted affluent transplants. The nearby Savannah River Site—a 310-square-mile federal weapons plant complex that for four decades produced tritium and plutonium that fueled America's nuclear arsenal—employed generations of highly trained engineers. More than 12,000 were laid off when the plant closed in 1992, though many were hired for the massive cleanup of nuclear waste stored at the site. Today, cleanup activity is still an important economic driver regionally. Savannah River employs 13,000 people and received one of the biggest pots of federal economic stimulus money in 2009, $1.6 billion. Interstate 85—once the Main Street of America's textile belt—travels through a booming southeastern corridor that runs from Raleigh-Durham to Atlanta. Clemson University was founded here by Calhoun's son-in-law and is one of the state's two land-grant institutions.

The 3rd Congressional District of South Carolina follows the Georgia border north from the Savannah River Site through the tree-harvesting country around McCormick County to mountains along the North Carolina border. The southern part of the 3rd has a few heavily African-American areas, like Edgefield County, where the late Sen. Strom Thurmond grew up and first won public office in the 1930s. (The former segregationist served until he was 100 years old, retiring in 2002.) Edgefield County has grown significantly as it became part of the metropolitan area around Aiken and Augusta, Ga. This part of South Carolina, ancestrally Democratic, began trending Republican in the 1950s as cultural issues became more important in this fervently religious region. The district today is solidly Republican. In 2008, Republican John McCain won 64% of the vote, his best showing in a South Carolina district.

Jeff Duncan (R)

The new congressman from South Carolina's 3rd District is Republican Jeff Duncan, elected in 2010 to succeed four-term GOP Rep. Gresham Barrett, who gave up the seat to run for governor.

Duncan was born in Greenville, S.C. His family moved frequently, mostly in the Carolinas, as they followed his father's job as a textile industry manager tasked with turning around underperforming plants. In his senior year in high school, Duncan met his future wife, Melody. After graduation, he went on to Clemson University, where he played wide receiver on a team coached by football legend Danny Ford. Duncan majored in political science and interned one summer for the late Sen. Strom Thurmond, R-S.C., which Duncan called a "tremendous experience." When he got his degree in 1988, he worked briefly for a bank and then for a real-estate auction company, which inspired him to start his own business. His company, J. Duncan & Associates, specialized in statewide real estate auctions.

When the state legislator who represented his neighborhood retired, Duncan ran for the seat in the South Carolina House and won. In office, he worked on updating the funding formula for education and lowering taxes. In 2007, he sponsored a bill allowing gun owners with concealed-carry permits to bring guns onto school campuses, arguing that if students had been armed at Virginia Tech that year, they could have returned fire on the deranged student responsible for the mass shooting of 33 people. The bill died on the House floor. In 2009, Duncan sponsored a bill creating an alternative state budget that did not use federal stimulus money, as a way of protesting President Barack Obama's $787 billion economic stimulus bill for the nation.

After Barrett announced his plans to run for governor, Duncan entered a six-candidate field for the GOP nomination for Barrett's House seat. He was endorsed by the anti-tax group Club for Growth and built a 2-to-1 fundraising advantage over businessman Richard Cash. Duncan prevailed in a runoff with 51% of the vote. In the general election, he faced token Democratic opposition from Air Force veteran Jane Dyer, a FedEx pilot, who had little chance in the solidly Republican district. He won, 62% to 36%.

In an interview, Duncan told *National Journal* that he believes in the "Jeffersonian principles of limited governments, free markets, and individual liberties," and thinks that the federal government has gone beyond its constitutional authority. He would shift some of the government's powers to the states. "If the government would get out of the way, business would come back," he said. "I don't believe that more government and more government spending is the answer to the problems we face." In Congress, Duncan said he would work to either suspend or eliminate the capital gains tax to encourage business growth. Illegal immigration has been a hot topic in his district, and Duncan said he favors a proposal pushed by conservatives to deny citizenship to children born to illegal immigrants living in the United States.

FOURTH DISTRICT

Trey Gowdy (R)

Elected 2010, 1st term; b. Aug. 22, 1964, Greenville; home, Spartanburg; Baylor U., B.A. 1986; U. of SC, J.D. 1989; Baptist; Married (Terri Dillard Gowdy); 2 children.

Elected Office: Solicitor, SC 7th Circuit, 2000-10.

Professional Career: Prosecutor, U.S. Atty. Office, SC, 1994-2000.

DC Office: 1237 LHOB, 20515, 202-225-6030; Fax: 202-226-1177; Web site: gowdy.house.gov.

State Offices: Greenville, 864-241-0175; Spartanburg, 864-583-3264.

Committees: *Education & the Workforce:* Workforce Protections. *Judiciary:* Courts, Commercial & Administrative Law (VChmn); Crime, Terrorism & Homeland Security; Immigration Policy & Enforcement. *Oversight & Government Reform:* Federal Workforce, U.S. Postal Service & Labor Policy; Health Care, District of Columbia, Census & the National Archives; TARP, Financial Services & Bailouts of Public & Private Programs.

Election Results

2010 general	Trey Gowdy (R)	137,586	(63%)	($942,672)
	Paul Corden (D)	62,438	(29%)	($25,327)
	Dave Edwards (C)	11,059	(5%)	
2010 runoff	Trey Gowdy (R)	54,412	(71%)	
	Bob Inglis (R)	22,590	(29%)	
2010 primary	Trey Gowdy (R)	34,103	(39%)	
	Bob Inglis (R)	23,877	(27%)	
	Jim Lee (R)	11,854	(14%)	
	David Thomas (R)	11,073	(13%)	
	Christina Jeffrey (R)	6,041	(7%)	

Population		Race/Ethnicity		Work	
Pop. 2010:	770,226	White:	70.0%	Private:	82.9%
Change since 2000:	Up 15.2%	Black:	19.3%	Government:	11.2%
Urban:	73.5%	Hispanic:	7.0%	Self-employed:	5.7%
Rural:	26.5%	Asian:	1.9%	Blue collar:	25.6%
Area size:	2,166 sq. mi.	Native Am.:	0.2%	White collar:	58.3%
		Hawaiian:	0.0%	Khaki collar:	0.2%
Age		Two+ races:	1.4%	Other:	15.9%
Median age:	37.4 yrs.				
More than 65 yrs:	12.8%	*Ancestry*		Median income:	$44,116
Less than 18 yrs:	24.6%	USA	11.6%	Median Home Value:	$132,200
		Irish	9.0%		
Education		English	8.8%	**Military Veterans**	
H.S. grad:	81.5%			% of Pop:	10.1%
College grad:	25.3%				
Grad degree:	8.5%				

Northern South Carolina; Greenville

A century ago, Northern investors seeking sites for textile mills looked at the Upstate of South Carolina and found what was described then as "mild climate, abundant water power, proximity to the cotton fields and plenty of native labor already accustomed to a low standard of living." As mills fled New England, textile factories settled along the Southern Railway and Seaboard Coast Line tracks between Charlotte and At-

2008 Presidential Vote		
John McCain (R) 190,004	(60%)
Barack Obama (D) 119,246	(38%)
2004 Presidential Vote		
George Bush (R) 181,255	(65%)
John Kerry (D) 94,760	(34%)
Cook Partisan Voting Index: R+15		

lanta, especially in the Piedmont of South Carolina. The textile country might look bucolic, but Greenville, Spartanburg and the dozens of mill towns thick in the surrounding countryside became as industrial as Lancashire or the Ruhr, with mills rising up on what were once twisting woodland paths. In the days before child labor laws, factory work sometimes began at age 6, condemning workers to a life of illiteracy. Escapes to a brighter future, such as the brilliant but brief baseball career of West Greenville's "Shoeless" Joe Jackson, were rare.

Today, this same stretch of land along Interstate 85, which parallels the Southern Railway, remains one of the largest textile-producing areas in the United States, even though most mills have shut down and the others are unlikely to survive. The state had 35,000 textile and apparel workers in 2008, but had lost more than 30,000 textile jobs since 2000. But there is much more to the local economy than textiles. Many former textile workers have taken jobs with the new companies that have moved to the area. So many other jobs have been created that the South Carolina Textile Manufacturers Alliance dropped "Textile" from its name. Financial sweeteners, tax incentives, the absence of unions and solid infrastructure—airports, interstate highways and the busy Port of Charleston—attracted an enormous BMW plant. (The plant suffered layoffs during the 2007-09 recession, but then added 1,000 people to its workforce in 2010 when sales revived.) The region also has the headquarters of Michelin and Extended Stay Hotels, among others. Greenville's revitalized downtown now boasts fancy hotels and restaurants, many featuring Korean, Thai and Vietnamese cuisine—each catering to the new corporate manager class.

The 4th Congressional District of South Carolina includes all of Greenville and Spartanburg counties, plus much smaller Union County and a sliver of Laurens County. Greenville is the most populous county in the state, and has grown 19% since 2000. Culturally, the 4th ranges from conservative to very conservative, with strong influence from Greenville's many evangelical and fundamentalist churches. Bob Jones University is here as well; it has dropped its longtime ban on interracial dating but students are still prohibited from smoking, drinking, dancing and wearing jeans or shorts to class. Here, the real political divide is between religious and economic conservatives. But large new subdivisions have sprouted between Greenville and Spartanburg, and newcomers have brought religious diversity. Greenville has growing populations not only of Catholics and Jews, but also Muslims, Buddhists, Hindus, Baha'is, and even one gay-oriented church. Still, this is a heavily Republican district, with the smallest African-American percentage in the state. In 2008, GOP presidential candidate John McCain won 60% of the vote in the district.

Trey Gowdy (R)

The new congressman from the 4th District is Republican Trey Gowdy, who upset six-term GOP Rep. Bob Inglis in an early summer primary in 2010 and then went on to win the seat in the fall.

Gowdy grew up in Spartanburg, S.C., where he still lives with his wife, Terri, and their two children. His father grew up poor but worked to become the first in his family to finish college, and eventually to put himself through medical school and became a pediatrician. The family was well-off financially, but Trey Gowdy was encouraged to get jobs mowing lawns and bagging groceries. He got his first car from his father, who made him pay for it with his earnings. His academic performance in his younger years was "extraordinarily average," Gowdy recalled in an interview with *National Journal*. But as a teenager, he was inspired by Ronald Reagan's campaign for president and by a stint as a Senate page, sponsored by then-Sen. Strom Thurmond, R-S.C. Gowdy fondly recalls bumping into then-Rep. Jack Kemp, R-N.Y., in a Capitol Hill elevator. Kemp, instrumental in enacting President Reagan's tax cuts, complimented Gowdy on the "Reagan for President" button on his lapel. Gowdy buckled down to his studies and earned a law degree from the University of South Carolina. He also was fascinated by psychology and Greek history, and particularly liked to read about Spartan culture.

In 1994, Gowdy became a prosecutor for the U.S. Attorney's Office in Greenville, where he worked on cases ranging from drug trafficking to murder. In 2000, he successfully ran for the county solicitor's post and was re-elected twice. In that role, he sought the death penalty in seven cases and won them all. Much of the job was managerial, but Gowdy says he tried about half of the cases that came through his office himself, focusing his efforts on preventing violence against women and drunken driving. Gowdy, who named his dogs Judge and Jury, says that being a prosecutor was "the best job I will ever have in my life."

He said he decided to challenge Inglis in the primary after the incumbent had tacked to the left on a number of issues. During the campaign, Gowdy portrayed his opponent as a Washington insider whose pragmatic positions on some issues were out of step with the district's conservative voters. He criticized Inglis for earmarking funds in appropriations bills, for his opposition to President George W. Bush's 2007 troop surge in Iraq, and for his stand against oil exploration in Alaska's Arctic National Wildlife Refuge. Inglis complained that he felt as if he was running against the "sins of Congress," rather than an individual. Gowdy finished ahead of Inglis in the initial balloting, and then soundly defeated him in a runoff, 71% to 29%. Inglis' defeat in the early summer primary was one of the first concrete signs that the restless mood of voters in 2010 would spell serious trouble for incumbents that fall.

In the general election, Gowdy breezed past Democrat Paul Corden, a retired businessman and Vietnam veteran, in the conservative district, 63% to 29%. Gowdy said that his top priorities in Congress are entitlement reform that drastically reduces federal spending and repeal of President Barack Obama's health care law of 2010.

FIFTH DISTRICT

Mick Mulvaney (R)

Elected 2010, 1st term; b. July 21, 1967, Alexandria, VA; home, Indian Land; Georgetown U., B.S. 1989; U. of NC-Chapel Hill, J.D. 1992; Catholic; Married (Pamela); 3 children.

Elected Office: SC House, 2006-08; SC Senate, 2008-10.

Professional Career: Practicing atty., 1993-2000; real estate firm owner, 2000-10.

DC Office: 1004 LHOB, 20515, 202-225-5501; Fax: 202-225-0464; Web site: mulvaney.house.gov.

State Offices: Rock Hill, 803-327-1114.

Committees: *Budget. Joint Economic Committee. Small Business:* Contracting & Workforce (Chmn); Economic Growth, Tax and Capital Access; Healthcare & Technology.

Election Results

2010 general	Mick Mulvaney (R)	125,834	(55%)	($1,647,870)
	John Spratt (D)	102,296	(45%)	($2,035,361)
2010 primary	Mick Mulvaney (R)	unopposed		

Population		Race/Ethnicity		Work	
Pop. 2010:	767,773	White:	63.0%	Private:	80.2%
Change since 2000:	Up 14.8%	Black:	30.4%	Government:	14.7%
Urban:	46.7%	Hispanic:	3.7%	Self-employed:	4.9%
Rural:	53.3%	Asian:	0.8%	Blue collar:	29.3%
Area size:	7,141 sq. mi.	Native Am.:	0.7%	White collar:	53.1%
		Hawaiian:	0.0%	Khaki collar:	0.5%
Age		Two+ races:	1.3%	Other:	17.1%
Median age:	37.9 yrs.				
More than 65 yrs:	13.0%	*Ancestry*		Median income:	$40,736
Less than 18 yrs:	25.1%	USA	11.8%	Median Home Value:	$111,400
		Irish	7.7%		
Education		German	7.5%	**Military Veterans**	
H.S. grad:	78.5%			% of Pop:	10.4%
College grad:	18.5%				
Grad degree:	6.2%				

Northern South Carolina; Rock Hill

Some of the fiercest battles of the Revolutionary War were fought in South Carolina's Upstate, on hilly lands just being settled by Scots-Irish farmers moving up from the Lowcountry or down the Virginia Piedmont valley. This was a country of violent passions and unclear lines. Carolinians argued for years over which side of the North and South Carolina boundary Andrew Jackson was born on in 1767, although they have agreed that his successor James K. Polk was born in North

2008 Presidential Vote		
John McCain (R) 166,948	(53%)
Barack Obama (D) 145,036	(46%)
2004 Presidential Vote		
George Bush (R) 143,001	(57%)
John Kerry (D) 104,850	(42%)
Cook Partisan Voting Index: R+7		

Carolina 1795. Ever since, the fighting spirit and Calvinist faith of Upstate Carolinians have not wavered. This "Olde English District" remains intensely religious and pro-military, but it is no longer impoverished. For many years, the dominant industry here was textiles, traditionally the first factory enterprise of industrializing countries, with low pay and poor working conditions. But over three decades, the number of textile jobs has declined markedly while more sophisticated manufacturing has boomed, most visibly in big plants like BMW's in Spartanburg and Michelin's in Greenville. Smaller towns suffered massive unemployment in the 2007-09 recession—over 20% in some small counties—but there has also been rapid growth south of Charlotte in York and Lancaster counties. (They are appropriately named for the royal dynasties that fought it out in England's 15th century Wars of the Roses.) Lancaster County is best known for the huge Sun City Carolina Lakes development.

The 5th Congressional District of South Carolina consists of all or part of 14 counties, mostly in the Upstate and some in the Midlands. About half the population is in Lancaster and York counties, and just to the west in Cherokee County, along Interstate 85. Another population center is around Sumter, with its Air Force base, and Kershaw County, with the charming county seat of Camden. The district also includes Dillon County and Darlington, site of the Southern 500 stock car race every Labor Day, and the lowland tobacco country, including Marlboro and Chesterfield counties. Dillon County is also the boyhood home of Federal Reserve Chairman Ben Bernanke. Politically, this homeland of Andrew Jackson is ancestrally Democratic, but has become increasingly Republican. Much of the population growth in York and Lancaster comes from Charlotte suburban commuters with no ancestral ties here and with strong conservative views. Overall, this has been a Republican district in presidential elections, though it voted only 53% for John McCain in 2008.

Mick Mulvaney (R)

The congressman from the 5th District is Mick Mulvaney, a Republican elected in 2010 by toppling 28-year Democratic incumbent John Spratt, the chairman of the House Budget Committee.

Mulvaney grew up in Charlotte, where his father left teaching to run a homebuilding business. His views were also shaped by listening to his grandparents' stories about economic hardships during the Great Depression and by his first political hero, Ronald Reagan. At age 13, he was inspired by Reagan's 1980 campaign for president. "I remember seeing Reagan on TV and being able to understand what he was talking about," said Mulvaney, who stuffed envelopes for Reagan's campaign. Mulvaney graduated from Georgetown's School of Foreign Service, where he took one of former Secretary of State Madeleine Albright's courses and where he was voted student body president. After graduation from the University of North Carolina's law school, he practiced at a large firm in Charlotte and then established his own practice in 1997. A year later, he married and he and his wife, Pamela, soon became parents of triplets. Mulvaney sold the firm in 2000 to join his father's homebuilding business. He also dabbled in politics, working in George W. Bush's presidential campaign in 2000. In 2002, Mulvaney settled with his family across the state line in Lancaster County.

In 2006, he won a seat in the South Carolina House covering parts of Lancaster and York counties. Two years later, he ran for the state Senate, also in a seat covering the two counties, and won. He was one of 10 state senators who supported Republican Gov. Mark Sanford's decision to reject federal economic stimulus money, and he generally tended to support Sanford's budget-cutting over the policies of Republican legislative leaders. He kept a Gadsden flag—"DONT TREAD ON ME"—on his Senate desk. In November 2009, he attended a town hall meeting where Spratt was jeered and booed when he explained his vote for the Democrats' health care bill. "I decided to run while sitting at the back of that meeting," Mulvaney told the Associated Press.

Despite his prominence in Washington, Spratt had been re-elected every two years with diminishing margins as the region grew out of its Southern Democratic roots and became more Republican. Spratt rose through the ranks in Washington, eventually becoming chairman of the Budget Committee, but that did not help him at home in the first two years of Barack Obama's presidency, as the area became a hotbed of dissent from the administration's agenda. Mulvaney slammed Spratt for his support of the Democrats' health care overhaul, the $787 billion economic stimulus bill, and cap-and-trade legislation limiting carbon emissions from industrial plants. He vowed to join Republican efforts to repeal the health care legislation.

Mulvaney insisted that he liked and respected Spratt, but said, "Times have changed, and I think it's time for us to change congressmen." He spent $1.6 million, not much more than Republican Ralph Norman had spent against Spratt in 2006. But groups allied with Republicans also stepped in to help this time, including the anti-tax Club for Growth, American Future Fund and the National Republican Congressional Committee. Republicans put up posters around the district with a photo of Spratt and President Barack Obama arriving in Charlotte on Air Force One.

Spratt spent $2 million on his campaign, while the Democratic Congressional Campaign Committee put in another $1 million. Democrats attacked Mulvaney for convincing Lancaster County to issue bonds to improve a property, which he promptly sold for a profit to someone who then abandoned the planned development. On the stump, Spratt told voters, "It makes sense to re-elect a seasoned old-timer like myself, who has been around the track a few times and knows how to get things done in Washington." But seniority and past service were not strong currency in the anti-incumbent year of 2010.

Mulvaney won by a solid 55%-45%. In the area closest to Charlotte—York, Lancaster and Cherokee counties—he won 63% of the votes, a stunning outcome against a longtime and respected incumbent. Spratt carried the tobacco counties area, while Mulvaney carried the counties around Camden and Sumter.

When Obama announced his budget in February 2011, Mulvaney left no doubt that he takes a different view from his predecessor. "Let me see if I can say this as politically correctly as I can. I thought it was a joke," Mulvaney told *Politico*. "It's hard to explain how detached from reality this is, to think that the country can spend another $1.6 trillion when it doesn't have the means."

SIXTH DISTRICT

James Clyburn (D)

Elected 1992, 10th term; b. July 21, 1940, Sumter; home, Columbia; SC St. U., B.A. 1962; African Methodist Episcopal; married (Emily); 3 children.

Professional Career: Teacher, 1962–66; Dir., Charleston Neighborhood Youth Corps, 1966–68; Exec. dir., SC Comm. for Farm Workers, 1968–71; Asst., SC Gov. West, 1971–74; SC Human Affairs Comm., 1974–92.

DC Office: 2135 RHOB, 20515, 202-225-3315; Fax: 202-225-2313; Web site: clyburn.house.gov.

State Offices: Columbia, 803-799-1100; Florence, 843-622-1212; Santee, 803-854-4700.

Group Ratings

	ACLU	ACU	ADA	CFG	AFS	FRC	LCV	ITIC	NTU	COC
2010	80	0	95	0	100	0	100	50	2	13
2009	–	0	100	4	100	–	93	–	1	29

National Journal Ratings

	2010 LIB	—	2010 CONS	2009 LIB	—	2009 CONS
Economic	84%	—	15%	91%	—	0%
Social	71%	—	25%	89%	—	0%
Foreign	66%	—	29%	84%	—	16%
Composite	75%	—	25%	91%	—	9%

Key Votes of the 111th Congress

1. Overturn Ledbetter	Y	5. Bar federal abortion funds	N	9. Stop detainee transfers	N
2. Pass $820 billion stimulus	Y	6. Pass health care bill	Y	10. Legalize immigrants' kids	Y
3. Let guns in national parks	N	7. Regulate financial firms	Y	11. Repeal don't ask, tell	Y
4. Pass cap-and-trade	Y	8. Pass tax cuts for some	Y	12. Limit campaign funds	Y

Election Results

2010 general	James Clyburn (D)	125,459	(63%)	($3,319,719)
	Jim Pratt (R)	72,661	(36%)	($66,703)
2010 primary	James Clyburn (D)	50,138	(90%)	
	Gregory Brown (D)	5,527	(10%)	

Prior Winning Percentages: 2008 (67%), 2006 (64%), 2004 (67%), 2002 (67%), 2000 (72%), 1998 (73%), 1996 (69%), 1994 (64%), 1992 (65%)

Population		Race/Ethnicity		Work	
Pop. 2010:	682,410	White:	41.1%	Private:	74.7%
Change since 2000:	Up 2.1%	Black:	53.9%	Government:	19.0%
Urban:	48.0%	Hispanic:	2.7%	Self-employed:	6.1%
Rural:	52.0%	Asian:	0.8%	Blue collar:	28.3%
Area size:	8,491 sq. mi.	Native Am.:	0.4%	White collar:	49.4%
		Hawaiian:	0.0%	Khaki collar:	0.4%
Age		Two+ races:	1.1%	Other:	21.9%
Median age:	35.9 yrs.				
More than 65 yrs:	12.9%	*Ancestry*		Median income:	$33,550
Less than 18 yrs:	23.5%	USA	7.4%	Median Home Value:	$94,000
		German	5.1%		
Education		English	5.0%	**Military Veterans**	
H.S. grad:	78.1%			% of Pop:	10.1%
College grad:	16.8%				
Grad degree:	5.8%				

Eastern South Carolina; Columbia

South Carolina was first settled by planters from Barbados, bringing with them a tropical plantation economy, which they transferred to the not-quite-tropical climate of the Carolina coastal lowlands. The flat Lowcountry and the coastal islands are laced with sluggish rivers and swamps. The planters brought thousands of slaves from Africa, and Colonial South Carolina quickly became one of the richest parts of North America, with dazzling Georgian architecture in

2008 Presidential Vote

Barack Obama (D)	188,098	(64%)
John McCain (R)	102,387	(35%)

2004 Presidential Vote

John Kerry (D)	151,061	(61%)
George Bush (R)	97,248	(39%)

Cook Partisan Voting Index: D+12

Charleston and classic plantation gardens. The planters built great irrigation systems and grew rice and cotton and the dye-plant indigo, all heavily in demand in Britain and elsewhere. All this wealth, of course, was built on the slave labor of countless African-Americans. In colonial times, a majority of South Carolinians were slaves, as were a majority of lowlands residents when Fort Sumter was fired upon. (There were also many free blacks in Charleston, a few of whom owned slaves themselves.) South Carolina's black heritage has left a lasting imprint on American culture. Gullah, a mixture of English, French and African dialects, is still spoken on the sea islands, and Gullah customs survive—oyster roasts and sweet potato feasts at Christmas, handmade dolls and sweetgrass baskets. The poverty that was the almost universal lot of lowland blacks after the Civil War has eased only in the last generation, as development came to the coast and cultural isolation dissipated. But many African-Americans decided not to wait for progress. They abandoned South Carolina for opportunities in the North.

The 6th Congressional District of South Carolina, created in 1992 as a black-majority district, includes only a bit of the South Carolina coast, which is increasingly lined with affluent retirement and recreational communities. The district's boundaries take in the black central city neighborhoods of Charleston, North Charleston and Columbia, but leave out their affluent white areas, both urban and suburban, in the adjacent 1st and 2nd Districts. The 6th includes most of Orangeburg County, home of the historically black South Carolina State University, and Florence, at the center of the Pee Dee tobacco-growing country in eastern South Carolina. Orangeburg was the scene of a massacre in February 1968, when three black students were killed and 27 were wounded by police while protesting a segregated bowling alley.

In recent years, the Pee Dee area has had substantial economic growth as a warehousing and distribution center, including a QVC home shopping network facility, although Honda in 2009 shut down its 1,600-worker, all-terrain vehicle plant there. In Orangeburg County, the Dubai-based Economic Zones World had a 1,300-acre industrial and warehouse facility under construction in 2011; it is expected to generate 8,000 jobs over the next decade. Most of the cargo would arrive through the Port of Charleston. The 6th's population in 2010 was 54% African-American. In 2008, Democratic presidential nominee Barack Obama got 64% of the vote, carrying every county except for Florence. This was the only South Carolina district he won.

James Clyburn (D)

The congressman from the 6th District is James Clyburn, a Democrat elected in 1992 who is the assistant minority leader, the third-ranking position in the House Democratic leadership. He is also the highest ranking African-American in Congress.

Clyburn grew up in Sumter, the son of a minister, and was educated at a private, all-black boarding school. As a young man, he joined the Student Nonviolent Coordinating Committee, which took its cues from the Rev. Martin Luther King Jr.'s Southern Christian Leadership Conference. In 1960, he was one of seven people who organized the state's first sit-ins, at a five-and-dime store in the Orangeburg town square. He met his wife while in jail for three days. Clyburn worked as a teacher, as an employment counselor and in government antipoverty programs. In 1970, he ran for the South Carolina House and lost narrowly. Democratic Gov. John West appointed Clyburn as state Human Affairs commissioner and he served 18 years, under two Democratic and two Republican governors. He ran twice for secretary of state, in 1978 and 1986, losing narrowly. Then the new, black-majority 6th District was created. Clyburn ran for the seat, and in the Democratic primary, won 56% of the vote against four African-American opponents, all with serious claims to the nomination. Clyburn was better known, ran first or second in every part of the district, and piled up 88% of the vote in his home county of Sumter. Clyburn became the only African-American to represent South Carolina in Congress since George Washington Murray (a distant relative of his) left in 1897.

In the House, he established a moderate-to-liberal voting record, and in his early years, focused on local priorities. He also joined the moderate New Democrat Coalition at its inception in 1997, the only African-American House member to do so. On the Appropriations Committee from 1998 to 2006, Clyburn focused on securing federal funds to develop the corridor around Interstate 95, which passes through rural counties in the district that historically were dependent on tobacco and cotton. Whenever cigarette tax increases were proposed, he urged safeguards for tobacco farmers. The House twice passed his bill to create a Gullah/Geechee Cultural Heritage Corridor from northern Florida to North Carolina.

Clyburn was chosen as chairman of the Congressional Black Caucus in 1999, and in that role, urged the Democratic National Committee to become more responsive to African-Americans. After the 2002 election, he ran for vice chairman of the Democratic Caucus, arguing that the leadership needed to better reflect the party's diversity. He prevailed with 95 votes to 56 for New York Rep. Gregory Meeks and 53 for California Rep. Zoe Lofgren. In 2006, he was elected Democratic Caucus chairman, the No. 4 position in the party leadership, and later that year, after Democrats won control of the House, he was chosen majority whip, moving up to the No. 3 post. Then-Rep. Rahm Emanuel of Illinois also wanted to be whip, but had less seniority than Clyburn and backed down at the urging of House Speaker Nancy Pelosi, who favored Clyburn. Emanuel took Clyburn's spot as Democratic Caucus chairman in recognition of his work raising money and successfully recruiting challengers in the pivotal 2006 election, when he chaired the Democratic Congressional Campaign Committee. Clyburn said, "I'm going to be leery of going away from seniority. African-Americans supported the seniority system and waited their turn. Now, we get nervous when people talk about changing the rules." He described his approach to leadership this way: "When it comes to working with the Democratic Caucus, I have to fish in a lot of ponds. I go fishing with the Blue Dogs. I go fishing with the New Dems. I go fishing with the Hispanics and I go fishing with the Asian Pacific Islanders, trying to cobble together the 218 votes I need. But a lot of times I have to be a hunter, and they tell me, even though I never hunt, they tell me that a good hunter knows how to work both sides of the ditch. I fish among my caucus, Democratic members, and I go hunting sometimes, among my Republican members."

Clyburn sought enhanced influence for his whip organization in crafting policy, a way of getting more points of view from across party factions into the process of drafting major legislation. In 2007, he held a series of "listening sessions" with Democrats to explore options for an immigration bill. He also coordinated the House's response to the devastation caused by Hurricane Katrina in 2005, leading the Hurricane Katrina Task Force, which made visits to the Gulf Coast and had regular meetings with local officials. "I truly believe that if the demographics of the affected areas had been different, the response of the federal government would have been different," he said in a 2007 speech in Baton Rouge, La. Clyburn also finessed a solution to a longstanding complaint by the CBC that they were prevented from advancing in the Democratic caucus because they couldn't pay their "dues" by raising large amounts of political donations in their disproportionately low-income districts. Clyburn convinced Pelosi to adopt a modified system that rewarded Democrats for non-financial contributions, such as making appearances for candidates and doing press interviews.

When Democrats lost the House majority in 2010, they no longer controlled the speakership, and so lost one spot in their leadership lineup. Pelosi became leader, the top job in the minority. But a battle shaped up for the No. 2 position of minority whip between Clyburn and former majority leader Steny Hoyer of Maryland. Both had a legitimate claim: Clyburn had already been doing the whip's job for four years in the majority and for his part, Hoyer had a right to expect to remain in a No. 2 role, as he had in the majority. An intense, behind-the-scenes rivalry unfolded, with each camp touting his greater level of support in the caucus. To avoid a divisive outcome, Pelosi created the new job of assistant leader and made it the No. 3 post in the minority hierarchy. Clyburn was named assistant leader and Hoyer became minority whip.

Back home, Clyburn has not faced serious opposition for re-election. He has been a player in the state's often pivotal Democratic presidential primary. African-Americans cast about half the votes in the primary, and Clyburn is the most prominent black politician in the state. In the 2004 presidential primary campaign, he first backed Rep. Dick Gephardt of Missouri, with whom he had worked in the House. But Gephardt withdrew after the Iowa caucuses, and Clyburn endorsed front-runner John Kerry rather than South Carolina native John Edwards. Throughout 2007, his support was eagerly sought by Democratic contenders, who attended his annual Fish Fry in Columbia. Although he did not take sides in the January 2008 primary, he clashed with Hillary Rodham Clinton when she seemed to suggest that President Lyndon Johnson, in signing the Civil Rights Act of 1964, had a more important role than King and other key civil rights figures at the time. "That bothered me a great deal," Clyburn told *The New York Times*. As the leader of an older generation of civil rights leaders, he was initially skeptical that Obama could win the nomination. When Obama clinched it in June 2008, Clyburn told a radio interviewer that he went home to watch it alone on television "because what I was feeling was indescribable and I was afraid that I would not be able to control my emotions."

After the election, Clyburn got into an unusual conflict with Republican Gov. Mark Sanford, who said that he would not use all of the money available to South Carolina in the Democrats' economic stimulus bill enacted in February 2009. Clyburn called the action a "slap in the face" to the predominately black constituents who would benefit. He also wrote a clause into the $787 billion stimulus bill that enabled state legislatures to bypass governors who rejected the money. Clyburn took on another South Carolina conservative, House colleague Joe Wilson, after Wilson infamously called out, "You lie!" during Obama's health care address to Congress in 2009. Clyburn pressed a resolution formally reproaching Wilson for a breach of House rules, which passed on a largely party-line vote.

★ SOUTH DAKOTA ★

One of the last great stretches of the American Wild West was the southern part of the Dakota Territory, admitted to the Union in 1889 as the state of South Dakota. This land had been inhabited by the Oglala Sioux, one of the largest Native American tribes, who had built a buffalo hunting civilization by becoming masters of the horses the Spaniards had imported to North America 350 years earlier. It was the Sioux warrior chief Sitting Bull, buried on a bluff above the Missouri River, who destroyed Custer at Little Big Horn in 1876. But many of the remaining Oglala Sioux Indians in South Dakota were massacred at Wounded Knee in 1890. After half a century of disease and a decade of defeat fighting the westward advance of white settlement, the Sioux were a traumatized people, and still are today, living on reservations with proud traditions but in terrible poverty: Four of the five American counties with the highest poverty rates are Indian reservation counties in South Dakota. Isolated from the mainstream economic marketplace, they are beset by high rates of crime, alcoholism and suicide, with life expectancy and disease rates akin to those of sub-Saharan Africa. Incremental progress has been made over the years, at least in preserving the vestiges of the Sioux culture and staunching some of the decline in standards of living. Infant mortality has been reduced and the state's Indian population grew 15% from 2000 to 2010. In 2007, the state added to school curricula units on the language and culture of the Lakota and other Indians. Indians account for 9% of the population in South Dakota, more than in any other state in the lower 48.

Once the Sioux were forced to surrender their territory, white settlement of South Dakota came fast. After the gold strikes in the Black Hills in 1876, the mountains swarmed with settlers. Deadwood became a city of 20,000 where Calamity Jane ruled the saloons and Wild Bill Hickok was shot in the back while holding two pair—aces and eights. Ranchers, knowing that the buffalo could not be contained by barbed wire fences, massacred them so thoroughly that when Teddy Roosevelt got to the Dakota Territory in 1884, he had a hard time finding one to shoot. It was not long before the railroad came through, and then permanent settlers, many of them German and Scandinavian immigrants recruited by the railroads. They built sod houses, broke the land and set down roots, a story told by Jon Lauck in *Prairie Republic: The Political Culture of Dakota Territory 1879-1889*.

There were 98,000 South Dakotans in 1880, 401,000 in 1900 and 636,000 in 1920. But demographically, South Dakota has never entirely filled up. In the 25 years between statehood and World War I, the eastern third of the state, sectioned off Midwestern-style into 640-acre square miles, was settled by farmers. But moving westward, before a traveler reaches the Missouri River in the middle of the state, green turns to brown, cultivation grows sparse and then stops. The West River plains are open grazing land, scarcely touched by the white men who were so eager to establish dominion over them a century ago. The land is punctuated, not by roads meeting every mile at precise angles, but by buttes, gullies and grasslands sweeping to the horizon with no sign of human habitation except the occasional missile silos that once pointed toward the Soviet Union. Far in the west, in Butte County, is the point designated as the Geographic Center of the United States after Alaska was admitted to the Union.

South Dakota's political patterns were fairly well set by the early 1900s. Its early settlers were mostly Midwesterners who brought their Republicanism with them, of New England Yankee and German stock primarily, and also some Norwegians. Voters here never had much use for the Non-Partisan League, which caught on in North Dakota, and there was never anything here comparable to the Farmer-Labor Party of Minnesota. But the nature of the farm economy—its dependence on the great railroads and milling companies, and on the vagaries of international markets—meant that South Dakota was subject to periodic farm revolts. It voted for Populists and William Jennings Bryan in the 1890s. It supported the early New Deal, and it revolted against the President Dwight Eisenhower administration in the 1950s by electing a young Democratic congressman named George McGovern, then a professor at Dakota Wesleyan University in Mitchell. South Dakota shared the isolationist impulse of much of the Great Plains. McGovern's opposition to the Vietnam War in the late 1960s was not a liability here. For a moment in the mid-1970s, Democrats seemed on the verge of becoming the majority party.

Then South Dakota moved sharply to the Republicans, beginning with the administration of Republican Gov. Bill Janklow, elected in 1978 and 1982 and then again in 1994 and 1998. In 1979, Sioux Falls banker Thomas Reardon suggested that the state get rid of its usury law limiting interest rates; inflation was driving market rates over most states' usury limits and choking off credit to

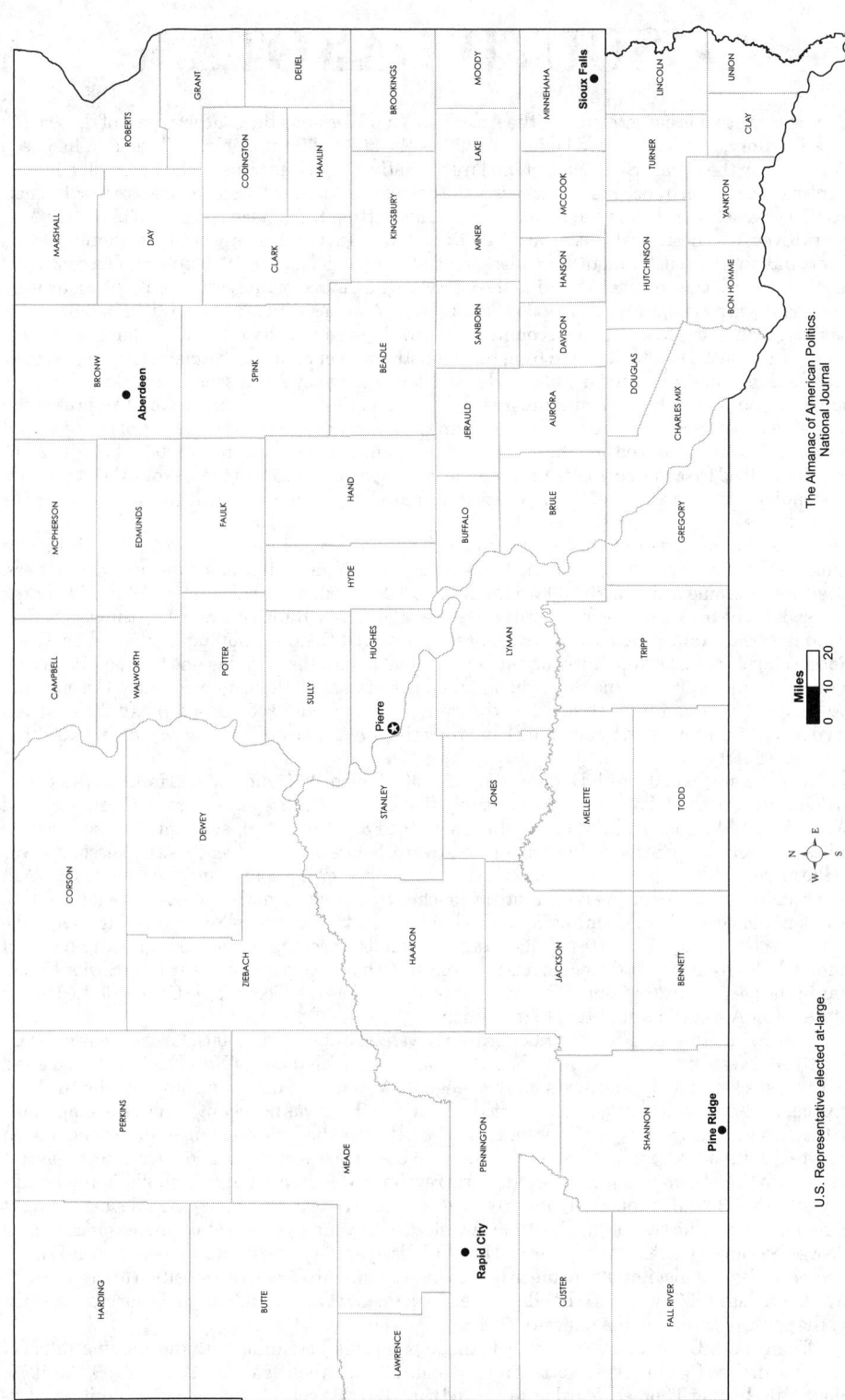

The Almanac of American Politics.
National Journal

U.S. Representative elected at-large.

consumers. Janklow and the legislature repealed the usury laws and in 1981 passed laws enabling Citibank to move its credit card operations to Sioux Falls, where it could charge market interest rates—all in a state with no corporate or personal income taxes, and a community with a literate, low-wage work force. The Citibank operation here has grown from 50 employees to 3,200, servicing some 118 million cardholders and replacing the meatpacker John Morrell as the biggest employer. Other banks and telemarketing followed. More than 15,000 people in the Sioux Falls area work in financial services.

All this has made South Dakota an unusually productive place economically. The state leads the nation in the percentage of young children in two-income families and has the highest rate of employed seniors—a third of people age 65 to 74 are working. It ranks high in credit ratings, low in foreclosures, and high in repaying college loans. It has relatively low wages, but also some of the nation's lowest unemployment and housing prices. Its residents and those in North Dakota spend less time commuting to work than Americans elsewhere. It leads the nation in the percentage of home-based businesses. Even as some big employers have disappeared—Gateway computer moved to San Diego, IBP was bought by Tyson Foods, NorthWestern Energy went bankrupt—other jobs have been created, and the National Science Foundation picked the Homestake gold mine in the Black Hills as the site of a new physics lab. Some meatpacking plants have closed, but others are manned now by a largely Hispanic work force, recruited from the Southwest and beyond. Some 40 languages are spoken on the floor of the John Morrell plant in Sioux Falls. The 2007-09 recession had a minimal impact here, with unemployment rates among the lowest in the nation and about half the national rate. South Dakota's population rose 7.9% from 2000 to 2010, the highest rate in the Midwest and not much lower than the national average of 9.7%.

South Dakota has long been thought of as a farm state, but farm counties have been losing population. The 1990 census counted 11% of the workforce as employed in farming, forestry or fishing; in the Census Bureau's 2006-08 American Community Survey, the figure was only 1%. One reason is increased productivity. South Dakota in 2008 had half as many dairy cows as it did in 1970 but produced more milk. Economically and demographically, South Dakota is coming to resemble the Rocky Mountain states, with most people concentrated around a few prosperous and growing cities and towns, while vast acreage remains vacant, punctuated by infrequent farm and ranch houses. The 2010 census showed most South Dakota counties losing population over the past decade, with two regions—metro Sioux Falls and the area around Rapid City and the Black Hills—accounting for all of the state's population gain and more. Both Sioux Falls' Minnehaha County and Lincoln County just to the south each gained more than 20,000 people. Lincoln County's growth rate of 86% was the fourth highest of any county over 10,000 in the nation.

Politically, South Dakota has been mostly Republican. But this is a small state where people expect to meet and chat with their elected officials repeatedly, and personal campaigning has enabled Democrats to be competitive in congressional elections. Back in 1977, 29-year-old Tom Daschle's personal campaigning enabled him to beat Congressional Medal of Honor recipient Leo Thorsness by exactly 139 votes in a House race. That led to Daschle's election to the Senate in 1986 and his elevation to Senate Democratic leader in 1995. Only the burden of having to defend his steadfast opposition to then-popular George W. Bush and the assiduous personal campaigning of John Thune ended his electoral career in 2004 by a grand total of 4,508 votes. South Dakota's other Senate seat was held by Democrat Tim Johnson, elected in 1996 by 8,579 votes over Republican Larry Pressler, who had been spending time shepherding a major telecommunications bill to passage. Helped by a major turnout drive on the Pine Ridge Indian Reservation, Johnson was re-

Population		Household Income		Work	
Pop. 2010:	814,180	Under $15k:	13.6%	Private:	74.5%
State rank:	46th	$15k to $50k:	41.1%	Government:	16.0%
Change since 2000:	Up 7.9%	$50k to $100k:	33.0%	Self-employed:	9.0%
Urban:	52.4%	$100k to $200k:	10.1%	Unemployment (3-yr. average):	3.0%
Rural:	47.6%	Over $200k:	2.1%	Poverty:	13.4%
Native of state:	66.6%	Median income:	$45,378	Blue collar:	22.2%
Not a citizen:	1.3%			White collar:	58.7%
Area size:	77,116 sq. mi.	**Home Value**		Khaki collar:	0.3%
		Under $100k:	39.7%	Other:	18.9%
Most populous cities		$100k to $300k:	51.6%		
Sioux Falls	153,888	$300k to $500k:	6.1%	**Age**	
Rapid City	67,956	$500k to $1 mil:	1.8%	Median age:	37.2 yrs.
Aberdeen	26,091	Over $1 million:	0.8%	More than 65 yrs:	14.4%
Brookings	22,056	Median:	$122,500	Less than 18 yrs:	24.4%

Race/Ethnicity				Military Veterans		Registered Voters in 2010	
White:	84.7%	*Language*		% of Pop:	11.8%	Democrats:	194,204
Black:	1.2%	English:	93.7%			Republicans:	237,809
Hispanic:	2.7%	Spanish:	1.8%	*Veterans by Period*		Ind./other:	87,348
Asian:	0.9%	Asian:	0.6%	WWII and before:	10.7%	Voter turnout:	319,426
Native Am.:	8.5%	Other European:	2.1%	Korea:	13.9%	Turnout as % of	
Hawaiian:	0.0%			Vietnam:	32.4%	voting age:	52.2%
Two+ races:	1.8%	**Education**		Gulf (pre-2001):	10.8%		
		H.S. grad:	89.3%	Gulf (post-2001):	8.5%	**Legislature**	
Ancestry		College grad:	24.9%	Peace time:	23.7%	Senate:	5 D 30 R
German	32.6%	Grad degree:	7.0%			House:	19 D 50 R 1 I
Norwegian	11.1%						
Irish	8.4%						

elected in 2002 over Thune by just 524 votes. Thune then came back as a strong challenger to Daschle two years later and ended Daschle's Senate career. Briefly, from June 2004 to January 2005, South Dakota had an all-Democratic congressional delegation—with Daschle and Johnson in the Senate and Stephanie Herseth Sandlin, granddaughter of a former governor, in the House—for only the second time in its history. (The other time was a period of five days in 1936-37.) Johnson suffered a disabling brain hemorrhage in December 2006 and his determined recovery generated wide sympathy. He was re-elected 62%-38% in 2008.

But aside from Johnson, Democrats seemed to run out of steam by 2010. Republican Gov. Mike Rounds generally got high marks for his two terms ending in 2011. He boosted spending by tourists significantly as he had promised to do, from $600 million in 2001 to $962 million in 2009, and the state's gross domestic product grew by $14 billion on his watch. He also lured to the state the National Science Foundation's new Deep Underground Science and Engineering Lab in 2007. But nationally, those efforts attracted less attention than the legislature's efforts to criminalize abortion in 2006. Opponents put the issue on the November 2006 ballot and repealed the law 56%-44%. The legislature responded with a more limited bill, but voters repealed it as well, 55%-45%, in November 2008. Amid this controversy, Rounds was re-elected 62%-36% in 2006 and Republicans held onto majorities in the legislature. The 2010 elections produced a Republican rout. Democrats who had won five of the last six U.S. Senate races in the state nominated no one at all to oppose Thune's bid for a second term. At large Rep. Herseth Sandlin lost the state's only House seat to Republican Kristi Noem, 48%-46%. Republican Dennis Daugaard was elected governor 62%-38%, losing only in counties with high Indian percentages and the University of South Dakota. Republicans won huge margins in the state Senate, 30-5, and state House, 50-19.

Presidential politics   South Dakota has voted Democratic for president just four times since statehood, in 1896, 1932, 1936 and 1964. But it was fairly close in five of the seven elections between 1972, when South Dakota's George McGovern was the Democratic nominee, and in 1996, when Democrat Bill Clinton came within 3% of winning. In 2000, Democrat Al Gore's environmental policies were unpopular here and Republican George W. Bush carried the state, 60%-38%. Gore carried only Indians, a rising but small percentage of the electorate, and ran even among the elderly, but the percentage of voters who became Democrats during President Franklin D. Roosevelt's time was on the wane. In 2004, Bush once again carried the state, 60%-38%, winning every county except those with Indian reservations and the University of South Dakota. In 2008, with no contest generating the interest that the Tom Daschle-John Thune Senate matchup had four years earlier, turnout was

2008 Presidential Vote		
John McCain (R)	203,054	(53%)
Barack Obama (D)	170,924	(45%)
2008 Presidential Primary		
Hillary Clinton (D)	54,128	(55%)
Barack Obama (D)	43,669	(45%)
2008 Presidential Primary		
John McCain (R)	42,788	(70%)
Ron Paul (R)	10,072	(17%)
Mike Huckabee (R)	4,328	(7%)
2004 Presidential Vote		
George W. Bush (R)	232,584	(60%)
John Kerry (D)	149,244	(38%)

down 2%, contrary to the national trend. Republican John McCain carried the state by just 53%-45%. Democrat Barack Obama won the Indian reservations, plus several counties in the northeast and southeast, and he won Sioux Falls' Minnehaha County by 587 votes out of 80,000 cast.

In 1988, South Dakota switched its presidential primary from the traditional June date to February, just one week after New Hampshire. It proved to be a boost for Great Plains candidates who did not fare well elsewhere: Republican Bob Dole in 1988 and 1996, Democrat Dick Gephardt in 1988, and Democrats Bob Kerrey and Tom Harkin in 1992. But in 1996, it attracted few candidates, and the South Dakota Legislature decided to save $400,000 in election costs by reverting to a June primary. In January 2007, a move to hold the 2008 primary on Feb. 5 was blocked by a 35-35 vote in the state House. As it turned out, there was a robust race for the Democratic nomination up through June 3, when South Dakota and Montana voted. Obama had long since won the endorsements of leading South Dakota Democrats—Sen. Tim Johnson and former senators Daschle and George McGovern. Rep. Stephanie Herseth Sandlin switched to Obama after her initial preference, John Edwards, dropped out. But Obama campaigned only briefly in South Dakota, while Hillary Rodham Clinton, Bill Clinton and Chelsea Clinton crisscrossed the state in the two weeks before the primary. It paid off. Clinton won 55%-45%. She ran especially strong in the eastern counties and lost on the Indian reservations. It was her only victory north of the 42nd parallel and west of Indiana and Michigan, and raised the question of whether she might have won the nomination if more states in the region had held primaries rather than the caucuses in which the better-organized Obama campaign prevailed.

Governor

Dennis Daugaard (R)

Elected 2010, term expires Jan. 2015, 1st term; b. June 11, 1953, Garretson; home, Pierre; U. of SD, B.S. 1975; Northwestern U., J.D. 1978; Lutheran; married (Linda); 3 children.

Elected Office: SD Senate, 1996-2002; SD lt. gov., 2002-10.

Professional Career: Business devel. and V.P., U.S. Bank, Sioux Falls, 1981-90; Devel. dir., Children's Home Foundation, 1990-2002; Exec. dir., Children's Home Society, 2002-09.

Office: 500 E. Capitol Ave, 57501, 605-773-3212; Web site: www.sd.gov/governor/.

Election Results

2010 general	Dennis Daugaard (R)	195,046	(62%)
	Scott Heidepriem (D)	122,037	(38%)
2010 primary	Dennis Daugaard (R)	42,261	(50%)
	Scott Munsterman (R)	14,726	(18%)
	Dave Knudson (R)	13,218	(16%)
	Gordon Howie (R)	10,426	(12%)

South Dakota's new governor is Dennis Daugaard, a Republican elected in 2010. He previously spent eight years as lieutenant governor under his predecessor, Mike Rounds, and six years in the state Senate before that. He shares Rounds' conservative views but describes himself as fiscally more to the right.

Daugaard (*DOO-gahrd*) grew up on his family's dairy farm near Garretson in eastern South Dakota. His grandparents, who emigrated from Denmark, started the farm in 1911. Both of his parents were born deaf, so he principally communicated with them through sign language. He graduated from the University of South Dakota in 1975, and earned his law degree from Northwestern University in 1978. He spent a year at a small law firm in Chicago, and then left the firm to concentrate on real estate and settlement negotiations. He returned to South Dakota in 1981, marrying his high school girlfriend, Linda, and working as a trust officer at U.S. Bank in Sioux Falls for nine years. In 1990, he became director of development at the Children's Home Foundation, the fundraising arm of the Children's Home Society providing help to young victims of abuse and neglect. He became the society's executive director in 2002.

Daugaard made his initial bid for public office in 1996, when he won a seat in the state Senate. He was re-elected easily in 1998 and 2000. He focused on issues affecting people with disabilities and children, sponsoring an unsuccessful bill in 1999 that would have charged youths under 21 if they were caught driving with any amount of alcohol in their blood. He told the Sioux Falls *Argus Leader* in 2000 that he supported the state's inheritance tax, which was repealed the following year. In 2002, Rounds, a former state Senate president, asked him to join his gubernatorial ticket as lieutenant governor. They won with 57% of the vote and were re-elected in 2006 with 62%. As lieutenant governor, Daugaard chaired the Worker's Compensation Advisory Board and a task force on health care, and also served on a commission to revise the state constitution.

He was widely seen as the front-runner to replace the term-limited Rounds. But a February 2010 poll showed he had less than 50% support and that one-third of voters remained unsure what they thought of him. He sought to boost his image by vowing not to raise taxes except to cope with the aftermath of a flood or other severe emergencies. He also called for increasing the value of the state's economic development fund providing low-interest loans to start-up companies expanding or relocating to the state while also continuing to expand wind, ethanol and other alternative energy sources. At the same time, he pushed for a strong increase in science and math education for students. He easily won the June GOP primary with just over 50% of the vote, having far outspent four opponents.

His general election opponent was Scott Heidepriem, the state Senate's minority leader. He campaigned as an independent Democrat who was skilled at building consensus, and in recognition of the uphill challenge facing his party, chose a Republican businessman as his running mate. Heidepriem repeatedly sought to tie Daugaard to Rounds' policies, which he asserted had led to a ballooning in government's size and cost. He also accused Rounds' administration of not doing enough to promote ethanol production and wind energy. He was able to remain competitive on fundraising, but the state's GOP political dominance proved too much of an obstacle, and Daugaard won a landslide 62%-38% victory.

With a more hands-on management style than Rounds, Daugaard focused on fiscal matters during his early months in office, proposing a budget cutting about 10% of almost every aspect of state government. His proposal went deeper than one Rounds had proposed in December that relied on reserve money to limit cuts to 5% for such programs as elementary education and Medicaid. But Daugaard rejected that approach. "The gun is at our head," he said. "Using reserves sounds good, but it's just kicking the can down the road." Lawmakers heeded his concerns and passed a budget in March making cuts of 10% or higher. Daugaard also vetoed a bill limiting the co-payments that insurance companies charge for visits to chiropractors, but the legislature overrode the veto.

But the issue that brought Daugaard the most public attention was his signing into law in March 2011 a bill instituting the nation's longest waiting period—three days—for women seeking an abortion after meeting with a doctor. The measure also required women to visit an anti-abortion counseling center. "I think everyone agrees with the goal of reducing abortion by encouraging consideration of other alternatives," he said in a statement. Abortion rights groups called the law unconstitutional and vowed to challenge it in court.

Senior Senator

Tim Johnson (D)

Elected 1996, term expires 2014, 3rd term; b. Dec. 28, 1946, Canton; home, Vermillion; U. of SD, B.A. 1969, M.A. 1970, J.D. 1975, MI St. U., 1970-71; Lutheran; married (Barbara); 3 children.

Elected Office: SD House of Reps., 1978–82; SD Senate, 1982–86; U.S. House of Reps., 1986–96.

Professional Career: Budget analyst, MI Senate, 1971–72; Practicing atty., 1975–85; Clay Cnty. dpty. atty., 1985.

DC Office: 136 HSOB, 20510, 202-224-5842; Fax: 202-228-5765; Web site: johnson.senate.gov.

State Offices: Aberdeen, 605-226-3440; Rapid City, 605-341-3990; Sioux Falls, 605-332-8896.

Committees: *Appropriations:* Agriculture, Rural Development, Food and Drug Administration & Related Agencies; Defense; Energy & Water Development; Interior, Environment & Related Agencies; Military Construction, Veterans Affairs & Related Agencies (Chmn); Transportation, HUD & Related Agencies. *Banking, Housing & Urban Affairs* (Chmn): Economic Policy; Securities, Insurance & Investment; Security & International Trade & Finance. *Energy & Natural Resources:* Energy; Public Lands & Forests; Water & Power. *Indian Affairs.*

Group Ratings

	ACLU	ACU	ADA	CFG	AFS	FRC	LCV	ITIC	NTU	COC
2010	93	0	85	5	94	0	71	67	7	27
2009	–	8	95	8	91	–	100	–	6	57

National Journal Ratings

	2010 LIB — 2010 CONS		2009 LIB — 2009 CONS	
Economic	74%	— 25%	67%	— 32%
Social	65%	— 0%	65%	— 34%
Foreign	47%	— 0%	55%	— 0%
Composite	77%	— 23%	70%	— 30%

Key Votes of the 111th Congress

1. Overturn Ledbetter	Y	5. Pass health care bill	Y	9. Ratify New START	Y
2. Pass $787 billion stimulus	Y	6. Regulate financial firms	Y	10. Confirm Elena Kagan	Y
3. Repeal DC gun laws	Y	7. Pass tax cuts for some	Y	11. Stop EPA climate regs	N
4. Confirm Sonia Sotomayor	Y	8. Legalize immigrants' kids	Y	12. Repeal don't ask, tell	Y

Election Results

2008 general	Tim Johnson (D)	237,889	(62%)	($6,423,536)
	Joel Dykstra (R)	142,784	(38%)	($906,630)
2008 primary	Tim Johnson (D)	unopposed		

Prior Winning Percentages: 2002 (50%); 1996 (51%); House: 1994 (60%); 1992 (69%); 1990 (68%); 1988 (72%); 1986 (59%)

Democrat Tim Johnson was first elected to the Senate in 1996. Most of the attention he has drawn has been for his health—he suffered a near-fatal brain hemorrhage in 2006 that led to a months-long recovery. But he now has the opportunity to make a larger mark as a legislator as chairman of the Banking, Housing and Urban Affairs Committee, overseeing the financial industry in the aftermath of the Troubled Asset Relief Program and Dodd-Frank industry overhaul law.

Johnson grew up in Canton, Flandreau and Vermillion in southeast South Dakota and went to the University of South Dakota, where he ultimately earned a law degree. Johnson served briefly in the Army, but was discharged because of a hearing problem. He opened a law practice in Vermillion, and then got increasingly involved in politics. He was elected to the state House in 1978, at age 31, and served four years. In 1982, he was elected to the state Senate for another four years. When Democratic U.S. Rep. Tom Daschle ran for the Senate in 1986, Johnson ran for the state's at-large House seat and won the general election 59%-41%. He was re-elected easily every two years. In the House, Johnson compiled a generally liberal voting record, though he sometimes voted for conservative fiscal proposals, such as the balanced budget amendment of the 1990s.

In 1996, Johnson challenged Republican Sen. Larry Pressler, then chairman of the influential Commerce, Science and Transportation Committee. This was a high-spending, high-stakes race.

Pressler spent $5.1 million, and Johnson spent almost $3 million. The race was neck-and-neck for 15 months. Since South Dakota television is relatively inexpensive, that meant one barrage of ads after another, plus seven debates. Pressler attacked Johnson as too liberal, going back to a 1981 vote in the legislature against workfare, the practice of requiring welfare recipients to work. Johnson attacked Pressler as a clone of Republican House Speaker Newt Gingrich and a Medicare-cutter. Pressler spent much time in 1995 and 1996 on the telecommunications bill, a heavily lobbied and complex bill. He succeeded in passing the bill, a significant accomplishment. But back home, Johnson charged that phone and cable rates were going up because of Pressler's work. The final result was a 51%-49% Johnson victory.

Johnson's voting record initially was toward the center of the Senate, though since Barack Obama became president he has become much more inclined to side with his party. In 2009, he was the only Senate Democrat to vote with Republicans against a bill imposing restrictions on credit card company lending practices, bowing to the concerns of credit card providers in his state such as Citigroup and First Premier Bank. He also opposed a bill that year allowing bankruptcy judges to write down the principal and interest rates of certain mortgages on primary homes, a controversial procedure known as "cramdown." But he voted with the majority of Democrats on most other major bills, and even drew headlines on occasion for sharply rebuking House Republicans. He said in April 2011 that House Budget Committee Chairman Paul Ryan's budget plans dealing with the financial industry involved "gutting consumer and investor protections and letting Wall Street run wild all over again."

Most of the time, however, Johnson seldom seeks or gets publicity as other senators do. "There are enough show horses in Washington to go around," he likes to say. His quiet style stands in sharp contrast to Connecticut Democrat Christopher Dodd, his voluble predecessor as Banking chairman. On substance, however, the two men share a great deal. Johnson said he would lead an aggressive focus on revamping the nation's housing finance system in addition to overseeing the Dodd-Frank regulatory reforms, which he helped get into law. He told *National Journal* in December 2010 that he wanted to look at the measure's impact on community banks, which face fewer burdens than large financial firms. Johnson also has been a chief proponent of legislation to allow insurance carriers to choose to be regulated under a new federal supervisor instead of at the state level. The measure has the support of large multinational carriers, but has drawn opposition from insurance agents and state regulators.

Johnson expressed a desire to let Banking subcommittee chairmen such as New Jersey's Robert Menendez and Rhode Island's Jack Reed play significant roles, and said he would seek cooperation with Republicans. However, he was not averse to putting his foot down. When House Republicans expressed an eagerness to overhaul mortgage giants Fannie Mae and Freddie Mac in early 2011, Johnson countered that lawmakers needed to take their time to do it right. "One of the things I learned never to do with Tim is to mistake his quietness or his very calm demeanor as any form of weakness or indecision," said Mike Thompson, who was Johnson's first legislative director and later became a lobbyist. "He is an extremely strong person, and very determined (that) whenever he sets his mind to accomplish things, he gets it done."

When Democrats gained a Senate majority in 2006, Johnson got the gavels of the Appropriations Subcommittee on Military Construction and Veterans Affairs, and the Banking Subcommittee on Financial Institutions. Then, on December 13, 2006, Johnson suffered a brain hemorrhage while working at the Capitol. Within hours, he had extensive brain surgery. With prospects of his survival unclear and the assumption that Republican Gov. Mike Rounds would appoint a Republican successor, speculation grew that Johnson's departure from the Senate could reverse the Democrats' expected majority control. Although Johnson survived the immediate crisis, his recovery was predicted to last for several months. Amid the uncertainty and also out of respect for Johnson, Democratic senators assisted him in fundraising for his 2008 re-election and potential Republican rivals such as Rounds delayed their decisions. On September 5, 2007, Johnson returned to the Senate and made his first floor speech of the year. "My speech is not 100 percent," he said. "But my thoughts are clear and my mind is sharp."

Johnson has continued to suffer lingering health effects such as slurred speech and partial paralysis on his right side, but they have not impaired his ability to work. He helped get more than $150 million in earmarks for South Dakota into an omnibus spending bill for fiscal 2011, ranging from $100,000 for a dialysis unit for the Yankton Sioux tribe to $28 million for a rural water system in southwest South Dakota. In November 2009, he amended an appropriations bill that became law to provide $50 million to convert unused buildings into housing for homeless veterans. He introduced a measure in April 2011 establishing an independent, bipartisan commission in each state to redraw congressional districts. On a personal level, he watched as the Senate confirmed his son, Brendan, in October 2009 as U.S. attorney for South Dakota. The senator stayed out of the nominating process for his son, a former Minnehaha County prosecutor who drew the support of Republicans such as former Gov. Bill Janklow, who also served in the U.S. House.

Earlier, on the 2008 farm bill, Johnson won passage of a provision requiring meat products to carry country-of-origin labeling, which he had worked on for several years. He also helped get passed country-of-origin meat labeling and a bill to provide more funding for housing on Indian reservations. In 2006, he supported funding for improved access to affordable health care in rural communities, and in the 2005 energy bill, he worked on increases for ethanol and other renewable fuels. South Dakota devotes more of its corn to ethanol than any other state. It also gets much of its energy from coal, and Johnson voted in favor of a failed proposal in April 2011 to block Environmental Protection Agency regulation of carbon emissions linked to climate change.

His support for the EPA ban illustrates the fine line Johnson has had to walk as a Democrat in a state where Republicans have become dominant. By early 2001, it was apparent that he would face a tough challenge in 2002. President George W. Bush talked popular Republican Rep. John Thune into running for the Senate. Daschle, by then the Senate majority leader, immediately made saving his friend and fellow home-state Democrat "the most important political effort for me" in 2002. Daschle helped Johnson get a seat on Appropriations, where he could secure federal money for South Dakota. And Johnson was careful to cast some moderate votes on big issues. The two candidates spent record amounts for a South Dakota race—about $6 million each—and the national parties and independent expenditure groups on both sides spent much more.

Thune was the more outgoing of the two, a candidate who loved shaking hands and seldom forgot a face. He attacked Johnson for voting against making the Bush tax cuts permanent. Johnson replied that he supported eliminating the estate tax for family farmers and ranchers and family-owned businesses. The biggest local issue was the drought that hit western South Dakota in 2002. Ranchers were selling off their herds for low prices, and business losses were estimated at $1.8 billion. Daschle and Johnson responded by sponsoring $5 billion in disaster aid for farmers and ranchers, arguing that if floods and tornadoes triggered disaster relief, then droughts should too. In mid-September, Agriculture Secretary Ann Veneman announced $750 million in aid for 30 states. On defense issues, Thune tried to make an issue of Johnson's opposition to the first Persian Gulf War in 1991, but the impact was mitigated when Johnson announced he would vote for the pending resolution authorizing war in Iraq.

The election turned out to be the closest in the nation that year. During most of election night, Thune was in the lead, but the last two precincts to be counted came in from Shannon County, which includes most of the Pine Ridge Indian Reservation. They put Johnson over the top by a margin of 524 votes. Many Republicans urged Thune to contest the election, but he declined. Thune got his revenge two years later, however, when he fulfilled his party's long-held goal of toppling Daschle.

Johnson sought a third term in 2008, and was challenged by Republican State Rep. Joel Dykstra. He suggested that Johnson was not physically up to the rigors of service in the Senate and criticized his vote against a 2005 bill that would have increased oversight of mortgage lending practices, an issue with potential resonance during the housing foreclosure crisis. But neither line of attack struck a chord with voters, and Johnson trounced Dykstra 62%-38%. Exit polls showed that he won support from about a third of the voters who identified themselves as Republicans.

Junior Senator

John Thune (R)

Elected 2004, term expires 2016, 2nd term; b. Jan. 7, 1961, Pierre; home, Sioux Falls; Biola U., B.A. 1983, U. of SD, M.B.A. 1984; Baptist; married (Kimberley); 2 children.

Elected Office: U.S. House of Reps., 1996-2002.

Professional Career: Legis. asst., U.S. Sen. James Abdnor, 1985–87; Special asst., U.S. Small Business Admin., 1987–89; Exec. dir., SD Republican Party, 1989–91; SD railroad dir., 1991–93; Exec. dir., SD Municipal League, 1993–96.

DC Office: 493 RSOB, 20510, 202-224-2321; Fax: 202-228-5429; Web site: thune.senate.gov.

State Offices: Aberdeen, 605-225-8823; Rapid City, 605-348-7551; Sioux Falls, 605-334-9596.

Committees: *Agriculture, Nutrition & Forestry:* Jobs, Rural Economic Growth & Energy Innovation (RMM); Livestock, Dairy, Poultry, Marketing & Ag Research. *Budget. Commerce, Science & Transportation:* Aviation Operations, Safety & Security (RMM); Communications, Technology & the Internet; Competitiveness, Innovation & Export Promotion; Consumer Protection, Product Safety & Insurance; Surface Transportation & Merchant Marine Infrastructure, Safety & Security (RMM). *Finance:* Energy, Natural Resources & Infrastructure; International Trade, Customs & Global Competitiveness (RMM); Taxation & IRS Oversight.

Group Ratings

	ACLU	ACU	ADA	CFG	AFS	FRC	LCV	ITIC	NTU	COC
2010	7	100	0	94	4	100	0	67	99	100
2009	–	100	10	99	0	–	0	–	91	86

National Journal Ratings

	2010 LIB — 2010 CONS		2009 LIB — 2009 CONS	
Economic	0%	— 87%	3%	— 95%
Social	0%	— 79%	17%	— 81%
Foreign	0%	— 72%	0%	— 84%
Composite	10%	— 90%	10%	— 90%

Key Votes of the 111th Congress

1. Overturn Ledbetter	N	5. Pass health care bill	N	9. Ratify New START	N
2. Pass $787 billion stimulus	N	6. Regulate financial firms	N	10. Confirm Elena Kagan	N
3. Repeal DC gun laws	Y	7. Pass tax cuts for some	N	11. Stop EPA climate regs	Y
4. Confirm Sonia Sotomayor	N	8. Legalize immigrants' kids	N	12. Repeal don't ask, tell	N

Election Results

2010 general	John Thune (R) .... unopposed	($12,518,942)
2010 primary	John Thune (R) .... unopposed	

Prior Winning Percentages: 2004 (51%); House: 2000 (73%); 1998 (75%); 1996 (58%)

John Thune, a Republican, was elected senator in a close contest in 2004 and re-elected without opposition in 2010. He grew up in Murdo, on the dusty plains west of the Missouri River, a small town with a cluster of restaurants and motels at the interchange of Interstate 94 and U.S. 83. His father, the son of a Norwegian immigrant and a Navy veteran of World War II, was a teacher and the family was Democratic. He graduated from Biola University in La Mirada, Calif., and from the business school at the University of South Dakota. As a high school freshman, he met Republican Rep. Jim Abdnor, who spotted Thune at a grocery checkout counter and recalled that the young man had missed only one of six free throws in his high school basketball game the previous night. They kept in touch, and years later, when Abdnor was in the Senate, he hired Thune on this Washington staff, where Thune worked from 1985 until Abdnor lost a bid for re-election to Democrat Tom Daschle in 1986.

Thune returned to South Dakota in 1989 and, at age 28, became executive director of the state Republican Party. In 1991, he was appointed state railroad director by Gov. George Mickelson and in 1993 he became director of the state Municipal League. In 1996, Thune entered a race for the state's open at large seat in the U.S. House. The favorite in the Republican primary was Lt. Gov. Carole Hillard. But Thune attracted the support of religious conservatives and won the primary 59%-41%. In the general election, he faced Democrat Rick Weiland, a former state director for Daschle. Thune opposed all tax increases and promised to serve only three terms. He won 58%-37%.

In the House, Thune was chosen as freshman class representative to the Republican leadership. He was re-elected, 75%-25%, in 1998, the largest percentage margin ever for a statewide candidate in South Dakota.

At a White House dinner in April 2001, President George W. Bush urged Thune to challenge Democratic Sen. Tim Johnson in 2002. Daschle, who had become Senate Democratic leader in 1995, pledged to do everything he could to protect Johnson and got him a seat on the Appropriations Committee. In his challenge to Johnson, Thune argued that South Dakota would be better off with a bipartisan Senate delegation. Johnson argued that he and Daschle made a uniquely powerful team and emphasized votes he had cast for Bush administration policies. The two candidates spent about $6 million each, a record amount for South Dakota, and the national parties and independent groups spent much more. On defense issues, Thune tried to make an issue of Johnson's opposition to the Gulf War in 1991, but the impact was mitigated when Johnson announced he would vote for the pending resolution authorizing war in Iraq. He also noted that his son, Brooks Johnson, served with the 101st Airborne Division in Afghanistan in 2001 and 2002 and could be sent to Iraq, which he later was.

The election was the closest in the nation that year. During most of election night and into the morning, Thune led in the count. Then the last two precincts came in, from Shannon County, which includes most of the Pine Ridge Indian Reservation. It voted 92%-8% for Johnson, putting him over the top by a margin of 524 votes—in percentage terms, 50.1%-49.9%. Many Republicans urged Thune to contest the election. But on Nov. 13, he said: "The people of South Dakota have been subjected to one of the longest and most expensive campaigns in South Dakota history. I choose not to subject them to more."

Thune went to work as a lobbyist and consultant in Washington. He was urged by Republican leaders and family members to run in 2004 against Daschle, who had beaten lightly funded opponents in 1992 and 1998. As minority leader in a 51-49 Republican-controlled Senate, Daschle remained a pivotal figure, a frequent but not strident critic of the Bush administration. Thune's favorable ratings remained high after his defeat, and early Republican polls showed him running slightly ahead of Daschle, and it was clear Thune would enjoy the full support of the Bush White House. Bush, who had carried South Dakota 60%-38% in 2000, was at the top of the ballot that year. In January 2004, Thune announced that he would take on Daschle.

He sought to portray Daschle as the chief obstructionist to the Bush agenda in the Senate. To underscore the idea, Majority Leader Bill Frist traveled to South Dakota to stump for Thune, breaking with Senate tradition of party leaders refraining from campaigning against each other. Daschle ran ads in the summer of 2003, arguing that a freshman senator could not hope to match his influence in Washington and emphasizing the federal largesse he had brought to South Dakota. He also emphasized his support of some Bush initiatives. Thune portrayed Daschle as a political insider who lived in a $2 million house in Washington and had lost touch with the folks back home. The state Republican Party sent a mailer attacking the work of Daschle's wife, an aviation industry lobbyist. One attack ad showed Daschle as a bobble-head doll, nodding in unison with bobble-head dolls of liberal Edward Kennedy of Massachusetts and Hillary Rodham Clinton of New York. It was the most expensive congressional election of the year, as both national parties and numerous third-party interest groups poured millions of dollars into South Dakota. By the end, they had spent $35 million.

The closely fought race brought a huge turnout, up 23% from 2000. Thune won 51%-49%, the first defeat for a Senate party leader since Democrat Ernest McFarland of Arizona lost to Republican Barry Goldwater in 1952. The popular vote margin was 4,508—small, but more than eight times the margin by which Thune had lost to Johnson two years earlier. The contours of the vote were similar. Thune narrowly lost Sioux Falls' Minnehaha County, but won fast-growing Lincoln County by a bigger margin. He carried Mitchell, North Sioux City, Pierre and Rapid City's Pennington County and the Black Hills counties around it. He also increased his share of the vote significantly in the Pine Ridge and Rosebud Indian reservations, where his decision not to challenge the election outcome two years earlier may have earned him goodwill. Daschle won most of the counties in eastern South Dakota. Nationally, Thune was celebrated by Republicans as a giant-killer. He became a talk show favorite, a fundraising star and a celebrity among Republican freshmen.

In the Senate, Thune established a mostly conservative voting record, especially on cultural issues. One of his first legislative efforts was intensely local. In May 2005, Ellsworth Air Force Base near Rapid City, with nearly 4,000 local jobs and half of the nation's B-1 bombers, was placed on the base closing list, despite Thune's campaign promise that a Republican senator with good relations with the Bush administration could protect Ellsworth. The initial news was "like a death in the family," he recounted. "In Washington, you can't count on anybody else to fight your battles."

With South Dakota colleagues Johnson and Democratic Rep. Stephanie Herseth Sandlin, Thune made the case to save the base to the commission, the Pentagon and White House officials. They generated a crowd of more than 10,000 and a pep-rally atmosphere at a base closing commission hearing in Rapid City, and the base survived.

Thune also helped author a section of the 2008 farm bill establishing a permanent disaster program to provide financial aid to farmers whose crops are harmed by natural disasters. He also successfully fought for the inclusion of a provision creating financial incentives for manufacturers that produce cellulosic ethanol from switchgrass, which is abundant in South Dakota. As gas prices climbed in the summer of 2008, Thune helped form a bipartisan group of senators that pushed for more offshore oil drilling. On an energy initiative helpful to his state, Thune in July 2009 won passage of an amendment to the defense bill requiring the Air Force to obtain half of its domestic jet fuel from synthetic blends produced in the United States. Earlier, he worked to get the Senate to agree to an annual mandate of 8 billion gallons of ethanol production by 2012.

He also has been active in issues involving Native Americans. In April 2009, Thune joined with Democrats Johnson and Indian Affairs Committee Chairman Byron Dorgan to successfully pass $400 million for the Emergency Fund for Indian Health and Safety as part of the omnibus appropriations bill. Decrying high murder rates on the reservations, Thune called on the Bureau of Indian Affairs to provide better law enforcement, and in July 2010, he won passage of his Tribal Law and Order Act, which paved the way for retired military personnel to be recruited as reservation police.

On national issues, Thune supports proposals for a biennial budget, a presidential line-item veto and a joint committee on deficit reduction, which would reduce spending by 10% of the previous year's budget deficit. Over the years, Thune has supported many earmarks for his state, but in 2010, he voted for the successful two-year moratorium on earmarks. In July 2009, Thune tried to amend the defense authorization bill with a provision allowing holders of concealed weapons permits in one state to carry their weapons to other states with similar laws. It received 58 votes, but not the 60 needed to stop a filibuster and pass. Thune spoke out against the labor unions' card check bill, which would effectively abolish the secret ballot in unionization elections, and voted against the 2005 Central American Free Trade Agreement. Although he opposed many of President Barack Obama initiatives, Thune supported the president on policy in Afghanistan, including his decision to send in additional troops in late 2009.

Thune was one of the first Senate Republicans to endorse John McCain's 2008 presidential campaign, and he was mentioned as a possible running mate after McCain won the party's nomination. Thune moved up the Republican leadership ladder in June 2009, when he became Republican Policy Committee chairman after the resignation of scandal-plagued John Ensign of Nevada.

After two close Senate races in two years, Thune prepared early for his 2010 re-election campaign, visiting the state often and raising $6 million by February 2010. Leading South Dakota Democrats took a pass on the contest, and the party did not field a candidate. He thus became only the third Republican senator to run unopposed since direct election of senators began in 1913. He ultimately raised $12.5 million, and used part of it to contribute to relatively moderate Republican Senate candidates like Kelly Ayotte in New Hampshire, Carly Fiorina in California, Mark Kirk in Illinois and Rob Portman in Ohio.

His leadership political action committee sent money to Republican gubernatorial nominees in Iowa and South Carolina, stirring speculation that Thune might run for president in 2012. And Thune indeed flirted with the idea during the closing months of 2010. Thune told *National Journal* that November, "We are taking a look at it....The one thing I know is that we need to get a candidate out there who can take on this president and hopefully defeat him and his agenda and get us back on a path." But in February 2011, Thune issued a statement saying that he would not run. "I feel that I am best positioned to fight for America's future here in the trenches of the United States Senate," he said.

REPRESENTATIVE-AT-LARGE
Kristi Noem (R)

Elected 2010, 1st term; b. Nov. 30, 1971, Hamlin County; home, Castlewood; Attended SD St. U., Northern St. U., Mount Marty Col.; Protestant; Married (Bryon); 3 children.

Elected Office: SD House, 2007-2010.

Professional Career: Farmer, rancher.

DC Office: 226 CHOB, 20515, 202-225-2801; Fax: 202-225-5823; Web site: noem.house.gov.

State Offices: Rapid City, 605-791-4673; Sioux Falls, 605-275-2868.

Committees: *Education & the Workforce:* Early Childhood, Elementary & Secondary Education; Health, Employment, Labor & Pensions; Workforce Protections. *Natural Resources:* Indian & Alaska Native Affairs; National Parks, Forests & Public Lands; Water & Power.

Election Results

2010 general	Kristi Noem (R)	153,703	(48%)	($2,295,249)
	Stephanie Herseth Sandlin (D)	146,589	(46%)	($2,086,660)
	B. Thomas Marking (I)	19,134	(6%)	($7,174)
2010 primary	Kristi Noem (R)	34,527	(42%)	
	Chris Nelson (R)	28,380	(35%)	
	Blake Curd (R)	19,134	(23%)	

The new congresswoman from South Dakota is Republican Kristi Noem, who prevailed in one of the most closely followed races of 2010. She eked out a narrow win over Democratic Rep. Stephanie Herseth Sandlin, even though the Democrat had won her last two elections with more than 70% of the vote.

Noem (*NOME*) was born in Hamlin County, S.D., and graduated from high school there. She attended college but came home to help run the family farm after her father died in a fall into a grain bin while trying to unclog a feeder line, an accident that she discussed in her first campaign advertisement. An avid hunter of elk, pheasant, and other game, Noem later owned a hunting lodge and also worked a variety of jobs, including a stint as a restaurant manager. When she was elected to Congress, the 38-year-old Noem raised Angus cattle and quarter horses on a ranch she shared with her husband, Byron. They have three children.

Noem became interested in conservative causes and decided to run for the South Dakota House. She narrowly won a seat in 2006 and established herself as a forceful figure in the legislature, earning her GOP colleagues' respect when she questioned a Democratic state senator's sponsorship of a bill to expand casino-style gambling in the state while the senator's law firm was representing an American Indian tribe. She was quickly promoted to assistant majority leader.

Noem said she decided to challenge Herseth Sandlin in February 2010 after becoming disenchanted with rising federal spending and the ballooning national debt. In the GOP primary, two-term Secretary of State Chris Nelson had more name recognition and experience, and state Rep. Blake Curd raised more money. But Noem, who emphasized that she didn't plan to make politics a career, struck a chord with voters. One of them told *The Washington Post*, "She's the mama grizzly that we hope for." She was often compared to former Alaska Gov. Sarah Palin, the 2008 GOP vice presidential nominee, but Noem regularly resisted such labeling and said she didn't want the Alaskan's help on the campaign trail. Noem won the June primary with 42%, compared with 35% for Nelson and 23% for Curd.

After her victory, Noem began collecting substantial campaign contributions from out-of-state Republican interests, enabling her to out-raise Herseth Sandlin in the early part of the campaign. She also drew campaign help from operatives associated with Sen. John Thune, a popular Republican who toppled Democrat Tom Daschle in 2004 when Daschle was the Senate minority leader. Outside conservative groups ended up pouring about $2 million into the race, more than three times what Herseth Sandlin collected from outside Democratic groups. Noem sought to tie her opponent to liberal House Speaker Nancy Pelosi and promised to cut spending and help small businesses create jobs.

The two candidates shared similar backgrounds and lifestyles—both had been raised on farms, had young families and are politically conservative. But Noem had one major advantage: the distinction of not being a Democrat in a Republican-dominated state. Herseth Sandlin, a leader of the Blue Dog Coalition of fiscally conservative House Democrats, touted her credentials as a moderate who opposed Pelosi on several high-profile measures, including the health care overhaul. She played down her party affiliation, leaving it out of her campaign literature entirely.

The incumbent did receive help from the state's Democratic Party, which sought to make an issue of Noem's 20 speeding tickets and other traffic violations over two decades—a sore point in a state where GOP Rep. Bill Janklow resigned in 2004 after he ran a stop sign and killed a motorcyclist. Herseth Sandlin succeeded Janklow. Noem was ticketed three times for stop-sign violations and once for driving 94 mph in a 75 mph zone; she also received six notices for failing to appear in court. She responded to the criticism by saying that she is not proud of her driving record and is working to be a better example to young drivers. The issue seemed to matter little to voters: Noem won 48%-46%, with independent B. Thomas Marking drawing 6%. Herseth Sandlin was competitive in many rural counties and took Sioux Falls-based Minnehaha County, which cast the largest number of votes, 50%-45%. But Noem won neighboring Lincoln County 52%-43% and Pennington County, which includes Rapid City, 58%-37%.

In Washington, Noem was named one of two freshman class representatives to the GOP leadership. She was given seats on the Natural Resources and Education and Workforce committees and joined fellow GOP freshman Stephen Fincher of Tennessee in leading a GOP effort against the Environmental Protection Agency's proposal to regulate dust as part of air quality standards, arguing it would hurt farmers and ranchers. She joined her party in backing a budget that eliminated an Agriculture Department flood control program, but later requested federal disaster aid to cope with South Dakota's spring flooding—a move that led state Democrats to accuse her of hypocrisy. She continued to win attention from activists on the right, drawing a cheer at the Conservative Political Action Conference in February when she declared, "A lot of us freshmen don't have a whole lot of knowledge, necessarily, about the way that Washington, D.C., is operated. And, frankly, we don't really care."

If Noem is re-elected in 2012—a good possibility in such a heavily Republican state—she is favored to run against Democratic Sen. Tim Johnson, who is up for re-election in 2014.

★ TENNESSEE ★

Tennessee is a battleground state, with a fighting temperament since it was settled more than 200 years ago. It produced so many soldiers for Andrew Jackson's wars with Indians and the British that it came to be known as the Volunteer State. In the 1860s, Yankee troops swept down the Tennessee and Cumberland rivers on their way to Mississippi, traveling through Chattanooga's Lookout Mountain on their way to Atlanta and the sea. But Tennessee is a battleground with a certain civility: Both Confederate and Union generals paid respectful calls on the widow of President James K. Polk, who stayed carefully neutral, in her Nashville mansion. Tennessee also was a cultural battleground for much of the 20th century. On one side were the Fugitives, writers like John Crowe Ransom and Allen Tate, who contributed to "I'll Take My Stand," a manifesto calling for retaining the South's rural economy and heritage. On the other side were business leaders and politicians who have made Tennessee the fastest-growing state of the interior South. The state gave birth to the first supermarket (Piggly Wiggly), the Holiday Inn, FedEx and Goo-Goo Clusters. Both of these major influences remain strong in this elongated state, despite the long distance between its two ends: Johnson City in East Tennessee is closer to Dover, Del., than it is to Memphis, and Memphis is closer to Dallas, Texas, than to Johnson City.

The state has also been a marshaling ground for the music traditions that have a large place in American lives. East Tennessee is one of the original homes of bluegrass music and mountain fiddling, with string bands and vocal harmony. Knoxville's *Tennessee Barn Dance* has been broadcast since 1942. Gospel music has long been centered in Nashville, which is also the nation's leading center of religious publishing, the headquarters of Thomas Nelson, FaithWorks, Integrity Books and LifeWay's Broadman & Holman. Country music got its commercial start in Nashville, with broadcasts of the Grand Ole Opry from Ryman Auditorium in 1925, and Nashville remains indisputably the capital of country music today. The Mississippi lowlands around Memphis, which is economically and culturally the metropolis of the Mississippi Delta, gave birth to the blues in the years from 1890 to 1920, and the blues were in turn the inspiration for the jazz musicians of Beale Street in the 1920s and for Elvis Presley's rock 'n' roll in the 1950s and 1960s. Presley's Graceland mansion is now a major tourist destination.

As Tennessee has expanded economically, it hasn't abandoned its cultural roots. If its economy lagged behind the nation's through much of the 20th century, its open climate for entrepreneurism enabled it to grow mightily over the last three decades. The expansion started in the early 1980s, when Republican Gov. Lamar Alexander (now a senator) helped bring big auto plants to Middle Tennessee. The absence of strong unions and of bitter racial divisions—Tennessee was mostly untouched by the civil rights battles of the 1950s and 1960s—and the presence of skilled labor made Tennessee attractive. Nissan opened a plant in Smyrna, south of Nashville, and in 2006, moved its American headquarters from the Los Angeles suburbs to Nashville. It is building a new plant in Smyrna to assemble the electric Leaf and its lithium ion batteries. General Motors located its Saturn division nearby in Spring Hill, but closed it in 2009 after the company's dire financial troubles. Compensating for this was Volkswagen's decision to build a $1 billion plant for its Passat in Chattanooga. Auto employment in Tennessee peaked in December 2006 at 159,000, and fell to 126,000 in 2008 and 107,000 in early 2011, but seemed to be rising again. Tennessee has also become a center for making polysilicon, an ingredient for the solar cells in solar power panels. Big investors here include Hemlock Semiconductor and Wacker Chemie. In addition, Nashville has long been a major health insurance center. Tennessee, unburdened by a state income tax, with business-friendly administrations led by Democrat Phil Bredesen from 2002 to 2010 and now by Republican Bill Haslam, has been growing faster than the national average over the past two decades, up 30%, while the nation grew 24%.

Tennessee has long been a political battleground, with political divisions rooted in Civil War loyalties. Tennessee had two referenda on secession, rejecting the idea 55%-45% in February 1861, but embracing it 69%-31% in June of that year, after the attack on Fort Sumter. Most East Tennessee counties voted heavily for the Union both times, and have remained heavily Republican ever since; the 1st Congressional District has never elected a Democratic congressman in all the years since. Pro-secession counties in Middle and West Tennessee long voted heavily Democratic, even for liberal candidates like George McGovern and Michael Dukakis. Within the limits of these enduring party loyalties, political entrepreneurs have set the tone for the state. From the 1920s to 1948, Edward Crump, longtime mayor of Memphis, used his total control of Democratic primary votes there to elect governors and senators. (Crump, unlike other Southern Democrats, allowed

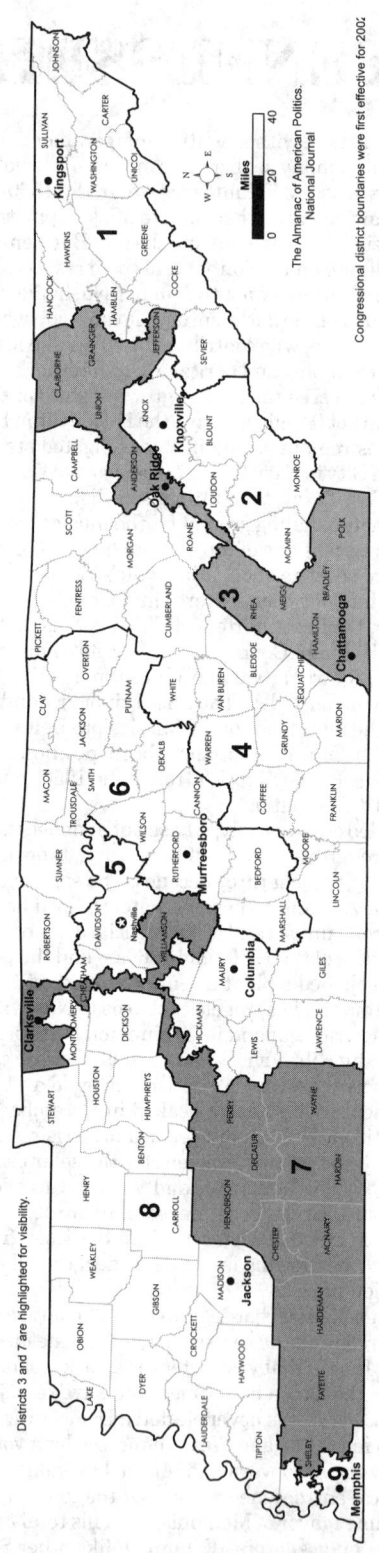

Districts 3 and 7 are highlighted for visibility.

The Almanac of American Politics.
National Journal

Congressional district boundaries were first effective for 2002

blacks to vote; they voted his way.) The Tennessee Valley Authority and the cheap electric power it generated provided an institutional base for reform-minded liberal Democrats Estes Kefauver and Albert Gore Sr., who beat incumbents in primaries when they were elected to the Senate in 1948 and 1952, respectively. They were soon national figures, with reliable enough backing from Tennessee's yellow-dog Democratic majority to vote for civil rights bills and to refuse to sign the segregationist Southern Manifesto. Kefauver died in 1963 and Gore was defeated in 1970, but he lived to see his son twice elected vice president before his death in 1998. Tennessee has never had a large African-American population—17% today, half of whom live in and around Memphis—and the state was not riven by the racial animosity that divided so much of the South in the 1950s and 1960s, thanks in large part to the actions of its leading politicians, but also thanks in part to the continuing hold of ancestral partisan preferences.

In the half-century since, the balance has shifted toward Republicans. Democrats' cultural liberalism strained the ancestral loyalties of rural voters in West and Middle Tennessee and the surging growth in the ring of counties around Nashville in the last two decades created a new voting bloc that is conservative on both economic and cultural issues. The first movement toward the Republicans occurred in the 1960s and 1970s, with the election of Sens. Howard Baker and Bill Brock in 1966 and 1970 and Alexander as governor in 1978. Then, as Georgia Democrat Jimmy Carter changed the image of the Democratic Party, Democrats rallied, electing Jim Sasser and Al Gore Jr. to the Senate in 1976 and 1984, respectively, and Ned Ray McWherter governor in 1986. The Clinton-Gore ticket carried Tennessee 47%-42% in 1992. But the narrowness of the margin was a warning. In 1994, Tennessee turned against the Clinton administration and produced a kind of political revolution. Fred Thompson, famous as a Watergate investigator and movie actor, won the remainder of Gore's Senate term by a landslide. Heart transplant surgeon Bill Frist beat Sasser in the Senate and Rep. Don Sundquist was elected governor. Republicans carried the popular vote for the U.S. House by 55%-43%, gaining two seats.

The Republican trend was strong enough in 1996 that only after extraordinary efforts—Gore made 16 appearances here and the campaign pumped in money for late ads—was the Clinton-Gore ticket able to win 48%-46%. In 2000, the tide was even stronger. Republican George W. Bush targeted the state early and worked it energetically. Headquartered in Nashville, the Gore campaign seemed to assume the state would come around in the end and campaigned hard here only in the last few days. Bush carried the state 51%-47%, and Gore became only the fifth major party nominee to lose his home state in 85 years. (The others were South Dakota's McGovern in 1972, Kansas' Alf Landon in 1936 and New Jersey's Woodrow Wilson in 1916; Thomas Dewey lost to fellow New Yorker Franklin Roosevelt in 1944.)

Over the past dozen years, Tennessee experienced the sort of voter backlash the rest of the country witnessed in 2010. In 1994, Democratic Gov. Ned Ray McWherter created TennCare, an extension of Medicaid, which accelerated spending far beyond projections in the next several years. Sundquist succeeded McWherter and was popular, until he tried to pass a state income tax. When the Democratic legislature seemed on the verge of approving the tax, protesters inspired by talk radio hosts drove to the Capitol and honked their horns. This earlier version of the tea party prevailed, and Tennessee, unlike all eight adjoining states, has no income tax—one reason for its above-average growth. In 2002, Sundquist was replaced by Bredesen, a former mayor of Nashville and a health care entrepreneur. He trimmed TennCare spending sharply and quashed all talk of an income tax. He was re-elected 69%-30% in 2006, carrying all 95 counties. But Bredesen's success did not rub off on his party. In 2002, when Thompson retired, Lamar Alexander, making a political comeback, beat Democratic Rep. Bob Clement, 54%-44%. And in 2006, when Frist retired, former Chattanooga Mayor Bob Corker beat Democratic Rep. Harold Ford Jr., 51%-48%. Bush carried Tennessee by 57%-43% in 2004, and for the first time since Reconstruction, voters elected a Republican majority in the state Senate.

Most of Tennessee is part of the Jacksonian belt of America running along the Appalachians and to the southwest, territory that seemed immune to Democrat Barack Obama's appeal in both the primary and general election in 2008. It was one of four states where Republican John McCain got a higher percentage of the vote than Bush had four years earlier. McCain carried seven of nine congressional districts and 89 of 95 counties, and Republicans won majorities in both houses of the legislature for the first time since Reconstruction. Alexander was re-elected to the Senate by, 65%-32%, carrying 94 of 95 counties, including Memphis' black-majority Shelby County. But this was only a prelude to 2010. At the top of the ticket, Republican Bill Haslam was elected governor 65%-33%, losing only the counties containing Memphis and Nashville and three rural counties. Republicans vaulted to a 64-33 margin in the state House. Longtime Democratic congressmen Bart Gordon and John Tanner retired and were replaced by Republicans who won by wide margins. And Rep.

Lincoln Davis, who since 2002 held a Middle Tennessee district carefully designed by Democratic redistricters, was swept aside as well. For the moment anyway, Tennessee seemed a solidly Republican state for the first time in its history.

A word should be said about the issue of water. Tennessee, crisscrossed twice by the Tennessee River and once by the Cumberland, both major tributaries of the Ohio and Mississippi, has plenty of it—sometimes too much. In May 2010, the Cumberland crested higher than any time since 1937 and there was devastating flooding in Nashville and Memphis. One year later, it seemed that the waters might rise even higher. Meanwhile, politicians in Atlanta, stricken by drought in 2006-08 and facing lawsuits from Alabama and Florida over the division of the waters of the Chattahoochee River, have looked toward Tennessee for help. In 2008, the Georgia legislature passed a resolution declaring that the border with Tennessee had been incorrectly drawn by a surveyor in 1818 and demanded that it be redrawn a mile north. This would mean that part of the Tennessee River would be in Georgia, and that its water could be diverted to parched Atlanta. The resolution directed Georgia Gov. Sonny Perdue to negotiate a settlement, but Gov. Bredesen, his spokesman said, "has made it clear he has no intention of moving Tennessee's border, nor will he give away Tennessee's natural resources." The Georgians have kept pressing, and in February 2011, the Coosa-North Georgia Water Planning Council called for the state to "explore opportunities for Georgia to expand use of the Tennessee River as a water supply source." But incoming Gov. Haslam stuck to his campaign pledge to "protect our state's precious resources" and said he would fight the effort.

Population			Household Income			Work		
Pop. 2010:	6,346,105		Under $15k:	16.3%		Private:		78.1%
State rank:	17th		$15k to $50k:	40.6%		Government:		14.3%
Change since 2000:	Up 11.5%		$50k to $100k:	29.2%		Self-employed:		7.4%
Urban:	62.2%		$100k to $200k:	11.1%		Unemployment (3-yr. average):	5.4%	
Rural:	37.8%		Over $200k:	2.7%		Poverty:		16.4%
Native of state:	61.9%		Median income:	$42,832		Blue collar:		25.0%
Not a citizen:	2.8%					White collar:		57.8%
Area size:	42,144 sq. mi.		**Home Value**			Khaki collar:		0.3%
			Under $100k:	33.7%		Other:		16.9%
Most populous cities			$100k to $300k:	53.5%				
Memphis	646,889		$300k to $500k:	8.6%		**Age**		
Nashville-Davidson	626,681		$500k to $1 mil:	3.3%		Median age:		37.5 yrs.
Knoxville	178,874		Over $1 million:	0.9%		More than 65 yrs:		13.1%
Chattanooga	167,674		Median:	$135,400		Less than 18 yrs:		23.9%

Race/Ethnicity				Military Veterans		Registered Voters in 2010	
White:	75.6%	*Language*		% of Pop:	10.6%	No Party registration	
Black:	16.5%	English:	94.0%			Voter turnout:	1,620,542
Hispanic:	4.6%	Spanish:	3.4%	*Veterans by Period*		Turnout as % of	
Asian:	1.4%	Asian:	1.0%	WWII and before:	8.7%	voting age:	33.4%
Native Am.:	0.3%	Other European:	1.2%	Korea:	10.2%		
Hawaiian:	0.0%			Vietnam:	34.6%	**Legislature**	
Two+ races:	1.4%	**Education**		Gulf (pre-2001):	12.7%	Senate:	13 D 19 R 1 V
		H.S. grad:	82.5%	Gulf (post-2001):	8.0%	House:	33 D 64 R
Ancestry		College grad:	22.6%	Peace time:	25.8%		1 Indep. 1 V
USA	14.4%	Grad degree:	7.9%				
Irish	9.8%						
German	9.2%						

Presidential politics   Tennessee is one of only two states—the other is Arkansas—that have given Republican presidential candidates increasing percentages of its votes in each of the last four elections. One reason is that Arkansas' Bill Clinton and Tennessee's Al Gore were running in 1992 and 1996 and ran unusually well for Democrats in their home states. But Gore's hometown status was not enough for him to carry Tennessee—which would have made him president regardless of Florida's outcome—because of the unpopularity here of the cultural liberalism that won Clinton and Gore so many suburban votes in the nation's largest metropolitan areas. Further Republican gains, such as George W. Bush's 56.8% of the vote here in 2004 and John McCain's 56.9% in 2008, probably owe something to attitudes on foreign policy and war.

Tennessee's most famous son is President Andrew Jackson, and much of the state was settled by his fellow Scots-Irish, who were famously ready to fight to the death when their families or

2008 Presidential Vote		
John McCain (R) 1,479,178	(57%)
Barack Obama (D) 1,087,437	(42%)

2008 Presidential Primary		
Hillary Clinton (D) 336,245	(54%)
Barack Obama (D) 252,874	(40%)

2008 Presidential Primary		
Mike Huckabee (R)................190,904	(34%)
John McCain (R) 176,091	(32%)
Mitt Romney (R)....................130,632	(24%)
Ron Paul (R) 31,026	(6%)

2004 Presidential Vote		
George W. Bush (R)............1,384,375	(57%)
John Kerry (D) 1,036,477	(43%)

their country were threatened. (Jackson killed two men in duels after they said unkind things about his wife.) The Jacksonian belt, throughout the Appalachian chain and running west from Tennessee to Arkansas and Oklahoma, seemed repelled by the antiwar policies of Democratic nominees John Kerry in 2004 and Barack Obama in 2008. Obama carried Memphis' Shelby County, which is about half African-American, and Nashville's Davidson County, but he won only four of the state's other 95 counties, each of them a declining-population rural area where Democratic loyalties go back to the Civil War. McCain carried white voters 63%-34% and white evangelical Protestants (52% of the electorate) 75%-22%. Bredesen said that Obama's strategy of concentrating on target states "that produced our national win came at a real cost to Democrats here in Tennessee."

For several election seasons, Tennessee held its presidential primary on Super Tuesday (though Tennessee holds its state primaries on Thursdays, the only state to do so). But it was far from the biggest state to vote that day, and received little attention. In 2004, it voted earlier, on Feb. 10, just two weeks after New Hampshire, and the only other primary that day was in Virginia. This was just a week after John Edwards had won in South Carolina and Wesley Clark had led Edwards and Kerry in a virtual three-way tie in Oklahoma. Both Edwards and Clark were from next-door states, but Kerry won with 41% to 27% for Edwards and 23% for Clark. Turnout was 369,000, far lower than the record Democratic primary turnout in 1988 of 576,000, when Gore was running. For 2008, Tennessee set its primary on Super Tuesday, Feb. 5. But it did not see much campaigning. Democrat Hillary Rodham Clinton was well ahead in polls, and won a solid 54%-40%. Turnout was a record high, 625,000, and 25% of voters were African-American. Obama carried Shelby and Davidson counties, plus four small rural counties. Clinton carried the rest, getting as much as 86% in yellow-dog Democratic Grundy County. Obama carried the Memphis- and Nashville-based 5th and 9th congressional districts by a 64%-34% margin; Clinton carried the other seven congressional districts 61%-32%, a margin similar to those she won in Kentucky, West Virginia and southwest Virginia's 9th District.

On the Republican side, everyone assumed that Fred Thompson, who announced his candidacy in September 2007, would carry his home state. But he dropped out of the race after his weak showing in South Carolina, and the remaining candidates started putting Tennessee on their schedules. Mike Huckabee carried most of rural Tennessee and Shelby County as well and won with 34% of the vote. John McCain carried Knoxville and its suburbs and got his highest percentage in the county that includes Fort Campbell, for a total of 32%. Mitt Romney carried most of metro Nashville and got 24%.

Congressional districting

112th Congress Lineup	
7 R	2 D
111th Congress Lineup	
5 D	4 R

Tennessee's Democratic Legislature controlled redistricting after the 2000 census. The plan provided critical votes to Democrat Lincoln Davis in the open Republican 4th district in 2002, and he held the district until he was defeated in 2010.

It appears that Republicans will control the redistricting process for 2012. They have a relatively narrow 19-13 margin in the state Senate and they have a larger 64-33 margin in the House. Vetoes are unlikely to be a problem: Gov. Haslam is a Republican and vetoes can be overridden by majority vote anyway. With Democrats holding only two seats, the 5th District in Nashville's Davidson County and the black-majority 9th in Memphis' Shelby County, redistricters may smooth out the highly irregular lines which resulted from successive Democratic redistrictings.

Governor

Bill Haslam (R)

Elected 2010, term expires Jan. 2015, 1st term; b. Aug. 23, 1958, Knoxville; home, Nashville; Emory U., B.A. 1980; Presbyterian; married (Crissy); 3 children.

Elected Office: Knoxville mayor, 2003-11.

Professional Career: Manager, dir., and pres., Pilot Corp., 1980-2003; Pres. of e-strategies, consultant, Saks Inc., 1999-2001.

Office: State Capitol, 1st Floor, Nashville, 37243, 615-741-2001; Web site: www.tn.gov/governor/.

Election Results

2010 general	Bill Haslam (R)	1,041,545	(65%)
	Mike McWherter (D)	529,851	(33%)
2010 primary	Bill Haslam (R)	343,817	(47%)
	Zach Wamp (R)	211,735	(29%)
	Ron Ramsey (R)	159,555	(22%)

The new governor of Tennessee is Bill Haslam, a Republican elected in 2010 after serving as mayor of Knoxville. He replaced the term-limited Democrat Phil Bredesen, who had held the job since 2002.

Haslam is a product of Knoxville's most influential and powerful family. His father, James, made a fortune by building a single gas station into a chain of Pilot stations, which expanded into an empire of more than 300 convenience stores and truck stops along many of the country's major roads in 41 states. It was the United States' 14th largest private company in 2008, according to *Forbes* magazine. The family has financed numerous projects around the state, many of them at the University of Tennessee. Tennessee's senior senator, Republican Lamar Alexander, once served on the company's board, and its junior senator, Republican Bob Corker, was college roommates with James Haslam III, Bill's older brother and Pilot's current chief executive officer. Bill Haslam attended Emory University, where he met his wife, Crissy. After graduating in 1980 with a history degree, he toyed with going into education or the clergy. But his father asked him to join the family business, and he stayed until taking a two-year leave in 1999 to serve as chief executive officer of Saks Direct, the online retail arm of Saks Fifth Avenue. He served as Pilot's president for 13 years.

At the urging of his brother, James, and Corker, who at the time was mayor of Chattanooga, Bill Haslam decided to run for Knoxville mayor in 2003. His Democratic opponent, Madeline Rogero, a nonprofit executive and former Knox County commissioner, depicted him as an inexperienced elitist. He squeaked into office by just 2,000 votes out of nearly 30,000 cast, even though he raised nearly four times as much money as his opponent. He responded to criticism by promising to involve the community in decision-making and to run an open government. He reached out to Rogero and her supporters and embraced some of the issues she championed, such as environmental sustainability. He brought together various groups to work out a plan for South Knoxville's waterfront and to end homelessness, and brought the city's finances under control, getting property taxes to the lowest levels in 50 years. He even ultimately hired Rogero to serve as the city's director of community development. He developed a reputation as a moderate with a hands-off management style and was re-elected in 2007 with 87% of the vote.

Haslam was one of several prominent Republicans interested in succeeding Bredesen as governor in 2010, but all waited to see whether former U.S. Senate Majority Bill Frist would run. As soon as Frist opted out in January 2009, Haslam announced his bid. "In these challenging economic times, Tennessee needs a leader who has experience managing a budget and prioritizing resources," he said. He became part of a Republican field that eventually included Chattanooga-area 3rd District Rep. Zach Wamp and Lt. Gov. Ron Ramsey, each of whom ran to Haslam's right. The Haslam family's company became a frequent political punching bag. In April 2009, state Attorney General Bob Cooper announced that Pilot was among 16 companies and individuals that settled claims of gasoline price gouging, prompting criticism from Democrats. "When you have that many employees, there are bound to be occasional issues," Haslam said in a statement. Wamp in particular went aggressively after Haslam, accusing him of a breach of ethics by mixing personal money with city funds to develop a movie theater. Haslam responded he was a buyer of last resort and that city legal and ethics officials agreed that the arrangement posed no conflict of interest. Wamp also questioned whether his opponent really was in charge of all that much at Pilot, telling a Memphis newspaper, "He didn't run Pilot Oil."

Neither Wamp nor Ramsey could match Haslam's financial advantages. He spent over $9 million, more than Wamp and Ramsey combined, and maintained a continuous double-digit lead in polls while collecting endorsements from the state's largest newspapers, which praised his pragmatism. He easily won the August primary with 47% of the vote, compared to 29% for Wamp and 22% for Ramsey. Wamp, who had developed a reputation for occasional hot-temperedness while in the House, chafed at the result. "The best candidate doesn't always win," he fumed on primary night.

Haslam was widely regarded as the favorite in the general election over Democrat Mike McWherter, a businessman and the son of former Gov. Ned McWherter. McWherter portrayed himself as a fresh-faced political outsider. Haslam outlined a platform that called for issuing annual report cards on progress in five key areas: jobs and economic development, education and workforce development, fiscal strength, health and public safety. McWherter criticized Haslam's plan as short on specifics on spending cuts, and he picked up where the primary candidates had left off in attacking Pilot, charging that the company was linked to a German firm that had done business in Iran and Libya. Haslam's campaign dismissed the charge as "desperate, silly and insulting." McWherter also jumped on Haslam's statement to the Tennessee Firearms Association that if the legislature abolished the state's handgun-carry permit system and allowed people to carry guns with permits, he would sign it into law. McWherter warned that such a move would scare off economic development from out-of-state companies.

Haslam again had the financial advantage, outspending McWherter by 6-to-1. He won a lopsided 65%-33%, the largest margin of victory for an open-seat race in Tennessee since the 1970s, and carried 90 of the state's 95 counties. And in three of the five he lost, Haslam was within a couple of percentage points of McWherter. The exceptions were Shelby, home of Memphis, and nearby Haywood County.

Haslam came into office determined to replicate the inclusive style he used as mayor. Unlike Republican governors in other states who demonized teachers' unions, he met with teachers over lunch around the state to seek their input. He promised to fully fund the Basic Education Program for elementary education, but asked state departments to provide cuts ranging from 1% to 3%. At the same time, however, he showed his affinity with conservatives by proposing new restrictions to the state's consumer protection law, including a ban on class action lawsuits. He also sought to develop a broad-based illegal immigration bill that would include enhanced powers for law enforcement modeled after the state of Arizona's controversial law.

Senior Senator

Lamar Alexander (R)

Elected 2002, term expires 2014, 2nd term; b. July 3, 1940, Maryville; home, Nashville; Vanderbilt U., B.A. 1962, N.Y.U., J.D. 1965; Presbyterian; married (Honey); 4 children.

Elected Office: TN governor, 1979-87.

Professional Career: Pres., Univ. of TN, 1988-91; U.S. Edu. Sect., 1991-93; Co-director, Empower America, 1994-95; Prof., Harvard U. JFK Schl. of Govt., 2001-02.

DC Office: 455 DSOB, 20510, 202-224-4944; Fax: 202-228-3398; Web site: alexander.senate.gov.

State Offices: Blountville, 423-325-6240; Chattanooga, 423-752-5337; Jackson, 731-423-9344; Knoxville, 865-545-4253; Memphis, 901-544-4224; Nashville, 615-736-5129.

Committees: *Appropriations:* Commerce, Justice, Science & Related Agencies; Defense; Energy & Water Development (RMM); Interior, Environment & Related Agencies; Labor, Health & Human Services, Education & Related Agencies; Transportation, HUD & Related Agencies. *Environment & Public Works:* Children's Health & Environmental Responsibility (RMM); Clean Air & Nuclear Safety; Superfund, Toxics & Environmental Health; Water & Wildlife. *Health, Education, Labor & Pensions:* Children & Families; Employment & Workplace Safety. *Rules & Administration* (RMM).

Group Ratings

	ACLU	ACU	ADA	CFG	AFS	FRC	LCV	ITIC	NTU	COC
2010	7	80	10	78	10	83	0	67	93	100
2009	–	68	25	64	36	–	27	–	72	86

National Journal Ratings

	2010 LIB	—	2010 CONS		2009 LIB	—	2009 CONS
Economic	33%	—	66%		33%	—	66%
Social	0%	—	79%		34%	—	65%
Foreign	36%	—	62%		32%	—	66%
Composite	27%	—	73%		34%	—	66%

Key Votes of the 111th Congress

1. Overturn Ledbetter	N	5. Pass health care bill	N
2. Pass $787 billion stimulus	N	6. Regulate financial firms	N
3. Repeal DC gun laws	Y	7. Pass tax cuts for some	N
4. Confirm Sonia Sotomayor	Y	8. Legalize immigrants' kids	N

9. Ratify New START	Y
10. Confirm Elena Kagan	N
11. Stop EPA climate regs	Y
12. Repeal don't ask, tell	N

Election Results

2008 general	Lamar Alexander (R)	1,579,477	(65%)	($8,309,683)
	Robert Tuke (D)	767,236	(32%)	($759,199)
2008 primary	Lamar Alexander (R)	unopposed		

Prior Winning Percentages: 2002 (54%); governor: 1978 (56%); 1982 (60%)

Lamar Alexander, former governor of Tennessee and U.S. Education secretary, was elected to the Senate in 2002 and re-elected in 2008. Alexander hails from a prominent Scots-Irish family that dates to the 18th century. He grew up Maryville, in East Tennessee between Knoxville and the Smoky Mountains, the son of a principal and a teacher. He started piano lessons at age 4 and still plays. Like former President Bill Clinton, he participated in Boys State, the high school summer leadership program run by the American Legion. He went to school at Vanderbilt University, where in the early 1960s he wrote editorials for the school newspaper *The Vanderbilt Hustler* urging integration. He went on to get a law degree from New York University, and then clerked for Judge John Minor Wisdom of the 5th U.S. Circuit Court of Appeals. In 1966, he wrote to Republican Howard Baker, volunteering to work in Baker's Senate campaign against Democrat Frank Clement. Instead, Baker gave him a job on his Washington staff. In 1969, on Baker's recommendation, Alexander got a job working for President Richard Nixon's congressional liaison, Bryce Harlow. On a trip back to Tennessee in 1970, he met Memphis dentist Winfield Dunn, who was running for governor, and Alexander agreed to manage his campaign. Dunn became the first Republican elected governor in 50 years. Tennessee governors were limited to one four-year term in those days, and Alexander decided that next time, he would be the candidate. So in 1974, at age 34, he ran for governor. He ran a conventional campaign and in that Watergate year, he lost 55%-44% to Democratic Rep. Ray Blanton.

He ran again in 1978, this time with a more colorful campaign strategy: Wearing a red plaid shirt, Alexander walked 1,000 miles across Tennessee. He faced Blanton—Tennessee had changed its law by then to allow two consecutive terms—and won 56%-44%. After the election, Blanton started issuing many pardons of criminals, who, it turned out, were paying him bribes. The U.S. attorney urged that Alexander be sworn in three days early, and Democratic legislative leaders and the state's chief justice agreed. In a hurried ceremony, Alexander took the oath and announced that he was naming Fred Thompson, famous for his work as Baker's chief counsel in the Senate Watergate hearings, as special prosecutor. In office, Alexander attended a White House meeting where President Jimmy Carter urged governors to get Japanese auto manufacturers to build cars in the United States; he responded by flying to Japan and persuading Nissan to build its first American plant in Rutherford County. He also persuaded General Motors to build its innovative Saturn plant in Williamson County. The plants became the sparkplugs of rapid growth in the counties around Nashville. Alexander was re-elected 60%-40% in 1982. After leaving office he spent six months living in Australia, writing a book called *Six Months Off*. In 1988, he became president of the University of Tennessee and in 1991, he was appointed George H.W. Bush's Education secretary. In these years, he also reaped big profits from small investments: An option to buy *The Knoxville Journal* was sold to Gannett and yielded $620,000; an option given for his consultant work at Whittle Communications earned him $330,000; he also started a company called Corporate Child Care.

The year 1994 turned out to be a good one for Tennessee Republicans. Thompson and Bill Frist were elected to the Senate and Don Sundquist was elected governor. Alexander was after a bigger prize: the White House. His 1996 campaign was keyed to the mood of 1994: He campaigned as an outsider, wore his red plaid shirt and called, as Baker often had, for citizen-politicians. Of members of Congress, he said, "Cut their pay and bring them home!" But he also had a sophisticated message, calling for a more decentralized government. He had a superb fundraising organization that made Nashville one of the leading Republican money sources in the nation. He hired top-notch political consultants and good organizers in Iowa and New Hampshire. Alexander finished third in the Iowa caucuses, behind Bob Dole and Pat Buchanan and ahead of Steve Forbes. New Hampshire was his best chance for a breakthrough. Five days before the primary, Dole ran ads attacking Alexander, a shrewd strategy. Buchanan was likely to do well in New Hampshire, but probably could never be nominated. The candidate who finished second in New Hampshire would likely be his chief rival and easily win the nomination. So it turned out. Buchanan won with 27% of the vote; Dole got 26% and the Republican nomination; Alexander, in third place with 23%, dropped by the wayside.

In 1999, Alexander started running for president again. But the plaid shirt and the 1994-style themes failed to resonate. George W. Bush, with his celebrity and his fundraising, dominated the race, and Forbes' extensive campaigning in Iowa left little room for Alexander. His fundraising faltered and after his disappointing sixth-place finish in the August 1999 straw poll, he dropped out and endorsed Bush. He was later interviewed by Dick Cheney as a possible vice presidential nominee, but the job went to Cheney. Critical of the frontloaded presidential primary calendar, Alexander in 2007 was a chief co-sponsor of legislation to implement a system of rotating regional primaries.

In March 2002, less than a month before the filing deadline, Thompson announced that he would not seek re-election to the Senate. He gave Alexander a heads-up on his decision, allowing Alexander to get his campaign underway shortly after the announcement. He started with 93% name recognition and 66% of voters had favorable feelings toward him. Republican Rep. Ed Bryant of suburban Memphis also got into the race, even though some Republicans tried to talk him out of it. He claimed to be the real conservative in the race. On talk radio shows, Alexander ran a series of "plain talk" ads taking conservative stands on taxes, charter schools and oil drilling in the Arctic National Wildlife Refuge. Bryant's ads urged, "Don't be plaid. Be solid for Bryant." And he emphasized that Alexander increased the sales and gasoline taxes as governor. But Alexander won 54%-43%.

In the general election, his opponent was Democratic Rep. Bob Clement, of Nashville, the center of the state's largest media market. Clement had a relatively moderate voting record, having supported the Bush tax cuts and the 2002 Iraq war resolution. Clement depicted Alexander as a political insider who became wealthy through political connections. Alexander charged that Clement, while public service commissioner in the 1970s, served on the board of one of the banks of Jake Butcher, whose banks imploded in scandal in the 1980s. Clement at first denied that he'd served on the board, and then said it was just an advisory board a decade before the scandal. Alexander prevailed 54%-44%. He won 63% in his native (and ancestrally Republican) East Tennessee, which cast nearly 40% of the vote. Clement carried Nashville's Davidson County and rural counties in Middle Tennessee, but Alexander carried the fast-growing ring of suburban counties around Nashville and held Clement to 53% in Middle Tennessee. In West Tennessee, Alexander made some inroads among Memphis blacks and carried the rural counties.

Alexander, who ran for governor at 34, became a senator at 62. On his office wall, he mounted not the usual array of framed photographs but a 27-foot authentic barn wall, with 40 antique items (a guitar made of matchsticks, a banjo made from a fruitcake tin) on loan from The Museum of Appalachia in Norris, Tenn.

On the Health, Education, Labor, and Pensions Committee, he worked on successful bills to help states ensure special education teachers meet federal standards, to give parents more choice in special education services, and to create summer academies for teachers and students to study American history. Another Alexander proposal was legislation creating $4,000 scholarships for private schools for students in failing public schools. As a former secretary of Education, Alexander opposed greater involvement by the federal government in federal student loans, comparing it to the "European-Soviet higher education model." But he has often found himself in agreement with Obama administration Education Secretary Arne Duncan, and in January 2011, urged a bipartisan update of the Bush-era No Child Left Behind law. On a key labor issue for their state, Alexander and fellow Tennessee Republican Bob Corker held up the Federal Aviation Administration authorization in spring 2010 over their opposition to a House provision increasing the power of labor unions to organize Memphis-based FedEx.

From his seat on the committee overseeing energy and public works programs, Alexander sometimes parts with his party on the environment. He joined Delaware Democrat Tom Carper's bill to limit emissions of carbon dioxide as well as other pollutants, and to create a system of emissions trading, both of which the Bush White House opposed. Air pollution had been high in Knoxville and threatening the tourism industry in the Great Smoky Mountains area. To counter the effects of a federal court ruling, he also pushed to restrict emissions from coal-fired power plants. For his ongoing support of the Great Smoky Mountains and its environmental quality, researchers in 2007 named a newly discovered bug in the park after Alexander, calling it the *Cosberalla lamaralexandrei*. Its checkerboard markings reminded them of Alexander's trademark red and black flannel shirts. Later, Alexander in 2009 actively opposed the Democrats' cap-and-trade bill to create a system of emissions trading, though it was similar to the one he had supported with Carper.

In the deliberations on the energy bill in 2005, Alexander proposed an amendment to give local governments a veto over wind power projects and to require environmental impact statements of such projects in offshore areas and within 20 miles of scenic areas and military bases. And he won passage of an amendment providing a 30% solar investment tax credit for homeowners. Alexander has continued to champion alternative energy, and even purchased a Toyota Prius with a special battery making the vehicle entirely electric. In 2009, he co-sponsored a bill to ban mountaintop mining, common in West Virginia and Kentucky, but not Tennessee. The same year, he called for 100 new nuclear power plants over the next 20 years, and conversion of half the country's automobiles to electric power.

In 2007, Alexander formed a Bipartisan Members Group with independent Joe Lieberman of Connecticut. On the Iraq war, he and Colorado Democrat Ken Salazar urged President Bush to set goals for troop withdrawals, and pushed for troops to transition into training Iraqi forces to defend themselves. He angered both sides in the debate because he didn't fit neatly into either camp. He told *The New York Times*, "We just can't keep shouting at one another. I think it is inexcusable for United States senators to be lecturing Baghdad about being in a political stalemate, yet we can't come up with a consensus ourselves." In the debate over the February 2008 economic stimulus bill, when Minority Leader Mitch McConnell tried to force Democratic Majority Leader Harry Reid to accept a simple tax rebate bill, Alexander promoted the idea that the plan should be bipartisan while also trying to hold together a diverse party. "We have 49 senators with very different points of view," Alexander told the *Knoxville News-Sentinel*. "My job is not to make us all sing the same note. It's to make us sing at least in some harmony."

He sounded bipartisan notes on other issues as well. He voted for President Barack Obama's Supreme Court nominee, Sonia Sotomayor, in August 2009, but voted against his other nominee to the high court, Elena Kagan, in August 2010. He cited Kagan's action as Harvard Law School dean barring military recruiters from the school. Alexander was the only member of the Republican leadership to favor a bill setting up a bipartisan fiscal commission in 2010. Also that year, his endorsement of the New START treaty insured there would be sufficient Republican votes to pass it.

However, Alexander continued to oppose comprehensive immigration reform. In the past, Alexander had supported measures to designate English as the national language, and in 2008, he introduced a bill to protect employers from language-based anti-discrimination lawsuits. He also opposed the Democrats' health care overhaul, telling the *Tennessee Tribune* that it was "arrogant in its dumping of 15 million low-income Americans into a medical ghetto called Medicaid that none of us or any of our families would ever want to be a part of for our health care."

At the start of the 112th Congress in 2011, Alexander worked with Democrats for modest changes in the rules governing filibusters and anonymous holds on legislation. He also supported the ban on earmarked spending, but said there should be an exception for emergencies, like the 2010 floods in Tennessee.

When Senate Republican Leader Frist decided to retire in 2005, GOP Whip Mitch McConnell of Kentucky was poised to replace him as leader. Alexander courted votes to take McConnell's spot as whip. But after the 2006 election, former majority leader Trent Lott of Mississippi got into the contest. Although Alexander claimed he had sufficient votes to win, Lott prevailed 25-24. "Senators, like most Americans, like a comeback. Trent proved he is a better vote counter," Alexander said. When Lott resigned from the Senate in December 2007, GOP Conference Chairman Jon Kyl was elected whip and Alexander ran for conference chairman. North Carolina's Richard Burr also ran, and pulled support from younger conservatives. Yet Alexander won 31-16. When Kyl announced in 2011 that he would retire in 2012, Alexander again expressed interest in the whip's job. But John Cornyn of Texas and John Thune of South Dakota also declared their interest, and the three agreed to put the contest on hold until summer 2012.

Alexander's path to re-election in 2008 was relatively easy. After more prominent Tennessee Democrats passed on the race, former state Democratic Chairman Robert Tuke got his party's nod, but raised only $700,000 compared to Alexander's $8.3 million. Alexander won 65%-32%, carrying 94 of 95 counties, including Memphis's black-majority Shelby County. It was the highest percentage for a Tennessee Republican senator ever and slightly higher than Frist's in 2000.

Junior Senator

Bob Corker (R)

Elected 2006, term expires 2012, 1st term; b. Aug. 24, 1952, Orangeburg, SC; home, Chattanooga; U. of TN, B.S. 1974; Protestant; married (Elizabeth); 2 children.

Elected Office: Chattanooga mayor, 2001-05.

Professional Career: Owner, Bencor Corp., 1978-90; Commissioner, TN Dept. of Fin. and Admin., 1995-96; Owner, Corker Group, 1982-2006.

DC Office: 185 DSOB, 20510, 202-224-3344; Fax: 202-228-0566; Web site: corker.senate.gov.

State Offices: Blountville, 423-323-1252; Chattanooga, 423-756-2757; Jackson, 731-424-9655; Knoxville, 865-637-4180; Memphis, 901-683-1910; Nashville, 615-279-8125.

Committees: *Aging (Special)* (RMM). *Banking, Housing & Urban Affairs:* Financial Institutions & Consumer Protection (RMM); Housing, Transportation & Community Development; Securities, Insurance & Investment. *Energy & Natural Resources:* Energy; National Parks; Water & Power. *Foreign Relations:* African Affairs; European Affairs; International Development & Foreign Assistance, Economic Affairs & International Environmental Protection (RMM); Near Eastern & South & Central Asian Affairs.

Group Ratings

	ACLU	ACU	ADA	CFG	AFS	FRC	LCV	ITIC	NTU	COC
2010	7	92	5	94	9	95	14	67	99	100
2009	–	84	10	84	18	–	9	–	83	71

National Journal Ratings

	2010 LIB	—	2010 CONS	2009 LIB	—	2009 CONS
Economic	0%	—	87%	29%	—	69%
Social	21%	—	74%	29%	—	70%
Foreign	40%	—	59%	41%	—	56%
Composite	24%	—	77%	34%	—	66%

Key Votes of the 111th Congress

1. Overturn Ledbetter	N	5. Pass health care bill	N	9. Ratify New START	Y
2. Pass $787 billion stimulus	N	6. Regulate financial firms	N	10. Confirm Elena Kagan	N
3. Repeal DC gun laws	Y	7. Pass tax cuts for some	N	11. Stop EPA climate regs	Y
4. Confirm Sonia Sotomayor	N	8. Legalize immigrants' kids	N	12. Repeal don't ask, tell	N

Election Results

2006 general	Bob Corker (R)	929,911	(51%)	($18,859,449)
	Harold Ford (D)	879,976	(48%)	($14,303,967)
2006 primary	Bob Corker (R)	231,541	(48%)	
	Ed Bryant (R)	161,189	(34%)	
	Van Hilleary (R)	83,078	(17%)	

Bob Corker, elected in 2006, is the junior senator from Tennessee. He was born in South Carolina, grew up in Chattanooga and graduated from the University of Tennessee in 1974 with a degree in industrial management. Just a few years out of college, he started his own successful construction company, which he sold before he turned 40. Before that, Corker took a church mission trip to Haiti, which inspired him to help create Chattanooga Neighborhood Enterprise, a non-profit organization designed to get low-income families into affordable housing. In 1994, he ran for the Senate, finishing second in the Republican primary to Bill Frist, who went on to defeat Democratic incumbent Jim Sasser that year and eventually became the Senate majority leader. After his defeat, Corker was named state finance commissioner by Republican Gov. Don Sundquist, giving him responsibility for state government spending. After 18 months, he returned to private business, purchasing two real estate and development companies in Chattanooga. In 2001, he won election as Chattanooga mayor and got credit for reducing violent crime and revitalizing the city's waterfront.

While still in his first term as mayor, Corker in October 2004 announced he would run to succeed Frist, who stuck to his initial campaign promise to serve just two terms. By the end of the year, Corker had raised $2 million. Two former Republican congressmen also ran, Ed Bryant, who lost to Lamar Alexander in the 2002 Senate primary, and Van Hilleary, who lost to Democrat Phil Bredesen in the 2002 governor's race. Corker drew on his personal wealth and spent $5 million through mid-July to introduce himself to voters and defend against attacks that he was insufficiently conservative. Bryant and Hilleary claimed Corker raised property taxes in Chattanooga and criticized his support for abortion rights during his 1994 Senate campaign. Corker responded by calling his opponents "ineffective career politicians" and talked about his background as a successful businessman and mayor. He said he was "wrong" on abortion in 1994 and that he opposed the right to abortion, although he agreed with exceptions in cases of rape and incest. Corker ended up winning by a comfortable margin as Bryant and Hilleary split the conservative vote. He carried nearly every county east of Nashville and a half-dozen west of it, winning 48% to Bryant's 34%; Hilleary finished third with 17%.

The Democratic nominee was Rep. Harold Ford of Memphis, who, in the absence of serious primary opposition, was able to conserve his resources for the general election. Youthful, ambitious and telegenic, Ford was an attractive candidate. The son of former Rep. Harold Ford Sr., he was first elected to the House in 1996, just months after graduating from law school, and his record was sufficiently moderate to make him a competitive statewide candidate. The national media took great interest in the race. Ford was seeking to become the first African-American senator popularly elected in the South and from a state that had never before elected a black candidate to statewide office. For much of the general election campaign, it appeared Corker might defy Tennessee's recent Republican trend in national elections and lose a seat that was critical to the party's hopes of retaining its Senate majority. Corker struggled to unify the party after the contentious primary and failed to gain traction in the two months following the August primary. Meanwhile, Ford ran a nearly flawless campaign. Corker's efforts to frame Ford as too liberal for Tennessee fell flat in the face of Ford's centrist positions on illegal immigration, the Iraq war, border security and gay marriage. Ford also put Corker on the defensive about his business dealings.

The last Democrat that Tennessee elected to the Senate was Al Gore in 1990, and in the 2000 presidential race, George W. Bush embarrassed Gore by defeating him 51%-47% in his home state. Plus, as the scion of a Memphis political dynasty, Ford had to weather distractions caused by several family members, including his uncle, former state Sen. John Ford, who was indicted on federal corruption charges the day after Harold Ford filed to run for the Senate. Then, John Ford's sister—Harold's aunt—won the special election to replace him but she was ousted by the state Senate in April amid allegations of vote fraud. Meanwhile, in the racially-charged House race to succeed Harold Ford, his brother, Jake, unexpectedly ran as an independent candidate against white Democratic nominee Steve Cohen.

Heading into the final weeks of the campaign, the election appeared to be a dead heat. But Corker gained momentum after Republicans launched a series of attack ads and zeroed in on Ford's personal story, characterizing it as a life of privilege and emphasizing that he went to preparatory school in Washington and graduated from an Ivy League university. Corker's ads described his rise from a laborer who poured concrete. In late October, the Republican National Committee weighed in with a controversial ad featuring purported on-the-street interviews with regular people, including an attractive young, blonde and white woman, claiming that she had "met Harold at the *Playboy* party," a reference to news stories that Ford had attended a Super Bowl party hosted by *Playboy* magazine. The commercial ended with the woman saying, "Harold, call me." Critics called the ad racial politicking, while Republicans insisted it was about values. Corker's campaign asked television stations not to air the spot.

Corker won 51%-48%. Whites voted 59%-40% for Corker and blacks voted 95%-4% for Ford. Ford won 61%-38% in the Memphis area, while Corker carried the Nashville area 50%-49%. Corker far outpaced Ford in East Tennessee, winning 58%-40%. Ford carried Middle and West Tennessee 52%-46%.

In the Senate, Corker tried to further separate himself from the controversial attack ads. He introduced a bill to allow candidates to approve commercials and direct mail pieces from political parties before they are released to the public. While he was a reliable vote for Republicans on issues such as opposing embryonic stem cell research and troop withdrawal timetables in Iraq, Corker broke with the party on some high-profile issues. He backed an energy bill to raise gas mileage standards for cars and trucks. He joined a bipartisan effort to promote a 2008 energy bill allowing offshore drilling while also emphasizing renewable energy sources. In 2007, he voted for a Democratic bill to expand the State Children's Health Insurance Program, and also played a crucial role in negotiations to renew federal funding for the state's TennCare Medicaid program.

In January 2008, Corker got a seat on the Banking Committee. When committee ranking Republican Richard Shelby of Alabama refused to participate in bipartisan talks about a bailout for the collapsing financial industry, Corker engaged in meetings with Democratic Chairman Christopher Dodd that produced the $700 billion Troubled Asset Relief Program. In late 2008, when the big three domestic auto makers sought a multi-billion-dollar bailout, Corker criticized auto executives who appeared before the committee, chiding their plans for securing government loans and waiting for mergers, and telling the head of Chrysler: "While this is happening, you're going to be going to spas and getting facials and hopefully finding someone to marry you." In December, Corker offered an alternative proposal that required retiring autoworkers to accept most of their benefits in stock rather than in cash, forced bondholders to accept a steep cut in the value of their bonds and required wages and benefits comparable to American employees of foreign automakers. Outrage was expressed in various quarters in Detroit. But Corker's conditions were in large part followed by President Barack Obama's task force on the auto companies. As General Motors and Chrysler at least partially recovered, United Auto Workers leaders called for organizing Southern plants. "I can't imagine any company wanting the UAW to be part of their company," Corker told the *Detroit News*. "It's the employees who decide. My sense is that they will view their economic self-interest being better served by not being affiliated with the UAW."

Corker was unusually active for a junior member on financial regulation, the big issue before the Banking Committee, in 2009 and 2010. By then, he had built a good working relationship with Dodd, who encouraged him to engage in informal meetings with Virginia Democrat Mark Warner. The two sought the views of top current and former regulators. When Corker saw the Obama administration plan, he said that its proposals for a systemic risk regulator and a consumer finance protection agency were not responsive to the causes of the financial crisis. "One question that needs to be asked is, if we had proper regulation at the various functioning levels, do we need a systemic risk regulator?" Corker told *American Banker*.

In early February 2010, when Dodd concluded that negotiations with Shelby on the bill were going nowhere, Corker once again agreed to work with Dodd, despite complaints from Shelby and Minority Leader Mitch McConnell. On the sensitive issue of creating a consumer finance protection agency, strongly backed by liberal Democrats, Corker, Dodd, Shelby and New Hampshire Republican Judd Gregg agreed to put the new CFPA under the authority of the Federal Reserve. But Corker continued to be troubled by what he regarded as the too-big-to-fail treatment of major banks and other financial institutions. He told *National Journal*: "What you want to do is create an orderly dissolution, an orderly unwinding. . . . a resolution mechanism like the one we have for the FDIC."

Yet it proved difficult to close the deal. And on March 11, Dodd announced that he would unveil his own bill without support from Corker or other Republicans. Corker complained that the unilateral action was ordered by the Obama White House, but he was also critical of fellow Republicans, saying they had made a major strategic error in not reaching a compromise and that GOP assertions that the bill would increase the likelihood of bailouts were overstated. Dodd's bill was passed in committee along party lines, with some provisions unacceptable to Corker and he ended up voting against the final version. He said on the Senate floor, "I don't think either side of the aisle deserves a badge of honor as it relates to the way this has been discussed." At a May 2010 meeting between Obama and Republican senators, Corker told the president that in his view the White House role in the legislation was "duplicitous." On another major financial issue, Corker in 2010 called for limiting the Federal Reserve to a single mandate—preventing inflation.

On energy issues, Corker sought unsuccessfully in May 2009 to bar draw-downs of the Strategic Petroleum Reserve to bring down the price of oil and in February 2011 he opposed a new regulation requiring the cost of transmission lines for alternative energy sources to be paid by utility ratepayers in states not served by them. On an issue of interest at home, he worked with fellow Tennessee Republican Lamar Alexander to strip from the 2010 Federal Aviation Administration bill a provision that would facilitate unionization of Memphis-based FedEx. In December 2010, he and Alexander cast key votes for ratification of the New START treaty after Corker got assurances from appropriators of funding for the modernization of nuclear weapons.

Corker jumped into the debate over cutting federal spending in 2011, and again, did so in a bipartisan way. He and Missouri Democrat Claire McCaskill sponsored a bill to require reductions of federal spending from 24.7% of gross domestic product to the 40-year historic average of 20.6%, with the White House budget office charged with making simultaneous cuts in entitlement and discretionary spending if Congress did not meet the targets.

After the 2010 elections, there was talk that Corker might get opposition from a tea party candidate in 2012. But a poll for Republican Gov. Bill Haslam showed that 72% of tea party sympathizers expressed favorable feelings toward Corker in spite of his work with Democrats on major issues.

FIRST DISTRICT

Phil Roe (R)

Elected 2008, 2nd term; b. July 21, 1945, Clarksville; home, Johnson City; Austin Peay St. U., B.S. 1967; U. of TN, M.D. 1970; Methodist; married (Pam); 3 children.

Military Career: Army, 1973-74.

Elected Office: Johnson City Commission, 2003-09, Vice mayor, 2005-07, Mayor, 2007-09.

Professional Career: Obstetrician/gynecologist, 1970-2008.

DC Office: 419 CHOB, 20515, 202-225-6356; Fax: 202-225-5714; Web site: roe.house.gov.

State Offices: Kingsport, 423-247-8161; Morristown, 423-254-1400.

Committees: *Education & the Workforce:* Health, Employment, Labor & Pensions (Chmn); Higher Education & Workforce Training. *Veterans' Affairs:* Health; Oversight & Investigations.

Group Ratings

	ACLU	ACU	ADA	CFG	AFS	FRC	LCV	ITIC	NTU	COC
2010	13	96	0	87	13	100	0	33	87	88
2009	–	92	5	88	22	–	7	–	84	87

National Journal Ratings

	2010 LIB	—	2010 CONS		2009 LIB	—	2009 CONS
Economic	22%	—	77%		23%	—	76%
Social	0%	—	85%		29%	—	68%
Foreign	12%	—	79%		0%	—	75%
Composite	16%	—	85%		22%	—	78%

Key Votes of the 111th Congress

1. Overturn Ledbetter	N	5. Bar federal abortion funds	Y	9. Stop detainee transfers	Y
2. Pass $820 billion stimulus	N	6. Pass health care bill	N	10. Legalize immigrants' kids	N
3. Let guns in national parks	Y	7. Regulate financial firms	N	11. Repeal don't ask, tell	N
4. Pass cap-and-trade	N	8. Pass tax cuts for some	N	12. Limit campaign funds	N

Election Results

2010 general	Phil Roe (R)	123,006	(81%)	($518,529)
	Michael Clark (D)	26,045	(17%)	
	Kermit Steck (I)	3,110	(2%)	
2010 primary	Phil Roe (R)	78,862	(96%)	

Prior Winning Percentages: 2008 (72%)

Population		Race/Ethnicity		Work	
Pop. 2010:	684,093	White:	92.4%	Private:	79.2%
Change since 2000:	Up 8.2%	Black:	2.2%	Government:	12.6%
Urban:	55.4%	Hispanic:	3.3%	Self-employed:	8.0%
Rural:	44.6%	Asian:	0.6%	Blue collar:	28.3%
Area size:	4,174 sq. mi.	Native Am.:	0.2%	White collar:	52.8%
		Hawaiian:	0.0%	Khaki collar:	0.0%
Age		Two+ races:	1.2%	Other:	18.9%
Median age:	40.8 yrs.				
More than 65 yrs:	16.3%	*Ancestry*		Median income:	$36,651
Less than 18 yrs:	21.2%	USA	23.1%	Median Home Value:	$115,800
		English	10.3%		
Education		Irish	10.2%	**Military Veterans**	
H.S. grad:	79.1%			% of Pop:	11.9%
College grad:	16.7%				
Grad degree:	6.0%				

Northeastern Tennessee; Tri-Cities

Between the corduroy-like ridges of the Appalachian chains, as they bend west and then south, the valley of Virginia extends far into northeastern Tennessee. The communities of this region are a hilly patchwork of industrial centers, small farms and federal land. The land rush immediately after the Revolutionary War populated the area. In tiny Jonesborough, the early settlers established the free state of Franklin in 1784, and many pioneer cabins, federal mansions and Greek Revival churches are lovingly preserved. It was the building of the railroads in the 1850s, however, that determined the winners and losers. The small industrial cities that developed—Johnson City, Kingsport and Bristol, Va., now collectively known as the Tri-Cities—were on the main lines of national commerce before the Civil War. The war had a different political effect here than in most of the South: Northeast Tennessee, the home of wartime governor and then Vice President Andrew Johnson had few slaves, and with its connection to northern industry, was Union and Republican territory. It remains heavily Republican to this day.

2008 Presidential Vote
John McCain (R) 181,898 (70%)
Barack Obama (D) 75,528 (29%)

2004 Presidential Vote
George Bush (R) 172,079 (68%)
John Kerry (D) 79,507 (31%)

Cook Partisan Voting Index: R+21

The political continuity may be surprising because this area had decades of continuous economic growth and developed the sort of industrial economy that produced unions and Democrats in the North. Its growth was helped by a skilled labor force, low electric power rates because of the Tennessee Valley Authority and good transportation routes (rail lines and now Interstate 81). Its small cities used to boast major paper and printing plants, but most of those industries are gone. One of the largest employers is Eastman Kodak in Kingsport, which announced in 2010 that it would boost production by about 70% of a material used in liquid crystal displays. This area fared reasonably well during the 2007-09 recession. In 2010, *Southern Business & Development* magazine ranked the Tri-Cities as the fourth best medium-sized market in the South for industry over the past decade. There also has been some economic growth in Sevier County near Knoxville, where Gatlinburg and Pigeon Forge (home of Dolly Parton's Dollywood theme park) have more than 10,000 hotel rooms at the entry point to the Great Smoky Mountains National Park, the nation's most-visited national park. However, the area surrounding the park has suffered from heavy acid rain and ozone pollution from nearby power plants and factories.

The 1st Congressional District takes in the far northeastern end of Tennessee, a district so heavily Republican that it has not elected a Democrat to the House for more than 100 years. Nonetheless, it has had turbulent politics on occasion. For almost 40 years, the seat was held by B. Carroll Reece, a fierce mountain politician who was the Republican national chairman from 1946 to 1948. After Reece died in 1961 and his widow was elected to fill out his term, there was a hotly contested primary. The winner, Republican Jimmy Quillen, was a bread-and-butter politician, homebuilder and former owner of the *Johnson City Times*. He represented the district for the next 34 years, a record tenure for the Tennessee congressional delegation. True to its roots, the district gave GOP nominee John McCain his highest percentage in Tennessee, 70%, in 2008. In the 2010 governor's race, Republican Bill Haslam did even better in all of the district's counties.

Phil Roe (R)

The congressman from the 1st District is Phil Roe, a conservative Republican elected in 2008. As one of the House's GOP physicians, he regularly appears on television talk shows to espouse the party's opposition to the Obama administration on health care.

Roe grew up in Clarksville and attended a one-room schoolhouse with no running water. He went on to receive degrees from Austin Peay State University and a medical degree from the University of Tennessee. He served in the Army Medical Corps and then relocated to Johnson City, setting up practice as an obstetrician/gynecologist for 30 years. In 2003, the political bug bit Roe, and he ran successfully for the Johnson City Commission. Roe was chosen by commission members to be vice mayor in 2005 and mayor 2007. When five-term U.S. Rep. Bill Jenkins retired in 2006, Roe competed in a crowded GOP primary but finished fourth with 17% of the vote, behind health care business owner David Davis, who went on to win the seat in the general election.

In his first term in the House, Davis quickly gained a reputation as a combative partisan. Roe decided to challenge Davis when he sought re-election in 2008, and embarked on a grass-roots campaign, personally visiting each county multiple times, talking to voters, stumping in restaurants and waving signs at busy intersections. In ads featuring an elderly grandmother trying to fill up her car with gas, Roe criticized Davis for accepting money from oil companies, attacks that resonated as gas prices spiked. Davis led in fundraising, outspending his challenger 3-to-1. But two years after finishing fourth behind Davis in a crowded Republican field, Roe rebounded to narrowly upset the one-term Davis, becoming the first challenger in more than 40 years to defeat an incumbent representative in Tennessee.

Roe's challenge to Davis was barely on the national radar, and his win surprised Davis as well, leading to one of the more unusual escapades of the congressional election season. As vote tallies trickled in from precincts across the rural eastern Tennessee district, Davis refused to emerge from his hotel room to greet supporters. With the unofficial vote tally the next morning at roughly 500 votes in Roe's favor, Davis refused to concede, despite winning the 2006 primary by only 573 votes himself. Instead, Davis tried to raise doubt on the validity of the outcome, issuing a statement saying Democrats had conspired to throw the election by voting in the Republican primary. The charge gained little traction considering Tennessee has an open primary system that does not require registration by party. Davis conceded a week later. Roe's margin of victory was 482 votes. He won the district's two largest counties, Washington and Sullivan, while Davis was strong along the western edge of the district, winning Sevier and Hawkins counties. In November, Roe easily beat Democrat Robert Russell with 72% of the vote.

Roe's positions are similar to Davis', mirroring the conservative bent of the district, but he has a more upbeat, folksy demeanor. He was among the first House Republicans to join the Tea Party Caucus in 2010 and posted the most conservative voting record in Tennessee's House delegation that year, according to *National Journal's* rankings. As a doctor, Roe says he is committed to reforming the medical insurance system, but opposes government-run health care. With the GOP takeover of the House, he was named chairman of the Education and Workforce Committee's health panel in 2011 and became involved in his party's free market alternatives to the current law. He introduced a bill in January 2011 seeking to repeal an advisory board that was created to rein in the growth of Medicare payments. "This board does not have a mandate to improve patient care—it has a mandate to meet a budget, and that harms patient care," he said.

Roe has been reliably conservative on other issues. He sponsored a bill in 2009 seeking to help create jobs in rural areas by broadening tax credits for employers, saying such efforts were preferable to providing states with federal stimulus money. He supports the fair tax, which would replace the federal income tax with a 23% national retail sales tax. Despite his support for banning earmarks, Roe was among the Republicans in 2010 who called for better defining the special interest spending provisions, noting that the ban prevented him from seeking a tariff waiver on behalf of Eastman Chemical for a chemical found only overseas.

He was easily re-elected in 2010.

SECOND DISTRICT

John Duncan (R)

Elected Nov. 1988, 12th full term; b. July 21, 1947, Lebanon; home, Knoxville; U. of TN, B.S. 1969, George Washington U., J.D. 1973; Presbyterian; married (Lynn); 4 children.

Military Career: Army Natl. Guard & Army Reserves, 1970–87.

Professional Career: Practicing atty., 1973–81; Knox Cnty. judge, 1981–88.

DC Office: 2207 RHOB, 20515, 202-225-5435; Fax: 202-225-6440; Web site: duncan.house.gov.

State Offices: Athens, 423-745-4671; Knoxville, 865-523-3772; Maryville, 865-984-5464.

Committees: *Natural Resources:* National Parks, Forests & Public Lands. *Transportation & Infrastructure:* Aviation; Highways & Transit (Chmn); Water Resources & Environment.

Group Ratings

	ACLU	ACU	ADA	CFG	AFS	FRC	LCV	ITIC	NTU	COC
2010	19	100	5	79	13	100	0	33	91	88
2009	–	92	10	85	0	–	7	–	88	67

National Journal Ratings

	2010 LIB	—	2010 CONS		2009 LIB	—	2009 CONS
Economic	27%	—	73%		29%	—	71%
Social	15%	—	84%		11%	—	87%
Foreign	39%	—	61%		40%	—	59%
Composite	27%	—	73%		27%	—	73%

Key Votes of the 111th Congress

1. Overturn Ledbetter	N	5. Bar federal abortion funds	Y	9. Stop detainee transfers	Y
2. Pass $820 billion stimulus	N	6. Pass health care bill	N	10. Legalize immigrants' kids	N
3. Let guns in national parks	Y	7. Regulate financial firms	N	11. Repeal don't ask, tell	N
4. Pass cap-and-trade	N	8. Pass tax cuts for some	Y	12. Limit campaign funds	N

Election Results

2010 general	John Duncan (R)	141,796	(82%)	($566,844)
	David Hancock (D)	24,500	(15%)	
2010 primary	John Duncan (R)	unopposed		

Prior Winning Percentages: 2008 (78%), 2006 (78%), 2004 (79%), 2002 (79%), 2000 (89%), 1998 (89%), 1996 (71%), 1994 (90%), 1992 (72%), 1990 (81%), 1988 (57%), 1988 special (56%)

Population		Race/Ethnicity		Work	
Pop. 2010:	723,798	White:	87.1%	Private:	80.4%
Change since 2000:	Up 14.5%	Black:	6.2%	Government:	13.1%
Urban:	71.4%	Hispanic:	3.5%	Self-employed:	6.4%
Rural:	28.6%	Asian:	1.4%	Blue collar:	21.5%
Area size:	2,492 sq. mi.	Native Am.:	0.3%	White collar:	62.0%
		Hawaiian:	0.0%	Khaki collar:	0.1%
Age		Two+ races:	1.5%	Other:	16.4%
Median age:	38.6 yrs.				
More than 65 yrs:	14.1%	*Ancestry*		Median income:	$45,166
Less than 18 yrs:	22.1%	German	13.0%	Median Home Value:	$151,700
		USA	12.4%		
Education		English	11.6%	**Military Veterans**	
H.S. grad:	85.8%			% of Pop:	10.4%
College grad:	27.0%				
Grad degree:	9.5%				

Eastern Tennessee; Knoxville

Knoxville, the largest city in East Tennessee, is nestled between mountain ridges where the Holston and French Broad rivers join to form the Tennessee River. It was established not long after the first wave of pioneers came through the gaps and down the mountains of the Appalachian chain. During the Civil War, it was Union territory, and it has remained Republican in allegiance and progressive on civil rights ever since. But its Republican heritage is tempered

2008 Presidential Vote		
John McCain (R) 195,423	(64%)
Barack Obama (D) 104,004	(34%)

2004 Presidential Vote		
George Bush (R) 185,450	(64%)
John Kerry (D) 100,032	(35%)

Cook Partisan Voting Index: R+16

by another tradition, that of the Tennessee Valley Authority. A venturesome program when created in the 1930s, it is now part of the fabric of life in East Tennessee, sometimes criticized as it has reached capacity to produce cheap hydroelectric power and began to rely more on expensive and sometimes poorly functioning nuclear power plants. The area's largest cash crop remains tobacco, though its importance has diminished. East Tennessee's five major health care systems announced in 2010 that they would all have smoke-free workplaces.

Both TVA and the region have undergone turbulent changes in recent years. In a competitive electricity market, and laboring under billions of dollars in debt mostly incurred in building its nuclear plants, TVA has cut its payroll sharply and held down rates. Heavy ozone pollution in Knoxville led the Environmental Protection Agency to impose growth limits. TVA spent several billion dollars to reduce pollution at its coal-fired power plants and the result has been marked improvement in recent years in local air quality due. The EPA announced in March 2011 that the Knoxville area had met its ozone standard. Delay in construction of a national nuclear-waste repository at Yucca Mountain in Nevada has forced TVA to spend tens of millions of dollars for new nuclear waste storage pools.

Yet Knoxville has overcome setbacks and grown, at times robustly. *Forbes* magazine ranked it the 10th best city in the country for business in 2008, though it fell to number 56 in 2010. That year, media company Scripps Networks Interactive dedicated a new $30 million expansion of its facility in west Knoxville and announced it would relocate its corporate headquarters there from Cincinnati. Knoxville's Republican mayor, Bill Haslam, touted his record of promoting economic growth as the centerpiece of his successful 2010 campaign for governor. His family runs the Pilot chain of convenience stores and roadside travel centers that are one of the city's economic mainstays. And the University of Tennessee's football complex, Neyland Stadium, on fall Saturdays contains one of the nation's largest crowds, cheering on the Vols. Women's basketball is nearly as popular as football here, and in 2009, Lady Vols' coach Pat Summitt became the only Division I basketball coach, men's or women's, to win 1,000 career games. Knoxville also hosts the Women's Basketball Hall of Fame.

The 2nd Congressional District of Tennessee includes Knoxville and Knox County, plus four mountainous counties and part of another to the south. Most of its people live within the Knoxville metro area. Its less populated areas span the foothills of the Great Smoky Mountains. The district is heavily Republican; it has not elected a Democratic congressman since the Civil War. GOP nominee John McCain won Knox County comfortably and the rest of the district with 64% in 2008.

John Duncan (R)

The congressman from the 2nd District is John (Jimmy) Duncan, a Republican first elected in 1988. He has been a frequent maverick on economic and foreign policy issues, something that has hindered his ascension up the House GOP ranks.

His father, who was the senior Republican on the House Ways and Means Committee, represented the 2nd District from 1964 until his death in May 1988. Jimmy Duncan got a bachelor's degree in journalism at the University of Tennessee and a law degree from George Washington University. He practiced law and was a trial judge in the 1980s. When his father died, he won the seat despite a spirited challenge from Democrat Dudley Taylor, a scion of another prominent East Tennessee political family. Taylor attacked Duncan for his ties to scandal-tarred banker and Democratic politician Jake Butcher. But Duncan won with 57% in November. He has not been seriously challenged since then.

While Duncan is known for his independence, he has become more inclined to side with his party in recent years. He was one of just 10 Republicans in April 2009 to vote in favor of the Democrats' bill to curb employee bonuses at financial companies receiving government bailout funds. In

July 2009, he was one of two Republicans to support expanded regulatory oversight of all executive compensation. In April 2011, he voted against the compromise that Republicans struck with President Obama on the fiscal 2011 budget to avert a shutdown. Duncan opposed normal trade relations with China and the Bush administration's 2001 No Child Left Behind education law that imposed mandatory testing on schools. In October 2002, he was one of six Republicans—and the only Tennessean—who voted against the use of force in Iraq. He argued that there was not sufficient proof that Iraqi Leader Saddam Hussein had weapons of mass destruction. He did please some anti-government conservatives in November 2010 when he took to the House floor to declaim the Transportation Security Administration's "very embarrassing, intrusive" procedures for pat-down searches of airport travelers.

But his contrariness has had its price. Duncan was a candidate for the chairmanship of the House Resources Committee in 2003, but Republican Speaker Dennis Hastert passed over him and five other senior Republicans to give the post to the more loyal Richard Pombo of California. When Republicans recaptured the House in 2010, the Resources chairmanship went to the more loyal Doc Hastings of Washington state. In 2006, Duncan made a big push for the top Republican position on the Transportation and Infrastructure Committee. But he lost to John Mica of Florida, who was more junior but, once again, more of a party regular. In 2011, Duncan became chairman of the committee's Subcommittee on Highways and Transit, where he sought to play a major role in getting a multi-year surface transportation bill into law. He has disdained "radical environmentalists" whom he accused in a June 2010 floor speech of being insensitive to rural Americans: "Most of them are city people, anyway. They probably think it would be good if everyone was forced to live in 25 or 30 urban areas, with the country left totally empty."

Before joining his caucus' push to ban earmarks, Duncan wasn't shy about seeking funding for local projects, from resurfacing the Foothills Parkway in the Great Smoky Mountains National Park to a rail and trolley system for downtown Knoxville. Another of his legislative interests has been a bill to require the disclosure of contributions to presidential libraries, which the House passed in 2009 by a 388-31 vote. The Senate did not act on it, and he reintroduced it in 2011.

In Knoxville, Duncan's annual barbecue dinner draws as many as 5,000 people and reinforces his local popularity. Although he shows no signs of retiring, when Duncan does decide to leave Congress, his son, John Duncan III, is said to be interested in the seat. The younger Duncan was elected Knox County trustee in 2010.

THIRD DISTRICT

Charles Fleischmann (R)

Elected 2010, 1st term; b. Oct. 12, 1962, New York, NY; home, Ooltewah; U. of IL, B.A. 1983; U. of TN, J.D. 1986. ; Catholic; Married (Brenda); 3 children.

Professional Career: Practicing atty., 1987-2010.

DC Office: 511 CHOB, 20515, 202-225-3271; Fax: 202-225-3494; Web site: fleischmann.house.gov.

State Offices: Chattanooga, 423-756-2342; Oak Ridge, 865-576-1976.

Committees: *Natural Resources:* Energy & Mineral Resources. *Science, Space & Technology:* Energy & Environment; Technology & Innovation. *Small Business:* Agriculture, Energy & Trade; Economic Growth, Tax and Capital Access; Healthcare & Technology.

Election Results

2010 general	Charles Fleischmann (R)	92,032	(57%)	($1,409,582)
	John Wolfe (D)	45,387	(28%)	
	Savas Kyriakidis (I)	17,077	(11%)	($128,660)
	Mark DeVol (I)	5,773	(4%)	($37,983)
2010 primary	Charles Fleischmann (R)	26,869	(30%)	
	Robin Smith (R)	25,454	(28%)	
	Tim Gobble (R)	14,274	(16%)	
	Van Irion (R)	10,492	(12%)	
	Tommy Crangle (R)	5,149	(6%)	
	Art Rhodes (R)	4,552	(5%)	

Population		Race/Ethnicity		Work	
Pop. 2010:	692,346	White:	82.3%	Private:	78.8%
Change since 2000:	Up 9.5%	Black:	11.1%	Government:	13.4%
Urban:	64.2%	Hispanic:	3.7%	Self-employed:	7.5%
Rural:	35.8%	Asian:	1.2%	Blue collar:	26.0%
Area size:	3,597 sq. mi.	Native Am.:	0.3%	White collar:	56.4%
		Hawaiian:	0.0%	Khaki collar:	0.1%
Age		Two+ races:	1.4%	Other:	17.5%
Median age:	39.5 yrs.				
More than 65 yrs:	14.9%	*Ancestry*		Median income:	$40,520
Less than 18 yrs:	22.3%	USA	16.2%	Median Home Value:	$130,700
		Irish	10.4%		
Education		German	9.5%	**Military Veterans**	
H.S. grad:	81.0%			% of Pop:	11.3%
College grad:	21.1%				
Grad degree:	7.4%				

Eastern Tennessee; Chattanooga

Etching its way through the serrated ridges of East Tennessee, with some of the most vivid scenery in the Appalachian Mountain chain, is the river that gave Tennessee its name. From Knoxville, the river cuts through a ridge and then plunges down a long valley to the city of Chattanooga at the Georgia line. There it switches course again, winding around the tabletop Lookout Mountain and then moving into northern Alabama. At the base of the mountain, Chatta-

2008 Presidential Vote		
John McCain (R)	174,696	(62%)
Barack Obama (D)	103,767	(37%)

2004 Presidential Vote		
George Bush (R)	163,612	(61%)
John Kerry (D)	102,390	(38%)

Cook Partisan Voting Index: R+13

nooga was just a village when it was a Civil War battlefield. It then became the industrial "Dynamo of Dixie." Four decades ago, it was labeled America's most polluted city. But regional political leaders, prodded by influential and civic-minded remnants of its Industrial Age aristocracy, used creative measures, such as a locally built electric shuttle bus, to reduce pollution and to spruce up the city's scenic river banks.

With big job cuts at the Tennessee Valley Authority, the region has pinned its hopes for growth more on the private sector, including a large food-service industry. The district is home to both the MoonPie and Little Debbie confectioners. Downtown Chattanooga is the home of the twelve-story, well-visited Tennessee Aquarium. Nearby are the 145-foot waterfall of Ruby Falls, as well as the rock formations and native gardens of Rock City. Grainger County, north of the Interstate 75 and Interstate 40 split, was the home of President Andrew Johnson and the South's first paper mill.

The 3rd Congressional District of Tennessee includes Chattanooga and runs northeasterly from the Tennessee-Georgia border to the Virginia border, making this one of three Tennessee districts that span the state from north to south. Most of the population is in Chattanooga and the counties around it. Chattanooga is the state's fourth-largest city, but in recent years it has been challenging Knoxville for third place. Chattanooga's population surged 8% between 2000 and 2010, even as the area lost more than 18,000 manufacturing, construction and transportation jobs between 2001 and 2009. Unemployment rates were lower here during the 2007-09 recession than in Tennessee's other large cities. Volkswagen opened a $1 billion plant there to build a new midsize sedan that is expected to add more than 11,000 jobs to the region. Amazon.com also announced plans to open two distribution centers in the area in summer 2011 to create more than 1,400 full-time positions and more than 2,000 seasonal slots.

The district's thin strip of land to the north includes Dayton, the "buckle of the Bible Belt" where John Scopes was tried for teaching evolution in 1925, defended by Clarence Darrow and prosecuted by William Jennings Bryan, events immortalized in the play *Inherit the Wind*. Farther north is Oak Ridge, which was secretly constructed in virgin Appalachian forest during World War II to house the nuclear facility that made uranium isotopes for the Hiroshima bomb and is now the Oak Ridge National Laboratory. For years, it did not appear on maps. Politically, this area was split historically, with Chattanooga voting Democratic and the mountain counties Republican. Today, it is solidly Republican, with none of its counties voting less than 57% for George W. Bush in 2004. In 2008, GOP nominee John McCain won the district with a comfortable 62%. In the 2010 governor's race, Republican Bill Haslam took 66% in Chattanooga's Hamilton County.

Charles Fleischmann (R)

The new congressman from the 3rd District is Charles Fleischmann, a Republican elected in 2010 to succeed GOP Rep. Zach Wamp, who ran unsuccessfully for governor. Fleischmann was born in New York City. His father, Max, worked in the food services business. The family moved often, following his father's job opportunities. Fleischmann, an only child, lived in Philadelphia and New Jersey before finishing high school in Chicago. His mother, Rose Marie, was diagnosed with terminal cancer when he was nine and died when he was 14. He excelled in school, graduating from the University of Illinois at Champaign-Urbana in three years with a bachelor's degree in political science in 1983. He went to the University of Tennessee, in Knoxville, for his law degree in the mid-1980s and adopted the state as his home. He clerked for Knoxville lawyer Foster Arnett, and then started his own firm with his wife, Brenda.

When Wamp announced he would leave Congress to run for governor in 2010, Fleischmann decided to run, saying he was "very, very upset with the way things were going in Washington, D.C." In the August primary, his most formidable opponent was health care consultant Robin Smith, a former Republican state party chairwoman. Fleischmann put $544,000 of his own money into the campaign and ran ads that accused Smith of mismanaging funds when she chaired the Tennessee GOP.

In late July, the Smith campaign went after Fleischmann's record as a personal injury lawyer, saying that he had sued gun clubs, Wal-Mart stores, and churches, all popular institutions with the state's conservative voters. It was a potentially fatal line of attack, but Fleischmann defended himself by saying, "I make a living standing up for the little guy, people who have traditionally not had a voice and who have been dealt injustices and harm." The *Chattanooga Times Free Press* ran a story that backed up his position, reporting that the gun club case in 2003 involved a man who was working on his own property when a bullet fired from a machine gun struck him in the abdomen. In the end, Fleischmann edged out Smith, 30%- 28%. His Democratic opponent, radio talk show personality John Wolfe, was the same unsuccessful challenger Wamp had faced in 2002 and 2004. Fleischmann refused to treat Wolfe as a serious opponent, steering clear of debates and candidate forums, and won an easy 67%-33% victory.

In the House, he joined the state's other GOP House members in supporting riders in the House's fiscal 2011 budget bill aimed at limiting the Environmental Protection Agency's authority, with one notable exception: He opposed an April amendment blocking the Environmental Protection Agency from tightening the standards governing particulate matter, a nod to Chattanooga's earlier efforts to clean its air. Unlike some of his fellow GOP freshman colleagues from outside the state,he backed the final budget deal for that year. He concentrated on keeping his visibility up in his district and launched a "Chuck on the Job" workday program that led him to sell milkshakes at a drugstore and mop floors at a farm-supply store. He also joined fellow Tennessee freshman Republican Scott DesJarlais in opposing an Energy Department plan to consolidate management of Oak Ridge's Y-12 weapons plant with the one at Texas' Pantex facility.

FOURTH DISTRICT

Scott DesJarlais (R)

Elected 2010, 1st term; b. Feb. 21, 1964, Sturgis, SD; home, Jasper; U. of SD, B.S. 1987, M.D. 1991; Episcopalian; Married (Amy); 3 children.

Professional Career: Practicing physician, 1993-2010.

DC Office: 413 CHOB, 20515, 202-225-6831; Fax: 202-226-5172; Web site: desjarlais.house.gov.

State Offices: Columbia, 931-381-9920; Crossville, 931-707-9091.

Committees: *Agriculture:* Livestock, Dairy & Poultry. *Education & the Workforce:* Health, Employment, Labor & Pensions. *Oversight & Government Reform:* Health Care, District of Columbia, Census & the National Archives; Regulatory Affairs, Stimulus Oversight & Government Spending.

Election Results

2010 general	Scott DesJarlais (R)	103,969	(57%)	($973,111)
	Lincoln Davis (D)	70,254	(39%)	($1,488,038)
2010 primary	Scott DesJarlais (R)	27,812	(37%)	
	Jack Bailey (R)	20,420	(27%)	
	Kent Greenough (R)	11,413	(15%)	
	Ronald Harwell (R)	9,237	(12%)	
	Donald Strong (R)	5,992	(8%)	

Population		Race/Ethnicity		Work	
Pop. 2010:	688,008	White:	91.1%	Private:	75.3%
Change since 2000:	Up 8.8%	Black:	4.1%	Government:	15.0%
Urban:	32.1%	Hispanic:	2.7%	Self-employed:	9.5%
Rural:	67.9%	Asian:	0.4%	Blue collar:	31.9%
Area size:	10,155 sq. mi.	Native Am.:	0.3%	White collar:	49.5%
		Hawaiian:	0.0%	Khaki collar:	0.1%
Age		Two+ races:	1.3%	Other:	18.5%
Median age:	40.3 yrs.				
More than 65 yrs:	16.1%	*Ancestry*		Median income:	$37,571
Less than 18 yrs:	23.0%	USA	19.9%	Median Home Value:	$112,500
		Irish	10.7%		
Education		English	9.6%	**Military Veterans**	
H.S. grad:	77.5%			% of Pop:	11.3%
College grad:	14.0%				
Grad degree:	5.0%				

Central Tennessee; Columbia

The invisible line between Civil War Republican and Civil War Democratic territory runs along the Cumberland Plateau, the westernmost swelling of the Appalachians, west of the valley where the Tennessee River runs south from Knoxville to Chattanooga. This is cave country. Under its green hills, Tennessee has 8,500 caves, more than any other state, with 15 species of bats and more than 100 species of rare insects. This invisible line separates the Tennessee Val-

2008 Presidential Vote		
John McCain (R)	173,022	(64%)
Barack Obama (D)	93,483	(35%)
2004 Presidential Vote		
George Bush (R)	154,457	(58%)
John Kerry (D)	109,802	(41%)
Cook Partisan Voting Index: R+13		

ley, which had few slaves and whose economic ties were with the North, from the rolling farmlands of middle Tennessee, first settled by Andrew Jackson in the 1790s and resolutely Democratic from

1829, when Jackson became the first president to call himself a Democrat. Sewanee is the pleasant home of the University of the South, and Bledsoe County, which grows pumpkins. Columbia is the home of former President James K. Polk.

General Motors launched its Saturn brand in Spring Hill in 1990, igniting growth in the region. When the erstwhile auto giant went bankrupt in 2009, it shut down the factory and furloughed most of its 2,700 employees. But it rebounded somewhat, as GM announced in September 2010 it would bring back more than 480 workers as part of a $483 million investment there by 2012. Decherd in Franklin County has a large Nissan engine assembly plant that was expected to get more business in 2011 and 2012. Lynchburg in dry Moore County produces Jack Daniel's sourmash whiskey at the nation's oldest registered distillery. It is every bit the idealized small town that the distillery's folksy, black-and-white advertisements make it out to be. Campbell County, where the construction of the Tennessee Valley Authority's Norris Dam once forced massive resettlements and low living standards, has rebounded as a retirement and tourist haven. Cattle, poultry and eggs are the district's leading commodities.

The 4th Congressional District of Tennessee crosses the state for some 200 miles. It reaches almost to Virginia in the northeast and almost to Mississippi in the southwest, bordering both Kentucky and Alabama. More than one-third of its households earn less than $25,000 a year. Republican nominee John McCain picked up 64% of the vote district-wide and won every county here in 2008. Two years later, GOP gubernatorial nominee Bill Haslam did the same.

Scott DesJarlais (R)

The new congressman from the 4th District is Scott DesJarlais, a Republican elected in 2010 following one of the year's most negative campaigns. He defeated four-term Democratic Rep. Lincoln Davis.

DesJarlais (*DAY-zhar-lay*) grew up in Sturgis, S.D. His father was a barber, and his mother was a registered nurse at a veterans' hospital. He earned a bachelor's degree in chemistry and psychology from the University of South Dakota in 1987. After receiving his medical degree from the school in 1991, DesJarlais moved to Jasper, Tenn., where he practiced medicine.

The House race was DesJarlais's first bid for elected office, and he said it was motivated by his patients' concerns about the foundering economy and their fears about losing their jobs. Davis had been considered the most conservative Democrat in the Tennessee delegation, and had earned the endorsements of the U.S. Chamber of Commerce, the National Rifle Association, and National Right to Life. DesJarlais, billed himself as a "doctor, not a politician." Davis made headlines with accusations made by DesJarlais's first wife, Susan, who claimed that he physically intimidated her during their 2000 divorce and threatened to commit suicide. The Republican's campaign called the charges "completely false," and the ad exposed Davis to accusations of mudslinging. Davis also tried to draw attention to his votes against the Democrats' health care overhaul and their cap-and-trade bill to limit greenhouse gas emissions. But even his limited cooperation with President Barack Obama in voting for the $787 billion economic stimulus bill cost him votes. DesJarlais won 57% to 39% for Davis, with minor candidates splitting the rest.

In the House, DesJarlais was among the GOP freshmen to back an unsuccessful $100 billion cut in the fiscal 2011 budget, but supported the final budget agreement cutting less than half that amount. He also held a series of forums on Tennessee's methamphetamine problems and joined fellow Tennessee freshman Republican Chuck Fleischmann in opposing an Energy Department plan to consolidate management of Oak Ridge's Y-12 weapons plant with the one at Texas' Pantex facility. He told *The News-Sentinel* of Knoxville after his first 100 days in office that "the process is even more broken than what I anticipated."

FIFTH DISTRICT

Jim Cooper (D)

Elected 2002, 11th term; b. June 19, 1954, Nashville; home, Nashville; U. of NC, B.A. 1975, Oxford U., B.A./M.A. 1977, Harvard U., J.D. 1980; Episcopalian; married (Martha); 3 children.

Elected Office: U.S. House of Reps., 1983-95.

Professional Career: Practicing atty., 1980-82; Investment banker, 1995-99; Founder and partner, investment bank, 1999-2002.

DC Office: 1536 LHOB, 20515, 202-225-4311; Fax: 202-226-1035; Web site: cooper.house.gov.

State Offices: Nashville, 615-736-5295.

Committees: *Armed Services:* Air & Land Forces; Oversight & Investigations (RMM). *Oversight & Government Reform:* Government Organization, Efficiency & Financial Management; Regulatory Affairs, Stimulus Oversight & Government Spending; TARP, Financial Services & Bailouts of Public & Private Programs.

Group Ratings

	ACLU	ACU	ADA	CFG	AFS	FRC	LCV	ITIC	NTU	COC
2010	81	35	55	24	25	6	90	67	38	63
2009	–	16	90	14	100	–	93	–	15	40

National Journal Ratings

	2010 LIB	—	2010 CONS	2009 LIB	—	2009 CONS
Economic	43%	—	57%	54%	—	46%
Social	52%	—	46%	57%	—	42%
Foreign	48%	—	51%	62%	—	35%
Composite	48%	—	52%	58%	—	42%

Key Votes of the 111th Congress

1. Overturn Ledbetter	Y	5. Bar federal abortion funds	Y	9. Stop detainee transfers	Y
2. Pass $820 billion stimulus	N	6. Pass health care bill	Y	10. Legalize immigrants' kids	Y
3. Let guns in national parks	N	7. Regulate financial firms	N	11. Repeal don't ask, tell	Y
4. Pass cap-and-trade	Y	8. Pass tax cuts for some	Y	12. Limit campaign funds	Y

Election Results

2010 general	Jim Cooper (D)	99,162	(56%)	($1,044,042)
	David Hall (R)	74,204	(42%)	($358,308)
2010 primary	Jim Cooper (D)	28,660	(89%)	
	Eric Pearson (D)	2,214	(7%)	

Prior Winning Percentages: 2008 (66%), 2006 (69%), 2004 (69%), 2002 (64%), 1992 (66%), 1990 (69%), 1988 (100%), 1986 (100%), 1984 (75%), 1982 (66%)

Population		Race/Ethnicity		Work	
Pop. 2010:	707,420	White:	61.5%	Private:	80.7%
Change since 2000:	Up 11.9%	Black:	24.6%	Government:	11.9%
Urban:	88.7%	Hispanic:	9.0%	Self-employed:	7.2%
Rural:	11.3%	Asian:	2.6%	Blue collar:	19.4%
Area size:	932 sq. mi.	Native Am.:	0.3%	White collar:	63.9%
		Hawaiian:	0.0%	Khaki collar:	0.1%
Age		Two+ races:	1.8%	Other:	16.6%
Median age:	34.7 yrs.				
More than 65 yrs:	10.8%	*Ancestry*		Median income:	$46,973
Less than 18 yrs:	22.7%	USA	9.3%	Median Home Value:	$165,400
		German	9.0%		
Education		Irish	8.7%	**Military Veterans**	
H.S. grad:	85.0%			% of Pop:	8.9%
College grad:	31.0%				
Grad degree:	10.6%				

Nashville, Suburbs

Nashville is the home of country music and is in almost every way the heart of Tennessee. It was one of the first American cities established west of the Appalachian Mountains. President Andrew Jackson built his Hermitage nearby above the banks of the Cumberland River, and his political home base has remained Democratic ever since. It was the capital of Tennessee early on, just as it was, and still is, the center of the state's political life and discourse, the so-called "Athens

2008 Presidential Vote		
Barack Obama (D) 166,867	(56%)
John McCain (R) 127,394	(43%)
2004 Presidential Vote		
John Kerry (D) 140,874	(52%)
George Bush (R) 129,455	(48%)
Cook Partisan Voting Index: D+3		

of the South," home to *The Tennessean,* a liberal newspaper by Southern standards where a young Al Gore once worked as a reporter, and the state's biggest television market. Nashville is proud of its universities: Christian liberal arts college Belmont University was the site of an October 2008 presidential debate between Democrat Barack Obama and Republican John McCain. With its columned Capitol and its Parthenon, Nashville is an outstanding center of Greek revival architecture in America.

Country music, an art form that emerged from the hardscrabble, mountainous counties of East Tennessee, is a more than $2 billion-a-year business. One of the nation's dominant radio formats, it generates a significant number of local jobs with music publishers and recording studios. Run from a series of deceptively modest homes-turned-offices on what's called Music Row, the industry congregated in Nashville because local radio station WSM had a clear channel in the 1920s from which to beam its weekly "barn dances" throughout the South. The broadcasts later became known as the Grand Ole Opry, the longest continuously running radio show (since 1925). An expanded Country Music Hall of Fame and Museum opened as part of a downtown revitalization in recent years, and the city now offers good music of all sorts, sushi bars and a lively cafe scene.

For years, both the city's elite and its religious leaders resented the growing local influence of country music. But all three groups made their peace in the 1970s, and since then, Nashville has become one of the South's boom cities—one of the fastest-growing metropolitan areas behind the still-larger Atlanta and the Dallas-Fort Worth metroplex. Nashville is also a center of the for-profit health industry, the area's largest and fastest-growing employer. An agreeable quality of life, plenty of high-skill labor, a central location, and absence of urban strife have all helped make Nashville the largest metropolitan area in the state, with suburban growth in all directions. It was one of the nation's 50 large best cities in recovering from the 2007-09 recession, according to the Brookings Institution. Devastating floods in May 2010, the worst natural disaster in city history, slowed that growth a bit. The dominant cultural tone remains conservative, and fast-growing surrounding counties have become increasingly Republican, but Nashville and Davidson County remain Democratic bulwarks.

The 5th Congressional District of Tennessee includes most of Nashville-Davidson County, plus the bulk of suburban Wilson County to the east and Cheatham County to the west. The 5th is reliably Democratic in statewide elections. It has elected rather liberal Democrats to Congress, and was Gore's pre- and post-Washington home. He and wife, Tipper, had a house in the elegant Belle Meade neighborhood before their surprise June 2010 announcement that they would amicably separate after 40 years of marriage. The 5th was one of only two districts in Tennessee to vote for Obama in 2008, 56%-43%. In the 2010 governor's race, Democrat Mike McWherter edged out eventual winner Bill Haslam in Davidson County, 49.3%-48.6%, while Haslam won Wilson and Cheatham in a landslide.

Jim Cooper (D)

The congressman from the 5th District is Jim Cooper, a Democrat elected in 2002 who also served from 1983 to 1995. A tart-tongued moderate, he seeks bipartisanship on fiscal matters and other issues in a polarized political climate. His father, Prentice Cooper, was governor for six years. Jim Cooper, educated at the University of North Carolina, Oxford and Harvard Law School, won the 4th District seat in 1982 by beating the bearer of another famous name, Republican Cissy Baker, the daughter of then-Senate Majority Leader Howard Baker. In recent years, he has focused on being a leader of the fiscally conservative Blue Dog Coalition and a consensus-builder within the national Democratic Party.

In 2011, he introduced a series of measures with GOP support. One, to impose an across-the-board spending cap, was advocated in the Senate by his Tennessee Republican colleague Bob

Corker; another would create a bipartisan commission to abolish unnecessary federal programs. He also sponsored a bill to have the Internal Revenue Service fill out citizens' tax returns with the income information that the agency gets from employers. He said finding Republicans to support him "is really not hard" but gets overlooked. "The press is only focused on the leaders," he told *National Journal*. "They barely know the names of the backbenchers, and those are the people who can make things happen if they choose to." It helps that Cooper eschews name-calling. When others in his party were savaging House Budget Committee Chairman Paul Ryan, R-Wis., for his budget-cutting proposals in 2011, Cooper defended Ryan as "genuinely smart and nice and humble and caring. I don't agree with all of his proposals, but they are not out of bounds." Cooper earlier had joined another conservative Republican, Virginia's Frank Wolf, in calling for a panel to examine entitlement spending—an idea that became reality with President Obama's creation of a commission on the national debt in 2010.

During the health care debate, Cooper was among the Blue Dogs who worked with Energy and Commerce Committee Chairman Henry Waxman, D-Calif., in 2009 to moderate some provisions that conservative Democrats considered government overreach. He has sought limits on spending earmarks—he has refused for years to seek such special-interest funding—and enforcement of pay-as-you-go rules that require tax cuts or spending increases to be offset elsewhere in the budget. Cooper also urged expanded powers for the president to veto specific items in the budget. A longtime proponent of increased government oversight, his bill to strengthen the independence of federal inspectors passed Congress and, despite a veto threat from President George W. Bush, became law in October 2008. One of his pet issues is changing the method of calculating the federal budget. He said in a January 2011 speech that the use of accrual accounting procedures that recognize statutory commitments to future spending would put the national debt about three times higher than its current $15 trillion.

Cooper was mentioned as a candidate to head the White House budget office, but he fell out of favor with the Obama administration after an incident during Congress' work on the $787 billion economic stimulus bill in 2009. Cooper was one of 11 Democrats to vote against the initial version of the bill and told a Nashville radio station he had gotten "quiet encouragement" from the White House to oppose it because Obama disagreed with changes in the legislation made by the House Democratic leadership. The White House denied urging Cooper to vote against the leadership-backed bill. Cooper also took at shot at liberal House Speaker Nancy Pelosi, saying, "We're just told how to vote. We are treated like mushrooms most of the time." He supported fellow Blue Dog Heath Shuler of North Carolina over Pelosi in the caucus-wide vote for minority leader in 2011.

Notable for his frankness, he spoke out against tobacco use and opposed the National Rifle Association in a state where both were popular. He participated actively in the "Group of Nine" Democrats on the Energy and Commerce Committee that produced a compromise between Michigan Democrat John Dingell, an ally of the auto industry, and Waxman, who was pro-environmental regulation, on the Clean Air Act of 1990. When, years later, Waxman successfully challenged Dingell for the chairmanship of Energy and Commerce in 2009, Cooper was a key ally of Waxman's. In 1994, Cooper ran against Republican Fred Thompson for the Senate seat Gore vacated when he was elected vice president and Cooper lost.

Cooper then went to work as an investment banker in Nashville and as a teacher at Vanderbilt University's business school. In 2002, when Democratic U.S. Rep. Bob Clement jumped into a Senate race, Cooper joined a flurry of Democratic candidates for his seat. His toughest opponent was Davidson County Sheriff Gayle Ray, the first female sheriff in Tennessee, who had support from the national fundraising group EMILY's List. Ray attacked Cooper's voting record on women's health issues. An abortion rights supporter, Cooper said that Ray's charges were inaccurate and ran positive ads showing his children describing what he does well—banjo playing, helping with homework, getting health care for senior citizens—and what he doesn't do well—cooking, playing basketball. The AFL-CIO and *The Tennessean* endorsed Ray. Cooper had support from the Sierra Club environmental group and several smaller newspapers, and raised twice as much money as Ray, including $700,000 of his own money. He won the primary with 47%. Ray got 23% in the seven-candidate field. Cooper won the general election easily.

In 2010, Cooper was re-elected with 56% of the vote.

SIXTH DISTRICT

Diane Black (R)

Elected 2010, 1st term; b. Jan. 16, 1951, Baltimore, MD; home, Gallatin; Anne Arundel Col., A.S. 1971; Belmont U., B.A. 1991; Lutheran; Married (David); 3 children.

Elected Office: TN House, 1998-2004; TN Senate, 2004-10.

Professional Career: Registered nurse, 1969-2010; dir., Sumner Regional Health Systems, 1993-98; owner, Ebon-Falcon.

DC Office: 1531 LHOB, 20515, 202-225-4231; Fax: 202-225-6887; Web site: black.house.gov.

State Offices: Cookeville, 931-854-0069; Murfreesboro, 615-896-1986.

Committees: *Budget. Ways & Means:* Human Resources; Oversight.

Election Results

2010 general	Diane Black (R)...128,517	(67%)	($2,364,211)
	Brett Carter (D) 56,145	(29%)	($215,355)
2010 primary	Diane Black (R)...24,374	(31%)	
	Lou Ann Zelenik (R)...24,091	(30%)	
	Jim Tracy (R) 23,808	(30%)	

Population		Race/Ethnicity		Work	
Pop. 2010:	788,754	White:	83.8%	Private:	77.9%
Change since 2000:	Up 24.8%	Black:	7.5%	Government:	13.9%
Urban:	53.2%	Hispanic:	5.4%	Self-employed:	8.1%
Rural:	46.8%	Asian:	1.5%	Blue collar:	28.7%
Area size:	5,576 sq. mi.	Native Am.:	0.3%	White collar:	56.3%
		Hawaiian:	0.0%	Khaki collar:	0.2%
Age		Two+ races:	1.5%	Other:	14.8%
Median age:	35.8 yrs.				
More than 65 yrs:	11.4%	*Ancestry*		Median income:	$46,683
Less than 18 yrs:	25.2%	USA	18.7%	Median Home Value:	$147,300
		Irish	10.2%		
Education		English	9.0%	**Military Veterans**	
H.S. grad:	81.9%			% of Pop:	9.9%
College grad:	19.9%				
Grad degree:	5.8%				

Central Tennessee; Murfreesboro

The rolling countryside of Middle Tennessee, west of the Cumberland Plateau and the last of the Appalachian Mountain chain, has been called "the dimple of the universe." This is hilly and fertile land, cut by deep, curvy rivers. It has long been a land of small farmers and small county-seat towns, nestled amid what people here regard as some of the loveliest scenery on earth. Middle Tennessee has also been one of the heartlands of the Democratic Party. It was the political home base of President Andrew Jackson and supported him nearly unanimously during the Civil War, and though it had very few slaves, it resisted the invading Union armies. For 140 years after Jackson, it voted solidly Democratic and elected as its representatives in Congress some of the luminaries of the national Democratic Party: James K. Polk (1825-39), speaker of the House and later president; Cordell Hull (1907-21, 1923-31), later senator and secretary of State; Albert Gore Sr. (1939-53), later senator; and Albert Gore Jr., (1977-85), later senator and vice president.

The 6th Congressional District includes 14 Middle Tennessee counties surrounding Nashville, plus the eastern half of Wilson County. The heritage here is rural, but economic growth has fanned out into the farmland from Nashville, evident in thousands of jobs created by Japanese companies and American startups, firms fleeing the North's high taxes and wages. Nearby is Smyrna and its Nissan plant, which has the largest automobile production capacity in the nation

2008 Presidential Vote		
John McCain (R) 189,726	(62%)
Barack Obama (D) 112,584	(37%)

2004 Presidential Vote		
George Bush (R) 167,372	(60%)
John Kerry (D) 111,203	(40%)

Cook Partisan Voting Index: R+13

and is the home of the Altima. Nissan plans to shift production of the compact Rogue from Japan to Smyrna in 2013. In Rutherford County, Murfreesboro, which is the district's largest city, has grown from a crumbling town in the 1980s to a thriving community and the home of Middle Tennessee State University, the second-largest in the state. General Mills in 2010 announced a $100 million investment in its production facility here. The district's new arrivals have given it a Republican flavor. George W. Bush carried the 6th District 60%-40% in 2004. Republican presidential nominee John McCain won it 62%-37%, carrying every county except Jackson.

Diane Black (R)

The new congresswoman from the 6th District is Diane Black, a Republican elected in 2010 to succeed conservative Democratic Rep. Bart Gordon, who retired after a 25-year career.

Black was born in Baltimore and lived in the area for most of her early life. She obtained an associate's degree in nursing from a local community college in 1971. In 1985, she and her husband, David Black —currently the president and CEO of Aegis Science, a Nashville company—moved to Tennessee. Black returned to school to get her bachelor's degree in nursing from Belmont University. She got into politics in 1998, when she was elected to the first of three terms in the Tennessee House. By 2001, she was involved in an anti-tax protest that foreshadowed her involvement in the tea party eight years later. In 2004, Black moved up to the state Senate. During her six-year tenure, she became the first woman to chair the Senate Republican Caucus. She also earned her stripes as a small-government conservative, repeatedly voting against a state income tax and increases to the state sales tax. Late in the 2010 General Assembly session, Black championed an unsuccessful bill to allow Tennessee residents to opt out of the federal health care law. She pushed for a traditional definition of marriage, a zero tolerance policy for illegal immigrants, and a balanced budget constitutional amendment.

She decided to run for the House after Gordon announced his retirement in December 2009. Black's campaign hit an initial bump when one of her legislative aides sent a racist e-mail from her government account portraying President Barack Obama as two eyes peering out of a black background in a presidential portrait. The incident received widespread media coverage, and Black reprimanded the staffer but did not fire her. Black subsequently survived a bruising three-way GOP primary with 31% of the vote, edging out second-place finisher Lou Ann Zelenik by 283 votes. Zelenik, the Rutherford County GOP chair, drew considerable attention for making her opposition to a local Muslim community center a top issue and accusing Black of not taking a strong enough stand against it.

In the general election, Black's conservative views made her a tea party favorite, and she racked up endorsement from Republican luminaries, including former Alaska Gov. Sarah Palin and Sen. Lamar Alexander of Tennessee. She also was backed by the National Rifle Association and the U.S. Chamber of Commerce. In calling for repeal of the health care law, Black invoked her experience a nurse in emergency rooms. She raised $2.4 million, with more than half coming from her own wallet and more than 10 times the amount mustered by her opponent, Iraq war veteran Brett Carter. She won 67%-to-29%, carrying every county in the district.

In the House, Black's health care background helped her land a coveted seat on the Ways and Means Committee, a rare assignment for a freshman. Her first piece of legislation was a bill to deny federal funding to Planned Parenthood in a fiscal 2011 spending bill because of the group's involvement with abortion —an issue that eventually became one of the main sticking points in a final budget deal between Obama and House Republicans that year. Black also was given a seat on the Budget Committee, where she staunchly defended GOP Chairman Paul Ryan's effort to cut more than $6 trillion in spending.

In recognition of her fundraising acumen, she was named as one of four freshmen regional directors of the National Republican Congressional Committee. Black is among the House's wealthiest members, with an average net worth of $49 million in 2009, according to the Center for Responsive Politics.

SEVENTH DISTRICT

Marsha Blackburn (R)

Elected 2002, 5th term; b. June 6, 1952, Laurel, MS; home, Brentwood; MS St. U., B.S. 1973; Presbyterian; married (Chuck); 2 children.

Elected Office: TN Senate, 1998-2002.

Professional Career: Retail marketing consultant, 1973-98.

DC Office: 217 CHOB, 20515, 202-225-2811; Fax: 202-225-3004; Web site: blackburn.house.gov.

State Offices: Clarksville, 931-503-0391; Franklin, 615-591-5161; Memphis, 901-382-5811.

Committees: *Energy & Commerce:* Commerce, Manufacturing & Trade (VChmn); Communications & Technology; Health; Oversight & Investigations.

Group Ratings

	ACLU	ACU	ADA	CFG	AFS	FRC	LCV	ITIC	NTU	COC
2010	6	100	0	97	0	100	0	33	93	88
2009	–	100	0	98	11	–	0	–	91	73

National Journal Ratings

	2010 LIB	—	2010 CONS	2009 LIB	—	2009 CONS
Economic	11%	—	88%	4%	—	95%
Social	0%	—	85%	0%	—	93%
Foreign	28%	—	71%	0%	—	75%
Composite	16%	—	84%	7%	—	93%

Key Votes of the 111th Congress

1. Overturn Ledbetter	N	5. Bar federal abortion funds	Y	9. Stop detainee transfers	Y
2. Pass $820 billion stimulus	N	6. Pass health care bill	N	10. Legalize immigrants' kids	N
3. Let guns in national parks	Y	7. Regulate financial firms	N	11. Repeal don't ask, tell	N
4. Pass cap-and-trade	N	8. Pass tax cuts for some	N	12. Limit campaign funds	N

Election Results

2010 general	Marsha Blackburn (R)	158,916	(72%)	($1,563,193)
	Greg Rabidoux (D)	54,347	(25%)	($74,930)
	J. W. (Bill) Stone (I)	6,320	(3%)	
2010 primary	Marsha Blackburn (R)	unopposed		

Prior Winning Percentages: 2008 (69%), 2006 (66%), 2004 (100%), 2002 (71%)

Population		Race/Ethnicity		Work	
Pop. 2010:	792,605	White:	77.0%	Private:	74.7%
Change since 2000:	Up 25.4%	Black:	14.3%	Government:	17.5%
Urban:	61.0%	Hispanic:	4.1%	Self-employed:	7.6%
Rural:	39.0%	Asian:	2.5%	Blue collar:	18.4%
Area size:	6,351 sq. mi.	Native Am.:	0.3%	White collar:	66.2%
		Hawaiian:	0.1%	Khaki collar:	1.7%
Age		Two+ races:	1.7%	Other:	13.7%
Median age:	37.1 yrs.				
More than 65 yrs:	10.7%	*Ancestry*		Median income:	$61,738
Less than 18 yrs:	26.5%	Irish	11.1%	Median Home Value:	$182,200
		English	10.7%		
Education		German	10.3%	**Military Veterans**	
H.S. grad:	89.1%			% of Pop:	11.8%
College grad:	34.1%				
Grad degree:	12.0%				

Memphis and Nashville Suburbs

Rural Tennessee north of Mississippi is one of the most sparsely settled areas in the state. Along each side of the Tennessee River, as it flows north and widens out into Kentucky Lake, are small rural communities. Many date to pre-Civil War days and have not grown much since. One of these is Waynesboro, where Davy Crockett delivered campaign speeches from the base of a huge natural stone double bridge overlooking the Buffalo River. Farther west is McNairy County, where Sheriff Buford Pusser of *Walking Tall* fame carried his big stick and fought organized crime until his death in a car crash 1974. In Fayette County, outside of Memphis, black sharecroppers in 1959 were removed from white-owned land and protested by creating a "tent city" that went on for a decade, the longest civil rights protest in the nation. This sparsely populated land is bounded on two sides by large metropolitan areas, Nashville to the east and Memphis to the west. South of Nashville is Williamson County, where the bedroom communities of Franklin and Brentwood are affluent, highly educated and fast growing. To the north, along the Cumberland River, is Clarksville, with many restored 19th century homes, a large industrial park. Just across the Kentucky border is the Army's sprawling Fort Campbell, home of the 101st Airborne Division.

2008 Presidential Vote		
John McCain (R)	233,645	(66%)
Barack Obama (D)	119,046	(33%)
2004 Presidential Vote		
George Bush (R)	206,410	(66%)
John Kerry (D)	104,792	(33%)
Cook Partisan Voting Index:	R+18	

The 7th Congressional District of Tennessee spans this territory, packing in Republican voters from Montgomery County's seat of Clarksville, south through the western half of Cheatham County and most of Williamson County plus a bite of Nashville-Davidson. It rambles west across the Tennessee River and south to the Mississippi border and finally to the east side of Memphis and Shelby County. On the map, this looks like a rural district. Demographically, it's mostly suburban. The 7th District grew by 16% between 2000 and 2009, making this the second fastest-growing district in the state after the neighboring 6th. Historically, the majority of votes are roughly split between metro Memphis and metro Nashville. The 7th is solidly Republican. In 2004, while Democratic presidential nominee John Kerry won Nashville 55%-45%, Republican George W. Bush carried the four rapidly growing counties in the southern and eastern suburbs of Nashville 66%-33%, with 72% in heavily Republican Williamson County. In 2008, GOP nominee John McCain won every county here except for Hardeman, losing it by only 694 votes. He won the district 66%-33%. Republican Bill Haslam won all but two of these counties in the 2010 governor's race and got more than 80% of the vote in Williamson.

Marsha Blackburn (R)

The congresswoman from the 7th District is Marsha Blackburn, a Republican elected in 2002 and a conservative firebrand who has become a frequent GOP presence on television.

Blackburn grew up in Laurel, Miss., where her father sold oil-field production equipment. Her interest in gardening and canning won her a 4-H college scholarship at Mississippi State University, where she majored in merchandising and clothing. She helped pay her way through college by selling books door-to-door. She then became a sales manager with Southwestern Company, which sells educational materials, and moved to Williamson County. Her hilltop home is known as "Up Yonder," named by its former owner, Grand Ole Opry star Minnie Pearl. Blackburn became director of retail fashion for a Nashville department store and was appointed by Republican Gov. Don Sundquist as executive director of the Tennessee Film, Entertainment and Music Commission. In 1992, she was the Republican nominee against Democrat Bart Gordon in the 6th District, and lost 57%-41%. Blackburn was elected in 1998 to the Tennessee Senate, where she became an outspoken opponent of Sundquist's proposed income tax.

When Republican Rep. Ed Bryant decided to run for the Senate, Blackburn ran for his seat. Seven candidates ran in the GOP primary, three of them familiar figures in the Memphis area. Blackburn was the only well-known candidate from the Nashville area. She benefited from financial support from the national anti-tax group Club for Growth, and from attacks by the Shelby County candidates on one another. She ran as anti-abortion rights, pro-gun and pro-military conservative and won with 40% of the vote, while the other candidates split the rest. She went on to easily win the general election.

In the House, Blackburn's voting record is among the most conservative. She is active on the Republican Study Committee, the caucus of the House's most right-leaning members, and in 2009 cosponsored the controversial "birther" bill requiring future presidential candidates to prove they were born in the United States, a measure that played off attacks on President Barack Obama's legal fitness to hold office. In February 2011, she sponsored an amendment to cut spending for most non-defense programs by 5.5%, but 92 members of her party joined Democrats in arguing that it went too far and it failed. In April 2011, she voted against the compromise that Republicans struck with President Obama on the fiscal 2011 budget to avert a shutdown. A champion of gun owners' rights, she has boasted about her perfect marksmanship score with her Smith & Wesson .38.

With her party controlling the House in 2011, Blackburn assumed a more prominent role on technology policy as a member of the Energy and Commerce Committee. A fervent advocate of the music industry central to her district, she has fought to protect intellectual property rights of artists against illegal music downloads. She also has been a fierce critic of the Obama administration's efforts to regulate the Internet, introducing a bill that would clarify that such a task is solely Congress' responsibility. She was also active in the failed effort in early 2011 to repeal Obama's health care legislation. On energy issues, she is a self-described skeptic of human-caused climate change and has called for more widespread use of nuclear power.

Blackburn was mentioned as a possible candidate for the Senate or governor in 2006 and again in 2010. But once she secured a seat on Energy and Commerce, she had sufficient incentive to remain in the House. After the 2006 election, she was one of four candidates for chairman of the Republican Conference, but she was eliminated on the second ballot. Instead, she became communications chair for the National Republican Congressional Committee.

In 2008, she faced a primary challenge from Shelby County Register of Deeds Tom Leatherwood, whose campaign gained ammunition when it was revealed Blackburn had misreported more than $440,000 on campaign finance disclosure forms dating to her first House campaign. Blackburn filed amended returns. The underdog Leatherwood, hoping to cement West Tennessee support, also charged that Blackburn had used her campaign funds to help her family's businesses and that she hadn't been effective in Washington. But Blackburn easily won the primary, 62%-38%, carrying every county except Shelby. She won easily in November.

In 2009, Blackburn wrote a book, *Life Equity: Realize Your True Value and Pursue Your Passions at Any Stage in Life*. She told the Nashville *Tennessean* that it was not intended to be political, but rather a "book of encouragement and empowerment for women."

EIGHTH DISTRICT

Stephen Fincher (R)

Elected 2010, 1st term; b. Feb. 7, 1973, Memphis; home, Frog Jump; Crockett Cnty. H.S., diploma, 1990; Methodist; Married (Lynn); 3 children.

Professional Career: Partner, Fincher Farms; singer, Fincher Family

DC Office: 1118 LHOB, 20515, 202-225-4714; Fax: 202-225-1765; Web site: fincher.house.gov.

State Offices: Dyersburg, 731-285-0910; Jackson, 731-423-4848; Martin, 731-588-5190.

Committees: *Agriculture:* Conservation, Energy & Forestry; Department Operations, Oversight & Credit; Livestock, Dairy & Poultry. *Transportation & Infrastructure:* Aviation; Economic Development, Public Buildings & Emergency Management; Railroads, Pipelines & Hazardous Materials.

Election Results

2010 general	Stephen Fincher (R)	98,759	(59%)	($2,974,526)
	Roy Herron (D)	64,960	(39%)	($2,604,121)
2010 primary	Stephen Fincher (R)	35,024	(48%)	
	Ron Kirkland (R)	17,637	(24%)	
	George Flinn (R)	17,308	(24%)	

Population		Race/Ethnicity		Work	
Pop. 2010:	658,258	White:	71.5%	Private:	75.5%
Change since 2000:	Up 4.1%	Black:	23.2%	Government:	16.9%
Urban:	47.0%	Hispanic:	3.0%	Self-employed:	7.4%
Rural:	53.0%	Asian:	0.5%	Blue collar:	30.5%
Area size:	8,529 sq. mi.	Native Am.:	0.3%	White collar:	51.3%
		Hawaiian:	0.0%	Khaki collar:	0.6%
Age		Two+ races:	1.4%	Other:	17.7%
Median age:	37.8 yrs.				
More than 65 yrs:	13.6%	*Ancestry*		Median income:	$37,440
Less than 18 yrs:	24.6%	USA	14.0%	Median Home Value:	$97,900
		Irish	10.0%		
Education		English	7.1%	**Military Veterans**	
H.S. grad:	80.7%			% of Pop:	11.6%
College grad:	15.5%				
Grad degree:	5.3%				

Western Tennessee; Jackson

West of Nashville and north of Memphis, the rivers roll lazily through flat or gently rolling land that almost could be the northern end of Mississippi. Cotton and soybeans are the main crops, and they often are abundant. African-Americans remain in rural areas here, a reminder of its old plantation economy. The towns are small, edged in by farm fields. Henning, the hometown of Alex Haley, is where he used to sit on his porch and listen to his aunts tell him stories about slave ships and the Civil War, which became his book *Roots*.

2008 Presidential Vote		
John McCain (R)	146,739	(56%)
Barack Obama (D)	112,243	(43%)

2004 Presidential Vote		
George Bush (R)	131,524	(53%)
John Kerry (D)	116,327	(47%)

Cook Partisan Voting Index: R+6

The 8th Congressional District of Tennessee includes much of this West Tennessee farmland, from the lakes west to the Mississippi. Its median income in 2009 was $37,644, almost $3,000 below the state's median level. Its largest city is Jackson, which was ranked 13th on the annual list of most dangerous American cities in 2010 by the Morgan Quitno Press, which publishes a variety of local and state statistical rankings. The district also includes the northern fringes of Memphis. Historically, this was Democratic country, but it has been increasingly Republican in recent elections. The district voted 51%-48% for Democrat Al Gore in 2000, switched to George W. Bush 53%-47% in 2004, and then voted for Republican John McCain, 56%-43%, in 2008. In 2010, Republican Bill Haslam easily carried every county except Lake and Haywood.

Stephen Fincher (R)

The new congressman from the 8th District is Republican Stephen Fincher, a gospel-singing farmer who was elected in 2010 to succeed the retiring Democratic Rep. John Tanner. Fincher grew up in Frog Jump, Tenn. Since the age of nine, he has made the rounds of the gospel-singing circuit as a member of the Fincher Family, performing with his father, a cousin, and an uncle at more than 100 events a year around the region. He worked most of his life on the family farm, which produces cotton, corn, soybeans, and wheat. Fincher has said he had his own crop at age 12 and was developing budgets at 13.

A friend asked him to run against Tanner in 2010, and he took on the challenge, even though he faced better-funded opponents for the Republican nomination. But using the theme "Plow Congress," he raised $300,000 so quickly, and without any staff, that his presence in the race was largely credited with prompting Tanner to retire. His primary fight against Shelby County Commissioner George Flinn and physician Ron Kirkland became one of the most expensive contests in the country: $7 million was spent in an area with one of the nation's lowest median incomes. Fincher won with 50% of the vote.

After Tanner's announcement, Democratic state Sen. Roy Herron decided to drop out of the gubernatorial race and run for the House seat. A farmer himself, as well as a Methodist preacher, an author, and a lawyer, Herron vowed that "No one will out-God me, no one will outgun me."

Democrats criticized Fincher for collecting millions of dollars in federal farm subsidies between 1995 and 2006. He responded that he needed to participate in the program to earn a living. Despite that, he won the endorsement of several key tea party organizations in Tennessee, and polls in the district had him continually leading Herron, even though he bypassed the traditional campaign rituals of releasing his tax returns, appearing before newspaper editorial boards, and debating Herron, whom he derided as a "career politician." The National Republican Congressional Committee spent more than $250,000 during October alone to help him, and Fincher kept apace with Herron in fundraising, $3 million to $2.6 million, respectively. He won a resounding 59%-39% victory. He lost four of the counties that Tanner had carried in his last contested election in 2006. But he won the other counties, including Madison, the most populous county which contains Jackson, 57%-41%.

In the House, Fincher joined the Tea Party Caucus. He supported the fiscal 2011 budget deal that President Barack Obama struck with House GOP leaders in April 2011, but earlier had been among the House lawmakers who rallied on the Senate steps in an effort to force the upper chamber to agree to larger spending cuts. "We were not sent here to go along and compromise," he said. "We were sent to come up here and lead." He also continued his fundraising prowess, bringing in more than $235,000 in the first quarter of 2011.

NINTH DISTRICT

Steve Cohen (D)

Elected 2006, 3rd term; b. May 24, 1949, Memphis; home, Memphis; Vanderbilt U., B.A. 1971, U. of Memphis, J.D. 1973; Jewish; single.

Elected Office: Shelby Cnty. Comm., 1977-78, TN Senate, 1982-2006.

Professional Career: Practicing atty., 1974-2006.

DC Office: 1005 LHOB, 20515, 202-225-3265; Fax: 202-225-5663; Web site: cohen.house.gov.

State Offices: Memphis, 901-544-4131.

Committees: *Judiciary:* Courts, Commercial & Administrative Law (RMM); Crime, Terrorism & Homeland Security. *Transportation & Infrastructure:* Aviation; Highways & Transit; Water Resources & Environment.

Group Ratings

	ACLU	ACU	ADA	CFG	AFS	FRC	LCV	ITIC	NTU	COC
2010	93	0	100	0	100	0	90	67	8	14
2009	–	0	100	0	100	–	100	–	2	33

National Journal Ratings

	2010 LIB	—	2010 CONS		2009 LIB	—	2009 CONS
Economic	71%	—	29%		82%	—	14%
Social	93%	—	0%		75%	—	20%
Foreign	91%	—	8%		67%	—	31%
Composite	86%	—	14%		77%	—	24%

Key Votes of the 111th Congress

1. Overturn Ledbetter	Y	5. Bar federal abortion funds	N	9. Stop detainee transfers	N
2. Pass $820 billion stimulus	Y	6. Pass health care bill	Y	10. Legalize immigrants' kids	*
3. Let guns in national parks	N	7. Regulate financial firms	Y	11. Repeal don't ask, tell	Y
4. Pass cap-and-trade	Y	8. Pass tax cuts for some	Y	12. Limit campaign funds	Y

Election Results

2010 general	Steve Cohen (D)	99,827	(74%)	($1,151,408)
	Charlotte Bergmann (R)	33,879	(25%)	($217,428)
2010 primary	Steve Cohen (D)	63,402	(79%)	
	Willie Herenton (D)	17,153	(21%)	

Prior Winning Percentages: 2008 (88%), 2006 (60%)

Population		Race/Ethnicity		Work	
Pop. 2010:	610,823	White:	26.9%	Private:	80.5%
Change since 2000:	Down 3.4%	Black:	63.2%	Government:	14.7%
Urban:	99.6%	Hispanic:	6.6%	Self-employed:	4.8%
Rural:	0.4%	Asian:	1.9%	Blue collar:	22.7%
Area size:	340 sq. mi.	Native Am.:	0.2%	White collar:	57.8%
		Hawaiian:	0.0%	Khaki collar:	0.1%
Age		Two+ races:	1.0%	Other:	19.5%
Median age:	33.0 yrs.				
More than 65 yrs:	10.3%	*Ancestry*		Median income:	$36,169
Less than 18 yrs:	27.1%	USA	5.1%	Median Home Value:	$104,700
		Irish	5.0%		
Education		English	4.8%	**Military Veterans**	
H.S. grad:	81.3%			% of Pop:	8.5%
College grad:	23.3%				
Grad degree:	9.1%				

Memphis

Memphis is the largest city in Tennessee, though its metropolitan area is second to Nashville. In the state's far southwestern corner, 20 miles from Mississippi's cotton fields and riverboat casinos, metropolitan Memphis has one of the highest percentages of African-Americans in the country, evidence of the city's economic heritage as a capital of the Cotton Kingdom. Big Missis-

2008 Presidential Vote		
Barack Obama (D) 199,915	(78%)
John McCain (R) 56,635	(22%)
2004 Presidential Vote		
John Kerry (D) 171,547	(70%)
George Bush (R) 74,020	(30%)
Cook Partisan Voting Index: D+23		

sippi planters used to come north to sell their crops in the courtyard of the Peabody Hotel, then make financial arrangements for the next growing season. According to tradition, ducks still famously march daily to the hotel's fountain for a dip.

The city's most celebrated tradition is the blues, a musical form separate from Nashville's country music, which emerged from mountainous, mainly white Middle and East Tennessee. The Memphis sound originated from the self-taught musical stylings of poor, rural blacks in the Mississippi Delta. Throughout the first half of the 20th century, talented black musicians migrated north to Memphis and congregated downtown on Beale Street. The blues sound was later adapted by Elvis Presley, a poor white from rural Mississippi, in pivotal sessions in July 1954 at Sam Phillips' Sun Studio in Memphis—the birth of rock 'n' roll. (*Million Dollar Quartet*, a musical inspired by a jam session there featuring Elvis, Phillips, Jerry Lee Lewis and Johnny Cash, opened on Broadway in 2010.) In the early 1960s, Memphis once again became the crucible of a new sound, soul music, which emerged as a counterpoint to rock, its increasingly white-dominated cousin. Otis Redding, Isaac Hayes, the Staple Singers and Sam & Dave made their records at the Stax studio. For some years, Memphis tried to downplay its musical heritage. Much of Beale Street was razed and set on a misguided path toward urban renewal. But the city came to recognize its history as an asset. Graceland, Presley's garishly decorated mansion, attracts hordes of musical pilgrims from all over the world, and a Museum of American Soul Music opened in 2003 on the site of the Stax studio, demolished in 1989.

Geographically central, Memphis is the home of the first supermarket chain: the Piggly Wiggly, founded in 1916 (its symbol, Mr. Pig, has slimmed down since then). It also hosted the first Holiday Inn. The biggest employer by far is FedEx, operating out of the world's busiest cargo airport. The airport pumps nearly $29 billion into the economy every year. For some years, racial discord scarred the political life of Memphis. The Rev. Martin Luther King Jr. was assassinated there in 1968, and the site, the Lorraine Motel, has been converted into a civil rights museum. Even today, resurgent Beale Street is one of the few racially integrated spaces in the city, a division that holds equally true in voting. Blacks vote almost unanimously Democratic, and whites vote Republican by margins almost as great. Many African-Americans have moved into the middle class, although Memphis continues to have the highest poverty rate in Tennessee. The city was hit hard by the 2007-09 recession and has been losing population, shrinking by 3,200 people between 2000 and 2010. The city's recovery has lagged behind that of Nashville and Knoxville.

The 9th Congressional District of Tennessee consists of most of the city of Memphis, some of its suburban fringe and about 30 precincts in east Shelby County. The black-majority 9th remains the strongest Democratic district in the state and is essential to the success of Democrats running statewide. In 2008, Democrat Barack Obama greatly improved on Al Gore's 63% in 2000 and John Kerry's 70% in 2004 by winning 78% in the district. Shelby County gave Democrat Mike McWherter 52% of the vote in the 2010 governor's race as Republican Bill Haslam ran away with the race statewide.

Steve Cohen (D)

The congressman from the 9th District is Steve Cohen, a Democrat elected in 2006. Though he is white, he has easily fended off primary challenges from the district's African-American majority by maintaining one of the House's most liberal voting records and concentrating on issues of strong interest to his constituents.

Cohen is a fourth-generation Memphian and the son of a psychiatrist. At age 5, Cohen was diagnosed with polio, an illness that would shift his focus from sports to politics. Cohen studied at Vanderbilt University and went on to law school at the University of Memphis. After graduation in 1973, he worked as a legal advisor for the Memphis Police Department and then started a law practice in 1978. He was elected to the Shelby County Commission and, in 1982, to a Memphis-based state Senate seat, where he served for the next 24 years. He became known as the father of the Tennessee State Lottery for his successful efforts in 2002 to pass a referendum repealing a lottery ban and for passing legislation that used the lottery revenue to fund college scholarships.

Cohen wanted to run for Congress in 1996 when 22-year veteran Rep. Harold Ford Sr. announced his retirement, but he found his path to Washington blocked by the incumbent's 26-year-old son, an African-American who secured the seat. But he got a second chance in 2006 when Ford Jr. ran unsuccessfully for the Senate. As the only serious white contender among the 15 candidates who filed to run, Cohen faced considerable criticism from local black leaders, who publicly asserted that an African-American should represent the district. Cohen's supporters charged that another primary foe paid for a push poll that asked, "Are you more likely to vote for a born-again Christian or a Jew?" Cohen quipped that his staunchly liberal record would make people mistake him for a black woman. The district's black leaders were unable to narrow the crowded field and the primary results splintered. Cohen won with 31%. Nikki Tinker, the former campaign manager for Ford Jr., finished second with 25%. The incumbent's cousin, Joe Ford Jr., finished third with 12%.

The Democratic primary is typically the only election that matters in this solidly Democratic district, but Cohen faced a challenge in November from yet another Ford—Jake Ford, the incumbent's younger brother, who ran as an independent candidate. Jake Ford was a high school dropout who had had a few scrapes with the law, but he had support from his father and other African-American leaders who opposed Cohen. He argued that he was in better sync with the community, noting that more than two-thirds of the primary vote went against Cohen. Cohen's critics also made an issue of the fact that Cohen supports same-sex marriage. He won the general election with 60% of the vote, ending the Ford family's 32-year hold on the district and becoming the only white member of Congress to represent a majority-black district. Cohen wanted to join the Congressional Black Caucus, but he backed off when CBC leaders made it clear he would not be allowed to join.

In his first term, Cohen worked to quickly secure his hold on the seat, knowing that he faced a near-certain primary challenge in 2008. Among his first moves was a resolution apologizing for slavery. While it seemed like a relatively harmless motion that easily passed the House on a voice vote, Cohen's office was slammed with constituent calls charging the measure was a political ploy. It was called up for a vote just days before the August 2008 primary. Cohen also succeeded in naming a Memphis federal building and post offices after prominent African-Americans.

Winning a plum seat on the Judiciary Committee, Cohen worked on bills to force radio broadcasters to pay money to performers whose music is played and on studying racial disparities in the criminal justice system. He got a measure into law in 2010 protecting authors and journalists from having foreign libel judgments honored in U.S. courts. On the Transportation and Infrastructure Committee, he opposed a bill that could have exposed FedEx to worker strikes. Cohen also made himself a fixture on C-SPAN, which covers floor proceedings. After a scandal at the University of Memphis involving a basketball player who stayed just one year, Cohen in 2009 urged the National Basketball Association to end the requirement that players must be at least 19 years old.

When Cohen was up for re-election in 2008, his race was his biggest obstacle. African-American leaders in the district coalesced around Tinker, who had come in second to Cohen two years earlier and who was back to challenge him in the Democratic primary. "He's not black and he can't represent me," one minister told the *Memphis Commercial Appeal.* "I don't care how people try to dress up, it always comes down to race and he can't know what it's like to be black." Tinker got financial help from the CBC and EMILY's list, the women's fundraising group. But prominent black leaders from outside the district, including Judiciary Chairman John Conyers of Michigan and Rep. Jesse Jackson Jr. of Illinois, made radio ads for Cohen and donated to his campaign. He outraised Tinker by more than 2-to-1 and crushed her, 79%-19%. Cohen faced three independent candidates in November and won with 88% of the vote.

He drew another primary challenge in 2010 from Willie Herenton, Memphis' first elected black mayor. But Cohen once again was ready—he snagged a rare written endorsement from President Barack Obama, a hugely popular figure in the district, as well as support from a dozen CBC members. He trounced Herenton, 79%-21%, in the August primary and again sailed to re-election.

★ TEXAS ★

Texas is a nation-sized state, one of four states that had been independent republics earlier in their histories (along with California, Vermont and Hawaii), and it comes as no surprise that Texas stuck with its independent status the longest. Today it is a state with an international image and international impact. In the 12 presidential elections since 1960, Americans have elected Texans four times and Californians four times. These two largest states have put their stamp on national politics in our time, just as New York did from 1900 to 1960, when it was the residence of five of the winners and eight of the losers in 15 presidential elections. Texas has been the second-largest state in area since Alaska was admitted to the Union in 1959, and it became the second-largest in population in 1994, when it surpassed New York. A formative strain in the state's history is that it is a society without an aristocratic past, a state not formed by plantation owners or plutocrats, but by dirt farmers. Texas was founded by Southerners, particularly Tennesseans, who wanted to establish their own republic within the borders of Mexico, a republic with Anglo-Saxon freedoms and black slavery. They defended their dream to the death at the Alamo and to a bloody victory at San Jacinto. They entered the Union willingly in 1845 and left it enthusiastically in 1861. The Texas that emerged from the Civil War was still young and poor. Not until 1901 was oil discovered at Spindletop, near Beaumont, setting Texas wildcatters on the road to riches.

Without the underpinnings and burdens of tradition, 20th century Texas produced fabulous wealth, generously rewarding success while being unforgiving of failure. It has respect for learning and style—think of its great universities and Neiman Marcus—and it revels in rough manners and western wear. Texans are prone to wild swings in fortune—think of Sam Houston and the wildcatters, or Lyndon B. Johnson and George W. Bush. In the 21st century, Texans, despite their history of slavery and segregation, have proved open to immigrants and friendly to their Mexican neighbors. The North American Free Trade Agreement, the opening up of the border and the coming together of these two countries that are at such different economic levels and have such different cultures, was a project mainly of Texans of both political parties, of Republican President George H.W. Bush and Democratic Treasury Secretary Lloyd Bentsen, of Democratic Gov. Ann Richards and Republican Gov. George W. Bush. At the same time, Texas has become a high-technology powerhouse with some of the nation's most creative businesses. But its success is not just economic. There are elements of heroism—some mythical, some genuine—in Texas history that every elementary and high school student learns.

Texas started off as a marchland on the border of the Third World, with an economy based on commodities, mainly cotton, when cotton prices were in long-term decline. Its farmers felt like they were part of a colonial economy controlled by bankers and Wall Street financiers. After Spindletop, Texas became the nation's—and for a time the world's—leading producer of oil. But oil prices, too, fell in free markets and were propped up by politicians. There was the 1936 "hot oil" act that Democrat Sam Rayburn, as chairman of the House Commerce Committee, pushed through and the oil depletion allowance maintained for years by Rayburn when he was speaker and by Johnson when he was Senate majority leader and later by Bentsen as Senate Finance Committee chairman. These politicians also secured subsidies for cotton growers and contracts for defense plants and space facilities in World War II and through the Cold War years. Most Texas voters stayed Democratic up to 1970 because of Confederate memories, New Deal affections and the clout and competence of Texas Democratic officeholders.

But the state's economy grew more complex. By the 1970s it was no longer dependent on raw commodities. The "awl bidness" here became less a matter of extracting oil than it was playing host to the greatest concentration of highly skilled specialists in extracting oil and natural gas in any part of the world. Also beginning in the 1960s, Texas became a center for technology with the critical mass of knowledge and finances needed to produce firms like Texas Instruments and Dell Computer and a university infrastructure in the University of Texas and Texas A&M. The Dallas-Fort Worth Metroplex is rich with defense contractors and with erstwhile small firms that grew large with exports to Mexico. Houston is home to firms like Schlumberger, the global oil services company, to many of the high-tech spinoffs from the space program and to the enormous Texas Medical Center. San Antonio, with the Air Force's prime hospital, has significant medical technology and biotech industries. As UT doubled its number of engineering professors, Austin became a high-tech center vying for second place after California's Silicon Valley. The federal court in Marshall, thanks to a fast discovery process and the willingness of juries to bring in big verdicts against patent violators, has become one of the nation's prime venues for patent cases. Texas' low taxes, and lack

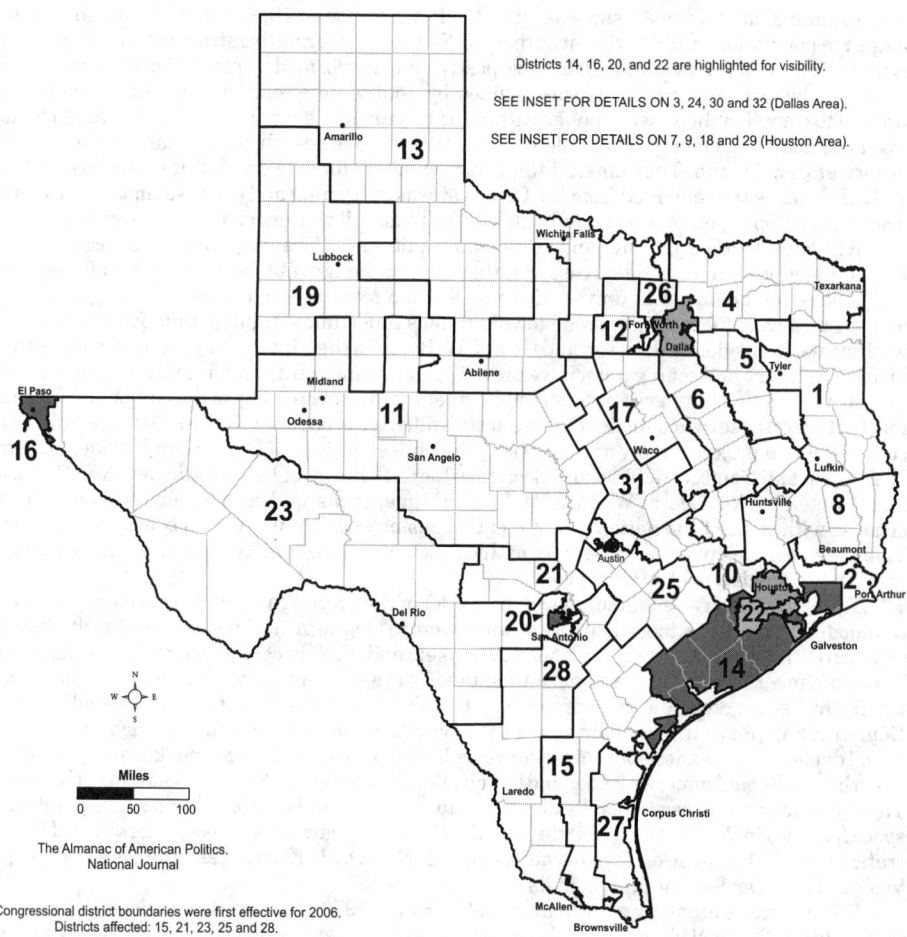

Districts 14, 16, 20, and 22 are highlighted for visibility.

SEE INSET FOR DETAILS ON 3, 24, 30 and 32 (Dallas Area).

SEE INSET FOR DETAILS ON 7, 9, 18 and 29 (Houston Area).

The Almanac of American Politics.
National Journal

Congressional district boundaries were first effective for 2006.
Districts affected: 15, 21, 23, 25 and 28.

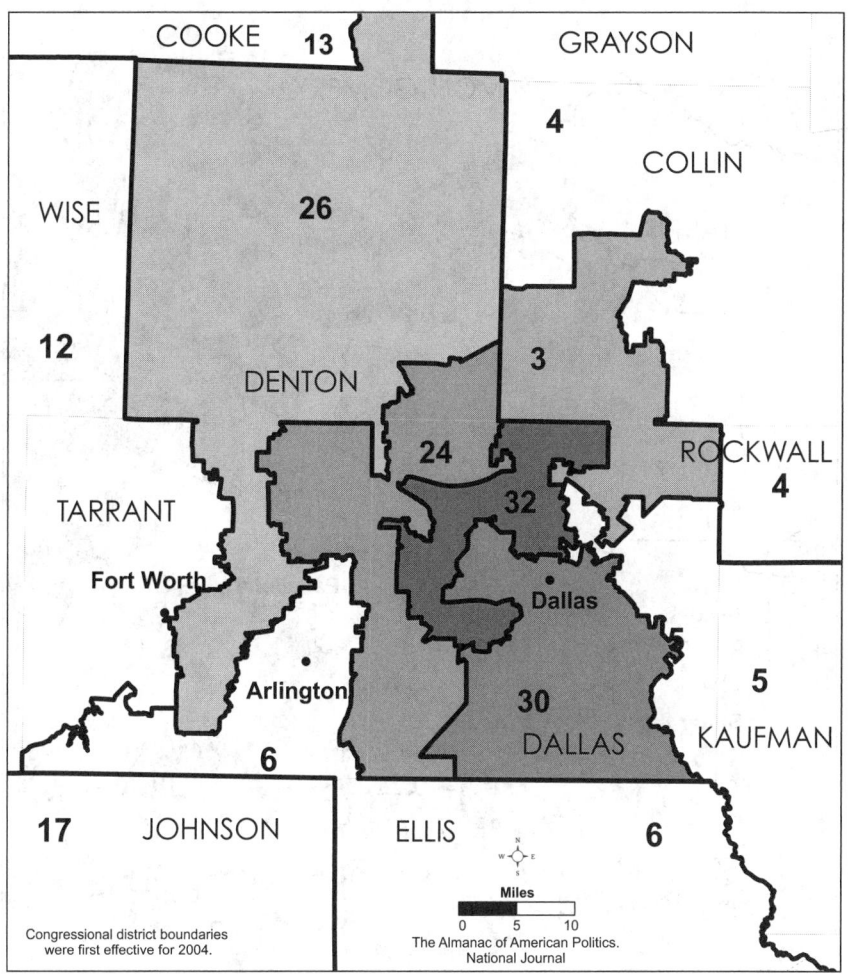

COOKE 13

GRAYSON

4

COLLIN

WISE

26

12

DENTON

3

24

ROCKWALL

4

TARRANT

32

Fort Worth

Dallas

Arlington

5

30

KAUFMAN

6

DALLAS

17   JOHNSON

ELLIS

6

Miles

0   5   10

Congressional district boundaries
were first effective for 2004.

The Almanac of American Politics.
National Journal

of a state income tax, helped attract corporate headquarters like American Airlines, GTE, J.C. Penney and Exxon Mobil. Oil is just a part of the Texas economy now. As a result, Dallas-Fort Worth and Houston are ahead of old industrial centers like Detroit, Cleveland, Pittsburgh and St. Louis on the Top 10 list of metropolitan areas, and they are in the process of overtaking Philadelphia and San Francisco.

Texas surged ahead despite the crash of oil prices in the early 1980s and the savings and loan crisis in the late 1980s, the defense cuts of the early 1990s and the World Trade Organization ruling against cotton subsidies in 2005. Its economy quietly boomed during the first seven years of the new century and it was hit late and only lightly by the 2007-09 recession. Low housing prices, tight lending practices and tough foreclosure laws meant that Texas did not have much of a housing bubble. Foreclosure rates were well below the national average and far below those in California, Nevada, Arizona and Florida. The state's unemployment rate remained well under the national average. Texas kept producing an increasing number of jobs during the recession and Republican Gov. Rick Perry bragged that Texas produced more than 70% of the nation's new jobs in late 2007 and much of 2008—true, because Texas was generating job growth when almost all other states weren't. A more revealing comparison is to consider the four calendar years 2007 through 2010. During that time, the nation lost nearly 7 million jobs, while Texas gained 300,000.

Texas is also a religious state, with 17 of the nation's 100 largest churches, according to one survey, and charitable giving is a widespread habit among rich and poor alike. Texas has developed a civic culture of adaptability and resilience, as it demonstrated by taking in thousands of Hurricane Katrina evacuees in 2005. Three years later, Houston weathered Hurricane Ike with orderly

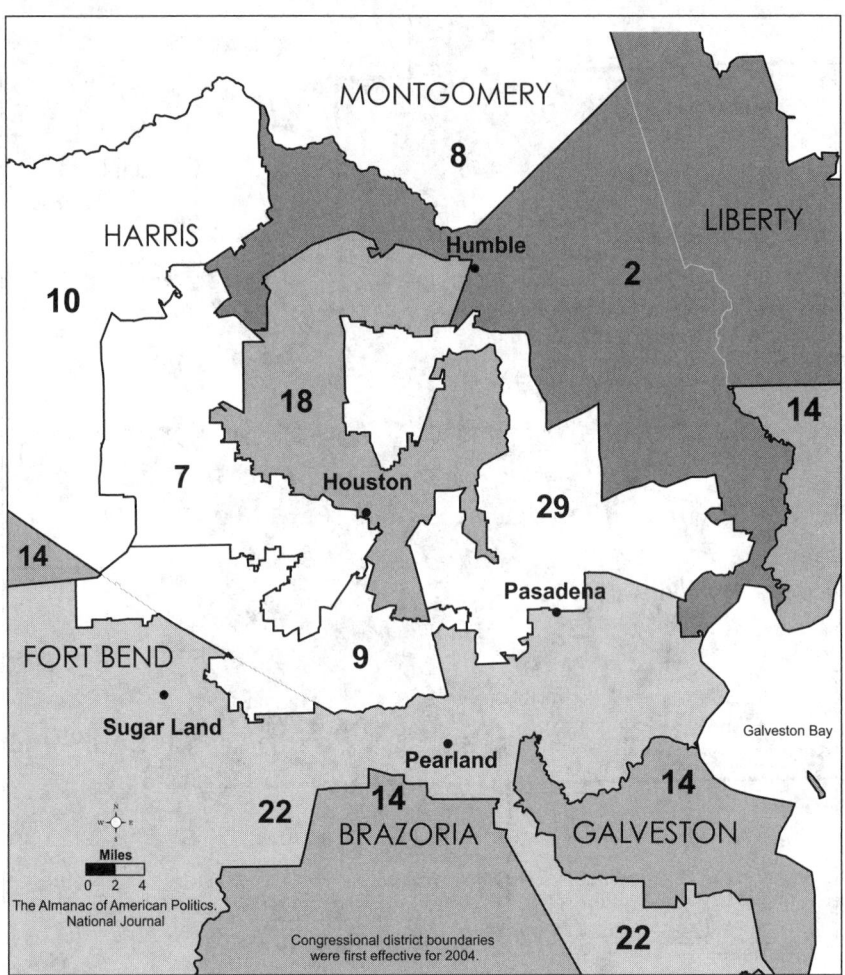

and timely evacuations. While other states pass laws requiring alternative energy sources in some distant year, Texas already produces more electricity from wind power than any other state—8% of its total electricity in 2010, up from 3% in 2007. State regulators in 2008 approved a $5 billion wind power transmission line project to quadruple production and to bring power from the windy and mostly empty west Texas plains to the heavy electricity users of the big metropolitan areas.

Texas is proud of its history and requires a year of Texas history in its high schools. In 1845, when the Republic of Texas was annexed by the United States, New Englander Edward Everett Hale wrote a pamphlet entitled *How to Conquer Texas Before It Conquers Us*, calling for emigration from the North to dilute "an unprincipled population of adventurers." But the newcomers joining ancestral Texans—think of the Bushes—have done much to put the stamp of Texas on the whole of the United States. And people have been voting for Texas with their feet. Texas's population grew from 21 million in 2000 to 25 million in 2010, a 21% increase. The state accounted for 16% of the population increase of the entire country. The reapportionment of House seats among the states reflects relative population growth; after the 2010 census, six states gained one seat, Florida gained two, California for the first time in its history gained none and Texas gained four. Growth came from both immigration and from domestic migration. The U.S. Census Bureau estimates that 933,000 immigrants came to the state between 2000 and 2009 and 849,000 people came from elsewhere in the United States.

Latino activists pointed out that Hispanics accounted for about half of the state's population increase, and immigration was particularly heavy in Dallas County and Houston's Harris County. It was not, interestingly, nearly so heavy in San Antonio, which is closer to the Mexican border, or in El Paso or the Lower Rio Grande Valley. But the biggest percentage population increases were in counties at the edge of big metro areas, where there was very little international immigration but more domestic migration—Collin and Denton counties north of Dallas and Fort Worth, Fort Bend and Montgomery counties southwest and north of Houston, and Williamson County north of Austin. The Dallas-Fort Worth Metroplex grew 23% in the decade, metro Houston 26%, metro Austin 37%—one of the highest figures of any 1 million-plus metro area—and metro San Antonio 25%. The Rio Grande counties grew 20%, while the rest of Texas, mostly small city and rural, grew by 8%, just a little under the national average of 9.7%.

Texas has surged in part because, in vivid contrast to that other onetime republic, California, it has nurtured and profited from its relationship with its southern neighbor, Mexico. California has been relatively indifferent to Mexico and even at times portrayed its southern neighbor as a burden, generating illegal immigrants that California taxpayers must pay for. Texas has taken a different course. Its border with Mexico is longer, some 1,200 miles, and more often crossed. Southern Texas along the Rio Grande is a transition zone between two very different economies. Despite a history of racial segregation, Texas has shown a friendly face to Mexicans, while Mexican immigrants have been happy to become Texans. Fewer Latinos have crossed the border here to take advantage of welfare programs, which are much less generous in Texas than in California. Political leadership has made a difference. Perry, who prepared for his office by taking Spanish lessons, followed the lead of predecessors Bush and Richards by maintaining good relations with Mexican leaders, and he has opposed putting up a border fence on the Rio Grande. Nearly half of U.S. merchandise exports to Mexico are from Texas, significantly more than California. The NAFTA secretariat of labor is in Dallas, the North American Development Bank is headquartered in San Antonio, the Border Environmental Cooperation Commission is in Juarez, across the Rio Grande from El Paso, and the busiest truck crossing between the countries is the new World Trade Bridge near Laredo and Nuevo Laredo.

Politically, Texas is now a predominantly Republican state. Republicans hold all 29 statewide elective offices, including the entire state Supreme Court, and have large margins in both houses of the state legislature. They have carried the state in the last eight presidential elections, starting in 1980, and have won every gubernatorial election but one since 1986 and every U.S. Senate election since 1990. The default result seems to be Republican by a 5-4 ratio. Perry won 55%-42% in 2010 and 58%-40% in 2002 (he won with 39% in a four-way race in 2006), not much different from Bush's first win in 1994 (53%-46%). In presidential contests, Republican John McCain carried the state 55%-44% in 2008, just about the same margin as George H. W. Bush carried it in 1988 (56%-43%) and Ronald Reagan in 1980 (55%-41%). John Cornyn was elected to the U.S. Senate by the identical margin of 55%-43% in 2002 and 2008. George W. Bush did run ahead of party lines for re-election as governor in 1998 and as a presidential candidate in 2000 and 2004, and Kay Bailey Hutchison ran ahead of party lines in her four races for the Senate in 1993 (a special election), 1994, 2000 and 2006.

But the patterns of support in these races have changed over time. Texas can be divided into four roughly equal-size parts for electoral analysis—the Dallas-Fort Worth Metroplex, metro Houston, the more Democratic parts of the state (metro Austin, metro San Antonio, the Rio Grande Valley) and the remainder, rural and small town Texas east, north, south and west. Back in 1988, George H.W. Bush received his biggest percentage margins in the Metroplex and metro Houston, 61% and 57%, respectively. He lost Austin, carried San Antonio and lost the Rio Grande Valley 56%-43%, and he carried rural, small-town Texas 57%-43%. That last number, by the way, was a sharp change from ancestral Democratic voting habits; rural, small-town Texas was a banner area for Democrat Bentsen in his four U.S. Senate races from 1970 to 1988. Fast forward 20 years, and McCain carried the Metroplex and metro Houston with lower percentages, 55% and 54%, respectively, as the central cities with their increasing black and Latino populations voted Democratic, while the rapidly growing suburban counties voted Republican. McCain lost metro Austin and carried metro San Antonio by percentages comparable to those in 1988, and he lost the Rio Grande Valley 63%-36%. But he carried rural, small-town Texas 69%-31%. Aside from a few lightly populated desert areas, McCain carried every single county in what had once been solidly Democratic country.

Many commentators have pointed out that demographic factors seem to threaten Republican dominance in the state. Rural, small-town Texas, now the Republican stronghold, is growing less than the rest of the state, and the Latino population is increasing. The 2010 census reported 38% of Texas' residents as Hispanic, and more than half its public school pupils are so classified. Yet Texas so far has remained as defiantly Republican as California—also 38% Hispanic—has remained definitely Democratic. The chief reason is that Anglo whites are still the large majority of voters in both states: They voted 52% for Democrat Barack Obama in California and 73% for McCain in Texas. But Texas Hispanics are different as well. They voted 49% or 39% (depending on which exit poll you believe) for George W. Bush in his 1998 re-election for governor, and 42% and 49% for Bush in his presidential races in 2000 and 2004. They voted 35% for McCain in 2008, a low number, but higher than the 23% he got in California. Hutchison got 44% of Latino votes in 2006, Cornyn won 36% in 2008 and Perry got 38% in 2010—not majorities, but not disastrously low percentages either.

The other potential pitfall for Republicans here is staleness: They have been visibly and sometimes controversially in control of state government and the state's congressional delegation for some time now, time enough to accumulate political baggage and to inspire creative campaigning by the opposition. In 2010, all of those factors seemed to be in play. Hutchison waged a fierce primary fight with Perry, whose 10 years in office, since he succeeded Bush, made him the longest-serving Texas governor in history. Perry had been re-elected with only 39% of the vote in 2006 against Democratic former Rep. Chris Bell and two independents. Perry had suffered setbacks as his ambitious transportation plan—a combined rail line and toll highway parallel to Interstate 35—was rejected and Republicans were reduced in 2008 to a 76-74 majority in the state House, which resulted in the election of a mostly Democrat-supported moderate Republican as speaker (a powerful position in Texas). But as opposition to the Obama administration polices grew, Perry's popularity increased. "Texas has yet to learn submission to oppression," he told *Time*, explaining that he rejected federal unemployment funds because they came with strings. He dubbed his opponent "Kay Bailout Hutchison" for her support of the federal government's rescue of the financial industry. Perry shot ahead in polls. Perry won the primary with 51% of the vote, to 30% for Hutchison and 19% for third candidate Debra Medina.

In the general election, Perry faced about as strong an opponent as Democrats could field, Bill White, whose moderate record as Houston mayor had won widespread praise. But Texas' basic partisan preferences prevailed; Perry won 55%-42%, losing the Rio Grande Valley and metro Austin, but carrying the Metroplex and metro Houston and winning rural, small-town Texas, 65%-32%. Republicans increased their margin in the state House to an unprecedented 101-49. The only check on Republican dominance was the party's 19-12 majority in the state Senate, where 21 votes are required to bring an issue to the floor.

Population		Household Income		Work	
Pop. 2010:	25,145,561	Under $15k:	13.7%	Private:	78.0%
State rank:	2nd	$15k to $50k:	37.4%	Government:	14.8%
Change since 2000:	Up 20.6%	$50k to $100k:	29.6%	Self-employed:	7.1%
Urban:	79.9%	$100k to $200k:	15.4%	Unemployment (3-yr. average):	4.3%
Rural:	20.1%	Over $200k:	4.0%	Poverty:	16.6%
Native of state:	60.7%	Median income:	$48,765	Blue collar:	23.4%
Not a citizen:	11.0%			White collar:	58.6%
Area size:	268,596 sq. mi.	**Home Value**		Khaki collar:	0.5%
		Under $100k:	37.9%	Other:	17.5%
Most populous cities		$100k to $300k:	51.0%		
Houston	2,099,451	$300k to $500k:	7.4%	**Age**	
San Antonio	1,327,407	$500k to $1 mil:	2.8%	Median age:	33.0 yrs.
Dallas	1,197,816	Over $1 million:	0.9%	More than 65 yrs:	10.1%
Austin	790,390	Median:	$124,400	Less than 18 yrs:	27.8%

Race/Ethnicity				Military Veterans		Registered Voters in 2010	
White:	45.3%	*Language*		% of Pop:	9.1%	No Party registration	
Black:	11.5%	English:	66.1%			Voter turnout:	4,979,870
Hispanic:	37.6%	Spanish:	29.1%	*Veterans by Period*		Turnout as % of	
Asian:	3.8%	Asian:	2.3%	WWII and before:	8.5%	voting age:	27.2%
Native Am.:	0.3%	Other European:	1.9%	Korea:	9.3%		
Hawaiian:	0.1%			Vietnam:	33.3%	**Legislature**	
Two+ races:	1.3%	**Education**		Gulf (pre-2001):	14.9%	Senate:	12 D 19 R
		H.S. grad:	79.6%	Gulf (post-2001):	10.4%	House:	49 D 101 R
Ancestry		College grad:	25.5%	Peace time:	23.7%		
German	9.7%	Grad degree:	8.4%				
Irish	6.9%						
English	6.5%						

Presidential politics In 2008, Texas was, for the first time in 20 years, a pivotal state in presidential politics, more so in the two parties' nomination contests than in the general election, although the result there was notably closer than many people had anticipated. In 1988, Texas' presidential primary was moved to March, for Super Tuesday. Then, Democrats dominated the legislature and far more Texans chose to vote in the Democratic than in the Republican primary. That year, 1.7 million voted in the Democratic primary, and Michael Dukakis led with 33% of the vote, Jesse Jackson got 25%, ahead of Al Gore, running as a Southern moderate, with 20%. Dukakis had support from urban liberals and Hispanics, Jackson from African-Americans, Gore from the dwindling number of rural and small-town yellow dog Democrats. Just over 1 million votes were cast on the Republican side, most of them for Texas' own George

2008 Presidential Vote		
John McCain (R) 4,479,328	(55%)
Barack Obama (D) 3,528,633	(44%)

2008 Presidential Primary		
Hillary Clinton (D).............1,462,734	(51%)
Barack Obama (D) 1,362,476	(47%)

2008 Presidential Primary		
John McCain (R) 697,767	(51%)
Mike Huckabee (R)................518,002	(38%)

2004 Presidential Vote		
George W. Bush (R)...........4,526,917	(61%)
John Kerry (D) 2,832,704	(38%)

H.W. Bush. In 1992, turnout was lower in both parties' primaries and in 1996, 2000 and 2004, both parties' nominations were determined by the time Texas voted.

Not so in 2008. After Barack Obama in February won 14 straight Democratic primaries and 11 caucuses, Texas and Ohio were must-wins for Hillary Rodham Clinton on March 4. On the Republican side, Mike Huckabee was still campaigning against John McCain. So Texas got a lot more attention than it would have if the legislature had chosen to set the primary for Super Tuesday, Feb. 5. Obama and Clinton debated and campaigned hard in Texas. Democratic turnout was nearly 2.9 million, more than triple the 839,000 who voted in 2004 and 70% above the peak in 1988. The primary was a closer contest than Ohio's. Clinton won by just 51%-47%. As in other states, Clinton carried women, older voters, downscale and rural whites and Latinos by wide margins. Obama carried men, younger voters, upscale and urban whites and blacks by wide margins. Clinton won 61% to 70% of the vote in San Antonio and border state Senate districts. (Texas Democrats elect delegates by state Senate districts.) Obama won 73% in heavily African-American state Senate districts in Houston and Dallas. Rural districts, except for one which includes exurban Austin's Williamson County voted for Clinton. Obama carried metro Dallas with 56%, metro Houston with 55%, and metro Austin with 60%. Clinton carried 18 Senate districts to Obama's 13, but Obama won more delegates overall because one-third of them were selected in caucuses held on primary night and more Obama voters took the trouble to show up.

Turnout on the Republican side was much lower, 1.3 million, less than half the Democratic turnout and only slightly above the 1.1 million Republicans who voted in the not seriously contested primary in 2000. McCain beat Huckabee, 51%-38%. Huckabee carried only one U.S. House district, the 4th, which includes Texarkana, right on the border with his native Arkansas. Half the primary voters were white evangelical Protestants, and Huckabee won more than 40% of the vote in the northern more, Baptist half of the state, including the Dallas-Fort Worth Metroplex. He won less than 40% in most parts of the southern half of the state. McCain's biggest majorities were in the border areas and in the most upscale districts in Houston and Dallas.

In general elections, Texas has not voted Democratic since 1976, when it narrowly backed Jimmy Carter. The best the Democratic ticket has done here since then was 43% in 1988, when Texas Sen. Lloyd Bentsen was Michael Dukakis' running mate, and 44% in 1996, when Texan Ross Perot split the opposition to Bill Clinton, and Republican Bob Dole carried the state with 49% of the vote.

In 2008, Obama got 44% of the vote, which left him well behind McCain's 55%, but not so far behind as to banish Democrats' hopes they may be competitive for Texas' 38 electoral votes in 2012. Obama carried the central city counties including Dallas, Houston, San Antonio and Austin, something no Democrat has done since Lyndon Johnson swept his home state in 1964. Republicans led in party identification by only 34%-33%, but conservatives outnumbered liberals, 46%-15%. Whites voted 73%-26% for McCain. He also won 83% among white evangelical Protestants and 69% among white voters under 30. African-Americans voted 98%-2% for Obama. Hispanics voted 63%-35% for Obama. Hispanics and upscale white voters were the most likely to have switched from Bush in 2004 to Obama in 2008. As a result, the coalitions supporting each candidate were very different in hue. More than 80% of McCain's votes were cast by whites. A little more than one-third of Obama voters were whites, with a little less than one-third African-American and about the same share Hispanic.

Congressional districting

Before 2001, redistricting in Texas had always been the prerogative of Democrats. For many years, it was not particularly partisan; there weren't enough Republicans to matter. By the 1990s there were, and in 1991, Democrats produced their masterpiece. Modified slightly by a 1996 court ruling, it clumped heavily Republican areas into hugely Republican districts and then carved out, with convoluted lines, three new districts for Democrats. Starting in 1994, Republicans outpolled Democrats in House races and Anglo Democrats found themselves increasingly imperiled. Still, Democrats held a 17-13 majority in the delegation after the 2000 election.

Texas gained two seats after the 2000 census, and Republicans like House Majority Whip Tom DeLay predicted that their party would pick up six to eight seats. But that didn't happen. The legislature was unable to agree on a map in 2001, and a three-judge federal court, with two Democratic judges and one Republican judge, took control and came up with a plan that protected all the incumbents and created two new Republican districts. In effect, the partisan Democratic plan of 1991 was given new life, with the Republicans given two new seats as a consolation prize. The result was, predictably, a 17-15 Democratic delegation.

In 2002, Republicans won big majorities in the legislature, and DeLay lost no time in urging passage of a new plan. Senate Republicans balked. But DeLay continued to press newly installed Republican House Speaker Tom Craddick. As the legislative session neared adjournment, the House Redistricting Committee approved a new map on May 6, 2003. The disciplined Republican majority ignored Democrats' protests. On the eve of the House's scheduled debate on the plan, 51 Democrats fled the state and settled in a Holiday Inn in Ardmore, Okla., to prevent the Republicans from getting the two-thirds required for a quorum. The state police were dispatched to track down the "Killer D's." Once their location was revealed, the Democrats insisted they would not return to Austin until after May 15, the final day the House could take up the bill in its regular session. The maneuver worked only temporarily. Republican Gov. Rick Perry convened a special session on June 30, and in late July, the House approved the redistricting plan and sent it to the Senate.

Once Republicans hammered out details of the plan, with lines drawn to satisfy DeLay and Craddick, the pro-Republican plan passed. The drafters attempted to comply with the Voting Rights Act by drawing safe districts for Texas' two African-American and five Hispanic incumbent Democrats. The new map in fact added a third heavily black district, in the Houston area, and increased from seven to eight the number of districts with Hispanic majorities. But it pointedly made what political insiders called WD-40s—white incumbent Democrats over 40—an endangered species. There were 15 of them in the Texas delegation in 1992, 11 in 2000, 10 in 2002 and only three in 2004.

On Dec. 19, 2003, the Justice Department ruled the plan was in compliance with the Voting Rights Act. And a federal court, after Democrats sued, ruled that it was permissible to redistrict more than once in the 10 years between censuses. On Jan. 6, 2004, the court approved the plan 2-1. (In September 2005, DeLay and three associates who pushed the redistricting plan were indicted on charges related to the 2002 state House elections. DeLay was convicted in 2010 and sentenced in early 2011 to three years in prison.) Elections were held under the new plan in 2004. That year, Republican George W. Bush carried Texas 61%-38%, and in the 32 House races, five WD-40s were defeated. Only three survived: Chet Edwards of Waco and Lloyd Doggett and Gene Green in majority Hispanic districts. The Texas delegation, 17-15 Democratic under the old map, was 21-11 Republican under the new map. Nationally, Republicans gained three seats in the House, with the help of Texas, to bring their total to 232, the most won by Republicans in any biennial election between 1946 and 2010.

In June 2005, the U.S. Supreme Court upheld the basic plan, rejecting 7-2 the charge that it was "an unconstitutional political gerrymander." But it also ruled, 5-4, that the fact that the 23rd District, held by Republican Henry Bonilla, had a population that was only 55% Hispanic violated the Voting Rights Act, and it suggested that the 25th District, stretching from Austin to the Rio Grande and 69% Hispanic (represented by Doggett), might also have to be redrawn. The three-judge district court adopted a new plan that gave a larger portion of San Antonio to the 23rd District and kept the 25th District within easy driving distance of Austin. Filing was reopened for the five altered districts with primaries to be held on Election Day and runoffs between the party nominees later in December.

The overall result was a victory for Republicans, but with two offsetting losses. Democrat Nick Lampson, ousted in the 2nd District in 2004, came back and won in DeLay's old 22nd District, despite its heavy Republican leanings, in a voter backlash against DeLay's problems with the law.

And Bonilla lost his 23rd District seat to Democrat Ciro Rodriguez. That left Republicans with a 19-13 majority in the delegation. In 2008, Pete Olson beat Lampson and restored the DeLay district to the Republicans, raising the Republican advantage to 20-12. In 2010, Edwards lost 62%-37% after 20 years in Congress and Republicans captured the Hispanic-majority 23rd and 27th districts, giving Republicans 23-9 dominance of the House delegation.

Texas gained four House seats from the reapportionment following the 2010 census. Republicans were in control of the redistricting process with Perry as governor and solid Republican margins in both houses of the legislature. Demographically, the most rapid growth in the state has been in exurban counties, almost all of them heavily Republican. But the prevailing interpretation of the Voting Rights Act seems to require maximizing the number of black- and Hispanic-majority seats, and Texas's plan is subject to review by the Obama administration's Justice Department.

There are currently three districts (the 9th and 18th in Houston, and the 30th in Dallas) with African-American representatives, though each had more Hispanic than black residents in 2000, and it is hard to see how a fourth district where blacks are the dominant voting bloc can be created without the kind of highly irregular boundary lines that the Supreme Court disapproved in North Carolina cases in the 1990s. Democrats may argue that the state should have 13 or 14 districts with Hispanic majorities instead of the current seven (the 15th, 16th, 20th, 23rd, 27th, 28th and 29th). But while it seems possible to create one such district each in the Metroplex and in the Rio Grande Valley, and perhaps possible to create another in metro Houston, it is hard to see how any more can be created without, again, drawing highly irregular boundaries. The current 23rd and 27th districts are represented by Republicans, and the 29th by an Anglo Democrat: Hispanics tend to be a substantially lower percentage of the electorate than of the total population because of the large number of Hispanic non-citizens and children. So prospects are for Texas to continue to have a majority-Republican delegation, but perhaps only after a protracted struggle in the legislature, the Justice Department and the courts.

Governor

Rick Perry (R)

Assumed office Dec. 2000, term expires Jan. 2015, 3rd full term; b. March 4, 1950, Paint Creek; home, Austin; Texas A&M U., B.S. 1972; United Methodist; married (Anita); 2 children.

Military Career: Air Force, 1972-77.

Elected Office: TX House of Reps., 1984-90; Comm., TX Dept. of Agriculture, 1990-98; Lt. gov., 1998-2000.

Professional Career: Farmer & rancher.

Office: State Capitol, P.O. Box 12428, Austin, 78711, 512-463-2000; Fax: 512-463-1849; Web site: www.governor.state.tx.us.

Election Results

2010 general	Rick Perry (R)	2,737,481	(55%)
	Bill White (D)	2,106,395	(42%)
	Kathy Glass (I)	109,211	(2%)
2010 primary	Rick Perry (R)	759,296	(51%)
	Kay Hutchison (R)	450,087	(30%)
	Debra Medina (R)	275,159	(19%)

Prior Winning Percentages: 2006 (39%); 2002 (58%)

Republican Rick Perry succeeded George W. Bush as governor of Texas on December 21, 2000, and was elected to full four-year terms in 2002, 2006 and 2010. In December 2008, he became the longest-serving governor in Texas history. His fervent state's-rights stance has made him one of the nation's highest-profile governors.

Perry grew up on his family's farm in Paint Creek, north of Abilene in Haskell County, near where his great-great grandfather settled after fighting in the Civil War; he was elected to the Texas House in the 1890s. Perry's family owns a 10,000-acre ranch, and his father served 28 years as a county commissioner, as a Democrat, like pretty much everyone in those parts at that time. Rick Perry was an Eagle Scout and went to Texas A&M University to study to be a veterinarian.

While working on a degree in animal science, he became a yell leader, or cheerleader, a coveted position at A&M. It was the late 1960s, a time of great student rebellions, but apparently not in College Station; Perry says he never saw a war protest. After college, he served five years in the Air Force, piloting C-130 transports. In 1977, he returned to work on the family ranch. In 1984, he was elected to the state House as a Democrat. Perry was part of a group called the Pit Bulls, who focused on trying to cut state agency budgets. In 1989, he was passed over for a leadership position by Democratic Speaker Gib Lewis and switched to the Republican Party.

In 1990, he ran for agriculture commissioner against the colorful populist incumbent Jim Hightower. With the help of Karl Rove, then working as a consultant in Texas, Perry got the support of the Texas Farm Bureau and won an upset victory with ads pointing out that Hightower had supported civil rights leader Jesse Jackson for president. In the increasingly Republican Texas, Perry was easily re-elected in 1994. Four years later, when storied Democratic Lt. Gov. Bob Bullock retired, Perry ran for that office, which in Texas is a powerful position. The lieutenant governor presides over the state Senate, controls its proceedings, and appoints its committee members and chairmen. Governors and lieutenant governors are elected separately in Texas, and George W. Bush and Perry ran separate campaigns in 1998. Perry had no Republican primary opposition, and his Democratic opponent was state Comptroller John Sharp, who Perry had known during college. (Sharp had been student-body president at A&M when Perry was a yell leader.) Perry won 50%-48%.

After Bush was elected president in 2000, Perry automatically ascended, becoming the first Aggie (as A&M graduates are known) to become governor of Texas. In 2002, when Perry had to run for the job, Democrats believed that he was vulnerable and gamely tried to put together a ticket. The chief organizer was Sharp, who decided to run for lieutenant governor again, not governor, and worked to get a gubernatorial candidate who could swell Democratic turnout among Latinos. His dream candidate was Tony Sanchez, chief shareholder of International Bank of Commerce and Sanchez Oil & Gas in Laredo, who was said to have a net worth of $600 million. Sanchez spent $18 million on ads and beat former Attorney General Dan Morales in the Democratic primary 61%-33%.

Perry and Sanchez agreed on many issues, but much of the campaign consisted of vitriolic ads. Sanchez charged that Perry was beholden to campaign contributors and did their bidding. Perry hit Sanchez for not voting in some elections and for his business practices. In the fall, he ran a number of hard-hitting ads linking Sanchez to drug kingpins' money laundering. It was undisputed that some $25 million had been laundered through Tesoro Savings & Loan, a company Sanchez owned, in the early 1980s. Sanchez said that he had not known of the transactions and pointed out that no one at the S&L had been charged with a crime. Nevertheless, Perry's ads linked the money laundering to the 1985 murder of a Drug Enforcement Administration agent in Mexico. An outraged Sanchez called Perry "by far the most disgusting human being I have ever known."

On election night, Republicans won up and down the line. Perry beat Sanchez 58%-40%, although Sanchez had spent $67 million to Perry's $28 million. Sharp also lost, as did Ron Kirk, the African-American former mayor of Dallas who ran for the Senate. The high Latino turnout that Democrats had hoped for materialized only in the Rio Grande Valley. Turnout in Latino neighborhoods in Houston, Dallas and San Antonio was not up by much. Rather, the big increases in turnout were in the fast-growing, heavily Republican counties at the edge of metro areas. Republicans also won big margins in the state legislature. Perry called his victory a mandate for restricting tort lawsuits, providing rate relief on homeowner insurance, changes in medical malpractice law, and government-paid vouchers for private school tuition.

Redistricting dominated the Texas political landscape in 2003. Early that year, U.S. House Majority Leader Tom DeLay urged the legislature to pass a new congressional district map. Senate Republicans were reluctant, but DeLay found an ally in GOP House Speaker Tom Craddick. As the legislative session neared adjournment, the House Redistricting Committee approved a new map that added five to seven new Republican seats and jeopardized each of the delegation's 10 Anglo Democrats, though it protected the five incumbent Latino Democrats and two African-Americans. On the eve of the House's scheduled May 12 debate, 51 Democrats fled the state and secretly settled at a Holiday Inn in Ardmore, Okla., to prevent the Republicans from getting the two-thirds required for a quorum. The spectacle attracted national attention, and the state police were dispatched to track down the "Killer D's." The maneuver worked, temporarily. But Perry convened a special session on June 30. After House Republicans passed their plan, the 30-day session deadlocked when senators abided by their traditional rule for two-thirds approval to debate legislation. Perry called a second 30-day session. When Republicans threatened to take action this time with a simple majority, 11 Senate Democrats fled to Albuquerque to prevent a quorum for legislative action. With cheers from Democrats nationwide and growing anger from Republicans, they remained there for the month of August. When Perry indicated in early September that he would call a third special session, Democratic state Sen. John Whitmire effectively broke the deadlock by returning to his legislative duties. On Oct. 9, DeLay's redistricting plan, with Perry's help, was passed by the legislature.

School finance has long been a major issue in Texas government and politics. In 1993, Democratic Gov. Ann Richards and the Democratic legislature passed a "Robin Hood" plan to distribute money from high-property-value school districts to poorer ones. By 2004, many school districts had reached their maximum taxing levels, and voters were complaining about high property taxes while parents complained about schools starved for money. In 2004, Perry advanced legislation with more spending on schools, a $1 cigarette-tax increase and property tax reductions. But it met fierce opposition from some Republicans and failed to pass.

In September 2004, a state trial judge ruled that the school finance system was unconstitutional and gave the legislature a year to come up with a solution. In 2005, Perry declared school financing a "legislative emergency," and he and the legislature struggled through several special sessions to find a solution, but ultimately failed. In November 2005, the state Supreme Court ruled the financing system unconstitutional, on the grounds that it amounted to a statewide property tax. In September, Perry appointed a commission headed by his old college friend and political foe Sharp. It recommended a plan that Perry brought before a special session in April 2006. The Senate passed a bill in May with a one-third property tax cut, a $2,000 pay raise for teachers, a 4% spending increase, new math and science initiatives and a cigarette tax increase. It also incorporated changes in business taxes and expanded the franchise tax to reach every significant business operation, with revenues to be used to finance property tax reductions.

Perry next tackled Texas's traffic-choked roads. Interstate 35 from the Dallas-Fort Worth Metroplex on south has been pounded by trucks headed for the border at Laredo, the busiest crossing point for truck traffic between the United States and Mexico. Perry argued that the state's 20-cent gas tax was no longer adequate to build needed infrastructure, and in 2005, the legislature authorized his Trans-Texas Corridor plan to build a network of toll highways, with freight and passenger rail corridors and utility zones for water and gas pipelines and electric transmission lines, at a cost of $184 billion or more. Another problem was border enforcement. In 2006, Perry ordered video surveillance cameras placed on the border and sent large numbers of state troopers to protect Texans from Mexican drug cartels operating just south of the border. "Enforcing the border is the federal government's responsibility, but Texas will not wait for them to act," he said.

Going into his 2006 re-election campaign, Perry had a job-approval rating of under 50%. Republican U.S. Sen. Kay Bailey Hutchison gave long thought to challenging him in the March 2006 primary, but decided against it. But Texas Comptroller Carole Keeton Strayhorn decided to challenge him, saying memorably: "I am not a weak leadin', ethics ignorin', pointin'-the-finger-at-everyone blamin', special session callin', public school slashin', slush fund spendin', toll road buildin', special interest panderin', rainy day fund raidin', fee increasin', no property tax cuttin', promise breakin', do-nothin' Rick Perry phony conservative." She called for repealing Perry's business tax and called the property tax reductions a "$23 billion hot check." Also entering the race was musician Kinky Friedman. "How hard could it be?" was his theme. Democrats had more difficulty coming up with a candidate. Finally Chris Bell, a one-term congressman from Houston who had been defeated as a result of the 2003 redistricting plan, stepped forward. Just before the filing deadline, Strayhorn said she would run as an independent rather than go up against Perry in the GOP Early 2006 polls showed Perry running around 40% and his three opponents each receiving about half as many votes.

Perry won 39% of the vote, to 30% for Bell, 18% for Strayhorn and 12% for Friedman. Perry carried metro Dallas 41%-31%, Houston 38%-31%, and San Antonio 36%-28%. Bell carried metro Austin 39%-31% and the border counties 38%-33%. Whites voted 44%-24% for Perry, African-Americans 63%-16% for Bell. Hispanics, who cast 15% of the votes, voted 41%-31% for Bell. Republicans gained one seat in the state Senate, for a 20-11 margin, and lost seats in the state House, leaving their majority at 81-69.

In June 2007, with a booming economy and a budget surplus, Perry signed a $152 billion, two-year budget. It raised spending 12% and included $3 billion in bonds for cancer research, a health insurance pool, a $146 million increase in college aid and a $100 million increase in funds for border security. But Perry opposed the border fence ordered by Congress. "We know how to deal with border security, and you don't do it by building a fence. You do it by putting boots on the ground," he said. However, he said a "strategic" fence might be useful in urban border areas. On other issues, Perry signed a bill barring confiscation of guns in a state of emergency and, after the Virginia Tech

University massacre of 32 students, supported repeal of the law prohibiting guns on campuses, saying, "It makes sense for Texans to be able to protect themselves from deranged individuals." He issued a widely criticized order requiring teenage girls to receive the HPV vaccine, which has shown promise in combating genital warts and cervical cancer.

By early 2009, the state government had no budget deficit and a $9 billion rainy day fund to draw on. Yet Perry faced some obstacles. In the 2008 elections, Democrats had reduced the Republican majority in the state House to 76-74 and Republicans forced out conservative Speaker Craddick and installed, mostly with Democratic votes, the more moderate Republican Joe Straus. In January, the Texas Department of Transportation officially abandoned the Trans-Texas Corridor project in the face of widespread opposition from landowners and suspicion of the foreign contractor, Cintra. Some of the roads would still be built, but not all of the 1,200-foot-wide corridor of toll roads, rail lines, pipelines and electrical transmission wires. Legislators also questioned Perry's 2005 mandate that at least 65% of school spending go to classroom instruction.

Despite those setbacks, Perry was building a national profile. He was the head of the Republican Governors Association, and in that role, was a leading critic of President Barack Obama's $787 billion economic stimulus bill. "I believe that our federal government has become oppressive in its size, its intrusion into the lives of our citizens and its interference with the affairs of our state," he said. In March 2009, Perry opposed taking $555 million in stimulus money that required Texas to expand its unemployment compensation program. Nonetheless, bipartisan coalitions in the legislature forced him to accept the money. Perry frequently touted Texas' economic strengths, and his own role developing them, seemingly with an eye on his future. "Our low taxes, controlled government spending and fair legal system give us a leg up on other states," he said, noting that Texas led the nation in exports and *Fortune* 500 company headquarters. With much of the nation suffering from recession, he said, "I can't imagine what Texas would look like if we had applied the same principles and the same decision-making in Texas that they're applying in Washington. Well, California." He published a book in 2010 titled, *"Fed Up! Our Fight to Save America from Washington,"* which called for giving states more power on issues ranging from taxes to gay marriage.

In seeking another four-year term in 2010, Perry this time had competition for the GOP nomination from Hutchison. She touted her record of delivering federal money for the state and criticized the Trans-Texas Corridor as Perry's "quest to cover our state with massive toll roads." She also attacked him for reducing the State Children's Health Insurance Program and called for more education funding. After Hutchison voted for the $700 billion government rescue of the financial services industry, Perry's campaign dubbed her "Kay Bailout." Perry also burnished his conservative credentials by supporting a "Choose Life" license plate in the 2009 legislative session and a bill requiring any woman seeking an abortion to first view an ultrasound of the fetus. He suggested that Texans disgusted by the economic stimulus might consider seceding from the United States. His anti-Washington rhetoric played well with tea party activists and other disgruntled Republicans, while most of the attention Hutchison got focused on her protracted equivocating over whether to resign her Senate seat to run for governor. Her initial double-digit lead over Perry in the polls vanished by early 2010. Though she outraised him $19.7 million to $16.7 million, he trounced her 51%-30% in the March GOP primary, with tea party activist Debra Medina drawing 19%.

Perry's general election opponent was former Houston Mayor Bill White, who had served in President Bill Clinton's Energy Department and chaired the Texas Democratic Party from 1996 to 1998. He won election as mayor in 2003 and was praised for his city's response to Hurricane Katrina; he also cut the city's property taxes five times. Democrats hoped that voters had had enough of Perry and were ready for a fresh face. But White was unable to find an issue that stuck against Perry, and he settled on trying to highlight cronyism in his administration. Perry unleashed a barrage of tough ads that raised questions about White's tenure as mayor while continuing to trumpet his anti-Washington message. He coasted to another term with a 55%-42% win. A CNN exit poll showed Perry getting 69% from white voters, while White got 88% from African-Americans and 61% from Hispanics. He racked up totals in excess of 70% in most rural counties and held White to just over 50% in Houston-based Harris County.

Perry made good on his state's rights rhetoric, refusing in January 2011 to let his state enforce federal climate change regulations and joining Attorney General Greg Abbott in launching a series of lawsuits against the Environmental Protection Agency's clean air rules. He also called for reducing funds by one-third for the state's Commission on Environmental Quality to help deal with the state's $15 billion budget deficit. Though Perry had come out against tapping the state's $9.4 billion rainy day fund, some lawmakers began discussing that possibility as an alternative to slashing other state services.

Senior Senator

Kay Bailey Hutchison (R)

Elected June 1993, term expires 2012, 3rd full term; b. July 22, 1943, Galveston; home, Dallas; U. of TX, B.A. 1962, J.D. 1967; Episcopalian; married (Ray); 2 children.

Elected Office: TX House of Reps., 1972–76; TX treasurer, 1990–93.

Professional Career: Political & legal corresp., KPRC–TV, 1967–70; Vice chmn., Natl. Transp. Safety Bd., 1976–78; V.P. & gen. cnsl., RepublicBank Corp., 1978–82; Owner, McCraw Candies, 1984–88.

DC Office: 284 RSOB, 20510, 202-224-5922; Fax: 202-224-0776; Web site: hutchison.senate.gov.

State Offices: Abilene, 325-676-2839; Austin, 512-916-5834; Dallas, 214-361-3500; Harlingen, 956-425-2253; Houston, 713-653-3456; San Antonio, 210-340-2885.

Committees: *Appropriations:* Commerce, Justice, Science & Related Agencies (RMM); Defense; Energy & Water Development; Labor, Health & Human Services, Education & Related Agencies; Military Construction, Veterans Affairs & Related Agencies; Transportation, HUD & Related Agencies. *Commerce, Science & Transportation* (RMM). *Rules & Administration.*

Group Ratings

	ACLU	ACU	ADA	CFG	AFS	FRC	LCV	ITIC	NTU	COC
2010	13	96	0	89	9	100	0	33	98	100
2009	–	96	25	81	27	–	18	–	81	57

National Journal Ratings

	2010 LIB — 2010 CONS		2009 LIB — 2009 CONS	
Economic	19%	— 80%	27%	— 72%
Social	0%	— 79%	27%	— 72%
Foreign	0%	— 72%	27%	— 72%
Composite	15%	— 85%	28%	— 73%

Key Votes of the 111th Congress

1. Overturn Ledbetter	Y	5. Pass health care bill	9. Ratify New START	N
2. Pass $787 billion stimulus	N	6. Regulate financial firms	10. Confirm Elena Kagan	N
3. Repeal DC gun laws	Y	7. Pass tax cuts for some	11. Stop EPA climate regs	Y
4. Confirm Sonia Sotomayor	N	8. Legalize immigrants' kids	12. Repeal don't ask, tell	N

Election Results

2006 general	Kay Bailey Hutchison (R)	2,661,789	(62%)	($9,248,720)
	Barbara Radnofsky (D)	1,555,202	(36%)	($1,482,207)
2006 primary	Kay Bailey Hutchison (R)	unopposed		

Prior Winning Percentages: 2000 (65%); 1994 (61%); 1993 special (67%)

Kay Bailey Hutchison, the senior senator from Texas, is a Republican who first won her seat in a June 1993 special election. She announced on Jan. 13, 2011 that she would not seek re-election when her term is up in 2012. Hutchison, who lost the GOP gubernatorial primary to incumbent Rick Perry on March 2, 2010, will have served 19 years in the Senate when her term is up and said that she wants to live year-round in Texas again. "The last two years have been particularly difficult, especially for my family, but I felt it would be wrong to leave the Senate during such a critical period," said Hutchison, the mother of two school-age children.

Hutchison is of old Texas stock, the great-great-granddaughter of Charles S. Taylor, a signer of the Texas Declaration of Independence. She grew up in La Marque, near the refinery town of Texas City, a prom queen who went to college and then to law school at the University of Texas. She went to work as a Houston television news reporter in 1967 because, as she later told *Esquire* magazine, "I couldn't get a job in law. The top Houston firms just did not hire women. It was very frustrating. I looked for four months. Nothing." In 1972, Hutchison won a seat in the Texas Legislature, its first Republican woman. In 1976, she went to Washington for a top job at the National Transportation Safety Board. She married Ray Hutchison, moved to Dallas, went into banking and became a small-business owner in 1978. In 1982, she lost a race for the U.S. House to Republican Steve Bartlett, later mayor of Dallas. But she stayed active in Republican politics and was elected state treasurer in 1990. This was a breakthrough year for state Republicans, who before that had not been successful in down-ballot statewide races. Hutchison began her political career when it was no advantage to be a woman and has been mocked by liberals for her prim manners and by Washington conservatives as a "Texas pom-pom girl." Her response: "This is what I have faced all my life—the trivialization of me—which I have not ever let bother me. I have always been able to rise above the expectations." Indeed, she is a senator from the nation's second-largest state and was re-elected in 2000 with more than 4 million votes.

Hutchison had a chance to run for Congress in January 1993, when Democrat Lloyd Bentsen resigned his Senate seat after 22 years to become President Bill Clinton's Treasury secretary. Democratic Gov. Ann Richards appointed Bob Krueger, a two-term U.S. representative from Texas in the 1970s who was then the state railroad commissioner. Running against him in the May 1993 all-party primary were three Republicans: Hutchison and Reps. Joe Barton and Jack Fields. Krueger opposed the Clinton budget and tax plan, but Democrats were so unpopular in Texas then—Clinton had a 73% negative job rating—that Krueger won only 29% of the total vote, just behind Hutchison, also with 29%. Barton and Fields won 14% each. Hutchison kept the focus on Clinton and won the June runoff by an astonishing 67%-33%. Three serious Democrats were running as she entered the race for the full term in 1994. The potentially strongest candidate, moderate U.S. Rep. Mike Andrews of Houston, was eliminated in the March primary. In the April runoff, former Attorney General Jim Mattox lost 54%-46% to Richard Fisher, a free-spending moderate who campaigned extensively in the border counties in Spanish. Hutchison cruised to a solid 61%-38% victory, and became the first woman to represent Texas in the Senate.

Hutchison has not had trouble being taken seriously by fellow Republicans in the Senate. She moved up quickly in the leadership, and in 2006, she was elected chairman of the Senate Republican Policy Committee, the No. 4 position in the leadership. The following year, she declined to run for the conference chairman, the No. 3 position. Currently, she is the ranking Republican on the influential Senate Commerce, Science and Transportation Committee.

For a long time, she has had her eye on the Texas governorship, and, after several false starts, decided to run even though the state had a Republican governor running for re-election in 2010, Rick Perry. He had been re-elected with only 39% in a four-candidate race in 2006, and polls in early 2009 showed Hutchison leading him in a primary matchup. By January 2009, she had banked $8 million for her challenge to Perry, more than his $6.6 million.

The contest between Hutchison and Perry was spirited and sometimes mean-spirited, but it never developed into the high theater that it was anticipated to be. As Dallas newspaper columnist Steve Blow put it, rather than a clash of titans, "it turned into a duel with squirt guns." In the early stages, Hutchison picked a fight with Perry on an important state issue: whether to impose tolls on Texas's interstate highways. Perry had proposed a toll-financed "Trans-Texas Corridor" paralleling Interstate 35 from Laredo to Dallas-Fort Worth. Hutchinson called it a "quest to cover our state with massive toll roads." But beyond that, she was unable to capitalize on issues where Perry was vulnerable, such as the state's jobless rate, which was at its highest since the 1980s, and its soaring insurance rates, utility costs and school dropout rates. While Texas voters told pollsters they were dissatisfied with the direction of the country, a majority expressed the belief that the state itself was on the right track. Hutchison was also hurt by her indecisiveness about whether or not she would keep her Senate seat during the campaign.

Perry's campaign portrayed Hutchison as a captive of Washington, hammering her for her vote in favor of the federal government's $700 billion rescue of the financial services industry in 2008. His campaign dubbed her "Kay Bailout." At the same time, the governor made a play for voters angry at President Barack Obama's government activism, attending events of tea party activists and winking at the notion of Texas seceding from the United States. Attributes that normally should have helped Hutchison, especially her work bringing home federal money and keeping open Texas military installations, were of little use in a hostile, anti-Washington political climate. Perry won with a large enough share of the vote in the March 2, 2010 primary—51%—to deny Hutchison a second shot at him in a runoff. She posted just 30%. Conservative activist Debra Medina, who tried to appeal to tea party voters, got 19%, and was probably hurt by campaign remarks sympathizing with fringe theories that Bush administration officials played a role in the September 11 attacks.

Once back in Washington, Hutchison dodged media inquiries about whether she intended to give up her seat, but ended up deciding to stay, at least until her current term ends in January 2013. Hutchison was re-elected 65%-32% in 2000, carrying 237 of 254 counties, and 62%-36% in 2006, carrying 238 of the counties. She has run about even in the heavily Democratic border counties, and her losses in Austin's Travis County have been offset by her margins in suburban Williamson County just to the north.

Hutchison has been an impressively productive senator on the legislative front, both in the majority and out, and especially in behalf of her state. In 2006, she worked successfully on a bill that sealed her popularity at home: a measure allowing taxpayers in Texas and other states with no state income taxes to continue to be able to deduct state sales taxes from their federal income taxes. She also supported the 2001 Bush tax cut and advanced her own version that included a homemakers' Individual Retirement Account.

On the Commerce committee, Hutchison has been an influential player on Internet and transportation issues. She has been willing to work with Democratic Chairman Jay Rockefeller of West Virginia on ambitious proposals to make broadband more accessible nationally, especially in poorer and rural parts of the country. But Hutchison is also a strong advocate for the Republican point of view on the committee, and has picked a number of battles with Obama's Federal Communications Commission chairman, Julius Genachowski. In 2009, Hutchison fought his proposal to toughen the agency's "network neutrality" guidelines, which are aimed at preventing large telephone and cable operators from discriminating against some kinds of content on their broadband networks. Hutchison and other Republicans generally prefer to let the marketplace resolve such issues and contend that regulation will stifle the robust growth in the broadband market. In February 2011, she and other Republicans introduced a resolution to halt the FCC's net neutrality rules, but it was unlikely to pass in the Democratically controlled Senate or to be signed by the president.

Hutchison rose to the top minority slot on the Commerce panel in 2008. Before that, she had been the senior Republican on the Aviation Subcommittee. With Democratic Chairman Rockefeller, she strongly supported federalization of airport security after September 11. Also with Rockefeller, she sought to add funding for upgrading the air traffic control system to the 2009 economic stimulus bill. She also had a hand in the repeal of the Wright amendment, which barred many interstate flights from Dallas's Love Field, the home base of Southwest Airlines. She has been a longtime supporter of the Amtrak system and has fought repeated attempts to slash its funding. Having grown up near what is now the Johnson Space Center, Hutchison is also a strong supporter of the manned space program.

On foreign policy, Hutchison was mostly supportive of the Bush administration's policies in Iraq, including the 2007 troop surge. She echoed the views of many congressional Republicans when she said, "It is critical that the initiative be given a chance to succeed. I respect the president for admitting mistakes, correcting the course."

In other recent legislative battles, Hutchison withdrew her support of immigration legislation in 2007 after the Senate rejected 53-45 her so-called "touch back" amendment, which required illegal immigrants who wished to stay in the United States to return first to their countries of origin. Also in 2007, she backed the DREAM Act, which would allow high school graduates and military volunteers who had illegally immigrated as children with their parents to become citizens. But she voted against the bill when Democrats brought it back up in December 2010. She said the bill had grown in scope since the first one, but some observers blamed her change of heart (and that of other Senate Republicans) on the conservative backlash against illegal immigrants since 2007.

In 2008, Hutchison filed a brief in support of a challenge to the D.C.'s ban on gun ownership. The U.S. Supreme Court came down on her side, ruling that the city's gun ban violated the Second Amendment. On another legal issue, she supported the Democrats' bill extending the statute of limitations on court cases involving gender pay discrimination, though she sought unsuccessfully to put a higher burden of proof on plaintiffs.

In 2011, Hutchison focused on trying to block spending to implement Obama's 2010 health care law, though the effort was unlikely to succeed. When she announced her retirement decision, *The Dallas Morning News* lauded her record in an editorial, crediting Hutchison with helping to improve math and science education in Texas, to build veterans hospitals, to improve living conditions in the colonias on the Mexican border, among other accomplishments. "Hutchison has helped resolve many problems that have challenged Texas," the newspaper said, and encouraged her eventual successor to follow her lead.

Junior Senator

John Cornyn (R)

Elected 2002, term expires 2014, 2nd term; b. Feb. 2, 1952, Houston; home, San Antonio; Trinity U., B.A. 1973, St. Mary's Law Schl., J.D. 1977, U. of VA, L.L.M. 1995; Church of Christ; married (Sandy); 2 children.

Elected Office: San Antonio dist. ct. judge, 1984-90; TX Sup. Ct., 1990-97; TX atty. gen., 1998-2002.

Professional Career: Practicing atty., 1977-84.

DC Office: 517 HSOB, 20510, 202-224-2934; Fax: 202-228-2856; Web site: cornyn.senate.gov.

State Offices: Austin, 512-469-6034; Dallas, 972-239-1310; Harlingen, 956-423-0162; Houston, 713-572-3337; Lubbock, 806-472-7533; San Antonio, 210-224-7485; Tyler, 903-593-0902.

Committees: *Armed Services:* Emerging Threats & Capabilities; Readiness & Management Support; Strategic Forces. *Budget. Finance:* Energy, Natural Resources & Infrastructure (RMM); Health Care; Taxation & IRS Oversight. *Judiciary:* Antitrust, Competition Policy & Consumer Rights; Constitution, Civil Rights & Human Rights; Immigration, Refugees & Border Security (RMM).

Group Ratings

	ACLU	ACU	ADA	CFG	AFS	FRC	LCV	ITIC	NTU	COC
2010	7	100	0	97	2	95	0	67	99	100
2009	–	100	5	95	0	–	0	–	89	71

National Journal Ratings

	2010 LIB — 2010 CONS		2009 LIB — 2009 CONS	
Economic	0%	87%	6%	91%
Social	0%	79%	21%	78%
Foreign	0%	72%	0%	84%
Composite	10%	90%	12%	88%

Key Votes of the 111th Congress

1. Overturn Ledbetter	N	5. Pass health care bill	N	9. Ratify New START	N
2. Pass $787 billion stimulus	N	6. Regulate financial firms	N	10. Confirm Elena Kagan	N
3. Repeal DC gun laws	Y	7. Pass tax cuts for some	N	11. Stop EPA climate regs	Y
4. Confirm Sonia Sotomayor	N	8. Legalize immigrants' kids	N	12. Repeal don't ask, tell	N

Election Results

2008 general	John Cornyn (R)	4,337,469	(55%)	($19,326,337)
	Richard Noriega (D)	3,389,365	(43%)	($4,116,286)
	Yvonne Schick (Lib)	185,241	(2%)	
2008 primary	John Cornyn (R)	997,216	(81%)	
	Larry Kilgore (R)	226,649	(19%)	

Prior Winning Percentages: 2002 (55%)

John Cornyn, a Republican, was elected to the Senate in 2002 and re-elected in 2008. He is a member of the minority leadership as the chairman of the National Republican Senatorial Committee.

Cornyn was born in Houston and spent much of his childhood in San Antonio. His father was an oral pathologist in the Air Force stationed in Japan, where Cornyn went to high school. After his father retired from the service, the family settled in San Antonio. Cornyn graduated from Trinity University and St. Mary's University School of Law, both in San Antonio, in the 1970s. He practiced law for five years with a firm that defended doctors and insurance companies in medical malpractice cases. In 1984, he ran for district court judge on the Republican ticket in Bexar County and, at age 32, upset a strong favorite in the race. In 1990, Cornyn was elected to the state Supreme Court. In 1995, he wrote a 5-4 decision upholding the "Robin Hood" school finance system, in which property-wealthy school districts had to send money to property-poor districts.

In 1997, he resigned from the court to run for attorney general, defeating two better-known opponents in the Republican primary. In the general election, he faced a grizzled veteran of Texas politics, Jim Mattox, a populist Democrat, a former U.S. House member from Dallas and the second-place finisher to Ann Richards in the 1990 runoff for Texas governor. Cornyn won 54%-44%, becoming the first Republican attorney general in Texas since Reconstruction. He argued two cases before the U. S. Supreme Court, including the Santa Fe Independent School District's defense of reading the Lord's Prayer at football games. (The high court nixed it.)

When Sen. Phil Gramm announced that he would not seek re-election in 2002, Cornyn got into the contest to succeed him. He had no serious opposition in the Republican primary. Democrats nominated Dallas Mayor Ron Kirk, the son of the first black mailman in Austin, a teacher and former aide to Sen. Lloyd Bentsen. He had been elected mayor of Dallas in 1995, and re-elected in 1999 by a wide margin. In the primary, he overcame challenges from former U.S. Rep. Ken Bentsen of Houston, the senator's nephew, and Victor Morales, a track coach from suburban Dallas who had been the Democratic nominee against Gramm in 1996. Morales finished just narrowly ahead of Kirk in the first round of balloting. Kirk was endorsed by Bentsen and won the runoff, 60%-40%.

In the general election, Cornyn ran as a supporter of President George W. Bush. He called for making Bush's 2001 tax cuts permanent, for extending the research and development tax credit, and for raising Texas' share of gas tax funds from 90.5 cents to 95 cents of each dollar of gas tax revenues. He supported government vouchers for private school tuition, individual investment accounts as part of Social Security and color-blind standards for college and university admissions. Kirk took opposite stands on most issues, but portrayed himself as a moderate Democrat who would support Bush on many issues.

Republicans ran ads linking him to Hillary Rodham Clinton, then a New York senator, and liberal out-of-state contributors. Kirk campaigned with a sense of humor and considerable charm, making fun of his bald pate and answering, when asked whether he owned a gun, "I have a wife and two little girls. You figure it out." But he made some mistakes. He opposed the nomination to a federal judgeship of Texas Supreme Court Justice Priscilla Owen, something Republicans seized on in ads. He refused to disclose his income tax returns, except for allowing reporters one peek at his 2001 return. Cornyn came out in favor of a bill in the Texas legislature requiring district attorneys to seek the death penalty for killers of law enforcement officials after the Austin-based district attorney had not sought the death penalty for the killer of a Travis County sheriff's deputy. Kirk said Cornyn was acting like he was running for district attorney, and then apologized to a convention of law enforcement officials a few days later. Meanwhile, Cornyn met with the deputy's widow. In the high-spending contest, Kirk spent $8.9 million to Cornyn's $9.5 million.

Texas Democrats considered their 2002 ticket of Kirk for senator and Tony Sanchez for governor the "Dream Team," and hoped it would draw a large turnout of African-Americans and Hispanics. Meanwhile, Republicans quietly registered thousands of new voters in the heavily Republican and fast-growing suburban counties around Dallas-Fort Worth, Houston, San Antonio and Austin. Polls showed the race close in the spring. Democrats operated on the assumption that Kirk had to win 85% of blacks, 65% of Hispanics and 35% of whites to win. He clearly achieved the first and probably achieved the second of those goals, but failed by a solid margin to achieve the third. Cornyn won 55%-43%—almost the same percentages as in his race for attorney general in 1998 and a fair reflection of basic party identification in Texas in recent years. Kirk carried historically Republican Dallas County 50%-49%. But Cornyn carried the entire Dallas-Fort Worth Metroplex, 58%-41%. Cornyn also won metro Houston, 55%-43%, and the combined San Antonio and Austin metro areas, 51%-47%. The border went 69%-29% for Kirk, a 148,000-vote margin. But rural and small-town Texas went 62%-37% for Cornyn. He won the seat that dates to Sam Houston, who won it shortly after Texas was annexed in 1845; it was later occupied by Lyndon Johnson and John Tower. Cornyn is also the first Texas senator to come from San Antonio, once the state's largest city.

In his first term, Cornyn chaired the Judiciary Committee's Constitution Subcommittee. He was a lead sponsor of a proposed constitutional amendment to ban same-sex marriage, which got less than 50 votes. He also supported amendments to expand the rights of crime victims and to overturn a federal court's decision banning the phrase "one nation under God" in the Pledge of Allegiance. He cosponsored the class action and bankruptcy bills opposed by trial lawyers but passed by the Senate and signed by Bush in 2005. He also took a lead role in seeking to confirm Bush appellate court appointees. Cornyn was initially critical of the "Gang of 14," a bipartisan group of senators who ultimately succeeded in hammering out a compromise on the explosive issue of changing Senate rules to stop filibusters. He later said, "In retrospect, I have to concede they actually broke the logjam that allowed us to get some very good people confirmed."

In more recent confirmation battles on the committee, Cornyn in May 2009 said it was "terrible" for former Republican House Speaker Newt Gingrich to characterize Supreme Court nominee Sonia Sotomayor's self-description, "wise Latina," as racist, but he voted against her confirmation in July, as he did against the nomination of Elena Kagan in 2010.

In a split with the Bush administration in 2007, Cornyn criticized Attorney General Alberto Gonzales for his handling of the firings of U.S. attorneys. He worked on a bipartisan basis with

Democratic Chairman Patrick Leahy of Vermont on strengthening the Freedom of Information Act, which guarantees the public the right to view public documents. He and Minnesota Democrat Amy Klobuchar collaborated successfully in August 2010 on a bill to create take-back programs to collect prescription medicines that would be run by the government and private firms.

One of Cornyn's first successful bills reduced, from three years to one year, the waiting period for citizenship for legal immigrants serving in the armed forces. He has opposed military patrols of the border and the building of a fence along most of its length, which he says would disrupt life in South Texas. In 2006, he voted for the 700-mile border fence pushed by House Republicans, though he questioned whether it would be a "practical use" of federal money. In spring 2007, as Republicans and Democrats in the Senate tried to negotiate an immigration bill, Cornyn took part in the talks but skipped the unveiling of the final bill. Arizona Republican John McCain angrily accused him of raising arcane legal issues to scuttle the bill. Cornyn said of the talks, "I didn't so much walk away as got chased away." His amendment to bar illegal immigrants convicted of identity theft from legalization processes was defeated 51-46. From then on, he opposed the larger immigration bill.

In 2010, as some conservatives called for abolishing the 14th Amendment's birthright citizenship, Cornyn was cool to the idea. He told the Associated Press that hearings on the issue would be "going after a symptom rather than the cause of the problem" of illegal immigration, and that he would rather emphasize getting the federal government to do a better job securing the border and enforcing immigration laws.

On the hot topic of earmarks in recent years, Cornyn supported the Republicans' 2010 ban on the special spending provisions. Democrats sought to embarrass him and other Republicans by including their earlier earmark requests in an omnibus appropriations bill. He has sponsored bills to compensate county governments for the cost of levee replacements in the Rio Grande Valley and to protect Texas citrus farmers against citrus greening disease, after it decimated 100,000 acres in Florida.

Cornyn began his campaign for re-election in 2008 with polls showing he was less popular than fellow Republican Kay Bailey Hutchison of Texas. But Democratic attempts to attract a well-known challenger failed. Their nominee was Houston state Rep. Rick Noriega, who had served with the Texas Army National Guard in Afghanistan. He set a goal of raising $10 million, but ultimately raised $4 million to Cornyn's $16.5 million. Polls consistently showed Cornyn ahead, and neither national party invested in the contest. Cornyn won 55%-43%, the same margin as in 2002. He won 36% of the Hispanic vote, an improvement over 2002. He carried 223 of the state's 254 counties, running behind only in the Rio Grande Valley and in the counties with the central cities of Houston, Dallas, Austin and San Antonio.

Cornyn had a major role in the Republican leadership in 2010 as chairman of the NRSC, the main political arm of the Senate GOP. Democrats had gained 14 Senate seats in the 2006 and 2008 campaign cycles, when their Senate campaign committee was headed by Chuck Schumer of New York; Cornyn wanted to reverse those results. Cornyn adopted Schumer's strategy of recruiting candidates who could win in states not naturally inclined to his party. He urged Gov. Charlie Crist to run in Florida and Rep. Mike Castle to run in Delaware. He opposed the candidacy of former Rep. Pat Toomey, who announced he was running again in Pennsylvania against Arlen Specter, who had won their 2004 primary by only 51%-49%. But as the tea party movement gained strength and opposition to Obama administration programs grew, conservatives criticized his treatment of Toomey, a staunch conservative. In April 2009, Specter announced he was switching parties, leaving Cornyn in the embarrassing position of having to support Toomey, now the obvious Republican nominee. Toomey went on to win the seat. In Florida, former state House Speaker Marco Rubio remained in the Republican race against Crist, Cornyn's chosen candidate, and Rubio proceeded to win endorsements from conservative groups and dozens of county Republican parties despite the governor's high job ratings.

Despite these setbacks, Cornyn succeeded in the chairman's major duty: raising large sums for the candidates. He brought in $115 million for the season, and came close to matching the $130 million raised for the 2010 election by the rival Democratic Senatorial Campaign Committee. In states carried by President Barack Obama in 2008, Cornyn recruited serious candidates like Dino Rossi in Washington and saw promising newcomers emerge, like Ron Johnson in Wisconsin. Cornyn managed to surf the conservative tide when it gained strength. When Crist fell behind Rubio in polls, Cornyn urged him not to leave the party; when he did, the NRSC backed Rubio. When Joe Miller upset Lisa Murkowski in the August primary in Alaska, the NRSC supported Miller against Murkowski's ultimately successful write-in campaign. When Christine O'Donnell upset Mike Castle in the September primary in Delaware, Cornyn sent in the technical maximum of $42,000 and then left her on her own, correctly calculating that she had no chance of making it a close race. Republicans ended up gaining six seats, many more than seemed likely in January 2009, when insiders were predicting further Democratic gains. O'Donnell lost in Delaware, where Castle would almost certainly have won. Sharron Angle lost in Nevada, and Ken Buck lost narrowly in Colorado.

After the election, Cornyn got another term as NRSC chairman for the 2012 contests without serious opposition. Plainly irritated by South Carolina Republican Jim DeMint's endorsements of candidates whose chances he thought dim in 2010, notably Angle and O'Donnell, he urged colleagues to bring concerns they had about candidates to him. DeMint pledged not to oppose any incumbent Republican senators, a pledge probably relevant to Olympia Snowe of Maine, Richard Lugar of Indiana and Orrin Hatch of Utah, who faced the possibility of conservative primary opponents in 2012. Cornyn in turn made it plain that he would be more wary of taking sides in primaries, as he did in the Pennsylvania contest. Hutchison has announced her retirement in 2012 and Cornyn will presumably stay neutral in what could be the first multi-candidate Republican primary for Senate in Texas since 1984.

Cornyn will be up for re-election himself in 2014. In February 2011, when Republican Whip Jon Kyl of Arizona announced that he would retire at the end of his term in 2012, Cornyn announced that he would run for whip. Lamar Alexander of Tennessee also said he would run, and they agreed to refrain from campaigning among colleagues for the secret ballot contest until summer 2012.

FIRST DISTRICT

Louie Gohmert (R)

Elected 2004, 4th term; b. Aug. 18, 1953, Pittsburg; home, Tyler; TX A&M U., B.A. 1975, Baylor U. Law Schl., J.D. 1977; Baptist; married (Kathy); 3 children.

Military Career: Army, 1978-82.

Elected Office: Smith Cnty. Dist. Ct. judge, 1992-2002.

Professional Career: Practicing atty., 1982-92; Chief justice, TX 12th Ct. of Appeals, 2002-03.

DC Office: 2440 RHOB, 20515, 202-225-3035; Fax: 202-226-1230; Web site: gohmert.house.gov.

State Offices: Longview, 903-236-8597; Lufkin, 936-632-3180; Marshall, 903-938-8386; Nacogdoches, 936-715-9514; Tyler, 903-561-6349.

Committees: *Judiciary:* Crime, Terrorism & Homeland Security (VChmn); Immigration Policy & Enforcement. *Natural Resources:* Energy & Mineral Resources; Water & Power.

Group Ratings

	ACLU	ACU	ADA	CFG	AFS	FRC	LCV	ITIC	NTU	COC
2010	13	96	5	92	0	100	10	0	89	75
2009	–	100	0	97	0	–	0	–	91	79

National Journal Ratings

	2010 LIB	—	2010 CONS	2009 LIB	—	2009 CONS
Economic	21%	—	78%	11%	—	89%
Social	0%	—	85%	0%	—	93%
Foreign	0%	—	88%	0%	—	75%
Composite	12%	—	88%	9%	—	91%

Key Votes of the 111th Congress

1. Overturn Ledbetter	N	5. Bar federal abortion funds	Y	9. Stop detainee transfers	Y
2. Pass $820 billion stimulus	N	6. Pass health care bill	N	10. Legalize immigrants' kids	N
3. Let guns in national parks	Y	7. Regulate financial firms	N	11. Repeal don't ask, tell	N
4. Pass cap-and-trade	N	8. Pass tax cuts for some	N	12. Limit campaign funds	N

Election Results

2010 general	Louie Gohmert (R)	129,398	(90%)	($793,679)
	Charles Parkes (Lib)	14,811	(10%)	
2010 primary	Louie Gohmert (R)	unopposed		

Prior Winning Percentages: 2008 (88%), 2006 (68%), 2004 (61%)

Population		Race/Ethnicity		Work	
Pop. 2010:	723,464	White:	64.8%	Private:	79.6%
Change since 2000:	Up 11.0%	Black:	17.5%	Government:	13.0%
Urban:	50.9%	Hispanic:	15.1%	Self-employed:	7.1%
Rural:	49.1%	Asian:	0.9%	Blue collar:	28.8%
Area size:	8,917 sq. mi.	Native Am.:	0.4%	White collar:	52.8%
		Hawaiian:	0.0%	Khaki collar:	0.0%
Age		Two+ races:	1.2%	Other:	18.3%
Median age:	36.2 yrs.				
More than 65 yrs:	14.3%	*Ancestry*		Median income:	$41,426
Less than 18 yrs:	25.5%	Irish	10.9%	Median Home Value:	$95,800
		USA	10.0%		
Education		English	9.3%	**Military Veterans**	
H.S. grad:	81.8%			% of Pop:	10.7%
College grad:	18.9%				
Grad degree:	5.9%				

East Texas; Tyler, Longview

The gently rolling land of East Texas was settled by Tennessee farmers in the years before the Civil War. It sits at the western edge of Scots-Irish America, a swath of land that starts in the Appalachian ridge and is inhabited by a combative, honor-bound and highly religious populace. A hundred years ago, this was one of the poorest parts of America, where farmers scratched a living off the land and hoped for good weather and good prices in the marketplace. When a peach

2008 Presidential Vote		
John McCain (R)	184,560	(69%)
Barack Obama (D)	81,749	(31%)
2004 Presidential Vote		
George Bush (R)	178,409	(69%)
John Kerry (D)	78,609	(31%)
Cook Partisan Voting Index: R+21		

blight in the early 20th century wiped out much of the local fruit industry, many farmers turned to growing roses, which proved ideally suited to the climate and soil of the area. By the 1940s, more than half the nation's rose bushes were grown within 10 miles of Tyler, which has become known for its annual Texas Rose Festival and the East Texas State Fair. Longview, which in the 1870s was the western terminus of the Southern Pacific Railroad, became a trading center for wagon trains and local cotton growers and timber cutters. In 1943, the Big Inch pipeline began sending millions of barrels of crude oil from the "Black Giant" oil field near Longview—the largest ever in the state—to the East for refining.

Since then, the Longview area has become an industrial center for earth-moving equipment and chemicals. A giant U.S. Steel pipe plant has been a mainstay in the community since the 1950s. In April 2009, the company idled the plant and fired most of its workforce. But as demand returned, production resumed in 2010. Eastman Chemical Co. also recently announced an expansion at its Longview site. Marshall was the hometown of the late Lady Bird Johnson. The fields and woodlands around Nacogdoches—the oldest city in Texas—have the distinction as the site where debris from the Space Shuttle Columbia fell in February 2003. An organized search by 25,000 people recovered more than 84,000 pieces—38% of the shuttle.

The 1st Congressional District of Texas, covering the heart of East Texas, is made up of 12 counties, the most populous being Tyler's Smith County and Longview's Gregg County. East Texas is ancestrally Democratic, a region that responded to the populist rhetoric of presidential candidate William Jennings Bryan in the 1890s and President Franklin D. Roosevelt in the 1930s and 1940s. But Republicans began making inroads in Tyler and Longview in the 1950s, and the GOP eventually gained dominance in the region. When Republican George H.W. Bush ran for the Senate against Democratic Sen. Lloyd Bentsen in 1970, East Texas was solidly Democratic. (Bentsen won.) By the time Republican George W. Bush ran for re-election as governor in 1998, it was solidly Republican.

Still, Democrats held onto the district until the 2003 redistricting, masterminded by former House Majority Leader Tom DeLay of Texas to give the GOP a strong advantage. Heavily Republican Smith and Gregg counties were added to the district. In 2008, Republican John McCain carried the district with 69% of the vote. GOP Gov. Rick Perry won at least 55% in each of the district's counties in his 2010 re-election, drawing 69% in Smith County and 68% in Gregg.

Louie Gohmert (R)

The congressman from the 1st District is Louie Gohmert, a Republican first elected in 2004. Gohmert *(GO-mert)* grew up in Mount Pleasant and got an Army scholarship at Texas A&M University, where he was class president. He went on get a law degree from Baylor University, and then served as a captain in the Army. He practiced law in Tyler and spent a decade as a district court judge. Republican Gov. Rick Perry named him chief justice of the Texas Appellate Court in 2002. He earned a reputation as a tough law-and-order judge with a knack for attracting attention. In 1996, he ordered an HIV-positive convicted car thief, as a condition of probation, to notify future sexual partners of his HIV status and to obtain written consent from them before engaging in sexual activity.

After the 2003 redistricting, Gohmert was one of six Republicans who got into the primary to challenge four-term Democratic Rep. Max Sandlin, who had a moderate voting record but was a close ally of liberal Democratic Minority Leader Nancy Pelosi. Gohmert led in the primary with 42% of the vote to 30% for lawyer John Graves. In the month-long runoff campaign, few differences separated the two conservatives. Gohmert prevailed 57%-43%. Graves carried nine of the 13 counties, but Gohmert won 77% of the vote in his home base of Smith County, where half the votes were cast.

In the general election, Gohmert linked Sandlin to the national Democratic Party and their 2004 presidential nominee, John Kerry. He frequently mentioned his strong support for President George W. Bush, while Sandlin criticized Gohmert for his support from DeLay. The result wasn't close. Gohmert beat Sandlin, 61%-38%, with 79% in Smith County and 64% in Gregg County.

In the House, Gohmert established a conservative voting record, with occasional dissents from the party line. In December 2009, he opposed a House-passed bill to permanently extend the estate tax at its 2009 level, saying, "Jesus never advocated the government go steal." When the bailout for the financial industry came to the House floor in 2008, he made a motion to adjourn the chamber "so we don't do this terrible thing to our nation." It was defeated 394-8.

Gohmert's legislative work has been mostly on the Judiciary Committee, where he often draws television talk show invitations and scorn from liberal blogs for his provocative views. He drew widespread attention for his appearance on Anderson Cooper's CNN show in August 2010 to discuss "terror babies"—an alleged effort to send pregnant women into the United States to give birth to children eligible for U.S. passports who could be trained to carry out attacks. Cooper pressed Gohmert to offer proof. "Had somebody done this in your courtroom, you would have asked for evidence, and you have none," Cooper said. An irate Gohmert replied: "This isn't a courtroom. We're trying to protect America."

After the assassination attempt on Arizona Rep. Gabrielle Giffords in January 2011, Gohmert called for allowing members of Congress to carry concealed weapons in the District of Columbia, which has strict gun control laws. Two months later, when a conservative website published footage of protesters at a Common Cause rally calling for the lynching of conservative Supreme Court members, he asked Attorney General Eric Holder to explore whether the group should lose its nonprofit status. He drew fury from Jewish members of Congress when, during a 2007 debate on a bill prohibiting hiring discrimination in government-funded charitable organizations, he argued that religious groups should be allowed to hire employees of their own faith, otherwise, he said, Jewish organizations would be forced to hire Nazis.

Gohmert has been re-elected easily. But his knack for stirring controversy may be a concern for GOP leaders. When House Republicans selected Judiciary subcommittee chairmen in January 2011, they removed Gohmert from his post as the ranking Republican on the crime and terrorism panel in favor of former Judiciary chairman James Sensenbrenner, R-Wis. He also lost a challenge to Ohio's Jim Jordan for the chairmanship of the Republican Study Committee, the caucus of House conservatives.

SECOND DISTRICT

Ted Poe (R)

Elected 2004, 4th term; b. Sept. 10, 1948, Temple; home, Humble; Abilene Christian U., B.A. 1970, U. of Houston, J.D. 1973; Church of Christ; married (Carol).

Military Career: Air Force Reserve, 1970-76.

Elected Office: Harris Cnty. judge, 1981-2003.

Professional Career: Asst. dist. atty., 1973-81.

DC Office: 430 CHOB, 20515, 202-225-6565; Fax: 202-225-5547; Web site: poe.house.gov.

State Offices: Beaumont, 409-212-1997; Kingwood, 281-446-0242.

Committees: *Foreign Affairs:* Europe and Eurasia; Oversight & Investigations (VChmn); Terrorism, Nonproliferation & Trade. *Judiciary:* Crime, Terrorism & Homeland Security; Immigration Policy & Enforcement; Intellectual Property, Competition & the Internet.

Group Ratings

	ACLU	ACU	ADA	CFG	AFS	FRC	LCV	ITIC	NTU	COC
2010	13	100	5	98	0	100	10	0	89	75
2009	–	92	5	90	11	–	0	–	87	73

National Journal Ratings

	2010 LIB	—	2010 CONS	2009 LIB	—	2009 CONS
Economic	6%	—	94%	17%	—	82%
Social	0%	—	85%	18%	—	81%
Foreign	0%	—	88%	0%	—	75%
Composite	7%	—	94%	16%	—	84%

Key Votes of the 111th Congress

1. Overturn Ledbetter	N	5. Bar federal abortion funds	Y	9. Stop detainee transfers	Y
2. Pass $820 billion stimulus	N	6. Pass health care bill	N	10. Legalize immigrants' kids	N
3. Let guns in national parks	Y	7. Regulate financial firms	N	11. Repeal don't ask, tell	N
4. Pass cap-and-trade	N	8. Pass tax cuts for some	N	12. Limit campaign funds	N

Election Results

2010 general	Ted Poe (R)	130,020	(89%)	($876,075)
	David Smith (Lib)	16,711	(11%)	
2010 primary	Ted Poe (R)	unopposed		

Prior Winning Percentages: 2008 (89%), 2006 (66%), 2004 (56%)

Population		Race/Ethnicity		Work	
Pop. 2010:	782,375	White:	51.1%	Private:	80.6%
Change since 2000:	Up 20.1%	Black:	21.2%	Government:	13.5%
Urban:	89.5%	Hispanic:	22.5%	Self-employed:	5.8%
Rural:	10.5%	Asian:	3.3%	Blue collar:	23.8%
Area size:	2,181 sq. mi.	Native Am.:	0.3%	White collar:	61.0%
		Hawaiian:	0.1%	Khaki collar:	0.1%
Age		Two+ races:	1.3%	Other:	15.1%
Median age:	34.3 yrs.				
More than 65 yrs:	9.9%	*Ancestry*		Median income:	$57,939
Less than 18 yrs:	27.3%	German	9.8%	Median Home Value:	$123,500
		Irish	7.6%		
Education		English	6.8%	**Military Veterans**	
H.S. grad:	84.8%			% of Pop:	9.6%
College grad:	24.1%				
Grad degree:	7.2%				

East Texas; Beaumont

The spongy land of the Texas Gulf Coast, where French explorer Robert de La Salle and Spanish conquistador Bernardo de Galvez dreamed of thriving settlements, remained mostly unsettled until well into the 19th century. When oil was found at the Spindletop field near Beaumont in 1901, the area all around it boomed, first with oil exploration, then petroleum refining, and then petrochemical production. The rig workers and mechanical engineers they attracted have given a kind of permanent roughneck air to the region, and it's the one of the few places in Texas where unions have any strength. The Humble oil field was once the largest in Texas and the local Humble Oil and Refining Company is now known as Exxon. But oil drilling has declined in this area. By the mid-2000s, annual production in East Texas from the Red River to the Gulf of Mexico fell by half. Hurricanes Gustav and Ike in 2008 shut down oil pipelines for months and toppled some platforms, but some local refineries have been expanding and adding jobs thanks to high oil prices in recent years.

2008 Presidential Vote		
John McCain (R)	159,165	(60%)
Barack Obama (D)	105,745	(40%)

2004 Presidential Vote		
George Bush (R)	160,365	(63%)
John Kerry (D)	92,842	(37%)
Cook Partisan Voting Index: R+13		

The 2nd Congressional District of Texas occupies much of this territory. About half of its people live in and around the highly polluted "Golden Triangle" industrial area that includes Beaumont and Port Arthur. Of the two, Port Arthur suffered more during the recession, with unemployment rates through 2010 in excess of 14%, one of the highest in the state. The BP oil spill disaster and subsequent offshore drilling moratorium hurt not only that industry but the local shrimping economy as well.

These cities increasingly are in the shadow of Houston, and the majority of the people in the district live in the city's north and east suburbs in Harris County, where oil is an important part of the local economy but hardly all of it. The district grew 20% from 2000 to 2010, largely because of minorities: The African-American population has increased to 21% and Hispanics are now 23% of the district's population. In 2008, Republican John McCain got 60% of the vote in the district.

Ted Poe (R)

The congressman from the 2nd District is Ted Poe, a Republican first elected in 2004 who is best known for his loquaciousness on the House floor. In the 111th Congress (2009-10), according to C-SPAN, he spoke on 234 of the 317 days that the chamber was in session—far ahead of second-place finisher Sheila Jackson Lee, D-Texas. "The people of Southeast Texas can't come up here and do it, so I speak for them," Poe told *The Houston Chronicle*.

A sixth-generation Texan, Poe got a bachelor's degree from Abilene Christian University and enlisted in the Air Force Reserves. He received his law degree from the University of Houston and became a prosecutor in Harris County where, he boasts, he never lost a jury trial. Poe then became a district court judge in the county, becoming a judicial celebrity during his 22 years on the bench for meting out humiliating "Poe-tic justice" punishments to criminals. He required murderers to hang pictures of their victims in their prison cells and ordered drunken drivers and shoplifters to stand at the entrances to taverns and stores carrying signs publicizing their offenses. He also gained national recognition as a legal commentator on national television.

In 2003, Poe stepped down as a judge to run for Congress. In a six-candidate Republican primary, Poe's high name recognition and bench experience earned him 61% of the vote and the right to challenge Democratic Rep. Nick Lampson. The incumbent was running in largely unfamiliar territory due to the 2003 Republican-engineered redistricting of congressional boundaries in the state. Lampson had a moderate voting record, a low-key style and was a big booster of NASA. At first, it was not clear whether Poe would be able to capitalize on the favorable redistricting. National Republicans fretted about his fundraising and his seemingly complacent campaign. Lampson outspent Poe nearly 2-to-1. But on Election Day, the new district's solid Republican bent was decisive. Lampson led 68%-31% in Jefferson County, the area he had previously represented and where 36% of votes were cast. But Poe won 70%-28% in Harris County, where 58% of the votes were cast. Overall, Poe won 56%-43%. He has not been seriously challenged for re-election.

In the House, Poe began with a relatively moderate voting record for a Republican from Texas, but has become a more loyal party vote since President Barack Obama took office. He was the House's 12th most conservative member in 2010, according to *National Journal's* rankings. He joined fellow Texas Republicans John Carter and Joe Barton in amending a temporary House-passed spending bill in January 2011 to prevent the Environmental Protection Agency from regulating greenhouse gas emissions. A month earlier, he refused to support the tax-cut deal that Obama struck with Republicans, saying it did not go far enough in reducing spending. For the same reason, he opposed a compromise that Obama struck with Republicans on the fiscal 2011 budget.

Poe has been a leader of the Immigration Reform Caucus, where he sought tighter enforcement at the border with Mexico. He introduced a bill in 2010 requiring the Pentagon to make National Guard troops available to states on request for border duty. He successfully lobbied President George W. Bush to commute the prison terms of two border agents who were convicted for wounding a drug smuggler. He also has been active on victim's rights, something he said stems partly from his maternal grandfather's death at the hands of a drunk driver.

Poe typically ends speeches on the House floor with his trademark, "And that's just the way it is." But he has also drawn negative attention for some of his remarks. In a February 2011 speech decrying foreign aid to Venezuela and other nations, he said that "we give money to (anti-American dictator Hugo) Chavez." The fact-checking website *PolitiFact* labeled the statement false, noting that the $5 million given to the country in 2010 went to outside organizations monitoring the government's performance.

THIRD DISTRICT

Sam Johnson (R)

Elected May 1991, 10th full term; b. Oct. 11, 1930, San Antonio; home, Dallas; S. Methodist U., B.B.A. 1951, George Washington U., M.S. 1974; Methodist; married (Shirley); 3 children.

Military Career: Air Force, 1950–79 (Korea & Vietnam).

Elected Office: TX House of Reps., 1984–91.

Professional Career: Home builder.

DC Office: 1211 LHOB, 20515, 202-225-4201; Fax: 202-225-1485; Web site: samjohnson.house.gov.

State Offices: Richardson, 972-470-0892.

Committees: *Joint Committee on Taxation. Ways & Means:* Health; Social Security (Chmn).

Group Ratings

	ACLU	ACU	ADA	CFG	AFS	FRC	LCV	ITIC	NTU	COC
2010	13	100	0	97	0	87	0	33	92	100
2009	–	100	0	97	0	–	0	–	92	79

National Journal Ratings

	2010 LIB	—	2010 CONS	2009 LIB	—	2009 CONS
Economic	0%	—	97%	0%	—	96%
Social	0%	—	85%	17%	—	82%
Foreign	0%	—	88%	0%	—	75%
Composite	5%	—	95%	11%	—	89%

Key Votes of the 111th Congress

1. Overturn Ledbetter	N	5. Bar federal abortion funds	Y	9. Stop detainee transfers	Y
2. Pass $820 billion stimulus	N	6. Pass health care bill	N	10. Legalize immigrants' kids	N
3. Let guns in national parks	Y	7. Regulate financial firms	N	11. Repeal don't ask, tell	N
4. Pass cap-and-trade	N	8. Pass tax cuts for some	N	12. Limit campaign funds	N

Election Results

2010 general	Sam Johnson (R)	101,180	(66%)	($1,110,253)
	John Lingenfelder (D)	47,848	(31%)	($157,001)
	Christopher Claytor (Lib)	3,602	(2%)	
2010 primary	Sam Johnson (R)	unopposed		

Prior Winning Percentages: 2008 (60%), 2006 (63%), 2004 (86%), 2002 (74%), 2000 (72%), 1998 (91%), 1996 (73%), 1994 (91%), 1992 (86%), 1991 special (53%)

Population		Race/Ethnicity		Work	
Pop. 2010:	842,449	White:	51.9%	Private:	85.1%
Change since 2000:	Up 29.3%	Black:	11.3%	Government:	8.3%
Urban:	99.0%	Hispanic:	22.2%	Self-employed:	6.4%
Rural:	1.0%	Asian:	12.1%	Blue collar:	15.9%
Area size:	266 sq. mi.	Native Am.:	0.4%	White collar:	70.2%
		Hawaiian:	0.0%	Khaki collar:	0.0%
Age		Two+ races:	1.9%	Other:	13.9%
Median age:	33.6 yrs.				
More than 65 yrs:	7.3%	*Ancestry*		Median income:	$68,448
Less than 18 yrs:	28.1%	German	10.4%	Median Home Value:	$190,500
		Irish	7.7%		
Education		English	7.3%	**Military Veterans**	
H.S. grad:	87.4%			% of Pop:	6.9%
College grad:	42.0%				
Grad degree:	13.7%				

North Dallas Suburbs; Plano

North Dallas, the putative location of the 1980s television program *Dallas,* conjures up a certain image of sudden affluence and of shady dealings and immoral trysts in an environment of outward embrace of traditional values. The caricature doesn't tell the whole story. Dallas got its start as a railroad junction and cotton-shipping center. In recent decades, it has been at the cutting edge of high technology, and is the home of

2008 Presidential Vote
John McCain (R) 171,119   (57%)
Barack Obama (D) 124,027   (42%)

2004 Presidential Vote
George Bush (R) 174,711   (67%)
John Kerry (D) 86,718   (33%)

Cook Partisan Voting Index: R+14

Texas Instruments, where an integrated circuit on a silicon chip was invented in 1958, and of Electronic Data Systems, the source of former independent presidential candidate Ross Perot's fortune. The high-tech, telecommunications and defense businesses are less robust than in the 1980s, but the Dallas-Fort Worth Metroplex continues to thrive. Growth has come from corporate headquarters relocated from less business-friendly precincts, from small businesses, and from companies making money trading with Mexico. Dallas is the nation's chief beneficiary of the North America Free Trade Agreement. Health care and universities have created many jobs as well.

Dallas' growth has extended far into the countryside. The home of the city's old elite may still be in the mansion-lined streets of Highland Park north of downtown, but Dallas' business and professional classes have moved farther in Dallas County and up into Collin County's scrub-covered hills. Back in 1960, Collin County was mostly rural. It had 41,000 people then, and actually lost population in the 1950s. Then the Dallas-Fort Worth area exploded, and Collin's population grew from 66,000 in 1970 to 791,000 in 2009. It is now the sixth-largest and third-wealthiest county in Texas. Its biggest city is Plano, with 273,000 people. This former farming community is now the corporate headquarters of Dr. Pepper, J.C. Penney and EDS, which was purchased by Hewlett-Packard in 2008 and became HP Enterprise Services. Even during the height of the recession in 2009, Plano ranked fifth in the country in household spending. The population of McKinney has more than doubled since 2000, to 127,000. Politically, Collin County has been very Republican, more Republican than Dallas County ever was. Republican Gov. Rick Perry beat Democrat Bill White in Collin, 64%-33%, in 2010.

The 3rd Congressional District of Texas includes most of Collin County and centers on Plano. It also covers the northeastern corner of Dallas County, beyond the LBJ Freeway, including much of Rowlett and Garland. In 2008, Republican John McCain got 60% of the vote in the Collin County portion of the district, and he trailed Democrat Barack Obama by 221 votes in Dallas County, which cast 27% of the total. Overall, McCain won 57%-42%, a big drop from President George W. Bush's favorite-son showing of 70%-30% in 2000.

Sam Johnson (R)

The congressman from the 3rd District is Sam Johnson, a conservative Republican first elected in 1991. He has a prominent perch from which to weigh in on Social Security as chairman of the Ways and Means Committee panel that oversees the program.

Johnson grew up in Dallas and graduated from Southern Methodist University and George Washington University. He was a director of the Air Force Fighter Weapons (Top Gun) School, and as a fighter pilot, flew 87 combat missions during the wars in Korea and Vietnam. After his F-4 was shot down over North Vietnam during his 25th mission, he was imprisoned from 1966 to 1973 in the "Hanoi Hilton," where he spent 42 months in solitary confinement. He weighed 120 pounds upon his release, having subsisted on river weeds and pig fat, and was left with a slight stoop in his walk and a disfigured hand. In 2009, the Congressional Medal of Honor Society gave him its highest civilian honor, the National Patriots Award. On his return, Johnson started a homebuilding company and was elected to the Texas House in 1984.

He was elected to Congress in a 1991 special election, after Republican Steve Bartlett resigned to become mayor of Dallas. Johnson ran second in the primary, behind former Peace Corps director Tom Pauken. In the runoff, he emphasized his war record and won 53%-47% over Pauken. He won the general election without difficulty.

Johnson was among the lawmakers tied for the House's most conservative member in 2010, according to *National Journal's* rankings. He was a founder of the Conservative Action Team, now known as the Republican Study Committee, which has pressed Republican leaders to support goals ranging from a balanced budget amendment to shutting down the National Endowment for the Arts.

His chief source of concern is taxation. Every two years, he offers a constitutional amendment to repeal the 16th Amendment, which authorized the federal income tax. On Ways and Means, where he is the third-most senior Republican, Johnson in January 2011 raised the specter of the U.S. "corporate structure" incrementally relocating overseas to avoid U.S. rates if the tax code is not reformed. He also suggested that one goal should be requiring everyone, including lower-income earners, to pay income tax. Earlier, he sponsored the successful repeal in 2000 of the earnings limit for Social Security recipients, and he was a leading proponent of pension reform that was enacted in 2006.

Johnson has also focused on military issues. He has staunchly opposed setting arbitrary troop withdrawal deadlines in Afghanistan. Johnson gained national attention in February 2007 when he spoke emotionally on the House floor against a plan by Democratic Speaker Nancy Pelosi to set a timetable to withdraw from Iraq. Invoking his memories of Vietnam, he said, "I know what it's like to be far from home and hear that your country and your Congress don't care about you." Even though he and McCain, who was also a Vietnam prisoner of war, shared a cell for 18 months, they have had a chilly political relationship. Johnson strongly backed Bush in the 2000 primaries, stating that McCain "cannot hold a candle to George Bush."

On other defense matters, he helped to enact the Military Family Tax Relief Act of 2003, which doubled the death benefit for families of active service members who pass away and also reduced taxes for those families. Johnson has been a defender of the F-22 fighter jet, partly produced at the Lockheed Martin plant in Fort Worth near his district and the subject of intense debates over whether the program should continue.

In 2008, Johnson was re-elected with 60% of the vote against a poorly financed foe. This was his smallest share of the vote since his first win. He rebounded with a 66%-31% win in 2010. He represents an overpopulated district whose lines will be redrawn for 2012, and though he's unlikely to face any political trouble, speculation about his retirement has increased since he entered his 80s.

FOURTH DISTRICT

Ralph Hall (R)

Elected 1980, 16th term; b. May 3, 1923, Fate; home, Rockwall; U. of TX, TX Christian U., S. Methodist U., LL.B. 1951; United Methodist; widowed; 3 children.

Military Career: Navy, 1942–45 (WWII).

Elected Office: Rockwall Cnty. judge, 1950-62; TX Senate, 1962–72.

Professional Career: Practicing atty., 1951-80; Pres. & CEO, TX Aluminum Corp., 1967-68; Spec. cnsl., Howmet Corp., 1970-74.

DC Office: 2405 RHOB, 20515, 202-225-6673; Fax: 202-225-3332; Web site: ralphhall.house.gov.

State Offices: McKinney, 214-726-9949; New Boston, 903-628-8309; Rockwall, 972-771-9118; Sherman, 903-892-1112; Sulphur Springs, 903-885-8138; Texarkana, 903-794-4445.

Committees: *Science & Technology* (Chmn).

Group Ratings

	ACLU	ACU	ADA	CFG	AFS	FRC	LCV	ITIC	NTU	COC
2010	13	96	0	95	0	93	10	33	87	88
2009	–	92	10	87	11	–	0	–	83	93

National Journal Ratings

	2010 LIB — 2010 CONS		2009 LIB — 2009 CONS	
Economic	25%	— 75%	25%	— 74%
Social	23%	— 76%	20%	— 78%
Foreign	0%	— 88%	0%	— 75%
Composite	18%	— 82%	20%	— 80%

Key Votes of the 111th Congress

1. Overturn Ledbetter	N	5. Bar federal abortion funds	Y
2. Pass $820 billion stimulus	N	6. Pass health care bill	N
3. Let guns in national parks	Y	7. Regulate financial firms	N
4. Pass cap-and-trade	N	8. Pass tax cuts for some	N

9. Stop detainee transfers	Y
10. Legalize immigrants' kids	N
11. Repeal don't ask, tell	N
12. Limit campaign funds	N

Election Results

2010 general	Ralph Hall (R)	136,338	(73%)	($664,579)
	VaLinda Hathcox (D)	40,975	(22%)	($13,693)
	Jim Prindle (Lib)	4,729	(3%)	($47,687)
2010 primary	Ralph Hall (R)	39,579	(57%)	
	Steve Clark (R)	20,496	(30%)	
	John Cooper (R)	3,748	(5%)	

Prior Winning Percentages: 2008 (69%), 2006 (64%), 2004 (68%), 2002 (58%), 2000 (60%), 1998 (58%), 1996 (64%), 1994 (59%), 1992 (58%), 1990 (100%), 1988 (66%), 1986 (72%), 1984 (58%), 1982 (74%), 1980 (52%)

Population		Race/Ethnicity		Work	
Pop. 2010:	846,142	White:	72.1%	Private:	78.0%
Change since 2000:	Up 29.9%	Black:	10.2%	Government:	14.9%
Urban:	49.6%	Hispanic:	13.1%	Self-employed:	6.8%
Rural:	50.4%	Asian:	2.0%	Blue collar:	24.2%
Area size:	9,839 sq. mi.	Native Am.:	0.7%	White collar:	59.1%
		Hawaiian:	0.1%	Khaki collar:	0.1%
Age		Two+ races:	1.7%	Other:	16.6%
Median age:	36.5 yrs.				
More than 65 yrs:	12.7%	*Ancestry*		Median income:	$51,112
Less than 18 yrs:	26.7%	German	11.0%	Median Home Value:	$122,200
		Irish	10.5%		
Education		USA	8.7%	**Military Veterans**	
H.S. grad:	84.3%			% of Pop:	11.3%
College grad:	22.4%				
Grad degree:	6.8%				

Northeast Texas; Sherman

The Red River Valley is hardscrabble farm country along an unnavigable river. First settled in
the 1830s, in the days of the Texas Republic,
many counties here reached their population
peak around 1900, when a large extended farm
family worked every 160 acres. It includes towns
like Denison, which was the birthplace of
Dwight Eisenhower and has become a manufacturing center, and Sherman, which was the site
of a major race riot in 1930 when a black farm

2008 Presidential Vote		
John McCain (R) 213,967	(69%)
Barack Obama (D) 93,439	(30%)
2004 Presidential Vote		
George Bush (R) 192,926	(70%)
John Kerry (D) 81,269	(30%)
Cook Partisan Voting Index: R+21		

worker accused of rape was attacked by an angry white mob. To the east is Texarkana, noteworthy
because its neat grid streets cross the Texas-Arkansas state line, which is straddled by the city's
downtown post office. This small city and its hinterland have produced three recent presidential
candidates: Ross Perot grew up in Texarkana, while Bill Clinton and Mike Huckabee hail from
Hope, Ark., just 30 miles east.

This part of Texas sent Democrat Sam Rayburn to Congress in 1912. He was the powerful
House speaker from 1940 until his death in 1961, except for two terms when Republicans had the
majority. The Red River Valley was one of the strongest Democratic parts of the country, with a
sentimental regard for Confederate veterans and a seething hatred of Wall Street bankers. This
was Rayburn's politics, and he arguably was the most skillful lawmaker of the 20th century. Today,
Rayburn's style of politics has almost completely vanished from the area. Rafael de la Garza, a
Republican-turned-Democrat who unsuccessfully ran for Collin County district attorney in 2010,
told *The Dallas Morning News* he had trouble getting his backers to put up yard signs or publicly
endorse him, because they feared neighbors would associate such moves with support for the
deeply unpopular President Obama.

The 4th Congressional District of Texas is the lineal descendant of the seat that Rayburn held,
and still includes his hometown of Bonham in Fannin County, which houses a Rayburn museum.
But it is quite a different district today. In Rayburn's time it was a farm district, separate and
distinct from citified Dallas. Today, it still has its farm counties, but they are only a short hop on
the interstate from the Dallas-Fort Worth Metroplex, and nearly half the district's people live in
the metropolitan area. The counties at the edge of the Metroplex, Collin and Rockwall, were among
the fastest-growing in the country in the last decade. Rockwall in 2008 passed a $100 million refer-
endum to improve congested roads. The two counties are home now to upwardly mobile families
who lean Republican. In 1940, the year Rayburn became speaker, his district voted 90% for Franklin D. Roosevelt. In 2008, the 4th District voted 69% for Republican John McCain. In the 2010
governor's election, incumbent Republican Rick Perry took 64% of the vote in Collin and 72% in
Rockwall.

Ralph Hall (R)

The congressman from the 4th District is Ralph Hall, who was born in 1923 and first elected in
1980. He turned 88 in 2011, and is the oldest member of the House; he is also the affable dean of
the Texas delegation in Congress.

Hall grew up in Rockwall County, served in the Navy during World War II as a lieutenant
and aircraft carrier pilot, and had a 30-year career in local politics and business before coming to
Washington. He got his law degree from Southern Methodist University, was a county judge in the
1950s, and from 1962 to 1972, served in the Texas Senate. In 1980, he was elected to the House as
a Democrat. His evolution to the Republican Party was a long time in gestation. He supported just
about everything in the GOP's Contract with America policy agenda in 1995 and was one of only five
House Democrats who voted to impeach President Bill Clinton. He voted for Bush administration
policies on taxes, trade and foreign policy. (But Hall is not a pure free marketer. He voted against
the North American Free Trade Agreement.) During the 2002 campaign, he promised to vote for
Republican Speaker Dennis Hastert if his vote decided which party would control the House.
And in January 2003, he voted "present" rather than vote for liberal Democrat Nancy Pelosi for
speaker, because, he said, "she just don't think like we do."

Republicans restlessly waited for years for Hall to join them. When he failed to switch after
the 2001 redistricting, local and national Republicans expressed interest in a serious challenge to
Hall. But they backed off after he met with President George W. Bush at the White House and the
president strongly opposed a challenge. In March 2003, Hall was the only Democrat to vote for the

Republican budget, which barely passed. The 2003 redistricting finally convinced Hall to change parties. With Republican candidates lined up to run against him, he switched parties on January 2, 2004, the final day for filing. He said that his Democratic Party affiliation was limiting his ability to get appropriations for his district. No one on either side stayed angry with him for long; he has a droll sense of humor and in 2010's *Washingtonian* survey of congressional staffers, Hall was named the House's second-funniest member behind perpetual winner Barney Frank, D-Mass.

When he joined their side, Republicans rewarded him with the chairmanship of the Energy and Air Quality Subcommittee of the Energy and Commerce Committee, an attractive perk for a Texan. Hall helped to enact the energy bill of 2005, and later fought Democratic proposals to raise taxes on oil companies. When Republicans lost the majority in 2007, Hall became the ranking Republican of a full committee, the Science and Technology Committee. He assumed the Science chairmanship in 2011, beating back a challenge from the more confrontational Dana Rohrabacher, R-Calif. (When asked why he should get the job over his much-younger colleague, Hall told a reporter: "I'm in better shape than he's in.") Hall is a strong champion of NASA's International Space Station, which is controlled from Houston, though he is less enthusiastic about the agency's climate change research and held hearings on the sharply partisan disputes over climate science.

Party-switching has played well for Hall at home. With support from Bush and then-Republican House Speaker Hastert, Hall won 77% against two opponents in the 2004 Republican primary and went on to win in the general, 68%-30%, his biggest victory in more than a decade. He won subsequent elections with more than 60% of the vote, and held off a 2010 primary challenge from five GOP contenders, one of whom filed to be on the ballot as Jerry Ray (Tea) Hall to court tea party support. When Hall retires, his son, Rockwall County District Judge Brett Hall, a Republican, is said to be interested in running for the seat.

FIFTH DISTRICT

Jeb Hensarling (R)

Elected 2002, 5th term; b. May 29, 1957, Stephenville; home, Dallas; TX A&M U., B.A. 1979, U. of TX, J.D. 1982; Christian; married (Melissa); 2 children.

Professional Career: Practicing atty., 1982-84; TX dir., U.S. Sen. Phil Gramm, 1985-90; Exec. dir., NRSC, 1991-93; Communications exec., 1993-02.

DC Office: 129 CHOB, 20515, 202-225-3484; Fax: 202-226-4888; Web site: hensarling.house.gov.

State Offices: Athens, 903-675-8288; Dallas, 214-349-9996.

Committees: *Financial Services* (VChmn): Capital Markets and Government Sponsored Enterprises; Financial Institutions & Consumer Credit.

Group Ratings

	ACLU	ACU	ADA	CFG	AFS	FRC	LCV	ITIC	NTU	COC
2010	13	100	0	100	0	100	0	33	94	88
2009	–	100	0	100	0	–	0	–	95	73

National Journal Ratings

	2010 LIB	—	2010 CONS	2009 LIB	—	2009 CONS
Economic	0%	—	97%	0%	—	96%
Social	0%	—	85%	0%	—	93%
Foreign	26%	—	72%	26%	—	68%
Composite	12%	—	88%	12%	—	89%

Key Votes of the 111th Congress

1. Overturn Ledbetter	N	5. Bar federal abortion funds	Y	9. Stop detainee transfers	Y
2. Pass $820 billion stimulus	N	6. Pass health care bill	N	10. Legalize immigrants' kids	N
3. Let guns in national parks	Y	7. Regulate financial firms	N	11. Repeal don't ask, tell	N
4. Pass cap-and-trade	N	8. Pass tax cuts for some	N	12. Limit campaign funds	N

Election Results

2010 general	Jeb Hensarling (R)	106,742	(71%)	($1,745,500)
	Tom Berry (D)	41,649	(28%)	
2010 primary	Jeb Hensarling (R)	unopposed		

Prior Winning Percentages: 2008 (84%), 2006 (62%), 2004 (64%), 2002 (58%)

Population		Race/Ethnicity		Work	
Pop. 2010:	725,642	White:	60.9%	Private:	78.6%
Change since 2000:	Up 11.4%	Black:	13.7%	Government:	13.7%
Urban:	67.7%	Hispanic:	21.6%	Self-employed:	7.5%
Rural:	32.3%	Asian:	1.9%	Blue collar:	26.6%
Area size:	5,610 sq. mi.	Native Am.:	0.4%	White collar:	56.3%
		Hawaiian:	0.0%	Khaki collar:	0.0%
Age		Two+ races:	1.3%	Other:	17.1%
Median age:	36.1 yrs.				
More than 65 yrs:	12.5%	*Ancestry*		Median income:	$48,010
Less than 18 yrs:	26.1%	USA	10.4%	Median Home Value:	$114,500
		German	8.9%		
Education		English	8.9%	**Military Veterans**	
H.S. grad:	79.9%			% of Pop:	10.1%
College grad:	19.8%				
Grad degree:	6.5%				

Part Dallas, Mesquite

Not all of Dallas is glitz and postmodern marble. East of downtown, on one of the three street grids that skew to each other, is an older Dallas with neighborhoods of old mansions, modest bungalows and shotgun houses. They extend past the old airport at Love Field, and past the State Fair Grounds and the Cotton Bowl in east Dallas. Some of this older section of Dallas is being renovated and rebuilt, with chic cafes and trendy stores. Other once middle-class neighbor-

2008 Presidential Vote
John McCain (R) 158,356   (63%)
Barack Obama (D) 90,135   (36%)

2004 Presidential Vote
George Bush (R) 160,240   (67%)
John Kerry (D) 77,952   (33%)

Cook Partisan Voting Index: R+17

hoods are filling up with immigrants from Mexico and are once again noisy with children as they were in the 1950s when people moved here not from Mexico or Central America, but from the almost all-Anglo counties of north and central Texas. With the economic downturn and the scarcity of jobs, some of them are returning to Mexico.

The 5th Congressional District includes much of east and southeast Dallas County, including neighborhoods in east Dallas and suburban Mesquite, which has become a destination for immigrants moving up the economic ladder. It also covers a more upscale slice of Dallas inside the freeway, including parts of Lakewood and White Rock Lake, which was rescued by President Franklin Roosevelt's Civilian Conservation Corps during the New Deal. Nearly half of the district's population is in Dallas County. It was 22% Hispanic in 2010, up from 16% in 2000. The 5th contains six counties in East Texas, the largest of which are Henderson and Kaufman, which are the next high-growth areas in the Metroplex. One of the booming small towns is Forney, which has become a destination for young families. Each of the outlying counties is more heavily Republican than the Dallas portion of the district. As rural areas have swung away from the Democrats, the district switched from being a battleground in the early 1990s to safely Republican. In 2008, GOP presidential nominee John McCain won 63% of the vote in the district and 53% in Dallas County. Two years later, Republican Gov. Rick Perry drew 65% in both Henderson and Kaufman counties while getting just 43% in Dallas County.

Jeb Hensarling (R)

The congressman from the 5th District is Jeb Hensarling, a Republican first elected in 2002. His disciplined brand of conservativism and political savvy have propelled him upward to become Republican conference chairman, the fourth-ranking House GOP leadership post.

Hensarling grew up in Morris County in East Texas. He worked on his father's poultry farm near College Station as a teenager and decided that he did not want to be a farmer. In high school, he started a Republican club and began organizing political events. He graduated from Texas A&M University and went on to get a law degree from the University of Texas law school. After a short stint practicing law, he got a job on the staff of U.S. Sen. Phil Gramm, a Republican. Hensarling rose quickly through the ranks of Gramm's staff and became his campaign manager in 1990. When Gramm's fellow senators chose him as chairman the National Republican Senatorial Committee, Gramm named Hensarling as his executive director. Hensarling later returned to Texas to become vice president of communications for Green Mountain Energy, a local utility, and was co-founder of Family Support Assurance, a firm that aided child support collections.

After the congressional redistricting in 2001, Republican Rep. Pete Sessions, who had represented the 5th District for the previous six years, decided to run in the new and more compact 32nd District on the north side of Dallas. Hensarling became the front-runner for the Republican nomination in the 5th District. Like his mentor, Gramm, he listed cutting taxes as his top priority. Against four opponents, he won the nomination with 54% of the vote. Democrats nominated Ron Chapman, a former Dallas County appellate judge who described himself as a loyal Democrat who could work with Republicans. Hensarling referred to his opponent as "Judge Softie" for his record on capital murder cases. The folksy Chapman emphasized his fiscal conservatism and deep local roots. He tried to paint Hensarling as too conservative and extreme for the district, but his message failed to take hold, especially as high-profile Republicans came through the district with Hensarling endorsements, including President George W. Bush, Vice President Dick Cheney, and Gramm. Hensarling won 58%-40%, and has been re-elected easily since.

In the House, Hensarling has a solidly conservative voting record. He has styled himself as a fiscal conservative in the mold of Gramm and has not been afraid to push Republican leaders to take more conservative positions, though he usually votes with them in the end when they don't. He served on the Simpson-Bowles deficit commission in 2010 and made clear from the outset that he preferred that it concentrate on federal spending. He opposed the commission's findings as insufficient in containing health care costs. He also disdained the 2011 budget-cutting deal that President Barack Obama struck with Republicans, saying it still did not cut spending enough and that "we probably all deserve to be tarred and feathered."

He joined the Republican Study Committee, a group of the most conservative House members and became its chairman in the 110th Congress (2007-08). As RSC chairman, Hensarling crafted a seven-point strategy for House Republicans that included a constitutional amendment to limit spending and a flat tax on goods and services to replace the federal income tax. The party embraced his platform, except for his call for a moratorium on spending earmarks in appropriations bills. After the 2008 election, Hensarling was named to head fundraising for the National Republican Congressional Committee, chaired by his Dallas-area conservative colleague Sessions.

Hensarling's adversarial approach did not endear him to Republicans on the Appropriations Committee and others in the party establishment, including—reportedly—then-Minority Leader John Boehner. It didn't help Hensarling that he managed Indiana Republican Mike Pence's unsuccessful challenge to Boehner for minority leader in 2006. But Hensarling developed a key ally in Boehner's similarly message-driven minority whip, Eric Cantor of Virginia. With Cantor's backing he easily won the conference chairmanship to succeed Pence following the November 2010 elections. Tea party favorite Michele Bachmann, R-Minn., threw her hat in the ring for the post, but abandoned her bid after Hensarling's staff trumpeted a long string of endorsements from other influential figures in the movement, including Rep. Ron Paul of Texas.

Hensarling also assumed the vice chairmanship of the Financial Services Committee, a position that enables him to keep watch on Chairman Spencer Bachus, a lawmaker with whom some conservatives remain suspicious. Hensarling has called for the abolition of the government-sponsored mortgage giants Fannie Mae and Freddie Mac, which he said abused their power. He was a prominent critic of the 2010 financial industry overhaul and helped lead the conservative revolt in 2008 against the Troubled Asset Relief Program, which Boehner was charged with selling to his caucus. His bill to kill the Emergency Homeowners' Relief Program, which was set up to provide loans to recently unemployed homeowners who have missed mortgage payments, prompted a rare veto threat from Obama in March 2011.

SIXTH DISTRICT

Joe Barton (R)

Elected 1984, 14th term; b. Sept. 15, 1949, Waco; home, Ennis; Texas A&M U., B.S. 1972, Purdue U., M.S. 1973; United Methodist; married (Terri); 4 children.

Professional Career: Asst. to V.P., Ennis Business Forms, 1973–81; White House Fellow, U.S. Dept. of Energy, 1981–82; Consultant, Atlantic Richfield Co., 1982–84.

DC Office: 2109 RHOB, 20515, 202-225-2002; Fax: 202-225-3052; Web site: joebarton.house.gov.

State Offices: Arlington, 817-543-1000; Crockett, 936-544-8488; Ennis, 972-875-8488.

Committees: *Energy & Commerce:* Commerce, Manufacturing & Trade; Communications & Technology; Energy & Power; Environment & the Economy; Health; Oversight & Investigations.

Group Ratings

	ACLU	ACU	ADA	CFG	AFS	FRC	LCV	ITIC	NTU	COC
2010	13	96	5	93	0	100	10	0	89	86
2009	–	96	5	85	11	–	0	–	84	92

National Journal Ratings

	2010 LIB	—	2010 CONS	2009 LIB	—	2009 CONS
Economic	15%	—	85%	30%	—	70%
Social	18%	—	77%	11%	—	87%
Foreign	29%	—	71%	0%	—	75%
Composite	22%	—	79%	18%	—	82%

Key Votes of the 111th Congress

1. Overturn Ledbetter	N	5. Bar federal abortion funds	Y	9. Stop detainee transfers	Y
2. Pass $820 billion stimulus	N	6. Pass health care bill	N	10. Legalize immigrants' kids	N
3. Let guns in national parks	Y	7. Regulate financial firms	N	11. Repeal don't ask, tell	N
4. Pass cap-and-trade	N	8. Pass tax cuts for some	N	12. Limit campaign funds	N

Election Results

2010 general	Joe Barton (R)	107,140	(66%)	($2,377,715)
	David Cozad (D)	50,717	(31%)	($25,145)
	Byron Severns (Lib)	4,700	(3%)	
2010 primary	Joe Barton (R)	unopposed		

Prior Winning Percentages: 2008 (62%), 2006 (60%), 2004 (66%), 2002 (70%), 2000 (88%), 1998 (73%), 1996 (77%), 1994 (76%), 1992 (72%), 1990 (66%), 1988 (68%), 1986 (56%), 1984 (57%)

Population		Race/Ethnicity		Work	
Pop. 2010:	809,095	White:	54.5%	Private:	80.0%
Change since 2000:	Up 24.2%	Black:	16.3%	Government:	13.5%
Urban:	80.0%	Hispanic:	22.9%	Self-employed:	6.4%
Rural:	20.0%	Asian:	4.0%	Blue collar:	24.7%
Area size:	6,335 sq. mi.	Native Am.:	0.4%	White collar:	59.6%
		Hawaiian:	0.1%	Khaki collar:	0.1%
Age		Two+ races:	1.6%	Other:	15.6%
Median age:	33.2 yrs.				
More than 65 yrs:	9.4%	*Ancestry*		Median income:	$53,820
Less than 18 yrs:	28.5%	German	10.0%	Median Home Value:	$129,800
		Irish	8.5%		
Education		English	7.1%	**Military Veterans**	
H.S. grad:	83.4%			% of Pop:	9.5%
College grad:	24.8%				
Grad degree:	7.5%				

Dallas Suburbs; Arlington

The Dallas-Fort Worth Metroplex—a name even the locals use—has spread outward from its historic nodes in downtown Dallas and downtown Fort Worth. Although Dallas is the larger population center, much of the development has moved west, across the plains and the barely perceptible Balcones Escarpment, the geologist's boundary between green and grassy East Texas and brown, barren and hilly West. The plains have been filled in with subdivisions and

2008 Presidential Vote		
John McCain (R) 172,061	(60%)
Barack Obama (D) 114,133	(40%)
2004 Presidential Vote		
George Bush (R) 173,476	(67%)
John Kerry (D) 87,454	(34%)
Cook Partisan Voting Index: R+15		

shopping centers under the enormous Texas sky. Among the larger suburbs is Arlington, right between Dallas and Fort Worth and an easy highway commute to both cities. Its location has made it ideal as a site for regional attractions like Six Flags over Texas and the Ballpark in Arlington, commissioned by the former part-owner of the Texas Rangers, George W. Bush. In 2009, the Dallas Cowboys football team opened a new $1.1 billion stadium in Arlington that hosted the 2011 Super Bowl. The city's population of 380,000 in 2009 was 29% Hispanic, 18% African-American and 7% Asian. The University of Texas' campus there reached an all-time high of almost 33,000 students in fall 2010, making it the second-largest in the UT system behind Austin. As Arlington has filled up, the big growth now is to the south in Mansfield, where the population increased 69% from 2000 to 2009, and in Crowley. Growth in the area has been so robust that Tarrant County, the third-largest county in Texas, was the 16th largest in the country in 2010.

The 6th Congressional District of Texas includes all of Arlington and the southern fringe of Fort Worth to the west. Two-thirds of its people live in Arlington and Tarrant County. Much of the rest are in Ellis County, directly south of Dallas County. Ellis has grown 34% since 2000. The district includes all or part of six counties to the southeast, reaching most of the way to Houston. Politically, this territory was ancestrally Democratic for many years, but no longer. It voted for Republican native son George W. Bush with 67% in 2004, and it voted for Republican nominee John McCain in 2008 with 60%. In 2010, GOP Gov. Rick Perry took 56% in Tarrant and 66% in Ellis.

Joe Barton (R)

The congressman from the 6th District is Joe Barton, a Republican first elected in 1984. Once a powerful House Republican, Barton's influence has waned, having lost his bid to chair the Energy and Commerce Committee following his unpopular defense of BP during its 2010 oil spill disaster. He remains an outspoken champion for the oil industry and, along with Oklahoma GOP Sen. James Inhofe, he is the leading global-warming skeptic on Capitol Hill.

Barton grew up in Ennis, in then-rural Ellis County. He graduated from Texas A&M and Purdue universities, worked as an oil company engineer and then was a White House fellow in the Energy Department. When Republican Rep. Phil Gramm ran successfully for the Senate in 1984, Barton ran for his 6th District House seat. Barton won the Republican runoff by only 10 votes, and he went on to win the general election with 57% of the vote.

Barton once sometimes strayed to the center on cultural issues, but since Democrat Barack Obama became president, he has been a rock-solid conservative. He chaired the Energy and Commerce Committee before his party lost its majority in 2006, and hoped to continue in the top spot in the 112th Congress (2011-12). After the election, Barton pushed the GOP leadership to ease term limits on chairmen, arguing that the rule wasn't intended to apply to the positions of both ranking member and committee chairman. He set up an aggressive operation to boost his chances against Michigan's Fred Upton, the Republican next in line on the panel. A 22-page critique of the moderate Upton's record was circulated that accused him of being a "part-time Republican." Though Barton said he wasn't behind the effort, many Republicans were skeptical. The leadership-driven GOP Steering Committee picked Upton in December, and Barton chose not to challenge its decision.

The chairmanship defeat capped what was already a tough year for Barton. News reports surfaced in February that Barton had earned nearly $100,000 from an interest in natural gas wells that he bought from a campaign donor who had given him advice on energy policy. He said his investment was legal and presented no conflict with his legislative responsibilities, but it provided ammunition to environmentalists who loath his unyielding pro-production stance. Then came the June committee hearing at which BP executives were grilled on the catastrophic spill in the Gulf of Mexico. Barton apologized to the executives for the Obama administration's decision to force it to establish a $20 billion fund to compensate people who lost their livelihoods in the aftermath. "I think it is a tragedy of the first proportion that a private corporation can be subjected to what I would characterize as a shakedown, in this case, a $20 billion shakedown, with the attorney general of the United States," Barton said. In light of the public's anger over the spill, his remarks sparked a political uproar. GOP leaders threatened to strip him of his ranking spot on the committee, and Barton issued a retraction.

It was not the first time Barton's contrariness had landed him in controversy. Discussing global warming with former Democratic Vice President Al Gore at hearings in 2007, Barton told Gore, who'd written a book on the topic, "You're not just off a little. You're totally wrong." In a December 2009 C-SPAN interview, Barton said, "There's ample evidence that warming generically, however it is caused, is a net benefit to mankind." He was the party's lead spokesman against the sweeping climate change bill passed by the House in June 2009. The bill established a cap on greenhouse gas emissions, aiming to reduce them by 80% from 2005 levels by 2050. Barton called it "a triumph of fear over good sense and science." He offered his own bill that would have set emission standards for new coal and natural gas plants, but would not have penalized existing plants. Barton's plan failed on a party-line vote. In March 2010, he introduced a bill to prevent the Environmental Protection Agency from regulating greenhouse gases; it passed the House in April 2011 with unanimous GOP support, but was unlikely to prevail in the Democratically controlled Senate.

Barton also fought the Democrats' health care proposals tooth-and-nail, but was often outgunned by California's Henry Waxman, who took over the top Energy and Commerce Democratic slot in 2009. He was the opposing voice on the committee when the Democrats unveiled a restructuring of the nation's health care delivery system. But on some issues, Barton sought common ground with Waxman, as he had with Waxman's predecessor as chairman, Democrat John Dingell of Michigan. He worked with committee Democrats on a proposal to approve generic versions of biologic drugs following a 12-year period of exclusivity for the inventor to recoup costs. And he worked with Dingell on a consensus approach to improved electronic medical records.

In earlier years, Barton had enjoyed a degree of success in the majority on the committee. In 1995, he became chairman of the panel's Oversight and Investigation Subcommittee and used the platform to conduct extensive hearings of the nation's food and drug laws. The result was enactment, with bipartisan support, of significant modernization of the Food and Drug Administration, encouraging the agency to more quickly review innovative drugs and medical devices. In 1999, he became chairman of the Energy and Power Subcommittee with jurisdiction over energy legislation. He managed to reach agreement in 2001 with Dingell on higher fuel economy standards. Barton pressed for action on electricity regulation, but he retreated from requiring utilities to join regional transmission organizations and sought to encourage them to do so. His bill passed the House but died in the Senate.

In 2004, after full commerce chairman Billy Tauzin, R-La., stepped down, Barton was selected to succeed him—the only Texan other than former Democratic speaker Sam Rayburn to hold the post. He aroused some partisan ire when in September of that year he blocked committee Democrats' demand for information about Vice President Dick Cheney's 2001 energy task force. But he also worked successfully to win Democratic votes on some issues and to defend and expand the committee's jurisdiction. Telecommunications issues are a major responsibility of Energy and Commerce. In 2006, the House passed Barton's bill to make it easier for telephone companies to enter the broadband market, but influential Democrats opposed the measure, and it died in the Senate. In 2010, Barton became one of the leading opponents of a Federal Communications Commission plan to increase regulation of broadband service companies. The FCC argued that the regulations were necessary to prevent companies from favoring some kinds of content over others, but Barton and other Republicans worried that the plan would harm competition and growth in the high speed internet industry.

On the 2005 energy bill, Barton insisted on retaining provisions protecting manufacturers of MTBE, a fuel additive that was discovered to be polluting groundwater. The bill became hung up over that provision as some lawmakers fought to hold the manufacturers responsible for expensive cleanup projects. Barton ultimately agreed to drop it in order to get a bill that could pass both chambers. With his help, the GOP majority was able to enact major energy legislation with $12 billion in incentives, an inventory of oil and natural gas reserves, and a one-month extension of daylight savings time. Also in 2005, the House narrowly passed Barton's bill to encourage the construction of new refineries, but it died in the Senate.

At home, Barton was criticized by Democrats for seeking in 2003 and 2004 to keep Ellis County outside the Environmental Protection Agency's Dallas region in applications of the stringent rules of the Clean Air Act. Ellis County is home to three cement producers and other companies whose political action committees and executives were big contributors to Barton's campaigns, and the county produces 40% of the industrial emissions in North Texas. Barton said there was no connection between the contributions and his action and argued that there was no scientific basis for Ellis County's inclusion. But in 2004 the EPA decided otherwise and that Ellis County must take steps to reduce air pollution.

Barton has had some political disappointments. He ran for the Senate in 1993 after Democrat Lloyd Bentsen resigned to become President Bill Clinton's Treasury secretary. He finished third with just 14% of the vote in the all-party primary. In September 2001, when Gramm announced his retirement from the Senate, Barton considered running for his seat. But the Bush White House favored Texas Attorney General John Cornyn and Barton stepped aside. After the 2006 election, he made a bid for minority leader, but discovered that John Boehner, R-Ohio, had wrapped up sufficient votes to win. Barton withdrew after six days.

He has been re-elected easily in the 6th District. He suffered a heart attack in December 2005 but made a full recovery. He reportedly got into a spat with fellow Texas Republican Lamar Smith, the Judiciary Committee chairman, in early 2011 over the racial makeup of the state's redistricted congressional boundaries in 2012. Smith sought to evenly split four new districts between Republicans and Democrats, giving Texas' booming Hispanic population minority-majority seats in the Dallas and Houston areas. But Barton wanted to keep Republican voters dominant in three or all four of the new districts.

SEVENTH DISTRICT

John Culberson (R)

Elected 2000, 6th term; b. Aug. 24, 1956, Houston; home, Houston; Southern Methodist U., B.A. 1981, S. TX Col. of Law, J.D. 1988; Methodist; married (Belinda); 1 child.

Elected Office: TX House of Reps., 1986-2000, Maj. whip, 1999-2000.

Professional Career: Jim Culberson Advertising, 1981-85; Practicing atty., 1988-2000.

DC Office: 2352 RHOB, 20515, 202-225-2571; Fax: 202-225-4381; Web site: culberson.house.gov.

State Offices: Houston, 713-682-8828.

Committees: *Appropriations:* Commerce, Justice, Science & Related Agencies; Homeland Security (VChmn); Military Construction, Veterans Affairs & Related Agencies (Chmn).

Group Ratings

	ACLU	ACU	ADA	CFG	AFS	FRC	LCV	ITIC	NTU	COC
2010	13	100	0	97	0	100	0	33	90	100
2009	–	100	0	97	0	–	0	–	90	73

National Journal Ratings

	2010 LIB — 2010 CONS		2009 LIB — 2009 CONS	
Economic	5%	95%	12%	87%
Social	0%	85%	13%	84%
Foreign	0%	88%	0%	75%
Composite	6%	94%	13%	87%

Key Votes of the 111th Congress

1. Overturn Ledbetter	N	5. Bar federal abortion funds	Y
2. Pass $820 billion stimulus	N	6. Pass health care bill	N
3. Let guns in national parks	Y	7. Regulate financial firms	N
4. Pass cap-and-trade	N	8. Pass tax cuts for some	N

9. Stop detainee transfers	Y
10. Legalize immigrants' kids	N
11. Repeal don't ask, tell	N
12. Limit campaign funds	N

Election Results

2010 general	John Culberson (R)	143,655	(81%)	($779,425)
	Bob Townsend (Lib)	31,704	(18%)	
2010 primary	John Culberson (R)	unopposed		

Prior Winning Percentages: 2008 (56%), 2006 (59%), 2004 (64%), 2002 (89%), 2000 (74%)

Population		Race/Ethnicity		Work	
Pop. 2010:	780,611	White:	52.7%	Private:	83.0%
Change since 2000:	Up 19.8%	Black:	9.7%	Government:	9.2%
Urban:	99.7%	Hispanic:	25.4%	Self-employed:	7.6%
Rural:	0.3%	Asian:	10.1%	Blue collar:	12.4%
Area size:	198 sq. mi.	Native Am.:	0.2%	White collar:	76.2%
		Hawaiian:	0.0%	Khaki collar:	0.0%
Age		Two+ races:	1.7%	Other:	11.4%
Median age:	35.5 yrs.				
More than 65 yrs:	10.0%	*Ancestry*		Median income:	$70,998
Less than 18 yrs:	23.8%	German	10.9%	Median Home Value:	$202,600
		English	8.5%		
Education		Irish	7.2%	**Military Veterans**	
H.S. grad:	91.4%			% of Pop:	7.1%
College grad:	50.8%				
Grad degree:	19.5%				

West Houston and Suburbs

When George H.W. Bush moved from Midland in West Texas to Houston in 1960, he bought a house in Briarwood in what was then the western outskirts of the fast-growing city. He returned to Houston in 1993 after losing his reelection bid for the presidency and built a new house one mile from his old one, near lush Memorial Park. Briarwood is not far from the retail and commercial epicenter of Houston. The lavish Galleria, one of the largest malls in the United States, draws more than 24 million visitors a year under its impressive glass atriums. Downtown Houston is sprouting residential apartments. Although the sale of high-priced homes fell in 2008, the economy of Houston is still relatively strong. Oil company revenues have been up and many businesses moved here from the New Orleans area following the devastation of Hurricane Katrina in 2005.

2008 Presidential Vote		
John McCain (R)	173,162	(58%)
Barack Obama (D)	121,472	(41%)

2004 Presidential Vote		
George Bush (R)	179,456	(64%)
John Kerry (D)	99,422	(36%)

Cook Partisan Voting Index: R+13

The 7th Congressional District of Texas is the lineal descendant of the House district that in 1966 elected Bush as the first Republican ever to represent Houston. It occupied far more territory then, half of Harris County. In successive redistrictings, its boundaries have been pared back, as the population of the west side of Houston has skyrocketed. Today, more than 1.5 million people live in an area where 350,000 lived when Bush was first elected. Between 2000 and 2010, the 7th District's population jumped 20%, to more than 780,000. It touches the western edge of downtown Houston and includes most of the land between the Katy Freeway (Interstate 10) and Westheimer running straight west to Highway 6. To the south, it includes the affluent neighborhoods southwest of downtown Houston, Rice University and the Texas Medical Center, Bellaire, some small Buffalo Bayou towns, and a swath of Houston west of the 610 highway loop. One extremely fast-growing stretch of U.S. 290 is expected to see its road usage more than double over the next 25 years, leading to a three-part construction project set to begin in 2011. Most of Houston's business and professional elite live within its boundaries: the partners of the big law firms, cutting-edge medical researchers, and society mavens. Since 2000, the Hispanic population has increased from 18% to 23%.

Back in the 1980s, the 7th District was one of the most Republican districts in the country, and it still is. But as with many precincts of the very elite, it did not take a liking to President George W. Bush's brand of Republicanism. Within these boundaries, he won 69% of the vote in 2000 but 64% in 2004. As with other close-in Texas suburbs, local Republican fortunes continued to slide in 2008, although it was still a safe GOP district; it voted 58% for Republican John McCain. Former Houston mayor Bill White, a Democrat, managed to draw just over 50% in Harris County against GOP Gov. Rick Perry in 2010.

John Culberson (R)

The congressman from the 7th District is John Culberson, a conservative Republican first elected in 2000. Culberson grew up in Houston, the son of the owner of an advertising agency. He graduated from Southern Methodist University, South Texas College of Law, and then worked as a civil defense lawyer. In 1986, at age 29, Culberson won a seat in the Texas House, where he served for 14 years. In 2000, Republican Rep. Bill Archer, Bush's successor in the House, retired after being forced to give up the chairmanship of the Ways and Means Committee by Republican term limits. The front-runners in the GOP primary were Culberson and Peter Wareing, a Houston merchant banker and son-in-law of Texas oilman Jack Blanton. Culberson led Wareing in the first round 38%-27%. Wareing spent nearly $4 million to Culberson's $650,000, but Culberson had an extensive grassroots campaign and won the runoff four weeks later 60%-40%. The general election was no contest in this GOP-dominant district.

Culberson calls himself a "Jeffersonian Republican" and is passionate about transferring power from the federal to local governments. He was the House's 10th most conservative member in 2010, according to *National Journal*'s rankings. He cosponsored Florida GOP Rep. Bill Posey's 2009 "birther" bill requiring future presidential candidates to offer proof of citizenship in response to far-right theories about President Barack Obama being born overseas. During the final days of the 2010 health care debate, he attended a Capitol Hill rally of the bill's opponents and tossed loose pages of the 2,000-page document to the crowd. Like his predecessor, Archer, he dreams of junking the current tax system and replacing it with a national sales tax. Culberson sometimes goes his own way. He ruffled feathers as one of only two Texas Republicans to oppose the $400 billion Medicare expansion of 2003.

An amateur astronomer and self-proclaimed science buff, Culberson is an enthusiast for NASA and has an interest in nanotechnology research, which is a specialty at Rice. He also is an avid fan of Twitter and in 2009 was the House's top user of the social media account, according to a University of Maryland study. He was an early proponent of requiring the House to post all non-emergency legislation online at least 72 hours before debate, a rules change that Republicans enacted in 2011. He joined several conservatives in getting a provision into a 2011 spending measure that banned NASA from collaborating with China's scientists.

Culberson has a coveted spot on the Appropriations Committee, which he has used to secure money for projects in his district, including medical research, flood control projects and funds for the Houston Ship Channel. He has fought with Houston officials who wanted money for local light rail projects, filing a formal objection with the Federal Transit Administration in December 2009 to stop a light-rail line because he said the local transit agency was in precarious financial shape—a charge agency officials said was based on outdated information.

In 2008, Culberson faced his first well-financed Democratic challenger. Wind energy executive Michael Skelly spent nearly $3.1 million, including $1 million from his own pocket. Culberson spent a relatively modest $1.8 million, which left some Republicans worried about a possible upset. Skelly criticized Culberson's lack of support for alternative energy and said he was not sufficiently helpful to the space program, citing Culberson's call to reduce the bureaucracy at NASA, which employs about 20,000 people locally. Culberson ran as a strong social and fiscal conservative, but suffered from discontent in the Republican grassroots over perceived weak enforcement of immigration law and a spike in deficit spending during the Bush years. Culberson won, 56%-42% Two years later, however, Democrats did not even bother to challenge him and he beat a Libertarian candidate 81%-18%.

EIGHTH DISTRICT

Kevin Brady (R)

Elected 1996, 8th term; b. April 11, 1955, Vermillion, SD; home, The Woodlands, TX; U. of SD, B.S. 1990; Catholic; married (Cathy); 2 children.

Elected Office: TX House of Reps., 1990–96.

Professional Career: Exec., The Woodlands Chamber of Commerce, 1978–96.

DC Office: 301 CHOB, 20515, 202-225-4901; Fax: 202-225-5524; Web site: house.gov/brady.

State Offices: Conroe, 936-441-5700; Huntsville, 936-439-9532; Orange, 409-883-4197.

Committees: *Joint Economic Committee* (VChmn). *Ways & Means:* Social Security; Trade (Chmn).

Group Ratings

	ACLU	ACU	ADA	CFG	AFS	FRC	LCV	ITIC	NTU	COC
2010	13	100	0	95	0	100	10	33	91	88
2009	–	100	0	97	0	–	0	–	91	73

National Journal Ratings

	2010 LIB — 2010 CONS		2009 LIB — 2009 CONS	
Economic	7%	—	92%	0%	—	96%
Social	16%	—	82%	11%	—	87%
Foreign	0%	—	88%	26%	—	68%
Composite	10%	—	90%	14%	—	86%

Key Votes of the 111th Congress

1. Overturn Ledbetter	N	5. Bar federal abortion funds	Y	9. Stop detainee transfers	Y
2. Pass $820 billion stimulus	N	6. Pass health care bill	N	10. Legalize immigrants' kids	N
3. Let guns in national parks	Y	7. Regulate financial firms	N	11. Repeal don't ask, tell	N
4. Pass cap-and-trade	N	8. Pass tax cuts for some	N	12. Limit campaign funds	N

Election Results

2010 general	Kevin Brady (R)	161,417	(80%)	($1,028,855)
	Kent Hargett (D)	34,694	(17%)	
	Bruce West (Lib)	4,988	(2%)	
2010 primary	Kevin Brady (R)	52,595	(79%)	
	Scott Baker (R)	8,614	(13%)	
	Tyler Russell (R)	3,542	(5%)	

Prior Winning Percentages: 2008 (73%), 2006 (67%), 2004 (69%), 2002 (93%), 2000 (92%), 1998 (93%); 1996 (59%)

Population		Race/Ethnicity		Work	
Pop. 2010:	833,770	White:	73.7%	Private:	77.3%
Change since 2000:	Up 28.0%	Black:	7.7%	Government:	14.4%
Urban:	49.6%	Hispanic:	15.4%	Self-employed:	8.2%
Rural:	50.4%	Asian:	1.4%	Blue collar:	26.1%
Area size:	8,415 sq. mi.	Native Am.:	0.5%	White collar:	57.0%
		Hawaiian:	0.0%	Khaki collar:	0.1%
Age		Two+ races:	1.2%	Other:	16.9%
Median age:	37.1 yrs.				
More than 65 yrs:	12.2%	*Ancestry*		Median income:	$52,019
Less than 18 yrs:	25.4%	German	12.3%	Median Home Value:	$118,000
		Irish	10.8%		
Education		English	9.0%	**Military Veterans**	
H.S. grad:	83.8%			% of Pop:	10.9%
College grad:	21.4%				
Grad degree:	6.4%				

East Texas; Montgomery County

Montgomery County, to the north of Houston, was once fenceless cattle country, dotted with roadside stands and barbecues and unpainted farmhouses. In 1931, wildcatter George Strake struck oil near Conroe. Thousands of other wildcatters and roughnecks quickly joined in the boom, and this became one of the richest oil-producing areas in the nation. Active production continues today. The oil boom centered on Conroe was followed by a population boom. In 1972,

2008 Presidential Vote		
John McCain (R) 215,845	(74%)
Barack Obama (D) 74,695	(26%)

2004 Presidential Vote		
George Bush (R) 194,696	(73%)
John Kerry (D) 73,946	(28%)

Cook Partisan Voting Index: R+25

construction began on a planned community called The Woodlands, 30 miles north of Houston and 15 miles south of Conroe. Development of this new city has barreled along since then, with corporate parks, glistening steel condos, pristine golf courses, and a man-made waterway. Greater Houston has spread far out into this countryside, past the now mislabeled Farm-Market Route 1960, past The Woodlands and even past Conroe. Montgomery County had 49,000 people in 1970 and 456,000 in 2010. It is the sixth fastest-growing county in Texas. The recession inflicted considerably less damage in this area than elsewhere—Montgomery's unemployment rate topped 8% just once in 2010. The rural counties further east bordering Louisiana did not fare as well, with Newton County's jobless rate hitting 14% in early 2011.

The 8th Congressional District includes all of Montgomery County, which contains slightly more than half of the district's people. The district extends east to the Sabine River on the Louisiana border, and takes in all of eight counties and parts of two others. It covers the Big Thicket National Preserve, a primeval swamp described as "America's Ark" because of its vast array of animals and plants. The district also includes Huntsville, with one of Texas's oldest prisons and "Big Sam," a 65-foot-tall statue of Sam Houston outside the town along Interstate 45. It takes in the oil refinery town of Orange on the Sabine River, which is popular for bass fishing. Redistricting changes in recent years have made the district less affluent and metropolitan, but it is still solidly Republican. President George W. Bush won 72% of the vote in the district in 2004. In 2008, Republican John McCain won 74% of the vote, his sixth-best district in the nation. GOP Gov. Rick Perry won Montgomery County two years later with 75%.

Kevin Brady (R)

The congressman from the 8th District is Kevin Brady, a Republican first elected in 1996 who has emerged as one of his party's key figures on trade.

Brady grew up and went to college in South Dakota, moved to Montgomery County in 1978 and headed The Woodlands Chamber of Commerce for 18 years. In 1990, he was elected to the Texas House. When Republican U.S. Rep. Jack Fields announced his retirement in 1995, Brady ran for the seat. His main opponent in the decisive Republican primary was Eugene Fontenot, a physician who said he wanted "to restore America to its Christian heritage." Brady was the choice of party regulars, while Fontenot was backed by religious conservatives. Fontenot attacked Brady for being one of two Republicans to vote against the state's concealed weapons law. Brady had opposed most gun control bills but not the concealed weapons bill. When he was 12 years old, his father, an attorney, was shot and killed while trying a case in a South Dakota courtroom. "I couldn't look Mom in the eye and vote for this," he told *The Houston Chronicle* after the vote. After Fontenot led Brady in the March primary, Brady won the April runoff by 53%-47%. After the U.S. Supreme Court in June ordered a redrawing of 13 districts, Brady led Fontenot 41%-39% in an all-party primary in November. Finally, in the December runoff, turnout was sharply down and Brady won 59%-41%. He has had no problem winning re-election since.

In the House, Brady has compiled a conservative voting record, though he has gained a reputation as more of a pragmatist than other Texas conservatives. Brady is also a deputy whip for the House Republican leadership. He is known for being easygoing and soft-spoken, but that doesn't mean he never gets mad. His November 2009 showdown with Treasury Secretary Timothy Geithner made national news when Brady savaged Geithner's handling of the Wall Street crisis, saying, "The public has lost all confidence in your ability to do the job." A year earlier, Brady was the only Houston-area member of the House in either party to vote for the financial industry rescue. "As much as I detest this bill, doing nothing is worse," he said.

Brady has focused on economic issues and has a coveted spot on the Ways and Means Committee, a panel he hopes to someday chair. He currently leads that panel's trade subcommittee and has adamantly fought for more free-trade agreements, which he contends are essential to the United States' economic recovery. He said in April 2010 that he supported easing restrictions on the sale of food and medicine to Cuba, but that such a move would look inconsistent without passing a free-trade pact with Colombia. He was also the chief House sponsor of the 2005 Central America Free Trade Agreement.

Brady was a central figure in the successful effort in 2004 to make state and local sales taxes deductible in the seven states, including Texas, that have no personal income tax. Like Houston-area lawmakers of both parties, Brady jealously guards NASA's Johnson Space Center. When the agency announced in April 2011 that it would not place any of its retired space shuttles at Johnson, he said, "With this White House, I always expect the worst and am rarely disappointed."

NINTH DISTRICT

Al Green (D)

Elected 2004, 4th term; b. Sept. 1, 1947, New Orleans, LA; home, Houston; TX Southern U., J.D. 1973; Baptist; single.

Elected Office: Harris Cnty. justice of the peace, 1977-2004.

Professional Career: Practicing atty., 1973-77; Pres., Houston NAACP, 1986-95.

DC Office: 2201 RHOB, 20515, 202-225-7508; Fax: 202-225-2947; Web site: house.gov/algreen.

State Offices: Houston, 713-383-9234.

Committees: *Financial Services:* Capital Markets and Government Sponsored Enterprises; Domestic Monetary Policy & Technology.

Group Ratings

	ACLU	ACU	ADA	CFG	AFS	FRC	LCV	ITIC	NTU	COC
2010	94	0	90	0	100	0	100	100	6	25
2009	–	0	100	0	100	–	100	–	2	33

National Journal Ratings

	2010 LIB — 2010 CONS		2009 LIB — 2009 CONS	
Economic	69% —	30%	88% —	9%
Social	77% —	21%	84% —	11%
Foreign	66% —	29%	70% —	24%
Composite	72% —	28%	83% —	17%

Key Votes of the 111th Congress

1. Overturn Ledbetter	Y	5. Bar federal abortion funds	N	9. Stop detainee transfers	N
2. Pass $820 billion stimulus	Y	6. Pass health care bill	Y	10. Legalize immigrants' kids	Y
3. Let guns in national parks	N	7. Regulate financial firms	Y	11. Repeal don't ask, tell	Y
4. Pass cap-and-trade	Y	8. Pass tax cuts for some	Y	12. Limit campaign funds	Y

Election Results

2010 general	Al Green (D)	80,107	(76%)	($443,131)
	Steve Mueller (R)	24,201	(23%)	($16,549)
2010 primary	Al Green (D)	unopposed		

Prior Winning Percentages: 2008 (94%), 2006 (100%), 2004 (72%)

Population		Race/Ethnicity		Work	
Pop. 2010:	733,796	White:	10.4%	Private:	82.0%
Change since 2000:	Up 12.6%	Black:	34.9%	Government:	9.9%
Urban:	99.8%	Hispanic:	42.4%	Self-employed:	7.9%
Rural:	0.2%	Asian:	10.8%	Blue collar:	26.9%
Area size:	154 sq. mi.	Native Am.:	0.1%	White collar:	48.5%
		Hawaiian:	0.0%	Khaki collar:	0.1%
Age		Two+ races:	1.1%	Other:	24.6%
Median age:	30.6 yrs.				
More than 65 yrs:	6.7%	*Ancestry*		Median income:	$37,120
Less than 18 yrs:	29.0%	Subsaharan	4.0%	Median Home Value:	$109,900
		German	2.6%		
Education		English	1.8%	**Military Veterans**	
H.S. grad:	72.3%			% of Pop:	4.8%
College grad:	21.0%				
Grad degree:	6.9%				

South Houston and Suburbs

Spreading out in all directions from its historic center at Allen's Landing on Buffalo Bayou, Houston has become one of the great metropolises of North America. A half-century ago, the steaming flatlands south of Houston running down to the Gulf of Mexico did not seem a likely site for one of the world's most advanced civilizations. But they are today. Most of the scientific work in NASA's early years was done in Houston, and the first word spoken when man landed

2008 Presidential Vote
Barack Obama (D) 137,619   (77%)
John McCain (R) 40,240   (23%)

2004 Presidential Vote
John Kerry (D) 112,065   (70%)
George Bush (R) 48,052   (30%)

Cook Partisan Voting Index: D+22

on the moon was "Houston." It is the undisputed center of expertise in the oil business. The recent recession slowed growth in the business, while many projects were put on hold, but by mid-2010, it had rebounded and companies began hiring again. Houston has also become a medical mecca, with the giant Texas Medical Center and its 14 hospitals leaving their mark on the health care statewide. Houston has become one of the great surprise growth cities, creating thousands of small businesses, many owned by immigrants. This success is testimony to human, and Texas, creativity, and to the triumph of air conditioning, which made Houston's five-month summer tolerable. Today, it is the fourth-largest city in the nation, with a population that grew 29% from 1990 to 2010.

The 9th Congressional District of Texas slices across the southern part of metropolitan Houston on the streets and freeways and waterways spreading out from the center of the city. It begins just southwest of where Interstate 45 crosses the I-610 Loop, continues west with a slight intrusion inside 610 near the Reliant Astrodome and Reliant Stadium, and then heads past Meadows Place and Mission Bend outside Beltway 8 toward the western end of Harris County. It includes two wedges of Fort Bend County, which form a crescent around the 22nd District.

The district includes many African-American neighborhoods, low-income and middle-income, in Harris and Fort Bend counties. In 2009, it was one of the bottom 30 districts in the nation in the number of people without health insurance. Its population is 35% black, and it also includes many Asians, who form 11% of the total population, many clustered along Belleaire Boulevard in the Chinese-American community. Entrepreneurial Vietnamese boat people settled in the Alief neighborhood of southwest Houston on Bray's Bayou and have created quality schools, an Asian-oriented shopping mall and businesses that serve the largest Vietnamese community in the nation outside of California. And of course, there are many Hispanics, who made up 42% of the district's population in 2010, though many are not citizens or do not vote. Half of the district's population speaks a language other than English at home. The devastation of Katrina that emptied out New Orleans moved approximately 200,000 residents to Houston, and tens of thousands have remained. Overall this is a heavily Democratic district, which voted 77% for Democrat Barack Obama for president in 2008.

Al Green (D)

The congressman from the 9th District is Al Green, a Democrat first elected in 2004 who champions the concerns of the homeless and poor. Green grew up in New Orleans. He attended college at Florida A&M University and graduated from Texas Southern University's law school, where he later taught. From 1986 to 1995, he was president of the Houston chapter of the NAACP. In 1977, he was elected justice of the peace and served 26 years. After new district boundaries were created in 2003, Green saw an opening to run for Congress. The representative from the old district that covered much of this area was Chris Bell, a white Democrat first elected in 2002. That year, he ran with liberal support and beat a more conservative black candidate. The primary against Green was a different matter. Green said that he wanted to fight racial profiling and discrimination in law enforcement, and used subtle racial references on the campaign trail, including his promise to bring "a mountain of soul" to the new district. He amassed an impressive roster of endorsements from prominent local and national black leaders. Bell responded by asking voters "not to focus on the color of my skin, but on the size of my heart." Bell was endorsed by the AFL-CIO, Texas teachers, abortion rights groups and Democratic Minority Leader Nancy Pelosi. But he struggled as a white candidate running in a district where minorities constituted two-thirds of the electorate.

As the primary neared, the racially charged atmosphere intensified. When state Democratic Chairman Charles Soechting endorsed Bell, Green said that it reminded him of "the double standards when African-Americans had to ride on the back of the bus and drink from colored-only water fountains." The Congressional Black Caucus was drawn into the campaign after California Rep. Maxine Waters suggested many CBC members backed Green while Bell claimed that caucus Chairman Elijah Cummings, D-Md., had promised to support him. Although the caucus itself never made a formal endorsement, its role in the primary angered other Democratic members. In the end, it may not have mattered. Green won the primary in a landslide, 66%-31%. Green faced no real opposition in the general election.

In the House, Green began with a relatively moderate voting record, but has become a loyal Democrat in recent years. On the Financial Services Committee, he has worked to eliminate housing practices that discriminated against minorities. In 2008, he teamed with then-Rep. Christopher Shays, R-Conn., on a plan to reduce the number of mortgage holders with unstable sub-prime loans, and he passed a bill in the House to expand housing assistance for low-income veterans. He defended that program from Republican budget-cutters in March 2011. He told *The Houston Chronicle* in 2010, "My mission in life seems to remain constant—doing what I can to be of service to the least, the last and the lost."

Like other Texas lawmakers, he has been protective of the oil and gas industry, joining a group of Democrats in 2009 warning that President Barack Obama's proposal to raise taxes and impose new fees on the oil and gas industry could hamper domestic production. Green broke with most House Democrats by voting in 2006 to permit oil drilling in the Arctic National Wildlife Refuge, probably the smart vote in a Houston-based district that relies on oil profits. He left the Homeland Security Committee after the GOP takeover in 2011, but attended a controversial panel hearing on Muslim extremism in March to passionately tell panel members that other groups using religion as the basis for their views, such as the Ku Klux Klan, also should be examined.

Green was re-elected twice without Republican opposition before easily beating GOP business analyst Steve Mueller 76%-23% in 2010.

TENTH DISTRICT

Michael McCaul (R)

Elected 2004, 4th term; b. Jan. 14, 1962, Dallas; home, Austin; Trinity U., B.A. 1984, St. Mary's U., J.D. 1987; Catholic; married (Linda); 5 children.

Professional Career: Fed. prosecutor, 1990-99; Dep. atty. gen., 1999-2003; Chief, Western Div. of TX., U.S. Attys. Office, 2003-04.

DC Office: 131 CHOB, 20515, 202-225-2401; Fax: 202-225-5955; Web site: mccaul.house.gov.

State Offices: Austin, 512-473-2357; Brenham, 979-830-8497; Katy, 281-398-1247; Tomball, 281-255-8372.

Committees: *Ethics. Foreign Affairs:* Middle East & South Asia; Western Hemisphere (VChmn). *Homeland Security:* Border & Maritime Security; Cybersecurity, Infrastructure Protection & Security Technologies; Oversight, Investigations & Management (Chmn). *Science & Technology:* Space & Aeronautics; Technology & Innovation.

Group Ratings

	ACLU	ACU	ADA	CFG	AFS	FRC	LCV	ITIC	NTU	COC
2010	13	96	0	95	0	100	10	67	85	100
2009	–	96	0	93	11	–	14	–	86	87

National Journal Ratings

	2010 LIB	—	2010 CONS	2009 LIB	—	2009 CONS
Economic	26%	—	74%	19%	—	81%
Social	29%	—	69%	29%	—	68%
Foreign	0%	—	88%	0%	—	75%
Composite	21%	—	79%	21%	—	79%

Key Votes of the 111th Congress

1. Overturn Ledbetter	N	5. Bar federal abortion funds	Y	9. Stop detainee transfers	Y
2. Pass $820 billion stimulus	N	6. Pass health care bill	N	10. Legalize immigrants' kids	N
3. Let guns in national parks	Y	7. Regulate financial firms	N	11. Repeal don't ask, tell	N
4. Pass cap-and-trade	N	8. Pass tax cuts for some	N	12. Limit campaign funds	N

Election Results

2010 general	Michael McCaul (R)	144,980	(65%)	($2,124,577)
	Ted Ankrum (D)	74,086	(33%)	($23,314)
	Jeremish Perkins (Lib)	5,105	(2%)	
2010 primary	Michael McCaul (R)	46,881	(83%)	
	Rick Martin (R)	5,038	(9%)	
	Joe Petronis (R)	4,656	(8%)	

Prior Winning Percentages: 2008 (54%), 2006 (55%), 2004 (79%)

Population		Race/Ethnicity		Work	
Pop. 2010:	981,367	White:	52.4%	Private:	77.8%
Change since 2000:	Up 50.6%	Black:	11.0%	Government:	15.0%
Urban:	80.8%	Hispanic:	28.8%	Self-employed:	7.0%
Rural:	19.2%	Asian:	5.7%	Blue collar:	19.6%
Area size:	3,846 sq. mi.	Native Am.:	0.3%	White collar:	65.8%
		Hawaiian:	0.1%	Khaki collar:	0.1%
Age		Two+ races:	1.6%	Other:	14.5%
Median age:	32.5 yrs.				
More than 65 yrs:	7.6%	*Ancestry*		Median income:	$62,199
Less than 18 yrs:	28.3%	German	12.6%	Median Home Value:	$160,600
		English	7.1%		
Education		Irish	7.0%	**Military Veterans**	
H.S. grad:	86.3%			% of Pop:	8.1%
College grad:	35.2%				
Grad degree:	11.3%				

Part Austin, Houston Suburbs

Two of Texas' major cities are named for leaders of the old Texas Republic, Sam Houston and Stephen Austin. They were not entirely attractive characters: Houston had episodes of alcoholic depression and Austin was a slaveholder who argued that Mexico infringed on Texas' liberty when it freed its slaves. But they were also men of courage and determination who built a distinctively American culture in what was then the northeast of Mexico. Today, the two metropolises named for them are quite different in character. Houston is about commerce, the capital of the oil business, an entrepreneurial hub spread out over the swampy, humid plains north of the Gulf of Mexico. Austin is the creature of the state government headquartered in the grand Capitol building and of the University of Texas with a huge endowment of land in West Texas that turned out to be full of oil.

2008 Presidential Vote		
John McCain (R) 187,496	(55%)
Barack Obama (D) 150,713	(44%)

2004 Presidential Vote		
George Bush (R) 177,555	(62%)
John Kerry (D) 109,287	(38%)
Cook Partisan Voting Index: R+10		

The historic Austin is a liberal enclave in the heart of a conservative state. But the area around north Austin and its suburbs has taken on some of Houston's character in recent years despite the continuing popularity of "Keep Austin Weird" bumper stickers. North of the Capitol and the university, on land that was vacant when Lyndon Johnson celebrated his 87-vote victory in the 1948 Senate primary in the Driskill Hotel, an entrepreneurial Austin has taken shape. It embraces technology and the free market and spreads out over the hills into adjacent Williamson County. IBM has a major research lab in Austin, and not far away, the J.J. Pickle Research Campus of UT-Austin conducts research in areas ranging from archaeology to robots. In nearby Pflugerville, developers broke ground in late 2010 on a $200 million solar farm, the largest of its kind in Texas. Curiously, there is no superhighway between Austin and Houston. To get from one to the other, one drives through rural counties with monuments and plaques recalling the days of the Texas Republic.

The 10th Congressional District of Texas connects the western edge of Houston with the northern precincts of Austin through a corridor of still mostly rural counties. It is split into three parts. Approximately 40% live in Austin and Travis County, where the district includes the northern third of Austin, with one tentacle reaching southwest beyond the city limits and another dropping south to Austin State Hospital. Another 40% are in the western edge of Houston's Harris County, a fast-growing area, with lots of young families, new subdivisions and mega churches. In between are the six lightly populated rural counties. In recent years, the 10th has been the fastest-growing district in the state. From 2000 to 2010, it grew 51%, and the Hispanic population increased from a 19% share to 29%. It's also a heavily Republican district. Republican President George W. Bush won the district with 62% in 2004. Republican candidate John McCain got 55% in 2008. Democratic candidate Barack Obama won the Travis County portion with 63%, while McCain got 68% in Harris County. In the 2010 governor's race, Democrat Bill White got 60% in Travis and 50% in Harris, but lost to GOP incumbent Rick Perry.

Michael McCaul (R)

The congressman from the 10th District is Michael McCaul, a Republican first elected in 2004 and a protégé of Texas GOP Sen. John Cornyn. McCaul grew up in Dallas, studied business and history at Trinity University and went to law school at St. Mary's University, both in San Antonio. He worked as a federal prosecutor and then moved to Austin in 1999 to be a deputy to then-Attorney General Cornyn in Austin. In 2002, he joined the U.S. attorney's office and was chief of the Terrorism and National Security Section for West Texas.

McCaul was one of eight candidates in the Republican primary for the newly created congressional district in 2004. The top Republican contenders were McCaul, mortgage company owner Ben Streusand and former Judge John Devine. McCaul focused on his anti-terrorism work in the U.S. attorney's office. "I'm the only candidate that's had a top-secret security clearance," he said. "I won't have a learning curve." Streusand, based in Harris County, called for less government regulation and opposed the Bush administration's immigration proposals. Devine, who had refused to remove a Ten Commandments display from his Harris County courtroom, had the support of Christian conservatives and called for a crackdown on illegal immigration. In the primary, Streusand carried seven of the eight counties to finish with 28% of the vote, to 24% for McCaul and 21% for Devine.

In the runoff campaign, McCaul and Streusand agreed on most issues. McCaul criticized Streusand's past donations to Democratic candidates, while Streusand questioned McCaul's service in the Clinton administration Justice Department. McCaul used his connections—his father-in-law is Clear Channel Communications chairman Lowry Mays—to collect major Republican endorsements, including from former President George H.W. Bush, Gov. Rick Perry and Sen. Kay Bailey Hutchison. (His connection to Mays helps explain McCaul's status as one of the House's wealthiest members.) McCaul won 63%-37%, carrying every county except one, which he lost by seven votes. He faced no major-party opposition in the general election.

In the House, McCaul has a voting record that is only slightly less conservative than the Texas delegation's other Republicans. He supported requiring insurers to treat mental illness the same as other health conditions in 2008 and allowing the Food and Drug Administration to regulate tobacco products in 2009.

He is on the Homeland Security Committee and chairs its Oversight, Investigations & Management Subcommittee. In 2011, he became a regular guest on television news shows to discuss Mexican drug cartel violence and the committee's high-profile hearings on Muslim extremism. Despite complaints from American Muslims that they were being unfairly singled out at the hearings, he told MSNBC: "I don't really understand the controversy when we talk about this, because of the 27 plots thwarted in the last two years, they were all radical Islam." As a freshman, he gained headlines with hearings that revealed more than $1 billion in fraud in Hurricane Katrina disaster relief. He also has repeatedly introduced legislation banning so-called "monuments to me," landmarks honoring incumbent lawmakers that he considers arrogant examples of earmarking.

Until 2010, his re-election performances suggested he needed to work harder in this once-solidly GOP district. In 2006, against retired Navy Captain Ted Ankrum, an underfunded challenger, McCaul won 55%-40%. His challenger in 2008 was Larry Joe Doherty, a Houston lawyer who stars as a judge in a courtroom reality television show called "Texas Justice." Doherty characterized McCaul as voting most of the time for the Republican agenda, including cuts in Medicare. McCaul accused Doherty of supporting a health care plan that would lead to rationing. McCaul won 54%-43%.

Two years later, wealthy Democratic entrepreneur Jack McDonald raised his party's hopes of a serious challenge, but McDonald dropped out. McCaul coasted in a return matchup against Ankrum, 65%-33%.

ELEVENTH DISTRICT

Mike Conaway (R)

Elected 2004, 4th term; b. June 11, 1948, Borger; home, Midland; E. TX St. U., B.B.A. 1970; Baptist; married (Suzanne); 4 children.

Military Career: Army, 1970-72.

Elected Office: Midland Schl. Bd., 1985-88.

Professional Career: Tax mgr., Price Waterhouse & Co., 1972-80; CFO, Keith G. Graham, 1980-81; CFO, Lantern Petroleum Comp., 1981; CFO, Arbusto Energy Inc./Bush Exploration Comp., 1982-84; CFO, Spectrum 7 Energy Corp., 1984-86; CFO, United Bank, 1987-90; Sr. VP, TX Comm. Bank, 1990-92; Owner, K. Michael Conaway, CPA, 1993-2004.

DC Office: 1527 LHOB, 20515, 202-225-3605; Fax: 202-225-1783; Web site: conaway.house.gov.

State Offices: Brownwood, 325-646-1950; Llano, 325-247-2826; Midland, 432-687-2390; Odessa, 432-331-9667; San Angelo, 325-659-4010.

Committees: *Agriculture:* General Farm Commodities & Risk Management (Chmn); Livestock, Dairy & Poultry. *Armed Services:* Emerging Threats & Capabilities; Oversight & Investigations. *Ethics. Permanent Select Committee on Intelligence:* Terrorism, HUMINT, Analysis & Counterintelligence.

Group Ratings

	ACLU	ACU	ADA	CFG	AFS	FRC	LCV	ITIC	NTU	COC
2010	13	100	0	95	0	100	0	33	90	88
2009	–	100	0	97	0	–	0	–	93	71

National Journal Ratings

	2010 LIB	—	2010 CONS	2009 LIB	—	2009 CONS
Economic	5%	—	94%	0%	—	96%
Social	0%	—	85%	11%	—	87%
Foreign	0%	—	88%	0%	—	75%
Composite	6%	—	94%	9%	—	91%

Key Votes of the 111th Congress

1. Overturn Ledbetter	N	5. Bar federal abortion funds	Y	9. Stop detainee transfers	Y
2. Pass $820 billion stimulus	N	6. Pass health care bill	N	10. Legalize immigrants' kids	N
3. Let guns in national parks	Y	7. Regulate financial firms	N	11. Repeal don't ask, tell	N
4. Pass cap-and-trade	N	8. Pass tax cuts for some	N	12. Limit campaign funds	N

Election Results

2010 general	Mike Conaway (R)	125,581	(81%)	($1,098,814)
	James Quillian (D)	23,989	(15%)	($13,024)
	James Powell (Lib)	4,321	(3%)	
2010 primary	Mike Conaway (R)	55,610	(77%)	
	Chris Younts (R)	9,586	(13%)	
	Al Cowan (R)	6,680	(9%)	

Prior Winning Percentages: 2008 (88%), 2006 (100%), 2004 (77%)

Population		Race/Ethnicity		Work	
Pop. 2010:	710,682	White:	57.8%	Private:	74.1%
Change since 2000:	Up 9.1%	Black:	3.7%	Government:	16.1%
Urban:	70.8%	Hispanic:	36.3%	Self-employed:	9.5%
Rural:	29.2%	Asian:	0.7%	Blue collar:	27.2%
Area size:	35,186 sq. mi.	Native Am.:	0.4%	White collar:	53.0%
		Hawaiian:	0.0%	Khaki collar:	1.0%
Age		Two+ races:	1.0%	Other:	18.9%
Median age:	36.6 yrs.				
More than 65 yrs:	15.0%	*Ancestry*		Median income:	$45,193
Less than 18 yrs:	25.9%	German	11.0%	Median Home Value:	$90,700
		English	8.5%		
Education		Irish	8.2%	**Military Veterans**	
H.S. grad:	78.7%			% of Pop:	10.8%
College grad:	18.1%				
Grad degree:	5.4%				

West Central Texas; Midland

More than 400 years ago, in the 1540s, the conquistador Francisco Coronado and his men rode
their horses over the plains of the land they
called the Llano Estacado, or "flat palisades,"
which is now West Texas. They saw a vast emptiness, gradually and imperceptibly rising in elevation to the west, with only scrub vegetation
and small bands of Comanche Indians. What
they did not see, lying far beneath the surface,
was oil, discovered in the 1940s in large amounts

2008 Presidential Vote		
John McCain (R) 185,350	(75%)
Barack Obama (D) 58,323	(24%)
2004 Presidential Vote		
George Bush (R) 188,929	(78%)
John Kerry (D) 52,174	(22%)
Cook Partisan Voting Index: R+28		

in the Permian Basin. When oil was found, two tiny county seats 25 miles apart suddenly became
small cities—Odessa, home of the roughneck oil well workers, and Midland, the more upscale town
where oil entrepreneurs lived and started their own Petroleum Club. The Permian Basin boomed
in the years just after World War II. In 1940, Ector and Midland counties had a population of
26,000. By 1960, they had grown to 159,000. Midland in the 1950s was an affluent town by west
Texas standards, but hardly a luxurious town. Air conditioning had not yet become standard in
homes or schools, and there were no mansions at the edge of town, just barren desert and oil derricks. George and Barbara Bush moved to the Permian Basin in 1948 in search of success in the
oil industry and room for a growing family. They rented houses in Odessa before upgrading to a
series of larger, but by no means grand, ranch houses in Midland. President George W. Bush's wife,
Laura, is also from Midland. Odessa is now perhaps best known as the high school football-crazed
town depicted in the 1990 book *Friday Night Lights*, later turned into a movie and hit TV series.

Growth has slowed as new discoveries have grown fewer, but the area still yields much of the
state's oil and more than one-quarter of its gas. Midland's unemployment rate in 2008 was among
the lowest in the nation following the oil-price boom, but the familiar boom-and-bust fears pervaded
as the subsequent price drop quickly led to the closing of dozens of rigs. Oil prices shot up again in
early 2011.

The 11th Congressional District of Texas covers much of West Texas and encompasses 36
counties. The district sweeps 400 miles across much of the state, beginning in the hills of fast-
growing Burnet County just north of Austin and Gillespie County, home to Democratic President
Lyndon Johnson. To the west is oil-producing Loving County, on the New Mexico border. With 82
people in 2010, it was the least populous county in the United States. Geographically, the district
is larger than 12 states; 53% of the population is in Midland, Ector and Tom Green (San Angelo)
counties. None of the other counties have more than 46,000 people. The district's Hispanic population is 36% and poverty is a bit above the national average, but no longer as pervasive as when
Lyndon Johnson was a kid.

Politically, West Texas in the 1940s was, like nearly every other part of Texas, almost totally
Democratic. That began to change in the 1950s as Midland moved toward Republicans. Newcomers
like the Bushes were an important part of this trend. The current 11th District is overwhelmingly
Republican. In 2004, it cast 78% of its votes for George W. Bush, his highest percentage in the
nation. In 2008, Republican John McCain did almost as well. He got 75%, making the 11th his
fifth-best district in the nation.

Mike Conaway (R)

The congressman from the 11th District is Mike Conaway, a Republican first elected in 2004. He
is a low-profile but well-regarded conservative; *The Houston Chronicle* in December 2010 called
him "the most important Texas lawmaker you don't yet know."

Conaway grew up in Odessa—he played offensive and defensive line on the Odessa Permian
High School team, and graduated from East Texas State University, before it became known as
Texas A&M-Commerce. He worked as a certified public accountant for, among others, George W.
Bush, and was chief financial officer in Arbusto/Bush Exploration during the 1980s. After Bush
became governor, he named Conaway to the state Board of Public Accountancy, and Conaway later
chaired the National Association of State Boards of Accountancy. In May 2003, he finished second
in the all-party special primary election in the old 19th District, which included nearly half of the
new 11th. In June, he lost by fewer than 600 votes in a hard-fought runoff with Republican Randy
Neugebauer of Lubbock, who later won the seat.

After state Republicans pushed through a new redistricting plan in October 2003, Conaway
was the obvious frontrunner for this seat. Democratic Rep. Charles Stenholm, who represented

much of the area in the old 17th District, decided to run against Neugebauer in the new 19th. Conaway's Republican primary opponent was Bill Lester, a political science professor who campaigned against Bush's proposed guest worker program. Lester called for the militarization of the border with helicopter patrols to stop illegal immigration. Conaway supported increased documentation of people crossing the border. He won 75%- 25%, carrying 33 of the 36 counties and losing only in the eastern part of the district. In the general election, he won easily, 77%-22%, and has been re-elected with ease ever since.

Conaway has a solidly conservative voting record. He voted against the original $700 billion bailout of the financial services industry in October 2008, but voted for the final version after his old friend President Bush called him to urge his support. Since Bush's departure, he has remained influential. He served in 2009 as the senior Republican on an Armed Services Committee panel looking at the Pentagon's problems in acquiring goods and services, and he worked closely with Democrats on identifying areas for improvement. After the GOP won control of the House in 2010, Conaway was named to a 22-member transition team helping his party adjust to its majority status. He also became chairman of the Agriculture Committee's panel on farm commodities and risk management. He has been willing to counter fellow conservatives who have criticized subsidies for mohair, a fabric yielded from Angora goats. Numerous Angora farmers live in his district.

In 2007, Conaway, a certified public accountant, joined the executive committee of the National Republican Congressional Committee to take charge of auditing. He uncovered an internal fraud scheme by the committee's longtime treasurer, who had embezzled almost $1 million. He is known for requiring his staff to read and understand the Constitution, and wants to see all congressional aides follow suit. "It's only 4,500 words—it's not like reading *War and Peace*," he told the *Chronicle*.

TWELFTH DISTRICT

Kay Granger (R)

Elected 1996, 8th term; b. Jan. 18, 1943, Greenville; home, Ft. Worth; TX Wesleyan Col., B.S. 1965; Methodist; divorced; 3 children.

Elected Office: Ft. Worth City Cncl., 1989–91; Ft. Worth mayor, 1991–96.

Professional Career: Teacher, 1965–78; Life Insurance agent, 1978–85; Chmn., Ft. Worth Zoning Comm., 1981–88; Founder & Pres., Kay Granger Insurance Co., Inc., 1985–present.

DC Office: 320 CHOB, 20515, 202-225-5071; Fax: 202-225-5683; Web site: kaygranger.house.gov.

State Offices: Ft. Worth, 817-338-0909.

Committees: *Appropriations:* Defense; Labor, HHS, Education & Related Agencies; State, Foreign Operations & Related Programs (Chmn).

Group Ratings

	ACLU	ACU	ADA	CFG	AFS	FRC	LCV	ITIC	NTU	COC
2010	10	100	0	93	0	93	20	0	92	100
2009	–	92	0	84	0	–	0	–	85	77

National Journal Ratings

	2010 LIB	—	2010 CONS	2009 LIB	—	2009 CONS
Economic	27%	—	73%	15%	—	85%
Social	0%	—	85%	11%	—	89%
Foreign	0%	—	88%	0%	—	75%
Composite	14%	—	87%	13%	—	87%

Key Votes of the 111th Congress

1. Overturn Ledbetter	*	5. Bar federal abortion funds		9. Stop detainee transfers	Y
2. Pass $820 billion stimulus	N	6. Pass health care bill	N	10. Legalize immigrants' kids	*
3. Let guns in national parks	Y	7. Regulate financial firms	N	11. Repeal don't ask, tell	*
4. Pass cap-and-trade	N	8. Pass tax cuts for some	N	12. Limit campaign funds	N

Election Results

2010 general	Kay Granger (R)..	109,882	(72%)	($1,341,260)
	Tracey Smith (D)..	38,434	(25%)	($8,397)
	Matthew Solodow (Lib).......................................	4,601	(3%)	
2010 primary	Kay Granger (R)..	40,325	(70%)	
	Mike Brasovan (R)...	10,943	(19%)	
	Matthew Kelly (R)	6,361	(11%)	

Prior Winning Percentages: 2008 (68%), 2006 (67%), 2004 (72%), 2002 (92%), 2000 (63%), 1998 (62%), 1996 (58%)

Population		Race/Ethnicity		Work	
Pop. 2010:	831,100	White:	59.8%	Private:	81.4%
Change since 2000:	Up 27.5%	Black:	6.5%	Government:	11.8%
Urban:	82.8%	Hispanic:	28.8%	Self-employed:	6.6%
Rural:	17.2%	Asian:	2.9%	Blue collar:	26.2%
Area size:	2,218 sq. mi.	Native Am.:	0.4%	White collar:	57.7%
		Hawaiian:	0.1%	Khaki collar:	0.1%
Age		Two+ races:	1.4%	Other:	16.0%
Median age:	33.5 yrs.				
More than 65 yrs:	9.5%	*Ancestry*		Median income:	$53,163
Less than 18 yrs:	27.3%	German	10.0%	Median Home Value:	$122,900
		USA	8.5%		
Education		Irish	8.1%	**Military Veterans**	
H.S. grad:	80.1%			% of Pop:	10.4%
College grad:	23.4%				
Grad degree:	7.3%				

Part Fort Worth, Suburbs

Fort Worth has a fair claim to being the quintessential mid-American city. It sits halfway across the continent, just west of the Balcones Escarpment that divides the dry, treeless grazing lands of West Texas from the humid green croplands of East Texas, "where the West begins," as its 19th century boosters proclaimed, coining the slogan that's still used by the city. This was the last stop for cattle drives before they returned to Kansas. It is Southern in heritage and Northern

2008 Presidential Vote

John McCain (R)	171,408	(63%)
Barack Obama (D)	99,083	(36%)

2004 Presidential Vote

George Bush (R)	162,192	(67%)
John Kerry (D)	79,862	(33%)

Cook Partisan Voting Index: R+16

in its advanced post-industrial economy. It has the nation's longest row of Western wear shops and one of the nation's richest families, the Basses, whose steel skyscrapers dominate the skyline. The family also developed Sundance Square, a 38-block entertainment, office and retail district that has helped revive the downtown district in recent years.

"Cowtown," as the city is sometimes called, is the 17th largest city in the nation, larger than Boston, Memphis and Baltimore. Fort Worth has a high-tech economy and has been an aviation center since the 1940s, though one hard hit by defense cuts. Defense-related spending accounts for about 5.3% of Tarrant County's gross product, *The Dallas Morning News* reported in 2010. The big Lockheed Martin (formerly General Dynamics) plant produces numerous bombers and fighter planes for the armed forces, including the F-35 fighter jet. Next door is the Naval Air Station Fort Worth Joint Reserve Base, formerly Carswell Air Force Base, the home of the B-52 bombers for years. Bell Helicopter Textron's nearby plant is building a new reconnaissance helicopter. *The New York Times* has called the city "an irresistible combination of cowboys and culture," in part because it has some of the nation's premier small museums, including the Amon Carter Museum, the Kimbell Art Museum, the Modern Art Museum of Fort Worth, and the Sid Richardson Museum. The city also has Texas-sized watering holes and eateries, like Billy Bob's Texas, billed as the world's largest honky-tonk.

The 12th Congressional District of Texas includes two-thirds of Fort Worth and western suburban Tarrant County, as well as all of Parker and Wise counties to the west and northwest. More than three-quarters of the population is in Tarrant, which has grown an impressive 25% since 2000. The district includes northern and western city neighborhoods and the affluent southwest quarter beyond Texas Christian University, downtown and the Stockyards. Parker County was once windswept open land around the courthouse town of Weatherford, where former U.S. House

Speaker Jim Wright, a Democrat, grew up and was first elected to the House in 1954. Today, it is sprouting subdivisions. Parker County grew 32% from 2000 to 2010, to a population of 117,000. Fort Worth and Tarrant County stayed Democratic in the 1950s when Dallas went Republican. With Dallas recently swinging back to Democrats, Fort Worth and Tarrant have remained Republican. The 12th District, which Wright represented until 1989, is now solidly Republican—67% of voters here backed Republican President George W. Bush in 2004 and 63% supported Republican candidate John McCain in 2008. GOP Gov. Rick Perry drew 56% in Tarrant in his 2010 re-election.

Kay Granger (R)

The congresswoman from the 12th District is Kay Granger, first elected in 1996 and the only Republican woman to represent the Lone Star State in the House. Granger grew up in Fort Worth, graduated from Texas Wesleyan College, and worked as a teacher in North Richland Hills. She raised three children and started her own insurance agency. In 1989, she was elected to the Fort Worth Council, and two years later, was elected as mayor. In 1995, when Rep. Pete Geren, a conservative Democrat who succeeded Wright, announced he would not seek re-election, both Republican and Democratic leaders tried to recruit Granger. She decided to run in the Republican primary. In a three-candidate race, she was attacked as a liberal, partly for her support of abortion rights. But she won with 69% of the vote. Her Democratic opponent was Hugh Parmer, a former Fort Worth mayor and the Democratic nominee against Republican Sen. Phil Gramm in 1990. Parmer attacked Republican cuts in Medicare and the stewardship of Republican House Speaker Newt Gingrich. Granger called for a balanced budget and tax cuts for business, and ran on her record as mayor. She won 58%-41%, a stunning victory for a Republican in Wright's old district.

In the House, Granger's voting record has tended to be moderate on cultural issues and more conservative on economic issues. In 2010, however, she was the least conservative Republican in Texas' House delegation on fiscal matters. In 2007 and 2008, she was vice-chair of the Republican Conference, where she worked on issues such as retirement planning and reducing the influence of gangs. One of Granger's legislative achievements was enactment of tax-free savings accounts for higher education expenses.

With a seat on the Appropriations Committee, Granger keeps a close eye on local Pentagon spending. She has worked to maintain production of Lockheed Martin planes that are produced in her district. In 2011, she became chairman of the Appropriations Committee's Subcommittee on State and Foreign Operations, where her experience with military spending and her interest in human rights are useful. She was among the members of her party warning freshman Republicans against cutting foreign aid too deeply. "I think that there is more pressure (to cut foreign aid) because there's this misunderstanding of how much that part of the budget is," she said on the PBS show *NewsHour*. However, she also opposes major increases in foreign aid spending. Despite personal lobbying from U2 singer and human rights activist Bono and former Bush White House Chief of Staff Joshua Bolten, she said that the U.S. Agency for International Development's request for a 22% increase for fiscal 2012 was "unrealistic in today's budget environment." She also rebuked Homeland Security Secretary Janet Napolitano about the violent state of the U.S-Mexico border, telling Fox News in April 2011, "It is a delusion she thinks the border is safe."

In January 2005, Granger traveled to Iraq, where she and then-Rep. Ellen Tauscher, D-Calif., conducted a training session for women candidates in their election. Granger continues to co-chair the Iraqi Women's Caucus. In late 2009, Granger visited U.S. troops in Afghanistan, and was among the Republicans who urged the Obama administration to step up pressure on Afghan President Hamid Karzai to establish a "functional, transparent government that does not condone corruption." She also has served on the Center for Strategic and International Studies' Commission on Smart Global Health Policy.

Granger has been re-elected by wide margins. Her moderate tendencies inspired challenges from her right in the 2010 Republican primary, from tea party activist and energy executive Mike Brasovan, and from wholesale grocery distributor Matthew Kelly. Both were underfunded, and she won with 70% of the vote. She went on to defeat Democratic opponent Tracey Smith, 72% to 25%. Granger is the author of a book, *What's Right About America: Celebrating Our Nation's Values*, published in 2006.

THIRTEENTH DISTRICT

Mac Thornberry (R)

Elected 1994, 9th term; b. July 15, 1958, Clarendon; home, Clarendon; TX Tech. U., B.A. 1980, U. of TX Law Schl., J.D. 1983; Presbyterian; married (Sally); 2 children.

Professional Career: Legis. cnsl., U.S. Rep. Tom Loeffler, 1983–85; Chief of staff, U.S. Rep. Larry Combest, 1985–88; Dpty. asst. secy. of state for Legis. Affairs, 1988–89; Practicing atty., 1989–94; Rancher 1989-94.

DC Office: 2209 RHOB, 20515, 202-225-3706; Fax: 202-225-3486; Web site: thornberry.house.gov.

State Offices: Amarillo, 806-371-8844; Wichita Falls, 940-692-1700.

Committees: *Armed Services* (VChmn): Emerging Threats & Capabilities (Chmn); Strategic Forces. *Permanent Select Committee on Intelligence:* Technical & Tactical Intelligence.

Group Ratings

	ACLU	ACU	ADA	CFG	AFS	FRC	LCV	ITIC	NTU	COC
2010	13	100	0	95	0	100	0	33	90	88
2009	–	100	0	97	0	–	0	–	92	73

National Journal Ratings

	2010 LIB — 2010 CONS	2009 LIB — 2009 CONS
Economic	7% — 92%	0% — 96%
Social	0% — 85%	0% — 93%
Foreign	0% — 88%	0% — 75%
Composite	7% — 93%	6% — 94%

Key Votes of the 111th Congress

1. Overturn Ledbetter	N	5. Bar federal abortion funds	Y
2. Pass $820 billion stimulus	N	6. Pass health care bill	N
3. Let guns in national parks	Y	7. Regulate financial firms	N
4. Pass cap-and-trade	N	8. Pass tax cuts for some	N

9. Stop detainee transfers	Y
10. Legalize immigrants' kids	N
11. Repeal don't ask, tell	N
12. Limit campaign funds	N

Election Results

2010 general	Mac Thornberry (R)	113,201	(87%)	($689,960)
	Keith Dyer (I)	11,192	(9%)	
	John Burwell (Lib)	5,650	(4%)	
2010 primary	Mac Thornberry (R)	unopposed		

Prior Winning Percentages: 2008 (78%), 2006 (74%), 2004 (92%), 2002 (79%), 2000 (68%), 1998 (68%), 1996 (67%), 1994 (55%)

Population		Race/Ethnicity		Work	
Pop. 2010:	672,781	White:	67.2%	Private:	72.4%
Change since 2000:	Up 3.2%	Black:	5.6%	Government:	19.0%
Urban:	69.9%	Hispanic:	23.4%	Self-employed:	8.3%
Rural:	30.1%	Asian:	1.7%	Blue collar:	26.4%
Area size:	40,404 sq. mi.	Native Am.:	0.6%	White collar:	51.5%
		Hawaiian:	0.0%	Khaki collar:	1.4%
Age		Two+ races:	1.3%	Other:	20.6%
Median age:	35.5 yrs.				
More than 65 yrs:	13.5%	*Ancestry*		Median income:	$42,938
Less than 18 yrs:	25.7%	German	12.6%	Median Home Value:	$84,900
		Irish	8.9%		
Education		USA	8.4%	**Military Veterans**	
H.S. grad:	80.8%			% of Pop:	10.4%
College grad:	18.3%				
Grad degree:	5.6%				

North Texas; Amarillo

The farther west one travels in Texas, the browner the land gets and the smaller the towns get, until you arrive at counties containing only a few hundred people each—plus quite a few more head of cattle. At that point, the land rises nearly 1,000 feet in elevation, up steep hillsides from the gullies along the rivers that for most of the year are just trickles, to the tilted tableland that makes up the High Plains of West Texas. The winds here sweep down from the Rockies, the

2008 Presidential Vote		
John McCain (R) 181,456	(76%)
Barack Obama (D) 53,837	(23%)
2004 Presidential Vote		
George Bush (R) 183,375	(78%)
John Kerry (D) 52,431	(22%)
Cook Partisan Voting Index: R+29		

land is barren except where irrigated, often with the now dangerously depleted waters of the Ogallala Aquifer. The land alternates between grazing areas and cotton fields. But here and there in this demanding environment—sticky-hot in the summer, swept by north winds from Canada in winter, always threatened by tornadoes—comfortable cities have been built to house the people and businesses that bring forth some of the nation's most abundant oil, natural gas, helium and other elements from the earth.

The 13th Congressional District of Texas covers more than 40,000 square miles, from the New Mexico border to just north of Dallas, and it includes 42 counties and parts of two others. The population of this region has been either in decline or stagnant for nearly three decades. In the 1990s, the district registered a population increase of just 5%, the smallest gain of any Texas district. From 2000 to 2010, the population grew by just 3%. Around Wichita Falls is the agricultural land of the Red River Valley and one of Bell Helicopter's V-22 Osprey plants. Sheppard Air Force Base, a medical facility and pilot training center, was hit hard by cutbacks in the 2005 base review.

The area produces cotton and milo, a variety of sorghum, and is home to one of the nation's oldest cattle auctions. The area was long dominated by Texas Anglos, but Latinos lately have been moving here in large numbers to work in the fields or in crop processing. Today, the district is 23% Hispanic. Much of the High Plains economy is based on natural resources. The largest city here is Amarillo in the heart of cowboy country. It—not Chicago—is the windiest city in the United States, and a large wind farm is proposed north of the city. Just outside town is the Pantex plant that secretly assembled the nation's thousands of nuclear warheads and was the epicenter of American defense in the Cold War.

Settled by Confederate veterans, the valley was heavily Democratic through the 1970s. The High Plains was for years more Republican. Both parts are now solidly Republican. The 78% that George W. Bush won here in 2004 was his third-best performance in the nation. GOP presidential nominee John McCain won 76.4% in 2008, his second-best district in the nation, behind Alabama's 6th District.

Mac Thornberry (R)

The congressman from the 13th District is Mac Thornberry, a Republican first elected in 1994. He is considered one of Congress' brainiest and most thoughtful Republicans on national and domestic security issues.

His great-great-grandfather, Amos Thornberry, a Union Army veteran and staunch Republican, moved to Clay County, just east of Wichita Falls, in the 1880s. A year after Amos died in 1925, his son bought the cattle ranch that Mac Thornberry, his brothers and father now run. After college and law school in Texas, Thornberry worked for Texas Republican Reps. Tom Loeffler and Larry Combest. He returned to practice law in West Texas, and in 1994, challenged Democratic Rep. Bill Sarpalius, whom he attacked for voting for President Bill Clinton's budget and tax legislation. He also profited from news stories that said Sarpalius failed to pay a company that moved him to Washington, and then accepted a fee for speaking at the company's convention in Las Vegas. Thornberry won 55%-45%, and has rolled up large re-election margins ever since.

In the House, Thornberry has compiled a solidly conservative voting record, though he has a pragmatic streak and is hardly the most ideological Republican in the Texas delegation. In keeping with his scholarly nature, his official website includes an essay explaining his philosophy and explaining his interest "in continuing to push government to work smarter and more efficiently."

Thornberry has often been at the forefront of security issues. In 2002, after the September 11 terrorist attacks, he played a key role in the establishment of the new Homeland Security Department. He took over in January 2011 as chairman of the Armed Services Committee's terrorism panel, and Speaker John Boehner also asked him to lead an effort to develop a cyber security strategy for the country. Earlier, as a member of the Intelligence Committee, Thornberry criticized delays in integrating computer networks and intelligence analyses at the Homeland Security Department. He also has championed missile defense and called for better coordination of military space programs.

Thornberry was critical of President Barack Obama's arms control deal with Russia in 2010 for precluding the use of nuclear weapons against non-nuclear nations. But he can be more pragmatic than other defense hawks. He served on a bipartisan commission in 2007 that drew up recommendations for winning the war in Iraq with both lethal and non-lethal approaches, such as diplomacy and foreign aid. Despite his expertise on security matters, he lost his bid in 2009 to chair the full Armed Services Committee to Buck McKeon, R-Calif., who had more seniority.

On domestic issues, Thornberry has pressed for repeal of the estate tax and also tax credits to encourage production of oil in marginal wells. In 2010, he got a bill into law expanding access to state veterans' homes to parents whose children died while serving in the military. He introduced a bill in January 2011 to help states set up special health care courts staffed by judges with expertise in the subject. The judges would serve as an alternative to juries that Republicans say are inclined to award unnecessarily large damage amounts in malpractice cases.

FOURTEENTH DISTRICT

Ron Paul (R)

Elected April 1996, 11th full term; b. Aug. 20, 1935, Pittsburgh, PA; home, Surfside; Gettysburg Col., B.A. 1957, Duke U., M.D. 1961; Protestant; married (Carol); 5 children.

Military Career: Flight surgeon, Air Force, 1963-68.

Elected Office: U.S. House of Reps., 1976–77, 1979–85.

Professional Career: Practicing physician, 1968–96.

DC Office: 203 CHOB, 20515, 202-225-2831; Web site: paul.house.gov.

State Offices: Lake Jackson, 979-285-0231; Victoria, 361-576-1231.

Committees: *Financial Services:* Domestic Monetary Policy & Technology (Chmn); International Monetary Policy & Trade. *Foreign Affairs:* Asia & the Pacific; Oversight & Investigations.

Group Ratings

	ACLU	ACU	ADA	CFG	AFS	FRC	LCV	ITIC	NTU	COC
2010	43	96	15	90	13	81	0	33	95	88
2009	–	91	5	97	0	–	0	–	96	67

National Journal Ratings

	2010 LIB — 2010 CONS		2009 LIB — 2009 CONS	
Economic	22%	— 78%	15%	— 85%
Social	34%	— 65%	27%	— 73%
Foreign	40%	— 60%	47%	— 53%
Composite	32%	— 68%	30%	— 70%

Key Votes of the 111th Congress

1. Overturn Ledbetter	N	5. Bar federal abortion funds	Y	9. Stop detainee transfers	N
2. Pass $820 billion stimulus	N	6. Pass health care bill	N	10. Legalize immigrants' kids	N
3. Let guns in national parks	Y	7. Regulate financial firms	N	11. Repeal don't ask, tell	Y
4. Pass cap-and-trade	N	8. Pass tax cuts for some	Y	12. Limit campaign funds	N

Election Results

2010 general	Ron Paul (R)	140,623	(76%)	($986,269)
	Robert Pruett (D)	44,431	(24%)	($28,008)
2010 primary	Ron Paul (R)	45,990	(81%)	
	Tim Graney (R)	5,499	(10%)	
	John Gay (R)	3,004	(5%)	

Prior Winning Percentages: 2008 (100%), 2006 (60%), 2004 (100%), 2002 (68%), 2000 (60%), 1998 (55%), 1996 (51%), 1982 (99%), 1980 (51%), 1978 (51%), 1976 special (56%)

Population		Race/Ethnicity		Work	
Pop. 2010:	779,704	White:	57.0%	Private:	77.1%
Change since 2000:	Up 19.7%	Black:	8.9%	Government:	15.6%
Urban:	71.1%	Hispanic:	29.0%	Self-employed:	7.1%
Rural:	28.9%	Asian:	3.5%	Blue collar:	25.5%
Area size:	9,380 sq. mi.	Native Am.:	0.3%	White collar:	57.8%
		Hawaiian:	0.0%	Khaki collar:	0.1%
Age		Two+ races:	1.2%	Other:	16.7%
Median age:	36.6 yrs.				
More than 65 yrs:	11.3%	*Ancestry*		Median income:	$54,537
Less than 18 yrs:	27.1%	German	13.5%	Median Home Value:	$126,600
		Irish	8.9%		
Education		English	7.0%	**Military Veterans**	
H.S. grad:	83.3%			% of Pop:	10.1%
College grad:	23.8%				
Grad degree:	7.4%				

North Gulf Coast; Victoria

Retreating east from the Alamo, the ragtag army led by Sam Houston passed over what would become, after their bloody and conclusive victory in 1836 at San Jacinto, some of the prime cropland in the Republic and later the state of Texas. The hilly and river-crossed land between Houston and Austin, named after Texas' first two leaders, was settled early. The flat coastal plains, steamy and humid much of the year, were settled later, when the railroads came in.

2008 Presidential Vote		
John McCain (R) 177,370	(66%)
Barack Obama (D) 88,532	(33%)
2004 Presidential Vote		
George Bush (R) 169,480	(67%)
John Kerry (D) 82,792	(33%)
Cook Partisan Voting Index:	R+18

Rice is grown along the coast, and cotton and cattle dominate inland. The Gulf of Mexico coastline, though it has plenty of inlets, never had any important ports in the stretch between Houston and Corpus Christi until the discovery of oil here made it worthwhile to build channels to ship the oil out.

This is the 14th Congressional District of Texas. With rural countryside and the cities of Victoria and El Campo, it runs along the Gulf coast between Corpus Christi and Port Arthur. Victoria is a rail hub that serves Gulf ports, and it also includes large industrial plants, such as DuPont, Union Carbide, Alcoa and BP Chemicals. Galveston, on a barrier island on the Gulf, was an immigrant port known as the Ellis Island of the West until a 1900 hurricane killed thousands. The city is now guarded by a 17-foot seawall and connected to the mainland by a hurricane-resistant bridge; its cruise ship port is the country's fourth largest. After the BP oil spill began in 2010, local officials feared tourists would stay away. But the area ended up benefitting from vacationers fleeing beaches in Louisiana, Mississippi and Florida, where the impact was worse.

This district is mostly small-city Texas, but much of it now surrounds the suburban fringes of metropolitan Houston. Like other parts of the state, it has seen a surge of Hispanics, whose population increased in Galveston County 45% from 2000 to 2010. The region is ancestrally Democratic, but is now Republican. The district voted 67% for President George W. Bush in 2004 and 66% for Republican John McCain in 2008. GOP Gov. Rick Perry won 57% in Galveston County in 2010.

Ron Paul (R)

The congressman from the 14th District is Ron Paul, a Republican first elected to Congress more than three decades ago. He failed in his only attempt to win statewide office, yet gained celebrity status in 2008 in his second run for president. One of the most proudly individualistic politicians on Capitol Hill, he functions as a sort of father figure to the tea party movement, which helped elect his son, Rand Paul, to the Senate in 2010. He announced a third presidential run in May 2011.

Paul grew up on a dairy farm in western Pennsylvania, and, with his four brothers, started helping out with the chores when he was still a boy. When he got older, he had a newspaper route, and then a job as a dairy truck driver. He was a track standout in high school, winning a state championship in the 220-yard dash his junior year. Paul was also student body president. He got a science degree from Gettysburg College in 1957 and a medical degree from Duke University. He served as an Air Force flight surgeon in the 1960s, and then moved with his wife, Carol, to Texas to practice obstetrics and gynecology in Brazoria County. Paul recalls that he was dismayed when

Republican President Richard Nixon cut the connection between the dollar and gold in 1971, and led to him becoming increasingly interested in politics, although he continued to practice medicine.

In 1976, he won the House seat in a special election by defeating Democratic state Rep. Bob Gammage. Seven months later, he lost the seat to Gammage in the regular general election. But he came back to reclaim the seat by defeating Gammage in 1978. Paul ran for the Senate in 1984 and lost the Republican primary to U.S. Rep. Phil Gramm 73%-16%. His House seat was won by a young legislator and exterminating company owner, Tom DeLay, a Republican who rose to become one of the most powerful members of Congress until an ethics scandal drove him from office. In 1988, Paul ran for president as a Libertarian candidate, finishing a distant third with 432,000 votes, 0.47% of the total.

Paul reentered electoral politics by challenging Rep. Greg Laughlin in 1996. Laughlin had switched from the Democratic to the Republican Party in June 1995. He had a moderate voting record, and Republicans offered him a seat on the powerful House Ways and Means Committee to make the switch. Paul raised money from a nationwide network of Libertarians, gold bugs and subscribers to the *Ron Paul Political Report*. Laughlin led in the primary with 43% of the vote, but Paul won the runoff, 54%-46%. In the general election, Democrats ran Charles "Lefty" Morris, a former president of the state trial lawyers' association. With the slogan "Lefty is right," Morris hit Paul for favoring abolition of the minimum wage, repeal of federal anti-drug laws and anti-prostitution laws. Paul won 51%-48%.

In his first stint in the House, Paul had advanced some ideas that by the mid-1990s, when he was returning to Congress, had become more widely accepted: term limits on lawmakers and abolition of the income tax. Other Paul ideas remained outside the political norm. He supported ending all government funding of education, cutting $150 billion from the defense budget, and returning to the gold standard. Paul practices what he preaches. As a physician, he did not accept payment by Medicare or Medicaid, he wouldn't let his children accept federal student loans and he refuses his congressional pension. He has written several books, the most recent being *Liberty Defined: The 50 Urgent Issues That Affect Our Freedom,* a summary of his positions on topics ranging from his opposition to abortion to his opposition to U.S. foreign aid to Israel.

With his libertarian views, Paul's voting record has been anything but rock-solid Republican. *National Journal's* ratings historically place him near the middle of the House. "Dr. No," as he is called, never votes for legislation that in his view is not expressly authorized by the Constitution. Frequently, his insistence on limited government makes Paul the House's lone dissenter. He has voted against bills to encourage people to participate in the census, to award Congressional Gold Medals to Rosa Parks and Pope John Paul II, to pass the USA PATRIOT Act after the September 11 attacks, and to spend money on homeland security. After his district in September 2005 was rocked by Hurricane Rita, he voted against hurricane relief. He favors relaxation of restrictions on illegal drugs, though he says that he has never even smoked a cigarette. More recently, he defended controversial WikiLeaks founder Julian Assange, whom many lawmakers condemned after his website released hundreds of thousands of sensitive U.S. military and diplomatic documents. "In a free society, we're supposed to know the truth," Paul said. Paul also opposed the constitutional ban on same-sex marriages, saying that the states should set such policy.

His isolationist views on foreign policy made his voting record on those issues indistinct from many liberal Democrats. He was the only Republican to vote "present" on the resolution expressing support for the military forces at the start of the war with Iraq. In June 2005, he co-sponsored with liberal Rep. Dennis Kucinich, D-Ohio, a resolution to withdraw from Iraq. Paul envisions virtually no role for the U.S. government overseas, from military defense to international trade. He calls himself a "non-interventionist," not an isolationist. His iconoclasm makes him probably the least dependable and persuadable Republican in the House and it explains why many liberals like him. Kucinich, during his abortive 2008 presidential bid, suggested he would consider Paul as his running mate "to balance the energies in this country." And he does offer alternatives. He has been among the most prolific legislators, sponsoring dozens of bills and amendments each year. Typically, none pass.

When Republicans regained control of the House in 2010, however, Paul emerged with a position of real authority as the new chairman of the Financial Services Committee's subcommittee on domestic monetary policy. Its jurisdiction includes the U.S. currency and the valuation of the dollar and the Federal Reserve, an agency that was the subject of his book, *End the Fed*. "Before two or three years ago, this could have never happened. . .But now people are looking for alternative answers," he told *National Review* of the GOP leadership's decision to give him a subcommittee gavel. He vowed to examine why monetary policy is, in his view, a major contributor to unemployment. He also reintroduced his bill to have the Government Accountability Office audit the Fed, a proposal that was included in the Dodd-Frank financial regulation overhaul of 2010 but removed in conference committee.

Given Paul's political isolation, his entry into the 2008 presidential campaign was not taken seriously. In March 2007, at age 71, he announced his candidacy for the Republican presidential nomination with the slogan, "The Taxpayers' Best Friend." Paul drew widespread attention, and the ire of former New York City Mayor Rudy Giuliani, when he suggested during a May 2007 primary debate that interventionist American foreign policy led to September 11. Despite being dismissed by party professionals and most of the news media, Paul's campaign generated grassroots interest and online support. His bloggers and other Internet backers sometimes flooded the dominant political websites. Paul raised $34 million, largely through the Internet, including a single-day fundraising record of $6 million in December 2007. He finished fifth in both the Iowa caucuses and the New Hampshire primary, though exit polls showed that he fared much better among young voters.

His well-organized and web-savvy supporters helped him to win many Internet polls, though that yielded scant impact on the official nominating contest. Nationwide, he received nearly 1.2 million Republican votes, or, 5.6% of the total cast. He won 12.3% of the total caucus vote, running second in Louisiana, Montana and Nevada. Despite his plodding speeches and self-effacing style, his popularity continued even after his campaign sputtered. In May 2008, his book *The Revolution: A Manifesto* was No. 1 on *The New York Times* best-seller list. Republican convention organizers refused to permit him to speak after he refused to endorse party nominee John McCain. So he sponsored his own events in Minneapolis-St. Paul, where the GOP convention was held, including a loud counter-rally for more than 10,000 in Minneapolis. Paul briefly considered a third-party run in the fall, but instead he urged support for other third-party candidates.

Back home, the national campaign raised speculation that the renewed attention to his views could weaken him in seeking to return to Congress. He was challenged by Chris Peden, a Friendswood city councilman who raised $268,000 and criticized Paul for failing to pass legislation or to vote with his party in Congress. On the day that McCain clinched the nomination, he won the primary for re-election to the House 70%-30%. Democrats ran no challenger in November.

Two years later, Paul beat a token Democratic opponent 76%-24%. During the 2010 election season, he instead focused on getting his son, Rand, elected to the Senate as a Republican from Kentucky. The younger Paul beat an establishment-backed challenger in the GOP primary and overcame questions about his past to win with massive tea party support. It marked the first time that a father has served in the House with a son in the Senate. (The roles were reversed for Democratic Sen. Edward Kennedy of Massachusetts and his son, Patrick.) The Pauls vowed to cooperate. "There will obviously be a lot of overlap," Ron Paul told *National Journal* in December 2010. "I don't think we have any disagreement about monetary policy."

FIFTEENTH DISTRICT

Rubén Hinojosa (D)

Elected 1996, 8th term; b. Aug. 20, 1940, Mercedes; home, Mercedes; U. of TX, B.B.A. 1962, M.B.A. 1980; Catholic; married (Marty); 5 children.

Elected Office: TX Bd. of Educ., 1974–84.

Professional Career: Pres. & CEO, H&H Foods Inc., 1962–present.

DC Office: 2262 RHOB, 20515, 202-225-2531; Fax: 202-225-5688; Web site: hinojosa.house.gov.

State Offices: Beeville, 361-358-8400; Edinburg, 956-682-5545.

Committees: *Education & the Workforce:* Health, Employment, Labor & Pensions; Higher Education & Workforce Training (RMM). *Financial Services:* Capital Markets and Government Sponsored Enterprises; Financial Institutions & Consumer Credit.

Group Ratings

	ACLU	ACU	ADA	CFG	AFS	FRC	LCV	ITIC	NTU	COC
2010	88	0	75	6	100	0	80	100	8	38
2009	–	0	90	6	100	–	79	–	2	31

National Journal Ratings

	2010 LIB — 2010 CONS	2009 LIB — 2009 CONS
Economic	61% — 38%	86% — 14%
Social	60% — 40%	71% — 29%
Foreign	56% — 44%	69% — 30%
Composite	59% — 41%	76% — 25%

Key Votes of the 111th Congress

1. Overturn Ledbetter	Y	5. Bar federal abortion funds	N	9. Stop detainee transfers	Y
2. Pass $820 billion stimulus	Y	6. Pass health care bill	Y	10. Legalize immigrants' kids	Y
3. Let guns in national parks	N	7. Regulate financial firms	Y	11. Repeal don't ask, tell	Y
4. Pass cap-and-trade	Y	8. Pass tax cuts for some	Y	12. Limit campaign funds	Y

Election Results

2010 general	Rubén Hinojosa (D)	53,546	(56%)	($609,898)
	Eddie Zamora (R)	39,964	(42%)	($87,768)
	Aaron Cohn (Lib)	2,570	(3%)	
2010 primary	Rubén Hinojosa (D)	37,430	(84%)	
	Doug Purl (D)	7,282	(16%)	

Prior Winning Percentages: 2008 (66%), 2006 (62%), 2004 (58%), 2002 (100%), 2000 (88%), 1998 (58%), 1996 (62%)

Population		Race/Ethnicity		Work	
Pop. 2010:	787,124	White:	15.0%	Private:	70.2%
Change since 2000:	Up 20.8%	Black:	1.3%	Government:	20.0%
Urban:	82.1%	Hispanic:	82.5%	Self-employed:	9.5%
Rural:	17.9%	Asian:	0.8%	Blue collar:	22.1%
Area size:	10,849 sq. mi.	Native Am.:	0.1%	White collar:	52.8%
		Hawaiian:	0.0%	Khaki collar:	0.1%
Age		Two+ races:	0.2%	Other:	25.0%
Median age:	30.0 yrs.				
More than 65 yrs:	11.3%	*Ancestry*		Median income:	$33,000
Less than 18 yrs:	32.9%	German	5.7%	Median Home Value:	$73,800
		Irish	2.9%		
Education		English	2.7%	**Military Veterans**	
H.S. grad:	65.1%			% of Pop:	7.3%
College grad:	14.9%				
Grad degree:	4.7%				

South Central Texas; McAllen

A century ago, there was little here but desert wilderness in the Lower Rio Grande Valley in South Texas. Only a handful of people lived anywhere near the shallow, sluggish Rio Grande. There was no U.S. Border Patrol because very few people wanted to venture across desert. Then came pioneers like Lloyd Bentsen Sr., father of the former senator and Treasury secretary, who arrived after World War I with $5 in his pocket and became one of the Valley's biggest

2008 Presidential Vote		
Barack Obama (D) 101,566	(60%)
John McCain (R) 67,650	(40%)
2004 Presidential Vote		
George Bush (R) 81,280	(51%)
John Kerry (D) 77,011	(49%)
Cook Partisan Voting Index: D+3		

landowners. Bentsen and others cleared the land and dug canals, hired Mexican and Mexican-American workers, and with irrigated water from the Rio Grande, planted citrus groves, cornfields and palm windbreaks, ran cattle and drilled for oil and gas. Along U.S. 83, north of the Rio Grande, these pioneers built a string of towns with Anglo names and storefronts. But most of the people here were Latino in culture and language. Wage levels higher than in Mexico, though low by U.S. standards, brought more Mexicans over the border.

The 15th Congressional District of Texas is one of three districts in the Lower Rio Grande Valley. It has gone through multiple iterations in this decade alone. A court-drawn redistricting plan in 2006 imposed modest changes, making the district more favorably Democratic and increasing its Hispanic population to 80%. The days are past when ranchers and oilmen wielded absolute political power here. There is instead a robust, mostly Hispanic, politics. Although the district reaches as far north as the rural area between Corpus Christi and San Antonio, about 75% of the district's residents live just north of the river in Hidalgo and Cameron counties, in or near the string of towns from McAllen to Harlingen.

Reasonably priced real estate contributed to fast-paced growth in the 15th District. Hidalgo and Cameron counties' populations rose 83% from 1990 to 2010, from 644,000 to 1.2 million. The local infrastructure has barely kept up as subdivisions have replaced citrus groves. A Gallup-Healthways survey of congressional districts in 2010 ranked this the nation's happiest. In the McAllen area, new suburbanites work just across the border as corporate managers in the low-wage "maquiladoras," or factories. But unemployment rates soared in the 2007-09 recession, and stayed above 11% in the area in 2010. There are also pockets of poverty here. Hidalgo County has the lowest median family income in Texas. The area is heavily Democratic in the border areas but more conservative elsewhere. In the 2010 governor's race, Democrat Bill White won 67% in Hidalgo and more than 73% in the two counties to the north, while GOP Gov. Rick Perry racked up similar totals in the areas farther to the east.

Rubén Hinojosa (D)

The congressman from the 15th District is Rubén Hinojosa, a Democrat first elected in 1996. He is known as a staunch advocate for improving education, housing and rural economic development for Hispanics.

Hinojosa (*Hee-no-HO-sa*) grew up in Mercedes, where his family owns H&H Foods, a company that produces Mexican foods and is one of the largest employers in the Valley. After earning his bachelor's and M.B.A. from the University of Texas, he went into the family business and was active in civic affairs, primarily in education and regional development. He served on the state Board of Education and led an effort to create three regional magnet schools.

After Democratic Rep. Kika de la Garza announced he would not seek re-election in 1996, Hinojosa decided to run. In the Democratic primary, he led Anglo lawyer Jim Selman 34%-33%. Selman questioned Hinojosa's Democratic credentials and said he profited from government contracts. Hinojosa emphasized his interest in improving educational opportunities and extending highways to the Lower Rio Grande Valley. Hinojosa took some moderate positions, calling for a reduction of the capital gains tax and investment tax credits for those making capital improvements. He won the runoff 52%-48% and easily won the general election.

Hinojosa once had a moderate voting record among House Democrats, especially on economic issues, but in recent years, has moved more in line with his party to back the Obama administration's major initiatives. He decried proposed GOP budget cuts in February 2011 that he contended would "stunt our economy and our means for creating better education for Americans." He also introduced a bill that month to provide more money for low-performing high schools to reduce dropout rates. He has sought to protect benefits for legal immigrants, to promote the North American

Free Trade Agreement and to demand that Mexico deliver on its agreement for water to South Texas farmers. He has a proclivity for holding out on votes to make last-minute legislative deals. He supported Republican President George W. Bush's proposal for broader authority to negotiate trade deals after he was promised a job training project for his district.

But Hinojosa has struggled to advance in the House. Despite support in 2003 from the Texas delegation for a spot on the Ways and Means Committee, Hinojosa was passed over in favor of Texas Rep. Max Sandlin, an ally of Minority Whip Nancy Pelosi. In early 2005, Hinojosa made an unsuccessful bid for a leadership post when he ran for vice-chairman of the Democratic Caucus, but he abandoned his candidacy after two weeks due to lack of support. After Democrats won control of the House in 2006, Hinojosa chaired the Higher Education, Life Long Learning and Competitiveness Subcommittee, where he focused on families traditionally left behind in American education. After the GOP victories in 2010, he became that panel's ranking Democrat. He also became the Congressional Hispanic Caucus' first vice chairman, its No. 2 position.

Hinojosa made headlines in February 2011 when, as a member of the Financial Services Committee, he filed for personal bankruptcy. He blamed the situation on a loan that he guaranteed for his family's food products company that led him to owe $2.6 million to Wells Fargo Bank. His troubles were compounded by a lackluster first quarter of fundraising in which he brought in less than $8,000. Redistricting in 2012 could affect his future political plans. After a series of easy election victories, Hinojosa had a scare in 2004, largely because of redistricting, but still won 58%-41%. The 2006 court-ordered redistricting returned Hinojosa to firmer footing. It removed four of the six troublesome northern counties Hinojosa lost in 2004.

SIXTEENTH DISTRICT

Silvestre Reyes (D)

Elected 1996, 8th term; b. Nov. 10, 1944, Canutillo; home, El Paso; El Paso Commun. Col., A.A. 1977; Catholic; married (Carolina); 3 children.

Military Career: Army, 1966–68 (Vietnam).

Elected Office: Canutillo Schl. Board, 1968–70.

Professional Career: Border Patrol agent, 1969–95.

DC Office: 2210 RHOB, 20515, 202-225-4831; Fax: 202-225-2016; Web site: reyes.house.gov.

State Offices: El Paso, 915-534-4400.

Committees: *Armed Services:* Air & Land Forces (RMM); Readiness. *Veterans' Affairs:* Health.

Group Ratings

	ACLU	ACU	ADA	CFG	AFS	FRC	LCV	ITIC	NTU	COC
2010	80	0	75	5	100	6	70	67	5	0
2009	–	4	95	4	100	–	93	–	3	40

National Journal Ratings

	2010 LIB — 2010 CONS		2009 LIB — 2009 CONS	
Economic	70%	30%	68%	30%
Social	70%	30%	58%	41%
Foreign	47%	53%	66%	33%
Composite	62%	38%	65%	35%

Key Votes of the 111th Congress

1. Overturn Ledbetter	Y	5. Bar federal abortion funds		9. Stop detainee transfers	Y
2. Pass $820 billion stimulus	Y	6. Pass health care bill	Y	10. Legalize immigrants' kids	Y
3. Let guns in national parks	Y	7. Regulate financial firms	Y	11. Repeal don't ask, tell	Y
4. Pass cap-and-trade	Y	8. Pass tax cuts for some	Y	12. Limit campaign funds	Y

Election Results

2010 general	Silvestre Reyes (D)	49,301	(58%)	($1,044,123)
	Tim Besco (R)	31,051	(37%)	($7,200)
	Bill Collins (Lib)	4,319	(5%)	
2010 primary	Silvestre Reyes (D)	unopposed		

Prior Winning Percentages: 2008 (82%), 2006 (79%), 2004 (68%), 2002 (100%), 2000 (68%), 1998 (88%), 1996 (71%)

Population		Race/Ethnicity		Work	
Pop. 2010:	757,427	White:	13.6%	Private:	69.6%
Change since 2000:	Up 16.2%	Black:	2.7%	Government:	23.5%
Urban:	98.3%	Hispanic:	81.5%	Self-employed:	6.7%
Rural:	1.7%	Asian:	1.0%	Blue collar:	22.4%
Area size:	582 sq. mi.	Native Am.:	0.3%	White collar:	56.0%
		Hawaiian:	0.1%	Khaki collar:	2.2%
Age		Two+ races:	0.7%	Other:	19.4%
Median age:	31.0 yrs.				
More than 65 yrs:	10.8%	*Ancestry*		Median income:	$36,272
Less than 18 yrs:	31.2%	German	3.6%	Median Home Value:	$107,000
		USA	3.2%		
Education		Irish	2.5%	**Military Veterans**	
H.S. grad:	72.0%			% of Pop:	9.2%
College grad:	20.2%				
Grad degree:	6.8%				

El Paso, Suburbs

El Paso, Texas, and Juarez, Mexico, face each other across the narrow Rio Grande, their tree-shaded streets spread out below the rough brown face of Comanche Peak. Downtown El Paso is only a few blocks from the bridge to Juarez. The two border cities are surrounded by hundreds of miles of some of North America's most rugged and desolate landscape. El Paso is closer to San Diego than to Houston, it's 600 miles from Dallas-Fort Worth, and it's in a differ-

2008 Presidential Vote
Barack Obama (D) 118,219   (66%)
John McCain (R) 60,306   (33%)

2004 Presidential Vote
John Kerry (D) 92,792   (57%)
George Bush (R) 71,454   (44%)
Cook Partisan Voting Index: D+10

ent time zone from the rest of the state. Still, the region has grown significantly. In the 1950s, El Paso and Juarez each had a population of 140,000. In 2010, there were 801,000 people in El Paso County, more than 80% of them Hispanic, and the Mexican census counted 1.3 million in metro Juarez. This is a bilingual, bicultural pair of cities, where most people have a Mexican heritage. El Paso is one of the lowest-wage and lowest-education locales in the United States, though statistically it also is one of the safest. Juarez, though struggling with drug cartel violence and crime, is one of the highest-wage cities in Mexico.

Maquiladora factories created a cross-border economy, bolstered by the North American Free Trade Agreement. Much of the local economy is built on cheap, low-skill labor. South of the border, there is a large General Motors technical center. Many factories on both sides of the border were shuttered during the 2007-09 recession, but trade with Mexico helped El Paso shield itself from the worst of the economic downturn. The other factor bolstering the city's economy was Fort Bliss, a big winner in the 2005 base closing review, with a $5 billion expansion and a net gain of nearly 30,000 soldiers. The Milken Institute in October 2010 ranked El Paso's economy as the 9th best-performing among 200 metro areas. That same month, *Portfolio* magazine ranked the city as having the highest per-capita income growth among large metro areas in the last 25 years.

The 16th Congressional District of Texas is made up of 96% of El Paso County—the city itself, the suburban fringe, giant Fort Bliss to the north and rural housing settlements known as colonias, most without electricity and running water, spreading out to the east and south. The district is overwhelmingly Democratic, though native son George W. Bush got 44% of the vote in the district in 2004. Republican John McCain got just 33% in 2008, and Democrat Barack Obama won it easily with 66%. Democrat Bill White beat Republican Rick Perry here, 61%-37%, in the 2010 gubernatorial race.

Silvestre Reyes (D)

The congressman from the 16th District is Silvestre Reyes, a Democrat first elected in 1996. Once the chairman of the House Intelligence Committee, he has a conspicuously lower profile in a Republican-controlled House and now focuses on issues of interest to his district instead of national security matters.

Reyes grew up on a farm in Canutillo, five miles north of El Paso, the oldest of 10 children. He went to college in El Paso and Austin, and then served in the Army in Vietnam, where he lost hearing in one ear during an enemy rocket attack. Once home, he "took as many civil service tests as I could, and the Border Patrol called" in 1969. He worked for the Immigration and Naturalization

Service in four cities in Texas and Glynco, Ga., before returning to El Paso in 1993 as a chief border patrol agent. When he got back, he found that the border was very porous, with people crossing wherever they wanted to. Reyes started "Operation Hold the Line," positioning 400 officers on the border instead of trying to intercept illegal aliens after they had already crossed into El Paso. (That had been firmly-rooted INS policy.) Mexico complained about threats to its sovereignty, merchants worried about the loss of sales, homeowners fretted about finding domestic help, and border agents feared losing credit for apprehending aliens. But the innovative Reyes reduced the flow of illegal immigrants in the area by more than half. The move was almost universally popular north of the border and ultimately was accepted to the south.

With local name recognition at 65%, Reyes retired from the INS in November 1995 and ran for Congress. He talked of the need for integrity and common sense in Washington against a vulnerable Democratic incumbent, Rep. Ron Coleman, who had 673 overdrafts at the House bank during a scandal that revealed widespread abuses by members of their tax-subsidized banking privileges. Coleman had also been accused by Texas Attorney General Dan Morales, a Democrat, of trying to block the prosecution of a local developer. In December, Coleman announced he was retiring, and he and labor unions backed Jose Luis Sanchez, his legislative assistant, as his successor. Sanchez accused Reyes of being a Republican in disguise for backing a cut in capital gains taxes. Reyes hewed to his moderate platform, promising more high technology jobs and more highways. He led in the primary 42%-28%, and despite a full court press by Sanchez and the unions in the runoff campaign, he won 51%-49%. He easily won the general election and has not been seriously challenged since then.

In the House, Reyes's voting record has been to the left of center, though more conservative on foreign policy. On immigration, he opposed the Republican plan for placing a fence along the border as unconstitutional, impractical and "a waste of federal dollars," and said he preferred an increase in federal personnel and resources. As violence increased in Mexico in 2009, Reyes discussed with Mexican leaders steps to decrease drug violence and to reduce gun smuggling from north of the border. He said that the permanent solution for the border is economic stabilization for Mexico.

Reyes moved into the national spotlight in December 2006, when incoming Democratic House Speaker Nancy Pelosi selected "Silver" to chair the Intelligence Committee, passing over Reps. Jane Harman, D-Calif., and Alcee Hastings, D-Fla. She cited his "impeccable national security credentials." But Reyes drew negative attention for an embarrassing gaffe in which he incorrectly told a reporter questioning him that al-Qaida was predominantly Shiite. He also could not identify whether Hezbollah was mostly Sunni or Shiite. As chairman, he got the Justice Department to turn over previously withheld documents from the surveillance program of the National Security Agency, and he voiced doubt about the "hyped" claims of the Bush administration that Iran was interfering in Iraq. But Reyes mostly kept a low profile and sought bipartisanship and cooperation with the Bush administration where possible. He distanced himself from liberal Democrats who opposed renewal of the Foreign Intelligence Surveillance Act and he sought to avoid a confrontation with the White House over the controversial use of water boarding in terrorism investigations. When President Barack Obama took office in early 2009, Reyes recommended additional intelligence resources in Iraq and Afghanistan. He also quarreled with Michigan's Pete Hoekstra, the Intelligence Committee's ranking Republican, about Hoekstra's push for full disclosure of what Pelosi and other congressional leaders knew about Bush-era interrogation techniques.

As a senior member on the Armed Services Committee, Reyes has been a supporter of the missile defense program and a critic of the Pentagon's system for putting critically needed equipment on the battlefield. He worked to protect Fort Bliss from possible base closing, and he claimed credit when additional soldiers were stationed there. He opposed the use of force in Iraq and criticized the intelligence failures in Iraq in the months before the war, but he later called for a troop increase in Iraq to dismantle local militias stirring up conflict.

When Republicans won majority control of the House in 2010, Reyes made a push to become the top Democrat on Armed Services to succeed Missouri's Ike Skelton, who lost his re-election bid that year. But Reyes finished third on the first ballot of the Democratic Steering and Policy Committee, and the job ultimately went to Washington state's Adam Smith, a rising star on the panel. Maryland's Dutch Ruppersberger took over Reyes' top slot on Intelligence, and Reyes left that panel to return to the Veterans' Affairs Committee, where he had served earlier.

SEVENTEENTH DISTRICT

Bill Flores (R)

Elected 2010, 1st term; b. Feb. 25, 1954, Cheyenne, WY; home, Bryan; TX A&M U., B.B.A. 1976; Houston Baptist U., M.B.A. 1985 ; Baptist; Married (Gina); 2 children.

Professional Career: Keyes Offshore, 1980-90; Marine Drilling, 1990-97; Western Atlas, 1997-98; Gryphon Exploration, 2001-05; accountant, financial mgr., Phoenix Exploration, 2006-09.

DC Office: 1505 LHOB, 20515, 202-225-6105; Fax: 202-225-0350; Web site: flores.house.gov.

State Offices: Bryan, 979-703-4037; Cleburne, 817-774-2551; Waco, 254-732-0748.

Committees: *Budget. Natural Resources:* Energy & Mineral Resources; Fisheries, Wildlife, Oceans & Insular Affairs. *Veterans' Affairs:* Oversight & Investigations.

Election Results

2010 general	Bill Flores (R)	106,696	(62%)	($3,433,415)
	Chet Edwards (D)	63,138	(37%)	($3,686,768)
2010 runoff	Bill Flores (R)	21,913	(65%)	
	Rob Curnock (R)	11,730	(35%)	
2010 primary	Bill Flores (R)	21,479	(33%)	
	Rob Curnock (R)	18,679	(29%)	
	Dave McIntyre (R)	11,870	(18%)	
	Chuck Wilson (R)	9,853	(15%)	

Population		Race/Ethnicity		Work	
Pop. 2010:	760,042	White:	66.0%	Private:	74.6%
Change since 2000:	Up 16.6%	Black:	9.6%	Government:	18.2%
Urban:	64.2%	Hispanic:	20.7%	Self-employed:	7.0%
Rural:	35.8%	Asian:	1.9%	Blue collar:	25.5%
Area size:	7,809 sq. mi.	Native Am.:	0.3%	White collar:	55.6%
		Hawaiian:	0.1%	Khaki collar:	0.1%
Age		Two+ races:	1.3%	Other:	18.7%
Median age:	31.6 yrs.				
More than 65 yrs:	12.0%	*Ancestry*		Median income:	$42,721
Less than 18 yrs:	24.4%	German	13.1%	Median Home Value:	$113,800
		Irish	10.1%		
Education		English	9.6%	**Military Veterans**	
H.S. grad:	80.7%			% of Pop:	9.5%
College grad:	21.6%				
Grad degree:	7.3%				

East Central Texas; Waco

Waco, about midway between Dallas to Austin, is deep in the heart of Texas. In the late 19th century, Waco was one of the largest cotton markets in the world, a rip-roaring town with legalized prostitution. In 1870, it opened a suspension bridge across the Brazos River, then the largest single-span suspension bridge in the United States, and it became the main depot along the Chisholm Trail, which cattlemen used to drive their longhorns north to Kansas shipyards. In

2008 Presidential Vote		
John McCain (R)	172,821	(67%)
Barack Obama (D)	82,326	(32%)
2004 Presidential Vote		
George Bush (R)	172,355	(70%)
John Kerry (D)	74,358	(30%)
Cook Partisan Voting Index: R+20		

1885, a Waco pharmacist concocted the first Dr. Pepper. Waco is the home of Baylor University, the oldest college in Texas and the largest Baptist university in the world. The city has embarked on an "Imagine Waco" program to restore a walkable downtown (much of it destroyed by a tornado in 1953) and is building an aerospace center at its technical college. Nearby are the ruins of David Koresh's Branch Dravidian compound, the scene of fatal standoff in 1993 between religious extremists and federal agents attempting to execute a search warrant. In Waco's McLennan County is the tiny town of Crawford, where the White House press corps huddled when President George W. Bush was staying at his 1,583-acre Prairie Chapel Ranch.

The 17th Congressional District of Texas includes all of nine counties and parts of three more, but is centered on Waco and McLennan County, which has 30% of the district's population. To the north, are fast-growing Johnson, Hood and Somervell counties just south of the Dallas-Fort Worth Metroplex. The other population center is Brazos County, whose largest city, College Station, is home to Texas A&M University. The school's agricultural and military tradition has given it a much more conservative atmosphere than the similarly selective University of Texas at Austin. College Station is the site of the George H.W. Bush Presidential Library; Defense Secretary Robert Gates was president of A&M until he left for Washington in December 2006. The political tradition in central Texas for more than a century after the Civil War was heavily Democratic. This area voted for Hubert Humphrey in 1968, while most of the rural South went for George Wallace and Richard Nixon. As recently as 1990, it voted Democratic for governor, supporting Waco native Ann Richards. Since then, the district has followed most of Texas and become Republican. George W. Bush carried the area in his two races for governor and two races for president. Republican John McCain won 67% of the vote in 2008.

Bill Flores (R)

The new congressman from the 17th District is Bill Flores, a Republican who toppled 10-term Democrat Chet Edwards in one of the big upsets of 2010.

The oldest of six children, Flores was born at Warren Air Force Base in Cheyenne, Wyo. After his father's military tour of duty, the family moved back to Stratford, a small town in the northern tip of the Texas Panhandle. From age 9, Flores helped work cattle on the family's ranch. Those early-life experiences made an impact. "I watched my Dad work real hard to put food on the table, and I got to see first hand what you can do when you start with nothing but you work really hard," Flores told *National Journal.* "I didn't want to be poor. I didn't want to be hungry." He said he also learned never to expect a handout. "I was always taught that you don't turn to the government for anything. You create your own opportunities," he said.

Flores helped pay his way through Texas A&M, where he was a member of the Corps of Cadets, the student body government and the honor guard. Flores counts his time at Texas A&M as formative and has remained active as an alumnus, donating millions of dollars to his alma mater to fund scholarships. He graduated in 1972, and went to work for the KPMG accounting firm. Over three decades, Flores built a career as a financial manager for several large corporations, eventually settling in the oil-and-gas industry in Houston. He was the president and chief executive officer of Phoenix Exploration until late 2009, when he left the job to run for Congress.

He had four opponents in the March 2010 Republican primary. He finished ahead of 2008 nominee Rob Curnock, 33%-29%. Curnock carried Waco and Johnson County, but Flores had a bigger margin over him in College Station and Brazos County, where another candidate, Dave McIntyre, finished second. Flores appears to have rallied other candidates' supporters for the April runoff, and beat Curnock 65%-35%.

In the general election, he faced Edwards, a 20-year incumbent with considerable political skills. A graduate of Harvard Business School, he served in the Texas state Senate and then won a seat in the U.S. House in 1990, when incumbent Democrat Marvin Leath retired. He retained the seat even as the district's voters became more Republican, taking care to cast conservative votes on some issues and to tend to the needs of sprawling Fort Hood. But his standing with conservatives was hurt in July 2008, when liberal House Speaker Nancy Pelosi mentioned him as a possible Democratic vice presidential candidate. That year, Republican Curnock held him to a 53%-46% victory, even though Edwards outspent him $2 million to $96,000.

Edwards had also taken some recent unpopular stands. Flores targeted his vote for the 2009 economic stimulus bill. And he emphasized his own business credentials, saying he would bring the discipline of a successful accountant to his work in government. In particular, Flores touted his role in the early 1990s helping to turn around a financially struggling oil and gas company called Marine Drilling. However, *The Dallas Morning News* reported that a Marine subsidiary filed for bankruptcy in 1992, leaving the government with $7.5 million in unpaid debt. Edwards assembled a "Vets for Chet" parade with retired generals attesting to his work for Fort Hood, and attacked Flores as a Houston interloper.

It was a high-dollar race, with Edwards spending $3.8 million and Flores $3.3 million (1.5 million of it his own money), with outside groups spending another $720,000 against Edwards and $1 million against Flores. By summer, Edwards was trailing badly; his own poll showed him behind 46%-42%, a disastrous result for a 20-year incumbent. And the Democratic Congressional Campaign Committee mostly pulled out of the race to focus resources on more winnable contests. Flores won 62%-37%, carrying all but one small county. He won with just 52% in Waco's McLennan County, but got 64% in College Station's Brazos County and 71% in Johnson County south of Fort Worth.

In the House, Flores' first bills were measures to set more stringent deadlines for government approval of offshore oil and gas drilling and to extend for 12 months all oil and gas leases in the Gulf of Mexico affected by the Interior Department's drilling moratoriums after the massive BP spill.

EIGHTEENTH DISTRICT

Sheila Jackson Lee (D)

Elected 1994, 9th term; b. Jan. 12, 1950, Queens, NY; home, Houston; Yale U., B.A. 1972, U. of VA Law Schl., J.D. 1975; Seventh Day Adventist; married (Elwyn); 2 children.

Elected Office: Houston City Cncl., 1990–94.

Professional Career: Practicing atty., 1975–77, 1978–87; Staff cnsl., U.S. House Select Assassinations Cmte., 1977–78; Houston assoc. municipal judge, 1987–90.

DC Office: 2160 RHOB, 20515; 202-225-3816; Fax: 202-225-3317; Web site: jacksonlee.house.gov.

State Offices: Acres Home, 713-691-4882; Fifth Ward, 713-227-7740; Heights, 713-861-4070; Houston, 713-691-4882; Houston, 713-655-0050.

Committees: *Homeland Security:* Border & Maritime Security; Transportation Security (RMM). *Judiciary:* Crime, Terrorism & Homeland Security; Immigration Policy & Enforcement; Intellectual Property, Competition & the Internet.

Group Ratings

	ACLU	ACU	ADA	CFG	AFS	FRC	LCV	ITIC	NTU	COC
2010	86	0	95	0	100	0	80	67	6	25
2009	–	0	95	0	100	–	100	–	2	33

National Journal Ratings

	2010 LIB	—	2010 CONS	2009 LIB	—	2009 CONS
Economic	63%	—	37%	91%	—	0%
Social	79%	—	20%	89%	—	0%
Foreign	97%	—	0%	83%	—	16%
Composite	80%	—	20%	91%	—	9%

Key Votes of the 111th Congress

1. Overturn Ledbetter	Y	5. Bar federal abortion funds	N	9. Stop detainee transfers	N
2. Pass $820 billion stimulus	Y	6. Pass health care bill	Y	10. Legalize immigrants' kids	Y
3. Let guns in national parks	N	7. Regulate financial firms	Y	11. Repeal don't ask, tell	Y
4. Pass cap-and-trade	Y	8. Pass tax cuts for some	Y	12. Limit campaign funds	Y

Election Results

2010 general	Sheila Jackson Lee (D)	85,108	(70%)	($825,310)
	John Faulk (R)	33,067	(27%)	($264,052)
	Mike Taylor (Lib)	3,118	(3%)	
2010 primary	Sheila Jackson Lee (D)	21,570	(67%)	
	Jarvis Johnson (D)	9,133	(28%)	
	Sean Roberts (D)	1,508	(5%)	

Prior Winning Percentages: 2008 (77%), 2006 (77%), 2004 (89%), 2002 (77%), 2000 (76%), 1998 (90%), 1996 (77%), 1994 (73%)

Population		Race/Ethnicity		Work	
Pop. 2010:	720,991	White:	15.8%	Private:	83.3%
Change since 2000:	Up 10.6%	Black:	36.1%	Government:	10.1%
Urban:	99.9%	Hispanic:	43.5%	Self-employed:	6.5%
Rural:	0.1%	Asian:	3.3%	Blue collar:	30.3%
Area size:	228 sq. mi.	Native Am.:	0.2%	White collar:	49.3%
		Hawaiian:	0.0%	Khaki collar:	0.0%
Age		Two+ races:	0.9%	Other:	20.4%
Median age:	30.9 yrs.				
More than 65 yrs:	8.5%	*Ancestry*		Median income:	$36,657
Less than 18 yrs:	28.6%	German	4.1%	Median Home Value:	$106,700
		Irish	2.7%		
Education		English	2.4%	**Military Veterans**	
H.S. grad:	68.8%			% of Pop:	5.9%
College grad:	17.9%				
Grad degree:	6.3%				

Downtown Houston

Within its sprawling boundaries, Houston contains income and wealth disparities as striking as any city in America, the product of an expanding city with dynamic economic growth, a high rate of immigration, and the absence of centralized planning. The contrast is most obvious at the edge of Houston's gleaming downtown. Just blocks from the Heritage Plaza, Pennzoil and Bank of America buildings, and the sports complexes for baseball's Astros and basketball's Rockets, are slums where many people live in unpainted frame houses with cracks wide enough to let in Houston's humid, smoggy air. But the contrasts are less obvious as one moves outward from the city's core.

2008 Presidential Vote
Barack Obama (D) 150,973   (77%)
John McCain (R) 43,292   (22%)

2004 Presidential Vote
John Kerry (D) 125,155   (72%)
George Bush (R) 48,753   (28%)

Cook Partisan Voting Index: D+24

Half a century ago, Houston had a Third World economy. It was a low-skill producer of basic commodities, where a few got rich and many lived near subsistence level. Since then, Houston has built a high-tech economy offering myriad opportunities and a wider range of economic outcomes. It has also greatly expanded its international trade. The Port of Houston brought in an estimated 220 million tons of cargo in 2010, the second most of any port in the United States. Many of Houston's blacks and Hispanics have moved to comfortable middle-class neighborhoods. In 2007, Hispanics for the first time outnumbered Anglos in Harris County, which has grown 20% since 2000. While the city has diversified economically, oil is still king. The city was shielded from the 2007-09 recession, with about 70% of the city's economic growth during this time coming from the energy industry. China's demand for fuel, along with that of other emerging nations, helped the expanding energy sector.

The 18th Congressional District of Texas contains Houston's downtown area and the African-American and Latino neighborhoods immediately south toward Loop 610. It has two spokes running beyond Loop 610—one is northeast, between the Eastex Freeway and Beaumont Highway, and the other is northwest between the Northwest Freeway and Hempstead. The district also includes George Bush Intercontinental Airport. African-Americans made up 35% of the district's population in 2009, a drop from previous years, while the Hispanic population continued to grow, increasing to 42%. This and the 30th District based in Dallas are the two most heavily Democratic districts in Texas.

Sheila Jackson Lee (D)

The congresswoman from the 18th District is Sheila Jackson Lee, a Democrat first elected in 1994. A native of Queens, N.Y., she was educated at Yale University and Virginia University's law school. She practiced law in Houston, where she was a local judge and won two terms as an at-large member of the Houston City Council. After a local term-limits law took effect in 1994, she ran for Congress. The incumbent was Democratic Rep. Craig Washington, a talented but iconoclastic legislator who voted against funding for the space station, a source of many local jobs, and against the 1993 North American Free Trade Agreement, which was a boon to Houston's port traffic. Jackson Lee supported NAFTA and raised a lot of money from business interests that favored it. She won the primary, 63%-37%, and she prevailed in the general election. She has been re-elected easily since.

In the House, Jackson Lee has a liberal voting record, though she has leaned toward the center on economic issues. She is prolific in proposing bills and offering amendments on the floor. Typically, her measures call for studies on one topic or another, add small amounts to spending bills, or are non-controversial, such as one that called on Afghanistan to prohibit the use of children as soldiers. Her more substantive proposals—for example, in favor of NASA funding and abortion rights—usually have been defeated. She also is known for regularly grabbing a prominent aisle seat for presidential State of the Union addresses, ensuring her a moment of national television time with the chief executive as he enters. In *Washingtonian* magazine's annual poll of House staffers, Jackson Lee has won best "Show Horse" every Congress since 2000, and she has routinely taken top honors in the poll's "Biggest Windbag" category.

Jackson Lee also draws negative reviews for her treatment of her staff. She used to have an aide drive her one block to and from her Capitol Hill apartment daily, and she has required aides to drive her to late-night hair appointments. The conservative website *Daily Caller*, citing disclosure forms on the website Legistorm, reported in March 2011 that in the previous decade, at least 39 staffers had left her office within a year, and during that time she had employed at least nine chiefs of staff. She told *The Houston Chronicle* that while she can ruffle feathers, she is unflagging in her desire to serve constituents. "I just want to be called an Energizer bunny that keeps on working for the people of this great district," she said.

Jackson Lee came into national prominence as an outspoken defender of Democratic President Bill Clinton during his impeachment in 1998. On the Judiciary Committee, she has faced conflicting desires from Latino constituents, who favor more generous treatment of immigrants, and African-American constituents, who see immigrants as competition for jobs. She frequently takes the pro-immigrant side. She favors an increase in visas and access to permanent resident status. She has vigilantly pursued alleged racial injustices in local courts; she called the Houston-area judicial system "tarnished" in 2008 after a grand jury failed to indict a white man who killed two black men after they robbed his neighbor.

She is the ranking Democrat on the Homeland Security Subcommittee on Transportation Security, an assignment that suits a port city. Jackson Lee got into a furious debate with Homeland Security Chairman Peter King, R-N.Y., at the panel's controversial March 2011 hearing on domestic Muslim extremism, waving a copy of the Constitution and denouncing the effort as "an outrage" to law-abiding Muslims. Meanwhile, King pounded his gavel to try to silence her.

Jackson Lee has been mindful to keep her name recognition in the district high, going so far as to have aides track constituents' deaths and then calling their grieving families to ask if she can speak at their funerals. Her most famous eulogy came in July 2009, when Jermaine Jackson asked her to speak at his famous brother Michael Jackson's memorial service in Los Angeles. She delivered a rambling speech to the crowd of 20,000 who gathered for the pop star's funeral, speaking for more time than many of the stars there who knew Jackson personally.

In 2010, Jackson Lee faced a primary challenge from Houston City Councilman Jarvis Johnson, who cited her reputation as difficult to work with, and local lawyer Sean Roberts. Neither, however, could come remotely close to her in fundraising, and in February, she unveiled her trump card—an endorsement from President Barack Obama calling her "a tireless champion for Houston's working families." She drew 67% of the vote to Johnson's 28% and Roberts' 5%, a victory that ensured her re-election.

NINETEENTH DISTRICT

Randy Neugebauer (R)

Elected June 2003, 4th full term; b. Dec. 24, 1949, Lubbock; home, Lubbock; TX Tech. U., B.B.A. 1972; Baptist; married (Dana); 2 children.

Elected Office: Lubbock City Cncl., 1992-98; Mayor pro tem, Lubbock, 1994-96.

Professional Career: Mgr., Sentry Property Mngt., 1972-75; Instructor, South Plains College, 1975-78; V.P., First National Bank, 1975-82; Pres., Prestige Homes, 1983-87; Pres., Lubbock Land Co., 1987-present.

DC Office: 1424 LHOB, 20515, 202-225-4005; Fax: 202-225-9615; Web site: randy.house.gov.

State Offices: Abilene, 325-675-9779; Big Spring, 432-264-0722; Lubbock, 806-763-1611.

Committees: *Agriculture:* General Farm Commodities & Risk Management; Livestock, Dairy & Poultry. *Financial Services:* Capital Markets and Government Sponsored Enterprises; Oversight & Investigations (Chmn). *Science & Technology:* Energy & Environment; Technology & Innovation.

Group Ratings

	ACLU	ACU	ADA	CFG	AFS	FRC	LCV	ITIC	NTU	COC
2010	13	100	0	100	0	93	0	33	92	88
2009	–	100	0	97	0	–	0	–	93	79

National Journal Ratings

	2010 LIB — 2010 CONS	2009 LIB — 2009 CONS
Economic	0% — 97%	0% — 96%
Social	0% — 85%	0% — 93%
Foreign	0% — 88%	0% — 75%
Composite	5% — 95%	6% — 94%

Key Votes of the 111th Congress

1. Overturn Ledbetter	N	5. Bar federal abortion funds	Y	9. Stop detainee transfers	Y
2. Pass $820 billion stimulus	N	6. Pass health care bill	N	10. Legalize immigrants' kids	N
3. Let guns in national parks	Y	7. Regulate financial firms	N	11. Repeal don't ask, tell	N
4. Pass cap-and-trade	N	8. Pass tax cuts for some	N	12. Limit campaign funds	N

Election Results

2010 general	Randy Neugebauer (R)	106,059	(78%)	($1,135,652)
	Andy Wilson (D)	25,984	(19%)	($42,097)
	Richard Peterson (Lib)	4,315	(3%)	
2010 primary	Randy Neugebauer (R)	unopposed		

Prior Winning Percentages: 2008 (72%), 2006 (68%), 2004 (58%), 2003 special (51%)

Population		Race/Ethnicity		Work	
Pop. 2010:	698,137	White:	58.0%	Private:	72.9%
Change since 2000:	Up 7.1%	Black:	5.4%	Government:	18.9%
Urban:	74.0%	Hispanic:	33.8%	Self-employed:	8.0%
Rural:	26.0%	Asian:	1.2%	Blue collar:	24.2%
Area size:	25,356 sq. mi.	Native Am.:	0.4%	White collar:	54.4%
		Hawaiian:	0.0%	Khaki collar:	0.7%
Age		Two+ races:	1.1%	Other:	20.7%
Median age:	32.6 yrs.				
More than 65 yrs:	13.1%	*Ancestry*		Median income:	$40,154
Less than 18 yrs:	25.8%	German	10.7%	Median Home Value:	$84,200
		Irish	8.2%		
Education		English	7.1%	**Military Veterans**	
H.S. grad:	78.6%			% of Pop:	9.2%
College grad:	20.8%				
Grad degree:	6.3%				

West Central Texas; Lubbock

Until water was discovered in the giant Ogallala Aquifer that lies under Lubbock and its environs, this was Indian country, then a land of Army forts and cattle ranches. When the water was tapped, well into the 20th century, what had been grazing land suddenly became cotton-growing territory, with green crops grown in circles where the sprinklers reached and parched ground beyond. Lubbock became a regional cen-

2008 Presidential Vote		
John McCain (R) 171,023	(72%)
Barack Obama (D) 65,034	(27%)
2004 Presidential Vote		
George Bush (R) 181,516	(78%)
John Kerry (D) 52,800	(23%)
Cook Partisan Voting Index: R+26		

ter, the home of Texas Tech University, and grew rapidly at mid-century. Lubbock County's population increased from 101,000 in 1950 to 156,000 in 1960. Since then, the regional economy has grown more slowly. Cotton growers have struggled with international competitors and adverse trade rulings, as well as pressure to reduce agricultural subsidies. However, wind power has become a source of energy and a new industry here, with hundreds of towers between Abilene and Sweetwater. In 2010, Lubbock County's population reached 279,000. The recession was relatively mild in Lubbock. Its 2010 unemployment rate of 6.1% was 31st lowest among U.S. metro areas. Lubbock also has made an outsized contribution to American popular culture. The city and nearby counties have produced a disproportionate share of renowned musicians: Buddy Holly, Tanya Tucker, Jimmy Dean, Waylon Jennings, Mac Davis, Joe Ely, Roy Orbison, Don Williams and the Dixie Chicks' Natalie Maines.

Lubbock is separated from the great metropolises of Texas by hundreds of miles of mostly, but not entirely, empty land. Nearly 200 miles southeast of Lubbock, over gully-ridden territory, are Abilene and the surrounding Big Country, with ranches specializing in Angora goats and sheep and exotic animals like ostriches, emus and aoudad sheep. There also are cotton fields, pecan trees, mesquite, and many oil wells. Archer City, the boyhood and current home of novelist Larry McMurtry, was chronicled in *The Last Picture Show* and *Texasville*. Some of the nation's B-1 bombers are stationed at Dyess Air Force Base near Abilene.

The 19th Congressional District of Texas takes in the Lubbock area and then travels east to take in the Abilene area. The two regions combined account for about 64% of the district's population. As recently as 1978, these parts of West Texas were Democratic enough that in an open-seat election, they rejected the candidacy of a young Midland oilman named George W. Bush in favor of Lubbock Democrat Kent Hance. Today, they are heavily Republican. Bush received 77% of the vote in his 2004 re-election, and Republican candidate John McCain won the district with 72% in 2008. GOP Gov. Rick Perry was re-elected with similarly large percentages here in 2010.

Randy Neugebauer (R)

The congressman from the 19th District is Randy Neugebauer, a Republican who won the seat in a June 2003 special election and who is one of the House's staunchest conservatives.

Neugebauer *(NAW-ga-bower)* graduated from Texas Tech, became a banker and then ran his own land development company that has made him one of the wealthiest members of Texas' delegation. From 1992 to 1998, he was a Lubbock city councilman. His chance for a House seat was prompted by the unexpected resignation, announced a week after the November 2002 election, of Republican Rep. Larry Combest. In the all-party primary, the four leading contenders to succeed Combest were all Republicans. They were Mike Conaway, a Midland accountant, plus three candidates from Lubbock: Neugebauer, state Rep. Carl Isett and former Lubbock Mayor David Langston. Neugebauer was the biggest spender and emphasized his positions on national defense and his business connections to oil and farming. He finished first, with 821 more votes than Conaway. He won in Lubbock while Conaway swept the Midland and Odessa areas. The runoff featured few differences on the issues, and regional patterns held firm. Neugebauer won 51%-49%. (Conaway won the neighboring 11th District seat in 2004.)

He barely had a chance to get settled in before the Texas Legislature drew up a new plan for congressional districts in October 2003. The new lines placed the home of 13-term Democratic Rep. Charlie Stenholm in the new 13th District, but that district was almost entirely unfamiliar territory for him and heavily Republican to boot, so Stenholm decided to run in the 19th against Neugebauer. Stenholm was arguably the last conservative Democrat from Texas in the House. He was one of only five Democrats who voted to impeach Democratic President Bill Clinton in 1998.

In the 2004 showdown, most of the advantages—the district's partisan tilt, the fact that Neugebauer had represented 58% of its residents and Stenholm only 31%—favored the Republican.

Both candidates promised to protect farm subsidies. Stenholm emphasized his social conservatism, his dedication to West Texas constituent services, and his independence as a Democrat. He criticized Neugebauer's ads that suggested he supported abortion rights and sought to link Neugebauer with then-Majority Leader Tom DeLay of Texas, who was increasingly mired in ethics controversies. The Texas Farm Bureau, which earlier honored Stenholm as "one of the giants of Texas agriculture," endorsed Neugebauer. He won 58%-40%, capturing 22 of the 27 counties. In Lubbock, Stenholm trailed 65%-33%. In his base of Abilene, which cast half as many votes as Lubbock, Stenholm led 50%-48%. Neugebauer has been easily re-elected.

In the House, Neugebauer tied for most conservative member of the House in 2009 and 2010, according to *National Journal's* rankings. He drew substantial attention in March 2010 when he acknowledged he was the lawmaker who shouted "baby killer" during Michigan Democratic Rep. Bart Stupak's speech on abortion during the final debate before passage of the health care overhaul bill. (Neugebauer apologized for his outburst and said it was not directed at Stupak, who opposes abortion.) A charter member of the Tea Party Caucus, Neugebauer also was among the co-sponsors of Florida Rep. Bill Posey's so-called "birther" bill in 2009 requiring future presidential candidates to provide a copy of their birth certificate. He unsuccessfully sought to strike everything but tax cuts from the 2009 economic stimulus bill.

On the Financial Services Committee, Neugebauer in 2011 became chairman of the oversight and investigations panel and promised to aggressively monitor the new consumer protection agency established in the Dodd-Frank financial overhaul law. He expressed the desire to change the agency's source of funding from the Federal Reserve to Congress, effectively giving his subcommittee more control over it. He also told an audience of housing experts in January 2011 that the federal government should get out of the foreclosure process, saying, "Markets aren't kind, but they're very efficient." His performance on the committee represents an audition of sorts for the full chairmanship in 2013, when term limits will force Alabama's Spencer Bachus to yield the gavel.

Neugebauer also has a seat on the Agriculture Committee, where he has defended farm subsidies for his district after the Environmental Working Group listed it as the nation's fourth-highest recipient of crop subsidies. On another farm issue, he added an amendment to the 2011 Federal Aviation Administration authorization bill requiring a study to create an online database of low-altitude aviation obstructions, something he said would help farmers using planes to spray crops. Before the House adopted a ban on earmarks in appropriations bills, he was the leading procurer of money for Texas Tech University's research. Defending the spending, he told *The Dallas Morning News* that its projects "must fit within the budget, not add to the budget."

TWENTIETH DISTRICT

Charles Gonzalez (D)

Elected 1998, 7th term; b. May 5, 1945, San Antonio; home, San Antonio; U. of TX, B. A. 1969; St. Mary's Law Schl., J.D. 1972.; Catholic; divorced; 1 child.

Military Career: TX Air Natl. Guard, 1969-75.

Elected Office: Judge, San Antonio Municipal Court; Judge, Bexar Cnty. Court at Law, 1983-87; Judge, 57th State Judicial Dist. Court, 1988-97.

Professional Career: Elem. schl. teacher, 1969-71; Practicing atty., 1972-82.

DC Office: 1436 LHOB, 20515, 202-225-3236; Fax: 202-225-1915; Web site: gonzalez.house.gov.

State Offices: San Antonio, 210-472-6195.

Committees: *Energy & Commerce:* Commerce, Manufacturing & Trade; Energy & Power; Health. *House Administration:* Elections; Oversight.

Group Ratings

	ACLU	ACU	ADA	CFG	AFS	FRC	LCV	ITIC	NTU	COC
2010	88	0	90	0	100	0	80	100	7	38
2009	–	0	100	4	100	–	100	–	3	36

National Journal Ratings

	2010 LIB — 2010 CONS		2009 LIB — 2009 CONS	
Economic	65%	— 34%	73%	— 27%
Social	80%	— 18%	72%	— 26%
Foreign	56%	— 38%	87%	— 9%
Composite	69%	— 32%	78%	— 22%

Key Votes of the 111th Congress

1. Overturn Ledbetter	Y	5. Bar federal abortion funds	N	9. Stop detainee transfers	Y
2. Pass $820 billion stimulus	Y	6. Pass health care bill	Y	10. Legalize immigrants' kids	Y
3. Let guns in national parks	N	7. Regulate financial firms	Y	11. Repeal don't ask, tell	Y
4. Pass cap-and-trade	Y	8. Pass tax cuts for some	Y	12. Limit campaign funds	Y

Election Results

2010 general	Charles Gonzalez (D)	58,645	(64%)	($921,601)
	Clayton Trotter (R)	31,757	(34%)	($162,679)
2010 primary	Charles Gonzalez (D)	unopposed		

Prior Winning Percentages: 2008 (72%), 2006 (87%), 2004 (65%), 2002 (100%), 2000 (88%), 1998 (63%)

Population		Race/Ethnicity		Work	
Pop. 2010:	711,705	White:	18.4%	Private:	77.7%
Change since 2000:	Up 9.2%	Black:	6.6%	Government:	16.3%
Urban:	99.8%	Hispanic:	71.5%	Self-employed:	5.8%
Rural:	0.2%	Asian:	1.8%	Blue collar:	23.3%
Area size:	184 sq. mi.	Native Am.:	0.2%	White collar:	52.6%
		Hawaiian:	0.1%	Khaki collar:	1.6%
Age		Two+ races:	1.1%	Other:	22.4%
Median age:	31.7 yrs.				
More than 65 yrs:	10.6%	*Ancestry*		Median income:	$35,846
Less than 18 yrs:	27.3%	German	6.2%	Median Home Value:	$91,600
		Irish	3.6%		
Education		USA	3.2%	**Military Veterans**	
H.S. grad:	74.6%			% of Pop:	11.6%
College grad:	15.5%				
Grad degree:	5.2%				

Downtown San Antonio

With its antique past and Hispanic heritage, San Antonio is unlike any other city in the United States. It is the home of the Alamo, preserved by the Daughters of the Republic of Texas, where Davy Crockett, Jim Bowie and 184 others were killed in 1836. (Crockett was a Tennessee congressman for three terms; if he had not lost his re-election in 1834, he presumably would not have left Tennessee for Texas.) Its Spanish architecture recalls San Antonio's days

2008 Presidential Vote		
Barack Obama (D) 115,739	(63%)
John McCain (R) 64,886	(36%)
2004 Presidential Vote		
John Kerry (D) 96,539	(55%)
George Bush (R) 78,757	(45%)
Cook Partisan Voting Index: D+8		

as the most important town in Texas, when the state was part of Mexico, and contrasts with the 31-story Tower Life Building, which contrasts with the armadillo-like Alamodome. And its Paseo del Rio, the Riverwalk along the tiny San Antonio River that was redeveloped in the 1970s, also recalls an earlier era. The city also has old neighborhoods that evoke the Germans who were its chief Anglo citizens for many years.

For most of the 20th century, San Antonio's economy was built on the military. What the locals call "Military City, U.S.A." remains the home of Lackland Air Force Base, Fort Sam Houston and a giant military hospital. In 1995, President Bill Clinton bent the rules of the base-closing process to keep in San Antonio the thousands of jobs at Kelly Air Force Base, a move so resented that Congress blocked new rounds of base closings until 2005. Kelly was finally closed in 2001. In the 2005 base review, Fort Sam's renowned Brooke Army Medical Center was transformed into a regional military medical center, for a net gain of more than 4,000 jobs in the area. The local health industry, which includes the Texas Health Science Center, has been thriving and is the largest local employer. It helped the city avoid the worst of the recent recession. San Antonio has many military retirees and is the largest tourist center in Texas. The city also is the Union Pacific rail hub and has a massive Toyota plant.

Since 2000, its population has grown 16%, and San Antonio has surpassed Dallas as Texas' second-largest city. (The largest is Houston.) However, its metropolitan-area population of 2.1 million is only about one-third the size of metro Houston and of the Dallas–Fort Worth Metroplex. Its low education and income levels are partially due to the high levels of new immigrants in the city. Yet it has mostly avoided polarized politics and ethnic strife as it has progressed as a low-wage, high-tech center that has some links to, and sometimes competes with, nearby Austin.

The 20th Congressional District of Texas includes most of central San Antonio and its lower-income west side. (Affluent neighborhoods are in the 21st and 23rd districts.) The district is wholly contained within Bexar County. On the west it extends beyond Lackland Air Force Base toward the county line. With an Hispanic population share of 70%, it is one of the state's seven Hispanic-majority districts. And it is Democratic. Republican favorite-son candidate George W. Bush won 45% of the vote here in 2004. Republican presidential nominee John McCain got 36% in 2008. GOP Gov. Rick Perry came within half a percentage point of beating Democrat Bill White in Bexar in 2010.

Charles Gonzalez (D)

The congressman from the 20th District is Charles Gonzalez, a Democrat first elected in 1998 and the chairman of the Congressional Hispanic Caucus. He is one of eight children of former U.S. Rep. Henry Gonzalez, who held the seat for 37 years.

Gonzalez grew up in San Antonio, graduated from the University of Texas and St. Mary's University School of Law, and served in the Texas Air National Guard. He was an elementary school teacher, practiced law and served as a judge from 1983 to 1997. When his father announced his retirement, Charles Gonzalez was the front-runner for the seat, but the contest was more competitive than many had expected. Gonzalez campaigned as a consensus-builder, emphasized his background in negotiation and compromise, and said he would work for the entire district, not simply its low-income groups. Taking a feistier tone was Maria Berriozabal, a former San Antonio City Council member, who called for more outspoken leadership. She displayed a picture of Henry Gonzalez in her campaign literature and claimed that she was more in his mold than was his son. Just before the March primary, Henry Gonzalez issued a brief statement endorsing his son, who wound up leading Berriozabal, 44%-22%. In the April runoff campaign, he benefited from a 2-to-1 fundraising advantage and mostly ignored his opponent. He won 62%-38% and went on to easily win the general election.

In the House, Gonzalez has a relatively moderate voting record, but during the years in which his party controlled the House, he became a much more reliable Democratic vote. He has a seat on the influential Energy and Commerce Committee, and in 2010 joined a minority of oil-state Democrats in opposing the House-passed bill to lift the $75 million liability cap for offshore spills. During the committee's debate on climate change legislation in 2009, he advocated incentives for the nuclear power industry. He also backed a requirement that satellite television operators end their policy that forced users to have two satellite dishes to receive channels in both English and Spanish.

As a member of both the Democratic Caucus and the Hispanic Caucus—which his father had refused to join—Gonzalez has been among those pushing for comprehensive immigration reform. He sought to persuade President Barack Obama in 2009 to reconsider a provision in the Senate health care bill that would bar illegal immigrants from buying insurance with their own money on the insurance exchanges created by the measure. In taking the helm of the Hispanic Caucus, he joined with leaders of the Congressional Black Caucus and the Asian and Pacific Islander-American Caucus to denounce the Republican-backed repeal of the health care law, arguing it would strip coverage from one-third of Latinos in the United States.

Gonzalez has been especially engaged on redistricting issues as they affect Hispanics. He has been a leading proponent of census sampling, which statistically estimates the number of members in a community for use in redistricting processes and generally increases population totals for immigrant communities. He also vowed to have at least two of the four new seats created through 2012 redistricting in Texas be Hispanic-dominated to correctly mirror population growth.

In 2004, Gonzalez's re-election challenge had unusual personal overtones. Initially, his ex-wife, Becky Whetstone, a marriage and family therapist, said that she would run against him so that voters would have a choice and he would be "held accountable." But she failed to get the 500 signatures required to get on the ballot as an independent. In the general election, Gonzalez beat Republican Roger Scott 65%-32%. He has not faced a serious challenge since then.

TWENTY-FIRST DISTRICT

Lamar Smith (R)

Elected 1986, 13th term; b. Nov. 19, 1947, San Antonio; home, San Antonio; Yale U., B.A. 1969, S. Methodist U., J.D. 1975; Christian Scientist; married (Beth); 2 children.

Elected Office: TX House of Reps., 1981–82; Bexar Cnty. comm., 1983–85.

Professional Career: U.S. Small Business Admin., 1969–70; Business writer, *Christian Science Monitor*, 1970–72; Practicing atty., 1975–78.

DC Office: 2409 RHOB, 20515, 202-225-4236; Fax: 202-225-8628; Web site: lamarsmith.house.gov.

State Offices: Austin, 512-306-0439; Kerrville, 830-896-0154; San Antonio, 210-821-5024.

Committees: *Homeland Security. Judiciary* (Chmn). *Science & Technology:* Space & Aeronautics; Technology & Innovation.

Group Ratings

	ACLU	ACU	ADA	CFG	AFS	FRC	LCV	ITIC	NTU	COC
2010	13	100	0	100	0	100	10	50	89	88
2009	–	96	5	89	13	–	7	–	84	87

National Journal Ratings

	2010 LIB	—	2010 CONS	2009 LIB	—	2009 CONS
Economic	17%	—	83%	22%	—	77%
Social	29%	—	69%	17%	—	83%
Foreign	0%	—	88%	0%	—	75%
Composite	18%	—	82%	17%	—	83%

Key Votes of the 111th Congress

1. Overturn Ledbetter	N	5. Bar federal abortion funds	Y	9. Stop detainee transfers	Y
2. Pass $820 billion stimulus	N	6. Pass health care bill	N	10. Legalize immigrants' kids	N
3. Let guns in national parks	Y	7. Regulate financial firms	N	11. Repeal don't ask, tell	N
4. Pass cap-and-trade	N	8. Pass tax cuts for some	N	12. Limit campaign funds	N

Election Results

2010 general	Lamar Smith (R)	162,924	(69%)	($1,312,958)
	Lainey Melnick (D)	65,927	(28%)	($34,987)
	James Strohm (Lib)	7,694	(3%)	($5,765)
2010 primary	Lamar Smith (R)	61,923	(81%)	
	Stephen Schoppe (R)	14,166	(19%)	

Prior Winning Percentages: 2008 (80%), 2006 (60%), 2004 (61%), 2002 (73%), 2000 (76%), 1998 (91%), 1996 (76%), 1994 (90%), 1992 (72%), 1990 (75%), 1988 (93%), 1986 (61%)

Population		Race/Ethnicity		Work	
Pop. 2010:	856,954	White:	59.8%	Private:	74.6%
Change since 2000:	Up 31.5%	Black:	6.3%	Government:	17.0%
Urban:	81.0%	Hispanic:	28.1%	Self-employed:	8.3%
Rural:	19.0%	Asian:	3.7%	Blue collar:	14.4%
Area size:	5,180 sq. mi.	Native Am.:	0.3%	White collar:	70.2%
		Hawaiian:	0.1%	Khaki collar:	0.9%
Age		Two+ races:	1.6%	Other:	14.5%
Median age:	36.0 yrs.				
More than 65 yrs:	11.9%	*Ancestry*		Median income:	$60,769
Less than 18 yrs:	25.3%	German	15.3%	Median Home Value:	$177,400
		English	8.8%		
Education		Irish	8.6%	**Military Veterans**	
H.S. grad:	91.4%			% of Pop:	13.4%
College grad:	39.2%				
Grad degree:	14.6%				

Central Texas; Part San Antonio

The Balcones Escarpment is a bulwark of cracked and weathered rock that crosses Texas diagonally from the Dallas-Fort Worth Metroplex southwest to Austin and San Antonio and all the way to the Rio Grande. It separates the flatlands of central Texas from the stony hills to the north and west. It is a boundary between cropland and grazing land, between acres rich with greenery and acres whose rolling brown hills blaze out in color when the wildflowers bloom in early spring. The Balcones Escarpment separates Dallas and Fort Worth; it runs through Austin and the western edge of San Antonio. But it is less familiar to Texans today than the highway that runs pretty much along the same line: Interstate 35. This is one of the most heavily traveled and congested interstates in America, thick with truck traffic in the populated stretches between the Metroplex and the Mexican border even as it passes through the lightly populated near-desert between San Antonio and Laredo. It is one of the great routes of commerce in America, or rather between the United States and Mexico. I-35 connects Austin and San Antonio, two booming Texan cities with very different beginnings and different characters now.

2008 Presidential Vote		
John McCain (R)	215,006	(59%)
Barack Obama (D)	148,477	(40%)

2004 Presidential Vote		
George Bush (R)	212,196	(66%)
John Kerry (D)	110,288	(34%)

Cook Partisan Voting Index: R+14

In the counties between these two cities and in the Hill Country to the west, is the Texas German country, originally settled by Germans fleeing the reaction against the failed revolutions of 1848. The Texas German country has always been a set of economically prosperous communities in rip-roaring Texas. It was anti-slavery and politically Republican in a state whose enthusiasm for the Democratic Party had roots in Confederate loyalties and populist rebellions. The Texas German heritage is still visible, as it introduced the long-barbecued beef brisket that has become synonymous with Lone Star State cuisine. An antique German is sometimes heard on the streets in towns like New Braunfels, Boerne and Fredericksburg. (There are about 10,000 speakers now, compared with 159,000 in the 1940s, and one scholar predicts it could vanish by 2050.) These communities, with their neat houses, low cost of living and Hill Country ambience, attract new residents to new subdivisions and lakeside developments.

The 21st Congressional District of Texas includes much of this territory. About half of its people are in San Antonio and Bexar County. It includes the northeast corner of the city and county, Fort Sam Houston plus some north-side neighborhoods, with many houses being bought by rich Mexicans from Monterrey. This is mostly Anglo San Antonio, though 35% of the Bexar County residents in the district are Hispanic. About one-fifth of the residents are in Austin and Travis County, including the downtown University of Texas campus. This is the most Republican part of a Democratic county. The district includes all of New Braunfels and Comal County just northeast of San Antonio as well as several Hill Country counties to the west: Blanco County, where Lyndon Johnson was born, in Johnson City, and where he lived when he was elected to the House in 1937 (but only a sliver of the LBJ Ranch near Fredericksburg, just to the west); Kendall County, a fast-growing area north of San Antonio; Kerr County, the most populous part of the Hill Country, and Bandera County. The political heritage of the district is mixed. While Travis County was always Democratic and the Texas German country was Republican, San Antonio was mixed. Overall, the district is heavily Republican. It voted 59% for Republican John McCain in 2008.

Lamar Smith (R)

The congressman from the 21st District is Lamar Smith, a Republican first elected in 1986. He chairs the House Judiciary Committee and has long been among his party's most influential figures on immigration.

Smith is from an old San Antonio and South Texas ranching family. Their Jim Wells County ranch has been in the family for four generations. Smith graduated from Texas Military Institute (now TMI, the Episcopal School of Texas), Yale University and Southern Methodist University's law school. He worked as a reporter for the *Christian Science Monitor* and as a lawyer in San Antonio. He was elected to the Texas House in 1980 and the Bexar County Commissioners Court in 1982. In 1986, when Republican U.S. Rep. Tom Loeffler ran for governor, Smith ran for the House seat. He won by beating two other San Antonio-based candidates in the primary and then winning the runoff 54%-46% against a religious conservative. His campaign was run by then little-known Texas political consultant Karl Rove, who became President George W. Bush's top political advisor. Smith has been easily re-elected by wide margins.

In the House, Smith has a conservative voting record and joined the Tea Party Caucus when it was formed in 2010. Taking the helm of Judiciary in 2011, he vowed to press for tougher enforcement of immigration laws as an alternative to comprehensive reform, which he and many Republicans insist cannot include provisions providing illegal immigrants a potential path to citizenship. He is a strong believer in stronger action to stop illegal immigration and to reduce legal immigration. Smith irked Democrats in December 2010 when he called the DREAM Act—which would have opened up legal status to some children of illegal immigrants—an "American nightmare."

He opposed Bush's guest worker proposal in 2004 and bipartisan proposals to provide a path to citizenship for illegal immigrants living in the United States. The guest worker program, Smith said, "opens up every job in America" to low-wage competition. Like other House Republican leaders, he insisted that better border enforcement must be in place before new guest worker programs or legalization policies were established. Smith's bill to split the Immigration and Naturalization Service into two agencies, one concentrating on law enforcement, the other on aid to immigrants, was passed as part of the homeland security bill in 2002. He drew attention in 2005 when one of his aides misdialed a fax number while intending to send a confidential memo to Rove at the White House, causing it to fall into Democratic hands. In the memo, Smith wrote that "liberals can easily and accurately be painted as opposing enforcement."

In the aftermath of a controversial law cracking down on illegal immigration in Arizona in 2010, Smith became a leading House Republican voice in support of the law, which allowed police to demand proof of citizenship from people stopped or questioned by police for other reasons. He criticized the Obama administration for suing to stop enforcement of the Arizona law. When President Barack Obama blamed Republicans for blocking comprehensive immigration reform in July 2010, Smith retorted that workplace enforcement of immigration laws under the president was in a free fall. He also stepped into the controversy stirred by South Carolina Republican Sen. Lindsey Graham's proposal to modify the 14th Amendment, which has formed the legal basis for granting citizenship to people born on U.S. soil. Smith argued that changing a constitutional amendment would be too difficult, and that the same end could be achieved by a statutory reinterpretation of the amendment by Congress to disallow citizenship to children born to illegal immigrants.

Despite deep partisan conflicts on the committee on immigration and other issues, Smith gets along with Democrats better than do many in his party, and in recent years, found common ground on bills to strengthen cyber security and intellectual property enforcement. Smith has worked closely with ranking Judiciary Democrat John Conyers of Michigan on patent reform issues. In April 2009, Smith and Conyers co-sponsored a bill to strengthen patent quality and to discourage frivolous lawsuits. He and Conyers also agreed with proposed structural changes made by the Patent and Trademark Office aimed at improving review quality and employee morale for an agency dealing with a heavy backlog of patent applications. Their bill also gave the PTO fee-setting authority on patents, and they sought a supplemental appropriation to hire more patent examiners. The measure did not become law in the 111th Congress (2009-10), so Smith moved a new version through the committee in April 2011.

On other issues, Smith parted with Conyers and held the Republican Party line. He opposed a committee proposal that eliminated mandatory minimum prison sentences for crack cocaine use. A modified version of the bill was eventually signed into law, making crack sentencing closer to the lighter penalties enforced for powder cocaine use. Smith also sharply criticized a Democratic proposal in February 2010 to impose criminal penalties of up to 20 years in jail for certain interrogation techniques in terrorism investigations. Smith in June 2009 announced the formation of a Media Fairness Caucus devoted to exposing what he considers the news media's liberal bias. During 2010, he spoke on the House floor about the issue 47 times.

In earlier years on the committee, Smith was chairman of what was then the Crime Subcommittee, where he focused on cyber crime and high technology issues. He also worked on bipartisan changes to the Freedom of Information Act to make it easier and faster for the public to obtain government information. Smith's bill creating a 20-year sentence for fraudulently obtaining consumer and business phone records and distributing them over the Internet became law in 2007. Smith created a new Judiciary subcommittee on intellectual property and the Internet in 2011 and vowed to work on curbing online child pornography.

TWENTY-SECOND DISTRICT

Pete Olson (R)

Elected 2008, 2nd term; b. Dec. 9, 1962, Fort Lewis, WA; home, Sugar Land; Rice U., B.A. 1985; U of TX, J.D. 1988; Methodist; married (Nancy); 2 children.

Military Career: Navy, 1988-98, Naval Reserves, 1998-Present.

Professional Career: Naval officer; Staffer, U.S. Sen. Phil Gramm.

DC Office: 312 CHOB, 20515, 202-225-5951; Fax: 202-225-5241; Web site: olson.house.gov.

State Offices: Clear Lake, 281-486-1095; Sugar Land, 281-494-2690.

Committees: *Energy & Commerce:* Commerce, Manufacturing & Trade; Energy & Power.

Group Ratings

	ACLU	ACU	ADA	CFG	AFS	FRC	LCV	ITIC	NTU	COC
2010	13	100	0	97	0	93	0	33	91	88
2009	–	100	0	91	0	–	0	–	89	80

National Journal Ratings

	2010 LIB	—	2010 CONS	2009 LIB	—	2009 CONS
Economic	3%	—	96%	0%	—	96%
Social	0%	—	85%	0%	—	93%
Foreign	0%	—	88%	0%	—	75%
Composite	6%	—	94%	6%	—	94%

Key Votes of the 111th Congress

1. Overturn Ledbetter	N	5. Bar federal abortion funds	Y	9. Stop detainee transfers	Y
2. Pass $820 billion stimulus	N	6. Pass health care bill	N	10. Legalize immigrants' kids	N
3. Let guns in national parks	Y	7. Regulate financial firms	N	11. Repeal don't ask, tell	N
4. Pass cap-and-trade	N	8. Pass tax cuts for some	N	12. Limit campaign funds	N

Election Results

2010 general	Pete Olson (R)	140,537	(67%)	($1,268,559)
	Kesha Rogers (D)	62,082	(30%)	($61,896)
	Steven Susman (Lib)	5,538	(3%)	
2010 primary	Pete Olson (R)	unopposed		

Prior Winning Percentages: 2008 (52%)

Population		Race/Ethnicity		Work	
Pop. 2010:	910,877	White:	44.5%	Private:	80.3%
Change since 2000:	Up 39.8%	Black:	13.9%	Government:	13.9%
Urban:	94.6%	Hispanic:	26.9%	Self-employed:	5.7%
Rural:	5.4%	Asian:	12.6%	Blue collar:	19.7%
Area size:	1,003 sq. mi.	Native Am.:	0.2%	White collar:	67.4%
		Hawaiian:	0.0%	Khaki collar:	0.1%
Age		Two+ races:	1.6%	Other:	12.8%
Median age:	34.3 yrs.				
More than 65 yrs:	8.0%	*Ancestry*		Median income:	$71,520
Less than 18 yrs:	28.4%	German	10.1%	Median Home Value:	$158,300
		English	6.5%		
Education		Irish	6.5%	**Military Veterans**	
H.S. grad:	87.2%			% of Pop:	8.4%
College grad:	34.8%				
Grad degree:	11.9%				

Houston and Suburbs; Sugar Land

Those seeking the story of Houston's booming growth over the past dozen years would be well advised to drive out the Southwest Freeway for about 45 minutes, if the traffic is not too bad, to Sugar Land. It is much changed from the days before the Civil War, when sugar plantations flourished here. In once-rural Fort Bend County, on the site of the old Imperial Sugar Mill, is a fast-growing, privately planned city of more than 80,000 people, with privatized water and

2008 Presidential Vote
John McCain (R) 183,172   (58%)
Barack Obama (D) 129,414   (41%)

2004 Presidential Vote
George Bush (R) 177,378   (64%)
John Kerry (D) 98,180   (36%)

Cook Partisan Voting Index: R+13

other services. (In 1990, its population was 33,000.) The county was fifth in the nation in job growth between 2000 and 2009. Since then, growth has slowed somewhat, but Sugar Land has continued to get positive economic news, including the arrival of a new minor league baseball team at a stadium to open in 2012. Its name, chosen by popular vote: the Sugar Land Skeeters, a reference to the area's uncomfortable proliferation of the biting insects. Suburban Sugar Land and Fort Bend County are also diverse. Some 21% of the county population is African-American, 23% is Hispanic, and 14% is Asian. Sugar Land has elected Daniel Wong, from Macao, to the City Council, and Dinesh Shah, from India, served on the board of the Chamber of Commerce.

The 22nd Congressional District of Texas covers more than two-thirds of Fort Bend County, including Sugar Land. It also includes one-quarter of Brazoria County, centering on fast-growing Pearland, just south of Houston, plus parts of Galveston County, including Santa Fe, La Marque and Hitchcock. Nearly one-half of its residents are in Harris County, which includes working-class Deer Park, Pasadena and LaPorte south of the Houston Ship Channel, and the more upscale Webster, Clear Lake and Taylor Lake Village surrounding the Johnson Space Center. Native son George W. Bush won here 67%-33% in 2000, and 64%-36% in 2004. GOP nominee John McCain won the district in 2008 with 58% of the vote. In 2010, Republican Gov. Rick Perry narrowly lost Harris County to former Houston Mayor Bill White, but won Fort Bend County 52%-47% and Brazoria County 61%-36%.

Pete Olson (R)

The congressman from the 22nd District is Pete Olson, a Republican elected in 2008. He ousted Democratic Rep. Nick Lampson, who was elected two years earlier in a voter backlash against Rep. Tom DeLay, who had become the symbol of influence-peddling and political corruption in the Republican majority in Congress.

The son of an Army veteran, Olson followed in his father's footsteps and entered the Navy on the same day he took the Texas bar exam. He served as a naval aviator, flew anti-submarine missions, and finished his military career as a liaison to the U.S. Senate. His next job was as a staff member for Republican Sen. Phil Gramm of Texas. After Gramm retired in 2002, Olson was the chief of staff to his successor, Republican Sen. John Cornyn.

In 2006, DeLay, after reaching the pinnacle of power as the House majority leader, resigned his seat after being indicted in Texas on criminal campaign-finance charges. Several of his aides and lobbyists close to him came under investigation for influence peddling. (DeLay was sentenced in January 2011 to three years in prison for money laundering and conspiracy stemming from his role funneling corporate contributions to Texas state races.) Houston City Council Member Shelley Sekula-Gibbs, a Republican, won a special election for the seat, served for several weeks, but then lost in the general election to Lampson. A legal technicality kept her name off the ballot, and she had to run as a write-in candidate, which, with the lingering taint of the DeLay scandal, doomed her candidacy.

Two years later, Republicans targeted Lampson for defeat. Olson, who had been living in the suburbs of Washington, moved back to the district in 2007 and joined a crowded primary field that included Sekula-Gibbs and Sugar Land Mayor Dean Hrbacek. Sekula-Gibbs won the primary, but failed to get the 50% share of the vote needed to avoid a runoff with second-place Olson. Republicans at the state and national levels regarded Sekula-Gibbs as a weak candidate and coalesced around Olson, who won the runoff with 69% of the vote.

In the general election campaign, Olson touted a conservative message, while Lampson tried to tar Olson with DeLay's image, charging that Olson employed consultants who had previously worked for DeLay. Democratic leaders also came to his aid, saying that if re-elected, Lampson would chair the House subcommittee with jurisdiction over NASA, an important local employer. But in the end, all of this could not stop the district from returning to its GOP roots on Election Day. Olson won 52% to 45%.

In the House, Olson has been a rock-solid conservative. In his freshman year, he was among the lawmakers who tied for the most conservative member of the House in *National Journal's* annual rankings. He got a plum seat on the Energy and Commerce Committee in 2011, and joined fellow Texas Republican Joe Barton on the panel as a staunch defender of their state's oil and gas industry. He was among lawmakers in February 2011 who accused the Interior Department of being too slow to approve new drilling permits. The same month, Olson spoke out against the Environmental Protection Agency's efforts to regulate greenhouse gas emissions blamed for global warming. "There is a proper role for oversight of air quality, but it must be balanced with economic impacts and again, that role is determined by Congress, not EPA," Olson said.

Olson has been a champion of NASA's Johnson Space Center and called President Barack Obama's flat budget request for the agency in fiscal 2012 "a non-starter" that ignored Congress' interest in human space flight. Earlier, as a member of the Science and Technology's space panel, he had urged continuation of the troubled Constellation program. "We've gotten ourselves in an unacceptable position of facing a large gap in our ability to send humans into space, and of tasking NASA to get back to the moon by 2020 with the necessary funding," he told *National Journal.*

In March 2009, Olson collapsed while lifting weights in the House gym. He was taken to George Washington University Hospital, where he underwent emergency surgery to install a pacemaker. He fully recovered. In his 2010 re-election bid, he trounced Democrat Kesha Rogers, a Lyndon LaRouche activist, 68%-30%. With his district having grown so rapidly, he is expected to lose part of it to redistricting in 2012, but he will remain a substantial favorite.

TWENTY-THIRD DISTRICT

Francisco Canseco (R)

Elected 2010, 1st term; b. July 30, 1949, Laredo; home, San Antonio; St. Louis U., B.A. 1972, J.D. 1975; Catholic; Married (Gloria); 3 children.

Professional Career: Practicing atty., 1975-2010; pres., dir., FMC Developers, 1992-2007; dir., Hondo National Bank, 1995-2009.

DC Office: 1339 LHOB, 20515, 202-225-4511; Fax: 202-225-4511.

State Offices: North San Antonio, 210-561-8855.

Committees: *Financial Services:* Financial Institutions & Consumer Credit; Oversight & Investigations.

Election Results

2010 general	Francisco Canseco (R)	74,853	(49%)	($1,931,186)
	Ciro Rodriguez (D)	67,348	(44%)	($1,616,735)
	Craig Stephens (I)	5,432	(4%)	
2010 runoff	Francisco Canseco (R)	7,210	(53%)	
	Will Hurd (R)	6,488	(47%)	
2010 primary	Will Hurd (R)	9,695	(34%)	
	Francisco Canseco (R)	9,250	(32%)	
	Robert Lowry (R)	6,369	(22%)	
	Mike Kueber (R)	1,990	(7%)	
	Joseph Gould (R)	1,459	(5%)	

Population		Race/Ethnicity		Work	
Pop. 2010:	847,651	White:	27.4%	Private:	74.6%
Change since 2000:	Up 30.1%	Black:	3.1%	Government:	18.8%
Urban:	76.4%	Hispanic:	66.4%	Self-employed:	6.3%
Rural:	23.6%	Asian:	1.8%	Blue collar:	22.6%
Area size:	48,567 sq. mi.	Native Am.:	0.3%	White collar:	57.2%
		Hawaiian:	0.1%	Khaki collar:	0.4%
Age		Two+ races:	0.9%	Other:	19.8%
Median age:	32.5 yrs.				
More than 65 yrs:	10.5%	*Ancestry*		Median income:	$43,165
Less than 18 yrs:	30.1%	German	8.0%	Median Home Value:	$102,700
		Irish	4.6%		
Education		English	4.4%	**Military Veterans**	
H.S. grad:	74.0%			% of Pop:	10.1%
College grad:	22.5%				
Grad degree:	7.9%				

San Antonio and Suburbs

The Mexican-American tradition in the part of South Texas radiating from San Antonio is anchored in two culturally conservative institutions, the Catholic Church and the United States military. Both are a major presence in San Antonio, just 150 miles north of the border, which for many years had the largest Mexican-American population of any American city and where Spanish has long been widely spoken. The church in San Antonio was led for years by liberal bishops. They also ran St. Mary's University, which educated many Hispanic politicians and leaders, including two longtime House Democratic committee chairmen, former Reps. Henry Gonzalez and Kika de la Garza, and Republican Sen. John Cornyn, who graduated from St. Mary's law school. Just as visible a presence in San Antonio are the Army and Air Force, with huge Fort Sam Houston, Lackland Air Force Base, and the Randolph Air Force Base, all in or near the city limits.

2008 Presidential Vote

Barack Obama (D)	124,936	(51%)
John McCain (R)	118,324	(48%)

2004 Presidential Vote

George Bush (R)	120,672	(57%)
John Kerry (D)	90,057	(43%)

Cook Partisan Voting Index: R+4

Mexican-Americans have long volunteered for military service in numbers higher than members of most other ethnic groups, and for many years, Mexican-Americans in San Antonio worked in civilian jobs for the military service. San Antonio's Mexican-American community also has produced many politicians who are liberal on economic issues and civil rights but also are pro-military and at home with traditional religious and cultural values.

Fifty or so miles west of San Antonio, the hills flatten out and become the parched uplands of West Texas. This is a borderland, just north of Mexico, where people are concentrated in tiny hamlets amid the empty ranchlands. Most residents are Latino. Once, Indians were the threat on this frontier. Now the challenge is a lack of water. The aquifers of West Texas are being drained, and state law still allows landowners to pump out as much water as they want. The Rio Grande, dried out by a dam in New Mexico, gets most of its water from the Rio Conchos in the Mexican state of Chihuahua. The mountains of Big Bend National Park rise above the Rio Grande, where in the clean air you can find dozens of species of birds and can see for 180 miles. Eccentrics have built an art colony in Marfa and stage a chili cook-off in Terlingua. Texas's frontier in many ways is thriving. Housing is cheap; Reeves County in 2009 had the nation's lowest median home values at $29,400. Huge wind farms have flowered along the interstate in Crockett County.

The 23rd Congressional District of Texas is geographically the largest in the state, stretching from the west side of San Antonio to the outskirts of El Paso, from Eagle Pass and Maverick County to the New Mexico border. About 60% of its population is in Bexar County, which includes many Latinos. The district's Latino population is 66%. Many of the border counties are Democratic. The district voted 57% for Republican President George W. Bush in 2004, and four years later, Democrat Barack Obama won the district 51%-48%.

Francisco Canseco (R)

The new congressman from the 23rd District is Republican Francisco (Quico) Canseco, one of five new Hispanic Republicans elected to the House in 2010. He won an expensive and negative contest by casting five-term Democratic Rep. Ciro Rodriguez as a career politician and a big-government liberal in an election that was hospitable to neither.

Canseco, the oldest of eight children born to Mexican immigrants, was raised in a devoutly Roman Catholic household. His father, a doctor, came to the border town of Laredo, Texas, as a teenager to wait out the Mexican Revolution. The family ultimately settled in Laredo. From an early age, Canseco embraced conservative ideals. When he was in seventh grade, he was beaten up at recess for wearing a Nixon-Lodge pin. His classmates preferred Democrat John F. Kennedy in the 1960 presidential election. "That was a year that I toughened up my spine. I knew, this is what I believe in and this is what I am," Canseco told *National Journal*. As a teenager, Canseco was sent to Indiana to attend Culver Military Academy, one of the nation's largest preparatory schools, where he played football and joined the debate team. Later, after graduating from law school, Canseco married his wife Gloria, whom he met at church.

Canseco practiced law for 30 years in Texas. He worked at a number of private firms, as a solo practitioner, and as in-house counsel for the Union National Bank. He took a brief sojourn in 1977 to teach law at the University of Paris. In the 1990s, Canseco delved into the real estate business, developing shopping centers in Laredo and elsewhere. He also got active in politics, serving as associate general counsel for the Texas Republican Party, on the board of directors of the Texas Federation of Republican Women, and as an at-large delegate to the Republican National Convention in 2008. He ran for Congress twice and failed, losing primaries in 2004 for the District 17 seat and in 2006 for the District 23 seat. "It's very important that I had lost, because in losing you learn a lot," he said.

Republicans had long hoped to oust Rodriguez, who was more moderate than most other Texans from his party but remained a strong liberal on economic issues. But the GOP previously had trouble finding a candidate who could win Hispanic votes beyond San Antonio, and from his position on the Appropriations Committee, Rodriguez was able to steer money back home. In his campaign, Canseco promised to bring private sector know-how to Washington, portraying Rodriguez as a politician who had overstayed his welcome.

Rodriguez and the Democratic Congressional Campaign Committee fired back with charges that Canseco incurred $715,000 in liens since the 1980s for unpaid payroll taxes and contracting fees. They dubbed him a "serial tax evader." Former President Bill Clinton stumped for Rodriguez in San Antonio, while Americans for Tax Reform stepped in with $332,000 on Canseco's behalf. Rodriguez spent $1.6 million defending the seat, while Canseco lent his campaign $235,000 of his own money and spent $1.9 million. He won 49%-44%, with three third-party candidates splitting the remaining votes. He carried 12 of the district's 19 counties, including Bexar, which cast by far the largest number of votes, 53%-41%. Rodriguez won most of the counties in the far western portion of the district, including the section of El Paso County.

In the House, Canseco received a seat on the Financial Services Committee in recognition of his background in banking. He added an amendment to a House-passed bill in March 2011 requiring that all unobligated savings from ending the Home Affordable Modification Program—the Obama administration's main foreclosure prevention program—be used to pay down the debt. He was among the House Republican freshmen who took a confrontational approach on forcing deep spending cuts in the fiscal 2011 budget. But Canseco drew some criticism at home when he contended inaccurately that car bombs were exploding in El Paso because of drug-related violence. He was the target of regular flyers from the Democratic Congressional Campaign Committee attacking his votes and their impact on his district.

TWENTY-FOURTH DISTRICT

Kenny Marchant (R)

Elected 2004, 4th term; b. Feb. 23, 1951, Bonham; home, Coppell; Southern Nazarene U., B.A. 1973, attended Nazarene Theol. Sem. 1975-76; Nazarene; married (Donna); 4 children.

Elected Office: Carrollton City Cncl., 1980-84; Mayor, 1984-86; TX House of Reps., 1986-2004.

Professional Career: Homebuilder, developer, 1975-2004.

DC Office: 1110 LHOB, 20515, 202-225-6605; Fax: 202-225-0074; Web site: marchant.house.gov.

State Offices: Irving, 972-556-0162.

Committees: *Ways and Means:* Social Security; Oversight; Select Revenue Measures.

Group Ratings

	ACLU	ACU	ADA	CFG	AFS	FRC	LCV	ITIC	NTU	COC
2010	14	95	5	100	0	100	0	0	90	100
2009	–	100	5	96	0	–	0	–	91	73

National Journal Ratings

	2010 LIB — 2010 CONS	2009 LIB — 2009 CONS
Economic	7% — 93%	7% — 92%
Social	0% — 85%	7% — 90%
Foreign	0% — 88%	0% — 75%
Composite	7% — 93%	10% — 91%

Key Votes of the 111th Congress

1. Overturn Ledbetter	N	5. Bar federal abortion funds	Y	9. Stop detainee transfers	Y
2. Pass $820 billion stimulus	N	6. Pass health care bill	N	10. Legalize immigrants' kids	*
3. Let guns in national parks	Y	7. Regulate financial firms	N	11. Repeal don't ask, tell	*
4. Pass cap-and-trade	N	8. Pass tax cuts for some	*	12. Limit campaign funds	N

Election Results

2010 general	Kenny Marchant (R)	100,078	(82%)	($542,265)
	David Sparks (Lib)	22,609	(18%)	
2010 primary	Kenny Marchant (R)	33,283	(84%)	
	Frank Roszell (R)	6,298	(16%)	

Prior Winning Percentages: 2008 (56%), 2006 (60%), 2004 (64%)

Population		Race/Ethnicity		Work	
Pop. 2010:	792,319	White:	46.5%	Private:	83.6%
Change since 2000:	Up 21.6%	Black:	14.4%	Government:	10.6%
Urban:	99.2%	Hispanic:	27.1%	Self-employed:	5.6%
Rural:	0.8%	Asian:	9.4%	Blue collar:	18.7%
Area size:	354 sq. mi.	Native Am.:	0.4%	White collar:	67.7%
		Hawaiian:	0.2%	Khaki collar:	0.1%
Age		Two+ races:	1.8%	Other:	13.6%
Median age:	33.1 yrs.				
More than 65 yrs:	7.1%	*Ancestry*		Median income:	$60,262
Less than 18 yrs:	27.2%	German	10.4%	Median Home Value:	$162,600
		English	7.9%		
Education		Irish	7.4%	**Military Veterans**	
H.S. grad:	87.0%			% of Pop:	7.7%
College grad:	36.5%				
Grad degree:	11.4%				

Dallas Suburbs; Grand Prairie

The gigantic (larger than Manhattan Island) Dallas–Fort Worth International Airport, the third-busiest in the world, bisects the Metroplex and its two adjacent counties with its large terminals and the Texas-sized highway network that feeds them. DFW, as the locals call it, also has been a focal point for the development in both Dallas and Tarrant counties. "DFW is no longer solely an airport. DFW is our home," the *Fort Worth Star-Telegram* wrote. New cities,

2008 Presidential Vote
John McCain (R) 153,758   (55%)
Barack Obama (D) 124,128   (44%)

2004 Presidential Vote
George Bush (R) 161,864   (65%)
John Kerry (D) 86,786   (35%)

Cook Partisan Voting Index: R+11

with as many people as Dallas and Fort Worth had in the 1950s—Grand Prairie and Irving—grew up around the airport during the next two decades in this once-impoverished region. For years, DFW and its supporters fiercely opposed efforts to repeal the Wright Amendment, which limited the number of cities that can be reached on flights out of the old Love Field in Dallas. In 2006, a political consensus in Texas and in Washington resulted in it being repealed, partly at the behest of locally based airlines seeking to throw off its anti-competitive shackles in a rapidly changing transportation world.

North of DFW are newer and more upscale suburbs: Grapevine and Southlake, with huge shopping malls and resort centers, in northeast Tarrant County. Across the International Parkway in northwest Dallas County are Coppell, Farmers Branch and Carrollton, which got a stop on an expanded light-rail system in 2010. To the north are the fast-growing suburbs and exurbs of Denton County. The Dallas-Fort Worth-Arlington Metropolitan Statistical Area has passed Philadelphia as the nation's fourth-largest MSA. It is 46% African-American, Asian or Hispanic, compared with 31% in the Philadelphia MSA. The MSA grew 25% from 2000 to 2009. The area's annual job growth in 2008 was the highest in the nation. A planned, seven-year, $2 billion upgrade of DFW's terminals augurs future growth.

The 24th Congressional District of Texas is based in this area and has three large spokes that reach out from DFW. The largest extends northeast through Dallas County and into Denton County, up to Route 121, including one-third of Irving and almost all of Farmers Branch, Coppell and Carrollton. To the west, another spoke reaches into Tarrant County out to Precinct Line Road and includes Grapevine, Bedford, Colleyville and Southlake. South of the airport it takes in Cedar Hill, part of Irving and almost all of Grand Prairie, where oil and gas drilling is common in residential neighborhoods. Half of the population is in Dallas County, nearly a third is in Tarrant County and the rest is in Denton County. After its transformation by the 2003 redistricting, the new 24th District voted 65% for President George W. Bush in 2004 and 55% for GOP nominee John McCain in 2008. GOP Gov. Rick Perry lost Dallas County to Democrat Bill White, but took Tarrant 56%-41% and Denton 64%-33%.

Kenny Marchant (R)

The congressman from the 24th District is Kenny Marchant, a Republican elected in 2004 whose loyalty to the GOP agenda landed him a prized seat on the Ways and Means Committee in March 2011.

Marchant graduated from Southern Nazarene University, and became a local homebuilder and successful developer. He was the House's 12th-richest member in 2009, according to the Center for Responsive Politics. Marchant served a quarter-century in elected offices before running for Congress, including stints on the Carrollton City Council, as Carrollton mayor, and then in the state House. He also has been active in private humanitarian projects around the world. The Ken Marchant Foundation funds church loans, mission projects and scholarships.

In contrast to other upwardly mobile Republicans in the state House, he enjoyed a reputation on both sides of the aisle as a levelheaded peacemaker. Despite serving in some of the legislature's most partisan leadership posts, the mild-mannered and deeply religious Marchant refrained from engaging in the acrimonious battles all around him. Marchant had been chairman and floor leader of the Texas House Republican caucus and served on the House Redistricting Committee during the bitter 2003 redistricting battle.

Unsurprisingly, the redistricting plan couldn't have been more favorable to him. The new 24th was heavily Republican and inhospitable to incumbent Rep. Martin Frost, an effective partisan who was targeted by then-Majority Leader Tom DeLay of Texas, the mastermind behind the redistricting effort. Frost opted to run in the new 32nd District in Dallas County and lost. Meanwhile, Marchant thrived in the new 24th, which incorporated nearly his entire state legislative district. In the primary, he defeated three other candidates with 73% of the vote, and in the general election, he won 64%-34%.

In the House, Marchant has a solidly conservative voting record. He was among the original members of the Tea Party Caucus and a co-sponsor of the so-called "birther" bill in 2009 requiring future presidential candidates to prove U.S. citizenship. But he does not have the sharp rhetorical edge of other hard-right conservatives. "He was a silver-tongued devil when he was a state legislator; he still is as a United States congressman," President George W. Bush once jokingly said of him.

In February 2011, Marchant introduced a bill to prevent the federal government from subsidizing illegal immigrants' housing purchases by requiring borrowers to submit to the E-Verify background check program. During debate on the Dodd-Frank financial overhaul bill in 2009, he unsuccessfully sought to have a new consumer protection agency's regulations be subject to review by the courts. He developed a fruitful relationship with Republican Speaker John Boehner; he joined the Education and the Workforce Committee that Boehner chaired in 2005 and was one of the few Texans to back Boehner in his bid to become majority leader when Republicans controlled the House in 2006.

Marchant has had no trouble winning re-election; Democrats didn't bother to field a candidate against him in 2010 and he defeated a Libertarian challenger, 82%-18%. Three weeks after the election, he underwent successful double-bypass heart surgery.

TWENTY-FIFTH DISTRICT
Lloyd Doggett (D)

Elected 1994, 9th term; b. Oct. 6, 1946, Austin; home, Austin; U. of TX, B.B.A. 1967, J.D. 1970; Methodist; married (Libby); 2 children.

Elected Office: TX Senate, 1972–84; TX Supreme Ct. justice, 1989-94.

Professional Career: Practicing atty., 1970–89; Adjunct prof., U. of TX Law Schl., 1989–94.

DC Office: 201 CHOB, 20515, 202-225-4865; Fax: 202-225-3073; Web site: doggett.house.gov.

State Offices: Austin, 512-916-5921.

Committees: *Budget. Ways & Means:* Human Resources (RMM); Social Security; Trade.

Group Ratings

	ACLU	ACU	ADA	CFG	AFS	FRC	LCV	ITIC	NTU	COC
2010	94	4	95	10	88	0	100	67	12	13
2009	–	12	95	13	100	–	100	–	12	33

National Journal Ratings

	2010 LIB — 2010 CONS		2009 LIB — 2009 CONS	
Economic	54% —	46%	58% —	42%
Social	67% —	31%	75% —	20%
Foreign	84% —	11%	57% —	42%
Composite	70% —	31%	64% —	36%

Key Votes of the 111th Congress

1. Overturn Ledbetter	Y	5. Bar federal abortion funds	N	9. Stop detainee transfers	N
2. Pass $820 billion stimulus	Y	6. Pass health care bill	Y	10. Legalize immigrants' kids	Y
3. Let guns in national parks	N	7. Regulate financial firms	Y	11. Repeal don't ask, tell	Y
4. Pass cap-and-trade	Y	8. Pass tax cuts for some	N	12. Limit campaign funds	Y

Election Results

2010 general	Lloyd Doggett (D)	99,967	(53%)	($1,200,342)
	Donna Campbell (R)	84,849	(45%)	($800,229)
	Jim Stutsman (Lib)	4,431	(2%)	
2010 primary	Lloyd Doggett (D)	unopposed		

Prior Winning Percentages: 2008 (66%), 2006 (67%), 2004 (68%), 2002 (84%), 2000 (85%), 1998 (85%), 1996 (56%), 1994 (56%)

Population		Race/Ethnicity		Work	
Pop. 2010:	814,381	White:	49.8%	Private:	74.2%
Change since 2000:	Up 25.0%	Black:	7.4%	Government:	18.0%
Urban:	75.2%	Hispanic:	38.8%	Self-employed:	7.6%
Rural:	24.8%	Asian:	2.2%	Blue collar:	21.1%
Area size:	6,184 sq. mi.	Native Am.:	0.3%	White collar:	60.4%
		Hawaiian:	0.1%	Khaki collar:	0.1%
Age		Two+ races:	1.4%	Other:	18.5%
Median age:	31.5 yrs.				
More than 65 yrs:	8.4%	*Ancestry*		Median income:	$48,554
Less than 18 yrs:	24.8%	German	13.7%	Median Home Value:	$164,200
		Irish	7.6%		
Education		English	7.3%	**Military Veterans**	
H.S. grad:	81.2%			% of Pop:	8.1%
College grad:	32.0%				
Grad degree:	10.7%				

Austin

Austin is the capital of the second-largest state in the United States and the site of the largest Capitol building, as well as perhaps the most rambunctious state legislature in the country. It has a first-rate university and its own musical tradition. Not long ago, Austin was laid-back and countrified. There had never been much commerce here, and state government provided much of the local employment. Its skies were un-tainted by industrial smoke and its downtown

2008 Presidential Vote		
Barack Obama (D) 176,935	(59%)
John McCain (R) 117,845	(39%)
2004 Presidential Vote		
John Kerry (D) 140,063	(54%)
George Bush (R) 120,715	(46%)
Cook Partisan Voting Index: D+6		

streets were lined not with business offices, but with buildings holding a few lobbyists and the antique Driskill Hotel. Its biggest industry was the University of Texas, with 50,000 students and an endowment of thousands of west Texas acres that turned out to sit on top of oil. The university has long had a distinguished faculty and some of the world's great scholarly collections, including the LBJ Presidential Library and its 35 million documents. Half a century ago, in Lyndon John-son's time, Austin had a metropolitan population of 132,000. The compact Austin that was John-son's headquarters in 1948, when the Duval County returns came in and gave him the 87-vote Senate victory that made his national career, is a very different Austin from the metropolitan cen-ter of 1.2 million that waited in the rain to hear the results of the election of native son George W. Bush as president in 2000.

For many years, Austin was the central focus of Texas' hardy but almost always outnumbered liberals, based in the university, state government and the *Texas Observer* magazine. They mocked the business lobbyists who called the shots when the "Leg" (pronounced *lej*) was in session. But as the Austin area grew, it became more conservative, especially as its private sector made up a larger share of the local economy. The techies who settled in the Silicon Hills from Austin's Travis County to once-rural Williamson County have tended to vote Republican. Some businesses cater to the old liberal bastions: the upscale organic-food chain, Whole Foods Market, is based in Austin. (Some of its progressive customers, however, have criticized founder John Mackey for his well-publicized skepticism of global warming.) The city core and the university area are still Democratic. But this is a state capital where Gov. Bush could feel at home, perhaps more so than he did 30 years earlier when his application for admission was rejected by UT's law school. Bush lost Austin and Travis County 59%-41% when he first ran for governor in 1994, but he carried the county 60%-38% in 1998 when he ran for re-election and 47%-42% in 2000 when he ran for president (10% went for Green Party nominee Ralph Nader). In 2004, Austin's liberal community registered large numbers of new voters, and Bush lost Travis County 56%-42%, even as he increased his margin statewide. Democratic nominee Barack Obama carried Travis County with 64% of the vote in 2008.

The 25th Congressional District of Texas encompasses nearly half of Travis County, including most of the east side of Austin and the city's heavily Latino and African-American neighborhoods. The increasingly settled Hispanic community includes many people moving toward the middle class, taking advantage of a job market that, according to *Forbes* magazine in 2010, tied Austin with Washington, D.C. as the nation's best cities to survive the recession. The Capitol and the UT campus are just outside the district, in the 21st, while the 10th District takes in most of the Republican northern part of the city and county. Seven rural counties that extend to the south and east now account for 40% of the 25th district. The largest of them are fast-growing Hays and Bas-trop counties. The district was 37% Hispanic and 8% African-American in 2009. In 2008, Demo-cratic presidential candidate Barack Obama carried the district 59%-39%. While Obama won Travis County, Republican nominee John McCain carried all the other seven counties, three of them by 2-to-1 or better. It was much the same story in the 2010 governor's race. Democrat Bill White won Travis 60%-37%, while GOP Gov. Rick Perry won the other seven counties, though not by margins as large as McCain's.

Lloyd Doggett (D)

The congressman from the 25th District is Lloyd Doggett, first elected in 1994 in the old 10th Dis-trict. He is a liberal Democrat and a respected voice in his party on tax and environmental issues.

Doggett grew up in Austin, finished first in his class at the University of Texas and was student body president in 1967. In 1972, at age 26, he was elected to the state Senate. In the 70s, as part of a large liberal bloc, he pushed for laws against job discrimination and cop-killer bullets and for generic drugs. He has long been a close ally of trial lawyers, the one strong institutional force supporting liberal Democrats in Texas. In the legislature, he was one of the "Killer Bees" who hid out to prevent a quorum on changing the rules in the Democratic primary and filibustered against what he called anti-consumer bills.

In 1984, he ran for the U.S. Senate, narrowly edging out two House members to win the Democratic nomination. Then, despite the campaign help of crack Democratic consultant James Carville, Doggett lost the general election 59%-41% to U.S. Rep. Phil Gramm, a Democrat who had switched to become a Republican. Doggett was elected to the Texas Supreme Court in 1988. When Democratic U.S. Rep. Jake Pickle retired after 31 years, Doggett ran for his seat. He won the Democratic primary with token opposition and in the general election won by a solid 56%-40%.

In the House, Doggett's voting record puts him among the most-liberal Texans and near the center of all Democrats. He has been a close ally of Nancy Pelosi of California, backing her against fellow Texan Martin Frost in her 2002 race for minority leader. In 2002, he was a leader in opposing the resolution authorizing the use of force in Iraq. He is at times highly partisan. When Republicans won a House majority in 1994, he was a frequent critic of Republican Speaker Newt Gingrich and a close ally of Minority Whip David Bonior of Michigan, who led an effort to diminish Gingrich's power by raising continual questions about his ethics.

In recent years, Doggett drew the most attention for a protracted standoff with Texas Republican Gov. Rick Perry in 2010 over a provision that Doggett added to a House-passed bill giving states aid to hire and retain teachers. The provision, which applied only to Texas, required the governor to maintain the state's current level of education funding over the next three years, State Attorney General Greg Abbott filed suit, arguing Texas was unfairly singled out. Doggett was unrepentant: "Instead of running to the courtroom, the governor should focus on our classrooms," he told *The Texas Tribune.* The requirement was eventually removed in the fiscal 2011 budget deal.

When Democrats controlled the House between 2007 and 2010, Doggett was active and often influential on the Ways and Means Committee. His priorities included eliminating tax shelters and loopholes and giving the federal government power to negotiate prescription drug prices for Medicare. He also sought tax incentives for purchasers of plug-in hybrid electric cars. In May 2009, when President Barack Obama announced his plan to reform international tax policy, he cited Doggett's input on proposals to crack down on overseas tax evasion. Doggett also pressed the president's Simpson-Bowles fiscal commission to scrutinize the more than $1 trillion a year that the Internal Revenue Service provides in the form of reduced taxes or refunds to companies and individuals. The commission's report called for eliminating most so-called "tax expenditures." Doggett refused to back Obama's tax-cut deal with Republicans in the 2010 lame-duck session for its inclusion of tax cuts for high-income taxpayers.

Reflecting his district's environmental activism, Doggett was among the Ways and Means Democrats who asserted the panel's role in global warming legislation, then dominated by the Energy and Commerce Committee. He initially announced he would oppose the Waxman-Markey cap-and-trade bill to limit carbon emissions in June 2009, but after lobbying from Pelosi ended up backing what he called "this flawed bill." On other issues, Doggett won House passage in 2008 and 2009 of a bill to create a "silver alert" modeled on the Texas program to track wandering senior citizens who may have Alzheimer's disease.

Republicans have long been giddy at the prospect that redistricting might end Doggett's congressional career. As the GOP determined how to add four congressional seats to Texas in 2012, there was discussion of hooking his district with the south side of San Antonio to give the district an Hispanic majority. The party tried a similar approach in 2004, stretching his district 300 miles south to the Mexican border. But he took up the challenge. As some other dislocated Texas Democrats took their fight to the courts, Doggett took his case to the voters of his new district. He started by working hard to get the support of elected officials and party activists along the border. Meanwhile, the best-known Hispanic challengers for a Democratic primary dropped out for various reasons. But Doggett's strong local base and relentless pursuit of new voters prevailed. If he lost, Doggett told voters, "Tom DeLay will have won," a reference to the powerful GOP majority leaders from Texas who had orchestrated the remap. Doggett won the primary 64%-36%. He led 88%-12% in Travis County and held Leticia Hinojosa, a former district court judge from McAllen, to a standoff in Hidalgo County.

Although the primary effectively sealed his re-election, Doggett faced a spirited challenge in the 2004 general from Becky Armendariz Klein. She called herself a conservative "new voice with new ideas" and cited her experience as policy director for Gov. George W. Bush and as chairwoman of the Texas Public Utility Commission. Doggett tweaked her for her bid for ethnic voters, saying she'd pulled out her "long forgotten maiden name" to run for the seat. He won 68%-31%, getting 79% in Travis County and 60% in Hidalgo County.

He had far less trouble in 2006 and 2008, winning with 67% and 66% respectively, after the Supreme Court ordered his district redrawn to include areas closer to Austin. In 2010, he drew a tough challenge from Republican Donna Campbell, a doctor and hospital emergency department director who raised more than $765,773. But Doggett spent $1.2 million and won 53%-45%, carrying Travis County by 2-to-1.

TWENTY-SIXTH DISTRICT

Michael Burgess (R)

Elected 2002, 5th term; b. Dec. 23, 1950, Rochester, MN; home, Lewisville; N. TX St. U., B.S. 1972, M.S. 1976, U. of TX Med. Schl., M.D. 1977, U. of TX Dallas, M.S. 2000; Episcopalian; married (Laura); 3 children.

Professional Career: Practicing obstetrician, 1981-2003.

DC Office: 2241 RHOB, 20515, 202-225-7772; Fax: 202-225-2919; Web site: burgess.house.gov.

State Offices: Ft. Worth, 817-531-8454; Lewisville, 972-434-9700.

Committees: *Energy & Commerce:* Energy & Power; Health (VChmn); Oversight & Investigations. *Joint Economic Committee.*

Group Ratings

	ACLU	ACU	ADA	CFG	AFS	FRC	LCV	ITIC	NTU	COC
2010	13	96	5	84	0	93	0	0	86	75
2009	–	100	0	90	11	–	0	–	88	71

National Journal Ratings

	2010 LIB — 2010 CONS		2009 LIB — 2009 CONS	
Economic	20%	— 80%	23%	— 77%
Social	25%	— 71%	19%	— 80%
Foreign	12%	— 79%	0%	— 75%
Composite	21%	— 79%	18%	— 82%

Key Votes of the 111th Congress

1. Overturn Ledbetter	N	5. Bar federal abortion funds	Y	9. Stop detainee transfers	Y
2. Pass $820 billion stimulus	N	6. Pass health care bill	N	10. Legalize immigrants' kids	N
3. Let guns in national parks	Y	7. Regulate financial firms	N	11. Repeal don't ask, tell	N
4. Pass cap-and-trade	N	8. Pass tax cuts for some	N	12. Limit campaign funds	N

Election Results

2010 general	Michael Burgess (R)...	120,984	(67%)	($1,019,693)
	Neil Durrance (D)	55,385	(31%)	($106,037)
	Mark Boler (Lib)	4,062	(2%)	
2010 primary	Michael Burgess (R)...	44,047	(86%)	
	James Herford (R)...	7,284	(14%)	

Prior Winning Percentages: 2008 (60%), 2006 (60%), 2004 (66%), 2002 (75%)

Population		Race/Ethnicity		Work	
Pop. 2010:	915,137	White:	59.4%	Private:	81.8%
Change since 2000:	Up 40.4%	Black:	13.1%	Government:	12.7%
Urban:	90.5%	Hispanic:	21.2%	Self-employed:	5.5%
Rural:	9.5%	Asian:	3.9%	Blue collar:	20.4%
Area size:	1,374 sq. mi.	Native Am.:	0.5%	White collar:	64.6%
		Hawaiian:	0.1%	Khaki collar:	0.0%
Age		Two+ races:	1.7%	Other:	15.0%
Median age:	32.7 yrs.				
More than 65 yrs:	8.1%	*Ancestry*		Median income:	$61,695
Less than 18 yrs:	28.7%	German	12.8%	Median Home Value:	$153,600
		Irish	9.0%		
Education		English	8.5%	**Military Veterans**	
H.S. grad:	85.5%			% of Pop:	9.1%
College grad:	30.4%				
Grad degree:	9.2%				

Fort Worth and Suburbs; Denton

Until the Texas Land and Immigration Company settled this portion of northeast Texas with a land grant from the Texas Congress in 1841, settlers were scarce and Indian raids were common. The area now known as Denton County takes its name from John Bunyan Denton, a Methodist pioneer preacher and lawyer killed in a skirmish with Indians. Today, this area on the northern edge of the Dallas-Fort Worth Metroplex is teeming with new arrivals and filling up

2008 Presidential Vote		
John McCain (R) 193,163	(58%)
Barack Obama (D) 137,622	(41%)

2004 Presidential Vote		
George Bush (R) 181,989	(65%)
John Kerry (D) 99,633	(35%)

Cook Partisan Voting Index: R+13

with young, well-educated, middle-class families. The University of North Texas, with more than 36,000 students, is the fourth-largest in the state. The county's chief cities are Denton and Lewisville, Carrollton and Flower Mound, all north of the DFW Airport. And there is plenty of room for more growth along Interstates 35E and 35W. Truck manufacturer Peterbilt Motors Company in Denton is one of the largest private employers and announced increases in production on two of its truck models in 2011. Near Justin, in the southwest corner of Denton County, a pipeline project was completed in 2010 allowing for the production of up to 1 billion cubic feet of natural gas daily. With sophisticated imaging and drilling technology, other natural gas wells operate within 10 miles of downtown Fort Worth. In 1940, there were 33,000 people in Denton County, and they voted 88% Democratic for president. In 2010, there were 662,614 people in the county, and they voted 62% for Republican John McCain in 2008 and 64% for GOP Gov. Rick Perry two years later.

The 26th Congressional District of Texas is at the heart of the northern expansion of the Dallas-Fort Worth Metroplex. It includes three-quarters of suburban and exurban Denton County, most of rural Cooke County on the Oklahoma border, and a large slice of urban Tarrant County. The Tarrant portion includes Fort Worth's African-American neighborhoods, its booming new subdivisions north of the downtown district, and the Alliance Airport business parks, founded and operated by Ross Perot Jr. and employing more than 28,000 people. Since 2000, the district's population has grown by 255,000 people, the second-largest overall population increase of any Texas district, behind only the 10th. President George W. Bush won the district 65%-35% in 2004, and Republican John McCain won it 58%-41% in 2008. In addition to nearly getting two-thirds of the Denton County vote, Perry in 2010 took Cooke County 68%-28% and Tarrant 56%-41%.

Michael Burgess (R)

The congressman from the 26th District is Michael Burgess, a conservative Republican physician first elected in 2002 and a spokesman for House Republicans on health care issues.

Burgess grew up in Denton County, the son of a physician, and graduated from the University of North Texas and the University of Texas Medical School in Houston. He trained at Parkland Hospital in Dallas and set up an obstetrics-gynecology practice in Lewisville. After 21 years in practice, Burgess decided to run for Congress, his first bid for elective office. When House Majority Leader Dick Armey announced in December 2001 that he would not run again, there was no doubt that a Republican would succeed him. But almost no one expected that the winner would be political novice Burgess. The widespread expectation was that the winner would be the majority leader's son, Scott Armey, 32, a former Denton County judge.

In the primary, Armey outspent Burgess by more than 6-to-1. But turnout was light—only 25,000 people out of 456,000 voting-age residents took part. There were no Republican primary contests at the top of the ticket, and there didn't seem to be much suspense about the outcome. Armey won 45% of the vote, which was not enough to avoid a runoff. Burgess won 23%. Then, in the four-week runoff campaign, Burgess benefited from a series of hard-hitting articles in the *The Dallas Morning News* about Scott Armey's record as a county judge. The paper reported that he had used his position to steer county jobs and contracts to close friends, including a $1.5 million transportation consulting contract.

Burgess focused on health care and taxes. He had helped to draft the Texas Patients' Bill of Rights and vowed to do the same on a national level. His campaign was helped by the support of medical societies and local physicians who urged their patients to vote for him. In another low-turnout affair, Burgess won 55%-45% in the runoff. Armey carried Collin and Tarrant counties, but tellingly lost 60%-40% in Denton County, where he was known best. After the runoff, his formerly powerful father spoke bitterly of the newspaper's "vicious unprofessionalism" and accused the paper of a vendetta against the Armey family. In the general election, Burgess won 75%-23% over his Democrat opponent. He has been re-elected comfortably since.

In the House, Burgess has a reliably conservative voting record. He joined the Tea Party Caucus when it formed in 2010. Also that year, he voted "present" on a resolution commemorating the 40th anniversary of the Vietnam-era shootings at Kent State University because he said the measure implied that the National Guard was at fault. He has for several years pushed legislation to implement a flat tax, a popular idea with conservatives that would replace the federal income tax with a 23% sales tax on goods and services. He was among those on the right in 2009 to issue calls for the resignation of Kevin Jennings, leader of the White House's safe and drug-free schools initiative. Burgess cited a *Washington Times* article that accused Jennings, who is gay, of giving sexual advice to minors.

Burgess is best known for his work on health care issues, especially since he joined the Energy and Commerce Committee, which has broad jurisdiction over the medical industry. As vice chairman of its health subcommittee and founding chairman of the Congressional Health Care Caucus, he emerged as one of the most effective inquisitors during the health care hearings in 2011, and fellow Republicans regularly yielded him their extra time so he could ask pointed questions of Obama administration officials. He was especially vocal about seeking to fully de-fund the health law in the fiscal 2011 budget, an idea that House Republican leaders sought to defuse. His nine-part plan for health care reform includes many of the ideas that successful GOP candidates espoused in the 2010, including allowing patients to shop for insurance across state lines and limiting damages in malpractice lawsuits.

But he has shown that he is not a reflexive partisan. In the 111th Congress (2009-10), he was the lone Republican to vote with House Democrats to permanently fix the formula determining Medicare reimbursements for doctors. He also was part of a bipartisan group that introduced legislation in April 2011 ensuring that seniors who show signs of Alzheimer's receive a formal diagnosis from their doctor. And in March 2009, he joined a bipartisan agreement to permit the Food and Drug Administration to approve generic versions of biologic drugs.

Burgess has made some inroads into the GOP leadership. He served as vice chairman of the Republican Policy Committee, which hammers out the party's positions on issues. In 2008, Burgess was GOP presidential candidate McCain's point person on health care policy.

TWENTY-SEVENTH DISTRICT

Blake Farenthold (R)

Elected 2010, 1st term; b. Dec. 12, 1961, Corpus Christi; home, Corpus Christi ; U. of TX, B.A. 1985; St. Mary's U., J.D. 1989. ; Episcopalian ; Married (Debbie); 2 children.

Professional Career: Practicing atty., 1989-95; owner, Farenthold LLC, 1995-2010; radio host, 1999-2010.

DC Office: 2110 RHOB, 20515, 202-225-7742; Fax: 202-226-1134; Web site: farenthold.house.gov.

State Offices: Brownsville, 956-544-8800; Corpus Christi, 361-884-2222.

Committees: *Homeland Security:* Emergency Preparedness, Response & Communications. *Oversight & Government Reform:* Government Organization, Efficiency & Financial Management; National Security, Homeland Defense & Foreign Operations; Technology, Information Policy, Intergovernmental Relations & Procurement Reform. *Transportation & Infrastructure:* Aviation; Coast Guard & Maritime Transportation; Highways & Transit.

Election Results

2010 general	Blake Farenthold (R)	51,001	(48%)	($619,018)
	Solomon Ortiz (D)	50,226	(47%)	($1,223,982)
	Ed Mishou (Lib)	5,372	(5%)	($32,863)
2010 runoff	Blake Farenthold (R)	4,742	(51%)	
	James Duerr (R)	4,496	(49%)	
2010 primary	James Duerr (R)	6,368	(32%)	
	Blake Farenthold (R)	5,921	(30%)	
	William Vaden (R)	4,268	(22%)	
	Jessica Puente-Bradshaw (R)	3,097	(16%)	

Population		Race/Ethnicity		Work	
Pop. 2010:	741,993	White:	22.8%	Private:	71.2%
Change since 2000:	Up 13.9%	Black:	2.0%	Government:	20.8%
Urban:	88.6%	Hispanic:	73.2%	Self-employed:	7.8%
Rural:	11.4%	Asian:	1.1%	Blue collar:	24.4%
Area size:	6,319 sq. mi.	Native Am.:	0.2%	White collar:	52.7%
		Hawaiian:	0.0%	Khaki collar:	0.4%
Age		Two+ races:	0.5%	Other:	22.5%
Median age:	31.3 yrs.				
More than 65 yrs:	10.7%	*Ancestry*		Median income:	$37,241
Less than 18 yrs:	30.8%	German	6.1%	Median Home Value:	$89,000
		Irish	3.7%		
Education		English	3.5%	**Military Veterans**	
H.S. grad:	70.8%			% of Pop:	9.6%
College grad:	17.4%				
Grad degree:	6.4%				

South Gulf Coast; Corpus Christi

Inland from the Laguna Madre in Kleberg County are the vast grazing and oil lands of the 825,000-acre—that's 1,289 square miles—King Ranch. This still seemingly vacant land between the Nueces River and the Rio Grande was the territory in contention during the Mexican-American War. Today, most people here are of Mexican ancestry, some from families who have lived for generations on the U.S. side of the border, some recent immigrants. The culture here

2008 Presidential Vote		
Barack Obama (D)	97,830	(53%)
John McCain (R)	84,366	(46%)
2004 Presidential Vote		
George Bush (R)	99,087	(55%)
John Kerry (D)	81,201	(45%)
Cook Partisan Voting Index: R+2		

is *Tejano*, proudly American but with Mexican flair and vitality. (Adjacent to the King Ranch is the Armstrong Ranch, where in February 2006, Vice President Dick Cheney accidentally shot a hunting partner.) Fronting the Gulf of Mexico is an altogether different bit of geography: the sand spit of Padre Island, an 80-mile barrier-reef island and national seashore, a magnet for college students on spring break.

The 27th Congressional District of Texas includes the area from Corpus Christi south to the Rio Grande. Its population is concentrated at the northern and southern ends of the district. In the north, Corpus Christi and surrounding Nueces County, with a 61% Hispanic population, is the southernmost natural port on Texas' Gulf Coast and the nation's fifth-largest in trading volume. There are big petrochemical plants here, but along the bay front, there are also palm trees and recreational areas. At the southern end is Cameron County, which includes South Padre Island. The population is 88% Hispanic. In addition to tourism, construction is under way on the nation's largest offshore wind farm; more than 100 turbines will generate power for 100,000 homes.

The biggest city in the district is Corpus Christi. It also includes Brownsville, on the Lower Rio Grande opposite Matamoros, Mexico, one of Texas' major border crossings. The 1993 North American Free Trade Agreement has lifted the economy in parts of this area, and there has been a boom in commercial construction. But pockets of poverty remain: Not far from the border is the *colonia* of Cameron Park, where people live in trailers or makeshift structures without water or sewer service. It is rated by the Census Bureau as one of the poorest places in the nation, with an annual per capita income of $5,600.

Politically, the 27th District is Democratic, but not as Democratic as one might expect from a 72% Hispanic district. In 2004, native son George W. Bush carried it with 55% of the vote. In 2008, Democrat Barack Obama won it 53%-46%. Democrat Bill White carried Cameron 57%-41% in the 2010 governor's race, while GOP Gov. Rick Perry took Nueces 53%-45%.

Blake Farenthold (R)

The new congressman from the 27th District is Republican Blake Farenthold, who edged out 14-term Democratic Rep. Solomon Ortiz after a post-election recount gave Farenthold a winning margin of just 799 votes in one of the most surprising GOP wins of 2010.

Farenthold was born and raised in Corpus Christi, where his family has farmed for three generations. His father died when Farenthold was 11 years old, and his mother raised him and his younger sister alone. "Growing up with a single mom, we learned independence," Farenthold told *National Journal*. His family is known for strong women. His grandfather's second wife is Sissy

Farenthold, a Democratic state legislator and a pioneer of the women's rights movement who was a serious contender to be George McGovern's presidential running mate in 1972.

Blake Farenthold studied radio, film, and television at the University of Texas in Austin. After earning his law degree, Farenthold joined his step-grandfather's law practice, focusing on agricultural law. He became dissatisfied with the legal profession, and in 1995, launched a computer consulting and website design firm. In the late 1990s, he also began dabbling in radio again, appearing as an occasional guest on a morning show to talk about computer-related issues. The job gradually became more regular until Farenthold became a sidekick on the program *Lago in the Morning* on Corpus Christi's news radio station KKTX. Farenthold aired many of his conservative views and gained local name recognition.

He began thinking seriously about running for Congress in November 2009 and decided to run to "stand up to the liberal special interests," as he said on his website. He was especially opposed to the national Democrats' health care overhaul law, which he deemed a bad case of government intrusion on the private sector. He faced a tough fight for the Republican nomination against Corpus Christi real estate agent James Duerr, who campaigned on a similarly conservative platform. Duerr edged out Farenthold in the March primary by 2 percentage points, but Farenthold prevailed in the April runoff, 51%-49%, after drawing on his personal wealth to outspend Duerr.

In the general election against Ortiz, Farenthold was a decided underdog. Ortiz had built a moderate voting record in a Hispanic-majority district, and he was a senior member of the Armed Services Committee who had shepherded money to local projects. The incumbent also had a considerable fundraising advantage. Farenthold raised $616,000, including about $150,000 from his own pocket, compared with Ortiz's $1.2 million.

The Republican's campaign also suffered a credibility deficit after images surfaced of Farenthold wearing pajamas featuring yellow ducks while out for a night on the town with a young woman wearing what appeared to be a sheer nightie. Ortiz touted the photograph, which was widely circulated on the Internet, in his campaign ads as evidence that his opponent could not be taken seriously. But Farenthold's campaign picked up steam with the support of local tea party activists. On Election Night, the contest was too close to call, and a recount was ordered. Ortiz conceded to Farenthold on Nov. 22.

In the House, the first bill Farenthold introduced would require federal agencies to display receipts and expenditures every two weeks on their websites. He also actively supported legislative riders attached to the fiscal 2011 funding bill, including one to ban funding for Planned Parenthood. His support of the Republican budget has made him one of the Democratic Congressional Campaign Committee's leading targets for defeat in 2012.

TWENTY-EIGHTH DISTRICT

Henry Cuellar (D)

Elected 2004, 4th term; b. Sept. 19, 1955, Laredo; home, Laredo; Georgetown U., B.S. 1976, U. of TX, J.D. 1981, Ph.D. 1998, TX A&M U., M.A. 1982; Catholic; married (Imelda); 2 children.

Elected Office: TX House of Reps., 1986-2000; TX secy. of state, 2001.

Professional Career: Practicing atty., 1981-2004.

DC Office: 2463 RHOB, 20515, 202-225-1640; Fax: 202-225-1641; Web site: cuellar.house.gov.

State Offices: Laredo, 956-725-0639; McAllen, 956-631-4826; Rio Grande City, 956-487-5603; San Antonio, 210-271-2851; Seguin, 830-401-0457.

Committees: *Agriculture:* Rural Development, Research, Biotechnology & Foreign Agriculture. *Homeland Security:* Border & Maritime Security (RMM); Counterterrorism & Intelligence.

Group Ratings

	ACLU	ACU	ADA	CFG	AFS	FRC	LCV	ITIC	NTU	COC
2010	69	13	75	29	88	12	70	100	14	63
2009	–	12	85	9	100	–	100	–	7	60

National Journal Ratings

	2010 LIB	—	2010 CONS	2009 LIB	—	2009 CONS
Economic	55%	—	44%	55%	—	44%
Social	61%	—	39%	51%	—	48%
Foreign	55%	—	45%	45%	—	53%
Composite	57%	—	43%	51%	—	49%

Key Votes of the 111th Congress

1. Overturn Ledbetter	Y	5. Bar federal abortion funds	Y
2. Pass $820 billion stimulus	Y	6. Pass health care bill	Y
3. Let guns in national parks	Y	7. Regulate financial firms	Y
4. Pass cap-and-trade	Y	8. Pass tax cuts for some	Y

9. Stop detainee transfers	Y
10. Legalize immigrants' kids	Y
11. Repeal don't ask, tell	N (Y)
12. Limit campaign funds	Y

Election Results

2010 general	Henry Cuellar (D)	62,773	(56%)	($1,247,643)
	Bryan Underwood (R)	46,740	(42%)	($149,432)
2010 primary	Henry Cuellar (D)	unopposed		

Prior Winning Percentages: 2008 (69%), 2006 (68%), 2004 (59%)

Population		Race/Ethnicity		Work	
Pop. 2010:	851,824	White:	18.4%	Private:	70.2%
Change since 2000:	Up 30.7%	Black:	1.3%	Government:	19.9%
Urban:	79.4%	Hispanic:	78.9%	Self-employed:	9.7%
Rural:	20.6%	Asian:	0.7%	Blue collar:	24.6%
Area size:	13,738 sq. mi.	Native Am.:	0.1%	White collar:	53.0%
		Hawaiian:	0.0%	Khaki collar:	0.2%
Age		Two+ races:	0.4%	Other:	22.1%
Median age:	29.5 yrs.				
More than 65 yrs:	9.9%	*Ancestry*		Median income:	$37,147
Less than 18 yrs:	34.2%	German	6.2%	Median Home Value:	$87,800
		Irish	3.2%		
Education		English	2.6%	**Military Veterans**	
H.S. grad:	65.4%			% of Pop:	7.5%
College grad:	16.1%				
Grad degree:	4.9%				

South Central Texas; Laredo

Hard by the Mexican border is the place where singer Johnny Cash, in "Streets of Laredo", summoned up images of lonely cowboys on dusty streets outside a row of saloons in a tiny town. But this is not the Laredo of today. On the Rio Grande River 150 miles south of San Antonio, Laredo is the busiest border crossing for U.S.-Mexico trade. Some 14,000 trucks and 1,200 railcars cross its three bridges daily. (Frustrated law enforcement agents contend that tons of

2008 Presidential Vote		
Barack Obama (D) 103,458	(56%)
John McCain (R) 80,741	(44%)
2004 Presidential Vote		
George Bush (R) 90,730	(54%)
John Kerry (D) 77,349	(46%)
Cook Partisan Voting Index: EVEN		

cocaine slip through with the legitimate traffic, often hidden on commercial buses.) Laredo was America's second-fastest-growing city in the 1990s, with more warehouse space than San Antonio and Austin combined. Its old downtown streets, with their bargain stores, are filled with Mexicans who cross the border on foot; those with cars head up the freeway to the Wal-Mart. Incomes and housing prices in greater Laredo, pop. 231,000, are low by U.S. standards but far above those of Nuevo Laredo across the Rio Grande, and there is money to be made here. Laredo's Tony Sanchez, proprietor of a family oil-and-gas business and owner of International Bank of Commerce, became rich enough here to spend $60 million on his unsuccessful 2002 campaign for governor. Webb County's natural gas production reached record levels in November 2010.

The border country along the Rio Grande is in some ways a region all its own, a mixture of the United States and Mexico, where many people have roots on both sides of the border. As former Laredo Mayor Betty Flores has said, "The river for us is more like some street that we cross. It's really not a border." Laredo's Webb County had a 95% Hispanic population in 2009. Local fast-food restaurants feature enchiladas more often than hamburgers. Years ago, movements like La Raza Unida—which had its beginnings here in 1969 when Hispanic youngsters pushed to be allowed to elect high school cheerleaders in Crystal City—wanted the border country to become more like Mexico, with its union and party apparatchiks. More recently, Mexico, with its economic reforms, has been trying to become more like the United States, and particularly like Texas, with its open markets and privatized companies and limited control by political or labor bosses. The region has its problems, including crime from the trade in illegal immigration and drugs. City officials in McAllen, however, have aggressively fought the perception that violence from Mexico is spilling over into their city, which is ranked among the country's safest.

The 28th Congressional District of Texas is centered in Laredo and Webb County and extends in two directions. South along the Rio Grande, it crosses Starr County, one of the poorest counties in Texas and home of many blatant and wealthy drug smugglers. It reaches Mission in a slice of the southwest corner of Hidalgo County. These border counties make up more than two-thirds of the district. It also includes thinly settled ranch and oil well country and a small piece of Bexar County. The district's per capita income of $15,322 is just 57% of the national average.

The redistricting plan imposed by a three-judge federal court in 2006 made major changes in the district. Historically, the 28th was based in Bexar County, anchored by the Hispanic community on the south side of San Antonio, but those neighborhoods were needed to ensure a sufficient number of Hispanic voters in the 23rd District. Yet the 28th is still 79% Hispanic. In the 2008 presidential contest, Democrat Barack Obama won the district 56%-44%, quite a change from Republican George W. Bush's 54%-46% win with the same district boundaries in 2004.

Henry Cuellar (D)

The congressman from the 28th District is Henry Cuellar, a Democrat elected in 2004. His ascension to the top Democratic slot on the Homeland Security Committee's border security panel in 2010 gave him greater prominence in debates over immigration.

Cuellar *(KWAY ar)* was the oldest of eight children of migrant workers who had only elementary school educations. He graduated from Georgetown University and the University of Texas law school, and he later got a Ph.D. in government from UT. From his base in Laredo, he served in the Texas House from 1986 to 2000, where he helped to author the Texas Grant college aid program. In 2001, Republican Gov. Rick Perry appointed him secretary of State even though he is a Democrat. Cuellar resigned in 2002 to run against veteran Republican Rep. Henry Bonilla in the old 23rd District. He got a big boost from a Bonilla gaffe; Bonilla claimed he didn't need Laredo to win, and in response, the Webb County Republican chairman endorsed Cuellar. Cuellar attacked Bonilla for his votes against funding the State Children's Health Insurance Program, the Family and Medical Leave Act, and funding for Pell grants. He also accused Bonilla of being insufficiently Hispanic. Bonilla had the money advantage. Cuellar carried Webb County 84%-15%, but only when the Bexar County votes were counted a few days later was it clear that Bonilla had won 52%-47%.

Redistricting in 2003 strengthened Bonilla in the 23rd District, but it also gave Cuellar an opportunity to run in the 28th against incumbent Democratic Rep. Ciro Rodriguez of San Antonio, who had the most liberal voting record of Texas' Hispanic Democrats in Congress and was chairman of the Hispanic Caucus. When Cuellar announced his candidacy, Rodriguez expressed disbelief that a friend and former legislative colleague for whom he had raised money in 2002 would run against him. The ambitious Cuellar explained that primary bids like his were a common political occurrence in South Texas. He sealed the end of the friendship when he told a local reporter, "Nobody died and made him king."

Rodriguez had little time to get acquainted with the new district, since the March primary took place just five months after the map became official. He had the support of the Hispanic Caucus in Washington, but that delivered few votes in Texas. Cuellar criticized Rodriguez for voting against the GOP's 2003 Medicare prescription drug bill, while Rodriguez pointed up Cuellar's collusion with Republicans as secretary of State. The initial vote count showed Rodriguez ahead by 145 votes, but a subsequent recount put Cuellar ahead by 203 votes. After a lawsuit, a second recount, and a state appellate court ruling in July, Cuellar was declared the Democratic nominee by 58 votes out of 49,000 cast. He went on to win in November 59%-39%. Later, in September 2007, the Federal Election Commission fined Cuellar $28,500 for failing to disclose a $200,000 bank loan in his 2004 campaign.

In the House, Cuellar's voting record is one of the most conservative of the Hispanic Democrats from Texas, putting him near the center of the House as a whole. Since President Barack Obama took office, however, he has been more inclined to join his party on major legislation—something that has boosted his popularity with his Democratic colleagues. The lone exception in the 111th Congress (2009-10) was the Dodd-Frank financial industry overhaul. Cuellar was one of 19 Democrats—many of them members of the fiscally conservative Blue Dog Coalition—to oppose it. He also joined other Texas delegation members in voting against lifting the financial liability cap on oil spills in 2010.

One result of Cuellar's increased loyalty was the chairmanship of Homeland Security's border security subcommittee in January 2010. He called for a new strategy to replace the Merida Initiative security agreement with Mexico that would improve the State Department's management and speed up money for training and equipment. He also helped broker a 2010 agreement between the Homeland Security Department and Federal Aviation Administration to use unmanned drones along the border for the first time. He has emphasized a bipartisan approach and shown a knack for getting legislation passed. With Republican help, he won passage of legislation to create a national gang intelligence center at the Federal Bureau of Investigation and to toughen penalties for sex offenders who break the terms of their release. He also got a bill into law in 2010 requiring federal agencies to establish measurable performance goals and devise systems for tracking them.

In Cuellar's first re-election bid in 2006, Rodriguez was back to challenge him in the primary, but struggled to match him in fundraising. Rodriguez said that Cuellar's votes in Washington had "sold out" the district. But the *San Antonio Express-News* endorsed Cuellar for his "independent non-partisan mindset" and said that his willingness to place the district ahead of his party was "refreshing." Cuellar won the primary comfortably this time, 53% to 40%. (With the court-ordered redistricting changes, Rodriguez had another opportunity to run for a House seat later in the year, in the 23rd District. He challenged Republican incumbent Henry Bonilla and won. He lost the seat in the 2010 election to Republican Francisco "Quico" Canseco.

In 2008, Cuellar easily won re-election. He faced a tougher challenge in 2010 from Republican building contractor Bryan Underwood, but Underwood could not compete with Cuellar's loyal base in the Rio Grande Valley, and Cuellar won 56%-42%. He is expected to lose a chunk of his district to redistricting in 2012 and he worked with Judiciary Committee Chairman Lamar Smith, R-Texas, in early 2011 on a potential compromise plan to ensure adequate Hispanic representation reflecting that community's population growth.

TWENTY-NINTH DISTRICT

Gene Green (D)

Elected 1992, 10th term; b. Oct. 17, 1947, Houston; home, Houston; U. of Houston, B.A., 1971, Bates Col. of Law at U. of Houston, 1973-77; Methodist; married (Helen); 2 children.

Elected Office: TX House of Reps., 1972–84; TX Senate, 1985–92.

Professional Career: Practicing atty., 1977–92.

DC Office: 2470 RHOB, 20515, 202-225-1688; Fax: 202-225-9903; Web site: house.gov/green.

State Offices: Baytown, 281-420-0502; Houston, 713-330-0761; Houston, 281-999-5879.

Committees: *Energy & Commerce:* Energy & Power; Environment & the Economy (RMM); Oversight & Investigations.

Group Ratings

	ACLU	ACU	ADA	CFG	AFS	FRC	LCV	ITIC	NTU	COC
2010	75	4	80	3	100	12	60	67	6	25
2009	–	0	100	0	100	–	100	–	3	40

National Journal Ratings

	2010 LIB — 2010 CONS		2009 LIB — 2009 CONS	
Economic	60%	40%	88%	12%
Social	58%	41%	59%	37%
Foreign	47%	53%	77%	22%
Composite	55%	45%	76%	25%

Key Votes of the 111th Congress

1. Overturn Ledbetter	Y	5. Bar federal abortion funds	N	9. Stop detainee transfers	Y
2. Pass $820 billion stimulus	Y	6. Pass health care bill	Y	10. Legalize immigrants' kids	Y
3. Let guns in national parks	Y	7. Regulate financial firms	Y	11. Repeal don't ask, tell	Y
4. Pass cap-and-trade	Y	8. Pass tax cuts for some	Y	12. Limit campaign funds	Y

Election Results

2010 general	Gene Green (D)	43,257	(65%)	($1,080,909)
	Roy Morales (R)	22,825	(34%)	($296,885)
2010 primary	Gene Green (D)	unopposed		

Prior Winning Percentages: 2008 (75%), 2006 (74%), 2004 (94%), 2002 (95%), 2000 (73%), 1998 (93%), 1996 (68%), 1994 (73%), 1992 (65%)

Population		Race/Ethnicity		Work	
Pop. 2010:	677,032	White:	12.5%	Private:	84.9%
Change since 2000:	Up 3.9%	Black:	9.6%	Government:	7.8%
Urban:	99.4%	Hispanic:	76.0%	Self-employed:	7.2%
Rural:	0.6%	Asian:	1.1%	Blue collar:	46.6%
Area size:	249 sq. mi.	Native Am.:	0.1%	White collar:	34.9%
		Hawaiian:	0.0%	Khaki collar:	0.0%
Age		Two+ races:	0.5%	Other:	18.4%
Median age:	28.6 yrs.				
More than 65 yrs:	7.0%	*Ancestry*		Median income:	$36,541
Less than 18 yrs:	32.9%	German	2.5%	Median Home Value:	$89,400
		Irish	2.1%		
Education		USA	1.8%	**Military Veterans**	
H.S. grad:	54.3%			% of Pop:	4.8%
College grad:	6.7%				
Grad degree:	1.9%				

Houston and Suburbs; Pasadena

"What built Houston," wrote John Gunther in *Inside U.S.A.* "was a combination of cotton, oil, and the ship canal." The cotton and oil were gifts of nature, though they required much human effort and ingenuity to produce in commercial quantities. The 54-mile Houston Ship Channel was almost totally man's creation. After the sand-spit port of Galveston was destroyed by a hurricane and tidal wave in 1900, Houston's elders decided to dredge out Buffalo Bayou and make their inland city a seaport. When the channel officially opened in November 1914, a sluggish, 6-foot-deep creek had become a 40-foot-deep waterway that would turn Houston into one of the nation's biggest ports. Today, the channel is 45 feet deep and 530 feet wide. More than 7,800 ships a year come through with an estimated $131 billion in foreign trade. The port also is the site of the largest petrochemical complex in the nation. On its west side, Houston seems entirely a white-collar, office-bound city. But on the east and north, around the port and through the maze of refinery towers and pipelines, Houston remains blue-collar and a job magnet for Mexican-Americans and workers from the rural South.

2008 Presidential Vote		
Barack Obama (D) 66,808	(62%)
John McCain (R) 40,884	(38%)

2004 Presidential Vote		
John Kerry (D) 59,897	(56%)
George Bush (R) 47,734	(44%)

Cook Partisan Voting Index: D+8

The 29th Congressional District of Texas covers much of the ship channel area and working-class Houston. Included is much of Houston's Northside, between the Eastex and North Freeways almost to George Bush Intercontinental Airport. Northside's residents began an effort in 2010 to build more affordable housing, parks, hiking and bike trails and other environmentally sustainable amenities. The district takes in blue-collar neighborhoods in northeast Houston as well. Neighborhoods in this area ballooned in size as more than 200,000 Hurricane Katrina refugees in 2005 temporarily or permanently relocated to Houston. From 2000 to 2010, the district's Hispanic population grew from 66% to 76%. Harris County has the second-largest Hispanic population in the U.S. (only Los Angeles County has more). This part of Houston has always been considered heavily Democratic. In 2004, President George W. Bush lost it 56%-44%, and in 2008, Democratic nominee Barack Obama won it 62%-38%.

Gene Green (D)

The congressman from the 29th District is Gene Green, a Democrat first elected in 1992 and a gregarious centrist with a bipartisan streak.

Green grew up in the largely Hispanic Lindale section of north Houston, the son of a home-improvement business owner who enlisted his sons to provide him with free labor. "The joke in our family was that nobody had enough money to be a Republican," he said. He worked as a printer's apprentice, and got business and law degrees from the University of Houston. He was elected to the state House in 1972, at age 25, and to the state Senate in a special election in 1985. He has been a friend to unions and trial lawyers in Austin and Washington, and an opponent of gun control, a politician whose natural political base is Texas's small, unionized blue-collar class.

In the 1992 primary for the House seat, he faced Ben Reyes, a tempestuous Houston councilman who once protested official inaction on crime by demolishing a crack house. Green, a compulsive campaigner, went door-to-door and carried lawn signs and a hammer in his trunk while appearing as a frequent guest on Spanish-language radio shows. In the primary, Reyes led 34%-28%. But in the runoff, Green came out ahead by 180 votes out of 31,508 cast. Reyes went to court and charged that Republican voters had illegally crossed over to vote in the runoff. That got him a July re-runoff, but to no avail. This time, Green won with 52%. He went on to win the general election with 65% of the vote.

In the House, Green has a moderate voting record, especially for a member of a heavily minority urban district. He has become more inclined to join Democrats since President Barack Obama took office, but he still goes his own way on occasion. In December 2010, he opposed repealing the military's "don't ask, don't tell" policy barring openly gay service members. He also voted against the tax cut deal that Obama reached with Republicans that month, having earlier opposed the original 2001 and 2003 tax cuts that were extended as part of the deal.

After a spirited fight with other Texas Democrats in 1996, Green won a seat on the influential Energy and Commerce Committee, where he naturally has focused on issues important to the oil industry. In 2008, he became chairman of the Environment and Hazardous Materials Subcommittee. But Democrat Henry Waxman of California eliminated the panel—and Green's chairmanship—soon after taking over as Energy and Commerce chairman in 2009. Green had been an ally of Michigan Democrat John Dingell in the pitched battle for control of the committee gavel in November 2008. He said he patched things up with Waxman after letting him know that he wouldn't stand for being retaliated against for backing Dingell. After the Republican takeover of the House in 2011, Green became ranking Democrat on the newly created Environment and Economy subcommittee.

Green has been active legislatively on the panel. In May 2009, he got significant concessions from Waxman for oil refineries in the climate change bill the committee produced, which capped emissions and created a system for companies to "trade" emissions limits. Green has had to strike a balance between the industry's desires and quality-of-life issues in the district. For example, he fought Republican proposals to encourage new oil refineries because the environmental exemptions could have jeopardized the clean air program in Houston. But he sided with other Texas delegation members after the 2010 BP oil spill in the Gulf of Mexico and opposed lifting the liability cap on spills for companies. He also joined Louisiana Republican Charles Boustany in March 2011 in sponsoring a resolution in support of continued deepwater drilling in the Gulf of Mexico.

One of Green's other main interests is health care. He backed the government-run "public option" to compete with private insurers that passed the House but was stripped from the Senate's health care overhaul. He has worked on array of related issues, getting bipartisan bills into law to upgrade states' trauma care systems and eliminate tuberculosis. In 2010, he worked with Pennsylvania Republican Tim Murphy on a House-passed bill to provide more doctors in underserved areas. On another issue, Green in 2009 took up the cause of local radio stations trying to preserve their long-standing exemption from paying royalties on the music they air. He said his goal was to prod stations to negotiate with performers. "I often tell industries, 'The last thing you want is to have Congress do something,'" he said.

Green has been re-elected easily and has had no significant primary challenges, despite the fact that the 29th remains an inviting opportunity for an ambitious Hispanic politician. He has paid close attention to constituent service—his office hosts an annual "Immunization Day" to provide free vaccines. His district has grown more slowly than the state average, making it more difficult to divide it into two for the purposes of adding another Hispanic-majority district in Texas as a result of 2012 redistricting.

THIRTIETH DISTRICT

Eddie Bernice Johnson (D)

Elected 1992, 10th term; b. Dec. 3, 1935, Waco; home, Dallas; St. Mary's at Notre Dame, B.A. 1955, TX Christian U., B.S. 1967, S. Methodist U., M.P.A. 1976; Baptist; divorced; 1 child.

Elected Office: TX House of Reps., 1972–1977; TX Senate, 1986–92.

Professional Career: Registered nurse; Regional dir., U.S. Dept. of HEW, 1977–80; Mgmt. consultant, Sammons Corp., 1979–81; Owner, Eddie Bernice Johnson & Assoc., 1981–present.

DC Office: 2468 RHOB, 20515, 202-225-8885; Fax: 202-226-1477; Web site: ebjohnson.house.gov.

State Offices: Dallas, 214-922-8885.

Committees: *Science, Space & Technology* (RMM). *Transportation & Infrastructure:* Aviation; Highways & Transit; Water Resources & Environment.

Group Ratings

	ACLU	ACU	ADA	CFG	AFS	FRC	LCV	ITIC	NTU	COC
2010	88	0	85	0	100	0	90	100	5	14
2009	–	0	95	0	100	–	100	–	1	29

National Journal Ratings

	2010 LIB	—	2010 CONS		2009 LIB	—	2009 CONS
Economic	76%	—	23%		91%	—	0%
Social	89%	—	7%		82%	—	17%
Foreign	77%	—	22%		70%	—	24%
Composite	82%	—	18%		84%	—	16%

Key Votes of the 111th Congress

1. Overturn Ledbetter	Y	5. Bar federal abortion funds	N	9. Stop detainee transfers	N
2. Pass $820 billion stimulus	Y	6. Pass health care bill	Y	10. Legalize immigrants' kids	Y
3. Let guns in national parks	N	7. Regulate financial firms	Y	11. Repeal don't ask, tell	Y
4. Pass cap-and-trade	Y	8. Pass tax cuts for some	Y	12. Limit campaign funds	Y

Election Results

2010 general	Eddie Bernice Johnson (D)	86,322	(76%)	($613,624)
	Stephen Broden (R)	24,668	(22%)	($701,889)
	J. B. Oswalt (Lib)	2,988	(3%)	
2010 primary	Eddie Bernice Johnson (D)	unopposed		

Prior Winning Percentages: 2008 (82%), 2006 (80%), 2004 (93%), 2002 (74%), 2000 (92%), 1998 (72%), 1996 (55%), 1994 (73%), 1992 (72%)

Population		Race/Ethnicity		Work	
Pop. 2010:	706,469	White:	16.7%	Private:	82.4%
Change since 2000:	Up 8.4%	Black:	41.0%	Government:	11.5%
Urban:	98.8%	Hispanic:	39.7%	Self-employed:	5.9%
Rural:	1.2%	Asian:	1.2%	Blue collar:	31.4%
Area size:	319 sq. mi.	Native Am.:	0.3%	White collar:	48.8%
		Hawaiian:	0.0%	Khaki collar:	0.2%
Age		Two+ races:	0.9%	Other:	19.6%
Median age:	30.6 yrs.				
More than 65 yrs:	7.8%	*Ancestry*		Median income:	$37,111
Less than 18 yrs:	28.6%	German	3.4%	Median Home Value:	$98,500
		Irish	2.8%		
Education		English	2.5%	**Military Veterans**	
H.S. grad:	67.7%			% of Pop:	6.0%
College grad:	18.4%				
Grad degree:	6.1%				

Downtown Dallas and Suburbs

Cotton was originally the major crop in northern Texas, and many of Dallas' first enterprising businessmen, after the railroad reached the Trinity River in the 1870s, were cotton brokers. Railroads made Dallas rich and helped it to grow. Geographically, Dallas is directly west of the Black Belt of Alabama and the Mississippi Delta, both heavy cotton-producing areas in the days before the boll weevil. Many blacks and whites came west on U.S. 80—and now Inter-

2008 Presidential Vote
Barack Obama (D) 170,826 (82%)
John McCain (R) 37,465 (18%)

2004 Presidential Vote
John Kerry (D) 136,116 (75%)
George Bush (R) 45,148 (25%)

Cook Partisan Voting Index: D+27

state 20—to the Dallas-Fort Worth Metroplex, now the largest metro area in the South and the nation's fourth-largest. The south side of Dallas is predominately African-American.

The 30th Congressional District of Texas, designed as the Dallas-Fort Worth Metroplex's black-majority district, includes most of the city's African-American neighborhoods. Its creation in 1991 was insisted on by the then-chairman of the Texas Senate's redistricting committee, and the result was a grotesquely shaped district. Its center was south and east Dallas, but it had tentacles as complex as a DNA molecule. Since then, lawsuits and two more rounds of redistricting have smoothed out the lines and left this as the only Democratic district in the Metroplex. Today, the 30th District includes two compact geographic units centered in downtown Dallas. One consists of most of the south side of Dallas; the other runs northwest out Stemmons Freeway. In between is the "mixmaster," where three busy interstates—Interstates 30, 35E and 45—come together within a square mile, surrounding many of the prominent sites in Dallas. The district includes The Cedars neighborhood, which is home to South Side on Lamar. A former 10-story Sears, Roebuck building that was transformed into a loft and retail development, it has become one of the foremost centers of Dallas' black community.

The district's population is 39% African-American and 41% Hispanic. The Hispanic population is mostly young and foreign-born, and 90% of the Latinos are from Mexico. Redistricting in 2012 could produce a Hispanic-majority district in the Dallas area, which would increase the current district's percentage of African-Americans. The growing influence of racial minorities in the city has been a major factor in the Democrats' recent capture of control of many Dallas County offices and seats in the Texas Legislature. In 2004, George W. Bush lost here 75%-25%, his worst performance in Texas. In 2008, Republican nominee John McCain lost 82%-18%, also his worst performance in the state.

Eddie Bernice Johnson (D)

The congresswoman from the 30th District is Eddie Bernice Johnson, a Democrat first elected in 1992. She became the ranking Democrat on the Science, Space and Technology Committee in 2011.

Johnson grew up in Texas, graduated from Texas Christian University with a nursing degree, and later got a master's degree in public administration at Southern Methodist University. She worked at St. Paul Hospital and was the chief psychiatric nurse at the Veterans Administration Hospital in Dallas. In 1972, she was elected to the Texas House, the first black woman elected to the legislature from Dallas. She became a regional director of the old Health, Education and Welfare Department under Democratic President Jimmy Carter. She was elected to the Texas Senate in 1986. As the Senate's Redistricting Committee chairman in 1991, she was instrumental in creating the new 30th District, and she went on to win the Democratic primary with 92% of the vote.

In the House, Johnson—known by her initials "EBJ" —has a mostly liberal voting record. A former chairman of the Congressional Black Caucus, she was more supportive of President Barack Obama in 2009 than other caucus members critical of his efforts for low-income and unemployed blacks. She has been attentive to business interests in Dallas, though her lifetime voting score from the U.S. Chamber of Commerce through 2010 was 41—third-lowest among Texas' House delegation. Johnson once pledged to labor unions to oppose the North American Free Trade Agreement, but she changed her mind and voted for it in 1993. Dallas probably exports more to Mexico than any other American city, and many jobs depend on those exports. Johnson also sided with business on normalizing trade relations with China.

On the Science Committee, Johnson has worked to develop cost-effective technologies for vehicle research and to help more women receive federal research grants. She shared credit for passing the Networking and Information Research and Development Act to double funding for information research. She also sought to double spending for the National Science Foundation. As a healthcare professional, she also takes an interest in minority health issues.

On the Transportation and Infrastructure Committee, Johnson has worked to secure funds for construction of the Interstate 30 suspension bridge over the Trinity River, and she continues to support Trinity River projects. The Trinity River Corridor project, in the works for decades and estimated to cost $2.5 billion, is moving toward reality, with its ambitious plans for flood control, recreational facilities, and transportation improvements, including three new suspension bridges. She also has sought to address the Dallas-Fort Worth area's mass transit needs to alleviate traffic congestion.

Johnson generally has sailed to re-election. But in the months before the 2010 election, *The Dallas Morning News* reported that she had awarded college scholarships to four relatives and the two children of a top aide who otherwise would have been ineligible under the Congressional Black Caucus Foundation's guidelines. Johnson said she had not been familiar with the rules and agreed to repay the foundation. But the scandal provided an opening for her Republican challenger, minister Stephen Broden. The *Morning News* endorsed Broden, and rebuked Johnson for being among the South Dallas leaders "who treat their districts as if they were their fiefdoms." But whatever chance Broden may have had for an upset vanished a few weeks later, when he told a television interviewer that an armed overthrow of the federal government is "on the table." Johnson chalked up another landslide, 76%-22%.

THIRTY-FIRST DISTRICT

John Carter (R)

Elected 2002, 5th term; b. Nov. 6, 1941, Houston; home, Round Rock; TX Tech. U., B.A. 1964, U. of TX, J.D. 1969; Christian; married (Erika); 4 children.

Elected Office: Dist. Ct. judge, 1982-2001.

Professional Career: Practicing atty., 1969-81.

DC Office: 409 CHOB, 20515, 202-225-3864; Fax: 202-225-5886; Web site: www.house.gov/carter/.

State Offices: Round Rock, 512-246-1600; Temple, 254-933-1392.

Committees: *Appropriations:* Homeland Security; Military Construction, Veterans Affairs & Related Agencies (VChmn); Transportation, HUD & Related Agencies.

Group Ratings

	ACLU	ACU	ADA	CFG	AFS	FRC	LCV	ITIC	NTU	COC
2010	13	100	0	95	0	100	10	33	90	88
2009	–	96	0	89	0	–	0	–	88	79

National Journal Ratings

	2010 LIB	—	2010 CONS	2009 LIB	—	2009 CONS
Economic	9%	—	90%	18%	—	82%
Social	0%	—	85%	0%	—	93%
Foreign	0%	—	88%	0%	—	75%
Composite	8%	—	92%	11%	—	89%

Key Votes of the 111th Congress

1. Overturn Ledbetter	N	5. Bar federal abortion funds	Y	9. Stop detainee transfers	Y
2. Pass $820 billion stimulus	N	6. Pass health care bill	N	10. Legalize immigrants' kids	N
3. Let guns in national parks	Y	7. Regulate financial firms	N	11. Repeal don't ask, tell	N
4. Pass cap-and-trade	N	8. Pass tax cuts for some	N	12. Limit campaign funds	N

Election Results

2010 general	John Carter (R)	126,384	(83%)	($997,508)
	Bill Oliver (Lib)	26,735	(17%)	
2010 primary	John Carter (R)	52,321	(90%)	
	Raymond Yamka (R)	5,910	(10%)	

Prior Winning Percentages: 2008 (60%), 2006 (58%), 2004 (65%), 2002 (69%)

Population		Race/Ethnicity		Work	
Pop. 2010:	902,101	White:	59.7%	Private:	69.0%
Change since 2000:	Up 38.4%	Black:	11.9%	Government:	25.1%
Urban:	77.9%	Hispanic:	21.7%	Self-employed:	5.8%
Rural:	22.1%	Asian:	3.3%	Blue collar:	19.4%
Area size:	7,194 sq. mi.	Native Am.:	0.4%	White collar:	59.6%
		Hawaiian:	0.4%	Khaki collar:	5.2%
Age		Two+ races:	2.4%	Other:	15.8%
Median age:	32.0 yrs.				
More than 65 yrs:	9.5%	*Ancestry*		Median income:	$54,894
Less than 18 yrs:	27.9%	German	14.5%	Median Home Value:	$144,800
		English	8.4%		
Education		Irish	8.2%	**Military Veterans**	
H.S. grad:	88.0%			% of Pop:	14.4%
College grad:	26.8%				
Grad degree:	8.1%				

East Central Texas; Austin Suburbs

Williamson County, long a rural backwater, has become a major population and business center deep in the heart of Texas. Its population has virtually doubled in every recent decade. It had 77,000 people in 1980, 140,000 in 1990, 250,000 in 2000, and 420,000 in 2010. Williamson County is just north of Austin, and much of this growth has been generated by the Austin area's high technology boom. Hugely successful computer producer Dell is headquartered in Round

2008 Presidential Vote		
John McCain (R) 172,570	(57%)
Barack Obama (D) 124,608	(41%)
2004 Presidential Vote		
George Bush (R) 170,234	(67%)
John Kerry (D) 85,574	(34%)
Cook Partisan Voting Index: R+14		

Rock, with 18,000 local employees, and is still expanding. As companies emerging from the recession ordered more computers in late 2010 and early 2011, Dell's earnings more than doubled during that period, to $927 million. Texas 130, a 49-mile 10-lane toll road that opened in 2008, has generated more growth. Georgetown has become a popular retirement destination.

Bell and Coryell counties, just north of Williamson County, are the site of Fort Hood, the largest U.S. military base in the world and the largest employer in Texas. The base is the only post in the United States capable of supporting two full armored divisions. It covers 218,000 acres—340 square miles, an area larger than New York's five boroughs. It became the center of national attention in November 2009 when a gunman killed 13 people and wounded 29 others. The suspect was Army Maj. Nidal Malik Hasan, a psychiatrist and Muslim of Palestinian descent whose alleged actions set off a fierce debate over domestic Islamic extremism. The fort's mission is maintaining readiness for combat missions, including training Army Reservists in urban combat. East of Fort Hood is Temple, a rail center. Decades ago, the freight carried from its rail yards was mostly cotton. Now, it serves a variety of industries, including plastics manufacturers.

The 31st Congressional District of Texas, created in the 2001 redistricting and sharply altered in the 2003 Republican redistricting, is dominated by Williamson, Bell and Coryell counties, which account for about 90% of its population. Historically this was solidly Democratic country, devoted to the party of the Confederacy and later, the New Deal. It was populated by cotton farmers who distrusted Wall Street and railroads and who trusted politicians like Sam Rayburn and Lyndon Johnson and later Gov. Ann Richards and Sen. Lloyd Bentsen. But people in this district took a shine to George W. Bush's brand of Republicanism, first as governor and then as president. In 2004, he carried the district 67%-33%. In 2008, GOP nominee John McCain did not fare as well, getting 57% to Democrat Barack Obama's 41%. In 2010, GOP Gov. Rick Perry won Williamson 59%-37%, Bell 57%-37% and Coryell 62%-38%.

John Carter (R)

The congressman from the 31st District is John Carter, a Republican first elected in 2002. He was re-elected in 2010 to a third term as House Republican Conference secretary, a position he has used to become a high-profile critic of Democrats.

Carter grew up in Houston and graduated from Texas Tech University and the University of Texas law school. He practiced law in Williamson County and served as a municipal judge in Round Rock. He was appointed a district judge in 1981 by Republican Gov. Bill Clements and in 1982 stood for election. Judicial elections are partisan in Texas, and Carter was the first Republican judge elected in Williamson County. Carter became known as the father of the county Republican Party. In 2001, after a three-judge district court created a new Republican 31st District stretching from Williamson County to Houston, Carter retired from the bench and ran for Congress. The real contest in this district was among the eight candidates for the Republican nomination. Carter's main rivals were Peter Wareing, the son-in-law of Texas oilman Jack Blanton, and Brad Barton, son of Rep. Joe Barton of the 6th District. In the primary, Wareing led with 37% to 26% for Carter and 16% for Barton.

In the four-week runoff campaign, Carter attacked Wareing as a liberal in disguise, pointing to his campaign contributions to Democrats like Rep. Sheila Jackson Lee of Houston. When Wareing proposed that each candidate sign a "clean campaign pledge," Carter offered what he called a "homestead pledge"—a ploy to highlight his charge that Wareing was a Houston carpetbagger who had rented an apartment in the district in order to run for the seat. Rep. Barton endorsed Carter as "the only true conservative in this race." Wareing outspent Carter more than 2-to-1, but Carter won 57%-43%. He got 78% of the vote in Williamson County, which cast 33% of the vote. Carter won the general election easily and has had little trouble winning re-election.

In the House, Carter has been a reliable conservative. He joined the Tea Party Caucus when it formed in July 2010 and was among the co-sponsors of the so-called "birther" bill in 2009 requiring future presidential candidates to provide proof of U.S. citizenship. He accused the Pentagon of watering down a 2010 report on the Fort Hood shootings to avoid discussing Islamic terrorism. When Republicans took over the majority in the House in January 2011, he introduced a resolution seeking to block the Environmental Protection Agency from issuing new air pollution regulations on cement kilns, drawing criticism from environmental groups. He also promised that his party would make frequent use of the Congressional Review Act—a measure requiring federal agencies to submit major proposed regulations for a 60-day review—to force votes on what he called "many of the heavy-handed regulations attempted by the Obama administration." But in addition to his attack dog role, Carter has had a few legislative accomplishments. On the Judiciary Committee, he won passage of a bill to establish penalties for identity theft and also was successful in passing his Terrorist Penalties Enhancement Act.

Carter became the chief antagonist of New York Democratic Rep. Charles Rangel in 2009. He introduced several resolutions seeking to remove Rangel as chairman of the House Ways and Means Committee during the investigation of ethics allegations against him. Rangel ultimately was removed as head of the committee and censured for his transgressions. But Carter himself drew Democrats' fire for an alleged ethical lapse after he reportedly failed to disclose nearly $300,000 in profits from sales of oil stocks in 2006 and 2007. Carter responded by taking the offensive, noting that he had paid all taxes on his stock transactions and had admitted his errors, and then challenged Rangel to do the same.

In 2005, with help from then-Majority Leader Tom DeLay of Texas, Carter got a coveted seat on the Appropriations Committee. He criticized Republican conservatives who objected to the appropriators' heavy use of earmarking, the practice of funding projects for individual lawmakers' districts rather than on a merit system. But he abided by the GOP's decision not to seek any earmarks in 2010 or 2011.

THIRTY-SECOND DISTRICT

Pete Sessions (R)

Elected 1996, 8th term; b. March 22, 1955, Waco; home, Dallas; SW U., B.S. 1978; Methodist; married (Juanita); 2 children.

Professional Career: District mgr., SW Bell Telephone Co., 1978–93; V.P., public policy, Natl. Center for Policy Analysis, 1994–95.

DC Office: 2233 RHOB, 20515, 202-225-2231; Fax: 202-225-5878; Web site: sessions.house.gov.

State Offices: Dallas, 972-392-0505.

Committees: *Rules* (VChmn).

Group Ratings

	ACLU	ACU	ADA	CFG	AFS	FRC	LCV	ITIC	NTU	COC
2010	13	100	0	97	0	100	10	33	91	88
2009	–	100	0	98	0	–	0	–	92	75

National Journal Ratings

	2010 LIB	—	2010 CONS		2009 LIB	—	2009 CONS
Economic	8%	—	91%		0%	—	96%
Social	0%	—	85%		7%	—	90%
Foreign	0%	—	88%		0%	—	75%
Composite	7%	—	93%		8%	—	92%

Key Votes of the 111th Congress

1. Overturn Ledbetter	N	5. Bar federal abortion funds	Y
2. Pass $820 billion stimulus	N	6. Pass health care bill	N
3. Let guns in national parks	Y	7. Regulate financial firms	Y
4. Pass cap-and-trade	N	8. Pass tax cuts for some	N

9. Stop detainee transfers	Y
10. Legalize immigrants' kids	N
11. Repeal don't ask, tell	N
12. Limit campaign funds	N

Election Results

2010 general	Pete Sessions (R)	79,433	(63%)	($2,153,120)
	Grier Raggio (D)	44,258	(35%)	($669,552)
	John Myers (Lib)	3,178	(3%)	($7,210)
2010 primary	Pete Sessions (R)	30,509	(84%)	
	David Smith (R)	5,937	(16%)	

Prior Winning Percentages: 2008 (57%), 2006 (56%), 2004 (54%), 2002 (68%), 2000 (54%), 1998 (56%), 1996 (53%)

Population		Race/Ethnicity		Work	
Pop. 2010:	640,419	White:	42.4%	Private:	85.7%
Change since 2000:	Down 1.7%	Black:	8.2%	Government:	7.3%
Urban:	99.9%	Hispanic:	42.4%	Self-employed:	6.8%
Rural:	0.1%	Asian:	5.2%	Blue collar:	23.0%
Area size:	161 sq. mi.	Native Am.:	0.3%	White collar:	60.5%
		Hawaiian:	0.0%	Khaki collar:	0.1%
Age		Two+ races:	1.2%	Other:	16.5%
Median age:	32.3 yrs.				
More than 65 yrs:	9.9%	*Ancestry*		Median income:	$49,692
Less than 18 yrs:	26.6%	German	7.9%	Median Home Value:	$180,000
		English	7.1%		
Education		Irish	6.2%	**Military Veterans**	
H.S. grad:	76.0%			% of Pop:	6.6%
College grad:	37.2%				
Grad degree:	13.3%				

North Dallas

North Dallas has long been the home of the city's elite, and indeed, of a slice of the nation's elite. Early in the 20th century, the city's richest citizens started moving away from old neighborhoods adjacent to downtown and out past Turtle Creek to the area around the suburbs of Highland Park and University Park—the Park Cities. Dallas grew lustily on from mid-century on, and beyond the Park Cities, miles of affluent neighborhoods were built, especially between

2008 Presidential Vote		
John McCain (R)	110,397	(53%)
Barack Obama (D)	96,203	(46%)
2004 Presidential Vote		
George Bush (R)	120,970	(60%)
John Kerry (D)	81,846	(40%)
Cook Partisan Voting Index:	R+8	

the Central Expressway and the Dallas North Tollway. Galleries and office complexes followed. There is an entertainment and singles apartment corridor along Greenville Avenue, working-class neighborhoods here and there, and pockets of Latino neighborhoods near the freeways. But overall, the tone has been set by the Dallas elite.

In the 1960s and 1970s, this was one of the most politically conservative parts of the country. People believed in unfettered free markets and the Republican Party. Since 1992, North Dallas has moved, like elite parts of other big metropolitan areas, toward the Democrats. The number of affluent women voting Democratic on the abortion issue is much smaller than in affluent quadrants of New York and Los Angeles, but there are some. In the 1990s, both Republicans George W. Bush and Dick Cheney lived in North Dallas, in or near the Park Cities. After eight years in the White House, George and Laura Bush returned to their Preston Hollow neighborhood, to an 8,500-square-foot home on an acre of land that's only a few miles from his planned presidential library at Southern Methodist University. Groundbreaking on the library took place in November 2010, and its scheduled opening is 2013.

The 32nd Congressional District of Texas includes most of the area commonly thought of as North Dallas: the Park Cities and affluent North Dallas neighborhoods extending to the Dallas County line. The district also includes some affluent suburbs in Dallas County: parts of racially diverse Richardson northeast of the city and Addison to the northwest. The median household income in 2009 was $50,145, slightly above the statewide level. The 2003 redistricting removed some suburban territory and added blue-collar and Democratic-tending Irving and the heavily Latino Oak Cliff neighborhoods south of the Trinity River, where Lee Harvey Oswald was captured inside the old Texas Theater on November 22, 1963, shortly after he killed President John F. Kennedy. Bush's vote declined here in 2004 to 60%, and the Republican vote dropped further in 2008, when John McCain got 53%, in part because of an increase in Democratic-voting Latino voters.

(Redistricting and an influx of Latinos had raised the Hispanic percentage from 27% to 42% by 2010.) With the adjacent 30th District also heavily Hispanic, redistricters after the 2010 census may create a new Hispanic district in this area as one of the four Texas is gaining.

Pete Sessions (R)

The congressman from the 32nd District is Pete Sessions, a Republican first elected in 1996. He is the chairman of the National Republican Congressional Committee, the No. 4 GOP leadership position in the House. After helping to guide his party back to control of the chamber in 2010, he now faces the challenge of holding it in 2012.

Sessions grew up in Waco, graduated from Southwestern University, then worked at Southwestern Bell in Dallas for 16 years. His father is William Sessions, a federal judge who served as director of the Federal Bureau of Investigation from 1987 to 1993. The vagaries of redistricting led Sessions to run for Congress in several different House districts. In 1991, he ran and finished sixth in the special election in the 3rd District, which then included much of North Dallas. In 1993, he resigned from the phone company to run against Democratic Rep. John Bryant in the 5th District, which included much of the east side of Dallas and several rural counties to the south. The district had been drawn to re-elect Bryant, a liberal Democrat. Sessions ran a vigorous campaign, making a two-day, 12-city tour of the district's rural portions with a livestock trailer full of horse manure and a sign saying, "The Clinton health care plan stinks worse than this trailer." Although he outspent Sessions 2-to-1 in 1994, Bryant won by just 50%-47%. Two years later, Bryant ran, unsuccessfully, for the Senate. Sessions ran again for the House seat and won the primary. In the general election, he faced John Pouland, a former regional General Services Administration director. Sessions charged that Pouland was a big-government liberal and would abandon U.S. military bases overseas. Pouland criticized Republican cuts in Medicare. Sessions won 53%-47%.

Sessions' voting record is among the most conservative in the House. In 1999, he got a seat on the leadership-run Rules Committee and has used it to forcefully articulate the Republican message. He sponsored the constitutional amendment to require a two-thirds vote to raise taxes, was a leading advocate of the Republican proposal to stop the government from spending Social Security and Medicare surpluses, and called for scrapping the income tax code. He contended in October 2010 that the economic stimulus law actually put Americans out of work, and in February 2011, sponsored an unsuccessful amendment to chop $447 million from the budget of Amtrak, the national passenger railroad. He is generally tightfisted but is apt to support government spending to help families with disabled children. Sessions and his wife have a son with Down syndrome.

Sessions sought to get on the House leadership track by running in 2006 for chairman of the National Republican Congressional Committee, which raises money for Republicans and recruits challengers in House races. But he lost to Republican Tom Cole of Oklahoma. After the 2008 election, Sessions succeeded in a second bid to head the NRCC. He had the strong support of Minority Leader John Boehner of Ohio—Sessions was among the few Texas Republicans who had backed Boehner for party leader against Roy Blunt of Missouri in 2006. Cole wanted a second term as NRCC chairman, but he carried the burden of the party's 21-seat loss in the November 2008 election.

Sessions had a rocky start as chairman. Republicans lost several special elections in 2009, including one in upstate New York that had long been in GOP hands. He drew criticism for holding fundraisers at risqué venues that were at odds with the party's family-values image. Sessions was lampooned by Democrats for his sometimes odd comments, including his statement that President Barack Obama was trying "to inflict damage and hardship on the free enterprise system, if not to kill it." Sessions set a challenging goal of gaining the 40 seats the party needed to recapture the majority in 2010, and reorganized the committee to improve fundraising, communications and candidate recruitment. He was not fully trusted with the job, as Boehner reportedly sat in on most major strategy meetings. Sessions let other NRCC figures, such as Oregon's Greg Walden, take on major roles. Sessions was among the first members to join the Tea Party Caucus and, sharing its members' anger at big spending, helped synchronize the Republican message to that theme. In the end, Republicans netted a gain of 63 seats in November 2010 to retake the majority.

Sessions considered using his accumulated political capital to run for majority whip, but decided against challenging California's politically savvy Kevin McCarthy. Boehner responded by giving Sessions added responsibilities as NRCC chairman to assist the new members coming into office in 2011. He was charged with advising first-termers on how to best coordinate their House work schedule with their re-election campaigns. His goal is to significantly add to the party's majority in 2012, but he faces a daunting task in doing so. In 2011, Republicans held 61 seats in districts that Obama had carried in 2008. Of those 61 seats, 31 of those were occupied by freshmen, many of whom were bolstered by tea party support. The GOP also held 99 of the 150 House seats with the highest proportion of senior citizens—a constituency that Democrats were confident they could mobilize in steadfast opposition to House Budget Committee Chairman Paul Ryan's ambitious and controversial budget blueprint that makes major changes in Medicare.

In 2001, redistricting made the 5th District more Republican. But Sessions surprised state politicos by leaving the 5th to run in the newly created 32nd, which had no incumbent but included only 16% of his old district. He said he wanted to spend less time traveling around his district—the new 32nd was considerably more compact—and he thought the new district was more compatible with his pro-business philosophy; the 32nd certainly has a stronger fundraising base. Sessions had only token primary opposition and won the seat in 2002, 68%-30%.

In 2003, Republican Tom DeLay of Texas, the powerful majority leader in the U.S. House, persuaded the Republican-controlled Texas Legislature to draw the lines yet again. Although most Republicans were well served by the new lines, Sessions wound up in a somewhat less Republican district and with a re-election challenge from 13-term Democratic incumbent Martin Frost, whose 24th District had been shorn of its most Democratic precincts in the DeLay remap. Frost chose to run in the 32nd because of its large, Democrat-friendly Jewish population in the Park Cities. Frost also felt Sessions was too conservative for the new district. From the start, Sessions voiced confidence that he would win, though he braced for negative attacks. Frost focused on his own legislative accomplishments and his work on local issues to help the Dallas business community; he rarely mentioned 2004 Democratic presidential nominee John Kerry.

This was the most expensive House campaign of 2004. Sessions spent $4.5 million and Frost $4.8 million, and more still was spent by party committees and independent groups. Sessions criticized Frost for scheduling a fundraiser with Peter Yarrow, the Peter, Paul and Mary singer who had been convicted of "taking indecent liberties" with a 14-year-old girl in 1969. Frost cited Sessions' vote against the establishment of new air-passenger security rules after the September 11 attacks and ran an ad with images of the World Trade Center in flames and the message "Protect America. Say No to Pete Sessions." Frost was endorsed by *The Dallas Morning News,* local police and firefighters groups, teachers' organizations, and the Sierra Club. Sessions had support from the national anti-tax group Club for Growth and the National Federation of Independent Business.

Sessions won 54%-44%, capturing more than 80% of the vote in some Park Cities precincts; Frost failed to get the higher turnout he needed in Oak Cliff. Sessions has not had great difficulty getting re-elected since. He did draw controversy in January 2011 when he and Republican Mike Fitzpatrick of Pennsylvania missed the swearing-in for House members, forcing the House to vote to expunge a series of votes they had taken. Democrats pounced on the snafu and said it did not augur well for Republicans regaining control.

★ UTAH ★

Utah is a triumph of man over nature, the creation of a productive and orderly civilization in a remote expanse of desert and mountain, arrayed around a desolate salt sea. Today's Utah and its ubiquitous Mormon Church have their roots in events that unfolded in Upstate New York some 180 years ago. There, farmer Joseph Smith said he experienced a vision in which the angel Moroni appeared and told him where to unearth several golden tablets inscribed with hieroglyphic writings. With the aid of special spectacles, Smith translated the tablets and published them as *The Book of Mormon* in 1830. He later declared himself to be a prophet and founded the Church of Jesus Christ of Latter-day Saints. The Mormons, as they were called, attracted thousands of converts and created their own communities. Persecuted for their beliefs, they moved west to Ohio, Missouri and then Illinois. In 1844, the Mormon colony at Nauvoo, Ill., had some 15,000 members living under Smith's theocratic rule. It was there that Smith received a revelation sanctioning the practice of polygamy, which led to his death at the hands of a mob. After the murder, the new church president, Brigham Young, decided to move the faithful, "the saints," farther west into territory that was still part of Mexico and far beyond white settlement. Young led a well-organized march across the Great Plains and into the Rocky Mountains. In 1847, the Mormons stopped on the western slope of the Wasatch Range and, as Young gazed over the valley of the Great Salt Lake spread out below, he said, "This is the place."

The place was Utah. Young was governor of the territory for many years. It is the only state that has continued, to varying degrees, to live by the teachings of a church. The early pioneers laid out towns foursquare to the points of the compass with huge city blocks. They built sturdy houses and planted dozens of trees. Young's home still stands a block away from Temple Square, where the Salt Lake LDS Temple, closed to non-Mormons, stands in gleaming marble, topped by the golden angel Moroni and situated across from the oval Mormon Tabernacle, where its great choir sings. For 160 years, this "Zion" has attracted thousands of converts from the Midwest, the north of England and Scandinavia. The object of religious fear and prejudice, Utah was not granted statehood until 1896, after the church renounced polygamy. Utah has grown steadily since then and remains heavily Mormon. Without the Mormons, Utah's inhospitable landscape would probably have remained as unpopulated as Nevada would have been without gambling.

The LDS Church remains distinctive in many ways. It cares deeply about its past. The church preserves America's most complete genealogical records in its Family History Library and has made them available on the Internet. It tries to spread the faith: Young Mormons, roughly 52,000 every year, work missionary years in the United States and abroad. (An ancillary result is that Utah has one of the lowest rates of Army enlistment in the country.) The missionaries' experiences give Utah the biggest inventory of people with knowledge of obscure foreign languages of any state in the union, a nice commercial advantage, and one that prompted the National Security Agency to set up language analyst offices in Utah in 2006.

The church prohibits the consumption of tobacco, alcohol and caffeine. It encourages hard work and large families. Mormons are healthier than the average American. They are also better educated, work longer hours and earn more money. In an individualist country, the church fosters communitarian attitudes. The LDS Church has no clergy, but members serve in positions for which they are chosen, conducting religious services but also keeping in touch with members and counseling them when they need help. The church also maintains its own social service organizations. While American mainline denominations have been losing members, the Mormon Church is growing. There were 2.9 million Mormons in 1970 and 14 million in 2010, including 120,000 new children of existing members and 272,000 converts. More than half of LDS members live outside the United States and only about 15% live in Utah. In 2010, new temples were dedicated in Gila Valley, Ariz.; Vancouver, B.C.; Cebu in the Philippines; and Kiev in Ukraine.

Mormons and Utahans are heavily Republican today, but this was not always so. In the 19th century, Republicans led the fight to keep Utah out of the union and Democratic President Grover Cleveland signed the statehood act. Before World War II, Utah saw itself as a colonial victim of East Coast bankers and financiers, and Mormons saw themselves as suffering religious discrimination and bigotry—all with some cause. Utah's income levels were well below the national average, its cost of living was higher and the prices paid for the things it produced seemed to be controlled elsewhere. In political terms, this perspective translated into a Democratic allegiance. In 1940, Utah was represented by staunch New Dealers in Congress and voted 62%-38% for Franklin Roosevelt. Since then, Utah has come to see itself as a busy generator of wealth, with a raft of

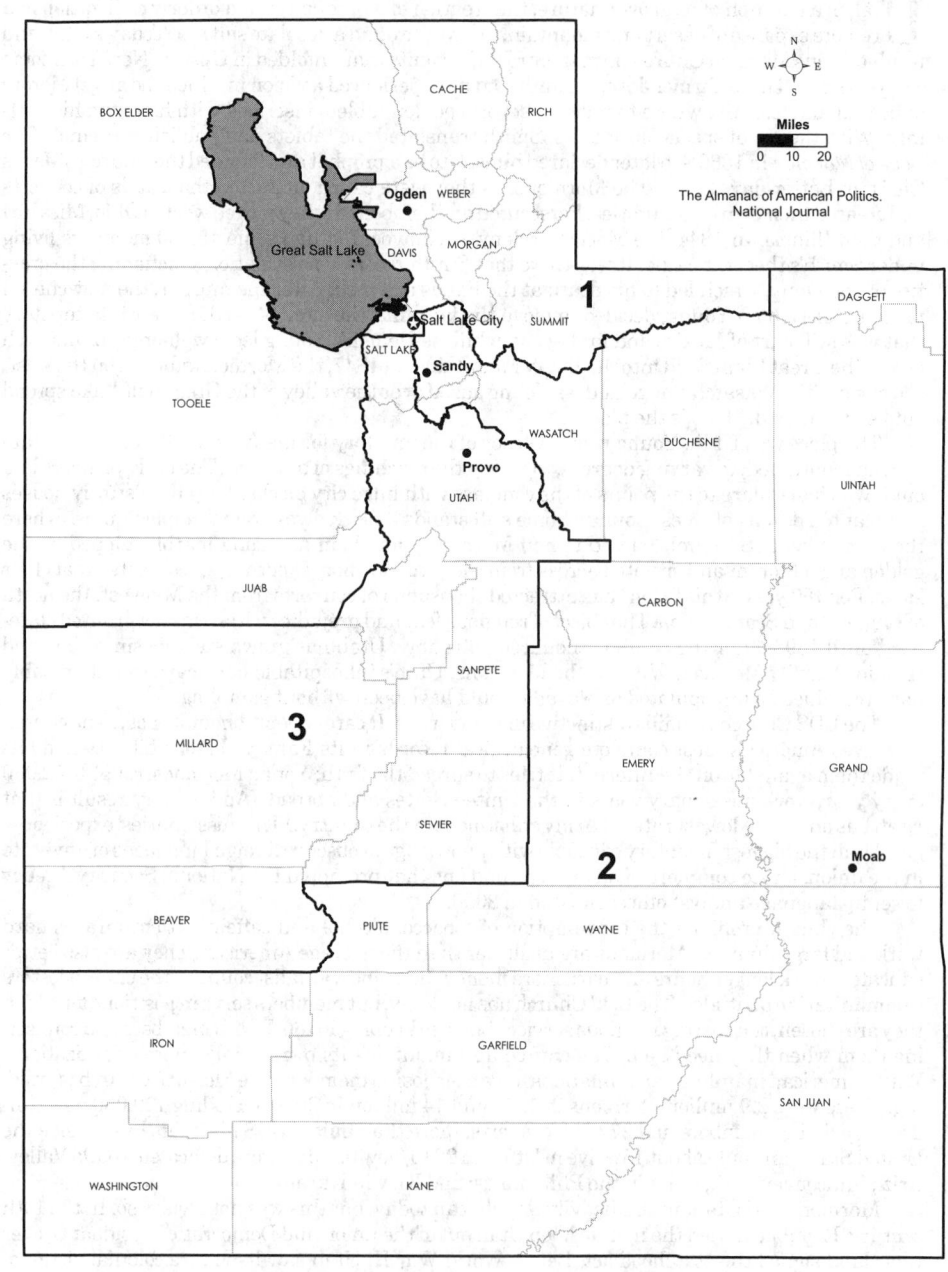

Congressional district boundaries were first effective for 2002.

successful businesses, a knack for high-tech innovation and longer workweeks than the rest of the nation. Politically, it has become increasingly Republican. In 1960, Utah voted for Richard Nixon by only 55%-45%. It voted 72%-20% for Ronald Reagan in 1980, and 67%-26% for George W. Bush in 2000. Utah does elect one Democratic congressman these days, Jim Matheson, who started off with the advantage of having a father who was a well-remembered Democratic governor. But it has not elected a Democratic governor since Scott Matheson won in 1980, or a Democratic senator since 1970, and it has not voted Democratic for president since 1964.

Utah has achieved all this with cultural attitudes and demographic patterns that resemble the America of the 1950s. The state has the highest percentage of households headed by married couples, the highest fertility rate for non-Hispanic whites, the youngest median age of first marriages and the lowest rate of birth to unmarried mothers. It has many more children per capita than any other state, and this can make its economic statistics misleading: Utah has a per capita income 21% below the national average (because all those kids aren't earning salaries), but a median household income 9% above the national average. It has the youngest population of any state, with the largest families and one of the longest life expectancies. It also has the highest rate of volunteerism. Some 75% of Utahans identified as Mormons in 2008 election exit polls, a percentage that has been declining but is still a solid majority.

And pervading the cultural atmosphere of the state is the LDS Church. Its opposition to abortion rights is widely shared and it has always discouraged gambling. It is one of only two states (Hawaii is the other) with no form of gambling, although many Mormons are employed in the gaming industry across the state line in Las Vegas. Utah has been way ahead of the rest of the nation in discouraging the use of tobacco and has had restrictive liquor laws. Only in July 2009 could you get a drink served at a bar without joining a private club, and then if beer is your preference, it will have a mere 3.2% alcohol by volume. Republican Gov. Jon Huntsman Jr. got the legislature to make that change by arguing that the old restrictions hurt tourism. Polls show that about 80% of Mormons usually vote Republican, but church leaders make a point of stating that "principles compatible with the gospel may be found in the platforms of all political parties."

Between 2000 and 2010, Utah's population grew 24% to nearly 2.8 million, the third-highest growth rate in the nation after Nevada, which was first, and Arizona, according to the U.S. Census Bureau. But Nevada and Arizona struggled far more economically as the real estate market crashed. With a much smaller housing bubble, Utah fell into recession later and less painfully, although state revenues tumbled sharply. Utah has also had substantial domestic inflow, especially from California Hispanics. Interestingly, the Salt Lake City neighborhoods close to the church headquarters, with gracious old houses and a smaller street grid that attract academic and professional newcomers, have become the most heavily "gentile" (the Mormon term for non-Mormons) and politically liberal part of the state. Just as the Yankee hub of Boston filled up with Irish Catholic Democrats in the 1890s, Salt Lake City has been getting secular liberal Democrats. Former Salt Lake City Mayor Rocky Anderson called George W. Bush a "war criminal" and in 2004 the city voted 58% for Democratic presidential nominee John Kerry. In 2008, all of Salt Lake County went for Democrat Barack Obama, albeit by only 296 votes out of 367,000 cast, and Democrats won control of the county government and elected most of its state legislators. But Democrats won almost no legislative seats in the rest of the state. And Utah County, which takes in Provo and Brigham Young University, voted 78%-19% for John McCain. And while Salt Lake County grew by 15% from 2000 to 2010, Utah County grew by 40%. There has been even faster growth in Washington County, in the far southwest corner of the state just northeast of Las Vegas, where polygamists like the prosecuted Warren Jeffs have been living in communities on the Utah-Arizona line.

The state population is now 13% Hispanic—far lower than in Arizona or Nevada, but still a sharp contrast with Utah's past—and there are an estimated 110,000 illegal immigrants in the state. This has evoked quite a different response from that in Arizona, where the legislature passed laws requiring employers to use the E-Verify system to validate employees' immigration statuses and authorizing law enforcement personnel to check the status of people stopped for other reasons. Utah businessmen interested in maintaining an immigrant work force, and LDS Church leaders with compassion for the unfortunate, urged a different approach, as did Huntsman before his resignation to become ambassador to China in 2009 and his successor, Republican Gary Herbert. They and others came together and formed a Utah Compact, which the legislature passed into law in March 2011. Law enforcement personnel were authorized to check the immigration status only of those arrested for felonies or serious misdemeanors. And illegal immigrants who pay a fine of $2,500 (or $1,000 if they had only overstayed a legal visa) and pass a criminal background check can get work permits. Other provisions allowed Utahans to sponsor an immigrant and established a partnership with the Mexican state of Nuevo Leon to facilitate visas for workers coming to

Population		Household Income		Work	
Pop. 2010:	2,763,885	Under $15k:	8.8%	Private:	78.9%
State rank:	34th	$15k to $50k:	34.6%	Government:	15.9%
Change since 2000:	Up 23.8%	$50k to $100k:	36.6%	Self-employed:	5.0%
Urban:	85.6%	$100k to $200k:	17.0%	Unemployment (3-yr. average):	3.7%
Rural:	14.4%	Over $200k:	3.0%	Poverty:	10.3%
Native of state:	62.3%	Median income:	$56,340	Blue collar:	22.1%
Not a citizen:	5.4%			White collar:	62.1%
Area size:	84,897 sq. mi.	**Home Value**		Khaki collar:	0.3%
		Under $100k:	7.5%	Other:	15.5%
Most populous cities		$100k to $300k:	62.9%		
Salt Lake City	186,440	$300k to $500k:	21.4%	**Age**	
West Valley City	129,480	$500k to $1 mil:	6.9%	Median age:	28.6 yrs.
Provo	112,488	Over $1 million:	1.4%	More than 65 yrs:	8.9%
West Jordan	103,712	Median:	$227,400	Less than 18 yrs:	31.2%

Race/Ethnicity				Military Veterans		Registered Voters in 2010	
White:	80.4%	*Language*		% of Pop:	8.0%	No Party registration	
Black:	0.9%	English:	86.1%			Voter turnout:	653,274
Hispanic:	13.0%	Spanish:	9.0%	*Veterans by Period*		Turnout as % of	
Asian:	2.0%	Asian:	2.0%	WWII and before:	12.0%	voting age:	34.5%
Native Am.:	1.0%	Other European:	2.1%	Korea:	12.0%		
Hawaiian:	0.9%			Vietnam:	31.1%	**Legislature**	
Two+ races:	1.8%	**Education**		Gulf (pre-2001):	11.9%	Senate:	7 D 22 R
		H.S. grad:	90.4%	Gulf (post-2001):	10.8%	House:	17 D 58 R
Ancestry		College grad:	28.8%	Peace time:	22.3%		
English	21.1%	Grad degree:	9.2%				
German	9.4%						
USA	5.1%						

Utah. The measures were attacked from both left and right and there was doubt that some provisions would survive legal scrutiny, but Herbert said he hoped Congress would follow Utah's example.

Presidential politics   Utah has been the most Republican state in six of the last nine presidential elections. George H.W. Bush won 66% here in 1988 and son George W. Bush 67% in 2000 and 72% in 2004. In 1992, this was also the least Democratic state: Third-party candidate Ross Perot finished ahead of Democratic nominee Bill Clinton, 27% to 25%. But in 2008, the movement toward Democrats in Salt Lake County and widespread enthusiasm for Barack Obama—some 600 Young Democrats campaigned for him at Brigham Young, and the campaign opened an office in Washington County during the primary—left Republican John McCain carrying the state by just 63%-34%, behind his showings in Oklahoma and Wyoming. This was the best Democratic showing since Hubert Humphrey won 37% of the vote in Utah in 1968. Obama carried Salt Lake County, if only by 296 votes. There was no gender gap at all,

2008 Presidential Vote		
John McCain (R)	596,030	(63%)
Barack Obama (D)	327,670	(34%)
2008 Presidential Primary		
Barack Obama (D)	74,538	(57%)
Hillary Clinton (D)	51,333	(39%)
2008 Presidential Primary		
Mitt Romney (R)	264,956	(89%)
John McCain (R)	15,931	(5%)
2004 Presidential Vote		
George W. Bush (R)	663,742	(72%)
John Kerry (D)	241,199	(26%)

and young voters went 62% for McCain. But Generation Xers, those 30 to 44, voted only 52%-44% for McCain. The exit poll showed Mormons voting 78%-19% for McCain, which suggests that "gentiles" actually voted for Obama.

Utah's attempts to become a force in presidential primaries have not been successful. Republican Gov. Mike Leavitt spent much time and effort promoting a Western regional primary for the Friday following the South-dominated Super Tuesday, March 10, 2000. But only Colorado and Wyoming (with a caucus, not a primary) adopted the date, and candidates paid less attention to Western issues than Leavitt had hoped. In 2004, Utah held a Democratic primary on Feb. 24, but the legislature would not pay for it, so the state Democratic Party footed the bill of $50,000; 35,000 people voted in a state of 2.3 million, and John Kerry beat John Edwards 55%-30%.

For the 2008 presidential contest, the legislature decided to hold state-financed primaries on Feb. 5, which turned out to be Super Tuesday, when many larger states voted. Nonetheless, Hillary Rodham Clinton and Obama ran television spots, perhaps the first Democratic presidential ads many native Utahans had ever seen. Chelsea Clinton and Michelle Obama came to campaign. Some 131,000 Utahans voted in the Democratic primary, 57% for Obama and 39% for Clinton. There was little suspense on the Republican side. Mitt Romney, as a Mormon and as the savior of the 2002 Winter Olympics, won 89% of the vote, with a robust turnout of 296,000, far higher than the 91,000 in 2000.

Congressional districting

112th Congress Lineup	
2 R	1 D
111th Congress Lineup	
2 R	1 D

Utahans expected that the 2000 census would give Utah a fourth seat in the House of Representatives. But, under the formula used for reapportionment, Utah fell 857 residents short of getting a new district. Instead, North Carolina got a 13th seat. Utah sued twice. The first lawsuit contended that if military personnel stationed abroad should be counted in their states of residence, so should Mormon missionaries, who also can be accurately tracked and matched with their home states. North Carolina had thousands of military personnel stationed abroad and only 107 Mormon missionaries. Utah had fewer military personnel stationed abroad but 11,176 Mormon missionaries. In April 2001, a three-judge federal court threw out Utah's case and the U.S. Supreme Court later affirmed the ruling.

Utah's other lawsuit charged that the Census Bureau violated the Constitution's injunction that it conduct an "actual enumeration" of the population when it employed what statisticians call "hot-deck imputation," when census-takers, after repeated failed efforts to contact residents of one housing unit, assume that it contains the same number of people in similar housing units nearby. Utah argued that this is "sampling," which, the Supreme Court ruled in another case, was prohibited for use in reapportionment. This argument did better in court. Utah lost by 2-to-1 in a three-judge district court in 2001, and by 5-4 on the Supreme Court in June 2002. But the upshot was that North Carolina, not Utah, got the 435th House district in the 2000 reapportionment. Utah conducted its 2002 election with the current three-district plan.

In 2006, Utah's quest for a fourth House seat got a boost with a bill by Republican Rep. Tom Davis of Virginia to award the District of Columbia a full voting member of the House. It balanced that obvious gain for Democrats by awarding another seat, until the next reapportionment after the 2010 census, to the state entitled to the 436th district under the statutory formula, which was Utah. But how would the new member from Utah be elected? House Republicans insisted that the Utah legislature draw up a plan with four congressional districts before the bill would be considered. The Utah legislature did so in December 2006, with a plan that allayed Democrats' fears and gave Jim Matheson, the only Democrat in the Utah congressional delegation, a much more Democratic district. But time was running out on the Republican Congress, and the D.C. bill never reached the floor.

With Democrats gaining solid majorities in both houses of Congress in 2008, it was widely expected that the D.C.-Utah bill would pass and be signed by President Barack Obama. The Senate did pass it 61-37 in February 2009, but in March, House Republicans managed to attach to the bill an amendment repealing D.C.'s strict gun control laws. Many Democrats from rural, pro-gun districts supported the move, but a large faction of Democrats who favor gun control opposed it, and House leaders shelved the bill.

Utah did gain a fourth district from the reapportionment following the 2010 census, and Republicans now hold the governorship and wide margins in the legislature. One strategy might be to create a Democratic-leaning district within Salt Lake County where Matheson, who survived the 2010 Republican sweep by a 50%-46% margin, could win easily, leaving three other solidly Republican seats. Another would be to attempt to create four districts that would be safely Republican.

Governor

Gary Herbert (R)

Assumed office Aug. 2009, term expires Jan. 2013, 1st term; b. May 7, 1947, American Fork; home, Orem; Attended Brigham Young U., 1968-1970; Mormon; Married (Jeanette); 6 children.

Military Career: UT National Guard, 1970-76.

Elected Office: UT Cnty. Commissioner, 1990-2004; UT Lt. Gov., 2005-09.

Professional Career: Realtor, Herbert & Associates Realtors; Co-owner, The Kids Connection, 1985-2008.

Office: 350 North State Street, Suite 200, PO Box 142220, Salt Lake City, 84114-2220, 801-538-1000; Fax: 801-538-1528; Web site: www.utah.gov/governor.

Election Results

2010 general	Gary Herbert (R)	412,151	(64%)
	Peter Corroon (D)	205,246	(32%)
	Farley Anderson (I)	13,038	(2%)
	W. Andrew McCullough (Lib)	12,871	(2%)
2010 primary	Gary Herbert (R)	unopposed	

Republican Gary Herbert became Utah's new governor on August 11, 2009. Herbert assumed office following the resignation of Republican Gov. Jon Huntsman Jr., who became U.S. ambassador to China in the Obama administration. Herbert was easily elected in 2010 to serve the remainder of Huntsman's term and will have to seek re-election in 2012. Herbert was born in American Fork, Utah, where his father owned a construction company. He studied engineering and accounting at Brigham Young University, but left school before graduating and established a real estate firm, Herbert and Associates Realtors. He ran for the Orem City Council in 1989, losing the election by just 32 votes. The next year, he was elected to the Utah County Commission and served as its chairman for 13 years. During his tenure, Utah County had one of the state's lowest tax rates. He entered the 1994 race to unseat Democratic U.S. Rep. Bill Orton in Utah's 3rd Congressional District but dropped out after struggling to raise money. Orton went on to win re-election.

In 2003, Herbert left the Utah County Commission to run for governor. The field for the 2004 Republican primary was crowded with better known politicians such as former U.S. Rep. Jim Hansen, former Utah House Speaker Nolan Karras and Huntsman, the son of the wealthiest man in Utah, industrialist Jon Huntsman. Herbert cast himself as a "David" in a field of "Goliaths," and stressed his rural roots and ties to local government. Unable to generate enough support for his candidacy, Herbert accepted Huntsman's invitation to join his ticket as the nominee for lieutenant governor. At the time, Huntsman was perceived as lacking credibility in state politics and rural affairs, two areas where Herbert was strong. The ticket won with 58% of the vote.

As lieutenant governor, Herbert made it clear that he would not be content performing the ceremonial duties often associated with the office. Under Utah's Constitution, the lieutenant governor's sole official duty is overseeing the state Elections Office, but Huntsman expanded Herbert's responsibilities to include overseeing the state's public lands policies, transportation plans and homeland security operations. That gave Herbert more influence than his predecessors. He pushed for the creation of a Public Lands Policy Coordination Office to help manage the state's role in land management issues. He also oversaw the state's transition from paper ballots to electronic voting and the transfer of candidate and lobbyist disclosure forms from paper to the Internet.

In 2008, Huntsman won a second term as governor, but then was courted by President Barack Obama to be the ambassador to China, a major diplomatic role at a time of unease in the West with the giant Asian economic powerhouse. When Huntsman announced his resignation, the conservative faction of Utah's Republican Party expressed excitement over Herbert, who is more conservative than Huntsman. But before taking office, Herbert said that he agreed with Huntsman on most issues and would not seek major policy changes.

Herbert attracted headlines during his first year as governor for some attention-grabbing comments. At a Western Governors' Association panel on global warming in June 2009, Herbert said the science behind the issue "is not necessarily conclusive." Two months later, he said he did not believe sexual orientation should be a protected class of discrimination similar to race, gender and religion. The Associated Press also reported in February 2010 that he met with a coal company embroiled in a dispute with state regulators over a strip-mining permit at about the same time that his campaign deposited a $10,000 check from the company. Herbert said he never ordered regulators to approve the permit and that he didn't know about the donation. Legislatively, Herbert made few changes to Huntsman's cabinet and continued a policy of opposing tax increases. He did, however, agree not to veto a bill that raised the state's cigarette tax by $1 a pack in order to cut an education budget shortfall from $300 million to around $10 million. He also retained a four-day workweek that his predecessor had started as a way to cut costs.

Herbert was strongly favored for election in 2010 and won the GOP nomination at the state party's convention in May with 71% of the vote. He ran on his state's fiscal stability during the 2007-09 recession, citing an economic development office that had created more than 3,000 jobs since he took office. His Democratic opponent was Salt Lake County Mayor Peter Corroon. A Roman Catholic in a state dominated by Mormon politicians, Corroon held conservative views on many social issues—he opposed abortion rights and same-sex marriage and backed gun owners' rights. He ran on his record in Salt Lake, which *Forbes* had rated the best location in the country for jobs in 2007 and 2008. In recognition of the tough challenge facing Democrats, he picked Republican state Rep. Sheryl Allen as his running mate and ran ads vowing to put "ideas ahead of ideology." He accused Herbert of leading the state into a "fiscal train wreck" by relying on "fuzzy math" to balance the budget, and he criticized Herbert's support of tougher immigration laws.

Herbert, however, maintained a dominating lead in fundraising and enjoyed the benefits of the national Republican wave that all but eliminated any chance for Democrats to win a statewide office in conservative Utah in 2010. He beat Corroon 64%-32%, carrying every county except Democratic-leaning Summit County.

Herbert returned to office in January 2011 vowing to "vigorously resist the increasing burden of federal intrusion into our lives." He enraged national open government advocates and the news media in March by signing into law a bill, HB 477, restricting disclosure of some state information, such as text messages and instant messages. It also required requesters to show with a preponderance of evidence that private information deserved release. Three days after the signing, activists filed a petition to start a referendum drive, and newspaper editorials condemned the measure. Herbert agreed to seek repeal, saying the public's response "just demands us to push the reset button." The law was swiftly and overwhelmingly repealed.

On immigration, Herbert in March signed four bills dubbed the "Utah Solution." The legislation authorized a guest worker program that would allow illegal immigrants to remain in the state if they paid fines. At the same time, it required police to check the legal status of people arrested on felony or serious misdemeanor charges; established a partnership with the Mexican state of Nuevo Leon to allow workers to come to Utah; and allowed Utah citizens to sponsor immigrants. Herbert said the legislation was intended to prod the federal government to act. "They've been on the sidelines way too long," he said. "They need to get in the game."

Senior Senator

Orrin Hatch (R)

Elected 1976, term expires 2012, 6th term; b. March 22, 1934, Pittsburgh, PA; home, Salt Lake City; Brigham Young U., B.S. 1959; U. of Pittsburgh, J.D. 1962; Mormon; married (Elaine); 6 children.

Professional Career: Practicing atty., 1962–76.

DC Office: 104 HSOB, 20510, 202-224-5251; Fax: 202-224-6331; Web site: hatch.senate.gov.

State Offices: Cedar City, 435-586-8435; Ogden, 801-625-5672; Provo, 801-375-7881; Salt Lake City, 801-524-4380; St. George, 435-634-1795.

Committees: *Aging (Special). Finance* (RMM): International Trade, Customs & Global Competitiveness; Social Security, Pensions & Family Policy. *Health, Education, Labor & Pensions:* Employment & Workplace Safety; Primary Health & Aging. *Joint Committee on Taxation. Judiciary:* Crime & Terrorism; Immigration, Refugees & Border Security; Privacy, Technology & the Law.

Group Ratings

	ACLU	ACU	ADA	CFG	AFS	FRC	LCV	ITIC	NTU	COC
2010	8	100	0	97	11	91	0	67	99	100
2009	–	88	20	88	9	–	18	–	83	86

National Journal Ratings

	2010 LIB	—	2010 CONS	2009 LIB	—	2009 CONS
Economic	0%	—	87%	32%	—	67%
Social	27%	—	72%	31%	—	67%
Foreign	0%	—	72%	26%	—	73%
Composite	16%	—	84%	30%	—	70%

Key Votes of the 111th Congress

1. Overturn Ledbetter	N	5. Pass health care bill	N	9. Ratify New START	N
2. Pass $787 billion stimulus	N	6. Regulate financial firms	N	10. Confirm Elena Kagan	N
3. Repeal DC gun laws	Y	7. Pass tax cuts for some	N	11. Stop EPA climate regs	Y
4. Confirm Sonia Sotomayor	N	8. Legalize immigrants' kids	*	12. Repeal don't ask, tell	*

Election Results

2006 general	Orrin Hatch (R)	356,238	(63%)	($6,580,325)
	Pete Ashdown (D)	177,459	(31%)	($256,010)
	Jeb Bradley (CNP)	21,526	(4%)	
2006 primary	Orrin Hatch (R)	unopposed		

Prior Winning Percentages: 2000 (66%); 1994 (69%); 1988 (67%); 1982 (58%); 1976 (54%)

Republican Orrin Hatch, Utah's senior senator, was first elected to the Senate in 1976. Like few others in Congress, he has been consistent in his inconsistency—he veers between collaborating enthusiastically with Democrats and attacking them with unusual vigor.

Hatch grew up in Pittsburgh, where his father was a metal lather. The family lost their home during the Depression, and lived for a time in a shelter made of salvaged wood and metal and without plumbing. He worked his way through Brigham Young University as a janitor and a metal lather, like his father. He went on to get a law degree from the University of Pittsburgh, and practiced law there. He and his wife and their young family moved to Salt Lake City, and the newly minted lawyer got interested in politics. In 1976, he ran for the U.S. Senate. An endorsement from Republican presidential candidate Ronald Reagan helped him get attention and he ultimately won the GOP nomination. In the general election, he upset three-term Democrat Frank Moss 54%-45%. His toughest re-election fight came in 1982, when he was opposed by Democratic Salt Lake City Mayor Ted Wilson. Hatch won 58%-41%.

Hatch has been in the Senate longer than any Republican except Richard Lugar of Indiana. His Senate career has been shaped by two impulses that are sometimes at odds with each other: a strong conservative philosophy and a sense of responsibility to pass legislation. When President Barack Obama took office in 2009, Hatch expressed a willingness to work with his longtime friend, the ailing liberal Massachusetts Democrat Edward Kennedy, on comprehensive health-care legislation. "I would like to do (health care reform) as a legacy issue for (Kennedy), if I can—this would mean a lot to him," Hatch told *The New Republic*. But even before Kennedy's death in August of that year, Hatch was assailing the measure as big-government overreach. In January 2011, he became the ranking Republican on the Finance Committee and took the lead on his party's efforts to repeal the law, sponsoring bills to end the individual mandate and the employer mandate for coverage.

In March, he was one of just nine senators to oppose a fiscal 2011 budget deal that staved off a government shutdown, arguing that it did not cut spending enough. He also called on the Treasury Department to delay implementation of the Dodd-Frank financial services overhaul law and ratcheted up criticism of the Justice Department for alleging not doing enough to fight obscenity and pornography. He also opposed the nomination of Supreme Court justice Elena Kagan, whom he had voted to confirm as solicitor general. In recent years, his unbroken streak of conservative positions was an acknowledgment that he was heeding the message Utah Republicans sent in 2010, when they dumped three-term Sen. Robert Bennett at their state party nominating convention after he was perceived to be insufficiently conservative on issues. The move paved the way for conservative Republican Mike Lee to win Bennett's seat that fall. With an eye toward the 2012 state party convention, Hatch told a conference of conservatives in Washington in February 2011, "I'm prepared to be the most hated man in this Godforsaken city in order to save this country."

But over the years, Hatch has taken some surprising and bipartisan positions. In 1997, he joined Kennedy in sponsoring a $24 billion program to get states to provide health insurance for children of low-income working parents who don't qualify for Medicaid. Hatch, however, voted against reauthorizing the State Children's Health Insurance Program in 2009, saying Democrats improperly modified it. In 2004, he gained wide bipartisan support for setting up a trust fund to handle asbestos cases, and two years later, the Senate passed a measure Hatch sponsored with Illinois Democrat Dick Durbin that toughened federal regulation of dietary supplements and over-the-counter drugs. Hatch has expressed doubts about the use of mandatory minimum sentences in some drug cases. And with then-Sen. Barack Obama, D-Ill., he got a provision in a tax bill to bar bankruptcy courts from preventing the carrying out of charitable and tithing pledges. The title of his 2002 autobiography summed up his idiosyncratic political style; it's called *Square Peg*.

Yet Hatch has also defended traditional Republican positions to the hilt, sponsoring bills to restrict class action lawsuits and to set limits on medical malpractice cases. He introduced his own comprehensive immigration bill in 2010 that focused heavily on enforcement and has repeatedly sponsored a constitutional balanced budget amendment resolution. As chairman of the Judiciary Committee from June 2001 to January 2003 and as the ranking minority member, Hatch defended the Bush Justice Department and judicial nominees against Democrats' attacks, and took them to task for refusing to hold hearings on many appointees. After same-sex couples in Massachusetts started obtaining marriage licenses, Hatch supported the amendment sponsored by Colorado Republican Wayne Allard that would ban same-sex marriage altogether. Hatch has opposed federal gun control measures and in 2003 sponsored a bill to make it easier to carry handguns in the District of Columbia.

Another of Hatch's preoccupations is the issue of protecting intellectual property in the face of technological advance. He supported the Digital Millennium Copyright Act of 1998 banning unlawful downloading of copyrighted music and movies and backed the record industry against the threat raised by Napster. In 2004, the Senate passed his bill, co-sponsored with Democrat Patrick Leahy of Vermont, to authorize the Justice Department to bring civil lawsuits as well as criminal actions for illegal downloading. He and Kirsten Gillibrand, D-N.Y., introduced a bill in 2010 creating an international group to police criminals using computers to steal or destroy information.

Hatch's interest in these issues is not just theoretical. He has long written poetry and in 1995 began writing songs. He has since written hundreds, some of which have been recorded by a Utah firm, including a 13-song album of Christmas music. Some of his songs have been recorded by singer Gladys Knight, a convert to the Mormon Church. His music has earned praise from Bono, the lead singer of the popular and politically-oriented rock band U2. In 2003, the two men met to discuss the AIDS crisis in Africa, and the singer suggested for Hatch the stage name "Johnny Trapdoor." One of his songs, "Souls Along the Way," was written for his friend Kennedy and was used in the movie *Ocean's 12*. In 2009, he even wrote a Jewish holiday tune called "Eight Days of Hannukah."

On the Judiciary Committee, he has fought abortion rights legislation and a civil rights bill that produced racial quotas and preferences. In earlier major battles over Supreme Court nominees, Hatch staunchly defended conservatives Robert Bork and Clarence Thomas. In 1995, when Hatch became chairman of the committee, he worked on limiting tort liability and regulatory law and managed the balanced budget amendment proposal to one-vote defeats in 1995 and 1997. He also helped draft the 2001 USA Patriot Act, the Bush administration's centerpiece anti-terrorism law, and in 2004 defended it against attempts to eliminate some of its main provisions. "It seems to me that we should not make it any harder to go after suspected terrorists than after suspected drug dealers," Hatch said. During negotiations to reauthorize the Foreign Intelligence Surveillance Act, Hatch supported a provision to grant retroactive immunity to phone companies that had participated in the administration's warrantless wiretapping program. Hatch described the phone companies as "patriotic" in a speech on the Senate floor. The FISA reauthorization passed the Senate in 2008 with retroactive immunity for the companies.

Every senator, it sometimes seems, feels compelled to run for president, and the time came for Hatch with the 2000 election. He conceded that it would take a "miracle" to win, but argued that he had more experience in federal office than the other candidates and that he had demonstrated he could work with Democrats and was not "beholden to the Republican establishment." In the Iowa caucuses in January 2000, he won only 1% of the vote, fewer than Republican John McCain, who did not campaign in the state. Two days later, he withdrew from the race and endorsed George W. Bush. In the 2008 presidential primaries, Hatch endorsed fellow Mormon Mitt Romney of Massachusetts. But after Romney dropped out, Hatch endorsed his colleague John McCain of Arizona and wrote a patriotic campaign song for him called "Together Forever."

In 2000, Hatch won 66%-31% and became the first Utahan popularly elected five times to the Senate. The only other five-term senator in Utah history, Reed Smoot, who served from 1903 to 1933, was elected to his first term by the legislature. In 2006, he won 63%-31% and after he was sworn into his sixth term, became the longest-serving senator in Utah history. But his 2008 vote in favor of the bailout of the financial industry—highly unpopular with the state's conservatives—and the thinking among some Republicans that he has been in office too long ensures his path to victory in 2012 may not be so easy.

Junior Senator

Mike Lee (R)

Elected 2010, term expires 2016, 1st term; b. June 4, 1971, Mesa, AZ; home, Alpine; Brigham Young U., B.A. 1994; J.D. 1997; Mormon; Married (Sharon); 3 children.

Professional Career: Law clerk, Judge Samuel Alito, U.S. Court of Appeals, Third Circuit, 1998-99; practicing atty., 1999-2002; asst. U.S. atty., 2002-05; gen. cnsl. Gov. Jon Huntsman, R-Utah., 2005-06; law clerk, Supreme Court Justice Samuel Alito, 2006-07; practicing atty., 2007-10.

DC Office: 825 HSOB, 20510, 202-224-5444; Fax: 202-228-1168; Web site: lee.senate.gov.

State Offices: Salt Lake City, 801-524-5933; St. George, 435-628-5514.

Committees: *Energy & Natural Resources:* Energy; Public Lands & Forests; Water & Power (RMM). *Foreign Relations:* African Affairs; Near Eastern & South & Central Asian Affairs; Western Hemisphere, Peace Corps & Global Narcotics Affairs. *Joint Economic Committee. Judiciary:* Administrative Oversight & the Courts; Antitrust, Competition Policy & Consumer Rights (RMM); Constitution, Civil Rights & Human Rights.

Election Results

2010 general	Mike Lee (R)	390,179	(62%)	($1,710,429)
	Sam Granato (D)	207,685	(33%)	($291,522)
	Scott Bradley (CNP)	35,937	(6%)	
2010 primary	Mike Lee (R)	98,512	(51%)	
	Tim Bridgewater (R)	93,905	(49%)	

Utah's junior senator is Republican Mike Lee, who toppled 18-year Senate veteran Robert Bennett in Utah's GOP convention in 2010, and went on to win the seat in the fall general election. His primary upset was a harbinger of potency of the tea party movement in that year's midterm elections.

Lee grew up in Provo, where his father, Rex Lee, was the founding dean of the Brigham Young University Law School. He also lived part of the time in McLean, Va., when Rex Lee served as an assistant attorney general from 1975 to 1976 and as solicitor general from 1981 to 1985. Democratic Sen. Robert Byrd of West Virginia lived three doors down from the Lees in McLean, a wealthy Washington, D.C. suburb. Senate Majority Leader Harry Reid, D-Nev., then a House member, was his LDS (Church of Jesus Christ of Latter-day Saints) "home teacher" and he was schoolmates with children of Sen. Strom Thurmond, R-S.C., and Rep. Dick Gephardt, D-Mo. As a teenager, Lee remembers watching his father argue cases before the Supreme Court. "It took me a while before I realized it wasn't entirely an ordinary experience to get to do that frequently," he recalled.

Lee returned to Provo at age 14, and later entered Brigham Young University, where he ran for student body president on a platform that the university should end the practice of vetting candidates for student government. "There were a number of people who called me a radical because of that. It's hardly radical to say students ought to be able to conduct their own elections," he said. He graduated from college and law school at Brigham Young, and then served as a law clerk to District Judge Dee Benson in Utah and Third Circuit Appeals Court Judge Samuel Alito in New Jersey. He then practiced law in Washington, D.C. and in Utah. In 2005, he was appointed legal counsel to Republican Gov. Jon Huntsman and in 2006, after Alito was appointed to the U.S. Supreme Court, Lee returned to Washington to clerk for him once again.

Lee had joined a Utah law firm by the time the 2010 election rolled around. He said he decided to challenge Bennett after Congress passed the $700 billion bailout of the financial industry and President Barack Obama's $787 billion stimulus bill. "The Republican Party had in so many ways deviated from what it professes," he said. Bennett was in his third term and regarded as a solid conservative. But he had voted for the Troubled Asset Relief Program for the financial industry, and he had been a chief supporter of a bipartisan approach to health care legislation with Oregon Democrat Ron Wyden. Their bill would have removed the tax preference for employer-provided health insurance.

Bennett was endorsed by Mitt Romney and fellow Utah GOP Sen. Orrin Hatch. But to get on the primary ballot, he had to finish first or second at the Utah Republican convention in May 2010. In the meantime, Lee had caught the fancy of tea party activists, who were beginning to make inroads with their attacks on government spending and the expanded reach of government into the health care system. He was endorsed by Sen. Jim DeMint of South Carolina, who was trying to influence the selection of a more conservative crop of GOP candidates in 2010.

At the convention, involving roughly 3,500 delegates from around the state, Bennett survived a first round of balloting, but was eliminated on the second round: Lee won 35% of the delegates; business consultant Tim Bridgewater came in first with 37 % and Bennett got 27%. The outcome ended Bennett's 18-year Senate career. In a third round of voting, neither Lee nor Bridgewater met the 60% threshold to win outright, and as a result, the contest went to a primary election. Bennett endorsed Bridgewater in his one-on-one primary match-up with Lee. But Lee prevailed, 51%-49%. Of the state's two most populous counties—Salt Lake and Utah—Bridgewater carried Salt Lake County, where relatively less conservative voters live, but Lee won in Utah County. The general election was anticlimactic in this heavily Republican state; Lee beat Democrat Sam Granato, 62%-33%.

At age 38, Lee was the youngest senator when he took office in January 2011. One of his first moves was to introduce a bill in February for a balanced budget amendment that would require a two-thirds vote of both houses of Congress to override the limitation on spending. It was not expected to go far in the Democratically-controlled Senate. Lee got some notice when he was one of the few Republicans to vote against extending the USA PATRIOT Act, the country's main terrorism investigation law, after expressing concern that it did not sufficiently protect civil liberties and privacy. He also sponsored a bill putting a two-year hold on the caps on fees that banks can charge for processing debit transactions, to the irritation of retailers. With other conservative Republicans, he co-sponsored a bill declaring that the 14th Amendment's birthright citizenship is limited to children of citizens, legal residents and members of the military, and does not extend to illegal immigrants.

FIRST DISTRICT

Rob Bishop (R)

Elected 2002, 5th term; b. July 13, 1951, Kaysville; home, Brigham City; U. of UT, B.A. 1974; Mormon; married (Jeralyn Hansen); 5 children.

Elected Office: UT House of Reps., 1978-94; Speaker, 1993-94.

Professional Career: H.S. teacher, 1974-2002; Chair, UT Rep. Party, 1997-2001.

DC Office: 123 CHOB, 20515, 202-225-0453; Fax: 202-225-5857; Web site: robbishop.house.gov.

State Offices: Ogden, 801-625-0107.

Committees: *Natural Resources:* National Parks, Forests & Public Lands (Chmn). *Rules.*

Group Ratings

	ACLU	ACU	ADA	CFG	AFS	FRC	LCV	ITIC	NTU	COC
2010	15	100	0	87	0	87	10	33	88	88
2009	–	100	0	91	0	–	0	–	90	79

National Journal Ratings

	2010 LIB	—	2010 CONS		2009 LIB	—	2009 CONS
Economic	17%	—	82%		0%	—	96%
Social	18%	—	77%		11%	—	89%
Foreign	21%	—	77%		0%	—	75%
Composite	20%	—	80%		9%	—	92%

Key Votes of the 111th Congress

1. Overturn Ledbetter	N	5. Bar federal abortion funds	Y	9. Stop detainee transfers	Y
2. Pass $820 billion stimulus	N	6. Pass health care bill	N	10. Legalize immigrants' kids	N
3. Let guns in national parks	Y	7. Regulate financial firms	N	11. Repeal don't ask, tell	N
4. Pass cap-and-trade	N	8. Pass tax cuts for some	N	12. Limit campaign funds	N

Election Results

2010 general	Rob Bishop (R)	135,247	(69%)	($278,327)
	Morgan Bowen (D)	46,765	(24%)	($11,550)
	Kirk Pearson (CNP)	9,143	(5%)	
	Jared Stratton (Lib)	4,307	(2%)	
2010 primary	Rob Bishop (R)	unopposed		

Prior Winning Percentages: 2008 (65%), 2006 (63%), 2004 (68%), 2002 (61%)

Population		Race/Ethnicity		Work	
Pop. 2010:	906,660	White:	79.9%	Private:	75.3%
Change since 2000:	Up 21.8%	Black:	1.2%	Government:	20.0%
Urban:	88.7%	Hispanic:	14.1%	Self-employed:	4.5%
Rural:	11.3%	Asian:	1.7%	Blue collar:	23.9%
Area size:	22,699 sq. mi.	Native Am.:	0.6%	White collar:	59.2%
		Hawaiian:	0.7%	Khaki collar:	0.6%
Age		Two+ races:	1.7%	Other:	16.3%
Median age:	29.2 yrs.				
More than 65 yrs:	8.8%	*Ancestry*		Median income:	$55,315
Less than 18 yrs:	31.1%	English	20.5%	Median Home Value:	$199,500
		German	9.2%		
Education		USA	8.1%	**Military Veterans**	
H.S. grad:	90.3%			% of Pop:	9.4%
College grad:	27.9%				
Grad degree:	8.6%				

Northern Utah; Salt Lake City

In May 1869, a motley crowd of Irish and Chinese laborers, teamsters, engineers, train crews, officials and guests from Salt Lake City gathered at Promontory Summit, Utah, to watch the opening of the transcontinental railroad. A photographer recorded the scene for posterity: United at last were the civilized East and the mostly untamed West. In Salt Lake City, the center of the Mormon Church—and of Utah—is Temple Square, illuminated by 300,000 lights during Christmas week and nestled beneath the towering mountains that flank Salt Lake City. The Mormon Tabernacle, home of the famous choir, is here, as is the Salt Lake LDS Temple itself, crowned with the golden angel Moroni. This area has been the focal point of Utah since Mormon leader Brigham Young, looking down at this valley, said, "This is the place." Ironically, this part of Salt Lake City is the least Mormon and most cosmopolitan part of Utah, with the state university and businesses bringing in outsiders who, flouting Mormon strictures, keep purveyors of alcohol and caffeine in business. (The state ended its private club system at bars in 2009, hoping to attract more people, but alcohol sales went up just 1% in the first year after elimination.) Salt Lake County voted 60% for George W. Bush in 2004, up from 55% in 2000, but Democrat Barack Obama narrowly carried the county by 296 votes in 2008. Republican Gov. Gary Herbert edged out Salt Lake County Mayor Peter Corroon here in 2010, 51%-46%.

2008 Presidential Vote		
John McCain (R)	197,433	(64%)
Barack Obama (D)	103,737	(33%)
2004 Presidential Vote		
George Bush (R)	220,869	(73%)
John Kerry (D)	75,728	(25%)
Cook Partisan Voting Index:	R+21	

The 1st Congressional District of Utah consists of the northern end of the state. It includes most of Salt Lake City's historic downtown, its distinctive Avenues District and the airport, but it takes in little of the fast-growing suburbia that stretches south of the city. However, new suburbs near Interstate 80 have made Tooele, where real estate remains affordable, one of the state's fastest growing counties. More than half the people in the district live in the stretch of the Wasatch Front, between the mountains and Great Salt Lake, just north of Salt Lake City, in Davis and Weber counties. Davis County is suburban and fairly affluent. Ogden in Weber County is an old, working-class railroad town, an industrial center that depends on nearby Hill Air Force Base, home of the advanced F-22A Raptor fighter jets.

Farther north in the Cache Valley is Logan, home of Utah State University. This is farming country and very heavily Mormon. Over the mountains to the east of Salt Lake City is Park City, the old mining town that is now a fashionable ski resort and home of actor Robert Redford's annual Sundance Film Festival. West of Salt Lake City is the desolate Bonneville Salt Flats, where land speed records have been set. This land of stark beauty, much of it federally owned, has been used roughly by man, as a repository for hazardous wastes at civilian and military dumps in Tooele County and as a place for military experimentation on the Dugway Proving Ground, where scientists test defenses against chemical and biological agents. The Skull Valley Band of Goshute Indians have pressed for a temporary nuclear waste storage site, near Dugway, but it has remained on hold for years because of Utah politicians' reluctance to take waste from other states.

Politically this is a heavily Republican area, with patches of Democratic strength. The district's portions of Salt Lake County are trendy and working-class Democratic, and Park City is also Democratic. But the Cache Valley is very heavily Republican, and overall the district voted 73% for Republican George W. Bush in 2004 and 64% for Republican John McCain in 2008.

Rob Bishop (R)

The congressman from the 1st District is Rob Bishop, a Republican first elected in 2002. He is a leading advocate of states' rights and a sharp critic of the federal government's management of its public lands, both hot-button issues in the rural West.

Bishop grew up in Davis County and graduated from the University of Utah. He became a high school history and government teacher in Box Elder County. In 1978, at age 27, he was elected to the state House. In 1993 and 1994, he was House speaker. He continued working as a teacher after leaving the legislature, and also worked as a lobbyist for state Republicans and for the National Rifle Association.

When the U.S. seat became open, both Bishop and former House Majority Leader Kevin Garn ran. As a former state party chair for four years, Bishop won 58% of the vote at the Republican nominating convention. With mostly similar conservative views, their chief difference was a contentious issue in Utah: the ongoing battle between banks and credit unions. The credit union lobby endorsed Bishop who, as a lobbyist in 1999, helped defeat legislation to curtail the credit unions' tax-exempt status. Garn, the wealthy chairman of a Layton bank, had the support of Utah bankers. The credit unions were the more valuable ally: They poured at least $100,000 in independent expenditures into an anti-Garn campaign, which helped even out the financial balance as Garn outspent Bishop by 4-to-1. Bishop won the primary 60%-40%. Democrats believed they had a chance in the general election with nominee Dave Thomas, a wealthy advertising executive and an anti-abortion rights Mormon bishop who presented himself as a fiscal conservative and "a regular guy" not tied to special interests. Bishop won more easily than expected, 61%-37%.

In the House, Bishop has been a reliable conservative vote and has a seat on the GOP leadership-driven Rules Committee. He joined the Tea Party Caucus in 2010, and the previous year he unsuccessfully offered a GOP resolution on the House floor calling for an investigation into Democratic Speaker Nancy Pelosi's claim that the Central Intelligence Agency misled her about the use of torture techniques on suspected terrorists. He started a "10th Amendment Task Force" to advocate for allowing states to assume control of federal programs. During his years in the Utah Legislature, "I learned to hate the federal government," he told *The Salt Lake Tribune* in May 2010. "I could point to (highway) overpasses that were made because there was a 10-to-1 (funding) match, or programs we ran simply because the government bribed us with money."

Bishop now is chairman of the National Parks, Forests and Public Lands Subcommittee of the House Natural Resources Committee—a useful assignment in a state where the federal government controls nearly two-thirds of the land. It also puts him in the middle of environment and energy issues. He introduced a bill in 2011 to exempt border immigration enforcement activities from some environmental laws within 100 miles of U.S. borders—a move critics called a thinly disguised attempt to bar any regulation of those lands. He long has been highly critical of attempts to designate new national monuments in the West, and in 2009 and 2011, introduced bills calling for oil drilling in Alaska's Arctic National Wildlife Refuge and other areas.

On local issues, Bishop has fought to save the Ares 1 rocket program, whose motor is built by Alliant Techsystems in his district. In 2005, Bishop won enactment of his bill to block private disposal of nuclear waste on the Skull Valley Band of Goshute Indian reservation and to convert the land to a wilderness area. He also helped protect Hill Air Force Base from the base closing review that year. He was criticized at home for supporting a change in federal law to permit Envirocare of Utah (now known as EnergySolutions) to dispose additional radioactive waste material from a bomb plant in Ohio. Envirocare, which was a client of his former lobbying firm, dropped the proposal after three months of controversy. Bishop later advocated recycling the waste.

Bishop has been comfortably re-elected every two years.

SECOND DISTRICT

Jim Matheson (D)

Elected 2000, 6th term; b. March 21, 1960, Salt Lake City; home, Salt Lake City; Harvard U., B.A. 1982, U.C.L.A., M.B.A. 1987; Mormon; married (Amy); 2 children.

Professional Career: Staff, Environmental Policy Inst., 1982-85; Project dev. mgr., Bonneville Pacific, 1987-91; Sr. assoc., Energy Strategies Inc., 1992-98; Founder & pres., The Matheson Group, 1998-99.

DC Office: 2434 RHOB, 20515, 202-225-3011; Fax: 202-225-5638; Web site: matheson.house.gov.

State Offices: Price, 435-636-3722; Salt Lake City, 801-486-1236; St. George, 435-627-0880.

Committees: *Energy & Commerce:* Commerce, Manufacturing & Trade; Energy & Power.

Group Ratings

	ACLU	ACU	ADA	CFG	AFS	FRC	LCV	ITIC	NTU	COC
2010	56	17	60	33	75	37	90	100	39	75
2009	–	24	55	49	67	–	64	–	30	80

National Journal Ratings

	2010 LIB	—	2010 CONS	2009 LIB	—	2009 CONS
Economic	45%	—	55%	44%	—	56%
Social	49%	—	49%	49%	—	50%
Foreign	52%	—	46%	52%	—	48%
Composite	49%	—	51%	49%	—	52%

Key Votes of the 111th Congress

1. Overturn Ledbetter	Y	5. Bar federal abortion funds	Y	9. Stop detainee transfers	Y
2. Pass $820 billion stimulus	Y	6. Pass health care bill	N	10. Legalize immigrants' kids	N
3. Let guns in national parks	Y	7. Regulate financial firms	Y	11. Repeal don't ask, tell	Y
4. Pass cap-and-trade	N	8. Pass tax cuts for some	N	12. Limit campaign funds	Y

Election Results

2010 general	Jim Matheson (D)	127,151	(50%)	($1,803,801)
	Morgan Philpot (R)	116,001	(46%)	($386,467)
2010 primary	Jim Matheson (D)	23,067	(67%)	
	Claudia Wright (D)	11,227	(33%)	

Prior Winning Percentages: 2008 (63%), 2006 (59%), 2004 (55%), 2002 (49%), 2000 (56%)

Population		**Race/Ethnicity**		**Work**	
Pop. 2010:	890,993	White:	84.2%	Private:	78.1%
Change since 2000:	Up 19.7%	Black:	0.8%	Government:	15.7%
Urban:	84.9%	Hispanic:	8.7%	Self-employed:	6.1%
Rural:	15.1%	Asian:	2.1%	Blue collar:	18.7%
Area size:	46,031 sq. mi.	Native Am.:	1.9%	White collar:	66.0%
		Hawaiian:	0.5%	Khaki collar:	0.1%
Age		Two+ races:	1.8%	Other:	15.2%
Median age:	31.3 yrs.				
More than 65 yrs:	11.5%	*Ancestry*		Median income:	$56,259
Less than 18 yrs:	28.8%	English	22.0%	Median Home Value:	$263,000
		German	10.4%		
Education		Irish	6.0%	**Military Veterans**	
H.S. grad:	91.6%			% of Pop:	8.5%
College grad:	33.1%				
Grad degree:	11.5%				

Eastern Utah

Demographically, Utah is an urban state. Geographically, it is not just rural but, over most of its acreage, scarcely inhabited. Three-quarters of its people live in the Wasatch Front, from Ogden south through Salt Lake City to Provo, between the Great Salt Lake and Utah Lake and the Wasatch Mountains. South of Provo, the natural landscape goes from simply beautiful to breathtaking. Much of southern Utah is preserved in five national parks, five national mon-

2008 Presidential Vote		
John McCain (R)	202,534	(58%)
Barack Obama (D)	138,790	(40%)
2004 Presidential Vote		
George Bush (R)	227,668	(66%)
John Kerry (D)	108,286	(31%)
Cook Partisan Voting Index: R+15		

uments and a national recreation area. The terrain ranges from the soaring cliffs of Zion National Park to the popsicle-like outcroppings of Bryce Canyon National Park to the red-walled river cuts of Canyonlands National Park to the surreal moonscape of Arches National Park. Visitation at these areas stagnated during the 2007-09 recession, but started to climb again as soon as the economy improved.

Monument Valley, on Navajo land in far southeastern Utah, has become familiar to Americans as the site of countless car commercials, and the land around Moab and Springdale is a tourist destination. The land is mostly owned by one agency or another of the federal government, and there have been bitter fights between locals dependent on mining and environmentalists who want to preserve the scenery. (You can see evidence of old uranium mines in some of the national parks.) President Bill Clinton's campaign-year creation of the Grand Staircase-Escalante National Monument in 1996, in a ceremony across the border in Arizona, enraged many Utahans. It effectively removed 1.7 million acres from mineral development, much of it land owned by the state that used the proceeds for schools.

The 2nd Congressional District of Utah includes this vast region of the state, but the majority of its people live in Salt Lake County, east of a wobbling line between Interstate 15 and the often dry Jordan River. The area includes most of the affluent neighborhoods in Salt Lake City and the suburbs of South Salt Lake, Murray (an old smelter city), Midvale, Sandy and Draper. In Washington County, St. George ranked as the second-fastest growing metro area in the nation from 2000 to 2010, with expensive homes and traffic jams and some spillover from Las Vegas. It is the headquarters for SkyWest Inc., which is United Airlines' main United Express carrier along the West Coast. Republican President George W. Bush won the district with 66% of the vote in 2004, and GOP nominee John McCain carried it with 58% in 2008.

Jim Matheson (D)

The congressman from the 2nd District is Jim Matheson, a Democrat first elected in 2000. His careful centrism has enabled him to survive as the only member of his party in Utah's congressional delegation.

Matheson grew up in Salt Lake City, graduated from Harvard University and interned on Capitol Hill for Democratic House Speaker Tip O'Neill. His father, Scott Matheson, was elected governor of Utah in 1976 and 1980. Jim Matheson worked for the Environmental Policy Institute and then earned an M.B.A. from the University of California at Los Angeles. He returned to Salt Lake City to join Bonneville Pacific, an energy development company, where he was a project development manager. He moved in 1992 to Energy Strategies, a consulting firm, where he was a senior associate. He served four years on the Salt Lake Public Utilities Board. In 1998, he started the Matheson Group to help businesses adapt to electricity deregulation, but he closed it a year later to run for the U.S. House.

From 1992 to 2000, district voters had elected two Democrats and two Republicans to Congress. When Matheson decided to run, the incumbent was Republican Rep. Merrill Cook. But Cook lost the primary to businessman Derek Smith. In the fall matchup, Matheson played down his party affiliation, while Smith denounced Clinton's creation of the Grand Staircase-Escalante National Monument and charged that Matheson was trying to look like a Republican. Matheson was vastly outspent by Smith, but still won 56%-41%.

Matheson has a voting record that is among the most conservative of the House Democrats. He has been a leader of the fiscally conservative Blue Dog Coalition and he backed fellow Blue Dog Heath Shuler of North Carolina over liberal Nancy Pelosi for minority leader in 2011. Also that year, he succeeded retired Tennessee Rep. John Tanner as the Blue Dog representative at the Democratic leadership table. In the 111th Congress (2009-10), Matheson opposed the Democrats' health care overhaul, their cap-and-trade bill to regulate greenhouse gas emissions, and the DREAM Act that provided a path to citizenship for some children of illegal immigrants. Earlier, he was one of only16 Democrats who voted for the GOP's Medicare prescription drug bill in 2003.

On the Energy and Commerce Committee, Matheson focuses on energy issues. He cosponsored a bipartisan bill in 2011 to accelerate production and usage of natural gas-powered cars and trucks. During the 110th Congress (2007-08), he was the only member of Utah's congressional delegation to cosponsor a bill to give the Nuclear Regulatory Commission authority to prevent foreign nuclear waste from being brought into the United States. At the time, the Salt Lake City-based company EnergySolutions, formerly known as Envirocare of Utah, was seeking a license to import nuclear waste from Italy, which Matheson opposed. He reintroduced the legislation in 2009 and 2011. In 2011, he also joined a bipartisan group pushing for increased compensation for radiation victims of atomic testing during the Cold War. Matheson's father died of cancer as the result of radioactive fallout from nuclear tests.

Showing his fiscal conservatism, Matheson worked with Rep. Harry Mitchell, D-Ariz., in 2010 to get a bill into law freezing salaries for members of Congress, and amended a fiscal 2011 spending bill to defund a program financing broadband projects in rural areas that he considered ineffective.

Over the years, Matheson has been a prime Republican target. In 2002, John Swallow, a three-term state legislator, emphasized his strong support for tax cuts and gun ownership rights, and reminded voters of Matheson's Democratic Party affiliation at every opportunity. Matheson reminded rural voters of his family's local connections and said that Swallow would harm public schools by giving tax money to parents to send their kids to private schools. Both national parties spent lavishly. Matheson won by 1,641 votes, 49.4%-48.7%, the narrowest victory for any House incumbent that year. In 2004, Swallow ran again with support from the national anti-tax group Club for Growth. Still, Matheson won 55%-43%. In 2006, he raised nearly $2 million and won against state Rep. LaVar Christensen, 59%-37%. He had his best winning percentage to date in 2008, 63% of the vote.

In 2010, Matheson faced a primary challenge on the left from retired teacher Claudia Wright, who answered a Craigslist ad placed by liberal activists incensed with Matheson's opposition to health care reform. He decisively trounced Wright, 67%-33%. His general election opponent, GOP former state Rep. Morgan Philpot, drew support from tea party groups and sought to link him with national Democratic figures. But Matheson fought back, calling attention to Philpot's frequent absences in the legislature, and managed a 50%-46% victory. As in the past, his key to victory was populous Salt Lake County, which he carried 62%-35%.

Matheson turned down Democrats urging him to run against Republican Sen. Orrin Hatch in 2006 and for the Senate or governorship in 2010; though he has left open the possibility of a future statewide bid. His brother, Scott Matheson, ran for governor in 2004 and lost to Republican Jon Huntsman Jr., but then was confirmed as a U.S. Court of Appeals judge in 2010.

THIRD DISTRICT

Jason Chaffetz (R)

Elected 2008, 2nd term; b. March 26, 1967, Los Gatos, CA; home, Alpine; Brigham Young U., B.A. 1989; Mormon; married (Julie); 3 children.

Professional Career: Spokesman & public relations, Nu Skin International; Chief of staff to Gov. Jon Huntsman, 2005-08.

DC Office: 1032 LHOB, 20515, 202-225-7751; Fax: 202-225-5629; Web site: chaffetz.house.gov.

State Offices: Provo, 801-851-2500; West Jordan, 801-282-5502.

Committees: *Budget. Judiciary:* Crime, Terrorism & Homeland Security; Intellectual Property, Competition & the Internet. *Oversight & Government Reform:* Federal Workforce, U.S. Postal Service & Labor Policy; National Security, Homeland Defense & Foreign Operations (Chmn); Technology, Information Policy, Intergovernmental Relations & Procurement Reform.

Group Ratings

	ACLU	ACU	ADA	CFG	AFS	FRC	LCV	ITIC	NTU	COC
2010	19	100	10	100	0	100	10	0	92	75
2009	–	100	0	98	11	–	0	–	93	80

National Journal Ratings

	2010 LIB	—	2010 CONS	2009 LIB	—	2009 CONS
Economic	20%	—	79%	0%	—	96%
Social	18%	—	77%	11%	—	87%
Foreign	32%	—	67%	0%	—	75%
Composite	25%	—	76%	9%	—	91%

Key Votes of the 111th Congress

1. Overturn Ledbetter	N	5. Bar federal abortion funds	Y	9. Stop detainee transfers	Y
2. Pass $820 billion stimulus	N	6. Pass health care bill	N	10. Legalize immigrants' kids	N
3. Let guns in national parks	Y	7. Regulate financial firms	N	11. Repeal don't ask, tell	N
4. Pass cap-and-trade	N	8. Pass tax cuts for some	N	12. Limit campaign funds	N

Election Results

2010 general	Jason Chaffetz (R)	139,721	(72%)	($647,194)
	Karen Hyer (D)	44,320	(23%)	($23,818)
	Douglas Slighting (CNP)	4,596	(2%)	
2010 primary	Jason Chaffetz (R)	unopposed		

Prior Winning Percentages: 2008 (66%)

Population		Race/Ethnicity		Work	
Pop. 2010:	966,232	White:	77.3%	Private:	83.0%
Change since 2000:	Up 29.8%	Black:	0.8%	Government:	12.3%
Urban:	91.2%	Hispanic:	15.9%	Self-employed:	4.6%
Rural:	8.8%	Asian:	2.1%	Blue collar:	23.5%
Area size:	16,167 sq. mi.	Native Am.:	0.6%	White collar:	61.2%
		Hawaiian:	1.4%	Khaki collar:	0.1%
Age		Two+ races:	1.8%	Other:	15.2%
Median age:	25.6 yrs.				
More than 65 yrs:	6.7%	*Ancestry*		Median income:	$57,500
Less than 18 yrs:	33.4%	English	20.9%	Median Home Value:	$222,900
		German	8.6%		
Education		Danish	4.7%	**Military Veterans**	
H.S. grad:	89.3%			% of Pop:	6.2%
College grad:	25.1%				
Grad degree:	7.5%				

Central Utah; Provo

Part of the heartland of the Mormon Church in America is in a geographically isolated valley between 11,000-foot peaks of the Wasatch Range and the shores of Utah Lake. It is Provo, the home of Brigham Young University, an institution long known for the conservative views of its faculty and the old-fashioned moral standards it encourages. Its student population in fall 2010 was 98.5% Mormon and 26% were married.

2008 Presidential Vote		
John McCain (R) 196,063	(67%)
Barack Obama (D) 85,143	(29%)
2004 Presidential Vote		
George Bush (R) 215,205	(77%)
John Kerry (D) 57,185	(21%)
Cook Partisan Voting Index: R+26		

BYU also is known for its welcoming of technological innovation. The Mormon commonwealth, after all, started off with a huge shortage of both labor and water, and its inhabitants were eager to use technology to compensate and prosper in this fearsome terrain. Provo produced Philo Farnsworth, the inventor of television, and Harvey Fletcher, inventor of the hearing aid. It has become one of America's high technology centers, the home of Novell and hundreds of other computer-related firms. Mormon Church-inspired overseas missionary work has bequeathed the area with unusual resources in foreign languages.

The 3rd Congressional District of Utah includes all or part of seven counties in central and western Utah. Many of them are remote, and the vast majority of its people live in Utah or Salt Lake counties. The 3rd includes the west side of Salt Lake City and the suburbs south of the city, including West Valley City (the state's second-largest city, home to many recent Mormon converts from Polynesia), West Jordan, South Jordan and Riverton. Kennecott Utah Copper, the old mining conglomerate that owns 90,000 acres in Salt Lake and Tooele counties, unloaded some of its land-holdings to real estate developers, who have built many subdivisions and "walkable" communities in South Jordan. The district includes almost all of Utah County, with Provo and the string of counties between high-jutting mountains and Utah Lake. Eagle Mountain and Saratoga Springs were created in the early 1990s and have grown rapidly. From 2000 to 2010, the youthful Provo was the sixth fastest-growing metro area in the nation. Politically, Utah County is overwhelmingly Republican; less than 5% of voters are registered Democrats. (Salt Lake County, by comparison, has 12% Democratic registration.) Republican President George W. Bush carried the district with 77% in 2004, and Republican John McCain won it with 67% of the vote in 2008.

Jason Chaffetz (R)

The congressman from the 3rd District is Republican Jason Chaffetz, a visible and media-savvy young conservative elected in 2008.

Born in Los Gatos, Calif., Chaffetz (*CHAY-fits*) grew up in Arizona and attended his senior year of high school in Colorado. His family's politics were Democratic, and they boasted one notable tie to the party: His father's first wife, Katharine Dickson, would later enter the national consciousness as "Kitty" while she stumped for votes with her second husband, Michael Dukakis, the 1988 Democratic presidential nominee. During college, Chaffetz was named an honorary co-chairman of the Dukakis campaign in Utah in 1988. Growing up, Chaffetz had a passion for soccer, but he switched to football when his high school discovered that he made a decent placekicker.

He won an athletic scholarship to Brigham Young University, where he converted to Mormonism and began what he views in hindsight as a natural gravitation toward the political right. After college, Chaffetz worked in public relations, first as an executive for Nu Skin Enterprises, a company that sells skin care products, and then at a firm he started with his brother. In 2003, Chaffetz took a brief hiatus from work to volunteer for Republican Jon Huntsman Jr.'s gubernatorial campaign. When his campaign manager abruptly resigned, Huntsman asked Chaffetz, who had barely any political experience, to replace him. After the election, Chaffetz served for one year as the new governor's chief of staff.

Although his residence in Alpine sits just outside the 3rd District, Chaffetz sensed an opportunity in early 2007 as perennial discontent with incumbent Republican Rep. Chris Cannon simmered within the Republican ranks. (The Constitution requires only that House members live in the state they represent, not in the district.) Chaffetz entered the race in October, at a steep disadvantage in both cash and name recognition. Chaffetz criticized Cannon's support of President George W. Bush's proposal for a guest worker program and a path to citizenship for illegal immigrants, both deeply unpopular in the conservative district. He called for immediate deportation of all illegal immigrants and the construction of tent cities, ringed by barbed-wire fences, to detain those who had committed crimes while in the United States. His staunchly conservative platform played well at the state Republican convention in May, where he came 10 votes short of the 60% needed to win the GOP nomination outright.

Bush and most of the state's Republican establishment endorsed Cannon, although Huntsman stayed neutral. Cannon attacked Chaffetz as an opportunist and raised more than $840,000. Chaffetz, by contrast, spent less than $200,000. In the low-turnout June contest, he stacked up big margins in the district's population centers in Salt Lake and Utah counties to win by a whopping 20 percentage points. Although Chaffetz came under fire nationally from some Japanese-American interest groups for his advocacy of tent cities, the outcome of the general election in this crimson segment of Utah was never truly in doubt after the primary. Chaffetz won with 66%.

In the House, Chaffetz typically votes the conservative line but is occasionally unpredictable. He was one of 36 House Republicans who refused to back the December 2010 deal extending the Bush-era tax cuts, contending the move would only contribute to the national debt. Earlier that year, he was one of just seven GOP lawmakers to unsuccessfully require that funds for military operations in Afghanistan be spent only on withdrawing troops. He quickly developed a reputation for his media accessibility and quotability, appearing in a CNN video project highlighting his freshman year and giving numerous interviews to publications, TV stations and websites. He also regularly posted videos on YouTube, collected thousands of followers on Twitter and agreed to a televised leg-wrestling match with conservative talk show satirist Stephen Colbert. (Chaffetz lost.)

Chaffetz has been an active member on the Oversight and Government Reform Committee. He got a bill through the House in 2009 to bar primary scanning at airports using whole body imaging machines, which he considered unnecessarily intrusive. He later was involved in a confrontation at Salt Lake's airport after trying to avoid an image scanner. He also was an outspoken opponent of the District of Columbia's 2009 legalization of same sex marriage. In 2011, Chaffetz took over the chairmanship of the panel's subcommittee on national security and introduced bills that would allow for the firing of federal workers who were delinquent paying taxes and bar such individuals from receiving government contracts or grants.

Chaffetz cruised to re-election in 2010 over Democrat Karen Hyer, a Brigham Young University professor. The more interesting question remains his future political plans. He hinted at a primary challenge in 2009 to Republican Sen. Robert Bennett, who subsequently lost his seat after angering tea party activists. Chaffetz then said he was considering a primary matchup to prevent GOP Sen. Orrin Hatch from winning a seventh term in 2012.

★ VERMONT ★

Early America and contemporary America come together in Vermont. The state is a mixture of the 19th and 21st centuries—maple syrup and Ben & Jerry's ice cream, tiny clapboard villages and carefully zoned towns with unobtrusively signed outlet malls, covered bridges and civil unions. Not so long ago, Vermont seemed an entirely antique state, almost as carefully preserved as its Shelburne Museum, with its barn and jail, railroad station and blacksmith shop, covered bridge, and 37 buildings of folk art. But in just a few decades, the state has been transformed by newcomers, who were attracted to its antique look but who have since transformed Vermont's culture in their own image.

Vermont was first settled by flinty Yankees from Connecticut, and the state showed an independent streak from the beginning. After Ethan Allen's Green Mountain Boys repulsed the British in 1777, this was an independent republic for 14 years, claimed by New York and by New Hampshire to no avail. Allen tried to persuade George Washington to make it a new state, but several histories argue that Vermont never voluntarily joined the United States. In any case, Vermont was admitted as the 14th state in 1791. The economy was almost entirely agricultural, as second sons and daughters from small New England farms struggled to scratch out livings from the rocky soil. Eventually, they quit that struggle and raised dairy cows, producing milk for the masses in New York City. Vermont developed commerce as well. With their legendary thriftiness, Vermonters accumulated capital that, invested wisely, was used to build the solid stone office buildings and courthouses, the thick-timbered houses, and gold-topped state Capitol that have remained long after ramshackle wooden buildings of the early 19th century crumbled. Vermont has made an economic asset of its maple trees and its quaintness. Beginning in the 1890s, state government promoted Vermont as a tourist destination and passed a law requiring Vermont maple syrup to be made only from local trees. But the state never developed labor-intensive industry, and so over the years, it exported people and its population aged. From 1850 to the 1960s, as a result of continuous out-migration, Vermont's population hovered between 300,000 and 400,000. Two presidents were born in Vermont, but both made their careers elsewhere—Chester Arthur in New York and Calvin Coolidge in Massachusetts. Two great foreign writers lived there for years—Rudyard Kipling and Aleksandr Solzhenitsyn—but neither ever wrote much about Vermont. In 2010, 626,000 people lived here, many of whom have no Vermont ancestry; 48% of current Vermonters were born outside the state.

Since the 1960s—perhaps the key date was 1963, when people first outnumbered cows—Vermont has changed rapidly. Its economy has boomed, led by leisure-time industries—ski resorts, summer homes—and high-tech companies in and around the Burlington area on the mostly undeveloped shores of glorious Lake Champlain. You can find big-box retailers in Williston, but also ethnic diversity—Vietnamese, Bosnians, Koreans—in Winooski. Sheldon has the highest representation of native Vermonters, 83%, and tiny Buels Gore, a sliver of land left out when the first settlers drew town lines, had a population boom in the 1990s, when it grew from two residents to 12. (It peaked in 1840, when it had 16 people and 3,516 sheep.) Homegrown firms started by baby boom rebels—Ben & Jerry's, founded in 1978, is the archetype—have flourished. The newcomers cherished what novelist Paul Greenberg calls "maple's homespun image." Vermont's population growth from 390,000 in 1960 to 626,000 today hasn't come from random settlement. Next-door New Hampshire, trumpeting its low taxes and aversion to government regulation, attracted right-leaning migrants from Massachusetts and elsewhere to settle spanking-new developments. Vermont, proclaiming its desire to preserve the environment and the past, attracted left-leaning migrants from New York and elsewhere who were willing to pay higher taxes and higher prices and submit to tough environmental restrictions for the privilege of living in a pristine setting. The state's greatest fans may be members of the 251 Club, the more than 4,000 people who have traveled to all 251 of Vermont's cities and towns.

Public policy played a part in the evolution of Vermont. Back in 1970, Republican Gov. Deane Davis (the last Vermont native to hold the job until Peter Shumlin was elected in 2010) pushed through Act 200, a sweeping land use law that helped give Vermont its environmental reputation. Housing developments and new ski resorts were required to meet 10 environmental criteria and get the approval of five different commissions, with opponents granted a right to appeal. Since then, Vermont has passed its own Clean Air Act that levies a tax on new cars that get less than 20 miles to the gallon. It bans billboards and rooftop air conditioning units. Residents also passed Act 60, which attempted to equalize property taxes throughout the state, and Act 200, which provided

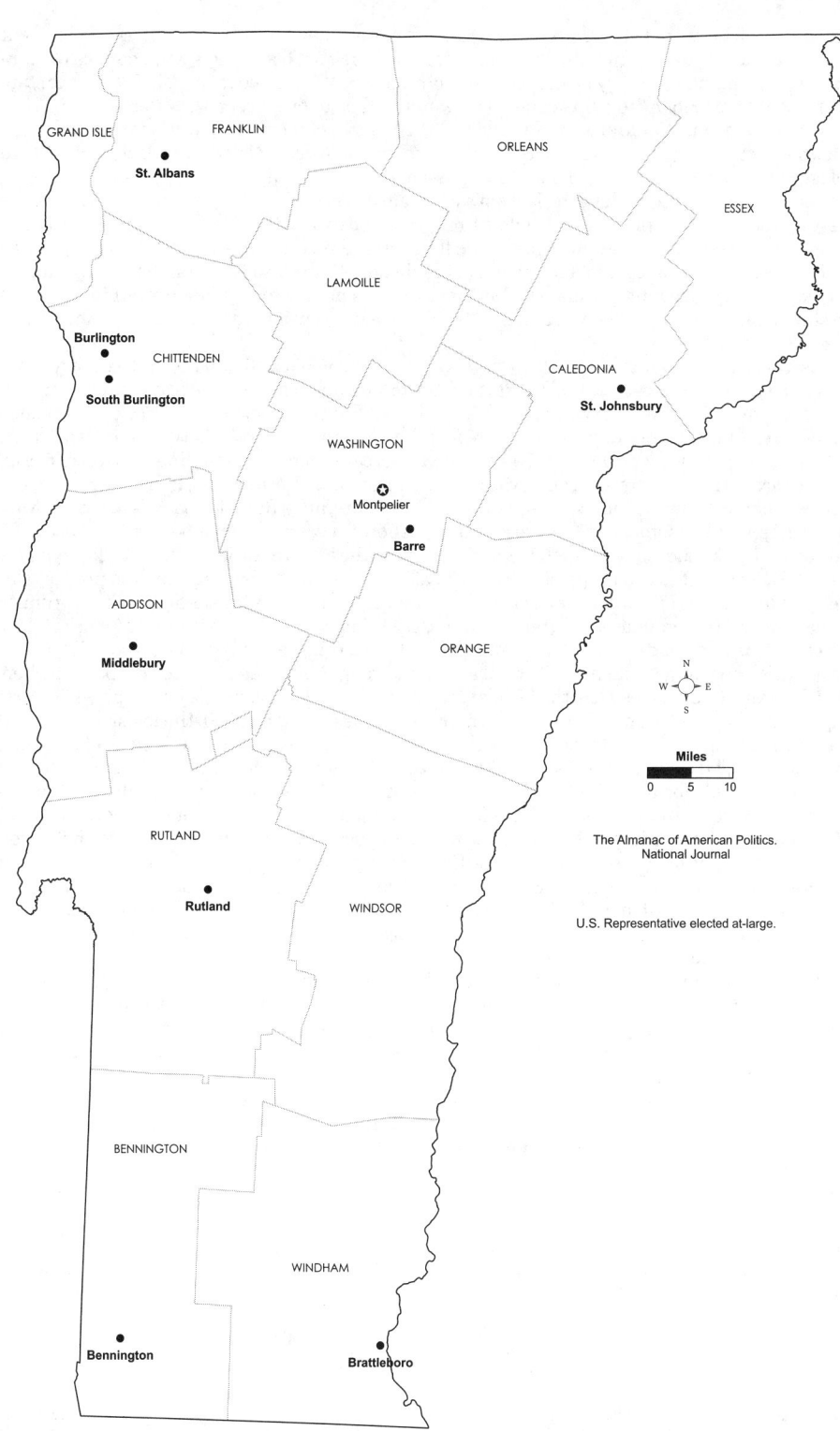

GRAND ISLE

FRANKLIN

ORLEANS

ESSEX

● St. Albans

LAMOILLE

CALEDONIA

● Burlington

CHITTENDEN

● St. Johnsbury

● South Burlington

WASHINGTON

✪ Montpelier

● Barre

ADDISON

ORANGE

● Middlebury

N
W ✦ E
S

Miles

0   5   10

RUTLAND

WINDSOR

● Rutland

The Almanac of American Politics.
National Journal

U.S. Representative elected at-large.

BENNINGTON

WINDHAM

● Bennington

● Brattleboro

state support for regional planning boards. The state maintains a land trust that buys development rights of farmland to stop the disappearance of family farms. Distressed by the demise of dairy farming—the number of dairy farms declined from 3,300 in 1983 to about 1,030 in 2009—the state government loans money to help farmers buy water buffalo to produce mozzarella.

There were four Wal-Marts in the state in 2011, but two of them are in pre-existing buildings. And when Home Depot tried to build a store in one town, the locals insisted on a vegetation-covered roof on which cows could graze; Home Depot passed. Some dairy farmers are processing their animals' solid waste, mixed with bacteria from their digestive systems, into methane fuel. The Grass Energy Collaborative is making fuel pellets from grass and corn. Other farmers are making biodiesel fuel from canola beans, sunflower seeds and flax. An organization called Rural Vermont is pressing for a certification process to allow farmers to sell more than the 50 quarts a day of raw unpasteurized milk that current law allows. But Vermont does not try to regulate everything. It is the one state with no gun control laws, and the state Senate has considered lowering the drinking age to 18.

As Vermont has changed culturally, it has also changed politically. In the 19th century, Yankee Vermont was the most Republican state in the nation; in 1936, Vermont and Maine were the only states to resist Franklin D. Roosevelt's landslide. For three decades thereafter, Vermont's Yankee Protestant Republicans outnumbered its French Canadian and Irish Catholic Democrats. In more recent decades, Vermont has been divided politically along different lines: between liberal, highly educated newcomers and conservative, less educated, old Vermonters. In the 2008 presidential election, Vermont was the second-most Democratic state, after Barack Obama's native Hawaii. Its last Republican member of Congress, James Jeffords, became an independent in May 2001 and voted to make the Democrats the majority party in the Senate. In January 2003, former Gov. Howard Dean set off to run for president. By July, his opposition to the Iraq war, and not his relatively moderate fiscal record in Vermont, made him the leading fundraiser and the front-runner for the Democratic nomination. Vermont, valuing tradition, had become a leader of America's left.

One issue that made Dean attractive to leftist Democrats was civil unions. Ironically, it was one on which he had not taken the lead. In a lawsuit brought by three same-sex couples, the Vermont Supreme Court ruled that the legislature had to pass a gay marriage law or give same-sex couples the same rights under state law as married couples. In April 2000, the legislature passed a law authorizing civil unions for same-sex couples, and Dean signed it out of sight of cameras. Opposition to civil unions was fierce and vocal, though seldom articulated in the state's liberal press. Groups were formed called Take Back Vermont and Who Would Have Thought, while backers of civil unions and other liberal policies formed a group called Move Vermont Forward. Republican gubernatorial candidate Ruth Dwyer vociferously opposed civil unions. Several pro-civil-union Republican legislators lost their seats in the September primary, and Republicans won control of the state House in November. But Dwyer lost, and Democrats held the state Senate. In subsequent years, the controversy abated. Both major party candidates for governor in 2002 opposed repeal, and legalization of same-sex marriage in neighboring Massachusetts and Connecticut has made Vermont seem moderate by comparison.

Vermont was only very marginally affected by the Republican swing in 2010, but Democrats face some challenges ahead on issues. Sen. Patrick Leahy was elected to a seventh term in 2010 by 64%-31%, a lower margin than in his last two elections but impressive nonetheless. His even more liberal colleague, Socialist Bernie Sanders, was elected in 2006 by 65%-32% and was considered certain to win a second term in 2012. Democratic Rep. Peter Welch, first elected in 2006, likewise seemed to have a safe seat. But Democrats were on the defensive in state politics in the past

Population		Household Income		Work	
Pop. 2010:	625,741	Under $15k:	11.6%	Private:	75.2%
State rank:	49th	$15k to $50k:	36.7%	Government:	14.3%
Change since 2000:	Up 2.8%	$50k to $100k:	34.3%	Self-employed:	10.2%
Urban:	37.3%	$100k to $200k:	14.7%	Unemployment (3-yr. average):	4.1%
Rural:	62.7%	Over $200k:	2.7%	Poverty:	10.9%
Native of state:	52.1%	Median income:	$51,555	Blue collar:	20.0%
Not a citizen:	1.6%			White collar:	61.9%
Area size:	9,616 sq. mi.	**Home Value**		Khaki collar:	0.1%
		Under $100k:	12.7%	Other:	18.0%
Most populous cities		$100k to $300k:	62.4%		
Burlington	42,417	$300k to $500k:	17.8%	**Age**	
Essex town	19,587	$500k to $1 mil:	5.8%	Median age:	40.9 yrs.
South Burlington	17,904	Over $1 million:	1.2%	More than 65 yrs:	14.1%
Colchester town	17,067	Median:	$211,800	Less than 18 yrs:	20.7%

Race/Ethnicity				Military Veterans		Registered Voters in 2010	
White:	94.3%	*Language*		% of Pop:	10.8%	No Party registration	
Black:	0.9%	English:	95.1%			Voter turnout:	243,617
Hispanic:	1.5%	Spanish:	1.0%	*Veterans by Period*		Turnout as % of	
Asian:	1.3%	Asian:	0.7%	WWII and before:	9.6%	voting age:	49.1%
Native Am.:	0.3%	Other European:	3.1%	Korea:	13.2%		
Hawaiian:	0.0%			Vietnam:	36.2%	**Legislature**	
Two+ races:	1.6%	**Education**		Gulf (pre-2001):	7.0%	Senate:	22 D 8 R
		H.S. grad:	90.6%	Gulf (post-2001):	5.9%	House:	95 D 48 R 7 I
Ancestry		College grad:	33.2%	Peace time:	28.1%		
English	13.3%	Grad degree:	12.9%				
Irish	13.2%						
French	11.4%						

decade, as Republican Jim Douglas won four, two-year terms as governor starting in 2002. (Vermont and New Hampshire are the last states with two-year gubernatorial terms.) The same year, Republicans won a majority in the state House and the legislature passed some changes in Act 250. Douglas retired in 2010, and Democrat Peter Shumlin beat Republican Brian Dubie in the governor's race by just 49%-48%. Under Vermont law, if no candidate gets a majority, the legislature elects the governor, but Democrats had huge majorities in both houses and Shumlin's election in January 2011 was a formality. Shumlin persuaded the state House and Senate to pass a single-payer health insurance plan, but the bill left the perhaps critical issue of financing to 2013. And while Vermont had no housing bubble or collapse—the state has had fewer foreclosures than any in the nation—job growth was only 3% between 2000 and 2007. IBM has been cutting back on local employment and has leased out part of its big Burlington campus. Vermont gets much of its electricity from the Vermont Yankee nuclear power plant, but the state has tried to shut it down because of safety concerns. IBM, which loses millions when electricity is cut off even for a minute, has demanded a totally reliable electricity supply. But five proposed wind power plants have been held up by local objections. Keeping Vermont green seems to be a proposition attended by some difficulties.

Presidential politics   Vermont was the most Republican state in the 1936 presidential election, when Franklin Roosevelt's campaign manager had a good laugh updating an old adage to say, "As goes Maine, so goes Vermont." Times have changed. In 2004, Vermont was the third most Democratic state, after Massachusetts and Rhode Island, and in 2008, the second most Democratic, after Hawaii. Vermont has become solidly liberal on cultural and foreign issues and it is not very conservative on economics. The state seems downright hostile to conservative national Republicans. Ronald Reagan got his seventh lowest percentage here in 1980, and in early 2007, some 29 town meetings voted to urge Congress to impeach President George W. Bush. It is the only state that Bush did not visit as president.

2008 Presidential Vote		
Barack Obama (D)	219,262	(67%)
John McCain (R)	98,974	(30%)
2008 Presidential Primary		
Barack Obama (D)	91,901	(59%)
Hillary Clinton (D)	59,806	(39%)
2008 Presidential Primary		
John McCain (R)	28,417	(71%)
Mike Huckabee (R)	5,698	(14%)
Ron Paul (R)	2,635	(7%)
2004 Presidential Vote		
John Kerry (D)	184,067	(59%)
George W. Bush (R)	121,180	(39%)

The conflict between the old and the new Vermont is apparent in the exit polls. Back in 2000, people without college degrees voted 48%-46% for Bush, but Democrat Al Gore carried college graduates 51%-36%, and those with postgraduate degrees 62%-29%. By 2008, the percentage for Obama among those with no college degree was 61%-38%, the split among those with college degrees was 67%-29%, and among those with postgraduate degrees, it was 80%-20%. The old divide between Protestants and Catholics has nearly vanished: Obama won 63% of Catholics and 58% of Protestants. He did even better, 82%, among the 24% of voters who said they had no religion.

The Vermont presidential primary, abolished for 1992, reappeared in 1996, but got little notice both that year and in 2000. Turnout in 2000 was light and tilted Republican because the Democratic race was over. Howard Dean's 2004 campaign was headquartered in Burlington, and although Dean was effectively eliminated by the time Vermont voted on March 2, Vermonters still came out in droves and gave him his only primary victory. Turnout was 83,000 for the Democrats and 27,000 in the uncontested Republican primary. In 2008, Vermont voted on March 4, when the Democratic race was still raging. Turnout was 155,000 in the Democratic primary, in which Obama beat Hillary Rodham Clinton 59%-39%, and each got more than twice as many votes as John McCain did in winning the light turnout (40,000) Republican primary, 71%-14%.

Governor

Peter Shumlin (D)

Elected 2010, term expires Jan. 2013, 1st term; b. March 24, 1956, Brattleboro; home, Montpelier; Wesleyan U., B.A. 1979; No religious affiliation; Separated; 2 children.

Elected Office: Putney Select Board, 1980-90; VT House, 1990-92; VT Senate, 1992-2002, 2006-11.

Professional Career: Co-dir., Putney Student Travel, 2003-06; Partner, dairy farm.

Office: 109 State Street, The Pavilion, Montpelier, 05609, 802-828-3333; Fax: 802-828-3339; Web site: governor.vermont.gov/.

Election Results

2010 general	Peter Shumlin (D)	119,543	(49%)
	Brian Dubie (R)	115,212	(48%)
2010 primary	Peter Shumlin (D)	18,276	(25%)
	Doug Racine (D)	18,079	(25%)
	Deb Markowitz (D)	17,579	(24%)
	Matt Dunne (D)	15,323	(21%)
	Susan Bartlett (D)	3,759	(5%)

Vermont's governor is Peter Shumlin, a Democrat elected in 2010. A longtime veteran of Vermont state politics, he eked out one of the closest wins of the political season after also prevailing by a hair in a contentious five-way primary. Shumlin succeeded Republican Jim Douglas, who declined to seek a fifth term.

Shumlin grew up in Putney, a small town in the state's southeast corner. His parents were educators who started a business matching high school students with academic and community service projects around the world. He suffered from dyslexia as a child, a problem that forced him to work on being articulate—something he said helped him later in politics. "I had to be the guy who was fastest with my tongue," he told *The Burlington Free Press*. After graduating from Wesleyan University, Shumlin and his brother took over their parents' business. In 1980, at age 24, he was elected to the Putney Selectboard. He was chosen in 1990 to fill an empty seat in the state House of Representatives, and then was elected to the seat the following year. He was elected in 1992 to represent Windham County in the state Senate, becoming the chamber's president pro-tempore within five years. He lost a three-way election in 2002 to Republican Brian Dubie. After taking four years off from politics, he returned to the Senate, where he was again elected president pro tempore. Around the Statehouse, he was known as a forceful advocate for Democratic causes and for being fast with a sound bite. He was a key sponsor of a comprehensive energy bill for the state in 2007 that sought to cut greenhouse gas emissions blamed for global warming.

Shumlin announced his candidacy for governor in November 2009, stressing that his record of running the family business and years as Senate leader made him the best candidate. "We need a governor who has experience," he said. He joined a crowded Democratic field that already included a number of political veterans, including state Senate Appropriations Committee Chairman Susan Bartlett, Secretary of State Deborah Markowitz and state Sen. Doug Racine, a former lieutenant governor who had lost a bid to Douglas in 2002. The candidates battled to stand out from the pack in the months leading up to the August 2010 primary. The race was so close that a winner couldn't be determined on Election Night, forcing a recount. Shumlin emerged with a 203-vote lead over Racine, who conceded more than two weeks after the polls closed. Shumlin finished with 24.8% to Racine's 24.6%, with Markowitz getting 23.9%. Former state Sen. Matt Dunne won 21% and Bartlett received 5%.

In the meantime, Dubie, by then the state's lieutenant governor, had the Republican field all to himself, and had raised nearly $1.2 million. By comparison, Shumlin had just $61,000 at the outset of the general election race. Dubie ran on the same small-government, anti-taxation platform as other Republicans around the country. Dubie called for a 2% growth cap on state spending; Shumlin advocated a single-payer health care system as a way of boosting the economy. With help from outside Democratic groups, Shumlin was able to close the financial gap with Dubie, but a Vermont Public Radio survey in October showed the Republican ahead by one percentage point.

A key issue that emerged in the closing weeks was the controversial Vermont Yankee nuclear power plant, which was blamed for contaminating nearby groundwater. Shumlin accused Dubie of being too friendly to the plant's operator, Entergy Corp. of New Orleans, while Dubie said that the plant's future status should be left to the state Public Service Board and federal Nuclear Regulatory Commission. The two men quarreled over other issues in a contest that was unusually negative by Vermont's placid political standards. On Election Night, the race was too close to call, but Shumlin pulled out a 49.5%-47.7% victory. He dominated the southern and central portions of Vermont, winning all but one county there, while Dubie carried the state's rural Northeast Kingdom. Under state law, since neither candidate received 50% plus one vote, the race could have been decided in the legislature. But with Democrats holding solid majorities in the House and Senate, Dubie chose to concede.

Shumlin presented an initial budget intended to reduce general funding more than $80 million, while keeping taxes stable. He named Racine to head the state Agency of Human Services and Bartlett as a special assistant. He also began to move the state toward a single-payer system, winning an agreement from the Obama administration in February 2011 that it would endorse a move to change the waiver date for federal reform requirements from 2017 to 2014. Shumlin did become the object of derision in March of that year, when he took a Caribbean vacation as Vermont was hit with two feet of snow during a severe storm. He did not bring along his security detail and did not inform the public of his whereabouts until he returned. He said he had no regrets about not returning sooner, saying his staff kept him abreast of emergency response developments.

Senior Senator

Patrick Leahy (D)

Elected 1974, term expires 2016, 7th term; b. March 31, 1940, Montpelier; home, Middlesex; St. Michael's Col., B.A. 1961, Georgetown U., J.D. 1964; Catholic; married (Marcelle); 3 children.

Elected Office: VT st. atty., Chittenden Cnty., 1966–74.

Professional Career: Practicing atty., 1964–74.

DC Office: 433 RSOB, 20510, 202-224-4242; Fax: 202-224-3479; Web site: leahy.senate.gov.

State Offices: Burlington, 802-863-2525; Montpelier, 802-229-0569.

Committees: *Agriculture, Nutrition & Forestry:* Conservation, Forestry & Natural Resources; Livestock, Dairy, Poultry, Marketing & Ag Research; Nutrition, Specialty Crops, Food & Ag Research. *Appropriations:* Commerce, Justice, Science & Related Agencies; Defense; Department of State, Foreign Operations & Related Programs; Homeland Security; Interior, Environment & Related Agencies; Transportation, HUD & Related Agencies. *Judiciary* (Chmn): Administrative Oversight & the Courts; Constitution, Civil Rights & Human Rights; Immigration, Refugees & Border Security. *Rules & Administration.*

Group Ratings

	ACLU	ACU	ADA	CFG	AFS	FRC	LCV	ITIC	NTU	COC
2010	93	0	100	0	92	0	100	33	2	0
2009	–	8	95	5	100	–	100	–	6	43

National Journal Ratings

	2010 LIB	—	2010 CONS		2009 LIB	—	2009 CONS
Economic	88%	—	0%		77%	—	22%
Social	65%	—	0%		66%	—	33%
Foreign	47%	—	0%		55%	—	0%
Composite	83%	—	17%		74%	—	26%

Key Votes of the 111th Congress

1. Overturn Ledbetter	Y	5. Pass health care bill	Y	9. Ratify New START	Y
2. Pass $787 billion stimulus	Y	6. Regulate financial firms	Y	10. Confirm Elena Kagan	Y
3. Repeal DC gun laws	N	7. Pass tax cuts for some	Y	11. Stop EPA climate regs	N
4. Confirm Sonia Sotomayor	Y	8. Legalize immigrants' kids	Y	12. Repeal don't ask, tell	Y

Election Results

2010 general	Patrick Leahy (D)	151,281	(64%)	($4,869,504)
	Len Britton (R)...	72,699	(31%)	($232,549)
2010 primary	Patrick Leahy (D)	64,515	(89%)	
	Daniel Freilich (D)	7,892	(11%)	

Prior Winning Percentages: 2004 (71%); 1998 (72%); 1992 (54%); 1986 (63%); 1980 (50%); 1974 (50%)

Patrick Leahy, Vermont's longest-serving senator, was first elected to the Senate in 1974 and is now the chamber's second most-senior member, behind Hawaii Democrat Daniel Inouye. As chairman of the Judiciary Committee, Leahy is as much of an influential ally of President Barack Obama as he was a stubborn antagonist of President George W. Bush.

Leahy grew up in Burlington, went to law school at Georgetown University, and then returned home to practice law. He was elected Chittenden County state's attorney in 1966, at age 26, and still often invokes his years in that job during hearings and in interviews. After eight years as state's attorney, he ran for the U.S. Senate at age 34. It was 1974, and Leahy had made a name for himself in the tiny state as the Burlington-area prosecutor who tried all major felony cases personally and who attacked the big oil companies during the 1970s energy crisis. He had a solid base in Democratic Burlington, together with the kind of quiet, thoughtful temperament that Vermonters like in their public officials. He outpolled Republican U.S. Rep. Richard Mallary by a narrow margin to win the Senate seat.

Leahy is a stalwart progressive—in 2010, he and his Vermont colleague, Independent Bernie Sanders, were among those tied for the Senate's most liberal member, according to *National Journal's* rankings. Over the years, Leahy has made his mark as Judiciary's chairman. He was formerly chairman of the Agriculture Committee, and he has a chance to chair the powerful Appropriations panel in the next few years, given his seniority. Judiciary handles many of the cultural issues—such as abortion and gun control—that have polarized the two parties and their constituencies, and the committee has been sharply divided at least since the hearings on Supreme Court nominee Robert Bork in 1987. Leahy was an early supporter of Barack Obama in the 2008 presidential primaries, and has largely been in sync with his administration. He helped guide Obama's first two Supreme Court nominees, Sonia Sotomayor and Elena Kagan, to swift confirmation, even while working with a new Judiciary ranking Republican, Alabama's Jeff Sessions, who was considerably more partisan than his predecessor in that role, Pennsylvania's Arlen Specter. Leahy accused Republicans of seeking to play the race card against Sotomayor, the court's first Latina justice, and of gender bias toward Kagan. He mused to reporters in May 2010 that if Obama nominated Moses to the panel, Republicans would find a way to oppose him.

Leahy had mixed results on other issues before Judiciary in Obama's first term. He was unable to get a long-delayed overhaul of the patent system into law, and he promised in January 2011 to redouble efforts on the issue with his House Judiciary counterpart, Texas Republican Lamar Smith. Leahy also pledged to revive failed legislation from 2010 aimed at cracking down on online piracy and counterfeiting as well as a measure to speed up the processing of Freedom of Information Act requests. He said he would look for ways to reduce government fraud with Judiciary's new ranking Republican, Iowa's Chuck Grassley.

In the 1990s, when Republicans were in the majority, Leahy criticized them for holding up President Bill Clinton's judicial appointments, and he stoutly defended Clinton during the impeachment proceedings in 1998 and 1999. When Leahy became chairman during the Democrats' 19 months in the majority in 2001 and 2003, he, in turn, held up the Republicans' judicial nominations. As ranking minority member of the committee from 2003 to 2007, Leahy led filibusters against 10 appeals court nominees, tactics that the Republicans bitterly attacked. Leahy noted that the committee had approved the vast majority of appellate nominees and almost every trial court nominee, and argued that he had been fairer to Bush's appointees than Republicans had been to Clinton's. Leahy's brass-knuckle tactics irked some Republicans, including Vice President Dick Cheney, who infamously cursed at the Democrat on the Senate floor during a 2004 photo shoot.

In 2005, Leahy led the minority's questioning of Bush's Supreme Court nominees, John Roberts and Samuel Alito, both of whom were ultimately confirmed by the Senate. The liberal senator surprised many when he voted to approve the conservative Roberts. "I know this will not be popular with many of my constituency, and I understand that," Leahy said. "I came here to do what I thought was right, and as a Vermonter I can do nothing different." He also asked tough questions of Alito, and that time he voted no. He said, "This president is in the midst of a radical realignment of the powers of government and its intrusiveness into the private lives of Americans. This nomination is part of that plan." When Alito appeared to mouth the words "not true" at the 2010 State of the Union address as Obama blasted the Supreme Court's decision allowing corporations to buy political attack ads, Leahy stood behind the president. He called the *Citizens United* ruling "the most partisan decision since *Bush v. Gore*" in 2000.

Another major chapter in Leahy's tenure as chairman was handling legislation that grew out of the September 11 terrorist attacks. He and his staff worked with the Bush administration to hammer out the USA Patriot Act, the sweeping law that sparked a national debate over whether government investigators should be given broader powers at the expense of individual liberties. It was essentially the Senate version, not the House bill, that was enacted in October 2001. But Leahy fought the administration when it sought to expand police powers in the wake of the attacks. He opposed a proposal to allow the government to detain and deport immigrants suspected of terrorism without presenting evidence in court. In 2002, he said that the Justice Department should be required to disclose the number of U.S. citizens being spied on, the number of secret foreign intelligence wiretaps that had become part of criminal proceedings, and the total number of persons targeted by foreign-intelligence surveillance warrants. In February 2010, he pushed for passage of an extension of the Patriot Act with additional civil liberty protections, but agreed to a one-year extension of several expiring provisions.

After the Abu Ghraib prison scandal broke in 2004, Leahy sharply criticized the administration, and he strongly disagreed with Bush's declaration that the Geneva Conventions did not apply to unlawful combatants in Afghanistan. In 2005, Leahy objected to the government's surveillance of communications between suspected Al Qaeda terrorists abroad and people in the United States. As chairman in 2007, he made life difficult for Attorney General Alberto Gonzales by requesting an internal investigation of whether Gonzales had told the truth about the warrantless wiretapping program. Leahy subsequently placed Gonzales's successor, Michael Mukasey, on the spot with demands that he denounce the use of water boarding, an interrogation tactic that simulates drowning and that has been used on terrorism suspects.

Around the Capitol, Leahy is known for his geniality. In 2010, he was named "nicest senator" in *Washingtonian* magazine's anonymous annual survey of Capitol Hill staff. He is a gadgeteer and an amateur photographer, whose work has been published in *The New York Times* and elsewhere. He is also an avid student of popular culture, and a huge fan of the *Batman* movies. (He appeared briefly in two of the films, with a speaking part in 2008's *The Dark Knight*. Leahy tells the Joker, "We're not intimidated by you thugs.") He can recite verses from Shakespeare and lyrics from the Grateful Dead rock band, and is friends with the Vermont band Phish. In 1995, he became the second senator, after Democrat Edward Kennedy of Massachusetts, to set up a personal website, and in 2003, he was the first member of Congress with a blog. Leahy's fascination with technology helps to explain his interest in patent issues.

Another Leahy cause is the elimination of land mines. Since 1989, he has been crusading against the export and use of land mines, which are easy and cheap to implant yet difficult and expensive to remove. In many places, land mines continue to injure and kill civilians long after hostilities have ended. In 1994, Leahy persuaded the United Nations to unanimously call for the eventual elimination of land mines. On a similar issue, he co-sponsored in 2006 an amendment to ban the use of cluster bombs near civilian sites in Iraq and Afghanistan, but it was defeated 70-30. He pushed Obama in 2010 to join an international treaty banning the mines. On other foreign policy and defense issues, Leahy tends to the left as well. He has been an outspoken critic of the Iraq war and expressed disappointment with Attorney General Eric Holder's decision in 2011 not to try suspected terrorists in federal court.

Leahy is one of the few members of the Agriculture Committee who is not from a state with heavily subsidized crops such as wheat, corn, soybeans, and cotton. As the ranking Democrat on the committee, he worked with Indiana Republican Richard Lugar in the 1990s to phase out the subsidy system. But after their success in passing the Freedom to Farm Act of 1996, crop prices fell, and lawmakers' resolve dissipated. Congress took to voting large annual subsidies in the form of emergency relief to farmers. The 2002 farm bill largely rolled back the 1996 act.

That is not to say that Leahy is not at times as parochial as the next senator. On Agriculture, he is a staunch defender of the interests of the 1,150 dairy farms in Vermont. In April 2011, he introduced a measure allowing dairy farmers in Vermont and elsewhere to issue H-2A visas long used by other sectors of agriculture to hire foreign workers. In 2010, he secured more than $57 million in solo spending earmarks for his state—the 10th highest total among senators, according to Taxpayers for Common Sense.

Leahy has had relatively easy re-election contests. His closest call was in 1980, when he narrowly survived that year's Republican sweep. He defeated Republican Stewart Ledbetter just 50%-49%. Six years later, he was completely rehabilitated politically. He defeated popular Gov. Richard Snelling, 63%-35%.

Junior Senator

Bernie Sanders (I)

Elected 2006, term expires 2012, 1st term; b. Sept. 8, 1941, New York, NY; home, Burlington; Attended Brooklyn Col., U. of Chicago, B.A. 1964; Jewish; married (Jane O'Meara Sanders); 4 children.

Elected Office: Burlington mayor, 1981-89; U.S. House of Reps., 1991-2007.

Professional Career: Writer; Dir., Amer. People's Historical Soc., 1977-81; Lecturer, Harvard U., 1989; Prof., Hamilton Col., 1990

DC Office: 332 DSOB, 20510, 202-224-5141; Fax: 202-228-0776; Web site: sanders.senate.gov.

State Offices: Brattleboro, 802-254-8732; Burlington, 802-862-0697; St. Johnsbury, 802-748-9269.

Committees: *Budget. Energy & Natural Resources:* Energy; National Parks; Water & Power. *Environment & Public Works:* Clean Air & Nuclear Safety; Green Jobs & the New Economy (Chmn); Oversight; Transportation & Infrastructure. *Health, Education, Labor & Pensions:* Children & Families; Primary Health & Aging (Chmn). *Joint Economic Committee. Veterans' Affairs.*

Group Ratings

	ACLU	ACU	ADA	CFG	AFS	FRC	LCV	ITIC	NTU	COC
2010	93	4	95	0	100	0	100	33	3	0
2009	–	12	100	6	100	–	100	–	9	29

National Journal Ratings

	2010 LIB	—	2010 CONS		2009 LIB	—	2009 CONS
Economic	88%	—	0%		68%	—	30%
Social	65%	—	0%		68%	—	31%
Foreign	47%	—	0%		49%	—	45%
Composite	83%	—	17%		63%	—	37%

Key Votes of the 111th Congress

1. Overturn Ledbetter	Y	5. Pass health care bill	Y	9. Ratify New START	Y
2. Pass $787 billion stimulus	Y	6. Regulate financial firms	Y	10. Confirm Elena Kagan	Y
3. Repeal DC gun laws	N	7. Pass tax cuts for some	Y	11. Stop EPA climate regs	N
4. Confirm Sonia Sotomayor	Y	8. Legalize immigrants' kids	Y	12. Repeal don't ask, tell	Y

Election Results

2006 general	Bernie Sanders (I)..	171,638	(65%)	($5,554,466)
	Richard Tarrant (I)...	84,924	(32%)	($7,315,854)
2006 primary	Bernie Sanders (D)	35,954	(94%)	

Prior Winning Percentages: House: 2004 (67%); 2002 (64%); 2000 (69%); 1998 (63%); 1996 (55%); 1994 (50%); 1992 (58%); 1990 (56%)

Vermont's junior senator is Bernie Sanders, a Socialist elected as an independent in 2006 but treated as a Democrat in the Senate. He is an ardent spokesman for the views of the political left.

Sanders grew up in the Flatbush section of Brooklyn, the son of a paint salesman who had emigrated from Poland; his mother died when he was a teenager. He became involved in radical leftist politics at the University of Chicago, and then moved to Vermont as part of the hippie migration of 1968 and worked as a carpenter. Four years later, he ran in a special U.S. Senate election to replace Republican Winston Prouty, who died in office in 1971. Sanders won just 2% of the vote as the candidate of the socialist Liberty Union Party. He went on to lose four more statewide races until his rumpled, tieless, sincere persona finally won over the people of Burlington, who elected him mayor in 1981 by just 10 votes.

In 1988, when Republican Rep. James Jeffords ran for the Senate, Sanders made a bid for the House but lost to Republican Peter Smith in a close, three-way race. Two years later, he ran again and reversed the result by capitalizing on Smith's support of the 1990 budget agreement and his vote to ban semiautomatic weapons. The National Rifle Association came out against Smith, and Sanders' opposition to gun control helped him carry 227 of Vermont's 251 cities and towns, plus three gores and one grant, as unincorporated areas in Vermont are known. Sanders became only the third Socialist elected to the House, after Victor Berger of Milwaukee (1911-13, 1923-29) and Meyer London of Manhattan's Lower East Side (1915-23). His views haven't changed much since his first election.

As a senator, he initially settled with surprising ease into the Senate's more structured ways, and grew more sensitive to his reputation as a troublemaker. Democrat Patrick Leahy, the state's senior senator, told a Vermont reporter that other senators confided to him "what a pleasant surprise (Sanders) has turned out to be" with his willingness to forge legislative deals. With seats on committees that deal with energy and environmental issues, Sanders worked for deep cuts in industrial pollution in the global warming bill. He sought to promote new technology to reduce emissions in the automobile and energy industries. In 2007, the Senate passed his amendment to the energy bill to encourage universities to support energy-efficient projects. Sanders also resumed his opposition to international trade deals, blaming them for lowering domestic wages and shuttering U.S. factories.

As the congressional focus moved to the economy following President Barack Obama's election, Sanders began showing signs of his older, feistier persona. When Obama renominated Ben Bernanke in 2009 as chairman of the Federal Reserve, Sanders bristled: "When the people voted for change in 2008, they did not vote to have one of the key architects of the Bush economy be reappointed." In 2010, Sanders got a provision into the Senate version of the Dodd-Frank financial industry overhaul bill ordering a one-time audit of the Fed, far less than what he had sought. He also introduced a bill imposing a 10% "billionaire's surtax" on inheritances worth more than $500 million per spouse. Sanders compared skeptics of human-caused global warming to those outside Germany who had denied the spread of Nazism before World War II. He was the Senate's 38th most liberal member in 2009, but the next year was among those tied for first in *National Journal's* annual rankings.

None of Sanders' efforts, though, drew as much attention as his apoplectic, marathon floor speech in December 2010 against extending the Bush tax cuts for the wealthy, which lasted more than eight hours and cemented his reputation on the left. He made a list beforehand of 10 key points he wanted to make, but said he set no time limit for himself. He repeatedly mocked how the rich sought cuts to finance what he called their unnecessarily extravagant lifestyles at the expense of the middle class. "How can I get by on one house?" Sanders said sarcastically at one point. "I need five houses, 10 houses! I need three jet planes to take me all over the world! Sorry, American people. We've got the money, we've got the power, we've got the lobbyists here and on Wall Street. Tough luck." The speech proved so popular that it temporarily shut down the Senate video server and put his name atop Twitter's list of trending topics. In early 2011, it was sold as a book, *The Speech: A Historic Filibuster on Corporate Greed and the Decline of Our Middle Class,* with the proceeds going to Vermont charities. "There have been filibusters," wrote columnist Stephen Herrington on the liberal *Huffington Post* website, "but not in the memory of any living American has such a rhyme to the ages and passion to justice been brought to the floor of the United States Senate."

In the months following the speech, Sanders made the rounds of television shows ranging from MSNBC to *The Daily Show with Jon Stewart.* He also was picked as the keynote speaker at California's Democratic Party convention. He inveighed against the fiscal 2011 budget deal that Obama reached with Republicans, calling it "Robin Hood in reverse." He also released a list of 10 large corporations that he said had paid disproportionately low taxes, including GE, Exxon-Mobil and Bank of America. And, after a visit to the Smithsonian's National Museum of American History, where he learned that its miniature souvenir statues of U.S. presidents were made in China, he persuaded the museum to have one of its gift shops sell exclusively American-made products.

During his years in the House (1991-2007), Sanders served as Vermont's single, at-large member. Democrats initially balked at accepting a Socialist in their caucus, but they granted him seniority as a Democrat when he arrived in 1991. He amassed a heavily liberal voting record and formed a Progressive Caucus with a somewhat quixotic agenda: progressive tax reform, a Canada-style single-payer health care system, a 50% cut in military spending, a national energy policy, and—a Vermont touch—support for family farms.

He was at times a practical and successful legislator, gaining Republican allies in targeting so-called corporate welfare—government benefits to well-heeled companies. With Republican Chris

Smith of New Jersey, he passed an amendment barring spending for defense contractor mergers. In 2001, he proposed a $300-per-person income tax rebate. It quickly became Democratic Party policy, and Republicans, in assembling majorities for the Bush tax cuts, included it in diluted form—a $300 rebate for income-tax-paying adults. Sanders and the Democrats noted ruefully that Bush took credit for a tax-cutting proposal that was initially theirs. As much as any member of Congress, Sanders made the cost of prescription drugs a national issue. Since the 1980s, he has called for government programs to pay for prescription drugs, and he was the first member of Congress to lead bus trips to Canada to buy drugs there. He has denounced "the insatiable greed that consumes this runaway (pharmaceutical) industry." With other liberals, he was a staunch opponent of going to war in Iraq.

All of this played well with Vermont voters, and by the late 1990s, Sanders began winning by large margins. Democratic candidates failed to gain support from the state party, if they filed to run against Sanders at all. Sanders twice gave serious consideration to challenging Jeffords for his Senate seat. But in May 2001, Jeffords left the Republican Party, an event that gave Democrats a majority in the Senate for 19 months. Like Sanders in the House, Jeffords called himself an independent, but caucused with the Democrats. In April 2005, Jeffords announced he would not run for another term in 2006. Sanders became the early front-runner and quickly amassed endorsements from top Vermont Democrats, including former Gov. Phil Hoff, Burlington Mayor Peter Clavelle, Senate President Pro Tempore Peter Welch, and House Speaker Gaye Symington. Ever the loner, Sanders said he would neither seek nor accept the Democratic nomination. But with his consent, Democrats ran his name on the primary ballot anyway. He won 94% of the vote, though he formally declined the nomination and petitioned the state to list him on the general election ballot as an independent. Still, Howard Dean, chairman of the Democratic National Committee and a former Vermont governor, declared, "A victory for Bernie Sanders is a win for Democrats."

On the Republican side, Gov. Jim Douglas was considered the strongest Republican candidate, but he declined to run. Richard Tarrant, a multi-millionaire businessman and former high school basketball star, became the nominee. His ads sought to portray Sanders as an ineffective radical who was soft on sexual predators and drug dealers. The strategy might have worked elsewhere, but not in Vermont, where voters were well acquainted with Sanders and his iconoclastic ways. Despite the harsh attacks—or perhaps because of them—Tarrant was never able to close the gap in the polls. He outspent Sanders, but Sanders also proved to be well-funded. He raised and spent over $6 million, many times more than ever before and enough to make this the costliest race in state history. Sanders won easily, 65%-32%. He will be a formidable opponent in 2012 in a state where Obama has remained popular, and his growing national following won't make defeating him any easier.

REPRESENTATIVE-AT-LARGE

Peter Welch (D)

Elected 2006, 3rd term; b. May 2, 1947, Springfield, MA; home, Hartland; Col. of the Holy Cross, A.B. 1969, U. of CA, J.D. 1973; Catholic; married (Margaret Cheney); 8 children.

Elected Office: VT Senate, 1980-88, 2001-2006; VT Senate min. ldr., 1982-84; VT Senate pres. pro tem, 1985-88, 2002-06.

Professional Career: Robert F. Kennedy fellow, 1969-70; Practicing atty., 1974-2006.

DC Office: 1404 LHOB, 20515, 202-225-4115; Web site: welch.house.gov.

State Offices: Burlington, 802-652-2450.

Committees: *Agriculture:* General Farm Commodities & Risk Management; Rural Development, Research, Biotechnology & Foreign Agriculture. *Oversight & Government Reform:* National Security, Homeland Defense & Foreign Operations; TARP, Financial Services & Bailouts of Public & Private Programs.

Group Ratings

	ACLU	ACU	ADA	CFG	AFS	FRC	LCV	ITIC	NTU	COC
2010	94	4	95	0	75	12	100	67	7	13
2009	–	0	90	4	100	–	93	–	6	33

National Journal Ratings

	2010 LIB — 2010 CONS		2009 LIB — 2009 CONS	
Economic	64%	— 35%	82%	— 14%
Social	82%	— 14%	66%	— 33%
Foreign	63%	— 35%	77%	— 23%
Composite	71%	— 29%	76%	— 24%

Key Votes of the 111th Congress

1. Overturn Ledbetter	Y	5. Bar federal abortion funds	N	9. Stop detainee transfers	N
2. Pass $820 billion stimulus	Y	6. Pass health care bill	Y	10. Legalize immigrants' kids	Y
3. Let guns in national parks	Y	7. Regulate financial firms	Y	11. Repeal don't ask, tell	Y
4. Pass cap-and-trade	Y	8. Pass tax cuts for some	Y	12. Limit campaign funds	Y

Election Results

2010 general	Peter Welch (D)	154,006	(65%)	($1,027,181)
	Paul Beaudry (R)	76,403	(32%)	($32,733)
2010 primary	Peter Welch (D)	unopposed		

Prior Winning Percentages: 2008 (83%), 2006 (53%)

Vermont's only House member is Peter Welch, a Democrat first elected in 2006. He grew up in Springfield, Mass., the son of a dentist, and graduated from College of the Holy Cross. The summer before his junior year, he worked for a Jesuit group that did community outreach in poor black neighborhoods in Chicago. While there, he was inspired by a speech by the Rev. Martin Luther King Jr., a leader of the growing civil rights movement in the 1960s. After graduating from law school at the University of California, Berkeley, Welch backpacked down the Pan-American Highway to Santiago, Chile, went overland to Brazil, then worked on a freighter that sailed to Portugal. After that, he was ready to settle down to practice law, and chose White River Junction, Vt. as his home. He married a professor at Dartmouth, just across the river, and became a stepfather to Joan Smith's five children.

In 1980, Welch was elected as only the second Democrat to represent Windsor County in the state Senate, and the first since the Civil War. In 1982, he became Senate minority leader. In 1984, after Democrats won a majority in the Senate for the first time ever, he was elected Senate president pro tem. He focused on environment, education, and tax issues and helped establish the Housing and Land Conservation Trust, which worked to create affordable housing and to conserve farmland and forests. In 1988, when Republican Rep. James Jeffords ran for the Senate, Welch aimed for the U.S. House but lost the Democratic primary by 266 votes. In 1990, Welch ran for governor, but lost 52%-46% to Republican Richard Snelling. For some years after that, Welch was out of political life. His wife, Joan, who had been his closest adviser and campaign manager, fought cancer for nine years, and Welch at times was her full-time caregiver. She died in 2004.

In 2001, Democratic Gov. Howard Dean appointed Welch to the state Senate to fill a vacancy in Windsor County. In 2003, he became president pro tem once again and focused on health care issues. He also helped negotiate a deal for the storage of spent nuclear fuel on the site of the Vermont Yankee nuclear power plant. In the spring of 2005, Sen. Jeffords announced he would not seek re-election in 2006. Socialist Rep. Bernie Sanders, after 15 years in the House, announced he would run for the Senate seat and attracted little opposition. So Welch decided to run again for the U.S. House, this time for the seat that Sanders was giving up.

He was supported by many Democratic leaders and, although other potential candidates canvassed for support, no one else ended up running, and Welch won the September 2006 primary unopposed. The winner of the Republican primary, by 71%-28%, was Martha Rainville, the commander of the Vermont National Guard, who had a sterling résumé. In 1997, she was chosen by the legislature to serve as state adjutant general, becoming the first woman to command a state's National Guard. Welch campaigned as an opponent of military action in Iraq from the start, and he condemned the "corrupt" Republicans in Washington. He supported a universal health care program and called for the resignation of Defense Secretary Donald Rumsfeld. Rainville said she would have voted for military action in Iraq in 2002 given what was known then, but she also criticized some of the Bush administration's decisions since. Both candidates favored access to abortion.

Both also pledged not to run negative campaigns, and this was probably the only seriously contested 2006 House race in the country without a single negative ad on the airwaves. But there was dispute. Welch called Rainville the "hand-picked" candidate of the by then unpopular national Republicans. Rainville countered that Vermont Republicans are "something very different," and insisted that "the party has a lot of room for diversity." Welch spent $1.7 million to Rainville's $1.1 million. But the House Republican campaign committee outspent its Democratic counterpart, $750,000 to $300,000. This was one of the few Democratic seats that Republicans thought they had a good chance of picking up. (Though technically not a Democrat, Sanders had caucused with the Democrats.) The contest was close in the polls throughout the summer, but by late September, Welch opened up a lead. Rainville was embarrassed when she was forced to fire a speechwriter in early October for plagiarizing from Democratic Sen. Hillary Rodham Clinton of New York. Welch won, 53%-45%.

In the House, Welch has become known for legislative skill, though he retains an understated and collegial style. With the GOP takeover of the House in 2011, he lost his prized seat on the Energy and Commerce Committee due to the majority's restructuring, but became a chief deputy for Minority Whip Steny Hoyer in recognition of his ability to work with others. He helped liberals articulate their opposition to both the tax cut extension deal between President Barack Obama and House Republicans in December 2010 as well as the GOP's vote to repeal health care reform the following month.

He also took a prominent position on the debate over extending the debt ceiling, circulating a letter in April 2011 calling on Democratic leaders to hold a special caucus meeting to discuss the issue and stick to a "clean" extension unencumbered by extraneous provisions. And he was among opponents turning up often on television to blast Budget Committee Chairman Paul Ryan's ambitious and controversial blueprint for a balanced budget. "There's an ideology that's at work with the Republican plan. And that is that revenues are always bad and a tax cut is always good, and it's better to cut rather than to invest," he told MSNBC in April 2011.

When he served on Energy and Commerce, Welch got a provision into House-passed energy and climate change legislation in 2009 to invest billions of dollars in energy efficiency efforts. A year later, he won committee passage of a measure to provide tax rebates to consumers for installing upgraded insulation, storm windows and other energy efficiency solutions. He sought to practice what he preached, making his office the first in the House to install new lights and water fixtures to reduce energy use.

Earlier, Welch was one of four freshman Democrats to get a seat on the Rules Committee, an influential, leadership-run panel that establishes the procedures for bills coming to the floor. With his legislative experience, he became a player on a range of issues. The House passed his amendment to require universities to report to Congress how they are using their endowments to reduce costs for middle-class families, and he won passage of his proposal to close a loophole that exempted overseas government contracts from federal reporting requirements.

At home, Welch secured his seat early and faced no serious re-election threats in 2008 or 2010. Shortly after his first term ended, Welch remarried. In 2009, he tied the knot with state Rep. Margaret Cheney.

★ VIRGINIA ★

Traditions endure in Virginia, even amid bustling high-tech growth. Through more than 400 years of history, Virginians have honored and sometimes been transfixed by traditions going back to the American Revolution and earlier. For the last half century, Virginia has grown lustily, sparked by an expanding federal government and, increasingly, by a vibrant private sector. But the first state in the nation to elect an African-American governor (Douglas Wilder in 1989) in some ways still hews to a course close to its roots. Colonial Virginia was a commonwealth ruled by a landed gentry that was, in the words of historian David Hackett Fischer, "elitist and libertarian." From this tobacco-growing region there emerged in the 1770s a group of leaders—George Washington, George Mason, Patrick Henry, Thomas Jefferson, Richard Henry Lee, and James Madison—that in learning, wisdom and strength of character equaled any such group from any polity since Periclean Athens or republican Rome. They were slaveholders who insisted on liberty, armed men who insisted on the rule of law, and believers in racial inequality who set forth principles of equality that would in time form the basis of a non-racist society. The Virginia they led into the American Revolution was not only the most populous and the richest of the 13 colonies, but it also was the indispensable creator of the republic and the Constitution that has held together the world's greatest democracy.

After the Revolutionary War, control by the gentry continued even as Virginia was eclipsed in population and wealth by Pennsylvania and New York. Its tobacco fields were all but exhausted, and were heavily dependent on slave labor. In the Civil War, Virginia had two great heroes, Robert E. Lee and Stonewall Jackson, who brilliantly fought for their state rather than the larger nation. Virginia's leadership class was impoverished and embittered by the Civil War, so much of which was fought on Virginia soil. Industrialization was haphazard. Railroads were constructed to ship cotton up from the South and coal east to the seaports. Textile mills were built in Southside towns and tobacco factories in Richmond. The giant Newport News Shipbuilding & Drydock Company was built by railroad magnate Collis Huntington. Politically, Virginia was ruled by local gentry who worshipped their revolutionary past and mourned their "Lost Cause" of the Confederacy. They were pessimists, looking not for economic growth but for stability, bent on maintaining Virginia's segregation and content with its second-class economy. County courthouse organizations were united in a political machine by Harry Byrd, who ran Virginia politics from 1925, when he was elected governor, to 1965, when he retired from the U.S. Senate. In national politics, this machine lost battles more often than Lee lost on the battlefield, and less gallantly. For years, the Byrd machine succeeded in keeping most vestiges of racial equality out of Virginia, to the point of closing public schools in Prince Edward County in the 1950s rather than obeying a federal court desegregation order.

This "massive resistance" collapsed in the late 1950s. Virginia's demographics were changing and its politics went through a quarter-century of flux. The many federal employees in the Northern Virginia suburbs of Washington, D.C. and the industrial Hampton Roads region around Norfolk and Newport News, plus the enfranchisement of blacks, provided a political base for liberal Democrats. In the years since, Virginia has undergone a demographic revolution. In 1970, its major metropolitan areas, as then defined, included only a minority of the state's residents: Northern Virginia had just 12%, Hampton Roads 17%, and metro Richmond 10%. The rest of Virginia—rural areas, small towns, and small industrial and textile-mill cities—had 61% of the state's population, and was solidly conservative. Most African-Americans didn't vote and the poll tax held down voting among whites. With less than half of Virginia's population, West Virginia cast more votes in 1960. Forty years later, in 2010, Virginia's population was 72% larger. Northern Virginia had spread out into once rural counties, some of which were the nation's fastest-growing exurbs in the 1990s and 2000s, and accounted for 33% of the state's population. Hampton Roads, growing out into swampy lands on either side of the James River, accounted for another 21%. Metropolitan Richmond expanded outward in every direction and accounted for 16% of the state's population. The traditional Virginia had shrunk geographically, limited to the Northern Neck, the two Eastern Shore counties, Southside Virginia, the Shenandoah Valley and the mountains of southwest Virginia.

Virginia's growth was accompanied by significant demographic change. Its population in 2010 was 19% black, not much changed over the years, but it was also 8% Hispanic and 5.5% Asian. Northern Virginia, which accounted for 55% of the 2000-10 population increase, now has large Hispanic populations in Fairfax County inside the Capital Beltway, around Dulles Airport and adjacent Loudoun County, and around Manassas and Dale City in Prince William County. It also

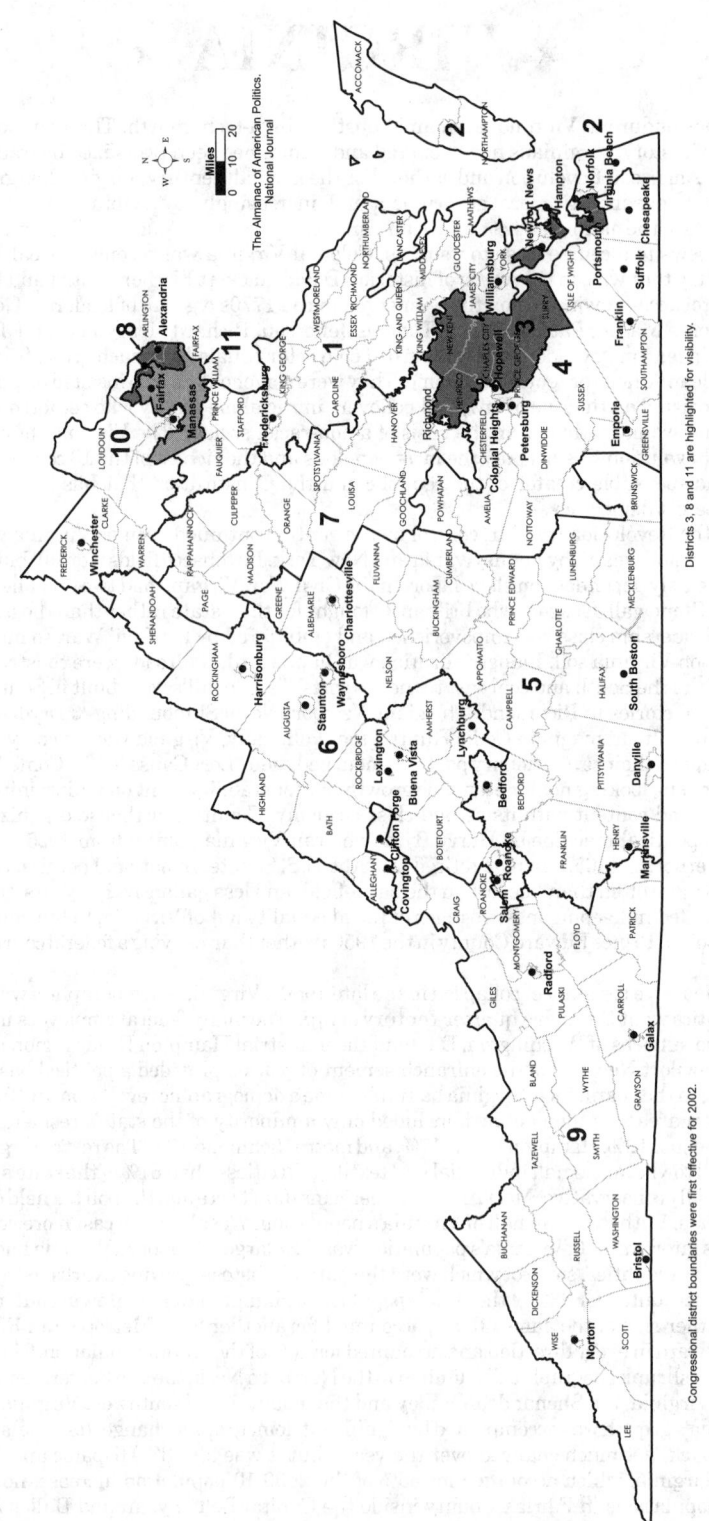

The Almanac of American Politics.
National Journal

Districts 3, 8 and 11 are highlighted for visibility.

Congressional district boundaries were first effective for 2002.

has large Asian concentrations outside the Beltway in Fairfax County and adjacent Loudoun County. Altogether, Fairfax County, whose years of rapid growth ended in the 1990s, was 17% Asian and 16% Hispanic in 2010. Loudoun County, one of the fastest growing counties in America in the 1990s and 2000s, was 15% Asian and 12% Hispanic.

Growth and change produced unstable politics. In the 1970s, conservatives who left the Democratic Party and ran as independents or Republicans held Democrats at bay. In the 1980s, three moderate Democrats were elected governor—Charles Robb in 1981, Gerald Baliles in 1985, and Douglas Wilder in 1989—who did not represent an attempt to impose a liberal agenda on an unwilling Virginia, but argued they could use government effectively to improve education and build the state's economy. Wilder's election was a national breakthrough, a successful attempt by an African-American politician to campaign and to govern on equal terms. His fiscal conservatism, which resulted in sharp spending cuts in the early 1990s, like his elegant manners and thick Richmond accent, echoed Virginia's elitist and libertarian tradition; his insistence on the rule of law helped him become the first elected mayor of Richmond in 60 years in 2004.

In the 1990s Virginia developed ideological politics along party lines, and Republicans made historic strides by winning majorities with traditional party platforms. George Allen was elected governor by a wide margin in 1993 as a Republican who believed in lower taxes, traditional cultural values, longer prison terms, and teaching basic skills. He combined confrontational issue positions with a sunny temperament. In the 1997 contest for governor (Virginia is the last state that bars its governors from running for re-election, another tradition that endures), Republican James Gilmore made his centerpiece issue the phasing-out of the property tax on automobiles and won a 56%-43% victory over Democrat Don Beyer. Republicans for the first time swept the top three statewide offices. In 1999, Gilmore led Republicans to legislative majorities in both chambers for the first time ever.

But the first decade of the 2000s belonged to the Democrats. The first Democratic winner was cell phone millionaire Mark Warner, who won the governorship in 2001 primarily due to an intensive 18-month campaign in rural Virginia, where he paid attention to the parts of the state not blessed by 1990s growth. Warner carried Northern Virginia and the Hampton Roads area only narrowly. But he also carried non-urban Virginia, which Republican George W. Bush had carried 56%-41% the year before. Warner's big success was persuading the legislature to raise taxes by a record amount in 2004. The Republican state Senate wanted to raise them even more, but a lot of arms had to be twisted to get the needed votes in the House of Delegates, also controlled by the GOP. The key impetus for raising taxes was the demand for more roads and mass transit in Northern Virginia and the Tidewater region. As it turned out, revenues poured in and produced a surplus. Warner left office with high ratings and, after considering a run for president in 2008, instead ran for Republican Sen. John Warner's open Senate seat and won in a 65%-34% landslide.

Warner's 2001 victory for governor was the first of several Democratic breakthroughs, fueled in large part by changes in the Northern Virginia electorate. Surges of Hispanic and Asian immigrants filled downscale neighborhoods inside the Capital Beltway, and singles apartment buildings went up in Arlington and Alexandria. Meanwhile, more conservative whites moved out to the exurbs. Young professionals moving into the suburbs, originally averse to higher taxes, embraced them as they languished for hours in rush hour traffic. And they were repelled by the Republicans' embrace of conservative rural values. Bush carried Northern Virginia in 2000, and then lost it four years later, 51%-48%; it was one of the few metropolitan areas in the nation where his vote fell off in 2004. That trend accelerated as Democrat Tim Kaine was elected governor in 2005, over Republican Jerry Kilgore, whose deep mountain accent and hard-line conservative stands were a tough sell in Northern Virginia.

In 2006, Allen was expected to win re-election to the Senate easily, and even contemplated a presidential campaign. But Democrat Jim Webb, a Navy secretary in the Reagan administration, campaigned against the Iraq war and carried Northern Virginia 57%-42% on his way to a 50%-49% statewide win. In 2008, Barack Obama became the first Democratic presidential candidate to carry Virginia since 1964, and he did so by his national average of 53%-46%. He carried Northern Virginia 59%-40% and Hampton Roads and metro Richmond by smaller margins. His campaign did brilliant work registering African-American voters all over the state, and new, young voters in Northern Virginia and in college towns. "Old Virginny is dead. We are a new and dynamic and exciting commonwealth," Kaine, an early Obama backer, proclaimed on election night. Obama installed him as Democratic National Committee chairman.

Virginia politics took a different turn in 2009, as the unpopularity of Obama's proposals among conservatives became apparent. Attorney General Bob McDonnell, elected in 2005 by just 323 votes over state Sen. Creigh Deeds, was the Republican nominee. Deeds won a three-way Democratic primary in June, but his campaign floundered afterwards. McDonnell deemphasized the crime and cultural issues he had worked on for years and ran as a jobs-creating candidate at a time when Virginia was hit fairly hard by the national recession. His low key demeanor and steady concentration on economic issues overshadowed issues the Democrats raised against him and he won a smashing 59%-41% victory, the biggest margin for any Virginia governor since the last big victory of the Byrd machine in 1961. In office, McDonnell was largely successful with the legislature in 2010, even though Democrats continued to have a narrow margin in the state Senate, and the state's economy, aided by the comparative prosperity of metro Washington, recovered smartly from the recession.

Population		Household Income		Work	
Pop. 2010:	8,001,024	Under $15k:	10.4%	Private:	72.2%
State rank:	12th	$15k to $50k:	31.2%	Government:	22.8%
Change since 2000:	Up 13.0%	$50k to $100k:	31.6%	Self-employed:	4.9%
Urban:	72.4%	$100k to $200k:	20.8%	Unemployment (3-yr. average):	3.9%
Rural:	27.6%	Over $200k:	6.1%	Poverty:	10.3%
Native of state:	50.4%	Median income:	$60,539	Blue collar:	19.2%
Not a citizen:	5.7%			White collar:	63.5%
Area size:	42,775 sq. mi.	**Home Value**		Khaki collar:	1.7%
		Under $100k:	13.5%	Other:	15.6%
Most populous cities		$100k to $300k:	43.8%		
Virginia Beach	437,994	$300k to $500k:	24.1%	**Age**	
Norfolk	242,803	$500k to $1 mil:	15.9%	Median age:	36.9 yrs.
Chesapeake	222,209	Over $1 million:	2.6%	More than 65 yrs:	11.9%
Arlington CDP	207,627	Median:	$260,100	Less than 18 yrs:	23.6%

Race/Ethnicity				Military Veterans		Registered Voters in 2010	
White:	64.8%	Language		% of Pop:	12.4%	No Party registration	
Black:	19.0%	English:	86.6%			Voter turnout:	2,189,841
Hispanic:	7.9%	Spanish:	6.0%	*Veterans by Period*		Turnout as % of	
Asian:	5.5%	Asian:	3.2%	WWII and before:	6.8%	voting age:	35.6%
Native Am.:	0.3%	Other European:	3.2%	Korea:	7.6%		
Hawaiian:	0.1%			Vietnam:	30.1%	**Legislature**	
Two+ races:	2.3%	**Education**		Gulf (pre-2001):	18.0%	Senate:	22 D 18 R
		H.S. grad:	86.1%	Gulf (post-2001):	15.9%	House of	39 D 59 R 2 I
Ancestry		College grad:	33.7%	Peace time:	21.6%	Delegates:	
German	10.7%	Grad degree:	13.9%				
English	9.9%						
Irish	9.2%						

Presidential politics   Long ignored in presidential politics, Virginia was a major battleground in 2008. In the first half of the 20th century it was part of the solid Democratic South. From 1952 to 1960, it obeyed the "golden silence" of Democratic Sen. Harry Byrd and voted Republican. It voted narrowly for Democrat Lyndon Johnson for president in 1964, and then voted Republican in the next 10 elections. But over time, the margins narrowed. Democrat Bill Clinton lost here by only 48%-46% in 1996. In 2000, Republican George W. Bush won 52%-44%. In 2004, Democrats, heartened by Mark Warner's election as governor in 2001, targeted the state early. John Kerry spent $1 million in advertising in the spring and early summer. But August polls showed Bush well ahead, and Virginia was dropped from the target list. Bush lost Northern Virginia 51%-48% and his statewide margin was reduced to 54%-45%, just 3 percentage points above his national average.

2008 Presidential Vote		
Barack Obama (D)	1,959,532	(53%)
John McCain (R)	1,725,005	(46%)

2008 Presidential Primary		
Barack Obama (D)	627,820	(64%)
Hillary Clinton (D)	349,766	(35%)

2008 Presidential Primary		
John McCain (R)	244,829	(50%)
Mike Huckabee (R)	199,003	(41%)

2004 Presidential Vote		
George W. Bush (R)	1,716,959	(54%)
John Kerry (D)	1,454,742	(45%)

In 2008, Democrat Barack Obama targeted Virginia from start to finish, with satisfying results. His organizing efforts for the Feb. 12 primary gave him a head start. He won the primary

64%-35% over Hillary Rodham Clinton. Still, Republicans had difficulty believing polls showing Obama leading throughout most of the summer and fall, but the polls proved accurate. Obama won the state 53%-46%, exactly at the national average, running 8 percentage points ahead of John Kerry's showing in 2004. Another way to look at it: Republican John McCain got 8,000 more votes than Bush did in 2004; Obama got almost 505,000 more votes than Kerry.

In Northern Virginia, the Obama campaign registered immigrants and young singles and carried the region 59%-40%. In Hampton Roads and metro Richmond, there was more emphasis on registering African-Americans, and turnout rose 19% and 20%, way ahead of population growth. Obama ran 10 percentage points ahead of Kerry in Hampton Roads, winning 56%-44%, and 9 points ahead of Kerry in metro Richmond, winning an area assumed to be staunchly Republican, 53%-46%. In the rest of the state, Obama ran only 5 percentage points ahead of Kerry. The county returns showed sharp improvement in areas with many African-Americans. The Obama campaign opened offices and canvassed in counties where no one had ever seen a Democratic operation before. But that was not effective everywhere. In the Shenandoah Valley, where there are few blacks, he ran only slightly ahead of Kerry, and in southwest Virginia, where there are almost none, turnout was down and Obama's percentages were lower than Kerry's, as was the case in adjacent Appalachian areas of West Virginia, Kentucky and Tennessee. The impact of Obama's organization was apparent from the exit poll showing that 22% of voters were contacted by his campaign, compared to 10% contacted by McCain's. Obama did not triumph everywhere. He lost non-college whites 66%-32% and young whites 56%-42%. But white Democrats stuck with him 86%-14%. Quite clearly the state that elected a black governor 19 years earlier was not averse to electing a black president.

Virginia has not had much of a tradition of presidential primaries, but that changed in 2008 as well. Virginia did hold presidential primaries on the original Super Tuesday in March 1988, when it voted for Republican George H.W. Bush and Democrat Jesse Jackson, but it then switched back to choosing delegates at state conventions. Republicans held a primary in 2000 in which George W. Bush beat McCain 53%-44%. In 2004, Virginia held its presidential primary in February in order to gain the attention of presidential candidates and the national media. But Wesley Clark concentrated on Tennessee and John Edwards split his time between Tennessee and southwest Virginia. They evidently concluded that Kerry had an insuperable lead in Northern Virginia. As it turned out, Kerry carried every part of the state and won 52% of the vote, to 27% for Edwards and 9% for Clark.

For 2008, Virginia scheduled primaries for Feb. 12, one week after Super Tuesday. Many people had expected both nominations to be settled by then, but the Democratic nomination was still very much in play and the Republican nomination, though obviously headed to McCain, was still being contested by Mike Huckabee. Obama showed his mettle in this contest, out-organizing the Clinton campaign and, with his big victories the same day in Maryland and the District of Columbia, generating an enthusiasm that proved to be contagious for the rest of the month, as he won 11 straight February contests. Turnout was 986,000, more than double the 396,000 in 2004. Obama won 64%-35%, his biggest percentage in any primary except for those in the District of Columbia (75%), Georgia (66%) and Illinois (65%). Obama carried Northern Virginia 61%-39%, running well in upscale areas as usual. But he also won over 70% of the vote in Hampton Roads and metro Richmond, reflecting a major effort at turning out black voters. He even prevailed 54%-45% in the rest of the state. Clinton carried only one of the 11 congressional districts, the "Fighting 9th" in southwest Virginia.

The Republican contest attracted less attention and, significantly in a state with no party registration, only about half as many voters, 489,000. McCain beat Mike Huckabee 50%-41%. Most of McCain's margin came from Northern Virginia, where he won 60% of the votes. He got 49% in Hampton Roads, 52% in metro Richmond and only 41% in the rest of the state, while Huckabee carried almost everything west of the big metro areas. McCain's high mark was in Alexandria, just outside Washington, where he got 70% of the vote. Huckabee's was in Campbell County, just outside of Lynchburg and within hailing distance of the late Rev. Jerry Falwell's Liberty University, where he got 71% of the vote.

Congressional districting

112th Congress Lineup	
8 R	3 D
111th Congress Lineup	
6 D	5 R

With control of both houses of the Virginia legislature in 1999 and with Jim Gilmore as governor, Republicans controlled the redistricting process in 2001 for the first time ever. Legislators promptly drew new lines, which made relatively minimal changes. They moved some black precincts from the 4th District to the 3rd and increased its black majority, while making the 4th more GOP-secure. Three Northern Virginia incumbents, two Republicans and one Democrat, were all strengthened. They made the 9th District, held for many years by Democrat Rick Boucher, a little more Republican, but it would have been difficult to do otherwise without drawing a geographical monstrosity. Bobby Scott, of the black-majority 3rd District, raised questions about the 3rd and 4th District lines, but the U.S. Justice Department approved the plan.

Despite above national average population growth, Virginia did not gain a seat in the reapportionment following the 2010 census. Efforts to promote non-political congressional redistricting foundered, as the Republican-controlled House of Delegates rejected such a proposal in 2007 and 2009. And legislators in early 2011 seemed to be ignoring the bipartisan advisory commission appointed by Gov. Bob McDonnell. Control is split between the parties: Republicans won a 59-39 majority in the House of Delegates in 2009, but Democrats won a 21-19 majority in the state Senate in 2007, which has four-year terms.

Democrats won a majority of U.S. House seats in 2008, but Republicans recaptured the 2nd and 5th district seats in 2010 and upset 28-year incumbent Rick Boucher in the "Fighting 9th." That left Republicans with an 8-3 advantage in the delegation, and in early 2011, all of the House incumbents agreed on a plan which would strengthen or protect each of them. The legislature, preoccupied with the intricacies of redrawing the boundaries of their own districts after a decade of major population shifts, seemed inclined to accept the House delegation's incumbent-protection plan or some close variant of it.

Governor

Bob McDonnell (R)

Elected 2009, term expires Jan. 2014, 1st term; b. June 15, 1954, Philadelphia, PA; home, Henrico County (outside Richmond); U. of Notre Dame, B.A. 1976; Boston University, M.B.A. 1980; Regent University, M.A., J.D. 1989; Catholic; married (Maureen McDonnell); 5 children.

Military Career: Army, 1976-81

Elected Office: VA House of Delegates, 1992-2006; VA attorney general, 2006-09

Professional Career: Manager, American Hospital Supply; sales manager, *The Virginian-Pilot*; practicing attorney, 1989-2006

Office: Patrick Henry Building, Third Floor, 1111 E. Broad St., Richmond, 23219, 804-786-2211; Fax: 804-371-6351; Web site: www.governor.virginia.gov.

Election Results

2009 general	Bob McDonnell (R)	1,163,523	(59%)
	Creigh Deeds (D)	818,950	(41%)
2009 primary	Bob McDonnell (R)	unopposed	

Bob McDonnell, a Republican, was elected governor of Virginia in November 2009 by the widest margin of any gubernatorial candidate of either party in the state since 1961. The son of an Air Force officer, McDonnell grew up near Mount Vernon in Fairfax County. He attended Catholic schools and was an altar boy at Sunday Mass. Although small for football, he was team captain for Bishop Ireton High School, playing wide receiver and defensive back. He graduated from the University of Notre Dame in 1976, with a degree in business management. That same year, he married a Redskins football team cheerleader from McLean, Va., and went on active duty in the Army, eventually rising to lieutenant colonel. He was stationed in Germany, where he ran the medical clinic for the 2nd Armored Division.

After he retired from active duty, McDonnell built a career as a manager with American Hospital Supply Corp., while he and Maureen McDonnell raised five children. He also pursued degrees in law and public policy at Christian Broadcasting Network University (now Regent University) in Virginia Beach, which was founded by televangelist and 1988 presidential candidate Pat Robertson. He also served a stint as an intern with the Republican Policy Committee in the U.S. House. In 1989, he wrote a public policy thesis that would become an issue in his gubernatorial campaign. In it, he argued that welfare programs, liberal court decisions and women entering the workforce in large numbers had undermined the American family. Federal support for child care programs, McDonnell wrote, subsidized "a dynamic trend of working women and feminists that is ultimately detrimental to the family by entrenching a status quo of non-parental primary nurture of children."

In 1989, after receiving his degrees, he worked as an assistant commonwealth's attorney in Virginia Beach, the second largest jurisdiction (after his native Fairfax County) in Virginia. In 1991, he ran for a seat in the House of Delegates from the area. Rallying social conservatives through his university network, McDonnell took on a 20-year Democratic incumbent and, with an effective grassroots effort, won. In the legislature, McDonnell pushed for curbs on abortion rights and helped shepherd to passage then-Republican Gov. George Allen's welfare reform, which restricted benefits to two years. He also tried but failed to pass tax changes that rewarded traditional families. On other issues, he opposed government regulation of financial markets and pushed to reform the state's drunk-driving statute. Although his ideology was to the far right of the spectrum, McDonnell, personally gracious and respectful in style, grew in popularity with colleagues and rose to become the assistant majority leader.

With his eye on a statewide run, McDonnell developed a knack for appearing to be a moderate without betraying his deeply held conservative views. He toned down his rhetoric and focused on issues that appealed to moderate and independent voters, or, as he called it, "policies that keep Virginia safe, strong and prosperous."

In 2005, he ran for Virginia attorney general. After easily winning the GOP nomination in June, he faced Democratic state Sen. Creigh Deeds, from Bath County in the mountains west of the Shenandoah Valley. Deeds had a reputation as a moderate and had the advantage of running on the same ticket as former Richmond Mayor Tim Kaine, who was elected governor 52%-46%. But McDonnell won, albeit narrowly—by just 323 votes, or 49.96%-49.95%. McDonnell lost Northern Virginia 56%-44%, but he carried the part of the state beyond the three major metro areas 54%-46%. He also carried his home area of Hampton Roads 50.0%-49.8% and metro Richmond 53%-47%, running 7% and 9% ahead of Republican gubernatorial candidate Jerry Kilgore there.

As attorney general, McDonnell won enactment of a 25-year mandatory minimum sentence for violent child sex predators, created an up-to-date sex offender registry and increased penalties for drug dealing. He also weighed in on the U.S. Supreme Court review of Washington D.C.'s ban on handguns, supporting a legal brief filed with the high court that argued the law should be overturned as an infringement on the Second Amendment right to bear arms, which it ultimately was.

McDonnell set out to run for governor in 2009. He resigned as attorney general and had no competition for the GOP nomination. Meanwhile, Democrats had a fierce primary battle between Deeds, McDonnell's 2005 opponent, and two other hopefuls: former Democratic National Chairman Terry McAuliffe and Alexandria Delegate Brian Moran, brother of 8th District Rep. Jim Moran. McAuliffe called on his old patron Bill Clinton and raised more money, but a late endorsement by *The Washington Post* enabled Deeds to win the primary with 50% of the vote, to 26% for McAuliffe and 24% for Moran.

In the general election campaign, Deeds seized on McDonnell's master's thesis to raise doubts about him among women and independent voters and *The Post* ran several stories on the topic. McDonnell stayed focused on his themes of creating jobs, improving transportation (in part by selling Virginia's state-owned liquor stores to raise revenue) and avoiding tax increases by creating an offshore oil-drilling industry in Virginia. He also carefully avoided divisive cultural issues, and he aggressively reached out to Asian and Hispanic voters in Northern Virginia. The Deeds campaign, meanwhile, seemed to be adrift, and at one point, the candidate suggested he would consider raising taxes to pay for road improvements. McDonnell stood foursquare against tax increases.

McDonnell raised over $21 million to Deeds' $16 million, some of which he spent on the primary race. President Barack Obama campaigned for Deeds, helped him raise money and lent him organizational help. Still, McDonnell won 59% to 41%. He carried Northern Virginia 53%-47%, Hampton Roads 56%-44%, metro Richmond 60%-40%, and the rest of the state by 65%. He lost only in Deeds' home area of Bath County, in some black-majority counties and cities, in college towns (Charlottesville, Lexington, and Williamsburg) and in the Washington suburbs of Arlington, Alexandria and Falls Church.

Republican Bill Bolling was re-elected lieutenant governor 57%-43%, and Republican Ken Cuccinelli was elected attorney general 58%-42%. Republicans gained six seats in the House of Delegates.

At the start of his term, McDonnell faced a projected two-year budget deficit of $4.2 billion. But he persuaded the legislature to balance the budget with significant spending cuts and no tax increases, and in July 2010, he announced that the state had a $220 million revenue surplus. However, the state also committed to borrowing $3 billion for transportation projects under a McDonnell proposal. Another of his initiatives sought to require state employees to contribute part of their salaries to the state pension fund. Virginia is one of four states without such a requirement.

He outlined an ambitious program to spur economic development and to boost education. To spur job creation, he called for doubling spending on incentives for new businesses and increasing funding to promote tourism and the wine and film industries. McDonnell also sought to promote offshore oil drilling in Virginia's Atlantic waters, but was frustrated when the Obama administration banned offshore drilling after the massive BP oil spill in the Gulf of Mexico in spring 2010. On education, he called for expansion of the number of charter schools and got a compromise bill through the Democratic state Senate.

McDonnell took up the cause against the Obama administration's health care overhaul of 2010, signing a bill that prohibited Virginians from being forced to purchase health insurance. The governor also supported Attorney General Cuccinelli's lawsuit challenging the constitutionality of the federal health care legislation. But at the same time, McDonnell accelerated preparation for setting up a state health insurance exchange as encouraged by the act. He also signed a bill requiring abortion clinics to meet the same standards as hospitals, and he demanded that agencies use the E-Verify system to check the immigration status of job applicants.

A low point in his first term was McDonnell's decision in April 2010 to issue a proclamation of Confederate History Month that made no mention of slavery. He then publicly apologized.

Senior Senator

Jim Webb (D)

Elected 2006, term expires 2012, 1st term; b. Feb. 9, 1946, St. Joseph, MO; home, Arlington; U.S. Naval Academy, B.S. 1968, Georgetown U., J.D. 1975; Christian; married (Hong Le); 6 children.

Military Career: Marine Corps, 1968-72 (Vietnam).

Professional Career: Writer/journalist; Counsel, U.S. House Cmte. on Veterans' Affairs, 1977-81; Asst. sec. of defense for Reserve Affairs, 1984-87; U.S. Navy secy., 1987-88.

DC Office: 248 RSOB, 20510, 202-224-4024; Fax: 202-228-6363; Web site: webb.senate.gov.

State Offices: Arlington, 703-807-0581; Danville, 434-792-0976; Norton, 276-679-4925; Richmond, 804-771-2221; Roanoke, 540-772-4236; Virginia Beach, 757-518-1674.

Committees: *Armed Services:* Personnel (Chmn); Readiness & Management Support; Seapower. *Foreign Relations:* African Affairs; East Asian & Pacific Affairs (Chmn); European Affairs; Western Hemisphere, Peace Corps & Global Narcotics Affairs. *Joint Economic Committee. Veterans' Affairs.*

Group Ratings

	ACLU	ACU	ADA	CFG	AFS	FRC	LCV	ITIC	NTU	COC
2010	87	13	85	8	94	0	57	67	21	36
2009	–	20	100	10	91	–	100	–	13	43

National Journal Ratings

	2010 LIB — 2010 CONS		2009 LIB — 2009 CONS	
Economic	47%	— 52%	46%	— 53%
Social	51%	— 47%	44%	— 55%
Foreign	47%	— 0%	49%	— 45%
Composite	58%	— 42%	48%	— 52%

Key Votes of the 111th Congress

1. Overturn Ledbetter	Y	5. Pass health care bill	Y	9. Ratify New START	Y
2. Pass $787 billion stimulus	Y	6. Regulate financial firms	Y	10. Confirm Elena Kagan	Y
3. Repeal DC gun laws	Y	7. Pass tax cuts for some	N	11. Stop EPA climate regs	N
4. Confirm Sonia Sotomayor	Y	8. Legalize immigrants' kids	Y	12. Repeal don't ask, tell	Y

Election Results

2006 general	Jim Webb (D)	1,175,606	(50%)	($8,529,224)
	George Allen (R)	1,166,277	(49%)	($16,850,512)
2006 primary	Jim Webb (D)	83,298	(53%)	
	Harris Miller (D)	72,486	(47%)	

Democrat Jim Webb, Virginia's senior senator, was elected to the Senate in 2006. He has established himself as a candid and independent voice on military matters as well as on other issues. Webb's seat comes open in 2012. He announced on Feb. 9, 2011 that he will not seek a second term.

Of Scots-Irish descent, Webb is the son of an Air Force colonel who enlisted after Pearl Harbor. The family moved at least a dozen times when he was a child. He enrolled in the University of

Southern California, and then a year later in the U.S. Naval Academy. He wanted to become a writer. But he was also a combative young man, and a boxing match in 1967 with future Iran-contra operative Oliver North at Annapolis became the subject of legend (North won). He graduated in 1968, and in 1969, went into combat in Vietnam as a Marine lieutenant. He commanded 170 men and earned the Navy Cross, a Silver Star and two Purple Hearts. He suffered wounds that left him with shrapnel in his body and a limp—and forced him to retire from active duty. He was one of the subjects of Robert Timberg's moving 1995 book, *The Nightingale's Song*. Webb entered Georgetown Law School in 1972 and was appalled by his antiwar schoolmates, whom he believed had shirked duty and then considered themselves morally superior because of their opposition to the war. He started writing, and his respected novel about Vietnam, *Fields of Fire*, was published in 1978. He has since written five other novels, a 2004 history-cum-memoir, *Born Fighting: How the Scots-Irish Shaped America*, and his 2008 memoir-cum-policy-book *A Time to Fight: Reclaiming a Fair and Just America*.

In the years after *Fields of Fire*, Webb wrote movie scripts and many articles. In the process, he made some controversial public statements. He praised Confederate heroes, attacked feminists and Hollywood, academics and the news media. In 1979, he wrote an article for *Washingtonian* magazine criticizing the new policy on women in the military. "I have never met a woman, including the dozens of female midshipmen I encountered during my recent semester as a professor at the Naval Academy, whom I would trust to provide those men with combat leadership." The Navy banned him from speaking at the academy. He helped lead the fights against Maya Lin's Vietnam War memorial and for an additional sculpture depicting soldiers. Disgusted with President Jimmy Carter's amnesty for draft law violators, he left the Democratic Party and became a Republican, and in 1980, supported Ronald Reagan for president. For 20 years he refused to shake the hand of Massachusetts Sen. John Kerry, another Vietnam War hero who criticized the war effort on his return from combat. In 1984, Webb won an Emmy for his coverage for PBS' *NewsHour* of the 1983 barracks bombing that killed 241 Marines in Lebanon. In 1987, President Reagan appointed him secretary of the Navy. He issued a directive that performance in combat be given greater weight in promotions, which was criticized by advocates of equality for women in the military. Webb publicly complained about budget cuts imposed by Congress, which angered Defense Secretary Frank Carlucci. Webb resigned in 1988, saying, "It's no secret that I'm not a person who wears a bridle well."

Nor did he wear a political label well. In the late 1980s and early 1990s, both major parties tried to recruit him to run for the Senate, but he turned them down. In 1994, he backed Democratic Sen. Charles Robb against his one-time sparring partner North, who lost the contest. In 2000, he backed Republican George Allen against Robb, arguing that Robb had not done enough oversight of his party's administration. He wrote an article in *The Wall Street Journal* in 2000 attacking racial quotas and preferences as "a permeating state-sponsored racism that is as odious as the Jim Crow laws it sought to countermand." Once the Republicans were in power, he began thinking more like a Democrat. His research for *Born Fighting* convinced him that Scots-Irish people of modest means who willingly served in the military might better be served by the Democrats, and he foresaw a coalition of Scots-Irish and African-Americans. "You measure the health of a society not at its apex, but at its base," he said. In 2002, Webb opposed military action in Iraq, asserting that it would destabilize the region and mire the United States in a long occupation. His opposition continued even as his son dropped out of Penn State University to join the Marines. In the 2004 presidential contest, despite his feelings about Kerry, Webb supported Kerry over George W. Bush. The "last straw for me" in this political odyssey was the response to Hurricane Katrina, he said, which reminded him how people of little means were treated.

So in 2006, Webb found himself running as a Democrat against Allen, whom he had supported six years before. Webb was encouraged to run by Kerry and by Democratic Senatorial Campaign Committee Chairman Charles Schumer, D-N.Y., who saw in Webb an opportunity to cut into the conservative vote. Webb announced his candidacy on March 7, 2006, late in the season for such things. Noting that his son was being deployed to Iraq, he reiterated his opposition to military action there. At the same time, he opposed a precipitous withdrawal. On cultural issues, he said, "My belief is that the power of government stops at the front door unless there is a compelling reason for it to come inside." He supported abortion rights and civil unions, and he argued that racial preferences should be limited to African-Americans, because of their unique heritage, and not accorded to women or other ethnic groups. He strongly opposed new gun control laws, noting that his father had given him his first gun when he was eight and that he had done the same with his son.

Webb's primary competition was Harris Miller, the head of the Information Technology Association of America. Miller outspent Webb 3-to-1. Prominent African-Americans, nettled by Webb's statements on racial preferences, supported Miller, as did women military veterans. Webb was not a natural candidate, reluctant to handshake his way across a room, stiff in his public speeches. "I don't wake up in the morning wanting to be a U.S. senator. I wake up every morning very concerned about the country," he grumbled. His prime asset turned out to be support from antiwar activists, especially bloggers, who argued that he was the only candidate who could beat Allen. He won the light turnout event 53%-47%.

Webb had no money left after the primary. Meanwhile, Allen began the contest on a high note. He raised $7.5 million and his popularity put him on the list of possible Republican presidential contenders for 2008. Allen ultimately outspent Webb 2-to-1. But money was not as decisive as an incident that unfolded on the campaign trail for Allen. On Aug. 11, Allen was speaking in Breaks, Va., in Buchanan County, near the Kentucky border. He pointed at S.R. Sidarth, a 20-year-old student of Indian descent, who had been following him around for the Webb campaign, taping everything he said. "This fellow over here," Allen said, "with the yellow shirt, Macaca or whatever his name is, he's with my opponent. ... Let's give a welcome to Macaca here. Welcome to America, and welcome to the real world of Virginia." The exchange exploded on YouTube, and *The Washington Post* ran several front-page stories on the incident. The subtext was that "macaca" was a racial epithet, evidence that Allen was a bigot. Allen's strange word choice came against the backdrop of an unflattering profile in *The New Republic* in 2006, which said Allen had hung a Confederate flag on his wall as a young lawyer and had used the "n-word" while a student. Former schoolmates of Allen's countered this barrage of negative publicity by saying they had never heard Allen use such language or show bigotry in any way.

Allen had expected to run a campaign based on taxes and support of the military, but he was now on the defensive. Webb was running closely behind or even with Allen in the polls by September. Allen went on the attack with an ad with quotes from Webb's 1979 *Washingtonian* article on women in the military and showing three female academy graduates criticizing Webb. Another Allen ad claimed that Webb wanted to raise taxes on married couples and families, costing the average Virginia family $2,000. Webb rebutted with an ad saying that Allen wanted to raise taxes on retirement savings, make college more expensive and give billions in tax cuts to oil companies. To charges that he was bigoted, Allen pointed to his pilgrimages to civil rights sites and to the work he had done to aid historically black colleges and universities. And Allen's campaign attacked Webb for the sexually racy passages in some of his novels.

This was one of the two closest Senate races in the nation, and the one which, when the result became clear two days after the election, gave the Senate majority to the Democrats. Webb won by 9,000 votes, 49.6%-49.2%. His victory was almost entirely due to Northern Virginia. Webb carried Hampton Roads 52%-46%, almost the same as Robb's 52%-48% there two years before. In the half of the state outside the two big metro areas, Allen won 55%-44%, down just slightly from his 56%-44% in 2000. Northern Virginia was a different story. Webb carried it 57%-42%. Robb's popular vote margin in the area had been 21,000. Webb's was 110,000, five times larger.

National Democrats were ecstatic to win a Virginia Senate seat but also curious as to what kind of Democrat Webb would be. Addressing the concerns, Webb said, "There are going to be times when I've got some strong ideas, but I'm not looking to simply be a renegade." He proved to be a fairly loyal vote for the party, especially on major legislation. There were a few exceptions: He voted in 2008 against permitting lawsuits against companies that participated in the Bush administration's warrantless wiretapping program. He also joined most Republicans in 2009 on voting to repeal most of the District of Columbia's gun control laws. He accused President Barack Obama of overreacting to the massive BP oil spill disaster in the Gulf in spring 2010 and called for more offshore drilling off the Atlantic coast.

Webb drew publicity for taking up a new and unglamorous cause—reforming the criminal justice system. He called in 2009 for creating a national commission to examine the discrepancy between the United States' large prison population and continued high crime. "We can be smarter about whom we incarcerate, improve public safety outcomes, make better use of taxpayer dollars and bring greater fairness to our justice system," he said. The measure passed the House and the Senate Judiciary Committee but was blocked from a final Senate vote in the 111th Congress (2009-10); he reintroduced it in February 2011.

On defense issues, he played antagonist to the Bush administration on the Iraq war. One incident in particular drew notice. When Webb attended a reception at the White House a few days after his election, Bush approached and asked about his son in Iraq: "How's your boy?" Webb responded, "I'd like to get them out of Iraq, Mr. President." "That's not what I asked you," said the president. "How's your boy?" "That's between me and my boy, Mr. President," Webb starchily replied. In January 2007, he called Bush "a failed president." And in April of that year, Webb sharply criticized Pentagon plans to extend troop tours in Iraq from 12 months to 15 months. With support from fellow Virginia Sen. John Warner, a Republican, Webb won passage of an amendment creating an independent commission to investigate wartime contracting in Iraq, and was angry when Bush refused to abide by it, saying it threatened executive authority.

In 2008, Webb won passage of a modified version of his new GI Bill of Rights, which paid for four years of college tuition for veterans with three years of service. It was signed into law as part of a military spending bill, a considerable achievement for a second-year senator. The victory came despite the opposition of Arizona Sen. John McCain, who backed an alternative. McCain claimed that his fellow veteran of Vietnam was trying to bully him into supporting the bill without giving him adequate time to examine it. But Webb, with characteristic bluntness, dismissed McCain's willingness to negotiate the details: "He's so full of it," he said of the Arizonan.

With Obama in the White House, Webb was a largely supportive voice on his conduct of the war in Afghanistan, though he called on the administration in December 2009 to clarify "how it defines success and how we reach an end point." A year later, he also backed repeal of the "don't ask, don't tell" policy allowing openly gay service members after getting assurances that the repeal could be sequenced in a way to protect cohesion in small military units. Webb did express strong misgivings about U.S. military involvement in Libya after anti-government insurgents tried to topple dictator Moammar Gadhafi. "We know we don't like the Gadhafi regime, but we do not have a clear picture of who the opposition movement really is," he told MSNBC in March 2011.

On a defense matter of local concern, Webb accused the Pentagon in September 2010 of "stonewalling" in providing a cost benefit analysis of plans announced by Defense Secretary Robert Gates to close the Joint Forces Command in Norfolk, Va. But he subsequently said his concerns about the lack of consultation had been met and that many of the command's most important functions would be preserved.

Webb weighed in on other issues. He co-sponsored bills giving technological grants to historically black colleges and universities and providing schools with many foreign students a one-year grace period for meeting the requirements of the 2001 No Child Left Behind act, which tied federal funding to student performance on tests. His amendment to the Senate's immigration bill to reduce the number of illegal immigrants eligible for eventual citizenship from 12 million to 4 million was opposed by the bill's sponsors and defeated 79-18. None of that got as much attention as a bizarre incident in March 2007, when Webb's top aide was arrested for attempting to carry a loaded handgun into a Senate office building. A month later, the charges were dropped. Webb later acknowledged that the gun was his and said that he often carried a gun to protect himself and his family.

Webb caused a minor stir in political circles when he gave the keynote speech at the October 2007 Jefferson-Jackson Day dinner in New Hampshire, an indication that he might have aspirations beyond the Senate. But it was clear he was uncomfortable with the elaborate niceties of politicking as well as the public spotlight. The Senate, he wrote in *A Time to Fight,* is "an odd kingdom with 100 fiercely protected fiefdoms. No, let me amend that, as they say in this place. In terms of volatility, behind all of its courtesies, the United States Senate is composed of 100 scorpions in a jar. And one should be very careful in deciding how and when to shake that jar." He was briefly mentioned as a potential running mate for Obama in 2008, as Democrats sought a national security counterweight to McCain, the GOP nominee. But Webb took himself out of the running.

Junior Senator

Mark Warner (D)

Elected 2008, term expires 2014, 1st term; b. Dec. 15, 1954, Indianapolis, IN; home, Alexandria; George Washington U., B.A. 1977; Harvard U., J.D. 1980; Presbyterian; married (Lisa Collis); 3 children.

Elected Office: VA gov., 2002-06.

Professional Career: Fundraiser, DNC, 1980-82; Venture capitalist, 1982-89; Mng. dir., Columbia Capital Corp., 1989-2001; Chairman, VA Democratic Party, 1993-95.

DC Office: 459A RSOB, 20510, 202-224-2023; Fax: 202-224-6295; Web site: warner.senate.gov.

State Offices: Abingdon, 276-628-8158; Norfolk, 757-441-3079; Richmond, 804-775-2314; Roanoke, 540-857-2676; Vienna, 703-442-0670.

Committees: *Banking, Housing & Urban Affairs:* Economic Policy; Securities, Insurance & Investment; Security & International Trade & Finance (Chmn). *Budget. Commerce, Science & Transportation:* Aviation Operations, Safety & Security; Communications, Technology & the Internet; Competitiveness, Innovation & Export Promotion; Oceans, Atmosphere, Fisheries & Coast Guard; Science & Space; Surface Transportation & Merchant Marine Infrastructure, Safety & Security. *Intelligence (Select). Joint Economic Committee. Rules & Administration.*

Group Ratings

	ACLU	ACU	ADA	CFG	AFS	FRC	LCV	ITIC	NTU	COC
2010	80	8	80	10	94	4	86	67	19	36
2009	–	24	95	13	100	–	100	–	11	43

National Journal Ratings

	2010 LIB	—	2010 CONS		2009 LIB	—	2009 CONS
Economic	53%	—	46%		56%	—	43%
Social	54%	—	43%		60%	—	39%
Foreign	41%	—	53%		55%	—	0%
Composite	51%	—	49%		65%	—	35%

Key Votes of the 111th Congress

1. Overturn Ledbetter	Y	5. Pass health care bill	Y	9. Ratify New START	Y
2. Pass $787 billion stimulus	Y	6. Regulate financial firms	Y	10. Confirm Elena Kagan	Y
3. Repeal DC gun laws	Y	7. Pass tax cuts for some	Y	11. Stop EPA climate regs	N
4. Confirm Sonia Sotomayor	Y	8. Legalize immigrants' kids	Y	12. Repeal don't ask, tell	Y

Election Results

2008 general	Mark Warner (D)	2,369,327	(65%)	($13,663,049)
	James Gilmore (R)	1,228,830	(34%)	($2,777,933)
2008 primary	Mark Warner (D)	unopposed		

Prior Winning Percentages: Governor: 2001 (52%)

Democrat Mark Warner, a former Virginia governor, was elected U.S. senator in 2008. He is considered one of his party's fast-rising stars, having found a way for Democrats to make inroads among Southern voters.

Warner was born in Indianapolis, where his father was a safety evaluator for Aetna Life & Casualty Inc. and his mother stayed at home with their two children. The family moved to Vernon, Conn., when Warner was in the eighth grade. He later recalled that he was influenced by a social studies teacher who encouraged his students to pay attention to the turbulent social change unfolding in the late 1960s. Warner told *The Christian Science Monitor*, "The world was transforming around the whole notion that you could make change. But I wasn't out marching because I was too young, and besides, my parents would have killed me."

He graduated from George Washington University, the first college graduate in his family, and from Harvard Law School. Although he has emphasized his business experience in his campaigns, his first love seems to have been politics. After law school, he worked in fundraising for the Democratic National Committee and in 1989, managed Douglas Wilder's successful campaign to become Virginia's first African-American governor. His business success in fact grew out of his political contacts. While working for the DNC, Warner met Rep. Tom McMillen, a Maryland Democrat, who told him about the potential of cell phone markets just as the Reagan administration was about to award 1,500 free licenses for metropolitan markets. Warner cobbled together investor groups and packaged their applications in exchange for a fee and a 5% ownership stake if they received the licenses. The best known of these ventures was Nextel, and Warner quickly became a wealthy man. His net worth in 2009 was estimated at $174 million, putting him among the richest members of Congress.

But politics was always on Warner's mind. From 1993 to 1995, he was the Virginia Democratic chairman. In 1996, he ran against Republican Sen. John Warner in what seemed a quixotic race: the senior Warner, elected narrowly in 1978, had won re-election in a landslide in 1984 and had no Democratic opponent in 1990. But the incumbent had antagonized conservatives by refusing to endorse Republican nominee Oliver North in his 1994 race against Democratic Sen. Charles Robb and by taking liberal stands on some cultural issues. Mark Warner pitched his campaign not to his home turf in Northern Virginia but to the Shenandoah Valley and southwest Virginia, where North had done well. He carried southwest Virginia and lost the part of the state outside the three big metropolitan areas by only 51%-49%, a considerable achievement for a Democrat. But John Warner's strength among moderates enabled him to carry Northern Virginia 55%-45%, and to carry Tidewater and metropolitan Richmond with smaller majorities. The result was a 52%-47% win for John Warner, but certainly not an end to upstart Mark Warner's political career.

In the late 1990s, Mark Warner put millions of dollars into philanthropic efforts and set up four regional business investment funds in southwest Virginia, Southside Virginia, Richmond and Tidewater. By 1999, he had an eye on running for governor in 2001 as an entrepreneur who could bring savvy business methods to government. He picked a good year. Incumbent Republican Gov. Jim Gilmore had succeeded in helping to elect Republican majorities in both houses of the legislature, but then battled with them over the budget. Gilmore wanted to fulfill his 1997 promise to cut the state's automobile tax, but revenues were coming in under projections. Republicans had a primary battle in 2001 between Lt. Gov. John Hager and former Attorney General Mark Earley. Earley won but had little money and no clear campaign strategy. Warner ultimately spent $5 million of his own money on the campaign, but used his fundraising skills to raise more in Virginia and around the nation.

Warner lived in a mansion in Old Town Alexandria, but avoided being typecast as an urban liberal. He called himself a fiscal conservative and pledged not to raise the income or sales taxes. Responding to complaints from traffic-choked Northern Virginia and Tidewater, he called for regional referenda on local sales tax increases for transportation. This pleased business interests and local legislators who feared congestion would stop growth, and it propitiated some tax opponents who felt they would get a chance to vote no. He opposed any new gun control laws and wooed the National Rifle Association, which remained neutral. Warner ran ads featuring old pickup trucks and bluegrass music, and he sponsored a NASCAR race truck. He traveled to all parts of rural Virginia, much as Wilder had in 1989, to show that he was in touch with everyday folks and to remind them of his investment funds and philanthropic initiatives. In October, Earley came out against the regional referenda, and he ran ads on taxes and abortion rights. But Warner had inoculated himself on taxes and Earley's opposition to abortion put off some suburban Republicans.

Warner won, but not resoundingly, by 52%-47%, a reversal of the numbers in the 1996 Senate race. He carried all major regions of the state, albeit by narrow margins. And he attracted notice from national Democrats for winning a Southern state through business-friendly, fiscally responsible policies along with cultural conservatism—a combination Warner dubbed "radical centrism."

Once in office, Warner got the legislature to approve transportation tax referenda in Northern Virginia and Tidewater, but the House of Delegates rejected his education initiative in 2002. As a budget shortfall grew, Warner cut $858 million in spending and laid off 1,800 state employees. In November 2003, after the legislative elections and when Virginia seemed to be in danger of losing its AAA bond rating, Warner presented his new fiscal plan: a $1 billion tax increase, with increases in the income, sales and cigarette taxes, and tax reductions for those with low incomes and in the car and food taxes. He argued that state government needed the revenue and that under his plan, 65% of Virginians would pay less. In early 2004, his plan was rejected by the heavily Republican House of Delegates, which increased taxes by just $520 million and provided few spending increases. But the state Senate passed a $3.8 billion tax increase, with $1.7 billion in new spending for schools and $1.6 billion for transportation. But GOP Speaker William Howell was unable to hold his Republicans in line, and 17 of them abandoned their anti-tax positions. The Senate agreed to a $1.3 billion tax increase, more than Warner had requested, and the House went along, a major victory for Warner.

By December 2004, the fiscal picture had changed. State government was facing a $1.2 billion surplus. Warner called for spending $32 million to offset state employees' health insurance premiums, $200 million more for Medicaid, $70 million to cover cost overruns in college construction, and $824 million in transportation spending. He also sought a larger national profile. He became chairman of the National Governors Association, urged Democratic presidential candidate John Kerry to target Virginia (which Kerry did, until August) and advised other Democrats around the country about how to win support in rural areas and among conservative voters on culture issues. He was viewed as a potential presidential candidate in 2008, as a Democrat who would appeal to moderates. But in October 2006, he announced he would not run, citing the impact a national campaign would have on his family.

Then, when Sen. John Warner announced in August 2007 that he would retire from the Senate after five terms, Mark Warner's next career move seemed obvious. He had no serious opposition for the Democratic nomination. On the Republican side, Jim Gilmore, Warner's predecessor as governor, decided to get into the race. At the state Republicans' nominating convention in June 2008, Gilmore barely prevailed after being challenged from the right by Delegate Robert Marshall because of Gilmore's support for abortion rights in some cases. He only narrowly secured the nomination.

It turned out not to be a seriously contested campaign. Warner led in the polls by 20 percentage points or more throughout 2008. Warner raised $13.6 million while Gilmore raised just $2.8 million. Warner argued that Gilmore left the state in poor fiscal shape and that he had been able to turn things around. Warner won 65%-34%, losing only two counties in the Shenandoah Valley, two exurban Richmond counties and two small independent cities. He got 2.37 million votes, the only candidate in Virginia history to win more than 2 million votes. He won 69% of the votes in Northern Virginia, 68% in Tidewater, 64% in Richmond and 62% in the rest of the state, running far ahead of Democratic presidential nominee Barack Obama even as Obama was carrying the state by six points. For the first time since 1970, when Harry Byrd Jr. declared himself an independent, Virginia had two Democratic senators.

In the Senate, Warner's voting habits have put him in the exact political center. He has supported the Obama administration on some major legislation, but he also has joined Republicans in backing caps on discretionary spending. In April 2011, he was one of 17 Democrats to support Oklahoma GOP Sen. Tom Coburn's amendment to force $5 billion in savings by requiring the administration to end duplication in various programs, an idea that Senate appropriators strongly opposed. In his early months in office, Warner was given the chairmanship of a Budget Committee task force on government performance. He advocated eliminating spending on 17 programs, from watershed infrastructure grants to brownfields redevelopment. His proposal won committee approval as part of a broader budget measure, but the full Senate never acted on it.

Warner also developed a reputation for bipartisanship. He and Tennesssee Republican Bob Corker worked in 2009 and 2010 on ways to prevent financial institutions from becoming "too big to fail" as part of the Wall Street overhaul. Later in 2010, Warner circulated a proposal to let tax cuts for the wealthy expire and to use the money to finance additional tax cuts for small business and investment. Warner also reached out to Georgia Republican Saxby Chambliss, with whom he shared friends in Atlanta's business community, in forming a "Gang of Six" that explored cutting the debt in ways other than slashing domestic spending. To keep the group's closed-door meetings from becoming too partisan, Warner reportedly would occasionally push a comic buzzer that sounded the message: "Bull---- detected. Take precautions."

Warner has worked on a range of other issues. He got a bill into law in 2010 creating a foundation to bring private sector resources to promote sports and nutrition as ways to fight obesity. He also pushed legislation authorizing the Federal Communications Commission to hold incentive auctions to free up the wireless spectrum. During the health care overhaul debate, he led 11 freshman Democrats in proposing a series of amendments intended to control costs and boost accountability of the new program. When serious management and record-keeping problems surfaced at Arlington National Cemetery in 2010, he organized a consortium of high-tech companies to help the cemetery organize its files free of charge.

After the 2010 elections, Warner was offered a chance to become part of the Senate leadership by taking the chairmanship of the Democratic Senatorial Campaign Committee. But he turned down the job, which would have required him to become much more of a partisan.

FIRST DISTRICT

Rob Wittman (R)

Elected Dec. 2007, 2nd full term; b. Feb. 3, 1959, Washington, D.C.; home, Montross; VA Tech., B.S., 1981, U. of NC, M.S., 1990, VA Commonwealth U., Ph.D., 2002; Episcopalian; married (Kathyrn); 2 children.

Elected Office: Montross Town Cncl., 1986-1996, Montross Mayor, 1992-1996, Westmoreland Cnt. Bd. of Supervisors, 1996-2005, VA House of Del., 2005-07.

Professional Career: Field dir., VA Health Dept.

DC Office: 1317 LHOB, 20515, 202-225-4261; Fax: 202-225-4382; Web site: wittman.house.gov.

State Offices: Fredericksburg, 540-548-1086; Tappahannock, 804-443-0668; Yorktown, 757-874-6687.

Committees: *Armed Services:* Oversight & Investigations (Chmn); Seapower & Projection Forces. *Natural Resources:* Fisheries, Wildlife, Oceans & Insular Affairs.

Group Ratings

	ACLU	ACU	ADA	CFG	AFS	FRC	LCV	ITIC	NTU	COC
2010	6	92	5	79	0	100	40	33	80	88
2009	–	92	5	80	33	–	21	–	79	87

National Journal Ratings

	2010 LIB — 2010 CONS		2009 LIB — 2009 CONS	
Economic	34% —	66%	30% —	70%
Social	25% —	71%	24% —	73%
Foreign	33% —	65%	0% —	75%
Composite	32% —	68%	23% —	77%

Key Votes of the 111th Congress

1. Overturn Ledbetter	N	5. Bar federal abortion funds	N
2. Pass $820 billion stimulus	N	6. Pass health care bill	N
3. Let guns in national parks	Y	7. Regulate financial firms	N
4. Pass cap-and-trade	N	8. Pass tax cuts for some	N

9. Stop detainee transfers	Y
10. Legalize immigrants' kids	N
11. Repeal don't ask, tell	N
12. Limit campaign funds	N

Election Results

2010 general	Rob Wittman (R)	135,564	(64%)	($1,292,243)
	Krystal Ball (D)	73,824	(35%)	($1,094,183)
2010 primary	Rob Wittman (R)	28,956	(88%)	
	Catherine Crabill (R)	3,963	(12%)	

Prior Winning Percentages: 2008 (57%); 2007 special (61%)

Population		Race/Ethnicity		Work	
Pop. 2010:	786,237	White:	67.8%	Private:	66.4%
Change since 2000:	Up 22.2%	Black:	19.5%	Government:	28.7%
Urban:	64.0%	Hispanic:	6.7%	Self-employed:	4.7%
Rural:	36.0%	Asian:	2.6%	Blue collar:	18.6%
Area size:	4,612 sq. mi.	Native Am.:	0.3%	White collar:	62.3%
		Hawaiian:	0.1%	Khaki collar:	3.3%
Age		Two+ races:	2.7%	Other:	15.9%
Median age:	37.3 yrs.				
More than 65 yrs:	12.2%	*Ancestry*		Median income:	$67,695
Less than 18 yrs:	24.9%	English	12.0%	Median Home Value:	$297,100
		German	11.7%		
Education		Irish	9.9%	**Military Veterans**	
H.S. grad:	89.2%			% of Pop:	16.4%
College grad:	30.8%				
Grad degree:	12.2%				

Eastern Virginia; Newport News

When the English first sailed up the estuaries that flow into the Chesapeake Bay, they were searching for gold. But they couldn't help noticing that the spot where the James River fed into the bay, now Hampton Roads, was a fine natural harbor with calm, deep water and good anchorages. So some of them stayed and established communities that achieved not only the high craftsmanship of restored Williamsburg, but endured the pitiless hardship brought to life by the

2008 Presidential Vote		
John McCain (R) 193,273	(51%)
Barack Obama (D) 179,442	(48%)
2004 Presidential Vote		
George Bush (R) 188,417	(60%)
John Kerry (D) 122,771	(39%)
Cook Partisan Voting Index: R+7		

four-century story of Jamestown and other early settlements. Tidewater Virginia brought slavery to America and tobacco to the world, and slave-raised tobacco was the center of its economy in the colonial era and in the years afterward. (Former Virginia Gov. Douglas Wilder has been trying for years to build a U.S. National Slavery Museum in Fredericksburg.) Now, the tone of life in Tidewater Virginia is set by the American military. More than six decades ago, as America faced world war, the Navy base at Norfolk and the shipbuilding centers in Newport News across Hampton Roads became the center of American naval might in the Atlantic. At the time, there were fewer than 370,000 people living on both sides of Hampton Roads. Today there are more than 1.6 million—a population collected from all over the country, making this a metropolitan area that is not so much Southern in atmosphere as it is, in the manner of military bases abroad, national.

The 1st Congressional District of Virginia contains much of this territory. The district ranges as far north from the Peninsula as rural Fauquier County, outside Washington, D.C., but the bulk of the population lives between the Potomac and James rivers. Most of the major Hampton Roads military installations are in surrounding congressional districts, but the 1st remains steeped in military culture, and the Department of Defense and NASA continue to be significant employers. Historic Yorktown is adjacent to a naval weapons station on the banks of the York River. To the north, in Caroline County, Fort A.P. Hill serves as a training site for active and reserve-component units. Not far from there is the Naval Surface Warfare Center in Dahlgren, located on the Potomac River, originally established as the Navy's main proving ground for large-caliber guns.

The 1st takes in all of 13 counties and parts of five others, including the cities of Fredericksburg and colonial Williamsburg, the Marine Corps Base at Quantico, and the Northern Neck between the Rappahannock and Potomac rivers. The areas closest to Washington are expected to reap some of the benefits of the D.C. area's continued future growth. Quantico already has seen hundreds of millions of dollars in construction in recent years. Ancestrally, much of this area was Democratic. But with a large military population plus growing retirement communities, the 1st District is now reliably Republican in most elections. In the 2009 governor's race, Republican Bob McDonnell lost tiny Charles City County to Democrat Creigh Deeds but easily carried the district's other counties, including five that Barack Obama won in 2008.

Rob Wittman (R)

The congressman from the 1st District is Rob Wittman, a Republican who won a special election in December 2007 to replace Republican Jo Ann Davis, who died of breast cancer two months earlier. His main interests are national security and environmental protection, a combination not often found among conservative Republicans.

Wittman was born in Washington, D.C., and became a marine scientist. He also has a Ph.D. in public policy and administration from Virginia Commonwealth University. Wittman served for many years as an environmental health specialist in the Northern Neck and Peninsula regions, including as field director for the state's shellfish sanitation division. His first public office was a seat on the Montross Town Council, where he served for 10 years, including four as mayor. In 1995, he began a decade on the Westmoreland County Board of Supervisors. In 2005, he was elected to the Virginia House of Delegates.

Five weeks after Davis' death, Republicans held a convention to choose their nominee. Wittman's chief opponent was Paul Jost, a businessman and anti-tax activist who lost to Davis 35%-30% in 2000. The low-key Wittman cited his experience in public office and "the basics of good government." With help from several busloads of supporters, Jost led in the earlier balloting, which began with 11 candidates. The key moment came after five ballots, when Davis' widower, Chuck Davis, threw his support to Wittman, who became the compromise candidate.

Democrats nominated Philip Forgit, a school teacher and Navy reservist who won a Bronze Star in Iraq. He described himself as a centrist and called for improved training to bring strategic change in Iraq. Wittman emphasized his conservative credentials, including his support for gun rights and his opposition to abortion. He also touted the fact that House Minority Leader John Boehner had pledged to give him a seat on the Armed Services Committee. The Democratic Congressional Campaign Committee paid little attention to the contest in this heavily Republican district. Wittman won the low-turnout contest 61%-37%, carrying all 18 counties.

In the House, Wittman got a seat on Armed Services as promised, and also a seat on the Natural Resources Committee, another good fit for his district. He generally sticks with Republicans on major issues but is not an automatic vote. He bucked his party as one of 33 House Republicans to support the creation of an office of congressional ethics, which for the first time would give an outside panel the power to investigate the misdeeds of lawmakers. He also voted in 2009 to allow the Food and Drug Administration to regulate tobacco, a sign of that crop's diminished importance to the region's economy. With so many commuters in his district, he has been active on legislation to encourage tele-working, and reintroduced a bill in 2011 to give tax breaks of up to $1,000 to cover tele-workers' expenses. The House, in September 2009, passed his bill to improve the management of efforts to clean the Chesapeake Bay. He took over the chairmanship of Armed Services' Oversight and Investigations Subcommittee in 2011 and delved into the management scandal at Arlington National Cemetery, where an Army report found mismarked graves and numerous other problems.

Wittman was elected to a full term in 2008 with a smaller share of 57%-42%, but with five times as many votes as in the special election. He coasted to re-election two years later, and some Virginia Republicans touted him as a possible Senate candidate in 2012. Republican-led redistricting is expected to add some of the Northern Virginia suburbs to his district to take the heat off more vulnerable GOP lawmakers while keeping it solidly Republican.

SECOND DISTRICT

Scott Rigell (R)

Elected 2010, 1st term; b. May 28, 1960, Titusville, FL; home, Virginia Beach; Mercer U., B.B.A. 1983; Regent U., M.B.A. 1990.; Christian; Married (Teri); 4 children.

Military Career: Marine Corps Reserve, 1978-84.

Professional Career: Salesman, Ford dealership, 1983-86; pres., Freedom Automotive, 1991-2010.

DC Office: 327 CHOB, 20515, 202-225-4215; Fax: 202-225-4218; Web site: rigell.house.gov.

State Offices: Eastern Shore, 757-789-5172; Virginia Beach, 757-687-8290.

Committees: *Armed Services:* Seapower & Projection Forces; Strategic Forces. *Homeland Security:* Border & Maritime Security; Counterterrorism & Intelligence; Emergency Preparedness, Response & Communications. *Science & Technology:* Space & Aeronautics; Technology & Innovation.

Election Results

2010 general	Scott Rigell (R)	88,340	(53%)	($4,757,947)
	Glenn Nye (D)	70,591	(42%)	($2,260,922)
	Kenneth Golden (I)	7,194	(4%)	($125,938)
2010 primary	Scott Rigell (R)	14,396	(40%)	
	Ben Loyola (R)	9,762	(27%)	
	Bert Mizusawa (R)	6,342	(17%)	
	Scott Taylor (R)	2,950	(8%)	

Population		Race/Ethnicity		Work	
Pop. 2010:	646,184	White:	62.8%	Private:	64.2%
Change since 2000:	Up 0.4%	Black:	21.4%	Government:	31.5%
Urban:	91.7%	Hispanic:	7.0%	Self-employed:	4.2%
Rural:	8.3%	Asian:	5.0%	Blue collar:	20.3%
Area size:	2,777 sq. mi.	Native Am.:	0.3%	White collar:	57.5%
		Hawaiian:	0.1%	Khaki collar:	7.0%
Age		Two+ races:	3.1%	Other:	15.3%
Median age:	33.8 yrs.				
More than 65 yrs:	10.9%	*Ancestry*		Median income:	$57,802
Less than 18 yrs:	23.9%	German	10.7%	Median Home Value:	$259,000
		Irish	9.5%		
Education		English	9.2%	**Military Veterans**	
H.S. grad:	90.3%			% of Pop:	17.2%
College grad:	28.7%				
Grad degree:	10.2%				

Eastern Virginia; Virginia Beach

The U.S. Navy Atlantic fleet berthed in its home port of Norfolk is one of the awe-inspiring sights in America, or anywhere. The aggregation of destructive power in the line of towering gray ships is probably greater than in any other single port in history. Several dozen ships are based here—aircraft carriers, cruisers, destroyers, large amphibious ships, submarines, supply and logistics ships—and many more aircraft. Nor-

2008 Presidential Vote		
Barack Obama (D)	142,257	(51%)
John McCain (R)	136,725	(49%)
2004 Presidential Vote		
George Bush (R)	141,097	(58%)
John Kerry (D)	101,576	(42%)
Cook Partisan Voting Index: R+5		

folk has been a Navy port since 1801 and has long been recognized as one of the best natural harbors on the East Coast, one that never freezes, has a channel 50 feet deep and is within 750 miles of three-quarters of U.S. manufacturing capacity. The Norfolk Naval Station is the world's largest naval base, situated on 4,300 acres on Sewell's Point, and in the Hampton Roads region; residents are always within minutes of one naval installation or another. Once a small city, Norfolk is now part of a metropolitan area (along with Virginia Beach) of 1.7 million people. The local Navy community— active duty and civilian personnel, dependents, retirees, and workers at the Newport News Shipbuilding & Drydock—is estimated at more than 300,000, and military spending pours some $11 billion annually into the local economy. The Port of Hampton Roads is the second-busiest port on the East Coast, and its cargo volume has grown steadily since 2000.

Virginia Beach, once a sleepy beach resort, is the state's largest city, with 435,000 people. It began attracting tourists when rail service to Norfolk began in 1883. It is home to the headquarters of evangelist Pat Robertson's Christian Broadcasting Network, which produces the *700 Club*. The city has a growing industrial base, including a large power tool plant of the German-based Stihl company. But like Norfolk, Virginia Beach is infused with military culture. It is home to four military installations with 32,000 service and civilian employees and an annual payroll of $1.8 billion. East Coast Navy SEAL teams are based in Virginia Beach; these elite commandos endure punishing training and take on some of the military's most secretive and daring missions in Iraq and Afghanistan, including participating in the Pakistan compound raid that ended with the killing of Osama bin Laden in May 2011.

The 2nd Congressional District of Virginia includes all of Virginia Beach, plus small parts of Norfolk and Hampton, including the Norfolk Navy base and Langley Air Force Base and, on a spit of land in the bay, Fort Monroe, where Jefferson Davis was confined after the Civil War. It covers more than 100 miles of Atlantic Ocean coastline and stretches from Maryland's Eastern Shore to North Carolina. Of the district's total labor force of 365,000 in 2009, 46,000 people were employed by the armed forces. The district also includes a more placid area, the two Virginia counties of the Delmarva Peninsula, and Virginia's Eastern Shore, the site of the annual roundup of wild Chincoteague ponies. These rural counties with their fishing villages are two of the state's poorest. The overwhelming majority of the district's population is in Virginia Beach. The district leans Republican. George W. Bush carried it handily twice, but Democrat Barack Obama beat former Navy aviator John McCain here 51%-49% in 2008.

Scott Rigell (R)

The new congressman from Virginia's 2nd District is Republican Scott Rigell, a car dealer who knocked off Democratic freshman Glenn Nye in 2010. Rigell hails from Titusville, Fla., near the Kennedy Space Center, where his father worked as an engineer and director of NASA's launch-vehicle operations. His mother drove a school bus. Rigell earned his undergraduate degree from Mercer University in Georgia, and shortly afterward, returned to Titusville to work at a Ford dealership run by his father-in-law. He also enrolled in business school at Regent University, a private Christian college founded by televangelist Pat Robertson. After getting a master's degree in business administration, Rigell purchased Freedom Automotive in 1991. Soon afterward, he met Bob McDonnell, now the Republican governor of Virginia, on the showroom floor of his auto dealership, and the two became friends. Over the years, Rigell helped McDonnell in his campaigns and contributed to other Republican candidates. He also gave $1,000 to Democrat Barack Obama's presidential campaign in 2008, which conservatives cited as proof that he is too moderate for the district.

When he decided to challenge Nye, Rigell had to compete against five other candidates in the GOP primary. He ran as the establishment candidate, with the most cash, in a field that included Iraq war veteran Bert Mizusawa and engineering contractor Ben Loyola, the local tea party favorite. Though McDonnell remained neutral in the race, his politically active daughter, Jeanine, ran an ad for Rigell calling him a "longtime friend" of the family. Rigell won with 40% of the vote.

In the general election, Rigell pledged to adhere to a 12-year term limit and to extend the Bush-era tax cuts for everyone, even the wealthiest taxpayers. He also hammered Nye for supporting the Obama administration's $787 billion economic-stimulus plan. Nye said he, too, favored extending the tax cuts for everyone, and he won the endorsement of the conservative U.S. Chamber of Commerce, which called him a "pro-business" Democrat. Nye raised more money on the campaign trail, but Rigell maintained a slight lead in the polls and rode the 2010 Republican wave to victory with 53% of the vote to 42% for Nye.

In Washington, Rigell landed a seat on the House Armed Services Committee, a high value position in a district with several military bases. He also was assigned to the Homeland Security Committee. His first official act was to unveil a 10-point proposal for scaling back congressional perks that he said have fostered "a culture of privilege." His plan included cutting congressional office budgets to 2008 levels, limiting franked mail to two pieces a year, replacing lawmakers' pensions with 401(k) plans, banning travel paid for by lobbyists for foundations, and prohibiting lawmakers and their staffs from working as lobbyists for five years after leaving their government employment. Even if Congress declined to adopt his proposal, Rigell said he would abide by its provisions himself.

THIRD DISTRICT

Bobby Scott (D)

Elected 1992, 10th term; b. April 30, 1947, Washington, D.C.; home, Newport News; Harvard U., B.A. 1969, Boston Col., J.D. 1973; Episcopalian; single.

Military Career: Army Natl. Guard, 1970–73; Army Reserves, 1973–76.

Elected Office: VA House of Delegates, 1977–82; VA Senate, 1983–92.

Professional Career: Practicing atty., 1973–91.

DC Office: 1201 LHOB, 20515, 202-225-8351; Fax: 202-225-8354; Web site: bobbyscott.house.gov.

State Offices: Newport News, 757-380-1000; Richmond, 804-644-4845.

Committees: *Education & the Workforce:* Early Childhood, Elementary & Secondary Education; Health, Employment, Labor & Pensions. *Judiciary:* Constitution; Crime, Terrorism & Homeland Security (RMM).

Group Ratings

	ACLU	ACU	ADA	CFG	AFS	FRC	LCV	ITIC	NTU	COC
2010	94	0	100	7	88	6	100	67	6	13
2009	–	4	95	4	100	–	93	–	4	33

National Journal Ratings

	2010 LIB	—	2010 CONS		2009 LIB	—	2009 CONS
Economic	73%	—	25%		88%	—	9%
Social	82%	—	14%		69%	—	30%
Foreign	92%	—	3%		87%	—	9%
Composite	84%	—	16%		83%	—	17%

Key Votes of the 111th Congress

1. Overturn Ledbetter	Y	5. Bar federal abortion funds	N	9. Stop detainee transfers	N
2. Pass $820 billion stimulus	Y	6. Pass health care bill	Y	10. Legalize immigrants' kids	Y
3. Let guns in national parks	N	7. Regulate financial firms	Y	11. Repeal don't ask, tell	Y
4. Pass cap-and-trade	Y	8. Pass tax cuts for some	N	12. Limit campaign funds	Y

Election Results

2010 general	Bobby Scott (D)	114,754	(70%)	($444,548)
	Chuck Smith (R)	44,553	(27%)	($91,136)
2010 primary	Bobby Scott (D)	unopposed		

Prior Winning Percentages: 2008 (97%), 2006 (96%), 2004 (69%), 2002 (96%), 2000 (100%), 1998 (76%), 1996 (82%), 1994 (79%), 1992 (79%)

Population		Race/Ethnicity		Work	
Pop. 2010:	663,390	White:	35.5%	Private:	72.0%
Change since 2000:	Up 3.1%	Black:	54.6%	Government:	24.5%
Urban:	92.2%	Hispanic:	4.9%	Self-employed:	3.4%
Rural:	7.8%	Asian:	1.9%	Blue collar:	24.0%
Area size:	1,306 sq. mi.	Native Am.:	0.4%	White collar:	53.7%
		Hawaiian:	0.1%	Khaki collar:	3.2%
Age		Two+ races:	2.4%	Other:	19.1%
Median age:	32.9 yrs.				
More than 65 yrs:	11.3%	*Ancestry*		Median income:	$41,143
Less than 18 yrs:	24.3%	USA	6.8%	Median Home Value:	$185,600
		German	6.4%		
Education		English	6.3%	**Military Veterans**	
H.S. grad:	82.1%			% of Pop:	12.9%
College grad:	20.7%				
Grad degree:	7.6%				

Norfolk, Hampton, Newport News

The history of American slavery literally began along the tidal expanse of the James River. In 1607, the first English colonists chose one of the marshiest, unhealthiest spots along the broad river as the site of their settlement at James-town. Only a dozen years later, the first slave ship sailed up the James and offloaded its human cargo, giving birth to the biracial society of the American South. In the 21st century, the great plantation houses of the Tidewater, once

2008 Presidential Vote		
Barack Obama (D)	229,822	(76%)
John McCain (R)	72,249	(24%)
2004 Presidential Vote		
John Kerry (D)	158,561	(66%)
George Bush (R)	79,302	(33%)
Cook Partisan Voting Index:	D+20	

adorned by the most impressive architecture of the day and attended by hundreds of slaves, still dot the banks of the James. Charles City County—the site of William Byrd II's Westover, Benjamin Harrison III's Berkeley, and John Carter's Shirley—also was the birthplace of two successive presidents, William Henry Harrison and John Tyler. The county's population continues to be heavily African-American, 48% in 2010.

The 3rd Congressional District of Virginia is the descendant of a black-majority district formed in 1992, and redrawn three times since then. The district jumps back and forth across the James River to string together black precincts and communities in Norfolk, Hampton and Newport News. It moves upriver on the Peninsula past Jamestown and Charles City County all the way to Richmond and eastern suburban Henrico County. It includes the Army's Fort Eustis and all of the majority-black city of Portsmouth, a Navy port and industrial town with a charming old section. The population of Hampton has shrunk since 2000, while nearby areas have grown.

Politically, the 3rd is the most Democratic district in Virginia and the state's only black-majority district. Its economy depends heavily on Newport News Shipbuilding & Drydock Company, the largest industrial employer in Virginia. Once an arm of Northrop Grumman, it effectively separated as a spinoff in March 2011 to become part of Huntington Ingalls Industries. The ships loom larger than life over nearby neighborhoods. During the Cold War, Newport News built two of the largest tankers ever made in the western hemisphere. In 2008, Democrat Barack Obama carried the 3rd District 76%-24%, one of Obama's best showings in the South.

Bobby Scott (D)

The congressman from the 3rd District is Bobby Scott, a Democrat first elected when the district was created in 1992. He is both an influential civil libertarian on the Judiciary Committee and an intellectual force in the Congressional Black Caucus.

Scott grew up in Newport News, the son of a doctor. He went to Harvard University, where he was a classmate of future Democratic Vice President Al Gore, and then to Boston College's law school. He served in the National Guard and Army Reserves, and returned home to practice law. In 1977, he was elected to the Virginia House of Delegates, and in 1983, to the state Senate, representing a multi-racial district in a community where, because of the military tradition of integration, biracial politics came more naturally than in other places. In 1986, he ran a credible race for Congress and lost to Republican Herb Bateman, 56%-44%. In 1992, with his base on the Peninsula, Scott won the crucial Democratic primary with 67% of the vote against two Richmond-based candidates. He won the general election easily to become the first African-American elected from Virginia since 1891.

Scott has a solidly liberal voting record, with occasional exceptions on economic and defense issues, and he is one of the House's most outspoken civil libertarians. When bipartisan coalitions passed legislation to permit states to display the Ten Commandments in schools or government buildings, he raised First Amendment objections. After the September 11 attacks, he opposed the USA Patriot Act, the nation's tough new anti-terrorism law, arguing that it might promote racial profiling. Scott was one of three lawmakers to oppose condemnation of a federal court decision declaring unconstitutional the words "one nation under God" in the Pledge of Allegiance. "We ought to be standing up for unpopular decisions" and not voting for a resolution that "everyone knows is stupid, but it sounds popular," he said. On April 2009, Scott joined 15 other Judiciary Committee Democrats in challenging the Obama administration's reluctance to prosecute former officials who allegedly tortured suspected terrorists in custody.

Scott is the top Democrat on the Judiciary Subcommittee on Crime, Terrorism and Homeland Security, where he conducts oversight of criminal laws with the goal of shifting the focus from enforcement to prevention. One of Scott's legislative successes was the bipartisan Death in Custody Reporting Act, which requires states to report deaths of arrestees and prisoners. He also got a bill into law in 2010 to narrow the discrepancies between sentences for powder and crack cocaine, an issue he had long contended led to blacks receiving disproportionately longer sentences. In May 2009, the CBC urged President Barack Obama to select Scott to replace retiring Supreme Court Justice David Souter, although Obama ultimately settled on federal appellate Judge Sonia Sotomayor.

In 2007, he joined with then senators Obama of Illinois and Joe Biden of Delaware in pushing for compensation for black farmers who had been victims of government discrimination. Congress passed the bill in the 2010 lame-duck session. Scott also has been the prime sponsor of the CBC's alternative budget plan, which would phase out the Bush-era tax cuts for upper-income taxpayers to finance more spending on domestic programs. The House has routinely defeated the annual proposals, voting 103-302 in April 2011. Scott was one of New York Democrat Charles Rangel's chief defenders against ethics violations in 2010.

In 2004, Scott faced his first Republican challenger since 1996, Winsome Sears, a former Marine and the first black Republican woman in the House of Delegates. Sears criticized Scott as "radical" on national security, education, gay rights and abortion. Scott focused on his record and criticized Republican policies. In this strongly Democratic district, he won 69%-31%. After being unopposed in 2006 and 2008, in 2010 he faced Republican Chuck Smith, who was recruited after initially declaring his candidacy in the 2nd District. Scott coasted to a 70%-27% victory.

FOURTH DISTRICT

Randy Forbes (R)

Elected June 2001, 5th full term; b. Feb. 17, 1952, Chesapeake; home, Chesapeake; Randolph-Macon Col., B.A. 1974, U. of VA, J.D. 1977; Baptist; married (Shirley); 4 children.

Elected Office: VA House of Del., 1989-97; VA Senate, 1997-2001.

Professional Career: Practicing atty., 1977-2001.

DC Office: 2438 RHOB, 20515, 202-225-6365; Fax: 202-226-1170; Web site: forbes.house.gov.

State Offices: Chesapeake, 757-382-0080; Chesterfield, 804-382-0080; Colonial Heights, 804-526-4969; Emporia, 434-634-5575.

Committees: *Armed Services:* Readiness (Chmn); Seapower & Projection Forces. *Judiciary:* Constitution; Crime, Terrorism & Homeland Security.

Group Ratings

	ACLU	ACU	ADA	CFG	AFS	FRC	LCV	ITIC	NTU	COC
2010	10	100	5	84	0	100	0	0	83	75
2009	–	96	0	81	22	–	7	–	82	86

National Journal Ratings

	2010 LIB	—	2010 CONS	2009 LIB	—	2009 CONS
Economic	27%	—	72%	21%	—	79%
Social	0%	—	85%	13%	—	84%
Foreign	12%	—	79%	0%	—	75%
Composite	17%	—	83%	16%	—	84%

Key Votes of the 111th Congress

1. Overturn Ledbetter	N	5. Bar federal abortion funds	Y	9. Stop detainee transfers	Y
2. Pass $820 billion stimulus	N	6. Pass health care bill	N	10. Legalize immigrants' kids	N
3. Let guns in national parks	Y	7. Regulate financial firms	N	11. Repeal don't ask, tell	N
4. Pass cap-and-trade	N	8. Pass tax cuts for some	N	12. Limit campaign funds	N

Election Results

2010 general	Randy Forbes (R)	123,659	(62%)	($987,976)
	Wynne LeGrow (D)	74,298	(37%)	($175,687)
2010 primary	Randy Forbes (R)	unopposed		

Prior Winning Percentages: 2008 (60%), 2006 (76%), 2004 (64%), 2002 (98%), 2001 special (52%)

Population		Race/Ethnicity		Work	
Pop. 2010:	738,639	White:	57.9%	Private:	70.3%
Change since 2000:	Up 14.8%	Black:	33.2%	Government:	25.6%
Urban:	70.9%	Hispanic:	4.5%	Self-employed:	4.1%
Rural:	29.1%	Asian:	1.9%	Blue collar:	23.1%
Area size:	4,575 sq. mi.	Native Am.:	0.3%	White collar:	59.0%
		Hawaiian:	0.1%	Khaki collar:	2.0%
Age		Two+ races:	2.0%	Other:	15.9%
Median age:	37.3 yrs.				
More than 65 yrs:	11.2%	*Ancestry*		Median income:	$58,249
Less than 18 yrs:	24.9%	USA	10.9%	Median Home Value:	$230,000
		English	10.9%		
Education		German	8.3%	**Military Veterans**	
H.S. grad:	83.9%			% of Pop:	14.2%
College grad:	22.9%				
Grad degree:	8.1%				

Hampton Roads, Chesapeake

The clash of arms resounds through much of the history of Tidewater Virginia. The region was the scene of the final victory of the Revolutionary War and saw bitter fighting more than 80 years later in the Civil War, as Union troops invested the battlements of the small industrial city of Petersburg, 25 miles south of Richmond. The Blackwater River was a prominent dividing line between Union and Confederate troops. Today, the Tidewater boasts one of the densest

2008 Presidential Vote		
Barack Obama (D) 178,795	(50%)
John McCain (R) 173,358	(49%)
2004 Presidential Vote		
George Bush (R) 166,689	(57%)
John Kerry (D) 125,164	(43%)
Cook Partisan Voting Index: R+4		

concentrations of military power in the world. The Hampton Roads area has the nation's largest accumulation of Navy bases, while Fort Lee, the big Army base near Petersburg, will double in size to 44,600 by fall 2011.

The 4th Congressional District of Virginia includes much of the Tidewater south of the James River. The district covers some of Richmond's suburbs, but about half of its people are in the Hampton Roads area, mostly in the fast-growing suburbs of Chesapeake and Suffolk. *Money* magazine in 2010 named Chesapeake one of the best places to live in the country, with its quality schools, open local government and ample green space; it is close to passing Norfolk as the state's second largest city. Suffolk is the original home of the Planters Nut and Chocolate Company on the eastern edge of Virginia's Peanut Belt, though production has dropped markedly. Virginia peanuts are most often used in candy and snacks, two areas where demand has dropped. Growth in Suffolk has centered on high-tech defense contracting firms, which were threatened by Defense Secretary Robert Gates' proposed cutbacks in 2010.

The district also takes in the flat lands of Southside Virginia, fanning south from the James River. These were tobacco lands after the English first settled them in the 17th century. Today, they also produce Smithfield hams in an area that calls itself the "Ham Capital of the World." The district includes all of Petersburg and Hopewell, with its Honeywell plant and 18th century plantations. Chemical company Ashland Inc. announced in January 2011 a $39 million expansion of its Hopewell facility. The district is 33% African-American, which sometimes helps Democrats here. The district voted twice for Republican George W. Bush, but Democrat Barack Obama narrowly carried it 50%-49% in 2008.

Randy Forbes (R)

The congressman from the 4th District is Randy Forbes, a Republican who came to office in a June 2001 special election. Today he is the chairman of the Armed Services Subcommittee on Readiness, giving him a prominent position from which to battle the Obama administration over defense spending in his district and elsewhere.

Forbes grew up in Chesapeake, majored in government at Randolph-Macon College, and graduated from the University of Virginia law school. He started a law firm in Chesapeake that later merged with a larger Norfolk firm. His first job in politics was as an aide to a Democratic member of the House of Delegates from Chesapeake. When his boss retired in 1989, Forbes ran and won the seat as a Republican. Four years later, when Republicans were still in the minority, he became the party's floor leader. In 1997, he was elected to the state Senate. Forbes was a classmate and friend of Govs. George Allen and Jim Gilmore in law school, and in 1996 Allen made him state Republican chairman. In that job, he helped engineer the historic Republican 1997 sweep of all three statewide offices.

When 10-term Democratic Rep. Norman Sisisky died after cancer surgery in 2001, national and state Republican leaders asked Forbes to run for the competitive seat. He was nominated at a party convention, and then caught a break when the strongest Democrat, Sisisky's son, Mark, declined to run. Democrats chose state Sen. Louise Lucas of Portsmouth, an African-American who held a majority-black seat. Both national parties and their interest-group allies spent heavily on the race. Republicans attacked Lucas for opposing repeal of the sales tax on non-prescription drugs and for supporting a gasoline tax increase. Democrats criticized Forbes for his position in support of President George W. Bush's plan to partially privatize Social Security. Lucas carried Portsmouth 63%-37%. But Forbes won in more populous Chesapeake, 61%-39%, and in rural counties for an overall victory of 52%-48%.

In the House, the conservative Forbes generally deviates from the party line on major legislation when he deems it too costly for the government. For that reason, he opposed the extension of the Bush-era tax cuts that passed Congress in the 2010 lame-duck session. Also a strong social conservative, he founded the Congressional Prayer Caucus, which has tried to halt the removal of references to God in public dialogue. He has been the main champion of a GOP effort to reaffirm "In God We Trust" as the national motto, noting that Obama, during a 2010 Indonesia trip, said that the national motto is "E Pluribus Unum." Forbes is also interested in energy issues. In 2008, he introduced a bill calling for cash awards for companies that meet certain goals such as designing a car that gets 70 miles per gallon of gasoline. It failed in the Democratic-controlled House, 172-255.

On Armed Services, Forbes has fought the Obama administration over its plans to close the Joint Forces Command in Norfolk, attaching a provision to a House-passed spending bill in February 2011 that delayed the move. Earlier, he was part of the Virginia delegation's efforts to try to stop the Navy's plans to shift an aircraft carrier from Norfolk to Jacksonville, Fla. He has cited China's increasing economic and military strength as a reason for a U.S. military buildup. "If they (the Chinese) perceive a power vacuum, they get more bold," he told a Hampton Roads audience in January 2011.

In 2008, Forbes was held to a 60%-40% re-election victory against poorly-funded Democrat Andrea Miller, a former regional director for MoveOn.org who benefited from the local strength of Obama and Senate candidate Mark Warner. He had an easier time in 2010, winning 62%-37% over retired physician Wynne LeGrow. Republican redistricters are expected to provide him with some additional GOP turf in 2012.

FIFTH DISTRICT

Robert Hurt (R)

Elected 2010, 1st term; b. June 16, 1969, New York, NY; home, Chatham; Hampden-Sydney Col., B.S. 1991; MS Col., J.D. 1995; Presbyterian; Married (Kathy); 3 children.

Elected Office: Chatham Town Cncl., 2001; VA House of Del., 2002-07; VA Senate, 2008-10.

Professional Career: Chief asst., Pittsylvania Cnty. Commonwealth's Atty., 1996-99; practicing atty., 1999-2010.

DC Office: 1516 LHOB, 20515, 202-225-4711; Fax: 202-225-5681; Web site: hurt.house.gov.

State Offices: Charlottesville, 434-973-9631; Danville, 434-791-2596.

Committees: *Financial Services:* Capital Markets and Government Sponsored Enterprises; Insurance, Housing & Community Opportunity (VChmn).

Election Results

2010 general	Robert Hurt (R)	119,560	(51%)	($2,600,708)
	Tom Perriello (D)	110,562	(47%)	($3,775,363)
	Jeffrey Clark (I)	4,992	(2%)	
2010 primary	Robert Hurt (R)	17,120	(48%)	
	James McKelvey (R)	9,153	(26%)	
	Mike McPadden (R)	3,460	(10%)	
	Kenneth Boyd (R)	2,608	(7%)	

Population		Race/Ethnicity		Work	
Pop. 2010:	685,859	White:	71.7%	Private:	73.7%
Change since 2000:	Up 6.6%	Black:	21.9%	Government:	19.4%
Urban:	36.0%	Hispanic:	3.1%	Self-employed:	6.7%
Rural:	64.0%	Asian:	1.5%	Blue collar:	25.6%
Area size:	9,054 sq. mi.	Native Am.:	0.2%	White collar:	56.3%
		Hawaiian:	0.0%	Khaki collar:	0.1%
Age		Two+ races:	1.5%	Other:	17.9%
Median age:	40.4 yrs.				
More than 65 yrs:	15.7%	*Ancestry*		Median income:	$42,517
Less than 18 yrs:	20.9%	USA	14.8%	Median Home Value:	$154,000
		English	10.8%		
Education		German	8.8%	**Military Veterans**	
H.S. grad:	79.5%			% of Pop:	10.7%
College grad:	21.7%				
Grad degree:	8.9%				

South Central Virginia; Danville

Southside Virginia is a geographic name that for years was shorthand for a state of mind. Located here is Appomattox Court House, in the serene little hamlet where Robert E. Lee surrendered to his onetime subordinate Ulysses S. Grant; and also Danville, where the tobacco auction originated in 1858. In Prince Edward County, Democratic Sen. Harry Byrd's massive resistance to a federal court desegregation order shut down public schools in 1957. The eastern counties are

2008 Presidential Vote		
John McCain (R) 164,874	(51%)
Barack Obama (D) 157,362	(48%)
2004 Presidential Vote		
George Bush (R) 158,568	(56%)
John Kerry (D) 121,960	(43%)
Cook Partisan Voting Index: R+5		

flat and humid—frontier in the late-colonial period, plantation country by 1800, and now peanut fields and pine forests. Along U.S. 58 are the vestiges of Virginia's Tobacco Road, and in South Hill, the Tobacco Farm Life Museum pays tribute to that heritage. To the west, into the Piedmont, the land gradually gets hillier. There is a D-Day memorial in Bedford, which lost more men per capita, 23 of its 35 soldiers, in the Normandy invasion than any other town in the country. Nearby are the abandoned textile mills and furniture factories of Danville and Martinsville, which had 20% unemployment in early 2011—the highest rate in Virginia. Signs of hope for better days ahead were a recent IKEA furniture factory, the nation's largest indoor fish farm called Blue Ridge Aquaculture, and biofuel and wind energy research centers financed by the state's tobacco settlement money.

Other new influences are taking root in Southside Virginia. Metro Richmond is reaching out and rural counties have sprouted subdivisions and shopping centers. Charlottesville, once a tiny town centered on Thomas Jefferson's lawn at the University of Virginia, and surrounding Albemarle County have attracted new residents to the college town atmosphere and the beauty of the rolling hills of the Piedmont. A half century ago, the politics of Southside were Democratic and segregationist, run by chain-smoking local bankers and courthouse lawyers. But they are long gone. UVA's Board of Visitors voted in 2007 to apologize for its treatment of slaves.

The 5th District of Virginia consists of much of Southside Virginia, west of metropolitan Richmond, and spreads out to the Blue Ridge Mountains. It includes all of liberal Charlottesville and Albemarle County and fast-growing Fluvanna County, but skirts around conservative Lynchburg. In recent decades, the district has mostly voted Republican. But Virginia's recent Democratic governors, Mark Warner and Tim Kaine, have energized Charlottesville and Albemarle County liberals, and Democrat Barack Obama's presidential campaign in 2008 registered thousands of Southside blacks. Still, Republican John McCain won the district that year, 51% to 48%.

Robert Hurt (R)

The new congressman from the 5th District is Republican Robert Hurt, a former state senator who reclaimed the seat for the GOP by ejecting Democrat Tom Perriello, who had the seat in 2009 and 2010.

Hurt was born in New York City, the son of Henry Hurt, a journalist, nonfiction author, and editor for *Reader's Digest*. In 1986, Henry Hurt wrote a book questioning the findings of the Warren Commission called *Reasonable Doubt: An Investigation into the Assassination of John F. Kennedy*. He did much of his writing in rural Chatham, Va., where he and his wife raised their three children. Robert Hurt went to Hargrave Military Academy and then on to Episcopal High School in Alexandria, Va. He earned an undergraduate degree in English and then a law degree at Mississippi College before returning to Chatham to practice law. Robert's brother, Charlie Hurt, became a journalist like their father and became the Washington bureau chief for the *New York Post*. Robert Hurt was the chief assistant attorney for Pittsylvania County, and in 2001, began his political career with his election to the Chatham Town Council. A year later, he successfully ran for the Virginia House of Delegates, where he served until 2007. Hurt ran successfully for the state Senate the following year.

When the 2010 congressional elections approached, Perriello was among the most vulnerable freshman lawmakers. In 2008, he had snatched the Republican-leaning district away by only 727 votes from then-Rep. Virgil Goode, a six-term conservative Republican who left the Democratic Party in 2000. Goode had been re-elected by comfortable margins every two years until the Obama presidential campaign brought a flood of new voters to the polls that year, including many African-American voters in the Southside counties. Hurt was eager to take on Perriello, but so were six other Republicans, especially after Goode indicated he would not be back for a rematch.

During the primary campaign, Hurt won the confidence of establishment Republicans, but also angered conservatives when he refused to debate a tea party candidate, businessman Jeff Clark, who called Hurt "a situational conservative." Hurt said Clark was "not serious about his campaign or his ability to win." Hurt won a convincing primary victory, getting 48% of the vote. Clark stayed in the race as an independent, setting up a three-way contest in November.

In his general election campaign, Hurt slammed Perriello for his votes in favor of Obama's $787 billion economic stimulus bill, the Democrats' health care overhaul, and their legislation to cap carbon emissions. He said he would try to reduce the size of the federal budget with free market solutions rather than stimulus programs. Hurt also vowed not to vote for any bill that contained earmarks. Perriello attacked Hurt for supporting then-Democratic Gov. Mark Warner's 2004 budget, which increased state taxes by $1.4 billion. Hurt responded that as a state legislator he had voted against more than two dozen tax increases.

Both candidates had robust fundraising operations, although with $3.8 million, Perriello raised considerably more than Hurt, who took in $2.6 million. Hurt also lost out on the endorsement of the National Rifle Association, which backed Perriello in accordance with its policy of supporting gun rights-friendly incumbents. Still, Hurt won, 51% to 47%. The closeness of the race prompted Democrats to put Hurt on their target list for 2012.

In Washington, one of Hurt's first amendments passed the House in March 2011. On a bill to terminate a mortgage aid program championed by the Obama administration, Hurt proposed that any savings go to deficit reduction. The measure was approved by the Republican controlled chamber. The bill was not expected to pass the Democratically controlled Senate.

SIXTH DISTRICT

Bob Goodlatte (R)

Elected 1992, 10th term; b. Sept. 22, 1952, Holyoke, MA; home, Roanoke; Bates Col., B.A. 1974, Washington & Lee Law Schl., J.D. 1977; Christian Scientist; married (Maryellen); 2 children.

Professional Career: Dist. dir., U.S. Rep. Caldwell Butler, 1977–79; Practicing atty., 1979–92.

DC Office: 2240 RHOB, 20515, 202-225-5431; Fax: 202-225-9681; Web site: goodlatte.house.gov.

State Offices: Harrisonburg, 540-432-2391; Lynchburg, 434-845-8306; Roanoke, 540-857-2672; Staunton, 540-885-3861.

Committees: *Agriculture* (VChmn): Conservation, Energy & Forestry; Livestock, Dairy & Poultry. *Judiciary:* Crime, Terrorism & Homeland Security; Intellectual Property, Competition & the Internet (Chmn); Education and the Workforce.

Group Ratings

	ACLU	ACU	ADA	CFG	AFS	FRC	LCV	ITIC	NTU	COC
2010	13	100	0	86	0	100	0	33	89	88
2009	–	100	0	99	0	–	14	–	90	73

National Journal Ratings

	2010 LIB — 2010 CONS		2009 LIB — 2009 CONS	
Economic	13%	— 87%	12%	— 88%
Social	0%	— 85%	7%	— 90%
Foreign	12%	— 79%	25%	— 74%
Composite	12%	— 88%	15%	— 85%

Key Votes of the 111th Congress

1. Overturn Ledbetter	N	5. Bar federal abortion funds	Y	9. Stop detainee transfers	Y
2. Pass $820 billion stimulus	N	6. Pass health care bill	N	10. Legalize immigrants' kids	N
3. Let guns in national parks	Y	7. Regulate financial firms	N	11. Repeal don't ask, tell	N
4. Pass cap-and-trade	N	8. Pass tax cuts for some	N	12. Limit campaign funds	N

Election Results

2010 general	Bob Goodlatte (R)	127,487	(76%)	($1,006,727)
	Jeffrey Vanke (I)	21,649	(13%)	($13,691)
	Stuart Bain (Lib)	15,309	(9%)	($12,509)
2010 primary	Bob Goodlatte (R)	unopposed		

Prior Winning Percentages: 2008 (62%), 2006 (75%), 2004 (97%), 2002 (97%), 2000 (100%), 1998 (69%), 1996 (67%), 1994 (100%), 1992 (60%)

Population		Race/Ethnicity		Work	
Pop. 2010:	704,056	White:	81.2%	Private:	79.5%
Change since 2000:	Up 9.4%	Black:	11.1%	Government:	15.0%
Urban:	64.7%	Hispanic:	4.3%	Self-employed:	5.3%
Rural:	35.3%	Asian:	1.5%	Blue collar:	25.2%
Area size:	5,663 sq. mi.	Native Am.:	0.2%	White collar:	57.8%
		Hawaiian:	0.0%	Khaki collar:	0.1%
Age		Two+ races:	1.6%	Other:	16.9%
Median age:	38.9 yrs.				
More than 65 yrs:	15.8%	*Ancestry*		Median income:	$45,699
Less than 18 yrs:	21.3%	USA	17.3%	Median Home Value:	$173,700
		German	13.7%		
Education		English	10.3%	**Military Veterans**	
H.S. grad:	82.8%			% of Pop:	11.1%
College grad:	24.2%				
Grad degree:	8.7%				

Western Virginia; Roanoke

The sturdy men and women who settled the Valley of Virginia west of the Blue Ridge were quite different from the "second sons" of the European aristocracy who cleared the marshy forests of the Tidewater and built grand plantations. Even before the Revolutionary War, Scots and Scots-Irish, German Protestants and Mennonites and Moravians—members of religious communities and fiercely independent farmers—poured down the Great Wagon Road from Pennsylva-

2008 Presidential Vote
John McCain (R) 182,573   (57%)
Barack Obama (D) 134,212   (42%)

2004 Presidential Vote
George Bush (R) 177,133   (63%)
John Kerry (D) 100,561   (36%)

Cook Partisan Voting Index: R+12

nia to the valley. They were looking not for the flat, mahogany colored land that eastern tobacco growers sought, but for land that could support wheat, corn, and hay—crops that could be rotated and that an individual farmer and his family could handle.

That same independent spirit nurtured the growth of higher education here. In Lexington alone are Washington & Lee University, which Robert E. Lee headed, and the Virginia Military Institute, where Stonewall Jackson taught philosophy and artillery tactics and which did not admit women until forced to do so by the U.S. Supreme Court in 1996. A trio of distinguished women's colleges is nearby: Mary Baldwin College at Staunton, Sweet Briar College at Sweet Briar, and Hollins University at Roanoke. Also nearby is the respected Randolph College, which is co-ed. President Woodrow Wilson's birthplace is in Staunton.

Industry flourished here more than in most of Virginia east of the Blue Ridge. In the 19th century, the Norfolk and Western Railway established its chief junction at Roanoke, and as the years passed, the city became the headquarters of the railroad, now Norfolk Southern, and many other companies. The city's population has remained flat over the last decade. The city suffered double-digit unemployment during the recession, but has since been inching upward.

The 6th Congressional District of Virginia covers the heart of the Valley of Virginia, from Strasburg south to Roanoke, and it crosses over the Blue Ridge to take in Lynchburg, the home of Liberty University, a fundamentalist Baptist college. In recent decades, the ancestral conservatism of the region and the feisty politics of the mountain rebels have melded into a single conservative Republicanism, more populist than elitist in tone, as concerned with moral values as economic freedom, and prickly about interference from Washington and Richmond. In 2004, the 6th District voted 63% for Republican President George W. Bush, his highest percentage in a Virginia district. In 2008, GOP nominee John McCain easily defeated Democrat Barack Obama here, 57%-42%. In the governor's race one year later, Republican Bob McDonnell did even better in most counties.

Bob Goodlatte (R)

The congressman from the 6th District is Bob Goodlatte, a Republican first elected in 1992. He has been a leader on agricultural issues and now focuses on technology, a subject where he has regularly managed to find common ground with Democrats.

Goodlatte grew up in Massachusetts, the son of a Friendly's ice cream store manager and a part-time retail clerk. He attended Bates College in Maine, where he was president of the College

Republicans, and then went on to law school at Washington & Lee University. After college, he got a job on the staff of Republican U.S. Rep. Caldwell Butler of Roanoke. Goodlatte practiced law in Roanoke and stayed active in politics. In 1992, when Democrat Jim Olin retired, Goodlatte was nominated by the Republican convention to run for the seat, and won the general election 60%-40%.

With his conservative voting record, Goodlatte edged out then-Minority Whip Eric Cantor as the Virginia delegation's most conservative member in the 111th Congress (2009-10), according to *National Journal's* rankings. He jumped into the "birther" controversy in 2009 by co-sponsoring a bill to require presidential candidates to make their birth certificates public, which seemed to be a reaction to unsubstantiated theories that Democrat Barack Obama was not born in the United States and therefore ineligible to serve as president. In early 2011, Goodlatte introduced bills to abolish the tax code and immigrant visa lottery program as well as to implement a constitutional balanced-budget amendment and to permit oil drilling off Virginia's coast.

But Goodlatte has another, less partisan side. The low-key, unassuming lawmaker co-chairs the bipartisan Congressional Internet Caucus, and often has worked with its Democratic members. He and California Democrat Anna Eshoo pushed for a permanent ban on Internet taxes, and failing to achieve that goal in 2007, he helped to broker an agreement for a four-year prohibition. He also often collaborated with 9th District Democrat Rick Boucher before Boucher's defeat in 2010. "I don't think there is a single issue related to tech that isn't bipartisan," Goodlatte told *National Journal* in 2010.

Goodlatte became chairman of the Judiciary Subcommittee on Intellectual Property, Competition and the Internet in 2011. He examined the Federal Communications Commission's controversial network neutrality order aimed at barring broadband providers from discriminating against online content and applications. He said he opposes the FCC's "one-size fits all approach" and prefers a "light-touch" style that punishes anti-competitive behavior and enforces antitrust laws. He holds a similar philosophy on cyber security, saying that he rejects "heavy-handed mandates" that can hamper the private sector's ability to find innovative solutions. Earlier, in 2003, he sponsored the House-passed bill to limit class-action lawsuits against tobacco companies, gun makers and other companies, and a separate bill to give federal courts jurisdiction over large class-action suits.

Goodlatte previously was best known for his work on the Agriculture Committee, which he chaired from 2003 to 2007. In the minority, he worked closely with committee Chairman Collin Peterson, D-Minn., to enact the 2008 farm bill, serving as the committee's informal liaison to the White House. He helped to broker a compromise on country-of-origin labeling of meat in the bill. In 2008, he joined 50 other House Republicans in urging the Environmental Protection Agency to reduce ethanol production requirements The House GOP's term limits forced Goodlatte to give up his leadership position on the committee in 2009.

Goodlatte has been consistently re-elected without difficulty, and encountered no problem when in 2002 he abandoned his pledge to serve no more than 12 years. He is likely to be forced to yield a portion of his district in 2012 to help protect 9th District freshman Rep. Morgan Griffith, Boucher's successor.

SEVENTH DISTRICT

Eric Cantor (R)

Elected 2000, 6th term; b. June 6, 1963, Richmond; home, Richmond; George Washington U., B.A. 1985, Col. of William & Mary, J.D. 1988, Columbia U., M.S., 1989; Jewish; married (Diana); 3 children.

Elected Office: VA House of Del., 1991-2000.

Professional Career: Practicing atty., 1990-2000.

DC Office: 303 CHOB, 20515, 202-225-2815; Fax: 202-225-0011; Web site: cantor.house.gov.

State Offices: Culpeper, 540-825-8960; Richmond, 804-747-4073.

Group Ratings

	ACLU	ACU	ADA	CFG	AFS	FRC	LCV	ITIC	NTU	COC
2010	6	100	0	100	0	100	0	33	90	88
2009	–	100	0	92	0	–	0	–	89	71

National Journal Ratings

	2010 LIB —	2010 CONS	2009 LIB —	2009 CONS
Economic	9% —	91%	8% —	92%
Social	18% —	82%	13% —	84%
Foreign	26% —	72%	0% —	75%
Composite	18% —	82%	12% —	88%

Key Votes of the 111th Congress

1. Overturn Ledbetter	N	5. Bar federal abortion funds	Y	9. Stop detainee transfers	Y
2. Pass $820 billion stimulus	N	6. Pass health care bill	N	10. Legalize immigrants' kids	N
3. Let guns in national parks	Y	7. Regulate financial firms	N	11. Repeal don't ask, tell	N
4. Pass cap-and-trade	N	8. Pass tax cuts for some	N	12. Limit campaign funds	N

Election Results

2010 general	Eric Cantor (R)	138,209	(59%)	($5,955,025)
	Rickard Waugh (D)	79,616	(34%)	($148,869)
	Floyd Bayne (Green)	15,164	(7%)	($19,685)
2010 primary	Eric Cantor (R)	unopposed		

Prior Winning Percentages: 2008 (63%), 2006 (64%), 2004 (75%), 2002 (69%), 2000 (67%)

Population		Race/Ethnicity		Work	
Pop. 2010:	757,917	White:	72.1%	Private:	78.1%
Change since 2000:	Up 17.8%	Black:	16.9%	Government:	16.4%
Urban:	70.0%	Hispanic:	4.9%	Self-employed:	5.3%
Rural:	30.0%	Asian:	3.9%	Blue collar:	17.4%
Area size:	3,557 sq. mi.	Native Am.:	0.2%	White collar:	67.3%
		Hawaiian:	0.0%	Khaki collar:	0.1%
Age		Two+ races:	1.8%	Other:	15.2%
Median age:	38.4 yrs.				
More than 65 yrs:	12.5%	*Ancestry*		Median income:	$64,648
Less than 18 yrs:	24.0%	English	13.1%	Median Home Value:	$265,500
		German	11.9%		
Education		Irish	10.1%	**Military Veterans**	
H.S. grad:	88.1%			% of Pop:	11.2%
College grad:	36.6%				
Grad degree:	13.2%				

Central Virginia; Richmond area

In the center of Virginia, on a hill in downtown Richmond above the James River, is Thomas Jefferson's Capitol, one of the first classical-style buildings in North America, chaste and simple in the Jeffersonian style. A mile or so west is Monument Avenue, Richmond's grand 140-foot-wide boulevard, punctuated by circles, each with a statue of a Confederate hero—Robert E. Lee, Jeb Stuart, Jefferson Davis, Stonewall Jackson and Matthew Fontaine Maury, the "Pathfinder

2008 Presidential Vote		
John McCain (R) 205,949	(53%)
Barack Obama (D) 177,789	(46%)
2004 Presidential Vote		
George Bush (R) 204,273	(61%)
John Kerry (D) 128,166	(38%)
Cook Partisan Voting Index: R+9		

of the Seas." Richmond itself is a monument to Jefferson and to the Confederacy. Its metropolitan area is only the third-largest in the state, but it still sets the tone for Virginia. It is home to many of the state's great institutions—Dominion Resources, Main Street banks, big law firms, and the *Richmond Times-Dispatch*. Richmond's metro area has grown far past its city borders, covering almost all of suburban Henrico and Chesterfield counties and spreading into what was, until recently, countryside.

For many years, Richmond was riven by racial differences. In the 1950s, Virginia's leaders gathered in Richmond and called for massive resistance to desegregation. When Richmond elected its first black-majority City Council in the 1970s, the outgoing Council deeded the statue of Lee to the state for fear it would be torn down. Today, Richmond is a more tolerant place. African-Americans have been a majority in the city for two decades now, and in 1989, Virginia elected a black governor, Douglas Wilder, who grew up on Church Hill in a segregated neighborhood overlooking the Capitol. In 2005, Wilder made a triumphant return as mayor, elected by a biracial majority. A statue of Richmond-born, African-American tennis champion Arthur Ashe has been added to Monument Avenue. Except for during the recession, when the city suffered double-digit unemployment, Richmond had been thriving economically with banking, securities, and health care corporate offices and the Philip Morris headquarters. Politically, the city is solidly Democratic. Henrico, Chesterfield and the counties beyond are heavily Republican.

The 7th Congressional District of Virginia includes some city precincts and most of the area surrounding Richmond. The black precincts in the city and Henrico County are mostly in the black-majority 3rd District. The 7th District extends past President James Madison's home at Montpelier to fast-growing Spotsylvania and Culpeper counties and as far north as Rappahannock County and the Blue Ridge Mountains. In Louisa County, Dominion Virginia Power has considered adding a third reactor at its nuclear plant to meet the region's future electricity needs. The 7th is 17% African-American, and 80% of its votes are cast in metro Richmond. This is one of the most Republican districts in Virginia. George W. Bush twice won 61% of the vote here. In 2008, Republican John McCain beat Democrat Barack Obama 53%-46%. (However, Obama won the Henrico County suburbs by 679 votes of the 116,000 cast.)

Eric Cantor (R)

The congressman from the 7th District is Eric Cantor, a Republican first elected in 2000 who has risen through the ranks to become majority leader, the second-highest leadership position in the House. His swift ascension is a testament to his aggressive networking and fundraising skills as well as his unwaveringly on-message articulation of conservative themes. His relationship with Speaker John Boehner, reportedly tense at times, is one of the most-watched barometers of how successfully Republicans maintain their grip on the chamber.

Cantor grew up in a well-to-do Richmond family. His father ran a real estate law firm and was the Virginia treasurer for Ronald Reagan in 1984. His mother served on philanthropic boards. He went to George Washington University and then on to William and Mary to get a law degree. Cantor also got a master's degree in real estate from Columbia University, and then joined the family firm. In 1991, he was elected to the first of five terms in Virginia's House of Delegates. In the legislature, Cantor was a leading ally of business, sponsoring a bill to limit the liability of Philip Morris in a Florida court decree and opposing restrictions on telemarketers.

When GOP Rep. Tom Bliley announced his retirement in 2000, after six years as chairman of the Energy and Commerce Committee, Cantor entered the race to succeed him. Cantor had interned for Bliley in college, had later served as his campaign chairman and had the backing of his political organization. Still, he faced a serious contest in the Republican primary from state Sen. Stephen Martin, who had a solid base of social and religious conservatives. Their contest turned negative. Cantor attacked Martin for supporting a backdoor pay raise for legislators, and Martin questioned Cantor's business dealings. Martin raised less than $200,000, a quarter of what Cantor spent in the primary. Cantor won the primary by only 263 votes. He got 74% of the vote in Henrico, while Martin got 77% in his Chesterfield County base. In the general election, Cantor won 67%-33%, assuming the seat that Madison once held.

In the House, Cantor has been reliably conservative, sponsoring legislation that often is aimed at making a political point. He introduced the 2011 bill repealing the health care overhaul, a measure with no chance of passage in the Democratically controlled Senate. In 2009, he sponsored a $5,000 refinancing tax credit to assist homeowners with mortgage problems, something he said was a way to put private capital into the housing market without relying on government. It drew no Democratic support and stalled. He has backed cuts in corporate taxes to spur economic growth, and in 2007, he opposed tax increases on hedge funds and private equity firms. Despite his desire to cut the federal budget, he was one of 92 Republicans who joined Democrats in February 2011 in defeating a Republican Study Committee proposal to return non-security discretionary spending for fiscal 2011 to 2008 levels.

The budget debate in 2011 led to considerable speculation about signs of strain in the Boehner-Cantor relationship. Under pressure to show Republicans could do more than just criticize President Barack Obama, the speaker regularly appeared before the microphones at the White House to issue assurances of progress toward a deal, stressing that both sides liked and trusted each other. Meanwhile, Cantor expressed impatience with the negotiations on the House floor. "We don't accept the status quo," he declared, as Republicans around him broke into applause. The final agreement came in around $38 billion below fiscal 2010 levels—less than what many conservatives had demanded. Both Cantor and Boehner denied any friction, and some political observers wondered if their good cop-bad cop approach was deliberate. But there was also talk that Cantor's playing to the tea-party wing of the GOP was intended to keep him in its good graces if a future insurrection led to Boehner's ouster as speaker.

Cantor is popular with fellow Republicans, in no small part because of his skill at fundraising. He raised more than $10 million in the 2010 election cycle. In the first quarter of 2011 alone, his personal campaign account took in $1.3 million, while his other campaign organizations raked in another $900,000. His largest donors included securities and investment firms as well as the insurance and real estate industries.

Cantor is the only Jewish House Republican. With his knowledge of the Middle East and his strong support for Israel, he chaired the Republican Task Force on Terrorism and Unconventional Warfare, and he praised President George W. Bush as more committed to Israel than any other president. In 2007, Cantor warned that anti-Semitism—including "Holocaust denial" —was increasing around the world and was a danger "for all people." When Navy SEALs killed Osama bin Laden after a nearly decade-long hunt in April 2011, Cantor pointedly refused to give the president credit, contending that Obama had "followed the vigilance of President Bush in bringing bin Laden to justice."

When Obama took office, Cantor moved quickly to establish his mark as a leader of the loyal opposition to the president's programs. With Boehner's encouragement in 2009, he prepared an alternative to the Democrats' $787 billion economic stimulus plan, which he said would create twice as many jobs at half the cost. At the time, Cantor was Republican whip. In part because of Cantor's efforts in that role, all House Republicans opposed Obama's stimulus plan when it came to a vote on the House floor. Also in 2009, Cantor, with Republican Sen. John Thune of South Dakota, led a Republican working group to focus on waste, fraud and abuse in the spending of the stimulus money. And he was among the first Republicans to voice specific doubts about Democratic proposals on the federal budget, reform of the financial services industry, and expanded health care coverage.

Cantor also was deeply involved in party efforts to rebrand itself after two consecutive disappointing elections in 2006 and 2008. Cantor modeled himself after former Republican House Speaker Newt Gingrich of Georgia, who led his party to take control of the House in 1994. Cantor's aggressive style has earned him the enmity of House Democrats, who derisively dubbed him "Dr. No" and accused him of spoiling any hope for bipartisanship. Unfazed, Cantor rallied his deputy whips to begin focusing on fundraising for the 2010 congressional elections. In May 2009, Cantor launched the National Council for a New America to spotlight Republican alternatives to Obama's proposals. But the group's policy statements made no mention of social issues, leading social conservatives such as former Arkansas Gov. Mike Huckabee, another potential contender in 2012, to criticize their approach to expanding the Republican tent.

Cantor's earlier efforts to assure support for Republican initiatives impressed House leaders and led to his meteoric rise to leadership. In December 2002, incoming Majority Whip Roy Blunt,

R-Mo., named Cantor as his chief deputy whip, giving him a seat at the party's leadership table and handing him the often thankless task of tracking his colleagues' sentiments on pending legislation. Cantor also won a seat on the powerful Ways and Means Committee, where he was a booster of the 2003 Medicare prescription drug bill and was an active proponent of health savings accounts.

When Blunt ran against Boehner to replace Texan Tom DeLay as majority leader in early 2006, Cantor backed Blunt and built an aggressive campaign to replace him as whip if Blunt won the contest. But Blunt lost to Boehner and remained as whip. Cantor had pledged not to challenge Blunt for the whip's post and kept his word. Arguably, Cantor's decision served the interests of both men. Blunt remained in the leadership for another two years, which prepared him to run successfully for a Senate seat in Missouri in 2010, while Cantor earned additional chits in his continued move up the leadership ladder. He was also able to rebuild his relationship with Boehner after backing his opponent in the leadership contest. In 2007, Cantor became finance chairman of the National Republican Congressional Committee, a testament to his prodigious fundraising skills. He raised more money for Republican candidates for the House than anyone except for Boehner. With Reps. Paul Ryan, R-Wis., and Kevin McCarthy, R-Calif., Cantor created the Young Guns program to identify and finance conservatives and "new blood" candidates for the House, in tandem with the NRCC.

Cantor's political rise was accompanied by his enthusiastic salesmanship for GOP presidential nominee John McCain during the 2008 campaign, when he was among McCain's most outspoken backers in Congress. He embraced McCain's centrist approach on issues such as global warming and immigration, and his more conservative views on national security. As chairman of the 2008 Victory Jewish Coalition, Cantor also was an aggressive fundraiser for McCain.

At home, Cantor has faced only nominal opposition since his 2000 election.

EIGHTH DISTRICT

Jim Moran (D)

Elected 1990, 11th term; b. May 16, 1945, Buffalo, NY; home, Alexandria; Col. of Holy Cross, B.A. 1967, attended City U. of NY, 1967-68, U. of Pittsburgh, M.P.A. 1970; Catholic; married (LuAnn); 4 children.

Elected Office: Alexandria City Cncl., 1979–82; Alexandria vice mayor, 1982–84, Alexandria mayor, 1985–90.

Professional Career: Budget analyst & auditor, U.S. Dept. of H.E.W., 1968–74; Fiscal policy spec., Library of Congress, 1974–76; Staff, U.S. Senate Approp. Cmte., 1976–80; Investment broker, 1980–88.

DC Office: 2239 RHOB, 20515, 202-225-4376; Fax: 202-225-0017; Web site: moran.house.gov.

State Offices: Alexandria, 703-971-4700.

Committees: *Appropriations:* Defense; Interior, Environment & Related Agencies (RMM); Military Construction, Veterans Affairs & Related Agencies.

Group Ratings

	ACLU	ACU	ADA	CFG	AFS	FRC	LCV	ITIC	NTU	COC
2010	88	8	100	13	88	0	100	67	8	13
2009	–	0	85	6	89	–	93	–	2	50

National Journal Ratings

	2010 LIB	—	2010 CONS	2009 LIB	—	2009 CONS
Economic	62%	—	37%	67%	—	33%
Social	82%	—	14%	89%	—	0%
Foreign	84%	—	11%	91%	—	0%
Composite	78%	—	22%	86%	—	14%

Key Votes of the 111th Congress

1. Overturn Ledbetter	Y	5. Bar federal abortion funds	N	9. Stop detainee transfers	N
2. Pass $820 billion stimulus	Y	6. Pass health care bill	Y	10. Legalize immigrants' kids	Y
3. Let guns in national parks	N	7. Regulate financial firms	Y	11. Repeal don't ask, tell	Y
4. Pass cap-and-trade	Y	8. Pass tax cuts for some	N	12. Limit campaign funds	Y

Election Results

2010 general	Jim Moran (D)	116,404	(61%)	($1,312,117)
	Jay Murray (R)	71,145	(37%)	($446,468)
2010 primary	Jim Moran (D)	unopposed		

Prior Winning Percentages: 2008 (68%), 2006 (66%), 2004 (60%), 2002 (60%), 2000 (63%), 1998 (67%), 1996 (66%), 1994 (59%), 1992 (56%), 1990 (52%)

Population		Race/Ethnicity		Work	
Pop. 2010:	701,010	White:	54.6%	Private:	69.5%
Change since 2000:	Up 8.9%	Black:	13.3%	Government:	26.0%
Urban:	100.0%	Hispanic:	18.2%	Self-employed:	4.4%
Rural:	0.0%	Asian:	10.6%	Blue collar:	9.9%
Area size:	125 sq. mi.	Native Am.:	0.2%	White collar:	75.5%
		Hawaiian:	0.1%	Khaki collar:	1.4%
Age		Two+ races:	2.7%	Other:	13.2%
Median age:	35.2 yrs.				
More than 65 yrs:	9.7%	*Ancestry*		Median income:	$89,605
Less than 18 yrs:	19.9%	German	10.1%	Median Home Value:	$484,400
		Irish	9.4%		
Education		English	8.6%	**Military Veterans**	
H.S. grad:	90.4%			% of Pop:	9.7%
College grad:	60.1%				
Grad degree:	29.4%				

Washington, D.C. Suburbs; Arlington

More than 200 years ago, when George Washington strolled the brick sidewalks of Alexandria on his way to market or court or church, it was the largest city in Northern Virginia, far larger than Georgetown, just up the Potomac River. The areas that are now Capitol Hill and downtown Washington, D.C., were hills above the river's mud flats. But Washington became the national capital, and as it grew, Northern Virginia seemed left behind. In 1846, the District of Co-

2008 Presidential Vote		
Barack Obama (D)	234,203	(69%)
John McCain (R)	100,234	(30%)

2004 Presidential Vote		
John Kerry (D)	189,525	(64%)
George Bush (R)	104,298	(35%)

Cook Partisan Voting Index: D+16

lumbia retroceded its land south of the Potomac—now Alexandria and Arlington—to Virginia because it seemed obvious that the federal government would never need it. It would be another 97 years before the first federal building was built on the Virginia side—the Pentagon. When the Pentagon was built, Alexandria and the rural countryside of Northern Virginia were represented in Congress by Judge Howard W. Smith, a Democrat who saw as his mission the maintenance of the standards of George Washington, Thomas Jefferson and Robert E. Lee. Yet by the 1960s, the area was changing around him.

New subdivision dwellers with white-collar jobs and lots of families with children wanted schools with good academic programs, not the segregated schoolhouses Judge Smith's friends were willing to finance. The new generation wanted freeways, parks and recreation facilities. As Smith's district was moved farther out into the countryside, two-party politics came to the suburbs. Now the onetime suburbs of Alexandria and Arlington are "edge cities." Arlington County has the seventh highest median income ($96,200) of any county in the nation and has a greater share of people with college degrees (69%) than any other county. Giant office developments sprang up from rail yards in Crystal City and from used car lots upriver in Rosslyn. Commuters find roads jammed: The Texas Transportation Institute ranked the Washington area in a tie with Chicago for the nation's worst traffic delays in 2009.

The 8th Congressional District of Virginia consists of all of Arlington County and the cities of Alexandria and Falls Church. It takes in two sections of Fairfax County: a stretch of land from Tysons Corner west to Reston, and several areas south of Alexandria's Old Town. It includes George Washington's Mount Vernon, lower-income Groveton, suburban Springfield and the more rural areas around Fort Belvoir. The district now is solidly Democratic. Democrat Creigh Deeds got 66% of the Arlington County vote in the 2009 governor's race, his best showing among the state's counties.

Jim Moran (D)

The congressman from the 8th District is Democrat Jim Moran, elected in 1990. He has worked his way up to a senior position on the Appropriations Committee to take care of his federally-dependent district, but his legislative work has been overshadowed at times by a combativeness that has landed him in headline-grabbing confrontations.

Moran was one of seven children in an Irish Catholic family in suburban Boston. His father was a professional boxer and Washington Redskins football player. Moran graduated from the College of the Holy Cross and got a master's degree from the University of Pittsburgh. He was elected to the Alexandria City Council in 1979 and became vice mayor in 1982. Then in 1984, the first of what would be many career controversies flared, and Morgan pleaded no contest to a conflict of interest charge and resigned from the Council. The charges were later dropped, and in 1985, Moran was elected mayor. In 1990, he ran for Congress against Republican incumbent Stanford Parris. It was a nasty race. Parris said Moran was a supporter of Iraqi Leader Saddam Hussein, and Moran responded that he wanted to "break (Parris') nose," and called him "a deceitful, fatuous jerk." The major substantive issue was abortion rights; Moran ran an ad portraying Lady Liberty behind bars to demonstrate his "pro-choice" position. With a big margin in Alexandria, he won 52%-45%.

In the House, Moran has styled himself as a moderate among Democrats, though he has shown more loyalty to his caucus since President Barack Obama took office. In 1997, he co-founded the New Democrat Coalition, made up of moderate Democrats to support alternatives to liberal policies. Unlike many liberals, Moran has supported free trade agreements, and, he is a strong ally of the high-tech industry. He got a bill into law in 2010 aimed at cracking down on the illegal dog and cat fur trade by enforcing rules requiring that all garments containing any amount of fur list the species of the animal used on the product's label.

With a district chock full of federal employees, Moran watches out for their interests. When several Virginia military installations saw an influx of new personnel as a result of the 2005 base realignment process, he worked on ways to ease traffic problems. He also has been an advocate for his district through earmarking. He secured $107 million in earmarks in 2010, the fourth-highest amount among House members, according to Taxpayers for Common Sense.

Moran's short temper and edgy remarks sometime land him in hot water. In 1995, he had a shoving match with California Republican Duke Cunningham on the House floor after Cunningham said that Moran had "turned his back on Desert Storm." At an anti-war forum in 2003, Moran seemed to blame the pro-Israel lobby for the war in Iraq. "If it were not for the strong support of the Jewish community for this war with Iraq, we would not be doing this," he said. The furious reaction prompted Moran to apologize. After Democrats lost their majority in 2010, he told an Arab television network that Republican gains came in part because "a lot of people in this country ... don't want to be governed by an African-American." At a town hall meeting several months later, he tangled with a disabled military veteran whom the congressman accused of making "caustic" comments, a videotaped exchange that made the rounds of conservative blogs and websites.

Moran's personal finances have raised eyebrows as well. In 2000, *The Washington Post* reported that a pharmaceutical company lobbyist gave Moran a $25,000 loan on generous terms. Moran quickly agreed to repay the loan and suffered no apparent political damage. More trouble followed in 2002 with reports that he borrowed $50,000 from the founder of America Online, and that MBNA, the big credit card company, had given him a favorable rate on a mortgage. The *Post* reported in 2010 that since his 2004 remarriage to a wealthy entrepreneur, he has had one of the most actively traded stock portfolios, and that in 2005, he personally made more than two dozen risky, short-term investments.

In 2004, his primary opponent was Alexandria attorney Andrew Rosenberg, a political newcomer who criticized Moran's character and rhetoric. Moran cited his advocacy for his district and prevailed 59%-41%. He went on to win the general election easily and has had uneventful re-elections since. Redistricting in 2012 is likely to cause him to yield some Democratic portions of his district to 11th District Democrat Gerald Connolly and to pick up some Republican-leaning precincts.

NINTH DISTRICT

Morgan Griffith (R)

Elected 2010, 1st term; b. March 15, 1958, Philadelphia, PA; home, Salem; Emory and Henry Col., B.A. 1980; Washington and Lee U., J.D. 1983; Episcopalian; Married (Hilary Davis Griffith); 3 children.

Elected Office: VA House of Del., 1994-2010, majority ldr., 2000-10.

Professional Career: Practicing atty., 2008-10.

DC Office: 1108 LHOB, 20515, 202-225-3861; Fax: 202-225-0076; Web site: morgangriffith.house.gov.

State Offices: Abingdon, 276-525-1405; Christiansburg, 540-381-5671.

Committees: *Energy & Commerce:* Energy & Power; Oversight & Investigations.

Election Results

2010 general	Morgan Griffith (R)	95,726	(51%)	($1,075,273)
	Rick Boucher (D)	86,743	(46%)	($2,639,353)
	Jeremiah Heaton (I)	4,282	(2%)	($23,306)
2010 primary	Morgan Griffith (R)	unopposed		

Population		Race/Ethnicity		Work	
Pop. 2010:	656,200	White:	92.0%	Private:	75.0%
Change since 2000:	Up 2.0%	Black:	3.8%	Government:	19.4%
Urban:	34.1%	Hispanic:	1.8%	Self-employed:	5.5%
Rural:	65.9%	Asian:	1.1%	Blue collar:	28.5%
Area size:	8,838 sq. mi.	Native Am.:	0.2%	White collar:	53.1%
		Hawaiian:	0.0%	Khaki collar:	0.1%
Age		Two+ races:	1.1%	Other:	18.3%
Median age:	40.0 yrs.				
More than 65 yrs:	16.0%	*Ancestry*		Median income:	$36,757
Less than 18 yrs:	19.6%	USA	13.8%	Median Home Value:	$102,900
		German	11.5%		
Education		Irish	10.4%	**Military Veterans**	
H.S. grad:	76.9%			% of Pop:	10.1%
College grad:	17.3%				
Grad degree:	6.4%				

Southwest Virginia; Blacksburg

As early as 1765, settlements were carved out of the great Valley of Virginia, which bends westward and south toward Tennessee and the Cumberland Gap. Most founders were of Scots-Irish lineage, and they moved to a mountainous area that developed almost apart from the rest of Virginia. The fiercely independent settlers were first farmers, and later coal miners, as in West Virginia, which wasn't a separate state until 1863. Politically, this virtually all-white area op-

2008 Presidential Vote		
John McCain (R)	160,430	(59%)
Barack Obama (D)	108,220	(40%)

2004 Presidential Vote		
George Bush (R)	153,868	(59%)
John Kerry (D)	101,662	(39%)

Cook Partisan Voting Index: R+11

posed slavery and was skeptical, if not hostile, to the Confederacy. Out of the crucible of struggle between secessionists and unionists, Southwest Virginia developed a robust two-party politics after the Civil War, with both parties resembling their national counterparts more closely than in the rest of Virginia. It is a long way from here to plantation country—the state's extreme southwest corner is closer to the Mississippi River than to the Potomac River.

The 9th Congressional District covers all of southwest Virginia west of Roanoke. Over the years, the district became known as the "Fighting Ninth," because of its taste for raucous politics, which by and large were culturally conservative and economically populist. In recent decades, as development has moved down Interstate 81, it has become somewhat more like the rest of Virginia. With encouragement from state officials, businesses have created jobs at high-tech companies and telephone call centers. Agriculture has been thriving, especially with produce and dairy. Mountain counties farther west continue to depend on coal and to lose population. In 1990, mining employed 10,300 people and produced 46.5 million tons of coal; by 2009, the figures had dropped by more than 50%. The district voted narrowly for Democrat Bill Clinton twice, but voted by much wider margins for Republican George W. Bush in 2000 and 2004. In 2008, the district went 59%-40% for Republican John McCain.

Morgan Griffith (R)

The new congressman from the 9th District is Republican Morgan Griffith, the former Virginia House majority leader who unseated Democratic Rep. Rick Boucher, a 28-year incumbent, in one of the major upsets of 2010.

Griffith was born in Philadelphia and moved to Salem, Va., as a child. He was president of his high school student body and an avid swimmer. He attended Emory & Henry College, in part because it had just completed a new pool. He graduated in 1980 and received a law degree three years later from Washington and Lee University. Griffith then opened his own private practice in Salem. He joined a statewide firm in 2008, managing its Roanoke/Salem branch. He married Hilary Davis Griffith, a prosecutor, in 2005.

After winning a seat in the state House of Delegates in 1994, Griffith led efforts to repeal restrictions on gun ownership and sought to restrict abortion rights. He pushed to increase penalties for sex offenders and led an unsuccessful attempt to block a $1.4 billion tax increase. Griffith rose to majority leader in 2000, and he earned a reputation as a skilled parliamentarian. But Griffith also bucked his party on occasion. In 2010, he helped draft a bill to legalize marijuana for medicinal use.

In the U.S. House race, Griffith easily won the Republican nomination on the first ballot at a party convention in May. In the general election, he was at a significant financial disadvantage, outspent by Boucher 3-to-1. But Boucher, though not a liberal Democrat, had been a leader on the party's cap-and-trade bill aimed at limiting greenhouse gas emissions, which passed the House in 2009. The bill was unpopular in Appalachia's coal country, and Griffith made Boucher's work on the bill a centerpiece of his campaign. He argued that the measure would have killed jobs and raised electricity costs. Boucher framed his support for the bill as a way to ensure that Congress, and not the conservatives' nemesis, the Environmental Protection Agency, had regulatory power over carbon emissions.

Griffith also sought to tie Boucher to President Barack Obama. One of his ads repeatedly showed a clip of Obama saying, "I love Rick Boucher." The ad helped offset Boucher's legitimate claims that he had opposed the Democrats' health care overhaul bill. Boucher also was endorsed by the National Rifle Association. Boucher attacked Griffith as a carpetbagger because he lived outside the district boundaries. In one of his television ads, the announcer said, "Morgan Griffith: He's not from here ... and it shows."

Many pre-election polls showed Boucher leading Griffith, but in a historic day for Republicans across the country, Griffith defeated the incumbent, 51% to 46%.

In Washington, Griffith got a plum seat on the House Energy and Commerce Committee, rare for a freshman and a sign that the GOP leadership wants to keep Griffith around. He also joined the Republican Study Committee, a group of the most conservative House members.

TENTH DISTRICT

Frank Wolf (R)

Elected 1980, 16th term; b. Jan. 30, 1939, Philadelphia, PA; home, Vienna; PA St. U., B.A. 1961, Georgetown U., LL.B. 1965; Presbyterian; married (Carolyn); 5 children.

Military Career: Army, 1962–63, Army Reserves 1963–67.

Professional Career: Legis. asst., U.S. Rep. Edward Biester, 1968–71; Asst., U.S. Interior Secy. Rogers Morton, 1971–74; Dep. asst. secy., U.S. Dept. of Interior, 1974–75; Practicing atty., 1975–80.

DC Office: 241 CHOB, 20515, 202-225-5136; Fax: 202-225-0437; Web site: wolf.house.gov.

State Offices: Herndon, 703-709-5800; Winchester, 540-667-0990.

Committees: *Appropriations:* Commerce, Justice, Science & Related Agencies (Chmn); State, Foreign Operations & Related Programs; Transportation, HUD & Related Agencies.

Group Ratings

	ACLU	ACU	ADA	CFG	AFS	FRC	LCV	ITIC	NTU	COC
2010	13	92	10	69	0	100	10	33	75	88
2009	–	80	10	72	44	–	21	–	67	93

National Journal Ratings

	2010 LIB	—	2010 CONS	2009 LIB	—	2009 CONS
Economic	36%	—	63%	36%	—	64%
Social	25%	—	71%	29%	—	68%
Foreign	12%	—	79%	0%	—	75%
Composite	27%	—	73%	26%	—	74%

Key Votes of the 111th Congress

1. Overturn Ledbetter	N	5. Bar federal abortion funds	Y	9. Stop detainee transfers	Y
2. Pass $820 billion stimulus	N	6. Pass health care bill	N	10. Legalize immigrants' kids	N
3. Let guns in national parks	Y	7. Regulate financial firms	N	11. Repeal don't ask, tell	N
4. Pass cap-and-trade	N	8. Pass tax cuts for some	N	12. Limit campaign funds	N

Election Results

2010 general	Frank Wolf (R)	131,116	(63%)	($1,365,313)
	Jeffery Barnett (D)	72,604	(35%)	($606,229)
	William Redpath (Lib)	4,607	(2%)	($10,537)
2010 primary	Frank Wolf (R)	unopposed		

Prior Winning Percentages: 2008 (59%), 2006 (57%), 2004 (64%), 2002 (72%), 2000 (84%), 1998 (72%), 1996 (72%), 1994 (87%), 1992 (64%), 1990 (62%), 1988 (68%), 1986 (60%), 1984 (63%), 1982 (53%), 1980 (51%)

Population		Race/Ethnicity		Work	
Pop. 2010:	869,437	White:	63.7%	Private:	77.7%
Change since 2000:	Up 35.1%	Black:	7.2%	Government:	17.3%
Urban:	83.3%	Hispanic:	13.5%	Self-employed:	4.9%
Rural:	16.7%	Asian:	12.4%	Blue collar:	14.4%
Area size:	1,865 sq. mi.	Native Am.:	0.2%	White collar:	71.7%
		Hawaiian:	0.1%	Khaki collar:	0.4%
Age		Two+ races:	2.7%	Other:	13.5%
Median age:	35.8 yrs.				
More than 65 yrs:	8.4%	*Ancestry*		Median income:	$95,448
Less than 18 yrs:	27.3%	German	12.5%	Median Home Value:	$442,500
		Irish	10.4%		
Education		English	9.7%	**Military Veterans**	
H.S. grad:	89.9%			% of Pop:	10.0%
College grad:	48.6%				
Grad degree:	20.3%				

Northern Virginia; McLean

When George Washington decided to place the new nation's capital on the Potomac just upriver from his estate at Mount Vernon, where the falls blocked navigation above the port of Georgetown, the area was buzzing with new settlers. The land above the fall line on the Virginia side of the river consisted of rolling green Piedmont and the fertile mountain-bound Shenandoah Valley. The settlers came up the Great Wagon Road from Pennsylvania and traveled the Potomac and the runs (a Virginia word for small rivers) that fed the valley. During the Civil War, this

2008 Presidential Vote		
Barack Obama (D) 205,964	(53%)
John McCain (R) 179,337	(46%)
2004 Presidential Vote		
George Bush (R) 182,210	(55%)
John Kerry (D) 145,741	(44%)
Cook Partisan Voting Index: R+2		

was some of the most heavily contested land on the continent. The Piedmont, historian C. Vann Woodward wrote, "soaked up more of the blood, sweat and tears of American history than any other part of the country." After the Civil War, the region was quiet. The frontier was very far to the west, and on these lands farmers quietly raised hay, grazed cattle, and kept horses and hounds for fox hunting. During World War II and immediately afterward, this was still open country. Gen. George Marshall, driving from his office in the Pentagon to the old house he bought in Leesburg 30 miles away, would pass a few gas stations and crossroads villages and hundreds of acres of farm fields.

If Marshall made the trip today, he would see something very different. Metropolitan Washington has consumed the countryside. There are still some horse farms in the Piedmont, long the first or second home of some of the richest people in America, but they are increasingly flanked by subdivisions that sprout up seemingly overnight. Fairfax County had 99,000 people in 1950 and passed the 1 million mark in 2002. The explosive growth for the last decade or so has been in Loudoun County, just past Dulles International Airport, the fifth fastest-growing county in the United States from 2000 to 2010. It increased 84%, from 169,600 people to 312,300 people. Loudoun and Fairfax ranked first and second, respectively, in the nation in median household income in 2009. The Washington metro area now extends past those counties and over the Blue Ridge into the Shenandoah Valley.

In the 1950s and 1960s, the Northern Virginia suburbs of Washington were bedroom communities where most commuters headed into the District of Columbia for work and where one-third of them were employed by the federal government. But in the 1980s and 1990s, Northern Virginia became an employment center and focus of innovation on its own. The Dulles Access Road, which ran through rural-looking territory 20 years ago, is now lined with office buildings holding high-tech firms and entrepreneurial startups, defense contractors and "Beltway bandit" lobbying firms. There have been growing pains: traffic is mightily congested and Loudoun County voters have swung pro-growth proposals to anti-growth regulations. Loudoun is family country—45% of households have children under 18. Unemployment has been far lower than the national average in Northern Virginia, and Fairfax and Loudoun have alternated as the county with the highest median household incomes ($114,000 in 2009) among counties with populations of more than 250,000. Immigrants have flocked in to work on construction sites. In 2007, gang graffiti and an uptick in crime prompted Loudoun voters to pass an ordinance denying services to illegal immigrants.

The 10th Congressional District covers much of Northern Virginia. It starts inside the Capital Beltway and includes most of well-heeled McLean, home of many of Washington's political and lawyer-lobbyist elites. It goes beyond the Beltway to include woodsy Great Falls, Herndon and the Route 28 corridor around Dulles Airport. It includes all of Loudoun County, which is heavily built-up in the east with some still-rural areas west of Leesburg, and the northern half of Fauquier County, which has limited development and is still mostly horse farms. It includes three counties in the northern end of the Shenandoah Valley, the country around Front Royal and Winchester.

In 2008, 32% of the district's votes were cast in Fairfax County, 36% in Loudoun County, 10% in Prince William and Manassas, and 17% in the Shenandoah Valley. The district was once reliably Republican; it voted for George W. Bush by 56% in 2000 and by 55% in 2004. With the influx of immigrants, and as a reaction against religious conservatives who have pursued bans on books and other controversial positions, Northern Virginia is becoming friendlier to the Democrats. The 10th District voted 53%-46% for Democrat Barack Obama in 2008. In the 2009 governor's race, however, Republican Bob McDonnell narrowly won Fairfax County over Democrat Creigh Deeds, 50.7%-49.1, and easily carried Loudoun and the rest of the district.

Frank Wolf (R)

The congressman from the 10th District is Frank Wolf, a Republican first elected in 1980. One of the House's leading crusaders for human rights, he is also an influential appropriator as chairman of the Appropriations' Commerce, Justice, Science Subcommittee.

Wolf grew up in Philadelphia, the son of a police officer. As a child, he developed a strong interest in American history and precociously consumed biographies of Thomas Jefferson and Abraham Lincoln. He majored in political science at Pennsylvania State University and went on to get a law degree from Georgetown University in Washington, D.C. He worked as an aide on Capitol Hill and was an Interior Department appointee in the Nixon and Ford administrations. In 1976, he ran for Congress and lost the Republican primary. In 1978, he won the nomination to run against Joseph Fisher, a liberal who had won the district (then not extending beyond Fairfax County) in 1974. Wolf lost, 53%-47%. In 1980, Wolf ran again and won 51%-49%.

Conservative but not ideologically rigid, Wolf voted in 2009 to expand the State Children's Health Insurance Program and in 2010 for a Democratic bill to overhaul the nation's food safety system. On the Appropriations Committee, he joined younger conservatives in sounding alarms about federal spending, and warned in January 2011 that he would oppose raising the statutory debt ceiling unless there was a commitment to a plan "to put America on a path to financial responsibility." He was one of the forces behind a bipartisan commission to look at looming U.S. fiscal problems, a panel that President Barack Obama created administratively in 2010 with former Republican Sen. Alan Simpson and former Democratic White House official Erskine Bowles as chairmen. Wolf opposed earmarking even before that position became popular with budget reformers in recent years.

Wolf started off his House career concentrating on issues affecting federal employees. With Democrat Steny Hoyer, who represents a suburban D.C. district in Maryland, he sponsored a bill in 2007 to increase the government contribution to federal employees' health insurance premiums. He has long promoted telecommuting for federal employees. In 2008, Congress enacted his 175-mile Journey Through Hallowed Ground National Heritage Area, which will run from Gettysburg to Charlottesville, passing six presidential houses, 13 national historic landmarks and many Revolutionary War and Civil War battlefields. For years he has sought funding for a Metro rail link to Dulles International Airport which, astonishingly, was not foreseen by the system's planners. In 2011, he pressured the agency that runs Dulles to drop plans for an expensive underground station at the airport in favor of a cheaper, above-ground facility.

Wolf traces his interest in human rights to a 1984 trip he took to Ethiopia with his best friend in Congress, liberal Ohio Rep. Tony Hall (1979-2002). The country was in the middle of a famine, and Wolf called his close-up view of the impact on the Ethiopian people "a life-changing experience." Since then, Wolf has been to El Salvador, Chechnya, the Sudan, Sierra Leone and other global trouble spots. In 1998, Wolf sponsored the law setting up a religious freedom office in the State Department and requiring annual reports on religious freedom throughout the world.

With Democrat Nancy Pelosi of California, he led the annual efforts in the 1990s to withdraw normalized trade relations with China because of human right violations, citing China's acts of jailing dissidents, persecuting Tibetan Buddhists, and aiming missiles at the United States. In June 2008, he and New Jersey Republican Chris Smith charged that the Chinese had hacked into their office computers searching for casework information involving Chinese dissidents. When he and Smith tried to meet with dissidents' lawyers in China, the lawyers were arrested. Wolf joined several lawmakers in criticizing NASA Administrator Charles Bolden's visit to China in 2010 and crusaded against the space agency's cooperation with that country. The following year, he called for the creation of a special U.S. envoy to promote freedom for religious minorities overseas.

Wolf has also had an impact on policy toward Iraq. After his third visit to the country in September 2005, he called for "fresh eyes" to look at American policy there and suggested a bipartisan study group. The result was the influential Iraq Study Group, headed by former Secretary of State James Baker and former Indiana Democratic Rep. Lee Hamilton. When President George W. Bush ordered a troop surge to try to restore order in Iraq rather than move toward withdrawal as the ISG recommended, Wolf sponsored a bill to implement its recommendations, but the Democratic leadership declined to bring it up. He introduced a bill in April 2011 calling for an Afghanistan-Pakistan study group. In 2009, Wolf became a vocal opponent of transferring prisoners from the detention camp at Guantanamo Bay, Cuba to prisons within the continental United States. Wolf also has long been one of Congress' leading opponents of gambling and has tried, so far unsuccessfully, to stop the proliferation of Indian-run casinos. He also pushed for passage of a national .08 blood-alcohol limit for drunken driving.

Wolf generally has been re-elected by wide margins, but the Democratic trend in Northern Virginia has produced well-financed challenges to him in several elections. In 2004, he faced a well-financed opponent and won 64%-36%. In 2006 and 2008, his opponent was Judy Feder, who worked in the Clinton administration. She spent $1.5 million the first time and $2.2 million the second, attacking him for supporting the Bush administration and for GOP inaction on the health care crisis. Wolf kept pace with her spending and criticized her for backing the 1993 Clinton health care plan. He won 57%-41% in 2006. Two years later, despite Obama's success in boosting Democratic turnout in Northern Virginia, Wolf won, 59%-39%, carrying every county. He sailed to victory in 2010 against an underfunded Democrat, retired Air Force Col. Jeff Barnett. Redistricting in 2012 is expected to add Republicans to his district, which would bolster GOP efforts to keep the seat when Wolf retires.

ELEVENTH DISTRICT

Gerald Connolly (D)

Elected 2008, 2nd term; b. March 30, 1950, Boston, MA; home, Mantua; Maryknoll Col., B.A. 1971; Harvard U., M.A. 1979; Catholic; married (Cathy); 1 child.

Elected Office: Fairfax Cnty. Bd. of Supervisors, 1995-2008, Chmn., 2004-08.

Professional Career: Non-profit executive; U.S. Senate aide; Defense contractor.

DC Office: 424 CHOB, 20515, 202-225-1492; Fax: 202-225-3071; Web site: connolly.house.gov.

State Offices: Annandale, 703-256-3071; Prince William, 703-670-4989.

Committees: *Foreign Affairs:* Middle East & South Asia; Terrorism, Nonproliferation & Trade. *Oversight & Government Reform:* Federal Workforce, U.S. Postal Service & Labor Policy; Government Organization, Efficiency & Financial Management; Technology, Information Policy, Intergovernmental Relations & Procurement Reform (RMM).

Group Ratings

	ACLU	ACU	ADA	CFG	AFS	FRC	LCV	ITIC	NTU	COC
2010	88	4	85	5	100	0	90	100	12	25
2009	–	0	95	9	78	–	100	–	6	47

National Journal Ratings

	2010 LIB — 2010 CONS			2009 LIB — 2009 CONS		
Economic	53%	—	47%	60%	—	40%
Social	61%	—	35%	83%	—	16%
Foreign	66%	—	29%	70%	—	24%
Composite	62%	—	39%	72%	—	28%

Key Votes of the 111th Congress

1. Overturn Ledbetter	Y	5. Bar federal abortion funds	N
2. Pass $820 billion stimulus	Y	6. Pass health care bill	Y
3. Let guns in national parks	N	7. Regulate financial firms	Y
4. Pass cap-and-trade	Y	8. Pass tax cuts for some	Y

9. Stop detainee transfers	Y
10. Legalize immigrants' kids	Y
11. Repeal don't ask, tell	Y
12. Limit campaign funds	Y

Election Results

2010 general	Gerald Connolly (D)	111,720	(49.2%)	($2,465,298)
	Keith Fimian (R)	110,739	(48.8%)	($2,948,493)
2010 primary	Gerald Connolly (D)	unopposed		

Prior Winning Percentages: 2008 (55%)

Population		Race/Ethnicity		Work	
Pop. 2010:	792,095	White:	54.9%	Private:	68.7%
Change since 2000:	Up 23.1%	Black:	11.1%	Government:	25.8%
Urban:	95.9%	Hispanic:	15.6%	Self-employed:	5.4%
Rural:	4.1%	Asian:	14.8%	Blue collar:	12.4%
Area size:	404 sq. mi.	Native Am.:	0.2%	White collar:	73.1%
		Hawaiian:	0.1%	Khaki collar:	1.3%
Age		Two+ races:	3.1%	Other:	13.2%
Median age:	36.4 yrs.				
More than 65 yrs:	9.0%	*Ancestry*		Median income:	$104,033
Less than 18 yrs:	26.8%	German	11.5%	Median Home Value:	$473,400
		Irish	9.6%		
Education		English	8.5%	**Military Veterans**	
H.S. grad:	92.0%			% of Pop:	12.9%
College grad:	52.6%				
Grad degree:	23.9%				

Fairfax and Prince William Counties

Rising on a hill west of Washington, D.C., Tysons Corner was a back-country intersection 50 years ago. By the late 1980s, it was an edge city, with the largest concentration of office space to be found anywhere between Washington and Atlanta, and with a modern skyline and busy multi-lane avenues that served as arteries to the Capital Beltway. Fairfax County, which includes Tysons Corner, had been a typical post-war suburb. It had only 99,000 people in 1950,

2008 Presidential Vote
Barack Obama (D) 211,466   (57%)
John McCain (R) 156,003   (42%)

2004 Presidential Vote
George Bush (R) 161,104   (50%)
John Kerry (D) 159,055   (49%)

Cook Partisan Voting Index: D+2

far fewer than Washington's 802,000, and fewer than the 197,000 people who lived in closer-in Arlington and Alexandria. But in the years that followed, the trickle moving into Fairfax became a gusher. In 2000, it had 991,000 people, nearly twice as many as D.C. and three times the 318,000 population of Arlington and Alexandria combined. They became mostly affluent communities, with dazzlingly high percentages of residents with college degrees and two or more cars.

In the last decade, Fairfax County has changed. Just as Tysons Corner made it a major commercial center, so it has taken on other characteristics traditionally associated with a central city. Population growth has slowed since 2000; the county passed the 1 million mark in 2005 and stopped for the most part. Meanwhile, suburban Loudoun County vaulted ahead of Fairfax in median household income, and Prince William County has been growing at a fast clip (43% between 2000 and 2010), attracting the young families that Fairfax once did. Some communities have remained unchanged, such as Clifton, which still resembles a quaint old Virginia village. But much has changed. Immigrants—Koreans and Vietnamese, Ethiopians and Afghans, Salvadorans and Mexicans—have put their stamp on what once were mostly white, heavily Protestant neighborhoods. George Mason University economist Tyler Cowen runs a popular website that reviews the area's best ethnic dining spots, including Burmese, Tunisian and Palestinian restaurants.

The 2007-09 recession hit Fairfax with less force than elsewhere in America. Although unemployment rose, it had fallen to under 5% by early 2011—about half the national jobless rate. The federal government still provides a solid base for the local economy and the Federal Transit Administration in August 2008 approved the nearly $5.2 billion extension of the Washington-area Metrorail system from Tysons Corner to Dulles Airport. Unlike Loudoun and Prince William counties, Fairfax has declined to pass ordinances denying services to illegal immigrants, though local law enforcement turned over more than 1,200 suspected illegal residents to federal immigration officials in 2009 and 2010.

The 11th Congressional District of Virginia consists of much of Fairfax County and most of Prince William County. It straddles the Capital Beltway and takes in sprawling Tysons Corner. Inside the Beltway is Annandale; beyond are Vienna, Fairfax, much of Springfield, Burke, Clifton, Centreville and part of Mount Vernon. In Prince William County, it includes Woodbridge and Dale City, areas with large Latino immigrant populations, and it stretches west to Haymarket. The district is 11% African-American, 16% Hispanic, and 15% Asian. Demographic change has produced political change. Immigrants have been voting more Democratic than the people they have replaced, and among non-immigrants, liberal attitudes on cultural issues moved voters against President George W. Bush and toward Democrats such as former Gov. Tim Kaine. In recent presidential contests, the district voted 52%-45% for Bush in 2000, but only 50%-49% for him in 2004. The district voted 57%-42% for Democrat Barack Obama in 2008, and the district seat also fell into Democratic hands in the congressional election that year. But in a low-turnout election a year later, Republican Bob McDonnell narrowly carried Fairfax in the governor's race.

Gerald Connolly (D)

The congressman from the 11th District is Gerald Connolly, a Democrat elected in 2008 to the open seat left by retiring Republican Rep. Tom Davis. Connolly was among the small group of Democratic freshmen to survive the 2010 GOP tidal wave, though just barely.

Connolly grew up in the Boston area. He considered joining the priesthood and studied for six years at a Catholic seminary. But his interest in public policy led him to Washington, D.C., after college, where in the 1970s he managed the American Freedom from Hunger Foundation and the U.S. Committee for Refugees. He got a master's degree from Harvard and worked for a decade on the staff of the Senate Foreign Relations Committee, where he specialized in Middle Eastern affairs and foreign aid. In 1989, he left Capitol Hill to run the Washington office of Stanford Research Institute International, and then became vice president of the San Diego-based defense contractor SAIC. In 1995, Connolly won a seat on the Fairfax County Board of Supervisors, whose former chairman, Davis, had been elected to the 11th District seat in 1994. In 2003, Connolly was elected board chairman, putting him in charge of a large local government at a time of rapid growth. Transportation was a major preoccupation, and his biggest project was the Metrorail extension from Tysons Corner to Dulles.

In these battles, Connolly worked with Davis, who paid close attention to local issues as well as playing a major national role as the chairman of National Republican Congressional Committee in the 2000 and 2002 election seasons. But Davis, an expert on political demographics, could see that Northern Virginia was changing, and in January 2008, he announced he would not seek re-election.

Connolly was obviously a prime candidate for the office. Also getting into the primary, however, was former U.S. Rep. Leslie Byrne, who was defeated in the 11th District in 1994 by Davis. She had the backing of the national women's fundraising group EMILY's List, but Connolly outpaced her in fundraising, in part because of his support from defense contractors. Both ran as solid liberals. In a low-turnout June primary—only 24,000 people voted—Connolly won by a solid 58%-33%. The Republican nominee was Keith Fimian, a businessman and newcomer to Northern Virginia politics who self-financed much of his campaign. Democrats attacked Fimian as a conservative on cultural issues, in contrast to Davis' moderate record, and Fimian got little help from national Republicans. Connolly won by a solid 55%-43%.

In the House, Connolly joined the centrist New Democrat Coalition and established a moderate voting record. In 2009, he was among 10 freshman Democrats who opposed release of the second half of the Troubled Asset Relief Program funds for the financial services industry. Connolly got a bill into law in 2010 to encourage tele-working, one method to reduce traffic congestion in his district. And to better serve his district's multiethnic residents, he hired aides who spoke Korean, Spanish, Urdu and Arabic. "I think the Democratic message resonates ... with a lot of new Americans," he told *National Journal* in 2009. "But we don't even have to work hard at it, frankly, because the other side is absolutely driving folks into our arms because of the 'You're not welcome' message up front."

Fimian returned for a 2010 rematch with Connolly that could not have been more different from their earlier contest. Fimian did not have to rely on self-financing and raised nearly $3 million to Connolly's $2.5 million. Fimian stuck to the national Republican message of "outrageous spending" and rising deficits and attacked Connolly as a "career politician." The Democrat's lead shrunk to single digits by the closing weeks of the race. The Democratic Congressional Campaign Committee shelled out $1 million in the final week to cast Fimian as an extremist on gun control and other social issues. The polls closed showing Connolly with a 480-vote lead, which grew as more ballots were counted. Five days after the election, Fimian conceded, having won 48.8% to his opponent's 49.2%—a margin of less than 1,000 votes out of 227,000 cast. Republican redistricting efforts in Virginia in early 2011 reportedly were concentrating on bolstering GOP strength in other areas at the expense of making the 11th District more Republican.

★ WASHINGTON ★

The state of Washington likes to think of itself as a national trendsetter. As the headquarters of Microsoft, Starbucks and Amazon.com, Washington has been on the cutting edge of innovation for the past two decades. What was for many years an odd far corner of America is in many ways today a model for the rest of the nation. An unusual environment and human creativity combined to produce these achievements. Seattle's cold, misty air and 225 overcast days a year stimulate the appetite for strong, aromatic coffee, and the shapeless blue jeans and sweatshirts worn year-round in this moist climate by professionals and teenagers alike have created a trend made famous by Nirvana, Soundgarden and other Seattle-based grunge artists. Boeing's airframe business took off during World War II because the Pacific Northwest's abundant hydroelectric power made cheap aluminum possible, and the boom in air travel in the 1980s and 1990s kept Boeing's huge assembly lines humming. Microsoft, founded by the usually tie-less and tousle-haired Bill Gates and based in Redmond, across Lake Washington from Seattle, became one of America's great success stories as its software became embedded in the vast majority of the world's computers. With flannel shirts and umbrellas, blue-collar types (as if in a Raymond Carver story) as well as white-collar professionals relaxing on woodsy acreage, Washington set a tone for the late 1990s, a style plainly Middle American but with attitude, an ordinariness so hip it is no longer ordinary. Grunge rock's moment has passed, but Washington's innovators have survived government lawsuits and rollicking business cycles. Similarly, this commonwealth of 6.7 million people has had its woes, but has bounced back, displaying strengths that have proved to be more durable than fashion.

Washington is not much more than a century old. In the two decades after it became a state in 1889, it built a new civilization as transcontinental railroads reached the great ports of Puget Sound, the wheat-processing city of Spokane, and the orchard towns, fishing ports and lumber settlements. Shielded from the storms of the Pacific Ocean by the Olympic Mountains and the Sound, Seattle quickly became a serious American city, a lusty town full of lumbermen and railroad workers. When gold was struck in the Klondike and in Alaska, Seattle became a metropolis of miners, prospectors and get-rich-quick operators, the site of the original "Skid Road," where logs were rolled downhill to the port. (Today it's part of gentrified Pioneer Square.) In the years before World War I, thriving young Seattle's politics were turbulent, as class warfare pitted the Industrial Workers of the World (the IWW or Wobblies) against city business and civic leaders. The businessmen, after some violence, prevailed. Adding to the area's distinctiveness was its large number of Scandinavian immigrants, with their favorable views of cooperative enterprises and government ownership.

Over time, Washington was transformed by a series of national decisions that set its course for decades. One was government development of hydroelectric power. The Columbia River and its tributary, the Snake River, falling thousands of feet in a relatively short distance, had far greater hydroelectric potential than any other American river system, and Franklin Roosevelt, who grew up in another scenic river valley, was always interested in these aqueous projects. In 1937, Bonneville Dam was completed on the lower Columbia. In 1940, Grand Coulee Dam, the largest man-made structure in the world at the time and still the nation's single greatest producer of electricity, was opened where the Columbia cut through the arid, surrealistically contoured plains of eastern Washington. Washington proved hospitable to the industrial union movement of the 1930s, and became one of the nation's most heavily unionized states. When war came, Washington's hydroelectric power—the cheapest electricity in the country—made it the natural site for huge aluminum plants, which required vast amounts of electricity. The Seattle area became the home not only of shipbuilders, but also of the biggest aircraft manufacturer in the country, Boeing. William Boeing founded the company in 1916 in a converted shipyard on the Duwamish River. During the war, the Hanford plant on the Columbia was secretly one of the government's main nuclear-weapons manufacturing sites; after the war, it was open about that status. Cheap power, aluminum, aircraft, nuclear weapons and high unionized wages—these became Washington's economic foundations in the post-World War II years.

Today's Washington lives less off the brawn of hydroelectric power and rail and ship tonnage, and more off the brains that made Boeing the world leader in aircraft and Microsoft the world leader in software. Yet trouble struck this misty paradise in late 1999. Seattle had the world's attention when it hosted the World Trade Organization meeting in December, at which point 50,000 demonstrators took control of the streets, smashing Starbucks windows and preventing leaders, from President Bill Clinton on down, from attending meetings. The city's police chief and

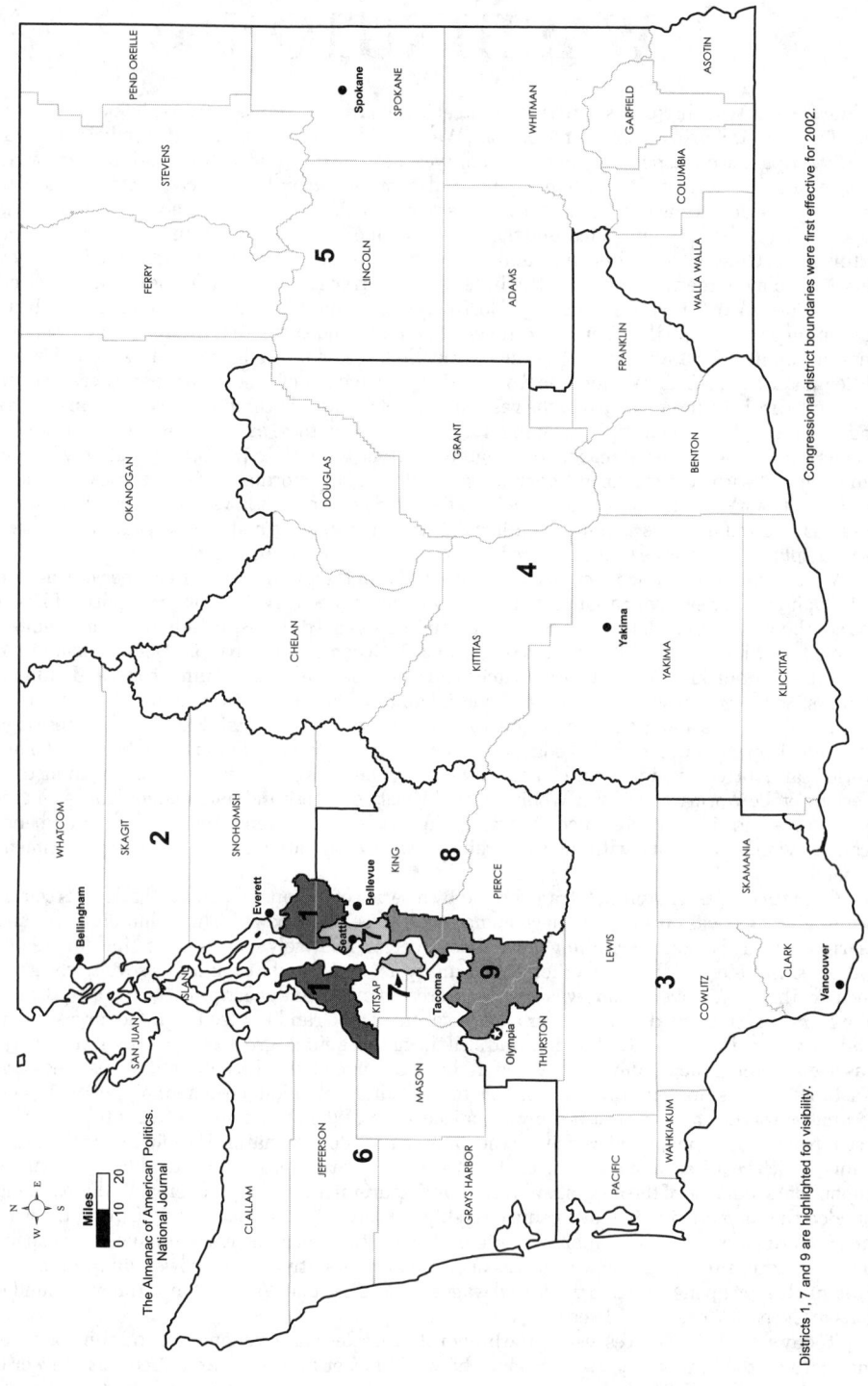

The Almanac of American Politics.
National Journal

Congressional district boundaries were first effective for 2002.

Districts 1, 7 and 9 are highlighted for visibility.

mayor, showing an excess of tolerance, did nothing to stop the violence. Three months later, the high-tech boom, stoked as businesses retooled to avoid Y2K problems, suddenly went bust. Microsoft was under attack from a government antitrust suit initiated in 1998, and Clinton administration proposals to breach the Snake River dams threatened to reduce hydroelectric supply and choke the agriculture of eastern Washington just as a court decision to protect the endangered spotted owl had largely shut down Washington's logging industry in the early 1990s. Boeing in March 2001 announced it was moving its headquarters to Chicago, and then saw its order book go blank after the September 11 attacks. In the recession of the early 2000s, Washington's unemployment was the second-highest in the nation, after Oregon's.

All these problems may turn out to be no more than footnotes. Look at a map that shows elevation of mountains and density of population. On both sides of the Pacific, vast numbers of people are squeezed into small margins of level land between steeply rising volcanic mountains and the sea or tucked into nearby valleys. These islands of settlement are surrounded by vast wildernesses—desert and mountains, open sea and Arctic lands. Yet in the past three decades, the inhabitants of these pockets along the Pacific Rim have produced more economic growth than anywhere else in the world, and though there have been occasional slumps, the Pacific Rim has always come surging back. By 2010, Boeing had 840 orders for its delayed 787 Dreamliner. (Some of which will be built in a new plant in North Charleston, S.C.) And it finally prevailed in the competition for the military's refueling tanker, which will add 11,000 to its current 58,000 jobs in Washington.

Microsoft survived the federal antitrust case, a huge fine from European Union antitrust authorities, Gates' retirement and vigorous competition from Apple and Google. It has spent $1 billion expanding its Redmond campus and opening offices in Bellevue and downtown Seattle. By 2010, it had 40,000 employees in the Puget Sound area. Starbucks, once the fastest-growing retail business of all time, hit problems in the 2007-09 recession but surged back in 2010 and 2011. And amazon.com has continued to make big profits, while brick-and-mortar booksellers struggle. Hydroelectric power may have reached its capacity, but Washington ranks fourth among the states in wind power, and a state Supreme Court ruling has barred local governments from banning wind farms. Washington may boost youth unemployment with the nation's highest minimum wage ($8.67 an hour)—unemployment tended to be a bit above the national average during the recession—but the Kauffman Foundation ranked it No. 2, behind Massachusetts, on its New Economy list.

Politically, Washington, with its Scandinavian and labor-union heritage, was one of the most Democratic northern states in the 1930s. Roosevelt's campaign manager, James Farley, used to refer to "the 47 states and the Soviet of Washington." Its mainstream Democrats—notably Warren Magnuson and Henry (Scoop) Jackson, who represented the state in Congress for a total of 87 years—believed in an active and compassionate federal government that built dams, fabricated aluminum and built nuclear weapons at the Hanford Works at home, and pursued an internationalist, anti-Communist foreign policy abroad. Their political strength came out of a blue-collar base, augmented by the respect big business had for their political clout. Today, the fulcrum of the electorate has moved from blue collar to white collar, from economic class warfare to culture wars, with the balance favoring the Democrats. In presidential races, Washington has voted exclusively Democratic since 1988, and has elected only Democratic governors since 1984. Washington's governor and both of its senators are Democratic women. And Democrats have had a secure hold on most of the state's U.S. House seats for a decade.

But there has been some significant competition and flux in Washington's politics. The 2004 governor race was especially close and the official count, after many shenanigans and legal challenges, declared Democrat Christine Gregoire the winner by 129 votes, even as Republican Rob McKenna was elected attorney general. Here as elsewhere, 2006 was a banner Democratic year, with Sen. Maria Cantwell re-elected by a solid 57%-40% and the party substantially increasing its majorities in the legislature. In 2008, Gregoire was re-elected in a rematch with Republican Dino Rossi by a not dazzling but not ambiguous 53%-47%, while Rob McKenna was re-elected 59%-41%. In 2010, the pendulum swung some distance toward the Republicans' way. Rossi ran against Sen. Patty Murray and, despite her work steering federal money to Washington, she won by only 52%-48%, while Republicans made significant gains in the legislature.

They may have been helped by two raging issues. One was the ballot proposition advanced by William Gates Sr. to impose a tax of 5% on income over $200,000 and 9% on income over $500,000. Gates argued that this so-called millionaire's tax would raise $2.9 billion for the education and public services Washington needs. It was supported by son Bill Gates, but opposed by his original partner, Paul Allen, Microsoft CEO Steve Ballmer and Amazon.com CEO Jeff Bezos, who argued that it would hurt business formation and talent recruitment. Others argued that once the state had an income tax, the legislature would not be able to resist extending it to others with lower incomes. Texas Gov. Rick Perry wrote to 90 Washington businesses, saying, "If Washington doesn't want your business, Texas does. Texas has no personal income tax and there's no interest in getting one." The anti-tax campaign prevailed by a crushing 64%-36%. It passed only in the central city of Seattle and in San Juan County. A measure to make it more difficult for the legislature to raise taxes passed by an identical margin.

The other looming issue was how to replace the Alaskan Way viaduct on Seattle's waterfront, which was damaged by the Nisqually earthquake in 2001. Civic leaders supported a tunnel 200 feet underground estimated to cost $2.8 billion. But legislators noted that Boston's Big Dig ended up costing six times more than estimated, and that those estimating the tunnel's cost said there was a 40% chance it would cost more. Seattle Mayor Mike McGinn opposed the tunnel and Speaker Frank Chopp led the House in passing a bill in April 2009 saying the state would not pay more than $2.8 billion, leaving overruns to "property owners in the Seattle area who benefit." The state signed a contract in January 2011 requiring that 90% of the work be performed for a fixed price of just over $1 billion. Cutbacks seemed to be the order of the day as the legislature in December 2010 cut $1.1 billion in spending by near-unanimous margins. Gregoire told the *The Seattle Times*, "I think it's historic, the bipartisan way in which they stood up to the most challenging time in 80 years."

The state's political divisions are fairly clear. The central city of Seattle and close-in suburbs are liberal bastions, heavy with singles and with most of Washington's small (3%) African-American and larger (7%) Asian populations. (The 11% who are Hispanic are found more in farming counties in eastern Washington, especially Yakima County). The more blue-collar and flannel-shirt areas in the western part of the state have been edging away from their historic Democratic allegiance. Seattle's King County, by far the most affluent county in the state, casts 30% of the state's votes, and it went 65% for John Kerry in 2004 and 70% for Barack Obama in 2008. Eastern Washington, the arid country east of the Cascades with much lower income levels, is heavily Republican and casts 20% of the state's votes. It voted 59% for George W. Bush in 2004 and 54% for John McCain in 2008. In 2010, King County voted 65%-35% for Murray and eastern Washington voted 61%-39% for Rossi. Western Washington outside Seattle, once predominantly Democratic, was almost precisely a tie, with Murray ahead 50.3%-49.7%. Demographics may be working marginally in the Republicans' favor. From 2000 to 2010, King County's population rose only 11%, while the heavily Republican Tri-Cities area (Benton and Franklin counties) gained 41% and Republican-trending Clark County, north of Portland, gained 23%. (Washington has no income tax and Oregon no sales tax, so you can create your own West Coast New Hampshire by living in Clark County and shopping across the line in Oregon.) Ironically, the Tri-Cities area was one of the chief beneficiaries of the 2009 economic stimulus bill because the government found it easy to ramp up spending on the multi-billion dollar, multi-year cleanup of nuclear waste at the Hanford Works.

A footnote on Washington's primaries: The state does not have party registration, and from 1935 to 2000, it allowed voters to choose candidates of various parties in its primaries. The top Democrat and top Republican in each constituency was deemed nominated, and the percentage of total votes won by incumbents in September primaries was often a harbinger of their performance in November general elections. But in 2000, the U.S. Supreme Court, in a 7-2 ruling, threw out a similar California primary system, and in 2003, a federal appeals court ruled Washington's system invalid. The Supreme Court's said that this arrangement violated the political parties' right to self-expression. In 2004, Washington voters passed Initiative 872, which allowed voters to select a candidate from either party, so that the two candidates with the most votes would move to the

Population		Household Income		Work	
Pop. 2010:	6,724,540	Under $15k:	10.5%	Private:	76.0%
State rank:	13th	$15k to $50k:	33.2%	Government:	17.4%
Change since 2000:	Up 14.1%	$50k to $100k:	33.3%	Self-employed:	6.4%
Urban:	81.2%	$100k to $200k:	18.9%	Unemployment (3-yr. average):	4.7%
Rural:	18.8%	Over $200k:	4.1%	Poverty:	11.8%
Native of state:	47.2%	Median income:	$57,125	Blue collar:	20.0%
Not a citizen:	6.9%			White collar:	61.3%
Area size:	71,298 sq. mi.	**Home Value**		Khaki collar:	0.8%
		Under $100k:	8.1%	Other:	17.9%
Most populous cities		$100k to $300k:	42.6%		
Seattle	608,660	$300k to $500k:	30.5%	**Age**	
Spokane	208,916	$500k to $1 mil:	15.8%	Median age:	36.9 yrs.
Tacoma	198,397	Over $1 million:	3.0%	More than 65 yrs:	11.9%
Vancouver	161,791	Median:	$297,000	Less than 18 yrs:	23.8%

Race/Ethnicity				Military Veterans		Registered Voters in 2010	
White:	72.5%	*Language*		% of Pop:	12.1%	No Party registration	
Black:	3.4%	English:	83.1%			Voter turnout:	2,565,589
Hispanic:	11.2%	Spanish:	7.4%	*Veterans by Period*		Turnout as % of	
Asian:	7.1%	Asian:	5.1%	WWII and before:	8.8%	voting age:	49.9%
Native Am.:	1.3%	Other European:	3.6%	Korea:	9.4%		
Hawaiian:	0.6%			Vietnam:	35.7%	**Legislature**	
Two+ races:	3.7%	**Education**		Gulf (pre-2001):	13.4%	Senate:	27 D 22 R
		H.S. grad:	89.6%	Gulf (post-2001):	8.9%	House:	56 D 42 R
Ancestry		College grad:	30.9%	Peace time:	23.9%		
German	15.5%	Grad degree:	11.0%				
Irish	9.5%						
English	9.2%						

general election, regardless of party. In 2005, a federal appeals court ruled the initiative invalid. That seemed to be the end of that, but in 2007, the U.S. Supreme Court agreed to hear a case on the validity of 872 and in March 2008, it upheld the law in a 7-2 ruling. That decision came after the February presidential caucuses and primaries, but the August 2008 primary was run under the rules of the 872 initiative. The result that some critics dreaded—two candidates of the same party facing off in the general election—occurred in only four of the 124 state legislative races in 2008, and in only nine in 2010. It happened in none of the congressional races. Instead, the effect seems to be marginalization of minor parties, since in almost every race, the primaries produced a Democratic and Republican nominee.

Presidential politics   For three decades, Washington was one of the most contrarian states in presidential politics, voting for Republican losers Richard Nixon in 1960 and Gerald Ford in 1976 and Democratic losers Hubert Humphrey in 1968 and Michael Dukakis in 1988. In the 1990s, it was more in sync with the nation, voting for Democrat Bill Clinton twice. Since then, it has moved significantly toward the Democrats, voting 50%-45% for Al Gore in 2000, 53%-46% for John Kerry in 2004 and 58%-40% for Barack Obama in 2008. In the first two contests, the winning margin and more came from just one of the state's nine congressional districts, the 7th District, which includes all of Seattle and close-in suburbs to the north and south in King County, where Democrats won more than 70% of the vote. In 2008, Obama carried the 7th district with 84% of the vote, but would have won even without it. Voting behavior seems to be a function more of cultural values than of economic status. High-income voters were not much

2008 Presidential Vote
Barack Obama (D) 1,750,848   (58%)
John McCain (R) 1,229,216   (40%)

2008 Presidential Primary
John McCain (R) 262,304   (50%)
Mike Huckabee (R)................127,657   (24%)
Mitt Romney (R).....................86,140   (16%)
Ron Paul (R) 40,539   (8%)

2008 Presidential Primary
Barack Obama (D) 354,112   (51%)
Hillary Clinton (D)................315,744   (46%)

2004 Presidential Vote
John Kerry (D) 1,510,201   (53%)
George W. Bush (R)............1,304,894   (46%)

less likely than others to vote for Obama, and his support was greater among college graduates than non-graduates, and even greater among those with graduate degrees. Some 24% of voters were white evangelical Protestants, and they voted 70% for John McCain; 19% reported their religion as "other" or "none," and they voted 71% for Obama.

Washington switched from a caucus system to primaries in 1992, after conservative evangelical candidate Pat Robertson won among Republicans and civil rights leader Jesse Jackson finished a solid second among Democrats in 1988. But Democrats have never chosen to allocate delegates according to the results, preferring to use the results from party caucuses. In 2000, Democrat Bill Bradley, having lost in Iowa and New Hampshire and having no other states to contest for five weeks, came to Washington for the Feb. 29 contest, to no avail; Al Gore won the caucus by about 2-to-1. On the GOP side, George W. Bush beat McCain by a razor-thin margin in a primary that counted a little toward delegate selection. In 2004, Washington Democrats held caucuses on Feb. 7, and Kerry defeated Howard Dean, despite the huge crowds Dean had attracted on his "Sleepless in Seattle" tour.

In early 2007, the parties were divided about what to do in 2008. Republicans, including Secretary of State Sam Reed, wanted to hold a primary on Feb. 5 that would count toward electing delegates. Democrats were divided, with many favoring eliminating the primary. In June, a bipartisan panel of state lawmakers and party leaders came to agreement and voted unanimously to hold the primary on Feb. 19, in hopes of being early enough to be relevant but not so early as to get lost amid the many states holding Feb. 5 contests. But both parties also held caucuses on Feb. 9. Republicans decided to allocate about half their delegates based on primary results; Democrats decided to use only caucus results to allocate delegates.

When Democrats caucused on the Saturday after Super Tuesday, Obama beat Hillary Rodham Clinton 68%-31%, and carried every county. In the primary 10 days later, Obama prevailed by a much narrower margin, 51%-46%, illustrating the huge advantage he and his organization had in caucus states. Turnout was 691,000; Obama got 56% of the vote in King County and barely won the rest of the state, running behind in less upscale areas like Pierce County (Tacoma) and Clark County (Vancouver, across the Columbia from Portland, Ore.)

The Republican contests produced murkier results. In the Feb. 9 caucus, McCain got 26% of the vote, Mike Huckabee 24%, and Ron Paul 22%. All three, unlike the Democrats, campaigned in the 10 days before the Feb. 19 primary, in which McCain won 50% of the vote, Huckabee 24%, Mitt Romney 16%, and Paul 8%. McCain carried every county. Turnout was 530,000; McCain did better in King County and the rest of western Washington than in the eastern part of the state.

Congressional districting   In 1983, Washington voters approved a constitutional amendment that provided that congressional and legislative districts be drawn by a bipartisan commission; the lines can be changed by a two-thirds vote in both houses of the legislature. If the commission is deadlocked, the issue goes to the state Supreme Court. In 1991, the commission created four districts that were pretty evenly divided between the parties. The one problem was that even minor alterations in the closely divided districts—the 1st, 2nd, 3rd and 9th—could turn out to be of partisan significance. A decade later, the 2002 plan followed pretty closely the lines drawn in 1991. The Washington plan has been lauded by many for taking partisanship out of the redistricting process and for creating more districts that both parties can win. But in Washington, where the commission is not bound by the mathematical requirements that in Iowa have resulted in districts not tailored to incumbents, incumbent protection has been the result.

112th Congress Lineup	
5 D	4 R
111th Congress Lineup	
6 D	3 R

Washington gained a House seat in the reapportionment following the 2010 census, as it did after the censuses of 1980 and 1990. Most or all of the new district will probably be west of the Cascade Range. The heavily Republican area east of the Cascades, which currently is carved into two districts, will be entitled to 2.22 districts.

Governor

Christine Gregoire (D)

Elected 2004, term expires Jan. 2013, 2nd term; b. March 24, 1947, Adrian, MI; home, Olympia; U. of WA, B.A. 1969; Gonzaga U., J.D. 1977; Catholic; married (Mike); 2 children.

Elected Office: WA atty. gen., 1992-2004.

Professional Career: Dep. atty. gen., 1982-88; Dir., WA Dept. of Ecology, 1988-92.

Office: 416 Sid Snyder Ave. SW, Suite 200, P.O. Box 40002, Olympia, 98504-0002, 360-902-4111; Fax: 360-753-4110; Web site: www.governor.-wa.gov.

Election Results

2008 general	Christine Gregoire (D)	1,598,738	(53%)
	Dino Rossi (R)	1,404,124	(47%)
2008 primary	Christine Gregoire (D)	696,306	(48%)
	Dino Rossi (R)	668,571	(46%)

Prior Winning Percentages: 2004 (49%)

Christine Gregoire is a Democrat elected governor in 2004 in the closest race in Washington history. She was re-elected in 2008 and gained prominence in late 2010 when she became chairman of the National Governors Association.

Gregoire (*Greg-WHAR*) grew up on a small farm in Auburn, just south of Seattle. Her mother was a short-order cook who moved west to escape an abusive husband. She graduated from the University of Washington and, unable to find a teaching position, took a job as a clerk-typist for the state parole board. She worked as a welfare caseworker, attended law school at Gonzaga University in eastern Washington, and then worked for Republican Sen. Slade Gorton in his Spokane office. There, she drew the attention of another Republican, Attorney General Ken Eikenberry, who hired her as a deputy attorney general in Olympia. In 1988, she was Democratic Gov. Booth Gardner's choice to head the Department of Ecology. Gregoire ran for attorney general in 1992, nationally a good year for women candidates but especially good in Washington state, where Democrat Patty Murray was elected to the Senate and Democrat Maria Cantwell to the House. Gregoire won the post and served three terms, getting national headlines in 1998 as the lead negotiator for the 46-state, $206 billion settlement with the tobacco industry.

With high name recognition from the tobacco case, Gregoire came to be viewed as a governor-in-waiting. When Democrat Gary Locke, elected governor in 1996 and 2000, announced in 2003 that he would not run for a third term, Gregoire became the front-runner to succeed him. She almost didn't run. She was diagnosed with an early form of breast cancer and had to have a mastectomy. She considered dropping out of the race, sought counsel from Democrats Janet Napolitano and Heidi Heitkamp, both former attorneys general and breast cancer survivors who had run for governor. (Napolitano won in Arizona in 2002; Heitkamp lost in North Dakota in 2000.) Gregoire decided to have the surgery, and she returned to the campaign trail a month later.

She had primary opposition from King County Executive Ron Sims, whose political base was in the state's most populous county and biggest media market. At the time, Washington was only slowly recovering from recession and had the nation's second-highest unemployment rate. Jobs, education, taxes and the environment were the major issues in the campaign. But the campaign was also sidetracked by the issue of Gregoire's sorority at the University of Washington, which excluded African-Americans. She charged that the Sims campaign was behind the story. Sims, who would have been the state's first black governor, denied being the source. When local black leaders harshly criticized Gregoire, she angrily defended her record on race issues and said that she had fought to eliminate the sorority's exclusionary policy. Voters didn't seem to hold it against her. She defeated Sims 66%-30%, carrying every county in the state, including Sims' King County base, 59%-38%.

Republicans nominated Dino Rossi, a former state senator and Ways and Means Committee chairman from the Seattle suburbs who billed himself as a "fiscal conservative with a social conscience." Business interests lined up with Rossi, who said he wanted to change the culture in Olympia to a "free-enterprise model," and who promised to create a cabinet-level office of regulatory reform. Gregoire ran as a fiscal moderate, and received strong support from the state's largest labor unions. Rossi's opposition to abortion spurred abortion-rights groups to donate heavily to Gregoire and led Democrats to characterize him as a right-wing extremist—the same tactic that had worked against the previous two Republican nominees. As a youthful suburban legislator with four children who focused on economic rather than social issues, Rossi was not so easily caricatured. But by October, Gregoire had built a double-digit lead in most polls. In the final weeks, Rossi's "change" theme gained traction against Gregoire, a cautious candidate who had spent nearly her entire career in government jobs.

Washington is one of just two states that allow absentee ballots to be postmarked as late as Election Day, so it took nearly three weeks to count all of the votes. The lead seesawed for days, and in the ensuing weeks, there were protests, legal challenges, allegations of ballot fraud and the intervention of national parties. On Nov. 12, the state Democratic Party sued the King County Elections Department over its handling of provisional ballots, seeking the names of those whose ballots had been invalidated. Three days later, King County, the state's Democratic stronghold, discovered 10,000 uncounted ballots, and Gregoire took a 158-vote lead. Republicans sought a restraining order to stop the counting of provisional ballots, but a King County judge denied the request. On Nov. 17, after all counties had reported their results, Rossi was the winner by just 261 votes out of 2.8 million cast.

Washington state law requires a machine recount if the margin of victory is under 2,000 votes and half of one percent. After a machine recount, Rossi on Nov. 24 was again the winner, this time by 42 votes. Rossi called on Gregoire to concede, but she refused. On Nov. 29, he was certified as governor-elect. Gregoire still had one more option. State election law allowed for a hand recount under such circumstances, provided that the party requesting it paid the cost. The state party agreed to pay, but only in the counties where Gregoire stood to gain the most votes. Republicans were quick to condemn the idea, and Gregoire said she would concede the race unless the party could raise enough money for a full, statewide recount.

With financial assistance from John Kerry's presidential campaign, MoveOn.org and the Democratic National Committee, the party raised the money for a $730,000 statewide hand recount. The vote-counting slogged on through December. King County discovered 561 wrongly disqualified ballots on Dec. 13. Then, the county found even more uncounted ballots. Republicans filed suit in neighboring Pierce County, which they said was a fairer venue than King County, to prevent the counting of all the newfound ballots. A Pierce County judge found in their favor and kept the votes out. Democrats appealed to the state Supreme Court, which unanimously ruled that the disputed ballots could be counted. The votes were enough to put Gregoire over the top. On Dec. 30, 58 days after the election, she was declared governor-elect by 129 votes. She won 48.873% to Rossi's 48.868%.

In January, just days before Gregoire's inauguration, Rossi and the Republican Party filed a lawsuit in Chelan County Superior Court in central Washington asking that Gregoire's victory be nullified and a new election held, presenting evidence of alleged improper votes. But the court upheld Gregoire's election, and Rossi decided not to appeal.

Gregoire was elected to chair the National Governors Association in November 2010, after West Virginia Democratic Gov. Joe Manchin won his Senate race. Gregoire took over as 29 new governors were elected to office, the largest such group in history. She warned them to put aside the harsh rhetoric of campaigns and move toward bipartisan solutions. "We are at a historic time in our country," she told a summit of governors. "We put the elephants and donkeys aside and we're prepared to govern." Despite the end of the recession, she noted that states faced massive fiscal challenges and that further cutbacks in federal grant programs could undermine their economic recovery. She called for greater flexibility for the states to tailor educational policies to their individual states' needs. And she also came out strongly against a Republican idea to permit states to seek bankruptcy protection as an alternative to bailouts.

Gregoire record as governor has been mixed. She has a reputation as a serious-minded manager who immerses herself in details and gives speeches that are heavy on substance. At the same time, she is often described as intense and stiff, and sometimes has had trouble connecting with voters. She told *The Seattle Times* in 2008 that she wanted to correct the misperception that she lacks a sense of humor. "I like to rib people and have fun, but we deal with very serious issues," she said.

Working with solid Democratic majorities in both the House and Senate, Gregoire had an accomplished first year. In one of her first acts as governor, she created an election reform task force, which eventually called for a statewide voter database, mandatory audits of local election systems and an earlier primary date. She signed a controversial, labor-backed unemployment insurance bill for seasonal workers, a mental health parity bill, and legislation requiring the state to adopt the same car-emissions standards used by California, which are stricter than the federal government's. She followed through on a campaign promise to create a $350 million Life Sciences Discovery Fund that would use tobacco settlement money for biotechnology research. But the big news was passage of a contentious $8.5 billion transportation bill that paid for scores of highway and bridge projects with a 9.5-cent increase in the gas tax over four years. The measure generated considerable hostility, and it didn't take long for opponents to get enough signatures to place a repeal initiative on the November 2005 ballot. But the initiative—opposed by Gregoire, big business, and labor and environmental groups—lost 55%-45%, thanks in large part to Seattle's King County, where nearly half the money was to be spent on crumbling transportation infrastructure.

Despite these successes, Gregoire's job-approval ratings remained low at the end of her first year, a vestige of her tainted victory, a reflection of a style not inclined toward glad-handing and a reaction to a record marked by several tax increases. There was talk that Gregoire needed a "makeover," and her press releases late in the year began to refer to her as "Chris."

In 2006, Gregoire helped pass a compromise medical malpractice bill and signed off on a landmark agreement for water storage in eastern Washington. She also signed a gay rights bill and a bill making Washington the first state with an electronics waste recycling mandate. The following year, she proposed a $30 billion budget, up $3 billion from her first two-year budget. There was significant criticism of spending increases on her watch, and she muted opposition by proposing a "rainy day fund" to put aside 1% of revenues each year as a hedge against future hard times. In 2008, Gregoire proposed a budget that put $1.2 billion of a projected $1.4 billion surplus in reserve, but also increased spending by $237 million. The legislature rejected her attempt to give Microsoft,

Yahoo and other high-tech companies tax exemptions on equipment used at computer data centers. Lawmakers also rejected her attempt to establish random drunk-driving checkpoints throughout the state. Gregoire signed a law giving couples in domestic partnerships benefits such as guardianship and powers of attorney previously accorded to only married couples. She also signed a law to reduce the state's greenhouse gas emissions to 25% of 1990 levels by the year 2035.

Her approval ratings slowly went up. Meanwhile, Rossi wrote a book and traveled the state giving speeches, gearing up for a rematch in 2008. Their second contest was even harder fought than the first. Gregoire touted her accomplishments in office, blamed the state's economic downturn on President George W. Bush, and painted Rossi as a social conservative out of touch with voters. Rossi criticized Gregoire's spending policies and emphasized the state's projected $3.2 billion deficit in coming years. In Washington's primary system, all candidates run on a single ballot, and the top two finishers advance. Gregoire beat Rossi, but only by 48%-46%.

In the campaign's final stretch, Democratic presidential nominee Barack Obama's popularity in Washington and a boost in voter turnout buoyed Gregoire's campaign, and she won, 53%-47%. Central Washington, typically viewed as Republican country, did not vote as strongly for Rossi as it had in 2004, and Gregoire improved her percentages throughout the state. The election ended up being the most expensive in state history. Gregoire and Rossi spent more than $12 million each, and outside groups spent a combined $20 million. Two years later, Rossi challenged Murray for her Senate seat, only to lose again.

In her second term, Gregoire proposed a budget that reduced state spending by $3.6 billion. It eliminated pay raises for teachers and state employees and canceled plans to expand health care for children. Many of her proposals had to be shelved during what she later called "the toughest legislative session in nearly 30 years, and maybe the toughest since the Great Depression." About $4 billion in cuts were made to close a $9 billion budget deficit. Though she called for a special session to wrap up work on several bills, House and Senate leaders were unable to agree on an agenda. Later that year, Gregoire made headlines for announcing her state would temporarily stop accepting paroled criminals from Arkansas. The decision came after Seattle police shot to death a man who had been granted clemency in Arkansas by then-Gov. Mike Huckabee.

Washington's economic picture wasn't much brighter in 2010. In May of that year, Gregoire signed into law a new operating budget that closed a $2.8 billion deficit through a variety of solutions that included tax increases on consumer products, including beer, soda and cigarettes. She praised lawmakers for preserving priorities such as financial aid for college students and the state's Basic Health Plan for low-income residents. Republicans, however, said the measure relied too much on short-term fixes. *The Seattle Times*' editorial page agreed, blasting Gregoire and Democratic lawmakers for "a failure of leadership." That fall, the state's voters defeated a proposed income tax on the top 1% of earners that would have raised money for education and health programs. She had endorsed the ballot initiative, telling reporters, "It may not be the best vehicle, but I don't have another vehicle."

Gregoire's proposed budget for the 2011-2013 biennium included more than $2 billion in cuts to public education while proposing to cleave another $2 billion from almost every other area. She said "the choices (the budget) reflects are the most difficult ones I've ever faced." Lawmakers dithered on passing a bill, forcing her to call a special session. Speculation began over whether she would seek a third term in 2012. Polls during 2010 showed her approval rating well below 50%. And in June 2011, Gregoire announced that she would not run for re-election.

Senior Senator

Patty Murray (D)

Elected 1992, term expires 2016, 4th term; b. Oct. 11, 1950, Seattle; home, Seattle; WA St. U., B.A. 1972; Catholic; married (Rob); 2 children.

Elected Office: Shoreline Schl. Bd., 1985–89, Pres., 1985–86; WA Senate, 1988–92.

DC Office: 448 RSOB, 20510, 202-224-2621; Fax: 202-224-0238; Web site: murray.senate.gov.

State Offices: Everett, 425-259-6515; Seattle, 206-553-5545; Spokane, 509-624-9515; Tacoma, 253-572-3636; Vancouver, 360-696-7797; Yakima, 509-453-7462.

Committees: *Appropriations:* Defense; Energy & Water Development; Homeland Security; Labor, Health & Human Services, Education & Related Agencies; Military Construction, Veterans Affairs & Related Agencies; Transportation, HUD & Related Agencies. *Budget. Health, Education, Labor & Pensions:* Children & Families; Employment & Workplace Safety (Chmn). *Rules & Administration. Veterans' Affairs* (Chmn).

Group Ratings

	ACLU	ACU	ADA	CFG	AFS	FRC	LCV	ITIC	NTU	COC
2010	93	0	95	0	95	0	86	67	6	27
2009	–	0	95	9	100	–	100	–	7	43

National Journal Ratings

	2010 LIB — 2010 CONS		2009 LIB — 2009 CONS	
Economic	79%	— 20%	66%	— 33%
Social	65%	— 0%	85%	— 0%
Foreign	47%	— 0%	55%	— 0%
Composite	79%	— 22%	79%	— 21%

Key Votes of the 111th Congress

1. Overturn Ledbetter	Y	5. Pass health care bill	Y	9. Ratify New START	Y
2. Pass $787 billion stimulus	Y	6. Regulate financial firms	Y	10. Confirm Elena Kagan	Y
3. Repeal DC gun laws	N	7. Pass tax cuts for some	Y	11. Stop EPA climate regs	N
4. Confirm Sonia Sotomayor	Y	8. Legalize immigrants' kids	Y	12. Repeal don't ask, tell	Y

Election Results

2010 general	Patty Murray (D)	1,314,930	(52%)	($17,124,667)
	Dino Rossi (R)	1,196,164	(48%)	($9,643,395)
2010 primary	Patty Murray (D)	670,284	(46%)	
	Dino Rossi (R)	483,305	(33%)	
	Clint Didier (R)	185,304	(13%)	

Prior Winning Percentages: 2004 (55%); 1998 (58%); 1992 (54%)

Patty Murray is the senior senator from Washington, first elected in 1992. She has come a long way from her entry in politics as a parent-activist. Murray is now a powerful Senate backroom player, with responsibility for ensuring that Democrats retain their majority in the 2012 elections.

Murray grew up in the Seattle suburb of Bothell, one of seven children of a disabled World War II veteran. She graduated from Washington State University in 1972, married and stayed home to raise her children. In 1980, she was in Olympia trying to save a parent education class she was teaching at Shoreline Community College, which was the target of budget cuts. A state legislator told her gruffly, "You're just a mom in tennis shoes. You can't make a difference." As she said later, "Almost every woman I've ever met in politics got into it because she was mad about something." She won her fight over the parents' class, and then ran for the Shoreline School District board. She eventually was chosen to be board president. In 1988, she challenged a Republican state senator, knocked on 17,000 doors and won the seat. Then in late 1991, Murray decided to run against U.S. Sen. Brock Adams, a Democrat who was under a cloud following charges of sexual harassment. He ultimately decided not to seek re-election.

Amid a crowd of better-known, conventional male politicians, Murray, with her flat, Midwestern-style accent and "mom in tennis shoes" line, attracted most of the attention. In the 1992 all-party primary, her main Democratic opponent was former U.S. Rep. Don Bonker, who had narrowly lost a Senate nomination in 1988. But Murray won 28% of the total vote to Bonker's 19%. She then sprinted to a big lead in polls against Republican U.S. Rep. Rod Chandler, winning 54%-46% in November.

In the Senate, Murray has had a largely liberal voting record. In the 111th Congress (2009-10) she was among the 20 most liberal senators, ahead of her Democratic Washington colleague Maria Cantwell, according to *National Journal's* annual rankings. Murray generally leaves the spotlight to others, but does not shy from openly taking on administration officials. In what she calls her "angry mom" voice, she has rebuked Republican and Democratic secretaries of the Department of Veterans Affairs for proposals that would make veterans pay more for health care. "Ask my kids about it," she said of such confrontations to *The Olympian* newspaper in October 2010. "There is a line they knew they shouldn't cross." That same year, she and Rep. Doc Hastings, R-Wash., led a protest against the Obama administration's plans to shutter the nuclear waste repository site at Nevada's Yucca Mountain, asserting that the decision violated the 1987 law that designated the site for study.

On the Appropriations Committee, Murray quickly ingratiated herself with more senior colleagues. After Alaska's Ted Stevens, the former GOP chairman, lost his bid for re-election in 2008, he gave Murray the desk that once belonged to legendary Washington Democrat Warren Magnuson (1944-81). And when West Virginia Democrat Robert Byrd was too ill in 2007 and 2008 to manage spending bills on the floor as chairman, he gave Murray the task ahead of more-senior members. Murray chairs the Appropriations subcommittee on transportation and housing and urban development. She has delivered for the state, and then some: $219 million in home-state projects in 2010, which was the ninth highest amount among senators that year. The Washington watchdog group Taxpayers for Common Sense dubbed her the "Queen of Pork." Murray is unapologetic about using her Appropriations seat to steer funding to her state, arguing that lawmakers, not bureaucrats, should make funding decisions. "Earmarks are how those of us who live 2,500 miles from the nation's capital ensure projects critical to our state are funded," she said.

Murray agreed in November 2010 to chair the Democratic Senatorial Campaign Committee, the Senate Democrats' campaign recruiting and fundraising arm, for the 2012 election. Several of her colleagues had reportedly turned down the post, prompting Majority Leader Harry Reid and others to persuade her that she was in the best position to succeed in the job. The assignment was a daunting one: Twenty-three Democratic senators face re-election in 2012. But even her political opponents predicted that she would not be outworked. "She's a mechanic, not a visionary. But she's really good at it," said Chris Vance, a former chairman of Washington's Republican Party. "And people have underestimated her for their entire career and they've always been wrong. She's a tremendous politician in the old-school, old-fashioned model."

Murray brought experience to the DSCC post, having held the job in the 2002 election cycle. She nearly doubled the committee's fundraising, bringing in $158 million during the cycle, and her recruiting efforts were mostly successful. But the results were disappointing, to say the least. Democrats lost more seats than they won that year, and they lost their Senate majority. Still, Murray's efforts got high marks. In 2004, Reid appointed Murray assistant floor leader, and after Democrats won back the majority in 2006, her colleagues elected her Democratic Conference Secretary, the fourth-ranking position in the leadership.

Murray also assumed the helm of the Veterans' Affairs Committee in 2011. She has long been one of the most persistent advocates for veterans' funding. She said in January 2011 that the new House Republican majority's "slash everything motive" did not recognize the many needs of veterans. "We cannot say, 'Gee, sorry,' to them," she told The Associated Press. "We have to say, 'Our country is there for you.'" She has sponsored bills for more benefits for National Guard and Reserve troops called up to active duty, and she successfully fought for more health care funding for veterans of the Iraq and Afghanistan conflicts. Republicans initially rejected her attempt to add $2 billion for veterans' health care, but relented and added $1.5 billion after it was revealed that the VA was using dated cost estimates and expected a shortfall.

In her first years, Murray was criticized as too staff reliant, but she grew into the role of senator. She immersed herself in Washington state issues, becoming one of the Senate's staunchest proponents of normal trade relations with China, a position strongly backed by Boeing. Murray also has worked to remove restrictions on abortion rights and has prevailed in the Senate on legislation allowing abortions in military hospitals. With then-Democratic Sen. Hillary Rodham Clinton of New York, she waged a fight with the Bush administration regarding the approval of over-the-counter sales of the Plan B contraceptive.

On defense issues, Murray voted in 2002 against using force in Iraq and was a vociferous critic of the Bush administration's war policy, accusing the administration of failing to plan for the full cost of the war. She has backed the Obama administration on Afghanistan. And like other Washington lawmakers, she worked diligently to ensure that Boeing won its protracted battle against a foreign competitor in 2011 for the right to build the next generation of Air Force aerial refueling tankers.

Murray has won re-election three times by steadily diminishing margins. In 1998, she was challenged by U.S. Rep. Linda Smith, a Republican and a strong opponent of abortion and free trade deals. Murray raised far more money than Smith and won 58%-42%. In 2004, she faced Republican George Nethercutt, another House member, who in 1994 earned a reputation as a giant killer by defeating Democratic House Speaker Tom Foley. But the former mom in tennis shoes had become a hardball fundraiser: An aide put out the word to lobbyists that the senator would regard contributions to Nethercutt as hostile, even if contributors gave to her too. Murray raised $11.5 million, much more than Nethercutt's $7.7 million. Nethercutt campaigned vigorously, and big-name Republicans came in for him. In September, Nethercutt ran an ad featuring Murray's controversial 2002 comments on Osama bin Laden's good works. But the ad did not seem to move votes. On Election Day, Murray won 55%-43%. It was almost as if the election had been held in two states: Nethercutt carried every county east of the Cascades, and Murray carried all but two counties to the west.

Republicans initially considered Murray vulnerable in 2010. They landed a top-tier recruit in former state Sen. Dino Rossi, a fiscal conservative who had twice run impressive but losing campaigns against Democratic Gov. Christine Gregoire. He easily captured the nomination to challenge Murray. He criticized her involvement in shaping the Democratic agenda. But Murray did not back down from her record and said Rossi would bankrupt the nation by giving tax breaks to the wealthy. She got a substantial boost from Boeing, whose machinists' union called her re-election its top priority.

Murray maintained a small lead in polls until October, when Rossi took the lead in two of them. The National Republican Senatorial Committee and outside conservative groups poured millions into the race on his behalf. But Murray also got help at campaign stops from Vice President Joe Biden and First Lady Michelle Obama, and she managed to pull out a 52%-48% victory. Although Republicans won the female vote nationally, exit polls showed Murray beating Rossi among women, 56%-44%. And even though national Republicans won the senior citizens' vote by 19 percentage points, Murray carried it by 10 points.

Junior Senator

Maria Cantwell (D)

Elected 2000, term expires 2012, 2nd term; b. Oct. 13, 1958, Indianapolis, IN; home, Edmonds; Miami U. (OH), B.A. 1980; Catholic; single.

Elected Office: WA House of Reps., 1986-92; U.S. House of Reps., 1993-95.

Professional Career: Owner, Cantwell & Assoc. PR firm, 1985-91; Real-Networks, 1995-2000.

DC Office: 311 HSOB, 20510, 202-224-3441; Fax: 202-228-0514; Web site: cantwell.senate.gov.

State Offices: Everett, 425-303-0114; Richland, 509-946-8106; Seattle, 206-220-6400; Spokane, 509-353-2507; Tacoma, 253-572-2281; Vancouver, 360-696-7838.

Committees: *Commerce, Science & Transportation:* Aviation Operations, Safety & Security (Chmn); Communications, Technology & the Internet; Competitiveness, Innovation & Export Promotion; Oceans, Atmosphere, Fisheries & Coast Guard; Science & Space; Surface Transportation & Merchant Marine Infrastructure, Safety & Security. *Energy & Natural Resources:* Energy (Chmn); Public Lands & Forests; Water & Power. *Finance:* Energy, Natural Resources & Infrastructure; Health Care; Taxation & IRS Oversight. *Indian Affairs. Small Business & Entrepreneurship.*

Group Ratings

	ACLU	ACU	ADA	CFG	AFS	FRC	LCV	ITIC	NTU	COC
2010	87	12	90	15	94	0	86	67	16	45
2009	–	8	95	15	100	–	100	–	10	43

National Journal Ratings

	2010 LIB	—	2010 CONS	2009 LIB	—	2009 CONS
Economic	58%	—	40%	53%	—	46%
Social	65%	—	0%	77%	—	22%
Foreign	47%	—	0%	49%	—	45%
Composite	72%	—	28%	61%	—	39%

Key Votes of the 111th Congress

1. Overturn Ledbetter	Y	5. Pass health care bill	Y	9. Ratify New START	Y
2. Pass $787 billion stimulus	Y	6. Regulate financial firms	N	10. Confirm Elena Kagan	Y
3. Repeal DC gun laws	N	7. Pass tax cuts for some	Y	11. Stop EPA climate regs	N
4. Confirm Sonia Sotomayor	Y	8. Legalize immigrants' kids	Y	12. Repeal don't ask, tell	Y

Election Results

2006 general	Maria Cantwell (D)	1,184,659	(57%)	($18,879,272)
	Mike McGavick (R)	832,106	(40%)	($10,852,230)
2006 primary	Maria Cantwell (D)	570,677	(91%)	
	Hong Tran (D)	33,124	(5%)	

Prior Winning Percentages: 2000 (49%); House: 1992 (55%)

Democrat Maria Cantwell, Washington's junior senator, was elected in 2000. She is active on energy, technology and tax matters, often working with Republicans, and is known for her persistence on issues.

Cantwell grew up in Indianapolis, where her father, Paul Cantwell, a construction worker, served as county commissioner, a city councilman and a state legislator. As a child, Cantwell observed politics firsthand as her father dispensed advice to the union members, laborers and politicians who stopped by to talk politics. During her father's stint as an aide to U.S. Rep. Andrew Jacobs, she awoke one morning to the distinctive Boston accent of Sen. Edward Kennedy of Massachusetts downstairs. Cantwell graduated from Miami University of Ohio in 1980, the first in her family to graduate from college. She worked in Ohio for television personality Jerry Springer's 1982 campaign for governor. (In 2003, when Springer was considering running for senator in Ohio, she said, "I think people will be surprised by his intellect. There's much more to him than his TV show.") Then she worked for Democratic Sen. Alan Cranston's presidential campaign, going to Seattle to set up a regional campaign office. The Cranston campaign went nowhere, but Cantwell loved the Pacific Northwest and decided to stay. She moved to Mountlake Terrace, a suburb in Snohomish County just north of Seattle, where she organized a coalition to build a new library. In 1986, at age 28, she was elected to the Washington state House.

In 1992 Cantwell ran for an open U.S. House seat and won a solid 55%-42% victory. In the House, she did not support President Bill Clinton's health care plan, and she was a strong supporter of abortion rights and of stands backed by environmental advocacy groups. But she lost her 1994 bid for re-election to Republican Rick White, 52%-48%.

Back in the Seattle area, she joined a start-up firm called Progressive Networks in 1995. Five years later, it had become RealNetworks, a leader in Internet-based audio and visual software. In late 1999, her stock was worth about $40 million, and she decided to run against Republican Sen. Slade Gorton. Gorton, Microsoft's leading advocate on Capitol Hill, had an increasingly conservative record on environmental and economic issues. Insurance Commissioner Deborah Senn, who also was running, was widely considered too liberal to win. The real difference was money. Cantwell, who liquidated more than $5 million in stock, spent freely, while Senn was on television only during the last two weeks before the September all-party primary. In the first round of balloting, Gorton got the most votes, 44% of the total, but short of a majority. Cantwell got 37%, and Senn got only 13%. As a result, Gorton and Cantwell faced off in the general election.

Cantwell said she would spend "whatever it takes" to win. At the same time, she made her support of McCain-Feingold-type campaign finance regulation a major issue and refused to take contributions from political action committees or large donations known as "soft money" from the Democratic Party (though it put $640,000 into the state before Cantwell won the primary). She charged that Gorton was beholden to special interest contributors, singling out his late-night amendment to open a cyanide-leach gold mine in Okanogan County. Gorton called Cantwell an old-style liberal Democrat who would have government meddling in health care, education and local environmental issues. Cantwell highlighted her experience in the high-tech private sector. Overall, she spent $11.5 million, $10.3 million of it her own money, to Gorton's $6.4 million.

Gorton led on election night, but not by much. That year, 54% of the votes were cast absentee, and it took three weeks to count them all. The last two days' worth of absentee ballots from heavily Democratic King County put Cantwell over the top by 1,953 votes. A mandated recount left the margin at 2,229 for Cantwell, out of 2.4 million cast, the closest Senate contest of 2000. Cantwell carried only five counties: King, Snohomish, Thurston, which includes the state capital of Olympia, and two small counties in the west. Gorton carried eastern Washington 61%-36%, not quite enough to win. Cantwell's victory created a tie in the Senate, until Vermont's James Jeffords became an independent in May 2001 and gave Democrats a razor-thin majority.

Cantwell is known for being intense, though some aides say she is as demanding of herself as she is of them. She generally takes her party's side, though she can show her independence. She was one of just nine Senate Democrats to oppose the 2008 law creating the Troubled Asset Relief Fund for ailing financial institutions, saying the government had no business getting so deeply involved with the private sector. She also showed distance from her party on the financial services issues that dominated the 111th Congress (2009-10). During the debate on overhauling the banking and financial services regulatory system, she pushed for more radical reforms. She co-sponsored a bill with Sen. John McCain, R-Ariz. that would have reinstated the Glass-Steagall Banking Act of 1933, which created a wall between commercial and investment banking. She also wanted to close loopholes on unregulated derivatives trading. Cantwell was one of only two Democrats to vote against the White House-backed banking reform bill in May 2010. However, she joined her party in July in voting for the final conference report version of the reform bill, reasoning that the updated bill offered at least tougher regulation and greater transparency of the derivatives market.

Cantwell chairs the Senate Energy and Natural Resources' Energy Subcommittee, and has been particularly active on those issues. When the Obama administration and Democrats in Congress pushed for legislation aimed at curbing greenhouse gases, Cantwell jumped into the debate. The Obama White House bill, which allowed energy efficient companies to trade credits to larger greenhouse gas emitters as a way to reduce overall levels of carbon dioxide emissions, proved a hard sell and by mid-2010, Cantwell and Sen. Susan Collins, R-Maine stepped up efforts to push their "cap-and-dividend" bill that skirted the idea of a carbon trading market. Instead, the bill would cap emissions from sources such as coal mines and oil refineries, and those emitters would be required to purchase carbon permits. The Senate failed to take final action on climate change bill before the November election. There was more political momentum for curbing offshore drilling in the aftermath of the BP Deepwater Horizon oil rig explosion in the Gulf of Mexico. Cantwell offered a bill in July 2010 requiring the oil drilling industry to continually integrate the latest technology into efforts at spill prevention. "We've seen over the past 20 years that the industry will not do it on its own," she said. She also joined Sen. Patty Murray, D-Wash. and the other four senators from Oregon and California in signing onto legislation that would permanently ban oil drilling off the West Coast.

An energy bill passed by Congress in December 2008 contained her provision giving the Federal Trade Commission authority to fine companies or individuals that manipulate petroleum markets. She has backed extending tax credits for wind, solar and other sources of renewable energy and told the *Tri-City Herald* in November 2010 that green energy could be a $6 trillion sector of the economy that is "bigger than the Internet." She brokered a land swap in 2011 to protect her state's Quileute Indian tribe from floods. A few years earlier, in 2005, Cantwell waged a series of floor fights with then-Senate Commerce Chairman Ted Stevens over drilling in the Arctic National Wildlife Refuge that antagonized the powerful Alaska senator. Republicans narrowly rebuffed attempts by Cantwell to remove ANWR drilling from a budget bill. Stevens retaliated by introducing a bill that would expand oil-tanker traffic in the environmentally sensitive Puget Sound. Washington politicians of both parties protested the move, and the Senate ultimately failed to pass the ANWR measure that year.

Cantwell also has a seat on the powerful Finance Committee, which she got in 2006. In that role, she secured passage of a 2008 measure to temporarily extend the deductibility of state sales taxes, a popular tax break in Washington. Cantwell had helped pass the original legislation in 2003 with Republican Sen. Kay Bailey Hutchison of Texas. It allows taxpayers to deduct state sales taxes as well as state income taxes on their federal income-tax forms. Washington, like Texas, has a sales tax but no income tax.

Although a strong supporter of campaign finance regulation, Cantwell has had campaign finance problems of her own. To fund her 2000 campaign, she had sold $5.6 million of her RealNetworks stock and had borrowed $3.8 million from a bank using the company's stock as collateral. That enabled her to run the last-minute ads that surely were essential to her victory. The Federal Election Commission ruled in January 2004 that she had violated the law by failing to disclose the terms of the loans, but it evidently saw the offense as minor because it took no punitive action. Paying off the loans should have been easy; Cantwell's net worth at one point was around $40 million. But RealNetworks, like other high-tech firms, saw its stock price plummet, from $80 per share in spring 2000 to $6 in spring 2001. Suddenly she owed far more than the collateral was worth. She negotiated another loan that would come due December 2001, guaranteed by the DSCC. By the end of 2004, she had reduced the debt to $2.5 million. With $435,000 in cash, she was able to pay off the remaining $130,000 in bank loans. Cantwell's top campaign contributor over the course of her career has been Microsoft.

Cantwell's narrow victory in 2000 placed her high on the Republicans target list for 2006. National Republicans recruited Mike McGavick, chairman and chief executive officer at Safeco insurance. He was a smart, successful businessman, with moderate positions, personal wealth and speaking ability. He also had political smarts, having managed Gorton's 1988 campaign and served as his chief of staff. But McGavick also acknowledged that he had been charged with drunken driving in 1993. Cantwell faced lingering discontent from liberals in the party for her 2002 vote in favor of the Iraq war resolution. But the earlier, well-publicized dustup with Stevens helped the reserved and cautious Cantwell, allowing her to show she could stand up to Stevens and the oil lobby in defense of Washington's environment. Stevens withdrew his tanker bill in March 2006, saying McGavick had persuaded him to pull the bill.

McGavick poured $2.5 million of own money into the race, but in the end, Cantwell outspent him $14 million to $10.8 million. In a Democratic year in a Democratic-leaning state, she won 57%-40%. Though her fundraising for 2012 was slow at the end of 2010, she was still regarded as a formidable opponent for Republicans in a year in which President Obama will also be on the ballot.

FIRST DISTRICT

Jay Inslee (D)

Elected 1998, 8th term; b. Feb. 9, 1951, Seattle; home, Bainbridge Island; Stanford U., 1969-70, U. of WA, B.A. 1973, Willamette U., J.D. 1976; Christian; married (Trudi); 3 children.

Elected Office: WA House of Reps., 1988-92; U.S. House of Reps., 1993-95.

Professional Career: Practicing atty., 1976-92, 1995-96; Regional dir., U.S. Dept. of H.H.S., 1997-98.

DC Office: 2329 RHOB, 20515, 202-225-6311; Fax: 202-226-1606; Web site: house.gov/inslee.

State Offices: Poulsbo, 360-598-2342; Shoreline, 206-361-0233.

Committees: *Energy & Commerce:* Energy & Power.

Group Ratings

	ACLU	ACU	ADA	CFG	AFS	FRC	LCV	ITIC	NTU	COC
2010	88	4	95	6	100	0	100	67	8	13
2009	–	0	100	6	100	–	100	–	5	36

National Journal Ratings

	2010 LIB — 2010 CONS			2009 LIB — 2009 CONS		
Economic	64%	—	35%	81%	—	18%
Social	71%	—	25%	64%	—	36%
Foreign	89%	—	10%	78%	—	17%
Composite	76%	—	24%	75%	—	25%

Key Votes of the 111th Congress

1. Overturn Ledbetter	Y	5. Bar federal abortion funds	N	9. Stop detainee transfers	N
2. Pass $820 billion stimulus	Y	6. Pass health care bill	Y	10. Legalize immigrants' kids	Y
3. Let guns in national parks	N	7. Regulate financial firms	Y	11. Repeal don't ask, tell	Y
4. Pass cap-and-trade	Y	8. Pass tax cuts for some	Y	12. Limit campaign funds	Y

Election Results

2010 general	Jay Inslee (D)	172,642	(58%)	($1,403,962)
	James Watkins (R)	126,737	(42%)	($351,477)
2010 primary	Jay Inslee (D)	90,208	(56%)	
	James Watkins (R)	44,269	(27%)	
	Matthew Burke (R)	20,185	(13%)	

Prior Winning Percentages: 2008 (68%), 2006 (68%), 2004 (62%), 2002 (56%), 2000 (55%), 1998 (50%), 1992 (51%)

Population		Race/Ethnicity		Work	
Pop. 2010:	739,455	White:	72.7%	Private:	78.6%
Change since 2000:	Up 12.9%	Black:	2.6%	Government:	15.0%
Urban:	95.4%	Hispanic:	7.6%	Self-employed:	6.2%
Rural:	4.6%	Asian:	11.9%	Blue collar:	15.5%
Area size:	616 sq. mi.	Native Am.:	0.7%	White collar:	70.2%
		Hawaiian:	0.4%	Khaki collar:	0.6%
Age		Two+ races:	3.9%	Other:	13.7%
Median age:	37.9 yrs.				
More than 65 yrs:	10.7%	*Ancestry*		Median income:	$73,696
Less than 18 yrs:	23.2%	German	14.8%	Median Home Value:	$406,200
		Irish	9.8%		
Education		English	9.7%	**Military Veterans**	
H.S. grad:	93.8%			% of Pop:	11.0%
College grad:	41.2%				
Grad degree:	14.1%				

Puget Sound; Seattle Suburbs

In the past 30 years, metropolitan Seattle grew to the north and to the east, as a wave of new-comers arrived seeking the area's distinctive blend of natural beauty, robust and creative eco-nomic expansion and freewheeling culture. In the process, some of the distinctiveness of the old Seattle was left behind. The fishy odor of its docks does not permeate new subdivisions built on vegetable fields and vineyards. The Scandi-navian heritage of old neighborhoods like Bal-

2008 Presidential Vote
Barack Obama (D) 226,292   (63%)
John McCain (R) 130,104   (36%)

2004 Presidential Vote
John Kerry (D) 189,566   (56%)
George Bush (R) 143,146   (43%)

Cook Partisan Voting Index: D+9

lard has been muted into a Pacific Northwest blend. The heart of new Seattle is east of Lake Washington, in the edge city of Redmond. Here are the turquoise, pine-shaded, low-rise buildings of the Microsoft campus—a tranquil environment for a booming and boisterously aggressive com-pany. With more than 40,000 employees in the Puget Sound area, the company has expanded its campus in Redmond and leased major chunks of office space in Seattle and Bellevue. Microsoft has fueled Redmond's transformation from a sleepy hamlet of 1,426 people in 1960 to a hip center of commerce with more than 52,000 people. Not far away, on the eastern shore of Lake Washington, are the homes and estates of the "Microsoft millionaires," who exercised company stock options before the economic bust.

The 1st Congressional District of Washington includes most of Redmond, many of the other suburbs east of Seattle, Shoreline in the northwest corner of King County, and Kirkland, where Google's research and development center came up with Google Maps. It also takes in Edmonds, Lynnwood, Mukilteo and biotech-heavy Bothell. Booming growth during the 1990s has been fol-lowed by some resistance to increased urbanization. Across Puget Sound, the 1st includes the northern tip of Kitsap County and Bainbridge Island, where residents commute by ferry to down-town Seattle. The district's median household income is more than $73,000, well above the state-wide figure.

Politically, this area has been torn by forces of roughly equal strength—cultural liberalism and economic conservatism—though the former seems predominant. It is impossible not to recog-nize the spectacular success of market economics in the 1st District. But most Seattle area resi-dents appreciate, and want to preserve, the region's unique natural aura: the evergreen smell of well-watered land and the regional style that is plainly American yet distinct. Democrat Barack Obama beat Republican John McCain here 62%-36% in 2008, improving on Al Gore's and John Kerry's showings in 2000 and 2004.

Jay Inslee (D)

The congressman from Washington's 1st Congressional District is Jay Inslee, a Democrat elected in 1998. A telegenic leader in his party on technology and environmental issues, he has had his eye on higher office.

Inslee grew up in north Seattle, the son of a high school biology teacher and football coach. He graduated from the University of Washington and Willamette University College of Law. He moved to Selah, in Yakima County east of the Cascades, to practice law and served on the State

Trial Lawyers Association board of directors. In 1988, at age 37, he was elected to the state House over a former Yakima mayor. In 1992, when 4th District Congressman Sid Morrison ran for governor, Inslee won the general election to succeed him 51%-49% over Doc Hastings, a conservative supported by the Christian Coalition. In the House, Inslee voted for the Clinton budget and tax increase and for a crime bill with a ban on assault weapons. In 1994, Hastings challenged Inslee and beat him, 53%-47%. After his defeat, Inslee moved to Bainbridge Island and practiced law in Seattle. In 1996, he ran for governor and finished fifth, with 10% of the total vote, in the all-party primary. He briefly served as regional director of the U.S. Health and Human Services Department.

In 1998, Inslee decided to run for Congress again, this time in the 1st District against Republican incumbent Rick White, an economic conservative with liberal votes on some cultural issues. Inslee attacked White for voting to reduce spending on education and the environment and for supporting electricity deregulation, claiming that White was "willing to sell our reasonably priced electricity to California." White painted Inslee as a carpetbagger. In the September all-party primary, White led 50%-44%. But by November, two issues changed the balance. One was White's divorce. Inslee ran ads claiming that White intended to spend 10 years in the House and then become a lobbyist, a charge his ex-wife had made in divorce papers. He also ran ads highlighting White's vote to impeach President Bill Clinton. In the acrimony, the primary numbers were reversed in November, and Inslee won 50%-44%.

Inslee is a moderate-to-liberal Democrat and likes to focus on technology issues. He joined in protecting the privacy of consumer financial records, an issue important to Microsoft. He and Sen. Maria Cantwell, D-Wash., pressed the Federal Communications Commission in December 2010 for stricter rules on the FCC's proposed net-neutrality order that some Republicans already said was too unfriendly to business. When security experts reported in 2011 that Apple's iPhone could secretly track its users' movements, Inslee called for greater government oversight of data collection.

On the Energy and Commerce Committee, Inslee has focused on conservation and increasing renewable energy sources. As early as 2005, he had introduced bills to address global warming and reduce U.S. dependence on foreign oil. When Republicans skeptical of climate change took control of the House, Inslee criticized what he called the GOP's "allergy to science," and toted a stack of more than 20 books to a March 2011 hearing, saying they contained irrefutable evidence of the problem. A book Inslee co-authored about ending the United States' dependence on foreign oil was published in 2007. He sponsored a provision in a 2009 bill to give rebates to certain industries, such as steel and cement, which face tough competition from international companies. Inslee joined Republicans in arguing against President Obama's decision to shelve the Yucca Mountain storage project in Nevada, which is destined to receive nuclear waste from Washington state. And in February 2011, he seconded the GOP's alarm about growing budget deficits and called for closing tax loopholes.

In 2000, Inslee won his first re-election in the district 55%-43%. He gave serious thought to running again for governor in 2004, but decided against it. But with Democratic Gov. Christine Gregoire deciding to retire, the job is open again in 2012.

SECOND DISTRICT

Rick Larsen (D)

Elected 2000, 6th term; b. June 15, 1965, Arlington; home, Lake Stevens; Pacific Lutheran U., B.A. 1987, U. of MN, M.P.A. 1990; Methodist; married (Tiia); 2 children.

Elected Office: Snohomish City Cncl., 1998-2000, Pres., 1999-2000.

Professional Career: Econ. dev. ofcl., Port of Everett, 1990-91; Dir., pub. affairs, WA St. Dental Assn., 1991-98.

DC Office: 108 CHOB, 20515, 202-225-2605; Fax: 202-225-4420; Web site: larsen.house.gov.

State Offices: Bellingham, 360-733-4500; Everett, 425-252-3188.

Committees: *Armed Services:* Seapower & Projection Forces; Strategic Forces. *Transportation & Infrastructure:* Coast Guard & Maritime Transportation (RMM); Railroads, Pipelines & Hazardous Materials.

Group Ratings

	ACLU	ACU	ADA	CFG	AFS	FRC	LCV	ITIC	NTU	COC
2010	88	0	90	11	100	0	100	100	6	25
2009	–	0	100	6	100	–	100	–	3	43

National Journal Ratings

	2010 LIB — 2010 CONS		2009 LIB — 2009 CONS	
Economic	88% —	10%	64% —	34%
Social	61% —	35%	84% —	11%
Foreign	63% —	35%	78% —	17%
Composite	72% —	28%	77% —	23%

Key Votes of the 111th Congress

1. Overturn Ledbetter	Y	5. Bar federal abortion funds	N	9. Stop detainee transfers	N
2. Pass $820 billion stimulus	Y	6. Pass health care bill	Y	10. Legalize immigrants' kids	Y
3. Let guns in national parks	N	7. Regulate financial firms	Y	11. Repeal don't ask, tell	Y
4. Pass cap-and-trade	Y	8. Pass tax cuts for some	Y	12. Limit campaign funds	Y

Election Results

2010 general	Rick Larsen (D)	155,241	(51%)	($2,028,596)
	John Koster (R)	148,722	(49%)	($1,114,868)
2010 primary	John Koster (R)	74,032	(42%)	
	Rick Larsen (D)	73,734	(42%)	
	Diana McGinness (D)	10,548	(6%)	
	John Carmack (R)	9,566	(5%)	

Prior Winning Percentages: 2008 (62%), 2006 (64%), 2004 (64%), 2002 (50%), 2000 (50%)

Population		Race/Ethnicity		Work	
Pop. 2010:	760,041	White:	80.2%	Private:	75.4%
Change since 2000:	Up 16.1%	Black:	1.3%	Government:	17.1%
Urban:	69.4%	Hispanic:	9.6%	Self-employed:	7.4%
Rural:	30.6%	Asian:	3.5%	Blue collar:	24.9%
Area size:	7,976 sq. mi.	Native Am.:	1.8%	White collar:	55.0%
		Hawaiian:	0.3%	Khaki collar:	0.9%
Age		Two+ races:	3.1%	Other:	19.3%
Median age:	37.5 yrs.				
More than 65 yrs:	12.8%	*Ancestry*		Median income:	$55,784
Less than 18 yrs:	23.6%	German	15.3%	Median Home Value:	$313,500
		English	9.6%		
Education		Irish	9.4%	**Military Veterans**	
H.S. grad:	90.0%			% of Pop:	13.4%
College grad:	25.1%				
Grad degree:	8.0%				

Northern Region; San Juan Islands

The 176 San Juan Islands, in the waters of Puget Sound at the far northwest corner of Washington, were the last part of the continental United States to be turned over to this country. These waters were great whaling grounds, and not until 1860 did the British relinquish them. Today, ferryboats ply the waters of the sound, connecting the islands to mainland Washington and to British Columbia, directly to the west.

2008 Presidential Vote		
Barack Obama (D) 202,452	(56%)
John McCain (R) 152,074	(42%)
2004 Presidential Vote		
John Kerry (D) 169,420	(51%)
George Bush (R) 156,632	(47%)
Cook Partisan Voting Index: D+3		

The publicly operated Washington State Ferries system has more than 26 million passengers annually. Whale watching is popular not only with tourists, but also among scientists on both sides of the border. This is some of the most beautiful coastline in North America: the steely blue sound with green forested hills rising behind, shielded from the full force of Pacific rains by the Olympic Mountains, though still seldom dry. The little towns, on bits of level land between the water and the mountains, have the look of pristine New England villages or Midwestern historic towns. The stores are full of fresh produce and local seafood.

The Seattle metropolitan area has marched north along the shore of Puget Sound, beyond the old lumber port and railroad terminus of Everett, where the huge Boeing plant produces 747s, 777s and the new long-range, twin-engine 787s. Sales of the 787 Dreamliner, which made its maiden flight in December 2009, have been especially strong. To the north of Seattle are Bellingham and Blaine (named for the House speaker and 1884 presidential nominee), on the 49th parallel, with America's most attractively landscaped border crossing and the International Peace Arch, just south of British Columbia. Local studies have aroused fears that global warming combined with shifting ocean wind patterns will raise the water level of the sound higher than in most other areas. The region's deepwater ports, two days closer to Asia than Southern California ports, also are nervous about the planned doubling of the competing Panama Canal's capacity. Economic growth in Whatcom County, home of Bellingham, remained sluggish in the early months of 2011, though the number of manufacturing jobs was increasing. To the south, unemployment in Snohomish and Skagit counties remained above 10%.

The 2nd Congressional District of Washington encompasses the San Juan Islands, including 45-mile-long Whidbey Island, and most of the margin of mainland along the sound and the huge Cascade Mountains, topped by snow-capped Mount Baker. The district has several military installations, including a Navy base at Everett and a naval air station on Whidbey Island. The political tradition in most of the lumbering and fishing areas here is Democratic, while the rich agricultural areas, like the flower-bulb-growing Skagit Valley, are more Republican. Everett tends to be Democratic, while some of the nearby new suburban towns are Republican. Overall, this is a nearly evenly balanced district that tends to vote close to the state average. President George W. Bush lost here 51%-47% in 2004. Democrat Barack Obama won the district 56%-42% in 2008.

Rick Larsen (D)

The congressman from the 2nd District is Rick Larsen, a Democrat first elected in 2000. Though considered a moderate, his backing of several of the Obama administration's biggest priorities nearly cost him his seat in one of 2010's most bruising elections.

Larsen grew up in Arlington, in Snohomish County, graduated from Pacific Lutheran University and got a master's degree at the University of Minnesota. He spent a year doing research on economic development for the Port of Everett. For six years, he was director of public affairs for the Washington State Dental Association. In 1998, he won a seat on the Snohomish County Council and later became its president. In 2000, Republican Jack Metcalf kept his promise to retire after three terms in Congress. The Democratic field was cleared for Larsen when a state legislator unpopular with labor leaders withdrew. The Republican field was cleared for conservative state Rep. John Koster when a moderate legislator failed to raise much money and dropped out. In the September all-party primary, Koster won 49%-46%. The general election became a battleground for political action committees and one of the premier contests in the nation. Anti-abortion rights groups and the National Rifle Association backed Koster, and unions and abortion rights groups fought for Larsen. Larsen said that the contest offered "a clear choice" on abortion, and he criticized Koster for referring to "our American holocaust." Larsen won 50%-46%, doing better than his primary performance in each major county.

In the House, Larsen joined the New Democrat Coalition and leans toward the center in his voting record, though he has been more reliably Democratic since President Barack Obama took office. He backed the 2009 economic stimulus law and the 2010 health care legislation. Earlier, he voted for the Bush tax cuts in 2001, but later expressed opposition to extending tax cuts for upper income taxpayers because it would add to the deficit. He voted reluctantly for President Barack Obama's 2010 tax-cut extension deal because, Larsen said, he was more concerned about "the needs of the unemployed and the potential for economic growth." After voting against the Iraq war resolution in 2002, Larsen became a staunch supporter of the military effort. He has generally supported the Obama administration's efforts in Afghanistan.

Larsen co-chairs the U.S.-China Working Group, a bipartisan group of House members that seeks to build lasting diplomatic ties with China. He joined then-Rep. Mark Kirk, R-Ill., in introducing a series of bills in 2009 aimed at boosting cooperation on trade, environmental, energy and language issues. Larsen said the group was founded as a way to give lawmakers of all political persuasions more information about the emerging nation. "We are neither 'panda huggers' nor 'dragon slayers,'" he said. The group met with Chinese military officials in May 2011 and was permitted to tour a Chinese navy attack submarine.

On local issues, Larsen has pushed to secure funds for upgraded border security at Bellingham and he helped get a pipeline safety bill into law in 2002 after a lethal explosion in his district. He joined other Washington delegation members in 2010 in seeking to ensure that Boeing received a lucrative contract to build the next generation of Air Force refueling tankers.

National Republicans made a play for the seat in 2006, raising money for retired Navy Capt. Doug Roulstone. But Roulstone turned out to be a weak candidate, and Larsen won 64%-36%. In 2008, Republicans recruited former Snohomish County Sheriff Rick Bart, but Bart entered the contest late, which hurt his ability to raise money. Larsen defeated him 62%-38%.

In 2010, he was challenged by Koster, his opponent of a decade earlier. Koster won endorsements from former Alaska Gov. Sarah Palin and Rep. Ron Paul, R-Texas, both favorites of tea party activists who pumped hundreds of thousands of dollars into the Republican's campaign. Their second battle was a microcosm of the two parties' skirmishes that year, as Koster blasted the Democrats' "socialist" health care bill and the rising federal debt, while Larsen stressed job creation and expanding credit for small business. On election night, Larsen trailed by about 1,200 votes but gained ground as more ballots were counted. He declared victory a week later with a 51%-49% edge.

THIRD DISTRICT

Jaime Herrera Beutler (R)

Elected 2010, 1st term; b. Nov. 3, 1978, Glendale, CA; home, Camas; U. of WA, B.A. 2004; Christian; Married (Daniel Beutler).

Elected Office: WA House, 2007-10.

Professional Career: Legis. aide, Rep. Cathy McMorris Rodgers, R-Wash., 2005-07.

DC Office: 1130 LHOB, 20515, 202-225-3536; Fax: 202-225-348; Web site: herrerabeutler.house.gov.

State Offices: Vancouver, 360-695-6292.

Committees: *Small Business:* Healthcare & Technology; Investigations, Oversight & Regulations. *Transportation & Infrastructure:* Highways & Transit; Railroads, Pipelines & Hazardous Materials; Water Resources & Environment (VChmn).

Election Results

2010 general	Jaime Herrera Beutler (R)	152,799	(53%)	($1,557,221)
	Denny Heck (D)	135,654	(47%)	($1,988,495)
2010 primary	Denny Heck (D)	51,895	(31%)	
	Jaime Herrera Beutler (R)	46,001	(28%)	
	David Hendrick (R)	22,621	(14%)	
	David Costillo (R)	19,995	(12%)	
	Cheryl Crist (D)	18,453	(11%)	

Population		Race/Ethnicity		Work	
Pop. 2010:	779,348	White:	83.1%	Private:	74.7%
Change since 2000:	Up 19.0%	Black:	1.5%	Government:	18.2%
Urban:	70.9%	Hispanic:	7.4%	Self-employed:	7.0%
Rural:	29.1%	Asian:	3.3%	Blue collar:	23.7%
Area size:	7,959 sq. mi.	Native Am.:	0.9%	White collar:	58.6%
		Hawaiian:	0.4%	Khaki collar:	0.3%
Age		Two+ races:	3.2%	Other:	17.4%
Median age:	37.8 yrs.				
More than 65 yrs:	12.3%	*Ancestry*		Median income:	$54,225
Less than 18 yrs:	25.1%	German	17.6%	Median Home Value:	$253,400
		Irish	10.2%		
Education		English	9.7%	**Military Veterans**	
H.S. grad:	89.5%			% of Pop:	13.0%
College grad:	24.0%				
Grad degree:	8.7%				

Southwest Washington; Vancouver

From the Pacific Ocean to the majestic row of active and inactive volcanoes, from Mount Rainier to Mount St. Helens, southwest Washington was long one of America's most productive lumber areas. The moist air and almost constant rain blown in from the Pacific keep the trees on the coast growing rapidly. Precipitation is heavy in the valleys just past the Coast Range, and the forests there are also fast growing. Then come the high mountains. The Cascades are a genuine

2008 Presidential Vote
Barack Obama (D) 188,888   (53%)
John McCain (R) 158,774   (45%)

2004 Presidential Vote
George Bush (R) 164,643   (50%)
John Kerry (D) 158,503   (48%)

Cook Partisan Voting Index: EVEN

divide, wringing almost all of the moisture out of the air and making the climate eastward for a thousand miles arid. Americans were reminded of the force of the volcanoes when Mount St. Helens, dormant for 123 years, erupted in 1980, killing 65 people, destroying its own peak and paving the land around it with lava. Americans had long been taught that the lower 48 states had no active volcanoes, but Mount St. Helens proved that wrong. Today, plants, animals and fish are surging back.

For many years, this part of Washington was sparsely settled, with lumber-mill and fishing-boat towns scattered between mountains and water. It was flannel-shirt country, Democratic since the New Deal days. In the early 1990s, its resource-based economy was threatened by the environmental movement, which restricted fishing practices and produced a court decision shutting down logging in old-growth forests to save spotted owl habitat. This roiled local politics and gave Republicans an opening. An important demographic shift has been the spread of two great metropolitan areas into these valleys. Clark County, across the Columbia from Portland, Ore., has filled up with new residents, eager to avoid Oregon's income tax but still make big purchases in Oregon free of sales tax. The county's population grew by 45% in the 1990s and by another 25% after 2000. Olympia, the increasingly trendy and steadily growing state capital, has added residents at a greater rate than the Seattle-Tacoma metro area in recent years. The region is one of America's great international trading areas, with big exports of logs and timber and imports arriving on the Puget Sound docks. The Columbia River Gorge features spectacular outdoor activities, including some of the finest windsurfing in the nation.

The 3rd Congressional District of Washington covers the southwestern corner of the state, between the ocean and the Cascades, from Olympia south to Vancouver. Economic growth and diversification and the coming of many new residents with no roots in the old industries have made the district politically marginal; George W. Bush won here with 48% of the vote in 2000 and 50% in 2004. Democrat Barack Obama won here with 53% of the vote in 2008. It is one of only nine districts in the country with a Cook Partisan Voting Index score of "Even," meaning its political performance closely approximates the national average. About two-thirds of the district's votes are cast near Vancouver in the Portland, Ore. market, where suburban dwellers are wary of high taxes. Liberals are more prevalent in the northern third of the district around Olympia, which is in the Seattle media market.

Jaime Herrera Beutler (R)

The new congresswoman from the 3rd District is Jaime Herrera Beutler, who as a young Latina is a rarity in the Republican Party. She succeeded retiring Democratic Rep. Brian Baird, who held the seat for six terms.

Herrera Beutler grew up in the region. Her father was a printer, and her parents raised six children, so finances were tight. It was a blended family—her parents took in an uncle's children to shelter them from the gangs and violence in Southern California. "My parents demonstrated it's better to sacrifice your own personal comfort at times," she told *National Journal*. She took a job as a nanny to help pay her way through college. She started out studying nursing at Seattle Pacific University, but took time off from her studies after concluding that nursing wasn't the right field for her. Herrera Beutler ultimately got a degree in communications from the University of Washington in 2004. She got involved in politics as a teenager, knocking on doors for Republican candidates in the 1994 campaign that resulted in the GOP capturing majorities in both chambers of Congress. While in college, she scored a prestigious White House internship.

After graduating, she worked as a legislative aide to Rep. Cathy McMorris Rodgers, R-Wash., who became her mentor. Herrera Beutler specialized in health care, education, and veterans and women's issues. When a seat unexpectedly opened up in the state legislature in fall 2007, she was appointed, and two years later, she won the election in her own right with 60% of the vote. She served on the health, transportation, and human services committees, and encouraged by colleagues to take on a greater role, she became the assistant floor leader, the only woman and minority on the Republican leadership team.

When Baird announced that he would retire at the end of his term in 2010, Herrera Beutler, age 31 and a newlywed, discussed getting into the race with her husband, Daniel Beutler, who was about to start law school. They decided to delay his plans so she could run. "We didn't want to look back in 10 or 20 years and say to our children we were too comfortable to do what was right," she said. Herrera Beutler beat out a crowded Republican primary field that included two tea party-backed candidates, winning 28% of the vote, 14 percentage points ahead of her closest competitor. She was the GOP establishment pick in the race and got help from the National Republican Congressional Committee, which put her on its "Young Guns" list of candidates worthy of funding and advertising.

In the general election campaign, Herrera Beutler was swamped by her opponent's fundraising. Media and technology entrepreneur Denny Heck raised $2 million, including $350,000 of his own money, to her $1.5 million. Still, she remained competitive. She criticized Heck for his support of the health care overhaul championed by Democrats in Congress and of President Barack Obama's $787 billion economic stimulus bill. "I may not have founder or CEO in my name," she said in a dig at her opponent, "but most of the folks in the 3rd Congressional District right now are having trouble with their family budget.... It allows me to truly understand why we're so frustrated at overspending." Her television ads concluded, "For fiscal sanity, Jaime Herrera for Congress."

Heck ran as a moderate Democrat and emphasized his experience in business creating jobs, launching a "jobs tour" of the district and supporting such Democratic measures as a bill creating $30 billion in loans for small business. Heck, who was endorsed by Baird, also favored exempting the highest-income taxpayers from a proposal to extend the Bush-era tax cuts. Herrera Beutler supported an extension for all taxpayers, and also opposed the small business bill. Herrera Buetler won 53% to 47%.

In Washington, she got a seat on the House Transportation and Infrastructure Committee, and said she would try to reform the way Congress funds transportation projects, which she called "archaic." On the Subcommittee on Water Resources and the Environment, Herrera Buetler in January 2011 joined 17 other lawmakers in a letter to the Council on Environmental Quality protesting a move to restrict the use of pesticides and herbicides in salmon watersheds.

FOURTH DISTRICT

Doc Hastings (R)

Elected 1994, 9th term; b. Feb. 7, 1941, Spokane; home, Pasco; Columbia Basin Col., 1959-61, Central Washington U., 1963-64; Protestant; married (Claire); 3 children.

Military Career: Army Reserves, 1964–69.

Elected Office: WA House of Reps., 1979–87.

Professional Career: Pres., Columbia Basin Paper & Supply, 1967–94.

DC Office: 1203 LHOB, 20515, 202-225-5816; Fax: 202-225-3251; Web site: hastings.house.gov.

State Offices: Pasco, 509-543-9396; Yakima, 509-452-3243.

Committees: *Natural Resources* (Chmn).

Group Ratings

	ACLU	ACU	ADA	CFG	AFS	FRC	LCV	ITIC	NTU	COC
2010	6	100	0	97	0	100	10	33	91	88
2009	–	96	0	91	0	–	0	–	87	80

National Journal Ratings

	2010 LIB — 2010 CONS		2009 LIB — 2009 CONS	
Economic	14%	86%	0%	96%
Social	25%	71%	11%	87%
Foreign	0%	88%	33%	63%
Composite	16%	84%	16%	84%

Key Votes of the 111th Congress

1. Overturn Ledbetter	N	5. Bar federal abortion funds	
2. Pass $820 billion stimulus	N	6. Pass health care bill	
3. Let guns in national parks	Y	7. Regulate financial firms	
4. Pass cap-and-trade	N	8. Pass tax cuts for some	N

9. Stop detainee transfers	Y
10. Legalize immigrants' kids	N
11. Repeal don't ask, tell	N
12. Limit campaign funds	N

Election Results

2010 general	Doc Hastings (R)	156,726	(68%)	($1,056,576)
	Jay Clough (D)	74,973	(32%)	($119,993)
2010 primary	Doc Hastings (R)	82,909	(59%)	
	Jay Clough (D)	31,782	(23%)	
	Rex Brocki (TEA)	9,826	(7%)	
	Shane Fast (R)	9,214	(7%)	

Prior Winning Percentages: 2008 (63%), 2006 (60%), 2004 (63%), 2002 (67%), 2000 (61%), 1998 (69%), 1996 (53%), 1994 (53%)

Population		Race/Ethnicity		Work	
Pop. 2010:	774,409	White:	60.2%	Private:	76.0%
Change since 2000:	Up 18.2%	Black:	0.8%	Government:	17.5%
Urban:	70.5%	Hispanic:	33.8%	Self-employed:	6.3%
Rural:	29.5%	Asian:	1.4%	Blue collar:	23.5%
Area size:	19,432 sq. mi.	Native Am.:	1.7%	White collar:	51.0%
		Hawaiian:	0.1%	Khaki collar:	0.0%
Age		Two+ races:	1.8%	Other:	25.4%
Median age:	33.5 yrs.				
More than 65 yrs:	11.8%	*Ancestry*		Median income:	$46,353
Less than 18 yrs:	29.1%	German	15.0%	Median Home Value:	$171,000
		English	8.3%		
Education		Irish	7.4%	**Military Veterans**	
H.S. grad:	78.4%			% of Pop:	10.8%
College grad:	19.6%				
Grad degree:	7.3%				

Central Washington; Yakima

The rugged peaks of the Cascade Mountains divide Washington state into two starkly different climate zones and two almost as starkly different political cultures. West of the Cascades, Washington is moist, green and crammed with watery inlets. To the east, it is barren and brown, except where irrigation ditches channel the water of the Columbia River into thirsty valleys and where the mountaintop waters fall east, as they do above the apple orchards in the Yakima

2008 Presidential Vote		
John McCain (R)	159,660	(58%)
Barack Obama (D)	111,374	(40%)
2004 Presidential Vote		
George Bush (R)	160,310	(63%)
John Kerry (D)	90,083	(36%)
Cook Partisan Voting Index: R+13		

Valley. The federal government has been a presence east of the Cascades since the 1930s, when it began to build dams to provide cheap power and boost economic development in this forbidding, often surreal, landscape. A giant bust of Franklin D. Roosevelt gazes out from a bluff on the Columbia over 550-foot-high Grand Coulee Dam, which Roosevelt initiated and which was one of his favorite projects. Other dams are strung like beads on the necklace of the Columbia most of the way downriver to Bonneville Dam near Portland, where the river breaks through the Cascades. In 1996, a 9,300-year-old skeleton was found on the banks of the Columbia River in Richland. It was named the Kennewick Man and is one of the oldest skeletons ever found in North America.

The last undammed, undeveloped stretch of the upper Columbia River is near the 640-square-mile Hanford Nuclear Reservation, north of the Tri-Cities of Richland, Kennewick and Pasco. Hanford was built by the Army to manufacture plutonium for the Manhattan Project and was where the Nagasaki bomb was constructed. After the war, the Hanford Works became the primary producer of materials for America's nuclear weapons and eastern Washington's largest employer. Then in 1989, Hanford's plutonium plant, which produced two-thirds of the nation's plutonium, was shut down because of hazardous leaks and contaminated waste. The spent fuel was scheduled to be shipped to a permanent repository at Yucca Mountain in Nevada, but that project has been delayed by stiff resistance from Nevada politicians who persuaded President Barack Obama to put it on hold, leaving the future of Hanford's high-level waste in doubt. In 2004, voters approved a referendum to prohibit the Energy Department from sending more radioactive waste into Washington until the existing sites were cleaned up. The effort at Hanford is expected to continue until 2047, and operational costs could reach $100 billion.

The 4th Congressional District of Washington covers much of the center of the state east of the Cascades, running from Grand Coulee and the Columbia River through the Hanford Works down to the Dalles Dam and the Columbia River Gorge. The region has suffered economically. Thirty-four percent of the district's residents are Hispanic, many of them farm workers or the children of farm workers who have picked fruit for generations. Farmers in the Yakima Valley, which produces most of the nation's apples and many other crops, were enraged when environmentalists proposed breaching the Snake River dams upriver to save salmon. Lumber towns in the Cascades responded angrily when the logging business was hurt by efforts to preserve the spotted owl. In an area that was once narrowly split between the parties, this has become the most Republican district in the state, with John McCain carrying it 58%-40% over Obama in 2008. The cultural liberalism of Seattle seems very far away from here.

Doc Hastings (R)

The congressman from the 4th District is Doc Hastings, a Republican first elected in 1994. A close friend and ally of Speaker John Boehner, he became chairman of the Natural Resources Committee in 2011, giving him an influential platform to lead the Republican Party's push for more domestic energy extraction.

Hastings grew up in the Tri-Cities, went to college in Ellensburg and is one of the few members of Congress without a college degree. He got his nickname from a brother who could not pronounce his given name, Richard, when they were kids. Hastings served in the Army Reserves and for 27 years ran the Columbia Basin Paper & Supply Company in Pasco, where he was also president of the Chamber of Commerce. In 1979, he was elected to the state House, served as a Republican leader, and then retired in 1987. In 1992, he won the Republican nomination for the U.S. House seat, but was beaten 51%-49% by Democrat Jay Inslee. In office, Inslee voted for the Clinton budget and tax package and for a crime bill with its gun-control provisions—big liabilities when he ran for re-election in 1994 and faced Hastings again. In their second contest, Hastings won 53%-47%. Since then, Democrats have not seriously competed here.

In the House, Hastings has had a mostly conservative voting record, especially on economic and environmental issues. Shortly after the 2010 elections handed Republicans control of the House, Hastings startled party veterans by formally demanding that his committee take jurisdiction over energy-related issues from the Energy and Commerce Committee, which he called "a Goliath" with an unequal share of power among committees. Not surprisingly, Republicans on Energy and Commerce fought the encroachment on their turf, and GOP leaders nixed the idea.

With gasoline prices rising in May 2011, the House passed Hastings' bill requiring the Obama administration to speed up sales of offshore oil leases in the Gulf of Mexico and off Virginia's coast. Hastings said the administration had "repeatedly blocked, hindered and raised the cost to access our American energy resources." The measure was one of several that Hastings had developed after holding face-to-face conversations with Republicans and energy lobbyists. Thirty-three Democrats joined a mostly unanimous GOP in supporting the bill, though senior Natural Resources Democrats complained that Hastings was ignoring the lessons of 2010's BP Deepwater Horizon oil spill disaster. He said earlier that he was open to considering oil spill legislation if the White House agreed to more offshore drilling. He also charged that Interior Secretary Ken Salazar was wrongfully designating federal lands as wilderness areas over other purposes, including energy development.

Until 2009, Hastings had a seat on the leadership-run Rules Committee, and he has been a prominent behind-the-scenes player in the House GOP caucus. As chairman of the investigating subcommittee of the House ethics committee, he had the thankless task of reviewing the case against Ohio Democrat James Traficant, who was convicted of bribery in federal court in 2002. The panel voted unanimously to expel Traficant from the House, only the second such action since the Civil War. Hastings also was part of the unanimous, 10-member panel in 2004 that voted to admonish Majority Leader Tom DeLay of Texas three times, the mildest possible sanction. In what was viewed as a ham-handed rebuke to the committee for even mildly punishing DeLay, then-Republican Speaker Dennis Hastert removed Colorado's Joel Hefley as chairman and replaced him with Hastings. The next year, Hastings was at the center of another dustup. He supported the GOP leadership's change in House rules to make it harder to launch investigations of members. He also ousted the ethics committee's top staff. When committee Democrats protested by refusing to attend committee meetings, Hastings and the Republicans agreed to restore the earlier rules.

Hastings is a vocal defender of Washington's apple and asparagus industries, and during the 110th Congress (2007-08), he voted against the United States-Peru Trade Promotion Agreement Implementation Act and an extension of the 1991 Andean Trade Preference Act, both of which he said hurt Washington growers. Much of his time has been spent on issues surrounding the Hanford Nuclear Reservation. When President George W. Bush proposed cuts in the Energy Department budget, Hastings protected the Hanford cleanup program from reductions. Congress enacted his bill requiring the Interior Department to study preservation of the Manhattan Project's historic sites at Hanford as part of the national park system. Hastings says that his proudest legislative achievement was the 2003 passage of the Citizens' Soldier Act, which makes legal immigrants serving in the military eligible for citizenship after one year in uniform.

FIFTH DISTRICT

Cathy McMorris Rodgers (R)

Elected 2004, 4th term; b. May 22, 1969, Salem, OR; home, Deer Lake; Pensacola Christian Col., B.A. 1990, U. of WA, M.B.A. 2002; Christian; married (Brian Rodgers); 1 child.

Elected Office: WA House of Reps., 1994-2004; Min. ldr. 2002-04.

Professional Career: Owner-operator, Peachcrest Fruit Basket orchard, 1984-98; State legislative aide, 1990-94.

DC Office: 2421 RHOB, 20515, 202-225-2006; Fax: 202-225-3392; Web site: mcmorris.house.gov.

State Offices: Colville, 509-684-3481; Spokane, 509-353-2374; Walla Walla, 509-529-9358.

Committees: *Energy & Commerce:* Energy & Power; Environment & the Economy; Health.

Group Ratings

	ACLU	ACU	ADA	CFG	AFS	FRC	LCV	ITIC	NTU	COC
2010	14	96	0	94	0	100	10	33	89	100
2009	–	96	0	82	22	–	0	–	84	80

National Journal Ratings

	2010 LIB	—	2010 CONS		2009 LIB	—	2009 CONS
Economic	17%	—	83%		9%	—	89%
Social	31%	—	69%		24%	—	73%
Foreign	0%	—	88%		33%	—	63%
Composite	18%	—	82%		24%	—	77%

Key Votes of the 111th Congress

1. Overturn Ledbetter	N	5. Bar federal abortion funds	Y	9. Stop detainee transfers	Y
2. Pass $820 billion stimulus	N	6. Pass health care bill	N	10. Legalize immigrants' kids	*
3. Let guns in national parks	Y	7. Regulate financial firms	N	11. Repeal don't ask, tell	*
4. Pass cap-and-trade	N	8. Pass tax cuts for some	*	12. Limit campaign funds	N

Election Results

2010 general	Cathy McMorris Rodgers (R)	177,235	(64%)	($1,453,240)
	Daryl Romeyn (D)	101,146	(36%)	($2,320)
2010 primary	Cathy McMorris Rodgers (R)	106,191	(63%)	
	Daryl Romeyn (D)	21,091	(12%)	
	Barbara Lampert (D)	15,538	(9%)	
	Clyde Cordero (D)	10,787	(6%)	
	Randall Yearout (CNP)	10,635	(6%)	

Prior Winning Percentages: 2008 (65%); 2006 (56%); 2004 (60%)

Population		Race/Ethnicity		Work	
Pop. 2010:	723,609	White:	84.7%	Private:	73.5%
Change since 2000:	Up 10.5%	Black:	1.4%	Government:	19.3%
Urban:	71.9%	Hispanic:	6.3%	Self-employed:	6.9%
Rural:	28.1%	Asian:	2.0%	Blue collar:	18.9%
Area size:	23,165 sq. mi.	Native Am.:	2.2%	White collar:	60.1%
		Hawaiian:	0.3%	Khaki collar:	0.4%
Age		Two+ races:	2.9%	Other:	20.6%
Median age:	37.2 yrs.				
More than 65 yrs:	13.7%	*Ancestry*		Median income:	$44,868
Less than 18 yrs:	23.2%	German	19.8%	Median Home Value:	$191,300
		Irish	11.0%		
Education		English	9.9%	**Military Veterans**	
H.S. grad:	90.7%			% of Pop:	13.6%
College grad:	25.9%				
Grad degree:	9.5%				

Eastern Washington; Spokane

Eastern Washington is a land of great rivers and bare parched land, where the Columbia, Spokane and Snake rivers wind among vast plateaus, bringing water from the Rockies to the desert. Spokane grew up at the falls of the Spokane River when the railroads first came through, and early in the 20th century, it became a major wheat, mining, electrical and railroad center. It celebrated with the 1974 World's Fair and Exposition on the downtown riverfront. Nearby are

2008 Presidential Vote		
John McCain (R) 171,670	(52%)
Barack Obama (D) 152,970	(46%)
2004 Presidential Vote		
George Bush (R) 177,311	(57%)
John Kerry (D) 127,162	(41%)
Cook Partisan Voting Index: R+7		

some of the most fascinating landscapes in the United States: undulating yellow wheat fields on the rolling ridges of the Palouse, where the wheat-growing topsoil is 200 feet deep; bare-rock coulees rising above dammed-up lakes and barren desert; and the vast wilderness of Okanogan County, which has long been gold country. A new mine began operating in 2008 after an agreement was reached with local conservation groups on water quality monitoring. This is remote and inhospitable land. The summers can be blazingly hot and the winters bitterly cold. But the water from the Grand Coulee and other dams irrigates some of the richest farmland in the country.

The 5th Congressional District of Washington covers the easternmost part of the state. Two-thirds of the people here live in greater Spokane, a city whose voting habits have grown apart from the Washington west of the Cascades, especially on natural resource issues. Several Spokane-area politicians have called for creating a 51st state of Eastern Washington, with 60% of the current state's land and 22% of its population. The city has grown slightly over the last decade and has more than 200,000 residents. But it has weathered hard times. After the 2007-09 recession, its unemployment remained above 10% in early 2011. Near the Oregon border is Walla Walla, long dependent on wheat and sweet onions but now attracting tourists with its budding wine industry. The district's political inclinations are Republican. Spokane County voted for Democrat Bill Clinton in 1992 and 1996, but Republican George W. Bush won the county 56%-44% in 2004. In 2008, Republican John McCain carried the county 49%-48% and won the district 52%-46%.

Cathy McMorris Rodgers (R)

The congresswoman from the 5th District is Cathy McMorris Rodgers, a Republican elected in 2004. She is in her second term as vice chairman of the Republican Conference and is the only woman among the top GOP leaders in the House.

McMorris Rodgers spent much of her childhood in northern British Columbia, but moved with her family to Kettle Falls, Wash., where her parents bought a fruit orchard and operated a stand selling apples, peaches, cherries and strawberries. She graduated from Pensacola Christian College in Florida and got an M.B.A. from the University of Washington. After college, she became a legislative assistant to a state House member. When he moved up to the state Senate, McMorris Rodgers was appointed to his House seat at age 24, and later, was elected in her own right. She served for 10 years and chaired the Commerce and Labor Committee. She eventually rose to minority leader, the first female House leader in state history. In 2004, George Nethercutt, who defeated Democratic House Speaker Tom Foley in 1994, ran for the Senate. McMorris Rodgers and two other Republicans filed to compete for his seat in the primary. The three primary candidates agreed on most major issues. Each opposed abortion and favored a constitutional amendment banning same-sex marriage. Each supported tort law changes and making the Bush administration tax cuts permanent, and each criticized the Endangered Species Act. McMorris Rodgers won 50% of the vote in the primary to 27% for state Sen. Larry Sheahan and 23% for Spokane lawyer Shaun Cross.

The Democratic nominee, Don Barbieri, a wealthy businessman, had a geographical edge over McMorris Rodgers. He was from Spokane, while she was from rural northeastern Washington. Barbieri also had a heavy financial advantage. He had no primary opposition and was well funded going into the general. The National Republican Congressional Committee spent heavily on McMorris Rodgers's behalf, including airing an ad charging that Barbieri had put "profits before jobs" when his hotel development company laid off workers following a merger. McMorris Rodgers highlighted her pro-business credentials and agricultural background as a farmer's daughter. That was enough to give her a comfortable victory, 60%-40%, a sign of how much has changed in Foley's old district.

In the House, McMorris Rodgers has a mostly conservative voting record, especially since President Barack Obama took office. Earlier, she leaned toward the center on some issues. In 2007, she voted to expand the State Children's Health Insurance Plan, a move favored by Democrats but opposed by President George W. Bush. (She opposed the final version that became law in 2009.) She backed Bush's Iraq war policies, but also criticized the administration on veterans' health care and on a delay in rules for country-of-origin meat labeling. During her first term, she won passage in the House a bill to increase the number of qualified teachers for advanced placement courses.

McMorris Rodgers quickly became an acolyte of Minority Leader John Boehner, with whom she served on the Education and Labor Committee. She won the conference vice chairmanship job with his backing and took on several tasks. He selected her in 2009 to head a GOP task force that unsuccessfully sought to develop a policy on earmarks. She also has served as a liaison to newly-elected female Republicans, and was charged with helping to recruit women to run in 2012. McMorris Rodgers also has sought to broaden her party's use of social media tools such as Twitter and Facebook. She became part of the new majority's push in 2011 to cut off money to implement the 2010 health care reform law, introducing a bill to block the Internal Revenue Service from hiring employees to enforce the requirement that all individuals obtain health insurance.

In 2007, the Citizens for Responsibility and Ethics in Washington listed McMorris Rodgers as one of 96 lawmakers who had hired family members for their congressional campaigns in the last six years. The following year, she faced five opponents in the primary, including two who campaigned for support among the district's conservatives. McMorris Rodgers won the primary with 56% of the vote and then won the general election by defeating Democrat Mark Mays, the primary runner-up, 65%-35%.

In April 2007, McMorris Rodgers and her husband had their first child, a boy, Cole McMorris Rodgers, who was born four weeks premature and was diagnosed with Down syndrome. Only eight women, all of them in the House, have given birth while serving in Congress, inclusive of McMorris Rodgers. She formed the Congressional Down Syndrome Caucus in the spring of 2008 to raise awareness about institutional barriers that individuals with Down syndrome face. In December 2010, she and her husband had a girl, making her the first woman in Congress to give birth twice while in office.

SIXTH DISTRICT

Norm Dicks (D)

Elected 1976, 18th term; b. Dec. 16, 1940, Bremerton; home, Belfair; U. of WA, B.A. 1963, J.D. 1968; Lutheran; married (Suzanne); 2 children.

Professional Career: Legis. asst., U.S. Sen. Warren Magnuson, 1968–73, A.A., 1973–76.

DC Office: 2467 RHOB, 20515, 202-225-5916; Web site: www.house.gov/dicks.

State Offices: Bremerton, 360-479-4011; Port Angeles, 360-452-3370; Tacoma, 253-593-6536.

Committees: *Appropriations* (RMM): Defense (RMM).

Group Ratings

	ACLU	ACU	ADA	CFG	AFS	FRC	LCV	ITIC	NTU	COC
2010	81	0	90	0	100	0	100	100	6	25
2009	–	0	100	6	100	–	100	–	3	40

National Journal Ratings

	2010 LIB	—	2010 CONS	2009 LIB	—	2009 CONS
Economic	86%	—	13%	75%	—	21%
Social	61%	—	35%	75%	—	20%
Foreign	56%	—	38%	70%	—	24%
Composite	70%	—	31%	76%	—	24%

Key Votes of the 111th Congress

1. Overturn Ledbetter	Y	5. Bar federal abortion funds	N	9. Stop detainee transfers	N
2. Pass $820 billion stimulus	Y	6. Pass health care bill	Y	10. Legalize immigrants' kids	Y
3. Let guns in national parks	N	7. Regulate financial firms	Y	11. Repeal don't ask, tell	Y
4. Pass cap-and-trade	Y	8. Pass tax cuts for some	Y	12. Limit campaign funds	Y

Election Results

2010 general	Norm Dicks (D)	151,873	(58%)	($1,412,760)
	Doug Cloud (R)	109,800	(42%)	($118,128)
2010 primary	Norm Dicks (D)	90,596	(57%)	
	Doug Cloud (R)	45,959	(29%)	
	Jesse Young (R)	23,410	(15%)	

Prior Winning Percentages: 2008 (67%); 2006 (71%); 2004 (69%); 2002 (64%); 2000 (65%); 1998 (68%); 1996 (66%); 1994 (58%); 1992 (64%); 1990 (61%); 1988 (68%); 1986 (71%); 1984 (66%); 1982 (63%); 1980 (54%); 1978 (61%); 1976 (74%)

Population		Race/Ethnicity		Work	
Pop. 2010:	709,570	White:	73.3%	Private:	70.7%
Change since 2000:	Up 8.3%	Black:	5.3%	Government:	22.2%
Urban:	78.8%	Hispanic:	8.5%	Self-employed:	7.0%
Rural:	21.2%	Asian:	4.8%	Blue collar:	22.8%
Area size:	8,590 sq. mi.	Native Am.:	2.1%	White collar:	55.3%
		Hawaiian:	1.0%	Khaki collar:	1.0%
Age		Two+ races:	5.0%	Other:	20.8%
Median age:	39.3 yrs.				
More than 65 yrs:	14.4%	*Ancestry*		Median income:	$48,538
Less than 18 yrs:	22.3%	German	15.1%	Median Home Value:	$249,700
		Irish	10.1%		
Education		English	9.2%	**Military Veterans**	
H.S. grad:	89.2%			% of Pop:	15.5%
College grad:	23.3%				
Grad degree:	8.4%				

Western Washington; Tacoma

The rainiest part of the continental United States is its far northwest corner, where the Olympic Mountains of Washington thrust into the Pacific Ocean. The waters of the Pacific evaporate, condense and then mist or rain down on the hills and mountains that jut up from the ocean and Puget Sound. The mountains here are always green, the trees that line the inlets towering, and during heavy rain falls, the rivers can rise six feet in a day. This has long been lumber-

2008 Presidential Vote		
Barack Obama (D)	182,789	(57%)
John McCain (R)	128,883	(41%)

2004 Presidential Vote		
John Kerry (D)	163,145	(53%)
George Bush (R)	137,891	(45%)

Cook Partisan Voting Index: D+5

ing and fishing country, where people start work at 6 a.m. and where the vagaries of nature and environmental laws—like the ban on old-growth logging to protect the habitat of the spotted owl—have strengthened a traditional surly independence and suspicion of authority. Still, respect for the beauty of nature endures, including at the 3,310-square-mile Olympic Coast National Marine Sanctuary, a vast underwater reserve. There are also some fears that too much land is being bought up to build subdivisions and second homes.

The many inlets of Puget Sound, winding sinuously through mountains, are among America's most picturesque waterways and strategically among its most important. During World War II, shipyards were built to shelter much of the U.S. Navy's Pacific fleet, and during the Cold War, much of the nuclear submarine fleet was anchored at the giant Kitsap Navy base. The Tacoma Narrows Bridge was built to replace the original bridge, in a scene preserved on newsreel and still viewed by civil engineering students, started vibrating on the wrong harmonic in high winds and collapsed in 1940. On the other side is Tacoma, long the second-ranking city on Puget Sound, with its massive docks, former pulp mills, pleasant hilly residential neighborhoods and recently revived waterfront.

The 6th Congressional District of Washington includes the Olympic Peninsula, Bremerton, much of surrounding Kitsap County and most of Tacoma. Like other parts of Washington, Tacoma was slow to recover from the 2007-09 recession, with unemployment still above 10% in early 2011.

In the Bremerton area, the jobless rate was far lower. Politically, the Olympic Peninsula and Bremerton are working-class Democratic. Tacoma also is traditionally Democratic. Seattle and King County were somewhat more Republican than Tacoma and Pierce County as late as the early 1980s, but now they are much more heavily Democratic. In 2004, the district voted 53%-45% for Democrat John Kerry, and in 2008, it voted 57%-41% for Democrat Barack Obama.

Norm Dicks (D)

The congressman from the 6th District is Norm Dicks, a Democrat first elected in 1976. He is the ranking Democrat on the Appropriations Committee and also serves in that capacity on the Defense Appropriations Subcommittee, a powerful posting with jurisdiction over the military budget.

Dicks grew up in Bremerton, the son of a shipyard worker at the Puget Sound Naval Shipyard. At the University of Washington, he was a 185-pound linebacker dubbed "Dizzy Dicks" for his manic style on the field. (For years afterward, he was known to bellow "Huskies!" to motivate himself on the tennis or basketball courts.) He played on the team that legendary UW Coach Jim Owens took to the Rose Bowl in 1960. Injuries, including a bad knee, kept Dicks from going pro, so he decided to pursue his second love, politics. After graduation from UW's law school, Dicks landed a job as a legislative aide and speechwriter for Democratic Sen. Warren Magnuson, one of the most prominent senators of his time. Before long, Dicks was on a fast track. In three years, he was running Magnuson's Senate office. Then, when 6th District Rep. Floyd Hicks, a Democrat, left Congress to accept a judgeship in 1976, Dicks got his chance to jump from staffer to legislator.

He ran a hard-charging campaign and, helped by Magnuson's political connections, prevailed in a four-candidate primary that included the mayor of Tacoma. He then cruised to a 74%-26% general election victory. For many years, Dicks had had his eye on the Senate, but the timing never seemed right, and his hawkish positions made him a tough sell in liberal Seattle, the state's largest city. Dicks stayed in the House.

In his first term, he succeeded in the unusual feat of winning a seat on the Appropriations Committee, over a fellow Democratic freshman named Al Gore. In his second term, he got a seat on the Defense Subcommittee, of vital interest not only to the military at large but to the 6th District's defense-fueled economy. His rise to the top job on the committee was stymied for three decades by Pennsylvania Rep. John Murtha's longevity. Dicks ultimately rose to chairman of the Interior and Environment Appropriations Subcommittee in 2007, while remaining active on the Defense panel. He took the helm of the defense subcommittee following Murtha's death in March 2010.

When Appropriations Chairman David Obey, D-Wis., announced his retirement two months later, Dicks swiftly launched a campaign to replace him and eventually got the Congressional Black Caucus' implicit backing over CBC member Chaka Fattah, D-Pa. Some lawmakers considered it unfair for the chairman or ranking member of a full committee to also hold the same slot on a subcommittee, but House Democrats voted in December 2010 to let the policy stand.

Dicks has a moderate voting record and has been considered more supportive of military spending and an interventionist foreign policy than most House Democrats, in the tradition of former Washington Sen. Henry (Scoop) Jackson. He often quotes Jackson saying, "I'm not a hawk or a dove. I just don't want my country to be a pigeon." In March 2011, he also applauded the Pentagon's efforts to find $78 billion in savings for fiscal years 2012 to 2016. On the major defense issue of the decade, Dicks voted for the Iraq war resolution in 2002 and rounded up support for it among Democrats. In 2005, he said he'd been misled by the Bush administration's claims of Iraqi weapons of mass destruction and regretted his past support.

From the committee, Dicks watches over the Naval Base Kitsap, a major nuclear submarine base and by far the largest employer in Kitsap County. And he certainly does not neglect the state's largest defense contractor, Boeing. On Capitol Hill, he is known as "Mr. Boeing" for his close association with the company that employs thousands in and around Everett, Wash., just outside his district. In the House, he was the prime promoter of a failed plan by Boeing to lease to the government 100 Boeing 767s to replace aging KC-135 tankers, which would have reaped $23 billion for the company. Sen. John McCain, R-Ariz., argued that it would be cheaper in the long run to design a new tanker. The deal finally came undone when a former top Air Force official admitted to trying to win the contract for Boeing while she was secretly negotiating for a job with the company. Dicks was bitterly disappointed by the turn of events. But he continued to push for Boeing when the Pentagon decided to build, rather than lease, the tankers, and the company jumped into competition with Northrop Grumman and its European partner, EADS.

In 2006, the contract went to Northrop, which planned to build the tankers in Alabama. With Dicks' backing, Boeing challenged the contract award on technical issues and won. The bidding was reopened, and the titanic battle between the two defense giants, with its political and regional undertones, raged on. Then, in early March 2010, Dicks was elevated to Defense Appropriations chairman, and Northrop abruptly withdrew from the competition, handing victory to Boeing. The project's estimated 9,000 jobs went to Everett. Dicks told the *Tri-City Herald* that the awarding of the $35 billion tanker contract to Boeing in February 2011 was "the happiest day in my professional life."

Dicks' ties to the defense-contracting establishment also have caused him some problems. In 2009, after the Federal Bureau of Investigation began investigating the Paul Magliocchetti and Associates (PMA) lobbying group, Dicks' campaign contributions from PMA and his work securing earmarks for the company's defense-related clients came under scrutiny by the House ethics investigators. (Several other appropriators came under scrutiny as well.) The Office of Congressional Ethics looked into Dicks' fundraising for the 2008 and 2010 elections, during which he collected $56,000 from PMA and its clients. In the same time period, he secured $19.8 million in earmarks for four of PMA's client companies. Although Dicks told investigators one of his criteria for his decisions was whether a project "would diversify the economy of his district," the four companies combined employed less than 85 people in the 6th, according to the OCE's report. But the OCE concluded in November 2009 that Dicks kept his fundraising operation sufficiently separate from his legislative office and that "there is not substantial reason to believe" that Dicks took contributions in exchange for earmarks.

When he chaired the interior subcommittee beginning in January 2007, Dicks was frequently at odds with the Bush administration, which wanted deep cuts in spending. Dicks, who had frequently worked with Republicans over the years, criticized the White House for refusing to negotiate spending proposals. In 2009, he shepherded through the House a $32 billion bill that included money for the Environmental Protection Agency's development of a greenhouse gas program. But he was forced to make concessions to lawmakers from farm states, including an exemption for large cattle, dairy and hog farmers from having to report their greenhouse gas emissions.

Over the years, Dicks has been an energetic practitioner of earmarking, in spite of the growing number of critics who say it results in wasteful spending. He sent $1.2 billion to mill towns when logging in old growth forests was banned in the campaign to save the spotted owl. He passed timber-salvage riders to keep mills going, and he found federal dollars for maintaining salmon runs in dammed rivers. He helped get funding for the multi-billion-dollar Hanford Nuclear Reservation cleanup and for revitalizing Tacoma's once-grimy waterfront. He hammered out a deal with the Skokomish tribe and a Bellingham seafood company to end the dumping of salmon carcasses into Hood Canal, which suffered from algae overgrowth and happened to be a favorite Dicks fishing hole. (He wants to designate Hood Canal as a critical habitat for orcas and other whales.)

During the Reagan era, Dicks worked with Armed Services Chairman Les Aspin of Wisconsin in support of development of the MX missile, which many fellow Democrats opposed. Later, Dicks pushed for expanded production of the B-2 stealth bomber, and was vindicated when the B-2 was used in the bombings of Serbia and Kosovo in 1999, Afghanistan in 2001 and Iraq in 2003. In the 1980s, Dicks helped Texas Rep. Charlie Wilson covertly send money and equipment to Afghans who were trying to repel invading Soviets. (Wilson's swashbuckling involvement was chronicled in a book and a 2007 movie, *Charlie Wilson's War.*) Also in the early 1980s, Dicks was an influential player in the nuclear weapons freeze debate. As the senior Democrat on the Intelligence Committee in the 1990s, he was at the forefront of efforts to improve inefficiencies and lack of coordination among intelligence agencies, problems that finally began to command attention after the September 11 attacks. He also worked with Republicans in a bipartisan investigation of China's attempts to buy sensitive U.S. technology, and pushed to expand the probe to include security lapses at U.S. weapons labs.

Dicks had something of a close election in 1980, but he has been re-elected by wide margins ever since. In four of his elections, his opponent has been Republican attorney Doug Cloud. In the 2010 election, Dicks had to battle a rumor spread by email among local Democrats that he was resigning for health reasons. The email was a hoax.

SEVENTH DISTRICT

Jim McDermott (D)

Elected 1988, 12th term; b. Dec. 28, 1936, Chicago, IL; home, Seattle; Wheaton Col., B.S. 1958, U. of IL, M.D. 1963; Episcopalian; married (Therese Hansen); 2 children.

Military Career: U.S. Navy Medical Corps., 1968–70.

Elected Office: WA House of Reps., 1970–72; WA Senate, 1974–87.

Professional Career: Asst. prof., U. of WA, Practicing psychiatrist, 1970–83; Medical officer, U.S. Foreign Svc., Zaire, 1987–88.

DC Office: 1035 LHOB, 20515, 202-225-3106; Fax: 202-225-6197; Web site: mcdermott.house.gov.

State Offices: Seattle, 206-553-7170.

Committees: *Ways & Means:* Human Resources; Oversight; Trade (RMM).

Group Ratings

	ACLU	ACU	ADA	CFG	AFS	FRC	LCV	ITIC	NTU	COC
2010	94	0	100	0	100	6	100	50	8	13
2009	–	4	95	6	100	–	93	–	5	36

National Journal Ratings

	2010 LIB — 2010 CONS		2009 LIB — 2009 CONS	
Economic	72%	— 27%	73%	— 25%
Social	93%	— 0%	89%	— 0%
Foreign	78%	— 17%	67%	— 31%
Composite	83%	— 17%	79%	— 21%

Key Votes of the 111th Congress

1. Overturn Ledbetter	Y	5. Bar federal abortion funds	N	9. Stop detainee transfers	N
2. Pass $820 billion stimulus	Y	6. Pass health care bill	Y	10. Legalize immigrants' kids	Y
3. Let guns in national parks	N	7. Regulate financial firms	Y	11. Repeal don't ask, tell	Y
4. Pass cap-and-trade	Y	8. Pass tax cuts for some	Y	12. Limit campaign funds	Y

Election Results

2010 general	Jim McDermot (D)	232,649	(83%)	($582,232)
	Bob Jeffers-Schroder (I)	47,741	(17%)	
2010 primary	Jim McDermot (D)	110,914	(80%)	
	Bob Jeffers-Schroder (I)	8,860	(6%)	

Prior Winning Percentages: 2008 (84%); 2006 (79%); 2004 (81%); 2002 (74%); 2000 (73%); 1998 (88%); 1996 (81%); 1994 (75%); 1992 (78%); 1990 (72%); 1988 (76%)

Population		Race/Ethnicity		Work	
Pop. 2010:	704,225	White:	63.8%	Private:	77.7%
Change since 2000:	Up 7.5%	Black:	8.2%	Government:	15.3%
Urban:	98.5%	Hispanic:	8.0%	Self-employed:	6.9%
Rural:	1.5%	Asian:	14.2%	Blue collar:	12.2%
Area size:	246 sq. mi.	Native Am.:	0.7%	White collar:	71.7%
		Hawaiian:	0.5%	Khaki collar:	0.1%
Age		Two+ races:	4.4%	Other:	16.0%
Median age:	36.6 yrs.				
More than 65 yrs:	10.7%	*Ancestry*		Median income:	$59,529
Less than 18 yrs:	16.0%	German	12.5%	Median Home Value:	$449,000
		Irish	9.1%		
Education		English	8.9%	**Military Veterans**	
H.S. grad:	91.5%			% of Pop:	7.4%
College grad:	51.5%				
Grad degree:	19.9%				

Seattle and Suburbs

Seattle rises from the Puget Sound harbor of Elliott Bay on steep hills once covered with 300-foot-high Douglas firs. Behind the hills and buildings on a clear day, you can see from almost anywhere the nimbus of Mount Rainier. On the picturesque waterfront, below gleaming high-rises, is Pike Place Market, where you can get fresh salmon and Dungeness crabs. Nearby is Pioneer Square, where stores and warehouses from the turn of the 20th century have been re-

stored. Yesler Way was America's original Skid Road—literally a path for skidding newly cut logs to transportation terminals—and it still has some homeless people. Seattle's upper class, like San Francisco's, continues to be anchored in downtown, with its upscale stores and busy sidewalks. Seattle first broke into the national consciousness with the 1897 Klondike gold strike and has been a major American city since around 1910. It hosted its own World's Fair in 1962.

In the 1990s, its combination of economic growth and creativity plus its physical beauty and distinctive style made it a national trendsetter. Seattle has some old ethnic neighborhoods, like the once heavily Scandinavian Ballard, which has been moving toward boutiques and nightspots, and the countercultural Capitol Hill, where shoppers jam busy stores, galleries and clubs. But it also has a new ethnic mix, with thousands of Asian immigrants. The dominant tone is set by highly educated, affluent, single professionals, who have made the Victorian houses overlooking the harbor and the 1940s houses in Capitol Hill among the nation's highest-priced residential real estate. There are still blue-collar workers on the south side of the city and in the valleys. Factories, warehouses and railroad yards are concentrated on a flat plain near Puget Sound and south of downtown. Boeing, still a major presence in the Seattle area since moving its headquarters to Chicago in 2001, is America's biggest exporter. But Seattle has had other exports, such as Nordstrom department stores with their famously attentive service and fashionable goods. Seattle remains the headquarters, in an old industrial district, of Starbucks coffee, which now has more than 17,000 stores.

Seattle ranks as one of the nation's most desirable, and liberal, cities. But it has suffered some black eyes in recent years. The U.S. Justice Department began a comprehensive investigation of the city's police in March 2011 after several episodes in which officers were accused of using unnecessary force and discriminating against minorities. During the 2007-09 recession, Starbucks not only ceased its rapid expansion, it closed stores and laid off baristas. The city's professional basketball team, the SuperSonics, moved to Oklahoma City after Starbucks owner Howard Schultz sold the team to a group of Oklahoma businessmen who broke a promise to keep the team in the Northwest. And in March 2009, Seattle's oldest running newspaper, the *Seattle Post-Intelligencer*, stopped its printing presses and began publishing exclusively online, leaving *The Seattle Times* as the city's only daily newspaper. But Seattle boasts a unique economic foundation. Amazon has expanded into a huge new campus in Seattle's South Lake Union area, and has remained robust. In March 2011 its online jobs board listed 1,900 openings in Seattle. Microsoft founder Bill Gates' decision to turn his attention to global health philanthropy has made Seattle the Davos of health care, drawing experts in malaria, tuberculosis, AIDS and other global scourges. Despite such assets, the Seattle area has been in the middle of the pack among large cities in emerging from the recession. Unemployment in the area remained above 9% in early 2011, and housing prices were far below their peak levels.

The 7th Congressional District of Washington includes nearly all of the city of Seattle, some industrial suburban fringe to the south, a white-collar suburban fringe to the north, and artsy, bucolic Vashon Island in Puget Sound. Seattle is one of the whitest major cities in the nation, so this district—14% Asian, 8% black and 8% Hispanic—is the closest thing to a minority district in the Seattle area. It shares more with San Francisco than hills and scenery. It is heavily populated by singles, gays, young professionals and elderly pensioners. It has one of the nation's lowest percentages of married couples and children. A generation ago, Seattle was roughly split between the parties. Today, it is heavily Democratic. John Kerry carried the district 79%-19% in 2004, and Barack Obama won it 84%-15% in 2008.

Jim McDermott (D)

The congressman from the 7th District is Jim McDermott, first elected in 1988. Long one of Congress' most liberal members, he is a persistent attack dog against Republican policies that he complains, often caustically, are unfair to the middle class.

McDermott grew up in the Chicago suburb of Downers Grove, one of three boys, and was the first in his family to attend college. His father, a fundamentalist Christian, ministered in a church run out of the garage. McDermott graduated from conservative Christian Wheaton College, the alma mater of the Rev. Billy Graham. He went on to get a medical degree from the University of Illinois and did the last two years of his psychiatric residency at the University of Washington. He fell in love with the area and decided to make it his home. But first, with the Vietnam War under way, McDermott volunteered for a stint in the Navy as a psychiatrist. The experience left him adamantly opposed to the war, and when he returned to Seattle, he got involved in politics. In 1970, while he was operating his medical practice, he was elected to the state House, and in 1974, he was elected to the state Senate. He ran for governor three times and lost every time. In 1987, he retired from the legislature and went to Zaire (now the Democratic Republic of the Congo) as a medical officer in the Foreign Service. When the House seat opened in 1988, he returned to Seattle and won easily, beating Norm Rice 38%-29% in the primary and taking 76% in the general. He is the only psychiatrist in the House.

McDermott is upfront about his legislative interests, which tend not to include the parochial matters and pork barrel spending that consume some of his congressional colleagues. He has promoted health issues overseas; he founded and chaired the Congressional Task Force on International HIV/AIDS. He also sponsored a measure that at first seemed quixotic but was enacted in 2000: The African Growth and Opportunity Act, which reduced import quotas and tariffs on African goods and included investment funds. More recently, he has introduced bills requiring the Internal Revenue Service to provide to taxpayers a detailed breakdown of how their money is spent.

McDermott is equally upfront in voicing his displeasure with the GOP. In April 2011, he said on the House floor: "The difference between a Boy Scout troop and this House of Representatives is that the Boy Scout troop has adult leadership." A day earlier, he complained that Republicans were "out to get the poor women in this country." He issued a video calling the tea party "the most nonsensical display of people not thinking" that he had seen in decades. McDermott also alleged that Republicans were deliberately "trying to create chaos in the economy" as a way of stopping President Barack Obama's agenda. He adamantly opposed Obama's December 2010 tax cut deal with Republicans that extended cuts to the top-income earners and accused the GOP of caring more about "trust-fund babies" than unemployed workers.

In his early years in the House, McDermott rose quickly in influence. Democratic leader Tom Foley of Washington state tapped him for influential assignments. His great cause has been health care, but he has shared the frustration many have felt in dealing with the issue. He has long backed a single-payer, Canadian-style national health insurance program. During the most recent health care debate in 2009 and 2010, he pushed for a government-run "public option" to compete with private insurers. Even after the bill became law without such an option, he cosponsored legislation for a public plan that he said would lower the deficit.

McDermott was harshly critical of the Bush administration on a number of fronts, especially the war in Iraq. In September 2002, with a congressional delegation in Baghdad, McDermott said in a statement broadcast on ABC's *This Week* that Bush was willing to "mislead the American people," and that he found Iraqi Leader Saddam Hussein to be more credible than Bush. This sparked harsh criticism from Republicans and dismay from those Democrats who felt his comments had gone too far. But McDermott was unbowed. In a 2007 floor speech, he said, "In less than one generation we have done what we vowed never to do again. We allowed a president to stampede the nation into a hopeless war, not because we had to, but because he wanted to."

His antiwar sentiments are not tied to party loyalty. He has also castigated the Obama administration for its Middle East policies. "No matter how many troops we commit, the United States cannot bring about the change necessary to stabilize Afghanistan," he said in December 2009.

With the Democrats' return to the majority in 2007, legislative life for McDermott was considerably more enjoyable. A longtime ally of House Speaker Nancy Pelosi, he again had a friendly ear in high places. In the opening days of the 110th Congress (2007-08), he helped shape the House-passed bill to rescind some tax breaks for oil companies. As a senior member of the Ways and Means Committee, he was the lead sponsor of bills between 2008 and 2010 that extended unemployment benefits for American workers. He also shepherded to enactment legislation aimed at improving foster care programs through initiatives such as allowing children to remain in foster care until age 21. In 2009 and 2010, he sponsored measures to tax online gambling and send the proceeds to foster care programs. He tends to reach for broad legislative fixes to entrenched social problems, even though Congress moves at best slowly and incrementally.

McDermott stirred controversy in 2004 when he omitted the words "under God" as he led the House in its daily Pledge of Allegiance to the flag. After leaders of both parties criticized him, he replied that his omission had not been deliberate. In 2007, he was attacked by conservatives for voting against a House resolution recognizing the importance of Christmas. They noted that he had previously voted for resolutions recognizing the Islamic holy month of Ramadan.

McDermott was also bogged down in a years-long partisan battle with House Republicans stemming from an incident when he was ranking minority member on the Ethics Committee, during its consideration in 1997 of charges against Republican Speaker Newt Gingrich. In that highly charged political atmosphere, two Democratic activists in Florida happened to tape from a police scanner a cell-phone conversation between Ohio Republican John Boehner and other GOP leaders. They gave the tape to McDermott. A few days later, excerpts from it appeared in newspapers. Boehner sued McDermott in federal court for invasion of privacy, and the case lingered in the courts for years. McDermott approached Boehner in 2002—they had not spoken in the 12 years they served together—and sought to settle the case. He agreed to one of Boehner's demands, that he apologize to the House. But he would not agree to the other two: admit that he was wrong and make a contribution to charity. In 2004, the judge found McDermott guilty of violating the federal wiretapping law and ordered him to pay $60,000 in damages and $500,000 in attorneys' fees. McDermott appealed the ruling. But the court case took yet another turn against him in 2007, when the divided D.C. Circuit Court concluded that House rules on confidentiality barred him from disclosing the contents of the tape. The judges ordered payment of the damages to Boehner. McDermott claimed the ruling infringed on his free speech rights and took his case to the U.S. Supreme Court, which refused to hear it. In April 2008, a federal judge ordered McDermott to pay Boehner over $1.2 million in legal fees.

His outspokenness has not hurt McDermott in Seattle, where he regularly wins re-election with more than 70% of the vote. He considered running against Republican Sen. Slade Gorton in 2000, but backed away soon after he underwent open heart surgery, saying he didn't want to raise the $8 million that would be required. Democrat Maria Cantwell defeated Gorton to capture the seat. Two months after his 2010 re-election, a Palm Springs, Calif., man was arrested for phone calls in which he allegedly threatened to kill McDermott as well as his friends and family.

EIGHTH DISTRICT

Dave Reichert (R)

Elected 2004, 4th term; b. Aug. 29, 1950, Detroit Lakes, MN; home, Auburn; Concordia Lutheran Col., A.A. 1970; Lutheran; married (Julie); 3 children.

Military Career: Air Force Reserve, 1971-76.

Elected Office: King Cnty. Sheriff, 1997-2004.

Professional Career: King Cnty. police officer, 1972-1997.

DC Office: 1730 LHOB, 20515, 202-225-7761; Fax: 202-225-4282; Web site: reichert.house.gov.

State Offices: Buckley, 206-498-8103; Mercer Island, 206-275-3438.

Committees: *Ways & Means:* Health; Trade.

Group Ratings

	ACLU	ACU	ADA	CFG	AFS	FRC	LCV	ITIC	NTU	COC
2010	33	67	20	86	25	68	70	67	74	100
2009	–	60	45	53	56	–	64	–	50	80

National Journal Ratings

	2010 LIB	—	2010 CONS	2009 LIB	—	2009 CONS
Economic	38%	—	61%	40%	—	60%
Social	37%	—	62%	40%	—	59%
Foreign	39%	—	61%	41%	—	59%
Composite	38%	—	62%	41%	—	60%

Key Votes of the 111th Congress

1. Overturn Ledbetter	N	5. Bar federal abortion funds	Y	9. Stop detainee transfers	Y
2. Pass $820 billion stimulus	N	6. Pass health care bill	N	10. Legalize immigrants' kids	N
3. Let guns in national parks	Y	7. Regulate financial firms	N	11. Repeal don't ask, tell	Y
4. Pass cap-and-trade	Y	8. Pass tax cuts for some	N	12. Limit campaign funds	N

Election Results

2010 general	Dave Reichert (R)..161,296	(52%)	($2,793,788)
	Suzan DelBene (D)...148,581	(48%)	($4,024,786)
2010 primary	Dave Reichert (R)..76,118	(47%)	
	Suzan DelBene (D)...43,272	(27%)	
	Tom Cramer (D)..15,313	(10%)	
	Ernest Hubert (R)...9,376	(6%)	
	Tim Dillon (R) 8,291	(5%)	

Prior Winning Percentages: 2008 (53%); 2006 (51%); 2004 (52%)

Population		Race/Ethnicity		Work	
Pop. 2010:	810,754	White:	71.2%	Private:	82.3%
Change since 2000:	Up 23.8%	Black:	2.9%	Government:	12.2%
Urban:	87.6%	Hispanic:	7.2%	Self-employed:	5.4%
Rural:	12.4%	Asian:	13.4%	Blue collar:	17.4%
Area size:	2,622 sq. mi.	Native Am.:	0.7%	White collar:	69.6%
		Hawaiian:	0.4%	Khaki collar:	0.2%
Age		Two+ races:	3.9%	Other:	12.8%
Median age:	37.0 yrs.				
More than 65 yrs:	9.6%	*Ancestry*		Median income:	$82,402
Less than 18 yrs:	26.5%	German	15.4%	Median Home Value:	$402,000
		English	9.6%		
Education		Irish	9.1%	**Military Veterans**	
H.S. grad:	93.4%			% of Pop:	10.3%
College grad:	41.4%				
Grad degree:	14.2%				

East Seattle Suburbs; Bellevue

The land east of Seattle's Lake Washington half a century ago was quiet countryside. Orchards and vineyards flourished in the rich, moist soil just below the rise of the Cascades Mountains, while farms and broad pasturelands spread toward 14,410-foot Mount Rainier like a living green quilt. But as Seattle has grown over the years, people have crossed the pontoon bridge across Mercer Island to Bellevue and have made this area one of the most vibrant parts of metro-

2008 Presidential Vote
Barack Obama (D) 211,045   (57%)
John McCain (R) 155,936   (42%)

2004 Presidential Vote
John Kerry (D) 177,601   (51%)
George Bush (R) 168,291   (48%)

Cook Partisan Voting Index: D+3

politan Seattle. With 122,000 people, more than a quarter of them of Asian descent, and enough office space to make it an edge city, Bellevue has grown out of the shadow of Seattle. Its tallest skyscraper has hit the city's 450-foot height limit, a departure from the strip malls and parking lots that defined its downtown a quarter century ago. Bellevue ranked fourth in 2010 on *Money* magazine's annual best small cities list. While downtown Seattle specialized in banks and law firms and trading companies, Bellevue and other communities in Overlake specialized in high-tech start-ups. The proximity of Redmond, the headquarters of Microsoft, and dozens of other firms here have fueled the growth in high tech and Bellevue's unemployment rate is lower than the Seattle area's.

The 8th Congressional District of Washington takes in most of the eastern edge of metro Seattle. It includes most of Bellevue, Mercer Island and the affluent suburbs on Lake Washington—Medina, Clyde Hill, Yarrow Point, Hunts Point, Beaux Arts. It includes Bill Gates' $60 million, 66,000-square-foot high-tech home with its trampoline room, video walls that can be electronically programmed with art from the world's great museums, and a garage large enough to hold 30 cars. According to the King County Assessor's office, annual property taxes on the house exceed $1 million. The 8th also includes the suburbs to the south in King and Pierce counties. It goes east to the crest of the Cascades Mountains and encompasses all of Mount Rainier and one of the nation's last inland old-growth rain forests. This is the most affluent district in Washington, rivaled only by the 1st District in suburban Seattle. Politically, it is a swing district that has become more Democratic. In 2004, John Kerry won it 51% to 48%, and in 2008, Barack Obama won it 57%-42%.

Dave Reichert (R)

The congressman from the 8th District is Dave Reichert, a Republican elected in 2004. He is a party loyalist on economic matters but regularly joins Democrats on environmental issues.

Reichert (*RY-kurt*) was born in Detroit Lakes, Minn., and his family moved to the Seattle area a year later. He graduated from Concordia Lutheran College in Portland and then joined the Air Force Reserves. He worked for 32 years in the King County sheriff's office and was elected sheriff in 1997. He was a national leader on gun crime reduction and methamphetamine prevention. During the riots that accompanied the 1999 international trade meeting in Seattle, he criticized city leaders and the police force for inadequate preparation. He gained national attention for his prominent role in capturing Gary Ridgway, the "Green River Killer" who had terrorized the Seattle area with a two-decade murder spree that left 48 women dead. After Ridgway's capture in 2001, Reichert was featured on television shows and in documentaries, and he published a book about the experience, *Chasing the Devil: My Twenty-Year Quest to Capture the Green River Killer*.

When Republican Rep. Jennifer Dunn announced that she was retiring after 12 years in the House, Republicans actively recruited Reichert to run. He defeated three opponents in the September Republican primary, winning the nomination with 43% of the vote. The Democratic nominee was Dave Ross, a longtime Seattle radio talk show host.

In the general election, Reichert argued that local law enforcement agencies should receive more money and equipment for homeland security. Ross said that he wanted to be the eyes and ears of the public, checking "into what's going on, who's making the trades, where the money is going and whether it's being wisely spent." The national parties stormed in, spending well over $5 million and organizing visits by prominent leaders. Each candidate tried to portray the other as lacking in public policy experience and holding views too extreme for the swing district. Both Seattle newspapers, with strong liberal traditions, endorsed Ross for his greater familiarity with issues and suggested that Reichert was too conservative for the district. Still, Reichert won 52%-47%.

He is one of the House's most green-friendly Republicans, earning a 67 out of 100 score on the League of Conservation Voters' scorecard for the 111th Congress (2009-10). He supported the 2009 House-passed bill to cap carbon dioxide emissions blamed for global warming, and in April 2011, he was the lone House Republican to support a Democratic amendment putting the chamber on record as accepting the scientific view that human beings are a major cause of global warming. He co-sponsored a 2005 bill to designate wilderness in Washington state as off-limits to development and he opposed oil drilling in Alaska's Arctic National Wildlife Refuge while backing tougher fuel economy standards for cars and trucks.

But Reichert has opposed President Barack Obama's major economic initiatives, and in 2009 was rewarded with a prized seat on the powerful Ways and Means Committee. He joined several Republicans in releasing a March 2011 report critical of AARP's venture into the for-profit insurance business as an argument for potentially revoking the giant senior organization's tax-exempt status. His district depends heavily on trade, and a year earlier he led several Ways and Means members in seeking to prod Obama to move on stalled free trade agreements.

When Reichert arrived in the House, he backed New York Rep. Peter King's bid to chair the Homeland Security Committee and was rewarded by King with the chairmanship of the Emergency Preparedness Subcommittee, making him the only freshman in his class to chair a subcommittee. He won enactment of a bill that established standards for interoperable communications. He later sponsored a successful bill to fund programs fostering intelligence sharing with state and local governments.

National Democrats have targeted Reichert since he first ran for re-election in 2006, but he has beaten well-financed Democrats who worked for Microsoft. In a competitive district where dissatisfaction with Bush would likely be a major liability in 2006, Reichert was unapologetic about inviting him to the district. Former Microsoft executive Darcy Burner, the Democratic nominee, dubbed him "Rubber Stamp Reichert." The candidates each spent $3 million, and together, the national parties poured in more than $4 million. Reichert won 51%-49%.

Burner was back for a rematch in 2008. She outraised Reichert $4.3 million to $3 million, but he won 53%-47%. Two years later, he drew a new Democratic opponent in Suzan DelBene, who had been a Microsoft executive for three years. She ran a strong campaign and got substantial national party help, but Reichert again won, 52%-48%.

NINTH DISTRICT

Adam Smith (D)

Elected 1996, 8th term; b. June 15, 1965, Washington, DC; home, Tacoma; Fordham U., B.A. 1987, U. of WA, J.D. 1990; Christian; married (Sara); 2 children.

Elected Office: WA Senate, 1990–96.

Professional Career: Practicing atty., 1991–92; City prosecutor, 1992–95.

DC Office: 2402 RHOB, 20515, 202-225-8901; Fax: 202-225-5893; Web site: adamsmith.house.gov.

State Offices: Tacoma, 253-593-6600.

Committees: *Armed Services* (RMM).

Group Ratings

	ACLU	ACU	ADA	CFG	AFS	FRC	LCV	ITIC	NTU	COC
2010	88	8	90	0	100	0	90	67	8	0
2009	–	0	95	11	89	–	100	–	8	47

National Journal Ratings

	2010 LIB	—	2010 CONS	2009 LIB	—	2009 CONS
Economic	52%	—	48%	55%	—	45%
Social	54%	—	42%	59%	—	37%
Foreign	84%	—	11%	58%	—	41%
Composite	65%	—	35%	58%	—	42%

Key Votes of the 111th Congress

1. Overturn Ledbetter	Y	5. Bar federal abortion funds	N	9. Stop detainee transfers	N
2. Pass $820 billion stimulus	Y	6. Pass health care bill	Y	10. Legalize immigrants' kids	Y
3. Let guns in national parks	Y	7. Regulate financial firms	Y	11. Repeal don't ask, tell	Y
4. Pass cap-and-trade	Y	8. Pass tax cuts for some	Y	12. Limit campaign funds	Y

Election Results

2010 general	Adam Smith (D)	123,743	(55%)	($948,533)
	Dick Muri (R)	101,851	(45%)	($243,210)
2010 primary	Adam Smith (D)	63,866	(51%)	
	Dick Muri (R)	32,116	(26%)	
	Jim Postma (R)	24,509	(20%)	

Prior Winning Percentages: 2008 (65%); 2006 (66%); 2004 (63%); 2002 (59%); 2000 (62%); 1998 (65%); 1996 (50%)

Population		Race/Ethnicity		Work	
Pop. 2010:	723,129	White:	63.1%	Private:	72.9%
Change since 2000:	Up 10.4%	Black:	7.5%	Government:	22.0%
Urban:	95.0%	Hispanic:	12.0%	Self-employed:	4.9%
Rural:	5.0%	Asian:	9.2%	Blue collar:	24.0%
Area size:	691 sq. mi.	Native Am.:	1.1%	White collar:	55.1%
		Hawaiian:	1.8%	Khaki collar:	3.2%
Age		Two+ races:	5.1%	Other:	17.7%
Median age:	35.5 yrs.				
More than 65 yrs:	11.4%	*Ancestry*		Median income:	$56,649
Less than 18 yrs:	24.0%	German	14.0%	Median Home Value:	$284,600
		Irish	9.0%		
Education		English	8.0%	**Military Veterans**	
H.S. grad:	88.8%			% of Pop:	13.9%
College grad:	22.5%				
Grad degree:	7.2%				

South Seattle Suburbs

The misty shores of Puget Sound have seen some of America's most vibrant economic growth over the past two decades. It has spread south and west from Seattle, over the suburban territory to the outskirts of the once-industrial city of Tacoma. The subdivisions along the sound, which have some of the loveliest views in America, tend to be high-income. But much of greater Seattle's prime industrial territory lies between the ridges that run north and south inland. Weyer-

2008 Presidential Vote		
Barack Obama (D) 166,812	(58%)
John McCain (R) 116,915	(41%)
2004 Presidential Vote		
John Kerry (D) 146,494	(53%)
George Bush (R) 126,428	(46%)
Cook Partisan Voting Index: D+5		

haeuser, the world's largest private owner of softwood timber, has its headquarters in Federal Way. Boeing is a major presence in Renton, on the south end of Lake Washington. Boeing's aircraft and electronic components plants have made it America's No. 1 exporter for many years. Renton, which gained renown as the home of 1960s guitarist Jimi Hendrix, manufactures 737s, the best-selling commercial jet in history. A host of smaller factories cluster near the rail lines that run from Minneapolis-St. Paul across the Great Plains to Puget Sound.

The 9th Congressional District of Washington covers much of this area. It includes Sea-Tac Airport, Burien and Renton, just south of Seattle, as well as Kent, Des Moines, and most of Auburn and Federal Way, which are farther south in King County. It includes the container port of Tacoma, though most of the rest of that city is in the 6th District. In Pierce County, it takes in Edgewood and Puyallup, plus an Army facility and an Air Force Base that merged in 2010 to become Joint Base Lewis-McChord, the largest military installation on the West Coast. It also includes a part of Thurston County outside the state capital of Olympia, including the Nisqually National Wildlife Refuge, an important transit point for migratory birds. The district was created after the 1990 census and, politically, was almost perfectly balanced in the mid-1990s. It elected a Democratic representative in 1992, a Republican in 1994 and a Democrat in 1996. But as the Seattle region trended toward the Democrats, the district has done likewise. Barack Obama got 58% of the vote here in 2008.

Adam Smith (D)

The congressman from the 9th District is Adam Smith, a Democrat first elected in 1996 who became the Armed Services Committee's ranking Democrat in December 2010, giving his state added clout on defense matters.

Smith grew up in the Sea-Tac area. His father, a baggage handler for United Airlines who was active in the Machinists Union, died when Smith was 17. The family went on welfare. Smith worked his way through Fordham University driving trucks for UPS, and then went to the University of Washington law school. He worked as a lawyer, and then as a Seattle prosecutor, handling drunk-driving and domestic-abuse cases. In 1990, at age 25, he was elected to the state Senate, beating an incumbent Republican by canvassing the district door-to-door.

In 1995, he decided to run against first-term U.S. Rep. Randy Tate, a Republican. The two had similar backgrounds. They were born in the same year to families of modest means, were first elected to office at young ages and were firm believers in grassroots campaigning. But Tate was a religious conservative and a strong supporter of Republican House Speaker Newt Gingrich, while Smith campaigned as a moderate Democrat, supporting the death penalty and tougher penalties for criminals. He attacked Tate for his support of Gingrich and for backing cuts in Medicare. Tate attacked Smith for his opposition to assigning youthful offenders to adult courts and prisons, and for voting for a tax increase in 1993. This was one of the closest races in the country. In the September all-party primary, Smith led 49%-48%. In November, he won 50%-47%.

In the House, Smith joined the New Democrat Coalition, established a moderate voting record and showed a willingness to take on established interests within his party. He voted to authorize military action in Iraq and sought to improve compensation and other quality-of-life benefits for military personnel. In 2004, he was one of four Democrats who opposed a provision in the USA Patriot Act to bar law enforcement access to library and bookstore records. He joined Republicans in 2011 in voting to extend several key expiring provisions of the controversial anti-terrorism law. He supported the House-passed health care overhaul in 2009, but remained neutral on the final version until the very end in March 2010, finally agreeing to back it after lobbying from President Barack Obama and others.

Smith reportedly joined the Armed Services Committee at the urging of his home-state Democratic colleague Norm Dicks, an influential figure on the Appropriations Defense Subcommittee. Smith rose quickly on the panel, winning praise for his work as chairman of two of its subcommittees. He also earned a seat on the Intelligence Committee, further bolstering his credentials on military and foreign affairs issues. When Armed Services Chairman Ike Skelton, D-Mo., lost his re-election bid in 2010, Smith jumped into the race to succeed Skelton on the panel. Intelligence Committee Chairman Silvestre Reyes of Texas was the early favorite for the job, and California Rep. Loretta Sanchez also got into the race. When the House Democratic Caucus voted, Sanchez and Smith tied at 64 votes apiece, while Reyes got 53. In a two-person runoff, Smith won by 11 votes. Skelton told *National Journal* in May 2011 that his successor would make an impact: "He is a scholar, he is precise in his judgments, he is a very hard worker and knows the subject matters very, very well."

Smith has generally supported the Obama administration's defense policies, though he said after a November 2010 trip to Afghanistan that he remained troubled "about the high cost of our efforts and the challenges we continue to face in developing a reliable partner in the Afghan government." He said Obama "could have done a better job" in working with Congress in the days before taking military action against Libya in March 2011 as part of a NATO coalition, but still backed the president's strategy. When the majority Republicans unveiled their fiscal 2012 defense authorization bill in May 2011, he expressed concerns over the bill's restrictions on the administration's ability to transfer terrorist detainees and over a provision barring Medicare-eligible retirees from enrolling in one of the military's health care programs.

Smith's independence has worked well for him back home. He has won re-election easily, and Republicans have quit targeting this district. In 2008, he chaired Obama's presidential campaign in Washington state. Smith briefly explored the possibility of taking a job with the Obama administration, but in February 2009, announced that he would keep his seat in the House. He is one of the closest friends in the House of Rep. Gabrielle Giffords, D-Ariz., and after she was shot in January 2011 by a mentally unstable constituent, he visited her congressional district and met with her supporters.

★ WEST VIRGINIA ★

Almost heaven—that's what the song says about West Virginia. And there's something to it, at least in the minds of West Virginians who have never lost their affection for the hills and mountains that make this the most unhorizontal state in the nation. The late Sen. Robert Byrd, working in a shipyard in Baltimore in 1944, once painted a landscape of the mountains. (Lithographs of it can still be found on eBay). But West Virginia has had more than its share of tragedy and heartbreak. It was first settled by Scots-Irish immigrants, fresh from internecine fighting in the British Isles and determined to stake out homesteads where they could do as they liked. The state slogan is *Montani semper liberi:* Mountaineers are always free. It was born out of the tragedy of the Civil War, when 55 mountain counties with few slaves seceded from Virginia and were admitted to the Union in 1863. It has made its living most of the years since from that cruelest of minerals, coal. West Virginia is laced with coal. There are coal seams in 53 of its 55 counties and today, even after many mines have closed, production continues in 26 counties. Coal kept the sons of large mountaineer families here for much of the 20th century, men who would otherwise have left for big cities. Coal brought immigrants in, a few from odd corners of Europe, but more from adjacent areas of the South where the local farming economies were stagnant as West Virginia's coal economy was booming. Fifty years ago, coal and local rock salt and brines brought the large concentration of chemical plants to the Kanawha Valley around Charleston. Steel mills and glass factories were established in the panhandle and in the Monongahela River valley south of Pittsburgh.

But for many years, coal did not build a reliable economy. When America was beleaguered abroad, demand for coal increased and energy prices rose. West Virginia boomed during World War II (the state reached its all-time population peak of 2 million in 1950) and during the oil shocks of the 1970s. Coal changed the state's politics too. West Virginia's heritage from the Civil War days was Republican, though some counties tilted toward the Confederacy and the Democrats. The United Mine Workers organized most of the West Virginia mines by 1902, and there were bloody strikes in 1912-13 and 1920-21. Under the UMW's John L. Lewis, the coal country shifted toward the New Deal Democrats, and West Virginia for more than half a century was one of the most Democratic states, deserting the national ticket only in Republican landslide years (1956, 1972, 1984) until George W. Bush carried it in 2000. Its legislature has been controlled by Democrats since 1930. But neither Democratic administrations nor the pensions and medical benefits the UMW negotiated for retired miners were able to provide the economic growth to keep thousands of West Virginians from leaving their mountains to find work elsewhere. As miners were replaced by strip-mining machines, coal tonnage went way up but coal mine employment dropped from 22% of the state's work force in 1950 to 10% in 1980 and to only 4% in the late 1990s. Coal mines employed 126,000 West Virginians in 1948 and 20,000 in 2009. The state's population, 2 million in 1950, fell to 1.85 million in 2010—the only state that lost population between those years. Of the state's 55 counties, 37 had fewer people in 2010 than they did in 1950. The only big population increases over that half-century have been in the eastern panhandle, the university town of Morgantown and several Ohio River counties below Charleston and around Parkersburg. West Virginia ranks at or near the bottom of states in household income, in median home value and in percentage of adults with a high school diploma. It has attracted few immigrants since the 1920s. Its population is only 3% black and 1% Hispanic. But West Virginia ranks very high in percentage of home ownership and married couples. And West Virginians who remained have a strong attachment to this unique state, where the accent sounds Southern and the early 20th century factories and houses look Northern, where the landscape is rural and the economy is industrial.

In the past two decades, however, West Virginia's aging population has finally built a steadier and at least slowly growing economy. The outflow of young people over the decades has left the state with the nation's third oldest population, behind Maine and Vermont—the median age is older than Florida's—and it is the only state with more deaths than births. But the number of jobs rose during most of the 1990s and 2000s, even as the number of manufacturing and underground mining jobs decreased. Unemployment stayed below the national average until December 2010, and the state still generated 9,000 new jobs that year. If West Virginia did not have a housing boom, except in a few eastern panhandle counties, it also did not have a housing bust. In contrast to the 1980s, when thousands left the state, West Virginia saw more people move in than move out from 2000 to 2010. And the demand for coal, despite the national debate about alternative energy sources, has been robust.

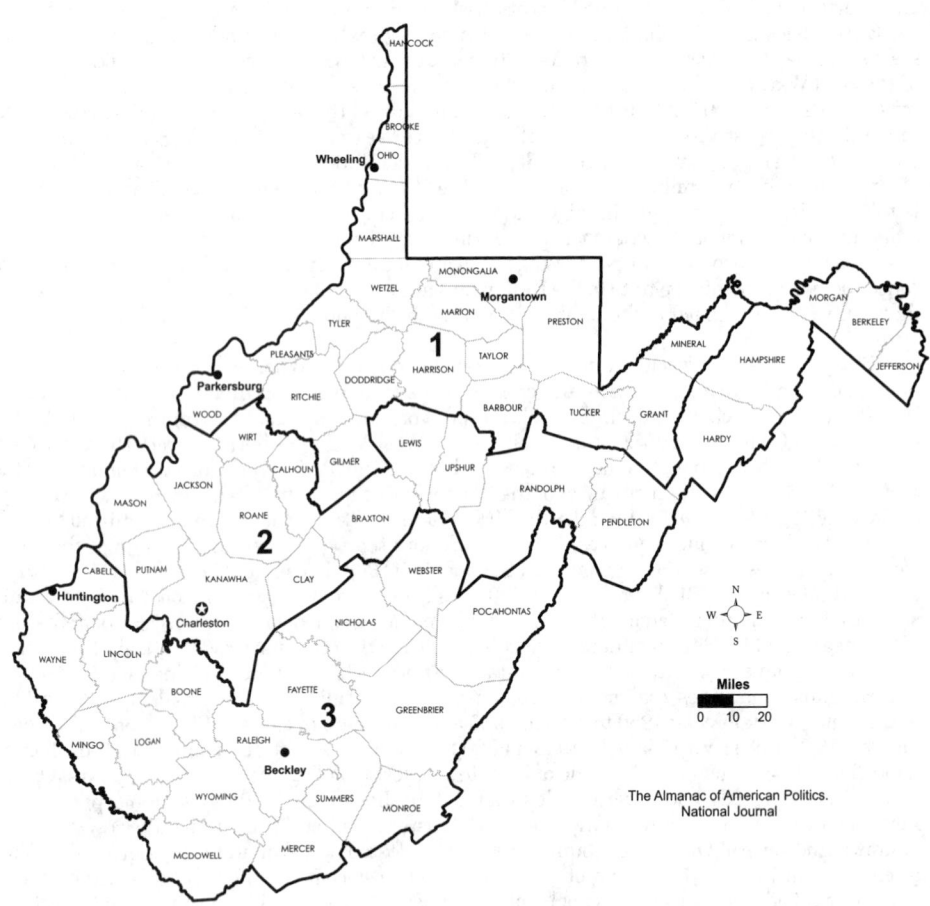

The Almanac of American Politics.
National Journal

Congressional district boundaries were first effective for 2002.

Bible." In 2008, Clinton, celebrating her victory on election night, proclaimed, "We all know from the Bible, faith can move mountains. My friends, the faith of the Mountain State has moved me."

Congressional districting

112th Congress Lineup	
2 R	1 D
111th Congress Lineup	
2 D	1 R

West Virginia's three congressional districts, created after the state lost one House seat in the 1990 census, were not significantly altered in redistricting after the 2000 census. The process was dominated by Democrats and the sole Republican, Shelley Moore Capito, who won an open seat in 2000, could have been harmed by a partisan redrawing of the lines. But one or both of the state's two Democratic incumbents might also have been weakened. Most state legislators, preoccupied with redrawing their own districts, were content to please all three congressional incumbents. In 2001, the legislature, with one dissenting vote, removed Gilmer County from the 2nd District and placed it in the 1st, and removed Nicholas County from the 2nd and placed it in the 3rd. Both are Democratic counties that had no significant impact on the 2002 election results.

West Virginia will have the same number of seats as a result of the reapportionment following the 2010 census. Democrats will control the redistricting process, with big margins in both houses of the legislature and Democrat Earl Ray Tomblin, a legislator from coal-mining Logan County, succeeded Joe Manchin after he was elected to the U.S. Senate in November 2010. But two of the three U.S. House seats are now held by Republicans. Capito was re-elected overwhelmingly in 2010, and David McKinley narrowly defeated Democrat Mike Oliverio in the 1st District. In the southern, 3rd District, Democrat Nick Joe Rahall won re-election 56%-44% in territory that was once as safely Democratic as any in the nation. Redistricters may try to strengthen Rahall and weaken McKinley, but that would only make Capito's 2nd District more Republican.

Governor

Earl Ray Tomblin (D)

Assumed office Nov. 2010, term expires Nov. 2011, 1st term; b. March 15, 1952, Chapmanville; home, Charleston; WV U., B.S. 1974; Marshall U., M.B.A. 1975; Presbyterian; married (Joanne); 1 child.

Elected Office: WV House, 1974-80; WV Senate, 1980-present; Senate pres., 1995-present.

Professional Career: Restaurant owner; farmer.

Office: State Capitol, 1900 Kanawha Boulevard, East, Charleston, 25305, 304-558-2000; Web site: www.governor.wv.gov.

West Virginia's acting governor is Earl Ray Tomblin, a Democrat. The former president of the state Senate, Tomblin assumed office on Nov. 15, 2010, the day that Democrat Joe Manchin stepped down as governor to take the late Sen. Robert Byrd's seat in the U.S. Senate. Tomblin won a May 2011 primary, giving him the right to run in an Oct. 4 special election to serve the remaining year of Manchin's unexpired term.

Tomblin was born in Logan County, in southwestern West Virginia's coal country. His parents ran a restaurant in Chapmanville, and he bussed tables there in addition to selling eggs and rabbits and mowing lawns for income. He attended West Virginia University and ran for the state House of Delegates as a college senior, winning election in 1974 at age 22. He served until 1980, when he was elected to the state Senate. He became the Senate's president in January 1995 after chairing its Finance Committee.

When Byrd died in June 2010 after a 51-year career, Manchin—who had easily been re-elected to a second term as governor in 2008—declined to appoint himself as Byrd's successor. Instead, the governor named his legal adviser, Carte Goodwin, to the job in a caretaker capacity, and then announced his candidacy four days later. Manchin beat Republican John Raese in the general election that November, and under state law, Tomblin was next in line of succession. But Manchin's vacancy as the state's chief executive immediately raised a series of legal questions. He ruled out the possibility of calling a special legislative session to resolve the issue of succession because he said there was no consensus among state officials about whether one was needed, though some citizens' watchdog groups argued that it was necessary. Tomblin contended that he could serve in the job until the next general election in 2012.

The matter went to the state Supreme Court, which issued a unanimous opinion in January 2011 that said the state constitution never intended for an acting governor to serve more than one year without an election. After the court's decision, Tomblin submitted a proposal to the legislature for the state to have an elected lieutenant governor, a position that was already in place in 43 states. A primary election was scheduled for May 2011.

Tomblin campaigned on his experience as a lawmaker and stressed his ability to work with members of both parties in much the same manner as Manchin had. "We have to stop playing partisan games, set aside personal ambition and put West Virginia first," he said. He promised to promote the state to attract large corporations while keeping taxes low and improving the state's schools, which have high dropout rates. Like many other West Virginia Democrats, he is culturally conservative and opposes abortion rights.

Tomblin drew five Democratic opponents, including Secretary of State Natalie Tennant, State Treasurer John Perdue, and state House Speaker Rick Thompson. While Tennant ran a positive campaign, Perdue and Thompson attacked Tomblin, accusing him of steering $2.5 million of greyhound breeders' funds to his family's greyhound farm. Tomblin said his opponents should be "ashamed" of making "false attacks." News media outlets pointed out holes in the accusation, noting that the breeders' funds are distributed based on the dogs' performances on the racetrack in the same fashion as racing purses. Tomblin easily won the special election primary with 40% of the vote; Thompson took 24%, Tennant got 17%, and Perdue won 13%.

Tomblin's victory set up a general election matchup with Morgantown GOP businessman Bill Maloney, who had never held elected office. Former Secretary of State Betty Ireland initially had been considered the frontrunner for the Republican nomination, but she struggled to raise money and ran into criticism from some in the party who questioned whether she was conservative enough. Maloney defeated her 45%-31%, with six other candidates dividing the rest of the vote. A third candidate planning to run in the general election was former Richwood Mayor Bob Henry Baber of the West Virginia Mountain Party. The election had not been held at press time for *The Almanac*.

Senior Senator

Jay Rockefeller (D)

Elected 1984, term expires 2014, 5th term; b. June 18, 1937, New York, NY; home, Charleston; Harvard U., B.A. 1961, Intl. Christian U., Tokyo, Japan, 1957-60; Presbyterian; married (Sharon); 4 children.

Elected Office: WV House of Delegates, 1966–68; WV secy. of state, 1968–72; WV gov., 1976–84.

Professional Career: Natl. Advisory Cncl., Peace Corps, 1961; Asst., Peace Corps Dir. Sargent Shriver, 1962–63; VISTA worker, 1964–66; Pres., WV Wesleyan Col., 1973–75.

DC Office: 531 HSOB, 20510, 202-224-6472; Fax: 202-224-7665; Web site: rockefeller.senate.gov.

State Offices: Beckley, 304-253-9704; Charleston, 304-347-5372; Fairmont, 304-367-0122; Martinsburg, 304-262-9285.

Committees: *Commerce, Science & Transportation* (Chmn). *Finance:* Energy, Natural Resources & Infrastructure; Health Care (Chmn); International Trade, Customs & Global Competitiveness; Social Security, Pensions & Family Policy. *Intelligence (Select). Joint Committee on Taxation. Veterans' Affairs.*

Group Ratings

	ACLU	ACU	ADA	CFG	AFS	FRC	LCV	ITIC	NTU	COC
2010	87	8	85	4	94	0	43	67	9	27
2009	–	0	85	3	100	–	91	–	5	40

National Journal Ratings

	2010 LIB	—	2010 CONS	2009 LIB	—	2009 CONS
Economic	61%	—	38%	78%	—	21%
Social	59%	—	38%	73%	—	26%
Foreign	47%	—	0%	55%	—	0%
Composite	65%	—	35%	77%	—	24%

Key Votes of the 111th Congress

1. Overturn Ledbetter	Y	5. Pass health care bill	Y	9. Ratify New START	Y
2. Pass $787 billion stimulus	Y	6. Regulate financial firms	Y	10. Confirm Elena Kagan	Y
3. Repeal DC gun laws	N	7. Pass tax cuts for some	Y	11. Stop EPA climate regs	Y
4. Confirm Sonia Sotomayor	Y	8. Legalize immigrants' kids	Y	12. Repeal don't ask, tell	Y

Election Results

2008 general	Jay Rockefeller (D)	447,560	(64%)	($5,972,208)
	Jay Wolfe (R)	254,629	(36%)	($123,862)
2008 primary	Jay Rockefeller (D)	271,425	(77%)	
	Sheirl Fletcher (D)	50,173	(14%)	
	Billy Hendricks (D)	29,707	(8%)	

Prior Winning Percentages: 2002 (63%); 1996 (77%); 1990 (68%); 1984 (52%)

Jay Rockefeller is a Democrat and the senior senator from West Virginia, having spent 25 years as the junior partner to fellow Democrat Robert Byrd until Byrd's death in 2010. Rockefeller chairs the Senate Commerce, Science and Transportation Committee and combines an abiding interest in modernizing health care and technology with an old-fashioned devotion to guarding his state's coal industry.

Rockefeller's full name, John D. Rockefeller IV, has a familiar ring to those who remember his great-grandfather as the oil billionaire who was America's richest man, and his grandfather as the heir who had more than enough money to build New York's Rockefeller Center, restore Colonial Williamsburg, and found the Museum of Modern Art during the Depression of the 1930s. Jay Rockefeller's father and uncles were men of impressive achievement in different fields. Father John D. Rockefeller III was the head of the family's philanthropic efforts and founder of the Asia Society. Uncle David Rockefeller was the head of Chase Manhattan Bank. Two uncles became governors—Nelson, governor of New York for 15 years and a man of great building projects and fitful presidential ambitions; and Winthrop, who moved to impoverished and out-of-the-way Arkansas and served four years as a reform governor when the state needed it most. At various points in his life, Jay Rockefeller has followed the example of each, with emphases and achievements of his own.

John D. Rockefeller IV grew up in New York, graduated from Harvard, and lived and studied in Japan for three years (evidence of his father's Asiaphilia). He worked for a year in Washington D.C. running the early Peace Corps program in the Philippines. Then, like so many of the elite of those years, he turned his attention from abroad to home, and in 1964 went to the impoverished hill country of West Virginia to work as a VISTA volunteer in Emmons on the Big Coal River. "Although I went to Emmons to help that community," he has reminisced. "They helped me much more. My experience in Emmons set the course for the rest of my life." He moved on, more quickly than his uncles Nelson and Winthrop, to electoral politics. He was elected to the state House of Delegates from Kanawha County in 1966 and as West Virginia secretary of state in 1968. Rockefeller then had the chastening experience of losing a 1972 race for governor to Republican Arch Moore. He served three years as president of West Virginia Wesleyan College in Buckhannon, and became more practical, dropping his opposition to strip mining. He was not shy about spending his own millions—his net worth was estimated at nearly $99 million in 2009—and was elected governor in 1976 and re-elected in 1980. In 1984, he ran for the U.S. Senate and beat Republican businessman John Raese by just 52%-48% after spending $12 million.

Rockefeller has been a consistent Democratic vote. He began his career inclined toward free trade because of his experience in East Asia, but is a strong supporter of organized labor who regularly earns 100% on the AFL-CIO's annual legislative scorecard. He is sensitive at times to the cultural conservatism of his state, supporting a 2006 constitutional flag desecration amendment and another proposed amendment to allow voluntary prayer in schools. Though he has done his share to shape the Democratic message as well as attack Republican policies, he is known in the Senate for his civility. He laments the extreme polarization of politics, especially as practiced by Republican-leaning Fox News and the liberally oriented MSNBC. "There's a little bug inside of me which wants the (Federal Communications Commission) to say to Fox and to MSNBC, 'Out. Off. End. Goodbye,'" he said at a November 2010 hearing. "It would be a big favor to our political discourse, to our ability to do our work here in Congress, and to the American people."

As Commerce Committee chairman, Rockefeller has championed consumers' rights. He helped secure $7.2 billion in economic stimulus money to upgrade broadband infrastructure, telling the *Charleston Daily Mail* in 2009, "It's a basic part of our belonging to the future of this world." He held hearings on electronic commerce practices that pass on customers' information to other companies and introduced legislation in 2010 to prohibit some Internet companies' misleading sales practices. In 2011, he sponsored a bill to give consumers the ability to block companies from tracking their online activity, a measure that privacy advocates hailed while Internet companies warned would hamper their ability to tailor services to customers. Rockefeller also spent much of 2010 working to eventually get a NASA authorization bill into law, laboring for months to bridge the substantial differences between the Obama administration and congressional Republicans. And in 2009 he pushed an unsuccessful bill—which he re-introduced in 2011—to re-regulate the railroad industry.

Rockefeller played a part in shaping the Democrats' health care overhaul of 2010, though not as central a role as he would have liked. As chairman of the Finance Committee's health subcommittee, he introduced his own bill in July 2009 creating an optional public health insurance plan to compete with private insurers. He sharply criticized the parallel efforts of the more centrist Finance Chairman Max Baucus, D-Mont., and Baucus ended up excluding Rockefeller from the bipartisan "Gang of Six" that fruitlessly met through the summer of 2009 trying to craft a deal. The Finance Committee rejected Rockefeller's proposal in September, but he remained confident that a public option would pass. When it became clear by December that that would not occur, he told the *Daily Mail* he felt "sadness and agony." He still got several provisions into the Senate-passed legislation that eventually became law, including requiring insurers to spend 80% to 85% of all premiums to pay for actual medical care and not other costs.

Health care has long been a passion of Rockefeller's. He is motivated in part by anger at his mother's treatment during a long terminal illness—an experience that would be much worse for people of ordinary incomes, he thought—and he has sought to increase the number of general practitioners, especially in states like West Virginia and Arkansas. As he was working on health issues, Rockefeller in 1991 gave serious consideration to running for president. He was 54, about the same age as his uncle, Nelson, when he made his second attempt at running; and, Rockefeller by then had developed an expertise on an issue that seemed likely to be a major domestic priority. After he decided against running, he warmly endorsed Democrat Bill Clinton and applauded his emphasis on health care. When the Clinton health care bill crashed and burned in September 1994, Rockefeller worked for incremental changes. One of his biggest legislative achievements was a 1992 law, passed over furious opposition from Western coal states, that forced union and non-union coal companies, as well as companies that had gone out of the coal business, to pay for the exploding cost of the United Mine Workers' health care trust funds. He also was at the fore of Democratic efforts to expand the State Children's Health Insurance Program.

Rockefeller's efforts on health care earned him deep admiration from liberals. But they have been less enthralled with his efforts to protect West Virginia's coal industry from legislation to curb global warming. In 2003, he supported cap-and-trade legislation to allow energy efficient companies to trade credits to larger greenhouse gas emitters as a way to reduce overall levels of carbon dioxide emissions. But after Democrats took control of the Senate and sought to craft a bill, Rockefeller was reluctant to back it. Then in 2010, he pushed legislation to stop the Environmental Protection Agency from regulating greenhouse gas emissions from some sources. In 2011, he differed publicly with Republican Sen. Lisa Murkowski of Alaska about the extent to which the EPA should be regulated under the bill. At the same time, he said in a February 2011 speech to the West Virginia Coal Association that the industry needed to stop "fighting for the status quo."

Steel has been another longtime preoccupation for Rockefeller. He helped Weirton Steel become employee-owned in 1984. In the late 1990s, he called for aid to steel makers in the face of what he regarded as a flood of subsidized steel imports, arguing that workers and companies that have "played by the book" should get government help to allow them to continue in their jobs and to stay in their homes. In 2002, he called for 40% tariffs for four years on steel imports. The Bush administration in 2002 imposed a 24% tariff in the second year and 18% in the third. Rockefeller complained loudly when the administration made exceptions and then dropped the quotas. He got a tax credit into law in 2008 providing an incentive for companies to recycle hazardous byproducts from steelmaking. His desire to put a moratorium on EPA regulation of greenhouse gas emissions is in part motivated by the fact that steel production plants would be among the facilities regulated.

During the Bush administration, Rockefeller was extremely active on the Intelligence Committee. Some Democrats criticized him in 1983 for not being a partisan team-player and for not countering Republican Chairman Pat Roberts' opposition to a far-ranging investigation of intelligence before the September 11 attacks. But the bipartisan working relationship between the two was not to last. In December 2005, after *The New York Times* revealed National Security Agency surveillance of communications between terrorist suspects abroad and people in the United States, and that Rockefeller had been informed of the program several years before, Rockefeller charged that administration officials were misstating the facts and that they never offered him the opportunity to approve or disapprove of the program. Rockefeller protested vigorously that month when Roberts adjourned a committee meeting after Democrats demanded an inquiry into the NSA surveillance program.

After Democrats won majority control of the Senate, Rockefeller in 2007 ascended to the chairmanship of Intelligence. Roberts rotated off the committee and the new vice chairman was Republican Christopher (Kit) Bond of Missouri. Rockefeller agreed to accept Bond's suggestions that it investigate shortcomings in human intelligence and radical Islamist ideology. In October 2007, Rockefeller produced a compromise on the issue of immunity for telecommunications companies who cooperated in the government's secret surveillance of people in the United States. It provided that the companies be able to assert as a defense that they were told by the administration that the surveillance was legal. After stepping down as chairman, Rockefeller told *The Charleston Gazette* in April 2011 that his earlier support for the Iraq war was "one of the worst votes in my life" and that U.S. troops should leave the country that year. He also expressed serious misgivings about military operations in Afghanistan and Libya.

Rockefeller has been in strong shape politically—strong enough that since 1984, he has not self-financed any of his campaigns and has still been re-elected by handsome margins. In 2008, he ran for a fifth term. He spent $5.9 million to his Republican opponent's $123,000 and won 64%-36%, carrying 52 of 55 counties.

Junior Senator

Joe Manchin (D)

Elected Nov. 2010, term expires 2012, 1st term; b. Aug. 24, 1947, Farmington; home, Marion County; WV U., B.S. 1970; Catholic; married (Gayle); 3 children.

Elected Office: WV House, 1982-84; WV Senate 1986-96; WV sec. of state, 2000-04; WV gov., 2005-10

Professional Career: Co-owner, Manchin's Carpet and Tile, 1968-82; owner, Enersystems, 1989-2000.

DC Office: 303 HSOB, 20510, 202-224-3954; Fax: 202-228-0002; Web site: manchin.senate.gov.

State Offices: Charleston, 304-342-5855; Martinsburg, 304-264-4626.

Committees: *Aging (Special). Armed Services:* Airland; Emerging Threats & Capabilities; Readiness & Management Support. *Energy & Natural Resources:* Energy; National Parks; Water & Power.

Election Results

2010 general	Joe Manchin (D)	283,358	(53%)	($4,395,107)
	John Raese (R)	230,013	(43%)	($6,288,292)
2010 primary	Joe Manchin (D)	unopposed		

Prior Winning Percentages: Governor: 2008 (70%); 2004 (64%)

The junior senator from West Virginia is Democrat Joe Manchin, a popular former governor who nonetheless had to fight to claim the seat of the late Democratic Sen. Robert Byrd in 2010, a tough year for Democrats everywhere.

Manchin hails from a prominent political family. He grew up in Farmington, a few miles up Buffalo Creek from the industrial city of Fairmont on the Monongahela River. He remembers working in his grandfather's grocery store, and later in his father's carpet and furniture store. Manchin took a semester off from college to help his father rebuild the store after a fire. His grandfather and father were both elected mayor of Farmington. His uncle, A. James Manchin, was elected to the West Virginia House of Delegates and was also secretary of state and state treasurer.

After graduating from West Virginia University, Joe Manchin went to work in the carpet and furniture business, helping to send his four siblings to college. Then he started a coal brokerage company and eventually moved to Fairmont. In 1982, at age 35, Manchin was elected to the House of Delegates and in 1986 to the state Senate. He then ran for governor, only to lose in the Democratic primary to legislator Charlotte Pritt. When Secretary of State Ken Hechler ran for the U.S. House in 2000, Manchin ran to succeed him, as did Pritt. This time, Manchin beat her in the primary, 51% to 29%, and went on to win the general election.

In May 2003, Manchin announced he would challenge Democratic Gov. Bob Wise in the 2004 primary. Later that month, Wise admitted that he had had an extramarital affair and would not seek re-election. Manchin worked successfully to get support from both unions and business. His stands on cultural issues were impeccably conservative: He was opposed to abortion rights, gun control and same sex marriage. Manchin won the Democratic primary with 53%. And he went on to easily defeat Republican Monty Warner in the general election, 64% to 34%, carrying 52 of 55 counties.

Manchin had been in office for just one year when he gained renown as the public face of desperate attempts to rescue 13 trapped coal miners after the January 2006 explosion at the Sago Mine in central West Virginia. Manchin, whose uncle was killed in a 1968 mine accident that claimed 78 lives, gave numerous televised interviews from the mine site. But he also mistakenly announced "the miracle of all miracles"—that 12 of the miners had survived—when in fact they had died. The blunder could have been career-ending. But Manchin's standing skyrocketed in the polls, partly because West Virginia Republicans decided that invoking the accident politically was a line that they would not cross. After two other deadly mining accidents, Manchin in early February ordered safety inspections at all mines in the state. In 2007, he signed new safety laws mandating certain ventilation practices and giving the state authority to temporarily shut down mines with violations.

Manchin had success on other issues as well. In 2006, he signed into law eight bills designed to improve health care in the state, including a low-income health care plan providing basic care at clinics, a catastrophic health care insurance program, and a new mental health commission. He also signed legislation restricting city governments' power to take property by eminent domain. Manchin did not have serious competition for re-election in 2008, and he won, 70% to 26%.

His popularity sparked speculation about his political future. When Byrd died in June 2010 after 50 years in office (the longest service of any member of Congress in history), Manchin was seen as the Democrats' best hope for keeping the seat, which Byrd had used to bring federal largesse to his economically hard-pressed state. Although empowered to appoint himself to the Senate pending a special election, Manchin declined to do so. Instead, he appointed his former chief counsel, Carte Goodwin, as a placeholder.

Republicans initially hadn't planned to invest in the race. In September, a Rasmussen survey showed Manchin with a soaring job approval rating of 69%. His GOP opponent was John Raese, a wealthy businessman whom Byrd defeated four years earlier by nearly 2-to-1. But Raese, who poured his own money into the contest, turned out to be a stronger challenger than expected in a highly favorable year for Republicans. He ran ads seeking to tie Manchin to President Barack Obama. The National Republican Senatorial Committee launched its own ads portraying Manchin as a rubber stamp for Obama's agenda, and the race became a toss-up.

Manchin distanced himself from the president, even at the expense of flip-flopping. After saying early in 2010 that he supported Obama's health care overhaul, by October Manchin was saying he would have voted against it as a senator. The health care legislation had proved to be highly unpopular in some quarters, especially among conservative voters. The Democrats' cap-and-trade bill to curb carbon emissions was also highly unpopular in West Virginia coal country, still an important economic driver in the state. Manchin ran an ad in which he shot a mock copy of the carbon emissions bill with a rifle. "This is the first campaign I've ever been in that you haven't been judged on your performance," Manchin complained to McClatchy News Service. "It doesn't matter, or doesn't seem to."

For his part, Manchin raised questions about Raese's commitment to the state, pointing out repeatedly that the steel and limestone magnate owned a home in Florida and that his wife was registered to vote there. Raese called the move "desperation." Manchin also hammered Raese for his support for eliminating the minimum wage and abolishing the Education Department. He began to pull ahead in the closing days of the contest, although he was outspent $6.3 million to $4.4 million. The closeness of the race was an indication of voter discontent with Obama and incumbent Democrats. "Under standard operating rules, it should've been a walk" for Manchin, West Virginia Wesleyan College history professor Robert Rupp told *The State Journal* newspaper. Still, Manchin won by 10 percentage points, 53% to 43%.

He went to Washington immediately after the election to begin serving the final two years of Byrd's term. Manchin voted on a proposal to extend the Bush-era tax cuts except for taxpayers earning over $1 million, although he had said during his campaign he favored the Republican position of extending them for all taxpayers. But he took a conservative position in voting no on a proposal to repeal the ban on openly gay members in the military, the only Democrat to join Republicans in opposing repeal of the so-called "don't ask, don't tell" policy of the Clinton era.

Still, Manchin could not seem to turn the vote in his favor. He was roundly criticized around the state for missing a final vote on repeal of "don't ask, don't tell," and also for missing a major vote on a bill to give legal status to the children of some illegal immigrants. The *Charleston Gazette* called him "absolutely gutless." Manchin apologized publicly, saying he missed the December votes to be with his grandchildren over the holidays.

FIRST DISTRICT

David McKinley (R)

Elected 2010, 1st term; b. March 28, 1947, Wheeling; home, Wheeling; Purdue U., B.S. 1969; Episcopalian; Married (Mary); 4 children.

Elected Office: WV House of Del., 1980-94.

Professional Career: Principal, McKinley & Assoc., 1981-2010.

DC Office: 313 CHOB, 20515, 202-225-4172; Fax: 202-225-7564; Web site: mckinley.house.gov.

State Offices: Wheeling, 304-232-3801; Morgantown, 304-284-8506; Parkersburg, 304-422-5972.

Committees: *Energy & Commerce:* Commerce, Manufacturing & Trade; Energy & Power.

Election Results

2010 general	David McKinley (R)	90,660	(50.4%)	($1,783,039)
	Michael Oliverio (D)	89,220	(49.6%)	($1,464,376)
2010 primary	David McKinley (R)	14,783	(35%)	
	Andrew Warner (R)	11,353	(27%)	
	Sarah Minear (R)	8,994	(21%)	
	Thomas Stark (R)	3,636	(9%)	

Population		Race/Ethnicity		Work	
Pop. 2010:	615,991	White:	94.5%	Private:	76.5%
Change since 2000:	Up 2.2%	Black:	2.1%	Government:	18.3%
Urban:	53.7%	Hispanic:	1.1%	Self-employed:	5.0%
Rural:	46.3%	Asian:	0.8%	Blue collar:	25.8%
Area size:	6,344 sq. mi.	Native Am.:	0.2%	White collar:	54.9%
		Hawaiian:	0.0%	Khaki collar:	0.1%
Age		Two+ races:	1.3%	Other:	19.1%
Median age:	40.5 yrs.				
More than 65 yrs:	16.2%	*Ancestry*		Median income:	$37,989
Less than 18 yrs:	20.4%	German	19.6%	Median Home Value:	$95,000
		Irish	13.2%		
Education		English	9.3%	**Military Veterans**	
H.S. grad:	85.2%			% of Pop:	11.5%
College grad:	18.6%				
Grad degree:	7.6%				

Northern West Virginia; Parkersburg

The northern part of West Virginia is in many ways an extension of the Pittsburgh metropolitan area. People here are Steelers and Pirates fans, they drink Iron City and Rolling Rock beer, they watch Pittsburgh television, and they live in the crevasses between hills cut by the Monongahela and Ohio Rivers, on terrain that seems to forbid industrial and urban development. Yet this has been one of America's prime industrial areas. Northern West Virginia is part of the

2008 Presidential Vote		
John McCain (R) 140,421	(57%)
Barack Obama (D) 102,826	(42%)
2004 Presidential Vote		
George Bush (R) 150,052	(58%)
John Kerry (D) 107,904	(42%)
Cook Partisan Voting Index: R+9		

same coal-and-steel economy that made Pittsburgh one of the nation's largest cities and filled the narrow bottomlands along the rivers with steel and glass factories, foundries and coal yards. These industries have been declining, and they have become far less labor-intensive. Since 1980, the 12,000 mining jobs in this part of the state have dropped by more than two-thirds, with comparable fall-offs in manufacturing. The Weirton tin and steel mill (now called ArcelorMittal), which employed 14,000 in the mid-1970s and was the subject of an employee buyout at one point, was down to fewer than 1,000 workers in 2011. Service jobs have replaced some of these losses. West Virginia's largest employer now is Wal-Mart, and the government has brought in thousands more jobs, compliments of the late Robert Byrd, the West Virginia Democrat and powerful Senate appropriator. One of the largest employers in Harrison County is the U.S. Department of Justice.

The 1st Congressional District of West Virginia is in the northern third of the state. It includes 20 of the state's 55 counties, and shares borders with Maryland, Ohio and Pennsylvania. On the panhandle along the Ohio River is Victorian Wheeling, once one of the richest cities in the country with its steel and glass companies. There is Weirton, named for Ernest T. Weir, the anti-union Pittsburgh industrialist who transformed it from a farming community to a steel town in the early 1900s. South of Pittsburgh on the Monongahela River is Morgantown, site of West Virginia University and a popular white-water rafting destination. With the university providing vital human capital, Morgantown routinely makes it onto *Forbes* magazine's top small cities for business. The city ranked 10th out of 184 small cities in 2010.

To the west, the district includes three lonely mountain counties—Doddridge, Ritchie and Tyler—that were never heavily industrialized and have remained firmly Republican since the Civil War. Doddridge was the only one of West Virginia's 55 counties to vote against Byrd in 2006, the last time he was up for re-election. West of these, on the Ohio River, is the former oil-refining and shipping center of Parkersburg, which has become a plastics and manufacturing hub. Parts of the district are stagnant while others are on a growth path. Morgantown's population grew nearly 11% from 2000 to 2010, while Wheeling's fell by 9% and Parkersburg's decreased by 5%. For most of the 20th century, much of this territory was solidly Democratic. But dissatisfaction with the Clinton-Gore policies on coal mining and the environment helped Republican George W. Bush carry the district twice. And in 2008, GOP nominee John McCain won all of the district's 20 counties except for the two based in Morgantown and Fairmont, and won 57%-42%.

David McKinley (R)

The new congressman from West Virginia's 1st District is David McKinley, who captured the seat for the GOP after it had been in Democratic hands for 40 years. McKinley succeeded Rep. Alan Mollohan, a scandal-plagued Democrat who lost the primary after serving nearly 28 years in the House.

McKinley is a seventh-generation native of Wheeling, W.Va. He was one of five boys, and his father was a civil engineer who taught him to read blueprints when he was in third grade. He attended Purdue University, majoring in civil engineering. To pay for room and board, McKinley worked in the kitchens of a sorority and a fraternity. After graduating, he married his high school sweetheart. They had three children but divorced in 1979. He married his second wife, a critical-care nurse, in 1981, and they had one child together. After college, McKinley worked for several engineering and construction companies until 1981, when he founded his own firm, McKinley & Associates, which restores historic properties and does other construction work. McKinley has suffered from hearing loss since his 20s; today he is deaf in one ear and has only partial hearing in the other.

McKinley comes from a Democratic family; his great-grandfather ran for West Virginia governor as a Democrat in 1908. McKinley switched parties in 1976 because he said he felt that the

Democratic Party did not support limited government. After he won a seat in the state House of Delegates in 1981, he pushed for a bill to allow school and prison cafeterias to donate unused food to homeless shelters, and authored a law that prohibits insurance companies from canceling policies of people diagnosed with HIV. Although in his campaign McKinley called for repeal of President Barack Obama's health care overhaul, he supported the provision that prohibits insurance companies from denying coverage to people with preexisting conditions. He retired from the legislature in 1994 and ran for governor in 1996; he lost the primary to Cecil Underwood, who went on to win the general election.

In his bid for the House, McKinley had the backing of national Republicans in the primary and got 35% of the vote, defeating former state Sen. Sarah Minear and businessman Mac Warner. In the general election, he faced a strong opponent in state Sen. Mike Oliverio, who had toppled Mollohan in the primary after several newspaper accounts raised questions about whether Mollohan profited personally from business deals with people and nonprofit groups that got federal funds that he earmarked in appropriations bills.

McKinley's ads labeled Oliverio as a "career politician" who supported "job-killing liberal Nancy Pelosi," a reference to the House speaker. McKinley emphasized his opposition to the Democrats' energy bill that would limit carbon emissions, arguing that it would hurt West Virginia's coal industry. But Oliverio also opposed the bill. And his backing from tea party activists made it difficult to tar him as a tax-and-spend liberal. Oliverio emphasized that he would be independent from the then-majority Democrats in the House. "I'm not going to Congress to get in step with the Washington leadership," he said in one debate.

Oliverio charged that McKinley got rich from government contracts even as he criticized government spending, citing federal economic stimulus money that McKinley's architectural and engineering firm received to design a Marshall County school. The Democratic Congressional Campaign Committee dubbed the Republican contender "Millionaire McKinley." Still, McKinley eked out a victory of 1,440 votes out of 179,880 cast, a split of 50.4% to 49.6%.

In Washington, McKinley got a plum seat on the House Energy and Commerce Committee. His first bill, introduced in early 2011, was aimed at curbing the power of the Environmental Protection Agency to stop permits for mountaintop-removal mining operations.

SECOND DISTRICT

Shelley Moore Capito (R)

Elected 2000, 6th term; b. Nov. 26, 1953, Glen Dale; home, Charleston; Duke U., B.S. 1975, U. of VA, M.Ed. 1976; Presbyterian; married (Charles); 3 children.

Elected Office: WV House of Del., 1996-2000.

Professional Career: Career counselor, WV State Col., 1976-78; Dir., Educ. Info. Center, WV Board of Regents, 1978-81.

DC Office: 2443 RHOB, 20515, 202-225-2711; Fax: 202-225-7856; Web site: capito.house.gov.

State Offices: Charleston, 304-925-5964; Martinsburg, 304-264-8810.

Committees: *Financial Services:* Financial Institutions & Consumer Credit (Chmn); Insurance, Housing & Community Opportunity. *Transportation & Infrastructure:* Highways & Transit; Railroads, Pipelines & Hazardous Materials; Water Resources & Environment.

Group Ratings

	ACLU	ACU	ADA	CFG	AFS	FRC	LCV	ITIC	NTU	COC
2010	7	82	10	74	17	75	40	67	76	100
2009	–	75	30	62	44	–	29	–	64	93

National Journal Ratings

	2010 LIB	—	2010 CONS	2009 LIB	—	2009 CONS
Economic	38%	—	62%	38%	—	62%
Social	36%	—	63%	35%	—	64%
Foreign	21%	—	77%	26%	—	68%
Composite	32%	—	68%	34%	—	66%

Key Votes of the 111th Congress

1. Overturn Ledbetter	N	5. Bar federal abortion funds	Y	9. Stop detainee transfers	Y
2. Pass $820 billion stimulus	N	6. Pass health care bill	N	10. Legalize immigrants' kids	N
3. Let guns in national parks	Y	7. Regulate financial firms	N	11. Repeal don't ask, tell	N
4. Pass cap-and-trade	N	8. Pass tax cuts for some	N	12. Limit campaign funds	N

Election Results

2010 general	Shelley Moore Capito (R)	...126,814	(68%)	($1,531,270)
	Virginia Graf (D)	...55,001	(30%)	($25,696)
2010 primary	Shelley Moore Capito (R)	...unopposed		

Prior Winning Percentages: 2008 (57%), 2006 (57%), 2004 (57%), 2002 (60%), 2000 (48%)

Population		Race/Ethnicity		Work	
Pop. 2010:	648,186	White:	91.6%	Private:	74.6%
Change since 2000:	Up 7.6%	Black:	4.1%	Government:	19.5%
Urban:	46.2%	Hispanic:	1.7%	Self-employed:	5.7%
Rural:	53.8%	Asian:	0.7%	Blue collar:	25.6%
Area size:	8,511 sq. mi.	Native Am.:	0.2%	White collar:	56.6%
		Hawaiian:	0.0%	Khaki collar:	0.2%
Age		Two+ races:	1.5%	Other:	17.6%
Median age:	40.3 yrs.				
More than 65 yrs:	15.0%	*Ancestry*		Median income:	$41,633
Less than 18 yrs:	22.4%	German	17.1%	Median Home Value:	$119,900
		Irish	11.4%		
Education		English	10.6%	**Military Veterans**	
H.S. grad:	83.9%			% of Pop:	12.2%
College grad:	19.2%				
Grad degree:	7.3%				

Central West Virginia; Charleston

Not all of West Virginia has been coal country, and not all of its hills are scarred with strip mining wounds or piled with tailings. It's true that for miles you can see gentle hills and rugged mountains, stands of green trees and vistas stretching to far horizons. Yet over another hill you may find, amid scenery primeval and rural, sudden evidence of industrialization: a pulp mill or charcoal factory in a clearing scraped out of the forest; a small factory town, built close to a river in a cleft bordered with hills, its houses built in the same 1910s style as in the factory suburbs of Pittsburgh; the entrance to an underground coal mine or a mountaintop blasted open to allow surface mining. Large parts of this naturally beautiful state look as verdant and unchanged as they must have when George Washington was speculating in land here or when John Brown was launching his assault on the federal arsenal at Harpers Ferry in 1859.

2008 Presidential Vote

John McCain (R)	...142,112	(55%)
Barack Obama (D)	...113,853	(44%)

2004 Presidential Vote

George Bush (R)	...151,019	(57%)
John Kerry (D)	...112,418	(42%)

Cook Partisan Voting Index: R+8

The 2nd Congressional District of West Virginia is a central slice of the state, a belt of land from Berkeley Springs and Harpers Ferry in the Washington exurbs, all the way west to the Ohio River town of Point Pleasant, where the Kanawha River flows into the Ohio. The district includes the few fast-growing parts of West Virginia: the eastern panhandle counties, which are part of the Washington, D.C., metropolitan area, and chemical-producing Putnam County, where Toyota built an engine plant that employs more than 1,000 people. The major urban center is Charleston, where on the banks of the Kanawha rises West Virginia's Capitol, built in 1932 and designed by Cass Gilbert with a dome higher than the U.S. Capitol and a chandelier with 10,000 pieces of cut glass. Charleston, with its two partisan newspapers, the Democratic *The Charleston Gazette* and the Republican *Charleston Daily Mail*, is the center of the state's political culture. It also is a major industrial center, with huge petrochemical plants that convert coal tar into everyday products.

In the 1940s, the area produced all of the nation's Lucite, polyethylenes and nylon, as well as much of its artificial rubber and antifreeze. Today, the state boasts it is home to more polymer producers than any other place on the planet; the chemical industry makes products used in the manufacturing of cosmetics, detergents, shampoo, rubber, paints and coatings, fire retardants and agricultural products. Charleston is also West Virginia's professional center, with a few downtown skyscrapers and some affluent residential districts. Kanawha County has continued to lose population, about 14,500 people between 2000 and 2010, as well as jobs. Politically, this is an ancestrally Democratic district now trending Republican. Berkeley County, which has grown 37% in population since 2000 to become the second-largest county in the state, votes like a Republican exurb. GOP presidential nominee John McCain won the district 55%-44% in 2008.

Shelley Moore Capito (R)

The congresswoman from the 2nd District is Shelley Moore Capito, a Republican first elected in 2000. She is widely mentioned in West Virginia as a candidate for future higher office.

Capito grew up in northern West Virginia and in the Washington, D.C., area, when her father, Arch Moore, served in the House from 1957 to 1969. He was elected governor in 1968 and 1972, and then again in 1984. He later was convicted and served three years in jail for fraud and extortion. Capito graduated from Duke University and the University of Virginia, and was the first Cherry Blossom Princess elected to Congress. She worked for two years as a career counselor at West Virginia State University, and then was director of the state's Educational Information Center from 1978 to 1981. She served two terms in the West Virginia House of Delegates.

Her opportunity to follow in her father's footsteps came when Democratic Rep. Bob Wise ran for governor in 2000. She benefited from a divisive Democratic primary that was won by Jim Humphreys, a former state senator and a lawyer who made a fortune in asbestos litigation. Capito, who supported abortion rights, started as the underdog, but Humphreys, who spent $6 million of his own money in the general election, proved to be a poor candidate. One of the few beneficiaries of Republican presidential candidate George W. Bush's coattails that year, she won 48%-46%, with big margins in the eastern panhandle counties.

In the House, Capito has a largely moderate voting record, though she has become more inclined to side with her party since President Barack Obama took office. She supported the State Children's Health Insurance Program expansion in 2009 and a bill in 2010 extending unemployment benefits. She has received special attention from Republican leaders because of her precarious district. She was one of the few House Republicans to get a free pass to vote against the president's position on free trade bills. After Democrats took control of Congress in 2007, Capito voted for five of the Democratic "Six for '06" agenda items.

In 2011, Capito took over as chairman of the Financial Services Subcommittee on Financial Institutions and Consumer Credit. She promised to focus on three areas: the Federal Deposit Insurance Corp.'s authority to unwind systemically vital institutions, the consumer protection bureau established in the Dodd-Frank financial regulation bill, and the tensions community banks face in tightening lending standards while making loans to small businesses. During conference negotiations on Dodd-Frank in 2010, she unsuccessfully sought to remove a $150 billion resolution fund to cover the cost of taking over a failing firm and to replace it with a streamlined bankruptcy process to ensure liquidation of companies. Her husband, Charles, is a longtime banking executive, something that has raised eyebrows among watchdog groups. She has said she makes her own decisions and told *Esquire* magazine in 2010, "No matter what your decisions are, no matter what your votes are, if you're not playing by the rules you're taking a big risk."

Capito also has a seat on the Transportation and Infrastructure Committee, where she seeks to authorize highway projects for the state. After a deadly accident at the Sago mine in 2006, Capito joined the West Virginia delegation in supporting legislation to improve mine safety by requiring that coal miners be given communications and tracking equipment and two-hour reserves of oxygen. After the Senate passed the bill, she persuaded House Republican leaders to schedule it for the floor; Bush signed the bill into law in 2006. After the April 2010 explosion that killed 29 miners at her state's Upper Big Branch Mine, she introduced her own mine safety bill and opposed the version that was brought to the floor (but failed to pass) in December, contending that it "imposes severe penalties on businesses, introduces dramatic regulatory changes and promotes unnecessary litigation."

Democrats repeatedly have been frustrated in trying to defeat Capito. In 2002, Democrats gave her a big break by again nominating Humphreys, who won another expensive primary and then ran an even more ineffective campaign than the one two years earlier. Capito won 60%-40%. In 2006, she had a well-funded opponent in attorney Mike Callaghan, a former state Democratic Party chairman. In a year when Bush was a drag for many Republicans, Capito was unafraid to align herself with Bush on issues like energy policy. Capito outspent her opponent by nearly 4-to-1 and won 57%-43%. In 2008, longtime Byrd aide Anne Barth was her Democratic challenger and raised $1.2 million, including support from the United Mine Workers and EMILY's List. Barth criticized Capito for her support of "big oil," while Capito cited Barth's backing from "anti-coal" politicians in Washington. Capito won, again by 57%-43%.

When Capito announced in July 2010 that she would not run in a special election for the late Democratic Sen. Robert Byrd's seat, she deprived Republicans of their best candidate. She coasted to a sixth term in November, 68%-30%, against Democrat Virginia Lynch Graf, a former Catholic nun. Capito is considered a possible candidate for governor or for the U.S. Senate when Democrat Jay Rockefeller retires.

THIRD DISTRICT

Nick Rahall (D)

Elected 1976, 18th term; b. May 20, 1949, Beckley; home, Beckley; Duke U., B.A. 1971; Presbyterian; married (Melinda); 3 children.

Professional Career: Civil Air Patrol, 1977–88; Staff asst., U.S. Sen. Robert Byrd, 1971–74; Bd. of Dir., Rahall Communications Corp. 1974–76; Pres., Mountaineer Tour & Travel Agency, 1974–76; Pres., WV Broadcasting Corp. 1980–2001.

DC Office: 2307 RHOB, 20515, 202-225-3452; Web site: rahall.house.gov.

State Offices: Beckley, 304-252-5000; Bluefield, 304-325-6222; Huntington, 304-522-6425; Logan, 304-752-4934.

Committees: *Transportation & Infrastructure* (RMM).

Group Ratings

	ACLU	ACU	ADA	CFG	AFS	FRC	LCV	ITIC	NTU	COC
2010	50	8	60	9	100	37	80	100	9	25
2009	–	12	85	10	100	–	86	–	7	53

National Journal Ratings

	2010 LIB	—	2010 CONS	2009 LIB	—	2009 CONS
Economic	67%	—	32%	62%	—	36%
Social	46%	—	54%	53%	—	47%
Foreign	44%	—	55%	57%	—	42%
Composite	53%	—	47%	58%	—	42%

Key Votes of the 111th Congress

1. Overturn Ledbetter	Y	5. Bar federal abortion funds	Y	9. Stop detainee transfers	Y
2. Pass $820 billion stimulus	Y	6. Pass health care bill	Y	10. Legalize immigrants' kids	N
3. Let guns in national parks	Y	7. Regulate financial firms	Y	11. Repeal don't ask, tell	N
4. Pass cap-and-trade	N	8. Pass tax cuts for some	Y	12. Limit campaign funds	Y

Election Results

2010 general	Nick Rahall (D)	83,636	(56%)	($1,261,182)
	Elliott Maynard (R)	65,611	(44%)	($1,017,206)
2010 primary	Nick Rahall (D)	44,929	(68%)	
	Bruce Barilla (D)	21,620	(32%)	

Prior Winning Percentages: 2008 (67%), 2006 (69%), 2004 (65%), 2002 (70%), 2000 (91%), 1998 (87%), 1996 (100%), 1994 (64%), 1992 (66%), 1990 (52%), 1988 (61%), 1986 (71%), 1984 (67%), 1982 (81%), 1980 (77%), 1978 (100%), 1976 (46%)

Population		Race/Ethnicity		Work	
Pop. 2010:	588,817	White:	93.4%	Private:	77.8%
Change since 2000:	Down 2.4%	Black:	3.8%	Government:	17.6%
Urban:	38.4%	Hispanic:	0.8%	Self-employed:	4.6%
Rural:	61.6%	Asian:	0.4%	Blue collar:	27.5%
Area size:	9,375 sq. mi.	Native Am.:	0.2%	White collar:	53.4%
		Hawaiian:	0.0%	Khaki collar:	0.1%
Age		Two+ races:	1.2%	Other:	19.0%
Median age:	40.8 yrs.				
More than 65 yrs:	15.8%	*Ancestry*		Median income:	$32,856
Less than 18 yrs:	21.1%	Irish	12.9%	Median Home Value:	$77,400
		USA	12.5%		
Education		German	11.8%	**Military Veterans**	
H.S. grad:	76.9%			% of Pop:	11.2%
College grad:	13.7%				
Grad degree:	5.2%				

Southern West Virginia; Huntington

Early in the 20th century, the coal fields of southern West Virginia were one of America's boom areas. Into rural farmland and hollows, inhabited by the same families that settled these mountains 100 years before, came coal company lawyers with mineral rights leases to sign, coal company engineers to design and sink mine shafts, and men from other mountain counties, as well as Europe, to work the mines.

2008 Presidential Vote		
John McCain (R) 114,933	(56%)	
Barack Obama (D) 87,178	(42%)	
2004 Presidential Vote		
George Bush (R) 122,707	(53%)	
John Kerry (D) 106,219	(46%)	
Cook Partisan Voting Index: R+6		

Company houses were built, company stores were stocked with goods as the company dictated, and company paymasters kept close tabs on the finances of every employee. These conditions bred dull discontent, which was ignited into the fire of industrial unionism by John L. Lewis, president of the United Mine Workers, who organized most of the mines in the 1930s. Lewis was not only a militant unionist, but also an isolationist. During and after World War II, he called out his coal miners on strikes, to the fury of Democratic Presidents Franklin Roosevelt and Harry Truman. The national war effort and postwar economic recovery were threatened by these labor stoppages involving some 300,000 workers, centered in back corners of the country like southern West Virginia.

All that is history now, but coal is still the dominant U.S. source of electricity and is likely to remain that way for a while. Use of coal for electricity is expected to rise 25% from 2009 to 2035. Most of the coal mining in this region is done in Boone, Logan, Raleigh and Mingo counties, each of which produced more than 10 million tons in 2009. The four counties employed more than 8,500 people in the industry. Raleigh County is the site of Massey Energy's Upper Big Branch Mine, where an April 2010 disaster killed 29 miners in the worst industry accident in four decades.

The 3rd Congressional District of West Virginia includes most of the mountainous coal country in the southern part of the state that for years was heavily Democratic. But the coal mining counties now make up less than half of the district. About a quarter of the population is in and around the industrial city of Huntington on the Ohio River, which includes Marshall University. Another quarter is to the east, in Beckley and the farming uplands. (Also located there is the Greenbrier Resort, where the government built a massive secret fallout shelter, code-named "Project Greek Island," to house the entire U.S. Congress in the event of nuclear war). The population of the 3rd District in 2010 was about 588,000, the lowest of the state's three districts and nearly 29,000 below the state's average district size. The district has shifted to Republicans in the past decade. In 2000, Democratic presidential nominee Al Gore won the district 51%-47%. Eight years later, Republican John McCain won the district 56%-42%.

Nick Rahall (D)

The congressman from the 3rd District is Nick Rahall, a Democrat first elected in 1976. After a long tenure as the top Democrat and chairman of the Natural Resources Committee, in 2011 he switched to the ranking member slot on the Transportation and Infrastructure Committee, another vital assignment for his state.

Rahall comes from the thin economic upper crust of the coal country. His family owned radio and television stations in Beckley and in St. Petersburg, Fla. He graduated from Duke University, worked on Democratic Sen. Robert Byrd's staff and then in his family's businesses. (When Byrd died at age 92 in 2010, Rahall said the senator had been like a father to him.) In 1976, when Democratic Rep. Ken Hechler ran for governor, Rahall ran for the House and won a five-candidate Democratic primary with 37% of the vote. Hechler, after losing the primary to Jay Rockefeller, returned to the district and ran as a write-in. Rahall spent $236,000 of his own money on his campaign—an enormous sum in those days—and beat Hechler 46%-37%.

Rahall got seats on the Interior and Public Works committees in his first term, fine assignments for a young member from a rural district with low incomes and poor roads. Rahall's voting record puts him near the center of the House. He is conservative on social issues—he opposes abortion rights and received an "A" rating from the National Rifle Association in 2010, one of the few Democrats to do so that year.

He predictably has worked to help the coal industry and coal miners over the years. He was the chief House sponsor of the law requiring union and non-union coal operators to bail out the United Mine Workers' health care funds and he has continued to secure federal funds for retired mine workers. In 2006, after the Sago Mine disaster in Upshur County, he and Rep. Shelley Moore

Capito, R-W.Va., co-sponsored legislation requiring companies to have updated mine emergency response plans, wireless two-way communication and electronic tracking systems. It quickly passed both houses and became law. He opposed the 2009 cap-and-trade bill aimed at curbing greenhouse gas emissions, saying he wanted more emphasis on clean coal technologies. He also sought to distance himself from some of the Obama administration's increased regulation of coal. After the Upper Big Branch Mine explosion, he worked in 2010 to get more money for mine safety.

Environmental groups were disappointed when Rahall in 2001 became the ranking Democrat on the Natural Resources Committee because he had shown little support for their views. But while he promotes the use of coal, he has by no means been a reliable supporter of measures sought by oil companies. He has opposed oil drilling in the Arctic National Wildlife Refuge and he has favored expanding wilderness areas in the West. When the issue of oil drilling took center stage following the massive 2010 BP oil spill in the Gulf of Mexico, he held hearings in which he sharply criticized Interior's Minerals Management Service. He also introduced a bill to create a new Interior Department agency to govern oil and gas leasing on federal lands, which narrowly passed the House in July 2010, but was blocked by Republicans in the Senate. Rahall noted in January 2011 that the recommendations of the independent commission that investigated the spill were largely consistent with his legislation. "Congress must reform the way Big Oil does business to prevent another disaster from occurring," he said.

On Transportation and Infrastructure, Rahall promised to work closely with new Chairman John Mica, R-Fla. But Rahall was critical of the House's decision in January 2011 to adopt new rules enabling lawmakers to control transportation appropriations year to year, something he said would hurt states' abilities to plan long-term. From 1993 to 2001, he was chairman and ranking minority member on the panel's Surface Transportation subcommittee, where he established the Rahall Appalachian Transportation Institute, a consortium of five colleges at Marshall University.

Rahall's family roots are in Lebanon, and he is often in the small minority of members voicing support for Arab causes and voting against pro-Israel resolutions. In 2002, he opposed military action in Iraq, saying, "I feel the Iraqis want to give peace a chance." His sister, Tanya Rahall, worked for several years as a lobbyist for Qatar before joining a D.C. lobbying firm in 2008 and 2009. The firm, RJI Government Strategies, filed a lawsuit in 2010 contending that Tanya Rahall had threatened to use her brother to ensure that "doors on Capitol Hill will be closed" to the firm after it fired her. The congressman's office dismissed the suit as politically motivated and said he does not let family members lobby him. The controversy wasn't the only one associated with the lawmaker that year. In August, he acknowledged that he should not have used his official congressional stationery five years earlier in asking a judge for leniency for his son, who was facing felony robbery charges at the time. His son was given a four-year suspended sentence.

Until 2010, Rahall had dropped below 61% of the vote only once, and had not been seriously challenged in 20 years. But Republicans made an aggressive run at his seat that year. Former Alaska Gov. Sarah Palin singled him out in March as one of 20 House Democrats on her target list. His opponent was former state Supreme Court Justice Elliott "Spike" Maynard, who had switched his voter registration from Democrat to Republican before entering the race.

Maynard blasted Rahall as a Washington insider who was insufficiently concerned with protecting the state's coal industry. Meanwhile, a West Virginia group led by tea party activists ran an ad trying to play up Rahall's Arab-American ancestry and connections to President Barack Obama, whom some activists believed to be Muslim. Maynard ran another ad on that theme, claiming the congressman was "good for the Middle East, good for Obama, bad for America." But those negative efforts appeared to backfire; Rahall won 56%-44%.

★ WISCONSIN ★

Wisconsin, tucked off north of the main east-west routes across the country, has been one of America's premier "laboratories of reform," in Justice Louis Brandeis' phrase, a state originating new public policies, observing whether or not they worked, and serving as an example for other states. Wisconsin's reputation for innovative public policy was established during the Progressive era that began around 1900 and owes its development to an extraordinary governor, Robert La Follette Sr., and the state's German heritage. Wisconsin was settled first by New England Yankees, and then by waves of immigrants from Germany and Scandinavia. The German language is seldom heard now, and the once plainly German beer and brat brands now seem quintessentially American. But in the late 19th and early 20th centuries, Germans were among America's most numerous immigrants, and until the 1890s, probably the most distinct. On the rolling dairy land of Wisconsin and the orderly streets of Milwaukee, they implanted their own religions, often retained their language, and maintained old customs, from country weddings to beer drinking—a source of friction in temperance-minded America. Wisconsin still has an orderliness and steadiness that owes something to its Germanic heritage, evident in its excellence in precision manufacturing, its low crime rates, its respect for higher learning, and its hold on its people—the state ranks No. 5 in the percentage of people born there who are still living there. In 2009, 44.5% of Wisconsin residents surveyed by the Census Bureau reported being of German descent.

Politically, the Germans were not monolithic. Their origins were diverse and they were spread too widely across the nation. But where they were concentrated, there was a distinctive politics, basically American, but with echoes of progressive ideas then popular in German-speaking countries in Europe. Nowhere were the politics of German-Americans more apparent than in Wisconsin. This is one of the two states that gave birth to the Republican Party in 1854 (the other is Michigan) and Germans, then arriving in America in vast numbers, heavily favored it. They abhorred slavery and welcomed the free lands Republicans delivered in the Homestead Act, the free education promised by setting up land grant colleges, and the transportation routes constructed by subsidized railroad builders. Then came the Progressive movement of La Follette, elected governor of Wisconsin in 1900. Up to that time a conventional Republican politician, La Follette completely revamped the state government before going to the U.S. Senate in 1906. At a time when Germany was the world's leader in graduate education and the application of science to government, La Follette had professors from the University of Wisconsin help develop the state workmen's compensation system and income tax. The Progressive movement favored rational use of government to improve the lot of ordinary citizens, an idea borrowed partly from German liberals and adopted by the New Dealers a generation later. All of these programs were an attempt to bring bureaucratic rationality—Germanic systematization—to the seemingly disordered America of free markets and multiple cultures, gigantic fortunes and vast open spaces.

La Follette became a national figure. He tried to run for president in 1912 as a Progressive, but was shoved aside by Theodore Roosevelt. He did run in 1924 on his Progressive ticket and won 18% of the vote, the best third-candidate showing between 1912 and 1992. He ran strongest in the northern tier of states from Wisconsin west and along the West Coast, the same area of strength of later liberal Democrats like George McGovern, Walter Mondale, Michael Dukakis and John Kerry. After La Follette died in 1925, his sons carried on his tradition, progressive at home and isolationist abroad. Robert La Follette Jr., served 22 years in the Senate; Philip La Follette was elected governor in 1930, 1934 and 1936. Robert Jr. ran for re-election in 1946 as a Republican but lost in the primary to Joseph McCarthy. McCarthy's charges that Communists were influencing American foreign policy fed on the inarticulate convictions of many in Wisconsin and elsewhere that the United States should have been fighting Russia as well as Germany in World War II. McCarthy's national prominence made Wisconsin seem like a Republican state. But he won only two elections in heavily Republican years by narrow margins, and the La Follette Progressive tradition was taken up by liberal Democrats such as Sens. William Proxmire and Gaylord Nelson and Gov. Patrick Lucey. Like most liberals of their era, these progressives saw Washington rather than Madison as the main site of their laboratory of reform. Wisconsin, a mostly Republican state in the mostly Democratic years from 1944 to 1964, became a mostly Democratic state in the mostly Republican years from 1968 to 1988.

Wisconsin's economy likewise has been an outgrowth of its immigrant heritage. Its high-skill, precision manufacturing economy jumped into gear in the late 1980s, and helped lead the nation's export boom of the 1990s. Yet much of the political focus remained on the dwindling number of

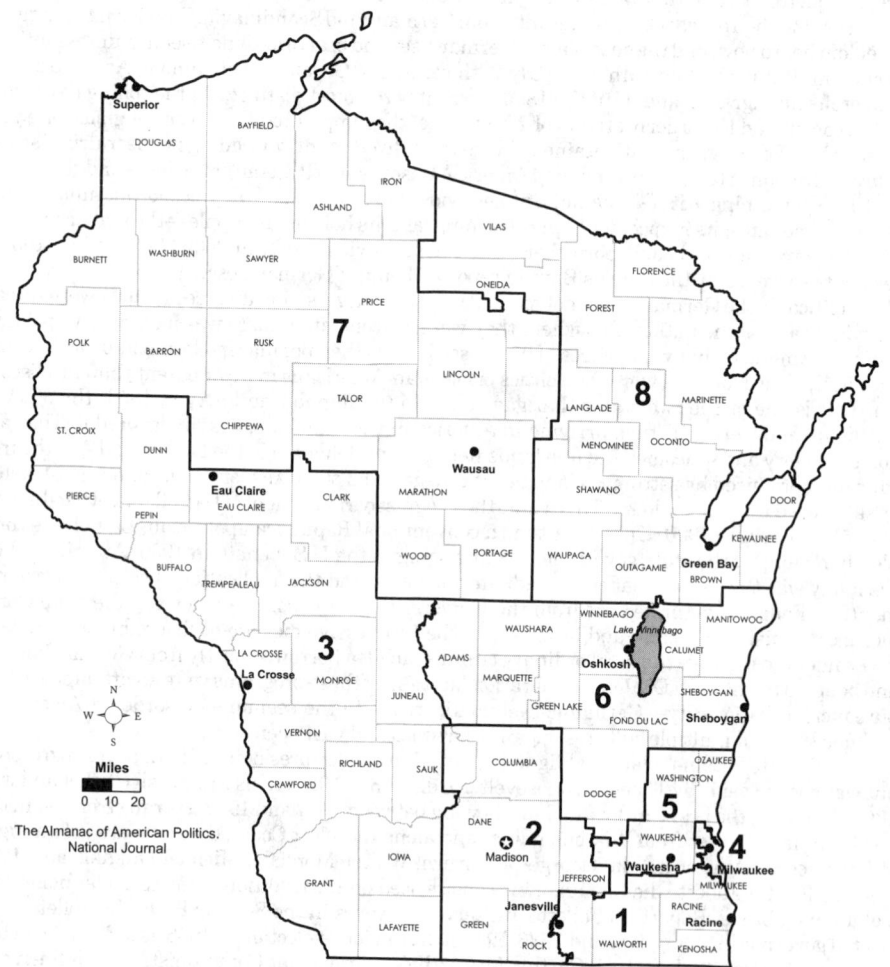

Congressional district boundaries were first effective for 2002.

dairy farmers. Wisconsin ranks No. 2 in milk and butter production and No. 1 in cheese. But thanks to improved productivity, the number of dairy farms has declined from 105,000 in 1960 to 12,700 in 2010. For years, the federal milk price-fixing system was biased against Wisconsin, with prices higher the farther a farm is from Eau Claire. The Milk Income Loss Contract program, adopted in 2002, is biased toward Wisconsin, with a limit on individual payments that works against big dairy farms in California. But in 2009 and 2010, dairy prices tended to hover below the cost of production in "America's dairy land." But Wisconsin feeds the country in other ways as well. It's No. 1 in the production of beans, cranberries and ginseng, No. 3 in carrots, peas and sweet corn and No. 4 in food processing—not to mention a prime source of beer and sausage.

In the 1990s, Wisconsin was a laboratory for reforms of a different nature. The motivating force was another Republican governor, Tommy Thompson, who beat a liberal Democrat in 1986 and was re-elected three times. He cut taxes, sponsored a school choice program and passed a series of welfare programs—the nation's most thoroughgoing—that dramatically cut caseloads by equipping recipients to work. Across the nation, other governors and Republicans in Congress watched Wisconsin's experiment with interest. It's a fair question whether the 1996 overhaul of federal welfare policy would have passed without Wisconsin's example to give its backers confidence. When Thompson left to become President George W. Bush's Health and Human Services secretary in 2001, Wisconsin moved back toward Democrats. It was a target state in the 2000 and 2004 presidential races, when Al Gore carried it 47.8%-47.6% and John Kerry carried it 49.7%-49.3%, respectively. In 2008, it gave a resounding 56%-42% majority to Democrat Barack Obama. From 1992 to 2006, it elected only Democratic senators, though sometimes by narrow margins, and Democrats gained a 5-3 edge in its U.S. House delegation in 2008. In 2002, Wisconsin elected as governor Democrat Jim Doyle, who went on to be re-elected 53%-45% in 2006. Democrats captured a majority in the state House that year and in the state Senate in 2008. Doyle expanded Wisconsin's Medicaid program, leaving it with one of the lowest rates of uninsured households, passed a Wisconsin Covenant guaranteeing state college admission and aid to eighth graders who continued to do well in high school, and raised taxes on high-income earners in 2009.

Wisconsin's political pattern is the opposite of most other Great Lakes states, where the big metro areas are heavily Democratic and the countryside is traditionally Republican. The three suburban counties around Milwaukee are so heavily Republican that metro Milwaukee voted for George W. Bush in 2004 and for Republicans Scott Walker and Ron Johnson in the 2010 races for governor and senator. Eastern Wisconsin—the counties along Lake Michigan and two or three counties inland, with small industrial cities like Kenosha, Sheboygan, Appleton, and Green Bay—is the most Republican part of the state, and voted 58% for Walker and Johnson in 2010. Western and northern Wisconsin—areas along the Mississippi River, the small inland cities such as Wausau and Eau Claire and the counties along Lake Superior—are somewhat more Democratic, voting for Doyle in 2006 when metro Milwaukee and eastern Wisconsin backed his Republican opponent. The *Milwaukee Journal Sentinel*'s Craig Gilbert, in his fine-grained analysis of Wisconsin election results, has suggested that this represents ethnic differences: Eastern Wisconsin is more German, and western and northern Wisconsin more Scandinavian. The most Democratic region by far is around Madison, the state capital and home of the huge University of Wisconsin, whose college town atmosphere and unionized state employees have spread to rural counties to the south, plus the industrial cities of Janesville and Beloit in Rock County. Greater Madison voted 62% for John Kerry in 2004, 66% for Doyle in 2006, 69% for Barack Obama in 2008, and 63% and 64% for Republicans Tom Barrett and Russ Feingold, respectively, in 2010.

The 2010 election ended, at least temporarily, Democratic dominance in Wisconsin. Scott Walker, after successful terms as Milwaukee County executive, called for reducing state spending, curbing the powers of public employee unions, and rejecting a proposed high-speed rail line between Milwaukee and Madison. Democrat Tom Barrett, after successful terms in Congress and as mayor of Milwaukee, took the opposite stands. Walker piled up big enough majorities in eastern Wisconsin, the west and north and in metro Milwaukee to overcome Barrett's 84,000-vote lead in greater Madison to win 52%-46%. In the Senate race, political insiders expected Sen. Russ Feingold to be a shoo-in for a fourth term after former Gov. Thompson announced he would not run. But in April 2010, a plastic manufacturer from Oshkosh named Ron Johnson entered the race out of opposition to Democratic policies in Washington. While national political reporters were chronicling the hopeless campaign of tea party favorite Christine O'Donnell in Delaware, Johnson, in his head-on television ads, showed something close to perfect political pitch in personifying the tea party. He charged to a lead in the polls over Feingold and went on to win 52%-47%, with the same regional patterns, except that Feingold ran a bit better than Barrett in greater Madison. These results were in part a response to economic conditions, although Wisconsin's unemployment rate was below the national average and the 2009 economic stimulus bill, fashioned in part by Wisconsin Democrat David Obey, chairman of the House Appropriations Committee, produced a large infusion of federal money into the state. Obey himself, after Republican Sean Duffy launched a spirited campaign against him, decided to retire after 41 years in the House; Duffy won Obey's northern Wisconsin 7th District and a Republican also captured the 8th District around Green Bay and Appleton. The GOP also captured majorities in both houses of the legislature.

Shortly after taking office, Walker started a firestorm with a proposal to restrict collective bargaining with public employee unions to the issue of wages and to end the practice of sending dues payments directly to the unions. He argued that the moves were necessary to address a looming $3.6 billion budget shortfall and shrink the size of government. Republicans had sufficient votes to pass Walker's measures, but were one vote short of the 20-vote quorum required to bring the bills to the floor of the state Senate. In February 2011, all 14 Democratic senators left the state for Illinois, a tactic used by Texas Democrats in a congressional redistricting fight in 2003. On Feb. 16, protesters packed the Capitol rotunda and held street demonstrations in Madison. But Republicans passed Walker's legislation in late February and early March, and Walker delivered layoff notices to 1,500 state workers.

The Senate Democrats returned to Madison, but the struggle was not over. With the legislation headed for a court challenge, a state Supreme Court election became the next battleground. Republican appointees had a 4-3 majority on the state Supreme Court, but in an April 5 local election, Democrat JoAnne Kloppenburg challenged Republican Judge David Prosser and let it be understood that she would look favorably on challenges to Walker's legislation. The outcome was close, and went to a recount, but Prosser prevailed and Republicans retained the edge on the high court. On yet another front in La Follette's Wisconsin, which pioneered the recall election, both Democrats and Republicans in the spring of 2011 filed multiple recall petitions against state senators of the opposite party.

Population		Household Income		Work	
Pop. 2010:	5,686,986	Under $15k:	11.5%	Private:	81.9%
State rank:	20th	$15k to $50k:	37.2%	Government:	12.2%
Change since 2000:	Up 6.0%	$50k to $100k:	34.5%	Self-employed:	5.6%
Urban:	67.1%	$100k to $200k:	14.3%	Unemployment (3-yr. average):	4.5%
Rural:	32.9%	Over $200k:	2.6%	Poverty:	11.4%
Native of state:	71.8%	Median income:	$51,257	Blue collar:	25.4%
Not a citizen:	2.6%			White collar:	57.5%
Area size:	65,496 sq. mi.	**Home Value**		Khaki collar:	0.1%
		Under $100k:	17.4%	Other:	17.0%
Most populous cities		$100k to $300k:	66.8%		
Milwaukee	594,833	$300k to $500k:	11.5%	**Age**	
Madison	233,209	$500k to $1 mil:	3.4%	Median age:	38.1 yrs.
Green Bay	104,057	Over $1 million:	0.8%	More than 65 yrs:	13.3%
Kenosha	99,218	Median:	$170,800	Less than 18 yrs:	23.4%

Race/Ethnicity				Military Veterans		Registered Voters in 2010	
White:	83.3%	*Language*		% of Pop:	10.2%	No Party registration	
Black:	6.2%	English:	91.7%			Voter turnout:	2,171,331
Hispanic:	5.9%	Spanish:	4.3%	*Veterans by Period*		Turnout as % of	
Asian:	2.3%	Asian:	1.5%	WWII and before:	11.5%	voting age:	49.9%
Native Am.:	0.9%	Other European:	2.2%	Korea:	12.0%		
Hawaiian:	0.0%			Vietnam:	33.4%	**Legislature**	
Two+ races:	1.4%	**Education**		Gulf (pre-2001):	9.3%	Senate:	14 D 19 R
		H.S. grad:	89.4%	Gulf (post-2001):	6.1%	Assembly:	38 D 60 R 1 I
Ancestry		College grad:	25.6%	Peace time:	27.6%		
German	32.2%	Grad degree:	8.5%				
Irish	8.6%						
Polish	7.0%						

Presidential politics Wisconsin has voted Democratic in the last six presidential elections, starting in 1988. But sometimes the margin has been quite narrow. Al Gore carried Wisconsin by only 5,708 votes in 2000, John Kerry by only 11,384 in 2004. In both elections, the state was heavily contested. Kerry stumbled when he came to Green Bay and referred to "Lambert Field" —it's Lambeau Field, as any Cheesehead can tell you. But Kerry perhaps atoned by abjuring the Northeast Dairy Compact. In both races, some historic patterns were reversed. Bush carried eastern Wisconsin and metro Milwaukee both times, while Gore and Kerry carried western and northern Wisconsin. Indeed, western and northern Wisconsin and adjacent eastern Iowa were the only rural parts of the country where Gore and Kerry carried large numbers of counties.

2008 Presidential Vote		
Barack Obama (D) 1,677,211	(56%)
John McCain (R) 1,262,393	(42%)

2008 Presidential Primary		
Barack Obama (D) 646,851	(58%)
Hillary Clinton (D)...............453,954	(41%)

2008 Presidential Primary		
John McCain (R) 224,755	(55%)
Mike Huckabee (R)...............151,707	(37%)

2004 Presidential Vote		
John Kerry (D) 1,489,504	(50%)
George W. Bush (R)...........1,478,120	(49%)

Then in 2008 Wisconsin fell off the target list. Although polls tightened after the Republican National Convention and there was speculation that Sarah Palin might attract votes in the rural north, it became apparent by early October that Barack Obama was far ahead. He ended up winning 56%-42%, carrying 59 of 72 counties. Republican John McCain carried only one of the eight congressional districts, in the heavily Republican Milwaukee suburbs, and he barely won the state's fastest-growing county, St. Croix, just east of St. Paul, Minn. Obama made especially large gains over previous Democrats in the Fox River Valley and in the rural southwestern counties.

Wisconsin once had one of the nation's most influential presidential primaries. It knocked Wendell Willkie out of the race in 1944, helped John Kennedy establish his lead over Hubert Humphrey in 1960, prompted Lyndon Johnson to withdraw as Eugene McCarthy was about to beat him here in 1968, gave George McGovern his first victory in 1972, and chose "New Democrat" Gary Hart over Minnesota neighbor Walter Mondale in 1984. Later, Wisconsin's primary, even after it was moved from April to March, tended to be ignored. So for the 2004 election, the legislature moved the date up another month, to Feb.17, the only primary held that day. Wisconsin saw heavier campaigning than it had in years, at least for a few days. It may have proved crucial. In the Democratic primary, Kerry led John Edwards 40%-34%, with Howard Dean in third place with 18%. Dean ended his campaign, while Edwards failed to get the momentum a victory here might have given him. Wisconsin does not have party registration and few people bothered to vote in the uncontested Republican primary.

Wisconsin scheduled its 2008 primary on Feb. 19. A week earlier, Obama swept the primaries in Maryland, Virginia and the District of Columbia. Gov. Jim Doyle campaigned actively for Obama and he was endorsed by longtime Rep. David Obey, the dean of the Wisconsin congressional delegation. Obama outspent Hillary Rodham Clinton on television ads 5-to-1 and won a smashing 58%-41% victory, demonstrating, as he did in the Iowa caucuses, that he could prevail among a mostly white electorate. He carried all eight congressional districts and lost only 10 counties, mostly at the edge of the state and presumably out of range of most Wisconsin television stations. Clinton got the votes of 50% of women, but Obama got the votes of 67% of men. He won 68% of the vote in Dane County, home to the University of Wisconsin at Madison, and 64% in Milwaukee County, with its large African-American population. Turnout topped 1 million, far above that in recent years, though just slightly below the turnout in 1972, when McGovern's 30% of the vote beat George Wallace's 22% and Hubert Humphrey's 21%.

There was less action on the Republican side. McCain had serious opposition only from Mike Huckabee, who was far behind in delegates. Turnout was 410,000, below that of the primaries in 1968, 1976, 1992, 1996 and 2000, and less than half the turnout in 1980. McCain beat Huckabee 55%-37%. Huckabee did well enough in the central and western parts of the state to carry the 3rd and 7th congressional districts. McCain ran best in the Milwaukee suburbs. On election night, McCain was able to say, "Thank you, Wisconsin, for bringing us to the point where even a superstitious military aviator can claim with confidence and humility that I will be our party's nominee for president of the United States."

Congressional districting

112th Congress Lineup	
5 R	3 D
111th Congress Lineup	
5 D	3 R

Wisconsin lost a congressional district in the 2000 census. Ordinarily, that might have triggered a fierce battle between a Republican governor and Assembly and a Democratic state Senate. But in May 2001, 5th District Democrat Tom Barrett announced he was running for governor. His north Milwaukee district had lost population and was easy to eliminate. The result was a consensus plan, passed by both houses of the legislature and signed by Gov. Scott McCallum. This is one state that produced a plan with regularly shaped districts with obvious communities of interest. It was also a plan that enabled all eight incumbents running to win re-election in the next two elections. There was change later, as Democrat Steve Kagen won the 8th District in 2006 (and then lost it in 2010) and as Republican Sean Duffy won the 7th District after House Appropriations Chairman David Obey retired in 2010.

Wisconsin did not lose a House seat in the reapportionment following the 2010 census. Republicans, with the governorship and majorities in the legislature, control the redistricting process and could conceivably try to weaken 3rd District Democrat Ron Kind and to bolster freshman Republicans Duffy and Reid Ribble in the 8th District. But most of the territory that could be shuffled between these districts is politically marginal. So, in the midst of Wisconsin's fierce partisan warfare, there may not be major changes in the current plan.

Governor

Scott Walker (R)

Elected 2010, term expires Jan. 2015, 1st term; b. Nov. 2, 1967, Colorado Springs, CO; home, Wauwatosa; Attended Marquette U., 1986-90; Christian; married (Tonette); 2 children.

Elected Office: WI Assembly, 1993-2002; Milwaukee Cnty. Exec., 2002-10.

Professional Career: Salesman, IBM Corp., 1988-90; Financial developer, American Red Cross, 1990-94.

Office: 115 East Capitol, Madison, 53702, 608-266-1212; Web site: www.wisgov.state.wi.us/.

Election Results

2010 general	Scott Walker (R)	1,128,941	(52%)
	Tom Barrett (D)	1,004,303	(46%)
2010 primary	Scott Walker (R)	362,913	(59%)
	Mark Neumann (R)	239,022	(39%)

Republican Scott Walker became Wisconsin's governor in January 2011, and he almost immediately became the nation's highest-profile chief executive when his tough budget-balancing initiative sparked a month-long protest at the state Capitol and led 14 Democratic senators to flee the state to stall passage.

Walker was born in Colorado Springs, Colo., and moved with his family at age 10 to Delavan, a small town 60 miles southeast of Madison. His father was a preacher at the local Baptist church and his mother kept the books for a department store. Walker was an Eagle Scout and represented Wisconsin at the Boys Nation student government program in Washington, D.C., in 1985, an achievement he says spurred his interest in politics. Republican Ronald Reagan was president at the time, and served as an inspiration to him. He attended Marquette University and left before graduating to take a job in his senior year with the American Red Cross doing marketing and development work. Walker ran for the state Assembly in 1990, but lost to Democratic incumbent Gwen Moore, who went on to serve in the U.S. House. Three years later, he tried again and won. He reportedly considered running for governor, but a pension scandal involving Milwaukee County Executive Tom Ament changed his plans. Walker was elected to that job in 2002 after promising to run a cleaner government.

The nonpartisan county executive's job had usually been held by liberal Democrats. But Walker put a fiscally conservative stamp on the job. He cut the workforce by 20% and used his veto more than 100 times to force $44 million in spending cuts. Each of his budgets held the property tax levy to the previous year's level, and he returned a portion of his personal paychecks to the county's coffers. Some Democrats accused him of being overly stingy in financing basic services. But others hailed his low-key personality and political skills. Walker "has that ability to disagree without being disagreeable, which is important," University of Wisconsin-Milwaukee political scientist Mordecai Lee told the *Wisconsin State Journal* in 2010. "He is probably the best politician I have seen in a generation."

Walker entered the race for governor in 2006, but backed out after 14 months, saying that he had trouble raising enough money to compete. In April 2009, he announced his second bid, criticizing Democratic Gov. Jim Doyle for increased spending and taxes; he vowed "to bring this state back." Walker said he was reminded of the early 1980s, when Republican Tommy Thompson beat incumbent Democratic Gov. Tony Earl, and called for tax cuts and a property tax freeze. He emphasized what he characterized as a common-sense, "brown bag" approach to making cutbacks, a philosophy he said was reflected in his habit of packing his own lunch most of the time. Four months after Walker entered the race, Doyle—who trailed Walker in some polls—announced he would not seek a third term.

Walker faced a GOP primary challenger in Mark Neumann, a homebuilder and developer who served two terms in the U.S. House in the 1990s. Despite Neumann's reputation as a budget hawk, Walker accused his opponent of having voted for a transportation bill that included $9 billion in pork-barrel spending—an attack that Neumann said he initially thought was a joke. Neumann remained ahead in fundraising throughout the race, drawing from his personal wealth. But Walker continued to blast Neumann as a "career politician," a charge that resonated in an anti-incumbent political climate. He handily beat Neumann in the September 2010 primary, 59%-39%.

Walker's Democratic opponent was another former House member—Tom Barrett, a representative from 1993 to 2003 before winning election as Milwaukee's mayor. He lost the 2002 Democratic primary for governor to Doyle. Barrett touted his economic proposals, which included targeted tax credits for companies hiring more workers as well as a proposal to commit $100 million in state money to private venture capital firms over five years, a move he said would raise at least $500 million. Walker scoffed at that idea, saying it would expand government and hike spending. Barrett began the race with a considerable fundraising edge, but Walker raised $2.8 million from September to mid-October. Wisconsin Republicans were clearly more energized than Democrats in the election, charged up by their efforts to oust veteran Democratic Sen. Russ Feingold, who was up for re-election. They propelled Walker to a 52%-47% victory on his 43rd birthday. Though Barrett carried Milwaukee County 62%-38% and Dane County—home of Madison—68%-31%, Walker won all but a handful of rural counties.

Walker's fiscal stands earned him headlines well before he was sworn in as governor. He vowed to block construction of a proposed high-speed train from Milwaukee to Madison, and announced changes in education that would tie teacher pay raises to performance. But the biggest issue remained finding ways to close an estimated $3.6 billion hole in the state's budget. A former state revenue secretary working on Walker's transition team floated a proposal to raise the state sales tax in exchange for reducing other taxes, but the governor-elect swiftly quashed that idea.

On his first official day in office, Walker called the legislature into session to address the state's economy and swiftly won two victories. Republicans passed and sent him bills to tighten personal injury laws and to provide tax breaks for people with health savings accounts. He also shuttered the state's Department of Commerce and replaced it with a public-private economic development corporation. But the attention those measures received paled in attention to his measure to close a $137 million gap in the current year's budget. He called for curtailing collective bargaining rights for many of the state's unionized workers, describing those rights as an obstacle to reducing state and local budget deficits. Outraged by the assault on unions, 14 Senate Democrats traveled to Illinois to stall a vote. Union workers showed up at the Capitol by the tens of thousands, carrying angry signs and inspiring similar protests against GOP governors' tactics in other states. Activists gathered petitions to recall eight GOP Wisconsin state senators. Walker became an instant political celebrity. Prospective presidential candidates stampeded to support him, he was invited on national television shows and he even was mentioned as a possible vice presidential candidate for 2012.

In the face of the noisy protests, Walker refused to back down from his hard-line stance, saying repeatedly that the state was "broke"—an assertion that the politics watchdog *PolitiFact* declared false, noting that the state still had money to pay its bills and enjoyed a high credit rating. State Senate Republicans in March passed a bill with the collective bargaining provisions without Democratic senators present. A *Milwaukee Journal Sentinel* poll that month showed just how polarizing the governor had become: 90% of Republicans approved of his job performance, while 91% of Democrats disapproved. His overall favorability rating was 43%.

Walker's administration went to the state Supreme Court to try to implement the collective bargaining measure. By coincidence, an April election for one of the judgeships was held, and voters flocked to the polls. The early results showed challenger JoAnne Kloppenburg edged out incumbent Justice David Prosser, a self-described judicial conservative, but the narrowness of the race prompted a recount that lasted more than a month. Prosser ultimately edged out Kloppenburg by 7,000 votes. Even so, Democrats said the election was a repudiation of Walker's philosophy. "The average Wisconsinite stood up to Gov. Scott Walker's overreach," state Democratic Party Chairman Mike Tate said. But Walker said the results only proved how divided the state was. "You've got a world driven by Madison," he told the *State Journal*, "and a world driven by everyone else out across the state."

Senior Senator

Herb Kohl (D)

Elected 1988, term expires 2012, 4th term; b. Feb. 7, 1935, Milwaukee; home, Milwaukee; U. of WI, B.A. 1956, Harvard U., M.B.A. 1958; Jewish; single.

Military Career: Army Reserves, 1958–64.

Professional Career: Businessman; Pres., Kohl Corp., 1970–79; Chmn., WI Dem. Party, 1975–77; Pres., Herbert Kohl Investments, 1979–88; Owner, Milwaukee Bucks pro basketball team, 1985–present.

DC Office: 330 HSOB, 20510, 202-224-5653; Fax: 202-224-9787; Web site: kohl.senate.gov.

State Offices: Appleton, 920-738-1640; Eau Claire, 715-832-8424; La-Crosse, 608-796-0045; Madison, 608-264-5338; Milwaukee, 414-297-4451.

Committees: *Aging (Special)* (Chmn). *Appropriations:* Agriculture, Rural Development, Food and Drug Administration & Related Agencies (Chmn); Commerce, Justice, Science & Related Agencies; Defense; Interior, Environment & Related Agencies; Labor, Health & Human Services, Education & Related Agencies; Transportation, HUD & Related Agencies. *Banking, Housing & Urban Affairs:* Financial Institutions & Consumer Protection; Housing, Transportation & Community Development; Securities, Insurance & Investment. *Judiciary:* Administrative Oversight & the Courts; Antitrust, Competition Policy & Consumer Rights (Chmn); Crime & Terrorism.

Group Ratings

	ACLU	ACU	ADA	CFG	AFS	FRC	LCV	ITIC	NTU	COC
2010	93	8	90	6	88	0	71	67	10	36
2009	–	8	100	10	100	–	100	–	9	43

National Journal Ratings

	2010 LIB	—	2010 CONS	2009 LIB	—	2009 CONS
Economic	64%	—	34%	65%	—	34%
Social	59%	—	38%	67%	—	32%
Foreign	47%	—	0%	55%	—	0%
Composite	66%	—	34%	70%	—	30%

Key Votes of the 111th Congress

1. Overturn Ledbetter	Y	5. Pass health care bill	Y	9. Ratify New START	Y
2. Pass $787 billion stimulus	Y	6. Regulate financial firms	Y	10. Confirm Elena Kagan	Y
3. Repeal DC gun laws	N	7. Pass tax cuts for some	N	11. Stop EPA climate regs	N
4. Confirm Sonia Sotomayor	Y	8. Legalize immigrants' kids	Y	12. Repeal don't ask, tell	Y

Election Results

2006 general	Herb Kohl (D)	1,439,214	(67%)	($6,089,212)
	Robert Lorge (R)	630,299	(29%)	($114,139)
2006 primary	Herb Kohl (D)	308,178	(86%)	
	Ben Masel (D)	51,245	(14%)	

Prior Winning Percentages: 2000 (62%); 1994 (58%); 1988 (52%)

Herb Kohl, Wisconsin's senior senator, is a Democrat elected in 1988. He announced in May 2011 that he would not seek re-election when his fourth term expires in 2012.

Kohl grew up in Milwaukee, where his parents had opened a food store after emigrating from Russia and Poland in the 1920s. Kohl got degrees from the University of Wisconsin and Harvard

Business School, then returned home and with his brothers, developed the family business into a department chain, which became the wildly successful Kohl's department stores. They sold the business in 1975, and Kohl followed his love of sports into a new business venture. In a city smarting over sports franchises with lousy records eager to move elsewhere, Kohl spent $18 million to buy the Milwaukee Bucks basketball team to keep it from leaving. His efforts to make the team respectable lost him money for several years, but he should turn a nice profit if he decides to sell the team—it was valued at $254 million by the Center for Responsive Politics in 2009. He has remained an active owner, involved in personnel decisions and pushing for a new stadium. "If we didn't have Herb Kohl, it would be a real challenge to keep an NBA team here," Marc Marotta, chairman of the Bradley Center board, told the *Milwaukee Journal Sentinel* in 2010. He personally funds the Herb Kohl Educational Foundation, which has given millions of dollars in scholarships and grants to Wisconsin students, teachers and schools. He donated $25 million to the University of Wisconsin for the Kohl Center arena, which opened in 1998.

Throughout his long career in business, Kohl was involved in Democratic politics as a campaign contributor, and in the mid-70s, he was chairman of the Wisconsin Democratic Party. When Democratic Sen. William Proxmire retired in 1988, Kohl decided to run for the Senate. He spent his own money liberally, running an extensive ad campaign with the theme, "Nobody's senator but yours." He won 47% of the vote in the primary to 38% for former Gov. Tony Earl. In the general election campaign against moderate Republican state Sen. Susan Engeleiter, Kohl stressed his support of defense cuts—popular in dovish Wisconsin—and for requiring businesses to provide health insurance. Engeleiter stressed her environmental stands, her legislative experience, and her status as a wife and mother. It turned out to be one of the closest Senate races in the country that year, with Kohl winning 52%-48% after spending $7 million of his own money.

Kohl is an earnest man of transparent good will, seemingly little guile and a natural tendency toward bipartisanship. He is highly regarded for his constituent service, and for generously doling out Wisconsin-made chocolate to office visitors and colleagues. He is also a political introvert who shows little interest in mingling with reporters in the Capitol hallways or for grabbing attention in other ways. "The typical politician will go for the biggest group because they like people and want to meet as many as they can," Wisconsin political activist Bill Kraus told *Milwaukee Magazine* in 2010. "I see none of that in Herb Kohl." In the Senate, Kohl once told the *Journal Sentinel*, "There's too much of the I-I-I-I, me-me-me-me, and these are my needs and you have to do them and you have to take care of me. When I see that in other people, I think it's a weakness." His voting record has been moderate to liberal, edging slightly toward the latter since 2007, when Democrats regained Senate control. In 2009, Kohl helped form the Moderate Dems Working Group, a coalition of 15 Democratic senators who, as Kohl put it, "still believe we need to be fiscally responsible and have a dialogue with amenable people of the other party."

Much of Kohl's focus has been Wisconsin-centric, particularly his work on the Appropriations Committee. With former House Appropriations Chairman David Obey, D-Wis., he added a provision to a fiscal 2010 omnibus spending bill to build a rail line in downtown Milwaukee as well as provide bus service to Milwaukee County. The same year, he worked to get a Wisconsin company a contract to build a fleet of Navy combat ships in a move estimated to create 6,000 direct and indirect jobs. Kohl ranked 12th among senators in solo earmarks for 2010 with nearly $95 million, according to Taxpayers for Common Sense. Despite his love of earmarks, he praised the work of the bipartisan Simpson-Bowles deficit commission and has backed several spending reduction measures, including a balanced budget amendment. However, the website *PolitiFact* rated his December 2010 assertion that he has always focused on cutting deficits as "barely true."

Kohl chairs Judiciary's Subcommittee on Antitrust, Competition Policy and Consumer Rights. He pushed in 2009 for a federal investigation of alleged anti-competitive practices in the wireless communications industry, and in 2011, expressed serious concerns about the proposed merger of AT&T and T-Mobile. Earlier, Kohl and former Republican Sen. Mike DeWine of Ohio ran the subcommittee on a bipartisan basis in both the Clinton and Bush years. Together, they stopped several proposed megamergers: the proposed AT&T-SBC merger in 1997, the proposed American Airlines-British Airways merger in 1998 and the U.S. Airways-United Airlines merger in 2001. In 2005, they co-sponsored a bill to allow the Justice Department to seek wiretaps of antitrust violators. As chairman of the panel beginning in 2007, Kohl introduced legislation that would repeal antitrust exemptions for the railroad industry, although the bill was dropped after President George W. Bush threatened to veto it. In 2009, Kohl worked with Republican ranking member Orrin Hatch of Utah to revise the bill, which passed without opposition in the committee after rail industry lobbyists accidentally emailed committee members their internal deliberations on how to kill the legislation.

Kohl, who chairs the Appropriations Committee's agriculture subcommittee, has fought with uncharacteristic fierceness to change what he considers the unfair treatment of Wisconsin dairy farmers. Since 1937, the Agriculture Department has fixed national milk prices using a formula that allows higher prices the farther a farmer is from Eau Claire, Wis. This increases prices to consumers, creates an oversupply of milk, and reduces dairy prices in the upper Midwest. Further aggravating the problem is the Northeast Dairy Compact, set up in the 1980s, which allows New England states to set even higher prices. During the debate on the 1996 Freedom to Farm Act, Kohl persuaded the Senate to vote 50-46 to end the Northeast Dairy Compact, but in conference it was extended to 1999, and the agriculture secretary was ordered to set new milk-marketing rules.

In October 1999, New England senators inserted into an appropriations bill a two-year extension of the compact and rejected then-Agriculture Secretary Dan Glickman's new rules. Kohl was outraged and filibustered the bill. He was forced to desist, but got verbal promises from leaders of both parties that the issue would be revisited. In 2001, he got 41 senators to sign a letter opposing the Northeast Dairy Compact, enough to threaten a filibuster if the issue was brought up, and on Sept. 30, the compact expired. To take its place, in 2002 Kohl helped pass the Milk Income Loss Contract program, which pays dairy farmers if market prices fall. In its first three years, it provided $2 billion to dairy farmers nationally, with $413 million going to Wisconsin farmers. In 2005, he and Republican Norm Coleman of Minnesota pushed for renewal of MILC. Kohl was pleased when the administration budget continued the program, though with a 5% funding decrease. He voted for the 2008 farm bill because it had provisions that would help Wisconsin's dairy farmers, including the extension of MILC and increased payments for farmers.

On another issue before the agriculture subcommittee, Kohl consistently has pushed for higher funding for the Food and Drug Administration. He championed a provision in the 2010 food safety law that allows the FDA to refuse imported food from a foreign facility that bars U.S. inspectors within 48 hours of a request to enter.

After Democrats won the majority in 2007, Kohl became chairman of the Special Committee on Aging, which he has used as a platform to push for the government to use its buying power to negotiate lower prescription drug prices. Kohl also introduced a bill that encourages businesses to retain employees beyond their retirement age. Kohl drew attention in 2010 when he blocked the nomination of Michele Leonhart to head the Drug Enforcement Administration. The DEA had increased its scrutiny of prescribing practices in long-term care facilities, and Kohl contended that some patients had been left in pain because of delays in receiving medication. He released his hold on Leonhart within a few weeks after Attorney General Eric Holder assured him he would seek to fix the problem.

Kohl has been re-elected easily, with the help of his personal fortune. He spent $6.5 million of his own money on his campaign in 1994 and $5 million in 2000. Kohl spent more than $6 million on his re-election in 2006 and sailed to a fourth term with 67% of the vote.

Junior Senator

Ron Johnson (R)

Elected 2010, term expires 2016, 1st term; b. April 8, 1955, Mankato, MN; home, Oshkosh; U. of MN, B.S. 1977; Lutheran; Married (Jane); 3 children.

Professional Career: Owner, PACUR; accountant, Josten's.

DC Office: 386 RSOB, 20510, 202-224-5323; Fax: 202-228-6965; Web site: ronjohnson.senate.gov.

State Offices: Milwaukee, 414-276-7282; Oshkosh, 920-230-7250.

Committees: *Aging (Special). Appropriations:* Commerce, Justice, Science & Related Agencies; Department of State, Foreign Operations & Related Programs; Interior, Environment & Related Agencies; Labor, Health & Human Services, Education & Related Agencies; Transportation, HUD & Related Agencies. *Budget. Homeland Security & Governmental Affairs:* Disaster Recovery & Intergovernmental Affairs (Ad Hoc); Federal Financial Management, Government Information, Federal Services & International Security; Oversight of Government Management, the Federal Workforce & the District of Columbia (RMM).

Election Results

2010 general	Ron Johnson (R)	1,125,999	(52%)	($15,235,898)
	Russ Feingold (D)	1,020,958	(47%)	($20,803,357)
2010 primary	Ron Johnson (R)	504,644	(85%)	
	Dave Westlake (R)	61,633	(10%)	

Republican Ron Johnson is the junior senator from Wisconsin. He won the seat in one of 2010's biggest upsets, dispatching 18-year Democratic Sen. Russell Feingold.

Johnson grew up in Mankato, Minn. He says he developed a strong work ethic at an early age, delivering newspapers, caddying at a golf course, and baling hay on his uncle's dairy farm. He was a restaurant dishwasher at 15 and within a year won a promotion to night manager. Although Johnson didn't finish high school, he still attended college, working full-time and managing to graduate with $7,000 in the bank. After graduation, he married his high school sweetheart. He and Jane Johnson now have three children.

While working as an accountant, Johnson went to night school to earn a master's in business administration. Just short of a degree in 1979, he decided to move to Oshkosh, Wis., to start a plastics company, PACUR, with his brother-in-law. Their first customer was a company co-founded by his father-in-law. Since then, the business has become a major producer of specialty packaging for medical devices, employing around 120 workers.

Johnson said his political views have been influenced by Ayn Rand's 1957 novel *Atlas Shrugged*, which argues that civilization cannot exist where men are slaves to society and government. He also has looked to Rep. Paul Ryan, R-Wis., author of the GOP "road map" for entitlement reform. Johnson said that his motivation to run against Feingold was the senator's support of the Democrats' 2010 health care overhaul, which he called "the single greatest assault to our freedom in my lifetime."

He entered the race in May, just days before the state Republican nominating convention. Three GOP candidates were already competing, including beer mogul and former state Commerce Secretary Dick Leinenkugel and Madison developer Terrence Wall. But Johnson's ability to self-finance made an immediate impact. At the convention, Leinenkugel surprised everyone, including Johnson, by taking his turn at the lectern to drop out and endorse Johnson, saying, "It's not my time····. It's Ron Johnson's time." Wall then reluctantly followed suit. Spending more than $4 million of his own money, Johnson went on to crush Watertown businessman Dave Westlake in the September primary with 85% of the vote.

In the general election contest, Johnson began with backing from tea party activists. "America needs to be pulled back from the brink of socialism and state control," Johnson told a tea party gathering in May 2010. Bu some conservative groups developed second thoughts about his readiness for the Senate. Early in the campaign, he acknowledged that he was still developing his views on issues. One state group, the Rock River Patriots, declined to endorse him, saying they were unimpressed with his knowledge of the Constitution. But the National Republican Senatorial Committee, sensing an opportunity, jumped in to help, as did conservative kingmaker Jim DeMint, a Republican senator from South Carolina.

The campaign between Feingold and Johnson was nasty, especially by Wisconsin's usually civil standards. Without a legislative record of his opponent to mine, Feingold sought to concentrate on Johnson's record in business, attempting to depict him as someone more concerned about profits than people, "with a country club view of reality." He was helped along by an Associated Press story just before the election revealing that five of Johnson's 120 employees relied on state-provided health coverage for low-income families. Feingold also called Johnson a hypocrite for opposing federal economic stimulus funds and then allegedly seeking those funds for renovation of an opera house.

Johnson fought back, noting in one ad that the Senate has 57 lawyers, including Feingold, but just one accountant and no manufacturers like himself. His GOP allies also did a textbook job of depicting the incumbent—who contemplated running for president in 2008—as an entrenched Washington insider supportive of deficit spending. Johnson called for a "hard spending cap" in the federal budget, while Feingold said he would support giving the president line-item veto power over appropriations bills. On the issue of climate change, Johnson took the position common among hard-right conservatives that global warming is "not settled science."

In spite of 18 years of service in the Senate and his independent stands on issues that appealed to Wisconsin voters, Feingold was surprisingly endangered, with polls revealing Johnson ahead and the incumbent on the defensive for his vote for the Democrats' health care overhaul. He fought back by making his own appeal to tea party groups, touting his vote against the Bush-era USA PATRIOT Act as an infringement on personal liberties. Labor unions, MoveOn.org, and other liberal groups made the race a priority, and Feingold raised $21 million compared to Johnson's $15 million, all to no avail. Johnson beat Feingold, 52% to 47%.

Once in Washington, Johnson declined to join the Tea Party Caucus, despite the help he got from tea party groups in his campaign. He said he wanted to unify Republicans, not further divide them. Johnson got seats on the Senate Appropriations and Budget committees, two important assignments in his quest to clamp down on government spending.

FIRST DISTRICT

Paul Ryan (R)

Elected 1998, 7th term; b. Jan. 29, 1970, Janesville; home, Janesville; Miami U. of OH, B.A., 1992; Catholic; married (Janna); 3 children.

Professional Career: Aide, U.S. Sen. Bob Kasten, 1992; Advisor & speechwriter, Empower America, 1993-95; Legis. dir., U.S. Sen. Sam Brownback, 1995-97; Mktg. consultant., Ryan Inc. Central, 1997-98.

DC Office: 1233 LHOB, 20515, 202-225-3031; Fax: 202-225-3393; Web site: paulryan.house.gov.

State Offices: Janesville, 608-752-4050; Kenosha, 262-654-1901; Racine, 262-637-0510.

Committees: *Budget* (Chmn). *Ways & Means:* Health.

Group Ratings

	ACLU	ACU	ADA	CFG	AFS	FRC	LCV	ITIC	NTU	COC
2010	13	96	0	97	0	87	20	50	92	88
2009	–	96	0	93	11	–	7	–	90	73

National Journal Ratings

	2010 LIB	—	2010 CONS	2009 LIB	—	2009 CONS
Economic	19%	—	80%	20%	—	79%
Social	0%	—	85%	7%	—	90%
Foreign	0%	—	88%	26%	—	68%
Composite	11%	—	89%	19%	—	81%

Key Votes of the 111th Congress

1. Overturn Ledbetter	N	5. Bar federal abortion funds	Y	9. Stop detainee transfers	*
2. Pass $820 billion stimulus	N	6. Pass health care bill	N	10. Legalize immigrants' kids	N
3. Let guns in national parks	Y	7. Regulate financial firms	N	11. Repeal don't ask, tell	N
4. Pass cap-and-trade	N	8. Pass tax cuts for some	N	12. Limit campaign funds	N

Election Results

2010 general	Paul Ryan (R)	179,819	(68%)	($3,922,760)
	John Heckenlively (D)	79,363	(30%)	($12,066)
2010 primary	Paul Ryan (R)	unopposed		

Population		Race/Ethnicity		Work	
Pop. 2010:	728,042	White:	82.2%	Private:	84.9%
Change since 2000:	Up 8.6%	Black:	5.2%	Government:	10.5%
Urban:	84.4%	Hispanic:	9.0%	Self-employed:	4.5%
Rural:	15.6%	Asian:	1.7%	Blue collar:	25.5%
Area size:	1,723 sq. mi.	Native Am.:	0.3%	White collar:	59.1%
		Hawaiian:	0.0%	Khaki collar:	0.1%
Age		Two+ races:	1.5%	Other:	15.4%
Median age:	38.5 yrs.				
More than 65 yrs:	12.7%	*Ancestry*		Median income:	$56,833
Less than 18 yrs:	24.6%	German	28.3%	Median Home Value:	$195,600
		Irish	9.4%		
Education		Polish	9.0%	**Military Veterans**	
H.S. grad:	89.0%			% of Pop:	10.6%
College grad:	25.2%				
Grad degree:	7.9%				

Southeast Wisconsin; Kenosha

With its rolling hills, blanketed by snow during most of the winter, gloriously green under blue skies in summer, the southern tier of Wisconsin, from Lake Michigan to the Rock River Valley, is some of America's prime industrial country. Settled by Yankee and German farmers 170 years ago, it was once primarily dairy land. By the early 20th century, the steady habits and high skills of the local dairy farmers had made them a good labor pool for factories. There are still major plants here, including the operations center for S. C. Johnson in Racine, with its Frank Lloyd Wright–designed tower. But the collapse of the domestic auto industry had a powerful impact on the local economy. In 2008, General Motors closed its Janesville plant, laying off 2,500 workers, and in 2010 Chrysler shuttered its Kenosha plant, which once employed 14,000. Things are slowly turning around. The Woodman's food market chain opened a new corporate headquarters in Janesville, while hospitals in the area broke ground for construction and expansion.

> **2008 Presidential Vote**
> Barack Obama (D) 191,901   (51%)
> John McCain (R) 177,162   (47%)
>
> **2004 Presidential Vote**
> George Bush (R) 197,970   (54%)
> John Kerry (D) 170,371   (46%)
>
> **Cook Partisan Voting Index:** R+2

Kenosha, once primarily a factory town, has undergone a bit of a transformation, with some of the old smokestacks and shipyards along its lakefront replaced with museums, a marina, restaurants and boutiques that attract weekending Chicagoans and Chicago-based businesses. Other towns in the area have tried to follow Kenosha's example in offering tax breaks and other enticements to lure Chicago businesses north. Most of this region is becoming metropolitan, part of the almost continuously suburban zone where metro Milwaukee melds into metro Chicago. But there are still some thriving old lake resorts, most notably Lake Geneva, a favorite of wealthy Chicagoans. In nearby Williams Bay is the University of Chicago's historic Yerkes Observatory, long one of the nation's largest astronomy research centers.

This is the 1st Congressional District of Wisconsin. It runs from Lake Michigan west to Janesville in Rock County and encompasses all of Racine and Kenosha counties on Lake Michigan as well as parts of Walworth County, including Lake Geneva. It also takes in the southern Milwaukee County suburbs of Oak Creek and Greenfield and the southern tier of townships in suburban Waukesha County, including New Berlin. Generally, it tilts Republican, and Waukesha and Walworth counties are heavily Republican. In this presidential battleground state, the district voted 54% for Republican George W. Bush in 2004 but broke narrowly for Democrat Barack Obama in 2008, 51%-47%.

Paul Ryan (R)

The congressman from the 1st District is Paul Ryan, a Republican elected in 1998 at age 28. Ryan took over as chairman of the Budget Committee in 2011, and is regarded as an intellectual leader in the GOP for his unrivaled influence on fiscal matters. Many Republicans embraced his controversial blueprint for controlling future spending, while dissatisfied Democrats made clear that its drastic proposal for overhauling Medicare would be among their leading campaign issues for 2012.

Ryan grew up in Janesville, where in 1884 his great-grandfather started a family construction firm, now run by his cousins. His father, a Republican lawyer, and former Democratic Sen. Russ Feingold's father had law offices in the same building, and the two sons were friends in Congress before Feingold's 2010 defeat. Ryan got started in politics early, as a staffer for Republican Sen. Bob Kasten while attending college at Miami University in Ohio. During summers, he was a salesman for Oscar Mayer and can boast that he once drove the company's incomparable Wienermobile. He planned to apply to the University of Chicago and eventually become an economist, but says he "just kept getting really interesting jobs" in politics.

Ryan was hired as a speechwriter for Republican Rep. Jack Kemp of New York and then worked for the think tank Empower America founded by Kemp and conservative pundit William Bennett. He later was legislative director for then-Sen. Sam Brownback, R-Kan. In his days as a poorly paid congressional staffer, Ryan moonlighted as a waiter and a fitness trainer. (His father and grandfather both died of heart attacks in their 50s, making Ryan, the father of three young children, particularly mindful of a healthy diet and an exercise regimen. *Washingtonian* magazine's survey of anonymous congressional staffers in 2010 named him the House's biggest "gym rat.")

In 1998, Ryan returned to the 1st District to run for the House when GOP Rep. Mark Neumann ran for the Senate (Neumann lost to Feingold). Ryan won the Republican primary with 81% of the vote. Democrats nominated Kenosha County official Lydia Spottswood, who had lost to Neumann in 1996. Ryan campaigned against tax increases and in favor of gun ownership rights. This was a strenuously contested election, one of the Democrats' top 10 priorities in the nation that year. Spottswood spent $1.33 million, and Ryan spent $1.24 million. However, the results were not close. Ryan won 57%-43%.

In the House, Ryan has been a loyal conservative, especially since Barack Obama became president. Previously he had a reputation as someone who occasionally bucked his party and took centrist positions on foreign policy and some social issues. In 2007, he voted for a bill to prohibit employment discrimination on the basis of sexual orientation and later said he supported the bill because he had friends "who didn't choose to be gay ... they were just created that way." He said he "took a lot of crap" for the vote from social conservatives. He also voted for the 2008 government bailout of the domestic auto industry, citing mounting hardships in his district because of factory layoffs.

Like his political mentor, the late supply-sider Kemp, Ryan advocates tax cuts to spur economic growth but says his views also have evolved to put equal weight on keeping deficits low and government growth in check. His beliefs drew widespread attention in 2009, when he began warning of future fiscal problems in dire terms. The debt, he told *The Washington Post*, was "completely unsustainable" and would "crash our economy." That year, Ryan helped write the Republicans' alternative to Obama's first budget, along with Republican Study Committee Chairman Mike Pence of Indiana and Minority Whip Eric Cantor of Virginia, a close ally of Ryan's. Ryan and Cantor pushed House Minority Leader John Boehner to include details about how the party would control spending and trim the deficit, but Boehner steered it away from specifics that could be picked apart by Democratic critics. The plan ultimately was panned in the press for lacking detail, and the effort was scrapped.

Undeterred, Ryan in 2010 produced a detailed "roadmap" to economic recovery as an alternative to the majority Democrats' budget, which he said was chock full of "reckless borrowing." His document called for a dramatically simpler tax code of two rates, 10% on annual income up to $100,000 for joint filers and 25% on income above that. Ryan's plan also would: break the link between employment and health insurance by switching from tax incentives for employer-provided insurance plans to tax credits for individual purchases of insurance; transform Medicare for Americans younger than 55 into a voucher system providing an average $11,000 for the purchase of government-approved policies; and allow younger people to invest a third or more of their Social Security savings in personal retirement accounts. While Obama and other leading Democrats said they disagreed with much of Ryan's proposal, the president lauded him for having "serious" ideas. Most of the Republicans who ran for and won House seats in 2010 campaigned on Ryan's message of immediate and bold action on the deficit.

Taking the helm of Budget, Ryan pronounced himself highly disappointed with Obama's fiscal 2012 budget proposal, contending it did little to rein in spending over 10 years. Answering Democratic taunts that Republicans had no detailed response of their own, Ryan promised again to offer an alternative, which was rolled out in April 2011 to much conservative fanfare. Titled "The Path to Prosperity," it called for freezing most domestic spending for five years and repealing the stimulus law in the course of cutting spending more than $6 trillion over 10 years, shrinking federal spending as a percentage of the economy to its lowest level since 1949. It proposed overhauling the tax code, lowering the top tax rates for individuals and corporations from the current 35% to 25%, and reducing the number of individual tax brackets. To raise revenues, it would reduce or eliminate an unspecified number of tax credits, deductions and other tax breaks. It also would repeal several tax increases in the 2010 health care law, such as the 3.8% surtax on higher earners' investment income. Medicaid would be cut by over $700 billion and would be replaced by block grants to the states. Defense spending would not be touched, and the budget itself would not be balanced until 2040.

The most immediately controversial feature of Ryan's budget was its plan for Medicare. Like his earlier "roadmap," individuals who turned 65 before 2022 would continue under the current program, while others would get a government subsidy to buy private insurance. Many Democrats and some economic commentators sharply questioned the disparity, as well as the impact its cuts would have on the poor and middle class. In an April speech, Obama said Ryan's approach would lead to a country that is "fundamentally different than what we've known throughout our history." The House passed the budget in April, with 235 of the chamber's 239 Republicans backing it and every single Democrat opposing it.

The political repercussions became apparent on Ryan's "listening tour" in Wisconsin during a congressional recess. Some audiences jeered him, while polls showed strong majorities of Americans opposed to the Medicare aspects of his budget. Democrats quickly began incorporating such sentiments into their effort to retake control of the House in 2012. Even some Republicans grew uneasy. Former Speaker Newt Gingrich, fresh from announcing his intention to run for president, called the budget "radical" in May and added, " I don't think right-wing social engineering is any more desirable than left-wing social engineering." Ryan responded to a conservative talk-radio host: "Hardly is that (budget) social engineering and radical. What's radical is kicking the can down the road."

Ryan has been the top Republican on Budget since 2007, when he vaulted over 12 more-senior Republicans on the committee. "We lost our brand as the party of fiscal responsibility, and we've got to get it back," Ryan said after his selection. "It's important that we give voters a very clear choice on fiscal policy." In late 2008, Ryan helped to almost derail negotiations on a $700 billion bailout of the financial services industry when he and other fiscal conservatives introduced an alternative plan to the one backed by Treasury Secretary Henry Paulson and Democratic leaders. Eventually, the Democrats included some of his provisions, and he supported the compromise bill. Ryan was once offered the job as President George W. Bush's budget director, in 2005, but turned it down to remain in Congress.

Unlike many of his conservative peers, Ryan refrains from culture war arguments over abortion rights, immigration and other hot-button issues. He backed versions of the DREAM Act giving some children of illegal immigrants a potential path to citizenship. But he refused to support the version that the Democratically-controlled House passed in December 2010, saying it went too far. After the 2008 election, a *Wall Street Journal* editorial called for Ryan to challenge Minority Leader Boehner, arguing that Ryan's "economic knowledge and youthful energy make him the best choice to pull his party in a more promising direction." Some Republican House members encouraged the move as well, but Ryan decided against a challenge.

Ryan is considerably more conservative than the balance of his district. Still, he seems secure in the seat, having cruised to re-election in 2010 with 68% of the vote. As his political stock rose, he was even mentioned as a possible 2012 presidential candidate, but Ryan told a Milwaukee television station in February 2010 he wasn't interested: "My head's not that big, and my kids are too small." An avid sportsman, Ryan enjoys fishing (walleye and muskie) and hunting, particularly bow hunting, and has been known to send emails from his BlackBerry while waiting in the brush for deer to appear.

SECOND DISTRICT

Tammy Baldwin (D)

Elected 1998, 7th term; b. Feb. 11, 1962, Madison; home, Madison; Smith Col., A.B. 1984; U. of WI Law Schl., J.D. 1989; No religious affiliation; Single.

Elected Office: Dane Cnty. Bd. of Supervisors, 1986-94; WI Assembly, 1992-98.

Professional Career: Practicing atty, 1989-92.

DC Office: 2446 RHOB, 20515, 202-225-2906; Fax: 202-225-6942; Web site: tammybaldwin.house.gov.

State Offices: Beloit, 608-362-2800; Madison, 608-258-9800.

Committees: *Energy & Commerce:* Environment & the Economy; Health.

Group Ratings

	ACLU	ACU	ADA	CFG	AFS	FRC	LCV	ITIC	NTU	COC
2010	94	0	100	0	100	0	90	67	6	13
2009	–	0	95	0	100	–	100	–	4	45

National Journal Ratings

	2010 LIB	—	2010 CONS		2009 LIB	—	2009 CONS
Economic	90%	—	0%		91%	—	0%
Social	93%	—	0%		89%	—	0%
Foreign	97%	—	0%		78%	—	17%
Composite	97%	—	3%		90%	—	10%

Key Votes of the 111th Congress

1. Overturn Ledbetter	Y	5. Bar federal abortion funds	N	9. Stop detainee transfers	N
2. Pass $820 billion stimulus	Y	6. Pass health care bill	Y	10. Legalize immigrants' kids	Y
3. Let guns in national parks	N	7. Regulate financial firms	Y	11. Repeal don't ask, tell	Y
4. Pass cap-and-trade	Y	8. Pass tax cuts for some	Y	12. Limit campaign funds	Y

Election Results

2010 general	Tammy Baldwin (D)	191,164	(62%)	($1,197,114)
	Chad Lee (R)	118,099	(38%)	($130,126)
2010 primary	Tammy Baldwin (D)	unopposed		

Prior Winning Percentages: 2008 (69%), 2006 (63%), 2004 (63%), 2002 (66%), 2000 (51%), 1998 (53%)

Population		Race/Ethnicity		Work	
Pop. 2010:	751,169	White:	84.1%	Private:	76.0%
Change since 2000:	Up 12.0%	Black:	4.3%	Government:	18.7%
Urban:	75.6%	Hispanic:	6.1%	Self-employed:	5.1%
Rural:	24.4%	Asian:	3.3%	Blue collar:	19.2%
Area size:	3,602 sq. mi.	Native Am.:	0.3%	White collar:	64.8%
		Hawaiian:	0.0%	Khaki collar:	0.1%
Age		Two+ races:	1.8%	Other:	15.9%
Median age:	35.4 yrs.				
More than 65 yrs:	11.1%	*Ancestry*		Median income:	$56,093
Less than 18 yrs:	21.8%	German	30.5%	Median Home Value:	$209,800
		Irish	10.2%		
Education		Norwegian	9.1%	**Military Veterans**	
H.S. grad:	92.2%			% of Pop:	8.8%
College grad:	35.3%				
Grad degree:	13.7%				

Southern Wisconsin; Madison

On a narrow isthmus between Lakes Mendota and Monona is the center of Madison, and in many ways, the center of Wisconsin. The state Capitol rises at one end of State Street, and at the other end is the main campus of the University of Wisconsin, in a beautiful, park-like setting above Lake Mendota. For most of the 20th century, Wisconsin politics was dominated by the Madison-based La Follettes and their liberal

2008 Presidential Vote		
Barack Obama (D) 286,089	(69%)
John McCain (R) 123,495	(30%)
2004 Presidential Vote		
John Kerry (D) 250,151	(62%)
George Bush (R) 151,024	(37%)
Cook Partisan Voting Index: D+15		

Democratic successors. University faculty were devoted to Robert La Follette's "Wisconsin idea" of an apolitical bureaucracy and to his Wisconsin Tax Commission and workmen's compensation law—both firsts in the nation and conceived of by the former governor and senator. Madison spawned an activist and sometimes violent student movement during the Vietnam War. A graduate student was killed in a laboratory by a bomb set off by a protester. In recent years, the liberal campus opposed the welfare reform and school choice laws enacted while Republican Tommy Thompson was governor, and it was not entirely happy with the centrist policies of his Democratic successor, Jim Doyle. But the city's deep animosity toward new Republican Gov. Scott Walker's proposal to end collective bargaining for most state workers drew substantial attention in 2011.

Madison is the center of Wisconsin's 2nd Congressional District, which is roughly equal parts urban, suburban and rural. It includes surrounding Dane County and dairy and alfalfa country to the north and south, as well several rural dairy counties that have traditionally been Republican. It takes in the birthplace of the Ringling Brothers Circus in Baraboo, and the Swiss-settled town of New Glarus, known statewide for the New Glarus Brewing Company and its Fat Squirrel and Spotted Cow beers. Prairie du Sac, to the north of Madison, is home to the corporate headquarters of the rapidly expanding Culver's fast-food chain, famous for its quintessentially Wisconsin butter burgers, with an optional side of fried cheese curds. The Wisconsin Dells, and its giant water park, has long been a family vacation destination for city dwellers.

Madison remains economically vibrant—its unemployment rate of 5.7% in early 2011 was the 22nd lowest among U.S. cities. Local industry, rooted in the university and the state government, proved to be recession resistant. The growth industries include health care (Madison is home to American Family Insurance) and biotechnology start-ups tied to the university. In the early 1990s, rural Dane County was open to Republicans like Thompson. But even the rural areas have become bluer as Madison-area liberals move to the countryside. The 2nd is now a very Democratic district. John Kerry carried it 62%-37% in 2004, and Barack Obama won it 69%-30% in 2008. In the 2010 governor's race, Democrat Tom Barrett carried Dane County over Walker 68%-31%. People take voting seriously here: In the 2010 election, 2nd District Rep. Tammy Baldwin got more votes (190,000) than any other Democratic House candidate.

Tammy Baldwin (D)

The congresswoman from the 2nd District is Tammy Baldwin, a Democrat elected in 1998 and the first woman to represent Wisconsin in Congress. True to her Madison constituents, she has a strongly liberal voting record, though she prefers to be called a progressive.

Baldwin grew up in Madison, where she was raised by her mother, a University of Wisconsin student when Tammy was born, and her maternal grandparents, a UW biochemist and the theater department's head costume designer. She graduated first in her class at Madison West High School and went on to Smith College and UW law school. In 1986, at age 24 and still in law school, she was elected to the Dane County Board of Supervisors. In 1992, she was elected to the Wisconsin Assembly, winning a heavily Democratic Madison seat. Six years later, when moderate Republican Scott Klug honored his promise to serve only four terms in the U.S. House, Baldwin got into the race, along with three other Democrats and six Republicans. As a woman who favored abortion rights, she was supported by EMILY's List, which helped raise about one-quarter of her $1.5 million campaign chest. As an openly gay woman, Baldwin had enthusiastic support from national gay and lesbian organizations, which also helped her raise money. With 86% of Democratic primary votes cast in Dane County, Baldwin won with 37% of the vote.

Republicans nominated former state Insurance Commissioner Jo Musser. Baldwin roused the enthusiasm of Madison liberals in a way not seen in years. She called for a single-payer health insurance system and suggested that Musser was captive to insurance companies. Musser, a nurse who had founded the Madison Employers Health Care Alliance, argued that a single-payer system would reduce choices and create long waiting periods for elective surgery. Both sides were well financed. Dane County went 57%-42% for Baldwin, and she won the district 53%-47%. Having come out as a lesbian during her college years, Baldwin became the first openly gay non-incumbent to win a seat in the House. (Democrat Barney Frank of Massachusetts, the first openly gay House member, revealed his sexual orientation after serving several terms.) The vast majority of voters, Baldwin has said, care more about her positions on issues that affect their lives than about her sexual orientation.

Baldwin was among those tied for the most liberal member of the House in 2010, according to *National Journal* rankings. She holds a coveted seat on the Energy and Commerce Committee, but with the House in Republican hands, her ability to accomplish many of her goals is limited. She has been sharply critical of many GOP proposals, including fellow Wisconsinite Paul Ryan's controversial budget blueprint and Gov. Scott Walker's equally controversial proposal to limit collective bargaining rights for many state workers. In April 2011, she asked Attorney General Eric Holder to open a federal investigation into voting irregularities in the state Supreme Court election that many regarded as a referendum on Walker's policies.

Baldwin's driving issue is guaranteed health care for all Americans. She sponsored the Health Security for All Americans Act to guarantee universal coverage. She supported the Democrats' 2010 overhaul of the health insurance system even though it dropped a government-run "public option" to compete with private insurers. She said she cast her vote with "hope in the promise of this health care reform bill." With Republican co-sponsors, she introduced a bill to encourage flexibility in how the states cover the uninsured. In 2007, the House passed her bill to expand breast and cervical-cancer screening for poor and uninsured women. Baldwin also has been a leader in urging additional federal support for embryonic stem cell research, some of which has been done at UW. And in 2010, she got a bill through the House aimed at stopping abusive mail, telemarketing, and Internet fraud targeting senior citizens.

Baldwin has been at the forefront of the opposition to a proposed constitutional amendment to bar same-sex marriages. She joined a bipartisan initiative to bar workplace discrimination against gays, reinserting a previously dropped provision in the bill to include transgender people. The provision threatened the bill's passage, and she eventually agreed to drop it. She also sought to broaden the definition of hate crimes to include people targeted because of gender, sexual orientation or disability. In 2008, she and Frank created the House Lesbian, Gay, Bisexual and Transgender Equality Caucus, starting with 52 members and reaching almost 100 in early 2011. Baldwin has faced discrimination, even as a member of Congress. In 2008, the Pentagon initially barred her partner from traveling with her on a military flight to Europe, citing a rule that allowed only congressional spouses on such trips. Baldwin's partner was allowed on the plane only after then-House Speaker Nancy Pelosi intervened. She joined in co-sponsoring a bill in 2011 to allow gay Americans to sponsor their foreign partners for U.S. residency.

An outspoken opponent of the Iraq war, Baldwin was one of only 13 House members to vote against the defense budget for fiscal 2008. She signed on as a cosponsor of Ohio Democrat Dennis Kucinich's 2007 resolution to impeach Vice President Dick Cheney for "deceptive actions leading up to the Iraq war," and other alleged crimes. And she supported Kucinich's failed attempt in March 2010 to withdraw troops from Afghanistan by the end of the year.

In 2000, in her first re-election campaign, Baldwin faced Republican John Sharpless, whose ads in UW newspapers called him "our professor, our congressman, our voice." He accused Baldwin of accomplishing little, ignoring farmers and raising most of her campaign money out of state. Baldwin won by only 51%-49%, a smaller margin than her first House election and a reversal of the usual pattern. Since then, she has secured the seat with victories of 62% or more.

THIRD DISTRICT

Ron Kind (D)

Elected 1996, 8th term; b. March 16, 1963, La Crosse; home, La Crosse; Harvard U., B.A. 1985, London Schl. of Econ., 1986, U. of MN, J.D. 1990; Lutheran; married (Tawni); 2 children.

Professional Career: Practicing atty., 1990–92; Asst. st. prosecutor, La Crosse Cnty., 1992–96.

DC Office: 1406 LHOB, 20515, 202-225-5506; Fax: 202-225-5739; Web site: kind.house.gov.

State Offices: Eau Claire, 715-831-9214; La Crosse, 608-782-2558.

Committees: *Ways & Means:* Health; Oversight.

Group Ratings

	ACLU	ACU	ADA	CFG	AFS	FRC	LCV	ITIC	NTU	COC
2010	88	4	95	6	100	6	90	67	7	13
2009	–	8	90	19	89	–	100	–	16	47

National Journal Ratings

	2010 LIB — 2010 CONS		2009 LIB — 2009 CONS	
Economic	60%	— 40%	49%	— 50%
Social	54%	— 42%	67%	— 31%
Foreign	56%	— 38%	78%	— 17%
Composite	58%	— 42%	66%	— 34%

Key Votes of the 111th Congress

1. Overturn Ledbetter	Y	5. Bar federal abortion funds	N	9. Stop detainee transfers	Y
2. Pass $820 billion stimulus	Y	6. Pass health care bill	Y	10. Legalize immigrants' kids	Y
3. Let guns in national parks	Y	7. Regulate financial firms	Y	11. Repeal don't ask, tell	Y
4. Pass cap-and-trade	Y	8. Pass tax cuts for some	Y	12. Limit campaign funds	Y

Election Results

2010 general	Ron Kind (D)	126,380	(50%)	($1,857,853)
	Dan Kapanke (R)	116,838	(46%)	($1,034,222)
	Michael Krsiean (I)	8,001	(3%)	
2010 primary	Ron Kind (D)	unopposed		

Prior Winning Percentages: 2008 (63%), 2006 (65%), 2004 (56%), 2002 (63%), 2000 (64%), 1998 (71%), 1996 (52%)

Population		Race/Ethnicity		Work	
Pop. 2010:	729,957	White:	93.8%	Private:	77.6%
Change since 2000:	Up 8.9%	Black:	0.8%	Government:	13.9%
Urban:	43.1%	Hispanic:	2.0%	Self-employed:	8.2%
Rural:	56.9%	Asian:	1.6%	Blue collar:	27.0%
Area size:	13,849 sq. mi.	Native Am.:	0.6%	White collar:	54.5%
		Hawaiian:	0.0%	Khaki collar:	0.1%
Age		Two+ races:	1.0%	Other:	18.4%
Median age:	37.4 yrs.				
More than 65 yrs:	13.6%	*Ancestry*		Median income:	$49,436
Less than 18 yrs:	22.8%	German	33.1%	Median Home Value:	$152,100
		Norwegian	13.4%		
Education		Irish	9.5%	**Military Veterans**	
H.S. grad:	90.3%			% of Pop:	10.5%
College grad:	22.7%				
Grad degree:	7.2%				

West Wisconsin; Eau Claire

On the rolling land of western Wisconsin, in the knobby hills just east of the Mississippi River, is some of the most beautiful river landscape in the country. This is where author Laura Ingalls Wilder's family built their little house in the big woods in the 1870s, before the first railroad came steaming up the narrow floodplain alongside the Mississippi River. Today, it is hard to imagine the big woods. The trees have long since been cut down, and the hillsides are covered with grass

2008 Presidential Vote		
Barack Obama (D) 213,211	(58%)
John McCain (R) 150,618	(41%)
2004 Presidential Vote		
John Kerry (D) 192,297	(51%)
George Bush (R) 178,367	(48%)
Cook Partisan Voting Index: D+4		

grazed by placid dairy cattle. Where the pioneers tried to scratch out diversified crops, later generations of farmers created America's premier dairy region, producing milk, butter and especially cheese. Some Amish communities from Pennsylvania have relocated here in recent years because land is cheaper. But since 1980, the area has been in flux. Numerous dairy farmers have gone out of business. Cows have become more productive, and demand for milk has decreased. Wisconsin has also had trouble competing against the European Economic Community's subsidized cheese and butter, and more recently, with products from California's large-scale agribusiness. Meanwhile, other businesses have thrived. Dodgeville, in Iowa County (which is not on the Iowa border), is the headquarters of Lands' End, the catalog retailer. In the 1980s, many communities here lost population, but there has been some growth since then. In commuter-oriented St. Croix County, part of the Minneapolis-St. Paul metro area, the population rose by almost one-third from 2000 to 2009, to more than 83,000. Eau Claire County's population also grew briskly.

The 3rd Congressional District of Wisconsin follows the Mississippi from the border with Illinois north to St. Croix County, just east of St. Paul, covering the western edge of the state. The district's two largest cities are Eau Claire, home to home-improvement giant Menards and ranked by *Money* magazine as the nation's 69th best small city in 2010, and La Crosse, which also has won recognition for its livability. This is the nation's No. 3 dairy district, with 5,000 dairy farms, but it is very different in character from the No. 1 district, California's 21st, which has more dairy cows concentrated on just 340 farms. The 3rd Congressional District is the top recipient of federal dairy subsidies, according to the Environmental Working Group. It was settled largely by German and Scandinavian immigrants, and it once consistently voted for Wisconsin's La Follette Progressives. More recently, the district has leaned Democratic. Western Wisconsin was the one segment of rural America where Democratic presidential nominees Al Gore and John Kerry ran even with historic Democratic percentages, which was vital to the narrow victory that each won in this state. The district produced solid victories for Democratic Gov. Jim Doyle in 2002 and 2006 and Sen. Russ Feingold in 2004. In 2008, Barack Obama carried the district 58%-41%, winning in every county except St. Croix.

Ron Kind (D)

The congressman from the 3rd District is Ron Kind, a Democrat elected in 1996. He is a moderate who focuses on health and agriculture issues from his perch on the Ways and Means Committee.

Kind grew up in a large family in La Crosse, the son of a telephone repairman and a secretary in the local schools. He went to Harvard University on a scholarship and played quarterback. He worked as a summer intern for Democratic Sen. William Proxmire, doing research for Proxmire's Golden Fleece awards pointing out wasteful government spending. Kind attended the London School of Economics and the University of Minnesota's law school, practiced law in a large firm in Milwaukee, and then returned home to La Crosse to work as an assistant prosecutor on rape and sexual abuse cases.

Kind started running for Congress soon after moderate Republican Steve Gunderson announced in 1994 that he would not seek re-election. Former state Sen. Jim Harsdorf won the Republican primary and made a case for a balanced budget and for Republican Gov. Tommy Thompson's "Wisconsin Works" welfare reform program. Kind presented his own balanced budget proposal and urged reform of the campaign finance system. Kind won, 52%-48%.

In the House, Kind is the vice chairman of the business-oriented New Democrat Coalition. He formerly co-chaired the Congressional Sportsmen's Caucus of pro-conservation hunters, and received the National Rifle Association's endorsement in 2010. He refused to support liberal Democrat Nancy Pelosi in her bid for minority leader in January 2011, casting his vote for Tennessee Democrat Jim Cooper, another moderate. Kind complained to the *Milwaukee Journal Sentinel* in

November 2010 that his party, in losing its majority, failed to retain many of the districts between the Appalachian Mountains and the Rockies, "yet we have a leadership that is East Coast, West Coast."

With dairy farming prominent in his district, Kind is vitally interested in issues affecting farmers. In 2007, he joined with conservative deficit hawks and suburban and urban Democrats in an attempt to add provisions to the farm bill that would have changed federal policy for agricultural subsidies and provided more funds for land conservation and school nutrition. "For too long, we've had large taxpayer subsidies going to a few very large farming entities to the disadvantage of family farmers," Kind said. "It ultimately distorts the marketplace and distorts trade policy, which also hurts agriculture." Kind won 200 votes for similar provisions in the 2002 farm bill, but this time around, the Democratic leadership was worried about angering farmers' groups in rural swing districts and refused to allow a vote by the full House. The plan died in committee. Kind voted against the final version of the farm bill, calling it a "nightmare." He said that congressional negotiators "managed to avoid every opportunity to reform wasteful, outdated subsidies while piling on additional layers of unnecessary spending."

Despite the farm subsidies that flow to the district, he said that the vast majority of producers he represents don't get huge agriculture subsidies because they're not large agribusinesses. When President Barack Obama unveiled a plan in April 2009 to save nearly $10 billion by putting strict limits on subsidies, Kind worked with the White House to revamp the measure. On Ways and Means, he also has championed tax credits aimed at encouraging farmers to control animal waste while producing renewable biogas energy. He has encouraged the development of alternative crops such as wheat and soybeans for farmers in Afghanistan, saying it could help create a stable society there.

Kind got an early start on the health care overhaul debate in 2009, co-sponsoring a bill to put greater emphasis on quality and coordination of care in reimbursing health care providers. He was dissatisfied with the version that passed Ways and Means the next month and was one of three Democrats who joined committee Republicans in opposing it. But after a series of lengthy meetings that he and others held with Pelosi on containing the spiraling costs of Medicare, he pronounced himself satisfied with the legislation. He ultimately succeeded in getting $800 million in immediate payments for doctors and hospitals as well as a commitment for a value-based system for paying providers, and backed the version that became law.

In 2004, Kind had his first credible challenger, Republican state Sen. Dale Schultz, a moderate in the Wisconsin legislature for more than two decades. Schultz ran with an unlikely Republican theme, criticizing Kind as a free trader who had sent jobs overseas. Kind affirmed his support for trade agreements, but he criticized the Bush administration for failing to enforce their labor and environmental protection terms. Kind won, 56%-43%, and two years later did even better, attaining 65% of the vote.

He passed on the opportunity to run for governor in 2010, saying he wanted to focus on passing health care legislation. But that year, another serious challenger emerged for his House seat, Dan Kapanke, a Republican state senator who lambasted Kind for his support of the health care bill and Obama's economic agenda. Less than a week before the election, Wisconsin Republicans alleged that a Kind staffer asked for campaign contributions in 2007 to arrange a meeting between the congressman and a group of doctors. Kind called the charge "blatant lies" and questioned the timing of the complaint. He survived with a 50.3%-46.5% win.

FOURTH DISTRICT

Gwen Moore (D)

Elected 2004, 4th term; b. April 18, 1951, Racine; home, Milwaukee; Marquette U., B.A. 1978; Baptist; single; 3 children.

Elected Office: WI Assembly, 1989-92; WI Senate, 1992-2004; Senate pres. pro tem, 1997-98.

Professional Career: Housing and urban dev. specialist, 1985-89.

DC Office: 2245 RHOB, 20515, 202-225-4572; Fax: 202-225-8135; Web site: gwenmoore.house.gov.

State Offices: Milwaukee, 414-297-1140.

Committees: *Budget. Financial Services:* Capital Markets and Government Sponsored Enterprises; International Monetary Policy & Trade.

Group Ratings

	ACLU	ACU	ADA	CFG	AFS	FRC	LCV	ITIC	NTU	COC
2010	93	0	100	7	88	6	100	67	8	13
2009	–	0	100	0	100	–	93	–	2	33

National Journal Ratings

	2010 LIB — 2010 CONS		2009 LIB — 2009 CONS	
Economic	65%	— 35%	91%	— 0%
Social	80%	— 18%	89%	— 0%
Foreign	78%	— 17%	91%	— 0%
Composite	76%	— 25%	95%	— 5%

Key Votes of the 111th Congress

1. Overturn Ledbetter	*	5. Bar federal abortion funds	N
2. Pass $820 billion stimulus	Y	6. Pass health care bill	Y
3. Let guns in national parks	N	7. Regulate financial firms	Y
4. Pass cap-and-trade	Y	8. Pass tax cuts for some	N

9. Stop detainee transfers	N
10. Legalize immigrants' kids	Y
11. Repeal don't ask, tell	Y
12. Limit campaign funds	Y

Election Results

2010 general	Gwen Moore (D)	143,559	(69%)	($603,253)
	Dan Sebring (R)	61,543	(30%)	($45,607)
2010 primary	Gwen Moore (D)	33,107	(84%)	
	Paul Morel (D)	6,430	(16%)	

Prior Winning Percentages: 2008 (88%), 2006 (71%), 2004 (70%)

Population		Race/Ethnicity		Work	
Pop. 2010:	669,015	White:	41.9%	Private:	84.2%
Change since 2000:	Down 0.2%	Black:	35.2%	Government:	12.3%
Urban:	100.0%	Hispanic:	16.7%	Self-employed:	3.4%
Rural:	0.0%	Asian:	3.2%	Blue collar:	24.3%
Area size:	113 sq. mi.	Native Am.:	0.6%	White collar:	54.0%
		Hawaiian:	0.0%	Khaki collar:	0.0%
Age		Two+ races:	2.2%	Other:	21.7%
Median age:	31.5 yrs.				
More than 65 yrs:	9.8%	*Ancestry*		Median income:	$37,500
Less than 18 yrs:	26.4%	German	19.1%	Median Home Value:	$148,300
		Polish	8.2%		
Education		Irish	6.0%	**Military Veterans**	
H.S. grad:	81.4%			% of Pop:	7.6%
College grad:	21.4%				
Grad degree:	7.0%				

Milwaukee

Milwaukee is America's most German city, with an ethnic heritage noticeable not just in the names of its beers and its old German restaurants, but in the sturdiness of its houses and the orderliness of its streets. Until World War I made this German character seem un-American, German was spoken on the streets and read in city newspapers; German beer was produced in dozens of breweries; and German cultural tra-

2008 Presidential Vote		
Barack Obama (D) 234,468	(75%)
John McCain (R) 73,447	(24%)
2004 Presidential Vote		
John Kerry (D) 219,636	(70%)
George Bush (R) 94,090	(30%)
Cook Partisan Voting Index: D+22		

ditions lived on in churches, union halls and parlors. The world's largest four-sided clock, nearly twice the size of London's Big Ben, rises above the Allen-Bradley factory, looking out over the industrial city. It is an apt symbol, a piece of precision engineering in this high-skill manufacturing town, with its skyline of smokestacks and church steeples—the closest thing in America to the German factory cities Milwaukee's early immigrants once knew well. The city has led the nation in beer brewing, industrial control equipment, mining gear, cranes and independent foundries. Harley-Davidson began manufacturing on the West Side a century ago. The city had large and efficiently run factories that paid good wages to highly-skilled and well-disciplined workers.

But like other Rust Belt cities, Milwaukee has lost its share of plants over the past three decades. It hemorrhaged population in the 1990s, though it has finally stopped shrinking, thanks in part to a rapidly expanding Hispanic population. For the most part, the city has embraced Latinos. A chorizo sausage now competes against the bratwurst, Polish sausage and Italian sausage mascots during the famous Sausage Race at Milwaukee Brewers baseball games, and plush chorizo dolls outsell the other mascots at stadium stores. Many Hispanics have settled in the old immigrant neighborhoods of the city's south side. The west side and north side are home to many of the city's African-American neighborhoods, such as Sherman Park and Bronzeville. Some of those areas are struggling against an unemployment rate that for black men shot to 53% in Milwaukee in 2009—a level second only to Detroit's, according to a 2010 University of Wisconsin-Milwaukee study.

The 4th District of Wisconsin covers the entire city of Milwaukee and a few of its working-class suburbs—St. Francis, Cudahy and South Milwaukee on Lake Michigan, West Milwaukee, and part of West Allis. Blacks make up 35% of the population, while Hispanics comprise another 17%. It is easily Wisconsin's most Democratic district, with Barack Obama getting 75% of the vote here in 2008. In the 2010 governor's race, the city's Democratic mayor, Tom Barrett, carried Milwaukee County 62%-38% over Republican Milwaukee County Executive Scott Walker, who won.

Gwen Moore (D)

The congresswoman from the 4th District is Gwen Moore, a Democrat elected in 2004 and Wisconsin's first African-American member of Congress. Moore was born in Racine, the eighth of nine children, and raised on the north side of Milwaukee. As an 18-year-old college freshman, she became a single mother who relied on welfare to help support her daughter. She graduated from Marquette University and worked as a housing and urban development specialist. Moore said she got active in politics when a rent-to-own center repossessed her washer and dryer even though she had paid three times their value in exorbitant interest rates. She led an effort to establish a community credit union. She was elected to the state Assembly in 1988 and to the state Senate in 1992, making her the state's first black woman senator. In winning re-election in 1990, she beat Republican Scott Walker, who later became Wisconsin's governor.

In 2003, when 4th District Democrat Gerald Kleczka announced that he was retiring after 20 years, Moore was the front-runner, but she had serious competition in the September 2004 Democratic primary from two political veterans, state Sen. Tim Carpenter and former state party Chairman Matt Flynn, both white. The candidates agreed on most issues: All three supported abortion rights, focused on jobs and economic concerns, and called for eliminating the Bush administration's tax cuts for people with incomes exceeding $200,000 a year. In the absence of significant ideological clashes, the fallout from Milwaukee's mayoral primary earlier that year played a role. The nonpartisan election had pitted former Rep. Tom Barrett, who is white, against acting Mayor Marvin Pratt, vying to become the city's first black elected mayor. Barrett won, but the vote was split along racial lines and caused hard feelings in the black community.

Moore took advantage of the energized black voter base, and she leveraged financial support from national women's organizations, teachers' unions and other liberal groups. Flynn was endorsed by Kleczka, and boasted that he had backed Pratt for mayor. But he was damaged politically by his work as general counsel for the local Roman Catholic archdiocese in a priest sex abuse scandal. Carpenter was the only openly gay member of the Senate and had the support of national gay rights groups. Moore won 64% of the vote to 25% for Flynn and 10% for Carpenter. Flynn won the five aldermanic districts and 49% of the vote on the south side, but Moore won about 80% of the vote north of Interstate 94. In the general election, Republican Gerald Boyle tried to win over Democrats disaffected with Moore. But he got no support from the national party and Moore won easily, 70%-28%.

Moore has a solidly liberal voting record and often is passionate in her criticism of Republicans. At a 2010 campaign rally, she poured what she said represented "lies" from a Thermos into a glass of "poison tea" marked with a skull, and invoked the 1978 Jonestown mass suicide in condemning tea party activism. "Remember the Kool-Aid? This tea is just as lethal," she said, according to the *Wisconsin State Journal*. When her onetime political opponent, Walker, reportedly considered turning down federal education funding in February 2011, Moore accused him of "channeling Sarah Palin." And when House Republicans sought that month to de-fund Planned Parenthood during the fiscal 2011 budget debate, Moore drew on her own unwelcome experience of an unplanned pregnancy at age 18. "I just want to tell you a little bit about what it's like to not have Planned Parenthood," she said on the House floor. "You have to add water to the (baby) formula to make it stretch. You have to give your kids Ramen noodles at the end of the month to fill up their little bellies so they won't cry. You have to give them mayonnaise sandwiches."

Much of the legislation she has introduced has dealt with helping the poor through expanding school lunch funding, cracking down on foreclosure fraud and providing grants to crime-ravaged communities. In 2005, the House incorporated provisions of her SHIELD Act into the reauthorization of the Violence Against Women Act that would protect the identity of domestic-violence victims who receive homeless assistance.

Moore has developed an interest in foreign relations and defense. She was one of only five House members to vote against a resolution expressing congressional support for Israel during its 2008 military actions in the Gaza Strip. She called Israel a "strong ally," but expressed concern about civilian Palestinian deaths and called for renewed diplomatic efforts in the region. She has been an ardent supporter of Liberia, the African nation founded by freed slaves, and added a provision to a spending bill in 2007 to speed up delivery of foreign aid to the country.

Moore, who said she is learning Spanish to help her reach out to the Hispanic population on Milwaukee's south side, is well-established in her district and was re-elected with 69% of the vote in 2010.

FIFTH DISTRICT

Jim Sensenbrenner (R)

Elected 1978, 17th term; b. June 14, 1943, Chicago, IL; home, Menomonee Falls; Stanford U., A.B. 1965, U. of WI, J.D. 1968; Episcopalian; married (Cheryl); 2 children.

Elected Office: WI Assembly, 1968–74; WI Senate, 1974–78.

Professional Career: Practicing atty., 1968–69; Staff asst., U.S. Rep. Arthur Younger, 1965.

DC Office: 2449 RHOB, 20515, 202-225-5101; Fax: 202-225-3190; Web site: sensenbrenner.house.gov.

State Offices: Brookfield, 262-784-1111.

Committees: *Judiciary:* Crime, Terrorism & Homeland Security (Chmn); Intellectual Property, Competition & the Internet. *Science, Space & Technology (VChmn):* Investigations & Oversight; Space & Aeronautics.

Group Ratings

	ACLU	ACU	ADA	CFG	AFS	FRC	LCV	ITIC	NTU	COC
2010	6	100	0	86	0	100	0	33	92	88
2009	–	100	0	95	11	–	7	–	95	73

National Journal Ratings

	2010 LIB — 2010 CONS		2009 LIB — 2009 CONS	
Economic	0% —	97%	4% —	95%
Social	0% —	85%	7% —	90%
Foreign	33% —	65%	33% —	67%
Composite	14% —	86%	15% —	85%

Key Votes of the 111th Congress

1. Overturn Ledbetter	N	5. Bar federal abortion funds	Y	9. Stop detainee transfers	Y
2. Pass $820 billion stimulus	N	6. Pass health care bill	N	10. Legalize immigrants' kids	N
3. Let guns in national parks	Y	7. Regulate financial firms	N	11. Repeal don't ask, tell	N
4. Pass cap-and-trade	N	8. Pass tax cuts for some	N	12. Limit campaign funds	N

Election Results

2010 general	Jim Sensenbrenner (R)	229,642	(69%)	($419,147)
	Todd Kolosso (D)	90,634	(27%)	($175,545)
	Robert Raymond (I)	10,813	(3%)	
2010 primary	Jim Sensenbrenner (R)	unopposed		

Prior Winning Percentages: 2008 (80%), 2006 (62%), 2004 (67%), 2002 (87%), 2000 (74%), 1998 (91%), 1996 (74%), 1994 (100%), 1992 (70%), 1990 (100%), 1988 (75%), 1986 (78%), 1984 (73%), 1982 (100%), 1980 (78%), 1978 (61%)

Population		Race/Ethnicity		Work	
Pop. 2010:	707,580	White:	89.9%	Private:	86.3%
Change since 2000:	Up 5.5%	Black:	2.3%	Government:	8.6%
Urban:	84.9%	Hispanic:	3.8%	Self-employed:	4.9%
Rural:	15.1%	Asian:	2.5%	Blue collar:	18.9%
Area size:	1,302 sq. mi.	Native Am.:	0.3%	White collar:	69.2%
		Hawaiian:	0.0%	Khaki collar:	0.1%
Age		Two+ races:	1.2%	Other:	11.9%
Median age:	41.2 yrs.				
More than 65 yrs:	14.7%	*Ancestry*		Median income:	$68,107
Less than 18 yrs:	23.5%	German	36.4%	Median Home Value:	$245,500
		Irish	10.1%		
Education		Polish	8.5%	**Military Veterans**	
H.S. grad:	94.3%			% of Pop:	9.8%
College grad:	38.9%				
Grad degree:	13.9%				

Milwaukee Suburbs; Waukesha

For decades, the orderly, heavily German-American factory city of Milwaukee has been spreading slowly, mostly west and north, into Wisconsin dairy country. There are high-income enclaves here, such as close-in Elm Grove and exurban Oconomowoc, halfway to Madison and tucked in around numerous lakes. There is office development in Brookfield, and subdivisions have spread to Mequon, Menomonee Falls and farther, reaching small towns with roots in the

2008 Presidential Vote		
John McCain (R) 243,597	(58%)
Barack Obama (D) 174,174	(41%)
2004 Presidential Vote		
George Bush (R) 265,537	(63%)
John Kerry (D) 151,968	(36%)
Cook Partisan Voting Index: R+12		

19th century. This is comfortable but not fancy territory, and the economy is still based heavily on skilled manufacturing. It felt the effects of the recession, but less than other areas. About 8.5% of Brookfield's retail space was unoccupied in January 2011, five points below the national average. Not far from Milwaukee are Port Washington, with Allen Edmonds shoes; West Bend, with West Bend kitchen appliances; and Pewaukee, with Harken sailboat hardware. Closer to Milwaukee are tonier, liberal suburbs along Lake Michigan, many with sizeable Jewish populations—Shorewood, Whitefish Bay, and Fox Point. Shorewood was the base of a 2011 recall campaign of a Republican state senator criticized for supporting Gov. Scott Walker's agenda.

The 5th Congressional District of Wisconsin includes most of the western, northwestern and northern suburbs of Milwaukee. Among them are the close-in lakefront suburbs in Milwaukee County and the suburbs in Ozaukee County north of Milwaukee and in Washington County to the west. It also takes in most of the Milwaukee County suburbs of Wauwatosa and West Allis, most of the northern three tiers of townships in Waukesha County just to the west, and a part of Jefferson County farther west. This is by far the most Republican district in the state, exemplified by Ozaukee County's response to Milwaukee Area Technical College's decision to endorse a boycott of Arizona after the state passed the nation's most stringent immigration law in 2010. The county supervisors voted to apologize to any Arizonans who were upset by the college's action. The district voted 62% and 63% for George W. Bush in 2000 and 2004, respectively. And it voted 58% for GOP nominee John McCain in 2008. It was the only district in Wisconsin that he carried. People here habitually turn out in large numbers for elections, and the district cast more Republican votes in 2010 than in any House race in the country—almost 230,000.

Jim Sensenbrenner (R)

The congressman from the 5th District is Jim Sensenbrenner, a Republican first elected in 1978. His prickly personality can rankle liberals, but he has racked up a number of legislative accomplishments.

Sensenbrenner grew up in the Milwaukee area, with strong Wisconsin roots. His great-grandfather was a founder of Kimberly-Clark, which invented the sanitary napkin, and Sensenbrenner is an heir to the paper and cellulose fortune. He reports a net worth of more than $14 million, and on top of that, he won $250,000 in the District of Columbia lottery after buying two tickets while picking up some beer for an office party at a Capitol Hill liquor store. He graduated from Stanford University and the University of Wisconsin Law School and has spent most of his adult life in politics. He served briefly as a staffer in the U.S. House, and then was elected to the Wisconsin Assembly in 1968 and to the Wisconsin Senate in 1974. When Republican Rep. Bob Kasten ran for governor, Sensenbrenner ran in this district and won the Republican primary by 589 votes.

Sensenbrenner has a rough and often partisan edge, which does not always wear well with his colleagues. Fellow Republican Dan Lungren of California told *The New York Times* in 2006 that Sensenbrenner "treats us all like dogs." But it has endeared him to conservatives—the right-wing magazine *Human Events* named him as its man of the year in 2006. And his legislative skills have won him respect on Capitol Hill. He has long been a stickler on ethics and was one of the first to urge that Congress apply to itself the same laws it imposes on the rest of the country. A former chairman of the Judiciary Committee, Sensenbrenner now heads the panel's Crime, Terrorism and Homeland Security Subcommittee.

When he chaired Judiciary in 2001, Sensenbrenner was instrumental in passing the first congressional authorization of the Department of Justice in many years, citing the vital role that it gave his committee in improving oversight of the department. "I am a hawk on oversight," he said. "I don't back down because the president is in my party." The watchdog group Citizens for Responsibility and Ethics in Washington criticized him, however, after the BP oil spill disaster in

2010 in the Gulf of Mexico. Sensenbrenner owned more than 3,600 shares of the company's stock, but did not recuse himself from an investigation into the company or votes relating to it. He was not required to do so under House rules, but the group said his involvement created an appearance of impropriety. He also has come under criticism for taking foreign trips financed by outside groups. The *Milwaukee Journal Sentinel* reported in 2009 that he had visited Liechtenstein five times since 2004.

Sensenbrenner is best known for his work on Judiciary after the September 11 attacks. He pressed for a thorough congressional review of Attorney General John Ashcroft's proposal for beefed-up investigative powers for law enforcement. Concerned about possible violations of civil liberties, he insisted on a sunset provision for the USA PATRIOT Act, the anti-terrorism law passed just after the attacks on New York and Washington, ensuring it would expire in four years and give Congress a chance to study its impact. By 2005, he decided that his concerns about civil liberties had been addressed and pushed to make most of the law permanent. Some questionable parliamentary maneuvering during one of his hearings on renewal of the act led Democrats to file an unusual resolution condemning Sensenbrenner for alleged abuse of power. The House rejected the resolution on a party-line vote, and Sensenbrenner refused demands for an apology.

After a difficult conference committee with the Senate, he won an extension of the PATRIOT Act for the Bush administration. But Sensenbrenner had differences with Attorney General Alberto Gonzales over the scope of the domestic surveillance program and demanded steps to protect "the freedoms we cherish." Sensenbrenner pushed in 2011 for a six-year extension of the act, as well as a permanent extension of its so-called "lone wolf" provision allowing the government to monitor terrorists even if they are not suspected of ties to a specific group.

Sensenbrenner worked steadily for years to pass some major bills. One of them was the bankruptcy bill, which passed in 2005 after being held up for years by a Democratic provision preventing abortion protesters from filing for bankruptcy to avoid fines and damages in attacks on abortion clinics. Sensenbrenner has backed limitations in tort law on class action, medical malpractice, and asbestos liability, and has sought to increase penalties for frivolous lawsuits. But he has not always followed the party line. In 2003, he said he saw no need to amend the Constitution to ban same-sex marriages. In 2004, after the Massachusetts Supreme Judicial Court ruled that such marriages were allowed by the state's constitution, the Republican leadership bypassed the committee and brought their amendment to the floor directly, but it fell well short of the required two-thirds majority.

Another of Sensenbrenner's focused efforts was on immigration. In 2004, he successfully added to the intelligence reorganization bill provisions setting national standards for driver's licenses. They denied licenses to illegal immigrants, prohibited the use of Mexican *matricula consular* cards for identification, tightened standards for asylum, and overrode state laws and regulations blocking border barriers. When Sensenbrenner objected to the conference report with the Senate, GOP Speaker Dennis Hastert promised that the immigration provisions would come to the floor in 2005. That year, the House approved Sensenbrenner's immigration bill 261-161, and it became law.

The House Republicans' six-year term limit for senior committee members forced Sensenbrenner to give up the Judiciary gavel in January 2007. In March, Minority Leader John Boehner named Sensenbrenner the ranking Republican on the Select Committee on Energy Independence and Global Warming. A global warming skeptic, Sensenbrenner had voted against the creation of the panel, saying it was nothing more than a publicity stunt, but he promised to participate in the debate. In 2008, he sponsored a bill to bolster research and development of hybrid-fuel utility and delivery trucks. He protested when Republicans abolished the committee—which he would have chaired—in late 2010, saying the panel was still needed as a check on the Obama administration. He continues to attack climate science as vice chairman of the Science, Space and Technology Committee, which he also chaired in the late 1990s.

Sensenbrenner has been re-elected easily every two years. In 2008, he faced an odd "tag-team" when two political science professors decided to run against him, one in the Republican primary and one in the general election as a Democrat. The two planned to make joint appearances, share a campaign website and even share fundraising, but the Democrat backed out of the race. Sensenbrenner easily won both contests. In 2009, he announced his re-election at the same time he made it known that he had prostate cancer. He prided himself on not missing votes, scheduling his cancer treatments around the House schedule, and holding more than 200 town meetings in 2009 and 2010. He cruised to a 69%-27% victory.

SIXTH DISTRICT

Tom Petri (R)

Elected April 1979, 16th full term; b. May 28, 1940, Marinette; home, Fond du Lac; Harvard U., B.A. 1962, J.D. 1965; Lutheran; married (Anne); 1 child.

Elected Office: WI Senate, 1972–79.

Professional Career: Peace Corps, Somalia, 1966–67; Law clerk, Fed. Judge James Doyle, 1965–66; White House aide, 1969; Practicing atty., 1970–79.

DC Office: 2462 RHOB, 20515, 202-225-2476; Fax: 202-225-2356; Web site: petri.house.gov.

State Offices: Fond du Lac, 920-922-1180; Oshkosh, 920-231-6333.

Committees: *Education & the Workforce:* Early Childhood, Elementary & Secondary Education; Higher Education & Workforce Training. *Transportation & Infrastructure:* Aviation (Chmn); Highways & Transit.

Group Ratings

	ACLU	ACU	ADA	CFG	AFS	FRC	LCV	ITIC	NTU	COC
2010	13	88	10	69	13	100	20	33	86	88
2009	–	92	10	84	33	–	36	–	80	80

National Journal Ratings

	2010 LIB	—	2010 CONS	2009 LIB	—	2009 CONS
Economic	30%	—	69%	35%	—	65%
Social	0%	—	85%	24%	—	73%
Foreign	29%	—	68%	33%	—	67%
Composite	23%	—	77%	31%	—	69%

Key Votes of the 111th Congress

1. Overturn Ledbetter	N	5. Bar federal abortion funds	Y	9. Stop detainee transfers	Y
2. Pass $820 billion stimulus	N	6. Pass health care bill	N	10. Legalize immigrants' kids	N
3. Let guns in national parks	Y	7. Regulate financial firms	N	11. Repeal don't ask, tell	N
4. Pass cap-and-trade	N	8. Pass tax cuts for some	N	12. Limit campaign funds	N

Election Results

2010 general	Tom Petri (R)	183,271	(71%)	($737,019)
	Joseph Kallas (D)	75,926	(29%)	($6,941)
2010 primary	Tom Petri (R) .... unopposed			

Prior Winning Percentages: 2008 (64%), 2006 (100%), 2004 (67%), 2002 (100%), 2000 (65%), 1998 (93%), 1996 (73%), 1994 (100%), 1992 (53%), 1990 (100%), 1988 (74%), 1986 (97%), 1984 (76%), 1982 (65%), 1980 (59%), 1979 special (50%)

Population		Race/Ethnicity		Work	
Pop. 2010:	705,102	White:	91.1%	Private:	84.1%
Change since 2000:	Up 5.2%	Black:	1.4%	Government:	10.1%
Urban:	60.7%	Hispanic:	4.0%	Self-employed:	5.6%
Rural:	39.3%	Asian:	1.9%	Blue collar:	31.2%
Area size:	5,816 sq. mi.	Native Am.:	0.4%	White collar:	50.5%
		Hawaiian:	0.0%	Khaki collar:	0.0%
Age		Two+ races:	1.0%	Other:	18.2%
Median age:	39.9 yrs.				
More than 65 yrs:	14.4%	*Ancestry*		Median income:	$50,592
Less than 18 yrs:	22.4%	German	42.0%	Median Home Value:	$146,300
		Irish	7.6%		
Education		Polish	6.0%	**Military Veterans**	
H.S. grad:	88.8%			% of Pop:	11.1%
College grad:	19.4%				
Grad degree:	5.7%				

East Central Wisconsin; Oshkosh

Central Wisconsin is solid country, a producer of basic commodities—milk, butter and cheese, Kleenex, Mercury Marine outboard motors, and military trucks. This is where the rolling hills and prairies of southern Wisconsin begin to give way to the pine and hardwood forests and glacial lakes of the Northwoods. Settled first by Yankee Protestants, it was one of the birthplaces of the Republican Party in February 1854, when a group of Whigs, Free Soilers and Democrats met

2008 Presidential Vote		
Barack Obama (D) 181,198	(50%)
John McCain (R) 176,871	(49%)

2004 Presidential Vote		
George Bush (R) 208,931	(56%)
John Kerry (D) 157,212	(43%)

Cook Partisan Voting Index: R+4

in a small white schoolhouse in Ripon, Wis., and proclaimed themselves Republicans. (A similar gathering took place in Jackson, Mich., which also claims to be the birthplace of the party.) The party grew rapidly, winning a near majority in the U.S. House in that year's elections. The 1850s brought the first surge of German migration into the United States, and central Wisconsin was a favorite destination. They built the dairy farms and factory towns that seemed steadfastly prosperous, and they developed a manufacturing economy. The German influence is still felt. Sheboygan is the Bratwurst Capital of the World, though these days the city and surrounding county also are home to more than 4,700 Asians, mostly Hmong, and 5,600 Hispanics. Fond du Lac County was the testing ground for former Republican Gov. Tommy Thompson's welfare-reform program. The county's welfare rolls, never high, fell to zero after the program began in 1994.

The 6th Congressional District is a slice of central Wisconsin from Lake Michigan to the Wisconsin River. It includes Sheboygan and Manitowoc on Lake Michigan, Oshkosh and Fond du Lac on Lake Winnebago in the Fox River Valley, and the towns of Menasha and Kimberly, just outside Appleton. It also takes in five rural counties to the west and south. Oshkosh, the largest city in the district, is no longer the place where children's clothing maker OshKosh B'Gosh manufactures its products. But it is home to the Oshkosh Corporation, which produces everything from dump trucks to military vehicles and employs about 4.5% of the area's total workforce. Unemployment in many of the district's counties remained well above 8% in early 2011. Politically, this had been Republican territory since that first meeting in Ripon, but its GOP leanings have waned as Southern conservatives increasingly have dominated the national party. In 2008, the district voted narrowly for Democrat Barack Obama, 50%-49%. Two years later, however, Republican Scott Walker easily captured the district's counties in the governor's race. Traditionally, the district has elected moderate Republicans.

Tom Petri (R)

The congressman from the 6th District is Tom Petri (*PEE try*), a Republican first elected in the 1979 contest to succeed veteran Republican William Steiger, who was instrumental in creating the all-volunteer army and the Occupational Safety and Health Administration. Petri is a moderate who has occasionally paid a price for his political independence.

Petri spent his early years in Puerto Rico, where his father, a Navy pilot, was stationed. After his father died in World War II, the family moved to Fond du Lac, where, as a teen, Petri was the host of a popular Wisconsin radio show called *Teen Time*. Petri got both his undergraduate and law degrees from Harvard University, and then was a Peace Corps volunteer in Somalia. In 1972, at age 32, he was elected to the state Senate. Two years later, he was the Republican nominee running against Democratic Sen. Gaylord Nelson. He walked across the state campaigning, but lost 62%-36%. When he ran for the House in 1979, Petri beat Republican Tommy Thompson, then a state legislator, in the primary 35%-19%; Petri won the special election with 50%.

Petri has a centrist voting record in the House, though he generally has aligned with his party against most of President Barack Obama's major fiscal initiatives. He bolted from the majority of Republicans in 2009 in supporting tougher regulations on credit card companies, setting mortgage standards and curbing predatory lending practices as well as expanding the State Children's Health Insurance Program. He also voted against an emergency supplemental spending bill in May 2009 to fund the wars in Afghanistan and Iraq, saying, "It is time to include such funding within the regular appropriations and budget process." He provides explanations for his dissenting votes on major legislation on his official website. Petri long supported the Earned Income Tax Credit, a policy most closely associated with Democrats that guarantees a tax credit to low-wage earners.

After Democrats won control of the House in 2006, Petri was the most senior member of the full Transportation and Infrastructure Committee and hoped that he would assume the ranking

Republican slot. The leadership passed him over for the more-partisan John Mica of Florida. "Maybe I'm missing something," Petri told the *Milwaukee Journal Sentinel.* "Sometimes I think you can be more effective by working with people." With the House GOP takeover in 2011, he became chairman of the Aviation Subcommittee and guided a Federal Aviation Administration reauthorization bill to passage in April. Though in 2009 he advocated a high-speed rail train from Madison to Milwaukee, he switched his position in 2010 after Republican Scott Walker made the project a symbol of wasteful spending in his campaign for governor. Petri signed onto a statement calling the project a "boondoggle."

After the 2000 elections, Petri hoped to become chairman of the Education and the Workforce Committee—he was the most senior Republican on the committee—but his party's leadership passed over him and installed the fourth-most-senior Republican, John Boehner of Ohio, who went on to become the majority leader and later, House speaker. Petri decried the "purge of moderate Republicans," and afterward, his voting record became even more moderate. Working with California Democrat George Miller in 2005, he sponsored a $1,000 increase in Pell college grants, to $5,050 a year. The same year, Petri was one of 12 House Republicans to vote against a proposed constitutional amendment to ban flag desecration, and in February 2007, he was one of 17 Republicans to oppose President George W. Bush's troop surge in Iraq. He backed Democratic efforts in 2009 to replace federal student lending subsidies with direct lending from the government. He also pushed legislation that year to make more schools eligible for the Troops to Teachers program recruiting veterans to teach in classrooms.

Petri has been re-elected easily and was among the few Republicans who ran without opposition in the Democratic year of 2006. In 2008, Petri won with 64% of the vote, outperforming GOP presidential nominee John McCain by 15 percentage points in the district. Two years later, he won with 71%.

SEVENTH DISTRICT

Sean Duffy (R)

Elected 2010, 1st term; b. Oct. 3, 1971, Hayward; home, Ashland; St. Mary's U., MN, B.A. 1994; William Mitchell Col. of Law, J.D. 1999; Catholic; Married (Rachel Campos-Duffy); 6 children.

Elected Office: District atty., Ashland Cnty., 2002-10.

Professional Career: Practicing atty., 1999-2000; special prosecutor, Ashland Cnty., 2000-02.

DC Office: 1208 LHOB, 20515, 202-225-3365; Fax: 202-225-3240; Web site: duffy.house.gov.

State Offices: Wausau, 715-298-9344.

Committees: *Financial Services:* Financial Institutions & Consumer Credit; Insurance, Housing & Community Opportunity. *Joint Economic Committee.*

Election Results

2010 general	Sean Duffy (R)	132,551	(52%)	($1,977,172)
	Julie Lassa (D)	113,018	(44%)	($1,271,594)
	Gary Kauther (I)	8,397	(3%)	
2010 primary	Sean Duffy (R)	41,032	(66%)	
	Dan Mielke (R)	21,075	(34%)	

Northwest Wisconsin; Wausau

In the late 19th century, thousands of migrants traveled the rail lines radiating northwest from Chicago and Milwaukee to settle the northern reaches of Wisconsin, the most thickly settled land this far north in the United States and east of the Mississippi. What attracted them was not cropland—there are no industrial-size wheat farms as in the Red River Valley of North Dakota—but trees, iron and cows. This was one of America's largest virgin timberlands, and the river towns are still dotted with paper mills. Farther north, iron brought Finns and Italians to the

2008 Presidential Vote		
Barack Obama (D)	200,562	(56%)
John McCain (R)	152,507	(42%)

2004 Presidential Vote		
John Kerry (D)	185,076	(50%)
George Bush (R)	179,963	(49%)

Cook Partisan Voting Index: D+3

Population		Race/Ethnicity		Work	
Pop. 2010:	689,279	White:	92.9%	Private:	80.2%
Change since 2000:	Up 2.8%	Black:	0.6%	Government:	12.0%
Urban:	42.0%	Hispanic:	1.9%	Self-employed:	7.6%
Rural:	58.0%	Asian:	1.8%	Blue collar:	30.3%
Area size:	19,391 sq. mi.	Native Am.:	1.5%	White collar:	51.7%
		Hawaiian:	0.0%	Khaki collar:	0.1%
Age		Two+ races:	1.2%	Other:	17.9%
Median age:	41.4 yrs.				
More than 65 yrs:	15.9%	*Ancestry*		Median income:	$45,610
Less than 18 yrs:	22.4%	German	33.2%	Median Home Value:	$138,200
		Polish	9.1%		
Education		Norwegian	7.7%	**Military Veterans**	
H.S. grad:	88.7%			% of Pop:	11.8%
College grad:	19.4%				
Grad degree:	6.3%				

port of Superior, Wis., next to Duluth, Minn., and to smaller towns on the chilly lake, such as Bay-field near the Apostle Islands. The cleared forest lands became dairy farms. Dairy cattle, properly cared for, thrived in these northern uplands, and the sons of Wisconsin dairymen, many of them immigrants from Germany and Norway, moved their dairy herds even farther north towards Canada. Small cities grew, and some became home to big enterprises.

Wausau has paper mills, Wisconsin Rapids has NewPage paper, and Stevens Point has Sentry Insurance. The three cities have continued to generate new businesses and jobs and have retained a highly skilled workforce. But the number of dairy farmers in the region is in sharp decline; some farmers have turned to potatoes, vegetables, cranberries, and even ginseng. Wausau, which the 1980 census found to be the most ethnically homogeneous city in the nation, now has a sizeable immigrant community. Many Hmong refugees moved there in the 1980s, and as of 2010, 11% of the city's population was Asian.

This area makes up Wisconsin's 7th Congressional District, which stretches from Stevens Point in the south to Lake Superior in the north. The politics of northern Wisconsin and the 7th District have a rough-hewn quality, a lumberjack-populist flavor. Ancestrally Republican, the area favored the progressivism of the La Follettes. Today, the Superior and Stevens Point areas are heavily Democratic, though Wausau's Marathon County and many of the smaller counties have leaned Republican. The district was closely divided in the 2000 and 2004 presidential elections. Democrat Al Gore carried it 47.5%-46.8%, Democrat John Kerry won 50.1%-48.7%. In 2008, Democrat Barack Obama beat Republican John McCain here 56%-42%, winning 18 of the 20 counties in the district.

Sean Duffy (R)

The new congressman from Wisconsin's 7th District is Republican Sean Duffy, who won the seat of Democratic stalwart David Obey in one of 2010's most bitterly disappointing races for the Democratic Party. Obey had represented the district for 40 years, rising to chairman of the House Appropriations Committee.

Duffy hails from the sparsely populated, thickly forested northern end of the state, the 10th of 11 children who enjoyed what he calls a "quintessential small-town childhood" in Hayward, Wis. He became adept at the local craft of lumberjacking, eventually earning multiple world-champion titles in the 60-foot and 90-foot pole speed climb. In college, he studied business marketing, earning a degree in 1994. On a lark after graduation, Duffy joined the cast of MTV's *The Real World: Boston*, one of the earliest reality-TV series. The program brought young people with diverse backgrounds together to live as roommates, with the aim of spurring lively confrontations. Duffy was cast as the conservative in the show, and he frequently sparred with a liberal roommate. Around that time, he met his future wife, Rachel Campos-Duffy, who had been cast as the conservative foil in the *Real World* season taped in San Francisco.

Eventually, Duffy enrolled in law school in Minnesota. With degree in hand, he moved back to Wisconsin to work for his family's law firm for a short time before becoming a prosecutor. In 2002, Republican Gov. Scott McCallum appointed Duffy as Ashland County district attorney. In that role, he boasted a 90% success rate in jury trials and prosecuting child sex offenders. Duffy was serving his fourth term when he resigned to challenge Obey.

Then, in May, Obey unexpectedly announced that he would not seek re-election, removing himself as a ready target for Duffy, a 38-year-old with a conservative, anti-government message.

Instead of facing the 72-year-old Obey, an old-time appropriator who had been in Washington for four decades, Duffy drew as an opponent a Washington outsider like himself, Democratic state Sen. Julie Lassa, 39. In his campaign, Duffy made an issue of the government's big-spending ways and, specifically, the $787 billion economic stimulus bill that Obey, as Appropriations chairman, had helped push to passage. Duffy was adept at raising money and he was endorsed by tea party favorite Sarah Palin, the former Republican governor of Alaska.

Duffy banked on a national mood favoring Republicans to carry him to victory in a district that has voted Democratic in every presidential election since 1988. He ran as an unabashedly family-values and small-government conservative. Rachel Campos-Duffy wrote a book in 2009 titled *Stay Home, Stay Happy: 10 Secrets to Loving At-Home Motherhood*, which she calls "a love letter to at-home moms." The couple has six young children.

Lassa accused Duffy of supporting deep cuts in entitlement spending after he embraced Wisconsin Rep. Paul Ryan's budget plan. She campaigned as a champion of the middle class, calling for a first-time home buyers' tax credit, a payroll tax holiday for businesses that hire new workers, and a 10% pay cut for members of Congress until the unemployment rate dropped. But Lassa, despite strong backing from national Democrats, had difficulty connecting with voters, giving stump speeches that were heavily reliant on notes.

By contrast, Duffy was at ease and even charming in a crowd, speaking extemporaneously about issues and defining his opponent better than she could define herself. At one debate, when Lassa accused him of supporting policies that sent American jobs overseas, he replied, "They're packin' up and goin' elsewhere because they can't do business in Wisconsin! ... And Senator Lassa has a leading role in developing those policies that make Wisconsin one of the worst places in the country to do business." Duffy even overcame an unflattering video clip that was circulated of him dancing on a pool table in his underwear at a "toga" party. On election day, Duffy won, 52% to 44%.

EIGHTH DISTRICT

Reid Ribble (R)

Elected 2010, 1st term; b. April 5, 1956, Neenah; home, De Pere; H.S., diploma, 1974; Grand Rapids Bible and Music Schl., attended; Baptist; Married (DeaNa); 2 children.

Professional Career: Pres., The Ribble Group, 1981-2009.

DC Office: 1513 LHOB, 20515, 202-225-5665; Fax: 202-225-5729; Web site: ribble.house.gov.

State Offices: Appleton, 920-380-0061; Green Bay, 920-471-1950.

Committees: *Agriculture:* Conservation, Energy & Forestry; Livestock, Dairy & Poultry. *Budget.*

Election Results

2010 general	Reid Ribble (R)	143,998	(55%)	($1,301,283)
	Steve Kagen (D)	118,646	(45%)	($2,096,971)
2010 primary	Reid Ribble (R)	38,521	(48%)	
	Roger Roth (R)	25,704	(32%)	
	Terri McCormick (R)	14,107	(18%)	

Northeast Wisconsin; Green Bay

In 1673, the French Catholic missionary and explorer Jacques Marquette sailed from the open waters of Lake Michigan into what is now Green Bay. He had hoped to find the Northwest Passage to the Pacific. He actually found the Fox River, which leads to Lake Winnebago and, after a not-too-difficult portage, the Wisconsin River, which flows into the Mississippi. Green Bay and the Fox River Valley remained mostly wilderness and Indian country for more than 150 years. But once settled by Europeans, they became, as Father Marquette would have liked, one of

2008 Presidential Vote		
Barack Obama (D)	195,608	(54%)
John McCain (R)	164,696	(45%)
2004 Presidential Vote		
George Bush (R)	202,238	(55%)
John Kerry (D)	162,793	(44%)
Cook Partisan Voting Index:	R+2	

Population		Race/Ethnicity		Work	
Pop. 2010:	706,840	White:	88.5%	Private:	83.4%
Change since 2000:	Up 5.4%	Black:	1.1%	Government:	10.8%
Urban:	56.0%	Hispanic:	4.3%	Self-employed:	5.6%
Rural:	44.0%	Asian:	1.9%	Blue collar:	28.3%
Area size:	10,117 sq. mi.	Native Am.:	2.8%	White collar:	54.3%
		Hawaiian:	0.0%	Khaki collar:	0.0%
Age		Two+ races:	1.3%	Other:	17.4%
Median age:	39.7 yrs.				
More than 65 yrs:	14.4%	*Ancestry*		Median income:	$49,997
Less than 18 yrs:	23.2%	German	33.7%	Median Home Value:	$153,300
		Irish	7.7%		
Education		Polish	7.3%	**Military Veterans**	
H.S. grad:	90.0%			% of Pop:	11.1%
College grad:	21.8%				
Grad degree:	6.2%				

the most heavily Catholic parts of the United States. The area has thrived economically, with paper mills, a busy port and high-skill manufacturing in Green Bay and Appleton in the Fox River Valley. While paper products have long been an economic mainstay, the industry has experienced some instability. The 2007-09 recession had a big impact on Port of Green Bay shipping as did lowered demand for the region's timber. But the port economy began to rebound in 2010 with an 8% increase in domestic cargo.

No reference to Green Bay is complete without a mention of professional football's Packers, owned by 110,000 shareholding Wisconsinites and unlikely ever to move. Under the team's charter, if the Packers were ever sold, the proceeds would go to the local Sullivan-Wallen American Legion Post 11 "for the purposes of erecting a proper soldier's memorial." The city is by far the smallest to have a National Football League franchise. It has earned the nickname Titletown for the Packers' numerous championships, including the 2011 Super Bowl championship. Thirty miles south is Appleton, which has produced a number of famous, and infamous, Americans—novelist Edna Ferber, escape artist Harry Houdini, and demagogue Sen. Joseph McCarthy, the central figure in the red scare of the 1950s. Both Green Bay and Appleton are growing, thanks in part to booming Hispanic populations. Green Bay's Latino community has increased from approximately 1,000 people in 1990 to nearly 14,000 today; the city is now more than 13% Hispanic.

The 8th Congressional District of Wisconsin includes Green Bay and the Fox River Valley south to Appleton. It also includes the inland dairy counties and the Northwoods, which has hundreds of pine-ringed lakes where city dwellers from Chicago and Milwaukee keep summer homes. The Door County peninsula, which juts out into Lake Michigan, is another popular summer destination that is closer to the big population centers and as a consequence is more upscale, with art galleries, boutiques and restaurants. Politically, this has often been malleable territory and is one of the must-win regions in this traditional swing state. Republican presidential nominee George W. Bush won 52% of the vote here in 2000 and 55% in 2004, but Democrat Barack Obama carried the district with 54% of the vote in 2008.

Reid Ribble (R)

The new congressman from the 8th District is Republican Reid Ribble, a political newcomer who defeated two-term Democratic Rep. Steve Kagen in 2010.

Ribble was raised in Appleton and was the youngest of eight children. He told *National Journal* that he got beaten up a lot as a youth, a consequence of his tendency to say exactly what was on his mind. His father was a World War II-era Marine who started a roofing business that still bears the family name. In high school, Ribble played volleyball and ran track. He also began dating DeaNa, the girl who would become his wife. After high school, Ribble enrolled in Grand Rapids Bible and Music School, planning to join the Baptist ministry. But in 1976, when he was 20 years old, his father asked him to take over the business. Ribble left school and spent the next five years learning the ropes from his father, and in 1981, he became president of the company. He said that his greatest challenges were overcoming his fear of heights and dealing with the volatile nature of the construction industry. Ribble ran the commercial and industrial roofing firm for almost 30 years, until he sold it to his nephew in 2009. An avid reader, he says he has read thousands of books. Another cherished pastime is taking trips with his wife on his BMW touring motorcycle.

In his first run for public office, Ribble got into the contest against Kagen as "just an American who is frustrated with the overall condition of the economy and state of the union," he said. He added that he was fed up with "out-of-control spending," the ballooning deficit, and illegal immigration. Ribble campaigned in the mold of Republicans Rep. Mike Pence of Indiana and Sen. Jim De-Mint of South Carolina, two of the most conservative members of Congress. His campaign website included detailed position papers, which he said his professional consultants advised against posting. "I decided to go out on a limb and be a different type of candidate, and trust people to make the decision," Ribble said.

He was an attractive prospect to GOP recruiters because of his lack of a voting record and his ability to self-fund his campaign. In the Republican primary, Ribble dispatched two more-seasoned candidates who served in the Wisconsin House, winning with a hefty 48% of the vote.

In the general-election campaign, Ribble criticized Kagen for his support of President Barack Obama's health care overhaul and the Democratic energy bill that would put limits on carbon emissions. The northeastern Wisconsin district has a history of giving Democratic representatives the boot after two terms. Kagen had served two terms and never gotten more than 54% of the vote. He raised $2 million and outspent Ribble 2-to-1.

The Democratic Congressional Campaign Committee also stepped in to help with an ad asserting that Ribble's construction firm had gotten $300,000 in federal stimulus money to replace a school roof, even though the candidate criticized Kagen's support for the bill. While some endangered Democrats that year ran away from the party's agenda in Congress, Kagen defended his vote for the health care bill, and he focused on reminding voters that Republican President George W. Bush was in charge when the economy went south in 2007.

Still, Kagen lost the seat to Ribble, 54.7% to 45%. *The Oshkosh Northwestern* blamed his defeat on high unemployment and voters' belief that Democrats in the majority in Congress were doing too little to fix the problem. Kagen's embrace of the health care bill also galvanized conservative voters in the district, the newspaper said.

★ WYOMING ★

Wyoming is "the land of the cowboy," as the *WPA Guide* said more than 70 years ago. "Its mountains, plains, and valleys are essentially livestock country. A cowboy astride a bucking bronco greets the visitor from enameled license plates, from newspapers, magazines and painted signs." The cowboy is still on the license plates, and Wyoming remains the most western of states in spirit—largely unsettled, relatively few people, and a thin veneer of civilization stretched over a forbidding and beautiful land. But it is more than the land of the cowboy now. It is the land of the oil and gas worker, of the coal mine operator, and of the tourism operator.

Wyoming's economy today depends not on cowboys and cattle but on mining and minerals. The state boomed with oil prospectors during the energy price surge of the 1970s, but was hit hard by steep drops in oil prices in the early 1980s and again in the late 1990s. As oil exploration slumped, the production of other minerals surged. The 1970 Clean Air Act put a premium on Wyoming's low-sulfur coal, and it is now the No. 1 coal state, producing more than one-third of the nation's coal, more than West Virginia and Kentucky combined. In the Powder River Basin, 30-story high machines blast away the topsoil and scoop out coal. It is then hauled away by 65 trains a day by the Burlington Northern Santa Fe and Union Pacific. Wyoming is also the nation's eighth largest oil producer—the first oil well here was drilled in 1884, six years before statehood—and its second largest natural gas producer. Much of the natural gas is coal-bed methane, mixed with water next to coal seams. Only in 1989 did engineers figure out how to separate the natural gas from the water. Now, 200-foot drilling rigs are sinking wells as deep as 25,000 feet, and production has spiked since 2000. It is also the top producer of the mineral bentonite, which is used in oil drilling and cosmetics, and it has the world's largest reserve of trona, which is transformed into 90% of U.S. soda ash, used in making glass. These are capital-intensive industries that produce relatively few jobs for highly educated young people. But they have a major impact in this small state, and nearly 10% of jobs are in mining, the highest percentage in the nation, compared to only 3% in manufacturing, one of the lowest rates in the country. The mineral industry has made Wyoming an unusually prosperous state. Its population grew 14% to 564,000 in the decade ending in 2010, and its unemployment rate remained far below the national average during the 2007-09 recession. Wyoming was ranked No. 2 in a feeling of "well-being" among its residents by a Gallup-Healthways study.

Wyoming's second industry is tourism. Yellowstone National Park continues to draw millions of people, and Jackson Hole, just to the south of the park, has become one of America's elite year-round resort areas. The Jackson Hole Airport is the state's busiest and the only one that accommodates jets. There has been growth as well in the scenic and pastoral country on the eastern slope of the Big Horn Mountains around Buffalo and Sheridan. The third industry is agriculture. Wyoming is second in the nation in wool production and third in sheep inventory. It also produces hay, sugar beets, barley, pinto beans and beef cattle. The state's mix of tourism and agriculture sometimes leads to a cultural clash. The movie *Brokeback Mountain*, based on a story by Wyoming resident Annie Proulx, premiered in Jackson Hole in December 2005, but played to mostly empty houses in the rest of the state.

The juxtaposition of civilization and wilderness also raises some difficult policy issues. Ozone levels have risen around natural gas wells and, as utilities try to buy easements to build electric transmission lines to deliver wind power to consumers in California and elsewhere, Wyoming ranchers are forming wind associations to assure that they will have some say in this development. For years, the state has run feeding grounds for elk near Jackson Hole, and the herd has grown to tens of thousands. Environmental groups, worried about the spread of chronic wasting disease, want the feeding stopped, though thousands of elk induced over generations to depend on the feeding grounds will die. Local ranchers want it continued, to keep the elk away from their cattle, especially in winter. Grizzly bears, once endangered and protected in Yellowstone, have now increased in number and have been removed from the endangered list, while the state sued the National Park Service when it cut in half the number of snowmobiles allowed in the park.

Reliance on high-tech mineral extraction and high-end tourism may seem a contradiction of Wyoming's Old West heritage. But the state has always depended on new technology to tame age-old nature. After the open range era, cattle ranches were made possible only by the barbed wire that could fence in roaming herds, and the steam locomotives that could carry cattle to markets in the East. This 19th century high technology was brought to Wyoming by large capitalist operators, some of them onetime Texas cowhands or second sons of English landed gentry, who started the first big operations after the Civil War. And, of course, mining depends on intricate machinery and

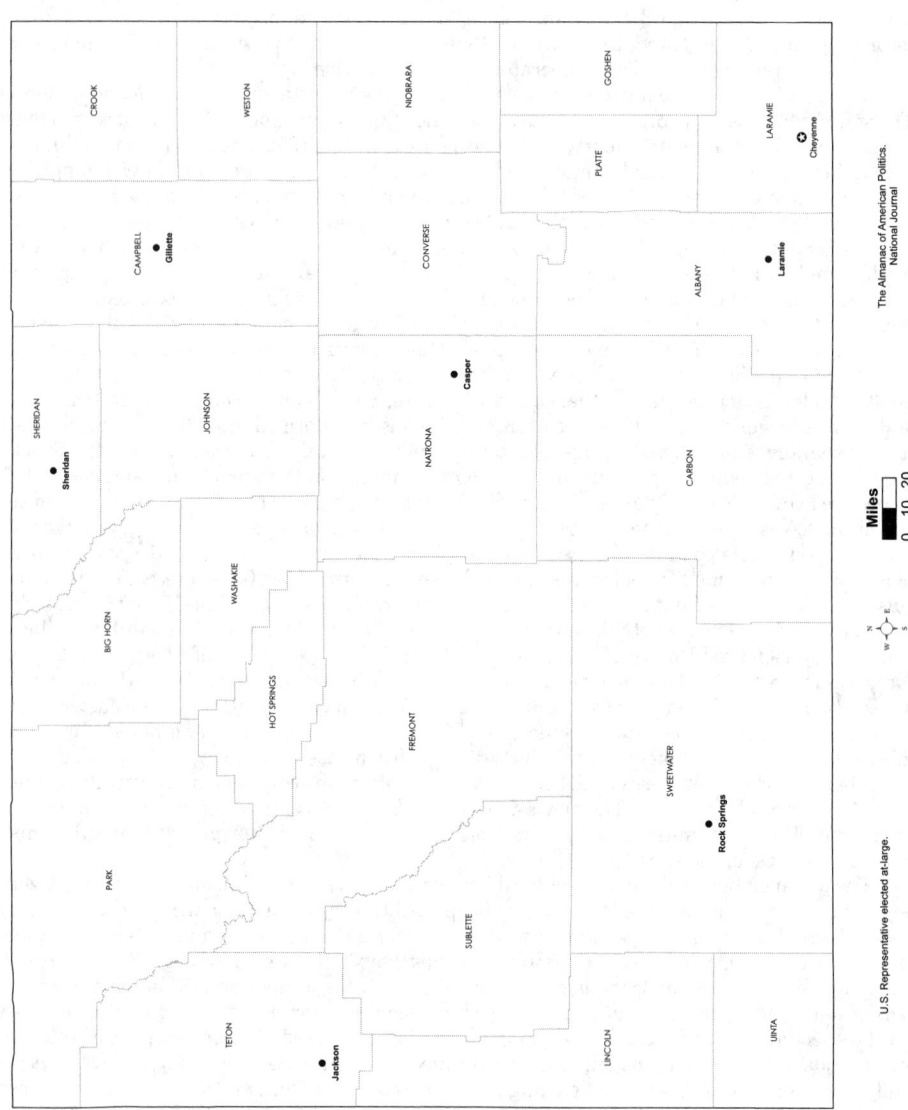

U.S. Representative elected at-large.

The Almanac of American Politics.
National Journal

responsiveness to markets that reward innovation and penalize stasis. At the same time, Wyoming still is a kind of frontier. It was, until recently, one of the few states with more men than women, which was one reason that Wyoming, when it was still a territory in 1869, was the first to give women the vote. (The exception: New Jersey allowed women with property to vote between 1776 and 1807, but there weren't many women with property.) Wyoming's amazing landscape has long elicited national notice. Yellowstone, established in 1872, was the nation's first national park.

The settled part of Wyoming consists of medium-sized towns, which are the state's largest cities, and settlements tucked among sheep and cattle ranches, and sugar beet and malting barley farms. It is a small state, a single community really, where people remember who played what position, when and how well, and for what high school football team. The locals set the tone of life in Wyoming. There was once a sharp economic and regional split reflected in its partisan politics. The big economic interests—cattle ranchers, organized in the Wyoming Stock Growers Association, and the Union Pacific Railroad management—favored the Republicans, as did the wildcatters, independent producers and oil company geologists. The main Democratic constituency was the Union Pacific Railroad workers who built the first transcontinental line across southern Wyoming in the 1860s. (Cheyenne was established because it was the midpoint between the UP's operations in Omaha and Ogden, Utah.) The southern tier of counties, from Cheyenne through Laramie to Evanston, once voted Democratic. But now the Democrats are strongest in Teton County, the home of Jackson Hole, which voted nearly 2-to-1 for Barack Obama in 2008, and in Albany County, home of Laramie and the University of Wyoming, the only other county Obama carried. All other counties gave John McCain between 59% (Cheyenne's Laramie County) and 81% (coal-mining Crook County). Wyoming hasn't elected a Democrat to the U.S. Senate since 1970 or to the House since 1976, though it has had mostly Democratic governors over that time. How to explain that anomaly? In a small state, voters expect to talk person-to-person with their governors, senators and congressmen every so often. Personal campaigning is important, and it enabled Democrats Ed Herschler, Mike Sullivan and Dave Freudenthal to win six of the last eight races for governor.

But elections in 2008 and 2010 reinforced Wyoming as a Republican state. In 2008, it cast the lowest percentage, 33%, for Barack Obama of any state, and in two Senate races, it voted 76% and 73% for Republicans Mike Enzi and John Barrasso, respectively. In 2010, Wyoming voted 70% for Republican at-large Rep. Cynthia Lummis, 66% for Republican Gov. Matt Mead and it elected 76 Republicans and 14 Democrats to the legislature. But Wyoming Republicans combine conservatism on spending—the legislature resisted Mead's proposal to spend part of $1 billion in unexpected revenue on roads and local governments—with a live-and-let-live attitude on cultural is-

Population		Household Income		Work	
Pop. 2010:	563,626	Under $15k:	10.5%	Private:	71.7%
State rank:	50th	$15k to $50k:	36.9%	Government:	20.4%
Change since 2000:	Up 14.1%	$50k to $100k:	33.8%	Self-employed:	7.5%
Urban:	64.5%	$100k to $200k:	16.1%	Unemployment (3-yr. average):	3.0%
Rural:	35.5%	Over $200k:	2.7%	Poverty:	9.7%
Native of state:	41.7%	Median income:	$52,951	Blue collar:	28.1%
Not a citizen:	2.0%			White collar:	53.0%
Area size:	97,813 sq. mi.	**Home Value**		Khaki collar:	0.5%
		Under $100k:	20.6%	Other:	18.4%
Most populous cities		$100k to $300k:	60.3%		
Cheyenne	59,466	$300k to $500k:	12.3%	**Age**	
Casper	55,316	$500k to $1 mil:	4.5%	Median age:	36.4 yrs.
Laramie	30,816	Over $1 million:	2.2%	More than 65 yrs:	12.2%
Gillette	29,087	Median:	$181,900	Less than 18 yrs:	24.0%

Race/Ethnicity				Military Veterans		Registered Voters in 2010	
White:	85.9%	*Language*		% of Pop:	12.7%	Democrats:	63,594
Black:	0.8%	English:	93.5%			Republicans:	170,719
Hispanic:	8.9%	Spanish:	4.5%	*Veterans by Period*		Ind./other:	35,770
Asian:	0.8%	Asian:	0.3%	WWII and before:	9.0%	Voter turnout:	190,822
Native Am.:	2.1%	Other European:	1.2%	Korea:	10.4%	Turnout as % of	
Hawaiian:	0.1%			Vietnam:	34.7%	voting age:	44.6%
Two+ races:	1.5%	**Education**		Gulf (pre-2001):	12.5%		
		H.S. grad:	91.3%	Gulf (post-2001):	11.0%	**Legislature**	
Ancestry		College grad:	23.5%	Peace time:	22.4%	Senate:	4 D 26 R
German	20.8%	Grad degree:	7.8%			House:	10 D 50 R
English	11.9%						
Irish	11.2%						

sues. A state House committee rejected a bill to authorize civil unions, but the state Senate rejected bills to bar recognition of same-sex marriages conducted in other states.

Presidential politics Wyoming is one of the least likely states in the nation to be seriously contested in presidential general elections. It is too Republican, too remote and has only three electoral votes. Candidates have seldom visited, except when Dick Cheney visited his home in Jackson. This was George W. Bush's best state in 2000, when he carried it 69%-28%, and it was his second best state in 2004, when he carried it 69%-29%. It was John McCain's No. 2 state in 2008 and Barack Obama's 50th, as McCain carried it 65%-33%. In Wyoming, Democrats tend to do better with the elite and Republicans with ordinary folks. Obama carried the richest county in the state, Jackson Hole's Teton County, and he won Albany County, which includes Laramie and the University of Wyoming. McCain won the votes of just 53% of college graduates, but he won 78% of those who did not graduate from college.

2008 Presidential Vote		
John McCain (R)	164,958	(65%)
Barack Obama (D)	82,868	(33%)

2004 Presidential Vote		
George W. Bush (R)	167,629	(69%)
John Kerry (D)	70,776	(29%)

Wyoming has typically held presidential caucuses in early March, with no significant impact on the presidential nominating process. In early 2007, Wyoming Republicans pledged to caucus on the same date as the New Hampshire Republican primary. With New Hampshire Secretary of State Bill Gardner holding his cards close until December (New Hampshire law gives him sole authority to set the date of its presidential primary), Wyoming Republicans blinked, and decided in August 2007 to hold their caucuses on Jan. 5, which turned out to be two days after the Iowa caucuses and three days before the New Hampshire primary. The date was against party rules and cost the state half of its 28 delegates, but state party leaders evidently decided it was a minimal price to pay.

As in most other Republican caucus states, Mitt Romney's well-organized campaign dominated here. Romney, his wife, Ann, and sons Josh and Craig campaigned in Wyoming. In county conventions Romney won 13 delegates, to four for Fred Thompson, two for Duncan Hunter, one for McCain and four for "uncommitted." (Each county got one delegate, except for Cheyenne's Laramie County, which got two.) In retrospect, it was a high watermark for the Thompson and Hunter campaigns. Wyoming Republicans in characteristic fashion assembled early in the morning and made quick work of it. The Albany County chairwoman made sure that the caucus was over by 10 a.m. because she had a funeral to attend.

Wyoming Democrats held their caucuses on March 8, a date on which most observers thought the nomination would be determined. Not so. Obama's brilliant February, with 11 straight primary and caucus wins, was followed by Hillary Clinton's victories in Ohio and Texas on March 4. Anticipating a prolonged campaign, Obama opened a Cheyenne office in mid-February and ran television ads. The Clinton campaign, caught short-funded, sent in Bill Clinton and daughter, Chelsea, and ran radio spots. The Wyoming media wrote stories about state Democrats being energized, and Obama half-filled the University of Wyoming's auditorium in Laramie.

Of the 59,000 registered Democrats, only 8,753 showed up at 23 county caucuses. Obama won 61%-38%, thanks in large part to big percentages in affluent Jackson Hole's Teton County (80%) and in the University of Wyoming's Albany County (74%). Clinton carried the Democrats' historical base, the Union Pacific Railroad worker counties of Carbon and Sweetwater that cover most of the southern half of the state.

Governor

Matt Mead (R)

Elected 2010, term expires Jan. 2015, 1st term; b. March 11, 1962, Jackson; home, Cheyenne; Trinity U., San Antonio, TX, B.A. 1984; U. of WY, J.D. 1987; Episcopalian; Married (Carol); 2 children.

Professional Career: Cnty. prosecutor, Campbell, 1987-90; Federal prosecutor, U.S. atty., Cheyenne, 1991-94; Special asst. U.S. atty., 1994-95; Special asst. atty. gen., St. of WY, 1998-2001; Practing atty., 1995-2001; U.S. atty., WY, 2001-07; Farm/ranch operator, 2007-present.

Office: State Capitol, 200 West 24th Street, Cheyenne, WY, 82002-0010, 307-777-7434; Fax: 307-632-3909; Web site: governor.wy.gov.

Election Results

2010 general	Matt Mead (R)	123,780	(66%)
	Leslie Petersen (D)	43,240	(23%)
	Taylor Haynes (I)	13,796	(7%)
	Mike Wheeler (Lib)	5,362	(3%)
2010 primary	Matt Mead (R)	30,308	(29%)
	Rita Meyer (R)	29,605	(28%)
	Ron Micheli (R)	27,630	(26%)
	Colin Simpson (R)	16,722	(16%)

Wyoming's governor is Matt Mead, a Republican elected in 2010. He succeeded two-term Democrat Dave Freudenthal, giving the GOP a pickup in a state where Republican presidential nominee John McCain won with 65% of the vote in 2008.

Mead was born in Jackson and raised on his family's Teton County ranch. He is the grandson of Clifford Hansen, a former Wyoming GOP governor (1963-67) and U.S. senator (1967-78). Mead's mother, Mary, also ran unsuccessfully for governor in 1990, six years before her death in a riding accident. After receiving a bachelor's degree from Trinity University in San Antonio, Matt Mead returned home to attend the University of Wyoming's law school. He worked as a prosecutor in Campbell County and in the U.S. Attorney's office in Cheyenne and practiced law for six years at a Cheyenne firm. He was chosen to serve as U.S. attorney for Wyoming in 2001 and spent nearly six years in the job. When Republican U.S. Sen. Craig Thomas died in 2007, Mead resigned his position to run for the Senate. But the Republican State Central Committee instead picked state Sen. John Barrasso, whom Democratic Gov. Dave Freudenthal subsequently appointed. Barrasso won a 2008 special election to serve the remaining four years of Thomas' term.

After the Senate loss, Mead returned to working in his family's ranching business. Meanwhile, Freudenthal—who had won re-election in 2006 with an impressive 70% of the vote—was giving serious thought to running for a third term. The state legislature had limited governors to two terms in the 1980s, prompting the state's voters to pass a 1992 ballot initiative imposing them on state lawmakers. In 2004, two lawmakers challenged the initiative, and the state Supreme Court agreed. The court's decision did not apply to the governorship, but some Wyoming political observers predicted that the popular Freudenthal could prevail if he said the law extended to him as well. The governor, however, decided in March 2010 not to seek a third term.

Even before Freudenthal's decision, Mead had given serious thought to a 2010 challenge, having formed an exploratory committee in November 2009. Three months later, he formally announced his candidacy, emphasizing his family's record of service. "Every generation of my family, they've stressed the value of giving back to the state because the state means so much to all of us, and I sense that as well," he said. He joined a crowded Republican field that included state Auditor Rita Meyer, who served as Gov. Jim Geringer's chief of staff; former state Rep. Ron Micheli; and state House Speaker Colin Simpson, son of former U.S. Sen. Alan Simpson. The candidates battled closely, all sharing similar conservative views. Meyer got the coveted endorsement of former Alaska Gov. Sarah Palin, while Simpson used his family connections to win the backing of former President George H.W. Bush. But Mead outraised them all, putting nearly $900,000 of his own money into the contest to give him a 2-to-1 advantage over the other candidates and helping him build name recognition in a field of better-known competitors. He won 28.7% of the vote in the September primary, to Meyer's 28%. Micheli took 26% and Simpson won 16%.

Mead entered the general election as the heavy favorite against Leslie Petersen, Wyoming's former state Democratic Party chairman. She promised to continue the conservative-minded policies of Freudenthal and told the *Wyoming Tribune-Eagle* that she had "a deep Libertarian streak." But she had the serious disadvantage of running in a Republican state at a time when feelings toward national Democrats were especially negative. Mead won 66%-23%, carrying every county. Independent Taylor Haynes drew 7% as a write-in candidate, running on a family values platform.

Taking office, Mead noted that Wyoming's relatively sound fiscal health made it the envy of other states coping with severe budget shortfalls. But he said he wanted to avoid complacency, "because when the nation remains under an economic cloud, the cloud moves our way." He sought to show his fiscal conservatism by trimming the payroll in the governor's office by about $100,000 a year. At the same time, he saw a need for greater state investment, and signed into law $15 million in incentives to entice large computer data centers to the state. He also proposed investing more state money in highways by taking a portion of the proceeds from Wyoming's statutory severance tax on minerals to contribute $52 million annually to the highways. The state legislature rejected the idea, but committed to an interim study to look at new non-tax and non-toll-based revenue sources to fund roads.

On other issues, Mead signed into law a bill that would eliminate the right of drivers suspected by police of driving while intoxicated to refuse testing, as well as a measure that enabled Wyoming to join Alaska, Arizona and Vermont in allowing residents to carry concealed guns without a permit. He called the latter "an appropriate law for Wyoming."

Senior Senator

Michael Enzi (R)

Elected 1996, term expires 2014, 3rd term; b. Feb. 1, 1944, Bremerton, WA; home, Gillette; George Washington U., B.S. 1966, Denver U., M.B.A. 1968; Presbyterian; married (Diana); 3 children.

Military Career: WY Natl. Guard, 1967–73.

Elected Office: Gillette mayor, 1975–82; WY House of Reps., 1986–90; WY Senate, 1990–96.

Professional Career: Owner, NZ Shoes, 1969–95; Dir. & chmn., First WY Bank of Gillette, 1978–88; Accounting mgr. & computer programmer, Dunbar Well Service, 1985–97; Educ. Comm. of States, 1989–93; Dir., Black Hills Corp., 1992–96; Western Interstate Comm. for Higher Educ., 1995–96.

DC Office: 379-A RSOB, 20510, 202-224-3424; Fax: 202-228-0359; Web site: enzi.senate.gov.

State Offices: Casper, 307-261-6572; Cheyenne, 307-772-2477; Cody, 307-527-9444; Gillette, 307-682-6268; Jackson, 307-739-9507.

Committees: *Budget. Finance:* Energy, Natural Resources & Infrastructure; Health Care; Taxation & IRS Oversight. *Health, Education, Labor & Pensions* (RMM): Primary Health & Aging. *Small Business & Entrepreneurship.*

Group Ratings

	ACLU	ACU	ADA	CFG	AFS	FRC	LCV	ITIC	NTU	COC
2010	7	96	5	84	3	95	14	67	97	100
2009	–	100	10	99	9	–	9	–	92	86

National Journal Ratings

	2010 LIB — 2010 CONS		2009 LIB — 2009 CONS	
Economic	16%	83%	14%	81%
Social	0%	79%	9%	90%
Foreign	0%	72%	16%	80%
Composite	14%	86%	15%	85%

Key Votes of the 111th Congress

1. Overturn Ledbetter	N	5. Pass health care bill		
2. Pass $787 billion stimulus	N	6. Regulate financial firms	N	9. Ratify New START	N
3. Repeal DC gun laws	Y	7. Pass tax cuts for some	N	10. Confirm Elena Kagan	N
4. Confirm Sonia Sotomayor	N	8. Legalize immigrants' kids	N	11. Stop EPA climate regs	Y
				12. Repeal don't ask, tell	N

Election Results

2008 general	Michael Enzi (R) 189,046	(76%)	($2,368,893)
	Chris Rothfuss (D) 60,631	(24%)	($32,326)
2008 primary	Michael Enzi (R) .... unopposed		

Prior Winning Percentages: 2002 (73%); 1996 (54%)

Michael Enzi, the senior senator from Wyoming, was elected in 1996. He is the ranking Republican on the Health, Education, Labor and Pensions Committee, and his mild-mannered demeanor masks deeply held conservative views.

Enzi grew up in Thermopolis and Sheridan, the son of a shoe salesman. He earned degrees in accounting and retail marketing, moved to Gillette and became an accountant for an oil well servicing company. He and his wife, Diana, started a small business, NZ Shoes. In the 1970s, at a Jaycees meeting, Enzi met Republican Sen. Alan Simpson, who was impressed by his volunteerism and suggested he run for public office. In 1975, Enzi was elected mayor of Gillette, the center of Wyoming's coal belt and its fastest-growing town. He was mayor for eight years. In 1986, he was elected to the Wyoming state House and in 1990 to the state Senate.

After Simpson announced his retirement in December 1995, Enzi was one of nine Republicans and two Democrats who ran for the seat. With support from a grassroots network of conservatives, Enzi finished first in a straw poll at the May 1996 Republican state convention. In second place was John Barrasso, an orthopedic surgeon from Casper who had statewide name recognition as a television commentator on health issues. Their chief difference was on abortion rights. Enzi opposed abortion rights, and Barrasso did not. Barrasso also had more money, but Enzi won 32%-30%. The Democratic nominee was former Secretary of State Kathy Karpan, who opposed gun control and abortion rights. But she had the liabilities of having supported the presidential candidacies of Bill Clinton, who was unpopular in conservative Wyoming, and Bruce Babbitt, who was unpopular in Wyoming as Clinton's Interior secretary. Enzi led in polls throughout the campaign and won 54%-42%.

In the Senate, he has been a reliable stalwart for the political right—his lifetime rating from the American Conservative Union through 2010 was above 93%, one of the highest among senators. He and Rep. Rob Bishop, R-Utah, pleased tea party activists in May 2011 when they introduced the "Repeal Amendment," a measure enabling states to repeal any federal law. They said in an op-ed article that their goal was "to restore the balance of power in our system of government as provided in the original Constitution."

Enzi also has a reputation as a hard worker who pays attention to the details of legislation and who looks for areas of compromise. He was a key negotiator in the Obama administration's early efforts to get a health care bill through Congress in 2009. His own health care proposal called for tax credits for buying health care, assistance to help small businesses provide coverage for their employees, and requirements for the states to reduce the cost of medical malpractice insurance. He was one of the "Gang of Six" senators that met during the summer of 2009 in an unsuccessful effort to hammer out a solution acceptable to both parties. He drew criticism from Democrats when he reportedly suggested to a town hall audience in Wyoming that his chief priority wasn't striking a deal. "It's not where I get them to compromise, it's what I get them to leave out," Enzi was quoted by the Associated Press as saying. White House spokesman Robert Gibbs said, "Sen. Enzi's clearly turned over his cards on bipartisanship and decided that it's time to walk away from the table."

Since then, Enzi has remained a vocal critic of the Obama administration's efforts on health care. In April 2011, he joined Republicans Olympia Snowe of Maine and Orrin Hatch of Utah in questioning the Small Business Administration in how the agency was protecting small companies who were overwhelmed in trying to meet the new law's regulations. He also joined Hatch, the Finance Committee's ranking Republican, in leading an ultimately unsuccessful GOP effort to block the nomination of Donald Berwick as administrator of the Centers for Medicare and Medicaid Services, contending Berwick lacked experience.

Enzi has teamed with Democrats on other issues, however. He and California Democrat Dianne Feinstein worked in 2010 to limit the use of the controversial chemical bisphenol A as part of food safety legislation, but the chemical industry successfully blocked the move. He also joined North Dakota's Byron Dorgan that year in pushing a bill to lift the U.S. travel ban on Cuba. And despite his ideological differences with the late liberal Edward M. Kennedy of Massachusetts, he forged a productive and largely bipartisan working relationship with him. When Kennedy chaired the HELP panel, the two established what they called the 80-20 principle: reach broad agreement on 80% of an issue and leave out the 20% where no agreement can be found. The two successfully pushed through the committee a bill requiring insurance companies to treat mental illness the same as other ailments in coverage decisions. And they agreed on reauthorization of Head Start early education programs and on renewal of college programs. Still, talks on reauthorization of No Child Left Behind, the Bush-era law tying federal education funding to school performance, stalled for several years. They also disagreed on Kennedy's bill requiring employers to provide workers with paid sick leave, with Enzi arguing the rule would have an adverse effect on employee health benefits. The bill stalled.

Enzi chaired the HELP panel in 2005 when Republicans held the majority, and did not always follow the Bush administration's lead. He put together the reauthorization of the Carl D. Perkins Vocational and Technical Education Act, which passed the Senate 99-0 and was enacted in August 2005. Enzi also won passage of renewed versions of a major jobs training bill and the higher education law. He sided with ranking minority member Kennedy in opposing a White House proposal to encourage more use of government vouchers for private school tuition in Gulf states recovering from Hurricane Katrina in 2005. Working with leaders of the Finance Committee, he also participated in the protracted negotiations with the House on pension reform. On an issue of special interest back home, Enzi helped to enact a bill to expedite the clean-up of abandoned coal mines. In the closing days of the Republican majority, he helped to resolve conflicts over the funding formula to renew domestic AIDS programs.

Earlier, he played a key role on a major corporate accountability bill in 2002. As the only accountant in the Senate, Enzi could claim special expertise. Enzi opposed a move by Securities and Exchange Commission Chairman Arthur Levitt to bar accounting firms from doing auditing and consulting work for the same corporation. Banking, Housing and Urban Affairs Committee Chairman Paul Sarbanes, D-Md., introduced a bill that did not go as far as Levitt's proposal, but included an accounting board independent of the SEC with power to set rules, investigate, punish violations and conduct regular inspections of accounting firms' work. Enzi worked closely with lobbyists for the big accounting firms, but also held negotiations with Sarbanes, and in June, the two negotiated a compromise. They agreed that two of the four members of the board would be accountants, that the board could adopt rules favored by the accounting industry and that the board would not be financed by accountants. Enzi led six of the 10 committee Republicans in voting for the Sarbanes bill. Disciplinary proceedings would be kept confidential. The Senate later passed the bill without a single no vote. It became known as the Sarbanes-Oxley corporate accounting law (after House Republican Michael Oxley of Ohio, who pushed it through the House).

Enzi briefly considered retirement after being passed over twice for appointment to the Finance Committee. In 2007, GOP Senate leaders gave a committee vacancy to the less-senior John Ensign of Nevada as a reward for his work leading the National Republican Senatorial Committee. He tried again when another seat opened in late 2007, but the spot instead went to New Hampshire Sen. John Sununu, who also had less seniority but was facing a difficult re-election in 2008. "That was a really down time in my life," Enzi told the Associated Press. Sununu lost in 2008, and Enzi finally got his appointment to the powerful Finance panel. He did not have serious opposition in either of his re-election races, winning both with at least 73% of the vote.

Junior Senator

John Barrasso (R)

Appointed June 2007, term expires 2012, 1st full term; b. July 21, 1952, Reading, PA.

Elected Office: WY Senate, 2002-07.

Professional Career: Orthopedic surgeon 1983-2007; RNC Committeeman, 1992-96; Chief of staff, WY Medical Center, 2003-05.

DC Office: 307 DSOB, 20510, 202-224-6441; Fax: 202-224-1724; Web site: barrasso.senate.gov.

State Offices: Casper, 307-261-6413; Cheyenne, 307-772-2451; Riverton, 307-856-6642; Rock Springs, 307-362-5012; Sheridan, 307-672-6456.

Committees: *Energy & Natural Resources:* Energy; National Parks (RMM); Public Lands & Forests (RMM). *Environment & Public Works:* Clean Air & Nuclear Safety (RMM); Transportation & Infrastructure; Water & Wildlife. *Foreign Relations:* East Asian & Pacific Affairs; European Affairs (RMM); International Operations & Organizations, Democracy & Global Women's Issues; Western Hemisphere, Peace Corps & Global Narcotics Affairs. *Indian Affairs* (VChmn).

Group Ratings

	ACLU	ACU	ADA	CFG	AFS	FRC	LCV	ITIC	NTU	COC
2010	7	100	0	89	3	100	14	67	98	100
2009	–	100	5	99	9	–	9	–	91	86

National Journal Ratings

	2010 LIB — 2010 CONS		2009 LIB — 2009 CONS	
Economic	0% —	87%	14% —	81%
Social	0% —	79%	0% —	94%
Foreign	0% —	72%	16% —	80%
Composite	10% —	90%	13% —	88%

Key Votes of the 111th Congress

1. Overturn Ledbetter	N	5. Pass health care bill	N
2. Pass $787 billion stimulus	N	6. Regulate financial firms	N
3. Repeal DC gun laws	Y	7. Pass tax cuts for some	N
4. Confirm Sonia Sotomayor	N	8. Legalize immigrants' kids	N

9. Ratify New START	N
10. Confirm Elena Kagan	N
11. Stop EPA climate regs	Y
12. Repeal don't ask, tell	N

Election Results

2008 general	John Barrasso (R)	183,063	(73%)	($2,585,977)
	Nick Carter (D)	66,202	(27%)	($210,914)
2008 primary	John Barrasso (R)	unopposed		

Republican John Barrasso, the junior senator from Wyoming, was appointed in June 2007 after Republican Sen. Craig Thomas died in office of leukemia. Barrasso was then elected in November 2008 to fill the remaining four years of Craig's unexpired term. Barrasso's intellect and unwavering conservatism have helped him quickly climb the GOP leadership ladder; he is vice chairman of the Senate Republican Conference.

Barrasso *(bah-RAH-soh)* grew up in Reading, Pa., the son of a World War II veteran who made a living as a cement finisher and who took his family to Washington every four years for the president's inauguration. John Barrasso got his undergraduate and medical degrees from Georgetown University, and then moved to Wyoming in the 1980s and set up practice as an orthopedic surgeon in Casper. Barrasso quickly made his name in local Republican politics, serving as a Republican national committeeman and as state party treasurer. He also was a local radio and television personality, dispensing practical medical advice on news programs and in public service announcements. He also hosted the annual Jerry Lewis telethon for muscular dystrophy.

In 1996, Barrasso ran for the U.S. Senate when Republican Alan Simpson retired. He faced then-state Sen. Michael Enzi in a crowded GOP primary where the abortion issue played a key role. Running as a moderate, Barrasso favored abortion rights and had opposed a 1994 constitutional amendment to ban most abortions. Enzi, who had support from social conservatives, opposed abortion rights and narrowly edged out Barrasso 32% to 30%. The two then joined forces for the general election, with Barrasso serving as Enzi's finance chairman in the fall.

In 2002, Barrasso won election to the state Senate, where he worked on health care issues and chaired the Transportation, Highways and Military Affairs Committee. He sponsored a bill to increase the criminal penalty for killing a pregnant woman, but then-Democratic Gov. Dave Freudenthal vetoed it. He occasionally crossed the political aisle to join with Democrats, backing a bill to exempt food from the state sales tax and supporting a ban on smoking in public buildings. He also sponsored a law enabling physicians to talk freely with patients about medical complications, without the risk that the conversations could be used against them in a lawsuit.

After Thomas died on June 4, 2007, the state Republican State Central Committee had 15 days to select three candidates to fill the vacancy, from which the governor was required to pick the successor under Wyoming law. That triggered a scramble by 31 candidates who applied for consideration. They conducted a week-long beauty pageant among the 71 members of the party committee. The roster of applicants included state Rep. Colin Simpson, the son of former U.S. Sen. Simpson, and numerous state legislators, attorneys, ranchers, and other professionals. Barrasso emphasized his strong conservative credentials, saying in a statement to the committee, "I believe in limited government, lower taxes, less spending, traditional family values, local control, and a strong national defense." He noted he had an "A" rating from the National Rifle Association and that he had voted for prayer in public schools, sponsored legislation "to protect the sanctity of life," and opposed gay marriage

The Republican committee named three finalists: Barrasso, Cynthia Lummis, who served 14 years in the legislature and two terms as state treasurer, and Tom Sansonetti, who had been Thomas' chief of staff and an assistant attorney general in the Bush administration. Barrasso's competitors had drawbacks: Lummis was not on good terms with the governor, and Sansonetti had been a lobbyist for mining, energy and ranching interests at a time lobbyists were unpopular with the public after a series of bribery and influence-peddling scandals involving lobbyists and members of Congress. Barrasso had worked with Freudenthal on health care issues in the legislature, and on June 22, the governor announced Barrasso as his choice.

In the Senate, Barrasso quickly won recognition from his peers. *Washingtonian* magazine's anonymous survey of Capitol Hill staffers named him "brainiest senator" in 2010, along with Rhode Island Democrat Sheldon Whitehouse. In May of that year, the Republican attacked the Democrats' health care law in a closed-door meeting that President Barack Obama held with Republicans. Obama became so irked by Barrasso's comments that he reportedly reminded him there were no TV cameras in the room, prompting the senator to answer, "I'm saying this out of my most firm beliefs." Barrasso became Republican Conference vice chairman in September, after Alaska Republican Lisa Murkowski stepped aside when she decided to run—successfully—as a write-in candidate for election that fall. He was re-elected to another term in the position in November.

National Journal's 2010 vote ratings tied Barrasso with six other Republicans as the most conservative members of the Senate. Although he opposed the Democratic proposal to extend the State Children's Health Insurance Program in 2009, he successfully included a provision in the bill to benefit rural doctors and hospitals. Among his first bills was a proposal to withhold 10% of highway funds from states that issue driver's licenses to illegal immigrants. He does break with some conservatives in calling for lifting the U.S. ban on travel to Cuba, saying citizens should be free to visit relatives in the Communist island nation.

Barrasso focuses heavily on energy and public lands issues. He has been a particularly vehement critic of the Environmental Protection Agency and introduced a bill in February 2011 to bar the EPA from regulating greenhouse gases blamed for global warming. "This is not your parents' EPA," he said in a May 2011 speech. " ... Your parents' EPA focused on rebuilding the environment. This EPA is focused on remaking society." In 2009, he and Oklahoma Republican James Inhofe, Congress' leading climate change skeptic, accused the Obama administration of suppressing an EPA memo that criticized the science behind labeling carbon dioxide a greenhouse gas. Agency officials responded that the memo's author was an economist, not a climate scientist, and denied it was kept under wraps.

Barrasso said the cap-and-trade bill regulating carbon emissions that failed to get through the Senate that year would unfairly punish his state's farmers and ranchers. In opposing similar legislation in 2008, he said the bill would harm Wyoming's coal industry, and he sought amendments to increase funding for states to implement the new standards and also to allow more types of coal to qualify for program incentives, benefiting Wyoming coal plants. On a bill to ban the exportation of elemental mercury, Barrasso got an exemption for mercury found in coal.

Continuing work on an issue that was dear to Thomas' heart, Barrasso pushed for more protection of Wyoming wilderness and wildlife. He proposed legislation to protect undeveloped areas of the Wyoming range from oil and gas development and to preserve 387 miles around the Snake River. It became law as part of a larger land management bill in March 2009. Barrasso also supported removing gray wolves from the Endangered Species List because of the danger they pose to livestock. He told the Associated Press, "This is a Wyoming concern that requires a Wyoming solution. It does not require interference from Washington." The U.S. Fish and Wildlife Service eventually removed gray wolves from the list.

After the BP oil spill disaster in the Gulf of Mexico in 2010, Barrasso sought to create an independent commission to investigate the spill after questioning the expertise of the Obama administration's bipartisan panel conducting its own probe. Also that year, Barrasso joined Senate Republicans in opposing the Interior Department's new oil and gas leasing regulations. He joined West Virginia Democrat Joe Manchin in 2011 on a bill seeking to expand use of alternative fuels, including those made from coal.

As the vice chairman of the Indian Affairs Committee, Barrasso also has been active on Indian-related issues. He introduced a bipartisan bill in April 2011 to pave the way for tribes to pursue homeownership and other economic development opportunities on tribal lands. A year earlier, he questioned a $3.4 billion settlement against the federal government for mismanaging Indian trust funds and suggested revisions to the settlement, including capping attorney fees and costs.

In 2008, Barrasso was unopposed in the Republican primary, and his eventual Democratic challenger was Gillette attorney Nick Carter, a political newcomer. Barrasso stressed his many years in public service in Wyoming and highlighted his early successes in the Senate. Carter tried to tie Barrasso to national Republicans and corporate special interests, but the assertions didn't stick. Barrasso vastly outspent Carter, $2 million to $273,000. Barrasso won easily 73%-27%, carrying every county.

REPRESENTATIVE-AT-LARGE
Cynthia Lummis (R)

Elected 2008, 2nd term; b. Sept. 10, 1954, Cheyenne; home, Cheyenne; U. of WY, B.S. 1976, B.S. 1978; J.D. 1985; Lutheran; married (Alvin Wiederspahn); 1 child.

Elected Office: WY House of Reps., 1979-83, 1985-93; WY Senate, 1994-95; WY treasurer 1998-2006.

Professional Career: WY Supreme Court law clerk, 1985-86; Wiederspahn, Lummis & Liepas, P.C., 1986-96; Lummis Livestock Co. LLC, 1976-present.

DC Office: 113 CHOB, 20510, 202-225-2311; Fax: 202-225-3057; Web site: lummis.house.gov.

State Offices: Casper, 307-261-6595; Cheyenne, 307-772-2595; Rock Springs, 307-362-4095; Sheridan, 307-673-4608.

Committees: *Appropriations:* Agriculture, Rural Development, FDA & Related Agencies; Interior, Environment & Related Agencies; Labor, HHS, Education & Related Agencies.

Group Ratings

	ACLU	ACU	ADA	CFG	AFS	FRC	LCV	ITIC	NTU	COC
2010	13	100	0	95	0	100	10	33	91	88
2009	–	100	0	97	0	–	0	–	93	80

National Journal Ratings

	2010 LIB	—	2010 CONS	2009 LIB	—	2009 CONS
Economic	19%	—	81%	0%	—	96%
Social	31%	—	67%	0%	—	93%
Foreign	0%	—	88%	26%	—	68%
Composite	19%	—	81%	12%	—	89%

Key Votes of the 111th Congress

1. Overturn Ledbetter	N	5. Bar federal abortion funds	Y	9. Stop detainee transfers	Y
2. Pass $820 billion stimulus	N	6. Pass health care bill	N	10. Legalize immigrants' kids	N
3. Let guns in national parks	Y	7. Regulate financial firms	N	11. Repeal don't ask, tell	N
4. Pass cap-and-trade	N	8. Pass tax cuts for some	N	12. Limit campaign funds	N

Election Results

2010 general	Cynthia Lummis (R)	131,661 (70%)	($780,426)
	David Wendt (D)	45,768 (24%)	($65,709)
	John Love (Lib)	9,253 (5%)	
2010 primary	Cynthia Lummis (R)	84,063 (83%)	
	Evan Slafter (R)	17,148 (17%)	

Prior Winning Percentages: 2008 (53%)

The congresswoman from Wyoming is Cynthia Lummis, a Republican elected in 2008. As the nation's least populous state, Wyoming has elected one representative-at-large since it was admitted to the Union in 1890.

Lummis *(LUM-iss)* grew up on her family's ranch in Cheyenne. She earned two bachelor's degrees and a law degree at the University of Wyoming. When she won a seat in the state House of Representatives at age 24, Lummis became the youngest woman ever elected to the Wyoming Legislature. She chaired the Revenue Committee and helped revise the state's taxation of the mining industry, which is the state's chief source of revenue. She served in the state Senate from 1994 to 1995, and went on to become state treasurer in 1998. In that office, she diversified the state's investment portfolio, which at the time was heavily invested in mortgage giants Fannie Mae and Freddie Mac, to include various equities totaling $8.5 billion. Lummis later said that the move helped Wyoming weather the 2007-09 economic downturn spurred by the credit crisis in the home mortgage market.

In 2007, the Wyoming Republican Party placed Lummis on a list of three potential candidates to succeed Sen. Craig Thomas, a Republican who died of leukemia in June of that year. Under Wyoming state law, if a senator leaves office prematurely, his political party must nominate three possible replacements. The governor then chooses a successor from among the candidates. Lummis' name was submitted along with state Sen. John Barrasso and ex-Justice Department lawyer Tom Sansonetti. Lummis' poor relationship with then-Gov. Dave Freudenthal made her a dark horse candidate. It was reported that during a private meeting in 2002, Freudenthal threatened her by saying, "Don't ever cross me or your head will be in your lap before you even know I've drawn my knife." Lummis verified this report, and Freudenthal did not deny it. Freudenthal selected Barrasso for the Senate seat, but Lummis says the experience encouraged her to seek federal office. She announced her candidacy for the state's at-large seat in the U.S. House, which came open in 2008 when Republican Barbara Cubin retired.

In the Republican primary, Lummis faced rancher Mark Gordon, who invested $1 million of his own money and outspent Lummis by 4-to-1. They shared similar political views, and the contest hinged on who was the more conservative candidate. Gordon ran as a political outsider, but Lummis criticized him for supporting Democratic presidential nominee John Kerry in 2004 and Democrat Gary Trauner in his 2006 race against Cubin. Lummis won with 46% of the vote to Gordon's 37%.

In the general election, Lummis faced Trauner, a businessman who came out of nowhere in 2006 and used a well-financed grassroots campaign to nearly unseat Cubin. The Democratic Congressional Campaign Committee put Trauner on their top priority "Red to Blue" list, but his chances of winning in a heavily Republican state diminished with the prospect of having to face a candidate other than Cubin, whose poor roll call attendance and penchant for outlandish comments had weakened her politically. Lummis ran as a staunch conservative, pledging to oppose new taxes and calling for making the Bush-era tax cuts permanent. Trauner claimed that Lummis would threaten the stability of the country's Social Security system by investing money from the program in unstable capital markets, which she denied. Several October polls showed the candidates in a statistical dead heat, but the numbers proved to be misleading. Lummis won 53%-43%, with Libertarian candidate David Herbert getting 4% of the vote.

In the House, Lummis joined the Republican Study Committee, a group of the most conservative members of the House, as well as the Tea Party Caucus. In 2011, she also was named communications chairman for the Congressional Western Caucus, giving her an added forum for her views on limited government interference on public lands. Her party loyalty landed her a spot on the Appropriations Committee after the House GOP takeover in 2010. She has called for reform of spending earmarks and promised she would not request them for her state. She also introduced a bill to slash the federal workforce by freezing the hiring of non-national security employees and requiring that only one replacement be hired for every two departing workers. Though she strongly opposed the Democrats' health care overhaul, she backed its provisions benefitting rural hospitals and allowing adults up to age 26 to remain on their parents' insurance plans.

Lummis sponsored a measure in 2010 and 2011 that prevented the State Department from interfering with imports of U.S.-made collectable firearms from overseas. Earlier, she co-sponsored a successful bill with other Wyoming members of Congress to allow gun owners to carry concealed weapons in national parks. It was signed into law by President Barack Obama as part of a credit card-holders consumer protection bill.

In 2010, Lummis faced competition in her first re-election bid from Democrat David Wendt, president of the Jackson Hole Center for Global Affairs. The *Wyoming Tribune-Eagle* of Cheyenne endorsed her candidacy, but also scolded Lummis for her "partisan stridency" and tea party affiliation. "We suggest Ms. Lummis find her way back to the Wyoming mainstream," the newspaper said. She soundly defeated Wendt, 70.4% to 24.4%.

THE INSULAR
★ TERRITORIES ★

PUERTO RICO

Puerto Rico has a unique history. For four centuries, from Columbus' landing in 1493 until the Spanish-American War of 1898, Puerto Rico was a Spanish colony. And for three centuries, the port of San Juan was the gathering place for its annual convoy of gold and silver from the Americas to Spain. Today, with 3.7 million people (more than Connecticut), it is the largest American territory. Sixty years ago, it was "the poorhouse of the Caribbean," heavily populated, and devoted almost entirely to sugar and coffee cultivation. Now Puerto Rico has a recognizably First World economy, although one hobbled by a five-year recession that resulted in a 13% job loss and nearly 17% unemployment. It also has a solidly democratic, if at times turbulent, politics.

Puerto Rico has elected a resident commissioner to Congress since 1900, the only member of Congress with a four-year term, and its residents have been American citizens since 1917. But it didn't elect its own governor until 1948. From the 1940s until the early 1960s, Puerto Rico was transformed by Gov. Luis Muñoz Marin and his Popular Democratic Party. Muñoz initiated "Operation Bootstrap" to lure businesses to Puerto Rico with promises of low-wage labor and government-built factories and tax exemptions. Muñoz also developed Puerto Rico's commonwealth form of government—in Spanish, Estado Libre Asociado (ELA): Free Associated State—that was approved by referendum in 1952. Under ELA, Puerto Rico is part of the United States for purposes of international trade, foreign policy and war, but has its own laws, taxes and representative government. It is not subject to federal income taxes and is not eligible for all federal benefits, though some have been approved by Congress. Puerto Rico has also developed its own political parties: Muñoz's Popular Democrats (the Spanish acronym is PPD), the New Progressives (PNP), who favor statehood, and two small independence parties.

The commonwealth solution, by its own terms, was open to amendment, and ever since Muñoz retired in 1964, the central issue in Puerto Rico's politics has been status: Should the island continue or modify ELA, should it seek statehood, or should it seek independence? For many years, there was indeed gradual movement toward statehood. In the 1967 referendum, Puerto Ricans voted for ELA over statehood 60%-39%. In a 1993 referendum, the vote was 48% for ELA, and 46% for statehood. In a 1998 referendum, the vote was 47% voted for statehood and 50% for "none of the above," the option favored by the PPD. Independence has low levels of support (4% in 2008), and it comes primarily from university students.

In 2005, a White House task force recommended a two-step referendum, with Puerto Ricans both on the island and on the mainland first voting on whether to consider a change in the current ELA status, and then, if they favored a change, choosing between statehood and independence. A bill to that effect was sponsored in 2006 by Rep. José Serrano and then-Resident Commissioner Luis Fortuño of the PNP. PPD Gov. Aníbal Acevedo Vilá argued that the two-step approach would frustrate the wishes of the majorities or pluralities that had voted for ELA in previous referenda and would produce a verdict for an option, statehood, that had never won majority support. Acevedo Vilá called for an "enhanced commonwealth," under which Puerto Rico could set its own foreign and trade policies and opt out of federal law as negotiated with Congress. In October 2007, the House Natural Resources Committee unanimously approved a bill requiring a referendum by the end of 2009 on whether Puerto Rico should maintain its current status. An amendment by Rep. Nydia Velázquez instructed that if the result was negative, then Congress would recognize the Puerto Rican government's "inherent authority" to decide between holding a constitutional convention and holding a second referendum on status. But the bill never came to the floor.

President Barack Obama pledged to "enable the question of Puerto Rico's status to be resolved" in his first term. In 2009, Resident Commissioner Pedro Pierluisi and Serrano introduced a bill with 147 co-sponsors that provided for two plebiscites. The first was whether to continue Puerto Rico's current status or to consider other options. The second, if voters chose the latter, presented four options—independence, statehood, free association, or the current ELA. It was supported by Serrano and opposed by Velázquez and passed the House in April 2010. But the Senate showed no disposition to act and the Obama administration was silent.

Possible consequences were daunting. A vote for statehood would raise the question of whether Congress would accept Puerto Rico as a state under the terms and conditions advocated by the

PNP, such as Spanish as an official language. Many Republicans worried that Puerto Rico as a state would be solidly Democratic with five House members, though Fortuño, a member of the PNP, and others have argued that it would actually lean Republican. There also may have been concern that the issue would be decided by a narrow majority. Over the past century, Congress has admitted new states only when there has been a widespread consensus for statehood.

In 2008, Puerto Rico held a primary on June 1. On the Democratic side, Hillary Clinton consistently led in the polls, but many Puerto Rico politicians of both parties endorsed Obama, including the PNP's Pierluisi and the PPD's Acevedo Vilá. Obama avoided taking a stance on the status issue. Clinton, the then-New York senator who had many constituents with roots in Puerto Rico, campaigned heavily around the island, and won a solid 68%-32% victory, securing 38 delegates to Obama's 17. This was far too few to overcome Obama's delegate lead, and her hopes of coming out ahead in the national popular vote were frustrated by the low turnout. Puerto Rico had 2.4 million registered voters, but only 384,000 voted in the primary. Still, the Democratic turnout dwarfed Republican participation: Only 208 people participated in the GOP caucus.

Governor   Luis Fortuño, a member of the New Progressive Party (PNP), was elected governor of Puerto Rico in 2008. Fortuño grew up in San Juan and graduated from Georgetown University and the University of Virginia law school. He practiced corporate law at a San Juan law firm until Gov. Pedro Rosselló appointed him executive director of the Puerto Rico Tourism Company in 1993. In 1994, he became Puerto Rico's first Economic Development and Commerce secretary. In 1996, he returned to private practice. Like some, but not all, members of the PNP, he identifies with the mainland Republican Party. In 2001, he became Puerto Rico's Republican National Committeeman and in 2004, he won an election to become Puerto Rico's resident commissioner, the island's representative in Congress.

Puerto Ricans tend to vote along party lines, and the results in 2004 were very close. Fortuño won 48.5%-48%, outperforming his party's candidate for governor (who narrowly lost) by only 0.5%. That made Fortuño the first Republican to represent Puerto Rico in the House since 1904. This was also the first time Puerto Rico has elected a split ticket, sharply divided on the key issue of Puerto Rico's status. The pro-statehood Fortuño frequently quarreled with the Popular Democratic Party's (PPD) Gov. Aníbal Acevedo Vilá, who has supported the island's current commonwealth status. Fortuño co-sponsored a bill with Rep. José Serrano for a two-step referendum, the first vote on whether to retain the current status, the second, if it is rejected, to choose between independence and statehood. Fortuño opposed Nydia Velázquez's bill for a constitutional convention in Puerto Rico, which was more likely to lead to Acevedo Vilá's choice of an "enhanced commonwealth," arguing that Acevedo Vilá's proposal that Puerto Rico set its own foreign and trade policies was unrealistic. "Three administrations have told you what you are proposing is unconstitutional. What part of 'no' don't you understand?" he said. But to get unanimous approval for his bill in the House Natural Resources Committee in 2007, Fortuño agreed to compromise between his bill and Velázquez's. But the bill never reached the floor.

In February 2007, Fortuño announced he would challenge Acevedo Vilá in 2008. Acevedo Vilá was in a difficult position. He had been elected by just 48.4%-48.2% after a lengthy court battle. In March 2008, Acevedo Vilá was indicted on 19 counts of violating federal election laws and defrauding the Internal Revenue Service. He was acquitted in March 2009, but the trial severely damaged his re-election chances. Fortuño won 53%-41%, the biggest victory in a Puerto Rico gubernatorial election since 1964.

RESIDENT COMMISSIONER

Pedro Pierluisi (D)

Elected 2008, 2nd term; b. April 26, 1959, San Juan; home, San Juan; Tulane U., B.A. 1981; George Washington U., J.D. 1984; Catholic; married (Maria-Elena Carrión); 4 children.

Elected Office: PR atty. gen., 1993-96

Professional Career: Practicing atty., 1997-2007

DC Office: 1213 LHOB, 20515, 202-225-2615; Fax: 202-225-2154; Web site: pierluisi.house.gov.

State Offices: Puerto Rico, 787-723-6333.

Committees: *Ethics. Judiciary:* Crime, Terrorism & Homeland Security; Immigration Policy & Enforcement. *Natural Resources:* Fisheries, Wildlife, Oceans & Insular Affairs.

Pedro Pierluisi, a member of the New Progressive Party (PNP), was elected Puerto Rico's resident commissioner in November 2008. Pierluisi grew up in San Juan, the son of former Puerto Rico Housing Secretary Jorge Pierluisi. Pedro Pierluisi graduated from Tulane University and George Washington University Law School in the early 1980s and served as an aide to Resident Commissioner Baltasar Corrada del Río of the PNP. He then practiced law for six years in Washington. In 1993, Gov. Pedro Rosselló of the PNP appointed him attorney general of Puerto Rico. He argued two constitutional cases before the Puerto Rico Supreme Court. He left Rosselló's scandal-plagued administration in 1996 and practiced law in Puerto Rico.

In February 2007, the PNP's Luis Fortuño, then the resident commissioner, announced he was running for governor. Three months later, Pierluisi decided to run for resident commissioner. Although the two had different mainland party affiliations (Fortuño is a Republican), both were strong backers of statehood for Puerto Rico and ran on a united ticket. Pierluisi spent $1.5 million, while his PPD opponent, Alfredo Salazar, spent $529,000. Pierluisi won 53%-42%, an almost identical result as Fortuño's victory, and carried 71 of Puerto Rico's 78 municipalities. It was the biggest win for the PNP ever, and the biggest win for either party in Puerto Rico since 1964.

In the House, Pierluisi caucuses with the Democrats and has seats on the Ethics, Judiciary, and Natural Resources committees. In 2009, Pierluisi introduced a bill on Puerto Rico status, similar to a bill introduced by Fortuño in 2007 that passed in committee but never received a floor vote. Pierluisi's bill calls for a referendum on maintaining Puerto Rico's current status and, if the vote is negative, authorizes the government of Puerto Rico to hold a referendum to choose among commonwealth, statehood or independence. Pierluisi assembled 123 co-sponsors, including several committee chairmen and ranking minority members. In April 2010, it passed the House 223-169. But the Senate declined to take up the bill.

VIRGIN ISLANDS

The Virgin Islands are a very different place from Puerto Rico, and the only place under the U.S. flag where people drive on the left. It is much smaller, with a resident population of only 109,000, mainly on the three islands of St. Thomas, St. John and St. Croix, purchased by the United States from Denmark in 1917. They were settled by Dutch and Danes and had a polyglot colonial society with one of the oldest Jewish communities in the Western Hemisphere. The islands' most famous son is Alexander Hamilton, who grew up on St. Croix. The Virgin Islands have lived primarily off tourism and oil refineries. The Hovensa refinery on St. Croix, half-owned by the Venezuelan government, is the largest refinery in the Western Hemisphere and one of the ten largest in the world. But in January 2011, after being hit with a $5 million Clean Air Act fine, it cut back capacity by 30%. St. Thomas is the No. 1 cruise ship destination in the world, with more than 2 million visitors a year, and tourism, together with shopping (visitors spend an average of $195 a day), accounts for 80% of the islands' economy. But hurricanes have cut tourism numbers sharply, as did the 2007-09 recession, but the numbers were up in late 2010.

Investment businesses are attracted to the Virgin Islands by tax breaks established by Congress and the Virgin Islands government. Individuals and businesses that qualify pay a maximum of 3.5% in income tax, which has yielded revenues of about $100 million a year to the island government. To qualify, taxpayers must live half the year in the islands and invest $100,000 there, buy computers and office supplies there and hire at least 10 local people. Since 2004, Congress has been gradually tightening restrictions on claims of residency, and the Internal Revenue Service has been auditing those who say they qualify.

Any loss of revenue is a problem. One-third of workers on the islands are employed by the government, and the territorial government has been running structural deficits of about one-eighth of spending. That's on top of the crushing burden of a $1 billion in bond debt, which requires millions of dollars in debt service. Some economic recovery has been spurred by rum sales. Rum-producing territories have been receiving $13.25 of the $13.50 federal tax on rum since 1999. In 2008, the Virgin Islands government made a deal with the British-based liquor company Diageo to move its Captain Morgan rum operations from Puerto Rico to a new $165 million distillery in the Virgin Islands. The Islands government estimated it would get $119 million annual revenue, of which $36 million would go to Diageo as an incentive to move. Not surprisingly, Puerto Rican politicians were unhappy with the plan and argued that it was illegitimate to use rum tax funds to lure a rum distillery operation from one territory to another.

In 2009, Puerto Rico Resident Commissioner Pedro Pierluisi sponsored a bill to limit payment to liquor companies to 10% of rum tax funds. The bill won bipartisan support, but Virgin Island Del. Donna Christensen, more experienced than the freshman Perluisi, rounded up support from the Congressional Black Caucus and the renewal of the $13.25 rebate passed.

The Virgin Islands plays a small role in the presidential selection process. It held a Democratic presidential primary on Feb. 9, 2008, in which Barack Obama beat Hillary Clinton 90%-8%, and got all three pledged delegates. Republicans held a tiny caucus in a local restaurant that April, after John McCain had already locked up the nomination.

Governor   John deJongh, a Democrat, has been governor of the Virgin Islands since 2006. De-Jongh (*dee YOUNG*) grew up in St. Thomas and in Detroit and attended Antioch College. He returned to St. Thomas, worked on the Tri-Island Development Council's historic redevelopment projects, then ran all consumer banking for Chase Bank in the U.S. and British Virgin Islands and St. Maarten. From 1987 to 1990, he was territorial commissioner of finance and headed the U.S. Virgin Islands Public Finance Authority. From 1990 to 1992, he was executive assistant to Democratic Gov. Alexander Farrelly. For the next dozen years, he worked in the private sector in the Virgin Islands, including a stint as president of the chamber of commerce. In 2002, deJongh ran for governor as an independent and finished second to incumbent Democratic Gov. Charles Turnbull. He ran again in 2006, after the term-limited Turnbull stepped down, and defeated Republican Kenneth Mapp 57%-43% in a runoff.

In office, deJongh has grappled with the Islands' fiscal problems. He revamped residential property taxes, eliminating the territory's single tax rate and replacing it with four property classes each with a different tax rate. He has tried to hold down borrowing, but the $831 million budget adopted in October 2010 had $125 million in borrowing. In 2010, he was re-elected with 56% of the vote.

DELEGATE

Donna Christensen (D)

Elected 1996, 8th term; b. Sept. 19, 1945, Teaneck, NJ; home, St. Croix; St. Mary's Col., B.S. 1966, George Washington U., M.D. 1970; Moravian; married (Christian); 6 children.

Professional Career: Practicing physician, 1975–97; Territorial Asst., Commissioner of Health, 1988–94; Acting Commissioner of Health, 1994–95.

DC Office: 1510 LHOB, 20515, 202-225-1790; Fax: 202-225-5517; Web site: donnachristensen.house.gov.

State Offices: St. Croix, 340-778-5900; St. Thomas, 340-774-4408; St. John, 340-776-1212.

Committees: *Energy & Commerce:* Communications & Technology; Oversight & Investigations.

The delegate from the Virgin Islands is Donna Christensen, a Democrat first elected in 1996. Christensen is from an old St. Croix family. Her father was Virgin Islands Chief District Court Judge Almeric Christian. She graduated from St. Mary's College and George Washington Medical School, and then practiced medicine for more than 20 years in the Virgin Islands. In 1996, she ran for delegate against incumbent independent Victor Frazer, and led 38%-34% on Nov. 5. She won in a runoff 52%-48%. In the House, Christensen has forged alliances with the Congressional Black Caucus, and she is the first woman physician to serve in Congress. In 2008, she got a seat on the Energy and Commerce Committee, making her the first territorial delegate to land a spot on one of the five "A-list" committees. She strongly supported the Democrats' health care bill in 2009-10, and sought more Medicaid funding for the territories. Christensen has been re-elected by wide margins. In 2010, she won 71% of the vote against three opponents.

Perhaps the most contentious issue she had to deal with was rum. She backed a deal allowing the Virgin Islands to issue bonds to pay for a new $165 million distillery for the British firm Diageo, producer of Captain Morgan rum, which planned to relocate from Puerto Rico. The Islands government estimated it would get $119 million annual revenue, of which $36 million would go to Diageo as an incentive to move. Not surprisingly, Puerto Rican politicians were unhappy with the plan, and they argued that it was illegitimate to use rum tax funds to lure a rum distillery operation from one territory to another.

GUAM

Some 7,800 miles west of Los Angeles and 3,800 miles west of Hawaii, 17 hours of flying time from Washington, D.C., is Guam, where America's day begins. Guam lies west of the International Date Line, and people there are in the early hours of Tuesday when the rest of us are still in Monday afternoon. Geographically, this island is in the center of the Marianas, but Guam is legally separate. It was ruled by Navy captains from 1898 to 1949, except for 32 months of Japanese occupation during World War II. In 1950, the Guam Organic Act made Guamanians U.S. citizens. Guam's first civilian governor, Carlton Skinner, who as a captain integrated the crew of his Navy ship in 1943, became the first civilian governor in 1949; he helped write the constitution, enshrined in the Organic Act of 1950. The local government is GovGuam, but Congress still retains final power over the territory. It gave Guam a non-voting delegate to the House in 1972.

Guam, as the *Washington Post's* Blaine Harden put it, "marries the beauty of Bali with the banality of Kmart." It is 36 miles long by four to nine miles wide, with about 180,000 people. Thirty-seven percent are Chamorro (descendants of the original islanders) or from elsewhere in Micronesia, 26% are Filipino, 11% other Pacific Islander, 6% other Asian, and 7% white. The territory is overwhelmingly Catholic. Guam is tropical, but not an easy environment. In August 1993, it lived through an earthquake rated at 8.2 on the Richter scale, comparable to San Francisco's in 1906. In 2002, a typhoon with winds up to 184 miles per hour caused hundreds of millions of dollars in damage. And Guam suffers from an invasive species, the semi-poisonous brown tree snake, which has killed off nearly all of the island's bird population and severely disrupted the island's ecosystem. The latest attempt at eradication of the 10-foot long snakes—dropping dead mice packed with acetaminophen from helicopters—has not been completely effective.

Economically, Guam depends on tourism and service businesses, but most of all on the U.S. military. Bases occupy one-third of the land, and 60% of income comes from the federal government.

Military spending here has risen to double the levels of the mid-1990s. The Navy has invested in dredging Apra Harbor to accommodate nuclear aircraft carriers; the Marine Corps is building an entire new base at Finegayan in a setting apt for tropical and jungle warfare training. Guam's population is expected to swell by as many as 60,000 people during construction, straining already near-capacity water and wastewater systems. GovGuam, which has been borrowing money to meet current expenses, is seeking $3 billion from the federal government to pay for roads and other infrastructure, and the Obama administration has budgeted as much as $1 billion a year.

Guam does not cast any electoral votes for president, but has a part in presidential politics. It elects delegates to national party conventions. In 2008, Guam Democrats scheduled a primary on May 3, when the Democratic contest was still raging between Hillary Clinton and Barack Obama. Former President Bill Clinton called in to a morning Guam radio show, while Obama opened an office in the capital of Hagåtña, with three paid staffers. Obama stressed his Hawaiian roots and ties to the Pacific islands. He won 2,264 votes to Clinton's 2,257. Under Democrats' proportional representation delegate allocation rules, they split evenly Guam's four delegate votes. Guam Republicans held a convention on March 8, after John McCain clinched the Republican nomination. All nine delegates supported him.

Governor   Eddie Calvo, a Republican, was elected governor of Guam in 2010. Calvo grew up in Guam and south of San Francisco, where he graduated from a Catholic high school in Mountain View and Notre Dame de Namur University in Belmont. His father, Paul Calvo, had many business interests in Guam and was elected governor in 1978. After school, Eddie Calvo returned to Guam and worked for the Pacific Construction Company and as general manager of the Pepsi Bottling Company of Guam. In 1998, he was elected senator in the Guam legislature as a Republican. In 2002, he ran for lieutenant governor as the running mate of Tony Unpingco, who lost to Felix Camacho, also a Republican.

In April 2010, with Camacho term-limited, Calvo announced he was running for governor and chose Sen. Ray Tenorio as his running mate. In the Republican primary, he was opposed by Lt. Gov. Mike Cruz. The Calvo-Tenorio ticket won 59%-41% out of 15,679 votes cast. Winning the Democratic nomination unopposed was former Gov. Carl Gutierrez, an independent.

The results of the general election were exceedingly close; Calvo won by just 487 votes, 20,066 to 19,579.

Taking office, Calvo faced major fiscal problems, including a $90 million budget shortfall. Guam Memorial Hospital was having trouble paying bills, and the Department of Administration had only enough cash for its payroll.

DELEGATE

Madeleine Bordallo (D)

Elected 2002, 5th term; b. May 31, 1933, Graceville, MN; home, Tamuning; St. Mary's Col., attended 1952, St. Catherine's Col., attended 1953; Catholic; widowed; 1 child.

Elected Office: GU Senate, 1981-82, 1986-94; GU Lt. Gov., 1994-2002.

DC Office: 2441 RHOB, 20515, 202-225-1188; Fax: 202-226-0341; Web site: www.house.gov/bordallo.

State Offices: Hagåtña, 671-477-4272.

Committees: *Armed Services:* Military Personnel; Readiness (RMM). *Natural Resources:* Energy & Mineral Resources; Fisheries, Wildlife, Oceans & Insular Affairs.

Madeleine Bordallo, a Democrat, was first elected as the delegate from Guam in 2002. She grew up in Minnesota and, after age 14, in Guam. She studied vocal music at St. Catherine's College in St. Paul and worked for a few Guam radio stations. She was elected to the Guam legislature in 1980. Her husband, Ricardo Bordallo, was elected governor in 1974, was defeated for re-election in 1978 by Paul Calvo, the father of current Gov. Eddie Calvo, and then elected governor again in 1982. Then, in a tragic turn of events, Ricardo Bordallo, facing a prison term for bribery in 1990, chained himself to the statue of Chief Quipuha and shot himself in the head, dying later that day. Madeleine Bordallo was a candidate for governor that year, and lost 57%-43% to incumbent Republican Joseph Ada. In 1994, she was elected lieutenant governor and was re-elected in 1998.

In 2002, when Del. Robert Underwood decided to run for governor, Bordallo ran for delegate. In the primary, she faced Judith Won Pat, daughter of Guam's first delegate, Antonio Borja Won Pat, after whom Guam's international airport is named. In this contest between longtime friends, Bordallo won 59%-41%. In the general election, she once again faced Ada. This time, Bordallo won 65%-35%. She has not had major party opposition since then.

With a seat on the House Armed Services Committee, Bordallo typically lobbies her colleagues for more military deployments and spending on military construction. Like other Guam delegates before her, Bordallo has sought reparations for Guamanians for human rights abuses suffered during Japan's occupation during World War II, even though the 1951 treaty between the United States and Japan absolved Japan of any claims. The House approved her bill for reparations for Guamanians, but it stalled in the Senate. She secured a commitment from incoming Armed Services Committee Chairman Buck McKeon, R-Calif., to include it in the House defense authorization in 2011.

NORTHERN MARIANA ISLANDS

The Commonwealth of the Northern Mariana Islands, in American hands since 1944, gained representation in Congress for the first time in January 2009. This is a chain of approximately 15 islands, only five inhabited, running north and south from Guam in the Western Pacific. The northern islands are volcanic and the southern islands are limestone and are fringed with coral reefs. They are much closer to mainland Asia than to the mainland U.S., and sit some 7,800 miles southwest of Los Angeles and 3,800 miles west of Hawaii. Typhoons are common from August to November.

The Northern Marianas were first peopled by Micronesians three millennia ago and were visited by Magellan in 1521. Spanish Jesuits arrived in 1668, and the islands were a possession of Spain until the Spanish-American War in 1898. In the treaty that followed, Guam was acquired by the United States, but the Northern Marianas were sold to Germany in 1899. They were seized by Japan in 1914 soon after it entered World War I, and the League of Nations gave Japan legal claim to them in 1920. They were occupied by U.S. forces in 1944. The Enola Gay took off in August 1945 from Tinian, on its mission to drop the atomic bomb on Hiroshima. In 1945, the Northern Marianas were put in the custody of the new United Nations Security Council, and in 1947, they were declared part of the U.S. Trust Territory of the Pacific Islands. While the other islands in time opted for independence, the Northern Marianas took a difference course.

In 1975, Islanders voted to approve a covenant with the United States creating the Commonwealth of the Northern Mariana Islands (C.N.M.I.), which went into effect in March 1976. Under its terms, the C.N.M.I. was not subject to federal immigration or labor laws and not obliged to pay U.S. taxes, but it deferred entirely to the United States in foreign and military affairs. Foreign investors were limited to a 49% share of businesses or property, and land could be owned only by "persons of Northern Marianas descent." The C.N.M.I. government started operating after the 1977 elections.

Then, the Northern Marianas in the early 1970s had only 12,000 people, about 90% of them on Saipan. There were no modern runways and only one rickety flight a day from Guam. The U.S. government discouraged development in the islands after World War II because the CIA operated a covert training base on half of Saipan until 1962. But the C.N.M.I. government began to make decisions which transformed the Northern Marianas. In the mid-1980s, the C.N.M.I. opened up its economy to foreign investment and wrote its immigration laws to permit a huge influx of guest workers. This resulted in heavy investment in garment factories that imported guest workers, mostly female, from low-wage countries like the Philippines, China and Vietnam. Products made here could be labeled "Made in U.S.A." and imported into the United States without being subject to textile import quotas. By the mid-1990s, there were some 34 garment factories, employing 17,000 guest workers. Japanese investors also began building tourist destinations, with many low-wage jobs for guest workers.

The result was a population boom. The 2000 census counted 69,000 people in the Northern Marianas, with more than 90% on Saipan. The population was 32% Chamorro (the original inhabitants) or other Micronesian, 56% Asian, 2% white and 10% other and mixed. Only 44% were U.S. citizens. The booming garment industry and tourism business were hailed by some free market conservatives as a triumph of free enterprise. Former House Majority Leader Tom DeLay, a Texas Republican, was a strong booster of the C.N.M.I.'s arrangements, particularly its exemption from federal immigration laws and minimum wage. Others members of Congress, notably Rep. George Miller, D-Calif., were appalled at the exploitation of the mostly female Chinese and Filipina guest workers, who were often forced to work long hours in sweat shops to pay off $7,000 in recruiting fees needed to get such jobs. Many were forced into prostitution by unmonitored recruiters. They had no legal recourse, they could not become U.S. citizens and they were subject to summary deportation. Members of Congress who wanted reform responded by trying to deny the "Made in U.S.A." label to clothing manufactured in the C.N.M.I. Alaska Republican Frank Murkowski got the Senate to vote unanimously to do so in 1995 and 2000. But DeLay kept the measure from coming to a vote in the House.

Two outside developments transformed the situation. In January 2005, the treaty that had set quotas on textile imports into the United States expired. Suddenly, the C.N.M.I.'s exemption from those quotas became irrelevant, and Saipan was subject to lower-wage competition from Vietnam, Cambodia and China. Then, in October 2005, Japan Airlines cancelled its daily flights to Saipan after nearly 30 years of direct service. Japanese investors sold three hotels, a golf course and shopping center. Tourism, which had employed half the workforce, nosedived.

The increase in the federal minimum wage that passed in 2007 included a gradual increase in the hourly minimum wage for the C.N.M.I. from $3.05 to $7.25 by 2014. This further destroyed the business model of the garment factories, which claimed they could not survive an hourly wage above $4. By January 2009, all of them were shuttered. Congress in 2008 brought the C.N.M.I. under federal immigration law, at the same time phasing out the current guest worker program by 2017 and providing worker protections. Most C.N.M.I. politicians opposed the bill, but had little power to stop it. It also gave the C.N.M.I. its first ever delegate in Congress.

The C.N.M.I. does not vote for president and plays less of a role in presidential politics than the other four territories represented in Congress. On Feb. 23, 2008, all nine of its delegates to the Republican National Convention "decided to vote as a team for McCain." The national Democratic Party does not recognize the C.N.M.I. Democratic Party.

Governor   Benigno Fitial was elected governor of the C.N.M.I. in November 2005 as a candidate of the Covenant Party. He is the first governor of Carolinian descent. The Carolinians immigrated to the Northern Marianas from Micronesia about a century ago. He grew up on Saipan and graduated from the University of Guam. He was elected to the first C.N.M.I. Legislature in 1977, served for the majority of the years since, and had much to do with fashioning the C.N.M.I. immigration and property laws that led to the vast growth in the garment and tourism industries in the 1980s and 1990s. He was also an active participant in the Bank of Saipan, Tan Holdings and various insurance, travel and home improvement companies. Long a Republican, he was head of the islands' 2000 campaign for George W. Bush and called himself a "good friend" of disgraced lobbyist Jack Abramoff, who took members of Congress on junkets to the islands. He won the contest for governor by only 99 votes.

Fitial opposes the imposition of federal immigration law on the C.N.M.I., and in September 2008, filed a lawsuit challenging it on the grounds that it violated the covenant agreed to by the Marianas and the United States in 1976, which allowed the commonwealth to pass its own labor laws. After Homeland Security Secretary Janet Napolitano agreed to delay implementation of federalized immigration from May 2009 to November 2009, he called for a further delay, and he pressed Congress to grant visa waivers for Chinese and Russian tourists, without which, he said, the C.N.M.I. would face "economic genocide."

Fitial attracted some attention when he had his 28-year-old masseuse released from jail to give him a massage, later claiming he didn't know she was jailed for federal human smuggling charges. The C.N.M.I.'s parlous fiscal condition resulted in a ten-day partial government shutdown when Fitial and the legislature could not agree on a budget in October 2010.

Still, Fitial won re-election in 2010 to a new five-year term. He defeated Republican Heinz Hofschneider.

DELEGATE

Gregorio Kilili Camacho Sablan (D)

Elected 2008, term expires 2010, 2nd term; b. Jan. 19, 1955, Saipan; home, Saipan; Attended U. of Guam, 1972; Attended Armstrong U., 1973-74; Attended U. of HI-Manoa, 1989-90; Catholic; married (Andrea); 6 children.

Military Career: Army Reserves, 1982-87.

Elected Office: Northern Marianas Commonwealth Legislature, 1982-86.

Professional Career: Governor's deputy chief admin. officer, CNMI government, 1980-81; Spec. asst. for mgmt. & budget, CNMI government, 1994-95; Exec. dir., Commonwealth Election Commission, 1999-2008.

DC Office: 423 CHOB, 20515, 202-225-2646; Fax: 202-226-4249; Web site: sablan.house.gov.

State Offices: Rota, 670-532-2647; Saipan, 670-323-2647/8; Tinian, 670-433-2647.

Committees: *Agriculture:* Conservation, Energy & Forestry; Nutrition & Horticulture. *Natural Resources:* Energy & Mineral Resources; Fisheries, Wildlife, Oceans & Insular Affairs (RMM).

The first delegate to the U.S. House of Representatives from the Commonwealth of the Northern Mariana Islands is Gregorio Kilili Camacho Sablan, elected in November 2008. He grew up in Saipan in an extended family much involved in politics. His grandfather was the first elected mayor of Saipan, and his uncle was the city's longest serving mayor. At age 11, he moved to the Federated States of Micronesia and attended boarding school, the only ethnic Chamorro there. He attended the University of Guam and the University of California at Berkeley, but did not get a degree. He went to work for Republican Gov. Carlos Camacho, the C.N.M.I.'s first elected governor, and then served in the legislature from 1982 to 1986. Sablan also worked for 18 months on the Washington staff of Hawaii Democratic Sen. Daniel Inouye, who has long taken an interest in the Pacific territories. When he returned to Saipan, Sablan was special assistant for management and budget for Democratic Gov. Froilan Tenorio. Later, he was appointed executive director of the Commonwealth Election Commission and won praise for his conduct of C.N.M.I.'s closely contested election in 2006.

After Congress voted in April 2008 to give the C.N.M.I. a non-voting delegate in Congress for the first time, Sablan ran for the office with eight others. Two of them spent large sums—large for the C.N.M.I., at least—on their campaigns. Retired Judge Juan Tudela Lizama spent $52,000 and seven-year C.N.M.I. Washington representative Pete A. Tenorio, a Republican, spent $37,000. Sablan ran as an independent rather than as a Democrat because, he said, the local Democratic Party was "not organized," and spent $15,000. Of 10,161 votes cast, Sablan received 2,474, edging his nearest competition, Tenorio, by 357 votes. In November 2010, Sablan was re-elected with 4,902 votes, to 2,744 for Joseph Camacho of the Covenant Party, 2,049 for former Republican Gov. Juan Babauta and 1,707 for former Democratic Lt. Gov. Jesse Borja.

AMERICAN SAMOA

American Samoa, the only American territory south of the Equator, has been little influenced by Western settlers and remains almost as Polynesian today as it was when the United States took possession of it in 1900 at the request of tribal chiefs. These seven hot, rainy islands are 2,300 miles southwest of Hawaii, 1,600 miles northeast of New Zealand, and have a land area slightly larger than the District of Columbia. Pago Pago, the largest town, has one of the finest natural harbors in the Pacific. American Samoa has 67,000 people, 90% of them on the island of Tutuila. They are U.S. nationals but not U.S. citizens; they can serve in the American military, and volunteer in large proportions, but not as officers. An estimated 50,000 Samoans live on the U.S. mainland and 20,000 in Hawaii, including former Honolulu Mayor Mufi Hannemann. The islands' population has doubled in the last 20 years, and fear that outsiders will change the culture has prompted some demands for stricter immigration standards. American Samoa is an unincorporated territory administered by the Interior Department. American Samoa elects a governor and a two-house legislature known as the Fono. It is a largely Christian and bilingual society and government. Government is mostly conducted in English, Fono proceedings are in Samoan, and court sessions are conducted in English with each sentence then translated into Samoan.

The market economy has not made much progress here. American Samoa lives primarily off the federal government, which contributes about 60% of its government revenues. For years, the private sector economy consisted of two big StarKist and Chicken of the Sea tuna canneries, which provided one-third of all U.S. canned tuna and employed over 5,000 workers. But demand for tuna has been stagnant in recent years, while tuna workers' wages have gone up. In 2007, congressional Democrats excluded American Samoa from their minimum wage increase (although Guam and the Commonwealth of the Northern Marianas Islands were included) at the request of American Samoa Delegate Eni Faleomavaega. But House Republicans attacked the Democrats as hypocritical, and so Democrats agreed that the minimum wage in American Samoa would rise to $7.25 an hour by 2014. In response, Chicken of the Sea announced in 2009 that it would close its Samoa packing plant, with 2,100 jobs, at the end of September. Then on Sept. 29, 2009, an offshore earthquake measuring 8.0 on the Richter scale produced a four-wave tsunami that struck American Samoa, killing 24 people.

Emergency aid poured in, but the tuna industry remained shaky. Faleomavaega managed to get a bill passed almost unanimously and signed in September 2010 rescinding scheduled minimum wage increases for 2011 and 2012. But StarKist, owned by the Korean firm Dongwon, laid off workers, reducing its workforce of 3,000 to 1,200 by late 2010. In the meantime, the bulwark of the economy remains the territorial government, which employs about 4,000, most at $8 an hour. Local agriculture is minimal. A government report summarized American Samoa's difficulty in finding alternatives to the tuna canneries. "Attempts by the government to develop a larger and broader economy are restrained by Samoa's remote location, its limited transportation and its devastating hurricanes.

American Samoa does not cast electoral votes for president, but it does send delegates to the major parties' national conventions. In 2008, Democrat Hillary Clinton edged out Barack Obama, receiving two convention votes split among four delegates, while Obama got one vote and two delegates. John McCain swept the Republican caucus, receiving all nine delegates. American Samoa also plays some role in national party politics.

Governor   Democrat Togiola T.A. Tulafono was sworn in as American Samoa's governor on April 7, 2003, after the sudden death of Gov. Tauese Sunia on March 26. Togiola grew up in American Samoa. He graduated from the Honolulu Police Academy and worked as a policeman for a year. After attending college and law school on the mainland, he returned home and practiced law for 20 years. He also was a judge and a senator. Togiola was elected lieutenant governor in 1996 and served under Tauese until his death.

In the 2008 election, Togiola won 41% of the votes in the first round to 31% for Utu Abe Malae and 27% for Afoa Moega Lutu, even though Togiola's lieutenant governor was facing federal corruption charges. In the runoff, he beat Malae, 56%-44%.

In 2008 and 2009, Togiola strongly opposed the six-month incremental increases in the minimum wage voted by Congress and called for reestablishing the administrative process for setting minimum wages for the territory. "The promise to have higher wages is now the demise of the very people that this law was supposed to help. This thing is killing us," he said in a statement. In June 2010, he called for full autonomy for American Samoa, so that it would not be bound by U.S. minimum wage laws.

DELEGATE

Eni F.H. Faleomavaega (D)

Elected 1988, 12th term; b. Aug. 15, 1943, Vailoatai; home, Pago Pago; Brigham Young U., B.A. 1966, U. of Houston, J.D. 1972, U. of CA, LL.M. 1973; Mormon; married (Hinanui); 5 children.

Military Career: Army, 1966–69 (Vietnam).

Elected Office: AS Lt. Gov., 1984–89.

Professional Career: A.A., U.S. Del. from AS, 1973–75; Cnsl., U.S. House Interior Cmte., 1975–81; AS Dpty. Atty. Gen., 1981–84.

DC Office: 2422 RHOB, 20515, 202-225-8577; Fax: 202-225-8757; Web site: www.house.gov/faleomavaega.

State Offices: Pago Pago, 684-633-1372.

Committees: *Foreign Affairs:* Asia & the Pacific (RMM); Western Hemisphere. *Natural Resources:* Fisheries, Wildlife, Oceans & Insular Affairs; Indian & Alaska Native Affairs.

Delegate Eni F. H. Faleomavaega, a Democrat elected in 1988, has represented American Samoa for most of the time since it first got a representative in 1980. A Mormon, he graduated from high school in Hawaii and from the Mormon-run Brigham Young University in Utah. He then attended law school in Houston and Berkeley. He served in the Army in Vietnam. In 1981, he became deputy attorney general of American Samoa, and in 1985, lieutenant governor.

In early 2011, he became the ranking member of the Subcommittee on Asia, the Pacific and the Global Environment on the Foreign Affairs Committee. He has taken a particular interest in the independence movement in Indonesia's West Papua, where his relatives were Christian missionaries in the late 1800s. The Indonesian government denied him entry to West Papua in 2007, on the grounds that it would spark demonstrations and violence. But that December, Indonesian President Susilo Bambang Yudhoyono allowed him limited, closely monitored access to the island.

For several years, Faleomavaega pressed for a bill to exempt interest on American Samoa bonds from state and local taxes—the same treatment given bonds issued by Puerto Rico, Guam and the Virgin Islands—and it was signed into law in 2004. He has also worked successfully for favorable tax treatment for tuna canneries. In 2007, Faleomavaega urged his fellow Democrats not to include American Samoa in their minimum wage increase. Faleaomavaega faced Republican Aumua Amata Coleman in the 2008 and 2010 elections. In 2008, he won 60%-35% and in 2010 he won 56%-40%. He is the senior representative from the territories.

LEADERSHIP

The 112th Congress
2011–2012

U.S. Senate

51 D, 47 R, 2 I

Democrats

Senate Majority Leader	Harry Reid (NV)
President Pro Tempore	Daniel Inouye (HI)
Senate Assistant Majority Leader and Whip	Richard Durbin (IL)
Senate Democratic Conference Vice Chairman & Policy Committee Chairman	Charles Schumer (NY)
Senate Democratic Conference Secretary	Patty Murray (WA)
Democratic Senatorial Campaign Committee Chairman	Patty Murray (WA)
Senate Democratic Steering and Outreach Committee Chairman	Debbie Stabenow (MI)

Republicans

Senate Minority Leader	Mitch McConnell (KY)
Senate Assistant Minority Leader and Whip	Jon Kyl (AZ)
Senate Republican Conference Chairman	Lamar Alexander (TN)
Senate Republican Conference Vice Chairman & Secretary	John Barrasso (WY)
Senate Republican Policy Committee Chairman	John Thune (SD)
National Republican Senatorial Committee Chairman	John Cornyn (TX)

U.S. House of Representatives

192 D, 240 R, 3 V

Republicans

House Speaker	John Boehner (OH-8)
Majority Leader	Eric Cantor (VA-7)
Majority Whip	Kevin McCarthy (CA-22)
House Chief Deputy Whip	Peter Roskam (IL-6)
House Republican Conference Chairman	Jeb Hensarling (TX-5)
National Republican Congressional Committee Chairman	Pete Sessions (TX-32)
House Republican Conference Vice Chairman	Cathy McMorris Rodgers (WA-5)
House Republican Conference Secretary	John Carter (TX-31)
House Republican Policy Committee Chairman	Tom Price (GA-6)

Democrats

House Minority Leader... Nancy Pelosi (CA-8)
House Minority Whip .... Steny Hoyer (MD-5)
House Democratic Caucus Chairman...................... John Larson (CT-1)
Assistant Democratic Leader .... James Clyburn (SC-6)
House Democratic Caucus Vice Chairman .... Xavier Becerra (CA-31)
Senior Chief Deputy Whip .... John Lewis (GA-5)
Chief Deputy Whip .... G.K. Butterfield (NC-1)
Chief Deputy Whip .... Joseph Crowley (NY-7)
Chief Deputy Whip .... Diana DeGette (CO-1)
Chief Deputy Whip .... Ed Pastor (AZ-4)
Chief Deputy Whip .... Jan Schakowsky (IL-9)
Chief Deputy Whip .... Debbie Wasserman
                                                                                        Schultz (FL-20)
Chief Deputy Whip .... Maxine Waters (CA-35)
Chief Deputy Whip .... Jim Matheson (UT-2)
Chief Deputy Whip .... Peter Welch (VT-AL)

Rosters and party breakdowns as of May 31, 2011

SENATE SENIORITY

This list of senators in order of their seniority was provided by the U.S. Senate Press Gallery and was compiled from U.S. Senate Historical Office records.

Democrats

Member (State)	Start of Service	Member (State)	Start of Service
Daniel Inouye (HI)	January 3, 1963	Ben Nelson (NE)	January 3, 2001
Patrick Leahy (VT)	January 3, 1975	Frank Lautenberg[1] (NJ)	January 7, 2003
Max Baucus (MT)	December 15, 1978	Mark Pryor (AR)	January 7, 2003
Carl Levin (MI)	January 3, 1979	Robert Menendez (NJ)	January 18, 2006
Jeff Bingaman (NM)	January 3, 1983	Ben Cardin (MD)	January 4, 2007
John Kerry (MA)	January 3, 1985	Sherrod Brown (OH)	January 4, 2007
Tom Harkin (IA)	January 3, 1985	Robert Casey (PA)	January 4, 2007
Jay Rockefeller (WV)	January 15, 1985	Jim Webb (VA)	January 4, 2007
Barbara Mikulski (MD)	January 3, 1987	Claire McCaskill (MO)	January 4, 2007
Harry Reid (NV)	January 3, 1987	Amy Klobuchar (MN)	January 4, 2007
Kent Conrad (ND)	January 3, 1987	Sheldon Whitehouse (RI)	January 4, 2007
Herb Kohl (WI)	January 3, 1989	Jon Tester (MT)	January 4, 2007
Daniel Akaka (HI)	May 16, 1990	Mark Udall (CO)	January 6, 2009
Dianne Feinstein (CA)	November 10, 1992	Tom Udall (NM)	January 6, 2009
Barbara Boxer (CA)	January 3, 1993	Jeanne Shaheen (NH)	January 6, 2009
Patty Murray (WA)	January 3, 1993	Mark Warner (VA)	January 6, 2009
Ron Wyden (OR)	February 6, 1996	Kay Hagan (NC)	January 6, 2009
Dick Durbin (IL)	January 7, 1997	Jeff Merkley (OR)	January 6, 2009
Tim Johnson (SD)	January 7, 1997	Mark Begich (AK)	January 6, 2009
Jack Reed (RI)	January 7, 1997	Michael Bennet (CO)	January 22, 2009
Mary Landrieu (LA)	January 7, 1997	Kirsten Gillibrand (NY)	January 27, 2009
Chuck Schumer (NY)	January 6, 1999	Al Franken (MN)	July 7, 2009
Bill Nelson (FL)	January 3, 2001	Joe Manchin(WV)	November 15, 2010
Thomas Carper (DE)	January 3, 2001	Christopher Coons (DE)	November 15, 2010
Debbie Stabenow (MI)	January 3, 2001	Richard Blumenthal (CT)	January 5, 2011
Maria Cantwell (WA)	January 3, 2001		

Republicans

Member (State)	Start of Service	Member (State)	Start of Service
Richard Lugar (IN)	January 4, 1977	Lamar Alexander (TN)	January 7, 2003
Orrin Hatch (UT)	January 4, 1977	John Cornyn (TX)	December 2, 2002
Thad Cochran (MS)	December 27, 1978	Richard Burr (NC)	January 3, 2005
Chuck Grassley (IA)	January 3, 1981	Jim DeMint (SC)	January 3, 2005
Mitch McConnell (KY)	January 3, 1985	Tom Coburn (OK)	January 3, 2005
Richard Shelby (AL)	January 3, 1987	John Thune (SD)	January 3, 2005
John McCain (AZ)	January 3, 1987	Johnny Isakson (GA)	January 3, 2005
Kay Bailey Hutchison (TX)	June 14, 1993	David Vitter (LA)	January 3, 2005
James Inhofe (OK)	November 16, 1994	Bob Corker (TN)	January 4, 2007
Olympia Snowe (ME)	January 4, 1995	John Barrasso (WY)	June 22, 2007
John Kyl (AZ)	January 4, 1995	Roger Wicker (MS)	December 31, 2007
Pat Roberts (KS)	January 7, 1997	Mike Johanns (NE)	January 6, 2009
Jeff Sessions (AL)	January 7, 1997	James Risch (ID)	January 6, 2009
Susan Collins (ME)	January 7, 1997	Scott Brown (MA)	February 4, 2010
Michael Enzi (WY)	January 7, 1997	Mark Kirk (IL)	November 29, 2010
Mike Crapo (ID)	January 6, 1999	Dan Coats (IN)	January 5, 2011
Lisa Murkowski (AK)	December 20, 2002	Roy Blunt (MO)	January 5, 2011
Saxby Chambliss (GA)	January 7, 2003	Jerry Moran (KS)	January 5, 2011
Lindsey Graham (SC)	January 7, 2003	Rob Portman (OH)	January 5, 2011

[1]First served Dec. 1982-Jan. 2001.

Member (State)	Start of Service	Member (State)	Start of Service
John Boozman (AR)	January 5, 2011	Rand Paul (KY)	January 5, 2011
Pat Toomey (PA)	January 5, 2011	Mike Lee (UT)	January 5, 2011
John Hoeven (ND)	January 5, 2011	Kelly Ayotte (N.H.)	January 5, 2011
Marco Rubio (FL)	January 5, 2011	Dean Heller (NV)	May 9, 2011
Ron Johnson (WI)	January 5, 2011		

Independents

Member (State)	Start of Service	Member (State)	Start of Service
Joe Lieberman (CT)	January 3, 1989	Bernie Sanders (VT)	January 4, 2007

HOUSE SENIORITY

Republicans

House Republicans base seniority on length of time in office. Members who return after previous House service are usually allowed to claim most of their earlier service for seniority purposes, although final decisions are made by the Republican leadership. Start of service dates are from the U.S. House clerk.

Member (State)	Start of Service	Member (State)	Start of Service
Bill Young (FL)	January 3, 1971	Buck McKeon (CA)	January 3, 1993
Don Young (AK)	March 6, 1973	Don Manzullo (IL)	January 3, 1993
Jerry Lewis (CA)	January 3, 1979	John Mica (FL)	January 3, 1993
Jim Sensenbrenner (WI)	January 3, 1979	Ed Royce (CA)	January 3, 1993
Thomas Petri (WI)	April 3, 1979	Frank Lucas (OK)	May 10, 1994
David Dreier (CA)	January 3, 1981	Rodney Frelinghuysen (NJ)	January 3, 1995
Ralph Hall (TX)	January 3, 1981	Doc Hastings (WA)	January 3, 1995
Harold Rogers (KY)	January 3, 1981	Walter Jones (NC)	January 3, 1995
Chris Smith (NJ)	January 3, 1981	Tom Latham (IA)	January 3, 1995
Frank Wolf (VA)	January 3, 1981	Steven LaTourette (OH)	January 3, 1995
Dan Burton (IN)	January 3, 1983	Frank LoBiondo (NJ)	January 3, 1995
Joe Barton (TX)	January 3, 1985	Sue Myrick (NC)	January 3, 1995
Howard Coble (NC)	January 3, 1985	Mac Thornberry (TX)	January 3, 1995
Elton Gallegly (CA)	January 3, 1987	Ed Whitfield (KY)	January 3, 1995
Wally Herger (CA)	January 3, 1987	Jo Ann Emerson (MO)	November 5, 1996
Lamar Smith (TX)	January 3, 1987	Dan Lungren[2] (CA)	January 3, 2005
Fred Upton (MI)	January 3, 1987	Robert Aderholt (AL)	January 3, 1997
John Duncan (TN)	November 8, 1988	Kevin Brady (TX)	January 3, 1997
Dana Rohrabacher (CA)	January 3, 1989	Kay Granger (TX)	January 3, 1997
Cliff Stearns (FL)	January 3, 1989	Joe Pitts (PA)	January 3, 1997
Ileana Ros-Lehtinen (FL)	August 29, 1989	Pete Sessions (TX)	January 3, 1997
Ron Paul[1] (TX)	January 3, 1997	John Shimkus (IL)	January 3, 1997
John Boehner (OH)	January 3, 1991	Mary Bono Mack (CA)	April 7, 1998
Dave Camp (MI)	January 3, 1991	Steve Chabot[3] (OH)	January 3, 2011
Sam Johnson (TX)	May 8, 1991	Judy Biggert (IL)	January 3, 1999
Spencer Bachus (AL)	January 3, 1993	Gary Miller (CA)	January 3, 1999
Roscoe Bartlett (MD)	January 3, 1993	Paul Ryan (WI)	January 3, 1999
Ken Calvert (CA)	January 3, 1993	Mike Simpson (ID)	January 3, 1999
Bob Goodlatte (VA)	January 3, 1993	Lee Terry (NE)	January 3, 1999
Peter King (NY)	January 3, 1993	Greg Walden (OR)	January 3, 1999
Jack Kingston (GA)	January 3, 1993	Charlie Bass[4] (NH)	January 3, 2001

---

[1] Also served 1976–1977; 1979–1985
[2] Also served 1979–1989
[3] Also served 1995–2009
[4] Also served 1995–2007

Member (State)	Start of Service	Member (State)	Start of Service
Brian Bilbray[5] (CA)	June 6, 2006	Ted Poe (TX)	January 3, 2005
Todd Akin (MO)	January 3, 2001	Tom Price (GA)	January 3, 2005
Eric Cantor (VA)	January 3, 2001	Dave Reichert (WA)	January 3, 2005
Shelley Moore Capito (WV)	January 3, 2001	Lynn Westmoreland (GA)	January 3, 2005
Ander Crenshaw (FL)	January 3, 2001	Jean Schmidt (OH)	August 2, 2005
John Culberson (TX)	January 3, 2001	John Campbell (CA)	December 6, 2005
Jeff Flake (AZ)	January 3, 2001	Steve Pearce[6] (NM)	January 3, 2011
Sam Graves (MO)	January 3, 2001	Michele Bachmann (MN)	January 3, 2007
Darrell Issa (CA)	January 3, 2001	Gus Bilirakis (FL)	January 3, 2007
Tim Johnson (IL)	January 3, 2001	Vern Buchanan (FL)	January 3, 2007
Mike Pence (IN)	January 3, 2001	Jim Jordan (OH)	January 3, 2007
Todd Platts (PA)	January 3, 2001	Doug Lamborn (CO)	January 3, 2007
Denny Rehberg (MT)	January 3, 2001	Kevin McCarthy (CA)	January 3, 2007
Mike Rogers (MI)	January 3, 2001	Peter Roskam (IL)	January 3, 2007
Pat Tiberi (OH)	January 3, 2001	Adrian Smith (NE)	January 3, 2007
Bill Shuster (PA)	May 15, 2001	Paul Broun (GA)	July 17, 2007
Randy Forbes (VA)	June 19, 2001	Bob Latta (OH)	December 11, 2007
Jeff Miller (FL)	October 16, 2001	Robert Wittman (VA)	December 11, 2007
Joe Wilson (SC)	December 18, 2001	Steve Scalise (LA)	May 3, 2008
John Sullivan (OK)	February 15, 2002	Steve Austria (OH)	January 3, 2009
Rodney Alexander (LA)	January 3, 2003	Bill Cassidy (LA)	January 3, 2009
Rob Bishop (UT)	January 3, 2003	Jason Chaffetz (UT)	January 3, 2009
Marsha Blackburn (TN)	January 3, 2003	Mike Coffman (CO)	January 3, 2009
Jo Bonner (AL)	January 3, 2003	John Fleming (LA)	January 3, 2009
Michael Burgess (TX)	January 3, 2003	Brett Guthrie (KY)	January 3, 2009
John Carter (TX)	January 3, 2003	Gregg Harper (MS)	January 3, 2009
Tom Cole (OK)	January 3, 2003	Duncan D. Hunter (CA)	January 3, 2009
Mario Diaz-Balart (FL)	January 3, 2003	Lynn Jenkins (KS)	January 3, 2009
Trent Franks (AZ)	January 3, 2003	Leonard Lance (NJ)	January 3, 2009
Scott Garrett (NJ)	January 3, 2003	Blaine Luetkemeyer (MO)	January 3, 2009
Jim Gerlach (PA)	January 3, 2003	Cynthia Lummis (WY)	January 3, 2009
Phil Gingrey (GA)	January 3, 2003	Tom McClintock (CA)	January 3, 2009
Jeb Hensarling (TX)	January 3, 2003	Pete Olson (TX)	January 3, 2009
Steve King (IA)	January 3, 2003	Erik Paulsen (MN)	January 3, 2009
John Kline (MN)	January 3, 2003	Bill Posey (FL)	January 3, 2009
Thaddeus McCotter (MI)	January 3, 2003	Phil Roe (TN)	January 3, 2009
Candice Miller (MI)	January 3, 2003	Tom Rooney (FL)	January 3, 2009
Tim Murphy (PA)	January 3, 2003	Aaron Schock (IL)	January 3, 2009
Devin Nunes (CA)	January 3, 2003	Glenn Thompson (PA)	January 3, 2009
Mike Rogers (AL)	January 3, 2003	Tom Graves (GA)	June 8, 2010
Mike Turner (OH)	January 3, 2003	Tom Reed (NY)	November 2, 2010
Randy Neugebauer (TX)	June 3, 2003	Marlin Stutzman (IN)	November 2, 2010
Charles Boustany (LA)	January 3, 2005	Mike Fitzpatrick[7] (PA)	January 3, 2011
Mike Conaway (TX)	January 3, 2005	Tim Walberg[8] (MI)	January 3, 2011
Geoff Davis (KY)	January 3, 2005	Sandy Adams (FL)	January 3, 2011
Charlie Dent (PA)	January 3, 2005	Justin Amash (MI)	January 3, 2011
Jeff Fortenberry (NE)	January 3, 2005	Lou Barletta (PA)	January 3, 2011
Virginia Foxx (NC)	January 3, 2005	Dan Benishek (MI)	January 3, 2011
Louie Gohmert (TX)	January 3, 2005	Rick Berg (ND)	January 3, 2011
Michael McCaul (TX)	January 3, 2005	Diane Black (TN)	January 3, 2011
Patrick McHenry (NC)	January 3, 2005	Mo Brooks (AL)	January 3, 2011
Cathy McMorris Rodgers (WA)	January 3, 2005	Larry Bucshon (IN)	January 3, 2011
Connie Mack (FL)	January 3, 2005	Ann Marie Buerkle (NY)	January 3, 2011
Kenny Marchant (TX)	January 3, 2005	Francisco (Quico) Canseco (TX)	January 3, 2011

[5]Also served 1995–2001
[6]Also served 2003–2009
[7]Also served 2005–2007
[8]Also served 2007–2009

Member (State)	Start of Service	Member (State)	Start of Service
Chip Cravaack (MN)	January 3, 2011	Jeff Landry (LA)	January 3, 2011
Rick Crawford (AR)	January 3, 2011	James Lankford (OK)	January 3, 2011
Jeff Denham (CA)	January 3, 2011	Billy Long (MO)	January 3, 2011
Scott DesJarlais (TN)	January 3, 2011	David McKinley (WV)	January 3, 2011
Robert Dold (IL)	January 3, 2011	Tom Marino (PA)	January 3, 2011
Sean Duffy (WI)	January 3, 2011	Pat Meehan (PA)	January 3, 2011
Jeff Duncan (SC)	January 3, 2011	Mick Mulvaney (SC)	January 3, 2011
Renee Ellmers (NC)	January 3, 2011	Kristi Noem (SD)	January 3, 2011
Blake Farenthold (TX)	January 3, 2011	Richard Nugent (FL)	January 3, 2011
Stephen Fincher (TN)	January 3, 2011	Alan Nunnelee (MS)	January 3, 2011
Chuck Fleischmann (TN)	January 3, 2011	Steven Palazzo (MS)	January 3, 2011
Bill Flores (TX)	January 3, 2011	Mike Pompeo (KS)	January 3, 2011
Cory Gardner (CO)	January 3, 2011	Ben Quayle (AZ)	January 3, 2011
Bob Gibbs (OH)	January 3, 2011	Jim Renacci (OH)	January 3, 2011
Chris Gibson (NY)	January 3, 2011	Reid Ribble (WI)	January 3, 2011
Paul Gosar (AZ)	January 3, 2011	Scott Rigell (VA)	January 3, 2011
Trey Gowdy (SC)	January 3, 2011	David Rivera (FL)	January 3, 2011
Tim Griffin (AR)	January 3, 2011	Martha Roby (AL)	January 3, 2011
Morgan Griffith (VA)	January 3, 2011	Todd Rokita (IN)	January 3, 2011
Michael Grimm (NY)	January 3, 2011	Dennis Ross (FL)	January 3, 2011
Frank Guinta (NH)	January 3, 2011	Jon Runyan (NJ)	January 3, 2011
Richard Hanna (NY)	January 3, 2011	Bobby Schilling (IL)	January 3, 2011
Andy Harris (MD)	January 3, 2011	David Schweikert (AZ)	January 3, 2011
Vicky Hartzler (MO)	January 3, 2011	Austin Scott (GA)	January 3, 2011
Nan Hayworth (NY)	January 3, 2011	Tim Scott (SC)	January 3, 2011
Joe Heck (NV)	January 3, 2011	Steve Southerland (FL)	January 3, 2011
Jaime Herrera Beutler (WA)	January 3, 2011	Steve Stivers (OH)	January 3, 2011
Tim Huelskamp (KS)	January 3, 2011	Scott Tipton (CO)	January 3, 2011
Bill Huizenga (MI)	January 3, 2011	Joe Walsh (IL)	January 3, 2011
Randy Hultgren (IL)	January 3, 2011	Daniel Webster (FL)	January 3, 2011
Robert Hurt (VA)	January 3, 2011	Allen West (FL)	January 3, 2011
Bill Johnson (OH)	January 3, 2011	Steve Womack (AR)	January 3, 2011
Mike Kelly (PA)	January 3, 2011	Rob Woodall (GA)	January 3, 2011
Adam Kinzinger (IL)	January 3, 2011	Kevin Yoder (KS)	January 3, 2011
Raul Labrador (ID)	January 3, 2011	Todd Young (IN)	January 3, 2011

Democrats

House Democrats base seniority on length of time in office. Democratic members who return after previous House service are given seniority over others elected at that time, but do not receive full credit for their earlier years in the house. Start of service dates provided by the U.S. House clerk.

Member (State)	Start of Service	Member (State)	Start of Service
John Dingell (MI)	December 13, 1955	Tim Holden (PA)	January 3, 1993
John Conyers (MI)	January 3, 1965	Eddie Bernice Johnson (TX)	January 3, 1993
Charles Rangel (NY)	January 3, 1971	Carolyn Maloney (NY)	January 3, 1993
Pete Stark (CA)	January 3, 1973	Lucille Roybal-Allard (CA)	January 3, 1993
George Miller (CA)	January 3, 1975	Bobby Rush (IL)	January 3, 1993
Henry Waxman (CA)	January 3, 1975	Bobby Scott (VA)	January 3, 1993
Edward Markey (MA)	November 2, 1976	Nydia Velázquez (NY)	January 3, 1993
Norm Dicks (WA)	January 3, 1977	Melvin Watt (NC)	January 3, 1993
Dale Kildee (MI)	January 3, 1977	Lynn Woolsey (CA)	January 3, 1993
Nick Rahall (WV)	January 3, 1977	Bennie Thompson (MS)	April 13, 1993
Barney Frank (MA)	January 3, 1981	Sam Farr (CA)	June 8, 1993
Steny Hoyer (MD)	May 19, 1981	Lloyd Doggett (TX)	January 3, 1995
Howard Berman (CA)	January 3, 1983	Mike Doyle (PA)	January 3, 1995
Marcy Kaptur (OH)	January 3, 1983	Chaka Fattah (PA)	January 3, 1995
Sander Levin (MI)	January 3, 1983	Sheila Jackson Lee (TX)	January 3, 1995
Edolphus Towns (NY)	January 3, 1983	Zoe Lofgren (CA)	January 3, 1995
Gary Ackerman (NY)	March 1, 1983	Jesse Jackson Jr. (IL)	December 12, 1995
Peter Visclosky (IN)	January 3, 1985	Elijah Cummings (MD)	April 16, 1996
Peter DeFazio (OR)	January 3, 1987	Earl Blumenauer (OR)	May 21, 1996
John Lewis (GA)	January 3, 1987	Leonard Boswell (IA)	January 3, 1997
Louise Slaughter (NY)	January 3, 1987	Danny Davis (IL)	January 3, 1997
Nancy Pelosi (CA)	June 2, 1987	Diana DeGette (CO)	January 3, 1997
Jerry Costello (IL)	August 9, 1988	Rubén Hinojosa (TX)	January 3, 1997
Frank Pallone (NJ)	November 8, 1988	Ron Kind (WI)	January 3, 1997
Eliot Engel (NY)	January 3, 1989	Dennis Kucinich (OH)	January 3, 1997
Nita Lowey (NY)	January 3, 1989	Carolyn McCarthy (NY)	January 3, 1997
Jim McDermott (WA)	January 3, 1989	Jim McGovern (MA)	January 3, 1997
Richard Neal (MA)	January 3, 1989	Mike McIntyre (NC)	January 3, 1997
Donald Payne (NJ)	January 3, 1989	Bill Pascrell (NJ)	January 3, 1997
José Serrano (NY)	March 20, 1990	Silvestre Reyes (TX)	January 3, 1997
Robert Andrews (NJ)	November 6, 1990	Steven Rothman (NJ)	January 3, 1997
David Price[9] (NC)	January 3, 1997	Loretta Sanchez (CA)	January 3, 1997
Rosa DeLauro (CT)	January 3, 1991	Brad Sherman (CA)	January 3, 1997
Jim Moran (VA)	January 3, 1991	Adam Smith (WA)	January 3, 1997
Collin Peterson (MN)	January 3, 1991	John Tierney (MA)	January 3, 1997
Maxine Waters (CA)	January 3, 1991	Gregory Meeks (NY)	February 3, 1998
John Olver (MA)	June 4, 1991	Lois Capps (CA)	March 10, 1998
Ed Pastor (AZ)	September 24, 1991	Barbara Lee (CA)	April 7, 1998
Jerrold Nadler (NY)	November 3, 1992	Robert Brady (PA)	May 19, 1998
Jim Cooper[10] (TN)	January 3, 2003	Jay Inslee[11] (WA)	January 3, 1999
Xavier Becerra (CA)	January 3, 1993	Tammy Baldwin (WI)	January 3, 1999
Sanford Bishop (GA)	January 3, 1993	Shelley Berkley (NV)	January 3, 1999
Corrine Brown (FL)	January 3, 1993	Michael Capuano (MA)	January 3, 1999
James Clyburn (SC)	January 3, 1993	Joseph Crowley (NY)	January 3, 1999
Anna Eshoo (CA)	January 3, 1993	Charles Gonzalez (TX)	January 3, 1999
Bob Filner (CA)	January 3, 1993	Rush Holt (NJ)	January 3, 1999
Gene Green (TX)	January 3, 1993	John Larson (CT)	January 3, 1999
Luis Gutierrez (IL)	January 3, 1993	Grace Napolitano (CA)	January 3, 1999
Alcee Hastings (FL)	January 3, 1993	Jan Schakowsky (IL)	January 3, 1999
Maurice Hinchey (NY)	January 3, 1993	Mike Thompson (CA)	January 3, 1999

[9]Also served 1987-1995
[10]Also served 1983-1995
[11]Also served 1993-1995

Member (State)	Start of Service	Member (State)	Start of Service
David Wu (OR)	January 3, 1999	Keith Ellison (MN)	January 3, 2007
Joe Baca (CA)	November 16, 1999	Gabrielle Giffords (AZ)	January 3, 2007
William Lacy Clay (MO)	January 3, 2001	Mazie Hirono (HI)	January 3, 2007
Susan Davis (CA)	January 3, 2001	Hank Johnson (GA)	January 3, 2007
Mike Honda (CA)	January 3, 2001	Dave Loebsack (IA)	January 3, 2007
Steve Israel (NY)	January 3, 2001	Jerry McNerney (CA)	January 3, 2007
Jim Langevin (RI)	January 3, 2001	Chris Murphy (CT)	January 3, 2007
Rick Larsen (WA)	January 3, 2001	Ed Perlmutter (CO)	January 3, 2007
Betty McCollum (MN)	January 3, 2001	John Sarbanes (MD)	January 3, 2007
Jim Matheson (UT)	January 3, 2001	Heath Shuler (NC)	January 3, 2007
Mike Ross (AR)	January 3, 2001	Betty Sutton (OH)	January 3, 2007
Adam Schiff (CA)	January 3, 2001	Tim Walz (MN)	January 3, 2007
Stephen Lynch (MA)	October 16, 2001	Peter Welch (VT)	January 3, 2007
Tim Bishop (NY)	January 3, 2003	John Yarmuth (KY)	January 3, 2007
Dennis Cardoza (CA)	January 3, 2003	Laura Richardson (CA)	August 21, 2007
Raúl Grijalva (AZ)	January 3, 2003	Niki Tsongas (MA)	October 16, 2007
Michael Michaud (ME)	January 3, 2003	André Carson (IN)	March 11, 2008
Brad Miller (NC)	January 3, 2003	Jackie Speier (CA)	April 8, 2008
Dutch Ruppersberger (MD)	January 3, 2003	Donna Edwards (MD)	June 17, 2008
Tim Ryan (OH)	January 3, 2003	Marcia Fudge (OH)	November 18, 2008
Linda Sánchez (CA)	January 3, 2003	Gerald Connolly (VA)	January 3, 2009
David Scott (GA)	January 3, 2003	Martin Heinrich (NM)	January 3, 2009
Chris Van Hollen (MD)	January 3, 2003	Jim Himes (CT)	January 3, 2009
Ben Chandler (KY)	February 17, 2004	Larry Kissell (NC)	January 3, 2009
G.K. Butterfield (NC)	July 20, 2004	Ben Ray Luján (NM)	January 3, 2009
John Barrow (GA)	January 3, 2005	Gary Peters (MI)	January 3, 2009
Dan Boren (OK)	January 3, 2005	Chellie Pingree (ME)	January 3, 2009
Russ Carnahan (MO)	January 3, 2005	Jared Polis (CO)	January 3, 2009
Emanuel Cleaver (MO)	January 3, 2005	Kurt Schrader (OR)	January 3, 2009
Jim Costa (CA)	January 3, 2005	Paul Tonko (NY)	January 3, 2009
Henry Cuellar (TX)	January 3, 2005	Mike Quigley (IL)	April 7, 2009
Al Green (TX)	January 3, 2005	Judy Chu (CA)	July 14, 2009
Brian Higgins (NY)	January 3, 2005	John Garamendi (CA)	November 3, 2009
Daniel Lipinski (IL)	January 3, 2005	Bill Owens (NY)	November 3, 2009
Gwen Moore (WI)	January 3, 2005	Ted Deutch (FL)	April 13, 2010
Allyson Schwartz (PA)	January 3, 2005	Mark Critz (PA)	May 18, 2010
Debbie Wasserman		Karen Bass (CA)	January 3, 2011
Schultz (FL)	January 3, 2005	John Carney (DE)	January 3, 2011
Doris Matsui (CA)	March 8, 2005	David Cicilline (RI)	January 3, 2011
Albio Sires (NJ)	November 7, 2006	Hansen Clarke (MI)	January 3, 2011
Jason Altmire (PA)	January 3, 2007	Colleen Hanabusa (HI)	January 3, 2011
Bruce Braley (IA)	January 3, 2007	William Keating (MA)	January 3, 2011
Kathy Castor (FL)	January 3, 2007	Cedric Richmond (LA)	January 3, 2011
Yvette Clarke (NY)	January 3, 2007	Terri Sewell (AL)	January 3, 2011
Steve Cohen (TN)	January 3, 2007	Frederica Wilson (FL)	January 3, 2011
Joe Courtney (CT)	January 3, 2007	Kathy Hochul (NY)	June 1, 2011
Joe Donnelly (IN)	January 3, 2007		

CONGRESSIONAL CLASS OF 2010

Senators

Kelly Ayotte (R-NH)
Richard Blumenthal (D-CT)
Roy Blunt (R-MO)
John Boozman (R-AR)
Scott Brown* (R-MA)
Dan Coats (R-IN)

Christopher Coons (D-DE)
John Hoeven (R-ND)
Ron Johnson (R-WI)
Mark Kirk (R-IL)
Mike Lee (R-UT)
Joe Manchin (D-WV)

Jerry Moran (R-KS)
Rand Paul (R-KY)
Rob Portman (R-OH)
Marco Rubio (R-FL)
Pat Toomey (R-PA)

Representatives

Sandy Adams (R-FL)
Justin Amash (R-MI)
Lou Barletta (R-PA)
Charlie Bass (R-NH)
Karen Bass (D-CA)
Dan Benishek (R-MI)
Rick Berg (R-ND)
Diane Black (R-TN)
Mo Brooks (R-AL)
Larry Bucshon (R-IN)
Ann Marie Buerkle (R-NY)
Francisco (Quico) Canseco (R-TX)
John Carney (D-DE)
Steve Chabot (R-OH)
David Cicilline (D-RI)
Hansen Clarke (D-MI)
Chip Cravaack (R-MN)
Rick Crawford (R-AR)
Mark Critz* (D-PA)
Jeff Denham (R-CA)
Scott DesJarlais (R-TN)
Ted Deutch* (D-FL)
Robert Dold (R-IL)
Sean Duffy (R-WI)
Jeff Duncan (R-SC)
Renee Ellmers (R-NC)
Blake Farenthold (R-TX)
Stephen Fincher (R-TN)
Mike Fitzpatrick (R-PA)
Chuck Fleischmann (R-TN)
Bill Flores (R-TX)
Cory Gardner (R-CO)
Bob Gibbs (R-OH)

Chris Gibson (R-NY)
Paul Gosar (R-AZ)
Trey Gowdy (R-SC)
Tom Graves* (R-GA)
Tim Griffin (R-AR)
Morgan Griffith (R-VA)
Michael Grimm (R-NY)
Frank Guinta (R-NH)
Colleen Hanabusa (D-HI)
Richard Hanna (R-NY)
Andy Harris (R-MD)
Vicky Hartzler (R-MO)
Nan Hayworth (R-NY)
Joe Heck (R-NV)
Jaime Herrera Beutler (R-WA)
Tim Huelskamp (R-KS)
Bill Huizenga (R-MI)
Randy Hultgren (R-IL)
Robert Hurt (R-VA)
Bill Johnson (R-OH)
William Keating (D-MA)
Mike Kelly (R-PA)
Adam Kinzinger (R-IL)
Raul Labrador (R-ID)
Jeffrey Landry (R-LA)
James Lankford (R-OK)
Billy Long (R-MO)
Tom Marino (R-PA)
David McKinley (R-WV)
Pat Meehan (R-PA)
Mick Mulvaney (R-SC)
Kristi Noem (R-SD)
Richard Nugent (R-FL)

Alan Nunnelee (R-MS)
Steven Palazzo (R-MS)
Steve Pearce (R-NM)
Mike Pompeo (R-KS)
Ben Quayle (R-AZ)
Tom Reed (R-NY)
Jim Renacci (R-OH)
Reid Ribble (R-WI)
Cedric Richmond (D-LA)
Scott Rigell (R-VA)
David Rivera (R-FL)
Martha Roby (R-AL)
Todd Rokita (R-IN)
Dennis Ross (R-FL)
Jon Runyan (R-NJ)
Bobby Schilling (R-IL)
David Schweikert (R-AZ)
Austin Scott (R-GA)
Tim Scott (R-SC)
Terri Sewell (D-AL)
Steve Southerland (R-FL)
Steve Stivers (R-OH)
Marlin Stutzman (R-IN)
Scott Tipton (R-CO)
Tim Walberg (R-MI)
Joe Walsh (R-IL)
Daniel Webster (R-FL)
Allen West (R-FL)
Frederica Wilson (D-FL)
Steve Womack (R-AR)
Rob Woodall (R-GA)
Kevin Yoder (R-KS)
Todd Young (R-IN)

*Won seat in special election in 2010

MINORITIES IN CONGRESS

African-American
House (42D, 2R)

Terri Sewell (D-Ala.)
Karen Bass (D-Calif)
Barbara Lee (D-Calif.)
Laura Richardson (D-Calif.)
Maxine Waters (D-Calif.)
Del. Eleanor Holmes Norton
   (D-D.C.)
Corrine Brown (D-Fla.)
Alcee Hastings (D-Fla.)
Allen West (R-Fla.)
Frederica Wilson (D-Fla.)
Sanford Bishop (D-Ga.)
Hank Johnson (D-Ga.)
John Lewis (D-Ga.)
David Scott (D-Ga.)
Danny Davis (D-Ill.)
Jesse Jackson Jr. (D-Ill.)
Bobby Rush (D-Ill.)
André Carson (D-Ind.)
Cedric Richmond (D-La.)
Elijah Cummings (D-Md.)
Donna Edwards (D-Md.)
Hansen Clarke (D-Mich.)

John Conyers (D-Mich.)
Keith Ellison (D-Minn.)
Bennie Thompson (D-Miss.)
William Lacy Clay (D-Mo.)
Emanuel Cleaver (D-Mo.)
G.K. Butterfield (D-N.C.)
Melvin Watt (D-N.C.)
Donald Payne (D-N.J.)
Yvette Clarke (D-N.Y.)
Gregory Meeks (D-N.Y.)
Charles Rangel (D-N.Y.)
Edolphus Towns (D-N.Y.)
Marcia Fudge (D-Ohio)
Chaka Fattah (D-Pa.)
James Clyburn (D-S.C.)
Tim Scott (R-S.C.)
Al Green (D-Texas)
Sheila Jackson Lee (D-Texas)
Eddie Bernice Johnson (D-Texas)
Del. Donna Christian-Christensen
   (D-V.I.)
Bobby Scott (D-Va.)
Gwen Moore (D-Wis.)

Hispanic
Senate (1 D, 1 R)

Marco Rubio (R-Fla.)

Robert Menendez (D-N.J.)

House (18D, 7R)

Raúl Grijalva (D-Ariz.)
Ed Pastor (D-Ariz.)
Joe Baca (D-Calif.)
Xavier Becerra (D-Calif.)
Grace Napolitano (D-Calif.)
Lucille Roybal-Allard
   (D-Calif.)
Linda Sánchez (D-Calif.)
Loretta Sanchez (D-Calif.)
Mario Diaz-Balart (R-Fla.)

David Rivera (R-Fla.)
Ileana Ros-Lehtinen (R-Fla.)
Raúl Labrador (R-Idaho)
Luis Gutierrez (D-Ill.)
Albio Sires (D-N.J.)
Ben Ray Luján (D-N.M.)
José Serrano (D-N.Y.)
Nydia Velázquez (D-N.Y.)
Res. Cmmsr. Pedro Pierluisi
   (D-P.R.)

Francisco (Quico) Canseco
(R-Texas)
Henry Cuellar (D-Texas)
Bill Flores (R-Texas)

Charles Gonzalez (D-Texas)
Rubén Hinojosa (D-Texas)
Silvestre Reyes (D-Texas)
Jaime Herrera Beutler (R-Wash.)

Asian-American

Senate (2 D)

Daniel Akaka (D-Hawaii)

Daniel Inouye (D-Hawaii)

House (9 D, 1 R)

Del. Eni F.H. Faleomavaega
(D-Am. Samoa)
Judy Chu (D-Calif.)
Mike Honda (D-Calif.)
Doris Matsui (D-Calif.)
Del. Gregorio Kilili Camacho
Sablan (D-CNMI)

Colleen Hanabusa (D-Hawaii)
Mazie Hirono (D-Hawaii)
Hansen Clarke (D-Mich.)
Steve Austria (R-Ohio)
David Wu (D-Ore.)

American Indian

House (1 R)

Tom Cole (R-Okla.)

Arab-American

House (4 R, 1 D)

Justin Amash (R-Mich.)
Charles Boustany (R-La.)
Darrell Issa (R-Calif)

Richard Hanna (R-N.Y.)
Nick Rahall (D-W.V.)

Minority Governors

Mitch Daniels (Arab-American)
(R-Ind.)
Bobby Jindal (Indian-American)
(R-La.)
Deval Patrick (African-American)
(D-Mass.)

Brian Sandoval (Hispanic)
(R-Nev.)
Susana Martinez (Hispanic)
(R-N.M.)
Nikki Haley (Indian-American)
(R-S.C.)

WOMEN IN CONGRESS

Senate (12 D, 5 R)

Lisa Murkowski (R-Alaska)
Barbara Boxer (D-Calif.)
Dianne Feinstein (D-Calif.)
Mary Landrieu (D-La.)
Susan Collins (R-Maine)
Olympia Snowe (R-Maine)
Barbara Mikulski (D-Md.)
Debbie Stabenow (D-Mich.)
Amy Klobuchar (D-Minn.)

Claire McCaskill (D-Mo.)
Kay Hagan (D-N.C.)
Kelly Ayotte (R-N.H.)
Jeanne Shaheen (D-N.H.)
Kirsten Gillibrand (D-N.Y.)
Kay Bailey Hutchison (R-Texas)
Maria Cantwell (D-Wash.)
Patty Murray (D-Wash.)

House (51 D, 24 R)

Martha Roby (R-Ala.)
Terri Sewell (D-Ala.)
Gabrielle Giffords (D-Ariz.)
Karen Bass (D-Calif.)
Mary Bono Mack (R-Calif)
Lois Capps (D-Calif.)
Judy Chu (D-Calif.)
Susan Davis (D-Calif.)
Anna Eshoo (D-Calif.)
Barbara Lee (D-Calif.)
Zoe Lofgren (D-Calif.)
Doris Matsui (D-Calif.)
Grace Napolitano (D-Calif.)
Nancy Pelosi (D-Calif.)
Laura Richardson (D-Calif.)
Lucille Roybal-Allard (D-Calif.)
Linda Sanchez (D-Calif.)
Loretta Sanchez (D-Calif.)
Jackie Speier (D-Calif.)
Maxine Waters (D-Calif.)
Lynn Woolsey (D-Calif.)
Diana DeGette (D-Colo.)
Rosa DeLauro (D-Conn.)
Del. Eleanor Holmes Norton (D-D.C.)
Sandy Adams (R-Fla.)
Corrine Brown (D-Fla.)
Kathy Castor (D-Fla.)
Ileana Ros-Lehtinen (R-Fla.)
Debbie Wasserman Schultz (D-Fla.)
Frederica Wilson (D-Fla.)
Del. Madeleine Bordallo (D-Guam)
Colleen Hanabusa (D-Hawaii)

Mazie Hirono (D-Hawaii)
Judy Biggert (R-Ill.)
Jan Schakowsky (D-Ill.)
Lynn Jenkins (R-Kan.)
Chellie Pingree (D-Maine)
Niki Tsongas (D-Mass.)
Donna Edwards (D-Md.)
Candice Miller (R-Mich.)
Michele Bachmann (R-Minn.)
Betty McCollum (D-Minn.)
Jo Ann Emerson (R-Mo.)
Vicky Hartzler (R-Mo.)
Renee Ellmers (R-N.C.)
Virginia Foxx (R-N.C.)
Sue Myrick (R-N.C.)
Ann Marie Buerkle (R-N.Y.)
Yvette Clarke (D-N.Y.)
Nan Hayworth (R-N.Y.)
Kathy Hochul (D-N.Y.)
Nita Lowey (D-N.Y.)
Carolyn Maloney (D-N.Y.)
Carolyn McCarthy (D-N.Y.)
Louise Slaughter (D-N.Y.)
Nydia Velazquez (D-N.Y.)
Shelley Berkley (D-Nev.)
Marcia Fudge (D-Ohio)
Marcy Kaptur (D-Ohio)
Jean Schmidt (R-Ohio)
Betty Sutton (D-Ohio)
Allyson Schwartz (D-Pa.)
Kristi Noem (R-S.D.)
Diane Black (R-Tenn.)

Kay Granger (R-Texas)
Sheila Jackson Lee (D-Texas)
Eddie Bernice Johnson (D-Texas)
Del. Donna Christian-Christensen
   (D-V.I.)
Shelley Moore Capito (R-W.Va.)
Jaime Herrera Beutler
   (R-Wash.)

Marsha Blackburn (R-Tenn.)
Cathy McMorris Rodgers
   (R-Wash.)
Tammy Baldwin (D-Wis.)
Gwen Moore (D-Wis.)
Cynthia Lummis (R-Wyo.)

Women Who Are Governors (2 D, 4 R)

Jan Brewer (R-Ariz.)
Bev Perdue (D-N.C.)
Susana Martinez (R-N.M.)

Mary Fallin (R-Okla.)
Nikki Haley (R-S.C.)
Christine Gregoire (D-Wash.)

MILITARY SERVICE

This is a list of members of Congress and governors who have served in the United States Army, Navy, Air Force, Marines, Coast Guard, National Guard or the Reserves.

Senate (12 R, 12 D)

Daniel Akaka	D-Hawaii	Army Corps of Engineers, 1945-47
Jeff Bingaman	D-N.M.	Army Res., 1968-74
Richard Blumenthal	D-Conn.	Marine Corps Res., 1970-76
Thomas Carper	D-Del.	Navy, 1968-73; Naval Res., 1973-91
Dan Coats	R-Ind.	Army Corps of Engineers, 1966-68
Thad Cochran	R-Miss.	Navy, 1959-61
Michael Enzi	R-Wyo.	Wyo. Natl. Guard, 1967-73
Lindsey Graham	R-S.C.	Air Force, 1982-88; S.C. Air Natl. Guard, 1989-94; Air Force Res., 1995-present
Tom Harkin	D-Iowa	Navy, 1962-67; Naval Res., 1969-72
James Inhofe	R-Okla.	Army, 1957-58
Daniel Inouye	D-Hawaii	Army, 1943-47
Johnny Isakson	R-Ga.	Ga. Air Natl. Guard, 1966-72
John Kerry	D-Mass.	Navy, 1966-70; Naval Res., 1970-78
Mark Kirk	R-Ill.	Naval Res., 1989-present
Herb Kohl	D-Wis.	Army Res., 1958-64
Frank Lautenberg	D-N.J.	Army Signal Corps, 1942-46
Richard Lugar	R-Ind.	Navy, 1957-60
John McCain	R-Ariz.	Navy, 1958-80
Bill Nelson	D-Fla.	Army, 1968-70; Army Res., 1965-71
Jack Reed	D-R.I.	Army, 1967-79; Army Res., 1979-91
Pat Roberts	R-Kan.	Marine Corps, 1958-62
Jeff Sessions	R-Ala.	Army Res., 1973-86
Jim Webb	D-Va.	Marine Corps, 1968-72
Roger Wicker	R-Miss.	Air Force, 1976-80; Air Force Res., 1980-present

House (63 R, 25 D)

Sandy Adams	R-Fla.	Air Force, 1974-75
Todd Akin	R-Mo.	Army Res., 1972-80
Rodney Alexander	R-La.	Air Force Res., 1965-71
Joe Baca	D-Calif.	Army, 1966-68
Spencer Bachus	R-Ala.	Natl. Guard, 1969-71
Sanford Bishop	D-Ga.	Army, 1970-71
John Boehner	R-Ohio	Navy, 1969
Leonard Boswell	D-Iowa	Army, 1956-76
Paul Broun	R-Ga.	Marine Corps Res., 1964-67; Naval Res., 1967-73; Ga. Air Natl. Guard, 1972-73; Air Force Res., 1973-88
Vern Buchanan	R-Fla.	Mich. Air Natl. Guard, 1970-76
Dan Burton	R-Ind.	Army, 1956-57; Army Res., 1957-62
Larry Bucshon	R-Ind.	Naval Res., 1989-98
G.K. Butterfield	D-N.C.	Army, 1968-70

Howard Coble	R-N.C.	Coast Guard, 1952-56, 1977-78; Coast Guard Res., 1960-81
Mike Coffman	R-Colo.	Army, 1972-79; Marine Corps, 1979-94, 2005-06
Mike Conaway	R-Texas	Army, 1970-72
John Conyers	D-Mich.	Natl. Guard, 1948-50; Army, 1950-54; Army Res., 1954-57
Chip Cravaack	R-Minn.	Navy, 1981-2005
Rick Crawford	R-Ark.	Army, 1985-89
Geoff Davis	R-Ky.	Army, 1976-87
Peter DeFazio	D-Ore.	Air Force, 1967-71
Jeff Denham	R-Calif.	Air Force, 1984-89; Air Force Res., 1989-2000
John Dingell	D-Mich.	Army, 1944-46
John Duncan	R-Tenn.	Army Natl. Guard & Army Res., 1970-87
Eni F.H. Faleomavaega	D-Am.Samoa	Army, 1966-69
John Fleming	R-La.	Navy, 1976-82
Rodney Frelinghuysen	R-N.J.	Army, 1969-71
Chris Gibson	R-N.Y.	Army Natl. Guard, 1981-86; Army, 1986-2010
Louie Gohmert	R-Texas	Army, 1978-82
Charles Gonzalez	D-Texas	Texas Air Natl. Guard, 1969-75
Tim Griffin	R-Ark.	Army Res., 1996-present
Michael Grimm	R-N.Y.	Marine Corps, 1991
Brett Guthrie	R-Ky.	Army, 1987-2001
Ralph Hall	R-Texas	Navy, 1942-45
Andy Harris	R-Md.	Naval Res., 1988-94
Doc Hastings	R-Wash.	Army Res., 1964-69
Joe Heck	R-Nev.	Army Res., 1991-present
Maurice Hinchey	D-N.Y.	Navy, 1956-59
Duncan D. Hunter	R-Calif.	Marine Corps, 2002-05; Marine Res., 2005-present
Darrell Issa	R-Calif.	Army, 1970-72, 1976-80
Bill Johnson	R-Ohio	Air Force, 1973-99
Sam Johnson	R-Texas	Air Force, 1950-79
Walter Jones	R-N.C.	N.C. Natl. Guard, 1967-71
Peter King	R-N.Y.	Army Natl. Guard, 1968-73
Adam Kinzinger	R-Ill.	Air Natl. Guard, 2003-present
John Kline	R-Minn.	Marine Corps, 1969-94
Jeffrey Landry	R-La.	La. Natl. Guard, 1987-98
Edward Markey	D-Mass.	Army Res., 1968-73
Jim McDermott	D-Wash.	Navy Medical Corps, 1968-70
Gary Miller	R-Calif.	Army, 1967
Richard Nugent	R-Fla.	Ill. Air Natl. Guard, 1969-75
Pete Olson	R-Texas	Navy, 1988-98; Naval Res., 1998-present
Steven Palazzo	R-Miss.	Marine Res., 1988-96; Miss. Army Natl. Guard, 1997-present
Bill Pascrell	D-N.J.	Army, 1961; Army Res., 1962-67
Ron Paul	R-Texas	Air Force, 1963-68
Steve Pearce	R-N.M.	Air Force, 1970-76
Gary Peters	D-Mich.	Naval Res., 1993-2005
Collin Peterson	D-Minn.	Army Natl. Guard, 1963-69

Joe Pitts	R-Pa.	Air Force, 1963-69
Ted Poe	R-Texas	Air Force Res., 1970-76
Mike Pompeo	R-Kan.	Army, 1986-91
Charles Rangel	D-N.Y.	Army, 1948-52
Dave Reichert	R-Wash.	Air Force Res., 1971-76
Silvestre Reyes	D-Texas	Army, 1966-68
Scott Rigell	R-Va.	Marine Corps Res., 1978-84
Phil Roe	R-Tenn.	Army, 1973-74
Harold Rogers	R-Ky.	Army Natl. Guard, 1957-64
Mike Rogers	R-Mich.	Army, 1985-88
Tom Rooney	R-Fla.	Army JAG, 2000-04; Army Res., 2004-07
Bobby Rush	D-Ill.	Army, 1963-68
Del. Gregorio Kilili Camacho Sablan	D-C.N.M.I.	Army, 1981-86
Bobby Scott	D-Va.	Army Natl. Guard, 1970-73; Army Res., 1973-76
José Serrano	D-N.Y.	Army Medical Corps, 1964-66
John Shimkus	R-Ill.	Army, 1980-85; Army Res., 1985-2008
Pete Stark	D-Calif.	Air Force, 1955-57
Cliff Stearns	R-Fla.	Air Force, 1963-67
Steve Stivers	R-Ohio	Ohio Army Natl. Guard, 1988-2008
Mike Thompson	D-Calif.	Army, 1969-73
Edolphus Towns	D-N.Y.	Army, 1956-58
Tim Walz	D-Minn.	Army Natl. Guard, 1981-2005
Allen West	R-Fla.	Army, 1982-2004
Ed Whitfield	R-Ky.	Army Res., 1967-73
Joe Wilson	R-S.C.	Army Res., 1972-75; S.C. Natl. Guard, 1975-2003
Frank Wolf	R-Va.	Army, 1962-63; Army Res., 1963-67
Steve Womack	R-Ark.	Ark. Army Natl. Guard, 1979-2009
Bill Young	R-Fla.	Army Natl. Guard, 1948-57
Don Young	R-Alaska	Army, 1955-57
Todd Young	R-Ind.	Marine Corps, 1996-2000

Governors (10 R, 2 D)

Mike Beebe	D-Ark.	Army Res., 1968-74
Robert Bentley	R-Ala.	Air Force, 1969-71
Steve Beshear	D-Ky.	Army Res., 1969-75
Terry Branstad	R-Iowa	Army, 1969-71
Tom Corbett	R-Pa.	Pa. Army Natl. Guard, 1971-84
Nathan Deal	R-Ga.	Army, 1966-68
Dave Heineman	R-Neb.	Army Ranger, 1970-75
Gary Herbert	R-Utah	Utah Army Natl. Guard, 1970-76
Bob McDonnell	R-Va.	Army, 1976-81
C.L. "Butch" Otter	R-Idaho	Idaho Natl. Guard, 1967-73
Rick Perry	R-Texas	Air Force, 1972-77
Rick Scott	R-Fla.	Navy, 1971-74

NATIONAL JOURNAL VOTE RATINGS

Most Liberal, Most Conservative

These are the members at the far ends of the ideological spectrum, based on *National Journal*'s 2010 vote ratings. Scores are a composite of ratings of economic, social and foreign policy votes. Members marked with an asterisk were no longer in Congress as of January 2011.

Senate

Most Liberal			Liberal Score
1st	(tie)	Sherrod Brown, D-Ohio	83.3
		Ben Cardin, D-Md.	83.3
		Patrick Leahy, D-Vt.	83.3
		Carl Levin, D-Mich.	83.3
		Barbara Mikulski, D-Md.	83.3
		Harry Reid, D-Nev.	83.3
		Bernie Sanders, I-Vt.	83.3
		Debbie Stabenow, D-Mich.	83.3
		Sheldon Whitehouse, D-R.I.	83.3
10th	(tie)	Kirsten Gillibrand, D-N.Y.	80.8
		Jack Reed, D-R.I.	80.8
		Chuck Schumer, D-N.Y.	80.8
13th		Robert Menendez, D-N.J.	80.2
14th		Frank Lautenberg, D-N.J.	79.8
15th	(tie)	Robert Casey, D-Pa.	79.2
		Al Franken, D-Minn.	79.2
		Tom Udall, D-N.M.	79.2

Most Conservative			Conservative Score
1st	(tie)	John Barrasso, R-Wyo.	89.7
		Saxby Chambliss, R-Ga.	89.7
		John Cornyn, R-Texas	89.7
		Mike Crapo, R-Idaho	89.7
		Jim DeMint, R-S.C.	89.7
		John McCain, R-Ariz.	89.7
		James Risch, R-Idaho	89.7
		John Thune, R-S.D.	89.7
9th		Tom Coburn, R-Okla.	87.3
10th		Roger Wicker, R-Miss.	86.8
11th		Michael Enzi, R-Wyo.	86.3
12th		Jim Bunning, R-Ky.*	86.0
13th		Pat Roberts, R-Kan.	85.7
14th	(tie)	Kay Bailey Hutchison, R-Texas	85.3
		Jeff Sessions, R-Ala.	85.3

House

Most Liberal			Liberal Score
1st	(tie)	Tammy Baldwin, D-Wis.	96.7
		Judy Chu, D-Calif.	96.7
		John Lewis, D-Ga.	96.7
		Jerrold Nadler, D-N.Y.	96.7

Most Liberal			Liberal Score
		John Olver, D-Mass.	96.7
		Linda Sánchez, D-Calif.	96.7
		Jan Schakowsky, D-Ill.	96.7
8th	(tie)	Edward Markey, D-Mass.	95.3
		Jim McGovern, D-Mass.	95.3
		George Miller, D-Calif.	95.3
11th		Niki Tsongas, D-Mass.	93.7
12th	(tie)	John Larson, D-Conn.	93.5
		Grace Napolitano, D-Calif.	93.5
14th		Keith Ellison, D-Minn.	92.7
		Barney Frank, D-Mass.	92.7
		Rush Holt, D-N.J.	92.7
		Zoe Lofgren, D-Calif.	92.7
18th		Joseph Crowley, D-N.Y.	92.5
19th		Mike Doyle, D-Pa.	92.0
20th		John Tierney, D-Mass.	91.7
21st		Chellie Pingree, D-Maine	91.5
22nd	(tie)	Richard Neal, D-Mass.	91.2
		Charles Rangel, D-N.Y.	91.2
		José Serrano, D-N.Y.	91.2
25th	(tie)	Elijah Cummings, D-Md.	90.8
		Mazie Hirono, D-Hawaii	90.8
		Doris Matsui, D-Calif.	90.8

Most Conservative			Conservative Score
1st	(tie)	Trent Franks, R-Ariz.	95.0
		Sam Johnson, R-Texas	95.0
		Jim Jordan, R-Ohio	95.0
		Doug Lamborn, R-Colo.	95.0
		Randy Neugebauer, R-Texas	95.0
6th		Jean Schmidt, R-Ohio	94.5
7th		Pete Olson, R-Texas	94.3
8th		John Boehner, R-Ohio	94.2
9th		Bob Latta, R-Ohio	94.0
10th		John Culberson, R-Texas	93.8
11th		Mike Conaway, R-Texas	93.7
12th	(tie)	Wally Herger, R-Calif.	93.5
		Ted Poe, R-Texas	93.5
14th		Kenny Marchant, R-Texas	93.2
15th		Mac Thornberry, R-Texas	93.0
16th	(tie)	Tom Price, R-Ga.	92.7
		Pete Sessions, R-Texas	92.7
18th		John Carter, R-Texas	92.3
19th	(tie)	Michele Bachmann, R-Minn.	92.2
		Paul Broun, R-Ga.	92.2
		Scott Garrett, R-N.J.	92.2
22nd		Jerry Lewis, R-Calif.	91.7
23rd	(tie)	Devin Nunes, R-Calif.	91.5
		Todd Tiahrt, R-Kan.*	91.5
25th		John Linder, R-Ga.*	91.0

The Centrists

Here are the members who made up the ideological center of Congress in 2010, according to *National Journal*'s vote ratings. The members with scores closest to 50 were at the exact center of the chamber. Members marked with an asterisk were no longer in Congress as of January 2011.

Senate

	Liberal Score	Conservative Score
Judd Gregg, R-N.H.*	35.0	65.0
Scott Brown, R-Mass.	35.2	64.8
Lisa Murkowski, R-Alaska	36.2	63.8
Richard Lugar, R-Ind.	36.3	63.7
Olympia Snowe, R-Maine	36.7	63.3
Susan Collins, R-Maine	38.0	62.0
George Voinovich, R-Ohio*	39.3	60.7
Ben Nelson, D-Neb.	42.3	57.7
Joe Lieberman, I-Conn.	46.8	53.2
Jon Tester, D-Mont.	47.5	52.5
Max Baucus, D-Mont.	48.5	51.5
Mark Warner, D-Va.	51.0	49.0
Blanche Lincoln, D-Ark.*	53.8	46.2
Mark Pryor, D-Ark.	53.8	46.2
Claire McCaskill, D-Mo.	56.5	43.5
Jim Webb, D-Va.	57.7	42.3
Michael Bennet, D-Colo.	59.7	40.3
Kay Hagan, D-N.C.	60.5	39.5
Mark Udall, D-Colo.	60.8	39.2
Bill Nelson, D-Fla.	62.2	37.8
Mary Landrieu, D-La.	63.8	36.2
Dianne Feinstein, D-Calif.	64.2	35.8
Mark Begich, D-Alaska	64.7	35.3
Amy Klobuchar, D-Minn.	65.0	35.0
Jay Rockefeller D-W.Va.	65.2	34.8

House

	Liberal Score	Conservative Score
Jeff Fortenberry, R-Neb.	35.0	65.0
Todd Platts, R-Pa.	35.7	64.3
Judy Biggert, R-Ill.	36.7	63.3
Steven LaTourette, R-Ohio	37.0	63.0
Mario Diaz-Balart, R-Fla.	37.8	62.2
Lincoln Diaz-Balart, R-Fla.*	38.0	62.0
Tim Johnson, R-Ill.	38.2	61.8
Don Young, R-Alaska	38.2	61.8
Dave Reichert, R-Wash.	38.3	61.7
Tim Murphy, R-Pa.	38.7	61.3
Ileana Ros-Lehtinen, R-Fla.	38.8	61.2
Mark Kirk, R-Ill.	39.2	60.8
Charlie Dent, R-Pa.	39.7	60.3
Gene Taylor, D-Miss.*	39.7	60.3
Bobby Bright, D-Ala.*	40.2	59.8

	Liberal Score	Conservative Score
Vernon Ehlers, R-Mich.*	40.3	59.7
Walter Jones, R-N.C.	40.3	59.7
Travis Childers, D-Miss.*	40.8	59.2
Michael Castle, R-Del.*	41.0	59.0
Charles Djou, R-Hawaii*	41.7	58.3
Jim Marshall, D-Ga.*	42.2	57.8
Joseph Cao, R-La.*	43.0	57.0
Walt Minnick, D-Idaho*	43.2	56.8
Dan Boren, D-Okla.	44.0	56.0
Mike McIntyre, D-N.C.	44.0	56.0
Bill Owens, D-N.Y.	44.0	56.0
Harry Mitchell, D-Ariz.*	44.3	55.7
Glenn Nye, D-Va.*	45.0	55.0
John Tanner, D-Tenn.*	45.2	54.8
Joe Donnelly, D-Ind.	45.3	54.7
Zack Space, D-Ohio*	45.3	54.7
Rick Boucher, D-Va*	45.5	54.5
Mark Critz, D-Pa.	45.5	54.5
Tim Holden, D-Pa.	45.5	54.5
Collin Peterson, D-Minn.	45.7	54.3
Jason Altmire, D-Pa.	45.8	54.2
Christopher Carney, D-Pa.*	46.0	54.0
Ike Skelton, D-Mo.*	46.2	53.8
Mike Ross, D-Ark.	46.3	53.7
Michael McMahon, D-N.Y.*	46.7	53.3
Gabrielle Giffords, D-Ariz.	46.8	53.2
Stephanie Herseth Sandlin, D-S.D.*	47.0	53.0
John Adler, D-N.J.*	47.5	52.5
Jim Cooper, D-Tenn.	48.2	51.8
Daniel Lipinski, D-Ill.	48.3	51.7
Chet Edwards, D-Texas*	49.0	51.0
Jerry Costello, D-Ill.	49.2	50.8
Ann Kirkpatrick, D-Ariz.*	49.2	50.8
John Barrow, D-Ga.	49.3	50.7
Jim Matheson, D-Utah	49.3	50.7
Ben Chandler, D-Ky.	49.8	50.2
Frank Kratovil, D-Md.*	50.2	49.8
Kathy Dahlkemper, D-Pa.*	50.3	49.7
Lincoln Davis, D-Tenn.*	50.5	49.5
Brad Ellsworth, D-Ind.*	51.0	49.0
Charlie Melancon, D-La.*	51.0	49.0
Melissa Bean, D-Ill.*	51.5	48.5
Michael Arcuri, D-N.Y.*	51.8	48.2
Bill Foster, D-Ill.*	51.8	48.2
Debbie Halvorson, D-Ill.*	51.8	48.2
Solomon Ortiz, D-Texas*	52.0	48.0
Jerry McNerney, D-Calif.	52.2	47.8
Baron Hill, D-Ind.*	52.3	47.7
Nick Rahall, D-W.Va.	52.7	47.3
John Salazar, D-Colo.*	52.7	47.3
Allen Boyd, D-Fla.*	53.0	47.0

	Liberal Score	Conservative Score
Jim Costa, D-Calif.	53.0	47.0
Tom Perriello, D-Va.*	53.3	46.7
Marion Berry, D-Ark.*	53.7	46.3
John Boccieri, D-Ohio*	53.7	46.3
Jim Himes, D-Conn.	53.8	46.2
Patrick Murphy, D-Pa.*	53.8	46.2
Harry Teague, D-N.M.*	53.8	46.2
Earl Pomeroy, D-N.D.*	54.0	46.0
Gary Peters, D-Mich.	54.7	45.3
Betsy Markey, D-Colo.*	55.0	45.0
Gene Green, D-Texas	55.2	44.8
Steve Driehaus, D-Ohio*	55.3	44.7
Heath Shuler, D-N.C.	55.3	44.7
Dina Titus, D-Nev.*	55.3	44.7
Paul Kanjorski, D-Pa.*	56.0	44.0
Larry Kissell, D-N.C.	56.0	44.0
David Wu, D-Ore.	56.5	43.5
Henry Cuellar, D-Texas	57.2	42.8
Suzanne Kosmas, D-Fla.*	57.3	42.7
Artur Davis, D-Ala.*	57.7	42.3
Paul Hodes, D-N.H.*	58.3	41.7
Ron Kind, D-Wis.	58.3	41.7
Scott Murphy, D-N.Y.*	58.3	41.7
Charlie Wilson, D-Ohio*	58.8	41.2
Ruben Hinojosa, D-Texas	59.2	40.8
Mark Schauer, D-Mich.*	59.2	40.8
Brian Baird, D-Wash.*	59.3	40.7
John Spratt, D-S.C.*	59.3	40.7
Peter Visclosky, D-Ind.	59.3	40.7
Kurt Schrader, D-Ore.	59.7	40.3
Sanford Bishop, D-Ga.	60.5	39.5
Bob Etheridge, D-N.C.*	61.3	38.7
Gerald Connolly, D-Va.	61.5	38.5
Joe Courtney, D-Conn.	61.5	38.5
Vic Snyder, D-Ark.*	61.5	38.5
Dennis Moore, D-Kan.*	61.7	38.3
Dennis Cardoza, D-Calif.	61.8	38.2
Bart Gordon, D-Tenn.*	62.0	38.0
Marcy Kaptur, D-Ohio	62.2	37.8
Alan Mollohan, D-W.Va.*	62.3	37.7
Silvestre Reyes, D-Texas	62.3	37.7
Dutch Ruppersberger, D-Md.	62.5	37.5
Joe Baca, D-Calif.	62.8	37.2
Ron Klein, D-Fla.*	63.3	36.7
Allyson Schwartz, D-Pa.	63.3	36.7
Ed Perlmutter, D-Colo.	63.7	36.3
Ciro Rodriguez, D-Texas*	64.0	36.0
Adam Smith, D-Wash.	64.8	35.2

DISTRICT DEMOGRAPHICS

African-American

Districts with highest percentages of African-Americans.

District	%	Member
IL-2	68.8	Jackson (D)
MS-2	66.2	Thompson (D)
TN-9	63.2	Cohen (D)
AL-7	62.6	Sewell (D)
IL-1	62.2	Rush (D)
OH-11	59.3	Fudge (D)
MI-14	58.9	Conyers (D)
MI-13	58.5	Clarke (D)
NY-10	58.4	Towns (D)
LA-2	58.2	Richmond (D)

Hispanic

Districts with highest percentages of Hispanics.

District	%	Member
TX-15	82.5	Hinojosa (D)
TX-16	81.5	Reyes (D)
TX-28	78.9	Cuellar (D)
CA-34	78.7	Roybal-Allard (D)
TX-29	76.0	Green (D)
FL-21	75.6	Diaz-Balart (R)
CA-38	75.4	Napolitano (D)
IL-4	73.5	Gutierrez (D)
TX-27	73.2	Farenthold (R)
FL-25	71.6	Rivera (R)

Asian-American

Districts with highest percentages of Asian-Americans.

District	%	Member
HI-1	51.4	Hanabusa (D)
CA-15	36.4	Honda (D)
CA-13	36.0	Stark (D)
CA-12	33.4	Speier (D)
NY-5	32.6	Ackerman (D)
CA-8	31.1	Pelosi (D)
CA-16	28.3	Lofgren (D)
CA-29	27.7	Schiff (D)
HI-2	24.9	Hirono (D)
CA-32	22.1	Chu (D)

American-Indian/Alaska Native

Districts with highest percentages of American-Indians and Alaska Natives.

District	%	Member
AZ-1	19.1	Gosar (R)
OK-2	18.4	Boren (D)
NM-3	17.3	Luján (D)
AK-AL	14.4	Young (R)
SD-AL	8.5	Noem (R)
NC-7	7.8	McIntyre (D)
OK-1	6.6	Sullivan (R)
OK-3	6.2	Lucas (R)
MT-AL	6.1	Rehberg (R)
OK-4	5.8	Cole (R)

Youngest

Disticts with lowest median age.

District	Median Age	Member
UT-3	25.6	Chaffetz (R)
CA-20	27.5	Costa (D)
AZ-4	28.0	Pastor (D)
CA-43	28.1	Baca (D)
TX-29	28.6	Green (D)
NY-16	29.1	Serrano (D)
UT-1	29.2	Bishop (R)
TX-28	29.5	Cuellar (D)
CA-47	29.7	Sanchez (D)
IL-4	29.7	Gutierrez (D)

Oldest

Districts with highest median age.

District	Median Age	Member
FL-13	47.9	Buchanan (R)
FL-14	46.4	Mack (R)
FL-10	45.7	Young (R)
FL-19	45.4	Deutch (D)
FL-5	45.3	Nugent (R)
FL-16	44.9	Rooney (R)
FL-22	44.4	West (R)
MI-1	44.3	Benishek (R)
MA-10	43.5	Keating (D)
PA-4	43.2	Altmire (D)

Wealthiest

Districts with highest median household incomes.

District	Median Income	Member
VA-11	$104,033	Connolly (D)
NJ-11	$98,542	Frelinghuysen (R)
VA-10	$95,448	Wolf (R)
CA-14	$94,547	Eshoo (D)
NJ-7	$93,739	Lance (R)
NJ-5	$91,702	Garrett (R)
NY-2	$91,515	Israel (D)
NY-3	$91,458	King (R)
VA-8	$89,605	Moran (D)
MD-8	$88,889	Van Hollen (D)

Poorest

Districts with highest percentages of people in poverty.

District	%	Member
NY-16	38.4	Serrano (D)
MI-13	32.3	Clarke (D)
TX-15	31.2	Hinojosa (D)
CA-20	29.5	Costa (D)
MS-2	29.2	Thompson (D)
AZ-4	29.2	Pastor (D)
KY-5	28.5	Rogers (R)
PA-1	28.4	Brady (D)
MI-14	27.3	Conyers (D)
TX-28	26.9	Cuellar (D)

Most Educated

Districts with highest percentages of post-graduate degrees.

District	%	Member
NY-14	30.2	Maloney (D)
MD-8	29.9	Van Hollen (D)
VA-8	29.4	Moran (D)
CA-14	28.2	Eshoo (D)
DC-AL	27.0	Norton (D)
NY-8	25.4	Nadler (D)
CA-30	24.6	Waxman (D)
NY-18	24.2	Lowey (D)
VA-11	23.9	Connolly (D)
MA-8	23.0	Capuano (D)

Least Educated

Districts with lowest percentages of high school graduates.

District	%	Member
TX-29	54.3	Green (D)
CA-34	55.0	Roybal-Allard (D)
CA-20	55.6	Costa (D)
CA-47	56.4	Sanchez (D)
NY-16	59.2	Serrano (D)
CA-31	59.6	Becerra (D)
AZ-4	63.6	Pastor (D)
IL-4	64.7	Gutierrez (D)
TX-15	65.1	Hinojosa (D)
TX-28	65.4	Cuellar (D)

Government Workers

Districts with highest percentages of government employees.

District	%	Member
NC-3	31.6	Jones (R)
VA-2	31.5	Rigell (R)
MD-5	30.6	Hoyer (D)
VA-1	28.7	Wittman (R)
AK-AL	28.2	Young (R)
FL-2	27.5	Southerland (R)
HI-1	27.3	Hanabusa (D)
MD-4	27.0	Edwards (D)
DC-AL	26.8	Norton (D)
VA-8	26	Moran (D)

Veterans

Districts with highest percentages of military veterans.

District	%	Member
FL-1	17.6	Miller (R)
VA-2	17.2	Rigell (R)
CO-5	17	Lamborn (R)
VA-1	16.4	Wittman (R)
FL-5	16.3	Nugent (R)
AZ-8	15.9	Giffords (D)
WA-6	15.5	Dicks (D)
FL-6	15.1	Stearns (R)
FL-13	14.9	Buchanan (R)
FL-14	14.8	Mack (R)

Demographic rankings provided by Polidata

SENATE SEATS

2012 ELECTION

Democrats (21)	Previous %	Republicans (10)	Previous %
Daniel Akaka (Hawaii)	61%	John Barrasso (Wyo.)	73%
Jeff Bingaman (N.M.)	71%	Scott Brown* (Mass.)	52%
Sherrod Brown (Ohio)	56%	Bob Corker (Tenn.)	51%
Maria Cantwell (Wash.)	57%	Orrin Hatch (Utah)	63%
Ben Cardin (Md.)	54%	Dean Heller** (Nev.)	Appointed
Thomas Carper (Del.)	70%	*Kay Bailey Hutchison (Texas)*	62%
Robert Casey (Penn.)	59%	*Jon Kyl (Ariz.)*	53%
Kent Conrad (N.D.)	69%	Richard Lugar (Ind.)	87%
Dianne Feinstein (Calif.)	59%	Olympia Snowe (Maine)	74%
Kirsten Gillibrand (N.Y.)	67%	Roger Wicker (Miss.)	55%
Amy Klobuchar (Minn.)	58%		
Herb Kohl (Wis.)	67%	**Independents (2)**	
Joe Manchin (W.Va.)	53%	*Joe Lieberman (Conn.)*	50%
Claire McCaskill (Mo.)	50%	Bernie Sanders (Vt.)	65%
Robert Menendez (N.J.)	53%		
Ben Nelson (Neb.)	64%		
Bill Nelson (Fla.)	60%		
Debbie Stabenow (Mich.)	57%		
Jon Tester (Mont.)	49%		
Jim Webb (Va.)	50%		
Sheldon Whitehouse (R.I.)	54%		

2014 ELECTION

Democrats (20)	Previous %	Republicans (13)	Previous %
Max Baucus (Mont.)	73%	Lamar Alexander (Tenn.)	65%
Mark Begich (Alaska)	48%	Saxby Chambliss (Ga.)	57%
Christopher Coons (Del.)	57%	Thad Cochran (Miss.)	61%
Dick Durbin (Ill.)	68%	Susan Collins (Maine)	61%
Al Franken (Minn.)	42%	John Cornyn (Texas)	55%
Kay Hagan (N.C.)	53%	Michael Enzi (Wyo.)	76%
Tom Harkin (Iowa)	63%	Lindsey Graham (S.C.)	58%
Tim Johnson (S.D.)	62%	James Inhofe (Okla.)	57%
John Kerry (Mass.)	66%	Mike Johanns (Neb.)	58%
Mary Landrieu (La.)	52%	Mitch McConnell (Ky.)	53%
Frank Lautenberg (N.J.)	56%	James Risch (Idaho)	58%
Carl Levin (Mich.)	63%	Pat Roberts (Kan.)	60%
Jeff Merkley (Ore.)	49%	Jeff Sessions (Ala.)	63%
Mark Pryor (Ark.)	80%		
Jack Reed (R.I.)	73%		
Jay Rockefeller (W.Va.)	64%		
Jeanne Shaheen (N.H.)	52%		
Mark Udall (Colo.)	53%		
Tom Udall (N.M.)	61%		
Mark Warner (Va.)	65%		

Senators not running for re-election are italicized.
*Won January 2010 special election.
**Appointed May 2011 to replace Republican Sen. John Ensign, who resigned.

GOVERNORSHIPS

2011, 4 states

Kentucky	(D)	**Mississippi**	**(R)**
Louisiana	(R)	West Virginia**	(D)

2012, 11 states

Delaware	(D)	North Dakota	(R)
Indiana	**(R)**	Utah	(R)
Missouri	(D)	Vermont*	(D)
Montana	**(D)**	Washington	(D)
New Hampshire*	(D)	West Virginia	(D)
North Carolina	(D)		

2013, 2 states

New Jersey	(R)	**Virginia**	**(R)**

2014, 36 states

Alabama	(R)	Minnesota	(D)
Alaska	(R)	**Nebraska**	**(R)**
Arizona	(R)	Nevada	(R)
Arkansas	**(D)**	New Hampshire*	(D)
California	(D)	New Mexico	(R)
Colorado	(D)	New York	(D)
Connecticut	(D)	Ohio	(R)
Florida	(R)	Oklahoma	(R)
Georgia	(R)	Oregon	(D)
Hawaii	(D)	Pennsylvania	(R)
Idaho	(R)	Rhode Island	(I)
Illinois	(D)	South Carolina	(R)
Iowa	(R)	South Dakota	(R)
Kansas	(R)	Tennessee	(R)
Maine	(R)	Texas	(R)
Maryland	**(D)**	Vermont*	(D)
Massachusetts	(D)	Wisconsin	(R)
Michigan	(R)	Wyoming	(R)

Boldface indicates states with term-limited incumbents.

*New Hampshire and Vermont have two-year terms. All other states have four-year terms.

** Special election scheduled Oct. 4, 2011 for the remainder of Democrat Joe Manchin's term as governor.

CLOSEST CONGRESSIONAL ELECTIONS

These are the contests decided by the smallest margins of victory in 2010, based on statistics from Polidata.

Senate

State	Winner	Loser	Vote Difference	% Difference
Colo.	Michael Bennet (D)	Ken Buck (R)	28,859	1.63
Ill.	Mark Kirk (R)	Alexi Giannoulias (D)	71,501	1.95
Pa.	Pat Toomey (R)	Joe Sestak (D)	80,229	2.02
Alaska	Lisa Murkowski (R)	Joe Miller (R)	10,252	4.00
Wash.	Patty Murray (D)	Dino Rossi (R)	118,766	4.72
Wis.	Ron Johnson (R)	Russell Feingold (D)	105,041	4.84
Nev.	Harry Reid (D)	Sharron Angle (R)	40,659	5.77
Calif.	Barbara Boxer (D)	Carly Fiorina (R)	1,001,075	10.01
W.Va.*	Joe Manchin (D)	John Raese (R)	53,345	10.07
Ky.	Rand Paul (R)	Jack Conway (D)	156,176	11.54

House

District	Winner	Loser	Vote Difference	% Difference
KY-6	Ben Chandler (D)	Andy Barr (R)	647	0.27
IL-8	Joe Walsh (R)	Melissa Bean (D)	553	0.28
NY-25	Ann Marie Buerkle (R)	Dan Maffei (D)	659	0.34
VA-11	Gerald Connolly (D)	Keith Fimian (R)	981	0.44
NV-3	Joe Heck (R)	Dina Titus (D)	1,922	0.76
TX-27	Blake Farenthold (R)	Solomon Ortiz (D)	799	0.80
WV-1	David McKinley (R)	Mike Oliverio (D)	1,440	0.80
CA-11	Jerry McNerney (D)	David Harmer (R)	2,658	1.11
NC-2	Renee Ellmers (R)	Bob Etheridge (D)	2,095	1.16
IN-2	Joe Donnelly (D)	Jackie Walorski (R)	2,543	1.42
AZ-8	Gabrielle Giffords (D)	Jesse Kelly (R)	4,156	1.46
PA-12	Mark Critz (D)	Tim Burns (R)	2,886	1.56
NH-2	Charlie Bass (R)	Ann McLane Kuster (D)	3,550	1.58
PA-4	Jason Altmire (D)	Keith Rothfus (R)	3,869	1.62
MN-8	Chip Cravaack (R)	Jim Oberstar (D)	4,407	1.68
NY-1	Tim Bishop (D)	Randy Altschuler (R)	3,461	1.92
IA-1	Bruce Braley (D)	Ben Lange (R)	4,209	1.99
WA-2	Rick Larsen (D)	John Koster (R)	6,101	2.12
AL-2	Martha Roby (R)	Bobby Bright (D)	4,780	2.18
MO-3	Russ Carnahan (D)	Ed Martin (R)	4,418	2.28

*November 2010 special election.

CAMPAIGN FINANCE

Here are the congressional candidates who raised and spent the most money on their 2010 races. The information is based on research by the Center for Responsive Politics (opensecrets.org), as of Dec. 31, 2010.

Senate

	State	Primary	General	Raised	Spent
Linda McMahon (R)	CT	W	L	$50,285,122	$50,181,464
Sharron Angle (R)	NV	W	L	$28,162,049	$28,262,487
Barbara Boxer (D)	CA	W	W	$23,401,332	$26,933,249
Jeff Greene (D)	FL	L		$23,777,064	$23,777,064
Harry Reid (D)	NV	W	W	$19,378,713	$22,534,460
Marco Rubio (R)	FL	W	W	$21,741,330	$21,638,315
Carly Fiorina (R)	CA	W	L	$21,521,397	$21,484,825
John McCain (R)	AZ	W	W	$18,414,247	$20,478,626
Chuck Schumer (D)	NY	W	W	$17,764,831	$18,143,841
Pat Toomey (R)	PA	W	W	$17,141,810	$16,945,137
Russell Feingold (D)	WI	W	L	$13,947,563	$15,544,093
Rob Portman (R)	OH	W	W	$16,540,629	$15,054,910
Ron Johnson (R)	WI	W	W	$15,235,898	$15,043,252
Patty Murray (D)	WA	W	W	$12,762,491	$14,873,696
Mark Kirk (R)	IL	W	W	$14,305,287	$14,079,356
Arlen Specter (D)	PA	L		$8,094,055	$13,835,564
Charlie Crist (I)	FL		L	$13,680,424	$13,608,676
Kirsten Gillibrand (D)	NY	W	W	$13,418,545	$13,007,808
Roy Blunt (R)	MO	W	W	$11,932,403	$12,095,571
Blanche Lincoln (D)	AR	W	L	$10,752,803	$11,545,776
Scott Brown (R)*	MA		W	$18,272,033	$11,085,821
Michael Bennet (D)	CO	W	W	$11,536,750	$10,875,565
David Vitter (R)	LA	W	W	$8,734,427	$10,572,617
Robin Carnahan (D)	MO	W	L	$10,331,090	$10,311,557
Alexi Giannoulias (D)	IL	W	L	$9,923,570	$9,902,006

House

	State	Primary	General	Raised	Spent
Michele Bachmann (R)	MN	W	W	$13,517,222	$11,647,656
John Boehner (R)	OH	W	W	$9,796,947	$9,876,911
Allen West (R)	FL	W	W	$6,542,738	$6,519,713
Alan Grayson (D)	FL	W	L	$5,928,282	$5,459,812
Eric Cantor (R)	VA	W	W	$5,955,025	$5,407,656
Scott Murphy (D)	NY	W	L	$5,366,128	$5,321,745
Ron Klein (D)	FL	W	L	$3,776,867	$5,319,671
William Russell (R)	PA	L		$5,085,382	$5,081,289
Joe Wilson (R)	SC	W	W	$4,739,095	$4,765,083
Tarryl Clark (D)	MN	W	L	$4,718,912	$4,691,807
Steny Hoyer (D)	MD	W	W	$4,511,873	$4,687,713
Randy Altschuler (R)	NY	W	L	$4,602,691	$4,593,405
Scott Rigell (R)	VA	W	W	$4,510,947	$4,352,653

	State	Primary	General	Raised	Spent
Patrick Murphy (D)	PA	W	L	$4,246,047	$4,287,244
Barney Frank (D)	MA	W	W	$4,052,944	$4,205,447
Charles Rangel (D)	NY	W	W	$2,937,509	$4,139,258
Suzan DelBene (D)	WA	W	L	$4,024,786	$3,942,493
Steve Israel (D)	NY	W	W	$2,547,657	$3,941,248
Gabrielle Giffords (D)	AZ	W	W	$3,504,410	$3,888,406
Chet Edwards (D)	TX	W	L	$3,686,768	$3,841,632
Allen Boyd (D)	FL	W	L	$2,690,989	$3,814,064
Tom Perriello (D)	VA	W	L	$3,775,363	$3,782,680
Bill Foster (D)	IL	W	L	$3,804,082	$3,737,519
George Flinn (R)	TN	L		$3,729,090	$3,723,239
Michael Capuano (D)	MA	W	W	$3,699,635	$3,699,584
Earl Pomeroy (D)	ND	W	L	$3,048,387	$3,690,646
Jim Himes (D)	CT	W	W	$3,660,498	$3,603,727
Carolyn Maloney (D)	NY	W	W	$3,052,944	$3,532,298
Betsy Markey (D)	CO	W	L	$3,505,293	$3,516,268
Allyson Schwartz (D)	PA	W	W	$2,906,212	$3,481,643
Matt Doheny (R)	NY	W	L	$3,448,912	$3,440,808
Rick Boucher (D)	VA	W	L	$2,639,353	$3,325,898
Bill Flores (R)	TX	W	W	$3,353,665	$3,309,747
James Clyburn (D)	SC	W	W	$3,319,719	$3,289,439
John Adler (D)	NJ	W	L	$3,301,321	$3,285,638
Mark Schauer (D)	MI	W	L	$3,255,382	$3,261,651
Gary Peters (D)	MI	W	W	$3,284,646	$3,236,452
Dan Maffei (D)	NY	W	L	$3,192,682	$3,114,128
Ike Skelton (D)	MO	W	L	$2,923,038	$3,107,552
Jerry McNerney (D)	CA	W	W	$3,208,078	$3,097,237
Tim Bishop (D)	NY	W	W	$3,066,831	$3,097,008
Chris Murphy (D)	CT		W	$3,034,971	$3,079,678
Mike Ross (D)	AR	W	W	$2,426,280	$3,012,727
Pat Meehan (R)	PA	W	W	$3,031,825	$2,986,713
Rush Holt (D)	NJ	W	W	$2,616,604	$2,958,135
Ed Perlmutter (D)	CO	W	W	$2,443,962	$2,943,593
Dan Seals (D)	IL	W	L	$2,935,284	$2,941,677
Ami Bera (D)	CA	W	L	$2,942,764	$2,935,828
Zack Space (D)	OH	W	L	$2,686,942	$2,931,978
Robert Dold (R)	IL	W	W	$2,985,088	$2,903,831

*Special election held in January 2010.

INDEX